Peterson's®
How to Get
Money
for College
2018

About Peterson's®

Peterson's® provides the accurate, dependable, high-quality education content and guidance you need to succeed. No matter where you are on your academic or professional path, you can rely on Peterson's publications and its online information at **www.petersons.com** for the most up-to-date education exploration data, expert test-prep tools, and top-notch career success resources—everything you need to achieve your goals.

For more information, contact Peterson's, 3 Columbia Circle, Albany, NY 12203-5158; 800-338-3282 Ext. 54229; or visit us online at **www.petersons.com**.

Previous editions published as *How to Get Money for College* © 2009, 2010, 2011, 2012, 2013, 2014, 2015, 2016; *Peterson's College Money Handbook* © 1983, 1984, 1985, 1986, 1987, 1988, 1989, 1990, 1991, 1997, 1998, 1999, 2000, 2001, 2002, 2003, 2004, 2005, 2006, 2007, 2008; and as *Paying Less for College* © 1992, 1993, 1994, 1995, 1996

FAFSA® is a registered trademark of the U.S. Department of Education.

Peterson's makes reasonable efforts to obtain accurate, complete, and timely data from reliable sources. Nevertheless, Peterson's and the third-party data suppliers make no representation or warranty, either expressed or implied, as to the accuracy, timeliness, or completeness of the data or the results to be obtained from using the data, including, but not limited to, its quality, performance, merchantability, or fitness for a particular purpose, non-infringement or otherwise.

Neither Peterson's nor the third-party data suppliers warrant, guarantee, or make any representations that the results from using the data will be successful or will satisfy users' requirements. The entire risk to the results and performance is assumed by the user.

ISSN 1544-2330
ISBN: 978-0-7689-4158-6

Printed in the United States of America

10 9 8 7 6 5 4 3 2 1   19 18 17

Thirty-fifth Edition

Contents

A Note from the Peterson's® Editors

The news media seem to constantly remind us that a college education is expensive. It certainly appears to be beyond the means of many Americans. The sticker price for four years at state-supported colleges can be more than $45,000, and private colleges and universities can cost more than $150,000. And these numbers continue to rise.

But there is good news. The system operates to provide the needed money so that most families and students are able to afford a college education while making only a reasonable financial sacrifice. However, because the college financial aid system is complex, finding the money is often easier said than done. That is why the process demands study, planning, calculation, flexibility, filling out forms, and meeting deadlines. Fortunately, for most people, it can produce positive results. There are many ways to manage college costs and many channels through which you can receive help. Be sure to take full advantage of the opportunities that have been opened up to students and their families by the many organizations, foundations, and businesses that have organized to help you with the burden of college expenses.

For nearly forty years, Peterson's has given students and parents the most comprehensive, up-to-date information on how to get their fair share of the financial aid pie. *Peterson's How to Get Money for College* is both a quick reference and a comprehensive resource that puts valuable information about college costs and financial aid opportunities at your fingertips.

- **The ABCs of Paying for College** provides insight into federal financial aid programs that are available, offers an overview of the financial aid landscape, walks you through the process of filing for aid, and provides proven tips on how to successfully navigate the financial aid process to obtain the federal, state, and institutional aid you deserve.

- The **Quick-Reference Chart** offers a snapshot comparison of the financial aid programs available at more than 2,400 four-year institutions across the country.

- The **Profiles of College Financial Aid Programs** provide unbiased financial aid data for each of the more than 2,400 four-year institutions listed.

- The **Appendix** lists the state scholarship and grant programs offered by all fifty states and the District of Columbia.

- The six **Indexes** included in the back of the book allow you to search for specific award programs based on a variety of criteria, including merit-based awards, athletic grants, ROTC programs, and much more.

Peterson's publishes a full line of books—financial aid, education exploration, test prep, and career preparation. Peterson's publications can be found at high school guidance offices, college libraries and career centers, and your local bookstore and library. Peterson's books are also available at www.petersonsbooks.com.

We welcome any comments or suggestions you may have about this publication. Your feedback will help us make educational dreams possible for you—and others like you.

The ABC's of Paying for College

What You Need to Know About the FAFSA®

The Free Application for Federal Student Aid or FAFSA® (https://fafsa.ed.gov/FAFSA/app/fafsa) is a critical form that anyone seeking college financial aid must complete.

WHY YOU MUST FILE THE FAFSA®

The FAFSA® is required in order for a student to be considered for any type of federal financial aid, including grants and loans. Even if you think your family makes too much for you to qualify for need-based aid, you should still complete the FAFSA®. For one thing, many people are surprised to find that they may actually qualify for need-based aid—the eligibility for which is determined by a number of factors, in addition to household income.

Also, the FAFSA® is required to apply for students loans (for which there is no need-based element such as income limits). If you don't initially think you want to apply for student loans but later change your mind, having a completed FAFSA® already on file will help speed up the process.

In addition, most schools will require a student to have a completed FAFSA® on file before the student can be considered for any school-based aid programs such as scholarships. A completed FAFSA® is also required for federal work study jobs.

IT'S EASIER TO FILE ONLINE

While you can opt to print and complete a paper version of the FAFSA®, it is much quicker and easier to complete the online version. The system walks you through the process and can alert you to sections you can skip if they don't apply to you.

If you have completed a FAFSA® in the past, some of your information will be automatically entered when you start to work on your newest one, giving you a head start. You will further save a lot of time by using the IRS data retrieval tool, which will be discussed later in this article.

Filing online means your form will be processed faster, and it also eliminates the worry that your paperwork will be lost or delayed in the mail.

For those who want or need to print and submit a paper version of the FAFSA®, you can print a PDF version of the FAFSA® online. Students and parents can request up to three copies of the paper FAFSA® (in English or Spanish) by calling the Federal Student Aid Information Center toll-free at 800-4-FED-AID.

THE NEW FEDERAL STUDENT AID ID

In order for a student to complete the online FAFSA®, he or she must obtain a Federal Student Aid (FSA) ID. You can get this online at https://fsaid.ed.gov/npas/index.htm. The FSA ID replaced the PIN system that was previously used prior to May 2015. Parents of dependent students also need to obtain their own FSA ID in order to sign their child's FAFSA® electronically online.

The FSA ID can be used to access several federal aid-related websites, including FAFSA.gov and StudentLoans.gov. It consists of a username and password and can be used to electronically sign Federal Student Aid documents, access your personal records, and make binding legal obligations. The FSA ID is beneficial in several ways:

- It removes your personally identifiable information (PII), such as your Social Security number, from your log-in credentials.

- It creates a more secure and efficient way to verify your information when you log in to access to your federal student aid information online.

- It gives you the ability to easily update your personal information.

- It allows you to easily retrieve your username and password by requesting a secure code be sent to your e-mail address or by answering challenge questions.

It's relatively simple to create an FSA ID and should only take a few minutes. In addition, you will have an opportunity to link your current Federal Student Aid PIN (if you already have one) to your FSA ID. The final step is to confirm your e-mail address. You will receive a secure code to the e-mail address you provided when you set up your FSA ID. Once you retrieve the code from your e-mail account and enter it—to confirm your e-mail address is valid—you will be able to use this e-mail address instead of your username to log in to any of the federal aid-related websites, making the log-in process even simpler for you and your parents.

When you initially create your FSA ID, your information will need to be verified with the Social Security Administration. This process can take anywhere from one to three days. For that reason, it's a good idea to take care of setting up your FSA ID as early as possible, so it will be all set when you are ready to begin completing your FAFSA®.

IMPORTANT NOTE: Since your FSA ID provides access to your personal information and is used to sign online documents, it's imperative that you protect this ID. Don't share it with *anyone* or write it down in an insecure location—you could place yourself at great risk for identify theft.

If your FSA ID is lost or stolen, you must do one of the following:

• Contact Federal Student Aid's Customer Service center at 800-433-3243 (toll-free).

• Update your username and password by selecting "Edit My FSA ID".

• Disable your FSA ID so that no one can use it by selecting "Edit My FSA ID" and then selecting Disable My FSA ID.

INFORMATION YOU WILL NEED

Completing your FAFSA® (or updating one you have already started) will be much easier if you have some basic information and documentation handy when you prepare to complete the form. The first section of the FAFSA® involves your basic personal information that you should know offhand, such as your name, address, and Social Security number. After that, you will need to provide details about your income, assets, and other financial issues. If you file taxes, much of this information will be taken from your tax return. If you haven't yet completed your taxes for that year, you can enter estimated figures and update the form with the final numbers later.

If you're a student who is married, you will also need to provide information about your spouse and their finances. If you're a dependent student, information about one or both or your parents and their finances will be required.

You will also need to provide information about the school(s) you attend or plan to attend. If you haven't made your final school choices yet, you can list the ones you know at this point and add others later.

BE MINDFUL OF DEADLINES

The new FAFSA® for the upcoming school year is available online starting on October 1. It is smart to complete your FAFSA® as early as possible. If you file taxes, you will need information from your tax return (and from your parents, too, if you are a dependent student). Beginning with the 2017–18 FAFSA®, students will be required to report income information from an earlier tax year. For example, on the 2017–18 FAFSA®, students (and parents, as appropriate) will report their 2015 income information, rather than their 2016 income information. However, you can complete your FAFSA® before you file your tax return by entering estimated information and then returning to the online system and making any necessary updates once you have filed your taxes.

For federal aid, the final deadline to submit your FAFSA® is June 30 at the end of the school year for which you are applying. So for the 2018–19 school year, the final deadline to submit your FAFSA® would be June 30, 2018. However, you would normally want to apply for aid before the start of a semester—and ideally, as far in advance as possible. That's because schools frequently require all of your financial aid to be

processed (or at least be in process) before your registration is considered official.

It can sometimes be tricky to keep track of other financial aid deadlines because the deadlines for different types of aid can vary by state and school. Be sure to check with your school—or the schools you are considering attending—to find out their financial aid deadlines so you can get all of your forms submitted in time.

Check the website for your state's department of education to find out the deadlines to submit the FAFSA® and other forms in order to be considered for any state-funded financial aid that may be available to you.

DEPENDENCY

One of the biggest misconceptions—or most misunderstood aspects of the FAFSA® and financial aid—is that a student can simply declare himself or herself independent, and then their parents' information will not be considered. In the past, dependency wasn't viewed in such strict terms, and it was easier for a student who lived on their own to be considered independent.

It's important to keep in mind that dependency for financial aid purposes has nothing to do with tax status or whether a student's parents claimed the student as a dependent on their tax return. Dependency for taxes and financial aid are two completely different and separate things.

There are now strict criteria that determine a student's dependency status. To be considered independent, a student must meet one of the following conditions:

• Age 24 or older by December 31 of the school year for which the student is applying for aid

• Married

• Have children or other dependents for whom the student provides more than half of their support

• Currently serving in the military

• Having been homeless, in foster care, or a ward of the court

Even if one of these conditions applies, that doesn't necessarily grant the student automatic independent status. There may still be additional required documentation or other conditions that must be met.

IRS DATA RETRIEVAL TOOL

A common complaint about the FAFSA® is that it takes too long to complete. But a fairly recent change has made the form considerably less time-consuming for many people. The IRS Data Retrieval tool now allows the tax information of students or parents to be automatically imported into the FAFSA®.

Once you reach the section of the online FAFSA® that deals with financial information of the student (and parent, if applicable), you will see a button that says "Link to IRS" if that option is available to you. You will then follow the steps to log into the IRS system and have your information transferred to your FAFSA®. In order to access the Data Retrieval Tool, the information you enter on the IRS login screen—including your name, address, and filing status—must exactly match the information on your most recent tax return.

Those who decide to skip this step for whatever reason should know that there's a good chance they will then be required to submit copies of their tax return and possibly even an IRS transcript in order to verify their tax information. (An IRS transcript is an official document that must be obtained from the IRS. That can be a time-consuming and inconvenient process, so you are usually better off just using the IRA data retrieval tool in the first place.)

There are certain situations in which the FAFSA® will not allow you to use the Data Retrieval Tool. This tool is not an option for students or parents who are married and filed as Married Filing Separately, are married and filed as Head of Household, filed a Form 1040X amended tax return, or filed a Puerto Rican or foreign tax return. If you fall into one of these categories, you will need to enter your tax information manually.

Also, if you have just filed your tax return within a few weeks prior to completing the FAFSA®, your current information may not be in the IRS system yet and may not be accessible by the Data Retrieval Tool.

PARENTS' MARITAL STATUS

For dependent students, their parents' marital status can have a big impact on financial aid eligibility. If the parents are married, financial information for both parents must be reported. If the parents are separated but still living together, they are still listed as "married or remarried" on the FAFSA®. Parents who are legally separated or living in separate households are classified as "divorced or separated."

If parents are divorced, the FAFSA® must be completed by the parent with whom the student lived with most during the previous twelve-month period. If the student lived equally with both parents, the form would be completed by the parent who provided the most support.

LISTING SCHOOL CHOICES

When completing the FAFSA®, you must specify which colleges should receive the report generated by your FAFSA® application. On the paper FAFSA®, you can only list four colleges. On the online version, you can list ten. If you complete the paper version and want to have your information provided to more than four schools, you can go online to the FAFSA® website after your form has been processed and add more schools to your list (up to a total of ten).

From a federal aid standpoint, it doesn't matter in what order you list the colleges. However, the FAFSA® instructions note that for state aid purposes, you may want to list the colleges in order of preference. Keep in mind that each school on your list will see everything on your FAFSA®—including the names of the other colleges you have listed. There have been reports that schools are using students' college listings to determine how likely a specific student is to attend their particular school (based on the theory that students tend to list colleges in the order of how much they want to attend each). The speculation is that a college may reserve its best financial aid offers for students who seem most interested in attending. While most schools won't confirm that practice, it is probably in your best interest to list your colleges in order of the ones you most want to attend.

Falsifying Information on Your FAFSA® Could Bring Big Problems

With the cost of college rising each year and college graduates saddled with more than $1 trillion in debt to pay for their postsecondary studies, more and more families are desperate to secure payment-free options for higher education. Nothing illuminates this fact better than the meteoric rise in applications for financial aid through the annually Free Application for Federal Student Aid (FAFSA). In the 2004–05 academic year, more than 11 million students sent in FAFSA applications. Less than seven years later, that number doubled to more than 22 million. With more and more students applying for federal financial aid, there is, unfortunately, an increased temptation to commit fraud. Parents try to do whatever they can to lower their Expected Family Contribution (EFC), and sometimes this can lead to falsifying information. This is a big no-no, but that doesn't stop people from trying.

A quick search on Google, and you can find parents and students asking boldly, "Do people lying on their FAFSA really get caught?" or "How do I hide the fact that I have money from FAFSA?" Cheating on the FAFSA seems as intuitive as forgetting to report that second job you have to the Internal Revenue Service.

A report released by the Government Accountability Office, the Congress-created financial watchdog, found that fifteen for-profit universities encouraged fraud and/or engaged in deceptive marketing practices. The report stated that one college admission worker encouraged an undercover applicant to not report $250,000 in savings on the student's FAFSA. Another college representative told an undercover applicant to falsify the number of dependents he had from 0 to 3.

It all seems so deceptively easy—giving thousands of dollars in savings to a student's uncle temporarily to hide that asset; writing down grandma's address to gain in-state tuition rates; forgetting to mention your true immigration status; or the extreme example of one Alaskan woman who used a false identity. In that situation, after claiming she suffered from years of child abuse, the woman used an obscure federal law to secure a new identity to hide from her accused abuser. (The abuser she named was never charged with a crime.) She received a new social security number and card. But instead of living a new life in anonymity, she used her *old* identity to apply for federal student loans—a lot of them. Arrested and convicted, the woman was sentenced to five years in prison and ordered to pay back nearly $1 million.

The prospect of going to jail for filling out false information on your FAFSA application may not have crossed your mind, but it is certainly a possibility. Falsifying information—knowingly or unknowingly—is a federal crime. It is punishable by up to $20,000 in fines and up to five years in prison. And though there are books offering tantalizing options to "game," the federal student aid system—do not be tempted.

You do not want to start your college career by committing a crime against the government. It's just not worth it. Your FAFSA is checked against your IRS documents by professionals who do not want to take the chance that they will use their precious scarce financial aid resources to support students who really do not need it. Students who falsify information to get financial aid leave deserving cash-strapped students out in the cold. Fortunately, though, fraud in the federal aid system is low—a recent government study found that about 5 percent of applications contain false information.

Even if you do not intend to defraud the government, inaccurate information on your FAFSA can get you into trouble. It is critical that you fill the application out as accurately as possible. It may look like an innocuous document, but it amounts to a partnership between you and the federal government, and it is essential that partnership is based upon trust.

Here are some tips to avoid making mistakes on your FAFSA that could cost you financial aid or even your freedom:

- Accurately report your assets, address, dependents, income, and so on. It just doesn't make sense to lie. All that information is easily verifiable. Income includes wages, tips, social security payments, child support payments, and other untaxed income. But retirement income such as those in a 401K or IRA does not have to be reported. Check with your tax advisor when filling out your FAFSA application.

- Fill out your FAFSA completely. Mistakes can cost you time as you might have to reapply, and that will literally cost you money.

- Avoid books, consultants, and websites that promise to lower your EFC by questionable means. Trying to "game," the federal aid system is just going to cause you headaches.

College is expensive, and families are smart to try to lower that expense as much as possible. But planning, saving, and focusing on academic pursuits to garner scholarships and grants is a much better way of acquiring money for college than trying to put one over on the federal government. Being honest is always the best policy—especially when applying for federal financial aid.

Tips for Financing Your Child's College Education

by Don Betterton

Given the lifelong benefit of a college degree (college graduates are projected to earn in a lifetime $1 million more than those with only a high school diploma), higher education is a worthwhile investment. However, it is also an expensive one made even more difficult to manage by cost increases that have outpaced both inflation and gains in family income. The reality of higher education economics is that paying for a child's college education is an issue that shows no sign of getting easier.

Because of the high cost involved (even the most inexpensive four-year education at a public institution costs about $10,000 a year), good information about college budgets and strategies for reducing the "sticker price" is essential. You have made a good start by taking the time to read *Peterson's How to Get Money for College*. In the pages that follow, you will find valuable information about the four main sources of aid—federal, state, institutional, and private. Before you learn about the various programs, however, it will be helpful if you have an overview of how the college financial aid system operates and what long-range financing strategies are available.

FINANCIAL AID

Financial aid refers to money that is awarded to a student, usually in a "package" that consists of gift aid (commonly called a scholarship or grant), a student loan, and/or a campus job.

COLLEGE COSTS

The starting point for organizing a plan to pay for your child's college education is to make a good estimate of the yearly cost of attendance. You can use the **College Cost Worksheet** on the next page to do this.

To estimate your college costs for 2017–18, refer to the tuition and fees and room and board figures shown in the **College Cost Worksheet**. If your child will commute from your home, use $2,500 instead of the college's room and board charges and $900 for transportation. We have used $800 for books and $1,500 for personal expenses. Finally, estimate the cost of two round trips if your home is more than a few hundred miles from the college. Add the items to calculate the total budget. You should now have a reasonably good estimate of college costs for 2017–18. (To determine the costs for later years, adding 4 percent per year will probably give you a fairly accurate estimate.)

DO YOU QUALIFY FOR NEED-BASED AID?

The next step is to evaluate whether or not you are likely to qualify for financial aid based on need. This step is critical, since more than 90 percent of the yearly total of $128 billion in student aid is awarded only after a determination is made that the family lacks sufficient financial resources to pay the full cost of college on its own. To judge your chance of receiving need-based aid, it is necessary to estimate an Expected Family Contribution (EFC) according to a government formula known as the Federal Methodology (FM). The official Federal Student Aid Website provides a FAFSA4caster tool (similar to an EFC calculator) that helps you get a head start on the financial aid process, including getting an early estimate of your eligibility for federal aid. The tool will also allow you to transfer the information provided into the actual Free Application for Federal Student Aid (FAFSA) form when you are ready to complete it. You can find the tool on the Fafsa.ed.gov website.

APPLYING FOR NEED-BASED AID

Because the federal government provides about 67 percent of all aid awarded, the application, FAFSA®, and need evaluation process is controlled by the U.S. Department of Education. In addition, nearly every state that offers student assistance uses the federal government's system to award its own aid. Furthermore, in addition to arranging for the payment of federal and state aid, many colleges use the FAFSA to award their own funds to eligible students. (Note: In addition to the FAFSA, many private colleges and universities also ask the family to complete the CSS/Financial Aid PROFILE® application.)

The FAFSA is your "passport" to receiving your share of the billions of dollars awarded annually in need-based aid. If you didn't read the first article in this section about the FAFSA, go back and take a look at it now. You will find the latest information on the FAFSA, including important details on the change from the PIN to the new FSA ID.

AWARDING AID

The colleges you list on the FAFSA will receive your information in order to calculate a financial aid award in a package that typi-

College Cost Worksheet

	College 1	College 2	College 3	Commuter College
Tuition and Fees	_____	_____	_____	_____
Room and Board	_____	_____	_____	$2,500
Books	$ 800	$ 800	$ 800	$ 750
Personal Expenses	$1,500	$1,500	$1,500	$1,500
Travel	_____	_____	_____	$ 900
Total Budget	_____	_____	_____	_____

cally includes aid from at least one of the major sources—federal, state, college, or private. In addition, the award will probably consist of a combination of a scholarship, grant, loan, or campus job. These last two pieces—loan and job—are called self-help aid because they require effort on your child's part (that is, the aid must be either earned through work or paid back later). Scholarships or grants are outright gifts that have no such obligation.

It is important that you understand each part of the package. You'll want to know, for example, how much aid is a gift, the interest rate and repayment terms of the student loan, or how many hours per week the campus job requires. There should be an enclosure with the award letter that answers these questions. If not, make a list of your questions and call or visit the financial aid office.

Once you understand the terms of each item in the award letter, you should turn your attention to the "bottom line"— how much you will have to pay at each college where your child is accepted. In addition to understanding the aid award, this means having a good estimate of the college budget so you can

accurately calculate how much you and your child will have to contribute. (Often, an aid package does not cover the entire need.) Colleges differ in how much detail they include in their award notifications. Many colleges provide full information— types and amounts of aid, yearly costs, and the EFC for the parent and student shares. If these important items are missing or incomplete, you can do the work on your own. (See the **Comparing Financial Aid Awards and Family Contribution Worksheet** on the next page.) For example, if the award letter only shows the college's direct charges—tuition, room, and board— you need to estimate indirect costs such as books, personal expenses, and travel. Then subtract the total aid awarded from the yearly cost to get the EFC. A portion of that amount may be your child's contribution (35 percent of student assets and 50 percent of student earnings over $2,200) and the remainder is the parental share. If you can afford this amount at your child's first-choice college, the financial aid system has worked well for you, and your child's college enrollment plans can go forward.

How Need Is Calculated and Aid Is Awarded

	College 1	College 2
Total Cost of Attendance	$10,000	$ 24,000
− Expected Family Contribution	− 5,500	− 5,500
= Financial Need	$ 4,500	$ 18,500
− Grant Aid Awarded	− 675	−14,575
− Campus Job (Work-Study) Awarded	− 1,400	− 1,300
− Student Loan Awarded	− 2,425	− 2,625
= Unmet Need	0	0

Note: Sometimes an institution is unable to meet all need. The amount of unmet need is called "the gap."

Comparing Financial Aid Awards and Family Contribution Worksheet

	College 1	College 2	College 3
Cost of Attendance	_____	_____	_____
Aid Awarded	_____	_____	_____
Grant/Scholarship	_____	_____	_____
Loan	_____	_____	_____
Job	_____	_____	_____
Total Aid	_____	_____	_____
Expected Family Contribution	_____	_____	_____
Student Contribution	_____	_____	_____
Parent Contribution	_____	_____	_____

But if you think your EFC is too high, you should contact the college's financial aid office and ask whether additional aid is available. Many private high-cost colleges are willing to work with families to help make attendance at their institutions possible. Most colleges also allow applicants to appeal their financial aid awards, the budget used for you, or any of the elements used to determine the family contribution, especially if there are extenuating circumstances or if the information has changed since the application was submitted. Some colleges may also reconsider an award based on a "competitive appeal," the submission of a more favorable award letter from another college.

If your appeal is unsuccessful and there is still a gap between the expected family contribution and what you feel you can pay from income and savings, you are left with two choices. One option is for your child to attend a college where paying your share of the bill will not be a problem. (This assumes that an affordable option was included on your child's original list of colleges, a wise admission application strategy.) The second is to look into alternate methods of financing. At this stage, parental loans and tuition payment plans are the best financing options. A parental loan can bring the yearly cost down to a manageable level by spreading payments over a number of years. This is the type of financing that families use when purchasing a home or automobile. A tuition payment plan is essentially a short-term loan and allows you to pay the costs over ten to twelve months. It is an option for families who have the resources available but need help with managing their cash flow.

NON-NEED-BASED AID

Regardless of whether you might qualify for a need-based award, it is always worthwhile to look into merit, or non-need, scholarships from sources such as foundations, agencies, religious groups, and service organizations. For a family that isn't eligible for need-based aid, merit scholarships are the only form of gift aid available. If your child later qualifies for a need-based award, a merit scholarship can be quite helpful in providing additional resources if the aid does not fully cover the costs. Even if the college meets 100 percent of need, a merit scholarship reduces the self-help (loan and job) portion of an award.

In searching for merit-based scholarships, keep in mind that there are relatively few awards (compared to those that are need-based), and most of them are highly competitive. Use the following checklist in your search.

- Take advantage of any scholarships for which your child is automatically eligible based on parents' employer benefits, military service, association or church membership, other affiliations, or student or parent attributes (ethnic background, nationality, and so on). Company or union tuition remissions are the most common examples of these awards.

- Look for other awards for which your child might be eligible based on the previous characteristics and affiliations but where there is a selection process and an application is required. Free computerized searches are available on the Internet. (You should not pay a fee for a scholarship search.) Peterson's free scholarship search can be accessed by logging on to www.petersons.com/finaid. Scholarship directories, such as *Peterson's Scholarships, Grants & Prizes*, which details more than 3,800 scholarship programs, and *Peterson's Best Scholarships for Best Students* are useful resources and can be found in bookstores, high school guidance offices, or your local library. You can also find these books at www.petersonsbooks.com.

- See if your state has a merit scholarship program.

- Look into national scholarship competitions. High school guidance counselors usually know about these scholarships. Examples of these awards are the National Meritt Scholarship Program, the Coca-Cola Scholarship, Gates Millennium Scholars, Intel Science Talent Search, and the U.S. Senate Youth Program.

- ROTC (Reserve Officers' Training Corps) scholarships are offered by the Army, Navy, Air Force, and Marine Corps. A full ROTC scholarship covers tuition, fees, textbook costs, and, in some cases, a stipend. Acceptance of an ROTC scholarship entails a commitment to take military science courses and to serve for a specific number of years as an officer in the sponsoring branch of the service. Competition is heavy, and preference may be given to students in certain fields of study, such as engineering, languages, science, and health professions. Application procedures vary by service. Contact an armed services recruiter or high school guidance counselor for further information.

- Investigate community scholarships. High school guidance counselors usually have a list of these awards, and announcements are published in local newspapers. Most common are awards given by service organizations like the American Legion, Rotary International, and the local women's club.

- If your child is strong academically or is very talented in fields such as athletics or performing/creative arts, you may want to consider colleges that offer their own merit awards to gifted students they wish to enroll. Refer to the Non-Need Scholarships for Undergraduates index in the back part of this guide.

In addition to merit scholarships, there are loan and job opportunities for students who do not qualify for need-based aid. Some of the organizations that sponsor scholarships—for example, the Air Force Aid Society—also provide loans.

Work opportunities during the academic year are another type of assistance that is not restricted to aid recipients. Many colleges will, after assigning jobs to students on aid, open campus positions to all students looking for work. In addition, there are usually off-campus employment opportunities available to everyone.

FINANCING YOUR CHILD'S COLLEGE EDUCATION

"Financing" means putting together resources to pay the balance due the college over and above payments from the primary sources of aid—grants, scholarships, student loans, and jobs. Financing strategies are important because the high cost of a college education today often requires a family, whether or not it receives aid, to think about stretching its college payment beyond the four-year period of enrollment. For high-cost colleges, it is not unreasonable to think about a 10-4-10 plan: ten years of saving; four years of paying college bills out of current income, savings, and borrowing; and ten years to repay a parental loan.

Note

A point of clarification about whether to put college savings in your name or your child's: If you are certain that your child will not be a candidate for need-based aid, there may be a tax advantage to accumulating money in his or her name. However, when it comes to maximizing aid eligibility, it is important to understand that student assets are assessed at a 20 percent rate and parental assets at about 5 percent. Therefore, if your college savings are in your child's name, it may be wise to reestablish title to these funds before applying for financial aid. You should contact your financial planner or accountant before making any modifications to your asset structure.

Savings

Although saving for college is always a good idea, many families are unclear about its advantages. Some families do not save because after normal living expenses have been covered, they do not have much money to set aside. An affordable but regular savings plan through a payroll deduction is usually the answer to the problem of spending your entire paycheck every month.

The second reason why saving for college is not a high priority is the belief that the financial aid system penalizes a family by lowering aid eligibility. The Federal Methodology of need determination is very kind to families that save. In fact, savings are ignored completely for most families that earn less than $50,000. Savings in the form of home equity, retirement plans, and most annuities are excluded from the calculation. And even when savings are counted, a maximum of 5 percent of the total is expected each year. In other words, if a family has $40,000 in savings after an asset protection allowance is considered, the contribution is no greater than $2,000. Given the impact of compound interest it is easy to see that a long-term savings plan can make paying for college much easier.

A sensible savings plan is important because of the financial advantage of saving compared to borrowing. The amount of money students borrow for college is now greater than the amount they receive in grants and scholarships. With loans becoming so widespread, savings should be carefully con-

What Is CSS/Financial Aid PROFILE

There are many complexities in the financial aid process: knowing which aid is merit-based and which aid is need-based; understanding the difference between grants, loans, and work-study; and determining whether funds are from federal, state, institutional, or private sources.

In addition, the aid application process itself can be confusing. It can involve more than the Free Application for Federal Student Aid (FAFSA) and the Federal Methodology (FM). Many colleges feel that the federal aid system (FAFSA and FM) does not collect or evaluate information thoroughly enough for them to award their own institutional funds. These colleges have made an arrangement with the College Scholarship Service, a branch of the College Board, to establish a separate application system.

The application is called the CSS/Financial Aid PROFILE®, and the need-analysis formula is referred to as the Institutional Methodology (IM). If you apply for financial aid at one of the colleges that uses the PROFILE, the admission material will state that the PROFILE is required in addition to the FAFSA. You should read the information carefully and file the PROFILE to meet the earliest college deadline. Before you can receive the PROFILE, however, you must register, either by phone or online at https://student.collegeboard.org/css-financial-aid-profile, providing enough basic information so the PROFILE package can be designed specifically for you. The FAFSA is free, but there is a charge for the PROFILE. As with the FAFSA, the PROFILE can be submitted via the Internet.

In addition to the requirement by certain colleges that you submit both the FAFSA and PROFILE (when used, the PROFILE is always in addition to the FAFSA; it does not replace it), you should understand that each system has its own method for analyzing a family's ability to pay for college. The main differences between PROFILE's Institutional Methodology and the FAFSA's Federal Methodology are:

- PROFILE includes equity in the family home as an asset; the FAFSA doesn't.

- PROFILE takes a broader look at assets not included on the FAFSA.

- PROFILE expects a minimum student contribution, usually in the form of summer earnings; the FAFSA has no such minimum.

- PROFILE may collect information on the noncustodial parent; the FAFSA does not.

- PROFILE allows for more professional judgment than the FAFSA. Medical expenses, private secondary school costs, and a variety of special circumstances are considered under PROFILE, subject to the discretion of the aid counselor on campus.

- PROFILE includes information on assets not reported on the FAFSA, including life insurance, annuities, retirement plans, etc.

To summarize: PROFILE's Institutional Methodology tends to be both more complete in its data collection and more rigorous in its analysis than the FAFSA's Federal Methodology. When IM results are compared to FM results for thousands of applicants, IM will usually come up with a somewhat higher expected parental contribution than FM.

Creditworthiness

If you will be borrowing to pay for your child's college education, making sure you qualify for a loan is critical. For the most part, that means your credit record must be free of default or delinquency. You can check your credit history with one or more of the following three major credit bureaus and clean up any adverse information that appears. The numbers below will offer specific information on what you need to provide to obtain a report. All of the credit bureaus accept credit report requests over their Web sites. You will usually be asked to provide your full name, phone number, social security number, birth date, and addresses for the last five years. You are entitled to a free report from each bureau.

Equifax Credit Information
P.O. Box 740241
Atlanta, GA 30374
800-685-1111
http://www.equifax.com

Trans Union
800-888-4213
http://www.transunion.com

Experian
888-397-3742
http://www.experian.com

sidered as an alternative to borrowing. Your incentive for saving is that a dollar saved is a dollar not borrowed.

Borrowing

Once you've calculated your "bottom-line" parental contribution and determined that the amount is not affordable out of your current income and assets, the most likely alternative is borrowing. Beginning July 1, 2010, as a result of the Health Care and Education Reconciliation Act, federal student loans are no longer made by private lenders under the Federal Family Education Loan (FFEL) Program. Instead, all new federal student loans come directly from the U.S. Department of Education under the Direct Loan Program, which offers subsidized and unsubsidized (Stafford) loans for students, PLUS loans for parents and graduate/professional students, and consolidation loans for both students and parents. For additional information, go online to https://studentloans.gov/myDirectLoan/index.action or call 800-4-FED-AID (toll-free).

For the Direct PLUS Loan, parents must complete a Direct PLUS Loan application and promissory note, contained in a single form that can be obtained from a school's financial aid office. The yearly limit on a PLUS Loan is equal to the student's cost of attendance minus any other financial aid the student receives. For example, if your cost of attendance is $6,000, and you receive $4,500 in other financial aid, your parents can borrow up to $1,500. Loans are disbursed between July 1 and June 30 of each year and have a fixed interest rate throughout the life of the loan. The rate for undergraduate students will never exceed 8.25%. Interest is charged on a PLUS Loan from the date of the first disbursement until the loan is paid in full. A PLUS Loan made to the parent cannot be transferred to the student. The parent is responsible for repaying the PLUS Loan. For more details about PLUS Loans, visit www.direct.ed.gov/about.html.

MAKE FINANCIAL AID WORK FOR YOU

If you are like millions of families that benefit from financial aid, it is likely that your child's college plans can go forward without undue worry about the costs involved. The key is to understand the financial aid system and to follow the best path for your family. The result of good information and good planning should be that you will receive your fair share of the billions of dollars available each year and that the cost of college will not prevent your child from attending.

Don Betterton is a former Director of Undergraduate Financial Aid at Princeton University and a Certified College Planner (CCP).

Residency: Its Impact on Tuition

When it comes to college tuition at a state school, a student's *in-state* or *out-of-state* status can often make a big difference. For those students who are unable to cover a school's price tag, it can often be quite frustrating. However, there is a legitimate reason why colleges charge more to out-of-state students, even if this happens to be thousands more. And here's why.

Public universities receive public funding by way of tax dollars paid by state residents. A large chunk of money that these public universities get each year are paid by taxpayers who live in that state. It only make sense then that in-state students should catch a break in tuition costs since their families, as residents, have helped pay for the public universities' operating costs.

Another reason for in-state tuition to be less expensive is because states want to offer an incentive to keep their residents in state. Their investment for keeping their students in-state pays off when a student graduates and starts working in-state as well, essentially helping boost the economy from within, and contributing to the social and cultural climate of the state.

RECIPROCITY

In some cases, a public college or university will offer in-state tuition to out-of-state students. Typically this happens when a program of study is not available to the student in his or her home state, or the states make an agreement with one another to offer in-state or close to in-state tuition to students from each other's states. For example, the Western Undergraduate Exchange (WUE) program offers out-of-state students tuition at 1.5 times as much as in-state tuition; states included are Alaska, Arizona, California, Colorado, Hawaii, Idaho, Montana, Nevada, New Mexico, North Dakota, South Dakota, Utah, Washington, and Wyoming.

Check with your high school guidance counselor and/or the financial aid office at your school(s) of interest to see if there are any options like this in your state

IN-STATE REQUIREMENTS

In-state requirements and establishing residency varies state to state, but you can always ask your prospective school what is required to establish residency. Typically it takes at least one year of living in the state, and you will be required to perform certain tasks, such as obtaining a driver's license in the state, filing taxes in the state, and so on. You may need to demonstrate that you are in the state for years to come—not only for the duration of your undergraduate education. It is important that you research this thoroughly and contact the school to be sure you are taking the right steps to obtain residency.

Although not easy, some students may find a way to move to the state they want to go to school in a year (or two) before they even apply. If you want to attend an out-of-state institution and cannot afford the out-of-state tuition, establishing residency is crucial to lowering your tuition cost and ensuring you will be able to afford to attend until graduation. Establishing residency might also open up other financial aid opportunities as well, so be sure to ask if there are any scholarships, grants, or other sources of funding available only to in-state students. Whether or not you want to obtain residency will have to do with your specific financial situation, so you should be sure to weigh your all of your options carefully before making your decision.

Federal Financial Aid Programs

There are a number of sources of financial aid available to students: federal and state governments, private agencies, and the colleges themselves. In addition, there are three different forms of aid: grants, earnings, and loans.

The federal government is the single largest source of financial aid for students. In recent years, the U.S. Department of Education's student financial aid programs made more than $80 billion available in loans, grants, and other aid to 14 million students. At present, there are four federal grant programs—Federal Pell Grant, Federal Supplemental Educational Opportunity Grant (FSEOG), Teacher Education Assistance for College and Higher Education (TEACH) Grant, and Iraq and Afghanistan Service Grant. There are two federal loan programs: Federal Perkins Loan Program and the William D. Ford Federal Direct Loan Program. The federal government also has a job program, Federal Work-Study Program (FWS), which helps colleges provide employment for students. In addition to the student aid programs, there are also tuition tax credits and deductions. They are the American Opportunity Credit, the Lifetime Learning Credit, the Tuition and Fees Tax Deduction, and the Student Loan Interest Tax Deduction. Also, there is AmeriCorps. AmeriCorps will pay the interest that is accrued on qualified student loans for members who complete the service program.

The majority of federal higher education loans are made in the Direct Loan Program, which makes available two kinds of loans: loans to students and PLUS loans to parents or to graduate or professional students. These loans are either subsidized or unsubsidized. Subsidized loans are made on the basis of demonstrated student need, and the interest is paid by the government during the time the student is in school or deferment. For the unsubsidized (non-need-based) loans and PLUS loans, interest begins to accrue as funds are disbursed.

All new federal student loans come directly from the U.S. Department of Education under the Direct Loan Program. Students interested in receiving federal student aid should continue to complete a Free Application for Federal Student Aid (FAFSA) for each school year that they wish to be considered for aid. For more information about applying for federal student aid, call 800-4-FED-AID (800-433-3243)(toll-free) or visit www.fafsa.ed.gov.

FEDERAL PELL GRANT

The Federal Pell Grant is the largest grant program; more than 9 million students receive Pell Grants annually. This grant is intended to be the starting point of assistance for lower-income families. Eligibility for a Pell Grant is based on the Expected Family Contribution. The amount you receive will depend on your EFC and the cost of education at the college you will attend. The highest award depends on how much funding the program receives from the government. For the 2017–18 award year (July 1, 2017 to June 30, 2018), the maximum award is $5,920. As of July 1, 2012, a student can not receive a Federal Pell Grant for more than 12 semesters or the equivalent. A student will receive notice when he/she is close to their limit.

FEDERAL SUPPLEMENTAL EDUCATIONAL OPPORTUNITY GRANT (FSEOG)

As its name implies, Federal Supplemental Educational Opportunity Grants provide additional need-based federal grant money to supplement the Federal Pell Grant Program. Each participating college is given funds to award to especially needy students. The maximum award is $4,000 per year, but the amount you receive depends on the college's awarding policy, the availability of FSEOG funds, the total cost of education, and the amount of other aid awarded.

FEDERAL WORK-STUDY PROGRAM (FWS)

This program provides jobs for students who demonstrate need. Salaries are paid by funds from the federal government as well as the college. Students work on an hourly basis on or off campus and must be paid at least the federal minimum wage. Students may earn only up to the amount awarded in the financial aid package.

FEDERAL PERKINS LOAN PROGRAM

This is a low-interest (5%) loan for students with exceptional financial need. Perkins Loans are made through the college's financial aid office with the college as the lender. Undergraduate students can borrow a maximum of $5,500 per year, and there is a cumulative limit of $27,500. The annual limit for graduate and professional-degree-seeking students is $8,500 with a total cumulative limit (including the $27,500) of $60,000. Borrowers may take up to ten years to repay the loan, beginning nine months after they graduate, leave school, or drop below half-time status. No interest accrues while they are in school, and, under certain conditions (e.g., they teach in low-income areas, work in law enforcement, are full-time nurses or medical technicians, serve as Peace Corps or VISTA volunteers, etc.), some or all of the loan can be cancelled. In addition, payments can be deferred under certain conditions such as unemployment.

FEDERAL DIRECT LOANS

A Direct Loan is borrowed directly from the U.S. Department of Education through the college's financial aid office.

Federal Financial Aid Programs

Name of Program	Type of Program	Maximum Award Per Year
Federal Pell Grant	need-based grant	$5,920
Federal Supplemental Educational Opportunity Grant (FSEOG)	need-based grant	$4,000
Teacher Education Assistance for College and Higher Education (TEACH) Grants	need/merit	up to $4,000 a year for undergraduates
Iraq and Afghanistan Service Grant	need/merit	$5,920 (based on strict criteria being met)
Federal Work-Study Program (FWS)	need-based part-time job	no maximum
Federal Perkins Loan Program	need-based loan	$5,500
Subsidized Federal Direct Loan	need-based grant student loan	$3,500 (first year)
Unsubsidized Federal Direct Loan	non-need based	$5,500 (first year, dependent student)

The interest rate on Direct Subsidized and Unsubsidized Loans for undergraduates with a first disbursement date between July 1, 2017, and June 30, 2018, is 4.29 percent. For those loans with a first disbursement date between July 1, 2016, and June 30, 2017, the interest rate was 3.76 percent.

The maximum amount dependent students may borrow in any one year is $5,500 for freshmen, $6,500 for sophomores, and $7,500 for juniors and seniors, with a maximum of $31,000 for the total undergraduate program (of which not more than $23,000 can be subsidized). The maximum amount independent students can borrow is $9,500 for freshmen (of which no more than $3,500 can be subsidized), $10,500 for sophomores (of which no more than $4,500 can be subsidized), and $12,500 for juniors and seniors (of which no more than $5,500 can be subsidized). Independent students can borrow up to $57,500 (of which no more than $23,000 can be subsidized) for the total undergraduate program. Borrowers may be charged a small origination fee, which is deducted from the loan proceeds. See the helpful, easy-to-read chart on the next page for maximum annual and total subsidized and unsubsidized loan limits.

To apply for a Federal Student Loan, you must first complete the FAFSA to determine eligibility for a subsidized loan and then complete a separate loan application that is submitted to the Department of Education. The Department of Education will send a master promissory for completion. The proceeds of the loan, less the origination fee, will be sent to the college to be either credited to your account or released to you directly. Direct loans are processed by the financial aid office as part of the overall financial aid package.

Once the repayment period starts, borrowers of both subsidized and unsubsidized Federal Direct Loans have to pay a combination of interest and principal monthly for up to a 25-year period. There are a number of repayment options as well as opportunities to consolidate federal loans. There are also provisions for extended repayments, deferments, and repayment forbearance, if needed. Note: If you received a Direct Subsidized Loan that was first disbursed between July 1, 2012, and July 1, 2014, you are responsible for paying any interest that accrued during your grace period (first six months after graduation). If you choose not to pay the interest that accrued during your grace period, the interest will be added to your principal balance.

DIRECT PLUS LOANS

PLUS loans are for parents of dependent students to help families with the cost of education. There is no needs test to qualify. For Direct PLUS Loans first disbursed on or after July 1, 2016, and before July 1, 2017, the interest rate is 6.31 percent. For Direct PLUS Loans first disbursed on or after July 1, 2017, and before July 1, 2018, the interest rate is 7%. There is no

Maximum Annual and Total Subsidized and Unsubsidized Loan Limits as of July 1, 2015

Year	Dependent Students (except students whose parents are unable to obtain PLUS Loans)	Independent Students (and dependent undergraduate students whose parents are unable to obtain PLUS Loans)
First-Year Undergraduate	$5,500—No more than $3,500 of this amount may be in subsidized loans.	$9,500—No more than $3,500 of this amount may be in subsidized loans.
Second-Year Undergraduate	$6,500—No more than $4,500 of this amount may be in subsidized loans.	$10,500—No more than $4,500 of this amount may be in subsidized loans.
Third-Year and Beyond Undergraduate	$7,500 per year—No more than $5,500 of this amount may be in subsidized loans.	$12,500 per year—No more than $5,500 of this amount may be in subsidized loans.
Graduate or Professional Degree Students	Not Applicable	$20,500
Maximum Total Debt from Subsidized and Unsubsidized Loans	$31,000—No more than $23,000 of this amount may be in subsidized loans.	$57,500 for undergraduates—No more than $23,000 of this amount may be in subsidized loans. $138,500 for graduate or professional students—No more than $65,500 of this amount may be in subsidized loans. The graduate debt limit includes all federal loans received for undergraduate study.

Source: https://studentaid.ed.gov/sa/types/loans/subsidized-unsubsidized

yearly limit; you can borrow up to the cost of your child's education, less other financial aid received. Repayment begins sixty days after the funds are disbursed. The origination fee is approximately 4 percent and may be subtracted from the proceeds. Parent borrowers must generally have a good credit record to qualify.

AMERICAN OPPORTUNITY CREDIT AND LIFETIME LEARNING CREDIT

Tuition tax credits allow families to reduce their tax bill by the out-of-pocket college tuition expense. Unlike a tax deduction, which is modified according to your tax bracket, a tax credit is a dollar-for-dollar reduction in taxes paid.

There are two programs: the American Opportunity Credit and the Lifetime Learning Credit. As is true of many federal programs, there are numerous rules and restrictions that apply. You should check with your tax preparer, financial adviser, or IRS Publication 970 for information about your own particular situation.

American Opportunity Credit

The American Opportunity Credit (formerly the Hope Credit) can be claimed for expenses for the first four years of postsecondary education. This is a change from the previous Hope Credit. The American Opportunity Credit can be claimed now through tax-year 2018 for expenses for course-related books, supplies, and equipment. It is a tax credit of up to $2,500 of the cost of qualifying tuition and expenses, and up to 40 percent of the credit is refundable (up to $1,000).

Eligibility also differs from the former Hope Credit. A taxpayer who pays qualified tuition and related expenses and whose federal income tax return has a modified adjusted gross income of $80,000 or less ($160,000 or less for joint filers) is eligible for the credit. The credit is reduced ratably if a taxpayer's modified adjusted gross income exceeds those amounts. A taxpayer whose modified adjusted gross income is greater than $90,000 ($180,000 for joint filers) cannot benefit from this credit.

For more information about the American Opportunity Tax Credit, go online to http://www.irs.gov/uac/American-Opportunity-Tax-Credit:-Questions-and-Answers.

Lifetime Learning Credit

The Lifetime Learning Credit is the counterpart of the American Opportunity Credit. The qualifying taxpayer can claim an annual tax credit of up to $2,000—20 percent of the first $10,000 of tuition. The credit is available for net tuition and fees, less grant aid. The total credit available is limited to $2,000 per year per taxpayer (or joint-filing couple). There is no limit on the number of years the lifetime learning credit can be claimed for each student. However, a taxpayer cannot claim both the American Opportunity Credit and Lifetime Learning Credit for the same student in one year. For more information, visit http://www.irs.gov/Individuals/LLC.

TUITION AND FEES TAX DEDUCTION

The Tuition and Fees Tax Deduction could reduce taxable income by as much as $4,000. This deduction is taken as an adjustment to income, which means you can claim this deduction even if you do not itemize deductions on Schedule A of Form 1040. This deduction may benefit taxpayers who do not qualify for either the American Opportunity Credit or Lifetime Learning Credit.

Up to $4,000 may be deducted for tuition and fees required for enrollment or attendance at an eligible postsecondary institution. Personal living and family expenses, including room and board, insurance, medical, and transportation, are not deductible expenses.

The exact amount of the Tuition and Fees Tax Deduction depends on the amount of qualified tuition and related expenses paid for one's self, spouse, or dependents, and your Adjusted Gross Income. Consult the IRS or your tax preparer for more information.

STUDENT LOAN INTEREST TAX DEDUCTION

If you made student loan interest payments, you may be able to reduce your taxable income by up to $2,500. You should check with your lender with regards to the amount of interest you paid if you did not receive an IRS Form 1098-E and your tax preparer or IRS Publication 970 for additional information, which can be found online at http://www.irs.gov/publications/p970/ch04.html.

AMERICORPS

AmeriCorps is a national umbrella group of service programs for students. Participants work in a public or private nonprofit agency and provide service to the community in one of four priority areas: education, human services, the environment, and public safety. For all AmeriCorps programs, members receive a modest living allowance, and some programs provide housing. Individuals may not save much money during their year of service, but most find the living allowance to be adequate to cover their needs. AmeriCorps members who complete a term of service also receive an AmeriCorps Education Award. Many student-loan lenders will postpone the repayment of student loans during service in AmeriCorps, and AmeriCorps will pay the interest that is accrued on qualified student loans for members who complete the service program. Participants can work before, during, or after college and can use the funds to either pay current educational expenses or repay federal student loans. For more information, visit http://www.nationalservice.gov/programs/americorps.

College Financial Aid: Impressing the Financial Aid Counselor

The best way to impress a financial aid counselor is to be prepared and do as much research as you can before your meeting. You want to build a positive relationship with the individuals in the financial aid office as they often are the ones who will ultimately help you receive the most financial aid possible, including scholarships and grants.

Here are some things to know and do:

- Be aware of the school's financial aid application deadline.
- Meet with the financial aid counselor as soon as possible.
- Keep copies of everything that will help complete your application.
- Check with the financial aid office to make sure your file is complete and that everything was filled out correctly.
- Speak with the financial aid officer about any scholarships you receive, whether they are from the school itself or from outside of the school.
- Never be late to an appointment, and call to cancel if you need to do so.

ACTION ITEMS

Be sure to gather and submit any documentation that will provide a truthful claim of your financial situation, and always ask for a confirmation of submission. Don't lie about anything in your financial aid application, and always be open to discussing your situation. Financial aid counselors are here to help.

Be patient. Financial aid decisions can take time. Appeals can typically take more time than usual, as well as the fact that committees usually only meet a couple of times a month to review appeal submissions. Ask your financial aid counselor about an expected date, and if you haven't heard from him/her in a couple of weeks at minimum, call them to follow up.

While you want to be assertive and make sure that your questions are answered to your satisfaction, you also want to be sure you are polite and respectful. Politeness goes a long way. Often financial aid counselors will work with you every year when applying for scholarships, grants, and loans, so you want to be sure you establish a good long-term relationship.

Keep these "DO" tips in mind:

- Do call ahead to make an appointment—otherwise you might be waiting all day to speak with the counselor.
- Do make a list of any questions or concerns you have.
- Do ask what requirements are needed in order to keep getting aid in the future, for example a minimum GPA.
- Do compare your family's expected contribution (EFC) with other schools, and ask the counselor to explain the differences.
- Do ask about employment opportunities on campus.
- Do fill out and submit all applications by the deadline.
- Do ask what changes in your financial situation can affect your award.
- Do ask if outside scholarships will affect your financial aid award.
- Do thank the counselor for helping you.

Remember, financial aid counselors are there to help you. While some may seem rude or be rushed, it doesn't mean that you have to be as well. Patience goes a long way in getting the help you need.

Keep these "DON'T" tips in mind:

- Don't try to compare your award with others as each situation is different. Ask your counselor if you have any questions.
- Don't discuss consumer debt with your counselor. Consumer debt will not be taken into account.
- Don't give up; you can always apply again the following year.
- Don't take out students loans just because you can. Loans HAVE to be repaid, usually with interest. Only take out loans that you absolutely need.
- Don't be ashamed to discuss your personal finances, including bankruptcy, child-support, medical expenses, and anything else that may affect your ability to pay for tuition.

Keep these tips in mind as you are meeting with your financial aid counselor, and always remember that they are there to help you find the best financial aid package as possible.

Inside the Federal Work-Study Program

If you're like millions of other families with college-age youth you may have had that moment. It's the stomach-churning wrinkle in time when you realize that the gap between the amount of money you've saved for your child's college education and the cost of that dream university seems as insurmountable as crossing the ocean on a surfboard. Even as you fill out the Free Application for Federal Student Aid (FAFSA) and your child gets the award letter from the college, the sticker shock can be depressing. But there is glimmer of hope, and it's called the Federal Work-Study Program (FWS).

The federally funded FWS, formerly known as the College Campus Work-Study Program, was a part of the anti-poverty legislation that swept the country in the 1960s. FWS partners with 3,400 institutions in the country to pay students to work on a college or university campus. Looking at the words "work study," may instill fear in some parent's hearts. They may think of nightmarish scenarios where their son or daughter spends so much time guarding the science building that they won't have time for their studies. This isn't necessarily true. There are several aspects to the federally supported work-study program that makes it an attractive option for students looking to lower their college bill.

WORK-STUDY CAN BE A VALUABLE EXPERIENCE

The Federal Work-Study (FWS) Program is a federal student aid program that provides part-time employment while you are enrolled in school to help pay your education expenses. The Federal Work-Study Program emphasizes, whenever possible, employment in civic education and work that is related to your course of study.

If you work on campus, you'll most likely work for your school. If you work off campus, your employer might be a private nonprofit organization or a public agency, and the work performed must be in the public interest.

Colleges and universities like that the FWS is federally subsidized, so they will offer this option as part of a financial aid package first because it saves them money. So send your FASFA as early as possible, especially if you want to beat out the millions of students who seek work-study jobs! Also, don't forget to indicate on your FASFA that you are interested in a work-study job.

In addition, it may be best to choose work-study over outside employment. You may believe that work is work, but when it comes to work-study jobs that sentiment is not true. Work-study jobs are usually better for students because the payment you receive is NOT counted against you when applying for financial aid. This could make a huge difference in how much aid you receive from your chosen institution.

WORK-STUDY JOBS—NOT ALWAYS "BORING"

Not all work-study jobs have to be through educational institutions. The program also funds jobs at a federal, state, or local public agency; a private nonprofit organization; or even a private for-profit organization. Check and see if your school has a partnership with an off-campus workplace. You might be able to find a work-study position in your field of study. This allows you to gain valuable experience and not just collect "man hours" while you pay down your college price tag.

Still, the type of job a student is privy to largely depends upon the intuition's work-study program. Some programs focus on interesting options such as janitorial services, cafeteria work, or even telemarketer. But with a little ingenuity, students can find a work-study assignment that fits their academic and financial need. For example, at Colorado College, a private school in Colorado Springs, work-study students can apply for jobs as diverse as stage manager for theater productions or work off campus at a nonprofit such as the Children's Literacy Center. To ensure you get a work-study position that fits your career goals, it's best to talk to officials at your institution early and often about available work-study options. For example, according to the U.S. Department of Education, a college must use 7 percent of its work-study funds to support students "working in community service jobs, including reading tutors for preschool age or elementary school children, mathematics tutors for students enrolled in elementary school through ninth grade, literacy tutors in a family literacy project performing family literacy activities, or emergency preparedness and response." When you talk to your institution's financial aid office you might mention your experience in any of these areas. This won't guarantee you a "better" work-study job, but it certainly can't hurt.

TAKE ANOTHER LOOK AT WORK-STUDY

With flexible hours, guaranteed pay and the ability to help your institution and community, the work-study option is an attractive way for students to pay for their college education. Do not over look its benefits. Indicate work-study on your FAFSA application, and apply early. Who knows? You could end up as a tennis racquet stringer at Colorado College. For more information about FWS, go to http://www2.ed.gov/programs/fws/index.html.

Analyzing Financial Aid Award Letters

by Richard Woodland

You have just received the financial aid award letters. Now what? This is the time to do a detailed analysis of each college's offer to help you pay for your child's education. Remember, accepting financial aid is a family matter. More often than not, parents need to borrow money to send their dependent children to college. You need to clearly understand the types of aid you and your child are being offered. How much is "free" money in the form of grants and/or scholarships that does not have to be repaid? If your financial aid award package includes loans, what are the terms and conditions for these loans? A good tool to have with you is the federal government's most recent issue of *Funding Your Education* or *Do You Need Money for College? Federal Student Aid at a Glance,* available from the school's financial aid office or at http://www.fsapubs.gov. This publication is very helpful in explaining the federal grant and loan programs that are usually a part of the aid package.

Let's take a minute to explain what is meant by "financial aid award package." A college will offer an aid applicant a combination of aid types, "packaged" in the form of grants and scholarships, loans, and a work-study job, based on the information provided on the FAFSA and/or another application. Many schools use a priority filing date, which guarantees that all applications received by this date will be considered for the full range of institutional aid programs available. Late applicants (by even one day!) often are only awarded the basic aid programs from state and federal sources. *It is important to apply on time.*

EVALUATE EACH LETTER

As each award letter comes in, read it through carefully. The following are some critical points to consider:

- **Does the Cost of Attendance (COA) include all projected costs?** Each award letter should state the school's academic year COA. Tuition, fees, room, board, books, transportation, and personal expenses are what normally make up the COA. Does the award letter itemize all these components? Or does it omit some? This is crucial because this is what you will need to budget for. If you need additional information, be sure to contact the financial aid office. They will be glad to provide you with information or answer any questions you may have about their costs.

- **What is your Expected Family Contribution (EFC)?** Is the school's—not just the federal government's—EFC listed on the award letter? Some schools may require a higher EFC than you expected. Be aware that the EFC may increase or decrease each year depending on the information you provide on the renewal FAFSA or other financial aid application.

- **Is there unmet need?** Does the aid package cover the difference between the COA and the EFC? Not every school can cover your full need. If the aid package does not cover your full need, does the information with the award letter provide you with alternative loan options? If not, contact the financial aid office for more information.

- **Is the scholarship renewable for four years?** If your child is awarded a scholarship based on scholastic achievement or talent, you need to ask these questions: Is there a minimum grade point average he has to maintain? Can he switch majors but keep the scholarship? Does he need to participate in an "honors college" program to maintain the scholarship? If he needs to change to part-time status, will the award amount be prorated, or does he need to maintain full-time status? If it is an athletic or "special talent" scholarship, will he continue to receive the award if for some reason he cannot continue with the specific program? Renewal of scholarship funds is often the biggest misunderstanding between families and colleges. Be sure you clearly understand the terms and conditions of all grants and scholarships.

- **What will the college do to your child's award if she receives outside, noninstitutional scholarships?** Will the award be used to cover unmet need or reduce her student loans? Will the college reduce her institutional grants or scholarships? Or will they reduce her work-study award? (This is a good time to compare each school's policy on this matter.) Remember, your overall aid cannot total more than the COA, and many programs cannot exceed your financial need.

- **What are the interest rates of the loans that are offered?** Did another school offer you more than one loan and why? *Do not* sign the award letter until you understand your loan obligations. Again, *Funding Education Beyond High School: The Guide to Federal Student Aid* can be very helpful with this part of the analysis.

- **Is the school likely to cover the same expenses every year?** In particular, ask if grant or scholarship funds are normally reduced or increased after the freshman year, even if family income and EFC remain the same. Some colleges will *increase* the self-help (loan, job) percentage every year but not necessarily the free money.

- **If work-study was awarded, how many hours a week will your child be expected to work?** If you feel working that many hours will have a negative impact on your child's academic performance, you may want to request that the awarded job funds be changed to a loan. You must ask immediately because funds are limited. Many schools are flexible with these funds early in the process.

- **What happens if (or more likely, when) tuition increases?** Check with the financial aid office to find out what its policy is for renewing an aid package. If, for example, tuition increases by 5 percent each of the next three years and your EFC remains the same, what will happen to your scholarships, grants, and loans?

You can always appeal your award letter if you feel that your needs are not being met, if your family situation has changed, or if you have received a better award from a competitive school. You have the right to ask for a reconsideration of your award. (Do not use the word *negotiate*.) When asking for reconsideration, be sure to provide the aid officer with all relevant information.

COMPARE LETTERS

After you have received and reviewed all the award letters from the schools your child is considering, the next step is to compare them and determine which schools are offering the best aid packages. Following are three sample award letters and a sample spreadsheet that shows you how to analyze and compare each school's awards.

(Note: These award letters are simply for discussion purposes. They should not be considered to be representative award letters with an EFC of $9,550.)

Once you have entered all the information into a spreadsheet of your own and come up with the balances, here are some things to consider for each school:

- **How much is the balance?** Ideally, your balance should be $0, but look to see which school has the lowest balance amount.

- **What part of the aid package comes in the form of grants and scholarships?** It is important to note this because these awards (gift aid) do not have to be paid back.

- **Look at the loans.** Usually, the best financial deal contains more money in scholarships and less in loan dollars. Based on expected freshman-year borrowing, determine the debt burden at each school once your child graduates. You have to multiply the amount of your loan by four or five years, depending on how long it will take for your child to graduate.

UNIVERSITY A
FINANCIAL AID AWARD LETTER
2017-2018

Date: 4/21/17
ID#: 0000000009

Dear Jane Smith,

We are pleased to inform you that you are eligible to receive the financial assistance indictate in the area labled "Your Financial Aid." We estimated your budget based on the following assumptions:

In-state resident and living on campus.

	FALL	SPRING	TOTAL
Tuition and Fees	$3,849	$3,849	$7,698
Room & Board	3,769	3,770	7,539
Books	420	420	840
Transportation	973	974	1,947
Personal expenses	369	369	738
Estimated Coast of Attendance	**$9,380**	**$9,382**	**$18,762**

Your Financial Aid

	FALL	SPRING	TOTAL
Federal Pell Grant	$1,950	$1,950	$3,900
Federal Direct Subsidized Loan	$1,750	$1,750	$3,500
State Grant	432	432	864
Total Financial Aid	**$4,132**	**$4,132**	**$8,264**
Unmet Need	**$5,248**	**$5,250**	**$10,498**

What to Do Next:
- Verify that accurate assumptions have been used to determine your awards.
- Carefully review and follow the instructions on the Data Changes Form.
- To reduce or decline all or part of your loans, you must complete and return the Data Changes Form.
- We will assume you fully accept the awards above unless you submit changes to us immediately.
- Return corrections and required documents promptly.
- Retain this letter for your records.

UNIVERSITY B
FINANCIAL AID AWARD LETTER
2017-2018

Date: 4/21/17
ID#: 0000000009

Dear Jane Smith,

We are pleased to inform you that you are eligible to receive the financial assistance indictate in the area labled "Your Financial Aid." We estimated your budget based on the following assumptions:

Nonresident and living on campus.

	FALL	SPRING	TOTAL
Tuition and Fees	$9,805	$9,085	$18,170
Room & Board	2,835	2,835	5,670
Books	410	410	820
Transportation	875	875	1,750
Personal Expenses	378	377	755
Estimated Coast of Attendance	**$13,583**	**$13,582**	**$27,165**

Your Financial Aid

	FALL	SPRING	TOTAL
Federal Pell Grant	$1,950	$1,950	$3,900
Federal SEOG Grant	225	225	450
Academic Excellence Scholarship	500	500	1,000
Federal Work-Study	1,050	1,050	2,100
Federal Perkins Loan Program	1,250	1,250	2,500
Subsidized Federal Stafford Student Loan	1,750	1,750	3,500
University Student Loan	2,000	2,000	4,000
Total Financial Aid	**$8,725**	**$8,725**	**$17,450**
Unmet Need	**$4,858**	**$4,857**	**$9,715**

What to Do Next:

■ Verify that accurate assumptions have been used to determine your awards.
■ Carefully review and follow the instructions on the Data Changes Form.
■ To reduce or decline all or part of your loans, you must complete and return the Data Changes Form.
■ We will assume you fully accept the awards above unless you submit changes to us immediately.
■ Return corrections and required documents promptly.
■ Retain this letter for your records.

UNIVERSITY C
FINANCIAL AID AWARD LETTER
2017-2018

Date: 4/21/17
ID#: 0000000009

Dear Jane Smith,

We are pleased to inform you that you are eligible to receive the financial assistance indictate in the area labled "Your Financial Aid." We estimated your budget based on the following assumptions:

Living on campus.

	FALL	SPRING	TOTAL
Tuition and Fees	$14,955	$14,955	$29,910
Room & Board	4,194	4,193	8,387
Books	450	450	900
Transportation	350	350	700
Personal Expenses	1,295	1,293	2,588
Estimated Coast of Attendance	**$21,244**	**$21,241**	**$42,485**

Your Financial Aid

	FALL	SPRING	TOTAL
Institutional Grant	$10,805	$10,805	$21,610
Federal Pell Grant	$1,950	$1,950	$3,900
Federal SEOG Grant	2,000	2,000	4,000
Federal Work-Study Program	1,713	1,712	3,425
Total Financial Aid	**$16,468**	**$16,467**	**$32,935**
Unmet Need	**$4,776**	**$4,774**	**$9,550**

What to Do Next:
- Verify that accurate assumptions have been used to determine your awards.
- Carefully review and follow the instructions on the Data Changes Form.
- To reduce or decline all or part of your loans, you must complete and return the Data Changes Form.
- We will assume you fully accept the awards above unless you submit changes to us immediately.
- Return corrections and required documents promptly.
- Retain this letter for your records.

Comparison Grid

	University A (State University)	University B (Nonresident State University)	University C (Private College)
Cost of Attendance	$18,762	$27,165	$42,485
Tuition and Fees	7,698	18,170	29,910
Room & Board	7,539	5,670	8,367
Books	840	820	900
Transportation	1,947	1,750	700
Personal Expenses	738	755	2,558
Grants and Scholarships	4,764	5,350	29,510
Loans	3,500	10,000	0
Work-Study	0	2,00	3,425
Expected Family Contribution	9,550	9,550	9,550
Balance	$948	$165	$0

Some things to notice:
- At all schools, the federal Pell Grant remains the same.
- The loan amounts varied greatly among these schools.
- Even though University C (a private college) has the highest "sticker price," the net cost is less than the state schools.
- University B is a state university, but you are classified as an out-of-state resident (or nonresident). Many Students in this situation find that the higher out-of-state costs combined with lower grant aid make this a costly decision.
- All schools assume that you will be residing in on-campus housing. But if you choose to commute to University A, you would save a substatial amount because you would not have the $7,539 room and board cost.

And remember that the loan amounts will probably increase each year. You also should take into consideration that you will have to borrow even more as the COA increases each year. To determine the best loan deal, consider:
— What are the terms of the loans?
— What are interest rates?
— Do you pay the yearly interest rate during enrollment or is the interest subsidized or paid by the government?
— Is any money due during enrollment or is it deferred until after graduation? Figuring out how much you will owe at each school at graduation will give you a clear picture of what your financial situation will be after graduation.

However, unless cost is your only concern, you shouldn't simply choose the school offering the lowest loan amounts. Many other factors need to be considered, such as academic and social environment. And you should never reject a school based solely on insufficient financial aid. Consult with an aid administrator to discuss possible alternatives.

Finally, if the college that costs the most is still the one your child wants to attend, there are a number of ways to find money to cover the gap between the aid package and your actual cost, including paying more than the EFC figure, increasing student borrowing, working more hours, and taking out a PLUS loan.

Richard Woodland is Vice President of Development for ProEd Solutions. He previously served as Director of Financial Aid at Rutgers University–Camden and as Director of Student Services and Financial Assistance at the Curtis Institute of Music.

The "Non-Offer"—Dealing With a Low Financial Aid Letter

by Ken O'Connor
Chief Impact Officer, Invite Education

When the last of college financial aid award letters are sent out, plenty of congratulations are in order to families that have their choice school lined up with their funding eligibility ready to go.

But there's a less publicized occurrence that's common as well: the disappointment of realizing that the financial aid awards cannot cover enough of the costs of a preferred college. In certain cases, I call it the "Non-Offer," when a family of modest means applies to a school with the hopes of gaining enough funding to make it affordable, and the school responds with limited awards.

GOING TO A STATE SCHOOL THAT IS OUT OF YOUR STATE

It's often discussed how affordable state schools are in comparison to private schools. But this is not the case when a person wants to attend a state school that is out of their state of residence. In an interesting twist of budgetary fate, state schools looking to boost their revenues may admit many students from out of state, charging them the full out-of-state tuition, plus requiring them to live on campus freshman year. For many state schools, pulling students from out of state is a financial win, practically doubling or even tripling the tuition costs but also leaving one less seat for an in-state student who was hoping to attend locally on discounted (in-state) tuition. Receiving an award letter with a $30,000+ shortfall in the first year adds up to a fair warning. Yes, you are invited to join this school—all you need is enough extra money over four years that could buy a 1-BR, mid-market condo.

UNDERSTANDING THE REAL COST OF STUDENT LOANS

Many 18 year olds are excited just to get away from their parents, and going away to college seems to provide the perfect venue until you take a step back and look at the real costs. I used the 1-BR condo example earlier to help illustrate in real terms *cost versus value*.[1]

Cost is an issue only in the absence of Value: What is most valuable to your child at 18?

Without real-world context, it's simply impossible for teenagers to understand the long-term implications of debt. But they do value independence—or at least the perception of it. To get around this, I use examples of property values, mortgage, and rent payments as the closest comparison to large student loan debt (!).

So, go ahead and run the numbers with a loan calculator. No fancy math required. $120k @ 6% would require payments of around $1,332 per month over ten years and cost about $40,000 in interest. Now look at the student's major. Question: Does this seem at all reasonable for an undergraduate degree from this particular institution? It's tough to justify, but once it's realized that the amount of debt used for their education would be enough to purchase real estate, then the young student at least has some context of their college costs. It's up to them to respond by evaluating this school option accordingly, while parents can more clearly see what they would be cosigning for.

RE-CHART THE COURSE

There's no time for optimism or pessimism when making the final school choice. It's time for *realism* in the decision-making process, given the short time ahead.

Here are three things to consider:

1. **Appeal for additional funding—if there is a legitimate reason to do so.** Real financial aid appeals are necessary due to specific circumstances including, but not limited to, a parent being laid-off, divorce, or a major medical issue and its ensuing expenses. In these types of appeals, documentation is required to prove that the financial need of the family has increased greatly due to such major life circumstances. If you are asking the school for more funding without one of these documentable circumstances, it will not go very far. If your student is looking at a $20,000–$30,000 gap per year without the cash to pay for it, you cannot expect a financial aid office to fund the difference.

2. **Eliminate the options that are not financially feasible.** It's time to say no and entertain the process of elimination. This is tough as some students grow quite attached to a preferred school choice, but they are going to have to get over it when it's simply unaffordable. Financial discipline is in short supply, but it's needed now more than ever during these uneasy economic times.

3. **Focus on your next simple step forward.** Take the pragmatic approach to affordability and value in higher education. Attend a school close by, and commute from home. Community college is still the go-to option to complete a substantial amount of required college credits while preparing to transfer to a four-year degree institution elsewhere.

What Long-Term Planners Learn From This

The last thing you want is to be stuck between a rock and a hard place, but that's exactly where most middle-income families are when financial aid award letters finally arrive. Avoid this by having these key areas well understood.

- Aptitude: Planning well for college also means honestly accounting for the student's aptitude. Early testing, excellent grades, and incredible mental acuity far above the average can be spotted rather quickly, even before starting high school. There will always be winners on the high end of the intelligence spectrum who have everything to gain from the college admissions process. This is a minority of students, so if your child is not on this level, it's not anyone's fault. It's better to be honest about your child's capabilities than to dream that somehow they will magically receive a perfect on the SAT® or ACT®. In such cases, expect college to remain an expense covered mainly by income, savings, student loans, and perhaps some need-based aid. If it turns out your child is able to earn a scholarship, it's an additional blessing, but good planners know well in advance the odds of qualifying and make up the difference by locating and applying for as many opportunities as they can find.

- Savings: It's cheaper to save than to borrow.[2] Planners remember this every month they contribute to their child's 529 plan by Kindergarten—or perhaps much earlier. They already know college is expensive, and if they, as a parent are already experienced with student loan debt, they may be even more motivated to save so their child can avoid it. College savings are up this past year,[3] with increases in assets and new accounts being opened. This is a good sign, as truly the entire higher education system is dealing with a flux of funding, where state support has dwindled, and the Parent Plus loan[4] may be subject to change in credit-approval criteria in the future. Without any savings, college options are just further limited to scholarship and financial aid eligibility that may or may not be robust when the child finally graduates high school.

REFERENCES

1. *http://www.theatlantic.com/education/archive/2015/10/the-allure-of-the-out-of-state-student/410656/*

2. *https://b2b.inviteeducation.com/2016/04/05/top-5-reasons-for-529/*

3. *http://time.com/money/4259055/saving-more-for-college-529-plan/*

4. *http://www.studentloanborrowerassistance.org/new-rules-plus-loan-credit-checks/*

Ken O'Connor has served parents and students for over fifteen years with high-quality knowledge and information about the college financing process. Ken developed his expertise as a financial aid officer, working face-to-face with families creating college payment strategies. At Invite Education, he continues to help thousands of families make smart college choices through the use of educational planning technology, blending his practical wisdom with in-depth knowledge of the financial aid process. He holds a B.S. an MBA in Finance from Fairleigh Dickinson University in New Jersey.

Parents' and Students' Common Questions Answered

Q *Are a student's chances of being admitted to a college reduced if the student applies for financial aid?*

A Generally no. Nearly all colleges have a policy of "need-blind" admissions, which means that a student's financial need is not taken into account in the admission decision. There are a few selective colleges, however, that do consider ability to pay before deciding whether or not to admit a student. Some colleges will mention this in their literature; others may not. The best advice is to apply for financial aid if the student needs assistance to attend college.

Q *Are parents penalized for saving money for college?*

A No. As a matter of fact, families that have made a concerted effort to save money for college are in a much better position than those that have not. For example, a student from a family that has saved money may not have to borrow as much. Furthermore, the "taxing rate" on savings is quite low—only about 5 percent of the parents' assets are assessed and neither the home equity nor retirement savings are included. For example, a single 40-year-old parent who saved $40,000 for college expenses will have about $1,900 counted as part of the parental contribution. Two parents, if the older one is 40 years old (a parent's age factors into the formulation), would have about $300 counted. (Note: The "taxing rate" for student assets is much higher—20 percent—compared to 5 percent for parents.)

Q *How does the financial aid system work in cases of divorce or separation? How are stepparents treated?*

A In cases of divorce or separation, the financial aid application(s) should be completed by the parent with whom the student lived for the longest period of time in the past twelve months (custodial parent). If the custodial parent has remarried, the stepparent is considered a family member and must complete the application along with the biological parent. If your family has any special circumstances, you should discuss these directly with the financial aid office. (Note: Colleges that award their own aid may ask the noncustodial biological parent to complete a separate aid application and a contribution will be calculated.)

Q *When are students considered independent of parental support in applying for financial aid?*

A The student must be at least 24 years of age in order to be considered independent. If younger than 24, the student must be married, be a graduate or professional student, have legal dependents other than a spouse, be an orphan or ward of the court, or be a veteran of the armed forces or on active military duty. However, in very unusual situations, students who can clearly document estrangement from their parents can appeal to the financial aid office for additional consideration.

Q *What can a family do if a job loss occurs?*

A Financial aid eligibility is based on the previous year's income. Currently, the family's 2016 income would be reported to determine eligibility for the 2017–18 academic year. It is possible that that income tax return may not reflect the family's current financial situation, due to a job loss or other hardship. So, families should discuss the situation directly with the financial aid office and be prepared to provide appropriate documentation.

Q *When my daughter first went to college, we applied for financial aid and were denied because our Expected Family Contribution was too high. Now, my son is a high school senior, and we will soon have two in college. Will we get the same results?*

A The results will definitely be different. Both your son and your daughter should apply. As described earlier, need-based financial aid is based on your Expected Family Contribution, or EFC. When you have two children in college, this amount is divided in half for each child.

Q *I've heard about the "middle-income squeeze" in regard to financial aid. What is it?*

A The so-called "middle-income squeeze" is the idea that low-income families qualify for aid, high-income families have adequate resources to pay for education, and those in the middle are not eligible for aid but do not have the ability to pay full college costs. There is no provision in the Federal Methodology that treats middle-income students differently than others (such as an income cutoff for eligibility). The Expected Family Contribution rises proportionately as income and assets increase. If a middle-income family does not qualify for aid, it is because the need analysis formula yields a contribution that exceeds college costs. But keep in mind that if a $65,000-income family does not qualify for grant aid at a public university with a $16,000 cost, the same family will likely be eligible for aid at a private college with a cost of $25,000 or more. Also, there are loan programs available to parents and students that are not based on need. Middle-income families should realize, however, that many of the grant programs funded by federal and state governments are directed at lower-income families. It is therefore likely that a larger share of an aid package for a middle-income student will consist of loans rather than grants.

Q *Given our financial condition, my daughter will be receiving financial aid. We will help out as much as we can, and, in fact, we ourselves will be borrowing. But I am concerned that she will have to take on a lot of loans in order to go to the college of her choice. Does she have any options?*

A She does. If offered a loan, she can decline all or part of it. One option is for her to ask in the financial aid office to have some of the loan changed to a work-study job. If this is not possible, she can find her own part-time work. Often there is an employment office on campus that can help her locate a job. In most cases, the more she works, the less she has to borrow. It is important to remember that the education loans offered to students have very attractive terms and conditions, with flexible repayment options. Students should look upon these loans as a long-term investment that will reap significant rewards.

Q *What are some easy ways to improve my chances of receiving aid?*

A When filling out your scholarship or financial aid application, it's important to remember that the smallest mistake could hurt your chances for landing free money, or even worse, it could disqualify you completely from an awards contest. Grants and scholarships are highly competitive, so it's a good idea to make a list of what's needed and make sure you have everything before submitting your application. If you are submitting an essay, have another pair of eyes look at it for any spelling and grammar errors. Keep a file on everything you're applying for so that you don't miss any elements of an application. Make sure you're using reputable sites to conduct your free scholarship searches. If you have to pay to apply for an award or look for scholarships, chances are you're being scammed. In a nutshell, the best advice is to follow all directions, and make sure that you meet all deadlines.

In addition, when filling out the FAFSA®, it's important to pay close attention to the details, since any errors may delay the application process. These days, it's preferable to fill out the FAFSA® online, since mailed forms can take weeks to process. If you're confused or concerned about something on the application, contact the Federal Student Aid Information Center at 1-800-4FED-AID; questions can also be asked through the FAFSA® Website. Your college's financial aid office should also be able to assist you. The FAFSA® is available this year starting October 1, and it's essential that you don't miss the deadline to apply. The sooner you apply, the sooner you'll know the kind of funding package you are likely to receive, and this will help you determine if you need to apply for any additional aid.

Q *Is it possible to change your financial aid package?*

A Yes. Most colleges have an appeal process. A request to change a need-based loan to a work-study job is usually approved if funds are available. A request to consider special financial circumstances may also be granted. At most colleges, a request for more grant money is rarely approved unless it is based on a change in the information reported. Applicants should speak with the financial aid office if they have concerns about their financial package. Some colleges may even respond to a competitive appeal, that is, a request to match another college's offer.

Q *The cost of attending college seems to be going up so much faster than the Consumer Price Index. Why is that, and how can I plan for my child's four years?*

A The cost of higher education cannot be compared to the Consumer Price Index (CPI). The CPI does not take into account most of the costs faced by colleges. For example, the dollars that universities spend on grants and scholarships have risen rapidly. Many universities have increased enrollment of students from less affluent families, further increasing the need for institutional financial aid. Colleges are expected to be on the cutting edge of technology, not only in research but also in the classroom and in the library. Many colleges have deferred needed maintenance and repairs that can now no longer be put off. In addition, there is market pressure to provide many expensive lifestyle amenities that were not expected ten years ago. In general, you can expect that college costs will rise at least 2 to 3 percent faster than inflation.

Q *I'm struggling with the idea that all students should apply to the college of their choice, regardless of cost, because financial aid will level the playing field. I feel I will be penalized because I have saved for college. My son has been required to save half of his allowance since age six for his college education. Will that count against him when he applies for financial aid? It's difficult to explain to him that his college choices may be limited because of the responsible choices and sacrifices we have made as a family. What can we do to make the most of our situation?*

A In general, it is always better to have planned ahead for college by saving. Families that have put away sufficient funds to pay for college will quickly realize that they have made the burden easier for themselves and their children. In today's college financing world, schools assume that paying for the cost of attendance is a ten-year commitment. So by saving when your child is young, you reap significant advantages from compound interest on the assets and reduce the need to borrow as much while in school. This should reduce the number of years after college that you will be burdened with loans. Families should spend the student's assets first, since the financial aid formulas count these more heavily than parental assets. Then, after the first year, you can explain to the college how you spent these assets, and why you might now need assistance. When looking at parental information, the income of the family is by far the most important component. Contrary to popular belief, parental assets play a minor role in the calculation of need. With this strategy, you have done the right thing, and in the long run, it should prove to be a wise financial plan.

Picking the right college also involves other factors. Students should select the colleges to which they are going to apply in two ways. First, and most important, is to look at colleges that meet your son's academic and lifestyle interests. Most experts will tell him to pick a few "reach" schools (i.e., schools where he is not sure he has the grades and scores required) and at least one or two academically "safe" schools. He should also select one or two financially "safe" schools that you are sure you can afford with either moderate or little financial aid. Most students do not get into all of their first-choice schools, and not everyone can afford the schools to which they are admitted. By working closely with the guidance office in high school and the admissions and financial aid offices at the college, you can maximize your options.

Q *My son was awarded a $2,500 scholarship. This can be split and used for two years. When filling out the FAFSA®, do we have to claim the full amount, or just the $1,250 he plans to use the first year?*

A Congratulations to your son on the scholarship. Nowhere on the FAFSA® should you report this scholarship. It is not considered income or an asset. However, once you choose a school to attend, you must notify the financial aid office for its advice on how to take the funds. But remember, do NOT report it on the FAFSA®.

Q *I will be receiving a scholarship from my local high school. How will this scholarship be treated in my financial aid award?*

A Federal student aid regulations specify that all forms of aid must be included within the defined level of need. This means that additional aid, such as outside scholarships, must be combined with any need-based aid you receive; it may not be kept separate and used to reduce your family's contribution. If the college has not filled 100 percent of your need, it will usually allow outside scholarships to close the gap. Once your total need has been met, the college must reduce other aid and replace it with the outside award. Most colleges will allow you to use some, if not all, of an outside scholarship to replace self-help aid (loans and Federal Work-Study Program awards) rather than grant aid.

Q *Is there enough aid available to make it worthwhile for me to consider colleges that are more expensive than I can afford?*

A Definitely. More than $100 billion in aid is awarded to undergraduates every year. With more than half of all enrolled students qualifying for some type of assistance, this totals more than $5,500 per student. You should view financial aid as a large, national system of tuition discounts, some given according to a student's ability and talent, others based on what a student's family can afford to pay. If you qualify for need-based financial aid, you will essentially pay only your calculated family contribution, regardless of the cost of the college. You will not pay the "sticker price" (the cost of attendance listed in the college catalog) but a lower rate that is reduced by the amount of aid you receive. No college should be ruled out until after financial aid is considered. In addition, when deciding which college to attend, consider that the short-term cost of a college education is only one criterion. If the college meets your educational needs and you are convinced it can launch you on an exciting career, a significant up-front investment may turn out to be a bargain over the long run.

Q *If I don't qualify for need-based aid, what options are available?*

A You should try to put together your own aid package to help reduce your parents' share. There are three sources to look into. First, search for merit scholarships. Second, seek employment, during both the summer and the academic year. The student employment office should be able to help you find a campus job. Third, look into borrowing. Even if you don't qualify for the need-based loan programs, the unsubsidized Federal Direct Loan is available to all students. The terms and conditions are the same as the subsidized loan programs except that interest accrues while you are in college.

After you have contributed what you can through scholarships, employment, and loans, your parents will be faced with their share of the college bill. Many colleges have monthly payment plans that allow families to spread their payments over the academic year. If these monthly payments turn out to be more than your parents can afford, they can take out a parent loan. By borrowing from the college itself, from a commercial agency or lender, or through PLUS, your parents can extend the payments over a ten-year period or longer. Borrowing reduces the monthly obligation to its lowest level, but the total amount paid will be the highest due to principal and interest payments. Before making a decision on where to borrow parental loan funds, be sure to first check with the financial aid office to determine what is the best source of alternative funds.

Q *After applying to college and receiving a financial award letter, am I able to back out of attending if I can't afford it?*

A Of course! This actually happens quite often. If you end up not being able to afford the college you applied to, don't worry. The first step would be to contact the financial aid office just to make sure the award is accurate and there aren't any other ways to cover the costs of attendance, for example a scholarship and/or grant. You never know what may have been missed in the initial application.

Second, if there aren't any other funds that can be awarded, send the admissions office an e-mail letting them know you won't be able to attend, thanking them for their time. They will greatly appreciate your e-mail, and it will help to stay on good terms with the school if you decide to apply again. Never burn bridges!

How to Use This Guide

QUICK-REFERENCE CHART

The amount of aid available at colleges can vary greatly. "College Costs At-a-Glance" lists the percent of freshmen who applied for and received need-based gift aid and the percent of those whose need was fully met. Also listed are the average freshman financial aid package, the average cost after aid, and the average indebtedness upon graduation.

PROFILES OF COLLEGE FINANCIAL AID PROGRAMS

After the federal government, colleges provide the largest amount of financial aid to students. In addition, they control most of the money channeled to students from the federal government. The amount and makeup of your financial aid package will depend on the institution's particular circumstances and its decisions concerning your application. The main section of this book shows you the pattern and extent of each college's current awards. The profiles present detailed factual and statistical data for each school in a uniform format to enable easy, quick references and comparisons. Items that could not be collected in time for publication for specific institutions do not appear in those institutions' profiles. Colleges that supplied no data are listed by name and address only so that you do not overlook them in your search for colleges.

There is much anecdotal evidence that students and their families fail to apply for financial aid under the misconception that student aid goes only to poor families. Financial need in the context of college expenses is not the same as being needy in the broad social context. Middle-class families typically qualify for need-based financial aid; at expensive schools, even upper-middle income families can qualify for need-based financial aid. Peterson's encourages you to apply for financial aid whether or not you think that you will qualify.

To help you understand the definition and significance of each item, the following outline of the profile format explains what is covered in each section. The term college or colleges is frequently used throughout to refer to any institution of higher education, regardless of its official definition.

The College

The name of the college is the official name as it appears on the institution's charter. The city and state listed are the official location of the school. The subhead line shows tuition and required fees, as they were charged to the majority of full-time undergraduate students in the 2016–17 academic year. Any exceptions to the 2016–17 academic year are so noted. For a public institution, the tuition and fees shown are for state residents, and this is noted. If a college's annual expenses are expressed as a comprehensive fee (including full-time tuition, mandatory fees, and college room and board), this is noted, as are any unusual definitions, such as tuition only. The average

undergraduate aid package is the average total package of grant, loan, and work-study aid that was awarded to meet the officially defined financial need of full-time undergraduates enrolled in fall 2016 (or fall 2015) who applied for financial aid, were determined to have need, and then actually received financial aid. This information appears in more detail in each profile.

About the Institution

This paragraph gives the reader a brief introduction to a college. It contains the following elements:

Institutional Control

Private institutions are designated as *independent* (nonprofit), *independent/religious* (sponsored by or affiliated with a religious group or having a nondenominational or interdenominational religious orientation), or *proprietary* (profit-making). Public institutions are designated by their primary source of support, such as *federal, state, commonwealth* (Puerto Rico), *territory* (U.S. territories), *county, district* (an administrative unit of public education, often having boundaries different from those of units of local government), *state-and locally-supported* ("locally" refers to county, district, or city), *state-supported* (funded by the state), or *state-related* (funded primarily by the state but administered autonomously).

Type of Student Body

The categories are *men* (100 percent of student body), *coed-primarily men, women* (100 percent of student body), *coed-primarily women,* and *coed.* A few schools are designated as *undergraduate: women only, graduate: coed* or *undergraduate: men only, graduate: coed.*

Degrees Awarded

Associate, bachelor's (baccalaureate), *master's, doctoral* (doctorate), and *first professional* (in such fields as law and medicine). There are no institutions in this book that award the associate degree only. Many award the bachelor's as the highest degree.

Number of Undergraduate Majors

This shows the number of academic fields in which the institution offers associate and/or bachelor's degrees. The purpose of this is to give you an indication of the range of subjects available.

Enrollment

These figures are based on the actual number of full-time and part-time students enrolled in degree programs as of fall 2016 (or 2015 if the 2016 figure was not available). In most instances, they are designated as *total enrollment* (for the specific college or university) and *freshmen.* If the institution is a university and its total enrollment figure includes graduate students, a separate figure for *undergraduates* may be provided. If the profiled institution is a subunit of a university, the figures may be designated *total university enrollment* for the entire university and *total unit enrollment* for the specific subunit.

Methodology Used for Determining Need

Private colleges usually have larger financial aid programs, but public colleges usually have lower sticker prices, especially for in-state or local students. At a public college, your financial need will be less, and you will receive a smaller financial aid package. This note on whether a college uses federal (FAFSA®) or institutional methodology (usually CSS/Financial Aid PRO-FILE®) will let you know whether you will have to complete one or two kinds of financial aid application forms. Federal Methodology is the needs-analysis formula used by the U.S. Department of Education to determine the Expected Family Contribution (EFC), which, when subtracted from the cost of attendance at an institution, determines the financial need of a student. There is no relative advantage or disadvantage to using one methodology over the other.

Undergraduate Expenses

If provided by the institution, the one-time application fee is listed. Costs are given for the 2017–18 academic year or for the 2016–17 academic year if 2017–18 figures were not yet available. (Peterson's collects information for freshmen specifically.) Annual expenses may be expressed as a comprehensive fee (including full-time tuition, mandatory fees, and college room and board) or may be given as separate figures for full-time tuition, fees, room and board, or room only. For public institutions where tuition differs according to state residence, separate figures are given for area or state residents and for nonresidents. Part-time tuition is expressed in terms of a per-unit rate (per credit, per semester hour, etc.), as specified by the institution.

The tuition structure at some institutions is complex. Freshmen and sophomores may be charged a different rate from that charged juniors and seniors, a professional or vocational division may have a different fee structure from the liberal arts division of the same institution, or part-time tuition may be prorated on a sliding scale according to the number of credit hours taken. Tuition and fees may vary according to academic program, campus/location, class time (day, evening, weekend), course/credit load, course level, degree level, reciprocity agreements, and student level. If tuition and fees differ for international students, the rate charged is listed.

Room and board charges are reported as a double occupancy and nineteen meals per week plan or the equivalent and may vary according to board plan selected, campus/location, gender, type of housing facility, or student level. If no college-owned or -operated housing facilities are offered, the phrase *college housing not available* will appear.

If a college offers a *guaranteed tuition* plan, it promises that the tuition rate of an entering student will not increase for the entire term of enrollment, from entrance to graduation. Other payment plans might include *tuition prepayment*, which allows an entering student to lock in the current tuition rate for the entire term of enrollment by paying the full amount in advance rather than year by year, and *installment* and *deferred*

payment plans, which allow students to delay the payment of the full tuition.

Guaranteed tuition and tuition prepayment help you to plan the total cost of education and can save you from the financial distress sometimes caused by tuition hikes. Colleges that offer such plans may also help you to arrange financing, which in the long run can cost less than the total of four years of increasing tuition rates. Deferred payment or installment payments may better fit your personal financial situation, especially if you do not qualify for financial aid and, due to other financial commitments, find that obtaining the entire amount due is burdensome. Carefully investigate these plans, however, to see what premium you may pay at the end to allow you to defer immediate payment.

Freshman Financial Aid

Usually, these are actual figures for the 2015–16 term, beginning in fall 2015; figures may also be estimated for the 2016–17 term. The particular term for which these data apply is indicated. The figures are for degree-seeking full-time freshman students. The first figure is the number of freshmen who applied for any kind of financial aid. The next figure is the percentage of those freshmen financial aid applicants who were determined to have financial need—that is, through the formal needs-assessment process, had a calculated expected family contribution that was less than the total college cost. The next figure is the percentage of this group of eligible freshmen who received any financial aid. The next figure is the percentage of this preceding group of eligible aid recipients whose need was fully met by financial aid. The *Average percent of need met* is the average percentage of financial need met for freshmen who received any need-based aid. The *Average financial aid package* is the average dollar amount awarded (need-based or non-need-based) to freshmen who applied for aid, were deemed eligible, and received any aid; awards used to reduce the expected family contribution are excluded from this average. The final line in most profiles is the percentage of freshmen who had no financial need but who received non-need-based aid other than athletic scholarships or special-group tuition benefits.

What do these data mean to you? If financial aid is important in your comparison of colleges, the relative percentage of students who received any aid, whose need was fully met, and the average percentage of need met have the most weight. These figures reflect the relative abundance of student aid available to the average eligible applicant. The average dollar amount of the aid package has real meaning, but only in relation to the college's expense; you will be especially interested in the difference between this figure and the costs figure, which is what the average student (in any given statistical group, there actually may be no average individual) will have to pay. Of course, if the financial aid package is largely loans rather than grants, you will have to pay this amount eventually. Relative differences in the figures of the number of students who apply for aid and who are deemed eligible can hinge on any number of factors: the relative sticker price of the college, the relative level of wealth of the students' families, the proportion of only children in college and students with siblings in college (families with two or more children in college are more likely to apply for aid and be considered eligible), or the relative sophistication in financial aid matters (or quality of college counseling they may have received) of the students and their families. While these may be interesting, they will not mean too much to most students and families. If you are among the unlucky (or, perhaps, lucky) families who do not qualify for need-based financial aid, the final sentence of this paragraph in the profile will be of interest because it reveals the relative policies that the college has in distributing merit-based aid to students who cannot demonstrate need.

Undergraduate Financial Aid

This is the parallel paragraph to the Freshman Financial Aid paragraph. The same definitions apply, except that the group being considered is degree-seeking full-time undergraduate students (including freshmen).

There are cases of students who chose a particular college because they received a really generous financial aid package in their freshman year and then had to scramble to pay the tuition bill in their later years. If a financial aid package is a key factor in the decision to attend a particular college, you want to be certain that the package offered to all undergraduates is not too far from that offered to freshmen. The key figures are those for the percentage of students who received any aid, the percentage of financial aid recipients whose need was fully met, the average percentage of need met, and the dollar figure of the average financial aid package. Generally, colleges assume that after the freshman year, students develop study habits and time-management skills that will allow them to take on part-time and summer employment without hurting their academic performance. So, the proportion of self-help aid (work-study and student loans) in the financial aid package tends to increase after the freshman year. This pattern, which is true of most colleges, can be verified in the freshman-undergraduate figures in the paragraph on Gift Aid (Need-Based).

Gift Aid (Need-Based)

Total amount is the total dollar figure in 2016–17 (estimated) or 2015–16 (actual) of need-based scholarships and grant (gift) aid awarded to degree-seeking full-time and part-time students that was used to meet financial need. The percentages of this aid from federal, state, institutional (college or university), and external (e.g., foundations, civic organizations, etc.) sources are shown. *Receiving aid* shows the percentages (and number, in parentheses) of freshmen and of all undergraduates who applied for aid, were considered eligible, and received any need-based gift aid. *Average award* is the average dollar amount of awards to freshmen and all undergraduates who applied for aid, were considered eligible, and received any need-based gift aid. *Scholarships, grants, and awards* cites major categories of need-based gift aid provided by the college; these include Federal Pell Grants, Federal Supplemental Educational Opportunity Grants (FSEOG), state scholarships, private scholarships, college/university gift aid from institutional funds,

United Negro College Fund aid, Federal Nursing Scholarships, and others.

Scholarships and grants are gifts awarded to students that do not need to be repaid. These are preferable to loans, which have to be repaid, or work-study wages, which may take time away from studies and personal pursuits. The total amount of need-based gift aid has to be placed into the context of the total number of undergraduate students (shown in the About the Institution paragraph) and the relative expense of the institution. Filing the FAFSA® automatically puts you in line to receive any available federal grants for which you may qualify. However, if the college being considered has a higher than usual proportion of gift aid coming from state, institutional, or external sources, be sure to check with the financial aid office to find out what these sources may be and how to apply for them. For almost all colleges, the percentage of freshmen receiving need-based gift aid will be higher than the percentage of all undergraduates receiving need-based gift aid. However, if you are dependent on need-based gift aid and the particular college under consideration shows a sharper drop from the freshman to undergraduate years than other colleges of a similar type, you might want to think about how this change will affect your ability to pay for later years at this college.

Gift Aid (Non-Need-Based)

Total amount is the total dollar figure in 2016–17 (estimated) or 2015–16 (actual) of non-need-based scholarships and grant (gift) aid awarded to degree-seeking full-time and part-time students. Non-need-based aid that was used to meet financial need is not included in this total. The percentages of this aid from federal, state, institutional (college or university), and external (e.g., National Merit Scholarships, civic, religious, fraternal organizations, etc.) sources are shown. *Receiving aid* shows the percentages (and number, in parentheses) of freshmen and of all undergraduates who were determined to have need and received non-need-based gift aid. *Average award* is the average dollar amount of awards to freshmen and all undergraduates determined to have no need but received non-need-based awards. *Scholarships, grants, and awards by category* cites the major categories in which non-need-based awards are available and the number of awards made in that category (in parentheses, the total dollar value of these awards). The categories listed are *Academic interests/achievement, Creative arts/ performance, Special achievements/activities,* and *Special characteristics. Tuition waivers* indicate special categories of students (minority students, children of alumni, college employees or children of employees, adult students, and senior citizens) who may qualify for a full or partial waiver of tuition. *ROTC* indicates Army, Naval, and Air Force ROTC programs that are offered on campus; a program offered by arrangement on another campus is indicated by the word *cooperative.*

This section covers college-administered scholarships awarded to undergraduates on the basis of merit or personal attributes without regard to need. If you do not qualify for financial aid but nevertheless lack the resources to pay for college, non-need-based awards will be of special interest to you. Some personal characteristics are completely beyond an individual's control, and talents and achievements take a number of years to develop or attain. However, certain criteria for these awards, such as religious involvement, community service, and special academic interests can be attained in a relatively brief period of time. ROTC programs offer such benefits as tuition, the cost of textbooks, and living allowances. In return, you must fulfill a service obligation after graduating from college. Because they can be a significant help in paying for college, these programs have become quite competitive. Certain subject areas, such as nursing, health care, or the technical fields, are in stronger demand than others. Among the obligations to consider about ROTC are that you must spend a regular portion of your available time in military training programs and that ROTC entails a multiyear commitment after your graduation to serve as an officer in the armed services branch sponsoring the program.

Loans

The figures here represent loans that are part of the financial aid award package. *Student loans* represents the total dollar amount of loans from all sources to full-time and part-time degree-seeking undergraduates or their parents. *Average need-based loan* represents the percentage of these loans that goes to meet financial need, and the percentage that goes to pay the non-need portion (the expected family contribution) are indicated. The percentage of a past graduating class who borrowed through any loan program (except parent loans) while enrolled at the college is shown, as is the average dollar figure per-borrower of cumulative undergraduate indebtedness (this does not include loans from other institutions). *Parent loans* shows the total amount borrowed through parent loan programs as well as the percentages that were applied to the need-based and non-needbased portions of financial need. *Programs* indicates the major loan programs available to undergraduates. These include Direct Student Loans (subsidized and unsubsidized and PLUS), Perkins Loans, Federal Nursing Loans, state loans, college/university loans, and other types.

Note: As a result of the Health Care and Education Reconciliation Act, as of July 1, 2010, federal student loans are no longer made by private lenders under the Federal Family Education Loan (FFEL) Program. Instead, all new federal student loans come directly from the U.S. Department of Education under the Direct Loan Program. Any FFEL loans noted in this section of an institution's profile are no longer available.

Loans are forms of aid that must be repaid with interest. Most people will borrow money to pay college costs. The loans available through financial aid programs are offered at very favorable interest rates. In comparing colleges, the dollar amount of total indebtedness is a factor to be considered. Typically, this amount would increase proportionate to the tuition. However, if it does not, this could mean that the college provides relatively generous grant or work-study aid rather than loans in its financial aid package.

Work-Study

The total dollar amounts, number, and average dollar amount of *Federal work-study* (FWS) jobs appear first. The total dollar figure of *State or other work-study/employment*, if available, is shown, as is the percentage of those dollars that go to meet financial need. The number of part-time jobs available on campus to undergraduates, other than work-study, is shown last.

FWS is a federally funded program that enables students with demonstrated need to earn money by working on or off campus, usually in a nonprofit organization. FWS jobs are a special category of jobs that are open to students only through the financial aid office. Other kinds of part-time jobs are routinely available at most colleges and may vary widely. In comparing colleges, you may find characteristic differences in how the "self-help" amounts (loans and work-study) are apportioned.

Athletic Awards

The total dollar amount of athletic scholarships given by the college to undergraduate students, including percentages that are need-based and non-need-based, is indicated.

Applying for Financial Aid

Required financial aid forms include the FAFSA® (Free Application for Federal Student Aid), the institution's own form, CSS/Financial Aid PROFILE, a state aid form, a noncustodial (divorced/separated) parent's statement, a business/farm supplement, and others. The college's financial aid application deadline is noted as the *Financial aid deadline* and is shown in one of three ways: as a specific date if it is an absolute deadline; noted as *continuous*, which means processing goes on without a deadline or until all available aid has been awarded; or as a date with the note *(priority)*, meaning that you are encouraged to apply before that date in order to have the best chance of obtaining aid. *Notification date* is listed as either a specific date or *continuous*. The date by which a reply to the college with the decision to accept or decline its financial aid package is listed as either a specific date or as a number of weeks from the date of notification.

Be prepared to check early with the colleges as to exactly which forms will be required. All colleges require the FAFSA® for students applying for federal aid. In most cases, colleges have a limited amount of funds set aside to use as financial aid. It is possible that the first eligible students will get a larger share of what is available.

Contact

The name, title, address, telephone and fax numbers, and e-mail address of the person to contact for further information (student financial aid contact) are given at the end of the profile. You should feel free to write or call for any materials you need or if you have questions.

APPENDIX

This section lists nearly 300 state-specific grants and loans. Award amounts, number of awards, eligibility requirements, application requirements, and deadlines are given for all programs.

INDEXES

Six indexes in the back of the book allow you to search for particular award programs based on the following criteria:

Non-Need Scholarships for Undergraduates

This index lists the colleges that report that they offer scholarships based on academic interests, abilities, achievements, or personal characteristics other than financial need. Specific categories appear in alphabetical order under the following broad groups:

- Academic Interests/Achievements
- Creative Arts/Performance
- Special Achievements/Activities
- Special Characteristics

See the index for specific categories in each group.

Athletic Grants for Undergraduates

This index lists the colleges that report offering scholarships on the basis of athletic abilities.

Co-op Programs

This index lists colleges that report offering cooperative education programs. These are formal arrangements with off-campus employers that are designed to allow students to combine study and work, often in a position related to the student's field of study. Salaries typically are set at regular marketplace levels, and academic credit is often given.

ROTC Programs

This index lists colleges that offer Reserve Officers' Training Corps programs. The index is arranged by the branch of service that sponsors the program.

Tuition Waivers

This index lists colleges that report offering full or partial tuition waivers for certain categories of students. A majority of colleges offer tuition waivers to employees or children of employees.

Because this benefit is so common and the affected employees usually are aware of it, no separate index of schools offering this option is provided. However, this information is included in the individual college profiles.

Tuition Payment Alternatives

This index lists colleges that report offering tuition payment alternatives. These payment alternatives include deferred payment plans, guaranteed tuition plans, installment payment plans, and prepayment plans.

DATA COLLECTION PROCEDURES

The data contained in the college chart, profiles, and indexes were collected in winter and spring 2017 through Peterson's *Annual Survey of Undergraduate Financial Aid* and *Peterson's Annual Survey of Undergraduate Institutions*. Questionnaires were sent to the more than 4,400 institutions of higher education that are accredited in the United States and U.S. territories and offer full four- or five-year baccalaureate degrees via full-time on-campus programs of study. Officials at the colleges—usually financial aid or admission officers but sometimes registrars or institutional research staff members—completed and returned the forms. Peterson's has every reason to believe that the data presented in this book are accurate. However, students should always confirm costs and other facts with a specific school at the time of application, since colleges can and do change policies and fees whenever necessary.

The state aid data presented in *Peterson's How to Get Money for College* was submitted by state officials (usually the director of the state scholarship commission) to Peterson's in the spring of 2017. Because regulations for any government-sponsored program may be changed at any time, you should request written descriptive materials from the office administering a program in which you are interested.

CRITERIA FOR INCLUSION IN THIS BOOK

To be included in this guide, an institution must have full accreditation or be a candidate for accreditation (preaccreditation) status by an institutional or specialized accrediting body recognized by the U.S. Department of Education or the Council for Higher Education Accreditation (CHEA). Institutional accrediting bodies, which review each institution as a whole, include the six regional associations of schools and colleges (Middle States, New England, North Central, Northwest, Southern, and Western), each of which is responsible for a specified portion of the United States and its territories. Other institutional accrediting bodies are national in scope and accredit specific kinds of institutions (e.g., Bible colleges, independent colleges, and rabbinical and Talmudic schools). Program registration by the New York State Board of Regents is considered to be the equivalent of institutional accreditation, since the board requires that all programs offered by an institution meet its standards before recognition is granted. There are recognized specialized or professional accrediting bodies in more than forty different fields, each of which is authorized to accredit institutions or specific programs in its particular field. For specialized institutions that offer programs in one field only, we designate this to be the equivalent of institutional accreditation. A full explanation of the accrediting process and complete information on recognized, institutional (regional and national) and specialized accrediting bodies can be found online at www.chea.org or at www.ed.gov/admins/finaid/accred/index.html.

Quick-Reference Chart

College Costs At-a-Glance

by Michael Steidel
Dean of Admission, Carnegie Mellon University

To help shed some light on the typical patterns of financial aid offered by colleges, we have prepared the following chart. This chart can help you to better understand financial aid practices in general, form realistic expectations about the amounts of aid that might be provided by specific colleges or universities, and prepare for meaningful discussions with the financial aid officers at colleges being considered. The data appearing in the chart have been supplied by the schools themselves and are also shown in the individual college profiles.

Tuition and fees are based on the total of full-time tuition and mandatory fees for the 2016–2017 academic year or for the 2015–2016 academic year if 2016–2017 figures are not available. More information about these costs, as well as the costs of room and board and the year for which they are current, can be found in the individual college profiles. For institutions that have two or more tuition rates for different categories of students or types of programs, the lowest rate is used in figuring the cost.

The colleges are listed alphabetically by state. An "NR" in any individual column indicates that the applicable data element was "Not Reported."

The chart is divided into eight columns of information for each college:

1. Institutional Control
Whether the school is independent (ind.), including independent, independent–religious, and proprietary, or public (pub.), including federal, state, commonwealth, territory, county, district, city, state, local, and state-related.

2. Tuition and Fees
Based on the total of full-time tuition and mandatory fees. An asterisk indicates that the school includes room and board in their mandatory fees.

3. Room and Board
If a school has room and board costs that vary according to the type of accommodation and meal plan, either the lowest figures are represented or the figures are for the most common room arrangement and a full meal plan. If a school has only housing arrangements, a dagger appears to the right of the number. An "NA" will appear in this column if no college-owned or -operated housing facilities are offered.

4. Percent of Eligible Freshmen Receiving Need-Based Gift Awards
Calculated by dividing the number of freshman students determined to have need who received need-based gift aid by the number of full-time freshmen.

5. Percent of Freshmen Whose Need Was Fully Met
Calculated by dividing the number of freshman students whose financial need was fully met by the number of freshmen with need.

6. Average Financial Aid Package for Freshmen
The average dollar amount from all sources, including *gift aid* (scholarships and grants) and *self-help* (jobs and loans), awarded to freshmen receiving aid. Note that this aid package may exceed tuition and fees if the average aid package included coverage of room and board expenses.

7. Average Net Cost After Aid
Average aid package subtracted from published costs (tuition, fees, room, and board) to produce what the average student will have to pay.

8. Average Indebtedness Upon Graduation
Average per-student indebtedness of graduating seniors.

Because personal situations vary widely, it is very important to note that an individual's aid package can be quite different from the averages. Moreover, the data shown for each school can fluctuate widely from year to year, depending on the number of applicants, the amount of need to be met, and the financial resources and policies of the college. Peterson's intent in presenting this chart is to provide you with useful facts and figures that can serve as general guidelines in the pursuit of financial aid. We caution you to use the data only as a jumping-off point for further investigation and analysis, not as a means to rank or select colleges.

After you have narrowed down the choice of colleges based on academic and personal criteria, we recommend that you carefully study this chart. From it, you can develop a list of questions for financial aid officers at the colleges under serious consideration. Here are just a few questions you might want to ask: About the Institution

- What are the specific types and sources of aid provided to freshmen at this school?

- What factors does this college consider in determining whether a financial aid applicant is qualified for its need-based aid programs?

- How does the college determine the combination of types of aid that make up an individual's package?

- How are non-need-based awards treated: as a part of the aid package or as a part of the parental/family contribution?

- Does this school "guarantee" financial aid and, if so, how is its policy implemented? Guaranteed aid means that, by policy, 100 percent of need is met for all students judged to have need. Implementation determines *how* need is met and varies widely from school to school. For example, grade point average may determine the apportioning of scholarship, loan, and work-study aid. Rules for freshmen may be different from those for upperclass students.

- To what degree is the admission process "need-blind"? Need-blind means that admission decisions are made without regard to the student's need for financial aid.

- What are the norms and practices for upperclass students? Peterson's chart presents information on *freshmen* financial aid only; however, the financial aid office should be able and willing to provide you with comparable figures for upper-

class students. A college might offer a wonderful package for the freshman year, then leave students mostly on their own to fund the remaining three years. Or the school may provide a higher proportion of scholarship money for freshmen, then rebalance its aid packages to contain more self-help aid (loans and work-study) in upperclass years. There is an assumption that, all other factors being equal, students who have settled into the pattern of college time management can handle more work-study hours than freshmen. Grade point average, tuition increases, changes in parental financial circumstances, and other factors may also affect the redistribution.

College Costs At-a-Glance

	Institutional Control ind.=independent; pub.=public	Tuition and Fees	Room and Board	Percent of Eligible Freshmen Receiving Need-Based Gift Awards	Percent of Freshmen Whose Need Was Fully Met	Average Financial Aid Package for Freshmen	Average Net Cost After Aid	Average Indebtedness Upon Graduation
Alabama								
Alabama State University	pub.	$9220	$5422	85%	34%	$15,869	—	$32,487
Amridge University	ind.	$10,860	NA	100%	100%	$5416	$5444	$11,179
Athens State University	pub.	$6480	NA	65%	4%	$10,341	—	NR
Auburn University	pub.	$10,696	$12,898	83%	18%	$11,758	$11,836	$28,170
Auburn University at Montgomery	pub.	$9640	$5650	72%	12%	$6421	$8869	$30,454
Faulkner University	ind.	$20,590	$8250	100%	12%	$14,144	$14,696	$29,000
Huntingdon College	ind.	$26,400	$9500	100%	12%	$19,204	$16,696	$33,503
Jacksonville State University	pub.	$9660	$7128	48%	NR	$9970	$6818	NR
Judson College	ind.	$17,376	$9978	NR	NR	NR	NR	NR
Samford University	ind.	$30,490	$10,280	99%	26%	$18,690	$22,080	$29,292
Spring Hill College	ind.	$35,798	$12,690	99%	25%	$33,531	$14,957	NR
Troy University	pub.	$11,199	$7853	56%	NR	$3655	$15,397	$5475
Tuskegee University	ind.	$20,320	$9320	72%	56%	$20,500	$9140	$26,500
United States Sports Academy	ind.	$10,280	NR	NR	NR	NR	NR	NR
The University of Alabama	pub.	$10,470	$9550	81%	28%	$15,376	$4644	$33,816
The University of Alabama at Birmingham	pub.	$9936	$9980	85%	14%	$9923	$9993	$34,950
The University of Alabama in Huntsville	pub.	$9842	$9603	91%	34%	$13,165	$6280	$35,009
University of Mobile	ind.	$21,400	$9600	63%	100%	$19,353	$11,647	$30,029
University of Montevallo	pub.	$12,040	$7462	93%	27%	$11,870	$7632	$28,848
University of North Alabama	pub.	$9920	$7284	70%	9%	$7334	$9870	NR
University of South Alabama	pub.	$9060	$7340	92%	11%	$9894	$6506	NR
The University of West Alabama	pub.	$8876	$6640	69%	1%	$10,478	$5038	$24,449
Alaska								
Alaska Bible College	ind.	$9300	$2700	100%	NR	NR	NR	NR
Alaska Pacific University	ind.	$20,830	$7140	68%	16%	$14,403	$13,567	$8922
University of Alaska Anchorage	pub.	N/R	NR	85%	20%	$9469	—	$26,951
University of Alaska Fairbanks	pub.	$8144	$8530	90%	14%	$7882	$8792	$25,344
University of Alaska Southeast	pub.	N/R	NR	92%	10%	$3205	—	$25,090
Arizona								
Arizona State University at the Downtown Phoenix campus	pub.	$10,370	$13,310	97%	21%	$16,307	$7373	$25,342
Arizona State University at the Polytechnic campus	pub.	$9886	$11,474	96%	20%	$14,288	$7072	$26,925
Arizona State University at the Tempe campus	pub.	$10,370	$11,386	98%	22%	$16,098	$5658	$22,903
Arizona State University at the West campus	pub.	$9886	$10,754	97%	25%	$14,949	$5691	$22,251
Dunlap-Stone University	ind.	$8000	NR	NR	NR	NR	NR	NR
Embry-Riddle Aeronautical University–Prescott	ind.	$34,662	$10,468	98%	NR	$19,324	$25,806	NR
Northern Arizona University	pub.	$10,764	$9482	67%	13%	$12,205	$8041	$26,279
Prescott College	ind.	$29,566	$7700	100%	4%	$23,691	$13,575	$27,130
The University of Arizona	pub.	$11,177	$11,300	95%	13%	$12,542	$9935	$23,273
Arkansas								
Arkansas Tech University	pub.	$8280	$7036	81%	5%	$9187	$6129	$27,156
Harding University	ind.	$18,440	$6756	96%	39%	$16,994	$8202	$30,570

NA = not applicable; NR = not reported; * = includes room and board; † = room only; — = not available.

College Costs At-a-Glance

	Institutional Control ind.=independent; pub.=public	Tuition and Fees	Room and Board	Percent of Eligible Freshmen Receiving Need-Based Gift Awards	Percent of Freshmen Whose Need Was Fully Met	Average Financial Aid Package for Freshmen	Average Net Cost After Aid	Average Indebtedness Upon Graduation
Hendrix College	ind.	$44,070	$11,926	100%	42%	$38,093	$17,903	$30,213
John Brown University	ind.	$25,324	$8840	98%	1%	$22,106	$12,058	$26,651
Lyon College	ind.	$26,290	$8440	100%	29%	$18,887	$15,843	$22,321
Ouachita Baptist University	ind.	$25,870	$7630	98%	29%	$22,721	$10,779	$29,298
Philander Smith College	ind.	N/R	NR	97%	5%	$12,280	—	$46,965
Southern Arkansas University–Magnolia	pub.	N/R	NR	73%	34%	$12,025	—	$21,092
University of Arkansas	pub.	$8820	$10,332	83%	13%	$8820	$10,332	$24,182
University of Arkansas at Little Rock	pub.	N/R	NR	99%	NR	$13,731	—	NR
University of Central Arkansas	pub.	$8224	$6248	NR	NR	NR	NR	NR
Williams Baptist College	ind.	$17,320	$7600	75%	NR	$14,263	$10,657	$19,295
California								
Academy of Art University	ind.	$26,490	$15,792	71%	3%	$10,073	$32,209	$27,020
Alliant International University–San Diego	ind.	$21,220	NA	100%	NR	$14,815	$6405	NR
American Jewish University	ind.	N/R	NR	100%	NR	$28,992	—	$30,000
Azusa Pacific University	ind.	$36,120	$5576†	98%	44%	$5904	$35,792	$24,338
California Baptist University	ind.	$32,566	$11,540	94%	22%	$20,833	$23,273	$20,693
California Christian College	ind.	$8990	$4950	NR	NR	NR	NR	NR
California College of the Arts	ind.	$45,466	$9370†	100%	8%	$33,021	$21,815	$32,434
California Institute of Technology	ind.	$47,577	$14,100	100%	100%	$46,283	$15,394	$18,219
California Institute of the Arts	ind.	$45,030	NR	98%	11%	$35,000	$10,030	$31,293
California Lutheran University	ind.	$39,780	$13,060	100%	17%	$32,833	$20,007	$32,030
California Polytechnic State University, San Luis Obispo	pub.	$9075	$12,507	94%	10%	$9585	$11,997	$22,413
California State Polytechnic University, Pomona	pub.	$7027	$14,514	82%	3%	$10,545	$10,996	$22,404
California State University, Bakersfield	pub.	$8249	NR	94%	14%	$4223	$4026	$11,437
California State University, Chico	pub.	$12,516	$12,824	78%	15%	$17,732	$7608	NR
California State University, Dominguez Hills	pub.	$6418	NR	89%	2%	$5604	$814	$16,370
California State University, East Bay	pub.	$7927	$14,184	98%	3%	$12,379	$9732	$19,149
California State University, Fresno	pub.	N/R	NR	94%	6%	$11,072	—	$18,221
California State University, Fullerton	pub.	$6560	$15,642	83%	81%	$6717	$15,485	$14,965
California State University, Long Beach	pub.	$6460	$12,398	80%	70%	$12,348	$6510	$15,917
California State University, Los Angeles	pub.	N/R	NR	95%	17%	$10,192	—	$16,362
California State University Maritime Academy	pub.	$8360	$12,807	96%	8%	NR	NR	$24,052
California State University, Monterey Bay	pub.	N/R	NR	83%	12%	$11,557	—	$20,869
California State University, Northridge	pub.	$6587	$10,272	84%	NR	$11,293	$5566	$16,956
California State University, Sacramento	pub.	$7204	$11,856	98%	14%	$10,651	$8409	$18,985
California State University, San Bernardino	pub.	$6601	$12,966	94%	10%	$9905	$9662	$22,452
California State University, San Marcos	pub.	$7364	$13,240	93%	10%	$10,682	$9922	$22,736
Chapman University	ind.	$50,594	$14,910	93%	11%	$31,342	$34,162	$25,959
Claremont McKenna College	ind.	$50,950	$15,740	100%	100%	$48,623	$18,067	$23,375
Cogswell Polytechnical College	ind.	$19,096	$8000†	NR	NR	NR	NR	NR
The Colburn School Conservatory of Music	ind.	$3000	$0	100%	NR	$1800	$1200	NR
Concordia University Irvine	ind.	$34,100	$10,760	98%	21%	$26,341	$18,519	$31,747

NA = not applicable; NR = not reported; * = includes room and board; † = room only; — = not available.

College Costs At-a-Glance

	Institutional Control ind.=independent; pub.=public	Tuition and Fees	Room and Board	Percent of Eligible Freshmen Receiving Need-Based Gift Awards	Percent of Freshmen Whose Need Was Fully Met	Average Financial Aid Package for Freshmen	Average Net Cost After Aid	Average Indebtedness Upon Graduation
Dominican University of California	ind.	$44,690	$14,060	100%	14%	$30,452	$28,298	$35,369
Fresno Pacific University	ind.	N/R	NR	80%	19%	$30,190	—	NR
Harvey Mudd College	ind.	$52,666	$17,051	97%	100%	$46,466	$23,251	$25,412
Hope International University	ind.	$31,800	$9930	69%	19%	$20,526	$21,204	$28,438
Humboldt State University	pub.	$7212	$12,638	95%	9%	$13,687	$6163	$24,337
John Paul the Great Catholic University	ind.	$24,900	$8100†	100%	2%	$18,914	$14,086	NR
Laguna College of Art & Design	ind.	$29,800	$9500†	NR	NR	NR	NR	$38,000
Loyola Marymount University	ind.	$44,230	$14,485	98%	20%	$27,843	$30,872	$30,698
Marymount California University	ind.	$35,884	$14,412	100%	33%	$34,769	$15,527	$32,470
The Master's University	ind.	$33,020	$10,850	100%	14%	$22,869	$21,001	$29,133
Mills College	ind.	$45,635	$13,528	89%	19%	$45,649	$13,514	$33,327
Mount Saint Mary's University	ind.	$37,722	$11,451	88%	2%	$30,636	$18,537	$32,805
Mt. Sierra College	ind.	N/R	NA	100%	NR	$12,100	—	$28,000
National University	ind.	$13,032	NA	67%	NR	$4936	$8096	$52,986
NewSchool of Architecture and Design	ind.	N/R	NR	97%	3%	$21,644	—	$40,000
Occidental College	ind.	$51,070	$14,460	98%	100%	$46,151	$19,379	$29,940
Pacific Union College	ind.	$28,629	$7827	100%	5%	$26,516	$9940	$40,263
Pepperdine University	ind.	$50,022	$14,330	100%	17%	$38,688	$25,664	$29,640
Pitzer College	ind.	N/R	NR	100%	100%	$47,280	—	$21,569
Point Loma Nazarene University	ind.	$34,600	$10,150	96%	16%	$23,119	$21,631	$34,844
Pomona College	ind.	$49,352	$15,605	100%	100%	$51,284	$13,673	$18,738
San Diego Christian College	ind.	$29,550	$10,974	75%	25%	$24,097	$16,427	$19,212
San Diego State University	pub.	$7084	$14,812	62%	8%	$9200	$12,696	$19,969
San Francisco Art Institute	ind.	$43,090	$15,415	90%	6%	$13,935	$44,570	$32,515
San Francisco Conservatory of Music	ind.	$43,410	$15,700	100%	8%	$45,000	$14,110	$36,113
San Francisco State University	pub.	$6484	$12,698	95%	34%	$15,973	$3209	$20,716
San Jose State University	pub.	$7417	$14,867	94%	55%	$17,379	$4905	$19,797
Santa Clara University	ind.	$47,112	$13,965	90%	46%	$36,762	$24,315	$27,385
Scripps College	ind.	$50,982	$15,682	100%	100%	$40,005	$26,659	$20,205
Shasta Bible College	ind.	$9280	$2700†	NR	NR	NR	NR	NR
Simpson University	ind.	$27,350	$8350	100%	14%	$22,370	$13,330	$26,938
Soka University of America	ind.	$31,776	$12,166	100%	89%	$33,399	$10,543	$22,409
Sonoma State University	pub.	$7330	$13,146	68%	4%	$10,004	$10,472	$20,797
Southern California Institute of Architecture	ind.	$42,900	NA	100%	NR	$27,752	$15,148	$39,287
Stanford University	ind.	$47,940	$14,601	98%	94%	$50,547	$11,994	$21,987
Thomas Aquinas College	ind.	$24,500	$7950	77%	100%	$18,959	$13,491	$16,901
University of California, Berkeley	pub.	$13,509	$16,042	99%	56%	$17,284	$12,267	$18,789
University of California, Davis	pub.	$14,100	$16,136	98%	19%	$23,648	$6588	$19,276
University of California, Irvine	pub.	$15,035	$13,661	98%	24%	$24,400	$4296	$20,628
University of California, Los Angeles	pub.	N/R	NR	96%	25%	$24,345	—	$21,323
University of California, Riverside	pub.	$13,581	$16,400	98%	25%	$26,537	$3444	$21,838
University of California, San Diego	pub.	$13,645	NR	96%	40%	$23,173	—	$21,830

NA = not applicable; NR = not reported; * = includes room and board; † = room only; — = not available.

College Costs At-a-Glance

	Institutional Control ind.=independent; pub.=public	Tuition and Fees	Room and Board	Percent of Eligible Freshmen Receiving Need-Based Gift Awards	Percent of Freshmen Whose Need Was Fully Met	Average Financial Aid Package for Freshmen	Average Net Cost After Aid	Average Indebtedness Upon Graduation
University of California, Santa Barbara	pub.	$14,069	$13,605	97%	22%	$24,479	$3195	$21,001
University of California, Santa Cruz	pub.	N/R	NR	97%	21%	$24,936	—	$22,582
University of La Verne	ind.	$41,450	$13,140	91%	7%	$31,855	$22,735	$31,445
University of Redlands	ind.	$46,570	$13,480	100%	49%	$34,212	$25,838	$32,662
University of San Diego	ind.	$47,708	$12,630	98%	14%	$32,725	$27,613	$29,646
University of San Francisco	ind.	$46,250	$14,330	83%	16%	$39,676	$20,904	$34,114
University of Southern California	ind.	$52,992	$14,348	87%	80%	$51,311	$16,029	$27,882
University of the Pacific	ind.	$44,588	$12,858	98%	20%	$32,756	$24,690	$28,810
Westmont College	ind.	$44,044	$13,886	100%	25%	$35,569	$22,361	$31,609
Whittier College	ind.	$46,110	$13,328	86%	17%	$36,933	$22,505	$31,826
William Jessup University	ind.	$28,700	$10,650	100%	18%	$23,226	$16,124	$24,656
Woodbury University	ind.	$37,906	$11,136	100%	2%	$25,843	$23,199	$41,211
Colorado								
Adams State University	pub.	$9153	$8550	94%	5%	$13,439	$4264	$17,808
The Colorado College	ind.	$50,892	$11,668	95%	100%	$46,960	$15,600	$20,742
Colorado Mesa University	pub.	$8395	$10,560	86%	22%	$8355	$10,600	$27,902
Colorado School of Mines	pub.	$17,842	$11,477	50%	27%	$15,787	$13,532	$32,901
Colorado State University	pub.	$11,052	$11,110	81%	35%	$10,664	$11,498	$25,155
Fort Lewis College	pub.	$8105	$9328	90%	16%	$15,627	$1806	$22,265
Metropolitan State University of Denver	pub.	$6929	NA	72%	3%	$7181	—	$28,380
Platt College	ind.	N/R	NA	50%	NR	$7500	—	$43,477
Regis University	ind.	$34,675	$10,420	100%	14%	$30,885	$14,210	$28,153
University of Colorado Boulder	pub.	$11,531	$13,590	78%	46%	$16,237	$8884	$27,405
University of Colorado Colorado Springs	pub.	$9863	$9800	58%	2%	$8049	$11,614	$22,228
University of Colorado Denver	pub.	$10,719	NA	83%	3%	$8836	$1883	$19,378
University of Denver	ind.	$48,669	$12,612	100%	31%	$37,209	$24,072	$31,077
University of Northern Colorado	pub.	$8888	$10,770	87%	38%	$11,863	$7795	$27,393
Western State Colorado University	pub.	$9193	$9446	90%	9%	$9105	$9534	$25,589
Connecticut								
Albertus Magnus College	ind.	$31,490	$14,016	96%	9%	$25,848	$19,658	$38,376
Central Connecticut State University	pub.	$9741	$11,462	74%	6%	$9250	$11,953	$28,016
Charter Oak State College	pub.	$9393	NA	NR	NR	NR	NR	NR
Connecticut College	ind.	$50,940	$14,060	97%	100%	$42,724	$22,276	$27,514
Eastern Connecticut State University	pub.	$10,500	$12,559	80%	9%	$10,848	$12,211	$30,566
Fairfield University	ind.	$46,000	$13,860	99%	29%	$34,622	$25,238	$37,910
Quinnipiac University	ind.	$46,100	$14,190	98%	18%	$27,621	$32,669	$47,217
Sacred Heart University	ind.	$38,300	$14,450	100%	18%	$19,822	$32,928	$40,240
Southern Connecticut State University	pub.	$10,054	$11,870	65%	21%	$15,069	$6855	$28,370
University of Bridgeport	ind.	$31,630	$13,320	86%	4%	$25,704	$19,246	$21,200
University of Hartford	ind.	$38,970	$12,346	99%	13%	$25,502	$25,814	NR
University of New Haven	ind.	$37,060	$15,130	100%	14%	$22,484	$29,706	$46,449
University of Saint Joseph	ind.	$38,033	$11,095	99%	19%	$26,686	$22,442	$29,028

NA = not applicable; NR = not reported; * = includes room and board; † = room only; — = not available.

College Costs At-a-Glance

	Institutional Control ind.=independent; pub.=public	Tuition and Fees	Room and Board	Percent of Eligible Freshmen Receiving Need-Based Gift Awards	Percent of Freshmen Whose Need Was Fully Met	Average Financial Aid Package for Freshmen	Average Net Cost After Aid	Average Indebtedness Upon Graduation
Wesleyan University	ind.	$52,474	$14,466	91%	100%	$44,344	$22,596	$22,495
Western Connecticut State University	pub.	$10,017	$11,884	93%	10%	$8443	$13,458	$31,229
Yale University	ind.	$49,480	$15,170	100%	100%	$54,590	$10,060	$13,625
Delaware								
University of Delaware	pub.	$12,830	$12,068	94%	13%	$13,812	$11,086	$33,150
District of Columbia								
American University	ind.	$44,853	$14,526	93%	49%	$36,320	$23,059	NR
The Catholic University of America	ind.	$42,536	$13,820	100%	47%	$31,783	$24,573	$46,779
Gallaudet University	ind.	$16,558	$14,038	100%	25%	$23,629	$6967	$15,767
Georgetown University	ind.	$50,547	$15,568	88%	100%	$48,620	$17,495	$23,412
The George Washington University	ind.	$53,518	$13,000	97%	47%	$42,555	$23,963	$33,305
Howard University	ind.	N/R	NR	64%	6%	$14,968	—	$26,181
University of the District of Columbia	pub.	N/R	NR	83%	1%	$9198	—	$22,964
Florida								
Ave Maria University	ind.	N/R	NR	100%	26%	$16,763	—	$25,962
The Baptist College of Florida	ind.	$11,100	$4138	100%	NR	$8856	$6382	$24,444
Barry University	ind.	$28,800	$10,800	88%	4%	$25,390	$14,210	$39,255
Bethune-Cookman University	ind.	$14,410	$8710	98%	6%	$13,227	$9893	$35,082
Carlos Albizu University, Miami Campus	ind.	$12,384	NA	100%	NR	$7837	$4547	NR
Eckerd College	ind.	$54,750*	$11,706	100%	46%	$34,048	$32,408	$33,979
Embry-Riddle Aeronautical University–Daytona	ind.	$34,822	$11,100	98%	NR	$18,189	$27,733	NR
Embry-Riddle Aeronautical University–Worldwide	ind.	$9076	NR	100%	NR	$8193	$883	NR
Everglades University	ind.	$16,648	NA	NR	NR	NR	NR	NR
Flagler College	ind.	$18,300	$10,688	100%	15%	$12,408	$16,580	$29,267
Florida Agricultural and Mechanical University	pub.	$5785	$10,058	88%	16%	$13,932	$1911	$33,568
Florida Atlantic University	pub.	$6039	$12,050	83%	17%	$13,551	$4538	$22,648
Florida College	ind.	$16,550	$8230	85%	11%	$10,026	$14,754	NR
Florida Gulf Coast University	pub.	N/R	NR	64%	6%	$9123	—	$24,763
Florida Institute of Technology	ind.	$41,240	$12,880	100%	48%	$36,771	$17,349	$36,678
Florida International University	pub.	$6558	$10,846	82%	6%	$7204	$10,200	$19,915
Florida National University	ind.	$13,250	NA	98%	NR	NR	NR	NR
Florida Southern College	ind.	$33,150	$10,680	100%	28%	$27,586	$16,244	$26,637
Florida State University	pub.	$6507	$10,304	94%	10%	$12,519	$4292	$23,679
Jacksonville University	ind.	$33,930	$13,550	100%	28%	$25,336	$22,144	NR
Keiser University	ind.	$15,498	NA	97%	100%	$3965	$11,533	NR
Lynn University	ind.	$37,510	$11,970	86%	100%	$24,185	$25,295	$33,689
Millennia Atlantic University	ind.	N/R	NR	NR	NR	NR	NR	$10,500
New College of Florida	pub.	$6916	$9264	93%	40%	$14,369	$1811	$15,173
Nova Southeastern University	ind.	$28,736	$11,540	100%	19%	$30,160	$10,116	$34,763
Palm Beach Atlantic University	ind.	$29,950	$9540	100%	23%	$21,274	$18,216	$28,862
Ringling College of Art and Design	ind.	$43,040	$14,390	100%	8%	$23,925	$33,505	$44,384

NA = not applicable; NR = not reported; * = includes room and board; † = room only; — = not available.

College Costs At-a-Glance

	Institutional Control ind.=independent; pub.=public	Tuition and Fees	Room and Board	Percent of Eligible Freshmen Receiving Need-Based Gift Awards	Percent of Freshmen Whose Need Was Fully Met	Average Financial Aid Package for Freshmen	Average Net Cost After Aid	Average Indebtedness Upon Graduation
Rollins College	ind.	$48,335	$14,730	100%	30%	$40,560	$22,505	$32,208
Saint Leo University	ind.	$21,970	$10,570	100%	13%	$20,841	$11,699	$28,542
St. Petersburg College	pub.	$14,214*	NA	NR	NR	NR	NR	NR
St. Thomas University	ind.	$28,800	$11,700	NR	NR	NR	NR	NR
Southeastern University	ind.	$24,160	$9450	80%	11%	$15,337	$18,273	$29,224
Stetson University	ind.	$43,240	$12,326	99%	22%	$35,646	$19,920	$31,457
Trinity College of Florida	ind.	$15,690	$6450	91%	5%	$13,237	$8903	$21,510
University of Central Florida	pub.	$6368	$9554	66%	9%	$8516	$7406	$21,911
University of Florida	pub.	$6381	$9910	63%	30%	$13,430	$2861	$21,645
University of Miami	ind.	$47,004	$13,310	56%	98%	$42,187	$18,127	$21,500
University of North Florida	pub.	$6394	$9772	66%	18%	$8777	$7389	$18,685
University of South Florida	pub.	$6410	$9700	91%	15%	$11,802	$4308	$22,276
The University of Tampa	ind.	$27,740	$10,196	97%	10%	$17,039	$20,897	$31,448
University of West Florida	pub.	$6360	$9580	97%	13%	$7782	$8158	NR
Warner University	ind.	$20,712	$8104	NR	NR	NR	NR	$22,618
Webber International University	ind.	$25,358	$8694	99%	8%	$20,396	$13,656	$25,135
Georgia								
Agnes Scott College	ind.	$39,960	$11,970	100%	30%	$35,471	$16,459	$34,022
Armstrong State University	pub.	$6332	$10,750	51%	NR	NR	NR	NR
Augusta University	pub.	$8282	$13,200	70%	5%	$2021	$19,461	NR
Berry College	ind.	$33,556	$11,730	100%	33%	$26,668	$18,618	$26,449
Brenau University	ind.	$27,152	$12,418	100%	16%	$24,035	$15,535	$33,375
Clark Atlanta University	ind.	$22,396	$10,800	92%	49%	$7742	$25,454	$40,393
Clayton State University	pub.	$6312	$10,156	91%	5%	$9801	$6667	$30,423
College of Coastal Georgia	pub.	$4434	$8458	89%	24%	$9875	$3017	$25,455
Columbus State University	pub.	$7076	$10,198	67%	19%	$9304	$7970	$31,676
Covenant College	ind.	$32,230	$9630	98%	32%	$25,833	$16,027	$24,484
Emmanuel College	ind.	$19,330	$7400	99%	14%	$15,493	$11,237	$25,609
Emory University	ind.	$49,392	$13,894	92%	100%	$41,301	$21,985	$29,217
Georgia College & State University	pub.	$9202	$11,946	39%	24%	$11,211	$9937	$29,138
Georgia Institute of Technology	pub.	$12,212	$13,640	91%	24%	$13,854	$11,998	$32,169
Georgia Southern University	pub.	$6796	$9650	92%	14%	$10,315	$6131	$28,098
Georgia Southwestern State University	pub.	$6234	$8952	68%	12%	$10,198	$4988	$28,469
Georgia State University	pub.	$10,686	$14,084	72%	10%	$12,561	$12,209	$29,959
Kennesaw State University	pub.	$8276	$11,467	45%	6%	$9249	$10,494	$25,613
LaGrange College	ind.	$28,490	$11,440	91%	18%	$23,680	$16,250	$29,301
Life University	ind.	$11,220	$14,400	55%	NR	$10,000	$15,620	$38,800
Mercer University	ind.	$35,130	$11,916	100%	46%	$36,478	$10,568	$28,194
Middle Georgia State University	pub.	$4542	$7870	95%	NR	$4309	$8103	NR
Morehouse College	ind.	$27,278	$13,557	83%	11%	$19,948	$20,887	$30,485
Oglethorpe University	ind.	$35,425	$12,710	100%	23%	$31,827	$16,308	$26,660
Piedmont College	ind.	$24,468	$9870	100%	26%	$20,504	$13,834	$30,187

NA = not applicable; NR = not reported; * = includes room and board; † = room only; — = not available.

College Costs At-a-Glance

	Institutional Control ind.=independent; pub.=public	Tuition and Fees	Room and Board	Percent of Eligible Freshmen Receiving Need-Based Gift Awards	Percent of Freshmen Whose Need Was Fully Met	Average Financial Aid Package for Freshmen	Average Net Cost After Aid	Average Indebtedness Upon Graduation
Savannah State University	pub.	$6616	NR	NR	NR	NR	NR	NR
Spelman College	ind.	$26,638	$12,363	76%	NR	$15,771	$23,230	$38,430
Thomas University	ind.	$16,940	$4800†	87%	NR	$83	$21,657	NR
Toccoa Falls College	ind.	$22,034	$7934	100%	13%	$17,959	$12,009	$27,567
Truett McConnell University	ind.	$19,230	$7400	99%	28%	$14,556	$12,074	$23,222
University of Georgia	pub.	$11,634	$9616	99%	29%	$13,514	$7736	$21,730
University of North Georgia	pub.	$7228	$9680	89%	62%	$9959	$6949	$10,062
University of West Georgia	pub.	$7188	$9652	66%	60%	$8591	$8249	$26,874
Valdosta State University	pub.	$6297	$7900	91%	19%	$16,340	—	$29,607
Wesleyan College	ind.	$22,370	$9570	100%	19%	$20,808	$11,132	$35,392
Young Harris College	ind.	N/R	NR	100%	20%	$22,731	—	$27,173
Hawaii								
Chaminade University of Honolulu	ind.	$24,514	$13,100	97%	21%	$21,080	$16,534	$31,145
Hawai`i Pacific University	ind.	$24,500	$14,204	95%	23%	$16,446	$22,258	$28,893
University of Hawaii at Manoa	pub.	$11,732	NR	98%	32%	$14,723	—	$24,665
Idaho								
Boise State University	pub.	$7080	$7076	74%	17%	$10,368	$3788	$28,127
The College of Idaho	ind.	$28,755	$9334	100%	30%	$26,538	$11,551	$7270
Idaho State University	pub.	$6956	$6663	76%	6%	$8065	$5554	$30,617
Lewis-Clark State College	pub.	$7224	$6570	75%	10%	$8033	$5761	$27,370
Northwest Nazarene University	ind.	$28,650	$6800	100%	20%	$23,388	$12,062	$31,318
University of Idaho	pub.	$7232	$8354	68%	36%	$13,894	$1692	$26,539
Illinois								
Augustana College	ind.	$40,908	$10,314	98%	25%	$30,778	$20,444	$33,547
Aurora University	ind.	$23,520	$11,470	95%	11%	$23,327	$11,663	$27,578
Benedictine University	ind.	N/R	NR	64%	NR	$24,062	—	$29,070
Blessing-Rieman College of Nursing & Health Sciences	ind.	$23,580	NR	NR	NR	NR	NR	NR
Bradley University	ind.	$32,120	$10,010	100%	14%	$24,549	$17,581	$25,725
Columbia College Chicago	ind.	$25,580	NR	NR	NR	NR	NR	NR
Concordia University Chicago	ind.	$31,562	$9448	100%	13%	$22,448	$18,562	$32,549
DePaul University	ind.	$37,626	$13,387	86%	13%	$24,454	$26,559	$29,829
Dominican University	ind.	$32,530	$9942	100%	6%	$24,562	$17,910	$28,533
Eastern Illinois University	pub.	$11,580	$9546	74%	9%	$10,546	$10,580	$31,382
Elmhurst College	ind.	$35,500	$10,078	100%	18%	$27,823	$17,755	$28,246
Eureka College	ind.	$25,390	$9370	100%	19%	$16,660	$18,100	$40,681
Governors State University	pub.	$10,516	$9868	89%	25%	$10,606	$9778	NR
Greenville College	ind.	$26,356	$9322	100%	15%	$20,851	$14,827	$32,860
Illinois College	ind.	$32,140	$9190	100%	15%	$29,911	$11,419	$32,000
Illinois Institute of Technology	ind.	$46,323	$12,818	99%	18%	$39,070	$20,071	$30,569
Illinois Wesleyan University	ind.	$45,856	$10,574	100%	53%	$34,845	$21,585	$34,999
Judson University	ind.	$29,434	$9840	44%	11%	$20,435	$18,839	NR

NA = not applicable; NR = not reported; * = includes room and board; † = room only; — = not available.

College Costs At-a-Glance

	Institutional Control ind.=independent; pub.=public	Tuition and Fees	Room and Board	Percent of Eligible Freshmen Receiving Need-Based Gift Awards	Percent of Freshmen Whose Need Was Fully Met	Average Financial Aid Package for Freshmen	Average Net Cost After Aid	Average Indebtedness Upon Graduation
Knox College	ind.	$44,958	$9666	98%	34%	$38,463	$16,161	$30,368
Lewis University	ind.	$31,250	$10,460	99%	21%	$26,765	$14,945	$36,073
Lincoln Christian University	ind.	$13,020	$7564	100%	6%	$9973	$10,611	$32,138
Loyola University Chicago	ind.	$42,828	$14,080	99%	16%	$36,209	$20,699	$33,319
MacMurray College	ind.	$26,100	$8925	100%	23%	$23,570	$11,455	$36,877
McKendree University	ind.	$29,640	$9350	100%	26%	$22,693	$16,297	$30,029
Millikin University	ind.	$31,824	$10,335	89%	23%	$25,400	$16,759	$32,924
Monmouth College	ind.	$36,400	$8620	100%	26%	$32,985	$12,035	$31,037
North Central College	ind.	$36,654	$10,356	100%	23%	$25,507	$21,503	$34,911
Northeastern Illinois University	pub.	$13,001	$11,424	100%	4%	$9090	$15,335	$16,247
Northern Illinois University	pub.	$12,212	$10,776	97%	9%	$13,947	$9041	$34,714
Northwestern University	ind.	$50,855	$15,489	98%	100%	$48,603	$17,741	$20,308
Olivet Nazarene University	ind.	$34,480	$7900	100%	26%	$25,886	$16,494	$32,754
Principia College	ind.	$28,920	$11,430	100%	56%	$31,528	$8822	$21,260
Robert Morris University Illinois	ind.	$27,180	$13,200	99%	4%	$17,285	$23,095	$30,985
Rockford University	ind.	$30,050	$8420	100%	13%	$19,125	$19,345	$40,313
Saint Anthony College of Nursing	ind.	N/R	NA	100%	100%	$10,191	—	NR
Saint Francis Medical Center College of Nursing	ind.	$20,854	$3600†	NR	NR	NR	NR	NR
School of the Art Institute of Chicago	ind.	$45,750	$15,190	100%	10%	$35,464	$25,476	$35,455
Southern Illinois University Carbondale	pub.	$13,481	$10,186	64%	10%	$16,329	$7338	$33,218
Southern Illinois University Edwardsville	pub.	$11,493	$9481	82%	44%	$11,553	$9421	$22,277
Trinity Christian College	ind.	$27,450	$9580	100%	17%	$22,583	$14,447	$31,321
University of Chicago	ind.	$52,491	$15,093	99%	100%	$52,659	$14,925	$23,852
University of Illinois at Chicago	pub.	$13,664	$10,882	89%	11%	$14,896	$9650	$24,601
University of Illinois at Springfield	pub.	$12,609	$11,600	98%	23%	$16,348	$7861	$24,652
University of Illinois at Urbana–Champaign	pub.	$15,698	$11,308	88%	14%	$16,886	$10,120	$25,222
University of St. Francis	ind.	$30,840	$9084	100%	46%	$24,374	$15,550	$31,506
Western Illinois University	pub.	$11,245	$9580	78%	25%	$12,676	$8149	$30,721
Wheaton College	ind.	$34,050	$9560	100%	23%	$24,703	$18,907	$27,354
Indiana								
Ball State University	pub.	$9848	$10,038	64%	40%	$13,496	$6390	$27,617
Bethel College	ind.	$27,930	$8800	NR	NR	NR	NR	$34,148
Butler University	ind.	$39,905	$13,030	99%	13%	$23,481	$29,454	$35,730
Calumet College of Saint Joseph	ind.	$17,920	NA	75%	22%	$15,867	$2053	$24,431
Crossroads Bible College	ind.	N/R	NR	100%	100%	$9694	—	$37,497
DePauw University	ind.	$47,838	$12,529	100%	27%	$40,923	$19,444	$22,770
Earlham College	ind.	$45,300	$9570	100%	28%	$41,876	$12,994	$25,784
Franklin College	ind.	$30,771	$9175	100%	17%	$24,293	$15,653	$34,884
Goshen College	ind.	$33,200	$10,500	100%	20%	$27,826	$15,874	$27,534
Hanover College	ind.	$36,520	$11,230	100%	28%	$28,162	$19,588	$29,745
Huntington University	ind.	$33,996*	$8456	76%	2%	$19,592	$22,860	$32,509
Indiana State University	pub.	$8746	$9696	68%	18%	$11,170	$7272	$27,705

NA = not applicable; NR = not reported; * = includes room and board; † = room only; — = not available.

College Costs At-a-Glance

	Institutional Control ind.=independent; pub.=public	Tuition and Fees	Room and Board	Percent of Eligible Freshmen Receiving Need-Based Gift Awards	Percent of Freshmen Whose Need Was Fully Met	Average Financial Aid Package for Freshmen	Average Net Cost After Aid	Average Indebtedness Upon Graduation
Indiana Tech	ind.	$26,370	$9580	87%	NR	$21,084	$14,866	$41,844
Indiana University Bloomington	pub.	$10,388	$10,041	85%	30%	$13,666	$6763	$28,039
Indiana University East	pub.	$7073	NA	93%	25%	$8589	—	$27,379
Indiana University Kokomo	pub.	$7073	NA	89%	15%	$8473	—	$25,675
Indiana University Northwest	pub.	$7073	NA	87%	14%	$7420	—	$29,701
Indiana University–Purdue University Fort Wayne	pub.	$8212	$6844†	66%	7%	$9480	$5576	$29,419
Indiana University–Purdue University Indianapolis	pub.	$9205	$8462	87%	25%	$10,900	$6767	$28,951
Indiana University South Bend	pub.	$7073	$7222†	93%	10%	$8243	$6052	$27,306
Indiana University Southeast	pub.	$7073	$6520†	91%	9%	$7724	$5869	$22,612
Indiana Wesleyan University	ind.	$25,346	$8148	86%	52%	$27,960	$5534	$28,907
Manchester University	ind.	$31,660	$9880	100%	24%	$30,084	$11,456	$33,011
Oakland City University	ind.	$23,700	$9450	80%	NR	$17,862	$15,288	NR
Purdue University	pub.	$10,002	$10,030	59%	52%	$13,088	$6944	$27,530
Rose-Hulman Institute of Technology	ind.	$44,010	$13,293	86%	21%	$31,060	$26,243	$59,113
Saint Mary-of-the-Woods College	ind.	$28,932	$10,700	100%	NR	$25,188	$14,444	NR
Saint Mary's College	ind.	$40,800	$12,100	100%	22%	$33,250	$19,650	$31,036
Taylor University	ind.	$31,472	$8845	100%	29%	$22,588	$17,729	$29,263
Trine University	ind.	$31,540	$10,570	100%	18%	$27,981	$14,129	$38,161
University of Evansville	ind.	$35,396	$12,160	100%	30%	$31,560	$15,996	$35,346
University of Indianapolis	ind.	$28,390	$9988	62%	15%	$19,900	$18,478	$36,304
University of Notre Dame	ind.	$49,685	$14,358	97%	99%	$48,322	$15,721	$28,406
University of Southern Indiana	pub.	$7165	$8896	89%	11%	$9908	$6153	$24,762
Valparaiso University	ind.	$38,760	$11,400	100%	59%	$31,139	$19,021	$37,294
Wabash College	ind.	$42,250	$9850	98%	76%	$36,118	$15,982	$37,495
Iowa								
Allen College	ind.	$18,536	NA	NR	NR	NR	NR	NR
Briar Cliff University	ind.	$29,786	$9086	99%	28%	$33,359	$5513	$29,484
Buena Vista University	ind.	$32,854	$9490	100%	22%	$29,833	$12,511	NR
Central College	ind.	$34,612	$9980	100%	23%	$28,395	$16,197	$36,363
Clarke University	ind.	$31,950	$9400	100%	25%	$27,454	$13,896	$39,907
Coe College	ind.	$42,430	$9140	100%	20%	$35,534	$16,036	$35,782
Cornell College	ind.	$39,900	$8900	100%	15%	$34,118	$14,682	$31,975
Dordt College	ind.	$29,130	$8730	100%	51%	$26,826	$11,034	$29,175
Drake University	ind.	$35,206	$9850	98%	29%	$26,153	$18,903	$33,649
Graceland University	ind.	$28,110	$8480	93%	19%	$24,666	$11,924	$30,676
Grand View University	ind.	$26,516	$8834	89%	36%	$23,261	$12,089	$37,158
Grinnell College	ind.	$50,464	$12,400	100%	100%	$46,431	$16,433	$18,780
Iowa State University of Science and Technology	pub.	$8420	$8356	100%	37%	$12,176	$4600	$28,617
Iowa Wesleyan University	ind.	$29,146	$10,054	70%	8%	$20,098	$19,102	$33,152
Loras College	ind.	$32,886	$7840	100%	34%	$27,644	$13,082	$34,775
Luther College	ind.	$41,020	$8970	100%	44%	$35,228	$14,762	$35,642
Morningside College	ind.	$29,094	$8590	65%	38%	$24,316	$13,368	$36,233

NA = not applicable; NR = not reported; * = includes room and board; † = room only; — = not available.

College Costs At-a-Glance

	Institutional Control ind.=independent; pub.=public	Tuition and Fees	Room and Board	Percent of Eligible Freshmen Receiving Need-Based Gift Awards	Percent of Freshmen Whose Need Was Fully Met	Average Financial Aid Package for Freshmen	Average Net Cost After Aid	Average Indebtedness Upon Graduation
Mount Mercy University	ind.	$30,582	$9166	100%	24%	$25,028	$14,720	$26,603
Northwestern College	ind.	$30,300	$9000	100%	62%	$24,357	$14,943	$28,501
St. Ambrose University	ind.	$30,016	$10,164	100%	23%	$22,362	$17,818	$27,929
Simpson College	ind.	$37,663	$7963	99%	28%	$32,435	$13,191	$37,228
University of Dubuque	ind.	$28,700	$9350	99%	12%	$24,153	$13,897	$26,674
The University of Iowa	pub.	N/R	NR	73%	36%	$17,645	—	$27,715
University of Northern Iowa	pub.	$8483	$8781	59%	19%	$8733	$8531	$24,325
Upper Iowa University	ind.	$29,600	$8370	95%	6%	$21,039	$16,931	$34,123
Waldorf University	ind.	$21,260	$7246	98%	16%	$18,337	$10,169	$33,494
Wartburg College	ind.	$39,730	$9748	100%	22%	$28,792	$20,686	$39,794
Kansas								
Baker University	ind.	$28,880	$8310	NR	NR	NR	NR	$26,869
Barclay College	ind.	$15,990	$8400	100%	21%	$17,420	$6970	NR
Benedictine College	ind.	$27,480	$9530	100%	24%	$22,754	$14,256	$29,602
Bethel College	ind.	$27,720	$9270	75%	21%	$22,512	$14,478	$5633
Emporia State University	pub.	$6178	$8391	93%	15%	$8956	$5613	$20,433
Fort Hays State University	pub.	N/R	NR	81%	9%	$6005	—	$26,820
Friends University	ind.	$27,465	$7740	88%	54%	$18,019	$17,186	$28,175
Kansas State University	pub.	$9874	$9150	54%	23%	$12,682	$6342	$27,198
Kansas Wesleyan University	ind.	$28,980	$8950	88%	12%	NR	NR	$34,526
McPherson College	ind.	$26,498	$8411	71%	25%	$25,862	$9047	$28,615
Pittsburg State University	pub.	N/R	NR	42%	NR	$6091	—	$24,384
Southwestern College	ind.	$28,750	$7520	100%	16%	$23,041	$13,229	$38,318
Sterling College	ind.	$24,485	$8580	95%	15%	$20,318	$12,747	$28,221
The University of Kansas	pub.	$10,549	$9586	87%	43%	$15,269	$4866	$27,479
Washburn University	pub.	$8300	$7527	57%	15%	$9828	$5999	$23,552
Wichita State University	pub.	$7895	$10,980	69%	70%	$7347	$11,528	$39,122
Kentucky								
Asbury University	ind.	$29,500	$6950	82%	NR	NR	NR	$30,123
Bellarmine University	ind.	$40,350	$12,182	100%	18%	$32,099	$20,433	$30,759
Berea College	ind.	$570	$6472	100%	NR	$34,366	—	$7062
Brescia University	ind.	$21,850	NR	70%	NR	$23,315	—	$19,060
Campbellsville University	ind.	$24,596	$7896	100%	16%	$21,711	$10,781	$24,224
Centre College	ind.	$40,500	$10,250	100%	39%	$34,106	$16,644	$26,740
Clear Creek Baptist Bible College	ind.	N/R	NR	100%	NR	$5806	—	NR
Eastern Kentucky University	pub.	$8568	$8466	60%	47%	$11,557	$5477	$34,358
Kentucky Mountain Bible College	ind.	$8070	$4850	100%	29%	$8941	$3979	$7370
Kentucky State University	pub.	$7796	$6690	94%	2%	$12,795	$1691	$36,323
Kentucky Wesleyan College	ind.	$3209	$8750	NR	NR	NR	NR	$24,150
Lindsey Wilson College	ind.	$24,246	$9300	100%	25%	NR	NR	$26,869
Morehead State University	pub.	$7031	$8900	65%	20%	$11,553	$4378	$28,125
Murray State University	pub.	$8400	$8588	92%	26%	$12,919	$4069	$27,564

NA = not applicable; NR = not reported; * = includes room and board; † = room only; — = not available.

College Costs At-a-Glance

	Institutional Control ind.=independent; pub.=public	Tuition and Fees	Room and Board	Percent of Eligible Freshmen Receiving Need-Based Gift Awards	Percent of Freshmen Whose Need Was Fully Met	Average Financial Aid Package for Freshmen	Average Net Cost After Aid	Average Indebtedness Upon Graduation
Northern Kentucky University	pub.	$9384	$6549	57%	27%	$11,586	$4347	$28,355
Thomas More College	ind.	$29,450	$7304	100%	27%	$23,134	$13,620	$31,235
Transylvania University	ind.	$37,290	$10,160	100%	25%	$27,139	$20,311	$30,514
Union College	ind.	$26,080	$7400	100%	8%	$21,809	$11,671	$32,691
University of Kentucky	pub.	$11,483	$12,184	42%	19%	$12,873	$10,794	$32,571
University of Louisville	pub.	$11,264	$8560	98%	24%	$12,815	$7009	$23,553
University of Pikeville	ind.	$20,200	$7500	100%	58%	$19,414	$8286	$26,013
Western Kentucky University	pub.	$9912	$7713	60%	36%	$13,586	$4039	$28,081
Louisiana								
Centenary College of Louisiana	ind.	$35,900	$13,150	98%	15%	$22,432	$26,618	$26,643
Grambling State University	pub.	$6256	$8954	86%	NR	$3450	$11,760	$49,648
Louisiana State University and Agricultural & Mechanical College	pub.	$10,814	$11,540	96%	24%	$16,340	$6014	$24,699
Louisiana State University in Shreveport	pub.	$7339	NR	49%	NR	NR	NR	NR
Louisiana Tech University	pub.	$9117	$5925	98%	27%	$12,283	$2759	$23,001
Loyola University New Orleans	ind.	$39,242	$13,214	100%	14%	$34,087	$18,369	$30,524
Nicholls State University	pub.	$7641	$9676	96%	20%	$11,512	$5805	NR
Northwestern State University of Louisiana	pub.	N/R	NR	95%	14%	$13,729	—	$41,500
Southeastern Louisiana University	pub.	$7773	$7510	65%	14%	$9379	$5904	$23,536
Tulane University	ind.	$51,010	$13,844	99%	67%	$45,312	$19,542	$31,642
University of Holy Cross	ind.	$11,632	NA	94%	16%	$8107	$3525	$43,123
University of Louisiana at Lafayette	pub.	N/R	NR	97%	16%	$10,481	—	NR
University of Louisiana at Monroe	pub.	$8282	$7304	87%	NR	$18,616	—	NR
University of New Orleans	pub.	$8694	$9730	65%	8%	$10,692	$7732	$21,767
Xavier University of Louisiana	ind.	$23,046	$9152	69%	NR	$22,835	$9363	$22,142
Maine								
Bates College	ind.	$50,310	$14,190	100%	100%	$46,647	$17,853	$22,845
Bowdoin College	ind.	$49,900	$13,600	100%	100%	$44,146	$19,354	$23,120
Colby College	ind.	$50,960	$13,100	100%	100%	$47,442	$16,618	$27,953
College of the Atlantic	ind.	$43,542	$9747	100%	52%	$45,334	$7955	$26,723
Husson University	ind.	$17,561	$9498	89%	27%	$13,131	$13,928	$33,412
Thomas College	ind.	$25,722	$10,228	99%	11%	$21,498	$14,452	$31,713
Unity College	ind.	$28,350	$10,400	100%	11%	$21,209	$17,541	NR
University of Maine	pub.	$10,628	$10,164	100%	20%	$17,759	$3033	$34,923
University of Maine at Augusta	pub.	$7448	NA	87%	5%	$7632	—	$30,457
University of Maine at Fort Kent	pub.	NR	$7910	95%	60%	$11,421	—	$29,910
University of Maine at Machias	pub.	$7480	$8466	100%	57%	$13,125	$2821	$23,734
University of Maine at Presque Isle	pub.	$7884	$8264	99%	53%	$11,908	$4240	$22,934
University of Southern Maine	pub.	$8920	$9200	96%	47%	$14,337	$3783	NR

NA = not applicable; NR = not reported; * = includes room and board; † = room only; — = not available.

College Costs At-a-Glance

	Institutional Control ind.=independent; pub.=public	Tuition and Fees	Room and Board	Percent of Eligible Freshmen Receiving Need-Based Gift Awards	Percent of Freshmen Whose Need Was Fully Met	Average Financial Aid Package for Freshmen	Average Net Cost After Aid	Average Indebtedness Upon Graduation
Maryland								
Frostburg State University	pub.	$8702	$8898	67%	17%	$10,044	$7556	$25,347
Goucher College	ind.	$43,440	$12,670	100%	25%	$36,465	$19,645	$33,446
Hood College	ind.	$37,960	$12,580	100%	16%	$32,632	$17,908	$30,554
Loyola University Maryland	ind.	$46,595	$13,870	73%	92%	$33,250	$27,215	$36,208
McDaniel College	ind.	$41,800	$11,110	100%	30%	$38,381	$14,529	$35,397
Morgan State University	pub.	$7636	$10,490	78%	11%	$9542	$8584	$52,622
Mount St. Mary's University	ind.	$40,550	$12,830	100%	26%	$28,795	$24,585	$33,894
Peabody Conservatory of The Johns Hopkins University	ind.	$44,872	$15,122	64%	46%	$8164	$51,830	$20,730
St. John's College	ind.	$51,670	$12,234	97%	25%	$42,952	$20,952	$34,212
St. Mary's College of Maryland	pub.	$14,192	$12,442	90%	7%	$13,772	$12,862	$24,213
Salisbury University	pub.	$9364	$11,350	85%	17%	$8395	$12,319	$26,940
Stevenson University	ind.	$30,884	$8718†	89%	16%	$24,074	$15,528	$34,324
Towson University	pub.	$9408	$11,754	55%	10%	$10,131	$11,031	$25,483
University of Maryland, Baltimore County	pub.	$11,264	$11,218	75%	18%	$10,253	$12,229	$25,505
University of Maryland, College Park	pub.	$10,181	$11,758	78%	23%	$12,005	$9934	$27,559
University of Maryland Eastern Shore	pub.	N/R	NR	77%	NR	$4835	—	$9861
University of Maryland University College	pub.	$7176	NA	85%	1%	$5534	$1642	NR
Washington College	ind.	$44,700	$11,040	99%	29%	$33,955	$21,785	$35,957
Massachusetts								
Amherst College	ind.	$52,476	$13,710	100%	100%	$52,877	$13,309	$18,662
Assumption College	ind.	$36,260	$11,660	100%	26%	$25,791	$22,129	NR
Babson College	ind.	N/R	NR	89%	56%	$39,384	—	$36,556
Bay Path University	ind.	$32,739	$12,610	100%	4%	$30,322	$15,027	$29,954
Bentley University	ind.	$45,760	$15,130	99%	41%	$34,352	$26,538	$31,046
Berklee College of Music	ind.	$41,398	$18,000	29%	11%	$16,827	$42,571	$48,331
Boston Architectural College	ind.	$20,666	NA	80%	NR	$14,667	$5999	NR
Boston College	ind.	$51,296	$13,818	86%	100%	$38,042	$27,072	$20,849
Boston University	ind.	$50,240	$14,870	99%	23%	$42,218	$22,892	$41,098
Brandeis University	ind.	$51,545	$14,380	96%	90%	$43,340	$22,585	$32,922
Bridgewater State University	pub.	$9870	$12,750	78%	9%	$5510	$17,110	$27,104
Clark University	ind.	$43,150	$8450	99%	61%	$36,552	$15,048	$26,870
College of the Holy Cross	ind.	$50,630	$13,690	82%	100%	$39,937	$24,383	$25,446
Curry College	ind.	$38,596	$15,415	100%	13%	$29,025	$24,986	$42,191
Dean College	ind.	$36,960	$15,732	88%	16%	$27,118	$25,574	$55,598
Elms College	ind.	$33,412	$12,236	100%	13%	$27,701	$17,947	$37,052
Emerson College	ind.	$42,908	$16,320	95%	14%	$24,576	$34,652	$23,225
Emmanuel College	ind.	$38,844	$14,628	91%	31%	$27,814	$25,658	$36,818
Endicott College	ind.	$31,312	$14,500	83%	10%	$21,538	$24,274	$41,901
Fisher College	ind.	$30,499	$15,768	98%	NR	$26,205	$20,062	$12,724
Fitchburg State University	pub.	$10,135	$9210	69%	NR	$9419	$9926	$26,684
Framingham State University	pub.	$9340	$11,250	82%	21%	$10,200	$10,390	$29,493

NA = not applicable; NR = not reported; * = includes room and board; † = room only; — = not available.

College Costs At-a-Glance

	Institutional Control ind.=independent; pub.=public	Tuition and Fees	Room and Board	Percent of Eligible Freshmen Receiving Need-Based Gift Awards	Percent of Freshmen Whose Need Was Fully Met	Average Financial Aid Package for Freshmen	Average Net Cost After Aid	Average Indebtedness Upon Graduation
Franklin W. Olin College of Engineering	ind.	$49,280	$16,300	100%	100%	$44,031	$21,549	$18,704
Gordon College	ind.	$36,740	$11,000	100%	14%	$24,811	$22,929	$36,557
Hampshire College	ind.	$50,030	$13,606	100%	10%	$45,654	$17,982	$21,758
Harvard University	ind.	$47,074	$15,951	100%	100%	$53,071	$9954	$16,702
Hellenic College	ind.	$22,490	NR	NR	NR	NR	NR	NR
Hult International Business School	ind.	N/R	NR	84%	NR	$14,470	—	$16,053
Lasell College	ind.	$34,600	$14,800	100%	15%	$27,698	$21,702	$41,100
Lesley University	ind.	$26,300	$15,750	100%	13%	$16,718	$25,332	$23,000
Massachusetts College of Art and Design	pub.	$12,200	$13,100	98%	NR	$11,838	$13,462	$26,792
Massachusetts College of Liberal Arts	pub.	$10,050	$10,078	87%	79%	$15,549	$4579	$29,933
Massachusetts Institute of Technology	ind.	$49,892	$14,720	97%	100%	$44,934	$19,678	$24,954
Massachusetts Maritime Academy	pub.	$8004	$11,978	67%	27%	$12,533	$7449	$37,414
MCPHS University	ind.	$31,670	$15,834	100%	46%	$10,459	$37,045	NR
Merrimack College	ind.	$38,825	$14,345	100%	12%	$23,779	$29,391	NR
Mount Holyoke College	ind.	$45,866	$13,440	100%	100%	$37,581	$21,725	$23,872
Mount Ida College	ind.	$35,720	$13,680	100%	10%	$25,304	$24,096	$44,963
New England Conservatory of Music	ind.	$44,755	$13,900	100%	26%	$29,114	$29,541	$31,039
Nichols College	ind.	$34,000	$13,800	100%	21%	$28,773	$19,027	$35,392
Northeastern University	ind.	$47,653	$15,600	98%	100%	$39,320	$23,933	NR
Simmons College	ind.	$39,610	$14,800	100%	17%	$31,648	$22,762	NR
Smith College	ind.	$50,044	$16,730	96%	100%	$48,887	$17,887	$23,857
Springfield College	ind.	N/R	NR	100%	9%	$27,824	—	$42,650
Stonehill College	ind.	$39,900	$15,230	99%	43%	$28,147	$26,983	$35,462
Suffolk University	ind.	$37,266	$16,576	87%	25%	$32,233	$21,609	$39,091
Tufts University	ind.	$52,430	$13,566	93%	100%	$43,518	$22,478	$24,267
University of Massachusetts Amherst	pub.	$14,971	$11,897	95%	14%	$16,388	$10,480	$31,397
University of Massachusetts Boston	pub.	$13,435	NA	96%	39%	$14,989	—	$28,368
University of Massachusetts Dartmouth	pub.	$13,188	$12,470	94%	42%	$16,917	$8741	$32,099
University of Massachusetts Lowell	pub.	$14,307	$12,073	93%	52%	$16,108	$10,272	$31,432
Wellesley College	ind.	$48,802	$15,114	96%	100%	$48,404	$15,512	$13,415
Wentworth Institute of Technology	ind.	$31,840	$12,570	87%	7%	$22,272	$22,138	NR
Western New England University	ind.	$34,874	$13,214	100%	14%	$26,179	$21,909	$44,013
Westfield State University	pub.	$9275	$10,396	74%	8%	$8371	$11,300	$29,602
Wheaton College	ind.	$50,850	$12,968	100%	61%	$41,456	$22,362	$33,040
Wheelock College	ind.	$36,200	$14,975	100%	10%	$26,673	$24,502	NR
Williams College	ind.	$51,790	$13,690	100%	100%	$52,512	$12,968	$15,496
Worcester Polytechnic Institute	ind.	$46,994	$13,736	100%	53%	$36,113	$24,617	NR
Worcester State University	pub.	$9202	$11,775	90%	37%	$12,541	$8436	$28,940
Michigan								
Albion College	ind.	$41,040	$11,610	100%	21%	$40,574	$12,076	$38,356
Alma College	ind.	$37,310	$10,238	100%	12%	$29,312	$18,236	$36,046
Andrews University	ind.	$27,684	$8742	58%	23%	$28,001	$8425	$36,708

NA = not applicable; NR = not reported; * = includes room and board; † = room only; — = not available.

College Costs At-a-Glance

	Institutional Control ind.=independent; pub.=public	Tuition and Fees	Room and Board	Percent of Eligible Freshmen Receiving Need-Based Gift Awards	Percent of Freshmen Whose Need Was Fully Met	Average Financial Aid Package for Freshmen	Average Net Cost After Aid	Average Indebtedness Upon Graduation
Aquinas College	ind.	$31,244	$9070	100%	18%	$25,225	$15,089	$30,503
Calvin College	ind.	$31,730	$9840	100%	20%	$24,924	$16,646	$30,998
Central Michigan University	pub.	$12,150	$9406	90%	56%	$13,990	$7566	$33,480
Concordia University Ann Arbor	ind.	$27,710	$9580	97%	22%	$22,573	$14,717	$20,641
Cornerstone University	ind.	$27,520	$9030	100%	15%	$21,902	$14,648	$32,191
Eastern Michigan University	pub.	$13,649	NR	69%	7%	$2068	$11,581	$30,588
Ferris State University	pub.	$11,760	$9651	85%	18%	$13,000	$8411	$35,710
Grand Valley State University	pub.	$11,520	$8400	87%	15%	$10,870	$9050	$29,675
Hillsdale College	ind.	$25,522	$10,200	64%	40%	$15,323	$20,399	$26,941
Hope College	ind.	$31,560	$9690	91%	26%	$26,468	$14,782	$33,969
Kalamazoo College	ind.	$46,692	$9390	98%	50%	$39,792	$16,290	$27,653
Kuyper College	ind.	$20,302	$6800	97%	12%	$17,306	$9796	$25,906
Lawrence Technological University	ind.	$31,140	$10,107	100%	23%	$24,465	$16,782	$40,976
Marygrove College	ind.	$22,064	$7100	NR	NR	NR	NR	NR
Michigan State University	pub.	$14,062	$9734	73%	18%	$13,208	$10,588	NR
Michigan Technological University	pub.	$14,634	$10,105	80%	23%	$15,282	$9457	$34,942
Northern Michigan University	pub.	N/R	NR	71%	22%	$10,070	—	$31,257
Oakland University	pub.	$11,970	$9620	81%	10%	$14,475	$7115	$27,669
Olivet College	ind.	$25,520	$8950	86%	24%	$18,990	$15,480	$26,872
Saginaw Valley State University	pub.	$9345	$7950	92%	NR	NR	NR	$31,695
Spring Arbor University	ind.	$26,730	$9270	100%	27%	$24,198	$11,802	$32,602
University of Detroit Mercy	ind.	$41,158	$9452	99%	12%	$36,737	$13,873	$33,631
University of Michigan	pub.	$14,402	$10,872	83%	81%	$24,025	$1249	$25,712
University of Michigan–Dearborn	pub.	$12,032	NA	78%	9%	$9940	$2092	$26,192
University of Michigan–Flint	pub.	$10,884	$8178	77%	1%	$12,080	$6982	$27,358
Walsh College of Accountancy and Business Administration	ind.	$16,590	NA	NR	NR	NR	NR	NR
Wayne State University	pub.	N/R	NR	78%	13%	$13,659	—	$28,439
Western Michigan University	pub.	$11,493	$9561	68%	30%	$15,083	$5971	$35,454
Minnesota								
Academy College	ind.	$17,129	NA	NR	NR	NR	NR	$14,476
Augsburg College	ind.	$37,615	$9939	100%	17%	$31,177	$16,377	$40,816
Bemidji State University	pub.	$8394	$7924	65%	13%	$7841	$8477	NR
Bethany Lutheran College	ind.	$25,890	$7960	100%	18%	$21,709	$12,141	$32,310
Bethel University	ind.	$36,210	$10,340	100%	18%	$27,448	$19,102	$36,132
Carleton College	ind.	$50,874	$13,197	100%	100%	$47,719	$16,352	$20,063
College of Saint Benedict	ind.	$42,271	$10,535	99%	39%	$36,984	$15,822	$39,536
The College of St. Scholastica	ind.	$35,326	$9314	76%	24%	$29,883	$14,757	$40,774
Concordia College	ind.	$36,878	$7810	99%	26%	$29,404	$15,284	NR
Concordia University, St. Paul	ind.	$21,750	$8750	98%	11%	$16,332	$14,168	$33,183
Crown College	ind.	N/R	NR	98%	10%	$18,757	—	$31,557
Gustavus Adolphus College	ind.	$42,550	$9400	100%	38%	$37,682	$14,268	$34,773
Hamline University	ind.	$40,332	$10,156	100%	22%	$32,000	$18,488	$34,935

NA = not applicable; NR = not reported; * = includes room and board; † = room only; — = not available.

College Costs At-a-Glance

	Institutional Control ind.=independent; pub.=public	Tuition and Fees	Room and Board	Percent of Eligible Freshmen Receiving Need-Based Gift Awards	Percent of Freshmen Whose Need Was Fully Met	Average Financial Aid Package for Freshmen	Average Net Cost After Aid	Average Indebtedness Upon Graduation
Macalester College	ind.	$52,464	$11,672	99%	100%	$43,701	$20,435	$23,875
Martin Luther College	ind.	$14,680	$5790	98%	10%	$11,379	$9091	$22,582
McNally Smith College of Music	ind.	N/R	NR	71%	NR	$14,729	—	$58,458
Minnesota State University Mankato	pub.	$8812	$8716	78%	24%	$9580	$7948	$31,453
Minnesota State University Moorhead	pub.	$7136	$8076	64%	NR	$2635	$12,577	$34,697
Saint John's University	ind.	$41,732	$9892	97%	40%	$33,080	$18,544	$40,272
Saint Mary's University of Minnesota	ind.	$33,560	$8880	100%	27%	$26,439	$16,001	$39,196
St. Olaf College	ind.	$46,000	$10,430	100%	97%	$38,733	$17,697	$27,945
University of Minnesota, Crookston	pub.	$11,700	$7658	96%	24%	$13,102	$6256	$30,018
University of Minnesota, Duluth	pub.	$13,082	NR	89%	27%	$12,396	$686	$30,579
University of Minnesota, Morris	pub.	$12,846	$7914	99%	29%	$12,768	$7992	$25,732
University of Minnesota, Twin Cities Campus	pub.	$14,142	$9377	87%	28%	$13,165	$10,354	$26,644
University of St. Thomas	ind.	$41,133	$10,054	99%	20%	$28,360	$22,827	$40,307
Winona State University	pub.	$9075	$8460	76%	10%	$7135	$10,400	$35,221
Mississippi								
Alcorn State University	pub.	$6552	$9356	100%	14%	$14,918	$990	$35,077
Belhaven University	ind.	$24,250	$8000	100%	5%	$19,281	$12,969	$29,738
Blue Mountain College	ind.	$11,212	$5764	99%	22%	$7783	$9193	$19,695
Delta State University	pub.	$6418	$7374	67%	NR	$7541	$6251	NR
Jackson State University	pub.	$7261	$8708	82%	7%	$13,483	$2486	$28,311
Millsaps College	ind.	$39,380	$13,400	100%	20%	$35,439	$17,341	$31,419
Mississippi State University	pub.	$7780	$9418	96%	30%	$16,024	$1174	$30,659
University of Mississippi	pub.	$7744	$10,002	91%	18%	$12,549	$5197	$28,162
University of Southern Mississippi	pub.	$7854	$9012	70%	34%	$14,818	$2048	$28,700
Missouri								
Calvary University	ind.	$9198	$5490	100%	20%	$12,646	$2042	$19,246
Central Methodist University	ind.	$23,770	$7730	61%	19%	$18,492	$13,008	$27,308
College of the Ozarks	ind.	$430	$6800	100%	17%	$19,871	—	$5339
Columbia College	ind.	$21,936	$7632	77%	19%	$17,653	$11,915	$21,934
Cox College	ind.	$10,270	NA	50%	NR	$6700	$3570	NR
Culver-Stockton College	ind.	$26,040	$8310	100%	18%	$18,715	$15,635	$28,605
Drury University	ind.	$27,005	$8036	100%	21%	$19,022	$16,019	$31,011
Evangel University	ind.	$22,707	$8118	100%	12%	$16,900	$13,925	$32,032
Goldfarb School of Nursing at Barnes-Jewish College	ind.	$20,188	NA	NR	NR	NR	NR	NR
Harris-Stowe State University	pub.	$5220	$6500†	82%	77%	$12,836	—	NR
Kansas City Art Institute	ind.	$37,550	$10,400	100%	10%	$25,957	$21,993	$25,000
Lincoln University	pub.	$7042	$6560	91%	7%	$12,542	$1060	$32,691
Lindenwood University	ind.	$16,332	$8800	89%	25%	$11,533	$13,599	$31,488
Logan University	ind.	$6760	NR	NR	NR	NR	NR	NR
Maryville University of Saint Louis	ind.	$27,958	$10,088	99%	16%	$21,739	$16,307	$19,266
Missouri Baptist University	ind.	$26,020	$10,380	84%	35%	$22,262	$14,138	$26,015
Missouri State University	pub.	$7060	$8288	90%	19%	$9620	$5728	$24,734

NA = not applicable; NR = not reported; * = includes room and board; † = room only; — = not available.

College Costs At-a-Glance

	Institutional Control ind.=independent; pub.=public	Tuition and Fees	Room and Board	Percent of Eligible Freshmen Receiving Need-Based Gift Awards	Percent of Freshmen Whose Need Was Fully Met	Average Financial Aid Package for Freshmen	Average Net Cost After Aid	Average Indebtedness Upon Graduation
Missouri University of Science and Technology	pub.	$9637	$9780	95%	19%	$17,252	$2165	$28,259
Missouri Western State University	pub.	$6652	$7834	NR	NR	NR	NR	NR
Northwest Missouri State University	pub.	$9178	$9612	89%	60%	$11,074	$7716	$28,332
Research College of Nursing	ind.	$35,700	$9350	NR	NR	NR	NR	NR
Rockhurst University	ind.	$35,670	$9680	100%	27%	$29,298	$16,052	$23,753
St. Louis College of Pharmacy	ind.	$28,620	$10,091	100%	16%	$20,446	$18,265	$112,161
Saint Louis University	ind.	$40,726	$10,640	95%	29%	$29,211	$22,155	$33,299
Southeast Missouri State University	pub.	$6990	$8508	97%	18%	$9797	$5701	$27,991
Southwest Baptist University	ind.	$22,440	$7460	76%	18%	$19,867	$10,033	$26,615
Stephens College	ind.	N/R	NR	100%	NR	$12,000	—	NR
Truman State University	pub.	$7456	$8558	100%	39%	$13,540	$2474	$24,811
University of Central Missouri	pub.	$7322	$8318	60%	12%	$8907	$6733	$28,673
University of Missouri	pub.	$9518	$10,298	88%	17%	$11,727	$8089	$26,685
University of Missouri–Kansas City	pub.	$9563	NR	96%	14%	$11,702	—	$25,912
Washington University in St. Louis	ind.	$51,533	$16,006	97%	100%	$46,548	$20,991	$23,577
Webster University	ind.	$26,300	$11,190	86%	5%	$26,788	$10,702	$28,479
Westminster College	ind.	$24,540	$9480	100%	53%	$23,607	$10,413	$30,805
William Jewell College	ind.	$33,620	$9640	100%	40%	$31,216	$12,044	$31,183
William Woods University	ind.	$23,260	$9400	99%	24%	$16,313	$16,347	$27,729
Montana								
Carroll College	ind.	$34,480	$9824	100%	25%	$23,966	$20,338	$32,768
Montana State University Billings	pub.	$5826	$7510	84%	25%	$8740	$4596	$28,337
Montana Tech of The University of Montana	pub.	$6881	$8932	88%	21%	$9696	$6117	$27,193
Rocky Mountain College	ind.	$27,566	$8210	100%	23%	$22,601	$13,175	$30,035
University of Great Falls	ind.	$25,050	$8500	74%	1%	$18,949	$14,601	$30,118
University of Montana	pub.	$6446	$8826	62%	12%	$14,821	$451	$38,008
The University of Montana Western	pub.	$4893	$7482	77%	NR	$2959	$9416	$29,779
Nebraska								
College of Saint Mary	ind.	$19,950	$7550	99%	28%	$24,112	$3388	$33,658
Concordia University, Nebraska	ind.	$31,000	$8100	100%	31%	$23,597	$15,503	$26,328
Creighton University	ind.	$38,750	$10,702	100%	30%	$27,658	$21,794	$35,921
Doane University	ind.	$30,434	$8750	100%	41%	$24,581	$14,603	$30,720
Nebraska Methodist College	ind.	$16,088	$6318†	96%	11%	$8748	$13,658	$28,461
Union College	ind.	$23,070	$6926	100%	21%	$18,067	$11,929	$35,893
University of Nebraska at Kearney	pub.	$6953	$9594	95%	27%	$11,564	$4983	$23,879
University of Nebraska at Omaha	pub.	N/R	NR	60%	30%	$9306	—	$26,728
University of Nebraska–Lincoln	pub.	$8538	$10,670	84%	24%	$14,543	$4665	$23,307
Wayne State College	pub.	$6427	$7110	61%	51%	$9388	$4149	NR
Nevada								
University of Nevada, Las Vegas	pub.	$7310	$10,806	68%	8%	$10,987	$7129	$25,374
University of Nevada, Reno	pub.	$7377	$10,868	72%	10%	$8293	$9952	$23,110

NA = not applicable; NR = not reported; * = includes room and board; † = room only; — = not available.

College Costs At-a-Glance

	Institutional Control ind.=independent; pub.=public	Tuition and Fees	Room and Board	Percent of Eligible Freshmen Receiving Need-Based Gift Awards	Percent of Freshmen Whose Need Was Fully Met	Average Financial Aid Package for Freshmen	Average Net Cost After Aid	Average Indebtedness Upon Graduation
New Hampshire								
Dartmouth College	ind.	$51,438	$14,736	95%	100%	$50,643	$15,531	$17,849
Franklin Pierce University	ind.	$34,050	$12,700	99%	22%	$26,074	$20,676	$36,614
Keene State College	pub.	$13,613	$10,390	76%	10%	$13,279	$10,724	$41,016
New England College	ind.	$36,954	$13,874	99%	12%	$34,662	$16,166	$35,230
Northeast Catholic College	ind.	N/R	NR	100%	100%	$24,638	—	$18,186
Plymouth State University	pub.	$13,472	$11,008	66%	22%	$10,951	$13,529	$37,801
Saint Anselm College	ind.	$39,990	$14,146	100%	30%	$26,931	$27,205	$35,601
Southern New Hampshire University	ind.	$31,136	$12,062	61%	15%	$23,900	$19,298	$41,028
Thomas More College of Liberal Arts	ind.	$20,400	$9700	NR	NR	NR	NR	$23,452
University of New Hampshire	pub.	$17,624	$10,938	77%	16%	$24,031	$4531	$38,799
University of New Hampshire at Manchester	pub.	$14,860	NA	62%	19%	$11,895	$2965	$39,034
New Jersey								
Bloomfield College	ind.	$29,300	$11,700	95%	13%	$28,719	$12,281	NR
Caldwell University	ind.	$32,800	$11,400	100%	12%	$29,017	$15,183	$25,114
The College of New Jersey	pub.	$15,794	$12,881	42%	11%	$11,002	$17,673	$35,798
College of Saint Elizabeth	ind.	$32,277	$12,744	NR	NR	NR	NR	NR
Drew University	ind.	$47,752	$13,296	100%	15%	$43,195	$17,853	$24,964
Felician University	ind.	$33,650	$12,630	82%	9%	$29,766	$16,514	$32,032
Georgian Court University	ind.	$31,618	$10,808	99%	27%	$29,822	$12,604	$40,267
Kean University	pub.	$11,870	$12,780	72%	1%	$10,100	$14,550	$33,693
Monmouth University	ind.	$36,732	$13,552	73%	13%	$25,579	$24,705	$29,483
Montclair State University	pub.	$12,116	$14,094	69%	2%	$9149	$17,061	$28,070
New Jersey City University	pub.	$11,431	$12,446	86%	2%	$11,020	$12,857	$26,093
New Jersey Institute of Technology	pub.	$16,430	$13,400	100%	16%	$14,168	$15,662	$40,967
Princeton University	ind.	$45,320	$14,770	100%	100%	$51,390	$8700	$8908
Ramapo College of New Jersey	pub.	$13,870	$12,030	42%	14%	$17,874	$8026	$33,300
Rider University	ind.	$39,820	$14,230	99%	14%	$31,784	$22,266	$36,032
Rowan University	pub.	$13,108	$11,688	53%	4%	$8834	$15,962	$30,899
Rutgers University–Camden	pub.	$14,238	$11,908	76%	2%	$14,016	$12,130	$29,624
Rutgers University–Newark	pub.	$13,829	$13,459	85%	2%	$14,424	$12,864	$27,881
Rutgers University–New Brunswick	pub.	$14,372	$12,260	98%	6%	$14,740	$11,892	$25,974
Saint Peter's University	ind.	N/R	NR	99%	11%	$33,205	—	$29,724
Stevens Institute of Technology	ind.	$50,554	$14,400	NR	NR	NR	NR	NR
Stockton University	pub.	$13,077	$11,942	64%	34%	$17,669	$7350	$33,201
Thomas Edison State University	pub.	$6350	NA	NR	NR	NR	NR	NR
William Paterson University of New Jersey	pub.	$12,574	$11,103	68%	33%	$10,798	$12,879	$32,949
New Mexico								
New Mexico Highlands University	pub.	$5550	$7235	79%	10%	$1553	$11,232	$17,312
New Mexico Institute of Mining and Technology	pub.	$6891	$7942	83%	15%	$12,388	$2445	$22,355

NA = not applicable; NR = not reported; * = includes room and board; † = room only; — = not available.

College Costs At-a-Glance

	Institutional Control ind.=independent; pub.=public	Tuition and Fees	Room and Board	Percent of Eligible Freshmen Receiving Need-Based Gift Awards	Percent of Freshmen Whose Need Was Fully Met	Average Financial Aid Package for Freshmen	Average Net Cost After Aid	Average Indebtedness Upon Graduation
New Mexico State University	pub.	$6094	$7988	99%	12%	$11,360	$2722	$21,402
St. John's College	ind.	$52,320	$11,486	100%	58%	$44,225	$19,581	$27,790
New York								
Adelphi University	ind.	$35,740	$14,052	99%	17%	$21,500	$28,292	$32,558
Alfred University	ind.	$32,264	$12,272	99%	12%	$29,584	$14,952	$37,437
Bard College	ind.	$52,915	$15,066	99%	30%	$47,604	$20,377	$27,816
Barnard College	ind.	$50,394	$15,598	99%	99%	$50,967	$15,025	$22,015
Baruch College of the City University of New York	pub.	$6861	NR	98%	31%	$5972	$889	$5642
Binghamton University, State University of New York	pub.	$9271	$13,590	79%	13%	$11,602	$11,259	$25,718
Canisius College	ind.	$36,454	$13,218	100%	25%	$33,160	$16,512	$33,973
Cazenovia College	ind.	$33,656	$14,210	100%	24%	$33,644	$14,222	$33,631
City College of the City University of New York	pub.	$6740	NR	86%	70%	$9499	—	$16,942
Clarkson University	ind.	$46,132	$14,260	100%	20%	$43,391	$17,001	$23,500
Colgate University	ind.	$51,955	$13,075	100%	100%	$51,521	$13,509	$21,427
The College at Brockport, State University of New York	pub.	$7928	$12,418	80%	17%	$11,571	$8775	$29,748
The College of New Rochelle	ind.	$34,960	$13,208	93%	2%	$29,183	$18,985	$35,430
The College of Saint Rose	ind.	$31,612	$12,356	71%	18%	$23,111	$20,857	$31,413
College of Staten Island of the City University of New York	pub.	$6889	$13,626†	94%	5%	$8489	$12,026	NR
Columbia University	ind.	$55,056	$13,244	99%	100%	$55,687	$12,613	NR
Columbia University, School of General Studies	ind.	$53,445	$13,586	96%	NR	$18,679	$48,352	NR
Cooper Union for the Advancement of Science and Art	ind.	$45,100	$16,270	100%	100%	$38,432	$22,938	$18,303
Cornell University	ind.	$50,953	$13,950	98%	100%	$46,569	$18,334	$23,389
The Culinary Institute of America	ind.	$31,616	$10,870	95%	9%	$18,382	$24,104	$51,200
Daemen College	ind.	$26,940	$12,425	98%	10%	$28,340	$11,025	$31,359
Davis College	ind.	$16,300	$7700	97%	47%	$9816	$14,184	$5360
Dominican College	ind.	$28,448	$12,670	95%	14%	$26,276	$14,842	$31,976
D'Youville College	ind.	$25,750	$11,808	99%	21%	$18,449	$19,109	$34,593
Elmira College	ind.	NR	NR	100%	20%	$30,560	—	$27,757
Farmingdale State College	pub.	$7860	$12,764	85%	9%	$7802	$12,822	NR
Fashion Institute of Technology	pub.	$7215	$13,386	74%	42%	$10,959	$9642	$24,850
Fordham University	ind.	$49,073	$16,845	98%	31%	$34,004	$31,914	$25,069
Hamilton College	ind.	$51,240	$13,010	100%	100%	$48,371	$15,879	$21,491
Hartwick College	ind.	$44,134	$12,093	100%	19%	$35,640	$20,587	$27,653
Hilbert College	ind.	$22,350	$9000	100%	16%	$16,676	$14,674	$19,233
Hobart and William Smith Colleges	ind.	$53,525	$13,525	100%	60%	$35,738	$31,312	$35,935
Hofstra University	ind.	$42,160	$14,460	98%	26%	$31,000	$25,620	NR
Iona College	ind.	$37,682	$14,832	43%	19%	$26,835	$25,679	$34,199
Ithaca College	ind.	$42,884	NR	97%	56%	$36,465	$6419	$40,595
John Jay College of Criminal Justice of the City University of New York	pub.	N/R	NA	92%	NR	$8437	—	NR
The Juilliard School	ind.	$41,660	$15,380	100%	26%	$32,580	$24,460	$32,493
Keuka College	ind.	$30,946	$11,452	84%	10%	$26,408	$15,990	NR

NA = not applicable; NR = not reported; * = includes room and board; † = room only; — = not available.

College Costs At-a-Glance

	Institutional Control ind.=independent; pub.=public	Tuition and Fees	Room and Board	Percent of Eligible Freshmen Receiving Need-Based Gift Awards	Percent of Freshmen Whose Need Was Fully Met	Average Financial Aid Package for Freshmen	Average Net Cost After Aid	Average Indebtedness Upon Graduation
The King's College	ind.	$34,720	$13,650†	100%	10%	$26,863	$21,507	$32,934
Lehman College of the City University of New York	pub.	$7010	NR	93%	93%	$7330	—	$8525
Le Moyne College	ind.	$33,030	$12,970	100%	25%	$26,507	$19,493	$37,337
LIM College	ind.	$26,350	$20,350	74%	7%	$10,954	$35,746	$34,717
Long Island University–LIU Brooklyn	ind.	$36,256	$13,426	84%	5%	$22,880	$26,802	$43,243
Long Island University–LIU Post	ind.	$36,256	$13,426	61%	19%	$23,466	$26,216	$35,102
Manhattan College	ind.	$40,639	$15,010	98%	51%	$23,453	$32,196	$39,443
Manhattanville College	ind.	$37,910	$14,520	75%	12%	$28,549	$23,881	$32,212
Maria College	ind.	$14,210	$7500	80%	7%	$12,127	$9583	NR
Marist College	ind.	$35,110	$16,163	72%	18%	$20,812	$30,461	$39,584
Marymount Manhattan College	ind.	$31,950	$16,400	100%	7%	$17,274	$31,076	$31,606
Medgar Evers College of the City University of New York	pub.	$6650	NA	97%	NR	$8729	—	NR
Mercy College	ind.	$18,392	$13,500	88%	3%	$14,650	$17,242	$29,197
Metropolitan College of New York	ind.	$19,180	NA	100%	NR	$14,593	$4587	$49,357
Molloy College	ind.	$29,100	$14,250	98%	8%	$18,731	$24,619	$33,826
Morrisville State College	pub.	$8023	$13,837	87%	NR	$9793	$12,067	$28,106
Mount Saint Mary College	ind.	$29,920	$14,528	100%	17%	$22,653	$21,795	$26,773
Nazareth College of Rochester	ind.	$32,424	$13,150	100%	42%	$26,585	$18,989	$40,567
New York Institute of Technology	ind.	$35,160	$13,570	79%	NR	$24,827	$23,903	NR
New York School of Interior Design	ind.	$30,945	$16,000†	80%	NR	$11,311	$35,634	$26,458
New York University	ind.	$49,062	$17,578	92%	9%	$37,805	$28,835	$31,210
Niagara University	ind.	$30,950	$12,700	97%	52%	$27,638	$16,012	$32,251
Paul Smith's College	ind.	$25,210	$11,290	95%	NR	NR	NR	$16,175
Purchase College, State University of New York	pub.	$8298	$12,952	98%	NR	$9087	$12,163	$31,188
Queens College of the City University of New York	pub.	$6938	$14,370	96%	5%	$8780	$12,528	$14,225
Rensselaer Polytechnic Institute	ind.	$52,305	$14,960	100%	22%	$41,926	$25,339	NR
Roberts Wesleyan College	ind.	$30,686	$10,430	100%	12%	$26,551	$14,565	$34,679
Rochester Institute of Technology	ind.	$38,568	$12,274	96%	82%	$25,200	$25,642	$38,198
The Sage Colleges	ind.	$28,805	$12,408	66%	NR	NR	NR	$31,699
St. Bonaventure University	ind.	$32,331	$11,473	100%	23%	$27,649	$16,155	$36,649
St. John Fisher College	ind.	$33,120	$12,150	100%	44%	$23,070	$22,200	$35,925
St. John's University	ind.	$39,460	$16,390	75%	15%	$28,216	$27,634	$34,234
St. Joseph's College, Long Island Campus	ind.	$25,930	NA	100%	37%	$17,511	$8419	$27,364
St. Joseph's College, New York	ind.	$25,930	NR	100%	20%	$19,674	$6256	$23,124
St. Lawrence University	ind.	$51,200	$13,190	99%	26%	$45,406	$18,984	$37,919
St. Thomas Aquinas College	ind.	$29,800	$12,390	100%	20%	$16,016	$26,174	$28,750
Sarah Lawrence College	ind.	$52,350	$14,836	98%	17%	$35,892	$31,294	$19,772
School of Visual Arts	ind.	$36,500	$18,300	88%	3%	$17,143	$37,657	$46,328
Siena College	ind.	$35,735	$14,550	100%	25%	$29,503	$20,782	$35,874
Skidmore College	ind.	$50,684	$13,530	100%	100%	$43,000	$21,214	$25,001
State University of New York at Fredonia	pub.	$8089	$12,730	79%	15%	$12,060	$8759	$32,083
State University of New York at New Paltz	pub.	$7754	$12,000	57%	7%	$11,489	$8265	$26,283

NA = not applicable; NR = not reported; * = includes room and board; † = room only; — = not available.

College Costs At-a-Glance

	Institutional Control ind.=independent; pub.=public	Tuition and Fees	Room and Board	Percent of Eligible Freshmen Receiving Need-Based Gift Awards	Percent of Freshmen Whose Need Was Fully Met	Average Financial Aid Package for Freshmen	Average Net Cost After Aid	Average Indebtedness Upon Graduation
State University of New York at Oswego	pub.	$7961	$13,390	95%	6%	$12,366	$8985	$28,676
State University of New York at Plattsburgh	pub.	$7906	$12,150	91%	18%	$13,814	$6242	$28,779
State University of New York College at Cortland	pub.	$8106	$12,600	75%	9%	$14,839	$5867	$29,674
State University of New York College at Geneseo	pub.	$8176	$12,264	78%	10%	$9147	$11,293	$24,784
State University of New York College at Potsdam	pub.	$7984	$12,420	86%	6%	$17,571	$2833	$28,582
State University of New York College of Agriculture and Technology at Cobleskill	pub.	$7929	$13,018	83%	1%	$7607	$13,340	$26,520
State University of New York College of Environmental Science and Forestry	pub.	$8103	$15,040	93%	48%	$14,200	$8943	$24,269
State University of New York College of Technology at Canton	pub.	$7881	$12,150	91%	21%	$11,458	$8573	$31,665
State University of New York College of Technology at Delhi	pub.	$8095	$11,680	NR	NR	NR	NR	$28,367
State University of New York Maritime College	pub.	$7834	$11,948	68%	28%	$4479	$15,303	NR
State University of New York Polytechnic Institute	pub.	$7890	$12,068	94%	100%	$6215	$13,743	NR
Stony Brook University, State University of New York	pub.	$8999	$12,882	92%	17%	$13,687	$8194	$24,656
Syracuse University	ind.	$45,022	$15,217	93%	51%	$36,040	$24,199	$37,753
Touro College	ind.	$16,980	$11,970	100%	35%	$8231	$20,719	NR
Union College	ind.	$53,490	$13,119	97%	100%	$41,185	$25,424	$33,045
University at Albany, State University of New York	pub.	$9223	$12,942	85%	6%	$11,352	$10,813	$21,217
University at Buffalo, the State University of New York	pub.	$9574	$13,548	82%	8%	$10,577	$12,545	$26,046
University of Rochester	ind.	$51,898	$15,338	100%	91%	$44,623	$22,613	$30,742
Utica College	ind.	$19,996	$10,434	98%	6%	$14,292	$16,138	$33,336
Vassar College	ind.	$53,090	$12,400	100%	100%	$51,083	$14,407	$18,462
Villa Maria College	ind.	$20,770	NA	NR	NR	NR	NR	$22,658
Wagner College	ind.	$43,980	$13,260	100%	29%	$30,427	$26,813	NR
Webb Institute	ind.	$48,775	$14,750	100%	NR	$49,330	$14,195	$15,000
Wells College	ind.	$39,600	$13,730	100%	12%	$37,677	$15,653	$34,735
York College of the City University of New York	pub.	$6747	NA	92%	2%	$8441	—	$4614
North Carolina								
Appalachian State University	pub.	$7136	$8100	79%	16%	$9177	$6059	$22,696
Barton College	ind.	$29,998	$9856	100%	10%	$23,395	$16,459	$28,018
Belmont Abbey College	ind.	$18,500	$10,094	100%	12%	$12,836	$15,758	$28,477
Brevard College	ind.	N/R	NR	100%	8%	$20,009	—	$28,511
Cabarrus College of Health Sciences	ind.	$12,268	NA	100%	NR	NR	NR	NR
Campbell University	ind.	$30,050	$10,760	77%	30%	$26,332	$14,478	$26,242
Carolina Christian College	ind.	$12,200	NA	NR	NR	NR	NR	$9500
Catawba College	ind.	$29,920	$10,488	73%	23%	$26,992	$13,416	$30,490
Charlotte Christian College and Theological Seminary	ind.	N/R	NA	NR	NR	NR	NR	$33,034
Chowan University	ind.	$22,480	NR	100%	5%	$20,641	$1839	$41,845
Davidson College	ind.	$50,444	$13,954	100%	100%	$46,079	$18,319	$20,431
Duke University	ind.	$51,265	$14,438	97%	100%	$49,774	$15,929	$22,256
East Carolina University	pub.	$6946	$9835	73%	10%	$9803	$6978	$29,391
Elizabeth City State University	pub.	$4888	$7479	96%	1%	$8641	$3726	$19,631

NA = not applicable; NR = not reported; * = includes room and board; † = room only; — = not available.

College Costs At-a-Glance

	Institutional Control ind.=independent; pub.=public	Tuition and Fees	Room and Board	Percent of Eligible Freshmen Receiving Need-Based Gift Awards	Percent of Freshmen Whose Need Was Fully Met	Average Financial Aid Package for Freshmen	Average Net Cost After Aid	Average Indebtedness Upon Graduation
Elon University	ind.	$33,104	$11,495	88%	14%	$19,363	$25,236	$30,170
Gardner-Webb University	ind.	$29,610	$9780	80%	20%	$24,926	$14,464	$31,901
Guilford College	ind.	$34,215	$10,222	82%	10%	$26,190	$18,247	$20,682
Heritage Bible College	ind.	N/R	NR	NR	NR	NR	NR	$15,000
High Point University	ind.	$34,005	$13,350	70%	18%	$16,330	$31,025	$35,897
Johnson C. Smith University	ind.	$18,236	$7100	95%	4%	$16,194	$9142	$38,732
John Wesley University	ind.	$11,230	$9280†	94%	4%	$8102	$12,408	$28,217
Lees-McRae College	ind.	$26,198	$10,758	82%	2%	$23,931	$13,025	NR
Lenoir-Rhyne University	ind.	$35,350	$12,150	100%	20%	$29,154	$18,346	$28,294
Meredith College	ind.	$34,907	$10,390	100%	19%	$25,635	$19,662	$33,993
Methodist University	ind.	N/R	NR	85%	8%	$23,494	—	$27,863
Mid-Atlantic Christian University	ind.	$13,600	$8200	73%	10%	$8414	$13,386	$26,414
Montreat College	ind.	$24,940	$8370	99%	19%	$20,724	$12,586	$24,512
North Carolina Agricultural and Technical State University	pub.	$6372	$7153	87%	9%	$11,393	$2132	$31,010
North Carolina State University	pub.	$9058	$10,854	95%	25%	$13,394	$6518	$21,507
Piedmont International University	ind.	$10,100	$7185	100%	9%	$8102	$9183	$19,784
Queens University of Charlotte	ind.	$32,560	$11,486	100%	25%	$22,842	$21,204	NR
St. Andrews University	ind.	$24,874	$10,396	99%	8%	$21,099	$14,171	$25,327
Saint Augustine's University	ind.	$17,890	$7692	NR	NR	NR	NR	$19,500
Salem College	ind.	$27,406	$11,500	NR	NR	NR	NR	NR
University of Mount Olive	ind.	N/R	NR	98%	18%	$16,089	—	$31,273
University of North Carolina at Asheville	pub.	$6977	$8746	96%	24%	$11,656	$4067	$22,026
The University of North Carolina at Chapel Hill	pub.	$9005	$11,556	91%	83%	$19,081	$1480	$20,852
The University of North Carolina at Charlotte	pub.	$6763	$10,470	77%	15%	$9875	$7358	$27,453
The University of North Carolina at Greensboro	pub.	$7042	$8580	70%	26%	$11,569	$4053	$27,073
The University of North Carolina at Pembroke	pub.	$5816	$8572	89%	7%	$9653	$4735	$25,263
University of North Carolina School of the Arts	pub.	$9211	$8977	84%	8%	$12,260	$5928	$28,551
The University of North Carolina Wilmington	pub.	$6952	$9489	95%	12%	$8252	$8189	$25,112
Wake Forest University	ind.	$51,400	$15,354	95%	100%	$46,337	$20,417	$33,797
Western Carolina University	pub.	$7027	$8864	95%	69%	$18,707	—	$20,201
William Peace University	ind.	$28,700	$10,800	NR	NR	$19,794	$19,706	$20,921
Wingate University	ind.	$31,120	$10,780	100%	33%	$24,556	$17,344	$31,997
North Dakota								
Dickinson State University	pub.	$6348	$6750	94%	41%	$10,046	$3052	$25,936
Mayville State University	pub.	$6254	$7107	97%	35%	$10,710	$2651	$32,424
Minot State University	pub.	$6568	NR	95%	55%	$9531	—	$25,110
University of Jamestown	ind.	$21,158	$7350	100%	26%	$16,219	$12,289	$25,368
Valley City State University	pub.	$7195	$6072	98%	54%	$13,133	$134	$24,281
Ohio								
Allegheny Wesleyan College	ind.	N/R	NR	100%	100%	NR	NR	NR
Art Academy of Cincinnati	ind.	N/R	NR	96%	13%	$12,000	—	$25,030
Baldwin Wallace University	ind.	$31,668	$9142	100%	20%	$24,408	$16,402	$34,423

NA = not applicable; NR = not reported; * = includes room and board; † = room only; — = not available.

College Costs At-a-Glance

	Institutional Control ind.=independent; pub.=public	Tuition and Fees	Room and Board	Percent of Eligible Freshmen Receiving Need-Based Gift Awards	Percent of Freshmen Whose Need Was Fully Met	Average Financial Aid Package for Freshmen	Average Net Cost After Aid	Average Indebtedness Upon Graduation
Bluffton University	ind.	$31,672	$10,484	100%	12%	$27,236	$14,920	$38,701
Bowling Green State University	pub.	$11,057	$8690	88%	15%	$13,820	$5927	$30,801
Capital University	ind.	$34,600	$10,178	99%	30%	$29,723	$15,055	$32,496
Case Western Reserve University	ind.	$46,006	$14,298	96%	61%	$37,695	$22,609	$30,561
Cedarville University	ind.	$29,156	$7088	63%	37%	$20,559	$15,685	$29,582
Cincinnati Christian University	ind.	N/R	NR	97%	13%	$12,827	—	$25,089
Cleveland Institute of Art	ind.	$40,655	$10,800	100%	8%	$28,654	$22,801	$35,136
Cleveland Institute of Music	ind.	N/R	NR	100%	25%	$34,990	—	$27,270
Cleveland State University	pub.	$9696	$12,000	83%	10%	$8902	$12,794	$25,504
The College of Wooster	ind.	$46,860	$11,040	96%	59%	$42,056	$15,844	$29,650
Columbus College of Art & Design	ind.	$35,375	$9370	99%	7%	$22,951	$21,794	$32,258
Defiance College	ind.	$32,190	$10,050	100%	9%	$23,891	$18,349	$19,554
Denison University	ind.	$48,960	$11,970	100%	40%	$39,755	$21,175	$28,833
Franciscan University of Steubenville	ind.	$26,430	$8400	100%	17%	$16,377	$18,453	NR
Heidelberg University	ind.	$30,200	$10,200	100%	22%	$24,888	$15,512	$35,872
John Carroll University	ind.	$39,790	NR	98%	29%	$31,492	$8298	$31,993
Kent State University	pub.	$10,012	$10,720	53%	13%	$11,097	$9635	$33,234
Kent State University at Geauga	pub.	$5664	NA	74%	5%	$6535	—	NR
Kent State University at Stark	pub.	$5664	NA	69%	11%	$6368	—	NR
Kenyon College	ind.	$51,200	$12,130	99%	100%	$41,728	$21,602	$27,000
Lake Erie College	ind.	$30,862	$9132	100%	21%	$25,607	$14,387	$38,234
Malone University	ind.	$29,900	$9300	100%	13%	$25,125	$14,075	$31,225
Marietta College	ind.	$36,060	$11,320	96%	22%	$30,481	$16,899	$40,196
Mercy College of Ohio	ind.	$14,610	$5460†	NR	NR	NR	NR	NR
Miami University	pub.	$14,288	$12,014	87%	27%	$13,219	$13,083	$30,015
Mount Carmel College of Nursing	ind.	$13,107	$5000†	78%	9%	$6516	$11,591	$35,713
Mount St. Joseph University	ind.	$29,100	$9266	99%	17%	$20,897	$17,469	NR
Mount Vernon Nazarene University	ind.	$28,090	$7854	100%	35%	$23,264	$12,680	$21,564
Muskingum University	ind.	$27,812	$11,040	100%	26%	$25,880	$12,972	$33,490
Oberlin College	ind.	$52,052	$14,010	100%	100%	$42,479	$23,583	$27,114
Ohio Northern University	ind.	$29,820	$11,050	100%	23%	$27,557	$13,313	NR
The Ohio State University	pub.	$10,037	$11,666	91%	28%	$14,399	$7304	$27,930
Ohio University	pub.	$11,744	$11,176	92%	42%	$10,034	$12,886	$27,879
Ohio University–Chillicothe	pub.	N/R	NA	85%	15%	$6473	—	$27,879
Ohio University–Eastern	pub.	$5150	NA	84%	12%	$5698	—	$27,879
Ohio University–Lancaster	pub.	N/R	NA	80%	15%	$6296	—	$27,879
Ohio University–Southern Campus	pub.	N/R	NA	87%	13%	$6840	—	$27,879
Ohio University–Zanesville	pub.	$5076	NR	86%	10%	$6206	—	$27,879
Ohio Wesleyan University	ind.	$44,090	$11,770	100%	17%	$35,757	$20,103	$34,666
Otterbein University	ind.	$31,874	$10,828	99%	23%	$25,048	$17,654	$40,397
Shawnee State University	pub.	$11,296	$10,116	72%	5%	$8662	$12,750	$30,554
Tiffin University	ind.	$23,850	$10,900	100%	16%	$18,876	$15,874	$37,834

NA = not applicable; NR = not reported; * = includes room and board; † = room only; — = not available.

College Costs At-a-Glance

	Institutional Control ind.=independent; pub.=public	Tuition and Fees	Room and Board	Percent of Eligible Freshmen Receiving Need-Based Gift Awards	Percent of Freshmen Whose Need Was Fully Met	Average Financial Aid Package for Freshmen	Average Net Cost After Aid	Average Indebtedness Upon Graduation
The University of Akron	pub.	$10,270	$10,684	55%	13%	$8658	$12,296	$32,372
University of Cincinnati	pub.	$11,000	$10,928	39%	7%	$8558	$13,370	$28,970
University of Dayton	ind.	$40,940	$12,680	100%	20%	$27,507	$26,113	$35,740
The University of Findlay	ind.	$33,320	$9720	100%	20%	$24,531	$18,509	$36,249
University of Mount Union	ind.	$29,890	$10,100	100%	12%	$23,612	$16,378	$32,680
The University of Toledo	pub.	$9560	$11,508	99%	14%	$11,808	$9260	$24,437
Ursuline College	ind.	$31,150	$10,362	100%	16%	$26,348	$15,164	$32,375
Wittenberg University	ind.	$38,730	$10,126	99%	21%	$28,689	$20,167	$35,034
Wright State University	pub.	$8730	$11,376	87%	17%	$10,111	$9995	$30,061
Wright State University–Lake Campus	pub.	$5842	$9674	88%	23%	$7441	$8075	$30,061
Xavier University	ind.	$36,150	$11,730	66%	10%	$22,548	$25,332	$32,108
Youngstown State University	pub.	$8317	$8990	77%	10%	$8750	$8557	$30,403
Oklahoma								
Cameron University	pub.	$5970	$5102	93%	14%	$9353	$1719	$20,019
East Central University	pub.	$6279	$5350	70%	NR	$5927	$5702	$19,170
Langston University	pub.	$5388	$10,050	94%	12%	$10,170	$5268	$39,681
Northeastern State University	pub.	$6207	$6650	94%	86%	$11,045	$1812	$23,840
Oklahoma Baptist University	ind.	$26,840	$7150	85%	30%	$22,070	$11,920	$24,451
Oklahoma Christian University	ind.	$21,670	$7590	65%	43%	$22,667	$6593	$27,793
Oklahoma City University	ind.	$30,726	$8624	100%	82%	$22,440	$16,910	$26,329
Oklahoma Panhandle State University	pub.	$7294	$5344	NR	NR	NR	NR	NR
Oklahoma State University	pub.	$8320	$8443	81%	18%	$14,732	$2031	$24,252
Oklahoma Wesleyan University	ind.	N/R	NR	100%	13%	$15,663	—	$25,234
Oral Roberts University	ind.	$26,792	$8750	99%	56%	$28,341	$7201	$32,970
Randall University	ind.	$13,040	$7360	67%	6%	$10,336	$10,064	$25,813
Rogers State University	pub.	$7000	$9512	89%	10%	$9200	$7312	$16,164
Southeastern Oklahoma State University	pub.	$6450	$6535	71%	10%	$11,434	$1551	$20,983
Southwestern Oklahoma State University	pub.	$6690	$5400	86%	17%	$5780	$6310	$18,809
University of Central Oklahoma	pub.	$6096	$7130	72%	16%	$11,430	$1796	$26,335
University of Oklahoma	pub.	$8631	$10,280	48%	80%	$13,032	$5879	$28,444
The University of Tulsa	ind.	$41,024	$11,116	30%	46%	$32,073	$20,067	$37,136
Oregon								
Corban University	ind.	$31,640	$10,060	100%	16%	$23,247	$18,453	$27,325
Eastern Oregon University	pub.	$8004	$8930	96%	20%	$10,157	$6777	$28,942
George Fox University	ind.	$34,866	$10,886	100%	44%	$24,260	$21,492	$22,799
Lewis & Clark College	ind.	$46,894	$11,540	99%	53%	$41,197	$17,237	$29,913
Linfield College	ind.	$41,576	$11,770	84%	20%	$34,943	$18,403	$34,320
Marylhurst University	ind.	$20,835	NA	100%	NR	$8266	$12,569	$51,833
Northwest Christian University	ind.	$28,680	$8800	100%	21%	$22,454	$15,026	$23,279
Oregon College of Art and Craft	ind.	$33,160	$9900	100%	27%	$15,902	$27,158	$20,793
Oregon State University	pub.	$10,366	$12,153	86%	10%	$11,816	$10,703	$26,453
Pacific University	ind.	$41,054	$11,822	73%	17%	$33,197	$19,679	$34,282

NA = not applicable; NR = not reported; * = includes room and board; † = room only; — = not available.

College Costs At-a-Glance

	Institutional Control ind.=independent; pub.=public	Tuition and Fees	Room and Board	Percent of Eligible Freshmen Receiving Need-Based Gift Awards	Percent of Freshmen Whose Need Was Fully Met	Average Financial Aid Package for Freshmen	Average Net Cost After Aid	Average Indebtedness Upon Graduation
Portland State University	pub.	$6933	$12,822	75%	8%	$9943	$9812	$27,213
Reed College	ind.	$52,150	$13,150	100%	89%	$41,643	$23,657	$19,627
Southern Oregon University	pub.	$8523	$12,756	82%	29%	$9406	$11,873	$27,375
University of Oregon	pub.	$10,762	$12,210	78%	7%	$10,812	$12,160	$25,542
University of Portland	ind.	N/R	NR	76%	10%	$27,296	—	$28,307
Warner Pacific College	ind.	$22,710	$8900	77%	17%	$18,992	$12,618	$36,916
Western Oregon University	pub.	$9285	$9798	97%	9%	$9792	$9291	$30,586
Willamette University	ind.	$48,164	$11,830	98%	26%	$37,016	$22,978	$29,958
Pennsylvania								
Albright College	ind.	$43,304	$11,606	100%	10%	$39,850	$15,060	$38,196
Allegheny College	ind.	$45,970	$11,650	100%	27%	$41,707	$15,913	NR
Alvernia University	ind.	$33,640	$11,890	100%	14%	$22,520	$23,010	$51,958
Arcadia University	ind.	$42,330	$13,660	100%	35%	$30,745	$25,245	NR
Bloomsburg University of Pennsylvania	pub.	$10,154	$8912	65%	9%	$8468	$10,598	$36,915
Bryn Mawr College	ind.	$50,500	$15,910	100%	100%	$46,357	$20,053	$23,081
Bucknell University	ind.	$51,960	$12,656	90%	100%	$35,500	$29,116	$22,600
Cabrini University	ind.	$31,350	$12,340	90%	21%	$17,185	$26,505	$43,437
Cairn University	ind.	$26,493	$9803	100%	16%	$23,175	$13,121	$31,166
California University of Pennsylvania	pub.	$10,339	$10,086	82%	9%	$9407	$11,018	$25,683
Carlow University	ind.	$27,764	$10,784	82%	NR	$25,130	$13,418	NR
Cedar Crest College	ind.	$38,092	$11,208	100%	15%	$30,222	$19,078	$38,726
Central Penn College	ind.	$18,174	$7416	NR	NR	NR	NR	NR
Chatham University	ind.	$35,475	$11,042	100%	31%	$28,841	$17,676	$37,734
Chestnut Hill College	ind.	$35,160	$10,400	99%	9%	$29,275	$16,285	$42,527
Clarion University of Pennsylvania	pub.	N/R	NR	80%	5%	$9204	—	$33,346
Clarks Summit University	ind.	N/R	NR	NR	NR	NR	NR	$29,483
Delaware Valley University	ind.	$36,750	$13,328	100%	14%	$28,389	$21,689	$47,640
DeSales University	ind.	$35,050	$12,400	100%	29%	$26,214	$21,236	$40,194
Dickinson College	ind.	$51,180	$12,794	98%	98%	$45,673	$18,301	$26,908
Drexel University	ind.	$52,002	$13,890	99%	31%	$42,995	$22,897	NR
Duquesne University	ind.	$35,062	$11,760	100%	21%	$25,358	$21,464	$41,272
Eastern University	ind.	$32,080	$10,980	83%	15%	$25,751	$17,309	$38,904
East Stroudsburg University of Pennsylvania	pub.	$9944	$8280	72%	47%	$7703	$10,521	$28,500
Elizabethtown College	ind.	$45,350	$10,990	100%	29%	$32,839	$23,501	$28,106
Franklin & Marshall College	ind.	$52,490	$13,120	97%	100%	$47,895	$17,715	$27,133
Gannon University	ind.	$30,042	$11,990	99%	22%	$25,699	$16,333	NR
Geneva College	ind.	$26,570	$9920	100%	22%	$20,500	$15,990	$10,549
Gettysburg College	ind.	$50,860	$12,140	97%	90%	$41,630	$21,370	$31,169
Grove City College	ind.	$16,630	$9062	99%	12%	$7804	$17,888	$37,655
Gwynedd Mercy University	ind.	$33,520	$11,630	100%	13%	$25,666	$19,484	$43,789
Haverford College	ind.	$51,024	$15,466	99%	100%	$49,928	$16,562	$13,000
Holy Family University	ind.	$29,338	$13,576	99%	20%	$26,244	$16,670	$39,664

NA = not applicable; NR = not reported; * = includes room and board; † = room only; — = not available.

College Costs At a Glance

	Institutional Control ind.=independent; pub.=public	Tuition and Fees	Room and Board	Percent of Eligible Freshmen Receiving Need-Based Gift Awards	Percent of Freshmen Whose Need Was Fully Met	Average Financial Aid Package for Freshmen	Average Net Cost After Aid	Average Indebtedness Upon Graduation
Indiana University of Pennsylvania	pub.	$11,368	$12,402	70%	10%	$11,192	$12,578	$36,514
Juniata College	ind.	$43,875	$12,040	97%	26%	$32,797	$23,118	$36,338
King's College	ind.	$34,720	$12,138	100%	18%	$25,853	$21,005	$37,874
Kutztown University of Pennsylvania	pub.	$9618	$9438	62%	6%	$8375	$10,681	$39,230
Lafayette College	ind.	$65,890*	NR	94%	100%	$45,502	$20,388	$29,324
Lancaster Bible College	ind.	N/R	NR	100%	26%	$17,408	—	$30,511
La Roche College	ind.	$27,000	$10,924	90%	33%	$32,150	$5774	$34,992
La Salle University	ind.	$29,500	$15,080	98%	12%	$31,471	$13,109	$36,907
Lebanon Valley College	ind.	$42,180	$11,410	99%	29%	$33,464	$20,126	$46,346
Lehigh University	ind.	$48,320	$12,690	97%	80%	$42,844	$18,166	$34,215
Lincoln University	pub.	$11,102	$9268	100%	5%	$11,351	$9019	$31,555
Lock Haven University of Pennsylvania	pub.	$10,229	$9588	71%	96%	$5916	$13,901	$34,192
Lycoming College	ind.	$37,162	$11,418	100%	16%	$36,681	$11,899	NR
Mansfield University of Pennsylvania	pub.	$11,908	$11,468	70%	6%	$9957	$13,419	$41,816
Marywood University	ind.	$33,000	$13,900	100%	20%	$25,698	$21,202	$42,603
Messiah College	ind.	$33,180	$9920	99%	21%	$24,666	$18,434	$39,617
Millersville University of Pennsylvania	pub.	$11,494	$12,228	72%	5%	$7350	$16,372	$29,481
Misericordia University	ind.	$31,660	$13,550	100%	21%	$23,823	$21,387	$42,686
Moravian College	ind.	$42,024	$12,694	100%	16%	$32,775	$21,943	$33,377
Mount Aloysius College	ind.	$21,850	$9940	100%	NR	$13,800	$17,990	NR
Muhlenberg College	ind.	$48,310	$11,090	99%	31%	$34,265	$25,135	$31,063
Neumann University	ind.	$28,580	$12,158	80%	NR	$23,340	$17,398	NR
Peirce College	ind.	$14,472	NA	94%	NR	$11,202	$3270	NR
Penn State Abington	pub.	$14,172	NA	81%	4%	$10,608	$3564	$35,758
Penn State Altoona	pub.	$14,828	$11,860	62%	4%	$9690	$16,998	$41,435
Penn State Beaver	pub.	$13,678	$11,860	69%	6%	$11,002	$14,536	$32,739
Penn State Berks	pub.	$14,828	$12,940	66%	4%	$9828	$17,940	$38,227
Penn State Brandywine	pub.	$14,134	NA	73%	5%	$10,170	$3964	$32,742
Penn State Erie, The Behrend College	pub.	$14,828	$11,860	66%	4%	$10,712	$15,976	$39,209
Penn State Greater Allegheny	pub.	$13,666	$11,860	88%	5%	$13,390	$12,136	$42,291
Penn State Harrisburg	pub.	$14,828	$13,460	67%	6%	$10,740	$17,548	$42,149
Penn State Hazleton	pub.	$14,072	$11,860	78%	3%	$11,406	$14,526	$43,579
Penn State Lehigh Valley	pub.	$14,134	NA	78%	4%	$10,604	$3530	$34,713
Penn State New Kensington	pub.	$13,616	NR	87%	15%	$10,771	$2845	$34,024
Penn State Schuylkill	pub.	$14,072	$8240	81%	6%	$12,159	$10,153	$41,345
Penn State University Park	pub.	$17,900	$11,860	43%	9%	$10,524	$19,236	$37,213
Penn State Wilkes-Barre	pub.	$13,540	NA	81%	8%	$10,737	$2803	$35,984
Penn State Worthington Scranton	pub.	$14,072	NA	90%	4%	$10,263	$3809	$37,098
Penn State York	pub.	$14,134	NA	77%	8%	$10,832	$3302	$36,176
Pennsylvania College of Technology	pub.	$18,570	$11,244	77%	NR	$12,327	$17,487	NR
Philadelphia University	ind.	$37,800	$12,570	100%	9%	$33,094	$17,276	$40,227
Point Park University	ind.	$30,130	$11,960	100%	16%	$26,242	$15,848	$26,729

NA = not applicable; NR = not reported; * = includes room and board; † = room only; — = not available.

College Costs At-a-Glance

	Institutional Control ind.=independent; pub.=public	Tuition and Fees	Room and Board	Percent of Eligible Freshmen Receiving Need-Based Gift Awards	Percent of Freshmen Whose Need Was Fully Met	Average Financial Aid Package for Freshmen	Average Net Cost After Aid	Average Indebtedness Upon Graduation
Robert Morris University	ind.	$28,250	$10,910	100%	13%	$24,242	$14,918	$39,431
Rosemont College	ind.	$19,480	NR	100%	12%	$14,549	$4931	$40,792
Saint Joseph's University	ind.	$43,020	$14,524	97%	23%	$30,163	$27,381	NR
Saint Vincent College	ind.	$33,814	$11,105	85%	31%	$30,476	$14,443	$38,493
Seton Hill University	ind.	$33,520	$11,000	100%	22%	$25,298	$19,222	$38,414
Shippensburg University of Pennsylvania	pub.	$11,452	$11,756	78%	5%	$8766	$14,442	$33,673
Slippery Rock University of Pennsylvania	pub.	$9862	$10,110	66%	10%	$9282	$10,690	$33,303
Susquehanna University	ind.	$45,470	$12,090	100%	24%	$35,083	$22,477	$36,882
Swarthmore College	ind.	$50,822	$14,952	100%	100%	$48,573	$17,201	$22,957
Temple University	pub.	$16,274	$11,298	85%	28%	$18,780	$8792	$37,708
Thiel College	ind.	$29,740	$11,700	92%	8%	$24,533	$16,907	$37,932
University of Pennsylvania	ind.	$53,534	$15,066	98%	100%	$47,992	$20,608	$24,536
University of Pittsburgh	pub.	$18,618	$10,950	80%	14%	$12,459	$17,109	$38,612
University of Pittsburgh at Bradford	pub.	$13,608	$8794	91%	14%	$17,581	$4821	$32,816
University of Pittsburgh at Greensburg	pub.	$13,618	$9990	90%	9%	$11,436	$12,172	$32,987
University of Pittsburgh at Johnstown	pub.	$13,388	$9684	90%	16%	$10,712	$12,360	$39,145
University of the Sciences	ind.	$38,850	$15,188	76%	60%	$18,444	$35,594	$24,191
University of Valley Forge	ind.	$21,270	$8610	100%	12%	$14,142	$15,738	$34,920
Ursinus College	ind.	$50,360	$12,560	100%	31%	$37,879	$25,041	$38,537
Villanova University	ind.	$49,280	$13,093	94%	19%	$35,801	$26,572	$35,545
Washington & Jefferson College	ind.	$44,900	$11,854	81%	16%	$35,711	$21,043	NR
Waynesburg University	ind.	$22,800	$9490	100%	32%	$18,999	$13,291	$30,850
West Chester University of Pennsylvania	pub.	$9720	$8736	52%	8%	$7063	$11,393	$33,814
Westminster College	ind.	$36,230	$11,020	100%	21%	$28,611	$18,639	$36,692
Widener University	ind.	$42,870	$13,616	99%	21%	$34,200	$22,286	NR
Wilkes University	ind.	$33,568	$13,746	99%	10%	$25,938	$21,376	$43,241
Wilson College	ind.	$24,430	$11,190	100%	23%	$20,934	$14,686	$31,613
York College of Pennsylvania	ind.	$18,780	$10,460	68%	17%	$13,354	$15,886	$40,617
Puerto Rico								
Carlos Albizu University	ind.	N/R	NA	100%	NR	$1166	—	NR
Inter American University of Puerto Rico, Bayamón Campus	ind.	$5178	$6114	99%	NR	$1311	$9981	NR
Inter American University of Puerto Rico, Guayama Campus	ind.	$6425	NA	99%	NR	$1399	$5026	NR
Polytechnic University of Puerto Rico	ind.	$8328	$11,837	100%	NR	$5339	$14,826	NR
Theological University of the Caribbean	ind.	$5168	$2400	100%	NR	NR	NR	NR
University of Puerto Rico in Bayamón	pub.	$2048	NA	NR	NR	NR	NR	NR
University of Puerto Rico, Mayagüez Campus	pub.	N/R	NR	100%	NR	$4979	—	$7550
Rhode Island								
Brown University	ind.	$53,419	$14,020	93%	100%	$46,043	$21,396	$23,810
Providence College	ind.	$46,970	$13,790	98%	30%	$32,374	$28,386	$39,775
Rhode Island College	pub.	$8206	$10,794	87%	12%	$10,242	$8758	$26,519
Rhode Island School of Design	ind.	$47,110	$12,850	86%	3%	$27,614	$32,346	$31,037
Roger Williams University	ind.	$31,850	$15,412	46%	7%	$19,829	$27,433	$41,632

NA = not applicable; NR = not reported; * = includes room and board; † = room only; — = not available.

College Costs At-a-Glance

	Institutional Control ind.=independent; pub.=public	Tuition and Fees	Room and Board	Percent of Eligible Freshmen Receiving Need-Based Gift Awards	Percent of Freshmen Whose Need Was Fully Met	Average Financial Aid Package for Freshmen	Average Net Cost After Aid	Average Indebtedness Upon Graduation
Salve Regina University	ind.	$37,820	$13,650	100%	12%	$27,009	$24,461	$29,192
University of Rhode Island	pub.	$12,884	$7622	96%	3%	$16,577	$3929	$32,750
South Carolina								
Anderson University	ind.	$25,880	$9174	100%	28%	$19,524	$15,530	$29,846
The Citadel, The Military College of South Carolina	pub.	$12,755	$7924	83%	19%	$14,144	$6535	$27,872
Claflin University	ind.	$16,158	$8932	99%	5%	$17,490	$7600	$31,688
Clemson University	pub.	$14,318	$9144	96%	19%	$13,045	$10,417	$26,335
Coastal Carolina University	pub.	$10,876	$8890	50%	8%	$9857	$9909	$38,897
College of Charleston	pub.	$11,846	$12,048	73%	19%	$13,421	$10,473	$26,203
Columbia International University	ind.	$22,390	$7990	100%	16%	$17,331	$13,049	$22,405
Converse College	ind.	$18,030	$10,610	98%	22%	$14,679	$13,961	$28,036
Francis Marion University	pub.	$10,428	$7716	99%	28%	$16,844	$1300	$36,587
Furman University	ind.	$47,164	$11,864	100%	35%	$40,141	$18,887	$36,846
Newberry College	ind.	$25,600	$9844	100%	13%	$22,048	$13,396	$18,566
Presbyterian College	ind.	$37,842	$10,298	100%	32%	$34,989	$13,151	$24,930
University of South Carolina	pub.	$11,854	$9700	36%	31%	$8614	$12,940	$29,012
University of South Carolina Aiken	pub.	$10,196	$7466	94%	16%	$10,692	$6970	$31,289
University of South Carolina Upstate	pub.	N/R	NR	70%	6%	$10,329	—	$27,338
Winthrop University	pub.	$14,510	$8572	99%	14%	$14,407	$8675	$30,061
Wofford College	ind.	$41,955	$12,140	100%	46%	$35,201	$18,894	$31,102
South Dakota								
Augustana University	ind.	$30,944	$7480	100%	28%	$28,520	$9904	$36,950
Black Hills State University	pub.	$8004	$6695	NR	NR	NR	NR	$25,628
Dakota State University	pub.	$8927	$6411	61%	13%	$7718	$7620	$24,444
Dakota Wesleyan University	ind.	$26,065	$6800	40%	17%	$21,889	$10,976	$37,564
Mount Marty College	ind.	$26,310	$7846	93%	42%	$28,743	$5413	$30,083
Northern State University	pub.	$8280	$7850	90%	27%	$10,752	$5378	$28,142
South Dakota School of Mines and Technology	pub.	$11,170	$7300	69%	39%	$14,379	$4091	$32,995
University of Sioux Falls	ind.	$27,160	$7140	97%	29%	$22,150	$12,150	$31,146
The University of South Dakota	pub.	$8457	$7535	NR	NR	NR	NR	NR
Tennessee								
Austin Peay State University	pub.	$7689	$8708	85%	NR	$11,153	$5244	$23,808
Belmont University	ind.	$32,820	$11,680	95%	13%	$19,939	$24,561	$31,020
Bryan College	ind.	$25,600	$7300	99%	31%	$23,944	$8956	NR
Carson-Newman University	ind.	$27,400	$8630	99%	23%	$23,773	$12,257	$27,418
Christian Brothers University	ind.	$30,860	$7000	99%	23%	$28,257	$9603	$22,527
Freed-Hardeman University	ind.	$21,950	$7950	98%	31%	$20,151	$9749	$32,899
King University	ind.	$27,276	$8180	99%	18%	$23,738	$11,718	$23,950
Lane College	ind.	$10,690	$4570†	99%	NR	$12,591	$2669	NR
Lee University	ind.	$16,730	$8080	96%	52%	$11,130	$13,680	$31,630
Lincoln Memorial University	ind.	N/R	NR	NR	NR	NR	NR	$19,987

NA = not applicable; NR = not reported; * = includes room and board; † = room only; — = not available.

College Costs At-a-Glance

	Institutional Control ind.=independent; pub.=public	Tuition and Fees	Room and Board	Percent of Eligible Freshmen Receiving Need-Based Gift Awards	Percent of Freshmen Whose Need Was Fully Met	Average Financial Aid Package for Freshmen	Average Net Cost After Aid	Average Indebtedness Upon Graduation
Lipscomb University	ind.	$30,932	$12,034	100%	25%	$23,179	$19,787	$31,082
Maryville College	ind.	$33,524	$10,868	100%	26%	$32,660	$11,732	NR
Memphis College of Art	ind.	$31,700	$8750	100%	3%	$23,909	$16,541	$34,828
Middle Tennessee State University	pub.	$8610	$8850	65%	12%	$10,478	$6982	$25,456
Milligan College	ind.	$31,450	$6700	100%	31%	$23,603	$14,547	$28,510
O'More College of Design	ind.	$28,176	NA	100%	20%	$18,902	$9274	$31,773
Rhodes College	ind.	$44,942	$11,068	100%	60%	$37,546	$18,464	$25,859
Sewanee: The University of the South	ind.	$45,120	$12,880	98%	29%	$34,638	$23,362	$24,431
Southern Adventist University	ind.	$21,150	$6450	93%	2%	$16,647	$10,953	$33,320
Tennessee State University	pub.	N/R	NR	85%	67%	$11,175	—	$35,214
Tennessee Technological University	pub.	N/R	NR	51%	12%	$11,219	—	$19,363
Tennessee Wesleyan University	ind.	$23,800	$7750	99%	20%	$19,231	$12,319	$20,649
Trevecca Nazarene University	ind.	$25,100	$8808	NR	NR	NR	NR	$29,291
Tusculum College	ind.	$23,700	$8700	82%	12%	$20,594	$11,806	$33,916
Union University	ind.	$31,780	$10,350	48%	36%	$31,100	$11,030	$31,784
University of Memphis	pub.	$9497	$9153	83%	6%	$10,501	$8149	$27,155
The University of Tennessee	pub.	$12,724	$10,238	95%	21%	$13,706	$9256	$24,420
The University of Tennessee at Chattanooga	pub.	$8544	$8676	96%	19%	$10,601	$6619	$22,917
The University of Tennessee at Martin	pub.	$9088	$5788	66%	21%	$12,298	$2578	$28,077
Vanderbilt University	ind.	$45,610	$14,962	87%	100%	$47,712	$12,860	$24,122
Texas								
Abilene Christian University	ind.	$32,070	$9730	100%	24%	$23,019	$18,781	NR
Angelo State University	pub.	$8038	$7666	84%	17%	$11,967	$3737	$24,099
Austin College	ind.	$39,010	$12,334	100%	45%	$35,826	$15,518	NR
Austin Graduate School of Theology	ind.	$8750	NA	NR	NR	NR	NR	NR
Baptist University of the Americas	ind.	$6240	$2500†	NR	NR	NR	NR	NR
Baylor University	ind.	$43,790	$12,163	100%	17%	$29,550	$26,403	$44,540
Concordia University Texas	ind.	$29,260	$9836	95%	23%	$26,347	$12,749	$30,699
Criswell College	ind.	$9858	NA	NR	NR	NR	NR	NR
Dallas Baptist University	ind.	$26,180	$7533	61%	36%	$15,619	$18,094	$22,568
East Texas Baptist University	ind.	$24,700	$8709	77%	10%	$18,914	$14,495	$34,048
Hardin-Simmons University	ind.	$27,440	$8420	72%	36%	$28,600	$7260	$39,597
Houston Baptist University	ind.	$30,800	$7858	100%	26%	$30,077	$8581	$32,027
Howard Payne University	ind.	$27,690	$8304	99%	18%	$19,362	$16,632	$34,875
Huston-Tillotson University	ind.	$14,346	$7568	NR	NR	NR	NR	NR
Lamar University	pub.	$9901	$8450	81%	14%	$9982	$8369	$11,878
LeTourneau University	ind.	$29,320	$9870	98%	23%	$25,035	$14,155	$38,988
Lubbock Christian University	ind.	$21,166	$7260	99%	11%	$15,219	$13,207	$31,089
Midland College	pub.	$2064	$5014	NR	NR	NR	NR	NR
Midwestern State University	pub.	N/R	NR	92%	53%	$10,955	—	$28,468
Our Lady of the Lake University	ind.	$28,192	$9388	100%	15%	$21,794	$15,786	$31,438
Paul Quinn College	ind.	N/R	NR	100%	100%	$7988	—	$6102

NA = not applicable; NR = not reported; * = includes room and board; † = room only; — = not available.

College Costs At-a-Glance

	Institutional Control ind.=independent; pub.=public	Tuition and Fees	Room and Board	Percent of Eligible Freshmen Receiving Need-Based Gift Awards	Percent of Freshmen Whose Need Was Fully Met	Average Financial Aid Package for Freshmen	Average Net Cost After Aid	Average Indebtedness Upon Graduation
Prairie View A&M University	pub.	$10,059	$8626	87%	7%	$16,160	$2525	$34,752
Rice University	ind.	$43,918	$13,750	97%	100%	$42,573	$15,095	$22,497
St. Edward's University	ind.	$43,050	$12,940	89%	13%	$35,885	$20,105	$37,377
St. Mary's University	ind.	N/R	NR	99%	13%	$25,269	—	$39,883
Sam Houston State University	pub.	$9516	$8780	88%	17%	$12,150	$6146	$26,135
Schreiner University	ind.	$26,750	$10,912	100%	19%	$18,806	$18,856	$29,020
Southern Methodist University	ind.	$52,498	$16,910	68%	40%	$43,984	$25,424	$29,601
Southwestern University	ind.	$40,560	$11,810	98%	36%	$34,827	$17,543	$32,801
Stephen F. Austin State University	pub.	$9537	$8868	72%	12%	$12,414	$5991	$29,574
Tarleton State University	pub.	$8703	$9970	91%	6%	$10,538	$8135	$25,725
Texas A&M International University	pub.	$11,456	$7882	98%	5%	$11,898	$7440	$17,394
Texas A&M University	pub.	$10,030	$10,368	93%	27%	$18,348	$2050	$24,072
Texas A&M University–Commerce	pub.	$7888	$8326	96%	8%	$11,756	$4458	$28,054
Texas A&M University–Corpus Christi	pub.	$8620	$9195	85%	3%	$9965	$7850	$17,804
Texas A&M University–Kingsville	pub.	$8050	$8530	82%	94%	$13,529	$3051	$29,307
Texas A&M University–Texarkana	pub.	N/R	NR	95%	15%	$11,823	—	$19,207
Texas Christian University	ind.	$42,670	$12,000	94%	40%	$29,339	$25,331	$36,550
Texas Lutheran University	ind.	$29,000	$9720	100%	NR	$27,403	$11,317	$37,337
Texas Southern University	pub.	N/R	NR	88%	88%	$14,500	—	$42,421
Texas State University	pub.	$10,620	$9490	84%	21%	$10,512	$9598	$27,840
Texas Tech University	pub.	$9781	$8505	89%	17%	$14,173	$4113	$29,214
Texas Wesleyan University	ind.	$27,684	$9630	100%	19%	$26,785	$10,529	$12,164
Texas Woman's University	pub.	$8790	$7578	94%	29%	$15,466	$902	$24,916
Trinity University	ind.	$41,344	$13,136	99%	62%	$37,524	$16,956	$38,605
University of Dallas	ind.	$37,230	$11,540	99%	27%	$31,642	$17,128	$32,921
University of Houston	pub.	$11,653	$9830	89%	18%	$12,922	$8561	$23,665
University of Houston–Clear Lake	pub.	N/R	NR	62%	12%	$9815	—	NR
University of Houston–Victoria	pub.	$7368	$7664	93%	16%	$12,367	$2665	NR
University of Mary Hardin-Baylor	ind.	$25,860	$7592	100%	11%	$18,476	$14,976	$38,726
University of North Texas	pub.	$10,520	$8679	74%	11%	$12,387	$6812	$25,249
University of North Texas at Dallas	pub.	$7848	NR	86%	8%	$8721	—	$6927
University of St. Thomas	ind.	$32,660	$8850	100%	13%	$28,300	$13,210	$26,455
The University of Texas at Arlington	pub.	$9616	$8397	71%	15%	$10,555	$7458	$15,559
The University of Texas at Austin	pub.	$10,144	$10,070	77%	20%	$11,349	$8865	$25,338
The University of Texas at Dallas	pub.	$12,162	$10,668	89%	23%	$13,429	$9401	$20,432
The University of Texas at El Paso	pub.	$7548	$9496	82%	7%	$14,633	$2411	$21,840
The University of Texas at San Antonio	pub.	$9044	$8074	88%	6%	$10,174	$6944	$26,763
The University of Texas of the Permian Basin	pub.	$7060	$10,800	79%	83%	$12,060	$5800	$17,578
The University of Texas Rio Grande Valley	pub.	$7438	$7950	99%	2%	$10,869	$4519	$15,731
University of the Incarnate Word	ind.	$29,990	$12,436	99%	21%	$21,365	$21,061	$19,243
Wayland Baptist University	ind.	$18,510	$7176	99%	9%	$14,350	$11,336	$23,764
West Texas A&M University	pub.	$7681	$7196	78%	21%	$29,694	—	$24,525

NA = not applicable; NR = not reported; * = includes room and board; † = room only; — = not available.

College Costs At-a-Glance

	Institutional Control ind.=independent; pub.=public	Tuition and Fees	Room and Board	Percent of Eligible Freshmen Receiving Need-Based Gift Awards	Percent of Freshmen Whose Need Was Fully Met	Average Financial Aid Package for Freshmen	Average Net Cost After Aid	Average Indebtedness Upon Graduation
Utah								
Brigham Young University	ind.	$5300	$7448	56%	2%	$6447	$6301	$15,158
Dixie State University	pub.	$5080	$5615	89%	8%	$8997	$1698	$15,882
Southern Utah University	pub.	$6530	$7067	58%	14%	$9641	$3956	$16,892
University of Utah	pub.	$8518	$9406	91%	19%	$19,868	—	$21,081
Utah State University	pub.	$6869	$5870	63%	16%	$10,341	$2398	$23,000
Utah Valley University	pub.	$5530	NA	69%	15%	$7902	—	$22,259
Weber State University	pub.	$5525	$5400	74%	60%	$5183	$5742	$22,029
Westminster College	ind.	$32,104	$9618	100%	24%	$27,834	$13,888	$30,442
Vermont								
Bennington College	ind.	$51,920	$15,040	100%	23%	$39,982	$26,978	$28,263
Champlain College	ind.	$38,660	$14,472	99%	16%	$27,978	$25,154	$34,582
Goddard College	ind.	N/R	NR	80%	NR	$10,090	—	NR
Marlboro College	ind.	$40,425	$11,930	96%	98%	$39,972	$12,383	$31,747
Middlebury College	ind.	$50,063	$14,269	99%	100%	$47,554	$16,778	$18,736
Saint Michael's College	ind.	$41,975	$11,300	100%	36%	$32,135	$21,140	$38,226
University of Vermont	pub.	$17,270	$11,608	100%	17%	$25,064	$3814	$26,964
Vermont Technical College	pub.	$15,000	$10,290	92%	8%	$12,492	$12,798	$29,988
Virginia								
Averett University	ind.	$31,980	$8990	100%	13%	$25,800	$15,170	$35,659
Bluefield College	ind.	$25,560	$8843	100%	13%	$19,071	$15,332	$30,487
Bridgewater College	ind.	$33,820	$12,440	100%	30%	$31,579	$14,681	$34,035
Christendom College	ind.	$24,840	$9730	100%	NR	$18,467	$16,103	$27,005
Christopher Newport University	pub.	$13,054	$10,914	68%	23%	$9117	$14,851	$30,451
The College of William and Mary	pub.	$21,234	$11,382	88%	24%	$21,252	$11,364	$26,400
Eastern Mennonite University	ind.	$34,200	$10,660	100%	12%	$31,857	$13,003	$36,132
Emory & Henry College	ind.	$33,700	$11,200	91%	20%	$31,237	$13,663	$30,514
George Mason University	pub.	$11,300	$10,730	84%	7%	$14,893	$7137	$30,132
Hampden-Sydney College	ind.	$43,940	$13,420	99%	30%	$31,743	$25,617	$34,344
Hampton University	ind.	$24,242	$10,684	100%	40%	$5641	$29,285	$34,367
Hollins University	ind.	$36,835	$12,800	100%	26%	$36,183	$13,452	$34,414
James Madison University	pub.	$10,342	$9334	60%	88%	$9593	$10,083	$28,407
Liberty University	ind.	$23,020	$9306	99%	14%	$14,427	$17,899	$21,474
Longwood University	pub.	$12,240	$10,685	86%	41%	$13,539	$9386	$28,047
Lynchburg College	ind.	$36,620	$10,120	100%	27%	$28,414	$18,326	$35,614
Mary Baldwin University	ind.	$31,085	$9410	100%	17%	$28,645	$11,850	$35,169
Marymount University	ind.	$30,426	$12,805	65%	17%	$24,041	$19,190	$35,545
Old Dominion University	pub.	$10,046	$10,864	81%	18%	$11,895	$9015	$30,410
Patrick Henry College	ind.	$28,172	$10,728	100%	NR	$14,200	$24,700	$44,000
Radford University	pub.	$10,081	$8946	66%	24%	$10,394	$8633	$29,103
Randolph College	ind.	$36,770	$12,580	100%	21%	$31,340	$18,010	$35,199

NA = not applicable; NR = not reported; * = includes room and board; † = room only; — = not available.

College Costs At-a-Glance

	Institutional Control ind.=independent; pub.=public	Tuition and Fees	Room and Board	Percent of Eligible Freshmen Receiving Need-Based Gift Awards	Percent of Freshmen Whose Need Was Fully Met	Average Financial Aid Package for Freshmen	Average Net Cost After Aid	Average Indebtedness Upon Graduation
Randolph-Macon College	ind.	$40,000	$11,480	100%	33%	$28,332	$23,148	$33,015
Regent University	ind.	$16,700	$8480	96%	17%	$12,457	$12,723	$28,780
Roanoke College	ind.	$42,694	$13,258	100%	28%	$33,990	$21,962	$39,175
Shenandoah University	ind.	$31,920	$10,180	71%	8%	$16,640	$25,460	$22,392
Sweet Briar College	ind.	$37,160	$12,900	96%	17%	$12,981	$37,079	$33,026
University of Mary Washington	pub.	$11,570	$11,118	69%	16%	$8868	$13,820	$19,444
University of Richmond	ind.	$50,910	$11,820	98%	88%	$46,348	$16,382	$27,670
University of Virginia	pub.	$15,162	$10,726	85%	100%	$28,084	—	$24,598
The University of Virginia's College at Wise	pub.	$9539	$10,346	88%	34%	$15,285	$4600	$14,478
Virginia Commonwealth University	pub.	$13,076	$9919	76%	13%	$11,333	$11,662	$31,512
Virginia Military Institute	pub.	$17,492	$8968	95%	25%	$22,640	$3820	$30,388
Virginia Polytechnic Institute and State University	pub.	$12,852	$8564	72%	21%	$17,742	$3674	$28,884
Virginia State University	pub.	$8472	$10,562	80%	34%	$10,985	$8049	$28,250
Virginia Wesleyan College	ind.	$36,660	$8944	100%	18%	$25,256	$20,348	$36,255
Washington and Lee University	ind.	$49,254	$11,380	100%	100%	$46,056	$14,578	$26,397
Washington								
Central Washington University	pub.	$7849	$10,684	87%	41%	$11,746	$6787	$22,827
DigiPen Institute of Technology	ind.	$30,000	NR	59%	2%	$9620	$20,380	$27,403
Eastern Washington University	pub.	$6951	$10,941	77%	16%	$13,873	$4019	$24,109
The Evergreen State College	pub.	$7239	$9360	95%	9%	$10,960	$5639	$21,215
Gonzaga University	ind.	$41,330	$11,550	100%	27%	$27,059	$25,821	$30,700
Northwest College of Art & Design	ind.	$19,075	NR	NR	NR	NR	NR	$20,426
Northwest University	ind.	$29,187	$7790	96%	13%	$17,809	$19,168	$23,516
Saint Martin's University	ind.	$35,656	$11,030	100%	28%	$25,672	$21,014	$27,807
Seattle Pacific University	ind.	$38,940	$10,824	100%	9%	$31,816	$17,948	$28,880
Seattle University	ind.	$41,265	$11,499	88%	12%	$32,663	$20,101	$28,297
University of Puget Sound	ind.	$48,090	$12,120	99%	16%	$32,274	$27,936	$34,140
University of Washington	pub.	$10,753	$11,691	90%	48%	$17,800	$4644	$21,900
University of Washington, Bothell	pub.	$10,690	$10,833	93%	24%	$13,100	$8423	$19,640
University of Washington, Tacoma	pub.	$10,831	$10,230	95%	33%	$13,400	$7661	$18,420
Walla Walla University	ind.	$27,495	$7350	73%	39%	$21,879	$12,966	$33,018
Washington State University	pub.	$11,041	$11,356	95%	15%	$13,745	$8652	$25,874
Western Washington University	pub.	$7653	$10,755	90%	20%	$13,714	$4694	$19,727
Whitman College	ind.	$49,766	$12,524	100%	20%	$36,324	$25,966	$18,089
Whitworth University	ind.	$42,186	$11,496	100%	16%	$37,108	$16,574	$28,294
West Virginia								
Alderson Broaddus University	ind.	$25,350	$7990	100%	27%	$23,207	$10,133	$24,079
Bethany College	ind.	$27,638	$9724	NR	NR	NR	NR	$27,057
Bluefield State College	pub.	$6408	NA	85%	15%	$3330	$3078	$29,000
Concord University	pub.	$7080	$8350	91%	43%	$7863	$7567	$21,176
Fairmont State University	pub.	$8684	$9640	88%	13%	$8592	$9732	$26,314
Glenville State College	pub.	$9096	$10,042	90%	16%	$14,552	$4586	$28,930

NA = not applicable; NR = not reported; * = includes room and board; † = room only; — = not available.

College Costs At-a-Glance

	Institutional Control ind.=independent; pub.=public	Tuition and Fees	Room and Board	Percent of Eligible Freshmen Receiving Need-Based Gift Awards	Percent of Freshmen Whose Need Was Fully Met	Average Financial Aid Package for Freshmen	Average Net Cost After Aid	Average Indebtedness Upon Graduation
Marshall University	pub.	$7154	$10,126	78%	33%	$11,418	$5862	$27,121
Ohio Valley University	ind.	$21,100	$7700	100%	14%	$16,026	$12,774	$23,841
Shepherd University	pub.	$7170	$10,054	74%	33%	$12,241	$4983	$30,526
West Virginia University	pub.	$7992	$10,218	71%	21%	$6616	$11,594	$27,993
West Virginia University Institute of Technology	pub.	$6648	$9814	84%	17%	$6706	$9756	$27,364
West Virginia Wesleyan College	ind.	$29,952	$4080	100%	29%	$28,400	$5632	$31,996
Wheeling Jesuit University	ind.	$28,110	$8996	77%	29%	$27,782	$9324	$37,762
Wisconsin								
Alverno College	ind.	$26,932	$7884	99%	NR	$25,752	$9064	$41,044
Beloit College	ind.	$47,060	$8146	97%	31%	$42,870	$12,336	$31,308
Cardinal Stritch University	ind.	$28,212	$7940	100%	12%	$26,451	$9701	$27,997
Carroll University	ind.	$30,388	$9264	100%	33%	$23,612	$16,040	$36,161
Concordia University Wisconsin	ind.	$28,600	$10,530	96%	33%	$24,318	$14,812	$33,298
Edgewood College	ind.	$27,530	$9870	99%	10%	$22,099	$15,301	$33,104
Lawrence University	ind.	$46,101	$10,032	98%	55%	$38,758	$17,375	$34,750
Maranatha Baptist University	ind.	$14,260	$6720	99%	11%	$10,213	$10,767	$20,965
Marian University	ind.	$27,370	$7000	100%	8%	$18,740	$15,630	$30,565
Marquette University	ind.	$39,800	NR	99%	27%	$29,842	$9958	$35,421
Milwaukee School of Engineering	ind.	$39,429	$9102	100%	25%	$28,091	$20,440	$38,745
Mount Mary University	ind.	$29,510	$8530	100%	13%	$27,107	$10,933	$27,811
Northland College	ind.	$35,157	$8886	93%	19%	$38,069	$5974	$34,144
St. Norbert College	ind.	$36,593	$9467	97%	22%	$25,870	$20,190	$33,948
University of Wisconsin–Eau Claire	pub.	$8813	$6984	85%	21%	$9092	$6705	$26,295
University of Wisconsin–Green Bay	pub.	$7948	$7200	77%	27%	$9977	$5171	$28,940
University of Wisconsin–La Crosse	pub.	$9091	$6156	65%	22%	$7593	$7654	$26,487
University of Wisconsin–Madison	pub.	$10,488	$10,446	80%	39%	$14,789	$6145	$27,831
University of Wisconsin–Milwaukee	pub.	$9534	$10,560	61%	30%	$7086	$13,008	$36,945
University of Wisconsin–Oshkosh	pub.	N/R	NR	50%	41%	$6455	—	$32,502
University of Wisconsin–Parkside	pub.	$7367	$7736	75%	16%	$9353	$5750	$29,362
University of Wisconsin–River Falls	pub.	$7981	$6576	65%	1%	$6828	$7729	$27,232
University of Wisconsin–Stevens Point	pub.	$9683	$7180	75%	16%	$8177	$8686	$25,646
University of Wisconsin–Stout	pub.	$9394	$6624	75%	13%	$10,611	$5407	$30,563
University of Wisconsin–Superior	pub.	$8087	$6520	63%	19%	$10,276	$4331	$27,382
University of Wisconsin–Whitewater	pub.	$7650	$7204	57%	41%	$7109	$7745	$28,345
Viterbo University	ind.	$26,920	$8760	NR	NR	NR	NR	NR
Wisconsin Lutheran College	ind.	$27,984	$9620	100%	24%	$22,291	$15,313	$28,476
Wyoming								
University of Wyoming	pub.	$5055	$10,320	59%	24%	$10,788	$4587	$25,378

NA = not applicable; NR = not reported; * = includes room and board; † = room only; — = not available.

Profiles of College Financial Aid Programs

ABILENE CHRISTIAN UNIVERSITY
Abilene, TX

Tuition & fees: $32,070	Average undergraduate aid package: $22,694

ABOUT THE INSTITUTION Independent Church of Christ, coed. *Awards:* certificates, associate, bachelor's, master's, and doctoral degrees. 66 undergraduate majors. *Total enrollment:* 4,910. Undergraduates: 3,758. Freshmen: 1,047. Federal methodology is used as a basis for awarding need-based institutional aid.

UNDERGRADUATE EXPENSES for 2016–2017 *Application fee:* $50. *Comprehensive fee:* $41,800 includes full-time tuition ($32,020), mandatory fees ($50), and room and board ($9730). *College room only:* $4690. Full-time tuition and fees vary according to course load. Room and board charges vary according to board plan and housing facility. *Part-time tuition:* $1334 per credit hour. Part-time tuition and fees vary according to course load. *Payment plan:* Tuition prepayment.

FRESHMAN FINANCIAL AID (Fall 2016, est.) 911 applied for aid; of those 83% were deemed to have need. 100% of freshmen with need received aid; of those 24% had need fully met. *Average percent of need met:* 68% (excluding resources awarded to replace EFC). *Average financial aid package:* $23,019 (excluding resources awarded to replace EFC). 28% of all full-time freshmen had no need and received non-need-based gift aid.

UNDERGRADUATE FINANCIAL AID (Fall 2016, est.) 2,770 applied for aid; of those 86% were deemed to have need. 100% of undergraduates with need received aid; of those 26% had need fully met. *Average percent of need met:* 68% (excluding resources awarded to replace EFC). *Average financial aid package:* $22,694 (excluding resources awarded to replace EFC). 34% of all full-time undergraduates had no need and received non-need-based gift aid.

GIFT AID (NEED-BASED) *Total amount:* $44,260,049 (9% federal, 8% state, 80% institutional, 3% external sources). *Receiving aid:* Freshmen: 76% (752); all full-time undergraduates: 67% (2,379). *Average award:* Freshmen: $20,728; Undergraduates: $19,776. *Scholarships, grants, and awards:* Federal Pell, FSEOG, state, private, college/university gift aid from institutional funds.

GIFT AID (NON-NEED-BASED) *Total amount:* $16,352,720 (98% institutional, 2% external sources). *Receiving aid:* Freshmen: 76% (752). Undergraduates: 67% (2,371). *Average award:* Freshmen: $12,937. Undergraduates: $12,246. *Scholarships, grants, and awards by category:* Academic interests/achievement: agriculture, biological sciences, business, communication, education, engineering/technologies, English, foreign languages, general academic interests/achievements, mathematics, physical sciences, religion/biblical studies, social sciences. Creative arts/performance: art/fine arts, debating, journalism/publications, music, theater/drama. Special achievements/activities: cheerleading/drum major, leadership. Special characteristics: children of faculty/staff, ethnic background, first-generation college students, local/state students, members of minority groups, out-of-state students, previous college experience, relatives of clergy, religious affiliation. *Tuition waivers:* Full or partial for employees or children of employees.

LOANS *Student loans:* $25,138,444 (28% need-based, 72% non-need-based). *Average need-based loan:* Freshmen: $3498. Undergraduates: $4404. *Parent loans:* $4,414,233 (100% non-need-based). *Programs:* Federal Direct (Subsidized and Unsubsidized Stafford, PLUS), Perkins, state.

WORK-STUDY *Federal work-study:* Total amount: $30,112; jobs available. *State or other work-study/employment:* Total amount: $2,206,634 (1% need-based, 99% non-need-based). Part-time jobs available.

ATHLETIC AWARDS Total amount: $5,616,001 (54% need-based, 46% non-need-based).

APPLYING FOR FINANCIAL AID *Required financial aid form:* FAFSA. *Financial aid deadline (priority):* 3/1. *Notification date:* Continuous beginning 4/1. Students must reply within 3 weeks of notification.

CONTACT Undergraduate Admissions, Abilene Christian University, ACU Box 29000, Abilene, TX 79699-9000, 325-674-2650 or toll-free 800-460-6228. *E-mail:* info@admissions.acu.edu.
Website: http://www.acu.edu/.

ABRAHAM BALDWIN AGRICULTURAL COLLEGE
Tifton, GA

CONTACT Michael Wright, Director of Student Financial Services, Abraham Baldwin Agricultural College, 2802 Moore Highway, ABAC 23, Tifton, GA 31793-2601, 229-391-4910 or toll-free 800-733-3653. *Fax:* 229-391-4871. *E-mail:* sfs@abac.edu. *Website:* http://www.abac.edu/.

ACADEMY COLLEGE
Bloomington, MN

Tuition & fees: $17,129	Average undergraduate aid package: N/A

ABOUT THE INSTITUTION Proprietary, coed. *Awards:* associate and bachelor's degrees. 25 undergraduate majors. *Total enrollment:* 116. Undergraduates: 116. Freshmen: 2. Federal methodology is used as a basis for awarding need-based institutional aid.

UNDERGRADUATE EXPENSES for 2017–2018 *Application fee:* $40. *One-time required fee:* $280. *Tuition:* full-time $17,009; part-time $450 per credit hour. *Required fees:* full-time $120; $40 per term. Full-time tuition and fees vary according to course load and program. Part-time tuition and fees vary according to course load and program.

FRESHMAN FINANCIAL AID (Fall 2015) 1 applied for aid; of those 100% were deemed to have need. 100% of freshmen with need received aid.

UNDERGRADUATE FINANCIAL AID (Fall 2015) 25 applied for aid; of those 100% were deemed to have need. 100% of undergraduates with need received aid.

GIFT AID (NEED-BASED) *Total amount:* $107,961 (24% federal, 76% state). *Receiving aid:* All full-time undergraduates: 30% (17). *Scholarships, grants, and awards:* Federal Pell, FSEOG, state, private, college/university gift aid from institutional funds.

GIFT AID (NON-NEED-BASED) *Total amount:* $1500 (100% institutional).

LOANS *Student loans:* $719,586 (44% need-based, 56% non-need-based). 71% of past graduating class borrowed through all loan programs. *Average indebtedness per student:* $14,476. *Parent loans:* $157,274 (100% non-need-based). *Programs:* Federal Direct (Subsidized and Unsubsidized Stafford, PLUS), state, alternative loans.

WORK-STUDY Federal work-study jobs available. *State or other work-study/employment:* Part-time jobs available.

APPLYING FOR FINANCIAL AID *Required financial aid forms:* FAFSA, institution's own form, state aid form. *Financial aid deadline:* Continuous. *Notification date:* Continuous.

CONTACT Kellye MacLeod, Director of Financial Aid, Academy College, 1101 East 78th Street, Bloomington, MN 55420, 952-851-0066 or toll-free 800-292-9149. *Fax:* 952-851-0093. *E-mail:* finaid@academycollege.edu.
Website: http://www.academycollege.edu/.

ACADEMY OF ART UNIVERSITY
San Francisco, CA

Tuition & fees: $26,490	Average undergraduate aid package: $11,209

ABOUT THE INSTITUTION Proprietary, coed. *Awards:* certificates, associate, bachelor's, and master's degrees. 40 undergraduate majors. *Total enrollment:* 12,608. Undergraduates: 8,303. Freshmen: 1,064. Federal methodology is used as a basis for awarding need-based institutional aid.

UNDERGRADUATE EXPENSES for 2017–2018 *Application fee:* $50. *Comprehensive fee:* $42,282 includes full-time tuition ($26,190), mandatory fees ($300), and room and board ($15,792). Full-time tuition and fees vary according to course load. Room and board charges vary according to board plan and housing facility. *Part-time tuition:* $873 per unit. Part-time tuition and fees vary according to course load.

FRESHMAN FINANCIAL AID (Fall 2015) 315 applied for aid; of those 91% were deemed to have need. 97% of freshmen with need received aid; of those 3% had need fully met. *Average percent of need met:* 29% (excluding resources awarded to replace EFC). *Average financial aid package:* $10,073 (excluding resources awarded to replace EFC). 2% of all full-time freshmen had no need and received non-need-based gift aid.

UNDERGRADUATE FINANCIAL AID (Fall 2015) 2,411 applied for aid; of those 92% were deemed to have need. 98% of undergraduates with need received aid; of those 2% had need fully met. *Average percent of need met:* 34% (excluding resources awarded to replace EFC). *Average financial aid package:* $11,209 (excluding resources awarded to replace EFC). 1% of all full-time undergraduates had no need and received non-need-based gift aid.

GIFT AID (NEED-BASED) Total amount: $21,999,407 (56% federal, 12% state, 3% institutional, 29% external sources). *Receiving aid:* Freshmen: 32% (196); all full-time undergraduates: 30% (1,603). *Average award:* Freshmen: $10,240; Undergraduates: $10,316. *Scholarships, grants, and awards:* Federal Pell, FSEOG, state, private, college/university gift aid from institutional funds.

GIFT AID (NON-NEED-BASED) Total amount: $5,177,688 (11% institutional, 89% external sources). *Receiving aid:* Freshmen: 3% (20). Undergraduates: 2% (122). *Average award:* Freshmen: $8243. Undergraduates: $8742.

LOANS Student loans: $38,208,364 (90% need-based, 10% non-need-based). 63% of past graduating class borrowed through all loan programs. *Average indebtedness per student:* $27,020. *Average need-based loan:* Freshmen: $3145. Undergraduates: $3887. *Parent loans:* $23,822,910 (71% need-based, 29% non-need-based). *Programs:* Federal Direct (Subsidized and Unsubsidized Stafford, PLUS), alternative loans.

WORK-STUDY Federal work-study: 107 jobs averaging $4370.

ATHLETIC AWARDS Total amount: $3,599,179 (49% need-based, 51% non-need-based).

APPLYING FOR FINANCIAL AID *Required financial aid forms:* FAFSA, institution's own form. *Financial aid deadline:* Continuous. *Notification date:* Continuous beginning 3/15. Students must reply within 2 weeks of notification.

CONTACT Mr. Joe Vollaro, Executive Vice President of Financial Aid and Compliance, Academy of Art University, 79 New Montgomery Street, San Francisco, CA 94105-3410, 415-618-6528 or toll-free 800-544-ARTS. *Fax:* 415-618-6273. *E-mail:* jvollaro@academyart.edu.
Website: http://www.academyart.edu/.

ADAMS STATE UNIVERSITY
Alamosa, CO

Tuition & fees (CO res): $9153	Average undergraduate aid package: $13,050

ABOUT THE INSTITUTION State-supported, coed. *Awards:* associate, bachelor's, master's, and doctoral degrees. 78 undergraduate majors. *Total enrollment:* 3,347. Undergraduates: 2,002. Freshmen: 462. Federal methodology is used as a basis for awarding need-based institutional aid.

UNDERGRADUATE EXPENSES for 2016–2017 Application fee: $30. *Tuition, state resident:* full-time $5736; part-time $239 per credit hour. *Tuition, nonresident:* full-time $16,752; part-time $698 per credit hour. *Required fees:* full-time $3417; $138.22 per credit hour. Full-time tuition and fees vary according to course load. Part-time tuition and fees vary according to course load. *College room and board:* $8550; *Room only:* $4000. Room and board charges vary according to board plan and housing facility. *Payment plan:* Guaranteed tuition.

FRESHMAN FINANCIAL AID (Fall 2016, est.) 435 applied for aid; of those 83% were deemed to have need. 100% of freshmen with need received aid; of those 5% had need fully met. *Average percent of need met:* 65% (excluding resources awarded to replace EFC). *Average financial aid package:* $13,439 (excluding resources awarded to replace EFC).

UNDERGRADUATE FINANCIAL AID (Fall 2016, est.) 1,629 applied for aid; of those 79% were deemed to have need. 99% of undergraduates with need received aid; of those 5% had need fully met. *Average percent of need met:* 62% (excluding resources awarded to replace EFC). *Average financial aid package:* $13,050 (excluding resources awarded to replace EFC).

GIFT AID (NEED-BASED) Total amount: $10,770,039 (47% federal, 16% state, 27% institutional, 10% external sources). *Receiving aid:* Freshmen: 79% (343); all full-time undergraduates: 75% (1,218). *Average award:* Freshmen: $9719; Undergraduates: $8356. *Scholarships, grants, and awards:* Federal Pell, FSEOG, state, private, college/university gift aid from institutional funds.

GIFT AID (NON-NEED-BASED) Total amount: $2,347,736 (1% federal, 45% institutional, 54% external sources). *Tuition waivers:* Full or partial for employees or children of employees, senior citizens.

LOANS Student loans: $8,085,761 (88% need-based, 12% non-need-based). 57% of past graduating class borrowed through all loan programs. *Average indebtedness per student:* $17,808. *Average need-based loan:* Freshmen: $3179. Undergraduates: $3907. *Parent loans:* $2,128,808 (78% need-based, 22% non-need-based). *Programs:* Federal Direct (Subsidized and Unsubsidized Stafford, PLUS), Perkins, alternative loans.

WORK-STUDY Federal work-study: Total amount: $682,020; jobs available. *State or other work-study/employment:* Total amount: $1,808,655 (87% need-based, 13% non-need-based). Part-time jobs available.

ATHLETIC AWARDS Total amount: $1,948,512 (64% need-based, 36% non-need-based).

APPLYING FOR FINANCIAL AID *Required financial aid form:* FAFSA. *Financial aid deadline:* Continuous. *Notification date:* Continuous beginning 3/1.

CONTACT Philip Schroeder, Director of Financial Aid, Adams State University, 208 Edgemont Boulevard, Alamosa, CO 81101, 719-587-7306 or toll-free 800-824-6494. *Fax:* 719-587-7366. *E-mail:* financialaid@adams.edu.
Website: http://www.adams.edu/.

ADELPHI UNIVERSITY
Garden City, NY

Tuition & fees: $35,740	Average undergraduate aid package: $21,500

ABOUT THE INSTITUTION Independent, coed. *Awards:* certificates, associate, bachelor's, master's, and doctoral degrees. 48 undergraduate majors. *Total enrollment:* 7,687. Undergraduates: 5,205. Freshmen: 1,226. Both federal and institutional methodology are used as a basis for awarding need-based institutional aid.

UNDERGRADUATE EXPENSES for 2016–2017 Application fee: $40. *Comprehensive fee:* $49,792 includes full-time tuition ($34,000), mandatory fees ($1740), and room and board ($14,052). Full-time tuition and fees vary according to course level, course load, location, program, and student level. Room and board charges vary according to board plan and housing facility. *Part-time tuition:* $1040 per credit hour. *Part-time fees:* $463 per term. Part-time tuition and fees vary according to course level, course load, location, program, and student level. *Payment plan:* Tuition prepayment.

FRESHMAN FINANCIAL AID (Fall 2016, est.) 1,080 applied for aid; of those 86% were deemed to have need. 100% of freshmen with need received aid; of those 17% had need fully met. *Average percent of need met:* 51% (excluding resources awarded to replace EFC). *Average financial aid package:* $21,500 (excluding resources awarded to replace EFC). 17% of all full-time freshmen had no need and received non-need-based gift aid.

UNDERGRADUATE FINANCIAL AID (Fall 2016, est.) 3,807 applied for aid; of those 84% were deemed to have need. 100% of undergraduates with need received aid; of those 14% had need fully met. *Average percent of need met:* 45% (excluding resources awarded to replace EFC). *Average financial aid package:* $21,500 (excluding resources awarded to replace EFC). 20% of all full-time undergraduates had no need and received non-need-based gift aid.

GIFT AID (NEED-BASED) Total amount: $51,951,204 (14% federal, 9% state, 77% institutional). *Receiving aid:* Freshmen: 76% (924); all full-time undergraduates: 66% (3,126). *Average award:* Freshmen: $21,071; Undergraduates: $15,855. *Scholarships, grants, and awards:* Federal Pell, FSEOG, state, private, college/university gift aid from institutional funds, United Negro College Fund, endowed and restricted scholarships and grants.

GIFT AID (NON-NEED-BASED) Total amount: $18,186,805 (94% institutional, 6% external sources). *Receiving aid:* Freshmen: 65% (792). Undergraduates: 59% (2,776). *Average award:* Freshmen: $18,535. Undergraduates: $15,467. *Scholarships, grants, and awards by category:* Academic interests/achievement: 3,496 awards ($48,861,637 total): business, communication, computer science, foreign languages, general academic interests/achievements, mathematics, physical sciences. *Creative arts/performance:* 66 awards ($535,080 total): art/fine arts, cinema/film/broadcasting, dance, music, performing arts, theater/drama. *Special achievements/activities:* 826 awards ($785,750 total): community service, general special achievements/activities, leadership, memberships. *Special characteristics:* 410 awards ($3,702,325 total): adult students, children and siblings of alumni, children of faculty/

staff, veterans. *Tuition waivers:* Full or partial for children of alumni, employees or children of employees, senior citizens. *ROTC:* Army cooperative, Air Force cooperative.

LOANS *Student loans:* $33,498,064 (38% need-based, 62% non-need-based). 64% of past graduating class borrowed through all loan programs. *Average indebtedness per student:* $32,558. *Average need-based loan:* Freshmen: $3812. Undergraduates: $4344. *Parent loans:* $12,375,988 (91% need-based, 9% non-need-based). *Programs:* Federal Direct (Subsidized and Unsubsidized Stafford, PLUS), Perkins, Federal Nursing.

WORK-STUDY *Federal work-study:* Total amount: $1,763,002; 378 jobs averaging $1719. *State or other work-study/employment:* Total amount: $2,441,909 (100% non-need-based). 1,163 part-time jobs averaging $2102.

ATHLETIC AWARDS Total amount: $3,212,137 (57% need-based, 43% non-need-based).

APPLYING FOR FINANCIAL AID *Required financial aid forms:* FAFSA, state aid form. *Financial aid deadline (priority):* 3/1. *Notification date:* 3/1.

CONTACT Ms. Debra Evans, Senior Associate Director of Student Financial Services, Adelphi University, 1 South Avenue, PO Box 701, Garden City, NY 11530, 516-877-3394 or toll-free 800-ADELPHI. *Fax:* 516-877-3380. *E-mail:* evans@adelphi.edu. *Website:* http://www.adelphi.edu/.

ADRIAN COLLEGE
Adrian, MI

CONTACT Mr. Matthew Rheinecker, Director of Financial Aid, Adrian College, 110 South Madison Street, Adrian, MI 49221-2575, 517-264-3109 or toll-free 800-877-2246. *Fax:* 517-264-3394. *E-mail:* mrheinecker@adrian.edu. *Website:* http://www.adrian.edu/.

ADVENTIST UNIVERSITY OF HEALTH SCIENCES
Orlando, FL

ABOUT THE INSTITUTION Independent, coed. *Awards:* certificates, associate, bachelor's, master's, and doctoral degrees. 10 undergraduate majors. *Total enrollment:* 1,912. Undergraduates: 1,659. Freshmen: 92.

GIFT AID (NEED-BASED) *Scholarships, grants, and awards:* Federal Pell, FSEOG, state, private, college/university gift aid from institutional funds.

LOANS *Programs:* Federal Direct (Subsidized and Unsubsidized Stafford, PLUS), private loans.

APPLYING FOR FINANCIAL AID *Required financial aid forms:* FAFSA, institution's own form.

CONTACT Rebecca Valencia, Director of Financial Aid, Adventist University of Health Sciences, 671 Winyah Drive, Orlando, FL 32803, 407-303-9203 or toll-free 800-500-7747. *Fax:* 407-303-7680. *E-mail:* rebecca.valencia@adu.edu. *Website:* http://www.adu.edu/.

AGNES SCOTT COLLEGE
Decatur, GA

Tuition & fees: $39,960	Average undergraduate aid package: $35,349

ABOUT THE INSTITUTION Independent Presbyterian Church (U.S.A.), women only. *Awards:* bachelor's degrees. 36 undergraduate majors. *Total enrollment:* 927. Undergraduates: 927. Freshmen: 272. Both federal and institutional methodology are used as a basis for awarding need-based institutional aid.

UNDERGRADUATE EXPENSES for 2017–2018 *Comprehensive fee:* $51,930 includes full-time tuition ($39,720), mandatory fees ($240), and room and board ($11,970). Room and board charges vary according to board plan and housing facility. *Part-time tuition:* $1655 per credit. Part-time tuition and fees vary according to course load.

FRESHMAN FINANCIAL AID (Fall 2016, est.) 233 applied for aid; of those 90% were deemed to have need. 100% of freshmen with need received aid; of those 30% had need fully met. *Average percent of need met:* 85% (excluding resources awarded to replace EFC). *Average financial aid package:* $35,471 (excluding resources awarded to replace EFC). 23% of all full-time freshmen had no need and received non-need-based gift aid.

UNDERGRADUATE FINANCIAL AID (Fall 2016, est.) 724 applied for aid; of those 90% were deemed to have need. 100% of undergraduates with need received aid; of those 25% had need fully met. *Average percent of need met:* 84% (excluding resources awarded to replace EFC). *Average financial aid package:* $35,349 (excluding resources awarded to replace EFC). 26% of all full-time undergraduates had no need and received non-need-based gift aid.

GIFT AID (NEED-BASED) *Total amount:* $18,871,308 (8% federal, 6% state, 83% institutional, 3% external sources). *Receiving aid:* Freshmen: 77% (210); all full-time undergraduates: 74% (655). *Average award:* Freshmen: $29,708; Undergraduates: $28,811. *Scholarships, grants, and awards:* Federal Pell, FSEOG, state, private, college/university gift aid from institutional funds.

GIFT AID (NON-NEED-BASED) *Total amount:* $7,147,787 (6% state, 89% institutional, 5% external sources). *Receiving aid:* Freshmen: 23% (62). Undergraduates: 18% (163). *Average award:* Freshmen: $26,447. Undergraduates: $26,029. *Scholarships, grants, and awards by category:* Academic interests/achievement: general academic interests/achievements. Creative arts/performance: music. Special achievements/activities: community service, leadership. Special characteristics: adult students, children of educators, children of faculty/staff, international students, local/state students, religious affiliation, veterans, veterans' children. *Tuition waivers:* Full or partial for employees or children of employees. *ROTC:* Army cooperative, Air Force cooperative.

LOANS *Student loans:* $4,733,602 (50% need-based, 50% non-need-based). 75% of past graduating class borrowed through all loan programs. *Average indebtedness per student:* $34,022. *Average need-based loan:* Freshmen: $3288. Undergraduates: $4391. *Parent loans:* $1,987,976 (53% need-based, 47% non-need-based). *Programs:* Federal Direct (Subsidized and Unsubsidized Stafford, PLUS).

WORK-STUDY *Federal work-study:* Total amount: $767,437; jobs available. *State or other work-study/employment:* Total amount: $43,700 (100% non-need-based). Part-time jobs available.

APPLYING FOR FINANCIAL AID *Required financial aid forms:* FAFSA, federal income tax form(s). *Financial aid deadline:* 5/1 (priority: 2/15). *Notification date:* Continuous beginning 3/1. Students must reply by 5/1.

CONTACT Patrick Bonones, Director of Financial Aid, Agnes Scott College, 141 East College Avenue, Decatur, GA 30030-3797, 404-471-6395 or toll-free 800-868-8602. *Fax:* 404-471-6159. *E-mail:* finaid@agnesscott.edu. *Website:* http://www.agnesscott.edu/.

ALABAMA AGRICULTURAL AND MECHANICAL UNIVERSITY
Huntsville, AL

CONTACT Ms. Deborah Gordon, Financial Aid Officer, Alabama Agricultural and Mechanical University, PO Box 907, Huntsville, AL 35762, 256-372-4853 or toll-free 800-553-0816. *Fax:* 256-372-5407. *E-mail:* deborah.gordon@aamu.edu. *Website:* http://www.aamu.edu/.

ALABAMA STATE UNIVERSITY
Montgomery, AL

Tuition & fees (AL res): $9220	Average undergraduate aid package: $19,409

ABOUT THE INSTITUTION State-supported, coed. *Awards:* certificates, bachelor's, master's, and doctoral degrees. 33 undergraduate majors. *Total enrollment:* 5,318. Undergraduates: 4,727. Freshmen: 1,163. Federal methodology is used as a basis for awarding need-based institutional aid.

UNDERGRADUATE EXPENSES for 2017–2018 *Application fee:* $25. *One-time required fee:* $150. *Tuition, state resident:* full-time $6936; part-time

$289 per credit hour. **Tuition, nonresident:** full-time $13,872; part-time $578 per credit hour. **Required fees:** full-time $2284; $446 per credit hour. Full-time tuition and fees vary according to class time, course level, course load, degree level, program, and student level. Part-time tuition and fees vary according to class time, course level, course load, degree level, program, and student level. **College room and board:** $5422; **Room only:** $3346. Room and board charges vary according to board plan and housing facility.

FRESHMAN FINANCIAL AID (Fall 2016, est.) 929 applied for aid; of those 99% were deemed to have need. 94% of freshmen with need received aid; of those 34% had need fully met. **Average percent of need met:** 79% (excluding resources awarded to replace EFC). **Average financial aid package:** $15,869 (excluding resources awarded to replace EFC). 2% of all full-time freshmen had no need and received non-need-based gift aid.

UNDERGRADUATE FINANCIAL AID (Fall 2016, est.) 4,206 applied for aid; of those 97% were deemed to have need. 99% of undergraduates with need received aid; of those 49% had need fully met. **Average percent of need met:** 81% (excluding resources awarded to replace EFC). **Average financial aid package:** $19,409 (excluding resources awarded to replace EFC). 2% of all full-time undergraduates had no need and received non-need-based gift aid.

GIFT AID (NEED-BASED) Total amount: $17,855,730 (96% federal, 1% state, 3% institutional). **Receiving aid:** Freshmen: 64% (733); all full-time undergraduates: 74% (3,496). **Average award:** Freshmen: $5327; Undergraduates: $5114. **Scholarships, grants, and awards:** Federal Pell, FSEOG, state, private, college/university gift aid from institutional funds, United Negro College Fund.

GIFT AID (NON-NEED-BASED) Total amount: $13,396,802 (2% federal, 34% state, 51% institutional, 13% external sources). **Receiving aid:** Freshmen: 29% (335). Undergraduates: 44% (2,056). **Average award:** Freshmen: $8789. Undergraduates: $8833. **Scholarships, grants, and awards by category:** Academic interests/achievement: general academic interests/achievements. Creative arts/performance: general creative arts/performance, music, theater/drama. Special achievements/activities: leadership. Special characteristics: general special characteristics, members of minority groups. **Tuition waivers:** Full or partial for employees or children of employees. **ROTC:** Army cooperative, Air Force.

LOANS Student loans: $27,876,378 (50% need-based, 50% non-need-based). 85% of past graduating class borrowed through all loan programs. **Average indebtedness per student:** $32,487. **Average need-based loan:** Freshmen: $3547. Undergraduates: $3976. **Parent loans:** $13,114,633 (86% need-based, 14% non-need-based). **Programs:** Federal Direct (Subsidized and Unsubsidized Stafford, PLUS), Perkins.

WORK-STUDY Federal work-study: Total amount: $1,273,620; 570 jobs averaging $1896. **State or other work-study/employment:** Total amount: $331,240 (100% non-need-based). 506 part-time jobs averaging $649.

ATHLETIC AWARDS Total amount: $3,702,778 (86% need-based, 14% non-need-based).

APPLYING FOR FINANCIAL AID Required financial aid form: FAFSA. **Financial aid deadline (priority):** 4/1. **Notification date:** Continuous beginning 5/1.

CONTACT Mr. Marcus Byrd, Interim Director of Financial Aid, Alabama State University, PO Box 271, Montgomery, AL 36101-0271, 334-229-4323 or toll-free 800-253-5037. Fax: 334-299-4924. E-mail: mbyrd@alasu.edu. Website: http://www.alasu.edu/.

ALASKA BIBLE COLLEGE
Palmer, AK

Tuition & fees: $9300	Average undergraduate aid package: N/A

ABOUT THE INSTITUTION Independent nondenominational, coed. **Awards:** certificates, associate, and bachelor's degrees. 1 undergraduate major. **Total enrollment:** 50. Undergraduates: 50. Freshmen: 6. Institutional methodology is used as a basis for awarding need-based institutional aid.

UNDERGRADUATE EXPENSES for 2017–2018 Application fee: $35. **Comprehensive fee:** $12,000 includes full-time tuition ($9000), mandatory fees ($300), and room and board ($2700). **Part-time tuition:** $375 per credit hour.

FRESHMAN FINANCIAL AID (Fall 2016, est.) 1 applied for aid; of those 100% were deemed to have need. 100% of freshmen with need received aid.

UNDERGRADUATE FINANCIAL AID (Fall 2016, est.) 11 applied for aid; of those 100% were deemed to have need. 100% of undergraduates with need received aid.

GIFT AID (NEED-BASED) Total amount: $97,778 (71% federal, 23% state, 3% institutional, 3% external sources). **Receiving aid:** Freshmen: 20% (1); all full-time undergraduates: 61% (11). **Scholarships, grants, and awards:** Federal Pell, FSEOG, private, college/university gift aid from institutional funds.

GIFT AID (NON-NEED-BASED) Receiving aid: Undergraduates: 6% (1). **Scholarships, grants, and awards by category:** Academic interests/achievement: general academic interests/achievements, religion/biblical studies. Creative arts/performance: music. Special achievements/activities: religious involvement. Special characteristics: children of faculty/staff, married students, spouses of current students. **Tuition waivers:** Full or partial for employees or children of employees, senior citizens.

LOANS Student loans: $76,025 (64% need-based, 36% non-need-based). **Parent loans:** $8914 (100% non-need-based). **Programs:** Federal Direct (Subsidized and Unsubsidized Stafford), state.

WORK-STUDY Federal work-study: Total amount: $5000; jobs available.

APPLYING FOR FINANCIAL AID Required financial aid form: FAFSA. **Financial aid deadline:** Continuous. **Notification date:** 9/1. Students must reply within 2 weeks of notification.

CONTACT Christy Coté, Financial Aid Administrator , Alaska Bible College, 248 East Elmwood Avenue, Palmer, AK 99645, 907-745-3201 or toll-free 800-478-7884. Fax: 907-745-3210. E-mail: financialaid@akbible.edu. Website: http://www.akbible.edu/.

ALASKA PACIFIC UNIVERSITY
Anchorage, AK

Tuition & fees: $20,830	Average undergraduate aid package: $10,522

ABOUT THE INSTITUTION Independent, coed. **Awards:** certificates, associate, bachelor's, master's, and doctoral degrees. 8 undergraduate majors. **Total enrollment:** 547. Undergraduates: 294. Freshmen: 41. Federal methodology is used as a basis for awarding need-based institutional aid.

UNDERGRADUATE EXPENSES for 2017–2018 Application fee: $25. **Comprehensive fee:** $27,970 includes full-time tuition ($20,350), mandatory fees ($480), and room and board ($7140). Full-time tuition and fees vary according to course load, degree level, program, and reciprocity agreements. Room and board charges vary according to board plan and housing facility. **Part-time tuition:** $848 per semester hour. **Part-time fees:** $130 per term. Part-time tuition and fees vary according to course load, degree level, and program.

FRESHMAN FINANCIAL AID (Fall 2015) 36 applied for aid; of those 86% were deemed to have need. 100% of freshmen with need received aid; of those 16% had need fully met. **Average percent of need met:** 45% (excluding resources awarded to replace EFC). **Average financial aid package:** $14,403 (excluding resources awarded to replace EFC). 15% of all full-time freshmen had no need and received non-need-based gift aid.

UNDERGRADUATE FINANCIAL AID (Fall 2015) 147 applied for aid; of those 88% were deemed to have need. 100% of undergraduates with need received aid; of those 23% had need fully met. **Average percent of need met:** 39% (excluding resources awarded to replace EFC). **Average financial aid package:** $10,522 (excluding resources awarded to replace EFC). 18% of all full-time undergraduates had no need and received non-need-based gift aid.

GIFT AID (NEED-BASED) Total amount: $1,102,559 (34% federal, 5% state, 52% institutional, 9% external sources). **Receiving aid:** Freshmen: 54% (21); all full-time undergraduates: 58% (114). **Average award:** Freshmen: $6926; Undergraduates: $5973. **Scholarships, grants, and awards:** Federal Pell, FSEOG, state, private, college/university gift aid from institutional funds, Bureau of Indian Affairs Grants, Yellow Ribbon Grant Program, Native Alaskan Scholarships.

GIFT AID (NON-NEED-BASED) Total amount: $1,118,121 (7% state, 80% institutional, 13% external sources). **Receiving aid:** Freshmen: 77% (30). Undergraduates: 57% (112). **Average award:** Freshmen: $4166. Undergraduates: $4635. **Scholarships, grants, and awards by category:** Academic interests/achievement: biological sciences, business, communication, education, English, general academic interests/achievements, health fields, humanities, mathematics, physical sciences, religion/biblical studies, social sciences. Creative arts/performance: art/fine arts, journalism/publications, music, theater/drama. Special achievements/activities: community service, general special achievements/activities, leadership, religious involvement. Special characteristics: adult students, children and siblings of alumni, children of faculty/staff, ethnic background, general special characteristics, international students, local/state students, members of minority groups, out-of-state students, previous college experience, religious affiliation. *Tuition waivers:* Full or partial for employees or children of employees. *ROTC:* Air Force cooperative.

LOANS *Student loans:* $1,152,141 (56% need-based, 44% non-need-based). 63% of past graduating class borrowed through all loan programs. *Average indebtedness per student:* $8922. *Average need-based loan:* Freshmen: $3479. Undergraduates: $4128. *Parent loans:* $141,885 (50% need-based, 50% non-need-based). *Programs:* Federal Direct (Subsidized and Unsubsidized Stafford, PLUS), state, alternative loans.

WORK-STUDY *Federal work-study:* jobs available. *State or other work-study/employment:* Total amount: $7380 (100% non-need-based). Part-time jobs available.

APPLYING FOR FINANCIAL AID *Required financial aid form:* FAFSA. *Financial aid deadline (priority):* 6/30. *Notification date:* Continuous beginning 2/1. Students must reply by 2/1 or within 4 weeks of notification.

CONTACT Mrs. Katie Bishop, Assistant Director of Financial Aid, Alaska Pacific University, 4101 University Drive, Carr-Gottstein Room 106, Anchorage, AK 99508-4672, 907-564-8354 or toll-free 800-252-7528. *Fax:* 907-564-8317. *E-mail:* kbishop@alaskapacific.edu.
Website: http://www.alaskapacific.edu/.

ALBANY COLLEGE OF PHARMACY AND HEALTH SCIENCES
Albany, NY

CONTACT Kathleen Montague, Director of Financial Aid, Albany College of Pharmacy and Health Sciences, 106 New Scotland Avenue, Albany, NY 12208-3425, 518-694-7256 or toll-free 888-203-8010. *Fax:* 518-694-7322.
E-mail: financial_aid@acphs.edu.
Website: http://www.acphs.edu/.

ALBANY STATE UNIVERSITY
Albany, GA

CONTACT Mr. Thomas A. Harris, Director of Financial Aid, Albany State University, 504 College Drive, Albany, GA 31705-2717, 229-430-4650 or toll-free 800-822-7267. *Fax:* 229-430-3936.
Website: http://www.asurams.edu/.

ALBERTUS MAGNUS COLLEGE
New Haven, CT

Tuition & fees: $31,490	Average undergraduate aid package: $15,110

ABOUT THE INSTITUTION Independent Roman Catholic, coed. *Awards:* certificates, diplomas, associate, bachelor's, and master's degrees. 45 undergraduate majors. *Total enrollment:* 1,555. Undergraduates: 1,220. Freshmen: 135. Federal methodology is used as a basis for awarding need-based institutional aid.

UNDERGRADUATE EXPENSES for 2017–2018 *Application fee:* $35. *Comprehensive fee:* $45,506 includes full-time tuition ($31,000), mandatory fees ($490), and room and board ($14,016). Full-time tuition and fees vary according to program. Room and board charges vary according to board plan. Part-time tuition and fees vary according to program.

FRESHMAN FINANCIAL AID (Fall 2016, est.) 127 applied for aid; of those 94% were deemed to have need. 100% of freshmen with need received aid; of those 9% had need fully met. *Average percent of need met:* 63% (excluding resources awarded to replace EFC). *Average financial aid package:* $25,848 (excluding resources awarded to replace EFC). 4% of all full-time freshmen had no need and received non-need-based gift aid.

UNDERGRADUATE FINANCIAL AID (Fall 2016, est.) 944 applied for aid; of those 96% were deemed to have need. 100% of undergraduates with need received aid; of those 5% had need fully met. *Average percent of need met:* 50% (excluding

resources awarded to replace EFC). *Average financial aid package:* $15,110 (excluding resources awarded to replace EFC). 3% of all full-time undergraduates had no need and received non-need-based gift aid.

GIFT AID (NEED-BASED) *Total amount:* $9,590,476 (30% federal, 5% state, 65% institutional). *Receiving aid:* Freshmen: 86% (114); all full-time undergraduates: 73% (755). *Average award:* Freshmen: $19,449; Undergraduates: $12,459. *Scholarships, grants, and awards:* Federal Pell, FSEOG, state, college/university gift aid from institutional funds.

GIFT AID (NON-NEED-BASED) *Total amount:* $2,065,913 (4% state, 91% institutional, 5% external sources). *Receiving aid:* Freshmen: 44% (58). Undergraduates: 20% (204). *Average award:* Freshmen: $11,510. Undergraduates: $5033. *Scholarships, grants, and awards by category:* Academic interests/achievement: biological sciences, business, communication, computer science, education, English, foreign languages, general academic interests/achievements, humanities, international studies, mathematics, physical sciences, premedicine, religion/biblical studies, social sciences. *Creative arts/performance:* art/fine arts, performing arts, theater/drama. *Special achievements/activities:* community service, leadership. *Special characteristics:* local/state students, religious affiliation, siblings of current students. *Tuition waivers:* Full or partial for employees or children of employees, senior citizens.

LOANS *Student loans:* $8,977,084 (43% need-based, 57% non-need-based). 94% of past graduating class borrowed through all loan programs. *Average indebtedness per student:* $38,376. *Average need-based loan:* Freshmen: $3273. Undergraduates: $4270. *Parent loans:* $861,865 (100% non-need-based). *Programs:* Federal Direct (Subsidized and Unsubsidized Stafford, PLUS), Perkins.

WORK-STUDY *Federal work-study:* Total amount: $130,769; jobs available.

APPLYING FOR FINANCIAL AID *Required financial aid form:* FAFSA. *Financial aid deadline (priority):* 3/15. *Notification date:* 4/15. Students must reply within 2 weeks of notification.

CONTACT Michelle Cochran, Director of Financial Aid, Albertus Magnus College, 700 Prospect Street, New Haven, CT 06511-1189, 203-773-8508 or toll-free 800-578-9160. *Fax:* 203-773-8972. *E-mail:* financial_aid@albertus.edu.
Website: http://www.albertus.edu/.

ALBION COLLEGE
Albion, MI

Tuition & fees: $41,040	Average undergraduate aid package: $35,866

ABOUT THE INSTITUTION Independent Methodist, coed. *Awards:* bachelor's degrees. 64 undergraduate majors. *Total enrollment:* 1,418. Undergraduates: 1,418. Freshmen: 394. Federal methodology is used as a basis for awarding need-based institutional aid.

UNDERGRADUATE EXPENSES for 2016–2017 *One-time required fee:* $185. *Comprehensive fee:* $52,650 includes full-time tuition ($40,570), mandatory fees ($470), and room and board ($11,610). *College room only:* $5680. Full-time tuition and fees vary according to course load. Room and board charges vary according to board plan and housing facility. *Part-time tuition:* $1720 per semester hour. Part-time tuition and fees vary according to course load.

FRESHMAN FINANCIAL AID (Fall 2016, est.) 374 applied for aid; of those 90% were deemed to have need. 100% of freshmen with need received aid; of those 21% had need fully met. *Average percent of need met:* 92% (excluding resources awarded to replace EFC). *Average financial aid package:* $40,574 (excluding resources awarded to replace EFC). 17% of all full-time freshmen had no need and received non-need-based gift aid.

UNDERGRADUATE FINANCIAL AID (Fall 2016, est.) 1,143 applied for aid; of those 92% were deemed to have need. 100% of undergraduates with need received aid; of those 19% had need fully met. *Average percent of need met:* 86% (excluding resources awarded to replace EFC). *Average financial aid package:* $35,866 (excluding resources awarded to replace EFC). 24% of all full-time undergraduates had no need and received non-need-based gift aid.

GIFT AID (NEED-BASED) *Total amount:* $33,035,757 (7% federal, 4% state, 87% institutional, 2% external sources). *Receiving aid:* Freshmen: 83% (335); all full-time undergraduates: 75% (1,047). *Average award:* Freshmen: $35,581; Undergraduates: $31,104. *Scholarships, grants, and awards:* Federal Pell, FSEOG, state, private, college/university gift aid from institutional funds.

GIFT AID (NON-NEED-BASED) *Total amount:* $7,298,767 (98% institutional, 2% external sources). *Receiving aid:* Freshmen: 82% (330). Undergraduates: 73% (1,022). *Average award:* Freshmen: $24,351. Undergraduates: $21,079. *Scholarships, grants, and awards by category:* Academic interests/achievement: 1,240 awards ($23,218,357 total): communication, general academic interests/achievements. *Creative arts/performance:* 56 awards ($108,620 total): art/fine arts, music, performing arts, theater/drama. *Special characteristics:* 308 awards ($1,588,435 total): children and siblings of alumni, international students, out-of-state students, relatives of clergy. *Tuition waivers:* Full or partial for employees or children of employees.

LOANS *Student loans:* $9,635,645 (43% need-based, 57% non-need-based). 68% of past graduating class borrowed through all loan programs. *Average indebtedness per student:* $38,356. *Average need-based loan:* Freshmen: $4604. Undergraduates: $4953. *Parent loans:* $2,990,060 (100% non-need-based). *Programs:* Federal Direct (Subsidized and Unsubsidized Stafford, PLUS), Perkins.

WORK-STUDY *Federal work-study:* Total amount: $378,815; 269 jobs averaging $1334. *State or other work-study/employment:* Total amount: $217,450 (99% need-based, 1% non-need-based). 120 part-time jobs averaging $1581.

APPLYING FOR FINANCIAL AID *Required financial aid form:* FAFSA. *Financial aid deadline (priority):* 12/1. *Notification date:* Continuous beginning 12/1.

CONTACT Ms. Ann Whitmer, Director of Student Financial Services, Albion College, Kellogg Center Box 4670, Albion, MI 49224-1831, 517-629-0440 or toll-free 800-858-6770. *Fax:* 517-629-0581. *E-mail:* financialaid@albion.edu. *Website:* http://www.albion.edu/.

ALBRIGHT COLLEGE
Reading, PA

Tuition & fees: $43,304	Average undergraduate aid package: $36,812

ABOUT THE INSTITUTION Independent United Methodist Church, coed. *Awards:* certificates, bachelor's, and master's degrees. 41 undergraduate majors. *Total enrollment:* 2,318. Undergraduates: 2,304. Freshmen: 596. Federal methodology is used as a basis for awarding need-based institutional aid.

UNDERGRADUATE EXPENSES for 2017–2018 *Application fee:* $35. *Comprehensive fee:* $54,910 includes full-time tuition ($42,404), mandatory fees ($900), and room and board ($11,606). *College room only:* $6408. Full-time tuition and fees vary according to degree level. Room and board charges vary according to board plan and housing facility. *Part-time tuition:* $5300 per course. Part-time tuition and fees vary according to degree level.

FRESHMAN FINANCIAL AID (Fall 2016, est.) 574 applied for aid; of those 98% were deemed to have need. 100% of freshmen with need received aid; of those 10% had need fully met. *Average percent of need met:* 85% (excluding resources awarded to replace EFC). *Average financial aid package:* $39,850 (excluding resources awarded to replace EFC). 6% of all full-time freshmen had no need and received non-need-based gift aid.

UNDERGRADUATE FINANCIAL AID (Fall 2016, est.) 1,742 applied for aid; of those 97% were deemed to have need. 100% of undergraduates with need received aid; of those 12% had need fully met. *Average percent of need met:* 80% (excluding resources awarded to replace EFC). *Average financial aid package:* $36,812 (excluding resources awarded to replace EFC). 8% of all full-time undergraduates had no need and received non-need-based gift aid.

GIFT AID (NEED-BASED) *Total amount:* $52,106,453 (8% federal, 5% state, 84% institutional, 3% external sources). *Receiving aid:* Freshmen: 94% (560); all full-time undergraduates: 90% (1,677). *Average award:* Freshmen: $34,162; Undergraduates: $31,045. *Scholarships, grants, and awards:* Federal Pell, FSEOG, state, private, college/university gift aid from institutional funds, United Negro College Fund.

GIFT AID (NON-NEED-BASED) *Total amount:* $4,559,370 (88% institutional, 12% external sources). *Receiving aid:* Freshmen: 7% (42). Undergraduates: 7% (136). *Average award:* Freshmen: $23,572. Undergraduates: $19,738. *Scholarships, grants, and awards by category:* Creative arts/performance: art/fine arts, journalism/publications, music, theater/drama. *Special achievements/activities:* memberships, religious involvement. *Special characteristics:* children and siblings of alumni, ethnic background, local/state students, siblings of current students. *Tuition waivers:* Full or partial for employees or children of employees, adult students, senior citizens. *ROTC:* Army cooperative.

LOANS *Student loans:* $15,950,865 (80% need-based, 20% non-need-based). 89% of past graduating class borrowed through all loan programs. *Average indebtedness per student:* $38,196. *Average need-based loan:* Freshmen: $4955. Undergraduates: $5224. *Parent loans:* $5,295,192 (100% non-need-based). *Programs:* Federal Direct (Subsidized and Unsubsidized Stafford, PLUS), Perkins.

WORK-STUDY *Federal work-study:* Total amount: $1,908,710; jobs available. *State or other work-study/employment:* Total amount: $2000 (100% non-need-based). Part-time jobs available.

APPLYING FOR FINANCIAL AID *Required financial aid form:* FAFSA. *Financial aid deadline:* 2/1 (priority: 2/1). *Notification date:* Continuous beginning 11/1.

CONTACT Chris Hanlon, Director of Financial Aid, Albright College, PO Box 15234, Reading, PA 19612-5234, 610-921-7515 or toll-free 800-252-1856. *Fax:* 610-921-7729. *E-mail:* chanlon@albright.edu. *Website:* http://www.albright.edu/.

ALCORN STATE UNIVERSITY
Lorman, MS

Tuition & fees (MS res): $6552	Average undergraduate aid package: $15,032

ABOUT THE INSTITUTION State-supported, coed. *Awards:* certificates, associate, bachelor's, and master's degrees. 29 undergraduate majors. *Total enrollment:* 3,420. Undergraduates: 2,825. Freshmen: 536. Both federal and institutional methodology are used as a basis for awarding need-based institutional aid.

UNDERGRADUATE EXPENSES for 2016–2017 *Tuition, state resident:* full-time $6552; part-time $546 per credit hour. *Tuition, nonresident:* full-time $6552; part-time $546 per credit hour. Full-time tuition and fees vary according to course load. Part-time tuition and fees vary according to course load. *College room and board:* $9356; *Room only:* $6384. Room and board charges vary according to board plan and housing facility.

FRESHMAN FINANCIAL AID (Fall 2016, est.) 525 applied for aid; of those 100% were deemed to have need. 100% of freshmen with need received aid; of those 14% had need fully met. *Average percent of need met:* 94% (excluding resources awarded to replace EFC). *Average financial aid package:* $14,918 (excluding resources awarded to replace EFC). 49% of all full-time freshmen had no need and received non-need-based gift aid.

UNDERGRADUATE FINANCIAL AID (Fall 2016, est.) 1,337 applied for aid; of those 96% were deemed to have need. 95% of undergraduates with need received aid; of those 11% had need fully met. *Average percent of need met:* 49% (excluding resources awarded to replace EFC). *Average financial aid package:* $15,032 (excluding resources awarded to replace EFC). 28% of all full-time undergraduates had no need and received non-need-based gift aid.

GIFT AID (NEED-BASED) *Total amount:* $16,380,443 (65% federal, 1% state, 34% institutional). *Receiving aid:* Freshmen: 100% (525); all full-time undergraduates: 45% (1,160). *Average award:* Freshmen: $6140; Undergraduates: $5902. *Scholarships, grants, and awards:* Federal Pell, FSEOG, state, private, college/university gift aid from institutional funds.

GIFT AID (NON-NEED-BASED) *Receiving aid:* Freshmen: 47% (246). Undergraduates: 16% (402). *Average award:* Freshmen: $8184. Undergraduates: $8158. *Scholarships, grants, and awards by category:* Academic interests/achievement: 427 awards ($4,124,133 total): general academic interests/achievements. *Creative arts/performance:* 244 awards ($1,458,402 total): music. *Special achievements/activities:* 2 awards ($23,630 total): leadership. *Special characteristics:* 55 awards ($157,248 total): children of faculty/staff. *Tuition waivers:* Full or partial for employees or children of employees. *ROTC:* Army.

LOANS *Student loans:* $23,276,824 (31% need-based, 69% non-need-based). 94% of past graduating class borrowed through all loan programs. *Average indebtedness per student:* $35,077. *Average need-based loan:* Freshmen: $3428. Undergraduates: $3892. *Parent loans:* $1,987,118 (100% non-need-based). *Programs:* Federal Direct (Subsidized and Unsubsidized Stafford, PLUS).

WORK-STUDY *Federal work-study:* Total amount: $312,135; 281 jobs averaging $1111. *State or other work-study/employment:* Part-time jobs available.

ATHLETIC AWARDS Total amount: $2,077,304 (100% non-need-based).

APPLYING FOR FINANCIAL AID *Required financial aid forms:* FAFSA, institution's own form. *Financial aid deadline (priority):* 3/15. *Notification date:* Continuous beginning 4/1. Students must reply within 4 weeks of notification.

CONTACT Mrs. Juanita M Edwards, Director of Financial Aid, Alcorn State University, 1000 ASU Drive #28, Alcorn State, MS 39096-7500, 601-877-6190 or toll-free 800-222-6790. *Fax:* 601-877-6110. *E-mail:* juanita@alcorn.edu. *Website:* http://www.alcorn.edu/.

ALDERSON BROADDUS UNIVERSITY
Philippi, WV

Tuition & fees: $25,350	Average undergraduate aid package: $22,284

ABOUT THE INSTITUTION Independent American Baptist Churches in the U.S.A., coed. *Awards:* associate, bachelor's, and master's degrees. 28 undergraduate majors. *Total enrollment:* 1,052. Undergraduates: 981. Freshmen: 261. Federal methodology is used as a basis for awarding need-based institutional aid.

UNDERGRADUATE EXPENSES for 2016–2017 *Comprehensive fee:* $33,340 includes full-time tuition ($25,140), mandatory fees ($210), and room and board ($7990). Room and board charges vary according to housing facility. *Part-time tuition:* $838 per credit hour. *Part-time fees:* $52.50 per term.

FRESHMAN FINANCIAL AID (Fall 2016, est.) 250 applied for aid; of those 91% were deemed to have need. 100% of freshmen with need received aid; of those 27% had need fully met. *Average percent of need met:* 91% (excluding resources awarded to replace EFC). *Average financial aid package:* $23,207 (excluding resources awarded to replace EFC). 11% of all full-time freshmen had no need and received non-need-based gift aid.

UNDERGRADUATE FINANCIAL AID (Fall 2016, est.) 887 applied for aid; of those 89% were deemed to have need. 100% of undergraduates with need received aid; of those 33% had need fully met. *Average percent of need met:* 90% (excluding resources awarded to replace EFC). *Average financial aid package:* $22,284 (excluding resources awarded to replace EFC). 13% of all full-time undergraduates had no need and received non-need-based gift aid.

GIFT AID (NEED-BASED) *Total amount:* $16,065,404 (17% federal, 6% state, 76% institutional, 1% external sources). *Receiving aid:* Freshmen: 87% (228); all full-time undergraduates: 83% (775). *Average award:* Freshmen: $22,405; Undergraduates: $20,274. *Scholarships, grants, and awards:* Federal Pell, FSEOG, state, private, college/university gift aid from institutional funds, Federal Nursing, Scholarships for Disadvantaged Students (SDS), National Health Service Corps Scholarships.

GIFT AID (NON-NEED-BASED) *Total amount:* $1,647,609 (1% federal, 7% state, 88% institutional, 4% external sources). *Receiving aid:* Freshmen: 20% (53). Undergraduates: 21% (196). *Average award:* Freshmen: $8761. Undergraduates: $9505. *Scholarships, grants, and awards by category:* Academic interests/achievement: 631 awards ($7,366,916 total): biological sciences, business, communication, computer science, education, general academic interests/achievements, health fields, mathematics, physical sciences, premedicine, religion/biblical studies, social sciences. *Creative arts/performance:* 6 awards ($13,000 total): applied art and design, debating, journalism/publications, music. *Special achievements/activities:* 680 awards ($1,491,924 total): general special achievements/activities, leadership. *Special characteristics:* 64 awards ($872,853 total): children and siblings of alumni, children of faculty/staff, ethnic background, general special characteristics, international students, religious affiliation. *Tuition waivers:* Full or partial for employees or children of employees.

LOANS *Student loans:* $8,490,126 (76% need-based, 24% non-need-based). 87% of past graduating class borrowed through all loan programs. *Average indebtedness per student:* $24,079. *Average need-based loan:* Freshmen: $3393. Undergraduates: $4047. *Parent loans:* $2,465,023 (45% need-based, 55% non-need-based). *Programs:* Federal Direct (Subsidized and Unsubsidized Stafford, PLUS), Perkins, Federal Nursing.

WORK-STUDY *Federal work-study:* Total amount: $608,441; 430 jobs averaging $1435. *State or other work-study/employment:* Total amount: $217,690 (36% need-based, 64% non-need-based). 95 part-time jobs averaging $2410.

ATHLETIC AWARDS Total amount: $3,289,046 (59% need-based, 41% non-need-based).

APPLYING FOR FINANCIAL AID *Required financial aid form:* FAFSA. *Financial aid deadline (priority):* 3/1. *Notification date:* Continuous beginning 3/1. Students must reply within 2 weeks of notification.

CONTACT Amy L. King, Director of Financial Aid, Alderson Broaddus University, College Hill Road, Philippi, WV 26416, 304-457-6354 or toll-free 800-263-1549. *Fax:* 304-457-6391. *Website:* http://www.ab.edu/.

ALFRED UNIVERSITY
Alfred, NY

Tuition & fees: $32,264	Average undergraduate aid package: $26,882

ABOUT THE INSTITUTION Independent, coed. *Awards:* certificates, bachelor's, master's, and doctoral degrees. 42 undergraduate majors. *Total enrollment:* 2,390. Undergraduates: 1,815. Freshmen: 417. Both federal and institutional methodology are used as a basis for awarding need-based institutional aid.

UNDERGRADUATE EXPENSES for 2017–2018 *Application fee:* $50. *Comprehensive fee:* $44,536 includes full-time tuition ($31,274), mandatory fees ($990), and room and board ($12,272). *College room only:* $6216. Full-time tuition and fees vary according to program. Room and board charges vary according to board plan and housing facility. *Part-time tuition:* $998 per credit hour. *Part-time fees:* $84 per term.

FRESHMAN FINANCIAL AID (Fall 2016, est.) 404 applied for aid; of those 90% were deemed to have need. 100% of freshmen with need received aid; of those 12% had need fully met. *Average percent of need met:* 87% (excluding resources awarded to replace EFC). *Average financial aid package:* $29,584 (excluding resources awarded to replace EFC). 3% of all full-time freshmen had no need and received non-need-based gift aid.

UNDERGRADUATE FINANCIAL AID (Fall 2016, est.) 1,528 applied for aid; of those 91% were deemed to have need. 100% of undergraduates with need received aid; of those 18% had need fully met. *Average percent of need met:* 84% (excluding resources awarded to replace EFC). *Average financial aid package:* $26,882 (excluding resources awarded to replace EFC). 8% of all full-time undergraduates had no need and received non-need-based gift aid.

GIFT AID (NEED-BASED) *Total amount:* $29,106,256 (12% federal, 8% state, 80% institutional). *Receiving aid:* Freshmen: 85% (362); all full-time undergraduates: 80% (1,370). *Average award:* Freshmen: $22,872; Undergraduates: $20,478. *Scholarships, grants, and awards:* Federal Pell, FSEOG, state, private, college/university gift aid from institutional funds.

GIFT AID (NON-NEED-BASED) *Total amount:* $2,768,615 (4% federal, 80% institutional, 16% external sources). *Receiving aid:* Freshmen: 46% (197). Undergraduates: 47% (801). *Average award:* Freshmen: $11,750. Undergraduates: $11,406. *Scholarships, grants, and awards by category:* Academic interests/achievement: 1,409 awards ($12,115,147 total): biological sciences, business, communication, education, engineering/technologies, English, foreign languages, general academic interests/achievements, humanities, international studies, mathematics, physical sciences, premedicine, social sciences. *Creative arts/performance:* 35 awards ($368,950 total): art/fine arts. *Special characteristics:* 54 awards ($1,012,802 total): children of educators, children of faculty/staff. *Tuition waivers:* Full or partial for employees or children of employees. *ROTC:* Army cooperative.

LOANS *Student loans:* $13,375,195 (55% need-based, 45% non-need-based). 86% of past graduating class borrowed through all loan programs. *Average indebtedness per student:* $37,437. *Average need-based loan:* Freshmen: $5463. Undergraduates: $5978. *Parent loans:* $3,428,468 (100% non-need-based). *Programs:* Federal Direct (Subsidized and Unsubsidized Stafford, PLUS), Perkins, college/university, alternative loans.

WORK-STUDY *Federal work-study:* Total amount: $1,785,778; 1,003 jobs averaging $1663.

APPLYING FOR FINANCIAL AID *Required financial aid forms:* FAFSA, institution's own form, state aid form, noncustodial (divorced/separated) parent's statement, business/farm supplement. *Financial aid deadline:* 3/15. *Notification date:* Continuous beginning 2/15. Students must reply by 5/1 or within 2 weeks of notification.

CONTACT Mr. Charles M. Scheetz, Director of Student Financial Aid, Alfred University, Alumni Hall, One Saxon Drive, Alfred, NY 14802-1205, 607-871-2159 or toll-free 800-541-9229. *Fax:* 607-871-2252. *E-mail:* scheetz@alfred.edu. *Website:* http://www.alfred.edu/.

ALICE LLOYD COLLEGE
Pippa Passes, KY

Tuition & fees: N/R	Average undergraduate aid package: $13,775

ABOUT THE INSTITUTION Independent, coed. *Awards:* bachelor's degrees. 15 undergraduate majors. *Total enrollment:* 599. Undergraduates: 599. Freshmen: 168. Federal methodology is used as a basis for awarding need-based institutional aid.

UNDERGRADUATE EXPENSES for 2017–2018 The cost of tuition is covered by a combination of scholarships and other other financial aid.

FRESHMAN FINANCIAL AID (Fall 2016, est.) 167 applied for aid; of those 91% were deemed to have need. 100% of freshmen with need received aid; of those 7% had need fully met. *Average percent of need met:* 67% (excluding resources awarded to replace EFC). *Average financial aid package:* $13,276 (excluding resources awarded to replace EFC). 13% of all full-time freshmen had no need and received non-need-based gift aid.

UNDERGRADUATE FINANCIAL AID (Fall 2016, est.) 572 applied for aid; of those 92% were deemed to have need. 100% of undergraduates with need received aid; of those 13% had need fully met. *Average percent of need met:* 71% (excluding resources awarded to replace EFC). *Average financial aid package:* $13,775 (excluding resources awarded to replace EFC). 10% of all full-time undergraduates had no need and received non-need-based gift aid.

GIFT AID (NEED-BASED) *Total amount:* $5,178,385 (29% federal, 45% state, 26% institutional). *Receiving aid:* Freshmen: 90% (151); all full-time undergraduates: 91% (521). *Average award:* Freshmen: $9550; Undergraduates: $9889. *Scholarships, grants, and awards:* Federal Pell, FSEOG, state, private, college/university gift aid from institutional funds.

GIFT AID (NON-NEED-BASED) *Total amount:* $668,975 (37% state, 63% institutional). *Receiving aid:* Freshmen: 5% (8). Undergraduates: 9% (53). *Average award:* Freshmen: $5090. Undergraduates: $5898. *Scholarships, grants, and awards by category:* Special achievements/activities: general special achievements/activities. Special characteristics: members of minority groups. *Tuition waivers:* Full or partial for employees or children of employees.

LOANS *Student loans:* $1,798,593 (81% need-based, 19% non-need-based). 68% of past graduating class borrowed through all loan programs. *Average indebtedness per student:* $10,714. *Average need-based loan:* Freshmen: $2062. Undergraduates: $2225. *Parent loans:* $37,000 (56% need-based, 44% non-need-based). *Programs:* Federal Direct (Subsidized and Unsubsidized Stafford, PLUS), college/university, Bagby Loans.

WORK-STUDY *Federal work-study:* Total amount: $1,000,580; 418 jobs averaging $2320. *State or other work-study/employment:* Total amount: $431,980 (16% need-based, 84% non-need-based). 168 part-time jobs averaging $2320.

ATHLETIC AWARDS Total amount: $171,881 (100% need-based).

APPLYING FOR FINANCIAL AID *Required financial aid form:* FAFSA. *Financial aid deadline (priority):* 11/1. *Notification date:* Continuous beginning 3/1. Students must reply by 7/1 or within 4 weeks of notification.

CONTACT Ms. Jacqueline Stewart, Director of Financial Aid, Alice Lloyd College, 100 Purpose Road, Pippa Passes, KY 41844, 606-368-6058 or toll-free 888-280-4252. *E-mail:* jacquelinestewart@alc.edu. *Website:* http://www.alc.edu/.

ALLEGHENY COLLEGE
Meadville, PA

Tuition & fees: $45,970	Average undergraduate aid package: $39,415

ABOUT THE INSTITUTION Independent, coed. *Awards:* bachelor's degrees. 47 undergraduate majors. *Total enrollment:* 1,920. Undergraduates: 1,920. Freshmen: 553. Federal methodology is used as a basis for awarding need-based institutional aid.

UNDERGRADUATE EXPENSES for 2017–2018 *Comprehensive fee:* $57,620 includes full-time tuition ($45,470), mandatory fees ($500), and room and board ($11,650). *College room only:* $6130. Room and board charges vary according to board plan and housing facility. *Part-time tuition:* $1895 per credit hour. *Part-time fees:* $250 per term. Part-time tuition and fees vary according to course load.

FRESHMAN FINANCIAL AID (Fall 2016, est.) 496 applied for aid; of those 90% were deemed to have need. 100% of freshmen with need received aid; of those 27% had need fully met. *Average percent of need met:* 91% (excluding resources awarded to replace EFC). *Average financial aid package:* $41,707 (excluding resources awarded to replace EFC). 19% of all full-time freshmen had no need and received non-need-based gift aid.

UNDERGRADUATE FINANCIAL AID (Fall 2016, est.) 1,529 applied for aid; of those 91% were deemed to have need. 100% of undergraduates with need received aid; of those 31% had need fully met. *Average percent of need met:* 90% (excluding resources awarded to replace EFC). *Average financial aid package:* $39,415 (excluding resources awarded to replace EFC). 24% of all full-time undergraduates had no need and received non-need-based gift aid.

GIFT AID (NEED-BASED) *Total amount:* $42,865,651 (8% federal, 3% state, 86% institutional, 3% external sources). *Receiving aid:* Freshmen: 81% (446); all full-time undergraduates: 74% (1,387). *Average award:* Freshmen: $35,455; Undergraduates: $31,814. *Scholarships, grants, and awards:* Federal Pell, FSEOG, state, private, college/university gift aid from institutional funds, Veterans Education Benefits (GI Bill), Yellow Ribbon Program.

GIFT AID (NON-NEED-BASED) *Total amount:* $10,288,064 (94% institutional, 6% external sources). *Receiving aid:* Freshmen: 12% (65). Undergraduates: 12% (231). *Average award:* Freshmen: $22,434. Undergraduates: $18,569. *Scholarships, grants, and awards by category:* Academic interests/achievement: 1,720 awards ($31,073,436 total): general academic interests/achievements. Special characteristics: 122 awards ($3,431,272 total): adult students, children of educators, children of faculty/staff, international students. *Tuition waivers:* Full or partial for employees or children of employees.

LOANS *Student loans:* $12,294,334 (46% need-based, 54% non-need-based). *Average need-based loan:* Freshmen: $3750. Undergraduates: $5259. *Parent loans:* $4,146,591 (100% non-need-based). *Programs:* Federal Direct (Subsidized and Unsubsidized Stafford, PLUS), Perkins, private loans.

WORK-STUDY *Federal work-study:* Total amount: $2,341,200; 948 jobs averaging $2470. *State or other work-study/employment:* Total amount: $686,675 (100% non-need-based). 130 part-time jobs averaging $5282.

APPLYING FOR FINANCIAL AID *Required financial aid form:* FAFSA. *Financial aid deadline (priority):* 2/15. *Notification date:* Continuous beginning 12/1. Students must reply by 5/1 or within 4 weeks of notification.

CONTACT Mr. Jonathan Boleratz, Director of Financial Aid, Allegheny College, 520 North Main Street, Meadville, PA 16335, 800-835-7780 or toll-free 800-521-5293. *Fax:* 814-332-2349. *E-mail:* fao@allegheny.edu. *Website:* http://www.allegheny.edu/.

ALLEGHENY WESLEYAN COLLEGE
Salem, OH

Tuition & fees: N/R	Average undergraduate aid package: N/A

ABOUT THE INSTITUTION Independent Wesleyan, coed. 2 undergraduate majors. Federal methodology is used as a basis for awarding need-based institutional aid.

FRESHMAN FINANCIAL AID (Fall 2015) 12 applied for aid; of those 100% were deemed to have need. 100% of freshmen with need received aid; of those 100% had need fully met.

UNDERGRADUATE FINANCIAL AID (Fall 2015) 7 applied for aid; of those 100% were deemed to have need. 100% of undergraduates with need received aid. 4% of all full-time undergraduates had no need and received non-need-based gift aid.

GIFT AID (NEED-BASED) *Total amount:* $234,161 (85% federal, 1% state, 8% institutional, 6% external sources). *Receiving aid:* Freshmen: 100% (12); all full-time undergraduates: 15% (7). *Scholarships, grants, and awards:* Federal Pell, FSEOG, private, college/university gift aid from institutional funds.

GIFT AID (NON-NEED-BASED) *Total amount:* $3700 (78% institutional, 22% external sources). *Receiving aid:* Freshmen: 100% (12). *Average award:* Freshmen: $3500. Undergraduates: $4500. *Scholarships, grants, and awards by category:* Creative arts/performance: music.

LOANS *Student loans:* $191,271 (100% need-based). *Programs:* Federal Direct (Subsidized and Unsubsidized Stafford, PLUS).

WORK-STUDY *State or other work-study/employment:* Total amount: $54,480 (100% need-based). 27 part-time jobs averaging $2000.

APPLYING FOR FINANCIAL AID *Required financial aid forms:* FAFSA, institution's own form. *Financial aid deadline (priority):* 7/31. *Notification date:* 8/15. Students must reply within 3 weeks of notification.

CONTACT Mrs. Esther Phelps, Financial Aid Director, Allegheny Wesleyan College, 2161 Woodsdale Road, Salem, OH 44460, 330-337-6403 Ext. 111 or toll-free 800-292-3153. *Fax:* 424-228-3006. *E-mail:* ephelps@awc.edu.
Website: http://www.awc.edu/.

ALLEN COLLEGE
Waterloo, IA

Tuition & fees: $18,536	Average undergraduate aid package: $11,217

ABOUT THE INSTITUTION Independent, coed, primarily women. *Awards:* certificates, associate, bachelor's, master's, and doctoral degrees (liberal arts and general education courses offered at either University of North Iowa or Wartburg College). 6 undergraduate majors. *Total enrollment:* 620. Undergraduates: 360. Federal methodology is used as a basis for awarding need-based institutional aid.
UNDERGRADUATE EXPENSES for 2017–2018 *Application fee:* $50. *Tuition:* full-time $16,876; part-time $603 per credit hour. Full-time tuition and fees vary according to course load, degree level, and program. Part-time tuition and fees vary according to course load, degree level, and program.
UNDERGRADUATE FINANCIAL AID (Fall 2015) 249 applied for aid; of those 82% were deemed to have need. 99% of undergraduates with need received aid; of those 5% had need fully met. *Average percent of need met:* 51% (excluding resources awarded to replace EFC). *Average financial aid package:* $11,217 (excluding resources awarded to replace EFC). 8% of all full-time undergraduates had no need and received non-need-based gift aid.
GIFT AID (NEED-BASED) *Total amount:* $2,335,082 (23% federal, 42% state, 25% institutional, 10% external sources). *Receiving aid:* All full-time undergraduates: 69% (197). *Average award:* Undergraduates: $8419. *Scholarships, grants, and awards:* Federal Pell, FSEOG, state, private, college/university gift aid from institutional funds, Federal Nursing, Scholarships for Disadvantaged Students (SDS).
GIFT AID (NON-NEED-BASED) *Total amount:* $64,322 (18% institutional, 82% external sources). *Receiving aid:* Undergraduates: 70% (201). *Average award:* Undergraduates: $1250. *Scholarships, grants, and awards by category:* Academic interests/achievement: health fields. *Special achievements/activities:* community service, general special achievements/activities, leadership. *Special characteristics:* children of faculty/staff, general special characteristics, local/state students, members of minority groups, out-of-state students. *ROTC:* Army cooperative.
LOANS *Student loans:* $2,611,645 (48% need-based, 52% non-need-based). *Average need-based loan:* Undergraduates: $5101. *Parent loans:* $706,611 (100% non-need-based). *Programs:* Federal Direct (Subsidized and Unsubsidized Stafford, PLUS), Perkins, Federal Nursing, state, college/university.
WORK-STUDY *Federal work-study:* 12 jobs averaging $5000.
APPLYING FOR FINANCIAL AID *Required financial aid form:* FAFSA. *Financial aid deadline:* Continuous. *Notification date:* Continuous beginning 4/1. Students must reply within 2 weeks of notification.

CONTACT Jobyna A. Johnston, Director of Finacial Aid, Allen College, Barrett Forum, 1825 Logan Avenue, Waterloo, IA 50703-1990, 319-226-2515. *Fax:* 319-226-2051. *E-mail:* jobyna.johnston@allencollege.edu.
Website: http://www.allencollege.edu/.

ALLEN UNIVERSITY
Columbia, SC

CONTACT Ms. Donna Foster, Director of Financial Aid, Allen University, 1530 Harden Street, Columbia, SC 29204-1085, 803-376-5736 or toll-free 877-625-5368. *E-mail:* donnaf@allenuniversity.edu.
Website: http://www.allenuniversity.edu/.

ALLIANT INTERNATIONAL UNIVERSITY–SAN DIEGO
San Diego, CA

Tuition & fees: $21,220	Average undergraduate aid package: $16,815

ABOUT THE INSTITUTION Independent, coed. *Awards:* certificates, bachelor's, master's, and doctoral degrees. 3 undergraduate majors. *Total enrollment:* 3,036. Undergraduates: 163. Federal methodology is used as a basis for awarding need-based institutional aid.
UNDERGRADUATE EXPENSES for 2016–2017 *Application fee:* $65. *Tuition:* full-time $21,000; part-time $700 per credit hour. *Required fees:* full-time $220; $70 per term.
FRESHMAN FINANCIAL AID (Fall 2015) 8 applied for aid; of those 100% were deemed to have need. 100% of freshmen with need received aid. *Average percent of need met:* 62% (excluding resources awarded to replace EFC). *Average financial aid package:* $14,815 (excluding resources awarded to replace EFC). 33% of all full-time freshmen had no need and received non-need-based gift aid.
UNDERGRADUATE FINANCIAL AID (Fall 2015) 118 applied for aid; of those 100% were deemed to have need. 100% of undergraduates with need received aid; of those 6% had need fully met. *Average percent of need met:* 62% (excluding resources awarded to replace EFC). *Average financial aid package:* $16,815 (excluding resources awarded to replace EFC). 13% of all full-time undergraduates had no need and received non-need-based gift aid.
GIFT AID (NEED-BASED) *Total amount:* $901,153 (80% federal, 20% state). *Receiving aid:* Freshmen: 67% (8); all full-time undergraduates: 12% (118). *Average award:* Freshmen: $12,315; Undergraduates: $14,315. *Scholarships, grants, and awards:* Federal Pell, FSEOG, state, private, college/university gift aid from institutional funds.
GIFT AID (NON-NEED-BASED) *Total amount:* $714,362 (100% institutional). *Receiving aid:* Freshmen: 67% (8). Undergraduates: 12% (118). *Average award:* Freshmen: $3000. Undergraduates: $4000. *Scholarships, grants, and awards by category:* Academic interests/achievement: business, communication, computer science, education, English, foreign languages, general academic interests/achievements, humanities, international studies, social sciences. *Special achievements/activities:* community service, general special achievements/activities, leadership. *Special characteristics:* children and siblings of alumni, children of faculty/staff, international students, local/state students, siblings of current students, spouses of current students, veterans, veterans' children. *Tuition waivers:* Full or partial for children of alumni, employees or children of employees.
LOANS *Student loans:* $775,394 (52% need-based, 48% non-need-based). *Average need-based loan:* Freshmen: $3500. Undergraduates: $5025. *Parent loans:* $77,302 (100% non-need-based). *Programs:* Federal Direct (Subsidized and Unsubsidized Stafford, PLUS), Perkins, alternative loans.
WORK-STUDY *Federal work-study:* 33 jobs averaging $4000. *State or other work-study/employment:* Part-time jobs available.
APPLYING FOR FINANCIAL AID *Required financial aid form:* FAFSA. *Financial aid deadline (priority):* 3/2. *Notification date:* 4/1. Students must reply within 3 weeks of notification.

CONTACT Ms. Deborah Spindler, Director of Financial Aid, Alliant International University–San Diego, 10455 Pomerado Road, San Diego, CA 92131-1799, 858-635-4559 Ext. 4700 or toll-free 866-825-5426. *Fax:* 858-635-4848. *E-mail:* dspindler@alliant.edu.
Website: http://www.alliant.edu/.

ALMA COLLEGE
Alma, MI

Tuition & fees: $37,310	Average undergraduate aid package: $26,369

ABOUT THE INSTITUTION Independent Presbyterian, coed. *Awards:* bachelor's degrees. 39 undergraduate majors. *Total enrollment:* 1,451. Undergraduates: 1,451. Freshmen: 447. Federal methodology is used as a basis for awarding need-based institutional aid.

UNDERGRADUATE EXPENSES for 2016–2017 *Application fee:* $25. *Comprehensive fee:* $47,548 includes full-time tuition ($36,890), mandatory fees ($420), and room and board ($10,238). *College room only:* $5119. Full-time tuition and fees vary according to student level. Room and board charges vary according to board plan and housing facility. *Part-time tuition:* $1150 per credit hour. Part-time tuition and fees vary according to course load and student level.

FRESHMAN FINANCIAL AID (Fall 2016, est.) 432 applied for aid; of those 91% were deemed to have need. 100% of freshmen with need received aid; of those 12% had need fully met. *Average percent of need met:* 72% (excluding resources awarded to replace EFC). *Average financial aid package:* $29,312 (excluding resources awarded to replace EFC). 9% of all full-time freshmen had no need and received non-need-based gift aid.

UNDERGRADUATE FINANCIAL AID (Fall 2016, est.) 1,268 applied for aid; of those 92% were deemed to have need. 99% of undergraduates with need received aid; of those 12% had need fully met. *Average percent of need met:* 68% (excluding resources awarded to replace EFC). *Average financial aid package:* $26,369 (excluding resources awarded to replace EFC). 8% of all full-time undergraduates had no need and received non-need-based gift aid.

GIFT AID (NEED-BASED) *Total amount:* $28,668,645 (7% federal, 5% state, 86% institutional, 2% external sources). *Receiving aid:* Freshmen: 88% (392); all full-time undergraduates: 83% (1,152). *Average award:* Freshmen: $28,254; Undergraduates: $25,234. *Scholarships, grants, and awards:* Federal Pell, FSEOG, state, private, college/university gift aid from institutional funds.

GIFT AID (NON-NEED-BASED) *Total amount:* $5,649,491 (97% institutional, 3% external sources). *Receiving aid:* Freshmen: 11% (47). Undergraduates: 10% (142). *Average award:* Freshmen: $21,225. Undergraduates: $19,008. *Scholarships, grants, and awards by category:* Academic interests/achievement: 1,304 awards ($20,546,465 total): general academic interests/achievements. *Creative arts/performance:* 307 awards ($754,310 total): art/fine arts, dance, music, performing arts, theater/drama. *Special achievements/activities:* 20 awards ($20,000 total): religious involvement. *Special characteristics:* 164 awards ($155,250 total): children and siblings of alumni, siblings of current students. *Tuition waivers:* Full or partial for employees or children of employees. *ROTC:* Army cooperative.

LOANS *Student loans:* $10,102,542 (72% need-based, 28% non-need-based). 83% of past graduating class borrowed through all loan programs. *Average indebtedness per student:* $36,046. *Average need-based loan:* Freshmen: $3552. Undergraduates: $4571. *Parent loans:* $3,802,479 (52% need-based, 48% non-need-based). *Programs:* Federal Direct (Subsidized and Unsubsidized Stafford, PLUS), Perkins, college/university, alternative loans.

WORK-STUDY *Federal work-study:* Total amount: $884,417; 592 jobs averaging $1500.

APPLYING FOR FINANCIAL AID *Required financial aid form:* FAFSA. *Financial aid deadline (priority):* 3/1. *Notification date:* Continuous beginning 3/1. Students must reply within 3 weeks of notification.

CONTACT Mrs. Michelle L. McNier, Director of Financial Aid, Alma College, 614 West Superior Street, Alma, MI 48801-1599, 989-463-7347 or toll-free 800-321-ALMA. *Fax:* 989-463-7993. *E-mail:* mcnierml@alma.edu.

Website: http://www.alma.edu/.

ALVERNIA UNIVERSITY
Reading, PA

Tuition & fees: $33,640	Average undergraduate aid package: $20,349

ABOUT THE INSTITUTION Independent Roman Catholic, coed. *Awards:* associate, bachelor's, master's, and doctoral degrees. 39 undergraduate majors. *Total enrollment:* 2,872. Undergraduates: 2,323. Freshmen: 345. Federal methodology is used as a basis for awarding need-based institutional aid.

UNDERGRADUATE EXPENSES for 2017–2018 *Application fee:* $25. *Comprehensive fee:* $45,530 includes full-time tuition ($32,840), mandatory fees ($800), and room and board ($11,890). *College room only:* $6030. Full-time tuition and fees vary according to class time and reciprocity agreements. Room and board charges vary according to board plan and housing facility. Part-time tuition and fees vary according to class time and course load.

FRESHMAN FINANCIAL AID (Fall 2016, est.) 333 applied for aid; of those 88% were deemed to have need. 100% of freshmen with need received aid; of those 14% had need fully met. *Average percent of need met:* 68% (excluding resources

awarded to replace EFC). *Average financial aid package:* $22,520 (excluding resources awarded to replace EFC). 15% of all full-time freshmen had no need and received non-need-based gift aid.

UNDERGRADUATE FINANCIAL AID (Fall 2016, est.) 1,582 applied for aid; of those 91% were deemed to have need. 100% of undergraduates with need received aid; of those 13% had need fully met. *Average percent of need met:* 65% (excluding resources awarded to replace EFC). *Average financial aid package:* $20,349 (excluding resources awarded to replace EFC). 12% of all full-time undergraduates had no need and received non-need-based gift aid.

GIFT AID (NEED-BASED) *Total amount:* $23,688,183 (16% federal, 11% state, 67% institutional, 6% external sources). *Receiving aid:* Freshmen: 85% (294); all full-time undergraduates: 83% (1,400). *Average award:* Freshmen: $18,943; Undergraduates: $16,212. *Scholarships, grants, and awards:* Federal Pell, FSEOG, state, private, college/university gift aid from institutional funds.

GIFT AID (NON-NEED-BASED) *Total amount:* $3,953,671 (1% federal, 80% institutional, 19% external sources). *Receiving aid:* Freshmen: 9% (31). Undergraduates: 7% (120). *Average award:* Freshmen: $13,419. Undergraduates: $13,054. *Scholarships, grants, and awards by category:* Academic interests/achievement: general academic interests/achievements. *Special achievements/activities:* community service, leadership, memberships, religious involvement. *Special characteristics:* children and siblings of alumni, children of faculty/staff, general special characteristics, local/state students, siblings of current students. *Tuition waivers:* Full or partial for employees or children of employees, senior citizens. *ROTC:* Army cooperative.

LOANS *Student loans:* $18,660,143 (74% need-based, 26% non-need-based). 84% of past graduating class borrowed through all loan programs. *Average indebtedness per student:* $51,958. *Average need-based loan:* Freshmen: $3211. Undergraduates: $4113. *Parent loans:* $5,491,000 (53% need-based, 47% non-need-based). *Programs:* Federal Direct (Subsidized and Unsubsidized Stafford, PLUS), Perkins.

WORK-STUDY *Federal work-study:* Total amount: $1,234,217; 981 jobs averaging $1592. *State or other work-study/employment:* Part-time jobs available.

APPLYING FOR FINANCIAL AID *Required financial aid forms:* FAFSA, state aid form. *Financial aid deadline (priority):* 5/1. *Notification date:* Continuous beginning 11/25. Students must reply by 5/1 or within 2 weeks of notification.

CONTACT Ms. Christine Saadi, Director of Student Financial Planning, Alvernia University, 400 Saint Bernardine Street, Reading, PA 19607-1799, 610-796-8213 or toll-free 888-ALVERNIA (in-state). *Fax:* 610-796-8336. *E-mail:* christine.saadi@alvernia.edu.

Website: http://www.alvernia.edu/.

ALVERNO COLLEGE
Milwaukee, WI

Tuition & fees: $26,932	Average undergraduate aid package: $23,988

ABOUT THE INSTITUTION Independent Roman Catholic, undergraduate: women only; graduate: coed. *Awards:* certificates, associate, bachelor's, and master's degrees (also offers weekend program with significant enrollment not reflected in profile). 41 undergraduate majors. *Total enrollment:* 2,017. Undergraduates: 1,413. Freshmen: 168. Federal methodology is used as a basis for awarding need-based institutional aid.

UNDERGRADUATE EXPENSES for 2016–2017 *Comprehensive fee:* $34,816 includes full-time tuition ($26,232), mandatory fees ($700), and room and board ($7884). Full-time tuition and fees vary according to program. Room and board charges vary according to board plan and housing facility. *Part-time tuition:* $1093 per credit hour. Part-time tuition and fees vary according to program.

FRESHMAN FINANCIAL AID (Fall 2016, est.) 157 applied for aid; of those 93% were deemed to have need. 99% of freshmen with need received aid. *Average financial aid package:* $25,752 (excluding resources awarded to replace EFC). 7% of all full-time freshmen had no need and received non-need-based gift aid.

UNDERGRADUATE FINANCIAL AID (Fall 2016, est.) 1,011 applied for aid; of those 95% were deemed to have need. 99% of undergraduates with need received aid. *Average financial aid package:* $23,988 (excluding resources awarded to replace EFC). 8% of all full-time undergraduates had no need and received non-need-based gift aid.

GIFT AID (NEED-BASED) *Total amount:* $17,232,321 (21% federal, 13% state, 64% institutional, 2% external sources). *Receiving aid:* Freshmen: 88% (144); all full-time undergraduates: 90% (950). *Average award:* Freshmen: $19,297; Undergrad-

uates: $15,461. *Scholarships, grants, and awards:* Federal Pell, FSEOG, state, private, college/university gift aid from institutional funds.

GIFT AID (NON-NEED-BASED) *Total amount:* $1,284,224 (97% institutional, 3% external sources). *Receiving aid:* Freshmen: 80% (131). Undergraduates: 79% (839). *Average award:* Freshmen: $13,363. Undergraduates: $10,670. *Scholarships, grants, and awards by category: Academic interests/achievement:* 1,800 awards ($8,504,091 total): general academic interests/achievements, library science. *Creative arts/performance:* 40 awards ($40,719 total): art/fine arts, music. *Special achievements/activities:* 3 awards ($77,196 total): community service. *Special characteristics:* 24 awards ($269,748 total): children of faculty/staff, ethnic background, international students, religious affiliation. *Tuition waivers:* Full or partial for employees or children of employees. **ROTC:** Army cooperative, Air Force cooperative.

LOANS *Student loans:* $16,799,101 (94% need-based, 6% non-need-based). 88% of past graduating class borrowed through all loan programs. *Average indebtedness per student:* $41,044. *Average need-based loan:* Freshmen: $3062. Undergraduates: $3830. *Parent loans:* $2,784,883 (85% need-based, 15% non-need-based). *Programs:* Federal Direct (Subsidized and Unsubsidized Stafford, PLUS), Perkins, state.

WORK-STUDY *Federal work-study:* Total amount: $215,967; 444 jobs averaging $1998. *State or other work-study/employment:* Total amount: $601,514 (100% non-need-based). Part-time jobs available.

APPLYING FOR FINANCIAL AID *Required financial aid forms:* FAFSA, institution's own form. *Financial aid deadline (priority):* 2/1. *Notification date:* Continuous beginning 11/1. Students must reply within 2 weeks of notification.

CONTACT Ms. Amy Christen, Director of Financial Aid, Alverno College, 3400 South 43rd Street, PO Box 343922, Milwaukee, WI 53234-3922, 414-382-6040 or toll-free 800-933-3401. *Fax:* 414-382-6354. *E-mail:* amy.christen@alverno.edu. *Website:* http://www.alverno.edu/.

AMERICAN ACADEMY OF ART
Chicago, IL

CONTACT Ms. Ione Fitzgerald, Director of Financial Aid, American Academy of Art, 332 South Michigan Avenue, Suite 300, Chicago, IL 60604, 312-461-0600 or toll-free 888-461-0600. *Fax:* 312-294-9570. *Website:* http://www.aaart.edu/.

AMERICAN BAPTIST COLLEGE
Nashville, TN

CONTACT Miss Sharonda Campbell, Financial Aid Administrator, American Baptist College, 1800 Baptist World Center Drive, Nashville, TN 37207, 615-687-6903. *Fax:* 615-226-7855. *E-mail:* scampbell@abcnash.edu. *Website:* http://www.abcnash.edu/.

AMERICAN BUSINESS & TECHNOLOGY UNIVERSITY
Saint Joseph, MO

CONTACT Financial Aid Office, American Business & Technology University, 2300 Frederick Avenue, Saint Joseph, MO 64506, 800-908-9329. *Website:* http://www.abtu.edu/.

AMERICAN COLLEGE FOR MEDICAL CAREERS
Orlando, FL

CONTACT Financial Aid Office, American College for Medical Careers, 5959 Lake Ellenor Drive, Orlando, FL 32809, 407-738-4488 or toll-free 888-599-7887. *Website:* http://www.acmc.edu/.

AMERICAN INTERCONTINENTAL UNIVERSITY ATLANTA
Atlanta, GA

CONTACT Financial Aid Office, American InterContinental University Atlanta, 6600 Peachtree-Dunwoody Road, 500 Embassy Row, Atlanta, GA 30328, 404-965-6500 or toll-free 800-353-1744. *Website:* http://www.aiuniv.edu/.

AMERICAN INTERCONTINENTAL UNIVERSITY HOUSTON
Houston, TX

CONTACT Financial Aid Office, American InterContinental University Houston, 9999 Richmond Avenue, Houston, TX 77042, 832-201-3600 or toll-free 888-607-9888. *Website:* http://www.aiuniv.edu/.

AMERICAN INTERCONTINENTAL UNIVERSITY ONLINE
Schaumburg, IL

CONTACT Financial Aid Office, American InterContinental University Online, 231 N. Martingale Road, 6th Floor, Schaumburg, IL 60173, 847-851-5000 or toll-free 877-701-3800. *Website:* http://www.aiuniv.edu/.

AMERICAN INTERNATIONAL COLLEGE
Springfield, MA

CONTACT Ms. Sage Stachowiak, Director of Financial Aid, American International College, 1000 State Street, Springfield, MA 01109-3189, 413-205-3521 or toll-free 800-242-3142. *Fax:* 413-205-3912. *E-mail:* sage.stachowiak@aic.edu. *Website:* http://www.aic.edu/.

AMERICAN JEWISH UNIVERSITY
Bel Air, CA

Tuition & fees: N/R	Average undergraduate aid package: $28,992

ABOUT THE INSTITUTION Independent Jewish, coed. 10 undergraduate majors. Both federal and institutional methodology are used as a basis for awarding need-based institutional aid.

FRESHMAN FINANCIAL AID (Fall 2015) 9 applied for aid; of those 100% were deemed to have need. 100% of freshmen with need received aid. *Average percent of need met:* 89% (excluding resources awarded to replace EFC). *Average* *financial aid package:* $28,992 (excluding resources awarded to replace EFC). 18% of all full-time freshmen had no need and received non-need-based gift aid.

UNDERGRADUATE FINANCIAL AID (Fall 2015) 70 applied for aid; of those 100% were deemed to have need. 100% of undergraduates with need received aid. *Average percent of need met:* 95% (excluding resources awarded to replace EFC). *Average financial aid package:* $28,992 (excluding resources awarded to replace EFC). 13% of all full-time undergraduates had no need and received non-need-based gift aid.

GIFT AID (NEED-BASED) *Total amount:* $572,291 (29% federal, 14% state, 57% institutional). *Receiving aid:* Freshmen: 82% (9); all full-time undergraduates: 91% (70). *Average award:* Freshmen: $9137; Undergraduates: $8973. *Scholarships, grants, and awards:* Federal Pell, FSEOG, state, private, college/university gift aid from institutional funds.

GIFT AID (NON-NEED-BASED) *Total amount:* $296,250 (100% institutional). *Receiving aid:* Freshmen: 82% (9). Undergraduates: 35% (27). *Average award:* Freshmen: $3000. Undergraduates: $5000. *Scholarships, grants, and awards by category:* Academic interests/achievement: business, general academic interests/achievements, premedicine. Special achievements/activities: leadership.

LOANS *Student loans:* $301,544 (47% need-based, 53% non-need-based). 90% of past graduating class borrowed through all loan programs. *Average indebtedness per student:* $30,000. *Average need-based loan:* Freshmen: $3500. Undergraduates: $3500. *Parent loans:* $167,139 (100% non-need-based). *Programs:* Federal Direct (Subsidized and Unsubsidized Stafford, PLUS), alternative loans.

WORK-STUDY *Federal work-study:* jobs available.

APPLYING FOR FINANCIAL AID *Required financial aid forms:* FAFSA, institution's own form, federal income tax form(s). *Financial aid deadline (priority):* 3/2. *Notification date:* Continuous beginning 3/15. Students must reply within 3 weeks of notification.

CONTACT Larisa Zadoyen, Director of Financial Aid, American Jewish University, 15600 Mulholland Drive, Bel Air, CA 90077-1599, 310-476-9777 Ext. 252 or toll-free 888-853-6763. *Fax:* 310-476-4613. *E-mail:* lzadoyen@aju.edu.
Website: http://www.aju.edu/.

AMERICAN MUSICAL AND DRAMATIC ACADEMY, LOS ANGELES
Los Angeles, CA

CONTACT Financial Aid Office, American Musical and Dramatic Academy, Los Angeles, 6305 Yucca Street, Los Angeles, CA 90028, 323-469-3300 or toll-free 888-474-9444.
Website: http://www.amda.edu/.

AMERICAN NATIONAL UNIVERSITY
Salem, VA

CONTACT Financial Aid Office, American National University, 1813 East Main Street, Salem, VA 24153, 540-986-1800 or toll-free 888-9-JOBREADY.
Website: http://www.an.edu/.

AMERICAN SENTINEL UNIVERSITY
Aurora, CO

CONTACT Financial Aid Office, American Sentinel University, 2260 South Xanadu Way, Suite 310, Aurora, CO 80014 or toll-free 800-729-2427.
Website: http://www.americansentinel.edu/.

AMERICAN UNIVERSITY
Washington, DC

Tuition & fees: $44,853	Average undergraduate aid package: $31,064

ABOUT THE INSTITUTION Independent Methodist, coed. *Awards:* certificates, associate, bachelor's, master's, and doctoral degrees. 69 undergraduate majors. *Total enrollment:* 13,347. Undergraduates: 7,901. Freshmen: 1,679. Institutional methodology is used as a basis for awarding need-based institutional aid.

UNDERGRADUATE EXPENSES for 2016–2017 *Application fee:* $70. *Comprehensive fee:* $59,379 includes full-time tuition ($44,046), mandatory fees ($807), and room and board ($14,526). *College room only:* $9800. Full-time tuition and fees vary according to course load. Room and board charges vary according to board plan, housing facility, and location. *Part-time tuition:* $1467 per credit hour. *Part-time fees:* $100 per term. *Payment plan:* Tuition prepayment.

FRESHMAN FINANCIAL AID (Fall 2016, est.) 1,235 applied for aid; of those 76% were deemed to have need. 100% of freshmen with need received aid; of those 49% had need fully met. *Average percent of need met:* 90% (excluding resources awarded to replace EFC). *Average financial aid package:* $36,320 (excluding resources awarded to replace EFC). 10% of all full-time freshmen had no need and received non-need-based gift aid.

UNDERGRADUATE FINANCIAL AID (Fall 2016, est.) 4,316 applied for aid; of those 86% were deemed to have need. 100% of undergraduates with need received aid; of those 19% had need fully met. *Average percent of need met:* 70% (excluding resources awarded to replace EFC). *Average financial aid package:* $31,064 (excluding resources awarded to replace EFC). 9% of all full-time undergraduates had no need and received non-need-based gift aid.

GIFT AID (NEED-BASED) *Total amount:* $88,732,789 (6% federal, 82% institutional, 12% external sources). *Receiving aid:* Freshmen: 52% (871); all full-time undergraduates: 46% (3,229). *Average award:* Freshmen: $30,045; Undergraduates: $25,024. *Scholarships, grants, and awards:* Federal Pell, FSEOG, private, college/university gift aid from institutional funds.

GIFT AID (NON-NEED-BASED) *Total amount:* $20,458,854 (100% institutional). *Receiving aid:* Freshmen: 15% (255). Undergraduates: 14% (1,003). *Average award:* Freshmen: $15,234. Undergraduates: $14,579. *Scholarships, grants, and awards by category:* Academic interests/achievement: general academic interests/achievements. Creative arts/performance: general creative arts/performance. Special achievements/activities: general special achievements/activities, leadership, memberships. Special characteristics: adult students, children and siblings of alumni, children of faculty/staff, ethnic background, first-generation college students, local/state students, members of minority groups, previous college experience, relatives of clergy, spouses of current students, veterans, veterans' children. *Tuition waivers:* Full or partial for employees or children of employees. *ROTC:* Army cooperative, Air Force cooperative.

LOANS *Student loans:* $23,768,134 (62% need-based, 38% non-need-based). *Average need-based loan:* Freshmen: $3712. Undergraduates: $4693. *Parent loans:* $24,807,394 (100% non-need-based). *Programs:* Federal Direct (Subsidized and Unsubsidized Stafford, PLUS), Perkins, college/university.

WORK-STUDY *Federal work-study:* Total amount: $2,185,761; jobs available.

ATHLETIC AWARDS Total amount: $4,720,914 (100% non-need-based).

APPLYING FOR FINANCIAL AID *Required financial aid forms:* FAFSA, CSS Financial Aid PROFILE. *Financial aid deadline:* 1/10. *Notification date:* 4/1. Students must reply within 4 weeks of notification.

CONTACT Brian Lee Sang, Assistant Vice Provost of Financial Aid, American University, 4400 Massachusetts Avenue, NW, Washington, DC 20016-8001, 202-885-6500. *Fax:* 202-885-1025. *E-mail:* facounselor@american.edu.
Website: http://www.american.edu/.

AMERICAN UNIVERSITY OF HEALTH SCIENCES
Signal Hill, CA

CONTACT Financial Aid Office, American University of Health Sciences, 1600 East Hill Street, Building #1, Signal Hill, CA 90755, 562-988-2278.
Website: http://www.auhs.edu/.

AMERICAN UNIVERSITY OF PUERTO RICO
Bayamon, PR

CONTACT Mr. Yahaira Melendez, Financial Aid Director, American University of Puerto Rico, PO Box 2037, Bayamón, PR 00960-2037, 787-620-2040 Ext. 2031. *Fax:* 787-785-7377. *E-mail:* melendezy@aupr.edu.
Website: http://www.aupr.edu/.

AMERICAN UNIVERSITY OF PUERTO RICO
Manati, PR

CONTACT Financial Aid Office, American University of Puerto Rico, Carretera Estatal #2 Km. 48.7, PO Box 1082, Manati, PR 00674-1082, 787-621-2835.
Website: http://www.aupr.edu/.

AMHERST COLLEGE
Amherst, MA

Tuition & fees: $52,476	Average undergraduate aid package: $51,775

ABOUT THE INSTITUTION Independent, coed. *Awards:* bachelor's degrees. 38 undergraduate majors. *Total enrollment:* 1,849. Undergraduates: 1,849. Freshmen: 471. Both federal and institutional methodology are used as a basis for awarding need-based institutional aid.
UNDERGRADUATE EXPENSES for 2016–2017 *Application fee:* $60. *Comprehensive fee:* $66,186 includes full-time tuition ($51,620), mandatory fees ($856), and room and board ($13,710). *College room only:* $7430.
FRESHMAN FINANCIAL AID (Fall 2016, est.) 318 applied for aid; of those 77% were deemed to have need. 100% of freshmen with need received aid; of those 100% had need fully met. *Average percent of need met:* 100% (excluding resources awarded to replace EFC). *Average financial aid package:* $52,877 (excluding resources awarded to replace EFC). 1% of all full-time freshmen had no need and received non-need-based gift aid.
UNDERGRADUATE FINANCIAL AID (Fall 2016, est.) 1,237 applied for aid; of those 86% were deemed to have need. 100% of undergraduates with need received aid; of those 100% had need fully met. *Average percent of need met:* 100% (excluding resources awarded to replace EFC). *Average financial aid package:* $51,775 (excluding resources awarded to replace EFC).
GIFT AID (NEED-BASED) *Total amount:* $54,016,376 (5% federal, 94% institutional, 1% external sources). *Receiving aid:* Freshmen: 52% (246); all full-time undergraduates: 55% (1,066). *Average award:* Freshmen: $51,513; Undergraduates: $50,380. *Scholarships, grants, and awards:* Federal Pell, FSEOG, state, private, college/university gift aid from institutional funds.
GIFT AID (NON-NEED-BASED) *Total amount:* $636,189 (100% external sources). *Average award:* Freshmen: $1000. *ROTC:* Army cooperative, Air Force cooperative.
LOANS *Student loans:* $1,780,363 (58% need-based, 42% non-need-based). 22% of past graduating class borrowed through all loan programs. *Average indebtedness per student:* $18,662. *Average need-based loan:* Freshmen: $352. Undergraduates: $478. *Parent loans:* $2,756,065 (100% non-need-based). *Programs:* Federal Direct (Subsidized and Unsubsidized Stafford, PLUS), Perkins, college/university.
WORK-STUDY *Federal work-study:* Total amount: $1,282,308; 834 jobs averaging $1482. *State or other work-study/employment:* Total amount: $385,370 (100% need-based). 230 part-time jobs averaging $2256.
APPLYING FOR FINANCIAL AID *Required financial aid forms:* FAFSA, CSS Financial Aid PROFILE, noncustodial (divorced/separated) parent's statement, business/farm supplement, federal income tax form(s), W-2 forms. *Financial aid deadline (priority):* 2/15. *Notification date:* 4/1. Students must reply by 5/1.

CONTACT Gail W. Holt, Dean of Financial Aid, Amherst College, B-5 Converse Hall, PO Box 5000, Amherst, MA 01002-5000, 413-542-2296. *Fax:* 413-542-2628. *E-mail:* finaid@amherst.edu.
Website: http://www.amherst.edu/.

AMRIDGE UNIVERSITY
Montgomery, AL

Tuition & fees: $10,860	Average undergraduate aid package: $9097

ABOUT THE INSTITUTION Independent Church of Christ, coed. *Awards:* associate, bachelor's, master's, and doctoral degrees. 4 undergraduate majors. *Total enrollment:* 636. Undergraduates: 315. Freshmen: 7. Federal methodology is used as a basis for awarding need-based institutional aid.
UNDERGRADUATE EXPENSES for 2016–2017 *Application fee:* $50. *Tuition:* full-time $9960; part-time $430 per semester hour. *Required fees:* full-time $900; $40 per semester hour or $110 per term. Full-time tuition and fees vary according to course load, program, and student level. Part-time tuition and fees vary according to course load, program, and student level. *Payment plans:* Guaranteed tuition, tuition prepayment.
FRESHMAN FINANCIAL AID (Fall 2016, est.) 4 applied for aid; of those 100% were deemed to have need. 100% of freshmen with need received aid; of those 100% had need fully met. *Average financial aid package:* $5416 (excluding resources awarded to replace EFC).
UNDERGRADUATE FINANCIAL AID (Fall 2016, est.) 131 applied for aid; of those 98% were deemed to have need. 100% of undergraduates with need received aid; of those 74% had need fully met. *Average financial aid package:* $9097 (excluding resources awarded to replace EFC).
GIFT AID (NEED-BASED) *Total amount:* $392,952 (93% federal, 6% state, 1% external sources). *Receiving aid:* Freshmen: 100% (4); all full-time undergraduates: 79% (103). *Average award:* Freshmen: $2188; Undergraduates: $2804. *Scholarships, grants, and awards:* Federal Pell, FSEOG, state, private, college/university gift aid from institutional funds.
GIFT AID (NON-NEED-BASED) *Total amount:* $1,241,987 (97% federal, 3% institutional). *Scholarships, grants, and awards by category:* Special achievements/activities: religious involvement. Special characteristics: children of educators, children of faculty/staff, veterans. *Tuition waivers:* Full or partial for employees or children of employees.
LOANS *Student loans:* $1,191,709 (100% non-need-based). *Average indebtedness per student:* $11,179. *Average need-based loan:* Freshmen: $4016. Undergraduates: $5280. *Parent loans:* $13,528 (100% non-need-based). *Programs:* Federal Direct (Subsidized and Unsubsidized Stafford, PLUS).
WORK-STUDY Federal work-study jobs available.
APPLYING FOR FINANCIAL AID *Required financial aid forms:* FAFSA, institution's own form, state aid form. *Financial aid deadline:* Continuous. *Notification date:* 7/30. Students must reply within 2 weeks of notification.

CONTACT Starr Fain, Director of Financial Aid, Amridge University, 1200 Taylor Road, Montgomery, AL 36117, 334-387-3877 Ext. 7523 or toll-free 888-790-8080. *Fax:* 334-387-3878. *E-mail:* starrfain@amridgeuniversity.edu.
Website: http://www.amridgeuniversity.edu/.

ANDERSON UNIVERSITY
Anderson, IN

CONTACT Mr. Kenneth Nieman, Director of Financial Aid, Anderson University, 1100 East Fifth Street, Anderson, IN 46012-3495, 765-641-4180 or toll-free 800-428-6414. *Fax:* 765-641-3831. *E-mail:* kfnieman@anderson.edu.
Website: http://www.anderson.edu/.

ANDERSON UNIVERSITY
Anderson, SC

Tuition & fees: $25,880	Average undergraduate aid package: $18,176

ABOUT THE INSTITUTION Independent Baptist, coed. *Awards:* bachelor's, master's, and doctoral degrees. 65 undergraduate majors. *Total enrollment:* 3,431. Undergraduates: 2,940. Freshmen: 670. Federal methodology is used as a basis for awarding need-based institutional aid.

UNDERGRADUATE EXPENSES for 2016–2017 *Application fee:* $25. *Comprehensive fee:* $35,054 includes full-time tuition ($23,470), mandatory fees ($2410), and room and board ($9174). *College room only:* $4670. Full-time tuition and fees vary according to course load and program. Room and board charges vary according to board plan and housing facility. *Part-time tuition:* $585 per credit hour. Part-time tuition and fees vary according to course load and program.

FRESHMAN FINANCIAL AID (Fall 2015) 610 applied for aid; of those 82% were deemed to have need. 100% of freshmen with need received aid; of those 28% had need fully met. *Average percent of need met:* 75% (excluding resources awarded to replace EFC). *Average financial aid package:* $19,524 (excluding resources awarded to replace EFC). 23% of all full-time freshmen had no need and received non-need-based gift aid.

UNDERGRADUATE FINANCIAL AID (Fall 2015) 2,221 applied for aid; of those 86% were deemed to have need. 100% of undergraduates with need received aid; of those 27% had need fully met. *Average percent of need met:* 70% (excluding resources awarded to replace EFC). *Average financial aid package:* $18,176 (excluding resources awarded to replace EFC). 18% of all full-time undergraduates had no need and received non-need-based gift aid.

GIFT AID (NEED-BASED) *Total amount:* $26,658,875 (13% federal, 28% state, 57% institutional, 2% external sources). *Receiving aid:* Freshmen: 77% (498); all full-time undergraduates: 79% (1,868). *Average award:* Freshmen: $16,925; Undergraduates: $14,959. *Scholarships, grants, and awards:* Federal Pell, FSEOG, state, private, college/university gift aid from institutional funds.

GIFT AID (NON-NEED-BASED) *Total amount:* $9,047,487 (1% federal, 33% state, 64% institutional, 2% external sources). *Receiving aid:* Freshmen: 19% (124). Undergraduates: 18% (424). *Average award:* Freshmen: $10,598. Undergraduates: $10,641. *Scholarships, grants, and awards by category: Academic interests/achievement:* business, education, general academic interests/achievements, religion/biblical studies. *Creative arts/performance:* art/fine arts, music, performing arts, theater/drama. *Special achievements/activities:* cheerleading/drum major, leadership, memberships. *Special characteristics:* children of faculty/staff, ethnic background, general special characteristics, international students, members of minority groups, out-of-state students, religious affiliation, veterans, veterans' children. *Tuition waivers:* Full or partial for employees or children of employees. *ROTC:* Army cooperative, Air Force cooperative.

LOANS *Student loans:* $15,358,637 (72% need-based, 28% non-need-based). 64% of past graduating class borrowed through all loan programs. *Average indebtedness per student:* $29,846. *Average need-based loan:* Freshmen: $3916. Undergraduates: $4993. *Parent loans:* $3,357,568 (48% need-based, 52% non-need-based). *Programs:* Federal Direct (Subsidized and Unsubsidized Stafford, PLUS), Perkins, state, private loans.

WORK-STUDY *Federal work-study:* 261 jobs averaging $2000. *State or other work-study/employment:* 317 part-time jobs averaging $3622.

ATHLETIC AWARDS Total amount: $1,756,092 (54% need-based, 46% non-need-based).

APPLYING FOR FINANCIAL AID *Required financial aid form:* FAFSA. *Financial aid deadline:* 7/30 (priority: 3/1). *Notification date:* Continuous beginning 3/15. Students must reply by 5/1 or within 2 weeks of notification.

CONTACT Nancy Tate, Director of Financial Aid Services, Anderson University, 316 Boulevard, Anderson, SC 29621-4035, 864-231-2181 or toll-free 800-542-3594. *Fax:* 864-231-2008. *E-mail:* ntate@andersonuniversity.edu. *Website:* http://www.andersonuniversity.edu/.

ANDREWS UNIVERSITY
Berrien Springs, MI

Tuition & fees: $27,684	Average undergraduate aid package: $29,204

ABOUT THE INSTITUTION Independent Seventh-day Adventist, coed. *Awards:* certificates, associate, bachelor's, master's, and doctoral degrees. 64 undergraduate majors. *Total enrollment:* 3,349. Undergraduates: 1,688. Freshmen: 304. Federal methodology is used as a basis for awarding need-based institutional aid.

UNDERGRADUATE EXPENSES for 2016–2017 *Application fee:* $30. *Comprehensive fee:* $36,426 includes full-time tuition ($26,790), mandatory fees ($894), and room and board ($8742). *College room only:* $4642. Full-time tuition and fees vary according to course load. Room and board charges vary according to board plan. *Part-time tuition:* $1116 per credit hour. Part-time tuition and fees vary according to course load.

FRESHMAN FINANCIAL AID (Fall 2016, est.) 294 applied for aid; of those 70% were deemed to have need. 100% of freshmen with need received aid; of those 23% had need fully met. *Average percent of need met:* 86% (excluding resources awarded to replace EFC). *Average financial aid package:* $28,001 (excluding resources awarded to replace EFC). 32% of all full-time freshmen had no need and received non-need-based gift aid.

UNDERGRADUATE FINANCIAL AID (Fall 2016, est.) 927 applied for aid; of those 92% were deemed to have need. 100% of undergraduates with need received aid; of those 18% had need fully met. *Average percent of need met:* 86% (excluding resources awarded to replace EFC). *Average financial aid package:* $29,204 (excluding resources awarded to replace EFC). 36% of all full-time undergraduates had no need and received non-need-based gift aid.

GIFT AID (NEED-BASED) *Total amount:* $22,100,587 (9% federal, 1% state, 72% institutional, 18% external sources). *Receiving aid:* Freshmen: 40% (119); all full-time undergraduates: 42% (584). *Average award:* Freshmen: $5273; Undergraduates: $6824. *Scholarships, grants, and awards:* Federal Pell, FSEOG, state, private, college/university gift aid from institutional funds.

GIFT AID (NON-NEED-BASED) *Receiving aid:* Freshmen: 70% (206). Undergraduates: 60% (840). *Average award:* Freshmen: $13,634. Undergraduates: $11,445. *Scholarships, grants, and awards by category: Academic interests/achievement:* 1,322 awards ($9,033,829 total): general academic interests/achievements. *Creative arts/performance:* 49 awards: music. *Special achievements/activities:* 196 awards ($265,472 total): leadership, religious involvement. *Special characteristics:* 104 awards ($1,181,134 total): children of faculty/staff, general special characteristics, international students. *Tuition waivers:* Full or partial for employees or children of employees, senior citizens.

LOANS *Student loans:* $15,695,878 (2% need-based, 98% non-need-based). 65% of past graduating class borrowed through all loan programs. *Average indebtedness per student:* $36,708. *Average need-based loan:* Freshmen: $3323. Undergraduates: $4620. *Parent loans:* $5,319,564 (100% non-need-based). *Programs:* Federal Direct (Subsidized and Unsubsidized Stafford, PLUS), Perkins.

WORK-STUDY *Federal work-study:* Total amount: $525,118; 571 jobs averaging $920. *State or other work-study/employment:* Part-time jobs available.

APPLYING FOR FINANCIAL AID *Required financial aid forms:* FAFSA, institution's own form, CSS Financial Aid PROFILE. *Financial aid deadline:* Continuous. *Notification date:* Continuous.

CONTACT Cynthia Gammon, Assistant Director of Student Financial Services, Andrews University, Student Financial Services Administration Building, Berrien Springs, MI 49104, 800-253-2874. *Fax:* 269-471-3228. *E-mail:* sfs@andrews.edu. *Website:* http://www.andrews.edu/.

ANGELES COLLEGE
Los Angeles, CA

CONTACT Financial Aid Office, Angeles College, 3440 Wilshire Boulevard, Suite 310, Los Angeles, CA 90010, 213-487-2211. *Website:* http://www.angelescollege.edu/.

ANGELO STATE UNIVERSITY
San Angelo, TX

Tuition & fees (TX res): $8038	Average undergraduate aid package: $11,500

ABOUT THE INSTITUTION State-supported, coed. *Awards:* bachelor's, master's, and doctoral degrees. 37 undergraduate majors. *Total enrollment:* 9,581. Undergraduates: 8,094. Freshmen: 1,583. Federal methodology is used as a basis for awarding need-based institutional aid.

UNDERGRADUATE EXPENSES for 2016–2017 *Application fee:* $35. *Tuition, state resident:* full-time $4956; part-time $165.20 per credit hour. *Tuition, nonresident:* full-time $17,196; part-time $573.20 per credit hour. *Required fees:* full-time $3082. Full-time tuition and fees vary according to course load. Part-time tuition and fees vary according to course load. *College room and board:* $7666. Room and board charges vary according to board plan and housing facility. *Payment plan:* Guaranteed tuition.

FRESHMAN FINANCIAL AID (Fall 2015) 1,175 applied for aid; of those 72% were deemed to have need. 100% of freshmen with need received aid; of those 17% had need fully met. *Average percent of need met:* 91% (excluding resources awarded to replace EFC). *Average financial aid package:* $11,967 (excluding resources awarded to replace EFC). 19% of all full-time freshmen had no need and received non-need-based gift aid.

UNDERGRADUATE FINANCIAL AID (Fall 2015) 3,675 applied for aid; of those 76% were deemed to have need. 99% of undergraduates with need received aid; of those 17% had need fully met. *Average percent of need met:* 83% (excluding resources awarded to replace EFC). *Average financial aid package:* $11,500 (excluding resources awarded to replace EFC). 19% of all full-time undergraduates had no need and received non-need-based gift aid.

GIFT AID (NEED-BASED) *Total amount:* $25,045,563 (52% federal, 48% state). *Receiving aid:* Freshmen: 53% (706); all full-time undergraduates: 51% (2,400). *Average award:* Freshmen: $3601; Undergraduates: $3220. *Scholarships, grants, and awards:* Federal Pell, FSEOG, state, private, college/university gift aid from institutional funds, Federal Nursing, Carr Academic Scholarships.

GIFT AID (NON-NEED-BASED) *Total amount:* $16,649,610 (1% state, 93% institutional, 6% external sources). *Receiving aid:* Freshmen: 43% (569). Undergraduates: 32% (1,489). *Average award:* Freshmen: $4177. Undergraduates: $3781. *Scholarships, grants, and awards by category:* Academic interests/achievement: agriculture, biological sciences, business, communication, computer science, education, English, foreign languages, general academic interests/achievements, humanities, international studies, mathematics, military science, physical sciences, premedicine, social sciences. *ROTC:* Air Force.

LOANS *Student loans:* $62,165,360 (28% need-based, 72% non-need-based). 50% of past graduating class borrowed through all loan programs. *Average indebtedness per student:* $24,099. *Average need-based loan:* Freshmen: $3231. Undergraduates: $3786. *Parent loans:* $22,585,159 (100% non-need-based). *Programs:* Federal Direct (Subsidized and Unsubsidized Stafford, PLUS), Perkins, Federal Nursing, state, college/university, alternative loans.

WORK-STUDY *Federal work-study:* jobs available. *State or other work-study/employment:* Total amount: $83,040 (100% need-based). Part-time jobs available.

ATHLETIC AWARDS Total amount: $2,055,330 (100% non-need-based).

APPLYING FOR FINANCIAL AID *Required financial aid form:* FAFSA. *Financial aid deadline:* Continuous. *Notification date:* Continuous beginning 4/1. Students must reply within 4 weeks of notification.

CONTACT Mr. William R. Bloom, Director of Financial Aid, Angelo State University, ASU Station #11015, San Angelo, TX 76909-1015, 325-942-2246 or toll-free 800-946-8627. *Fax:* 325-942-2082. *E-mail:* william.bloom@angelo.edu. *Website:* http://www.angelo.edu/.

ANNA MARIA COLLEGE
Paxton, MA

ABOUT THE INSTITUTION Independent Roman Catholic, coed. *Awards:* certificates, bachelor's, master's, and doctoral degrees. 58 undergraduate majors. *Total enrollment:* 1,468. Undergraduates: 1,128. Freshmen: 235.

GIFT AID (NEED-BASED) *Scholarships, grants, and awards:* Federal Pell, FSEOG, state, private, college/university gift aid from institutional funds.

GIFT AID (NON-NEED-BASED) *Scholarships, grants, and awards by category:* Academic interests/achievement: general academic interests/achievements. Creative arts/performance: music. Special achievements/activities: religious involvement. Special characteristics: children of faculty/staff, general special characteristics, local/state students, previous college experience.

LOANS *Programs:* Federal Direct (Subsidized and Unsubsidized Stafford, PLUS), Perkins, state.

APPLYING FOR FINANCIAL AID *Required financial aid form:* FAFSA.

CONTACT Sandra J. Pereira, Director of Financial Aid, Anna Maria College, 50 Sunset Lane, Paxton, MA 01612-1198, 508-849-3363. *Fax:* 508-849-3735. *E-mail:* spereira@annamaria.edu. *Website:* http://www.annamaria.edu/.

ANTIOCH UNIVERSITY MIDWEST
Yellow Springs, OH

CONTACT Tricia Webb, Assistant Director of Financial Aid , Antioch University Midwest, 900 Dayton Street, Yellow Springs, OH 45387, 937-769-1883. *Fax:* 937-769-1804. *E-mail:* twebb@antioch.edu. *Website:* http://midwest.antioch.edu/.

ANTIOCH UNIVERSITY SANTA BARBARA
Santa Barbara, CA

ABOUT THE INSTITUTION Independent, coed. *Awards:* certificates, bachelor's, master's, and doctoral degrees. 1 undergraduate major. *Total enrollment:* 210. Undergraduates: 128.

GIFT AID (NEED-BASED) *Scholarships, grants, and awards:* Federal Pell, FSEOG, state, college/university gift aid from institutional funds.

GIFT AID (NON-NEED-BASED) *Scholarships, grants, and awards by category:* Academic interests/achievement: general academic interests/achievements. Special achievements/activities: community service. Special characteristics: first-generation college students, veterans.

LOANS *Programs:* Federal Direct (Subsidized and Unsubsidized Stafford, PLUS), Perkins.

CONTACT Heather Nguyen, Assistant Director of Financial Aid, Antioch University Santa Barbara, 602 Anacapa Street, Santa Barbara, CA 93101, 805-962-8179 Ext. 5219 or toll-free 866-526-8462. *Fax:* 805-879-7062. *E-mail:* financialaid.ausb@antioch.edu. *Website:* http://www.antiochsb.edu/.

ANTIOCH UNIVERSITY SEATTLE
Seattle, WA

CONTACT Katy Stahl, Director of Financial Aid, Antioch University Seattle, 2326 Sixth Avenue, Seattle, WA 98121-1814, 206-268-4004 or toll-free 888-268-4477. *Fax:* 206-268-4242. *E-mail:* kstahl@antiochseattle.edu. *Website:* http://www.antiochsea.edu/.

APEX SCHOOL OF THEOLOGY
Durham, NC

CONTACT Financial Aid Office, Apex School of Theology, 2945 South Miami Boulevard, Suite 114, Durham, NC 27703, 919-572-1625. *Website:* http://www.apexsot.edu/.

APPALACHIAN BIBLE COLLEGE
Mount Hope, WV

CONTACT Deana Steinke, Director of Financial Aid, Appalachian Bible College, 161 College Drive, Mount Hope, WV 25880, 304-877-6428 Ext. 3247 or toll-free 800-678-9ABC. *Fax:* 304-877-5082. *E-mail:* deana.steinke@abc.edu.
Website: http://www.abc.edu/.

APPALACHIAN STATE UNIVERSITY
Boone, NC

Tuition & fees (NC res): $7136	Average undergraduate aid package: $9759

ABOUT THE INSTITUTION State-supported, coed. *Awards:* certificates, bachelor's, master's, and doctoral degrees. 72 undergraduate majors. *Total enrollment:* 18,295. Undergraduates: 16,595. Freshmen: 3,125. Federal methodology is used as a basis for awarding need-based institutional aid.

UNDERGRADUATE EXPENSES for 2016–2017 Application fee: $55. *Tuition, state resident:* full-time $4159; part-time $140.50 per credit hour. *Tuition, nonresident:* full-time $18,675; part-time $631 per credit hour. *Required fees:* full-time $2977; $19.14 per credit hour. Part-time tuition and fees vary according to course load. *College room and board:* $8100; *Room only:* $4340. Room and board charges vary according to board plan and housing facility.

FRESHMAN FINANCIAL AID (Fall 2015) 2,455 applied for aid; of those 66% were deemed to have need. 92% of freshmen with need received aid; of those 16% had need fully met. *Average percent of need met:* 68% (excluding resources awarded to replace EFC). *Average financial aid package:* $9177 (excluding resources awarded to replace EFC). 3% of all full-time freshmen had no need and received non-need-based gift aid.

UNDERGRADUATE FINANCIAL AID (Fall 2015) 10,616 applied for aid; of those 74% were deemed to have need. 94% of undergraduates with need received aid; of those 17% had need fully met. *Average percent of need met:* 71% (excluding resources awarded to replace EFC). *Average financial aid package:* $9759 (excluding resources awarded to replace EFC). 3% of all full-time undergraduates had no need and received non-need-based gift aid.

GIFT AID (NEED-BASED) Total amount: $47,879,638 (41% federal, 28% state, 26% institutional, 5% external sources). *Receiving aid:* Freshmen: 39% (1,183); all full-time undergraduates: 38% (5,861). *Average award:* Freshmen: $8447; Undergraduates: $8238. *Scholarships, grants, and awards:* Federal Pell, FSEOG, state, private, college/university gift aid from institutional funds.

GIFT AID (NON-NEED-BASED) Total amount: $3,545,116 (1% federal, 16% state, 43% institutional, 40% external sources). *Receiving aid:* Freshmen: 3% (79). Undergraduates: 2% (246). *Average award:* Freshmen: $3648. Undergraduates: $2806. *Scholarships, grants, and awards by category: Academic interests/achievement:* general academic interests/achievements. *Creative arts/performance:* general creative arts/performance. *Special achievements/activities:* general special achievements/activities. *Special characteristics:* general special characteristics. *Tuition waivers:* Full or partial for employees or children of employees. *ROTC:* Army.

LOANS Student loans: $51,444,866 (74% need-based, 26% non-need-based). 56% of past graduating class borrowed through all loan programs. *Average indebtedness per student:* $22,696. *Average need-based loan:* Freshmen: $3291. Undergraduates: $4201. *Parent loans:* $28,395,193 (63% need-based, 37% non-need-based). *Programs:* Federal Direct (Subsidized and Unsubsidized Stafford, PLUS), Perkins.

WORK-STUDY Federal work-study: jobs available.

ATHLETIC AWARDS Total amount: $24,374,476 (89% need-based, 11% non-need-based).

APPLYING FOR FINANCIAL AID Required financial aid form: FAFSA. *Financial aid deadline:* Continuous. *Notification date:* Continuous beginning 3/15. Students must reply within 3 weeks of notification.

CONTACT Office of Student Financial Aid, Appalachian State University, John E. Thomas Hall, ASU Box 32059, Boone, NC 28608-2059, 828-262-2190. *Fax:* 828-262-2585. *E-mail:* financialaid@appstate.edu.
Website: http://www.appstate.edu/.

AQUINAS COLLEGE
Grand Rapids, MI

Tuition & fees: $31,244	Average undergraduate aid package: $22,824

ABOUT THE INSTITUTION Independent Roman Catholic, coed. *Awards:* associate, bachelor's, and master's degrees. 52 undergraduate majors. *Total enrollment:* 1,764. Undergraduates: 1,654. Freshmen: 299. Federal methodology is used as a basis for awarding need-based institutional aid.

UNDERGRADUATE EXPENSES for 2017–2018 Comprehensive fee: $40,314 includes full-time tuition ($30,746), mandatory fees ($498), and room and board ($9070). *College room only:* $4254. Full-time tuition and fees vary according to course load. Room and board charges vary according to board plan and housing facility. *Part-time tuition:* $498 per credit hour. *Part-time fees:* $60 per term. Part-time tuition and fees vary according to course load.

FRESHMAN FINANCIAL AID (Fall 2016, est.) 273 applied for aid; of those 87% were deemed to have need. 100% of freshmen with need received aid; of those 18% had need fully met. *Average percent of need met:* 83% (excluding resources awarded to replace EFC). *Average financial aid package:* $25,225 (excluding resources awarded to replace EFC). 19% of all full-time freshmen had no need and received non-need-based gift aid.

UNDERGRADUATE FINANCIAL AID (Fall 2016, est.) 1,313 applied for aid; of those 82% were deemed to have need. 100% of undergraduates with need received aid; of those 21% had need fully met. *Average percent of need met:* 79% (excluding resources awarded to replace EFC). *Average financial aid package:* $22,824 (excluding resources awarded to replace EFC). 21% of all full-time undergraduates had no need and received non-need-based gift aid.

GIFT AID (NEED-BASED) Total amount: $20,703,507 (11% federal, 7% state, 82% institutional). *Receiving aid:* Freshmen: 80% (238); all full-time undergraduates: 76% (1,081). *Average award:* Freshmen: $23,104; Undergraduates: $19,974. *Scholarships, grants, and awards:* Federal Pell, FSEOG, state, private, college/university gift aid from institutional funds.

GIFT AID (NON-NEED-BASED) Total amount: $4,692,979 (100% institutional). *Receiving aid:* Freshmen: 29% (85). Undergraduates: 23% (332). *Average award:* Freshmen: $15,200. Undergraduates: $13,789. *Scholarships, grants, and awards by category: Academic interests/achievement:* general academic interests/achievements. *Creative arts/performance:* general creative arts/performance. *Special achievements/activities:* general special achievements/activities, leadership. *Special characteristics:* children and siblings of alumni, children of faculty/staff. *Tuition waivers:* Full or partial for employees or children of employees.

LOANS Student loans: $6,318,941 (94% need-based, 6% non-need-based). 76% of past graduating class borrowed through all loan programs. *Average indebtedness per student:* $30,503. *Average need-based loan:* Freshmen: $2121. Undergraduates: $2850. *Parent loans:* $1,538,482 (94% need-based, 6% non-need-based). *Programs:* Federal Direct (Subsidized and Unsubsidized Stafford, PLUS), Perkins.

WORK-STUDY Federal work-study: Total amount: $122,090; jobs available. *State or other work-study/employment:* Part-time jobs available.

ATHLETIC AWARDS Total amount: $1,555,076 (78% need-based, 22% non-need-based).

APPLYING FOR FINANCIAL AID Required financial aid form: FAFSA. *Financial aid deadline (priority):* 3/1. *Notification date:* Continuous beginning 2/15. Students must reply within 2 weeks of notification.

CONTACT Darcy Kampfschulte, Director of Financial Aid, Aquinas College, 1700 Fulton Street E, Grand Rapids, MI 49506-1801, 616-632-2894 or toll-free 800-678-9593. *Fax:* 616-732-4547. *E-mail:* kampfdar@aquinas.edu.
Website: http://www.aquinas.edu/.

AQUINAS COLLEGE
Nashville, TN

CONTACT Mrs. Kylie Pruitt, Director of Financial Aid, Aquinas College, 4210 Harding Road, Nashville, TN 37205-2005, 615-297-7545 Ext. 431 or toll-free 800-649-9956. *Fax:* 615-279-3891. *E-mail:* pruittk@aquinascollege.edu.
Website: http://www.aquinascollege.edu/.

ARCADIA UNIVERSITY
Glenside, PA

Tuition & fees: $42,330	Average undergraduate aid package: $30,072

ABOUT THE INSTITUTION Independent Presbyterian Church (U.S.A.), coed. *Awards:* certificates, bachelor's, master's, and doctoral degrees. 71 undergraduate majors. *Total enrollment:* 3,785. Undergraduates: 2,473. Freshmen: 606. Federal methodology is used as a basis for awarding need-based institutional aid.

UNDERGRADUATE EXPENSES for 2017–2018 *Application fee:* $30. *Comprehensive fee:* $55,990 includes full-time tuition ($41,630), mandatory fees ($700), and room and board ($13,660). *College room only:* $9000. Room and board charges vary according to board plan and housing facility. *Part-time tuition:* $700 per credit hour.

FRESHMAN FINANCIAL AID (Fall 2016, est.) 579 applied for aid; of those 98% were deemed to have need. 100% of freshmen with need received aid; of those 35% had need fully met. *Average percent of need met:* 86% (excluding resources awarded to replace EFC). *Average financial aid package:* $30,745 (excluding resources awarded to replace EFC). 20% of all full-time freshmen had no need and received non-need-based gift aid.

UNDERGRADUATE FINANCIAL AID (Fall 2016, est.) 2,054 applied for aid; of those 91% were deemed to have need. 100% of undergraduates with need received aid; of those 30% had need fully met. *Average percent of need met:* 83% (excluding resources awarded to replace EFC). *Average financial aid package:* $30,072 (excluding resources awarded to replace EFC). 15% of all full-time undergraduates had no need and received non-need-based gift aid.

GIFT AID (NEED-BASED) *Total amount:* $48,976,914 (8% federal, 5% state, 86% institutional, 1% external sources). *Receiving aid:* Freshmen: 95% (569); all full-time undergraduates: 80% (1,859). *Average award:* Freshmen: $28,059; Undergraduates: $26,516. *Scholarships, grants, and awards:* Federal Pell, FSEOG, state, private, college/university gift aid from institutional funds, Academic Competitiveness Grants, National SMART Grants, TEACH Grants.

GIFT AID (NON-NEED-BASED) *Total amount:* $8,615,695 (97% institutional, 3% external sources). *Receiving aid:* Freshmen: 20% (122). Undergraduates: 15% (339). *Average award:* Freshmen: $17,183. Undergraduates: $17,060. *Scholarships, grants, and awards by category: Academic interests/achievement:* 2,265 awards ($36,114,329 total): general academic interests/achievements. *Creative arts/performance:* applied art and design, art/fine arts, theater/drama. *Special achievements/activities:* community service, general special achievements/activities, leadership, memberships. *Special characteristics:* 34 awards ($66,000 total): children and siblings of alumni, relatives of clergy, religious affiliation. *Tuition waivers:* Full or partial for employees or children of employees.

LOANS *Student loans:* $20,320,501 (52% need-based, 48% non-need-based). 78% of past graduating class borrowed through all loan programs. *Average need-based loan:* Freshmen: $3023. Undergraduates: $3894. *Parent loans:* $6,106,465 (29% need-based, 71% non-need-based). *Programs:* Federal Direct (Subsidized and Unsubsidized Stafford, PLUS), Perkins.

WORK-STUDY *Federal work-study:* Total amount: $849,342; jobs available. *State or other work-study/employment:* Total amount: $225,675 (100% non-need-based). 140 part-time jobs averaging $1671.

APPLYING FOR FINANCIAL AID *Required financial aid forms:* FAFSA, institution's own form. *Financial aid deadline (priority):* 3/1. *Notification date:* 11/1. Students must reply by 5/1.

CONTACT Alison Venditti, Assistant Director of Financial Aid, Arcadia University, 450 South Easton Road, Glenside, PA 19038, 215-572-2837 or toll-free 877-ARCADIA. *Fax:* 215-572-4049. *E-mail:* venditta@arcadia.edu. *Website:* http://www.arcadia.edu/.

ARGOSY UNIVERSITY, ATLANTA
Atlanta, GA

CONTACT Financial Aid Office, Argosy University, Atlanta, 980 Hammond Drive, Suite 100, Atlanta, GA 30328, 770-671-1200 or toll-free 888-671-4777. *Website:* http://www.argosy.edu/locations/atlanta/.

ARGOSY UNIVERSITY, CHICAGO
Chicago, IL

CONTACT Financial Aid Office, Argosy University, Chicago, 225 North Michigan Avenue, Suite 1300, Chicago, IL 60601, 312-777-7600 or toll-free 800-626-4123. *Website:* http://www.argosy.edu/chicago-illinois/default.aspx.

ARGOSY UNIVERSITY, DALLAS
Farmers Branch, TX

CONTACT Financial Aid Office, Argosy University, Dallas, 5001 Lyndon B. Johnson Freeway, Heritage Square, Farmers Branch, TX 75244, 214-890-9900 or toll-free 866-954-9900. *Website:* http://www.argosy.edu/dallas-texas/default.aspx.

ARGOSY UNIVERSITY, DENVER
Denver, CO

CONTACT Financial Aid Office, Argosy University, Denver, 7600 East Eastman Avenue, Denver, CO 80231, 303-923-4110 or toll-free 866-431-5981. *Website:* http://www.argosy.edu/locations/denver/.

ARGOSY UNIVERSITY, HAWAII
Honolulu, HI

CONTACT Financial Aid Office, Argosy University, Hawaii, 1001 Bishop Street, Suite 400, Honolulu, HI 96813, 808-536-5555 or toll-free 888-323-2777. *Website:* http://www.argosy.edu/locations/hawaii/.

ARGOSY UNIVERSITY, INLAND EMPIRE
Ontario, CA

CONTACT Financial Aid Office, Argosy University, Inland Empire, 3401 Centre Lake Drive, Suite 200, Ontario, CA 91761, 909-472-0800 or toll-free 866-217-9075. *Website:* http://www.argosy.edu/locations/inland-empire/.

ARGOSY UNIVERSITY, NASHVILLE
Nashville, TN

CONTACT Financial Aid Office, Argosy University, Nashville, 100 Centerview Drive, Suite 225, Nashville, TN 37214, 615-525-2800 or toll-free 866-833-6598. *Website:* http://www.argosy.edu/locations/nashville/.

ARGOSY UNIVERSITY, NORTHERN VIRGINIA
Arlington, VA

CONTACT Financial Aid Office, Argosy University, Northern Virginia, 1550 Wilson Boulevard, Suite 600, Arlington, VA 22209, 703-526-5800 or toll-free 866-703-2777. *Website:* http://www.argosy.edu/locations/washington-dc/.

ARGOSY UNIVERSITY, ORANGE COUNTY

Orange, CA

CONTACT Financial Aid Office, Argosy University, Orange County, 601 South Lewis Street, Orange, CA 92868, 714-620-3700 or toll-free 800-716-9598.
Website: http://www.argosy.edu/locations/los-angeles-orange-county/.

ARGOSY UNIVERSITY, PHOENIX

Phoenix, AZ

CONTACT Financial Aid Office, Argosy University, Phoenix, 2233 West Dunlap Avenue, Phoenix, AZ 85021, 602-216-2600 or toll-free 866-216-2777.
Website: http://www.argosy.edu/phoenix-arizona/default.aspx.

ARGOSY UNIVERSITY, SALT LAKE CITY

Draper, UT

CONTACT Financial Aid Office, Argosy University, Salt Lake City, 121 Election Road, Suite 300, Draper, UT 84020, 801-601-5000 or toll-free 888-639-4756.
Website: http://www.argosy.edu/locations/salt-lake-city/.

ARGOSY UNIVERSITY, SAN DIEGO

San Diego, CA

CONTACT Financial Aid Office, Argosy University, San Diego, 1615 Murray Canyon Road, Suite 100, San Diego, CA 92108, 619-321-3000 or toll-free 866-505-0333.
Website: http://www.argosy.edu/locations/san-diego/.

ARGOSY UNIVERSITY, SAN FRANCISCO BAY AREA

Alameda, CA

CONTACT Financial Aid Office, Argosy University, San Francisco Bay Area, 1005 Atlantic Avenue, Alameda, CA 94501, 510-217-4700 or toll-free 866-215-2777.
Website: http://www.argosy.edu/locations/san-francisco/.

ARGOSY UNIVERSITY, SARASOTA

Sarasota, FL

CONTACT Financial Aid Office, Argosy University, Sarasota, 5250 17th Street, Sarasota, FL 34235, 941-379-0404 or toll-free 800-331-5995.
Website: http://www.argosy.edu/locations/sarasota/.

ARGOSY UNIVERSITY, SCHAUMBURG

Schaumburg, IL

CONTACT Financial Aid Office, Argosy University, Schaumburg, 999 North Plaza Drive, Suite 111, Schaumburg, IL 60173-5403, 847-969-4900 or toll-free 866-290-2777.
Website: http://www.argosy.edu/locations/chicago-schaumburg/.

ARGOSY UNIVERSITY, SEATTLE

Seattle, WA

CONTACT Financial Aid Office, Argosy University, Seattle, 2601-A Elliott Avenue, Seattle, WA 98121, 206-283-4500 or toll-free 866-283-2777.
Website: http://www.argosy.edu/locations/seattle/.

ARGOSY UNIVERSITY, TAMPA

Tampa, FL

CONTACT Financial Aid Office, Argosy University, Tampa, 1403 North Howard Avenue, Tampa, FL 33607, 813-393-5290 or toll-free 800-850-6488.
Website: http://www.argosy.edu/locations/tampa/.

ARGOSY UNIVERSITY, TWIN CITIES

Eagan, MN

CONTACT Financial Aid Office, Argosy University, Twin Cities, 1515 Central Parkway, Eagan, MN 55121, 651-846-2882 or toll-free 888-844-2004.
Website: http://www.argosy.edu/locations/twin-cities/.

ARIZONA CHRISTIAN UNIVERSITY

Phoenix, AZ

CONTACT Mr. Steven Young, Director of Financial Aid, Arizona Christian University, 2625 East Cactus Road, Phoenix, AZ 85032-7042, 602-386-4115 or toll-free 800-247-2697. *Fax:* 602-404-2159. *E-mail:* steven.young@arizonachristian.edu.
Website: http://arizonachristian.edu/.

ARIZONA COLLEGE–MESA

Mesa, AZ

CONTACT Financial Aid Office, Arizona College–Mesa, 163 N Dobson Road, Mesa, AZ 85201.
Website: http://www.arizonacollege.edu/.

ARIZONA STATE UNIVERSITY AT THE DOWNTOWN PHOENIX CAMPUS

Phoenix, AZ

Tuition & fees (AZ res): $10,370	Average undergraduate aid package: $13,859

ABOUT THE INSTITUTION State-supported, coed. *Awards:* certificates, bachelor's, master's, and doctoral degrees. 27 undergraduate majors. *Total enrollment:* 11,737. Undergraduates: 9,238. Federal methodology is used as a basis for awarding need-based institutional aid.

UNDERGRADUATE EXPENSES for 2016–2017 *Application fee:* $50. *Tuition, state resident:* full-time $9684; part-time $692 per credit hour. *Tuition, nonresident:* full-time $25,784; part-time $1074 per credit hour. *Required fees:* full-time $686. Full-time tuition and fees vary according to program. Part-time tuition and fees vary according to program. *College room and board:* $13,310; *Room only:* $8710. Room and board charges vary according to board plan and housing facility.

FRESHMAN FINANCIAL AID (Fall 2015) 1,127 applied for aid; of those 77% were deemed to have need. 100% of freshmen with need received aid; of those 21% had need fully met. *Average percent of need met:* 67% (excluding resources awarded to replace EFC). *Average financial aid package:* $16,307 (excluding

resources awarded to replace EFC). 23% of all full-time freshmen had no need and received non-need-based gift aid.

UNDERGRADUATE FINANCIAL AID (Fall 2015) 6,689 applied for aid; of those 86% were deemed to have need. 100% of undergraduates with need received aid; of those 16% had need fully met. *Average percent of need met:* 57% (excluding resources awarded to replace EFC). *Average financial aid package:* $13,859 (excluding resources awarded to replace EFC). 14% of all full-time undergraduates had no need and received non-need-based gift aid.

GIFT AID (NEED-BASED) *Total amount:* $52,043,256 (37% federal, 54% institutional, 9% external sources). *Receiving aid:* Freshmen: 69% (841); all full-time undergraduates: 63% (5,210). *Average award:* Freshmen: $12,702; Undergraduates: $9607. *Scholarships, grants, and awards:* Federal Pell, FSEOG, state, private, college/university gift aid from institutional funds, United Negro College Fund, Federal Nursing.

GIFT AID (NON-NEED-BASED) *Total amount:* $14,824,083 (7% federal, 68% institutional, 25% external sources). *Receiving aid:* Freshmen: 8% (103). Undergraduates: 4% (348). *Average award:* Freshmen: $8462. Undergraduates: $7886. *Scholarships, grants, and awards by category:* Academic interests/achievement: general academic interests/achievements. *Special achievements/activities:* leadership. *Special characteristics:* children of faculty/staff, international students, local/state students, out-of-state students. *Tuition waivers:* Full or partial for employees or children of employees. *ROTC:* Army cooperative, Naval cooperative, Air Force cooperative.

LOANS *Student loans:* $42,010,254 (76% need-based, 24% non-need-based). 61% of past graduating class borrowed through all loan programs. *Average indebtedness per student:* $25,342. *Average need-based loan:* Freshmen: $3015. Undergraduates: $4109. *Parent loans:* $21,457,254 (44% need-based, 56% non-need-based). *Programs:* Federal Direct (Subsidized and Unsubsidized Stafford, PLUS), Perkins, state, college/university, private loans from endowment funds.

WORK-STUDY *Federal work-study:* 396 jobs averaging $2613. *State or other work-study/employment:* Total amount: $4,249,061 (35% need-based, 65% non-need-based). 1,252 part-time jobs averaging $3393.

ATHLETIC AWARDS Total amount: $1,795,167 (41% need-based, 59% non-need-based).

APPLYING FOR FINANCIAL AID *Required financial aid form:* FAFSA. *Financial aid deadline (priority):* 3/1. *Notification date:* Continuous beginning 3/1.

CONTACT Office of Student Financial Assistance, Arizona State University at the Downtown Phoenix campus, PO Box 870412, Tempe, AZ 85287-0412, 855-278-5080. *Fax:* 480-965-9484.

Website: http://campus.asu.edu/downtown/.

ARIZONA STATE UNIVERSITY AT THE POLYTECHNIC CAMPUS
Mesa, AZ

Tuition & fees (AZ res): $9886	Average undergraduate aid package: $14,073

ABOUT THE INSTITUTION State-supported, coed. *Awards:* certificates, bachelor's, master's, and doctoral degrees. 34 undergraduate majors. *Total enrollment:* 4,380. Undergraduates: 3,869. Federal methodology is used as a basis for awarding need-based institutional aid.

UNDERGRADUATE EXPENSES for 2016–2017 *Application fee:* $50. *Tuition, state resident:* full-time $9200; part-time $692 per credit hour. *Tuition, nonresident:* full-time $24,495; part-time $1074 per credit hour. *Required fees:* full-time $686. Full-time tuition and fees vary according to program. Part-time tuition and fees vary according to program. *College room and board:* $11,474; *Room only:* $6874. Room and board charges vary according to board plan and housing facility.

FRESHMAN FINANCIAL AID (Fall 2015) 396 applied for aid; of those 77% were deemed to have need. 100% of freshmen with need received aid; of those 20% had need fully met. *Average percent of need met:* 64% (excluding resources awarded to replace EFC). *Average financial aid package:* $14,288 (excluding resources awarded to replace EFC). 23% of all full-time freshmen had no need and received non-need-based gift aid.

UNDERGRADUATE FINANCIAL AID (Fall 2015) 2,385 applied for aid; of those 86% were deemed to have need. 100% of undergraduates with need received aid; of those 20% had need fully met. *Average percent of need met:* 57% (excluding resources awarded to replace EFC). *Average financial aid package:* $14,073 (excluding resources awarded to replace EFC). 12% of all full-time undergraduates had no need and received non-need-based gift aid.

GIFT AID (NEED-BASED) *Total amount:* $17,921,637 (46% federal, 45% institutional, 9% external sources). *Receiving aid:* Freshmen: 61% (294); all full-time undergraduates: 58% (1,864). *Average award:* Freshmen: $11,152; Undergraduates: $8984. *Scholarships, grants, and awards:* Federal Pell, FSEOG, state, private, college/university gift aid from institutional funds, United Negro College Fund.

GIFT AID (NON-NEED-BASED) *Total amount:* $8,238,699 (8% federal, 36% institutional, 56% external sources). *Receiving aid:* Freshmen: 7% (32). Undergraduates: 4% (137). *Average award:* Freshmen: $7254. Undergraduates: $6849. *Scholarships, grants, and awards by category:* Academic interests/achievement: general academic interests/achievements. *Special achievements/activities:* leadership. *Special characteristics:* children of faculty/staff, international students, local/state students, out-of-state students. *Tuition waivers:* Full or partial for employees or children of employees. *ROTC:* Army cooperative, Naval cooperative, Air Force cooperative.

LOANS *Student loans:* $16,317,228 (77% need-based, 23% non-need-based). 59% of past graduating class borrowed through all loan programs. *Average indebtedness per student:* $26,925. *Average need-based loan:* Freshmen: $2824. Undergraduates: $4315. *Parent loans:* $6,824,893 (49% need-based, 51% non-need-based). *Programs:* Federal Direct (Subsidized and Unsubsidized Stafford, PLUS), Perkins, state, college/university, private loans from endowment funds.

WORK-STUDY *Federal work-study:* 150 jobs averaging $3016. *State or other work-study/employment:* Total amount: $2,948,816 (37% need-based, 63% non-need-based). 742 part-time jobs averaging $3963.

ATHLETIC AWARDS Total amount: $137,151 (42% need-based, 58% non-need-based).

APPLYING FOR FINANCIAL AID *Required financial aid form:* FAFSA. *Financial aid deadline (priority):* 3/1. *Notification date:* Continuous beginning 3/1.

CONTACT Office of Student Financial Assistance, Arizona State University at the Polytechnic campus, PO Box 870412, Tempe, AZ 85287-0412, 855-278-5080. *Fax:* 480-965-9484.

Website: http://campus.asu.edu/polytechnic.

ARIZONA STATE UNIVERSITY AT THE TEMPE CAMPUS
Tempe, AZ

Tuition & fees (AZ res): $10,370	Average undergraduate aid package: $14,528

ABOUT THE INSTITUTION State-supported, coed. *Awards:* certificates, bachelor's, master's, and doctoral degrees (profile includes data for the West, Polytechnic and Downtown Phoenix campuses). 93 undergraduate majors. *Total enrollment:* 51,869. Undergraduates: 42,477. Freshmen: 8,230. Federal methodology is used as a basis for awarding need-based institutional aid.

UNDERGRADUATE EXPENSES for 2016–2017 *Application fee:* $50. *Tuition, state resident:* full-time $9684; part-time $692 per credit hour. *Tuition, nonresident:* full-time $25,784; part-time $1074 per credit hour. *Required fees:* full-time $686. Full-time tuition and fees vary according to program. Part-time tuition and fees vary according to program. *College room and board:* $11,386; *Room only:* $6786. Room and board charges vary according to board plan and housing facility.

FRESHMAN FINANCIAL AID (Fall 2015) 6,440 applied for aid; of those 74% were deemed to have need. 100% of freshmen with need received aid; of those 22% had need fully met. *Average percent of need met:* 68% (excluding resources awarded to replace EFC). *Average financial aid package:* $16,098 (excluding resources awarded to replace EFC). 31% of all full-time freshmen had no need and received non-need-based gift aid.

UNDERGRADUATE FINANCIAL AID (Fall 2015) 25,678 applied for aid; of those 81% were deemed to have need. 100% of undergraduates with need received aid; of those 19% had need fully met. *Average percent of need met:* 61%

(excluding resources awarded to replace EFC). **Average financial aid package:** $14,528 (excluding resources awarded to replace EFC). 21% of all full-time undergraduates had no need and received non-need-based gift aid.

GIFT AID (NEED-BASED) Total amount: $201,896,545 (33% federal, 60% institutional, 7% external sources). **Receiving aid:** Freshmen: 57% (4,695); all full-time undergraduates: 52% (19,467). **Average award:** Freshmen: $12,360; Undergraduates: $10,074. **Scholarships, grants, and awards:** Federal Pell, FSEOG, state, private, college/university gift aid from institutional funds, United Negro College Fund.

GIFT AID (NON-NEED-BASED) Total amount: $129,835,098 (2% federal, 55% institutional, 43% external sources). **Receiving aid:** Freshmen: 8% (642). Undergraduates: 5% (1,841). **Average award:** Freshmen: $8008. Undergraduates: $7968. **Scholarships, grants, and awards by category:** Academic interests/achievement: general academic interests/achievements. Creative arts/performance: art/fine arts, dance, music, theater/drama. Special achievements/activities: leadership. Special characteristics: children of faculty/staff, international students, local/state students, out-of-state students. **Tuition waivers:** Full or partial for employees or children of employees. **ROTC:** Army, Naval, Air Force.

LOANS Student loans: $139,373,605 (74% need-based, 26% non-need-based). 49% of past graduating class borrowed through all loan programs. Average indebtedness per student: $22,903. **Average need-based loan:** Freshmen: $2953. Undergraduates: $4060. **Parent loans:** $71,338,204 (41% need-based, 59% non-need-based). **Programs:** Federal Direct (Subsidized and Unsubsidized Stafford, PLUS), Perkins, state, college/university, private loans from endowment funds.

WORK-STUDY Federal work-study: 1,279 jobs averaging $2402. **State or other work-study/employment:** Total amount: $20,046,443 (34% need-based, 66% non-need-based). 6,103 part-time jobs averaging $3284.

ATHLETIC AWARDS Total amount: $7,557,316 (38% need-based, 62% non-need-based).

APPLYING FOR FINANCIAL AID Required financial aid form: FAFSA. **Financial aid deadline (priority):** 3/1. **Notification date:** Continuous beginning 3/1.

CONTACT Office of Student Financial Assistance, Arizona State University at the Tempe campus, PO Box 870412, Tempe, AZ 85287-0412, 855-278-5080. Fax: 480-965-9484.

Website: http://www.asu.edu/.

ARIZONA STATE UNIVERSITY AT THE WEST CAMPUS
Glendale, AZ

Tuition & fees (AZ res): $9886	Average undergraduate aid package: $12,783

ABOUT THE INSTITUTION State-supported, coed. **Awards:** certificates, bachelor's, master's, and doctoral degrees. 36 undergraduate majors. **Total enrollment:** 3,663. Undergraduates: 3,264. Federal methodology is used as a basis for awarding need-based institutional aid.

UNDERGRADUATE EXPENSES for 2016–2017 **Application fee:** $50. **Tuition, state resident:** full-time $9200; part-time $692 per credit hour. **Tuition, nonresident:** full-time $24,495; part-time $1074 per credit hour. **Required fees:** full-time $686. Full-time tuition and fees vary according to program. Part-time tuition and fees vary according to program. **College room and board:** $10,754; **Room only:** $6154. Room and board charges vary according to board plan and housing facility.

FRESHMAN FINANCIAL AID (Fall 2015) 295 applied for aid; of those 80% were deemed to have need. 100% of freshmen with need received aid; of those 25% had need fully met. **Average percent of need met:** 69% (excluding resources awarded to replace EFC). **Average financial aid package:** $14,949 (excluding resources awarded to replace EFC). 18% of all full-time freshmen had no need and received non-need-based gift aid.

UNDERGRADUATE FINANCIAL AID (Fall 2015) 2,239 applied for aid; of those 90% were deemed to have need. 100% of undergraduates with need received aid; of those 16% had need fully met. **Average percent of need met:** 59% (excluding resources awarded to replace EFC). **Average financial aid package:** $12,783 (excluding resources awarded to replace EFC). 8% of all full-time undergraduates had no need and received non-need-based gift aid.

GIFT AID (NEED-BASED) Total amount: $17,101,232 (46% federal, 45% institutional, 9% external sources). **Receiving aid:** Freshmen: 71% (228); all full-time

undergraduates: 68% (1,849). **Average award:** Freshmen: $11,298; Undergraduates: $8605. **Scholarships, grants, and awards:** Federal Pell, FSEOG, state, private, college/university gift aid from institutional funds, United Negro College Fund.

GIFT AID (NON-NEED-BASED) Total amount: $2,947,707 (16% federal, 59% institutional, 25% external sources). **Receiving aid:** Freshmen: 9% (30). Undergraduates: 4% (97). **Average award:** Freshmen: $6400. Undergraduates: $6689. **Scholarships, grants, and awards by category:** Academic interests/achievement: general academic interests/achievements. Special achievements/activities: leadership. Special characteristics: children of faculty/staff, international students, local/state students, out-of-state students. **Tuition waivers:** Full or partial for employees or children of employees. **ROTC:** Army cooperative, Naval cooperative, Air Force cooperative.

LOANS Student loans: $14,701,855 (82% need-based, 18% non-need-based). 56% of past graduating class borrowed through all loan programs. Average indebtedness per student: $22,251. **Average need-based loan:** Freshmen: $2986. Undergraduates: $4420. **Parent loans:** $3,936,035 (41% need-based, 59% non-need-based). **Programs:** Federal Direct (Subsidized and Unsubsidized Stafford, PLUS), Perkins, state, college/university, private loans from endowment funds.

WORK-STUDY Federal work-study: 125 jobs averaging $2613. **State or other work-study/employment:** Total amount: $1,763,528 (41% need-based, 59% non-need-based). 498 part-time jobs averaging $3541.

APPLYING FOR FINANCIAL AID Required financial aid form: FAFSA. **Financial aid deadline (priority):** 3/1. **Notification date:** Continuous beginning 3/1.

CONTACT Office of Student Financial Assistance, Arizona State University at the West campus, PO Box 870412, Tempe, AZ 85287-0412, 855-278-5080. Fax: 480-965-9484.

Website: http://campus.asu.edu/west.

ARKANSAS BAPTIST COLLEGE
Little Rock, AR

CONTACT Office of Financial Aid, Arkansas Baptist College, 1600 Bishop Street, Little Rock, AR 72202-6067, 501-374-7856.

Website: http://www.arkansasbaptist.edu/.

ARKANSAS STATE UNIVERSITY
Jonesboro, AR

ABOUT THE INSTITUTION State-supported, coed. **Awards:** certificates, associate, bachelor's, master's, and doctoral degrees. 74 undergraduate majors. **Total enrollment:** 13,410. Undergraduates: 9,592. Freshmen: 1,577.

GIFT AID (NEED-BASED) Scholarships, grants, and awards: Federal Pell, FSEOG, state, private, college/university gift aid from institutional funds.

GIFT AID (NON-NEED-BASED) Scholarships, grants, and awards by category: Academic interests/achievement: agriculture, area/ethnic studies, biological sciences, business, communication, computer science, education, engineering/technologies, English, general academic interests/achievements, health fields, humanities, library science, mathematics, military science, physical sciences, premedicine, social sciences. Creative arts/performance: art/fine arts, cinema/film/broadcasting, debating, journalism/publications, music, performing arts, theater/drama. Special achievements/activities: cheerleading/drum major, community service, general special achievements/activities, leadership. Special characteristics: adult students, children and siblings of alumni, children of faculty/staff, ethnic background, first-generation college students, general special characteristics, handicapped students, local/state students, members of minority groups, out-of-state students, veterans, veterans' children.

LOANS Programs: Federal Direct (Subsidized and Unsubsidized Stafford, PLUS), Perkins.

WORK-STUDY Federal work-study: 190 jobs averaging $3500. **State or other work-study/employment:** Total amount: $2,500,000 (100% non-need-based). 380 part-time jobs averaging $3900.

APPLYING FOR FINANCIAL AID Required financial aid forms: FAFSA, institution's own form.

CONTACT Mr. Terry Finney, Director of Financial Aid, Arkansas State University, PO Box 1620, State University, AR 72467, 870-972-2310 or toll-free 800-382-3030. *Fax:* 870-972-2794. *E-mail:* finaid@astate.edu. *Website:* http://www.astate.edu/.

ARKANSAS TECH UNIVERSITY
Russellville, AR

Tuition & fees (AR res): $8280	Average undergraduate aid package: $9302

ABOUT THE INSTITUTION State-supported, coed. *Awards:* certificates, associate, bachelor's, master's, and doctoral degrees. 80 undergraduate majors. *Total enrollment:* 11,894. Undergraduates: 11,053. Freshmen: 1,892. Federal methodology is used as a basis for awarding need-based institutional aid.

UNDERGRADUATE EXPENSES for 2016–2017 *Tuition, state resident:* full-time $6570; part-time $219 per credit hour. *Tuition, nonresident:* full-time $13,140; part-time $438 per credit hour. *Required fees:* full-time $1710; $57 per credit hour. Full-time tuition and fees vary according to course load and location. Part-time tuition and fees vary according to course load and location. *College room and board:* $7036; *Room only:* $4296. Room and board charges vary according to board plan, housing facility, and location.

FRESHMAN FINANCIAL AID (Fall 2015) 1,867 applied for aid; of those 72% were deemed to have need. 99% of freshmen with need received aid; of those 5% had need fully met. *Average percent of need met:* 59% (excluding resources awarded to replace EFC). *Average financial aid package:* $9187 (excluding resources awarded to replace EFC). 18% of all full-time freshmen had no need and received non-need-based gift aid.

UNDERGRADUATE FINANCIAL AID (Fall 2015) 6,343 applied for aid; of those 77% were deemed to have need. 99% of undergraduates with need received aid; of those 6% had need fully met. *Average percent of need met:* 58% (excluding resources awarded to replace EFC). *Average financial aid package:* $9302 (excluding resources awarded to replace EFC). 12% of all full-time undergraduates had no need and received non-need-based gift aid.

GIFT AID (NEED-BASED) *Total amount:* $21,335,286 (97% federal, 3% state). *Receiving aid:* Freshmen: 56% (1,080); all full-time undergraduates: 55% (3,898). *Average award:* Freshmen: $4467; Undergraduates: $4458. *Scholarships, grants, and awards:* Federal Pell, FSEOG, state, private.

GIFT AID (NON-NEED-BASED) *Total amount:* $27,459,453 (38% state, 45% institutional, 17% external sources). *Receiving aid:* Freshmen: 48% (933). Undergraduates: 35% (2,468). *Average award:* Freshmen: $6728. Undergraduates: $6804. *Scholarships, grants, and awards by category:* Academic interests/achievement: agriculture, biological sciences, business, communication, computer science, education, engineering/technologies, English, foreign languages, general academic interests/achievements, health fields, home economics, humanities, mathematics, military science, physical sciences, premedicine, social sciences. *Creative arts/performance:* art/fine arts, cinema/film/broadcasting, creative writing, journalism/publications, music, theater/drama. *Special achievements/activities:* cheerleading/drum major, general special achievements/activities, junior miss. *Special characteristics:* children of faculty/staff, general special characteristics, international students, out-of-state students, parents of current students, public servants, veterans, veterans' children. *Tuition waivers:* Full or partial for employees or children of employees, senior citizens. *ROTC:* Army cooperative.

LOANS *Student loans:* $41,814,201 (39% need-based, 61% non-need-based). 58% of past graduating class borrowed through all loan programs. *Average indebtedness per student:* $27,156. *Average need-based loan:* Freshmen: $2913. Undergraduates: $3640. *Parent loans:* $1,961,764 (100% non-need-based). *Programs:* Federal Direct (Subsidized and Unsubsidized Stafford, PLUS).

WORK-STUDY *Federal work-study:* jobs available. *State or other work-study/employment:* Total amount: $565,854 (18% need-based, 82% non-need-based). Part-time jobs available.

ATHLETIC AWARDS Total amount: $1,432,279 (100% non-need-based).

APPLYING FOR FINANCIAL AID *Required financial aid forms:* FAFSA, institution's own form. *Financial aid deadline (priority):* 3/15. *Notification date:* Continuous beginning 3/15. Students must reply within 4 weeks of notification.

CONTACT Financial Aid Office, Arkansas Tech University, 1605 Coliseum Drive, Suite 117, Russellville, AR 72801, 479-968-0399 or toll-free 800-582-6953. *Fax:* 479-964-0857. *E-mail:* fa.help@atu.edu. *Website:* http://www.atu.edu/.

ARLINGTON BAPTIST COLLEGE
Arlington, TX

CONTACT Mr. David B. Clogston Jr., Business Manager, Arlington Baptist College, 3001 West Division Street, Arlington, TX 76012-3425, 817-461-8741 Ext. 110. *Fax:* 817-274-1138. *Website:* http://www.arlingtonbaptistcollege.edu/.

ARMSTRONG STATE UNIVERSITY
Savannah, GA

Tuition & fees (GA res): $6332	Average undergraduate aid package: N/A

ABOUT THE INSTITUTION State-supported, coed. *Awards:* certificates, associate, bachelor's, master's, and doctoral degrees. 42 undergraduate majors. *Total enrollment:* 7,157. Undergraduates: 6,397. Freshmen: 1,010. Federal methodology is used as a basis for awarding need-based institutional aid.

UNDERGRADUATE EXPENSES for 2016–2017 *Tuition, state resident:* full-time $4858; part-time $161.93 per credit hour. *Tuition, nonresident:* full-time $17,678; part-time $589.27 per credit hour. *Required fees:* full-time $1474; $612 per term. Full-time tuition and fees vary according to course load, location, and program. Part-time tuition and fees vary according to course load, location, and program. *College room and board:* $10,750; *Room only:* $6592. Room and board charges vary according to board plan and housing facility.

FRESHMAN FINANCIAL AID (Fall 2015) 522 applied for aid; of those 98% were deemed to have need. 100% of freshmen with need received aid. 4% of all full-time freshmen had no need and received non-need-based gift aid.

UNDERGRADUATE FINANCIAL AID (Fall 2015) 4,018 applied for aid; of those 99% were deemed to have need. 100% of undergraduates with need received aid. 3% of all full-time undergraduates had no need and received non-need-based gift aid.

GIFT AID (NEED-BASED) *Total amount:* $12,986,950 (98% federal, 2% institutional). *Receiving aid:* Freshmen: 45% (262); all full-time undergraduates: 49% (2,289). *Average award:* Freshmen: $1500; Undergraduates: $1500. *Scholarships, grants, and awards:* Federal Pell, FSEOG, state, private, college/university gift aid from institutional funds, United Negro College Fund, Federal Nursing.

GIFT AID (NON-NEED-BASED) *Total amount:* $7,126,798 (93% state, 3% institutional, 4% external sources). *Receiving aid:* Freshmen: 66% (379). Undergraduates: 43% (1,997). *Average award:* Freshmen: $688. Undergraduates: $1515. *Scholarships, grants, and awards by category:* Academic interests/achievement: biological sciences, computer science, education, engineering/technologies, English, foreign languages, general academic interests/achievements, health fields, humanities, international studies, mathematics, military science, physical sciences. *Creative arts/performance:* art/fine arts, general creative arts/performance, music. *Special achievements/activities:* community service. *Special characteristics:* ethnic background, international students, religious affiliation. *Tuition waivers:* Full or partial for employees or children of employees, senior citizens. *ROTC:* Army, Naval cooperative.

LOANS *Student loans:* $39,212,709 (33% need-based, 67% non-need-based). 57% of past graduating class borrowed through all loan programs. *Average need-based loan:* Freshmen: $3500. Undergraduates: $3500. *Parent loans:* $4,502,421 (100% non-need-based). *Programs:* Federal Direct (Subsidized and Unsubsidized Stafford, PLUS), state, alternative loans.

WORK-STUDY *Federal work-study:* jobs available. *State or other work-study/employment:* Part-time jobs available.

ATHLETIC AWARDS Total amount: $1,246,311 (100% non-need-based).

APPLYING FOR FINANCIAL AID *Required financial aid forms:* FAFSA, general scholarship application form. *Financial aid deadline:* 4/20 (priority: 3/15). *Notification date:* Continuous beginning 2/1. Students must reply by 4/15 or within 2 weeks of notification.

CONTACT Office of Financial Aid, Armstrong State University, 11935 Abercorn Street, Victor Hall, 2nd Floor, Savannah, GA 31419-1997, 912-344-3266 or toll-free 800-633-2349. *Fax:* 912-344-3448. *E-mail:* fin.aid@armstrong.edu. *Website:* http://www.armstrong.edu/.

ART ACADEMY OF CINCINNATI
Cincinnati, OH

Tuition & fees: N/R	Average undergraduate aid package: $14,000

ABOUT THE INSTITUTION Independent, coed. 11 undergraduate majors. Federal methodology is used as a basis for awarding need-based institutional aid.
FRESHMAN FINANCIAL AID (Fall 2016, est.) 52 applied for aid; of those 100% were deemed to have need. 100% of freshmen with need received aid; of those 13% had need fully met. *Average percent of need met:* 60% (excluding resources awarded to replace EFC). *Average financial aid package:* $12,000 (excluding resources awarded to replace EFC). 9% of all full-time freshmen had no need and received non-need-based gift aid.
UNDERGRADUATE FINANCIAL AID (Fall 2016, est.) 173 applied for aid; of those 100% were deemed to have need. 100% of undergraduates with need received aid; of those 11% had need fully met. *Average percent of need met:* 64% (excluding resources awarded to replace EFC). *Average financial aid package:* $14,000 (excluding resources awarded to replace EFC). 13% of all full-time undergraduates had no need and received non-need-based gift aid.
GIFT AID (NEED-BASED) *Total amount:* $1,593,527 (26% federal, 6% state, 64% institutional, 4% external sources). *Receiving aid:* Freshmen: 94% (50); all full-time undergraduates: 83% (153). *Average award:* Freshmen: $9400; Undergraduates: $9100. *Scholarships, grants, and awards:* Federal Pell, FSEOG, state, private, college/university gift aid from institutional funds.
GIFT AID (NON-NEED-BASED) *Receiving aid:* Freshmen: 11% (6). Undergraduates: 8% (15). *Average award:* Freshmen: $9700. Undergraduates: $8264. *Scholarships, grants, and awards by category:* Creative arts/performance: applied art and design, art/fine arts.
LOANS *Student loans:* $1,192,777 (100% need-based). *Average indebtedness per student:* $25,030. *Average need-based loan:* Freshmen: $4000. Undergraduates: $6000. *Parent loans:* $1,180,861 (100% need-based). *Programs:* college/university, alternative loans.
WORK-STUDY *Federal work-study:* Total amount: $18,286; jobs available. *State or other work-study/employment:* Part-time jobs available.
APPLYING FOR FINANCIAL AID *Required financial aid form:* FAFSA. *Financial aid deadline:* Continuous. *Notification date:* Continuous beginning 2/1. Students must reply within 2 weeks of notification.
CONTACT Ms. Dawn Reck, Director of Financial Aid, Art Academy of Cincinnati, 1212 Jackson Street, Cincinnati, OH 45202, 513-562-8773 or toll-free 800-323-5692. *Fax:* 513-562-8778. *E-mail:* financialaid@artacademy.edu. *Website:* http://www.artacademy.edu/.

ART CENTER COLLEGE OF DESIGN
Pasadena, CA

CONTACT Clema McKenzie, Director of Financial Aid, Art Center College of Design, 1700 Lida Street, Pasadena, CA 91103-1999, 626-396-2215. *Fax:* 626-683-8684. *Website:* http://www.artcenter.edu/.

THE ART INSTITUTE OF ATLANTA
Atlanta, GA

CONTACT Financial Aid Office, The Art Institute of Atlanta, 6600 Peachtree Dunwoody Road, NE, 100 Embassy Row, Atlanta, GA 30328, 770-394-8300 or toll-free 800-275-4242. *Website:* http://www.artinstitutes.edu/atlanta/.

THE ART INSTITUTE OF AUSTIN, A BRANCH OF THE ART INSTITUTE OF HOUSTON
Austin, TX

CONTACT Financial Aid Office, The Art Institute of Austin, a branch of The Art Institute of Houston, 101 W. Louis Henna Boulevard, Suite 100, Austin, TX 78728, 512-691-1707 or toll-free 866-583-7952. *Website:* http://www.artinstitutes.edu/austin.

THE ART INSTITUTE OF CALIFORNIA–HOLLYWOOD, A CAMPUS OF ARGOSY UNIVERSITY
North Hollywood, CA

Financial Aid Office, The Art Institute of California–Hollywood, a campus of Argosy University, 5250 Lankershim Boulevard, North Hollywood, CA 91601, 818-299-5100 or toll-free 877-468-6232.

THE ART INSTITUTE OF CALIFORNIA–INLAND EMPIRE, A CAMPUS OF ARGOSY UNIVERSITY
San Bernardino, CA

CONTACT Financial Aid Office, The Art Institute of California–Inland Empire, a campus of Argosy University, 674 East Brier Drive, San Bernardino, CA 92408, 909-915-2100 or toll-free 800-353-0812. *Website:* http://www.artinstitutes.edu/inlandempire/.

THE ART INSTITUTE OF CALIFORNIA–LOS ANGELES, A CAMPUS OF ARGOSY UNIVERSITY
Santa Monica, CA

CONTACT Financial Aid Office, The Art Institute of California–Los Angeles, a campus of Argosy University, 2900 31st Street, Santa Monica, CA 90405-3035, 310-752-4700 or toll-free 888-646-4610. *Website:* http://www.artinstitutes.edu/losangeles/.

THE ART INSTITUTE OF CALIFORNIA–ORANGE COUNTY, A CAMPUS OF ARGOSY UNIVERSITY
Santa Ana, CA

CONTACT Financial Aid Office, The Art Institute of California–Orange County, a campus of Argosy University, 3601 West Sunflower Avenue, Santa Ana, CA 92704, 714-830-0200 or toll-free 888-549-3055. *Website:* http://www.artinstitutes.edu/orangecounty/.

THE ART INSTITUTE OF CALIFORNIA–SACRAMENTO, A CAMPUS OF ARGOSY UNIVERSITY
Sacramento, CA

CONTACT Financial Aid Office, The Art Institute of California–Sacramento, a campus of Argosy University, 2850 Gateway Oaks Drive, Suite 100, Sacramento, CA 95833, 916-830-6320 or toll-free 800-477-1957.
Website: http://www.artinstitutes.edu/sacramento/.

THE ART INSTITUTE OF CALIFORNIA–SAN DIEGO, A CAMPUS OF ARGOSY UNIVERSITY
San Diego, CA

Financial Aid Office, The Art Institute of California–San Diego, a campus of Argosy University, 10025 Mesa Rim Road, San Diego, CA 92121, 619-546-0602 or toll-free 866-275-2422.

THE ART INSTITUTE OF CALIFORNIA–SAN FRANCISCO, A CAMPUS OF ARGOSY UNIVERSITY
San Francisco, CA

Financial Aid Office, The Art Institute of California–San Francisco, a campus of Argosy University, 1170 Market Street, San Francisco, CA 94102-4908, 415-865-0198 or toll-free 888-493-3261. *Fax:* 415-863-5831.

THE ART INSTITUTE OF CHARLESTON, A BRANCH OF THE ART INSTITUTE OF ATLANTA
Charleston, SC

CONTACT Financial Aid Office, The Art Institute of Charleston, a branch of The Art Institute of Atlanta, 24 North Market Street, Charleston, SC 29401, 843-727-3500 or toll-free 866-211-0107.
Website: http://www.artinstitutes.edu/charleston/.

THE ART INSTITUTE OF CHARLOTTE, A BRANCH OF MIAMI INTERNATIONAL UNIVERSITY OF ART & DESIGN
Charlotte, NC

CONTACT Financial Aid Office, The Art Institute of Charlotte, a branch of Miami International University of Art & Design, Three LakePointe Plaza, 2110 Water Ridge Parkway, Charlotte, NC 28217, 704-357-8020 or toll-free 800-872-4417.
Website: http://www.artinstitutes.edu/charlotte/.

THE ART INSTITUTE OF COLORADO
Denver, CO

CONTACT Financial Aid Office, The Art Institute of Colorado, 1200 Lincoln Street, Denver, CO 80203, 303-837-0825 or toll-free 800-275-2420.
Website: http://www.artinstitutes.edu/denver/.

THE ART INSTITUTE OF DALLAS, A BRANCH OF MIAMI INTERNATIONAL UNIVERSITY OF ART & DESIGN
Dallas, TX

CONTACT Financial Aid Office, The Art Institute of Dallas, a branch of Miami International University of Art & Design, 8080 Park Lane, Suite 100, Dallas, TX 75231-5993, 214-692-8080 or toll-free 800-275-4243.
Website: http://www.artinstitutes.edu/dallas/.

THE ART INSTITUTE OF FORT LAUDERDALE
Fort Lauderdale, FL

Financial Aid Office, The Art Institute of Fort Lauderdale, 1799 Southeast 17th Street Causeway, Fort Lauderdale, FL 33316-3000, 954-527-1799 or toll-free 800-275-7603.

THE ART INSTITUTE OF HOUSTON
Houston, TX

Financial Aid Office, The Art Institute of Houston, 4140 Southwest Freeway, Houston, TX 77027, 713-623-2040 or toll-free 800-275-4244.

THE ART INSTITUTE OF INDIANAPOLIS
Indianapolis, IN

CONTACT Financial Aid Office, The Art Institute of Indianapolis, 3500 Depauw Boulevard, Suite 1010, Indianapolis, IN 46268, 317-613-4800 or toll-free 866-441-9031.
Website: http://www.artinstitutes.edu/indianapolis/.

THE ART INSTITUTE OF LAS VEGAS
Henderson, NV

CONTACT Financial Aid Office, The Art Institute of Las Vegas, 2350 Corporate Circle Drive, Henderson, NV 89074, 702-369-9944 or toll-free 800-833-2678.
Website: http://www.artinstitutes.edu/lasvegas/.

THE ART INSTITUTE OF MICHIGAN
Novi, MI

CONTACT Financial Aid Office, The Art Institute of Michigan, 28125 Cabot Drive, Suite 120, Novi, MI 48377, 248-675-3800 or toll-free 800-479-0087.
Website: http://www.artinstitutes.edu/detroit/.

THE ART INSTITUTE OF PHILADELPHIA
Philadelphia, PA

Financial Aid Office, The Art Institute of Philadelphia, 1622 Chestnut Street, Philadelphia, PA 19103, 215-567-7080 or toll-free 800-275-2474.

THE ART INSTITUTE OF PHOENIX
Phoenix, AZ

CONTACT Financial Aid Office, The Art Institute of Phoenix, 2233 West Dunlap Avenue, Phoenix, AZ 85021-2859, 602-331-7500 or toll-free 800-474-2479.
Website: http://www.artinstitutes.edu/phoenix/.

THE ART INSTITUTE OF PITTSBURGH
Pittsburgh, PA

Financial Aid Office, The Art Institute of Pittsburgh, 420 Boulevard of the Allies, Pittsburgh, PA 15219, 412-263-6600 or toll-free 800-275-2470.

THE ART INSTITUTE OF PORTLAND
Portland, OR

CONTACT Financial Aid Office, The Art Institute of Portland, 1122 NW Davis Street, Portland, OR 97209, 503-228-6528 or toll-free 888-228-6528.
Website: http://www.artinstitutes.edu/portland/.

THE ART INSTITUTE OF RALEIGH-DURHAM, A BRANCH OF MIAMI INTERNATIONAL UNIVERSITY OF ART & DESIGN
Durham, NC

CONTACT Financial Aid Office, The Art Institute of Raleigh-Durham, a branch of Miami International University of Art & Design, 410 Blackwell Street, Suite 200, Durham, NC 27701, 919-317-3050 or toll-free 888-245-9593.
Website: http://www.artinstitutes.edu/raleigh-durham.

THE ART INSTITUTE OF ST. LOUIS
St. Charles, MO

CONTACT Financial Aid Office, The Art Institute of St. Louis, 1520 South Fifth Street, St. Charles, MO 63303, 636-688-3010.
Website: http://www.artinstitutes.edu/st-louis/.

THE ART INSTITUTE OF SAN ANTONIO, A BRANCH OF THE ART INSTITUTE OF HOUSTON
San Antonio, TX

CONTACT Financial Aid Office, The Art Institute of San Antonio, a branch of The Art Institute of Houston, 1000 IH-10 West, Suite 200, San Antonio, TX 78230, 210-338-7320 or toll-free 888-222-0040.
Website: http://www.artinstitutes.edu/san-antonio/.

THE ART INSTITUTE OF SEATTLE
Seattle, WA

Financial Aid Office, The Art Institute of Seattle, 2323 Elliott Avenue, Seattle, WA 98121-1642, 206-448-6600 or toll-free 800-275-2471.

THE ART INSTITUTE OF TAMPA, A BRANCH OF MIAMI INTERNATIONAL UNIVERSITY OF ART & DESIGN
Tampa, FL

CONTACT Financial Aid Office, The Art Institute of Tampa, a branch of Miami International University of Art & Design, Parkside at Tampa Bay Park, 4401 North Himes Avenue, Suite 150, Tampa, FL 33614, 813-873-2112 or toll-free 866-703-3277.
Website: http://www.artinstitutes.edu/tampa/.

THE ART INSTITUTE OF TENNESSEE-NASHVILLE, A BRANCH OF THE ART INSTITUTE OF ATLANTA
Nashville, TN

CONTACT Financial Aid Office, The Art Institute of Tennessee-Nashville, a branch of The Art Institute of Atlanta, 100 Centerview Drive, Suite 250, Nashville, TN 37214, 615-874-1067 or toll-free 866-747-5770.
Website: http://www.artinstitutes.edu/nashville/.

THE ART INSTITUTE OF TUCSON
Tucson, AZ

CONTACT Financial Aid Office, The Art Institute of Tucson, 5099 East Grant Road, Suite 100, Tucson, AZ 85712, 520-318-2700 or toll-free 866-690-8850.
Website: http://www.artinstitutes.edu/tucson/.

THE ART INSTITUTE OF VIRGINIA BEACH, A BRANCH OF THE ART INSTITUTE OF ATLANTA
Virginia Beach, VA

CONTACT Financial Aid Office, The Art Institute of Virginia Beach, a branch of The Art Institute of Atlanta, Two Columbus Center, 4500 Main Street, Suite 100, Virginia Beach, VA 23462, 757-493-6700 or toll-free 877-437-4428.
Website: http://www.artinstitutes.edu/virginia-beach/.

THE ART INSTITUTE OF WASHINGTON, A BRANCH OF THE ART INSTITUTE OF ATLANTA
Arlington, VA

Financial Aid Office, The Art Institute of Washington, a branch of The Art Institute of Atlanta, 1820 North Fort Myer Drive, Arlington, VA 22209, 703-247-6849 or toll-free 877-303-3771. Fax: 703-247-6829.

ASBURY UNIVERSITY
Wilmore, KY

Tuition & fees: $29,500	Average undergraduate aid package: N/A

ABOUT THE INSTITUTION Independent nondenominational, coed. *Awards:* associate, bachelor's, and master's degrees. 47 undergraduate majors. *Total enrollment:* 1,030. Undergraduates: 1,021. Freshmen: 306. Both federal and institutional methodology are used as a basis for awarding need-based institutional aid.

UNDERGRADUATE EXPENSES for 2017–2018 *Comprehensive fee:* $36,450 includes full-time tuition ($29,302), mandatory fees ($198), and room and board ($6950). Full-time tuition and fees vary according to course load and program. Room and board charges vary according to board plan and housing facility. *Part-time tuition:* $1127 per credit hour. Part-time tuition and fees vary according to course load and program.

FRESHMAN FINANCIAL AID (Fall 2015) 283 applied for aid; of those 85% were deemed to have need. 98% of freshmen with need received aid.

UNDERGRADUATE FINANCIAL AID (Fall 2015) 1,127 applied for aid; of those 90% were deemed to have need. 94% of undergraduates with need received aid.

GIFT AID (NEED-BASED) *Total amount:* $14,238,094 (16% federal, 17% state, 63% institutional, 4% external sources). *Receiving aid:* Freshmen: 63% (194); all full-time undergraduates: 54% (699). *Scholarships, grants, and awards:* Federal Pell, FSEOG, state, private, college/university gift aid from institutional funds.

GIFT AID (NON-NEED-BASED) *Total amount:* $3,591,248 (2% federal, 7% state, 83% institutional, 8% external sources). *Receiving aid:* Freshmen: 29% (90). Undergraduates: 24% (308). *Scholarships, grants, and awards by category:* Academic interests/achievement: business, general academic interests/achievements. Creative arts/performance: art/fine arts, music, theater/drama. Special achievements/activities: leadership. Special characteristics: children and siblings of alumni, children of faculty/staff, ethnic background, international students, out-of-state students, relatives of clergy, siblings of current students. *Tuition waivers:* Full or partial for employees or children of employees, senior citizens. *ROTC:* Army cooperative, Air Force cooperative.

LOANS *Student loans:* $8,630,452 (90% need-based, 10% non-need-based). 91% of past graduating class borrowed through all loan programs. *Average indebtedness per student:* $30,123. *Parent loans:* $1,841,452 (87% need-based, 13% non-need-based). *Programs:* Federal Direct (Subsidized and Unsubsidized Stafford, PLUS), Perkins, college/university, private loans.

WORK-STUDY *Federal work-study:* 326 jobs averaging $1711.

ATHLETIC AWARDS Total amount: $1,284,476 (72% need-based, 28% non-need-based).

APPLYING FOR FINANCIAL AID *Financial aid deadline:* Continuous. *Notification date:* Continuous beginning 10/31.

CONTACT Mr. Ronald Anderson, Director of Financial Aid, Asbury University, One Macklem Drive, Wilmore, KY 40390, 859-858-3511 Ext. 2195 or toll-free 800-888-1818. *Fax:* 859-858-9149. *E-mail:* ron.anderson@asbury.edu.
Website: http://www.asbury.edu/.

ASHFORD UNIVERSITY
San Diego, CA

CONTACT Lisa Kramer, Director of Financial Aid, Ashford University, 400 North Bluff Boulevard, PO Box 2967, Clinton, IA 52733-2967, 563-242-4023 Ext. 1243 or toll-free 866-711-1700. *Fax:* 563-242-8684.
Website: http://www.ashford.edu/.

ASHLAND UNIVERSITY
Ashland, OH

CONTACT Mr. Stephen C. Howell, Director of Financial Aid, Ashland University, 401 College Avenue, Ashland, OH 44805-3702, 419-289-5944 or toll-free 800-882-1548. *Fax:* 419-289-5976. *E-mail:* showell@ashland.edu.
Website: http://www.ashland.edu/.

ASHWORTH COLLEGE
Norcross, GA

CONTACT Financial Aid Office, Ashworth College, 6625 The Corners Parkway, Suite 500, Norcross, GA 30092, 770-729-8400 or toll-free 800-957-5412.
Website: http://www.ashworthcollege.edu/.

ASPEN UNIVERSITY
Denver, CO

CONTACT Jennifer Quinn, Director of Financial Aid, Aspen University, 720 South Colorado Bouleavrd #1150N, Denver, CO 80246, 800-441-4746. *Fax:* 303-336-1144. *E-mail:* jquinn@aspen.edu.
Website: http://www.aspen.edu/.

ASSUMPTION COLLEGE
Worcester, MA

Tuition & fees: $36,260	Average undergraduate aid package: $26,539

ABOUT THE INSTITUTION Independent Roman Catholic, coed. *Awards:* certificates, bachelor's, and master's degrees. 34 undergraduate majors. *Total enrollment:* 2,407. Undergraduates: 1,989. Freshmen: 579. Federal methodology is used as a basis for awarding need-based institutional aid.

UNDERGRADUATE EXPENSES for 2016–2017 *Application fee:* $50. *Comprehensive fee:* $47,920 includes full-time tuition ($35,510), mandatory fees ($750), and room and board ($11,660). *College room only:* $7356. Full-time tuition and fees vary according to course load and reciprocity agreements. Room and board charges vary according to housing facility. *Part-time tuition:* $1183.67 per credit hour. Part-time tuition and fees vary according to course load. *Payment plan:* Guaranteed tuition.

FRESHMAN FINANCIAL AID (Fall 2016, est.) 512 applied for aid; of those 89% were deemed to have need. 100% of freshmen with need received aid; of those 26% had need fully met. *Average percent of need met:* 74% (excluding resources awarded to replace EFC). *Average financial aid package:* $25,791 (excluding resources awarded to replace EFC). 19% of all full-time freshmen had no need and received non-need-based gift aid.

UNDERGRADUATE FINANCIAL AID (Fall 2016, est.) 1,623 applied for aid; of those 90% were deemed to have need. 100% of undergraduates with need received aid; of those 26% had need fully met. *Average percent of need met:* 76% (excluding resources awarded to replace EFC). *Average financial aid package:* $26,539 (excluding resources awarded to replace EFC). 21% of all full-time undergraduates had no need and received non-need-based gift aid.

GIFT AID (NEED-BASED) *Total amount:* $29,392,941 (6% federal, 3% state, 89% institutional, 2% external sources). *Receiving aid:* Freshmen: 79% (457); all full-time undergraduates: 74% (1,456). *Average award:* Freshmen: $21,789; Undergraduates: $21,546. *Scholarships, grants, and awards:* Federal Pell, FSEOG, state, private, college/university gift aid from institutional funds, Academic Competitiveness Grants, National SMART Grants.

GIFT AID (NON-NEED-BASED) *Total amount:* $7,768,051 (98% institutional, 2% external sources). *Receiving aid:* Freshmen: 13% (74). Undergraduates: 12% (232). *Average award:* Freshmen: $15,148. Undergraduates: $15,079. *Scholarships, grants, and awards by category:* Academic interests/achievement: 1,522 awards ($22,278,126 total): general academic interests/achievements. Creative arts/performance: 19 awards ($151,010 total). Special characteristics: members of minority groups. *Tuition waivers:* Full or partial for employees or children of employees. *ROTC:* Army cooperative, Air Force cooperative.

LOANS *Student loans:* $14,786,973 (60% need-based, 40% non-need-based). *Average need-based loan:* Freshmen: $3361. Undergraduates: $4674. *Parent loans:* $6,057,869 (39% need-based, 61% non-need-based). *Programs:* Federal Direct (Subsidized and Unsubsidized Stafford, PLUS), Perkins, state, college/university.

WORK-STUDY *Federal work-study:* Total amount: $414,500; 309 jobs averaging $1341.

ATHLETIC AWARDS Total amount: $2,533,140 (42% need-based, 58% non-need-based).

APPLYING FOR FINANCIAL AID *Required financial aid form:* FAFSA. *Financial aid deadline:* 2/15. *Notification date:* Continuous beginning 2/16. Students must reply by 5/1.

CONTACT William C. Smith, Director of Financial Aid, Assumption College, 500 Salisbury Street, Worcester, MA 01609-1296, 508-767-7157 or toll-free 866-477-7776. *Fax:* 508-767-7376. *E-mail:* fa@assumption.edu.

Website: http://www.assumption.edu/.

ATENAS COLLEGE
Manati, PR

CONTACT Financial Aid Office, Atenas College, Paseo de La Atenas #101 Altos, Manati, PR 00674, 787-884-3838.

Website: http://www.atenascollege.edu/.

ATHENS STATE UNIVERSITY
Athens, AL

Tuition & fees (AL res): $6480	Average undergraduate aid package: $8599

ABOUT THE INSTITUTION State-supported, coed. *Awards:* certificates, bachelor's, and master's degrees. 35 undergraduate majors. *Total enrollment:* 3,063. Undergraduates: 3,025. Federal methodology is used as a basis for awarding need-based institutional aid.

UNDERGRADUATE EXPENSES for 2016–2017 *Application fee:* $30. *Tuition, state resident:* full-time $5730. *Tuition, nonresident:* full-time $11,460. *Required fees:* full-time $750.

UNDERGRADUATE FINANCIAL AID (Fall 2015) 1,073 applied for aid; of those 91% were deemed to have need. 98% of undergraduates with need received aid; of those 2% had need fully met. *Average percent of need met:* 2% (excluding resources awarded to replace EFC). *Average financial aid package:* $8599 (excluding resources awarded to replace EFC). 1% of all full-time undergraduates had no need and received non-need-based gift aid.

GIFT AID (NEED-BASED) *Total amount:* $5,172,418 (99% federal, 1% external sources). *Receiving aid:* Entering class: 47% (574); all full-time undergraduates: 34% (563). *Average award:* Freshmen: $4190; Undergraduates: $2976. *Scholarships, grants, and awards:* Federal Pell, FSEOG, state, private, college/university gift aid from institutional funds.

GIFT AID (NON-NEED-BASED) *Total amount:* $589,954 (12% federal, 88% institutional). *Receiving aid:* Freshmen: 12% (153). Undergraduates: 7% (121). *Average award:* Freshmen: $3730. Undergraduates: $2060. *Tuition waivers:* Full or partial for employees or children of employees, senior citizens.

LOANS *Student loans:* $14,039,090 (44% need-based, 56% non-need-based). *Average need-based loan:* Freshmen: $3345. Undergraduates: $2925. *Programs:* Federal Direct (Subsidized and Unsubsidized Stafford, PLUS), college/university.

WORK-STUDY *Federal work-study:* jobs available.

APPLYING FOR FINANCIAL AID *Required financial aid form:* FAFSA. *Financial aid deadline:* Continuous. *Notification date:* Continuous beginning 5/1. Students must reply within 2 weeks of notification.

CONTACT Mary Chambliss, Financial Aid Director, Athens State University, 300 North Beaty Street, Athens, AL 35611, 256-233-8161 or toll-free 800-522-0272. *Fax:* 256-233-8161. *E-mail:* finaid@athens.edu.

Website: http://www.athens.edu/.

ATLANTIC UNIVERSITY COLLEGE
Guaynabo, PR

CONTACT Mrs. Velma Aponte, Financial Aid Coordinator, Atlantic University College, Calle Colton #9, Guaynabo, PR 00970, 787-720-1092. *E-mail:* atlaneco@coqui.net.

Website: http://www.atlanticu.edu/.

AUBURN UNIVERSITY
Auburn University, AL

Tuition & fees (AL res): $10,696	Average undergraduate aid package: $10,411

ABOUT THE INSTITUTION State-supported, coed. *Awards:* certificates, bachelor's, master's, and doctoral degrees. 148 undergraduate majors. *Total enrollment:* 28,290. Undergraduates: 22,658. Freshmen: 4,529. Federal methodology is used as a basis for awarding need-based institutional aid.

UNDERGRADUATE EXPENSES for 2016–2017 *Application fee:* $50. *Tuition, state resident:* full-time $9072; part-time $378 per semester hour. *Tuition, nonresident:* full-time $27,216; part-time $1134 per semester hour. *Required fees:* full-time $1624; $812 per term. Full-time tuition and fees vary according to program and reciprocity agreements. Part-time tuition and fees vary according to course load, program, and reciprocity agreements. *College room and board:* $12,898; *Room only:* $7538. Room and board charges vary according to board plan and housing facility.

FRESHMAN FINANCIAL AID (Fall 2015) 3,037 applied for aid; of those 58% were deemed to have need. 100% of freshmen with need received aid; of those 18% had need fully met. *Average percent of need met:* 52% (excluding resources awarded to replace EFC). *Average financial aid package:* $11,758 (excluding resources awarded to replace EFC). 30% of all full-time freshmen had no need and received non-need-based gift aid.

UNDERGRADUATE FINANCIAL AID (Fall 2015) 12,895 applied for aid; of those 55% were deemed to have need. 100% of undergraduates with need received aid; of those 13% had need fully met. *Average percent of need met:* 45% (excluding resources awarded to replace EFC). *Average financial aid package:* $10,411 (excluding resources awarded to replace EFC). 22% of all full-time undergraduates had no need and received non-need-based gift aid.

GIFT AID (NEED-BASED) *Total amount:* $40,650,239 (36% federal, 5% state, 48% institutional, 11% external sources). *Receiving aid:* Freshmen: 30% (1,456); all full-time undergraduates: 26% (5,069). *Average award:* Freshmen: $9078; Undergraduates: $7690. *Scholarships, grants, and awards:* Federal Pell, FSEOG, state, private, college/university gift aid from institutional funds.

GIFT AID (NON-NEED-BASED) *Total amount:* $51,289,983 (12% state, 70% institutional, 18% external sources). *Receiving aid:* Freshmen: 5% (249). Undergraduates: 3% (602). *Average award:* Freshmen: $7397. Undergraduates: $7083. *Scholarships, grants, and awards by category:* Academic interests/achievement: agriculture, architecture, biological sciences, business, communication, computer science, education, engineering/technologies, English, foreign languages, general academic interests/achievements, health fields, home economics, humanities, mathematics, physical sciences, premedicine, social sciences. Creative arts/performance: applied art and design, art/fine arts, cinema/film/broadcasting, creative writing, journalism/publications, music, performing arts, theater/drama. Special achievements/activities: cheerleading/drum major, leadership, memberships. Special characteristics: children and siblings of alumni, children of faculty/staff, children of union members/company employees, ethnic background, local/state students, married students, out-of-state students. *Tuition waivers:* Full or partial for employees or children of employees. *ROTC:* Army, Naval, Air Force.

LOANS *Student loans:* $70,086,975 (69% need-based, 31% non-need-based). 41% of past graduating class borrowed through all loan programs. *Average indebtedness per student:* $28,170. *Average need-based loan:* Freshmen: $3670. Undergraduates: $4594. *Parent loans:* $34,577,488 (56% need-based, 44% non-need-based). *Programs:* Federal Direct (Subsidized and Unsubsidized Stafford, PLUS), Perkins, Federal Nursing, college/university.

WORK-STUDY *Federal work-study:* 189 jobs averaging $4115.

ATHLETIC AWARDS Total amount: $14,310,234 (2% need-based, 98% non-need-based).

APPLYING FOR FINANCIAL AID *Required financial aid form:* FAFSA. *Financial aid deadline (priority):* 3/1. *Notification date:* Continuous beginning 10/2. Students must reply by 5/1.

CONTACT Mr. Mike Reynolds, Director of Student Financial Services, Auburn University, 203 Mary Martin Hall, Auburn University, AL 36849, 334-844-4634 or toll-free 800-AUBURN9. *Fax:* 334-844-6085. *E-mail:* finaid7@auburn.edu.

Website: http://www.auburn.edu/.

AUBURN UNIVERSITY AT MONTGOMERY
Montgomery, AL

Tuition & fees (AL res): $9640	Average undergraduate aid package: $6970

ABOUT THE INSTITUTION State-supported, coed. **Awards:** certificates, bachelor's, master's, and doctoral degrees. 36 undergraduate majors. **Total enrollment:** 4,878. Undergraduates: 4,273. Freshmen: 594. Federal methodology is used as a basis for awarding need-based institutional aid.

UNDERGRADUATE EXPENSES for 2016–2017 Tuition, state resident: full-time $8880; part-time $296 per credit hour. **Tuition, nonresident:** full-time $19,950; part-time $665 per credit hour. **Required fees:** full-time $760; $10 per credit hour or $230 per term. Full-time tuition and fees vary according to course load and degree level. Part-time tuition and fees vary according to course load and degree level. **College room and board:** $5650; **Room only:** $4450. Room and board charges vary according to housing facility.

FRESHMAN FINANCIAL AID (Fall 2015) 450 applied for aid; of those 88% were deemed to have need. 100% of freshmen with need received aid; of those 12% had need fully met. **Average financial aid package:** $6421 (excluding resources awarded to replace EFC). 10% of all full-time freshmen had no need and received non-need-based gift aid.

UNDERGRADUATE FINANCIAL AID (Fall 2015) 2,340 applied for aid; of those 88% were deemed to have need. 100% of undergraduates with need received aid; of those 12% had need fully met. **Average financial aid package:** $6970 (excluding resources awarded to replace EFC). 7% of all full-time undergraduates had no need and received non-need-based gift aid.

GIFT AID (NEED-BASED) Total amount: $8,841,183 (99% federal, 1% state). **Receiving aid:** Freshmen: 50% (286); all full-time undergraduates: 49% (1,521). **Average award:** Freshmen: $4505; Undergraduates: $4538. **Scholarships, grants, and awards:** Federal Pell, FSEOG, state, college/university gift aid from institutional funds.

GIFT AID (NON-NEED-BASED) Total amount: $3,356,454 (85% institutional, 15% external sources). **Receiving aid:** Freshmen: 25% (140). Undergraduates: 15% (474). **Average award:** Freshmen: $4626. Undergraduates: $6485. **Scholarships, grants, and awards by category:** Academic interests/achievement: general academic interests/achievements. **Tuition waivers:** Full or partial for employees or children of employees, senior citizens. **ROTC:** Army, Air Force cooperative.

LOANS Student loans: $16,405,540 (51% need-based, 49% non-need-based). 69% of past graduating class borrowed through all loan programs. **Average indebtedness per student:** $30,454. **Average need-based loan:** Freshmen: $3196. Undergraduates: $3934. **Parent loans:** $1,865,484 (100% non-need-based). **Programs:** Federal Direct (Subsidized and Unsubsidized Stafford, PLUS), Perkins.

WORK-STUDY Federal work-study: jobs available.

ATHLETIC AWARDS Total amount: $2,220,576 (100% non-need-based).

APPLYING FOR FINANCIAL AID Required financial aid form: FAFSA. **Financial aid deadline (priority):** 3/1. **Notification date:** Continuous beginning 4/15.

CONTACT Mr. Anthony Richey, Senior Director of Financial Aid, Auburn University at Montgomery, PO Box 244023, Montgomery, AL 36124-4023, 334-244-3571 or toll-free 800-227-2649. *Fax:* 334-244-3913. *E-mail:* aumfinancialaidoffice@aum.edu. *Website:* http://www.aum.edu/.

AUGSBURG COLLEGE
Minneapolis, MN

Tuition & fees: $37,615	Average undergraduate aid package: $28,485

ABOUT THE INSTITUTION Independent Lutheran, coed. **Awards:** certificates, bachelor's, master's, and doctoral degrees. 70 undergraduate majors. **Total enrollment:** 3,640. Undergraduates: 2,550. Freshmen: 477. Federal methodology is used as a basis for awarding need-based institutional aid.

UNDERGRADUATE EXPENSES for 2017–2018 Comprehensive fee: $47,554 includes full-time tuition ($36,950), mandatory fees ($665), and room and board ($9939). **College room only:** $5154. Full-time tuition and fees vary according to class time and location. Room and board charges vary according to board plan and housing facility. **Part-time tuition:** $1155 per credit hour. Part-time tuition and fees vary according to class time and location.

FRESHMAN FINANCIAL AID (Fall 2015) 426 applied for aid; of those 92% were deemed to have need. 99% of freshmen with need received aid; of those 17% had need fully met. **Average percent of need met:** 81% (excluding resources awarded to replace EFC). **Average financial aid package:** $31,177 (excluding resources awarded to replace EFC). 18% of all full-time freshmen had no need and received non-need-based gift aid.

UNDERGRADUATE FINANCIAL AID (Fall 2015) 1,790 applied for aid; of those 93% were deemed to have need. 100% of undergraduates with need received aid; of those 11% had need fully met. **Average percent of need met:** 72% (excluding resources awarded to replace EFC). **Average financial aid package:** $28,485 (excluding resources awarded to replace EFC). 16% of all full-time undergraduates had no need and received non-need-based gift aid.

GIFT AID (NEED-BASED) Total amount: $37,875,546 (14% federal, 12% state, 66% institutional, 8% external sources). **Receiving aid:** Freshmen: 81% (387); all full-time undergraduates: 81% (1,639). **Average award:** Freshmen: $26,314; Undergraduates: $22,652. **Scholarships, grants, and awards:** Federal Pell, FSEOG, state, private, college/university gift aid from institutional funds, Federal Nursing.

GIFT AID (NON-NEED-BASED) Total amount: $6,588,048 (4% state, 82% institutional, 14% external sources). **Receiving aid:** Freshmen: 8% (38). Undergraduates: 5% (107). **Average award:** Freshmen: $15,834. Undergraduates: $14,342. **Scholarships, grants, and awards by category:** Academic interests/achievement: biological sciences, business, communication, computer science, education, English, foreign languages, general academic interests/achievements, health fields, international studies, mathematics, physical sciences, religion/biblical studies, social sciences. Creative arts/performance: art/fine arts, music, performing arts, theater/drama. Special achievements/activities: community service, general special achievements/activities, junior miss, leadership, religious involvement. Special characteristics: children and siblings of alumni, international students, members of minority groups, relatives of clergy, siblings of current students. **Tuition waivers:** Full or partial for employees or children of employees. **ROTC:** Army cooperative, Naval cooperative, Air Force cooperative.

LOANS Student loans: $19,237,152 (78% need-based, 22% non-need-based). 89% of past graduating class borrowed through all loan programs. **Average indebtedness per student:** $40,816. **Average need-based loan:** Freshmen: $3804. Undergraduates: $4824. **Parent loans:** $3,611,622 (100% non-need-based). **Programs:** Federal Direct (Subsidized and Unsubsidized Stafford, PLUS), Perkins, Federal Nursing, state.

WORK-STUDY Federal work-study: jobs available. **State or other work-study/employment:** Total amount: $672,191 (37% need-based, 63% non-need-based). Part-time jobs available.

APPLYING FOR FINANCIAL AID Required financial aid form: FAFSA. **Financial aid deadline:** 8/1 (priority: 3/15). **Notification date:** Continuous beginning 3/1. Students must reply within 3 weeks of notification.

CONTACT Mr. Paul L. Terrio, Director of Student Financial Services, Augsburg College, 2211 Riverside Avenue, Minneapolis, MN 55454-1351, 612-330-1049 or toll-free 800-788-5678. *Fax:* 612-330-1308. *E-mail:* terriop@augsburg.edu. *Website:* http://www.augsburg.edu/.

AUGUSTANA COLLEGE
Rock Island, IL

Tuition & fees: $40,908	Average undergraduate aid package: $29,389

ABOUT THE INSTITUTION Independent Evangelical Lutheran Church in America, coed. **Awards:** bachelor's degrees. 61 undergraduate majors. **Total enrollment:** 2,537. Undergraduates: 2,537. Freshmen: 697. Federal methodology is used as a basis for awarding need-based institutional aid.

UNDERGRADUATE EXPENSES for 2017–2018 Comprehensive fee: $51,222 includes full-time tuition ($39,690), mandatory fees ($1218), and room and board ($10,314). **College room only:** $5220. Room and board charges vary according to board plan and housing facility. **Part-time tuition:** $1755 per credit. Part-time tuition and fees vary according to course load. **Payment plan:** Tuition prepayment.

FRESHMAN FINANCIAL AID (Fall 2015) 645 applied for aid; of those 85% were deemed to have need. 100% of freshmen with need received aid; of those 25% had need fully met. *Average percent of need met:* 88% (excluding resources awarded to replace EFC). *Average financial aid package:* $30,778 (excluding resources awarded to replace EFC). 20% of all full-time freshmen had no need and received non-need-based gift aid.

UNDERGRADUATE FINANCIAL AID (Fall 2015) 2,216 applied for aid; of those 85% were deemed to have need. 100% of undergraduates with need received aid; of those 22% had need fully met. *Average percent of need met:* 85% (excluding resources awarded to replace EFC). *Average financial aid package:* $29,389 (excluding resources awarded to replace EFC). 22% of all full-time undergraduates had no need and received non-need-based gift aid.

GIFT AID (NEED-BASED) *Total amount:* $43,436,125 (7% federal, 7% state, 85% institutional, 1% external sources). *Receiving aid:* Freshmen: 79% (537); all full-time undergraduates: 76% (1,852). *Average award:* Freshmen: $25,473; Undergraduates: $23,444. *Scholarships, grants, and awards:* Federal Pell, FSEOG, state, private, college/university gift aid from institutional funds.

GIFT AID (NON-NEED-BASED) *Total amount:* $13,947,850 (99% institutional, 1% external sources). *Receiving aid:* Freshmen: 15% (102). Undergraduates: 13% (313). *Average award:* Freshmen: $21,640. Undergraduates: $19,404. *Scholarships, grants, and awards by category: Academic interests/achievement:* 2,453 awards ($37,577,343 total): area/ethnic studies, biological sciences, business, communication, computer science, education, English, foreign languages, general academic interests/achievements, humanities, mathematics, physical sciences, religion/biblical studies, social sciences. *Creative arts/performance:* 359 awards ($1,017,159 total): art/fine arts, creative writing, debating, music, theater/drama. *Special achievements/activities:* 45 awards ($52,974 total): leadership, religious involvement. *Special characteristics:* 499 awards ($4,583,187 total): children and siblings of alumni, children of faculty/staff, ethnic background, international students, members of minority groups, out-of-state students, religious affiliation, siblings of current students. *Tuition waivers:* Full or partial for employees or children of employees.

LOANS *Student loans:* $15,466,060 (69% need-based, 31% non-need-based). 75% of past graduating class borrowed through all loan programs. *Average indebtedness per student:* $33,547. *Average need-based loan:* Freshmen: $3709. Undergraduates: $4732. *Parent loans:* $5,667,713 (34% need-based, 66% non-need-based). *Programs:* Federal Direct (Subsidized and Unsubsidized Stafford, PLUS), Perkins.

WORK-STUDY *Federal work-study:* 1,281 jobs averaging $2364.

APPLYING FOR FINANCIAL AID *Required financial aid forms:* FAFSA, institution's own form. *Financial aid deadline (priority):* 11/1. *Notification date:* Continuous beginning 12/15. Students must reply by 5/1.

CONTACT Ms. Sue Standley, Director of Financial Aid, Augustana College, 639 38th Street, Rock Island, IL 61201-2296, 309-794-7207 Ext. 7447 or toll-free 800-798-8100. *Fax:* 309-794-7174. *E-mail:* suestandley@augustana.edu. *Website:* http://www.augustana.edu/.

aid; of those 19% had need fully met. *Average percent of need met:* 94% (excluding resources awarded to replace EFC). *Average financial aid package:* $25,553 (excluding resources awarded to replace EFC). 37% of all full-time undergraduates had no need and received non-need-based gift aid.

GIFT AID (NEED-BASED) *Total amount:* $16,023,234 (12% federal, 83% institutional, 5% external sources). *Receiving aid:* Freshmen: 66% (276); all full-time undergraduates: 58% (929). *Average award:* Freshmen: $25,013; Undergraduates: $21,864. *Scholarships, grants, and awards:* Federal Pell, FSEOG, state, private, college/university gift aid from institutional funds, need-linked special talent scholarships, minority scholarships.

GIFT AID (NON-NEED-BASED) *Total amount:* $11,026,608 (1% federal, 5% state, 91% institutional, 3% external sources). *Receiving aid:* Freshmen: 64% (270). Undergraduates: 57% (908). *Average award:* Freshmen: $18,052. Undergraduates: $15,673. *Scholarships, grants, and awards by category: Academic interests/achievement:* biological sciences, business, communication, computer science, education, English, foreign languages, general academic interests/achievements, health fields, home economics, humanities, international studies, mathematics, physical sciences, premedicine, religion/biblical studies, social sciences. *Creative arts/performance:* art/fine arts, creative writing, dance, journalism/publications, music, performing arts, theater/drama. *Special achievements/activities:* cheerleading/drum major, community service, general special achievements/activities, leadership, religious involvement. *Special characteristics:* adult students, children and siblings of alumni, children of current students, children of faculty/staff, ethnic background, international students, local/state students, members of minority groups, religious affiliation, siblings of current students, spouses of current students, veterans. *Tuition waivers:* Full or partial for employees or children of employees. *ROTC:* Army cooperative, Air Force cooperative.

LOANS *Student loans:* $8,884,539 (53% need-based, 47% non-need-based). 67% of past graduating class borrowed through all loan programs. *Average indebtedness per student:* $36,950. *Average need-based loan:* Freshmen: $4460. Undergraduates: $5002. *Parent loans:* $648,816 (24% need-based, 76% non-need-based). *Programs:* Federal Direct (Subsidized and Unsubsidized Stafford, PLUS), Perkins, Federal Nursing, college/university, private loans, Minnesota SELF Loans.

WORK-STUDY *Federal work-study:* Total amount: $609,619; 327 jobs averaging $1815. *State or other work-study/employment:* Total amount: $103,779 (2% need-based, 98% non-need-based). 117 part-time jobs averaging $922.

ATHLETIC AWARDS Total amount: $3,705,007 (34% need-based, 66% non-need-based).

APPLYING FOR FINANCIAL AID *Required financial aid form:* FAFSA. *Financial aid deadline (priority):* 3/1. *Notification date:* Continuous beginning 4/1. Students must reply by 5/1 or within 4 weeks of notification.

CONTACT Ms. Tresse J. Evenson, Director of Financial Aid, Augustana University, 2001 South Summit Avenue, Sioux Falls, SD 57197, 605-274-5216 or toll-free 800-727-2844. *Fax:* 605-274-5295. *E-mail:* tresse.evenson@augie.edu. *Website:* http://www.augie.edu/.

AUGUSTANA UNIVERSITY
Sioux Falls, SD

Tuition & fees: $30,944	Average undergraduate aid package: $25,553

ABOUT THE INSTITUTION Independent Evangelical Lutheran Church in America, coed. *Awards:* bachelor's and master's degrees. 64 undergraduate majors. *Total enrollment:* 1,937. Undergraduates: 1,665. Freshmen: 424. Federal methodology is used as a basis for awarding need-based institutional aid.

UNDERGRADUATE EXPENSES for 2016–2017 *Comprehensive fee:* $38,424 includes full-time tuition ($30,454), mandatory fees ($490), and room and board ($7480). *College room only:* $3360. Full-time tuition and fees vary according to course load and degree level. Room and board charges vary according to board plan and housing facility. *Part-time tuition:* $450 per credit hour. Part-time tuition and fees vary according to course load and degree level.

FRESHMAN FINANCIAL AID (Fall 2016, est.) 337 applied for aid; of those 82% were deemed to have need. 100% of freshmen with need received aid; of those 28% had need fully met. *Average percent of need met:* 100% (excluding resources awarded to replace EFC). *Average financial aid package:* $28,520 (excluding resources awarded to replace EFC). 34% of all full-time freshmen had no need and received non-need-based gift aid.

UNDERGRADUATE FINANCIAL AID (Fall 2016, est.) 1,108 applied for aid; of those 85% were deemed to have need. 100% of undergraduates with need received

AUGUSTA UNIVERSITY
Augusta, GA

Tuition & fees (GA res): $8282	Average undergraduate aid package: $2390

ABOUT THE INSTITUTION State-supported, coed. *Awards:* certificates, associate, bachelor's, master's, and doctoral degrees. 40 undergraduate majors. *Total enrollment:* 7,918. Undergraduates: 5,133. Freshmen: 788. Federal methodology is used as a basis for awarding need-based institutional aid.

UNDERGRADUATE EXPENSES for 2017–2018 *Application fee:* $50. *Tuition, state resident:* full-time $6592; part-time $220 per credit hour. *Tuition, nonresident:* full-time $21,300; part-time $710 per credit hour. *Required fees:* full-time $1690. Full-time tuition and fees vary according to course load, location, and program. Part-time tuition and fees vary according to course load, location, and program. *College room and board:* $13,200. Room and board charges vary according to board plan and housing facility.

FRESHMAN FINANCIAL AID (Fall 2016, est.) 711 applied for aid; of those 78% were deemed to have need. 98% of freshmen with need received aid; of those 5% had need fully met. *Average financial aid package:* $2021 (excluding resources awarded to replace EFC). 1% of all full-time freshmen had no need and received non-need-based gift aid.

UNDERGRADUATE FINANCIAL AID (Fall 2016, est.) 3,070 applied for aid; of those 80% were deemed to have need. 97% of undergraduates with need received aid; of those 7% had need fully met. *Average financial aid package:* $2390 (excluding resources awarded to replace EFC). 1% of all full-time undergraduates had no need and received non-need-based gift aid.

GIFT AID (NEED-BASED) *Total amount:* $11,216,659 (88% federal, 12% external sources). *Receiving aid:* Freshmen: 48% (375); all full-time undergraduates: 40% (1,631). *Average award:* Freshmen: $2097; Undergraduates: $2216. *Scholarships, grants, and awards:* Federal Pell, FSEOG, state, private, college/university gift aid from institutional funds, Federal Nursing.

GIFT AID (NON-NEED-BASED) *Total amount:* $11,848,057 (87% state, 10% institutional, 3% external sources). *Receiving aid:* Freshmen: 50% (387). Undergraduates: 22% (903). *Average award:* Freshmen: $456. Undergraduates: $1421. *Scholarships, grants, and awards by category: Academic interests/achievement:* business, computer science, education, general academic interests/achievements, mathematics. *Creative arts/performance:* art/fine arts, music. *Special achievements/activities:* leadership. *Special characteristics:* local/state students, members of minority groups, religious affiliation, veterans. *Tuition waivers:* Full or partial for employees or children of employees, senior citizens. *ROTC:* Army.

LOANS *Student loans:* $18,881,775 (48% need-based, 52% non-need-based). *Average need-based loan:* Freshmen: $1881. Undergraduates: $2159. *Parent loans:* $1,622,782 (100% need-based). *Programs:* Federal Direct (Subsidized and Unsubsidized Stafford, PLUS), Perkins, Federal Nursing, state, college/university.

WORK-STUDY *Federal work-study:* Total amount: $437,791; 169 jobs averaging $2931.

ATHLETIC AWARDS Total amount: $940,286 (100% non-need-based).

APPLYING FOR FINANCIAL AID *Required financial aid form:* FAFSA. *Financial aid deadline:* 3/1 (priority: 3/1). *Notification date:* 5/1. Students must reply within 20 weeks of notification.

CONTACT Victoria Saraceno, Interim Director of Financial Aid, Augusta University, 1120 Fifteenth Street, Fanning Hall, Augusta, GA 30912-7320, 706-667-4199 or toll-free 800-519-3388. *Fax:* 706-737-1777. *E-mail:* vsaraceno@augusta.edu. *Website:* http://www.augusta.edu/.

AULTMAN COLLEGE OF NURSING AND HEALTH SCIENCES
Canton, OH

CONTACT Financial Aid Office, Aultman College of Nursing and Health Sciences, 2600 6th Street, SW, Canton, OH 44710, 330-363-6347. *Website:* http://www.aultmancollege.edu/.

AURORA UNIVERSITY
Aurora, IL

Tuition & fees: $23,520	Average undergraduate aid package: $20,413

ABOUT THE INSTITUTION Independent, coed. *Awards:* certificates, bachelor's, master's, and doctoral degrees. 40 undergraduate majors. *Total enrollment:* 5,643. Undergraduates: 3,796. Freshmen: 654. Federal methodology is used as a basis for awarding need-based institutional aid.

UNDERGRADUATE EXPENSES for 2017–2018 *Comprehensive fee:* $34,990 includes full-time tuition ($23,260), mandatory fees ($260), and room and board ($11,470). Full-time tuition and fees vary according to course load, location, and program. Room and board charges vary according to board plan, housing facility, and location. *Part-time tuition:* $670 per semester hour. Part-time tuition and fees vary according to course load, location, and program.

FRESHMAN FINANCIAL AID (Fall 2016, est.) 652 applied for aid; of those 86% were deemed to have need. 100% of freshmen with need received aid; of those 11% had need fully met. *Average percent of need met:* 81% (excluding resources awarded to replace EFC). *Average financial aid package:* $23,327 (excluding resources awarded to replace EFC). 14% of all full-time freshmen had no need and received non-need-based gift aid.

UNDERGRADUATE FINANCIAL AID (Fall 2016, est.) 2,869 applied for aid; of those 91% were deemed to have need. 100% of undergraduates with need received aid; of those 10% had need fully met. *Average percent of need met:* 79% (excluding resources awarded to replace EFC). *Average financial aid package:* $20,413 (excluding resources awarded to replace EFC). 18% of all full-time undergraduates had no need and received non-need-based gift aid.

GIFT AID (NEED-BASED) *Total amount:* $34,857,823 (21% federal, 19% state, 60% institutional). *Receiving aid:* Freshmen: 81% (531); all full-time undergraduates: 72% (2,381). *Average award:* Freshmen: $17,131; Undergraduates: $14,405. *Scholarships, grants, and awards:* Federal Pell, FSEOG, state, private, college/university gift aid from institutional funds.

GIFT AID (NON-NEED-BASED) *Total amount:* $9,476,526 (3% federal, 1% state, 93% institutional, 3% external sources). *Receiving aid:* Freshmen: 15% (99). Undergraduates: 14% (452). *Average award:* Freshmen: $11,637. Undergraduates: $9570. *Scholarships, grants, and awards by category: Academic interests/achievement:* 2,923 awards ($26,252,202 total): business, education, general academic interests/achievements. *Creative arts/performance:* 41 awards ($87,850 total): art/fine arts, music, theater/drama. *Special achievements/activities:* 13 awards ($25,000 total): leadership. *Special characteristics:* 749 awards ($1,245,756 total): children and siblings of alumni, children of current students, children of faculty/staff, out-of-state students, parents of current students, religious affiliation, siblings of current students, spouses of current students, veterans, veterans' children. *Tuition waivers:* Full or partial for children of alumni, employees or children of employees. *ROTC:* Army cooperative.

LOANS *Student loans:* $21,244,176 (73% need-based, 27% non-need-based). 83% of past graduating class borrowed through all loan programs. *Average indebtedness per student:* $27,578. *Average need-based loan:* Freshmen: $2707. Undergraduates: $3682. *Parent loans:* $3,754,567 (26% need-based, 74% non-need-based). *Programs:* Federal Direct (Subsidized and Unsubsidized Stafford, PLUS), private loans.

WORK-STUDY *Federal work-study:* Total amount: $3,708,745; 1,890 jobs averaging $1960. *State or other work-study/employment:* Total amount: $365,929 (48% need-based, 52% non-need-based). 35 part-time jobs averaging $9535.

APPLYING FOR FINANCIAL AID *Required financial aid form:* FAFSA. *Financial aid deadline:* Continuous. *Notification date:* Continuous beginning 3/1. Students must reply by 5/1.

CONTACT Ms. Heather Granart, Dean of Student Financial Services, Aurora University, 347 South Gladstone Avenue, Aurora, IL 60506-4892, 630-844-6190 or toll-free 800-742-5281. *Fax:* 630-844-6191. *E-mail:* finaid@aurora.edu. *Website:* http://www.aurora.edu/.

AUSTIN COLLEGE
Sherman, TX

Tuition & fees: $39,010	Average undergraduate aid package: $34,859

ABOUT THE INSTITUTION Independent Presbyterian, coed. *Awards:* bachelor's and master's degrees. 55 undergraduate majors. *Total enrollment:* 1,294. Undergraduates: 1,278. Freshmen: 345. Federal methodology is used as a basis for awarding need-based institutional aid.

UNDERGRADUATE EXPENSES for 2017–2018 *One-time required fee:* $25. *Comprehensive fee:* $51,344 includes full-time tuition ($38,825), mandatory fees ($185), and room and board ($12,334). Full-time tuition and fees vary according to student level. Room and board charges vary according to board plan and housing facility.

FRESHMAN FINANCIAL AID (Fall 2016, est.) 298 applied for aid; of those 85% were deemed to have need. 100% of freshmen with need received aid; of those 45% had need fully met. *Average percent of need met:* 95% (excluding resources awarded to replace EFC). *Average financial aid package:* $35,826 (excluding resources awarded to replace EFC). 26% of all full-time freshmen had no need and received non-need-based gift aid.

UNDERGRADUATE FINANCIAL AID (Fall 2016, est.) 952 applied for aid; of those 88% were deemed to have need. 100% of undergraduates with need received aid; of those 42% had need fully met. *Average percent of need met:* 94% (excluding resources awarded to replace EFC). *Average financial aid package:* $34,859 (excluding resources awarded to replace EFC). 33% of all full-time undergraduates had no need and received non-need-based gift aid.

GIFT AID (NEED-BASED) *Total amount:* $24,004,046 (9% federal, 6% state, 83% institutional, 2% external sources). *Receiving aid:* Freshmen: 74% (254); all full-time undergraduates: 65% (834). *Average award:* Freshmen: $30,923; Undergraduates: $29,091. *Scholarships, grants, and awards:* Federal Pell, FSEOG, state, private, college/university gift aid from institutional funds.

GIFT AID (NON-NEED-BASED) *Total amount:* $10,130,407 (99% institutional, 1% external sources). *Receiving aid:* Freshmen: 16% (55). Undergraduates: 11% (146). *Average award:* Freshmen: $24,248. Undergraduates: $22,355. *Scholarships, grants, and awards by category:* Academic interests/achievement: 88 awards: biological sciences, business, communication, education, engineering/technologies, English, foreign languages, general academic interests/achievements, home economics, humanities, international studies, physical sciences, premedicine, religion/biblical studies, social sciences. *Creative arts/performance:* 3 awards: art/fine arts, music, theater/drama. *Special achievements/activities:* 5 awards: community service, general special achievements/activities, leadership, religious involvement. *Special characteristics:* 20 awards: children of faculty/staff, first-generation college students, general special characteristics, international students, local/state students, out-of-state students, previous college experience, relatives of clergy, religious affiliation, veterans. *Tuition waivers:* Full or partial for employees or children of employees.

LOANS *Student loans:* $6,342,151 (66% need-based, 34% non-need-based). *Average need-based loan:* Freshmen: $3528. Undergraduates: $4792. *Parent loans:* $3,166,155 (27% need-based, 73% non-need-based). *Programs:* Federal Direct (Subsidized and Unsubsidized Stafford, PLUS), Perkins, state, private loans.

WORK-STUDY *Federal work-study:* Total amount: $638,890; 345 jobs averaging $1844. *State or other work-study/employment:* Total amount: $162,039 (23% need-based, 77% non-need-based). 119 part-time jobs averaging $1464.

APPLYING FOR FINANCIAL AID *Required financial aid form:* FAFSA. *Financial aid deadline (priority):* 3/1. *Notification date:* Continuous beginning 12/1. Students must reply by 5/1.

CONTACT Mrs. Laurie Coulter, Executive Director of Financial Aid, Austin College, 900 North Grand Avenue, Sherman, TX 75090, 903-813-2900 or toll-free 800-596-4276 (in-state), 800-526.4276 (out-of-state). *Fax:* 903-813-3198. *E-mail:* finaid@austincollege.edu.
Website: http://www.austincollege.edu/.

AUSTIN GRADUATE SCHOOL OF THEOLOGY
Austin, TX

Tuition & fees: $8750	Average undergraduate aid package: N/A

ABOUT THE INSTITUTION Independent Church of Christ, coed. *Awards:* bachelor's and master's degrees. 1 undergraduate major. *Total enrollment:* 41. Undergraduates: 20. Both federal and institutional methodology are used as a basis for awarding need-based institutional aid.

UNDERGRADUATE EXPENSES for 2017–2018 *Tuition:* full-time $8400; part-time $350 per credit hour. *Required fees:* full-time $350; $175 per term.

GIFT AID (NEED-BASED) *Scholarships, grants, and awards:* Federal Pell, FSEOG, college/university gift aid from institutional funds.

GIFT AID (NON-NEED-BASED) *Scholarships, grants, and awards by category:* Academic interests/achievement: religion/biblical studies. *Special achievements/activities:* religious involvement.

LOANS *Programs:* Federal Direct (Subsidized and Unsubsidized Stafford, PLUS).

WORK-STUDY Federal work-study jobs available.

APPLYING FOR FINANCIAL AID *Required financial aid forms:* FAFSA, institution's own form. *Financial aid deadline:* Continuous. *Notification date:* Continuous.

CONTACT David Arthur, Director of Financial Aid, Austin Graduate School of Theology, 7640 Guadalupe Street, Austin, TX 78752, 512-476-2772 Ext. 105 or toll-free 866-AUS-GRAD. *Fax:* 512-476-3919. *E-mail:* darthur@austingrad.edu.
Website: http://www.austingrad.edu/.

AUSTIN PEAY STATE UNIVERSITY
Clarksville, TN

Tuition & fees (TN res): $7689	Average undergraduate aid package: $10,840

ABOUT THE INSTITUTION State-supported, coed. *Awards:* certificates, associate, bachelor's, and master's degrees. 36 undergraduate majors. *Total enrollment:* 10,344. Undergraduates: 9,513. Freshmen: 1,963. Federal methodology is used as a basis for awarding need-based institutional aid.

UNDERGRADUATE EXPENSES for 2017–2018 *Application fee:* $25. *One-time required fee:* $75. *Tuition, state resident:* full-time $6216; part-time $259 per credit hour. *Tuition, nonresident:* full-time $21,456; part-time $894 per credit hour. *Required fees:* full-time $1473. Full-time tuition and fees vary according to location and program. Part-time tuition and fees vary according to location and program. *College room and board:* $8708; *Room only:* $5360. Room and board charges vary according to board plan and housing facility.

FRESHMAN FINANCIAL AID (Fall 2015) 1,247 applied for aid; of those 87% were deemed to have need. 99% of freshmen with need received aid. *Average financial aid package:* $11,153 (excluding resources awarded to replace EFC). 11% of all full-time freshmen had no need and received non-need-based gift aid.

UNDERGRADUATE FINANCIAL AID (Fall 2015) 6,267 applied for aid; of those 88% were deemed to have need. 97% of undergraduates with need received aid. *Average financial aid package:* $10,840 (excluding resources awarded to replace EFC). 8% of all full-time undergraduates had no need and received non-need-based gift aid.

GIFT AID (NEED-BASED) *Total amount:* $26,909,365 (82% federal, 18% state). *Receiving aid:* Freshmen: 71% (911); all full-time undergraduates: 70% (4,736). *Average award:* Freshmen: $7329; Undergraduates: $7480. *Scholarships, grants, and awards:* Federal Pell, FSEOG, state, private, college/university gift aid from institutional funds.

GIFT AID (NON-NEED-BASED) *Total amount:* $27,299,052 (38% state, 14% institutional, 48% external sources). *Receiving aid:* Freshmen: 69% (884). Undergraduates: 48% (3,233). *Average award:* Freshmen: $4869. Undergraduates: $4808. *Scholarships, grants, and awards by category:* Academic interests/achievement: 800 awards ($1,513,386 total): agriculture, biological sciences, business, communication, computer science, education, English, foreign languages, general academic interests/achievements, health fields, humanities, international studies, mathematics, military science, physical sciences, social sciences. *Creative arts/performance:* 530 awards ($301,970 total): art/fine arts, creative writing, debating, journalism/publications, music, performing arts, theater/drama. *Special achievements/activities:* 166 awards ($135,430 total): general special achievements/activities, leadership, memberships. *Special characteristics:* 108 awards ($124,799 total): children of educators, children of faculty/staff, ethnic background, general special characteristics, members of minority groups, veterans. *Tuition waivers:* Full or partial for employees or children of employees, senior citizens. *ROTC:* Army, Air Force cooperative.

LOANS *Student loans:* $37,517,045 (48% need-based, 52% non-need-based). 69% of past graduating class borrowed through all loan programs. *Average indebtedness per student:* $23,808. *Average need-based loan:* Freshmen: $3081. Undergraduates: $3863. *Parent loans:* $5,753,012 (100% non-need-based). *Programs:* Federal Direct (Subsidized and Unsubsidized Stafford, PLUS), Perkins.

WORK-STUDY *Federal work-study:* 137 jobs averaging $2482. *State or other work-study/employment:* Total amount: $753,905 (100% non-need-based). 486 part-time jobs averaging $1551.

ATHLETIC AWARDS Total amount: $3,835,574 (100% non-need-based).

APPLYING FOR FINANCIAL AID *Required financial aid form:* FAFSA. *Financial aid deadline:* Continuous. *Notification date:* Continuous beginning 4/7.

CONTACT Ms. Donna Price, Director of Student Financial Aid, Austin Peay State University, PO Box 4546, Clarksville, TN 37044, 931-221-7907 or toll-free 800-844-2778. *Fax:* 931-221-6329. *E-mail:* priced@apsu.edu.
Website: http://www.apsu.edu/.

AVE MARIA UNIVERSITY
Ave Maria, FL

Tuition & fees: N/R	Average undergraduate aid package: $17,812

ABOUT THE INSTITUTION Independent Roman Catholic, coed. *Awards:* bachelor's, master's, and doctoral degrees. 30 undergraduate majors. *Total enrollment:* 1,108. Undergraduates: 1,068. Freshmen: 303. Federal methodology is used as a basis for awarding need-based institutional aid.

FRESHMAN FINANCIAL AID (Fall 2016, est.) 221 applied for aid; of those 84% were deemed to have need. 100% of freshmen with need received aid; of those 26% had need fully met. *Average percent of need met:* 75% (excluding resources awarded to replace EFC). *Average financial aid package:* $16,763 (excluding resources awarded to replace EFC). 29% of all full-time freshmen had no need and received non-need-based gift aid.

UNDERGRADUATE FINANCIAL AID (Fall 2016, est.) 721 applied for aid; of those 84% were deemed to have need. 100% of undergraduates with need received aid; of those 24% had need fully met. *Average percent of need met:* 76% (excluding resources awarded to replace EFC). *Average financial aid package:* $17,812 (excluding resources awarded to replace EFC). 37% of all full-time undergraduates had no need and received non-need-based gift aid.

GIFT AID (NEED-BASED) *Total amount:* $7,057,381 (18% federal, 11% state, 69% institutional, 2% external sources). *Receiving aid:* Freshmen: 70% (186); all full-time undergraduates: 58% (602). *Average award:* Freshmen: $13,394; Undergraduates: $13,683. *Scholarships, grants, and awards:* Federal Pell, FSEOG, state, private, college/university gift aid from institutional funds.

GIFT AID (NON-NEED-BASED) *Total amount:* $4,366,729 (14% state, 84% institutional, 2% external sources). *Receiving aid:* Freshmen: 14% (36). Undergraduates: 9% (95). *Average award:* Freshmen: $7843. Undergraduates: $8957. *Scholarships, grants, and awards by category:* Creative arts/performance: 29 awards ($50,844 total): music. *Special achievements/activities:* 272 awards ($606,500 total): leadership. *Special characteristics:* 507 awards ($1,122,628 total): children of faculty/staff, religious affiliation, siblings of current students.

LOANS *Student loans:* $4,375,601 (61% need-based, 39% non-need-based). 66% of past graduating class borrowed through all loan programs. *Average indebtedness per student:* $25,962. *Average need-based loan:* Freshmen: $3155. Undergraduates: $3986. *Parent loans:* $1,288,735 (36% need-based, 64% non-need-based). *Programs:* Federal Direct (Subsidized and Unsubsidized Stafford, PLUS), college/university.

WORK-STUDY *Federal work-study:* Total amount: $131,361; 90 jobs averaging $1459. *State or other work-study/employment:* Total amount: $6260 (100% need-based). 3 part-time jobs averaging $2087.

ATHLETIC AWARDS Total amount: $3,428,804 (64% need-based, 36% non-need-based).

APPLYING FOR FINANCIAL AID *Required financial aid forms:* FAFSA, state aid form. *Financial aid deadline (priority):* 4/1. *Notification date:* Continuous beginning 11/1.

CONTACT Anne Hart, Director of Financial Aid, Ave Maria University, 5050 Ave Maria Boulevard, Ave Maria, FL 34142, 239-280-1669 or toll-free 877-283-8648. *Fax:* 239-280-2566. *E-mail:* amufinancialaid@avemaria.edu. *Website:* http://www.avemaria.edu/.

AVERETT UNIVERSITY
Danville, VA

Tuition & fees: $31,980	Average undergraduate aid package: $25,270

ABOUT THE INSTITUTION Independent Baptist General Association of Virginia, coed. *Awards:* bachelor's and master's degrees. 55 undergraduate majors. *Total enrollment:* 859. Undergraduates: 859. Freshmen: 237. Both federal and institutional methodology are used as a basis for awarding need-based institutional aid.

UNDERGRADUATE EXPENSES for 2016–2017 *Comprehensive fee:* $40,970 includes full-time tuition ($31,980) and room and board ($8990). *College room only:* $6070. Full-time tuition and fees vary according to class time, course load, degree level, location, and program. Room and board charges vary according to

board plan and housing facility. *Part-time tuition:* $1000 per credit. Part-time tuition and fees vary according to class time, course load, degree level, location, and program.

FRESHMAN FINANCIAL AID (Fall 2016, est.) 216 applied for aid; of those 96% were deemed to have need. 100% of freshmen with need received aid; of those 13% had need fully met. *Average percent of need met:* 71% (excluding resources awarded to replace EFC). *Average financial aid package:* $25,800 (excluding resources awarded to replace EFC). 12% of all full-time freshmen had no need and received non-need-based gift aid.

UNDERGRADUATE FINANCIAL AID (Fall 2016, est.) 749 applied for aid; of those 95% were deemed to have need. 100% of undergraduates with need received aid; of those 15% had need fully met. *Average percent of need met:* 73% (excluding resources awarded to replace EFC). *Average financial aid package:* $25,270 (excluding resources awarded to replace EFC). 14% of all full-time undergraduates had no need and received non-need-based gift aid.

GIFT AID (NEED-BASED) *Total amount:* $15,419,320 (13% federal, 9% state, 69% institutional, 9% external sources). *Receiving aid:* Freshmen: 88% (207); all full-time undergraduates: 86% (715). *Average award:* Freshmen: $22,289; Undergraduates: $21,485. *Scholarships, grants, and awards:* Federal Pell, FSEOG, state, private, college/university gift aid from institutional funds.

GIFT AID (NON-NEED-BASED) *Total amount:* $2,411,948 (9% state, 80% institutional, 11% external sources). *Receiving aid:* Freshmen: 10% (23). Undergraduates: 10% (84). *Average award:* Freshmen: $17,037. Undergraduates: $14,110. *Scholarships, grants, and awards by category:* Academic interests/achievement: 294 awards ($584,593 total): biological sciences, business, education, engineering/technologies, English, foreign languages, general academic interests/achievements, health fields, home economics, humanities, mathematics, physical sciences, premedicine, religion/biblical studies. *Creative arts/performance:* 10 awards ($15,000 total): art/fine arts, journalism/publications, music, theater/drama. *Special achievements/activities:* 79 awards ($96,626 total): general special achievements/activities, leadership, memberships, religious involvement. *Special characteristics:* 245 awards ($346,758 total): adult students, children and siblings of alumni, children of union members/company employees, first-generation college students, general special characteristics, international students, local/state students, out-of-state students, relatives of clergy, religious affiliation. *Tuition waivers:* Full or partial for employees or children of employees, senior citizens.

LOANS *Student loans:* $5,663,653 (82% need-based, 18% non-need-based). 81% of past graduating class borrowed through all loan programs. *Average indebtedness per student:* $35,659. *Average need-based loan:* Freshmen: $3783. Undergraduates: $4358. *Parent loans:* $4,013,393 (54% need-based, 46% non-need-based). *Programs:* Federal Direct (Subsidized and Unsubsidized Stafford, PLUS), Perkins, state, alternative loans.

WORK-STUDY *Federal work-study:* Total amount: $156,446; 163 jobs averaging $918. *State or other work-study/employment:* Part-time jobs available.

APPLYING FOR FINANCIAL AID *Required financial aid forms:* FAFSA, state aid form. *Financial aid deadline (priority):* 4/1. *Notification date:* Continuous beginning 11/1. Students must reply by 4/1 or within 2 weeks of notification.

CONTACT Carl Bradsher, Dean of Financial Assistance, Averett University, 420 West Main Street, Danville, VA 24541-3692, 434-791-5646 or toll-free 800-AVERETT. *Fax:* 434-791-5647. *E-mail:* carl.bradsher@averett.edu. *Website:* http://www.averett.edu/.

AVILA UNIVERSITY
Kansas City, MO

CONTACT Nancy Merz, Director of Financial Aid, Avila University, 11901 Wornall Road, Kansas City, MO 64145, 816-501-3782 or toll-free 800-GO-AVILA. *Fax:* 816-501-2462. *E-mail:* nancy.merz@avila.edu. *Website:* http://www.avila.edu/.

AZUSA PACIFIC UNIVERSITY
Azusa, CA

Tuition & fees: $36,120	Average undergraduate aid package: $7071

ABOUT THE INSTITUTION Independent nondenominational, coed. *Awards:* certificates, bachelor's, master's, and doctoral degrees. 36 undergraduate majors. *Total enrollment:* 10,020. Undergraduates: 5,770. Freshmen: 1,137. Federal methodology is used as a basis for awarding need-based institutional aid.

UNDERGRADUATE EXPENSES for 2016–2017 Tuition: full-time $35,540; part-time $1481 per credit hour. Full-time tuition and fees vary according to course load and degree level. Part-time tuition and fees vary according to course load and degree level. Room and board charges vary according to board plan and housing facility.

FRESHMAN FINANCIAL AID (Fall 2015) 1,163 applied for aid; of those 79% were deemed to have need. 100% of freshmen with need received aid; of those 44% had need fully met. *Average percent of need met:* 66% (excluding resources awarded to replace EFC). *Average financial aid package:* $5904 (excluding resources awarded to replace EFC). 10% of all full-time freshmen had no need and received non-need-based gift aid.

UNDERGRADUATE FINANCIAL AID (Fall 2015) 5,149 applied for aid; of those 79% were deemed to have need. 100% of undergraduates with need received aid; of those 42% had need fully met. *Average percent of need met:* 64% (excluding resources awarded to replace EFC). *Average financial aid package:* $7071 (excluding resources awarded to replace EFC). 10% of all full-time undergraduates had no need and received non-need-based gift aid.

GIFT AID (NEED-BASED) Total amount: $76,303,573 (13% federal, 15% state, 68% institutional, 4% external sources). *Receiving aid:* Freshmen: 76% (907); all full-time undergraduates: 74% (3,959). *Average award:* Freshmen: $3501; Undergraduates: $3604. *Scholarships, grants, and awards:* Federal Pell, FSEOG, state, private, college/university gift aid from institutional funds.

GIFT AID (NON-NEED-BASED) Total amount: $12,660,798 (85% institutional, 15% external sources). *Receiving aid:* Freshmen: 8% (95). Undergraduates: 5% (268). *Average award:* Freshmen: $11,405. Undergraduates: $8198. *ROTC:* Army, Air Force cooperative.

LOANS Student loans: $35,899,620 (80% need-based, 20% non-need-based). 66% of past graduating class borrowed through all loan programs. *Average indebtedness per student:* $24,338. *Average need-based loan:* Freshmen: $3592. Undergraduates: $4800. *Parent loans:* $15,512,058 (57% need-based, 43% non-need-based).

WORK-STUDY Federal work-study: jobs available.

ATHLETIC AWARDS Total amount: $5,013,703 (60% need-based, 40% non-need-based).

APPLYING FOR FINANCIAL AID Notification date: Continuous.

CONTACT Todd Ross, Associate Vice-President for Undergraduate Academic and Financial Services, Azusa Pacific University, 901 East Alosta Avenue, PO Box 7000, Azusa, CA 91702-7000, 626-812-3009 or toll-free 800-TALK-APU. *E-mail:* tross@apu.edu.
Website: http://www.apu.edu/.

BABSON COLLEGE
Wellesley, MA

Tuition & fees: N/R	Average undergraduate aid package: $40,358

ABOUT THE INSTITUTION Independent, coed. *Awards:* certificates, bachelor's, and master's degrees. 24 undergraduate majors. *Total enrollment:* 3,057. Undergraduates: 2,141. Freshmen: 528. Both federal and institutional methodology are used as a basis for awarding need-based institutional aid.

FRESHMAN FINANCIAL AID (Fall 2016, est.) 308 applied for aid; of those 77% were deemed to have need. 100% of freshmen with need received aid; of those 56% had need fully met. *Average percent of need met:* 97% (excluding resources awarded to replace EFC). *Average financial aid package:* $39,384 (excluding resources awarded to replace EFC). 5% of all full-time freshmen had no need and received non-need-based gift aid.

UNDERGRADUATE FINANCIAL AID (Fall 2016, est.) 1,072 applied for aid; of those 89% were deemed to have need. 100% of undergraduates with need received aid; of those 53% had need fully met. *Average percent of need met:* 97%

(excluding resources awarded to replace EFC). *Average financial aid package:* $40,358 (excluding resources awarded to replace EFC). 7% of all full-time undergraduates had no need and received non-need-based gift aid.

GIFT AID (NEED-BASED) Total amount: $33,869,000 (5% federal, 1% state, 94% institutional). *Receiving aid:* Freshmen: 36% (211); all full-time undergraduates: 40% (906). *Average award:* Freshmen: $37,126; Undergraduates: $37,388. *Scholarships, grants, and awards:* Federal Pell, FSEOG, state, college/university gift aid from institutional funds.

GIFT AID (NON-NEED-BASED) Total amount: $3,293,000 (82% institutional, 18% external sources). *Receiving aid:* Freshmen: 5% (29). Undergraduates: 7% (168). *Average award:* Freshmen: $21,646. Undergraduates: $17,687. *Scholarships, grants, and awards by category:* Academic interests/achievement: business, general academic interests/achievements. Special achievements/activities: leadership. Special characteristics: veterans. *ROTC:* Army cooperative, Naval cooperative, Air Force cooperative.

LOANS Student loans: $8,138,000 (41% need-based, 59% non-need-based). 44% of past graduating class borrowed through all loan programs. *Average indebtedness per student:* $36,556. *Average need-based loan:* Freshmen: $3557. Undergraduates: $5041. *Parent loans:* $2,902,000 (100% non-need-based). *Programs:* Federal Direct (Subsidized and Unsubsidized Stafford, PLUS), state.

WORK-STUDY Federal work-study: Total amount: $1,429,000; jobs available. *State or other work-study/employment:* Total amount: $202,000 (100% non-need-based). Part-time jobs available.

APPLYING FOR FINANCIAL AID Required financial aid forms: FAFSA, CSS Financial Aid PROFILE, noncustodial (divorced/separated) parent's statement, federal income tax form(s), W-2 forms, verification worksheet. *Financial aid deadline:* 2/1. *Notification date:* 4/1. Students must reply by 5/1.

CONTACT Ms. Meredith Stover, Director of Financial Aid, Babson College, Hollister Hall, Third Floor, Babson Park, MA 02457-0310, 781-239-4219 or toll-free 800-488-3696. *Fax:* 781-239-5510. *E-mail:* stoverm@babson.edu.
Website: http://www.babson.edu/.

BACONE COLLEGE
Muskogee, OK

ABOUT THE INSTITUTION Independent American Baptist Churches in the U.S.A., coed. 26 undergraduate majors.

GIFT AID (NEED-BASED) Scholarships, grants, and awards: Federal Pell, FSEOG, state, private, college/university gift aid from institutional funds.

WORK-STUDY Federal work-study jobs available.

APPLYING FOR FINANCIAL AID Required financial aid forms: FAFSA, institution's own form.

CONTACT Mrs. Misty Oleson, Assistant Director of Financial Aid, Bacone College, 2299 Old Bacone Road, Muskogee, OK 74403-1597, 918-781-7225 or toll-free 888-682-5514 Ext. 7340. *Fax:* 866-498-1487. *E-mail:* finaid@bacone.edu.
Website: http://www.bacone.edu/.

BAIS BINYOMIN ACADEMY
Stamford, CT

CONTACT Financial Aid Office, Bais Binyomin Academy, 132 Prospect Street, Stamford, CT 06901-1202, 203-325-4351.

BAIS HAMEDRASH AND MESIVTA OF BALTIMORE
Baltimore, MD

CONTACT Financial Aid Office, Bais HaMedrash and Mesivta of Baltimore, 6823 Old Pimlico Road, Baltimore, MD 21209, 410-486-0006.

BAKER COLLEGE
Flint, MI

CONTACT Financial Aid Office, Baker College, Baker College System Headquarters, 1050 West Bristol Road, Flint, MI 48507, 810-766-4000 or toll-free 800-964-4299. *Website:* http://www.baker.edu/.

BAKER UNIVERSITY
Baldwin City, KS

Tuition & fees: $28,880	Average undergraduate aid package: N/A

ABOUT THE INSTITUTION Independent United Methodist, coed. *Awards:* bachelor's, master's, and doctoral degrees (profile includes information primarily for undergraduate residential campus in Baldwin City, KS). 34 undergraduate majors. *Total enrollment:* 1,144. Undergraduates: 1,144. Freshmen: 238. Federal methodology is used as a basis for awarding need-based institutional aid.

UNDERGRADUATE EXPENSES for 2017–2018 *One-time required fee:* $80. *Comprehensive fee:* $37,190 includes full-time tuition ($28,430), mandatory fees ($450), and room and board ($8310). *College room only:* $3910. Full-time tuition and fees vary according to course load, degree level, location, and program. Room and board charges vary according to board plan and housing facility. *Part-time tuition:* $890 per credit hour. *Part-time fees:* $200 per year. Part-time tuition and fees vary according to course load, degree level, location, and program.

GIFT AID (NEED-BASED) *Scholarships, grants, and awards:* Federal Pell, FSEOG, state, private, college/university gift aid from institutional funds.

GIFT AID (NON-NEED-BASED) *Scholarships, grants, and awards by category: Academic interests/achievement:* general academic interests/achievements. *Creative arts/performance:* art/fine arts, cinema/film/broadcasting, dance, debating, journalism/publications, music, theater/drama. *Special achievements/activities:* cheerleading/drum major, leadership, religious involvement. *Special characteristics:* children and siblings of alumni, children of faculty/staff, ethnic background, international students, members of minority groups, out-of-state students, relatives of clergy, religious affiliation. *Tuition waivers:* Full or partial for employees or children of employees, senior citizens. *ROTC:* Army cooperative, Air Force cooperative.

LOANS *Student loans:* 81% of past graduating class borrowed through all loan programs. *Average indebtedness per student:* $26,869. *Programs:* Perkins, alternative loans.

WORK-STUDY Federal work-study jobs available. *State or other work-study/ employment:* Part-time jobs available.

APPLYING FOR FINANCIAL AID *Required financial aid forms:* FAFSA, institution's own form. *Financial aid deadline (priority):* 3/1. *Notification date:* Continuous. Students must reply by 5/1 or within 6 weeks of notification.

CONTACT Mrs. Jeanne Mott, Financial Aid Director, Baker University, Box 65, Baldwin City, KS 66006-0065, 785-594-4595 or toll-free 800-873-4282. *Fax:* 785-594-8358. *Website:* http://www.bakeru.edu/.

BALDWIN WALLACE UNIVERSITY
Berea, OH

Tuition & fees: $31,668	Average undergraduate aid package: $23,841

ABOUT THE INSTITUTION Independent Methodist, coed. *Awards:* certificates, bachelor's, and master's degrees. 77 undergraduate majors. *Total enrollment:* 3,951. Undergraduates: 3,305. Freshmen: 706. Federal methodology is used as a basis for awarding need-based institutional aid.

UNDERGRADUATE EXPENSES for 2017–2018 *Application fee:* $25. *Comprehensive fee:* $40,810 includes full-time tuition ($31,668) and room and board ($9142). *College room only:* $5280. Full-time tuition and fees vary according to class time, course level, course load, degree level, program, and reciprocity agreements. Room and board charges vary according to housing facility. *Part-time tuition:* $984 per credit hour. Part-time tuition and fees vary according to class time, course level, course load, degree level, program, and reciprocity agreements.

FRESHMAN FINANCIAL AID (Fall 2016, est.) 674 applied for aid; of those 86% were deemed to have need. 100% of freshmen with need received aid; of those 20% had need fully met. *Average percent of need met:* 87% (excluding resources awarded to replace EFC). *Average financial aid package:* $24,408 (excluding resources awarded to replace EFC). 18% of all full-time freshmen had no need and received non-need-based gift aid.

UNDERGRADUATE FINANCIAL AID (Fall 2016, est.) 2,557 applied for aid; of those 87% were deemed to have need. 100% of undergraduates with need received aid; of those 43% had need fully met. *Average percent of need met:* 86% (excluding resources awarded to replace EFC). *Average financial aid package:* $23,841 (excluding resources awarded to replace EFC). 11% of all full-time undergraduates had no need and received non-need-based gift aid.

GIFT AID (NEED-BASED) *Total amount:* $41,110,274 (12% federal, 4% state, 82% institutional, 2% external sources). *Receiving aid:* Freshmen: 82% (578); all full-time undergraduates: 73% (2,221). *Average award:* Freshmen: $20,749; Undergraduates: $19,305. *Scholarships, grants, and awards:* Federal Pell, FSEOG, state, private, college/university gift aid from institutional funds.

GIFT AID (NON-NEED-BASED) *Total amount:* $8,318,277 (1% state, 98% institutional, 1% external sources). *Receiving aid:* Freshmen: 16% (113). Undergraduates: 32% (956). *Average award:* Freshmen: $14,011. Undergraduates: $13,832. *Scholarships, grants, and awards by category: Academic interests/ achievement:* 2,589 awards ($24,444,000 total): general academic interests/achievements. *Creative arts/performance:* 211 awards ($925,000 total): music. *Special achievements/activities:* leadership. *Special characteristics:* 1,479 awards ($4,479,000 total): children and siblings of alumni, members of minority groups, religious affiliation, siblings of current students. *Tuition waivers:* Full or partial for children of alumni, employees or children of employees. *ROTC:* Army cooperative, Air Force cooperative.

LOANS *Student loans:* $18,876,870 (61% need-based, 39% non-need-based). 80% of past graduating class borrowed through all loan programs. *Average indebtedness per student:* $34,423. *Average need-based loan:* Freshmen: $4167. Undergraduates: $4678. *Parent loans:* $4,830,217 (68% need-based, 32% non-need-based). *Programs:* Federal Direct (Subsidized and Unsubsidized Stafford, PLUS), Perkins.

WORK-STUDY *Federal work-study:* Total amount: $466,000; 919 jobs averaging $1449. *State or other work-study/employment:* Total amount: $1,387,682 (62% need-based, 38% non-need-based). 527 part-time jobs averaging $1446.

APPLYING FOR FINANCIAL AID *Required financial aid form:* FAFSA. *Financial aid deadline (priority):* 8/15. *Notification date:* Continuous beginning 1/23.

CONTACT Dr. George L. Rolleston, Director of Financial Aid, Baldwin Wallace University, 275 Eastland Road, Berea, OH 44017-2088, 440-826-2108 or toll-free 877-BW-APPLY. *Fax:* 440-826-8048. *E-mail:* grollest@bw.edu. *Website:* http://www.bw.edu/.

BALL STATE UNIVERSITY
Muncie, IN

Tuition & fees (IN res): $9848	Average undergraduate aid package: $12,659

ABOUT THE INSTITUTION State-supported, coed. *Awards:* certificates, bachelor's, master's, and doctoral degrees. 95 undergraduate majors. *Total enrollment:* 21,998. Undergraduates: 17,011. Freshmen: 3,877. Federal methodology is used as a basis for awarding need-based institutional aid.

UNDERGRADUATE EXPENSES for 2017–2018 *Tuition, state resident:* full-time $9172; part-time $302 per credit hour. *Tuition, nonresident:* full-time $25,262; part-time $1000 per credit hour. *Required fees:* full-time $676. Full-time tuition and fees vary according to program and reciprocity agreements. Part-time tuition and fees vary according to course load, program, and reciprocity agreements. *College room and board:* $10,038. Room and board charges vary according to board plan and housing facility.

FRESHMAN FINANCIAL AID (Fall 2016, est.) 3,681 applied for aid; of those 77% were deemed to have need. 100% of freshmen with need received aid; of those 40% had need fully met. *Average percent of need met:* 71% (excluding resources awarded to replace EFC). *Average financial aid package:* $13,496 (excluding resources awarded to replace EFC). 14% of all full-time freshmen had no need and received non-need-based gift aid.

UNDERGRADUATE FINANCIAL AID (Fall 2016, est.) 12,927 applied for aid; of those 79% were deemed to have need. 100% of undergraduates with need received aid; of those 41% had need fully met. *Average percent of need met:* 68% (excluding resources awarded to replace EFC). *Average financial aid package:* $12,659 (excluding resources awarded to replace EFC). 13% of all full-time undergraduates had no need and received non-need-based gift aid.

GIFT AID (NEED-BASED) *Total amount:* $35,069,400 (70% federal, 16% state, 14% institutional). *Receiving aid:* Freshmen: 47% (1,810); all full-time undergraduates: 40% (5,959). *Average award:* Freshmen: $6006; Undergraduates: $5742. *Scholarships, grants, and awards:* Federal Pell, FSEOG, state, private, college/university gift aid from institutional funds.

GIFT AID (NON-NEED-BASED) *Total amount:* $68,134,812 (2% federal, 34% state, 52% institutional, 12% external sources). *Receiving aid:* Freshmen: 52% (1,999). Undergraduates: 38% (5,679). *Average award:* Freshmen: $7594. Undergraduates: $8386. *Scholarships, grants, and awards by category: Academic interests/achievement:* 6,157 awards ($23,967,584 total): architecture, biological sciences, business, communication, education, engineering/technologies, English, foreign languages, general academic interests/achievements, health fields, humanities, international studies, mathematics, military science, physical sciences, social sciences. *Creative arts/performance:* 189 awards ($212,799 total): cinema/film/broadcasting, dance, debating, general creative arts/performance, journalism/publications, music, performing arts, theater/drama. *Special achievements/activities:* 46 awards ($227,171 total): community service, general special achievements/activities, leadership. *Special characteristics:* 1,531 awards ($13,781,434 total): adult students, children of faculty/staff, ethnic background, general special characteristics, international students, local/state students, members of minority groups, out-of-state students, veterans, veterans' children. *Tuition waivers:* Full or partial for employees or children of employees, senior citizens. *ROTC:* Army.

LOANS *Student loans:* $104,138,471 (39% need-based, 61% non-need-based). 72% of past graduating class borrowed through all loan programs. *Average indebtedness per student:* $27,617. *Average need-based loan:* Freshmen: $3728. Undergraduates: $4434. *Parent loans:* $25,953,594 (100% non-need-based). *Programs:* Federal Direct (Subsidized and Unsubsidized Stafford, PLUS), Perkins, college/university.

WORK-STUDY *Federal work-study:* Total amount: $3,620,091; 748 jobs averaging $2500. *State or other work-study/employment:* Total amount: $9,341,522 (100% non-need-based). Part-time jobs available.

ATHLETIC AWARDS Total amount: $7,595,999 (100% non-need-based).

APPLYING FOR FINANCIAL AID *Required financial aid form:* FAFSA. *Financial aid deadline (priority):* 3/10. *Notification date:* Continuous beginning 4/1.

CONTACT Dr. John McPherson, Assistant Vice President of Enrollment Services/Executive Director of Financial Aid and Scholarships, Ball State University, Lucina Hall, Room 245, Muncie, IN 47306, 765-285-8894 or toll-free 800-482-4BSU. *Fax:* 765-285-4247. *E-mail:* finaid@bsu.edu. *Website:* http://www.bsu.edu/.

UNDERGRADUATE EXPENSES for 2017–2018 *Application fee:* $25. *Comprehensive fee:* $15,238 includes full-time tuition ($10,200), mandatory fees ($900), and room and board ($4138). Full-time tuition and fees vary according to location and program. Room and board charges vary according to board plan and housing facility. *Part-time tuition:* $340 per credit hour. *Part-time fees:* $30 per credit. Part-time tuition and fees vary according to location and program.

FRESHMAN FINANCIAL AID (Fall 2016, est.) 45 applied for aid; of those 78% were deemed to have need. 77% of freshmen with need received aid. *Average percent of need met:* 41% (excluding resources awarded to replace EFC). *Average financial aid package:* $8856 (excluding resources awarded to replace EFC). 4% of all full-time freshmen had no need and received non-need-based gift aid.

UNDERGRADUATE FINANCIAL AID (Fall 2016, est.) 336 applied for aid; of those 88% were deemed to have need. 86% of undergraduates with need received aid; of those 4% had need fully met. *Average percent of need met:* 41% (excluding resources awarded to replace EFC). *Average financial aid package:* $8517 (excluding resources awarded to replace EFC). 5% of all full-time undergraduates had no need and received non-need-based gift aid.

GIFT AID (NEED-BASED) *Total amount:* $1,635,534 (58% federal, 22% state, 16% institutional, 4% external sources). *Receiving aid:* Freshmen: 57% (27); all full-time undergraduates: 65% (246). *Average award:* Freshmen: $7152; Undergraduates: $5993. *Scholarships, grants, and awards:* Federal Pell, FSEOG, state, private, college/university gift aid from institutional funds.

GIFT AID (NON-NEED-BASED) *Total amount:* $92,980 (45% state, 46% institutional, 9% external sources). *Receiving aid:* Undergraduates: 1% (3). *Average award:* Freshmen: $1807. Undergraduates: $1872. *Scholarships, grants, and awards by category: Academic interests/achievement:* 177 awards ($277,700 total): education, religion/biblical studies. *Creative arts/performance:* music. *Special characteristics:* 165 awards ($225,229 total): children with a deceased or disabled parent, religious affiliation, spouses of current students. *Tuition waivers:* Full or partial for employees or children of employees.

LOANS *Student loans:* $1,234,405 (90% need-based, 10% non-need-based). 61% of past graduating class borrowed through all loan programs. *Average indebtedness per student:* $24,444. *Average need-based loan:* Freshmen: $2999. Undergraduates: $3520. *Parent loans:* $76,808 (33% need-based, 67% non-need-based). *Programs:* Federal Direct (Subsidized and Unsubsidized Stafford, PLUS).

WORK-STUDY *Federal work-study:* Total amount: $51,972; 24 jobs averaging $2163.

APPLYING FOR FINANCIAL AID *Required financial aid forms:* FAFSA, institution's own form, state aid form, business/farm supplement, student authorization form. *Financial aid deadline:* 4/15 (priority: 4/1). *Notification date:* Continuous beginning 6/15. Students must reply within 2 weeks of notification.

CONTACT Stephanie E. Powell, Director of Financial Aid, The Baptist College of Florida, 5400 College Drive, Graceville, FL 32440-3306, 850-263-3261 Ext. 461 or toll-free 800-328-2660 Ext. 460. *Fax:* 850-263-2141. *E-mail:* finaid@baptistcollege.edu. *Website:* http://www.baptistcollege.edu/.

BAPTIST BIBLE COLLEGE
Springfield, MO

CONTACT Bob Kotulski, Director of Financial Aid, Baptist Bible College, 628 East Kearney, Springfield, MO 65803-3498, 417-268-6036 or toll-free 800-228-5754. *Fax:* 417-268-6694. *Website:* http://www.gobbc.edu/.

THE BAPTIST COLLEGE OF FLORIDA
Graceville, FL

Tuition & fees: $11,100	Average undergraduate aid package: $8517

ABOUT THE INSTITUTION Independent Southern Baptist, coed. *Awards:* associate, bachelor's, and master's degrees. 9 undergraduate majors. *Total enrollment:* 456. Undergraduates: 440. Freshmen: 34. Federal methodology is used as a basis for awarding need-based institutional aid.

BAPTIST COLLEGE OF HEALTH SCIENCES
Memphis, TN

Tuition & fees: N/R	Average undergraduate aid package: N/A

ABOUT THE INSTITUTION Independent Southern Baptist, coed, primarily women. 7 undergraduate majors. Federal methodology is used as a basis for awarding need-based institutional aid.

GIFT AID (NEED-BASED) *Scholarships, grants, and awards:* Federal Pell, FSEOG, state, private, college/university gift aid from institutional funds.

APPLYING FOR FINANCIAL AID *Required financial aid form:* FAFSA. *Financial aid deadline:* Continuous. *Notification date:* Continuous.

CONTACT Joanna Darden, Director of Financial Aid, Baptist College of Health Sciences, 1003 Monroe Avenue, Memphis, TN 38104, 901-227-4330 or toll-free 866-575-2247. *E-mail:* joanna.darden@bchs.edu. *Website:* http://www.bchs.edu/.

BAPTIST HEALTH SYSTEM SCHOOL OF HEALTH PROFESSIONS
San Antonio, TX

CONTACT Financial Aid Office, Baptist Health System School of Health Professions, 8400 Datapoint Drive, San Antonio, TX 78229, 210-297-9636. *Website:* http://www.bshp.edu/.

BAPTIST MISSIONARY ASSOCIATION THEOLOGICAL SEMINARY
Jacksonville, TX

CONTACT Dr. Philip Attebery, Dean/Registrar, Baptist Missionary Association Theological Seminary, 1530 East Pine Street, PO Box 670, Jacksonville, TX 75766-5407, 903-586-2501 or toll-free 800-259-5673. *Fax:* 903-586-0378. *E-mail:* bmatsem@bmats.edu.
Website: http://www.bmats.edu/.

BAPTIST UNIVERSITY OF THE AMERICAS
San Antonio, TX

Tuition & fees: $6240	Average undergraduate aid package: N/A

ABOUT THE INSTITUTION Independent Baptist, coed. *Awards:* certificates, diplomas, associate, and bachelor's degrees (associate degree in Cross-Cultural Studies). 7 undergraduate majors. *Total enrollment:* 195. Undergraduates: 195. Freshmen: 30.
UNDERGRADUATE EXPENSES for 2017–2018 Tuition: full-time $5520; part-time $230 per credit hour. *Required fees:* full-time $720; $30 per credit hour. Room and board charges vary according to housing facility.
GIFT AID (NEED-BASED) *Scholarships, grants, and awards:* Federal Pell, FSEOG, private, college/university gift aid from institutional funds.
GIFT AID (NON-NEED-BASED) *Tuition waivers:* Full or partial for employees or children of employees.
LOANS *Programs:* Federal Direct (Subsidized and Unsubsidized Stafford).
WORK-STUDY *Federal work-study:* 4 jobs averaging $1265. *State or other work-study/employment:* 114 part-time jobs averaging $2740.
APPLYING FOR FINANCIAL AID *Required financial aid forms:* FAFSA, institution's own form. *Financial aid deadline:* Continuous. *Notification date:* Continuous.
CONTACT Mrs. Araceli G. Acosta, Financial Aid Director, Baptist University of the Americas, 7838 Barlite Boulevard, San Antonio, TX 78224, 210-924-4338 Ext. 214 or toll-free 800-721-1396. *Fax:* 210-924-2701. *E-mail:* araceli.acosta@bua.edu. *Website:* http://www.bua.edu/.

BARCLAY COLLEGE
Haviland, KS

Tuition & fees: $15,990	Average undergraduate aid package: $17,338

ABOUT THE INSTITUTION Independent Society of Friends, coed. *Awards:* certificates, associate, bachelor's, and master's degrees. 10 undergraduate majors. *Total enrollment:* 292. Undergraduates: 250. Freshmen: 52. Federal methodology is used as a basis for awarding need-based institutional aid.
UNDERGRADUATE EXPENSES for 2016–2017 Application fee: $15. *Comprehensive fee:* $24,390 includes full-time tuition ($12,500), mandatory fees ($3490), and room and board ($8400). Room and board charges vary according to board plan and housing facility. *Part-time tuition:* $295 per credit hour. Part-time tuition and fees vary according to course load.

FRESHMAN FINANCIAL AID (Fall 2016, est.) 29 applied for aid; of those 100% were deemed to have need. 100% of freshmen with need received aid; of those 21% had need fully met. *Average percent of need met:* 56% (excluding resources awarded to replace EFC). *Average financial aid package:* $17,420 (excluding resources awarded to replace EFC). 8% of all full-time freshmen had no need and received non-need-based gift aid.
UNDERGRADUATE FINANCIAL AID (Fall 2016, est.) 179 applied for aid; of those 100% were deemed to have need. 100% of undergraduates with need received aid; of those 3% had need fully met. *Average percent of need met:* 91% (excluding resources awarded to replace EFC). *Average financial aid package:* $17,338 (excluding resources awarded to replace EFC). 8% of all full-time undergraduates had no need and received non-need-based gift aid.
GIFT AID (NEED-BASED) *Total amount:* $2,164,319 (30% federal, 1% state, 67% institutional, 2% external sources). *Receiving aid:* Freshmen: 78% (29); all full-time undergraduates: 76% (179). *Average award:* Freshmen: $10,243; Undergraduates: $9402. *Scholarships, grants, and awards:* Federal Pell, FSEOG, state, private, college/university gift aid from institutional funds.
GIFT AID (NON-NEED-BASED) *Total amount:* $240,620 (2% state, 96% institutional, 2% external sources). *Receiving aid:* Freshmen: 78% (29). Undergraduates: 76% (179). *Average award:* Freshmen: $12,500. Undergraduates: $12,500. *Scholarships, grants, and awards by category:* Academic interests/achievement: education, general academic interests/achievements, religion/biblical studies. *Creative arts/performance:* art/fine arts, music. *Special achievements/activities:* general special achievements/activities, leadership. *Special characteristics:* children and siblings of alumni, children of current students, children of faculty/staff, international students, local/state students, married students, parents of current students, relatives of clergy, religious affiliation, siblings of current students, spouses of current students. *Tuition waivers:* Full or partial for employees or children of employees.
LOANS *Student loans:* $1,585,929 (89% need-based, 11% non-need-based). *Average need-based loan:* Freshmen: $1264. Undergraduates: $1988. *Parent loans:* $6110 (100% need-based).
WORK-STUDY *Federal work-study:* Total amount: $46,000; jobs available. *State or other work-study/employment:* Part-time jobs available.
APPLYING FOR FINANCIAL AID *Required financial aid form:* FAFSA. *Financial aid deadline (priority):* 3/15. *Notification date:* Continuous. Students must reply by 8/1 or within 4 weeks of notification.
CONTACT Ryan Haase, Financial Aid Coordinator, Barclay College, 607 North Kingman, Haviland, KS 67059, 800-862-0226. *Fax:* 620-862-5403. *E-mail:* financialaid@barclaycollege.edu. *Website:* http://www.barclaycollege.edu/.

BARD COLLEGE
Annandale-on-Hudson, NY

Tuition & fees: $52,915	Average undergraduate aid package: $44,760

ABOUT THE INSTITUTION Independent, coed. *Awards:* bachelor's, master's, and doctoral degrees. 57 undergraduate majors. *Total enrollment:* 2,335. Undergraduates: 1,995. Freshmen: 508. Both federal and institutional methodology are used as a basis for awarding need-based institutional aid.
UNDERGRADUATE EXPENSES for 2017–2018 Application fee: $50. *One-time required fee:* $1635. *Comprehensive fee:* $67,981 includes full-time tuition ($52,226), mandatory fees ($689), and room and board ($15,066). Full-time tuition and fees vary according to degree level and location. Room and board charges vary according to location. *Part-time tuition:* $1635 per credit hour. Part-time tuition and fees vary according to degree level and location. *Payment plan:* Tuition prepayment.
FRESHMAN FINANCIAL AID (Fall 2016, est.) 365 applied for aid; of those 96% were deemed to have need. 100% of freshmen with need received aid; of those 30% had need fully met. *Average percent of need met:* 88% (excluding resources awarded to replace EFC). *Average financial aid package:* $47,604 (excluding resources awarded to replace EFC). 1% of all full-time freshmen had no need and received non-need-based gift aid.
UNDERGRADUATE FINANCIAL AID (Fall 2016, est.) 1,362 applied for aid; of those 95% were deemed to have need. 100% of undergraduates with need received aid; of those 26% had need fully met. *Average percent of need met:* 87% (excluding resources awarded to replace EFC). *Average financial aid package:*

$44,760 (excluding resources awarded to replace EFC). 2% of all full-time undergraduates had no need and received non-need-based gift aid.

GIFT AID (NEED-BASED) *Total amount:* $49,023,280 (5% federal, 1% state, 92% institutional, 2% external sources). *Receiving aid:* Freshmen: 68% (345); all full-time undergraduates: 67% (1,272). *Average award:* Freshmen: $42,292; Undergraduates: $39,616. *Scholarships, grants, and awards:* Federal Pell, FSEOG, state, private, college/university gift aid from institutional funds.

GIFT AID (NON-NEED-BASED) *Total amount:* $1,090,848 (95% institutional, 5% external sources). *Average award:* Freshmen: $16,625. Undergraduates: $22,045. *Scholarships, grants, and awards by category: Special characteristics:* 12 awards ($491,224 total): children of educators, children of faculty/staff. *Tuition waivers:* Full or partial for employees or children of employees.

LOANS *Student loans:* $7,594,847 (95% need-based, 5% non-need-based). 52% of past graduating class borrowed through all loan programs. *Average indebtedness per student:* $27,816. *Average need-based loan:* Freshmen: $5898. Undergraduates: $6630. *Parent loans:* $3,682,149 (86% need-based, 14% non-need-based). *Programs:* Federal Direct (Subsidized and Unsubsidized Stafford, PLUS), Perkins.

WORK-STUDY *Federal work-study:* Total amount: $1,473,090; 890 jobs averaging $1606.

APPLYING FOR FINANCIAL AID *Required financial aid forms:* FAFSA, CSS Financial Aid PROFILE, state aid form, noncustodial (divorced/separated) parent's statement. *Financial aid deadline:* 2/15. *Notification date:* 4/1. Students must reply by 5/1 or within 2 weeks of notification.

CONTACT Denise Ann Ackerman, Director of Financial Aid, Bard College, Annandale Road, Annandale-on-Hudson, NY 12504, 845-758-7525. *Fax:* 845-758-7336. *E-mail:* finaid@bard.edu.
Website: http://www.bard.edu/.

BARD COLLEGE AT SIMON'S ROCK
Great Barrington, MA

CONTACT Ms. Ann Murtagh Gitto, Director of Financial Aid, Bard College at Simon's Rock, 84 Alford Road, Great Barrington, MA 01230-9702, 413-528-7297 or toll-free 800-235-7186. *Fax:* 413-528-7339. *E-mail:* agitto@simons-rock.edu. *Website:* http://www.simons-rock.edu/.

BARNARD COLLEGE
New York, NY

Tuition & fees: $50,394	Average undergraduate aid package: $49,012

ABOUT THE INSTITUTION Independent, women only. *Awards:* bachelor's degrees. 51 undergraduate majors. *Total enrollment:* 2,548. Undergraduates: 2,548. Freshmen: 635. Both federal and institutional methodology are used as a basis for awarding need-based institutional aid.

UNDERGRADUATE EXPENSES for 2016–2017 *Application fee:* $75. *Comprehensive fee:* $65,992 includes full-time tuition ($48,614), mandatory fees ($1780), and room and board ($15,598). *College room only:* $9230. Room and board charges vary according to board plan and housing facility. *Part-time tuition:* $1620 per credit hour. *Payment plan:* Tuition prepayment.

FRESHMAN FINANCIAL AID (Fall 2016, est.) 302 applied for aid; of those 73% were deemed to have need. 100% of freshmen with need received aid; of those 99% had need fully met. *Average percent of need met:* 100% (excluding resources awarded to replace EFC). *Average financial aid package:* $50,967 (excluding resources awarded to replace EFC).

UNDERGRADUATE FINANCIAL AID (Fall 2016, est.) 1,155 applied for aid; of those 87% were deemed to have need. 100% of undergraduates with need received aid; of those 99% had need fully met. *Average percent of need met:* 100% (excluding resources awarded to replace EFC). *Average financial aid package:* $49,012 (excluding resources awarded to replace EFC).

GIFT AID (NEED-BASED) *Total amount:* $43,286,377 (5% federal, 2% state, 90% institutional, 3% external sources). *Receiving aid:* Freshmen: 36% (217); all full-time undergraduates: 39% (998). *Average award:* Freshmen: $46,876; Undergraduates: $43,183. *Scholarships, grants, and awards:* Federal Pell, FSEOG, state, private, college/university gift aid from institutional funds.

GIFT AID (NON-NEED-BASED) *Total amount:* $1,522,528 (1% state, 99% external sources). *Tuition waivers:* Full or partial for employees or children of employees. *ROTC:* Army cooperative, Naval cooperative, Air Force cooperative.

LOANS *Student loans:* $5,970,441 (60% need-based, 40% non-need-based). 42% of past graduating class borrowed through all loan programs. *Average indebtedness per student:* $22,015. *Average need-based loan:* Freshmen: $3323. Undergraduates: $4557. *Parent loans:* $5,540,176 (100% non-need-based). *Programs:* Federal Direct (Subsidized and Unsubsidized Stafford, PLUS), Perkins, state, college/university.

WORK-STUDY *Federal work-study:* Total amount: $394,151; 189 jobs averaging $2270. *State or other work-study/employment:* Total amount: $1,724,988 (85% need-based, 15% non-need-based). 716 part-time jobs averaging $2100.

APPLYING FOR FINANCIAL AID *Required financial aid forms:* FAFSA, CSS Financial Aid PROFILE, state aid form, noncustodial (divorced/separated) parent's statement, federal income tax form(s). *Financial aid deadline:* 2/1. *Notification date:* 3/31. Students must reply by 5/1.

CONTACT Nanette DiLauro, Director of Financial Aid, Barnard College, 3009 Broadway, New York, NY 10027-6598, 212-854-2154. *Fax:* 212-280-8794. *E-mail:* finaid@barnard.edu.
Website: http://www.barnard.edu/.

BARRY UNIVERSITY
Miami Shores, FL

Tuition & fees: $28,800	Average undergraduate aid package: $20,983

ABOUT THE INSTITUTION Independent Roman Catholic, coed. *Awards:* certificates, bachelor's, master's, and doctoral degrees. 58 undergraduate majors. *Total enrollment:* 7,404. Undergraduates: 3,541. Freshmen: 480. Federal methodology is used as a basis for awarding need-based institutional aid.

UNDERGRADUATE EXPENSES for 2017–2018 *Application fee:* $30. *Comprehensive fee:* $39,600 includes full-time tuition ($28,800) and room and board ($10,800). Room and board charges vary according to housing facility. *Part-time tuition:* $865 per credit hour. Part-time tuition and fees vary according to course load.

FRESHMAN FINANCIAL AID (Fall 2016, est.) 423 applied for aid; of those 96% were deemed to have need. 100% of freshmen with need received aid; of those 4% had need fully met. *Average percent of need met:* 65% (excluding resources awarded to replace EFC). *Average financial aid package:* $25,390 (excluding resources awarded to replace EFC). 12% of all full-time freshmen had no need and received non-need-based gift aid.

UNDERGRADUATE FINANCIAL AID (Fall 2016, est.) 2,319 applied for aid; of those 96% were deemed to have need. 100% of undergraduates with need received aid; of those 3% had need fully met. *Average percent of need met:* 52% (excluding resources awarded to replace EFC). *Average financial aid package:* $20,983 (excluding resources awarded to replace EFC). 12% of all full-time undergraduates had no need and received non-need-based gift aid.

GIFT AID (NEED-BASED) *Total amount:* $16,092,742 (47% federal, 8% state, 45% institutional). *Receiving aid:* Freshmen: 74% (356); all full-time undergraduates: 61% (1,779). *Average award:* Freshmen: $9869; Undergraduates: $8811. *Scholarships, grants, and awards:* Federal Pell, FSEOG, state, private, college/university gift aid from institutional funds, Federal Nursing.

GIFT AID (NON-NEED-BASED) *Total amount:* $25,393,793 (17% state, 82% institutional, 1% external sources). *Receiving aid:* Freshmen: 83% (396). Undergraduates: 71% (2,076). *Average award:* Freshmen: $11,719. Undergraduates: $8629. *Tuition waivers:* Full or partial for employees or children of employees. *ROTC:* Army cooperative, Air Force cooperative.

LOANS *Student loans:* $19,829,381 (44% need-based, 56% non-need-based). 72% of past graduating class borrowed through all loan programs. *Average indebtedness per student:* $39,255. *Average need-based loan:* Freshmen: $3101. Undergraduates: $4488. *Parent loans:* $2,951,697 (100% non-need-based). *Programs:* Perkins, Federal Nursing, college/university, alternative loans.

WORK-STUDY *Federal work-study:* Total amount: $1,561,571; jobs available. *State or other work-study/employment:* Total amount: $351,556 (100% non-need-based). Part-time jobs available.

ATHLETIC AWARDS Total amount: $2,973,343 (100% non-need-based).

APPLYING FOR FINANCIAL AID *Required financial aid form:* FAFSA. *Financial aid deadline:* Continuous. *Notification date:* Continuous beginning 1/25.

CONTACT Mr. Dart Humeston, Director of Financial Aid, Barry University, 11300 Northeast Second Avenue, Miami Shores, FL 33161-6695, 305-899-3673 or toll-free 800-695-2279. *E-mail:* finaid@mail.barry.edu. *Website:* http://www.barry.edu/.

BARTON COLLEGE
Wilson, NC

Tuition & fees: $29,998	Average undergraduate aid package: $22,528

ABOUT THE INSTITUTION Independent Christian Church (Disciples of Christ), coed. *Awards:* bachelor's and master's degrees. 33 undergraduate majors. *Total enrollment:* 1,051. Undergraduates: 988. Freshmen: 241. Federal methodology is used as a basis for awarding need-based institutional aid.

UNDERGRADUATE EXPENSES for 2017–2018 *Comprehensive fee:* $39,854 includes full-time tuition ($27,536), mandatory fees ($2462), and room and board ($9856). *College room only:* $4256. Full-time tuition and fees vary according to class time, course load, and program. Room and board charges vary according to board plan and housing facility. *Part-time tuition:* $507 per credit hour. *Part-time fees:* $75 per credit hour. Part-time tuition and fees vary according to class time, course load, and program.

FRESHMAN FINANCIAL AID (Fall 2016, est.) 225 applied for aid; of those 96% were deemed to have need. 100% of freshmen with need received aid; of those 10% had need fully met. *Average percent of need met:* 64% (excluding resources awarded to replace EFC). *Average financial aid package:* $23,395 (excluding resources awarded to replace EFC). 11% of all full-time freshmen had no need and received non-need-based gift aid.

UNDERGRADUATE FINANCIAL AID (Fall 2016, est.) 828 applied for aid; of those 94% were deemed to have need. 100% of undergraduates with need received aid; of those 9% had need fully met. *Average percent of need met:* 62% (excluding resources awarded to replace EFC). *Average financial aid package:* $22,528 (excluding resources awarded to replace EFC). 13% of all full-time undergraduates had no need and received non-need-based gift aid.

GIFT AID (NEED-BASED) *Total amount:* $13,236,081 (18% federal, 18% state, 60% institutional, 4% external sources). *Receiving aid:* Freshmen: 89% (215); all full-time undergraduates: 86% (777). *Average award:* Freshmen: $20,094; Undergraduates: $18,370. *Scholarships, grants, and awards:* Federal Pell, FSEOG, state, private, college/university gift aid from institutional funds.

GIFT AID (NON-NEED-BASED) *Total amount:* $1,583,037 (92% institutional, 8% external sources). *Receiving aid:* Freshmen: 7% (16). Undergraduates: 5% (48). *Average award:* Freshmen: $11,557. Undergraduates: $10,579. *Scholarships, grants, and awards by category: Academic interests/achievement:* biological sciences, business, communication, education, English, general academic interests/achievements, humanities, mathematics, physical sciences, religion/biblical studies, social sciences. *Creative arts/performance:* art/fine arts, music, theater/drama. *Special achievements/activities:* general special achievements/activities, leadership, religious involvement. *Special characteristics:* adult students, children and siblings of alumni, children of faculty/staff, international students, local/state students, relatives of clergy, religious affiliation, siblings of current students, veterans. *Tuition waivers:* Full or partial for employees or children of employees, adult students.

LOANS *Student loans:* $7,272,303 (85% need-based, 15% non-need-based). 95% of past graduating class borrowed through all loan programs. *Average indebtedness per student:* $28,018. *Average need-based loan:* Freshmen: $3459. Undergraduates: $4325. *Parent loans:* $2,949,869 (64% need-based, 36% non-need-based). *Programs:* Federal Direct (Subsidized and Unsubsidized Stafford, PLUS), Perkins, state.

WORK-STUDY *Federal work-study:* Total amount: $248,349; jobs available. *State or other work-study/employment:* Part-time jobs available.

ATHLETIC AWARDS Total amount: $2,067,686 (51% need-based, 49% non-need-based).

APPLYING FOR FINANCIAL AID *Required financial aid forms:* FAFSA, noncustodial (divorced/separated) parent's statement. *Financial aid deadline:* 8/19. *Notification date:* Continuous beginning 12/12. Students must reply by 8/19.

CONTACT Mr. Thomas Welch, Director of Financial Aid, Barton College, Box 5000, Wilson, NC 27893, 252-399-6371 or toll-free 800-345-4973. *Fax:* 252-399-6572. *E-mail:* twelch@barton.edu. *Website:* http://www.barton.edu/.

BARUCH COLLEGE OF THE CITY UNIVERSITY OF NEW YORK
New York, NY

Tuition & fees (NY res): $6861	Average undergraduate aid package: $5572

ABOUT THE INSTITUTION State and locally supported, coed. *Awards:* certificates, bachelor's, and master's degrees. 25 undergraduate majors. *Total enrollment:* 18,286. Undergraduates: 15,210. Freshmen: 1,404. Federal methodology is used as a basis for awarding need-based institutional aid.

UNDERGRADUATE EXPENSES for 2016–2017 *Application fee:* $65. *Tuition, state resident:* full-time $6330; part-time $275 per credit hour. *Tuition, nonresident:* full-time $16,800; part-time $560 per credit hour. *Required fees:* full-time $531. Full-time tuition and fees vary according to course load. Part-time tuition and fees vary according to course load. Room and board charges vary according to housing facility.

FRESHMAN FINANCIAL AID (Fall 2016, est.) 1,148 applied for aid; of those 35% were deemed to have need. 92% of freshmen with need received aid; of those 31% had need fully met. *Average percent of need met:* 42% (excluding resources awarded to replace EFC). *Average financial aid package:* $5972 (excluding resources awarded to replace EFC). 18% of all full-time freshmen had no need and received non-need-based gift aid.

UNDERGRADUATE FINANCIAL AID (Fall 2016, est.) 8,334 applied for aid; of those 90% were deemed to have need. 93% of undergraduates with need received aid; of those 12% had need fully met. *Average percent of need met:* 21% (excluding resources awarded to replace EFC). *Average financial aid package:* $5572 (excluding resources awarded to replace EFC). 11% of all full-time undergraduates had no need and received non-need-based gift aid.

GIFT AID (NEED-BASED) *Total amount:* $67,849,141 (48% federal, 47% state, 4% institutional, 1% external sources). *Receiving aid:* Freshmen: 20% (363); all full-time undergraduates: 66% (6,655). *Average award:* Freshmen: $5398; Undergraduates: $5120. *Scholarships, grants, and awards:* Federal Pell, FSEOG, state, college/university gift aid from institutional funds.

GIFT AID (NON-NEED-BASED) *Receiving aid:* Freshmen: 15% (282). Undergraduates: 9% (943). *Average award:* Freshmen: $4593. Undergraduates: $4875. *Scholarships, grants, and awards by category: Academic interests/achievement:* general academic interests/achievements. *Tuition waivers:* Full or partial for employees or children of employees, senior citizens. *ROTC:* Army cooperative.

LOANS *Student loans:* $25,783,057 (24% need-based, 76% non-need-based). 22% of past graduating class borrowed through all loan programs. *Average indebtedness per student:* $5642. *Average need-based loan:* Freshmen: $3005. Undergraduates: $4921. *Parent loans:* $1,204,587 (100% non-need-based). *Programs:* Federal Direct (Subsidized and Unsubsidized Stafford, PLUS), Perkins.

WORK-STUDY *Federal work-study:* Total amount: $735,355; 299 jobs averaging $2459. *State or other work-study/employment:* Total amount: $125,453 (100% need-based). 69 part-time jobs averaging $1818.

APPLYING FOR FINANCIAL AID *Required financial aid forms:* FAFSA, state aid form. *Financial aid deadline (priority):* 4/15. *Notification date:* Continuous beginning 4/21. Students must reply by 6/1 or within 2 weeks of notification.

CONTACT Ms. Elizabeth Riquez, Financial Aid Services, Baruch College of the City University of New York, One Bernard Baruch Way, Box H-880, New York, NY 10010-5585, 646-312-1399. *Fax:* 646-312-1361. *E-mail:* elizabeth.riquez@baruch.cuny.edu. *Website:* http://www.baruch.cuny.edu/.

BASTYR UNIVERSITY
Kenmore, WA

ABOUT THE INSTITUTION Independent, coed. **Awards:** certificates, bachelor's, master's, and doctoral degrees. 7 undergraduate majors. **Total enrollment:** 1,266. Undergraduates: 287.

GIFT AID (NEED-BASED) Scholarships, grants, and awards: Federal Pell, FSEOG, state, private, college/university gift aid from institutional funds.

GIFT AID (NON-NEED-BASED) Scholarships, grants, and awards by category: Academic interests/achievement: health fields.

LOANS Programs: Federal Direct (Subsidized and Unsubsidized Stafford, PLUS), Perkins.

APPLYING FOR FINANCIAL AID Required financial aid forms: FAFSA, institution's own form.

CONTACT Danette Carter, Director of Financial Aid, Bastyr University, 14500 Juanita Drive NE, Kenmore, WA 98028-4966, 425-602-3083. Fax: 425-602-3094. E-mail: finaid@bastyr.edu.

Website: http://www.bastyr.edu/.

BATES COLLEGE
Lewiston, ME

Tuition & fees: $50,310	Average undergraduate aid package: $45,494

ABOUT THE INSTITUTION Independent, coed. **Awards:** bachelor's degrees. 36 undergraduate majors. **Total enrollment:** 1,780. Undergraduates: 1,780. Freshmen: 498. Institutional methodology is used as a basis for awarding need-based institutional aid.

UNDERGRADUATE EXPENSES for 2016–2017 Application fee: $60. **Comprehensive fee:** $64,500 includes full-time tuition ($50,310) and room and board ($14,190). **Payment plan:** Tuition prepayment.

FRESHMAN FINANCIAL AID (Fall 2016, est.) 245 applied for aid; of those 86% were deemed to have need. 100% of freshmen with need received aid; of those 100% had need fully met. **Average percent of need met:** 100% (excluding resources awarded to replace EFC). **Average financial aid package:** $46,647 (excluding resources awarded to replace EFC).

UNDERGRADUATE FINANCIAL AID (Fall 2016, est.) 849 applied for aid; of those 91% were deemed to have need. 100% of undergraduates with need received aid; of those 100% had need fully met. **Average percent of need met:** 100% (excluding resources awarded to replace EFC). **Average financial aid package:** $45,494 (excluding resources awarded to replace EFC).

GIFT AID (NEED-BASED) Total amount: $32,104,180 (4% federal, 96% institutional). **Receiving aid:** Freshmen: 42% (210); all full-time undergraduates: 43% (774). **Average award:** Freshmen: $43,506; Undergraduates: $41,478. **Scholarships, grants, and awards:** Federal Pell, FSEOG, state, private, college/university gift aid from institutional funds.

GIFT AID (NON-NEED-BASED) Total amount: $415,362 (100% external sources). **Tuition waivers:** Full or partial for employees or children of employees.

LOANS Student loans: $4,066,803 (44% need-based, 56% non-need-based). 34% of past graduating class borrowed through all loan programs. **Average indebtedness per student:** $22,845. **Average need-based loan:** Freshmen: $2235. Undergraduates: $3064. **Parent loans:** $1,922,651 (100% non-need-based). **Programs:** Federal Direct (Subsidized and Unsubsidized Stafford, PLUS), Perkins.

WORK-STUDY Federal work-study: Total amount: $780,675; 446 jobs averaging $1750. **State or other work-study/employment:** Total amount: $541,360 (100% need-based). 309 part-time jobs averaging $1757.

APPLYING FOR FINANCIAL AID Required financial aid forms: FAFSA, CSS Financial Aid PROFILE, noncustodial (divorced/separated) parent's statement. **Financial aid deadline:** 2/1. **Notification date:** 4/1. Students must reply by 5/1.

CONTACT Ms. Wendy G. Glass, Director of Student Financial Services, Bates College, 44 Mountain Avenue, Lewiston, ME 04240, 207-786-6096 or toll-free 855-228-3755. Fax: 207-786-8350. E-mail: wglass@bates.edu.

Website: http://www.bates.edu/.

BAYAMÓN CENTRAL UNIVERSITY
Bayamón, PR

CONTACT Financial Aid Director, Bayamón Central University, PO Box 1725, Bayamón, PR 00960-1725, 787-786-3030 Ext. 2115. Fax: 787-785-4365.

Website: http://www.ucb.edu.pr/.

BAYLOR UNIVERSITY
Waco, TX

Tuition & fees: $43,790	Average undergraduate aid package: $28,278

ABOUT THE INSTITUTION Independent Baptist, coed. **Awards:** certificates, bachelor's, master's, and doctoral degrees. 128 undergraduate majors. **Total enrollment:** 16,959. Undergraduates: 14,348. Freshmen: 3,503. Federal methodology is used as a basis for awarding need-based institutional aid.

UNDERGRADUATE EXPENSES for 2017–2018 Comprehensive fee: $55,953 includes full-time tuition ($39,610), mandatory fees ($4180), and room and board ($12,163). **College room only:** $6650. Room and board charges vary according to board plan and housing facility. **Part-time tuition:** $1650 per semester hour. **Part-time fees:** $174 per semester hour.

FRESHMAN FINANCIAL AID (Fall 2016, est.) 2,687 applied for aid; of those 76% were deemed to have need. 100% of freshmen with need received aid; of those 17% had need fully met. **Average percent of need met:** 69% (excluding resources awarded to replace EFC). **Average financial aid package:** $29,550 (excluding resources awarded to replace EFC). 38% of all full-time freshmen had no need and received non-need-based gift aid.

UNDERGRADUATE FINANCIAL AID (Fall 2016, est.) 9,090 applied for aid; of those 84% were deemed to have need. 100% of undergraduates with need received aid; of those 15% had need fully met. **Average percent of need met:** 65% (excluding resources awarded to replace EFC). **Average financial aid package:** $28,278 (excluding resources awarded to replace EFC). 37% of all full-time undergraduates had no need and received non-need-based gift aid.

GIFT AID (NEED-BASED) Total amount: $162,502,035 (7% federal, 6% state, 84% institutional, 3% external sources). **Receiving aid:** Freshmen: 58% (2,031); all full-time undergraduates: 53% (7,440). **Average award:** Freshmen: $24,060; Undergraduates: $22,291. **Scholarships, grants, and awards:** Federal Pell, FSEOG, state, college/university gift aid from institutional funds.

GIFT AID (NON-NEED-BASED) Total amount: $79,662,402 (98% institutional, 2% external sources). **Receiving aid:** Freshmen: 58% (2,017). Undergraduates: 51% (7,123). **Average award:** Freshmen: $14,716. Undergraduates: $13,976. **Scholarships, grants, and awards by category:** Academic interests/achievement: 13,781 awards ($146,178,622 total): business, communication, computer science, education, engineering/technologies, English, foreign languages, general academic interests/achievements, health fields, home economics, humanities, international studies, mathematics, military science, physical sciences, premedicine, religion/biblical studies, social sciences. Creative arts/performance: 483 awards ($2,832,733 total): art/fine arts, cinema/film/broadcasting, debating, journalism/publications, music, theater/drama. Special achievements/activities: 320 awards ($602,062 total): community service, leadership, religious involvement. Special characteristics: 222 awards ($6,180,926 total): children of faculty/staff, veterans, veterans' children. **Tuition waivers:** Full or partial for employees or children of employees. **ROTC:** Army, Air Force.

LOANS Student loans: $92,103,346 (65% need-based, 35% non-need-based). 53% of past graduating class borrowed through all loan programs. **Average indebtedness per student:** $44,540. **Average need-based loan:** Freshmen: $2564. Undergraduates: $3537. **Parent loans:** $34,602,951 (50% need-based, 50% non-need-based). **Programs:** Federal Direct (Subsidized and Unsubsidized Stafford, PLUS), Perkins, Federal Nursing, state, private loans.

WORK-STUDY Federal work-study: Total amount: $15,103,491; 5,154 jobs averaging $2930. **State or other work-study/employment:** Part-time jobs available.

ATHLETIC AWARDS Total amount: $13,285,265 (36% need-based, 64% non-need-based).

APPLYING FOR FINANCIAL AID Required financial aid forms: FAFSA, State Residency Affirmation (TX residents only). **Financial aid deadline (priority):** 2/1. **Notification date:** Continuous beginning 12/15. Students must reply by 5/1 or within 2 weeks of notification.

CONTACT Mrs. Jennifer L. Carron, Office of Admission Services, Baylor University, PO Box 97056, Waco, TX 76798-7056, 254-710-3435 or toll-free 800-BAYLORU. *Fax:* 254-710-3436. *E-mail:* admissions@baylor.edu. *Website:* http://www.baylor.edu/.

BAY PATH UNIVERSITY
Longmeadow, MA

Tuition & fees: $32,739	Average undergraduate aid package: $26,392

ABOUT THE INSTITUTION Independent, undergraduate: women only; graduate: coed. *Awards:* certificates, associate, bachelor's, master's, and doctoral degrees. 30 undergraduate majors. *Total enrollment:* 3,224. Undergraduates: 1,893. Freshmen: 153. Both federal and institutional methodology are used as a basis for awarding need-based institutional aid.

UNDERGRADUATE EXPENSES for 2017–2018 *Comprehensive fee:* $45,349 includes full-time tuition ($32,739) and room and board ($12,610). Room and board charges vary according to board plan. *Part-time tuition:* $500 per credit hour. Part-time tuition and fees vary according to course load.

FRESHMAN FINANCIAL AID (Fall 2016, est.) 148 applied for aid; of those 96% were deemed to have need. 99% of freshmen with need received aid; of those 4% had need fully met. *Average percent of need met:* 74% (excluding resources awarded to replace EFC). *Average financial aid package:* $30,322 (excluding resources awarded to replace EFC). 8% of all full-time freshmen had no need and received non-need-based gift aid.

UNDERGRADUATE FINANCIAL AID (Fall 2016, est.) 624 applied for aid; of those 94% were deemed to have need. 100% of undergraduates with need received aid; of those 8% had need fully met. *Average percent of need met:* 72% (excluding resources awarded to replace EFC). *Average financial aid package:* $26,392 (excluding resources awarded to replace EFC). 10% of all full-time undergraduates had no need and received non-need-based gift aid.

GIFT AID (NEED-BASED) *Total amount:* $12,400,567 (15% federal, 3% state, 81% institutional, 1% external sources). *Receiving aid:* Freshmen: 92% (141); all full-time undergraduates: 90% (587). *Average award:* Freshmen: $25,036; Undergraduates: $21,203. *Scholarships, grants, and awards:* Federal Pell, FSEOG, state, private, college/university gift aid from institutional funds.

GIFT AID (NON-NEED-BASED) *Total amount:* $1,096,756 (99% institutional, 1% external sources). *Receiving aid:* Freshmen: 3% (5). Undergraduates: 5% (33). *Average award:* Freshmen: $18,843. Undergraduates: $14,176. *Scholarships, grants, and awards by category:* Academic interests/achievement: 677 awards ($7,013,964 total): general academic interests/achievements. *Special characteristics:* adult students, children of faculty/staff, children with a deceased or disabled parent, general special characteristics, international students, siblings of current students. *Tuition waivers:* Full or partial for employees or children of employees. *ROTC:* Army cooperative, Air Force cooperative.

LOANS *Student loans:* $6,197,125 (81% need-based, 19% non-need-based). 51% of past graduating class borrowed through all loan programs. *Average indebtedness per student:* $29,954. *Average need-based loan:* Freshmen: $4238. Undergraduates: $4886. *Parent loans:* $1,553,356 (59% need-based, 41% non-need-based). *Programs:* Federal Direct (Subsidized and Unsubsidized Stafford, PLUS), Perkins.

WORK-STUDY *Federal work-study:* Total amount: $445,393; 113 jobs averaging $2500. *State or other work-study/employment:* 72 part-time jobs averaging $2500.

APPLYING FOR FINANCIAL AID *Required financial aid form:* FAFSA. *Financial aid deadline (priority):* 10/1. *Notification date:* Continuous beginning 12/1. Students must reply within 2 weeks of notification.

CONTACT Stephanie King, Director of Student Financial Services, Bay Path University, 588 Longmeadow Street, Longmeadow, MA 01106-2292, 413-565-1345 or toll-free 800-782-7284 Ext. 1331. *Fax:* 413-565-1101. *E-mail:* sking@baypath.edu. *Website:* http://www.baypath.edu/.

BEACON COLLEGE
Leesburg, FL

ABOUT THE INSTITUTION Independent, coed. *Awards:* associate and bachelor's degrees. 9 undergraduate majors. *Total enrollment:* 314. Undergraduates: 314. Freshmen: 66.

GIFT AID (NEED-BASED) *Scholarships, grants, and awards:* Federal Pell, FSEOG, state, private, college/university gift aid from institutional funds.

LOANS *Programs:* Federal Direct (Subsidized and Unsubsidized Stafford, PLUS).

WORK-STUDY *Federal work-study:* jobs available. *State or other work-study/employment:* Total amount: $3510 (100% need-based). Part-time jobs available.

APPLYING FOR FINANCIAL AID *Required financial aid forms:* FAFSA, state aid form.

CONTACT Mrs. Shawna L. Wells-Booth, Director of Financial Aid, Beacon College, 105 East Main Street, Leesburg, FL 34788, 352-638-9733. *Fax:* 800-360-1974. *E-mail:* financialaid@beaconcollege.edu. *Website:* http://www.beaconcollege.edu/.

BECKER COLLEGE
Worcester, MA

ABOUT THE INSTITUTION Independent, coed. *Awards:* certificates, associate, bachelor's, and master's degrees (also includes Leicester, MA small town campus). 33 undergraduate majors. *Total enrollment:* 2,189. Undergraduates: 2,178. Freshmen: 421.

GIFT AID (NEED-BASED) *Scholarships, grants, and awards:* Federal Pell, FSEOG, state, private, college/university gift aid from institutional funds.

GIFT AID (NON-NEED-BASED) *Scholarships, grants, and awards by category:* Academic interests/achievement: general academic interests/achievements. Special achievements/activities: leadership. Special characteristics: children of faculty/staff, siblings of current students.

LOANS *Programs:* Federal Direct (Subsidized and Unsubsidized Stafford, PLUS), state, alternative loans.

WORK-STUDY *Federal work-study:* jobs available.

APPLYING FOR FINANCIAL AID *Required financial aid form:* FAFSA.

CONTACT Mr. Heather Ruland, Director of Financial Aid, Becker College, 61 Sever Street, Worcester, MA 01615-0071, 508-373-9430 or toll-free 877-5BECKER. *Fax:* 508-890-1511. *E-mail:* financialaid@becker.edu. *Website:* http://www.becker.edu/.

BE'ER YAAKOV TALMUDIC SEMINARY
Spring Valley, NY

CONTACT Financial Aid Office, Be'er Yaakov Talmudic Seminary, 12 Jefferson Avenue, Spring Valley, NY 10977, 845-406-9699.

BEIS MEDRASH HEICHAL DOVID
Far Rockaway, NY

CONTACT Financial Aid Office, Beis Medrash Heichal Dovid, 257 Beach 17th Street, Far Rockaway, NY 11691, 718-868-2300.

BELHAVEN UNIVERSITY
Jackson, MS

Tuition & fees: $24,250	Average undergraduate aid package: $15,764

ABOUT THE INSTITUTION Independent Presbyterian, coed. *Awards:* certificates, associate, bachelor's, and master's degrees. 38 undergraduate majors. *Total*

enrollment: 4,759. Undergraduates: 2,715. Freshmen: 237. Federal methodology is used as a basis for awarding need-based institutional aid.

UNDERGRADUATE EXPENSES for 2017–2018 *Application fee:* $25. *Comprehensive fee:* $32,250 includes full-time tuition ($23,900), mandatory fees ($350), and room and board ($8000). Room and board charges vary according to housing facility. *Part-time tuition:* $425 per credit hour. Part-time tuition and fees vary according to course load.

FRESHMAN FINANCIAL AID (Fall 2015) 215 applied for aid; of those 89% were deemed to have need. 100% of freshmen with need received aid; of those 5% had need fully met. *Average percent of need met:* 68% (excluding resources awarded to replace EFC). *Average financial aid package:* $19,281 (excluding resources awarded to replace EFC). 19% of all full-time freshmen had no need and received non-need-based gift aid.

UNDERGRADUATE FINANCIAL AID (Fall 2015) 1,136 applied for aid; of those 93% were deemed to have need. 99% of undergraduates with need received aid; of those 6% had need fully met. *Average percent of need met:* 59% (excluding resources awarded to replace EFC). *Average financial aid package:* $15,764 (excluding resources awarded to replace EFC). 21% of all full-time undergraduates had no need and received non-need-based gift aid.

GIFT AID (NEED-BASED) *Total amount:* $4,248,681 (60% federal, 5% state, 35% institutional). *Receiving aid:* Freshmen: 80% (192); all full-time undergraduates: 74% (997). *Average award:* Freshmen: $16,268; Undergraduates: $12,671. *Scholarships, grants, and awards:* Federal Pell, FSEOG, state, private, college/university gift aid from institutional funds.

GIFT AID (NON-NEED-BASED) *Total amount:* $9,308,088 (2% state, 94% institutional, 4% external sources). *Receiving aid:* Freshmen: 80% (192). Undergraduates: 61% (818). *Average award:* Freshmen: $13,765. Undergraduates: $14,171. *Scholarships, grants, and awards by category:* Academic interests/achievement: biological sciences, business, communication, education, English, foreign languages, general academic interests/achievements, humanities, international studies, mathematics, premedicine, religion/biblical studies, social sciences. *Creative arts/performance:* applied art and design, art/fine arts, cinema/film/broadcasting, creative writing, dance, general creative arts/performance, journalism/publications, music, performing arts, theater/drama. *Special achievements/activities:* cheerleading/drum major, general special achievements/activities, junior miss, leadership. *Special characteristics:* children and siblings of alumni, children of faculty/staff, general special characteristics, international students, local/state students, religious affiliation, siblings of current students, veterans, veterans' children. *Tuition waivers:* Full or partial for employees or children of employees. *ROTC:* Army cooperative, Air Force cooperative.

LOANS *Student loans:* $5,770,498 (51% need-based, 49% non-need-based). 79% of past graduating class borrowed through all loan programs. *Average indebtedness per student:* $29,738. *Average need-based loan:* Freshmen: $3313. Undergraduates: $4298. *Parent loans:* $2,028,570 (100% non-need-based). *Programs:* Federal Direct (Subsidized and Unsubsidized Stafford, PLUS), Perkins, state.

WORK-STUDY *Federal work-study:* 215 jobs averaging $1500. *State or other work-study/employment:* Total amount: $45,050 (100% non-need-based). 42 part-time jobs averaging $2000.

APPLYING FOR FINANCIAL AID *Required financial aid form:* FAFSA. *Financial aid deadline (priority):* 3/1. *Notification date:* Continuous.

CONTACT Mrs. Debbi Braswell, Director of Financial Aid, Belhaven University, 1500 Peachtree Street, Box 159, Jackson, MS 39202-1789, 601-968-5933 or toll-free 800-960-5940. *E-mail:* dbraswell@belhaven.edu.
Website: http://www.belhaven.edu/.

BELLARMINE UNIVERSITY
Louisville, KY

Tuition & fees: $40,350	Average undergraduate aid package: $30,651

ABOUT THE INSTITUTION Independent Roman Catholic, coed. *Awards:* certificates, bachelor's, master's, and doctoral degrees. 42 undergraduate majors. *Total enrollment:* 3,971. Undergraduates: 2,650. Freshmen: 636. Both federal and institutional methodology are used as a basis for awarding need-based institutional aid.

UNDERGRADUATE EXPENSES for 2017–2018 *Application fee:* $25. *One-time required fee:* $400. *Comprehensive fee:* $52,532 includes full-time tuition ($38,800), mandatory fees ($1550), and room and board ($12,182). *College room*

only: $7652. Room and board charges vary according to board plan and housing facility. *Part-time tuition:* $905 per credit hour.

FRESHMAN FINANCIAL AID (Fall 2016, est.) 610 applied for aid; of those 88% were deemed to have need. 100% of freshmen with need received aid; of those 18% had need fully met. *Average percent of need met:* 72% (excluding resources awarded to replace EFC). *Average financial aid package:* $32,099 (excluding resources awarded to replace EFC). 15% of all full-time freshmen had no need and received non-need-based gift aid.

UNDERGRADUATE FINANCIAL AID (Fall 2016, est.) 2,192 applied for aid; of those 88% were deemed to have need. 98% of undergraduates with need received aid; of those 21% had need fully met. *Average percent of need met:* 74% (excluding resources awarded to replace EFC). *Average financial aid package:* $30,651 (excluding resources awarded to replace EFC). 20% of all full-time undergraduates had no need and received non-need-based gift aid.

GIFT AID (NEED-BASED) *Total amount:* $47,643,322 (6% federal, 12% state, 79% institutional, 3% external sources). *Receiving aid:* Freshmen: 84% (535); all full-time undergraduates: 77% (1,901). *Average award:* Freshmen: $24,796; Undergraduates: $23,040. *Scholarships, grants, and awards:* Federal Pell, FSEOG, state, private, college/university gift aid from institutional funds.

GIFT AID (NON-NEED-BASED) *Total amount:* $13,191,047 (5% state, 90% institutional, 5% external sources). *Receiving aid:* Freshmen: 23% (147). Undergraduates: 25% (607). *Average award:* Freshmen: $25,298. Undergraduates: $21,948. *Scholarships, grants, and awards by category:* Academic interests/achievement: biological sciences, business, education, general academic interests/achievements, physical sciences. *Creative arts/performance:* art/fine arts, music. *Special achievements/activities:* cheerleading/drum major, community service, general special achievements/activities, leadership, religious involvement. *Special characteristics:* adult students, children and siblings of alumni, children of faculty/staff, ethnic background, international students, local/state students, members of minority groups, out-of-state students, previous college experience, religious affiliation. *Tuition waivers:* Full or partial for employees or children of employees. *ROTC:* Army cooperative, Air Force cooperative.

LOANS *Student loans:* $14,313,640 (75% need-based, 25% non-need-based). 69% of past graduating class borrowed through all loan programs. *Average indebtedness per student:* $30,759. *Average need-based loan:* Freshmen: $3468. Undergraduates: $4475. *Parent loans:* $3,739,671 (58% need-based, 42% non-need-based). *Programs:* Federal Direct (Subsidized and Unsubsidized Stafford, PLUS), Perkins, college/university.

WORK-STUDY *Federal work-study:* Total amount: $457,523; jobs available. *State or other work-study/employment:* Total amount: $231,775 (71% need-based, 29% non-need-based). Part-time jobs available.

ATHLETIC AWARDS Total amount: $2,842,811 (52% need-based, 48% non-need-based).

APPLYING FOR FINANCIAL AID *Required financial aid form:* FAFSA. *Financial aid deadline (priority):* 11/1. *Notification date:* Continuous beginning 12/15. Students must reply by 5/1.

CONTACT Ms. Heather Boutell, Director of Financial Aid, Bellarmine University, 2001 Newburg Road, Louisville, KY 40205-0671, 502-272-7300 or toll-free 800-274-4723 Ext. 8131. *Fax:* 502-272-8486. *E-mail:* hboutell@bellarmine.edu.
Website: http://www.bellarmine.edu/.

BELLEVUE UNIVERSITY
Bellevue, NE

CONTACT Ms. Janet Yale, Director of Financial Aid, Bellevue University, 1000 Galvin Road South, Bellevue, NE 68005, 402-293-2000 or toll-free 800-756-7920. *Fax:* 402-557-5425.
Website: http://www.bellevue.edu/.

BELLIN COLLEGE
Green Bay, WI

CONTACT Mrs. Lena C. Goodman, Director of Financial Aid, Bellin College, 3201 Eaton Road, Green Bay, WI 54311, 920-433-6638 or toll-free 800-236-8707. *Fax:* 920-433-1922. *E-mail:* lena.goodman@bellincollege.edu.
Website: http://www.bellincollege.edu/.

BELMONT ABBEY COLLEGE
Belmont, NC

Tuition & fees: $18,500	Average undergraduate aid package: $11,710

ABOUT THE INSTITUTION Independent Roman Catholic, coed. *Awards:* bachelor's degrees. 16 undergraduate majors. *Total enrollment:* 1,524. Undergraduates: 1,524. Federal methodology is used as a basis for awarding need-based institutional aid.

UNDERGRADUATE EXPENSES for 2016–2017 *Comprehensive fee:* $28,594 includes full-time tuition ($18,500) and room and board ($10,094). *College room only:* $5828. Full-time tuition and fees vary according to course load and reciprocity agreements. Room and board charges vary according to board plan and housing facility. *Part-time tuition:* $617 per credit hour. Part-time tuition and fees vary according to course load and reciprocity agreements. *Payment plan:* Guaranteed tuition.

FRESHMAN FINANCIAL AID (Fall 2015) 265 applied for aid; of those 78% were deemed to have need. 100% of freshmen with need received aid; of those 12% had need fully met. *Average percent of need met:* 54% (excluding resources awarded to replace EFC). *Average financial aid package:* $12,836 (excluding resources awarded to replace EFC). 33% of all full-time freshmen had no need and received non-need-based gift aid.

UNDERGRADUATE FINANCIAL AID (Fall 2015) 1,143 applied for aid; of those 87% were deemed to have need. 96% of undergraduates with need received aid; of those 10% had need fully met. *Average percent of need met:* 51% (excluding resources awarded to replace EFC). *Average financial aid package:* $11,710 (excluding resources awarded to replace EFC). 20% of all full-time undergraduates had no need and received non-need-based gift aid.

GIFT AID (NEED-BASED) *Total amount:* $7,064,928 (35% federal, 25% state, 31% institutional, 9% external sources). *Receiving aid:* Freshmen: 67% (207); all full-time undergraduates: 71% (956). *Average award:* Freshmen: $9526; Undergraduates: $8048. *Scholarships, grants, and awards:* Federal Pell, FSEOG, state, private, college/university gift aid from institutional funds.

GIFT AID (NON-NEED-BASED) *Total amount:* $1,378,041 (100% institutional). *Receiving aid:* Freshmen: 5% (16). Undergraduates: 3% (45). *Average award:* Freshmen: $4452. Undergraduates: $5290. *Scholarships, grants, and awards by category:* Academic interests/achievement: 727 awards ($3,943,740 total): business, education, general academic interests/achievements, humanities. *Creative arts/performance:* 10 awards ($80,000 total): theater/drama. *Special achievements/activities:* 25 awards ($225,000 total): cheerleading/drum major, leadership, religious involvement. *Special characteristics:* 27 awards ($260,415 total): children of faculty/staff. *Tuition waivers:* Full or partial for employees or children of employees.

LOANS *Student loans:* $9,355,175 (80% need-based, 20% non-need-based). 76% of past graduating class borrowed through all loan programs. *Average indebtedness per student:* $28,477. *Average need-based loan:* Freshmen: $3667. Undergraduates: $4214. *Parent loans:* $7,201,479 (31% need-based, 69% non-need-based). *Programs:* Federal Direct (Subsidized and Unsubsidized Stafford, PLUS).

WORK-STUDY *Federal work-study:* 72 jobs averaging $2000.

ATHLETIC AWARDS Total amount: $1,369,004 (53% need-based, 47% non-need-based).

APPLYING FOR FINANCIAL AID *Required financial aid form:* FAFSA. *Financial aid deadline (priority):* 3/1. *Notification date:* Continuous beginning 12/5. Students must reply within 2 weeks of notification.

CONTACT Ms. Julie Hodge, Associate Director of Financial Aid, Belmont Abbey College, 100 Belmont Mt. Holly Road, Belmont, NC 28012-1802, 704-461-7000 or toll-free 888-BAC-0110. *Fax:* 704-461-6882. *E-mail:* juliehodge@bac.edu.
Website: http://www.belmontabbeycollege.edu/.

BELMONT UNIVERSITY
Nashville, TN

Tuition & fees: $32,820	Average undergraduate aid package: $18,276

ABOUT THE INSTITUTION Independent Christian, coed. *Awards:* certificates, bachelor's, master's, and doctoral degrees. 78 undergraduate majors. *Total* enrollment: 7,723. Undergraduates: 6,293. Freshmen: 1,568. Federal methodology is used as a basis for awarding need-based institutional aid.

UNDERGRADUATE EXPENSES for 2017–2018 *Application fee:* $50. *Comprehensive fee:* $44,500 includes full-time tuition ($31,300), mandatory fees ($1520), and room and board ($11,680). *College room only:* $6440. Full-time tuition and fees vary according to course load. Room and board charges vary according to board plan and housing facility. *Part-time tuition:* $1190 per credit hour. Part-time tuition and fees vary according to course load.

FRESHMAN FINANCIAL AID (Fall 2016, est.) 1,274 applied for aid; of those 68% were deemed to have need. 100% of freshmen with need received aid; of those 13% had need fully met. *Average percent of need met:* 52% (excluding resources awarded to replace EFC). *Average financial aid package:* $19,939 (excluding resources awarded to replace EFC). 32% of all full-time freshmen had no need and received non-need-based gift aid.

UNDERGRADUATE FINANCIAL AID (Fall 2016, est.) 3,990 applied for aid; of those 76% were deemed to have need. 100% of undergraduates with need received aid; of those 10% had need fully met. *Average percent of need met:* 50% (excluding resources awarded to replace EFC). *Average financial aid package:* $18,276 (excluding resources awarded to replace EFC). 33% of all full-time undergraduates had no need and received non-need-based gift aid.

GIFT AID (NEED-BASED) *Total amount:* $36,768,678 (13% federal, 1% state, 86% institutional). *Receiving aid:* Freshmen: 52% (822); all full-time undergraduates: 61% (2,677). *Average award:* Freshmen: $16,826; Undergraduates: $14,857. *Scholarships, grants, and awards:* Federal Pell, FSEOG, state, private, college/university gift aid from institutional funds.

GIFT AID (NON-NEED-BASED) *Total amount:* $10,974,228 (10% state, 90% institutional). *Receiving aid:* Freshmen: 7% (112). Undergraduates: 7% (304). *Average award:* Freshmen: $7515. Undergraduates: $7561. *Scholarships, grants, and awards by category:* Academic interests/achievement: biological sciences, business, general academic interests/achievements, health fields, religion/biblical studies, social sciences. *Creative arts/performance:* applied art and design, art/fine arts, cinema/film/broadcasting, creative writing, dance, general creative arts/performance, journalism/publications, music, performing arts, theater/drama. *Special achievements/activities:* cheerleading/drum major, community service, general special achievements/activities, leadership, religious involvement. *Special characteristics:* children and siblings of alumni, children of faculty/staff, local/state students, members of minority groups, siblings of current students, veterans, veterans' children. *Tuition waivers:* Full or partial for employees or children of employees, senior citizens. *ROTC:* Army cooperative, Naval cooperative, Air Force cooperative.

LOANS *Student loans:* $8,583,941 (100% need-based). 53% of past graduating class borrowed through all loan programs. *Average indebtedness per student:* $31,020. *Average need-based loan:* Freshmen: $3671. Undergraduates: $4501. *Parent loans:* $29,343,512 (82% need-based, 18% non-need-based). *Programs:* Federal Direct (Subsidized and Unsubsidized Stafford, PLUS), Perkins.

WORK-STUDY *Federal work-study:* Total amount: $2,617,805; jobs available.

ATHLETIC AWARDS Total amount: $4,989,767 (36% need-based, 64% non-need-based).

APPLYING FOR FINANCIAL AID *Required financial aid form:* FAFSA. *Financial aid deadline (priority):* 3/1. *Notification date:* Continuous beginning 3/15. Students must reply by 5/1 or within 2 weeks of notification.

CONTACT Mrs. Pat Smedley, Director of Student Financial Services, Belmont University, 1900 Belmont Boulevard, Nashville, TN 37212-3757, 615-460-6403. *E-mail:* pat.smedley@belmont.edu.
Website: http://www.belmont.edu/.

BELOIT COLLEGE
Beloit, WI

Tuition & fees: $47,060	Average undergraduate aid package: $39,976

ABOUT THE INSTITUTION Independent, coed. *Awards:* bachelor's degrees. 50 undergraduate majors. *Total enrollment:* 1,394. Undergraduates: 1,394. Freshmen: 382. Both federal and institutional methodology are used as a basis for awarding need-based institutional aid.

UNDERGRADUATE EXPENSES for 2016–2017 *Comprehensive fee:* $55,206 includes full-time tuition ($46,596), mandatory fees ($464), and room and board ($8146). **College room only:** $4626. Room and board charges vary according to board plan. **Part-time tuition:** $1456 per credit hour.

FRESHMAN FINANCIAL AID (Fall 2016, est.) 275 applied for aid; of those 86% were deemed to have need. 100% of freshmen with need received aid; of those 31% had need fully met. **Average percent of need met:** 95% (excluding resources awarded to replace EFC). **Average financial aid package:** $42,870 (excluding resources awarded to replace EFC). 38% of all full-time freshmen had no need and received non-need-based gift aid.

UNDERGRADUATE FINANCIAL AID (Fall 2016, est.) 925 applied for aid; of those 90% were deemed to have need. 100% of undergraduates with need received aid; of those 34% had need fully met. **Average percent of need met:** 94% (excluding resources awarded to replace EFC). **Average financial aid package:** $39,976 (excluding resources awarded to replace EFC). 34% of all full-time undergraduates had no need and received non-need-based gift aid.

GIFT AID (NEED-BASED) Total amount: $24,525,986 (7% federal, 1% state, 91% institutional, 1% external sources). **Receiving aid:** Freshmen: 60% (229); all full-time undergraduates: 62% (812). **Average award:** Freshmen: $32,586; Undergraduates: $30,133. **Scholarships, grants, and awards:** Federal Pell, FSEOG, state, private, college/university gift aid from institutional funds.

GIFT AID (NON-NEED-BASED) Total amount: $12,376,665 (99% institutional, 1% external sources). **Receiving aid:** Freshmen: 31% (120). Undergraduates: 33% (431). **Average award:** Freshmen: $25,897. Undergraduates: $22,962. **Scholarships, grants, and awards by category:** Academic interests/achievement: general academic interests/achievements. Creative arts/performance: music. Special achievements/activities: community service, general special achievements/activities, leadership. Special characteristics: siblings of current students, veterans. **Tuition waivers:** Full or partial for employees or children of employees.

LOANS Student loans: $7,476,133 (71% need-based, 29% non-need-based). 70% of past graduating class borrowed through all loan programs. **Average indebtedness per student:** $31,308. **Average need-based loan:** Freshmen: $5966. Undergraduates: $6497. **Parent loans:** $1,365,420 (43% need-based, 57% non-need-based). **Programs:** Federal Direct (Subsidized and Unsubsidized Stafford, PLUS), Perkins, college/university.

WORK-STUDY Federal work-study: Total amount: $909,336; jobs available. **State or other work-study/employment:** Total amount: $462,809 (11% need-based, 89% non-need-based). Part-time jobs available.

APPLYING FOR FINANCIAL AID Required financial aid form: FAFSA. **Financial aid deadline:** 3/1 (priority: 3/1). **Notification date:** Continuous beginning 3/1. Students must reply by 5/1.

CONTACT Ms. Victoria Gack, Director of Financial Aid, Beloit College, 700 College Street, Beloit, WI 53511-5596, 608-363-2696 or toll-free 800-9-BELOIT. *Fax:* 608-363-7139. *E-mail:* gackv@beloit.edu. *Website:* http://www.beloit.edu/.

BEMIDJI STATE UNIVERSITY
Bemidji, MN

Tuition & fees (MN res): $8394	Average undergraduate aid package: $9028

ABOUT THE INSTITUTION State-supported, coed. **Awards:** certificates, associate, bachelor's, and master's degrees. 70 undergraduate majors. **Total enrollment:** 5,120. Undergraduates: 4,795. Freshmen: 817. Federal methodology is used as a basis for awarding need-based institutional aid.

UNDERGRADUATE EXPENSES for 2016–2017 Application fee: $20. **Tuition, state resident:** full-time $7360; part-time $257.35 per credit. **Tuition, nonresident:** full-time $7360; part-time $257.35 per credit. **Required fees:** full-time $1034; $17.93 per credit. Full-time tuition and fees vary according to course load, location, program, and reciprocity agreements. Part-time tuition and fees vary according to course load, location, program, and reciprocity agreements. **College room and board:** $7924. Room and board charges vary according to board plan and housing facility.

FRESHMAN FINANCIAL AID (Fall 2015) 396 applied for aid; of those 68% were deemed to have need. 100% of freshmen with need received aid; of those 13% had need fully met. **Average percent of need met:** 57% (excluding resources awarded to replace EFC). **Average financial aid package:** $7841 (excluding resources awarded to replace EFC). 23% of all full-time freshmen had no need and received non-need-based gift aid.

UNDERGRADUATE FINANCIAL AID (Fall 2015) 2,765 applied for aid; of those 74% were deemed to have need. 99% of undergraduates with need received aid; of those 17% had need fully met. **Average percent of need met:** 61% (excluding resources awarded to replace EFC). **Average financial aid package:** $9028 (excluding resources awarded to replace EFC). 20% of all full-time undergraduates had no need and received non-need-based gift aid.

GIFT AID (NEED-BASED) Total amount: $10,400,351 (67% federal, 31% state, 1% institutional, 1% external sources). **Receiving aid:** Freshmen: 37% (175); all full-time undergraduates: 42% (1,421). **Average award:** Freshmen: $5647; Undergraduates: $5474. **Scholarships, grants, and awards:** Federal Pell, FSEOG, state, private, college/university gift aid from institutional funds.

GIFT AID (NON-NEED-BASED) Total amount: $6,166,087 (10% federal, 9% state, 64% institutional, 17% external sources). **Receiving aid:** Freshmen: 44% (208). Undergraduates: 42% (1,408). **Average award:** Freshmen: $9186. Undergraduates: $10,488. **Scholarships, grants, and awards by category:** Academic interests/achievement: 1,107 awards ($1,434,416 total): biological sciences, business, communication, computer science, education, engineering/technologies, English, foreign languages, general academic interests/achievements, health fields, humanities, international studies, mathematics, physical sciences, premedicine, social sciences. Creative arts/performance: 78 awards ($130,345 total): applied art and design, art/fine arts, cinema/film/broadcasting, creative writing, general creative arts/performance, journalism/publications, music, performing arts. Special achievements/activities: 18 awards ($24,400 total): general special achievements/activities, leadership. Special characteristics: 259 awards ($495,403 total): children and siblings of alumni, children of faculty/staff, handicapped students, international students, members of minority groups, out-of-state students, previous college experience. **Tuition waivers:** Full or partial for employees or children of employees, senior citizens.

LOANS Student loans: $1,498,249,271 (1% need-based, 99% non-need-based). **Average need-based loan:** Freshmen: $3448. Undergraduates: $4060. **Parent loans:** $978,341 (100% non-need-based). **Programs:** Federal Direct (Subsidized and Unsubsidized Stafford, PLUS), Perkins, state, alternative loans.

WORK-STUDY Federal work-study: 278 jobs averaging $1624. **State or other work-study/employment:** Total amount: $376,162 (100% need-based). 218 part-time jobs averaging $1737.

ATHLETIC AWARDS Total amount: $1,455,093 (100% non-need-based).

APPLYING FOR FINANCIAL AID Required financial aid form: FAFSA. **Financial aid deadline (priority):** 3/15. **Notification date:** Continuous beginning 6/15.

CONTACT Financial Aid Office, Bemidji State University, 1500 Birchmont Drive NE #14, Bemidji, MN 56601-2699, 218-755-2034 or toll-free 800-475-2001. *Fax:* 218-755-4361. *E-mail:* financialaid@bemidjistate.edu. *Website:* http://www.bemidjistate.edu/.

BENEDICT COLLEGE
Columbia, SC

CONTACT Mrs. Bichevia Green, Associate Director of Financial Aid, Benedict College, 1600 Harden Street, Columbia, SC 29204, 803-705-4418 or toll-free 800-868-6598. *Fax:* 803-705-6629. *E-mail:* greenb@benedict.edu. *Website:* http://www.benedict.edu/.

BENEDICTINE COLLEGE
Atchison, KS

Tuition & fees: $27,480	Average undergraduate aid package: $22,440

ABOUT THE INSTITUTION Independent Roman Catholic, coed. **Awards:** certificates, diplomas, associate, bachelor's, and master's degrees. 48 undergraduate majors. **Total enrollment:** 2,189. Undergraduates: 2,133. Freshmen: 508. Federal methodology is used as a basis for awarding need-based institutional aid.

UNDERGRADUATE EXPENSES for 2016–2017 Application fee: $50. **Comprehensive fee:** $37,010 includes full-time tuition ($26,730), mandatory fees ($750), and room and board ($9530). **College room only:** $5140. Full-time tuition and fees vary according to course load and degree level. Room and board charges vary according to board plan and housing facility. **Part-time tuition:** $775 per credit hour. *Part-time fees:* $50 per credit hour. Part-time tuition and fees vary according to course load and degree level.

FRESHMAN FINANCIAL AID (Fall 2016, est.) 421 applied for aid; of those 83% were deemed to have need. 100% of freshmen with need received aid; of those 24% had need fully met. *Average percent of need met:* 80% (excluding resources awarded to replace EFC). *Average financial aid package:* $22,754 (excluding resources awarded to replace EFC). 32% of all full-time freshmen had no need and received non-need-based gift aid.

UNDERGRADUATE FINANCIAL AID (Fall 2016, est.) 1,474 applied for aid; of those 84% were deemed to have need. 100% of undergraduates with need received aid; of those 24% had need fully met. *Average percent of need met:* 78% (excluding resources awarded to replace EFC). *Average financial aid package:* $22,440 (excluding resources awarded to replace EFC). 35% of all full-time undergraduates had no need and received non-need-based gift aid.

GIFT AID (NEED-BASED) *Total amount:* $17,680,408 (11% federal, 3% state, 80% institutional, 6% external sources). *Receiving aid:* Freshmen: 68% (349); all full-time undergraduates: 64% (1,232). *Average award:* Freshmen: $18,227; Undergraduates: $17,185. *Scholarships, grants, and awards:* Federal Pell, FSEOG, state, private, college/university gift aid from institutional funds.

GIFT AID (NON-NEED-BASED) *Total amount:* $9,290,051 (95% institutional, 5% external sources). *Receiving aid:* Freshmen: 12% (63). Undergraduates: 10% (195). *Average award:* Freshmen: $13,295. Undergraduates: $12,021. *Scholarships, grants, and awards by category:* Academic interests/achievement: 802 awards ($8,869,082 total): general academic interests/achievements. *Creative arts/performance:* 168 awards ($165,359 total): dance, journalism/publications, music, theater/drama. *Special achievements/activities:* 81 awards ($119,890 total): cheerleading/drum major, leadership. *Special characteristics:* 48 awards ($1,193,251 total): children of faculty/staff, general special characteristics. *Tuition waivers:* Full or partial for employees or children of employees, senior citizens. *ROTC:* Army cooperative.

LOANS *Student loans:* $9,072,933 (74% need-based, 26% non-need-based). 73% of past graduating class borrowed through all loan programs. *Average indebtedness per student:* $29,602. *Average need-based loan:* Freshmen: $3086. Undergraduates: $4734. *Parent loans:* $4,965,201 (39% need-based, 61% non-need-based). *Programs:* Federal Direct (Subsidized and Unsubsidized Stafford, PLUS), Perkins, alternative loans.

WORK-STUDY *Federal work-study:* Total amount: $1,022,443; 290 jobs averaging $725. *State or other work-study/employment:* Part-time jobs available.

ATHLETIC AWARDS Total amount: $4,484,698 (63% need-based, 37% non-need-based).

APPLYING FOR FINANCIAL AID *Required financial aid form:* FAFSA. *Financial aid deadline (priority):* 3/15. *Notification date:* Continuous beginning 3/1. Students must reply within 2 weeks of notification.

CONTACT Mr. Tony Tanking, Director of Financial Aid, Benedictine College, 1020 North Second Street, Atchison, KS 66002-1499, 913-360-7484 or toll-free 800-467-5340. *Fax:* 913-367-5462. *E-mail:* ttanking@benedictine.edu. *Website:* http://www.benedictine.edu/.

BENEDICTINE UNIVERSITY
Lisle, IL

Tuition & fees: N/R	Average undergraduate aid package: $21,842

ABOUT THE INSTITUTION Independent Roman Catholic, coed. *Awards:* certificates, diplomas, associate, bachelor's, master's, and doctoral degrees. 51 undergraduate majors. *Total enrollment:* 5,954. Undergraduates: 3,347. Freshmen: 451. Federal methodology is used as a basis for awarding need-based institutional aid.

FRESHMAN FINANCIAL AID (Fall 2016, est.) 511 applied for aid; of those 92% were deemed to have need. 100% of freshmen with need received aid. *Average financial aid package:* $24,062 (excluding resources awarded to replace EFC). 10% of all full-time freshmen had no need and received non-need-based gift aid.

UNDERGRADUATE FINANCIAL AID (Fall 2016, est.) 2,292 applied for aid; of those 94% were deemed to have need. 99% of undergraduates with need received aid. *Average financial aid package:* $21,842 (excluding resources awarded to replace EFC). 15% of all full-time undergraduates had no need and received non-need-based gift aid.

GIFT AID (NEED-BASED) *Total amount:* $11,549,187 (48% federal, 36% state, 16% institutional). *Receiving aid:* Freshmen: 54% (300); all full-time undergraduates:

53% (1,433). *Average award:* Freshmen: $9133; Undergraduates: $7892. *Scholarships, grants, and awards:* Federal Pell, FSEOG, state, college/university gift aid from institutional funds.

GIFT AID (NON-NEED-BASED) *Total amount:* $27,745,094 (99% institutional, 1% external sources). *Receiving aid:* Freshmen: 82% (455). Undergraduates: 69% (1,869). *Average award:* Freshmen: $12,278. Undergraduates: $12,106. *Scholarships, grants, and awards by category:* Academic interests/achievement: general academic interests/achievements. *Creative arts/performance:* music. *Special achievements/activities:* community service, general special achievements/activities, leadership, memberships. *Special characteristics:* children and siblings of alumni, children of faculty/staff, general special characteristics, international students, local/state students, out-of-state students, relatives of clergy, siblings of current students, veterans, veterans' children. *ROTC:* Army cooperative.

LOANS *Student loans:* $15,285,227 (51% need-based, 49% non-need-based). 79% of past graduating class borrowed through all loan programs. *Average indebtedness per student:* $29,070. *Average need-based loan:* Freshmen: $3422. Undergraduates: $4698. *Parent loans:* $5,547,232 (100% non-need-based). *Programs:* Federal Direct (Subsidized and Unsubsidized Stafford, PLUS), Perkins.

WORK-STUDY *Federal work-study:* Total amount: $333,617; jobs available. *State or other work-study/employment:* Part-time jobs available.

APPLYING FOR FINANCIAL AID *Required financial aid form:* FAFSA. *Financial aid deadline:* Continuous. *Notification date:* Continuous beginning 11/1.

CONTACT Diane Battistella, Senior Associate Dean of Financial Aid, Benedictine University, 5700 College Road, Lisle, IL 60532, 630-829-6415 or toll-free 888-829-6363 (out-of-state). *Fax:* 630-829-6101. *E-mail:* dbattistella@ben.edu. *Website:* http://www.ben.edu/.

BENNETT COLLEGE
Greensboro, NC

CONTACT Ms. Keisha Ragsdale, Director of Financial Aid, Bennett College, 900 East Washington Street, Greensboro, NC 27401, 336-370-8678 or toll-free 800-413-5323. *Fax:* 336-517-2204. *E-mail:* kragsdale@bennett.edu. *Website:* http://www.bennett.edu/.

BENNINGTON COLLEGE
Bennington, VT

Tuition & fees: $51,920	Average undergraduate aid package: $38,260

ABOUT THE INSTITUTION Independent, coed. *Awards:* certificates, bachelor's, and master's degrees. 87 undergraduate majors. *Total enrollment:* 805. Undergraduates: 711. Freshmen: 216. Both federal and institutional methodology are used as a basis for awarding need-based institutional aid.

UNDERGRADUATE EXPENSES for 2017–2018 *One-time required fee:* $2135. *Comprehensive fee:* $66,960 includes full-time tuition ($51,240), mandatory fees ($680), and room and board ($15,040). *College room only:* $8150. Full-time tuition and fees vary according to degree level and program. Room and board charges vary according to board plan. *Part-time tuition:* $2135 per credit hour.

FRESHMAN FINANCIAL AID (Fall 2015) 192 applied for aid; of those 74% were deemed to have need. 100% of freshmen with need received aid; of those 23% had need fully met. *Average percent of need met:* 84% (excluding resources awarded to replace EFC). *Average financial aid package:* $39,982 (excluding resources awarded to replace EFC). 23% of all full-time freshmen had no need and received non-need-based gift aid.

UNDERGRADUATE FINANCIAL AID (Fall 2015) 650 applied for aid; of those 65% were deemed to have need. 100% of undergraduates with need received aid; of those 14% had need fully met. *Average percent of need met:* 79% (excluding resources awarded to replace EFC). *Average financial aid package:* $38,260 (excluding resources awarded to replace EFC). 21% of all full-time undergraduates had no need and received non-need-based gift aid.

GIFT AID (NEED-BASED) *Total amount:* $11,809,049 (7% federal, 90% institutional, 3% external sources). *Receiving aid:* Freshmen: 66% (142); all full-time undergraduates: 61% (417). *Average award:* Freshmen: $36,264; Undergraduates: $33,968. *Scholarships, grants, and awards:* Federal Pell, FSEOG, state, private, college/university gift aid from institutional funds.

GIFT AID (NON-NEED-BASED) *Total amount:* $8,021,645 (99% institutional, 1% external sources). *Receiving aid:* Freshmen: 6% (12). Undergraduates: 5% (32). *Average award:* Freshmen: $10,285. Undergraduates: $10,098. *Scholarships, grants, and awards by category: Academic interests/achievement:* 146 awards ($1,473,282 total): general academic interests/achievements. *Tuition waivers:* Full or partial for employees or children of employees.

LOANS *Student loans:* $2,835,730 (69% need-based, 31% non-need-based). 74% of past graduating class borrowed through all loan programs. *Average indebtedness per student:* $28,263. *Average need-based loan:* Freshmen: $2293. Undergraduates: $3601. *Parent loans:* $1,338,691 (8% need-based, 92% non-need-based). *Programs:* Federal Direct (Subsidized and Unsubsidized Stafford, PLUS).

WORK-STUDY *Federal work-study:* 310 jobs averaging $1713. *State or other work-study/employment:* Total amount: $185,150 (100% non-need-based). 82 part-time jobs averaging $2300.

APPLYING FOR FINANCIAL AID *Required financial aid forms:* FAFSA, institution's own form, CSS Financial Aid PROFILE, state aid form, noncustodial (divorced/separated) parent's statement, business/farm supplement, federal income tax form(s), W-2 forms. *Financial aid deadline:* 2/15 (priority: 1/15). *Notification date:* 4/1. Students must reply by 5/1 or within 4 weeks of notification.

CONTACT Heather Clifford, Director of Financial Aid, Bennington College, One College Drive, Bennington, VT 05201, 802-440-4325 or toll-free 800-833-6845. *Fax:* 802-440-4880. *E-mail:* finaid@bennington.edu. *Website:* http://www.bennington.edu/.

BENTLEY UNIVERSITY
Waltham, MA

Tuition & fees: $45,760	Average undergraduate aid package: $35,525

ABOUT THE INSTITUTION Independent, coed. *Awards:* certificates, bachelor's, master's, and doctoral degrees. 24 undergraduate majors. *Total enrollment:* 5,508. Undergraduates: 4,222. Freshmen: 1,041. Both federal and institutional methodology are used as a basis for awarding need-based institutional aid.

UNDERGRADUATE EXPENSES for 2016–2017 *Application fee:* $50. *Comprehensive fee:* $60,890 includes full-time tuition ($44,210), mandatory fees ($1550), and room and board ($15,130). *College room only:* $9180. Room and board charges vary according to board plan and housing facility. *Part-time tuition:* $2250 per course. *Part-time fees:* $25 per term. Part-time tuition and fees vary according to class time and course load.

FRESHMAN FINANCIAL AID (Fall 2015) 618 applied for aid; of those 68% were deemed to have need. 100% of freshmen with need received aid; of those 41% had need fully met. *Average percent of need met:* 94% (excluding resources awarded to replace EFC). *Average financial aid package:* $34,352 (excluding resources awarded to replace EFC). 20% of all full-time freshmen had no need and received non-need-based gift aid.

UNDERGRADUATE FINANCIAL AID (Fall 2015) 2,387 applied for aid; of those 74% were deemed to have need. 100% of undergraduates with need received aid; of those 42% had need fully met. *Average percent of need met:* 93% (excluding resources awarded to replace EFC). *Average financial aid package:* $35,525 (excluding resources awarded to replace EFC). 21% of all full-time undergraduates had no need and received non-need-based gift aid.

GIFT AID (NEED-BASED) *Total amount:* $49,682,097 (7% federal, 2% state, 91% institutional). *Receiving aid:* Freshmen: 45% (414); all full-time undergraduates: 42% (1,730). *Average award:* Freshmen: $30,336; Undergraduates: $30,600. *Scholarships, grants, and awards:* Federal Pell, FSEOG, state, private, college/university gift aid from institutional funds.

GIFT AID (NON-NEED-BASED) *Total amount:* $18,902,289 (94% institutional, 6% external sources). *Receiving aid:* Freshmen: 10% (88). Undergraduates: 6% (252). *Average award:* Freshmen: $1801. Undergraduates: $18,705. *Scholarships, grants, and awards by category: Academic interests/achievement:* 1,598 awards ($29,592,032 total): general academic interests/achievements. *Special achievements/activities:* 24 awards ($220,000 total): community service, leadership. *Special characteristics:* 108 awards ($1,976,698 total): international students, members of

minority groups. *Tuition waivers:* Full or partial for employees or children of employees. *ROTC:* Army cooperative, Air Force cooperative.

LOANS *Student loans:* $18,637,374 (50% need-based, 50% non-need-based). 56% of past graduating class borrowed through all loan programs. *Average indebtedness per student:* $31,046. *Average need-based loan:* Freshmen: $3767. Undergraduates: $5106. *Parent loans:* $8,455,030 (100% non-need-based). *Programs:* Federal Direct (Subsidized and Unsubsidized Stafford, PLUS), Perkins, state.

WORK-STUDY *Federal work-study:* 761 jobs averaging $1794. *State or other work-study/employment:* Total amount: $709,875 (100% non-need-based). 900 part-time jobs averaging $1077.

ATHLETIC AWARDS *Total amount:* $2,816,852 (24% need-based, 76% non-need-based).

APPLYING FOR FINANCIAL AID *Required financial aid forms:* FAFSA, CSS Financial Aid PROFILE, noncustodial (divorced/separated) parent's statement, business/farm supplement, student tax returns (including W-2 and all schedules filed). *Financial aid deadline:* 1/7. *Notification date:* 3/31.

CONTACT Donna Kendall, Associate Vice President of Enrollment Management, Bentley University, 175 Forest Street, Waltham, MA 02452-4705, 781-891-3441 or toll-free 800-523-2354. *Fax:* 781-891-2448. *E-mail:* finaid@bentley.edu. *Website:* http://www.bentley.edu/.

BEREA COLLEGE
Berea, KY

Tuition & fees: $570	Average undergraduate aid package: $32,460

ABOUT THE INSTITUTION Independent, coed. *Awards:* bachelor's degrees. 38 undergraduate majors. *Total enrollment:* 1,665. Undergraduates: 1,665. Freshmen: 418. Federal methodology is used as a basis for awarding need-based institutional aid.

UNDERGRADUATE EXPENSES for 2016–2017 Room and board charges vary according to board plan. Financial aid is provided to all students for tuition costs.

FRESHMAN FINANCIAL AID (Fall 2016, est.) 418 applied for aid; of those 100% were deemed to have need. 100% of freshmen with need received aid. *Average percent of need met:* 98% (excluding resources awarded to replace EFC). *Average financial aid package:* $34,366 (excluding resources awarded to replace EFC).

UNDERGRADUATE FINANCIAL AID (Fall 2016, est.) 1,612 applied for aid; of those 100% were deemed to have need. 100% of undergraduates with need received aid. *Average percent of need met:* 93% (excluding resources awarded to replace EFC). *Average financial aid package:* $32,460 (excluding resources awarded to replace EFC).

GIFT AID (NEED-BASED) *Total amount:* $48,600,452 (15% federal, 8% state, 77% institutional). *Receiving aid:* Freshmen: 100% (418); all full-time undergraduates: 100% (1,612). *Average award:* Freshmen: $31,803; Undergraduates: $30,149. *Scholarships, grants, and awards:* Federal Pell, FSEOG, state, private, college/university gift aid from institutional funds.

LOANS *Student loans:* $623,284 (33% need-based, 67% non-need-based). 65% of past graduating class borrowed through all loan programs. *Average indebtedness per student:* $7062. *Average need-based loan:* Freshmen: $755. Undergraduates: $1147. *Parent loans:* $8000 (100% non-need-based). *Programs:* Federal Direct (Subsidized and Unsubsidized Stafford, PLUS), Perkins, college/university.

WORK-STUDY *Federal work-study:* Total amount: $3,054,311; jobs available. *State or other work-study/employment:* Total amount: $587,070 (100% need-based). Part-time jobs available.

APPLYING FOR FINANCIAL AID *Required financial aid form:* FAFSA. *Financial aid deadline:* 5/1 (priority: 2/1). *Notification date:* Continuous beginning 3/1. Students must reply within 2 weeks of notification.

CONTACT Theresa Lowder, Director of Student Financial Aid Services, Berea College, CPO 2172, Berea, KY 40404, 859-985-3313 or toll-free 800-326-5948. *Fax:* 859-985-3914. *E-mail:* lowdert@berea.edu. *Website:* http://www.berea.edu/.

BERGIN UNIVERSITY OF CANINE STUDIES
Rohnert Park, CA

CONTACT Financial Aid Office, Bergin University of Canine Studies, 5860 Labath Avenue, Rohnert Park, CA 94928, 707-545-3647. *Website:* http://www.berginu.edu/.

BERKELEY COLLEGE–NEW YORK CITY CAMPUS
New York, NY

CONTACT Office of Financial Aid, Berkeley College–New York City Campus, 3 East 43rd Street, New York, NY 10017, 800-446-5400. *E-mail:* financialaid@berkeleycollege.edu.
Website: http://www.berkeleycollege.edu/.

BERKELEY COLLEGE–WHITE PLAINS CAMPUS
White Plains, NY

CONTACT Office of Financial Aid, Berkeley College–White Plains Campus, 99 Church Street, White Plains, NY 10601, 800-446-5400. *E-mail:* financialaid@berkeleycollege.edu.
Website: http://www.berkeleycollege.edu/.

BERKELEY COLLEGE–WOODLAND PARK CAMPUS
Woodland Park, NJ

CONTACT Office of Financial Aid, Berkeley College–Woodland Park Campus, 44 Rifle Camp Road, Woodland Park, NJ 07424, 800-446-5400. *E-mail:* financialaid@berkeleycollege.edu.
Website: http://www.berkeleycollege.edu/.

BERKLEE COLLEGE OF MUSIC
Boston, MA

Tuition & fees: $41,398	Average undergraduate aid package: $18,827

ABOUT THE INSTITUTION Independent, coed. *Awards:* diplomas, bachelor's, and master's degrees. 13 undergraduate majors. *Total enrollment:* 5,272. Undergraduates: 5,112. Freshmen: 959. Both federal and institutional methodology are used as a basis for awarding need-based institutional aid.

UNDERGRADUATE EXPENSES for 2016–2017 *Application fee:* $150. *Comprehensive fee:* $59,398 includes full-time tuition ($40,220), mandatory fees ($1178), and room and board ($18,000). *Part-time tuition:* $1461 per credit. *Payment plan:* Tuition prepayment.

FRESHMAN FINANCIAL AID (Fall 2016, est.) 657 applied for aid; of those 82% were deemed to have need. 93% of freshmen with need received aid; of those 11% had need fully met. *Average percent of need met:* 35% (excluding resources awarded to replace EFC). *Average financial aid package:* $16,827 (excluding resources awarded to replace EFC). 20% of all full-time freshmen had no need and received non-need-based gift aid.

UNDERGRADUATE FINANCIAL AID (Fall 2016, est.) 2,120 applied for aid; of those 87% were deemed to have need. 95% of undergraduates with need received aid; of those 12% had need fully met. *Average percent of need met:* 38% (excluding resources awarded to replace EFC). *Average financial aid package:* $18,827 (excluding resources awarded to replace EFC). 24% of all full-time undergraduates had no need and received non-need-based gift aid.

GIFT AID (NEED-BASED) *Total amount:* $28,279,370 (12% federal, 1% state, 83% institutional, 4% external sources). *Receiving aid:* Freshmen: 11% (147); all full-time undergraduates: 12% (652). *Average award:* Freshmen: $1624; Undergraduates: $1892. *Scholarships, grants, and awards:* Federal Pell, FSEOG, state, private, college/university gift aid from institutional funds.

GIFT AID (NON NEED BASED) *Total amount:* $30,523,703 (95% institutional, 5% external sources). *Receiving aid:* Freshmen: 21% (279). Undergraduates: 20% (1,158). *Average award:* Freshmen: $19,354. Undergraduates: $18,776. *Scholarships, grants, and awards by category: Academic interests/achievement:* education, engineering/technologies, general academic interests/achievements. *Creative arts/performance:* music. *Special characteristics:* children and siblings of alumni, children of faculty/staff. *Tuition waivers:* Full or partial for employees or children of employees.

LOANS *Student loans:* $25,598,881 (53% need-based, 47% non-need-based). 41% of past graduating class borrowed through all loan programs. *Average indebtedness per student:* $48,331. *Average need-based loan:* Freshmen: $3418. Undergraduates: $4548. *Parent loans:* $20,869,483 (19% need-based, 81% non-need-based). *Programs:* Federal Direct (Subsidized and Unsubsidized Stafford, PLUS), Perkins, college/university, private loans.

WORK-STUDY *Federal work-study:* Total amount: $760,391; jobs available. *State or other work-study/employment:* Part-time jobs available.

APPLYING FOR FINANCIAL AID *Required financial aid forms:* FAFSA, CSS Financial Aid PROFILE, noncustodial (divorced/separated) parent's statement. *Financial aid deadline (priority):* 12/1. *Notification date:* Continuous beginning 12/31.

CONTACT Office of Financial Aid, Berklee College of Music, 921 Boylston Street, Boston, MA 02215-3693, 617-747-2274 or toll-free 800-BERKLEE. *Fax:* 617-747-2073. *E-mail:* financialaid@berklee.edu.
Website: http://www.berklee.edu/.

BERRY COLLEGE
Mount Berry, GA

Tuition & fees: $33,556	Average undergraduate aid package: $27,248

ABOUT THE INSTITUTION Independent interdenominational, coed. *Awards:* bachelor's and master's degrees. 47 undergraduate majors. *Total enrollment:* 2,174. Undergraduates: 2,073. Freshmen: 534. Federal methodology is used as a basis for awarding need-based institutional aid.

UNDERGRADUATE EXPENSES for 2016–2017 *Comprehensive fee:* $45,286 includes full-time tuition ($33,330), mandatory fees ($226), and room and board ($11,730). *College room only:* $6630. Room and board charges vary according to board plan and housing facility. *Part-time tuition:* $1111 per credit hour.

FRESHMAN FINANCIAL AID (Fall 2016, est.) 495 applied for aid; of those 79% were deemed to have need. 100% of freshmen with need received aid; of those 33% had need fully met. *Average percent of need met:* 84% (excluding resources awarded to replace EFC). *Average financial aid package:* $26,668 (excluding resources awarded to replace EFC). 27% of all full-time freshmen had no need and received non-need-based gift aid.

UNDERGRADUATE FINANCIAL AID (Fall 2016, est.) 1,756 applied for aid; of those 81% were deemed to have need. 100% of undergraduates with need received aid; of those 29% had need fully met. *Average percent of need met:* 83% (excluding resources awarded to replace EFC). *Average financial aid package:* $27,248 (excluding resources awarded to replace EFC). 30% of all full-time undergraduates had no need and received non-need-based gift aid.

GIFT AID (NEED-BASED) *Total amount:* $32,077,607 (6% federal, 9% state, 83% institutional, 2% external sources). *Receiving aid:* Freshmen: 73% (389); all full-time undergraduates: 70% (1,426). *Average award:* Freshmen: $23,045; Undergraduates: $22,585. *Scholarships, grants, and awards:* Federal Pell, FSEOG, state, private, college/university gift aid from institutional funds.

GIFT AID (NON-NEED-BASED) *Total amount:* $12,297,306 (17% state, 80% institutional, 3% external sources). *Receiving aid:* Freshmen: 18% (95). Undergraduates: 14% (284). *Average award:* Freshmen: $14,323. Undergraduates: $13,767.

Scholarships, grants, and awards by category: *Academic interests/ achievement:* agriculture, business, communication, education, English, general academic interests/achievements, humanities, religion/biblical studies. *Creative arts/performance:* art/fine arts, debating, journalism/publications, music, theater/drama. *Special achievements/activities:* community service, leadership, religious involvement. *Special characteristics:* adult students, children of faculty/staff, ethnic background, first-generation college students, international students, local/state students, members of minority groups, out-of-state students, veterans, veterans' children. **Tuition waivers:** Full or partial for employees or children of employees, senior citizens.

LOANS Student loans: $13,459,209 (56% need-based, 44% non-need-based). 71% of past graduating class borrowed through all loan programs. *Average indebtedness per student:* $26,449. **Average need-based loan:** Freshmen: $4091. Undergraduates: $4976. **Parent loans:** $4,086,157 (33% need-based, 67% non-need-based). **Programs:** Federal Direct (Subsidized and Unsubsidized Stafford, PLUS), Perkins, state, college/university.

WORK-STUDY Federal work-study: Total amount: $697,433; 358 jobs averaging $2270. **State or other work-study/employment:** Total amount: $572,007 (60% need-based, 40% non-need-based). 91 part-time jobs averaging $6294.

APPLYING FOR FINANCIAL AID Required financial aid forms: FAFSA, CSS Financial Aid PROFILE, state aid form. **Financial aid deadline (priority):** 1/15. **Notification date:** Continuous beginning 12/1. Students must reply by 5/1.

CONTACT Mrs. Donna Childres, Director of Financial Aid, Berry College, 2277 Martha Berry Highway, NW, Mount Berry, GA 30149-5007, 706-236-1714 or toll-free 800-237-7942. *Fax:* 706-290-2160. *E-mail:* financialaid@berry.edu. *Website:* http://www.berry.edu/.

BETHANY COLLEGE
Lindsborg, KS

CONTACT Ms. Amber Maneth, Office of Financial Aid, Bethany College, 335 East Swensson, Lindsborg, KS 67456-1897, 785-227-3311 Ext. 8248 or toll-free 800-826-2281. *Fax:* 785-227-2004. *E-mail:* manetha@bethanylb.edu. *Website:* http://www.bethanylb.edu/.

BETHANY COLLEGE
Bethany, WV

Tuition & fees: $27,638	Average undergraduate aid package: N/A

ABOUT THE INSTITUTION Independent Christian Church (Disciples of Christ), coed. **Awards:** bachelor's and master's degrees. 59 undergraduate majors. **Total enrollment:** 737. Undergraduates: 710. Freshmen: 208. Both federal and institutional methodology are used as a basis for awarding need-based institutional aid.

UNDERGRADUATE EXPENSES for 2016–2017 One-time required fee: $125. **Comprehensive fee:** $37,362 includes full-time tuition ($26,496), mandatory fees ($1142), and room and board ($9724). **College room only:** $4800. Full-time tuition and fees vary according to course load. Room and board charges vary according to board plan and housing facility. **Part-time tuition:** $1104 per credit hour. **Part-time fees:** $38.75 per credit hour. Part-time tuition and fees vary according to course load.

GIFT AID (NEED-BASED) Scholarships, grants, and awards: Federal Pell, FSEOG, state, private, college/university gift aid from institutional funds.

GIFT AID (NON-NEED-BASED) Scholarships, grants, and awards by category: *Academic interests/achievement:* general academic interests/achievements. *Creative arts/performance:* music. *Special achievements/activities:* community service, hobbies/interests, leadership, religious involvement. *Special characteristics:* children and siblings of alumni, children of faculty/staff, international students, local/state students, out-of-state students, relatives of clergy, religious affiliation. **Tuition waivers:** Full or partial for employees or children of employees.

LOANS Student loans: 95% of past graduating class borrowed through all loan programs. *Average indebtedness per student:* $27,057. **Programs:** Federal Direct (Subsidized and Unsubsidized Stafford, PLUS), Perkins, alternative loans.

WORK-STUDY Federal work-study: 141 jobs averaging $2000. **State or other work-study/employment:** 166 part-time jobs averaging $1500.

APPLYING FOR FINANCIAL AID Required financial aid form: FAFSA. **Financial aid deadline:** Continuous. **Notification date:** Continuous beginning 2/15. Students must reply within 2 weeks of notification.

CONTACT Jason McClain, Assistant Vice President of Financial Aid, Bethany College, Center for Enrollment and Financial Aid #4, 31 East Campus Drive, Bethany, WV 26032, 304-829-7611 or toll-free 800-922-7611. *Fax:* 304-829-7142. *E-mail:* financialaid@bethanywv.edu. *Website:* http://www.bethanywv.edu/.

BETHANY GLOBAL UNIVERSITY
Bloomington, MN

CONTACT Financial Aid Office, Bethany Global University, 6820 Auto Club Road, Suite C, Bloomington, MN 55438, 952-944-2121 or toll-free 800-323-3417. *Website:* http://www.bethanygu.edu/.

BETHANY LUTHERAN COLLEGE
Mankato, MN

Tuition & fees: $25,890	Average undergraduate aid package: $20,972

ABOUT THE INSTITUTION Independent Lutheran, coed. **Awards:** bachelor's degrees. 25 undergraduate majors. **Total enrollment:** 587. Undergraduates: 587. Freshmen: 138. Federal methodology is used as a basis for awarding need-based institutional aid.

UNDERGRADUATE EXPENSES for 2016–2017 One-time required fee: $130. **Comprehensive fee:** $33,850 includes full-time tuition ($25,440), mandatory fees ($450), and room and board ($7960). Room and board charges vary according to board plan, housing facility, and student level. **Part-time tuition:** $1080 per credit hour. **Part-time fees:** $225 per term. Part-time tuition and fees vary according to course load.

FRESHMAN FINANCIAL AID (Fall 2015) 122 applied for aid; of those 90% were deemed to have need. 100% of freshmen with need received aid; of those 18% had need fully met. **Average percent of need met:** 86% (excluding resources awarded to replace EFC). **Average financial aid package:** $21,709 (excluding resources awarded to replace EFC). 13% of all full-time freshmen had no need and received non-need-based gift aid.

UNDERGRADUATE FINANCIAL AID (Fall 2015) 422 applied for aid; of those 92% were deemed to have need. 100% of undergraduates with need received aid; of those 16% had need fully met. **Average percent of need met:** 84% (excluding resources awarded to replace EFC). **Average financial aid package:** $20,972 (excluding resources awarded to replace EFC). 14% of all full-time undergraduates had no need and received non-need-based gift aid.

GIFT AID (NEED-BASED) Total amount: $5,798,124 (13% federal, 15% state, 70% institutional, 2% external sources). **Receiving aid:** Freshmen: 82% (110); all full-time undergraduates: 82% (389). **Average award:** Freshmen: $17,927; Undergraduates: $16,242. **Scholarships, grants, and awards:** Federal Pell, FSEOG, state, private, college/university gift aid from institutional funds.

GIFT AID (NON-NEED-BASED) Total amount: $827,460 (1% state, 95% institutional, 4% external sources). **Receiving aid:** Freshmen: 9% (12). Undergraduates: 8% (38). **Average award:** Freshmen: $10,707. Undergraduates: $7783. **Scholarships, grants, and awards by category:** *Creative arts/performance:* 43 awards ($80,000 total): art/fine arts, debating, journalism/publications, music, theater/drama. *Special characteristics:* 21 awards ($418,892 total): children of faculty/staff. **Tuition waivers:** Full or partial for employees or children of employees, senior citizens. **ROTC:** Army cooperative.

LOANS Student loans: $3,383,436 (64% need-based, 36% non-need-based). 76% of past graduating class borrowed through all loan programs. *Average indebtedness per student:* $32,310. **Average need-based loan:** Freshmen: $4377. Undergraduates: $5046. **Parent loans:** $185,331 (24% need-based, 76% non-need-based). **Programs:** Federal Direct (Subsidized and Unsubsidized Stafford, PLUS), Perkins, state, alternative loans.

WORK-STUDY Federal work-study: 26 jobs averaging $1705. **State or other work-study/employment:** Total amount: $280,576 (53% need-based, 47% non-need-based). 276 part-time jobs averaging $1028.

APPLYING FOR FINANCIAL AID *Required financial aid forms:* FAFSA, institution's own form. *Financial aid deadline (priority):* 4/15. *Notification date:* Continuous beginning 12/15. Students must reply within 4 weeks of notification.

CONTACT Financial Aid Office, Bethany Lutheran College, 700 Luther Drive, Mankato, MN 56001-6163, 507-344-7328 or toll-free 800-944-3066. *Fax:* 507-344-7376. *E-mail:* finaid@blc.edu. *Website:* http://www.blc.edu/.

BETHEL COLLEGE
Mishawaka, IN

Tuition & fees: $27,930	Average undergraduate aid package: N/A

ABOUT THE INSTITUTION Independent Missionary Church, coed. *Awards:* associate, bachelor's, and master's degrees. 59 undergraduate majors. *Total enrollment:* 1,639. Undergraduates: 1,388. Freshmen: 243. Federal methodology is used as a basis for awarding need-based institutional aid.

UNDERGRADUATE EXPENSES for 2017–2018 *Comprehensive fee:* $36,730 includes full-time tuition ($27,580), mandatory fees ($350), and room and board ($8800). *College room only:* $4160. Full-time tuition and fees vary according to program. Room and board charges vary according to board plan and housing facility. *Part-time tuition:* $880 per credit hour. *Part-time fees:* $150 per year. Part-time tuition and fees vary according to course load and program.

GIFT AID (NEED-BASED) *Scholarships, grants, and awards:* Federal Pell, FSEOG, state, private, college/university gift aid from institutional funds, Federal Nursing.

GIFT AID (NON-NEED-BASED) *Average award:* Freshmen: $11,141. Undergraduates: $11,697. *Scholarships, grants, and awards by category:* Academic interests/achievement: 674 awards ($6,240,000 total): general academic interests/achievements. Creative arts/performance: art/fine arts, music, theater/drama. Special achievements/activities: general special achievements/activities, leadership. Special characteristics: children of faculty/staff, general special characteristics, international students, members of minority groups. *Tuition waivers:* Full or partial for employees or children of employees. *ROTC:* Army cooperative, Air Force cooperative.

LOANS *Student loans:* 70% of past graduating class borrowed through all loan programs. *Average indebtedness per student:* $34,148. *Programs:* Federal Direct (Subsidized and Unsubsidized Stafford, PLUS), Perkins, Federal Nursing.

WORK-STUDY Federal work-study jobs available.

APPLYING FOR FINANCIAL AID *Required financial aid form:* FAFSA. *Financial aid deadline:* 3/10 (priority: 3/1). *Notification date:* Continuous beginning 2/1.

CONTACT Mrs. Cindi Pedersen, Director of Financial Aid, Bethel College, 1001 Bethel Circle, Mishawaka, IN 46545-5591, 574-807-7239 or toll-free 800-422-4101. *Fax:* 574-807-7122. *E-mail:* pedersc@bethelcollege.edu. *Website:* http://www.bethelcollege.edu/.

BETHEL COLLEGE
North Newton, KS

Tuition & fees: $27,720	Average undergraduate aid package: $24,435

ABOUT THE INSTITUTION Independent Mennonite Church USA, coed. *Awards:* certificates and bachelor's degrees. 17 undergraduate majors. *Total enrollment:* 460. Undergraduates: 460. Freshmen: 99. Federal methodology is used as a basis for awarding need-based institutional aid.

UNDERGRADUATE EXPENSES for 2017–2018 *Application fee:* $20. *Comprehensive fee:* $36,990 includes full-time tuition ($27,480), mandatory fees ($240), and room and board ($9270). *College room only:* $4890. Room and board charges vary according to board plan, housing facility, and student level. *Part-time tuition:* $985 per credit hour. *Part-time fees:* $10 per credit hour. Part-time tuition and fees vary according to course load.

FRESHMAN FINANCIAL AID (Fall 2015) 116 applied for aid; of those 100% were deemed to have need. 100% of freshmen with need received aid; of those 21% had need fully met. *Average percent of need met:* 75% (excluding resources

awarded to replace EFC). *Average financial aid package:* $22,512 (excluding resources awarded to replace EFC). 5% of all full-time freshmen had no need and received non-need-based gift aid.

UNDERGRADUATE FINANCIAL AID (Fall 2015) 452 applied for aid; of those 96% were deemed to have need. 100% of undergraduates with need received aid; of those 20% had need fully met. *Average percent of need met:* 80% (excluding resources awarded to replace EFC). *Average financial aid package:* $24,435 (excluding resources awarded to replace EFC). 13% of all full-time undergraduates had no need and received non-need-based gift aid.

GIFT AID (NEED-BASED) *Total amount:* $1,731,224 (69% federal, 29% state, 2% institutional). *Receiving aid:* Freshmen: 70% (87); all full-time undergraduates: 67% (344). *Average award:* Freshmen: $5027; Undergraduates: $5498. *Scholarships, grants, and awards:* Federal Pell, FSEOG, state, college/university gift aid from institutional funds.

GIFT AID (NON-NEED-BASED) *Total amount:* $5,215,964 (96% institutional, 4% external sources). *Receiving aid:* Freshmen: 94% (116). Undergraduates: 84% (434). *Average award:* Freshmen: $12,083. Undergraduates: $10,892. *Scholarships, grants, and awards by category:* Academic interests/achievement: biological sciences, business, communication, general academic interests/achievements, mathematics, premedicine, social sciences. Creative arts/performance: art/fine arts, debating, music, theater/drama. Special achievements/activities: cheerleading/drum major. Special characteristics: children and siblings of alumni, children of current students, children of faculty/staff, ethnic background, general special characteristics, international students, local/state students, previous college experience, relatives of clergy, religious affiliation, siblings of current students, spouses of current students. *Tuition waivers:* Full or partial for minority students, children of alumni, employees or children of employees, senior citizens.

LOANS *Student loans:* $3,238,246 (100% need-based). 72% of past graduating class borrowed through all loan programs. *Average indebtedness per student:* $5633. *Average need-based loan:* Freshmen: $5755. Undergraduates: $8251. *Parent loans:* $951,433 (100% non-need-based). *Programs:* Federal Direct (Subsidized and Unsubsidized Stafford, PLUS), Perkins.

WORK-STUDY *Federal work-study:* jobs available. *State or other work-study/employment:* 150 part-time jobs averaging $1026.

ATHLETIC AWARDS Total amount: $1,317,263 (100% non-need-based).

APPLYING FOR FINANCIAL AID *Required financial aid form:* FAFSA. *Financial aid deadline (priority):* 4/1. *Notification date:* Continuous beginning 2/1. Students must reply by 5/1 or within 2 weeks of notification.

CONTACT Mr. Clark Oswald, Director of Financial Aid, Bethel College, 300 East 27th Street, North Newton, KS 67117, 316-284-5232 or toll-free 800-522-1887 Ext. 230. *Fax:* 316-284-5845. *E-mail:* coswald@bethelks.edu. *Website:* http://www.bethelks.edu/.

BETHEL COLLEGE
Hampton, VA

CONTACT Financial Aid Office, Bethel College, 1705 Todds Lane, Hampton, VA 23666, 757-826-1426. *Website:* http://www.bcva.edu/.

BETHEL UNIVERSITY
St. Paul, MN

Tuition & fees: $36,210	Average undergraduate aid package: $27,371

ABOUT THE INSTITUTION Independent Baptist General Conference, coed. *Awards:* certificates, associate, bachelor's, master's, and doctoral degrees. 50 undergraduate majors. *Total enrollment:* 4,615. Undergraduates: 2,965. Freshmen: 565. Federal methodology is used as a basis for awarding need-based institutional aid.

UNDERGRADUATE EXPENSES for 2017–2018 *Comprehensive fee:* $46,550 includes full-time tuition ($36,060), mandatory fees ($150), and room and board ($10,340). *College room only:* $5830. Room and board charges vary according to board plan. *Part-time tuition:* $1510 per credit. Part-time tuition and fees vary according to course load. *Payment plan:* Tuition prepayment.

FRESHMAN FINANCIAL AID (Fall 2016, est.) 502 applied for aid; of those 86% were deemed to have need. 100% of freshmen with need received aid; of those 18% had need fully met. *Average percent of need met:* 81% (excluding resources awarded to replace EFC). *Average financial aid package:* $27,448 (excluding resources awarded to replace EFC). 22% of all full-time freshmen had no need and received non-need-based gift aid.

UNDERGRADUATE FINANCIAL AID (Fall 2016, est.) 2,005 applied for aid; of those 85% were deemed to have need. 100% of undergraduates with need received aid; of those 20% had need fully met. *Average percent of need met:* 81% (excluding resources awarded to replace EFC). *Average financial aid package:* $27,371 (excluding resources awarded to replace EFC). 26% of all full-time undergraduates had no need and received non-need-based gift aid.

GIFT AID (NEED-BASED) *Total amount:* $35,697,294 (8% federal, 11% state, 79% institutional, 2% external sources). *Receiving aid:* Freshmen: 78% (433); all full-time undergraduates: 72% (1,704). *Average award:* Freshmen: $21,689; Undergraduates: $21,019. *Scholarships, grants, and awards:* Federal Pell, FSEOG, state, private, college/university gift aid from institutional funds.

GIFT AID (NON-NEED-BASED) *Total amount:* $9,300,868 (1% federal, 94% institutional, 5% external sources). *Receiving aid:* Freshmen: 10% (57). Undergraduates: 10% (227). *Average award:* Freshmen: $12,687. Undergraduates: $12,232. *Scholarships, grants, and awards by category: Academic interests/ achievement:* 2,228 awards ($22,263,683 total): general academic interests/achievements. *Creative arts/performance:* 115 awards ($370,000 total): art/fine arts, debating, music, theater/drama. *Special achievements/activities:* 368 awards ($511,750 total): community service, leadership, religious involvement. *Special characteristics:* 758 awards ($3,177,322 total): children and siblings of alumni, children of faculty/staff, out-of-state students, relatives of clergy, veterans, veterans' children. *Tuition waivers:* Full or partial for employees or children of employees. *ROTC:* Army cooperative, Air Force cooperative.

LOANS *Student loans:* $17,945,970 (60% need-based, 40% non-need-based). 77% of past graduating class borrowed through all loan programs. *Average indebtedness per student:* $36,132. *Average need-based loan:* Freshmen: $3151. Undergraduates: $3971. *Parent loans:* $4,655,558 (42% need-based, 58% non-need-based). *Programs:* Federal Direct (Subsidized and Unsubsidized Stafford, PLUS), state, alternative loans.

WORK-STUDY *Federal work-study:* Total amount: $600,000; jobs available. *State or other work-study/employment:* Total amount: $3,007,540 (71% need-based, 29% non-need-based). Part-time jobs available.

APPLYING FOR FINANCIAL AID *Required financial aid form:* FAFSA. *Financial aid deadline (priority):* 4/15. *Notification date:* Continuous beginning 3/1.

CONTACT Mr. Jeffrey D. Olson, Director of Financial Aid, Bethel University, 3900 Bethel Drive, St. Paul, MN 55112-6999, 651-638-6241 or toll-free 800-255-8706 Ext. 6242. *Fax:* 651-635-1491. *E-mail:* finaid@bethel.edu. *Website:* http://www.bethel.edu/.

BETHEL UNIVERSITY
McKenzie, TN

CONTACT Laura Bateman, Office of Financial Aid, Bethel University, 325 Cherry Avenue, McKenzie, TN 38201, 901-352-4007. *Fax:* 901-352-4069. *Website:* http://www.bethelu.edu/.

BETHESDA UNIVERSITY
Anaheim, CA

CONTACT Ms. Grace Choi, Financial Aid Administrator, Bethesda University, 730 North Euclid Street, Anaheim, CA 92801, 714-683-1413. *Fax:* 714-517-1948. *E-mail:* financialaid@bcu.edu. *Website:* http://www.buc.edu/.

BETH HAMEDRASH SHAAREI YOSHER INSTITUTE
Brooklyn, NY

CONTACT Financial Aid Office, Beth HaMedrash Shaarei Yosher Institute, 4102-10 16th Avenue, Brooklyn, NY 11204, 718-854-2290.

BETH HATALMUD RABBINICAL COLLEGE
Brooklyn, NY

CONTACT Financial Aid Office, Beth Hatalmud Rabbinical College, 2127 82nd Street, Brooklyn, NY 11204, 718-259-2525.

BETH MEDRASH GOVOHA
Lakewood, NJ

CONTACT Financial Aid Office, Beth Medrash Govoha, 617 Sixth Street, Lakewood, NJ 08701-2797, 732-367-1060.

BETHUNE-COOKMAN UNIVERSITY
Daytona Beach, FL

Tuition & fees: $14,410	Average undergraduate aid package: $13,302

ABOUT THE INSTITUTION Independent Methodist, coed. *Awards:* bachelor's and master's degrees. 38 undergraduate majors. *Total enrollment:* 3,934. Undergraduates: 3,796. Freshmen: 1,167. Federal methodology is used as a basis for awarding need-based institutional aid.

UNDERGRADUATE EXPENSES for 2016–2017 *Application fee:* $25. *Comprehensive fee:* $23,120 includes full-time tuition ($13,440), mandatory fees ($970), and room and board ($8710). *College room only:* $6710. Full-time tuition and fees vary according to course load and degree level. Room and board charges vary according to housing facility. *Part-time tuition:* $560 per credit hour. *Part-time fees:* $50 per credit hour. Part-time tuition and fees vary according to course load and degree level.

FRESHMAN FINANCIAL AID (Fall 2016, est.) 1,262 applied for aid; of those 98% were deemed to have need. 100% of freshmen with need received aid; of those 6% had need fully met. *Average percent of need met:* 49% (excluding resources awarded to replace EFC). *Average financial aid package:* $13,227 (excluding resources awarded to replace EFC). 2% of all full-time freshmen had no need and received non-need-based gift aid.

UNDERGRADUATE FINANCIAL AID (Fall 2016, est.) 3,436 applied for aid; of those 97% were deemed to have need. 100% of undergraduates with need received aid; of those 5% had need fully met. *Average percent of need met:* 48% (excluding resources awarded to replace EFC). *Average financial aid package:* $13,302 (excluding resources awarded to replace EFC). 2% of all full-time undergraduates had no need and received non-need-based gift aid.

GIFT AID (NEED-BASED) *Total amount:* $29,061,999 (52% federal, 25% state, 21% institutional, 2% external sources). *Receiving aid:* Freshmen: 93% (1,201); all full-time undergraduates: 90% (3,185). *Average award:* Freshmen: $10,177; Undergraduates: $9982. *Scholarships, grants, and awards:* Federal Pell, FSEOG, state, private, college/university gift aid from institutional funds, United Negro College Fund.

GIFT AID (NON-NEED-BASED) *Total amount:* $1,486,403 (17% state, 73% institutional, 10% external sources). *Receiving aid:* Freshmen: 4% (48). Undergraduates: 3% (113). *Average award:* Freshmen: $12,141. Undergraduates: $10,915. *Scholarships, grants, and awards by category: Academic interests/ achievement:* 180 awards ($1,109,670 total): general academic interests/achievements. *Tuition waivers:* Full or partial for employees or children of employees. *ROTC:* Army cooperative, Air Force cooperative.

LOANS *Student loans:* $25,730,919 (94% need-based, 6% non-need-based). 85% of past graduating class borrowed through all loan programs. *Average indebtedness*

per student: $35,082. *Average need-based loan:* Freshmen: $3575. Undergraduates: $4027. *Parent loans:* $13,236,217 (87% need-based, 13% non-need-based). *Programs:* Federal Direct (Subsidized and Unsubsidized Stafford, PLUS), alternative loans.
WORK-STUDY *Federal work-study:* Total amount: $301,323; 200 jobs averaging $2500. *State or other work-study/employment:* Total amount: $19,750 (82% need-based, 18% non-need-based). 100 part-time jobs averaging $2000.
ATHLETIC AWARDS Total amount: $4,496,158 (71% need-based, 29% non-need-based).
APPLYING FOR FINANCIAL AID *Required financial aid form:* FAFSA. *Financial aid deadline (priority):* 4/1. *Notification date:* Continuous beginning 3/1. Students must reply within 3 weeks of notification.
CONTACT Ms. Salina Hamilton, Director of Financial Aid, Bethune-Cookman University, 640 Dr. Mary McLeod Bethune Boulevard, Daytona Beach, FL 32114-3099, 386-481-2628 or toll-free 800-448-0228. *Fax:* 386-481-2621. *E-mail:* hamiltonsd@cookman.edu.
Website: http://www.cookman.edu/.

BEULAH HEIGHTS UNIVERSITY
Atlanta, GA

CONTACT Ms. Patricia Banks, Director of Financial Aid, Beulah Heights University, 892 Berne Street, SE, Atlanta, GA 30316, 404-627-2681 or toll-free 888-777-BHBC. *Fax:* 404-627-0702. *E-mail:* pat.banks@beulah.org.
Website: http://www.beulah.org/.

BINGHAMTON UNIVERSITY, STATE UNIVERSITY OF NEW YORK
Binghamton, NY

Tuition & fees (NY res): $9271	Average undergraduate aid package: $12,986

ABOUT THE INSTITUTION State-supported, coed. *Awards:* certificates, bachelor's, master's, and doctoral degrees. 76 undergraduate majors. *Total enrollment:* 17,292. Undergraduates: 13,632. Freshmen: 2,708. Institutional methodology is used as a basis for awarding need-based institutional aid.
UNDERGRADUATE EXPENSES for 2016–2017 *Application fee:* $50. *Tuition, state resident:* full-time $6470; part-time $270 per credit hour. *Tuition, nonresident:* full-time $21,550; part-time $898 per credit hour. *Required fees:* full-time $2801; $113.75 per credit hour or $29.50 per term. Full-time tuition and fees vary according to program. Part-time tuition and fees vary according to course load and program. *College room and board:* $13,590; *Room only:* $8804. Room and board charges vary according to board plan and housing facility.
FRESHMAN FINANCIAL AID (Fall 2016, est.) 2,181 applied for aid; of those 58% were deemed to have need. 100% of freshmen with need received aid; of those 13% had need fully met. *Average percent of need met:* 63% (excluding resources awarded to replace EFC). *Average financial aid package:* $11,602 (excluding resources awarded to replace EFC). 4% of all full-time freshmen had no need and received non-need-based gift aid.
UNDERGRADUATE FINANCIAL AID (Fall 2016, est.) 8,696 applied for aid; of those 72% were deemed to have need. 100% of undergraduates with need received aid; of those 15% had need fully met. *Average percent of need met:* 72% (excluding resources awarded to replace EFC). *Average financial aid package:* $12,986 (excluding resources awarded to replace EFC). 3% of all full-time undergraduates had no need and received non-need-based gift aid.
GIFT AID (NEED-BASED) *Total amount:* $44,914,242 (42% federal, 49% state, 7% institutional, 2% external sources). *Receiving aid:* Freshmen: 37% (989); all full-time undergraduates: 40% (5,227). *Average award:* Freshmen: $9067; Undergraduates: $8667. *Scholarships, grants, and awards:* Federal Pell, FSEOG, private, college/university gift aid from institutional funds.
GIFT AID (NON-NEED-BASED) *Total amount:* $5,317,699 (53% state, 32% institutional, 15% external sources). *Receiving aid:* Freshmen: 6% (169). Undergraduates: 3% (416). *Average award:* Freshmen: $6126. Undergraduates: $7250. *Scholarships, grants, and awards by category:* Academic interests/achievement: 410

awards ($1,915,484 total): area/ethnic studies, biological sciences, business, computer science, education, engineering/technologies, English, foreign languages, general academic interests/achievements, home economics, humanities, international studies, mathematics, physical sciences, premedicine, social sciences. *Creative arts/performance:* 27 awards ($31,475 total): art/fine arts, cinema/film/broadcasting, creative writing, dance, general creative arts/performance, journalism/publications, music, performing arts, theater/drama. *Special achievements/activities:* 65 awards ($122,050 total): community service, general special achievements/activities, leadership. *Special characteristics:* 161 awards ($819,700 total): adult students, children and siblings of alumni, children of faculty/staff, ethnic background, first-generation college students, handicapped students, international students, local/state students, married students, members of minority groups, out-of-state students, veterans, veterans' children.
ROTC: Army cooperative, Air Force cooperative.
LOANS *Student loans:* $77,747,195 (72% need-based, 28% non-need-based). 50% of past graduating class borrowed through all loan programs. *Average indebtedness per student:* $25,718. *Average need-based loan:* Freshmen: $3777. Undergraduates: $5010. *Parent loans:* $14,301,658 (69% need-based, 31% non-need-based). *Programs:* Federal Direct (Subsidized and Unsubsidized Stafford, PLUS), Perkins, college/university.
WORK-STUDY *Federal work-study:* Total amount: $543,933; 296 jobs averaging $1444.
ATHLETIC AWARDS Total amount: $4,846,122 (100% non-need-based).
APPLYING FOR FINANCIAL AID *Required financial aid forms:* FAFSA, state aid form. *Financial aid deadline (priority):* 1/1. *Notification date:* Continuous beginning 1/31. Students must reply within 2 weeks of notification.
CONTACT Ms. Patricia Donahue, Director of Student Financial Aid and Student Records, Binghamton University, State University of New York, PO Box 6000, Binghamton, NY 13902-6000, 607-777-2428. *Fax:* 607-777-6897. *E-mail:* finaid@binghamton.edu.
Website: http://www.binghamton.edu/.

BIOLA UNIVERSITY
La Mirada, CA

Tuition & fees: N/R	Average undergraduate aid package: $18,943

ABOUT THE INSTITUTION Independent interdenominational, coed. *Awards:* certificates, diplomas, bachelor's, master's, and doctoral degrees. 98 undergraduate majors. *Total enrollment:* 6,095. Undergraduates: 4,091. Freshmen: 872. Institutional methodology is used as a basis for awarding need-based institutional aid.
UNDERGRADUATE EXPENSES for 2017–2018 *Application fee:* $45.
FRESHMAN FINANCIAL AID (Fall 2015) 767 applied for aid; of those 87% were deemed to have need. 98% of freshmen with need received aid; of those 7% had need fully met. *Average percent of need met:* 51% (excluding resources awarded to replace EFC). *Average financial aid package:* $19,726 (excluding resources awarded to replace EFC). 25% of all full-time freshmen had no need and received non-need-based gift aid.
UNDERGRADUATE FINANCIAL AID (Fall 2015) 3,256 applied for aid; of those 88% were deemed to have need. 99% of undergraduates with need received aid; of those 6% had need fully met. *Average percent of need met:* 49% (excluding resources awarded to replace EFC). *Average financial aid package:* $18,943 (excluding resources awarded to replace EFC). 23% of all full-time undergraduates had no need and received non-need-based gift aid.
GIFT AID (NEED-BASED) *Total amount:* $38,442,506 (16% federal, 19% state, 65% institutional). *Receiving aid:* Freshmen: 70% (652); all full-time undergraduates: 67% (2,811). *Average award:* Freshmen: $15,270; Undergraduates: $13,487. *Scholarships, grants, and awards:* Federal Pell, FSEOG, state, private, college/university gift aid from institutional funds.
GIFT AID (NON-NEED-BASED) *Total amount:* $7,774,694 (99% institutional, 1% external sources). *Receiving aid:* Freshmen: 3% (28). Undergraduates: 2% (101). *Average award:* Freshmen: $8052. Undergraduates: $7392. *Scholarships, grants, and awards by category:* Academic interests/achievement: biological sciences, communication, general academic interests/achievements. *Creative arts/performance:* cinema/film/broadcasting, journalism/publications, music, theater/drama. *Special achievements/activities:* community service, leadership. *Special characteristics:* children of faculty/staff, ethnic background, international students, members of

minority groups, relatives of clergy. *Tuition waivers:* Full or partial for employees or children of employees. *ROTC:* Army cooperative, Air Force cooperative.

LOANS *Student loans:* $25,948,569 (80% need-based, 20% non-need-based). 68% of past graduating class borrowed through all loan programs. *Average indebtedness per student:* $35,630. *Average need-based loan:* Freshmen: $3123. Undergraduates: $3958. *Parent loans:* $13,684,242 (61% need-based, 39% non-need-based). *Programs:* Federal Direct (Subsidized and Unsubsidized Stafford, PLUS), Perkins, Federal Nursing, college/university, alternative loans.

WORK-STUDY *Federal work-study:* 340 jobs averaging $1682.

ATHLETIC AWARDS Total amount: $2,178,333 (52% need-based, 48% non-need-based).

APPLYING FOR FINANCIAL AID *Required financial aid form:* FAFSA. *Financial aid deadline (priority):* 3/1. *Notification date:* Continuous beginning 3/1.

CONTACT Office of Financial Aid, Biola University, 13800 Biola Avenue, La Mirada, CA 90639-0001, 562-903-4742 or toll-free 800-652-4652. *Fax:* 562-906-4541. *E-mail:* finaid@biola.edu.
Website: http://www.biola.edu/.

BIRMINGHAM-SOUTHERN COLLEGE
Birmingham, AL

ABOUT THE INSTITUTION Independent Methodist, coed. 42 undergraduate majors.

GIFT AID (NEED-BASED) *Scholarships, grants, and awards:* Federal Pell, FSEOG, state, private, college/university gift aid from institutional funds.

GIFT AID (NON-NEED-BASED) *Scholarships, grants, and awards by category: Academic interests/achievement:* area/ethnic studies, biological sciences, business, communication, computer science, education, engineering/technologies, English, foreign languages, general academic interests/achievements, health fields, humanities, international studies, mathematics, physical sciences, premedicine, religion/biblical studies, social sciences. *Creative arts/performance:* art/fine arts, dance, music, performing arts, theater/drama. *Special achievements/activities:* junior miss, leadership, memberships, religious involvement. *Special characteristics:* adult students, children and siblings of alumni, children of faculty/staff, ethnic background, first-generation college students, general special characteristics, international students, local/state students, previous college experience, relatives of clergy, religious affiliation, veterans, veterans' children.

LOANS *Programs:* Federal Direct (Subsidized and Unsubsidized Stafford, PLUS), Perkins, college/university.

WORK-STUDY *Federal work-study:* jobs available. *State or other work-study/employment:* Total amount: $138,221 (100% non-need-based). Part-time jobs available.

APPLYING FOR FINANCIAL AID *Required financial aid forms:* FAFSA, state aid form.

CONTACT Financial Aid Office, Birmingham-Southern College, 900 Arkadelphia Road, Birmingham, AL 35254, 205-226-4688 or toll-free 800-523-5793. *Fax:* 205-226-3082. *E-mail:* finaid@bsc.edu.
Website: http://www.bsc.edu/.

BIRTHINGWAY COLLEGE OF MIDWIFERY
Portland, OR

CONTACT Financial Aid Office, Birthingway College of Midwifery, 12113 SE Foster Road, Portland, OR 97299, 503-760-3131.
Website: http://www.birthingway.edu/.

BLACKBURN COLLEGE
Carlinville, IL

CONTACT Mrs. Jane Kelsey, Financial Aid Administrator, Blackburn College, 700 College Avenue, Carlinville, IL 62626-1498, 217-854-3231 Ext. 4227 or toll-free 800-233-3550. *Fax:* 217-854-3731.
Website: http://www.blackburn.edu/.

BLACK HILLS STATE UNIVERSITY
Spearfish, SD

Tuition & fees (SD res): $8004	Average undergraduate aid package: N/A

ABOUT THE INSTITUTION State-supported, coed. *Awards:* certificates, associate, bachelor's, and master's degrees. 47 undergraduate majors. *Total enrollment:* 4,489. Undergraduates: 4,020. Freshmen: 507. Federal methodology is used as a basis for awarding need-based institutional aid.

UNDERGRADUATE EXPENSES for 2017–2018 *Tuition, state resident:* full-time $6984; part-time $266.80 per credit hour. *Tuition, nonresident:* full-time $9900; part-time $364 per credit hour. *Required fees:* full-time $1020. Full-time tuition and fees vary according to course load, location, program, and reciprocity agreements. Part-time tuition and fees vary according to course load, location, program, and reciprocity agreements. *College room and board:* $6695. Room and board charges vary according to board plan and housing facility.

GIFT AID (NEED-BASED) *Scholarships, grants, and awards:* Federal Pell, FSEOG, state, private, college/university gift aid from institutional funds, Academic Competitiveness Grants, National SMART Grants, TEACH Grants.

GIFT AID (NON-NEED-BASED) *Scholarships, grants, and awards by category: Academic interests/achievement:* biological sciences, business, communication, computer science, education, English, foreign languages, general academic interests/achievements, health fields, humanities, mathematics, military science, physical sciences, social sciences. *Creative arts/performance:* art/fine arts, music, theater/drama. *Tuition waivers:* Full or partial for children of alumni, employees or children of employees, senior citizens. *ROTC:* Army.

LOANS *Student loans: Average indebtedness per student:* $25,628. *Programs:* Perkins.

WORK-STUDY Federal work-study jobs available. *State or other work-study/employment:* Part-time jobs available.

APPLYING FOR FINANCIAL AID *Required financial aid form:* FAFSA. *Financial aid deadline (priority):* 3/1. *Notification date:* Continuous beginning 5/1. Students must reply within 3 weeks of notification.

CONTACT Ms. Deb Henriksen, Director of Financial Aid, Black Hills State University, 1200 University Street, Spearfish, SD 57799-9670, 605-642-6581 or toll-free 800-255-2478. *Fax:* 605-642-6913. *E-mail:* deb.henriksen@bhsu.edu.
Website: http://www.bhsu.edu/.

BLESSING-RIEMAN COLLEGE OF NURSING & HEALTH SCIENCES
Quincy, IL

Tuition & fees: $23,580	Average undergraduate aid package: $14,625

ABOUT THE INSTITUTION Independent, coed, primarily women. *Awards:* bachelor's and master's degrees. 1 undergraduate major. *Total enrollment:* 251. Undergraduates: 233. Federal methodology is used as a basis for awarding need-based institutional aid.

UNDERGRADUATE EXPENSES for 2016–2017 *Tuition:* full-time $22,900; part-time $763 per credit hour. Full-time tuition and fees vary according to course load, degree level, program, and student level. Part-time tuition and fees vary according to course load, degree level, program, and student level. Room and board charges vary according to student level.

UNDERGRADUATE FINANCIAL AID (Fall 2015) 105 applied for aid; of those 100% were deemed to have need. 100% of undergraduates with need received aid; of those 100% had need fully met. *Average percent of need met:* 100% (excluding resources awarded to replace EFC). *Average financial aid package:* $14,625 (excluding resources awarded to replace EFC).

GIFT AID (NEED-BASED) *Total amount:* $1,049,527 (23% federal, 13% state, 56% institutional, 8% external sources). *Receiving aid:* All full-time undergraduates: 100% (105). *Average award:* Undergraduates: $3631. *Scholarships, grants, and awards:* Federal Pell, state, private, college/university gift aid from institutional funds.

GIFT AID (NON-NEED-BASED) *Receiving aid:* Undergraduates: 100% (105). *Scholarships, grants, and awards by category:* Academic interests/ achievement: general academic interests/achievements. *Tuition waivers:* Full or partial for employees or children of employees.

LOANS *Student loans:* $804,561 (100% need-based). *Parent loans:* $54,517 (100% need-based). *Programs:* Federal Direct (Subsidized and Unsubsidized Stafford, PLUS), Federal Nursing, college/university.

APPLYING FOR FINANCIAL AID *Required financial aid form:* FAFSA. *Financial aid deadline:* Continuous. *Notification date:* Continuous beginning 4/1.

CONTACT Mrs. Erin McHargue, Financial Aid Coordinator, Blessing-Rieman College of Nursing & Health Sciences, Broadway at 11th Street, PO Box 7005, Quincy, IL 62301, 217-223-8400 Ext. 6993 or toll-free 800-877-9140. *Fax:* 217-223-1781. *E-mail:* mcharguee@brcn.edu. *Website:* http://www.brcn.edu/.

BLOOMFIELD COLLEGE
Bloomfield, NJ

Tuition & fees: $29,300	Average undergraduate aid package: $27,426

ABOUT THE INSTITUTION Independent Presbyterian Church (U.S.A.), coed. *Awards:* certificates, bachelor's, and master's degrees. 22 undergraduate majors. *Total enrollment:* 2,000. Undergraduates: 1,947. Freshmen: 507. Federal methodology is used as a basis for awarding need-based institutional aid.

UNDERGRADUATE EXPENSES for 2017–2018 *Application fee:* $40. *Comprehensive fee:* $41,000 includes full-time tuition ($29,300) and room and board ($11,700). *College room only:* $5850. Full-time tuition and fees vary according to degree level. Room and board charges vary according to housing facility. *Part-time tuition:* $3670 per course. Part-time tuition and fees vary according to course load and degree level.

FRESHMAN FINANCIAL AID (Fall 2016, est.) 503 applied for aid; of those 95% were deemed to have need. 100% of freshmen with need received aid; of those 13% had need fully met. *Average percent of need met:* 69% (excluding resources awarded to replace EFC). *Average financial aid package:* $28,719 (excluding resources awarded to replace EFC). 3% of all full-time freshmen had no need and received non-need-based gift aid.

UNDERGRADUATE FINANCIAL AID (Fall 2016, est.) 1,767 applied for aid; of those 93% were deemed to have need. 100% of undergraduates with need received aid; of those 15% had need fully met. *Average percent of need met:* 65% (excluding resources awarded to replace EFC). *Average financial aid package:* $27,426 (excluding resources awarded to replace EFC). 5% of all full-time undergraduates had no need and received non-need-based gift aid.

GIFT AID (NEED-BASED) *Total amount:* $26,691,596 (25% federal, 41% state, 34% institutional). *Receiving aid:* Freshmen: 90% (451); all full-time undergraduates: 89% (1,569). *Average award:* Freshmen: $18,699; Undergraduates: $16,703. *Scholarships, grants, and awards:* Federal Pell, FSEOG, state, private, college/university gift aid from institutional funds.

GIFT AID (NON-NEED-BASED) *Total amount:* $8,117,551 (93% institutional, 7% external sources). *Receiving aid:* Freshmen: 41% (206). Undergraduates: 43% (764). *Average award:* Freshmen: $19,010. Undergraduates: $14,208. *Scholarships, grants, and awards by category:* Academic interests/achievement: biological sciences, business, communication, computer science, education, English, general academic interests/achievements, health fields, home economics, humanities, mathematics, physical sciences, premedicine, religion/biblical studies, social sciences. *Creative arts/performance:* art/fine arts, cinema/film/broadcasting, creative writing, general creative arts/performance, journalism/publications, performing arts. *Special achievements/activities:* community service, general special achievements/activities, leadership. *Special characteristics:* children and siblings of alumni, children of current students, general special characteristics, international students, local/state students, previous college experience, relatives of clergy, siblings of current students, spouses of

current students, veterans. *Tuition waivers:* Full or partial for employees or children of employees, senior citizens. *ROTC:* Army cooperative.

LOANS *Student loans:* $12,104,316 (46% need-based, 54% non-need-based). *Average need-based loan:* Freshmen: $3281. Undergraduates: $3896. *Parent loans:* $4,003,146 (100% non-need-based). *Programs:* Federal Direct (Subsidized and Unsubsidized Stafford, PLUS), private loans.

WORK-STUDY *Federal work-study:* Total amount: $384,607; 179 jobs averaging $2169. *State or other work-study/employment:* Part-time jobs available.

ATHLETIC AWARDS Total amount: $2,105,602 (100% non-need-based).

APPLYING FOR FINANCIAL AID *Required financial aid form:* FAFSA. *Financial aid deadline:* 4/15 (priority: 3/15). *Notification date:* Continuous beginning 4/15. Students must reply within 2 weeks of notification.

CONTACT Office of Financial Aid, Bloomfield College, 467 Franklin Street, Bloomfield, NJ 07003-9981, 973-748-9000 Ext. 1213 or toll-free 800-848-4555 Ext. 230. *Fax:* 973-748-9735. *Website:* http://www.bloomfield.edu/.

BLOOMSBURG UNIVERSITY OF PENNSYLVANIA
Bloomsburg, PA

Tuition & fees (PA res): $10,154	Average undergraduate aid package: $9232

ABOUT THE INSTITUTION State-supported, coed. *Awards:* certificates, bachelor's, master's, and doctoral degrees. 42 undergraduate majors. *Total enrollment:* 9,658. Undergraduates: 8,995. Freshmen: 1,902. Federal methodology is used as a basis for awarding need-based institutional aid.

UNDERGRADUATE EXPENSES for 2016–2017 *Application fee:* $35. *Tuition, state resident:* full-time $7238; part-time $302 per credit. *Tuition, non-resident:* full-time $18,096; part-time $754 per credit. *Required fees:* full-time $2916; $106 per credit or $75 per term. Full-time tuition and fees vary according to course load and location. Part-time tuition and fees vary according to course load and location. *College room and board:* $8912; *Room only:* $5736. Room and board charges vary according to board plan and housing facility.

FRESHMAN FINANCIAL AID (Fall 2016, est.) 1,766 applied for aid; of those 72% were deemed to have need. 98% of freshmen with need received aid; of those 9% had need fully met. *Average percent of need met:* 50% (excluding resources awarded to replace EFC). *Average financial aid package:* $8468 (excluding resources awarded to replace EFC). 3% of all full-time freshmen had no need and received non-need-based gift aid.

UNDERGRADUATE FINANCIAL AID (Fall 2016, est.) 7,363 applied for aid; of those 72% were deemed to have need. 99% of undergraduates with need received aid; of those 12% had need fully met. *Average percent of need met:* 57% (excluding resources awarded to replace EFC). *Average financial aid package:* $9232 (excluding resources awarded to replace EFC). 3% of all full-time undergraduates had no need and received non-need-based gift aid.

GIFT AID (NEED-BASED) *Total amount:* $22,261,374 (58% federal, 40% state, 2% institutional). *Receiving aid:* Freshmen: 43% (817); all full-time undergraduates: 42% (3,406). *Average award:* Freshmen: $6358; Undergraduates: $5924. *Scholarships, grants, and awards:* Federal Pell, FSEOG, state, private, college/university gift aid from institutional funds.

GIFT AID (NON-NEED-BASED) *Total amount:* $4,051,323 (20% state, 43% institutional, 37% external sources). *Receiving aid:* Freshmen: 18% (342). Undergraduates: 13% (1,036). *Average award:* Freshmen: $2603. Undergraduates: $2269. *Scholarships, grants, and awards by category:* Academic interests/ achievement: 715 awards ($1,436,175 total): biological sciences, business, communication, computer science, education, English, foreign languages, general academic interests/achievements, health fields, humanities, international studies, mathematics, physical sciences, religion/biblical studies, social sciences. *Special characteristics:* 251 awards ($1,071,852 total): children of faculty/staff, international students. *Tuition waivers:* Full or partial for employees or children of employees, senior citizens. *ROTC:* Army, Air Force cooperative.

LOANS *Student loans:* $63,377,138 (35% need-based, 65% non-need-based). 78% of past graduating class borrowed through all loan programs. *Average indebtedness per student:* $36,915. *Average need-based loan:* Freshmen: $3248. Undergraduates: $4172. *Parent loans:* $15,897,622 (100% non-need-based). *Programs:*

Federal Direct (Subsidized and Unsubsidized Stafford, PLUS), Perkins, state, alternative loans.

WORK-STUDY *Federal work-study:* Total amount: $3,006,327; 907 jobs averaging $3251. *State or other work-study/employment:* Total amount: $4,690,183 (100% non-need-based). 1,195 part-time jobs averaging $3834.

ATHLETIC AWARDS Total amount: $353,695 (100% non-need-based).

APPLYING FOR FINANCIAL AID *Required financial aid form:* FAFSA. *Financial aid deadline (priority):* 3/15. *Notification date:* Continuous beginning 12/1.

CONTACT Mrs. Amanda L. Kishbaugh, Interim Director of Financial Aid, Bloomsburg University of Pennsylvania, 119 Warren Student Services Center, 400 East 2nd Street, Bloomsburg, PA 17815-1301, 570-389-4279. *Fax:* 570-389-4795. *E-mail:* akishba2@bloomu.edu.

Website: http://www.bloomu.edu/.

BLUEFIELD COLLEGE
Bluefield, VA

Tuition & fees: $25,560	Average undergraduate aid package: $16,515

ABOUT THE INSTITUTION Independent Southern Baptist, coed. *Awards:* bachelor's and master's degrees. 43 undergraduate majors. *Total enrollment:* 982. Undergraduates: 969. Freshmen: 179. Federal methodology is used as a basis for awarding need-based institutional aid.

UNDERGRADUATE EXPENSES for 2017–2018 *Comprehensive fee:* $34,403 includes full-time tuition ($24,800), mandatory fees ($760), and room and board ($8843). *College room only:* $3692. Full-time tuition and fees vary according to course load and program. Room and board charges vary according to housing facility. *Part-time tuition:* $970 per credit. *Part-time fees:* $28 per credit hour. Part-time tuition and fees vary according to course load and program.

FRESHMAN FINANCIAL AID (Fall 2016, est.) 169 applied for aid; of those 96% were deemed to have need. 100% of freshmen with need received aid; of those 13% had need fully met. *Average percent of need met:* 64% (excluding resources awarded to replace EFC). *Average financial aid package:* $19,071 (excluding resources awarded to replace EFC). 11% of all full-time freshmen had no need and received non-need-based gift aid.

UNDERGRADUATE FINANCIAL AID (Fall 2016, est.) 728 applied for aid; of those 94% were deemed to have need. 100% of undergraduates with need received aid; of those 10% had need fully met. *Average percent of need met:* 62% (excluding resources awarded to replace EFC). *Average financial aid package:* $16,515 (excluding resources awarded to replace EFC). 11% of all full-time undergraduates had no need and received non-need-based gift aid.

GIFT AID (NEED-BASED) *Total amount:* $7,056,208 (28% federal, 20% state, 43% institutional, 9% external sources). *Receiving aid:* Freshmen: 89% (163); all full-time undergraduates: 85% (674). *Average award:* Freshmen: $16,030; Undergraduates: $12,876. *Scholarships, grants, and awards:* Federal Pell, FSEOG, state, private, college/university gift aid from institutional funds.

GIFT AID (NON-NEED-BASED) *Total amount:* $800,901 (26% state, 68% institutional, 6% external sources). *Receiving aid:* Freshmen: 9% (16). Undergraduates: 6% (51). *Average award:* Freshmen: $5931. Undergraduates: $5819. *Scholarships, grants, and awards by category:* Academic interests/achievement: 473 awards ($2,648,279 total): general academic interests/achievements, library science. *Creative arts/performance:* 44 awards ($136,100 total): art/fine arts, music, performing arts, theater/drama. *Special achievements/activities:* 9 awards ($28,000 total): cheerleading/drum major. *Special characteristics:* adult students, children of faculty/staff, first-generation college students, general special characteristics, local/state students, out-of-state students, religious affiliation, veterans, veterans' children. *Tuition waivers:* Full or partial for employees or children of employees, senior citizens.

LOANS *Student loans:* $6,002,742 (83% need-based, 17% non-need-based). 66% of past graduating class borrowed through all loan programs. *Average indebtedness per student:* $30,487. *Average need-based loan:* Freshmen: $3468. Undergraduates: $4343. *Parent loans:* $989,194 (69% need-based, 31% non-need-based). *Programs:* Federal Direct (Subsidized and Unsubsidized Stafford, PLUS), alternative loans.

WORK-STUDY *Federal work-study:* Total amount: $64,800; 57 jobs averaging $1137. *State or other work-study/employment:* Total amount: $6000 (25% need-based, 75% non-need-based). 16 part-time jobs averaging $375.

ATHLETIC AWARDS Total amount: $2,342,633 (71% need-based, 29% non-need-based).

APPLYING FOR FINANCIAL AID *Required financial aid forms:* FAFSA, state aid form. *Financial aid deadline (priority):* 6/1. *Notification date:* Continuous. Students must reply by 8/24.

CONTACT Ms. Carly Jean Kestner, Director of Financial Aid, Bluefield College, 3000 College Avenue, Bluefield, VA 24605, 276-326-4215 or toll-free 800-872-0175. *Fax:* 276-326-4356. *E-mail:* ckestner@bluefield.edu.

Website: http://www.bluefield.edu/.

BLUEFIELD STATE COLLEGE
Bluefield, WV

Tuition & fees (WV res): $6408	Average undergraduate aid package: $3600

ABOUT THE INSTITUTION State-supported, coed. *Awards:* associate and bachelor's degrees. 18 undergraduate majors. *Total enrollment:* 1,362. Undergraduates: 1,362. Freshmen: 226. Federal methodology is used as a basis for awarding need-based institutional aid.

UNDERGRADUATE EXPENSES for 2016–2017 *Tuition, state resident:* full-time $6408; part-time $267 per credit hour. *Tuition, nonresident:* full-time $12,876; part-time $537 per credit hour.

FRESHMAN FINANCIAL AID (Fall 2016, est.) 280 applied for aid; of those 84% were deemed to have need. 98% of freshmen with need received aid; of those 15% had need fully met. *Average percent of need met:* 65% (excluding resources awarded to replace EFC). *Average financial aid package:* $3330 (excluding resources awarded to replace EFC). 1% of all full-time freshmen had no need and received non-need-based gift aid.

UNDERGRADUATE FINANCIAL AID (Fall 2016, est.) 1,300 applied for aid; of those 92% were deemed to have need. 92% of undergraduates with need received aid; of those 13% had need fully met. *Average percent of need met:* 67% (excluding resources awarded to replace EFC). *Average financial aid package:* $3600 (excluding resources awarded to replace EFC). 1% of all full-time undergraduates had no need and received non-need-based gift aid.

GIFT AID (NEED-BASED) *Total amount:* $5,950,000 (77% federal, 23% state). *Receiving aid:* Freshmen: 67% (195); all full-time undergraduates: 70% (980). *Average award:* Freshmen: $3800; Undergraduates: $3800. *Scholarships, grants, and awards:* Federal Pell, FSEOG, state.

GIFT AID (NON-NEED-BASED) *Total amount:* $1,080,000 (37% state, 26% institutional, 37% external sources). *Receiving aid:* Freshmen: 24% (69). Undergraduates: 13% (179). *Average award:* Freshmen: $900. Undergraduates: $900. *Scholarships, grants, and awards by category:* Academic interests/achievement: engineering/technologies, general academic interests/achievements. *Special achievements/activities:* cheerleading/drum major, general special achievements/activities, junior miss, leadership. *Tuition waivers:* Full or partial for adult students, senior citizens.

LOANS *Student loans:* $6,900,000 (45% need-based, 55% non-need-based). 72% of past graduating class borrowed through all loan programs. *Average indebtedness per student:* $29,000. *Average need-based loan:* Freshmen: $3400. Undergraduates: $4300. *Parent loans:* $100,000 (100% non-need-based). *Programs:* Federal Direct (Subsidized and Unsubsidized Stafford, PLUS).

WORK-STUDY *Federal work-study:* Total amount: $130,000; 50 jobs averaging $2950. *State or other work-study/employment:* Total amount: $300 (100% non-need-based). Part-time jobs available.

ATHLETIC AWARDS Total amount: $300,000 (100% non-need-based).

APPLYING FOR FINANCIAL AID *Required financial aid forms:* FAFSA, institution's own form. *Financial aid deadline (priority):* 3/1. *Notification date:* 6/1.

CONTACT Mr. Tom Ilse, Director of Financial Aid, Bluefield State College, 219 Rock Street, Bluefield, WV 24701-2198, 304-327-4020 or toll-free 800-344-8892 Ext. 4065 (in-state), 800-654-7798 Ext. 4065 (out-of-state). *Fax:* 304-325-7747. *E-mail:* tilse@bluefieldstate.edu.

Website: http://www.bluefieldstate.edu/.

BLUE MOUNTAIN COLLEGE
Blue Mountain, MS

Tuition & fees: $11,212	Average undergraduate aid package: $8869

ABOUT THE INSTITUTION Independent Southern Baptist, coed. *Awards:* bachelor's and master's degrees. 21 undergraduate majors. *Total enrollment:* 571. Undergraduates: 544. Freshmen: 112. Federal methodology is used as a basis for awarding need-based institutional aid.

UNDERGRADUATE EXPENSES for 2016–2017 *Comprehensive fee:* $16,976 includes full-time tuition ($9518), mandatory fees ($1694), and room and board ($5764). Full-time tuition and fees vary according to course load, degree level, and program. Room and board charges vary according to gender, housing facility, and location. *Part-time tuition:* $317 per semester hour. *Part-time fees:* $511 per term. Part-time tuition and fees vary according to course load, degree level, and program.

FRESHMAN FINANCIAL AID (Fall 2016, est.) 106 applied for aid; of those 81% were deemed to have need. 100% of freshmen with need received aid; of those 22% had need fully met. *Average percent of need met:* 68% (excluding resources awarded to replace EFC). *Average financial aid package:* $7783 (excluding resources awarded to replace EFC). 6% of all full-time freshmen had no need and received non-need-based gift aid.

UNDERGRADUATE FINANCIAL AID (Fall 2016, est.) 487 applied for aid; of those 84% were deemed to have need. 100% of undergraduates with need received aid; of those 21% had need fully met. *Average percent of need met:* 78% (excluding resources awarded to replace EFC). *Average financial aid package:* $8869 (excluding resources awarded to replace EFC). 8% of all full-time undergraduates had no need and received non-need-based gift aid.

GIFT AID (NEED-BASED) *Total amount:* $2,933,159 (39% federal, 10% state, 46% institutional, 5% external sources). *Receiving aid:* Freshmen: 78% (85); all full-time undergraduates: 64% (312). *Average award:* Freshmen: $7783; Undergraduates: $8869. *Scholarships, grants, and awards:* Federal Pell, FSEOG, state, private, college/university gift aid from institutional funds.

GIFT AID (NON-NEED-BASED) *Receiving aid:* Freshmen: 39% (43). Undergraduates: 32% (156). *Average award:* Freshmen: $6369. Undergraduates: $4835. *Scholarships, grants, and awards by category: Academic interests/achievement:* biological sciences, business, education, English, general academic interests/achievements, humanities, mathematics, physical sciences, premedicine, religion/biblical studies, social sciences. *Creative arts/performance:* art/fine arts, music, theater/drama. *Special achievements/activities:* cheerleading/drum major, general special achievements/activities, leadership, memberships, religious involvement. *Special characteristics:* adult students, children and siblings of alumni, children of current students, children of faculty/staff, married students, parents of current students, relatives of clergy, religious affiliation, siblings of current students, spouses of current students, twins. *Tuition waivers:* Full or partial for employees or children of employees.

LOANS *Student loans:* $2,029,972 (51% need-based, 49% non-need-based). 65% of past graduating class borrowed through all loan programs. *Average indebtedness per student:* $19,695. *Average need-based loan:* Freshmen: $2946. Undergraduates: $3676. *Parent loans:* $103,833 (100% non-need-based). *Programs:* Federal Direct (Subsidized and Unsubsidized Stafford, PLUS).

WORK-STUDY *Federal work-study:* Total amount: $64,000; 46 jobs averaging $841. *State or other work-study/employment:* Total amount: $64,000 (100% non-need-based). 55 part-time jobs averaging $868.

ATHLETIC AWARDS Total amount: $1,321,717 (100% need-based).

APPLYING FOR FINANCIAL AID *Required financial aid form:* FAFSA. *Financial aid deadline (priority):* 3/1. *Notification date:* Continuous beginning 4/1. Students must reply within 2 weeks of notification.

CONTACT Mrs. Beverly K. Hickey, Director of Financial Aid, Blue Mountain College, PO Box 160, Blue Mountain, MS 38610-0160, 662-685-4771 Ext. 141 or toll-free 800-235-0136. *Fax:* 662-685-4776. *E-mail:* bhickey@bmc.edu. *Website:* http://www.bmc.edu/.

BLUFFTON UNIVERSITY
Bluffton, OH

Tuition & fees: $31,672	Average undergraduate aid package: $26,316

ABOUT THE INSTITUTION Independent Mennonite, coed. *Awards:* certificates, bachelor's, and master's degrees. 41 undergraduate majors. *Total enrollment:* 952. Undergraduates: 865. Freshmen: 208. Both federal and institutional methodology are used as a basis for awarding need-based institutional aid.

UNDERGRADUATE EXPENSES for 2017–2018 *Comprehensive fee:* $42,156 includes full-time tuition ($31,222), mandatory fees ($450), and room and board ($10,484). *College room only:* $5160. Room and board charges vary according to board plan and housing facility. *Part-time tuition:* $1301 per credit hour. *Part-time fees:* $113 per term.

FRESHMAN FINANCIAL AID (Fall 2016, est.) 196 applied for aid; of those 93% were deemed to have need. 100% of freshmen with need received aid; of those 12% had need fully met. *Average percent of need met:* 77% (excluding resources awarded to replace EFC). *Average financial aid package:* $27,236 (excluding resources awarded to replace EFC). 12% of all full-time freshmen had no need and received non-need-based gift aid.

UNDERGRADUATE FINANCIAL AID (Fall 2016, est.) 666 applied for aid; of those 94% were deemed to have need. 100% of undergraduates with need received aid; of those 14% had need fully met. *Average percent of need met:* 77% (excluding resources awarded to replace EFC). *Average financial aid package:* $26,316 (excluding resources awarded to replace EFC). 12% of all full-time undergraduates had no need and received non-need-based gift aid.

GIFT AID (NEED-BASED) *Total amount:* $12,977,316 (12% federal, 4% state, 81% institutional, 3% external sources). *Receiving aid:* Freshmen: 88% (183); all full-time undergraduates: 85% (621). *Average award:* Freshmen: $21,909; Undergraduates: $20,842. *Scholarships, grants, and awards:* Federal Pell, FSEOG, state, private, college/university gift aid from institutional funds.

GIFT AID (NON-NEED-BASED) *Total amount:* $1,758,968 (91% institutional, 9% external sources). *Receiving aid:* Freshmen: 8% (17). Undergraduates: 8% (61). *Average award:* Freshmen: $15,631. Undergraduates: $14,816. *Scholarships, grants, and awards by category: Academic interests/achievement:* 656 awards ($6,789,836 total): biological sciences, general academic interests/achievements, mathematics, physical sciences, premedicine. *Creative arts/performance:* 53 awards ($109,425 total): art/fine arts, music, performing arts. *Special achievements/activities:* 7 awards ($17,000 total): leadership. *Special characteristics:* 415 awards ($999,252 total): children and siblings of alumni, children of faculty/staff, international students, members of minority groups, out-of-state students, religious affiliation. *Tuition waivers:* Full or partial for employees or children of employees.

LOANS *Student loans:* $6,209,260 (78% need-based, 22% non-need-based). 85% of past graduating class borrowed through all loan programs. *Average indebtedness per student:* $38,701. *Average need-based loan:* Freshmen: $4775. Undergraduates: $4880. *Parent loans:* $2,516,530 (57% need-based, 43% non-need-based). *Programs:* Federal Direct (Subsidized and Unsubsidized Stafford, PLUS), Perkins, alternative loans.

WORK-STUDY *Federal work-study:* Total amount: $798,379; 520 jobs averaging $2247. *State or other work-study/employment:* Total amount: $463,175 (4% need-based, 96% non-need-based). 194 part-time jobs averaging $2303.

APPLYING FOR FINANCIAL AID *Required financial aid form:* FAFSA. *Financial aid deadline:* 10/1 (priority: 5/1). *Notification date:* Continuous beginning 3/1.

CONTACT Chris Fowler, Director of Financial Aid, Bluffton University, 1 University Drive, Bluffton, OH 45817-2104, 419-358-3266 or toll-free 800-488-3257. *Fax:* 419-358-3073. *E-mail:* fowlerc@bluffton.edu. *Website:* http://www.bluffton.edu/.

BOB JONES UNIVERSITY
Greenville, SC

CONTACT Office of Financial Aid, Bob Jones University, 1700 Wade Hampton Boulevard, Greenville, SC 29614, 864-242-5100 Ext. 3040 or toll-free 800-252-6363. *E-mail:* finaid@bju.edu. *Website:* http://www.bju.edu/.

BOISE BIBLE COLLEGE
Boise, ID

CONTACT Beth Turner, Financial Aid Counselor, Boise Bible College, 8695 West Marigold Street, Boise, ID 83714-1220, 208-376-7731 Ext. 12 or toll-free 800-893-7755. *Fax:* 208-376-7743. *E-mail:* betht@boisebible.edu.
Website: http://www.boisebible.edu/.

BOISE STATE UNIVERSITY
Boise, ID

Tuition & fees (ID res): $7080	Average undergraduate aid package: $9361

ABOUT THE INSTITUTION State-supported, coed. *Awards:* certificates, associate, bachelor's, master's, and doctoral degrees. 89 undergraduate majors. *Total enrollment:* 23,886. Undergraduates: 20,209. Freshmen: 2,627. Federal methodology is used as a basis for awarding need-based institutional aid.

UNDERGRADUATE EXPENSES for 2016–2017 *Application fee:* $50. *One-time required fee:* $175. *Tuition, state resident:* full-time $4872; part-time $200 per credit hour. *Tuition, nonresident:* full-time $19,322; part-time $470 per credit hour. *Required fees:* full-time $2208; $97 per credit hour. Full-time tuition and fees vary according to course load, program, and reciprocity agreements. Part-time tuition and fees vary according to course load and program. *College room and board:* $7076; *Room only:* $3756. Room and board charges vary according to board plan and housing facility.

FRESHMAN FINANCIAL AID (Fall 2015) 1,331 applied for aid; of those 97% were deemed to have need. 95% of freshmen with need received aid; of those 17% had need fully met. *Average percent of need met:* 6% (excluding resources awarded to replace EFC). *Average financial aid package:* $10,368 (excluding resources awarded to replace EFC). 5% of all full-time freshmen had no need and received non-need-based gift aid.

UNDERGRADUATE FINANCIAL AID (Fall 2015) 7,360 applied for aid; of those 98% were deemed to have need. 97% of undergraduates with need received aid; of those 12% had need fully met. *Average percent of need met:* 57% (excluding resources awarded to replace EFC). *Average financial aid package:* $9361 (excluding resources awarded to replace EFC). 2% of all full-time undergraduates had no need and received non-need-based gift aid.

GIFT AID (NEED-BASED) *Total amount:* $31,934,847 (74% federal, 5% state, 14% institutional, 7% external sources). *Receiving aid:* Freshmen: 34% (901); all full-time undergraduates: 42% (5,228). *Average award:* Freshmen: $5626; Undergraduates: $5116. *Scholarships, grants, and awards:* Federal Pell, FSEOG, state, private, college/university gift aid from institutional funds, Federal Nursing, Leveraging Educational Assistance Program (LEAP).

GIFT AID (NON-NEED-BASED) *Total amount:* $1,802,351 (1% federal, 2% state, 64% institutional, 33% external sources). *Receiving aid:* Freshmen: 3% (90). Undergraduates: 2% (235). *Average award:* Freshmen: $3024. Undergraduates: $1919. *Scholarships, grants, and awards by category: Academic interests/achievement:* architecture, area/ethnic studies, biological sciences, business, communication, computer science, education, engineering/technologies, English, foreign languages, general academic interests/achievements, health fields, home economics, humanities, international studies, mathematics, military science, physical sciences, pre-medicine, religion/biblical studies, social sciences. *Creative arts/performance:* art/fine arts, dance, debating, general creative arts/performance, journalism/publications, music, performing arts, theater/drama. *Special achievements/activities:* cheerleading/drum major, community service, leadership, rodeo. *Special characteristics:* ethnic background, first-generation college students, general special characteristics, handicapped students, international students, local/state students, members of minority groups, out-of-state students, previous college experience, spouses of current students, veterans, veterans' children. *Tuition waivers:* Full or partial for employees or children of employees, senior citizens. *ROTC:* Army.

LOANS *Student loans:* $58,773,561 (79% need-based, 21% non-need-based). 65% of past graduating class borrowed through all loan programs. *Average indebtedness per student:* $28,127. *Average need-based loan:* Freshmen: $3455. Undergraduates: $4408. *Parent loans:* $6,490,349 (37% need-based, 63% non-need-based). *Programs:* Federal Direct (Subsidized and Unsubsidized Stafford, PLUS), Perkins, Federal Nursing, college/university.

WORK-STUDY *Federal work-study:* 256 jobs averaging $2126. *State or other work-study/employment:* Total amount: $401,532 (100% need-based). 213 part-time jobs averaging $2289.
ATHLETIC AWARDS Total amount: $7,493,935 (88% need-based, 12% non-need-based).
APPLYING FOR FINANCIAL AID *Required financial aid form:* FAFSA. *Financial aid deadline:* 6/30 (priority: 2/15). *Notification date:* Continuous beginning 3/15. Students must reply by 4/12 or within 4 weeks of notification.
CONTACT Office of Financial Aid and Scholarships, Boise State University, Administration Building, Room 113, Boise, ID 83725-1315, 800-824-7017 Ext. 1664 or toll-free 800-824-7017. *Fax:* 208-426-1305. *E-mail:* financialaid@boisestate.edu. *Website:* http://www.boisestate.edu/.

BON SECOURS MEMORIAL COLLEGE OF NURSING
Richmond, VA

CONTACT Financial Aid Office, Bon Secours Memorial College of Nursing, 8550 Magellan Parkway, Suite 1100, Richmond, VA 23227-1149, 804-627-5300 or toll-free 866-238-7414.
Website: http://www.bsmcon.edu/.

BORICUA COLLEGE
New York, NY

CONTACT Ms. Rosalia Cruz, Financial Aid Administrator, Boricua College, 3755 Broadway, New York, NY 10032-1560, 212-694-1000 Ext. 611. *Fax:* 212-694-1015. *E-mail:* rcruz@boricuacollege.edu.
Website: http://www.boricuacollege.edu/.

BOSTON ARCHITECTURAL COLLEGE
Boston, MA

Tuition & fees: $20,666	Average undergraduate aid package: $11,288

ABOUT THE INSTITUTION Independent, coed. *Awards:* certificates, bachelor's, and master's degrees. 4 undergraduate majors. *Total enrollment:* 878. Undergraduates: 472. Freshmen: 24. Federal methodology is used as a basis for awarding need-based institutional aid.

UNDERGRADUATE EXPENSES for 2017–2018 *Tuition:* full-time $20,016; part-time $1668 per credit hour. *Required fees:* full-time $650; $175 per term. Full-time tuition and fees vary according to course load, degree level, and program. Part-time tuition and fees vary according to course load, degree level, and program.

FRESHMAN FINANCIAL AID (Fall 2016, est.) 5 applied for aid; of those 100% were deemed to have need. 100% of freshmen with need received aid. *Average percent of need met:* 51% (excluding resources awarded to replace EFC). *Average financial aid package:* $14,667 (excluding resources awarded to replace EFC).

UNDERGRADUATE FINANCIAL AID (Fall 2016, est.) 93 applied for aid; of those 95% were deemed to have need. 100% of undergraduates with need received aid; of those 2% had need fully met. *Average percent of need met:* 35% (excluding resources awarded to replace EFC). *Average financial aid package:* $11,288 (excluding resources awarded to replace EFC). 6% of all full-time undergraduates had no need and received non-need-based gift aid.

GIFT AID (NEED-BASED) *Total amount:* $850,825 (50% federal, 4% state, 41% institutional, 5% external sources). *Receiving aid:* Freshmen: 50% (4); all full-time undergraduates: 64% (71). *Average award:* Freshmen: $8665; Undergraduates: $6793. *Scholarships, grants, and awards:* Federal Pell, FSEOG, state, private, college/university gift aid from institutional funds.

GIFT AID (NON-NEED-BASED) *Total amount:* $160,632 (91% institutional, 9% external sources). *Receiving aid:* Undergraduates: 2% (2). *Average award:* Undergraduates: $3189. *Scholarships, grants, and awards by category: Academic interests/achievement:* 71 awards ($220,857 total): architecture, general academic interests/achievements. *Special characteristics:* 71 awards ($220,857 total). *Tuition waivers:* Full or partial for employees or children of employees.

LOANS *Student loans:* $1,929,106 (85% need-based, 15% non-need-based). *Average need-based loan:* Freshmen: $6999. Undergraduates: $5589. *Parent loans:* $587,594 (81% need-based, 19% non-need-based). *Programs:* Federal Direct (Subsidized and Unsubsidized Stafford, PLUS), private loans.

WORK-STUDY *Federal work-study:* Total amount: $57,506; 20 jobs averaging $2875.

APPLYING FOR FINANCIAL AID *Required financial aid form:* FAFSA. *Financial aid deadline (priority):* 4/15. *Notification date:* Continuous beginning 5/1. Students must reply within 2 weeks of notification.

CONTACT Ms. Janice Wilkos-Greenberg, Director of Financial Aid, Boston Architectural College, 320 Newbury Street, Boston, MA 02115, 617-585-0183. *Fax:* 617-585-0131. *E-mail:* janice.greenberg@the-bac.edu. *Website:* http://www.the-bac.edu/.

BOSTON BAPTIST COLLEGE
Boston, MA

CONTACT Financial Aid Office, Boston Baptist College, 950 Metropolitan Avenue, Boston, MA 02136, 617-364-3510 or toll-free 888-235-2014. *Website:* http://www.boston.edu/.

BOSTON COLLEGE
Chestnut Hill, MA

Tuition & fees: $51,296	Average undergraduate aid package: $39,942

ABOUT THE INSTITUTION Independent Roman Catholic (Jesuit), coed. *Awards:* certificates, bachelor's, master's, and doctoral degrees (also offers continuing education program with significant enrollment not reflected in profile). 48 undergraduate majors. *Total enrollment:* 13,851. Undergraduates: 9,309. Freshmen: 2,316. Institutional methodology is used as a basis for awarding need-based institutional aid.

UNDERGRADUATE EXPENSES for 2016–2017 *Application fee:* $75. *One-time required fee:* $530. *Comprehensive fee:* $65,114 includes full-time tuition ($50,480), mandatory fees ($816), and room and board ($13,818). *College room only:* $8610. Room and board charges vary according to housing facility.

FRESHMAN FINANCIAL AID (Fall 2015) 1,008 applied for aid; of those 85% were deemed to have need. 100% of freshmen with need received aid; of those 100% had need fully met. *Average percent of need met:* 100% (excluding resources awarded to replace EFC). *Average financial aid package:* $38,042 (excluding resources awarded to replace EFC). 1% of all full-time freshmen had no need and received non-need-based gift aid.

UNDERGRADUATE FINANCIAL AID (Fall 2015) 4,136 applied for aid; of those 90% were deemed to have need. 100% of undergraduates with need received aid; of those 100% had need fully met. *Average percent of need met:* 100% (excluding resources awarded to replace EFC). *Average financial aid package:* $39,942 (excluding resources awarded to replace EFC). 2% of all full-time undergraduates had no need and received non-need-based gift aid.

GIFT AID (NEED-BASED) *Total amount:* $120,221,719 (6% federal, 1% state, 91% institutional, 2% external sources). *Receiving aid:* Freshmen: 34% (739); all full-time undergraduates: 36% (3,271). *Average award:* Freshmen: $35,591; Undergraduates: $36,755. *Scholarships, grants, and awards:* Federal Pell, FSEOG, state, private, college/university gift aid from institutional funds.

GIFT AID (NON-NEED-BASED) *Total amount:* $8,105,305 (31% federal, 54% institutional, 15% external sources). *Receiving aid:* Freshmen: 1% (25). Undergraduates: 1% (84). *Average award:* Freshmen: $21,093. Undergraduates: $19,645. *Scholarships, grants, and awards by category:* Academic interests/achievement: general academic interests/achievements, military science. *Tuition waivers:* Full or partial for employees or children of employees. *ROTC:* Army cooperative, Naval cooperative, Air Force cooperative.

LOANS *Student loans:* $16,536,236 (77% need-based, 23% non-need-based). 49% of past graduating class borrowed through all loan programs. *Average indebtedness*

---

per student: $20,849. *Average need-based loan:* Freshmen: $3503. Undergraduates: $4035. *Parent loans:* $33,206,470 (100% non-need-based). *Programs:* Perkins, Federal Nursing, state.

WORK-STUDY *Federal work-study:* jobs available.

ATHLETIC AWARDS Total amount: $17,844,656 (14% need-based, 86% non-need-based).

APPLYING FOR FINANCIAL AID *Required financial aid forms:* FAFSA, CSS Financial Aid PROFILE, business/farm supplement, federal income tax form(s), W-2 forms. *Financial aid deadline (priority):* 2/1. *Notification date:* 4/1. Students must reply by 5/1.

CONTACT Office of Student Services, Boston College, Lyons Hall, 140 Commonwealth Avenue, Chestnut Hill, MA 02467, 617-552-3300 or toll-free 800-360-2522. *Fax:* 617-552-4889. *E-mail:* studentservices@bc.edu. *Website:* http://www.bc.edu/.

BOSTON UNIVERSITY
Boston, MA

Tuition & fees: $50,240	Average undergraduate aid package: $40,232

ABOUT THE INSTITUTION Independent, coed. *Awards:* certificates, bachelor's, master's, and doctoral degrees. 119 undergraduate majors. *Total enrollment:* 32,695. Undergraduates: 17,944. Freshmen: 3,552. Institutional methodology is used as a basis for awarding need-based institutional aid.

UNDERGRADUATE EXPENSES for 2017–2018 *Application fee:* $80. *Comprehensive fee:* $65,110 includes full-time tuition ($49,176), mandatory fees ($1064), and room and board ($14,870). *College room only:* $9810. Full-time tuition and fees vary according to class time and course load. Room and board charges vary according to board plan, housing facility, and location. *Part-time tuition:* $1537 per credit hour. *Part-time fees:* $60 per term. Part-time tuition and fees vary according to class time, course level, and course load. *Payment plan:* Tuition prepayment.

FRESHMAN FINANCIAL AID (Fall 2016, est.) 1,675 applied for aid; of those 79% were deemed to have need. 100% of freshmen with need received aid; of those 23% had need fully met. *Average percent of need met:* 88% (excluding resources awarded to replace EFC). *Average financial aid package:* $42,218 (excluding resources awarded to replace EFC). 7% of all full-time freshmen had no need and received non-need-based gift aid.

UNDERGRADUATE FINANCIAL AID (Fall 2016, est.) 6,587 applied for aid; of those 89% were deemed to have need. 100% of undergraduates with need received aid; of those 21% had need fully met. *Average percent of need met:* 85% (excluding resources awarded to replace EFC). *Average financial aid package:* $40,232 (excluding resources awarded to replace EFC). 8% of all full-time undergraduates had no need and received non-need-based gift aid.

GIFT AID (NEED-BASED) *Total amount:* $201,251,445 (7% federal, 1% state, 90% institutional, 2% external sources). *Receiving aid:* Freshmen: 37% (1,303); all full-time undergraduates: 36% (5,838). *Average award:* Freshmen: $35,861; Undergraduates: $33,521. *Scholarships, grants, and awards:* Federal Pell, FSEOG, state, private, college/university gift aid from institutional funds, Federal Nursing.

GIFT AID (NON-NEED-BASED) *Total amount:* $23,481,120 (1% federal, 86% institutional, 13% external sources). *Receiving aid:* Freshmen: 4% (139). Undergraduates: 3% (434). *Average award:* Freshmen: $23,169. Undergraduates: $19,975. *Scholarships, grants, and awards by category:* Academic interests/achievement: 1,263 awards ($18,022,566 total): engineering/technologies, general academic interests/achievements, military science. Creative arts/performance: 278 awards ($4,130,626 total): art/fine arts, music, theater/drama. Special achievements/activities: 41 awards ($1,976,104 total): general special achievements/activities, memberships. Special characteristics: 324 awards ($7,913,283 total): children and siblings of alumni, children of faculty/staff, general special characteristics, local/state students, members of minority groups, relatives of clergy, religious affiliation, veterans, veterans' children. *Tuition waivers:* Full or partial for employees or children of employees. *ROTC:* Army, Naval, Air Force.

LOANS *Student loans:* $72,976,835 (49% need-based, 51% non-need-based). 51% of past graduating class borrowed through all loan programs. *Average indebtedness per student:* $41,098. *Average need-based loan:* Freshmen: $4034. Undergraduates: $4694. *Parent loans:* $36,437,954 (30% need-based, 70% non-need-based).

Programs: Federal Direct (Subsidized and Unsubsidized Stafford, PLUS), Perkins, state.

WORK-STUDY *Federal work-study:* Total amount: $6,557,515; 2,880 jobs averaging $2277. *State or other work-study/employment:* Part-time jobs available.

ATHLETIC AWARDS Total amount: $15,380,448 (22% need-based, 78% non-need-based).

APPLYING FOR FINANCIAL AID *Required financial aid forms:* FAFSA, CSS Financial Aid PROFILE, noncustodial (divorced/separated) parent's statement. *Financial aid deadline:* 2/1. *Notification date:* 3/25. Students must reply by 5/1 or within 2 weeks of notification.

CONTACT Julie Wickstrom, Director of Financial Assistance, Boston University, 881 Commonwealth Avenue, Boston, MA 02215, 617-353-4176. *Fax:* 617-353-8200. *E-mail:* finaid@bu.edu.
Website: http://www.bu.edu/.

BOWDOIN COLLEGE
Brunswick, ME

Tuition & fees: $49,900	Average undergraduate aid package: $44,088

ABOUT THE INSTITUTION Independent, coed. *Awards:* bachelor's degrees. 47 undergraduate majors. *Total enrollment:* 1,806. Undergraduates: 1,806. Freshmen: 503. Institutional methodology is used as a basis for awarding need-based institutional aid.

UNDERGRADUATE EXPENSES for 2016–2017 *Application fee:* $65. *Comprehensive fee:* $63,500 includes full-time tuition ($49,416), mandatory fees ($484), and room and board ($13,600). *College room only:* $6356. Room and board charges vary according to board plan. *Part-time tuition:* $965 per credit hour.

FRESHMAN FINANCIAL AID (Fall 2016, est.) 290 applied for aid; of those 81% were deemed to have need. 100% of freshmen with need received aid; of those 100% had need fully met. *Average percent of need met:* 100% (excluding resources awarded to replace EFC). *Average financial aid package:* $44,146 (excluding resources awarded to replace EFC). 1% of all full-time freshmen had no need and received non-need-based gift aid.

UNDERGRADUATE FINANCIAL AID (Fall 2016, est.) 887 applied for aid; of those 91% were deemed to have need. 100% of undergraduates with need received aid; of those 100% had need fully met. *Average percent of need met:* 100% (excluding resources awarded to replace EFC). *Average financial aid package:* $44,088 (excluding resources awarded to replace EFC). 2% of all full-time undergraduates had no need and received non-need-based gift aid.

GIFT AID (NEED-BASED) *Total amount:* $33,883,975 (5% federal, 95% institutional). *Receiving aid:* Freshmen: 47% (235); all full-time undergraduates: 45% (806). *Average award:* Freshmen: $42,254; Undergraduates: $42,206. *Scholarships, grants, and awards:* Federal Pell, FSEOG, state, private, college/university gift aid from institutional funds.

GIFT AID (NON-NEED-BASED) *Total amount:* $1,262,456 (4% institutional, 96% external sources). *Average award:* Freshmen: $1000. Undergraduates: $1000. *Scholarships, grants, and awards by category:* Academic interests/achievement: 39 awards ($39,000 total): general academic interests/achievements. Special achievements/activities: leadership. Special characteristics: children of faculty/staff. *Tuition waivers:* Full or partial for employees or children of employees.

LOANS *Student loans:* 27% of past graduating class borrowed through all loan programs. *Average indebtedness per student:* $23,120. *Programs:* Federal Direct (Subsidized and Unsubsidized Stafford), Perkins, state.

WORK-STUDY *Federal work-study:* Total amount: $1,029,150; 542 jobs averaging $1899. *State or other work-study/employment:* Total amount: $488,300 (100% need-based). 257 part-time jobs averaging $1900.

APPLYING FOR FINANCIAL AID *Required financial aid forms:* FAFSA, CSS Financial Aid PROFILE, noncustodial (divorced/separated) parent's statement, business/farm supplement. *Financial aid deadline:* 2/15. *Notification date:* 3/20. Students must reply by 5/1 or within 1 week of notification.

CONTACT Mr. Michael D. Bartini, Director of Student Aid, Bowdoin College, 5300 College Station, Brunswick, ME 04011-8444, 207-725-3146. *Fax:* 207-725-3864. *E-mail:* mbartini@bowdoin.edu.
Website: http://www.bowdoin.edu/.

BOWIE STATE UNIVERSITY
Bowie, MD

ABOUT THE INSTITUTION State-supported, coed. *Awards:* certificates, bachelor's, master's, and doctoral degrees. 29 undergraduate majors. *Total enrollment:* 5,669. Undergraduates: 4,711. Freshmen: 967.

GIFT AID (NEED-BASED) *Scholarships, grants, and awards:* Federal Pell, FSEOG, state, private, college/university gift aid from institutional funds, United Negro College Fund, Federal Nursing.

GIFT AID (NON-NEED-BASED) *Scholarships, grants, and awards by category:* Academic interests/achievement: biological sciences, business, communication, computer science, engineering/technologies, mathematics, military science. Creative arts/performance: applied art and design, art/fine arts, general creative arts/performance, music. Special achievements/activities: general special achievements/activities. Special characteristics: first-generation college students, general special characteristics.

LOANS *Programs:* Federal Direct (Subsidized and Unsubsidized Stafford, PLUS), Perkins, Federal Nursing, state, college/university.

APPLYING FOR FINANCIAL AID *Required financial aid forms:* FAFSA, institution's own form.

CONTACT Linda Gayton, Director of Financial Aid, Bowie State University, 14000 Jericho Park Road, Bowie, MD 20715, 301-860-3543 or toll-free 877-772-6943. *Fax:* 301-860-3549. *E-mail:* lgayton@bowiestate.edu.
Website: http://www.bowiestate.edu/.

BOWLING GREEN STATE UNIVERSITY
Bowling Green, OH

Tuition & fees (OH res): $11,057	Average undergraduate aid package: $14,013

ABOUT THE INSTITUTION State-supported, coed. *Awards:* certificates, bachelor's, master's, and doctoral degrees. 221 undergraduate majors. *Total enrollment:* 17,644. Undergraduates: 14,852. Freshmen: 3,545. Federal methodology is used as a basis for awarding need-based institutional aid.

UNDERGRADUATE EXPENSES for 2016–2017 *Application fee:* $45. *Tuition, state resident:* full-time $9096; part-time $379 per credit hour. *Tuition, nonresident:* full-time $16,632; part-time $693 per credit hour. *Required fees:* full-time $1961; $70.15 per credit hour. Full-time tuition and fees vary according to course load and location. Part-time tuition and fees vary according to course load and location. *College room and board:* $8690. Room and board charges vary according to board plan and housing facility.

FRESHMAN FINANCIAL AID (Fall 2016, est.) 3,208 applied for aid; of those 75% were deemed to have need. 99% of freshmen with need received aid; of those 15% had need fully met. *Average percent of need met:* 81% (excluding resources awarded to replace EFC). *Average financial aid package:* $13,820 (excluding resources awarded to replace EFC). 22% of all full-time freshmen had no need and received non-need-based gift aid.

UNDERGRADUATE FINANCIAL AID (Fall 2016, est.) 10,767 applied for aid; of those 79% were deemed to have need. 98% of undergraduates with need received aid; of those 15% had need fully met. *Average percent of need met:* 80% (excluding resources awarded to replace EFC). *Average financial aid package:* $14,013 (excluding resources awarded to replace EFC). 20% of all full-time undergraduates had no need and received non-need-based gift aid.

GIFT AID (NEED-BASED) *Total amount:* $46,411,925 (40% federal, 8% state, 46% institutional, 6% external sources). *Receiving aid:* Freshmen: 59% (2,090); all full-time undergraduates: 53% (6,983). *Average award:* Freshmen: $6597; Undergraduates: $6920. *Scholarships, grants, and awards:* Federal Pell, FSEOG, state, private, college/university gift aid from institutional funds.

GIFT AID (NON-NEED-BASED) *Total amount:* $18,932,376 (3% state, 83% institutional, 14% external sources). *Receiving aid:* Freshmen: 7% (264). Undergraduates: 6% (763). *Average award:* Freshmen: $4894. Undergraduates: $5186. *Scholarships, grants, and awards by category:* Academic interests/achievement: biological sciences, business, communication, computer science, education, engineering/technologies, English, foreign languages, general academic interests/achievements, health fields, home economics, humanities, international studies, mathematics, military science, physical sciences, social sciences. Creative arts/performance: art/fine arts, cinema/film/broadcasting, creative writing, dance, debating, journalism/publications, music, performing arts, theater/drama. *Special achievements/activities:* general special achievements/activities, leadership. *Special characteristics:* children and siblings of alumni, children of faculty/staff, general special characteristics, international students, members of minority groups. *Tuition waivers:* Full or partial for employees or children of employees, senior citizens. *ROTC:* Army, Air Force.

LOANS *Student loans:* $75,351,187 (69% need-based, 31% non-need-based). 77% of past graduating class borrowed through all loan programs. *Average indebtedness per student:* $30,801. *Average need-based loan:* Freshmen: $3385. Undergraduates: $4143. *Parent loans:* $38,282,342 (43% need-based, 57% non-need-based).

Programs: Federal Direct (Subsidized and Unsubsidized Stafford, PLUS), Perkins, Federal Nursing, state, college/university, alternative loans.

WORK-STUDY *Federal work-study:* Total amount: $452,456; 371 jobs averaging $1220.

ATHLETIC AWARDS Total amount: $6,505,981 (32% need-based, 68% non-need-based).

APPLYING FOR FINANCIAL AID *Required financial aid form:* FAFSA. *Financial aid deadline:* Continuous. *Notification date:* Continuous beginning 4/15. Students must reply within 3 weeks of notification.

CONTACT Eric Bucks, Bowling Green State University, 231 Administration Building, Bowling Green, OH 43403, 419-372-2651. *Fax:* 419-372-0404. *Website:* http://www.bgsu.edu/.

BRADLEY UNIVERSITY
Peoria, IL

Tuition & fees: $32,120	Average undergraduate aid package: $22,141

ABOUT THE INSTITUTION Independent, coed. *Awards:* certificates, bachelor's, master's, and doctoral degrees. 119 undergraduate majors. *Total enrollment:* 5,598. Undergraduates: 4,473. Freshmen: 1,023. Federal methodology is used as a basis for awarding need-based institutional aid.

UNDERGRADUATE EXPENSES for 2016–2017 *Application fee:* $35. *One-time required fee:* $200. *Comprehensive fee:* $42,130 includes full-time tuition ($31,740), mandatory fees ($380), and room and board ($10,010). *College room only:* $5790. Full-time tuition and fees vary according to course load and program. Room and board charges vary according to board plan and housing facility. *Part-time tuition:* $850 per credit hour. *Part-time fees:* $380 per year. Part-time tuition and fees vary according to course load and program.

FRESHMAN FINANCIAL AID (Fall 2016, est.) 1,013 applied for aid; of those 83% were deemed to have need. 100% of freshmen with need received aid; of those 14% had need fully met. *Average percent of need met:* 75% (excluding resources awarded to replace EFC). *Average financial aid package:* $24,549 (excluding resources awarded to replace EFC). 22% of all full-time freshmen had no need and received non-need-based gift aid.

UNDERGRADUATE FINANCIAL AID (Fall 2016, est.) 3,505 applied for aid; of those 85% were deemed to have need. 99% of undergraduates with need received aid; of those 15% had need fully met. *Average percent of need met:* 70% (excluding resources awarded to replace EFC). *Average financial aid package:* $22,141 (excluding resources awarded to replace EFC). 28% of all full-time undergraduates had no need and received non-need-based gift aid.

GIFT AID (NEED-BASED) *Total amount:* $53,832,468 (9% federal, 9% state, 80% institutional, 2% external sources). *Receiving aid:* Freshmen: 77% (840); all full-time undergraduates: 63% (2,858). *Average award:* Freshmen: $20,264; Undergraduates: $17,049. *Scholarships, grants, and awards:* Federal Pell, FSEOG, state, private, college/university gift aid from institutional funds.

GIFT AID (NON-NEED-BASED) *Total amount:* $10,755,611 (93% institutional, 7% external sources). *Receiving aid:* Freshmen: 8% (92). Undergraduates: 7% (315). *Average award:* Freshmen: $12,111. Undergraduates: $11,042. *Scholarships, grants, and awards by category:* Academic interests/achievement: general academic interests/achievements. *Creative arts/performance:* art/fine arts, music, theater/drama. *Special achievements/activities:* community service, leadership. *Special characteristics:* children and siblings of alumni, children of faculty/staff. *Tuition waivers:* Full or partial for employees or children of employees, senior citizens. *ROTC:* Army.

LOANS *Student loans:* $29,543,367 (53% need-based, 47% non-need-based). 72% of past graduating class borrowed through all loan programs. *Average indebtedness*

per student: $25,725. *Average need-based loan:* Freshmen: $5042. Undergraduates: $6662. *Parent loans:* $14,236,638 (43% need-based, 57% non-need-based).

Programs: Federal Direct (Subsidized and Unsubsidized Stafford, PLUS), Perkins, Federal Nursing.

WORK-STUDY *Federal work-study:* Total amount: $524,245; 290 jobs averaging $1953.

ATHLETIC AWARDS Total amount: $3,846,371 (28% need-based, 72% non-need-based).

APPLYING FOR FINANCIAL AID *Required financial aid form:* FAFSA *Financial aid deadline:* Continuous. *Notification date:* Continuous beginning 11/15. Students must reply by 5/1 or within 2 weeks of notification.

CONTACT Debra Jackson, Director of Financial Assistance, Bradley University, 1501 West Bradley Avenue, Peoria, IL 61625, 309-677-3089 or toll-free 800-447-6460. *Fax:* 309-677-2798. *E-mail:* bufinaid@bradley.edu. *Website:* http://www.bradley.edu/.

BRANDEIS UNIVERSITY
Waltham, MA

Tuition & fees: $51,545	Average undergraduate aid package: $41,876

ABOUT THE INSTITUTION Independent, coed. *Awards:* bachelor's, master's, and doctoral degrees. 43 undergraduate majors. *Total enrollment:* 5,729. Undergraduates: 3,608. Freshmen: 841. Institutional methodology is used as a basis for awarding need-based institutional aid.

UNDERGRADUATE EXPENSES for 2016–2017 *Application fee:* $80. *Comprehensive fee:* $65,925 includes full-time tuition ($49,586), mandatory fees ($1959), and room and board ($14,380). *College room only:* $8060. Full-time tuition and fees vary according to student level. Room and board charges vary according to board plan and housing facility. *Part-time tuition:* $1549 per credit. *Part-time fees:* $1959 per year. Part-time tuition and fees vary according to course load.

FRESHMAN FINANCIAL AID (Fall 2015) 478 applied for aid; of those 78% were deemed to have need. 99% of freshmen with need received aid; of those 90% had need fully met. *Average percent of need met:* 95% (excluding resources awarded to replace EFC). *Average financial aid package:* $43,340 (excluding resources awarded to replace EFC). 13% of all full-time freshmen had no need and received non-need-based gift aid.

UNDERGRADUATE FINANCIAL AID (Fall 2015) 2,010 applied for aid; of those 90% were deemed to have need. 99% of undergraduates with need received aid; of those 69% had need fully met. *Average percent of need met:* 96% (excluding resources awarded to replace EFC). *Average financial aid package:* $41,876 (excluding resources awarded to replace EFC). 8% of all full-time undergraduates had no need and received non-need-based gift aid.

GIFT AID (NEED-BASED) *Total amount:* $63,618,568 (6% federal, 1% state, 90% institutional, 3% external sources). *Receiving aid:* Freshmen: 44% (356); all full-time undergraduates: 47% (1,694). *Average award:* Freshmen: $40,150; Undergraduates: $37,351. *Scholarships, grants, and awards:* Federal Pell, FSEOG, state, private, college/university gift aid from institutional funds.

GIFT AID (NON-NEED-BASED) *Total amount:* $6,433,389 (73% institutional, 27% external sources). *Receiving aid:* Freshmen: 3% (27). Undergraduates: 2% (87). *Average award:* Freshmen: $14,805. Undergraduates: $15,200. *Tuition waivers:* Full or partial for employees or children of employees. *ROTC:* Army cooperative, Air Force cooperative.

LOANS *Student loans:* $13,980,310 (77% need-based, 23% non-need-based). 55% of past graduating class borrowed through all loan programs. *Average indebtedness per student:* $32,922. *Average need-based loan:* Freshmen: $3335. Undergraduates: $4983. *Parent loans:* $4,745,650 (32% need-based, 68% non-need-based).

Programs: Federal Direct (Subsidized and Unsubsidized Stafford, PLUS), Perkins, state, college/university.

WORK-STUDY *Federal work-study:* 291 jobs averaging $2707. *State or other work-study/employment:* Total amount: $825,160 (58% need-based, 42% non-need-based). 16 part-time jobs averaging $2874.

APPLYING FOR FINANCIAL AID *Required financial aid forms:* FAFSA, CSS Financial Aid PROFILE, noncustodial (divorced/separated) parent's statement, business/farm supplement. *Financial aid deadline:* 1/1. *Notification date:* 4/1. Students must reply by 5/1.

CONTACT Tim Brown, Assistant Director for Student Services, Brandeis University, Usdan Student Center, 415 South Street, Waltham, MA 02454-9110, 781-736-3700 or toll-free 800-622-0622 (out-of-state). *Fax:* 781-736-3719. *E-mail:* sfs@brandeis.edu. *Website:* http://www.brandeis.edu/.

BRANDMAN UNIVERSITY
Irvine, CA

CONTACT Financial Aid Office, Brandman University, 16355 Laguna Canyon Road, Irvine, CA 92618, 949-753-4774 or toll-free 800-746-0082. *Website:* http://www.brandman.edu/irvine/.

BRENAU UNIVERSITY
Gainesville, GA

Tuition & fees: $27,152	Average undergraduate aid package: $21,389

ABOUT THE INSTITUTION Independent, coed, primarily women. *Awards:* certificates, associate, bachelor's, master's, and doctoral degrees (also offers coed evening and weekend programs with significant enrollment not reflected in profile). 37 undergraduate majors. *Total enrollment:* 2,899. Undergraduates: 1,653. Freshmen: 177. Both federal and institutional methodology are used as a basis for awarding need-based institutional aid.

UNDERGRADUATE EXPENSES for 2016–2017 *Comprehensive fee:* $39,570 includes full-time tuition ($26,752), mandatory fees ($400), and room and board ($12,418). Full-time tuition and fees vary according to course load, location, and program. *Part-time tuition:* $892 per credit hour. *Part-time fees:* $200 per term. Part-time tuition and fees vary according to course load, location, and program.

FRESHMAN FINANCIAL AID (Fall 2016, est.) 140 applied for aid; of those 89% were deemed to have need. 98% of freshmen with need received aid; of those 16% had need fully met. *Average percent of need met:* 70% (excluding resources awarded to replace EFC). *Average financial aid package:* $24,035 (excluding resources awarded to replace EFC). 6% of all full-time freshmen had no need and received non-need-based gift aid.

UNDERGRADUATE FINANCIAL AID (Fall 2016, est.) 922 applied for aid; of those 92% were deemed to have need. 99% of undergraduates with need received aid; of those 11% had need fully met. *Average percent of need met:* 73% (excluding resources awarded to replace EFC). *Average financial aid package:* $21,389 (excluding resources awarded to replace EFC). 11% of all full-time undergraduates had no need and received non-need-based gift aid.

GIFT AID (NEED-BASED) *Total amount:* $11,719,488 (26% federal, 14% state, 59% institutional, 1% external sources). *Receiving aid:* Freshmen: 80% (122); all full-time undergraduates: 80% (832). *Average award:* Freshmen: $20,648; Undergraduates: $13,418. *Scholarships, grants, and awards:* Federal Pell, FSEOG, state, private, college/university gift aid from institutional funds.

GIFT AID (NON-NEED-BASED) *Total amount:* $1,045,489 (32% state, 66% institutional, 2% external sources). *Receiving aid:* Freshmen: 11% (17). Undergraduates: 6% (58). *Average award:* Freshmen: $18,829. Undergraduates: $11,759. *Scholarships, grants, and awards by category:* Academic interests/achievement: biological sciences, business, communication, education, English, general academic interests/achievements, home economics, humanities. *Creative arts/performance:* applied art and design, art/fine arts, creative writing, dance, journalism/publications, music, performing arts, theater/drama. *Special achievements/activities:* cheerleading/drum major, community service, general special achievements/activities, leadership. *Special characteristics:* children and siblings of alumni, children of faculty/staff, first-generation college students, general special characteristics, international students, members of minority groups, out-of-state students. *Tuition waivers:* Full or partial for employees or children of employees.

LOANS *Student loans:* $11,464,221 (89% need-based, 11% non-need-based). 79% of past graduating class borrowed through all loan programs. *Average indebtedness per student:* $33,375. *Average need-based loan:* Freshmen: $4157. Undergraduates: $8830. *Parent loans:* $1,361,307 (57% need-based, 43% non-need-based). *Programs:* Federal Direct (Subsidized and Unsubsidized Stafford, PLUS), Perkins, Federal Nursing, state.

WORK-STUDY *Federal work-study:* Total amount: $248,143; 134 jobs averaging $1852.

ATHLETIC AWARDS Total amount: $1,855,803 (70% need-based, 30% non-need-based).

APPLYING FOR FINANCIAL AID *Required financial aid forms:* FAFSA, state aid form. *Financial aid deadline (priority):* 3/1. *Notification date:* Continuous beginning 3/1.

CONTACT Mrs. Pam Barrett, Associate Vice President and Director of Financial Aid, Brenau University, 500 Washington Street, SE, Gainesville, GA 30501-3697, 770-534-6176 or toll-free 800-252-5119. *Fax:* 770-538-4306. *E-mail:* pbarrett@brenau.edu. *Website:* http://www.brenau.edu/.

BRESCIA UNIVERSITY
Owensboro, KY

Tuition & fees: $21,850	Average undergraduate aid package: $25,489

ABOUT THE INSTITUTION Independent Roman Catholic, coed. *Awards:* certificates, associate, bachelor's, and master's degrees. 31 undergraduate majors. *Total enrollment:* 1,292. Undergraduates: 1,272. Freshmen: 129. Federal methodology is used as a basis for awarding need-based institutional aid.

UNDERGRADUATE EXPENSES for 2017–2018 *Application fee:* $25. *One-time required fee:* $200. *Tuition:* full-time $20,960; part-time $590 per credit hour. Full-time tuition and fees vary according to course load and degree level. Part-time tuition and fees vary according to course load and degree level. Room and board charges vary according to board plan and housing facility.

FRESHMAN FINANCIAL AID (Fall 2015) 193 applied for aid; of those 100% were deemed to have need. 100% of freshmen with need received aid. *Average financial aid package:* $23,315 (excluding resources awarded to replace EFC). 9% of all full-time freshmen had no need and received non-need-based gift aid.

UNDERGRADUATE FINANCIAL AID (Fall 2015) 925 applied for aid; of those 97% were deemed to have need. 100% of undergraduates with need received aid. *Average financial aid package:* $25,489 (excluding resources awarded to replace EFC). 6% of all full-time undergraduates had no need and received non-need-based gift aid.

GIFT AID (NEED-BASED) *Total amount:* $6,679,272 (74% federal, 26% state). *Receiving aid:* Freshmen: 70% (136); all full-time undergraduates: 75% (735). *Average award:* Freshmen: $7904; Undergraduates: $7811. *Scholarships, grants, and awards:* Federal Pell, FSEOG, state, private, college/university gift aid from institutional funds.

GIFT AID (NON-NEED-BASED) *Total amount:* $1,611,773 (53% state, 28% institutional, 19% external sources). *Receiving aid:* Freshmen: 89% (174). Undergraduates: 34% (330). *Average award:* Freshmen: $10,102. Undergraduates: $16,191. *Scholarships, grants, and awards by category:* Academic interests/achievement: 330 awards ($3,400,916 total): general academic interests/achievements. *Creative arts/performance:* 21 awards ($27,800 total): art/fine arts, creative writing, journalism/publications, music. *Special achievements/activities:* 17 awards ($82,400 total): leadership. *Tuition waivers:* Full or partial for employees or children of employees, senior citizens.

LOANS *Student loans:* $14,902,363 (36% need-based, 64% non-need-based). 66% of past graduating class borrowed through all loan programs. *Average indebtedness per student:* $19,060. *Average need-based loan:* Freshmen: $3116. Undergraduates: $3414. *Parent loans:* $1,915,993 (100% non-need-based). *Programs:* Federal Direct (Subsidized and Unsubsidized Stafford, PLUS), Perkins, college/university, private loans.

WORK-STUDY *Federal work-study:* 50 jobs averaging $909. *State or other work-study/employment:* Total amount: $121,341 (100% non-need-based). 48 part-time jobs averaging $849.

ATHLETIC AWARDS Total amount: $594,927 (100% non-need-based).

APPLYING FOR FINANCIAL AID *Required financial aid form:* FAFSA. *Financial aid deadline:* Continuous. *Notification date:* Continuous beginning 2/15. Students must reply by 8/20.

CONTACT Ms. Kristi Eidson, Director of Financial Aid, Brescia University, 717 Frederica Street, Owensboro, KY 42301-3023, 270-686-4356 or toll-free 877-273-7242. *Fax:* 270-689-9563. *E-mail:* financial.aid@brescia.edu. *Website:* http://www.brescia.edu/.

BREVARD COLLEGE
Brevard, NC

Tuition & fees: N/R	Average undergraduate aid package: $22,027

ABOUT THE INSTITUTION Independent United Methodist, coed. 21 undergraduate majors. Federal methodology is used as a basis for awarding need-based institutional aid.

FRESHMAN FINANCIAL AID (Fall 2015) 246 applied for aid; of those 80% were deemed to have need. 100% of freshmen with need received aid; of those 8% had need fully met. *Average percent of need met:* 61% (excluding resources awarded to replace EFC). *Average financial aid package:* $20,009 (excluding resources awarded to replace EFC). 18% of all full-time freshmen had no need and received non-need-based gift aid.

UNDERGRADUATE FINANCIAL AID (Fall 2015) 699 applied for aid; of those 78% were deemed to have need. 100% of undergraduates with need received aid; of those 13% had need fully met. *Average percent of need met:* 68% (excluding resources awarded to replace EFC). *Average financial aid package:* $22,027 (excluding resources awarded to replace EFC). 21% of all full-time undergraduates had no need and received non-need-based gift aid.

GIFT AID (NEED-BASED) *Total amount:* $8,495,503 (17% federal, 14% state, 65% institutional, 4% external sources). *Receiving aid:* Freshmen: 80% (198); all full-time undergraduates: 76% (540). *Average award:* Freshmen: $16,493; Undergraduates: $17,620. *Scholarships, grants, and awards:* Federal Pell, FSEOG, state, private, college/university gift aid from institutional funds.

GIFT AID (NON-NEED-BASED) *Total amount:* $1,532,504 (91% institutional, 9% external sources). *Receiving aid:* Freshmen: 5% (13). Undergraduates: 7% (52). *Average award:* Freshmen: $8748. Undergraduates: $8462. *Scholarships, grants, and awards by category:* Academic interests/achievement: general academic interests/achievements. Creative arts/performance: art/fine arts, music, theater/drama. Special achievements/activities: cheerleading/drum major, community service, general special achievements/activities, leadership. Special characteristics: children of faculty/staff, international students, local/state students, previous college experience, veterans' children.

LOANS *Student loans:* $3,727,554 (84% need-based, 16% non-need-based). 61% of past graduating class borrowed through all loan programs. *Average indebtedness per student:* $28,511. *Average need-based loan:* Freshmen: $3038. Undergraduates: $3885. *Parent loans:* $1,674,990 (72% need-based, 28% non-need-based). *Programs:* Federal Direct (Subsidized and Unsubsidized Stafford, PLUS), Perkins.

WORK-STUDY *Federal work-study:* jobs available. *State or other work-study/employment:* Total amount: $131,590 (57% need-based, 43% non-need-based). Part-time jobs available.

ATHLETIC AWARDS Total amount: $2,305,172 (65% need-based, 35% non-need-based).

APPLYING FOR FINANCIAL AID *Required financial aid form:* FAFSA. *Financial aid deadline (priority):* 2/1. *Notification date:* Continuous beginning 2/1. Students must reply by 5/1 or within 4 weeks of notification.

CONTACT Ms. Caron Surrett, Director of Financial Aid, Brevard College, 1 Brevard College Drive, Brevard, NC 28712, 828-884-8261 or toll-free 800-527-9090. *Fax:* 828-884-3790. *E-mail:* finaid@brevard.edu. *Website:* http://www.brevard.edu/.

BREWTON-PARKER COLLEGE
Mt. Vernon, GA

CONTACT Mrs. Shannon Mullins, Executive Director of Financial Aid, Brewton-Parker College, PO Box 197, Mt. Vernon, GA 30445-0197, 800-342-1087 Ext. 213 or toll-free 800-342-1087. *Fax:* 912-583-3598. *E-mail:* smullins@bpc.edu. *Website:* http://www.bpc.edu/.

BRIAR CLIFF UNIVERSITY
Sioux City, IA

Tuition & fees: $29,786	Average undergraduate aid package: $30,582

ABOUT THE INSTITUTION Independent Roman Catholic, coed. *Awards:* certificates, associate, bachelor's, master's, and doctoral degrees. 29 undergraduate majors. *Total enrollment:* 1,316. Undergraduates: 1,117. Freshmen: 210. Federal methodology is used as a basis for awarding need-based institutional aid.

UNDERGRADUATE EXPENSES for 2017–2018 *Application fee:* $20. *Comprehensive fee:* $38,872 includes full-time tuition ($28,650), mandatory fees ($1136), and room and board ($9086). *College room only:* $4300. Full-time tuition and fees vary according to class time, course load, degree level, location, and program. Room and board charges vary according to board plan, housing facility, and location. *Part-time tuition:* $956 per credit hour. Part-time tuition and fees vary according to class time, course load, degree level, location, and program.

FRESHMAN FINANCIAL AID (Fall 2015) 184 applied for aid; of those 86% were deemed to have need. 100% of freshmen with need received aid; of those 28% had need fully met. *Average percent of need met:* 30% (excluding resources awarded to replace EFC). *Average financial aid package:* $33,359 (excluding resources awarded to replace EFC). 14% of all full-time freshmen had no need and received non-need-based gift aid.

UNDERGRADUATE FINANCIAL AID (Fall 2015) 778 applied for aid; of those 84% were deemed to have need. 100% of undergraduates with need received aid; of those 24% had need fully met. *Average percent of need met:* 26% (excluding resources awarded to replace EFC). *Average financial aid package:* $30,582 (excluding resources awarded to replace EFC). 17% of all full-time undergraduates had no need and received non-need-based gift aid.

GIFT AID (NEED-BASED) *Total amount:* $10,929,963 (19% federal, 12% state, 65% institutional, 4% external sources). *Receiving aid:* Freshmen: 85% (157); all full-time undergraduates: 82% (648). *Average award:* Freshmen: $16,633; Undergraduates: $14,647. *Scholarships, grants, and awards:* Federal Pell, FSEOG, state, private, college/university gift aid from institutional funds.

GIFT AID (NON-NEED-BASED) *Total amount:* $587,567 (13% federal, 20% state, 57% institutional, 10% external sources). *Receiving aid:* Freshmen: 21% (38). Undergraduates: 20% (160). *Average award:* Freshmen: $1324. Undergraduates: $2524. *Scholarships, grants, and awards by category:* Academic interests/achievement: biological sciences, business, communication, computer science, education, English, foreign languages, general academic interests/achievements, health fields, humanities, mathematics, physical sciences, religion/biblical studies, social sciences. Creative arts/performance: art/fine arts, music, theater/drama. Special achievements/activities: leadership, religious involvement. Special characteristics: children and siblings of alumni, first-generation college students, international students, members of minority groups. *Tuition waivers:* Full or partial for employees or children of employees. *ROTC:* Army cooperative.

LOANS *Student loans:* $5,976,772 (51% need-based, 49% non-need-based). 92% of past graduating class borrowed through all loan programs. *Average indebtedness per student:* $29,484. *Average need-based loan:* Freshmen: $4669. Undergraduates: $4837. *Parent loans:* $962,216 (100% non-need-based). *Programs:* Federal Direct (Subsidized and Unsubsidized Stafford, PLUS), Perkins, alternative loans, partnership loans, Minnesota SELF Loans.

WORK-STUDY *Federal work-study:* jobs available. *State or other work-study/employment:* Total amount: $319,161 (100% non-need-based). Part-time jobs available.

ATHLETIC AWARDS Total amount: $3,635,708 (100% non-need-based).

APPLYING FOR FINANCIAL AID *Required financial aid form:* FAFSA. *Financial aid deadline:* 3/15. *Notification date:* Continuous beginning 2/1. Students must reply within 4 weeks of notification.

CONTACT Brian K. Eben, Office of Student Financial Aid, Briar Cliff University, 3303 Rebecca Street, PO Box 2100, Sioux City, IA 51104-2100, 712-279-5239 or toll-free 800-662-3303. *Fax:* 712-279-1632. *Website:* http://www.briarcliff.edu/.

BRIDGEWATER COLLEGE
Bridgewater, VA

Tuition & fees: $33,820	Average undergraduate aid package: $29,897

ABOUT THE INSTITUTION Independent Church of the Brethren, coed. **Awards:** bachelor's degrees. 30 undergraduate majors. **Total enrollment:** 1,882. Undergraduates: 1,882. Freshmen: 600. Federal methodology is used as a basis for awarding need-based institutional aid.

UNDERGRADUATE EXPENSES for 2017–2018 Comprehensive fee: $46,260 includes full-time tuition ($33,000), mandatory fees ($820), and room and board ($12,440). Room and board charges vary according to housing facility. **Part-time tuition:** $1150 per credit hour. **Part-time fees:** $40 per term.

FRESHMAN FINANCIAL AID (Fall 2016, est.) 569 applied for aid; of those 91% were deemed to have need. 100% of freshmen with need received aid; of those 30% had need fully met. **Average percent of need met:** 87% (excluding resources awarded to replace EFC). **Average financial aid package:** $31,579 (excluding resources awarded to replace EFC). 14% of all full-time freshmen had no need and received non-need-based gift aid.

UNDERGRADUATE FINANCIAL AID (Fall 2016, est.) 1,661 applied for aid; of those 91% were deemed to have need. 100% of undergraduates with need received aid; of those 29% had need fully met. **Average percent of need met:** 85% (excluding resources awarded to replace EFC). **Average financial aid package:** $29,897 (excluding resources awarded to replace EFC). 19% of all full-time undergraduates had no need and received non-need-based gift aid.

GIFT AID (NEED-BASED) Total amount: $33,391,488 (8% federal, 10% state, 81% institutional, 1% external sources). **Receiving aid:** Freshmen: 86% (517); all full-time undergraduates: 81% (1,508). **Average award:** Freshmen: $28,113; Undergraduates: $26,156. **Scholarships, grants, and awards:** Federal Pell, FSEOG, state, private, college/university gift aid from institutional funds.

GIFT AID (NON-NEED-BASED) Total amount: $13,918,509 (6% state, 93% institutional, 1% external sources). **Receiving aid:** Freshmen: 86% (517). Undergraduates: 81% (1,508). **Average award:** Freshmen: $21,809. Undergraduates: $19,563. **Scholarships, grants, and awards by category:** Academic interests/achievement: 1,709 awards ($30,785,243 total): general academic interests/achievements. Creative arts/performance: 66 awards ($123,681 total): music. **Special characteristics:** 977 awards ($4,500,496 total): children of educators, children of faculty/staff, international students, members of minority groups, out-of-state students, previous college experience, religious affiliation. **Tuition waivers:** Full or partial for employees or children of employees.

LOANS Student loans: $12,169,385 (60% need-based, 40% non-need-based). 75% of past graduating class borrowed through all loan programs. **Average indebtedness per student:** $34,035. **Average need-based loan:** Freshmen: $4168. Undergraduates: $4579. **Parent loans:** $5,281,148 (11% need-based, 89% non-need-based). **Programs:** Federal Direct (Subsidized and Unsubsidized Stafford, PLUS), Perkins.

WORK-STUDY Federal work-study: Total amount: $591,650; 407 jobs averaging $1454. **State or other work-study/employment:** 103 part-time jobs averaging $1145.

APPLYING FOR FINANCIAL AID Required financial aid forms: FAFSA, state aid form. **Financial aid deadline (priority):** 3/1. **Notification date:** Continuous beginning 12/1. Students must reply by 5/1 or within 2 weeks of notification.

CONTACT Mr. Scott Morrison, Director of Financial Aid, Bridgewater College, 402 East College Street, Bridgewater, VA 22812-1599, 540-828-5377 or toll-free 800-759-8328. Fax: 540-828-5671. E-mail: smorriso@bridgewater.edu. Website: http://www.bridgewater.edu/.

BRIDGEWATER STATE UNIVERSITY
Bridgewater, MA

Tuition & fees (MA res): $9870	Average undergraduate aid package: $8186

ABOUT THE INSTITUTION State-supported, coed. **Awards:** certificates, bachelor's, and master's degrees. 80 undergraduate majors. **Total enrollment:** 10,998. Undergraduates: 9,562. Freshmen: 1,420. Federal methodology is used as a basis for awarding need-based institutional aid.

UNDERGRADUATE EXPENSES for 2017–2018 Application fee: $50. **Tuition, state resident:** full-time $910; part-time $38 per credit hour. **Tuition, nonresident:** full-time $7050; part-time $294 per credit hour. **Required fees:** full-time $8960; $373.30 per credit hour. Full-time tuition and fees vary according to course load. **College room and board:** $12,750; **Room only:** $8400. Room and board charges vary according to board plan and housing facility.

FRESHMAN FINANCIAL AID (Fall 2015) 1,389 applied for aid; of those 75% were deemed to have need. 100% of freshmen with need received aid; of those 9% had need fully met. **Average financial aid package:** $5510 (excluding resources awarded to replace EFC). 1% of all full-time freshmen had no need and received non-need-based gift aid.

UNDERGRADUATE FINANCIAL AID (Fall 2015) 7,161 applied for aid; of those 77% were deemed to have need. 99% of undergraduates with need received aid; of those 8% had need fully met. **Average financial aid package:** $8186 (excluding resources awarded to replace EFC). 1% of all full-time undergraduates had no need and received non-need-based gift aid.

GIFT AID (NEED-BASED) Total amount: $22,521,640 (61% federal, 19% state, 20% institutional). **Receiving aid:** Freshmen: 54% (811); all full-time undergraduates: 52% (4,127). **Average award:** Freshmen: $3289; Undergraduates: $5420. **Scholarships, grants, and awards:** Federal Pell, FSEOG, state, college/university gift aid from institutional funds.

GIFT AID (NON-NEED-BASED) Total amount: $3,294,053 (4% federal, 41% state, 14% institutional, 41% external sources). **Receiving aid:** Freshmen: 16% (243). Undergraduates: 12% (923). **Average award:** Freshmen: $2195. Undergraduates: $5883. **Scholarships, grants, and awards by category:** Academic interests/achievement: general academic interests/achievements. **Special characteristics:** local/state students, members of minority groups. **Tuition waivers:** Full or partial for employees or children of employees, senior citizens. **ROTC:** Army cooperative, Air Force cooperative.

LOANS Student loans: $47,997,349 (45% need-based, 55% non-need-based). 78% of past graduating class borrowed through all loan programs. **Average indebtedness per student:** $27,104. **Average need-based loan:** Freshmen: $1860. Undergraduates: $4143. **Parent loans:** $8,716,018 (100% non-need-based). **Programs:** Federal Direct (Subsidized and Unsubsidized Stafford, PLUS), state.

WORK-STUDY Federal work-study: 406 jobs averaging $1371.

APPLYING FOR FINANCIAL AID Required financial aid form: FAFSA. **Financial aid deadline (priority):** 3/1. **Notification date:** Continuous beginning 4/1.

CONTACT Janet Gumbris, Office of Financial Aid, Bridgewater State University, Tillinghast Hall, Room 100, 45 School Street, Bridgewater, MA 02325-0001, 508-531-1341. Fax: 508-531-1728. E-mail: finaid@bridgew.edu. Website: http://www.bridgew.edu/.

BRIGHAM YOUNG UNIVERSITY
Provo, UT

Tuition & fees: $5300	Average undergraduate aid package: $7436

ABOUT THE INSTITUTION Independent The Church of Jesus Christ of Latter-day Saints, coed. **Awards:** certificates, bachelor's, master's, and doctoral degrees. 102 undergraduate majors. **Total enrollment:** 34,240. Undergraduates: 30,979. Freshmen: 5,246. Both federal and institutional methodology are used as a basis for awarding need-based institutional aid.

UNDERGRADUATE EXPENSES for 2016–2017 Application fee: $35. **Comprehensive fee:** $12,748 includes full-time tuition ($5300) and room and board ($7448). Room and board charges vary according to board plan, housing facility, and location. **Part-time tuition:** $276 per credit hour. Part-time tuition and fees vary according to course load.

FRESHMAN FINANCIAL AID (Fall 2015) 2,539 applied for aid; of those 64% were deemed to have need. 90% of freshmen with need received aid; of those 2% had need fully met. **Average percent of need met:** 26% (excluding resources awarded to replace EFC). **Average financial aid package:** $6447 (excluding resources awarded to replace EFC). 39% of all full-time freshmen had no need and received non-need-based gift aid.

UNDERGRADUATE FINANCIAL AID (Fall 2015) 15,451 applied for aid; of those 84% were deemed to have need. 95% of undergraduates with need received aid; of those 2% had need fully met. **Average percent of need met:** 33% (excluding resources awarded to replace EFC). **Average financial aid package:** $7436

(excluding resources awarded to replace EFC). 26% of all full-time undergraduates had no need and received non-need-based gift aid.

GIFT AID (NEED-BASED) *Total amount:* $54,444,186 (85% federal, 15% institutional). *Receiving aid:* Freshmen: 16% (830); all full-time undergraduates: 38% (10,452). *Average award:* Freshmen: $4263; Undergraduates: $4874. *Scholarships, grants, and awards:* Federal Pell, private, college/university gift aid from institutional funds.

GIFT AID (NON-NEED-BASED) *Total amount:* $65,093,894 (84% institutional, 16% external sources). *Receiving aid:* Freshmen: 20% (1,002). Undergraduates: 21% (5,853). *Average award:* Freshmen: $4216. Undergraduates: $4338. *Scholarships, grants, and awards by category: Academic interests/ achievement:* general academic interests/achievements. *Creative arts/performance:* art/fine arts, music, theater/drama. *Special achievements/activities:* leadership, religious involvement. *Special characteristics:* local/state students, members of minority groups, religious affiliation. *Tuition waivers:* Full or partial for employees or children of employees. *ROTC:* Army, Air Force.

LOANS *Student loans:* $29,503,238 (56% need-based, 44% non-need-based). 26% of past graduating class borrowed through all loan programs. *Average indebtedness per student:* $15,158. *Average need-based loan:* Freshmen: $3151. Undergraduates: $4111. *Parent loans:* $872,094 (100% non-need-based). *Programs:* Federal Direct (Subsidized and Unsubsidized Stafford, PLUS).

WORK-STUDY *State or other work-study/employment:* Part-time jobs available.

ATHLETIC AWARDS Total amount: $6,572,015 (100% non-need-based).

APPLYING FOR FINANCIAL AID *Required financial aid form:* FAFSA. *Financial aid deadline (priority):* 4/15. *Notification date:* Continuous beginning 4/1.

CONTACT Stephen E. Hill, Director of Financial Aid, Brigham Young University, C-144 ASB, Provo, UT 84602, 801-422-4104. *Fax:* 801-422-0234. *Website:* http://www.byu.edu/.

BRIGHAM YOUNG UNIVERSITY–HAWAII
Laie, HI

CONTACT Mr. Wes Duke, Director of Financial Aid, Brigham Young University–Hawaii, BYUH #1980, 55-220 Kulanui Street, Laie, HI 96762, 808-293-3530. *Fax:* 808-293-3349. *E-mail:* duekw@byuh.edu. *Website:* http://www.byuh.edu/.

BRIGHAM YOUNG UNIVERSITY–IDAHO
Rexburg, ID

CONTACT Financial Aid Office, Brigham Young University–Idaho, 525 South Center Street, Rexburg, ID 83460, 208-496-2011. *Website:* http://www.byui.edu/.

BRISTOL UNIVERSITY
Anaheim, CA

CONTACT Financial Aid Office, Bristol University, 2390 Orangewood Avenue, Suite 485, Anaheim, CA 92806, 714-542-8086. *Website:* http://bristoluniversity.edu/.

BROADVIEW ENTERTAINMENT ARTS UNIVERSITY
Salt Lake City, UT

CONTACT Office of Financial Aid, Broadview Entertainment Arts University, 240 East Morris Avenue, Salt Lake City, UT 84115, 801-300-4300 or toll-free 877-801-8889. *Fax:* 801-300-4301. *Website:* http://www.broadviewuniversity.edu/.

BROADVIEW UNIVERSITY–WEST JORDAN
West Jordan, UT

CONTACT Office of Financial Aid, Broadview University–West Jordan, 1902 West 7800 South, West Jordan, UT 84088, 801-304-4224 or toll-free 866-304-4224. *Fax:* 801-304-4229. *Website:* http://www.broadviewuniversity.edu/.

BROOKLINE COLLEGE
Phoenix, AZ

CONTACT Financial Aid Office, Brookline College, 2445 West Dunlap Avenue, Suite 100, Phoenix, AZ 85021, 602-242-6265 or toll-free 800-793-2428. *Website:* http://brooklinecollege.edu/.

BROOKLINE COLLEGE
Tempe, AZ

CONTACT Financial Aid Office, Brookline College, 1140 South Priest Drive, Tempe, AZ 85281, 480-545-8755 or toll-free 888-886-2428. *Website:* http://brooklinecollege.edu/.

BROOKLINE COLLEGE
Tucson, AZ

CONTACT Financial Aid Office, Brookline College, 5441 East 22nd Street, Suite 125, Tucson, AZ 85711, 520-748-9799 or toll-free 888-292-2428. *Website:* http://brooklinecollege.edu/.

BROOKLINE COLLEGE
Albuquerque, NM

CONTACT Financial Aid Office, Brookline College, 4201 Central Avenue NW, Suite J, Albuquerque, NM 87105-1649, 505-880-2877 or toll-free 888-660-2428. *Website:* http://brooklinecollege.edu/.

BROOKLYN COLLEGE OF THE CITY UNIVERSITY OF NEW YORK
Brooklyn, NY

ABOUT THE INSTITUTION State and locally supported, coed. *Awards:* certificates, bachelor's, and master's degrees. 76 undergraduate majors. *Total enrollment:* 17,580. Undergraduates: 14,406. Freshmen: 1,330.

GIFT AID (NEED-BASED) *Scholarships, grants, and awards:* Federal Pell, FSEOG, state, private, college/university gift aid from institutional funds.

LOANS *Programs:* Federal Direct (Subsidized and Unsubsidized Stafford, PLUS), Perkins.
WORK-STUDY *Federal work-study:* 407 jobs averaging $2613.
APPLYING FOR FINANCIAL AID *Required financial aid forms:* FAFSA, state aid form.

CONTACT Mr. Ahad Farhang, Director of Financial Aid, Brooklyn College of the City University of New York, 2900 Bedford Avenue, Brooklyn, NY 11210-2889, 718-951-5669. *Fax:* 718-951-4778. *E-mail:* afarhang@brooklyn.cuny.edu.
Website: http://www.brooklyn.cuny.edu/.

BROWN UNIVERSITY
Providence, RI

Tuition & fees: $53,419	Average undergraduate aid package: $48,420

ABOUT THE INSTITUTION Independent, coed. *Awards:* bachelor's, master's, and doctoral degrees. 69 undergraduate majors. *Total enrollment:* 9,781. Undergraduates: 6,926. Freshmen: 1,679. Both federal and institutional methodology are used as a basis for awarding need-based institutional aid.
UNDERGRADUATE EXPENSES for 2017–2018 *Application fee:* $75. *One-time required fee:* $1188. *Comprehensive fee:* $67,439 includes full-time tuition ($52,231), mandatory fees ($1188), and room and board ($14,020). *College room only:* $8784. Room and board charges vary according to board plan. *Part-time tuition:* $6528 per course. Part-time tuition and fees vary according to course load.
FRESHMAN FINANCIAL AID (Fall 2016, est.) 955 applied for aid; of those 77% were deemed to have need. 100% of freshmen with need received aid; of those 100% had need fully met. *Average percent of need met:* 100% (excluding resources awarded to replace EFC). *Average financial aid package:* $46,043 (excluding resources awarded to replace EFC). 1% of all full-time freshmen had no need and received non-need-based gift aid.
UNDERGRADUATE FINANCIAL AID (Fall 2016, est.) 3,291 applied for aid; of those 87% were deemed to have need. 100% of undergraduates with need received aid; of those 100% had need fully met. *Average percent of need met:* 100% (excluding resources awarded to replace EFC). *Average financial aid package:* $48,420 (excluding resources awarded to replace EFC). 1% of all full-time undergraduates had no need and received non-need-based gift aid.
GIFT AID (NEED-BASED) *Total amount:* $128,869,648 (4% federal, 92% institutional, 4% external sources). *Receiving aid:* Freshmen: 41% (682); all full-time undergraduates: 41% (2,702). *Average award:* Freshmen: $43,186; Undergraduates: $44,105. *Scholarships, grants, and awards:* Federal Pell, FSEOG, state, private, college/university gift aid from institutional funds.
GIFT AID (NON-NEED-BASED) *Total amount:* $5,350,211 (1% institutional, 99% external sources). *Average award:* Freshmen: $8889. Undergraduates: $8704. *Scholarships, grants, and awards by category:* Special characteristics: 18 awards ($160,645 total): veterans, veterans' children. *Tuition waivers:* Full or partial for employees or children of employees. *ROTC:* Army cooperative, Naval cooperative, Air Force cooperative.
LOANS *Student loans:* $14,050,188 (56% need-based, 44% non-need-based). 37% of past graduating class borrowed through all loan programs. *Average indebtedness per student:* $23,810. *Average need-based loan:* Freshmen: $3270. Undergraduates: $4059. *Parent loans:* $9,365,225 (4% need-based, 96% non-need-based). *Programs:* Federal Direct (Subsidized and Unsubsidized Stafford, PLUS), Perkins, college/university.
WORK-STUDY *Federal work-study:* Total amount: $4,194,842; 1,646 jobs averaging $2489. *State or other work-study/employment:* Total amount: $1,035,940 (100% need-based). 395 part-time jobs averaging $2564.
APPLYING FOR FINANCIAL AID *Required financial aid forms:* FAFSA, CSS Financial Aid PROFILE, noncustodial (divorced/separated) parent's statement. *Financial aid deadline:* 2/1. *Notification date:* 4/1. Students must reply by 5/1.
CONTACT Office of Financial Aid, Brown University, PO Box 1827, Providence, RI 02912, 401-863-2721. *Fax:* 401-863-7575. *E-mail:* financial_aid@brown.edu.
Website: http://www.brown.edu/.

BRYAN COLLEGE
Dayton, TN

Tuition & fees: $25,600	Average undergraduate aid package: $23,175

ABOUT THE INSTITUTION Independent interdenominational, coed. *Awards:* certificates, associate, bachelor's, and master's degrees. 27 undergraduate majors. *Total enrollment:* 1,582. Undergraduates: 1,422. Freshmen: 201. Federal methodology is used as a basis for awarding need-based institutional aid.
UNDERGRADUATE EXPENSES for 2017–2018 *Application fee:* $35. *Comprehensive fee:* $32,900 includes full-time tuition ($25,600) and room and board ($7300). *College room only:* $4550. Room and board charges vary according to housing facility. *Part-time tuition:* $1100 per credit hour.
FRESHMAN FINANCIAL AID (Fall 2016, est.) 195 applied for aid; of those 90% were deemed to have need. 100% of freshmen with need received aid; of those 31% had need fully met. *Average financial aid package:* $23,944 (excluding resources awarded to replace EFC).
UNDERGRADUATE FINANCIAL AID (Fall 2016, est.) 603 applied for aid; of those 90% were deemed to have need. 99% of undergraduates with need received aid; of those 29% had need fully met. *Average financial aid package:* $23,175 (excluding resources awarded to replace EFC).
GIFT AID (NEED-BASED) *Total amount:* $9,445,558 (23% federal, 22% state, 54% institutional, 1% external sources). *Receiving aid:* Freshmen: 86% (175); all full-time undergraduates: 70% (477). *Average award:* Freshmen: $13,655; Undergraduates: $12,382. *Scholarships, grants, and awards:* Federal Pell, FSEOG, state, private, college/university gift aid from institutional funds.
GIFT AID (NON-NEED-BASED) *Total amount:* $638,149 (19% state, 81% institutional). *Receiving aid:* Freshmen: 83% (169). Undergraduates: 59% (404). *Scholarships, grants, and awards by category:* Academic interests/achievement: biological sciences, business, communication, computer science, education, English, foreign languages, general academic interests/achievements, humanities, mathematics, physical sciences, premedicine, religion/biblical studies, social sciences. *Creative arts/performance:* journalism/publications, music, performing arts, theater/drama. *Special achievements/activities:* community service, general special achievements/activities, leadership, religious involvement. *Special characteristics:* children and siblings of alumni, children of current students, children of educators, children of faculty/staff, general special characteristics, handicapped students, international students, local/state students, members of minority groups, relatives of clergy, spouses of current students. *Tuition waivers:* Full or partial for employees or children of employees.
LOANS *Student loans:* $5,348,073 (94% need-based, 6% non-need-based). *Average need-based loan:* Freshmen: $3451. Undergraduates: $4105. *Parent loans:* $711,336 (88% need-based, 12% non-need-based). *Programs:* Federal Direct (Subsidized and Unsubsidized Stafford, PLUS), Perkins, college/university.
WORK-STUDY *Federal work-study:* Total amount: $208,133; jobs available.
ATHLETIC AWARDS Total amount: $2,246,052 (91% need-based, 9% non-need-based).
APPLYING FOR FINANCIAL AID *Required financial aid form:* FAFSA. *Financial aid deadline (priority):* 1/31. *Notification date:* Continuous beginning 11/1.
CONTACT David Haggard, Director of Financial Aid, Bryan College, PO Box 7000, Dayton, TN 37321-7000, 423-775-7339 or toll-free 800-277-9522. *Fax:* 423-775-7300. *E-mail:* finaid@bryan.edu.
Website: http://www.bryan.edu/.

BRYAN COLLEGE OF HEALTH SCIENCES
Lincoln, NE

CONTACT Financial Aid Office, Bryan College of Health Sciences, 5035 Everett Street, Lincoln, NE 68506-1398, 402-481 3801.
Website: http://www.bryanhealth.com/CollegeofHealthSciences.

BRYANT & STRATTON COLLEGE–AKRON CAMPUS
Akron, OH

CONTACT Financial Aid Office, Bryant & Stratton College–Akron Campus, 190 Montrose West Avenue, Akron, OH 44321, 330-598-2500.
Website: http://www.bryantstratton.edu/.

BRYANT & STRATTON COLLEGE–CLEVELAND CAMPUS
Cleveland, OH

CONTACT Bill Davenport, Financial Aid Supervisor, Bryant & Stratton College–Cleveland Campus, 1700 East 13th Street, Cleveland, OH 44114-3203, 216-771-1700. *Fax:* 216-771-7787.
Website: http://www.bryantstratton.edu/.

BRYANT & STRATTON COLLEGE–HAMPTON CAMPUS
Hampton, VA

CONTACT Financial Aid Office, Bryant & Stratton College–Hampton Campus, 4410 East Claiborne Square, Suite 233, Hampton, VA 23666, 757-896-6001.
Website: http://www.bryantstratton.edu/.

BRYANT & STRATTON COLLEGE–WAUWATOSA CAMPUS
Wauwatosa, WI

CONTACT Financial Aid Office, Bryant & Stratton College–Wauwatosa Campus, 10950 West Potter Road, Wauwatosa, WI 53226, 414-302-7000.
Website: http://www.bryantstratton.edu/.

BRYANT UNIVERSITY
Smithfield, RI

ABOUT THE INSTITUTION Independent, coed. *Awards:* certificates, bachelor's, and master's degrees. 60 undergraduate majors. *Total enrollment:* 3,698. Undergraduates: 3,462. Freshmen: 843.
GIFT AID (NEED-BASED) *Scholarships, grants, and awards:* Federal Pell, FSEOG, state, private, college/university gift aid from institutional funds.
GIFT AID (NON-NEED-BASED) *Scholarships, grants, and awards by category: Academic interests/achievement:* general academic interests/achievements. *Special characteristics:* international students, members of minority groups, siblings of current students, veterans.
LOANS *Programs:* Federal Direct (Subsidized and Unsubsidized Stafford, PLUS), Perkins, private loans.
WORK-STUDY *Federal work-study:* jobs available. *State or other work-study/employment:* Total amount: $1,253,989 (30% need-based, 70% non-need-based). Part-time jobs available.
APPLYING FOR FINANCIAL AID *Required financial aid form:* FAFSA.
CONTACT Mr. John B. Canning, Director of Financial Aid, Bryant University, 1150 Douglas Pike, Smithfield, RI 02917-1284, 401-232-6020 or toll-free 800-622-7001. *Fax:* 401-232-6293. *E-mail:* jcanning@bryant.edu.
Website: http://www.bryant.edu/.

BRYAN UNIVERSITY
Springfield, MO

CONTACT Financial Aid Office, Bryan University, 4255 South Nature Center Way, Springfield, MO 65804, 417-862-5700 or toll-free 855-566-0650.
Website: http://www.bryanu.edu/.

BRYN ATHYN COLLEGE OF THE NEW CHURCH
Bryn Athyn, PA

CONTACT Wendy Cooper, Associate Director of Financial Aid, Bryn Athyn College of the New Church, Box 717, Bryn Athyn, PA 19009, 267-502-2630 or toll-free 800-767-9552. *Fax:* 267-502-4866. *E-mail:* financialaid@brynathyn.edu.
Website: http://www.brynathyn.edu/.

BRYN MAWR COLLEGE
Bryn Mawr, PA

Tuition & fees: $50,500	Average undergraduate aid package: $45,900

ABOUT THE INSTITUTION Independent, undergraduate: women only; graduate: coed. *Awards:* certificates, bachelor's, master's, and doctoral degrees. 37 undergraduate majors. *Total enrollment:* 1,708. Undergraduates: 1,381. Freshmen: 407. Institutional methodology is used as a basis for awarding need-based institutional aid.
UNDERGRADUATE EXPENSES for 2017–2018 *Application fee:* $50. *Comprehensive fee:* $66,410 includes full-time tuition ($49,310), mandatory fees ($1190), and room and board ($15,910). *College room only:* $9080. *Part-time tuition:* $6165 per course.
FRESHMAN FINANCIAL AID (Fall 2016, est.) 288 applied for aid; of those 89% were deemed to have need. 100% of freshmen with need received aid; of those 100% had need fully met. *Average percent of need met:* 100% (excluding resources awarded to replace EFC). *Average financial aid package:* $46,357 (excluding resources awarded to replace EFC). 12% of all full-time freshmen had no need and received non-need-based gift aid.
UNDERGRADUATE FINANCIAL AID (Fall 2016, est.) 803 applied for aid; of those 91% were deemed to have need. 98% of undergraduates with need received aid; of those 100% had need fully met. *Average percent of need met:* 100% (excluding resources awarded to replace EFC). *Average financial aid package:* $45,900 (excluding resources awarded to replace EFC). 17% of all full-time undergraduates had no need and received non-need-based gift aid.
GIFT AID (NEED-BASED) *Total amount:* $29,150,891 (4% federal, 1% state, 94% institutional, 1% external sources). *Receiving aid:* Freshmen: 63% (257); all full-time undergraduates: 53% (721). *Average award:* Freshmen: $41,321; Undergraduates: $40,315. *Scholarships, grants, and awards:* Federal Pell, FSEOG, state, college/university gift aid from institutional funds.
GIFT AID (NON-NEED-BASED) *Total amount:* $4,515,279 (99% institutional, 1% external sources). *Receiving aid:* Freshmen: 4% (15). Undergraduates: 3% (36). *Average award:* Freshmen: $19,833. Undergraduates: $14,533. *Scholarships, grants, and awards by category: Academic interests/achievement:* general academic interests/achievements. *Special achievements/activities:* leadership. *ROTC:* Air Force cooperative.
LOANS *Student loans:* $4,809,682 (51% need-based, 49% non-need-based). 52% of past graduating class borrowed through all loan programs. *Average indebtedness per student:* $23,081. *Average need-based loan:* Freshmen: $3675. Undergraduates: $4437. *Parent loans:* $1,595,719 (100% non-need-based). *Programs:* Federal Direct (Subsidized and Unsubsidized Stafford, PLUS), Perkins, college/university.
WORK-STUDY *Federal work-study:* Total amount: $865,709; jobs available. *State or other work-study/employment:* Total amount: $470,325 (100% need-based). Part-time jobs available.
APPLYING FOR FINANCIAL AID *Required financial aid forms:* FAFSA, CSS Financial Aid PROFILE, noncustodial (divorced/separated) parent's statement,

parent and student tax returns or non-filer statements. *Financial aid deadline:* 1/15. *Notification date:* Continuous. Students must reply by 5/1.

CONTACT Ethel M. Desmarais, Director of Student Financial Services, Bryn Mawr College, 101 North Merion Avenue, Bryn Mawr, PA 19010-2899, 610-526-7922 or toll-free 800-BMC-1885. *Fax:* 610-526-5249. *E-mail:* edesmara@brynmawr.edu. *Website:* http://www.brynmawr.edu/.

BUCKNELL UNIVERSITY
Lewisburg, PA

Tuition & fees: $51,960	Average undergraduate aid package: $32,500

ABOUT THE INSTITUTION Independent, coed. *Awards:* bachelor's and master's degrees. 68 undergraduate majors. *Total enrollment:* 3,626. Undergraduates: 3,571. Freshmen: 950. Both federal and institutional methodology are used as a basis for awarding need-based institutional aid.

UNDERGRADUATE EXPENSES for 2016–2017 *Application fee:* $40. *Comprehensive fee:* $64,616 includes full-time tuition ($51,676), mandatory fees ($284), and room and board ($12,656). *College room only:* $7718. Room and board charges vary according to board plan and housing facility. *Part-time tuition:* $5672 per course. *Payment plan:* Tuition prepayment.

FRESHMAN FINANCIAL AID (Fall 2016, est.) 496 applied for aid; of those 68% were deemed to have need. 100% of freshmen with need received aid; of those 100% had need fully met. *Average percent of need met:* 91% (excluding resources awarded to replace EFC). *Average financial aid package:* $35,500 (excluding resources awarded to replace EFC). 11% of all full-time freshmen had no need and received non-need-based gift aid.

UNDERGRADUATE FINANCIAL AID (Fall 2016, est.) 1,490 applied for aid; of those 89% were deemed to have need. 100% of undergraduates with need received aid; of those 92% had need fully met. *Average percent of need met:* 91% (excluding resources awarded to replace EFC). *Average financial aid package:* $32,500 (excluding resources awarded to replace EFC). 12% of all full-time undergraduates had no need and received non-need-based gift aid.

GIFT AID (NEED-BASED) *Total amount:* $54,477,074 (4% federal, 1% state, 91% institutional, 4% external sources). *Receiving aid:* Freshmen: 32% (302); all full-time undergraduates: 35% (1,262). *Average award:* Freshmen: $29,200; Undergraduates: $28,900. *Scholarships, grants, and awards:* Federal Pell, FSEOG, state, private, college/university gift aid from institutional funds.

GIFT AID (NON-NEED-BASED) *Total amount:* $4,900,000 (100% institutional). *Receiving aid:* Freshmen: 10% (91). Undergraduates: 8% (302). *Average award:* Freshmen: $13,676. Undergraduates: $11,817. *Scholarships, grants, and awards by category: Academic interests/achievement:* 312 awards ($3,884,712 total): business, engineering/technologies, general academic interests/achievements, mathematics, physical sciences. *Creative arts/performance:* 117 awards ($747,000 total): art/fine arts, creative writing, dance, music, performing arts, theater/drama. *Special achievements/activities:* 115 awards ($5,917,709 total): general special achievements/activities, leadership. *Tuition waivers:* Full or partial for employees or children of employees. *ROTC:* Army.

LOANS *Student loans:* $12,213,092 (100% need-based). 53% of past graduating class borrowed through all loan programs. *Average indebtedness per student:* $22,600. *Average need-based loan:* Freshmen: $3500. Undergraduates: $5500. *Parent loans:* $5,755,853 (100% non-need-based). *Programs:* Federal Direct (Subsidized and Unsubsidized Stafford, PLUS), Perkins.

WORK-STUDY *Federal work-study:* Total amount: $365,249; 600 jobs averaging $1500. *State or other work-study/employment:* Total amount: $30,000 (100% need-based). 50 part-time jobs averaging $1500.

ATHLETIC AWARDS Total amount: $11,362,808 (32% need-based, 68% non-need-based).

APPLYING FOR FINANCIAL AID *Required financial aid forms:* FAFSA, CSS Financial Aid PROFILE, institution's own non-custodial form. *Financial aid deadline:* 1/15. *Notification date:* 4/1. Students must reply by 5/1.

CONTACT Andrea Leithner Stauffer, Director of Financial Aid, Bucknell University, 1 Dent Drive, Lewisburg, PA 17837, 570-577-1331. *Fax:* 570-577-1481. *E-mail:* finaid@bucknell.edu. *Website:* http://www.bucknell.edu/.

BUENA VISTA UNIVERSITY
Storm Lake, IA

Tuition & fees: $32,854	Average undergraduate aid package: $28,121

ABOUT THE INSTITUTION Independent Presbyterian Church (U.S.A.), coed. *Awards:* bachelor's and master's degrees. 57 undergraduate majors. *Total enrollment:* 829. Undergraduates: 795. Freshmen: 183. Federal methodology is used as a basis for awarding need-based institutional aid.

UNDERGRADUATE EXPENSES for 2017–2018 *Comprehensive fee:* $42,344 includes full-time tuition ($32,854) and room and board ($9490). *College room only:* $4774. Full-time tuition and fees vary according to location. Room and board charges vary according to board plan and housing facility. *Part-time tuition:* $1105 per credit hour. Part-time tuition and fees vary according to location.

FRESHMAN FINANCIAL AID (Fall 2016, est.) 171 applied for aid; of those 89% were deemed to have need. 100% of freshmen with need received aid; of those 22% had need fully met. *Average percent of need met:* 86% (excluding resources awarded to replace EFC). *Average financial aid package:* $29,833 (excluding resources awarded to replace EFC). 16% of all full-time freshmen had no need and received non-need-based gift aid.

UNDERGRADUATE FINANCIAL AID (Fall 2016, est.) 690 applied for aid; of those 91% were deemed to have need. 100% of undergraduates with need received aid; of those 25% had need fully met. *Average percent of need met:* 84% (excluding resources awarded to replace EFC). *Average financial aid package:* $28,121 (excluding resources awarded to replace EFC). 19% of all full-time undergraduates had no need and received non-need-based gift aid.

GIFT AID (NEED-BASED) *Total amount:* $14,208,999 (11% federal, 15% state, 72% institutional, 2% external sources). *Receiving aid:* Freshmen: 84% (153); all full-time undergraduates: 80% (621). *Average award:* Freshmen: $25,253; Undergraduates: $22,862. *Scholarships, grants, and awards:* Federal Pell, FSEOG, state, private, college/university gift aid from institutional funds.

GIFT AID (NON-NEED-BASED) *Total amount:* $3,822,596 (7% federal, 1% state, 89% institutional, 3% external sources). *Receiving aid:* Freshmen: 13% (23). Undergraduates: 13% (103). *Average award:* Freshmen: $18,668. Undergraduates: $18,724. *Scholarships, grants, and awards by category: Academic interests/achievement:* biological sciences, business, computer science, education, general academic interests/achievements, humanities, international studies, mathematics. *Creative arts/performance:* art/fine arts, music, theater/drama. *Special achievements/activities:* general special achievements/activities, leadership. *Special characteristics:* children of faculty/staff, ethnic background, international students, out-of-state students, religious affiliation, siblings of current students. *Tuition waivers:* Full or partial for employees or children of employees. *ROTC:* Army.

LOANS *Student loans:* $5,814,956 (46% need-based, 54% non-need-based). 86% of past graduating class borrowed through all loan programs. *Average need-based loan:* Freshmen: $4435. Undergraduates: $5316. *Parent loans:* $1,209,406 (100% non-need-based). *Programs:* Federal Direct (Subsidized and Unsubsidized Stafford, PLUS), Perkins, college/university.

WORK-STUDY *Federal work-study:* Total amount: $386,050; jobs available. *State or other work-study/employment:* Total amount: $426,746 (75% need-based, 25% non-need-based). Part-time jobs available.

APPLYING FOR FINANCIAL AID *Required financial aid form:* FAFSA. *Financial aid deadline (priority):* 6/1. *Notification date:* Continuous beginning 2/1.

CONTACT Mrs. Leanne Valentine, Director of Financial Assistance, Buena Vista University, 610 West Fourth Street, Storm Lake, IA 50588, 712-749-2164 or toll-free 800-383-9600. *Fax:* 712-749-1451. *E-mail:* valentinel@bvu.edu. *Website:* http://www.bvu.edu/.

BUFFALO STATE COLLEGE, STATE UNIVERSITY OF NEW YORK
Buffalo, NY

ABOUT THE INSTITUTION State-supported, coed. *Awards:* certificates, bachelor's, and master's degrees. 79 undergraduate majors. *Total enrollment:* 9,475. Undergraduates: 8,482. Freshmen: 1,628.

GIFT AID (NEED-BASED) *Scholarships, grants, and awards:* Federal Pell, FSEOG, state, private.
GIFT AID (NON-NEED-BASED) *Scholarships, grants, and awards by category: Academic interests/achievement:* biological sciences, business, communication, computer science, education, engineering/technologies, foreign languages, general academic interests/achievements, health fields, home economics, mathematics, physical sciences, social sciences. *Creative arts/performance:* applied art and design, art/fine arts, general creative arts/performance, music, performing arts, theater/drama. *Special achievements/activities:* general special achievements/activities. *Special characteristics:* general special characteristics, international students, veterans, veterans' children.
LOANS *Programs:* Federal Direct (Subsidized and Unsubsidized Stafford, PLUS), Perkins.
WORK-STUDY *Federal work-study:* 251 jobs averaging $3155. *State or other work-study/employment:* Part-time jobs available.
APPLYING FOR FINANCIAL AID *Required financial aid form:* FAFSA.
CONTACT Connie F. Cooke, Director of Financial Aid, Buffalo State College, State University of New York, 1300 Elmwood Avenue, Buffalo, NY 14222-1095, 716-878-4902. *Fax:* 716-878-4903. *E-mail:* finaid@buffalostate.edu.
Website: http://www.buffalostate.edu/.

BUTLER UNIVERSITY
Indianapolis, IN

Tuition & fees: $39,905	Average undergraduate aid package: $24,536

ABOUT THE INSTITUTION Independent, coed. *Awards:* certificates, bachelor's, master's, and doctoral degrees. 67 undergraduate majors. *Total enrollment:* 5,095. Undergraduates: 4,290. Freshmen: 1,256. Federal methodology is used as a basis for awarding need-based institutional aid.
UNDERGRADUATE EXPENSES for 2017–2018 *Comprehensive fee:* $52,935 includes full-time tuition ($38,900), mandatory fees ($1005), and room and board ($13,030). *College room only:* $6740. Full-time tuition and fees vary according to course level, course load, degree level, and program. Room and board charges vary according to board plan and housing facility. *Part-time tuition:* $1558 per credit hour. Part-time tuition and fees vary according to course level, course load, degree level, and program.
FRESHMAN FINANCIAL AID (Fall 2016, est.) 1,229 applied for aid; of those 63% were deemed to have need. 100% of freshmen with need received aid; of those 13% had need fully met. *Average percent of need met:* 63% (excluding resources awarded to replace EFC). *Average financial aid package:* $23,481 (excluding resources awarded to replace EFC). 36% of all full-time freshmen had no need and received non-need-based gift aid.
UNDERGRADUATE FINANCIAL AID (Fall 2016, est.) 4,172 applied for aid; of those 64% were deemed to have need. 100% of undergraduates with need received aid; of those 12% had need fully met. *Average percent of need met:* 67% (excluding resources awarded to replace EFC). *Average financial aid package:* $24,536 (excluding resources awarded to replace EFC). 33% of all full-time undergraduates had no need and received non-need-based gift aid.
GIFT AID (NEED-BASED) *Total amount:* $50,877,195 (6% federal, 6% state, 80% institutional, 8% external sources). *Receiving aid:* Freshmen: 61% (760); all full-time undergraduates: 59% (2,635). *Average award:* Freshmen: $19,085; Undergraduates: $20,022. *Scholarships, grants, and awards:* Federal Pell, FSEOG, state, private, college/university gift aid from institutional funds.
GIFT AID (NON-NEED-BASED) *Total amount:* $22,209,277 (91% institutional, 9% external sources). *Receiving aid:* Freshmen: 11% (132). Undergraduates: 8% (351). *Average award:* Freshmen: $14,998. Undergraduates: $13,570. *Scholarships, grants, and awards by category: Academic interests/achievement:* biological sciences, business, communication, computer science, education, engineering/technologies, English, foreign languages, general academic interests/achievements, home economics, humanities, international studies, mathematics, physical sciences, premedicine, religion/biblical studies, social sciences. *Creative arts/performance:* applied art and design, art/fine arts, cinema/film/broadcasting, dance, journalism/publications, music, performing arts, theater/drama. *Special characteristics:* veterans, veterans' children. *Tuition waivers:* Full or partial for employees or children of employees. *ROTC:* Army cooperative, Air Force cooperative.

LOANS *Student loans:* $30,796,755 (70% need-based, 30% non-need-based). 63% of past graduating class borrowed through all loan programs. *Average indebtedness per student:* $35,730. *Average need-based loan:* Freshmen: $4030. Undergraduates: $5124. *Parent loans:* $10,637,401 (44% need-based, 56% non-need-based). *Programs:* Federal Direct (Subsidized and Unsubsidized Stafford, PLUS), Perkins.
WORK-STUDY *Federal work-study:* Total amount: $394,459; 153 jobs averaging $925.
ATHLETIC AWARDS Total amount: $4,941,982 (40% need-based, 60% non-need-based)
APPLYING FOR FINANCIAL AID *Required financial aid form:* FAFSA. *Financial aid deadline (priority):* 12/1. *Notification date:* 1/20. Students must reply within 3 weeks of notification.
CONTACT Mrs. Leslie Middleton, Associate Director of Financial Aid, Butler University, 4600 Sunset Avenue, Indianapolis, IN 46208-3485, 317-940-8200 or toll-free 888-940-8100. *Fax:* 317-940-8250. *E-mail:* lmmiddle@butler.edu.
Website: http://www.butler.edu/.

CABARRUS COLLEGE OF HEALTH SCIENCES
Concord, NC

Tuition & fees: $12,268	Average undergraduate aid package: N/A

ABOUT THE INSTITUTION Independent, coed, primarily women. *Awards:* certificates, diplomas, associate, bachelor's, and master's degrees. 8 undergraduate majors. *Total enrollment:* 470. Undergraduates: 443. Freshmen: 23. Federal methodology is used as a basis for awarding need-based institutional aid.
UNDERGRADUATE EXPENSES for 2016–2017 *Application fee:* $50. *Tuition:* full-time $11,948; part-time $384 per credit hour. *Required fees:* full-time $320; $125 per term. Full-time tuition and fees vary according to course load. Part-time tuition and fees vary according to course load.
FRESHMAN FINANCIAL AID (Fall 2015) 17 applied for aid; of those 100% were deemed to have need. 100% of freshmen with need received aid.
GIFT AID (NEED-BASED) *Total amount:* $1,302,535 (40% federal, 44% state, 16% institutional). *Receiving aid:* Freshmen: 89% (17). *Scholarships, grants, and awards:* Federal Pell, FSEOG, state, college/university gift aid from institutional funds.
GIFT AID (NON-NEED-BASED) *Total amount:* $52,547 (94% institutional, 6% external sources). *Scholarships, grants, and awards by category: Special characteristics:* first-generation college students.
LOANS *Student loans:* $3,599,992 (36% need-based, 64% non-need-based). *Parent loans:* $60,592 (100% non-need-based). *Programs:* Federal Direct (Subsidized and Unsubsidized Stafford, PLUS), state.
WORK-STUDY *Federal work-study:* jobs available. *State or other work-study/employment:* Total amount: $177,750 (100% non-need-based). Part-time jobs available.
APPLYING FOR FINANCIAL AID *Required financial aid forms:* FAFSA, state aid form. *Financial aid deadline (priority):* 4/15. *Notification date:* Continuous beginning 6/1. Students must reply within 2 weeks of notification.
CONTACT Valerie Richard, Director of Financial Aid, Cabarrus College of Health Sciences, 401 Medical Park Drive, Concord, NC 28025, 704-403-3507. *Fax:* 704-403-2077. *E-mail:* valerie.richard@carolinashealthcare.org.
Website: http://www.cabarruscollege.edu/.

CABRINI UNIVERSITY
Radnor, PA

Tuition & fees: $31,350	Average undergraduate aid package: $16,988

ABOUT THE INSTITUTION Independent Roman Catholic, coed. *Awards:* bachelor's, master's, and doctoral degrees. 39 undergraduate majors. *Total enrollment:* 2,436. Undergraduates: 1,650. Freshmen: 486. Federal methodology is used as a basis for awarding need-based institutional aid.

UNDERGRADUATE EXPENSES for 2017–2018 *Application fee:* $20. *Comprehensive fee:* $43,690 includes full-time tuition ($30,400), mandatory fees ($950), and room and board ($12,340). Room and board charges vary according to board plan and housing facility. *Part-time tuition:* $550 per credit hour. *Part-time fees:* $45 per term. Part-time tuition and fees vary according to course load.
FRESHMAN FINANCIAL AID (Fall 2015) 383 applied for aid; of those 87% were deemed to have need. 100% of freshmen with need received aid; of those 21% had need fully met. *Average financial aid package:* $17,185 (excluding resources awarded to replace EFC). 15% of all full-time freshmen had no need and received non-need-based gift aid.
UNDERGRADUATE FINANCIAL AID (Fall 2015) 1,197 applied for aid; of those 84% were deemed to have need. 100% of undergraduates with need received aid; of those 26% had need fully met. *Average financial aid package:* $16,988 (excluding resources awarded to replace EFC). 17% of all full-time undergraduates had no need and received non-need-based gift aid.
GIFT AID (NEED-BASED) *Total amount:* $20,121,572 (13% federal, 9% state, 76% institutional, 2% external sources). *Receiving aid:* Freshmen: 76% (302); all full-time undergraduates: 77% (1,006). *Average award:* Freshmen: $7932; Undergraduates: $7627. *Scholarships, grants, and awards:* Federal Pell, FSEOG, state, private, college/university gift aid from institutional funds.
GIFT AID (NON-NEED-BASED) *Total amount:* $2,271,545 (99% institutional, 1% external sources). *Receiving aid:* Freshmen: 84% (335). Undergraduates: 77% (1,006). *Average award:* Freshmen: $9892. Undergraduates: $10,210. *Scholarships, grants, and awards by category:* Academic interests/achievement: 1,248 awards ($13,832,075 total): general academic interests/achievements. *Special characteristics:* 719 awards ($1,083,050 total): children and siblings of alumni, out-of-state students, religious affiliation, siblings of current students. *Tuition waivers:* Full or partial for children of alumni, employees or children of employees, senior citizens. *ROTC:* Army cooperative, Naval cooperative, Air Force cooperative.
LOANS *Student loans:* $9,538,033 (95% need-based, 5% non-need-based). 94% of past graduating class borrowed through all loan programs. *Average indebtedness per student:* $43,437. *Average need-based loan:* Freshmen: $2973. Undergraduates: $3257. *Parent loans:* $3,835,537 (92% need-based, 8% non-need-based). *Programs:* Federal Direct (Subsidized and Unsubsidized Stafford, PLUS), Perkins.
WORK-STUDY *Federal work-study:* 226 jobs averaging $1141.
APPLYING FOR FINANCIAL AID *Required financial aid form:* FAFSA. *Financial aid deadline (priority):* 2/15. *Notification date:* Continuous beginning 3/1. Students must reply by 5/1.
CONTACT Ms. Elizabeth Gingerich, Director of Financial Aid, Cabrini University, 610 King of Prussia Road, Grace Hall, First Floor, Radnor, PA 19087-3698, 610-902-8424 or toll-free 800-848-1003. *Fax:* 610-902-8426. *E-mail:* egs34@cabrini.edu. *Website:* http://www.cabrini.edu/.

CAIRN UNIVERSITY
Langhorne, PA

Tuition & fees: $26,493	Average undergraduate aid package: $20,983

ABOUT THE INSTITUTION Independent nondenominational, coed. *Awards:* certificates, bachelor's, and master's degrees. 25 undergraduate majors. *Total enrollment:* 1,042. Undergraduates: 744. Freshmen: 147. Federal methodology is used as a basis for awarding need-based institutional aid.
UNDERGRADUATE EXPENSES for 2017–2018 *Application fee:* $25. *Comprehensive fee:* $36,296 includes full-time tuition ($26,193), mandatory fees ($300), and room and board ($9803). *College room only:* $5132. Full-time tuition and fees vary according to course load. Room and board charges vary according to board plan and location. *Part-time tuition:* $777 per credit. Part-time tuition and fees vary according to course load.
FRESHMAN FINANCIAL AID (Fall 2016, est.) 133 applied for aid; of those 92% were deemed to have need. 100% of freshmen with need received aid; of those 16% had need fully met. *Average percent of need met:* 80% (excluding resources awarded to replace EFC). *Average financial aid package:* $23,175 (excluding resources awarded to replace EFC). 15% of all full-time freshmen had no need and received non-need-based gift aid.
UNDERGRADUATE FINANCIAL AID (Fall 2016, est.) 623 applied for aid; of those 91% were deemed to have need. 100% of undergraduates with need received aid; of those 13% had need fully met. *Average percent of need met:* 75% (excluding resources awarded to replace EFC). *Average financial aid package:*

$20,983 (excluding resources awarded to replace EFC). 18% of all full-time undergraduates had no need and received non-need-based gift aid.
GIFT AID (NEED-BASED) *Total amount:* $8,799,360 (16% federal, 9% state, 74% institutional, 1% external sources). *Receiving aid:* Freshmen: 85% (123); all full-time undergraduates: 79% (559). *Average award:* Freshmen: $18,778; Undergraduates: $16,025. *Scholarships, grants, and awards:* Federal Pell, FSEOG, state, private, college/university gift aid from institutional funds.
GIFT AID (NON-NEED-BASED) *Total amount:* $1,655,737 (98% institutional, 2% external sources). *Receiving aid:* Freshmen: 9% (13). Undergraduates: 7% (52). *Average award:* Freshmen: $13,011. Undergraduates: $11,286. *Scholarships, grants, and awards by category:* Academic interests/achievement: general academic interests/achievements. *Creative arts/performance:* music. *Special achievements/activities:* general special achievements/activities. *Special characteristics:* children of faculty/staff, relatives of clergy. *Tuition waivers:* Full or partial for employees or children of employees. *ROTC:* Air Force cooperative.
LOANS *Student loans:* $5,391,971 (77% need-based, 23% non-need-based). 83% of past graduating class borrowed through all loan programs. *Average indebtedness per student:* $31,166. *Average need-based loan:* Freshmen: $4092. Undergraduates: $4991. *Parent loans:* $869,735 (54% need-based, 46% non-need-based). *Programs:* Federal Direct (Subsidized and Unsubsidized Stafford, PLUS).
WORK-STUDY *Federal work-study:* Total amount: $276,630; jobs available.
APPLYING FOR FINANCIAL AID *Required financial aid form:* FAFSA. *Financial aid deadline (priority):* 3/1. *Notification date:* Continuous beginning 2/1. Students must reply within 2 weeks of notification.
CONTACT Mr. Stephen Cassel, Director of Financial Aid, Cairn University, 200 Manor Avenue, Langhorne, PA 19047-2990, 215-702-4243 or toll-free 800-366-0049. *Fax:* 215-702-4248. *E-mail:* scassel@cairn.edu. *Website:* http://cairn.edu/.

CALDWELL UNIVERSITY
Caldwell, NJ

Tuition & fees: $32,800	Average undergraduate aid package: $26,220

ABOUT THE INSTITUTION Independent Roman Catholic, coed. *Awards:* certificates, bachelor's, master's, and doctoral degrees. 33 undergraduate majors. *Total enrollment:* 2,214. Undergraduates: 1,633. Freshmen: 400. Federal methodology is used as a basis for awarding need-based institutional aid.
UNDERGRADUATE EXPENSES for 2016–2017 *Application fee:* $50. *Comprehensive fee:* $44,200 includes full-time tuition ($31,150), mandatory fees ($1650), and room and board ($11,400). Full-time tuition and fees vary according to course load, location, and program. Room and board charges vary according to housing facility. *Part-time tuition:* $865 per credit. *Part-time fees:* $200 per term. Part-time tuition and fees vary according to course load, location, and program.
FRESHMAN FINANCIAL AID (Fall 2016, est.) 330 applied for aid; of those 92% were deemed to have need. 100% of freshmen with need received aid; of those 12% had need fully met. *Average percent of need met:* 79% (excluding resources awarded to replace EFC). *Average financial aid package:* $29,017 (excluding resources awarded to replace EFC). 23% of all full-time freshmen had no need and received non-need-based gift aid.
UNDERGRADUATE FINANCIAL AID (Fall 2016, est.) 1,163 applied for aid; of those 93% were deemed to have need. 100% of undergraduates with need received aid; of those 11% had need fully met. *Average percent of need met:* 74% (excluding resources awarded to replace EFC). *Average financial aid package:* $26,220 (excluding resources awarded to replace EFC). 21% of all full-time undergraduates had no need and received non-need-based gift aid.
GIFT AID (NEED-BASED) *Total amount:* $23,448,785 (13% federal, 23% state, 61% institutional, 3% external sources). *Receiving aid:* Freshmen: 75% (303); all full-time undergraduates: 76% (1,070). *Average award:* Freshmen: $25,733; Undergraduates: $22,707. *Scholarships, grants, and awards:* Federal Pell, FSEOG, state, private, college/university gift aid from institutional funds.
GIFT AID (NON-NEED-BASED) *Total amount:* $6,246,726 (95% institutional, 5% external sources). *Receiving aid:* Freshmen: 8% (31). Undergraduates: 7% (99). *Average award:* Freshmen: $20,781. Undergraduates: $18,770. *Scholarships, grants, and awards by category:* Academic interests/achievement: 683 awards ($11,393,722 total): general academic interests/achievements, home economics. *Creative arts/performance:* 52 awards ($62,950 total): art/fine arts, music. *Special*

achievements/activities: 176 awards ($364,828 total): community service, general special achievements/activities, leadership, memberships, religious involvement. *Special characteristics:* 189 awards ($1,020,161 total): adult students, children and siblings of alumni, children of current students, children of educators, children of faculty/staff, general special characteristics, local/state students, parents of current students, previous college experience, public servants, relatives of clergy, religious affiliation, siblings of current students, spouses of current students, twins, veterans, veterans' children. *Tuition waivers:* Full or partial for children of alumni, employees or children of employees, adult students, senior citizens. *ROTC:* Army cooperative.

LOANS *Student loans:* $10,169,334 (75% need-based, 25% non-need-based). 81% of past graduating class borrowed through all loan programs. *Average indebtedness per student:* $25,114. *Average need-based loan:* Freshmen: $3269. Undergraduates: $4080. *Parent loans:* $8,363,207 (47% need-based, 53% non-need-based). *Programs:* Federal Direct (Subsidized and Unsubsidized Stafford, PLUS), state, private loans.

WORK-STUDY *Federal work-study:* Total amount: $142,577; 120 jobs averaging $1600. *State or other work-study/employment:* 130 part-time jobs averaging $2500.

ATHLETIC AWARDS Total amount: $1,710,738 (53% need-based, 47% non-need-based).

APPLYING FOR FINANCIAL AID *Required financial aid forms:* FAFSA, state aid form. *Financial aid deadline (priority):* 3/15. *Notification date:* Continuous beginning 11/15.

CONTACT Ms. Eileen Felske, Director of Financial Aid, Caldwell University, 120 Bloomfield Avenue, Caldwell, NJ 07006, 973-618-3419. *Fax:* 973-618-3650. *E-mail:* efelske@caldwell.edu.
Website: http://www.caldwell.edu/.

CALIFORNIA BAPTIST UNIVERSITY
Riverside, CA

Tuition & fees: $32,566	Average undergraduate aid package: $17,879

ABOUT THE INSTITUTION Independent Southern Baptist, coed. *Awards:* associate, bachelor's, master's, and doctoral degrees. 74 undergraduate majors. *Total enrollment:* 9,157. Undergraduates: 6,937. Freshmen: 1,146. Federal methodology is used as a basis for awarding need-based institutional aid.

UNDERGRADUATE EXPENSES for 2017–2018 *Application fee:* $45. *One-time required fee:* $310. *Comprehensive fee:* $44,106 includes full-time tuition ($30,446), mandatory fees ($2120), and room and board ($11,540). *College room only:* $5630. Full-time tuition and fees vary according to course load, location, and program. Room and board charges vary according to board plan and housing facility. *Part-time tuition:* $1171 per unit. *Part-time fees:* $175 per term. Part-time tuition and fees vary according to course load, location, and program.

FRESHMAN FINANCIAL AID (Fall 2016, est.) 1,034 applied for aid; of those 89% were deemed to have need. 99% of freshmen with need received aid; of those 22% had need fully met. *Average percent of need met:* 63% (excluding resources awarded to replace EFC). *Average financial aid package:* $20,833 (excluding resources awarded to replace EFC). 8% of all full-time freshmen had no need and received non-need-based gift aid.

UNDERGRADUATE FINANCIAL AID (Fall 2016, est.) 5,293 applied for aid; of those 96% were deemed to have need. 94% of undergraduates with need received aid; of those 8% had need fully met. *Average percent of need met:* 56% (excluding resources awarded to replace EFC). *Average financial aid package:* $17,879 (excluding resources awarded to replace EFC). 5% of all full-time undergraduates had no need and received non-need-based gift aid.

GIFT AID (NEED-BASED) *Total amount:* $66,822,304 (20% federal, 23% state, 56% institutional, 1% external sources). *Receiving aid:* Freshmen: 77% (852); all full-time undergraduates: 65% (3,809). *Average award:* Freshmen: $18,487; Undergraduates: $14,409. *Scholarships, grants, and awards:* Federal Pell, FSEOG, state, private, college/university gift aid from institutional funds, Federal Nursing.

GIFT AID (NON-NEED-BASED) *Total amount:* $2,791,534 (97% institutional, 3% external sources). *Receiving aid:* Freshmen: 69% (773). Undergraduates: 50% (2,946). *Average award:* Freshmen: $11,827. Undergraduates: $9129. *Scholarships, grants, and awards by category:* Academic interests/achievement: 861 awards ($6,367,328 total): architecture, engineering/technologies, general academic interests/achievements, home economics, religion/biblical studies. *Creative arts/perfor-*

mance: 941 awards ($2,360,377 total): applied art and design, art/fine arts, cinema/film/broadcasting, debating, journalism/publications, music, theater/drama. *Special achievements/activities:* 50 awards ($182,750 total): cheerleading/drum major. *Special characteristics:* 717 awards ($6,924,408 total): adult students, children of faculty/staff, international students, relatives of clergy, religious affiliation, siblings of current students, veterans, veterans' children. *Tuition waivers:* Full or partial for employees or children of employees. *ROTC:* Army, Air Force cooperative.

LOANS *Student loans:* $50,593,917 (94% need-based, 6% non-need-based). 77% of past graduating class borrowed through all loan programs. *Average indebtedness per student:* $20,693. *Average need-based loan:* Freshmen: $3636. Undergraduates: $4686. *Parent loans:* $19,256,740 (90% need-based, 10% non-need-based). *Programs:* Federal Direct (Subsidized and Unsubsidized Stafford, PLUS), Perkins, alternative loans.

WORK-STUDY *Federal work-study:* Total amount: $325,000; 255 jobs averaging $1400.

ATHLETIC AWARDS Total amount: $3,977,323 (89% need-based, 11% non-need-based).

APPLYING FOR FINANCIAL AID *Required financial aid forms:* FAFSA, state aid form. *Financial aid deadline (priority):* 3/2. *Notification date:* Continuous beginning 3/2. Students must reply by 6/1.

CONTACT Mr. Joshua Morey, Director of Financial Aid, California Baptist University, 8432 Magnolia Avenue, Riverside, CA 92504-3297, 951-343-4235 or toll-free 877-228-8866. *E-mail:* finaid@calbaptist.edu.
Website: http://www.calbaptist.edu/.

CALIFORNIA CHRISTIAN COLLEGE
Fresno, CA

Tuition & fees: $8990	Average undergraduate aid package: $12,138

ABOUT THE INSTITUTION Independent Free Will Baptist, coed. *Awards:* associate and bachelor's degrees. 2 undergraduate majors. *Total enrollment:* 18. Undergraduates: 18. Freshmen: 2. Federal methodology is used as a basis for awarding need-based institutional aid.

UNDERGRADUATE EXPENSES for 2016–2017 *Application fee:* $40. *Comprehensive fee:* $13,940 includes full-time tuition ($8400), mandatory fees ($590), and room and board ($4950). *Part-time tuition:* $350 per unit.

FRESHMAN FINANCIAL AID (Fall 2015) 1 applied for aid.

UNDERGRADUATE FINANCIAL AID (Fall 2015) 10 applied for aid; of those 90% were deemed to have need. 100% of undergraduates with need received aid. *Average percent of need met:* 55% (excluding resources awarded to replace EFC). *Average financial aid package:* $12,138 (excluding resources awarded to replace EFC).

GIFT AID (NEED-BASED) *Total amount:* $62,534 (100% federal). *Receiving aid:* All full-time undergraduates: 73% (8). *Average award:* Undergraduates: $5228. *Scholarships, grants, and awards:* Federal Pell, FSEOG, state, private.

LOANS *Student loans:* $76,379 (100% need-based). *Average need-based loan:* Undergraduates: $4277. *Programs:* Federal Direct (Subsidized and Unsubsidized Stafford, PLUS).

WORK-STUDY *Federal work-study:* 3 jobs averaging $1623.

APPLYING FOR FINANCIAL AID *Required financial aid forms:* FAFSA, institution's own form. *Financial aid deadline (priority):* 3/2. *Notification date:* 8/15.

CONTACT Mindy Scroggins, Financial Aid Coordinator, California Christian College, 5364 East Belmont Avenue, Fresno, CA 93727, 559-251-4215 Ext. 1006. *Fax:* 559-385-2329. *E-mail:* financialaid@calchristiancollege.edu.
Website: http://www.calchristiancollege.edu/.

CALIFORNIA COAST UNIVERSITY
Santa Ana, CA

CONTACT Financial Aid Office, California Coast University, 925 North Spurgeon Street, Santa Ana, CA 92701, 714-547-9625 or toll-free 888-CCU-UNIV.
Website: http://www.calcoast.edu/.

CALIFORNIA COLLEGE OF THE ARTS
San Francisco, CA

Tuition & fees: $45,466	Average undergraduate aid package: $30,706

ABOUT THE INSTITUTION Independent, coed. *Awards:* bachelor's and master's degrees. 22 undergraduate majors. *Total enrollment:* 1,983. Undergraduates: 1,528. Freshmen: 256. Federal methodology is used as a basis for awarding need-based institutional aid.

UNDERGRADUATE EXPENSES for 2017–2018 *Tuition:* full-time $44,976. Full-time tuition and fees vary according to degree level. Part-time tuition and fees vary according to degree level. Room and board charges vary according to housing facility.

FRESHMAN FINANCIAL AID (Fall 2016, est.) 131 applied for aid; of those 89% were deemed to have need. 100% of freshmen with need received aid; of those 8% had need fully met. *Average percent of need met:* 66% (excluding resources awarded to replace EFC). *Average financial aid package:* $33,021 (excluding resources awarded to replace EFC). 31% of all full-time freshmen had no need and received non-need-based gift aid.

UNDERGRADUATE FINANCIAL AID (Fall 2016, est.) 774 applied for aid; of those 93% were deemed to have need. 100% of undergraduates with need received aid; of those 4% had need fully met. *Average percent of need met:* 59% (excluding resources awarded to replace EFC). *Average financial aid package:* $30,706 (excluding resources awarded to replace EFC). 24% of all full-time undergraduates had no need and received non-need-based gift aid.

GIFT AID (NEED-BASED) *Total amount:* $20,019,155 (11% federal, 8% state, 75% institutional, 6% external sources). *Receiving aid:* Freshmen: 46% (117); all full-time undergraduates: 50% (718). *Average award:* Freshmen: $29,575; Undergraduates: $25,984. *Scholarships, grants, and awards:* Federal Pell, FSEOG, state, private, college/university gift aid from institutional funds.

GIFT AID (NON-NEED-BASED) *Total amount:* $4,854,729 (88% institutional, 12% external sources). *Receiving aid:* Freshmen: 43% (109). Undergraduates: 35% (505). *Average award:* Freshmen: $12,963. Undergraduates: $11,043. *Scholarships, grants, and awards by category:* Academic interests/achievement: 344 awards ($3,798,875 total): general academic interests/achievements. *Tuition waivers:* Full or partial for employees or children of employees.

LOANS *Student loans:* $2,990,689 (81% need-based, 19% non-need-based). 54% of past graduating class borrowed through all loan programs. *Average indebtedness per student:* $32,434. *Average need-based loan:* Freshmen: $3479. Undergraduates: $4776. *Parent loans:* $5,543,675 (76% need-based, 24% non-need-based). *Programs:* Federal Direct (Subsidized and Unsubsidized Stafford, PLUS), Perkins, private loans.

WORK-STUDY *Federal work-study:* Total amount: $352,065; jobs available. *State or other work-study/employment:* Total amount: $1,107,820 (100% non-need-based). 114 part-time jobs averaging $3000.

APPLYING FOR FINANCIAL AID *Required financial aid form:* FAFSA. *Financial aid deadline (priority):* 2/1. *Notification date:* Continuous beginning 2/15. Students must reply by 5/1 or within 3 weeks of notification.

CONTACT Mr. Dewayne J. Barnes, Director of Financial Aid, California College of the Arts, 1111 Eighth Street, San Francisco, CA 94107, 415-703-9528 or toll-free 800-447-1ART. *Fax:* 415-551-9261. *E-mail:* finaid@cca.edu. *Website:* http://www.cca.edu/.

CALIFORNIA COLLEGE SAN DIEGO
National City, CA

CONTACT Financial Aid Office, California College San Diego, 700 Bay Marina Drive, Suite 100, National City, CA 91950, 619-680-4421 or toll-free 800-622-3188. *Website:* http://www.cc-sd.edu/.

CALIFORNIA COLLEGE SAN DIEGO
San Diego, CA

CONTACT Raul Rivera, Senior Financial Aid Officer, California College San Diego, 6602 Convoy Court, #100, San Diego, CA 92111, 619-680-4430 Ext. 1507 or toll-free 800-622-3188. *Fax:* 619-695-5793. *E-mail:* raul.rivera@cc-sd.edu. *Website:* http://www.cc-sd.edu/.

CALIFORNIA COLLEGE SAN DIEGO
San Marcos, CA

CONTACT Financial Aid Office, California College San Diego, 277 Rancheros Drive, Suite 200, San Marcos, CA 92069, 760- 621-4333 or toll-free 800-622-3188. *Website:* http://www.cc-sd.edu/.

CALIFORNIA INSTITUTE OF INTEGRAL STUDIES
San Francisco, CA

ABOUT THE INSTITUTION Independent, coed. *Awards:* certificates, bachelor's, master's, and doctoral degrees. 1 undergraduate major. *Total enrollment:* 1,495. Undergraduates: 102. Entering class: 55.

GIFT AID (NEED-BASED) *Scholarships, grants, and awards:* Federal Pell, FSEOG, state, private, college/university gift aid from institutional funds, Yellow Ribbon Grant Program.

GIFT AID (NON-NEED-BASED) *Scholarships, grants, and awards by category:* Special characteristics: international students.

LOANS *Programs:* Federal Direct (Subsidized and Unsubsidized Stafford, PLUS), private loans.

WORK-STUDY *Federal work-study:* 6 jobs averaging $3208. *State or other work-study/employment:* Total amount: $16,000 (100% non-need-based). Part-time jobs available.

CONTACT Financial Aid Office, California Institute of Integral Studies, 1453 Mission Street, San Francisco, CA 94103, 415-575-6122. *Fax:* 415-575-1268. *E-mail:* finaid@ciis.edu. *Website:* http://www.ciis.edu/.

CALIFORNIA INSTITUTE OF TECHNOLOGY
Pasadena, CA

Tuition & fees: $47,577	Average undergraduate aid package: $46,095

ABOUT THE INSTITUTION Independent, coed. *Awards:* certificates, bachelor's, master's, and doctoral degrees. 28 undergraduate majors. *Total enrollment:* 2,240. Undergraduates: 979. Freshmen: 235. Both federal and institutional methodology are used as a basis for awarding need-based institutional aid.

UNDERGRADUATE EXPENSES for 2016–2017 *Application fee:* $75. *Comprehensive fee:* $61,677 includes full-time tuition ($45,846), mandatory fees ($1731), and room and board ($14,100). *College room only:* $7914. Room and board charges vary according to housing facility.

FRESHMAN FINANCIAL AID (Fall 2016, est.) 168 applied for aid; of those 73% were deemed to have need. 100% of freshmen with need received aid; of those 100% had need fully met. *Average percent of need met:* 100% (excluding resources awarded to replace EFC). *Average financial aid package:* $46,283 (excluding resources awarded to replace EFC). 1% of all full-time freshmen had no need and received non-need-based gift aid.

UNDERGRADUATE FINANCIAL AID (Fall 2016, est.) 587 applied for aid; of those 85% were deemed to have need. 100% of undergraduates with need received aid; of those 100% had need fully met. *Average percent of need met:* 100% (excluding resources awarded to replace EFC). *Average financial aid package:*

$46,095 (excluding resources awarded to replace EFC). 1% of all full-time undergraduates had no need and received non-need-based gift aid.

GIFT AID (NEED-BASED) *Total amount:* $20,276,483 (4% federal, 1% state, 94% institutional, 1% external sources). *Receiving aid:* Freshmen: 52% (122); all full-time undergraduates: 51% (500). *Average award:* Freshmen: $44,074; Undergraduates: $41,901. *Scholarships, grants, and awards:* Federal Pell, FSEOG, state, private, college/university gift aid from institutional funds.

GIFT AID (NON-NEED-BASED) *Total amount:* $339,001 (3% institutional, 97% external sources). *Average award:* Freshmen: $5000. Undergraduates: $5000. *Tuition waivers:* Full or partial for employees or children of employees. *ROTC:* Army cooperative, Air Force cooperative.

LOANS *Student loans:* $1,522,528 (79% need-based, 21% non-need-based). 33% of past graduating class borrowed through all loan programs. *Average indebtedness per student:* $18,219. *Average need-based loan:* Freshmen: $2702. Undergraduates: $3449. *Parent loans:* $348,621 (5% need-based, 95% non-need-based). *Programs:* Federal Direct (Subsidized and Unsubsidized Stafford, PLUS), college/university.

WORK-STUDY *Federal work-study:* Total amount: $856,385; 267 jobs averaging $3207. *State or other work-study/employment:* Total amount: $113,500 (82% need-based, 18% non-need-based). 44 part-time jobs averaging $2580.

APPLYING FOR FINANCIAL AID *Required financial aid forms:* FAFSA, institution's own form, CSS Financial Aid PROFILE, state aid form, noncustodial (divorced/separated) parent's statement, business/farm supplement. *Financial aid deadline (priority):* 2/1. *Notification date:* Continuous beginning 3/30. Students must reply by 5/1 or within 2 weeks of notification.

CONTACT Don Crewell, Director of Financial Aid, California Institute of Technology, 1200 East California Boulevard, MC 20-90, Pasadena, CA 91125-3405, 626-395-6280. *Fax:* 626-564-8136. *E-mail:* dcrewell@caltech.edu. *Website:* http://www.caltech.edu/.

CALIFORNIA INSTITUTE OF THE ARTS
Valencia, CA

Tuition & fees: $45,030	Average undergraduate aid package: $35,000

ABOUT THE INSTITUTION Independent, coed. *Awards:* certificates, bachelor's, master's, and doctoral degrees. 10 undergraduate majors. *Total enrollment:* 1,448. Undergraduates: 949. Freshmen: 193. Federal methodology is used as a basis for awarding need-based institutional aid.

UNDERGRADUATE EXPENSES for 2016–2017 *Application fee:* $70. *Tuition:* full-time $45,030.

FRESHMAN FINANCIAL AID (Fall 2016, est.) 138 applied for aid; of those 78% were deemed to have need. 100% of freshmen with need received aid; of those 11% had need fully met. *Average percent of need met:* 75% (excluding resources awarded to replace EFC). *Average financial aid package:* $35,000 (excluding resources awarded to replace EFC). 14% of all full-time freshmen had no need and received non-need-based gift aid.

UNDERGRADUATE FINANCIAL AID (Fall 2016, est.) 637 applied for aid; of those 87% were deemed to have need. 100% of undergraduates with need received aid; of those 12% had need fully met. *Average percent of need met:* 75% (excluding resources awarded to replace EFC). *Average financial aid package:* $35,000 (excluding resources awarded to replace EFC). 8% of all full-time undergraduates had no need and received non-need-based gift aid.

GIFT AID (NEED-BASED) *Total amount:* $10,721,064 (13% federal, 10% state, 74% institutional, 3% external sources). *Receiving aid:* Freshmen: 52% (106); all full-time undergraduates: 57% (546). *Average award:* Freshmen: $17,500; Undergraduates: $17,500. *Scholarships, grants, and awards:* Federal Pell, FSEOG, state, private, college/university gift aid from institutional funds.

GIFT AID (NON-NEED-BASED) *Total amount:* $1,936,951 (100% institutional). *Average award:* Freshmen: $6250. Undergraduates: $8800. *Scholarships, grants, and awards by category:* Creative arts/performance: applied art and design, art/fine arts, cinema/film/broadcasting, creative writing, dance, music, performing arts, theater/drama. *Tuition waivers:* Full or partial for employees or children of employees.

LOANS *Student loans:* $6,818,313 (91% need-based, 9% non-need-based). 93% of past graduating class borrowed through all loan programs. *Average indebtedness per student:* $31,293. *Average need-based loan:* Freshmen: $8500. Undergraduates: $10,500. *Parent loans:* $4,279,586 (91% need-based, 9% non-need-based). *Programs:* Federal Direct (Subsidized and Unsubsidized Stafford, PLUS), Perkins, college/university, private loans.

WORK-STUDY *Federal work-study:* Total amount: $612,554; 280 jobs averaging $2188.

APPLYING FOR FINANCIAL AID *Required financial aid form:* FAFSA *Financial aid deadline (priority):* 2/15. *Notification date:* Continuous beginning 4/1. Students must reply by 5/1 or within 3 weeks of notification.

CONTACT Dr. Robin Bailey-Chen, Director of Financial Aid, California Institute of the Arts, 24700 McBean Parkway, Valencia, CA 91355-2340, 661-253-7869 or toll-free 800-545-2787. *Fax:* 661-287-3816. *E-mail:* rbaileychen@calarts.edu. *Website:* http://www.calarts.edu/.

CALIFORNIA INTERCONTINENTAL UNIVERSITY
Irvine, CA

CONTACT Financial Aid Office, California Intercontinental University, 17310 Red Hill Avenue, #200, Irvine, CA 92614, 909-396-6090 or toll-free 866-687-2258. *Website:* http://caluniversity.edu/.

CALIFORNIA LUTHERAN UNIVERSITY
Thousand Oaks, CA

Tuition & fees: $39,780	Average undergraduate aid package: $30,415

ABOUT THE INSTITUTION Independent Lutheran, coed. *Awards:* certificates, bachelor's, master's, and doctoral degrees. 52 undergraduate majors. *Total enrollment:* 4,173. Undergraduates: 2,892. Freshmen: 639. Both federal and institutional methodology are used as a basis for awarding need-based institutional aid.

UNDERGRADUATE EXPENSES for 2016–2017 *Application fee:* $25. *Comprehensive fee:* $52,840 includes full-time tuition ($39,310), mandatory fees ($470), and room and board ($13,060). *College room only:* $7010. Room and board charges vary according to board plan and housing facility. *Part-time tuition:* $1265 per unit.

FRESHMAN FINANCIAL AID (Fall 2016, est.) 626 applied for aid; of those 78% were deemed to have need. 100% of freshmen with need received aid; of those 17% had need fully met. *Average percent of need met:* 76% (excluding resources awarded to replace EFC). *Average financial aid package:* $32,833 (excluding resources awarded to replace EFC). 23% of all full-time freshmen had no need and received non-need-based gift aid.

UNDERGRADUATE FINANCIAL AID (Fall 2016, est.) 2,509 applied for aid; of those 72% were deemed to have need. 100% of undergraduates with need received aid; of those 10% had need fully met. *Average percent of need met:* 72% (excluding resources awarded to replace EFC). *Average financial aid package:* $30,415 (excluding resources awarded to replace EFC). 30% of all full-time undergraduates had no need and received non-need-based gift aid.

GIFT AID (NEED-BASED) *Total amount:* $47,999,858 (7% federal, 12% state, 78% institutional, 3% external sources). *Receiving aid:* Freshmen: 76% (488); all full-time undergraduates: 69% (1,800). *Average award:* Freshmen: $29,971; Undergraduates: $26,191. *Scholarships, grants, and awards:* Federal Pell, FSEOG, state, private, college/university gift aid from institutional funds.

GIFT AID (NON-NEED-BASED) *Total amount:* $12,507,262 (97% institutional, 3% external sources). *Receiving aid:* Freshmen: 11% (69). Undergraduates: 7% (182). *Average award:* Freshmen: $19,445. Undergraduates: $17,885. *Scholarships, grants, and awards by category:* Academic interests/achievement: biological sciences, business, communication, computer science, education, English, foreign languages, general academic interests/achievements, humanities, international studies, mathematics, physical sciences, religion/biblical studies, social sciences. *Creative arts/performance:* art/fine arts, creative writing, journalism/publications, music, performing arts, theater/drama. *Special achievements/activities:* community service, general special achievements/activities, leadership, religious involvement. *Special characteristics:* adult students, children and siblings of alumni, children of faculty/staff, international students, relatives of clergy, religious affiliation, veterans, veterans' children. *ROTC:* Army cooperative, Air Force cooperative.

LOANS *Student loans:* $12,861,454 (91% need-based, 9% non-need-based). 66% of past graduating class borrowed through all loan programs. *Average indebtedness per student:* $32,030. *Average need-based loan:* Freshmen: $3612. Undergraduates: $4739. *Parent loans:* $10,018,170 (92% need-based, 8% non-need-based). *Programs:* Federal Direct (Subsidized and Unsubsidized Stafford, PLUS), Perkins.

WORK-STUDY *Federal work-study:* Total amount: $565,000; 261 jobs averaging $2500. *State or other work-study/employment:* Part-time jobs available.

APPLYING FOR FINANCIAL AID *Required financial aid forms:* FAFSA, Cal Grant forms, GPA verification form (CA residents only). *Financial aid deadline (priority):* 3/1. *Notification date:* Continuous beginning 3/15. Students must reply by 5/1 or within 2 weeks of notification.

CONTACT Jerry McKeen, Director of Financial Aid, California Lutheran University, 60 West Olsen Road, Thousand Oaks, CA 91360-2787, 805-493-3115 or toll-free 877-258-3678. *Fax:* 805-493-3114. *E-mail:* jmckeen@callutheran.edu. *Website:* http://www.callutheran.edu/.

CALIFORNIA MIRAMAR UNIVERSITY
San Diego, CA

CONTACT Financial Aid Office, California Miramar University, 3550 Camino Del Rio North, Suite 208, San Diego, CA 92108, 858-653-3000 or toll-free 877-570-5678. *Website:* http://www.calmu.edu/.

CALIFORNIA NATIONAL UNIVERSITY FOR ADVANCED STUDIES
Torrance, CA

Tuition & fees: N/R	Average undergraduate aid package: N/A

ABOUT THE INSTITUTION Proprietary, coed. 4 undergraduate majors.
LOANS *Programs:* Sallie Mae Smart Option Loans.
APPLYING FOR FINANCIAL AID *Notification date:* Continuous.

CONTACT Office of Financial Aid, California National University for Advanced Studies, 18520 Hawthorne Boulevard, Torrance, CA 90504, 800-782-2422. *Website:* http://www.cnuas.edu/.

CALIFORNIA POLYTECHNIC STATE UNIVERSITY, SAN LUIS OBISPO
San Luis Obispo, CA

Tuition & fees (CA res): $9075	Average undergraduate aid package: $10,141

ABOUT THE INSTITUTION State-supported, coed. *Awards:* certificates, bachelor's, and master's degrees. 64 undergraduate majors. *Total enrollment:* 21,306. Undergraduates: 20,426. Freshmen: 4,341. Federal methodology is used as a basis for awarding need-based institutional aid.

UNDERGRADUATE EXPENSES for 2017–2018 *Application fee:* $55. *Tuition, state resident:* full-time $5472; part-time $3174 per year. *Tuition, nonresident:* full-time $16,632; part-time $7638 per year. *Required fees:* full-time $3603; $3141 per year. Full-time tuition and fees vary according to course load, degree level, and program. Part-time tuition and fees vary according to course load, degree level, and program. *College room and board:* $12,507; *Room only:* $7360. Room and board charges vary according to housing facility.

FRESHMAN FINANCIAL AID (Fall 2015) 3,866 applied for aid; of those 53% were deemed to have need. 93% of freshmen with need received aid; of those 10% had need fully met. *Average percent of need met:* 56% (excluding resources awarded to replace EFC). *Average financial aid package:* $9585 (excluding resources

---

awarded to replace EFC). 14% of all full-time freshmen had no need and received non-need-based gift aid.

UNDERGRADUATE FINANCIAL AID (Fall 2015) 12,054 applied for aid; of those 67% were deemed to have need. 94% of undergraduates with need received aid; of those 8% had need fully met. *Average percent of need met:* 57% (excluding resources awarded to replace EFC). *Average financial aid package:* $10,141 (excluding resources awarded to replace EFC). 13% of all full-time undergraduates had no need and received non-need-based gift aid.

GIFT AID (NEED-BASED) *Total amount:* $54,313,429 (32% federal, 33% state, 27% institutional, 8% external sources). *Receiving aid:* Freshmen: 37% (1,804); all full-time undergraduates: 37% (7,065). *Average award:* Freshmen: $3287; Undergraduates: $3524. *Scholarships, grants, and awards:* Federal Pell, FSEOG, state, private, college/university gift aid from institutional funds, TEACH Grants, California Dream Grants.

GIFT AID (NON-NEED-BASED) *Total amount:* $9,062,492 (3% state, 60% institutional, 37% external sources). *Receiving aid:* Freshmen: 2% (77). Undergraduates: 1% (212). *Average award:* Freshmen: $2303. Undergraduates: $1890. *Scholarships, grants, and awards by category: Academic interests/achievement:* agriculture, architecture, biological sciences, business, communication, computer science, education, engineering/technologies, English, foreign languages, general academic interests/achievements, health fields, home economics, humanities, international studies, library science, mathematics, military science, physical sciences, social sciences. *Creative arts/performance:* applied art and design, art/fine arts, cinema/film/broadcasting, creative writing, dance, debating, general creative arts/performance, journalism/publications, music, performing arts, theater/drama. *Special achievements/activities:* community service, leadership, rodeo. *Special characteristics:* children and siblings of alumni, general special characteristics, local/state students. *Tuition waivers:* Full or partial for employees or children of employees. *ROTC:* Army.

LOANS *Student loans:* $46,795,617 (64% need-based, 36% non-need-based). 40% of past graduating class borrowed through all loan programs. *Average indebtedness per student:* $22,413. *Average need-based loan:* Freshmen: $3291. Undergraduates: $3995. *Parent loans:* $33,537,329 (26% need-based, 74% non-need-based). *Programs:* Federal Direct (Subsidized and Unsubsidized Stafford, PLUS), Perkins, college/university, alternative loans.

WORK-STUDY *Federal work-study:* jobs available.

ATHLETIC AWARDS Total amount: $4,572,710 (32% need-based, 68% non-need-based).

APPLYING FOR FINANCIAL AID *Required financial aid form:* FAFSA. *Financial aid deadline (priority):* 3/2. *Notification date:* Continuous beginning 3/15.

CONTACT Gerrie Hatten, Interim Director of Financial Aid, California Polytechnic State University, San Luis Obispo, Administration Building, Room 212, San Luis Obispo, CA 93407, 805-756-5878. *Fax:* 805-756-7243. *E-mail:* financialaid@calpoly.edu. *Website:* http://www.calpoly.edu/.

CALIFORNIA STATE POLYTECHNIC UNIVERSITY, POMONA
Pomona, CA

Tuition & fees (CA res): $7027	Average undergraduate aid package: $11,105

ABOUT THE INSTITUTION State-supported, coed. *Awards:* bachelor's, master's, and doctoral degrees. 55 undergraduate majors. *Total enrollment:* 25,326. Undergraduates: 23,733. Freshmen: 4,204. Federal methodology is used as a basis for awarding need-based institutional aid.

UNDERGRADUATE EXPENSES for 2017–2018 *Application fee:* $55. *Tuition, state resident:* full-time $5472. *Tuition, nonresident:* full-time $16,632; part-time $248 per credit hour. *Required fees:* full-time $1555. Full-time tuition and fees vary according to course load, degree level, and program. Part-time tuition and fees vary according to course load, degree level, and program. *College room and board:* $14,514; *Room only:* $9027. Room and board charges vary according to board plan and housing facility.

FRESHMAN FINANCIAL AID (Fall 2016, est.) 3,478 applied for aid; of those 79% were deemed to have need. 94% of freshmen with need received aid; of those 3% had need fully met. *Average percent of need met:* 59% (excluding resources awarded to replace EFC). *Average financial aid package:* $10,545 (excluding resources awarded to replace EFC).

UNDERGRADUATE FINANCIAL AID (Fall 2016, est.) 16,552 applied for aid; of those 87% were deemed to have need. 95% of undergraduates with need received aid; of those 6% had need fully met. **Average percent of need met:** 55% (excluding resources awarded to replace EFC). **Average financial aid package:** $11,105 (excluding resources awarded to replace EFC). 1% of all full-time undergraduates had no need and received non-need-based gift aid.

GIFT AID (NEED-BASED) Total amount: $146,233,362 (45% federal, 27% state, 28% institutional). **Receiving aid:** Freshmen: 52% (2,133); all full-time undergraduates: 51% (11,111). **Average award:** Freshmen: $9695; Undergraduates: $9805. **Scholarships, grants, and awards:** Federal Pell, FSEOG, state, private, college/university gift aid from institutional funds.

GIFT AID (NON-NEED-BASED) Total amount: $6,379,236 (55% state, 4% institutional, 41% external sources). **Receiving aid:** Freshmen: 15% (607). Undergraduates: 13% (2,678). **Average award:** Undergraduates: $1262. **Scholarships, grants, and awards by category:** Academic interests/achievement: agriculture, architecture, area/ethnic studies, biological sciences, business, communication, computer science, education, engineering/technologies, English, foreign languages, general academic interests/achievements, humanities, international studies, mathematics, physical sciences, social sciences. Special achievements/activities: hobbies/interests, leadership. Special characteristics: children and siblings of alumni, children of current students, first-generation college students, members of minority groups. **Tuition waivers:** Full or partial for employees or children of employees. **ROTC:** Army.

LOANS Student loans: $69,887,942 (54% need-based, 46% non-need-based). 53% of past graduating class borrowed through all loan programs. Average indebtedness per student: $22,404. **Average need-based loan:** Freshmen: $3767. Undergraduates: $4722. **Parent loans:** $4,322,194 (100% non-need-based). **Programs:** Federal Direct (Subsidized and Unsubsidized Stafford, PLUS), Perkins, college/university, alternative loans.

WORK-STUDY Federal work-study: Total amount: $973,400; 393 jobs averaging $2477.

ATHLETIC AWARDS Total amount: $718,520 (100% non-need-based).

APPLYING FOR FINANCIAL AID Required financial aid form: FAFSA. **Financial aid deadline:** Continuous. **Notification date:** Continuous beginning 4/1. Students must reply within 6 weeks of notification.

CONTACT Diana Minor, Director of Financial Aid and Scholarships, California State Polytechnic University, Pomona, 3801 West Temple Avenue, Pomona, CA 91768-2557, 909-869-3704. Fax: 909-869-4757. E-mail: dyminor@cpp.edu. Website: http://www.cpp.edu/.

CALIFORNIA STATE UNIVERSITY, BAKERSFIELD
Bakersfield, CA

Tuition & fees (CA res): $8249	Average undergraduate aid package: $4278

ABOUT THE INSTITUTION State-supported, coed. **Awards:** bachelor's, master's, and doctoral degrees. 30 undergraduate majors. **Total enrollment:** 9,341. Undergraduates: 8,093. Freshmen: 1,356. Federal methodology is used as a basis for awarding need-based institutional aid.

UNDERGRADUATE EXPENSES for 2016–2017 Application fee: $55. **Tuition, state resident:** full-time $5472; part-time $3174 per year. **Tuition, nonresident:** full-time $16,632; part-time $12,102 per year. **Required fees:** full-time $2777; $1388 per year. Full-time tuition and fees vary according to course load and degree level. Part-time tuition and fees vary according to course load and degree level. Room and board charges vary according to board plan and housing facility.

FRESHMAN FINANCIAL AID (Fall 2016, est.) 1,372 applied for aid; of those 88% were deemed to have need. 97% of freshmen with need received aid; of those 14% had need fully met. **Average percent of need met:** 15% (excluding resources awarded to replace EFC). **Average financial aid package:** $4223 (excluding resources awarded to replace EFC).

UNDERGRADUATE FINANCIAL AID (Fall 2016, est.) 6,591 applied for aid; of those 89% were deemed to have need. 97% of undergraduates with need received aid; of those 15% had need fully met. **Average percent of need met:** 15% (excluding resources awarded to replace EFC). **Average financial aid package:** $4278 (excluding resources awarded to replace EFC).

GIFT AID (NEED-BASED) Total amount: $56,960,148 (42% federal, 54% state, 2% institutional, 2% external sources). **Receiving aid:** Freshmen: 76% (1,098); all full-

time undergraduates: 73% (5,330). **Average award:** Freshmen: $3657; Undergraduates: $3397. **Scholarships, grants, and awards:** Federal Pell, FSEOG, state, private, college/university gift aid from institutional funds, Federal Nursing.

GIFT AID (NON-NEED-BASED) Total amount: $311,757 (11% federal, 89% state). **Receiving aid:** Freshmen: 12% (175). Undergraduates: 9% (650). **Scholarships, grants, and awards by category:** Academic interests/achievement: agriculture, architecture, biological sciences, business, communication, education, foreign languages, general academic interests/achievements, health fields, humanities, mathematics, physical sciences, premedicine, religion/biblical studies, social sciences. Creative arts/performance: art/fine arts, dance, music, theater/drama. Special achievements/activities: community service, general special achievements/activities, leadership. Special characteristics: children of faculty/staff, children of union members/company employees, ethnic background, first-generation college students, local/state students, veterans. **Tuition waivers:** Full or partial for employees or children of employees, senior citizens.

LOANS Student loans: $19,364,053 (100% need-based). 91% of past graduating class borrowed through all loan programs. Average indebtedness per student: $11,437. **Average need-based loan:** Freshmen: $1088. Undergraduates: $1410. **Parent loans:** $509,452 (100% need-based). **Programs:** Federal Direct (Subsidized and Unsubsidized Stafford, PLUS), Perkins, Federal Nursing, college/university.

WORK-STUDY Federal work-study: Total amount: $319,131; jobs available.

ATHLETIC AWARDS Total amount: $1,928,761 (100% need-based).

APPLYING FOR FINANCIAL AID Required financial aid forms: FAFSA, state aid form. **Financial aid deadline (priority):** 3/2. **Notification date:** Continuous beginning 4/15. Students must reply within 3 weeks of notification.

CONTACT Dr. Ron Radney, Director of Financial Aid and Scholarships, California State University, Bakersfield, 9001 Stockdale Highway, Bakersfield, CA 93311-1022, 661-654-3271 or toll-free 800-788-2782. Fax: 661-654-6800. E-mail: rradney@csub.edu. Website: http://www.csub.edu/.

CALIFORNIA STATE UNIVERSITY CHANNEL ISLANDS
Camarillo, CA

CONTACT Financial Aid Office, California State University Channel Islands, One University Drive, Camarillo, CA 93012, 805-437-8400. Website: http://www.csuci.edu/.

CALIFORNIA STATE UNIVERSITY, CHICO
Chico, CA

Tuition & fees (CA res): $12,516	Average undergraduate aid package: $16,081

ABOUT THE INSTITUTION State-supported, coed. **Awards:** certificates, bachelor's, and master's degrees. 48 undergraduate majors. **Total enrollment:** 17,557. Undergraduates: 16,471. Freshmen: 2,762. Federal methodology is used as a basis for awarding need-based institutional aid.

UNDERGRADUATE EXPENSES for 2016–2017 Application fee: $55. **Tuition, state resident:** full-time $7044. **Tuition, nonresident:** full-time $18,204. **Required fees:** full-time $5472. Full-time tuition and fees vary according to degree level. Part-time tuition and fees vary according to course load and degree level. **College room and board:** $12,824. Room and board charges vary according to board plan and housing facility.

FRESHMAN FINANCIAL AID (Fall 2015) 2,331 applied for aid; of those 80% were deemed to have need. 97% of freshmen with need received aid; of those 15% had need fully met. **Average percent of need met:** 79% (excluding resources awarded to replace EFC). **Average financial aid package:** $17,732 (excluding resources awarded to replace EFC). 6% of all full-time freshmen had no need and received non-need-based gift aid.

UNDERGRADUATE FINANCIAL AID (Fall 2015) 12,000 applied for aid; of those 86% were deemed to have need. 97% of undergraduates with need received aid; of those 16% had need fully met. **Average percent of need met:** 76% (excluding resources awarded to replace EFC). *Average financial aid package:* $16,081 (excluding resources awarded to replace EFC). 3% of all full-time undergraduates had no need and received non-need-based gift aid.

GIFT AID (NEED-BASED) *Total amount:* $135,629,876 (26% federal, 29% state, 45% institutional). *Receiving aid:* Freshmen: 61% (1,418); all full-time undergraduates: 52% (8,038). *Average award:* Freshmen: $10,733; Undergraduates: $9941. *Scholarships, grants, and awards:* Federal Pell, FSEOG, state, private, college/university gift aid from institutional funds, United Negro College Fund.

GIFT AID (NON-NEED-BASED) *Total amount:* $3,562,112 (2% federal, 4% state, 39% institutional, 55% external sources). *Receiving aid:* Freshmen: 18% (411). Undergraduates: 8% (1,281). *Average award:* Freshmen: $1488. Undergraduates: $1226. *Scholarships, grants, and awards by category: Academic interests/achievement:* agriculture, area/ethnic studies, biological sciences, business, communication, computer science, education, engineering/technologies, English, foreign languages, general academic interests/achievements, health fields, humanities, international studies, mathematics, physical sciences, social sciences. *Creative arts/performance:* applied art and design, art/fine arts, cinema/film/broadcasting, creative writing, dance, debating, general creative arts/performance, journalism/publications, music, performing arts, theater/drama. *Special achievements/activities:* community service, general special achievements/activities, hobbies/interests, leadership, memberships. *Special characteristics:* adult students, children of faculty/staff, ethnic background, first-generation college students, handicapped students, international students, local/state students, married students, members of minority groups, out-of-state students. *Tuition waivers:* Full or partial for employees or children of employees, senior citizens.

LOANS *Student loans:* $49,615,826 (58% need-based, 42% non-need-based). 66% of past graduating class borrowed through all loan programs. *Average need-based loan:* Freshmen: $3453. Undergraduates: $4534. *Parent loans:* $4,160,046 (100% non-need-based). *Programs:* Federal Direct (Subsidized and Unsubsidized Stafford, PLUS), Perkins, college/university.

WORK-STUDY *Federal work-study:* jobs available.

ATHLETIC AWARDS Total amount: $674,377 (100% need-based).

APPLYING FOR FINANCIAL AID *Required financial aid forms:* FAFSA, institution's own form. *Financial aid deadline:* Continuous. *Notification date:* Continuous beginning 3/2.

CONTACT Dan Reed, Director of Financial Aid and Scholarships, California State University, Chico, 400 West First Street, Student Services Center, Room 250, Chico, CA 95929-0705, 530-898-6451 or toll-free 800-542-4426 (out-of-state). *Fax:* 530-898-6883. *E-mail:* finaid@csuchico.edu. *Website:* http://www.csuchico.edu/.

CALIFORNIA STATE UNIVERSITY, DOMINGUEZ HILLS
Carson, CA

Tuition & fees (CA res): $6418	Average undergraduate aid package: $6320

ABOUT THE INSTITUTION State-supported, coed. *Awards:* certificates, bachelor's, and master's degrees. 67 undergraduate majors. *Total enrollment:* 14,635. Undergraduates: 12,562. Freshmen: 1,305. Federal methodology is used as a basis for awarding need-based institutional aid.

UNDERGRADUATE EXPENSES for 2016–2017 *Application fee:* $55. *Tuition, state resident:* full-time $5472; part-time $3174 per year. *Tuition, nonresident:* full-time $16,632; part-time $372 per unit. *Required fees:* full-time $946; $946 per year. Room and board charges vary according to housing facility.

FRESHMAN FINANCIAL AID (Fall 2015) 1,184 applied for aid; of those 93% were deemed to have need. 100% of freshmen with need received aid; of those 2% had need fully met. *Average percent of need met:* 36% (excluding resources awarded to replace EFC). *Average financial aid package:* $5604 (excluding resources awarded to replace EFC). 3% of all full-time freshmen had no need and received non-need-based gift aid.

UNDERGRADUATE FINANCIAL AID (Fall 2015) 6,989 applied for aid; of those 96% were deemed to have need. 98% of undergraduates with need received aid; of those 2% had need fully met. *Average percent of need met:* 34% (excluding resources awarded to replace EFC). *Average financial aid package:* $6320 (excluding resources awarded to replace EFC). 2% of all full-time undergraduates had no need and received non-need-based gift aid.

GIFT AID (NEED-BASED) *Total amount:* $43,695,217 (42% federal, 56% state, 1% institutional, 1% external sources). *Receiving aid:* Freshmen: 78% (984); all full-time undergraduates: 63% (5,792). *Average award:* Freshmen: $5424; Undergraduates: $5240. *Scholarships, grants, and awards:* Federal Pell, FSEOG, state, private, college/university gift aid from institutional funds.

GIFT AID (NON-NEED-BASED) *Total amount:* $30,188 (100% institutional). *Receiving aid:* Freshmen: 15% (182). Undergraduates: 18% (1,639). *Average award:* Freshmen: $4322. Undergraduates: $4022. *Tuition waivers:* Full or partial for employees or children of employees, senior citizens. *ROTC:* Army, Air Force cooperative.

LOANS *Student loans:* $15,982,863 (94% need-based, 6% non-need-based). 58% of past graduating class borrowed through all loan programs. *Average indebtedness per student:* $16,370. *Average need-based loan:* Freshmen: $1643. Undergraduates: $2354. *Parent loans:* $200,110 (68% need-based, 32% non-need-based). *Programs:* Federal Direct (Subsidized and Unsubsidized Stafford, PLUS), Perkins, college/university.

WORK-STUDY *Federal work-study:* 194 jobs averaging $1424.

ATHLETIC AWARDS Total amount: $254,974 (88% need-based, 12% non-need-based).

APPLYING FOR FINANCIAL AID *Required financial aid form:* FAFSA. *Financial aid deadline:* 5/15 (priority: 3/2). *Notification date:* Continuous beginning 3/15. Students must reply within 2 weeks of notification.

CONTACT Mrs. Delores S. Lee, Director of Financial Aid, California State University, Dominguez Hills, 1000 East Victoria Street, Carson, CA 90747-0001, 310-243-3189. *Fax:* 310-516-4498. *E-mail:* dslee@csudh.edu. *Website:* http://www.csudh.edu/.

CALIFORNIA STATE UNIVERSITY, EAST BAY
Hayward, CA

Tuition & fees (CA res): $7927	Average undergraduate aid package: $10,778

ABOUT THE INSTITUTION State-supported, coed. *Awards:* certificates, bachelor's, master's, and doctoral degrees. 90 undergraduate majors. *Total enrollment:* 15,885. Undergraduates: 13,761. Freshmen: 1,596. Federal methodology is used as a basis for awarding need-based institutional aid.

UNDERGRADUATE EXPENSES for 2017–2018 *Application fee:* $55. *Tuition, state resident:* full-time $6834. *Tuition, nonresident:* full-time $18,714; part-time $264 per credit hour. *Required fees:* full-time $1093. Full-time tuition and fees vary according to course load, program, and reciprocity agreements. Part-time tuition and fees vary according to course load, program, and reciprocity agreements. *College room and board:* $14,184. Room and board charges vary according to board plan and housing facility.

FRESHMAN FINANCIAL AID (Fall 2016, est.) 1,206 applied for aid; of those 96% were deemed to have need. 99% of freshmen with need received aid; of those 3% had need fully met. *Average percent of need met:* 61% (excluding resources awarded to replace EFC). *Average financial aid package:* $12,379 (excluding resources awarded to replace EFC).

UNDERGRADUATE FINANCIAL AID (Fall 2016, est.) 7,847 applied for aid; of those 98% were deemed to have need. 98% of undergraduates with need received aid; of those 3% had need fully met. *Average percent of need met:* 55% (excluding resources awarded to replace EFC). *Average financial aid package:* $10,778 (excluding resources awarded to replace EFC).

GIFT AID (NEED-BASED) *Total amount:* $67,450,806 (41% federal, 29% state, 29% institutional, 1% external sources). *Receiving aid:* Freshmen: 71% (1,120); all full-time undergraduates: 56% (7,178). *Average award:* Freshmen: $9758; Undergraduates: $8545. *Scholarships, grants, and awards:* Federal Pell, FSEOG, state, private, college/university gift aid from institutional funds.

GIFT AID (NON-NEED-BASED) *Scholarships, grants, and awards by category: Academic interests/achievement:* general academic interests/achievements. *Creative arts/performance:* music. *Tuition waivers:* Full or partial for employees or children of employees, senior citizens.

LOANS *Student loans:* $32,862,284 (87% need-based, 13% non-need-based). 47% of past graduating class borrowed through all loan programs. *Average indebtedness per student:* $19,149. *Average need-based loan:* Freshmen: $4836. Undergraduates: $6352. *Parent loans:* $5,399,588 (40% need-based, 60% non-need-based).

Programs: Federal Direct (Subsidized and Unsubsidized Stafford, PLUS), Perkins, college/university.

WORK-STUDY Federal work-study: Total amount: $2,044,456; jobs available.

APPLYING FOR FINANCIAL AID Required financial aid form: FAFSA. **Financial aid deadline (priority):** 3/2. **Notification date:** Continuous beginning 3/31. Students must reply within 4 weeks of notification.

CONTACT Office of Financial Aid, California State University, East Bay, 25800 Carlos Bee Boulevard, Hayward, CA 94542-3028, 510-885-2784. *Fax:* 510-885-2161. *E-mail:* finaid@csueastbay.edu.

Website: http://www.csueastbay.edu/.

CALIFORNIA STATE UNIVERSITY, FRESNO
Fresno, CA

Tuition & fees: N/R	Average undergraduate aid package: $10,923

ABOUT THE INSTITUTION State-supported, coed. **Awards:** certificates, bachelor's, master's, and doctoral degrees. 87 undergraduate majors. **Total enrollment:** 21,148. Undergraduates: 21,528. Freshmen: 3,194. Federal methodology is used as a basis for awarding need-based institutional aid.

FRESHMAN FINANCIAL AID (Fall 2016, est.) 2,777 applied for aid; of those 88% were deemed to have need. 96% of freshmen with need received aid; of those 6% had need fully met. **Average percent of need met:** 72% (excluding resources awarded to replace EFC). **Average financial aid package:** $11,072 (excluding resources awarded to replace EFC).

UNDERGRADUATE FINANCIAL AID (Fall 2016, est.) 15,326 applied for aid; of those 92% were deemed to have need. 97% of undergraduates with need received aid; of those 5% had need fully met. **Average percent of need met:** 70% (excluding resources awarded to replace EFC). **Average financial aid package:** $10,923 (excluding resources awarded to replace EFC).

GIFT AID (NEED-BASED) Total amount: $135,965,624 (46% federal, 54% state). **Receiving aid:** Freshmen: 2,210; all full-time undergraduates: 12,409. **Average award:** Freshmen: $10,573; Undergraduates: $10,108. **Scholarships, grants, and awards:** Federal Pell, FSEOG, state, private, college/university gift aid from institutional funds.

GIFT AID (NON-NEED-BASED) Total amount: $7,812,348 (25% state, 60% institutional, 15% external sources). **Receiving aid:** Freshmen: 519. Undergraduates: 2,693. **Average award:** Freshmen: $2880. Undergraduates: $2546. **Scholarships, grants, and awards by category:** Academic interests/achievement: 1,142 awards ($2,678,174 total): agriculture, area/ethnic studies, biological sciences, business, communication, education, engineering/technologies, English, foreign languages, general academic interests/achievements, health fields, humanities, mathematics, physical sciences, social sciences. Creative arts/performance: 135 awards ($165,429 total): art/fine arts, journalism/publications, music, theater/drama. Special achievements/activities: 17 awards ($25,750 total): community service, leadership. Special characteristics: 3 awards ($2717 total): handicapped students, local/state students. **ROTC:** Army, Air Force.

LOANS Student loans: $45,817,317 (56% need-based, 44% non-need-based). 51% of past graduating class borrowed through all loan programs. *Average indebtedness per student:* $18,221. **Average need-based loan:** Freshmen: $3126. Undergraduates: $4152. **Parent loans:** $1,387,347 (100% non-need-based). **Programs:** Federal Direct (Subsidized and Unsubsidized Stafford, PLUS), Perkins, Federal Nursing, college/university, alternative loans.

WORK-STUDY Federal work-study: Total amount: $921,424; 182 jobs averaging $4821.

ATHLETIC AWARDS Total amount: $5,651,623 (100% non-need-based).

APPLYING FOR FINANCIAL AID Required financial aid form: FAFSA. **Financial aid deadline (priority):** 3/2. **Notification date:** Continuous beginning 4/1. Students must reply within 3 weeks of notification.

CONTACT Kelly Russell, Director of Financial Aid, California State University, Fresno, 5150 North Maple Avenue, JA64, Fresno, CA 93740, 559-278-2182. *Fax:* 559-278-4833. *E-mail:* kellyr@csufresno.edu.

Website: http://www.csufresno.edu/.

CALIFORNIA STATE UNIVERSITY, FULLERTON
Fullerton, CA

Tuition & fees (CA res): $6560	Average undergraduate aid package: $7772

ABOUT THE INSTITUTION State-supported, coed. **Awards:** certificates, bachelor's, master's, and doctoral degrees. 66 undergraduate majors. **Total enrollment:** 40,235. Undergraduates: 34,576. Freshmen: 4,426. Federal methodology is used as a basis for awarding need-based institutional aid.

UNDERGRADUATE EXPENSES for 2016–2017 Application fee: $55. **Tuition, state resident:** full-time $5472; part-time $3174 per year. **Tuition, non-resident:** full-time $16,632; part-time $7638 per year. **Required fees:** full-time $1088; $1088 per year. Full-time tuition and fees vary according to course load, degree level, and program. Part-time tuition and fees vary according to course load, degree level, and program. **College room and board:** $15,642. Room and board charges vary according to board plan and housing facility.

FRESHMAN FINANCIAL AID (Fall 2015) 3,807 applied for aid; of those 78% were deemed to have need. 99% of freshmen with need received aid; of those 81% had need fully met. **Average percent of need met:** 81% (excluding resources awarded to replace EFC). **Average financial aid package:** $6717 (excluding resources awarded to replace EFC). 1% of all full-time freshmen had no need and received non-need-based gift aid.

UNDERGRADUATE FINANCIAL AID (Fall 2015) 18,107 applied for aid; of those 89% were deemed to have need. 100% of undergraduates with need received aid; of those 75% had need fully met. **Average percent of need met:** 75% (excluding resources awarded to replace EFC). **Average financial aid package:** $7772 (excluding resources awarded to replace EFC). 1% of all full-time undergraduates had no need and received non-need-based gift aid.

GIFT AID (NEED-BASED) Total amount: $185,811,596 (38% federal, 28% state, 33% institutional, 1% external sources). **Receiving aid:** Freshmen: 55% (2,436); all full-time undergraduates: 51% (12,262). **Average award:** Freshmen: $3615; Undergraduates: $3897. **Scholarships, grants, and awards:** Federal Pell, FSEOG, state, private, college/university gift aid from institutional funds, Federal Nursing.

GIFT AID (NON-NEED-BASED) Total amount: $631,722 (100% external sources). **Receiving aid:** Freshmen: 9% (412). Undergraduates: 6% (1,361). **Average award:** Freshmen: $1287. Undergraduates: $1683. **Scholarships, grants, and awards by category:** Academic interests/achievement: 780 awards ($818,656 total): area/ethnic studies, biological sciences, business, communication, computer science, education, engineering/technologies, English, foreign languages, general academic interests/achievements, health fields, home economics, humanities, international studies, mathematics, military science, physical sciences, religion/biblical studies, social sciences. Creative arts/performance: 139 awards ($188,472 total): art/fine arts, cinema/film/broadcasting, dance, journalism/publications, music, performing arts, theater/drama. Special achievements/activities: 220 awards ($281,542 total): general special achievements/activities, leadership. Special characteristics: 148 awards ($139,225 total): general special characteristics. **Tuition waivers:** Full or partial for employees or children of employees, senior citizens. **ROTC:** Army.

LOANS Student loans: $101,719,734 (41% need-based, 59% non-need-based). 42% of past graduating class borrowed through all loan programs. *Average indebtedness per student:* $14,965. **Average need-based loan:** Freshmen: $2640. Undergraduates: $2208. **Parent loans:** $5,375,245 (100% non-need-based). **Programs:** Federal Direct (Subsidized and Unsubsidized Stafford, PLUS), Perkins, college/university, private loans.

WORK-STUDY Federal work-study: 387 jobs averaging $1273.

ATHLETIC AWARDS Total amount: $973,711 (100% need-based).

APPLYING FOR FINANCIAL AID Required financial aid form: FAFSA. **Financial aid deadline (priority):** 3/2. **Notification date:** Continuous beginning 4/22. Students must reply within 4 weeks of notification.

CONTACT Ms. Kelly England, Interim Director of Financial Aid, California State University, Fullerton, 800 North State College Boulevard, Fullerton, CA 92831-3599, 657-278-3128. *Fax:* 657-278-7090. *E-mail:* kengland@fullerton.edu.

Website: http://www.fullerton.edu/.

CALIFORNIA STATE UNIVERSITY, LONG BEACH
Long Beach, CA

Tuition & fees (CA res): $6460	Average undergraduate aid package: $13,529

ABOUT THE INSTITUTION State-supported, coed. **Awards:** certificates, bachelor's, master's, and doctoral degrees. 148 undergraduate majors. **Total enrollment:** 37,776. Undergraduates: 32,246. Institutional methodology is used as a basis for awarding need-based institutional aid.

UNDERGRADUATE EXPENSES for 2016–2017 Application fee: $55. **Tuition, state resident:** full-time $5472; part-time $3174 per year. **Tuition, non-resident:** full-time $15,144. **Required fees:** full-time $988. Full-time tuition and fees vary according to degree level and program. Part-time tuition and fees vary according to course load, degree level, and program. **College room and board:** $12,398. Room and board charges vary according to board plan.

FRESHMAN FINANCIAL AID (Fall 2016, est.) 3,681 applied for aid; of those 79% were deemed to have need. 97% of freshmen with need received aid; of those 70% had need fully met. **Average percent of need met:** 82% (excluding resources awarded to replace EFC). **Average financial aid package:** $12,348 (excluding resources awarded to replace EFC).

UNDERGRADUATE FINANCIAL AID (Fall 2016, est.) 24,042 applied for aid; of those 89% were deemed to have need. 96% of undergraduates with need received aid; of those 48% had need fully met. **Average percent of need met:** 80% (excluding resources awarded to replace EFC). **Average financial aid package:** $13,529 (excluding resources awarded to replace EFC).

GIFT AID (NEED-BASED) Total amount: $182,290,937 (42% federal, 54% state, 3% institutional, 1% external sources). **Receiving aid:** Freshmen: 53% (2,254); all full-time undergraduates: 61% (17,295). **Average award:** Freshmen: $7731; Undergraduates: $6517. **Scholarships, grants, and awards:** Federal Pell, FSEOG, state, private, college/university gift aid from institutional funds.

GIFT AID (NON-NEED-BASED) Total amount: $27,709 (100% federal). **Receiving aid:** Freshmen: 15% (654). Undergraduates: 22% (6,187). **Tuition waivers:** Full or partial for employees or children of employees, senior citizens. **ROTC:** Army, Air Force cooperative.

LOANS Student loans: $66,497,110 (100% need-based). 44% of past graduating class borrowed through all loan programs. **Average indebtedness per student:** $15,917. **Average need-based loan:** Freshmen: $3351. Undergraduates: $3877. **Programs:** Federal Direct (Subsidized and Unsubsidized Stafford, PLUS), Perkins.

WORK-STUDY Federal work-study: Total amount: $3,117,785; jobs available.

APPLYING FOR FINANCIAL AID Required financial aid form: FAFSA. **Financial aid deadline (priority):** 3/2. **Notification date:** 4/1. Students must reply within 4 weeks of notification.

CONTACT Nicolas Valdivia, Office of Financial Aid, California State University, Long Beach, 1250 Bellflower Boulevard, Long Beach, CA 90840, 562-985-8403. *Website:* http://www.csulb.edu/.

CALIFORNIA STATE UNIVERSITY, LOS ANGELES
Los Angeles, CA

Tuition & fees: N/R	Average undergraduate aid package: $10,811

ABOUT THE INSTITUTION State-supported, coed. 62 undergraduate majors. Federal methodology is used as a basis for awarding need-based institutional aid.

FRESHMAN FINANCIAL AID (Fall 2016, est.) 2,207 applied for aid; of those 94% were deemed to have need. 98% of freshmen with need received aid; of those 17% had need fully met. **Average percent of need met:** 65% (excluding resources awarded to replace EFC). **Average financial aid package:** $10,192 (excluding resources awarded to replace EFC). 1% of all full-time freshmen had no need and received non-need-based gift aid.

UNDERGRADUATE FINANCIAL AID (Fall 2016, est.) 18,428 applied for aid; of those 95% were deemed to have need. 98% of undergraduates with need received aid; of those 18% had need fully met. **Average percent of need met:** 65% (excluding resources awarded to replace EFC). **Average financial aid package:** $10,811 (excluding resources awarded to replace EFC). 1% of all full-time undergraduates had no need and received non-need-based gift aid.

GIFT AID (NEED-BASED) Total amount: $174,452,740 (47% federal, 52% state, 1% institutional). **Receiving aid:** Freshmen: 52% (1,923); all full-time undergraduates: 83% (16,701). **Average award:** Freshmen: $8622; Undergraduates: $8293. **Scholarships, grants, and awards:** Federal Pell, FSEOG, state, private, college/university gift aid from institutional funds.

GIFT AID (NON-NEED-BASED) Total amount: $528,761 (67% state, 33% institutional). **Average award:** Freshmen: $2590. Undergraduates: $2313. **Scholarships, grants, and awards by category:** Academic interests/achievement: biological sciences, business, communication, computer science, education, engineering/technologies, English, foreign languages, general academic interests/achievements, health fields, mathematics, physical sciences, social sciences. Creative arts/performance: art/fine arts, general creative arts/performance, journalism/publications, music, theater/drama. Special achievements/activities: community service, general special achievements/activities. Special characteristics: general special characteristics.

LOANS Student loans: $99,559,629 (96% need-based, 4% non-need-based). 50% of past graduating class borrowed through all loan programs. **Average indebtedness per student:** $16,362. **Average need-based loan:** Freshmen: $3541. Undergraduates: $4084. **Parent loans:** $750,280 (60% need-based, 40% non-need-based). **Programs:** Federal Direct (Subsidized and Unsubsidized Stafford, PLUS), Perkins, Federal Nursing.

WORK-STUDY Federal work-study: Total amount: $1,048,760; jobs available.

ATHLETIC AWARDS Total amount: $849,802 (97% need-based, 3% non-need-based).

APPLYING FOR FINANCIAL AID Required financial aid form: FAFSA. **Financial aid deadline (priority):** 3/3. **Notification date:** Continuous beginning 4/1.

CONTACT Tamie L. Nguyen, Director of Financial Aid, California State University, Los Angeles, 5151 State University Drive, Los Angeles, CA 90032, 323-343-6260. *Fax:* 323-343-3166. *E-mail:* tnguyen10@cslanet.calstatela.edu. *Website:* http://www.calstatela.edu/.

CALIFORNIA STATE UNIVERSITY MARITIME ACADEMY
Vallejo, CA

Tuition & fees (CA res): $8360	Average undergraduate aid package: N/A

ABOUT THE INSTITUTION State-supported, coed. **Awards:** bachelor's and master's degrees. 4 undergraduate majors. **Total enrollment:** 1,150. Undergraduates: 1,107. Freshmen: 241. Federal methodology is used as a basis for awarding need-based institutional aid.

UNDERGRADUATE EXPENSES for 2017–2018 Application fee: $55. **Tuition, state resident:** full-time $5472. **Tuition, nonresident:** full-time $11,160; part-time $372 per credit hour. **Required fees:** full-time $2888. Full-time tuition and fees vary according to course load and reciprocity agreements. Part-time tuition and fees vary according to course load and reciprocity agreements. **College room and board:** $12,807. Room and board charges vary according to board plan.

FRESHMAN FINANCIAL AID (Fall 2016, est.) 137 applied for aid; of those 88% were deemed to have need. 100% of freshmen with need received aid; of those 8% had need fully met.

UNDERGRADUATE FINANCIAL AID (Fall 2016, est.) 575 applied for aid; of those 91% were deemed to have need. 100% of undergraduates with need received aid; of those 8% had need fully met.

GIFT AID (NEED-BASED) Receiving aid: Freshmen: 49% (116); all full-time undergraduates: 49% (526). **Average award:** Freshmen: $8030; Undergraduates: $8575. **Scholarships, grants, and awards:** Federal Pell, FSEOG, state, private, college/university gift aid from institutional funds.

GIFT AID (NON-NEED-BASED) Total amount: $4,569,494 (36% federal, 48% state, 7% institutional, 9% external sources). **Scholarships, grants, and awards by category:** Academic interests/achievement: business, engineering/technologies, general academic interests/achievements. **Tuition waivers:** Full or partial for employees or children of employees. **ROTC:** Naval cooperative, Air Force cooperative.

LOANS Student loans: $2,027,108 (100% non-need-based). 74% of past graduating class borrowed through all loan programs. **Average indebtedness per student:**

$24,052. **Average need-based loan:** Freshmen: $3613. Undergraduates: $4588.
Parent loans: $2,568,767 (100% non-need-based). **Programs:** Federal Direct (Subsidized and Unsubsidized Stafford, PLUS), Perkins.
WORK-STUDY Federal work-study: Total amount: $53,000; jobs available.
ATHLETIC AWARDS Total amount: $60,925 (100% non-need-based).
APPLYING FOR FINANCIAL AID Required financial aid forms: FAFSA, state aid form. **Financial aid deadline (priority):** 3/2. **Notification date:** Continuous beginning 4/15. Students must reply by 6/1 or within 2 weeks of notification.
CONTACT Priscilla Muha, Director of Financial Aid, California State University Maritime Academy, 200 Maritime Academy Drive, Vallejo, CA 94590-0644, 707-654-1275 or toll-free 800-561-1945. Fax: 707-654-1007. E-mail: pmuha@csum.edu.
Website: http://www.csum.edu/.

CALIFORNIA STATE UNIVERSITY, MONTEREY BAY
Seaside, CA

Tuition & fees: N/R — Average undergraduate aid package: $11,277

ABOUT THE INSTITUTION State-supported, coed. **Awards:** bachelor's and master's degrees. 23 undergraduate majors. **Total enrollment:** 7,634. Undergraduates: 6,923. Freshmen: 802. Federal methodology is used as a basis for awarding need-based institutional aid.
FRESHMAN FINANCIAL AID (Fall 2016, est.) 730 applied for aid; of those 88% were deemed to have need. 88% of freshmen with need received aid; of those 12% had need fully met. **Average percent of need met:** 65% (excluding resources awarded to replace EFC). **Average financial aid package:** $11,557 (excluding resources awarded to replace EFC). 1% of all full-time freshmen had no need and received non-need-based gift aid.
UNDERGRADUATE FINANCIAL AID (Fall 2016, est.) 4,847 applied for aid; of those 89% were deemed to have need. 88% of undergraduates with need received aid; of those 11% had need fully met. **Average percent of need met:** 69% (excluding resources awarded to replace EFC). **Average financial aid package:** $11,277 (excluding resources awarded to replace EFC). 1% of all full-time undergraduates had no need and received non-need-based gift aid.
GIFT AID (NEED-BASED) Total amount: $33,218,944 (44% federal, 28% state, 28% institutional). **Receiving aid:** Freshmen: 59% (468); all full-time undergraduates: 52% (3,233). **Average award:** Freshmen: $10,744; Undergraduates: $9706. **Scholarships, grants, and awards:** Federal Pell, FSEOG, state, private, college/university gift aid from institutional funds.
GIFT AID (NON-NEED-BASED) Total amount: $701,162 (10% federal, 21% institutional, 69% external sources). **Receiving aid:** Freshmen: 10% (81). Undergraduates: 5% (311). **Average award:** Freshmen: $700. Undergraduates: $1626. **Scholarships, grants, and awards by category:** Academic interests/achievement: business, general academic interests/achievements. Special achievements/activities: leadership. Special characteristics: children and siblings of alumni, general special characteristics, local/state students.
LOANS Student loans: $16,099,553 (68% need-based, 32% non-need-based). 69% of past graduating class borrowed through all loan programs. Average indebtedness per student: $20,869. **Average need-based loan:** Freshmen: $3400. Undergraduates: $4470. **Parent loans:** $2,452,944 (100% non-need-based). **Programs:** Federal Direct (Subsidized and Unsubsidized Stafford, PLUS), Perkins, private loans.
WORK-STUDY Federal work-study: Total amount: $110,526; jobs available. **State or other work-study/employment:** Part-time jobs available.
ATHLETIC AWARDS Total amount: $463,134 (100% non-need-based).
APPLYING FOR FINANCIAL AID Required financial aid forms: FAFSA, state aid form. **Financial aid deadline:** 5/20 (priority: 3/2). **Notification date:** Continuous beginning 4/1. Students must reply by 7/30.
CONTACT Office of Financial Aid, California State University, Monterey Bay, 100 Campus Center, Building 47, Seaside, CA 93955-8001, 831-582-5100. Fax: 831-582-3782.
Website: http://www.csumb.edu/.

CALIFORNIA STATE UNIVERSITY, NORTHRIDGE
Northridge, CA

Tuition & fees (CA res): $6587 — Average undergraduate aid package: $18,142

ABOUT THE INSTITUTION State-supported, coed. **Awards:** bachelor's, master's, and doctoral degrees. 59 undergraduate majors. **Total enrollment:** 39,916. Undergraduates: 35,552. Freshmen: 4,499. Federal methodology is used as a basis for awarding need-based institutional aid.
UNDERGRADUATE EXPENSES for 2016–2017 Application fee: $55. **Tuition, state resident:** full-time $5472. **Tuition, nonresident:** full-time $16,632; part-time $372 per credit hour. **Required fees:** full-time $1115. **College room and board:** $10,272. Room and board charges vary according to board plan and housing facility.
FRESHMAN FINANCIAL AID (Fall 2016, est.) 4,920 applied for aid; of those 95% were deemed to have need. 100% of freshmen with need received aid. **Average financial aid package:** $11,293 (excluding resources awarded to replace EFC). 12% of all full-time freshmen had no need and received non-need-based gift aid.
UNDERGRADUATE FINANCIAL AID (Fall 2016, est.) 24,211 applied for aid; of those 97% were deemed to have need. 100% of undergraduates with need received aid. **Average financial aid package:** $18,142 (excluding resources awarded to replace EFC). 17% of all full-time undergraduates had no need and received non-need-based gift aid.
GIFT AID (NEED-BASED) Total amount: $208,963,674 (45% federal, 54% state, 1% institutional). **Receiving aid:** Freshmen: 71% (3,920); all full-time undergraduates: 66% (19,905). **Average award:** Freshmen: $10,802; Undergraduates: $15,987. **Scholarships, grants, and awards:** Federal Pell, FSEOG, state, private, college/university gift aid from institutional funds.
GIFT AID (NON-NEED-BASED) Total amount: $7,131,129 (87% institutional, 13% external sources). **Receiving aid:** Freshmen: 12% (672). Undergraduates: 17% (5,249). **Average award:** Freshmen: $1466. Undergraduates: $1693. **Scholarships, grants, and awards by category:** Academic interests/achievement: business, communication, computer science, education, engineering/technologies, English, general academic interests/achievements, mathematics, social sciences. Creative arts/performance: journalism/publications, music. Special achievements/activities: leadership. **Tuition waivers:** Full or partial for employees or children of employees, senior citizens. **ROTC:** Army cooperative, Air Force cooperative.
LOANS Student loans: $80,831,489 (57% need-based, 43% non-need-based). 49% of past graduating class borrowed through all loan programs. Average indebtedness per student: $16,956. **Average need-based loan:** Freshmen: $4686. Undergraduates: $5893. **Parent loans:** $2,410,489 (100% non-need-based). **Programs:** Perkins.
WORK-STUDY Federal work-study: Total amount: $1,742,072; jobs available.
ATHLETIC AWARDS Total amount: $2,931,953 (100% non-need-based).
APPLYING FOR FINANCIAL AID Required financial aid form: FAFSA. **Financial aid deadline (priority):** 3/2. **Notification date:** Continuous beginning 4/1.
CONTACT Lili Vidal, Director of Financial Aid and Scholarships, California State University, Northridge, 18111 Nordhoff Street, Northridge, CA 91330-8307, 818-677-4085. Fax: 818-677-6787. E-mail: financial.aid@csun.edu.
Website: http://www.csun.edu/.

CALIFORNIA STATE UNIVERSITY, SACRAMENTO
Sacramento, CA

Tuition & fees (CA res): $7204 — Average undergraduate aid package: $10,618

ABOUT THE INSTITUTION State-supported, coed. **Awards:** bachelor's, master's, and doctoral degrees. 55 undergraduate majors. **Total enrollment:** 30,510. Undergraduates: 27,876. Freshmen: 3,760. Federal methodology is used as a basis for awarding need-based institutional aid.

UNDERGRADUATE EXPENSES for 2017–2018 Application fee: $55. **Tuition, state resident:** full-time $5742. **Tuition, nonresident:** full-time $17,622; part-time $372 per credit hour. **Required fees:** full-time $1462. **College room and board:** $11,856; **Room only:** $7226. Room and board charges vary according to board plan and housing facility.

FRESHMAN FINANCIAL AID (Fall 2015) 3,268 applied for aid; of those 84% were deemed to have need. 98% of freshmen with need received aid; of those 14% had need fully met. **Average percent of need met:** 62% (excluding resources awarded to replace EFC). **Average financial aid package:** $10,651 (excluding resources awarded to replace EFC). 1% of all full-time freshmen had no need and received non-need-based gift aid.

UNDERGRADUATE FINANCIAL AID (Fall 2015) 18,515 applied for aid; of those 90% were deemed to have need. 96% of undergraduates with need received aid; of those 11% had need fully met. **Average percent of need met:** 60% (excluding resources awarded to replace EFC). **Average financial aid package:** $10,618 (excluding resources awarded to replace EFC). 1% of all full-time undergraduates had no need and received non-need-based gift aid.

GIFT AID (NEED-BASED) Total amount: $159,842,996 (42% federal, 31% state, 27% institutional). **Receiving aid:** Freshmen: 73% (2,647); all full-time undergraduates: 72% (15,906). **Average award:** Freshmen: $8867; Undergraduates: $8469. **Scholarships, grants, and awards:** Federal Pell, FSEOG, state, private, college/university gift aid from institutional funds, Federal Nursing.

GIFT AID (NON-NEED-BASED) Total amount: $7,115,326 (3% federal, 45% institutional, 52% external sources). **Receiving aid:** Freshmen: 10% (372). Undergraduates: 5% (1,214). **Average award:** Freshmen: $1175. Undergraduates: $1497. **ROTC:** Army cooperative, Air Force.

LOANS Student loans: $89,220,942 (45% need-based, 55% non-need-based). 56% of past graduating class borrowed through all loan programs. **Average indebtedness per student:** $18,985. **Average need-based loan:** Freshmen: $3240. Undergraduates: $4221. **Parent loans:** $11,427,292 (100% non-need-based). **Programs:** Federal Direct (Subsidized and Unsubsidized Stafford, PLUS), Perkins, Federal Nursing, college/university.

WORK-STUDY Federal work-study: jobs available. **State or other work-study/employment:** Part-time jobs available.

ATHLETIC AWARDS Total amount: $4,533,329 (100% need-based).

APPLYING FOR FINANCIAL AID Required financial aid form: FAFSA. **Financial aid deadline (priority):** 3/2. **Notification date:** Continuous beginning 4/6.

CONTACT Caryl Vickers-Harper, Director of Financial Aid, California State University, Sacramento, 6000 J Street, Sacramento, CA 95819-6044, 916-278-6559. Fax: 916-278-6082.

Website: http://www.csus.edu/.

CALIFORNIA STATE UNIVERSITY, SAN BERNARDINO
San Bernardino, CA

Tuition & fees (CA res): $6601	Average undergraduate aid package: $9430

ABOUT THE INSTITUTION State-supported, coed. **Awards:** certificates, bachelor's, master's, and doctoral degrees. 42 undergraduate majors. **Total enrollment:** 20,767. Undergraduates: 18,453. Freshmen: 2,791. Federal methodology is used as a basis for awarding need-based institutional aid.

UNDERGRADUATE EXPENSES for 2017–2018 Application fee: $55. **Tuition, state resident:** full-time $5472. **Tuition, nonresident:** full-time $11,160; part-time $248 per credit hour. **Required fees:** full-time $1129. **College room and board:** $12,966. Room and board charges vary according to board plan and housing facility.

FRESHMAN FINANCIAL AID (Fall 2016, est.) 2,553 applied for aid; of those 93% were deemed to have need. 95% of freshmen with need received aid; of those 10% had need fully met. **Average percent of need met:** 62% (excluding resources awarded to replace EFC). **Average financial aid package:** $9905 (excluding resources awarded to replace EFC). 1% of all full-time freshmen had no need and received non-need-based gift aid.

UNDERGRADUATE FINANCIAL AID (Fall 2016, est.) 14,696 applied for aid; of those 94% were deemed to have need. 96% of undergraduates with need received aid; of those 10% had need fully met. **Average percent of need met:** 64%

(excluding resources awarded to replace EFC). **Average financial aid package:** $9430 (excluding resources awarded to replace EFC). 1% of all full-time undergraduates had no need and received non-need-based gift aid.

GIFT AID (NEED-BASED) Total amount: $131,039,309 (43% federal, 29% state, 27% institutional, 1% external sources). **Receiving aid:** Freshmen: 78% (2,103); all full-time undergraduates: 75% (12,401). **Average award:** Freshmen: $10,298; Undergraduates: $9944. **Scholarships, grants, and awards:** Federal Pell, FSEOG, state, private, college/university gift aid from institutional funds.

GIFT AID (NON-NEED-BASED) Total amount: $2,344,589 (93% institutional, 7% external sources). **Receiving aid:** Freshmen: 63% (1,688). Undergraduates: 42% (6,893). **Average award:** Freshmen: $3125. Undergraduates: $3690. **Scholarships, grants, and awards by category:** Academic interests/achievement: 436 awards ($757,065 total): biological sciences, business, computer science, education, foreign languages, general academic interests/achievements, health fields, international studies, mathematics, physical sciences, social sciences. Creative arts/performance: 26 awards ($25,666 total): art/fine arts, general creative arts/performance, journalism/publications, music, theater/drama. Special achievements/activities: 80 awards ($91,114 total): community service, general special achievements/activities, hobbies/interests, memberships. Special characteristics: 60 awards ($84,698 total): children of public servants, children with a deceased or disabled parent, first-generation college students, handicapped students, veterans, veterans' children. **Tuition waivers:** Full or partial for employees or children of employees, senior citizens. **ROTC:** Army, Air Force.

LOANS Student loans: $38,494,647 (74% need-based, 26% non-need-based). 66% of past graduating class borrowed through all loan programs. **Average indebtedness per student:** $22,452. **Average need-based loan:** Freshmen: $3281. Undergraduates: $4165. **Parent loans:** $3,617,749 (14% need-based, 86% non-need-based). **Programs:** Federal Direct (Subsidized and Unsubsidized Stafford, PLUS), Perkins.

WORK-STUDY Federal work-study: Total amount: $1,667,168; 326 jobs averaging $4073.

ATHLETIC AWARDS Total amount: $722,425 (78% need-based, 22% non-need-based).

APPLYING FOR FINANCIAL AID Required financial aid forms: FAFSA, state aid form. **Financial aid deadline (priority):** 3/2. **Notification date:** Continuous beginning 4/1.

CONTACT Ms. Roseanna Ruiz, Director of Financial Aid, California State University, San Bernardino, 5500 University Parkway, San Bernardino, CA 92407-2397, 909-537-5227. Fax: 909-537-4024.

Website: http://www.csusb.edu/.

CALIFORNIA STATE UNIVERSITY, SAN MARCOS
San Marcos, CA

Tuition & fees (CA res): $7364	Average undergraduate aid package: $10,677

ABOUT THE INSTITUTION State-supported, coed. **Awards:** bachelor's and master's degrees. 41 undergraduate majors. **Total enrollment:** 13,144. Undergraduates: 12,562. Freshmen: 2,152. Federal methodology is used as a basis for awarding need-based institutional aid.

UNDERGRADUATE EXPENSES for 2016–2017 Application fee: $65. **Tuition, state resident:** full-time $0. **Tuition, nonresident:** full-time $16,292; part-time $372 per unit. **Required fees:** full-time $7364; $2433 per term. Part-time tuition and fees vary according to course load. **College room and board:** $13,240. Room and board charges vary according to housing facility.

FRESHMAN FINANCIAL AID (Fall 2015) 1,809 applied for aid; of those 81% were deemed to have need. 95% of freshmen with need received aid; of those 10% had need fully met. **Average percent of need met:** 66% (excluding resources awarded to replace EFC). **Average financial aid package:** $10,682 (excluding resources awarded to replace EFC). 1% of all full-time freshmen had no need and received non-need-based gift aid.

UNDERGRADUATE FINANCIAL AID (Fall 2015) 8,037 applied for aid; of those 87% were deemed to have need. 97% of undergraduates with need received aid; of those 9% had need fully met. **Average percent of need met:** 46% (excluding resources awarded to replace EFC). **Average financial aid package:** $10,677 (excluding resources awarded to replace EFC). 1% of all full-time undergraduates had no need and received non-need-based gift aid.

GIFT AID (NEED-BASED) *Total amount:* $63,573,285 (42% federal, 30% state, 26% institutional, 2% external sources). *Receiving aid:* Freshmen: 61% (1,300); all full-time undergraduates: 62% (6,322). *Average award:* Freshmen: $9343; Undergraduates: $8873. *Scholarships, grants, and awards:* Federal Pell, FSEOG, state, private, college/university gift aid from institutional funds.

GIFT AID (NON-NEED-BASED) *Total amount:* $353,424 (50% state, 7% institutional, 43% external sources). *Receiving aid:* Freshmen: 1% (14). Undergraduates: 1% (51). *Average award:* Freshmen: $2250. Undergraduates: $1669. *Scholarships, grants, and awards by category:* Academic interests/achievement: general academic interests/achievements, mathematics. *Creative arts/performance:* art/fine arts. *Special achievements/activities:* leadership. *Special characteristics:* local/state students. *Tuition waivers:* Full or partial for employees or children of employees, senior citizens. *ROTC:* Army, Naval cooperative, Air Force cooperative.

LOANS *Student loans:* $35,137,674 (86% need-based, 14% non-need-based). 53% of past graduating class borrowed through all loan programs. *Average indebtedness per student:* $22,736. *Average need-based loan:* Freshmen: $3246. Undergraduates: $4061. *Parent loans:* $2,340,525 (71% need-based, 29% non-need-based). *Programs:* Federal Direct (Subsidized and Unsubsidized Stafford, PLUS), Perkins.

WORK-STUDY *Federal work-study:* jobs available. *State or other work-study/employment:* Part-time jobs available.

ATHLETIC AWARDS Total amount: $673,424 (85% need-based, 15% non-need-based).

APPLYING FOR FINANCIAL AID *Required financial aid form:* FAFSA. *Financial aid deadline (priority):* 3/2. *Notification date:* Continuous beginning 3/2. Students must reply by 3/2 or within 2 weeks of notification.

CONTACT Financial Aid and Scholarships Office, California State University, San Marcos, 333 South Twin Oaks Valley Road, San Marcos, CA 92096-0001, 760-750-4850. *Fax:* 760-750-3047. *E-mail:* finaid@csusm.edu.
Website: http://www.csusm.edu/.

CALIFORNIA STATE UNIVERSITY, STANISLAUS
Turlock, CA

ABOUT THE INSTITUTION State-supported, coed. *Awards:* bachelor's, master's, and doctoral degrees. 50 undergraduate majors. *Total enrollment:* 9,282. Undergraduates: 8,099. Freshmen: 1,270.

GIFT AID (NEED-BASED) *Scholarships, grants, and awards:* Federal Pell, FSEOG, state, private, college/university gift aid from institutional funds.

GIFT AID (NON-NEED-BASED) *Scholarships, grants, and awards by category:* Academic interests/achievement: agriculture, area/ethnic studies, biological sciences, business, communication, computer science, education, English, foreign languages, general academic interests/achievements, health fields, humanities, international studies, mathematics, physical sciences, premedicine, social sciences. *Creative arts/performance:* art/fine arts, music. *Special achievements/activities:* community service, general special achievements/activities, leadership, memberships. *Special characteristics:* children of faculty/staff, first-generation college students, general special characteristics, local/state students.

LOANS *Programs:* Federal Direct (Subsidized and Unsubsidized Stafford, PLUS), Perkins, private loans.

WORK-STUDY *Federal work-study:* 193 jobs averaging $3815. *State or other work-study/employment:* Part-time jobs available.

APPLYING FOR FINANCIAL AID *Required financial aid forms:* FAFSA, state aid form.

CONTACT Office of Financial Aid and Scholarships, California State University, Stanislaus, One University Circle, Turlock, CA 95382, 209-667-3336 or toll-free 800-300-7420. *Fax:* 209-664-7064. *E-mail:* financial_aid@csustan.edu.
Website: http://www.csustan.edu/.

CALIFORNIA UNIVERSITY OF MANAGEMENT AND SCIENCES
Anaheim, CA

CONTACT Financial Aid Office, California University of Management and Sciences, 721 North Euclid Street, Anaheim, CA 92801, 714-533-3946.
Website: http://www.calums.edu/.

CALIFORNIA UNIVERSITY OF PENNSYLVANIA
California, PA

Tuition & fees (PA res): $10,339	Average undergraduate aid package: $9863

ABOUT THE INSTITUTION State-supported, coed. *Awards:* certificates, associate, bachelor's, master's, and doctoral degrees. 50 undergraduate majors. *Total enrollment:* 7,553. Undergraduates: 5,522. Freshmen: 904. Federal methodology is used as a basis for awarding need-based institutional aid.

UNDERGRADUATE EXPENSES for 2016–2017 *Application fee:* $25. *Tuition, state resident:* full-time $7238; part-time $302 per credit hour. *Tuition, nonresident:* full-time $10,858; part-time $452 per credit hour. *Required fees:* full-time $3101. Full-time tuition and fees vary according to course load, location, and student level. Part-time tuition and fees vary according to course load, location, and student level. *College room and board:* $10,086; *Room only:* $6592. Room and board charges vary according to board plan and housing facility.

FRESHMAN FINANCIAL AID (Fall 2015) 862 applied for aid; of those 83% were deemed to have need. 100% of freshmen with need received aid; of those 9% had need fully met. *Average percent of need met:* 52% (excluding resources awarded to replace EFC). *Average financial aid package:* $9407 (excluding resources awarded to replace EFC). 3% of all full-time freshmen had no need and received non-need-based gift aid.

UNDERGRADUATE FINANCIAL AID (Fall 2015) 4,510 applied for aid; of those 83% were deemed to have need. 100% of undergraduates with need received aid; of those 7% had need fully met. *Average percent of need met:* 53% (excluding resources awarded to replace EFC). *Average financial aid package:* $9863 (excluding resources awarded to replace EFC). 2% of all full-time undergraduates had no need and received non-need-based gift aid.

GIFT AID (NEED-BASED) *Total amount:* $19,440,086 (52% federal, 34% state, 10% institutional, 4% external sources). *Receiving aid:* Freshmen: 64% (582); all full-time undergraduates: 62% (3,118). *Average award:* Freshmen: $6565; Undergraduates: $6145. *Scholarships, grants, and awards:* Federal Pell, FSEOG, state, private, college/university gift aid from institutional funds.

GIFT AID (NON-NEED-BASED) *Total amount:* $2,741,123 (11% federal, 1% state, 54% institutional, 34% external sources). *Receiving aid:* Freshmen: 27% (244). Undergraduates: 17% (837). *Average award:* Freshmen: $2923. Undergraduates: $3943. *Scholarships, grants, and awards by category:* Academic interests/achievement: general academic interests/achievements. *Creative arts/performance:* general creative arts/performance. *Special achievements/activities:* general special achievements/activities. *Special characteristics:* ethnic background, international students, members of minority groups, veterans. *Tuition waivers:* Full or partial for employees or children of employees. *ROTC:* Army.

LOANS *Student loans:* $37,672,168 (40% need-based, 60% non-need-based). 88% of past graduating class borrowed through all loan programs. *Average indebtedness per student:* $25,683. *Average need-based loan:* Freshmen: $3186. Undergraduates: $4043. *Parent loans:* $7,876,556 (100% non-need-based). *Programs:* Federal Direct (Subsidized and Unsubsidized Stafford, PLUS), Perkins.

WORK-STUDY *Federal work-study:* 400 jobs averaging $900. *State or other work-study/employment:* Total amount: $1,807,437 (34% need-based, 66% non-need-based). 1,035 part-time jobs averaging $1400.

ATHLETIC AWARDS Total amount: $1,548,725 (100% non-need-based).

APPLYING FOR FINANCIAL AID *Required financial aid form:* FAFSA. *Financial aid deadline:* 3/1. *Notification date:* Continuous beginning 4/1.

CONTACT Jill Fernandes, Director of Financial Aid, California University of Pennsylvania, 250 University Avenue, California, PA 15419-1394, 724-938-4415 or toll-free 888-412-0479. *E-mail:* fernandes@calu.edu. *Website:* http://www.calu.edu/.

CALUMET COLLEGE OF SAINT JOSEPH
Whiting, IN

Tuition & fees: $17,920	Average undergraduate aid package: $12,971

ABOUT THE INSTITUTION Independent Roman Catholic, coed. *Awards:* certificates, associate, bachelor's, and master's degrees. 12 undergraduate majors. *Total enrollment:* 1,035. Undergraduates: 784. Freshmen: 113. Both federal and institutional methodology are used as a basis for awarding need-based institutional aid.

UNDERGRADUATE EXPENSES for 2017–2018 *Tuition:* full-time $17,650; part-time $560 per credit hour. *Required fees:* full-time $270; $135 per term. Full-time tuition and fees vary according to course load and program. Part-time tuition and fees vary according to course load and program. *Payment plan:* Guaranteed tuition.

FRESHMAN FINANCIAL AID (Fall 2016, est.) 100 applied for aid; of those 98% were deemed to have need. 89% of freshmen with need received aid; of those 22% had need fully met. *Average percent of need met:* 39% (excluding resources awarded to replace EFC). *Average financial aid package:* $15,867 (excluding resources awarded to replace EFC). 14% of all full-time freshmen had no need and received non-need-based gift aid.

UNDERGRADUATE FINANCIAL AID (Fall 2016, est.) 458 applied for aid; of those 91% were deemed to have need. 98% of undergraduates with need received aid; of those 15% had need fully met. *Average percent of need met:* 46% (excluding resources awarded to replace EFC). *Average financial aid package:* $12,971 (excluding resources awarded to replace EFC). 23% of all full-time undergraduates had no need and received non-need-based gift aid.

GIFT AID (NEED-BASED) *Total amount:* $3,468,270 (43% federal, 27% state, 27% institutional, 3% external sources). *Receiving aid:* Freshmen: 60% (65); all full-time undergraduates: 58% (296). *Average award:* Freshmen: $8254; Undergraduates: $8682. *Scholarships, grants, and awards:* Federal Pell, FSEOG, state, private, college/university gift aid from institutional funds, United Negro College Fund.

GIFT AID (NON-NEED-BASED) *Receiving aid:* Freshmen: 69% (74). Undergraduates: 55% (279). *Average award:* Freshmen: $3508. Undergraduates: $2766. *Scholarships, grants, and awards by category:* Academic interests/achievement: 39 awards ($111,843 total): general academic interests/achievements. Creative arts/performance: art/fine arts, creative writing, general creative arts/performance, theater/drama. Special achievements/activities: 29 awards ($19,025 total): leadership. Special characteristics: 68 awards ($168,966 total): children and siblings of alumni, children of faculty/staff, general special characteristics, previous college experience, religious affiliation. *Tuition waivers:* Full or partial for children of alumni, employees or children of employees, senior citizens.

LOANS *Student loans:* $2,838,145 (92% need-based, 8% non-need-based). 80% of past graduating class borrowed through all loan programs. *Average indebtedness per student:* $24,431. *Average need-based loan:* Freshmen: $3017. Undergraduates: $3971. *Parent loans:* $392,999 (85% need-based, 15% non-need-based). *Programs:* Federal Direct (Subsidized and Unsubsidized Stafford, PLUS).

WORK-STUDY *Federal work-study:* Total amount: $29,961; 20 jobs averaging $1165. *State or other work-study/employment:* Part-time jobs available.

ATHLETIC AWARDS Total amount: $1,852,267 (72% need-based, 28% non-need-based).

APPLYING FOR FINANCIAL AID *Required financial aid form:* FAFSA. *Financial aid deadline (priority):* 3/10. *Notification date:* Continuous beginning 4/1.

CONTACT Gina Pirtle, Director of Financial Aid and Business Office Operations, Calumet College of Saint Joseph, 2400 New York Avenue, Whiting, IN 46394, 219-473-4379 or toll-free 877-700-9100. *E-mail:* gpirtle@ccsj.edu. *Website:* http://www.ccsj.edu/.

CALVARY UNIVERSITY
Kansas City, MO

Tuition & fees: $9198	Average undergraduate aid package: $12,774

ABOUT THE INSTITUTION Independent nondenominational, coed. *Awards:* certificates, associate, bachelor's, and master's degrees. 34 undergraduate majors. *Total enrollment:* 271. Undergraduates: 231. Freshmen: 32. Both federal and institutional methodology are used as a basis for awarding need-based institutional aid.

UNDERGRADUATE EXPENSES for 2017–2018 *One-time required fee:* $100. *Comprehensive fee:* $14,688 includes full-time tuition ($8760), mandatory fees ($438), and room and board ($5490). *College room only:* $2600. Full-time tuition and fees vary according to location and program. Room and board charges vary according to board plan and housing facility. *Part-time tuition:* $365 per credit hour. Part-time tuition and fees vary according to location and program.

FRESHMAN FINANCIAL AID (Fall 2016, est.) 17 applied for aid; of those 88% were deemed to have need. 100% of freshmen with need received aid; of those 20% had need fully met. *Average percent of need met:* 75% (excluding resources awarded to replace EFC). *Average financial aid package:* $12,646 (excluding resources awarded to replace EFC). 4% of all full-time freshmen had no need and received non-need-based gift aid.

UNDERGRADUATE FINANCIAL AID (Fall 2016, est.) 101 applied for aid; of those 94% were deemed to have need. 100% of undergraduates with need received aid; of those 7% had need fully met. *Average percent of need met:* 66% (excluding resources awarded to replace EFC). *Average financial aid package:* $12,774 (excluding resources awarded to replace EFC). 3% of all full-time undergraduates had no need and received non-need-based gift aid.

GIFT AID (NEED-BASED) *Total amount:* $608,540 (69% federal, 25% institutional, 6% external sources). *Receiving aid:* Freshmen: 58% (15); all full-time undergraduates: 65% (86). *Average award:* Freshmen: $6196; Undergraduates: $5694. *Scholarships, grants, and awards:* Federal Pell, FSEOG, private, college/university gift aid from institutional funds.

GIFT AID (NON-NEED-BASED) *Total amount:* $34,160 (55% institutional, 45% external sources). *Receiving aid:* Freshmen: 12% (3). Undergraduates: 3% (4). *Average award:* Freshmen: $1000. Undergraduates: $2543. *Scholarships, grants, and awards by category:* Academic interests/achievement: general academic interests/achievements, religion/biblical studies. Creative arts/performance: general creative arts/performance. Special achievements/activities: general special achievements/activities, religious involvement. Special characteristics: children and siblings of alumni, children of educators, children of faculty/staff, relatives of clergy, religious affiliation, siblings of current students, spouses of current students. *Tuition waivers:* Full or partial for employees or children of employees. *ROTC:* Army cooperative.

LOANS *Student loans:* $1,061,238 (79% need-based, 21% non-need-based). 67% of past graduating class borrowed through all loan programs. *Average indebtedness per student:* $19,246. *Average need-based loan:* Freshmen: $3591. Undergraduates: $4265. *Parent loans:* $22,234 (100% non-need-based). *Programs:* Federal Direct (Subsidized and Unsubsidized Stafford, PLUS).

WORK-STUDY *Federal work-study:* Total amount: $14,091; 8 jobs averaging $1687. *State or other work-study/employment:* Part-time jobs available.

APPLYING FOR FINANCIAL AID *Required financial aid forms:* FAFSA, scholarship application. *Financial aid deadline:* Continuous. *Notification date:* Continuous beginning 5/1. Students must reply within 2 weeks of notification.

CONTACT Mr. Charles Kurtz, Assistant Director of Financial Aid, Calvary University, 15800 Calvary Road, Kansas City, MO 64147-1341, 816-425-6136 or toll-free 800-326-3960. *Fax:* 816-425-6134. *E-mail:* finaid@calvary.edu. *Website:* http://www.calvary.edu/.

CALVIN COLLEGE
Grand Rapids, MI

Tuition & fees: $31,730	Average undergraduate aid package: $22,838

ABOUT THE INSTITUTION Independent Christian Reformed, coed. *Awards:* bachelor's and master's degrees. 103 undergraduate majors. *Total enrollment:* 3,918. Undergraduates: 3,807. Freshmen: 925. Both federal and institutional methodology are used as a basis for awarding need-based institutional aid.

UNDERGRADUATE EXPENSES for 2016–2017 *Application fee:* $35. *Comprehensive fee:* $41,570 includes full-time tuition ($31,730) and room and board ($9840). Full-time tuition and fees vary according to degree level, program, and student level. Room and board charges vary according to board plan and housing facility. *Part-time tuition:* $760 per credit hour. Part-time tuition and fees vary according to course load, degree level, and student level. *Payment plan:* Tuition prepayment.

FRESHMAN FINANCIAL AID (Fall 2015) 855 applied for aid; of those 77% were deemed to have need. 100% of freshmen with need received aid; of those 20% had need fully met. *Average percent of need met:* 77% (excluding resources awarded to replace EFC). *Average financial aid package:* $24,924 (excluding resources awarded to replace EFC). 29% of all full-time freshmen had no need and received non-need-based gift aid.

UNDERGRADUATE FINANCIAL AID (Fall 2015) 3,402 applied for aid; of those 69% were deemed to have need. 100% of undergraduates with need received aid; of those 18% had need fully met. *Average percent of need met:* 73% (excluding resources awarded to replace EFC). *Average financial aid package:* $22,838 (excluding resources awarded to replace EFC). 32% of all full-time undergraduates had no need and received non-need-based gift aid.

GIFT AID (NEED-BASED) *Total amount:* $38,885,240 (11% federal, 5% state, 81% institutional, 3% external sources). *Receiving aid:* Freshmen: 69% (655); all full-time undergraduates: 63% (2,324). *Average award:* Freshmen: $18,804; Undergraduates: $16,111. *Scholarships, grants, and awards:* Federal Pell, FSEOG, state, private, college/university gift aid from institutional funds.

GIFT AID (NON-NEED-BASED) *Total amount:* $15,592,054 (92% institutional, 8% external sources). *Receiving aid:* Freshmen: 10% (97). Undergraduates: 7% (272). *Average award:* Freshmen: $10,575. Undergraduates: $8421. *Scholarships, grants, and awards by category:* Academic interests/achievement: architecture, area/ethnic studies, biological sciences, business, communication, computer science, education, engineering/technologies, English, foreign languages, general academic interests/achievements, health fields, humanities, international studies, mathematics, physical sciences, premedicine, religion/biblical studies, social sciences. *Creative arts/performance:* applied art and design, art/fine arts, cinema/film/broadcasting, creative writing, journalism/publications, music, performing arts, theater/drama. *Special achievements/activities:* community service, leadership, religious involvement. *Special characteristics:* adult students, children and siblings of alumni, children of faculty/staff, children of union members/company employees, children of workers in trades, children with a deceased or disabled parent, ethnic background, first-generation college students, handicapped students, international students, local/state students, members of minority groups, out-of-state students, religious affiliation, twins, veterans, veterans' children. *Tuition waivers:* Full or partial for employees or children of employees. *ROTC:* Army cooperative.

LOANS *Student loans:* $22,017,243 (70% need-based, 30% non-need-based). 60% of past graduating class borrowed through all loan programs. *Average indebtedness per student:* $30,998. *Average need-based loan:* Freshmen: $4069. Undergraduates: $6494. *Parent loans:* $3,288,665 (52% need-based, 48% non-need-based). *Programs:* Federal Direct (Subsidized and Unsubsidized Stafford, PLUS), Perkins, state, college/university, alternative loans.

WORK-STUDY *Federal work-study:* 1,079 jobs averaging $1550. *State or other work-study/employment:* Total amount: $2,002,210 (100% non-need-based). 1,032 part-time jobs averaging $1413.

APPLYING FOR FINANCIAL AID *Required financial aid form:* FAFSA. *Financial aid deadline (priority):* 2/1. *Notification date:* Continuous beginning 12/15.

CONTACT Mr. Craig Heerema, Financial Aid Administrator, Calvin College, Spoelhof Center 263, Grand Rapids, MI 49546, 616-526-6134 or toll-free 800-688-0122. *Fax:* 616-526-6883. *E-mail:* cheerema@calvin.edu.
Website: http://www.calvin.edu/.

CAMBRIDGE COLLEGE
Cambridge, MA

CONTACT Dr. Frank Lauder, Director of Financial Aid, Cambridge College, 1000 Massachusetts Avenue, Cambridge, MA 02138, 617-868-1000 Ext. 1440 or toll-free 800-877-4723. *Fax:* 617-349-3561. *E-mail:* francis.lauder@cambridgecollege.edu.
Website: http://www.cambridgecollege.edu/.

CAMERON UNIVERSITY
Lawton, OK

Tuition & fees (OK res): $5970	Average undergraduate aid package: $9499

ABOUT THE INSTITUTION State-supported, coed. *Awards:* associate, bachelor's, and master's degrees. 34 undergraduate majors. *Total enrollment:* 4,846. Undergraduates: 4,444. Freshmen: 726. Federal methodology is used as a basis for awarding need-based institutional aid.

UNDERGRADUATE EXPENSES for 2016–2017 *Application fee:* $25. *Tuition, state resident:* full-time $4260; part-time $142 per credit hour. *Tuition, nonresident:* full-time $13,500; part-time $450 per credit hour. *Required fees:* full-time $1710; $57 per credit hour. Full-time tuition and fees vary according to course level, course load, location, and program. Part-time tuition and fees vary according to course level, course load, location, and program. *College room and board:* $5102; *Room only:* $1872. Room and board charges vary according to board plan and housing facility.

FRESHMAN FINANCIAL AID (Fall 2015) 593 applied for aid; of those 80% were deemed to have need. 94% of freshmen with need received aid; of those 14% had need fully met. *Average percent of need met:* 64% (excluding resources awarded to replace EFC). *Average financial aid package:* $9353 (excluding resources awarded to replace EFC). 9% of all full-time freshmen had no need and received non-need-based gift aid.

UNDERGRADUATE FINANCIAL AID (Fall 2015) 2,399 applied for aid; of those 86% were deemed to have need. 95% of undergraduates with need received aid; of those 11% had need fully met. *Average percent of need met:* 61% (excluding resources awarded to replace EFC). *Average financial aid package:* $9499 (excluding resources awarded to replace EFC). 8% of all full-time undergraduates had no need and received non-need-based gift aid.

GIFT AID (NEED-BASED) *Total amount:* $13,785,834 (79% federal, 15% state, 3% institutional, 3% external sources). *Receiving aid:* Freshmen: 54% (410); all full-time undergraduates: 56% (1,788). *Average award:* Freshmen: $6238; Undergraduates: $6296. *Scholarships, grants, and awards:* Federal Pell, FSEOG, state, private, college/university gift aid from institutional funds.

GIFT AID (NON-NEED-BASED) *Total amount:* $1,461,008 (28% federal, 22% state, 24% institutional, 26% external sources). *Receiving aid:* Freshmen: 3% (26). Undergraduates: 3% (83). *Average award:* Freshmen: $1749. Undergraduates: $2139. *Scholarships, grants, and awards by category:* Academic interests/achievement: agriculture, biological sciences, business, communication, computer science, education, engineering/technologies, English, foreign languages, general academic interests/achievements, home economics, mathematics, military science, physical sciences, social sciences. *Creative arts/performance:* art/fine arts, cinema/film/broadcasting, creative writing, debating, journalism/publications, music, performing arts, theater/drama. *Special achievements/activities:* cheerleading/drum major, general special achievements/activities, leadership. *Special characteristics:* children of faculty/staff, international students, members of minority groups, out-of-state students, veterans, veterans' children. *Tuition waivers:* Full or partial for employees or children of employees, senior citizens. *ROTC:* Army.

LOANS *Student loans:* $13,303,576 (77% need-based, 23% non-need-based). 37% of past graduating class borrowed through all loan programs. *Average indebtedness per student:* $20,019. *Average need-based loan:* Freshmen: $3490. Undergraduates: $3902. *Parent loans:* $122,703 (16% need-based, 84% non-need-based). *Programs:* Federal Direct (Subsidized and Unsubsidized Stafford, PLUS).

WORK-STUDY *Federal work-study:* 65 jobs averaging $1944. *State or other work-study/employment:* Total amount: $968,743 (3% need-based, 97% non-need-based). 309 part-time jobs averaging $2909.

ATHLETIC AWARDS *Total amount:* $761,559 (32% need-based, 68% non-need-based).

APPLYING FOR FINANCIAL AID *Required financial aid form:* FAFSA. *Financial aid deadline:* Continuous. *Notification date:* Continuous beginning 4/1. Students must reply by 8/1 or within 2 weeks of notification.

CONTACT Mr. Gary Garoffolo, Director of Financial Aid, Cameron University, 2800 West Gore Boulevard, Lawton, OK 73505-6377, 580-581-2221 or toll-free 888-454-7600. *Fax:* 580-581-2556. *E-mail:* ggaroffo@cameron.edu.
Website: http://www.cameron.edu/.

CAMPBELLSVILLE UNIVERSITY
Campbellsville, KY

Tuition & fees: $24,596	Average undergraduate aid package: $19,624

ABOUT THE INSTITUTION Independent Kentucky Baptist Convention, coed. *Awards:* certificates, associate, bachelor's, and master's degrees. 55 undergraduate majors. *Total enrollment:* 4,305. Undergraduates: 3,349. Freshmen: 595. Federal methodology is used as a basis for awarding need-based institutional aid.

UNDERGRADUATE EXPENSES for 2016–2017 *Application fee:* $20. *Comprehensive fee:* $32,492 includes full-time tuition ($24,096), mandatory fees ($500), and room and board ($7896). Full-time tuition and fees vary according to course load, location, and program. Room and board charges vary according to housing facility. *Part-time tuition:* $1004 per credit hour. *Part-time fees:* $250 per year. Part-time tuition and fees vary according to class time, course load, location, and program.

FRESHMAN FINANCIAL AID (Fall 2015) 456 applied for aid; of those 95% were deemed to have need. 99% of freshmen with need received aid; of those 16% had need fully met. *Average percent of need met:* 74% (excluding resources awarded to replace EFC). *Average financial aid package:* $21,711 (excluding resources awarded to replace EFC). 5% of all full-time freshmen had no need and received non-need-based gift aid.

UNDERGRADUATE FINANCIAL AID (Fall 2015) 1,589 applied for aid; of those 94% were deemed to have need. 100% of undergraduates with need received aid; of those 15% had need fully met. *Average percent of need met:* 74% (excluding resources awarded to replace EFC). *Average financial aid package:* $19,624 (excluding resources awarded to replace EFC). 7% of all full-time undergraduates had no need and received non-need-based gift aid.

GIFT AID (NEED-BASED) *Total amount:* $22,804,209 (19% federal, 22% state, 55% institutional, 4% external sources). *Receiving aid:* Freshmen: 91% (429); all full-time undergraduates: 88% (1,477). *Average award:* Freshmen: $19,265; Undergraduates: $16,723. *Scholarships, grants, and awards:* Federal Pell, FSEOG, state, private, college/university gift aid from institutional funds.

GIFT AID (NON-NEED-BASED) *Total amount:* $2,701,409 (14% state, 70% institutional, 16% external sources). *Receiving aid:* Freshmen: 11% (52). Undergraduates: 10% (167). *Average award:* Freshmen: $12,954. Undergraduates: $11,286. *Scholarships, grants, and awards by category: Academic interests/achievement:* biological sciences, business, communication, computer science, education, English, general academic interests/achievements, health fields, humanities, mathematics, physical sciences, premedicine, religion/biblical studies, social sciences. *Creative arts/performance:* art/fine arts, journalism/publications, music, theater/drama. *Special achievements/activities:* cheerleading/drum major, junior miss, leadership, religious involvement. *Special characteristics:* adult students, children of educators, children of faculty/staff, international students, relatives of clergy, religious affiliation, veterans. *Tuition waivers:* Full or partial for employees or children of employees, adult students, senior citizens. *ROTC:* Army cooperative.

LOANS *Student loans:* $8,990,920 (78% need-based, 22% non-need-based). 63% of past graduating class borrowed through all loan programs. *Average indebtedness per student:* $24,224. *Average need-based loan:* Freshmen: $2955. Undergraduates: $3690. *Parent loans:* $1,566,812 (53% need-based, 47% non-need-based). *Programs:* Federal Direct (Subsidized and Unsubsidized Stafford, PLUS), Perkins, college/university.

WORK-STUDY *Federal work-study:* 265 jobs averaging $1500. *State or other work-study/employment:* Total amount: $39,674 (61% need-based, 39% non-need-based). 30 part-time jobs averaging $1200.

ATHLETIC AWARDS Total amount: $3,275,789 (57% need-based, 43% non-need-based).

APPLYING FOR FINANCIAL AID *Required financial aid form:* FAFSA. *Financial aid deadline (priority):* 1/30. *Notification date:* Continuous beginning 3/15. Students must reply by 5/1 or within 2 weeks of notification.

CONTACT Chris Mapes, Director of Financial Aid, Campbellsville University, 1 University Drive, Campbellsville, KY 42718, 270-789-5013 or toll-free 800-264-6014. *Fax:* 270-789-5079. *E-mail:* finaid@campbellsville.edu. *Website:* http://www.campbellsville.edu/.

CAMPBELL UNIVERSITY
Buies Creek, NC

Tuition & fees: $30,050	Average undergraduate aid package: $22,874

ABOUT THE INSTITUTION Independent North Carolina Baptist State Convention, coed. 85 undergraduate majors. Federal methodology is used as a basis for awarding need-based institutional aid.

UNDERGRADUATE EXPENSES for 2016–2017 *Comprehensive fee:* $40,810 includes full-time tuition ($28,800), mandatory fees ($1250), and room and board ($10,760). *College room only:* $5300. Full-time tuition and fees vary according to class time, course load, location, and program. Room and board charges vary according to board plan and housing facility. *Part-time tuition:* $575 per credit hour. Part-time tuition and fees vary according to class time, course load, location, and program.

FRESHMAN FINANCIAL AID (Fall 2016, est.) 813 applied for aid; of those 76% were deemed to have need. 100% of freshmen with need received aid; of those 30% had need fully met. *Average percent of need met:* 81% (excluding resources awarded to replace EFC). *Average financial aid package:* $26,332 (excluding resources awarded to replace EFC). 22% of all full-time freshmen had no need and received non-need-based gift aid.

UNDERGRADUATE FINANCIAL AID (Fall 2016, est.) 3,148 applied for aid; of those 78% were deemed to have need. 100% of undergraduates with need received aid; of those 26% had need fully met. *Average percent of need met:* 81% (excluding resources awarded to replace EFC). *Average financial aid package:* $22,874 (excluding resources awarded to replace EFC). 16% of all full-time undergraduates had no need and received non-need-based gift aid.

GIFT AID (NEED-BASED) *Total amount:* $52,307,200 (15% federal, 14% state, 69% institutional, 2% external sources). *Receiving aid:* Freshmen: 53% (472); all full-time undergraduates: 54% (2,005). *Average award:* Freshmen: $7430; Undergraduates: $6882. *Scholarships, grants, and awards:* Federal Pell, FSEOG, state, private, college/university gift aid from institutional funds.

GIFT AID (NON-NEED-BASED) *Total amount:* $10,973,143 (98% institutional, 2% external sources). *Receiving aid:* Freshmen: 68% (601). Undergraduates: 63% (2,344). *Average award:* Freshmen: $17,335. Undergraduates: $16,442. *Scholarships, grants, and awards by category: Academic interests/achievement:* 2,865 awards ($35,309,613 total): general academic interests/achievements. *Creative arts/performance:* 38 awards ($10,200 total): art/fine arts, creative writing, journalism/publications, music, theater/drama. *Special achievements/activities:* 184 awards ($317,622 total): cheerleading/drum major, leadership, religious involvement. *Special characteristics:* 901 awards ($2,421,792 total): children of faculty/staff, international students, local/state students, out-of-state students, siblings of current students, veterans. *Tuition waivers:* Full or partial for employees or children of employees.

LOANS *Student loans:* $28,288,131 (91% need-based, 9% non-need-based). 73% of past graduating class borrowed through all loan programs. *Average indebtedness per student:* $26,242. *Average need-based loan:* Freshmen: $3230. Undergraduates: $4249. *Parent loans:* $8,025,667 (42% need-based, 58% non-need-based). *Programs:* Federal Direct (Subsidized and Unsubsidized Stafford, PLUS), Perkins, state.

WORK-STUDY *Federal work-study:* Total amount: $337,225; 253 jobs averaging $1353. *State or other work-study/employment:* Part-time jobs available.

ATHLETIC AWARDS Total amount: $4,428,518 (19% need-based, 81% non-need-based).

APPLYING FOR FINANCIAL AID *Required financial aid form:* FAFSA. *Financial aid deadline (priority):* 2/15. *Notification date:* Continuous. Students must reply within 2 weeks of notification.

CONTACT Merry M Taylor, Financial Aid Office, Campbell University, PO Box 36, Buies Creek, NC 27506, 910-893-1310 or toll-free 800-334-4111. *Fax:* 910-814-5788. *E-mail:* taylorm@campbell.edu. *Website:* http://www.campbell.edu/.

CANISIUS COLLEGE
Buffalo, NY

Tuition & fees: $36,454	Average undergraduate aid package: $30,597

ABOUT THE INSTITUTION Independent Roman Catholic (Jesuit), coed. **Awards:** certificates, associate, bachelor's, and master's degrees. 112 undergraduate majors. **Total enrollment:** 3,734. Undergraduates: 2,595. Freshmen: 600. Federal methodology is used as a basis for awarding need-based institutional aid.

UNDERGRADUATE EXPENSES for 2017–2018 Application fee: $40. **Comprehensive fee:** $49,672 includes full-time tuition ($34,966), mandatory fees ($1488), and room and board ($13,218). **College room only:** $7764. Room and board charges vary according to board plan and housing facility. **Part-time tuition:** $999 per credit hour.

FRESHMAN FINANCIAL AID (Fall 2016, est.) 566 applied for aid; of those 90% were deemed to have need. 100% of freshmen with need received aid; of those 25% had need fully met. **Average percent of need met:** 86% (excluding resources awarded to replace EFC). **Average financial aid package:** $33,160 (excluding resources awarded to replace EFC). 14% of all full-time freshmen had no need and received non-need-based gift aid.

UNDERGRADUATE FINANCIAL AID (Fall 2016, est.) 2,072 applied for aid; of those 91% were deemed to have need. 100% of undergraduates with need received aid; of those 23% had need fully met. **Average percent of need met:** 80% (excluding resources awarded to replace EFC). **Average financial aid package:** $30,597 (excluding resources awarded to replace EFC). 20% of all full-time undergraduates had no need and received non-need-based gift aid.

GIFT AID (NEED-BASED) Total amount: $43,507,121 (9% federal, 8% state, 82% institutional, 1% external sources). **Receiving aid:** Freshmen: 85% (511); all full-time undergraduates: 76% (1,880). **Average award:** Freshmen: $26,387; Undergraduates: $23,879. **Scholarships, grants, and awards:** Federal Pell, FSEOG, state, private, college/university gift aid from institutional funds.

GIFT AID (NON-NEED-BASED) Total amount: $4,709,990 (1% state, 98% institutional, 1% external sources). **Receiving aid:** Freshmen: 22% (135). Undergraduates: 18% (438). **Average award:** Freshmen: $20,100. Undergraduates: $17,387. **Scholarships, grants, and awards by category:** Academic interests/achievement: 1,871 awards ($26,470,567 total): general academic interests/achievements. Creative arts/performance: 55 awards ($105,000 total): art/fine arts, music. Special characteristics: 398 awards ($3,386,002 total): children and siblings of alumni, children of educators, children of faculty/staff, international students, religious affiliation, veterans. **Tuition waivers:** Full or partial for employees or children of employees. **ROTC:** Army.

LOANS Student loans: $16,505,493 (70% need-based, 30% non-need-based). 74% of past graduating class borrowed through all loan programs. Average indebtedness per student: $33,973. **Average need-based loan:** Freshmen: $4365. Undergraduates: $4789. **Parent loans:** $3,524,707 (42% need-based, 58% non-need-based). **Programs:** Federal Direct (Subsidized and Unsubsidized Stafford, PLUS), Perkins.

WORK-STUDY Federal work-study: Total amount: $1,184,253; 379 jobs averaging $1793. **State or other work-study/employment:** Total amount: $44,331 (94% need-based, 6% non-need-based). Part-time jobs available.

ATHLETIC AWARDS Total amount: $1,877,113 (44% need-based, 56% non-need-based).

APPLYING FOR FINANCIAL AID Required financial aid forms: FAFSA, state aid form. **Financial aid deadline (priority):** 2/15. **Notification date:** Continuous beginning 3/1. Students must reply by 5/1.

CONTACT Ms. Mary Koehneke, Associate Director of Student Records and Financial Services, Canisius College, 2001 Main Street, Buffalo, NY 14208-1098, 716-888-2600 or toll-free 800-843-1517. *Fax:* 716-888-2377. *E-mail:* mkoehnek@canisius.edu. *Website:* http://www.canisius.edu/.

CAPELLA UNIVERSITY
Minneapolis, MN

CONTACT University Services, Capella University, 222 South Ninth Street, Minneapolis, MN 55402, 888-227-3552 or toll-free 866-283-7921. *Website:* http://www.capella.edu/.

CAPITAL UNIVERSITY
Columbus, OH

Tuition & fees: $34,600	Average undergraduate aid package: $27,527

ABOUT THE INSTITUTION Independent Evangelical Lutheran Church in America, coed. **Awards:** certificates, bachelor's, master's, and doctoral degrees. 60 undergraduate majors. **Total enrollment:** 3,367. Undergraduates: 2,718. Freshmen: 613. Federal methodology is used as a basis for awarding need-based institutional aid.

UNDERGRADUATE EXPENSES for 2017–2018 Application fee: $25. **Comprehensive fee:** $44,778 includes full-time tuition ($34,280), mandatory fees ($320), and room and board ($10,178). Full-time tuition and fees vary according to course load. Room and board charges vary according to board plan and housing facility. **Part-time tuition:** $1144 per credit hour. Part-time tuition and fees vary according to course load.

FRESHMAN FINANCIAL AID (Fall 2015) 637 applied for aid; of those 92% were deemed to have need. 100% of freshmen with need received aid; of those 30% had need fully met. **Average percent of need met:** 86% (excluding resources awarded to replace EFC). **Average financial aid package:** $29,723 (excluding resources awarded to replace EFC). 11% of all full-time freshmen had no need and received non-need-based gift aid.

UNDERGRADUATE FINANCIAL AID (Fall 2015) 2,175 applied for aid; of those 93% were deemed to have need. 100% of undergraduates with need received aid; of those 27% had need fully met. **Average percent of need met:** 81% (excluding resources awarded to replace EFC). **Average financial aid package:** $27,527 (excluding resources awarded to replace EFC). 17% of all full-time undergraduates had no need and received non-need-based gift aid.

GIFT AID (NEED-BASED) Total amount: $50,926,276 (7% federal, 3% state, 90% institutional). **Receiving aid:** Freshmen: 86% (580); all full-time undergraduates: 78% (1,934). **Average award:** Freshmen: $24,756; Undergraduates: $22,547. **Scholarships, grants, and awards:** Federal Pell, FSEOG, state, private, college/university gift aid from institutional funds.

GIFT AID (NON-NEED-BASED) Total amount: $1,629,832 (3% institutional, 97% external sources). **Receiving aid:** Freshmen: 86% (579). Undergraduates: 76% (1,888). **Average award:** Freshmen: $21,467. Undergraduates: $19,223. **Scholarships, grants, and awards by category:** Academic interests/achievement: general academic interests/achievements. Creative arts/performance: music, performing arts. Special achievements/activities: hobbies/interests, leadership, religious involvement. Special characteristics: children and siblings of alumni, children of faculty/staff, ethnic background, international students, members of minority groups, out-of-state students, relatives of clergy, religious affiliation, siblings of current students. **Tuition waivers:** Full or partial for employees or children of employees, senior citizens. **ROTC:** Army, Air Force cooperative.

LOANS Student loans: $19,495,869 (40% need-based, 60% non-need-based). 80% of past graduating class borrowed through all loan programs. Average indebtedness per student: $32,496. **Average need-based loan:** Freshmen: $3973. Undergraduates: $4681. **Parent loans:** $6,979,085 (100% non-need-based). **Programs:** Federal Direct (Subsidized and Unsubsidized Stafford, PLUS), Perkins, Federal Nursing, college/university.

WORK-STUDY Federal work-study: jobs available. **State or other work-study/employment:** Part-time jobs available.

APPLYING FOR FINANCIAL AID Required financial aid form: FAFSA. **Financial aid deadline (priority):** 3/1. **Notification date:** Continuous beginning 12/15. Students must reply by 3/1.

CONTACT Ms. Susan Kannenwischer, Director, Office of Financial Aid, Capital University, 1 College and Main Street, Columbus, OH 43209-2394, 614-236-6511 or toll-free 866-544-6175. *Fax:* 614-236-6926. *E-mail:* finaid@capital.edu. *Website:* http://www.capital.edu/.

CAPITOL TECHNOLOGY UNIVERSITY
Laurel, MD

CONTACT Suzanne Thompson, Director of Financial Aid, Capitol Technology University, 11301 Springfield Road, Laurel, MD 20708-9759, 301-369-2800 Ext. 3037 or toll-free 800-950-1992. *Fax:* 301-369-2328. *E-mail:* sthompson@capitol-college.edu.
Website: http://www.captechu.edu/.

CARDINAL STRITCH UNIVERSITY
Milwaukee, WI

Tuition & fees: $28,212	Average undergraduate aid package: $20,277

ABOUT THE INSTITUTION Independent Roman Catholic, coed. **Awards:** certificates, associate, bachelor's, master's, and doctoral degrees. 40 undergraduate majors. **Total enrollment:** 2,464. Undergraduates: 1,534. Freshmen: 155. Both federal and institutional methodology are used as a basis for awarding need-based institutional aid.

UNDERGRADUATE EXPENSES for 2016–2017 Comprehensive fee: $36,152 includes full-time tuition ($28,212) and room and board ($7940). Full-time tuition and fees vary according to degree level, program, and reciprocity agreements. Room and board charges vary according to board plan and housing facility. **Part-time tuition:** $880 per credit. Part-time tuition and fees vary according to course load, degree level, program, and reciprocity agreements.

FRESHMAN FINANCIAL AID (Fall 2016, est.) 109 applied for aid; of those 95% were deemed to have need. 100% of freshmen with need received aid; of those 12% had need fully met. **Average percent of need met:** 81% (excluding resources awarded to replace EFC). **Average financial aid package:** $26,451 (excluding resources awarded to replace EFC). 35% of all full-time freshmen had no need and received non-need-based gift aid.

UNDERGRADUATE FINANCIAL AID (Fall 2016, est.) 882 applied for aid; of those 85% were deemed to have need. 100% of undergraduates with need received aid; of those 12% had need fully met. **Average percent of need met:** 67% (excluding resources awarded to replace EFC). **Average financial aid package:** $20,277 (excluding resources awarded to replace EFC). 21% of all full-time undergraduates had no need and received non-need-based gift aid.

GIFT AID (NEED-BASED) Total amount: $12,088,832 (21% federal, 10% state, 66% institutional, 3% external sources). **Receiving aid:** Freshmen: 63% (104); all full-time undergraduates: 65% (709). **Average award:** Freshmen: $22,013; Undergraduates: $16,610. **Scholarships, grants, and awards:** Federal Pell, FSEOG, state, private, college/university gift aid from institutional funds.

GIFT AID (NON-NEED-BASED) Total amount: $4,663,087 (3% federal, 94% institutional, 3% external sources). **Receiving aid:** Freshmen: 7% (11). Undergraduates: 5% (58). **Average award:** Freshmen: $22,695. Undergraduates: $17,945. **Scholarships, grants, and awards by category:** Academic interests/achievement: 783 awards ($8,027,300 total): general academic interests/achievements. Creative arts/performance: 37 awards ($65,450 total): art/fine arts, music, theater/drama. Special characteristics: 269 awards ($674,812 total): children and siblings of alumni, children of current students, children of faculty/staff, international students, religious affiliation, siblings of current students, spouses of current students. **Tuition waivers:** Full or partial for employees or children of employees.

LOANS Student loans: $8,561,482 (83% need-based, 17% non-need-based). 91% of past graduating class borrowed through all loan programs. *Average indebtedness per student:* $27,997. *Average need-based loan:* Freshmen: $3317. Undergraduates: $4055. **Parent loans:** $735,088 (61% need-based, 39% non-need-based). **Programs:** Federal Direct (Subsidized and Unsubsidized Stafford, PLUS), Perkins, state.

WORK-STUDY Federal work-study: Total amount: $814,053; 380 jobs averaging $2168. **State or other work-study/employment:** Total amount: $179,852 (60% need-based, 40% non-need-based). Part-time jobs available.

ATHLETIC AWARDS Total amount: $987,768 (43% need-based, 57% non-need-based).

APPLYING FOR FINANCIAL AID Required financial aid forms: FAFSA, institution's own form. **Financial aid deadline:** Continuous. **Notification date:** Continuous beginning 2/24. Students must reply within 2 weeks of notification.

CONTACT Financial Aid Office, Cardinal Stritch University, 6801 North Yates Road, Milwaukee, WI 53217-3985, 414-410-4048 or toll-free 800-347-8822 Ext. 4040. *E-mail:* finaid@stritch.edu.
Website: http://www.stritch.edu/.

CAREERS UNLIMITED
Orem, UT

CONTACT Financial Aid Office, Careers Unlimited, 1176 South 1480 West, Orem, UT 84058, 801-426-8234.
Website: http://www.ucdh.edu/.

CARIBBEAN UNIVERSITY
Bayamón, PR

CONTACT Financial Aid Office, Caribbean University, Box 493, Bayamón, PR 00960-0493, 787-780-0070.
Website: http://www.caribbean.edu/.

CARIBBEAN UNIVERSITY–CAROLINA
Carolina, PR

CONTACT Financial Aid Office, Caribbean University–Carolina, Calle Ignacio Arzuaga #208, Carolina, PR 00985, 787-769-0007.
Website: http://www.caribbean.edu/.

CARIBBEAN UNIVERSITY–PONCE
Ponce, PR

CONTACT Financial Aid Office, Caribbean University–Ponce, Ave. Ednita Nazario #1015, Ponce, PR 00716-7733, 787-840-2955.
Website: http://www.caribbean.edu/.

CARIBBEAN UNIVERSITY–VEGA BAJA
Vega Baja, PR

CONTACT Financial Aid Office, Caribbean University–Vega Baja, Carr 671 K.M. 5, Sector El Criollo, Bo. Algarrobo, Vega Baja, PR 00964, 787-858-3668.
Website: http://www.caribbean.edu/.

CARLETON COLLEGE
Northfield, MN

Tuition & fees: $50,874	Average undergraduate aid package: $45,763

ABOUT THE INSTITUTION Independent, coed. **Awards:** bachelor's degrees. 39 undergraduate majors. **Total enrollment:** 2,105. Undergraduates: 2,105. Both federal and institutional methodology are used as a basis for awarding need-based institutional aid.

UNDERGRADUATE EXPENSES for 2016–2017 Application fee: $30. **Comprehensive fee:** $64,071 includes full-time tuition ($50,580), mandatory fees ($294), and room and board ($13,197). **College room only:** $6864. Room and board charges vary according to board plan.

FRESHMAN FINANCIAL AID (Fall 2015) 438 applied for aid; of those 71% were deemed to have need. 100% of freshmen with need received aid; of those 100% had need fully met. **Average percent of need met:** 100% (excluding resources awarded to replace EFC). **Average financial aid package:** $47,719 (excluding

resources awarded to replace EFC). 3% of all full-time freshmen had no need and received non-need-based gift aid.

UNDERGRADUATE FINANCIAL AID (Fall 2015) 1,757 applied for aid; of those 65% were deemed to have need. 100% of undergraduates with need received aid; of those 100% had need fully met. *Average percent of need met:* 100% (excluding resources awarded to replace EFC). *Average financial aid package:* $45,763 (excluding resources awarded to replace EFC). 5% of all full-time undergraduates had no need and received non-need-based gift aid.

GIFT AID (NEED-BASED) *Total amount:* $38,756,171 (3% federal, 1% state, 92% institutional, 4% external sources). *Receiving aid:* Freshmen: 55% (312); all full-time undergraduates: 56% (1,147). *Average award:* Freshmen: $42,019; Undergraduates: $38,382. *Scholarships, grants, and awards:* Federal Pell, FSEOG, state, private, college/university gift aid from institutional funds.

GIFT AID (NON-NEED-BASED) *Total amount:* $1,349,857 (29% institutional, 71% external sources). *Receiving aid:* Freshmen: 8% (44). Undergraduates: 9% (183). *Average award:* Freshmen: $1906. Undergraduates: $4584. *Scholarships, grants, and awards by category:* Academic interests/achievement: 236 awards ($389,695 total): general academic interests/achievements. *Creative arts/performance:* 9 awards ($1008 total): music. *Tuition waivers:* Full or partial for employees or children of employees.

LOANS *Student loans:* $5,871,981 (96% need-based, 4% non-need-based). 41% of past graduating class borrowed through all loan programs. *Average indebtedness per student:* $20,063. *Average need-based loan:* Freshmen: $4089. Undergraduates: $5201. *Parent loans:* $944,183 (88% need-based, 12% non-need-based). *Programs:* Federal Direct (Subsidized and Unsubsidized Stafford, PLUS), Perkins, state, college/university.

WORK-STUDY *Federal work-study:* 377 jobs averaging $2556. *State or other work-study/employment:* Total amount: $3,358,286 (57% need-based, 43% non-need-based). 1,327 part-time jobs averaging $2530.

APPLYING FOR FINANCIAL AID *Required financial aid forms:* FAFSA, CSS Financial Aid PROFILE, noncustodial (divorced/separated) parent's statement. *Financial aid deadline:* 1/15. *Notification date:* 3/31. Students must reply by 5/1 or within 2 weeks of notification.

CONTACT Mr. Rodney M. Oto, Director of Student Financial Services, Carleton College, One North College Street, Northfield, MN 55057-4001, 507-222-4138 or toll-free 800-995-2275. *Fax:* 507-222-4269.

Website: http://www.carleton.edu/.

CARLOS ALBIZU UNIVERSITY
San Juan, PR

Tuition & fees: N/R	Average undergraduate aid package: $3958

ABOUT THE INSTITUTION Independent, coed. 3 undergraduate majors. Federal methodology is used as a basis for awarding need-based institutional aid.

FRESHMAN FINANCIAL AID (Fall 2016, est.) 13 applied for aid; of those 100% were deemed to have need. 100% of freshmen with need received aid. *Average percent of need met:* 100% (excluding resources awarded to replace EFC). *Average financial aid package:* $1166 (excluding resources awarded to replace EFC).

UNDERGRADUATE FINANCIAL AID (Fall 2016, est.) 147 applied for aid; of those 100% were deemed to have need. 100% of undergraduates with need received aid. *Average percent of need met:* 100% (excluding resources awarded to replace EFC). *Average financial aid package:* $3958 (excluding resources awarded to replace EFC).

GIFT AID (NEED-BASED) *Total amount:* $641,964 (100% federal). *Receiving aid:* Freshmen: 100% (13); all full-time undergraduates: 100% (147). *Average award:* Freshmen: $3209; Undergraduates: $3235. *Scholarships, grants, and awards:* Federal Pell, FSEOG, state, college/university gift aid from institutional funds.

GIFT AID (NON-NEED-BASED) *Scholarships, grants, and awards by category:* Academic interests/achievement: social sciences.

LOANS *Student loans:* $243,139 (100% need-based). *Average need-based loan:* Freshmen: $3166. Undergraduates: $3500. *Programs:* Federal Direct (Subsidized and Unsubsidized Stafford, PLUS).

WORK-STUDY *Federal work-study:* Total amount: $7040; 1 job averaging $1040.

APPLYING FOR FINANCIAL AID *Notification date:* Continuous.

CONTACT Mrs. Doris J. Quero, Director of Financial Aid, Carlos Albizu University, PO Box 9023711, San Juan, PR 00901, 787-725-6500 Ext. 1529. *Fax:* 787-721-4008. *E-mail:* dquero@albizu.edu.

Website: http://www.albizu.edu/.

CARLOS ALBIZU UNIVERSITY, MIAMI CAMPUS
Miami, FL

Tuition & fees: $12,384	Average undergraduate aid package: $7837

ABOUT THE INSTITUTION Independent, coed. *Awards:* certificates, diplomas, bachelor's, master's, and doctoral degrees. 6 undergraduate majors. *Total enrollment:* 1,046. Undergraduates: 356. Freshmen: 8. Federal methodology is used as a basis for awarding need-based institutional aid.

UNDERGRADUATE EXPENSES for 2016–2017 *Application fee:* $25. *Tuition:* full-time $11,628; part-time $323 per credit. *Required fees:* full-time $756; $252 per term. Full-time tuition and fees vary according to course load, degree level, and program. Part-time tuition and fees vary according to course load, degree level, and program.

FRESHMAN FINANCIAL AID (Fall 2015) 5 applied for aid; of those 100% were deemed to have need. 100% of freshmen with need received aid. *Average percent of need met:* 65% (excluding resources awarded to replace EFC). *Average financial aid package:* $7837 (excluding resources awarded to replace EFC).

UNDERGRADUATE FINANCIAL AID (Fall 2015) 137 applied for aid; of those 100% were deemed to have need. 100% of undergraduates with need received aid. *Average percent of need met:* 52% (excluding resources awarded to replace EFC). *Average financial aid package:* $7837 (excluding resources awarded to replace EFC).

GIFT AID (NEED-BASED) *Total amount:* $1,104,442 (69% federal, 28% state, 3% institutional). *Receiving aid:* Freshmen: 83% (5); all full-time undergraduates: 75% (128). *Average award:* Freshmen: $4720; Undergraduates: $4720. *Scholarships, grants, and awards:* Federal Pell, FSEOG, state, college/university gift aid from institutional funds.

GIFT AID (NON-NEED-BASED) *Scholarships, grants, and awards by category:* Special characteristics: children of faculty/staff. *Tuition waivers:* Full or partial for employees or children of employees.

LOANS *Student loans:* $2,056,513 (32% need-based, 68% non-need-based). *Average need-based loan:* Freshmen: $4250. Undergraduates: $4250. *Parent loans:* $36,354 (100% need-based). *Programs:* Federal Direct (Subsidized and Unsubsidized Stafford, PLUS), college/university.

WORK-STUDY *Federal work-study:* jobs available.

APPLYING FOR FINANCIAL AID *Required financial aid forms:* FAFSA, institution's own form. *Financial aid deadline (priority):* 6/1. *Notification date:* Continuous.

CONTACT Violeta Velasquez, Financial Aid Officer, Carlos Albizu University, Miami Campus, 2173 Northwest 99th Avenue, Miami, FL 33172, 305-593-1223 Ext. 3179 or toll-free 888-GO-TO-CAU (in-state), 800-GO-TO-CAU (out-of-state). *Fax:* 305-593-8902. *E-mail:* smenendez@albizu.edu.

Website: http://www.albizu.edu/.

CARLOW UNIVERSITY
Pittsburgh, PA

Tuition & fees: $27,764	Average undergraduate aid package: $20,295

ABOUT THE INSTITUTION Independent Roman Catholic, coed, primarily women. *Awards:* certificates, bachelor's, master's, and doctoral degrees. 28 undergraduate majors. *Total enrollment:* 2,255. Undergraduates: 1,408. Freshmen: 219. Both federal and institutional methodology are used as a basis for awarding need-based institutional aid.

UNDERGRADUATE EXPENSES for 2016–2017 *Comprehensive fee:* $38,548 includes full-time tuition ($27,136), mandatory fees ($628), and room and board ($10,784). **College room only:** $5514. Full-time tuition and fees vary according to course load, program, and reciprocity agreements. Room and board charges vary according to board plan. **Part-time tuition:** $863 per credit hour. **Part-time fees:** $13 per credit hour. Part-time tuition and fees vary according to course load, program, and reciprocity agreements.

FRESHMAN FINANCIAL AID (Fall 2015) 225 applied for aid; of those 95% were deemed to have need. 100% of freshmen with need received aid. **Average financial aid package:** $25,130 (excluding resources awarded to replace EFC).

UNDERGRADUATE FINANCIAL AID (Fall 2015) 1,065 applied for aid; of those 95% were deemed to have need. 100% of undergraduates with need received aid. **Average financial aid package:** $20,295 (excluding resources awarded to replace EFC).

GIFT AID (NEED-BASED) Total amount: $7,586,137 (41% federal, 32% state, 10% institutional, 17% external sources). **Receiving aid:** Freshmen: 75% (174); all full-time undergraduates: 73% (824). **Average award:** Freshmen: $3909; Undergraduates: $3739. **Scholarships, grants, and awards:** Federal Pell, FSEOG, state, private, college/university gift aid from institutional funds, Federal Nursing.

GIFT AID (NON-NEED-BASED) Total amount: $1,291,692 (1% federal, 3% state, 62% institutional, 34% external sources). **Receiving aid:** Freshmen: 84% (196). Undergraduates: 69% (772). **Scholarships, grants, and awards by category:** *Academic interests/achievement:* biological sciences, business, communication, computer science, education, English, general academic interests/achievements, humanities, mathematics, social sciences. *Special achievements/activities:* leadership, religious involvement. *Special characteristics:* children and siblings of alumni, children of educators, children of faculty/staff, international students, religious affiliation, siblings of current students. **Tuition waivers:** Full or partial for children of alumni, employees or children of employees, adult students. **ROTC:** Army cooperative, Naval cooperative, Air Force cooperative.

LOANS Student loans: $13,014,263 (81% need-based, 19% non-need-based). **Average need-based loan:** Freshmen: $3101. Undergraduates: $3442. **Parent loans:** $2,164,430 (55% need-based, 45% non-need-based). **Programs:** Federal Direct (Subsidized and Unsubsidized Stafford, PLUS), Perkins, Federal Nursing.

WORK-STUDY Federal work-study: jobs available.

ATHLETIC AWARDS Total amount: $616,750 (85% need-based, 15% non-need-based).

APPLYING FOR FINANCIAL AID Required financial aid forms: FAFSA, state aid form. **Financial aid deadline:** 5/1 (priority: 3/15). **Notification date:** Continuous beginning 12/1.

CONTACT Office of Financial Aid, Carlow University, 3333 Fifth Avenue, Pittsburgh, PA 15213-3165, 412-578-6171 or toll-free 800-333-CARLOW. *E-mail:* finaid@carlow.edu.

Website: http://www.carlow.edu/.

CARNEGIE MELLON UNIVERSITY
Pittsburgh, PA

Tuition & fees: N/R	Average undergraduate aid package: $40,347

ABOUT THE INSTITUTION Independent, coed. **Awards:** certificates, bachelor's, master's, and doctoral degrees. 75 undergraduate majors. **Total enrollment:** 13,961. Undergraduates: 6,673. Freshmen: 1,552. Both federal and institutional methodology are used as a basis for awarding need-based institutional aid.

UNDERGRADUATE EXPENSES for 2017–2018 Application fee: $75. **Tuition:** part-time $733 per unit. Room and board charges vary according to board plan and housing facility.

FRESHMAN FINANCIAL AID (Fall 2016, est.) 1,028 applied for aid; of those 74% were deemed to have need. 99% of freshmen with need received aid; of those 32% had need fully met. **Average percent of need met:** 86% (excluding resources awarded to replace EFC). **Average financial aid package:** $41,636 (excluding resources awarded to replace EFC). 2% of all full-time freshmen had no need and received non-need-based gift aid.

UNDERGRADUATE FINANCIAL AID (Fall 2016, est.) 3,243 applied for aid; of those 84% were deemed to have need. 99% of undergraduates with need received aid; of those 27% had need fully met. **Average percent of need met:** 85% (excluding resources awarded to replace EFC). **Average financial aid package:** $40,347 (excluding resources awarded to replace EFC). 4% of all full-time undergraduates had no need and received non-need-based gift aid.

GIFT AID (NEED-BASED) Total amount: $89,384,837 (6% federal, 1% state, 91% institutional, 2% external sources). **Receiving aid:** Freshmen: 46% (709); all full-time undergraduates: 40% (2,604). **Average award:** Freshmen: $39,061; Undergraduates: $34,632. **Scholarships, grants, and awards:** Federal Pell, FSEOG, state, private, college/university gift aid from institutional funds.

GIFT AID (NON-NEED-BASED) Total amount: $5,890,352 (70% institutional, 30% external sources). **Receiving aid:** Freshmen: 5% (71). Undergraduates: 4% (251). **Average award:** Freshmen: $12,312. Undergraduates: $11,763. **Scholarships, grants, and awards by category:** *Academic interests/achievement:* general academic interests/achievements. *Creative arts/performance:* general creative arts/performance. *Special achievements/activities:* general special achievements/activities. *Special characteristics:* general special characteristics. **Tuition waivers:** Full or partial for employees or children of employees. **ROTC:** Army cooperative, Naval, Air Force cooperative.

LOANS Student loans: $22,872,106 (69% need-based, 31% non-need-based). 51% of past graduating class borrowed through all loan programs. **Average indebtedness per student:** $30,866. **Average need-based loan:** Freshmen: $2841. Undergraduates: $5764. **Parent loans:** $7,452,826 (20% need-based, 80% non-need-based). **Programs:** Federal Direct (Subsidized and Unsubsidized Stafford, PLUS), Perkins.

WORK-STUDY Federal work-study: Total amount: $5,335,448; jobs available. **State or other work-study/employment:** Part-time jobs available.

APPLYING FOR FINANCIAL AID Required financial aid forms: FAFSA, CSS Financial Aid PROFILE, noncustodial (divorced/separated) parent's statement, federal income tax form(s). **Financial aid deadline (priority):** 2/15. **Notification date:** 4/15.

CONTACT Brian Hill, Director of Student Financial Services, Carnegie Mellon University, 5000 Forbes Avenue, Pittsburgh, PA 15213-3890, 412-268-8186. *Fax:* 412-268-8084. *E-mail:* thehub@andrew.cmu.edu.

Website: http://www.cmu.edu/.

CAROLINA CHRISTIAN COLLEGE
Winston-Salem, NC

Tuition & fees: $12,200	Average undergraduate aid package: $9500

ABOUT THE INSTITUTION Independent nondenominational, coed. **Awards:** associate, bachelor's, and master's degrees. 1 undergraduate major. **Total enrollment:** 44. Undergraduates: 36. Freshmen: 2. Federal methodology is used as a basis for awarding need-based institutional aid.

UNDERGRADUATE EXPENSES for 2017–2018 Application fee: $50. **One-time required fee:** $75. **Tuition:** full-time $11,000; part-time $2750 per term. **Required fees:** full-time $1200; $600 per term.

UNDERGRADUATE FINANCIAL AID (Fall 2016, est.) 15 applied for aid; of those 100% were deemed to have need. 100% of undergraduates with need received aid; of those 73% had need fully met. **Average percent of need met:** 90% (excluding resources awarded to replace EFC). **Average financial aid package:** $9500 (excluding resources awarded to replace EFC).

GIFT AID (NEED-BASED) Total amount: $86,640 (100% federal). **Receiving aid:** All full-time undergraduates: 100% (15). **Average award:** Undergraduates: $5775. **Scholarships, grants, and awards:** Federal Pell, FSEOG.

GIFT AID (NON-NEED-BASED) Scholarships, grants, and awards by category: *Academic interests/achievement:* 2 awards ($7000 total): religion/biblical studies. **Tuition waivers:** Full or partial for employees or children of employees.

LOANS Student loans: $142,500 (37% need-based, 63% non-need-based). 90% of past graduating class borrowed through all loan programs. **Average indebtedness per student:** $9500. **Average need-based loan:** Undergraduates: $2000. **Programs:** Federal Direct (Subsidized and Unsubsidized Stafford).

APPLYING FOR FINANCIAL AID Required financial aid forms: FAFSA, institution's own form. **Financial aid deadline:** Continuous. **Notification date:** Continuous.

CONTACT LaTanya V. Tyson, President, Carolina Christian College, 4209 Indiana Avenue, Winston-Salem, NC 27105, 336-744-0900 Ext. 204. *E-mail:* latanya@carolina.edu.

Website: http://www.carolina.edu/.

CAROLINA COLLEGE OF BIBLICAL STUDIES
Fayetteville, NC

CONTACT Financial Aid Office, Carolina College of Biblical Studies, 817 South McPherson Church Road, Fayetteville, NC 28303, 910-323-5614. *Website:* http://carolinabiblecollege.org/.

CARROLL COLLEGE
Helena, MT

Tuition & fees: $34,480	Average undergraduate aid package: $22,667

ABOUT THE INSTITUTION Independent Roman Catholic, coed. *Awards:* associate and bachelor's degrees. 50 undergraduate majors. *Total enrollment:* 1,373. Undergraduates: 1,373. Freshmen: 339. Federal methodology is used as a basis for awarding need-based institutional aid.
UNDERGRADUATE EXPENSES for 2017–2018 *Application fee:* $35. *Comprehensive fee:* $44,304 includes full-time tuition ($33,500), mandatory fees ($980), and room and board ($9824). Full-time tuition and fees vary according to program. Room and board charges vary according to board plan. *Part-time tuition:* $1395 per credit hour. Part-time tuition and fees vary according to program.
FRESHMAN FINANCIAL AID (Fall 2015) 329 applied for aid; of those 82% were deemed to have need. 100% of freshmen with need received aid; of those 25% had need fully met. *Average percent of need met:* 79% (excluding resources awarded to replace EFC). *Average financial aid package:* $23,966 (excluding resources awarded to replace EFC). 29% of all full-time freshmen had no need and received non-need-based gift aid.
UNDERGRADUATE FINANCIAL AID (Fall 2015) 1,063 applied for aid; of those 87% were deemed to have need. 100% of undergraduates with need received aid; of those 19% had need fully met. *Average percent of need met:* 75% (excluding resources awarded to replace EFC). *Average financial aid package:* $22,667 (excluding resources awarded to replace EFC). 32% of all full-time undergraduates had no need and received non-need-based gift aid.
GIFT AID (NEED-BASED) *Total amount:* $32,165,921 (59% federal, 38% institutional, 3% external sources). *Receiving aid:* Freshmen: 70% (270); all full-time undergraduates: 65% (916). *Average award:* Freshmen: $19,474; Undergraduates: $17,608. *Scholarships, grants, and awards:* Federal Pell, FSEOG, state, private, college/university gift aid from institutional funds.
GIFT AID (NON-NEED-BASED) *Total amount:* $7,429,176 (8% federal, 84% institutional, 8% external sources). *Receiving aid:* Freshmen: 17% (66). Undergraduates: 12% (169). *Average award:* Freshmen: $14,929. Undergraduates: $12,983. *Scholarships, grants, and awards by category:* Academic interests/achievement: 1,316 awards ($16,259,043 total): general academic interests/achievements. Creative arts/performance: 70 awards ($101,938 total): art/fine arts, creative writing, debating, music, performing arts, theater/drama. Special achievements/activities: 38 awards ($97,515 total): cheerleading/drum major, general special achievements/activities, leadership, religious involvement. Special characteristics: 108 awards ($2,326,182 total): children of faculty/staff, children of union members/company employees, international students, religious affiliation, siblings of current students, spouses of current students, veterans. *Tuition waivers:* Full or partial for employees or children of employees, senior citizens. *ROTC:* Army.
LOANS *Student loans:* $6,832,779 (55% need-based, 45% non-need-based). 66% of past graduating class borrowed through all loan programs. *Average indebtedness per student:* $32,768. *Average need-based loan:* Freshmen: $3041. Undergraduates: $4079. *Parent loans:* $3,370,386 (47% need-based, 53% non-need-based). *Programs:* Federal Direct (Subsidized and Unsubsidized Stafford, PLUS), Perkins, private loans.
WORK-STUDY *Federal work-study:* 209 jobs averaging $1175. *State or other work-study/employment:* Part-time jobs available.
ATHLETIC AWARDS *Total amount:* $2,790,159 (42% need-based, 58% non-need-based).
APPLYING FOR FINANCIAL AID *Required financial aid form:* FAFSA. *Financial aid deadline (priority):* 3/1. *Notification date:* Continuous. Students must reply within 2 weeks of notification.

CONTACT Ms. Janet Riis, Director of Financial Aid, Carroll College, 1601 North Benton Avenue, Helena, MT 59625-0002, 406-447-5423 or toll-free 800-992-3648. *Fax:* 406-447-4533. *E-mail:* jriis@carroll.edu. *Website:* http://www.carroll.edu/.

CARROLL UNIVERSITY
Waukesha, WI

Tuition & fees: $30,388	Average undergraduate aid package: $22,332

ABOUT THE INSTITUTION Independent Presbyterian, coed. 77 undergraduate majors. Federal methodology is used as a basis for awarding need-based institutional aid.
UNDERGRADUATE EXPENSES for 2016–2017 *One-time required fee:* $270. *Comprehensive fee:* $39,652 includes full-time tuition ($29,662), mandatory fees ($726), and room and board ($9264). *College room only:* $4930. Full-time tuition and fees vary according to program. Room and board charges vary according to board plan and housing facility. *Part-time tuition:* $381 per credit hour. Part-time tuition and fees vary according to course load and program.
FRESHMAN FINANCIAL AID (Fall 2016, est.) 606 applied for aid; of those 89% were deemed to have need. 100% of freshmen with need received aid; of those 33% had need fully met. *Average percent of need met:* 88% (excluding resources awarded to replace EFC). *Average financial aid package:* $23,612 (excluding resources awarded to replace EFC). 20% of all full-time freshmen had no need and received non-need-based gift aid.
UNDERGRADUATE FINANCIAL AID (Fall 2016, est.) 2,476 applied for aid; of those 87% were deemed to have need. 100% of undergraduates with need received aid; of those 34% had need fully met. *Average percent of need met:* 86% (excluding resources awarded to replace EFC). *Average financial aid package:* $22,332 (excluding resources awarded to replace EFC). 22% of all full-time undergraduates had no need and received non-need-based gift aid.
GIFT AID (NEED-BASED) *Total amount:* $38,151,126 (8% federal, 6% state, 83% institutional, 3% external sources). *Receiving aid:* Freshmen: 81% (539); all full-time undergraduates: 78% (2,142). *Average award:* Freshmen: $20,001; Undergraduates: $18,021. *Scholarships, grants, and awards:* Federal Pell, FSEOG, state, private, college/university gift aid from institutional funds.
GIFT AID (NON-NEED-BASED) *Total amount:* $8,913,611 (1% federal, 3% state, 94% institutional, 2% external sources). *Receiving aid:* Freshmen: 11% (72). Undergraduates: 12% (333). *Average award:* Freshmen: $16,349. Undergraduates: $14,269. *Scholarships, grants, and awards by category:* Academic interests/achievement: 2,442 awards ($31,913,392 total): biological sciences, business, communication, computer science, education, general academic interests/achievements, health fields, humanities, international studies, mathematics, physical sciences, premedicine, social sciences. Creative arts/performance: 65 awards ($71,625 total): art/fine arts, journalism/publications, music, performing arts, theater/drama. Special achievements/activities: 80 awards ($85,938 total): general special achievements/activities, junior miss, leadership, memberships, religious involvement. Special characteristics: 451 awards ($1,541,916 total): adult students, children and siblings of alumni, children of current students, children of faculty/staff, general special characteristics, international students, siblings of current students, spouses of current students. *Tuition waivers:* Full or partial for employees or children of employees.
LOANS *Student loans:* $19,343,759 (38% need-based, 62% non-need-based). 79% of past graduating class borrowed through all loan programs. *Average indebtedness per student:* $36,161. *Average need-based loan:* Freshmen: $3625. Undergraduates: $4643. *Parent loans:* $3,794,319 (91% need-based, 9% non-need-based). *Programs:* Federal Direct (Subsidized and Unsubsidized Stafford, PLUS), Perkins, state, college/university.
WORK-STUDY *Federal work-study:* Total amount: $745,862; 346 jobs averaging $2247. *State or other work-study/employment:* Total amount: $3,428,747 (100% non-need-based). 1,719 part-time jobs averaging $2286.
APPLYING FOR FINANCIAL AID *Required financial aid form:* FAFSA. *Financial aid deadline:* Continuous. *Notification date:* Continuous beginning 2/15. Students must reply by 5/1 or within 2 weeks of notification.

CONTACT Dawn Scott, Director of Financial Aid, Carroll University, 100 North East Avenue, Waukesha, WI 53186-5593, 262-524-7297 or toll-free 800-CARROLL. *Fax:* 262-951-3037. *E-mail:* dscott@carrollu.edu. *Website:* http://www.carrollu.edu/.

CARSON-NEWMAN UNIVERSITY
Jefferson City, TN

Tuition & fees: $27,400	Average undergraduate aid package: $23,514

ABOUT THE INSTITUTION Independent Southern Baptist, coed. **Awards:** certificates, associate, bachelor's, master's, and doctoral degrees. 76 undergraduate majors. **Total enrollment:** 2,659. Undergraduates: 1,812. Freshmen: 505. Federal methodology is used as a basis for awarding need-based institutional aid.

UNDERGRADUATE EXPENSES for 2017–2018 Comprehensive fee: $36,030 includes full-time tuition ($26,200), mandatory fees ($1200), and room and board ($8630). **College room only:** $4030. Full-time tuition and fees vary according to class time and course load. Room and board charges vary according to board plan, gender, and housing facility. **Part-time tuition:** $1092 per credit hour.

FRESHMAN FINANCIAL AID (Fall 2015) 426 applied for aid; of those 100% were deemed to have need. 100% of freshmen with need received aid; of those 23% had need fully met. **Average percent of need met:** 81% (excluding resources awarded to replace EFC). **Average financial aid package:** $23,773 (excluding resources awarded to replace EFC). 8% of all full-time freshmen had no need and received non-need-based gift aid.

UNDERGRADUATE FINANCIAL AID (Fall 2015) 1,366 applied for aid; of those 100% were deemed to have need. 100% of undergraduates with need received aid; of those 24% had need fully met. **Average percent of need met:** 79% (excluding resources awarded to replace EFC). **Average financial aid package:** $23,514 (excluding resources awarded to replace EFC). 11% of all full-time undergraduates had no need and received non-need-based gift aid.

GIFT AID (NEED-BASED) Total amount: $24,004,635 (14% federal, 20% state, 64% institutional, 2% external sources). **Receiving aid:** Freshmen: 84% (419); all full-time undergraduates: 81% (1,338). **Average award:** Freshmen: $18,638; Undergraduates: $17,873. **Scholarships, grants, and awards:** Federal Pell, FSEOG, state, private, college/university gift aid from institutional funds, Federal Nursing.

GIFT AID (NON-NEED-BASED) Total amount: $3,111,967 (14% state, 81% institutional, 5% external sources). **Receiving aid:** Freshmen: 14% (69). Undergraduates: 16% (258). **Average award:** Freshmen: $11,089. Undergraduates: $10,223. **Scholarships, grants, and awards by category:** Academic interests/achievement: biological sciences, business, education, general academic interests/achievements, home economics, mathematics, military science, religion/biblical studies. Creative arts/performance: art/fine arts, debating, journalism/publications, music. Special achievements/activities: leadership, memberships. Special characteristics: children and siblings of alumni, members of minority groups, relatives of clergy, siblings of current students. **Tuition waivers:** Full or partial for employees or children of employees, senior citizens. **ROTC:** Army.

LOANS Student loans: $8,099,114 (93% need-based, 7% non-need-based). 73% of past graduating class borrowed through all loan programs. **Average indebtedness per student:** $27,418. **Average need-based loan:** Freshmen: $2839. Undergraduates: $3623. **Parent loans:** $2,180,663 (93% need-based, 7% non-need-based). **Programs:** Federal Direct (Subsidized and Unsubsidized Stafford, PLUS), Perkins, state, alternative loans.

WORK-STUDY Federal work-study: 188 jobs averaging $1899. **State or other work-study/employment:** Total amount: $2400 (50% need-based, 50% non-need-based). 5 part-time jobs averaging $1280.

ATHLETIC AWARDS Total amount: $4,366,775 (68% need-based, 32% non-need-based).

APPLYING FOR FINANCIAL AID Required financial aid forms: FAFSA, institution's own form. **Financial aid deadline (priority):** 2/1. **Notification date:** Continuous beginning 2/1. Students must reply by 5/1 or within 2 weeks of notification.

CONTACT Mrs. Danette Seale, Director of Financial Aid, Carson-Newman University, 1646 Russell Avenue, Jefferson City, TN 37760, 865-471-3247 or toll-free 800-678-9061. Fax: 865-471-3502. E-mail: dseale@cn.edu. Website: http://www.cn.edu/.

CARTHAGE COLLEGE
Kenosha, WI

CONTACT Vatistas Vatistas, Director of Financial Aid, Carthage College, 2001 Alford Park Drive, Kenosha, WI 53140, 262-551-6001 or toll-free 800-351-4058. Fax: 262-551-5762. E-mail: vvatistas@carthage.edu. Website: http://www.carthage.edu/.

CARVER COLLEGE
Atlanta, GA

CONTACT Financial Aid Office, Carver College, 3870 Cascade Road SW, Atlanta, GA 30331, 404-527-4520. Website: http://www.carver.edu/.

CASE WESTERN RESERVE UNIVERSITY
Cleveland, OH

Tuition & fees: $46,006	Average undergraduate aid package: $38,928

ABOUT THE INSTITUTION Independent, coed. **Awards:** certificates, bachelor's, master's, and doctoral degrees. 72 undergraduate majors. **Total enrollment:** 11,664. Undergraduates: 5,152. Freshmen: 1,264. Federal methodology is used as a basis for awarding need-based institutional aid.

UNDERGRADUATE EXPENSES for 2016–2017 One-time required fee: $525. **Comprehensive fee:** $60,304 includes full-time tuition ($45,592), mandatory fees ($414), and room and board ($14,298). **College room only:** $8280. Room and board charges vary according to board plan, housing facility, and student level. **Part-time tuition:** $1900 per credit hour. Part-time tuition and fees vary according to course load.

FRESHMAN FINANCIAL AID (Fall 2016, est.) 841 applied for aid; of those 76% were deemed to have need. 100% of freshmen with need received aid; of those 61% had need fully met. **Average percent of need met:** 86% (excluding resources awarded to replace EFC). **Average financial aid package:** $37,695 (excluding resources awarded to replace EFC). 33% of all full-time freshmen had no need and received non-need-based gift aid.

UNDERGRADUATE FINANCIAL AID (Fall 2016, est.) 2,858 applied for aid; of those 86% were deemed to have need. 100% of undergraduates with need received aid; of those 61% had need fully met. **Average percent of need met:** 83% (excluding resources awarded to replace EFC). **Average financial aid package:** $38,928 (excluding resources awarded to replace EFC). 32% of all full-time undergraduates had no need and received non-need-based gift aid.

GIFT AID (NEED-BASED) Total amount: $71,981,045 (6% federal, 1% state, 89% institutional, 4% external sources). **Receiving aid:** Freshmen: 48% (612); all full-time undergraduates: 48% (2,392). **Average award:** Freshmen: $29,620; Undergraduates: $28,156. **Scholarships, grants, and awards:** Federal Pell, FSEOG, state, private, college/university gift aid from institutional funds.

GIFT AID (NON-NEED-BASED) Total amount: $42,368,476 (94% institutional, 6% external sources). **Receiving aid:** Freshmen: 15% (190). Undergraduates: 7% (336). **Average award:** Freshmen: $24,854. Undergraduates: $23,479. **Scholarships, grants, and awards by category:** Academic interests/achievement: 3,630 awards ($77,344,020 total): biological sciences, business, communication, computer science, engineering/technologies, English, foreign languages, general academic interests/achievements, health fields, home economics, humanities, international studies, mathematics, physical sciences, premedicine, religion/biblical studies, social sciences. Creative arts/performance: 48 awards ($1,528,012 total): art/fine arts, creative writing, dance, general creative arts/performance, music, performing arts, theater/drama. Special achievements/activities: 65 awards ($247,166 total): leadership. Special characteristics: 130 awards ($5,424,240 total): children of faculty/staff. **Tuition waivers:** Full or partial for employees or children of employees. **ROTC:** Army, Air Force cooperative.

LOANS Student loans: $22,493,943 (69% need-based, 31% non-need-based). 51% of past graduating class borrowed through all loan programs. Average indebtedness per student: $30,561. **Average need-based loan:** Freshmen: $3273. Undergraduates: $4859. **Parent loans:** $13,326,777 (56% need-based, 44% non-need-based). **Programs:** Federal Direct (Subsidized and Unsubsidized Stafford, PLUS), Perkins, college/university, alternative loans.

WORK-STUDY Federal work-study: Total amount: $3,953,971; 1,504 jobs averaging $2629.

APPLYING FOR FINANCIAL AID Required financial aid forms: FAFSA, institution's own form, CSS Financial Aid PROFILE, noncustodial (divorced/separated) parent's statement. **Financial aid deadline:** 2/1. **Notification date:** Continuous beginning 3/20. Students must reply by 5/1 or within 2 weeks of notification.

CONTACT Mrs. Venus M. Puliafico, Director of University Financial Aid, Case Western Reserve University, 2049 Martin Luther King Jr. Drive, Cleveland, OH 44106-7049, 216-368-4530. *Fax:* 216-368-5054. *E-mail:* vxp4@case.edu. *Website:* http://www.case.edu/.

CASTLETON UNIVERSITY
Castleton, VT

CONTACT Kathleen O'Meara, Director of Financial Aid, Castleton University, Castleton, VT 05735, 802-468-1292 or toll-free 800-639-8521. *Fax:* 802-468-5237. *E-mail:* kathy.omeara@castleton.edu. *Website:* http://www.castleton.edu/.

CATAWBA COLLEGE
Salisbury, NC

Tuition & fees: $29,920	Average undergraduate aid package: $23,873

ABOUT THE INSTITUTION Independent United Church of Christ, coed. **Awards:** bachelor's and master's degrees. 42 undergraduate majors. **Total enrollment:** 1,306. Undergraduates: 1,297. Freshmen: 329. Federal methodology is used as a basis for awarding need-based institutional aid.

UNDERGRADUATE EXPENSES for 2017–2018 Comprehensive fee: $40,408 includes full-time tuition ($29,920) and room and board ($10,488). **College room only:** $6188. Full-time tuition and fees vary according to class time, course load, and degree level. **Part-time tuition:** $785 per credit hour. Part-time tuition and fees vary according to class time, course load, and degree level.

FRESHMAN FINANCIAL AID (Fall 2015) 282 applied for aid; of those 89% were deemed to have need. 100% of freshmen with need received aid; of those 23% had need fully met. **Average percent of need met:** 78% (excluding resources awarded to replace EFC). **Average financial aid package:** $26,992 (excluding resources awarded to replace EFC). 16% of all full-time freshmen had no need and received non-need-based gift aid.

UNDERGRADUATE FINANCIAL AID (Fall 2015) 1,075 applied for aid; of those 92% were deemed to have need. 100% of undergraduates with need received aid; of those 23% had need fully met. **Average percent of need met:** 75% (excluding resources awarded to replace EFC). **Average financial aid package:** $23,873 (excluding resources awarded to replace EFC). 14% of all full-time undergraduates had no need and received non-need-based gift aid.

GIFT AID (NEED-BASED) Total amount: $5,699,645 (42% federal, 49% state, 5% institutional, 4% external sources). **Receiving aid:** Freshmen: 59% (184); all full-time undergraduates: 64% (764). **Average award:** Freshmen: $7157; Undergraduates: $6855. **Scholarships, grants, and awards:** Federal Pell, FSEOG, state, private, college/university gift aid from institutional funds.

GIFT AID (NON-NEED-BASED) Total amount: $14,126,703 (100% institutional). **Receiving aid:** Freshmen: 80% (249). Undergraduates: 71% (848). **Average award:** Freshmen: $17,184. Undergraduates: $14,318. **Scholarships, grants, and awards by category:** Academic interests/achievement: business, education, general academic interests/achievements, physical sciences. Creative arts/performance: music, theater/drama. Special achievements/activities: cheerleading/drum major, general special achievements/activities, leadership. Special characteristics: children of faculty/staff, siblings of current students. **Tuition waivers:** Full or partial for employees or children of employees. **ROTC:** Army cooperative, Air Force cooperative.

LOANS Student loans: $7,529,749 (50% need-based, 50% non-need-based). 77% of past graduating class borrowed through all loan programs. *Average indebtedness per student:* $30,490. **Average need-based loan:** Freshmen: $3177. Undergraduates: $4520. **Parent loans:** $2,568,992 (100% non-need-based). **Programs:** Federal Direct (Subsidized and Unsubsidized Stafford, PLUS), state, college/university, alternative loans.

WORK-STUDY Federal work-study: 111 jobs averaging $1510. **State or other work-study/employment:** Total amount: $219,885 (100% need-based). 153 part-time jobs averaging $1437.

ATHLETIC AWARDS Total amount: $3,244,674 (100% non-need-based).

APPLYING FOR FINANCIAL AID Required financial aid forms: FAFSA, state aid form. **Financial aid deadline (priority):** 3/15. **Notification date:** Continuous beginning 12/15. Students must reply by 5/1 or within 2 weeks of notification.

CONTACT Kelli Hand, Director of Financial Aid, Catawba College, 2300 West Innes Street, Salisbury, NC 28144-2488, 704-637-4416 or toll-free 800-CATAWBA. *Fax:* 704-637-4252. *E-mail:* kmhand@catawba.edu. *Website:* http://www.catawba.edu/.

THE CATHOLIC UNIVERSITY OF AMERICA
Washington, DC

Tuition & fees: $42,536	Average undergraduate aid package: $29,024

ABOUT THE INSTITUTION Independent Roman Catholic Church, coed. **Awards:** certificates, bachelor's, master's, and doctoral degrees. 64 undergraduate majors. **Total enrollment:** 6,060. Undergraduates: 3,238. Freshmen: 723. Federal methodology is used as a basis for awarding need-based institutional aid.

UNDERGRADUATE EXPENSES for 2016–2017 One-time required fee: $425. **Comprehensive fee:** $56,356 includes full-time tuition ($41,800), mandatory fees ($736), and room and board ($13,820). Full-time tuition and fees vary according to program. Room and board charges vary according to board plan and housing facility. **Part-time tuition:** $1655 per credit hour. **Part-time fees:** $420 per year. Part-time tuition and fees vary according to course load and program.

FRESHMAN FINANCIAL AID (Fall 2016, est.) 579 applied for aid; of those 80% were deemed to have need. 100% of freshmen with need received aid; of those 47% had need fully met. **Average percent of need met:** 83% (excluding resources awarded to replace EFC). **Average financial aid package:** $31,783 (excluding resources awarded to replace EFC). 29% of all full-time freshmen had no need and received non-need-based gift aid.

UNDERGRADUATE FINANCIAL AID (Fall 2016, est.) 2,014 applied for aid; of those 85% were deemed to have need. 100% of undergraduates with need received aid; of those 43% had need fully met. **Average percent of need met:** 80% (excluding resources awarded to replace EFC). **Average financial aid package:** $29,024 (excluding resources awarded to replace EFC). 33% of all full-time undergraduates had no need and received non-need-based gift aid.

GIFT AID (NEED-BASED) Total amount: $42,086,497 (5% federal, 94% institutional, 1% external sources). **Receiving aid:** Freshmen: 64% (463); all full-time undergraduates: 54% (1,673). **Average award:** Freshmen: $28,319; Undergraduates: $24,944. **Scholarships, grants, and awards:** Federal Pell, FSEOG, state, private, college/university gift aid from institutional funds.

GIFT AID (NON-NEED-BASED) Total amount: $18,343,824 (99% institutional, 1% external sources). **Average award:** Freshmen: $18,182. Undergraduates: $18,038. **Scholarships, grants, and awards by category:** Academic interests/achievement: general academic interests/achievements. Creative arts/performance: music, theater/drama. Special characteristics: children and siblings of alumni, children of faculty/staff, religious affiliation, siblings of current students, twins, veterans, veterans' children. **Tuition waivers:** Full or partial for children of alumni, employees or children of employees. **ROTC:** Army cooperative, Naval cooperative, Air Force cooperative.

LOANS Student loans: $17,727,017 (86% need-based, 14% non-need-based). 70% of past graduating class borrowed through all loan programs. *Average indebtedness per student:* $46,779. **Average need-based loan:** Freshmen: $4326. Undergraduates: $5245. **Parent loans:** $8,243,237 (91% need-based, 9% non-need-based). **Pro-**

grams: Federal Direct (Subsidized and Unsubsidized Stafford, PLUS), Federal Nursing, alternative loans.

WORK-STUDY *Federal work-study:* Total amount: $779,078; 407 jobs averaging $1914.

APPLYING FOR FINANCIAL AID *Required financial aid forms:* FAFSA, CSS Financial Aid PROFILE, noncustodial (divorced/separated) parent's statement, alumni and parish scholarship application form. *Financial aid deadline:* 4/10 (priority: 2/1). *Notification date:* Continuous beginning 3/20. Students must reply by 5/1 or within 2 weeks of notification.

CONTACT Ms. Jo Ann Humphreys, Director of Financial Aid, The Catholic University of America, 620 Michigan Avenue, NE, Washington, DC 20064, 202-319-6552 or toll-free 800-673-2772. *Fax:* 202-319-5573. *E-mail:* humphrej@cua.edu. *Website:* http://www.cua.edu/.

CAZENOVIA COLLEGE
Cazenovia, NY

Tuition & fees: $33,656	Average undergraduate aid package: $31,152

ABOUT THE INSTITUTION Independent, coed. *Awards:* certificates, associate, and bachelor's degrees. 22 undergraduate majors. *Total enrollment:* 1,042. Undergraduates: 1,042. Freshmen: 209. Federal methodology is used as a basis for awarding need-based institutional aid.

UNDERGRADUATE EXPENSES for 2017–2018 *Comprehensive fee:* $47,866 includes full-time tuition ($33,068), mandatory fees ($588), and room and board ($14,210). *College room only:* $7620. Full-time tuition and fees vary according to class time, course load, and program. Room and board charges vary according to board plan and housing facility. *Part-time tuition:* $700 per credit hour. Part-time tuition and fees vary according to class time and course load.

FRESHMAN FINANCIAL AID (Fall 2015) 238 applied for aid; of those 95% were deemed to have need. 100% of freshmen with need received aid; of those 24% had need fully met. *Average percent of need met:* 83% (excluding resources awarded to replace EFC). *Average financial aid package:* $33,644 (excluding resources awarded to replace EFC). 9% of all full-time freshmen had no need and received non-need-based gift aid.

UNDERGRADUATE FINANCIAL AID (Fall 2015) 899 applied for aid; of those 95% were deemed to have need. 100% of undergraduates with need received aid; of those 18% had need fully met. *Average percent of need met:* 80% (excluding resources awarded to replace EFC). *Average financial aid package:* $31,152 (excluding resources awarded to replace EFC). 8% of all full-time undergraduates had no need and received non-need-based gift aid.

GIFT AID (NEED-BASED) *Total amount:* $22,799,677 (10% federal, 9% state, 80% institutional, 1% external sources). *Receiving aid:* Freshmen: 91% (227); all full-time undergraduates: 91% (857). *Average award:* Freshmen: $30,445; Undergraduates: $27,096. *Scholarships, grants, and awards:* Federal Pell, FSEOG, state, private, college/university gift aid from institutional funds.

GIFT AID (NON-NEED-BASED) *Total amount:* $2,132,384 (1% state, 99% institutional). *Receiving aid:* Freshmen: 9% (22). Undergraduates: 8% (79). *Average award:* Freshmen: $19,393. Undergraduates: $18,424. *Scholarships, grants, and awards by category:* Academic interests/achievement: general academic interests/achievements. *Tuition waivers:* Full or partial for employees or children of employees. *ROTC:* Army cooperative, Air Force cooperative.

LOANS *Student loans:* $8,621,705 (81% need-based, 19% non-need-based). 94% of past graduating class borrowed through all loan programs. *Average indebtedness per student:* $33,631. *Average need-based loan:* Freshmen: $3068. Undergraduates: $4119. *Parent loans:* $3,122,421 (68% need-based, 32% non-need-based). *Programs:* Federal Direct (Subsidized and Unsubsidized Stafford, PLUS).

WORK-STUDY *Federal work-study:* jobs available.

APPLYING FOR FINANCIAL AID *Required financial aid forms:* FAFSA, state aid form. *Financial aid deadline (priority):* 3/1. *Notification date:* Continuous beginning 11/1. Students must reply by 5/1 or within 2 weeks of notification.

CONTACT Christine L. Mandel, Director of Financial Aid, Cazenovia College, 3 Sullivan Street, Cazenovia, NY 13035, 315-655-7887 or toll-free 800-654-3210. *Fax:* 315-655-7219. *E-mail:* finaid@cazenovia.edu. *Website:* http://www.cazenovia.edu/.

CEDAR CREST COLLEGE
Allentown, PA

Tuition & fees: $38,092	Average undergraduate aid package: $29,244

ABOUT THE INSTITUTION Independent United Church of Christ, coed, primarily women. *Awards:* certificates, bachelor's, and master's degrees. 38 undergraduate majors. *Total enrollment:* 1,669. Undergraduates: 1,428. Freshmen: 181. Federal methodology is used as a basis for awarding need-based institutional aid.

UNDERGRADUATE EXPENSES for 2017–2018 *Comprehensive fee:* $49,300 includes full-time tuition ($37,492), mandatory fees ($600), and room and board ($11,208). *College room only:* $5262. Full-time tuition and fees vary according to class time, course load, and program. Room and board charges vary according to board plan and housing facility. *Part-time tuition:* $1250 per credit hour. *Part-time fees:* $150 per term. Part-time tuition and fees vary according to class time, course load, and program.

FRESHMAN FINANCIAL AID (Fall 2016, est.) 175 applied for aid; of those 94% were deemed to have need. 100% of freshmen with need received aid; of those 15% had need fully met. *Average percent of need met:* 78% (excluding resources awarded to replace EFC). *Average financial aid package:* $30,222 (excluding resources awarded to replace EFC). 7% of all full-time freshmen had no need and received non-need-based gift aid.

UNDERGRADUATE FINANCIAL AID (Fall 2016, est.) 606 applied for aid; of those 94% were deemed to have need. 100% of undergraduates with need received aid; of those 13% had need fully met. *Average percent of need met:* 75% (excluding resources awarded to replace EFC). *Average financial aid package:* $29,244 (excluding resources awarded to replace EFC). 8% of all full-time undergraduates had no need and received non-need-based gift aid.

GIFT AID (NEED-BASED) *Total amount:* $14,222,530 (11% federal, 8% state, 79% institutional, 2% external sources). *Receiving aid:* Freshmen: 91% (164); all full-time undergraduates: 91% (570). *Average award:* Freshmen: $27,141; Undergraduates: $25,125. *Scholarships, grants, and awards:* Federal Pell, FSEOG, state, private, college/university gift aid from institutional funds.

GIFT AID (NON-NEED-BASED) *Total amount:* $1,161,289 (93% institutional, 7% external sources). *Receiving aid:* Freshmen: 10% (19). Undergraduates: 8% (53). *Average award:* Freshmen: $21,741. Undergraduates: $16,296. *Scholarships, grants, and awards by category:* Academic interests/achievement: biological sciences, communication, English, general academic interests/achievements, home economics, mathematics. Creative arts/performance: art/fine arts, dance, performing arts, theater/drama. Special achievements/activities: community service, general special achievements/activities, junior miss, religious involvement. Special characteristics: children and siblings of alumni, general special characteristics, relatives of clergy, siblings of current students. *Tuition waivers:* Full or partial for employees or children of employees. *ROTC:* Army cooperative.

LOANS *Student loans:* $6,360,720 (73% need-based, 27% non-need-based). 94% of past graduating class borrowed through all loan programs. *Average indebtedness per student:* $38,726. *Average need-based loan:* Freshmen: $3303. Undergraduates: $4461. *Parent loans:* $2,190,983 (58% need-based, 42% non-need-based). *Programs:* Federal Direct (Subsidized and Unsubsidized Stafford, PLUS), Perkins, Federal Nursing.

WORK-STUDY *Federal work-study:* Total amount: $144,000; jobs available. *State or other work-study/employment:* Total amount: $20,880 (77% need-based, 23% non-need-based). Part-time jobs available.

APPLYING FOR FINANCIAL AID *Required financial aid form:* FAFSA. *Financial aid deadline (priority):* 5/1. *Notification date:* Continuous beginning 9/15.

CONTACT Ms. Valerie D. Kreiser, Director of Student Financial Services, Cedar Crest College, Room 212 Blaney Hall, 100 College Drive, Allentown, PA 18104-6196, 610-606-4666 Ext. 3314 or toll-free 800-360-1222. *Fax:* 610-606-4653. *E-mail:* financialservices@cedarcrest.edu. *Website:* http://www.cedarcrest.edu/.

CEDARVILLE UNIVERSITY
Cedarville, OH

Tuition & fees: $29,156	Average undergraduate aid package: $20,654

ABOUT THE INSTITUTION Independent Baptist, coed. *Awards:* certificates, bachelor's, master's, and doctoral degrees. 73 undergraduate majors. *Total enrollment:* 3,717. Undergraduates: 3,380. Freshmen: 769. Federal methodology is used as a basis for awarding need-based institutional aid.

UNDERGRADUATE EXPENSES for 2017–2018 *Application fee:* $30. *Comprehensive fee:* $36,244 includes full-time tuition ($28,956), mandatory fees ($200), and room and board ($7088). *College room only:* $4018. Room and board charges vary according to board plan and housing facility. *Part-time tuition:* $1096 per credit hour. *Part-time fees:* $50 per term. Part-time tuition and fees vary according to course load.

FRESHMAN FINANCIAL AID (Fall 2016, est.) 695 applied for aid; of those 83% were deemed to have need. 100% of freshmen with need received aid; of those 37% had need fully met. *Average percent of need met:* 28% (excluding resources awarded to replace EFC). *Average financial aid package:* $20,559 (excluding resources awarded to replace EFC). 21% of all full-time freshmen had no need and received non-need-based gift aid.

UNDERGRADUATE FINANCIAL AID (Fall 2016, est.) 2,405 applied for aid; of those 85% were deemed to have need. 100% of undergraduates with need received aid; of those 35% had need fully met. *Average percent of need met:* 34% (excluding resources awarded to replace EFC). *Average financial aid package:* $20,654 (excluding resources awarded to replace EFC). 27% of all full-time undergraduates had no need and received non-need-based gift aid.

GIFT AID (NEED-BASED) *Total amount:* $10,297,557 (27% federal, 5% state, 67% institutional, 1% external sources). *Receiving aid:* Freshmen: 47% (363); all full-time undergraduates: 53% (1,609). *Average award:* Freshmen: $5252; Undergraduates: $5777. *Scholarships, grants, and awards:* Federal Pell, FSEOG, state, private, college/university gift aid from institutional funds, Federal Nursing.

GIFT AID (NON-NEED-BASED) *Total amount:* $33,076,235 (85% institutional, 15% external sources). *Receiving aid:* Freshmen: 72% (550). Undergraduates: 63% (1,905). *Average award:* Freshmen: $18,381. Undergraduates: $16,231. *Scholarships, grants, and awards by category:* Academic interests/achievement: 2,090 awards ($15,655,901 total): general academic interests/achievements. *Creative arts/performance:* 112 awards ($430,100 total): debating, music. *Special achievements/activities:* 245 awards ($484,300 total): leadership. *Special characteristics:* 449 awards ($4,553,886 total): children of faculty/staff, ethnic background, general special characteristics, religious affiliation, veterans. *Tuition waivers:* Full or partial for employees or children of employees, adult students, senior citizens. *ROTC:* Army cooperative, Air Force cooperative.

LOANS *Student loans:* $17,464,265 (39% need-based, 61% non-need-based). 61% of past graduating class borrowed through all loan programs. *Average indebtedness per student:* $29,582. *Average need-based loan:* Freshmen: $4642. Undergraduates: $5577. *Parent loans:* $12,917,219 (100% non-need-based). *Programs:* Federal Direct (Subsidized and Unsubsidized Stafford, PLUS), Perkins, Federal Nursing, college/university.

WORK-STUDY *Federal work-study:* Total amount: $256,855; 276 jobs averaging $2369. *State or other work-study/employment:* Total amount: $1,879,520 (100% non-need-based). 1,433 part-time jobs averaging $1312.

ATHLETIC AWARDS Total amount: $1,527,388 (100% non-need-based).

APPLYING FOR FINANCIAL AID *Required financial aid form:* FAFSA. *Financial aid deadline (priority):* 3/1. *Notification date:* Continuous beginning 3/1. Students must reply within 3 weeks of notification.

CONTACT Mr. Russell Kim Jenerette, Executive Director of Financial Aid, Cedarville University, 251 North Main Street, Cedarville, OH 45314-0601, 937-766-7866 or toll-free 800-233-2784. *Fax:* 937-766-7639. *E-mail:* kimjenerette@cedarville.edu. *Website:* http://www.cedarville.edu/.

CENTENARY COLLEGE OF LOUISIANA
Shreveport, LA

Tuition & fees: $35,900	Average undergraduate aid package: $27,996

ABOUT THE INSTITUTION Independent United Methodist, coed. *Awards:* bachelor's and master's degrees. 24 undergraduate majors. *Total enrollment:* 540. Undergraduates: 481. Freshmen: 130. Federal methodology is used as a basis for awarding need-based institutional aid.

UNDERGRADUATE EXPENSES for 2017–2018 *One-time required fee:* $250. *Comprehensive fee:* $49,050 includes full-time tuition ($35,900) and room and board ($13,150). Full-time tuition and fees vary according to course load, degree level, and student level. Room and board charges vary according to board plan, housing facility, and student level. *Part-time tuition:* $1455 per credit hour. Part-time tuition and fees vary according to course load, degree level, and student level.

FRESHMAN FINANCIAL AID (Fall 2016, est.) 124 applied for aid; of those 87% were deemed to have need. 100% of freshmen with need received aid; of those 15% had need fully met. *Average percent of need met:* 60% (excluding resources awarded to replace EFC). *Average financial aid package:* $22,432 (excluding resources awarded to replace EFC). 15% of all full-time freshmen had no need and received non-need-based gift aid.

UNDERGRADUATE FINANCIAL AID (Fall 2016, est.) 409 applied for aid; of those 91% were deemed to have need. 99% of undergraduates with need received aid; of those 22% had need fully met. *Average percent of need met:* 73% (excluding resources awarded to replace EFC). *Average financial aid package:* $27,996 (excluding resources awarded to replace EFC). 17% of all full-time undergraduates had no need and received non-need-based gift aid.

GIFT AID (NEED-BASED) *Total amount:* $9,218,137 (9% federal, 11% state, 79% institutional, 1% external sources). *Receiving aid:* Freshmen: 82% (106); all full-time undergraduates: 79% (372). *Average award:* Freshmen: $19,469; Undergraduates: $24,252. *Scholarships, grants, and awards:* Federal Pell, FSEOG, state, private, college/university gift aid from institutional funds.

GIFT AID (NON-NEED-BASED) *Total amount:* $2,501,469 (6% state, 93% institutional, 1% external sources). *Receiving aid:* Freshmen: 12% (16). Undergraduates: 15% (70). *Average award:* Freshmen: $17,544. Undergraduates: $21,080. *Scholarships, grants, and awards by category:* Academic interests/achievement: 513 awards ($5,743,868 total): biological sciences, business, communication, education, engineering/technologies, English, foreign languages, general academic interests/achievements, humanities, mathematics, physical sciences, premedicine, religion/biblical studies, social sciences. *Creative arts/performance:* 76 awards ($305,335 total): art/fine arts, dance, general creative arts/performance, music, performing arts, theater/drama. *Special achievements/activities:* 56 awards ($129,152 total): community service, general special achievements/activities, hobbies/interests, religious involvement. *Special characteristics:* 84 awards ($2,466,203 total): children and siblings of alumni, children of educators, children of faculty/staff, ethnic background, first-generation college students, general special characteristics, international students, local/state students, members of minority groups, out-of-state students, relatives of clergy, religious affiliation, siblings of current students, veterans, veterans' children. *Tuition waivers:* Full or partial for employees or children of employees.

LOANS *Student loans:* $2,032,613 (50% need-based, 50% non-need-based). 58% of past graduating class borrowed through all loan programs. *Average indebtedness per student:* $26,643. *Average need-based loan:* Freshmen: $3403. Undergraduates: $4442. *Parent loans:* $1,324,939 (90% need-based, 10% non-need-based). *Programs:* Federal Direct (Subsidized and Unsubsidized Stafford, PLUS), Perkins.

WORK-STUDY *Federal work-study:* Total amount: $373,200; 171 jobs averaging $2182. *State or other work-study/employment:* Total amount: $58,250 (100% non-need-based). 38 part-time jobs averaging $1533.

APPLYING FOR FINANCIAL AID *Required financial aid form:* FAFSA. *Financial aid deadline (priority):* 11/1. *Notification date:* Continuous beginning 12/1. Students must reply by 5/1.

CONTACT Mrs. Lynette Viskozki, Director of Financial Aid, Centenary College of Louisiana, PO Box 41188, Shreveport, LA 71134-1188, 318-869-5137 or toll-free 800-234-4448. *Fax:* 318-841-7266. *E-mail:* lviskozk@centenary.edu. *Website:* http://www.centenary.edu/.

CENTENARY UNIVERSITY
Hackettstown, NJ

CONTACT Michelle Burwell, Associate Director of Financial Aid, Centenary University, 400 Jefferson Street, Hackettstown, NJ 07840-2100, 908-852-1400 Ext. 2240 or toll-free 800-236-8679. *Fax:* 908-813-2632. *E-mail:* burwellm@centenarycollege.edu.
Website: http://www.centenaryuniversity.edu/.

CENTRAL BAPTIST COLLEGE
Conway, AR

CONTACT Christi Bell, Financial Aid Director, Central Baptist College, 1501 College Avenue, Conway, AR 72032-6470, 800-205-6872 Ext. 185 or toll-free 800-205-6872. *Fax:* 501-329-2941. *E-mail:* financialaid@cbc.edu.
Website: http://www.cbc.edu/.

CENTRAL CHRISTIAN COLLEGE OF KANSAS
McPherson, KS

CONTACT Mike Reimer, Financial Aid Director, Central Christian College of Kansas, 1200 South Main, PO Box 1403, McPherson, KS 67460, 620-241-0723 Ext. 333 or toll-free 800-835-0078. *Fax:* 620-241-6032. *E-mail:* miker@centralchristian.edu.
Website: http://www.centralchristian.edu/.

CENTRAL CHRISTIAN COLLEGE OF THE BIBLE
Moberly, MO

CONTACT Ms. Rhonda Dunham, Financial Aid Director, Central Christian College of the Bible, 911 East Urbandale Drive, Moberly, MO 65270-1997, 660-263-3900 Ext. 121 or toll-free 888-263-3900. *Fax:* 660-263-3936. *E-mail:* rdunham@cccb.edu.
Website: http://www.cccb.edu/.

CENTRAL COLLEGE
Pella, IA

Tuition & fees: $34,612	Average undergraduate aid package: $30,404

ABOUT THE INSTITUTION Independent Reformed Church in America, coed. *Awards:* bachelor's degrees. 38 undergraduate majors. *Total enrollment:* 1,274. Undergraduates: 1,274. Freshmen: 317. Federal methodology is used as a basis for awarding need-based institutional aid.
UNDERGRADUATE EXPENSES for 2016–2017 Application fee: $25. *Comprehensive fee:* $44,592 includes full-time tuition ($34,612) and room and board ($9980). *College room only:* $4892. Room and board charges vary according to board plan. *Part-time tuition:* $1442 per credit hour. Part-time tuition and fees vary according to course load.
FRESHMAN FINANCIAL AID (Fall 2016, est.) 311 applied for aid; of those 90% were deemed to have need. 100% of freshmen with need received aid; of those 23% had need fully met. *Average percent of need met:* 87% (excluding resources awarded to replace EFC). *Average financial aid package:* $28,395 (excluding resources awarded to replace EFC). 14% of all full-time freshmen had no need and received non-need-based gift aid.
UNDERGRADUATE FINANCIAL AID (Fall 2016, est.) 1,042 applied for aid; of those 91% were deemed to have need. 100% of undergraduates with need received aid; of those 19% had need fully met. *Average percent of need met:* 85% (excluding resources awarded to replace EFC). *Average financial aid package:*

$30,404 (excluding resources awarded to replace EFC). 19% of all full-time undergraduates had no need and received non-need-based gift aid.
GIFT AID (NEED-BASED) Total amount: $23,348,317 (6% federal, 10% state, 83% institutional, 1% external sources). *Receiving aid:* Freshmen: 86% (279); all full-time undergraduates: 81% (952). *Average award:* Freshmen: $25,511; Undergraduates: $25,629. *Scholarships, grants, and awards:* Federal Pell, FSEOG, state, private, college/university gift aid from institutional funds.
GIFT AID (NON-NEED-BASED) Total amount: $5,865,793 (4% federal, 1% state, 93% institutional, 2% external sources). *Receiving aid:* Freshmen: 76% (247). Undergraduates: 11% (125). *Average award:* Freshmen: $12,893. Undergraduates: $19,758. *Scholarships, grants, and awards by category: Academic interests/achievement:* biological sciences, business, computer science, education, engineering/technologies, foreign languages, general academic interests/achievements, health fields, humanities, international studies, mathematics, physical sciences, premedicine, religion/biblical studies, social sciences. *Creative arts/performance:* art/fine arts, creative writing, music, theater/drama. *Special achievements/activities:* community service, religious involvement. *Special characteristics:* children and siblings of alumni, children of current students, children of faculty/staff, general special characteristics, handicapped students, international students, local/state students, members of minority groups, out-of-state students, previous college experience, religious affiliation, siblings of current students, twins, veterans, veterans' children. *Tuition waivers:* Full or partial for employees or children of employees.
LOANS Student loans: $8,216,080 (71% need-based, 29% non-need-based). 82% of past graduating class borrowed through all loan programs. *Average indebtedness per student:* $36,363. *Average need-based loan:* Freshmen: $2352. Undergraduates: $4025. *Parent loans:* $2,415,811 (31% need-based, 69% non-need-based). *Programs:* Federal Direct (Subsidized and Unsubsidized Stafford, PLUS), Perkins, college/university, alternative loans.
WORK-STUDY Federal work-study: Total amount: $714,900; jobs available. *State or other work-study/employment:* Total amount: $565,150 (100% non-need-based). Part-time jobs available.
APPLYING FOR FINANCIAL AID Required financial aid form: FAFSA. *Financial aid deadline (priority):* 1/15. *Notification date:* Continuous beginning 11/15. Students must reply by 5/1 or within 2 weeks of notification.
CONTACT Wayne Dille, Director of Financial Aid, Central College, 812 University Street, Campus Box 5800, Pella, IA 50219-1999, 641-628-5336 or toll-free 877-462-3687. *Fax:* 641-628-7199. *E-mail:* dillew@central.edu.
Website: http://www.central.edu/.

CENTRAL CONNECTICUT STATE UNIVERSITY
New Britain, CT

Tuition & fees (CT res): $9741	Average undergraduate aid package: $9350

ABOUT THE INSTITUTION State-supported, coed. *Awards:* certificates, bachelor's, master's, and doctoral degrees. 62 undergraduate majors. *Total enrollment:* 11,784. Undergraduates: 9,538. Freshmen: 1,269. Federal methodology is used as a basis for awarding need-based institutional aid.
UNDERGRADUATE EXPENSES for 2016–2017 Application fee: $50. *Tuition, state resident:* full-time $5216; part-time $217 per credit. *Tuition, nonresident:* full-time $16,882; part-time $223 per credit. *Required fees:* full-time $4525; $265 per credit or $58 per term. Full-time tuition and fees vary according to course level, course load, and program. Part-time tuition and fees vary according to course level, course load, and program. *College room and board:* $11,462; *Room only:* $6636. Room and board charges vary according to board plan and housing facility.
FRESHMAN FINANCIAL AID (Fall 2016, est.) 1,125 applied for aid; of those 79% were deemed to have need. 94% of freshmen with need received aid; of those 6% had need fully met. *Average percent of need met:* 63% (excluding resources awarded to replace EFC). *Average financial aid package:* $9250 (excluding resources awarded to replace EFC). 9% of all full-time freshmen had no need and received non-need-based gift aid.
UNDERGRADUATE FINANCIAL AID (Fall 2016, est.) 6,792 applied for aid; of those 86% were deemed to have need. 89% of undergraduates with need received aid; of those 6% had need fully met. *Average percent of need met:* 64% (excluding resources awarded to replace EFC). *Average financial aid package:* $9350

(excluding resources awarded to replace EFC). 4% of all full-time undergraduates had no need and received non-need-based gift aid.

GIFT AID (NEED-BASED) Total amount: $23,992,360 (57% federal, 15% state, 28% institutional). **Receiving aid:** Freshmen: 49% (621); all full-time undergraduates: 47% (3,535). **Average award:** Freshmen: $5650; Undergraduates: $5725. **Scholarships, grants, and awards:** Federal Pell, FSEOG, state, college/university gift aid from institutional funds.

GIFT AID (NON-NEED-BASED) Total amount: $4,130,432 (68% institutional, 32% external sources). **Receiving aid:** Freshmen: 17% (213). Undergraduates: 12% (924). **Average award:** Freshmen: $3050. Undergraduates: $3075. **Scholarships, grants, and awards by category:** Academic interests/achievement: general academic interests/achievements. Special characteristics: members of minority groups. **Tuition waivers:** Full or partial for employees or children of employees, senior citizens. **ROTC:** Army cooperative, Air Force cooperative.

LOANS Student loans: $58,000,000 (36% need-based, 64% non-need-based). 74% of past graduating class borrowed through all loan programs. Average indebtedness per student: $28,016. **Average need-based loan:** Freshmen: $3255. Undergraduates: $4291. **Parent loans:** $7,100,000 (100% non-need-based). **Programs:** Federal Direct (Subsidized and Unsubsidized Stafford, PLUS), Perkins.

WORK-STUDY Federal work-study: Total amount: $386,480; 269 jobs averaging $1500. **State or other work-study/employment:** Part-time jobs available.

ATHLETIC AWARDS Total amount: $3,528,642 (100% non-need-based).

APPLYING FOR FINANCIAL AID Required financial aid form: FAFSA. **Financial aid deadline:** 9/15 (priority: 3/1). **Notification date:** Continuous beginning 1/31.

CONTACT Mr. Dennis Williams, Associate Director of Financial Aid, Central Connecticut State University, Davidson Hall, Room 221, New Britain, CT 06050-4010, 860-832-2200 or toll-free 888-733-2278 (in-state). Fax: 860-832-3330. E-mail: finaid@ccsu.edu.

Website: http://www.ccsu.edu/.

CENTRAL METHODIST UNIVERSITY
Fayette, MO

Tuition & fees: $23,770	Average undergraduate aid package: $19,890

ABOUT THE INSTITUTION Independent Methodist, coed. **Awards:** associate, bachelor's, and master's degrees. 45 undergraduate majors. **Total enrollment:** 1,094. Undergraduates: 1,094. Freshmen: 264. Federal methodology is used as a basis for awarding need-based institutional aid.

UNDERGRADUATE EXPENSES for 2017–2018 Comprehensive fee: $31,500 includes full-time tuition ($23,000), mandatory fees ($770), and room and board ($7730). **College room only:** $3780. Full-time tuition and fees vary according to program and reciprocity agreements. Room and board charges vary according to board plan and housing facility. **Part-time tuition:** $210 per credit hour. Part-time tuition and fees vary according to course load and program.

FRESHMAN FINANCIAL AID (Fall 2016, est.) 246 applied for aid; of those 93% were deemed to have need. 100% of freshmen with need received aid; of those 19% had need fully met. **Average percent of need met:** 71% (excluding resources awarded to replace EFC). **Average financial aid package:** $18,492 (excluding resources awarded to replace EFC). 8% of all full-time freshmen had no need and received non-need-based gift aid.

UNDERGRADUATE FINANCIAL AID (Fall 2016, est.) 925 applied for aid; of those 92% were deemed to have need. 100% of undergraduates with need received aid; of those 21% had need fully met. **Average percent of need met:** 75% (excluding resources awarded to replace EFC). **Average financial aid package:** $19,890 (excluding resources awarded to replace EFC). 14% of all full-time undergraduates had no need and received non-need-based gift aid.

GIFT AID (NEED-BASED) Total amount: $3,009,209 (69% federal, 29% state, 2% institutional). **Receiving aid:** Freshmen: 53% (139); all full-time undergraduates: 50% (533). **Average award:** Freshmen: $5325; Undergraduates: $5384. **Scholarships, grants, and awards:** Federal Pell, FSEOG, state, private, college/university gift aid from institutional funds.

GIFT AID (NON-NEED-BASED) Total amount: $9,245,268 (93% institutional, 7% external sources). **Receiving aid:** Freshmen: 87% (229). Undergraduates: 80% (847). **Average award:** Freshmen: $11,470. Undergraduates: $11,840. **Scholarships, grants, and awards by category:** Academic interests/achievement: bio-

logical sciences, business, communication, computer science, education, English, foreign languages, general academic interests/achievements, health fields, humanities, mathematics, physical sciences, premedicine, religion/biblical studies, social sciences. **Creative arts/performance:** music, theater/drama. **Special achievements/activities:** cheerleading/drum major, leadership, religious involvement. **Special characteristics:** children and siblings of alumni, children of faculty/staff, general special characteristics, international students, relatives of clergy, religious affiliation, siblings of current students, spouses of current students. **Tuition waivers:** Full or partial for children of alumni, employees or children of employees. **ROTC:** Army cooperative, Air Force cooperative.

LOANS Student loans: $6,816,479 (42% need-based, 58% non-need-based). 91% of past graduating class borrowed through all loan programs. Average indebtedness per student: $27,308. **Average need-based loan:** Freshmen: $3462. Undergraduates: $4336. **Parent loans:** $1,863,722 (100% non-need-based). **Programs:** Federal Direct (Subsidized and Unsubsidized Stafford, PLUS), Perkins.

WORK-STUDY Federal work-study: Total amount: $185,983; jobs available. **State or other work-study/employment:** Total amount: $110,739 (100% non-need-based). Part-time jobs available.

ATHLETIC AWARDS Total amount: $4,662,604 (100% non-need-based).

APPLYING FOR FINANCIAL AID Required financial aid form: FAFSA. **Financial aid deadline:** Continuous. **Notification date:** Continuous beginning 11/1. Students must reply by 8/5.

CONTACT Mrs. Kristen M. Gibbs, Director of Financial Assistance, Central Methodist University, 411 Central Methodist Square, Fayette, MO 65248-1198, 660-248-6244 or toll-free 888-CMU-1854 (in-state), 877-CMU-1854 (out-of-state). Fax: 660-248-6288. E-mail: kgibbs@centralmethodist.edu.

Website: http://www.centralmethodist.edu/.

CENTRAL MICHIGAN UNIVERSITY
Mount Pleasant, MI

Tuition & fees (MI res): $12,150	Average undergraduate aid package: $13,708

ABOUT THE INSTITUTION State-supported, coed. **Awards:** certificates, bachelor's, master's, and doctoral degrees. 121 undergraduate majors. **Total enrollment:** 26,080. Undergraduates: 19,923. Freshmen: 3,519. Federal methodology is used as a basis for awarding need-based institutional aid.

UNDERGRADUATE EXPENSES for 2016–2017 Application fee: $35. **Tuition, state resident:** full-time $12,150; part-time $405 per credit hour. **Tuition, nonresident:** full-time $23,670; part-time $789 per credit hour. Full-time tuition and fees vary according to location. Part-time tuition and fees vary according to location. **College room and board:** $9406; **Room only:** $4703. Room and board charges vary according to board plan and housing facility.

FRESHMAN FINANCIAL AID (Fall 2015) 3,062 applied for aid; of those 75% were deemed to have need. 97% of freshmen with need received aid; of those 56% had need fully met. **Average percent of need met:** 84% (excluding resources awarded to replace EFC). **Average financial aid package:** $13,990 (excluding resources awarded to replace EFC). 22% of all full-time freshmen had no need and received non-need-based gift aid.

UNDERGRADUATE FINANCIAL AID (Fall 2015) 13,178 applied for aid; of those 78% were deemed to have need. 98% of undergraduates with need received aid; of those 50% had need fully met. **Average percent of need met:** 79% (excluding resources awarded to replace EFC). **Average financial aid package:** $13,708 (excluding resources awarded to replace EFC). 12% of all full-time undergraduates had no need and received non-need-based gift aid.

GIFT AID (NEED-BASED) Total amount: $52,788,294 (45% federal, 3% state, 48% institutional, 4% external sources). **Receiving aid:** Freshmen: 58% (1,997); all full-time undergraduates: 46% (8,010). **Average award:** Freshmen: $8560; Undergraduates: $6661. **Scholarships, grants, and awards:** Federal Pell, FSEOG, state, private, college/university gift aid from institutional funds.

GIFT AID (NON-NEED-BASED) Total amount: $13,215,243 (90% institutional, 10% external sources). **Receiving aid:** Freshmen: 7% (239). Undergraduates: 3% (586). **Average award:** Freshmen: $5127. Undergraduates: $4908. **Scholarships, grants, and awards by category:** Academic interests/achievement: 1,707 awards ($5,411,681 total): biological sciences, business, communication, computer science, education, engineering/technologies, English, foreign languages, general academic interests/achievements, health fields, home economics, humanities, international studies, mathematics, military science, physical sciences, premedicine, religion/biblical studies, social sciences. *Creative arts/performance:* 136 awards ($324,878 total): applied art and design, art/fine arts, cinema/film/broadcasting, creative writing, dance, general creative arts/performance, journalism/publications, music, performing arts, theater/drama. *Special achievements/activities:* 756 awards ($6,621,788 total): general special achievements/activities, leadership. *Special characteristics:* 206 awards ($1,445,646 total): children and siblings of alumni, children of faculty/staff, ethnic background, international students, local/state students, out-of-state students. *Tuition waivers:* Full or partial for children of alumni, employees or children of employees, senior citizens. *ROTC:* Army, Air Force cooperative.

LOANS *Student loans:* $95,311,655 (71% need-based, 29% non-need-based). 70% of past graduating class borrowed through all loan programs. *Average indebtedness per student:* $33,480. *Average need-based loan:* Freshmen: $5859. Undergraduates: $7824. *Parent loans:* $36,122,198 (34% need-based, 66% non-need-based). *Programs:* Federal Direct (Subsidized and Unsubsidized Stafford, PLUS), state, college/university.

WORK-STUDY *Federal work-study:* 974 jobs averaging $1776. *State or other work-study/employment:* Total amount: $774,441 (78% need-based, 22% non-need-based). 490 part-time jobs averaging $2448.

ATHLETIC AWARDS Total amount: $5,248,527 (33% need-based, 67% non-need-based).

APPLYING FOR FINANCIAL AID *Required financial aid form:* FAFSA. *Financial aid deadline (priority):* 3/1. *Notification date:* Continuous beginning 3/31. Students must reply by 5/15.

CONTACT Mr. Kirk M. Yats, Director of Scholarships and Financial Aid, Central Michigan University, Mount Pleasant, MI 48859, 989-774-3674 or toll-free 888-292-5366. *Fax:* 989-774-3634. *E-mail:* cmuosfa@cmich.edu.
Website: http://www.cmich.edu/.

CENTRAL PENN COLLEGE
Summerdale, PA

Tuition & fees: $18,174	Average undergraduate aid package: N/A

ABOUT THE INSTITUTION Proprietary, coed. *Awards:* associate, bachelor's, and master's degrees. 23 undergraduate majors. *Total enrollment:* 1,370. Undergraduates: 1,337. Freshmen: 239. Federal methodology is used as a basis for awarding need-based institutional aid.

UNDERGRADUATE EXPENSES for 2017–2018 *One-time required fee:* $100. *Comprehensive fee:* $25,590 includes full-time tuition ($17,280), mandatory fees ($894), and room and board ($7416). *College room only:* $5346. Room and board charges vary according to board plan and housing facility. *Part-time tuition:* $480 per credit hour. *Part-time fees:* $290 per term.

GIFT AID (NEED-BASED) *Total amount:* $4,714,391 (55% federal, 45% state). *Scholarships, grants, and awards:* Federal Pell, FSEOG, state, private, college/university gift aid from institutional funds.

GIFT AID (NON-NEED-BASED) *Total amount:* $551,062 (100% institutional). *Scholarships, grants, and awards by category: Academic interests/achievement:* general academic interests/achievements. *Special achievements/activities:* leadership, memberships. *Special characteristics:* general special characteristics, out-of-state students. *Tuition waivers:* Full or partial for employees or children of employees.

LOANS *Student loans:* $55,018,108 (5% need-based, 95% non-need-based). *Parent loans:* $11,492,160 (100% non-need-based). *Programs:* Federal Direct (Subsidized and Unsubsidized Stafford, PLUS).

WORK-STUDY *Federal work-study:* Total amount: $77,394; jobs available. *State or other work-study/employment:* Total amount: $1,693,028 (100% non-need-based). Part-time jobs available.

APPLYING FOR FINANCIAL AID *Required financial aid forms:* FAFSA, institution's own form, state aid form. *Financial aid deadline:* 5/1 (priority: 3/15). *Notification date:* Continuous beginning 1/1. Students must reply by 3/15 or within 2 weeks of notification.

CONTACT Kathy Shepard, Financial Aid Director, Central Penn College, College Hill and Valley Roads, Summerdale, PA 17093, 717-728-2261 or toll-free 800-759-2727. *Fax:* 717-728-2350. *E-mail:* financial-aid@centralpenn.edu.
Website: http://www.centralpenn.edu/.

CENTRAL STATE UNIVERSITY
Wilberforce, OH

CONTACT Sonia Slomba, Director of Student Financial Aid, Central State University, PO Box 1004, Wilberforce, OH 45384, 937-376-6579 or toll-free 800-388-CSU1 (in-state), 800-388-2781 (out-of-state). *Fax:* 937-376-6519. *E-mail:* sslomba@centralstate.edu.
Website: http://www.centralstate.edu/.

CENTRAL WASHINGTON UNIVERSITY
Ellensburg, WA

Tuition & fees (WA res): $7849	Average undergraduate aid package: $11,434

ABOUT THE INSTITUTION State-supported, coed. *Awards:* certificates, bachelor's, and master's degrees. 138 undergraduate majors. *Total enrollment:* 11,971. Undergraduates: 11,047. Freshmen: 1,665. Federal methodology is used as a basis for awarding need-based institutional aid.

UNDERGRADUATE EXPENSES for 2017–2018 *Application fee:* $50. *Tuition, state resident:* full-time $6037. *Tuition, nonresident:* full-time $20,144. *Required fees:* full-time $1812. Full-time tuition and fees vary according to course load, degree level, location, and reciprocity agreements. Part-time tuition and fees vary according to course load, degree level, location, and reciprocity agreements. *College room and board:* $10,684. Room and board charges vary according to board plan, housing facility, and location.

FRESHMAN FINANCIAL AID (Fall 2015) 1,341 applied for aid; of those 73% were deemed to have need. 99% of freshmen with need received aid; of those 41% had need fully met. *Average percent of need met:* 84% (excluding resources awarded to replace EFC). *Average financial aid package:* $11,746 (excluding resources awarded to replace EFC). 1% of all full-time freshmen had no need and received non-need-based gift aid.

UNDERGRADUATE FINANCIAL AID (Fall 2015) 7,422 applied for aid; of those 79% were deemed to have need. 98% of undergraduates with need received aid; of those 29% had need fully met. *Average percent of need met:* 80% (excluding resources awarded to replace EFC). *Average financial aid package:* $11,434 (excluding resources awarded to replace EFC). 1% of all full-time undergraduates had no need and received non-need-based gift aid.

GIFT AID (NEED-BASED) *Total amount:* $38,056,103 (46% federal, 46% state, 8% institutional). *Receiving aid:* Freshmen: 57% (838); all full-time undergraduates: 55% (4,950). *Average award:* Freshmen: $9959; Undergraduates: $8841. *Scholarships, grants, and awards:* Federal Pell, FSEOG, state, private, college/university gift aid from institutional funds.

GIFT AID (NON-NEED-BASED) *Total amount:* $3,440,328 (9% state, 3% institutional, 88% external sources). *Receiving aid:* Freshmen: 8% (124). Undergraduates: 3% (235). *Average award:* Freshmen: $708. Undergraduates: $821. *Scholarships, grants, and awards by category: Academic interests/achievement:* general academic interests/achievements. *Creative arts/performance:* art/fine arts, general creative arts/performance, music, theater/drama. *Special achievements/activities:* leadership. *Special characteristics:* children and siblings of alumni, children of faculty/staff, children of public servants, local/state students, members of minority groups, out-of-state students, public servants, veterans, veterans' children. *Tuition waivers:* Full or partial for employees or children of employees, senior citizens. *ROTC:* Army, Air Force.

LOANS *Student loans:* $41,909,791 (46% need-based, 54% non-need-based). 77% of past graduating class borrowed through all loan programs. *Average indebtedness per student:* $22,827. *Average need-based loan:* Freshmen: $3137. Undergraduates: $4376. *Parent loans:* $18,574,734 (28% need-based, 72% non-need-based). *Programs:* Federal Direct (Subsidized and Unsubsidized Stafford, PLUS), Perkins, college/university.

WORK-STUDY *Federal work-study:* jobs available. *State or other work-study/employment:* Total amount: $299,045 (100% need-based). Part-time jobs available.

ATHLETIC AWARDS Total amount: $1,493,998 (66% need-based, 34% non-need-based).

APPLYING FOR FINANCIAL AID *Required financial aid form:* FAFSA. *Financial aid deadline (priority):* 3/1. *Notification date:* Continuous beginning 5/15. Students must reply within 4 weeks of notification.

CONTACT Mr. Adrian Naranjo, Director of Student Financial Services, Central Washington University, 400 East University Way, Ellensburg, WA 98926-7495, 509-963-2091. *Fax:* 509-963-1788. *E-mail:* finaid@cwu.edu. *Website:* http://www.cwu.edu/.

CENTRAL YESHIVA TOMCHEI TMIMIM-LUBAVITCH
Brooklyn, NY

CONTACT Rabbi Moshe M. Gluckowsky, Director of Financial Aid , Central Yeshiva Tomchei Tmimim-Lubavitch, 841-853 Ocean Parkway, Brooklyn, NY 11230, 718-859-2277.

CENTRE COLLEGE
Danville, KY

Tuition & fees: $40,500	Average undergraduate aid package: $32,001

ABOUT THE INSTITUTION Independent Presbyterian Church (U.S.A.), coed. *Awards:* bachelor's degrees. 28 undergraduate majors. *Total enrollment:* 1,430. Undergraduates: 1,430. Freshmen: 400. Federal methodology is used as a basis for awarding need-based institutional aid.

UNDERGRADUATE EXPENSES for 2017–2018 *Comprehensive fee:* $50,750 includes full-time tuition ($40,500) and room and board ($10,250). *College room only:* $5125. Room and board charges vary according to housing facility. *Part-time tuition:* $1455 per credit hour.

FRESHMAN FINANCIAL AID (Fall 2016, est.) 332 applied for aid; of those 73% were deemed to have need. 100% of freshmen with need received aid; of those 39% had need fully met. *Average percent of need met:* 90% (excluding resources awarded to replace EFC). *Average financial aid package:* $34,106 (excluding resources awarded to replace EFC). 37% of all full-time freshmen had no need and received non-need-based gift aid.

UNDERGRADUATE FINANCIAL AID (Fall 2016, est.) 1,021 applied for aid; of those 77% were deemed to have need. 100% of undergraduates with need received aid; of those 32% had need fully met. *Average percent of need met:* 86% (excluding resources awarded to replace EFC). *Average financial aid package:* $32,001 (excluding resources awarded to replace EFC). 41% of all full-time undergraduates had no need and received non-need-based gift aid.

GIFT AID (NEED-BASED) *Total amount:* $22,691,480 (4% federal, 10% state, 83% institutional, 3% external sources). *Receiving aid:* Freshmen: 61% (243); all full-time undergraduates: 55% (785). *Average award:* Freshmen: $31,508; Undergraduates: $28,880. *Scholarships, grants, and awards:* Federal Pell, FSEOG, state, private, college/university gift aid from institutional funds.

GIFT AID (NON-NEED-BASED) *Total amount:* $12,118,645 (5% state, 93% institutional, 2% external sources). *Average award:* Freshmen: $21,908. Undergraduates: $20,689. *Scholarships, grants, and awards by category:* Academic interests/achievement: 1,210 awards ($20,759,990 total): foreign languages, general academic interests/achievements. *Creative arts/performance:* 76 awards ($220,000 total): music, theater/drama. *Special achievements/activities:* 31 awards ($75,000 total): community service. *Special characteristics:* 245 awards ($3,918,958 total): children and siblings of alumni, children of faculty/staff, ethnic background, first-generation college students. *Tuition waivers:* Full or partial for employees or children of employees. *ROTC:* Army cooperative, Air Force cooperative.

LOANS *Student loans:* $5,225,083 (55% need-based, 45% non-need-based). 48% of past graduating class borrowed through all loan programs. *Average indebtedness per student:* $26,740. *Average need-based loan:* Freshmen: $3368. Undergraduates: $4512. *Parent loans:* $1,728,098 (100% non-need-based). *Programs:* Federal Direct (Subsidized and Unsubsidized Stafford, PLUS), Perkins, college/university.

WORK-STUDY *Federal work-study:* Total amount: $546,620; 334 jobs averaging $1665. *State or other work-study/employment:* Total amount: $7600 (100% non-need-based). Part-time jobs available.

APPLYING FOR FINANCIAL AID *Required financial aid forms:* FAFSA, institution's own form. *Financial aid deadline:* 1/31. *Notification date:* Continuous beginning 2/19. Students must reply by 5/1.

CONTACT Mr. Kevin Lamb, Associate Dean of Admission and Financial Aid, Centre College, 600 West Walnut Street, Danville, KY 40422-1394, 859-238-5365 or toll-free 800-423-6236. *Fax:* 859-238-8719. *E-mail:* finaid@centre.edu. *Website:* http://www.centre.edu/.

CENTRO DE ESTUDIOS MULTIDISCIPLINARIOS
Bayamon, PR

CONTACT Financial Aid Office, Centro de Estudios Multidisciplinarios, Calle Degetau #25, Bayamon, PR 00961, 787-780-8900. *Website:* http://www.cempr.edu/.

CENTRO DE ESTUDIOS MULTIDISCIPLINARIOS
Humacao, PR

CONTACT Financial Aid Office, Centro de Estudios Multidisciplinarios, Calle Dr. Vidal #8 y #53, Humacao, PR 00791, 809-852-5505. *Website:* http://www.cempr.edu/.

CHADRON STATE COLLEGE
Chadron, NE

CONTACT Ms. Sherry Douglas, Director of Financial Aid, Chadron State College, 1000 Main Street, Chadron, NE 69337, 308-432-6230 or toll-free 800-242-3766. *Fax:* 308-432-6229. *E-mail:* finaid@csc.edu. *Website:* http://www.csc.edu/.

CHAMBERLAIN COLLEGE OF NURSING
Phoenix, AZ

CONTACT Financial Aid Office, Chamberlain College of Nursing, 2149 West Dunlap Avenue, Phoenix, AZ 85021, 602-331-2720 or toll-free 877-751-5783. *Website:* http://www.chamberlain.edu/.

CHAMBERLAIN COLLEGE OF NURSING
Jacksonville, FL

CONTACT Financial Aid Office, Chamberlain College of Nursing, 5200 Belfort Road, Jacksonville, FL 32256, 904-251-8110 or toll-free 877-751-5783. *Website:* http://www.chamberlain.edu/.

CHAMBERLAIN COLLEGE OF NURSING
Miramar, FL

CONTACT Financial Aid Office, Chamberlain College of Nursing, 2300 SW 145th Avenue, Miramar, FL 33027, 954-885-3510 or toll-free 877-751-5783. *Website:* http://www.chamberlain.edu/.

CHAMBERLAIN COLLEGE OF NURSING
Atlanta, GA

CONTACT Financial Aid Office, Chamberlain College of Nursing, 5775 Peachtree Dunwoody Road NE, Suite A-100, Atlanta, GA 30342, 404-250-8500 or toll-free 877-751-5783.
Website: http://www.chamberlain.edu/.

CHAMBERLAIN COLLEGE OF NURSING
Addison, IL

CONTACT Financial Aid Office, Chamberlain College of Nursing, 1221 North Swift Road, Addison, IL 60101, 630-953-3660 or toll-free 877-751-5783.
Website: http://www.chamberlain.edu/.

CHAMBERLAIN COLLEGE OF NURSING
Chicago, IL

CONTACT Financial Aid Office, Chamberlain College of Nursing, 3300 North Campbell Avenue, Chicago, IL 60618, 773-961-3000 or toll-free 877-751-5783.
Website: http://www.chamberlain.edu/.

CHAMBERLAIN COLLEGE OF NURSING
Tinley Park, IL

CONTACT Financial Aid Office, Chamberlain College of Nursing, 18624 West Creek Drive, Tinley Park, IL 60477, 708-560-2000 or toll-free 877-751-5783.
Website: http://www.chamberlain.edu/.

CHAMBERLAIN COLLEGE OF NURSING
Indianapolis, IN

CONTACT Financial Aid Office, Chamberlain College of Nursing, 9100 Keystone Crossing, Indianapolis, IN 46240, 317-816-7335 or toll-free 877-751-5783.
Website: http://www.chamberlain.edu/.

CHAMBERLAIN COLLEGE OF NURSING
Troy, MI

CONTACT Financial Aid Office, Chamberlain College of Nursing, 200 Kirts Boulevard, Troy, MI 48084, 248-817-4140 or toll-free 877-751-5783.
Website: http://www.chamberlain.edu/.

CHAMBERLAIN COLLEGE OF NURSING
St. Louis, MO

CONTACT Financial Aid Counselor, Chamberlain College of Nursing, 11830 Westline Industrial Drive, Suite 106, St. Louis, MO 63146, 314-991-6200 or toll-free 877-751-5783.
Website: http://www.chamberlain.edu/.

CHAMBERLAIN COLLEGE OF NURSING
Las Vegas, NV

CONTACT Financial Aid Office, Chamberlain College of Nursing, 9901 Covington Cross Drive, Las Vegas, NV 89144, 702-786-1660 or toll-free 877-751-5783.
Website: http://www.chamberlain.edu/.

CHAMBERLAIN COLLEGE OF NURSING
North Brunswick, NJ

CONTACT Financial Aid Office, Chamberlain College of Nursing, 630 U.S. Highway 1, North Brunswick, NJ 08902, 732-875-1300 or toll-free 877-751-5783.
Website: http://www.chamberlain.edu/.

CHAMBERLAIN COLLEGE OF NURSING
Cleveland, OH

CONTACT Financial Aid Office, Chamberlain College of Nursing, 6700 Euclid Avenue, Cleveland, OH 44103, 216-361-6005 or toll-free 877-751-5783.
Website: http://www.chamberlain.edu/.

CHAMBERLAIN COLLEGE OF NURSING
Columbus, OH

CONTACT Financial Aid Office, Chamberlain College of Nursing, 1350 Alum Creek Drive, Columbus, OH 43209, 614-252-8890 or toll-free 877-751-5783.
Website: http://www.chamberlain.edu/.

CHAMBERLAIN COLLEGE OF NURSING
Houston, TX

CONTACT Financial Aid Office, Chamberlain College of Nursing, 11025 Equity Drive, Houston, TX 77041, 713-277-9800 or toll-free 877-751-5783.
Website: http://www.chamberlain.edu/.

CHAMBERLAIN COLLEGE OF NURSING
Pearland, TX

CONTACT Financial Aid Office, Chamberlain College of Nursing, 12000 Shadow Creek Parkway, Pearland, TX 77584, 832-664-7000 or toll-free 877-751-5783. *Website:* http://www.chamberlain.edu/.

CHAMBERLAIN COLLEGE OF NURSING
Arlington, VA

CONTACT Financial Aid Office, Chamberlain College of Nursing, 2450 Crystal Drive, Suite 319, Arlington, VA 22202, 703-416-7300 or toll-free 877-751-5783. *Website:* http://www.chamberlain.edu/.

CHAMINADE UNIVERSITY OF HONOLULU
Honolulu, HI

Tuition & fees: $24,514	Average undergraduate aid package: $19,111

ABOUT THE INSTITUTION Independent Roman Catholic, coed. *Awards:* certificates, associate, bachelor's, and master's degrees. 23 undergraduate majors. *Total enrollment:* 1,769. Undergraduates: 1,183. Freshmen: 256. Federal methodology is used as a basis for awarding need-based institutional aid.
UNDERGRADUATE EXPENSES for 2017–2018 *Application fee:* $50. *One-time required fee:* $180. *Comprehensive fee:* $37,614 includes full-time tuition ($24,400), mandatory fees ($114), and room and board ($13,100). Full-time tuition and fees vary according to course load, location, and program. Room and board charges vary according to board plan and housing facility. *Part-time tuition:* $813 per credit. Part-time tuition and fees vary according to course load, location, and program.
FRESHMAN FINANCIAL AID (Fall 2015) 196 applied for aid; of those 82% were deemed to have need. 100% of freshmen with need received aid; of those 21% had need fully met. *Average percent of need met:* 77% (excluding resources awarded to replace EFC). *Average financial aid package:* $21,080 (excluding resources awarded to replace EFC). 24% of all full-time freshmen had no need and received non-need-based gift aid.
UNDERGRADUATE FINANCIAL AID (Fall 2015) 951 applied for aid; of those 88% were deemed to have need. 100% of undergraduates with need received aid; of those 14% had need fully met. *Average percent of need met:* 66% (excluding resources awarded to replace EFC). *Average financial aid package:* $19,111 (excluding resources awarded to replace EFC). 26% of all full-time undergraduates had no need and received non-need-based gift aid.
GIFT AID (NEED-BASED) *Receiving aid:* Freshmen: 72% (155); all full-time undergraduates: 66% (783). *Average award:* Freshmen: $5138; Undergraduates: $4943. *Scholarships, grants, and awards:* Federal Pell, FSEOG, private, college/university gift aid from institutional funds, TEACH Grants.
GIFT AID (NON-NEED-BASED) *Receiving aid:* Freshmen: 74% (159). Undergraduates: 68% (811). *Average award:* Freshmen: $11,378. Undergraduates: $7827. *Scholarships, grants, and awards by category: Academic interests/achievement:* 986 awards ($6,861,770 total): general academic interests/achievements. *Special achievements/activities:* 73 awards ($943,327 total): community service, memberships, religious involvement. *Special characteristics:* 113 awards ($1,412,538 total): children of faculty/staff, ethnic background, religious affiliation, siblings of current students. *Tuition waivers:* Full or partial for employees or children of employees. *ROTC:* Army cooperative, Air Force cooperative.
LOANS *Student loans:* 64% of past graduating class borrowed through all loan programs. *Average indebtedness per student:* $31,145. *Average need-based loan:* Freshmen: $3249. Undergraduates: $4234. *Programs:* Federal Direct (Subsidized and Unsubsidized Stafford, PLUS), alternative loans.
WORK-STUDY Federal work-study jobs available.

APPLYING FOR FINANCIAL AID *Required financial aid form:* FAFSA. *Financial aid deadline:* Continuous. *Notification date:* Continuous.
CONTACT Amy Takiguchi, Director of Financial Aid, Chaminade University of Honolulu, 3140 Waialae Avenue, Honolulu, HI 96816-1578, 808-735-4780 or toll-free 800-735-3733. *Fax:* 808-739-8362. *E-mail:* finaid@chaminade.edu. *Website:* http://www.chaminade.edu/.

CHAMPLAIN COLLEGE
Burlington, VT

Tuition & fees: $38,660	Average undergraduate aid package: $25,134

ABOUT THE INSTITUTION Independent, coed. *Awards:* certificates, associate, bachelor's, and master's degrees. 38 undergraduate majors. *Total enrollment:* 3,133. Undergraduates: 2,267. Freshmen: 650. Federal methodology is used as a basis for awarding need-based institutional aid.
UNDERGRADUATE EXPENSES for 2016–2017 *Comprehensive fee:* $53,132 includes full-time tuition ($38,560), mandatory fees ($100), and room and board ($14,472). Room and board charges vary according to housing facility. *Part-time tuition:* $1608 per credit hour. *Payment plan:* Tuition prepayment.
FRESHMAN FINANCIAL AID (Fall 2016, est.) 556 applied for aid; of those 87% were deemed to have need. 100% of freshmen with need received aid; of those 16% had need fully met. *Average percent of need met:* 71% (excluding resources awarded to replace EFC). *Average financial aid package:* $27,978 (excluding resources awarded to replace EFC). 25% of all full-time freshmen had no need and received non-need-based gift aid.
UNDERGRADUATE FINANCIAL AID (Fall 2016, est.) 2,028 applied for aid; of those 88% were deemed to have need. 99% of undergraduates with need received aid; of those 14% had need fully met. *Average percent of need met:* 67% (excluding resources awarded to replace EFC). *Average financial aid package:* $25,134 (excluding resources awarded to replace EFC). 23% of all full-time undergraduates had no need and received non-need-based gift aid.
GIFT AID (NEED-BASED) *Total amount:* $34,088,761 (13% federal, 4% state, 82% institutional, 1% external sources). *Receiving aid:* Freshmen: 74% (476); all full-time undergraduates: 66% (1,713). *Average award:* Freshmen: $21,918; Undergraduates: $19,364. *Scholarships, grants, and awards:* Federal Pell, FSEOG, state, private, college/university gift aid from institutional funds.
GIFT AID (NON-NEED-BASED) *Total amount:* $8,166,991 (7% federal, 1% state, 90% institutional, 2% external sources). *Receiving aid:* Freshmen: 8% (53). Undergraduates: 6% (165). *Average award:* Freshmen: $10,729. Undergraduates: $10,330. *Scholarships, grants, and awards by category: Academic interests/achievement:* business, communication, computer science, education, general academic interests/achievements, social sciences. *Special achievements/activities:* leadership. *Special characteristics:* first-generation college students, general special characteristics, international students, members of minority groups. *Tuition waivers:* Full or partial for employees or children of employees. *ROTC:* Army cooperative.
LOANS *Student loans:* $21,571,407 (73% need-based, 27% non-need-based). 73% of past graduating class borrowed through all loan programs. *Average indebtedness per student:* $34,582. *Average need-based loan:* Freshmen: $3547. Undergraduates: $4230. *Parent loans:* $13,479,984 (51% need-based, 49% non-need-based). *Programs:* Federal Direct (Subsidized and Unsubsidized Stafford, PLUS), Perkins, state.
WORK-STUDY *Federal work-study:* Total amount: $2,956,543; jobs available.
APPLYING FOR FINANCIAL AID *Required financial aid form:* FAFSA. *Financial aid deadline:* 1/15. *Notification date:* 3/30. Students must reply by 5/1 or within 2 weeks of notification.
CONTACT Kristi Jovell, Director of Financial Aid, Champlain College, 163 South Willard Street, Burlington, VT 05401, 802-860-2777 or toll-free 800-570-5858. *Fax:* 802-860-2775. *E-mail:* kjovell@champlain.edu. *Website:* http://www.champlain.edu/.

CHAPMAN UNIVERSITY
Orange, CA

Tuition & fees: $50,594	Average undergraduate aid package: $30,329

ABOUT THE INSTITUTION Independent Christian Church (Disciples of Christ), coed. *Awards:* bachelor's, master's, and doctoral degrees. 50 undergraduate majors. *Total enrollment:* 8,542. Undergraduates: 6,410. Freshmen: 1,492. Federal methodology is used as a basis for awarding need-based institutional aid.

UNDERGRADUATE EXPENSES for 2017–2018 *Application fee:* $70. *Comprehensive fee:* $65,504 includes full-time tuition ($50,210), mandatory fees ($384), and room and board ($14,910). *College room only:* $10,176. Room and board charges vary according to board plan and housing facility. *Part-time tuition:* $1560 per credit hour. Part-time tuition and fees vary according to course load. *Payment plan:* Tuition prepayment.

FRESHMAN FINANCIAL AID (Fall 2015) 1,037 applied for aid; of those 80% were deemed to have need. 100% of freshmen with need received aid; of those 11% had need fully met. *Average percent of need met:* 72% (excluding resources awarded to replace EFC). *Average financial aid package:* $31,342 (excluding resources awarded to replace EFC). 12% of all full-time freshmen had no need and received non-need-based gift aid.

UNDERGRADUATE FINANCIAL AID (Fall 2015) 3,917 applied for aid; of those 88% were deemed to have need. 100% of undergraduates with need received aid; of those 9% had need fully met. *Average percent of need met:* 66% (excluding resources awarded to replace EFC). *Average financial aid package:* $30,329 (excluding resources awarded to replace EFC). 6% of all full-time undergraduates had no need and received non-need-based gift aid.

GIFT AID (NEED-BASED) *Total amount:* $102,775,880 (6% federal, 5% state, 88% institutional, 1% external sources). *Receiving aid:* Freshmen: 54% (769); all full-time undergraduates: 51% (3,082). *Average award:* Freshmen: $16,741; Undergraduates: $16,243. *Scholarships, grants, and awards:* Federal Pell, FSEOG, state, private, college/university gift aid from institutional funds.

GIFT AID (NON-NEED-BASED) *Total amount:* $6,359,534 (99% institutional, 1% external sources). *Receiving aid:* Freshmen: 44% (621). Undergraduates: 37% (2,249). *Average award:* Freshmen: $17,318. Undergraduates: $16,367. *Scholarships, grants, and awards by category:* Academic interests/achievement: 3,500 awards ($55,534,586 total): biological sciences, general academic interests/achievements, physical sciences. Creative arts/performance: 321 awards ($1,139,032 total): art/fine arts, cinema/film/broadcasting, creative writing, dance, music, performing arts, theater/drama. Special characteristics: 54 awards ($52,884 total): children and siblings of alumni. *Tuition waivers:* Full or partial for employees or children of employees. *ROTC:* Army cooperative, Air Force cooperative.

LOANS *Student loans:* $24,007,251 (91% need-based, 9% non-need-based). 54% of past graduating class borrowed through all loan programs. *Average indebtedness per student:* $25,959. *Average need-based loan:* Freshmen: $3431. Undergraduates: $4568. *Parent loans:* $23,702,330 (85% need-based, 15% non-need-based). *Programs:* Federal Direct (Subsidized and Unsubsidized Stafford, Perkins.

WORK-STUDY *Federal work-study:* 2,964 jobs averaging $2700.

APPLYING FOR FINANCIAL AID *Required financial aid forms:* FAFSA, state aid form. *Financial aid deadline (priority):* 3/2. *Notification date:* Continuous beginning 3/15. Students must reply within 3 weeks of notification.

CONTACT Mr. Jim Whitaker, Associate Vice Chancellor of Enrollment Management, Chapman University, One University Drive, Orange, CA 92866, 714-532-6050 or toll-free 888-CUAPPLY. *Fax:* 714-997-6743. *E-mail:* whitaker@chapman.edu. *Website:* http://www.chapman.edu/.

CHARLES R. DREW UNIVERSITY OF MEDICINE AND SCIENCE
Los Angeles, CA

CONTACT Financial Aid Office, Charles R. Drew University of Medicine and Science, 1731 East 120th Street, Los Angeles, CA 90059, 323-563-4824. *Fax:* 323-569-0597. *Website:* http://www.cdrewu.edu/.

CHARLESTON SOUTHERN UNIVERSITY
Charleston, SC

CONTACT Mr. Jim Rhoden, Director of Admissions, Charleston Southern University, PO Box 118087, 9200 University Boulevard, Charleston, SC 29423-8087, 843-863-7050 or toll-free 800-947-7474. *Fax:* 843-863-7070. *Website:* http://www.charlestonsouthern.edu/.

CHARLOTTE CHRISTIAN COLLEGE AND THEOLOGICAL SEMINARY
Charlotte, NC

Tuition & fees: N/R	Average undergraduate aid package: $6388

ABOUT THE INSTITUTION Independent Christian, coed. 2 undergraduate majors. Federal methodology is used as a basis for awarding need-based institutional aid.

UNDERGRADUATE FINANCIAL AID (Fall 2015) 18 applied for aid; of those 100% were deemed to have need. 100% of undergraduates with need received aid; of those 100% had need fully met. *Average percent of need met:* 100% (excluding resources awarded to replace EFC). *Average financial aid package:* $6388 (excluding resources awarded to replace EFC).

GIFT AID (NEED-BASED) *Total amount:* $180,530 (79% federal, 21% institutional). *Receiving aid:* All full-time undergraduates: 86% (18). *Average award:* Undergraduates: $2908. *Scholarships, grants, and awards:* Federal Pell, FSEOG, private, college/university gift aid from institutional funds, Veterans Education Benefits (GI Bill).

GIFT AID (NON-NEED-BASED) *Total amount:* $15,377 (100% institutional). *Receiving aid:* Undergraduates: 29% (6). *Scholarships, grants, and awards by category:* Academic interests/achievement: 4 awards ($6550 total): education, foreign languages, general academic interests/achievements, religion/biblical studies. Special achievements/activities: memberships, religious involvement. Special characteristics: religious affiliation.

LOANS *Student loans:* $267,361 (100% need-based). 100% of past graduating class borrowed through all loan programs. *Average indebtedness per student:* $33,034. *Average need-based loan:* Undergraduates: $3500. *Programs:* Federal Direct (Subsidized and Unsubsidized Stafford, PLUS).

WORK-STUDY *Federal work-study:* 2 jobs averaging $4274.

APPLYING FOR FINANCIAL AID *Required financial aid form:* FAFSA. *Financial aid deadline:* Continuous. *Notification date:* Continuous beginning 1/15. Students must reply within 2 weeks of notification.

CONTACT Mr. Kenneth Neal Roach, Financial Aid Officer, Charlotte Christian College and Theological Seminary, 3117 Whiting Avenue, PO Box 790106, Charlotte, NC 28206-7901, 704-334-6882 Ext. 114. *Fax:* 704-334-6885. *E-mail:* kroach@charlottechristian.edu. *Website:* http://www.charlottechristian.edu/.

CHARTER OAK STATE COLLEGE
New Britain, CT

Tuition & fees (CT res): $9393	Average undergraduate aid package: $7454

ABOUT THE INSTITUTION State-supported, coed. *Awards:* certificates, associate, bachelor's, and master's degrees (offers only external degree programs). 6 undergraduate majors. *Total enrollment:* 1,583. Undergraduates: 1,533. Federal methodology is used as a basis for awarding need-based institutional aid.

UNDERGRADUATE EXPENSES for 2016–2017 *Application fee:* $75. *Tuition, state resident:* full-time $8610; part-time $287 per credit. *Tuition, nonresident:* full-time $11,310; part-time $377 per credit. *Required fees:* full-time $783; $261 per term. Full-time tuition and fees vary according to course load. Part-time tuition and fees vary according to course load.

UNDERGRADUATE FINANCIAL AID (Fall 2015) 261 applied for aid; of those 92% were deemed to have need. 99% of undergraduates with need received aid; of those 3% had need fully met. *Average percent of need met:* 47% (excluding resources awarded to replace EFC). *Average financial aid package:* $7454 (excluding resources awarded to replace EFC). 1% of all full-time undergraduates had no need and received non-need-based gift aid.

GIFT AID (NEED-BASED) *Total amount:* $2,393,413 (71% federal, 11% state, 5% institutional, 13% external sources). *Receiving aid:* All full-time undergraduates: 64% (212). *Average award:* Undergraduates: $1106. *Scholarships, grants, and awards:* Federal Pell, FSEOG, state, college/university gift aid from institutional funds, foundation grants.

GIFT AID (NON-NEED-BASED) *Total amount:* $121,900 (1% federal, 55% state, 9% institutional, 35% external sources). *Receiving aid:* Undergraduates: 1% (2). *Average award:* Undergraduates: $922. *Scholarships, grants, and awards by category:* Academic interests/achievement: general academic interests/achievements.

LOANS *Student loans:* $5,716,279 (77% need-based, 23% non-need-based). *Average need-based loan:* Undergraduates: $4280. *Programs:* Federal Direct (Subsidized and Unsubsidized Stafford, PLUS), state, alternative loans.

APPLYING FOR FINANCIAL AID *Required financial aid form:* FAFSA. *Financial aid deadline (priority):* 7/1. *Notification date:* Continuous beginning 8/1.

CONTACT Ralph Brasure, Director of Financial Aid, Charter Oak State College, 55 Paul Manafort Drive, New Britain, CT 06053-2142, 860-515-3703. Fax: 860-760-6540. E-mail: sfa@charteroak.edu.

Website: http://www.charteroak.edu/.

CHATHAM UNIVERSITY
Pittsburgh, PA

Tuition & fees: $35,475	Average undergraduate aid package: $25,627

ABOUT THE INSTITUTION Independent, coed, primarily women. *Awards:* certificates, bachelor's, master's, and doctoral degrees. 44 undergraduate majors. *Total enrollment:* 2,110. Undergraduates: 1,002. Freshmen: 194. Both federal and institutional methodology are used as a basis for awarding need-based institutional aid.

UNDERGRADUATE EXPENSES for 2016–2017 *Application fee:* $35. *Comprehensive fee:* $46,517 includes full-time tuition ($34,195), mandatory fees ($1280), and room and board ($11,042). *College room only:* $5634. Room and board charges vary according to board plan and housing facility. *Part-time tuition:* $829 per credit. Part-time tuition and fees vary according to course load.

FRESHMAN FINANCIAL AID (Fall 2016, est.) 188 applied for aid; of those 85% were deemed to have need. 100% of freshmen with need received aid; of those 31% had need fully met. *Average percent of need met:* 74% (excluding resources awarded to replace EFC). *Average financial aid package:* $28,841 (excluding resources awarded to replace EFC). 6% of all full-time freshmen had no need and received non-need-based gift aid.

UNDERGRADUATE FINANCIAL AID (Fall 2016, est.) 687 applied for aid; of those 84% were deemed to have need. 100% of undergraduates with need received aid; of those 22% had need fully met. *Average percent of need met:* 83% (excluding resources awarded to replace EFC). *Average financial aid package:* $25,627 (excluding resources awarded to replace EFC). 4% of all full-time undergraduates had no need and received non-need-based gift aid.

GIFT AID (NEED-BASED) *Total amount:* $12,973,311 (11% federal, 9% state, 79% institutional, 1% external sources). *Receiving aid:* Freshmen: 82% (160); all full-time undergraduates: 69% (505). *Average award:* Freshmen: $8321; Undergraduates: $8938. *Scholarships, grants, and awards:* Federal Pell, FSEOG, state, private, college/university gift aid from institutional funds.

GIFT AID (NON-NEED-BASED) *Total amount:* $2,754,328 (93% institutional, 7% external sources). *Receiving aid:* Freshmen: 82% (160). Undergraduates: 69% (505). *Average award:* Freshmen: $15,637. Undergraduates: $15,576. *Scholarships, grants, and awards by category:* Academic interests/achievement: 647 awards ($10,009,202 total): general academic interests/achievements. *Creative arts/performance:* 16 awards ($38,600 total): applied art and design, art/fine arts, music. *Special achievements/activities:* 411 awards ($1,129,000 total): leadership. *Special characteristics:* 64 awards ($264,147 total): children and siblings of alumni, children of faculty/staff, siblings of current students. *Tuition waivers:* Full or partial for

employees or children of employees. *ROTC:* Army cooperative, Naval cooperative, Air Force cooperative.

LOANS *Student loans:* $5,368,626 (69% need-based, 31% non-need-based). 83% of past graduating class borrowed through all loan programs. *Average indebtedness per student:* $37,734. *Average need-based loan:* Freshmen: $3500. Undergraduates: $4670. *Parent loans:* $2,147,777 (92% need-based, 8% non-need-based). *Programs:* Federal Direct (Subsidized and Unsubsidized Stafford, PLUS), Perkins.

WORK-STUDY *Federal work-study:* Total amount: $521,432; 220 jobs averaging $2200. *State or other work-study/employment:* Total amount: $200,000 (100% non-need-based). Part-time jobs available.

APPLYING FOR FINANCIAL AID *Required financial aid form:* FAFSA. *Financial aid deadline:* 3/1 (priority: 3/1). *Notification date:* 3/1. Students must reply within 3 weeks of notification.

CONTACT Dr. Jennifer Burns, Director of Financial Aid, Chatham University, Woodland Road, Pittsburgh, PA 15232-2826, 412-365-1849 or toll-free 800-837-1290. Fax: 412-365-1643. E-mail: jburns@chatham.edu.

Website: http://www.chatham.edu/.

CHESTNUT HILL COLLEGE
Philadelphia, PA

Tuition & fees: $35,160	Average undergraduate aid package: $23,919

ABOUT THE INSTITUTION Independent Roman Catholic, coed. *Awards:* certificates, associate, bachelor's, master's, and doctoral degrees (profile includes figures from both traditional and accelerated (part-time) programs). 45 undergraduate majors. *Total enrollment:* 1,838. Undergraduates: 1,369. Freshmen: 244. Federal methodology is used as a basis for awarding need-based institutional aid.

UNDERGRADUATE EXPENSES for 2017–2018 *Application fee:* $35. *One-time required fee:* $425. *Comprehensive fee:* $45,560 includes full-time tuition ($34,950), mandatory fees ($210), and room and board ($10,400). Room and board charges vary according to board plan and housing facility. *Part-time tuition:* $745 per credit hour.

FRESHMAN FINANCIAL AID (Fall 2016, est.) 223 applied for aid; of those 94% were deemed to have need. 100% of freshmen with need received aid; of those 9% had need fully met. *Average percent of need met:* 67% (excluding resources awarded to replace EFC). *Average financial aid package:* $29,275 (excluding resources awarded to replace EFC). 10% of all full-time freshmen had no need and received non-need-based gift aid.

UNDERGRADUATE FINANCIAL AID (Fall 2016, est.) 972 applied for aid; of those 95% were deemed to have need. 100% of undergraduates with need received aid; of those 7% had need fully met. *Average percent of need met:* 56% (excluding resources awarded to replace EFC). *Average financial aid package:* $23,919 (excluding resources awarded to replace EFC). 10% of all full-time undergraduates had no need and received non-need-based gift aid.

GIFT AID (NEED-BASED) *Total amount:* $17,813,592 (18% federal, 9% state, 70% institutional, 3% external sources). *Receiving aid:* Freshmen: 87% (207); all full-time undergraduates: 83% (891). *Average award:* Freshmen: $25,285; Undergraduates: $19,979. *Scholarships, grants, and awards:* Federal Pell, FSEOG, state, private, college/university gift aid from institutional funds.

GIFT AID (NON-NEED-BASED) *Total amount:* $2,038,008 (99% institutional, 1% external sources). *Receiving aid:* Freshmen: 7% (16). Undergraduates: 4% (46). *Average award:* Freshmen: $16,940. Undergraduates: $14,926. *Scholarships, grants, and awards by category:* Creative arts/performance: music. *Special characteristics:* 13 awards ($239,219 total): children of educators, children of faculty/staff, international students, veterans, veterans' children. *Tuition waivers:* Full or partial for employees or children of employees, senior citizens.

LOANS *Student loans:* $12,269,718 (86% need-based, 14% non-need-based). 87% of past graduating class borrowed through all loan programs. *Average indebtedness per student:* $42,527. *Average need-based loan:* Freshmen: $3393. Undergraduates: $4298. *Parent loans:* $2,961,443 (66% need-based, 34% non-need-based). *Programs:* Federal Direct (Subsidized and Unsubsidized Stafford, PLUS), Perkins, state.

WORK-STUDY *Federal work-study:* Total amount: $272,250; 386 jobs averaging $1224.

ATHLETIC AWARDS Total amount: $1,460,317 (58% need-based, 42% non-need-based).

APPLYING FOR FINANCIAL AID *Required financial aid form:* FAFSA. *Financial aid deadline:* Continuous. *Notification date:* Continuous beginning 11/1.
CONTACT Ms. Dawn Snook, Director of Financial Aid, Chestnut Hill College, 9601 Germantown Avenue, Philadelphia, PA 19118-2693, 215-248-7076 or toll-free 800-248-0052. *Fax:* 215-248-7217. *E-mail:* snookd@chc.edu.
Website: http://www.chc.edu/.

CHEYNEY UNIVERSITY OF PENNSYLVANIA
Cheyney, PA

CONTACT Mr. James Brown, Director of Financial Aid, Cheyney University of Pennsylvania, 1837 University Circle, Cheyney, PA 19319, 610-399-2302 or toll-free 800-CHEYNEY. *Fax:* 610-399-2411. *E-mail:* jbrown@cheyney.edu.
Website: http://www.cheyney.edu/.

CHICAGO STATE UNIVERSITY
Chicago, IL

CONTACT Ms. Cathy Davis, Director of Student Financial Aid, Chicago State University, 9501 South Martin Luther King Drive, Chicago, IL 60628, 773-995-2304. *E-mail:* cdavis58@csu.edu.
Website: http://www.csu.edu/.

CHOWAN UNIVERSITY
Murfreesboro, NC

Tuition & fees: $22,480	Average undergraduate aid package: $21,012

ABOUT THE INSTITUTION Independent Baptist, coed. *Awards:* associate, bachelor's, and master's degrees. 39 undergraduate majors. *Total enrollment:* 1,534. Undergraduates: 1,525. Freshmen: 494. Federal methodology is used as a basis for awarding need-based institutional aid.
UNDERGRADUATE EXPENSES for 2017–2018 *Application fee:* $20. *Tuition:* full-time $22,480; part-time $400 per credit hour. Room and board charges vary according to board plan.
FRESHMAN FINANCIAL AID (Fall 2016, est.) 489 applied for aid; of those 98% were deemed to have need. 100% of freshmen with need received aid; of those 5% had need fully met. *Average percent of need met:* 64% (excluding resources awarded to replace EFC). *Average financial aid package:* $20,641 (excluding resources awarded to replace EFC). 3% of all full-time freshmen had no need and received non-need-based gift aid.
UNDERGRADUATE FINANCIAL AID (Fall 2016, est.) 1,404 applied for aid; of those 98% were deemed to have need. 100% of undergraduates with need received aid; of those 10% had need fully met. *Average percent of need met:* 66% (excluding resources awarded to replace EFC). *Average financial aid package:* $21,012 (excluding resources awarded to replace EFC). 7% of all full-time undergraduates had no need and received non-need-based gift aid.
GIFT AID (NEED-BASED) *Total amount:* $22,672,067 (25% federal, 13% state, 60% institutional, 2% external sources). *Receiving aid:* Freshmen: 97% (480); all full-time undergraduates: 93% (1,369). *Average award:* Freshmen: $17,316; Undergraduates: $16,719. *Scholarships, grants, and awards:* Federal Pell, FSEOG, state, private, college/university gift aid from institutional funds.
GIFT AID (NON-NEED-BASED) *Total amount:* $120,257 (6% federal, 94% state). *Receiving aid:* Undergraduates: 1% (10). *Average award:* Freshmen: $6792. Undergraduates: $7512. *Scholarships, grants, and awards by category:* Academic interests/achievement: 1,468 awards ($6,278,202 total): general academic interests/achievements. Creative arts/performance: 33 awards ($78,523 total): music. Special achievements/activities: 632 awards ($1,733,295 total): leadership. Special characteristics: 26 awards ($281,935 total): children of educators, children of faculty/staff, children of public servants, children of union members/company employees, first-generation college students, general special characteristics, handicapped students,

international students, local/state students, out-of-state students, public servants, relatives of clergy, religious affiliation, veterans, veterans' children. *Tuition waivers:* Full or partial for employees or children of employees.
LOANS *Student loans:* $10,515,354 (48% need-based, 52% non-need-based). 88% of past graduating class borrowed through all loan programs. *Average indebtedness per student:* $41,845. *Average need-based loan:* Freshmen: $3124. Undergraduates: $4048. *Parent loans:* $5,394,894 (100% non-need-based). *Programs:* Federal Direct (Subsidized and Unsubsidized Stafford, PLUS), Perkins, state, alternative loans.
WORK-STUDY *Federal work-study:* Total amount: $454,169; 315 jobs averaging $1441. *State or other work-study/employment:* Total amount: $7000 (100% non-need-based). 173 part-time jobs averaging $1977.
ATHLETIC AWARDS Total amount: $2,811,858 (100% need-based).
APPLYING FOR FINANCIAL AID *Required financial aid form:* FAFSA. *Financial aid deadline (priority):* 5/1. *Notification date:* Continuous beginning 4/1. Students must reply within 2 weeks of notification.
CONTACT Mrs. Sharon W. Rose, Director of Financial Aid, Chowan University, One University Place, Murfreesboro, NC 27855, 252-398-6535 or toll-free 888-4-CHOWAN. *Fax:* 252-398-6513. *E-mail:* roses1@chowan.edu.
Website: http://www.chowan.edu/.

CHRISTENDOM COLLEGE
Front Royal, VA

Tuition & fees: $24,840	Average undergraduate aid package: $19,472

ABOUT THE INSTITUTION Independent Roman Catholic, coed. *Awards:* associate, bachelor's, and master's degrees. 8 undergraduate majors. *Total enrollment:* 583. Undergraduates: 477. Freshmen: 119. Institutional methodology is used as a basis for awarding need-based institutional aid.
UNDERGRADUATE EXPENSES for 2016–2017 *Comprehensive fee:* $34,570 includes full-time tuition ($23,990), mandatory fees ($850), and room and board ($9730).
FRESHMAN FINANCIAL AID (Fall 2016, est.) 88 applied for aid; of those 77% were deemed to have need. 100% of freshmen with need received aid. *Average percent of need met:* 72% (excluding resources awarded to replace EFC). *Average financial aid package:* $18,467 (excluding resources awarded to replace EFC). 24% of all full-time freshmen had no need and received non-need-based gift aid.
UNDERGRADUATE FINANCIAL AID (Fall 2016, est.) 287 applied for aid; of those 90% were deemed to have need. 100% of undergraduates with need received aid. *Average percent of need met:* 75% (excluding resources awarded to replace EFC). *Average financial aid package:* $19,472 (excluding resources awarded to replace EFC). 19% of all full-time undergraduates had no need and received non-need-based gift aid.
GIFT AID (NEED-BASED) *Total amount:* $4,108,554 (100% institutional). *Receiving aid:* Freshmen: 57% (68); all full-time undergraduates: 54% (258). *Average award:* Freshmen: $12,292; Undergraduates: $12,511. *Scholarships, grants, and awards:* state, private, college/university gift aid from institutional funds.
GIFT AID (NON-NEED-BASED) *Total amount:* $1,557,458 (31% state, 65% institutional, 4% external sources). *Receiving aid:* Freshmen: 2% (2). Undergraduates: 2% (8). *Average award:* Freshmen: $10,527. Undergraduates: $10,452. *Scholarships, grants, and awards by category:* Academic interests/achievement: 284 awards ($2,467,478 total): general academic interests/achievements. Special characteristics: 91 awards ($591,000 total): siblings of current students. *Tuition waivers:* Full or partial for employees or children of employees.
LOANS *Student loans:* $2,917,281 (73% need-based, 27% non-need-based). 69% of past graduating class borrowed through all loan programs. *Average indebtedness per student:* $27,005. *Average need-based loan:* Freshmen: $6753. Undergraduates: $7343. *Programs:* college/university.
WORK-STUDY *State or other work-study/employment:* Total amount: $325,247 (100% non-need-based). 150 part-time jobs averaging $2168.
APPLYING FOR FINANCIAL AID *Required financial aid form:* institution's own form. *Financial aid deadline (priority):* 4/15. *Notification date:* Continuous beginning 2/1. Students must reply within 4 weeks of notification.
CONTACT Ms. Alisa Polk, Financial Aid Officer, Christendom College, 134 Christendom Drive, Front Royal, VA 22630-5103, 800-877-5456 Ext. 1214 or toll-free 800-877-5456. *Fax:* 540-631-0297. *E-mail:* apolk@christendom.edu.
Website: http://www.christendom.edu/.

CHRISTIAN BROTHERS UNIVERSITY
Memphis, TN

Tuition & fees: $30,860	Average undergraduate aid package: $24,503

ABOUT THE INSTITUTION Independent Roman Catholic, coed. *Awards:* associate, bachelor's, and master's degrees. 39 undergraduate majors. *Total enrollment:* 1,842. Undergraduates: 1,410. Freshmen: 312. Both federal and institutional methodology are used as a basis for awarding need-based institutional aid.

UNDERGRADUATE EXPENSES for 2017–2018 *Application fee:* $25. *Comprehensive fee:* $37,860 includes full-time tuition ($29,990), mandatory fees ($870), and room and board ($7000). Full-time tuition and fees vary according to class time, course load, and program. Room and board charges vary according to board plan and housing facility. *Part-time tuition:* $1070 per credit hour. *Part-time fees:* $205 per term. Part-time tuition and fees vary according to class time, course load, and program.

FRESHMAN FINANCIAL AID (Fall 2016, est.) 336 applied for aid; of those 73% were deemed to have need. 100% of freshmen with need received aid; of those 23% had need fully met. *Average percent of need met:* 80% (excluding resources awarded to replace EFC). *Average financial aid package:* $28,257 (excluding resources awarded to replace EFC). 26% of all full-time freshmen had no need and received non-need-based gift aid.

UNDERGRADUATE FINANCIAL AID (Fall 2016, est.) 1,319 applied for aid; of those 71% were deemed to have need. 100% of undergraduates with need received aid; of those 21% had need fully met. *Average percent of need met:* 72% (excluding resources awarded to replace EFC). *Average financial aid package:* $24,503 (excluding resources awarded to replace EFC). 25% of all full-time undergraduates had no need and received non-need-based gift aid.

GIFT AID (NEED-BASED) *Total amount:* $17,695,543 (15% federal, 15% state, 68% institutional, 2% external sources). *Receiving aid:* Freshmen: 72% (243); all full-time undergraduates: 67% (897). *Average award:* Freshmen: $23,071; Undergraduates: $19,446. *Scholarships, grants, and awards:* Federal Pell, FSEOG, state, private, college/university gift aid from institutional funds.

GIFT AID (NON-NEED-BASED) *Total amount:* $2,480,029 (25% state, 25% institutional, 50% external sources). *Receiving aid:* Freshmen: 13% (44). Undergraduates: 10% (138). *Average award:* Freshmen: $17,981. Undergraduates: $16,735. *Scholarships, grants, and awards by category:* Academic interests/achievement: engineering/technologies, general academic interests/achievements, mathematics. Creative arts/performance: art/fine arts, performing arts. Special achievements/activities: general special achievements/activities, leadership, memberships. Special characteristics: adult students, children and siblings of alumni, ethnic background, general special characteristics, local/state students, out-of-state students, veterans, veterans' children. *Tuition waivers:* Full or partial for employees or children of employees. *ROTC:* Army cooperative, Naval cooperative, Air Force cooperative.

LOANS *Student loans:* $6,604,236 (76% need-based, 24% non-need-based). 68% of past graduating class borrowed through all loan programs. *Average indebtedness per student:* $22,527. *Average need-based loan:* Freshmen: $3471. Undergraduates: $4177. *Parent loans:* $1,167,257 (52% need-based, 48% non-need-based). *Programs:* Federal Direct (Subsidized and Unsubsidized Stafford, PLUS), Perkins, college/university, alternative loans.

WORK-STUDY *Federal work-study:* Total amount: $183,324; 172 jobs averaging $1066. *State or other work-study/employment:* Total amount: $146,050 (17% need-based, 83% non-need-based). 118 part-time jobs averaging $1238.

ATHLETIC AWARDS Total amount: $1,998,230 (33% need-based, 67% non-need-based).

APPLYING FOR FINANCIAL AID *Required financial aid forms:* FAFSA, institution's own form. *Financial aid deadline (priority):* 2/15. *Notification date:* Continuous beginning 2/28. Students must reply by 5/1 or within 2 weeks of notification.

CONTACT Dr. John H. Lewis, IV, Director of Financial Aid, Christian Brothers University, 650 East Parkway South, Memphis, TN 38104, 901-321-3305 or toll-free 877-321-4CBU. *Fax:* 901-321-3327. *E-mail:* john.lewis@cbu.edu. *Website:* http://www.cbu.edu/.

CHRISTIAN LIFE COLLEGE
Mount Prospect, IL

CONTACT Christina Bell, Office of Financial Aid, Christian Life College, 400 East Gregory Street, Mt. Prospect, IL 60056, 847-259-1840. *Fax:* 847-259-3888. *Website:* http://www.christianlifecollege.edu/.

CHRISTOPHER NEWPORT UNIVERSITY
Newport News, VA

Tuition & fees (VA res): $13,054	Average undergraduate aid package: $9195

ABOUT THE INSTITUTION State-supported, coed. *Awards:* bachelor's and master's degrees. 39 undergraduate majors. *Total enrollment:* 5,042. Undergraduates: 4,930. Freshmen: 1,228. Federal methodology is used as a basis for awarding need-based institutional aid.

UNDERGRADUATE EXPENSES for 2016–2017 *Application fee:* $65. *Tuition, state resident:* full-time $7836; part-time $327 per credit hour. *Tuition, nonresident:* full-time $19,062; part-time $794 per credit hour. *Required fees:* full-time $5218; $217 per credit hour. Full-time tuition and fees vary according to course load. Part-time tuition and fees vary according to course load. *College room and board:* $10,914; *Room only:* $6764. Room and board charges vary according to board plan and housing facility.

FRESHMAN FINANCIAL AID (Fall 2016, est.) 985 applied for aid; of those 59% were deemed to have need. 96% of freshmen with need received aid; of those 23% had need fully met. *Average percent of need met:* 72% (excluding resources awarded to replace EFC). *Average financial aid package:* $9117 (excluding resources awarded to replace EFC). 18% of all full-time freshmen had no need and received non-need-based gift aid.

UNDERGRADUATE FINANCIAL AID (Fall 2016, est.) 3,150 applied for aid; of those 69% were deemed to have need. 97% of undergraduates with need received aid; of those 21% had need fully met. *Average percent of need met:* 69% (excluding resources awarded to replace EFC). *Average financial aid package:* $9195 (excluding resources awarded to replace EFC). 14% of all full-time undergraduates had no need and received non-need-based gift aid.

GIFT AID (NEED-BASED) *Total amount:* $9,469,966 (33% federal, 51% state, 16% institutional). *Receiving aid:* Freshmen: 31% (380); all full-time undergraduates: 29% (1,407). *Average award:* Freshmen: $6954; Undergraduates: $6731. *Scholarships, grants, and awards:* Federal Pell, FSEOG, state, private, college/university gift aid from institutional funds.

GIFT AID (NON-NEED-BASED) *Total amount:* $4,249,345 (1% state, 72% institutional, 27% external sources). *Receiving aid:* Freshmen: 22% (273). Undergraduates: 14% (692). *Average award:* Freshmen: $3369. Undergraduates: $2460. *Scholarships, grants, and awards by category:* Academic interests/achievement: 64 awards ($125,380 total): biological sciences, business, communication, computer science, education, engineering/technologies, English, foreign languages, general academic interests/achievements, humanities, mathematics, military science, physical sciences, premedicine, social sciences. Creative arts/performance: 90 awards ($158,150 total): art/fine arts, music, performing arts, theater/drama. Special achievements/activities: 1,130 awards ($2,701,800 total): community service, general special achievements/activities, leadership. Special characteristics: 8 awards ($34,300 total): adult students, first-generation college students, general special characteristics, local/state students, members of minority groups, religious affiliation. *Tuition waivers:* Full or partial for employees or children of employees, senior citizens. *ROTC:* Army.

LOANS *Student loans:* $23,062,367 (32% need-based, 68% non-need-based). 60% of past graduating class borrowed through all loan programs. *Average indebtedness per student:* $30,451. *Average need-based loan:* Freshmen: $3349. Undergraduates: $4279. *Parent loans:* $8,758,068 (100% non-need-based). *Programs:* Federal Direct (Subsidized and Unsubsidized Stafford, PLUS).

WORK-STUDY *Federal work-study:* Total amount: $105,691; 58 jobs averaging $1822. *State or other work-study/employment:* Total amount: $2,540,481 (100% non-need-based). 1,629 part-time jobs averaging $1849.

APPLYING FOR FINANCIAL AID *Required financial aid form:* FAFSA. *Financial aid deadline (priority):* 3/1. *Notification date:* Continuous beginning 3/1. Students must reply by 5/1.

CONTACT Christina Russell, Director of Financial Aid, Christopher Newport University, 1 Avenue of the Arts, Newport News, VA 23606, 757-594-7170 or toll-free 800-333-4268. *Fax:* 757-594-7113. *E-mail:* christina.russell@cnu.edu. *Website:* http://www.cnu.edu/.

CINCINNATI CHRISTIAN UNIVERSITY
Cincinnati, OH

Tuition & fees: N/R	Average undergraduate aid package: $12,945

ABOUT THE INSTITUTION Independent Church of Christ, coed. 11 undergraduate majors. Federal methodology is used as a basis for awarding need-based institutional aid.

FRESHMAN FINANCIAL AID (Fall 2015) 104 applied for aid; of those 90% were deemed to have need. 100% of freshmen with need received aid; of those 13% had need fully met. *Average percent of need met:* 60% (excluding resources awarded to replace EFC). *Average financial aid package:* $12,827 (excluding resources awarded to replace EFC). 4% of all full-time freshmen had no need and received non-need-based gift aid.

UNDERGRADUATE FINANCIAL AID (Fall 2015) 475 applied for aid; of those 91% were deemed to have need. 100% of undergraduates with need received aid; of those 9% had need fully met. *Average percent of need met:* 57% (excluding resources awarded to replace EFC). *Average financial aid package:* $12,945 (excluding resources awarded to replace EFC). 11% of all full-time undergraduates had no need and received non-need-based gift aid.

GIFT AID (NEED-BASED) *Total amount:* $3,232,448 (33% federal, 8% state, 53% institutional, 6% external sources). *Receiving aid:* Freshmen: 86% (91); all full-time undergraduates: 78% (404). *Average award:* Freshmen: $9376; Undergraduates: $9374. *Scholarships, grants, and awards:* Federal Pell, FSEOG, state, private, college/university gift aid from institutional funds.

GIFT AID (NON-NEED-BASED) *Total amount:* $592,403 (85% institutional, 15% external sources). *Receiving aid:* Freshmen: 9% (10). Undergraduates: 6% (31). *Average award:* Freshmen: $7929. Undergraduates: $6966. *Scholarships, grants, and awards by category:* Academic interests/achievement: education, general academic interests/achievements, religion/biblical studies. Creative arts/performance: music. Special achievements/activities: general special achievements/activities, leadership, religious involvement. Special characteristics: children of faculty/staff, international students, members of minority groups, parents of current students, siblings of current students, spouses of current students.

LOANS *Student loans:* $3,653,410 (79% need-based, 21% non-need-based). 79% of past graduating class borrowed through all loan programs. *Average indebtedness per student:* $25,089. *Average need-based loan:* Freshmen: $3335. Undergraduates: $3758. *Parent loans:* $1,090,448 (61% need-based, 39% non-need-based). *Programs:* Federal Direct (Subsidized and Unsubsidized Stafford, PLUS), college/university, private loans.

WORK-STUDY *Federal work-study:* jobs available.

ATHLETIC AWARDS Total amount: $871,774 (75% need-based, 25% non-need-based).

APPLYING FOR FINANCIAL AID *Required financial aid form:* FAFSA. *Financial aid deadline (priority):* 3/1. *Notification date:* Continuous beginning 2/1. Students must reply by 8/1.

CONTACT Marcella Farmer, Associate Director of Financial Aid, Cincinnati Christian University, 2700 Glenway Avenue, Cincinnati, OH 45204-1799, 513-244-8130 or toll-free 800-949-4228 (in-state), 800-949-4CCU (out-of-state). *Fax:* 513-244-8453. *E-mail:* financialaid@ccuniversity.edu. *Website:* http://www.ccuniversity.edu/.

CINCINNATI COLLEGE OF MORTUARY SCIENCE
Cincinnati, OH

CONTACT Ms. Pat Leon, Financial Aid Officer , Cincinnati College of Mortuary Science, 645 West North Bend Road, Cincinnati, OH 45224-1428, 513-761-2020 or toll-free 888-377-8433. *Website:* http://www.ccms.edu/.

THE CITADEL, THE MILITARY COLLEGE OF SOUTH CAROLINA
Charleston, SC

Tuition & fees (SC res): $12,755	Average undergraduate aid package: $16,428

ABOUT THE INSTITUTION State-supported, coed, primarily men. *Awards:* certificates, bachelor's, and master's degrees. 20 undergraduate majors. *Total enrollment:* 3,602. Undergraduates: 2,773. Freshmen: 734. Federal methodology is used as a basis for awarding need-based institutional aid.

UNDERGRADUATE EXPENSES for 2017–2018 *Application fee:* $40. *Tuition, state resident:* full-time $12,755. *Tuition, nonresident:* full-time $34,518. Full-time tuition and fees vary according to class time, degree level, program, and student level. Part-time tuition and fees vary according to class time and program. *College room and board:* $7924.

FRESHMAN FINANCIAL AID (Fall 2016, est.) 644 applied for aid; of those 77% were deemed to have need. 95% of freshmen with need received aid; of those 19% had need fully met. *Average percent of need met:* 52% (excluding resources awarded to replace EFC). *Average financial aid package:* $14,144 (excluding resources awarded to replace EFC). 21% of all full-time freshmen had no need and received non-need-based gift aid.

UNDERGRADUATE FINANCIAL AID (Fall 2016, est.) 1,869 applied for aid; of those 76% were deemed to have need. 97% of undergraduates with need received aid; of those 27% had need fully met. *Average percent of need met:* 61% (excluding resources awarded to replace EFC). *Average financial aid package:* $16,428 (excluding resources awarded to replace EFC). 24% of all full-time undergraduates had no need and received non-need-based gift aid.

GIFT AID (NEED-BASED) *Total amount:* $15,534,312 (18% federal, 17% state, 27% institutional, 38% external sources). *Receiving aid:* Freshmen: 53% (391); all full-time undergraduates: 45% (1,126). *Average award:* Freshmen: $13,821; Undergraduates: $16,154. *Scholarships, grants, and awards:* Federal Pell, FSEOG, state, private, college/university gift aid from institutional funds.

GIFT AID (NON-NEED-BASED) *Total amount:* $7,993,104 (23% state, 23% institutional, 54% external sources). *Receiving aid:* Freshmen: 10% (73). Undergraduates: 11% (267). *Average award:* Freshmen: $7300. Undergraduates: $13,354. *Scholarships, grants, and awards by category:* Academic interests/achievement: biological sciences, business, engineering/technologies, general academic interests/achievements, humanities, military science, religion/biblical studies. Creative arts/performance: journalism/publications, music. Special achievements/activities: community service, leadership, religious involvement. Special characteristics: children and siblings of alumni, children with a deceased or disabled parent, local/state students, out-of-state students, veterans, veterans' children. *Tuition waivers:* Full or partial for employees or children of employees, senior citizens. *ROTC:* Army, Naval, Air Force.

LOANS *Student loans:* $14,269,609 (78% need-based, 22% non-need-based). 59% of past graduating class borrowed through all loan programs. *Average indebtedness per student:* $27,872. *Average need-based loan:* Freshmen: $3447. Undergraduates: $4314. *Parent loans:* $9,917,896 (85% need-based, 15% non-need-based). *Programs:* Federal Direct (Subsidized and Unsubsidized Stafford, PLUS), Perkins, state.

WORK-STUDY *Federal work-study:* Total amount: $143,383; jobs available. *State or other work-study/employment:* Part-time jobs available.

ATHLETIC AWARDS Total amount: $5,380,024 (53% need-based, 47% non-need-based).

APPLYING FOR FINANCIAL AID *Required financial aid form:* FAFSA. *Financial aid deadline (priority):* 3/1. *Notification date:* 4/1. Students must reply within 2 weeks of notification.

CONTACT Lt. Col. Hank M. Fuller, Director of Financial Aid and Scholarships, The Citadel, The Military College of South Carolina, 171 Moultrie Street, Charleston, SC 29409, 843-953-5187 or toll-free 800-868-1842. *Fax:* 843-953-6759. *E-mail:* hank.fuller@citadel.edu.
Website: http://www.citadel.edu/.

CITY COLLEGE OF THE CITY UNIVERSITY OF NEW YORK
New York, NY

Tuition & fees (NY res): $6740	Average undergraduate aid package: $9597

ABOUT THE INSTITUTION State and locally supported, coed. *Awards:* certificates, bachelor's, master's, and doctoral degrees. 66 undergraduate majors. *Total enrollment:* 16,161. Undergraduates: 13,508. Federal methodology is used as a basis for awarding need-based institutional aid.

UNDERGRADUATE EXPENSES for 2016–2017 *Application fee:* $65. *Tuition, state resident:* full-time $6330. *Tuition, nonresident:* full-time $16,800. *Required fees:* full-time $410. Full-time tuition and fees vary according to course load and program. Part-time tuition and fees vary according to course load and program. Room and board charges vary according to housing facility.

FRESHMAN FINANCIAL AID (Fall 2016, est.) 1,613 applied for aid; of those 95% were deemed to have need. 100% of freshmen with need received aid; of those 70% had need fully met. *Average percent of need met:* 85% (excluding resources awarded to replace EFC). *Average financial aid package:* $9499 (excluding resources awarded to replace EFC). 12% of all full-time freshmen had no need and received non-need-based gift aid.

UNDERGRADUATE FINANCIAL AID (Fall 2016, est.) 8,263 applied for aid; of those 96% were deemed to have need. 91% of undergraduates with need received aid; of those 95% had need fully met. *Average percent of need met:* 84% (excluding resources awarded to replace EFC). *Average financial aid package:* $9597 (excluding resources awarded to replace EFC). 8% of all full-time undergraduates had no need and received non-need-based gift aid.

GIFT AID (NEED-BASED) *Total amount:* $88,247,871 (52% federal, 43% state, 4% institutional, 1% external sources). *Receiving aid:* Freshmen: 73% (1,315); all full-time undergraduates: 59% (5,925). *Average award:* Freshmen: $8589; Undergraduates: $8552. *Scholarships, grants, and awards:* Federal Pell, FSEOG, state, private, college/university gift aid from institutional funds.

GIFT AID (NON-NEED-BASED) *Total amount:* $6,087,240 (7% state, 79% institutional, 14% external sources). *Receiving aid:* Freshmen: 13% (231). Undergraduates: 30% (3,036). *Average award:* Freshmen: $3486. Undergraduates: $4413. *Scholarships, grants, and awards by category: Academic interests/achievement:* architecture, area/ethnic studies, biological sciences, communication, computer science, education, engineering/technologies, English, foreign languages, general academic interests/achievements, humanities, international studies, mathematics, premedicine, social sciences. *Creative arts/performance:* applied art and design, art/fine arts, cinema/film/broadcasting, creative writing, general creative arts/performance, music, performing arts. *Special achievements/activities:* community service, general special achievements/activities, leadership. *Special characteristics:* children and siblings of alumni, local/state students. *Tuition waivers:* Full or partial for senior citizens. *ROTC:* Army.

LOANS *Student loans:* $12,178,932 (47% need-based, 53% non-need-based). 22% of past graduating class borrowed through all loan programs. *Average indebtedness per student:* $16,942. *Average need-based loan:* Freshmen: $3080. Undergraduates: $4347. *Parent loans:* $934,104 (100% need-based). *Programs:* Federal Direct (Subsidized and Unsubsidized Stafford, PLUS), Perkins.

WORK-STUDY *Federal work-study:* Total amount: $872,445; jobs available. *State or other work-study/employment:* Part-time jobs available.

APPLYING FOR FINANCIAL AID *Required financial aid forms:* FAFSA, state aid form. *Financial aid deadline (priority):* 3/15. *Notification date:* Continuous beginning 4/1.

CONTACT Thelma Mason, Director of Financial Aid, City College of the City University of New York, 160 Convent Avenue, Wille Administration Building, Room 104, New York, NY 10031, 212-650-5816. *Fax:* 212-650-5829. *E-mail:* tmason@ccny.cuny.edu.
Website: http://www.ccny.cuny.edu/.

CITY VISION UNIVERSITY
Kansas City, MO

ABOUT THE INSTITUTION Independent Christian, coed. *Awards:* associate, bachelor's, and master's degrees. 4 undergraduate majors. *Total enrollment:* 106. Undergraduates: 96. Freshmen: 5.

GIFT AID (NEED-BASED) *Scholarships, grants, and awards:* Federal Pell, college/university gift aid from institutional funds.

GIFT AID (NON-NEED-BASED) *Scholarships, grants, and awards by category: Special achievements/activities:* memberships. *Special characteristics:* international students, veterans.

LOANS *Programs:* Federal Direct (Subsidized and Unsubsidized Stafford), private loans.

APPLYING FOR FINANCIAL AID *Required financial aid forms:* FAFSA, institution's own form.

CONTACT Mrs. Ann Marie Cameron-Thompson, Director of Financial Aid, City Vision University, City Vision Financial Aid, 48 Pleasant Street, Dorchester, MA 02125, 617-282-9798 Ext. 108. *Fax:* 816-256-8471. *E-mail:* financialaid@cityvision.edu .
Website: http://www.cityvision.edu/.

CLAFLIN UNIVERSITY
Orangeburg, SC

Tuition & fees: $16,158	Average undergraduate aid package: $15,615

ABOUT THE INSTITUTION Independent United Methodist, coed. 36 undergraduate majors. Federal methodology is used as a basis for awarding need-based institutional aid.

UNDERGRADUATE EXPENSES for 2016–2017 *Comprehensive fee:* $25,090 includes full-time tuition ($15,528), mandatory fees ($630), and room and board ($8932). Full-time tuition and fees vary according to class time and course load. Room and board charges vary according to housing facility. *Part-time tuition:* $647 per credit hour. *Part-time fees:* $227 per term. Part-time tuition and fees vary according to class time.

FRESHMAN FINANCIAL AID (Fall 2016, est.) 473 applied for aid; of those 99% were deemed to have need. 99% of freshmen with need received aid; of those 5% had need fully met. *Average percent of need met:* 40% (excluding resources awarded to replace EFC). *Average financial aid package:* $17,490 (excluding resources awarded to replace EFC). 3% of all full-time freshmen had no need and received non-need-based gift aid.

UNDERGRADUATE FINANCIAL AID (Fall 2016, est.) 1,827 applied for aid; of those 98% were deemed to have need. 98% of undergraduates with need received aid; of those 6% had need fully met. *Average percent of need met:* 37% (excluding resources awarded to replace EFC). *Average financial aid package:* $15,615 (excluding resources awarded to replace EFC). 3% of all full-time undergraduates had no need and received non-need-based gift aid.

GIFT AID (NEED-BASED) *Total amount:* $18,507,078 (39% federal, 37% state, 15% institutional, 9% external sources). *Receiving aid:* Freshmen: 94% (463); all full-time undergraduates: 89% (1,704). *Average award:* Freshmen: $14,323; Undergraduates: $12,191. *Scholarships, grants, and awards:* Federal Pell, FSEOG, state, private, college/university gift aid from institutional funds, United Negro College Fund.

GIFT AID (NON-NEED-BASED) *Total amount:* $1,149,819 (1% federal, 23% state, 47% institutional, 29% external sources). *Receiving aid:* Freshmen: 3% (14). Undergraduates: 4% (69). *Average award:* Freshmen: $8442. Undergraduates: $8417. *Scholarships, grants, and awards by category: Academic interests/achievement:* general academic interests/achievements. *Creative arts/performance:* applied art and design, art/fine arts, music. *Special achievements/activities:* cheerleading/drum major. *Special characteristics:* adult students, children of faculty/staff, ethnic background, first-generation college students, international students, local/state students, relatives of clergy, religious affiliation, veterans, veterans' children. *Tuition waivers:* Full or partial for employees or children of employees.

LOANS *Student loans:* $13,442,716 (94% need-based, 6% non-need-based). 88% of past graduating class borrowed through all loan programs. *Average indebtedness per student:* $31,688. *Average need-based loan:* Freshmen: $3287. Undergraduates: $4068. *Parent loans:* $6,385,655 (84% need-based, 16% non-need-based). *Programs:* Federal Direct (Subsidized and Unsubsidized Stafford, PLUS).

WORK-STUDY *Federal work-study:* Total amount: $171,430; 197 jobs averaging $896. *State or other work-study/employment:* Total amount: $30,036 (100% need-based). Part-time jobs available.

ATHLETIC AWARDS Total amount: $613,229 (86% need-based, 14% non-need-based).

APPLYING FOR FINANCIAL AID *Required financial aid forms:* FAFSA, institution's own form. *Financial aid deadline:* 7/15 (priority: 4/15). *Notification date:* Continuous beginning 2/1. Students must reply by 7/15 or within 2 weeks of notification.

CONTACT Ms. Terria C. Williams, Director of Financial Aid, Claflin University, Corson Hall, 400 Magnolia Street, Orangeburg, SC 29115, 803-535-5720 or toll-free 800-922-1276. *Fax:* 803-535-5383. *E-mail:* twilliams@claflin.edu. *Website:* http://www.claflin.edu/.

CLAREMONT MCKENNA COLLEGE
Claremont, CA

Tuition & fees: $50,950	Average undergraduate aid package: $46,129

ABOUT THE INSTITUTION Independent, coed. *Awards:* bachelor's and master's degrees. 32 undergraduate majors. *Total enrollment:* 1,347. Undergraduates: 1,347. Freshmen: 321. Both federal and institutional methodology are used as a basis for awarding need-based institutional aid.

UNDERGRADUATE EXPENSES for 2016–2017 *Application fee:* $70. *One-time required fee:* $500. *Comprehensive fee:* $66,690 includes full-time tuition ($50,700), mandatory fees ($250), and room and board ($15,740). *College room only:* $8470. Room and board charges vary according to board plan and housing facility. *Part-time tuition:* $8450 per course. Part-time tuition and fees vary according to course load.

FRESHMAN FINANCIAL AID (Fall 2016, est.) 127 applied for aid; of those 93% were deemed to have need. 100% of freshmen with need received aid; of those 100% had need fully met. *Average percent of need met:* 100% (excluding resources awarded to replace EFC). *Average financial aid package:* $48,623 (excluding resources awarded to replace EFC). 4% of all full-time freshmen had no need and received non-need-based gift aid.

UNDERGRADUATE FINANCIAL AID (Fall 2016, est.) 643 applied for aid; of those 83% were deemed to have need. 100% of undergraduates with need received aid; of those 100% had need fully met. *Average percent of need met:* 100% (excluding resources awarded to replace EFC). *Average financial aid package:* $46,129 (excluding resources awarded to replace EFC). 6% of all full-time undergraduates had no need and received non-need-based gift aid.

GIFT AID (NEED-BASED) *Total amount:* $22,260,495 (4% federal, 4% state, 88% institutional, 4% external sources). *Receiving aid:* Freshmen: 37% (118); all full-time undergraduates: 39% (523). *Average award:* Freshmen: $44,850; Undergraduates: $42,445. *Scholarships, grants, and awards:* Federal Pell, FSEOG, state, private, college/university gift aid from institutional funds.

GIFT AID (NON-NEED-BASED) *Total amount:* $1,371,385 (90% institutional, 10% external sources). *Receiving aid:* Freshmen: 21% (66). Undergraduates: 22% (294). *Average award:* Freshmen: $18,590. Undergraduates: $15,744. *Scholarships, grants, and awards by category: Academic interests/achievement:* general academic interests/achievements, military science. *Special achievements/activities:* leadership. *Special characteristics:* veterans, veterans' children. *Tuition waivers:* Full or partial for employees or children of employees. *ROTC:* Army, Air Force cooperative.

LOANS *Student loans:* $2,323,184 (55% need-based, 45% non-need-based). 27% of past graduating class borrowed through all loan programs. *Average indebtedness per student:* $23,375. *Average need-based loan:* Freshmen: $3491. Undergraduates: $4266. *Parent loans:* $1,123,458 (100% non-need-based). *Programs:* Federal Direct (Subsidized and Unsubsidized Stafford, PLUS), Perkins, college/university, alternative loans.

WORK-STUDY *Federal work-study:* Total amount: $813,223; jobs available. *State or other work-study/employment:* Total amount: $252,737 (99% need-based, 1% non-need-based). Part-time jobs available.

APPLYING FOR FINANCIAL AID *Required financial aid forms:* FAFSA, CSS Financial Aid PROFILE, state aid form, noncustodial (divorced/separated) parent's statement, business/farm supplement. *Financial aid deadline:* 2/1 (priority: 1/1). *Notification date:* 4/1. Students must reply by 5/1.

CONTACT Ms. Georgette R. DeVeres, Associate Vice President and Dean of Admission and Financial Aid, Claremont McKenna College, Kravis Center, Lower Court, 888 Columbia Avenue, Claremont, CA 91711, 909-621-8356. *Fax:* 909-607-0661. *E-mail:* georgette.deveres@claremontmckenna.edu. *Website:* http://www.claremontmckenna.edu/.

CLARION UNIVERSITY OF PENNSYLVANIA
Clarion, PA

Tuition & fees: N/R	Average undergraduate aid package: $9580

ABOUT THE INSTITUTION State-supported, coed. *Awards:* certificates, associate, bachelor's, master's, and doctoral degrees. 59 undergraduate majors. *Total enrollment:* 5,224. Undergraduates: 4,330. Freshmen: 941. Federal methodology is used as a basis for awarding need-based institutional aid.

FRESHMAN FINANCIAL AID (Fall 2016, est.) 895 applied for aid; of those 86% were deemed to have need. 99% of freshmen with need received aid; of those 5% had need fully met. *Average percent of need met:* 41% (excluding resources awarded to replace EFC). *Average financial aid package:* $9204 (excluding resources awarded to replace EFC). 7% of all full-time freshmen had no need and received non-need-based gift aid.

UNDERGRADUATE FINANCIAL AID (Fall 2016, est.) 3,263 applied for aid; of those 87% were deemed to have need. 98% of undergraduates with need received aid; of those 5% had need fully met. *Average percent of need met:* 45% (excluding resources awarded to replace EFC). *Average financial aid package:* $9580 (excluding resources awarded to replace EFC). 5% of all full-time undergraduates had no need and received non-need-based gift aid.

GIFT AID (NEED-BASED) *Total amount:* $15,729,942 (45% federal, 33% state, 14% institutional, 8% external sources). *Receiving aid:* Freshmen: 66% (607); all full-time undergraduates: 58% (2,056). *Average award:* Freshmen: $5655; Undergraduates: $5716. *Scholarships, grants, and awards:* Federal Pell, FSEOG, state, private, college/university gift aid from institutional funds, United Negro College Fund.

GIFT AID (NON-NEED-BASED) *Total amount:* $816,587 (10% state, 78% institutional, 12% external sources). *Receiving aid:* Freshmen: 27% (250). Undergraduates: 21% (759). *Average award:* Freshmen: $2197. Undergraduates: $2187. *Scholarships, grants, and awards by category: Academic interests/achievement:* biological sciences, business, communication, computer science, education, English, foreign languages, general academic interests/achievements, health fields, humanities, international studies, library science, mathematics, military science, physical sciences, premedicine, social sciences. *Creative arts/performance:* art/fine arts, debating, general creative arts/performance, music, theater/drama. *Special achievements/activities:* community service, leadership. *Special characteristics:* children of faculty/staff, children of union members/company employees, children with a deceased or disabled parent, first-generation college students, local/state students, members of minority groups, previous college experience, spouses of current students, veterans, veterans' children. *ROTC:* Army.

LOANS *Student loans:* $29,964,592 (88% need-based, 12% non-need-based). 81% of past graduating class borrowed through all loan programs. *Average indebtedness per student:* $33,346. *Average need-based loan:* Freshmen: $3320. Undergraduates: $4159. *Parent loans:* $7,493,302 (91% need-based, 9% non-need-based). *Programs:* Federal Direct (Subsidized and Unsubsidized Stafford, PLUS), Perkins, alternative loans.

WORK-STUDY *Federal work-study:* Total amount: $310,771; 139 jobs averaging $2442. *State or other work-study/employment:* Total amount: $1,094,289 (55% need-based, 45% non-need-based). 634 part-time jobs averaging $1726.

ATHLETIC AWARDS Total amount: $761,252 (72% need-based, 28% non-need-based).

APPLYING FOR FINANCIAL AID *Required financial aid forms:* FAFSA, state aid form. *Financial aid deadline (priority):* 5/1. *Notification date:* Continuous beginning 12/23.

CONTACT Ms. Sue A. Bloom, Student Financial Services, Clarion University of Pennsylvania, 122 Becht Hall, Clarion, PA 16214, 814-393-2315 or toll-free 800-672-7171. *Fax:* 814-393-2520. *E-mail:* stfinservice@clarion.edu. *Website:* http://www.clarion.edu/.

CLARK ATLANTA UNIVERSITY
Atlanta, GA

Tuition & fees: $22,396	Average undergraduate aid package: $7324

ABOUT THE INSTITUTION Independent United Methodist, coed. *Awards:* certificates, bachelor's, master's, and doctoral degrees. 28 undergraduate majors. *Total enrollment:* 3,884. Undergraduates: 3,093. Freshmen: 999. Federal methodology is used as a basis for awarding need-based institutional aid.

UNDERGRADUATE EXPENSES for 2016–2017 *Application fee:* $35. *Comprehensive fee:* $33,196 includes full-time tuition ($19,880), mandatory fees ($2516), and room and board ($10,800). Room and board charges vary according to board plan and housing facility. *Part-time tuition:* $828 per credit hour. *Part-time fees:* $1162 per term.

FRESHMAN FINANCIAL AID (Fall 2016, est.) 940 applied for aid; of those 96% were deemed to have need. 99% of freshmen with need received aid; of those 49% had need fully met. *Average percent of need met:* 48% (excluding resources awarded to replace EFC). *Average financial aid package:* $7742 (excluding resources awarded to replace EFC).

UNDERGRADUATE FINANCIAL AID (Fall 2016, est.) 2,780 applied for aid; of those 95% were deemed to have need. 99% of undergraduates with need received aid; of those 48% had need fully met. *Average percent of need met:* 45% (excluding resources awarded to replace EFC). *Average financial aid package:* $7324 (excluding resources awarded to replace EFC).

GIFT AID (NEED-BASED) *Total amount:* $12,643,020 (45% federal, 4% state, 39% institutional, 12% external sources). *Receiving aid:* Freshmen: 84% (832); all full-time undergraduates: 80% (2,378). *Average award:* Freshmen: $5987; Undergraduates: $5425. *Scholarships, grants, and awards:* Federal Pell, FSEOG, state, private, college/university gift aid from institutional funds, United Negro College Fund.

GIFT AID (NON-NEED-BASED) *Total amount:* $189,900 (100% external sources). *Receiving aid:* Freshmen: 15% (149). Undergraduates: 14% (405). *Scholarships, grants, and awards by category:* Academic interests/achievement: general academic interests/achievements. *Creative arts/performance:* music. *Special achievements/activities:* general special achievements/activities, leadership. *Special characteristics:* general special characteristics. *Tuition waivers:* Full or partial for employees or children of employees. *ROTC:* Army cooperative, Naval cooperative.

LOANS *Student loans:* $10,000,452 (98% need-based, 2% non-need-based). 91% of past graduating class borrowed through all loan programs. *Average indebtedness per student:* $40,393. *Average need-based loan:* Freshmen: $2227. Undergraduates: $2453. *Parent loans:* $16,940,198 (100% non-need-based). *Programs:* Federal Direct (Subsidized and Unsubsidized Stafford, PLUS), Perkins.

WORK-STUDY *Federal work-study:* Total amount: $349,786; 201 jobs averaging $1740.

ATHLETIC AWARDS Total amount: $899,779 (100% non-need-based).

APPLYING FOR FINANCIAL AID *Required financial aid forms:* FAFSA, state aid form. *Financial aid deadline (priority):* 4/1. *Notification date:* Continuous beginning 2/15. Students must reply within 2 weeks of notification.

CONTACT Office of Financial Aid, Clark Atlanta University, 223 James P. Brawley Drive, Atlanta, GA 30314, 404-880-8992 or toll-free 800-688-3228. *Fax:* 404-880-8070. *E-mail:* studentfinancialaid@cau.edu.
Website: http://www.cau.edu/.

CLARKE UNIVERSITY
Dubuque, IA

Tuition & fees: $31,950	Average undergraduate aid package: $26,183

ABOUT THE INSTITUTION Independent Roman Catholic, coed. *Awards:* associate, bachelor's, master's, and doctoral degrees. 31 undergraduate majors. *Total enrollment:* 1,043. Undergraduates: 801. Freshmen: 158. Federal methodology is used as a basis for awarding need-based institutional aid.

UNDERGRADUATE EXPENSES for 2017–2018 *Application fee:* $25. *Comprehensive fee:* $41,350 includes full-time tuition ($30,950), mandatory fees ($1000), and room and board ($9400). *College room only:* $4500. Room and board charges vary according to board plan. *Part-time tuition:* $720 per credit hour.

FRESHMAN FINANCIAL AID (Fall 2016, est.) 146 applied for aid; of those 90% were deemed to have need. 100% of freshmen with need received aid; of those 25% had need fully met. *Average percent of need met:* 78% (excluding resources awarded to replace EFC). *Average financial aid package:* $27,454 (excluding resources awarded to replace EFC). 13% of all full-time freshmen had no need and received non-need-based gift aid.

UNDERGRADUATE FINANCIAL AID (Fall 2016, est.) 658 applied for aid; of those 92% were deemed to have need. 100% of undergraduates with need received aid; of those 25% had need fully met. *Average percent of need met:* 75% (excluding resources awarded to replace EFC). *Average financial aid package:* $26,183 (excluding resources awarded to replace EFC). 13% of all full-time undergraduates had no need and received non-need-based gift aid.

GIFT AID (NEED-BASED) *Total amount:* $9,651,360 (13% federal, 12% state, 73% institutional, 2% external sources). *Receiving aid:* Freshmen: 87% (132); all full-time undergraduates: 87% (607). *Average award:* Freshmen: $23,381; Undergraduates: $20,957. *Scholarships, grants, and awards:* Federal Pell, FSEOG, state, private, college/university gift aid from institutional funds.

GIFT AID (NON-NEED-BASED) *Total amount:* $978,183 (98% institutional, 2% external sources). *Receiving aid:* Freshmen: 87% (132). Undergraduates: 85% (596). *Average award:* Freshmen: $24,955. Undergraduates: $20,424. *Scholarships, grants, and awards by category:* Academic interests/achievement: 698 awards ($4,799,813 total): general academic interests/achievements. *Creative arts/performance:* 42 awards ($107,977 total): art/fine arts, music, theater/drama. *Special achievements/activities:* 211 awards ($203,825 total): leadership, religious involvement. *Special characteristics:* 34 awards ($523,967 total): children and siblings of alumni, children of faculty/staff, relatives of clergy, siblings of current students. *Tuition waivers:* Full or partial for employees or children of employees. *ROTC:* Army cooperative.

LOANS *Student loans:* $7,643,057 (34% need-based, 66% non-need-based). 84% of past graduating class borrowed through all loan programs. *Average indebtedness per student:* $39,907. *Average need-based loan:* Freshmen: $3105. Undergraduates: $4586. *Parent loans:* $1,465,467 (99% need-based, 1% non-need-based). *Programs:* Federal Direct (Subsidized and Unsubsidized Stafford, PLUS), Perkins, Federal Nursing, college/university, private loans.

WORK-STUDY *Federal work-study:* Total amount: $799,700; 428 jobs averaging $2000.

ATHLETIC AWARDS Total amount: $1,669,322 (100% non-need-based).

APPLYING FOR FINANCIAL AID *Financial aid deadline:* Continuous. *Notification date:* Continuous beginning 3/15. Students must reply by 5/1 or within 2 weeks of notification.

CONTACT Amy Norton, Director of Financial Aid, Clarke University, 1550 Clarke Drive, Dubuque, IA 52001-3198, 563-588-6327 or toll-free 800-383-2345. *Fax:* 563-584-8605. *E-mail:* amy.norton@clarke.edu.
Website: http://www.clarke.edu/.

CLARKSON COLLEGE
Omaha, NE

CONTACT Pam Shelton, Director of Financial Aid, Clarkson College, 101 South 42nd Street, Omaha, NE 68131-2739, 402-552-2749 or toll-free 800-647-5500. *Fax:* 402-552-6165. *E-mail:* shelton@clarksoncollege.edu.
Website: http://www.clarksoncollege.edu/.

CLARKSON UNIVERSITY
Potsdam, NY

Tuition & fees: $46,132	Average undergraduate aid package: $41,810

ABOUT THE INSTITUTION Independent, coed. *Awards:* certificates, bachelor's, master's, and doctoral degrees. 34 undergraduate majors. *Total enrollment:* 4,384. Undergraduates: 3,268. Freshmen: 797. Federal methodology is used as a basis for awarding need-based institutional aid.

UNDERGRADUATE EXPENSES for 2016–2017 *Application fee:* $50. *Comprehensive fee:* $60,392 includes full-time tuition ($45,132), mandatory fees

($1000), and room and board ($14,260). *College room only:* $7554. Full-time tuition and fees vary according to course load. Room and board charges vary according to board plan and housing facility. *Part-time tuition:* $1505 per credit hour. Part-time tuition and fees vary according to course load.

FRESHMAN FINANCIAL AID (Fall 2016, est.) 724 applied for aid; of those 89% were deemed to have need. 100% of freshmen with need received aid; of those 20% had need fully met. *Average percent of need met:* 89% (excluding resources awarded to replace EFC). *Average financial aid package:* $43,391 (excluding resources awarded to replace EFC). 17% of all full-time freshmen had no need and received non-need-based gift aid.

UNDERGRADUATE FINANCIAL AID (Fall 2016, est.) 2,769 applied for aid; of those 92% were deemed to have need. 100% of undergraduates with need received aid; of those 21% had need fully met. *Average percent of need met:* 90% (excluding resources awarded to replace EFC). *Average financial aid package:* $41,810 (excluding resources awarded to replace EFC). 18% of all full-time undergraduates had no need and received non-need-based gift aid.

GIFT AID (NEED-BASED) *Total amount:* $76,861,259 (8% federal, 3% state, 88% institutional, 1% external sources). *Receiving aid:* Freshmen: 80% (640); all full-time undergraduates: 79% (2,510). *Average award:* Freshmen: $33,293; Undergraduates: $30,647. *Scholarships, grants, and awards:* Federal Pell, FSEOG, state, private, college/university gift aid from institutional funds, Higher Education Opportunity Program (HEOP).

GIFT AID (NON-NEED-BASED) *Total amount:* $18,267,477 (10% federal, 1% state, 87% institutional, 2% external sources). *Receiving aid:* Freshmen: 12% (93). Undergraduates: 11% (355). *Average award:* Freshmen: $23,918. Undergraduates: $22,172. *Scholarships, grants, and awards by category:* Academic interests/achievement: $52,525,347 total: biological sciences, business, communication, computer science, engineering/technologies, general academic interests/achievements, humanities, mathematics, military science, physical sciences, social sciences. *Special achievements/activities:* $9,339,255 total: general special achievements/activities, leadership. *Special characteristics:* $6,331,108 total: children and siblings of alumni, children of faculty/staff, general special characteristics, international students, local/state students, members of minority groups, veterans. *Tuition waivers:* Full or partial for employees or children of employees. *ROTC:* Army, Air Force.

LOANS *Student loans:* $25,765,900 (71% need-based, 29% non-need-based). 85% of past graduating class borrowed through all loan programs. *Average indebtedness per student:* $23,500. *Average need-based loan:* Freshmen: $3449. Undergraduates: $5193. *Parent loans:* $8,978,195 (49% need-based, 51% non-need-based). *Programs:* Federal Direct (Subsidized and Unsubsidized Stafford, PLUS), Perkins, college/university, private loans.

WORK-STUDY *Federal work-study:* Total amount: $613,525; jobs available. *State or other work-study/employment:* Total amount: $545,738 (58% need-based, 42% non-need-based). 65 part-time jobs averaging $10,907.

ATHLETIC AWARDS Total amount: $2,042,937 (3% need-based, 97% non-need-based).

APPLYING FOR FINANCIAL AID *Required financial aid forms:* FAFSA, state aid form. *Financial aid deadline:* 3/1 (priority: 2/15). *Notification date:* Continuous beginning 3/14. Students must reply by 5/1 or within 2 weeks of notification.

CONTACT Mrs. Pamela A. Nichols, Director of Financial Aid, Clarkson University, 8 Clarkson Avenue, Box 5615, Potsdam, NY 13699, 315-268-6413 or toll-free 800-527-6577. *Fax:* 315-268-3899. *E-mail:* pnichols@clarkson.edu. *Website:* http://www.clarkson.edu/.

CLARKS SUMMIT UNIVERSITY
South Abington Township, PA

Tuition & fees: N/R	Average undergraduate aid package: N/A

ABOUT THE INSTITUTION Independent Baptist, coed. 28 undergraduate majors. Both federal and institutional methodology are used as a basis for awarding need-based institutional aid.

GIFT AID (NEED-BASED) *Total amount:* $2,766,584 (48% federal, 10% state, 42% institutional). *Receiving aid:* Freshmen: 79% (58). *Scholarships, grants, and awards:* Federal Pell, FSEOG, state, private, college/university gift aid from institutional funds.

GIFT AID (NON-NEED-BASED) *Total amount:* $2,048,516 (97% institutional, 3% external sources). *Scholarships, grants, and awards by category:* Academic interests/achievement: education, general academic interests/achievements,

religion/biblical studies. *Creative arts/performance:* general creative arts/performance, music. *Special achievements/activities:* general special achievements/activities, leadership, religious involvement. *Special characteristics:* children of faculty/staff, general special characteristics, married students.

LOANS *Student loans:* $2,431,210 (50% need-based, 50% non-need-based). 38% of past graduating class borrowed through all loan programs. *Average indebtedness per student:* $29,483. *Parent loans:* $287,617 (100% non-need-based). *Programs:* Federal Direct (Subsidized and Unsubsidized Stafford, PLUS), alternative loans.

WORK-STUDY *Federal work-study:* 72 jobs averaging $1457. *State or other work-study/employment:* Part-time jobs available.

APPLYING FOR FINANCIAL AID *Required financial aid form:* FAFSA. *Financial aid deadline (priority):* 5/1. *Notification date:* Continuous beginning 12/1.

CONTACT Mrs. Deborah Cragle, Director of Financial Aid, Clarks Summit University, 538 Venard Road, South Abington Township, PA 18411, 570-586-2400 Ext. 9272 or toll-free 800-451-7664. *Fax:* 570-585-9470. *E-mail:* dcragle@clarkssummitu.edu. *Website:* http://www.clarkssummitu.edu/.

CLARK UNIVERSITY
Worcester, MA

Tuition & fees: $43,150	Average undergraduate aid package: $36,022

ABOUT THE INSTITUTION Independent, coed. *Awards:* certificates, bachelor's, master's, and doctoral degrees. 48 undergraduate majors. *Total enrollment:* 3,298. Undergraduates: 2,289. Freshmen: 548. Institutional methodology is used as a basis for awarding need-based institutional aid.

UNDERGRADUATE EXPENSES for 2016–2017 *Application fee:* $60. *Comprehensive fee:* $51,600 includes full-time tuition ($42,800), mandatory fees ($350), and room and board ($8450). *College room only:* $4900. Room and board charges vary according to board plan and housing facility. *Part-time tuition:* $1338 per credit. *Payment plan:* Tuition prepayment.

FRESHMAN FINANCIAL AID (Fall 2016, est.) 433 applied for aid; of those 79% were deemed to have need. 99% of freshmen with need received aid; of those 61% had need fully met. *Average percent of need met:* 91% (excluding resources awarded to replace EFC). *Average financial aid package:* $36,552 (excluding resources awarded to replace EFC). 25% of all full-time freshmen had no need and received non-need-based gift aid.

UNDERGRADUATE FINANCIAL AID (Fall 2016, est.) 1,700 applied for aid; of those 84% were deemed to have need. 98% of undergraduates with need received aid; of those 41% had need fully met. *Average percent of need met:* 82% (excluding resources awarded to replace EFC). *Average financial aid package:* $36,022 (excluding resources awarded to replace EFC). 33% of all full-time undergraduates had no need and received non-need-based gift aid.

GIFT AID (NEED-BASED) *Total amount:* $35,817,187 (8% federal, 1% state, 91% institutional). *Receiving aid:* Freshmen: 62% (334); all full-time undergraduates: 62% (1,386). *Average award:* Freshmen: $26,277; Undergraduates: $25,648. *Scholarships, grants, and awards:* Federal Pell, FSEOG, state, college/university gift aid from institutional funds.

GIFT AID (NON-NEED-BASED) *Total amount:* $11,887,270 (100% institutional). *Receiving aid:* Freshmen: 13% (68). Undergraduates: 11% (254). *Average award:* Freshmen: $18,798. Undergraduates: $18,160. *Scholarships, grants, and awards by category:* Academic interests/achievement: general academic interests/achievements. *Special achievements/activities:* general special achievements/activities. *Tuition waivers:* Full or partial for employees or children of employees. *ROTC:* Army cooperative, Air Force cooperative.

LOANS *Student loans:* $10,703,496 (78% need-based, 22% non-need-based). 90% of past graduating class borrowed through all loan programs. *Average indebtedness per student:* $26,870. *Average need-based loan:* Freshmen: $4033. Undergraduates: $5298. *Parent loans:* $2,788,637 (50% need-based, 50% non-need-based). *Programs:* Federal Direct (Subsidized and Unsubsidized Stafford, PLUS), Perkins, state.

WORK-STUDY *Federal work-study:* Total amount: $1,437,908; jobs available.

APPLYING FOR FINANCIAL AID *Required financial aid forms:* FAFSA, CSS Financial Aid PROFILE, noncustodial (divorced/separated) parent's statement. *Financial aid deadline:* 2/1. *Notification date:* 3/31. Students must reply by 5/1.

CONTACT Ms. Mary Ellen Severance, Director of Financial Assistance, Clark University, 950 Main Street, Worcester, MA 01610-1477, 508-793-7478 or toll-free 800-GO-CLARK. *Fax:* 508-793-8802. *E-mail:* finaid@clarku.edu. *Website:* http://www.clarku.edu/.

CLAYTON STATE UNIVERSITY
Morrow, GA

Tuition & fees (GA res): $6312	Average undergraduate aid package: $9259

ABOUT THE INSTITUTION State-supported, coed. *Awards:* certificates, associate, bachelor's, and master's degrees. 32 undergraduate majors. *Total enrollment:* 6,996. Undergraduates: 6,555. Freshmen: 588. Federal methodology is used as a basis for awarding need-based institutional aid.

UNDERGRADUATE EXPENSES for 2016–2017 *Application fee:* $40. *Tuition, state resident:* full-time $4858; part-time $161.93 per credit hour. *Tuition, nonresident:* full-time $17,678; part-time $589.27 per credit hour. *Required fees:* full-time $1454; $727 per term. Full-time tuition and fees vary according to course load. Part-time tuition and fees vary according to course load. *College room and board:* $10,156. Room and board charges vary according to board plan and housing facility.

FRESHMAN FINANCIAL AID (Fall 2016, est.) 410 applied for aid; of those 91% were deemed to have need. 100% of freshmen with need received aid; of those 5% had need fully met. *Average percent of need met:* 51% (excluding resources awarded to replace EFC). *Average financial aid package:* $9801 (excluding resources awarded to replace EFC). 1% of all full-time freshmen had no need and received non-need-based gift aid.

UNDERGRADUATE FINANCIAL AID (Fall 2016, est.) 3,224 applied for aid; of those 93% were deemed to have need. 100% of undergraduates with need received aid; of those 3% had need fully met. *Average percent of need met:* 44% (excluding resources awarded to replace EFC). *Average financial aid package:* $9259 (excluding resources awarded to replace EFC). 1% of all full-time undergraduates had no need and received non-need-based gift aid.

GIFT AID (NEED-BASED) *Total amount:* $17,194,726 (100% federal). *Receiving aid:* Freshmen: 77% (339); all full-time undergraduates: 75% (2,604). *Average award:* Freshmen: $7335; Undergraduates: $6156. *Scholarships, grants, and awards:* Federal Pell, FSEOG, state, private, college/university gift aid from institutional funds, Federal Nursing.

GIFT AID (NON-NEED-BASED) *Receiving aid:* Freshmen: 8% (34). Undergraduates: 4% (131). *Average award:* Freshmen: $1353. Undergraduates: $1862. *Tuition waivers:* Full or partial for employees or children of employees, senior citizens. *ROTC:* Army cooperative, Naval cooperative, Air Force cooperative.

LOANS *Student loans:* 84% of past graduating class borrowed through all loan programs. *Average indebtedness per student:* $30,423. *Average need-based loan:* Freshmen: $3391. Undergraduates: $4233. *Programs:* Federal Direct (Subsidized and Unsubsidized Stafford, PLUS), state.

WORK-STUDY *Federal work-study:* Total amount: $297,183; 73 jobs averaging $4071.

APPLYING FOR FINANCIAL AID *Required financial aid form:* FAFSA. *Financial aid deadline (priority):* 7/15. *Notification date:* Continuous beginning 4/15.

CONTACT Lakisha Sanders, Director of Financial Aid, Clayton State University, 2000 Clayton State Boulevard, Morrow, GA 30260, 678-466-4185. *Fax:* 678-466-4189. *E-mail:* financialaid@mail.clayton.edu. *Website:* http://www.clayton.edu/.

CLEAR CREEK BAPTIST BIBLE COLLEGE
Pineville, KY

Tuition & fees: N/R	Average undergraduate aid package: $5543

ABOUT THE INSTITUTION Independent Southern Baptist, coed, primarily men. 2 undergraduate majors. Institutional methodology is used as a basis for awarding need-based institutional aid.

FRESHMAN FINANCIAL AID (Fall 2016, est.) 6 applied for aid; of those 100% were deemed to have need. 100% of freshmen with need received aid. *Average percent of need met:* 49% (excluding resources awarded to replace EFC). *Average financial aid package:* $5806 (excluding resources awarded to replace EFC). 29% of all full-time freshmen had no need and received non-need-based gift aid.

UNDERGRADUATE FINANCIAL AID (Fall 2016, est.) 127 applied for aid; of those 100% were deemed to have need. 100% of undergraduates with need received aid. *Average percent of need met:* 44% (excluding resources awarded to replace EFC). *Average financial aid package:* $5543 (excluding resources awarded to replace EFC). 10% of all full-time undergraduates had no need and received non-need-based gift aid.

GIFT AID (NEED-BASED) *Total amount:* $773,906 (46% federal, 45% institutional, 9% external sources). *Receiving aid:* Freshmen: 86% (6); all full-time undergraduates: 93% (127). *Average award:* Freshmen: $5806; Undergraduates: $5543. *Scholarships, grants, and awards:* Federal Pell, FSEOG, state, private, college/university gift aid from institutional funds.

GIFT AID (NON-NEED-BASED) *Total amount:* $141,956 (30% federal, 70% institutional). *Receiving aid:* Freshmen: 57% (4). Undergraduates: 34% (47). *Average award:* Freshmen: $6115. Undergraduates: $1445. *Scholarships, grants, and awards by category:* Academic interests/achievement: 3 awards ($1950 total): general academic interests/achievements. *Creative arts/performance:* music. *Special characteristics:* 2 awards ($1214 total): handicapped students, international students.

WORK-STUDY *Federal work-study:* Total amount: $38,081; 35 jobs averaging $1088.

APPLYING FOR FINANCIAL AID *Required financial aid forms:* FAFSA, institution's own form. *Financial aid deadline:* Continuous. *Notification date:* Continuous beginning 6/1.

CONTACT Mr. Sam Risner, Director of Financial Aid, Clear Creek Baptist Bible College, 300 Clear Creek Road, Pineville, KY 40977-9754, 606-337-3196 Ext. 142. *Fax:* 606-337-1631. *E-mail:* srisner@ccbbc.edu. *Website:* http://www.ccbbc.edu/.

CLEARY UNIVERSITY
Howell, MI

ABOUT THE INSTITUTION Independent, coed. *Awards:* certificates, associate, bachelor's, and master's degrees. 11 undergraduate majors. *Total enrollment:* 704. Undergraduates: 618. Freshmen: 30.

GIFT AID (NEED-BASED) *Scholarships, grants, and awards:* Federal Pell, FSEOG, state, private, college/university gift aid from institutional funds.

GIFT AID (NON-NEED-BASED) *Scholarships, grants, and awards by category:* Academic interests/achievement: business, general academic interests/achievements. *Special achievements/activities:* leadership. *Special characteristics:* children and siblings of alumni, children of faculty/staff, veterans.

LOANS *Programs:* Federal Direct (Subsidized and Unsubsidized Stafford, PLUS).

WORK-STUDY *Federal work-study:* 11 jobs averaging $3209. *State or other work-study/employment:* Part-time jobs available.

APPLYING FOR FINANCIAL AID *Required financial aid form:* FAFSA.

CONTACT Vesta Smith-Campbell, Director of Financial Aid, Cleary University, 3750 Cleary Drive, Howell, MI 48843, 517-338-3042 or toll-free 800-686-1883. *Fax:* 517-552-8022. *E-mail:* vscampbell@cleary.edu. *Website:* http://www.cleary.edu/.

CLEMSON UNIVERSITY
Clemson, SC

Tuition & fees (SC res): $14,318	Average undergraduate aid package: $11,511

ABOUT THE INSTITUTION State-supported, coed. *Awards:* certificates, bachelor's, master's, and doctoral degrees. 71 undergraduate majors. *Total enrollment:* 23,406. Undergraduates: 18,599. Freshmen: 3,684. Federal methodology is used as a basis for awarding need-based institutional aid.
UNDERGRADUATE EXPENSES for 2016–2017 *Application fee:* $70. *Tuition, state resident:* full-time $13,186; part-time $613 per credit hour. *Tuition, nonresident:* full-time $32,738; part-time $1477 per credit hour. *Required fees:* full-time $1132. Full-time tuition and fees vary according to course level, course load, location, program, and student level. Part-time tuition and fees vary according to course level, course load, location, program, and student level. *College room and board:* $9144. Room and board charges vary according to board plan, housing facility, and location.
FRESHMAN FINANCIAL AID (Fall 2016, est.) 3,063 applied for aid; of those 66% were deemed to have need. 99% of freshmen with need received aid; of those 19% had need fully met. *Average percent of need met:* 61% (excluding resources awarded to replace EFC). *Average financial aid package:* $13,045 (excluding resources awarded to replace EFC). 32% of all full-time freshmen had no need and received non-need-based gift aid.
UNDERGRADUATE FINANCIAL AID (Fall 2016, est.) 11,865 applied for aid; of those 72% were deemed to have need. 97% of undergraduates with need received aid; of those 17% had need fully met. *Average percent of need met:* 55% (excluding resources awarded to replace EFC). *Average financial aid package:* $11,511 (excluding resources awarded to replace EFC). 26% of all full-time undergraduates had no need and received non-need-based gift aid.
GIFT AID (NEED-BASED) *Total amount:* $67,755,991 (21% federal, 42% state, 31% institutional, 6% external sources). *Receiving aid:* Freshmen: 52% (1,917); all full-time undergraduates: 38% (6,963). *Average award:* Freshmen: $10,441; Undergraduates: $9062. *Scholarships, grants, and awards:* Federal Pell, FSEOG, state, private, college/university gift aid from institutional funds, Federal Nursing.
GIFT AID (NON-NEED-BASED) *Total amount:* $56,812,580 (51% state, 43% institutional, 6% external sources). *Receiving aid:* Freshmen: 43% (1,576). Undergraduates: 23% (4,323). *Average award:* Freshmen: $5754. Undergraduates: $5122. *Scholarships, grants, and awards by category: Academic interests/achievement:* agriculture, architecture, biological sciences, business, communication, computer science, education, engineering/technologies, English, foreign languages, general academic interests/achievements, health fields, humanities, international studies, mathematics, military science, physical sciences, premedicine, social sciences. *Creative arts/performance:* applied art and design, art/fine arts, performing arts, theater/drama. *Special achievements/activities:* community service, general special achievements/activities, leadership. *Special characteristics:* children of faculty/staff, ethnic background, local/state students, members of minority groups, veterans. *Tuition waivers:* Full or partial for senior citizens. *ROTC:* Army, Air Force.
LOANS *Student loans:* $79,506,220 (77% need-based, 23% non-need-based). 49% of past graduating class borrowed through all loan programs. *Average indebtedness per student:* $26,335. *Average need-based loan:* Freshmen: $3787. Undergraduates: $4544. *Parent loans:* $30,923,955 (81% need-based, 19% non-need-based). *Programs:* Federal Direct (Subsidized and Unsubsidized Stafford, PLUS), Perkins, state, college/university.
WORK-STUDY *Federal work-study:* Total amount: $3,904,256; 1,177 jobs averaging $3337. *State or other work-study/employment:* Part-time jobs available.
ATHLETIC AWARDS Total amount: $7,932,471 (44% need-based, 56% non-need-based).
APPLYING FOR FINANCIAL AID *Required financial aid form:* FAFSA. *Financial aid deadline (priority):* 3/1. *Notification date:* Continuous beginning 4/1. Students must reply within 3 weeks of notification.
CONTACT Mrs. Jennifer Williams, Assistant Director of Financial Aid, Clemson University, G-01 Sikes Hall, Box 345123, Clemson, SC 29634-5123, 864-656-2280. *Fax:* 864-656-1831. *E-mail:* finaid@clemson.edu.
Website: http://www.clemson.edu/.

CLEVELAND INSTITUTE OF ART
Cleveland, OH

Tuition & fees: $40,655	Average undergraduate aid package: $27,354

ABOUT THE INSTITUTION Independent, coed. *Awards:* bachelor's degrees. 15 undergraduate majors. *Total enrollment:* 625. Undergraduates: 626. Freshmen: 161. Federal methodology is used as a basis for awarding need-based institutional aid.
UNDERGRADUATE EXPENSES for 2017–2018 *Application fee:* $40. *Comprehensive fee:* $51,455 includes full-time tuition ($37,980), mandatory fees ($2675), and room and board ($10,800). *College room only:* $8150. Full-time tuition and fees vary according to reciprocity agreements. Room and board charges vary according to board plan and housing facility. *Part-time tuition:* $1585 per credit. *Part-time fees:* $73 per semester hour; $115 per semester hour. Part-time tuition and fees vary according to course load and reciprocity agreements.
FRESHMAN FINANCIAL AID (Fall 2015) 158 applied for aid; of those 97% were deemed to have need. 100% of freshmen with need received aid; of those 8% had need fully met. *Average percent of need met:* 62% (excluding resources awarded to replace EFC). *Average financial aid package:* $28,654 (excluding resources awarded to replace EFC). 12% of all full-time freshmen had no need and received non-need-based gift aid.
UNDERGRADUATE FINANCIAL AID (Fall 2015) 504 applied for aid; of those 94% were deemed to have need. 100% of undergraduates with need received aid; of those 7% had need fully met. *Average percent of need met:* 61% (excluding resources awarded to replace EFC). *Average financial aid package:* $27,354 (excluding resources awarded to replace EFC). 15% of all full-time undergraduates had no need and received non-need-based gift aid.
GIFT AID (NEED-BASED) *Total amount:* $10,615,339 (12% federal, 4% state, 82% institutional, 2% external sources). *Receiving aid:* Freshmen: 96% (154); all full-time undergraduates: 78% (474). *Average award:* Freshmen: $24,745; Undergraduates: $22,663. *Scholarships, grants, and awards:* Federal Pell, FSEOG, state, private, college/university gift aid from institutional funds.
GIFT AID (NON-NEED-BASED) *Total amount:* $1,497,321 (99% institutional, 1% external sources). *Receiving aid:* Freshmen: 4% (7). Undergraduates: 4% (23). *Average award:* Freshmen: $17,459. Undergraduates: $13,768. *Scholarships, grants, and awards by category: Creative arts/performance:* general creative arts/performance. *Special achievements/activities:* 7 awards ($73,252 total): leadership. *Tuition waivers:* Full or partial for employees or children of employees.
LOANS *Student loans:* $4,928,663 (85% need-based, 15% non-need-based). 88% of past graduating class borrowed through all loan programs. *Average indebtedness per student:* $35,136. *Average need-based loan:* Freshmen: $3947. Undergraduates: $4627. *Parent loans:* $2,209,239 (80% need-based, 20% non-need-based). *Programs:* Federal Direct (Subsidized and Unsubsidized Stafford, PLUS), Perkins.
WORK-STUDY *Federal work-study:* 139 jobs averaging $1203.
APPLYING FOR FINANCIAL AID *Required financial aid form:* FAFSA. *Notification date:* Continuous. Students must reply by 5/1 or within 3 weeks of notification.
CONTACT Mr. Martin Joseph Carney Jr., Director of Financial Aid, Cleveland Institute of Art, 11610 Euclid Avenue, Cleveland, OH 44106-4387, 216-421-7425 or toll-free 800-223-4700. *Fax:* 216-754-3634. *E-mail:* financialaid@cia.edu. *Website:* http://www.cia.edu/.

CLEVELAND INSTITUTE OF MUSIC
Cleveland, OH

Tuition & fees: N/R	Average undergraduate aid package: $33,332

ABOUT THE INSTITUTION Independent, coed. 3 undergraduate majors. Both federal and institutional methodology are used as a basis for awarding need-based institutional aid.
FRESHMAN FINANCIAL AID (Fall 2015) 61 applied for aid; of those 87% were deemed to have need. 100% of freshmen with need received aid; of those 25% had need fully met. *Average percent of need met:* 77% (excluding resources awarded to replace EFC). *Average financial aid package:* $34,990 (excluding resources awarded to replace EFC). 18% of all full-time freshmen had no need and received non-need-based gift aid.

UNDERGRADUATE FINANCIAL AID (Fall 2015) 163 applied for aid; of those 90% were deemed to have need. 100% of undergraduates with need received aid; of those 22% had need fully met. *Average percent of need met:* 75% (excluding resources awarded to replace EFC). *Average financial aid package:* $33,332 (excluding resources awarded to replace EFC). 39% of all full-time undergraduates had no need and received non-need-based gift aid.

GIFT AID (NEED-BASED) *Total amount:* $4,171,994 (4% federal, 93% institutional, 3% external sources). *Receiving aid:* Freshmen: 82% (53); all full-time undergraduates: 61% (146). *Average award:* Freshmen: $30,789; Undergraduates: $28,763. *Scholarships, grants, and awards:* Federal Pell, FSEOG, state, private, college/university gift aid from institutional funds.

GIFT AID (NON-NEED-BASED) *Total amount:* $2,556,798 (96% institutional, 4% external sources). *Receiving aid:* Freshmen: 17% (11). Undergraduates: 11% (26). *Average award:* Freshmen: $20,333. Undergraduates: $23,841. *Scholarships, grants, and awards by category:* Creative arts/performance: music. *Special characteristics:* children of faculty/staff.

LOANS *Student loans:* $947,530 (77% need-based, 23% non-need-based). 51% of past graduating class borrowed through all loan programs. *Average indebtedness per student:* $27,270. *Average need-based loan:* Freshmen: $4604. Undergraduates: $5179. *Parent loans:* $862,330 (35% need-based, 65% non-need-based). *Programs:* Federal Direct (Subsidized and Unsubsidized Stafford, PLUS), Perkins, college/university, private loans.

WORK-STUDY *Federal work-study:* jobs available. *State or other work-study/employment:* Total amount: $66,610 (29% need-based, 71% non-need-based). Part-time jobs available.

APPLYING FOR FINANCIAL AID *Required financial aid forms:* FAFSA, CSS Financial Aid PROFILE. *Financial aid deadline (priority):* 2/15. *Notification date:* 4/1. Students must reply by 5/1.

CONTACT Ms. Kristie Gripp, Director of Financial Aid, Cleveland Institute of Music, 11021 East Boulevard, Cleveland, OH 44106-1776, 216-795-3192. *Fax:* 216-707-4519. *E-mail:* kristine.gripp@cim.edu. *Website:* http://www.cim.edu/.

CLEVELAND STATE UNIVERSITY
Cleveland, OH

Tuition & fees (OH res): $9696	Average undergraduate aid package: $8777

ABOUT THE INSTITUTION State-supported, coed. *Awards:* certificates, bachelor's, master's, and doctoral degrees. 77 undergraduate majors. *Total enrollment:* 16,949. Undergraduates: 12,433. Freshmen: 1,918. Federal methodology is used as a basis for awarding need-based institutional aid.

UNDERGRADUATE EXPENSES for 2016–2017 *Application fee:* $30. *Tuition, state resident:* full-time $9636; part-time $401.50 per credit hour. *Tuition, nonresident:* full-time $13,687; part-time $570.30 per credit hour. *Required fees:* full-time $60; $30 per term. Full-time tuition and fees vary according to course load, degree level, and program. Part-time tuition and fees vary according to course load, degree level, and program. *College room and board:* $12,000; *Room only:* $8600. Room and board charges vary according to board plan and housing facility.

FRESHMAN FINANCIAL AID (Fall 2016, est.) 1,700 applied for aid; of those 84% were deemed to have need. 98% of freshmen with need received aid; of those 10% had need fully met. *Average percent of need met:* 37% (excluding resources awarded to replace EFC). *Average financial aid package:* $8902 (excluding resources awarded to replace EFC). 9% of all full-time freshmen had no need and received non-need-based gift aid.

UNDERGRADUATE FINANCIAL AID (Fall 2016, est.) 7,634 applied for aid; of those 88% were deemed to have need. 97% of undergraduates with need received aid; of those 9% had need fully met. *Average percent of need met:* 43% (excluding resources awarded to replace EFC). *Average financial aid package:* $8777 (excluding resources awarded to replace EFC). 7% of all full-time undergraduates had no need and received non-need-based gift aid.

GIFT AID (NEED-BASED) *Total amount:* $36,747,045 (60% federal, 15% state, 21% institutional, 4% external sources). *Receiving aid:* Freshmen: 61% (1,156); all full-time undergraduates: 56% (5,089). *Average award:* Freshmen: $6986; Undergraduates: $6600. *Scholarships, grants, and awards:* Federal Pell, FSEOG, state, private, college/university gift aid from institutional funds.

GIFT AID (NON-NEED-BASED) *Total amount:* $4,473,524 (1% federal, 5% state, 86% institutional, 8% external sources). *Receiving aid:* Freshmen: 4% (76). Undergraduates: 3% (236). *Average award:* Freshmen: $5560. Undergraduates: $5145. *Scholarships, grants, and awards by category:* Academic interests/achievement: biological sciences, business, communication, computer science, education, engineering/technologies, English, general academic interests/achievements, home economics, humanities, mathematics, physical sciences, premedicine, social sciences. *Creative arts/performance:* art/fine arts, creative writing, dance, journalism/publications, music, performing arts, theater/drama. *Special achievements/activities:* cheerleading/drum major. *Special characteristics:* children of faculty/staff, general special characteristics, out-of-state students. *Tuition waivers:* Full or partial for employees or children of employees, senior citizens. *ROTC:* Army cooperative, Air Force cooperative.

LOANS *Student loans:* $58,547,605 (84% need-based, 16% non-need-based). 64% of past graduating class borrowed through all loan programs. *Average indebtedness per student:* $25,504. *Average need-based loan:* Freshmen: $3420. Undergraduates: $4209. *Parent loans:* $7,097,785 (46% need-based, 54% non-need-based). *Programs:* Federal Direct (Subsidized and Unsubsidized Stafford, PLUS), Perkins, state, alternative loans.

WORK-STUDY *Federal work-study:* Total amount: $1,487,029; 233 jobs averaging $3448. *State or other work-study/employment:* Part-time jobs available.

ATHLETIC AWARDS Total amount: $2,898,081 (32% need-based, 68% non-need-based).

APPLYING FOR FINANCIAL AID *Required financial aid forms:* FAFSA, federal income tax form(s). *Financial aid deadline (priority):* 2/15. *Notification date:* Continuous beginning 3/15. Students must reply within 4 weeks of notification.

CONTACT Financial Aid Office, Cleveland State University, 1621 Euclid Avenue, Cleveland, OH 44115, 216-687-5594 or toll-free 888-CSU-OHIO. *E-mail:* campus411@csuohio.edu. *Website:* http://www.csuohio.edu/.

COASTAL CAROLINA UNIVERSITY
Conway, SC

Tuition & fees (SC res): $10,876	Average undergraduate aid package: $10,093

ABOUT THE INSTITUTION State-supported, coed. *Awards:* certificates, bachelor's, master's, and doctoral degrees. 44 undergraduate majors. *Total enrollment:* 10,479. Undergraduates: 9,747. Freshmen: 2,249. Federal methodology is used as a basis for awarding need-based institutional aid.

UNDERGRADUATE EXPENSES for 2016–2017 *Application fee:* $45. *Tuition, state resident:* full-time $10,696; part-time $451 per credit hour. *Tuition, nonresident:* full-time $24,940; part-time $1039 per credit hour. *Required fees:* full-time $180; $5 per credit hour. Full-time tuition and fees vary according to course load, degree level, and reciprocity agreements. Part-time tuition and fees vary according to course load, degree level, and reciprocity agreements. *College room and board:* $8890; *Room only:* $5440. Room and board charges vary according to board plan and housing facility.

FRESHMAN FINANCIAL AID (Fall 2015) 2,112 applied for aid; of those 81% were deemed to have need. 98% of freshmen with need received aid; of those 8% had need fully met. *Average percent of need met:* 44% (excluding resources awarded to replace EFC). *Average financial aid package:* $9857 (excluding resources awarded to replace EFC). 19% of all full-time freshmen had no need and received non-need-based gift aid.

UNDERGRADUATE FINANCIAL AID (Fall 2015) 7,324 applied for aid; of those 84% were deemed to have need. 99% of undergraduates with need received aid; of those 8% had need fully met. *Average percent of need met:* 47% (excluding resources awarded to replace EFC). *Average financial aid package:* $10,093 (excluding resources awarded to replace EFC). 18% of all full-time undergraduates had no need and received non-need-based gift aid.

GIFT AID (NEED-BASED) *Total amount:* $16,713,974 (90% federal, 10% state). *Receiving aid:* Freshmen: 35% (835); all full-time undergraduates: 38% (3,331). *Average award:* Freshmen: $4894; Undergraduates: $4846. *Scholarships, grants, and awards:* Federal Pell, FSEOG, state, private, college/university gift aid from institutional funds.

GIFT AID (NON-NEED-BASED) *Total amount:* $15,606,643 (65% state, 22% institutional, 13% external sources). *Receiving aid:* Freshmen: 32% (755). Undergraduates: 22% (1,883). *Average award:* Freshmen: $12,165. Undergraduates: $13,723. *Scholarships, grants, and awards by category: Academic interests/ achievement:* 3,220 awards ($9,498,099 total): biological sciences, business, communication, computer science, education, English, foreign languages, general academic interests/achievements, humanities, international studies, mathematics, physical sciences, social sciences. *Creative arts/performance:* 86 awards ($109,879 total): art/fine arts, music, performing arts, theater/drama. *Special achievements/activities:* 37 awards ($32,500 total): cheerleading/drum major. *Special characteristics:* 2,478 awards ($7,426,528 total): children of faculty/staff, general special characteristics, international students, local/state students, out-of-state students, veterans' children. *Tuition waivers:* Full or partial for employees or children of employees, senior citizens. *ROTC:* Army.
LOANS *Student loans:* $66,297,539 (32% need-based, 68% non-need-based). 77% of past graduating class borrowed through all loan programs. *Average indebtedness per student:* $38,897. *Average need-based loan:* Freshmen: $8612. Undergraduates: $9136. *Parent loans:* $27,801,503 (100% non-need-based). *Programs:* Federal Direct (Subsidized and Unsubsidized Stafford, PLUS), Perkins, state.
WORK-STUDY *Federal work-study:* 184 jobs averaging $2335. *State or other work-study/employment:* Total amount: $2,824,782 (100% non-need-based). 1,404 part-time jobs averaging $2012.
ATHLETIC AWARDS Total amount: $4,307,512 (100% non-need-based).
APPLYING FOR FINANCIAL AID *Required financial aid form:* FAFSA. *Financial aid deadline (priority):* 3/1. *Notification date:* Continuous beginning 3/1. Students must reply by 5/15.
CONTACT Ms. Wendy H. Watts, Director of Financial Aid and Scholarships, Coastal Carolina University, PO Box 261954, Conway, SC 29528-6054, 843-349-2544 or toll-free 800-277-7000. *Fax:* 843-349-2347. *E-mail:* wwatts@coastal.edu.
Website: http://www.coastal.edu/.

COE COLLEGE
Cedar Rapids, IA

Tuition & fees: $42,430	Average undergraduate aid package: $33,486

ABOUT THE INSTITUTION Independent Presbyterian Church, coed. *Awards:* bachelor's degrees. 64 undergraduate majors. *Total enrollment:* 1,409. Undergraduates: 1,409. Freshmen: 374. Federal methodology is used as a basis for awarding need-based institutional aid.
UNDERGRADUATE EXPENSES for 2017–2018 *Application fee:* $30. *Comprehensive fee:* $51,570 includes full-time tuition ($42,090), mandatory fees ($340), and room and board ($9140). *College room only:* $4350. Room and board charges vary according to board plan and housing facility. *Part-time tuition:* $5261 per course. Part-time tuition and fees vary according to course load.
FRESHMAN FINANCIAL AID (Fall 2016, est.) 351 applied for aid; of those 93% were deemed to have need. 100% of freshmen with need received aid; of those 20% had need fully met. *Average percent of need met:* 85% (excluding resources awarded to replace EFC). *Average financial aid package:* $35,534 (excluding resources awarded to replace EFC). 12% of all full-time freshmen had no need and received non-need-based gift aid.
UNDERGRADUATE FINANCIAL AID (Fall 2016, est.) 1,174 applied for aid; of those 93% were deemed to have need. 100% of undergraduates with need received aid; of those 21% had need fully met. *Average percent of need met:* 83% (excluding resources awarded to replace EFC). *Average financial aid package:* $33,486 (excluding resources awarded to replace EFC). 15% of all full-time undergraduates had no need and received non-need-based gift aid.
GIFT AID (NEED-BASED) *Total amount:* $30,624,703 (6% federal, 6% state, 86% institutional, 2% external sources). *Receiving aid:* Freshmen: 87% (325); all full-time undergraduates: 83% (1,095). *Average award:* Freshmen: $31,524; Undergraduates: $28,610. *Scholarships, grants, and awards:* Federal Pell, FSEOG, state, private, college/university gift aid from institutional funds, Federal Nursing, ROTC Scholarships.
GIFT AID (NON-NEED-BASED) *Total amount:* $6,493,598 (2% federal, 94% institutional, 4% external sources). *Receiving aid:* Freshmen: 12% (44). Undergraduates: 12% (157). *Average award:* Freshmen: $25,905. Undergraduates: $23,175. *Scholarships, grants, and awards by category: Academic interests/*

achievement: 1,911 awards ($22,273,486 total): general academic interests/achievements. *Creative arts/performance:* 126 awards ($680,470 total): art/fine arts, creative writing, music, performing arts, theater/drama. *Special achievements/activities:* community service. *Special characteristics:* 417 awards ($2,564,139 total): adult students, children and siblings of alumni, children of educators, children of faculty/staff, ethnic background, general special characteristics, international students, members of minority groups, religious affiliation, siblings of current students, veterans, veterans' children. *Tuition waivers:* Full or partial for employees or children of employees, adult students, senior citizens. *ROTC:* Army, Air Force cooperative.
LOANS *Student loans:* $9,222,382 (73% need-based, 27% non-need-based). 82% of past graduating class borrowed through all loan programs. *Average indebtedness per student:* $35,782. *Average need-based loan:* Freshmen: $3808. Undergraduates: $5122. *Parent loans:* $2,852,264 (39% need-based, 61% non-need-based). *Programs:* Federal Direct (Subsidized and Unsubsidized Stafford, PLUS), Perkins, college/university.
WORK-STUDY *Federal work-study:* Total amount: $713,962; 584 jobs averaging $2565. *State or other work-study/employment:* Total amount: $312,800 (15% need-based, 85% non-need-based). 215 part-time jobs averaging $1431.
APPLYING FOR FINANCIAL AID *Required financial aid form:* FAFSA. *Financial aid deadline (priority):* 3/1. *Notification date:* Continuous beginning 3/15. Students must reply by 5/1 or within 2 weeks of notification.
CONTACT Ms. Barbara Hoffman, Director of Financial Aid, Coe College, 1220 First Avenue, NE, Cedar Rapids, IA 52402-5070, 319-399-8540 or toll-free 877-225-5263. *Fax:* 319-399-8886.
Website: http://www.coe.edu/.

COGSWELL POLYTECHNICAL COLLEGE
San Jose, CA

Tuition & fees: $19,096	Average undergraduate aid package: N/A

ABOUT THE INSTITUTION Proprietary, coed. *Awards:* bachelor's and master's degrees. 6 undergraduate majors. *Total enrollment:* 656. Undergraduates: 656. Freshmen: 114. Federal methodology is used as a basis for awarding need-based institutional aid.
UNDERGRADUATE EXPENSES for 2016–2017 *Tuition:* full-time $18,096; part-time $754 per credit. Full-time tuition and fees vary according to course load, degree level, and program. Part-time tuition and fees vary according to course load, degree level, and program. Room and board charges vary according to housing facility.
GIFT AID (NEED-BASED) *Total amount:* $2,419,752 (51% federal, 48% state, 1% institutional). *Scholarships, grants, and awards:* Federal Pell, FSEOG, state, private, college/university gift aid from institutional funds.
GIFT AID (NON-NEED-BASED) *Total amount:* $824,992 (94% institutional, 6% external sources). *Tuition waivers:* Full or partial for employees or children of employees.
LOANS *Student loans:* $3,956,914 (46% need-based, 54% non-need-based). *Parent loans:* $2,074,311 (100% non-need-based). *Programs:* Federal Direct (Subsidized and Unsubsidized Stafford, PLUS), private loans.
WORK-STUDY *Federal work-study:* 17 jobs averaging $2328.
APPLYING FOR FINANCIAL AID *Required financial aid forms:* FAFSA, state aid form. *Financial aid deadline (priority):* 3/1. *Notification date:* Continuous. Students must reply by 5/1 or within 2 weeks of notification.
CONTACT Yariela Perez, Director of Financial Aid, Cogswell Polytechnical College, 191 Baypointe Parkway, San Jose, CA 95134, 408-498-5100 or toll-free 800-264-7955. *E-mail:* yperez@cogswell.edu.
Website: http://www.cogswell.edu/.

COKER COLLEGE
Hartsville, SC

CONTACT Mrs. Betty Williams, Director of Financial Aid, Coker College, 300 East College Avenue, Hartsville, SC 29550, 843-383-8055 or toll-free 800-950-1908. *Fax:* 843-383-8056. *E-mail:* bwilliams@coker.edu.
Website: http://www.coker.edu/.

THE COLBURN SCHOOL CONSERVATORY OF MUSIC
Los Angeles, CA

Tuition & fees: $3000	Average undergraduate aid package: $2667

ABOUT THE INSTITUTION Independent, coed. *Awards:* certificates, diplomas, bachelor's, and master's degrees. 5 undergraduate majors. *Total enrollment:* 115. Undergraduates: 55. Freshmen: 9. Institutional methodology is used as a basis for awarding need-based institutional aid.

UNDERGRADUATE EXPENSES for 2016–2017 *Application fee:* $120. Full scholarships covering tuition, room and board are awarded to all students enrolled in the Conservatory (to the extent that this amount is not underwritten by outside scholarships).

FRESHMAN FINANCIAL AID (Fall 2016, est.) 3 applied for aid; of those 100% were deemed to have need. 100% of freshmen with need received aid. *Average percent of need met:* 92% (excluding resources awarded to replace EFC). *Average financial aid package:* $1800 (excluding resources awarded to replace EFC).

UNDERGRADUATE FINANCIAL AID (Fall 2016, est.) 19 applied for aid; of those 95% were deemed to have need. 100% of undergraduates with need received aid. *Average percent of need met:* 92% (excluding resources awarded to replace EFC). *Average financial aid package:* $2667 (excluding resources awarded to replace EFC).

GIFT AID (NEED-BASED) *Total amount:* $45,000 (100% institutional). *Receiving aid:* Freshmen: 23% (3); all full-time undergraduates: 35% (18). *Average award:* Freshmen: $1800; Undergraduates: $2667. *Scholarships, grants, and awards:* college/university gift aid from institutional funds.

GIFT AID (NON-NEED-BASED) *Receiving aid:* Freshmen: 15% (2). Undergraduates: 35% (18). *Scholarships, grants, and awards by category:* Creative arts/performance: 11 awards ($22,150 total): music.

APPLYING FOR FINANCIAL AID *Required financial aid form:* institution's own form. *Financial aid deadline:* 9/1. *Notification date:* 9/15. Students must reply by 10/1.

CONTACT Ms. Misha Starks, Registrar, The Colburn School Conservatory of Music, 200 South Grand Avenue, Los Angeles, CA 90012, 213-621-4788. *Fax:* 213-625-0371. *E-mail:* mstarks@colburnschool.edu.
Website: http://www.colburnschool.edu/.

COLBY COLLEGE
Waterville, ME

Tuition & fees: $50,960	Average undergraduate aid package: $45,306

ABOUT THE INSTITUTION Independent, coed. *Awards:* bachelor's degrees. 47 undergraduate majors. *Total enrollment:* 1,857. Undergraduates: 1,857. Freshmen: 508. Both federal and institutional methodology are used as a basis for awarding need-based institutional aid.

UNDERGRADUATE EXPENSES for 2016–2017 *Comprehensive fee:* $64,060 includes full-time tuition ($48,820), mandatory fees ($2140), and room and board ($13,100). Room and board charges vary according to housing facility. *Part-time tuition:* $1880 per credit hour. Part-time tuition and fees vary according to course load.

FRESHMAN FINANCIAL AID (Fall 2016, est.) 293 applied for aid; of those 81% were deemed to have need. 100% of freshmen with need received aid; of those 100% had need fully met. *Average percent of need met:* 100% (excluding resources awarded to replace EFC). *Average financial aid package:* $47,442 (excluding resources awarded to replace EFC).

UNDERGRADUATE FINANCIAL AID (Fall 2016, est.) 907 applied for aid; of those 86% were deemed to have need. 100% of undergraduates with need received aid; of those 100% had need fully met. *Average percent of need met:* 100% (excluding resources awarded to replace EFC). *Average financial aid package:* $45,306 (excluding resources awarded to replace EFC). 2% of all full-time undergraduates had no need and received non-need-based gift aid.

GIFT AID (NEED-BASED) *Total amount:* $33,495,842 (4% federal, 95% institutional, 1% external sources). *Receiving aid:* Freshmen: 46% (237); all full-time undergraduates: 42% (783). *Average award:* Freshmen: $46,261; Undergraduates: $43,906. *Scholarships, grants, and awards:* Federal Pell, FSEOG, state, private, college/university gift aid from institutional funds, Colby National Merit Scholarships.

GIFT AID (NON-NEED-BASED) *Total amount:* $584,119 (27% federal, 60% institutional, 13% external sources). *Receiving aid:* Freshmen: 1% (6). Undergraduates: 9. *Average award:* Undergraduates: $9595. *Scholarships, grants, and awards by category:* Academic interests/achievement: general academic interests/achievements. *Special characteristics:* general special characteristics. *Tuition waivers:* Full or partial for employees or children of employees. *ROTC:* Army cooperative.

LOANS *Student loans:* $3,368,847 (26% need-based, 74% non-need-based). 28% of past graduating class borrowed through all loan programs. *Average indebtedness per student:* $27,953. *Average need-based loan:* Freshmen: $2838. Undergraduates: $3689. *Parent loans:* $1,990,592 (100% non-need-based). *Programs:* Federal Direct (Subsidized and Unsubsidized Stafford, PLUS), Perkins, state, alternative loans.

WORK-STUDY *Federal work-study:* Total amount: $609,851; jobs available. *State or other work-study/employment:* Total amount: $359,715 (100% need-based). Part-time jobs available.

APPLYING FOR FINANCIAL AID *Required financial aid forms:* FAFSA, CSS Financial Aid PROFILE, business/farm supplement, federal income tax form(s). *Financial aid deadline:* 2/1. *Notification date:* 4/1. Students must reply by 5/1.

CONTACT Elreo Campbell, Associate Dean and Director of Financial Aid, Colby College, 4850 Mayflower Hill, Waterville, ME 04901-8848, 800-723-3032. *Fax:* 207-859-4828. *E-mail:* finaid@colby.edu.
Website: http://www.colby.edu/.

COLBY-SAWYER COLLEGE
New London, NH

CONTACT Ms. Beth Renzulli, Director of Financial Aid, Colby-Sawyer College, 541 Main Street, New London, NH 03257-7835, 603-526-3717 or toll-free 800-272-1015. *Fax:* 603-526-3737. *E-mail:* cscfinaid@colby-sawyer.edu.
Website: http://www.colby-sawyer.edu/.

COLEGIO UNIVERSITARIO DE SAN JUAN
San Juan, PR

CONTACT Ken Lira, Director of Financial Aid, Colegio Universitario de San Juan, 43-500 Monterey Avenue, Palm Desert, AB 92260, 760-776-7428. *Fax:* 760-776-7338. *E-mail:* klira@collegeofthedesert.edu.
Website: http://www.cunisanjuan.edu/.

COLEMAN UNIVERSITY
San Diego, CA

CONTACT Financial Aid Office, Coleman University, 8888 Balboa Avenue, San Diego, CA 92123, 858-499-0202 or toll-free 800-430-2030. *Fax:* 858-499-0233. *E-mail:* faoffice@coleman.edu.
Website: http://www.coleman.edu/.

COLGATE UNIVERSITY
Hamilton, NY

Tuition & fees: $51,955 | **Average undergraduate aid package:** $49,912

ABOUT THE INSTITUTION Independent, coed. **Awards:** bachelor's and master's degrees. 53 undergraduate majors. **Total enrollment:** 2,861. Undergraduates: 2,853. Freshmen: 773. Institutional methodology is used as a basis for awarding need-based institutional aid.

UNDERGRADUATE EXPENSES for 2016–2017 **Application fee:** $60. **One-time required fee:** $50. **Comprehensive fee:** $65,030 includes full-time tuition ($51,635), mandatory fees ($320), and room and board ($13,075). **College room only:** $6310. Full-time tuition and fees vary according to course load. Room and board charges vary according to board plan and housing facility. Part-time tuition and fees vary according to course load. **Payment plan:** Tuition prepayment.

FRESHMAN FINANCIAL AID (Fall 2016, est.) 284 applied for aid; of those 85% were deemed to have need. 100% of freshmen with need received aid; of those 100% had need fully met. **Average percent of need met:** 100% (excluding resources awarded to replace EFC). **Average financial aid package:** $51,521 (excluding resources awarded to replace EFC).

UNDERGRADUATE FINANCIAL AID (Fall 2016, est.) 1,134 applied for aid; of those 93% were deemed to have need. 100% of undergraduates with need received aid; of those 100% had need fully met. **Average percent of need met:** 100% (excluding resources awarded to replace EFC). **Average financial aid package:** $49,912 (excluding resources awarded to replace EFC).

GIFT AID (NEED-BASED) Total amount: $47,901,841 (4% federal, 1% state, 93% institutional, 2% external sources). **Receiving aid:** Freshmen: 31% (239); all full-time undergraduates: 37% (1,047). **Average award:** Freshmen: $48,355; Undergraduates: $45,724. **Scholarships, grants, and awards:** Federal Pell, FSEOG, state, college/university gift aid from institutional funds.

GIFT AID (NON-NEED-BASED) Total amount: $1,192,854 (14% state, 17% institutional, 69% external sources). **Scholarships, grants, and awards by category:** Special characteristics: 12 awards ($190,616 total): veterans, veterans' children. **Tuition waivers:** Full or partial for employees or children of employees. **ROTC:** Army cooperative.

LOANS Student loans: $5,480,255 (40% need-based, 60% non-need-based). 34% of past graduating class borrowed through all loan programs. **Average indebtedness per student:** $21,427. **Average need-based loan:** Freshmen: $1360. Undergraduates: $3660. **Parent loans:** $3,404,514 (100% non-need-based). **Programs:** Federal Direct (Subsidized and Unsubsidized Stafford, PLUS).

WORK-STUDY Federal work-study: Total amount: $1,314,837; 572 jobs averaging $2272. **State or other work-study/employment:** Total amount: $620,847 (98% need-based, 2% non-need-based). 295 part-time jobs averaging $2091.

ATHLETIC AWARDS Total amount: $12,279,223 (100% non-need-based).

APPLYING FOR FINANCIAL AID Required financial aid forms: CSS Financial Aid PROFILE, noncustodial (divorced/separated) parent's statement. **Financial aid deadline:** 1/15. **Notification date:** 4/1. Students must reply by 5/1 or within 2 weeks of notification.

CONTACT Office of Financial Aid, Colgate University, 13 Oak Drive, Hamilton, NY 13346, 315-228-7431. **Fax:** 315-228-7050. **E-mail:** finaid@colgate.edu. **Website:** http://www.colgate.edu/.

COLLEGEAMERICA–CHEYENNE
Cheyenne, WY

CONTACT Financial Aid Office, CollegeAmerica–Cheyenne, 6101 Yellowstone Road, Cheyenne, WY 82009, 307-632-7048. **Website:** http://www.collegeamerica.edu/.

THE COLLEGE AT BROCKPORT, STATE UNIVERSITY OF NEW YORK
Brockport, NY

Tuition & fees (NY res): $7928 | **Average undergraduate aid package:** $10,736

ABOUT THE INSTITUTION State-supported, coed. **Awards:** certificates, bachelor's, and master's degrees. 44 undergraduate majors. **Total enrollment:** 8,243. Undergraduates: 7,128. Freshmen: 1,205. Federal methodology is used as a basis for awarding need-based institutional aid.

UNDERGRADUATE EXPENSES for 2016–2017 **Application fee:** $50. **Tuition, state resident:** full-time $6470; part-time $270 per credit. **Tuition, nonresident:** full-time $16,320; part-time $680 per credit. **Required fees:** full-time $1458; $60.42 per credit hour. Part-time tuition and fees vary according to course load. **College room and board:** $12,418; **Room only:** $7682. Room and board charges vary according to board plan and housing facility.

FRESHMAN FINANCIAL AID (Fall 2015) 967 applied for aid; of those 80% were deemed to have need. 98% of freshmen with need received aid; of those 17% had need fully met. **Average percent of need met:** 72% (excluding resources awarded to replace EFC). **Average financial aid package:** $11,571 (excluding resources awarded to replace EFC). 5% of all full-time freshmen had no need and received non-need-based gift aid.

UNDERGRADUATE FINANCIAL AID (Fall 2015) 4,691 applied for aid; of those 82% were deemed to have need. 99% of undergraduates with need received aid; of those 17% had need fully met. **Average percent of need met:** 72% (excluding resources awarded to replace EFC). **Average financial aid package:** $10,736 (excluding resources awarded to replace EFC). 2% of all full-time undergraduates had no need and received non-need-based gift aid.

GIFT AID (NEED-BASED) Total amount: $23,741,625 (54% federal, 45% state, 1% external sources). **Receiving aid:** Freshmen: 58% (605); all full-time undergraduates: 59% (3,112). **Average award:** Freshmen: $7013; Undergraduates: $6685. **Scholarships, grants, and awards:** Federal Pell, FSEOG, state, private, college/university gift aid from institutional funds.

GIFT AID (NON-NEED-BASED) Total amount: $5,500,514 (9% federal, 8% state, 60% institutional, 23% external sources). **Receiving aid:** Freshmen: 27% (284). Undergraduates: 15% (813). **Average award:** Freshmen: $4662. Undergraduates: $5181. **Scholarships, grants, and awards by category:** Academic interests/achievement: 857 awards ($2,839,966 total): biological sciences, business, communication, computer science, education, English, foreign languages, general academic interests/achievements, home economics, humanities, international studies, mathematics, military science, physical sciences, premedicine, social sciences. Creative arts/performance: 36 awards ($26,800 total): art/fine arts, cinema/film/broadcasting, creative writing, dance, general creative arts/performance, journalism/publications, music, theater/drama. Special achievements/activities: 31 awards ($35,625 total): community service, general special achievements/activities, hobbies/interests, leadership, religious involvement. Special characteristics: 26 awards ($34,213 total): adult students, children and siblings of alumni, children of faculty/staff, ethnic background, first-generation college students, general special characteristics, international students, married students, members of minority groups, previous college experience, religious affiliation, veterans. **Tuition waivers:** Full or partial for employees or children of employees. **ROTC:** Army, Naval cooperative, Air Force cooperative.

LOANS Student loans: $41,332,614 (45% need-based, 55% non-need-based). 80% of past graduating class borrowed through all loan programs. **Average indebtedness per student:** $29,748. **Average need-based loan:** Freshmen: $4830. Undergraduates: $4879. **Parent loans:** $5,074,721 (100% non-need-based). **Programs:** Federal Direct (Subsidized and Unsubsidized Stafford, PLUS), Perkins, Federal Nursing, alternative loans.

WORK-STUDY Federal work-study: 488 jobs averaging $2166. **State or other work-study/employment:** Total amount: $1,667,545 (100% non-need-based). 750 part-time jobs averaging $2223.

APPLYING FOR FINANCIAL AID Required financial aid forms: FAFSA, state aid form. **Financial aid deadline (priority):** 1/1. **Notification date:** Continuous beginning 1/1. Students must reply by 2/1.

CONTACT Office of Financial Aid, The College at Brockport, State University of New York, 350 New Campus Drive, Brockport, NY 14420-2937, 585-395-2501. **Fax:** 585-395-5445. **Website:** http://www.brockport.edu/.

COLLEGE FOR CREATIVE STUDIES
Detroit, MI

CONTACT Office of Financial Aid, College for Creative Studies, 201 East Kirby, Detroit, MI 48202-4034, 313-664-7495 or toll-free 800-952-ARTS. *Fax:* 313-872-1521. *E-mail:* finaid@collegeforcreativestudies.edu. *Website:* http://www.collegeforcreativestudies.edu/.

COLLEGE OF BIBLICAL STUDIES–HOUSTON
Houston, TX

CONTACT Roshanna Hardison, Director of Student Financial Services, College of Biblical Studies–Houston, 7000 Regency Square Boulevard, Houston, TX 77036, 832-252-0728 or toll-free 844-227-9673. *E-mail:* roshanna.hardison@cbshouston.edu. *Website:* http://www.cbshouston.edu/.

COLLEGE OF CHARLESTON
Charleston, SC

Tuition & fees (SC res): $11,846	Average undergraduate aid package: $13,505

ABOUT THE INSTITUTION State-supported, coed. *Awards:* certificates, bachelor's, and master's degrees (also offers graduate degree programs through University of Charleston, South Carolina). 57 undergraduate majors. *Total enrollment:* 11,294. Undergraduates: 10,375. Freshmen: 2,349. Federal methodology is used as a basis for awarding need-based institutional aid.

UNDERGRADUATE EXPENSES for 2016–2017 Application fee: $50. *Tuition, state resident:* full-time $11,386; part-time $474 per credit hour. *Tuition, nonresident:* full-time $29,544; part-time $1231 per credit hour. *Required fees:* full-time $460; $16.25 per term or $15 per term. Full-time tuition and fees vary according to student level. Part-time tuition and fees vary according to course load and student level. *College room and board:* $12,048; *Room only:* $7828. Room and board charges vary according to board plan and housing facility.

FRESHMAN FINANCIAL AID (Fall 2016, est.) 1,840 applied for aid; of those 71% were deemed to have need. 95% of freshmen with need received aid; of those 19% had need fully met. *Average percent of need met:* 53% (excluding resources awarded to replace EFC). *Average financial aid package:* $13,421 (excluding resources awarded to replace EFC). 23% of all full-time freshmen had no need and received non-need-based gift aid.

UNDERGRADUATE FINANCIAL AID (Fall 2016, est.) 6,219 applied for aid; of those 77% were deemed to have need. 96% of undergraduates with need received aid; of those 17% had need fully met. *Average percent of need met:* 54% (excluding resources awarded to replace EFC). *Average financial aid package:* $13,505 (excluding resources awarded to replace EFC). 19% of all full-time undergraduates had no need and received non-need-based gift aid.

GIFT AID (NEED-BASED) Total amount: $28,738,747 (38% federal, 32% state, 25% institutional, 5% external sources). *Receiving aid:* Freshmen: 39% (908); all full-time undergraduates: 34% (3,223). *Average award:* Freshmen: $2775; Undergraduates: $2609. *Scholarships, grants, and awards:* Federal Pell, FSEOG, state, private, college/university gift aid from institutional funds.

GIFT AID (NON-NEED-BASED) Total amount: $19,851,774 (56% state, 38% institutional, 6% external sources). *Receiving aid:* Freshmen: 42% (972). Undergraduates: 24% (2,274). *Average award:* Freshmen: $10,982. Undergraduates: $11,630. *Scholarships, grants, and awards by category:* Academic interests/achievement: biological sciences, business, communication, computer science, education, engineering/technologies, English, foreign languages, general academic interests/achievements, health fields, humanities, mathematics, physical sciences, premedicine, social sciences. *Creative arts/performance:* art/fine arts, music, performing arts, theater/drama. *Special characteristics:* general special characteristics. *Tuition waivers:* Full or partial for employees or children of employees, senior citizens. *ROTC:* Air Force cooperative.

LOANS Student loans: $40,250,952 (63% need-based, 37% non-need-based). 48% of past graduating class borrowed through all loan programs. *Average indebtedness per student:* $26,203. *Average need-based loan:* Freshmen: $3019. Undergraduates: $3587. *Parent loans:* $35,166,382 (61% need-based, 39% non-need-based). *Programs:* Federal Direct (Subsidized and Unsubsidized Stafford, PLUS), Perkins.

WORK-STUDY Federal work-study: Total amount: $501,471; jobs available. *State or other work-study/employment:* Part-time jobs available.

ATHLETIC AWARDS Total amount: $4,699,722 (24% need-based, 76% non-need-based).

APPLYING FOR FINANCIAL AID Required financial aid form: FAFSA. *Financial aid deadline (priority):* 3/1. *Notification date:* Continuous beginning 4/1. Students must reply within 8 weeks of notification.

CONTACT Derwin Simpson, Student Services Manager, College of Charleston, 66 George Street, Charleston, SC 29424, 843-953-5540. *Fax:* 843-953-7192. *E-mail:* financialaid@cofc.edu. *Website:* http://www.cofc.edu/.

COLLEGE OF COASTAL GEORGIA
Brunswick, GA

Tuition & fees (GA res): $4434	Average undergraduate aid package: $9875

ABOUT THE INSTITUTION State-supported, coed. *Awards:* associate and bachelor's degrees. 28 undergraduate majors. *Total enrollment:* 3,529. Undergraduates: 3,529. Freshmen: 861. Federal methodology is used as a basis for awarding need-based institutional aid.

UNDERGRADUATE EXPENSES for 2017–2018 Application fee: $25. *Tuition, state resident:* full-time $3064; part-time $102.13 per semester hour. *Tuition, nonresident:* full-time $11,322; part-time $377.40 per semester hour. *Required fees:* full-time $1370; $685 per term. Full-time tuition and fees vary according to course load. Part-time tuition and fees vary according to course load. *College room and board:* $8458; *Room only:* $5008. Room and board charges vary according to board plan, housing facility, and location.

FRESHMAN FINANCIAL AID (Fall 2015) 430 applied for aid; of those 94% were deemed to have need. 100% of freshmen with need received aid; of those 24% had need fully met. *Average percent of need met:* 21% (excluding resources awarded to replace EFC). *Average financial aid package:* $9875 (excluding resources awarded to replace EFC).

UNDERGRADUATE FINANCIAL AID (Fall 2015) 1,627 applied for aid; of those 85% were deemed to have need. 100% of undergraduates with need received aid; of those 47% had need fully met. *Average percent of need met:* 38% (excluding resources awarded to replace EFC). *Average financial aid package:* $9875 (excluding resources awarded to replace EFC).

GIFT AID (NEED-BASED) Total amount: $1,695,371 (91% federal, 9% institutional). *Receiving aid:* Freshmen: 75% (360); all full-time undergraduates: 70% (1,201). *Average award:* Freshmen: $7875; Undergraduates: $7875. *Scholarships, grants, and awards:* Federal Pell, FSEOG, state, private, college/university gift aid from institutional funds.

GIFT AID (NON-NEED-BASED) Total amount: $855,554 (76% state, 24% external sources). *Scholarships, grants, and awards by category:* Academic interests/achievement: 163 awards ($139,160 total): biological sciences, business, education, home economics, mathematics. *Special achievements/activities:* 12 awards ($14,050 total): leadership. *Special characteristics:* 12 awards ($27,300 total): international students, local/state students. *Tuition waivers:* Full or partial for employees or children of employees, senior citizens.

LOANS Student loans: $1,468,053 (47% need-based, 53% non-need-based). 64% of past graduating class borrowed through all loan programs. *Average indebtedness per student:* $25,455. *Average need-based loan:* Freshmen: $3500. Undergraduates: $3500. *Parent loans:* $275,273 (100% non-need-based). *Programs:* Federal Direct (Subsidized and Unsubsidized Stafford, PLUS), state.

WORK-STUDY Federal work-study: 29 jobs averaging $3900.

ATHLETIC AWARDS Total amount: $78,000 (100% non-need-based).

APPLYING FOR FINANCIAL AID Required financial aid forms: FAFSA, state aid form. *Financial aid deadline:* 6/1 (priority: 5/1). *Notification date:* Continuous beginning 9/15.

CONTACT Financial Aid Office, College of Coastal Georgia, One College Drive, Brunswick, GA 31520, 912-279-5722 or toll-free 800-675-7235. *Fax:* 912-264-7320. *E-mail:* finaid@ccga.edu.
Website: http://www.ccga.edu/.

THE COLLEGE OF IDAHO
Caldwell, ID

Tuition & fees: $28,755	Average undergraduate aid package: $23,822

ABOUT THE INSTITUTION Independent, coed. *Awards:* bachelor's and master's degrees. 36 undergraduate majors. *Total enrollment:* 980. Undergraduates: 962. Freshmen: 238. Federal methodology is used as a basis for awarding need-based institutional aid.

UNDERGRADUATE EXPENSES for 2017–2018 Comprehensive fee: $38,089 includes full-time tuition ($28,000), mandatory fees ($755), and room and board ($9334). Room and board charges vary according to board plan and housing facility. *Part-time tuition:* $1165 per credit.

FRESHMAN FINANCIAL AID (Fall 2016, est.) 158 applied for aid; of those 100% were deemed to have need. 100% of freshmen with need received aid; of those 30% had need fully met. *Average percent of need met:* 66% (excluding resources awarded to replace EFC). *Average financial aid package:* $26,538 (excluding resources awarded to replace EFC). 24% of all full-time freshmen had no need and received non-need-based gift aid.

UNDERGRADUATE FINANCIAL AID (Fall 2016, est.) 618 applied for aid; of those 100% were deemed to have need. 100% of undergraduates with need received aid; of those 22% had need fully met. *Average percent of need met:* 60% (excluding resources awarded to replace EFC). *Average financial aid package:* $23,822 (excluding resources awarded to replace EFC). 34% of all full-time undergraduates had no need and received non-need-based gift aid.

GIFT AID (NEED-BASED) Total amount: $4,722,539 (30% federal, 6% state, 30% institutional, 34% external sources). *Receiving aid:* Freshmen: 67% (158); all full-time undergraduates: 67% (618). *Average award:* Freshmen: $5203; Undergraduates: $6291. *Scholarships, grants, and awards:* Federal Pell, FSEOG, state, private, college/university gift aid from institutional funds.

GIFT AID (NON-NEED-BASED) Total amount: $12,463,904 (98% institutional, 2% external sources). *Receiving aid:* Freshmen: 66% (156). Undergraduates: 67% (618). *Average award:* Freshmen: $15,745. Undergraduates: $13,324. *Scholarships, grants, and awards by category:* Academic interests/achievement: biological sciences, business, education, English, foreign languages, general academic interests/achievements, humanities, mathematics, physical sciences, premedicine, religion/biblical studies, social sciences. *Creative arts/performance:* art/fine arts, debating, music, performing arts, theater/drama. *Special achievements/activities:* leadership. *Special characteristics:* children and siblings of alumni, children of educators, children of faculty/staff, first-generation college students, international students, local/state students, married students, members of minority groups, out-of-state students, siblings of current students, veterans' children. *Tuition waivers:* Full or partial for employees or children of employees. *ROTC:* Army cooperative.

LOANS Student loans: $2,490,742 (100% need-based). 59% of past graduating class borrowed through all loan programs. *Average indebtedness per student:* $7270. *Average need-based loan:* Freshmen: $3241. Undergraduates: $4663. *Parent loans:* $999,445 (100% need-based). *Programs:* Federal Direct (Subsidized and Unsubsidized Stafford, PLUS), Perkins, private loans.

WORK-STUDY Federal work-study: Total amount: $11,400; jobs available. *State or other work-study/employment:* Total amount: $37,800 (100% need-based). Part-time jobs available.

ATHLETIC AWARDS Total amount: $2,258,812 (100% non-need-based).

APPLYING FOR FINANCIAL AID Required financial aid form: FAFSA. *Financial aid deadline (priority):* 2/1. *Notification date:* Continuous beginning 3/15.

CONTACT Jennifer Worden, Director of Financial Aid Services, The College of Idaho, 2112 Cleveland Boulevard, Caldwell, ID 83605, 208-459-5307 or toll-free 800-244-3246. *Fax:* 208-459-5844. *E-mail:* jworden@collegeofidaho.edu.
Website: http://www.collegeofidaho.edu/.

COLLEGE OF MOUNT SAINT VINCENT
Riverdale, NY

CONTACT Mr. Emmett Cooper, Director of Financial Aid, College of Mount Saint Vincent, 6301 Riverdale Avenue, Riverdale, NY 10471, 718-405-3309 or toll-free 800-665-CMSV. *Fax:* 718-405-3490. *E-mail:* emmett.cooper@mountsaintvincent.edu.
Website: http://www.mountsaintvincent.edu/.

THE COLLEGE OF NEW JERSEY
Ewing, NJ

Tuition & fees (NJ res): $15,794	Average undergraduate aid package: $10,955

ABOUT THE INSTITUTION State-supported, coed. *Awards:* certificates, bachelor's, and master's degrees. 53 undergraduate majors. *Total enrollment:* 7,396. Undergraduates: 6,787. Freshmen: 1,457. Federal methodology is used as a basis for awarding need-based institutional aid.

UNDERGRADUATE EXPENSES for 2017–2018 Application fee: $75. *Tuition, state resident:* full-time $11,124; part-time $394.19 per credit hour. *Tuition, nonresident:* full-time $22,301; part-time $789.34 per credit hour. *Required fees:* full-time $4670; $186.86 per credit hour. Part-time tuition and fees vary according to course load. *College room and board:* $12,881; *Room only:* $8794. Room and board charges vary according to board plan.

FRESHMAN FINANCIAL AID (Fall 2016, est.) 1,238 applied for aid; of those 67% were deemed to have need. 93% of freshmen with need received aid; of those 11% had need fully met. *Average percent of need met:* 40% (excluding resources awarded to replace EFC). *Average financial aid package:* $11,002 (excluding resources awarded to replace EFC). 12% of all full-time freshmen had no need and received non-need-based gift aid.

UNDERGRADUATE FINANCIAL AID (Fall 2016, est.) 4,588 applied for aid; of those 72% were deemed to have need. 96% of undergraduates with need received aid; of those 11% had need fully met. *Average percent of need met:* 43% (excluding resources awarded to replace EFC). *Average financial aid package:* $10,955 (excluding resources awarded to replace EFC). 8% of all full-time undergraduates had no need and received non-need-based gift aid.

GIFT AID (NEED-BASED) Total amount: $21,342,150 (25% federal, 31% state, 35% institutional, 9% external sources). *Receiving aid:* Freshmen: 22% (324); all full-time undergraduates: 20% (1,281). *Average award:* Freshmen: $13,272; Undergraduates: $11,951. *Scholarships, grants, and awards:* Federal Pell, FSEOG, state, private, college/university gift aid from institutional funds, Federal Nursing.

GIFT AID (NON-NEED-BASED) Total amount: $5,223,799 (84% institutional, 16% external sources). *Receiving aid:* Freshmen: 20% (292). Undergraduates: 13% (841). *Average award:* Freshmen: $5241. Undergraduates: $5018. *Scholarships, grants, and awards by category:* Academic interests/achievement: general academic interests/achievements. *Creative arts/performance:* art/fine arts, music. *Special characteristics:* children with a deceased or disabled parent, members of minority groups. *Tuition waivers:* Full or partial for employees or children of employees, senior citizens. *ROTC:* Army cooperative, Air Force cooperative.

LOANS Student loans: $37,128,477 (77% need-based, 23% non-need-based). 63% of past graduating class borrowed through all loan programs. *Average indebtedness per student:* $35,798. *Average need-based loan:* Freshmen: $3511. Undergraduates: $4564. *Parent loans:* $7,278,813 (77% need-based, 23% non-need-based). *Programs:* Federal Direct (Subsidized and Unsubsidized Stafford, PLUS), Perkins, Federal Nursing, private loans.

WORK-STUDY Federal work-study: Total amount: $153,381; jobs available.

APPLYING FOR FINANCIAL AID Required financial aid form: FAFSA. *Financial aid deadline:* 10/1 (priority: 3/1). *Notification date:* Continuous beginning 6/1. Students must reply within 2 weeks of notification.

CONTACT Mr. Wilbert Casaine, Executive Director of Financial Aid and Student Success, The College of New Jersey, PO Box 7718, Ewing, NJ 08628, 609-771-2602. *Fax:* 609-637-5154. *E-mail:* casainew@tcnj.edu.
Website: http://www.tcnj.edu/.

THE COLLEGE OF NEW ROCHELLE
New Rochelle, NY

Tuition & fees: $34,960	Average undergraduate aid package: $22,905

ABOUT THE INSTITUTION Independent, coed, primarily women. *Awards:* certificates, bachelor's, and master's degrees (also offers a non-traditional adult program with significant enrollment not reflected in profile). 35 undergraduate majors. *Total enrollment:* 1,551. Undergraduates: 936. Freshmen: 90. Federal methodology is used as a basis for awarding need-based institutional aid.

UNDERGRADUATE EXPENSES for 2016–2017 *Application fee:* $35. *Comprehensive fee:* $48,168 includes full-time tuition ($33,748), mandatory fees ($1212), and room and board ($13,208). Full-time tuition and fees vary according to course load, degree level, location, and program. Room and board charges vary according to housing facility. *Part-time tuition:* $1125 per credit. *Part-time fees:* $350 per term. Part-time tuition and fees vary according to course load, degree level, location, and program.

FRESHMAN FINANCIAL AID (Fall 2015) 88 applied for aid; of those 95% were deemed to have need. 100% of freshmen with need received aid; of those 2% had need fully met. *Average percent of need met:* 69% (excluding resources awarded to replace EFC). *Average financial aid package:* $29,183 (excluding resources awarded to replace EFC). 3% of all full-time freshmen had no need and received non-need-based gift aid.

UNDERGRADUATE FINANCIAL AID (Fall 2015) 564 applied for aid; of those 93% were deemed to have need. 100% of undergraduates with need received aid; of those 2% had need fully met. *Average percent of need met:* 57% (excluding resources awarded to replace EFC). *Average financial aid package:* $22,905 (excluding resources awarded to replace EFC). 6% of all full-time undergraduates had no need and received non-need-based gift aid.

GIFT AID (NEED-BASED) *Total amount:* $10,287,342 (19% federal, 9% state, 72% institutional). *Receiving aid:* Freshmen: 89% (78); all full-time undergraduates: 84% (474). *Average award:* Freshmen: $13,761; Undergraduates: $9705. *Scholarships, grants, and awards:* Federal Pell, FSEOG, state, private, college/university gift aid from institutional funds.

GIFT AID (NON-NEED-BASED) *Total amount:* $499,864 (1% state, 98% institutional, 1% external sources). *Receiving aid:* Freshmen: 94% (83). Undergraduates: 85% (481). *Average award:* Freshmen: $14,385. Undergraduates: $13,685. *Scholarships, grants, and awards by category:* Academic interests/achievement: 255 awards ($325,000 total): area/ethnic studies, biological sciences, business, communication, education, English, general academic interests/achievements, health fields, humanities, mathematics, physical sciences, premedicine, religion/biblical studies, social sciences. *Creative arts/performance:* 45 awards ($300,000 total): art/fine arts, creative writing, journalism/publications, music. *Special achievements/activities:* 75 awards ($95,000 total): community service, general special achievements/activities, hobbies/interests, leadership, memberships, religious involvement. *Special characteristics:* 56 awards ($255,000 total): children and siblings of alumni, children of faculty/staff, children of union members/company employees, children of workers in trades, general special characteristics, out-of-state students, parents of current students, previous college experience, siblings of current students, spouses of current students, spouses of deceased or disabled public servants, twins, veterans, veterans' children. *Tuition waivers:* Full or partial for employees or children of employees, senior citizens.

LOANS *Student loans:* $5,619,174 (45% need-based, 55% non-need-based). 87% of past graduating class borrowed through all loan programs. *Average indebtedness per student:* $35,430. *Average need-based loan:* Freshmen: $3261. Undergraduates: $5172. *Parent loans:* $807,438 (100% need-based). *Programs:* Federal Direct (Subsidized and Unsubsidized Stafford, PLUS), Perkins, Federal Nursing.

WORK-STUDY *Federal work-study:* 400 jobs averaging $2598. *State or other work-study/employment:* Part-time jobs available.

APPLYING FOR FINANCIAL AID *Required financial aid forms:* FAFSA, institution's own form. *Financial aid deadline:* Continuous. *Notification date:* Continuous beginning 1/1. Students must reply within 2 weeks of notification.

CONTACT Anne Pelak, Director of Financial Aid, The College of New Rochelle, 29 Castle Place, New Rochelle, NY 10805-2339, 914-654-5225 or toll-free 800-933-5923. *Fax:* 914-654-5420. *E-mail:* apelak@cnr.edu.
Website: http://www.cnr.edu/.

COLLEGE OF SAINT BENEDICT
Saint Joseph, MN

Tuition & fees: $42,271	Average undergraduate aid package: $35,174

ABOUT THE INSTITUTION Independent Roman Catholic, women only. *Awards:* bachelor's degrees (coordinate with Saint John's University for men). 50 undergraduate majors. *Total enrollment:* 1,950. Undergraduates: 1,950. Freshmen: 503. Federal methodology is used as a basis for awarding need-based institutional aid.

UNDERGRADUATE EXPENSES for 2016–2017 *Comprehensive fee:* $52,806 includes full-time tuition ($41,245), mandatory fees ($1026), and room and board ($10,535). *College room only:* $5098. Room and board charges vary according to board plan and housing facility. *Part-time tuition:* $1719 per credit hour. Part-time tuition and fees vary according to course load.

FRESHMAN FINANCIAL AID (Fall 2016, est.) 451 applied for aid; of those 88% were deemed to have need. 100% of freshmen with need received aid; of those 39% had need fully met. *Average percent of need met:* 92% (excluding resources awarded to replace EFC). *Average financial aid package:* $36,984 (excluding resources awarded to replace EFC). 19% of all full-time freshmen had no need and received non-need-based gift aid.

UNDERGRADUATE FINANCIAL AID (Fall 2016, est.) 1,617 applied for aid; of those 89% were deemed to have need. 100% of undergraduates with need received aid; of those 34% had need fully met. *Average percent of need met:* 90% (excluding resources awarded to replace EFC). *Average financial aid package:* $35,174 (excluding resources awarded to replace EFC). 22% of all full-time undergraduates had no need and received non-need-based gift aid.

GIFT AID (NEED-BASED) *Total amount:* $40,608,001 (6% federal, 8% state, 83% institutional, 3% external sources). *Receiving aid:* Freshmen: 78% (391); all full-time undergraduates: 71% (1,378). *Average award:* Freshmen: $30,440; Undergraduates: $28,598. *Scholarships, grants, and awards:* Federal Pell, FSEOG, state, private, college/university gift aid from institutional funds.

GIFT AID (NON-NEED-BASED) *Total amount:* $9,958,118 (95% institutional, 5% external sources). *Receiving aid:* Freshmen: 76% (380). Undergraduates: 69% (1,335). *Average award:* Freshmen: $19,922. Undergraduates: $17,814. *Scholarships, grants, and awards by category:* Academic interests/achievement: 1,776 awards ($28,094,677 total): computer science, engineering/technologies, general academic interests/achievements, mathematics, military science, physical sciences. *Creative arts/performance:* 222 awards ($574,800 total): art/fine arts, music, theater/drama. *Special characteristics:* 619 awards ($2,710,650 total): children and siblings of alumni, international students, out-of-state students. *Tuition waivers:* Full or partial for employees or children of employees. *ROTC:* Army cooperative.

LOANS *Student loans:* $16,738,695 (90% need-based, 10% non-need-based). 71% of past graduating class borrowed through all loan programs. *Average indebtedness per student:* $39,536. *Average need-based loan:* Freshmen: $4604. Undergraduates: $5208. *Parent loans:* $1,204,354 (90% need-based, 10% non-need-based). *Programs:* Federal Direct (Subsidized and Unsubsidized Stafford, PLUS), Perkins, state, private loans.

WORK-STUDY *Federal work-study:* Total amount: $949,055; 344 jobs averaging $2751. *State or other work-study/employment:* Total amount: $3,418,276 (79% need-based, 21% non-need-based). 1,202 part-time jobs averaging $2891.

APPLYING FOR FINANCIAL AID *Required financial aid form:* FAFSA. *Financial aid deadline (priority):* 3/15. *Notification date:* Continuous beginning 3/15. Students must reply by 5/1.

CONTACT Mr. Stuart Perry, Executive Director of Financial Aid, College of Saint Benedict, 37 South College Avenue, Saint Joseph, MN 56374-2099, 320-363-5388 or toll-free 800-544-1489. *Fax:* 320-363-6090. *E-mail:* sperry@csbsju.edu.
Website: http://www.csbsju.edu/.

COLLEGE OF SAINT ELIZABETH
Morristown, NJ

Tuition & fees: $32,277	Average undergraduate aid package: N/A

ABOUT THE INSTITUTION Independent Roman Catholic, coed, primarily women. *Awards:* certificates, bachelor's, master's, and doctoral degrees (also offers coed adult undergraduate degree program and coed graduate programs). 18 undergraduate majors. **Total enrollment:** 1,200. Undergraduates: 763. Freshmen: 167. Both federal and institutional methodology are used as a basis for awarding need-based institutional aid.

UNDERGRADUATE EXPENSES for 2017–2018 *Application fee:* $35. *Comprehensive fee:* $45,021 includes full-time tuition ($30,326), mandatory fees ($1951), and room and board ($12,744). Room and board charges vary according to board plan. *Part-time tuition:* $843 per credit hour. Part-time tuition and fees vary according to course load and location.

GIFT AID (NEED-BASED) *Scholarships, grants, and awards:* Federal Pell, FSEOG, state, private, college/university gift aid from institutional funds.

GIFT AID (NON-NEED-BASED) *Scholarships, grants, and awards by category:* Academic interests/achievement: 453 awards ($7,647,733 total): general academic interests/achievements. *Special characteristics:* adult students, children and siblings of alumni. *Tuition waivers:* Full or partial for children of alumni, employees or children of employees, senior citizens.

LOANS *Programs:* Federal Direct (Subsidized and Unsubsidized Stafford), Perkins.

WORK-STUDY Federal work-study jobs available.

APPLYING FOR FINANCIAL AID *Required financial aid form:* FAFSA. *Financial aid deadline:* Continuous. *Notification date:* Continuous beginning 11/15. Students must reply by 5/1 or within 2 weeks of notification.

CONTACT James Kulhawy, Assistant Director of Financial Aid, College of Saint Elizabeth, 2 Convent Road, Morristown, NJ 07960-6989, 973-290-4432 or toll-free 800-210-7900. *E-mail:* jkulhaway@cse.edu.
Website: http://www.cse.edu/.

COLLEGE OF ST. JOSEPH
Rutland, VT

CONTACT Julie Rosmus, Director of Financial Aid, College of St. Joseph, 71 Clement Road, Rutland, VT 05701-3899, 802-773-5900 Ext. 3274 or toll-free 877-270-9998. *Fax:* 802-776-5275. *E-mail:* jrosmus@csj.edu.
Website: http://www.csj.edu/.

COLLEGE OF SAINT MARY
Omaha, NE

Tuition & fees: $19,950	Average undergraduate aid package: $21,185

ABOUT THE INSTITUTION Independent Roman Catholic, women only. *Awards:* certificates, associate, bachelor's, master's, and doctoral degrees. 29 undergraduate majors. **Total enrollment:** 1,043. Undergraduates: 760. Freshmen: 103. Both federal and institutional methodology are used as a basis for awarding need-based institutional aid.

UNDERGRADUATE EXPENSES for 2017–2018 *Application fee:* $30. *Comprehensive fee:* $27,500 includes full-time tuition ($19,950) and room and board ($7550). Full-time tuition and fees vary according to program. *Part-time tuition:* $985 per credit. Part-time tuition and fees vary according to course load and program.

FRESHMAN FINANCIAL AID (Fall 2016, est.) 79 applied for aid; of those 86% were deemed to have need. 100% of freshmen with need received aid; of those 28% had need fully met. *Average percent of need met:* 78% (excluding resources awarded to replace EFC). *Average financial aid package:* $24,112 (excluding resources awarded to replace EFC). 28% of all full-time freshmen had no need and received non-need-based gift aid.

UNDERGRADUATE FINANCIAL AID (Fall 2016, est.) 640 applied for aid; of those 90% were deemed to have need. 100% of undergraduates with need received aid; of those 11% had need fully met. *Average percent of need met:* 66% (excluding resources awarded to replace EFC). *Average financial aid package:* $21,185 (excluding resources awarded to replace EFC). 17% of all full-time undergraduates had no need and received non-need-based gift aid.

GIFT AID (NEED-BASED) *Total amount:* $7,739,175 (18% federal, 3% state, 76% institutional, 3% external sources). *Receiving aid:* Freshmen: 71% (67); all full-time undergraduates: 81% (568). *Average award:* Freshmen: $19,963; Undergraduates: $15,036. *Scholarships, grants, and awards:* Federal Pell, FSEOG, state, private, college/university gift aid from institutional funds, Federal Nursing.

GIFT AID (NON-NEED-BASED) *Total amount:* $2,033,130 (97% institutional, 3% external sources). *Receiving aid:* Freshmen: 11% (10). Undergraduates: 6% (39).

Average award: Freshmen: $19,422. Undergraduates: $16,024. *Scholarships, grants, and awards by category:* Academic interests/achievement: 700 awards ($5,290,750 total): biological sciences, education, general academic interests/achievements, mathematics. *Creative arts/performance:* 2 awards ($4000 total): art/fine arts, debating, music. *Special achievements/activities:* 26 awards ($22,875 total): community service, general special achievements/activities, leadership, religious involvement. *Special characteristics:* 15 awards ($137,478 total): children of faculty/staff, first-generation college students, general special characteristics, international students. *Tuition waivers:* Full or partial for employees or children of employees, senior citizens. *ROTC:* Army cooperative, Air Force cooperative.

LOANS *Student loans:* $6,151,171 (83% need-based, 17% non-need-based). 74% of past graduating class borrowed through all loan programs. *Average indebtedness per student:* $33,658. *Average need-based loan:* Freshmen: $3954. Undergraduates: $5820. *Parent loans:* $1,599,041 (43% need-based, 57% non-need-based). *Programs:* Federal Direct (Subsidized and Unsubsidized Stafford, PLUS), Perkins, Federal Nursing.

WORK-STUDY *Federal work-study:* Total amount: $504,842; 173 jobs averaging $2918. *State or other work-study/employment:* Total amount: $59,250 (67% need-based, 33% non-need-based). 12 part-time jobs averaging $5063.

ATHLETIC AWARDS Total amount: $950,380 (69% need-based, 31% non-need-based).

APPLYING FOR FINANCIAL AID *Required financial aid form:* FAFSA. *Financial aid deadline (priority):* 3/15. *Notification date:* Continuous beginning 12/15. Students must reply within 2 weeks of notification.

CONTACT Beth Sisk, Director of Financial Aid and the Express Center, College of Saint Mary, 7000 Mercy Road, Omaha, NE 68106, 402-399-2362 or toll-free 800-926-5534. *Fax:* 402-399-2480. *E-mail:* finaid@csm.edu.
Website: http://www.csm.edu/.

THE COLLEGE OF SAINT ROSE
Albany, NY

Tuition & fees: $31,612	Average undergraduate aid package: $20,353

ABOUT THE INSTITUTION Independent, coed. *Awards:* certificates, bachelor's, and master's degrees. 41 undergraduate majors. **Total enrollment:** 4,211. Undergraduates: 2,602. Freshmen: 641. Federal methodology is used as a basis for awarding need-based institutional aid.

UNDERGRADUATE EXPENSES for 2017–2018 *One-time required fee:* $469. *Comprehensive fee:* $43,968 includes full-time tuition ($30,546), mandatory fees ($1066), and room and board ($12,356). *College room only:* $6214. Full-time tuition and fees vary according to course load. Room and board charges vary according to board plan and housing facility. *Part-time tuition:* $1016 per credit hour. *Part-time fees:* $37 per credit hour; $128 per term. Part-time tuition and fees vary according to course load.

FRESHMAN FINANCIAL AID (Fall 2015) 610 applied for aid; of those 94% were deemed to have need. 100% of freshmen with need received aid; of those 18% had need fully met. *Average percent of need met:* 82% (excluding resources awarded to replace EFC). *Average financial aid package:* $23,111 (excluding resources awarded to replace EFC). 8% of all full-time freshmen had no need and received non-need-based gift aid.

UNDERGRADUATE FINANCIAL AID (Fall 2015) 2,326 applied for aid; of those 92% were deemed to have need. 100% of undergraduates with need received aid; of those 17% had need fully met. *Average percent of need met:* 77% (excluding resources awarded to replace EFC). *Average financial aid package:* $20,353 (excluding resources awarded to replace EFC). 10% of all full-time undergraduates had no need and received non-need-based gift aid.

GIFT AID (NEED-BASED) *Total amount:* $16,095,602 (30% federal, 19% state, 49% institutional, 2% external sources). *Receiving aid:* Freshmen: 65% (409); all full-time undergraduates: 68% (1,726). *Average award:* Freshmen: $7313; Undergraduates: $8532. *Scholarships, grants, and awards:* Federal Pell, FSEOG, state, private, college/university gift aid from institutional funds.

GIFT AID (NON-NEED-BASED) *Total amount:* $24,923,062 (1% federal, 98% institutional, 1% external sources). *Receiving aid:* Freshmen: 90% (565). Undergraduates: 69% (1,748). *Average award:* Freshmen: $14,923. Undergraduates: $11,356. *Scholarships, grants, and awards by category:* Academic interests/achievement: business, communication, education, engineering/technologies, English, foreign languages, general academic interests/achievements, humanities, mathematics, premedicine, social sciences. *Creative arts/performance:* art/fine arts, music. *Special achievements/activities:* community service. *Special characteristics:* adult students, children and siblings of alumni, children of faculty/staff, children of union members/company employees, ethnic background, general special characteristics, members of minority groups, out-of-state students, siblings of current students, twins. *Tuition waivers:* Full or partial for employees or children of employees. *ROTC:* Army cooperative, Naval cooperative, Air Force cooperative.

LOANS *Student loans:* $13,456,692 (55% need-based, 45% non-need-based). 84% of past graduating class borrowed through all loan programs. *Average indebtedness per student:* $31,413. *Average need-based loan:* Freshmen: $3509. Undergraduates: $4370. *Parent loans:* $7,396,705 (74% need-based, 26% non-need-based). *Programs:* Federal Direct (Subsidized and Unsubsidized Stafford, PLUS), Perkins.

WORK-STUDY *Federal work-study:* jobs available. *State or other work-study/employment:* Total amount: $20,423 (100% non-need-based). Part-time jobs available.

ATHLETIC AWARDS Total amount: $2,374,203 (27% need-based, 73% non-need-based).

APPLYING FOR FINANCIAL AID *Required financial aid form:* FAFSA. *Financial aid deadline:* 4/1 (priority: 12/1). *Notification date:* 1/1. Students must reply by 5/1 or within 2 weeks of notification.

CONTACT Steven Dwire, Assistant Vice President of Financial Aid and Enrollment Management, The College of Saint Rose, 432 Western Avenue, Albertus Hall, Room 206, Albany, NY 12203-1419, 518-458-4915 or toll-free 800-637-8556. *Fax:* 518-454-2802. *E-mail:* finaid@strose.edu.
Website: http://www.strose.edu/.

THE COLLEGE OF ST. SCHOLASTICA
Duluth, MN

Tuition & fees: $35,326	Average undergraduate aid package: $24,815

ABOUT THE INSTITUTION Independent Roman Catholic Church, coed. *Awards:* certificates, bachelor's, master's, and doctoral degrees. 38 undergraduate majors. *Total enrollment:* 4,406. Undergraduates: 2,841. Freshmen: 451. Federal methodology is used as a basis for awarding need-based institutional aid.

UNDERGRADUATE EXPENSES for 2016–2017 *Comprehensive fee:* $44,640 includes full-time tuition ($34,764), mandatory fees ($562), and room and board ($9314). *College room only:* $5150. Full-time tuition and fees vary according to class time and program. Room and board charges vary according to board plan and housing facility. *Part-time tuition:* $1088 per credit. Part-time tuition and fees vary according to class time, course load, and program.

FRESHMAN FINANCIAL AID (Fall 2016, est.) 406 applied for aid; of those 90% were deemed to have need. 100% of freshmen with need received aid; of those 24% had need fully met. *Average percent of need met:* 83% (excluding resources awarded to replace EFC). *Average financial aid package:* $29,883 (excluding resources awarded to replace EFC). 9% of all full-time freshmen had no need and received non-need-based gift aid.

UNDERGRADUATE FINANCIAL AID (Fall 2016, est.) 1,929 applied for aid; of those 91% were deemed to have need. 99% of undergraduates with need received aid; of those 21% had need fully met. *Average percent of need met:* 71% (excluding resources awarded to replace EFC). *Average financial aid package:* $24,815 (excluding resources awarded to replace EFC). 6% of all full-time undergraduates had no need and received non-need-based gift aid.

GIFT AID (NEED-BASED) *Total amount:* $10,632,991 (35% federal, 39% state, 26% institutional). *Receiving aid:* Freshmen: 62% (279); all full-time undergraduates: 58% (1,307). *Average award:* Freshmen: $7000; Undergraduates: $7593. *Scholarships, grants, and awards:* Federal Pell, FSEOG, state, private, college/university gift aid from institutional funds.

GIFT AID (NON-NEED-BASED) *Total amount:* $31,922,439 (1% federal, 96% institutional, 3% external sources). *Receiving aid:* Freshmen: 81% (365). Undergraduates: 62% (1,401). *Average award:* Freshmen: $20,080. Undergraduates: $17,321. *Scholarships, grants, and awards by category:* Academic interests/achievement: general academic interests/achievements. *Creative arts/performance:* music. *Special characteristics:* children and siblings of alumni, children of faculty/staff, handicapped students, international students, local/state students, previous college experience, religious affiliation, siblings of current students, spouses of current stu-

dents. *Tuition waivers:* Full or partial for employees or children of employees, senior citizens. *ROTC:* Air Force cooperative.

LOANS *Student loans:* $21,557,828 (32% need-based, 68% non-need-based). 77% of past graduating class borrowed through all loan programs. *Average indebtedness per student:* $40,774. *Average need-based loan:* Freshmen: $3623. Undergraduates: $4717. *Parent loans:* $1,693,287 (100% non-need-based). *Programs:* Federal Direct (Subsidized and Unsubsidized Stafford, PLUS), Perkins, Federal Nursing, state.

WORK-STUDY *Federal work-study:* Total amount: $514,672; jobs available. *State or other work-study/employment:* Total amount: $1,816,892 (21% need based, 79% non-need-based). Part-time jobs available.

APPLYING FOR FINANCIAL AID *Required financial aid form:* FAFSA. *Financial aid deadline (priority):* 3/1. *Notification date:* Continuous beginning 3/1. Students must reply within 2 weeks of notification.

CONTACT Mr. Jon P. Erickson, Director of Financial Aid, The College of St. Scholastica, 1200 Kenwood Avenue, Duluth, MN 55811-4199, 218-723-6725 or toll-free 800-249-6412. *Fax:* 218-733-2229. *E-mail:* jerickso@css.edu.
Website: http://www.css.edu/.

COLLEGE OF STATEN ISLAND OF THE CITY UNIVERSITY OF NEW YORK
Staten Island, NY

Tuition & fees (NY res): $6889	Average undergraduate aid package: $8225

ABOUT THE INSTITUTION State and locally supported, coed. *Awards:* certificates, associate, bachelor's, master's, and doctoral degrees. 46 undergraduate majors. *Total enrollment:* 13,775. Undergraduates: 12,806. Freshmen: 2,569. Federal methodology is used as a basis for awarding need-based institutional aid.

UNDERGRADUATE EXPENSES for 2016–2017 *Tuition, state resident:* full-time $6330; part-time $275 per credit hour. *Tuition, nonresident:* full-time $16,800; part-time $560 per credit hour. *Required fees:* full-time $559; $181.10 per term. *Room only:* $13,626. Room and board charges vary according to board plan and housing facility.

FRESHMAN FINANCIAL AID (Fall 2016, est.) 2,223 applied for aid; of those 89% were deemed to have need. 92% of freshmen with need received aid; of those 5% had need fully met. *Average percent of need met:* 40% (excluding resources awarded to replace EFC). *Average financial aid package:* $8489 (excluding resources awarded to replace EFC). 4% of all full-time freshmen had no need and received non-need-based gift aid.

UNDERGRADUATE FINANCIAL AID (Fall 2016, est.) 7,704 applied for aid; of those 90% were deemed to have need. 93% of undergraduates with need received aid; of those 6% had need fully met. *Average percent of need met:* 39% (excluding resources awarded to replace EFC). *Average financial aid package:* $8225 (excluding resources awarded to replace EFC). 2% of all full-time undergraduates had no need and received non-need-based gift aid.

GIFT AID (NEED-BASED) *Total amount:* $47,802,970 (58% federal, 42% state). *Receiving aid:* Freshmen: 69% (1,706); all full-time undergraduates: 62% (5,983). *Average award:* Freshmen: $8140; Undergraduates: $7674. *Scholarships, grants, and awards:* Federal Pell, FSEOG, state, private, college/university gift aid from institutional funds.

GIFT AID (NON-NEED-BASED) *Total amount:* $2,852,907 (10% state, 66% institutional, 24% external sources). *Receiving aid:* Freshmen: 29% (718). Undergraduates: 13% (1,227). *Average award:* Freshmen: $1999. Undergraduates: $3124. *Scholarships, grants, and awards by category:* Academic interests/achievement: 13 awards ($21,140 total): area/ethnic studies, biological sciences, business, communication, computer science, education, engineering/technologies, English, foreign languages, general academic interests/achievements, home economics, humanities, international studies, mathematics, physical sciences, premedicine, social sciences. *Creative arts/performance:* 9 awards ($7480 total): applied art and design, art/fine arts, cinema/film/broadcasting, creative writing, dance, debating, general creative arts/performance, journalism/publications, music, performing arts, theater/drama. *Special achievements/activities:* 13 awards ($40,130 total): community service, general special achievements/activities, hobbies/interests, leadership. *Special characteristics:* 27 awards ($64,780 total): adult students, children and siblings of alumni, children of current students, children of educators, children of faculty/staff, children of public servants, children of union members/company employees, children of workers in trades, children with a deceased or disabled parent, ethnic background, first-generation college students, general special characteristics, handicapped students, international students, local/state students, married students, members of minority groups, out-of-state students, parents of current students, previous college experience, public servants, siblings of current students, spouses of current students, spouses of deceased or disabled public servants, veterans, veterans' children. *Tuition waivers:* Full or partial for employees or children of employees, senior citizens.

LOANS *Student loans:* $13,537,570 (43% need-based, 57% non-need-based). 76% of past graduating class borrowed through all loan programs. *Average need-based loan:* Freshmen: $9535. Undergraduates: $8970. *Parent loans:* $1,047,473 (100% non-need-based). *Programs:* Federal Direct (Subsidized and Unsubsidized Stafford, PLUS), Perkins.

WORK-STUDY *Federal work-study:* Total amount: $581,852; jobs available. *State or other work-study/employment:* Part-time jobs available.

APPLYING FOR FINANCIAL AID *Required financial aid forms:* FAFSA, state aid form. *Financial aid deadline (priority):* 1/31. *Notification date:* 2/15.

CONTACT Dr. Philippe Marius, Director of Student Financial Aid, College of Staten Island of the City University of New York, 2800 Victory Boulevard, 2A-401A, Staten Island, NY 10314-6600, 718-982-2030. *Fax:* 718-982-2037. *E-mail:* financialaid@csi.cuny.edu.
Website: http://www.csi.cuny.edu/.

COLLEGE OF THE ATLANTIC
Bar Harbor, ME

Tuition & fees: $43,542	Average undergraduate aid package: $40,946

ABOUT THE INSTITUTION Independent, coed. *Awards:* bachelor's and master's degrees. 42 undergraduate majors. *Total enrollment:* 345. Undergraduates: 338. Freshmen: 79. Both federal and institutional methodology are used as a basis for awarding need-based institutional aid.

UNDERGRADUATE EXPENSES for 2017–2018 *Application fee:* $50. *Comprehensive fee:* $53,289 includes full-time tuition ($42,993), mandatory fees ($549), and room and board ($9747). *College room only:* $6210. Full-time tuition and fees vary according to course load and degree level. Room and board charges vary according to board plan. *Part-time tuition:* $4777 per credit. *Part-time fees:* $183 per term. Part-time tuition and fees vary according to course load and degree level.

FRESHMAN FINANCIAL AID (Fall 2016, est.) 75 applied for aid; of those 95% were deemed to have need. 100% of freshmen with need received aid; of those 52% had need fully met. *Average percent of need met:* 97% (excluding resources awarded to replace EFC). *Average financial aid package:* $45,334 (excluding resources awarded to replace EFC). 6% of all full-time freshmen had no need and received non-need-based gift aid.

UNDERGRADUATE FINANCIAL AID (Fall 2016, est.) 284 applied for aid; of those 92% were deemed to have need. 100% of undergraduates with need received aid; of those 44% had need fully met. *Average percent of need met:* 96% (excluding resources awarded to replace EFC). *Average financial aid package:* $40,946 (excluding resources awarded to replace EFC). 12% of all full-time undergraduates had no need and received non-need-based gift aid.

GIFT AID (NEED-BASED) *Total amount:* $9,530,362 (5% federal, 1% state, 93% institutional, 1% external sources). *Receiving aid:* Freshmen: 90% (71); all full-time undergraduates: 83% (259). *Average award:* Freshmen: $39,592; Undergraduates: $35,189. *Scholarships, grants, and awards:* Federal Pell, FSEOG, state, private, college/university gift aid from institutional funds.

GIFT AID (NON-NEED-BASED) *Total amount:* $581,520 (97% institutional, 3% external sources). *Receiving aid:* Freshmen: 1% (1). Undergraduates: 1% (3). *Average award:* Freshmen: $16,279. Undergraduates: $13,444. *Scholarships, grants, and awards by category:* Academic interests/achievement: 38 awards ($496,500 total): general academic interests/achievements. *Tuition waivers:* Full or partial for employees or children of employees.

LOANS *Student loans:* $1,826,113 (53% need-based, 47% non-need-based). 70% of past graduating class borrowed through all loan programs. *Average indebtedness per student:* $26,723. *Average need-based loan:* Freshmen: $4183. Undergraduates: $4877. *Parent loans:* $253,837 (100% non-need-based). *Programs:* Federal Direct (Subsidized and Unsubsidized Stafford, PLUS), Perkins.

WORK-STUDY *Federal work-study:* Total amount: $524,338; 189 jobs averaging $2774. *State or other work-study/employment:* Total amount: $224,633 (86% need-based, 14% non-need-based). 81 part-time jobs averaging $2773.

APPLYING FOR FINANCIAL AID *Required financial aid forms:* FAFSA, institution's own form, noncustodial (divorced/separated) parent's statement. *Financial aid deadline:* 2/1 (priority: 2/1). *Notification date:* 4/1. Students must reply by 5/1 or within 2 weeks of notification.

CONTACT Bruce Hazam, Director of Financial Aid, College of the Atlantic, 105 Eden Street, Bar Harbor, ME 04609-1198, 207-801-5645 or toll-free 800-528-0025. *Fax:* 207-288-4126. *E-mail:* bhazam@coa.edu.
Website: http://www.coa.edu/.

COLLEGE OF THE HOLY CROSS
Worcester, MA

Tuition & fees: $50,630	Average undergraduate aid package: $39,079

ABOUT THE INSTITUTION Independent Roman Catholic (Jesuit), coed. *Awards:* bachelor's degrees. 34 undergraduate majors. *Total enrollment:* 2,941. Undergraduates: 2,941. Freshmen: 764. Both federal and institutional methodology are used as a basis for awarding need-based institutional aid.

UNDERGRADUATE EXPENSES for 2017–2018 *Application fee:* $60. *Comprehensive fee:* $64,320 includes full-time tuition ($49,980), mandatory fees ($650), and room and board ($13,690). *College room only:* $7390. Room and board charges vary according to board plan and housing facility.

FRESHMAN FINANCIAL AID (Fall 2016, est.) 546 applied for aid; of those 77% were deemed to have need. 100% of freshmen with need received aid; of those 100% had need fully met. *Average percent of need met:* 100% (excluding resources awarded to replace EFC). *Average financial aid package:* $39,937 (excluding resources awarded to replace EFC). 1% of all full-time freshmen had no need and received non-need-based gift aid.

UNDERGRADUATE FINANCIAL AID (Fall 2016, est.) 1,823 applied for aid; of those 80% were deemed to have need. 100% of undergraduates with need received aid; of those 100% had need fully met. *Average percent of need met:* 100% (excluding resources awarded to replace EFC). *Average financial aid package:* $39,079 (excluding resources awarded to replace EFC). 1% of all full-time undergraduates had no need and received non-need-based gift aid.

GIFT AID (NEED-BASED) *Total amount:* $42,407,741 (6% federal, 2% state, 92% institutional). *Receiving aid:* Freshmen: 45% (344); all full-time undergraduates: 41% (1,194). *Average award:* Freshmen: $38,039; Undergraduates: $35,521. *Scholarships, grants, and awards:* Federal Pell, FSEOG, state, private, college/university gift aid from institutional funds.

GIFT AID (NON-NEED-BASED) *Total amount:* $4,557,860 (58% institutional, 42% external sources). *Receiving aid:* Freshmen: 2% (13). Undergraduates: 2% (49). *Average award:* Freshmen: $30,908. Undergraduates: $40,213. *Scholarships, grants, and awards by category:* Academic interests/achievement: general academic interests/achievements, humanities, military science. *Creative arts/performance:* music. *Special characteristics:* children of faculty/staff. *Tuition waivers:* Full or partial for employees or children of employees. *ROTC:* Army cooperative, Naval, Air Force cooperative.

LOANS *Student loans:* $12,352,295 (81% need-based, 19% non-need-based). 62% of past graduating class borrowed through all loan programs. *Average indebtedness per student:* $25,446. *Average need-based loan:* Freshmen: $4850. Undergraduates: $5363. *Parent loans:* $9,736,666 (100% non-need-based). *Programs:* Federal Direct (Subsidized and Unsubsidized Stafford, PLUS), Perkins.

WORK-STUDY *Federal work-study:* Total amount: $1,685,089; jobs available.

ATHLETIC AWARDS Total amount: $10,934,682 (34% need-based, 66% non-need-based).

APPLYING FOR FINANCIAL AID *Required financial aid forms:* FAFSA, CSS Financial Aid PROFILE, noncustodial (divorced/separated) parent's statement, business/farm supplement, federal income tax form(s). *Financial aid deadline:* 1/15. *Notification date:* 4/1. Students must reply by 5/1.

CONTACT Ms. Lynne Myers, Director of Financial Aid, College of the Holy Cross, One College Street, Worcester, MA 01610-2395, 508-793-2265 or toll-free 800-442-2421. *Fax:* 508-793-2527.
Website: http://www.holycross.edu/.

COLLEGE OF THE OZARKS
Point Lookout, MO

Tuition & fees: $430	Average undergraduate aid package: $20,163

ABOUT THE INSTITUTION Independent Presbyterian, coed. *Awards:* bachelor's degrees. 71 undergraduate majors. *Total enrollment:* 1,512. Undergraduates: 1,512. Freshmen: 385. Federal methodology is used as a basis for awarding need-based institutional aid.

UNDERGRADUATE EXPENSES for 2016–2017 *College room only:* $3400. *Part-time tuition:* $310 per credit hour. Part-time tuition and fees vary according to course load. Each student participates in the on-campus work program for 15 hours per week and two forty-hour work weeks. Earnings from participation in the work program, plus any federal and/or state aid for which students qualify, plus a College of the Ozarks Cost of Education Scholarship combine to meet each student's full tuition charge.

FRESHMAN FINANCIAL AID (Fall 2015) 345 applied for aid; of those 97% were deemed to have need. 100% of freshmen with need received aid; of those 17% had need fully met. *Average percent of need met:* 78% (excluding resources awarded to replace EFC). *Average financial aid package:* $19,871 (excluding resources awarded to replace EFC). 3% of all full-time freshmen had no need and received non-need-based gift aid.

UNDERGRADUATE FINANCIAL AID (Fall 2015) 1,354 applied for aid; of those 95% were deemed to have need. 100% of undergraduates with need received aid; of those 32% had need fully met. *Average percent of need met:* 83% (excluding resources awarded to replace EFC). *Average financial aid package:* $20,163 (excluding resources awarded to replace EFC). 8% of all full-time undergraduates had no need and received non-need-based gift aid.

GIFT AID (NEED-BASED) *Total amount:* $18,577,549 (18% federal, 6% state, 76% institutional). *Receiving aid:* Freshmen: 97% (333); all full-time undergraduates: 92% (1,287). *Average award:* Freshmen: $15,086; Undergraduates: $15,488. *Scholarships, grants, and awards:* Federal Pell, FSEOG, state, private, college/university gift aid from institutional funds.

GIFT AID (NON-NEED-BASED) *Total amount:* $1,974,504 (3% state, 47% institutional, 50% external sources). *Receiving aid:* Freshmen: 7% (24). Undergraduates: 12% (162). *Average award:* Freshmen: $14,492. Undergraduates: $14,956. *ROTC:* Army.

LOANS *Student loans:* 7% of past graduating class borrowed through all loan programs. *Average indebtedness per student:* $5339.

WORK-STUDY *Federal work-study:* jobs available. *State or other work-study/employment:* Total amount: $2,925,045 (10% need-based, 90% non-need-based). Part-time jobs available.

ATHLETIC AWARDS Total amount: $295,896 (100% non-need-based).

APPLYING FOR FINANCIAL AID *Required financial aid form:* FAFSA. *Financial aid deadline (priority):* 11/15. *Notification date:* 7/1.

CONTACT Office of Financial Aid, College of the Ozarks, PO Box 17, Point Lookout, MO 65726, 417-690-3290 or toll-free 800-222-0525. *Fax:* 417-690-3286. *Website:* http://www.cofo.edu/.

THE COLLEGE OF WILLIAM AND MARY
Williamsburg, VA

Tuition & fees (VA res): $21,234	Average undergraduate aid package: $21,243

ABOUT THE INSTITUTION State-supported, coed. *Awards:* certificates, bachelor's, master's, and doctoral degrees. 41 undergraduate majors. *Total enrollment:* 8,617. Undergraduates: 6,276. Freshmen: 1,507. Federal methodology is used as a basis for awarding need-based institutional aid.

UNDERGRADUATE EXPENSES for 2016–2017 *Application fee:* $70. *Tuition, state resident:* full-time $15,674; part-time $400 per credit hour. *Tuition, nonresident:* full-time $36,158; part-time $1150 per credit hour. *Required fees:* full-time $5560. *College room and board:* $11,382; *Room only:* $6944. Room and board charges vary according to board plan and housing facility.

FRESHMAN FINANCIAL AID (Fall 2015) 1,009 applied for aid; of those 54% were deemed to have need. 94% of freshmen with need received aid; of those 24% had need fully met. *Average percent of need met:* 79% (excluding resources awarded to replace EFC). *Average financial aid package:* $21,252 (excluding resources awarded to replace EFC). 3% of all full-time freshmen had no need and received non-need-based gift aid.

UNDERGRADUATE FINANCIAL AID (Fall 2015) 3,090 applied for aid; of those 69% were deemed to have need. 96% of undergraduates with need received aid; of those 23% had need fully met. *Average percent of need met:* 80% (excluding resources awarded to replace EFC). *Average financial aid package:* $21,243 (excluding resources awarded to replace EFC). 7% of all full-time undergraduates had no need and received non-need-based gift aid.

GIFT AID (NEED-BASED) *Total amount:* $32,122,809 (11% federal, 10% state, 76% institutional, 3% external sources). *Receiving aid:* Freshmen: 30% (452); all full-time undergraduates: 30% (1,835). *Average award:* Freshmen: $15,468; Undergraduates: $15,892. *Scholarships, grants, and awards:* Federal Pell, FSEOG, state, private, college/university gift aid from institutional funds.

GIFT AID (NON-NEED-BASED) *Total amount:* $4,021,463 (3% federal, 1% state, 72% institutional, 24% external sources). *Receiving aid:* Freshmen: 16% (245). Undergraduates: 13% (788). *Average award:* Freshmen: $9893. Undergraduates: $6288. *Scholarships, grants, and awards by category:* Academic interests/achievement: general academic interests/achievements. Creative arts/performance: 43 awards ($54,551 total): music, theater/drama. Special characteristics: 139 awards ($2,561,114 total): general special characteristics. *Tuition waivers:* Full or partial for employees or children of employees, senior citizens. *ROTC:* Army.

LOANS *Student loans:* $15,290,646 (69% need-based, 31% non-need-based). 35% of past graduating class borrowed through all loan programs. *Average indebtedness per student:* $26,400. *Average need-based loan:* Freshmen: $3415. Undergraduates: $3946. *Parent loans:* $5,601,007 (61% need-based, 39% non-need-based). *Programs:* Federal Direct (Subsidized and Unsubsidized Stafford, PLUS), Perkins.

WORK-STUDY *Federal work-study:* 297 jobs averaging $990.

ATHLETIC AWARDS Total amount: $7,646,028 (22% need-based, 78% non-need-based).

APPLYING FOR FINANCIAL AID *Required financial aid forms:* FAFSA, CSS Financial Aid PROFILE. *Financial aid deadline (priority):* 3/1. *Notification date:* Continuous beginning 3/15. Students must reply by 5/1 or within 2 weeks of notification.

CONTACT Mr. Joe Dobrota, Director of Financial Aid, The College of William and Mary, PO Box 8795, Williamsburg, VA 23187, 757-221-2425. *Fax:* 757-221-2515. *E-mail:* jdobrota@wm.edu. *Website:* http://www.wm.edu/.

THE COLLEGE OF WOOSTER
Wooster, OH

Tuition & fees: $46,860	Average undergraduate aid package: $41,286

ABOUT THE INSTITUTION Independent Presbyterian Church (U.S.A.), coed. *Awards:* bachelor's degrees. 46 undergraduate majors. *Total enrollment:* 2,003. Undergraduates: 2,003. Freshmen: 545. Both federal and institutional methodology are used as a basis for awarding need-based institutional aid.

UNDERGRADUATE EXPENSES for 2016–2017 *Comprehensive fee:* $57,900 includes full-time tuition ($46,430), mandatory fees ($430), and room and board ($11,040). *College room only:* $5330. Full-time tuition and fees vary according to course load. Room and board charges vary according to board plan and housing facility. *Part-time tuition:* $1440 per credit hour. Part-time tuition and fees vary according to course load.

FRESHMAN FINANCIAL AID (Fall 2016, est.) 399 applied for aid; of those 83% were deemed to have need. 100% of freshmen with need received aid; of those 59% had need fully met. *Average percent of need met:* 95% (excluding resources awarded to replace EFC). *Average financial aid package:* $42,056 (excluding resources awarded to replace EFC). 25% of all full-time freshmen had no need and received non-need-based gift aid.

UNDERGRADUATE FINANCIAL AID (Fall 2016, est.) 1,218 applied for aid; of those 89% were deemed to have need. 100% of undergraduates with need received aid; of those 50% had need fully met. *Average percent of need met:* 92% (excluding resources awarded to replace EFC). *Average financial aid package:*

$41,286 (excluding resources awarded to replace EFC). 36% of all full-time undergraduates had no need and received non-need-based gift aid.

GIFT AID (NEED-BASED) *Total amount:* $33,147,302 (5% federal, 1% state, 92% institutional, 2% external sources). *Receiving aid:* Freshmen: 59% (321); all full-time undergraduates: 53% (1,049). *Average award:* Freshmen: $32,506; Undergraduates: $31,599. *Scholarships, grants, and awards:* Federal Pell, FSEOG, state, private, college/university gift aid from institutional funds.

GIFT AID (NON-NEED-BASED) *Total amount:* $20,534,704 (98% institutional, 2% external sources). *Receiving aid:* Freshmen: 11% (60). Undergraduates: 7% (138). *Average award:* Freshmen: $25,680. Undergraduates: $22,828. *Scholarships, grants, and awards by category:* Academic interests/achievement: 1,491 awards ($31,002,040 total): general academic interests/achievements. *Creative arts/performance:* 137 awards ($571,500 total): dance, music, theater/drama. *Special achievements/activities:* 184 awards ($1,337,875 total): community service, religious involvement. *Special characteristics:* 321 awards ($9,084,050 total): children of educators, children of faculty/staff, international students, members of minority groups. *Tuition waivers:* Full or partial for employees or children of employees.

LOANS *Student loans:* $8,464,218 (67% need-based, 33% non-need-based). 61% of past graduating class borrowed through all loan programs. *Average indebtedness per student:* $29,650. *Average need-based loan:* Freshmen: $5948. Undergraduates: $6930. *Parent loans:* $3,563,150 (24% need-based, 76% non-need-based). *Programs:* Federal Direct (Subsidized and Unsubsidized Stafford, PLUS), Perkins.

WORK-STUDY *Federal work-study:* Total amount: $1,750,135; 820 jobs averaging $2134. *State or other work-study/employment:* Total amount: $473,500 (100% non-need-based). 145 part-time jobs averaging $3265.

APPLYING FOR FINANCIAL AID *Required financial aid forms:* FAFSA, institution's own form. *Financial aid deadline (priority):* 2/15. *Notification date:* Continuous beginning 3/15. Students must reply by 5/1.

CONTACT Dana Kennedy, Director of Financial Aid, The College of Wooster, Pearl House, 804 Beall Avenue, Wooster, OH 44691, 800-877-3688 or toll-free 800-877-9905. *Fax:* 330-263-2634. *E-mail:* financialaid@wooster.edu. *Website:* http://www.wooster.edu/.

COLORADO CHRISTIAN UNIVERSITY
Lakewood, CO

CONTACT Mr. Steve Woodburn, Director of Financial Aid, Colorado Christian University, 180 South Garrison Street, Lakewood, CO 80226-7499, 303-963-3230 or toll-free 800-44-FAITH. *Fax:* 303-963-3231. *E-mail:* sfs@ccu.edu. *Website:* http://www.ccu.edu/.

THE COLORADO COLLEGE
Colorado Springs, CO

Tuition & fees: $50,892	Average undergraduate aid package: $46,024

ABOUT THE INSTITUTION Independent, coed. *Awards:* certificates, bachelor's, and master's degrees (master's degree in education only). 48 undergraduate majors. *Total enrollment:* 2,114. Undergraduates: 2,101. Freshmen: 533. Both federal and institutional methodology are used as a basis for awarding need-based institutional aid.

UNDERGRADUATE EXPENSES for 2016–2017 *Application fee:* $60. *One-time required fee:* $150. *Comprehensive fee:* $62,560 includes full-time tuition ($50,472), mandatory fees ($420), and room and board ($11,668). *College room only:* $6902. Room and board charges vary according to board plan and housing facility. *Part-time tuition:* $8482 per course. *Part-time fees:* $2120 per credit hour. Part-time tuition and fees vary according to course load.

FRESHMAN FINANCIAL AID (Fall 2016, est.) 229 applied for aid; of those 75% were deemed to have need. 100% of freshmen with need received aid; of those 100% had need fully met. *Average percent of need met:* 100% (excluding resources awarded to replace EFC). *Average financial aid package:* $46,960 (excluding resources awarded to replace EFC). 7% of all full-time freshmen had no need and received non-need-based gift aid.

UNDERGRADUATE FINANCIAL AID (Fall 2016, est.) 808 applied for aid; of those 84% were deemed to have need. 100% of undergraduates with need received

aid; of those 100% had need fully met. *Average percent of need met:* 100% (excluding resources awarded to replace EFC). *Average financial aid package:* $46,024 (excluding resources awarded to replace EFC). 7% of all full-time undergraduates had no need and received non-need-based gift aid.

GIFT AID (NEED-BASED) *Total amount:* $29,484,608 (4% federal, 96% institutional). *Receiving aid:* Freshmen: 30% (162); all full-time undergraduates: 31% (647). *Average award:* Freshmen: $45,278; Undergraduates: $42,451. *Scholarships, grants, and awards:* Federal Pell, FSEOG, state, private, college/university gift aid from institutional funds.

GIFT AID (NON-NEED-BASED) *Total amount:* $3,790,146 (58% institutional, 42% external sources). *Receiving aid:* Freshmen: 9% (46). Undergraduates: 6% (125). *Average award:* Freshmen: $10,950. Undergraduates: $10,193. *Scholarships, grants, and awards by category:* Academic interests/achievement: 164 awards ($2,049,705 total): biological sciences, general academic interests/achievements, mathematics, physical sciences. *Special characteristics:* 18 awards ($746,766 total): children of faculty/staff. *Tuition waivers:* Full or partial for employees or children of employees. *ROTC:* Army cooperative.

LOANS *Student loans:* $5,516,222 (40% need-based, 60% non-need-based). 41% of past graduating class borrowed through all loan programs. *Average indebtedness per student:* $20,742. *Average need-based loan:* Freshmen: $2999. Undergraduates: $5267. *Parent loans:* $1,514,264 (100% non-need-based). *Programs:* Federal Direct (Subsidized and Unsubsidized Stafford, PLUS), Perkins.

WORK-STUDY *Federal work-study:* Total amount: $663,154; 333 jobs averaging $1930. *State or other work-study/employment:* Total amount: $395,584 (99% need-based, 1% non-need-based). 206 part-time jobs averaging $2017.

ATHLETIC AWARDS Total amount: $2,122,153 (11% need-based, 89% non-need-based).

APPLYING FOR FINANCIAL AID *Required financial aid forms:* FAFSA, CSS Financial Aid PROFILE, noncustodial (divorced/separated) parent's statement, federal income tax form(s), W-2 forms. *Financial aid deadline:* 2/15. *Notification date:* 3/20. Students must reply by 5/1.

CONTACT Ms. Shannon L. Amundson, Director of Financial Aid, The Colorado College, 14 East Cache La Poudre Street, Colorado Springs, CO 80903-3294, 719-389-6651 or toll-free 800-542-7214. *Fax:* 719-389-6173. *E-mail:* financialaid@coloradocollege.edu. *Website:* http://www.coloradocollege.edu/.

COLORADO MESA UNIVERSITY
Grand Junction, CO

Tuition & fees (CO res): $8395	Average undergraduate aid package: $9026

ABOUT THE INSTITUTION State-supported, coed. *Awards:* certificates, associate, bachelor's, master's, and doctoral degrees. 55 undergraduate majors. *Total enrollment:* 9,735. Undergraduates: 9,595. Freshmen: 2,023. Federal methodology is used as a basis for awarding need-based institutional aid.

UNDERGRADUATE EXPENSES for 2016–2017 *Application fee:* $30. *Tuition, state resident:* full-time $7572; part-time $252.40 per credit hour. *Tuition, nonresident:* full-time $19,530; part-time $651 per credit hour. *Required fees:* full-time $823; $27.43 per credit hour. Full-time tuition and fees vary according to course load. Part-time tuition and fees vary according to course load. *College room and board:* $10,560; *Room only:* $5850. Room and board charges vary according to board plan and housing facility.

FRESHMAN FINANCIAL AID (Fall 2015) 1,803 applied for aid; of those 74% were deemed to have need. 99% of freshmen with need received aid; of those 22% had need fully met. *Average percent of need met:* 64% (excluding resources awarded to replace EFC). *Average financial aid package:* $8355 (excluding resources awarded to replace EFC). 10% of all full-time freshmen had no need and received non-need-based gift aid.

UNDERGRADUATE FINANCIAL AID (Fall 2015) 5,876 applied for aid; of those 79% were deemed to have need. 99% of undergraduates with need received aid; of those 19% had need fully met. *Average percent of need met:* 65% (excluding resources awarded to replace EFC). *Average financial aid package:* $9026 (excluding resources awarded to replace EFC). 7% of all full-time undergraduates had no need and received non-need-based gift aid.

GIFT AID (NEED-BASED) *Total amount:* $27,799,317 (55% federal, 24% state, 11% institutional, 10% external sources). *Receiving aid:* Freshmen: 56% (1,136); all full-time undergraduates: 53% (3,809). *Average award:* Freshmen: $6539; Undergraduates: $6813. *Scholarships, grants, and awards:* Federal Pell, FSEOG, state, private, college/university gift aid from institutional funds.

GIFT AID (NON-NEED-BASED) *Total amount:* $4,946,825 (10% federal, 72% institutional, 18% external sources). *Receiving aid:* Freshmen: 8% (163). Undergraduates: 6% (400). *Average award:* Freshmen: $3123. Undergraduates: $3641. *Scholarships, grants, and awards by category: Academic interests/achievement:* biological sciences, business, communication, computer science, education, engineering/technologies, English, foreign languages, general academic interests/achievements, health fields, humanities, mathematics, physical sciences, social sciences. *Creative arts/performance:* art/fine arts, creative writing, dance, journalism/publications, music, performing arts, theater/drama. *Special achievements/activities:* general special achievements/activities, hobbies/interests, leadership. *Special characteristics:* adult students, first-generation college students, local/state students, out-of-state students. *Tuition waivers:* Full or partial for employees or children of employees.

LOANS *Student loans:* $40,762,985 (81% need-based, 19% non-need-based). 65% of past graduating class borrowed through all loan programs. *Average indebtedness per student:* $27,902. *Average need-based loan:* Freshmen: $3134. Undergraduates: $3790. *Parent loans:* $16,356,090 (59% need-based, 41% non-need-based). *Programs:* Federal Direct (Subsidized and Unsubsidized Stafford, PLUS), Perkins.

WORK-STUDY *Federal work-study:* jobs available. *State or other work-study/employment:* Total amount: $4,527,938 (33% need-based, 67% non-need-based). Part-time jobs available.

ATHLETIC AWARDS Total amount: $2,052,380 (50% need-based, 50% non-need-based).

APPLYING FOR FINANCIAL AID *Required financial aid form:* FAFSA. *Financial aid deadline:* Continuous. *Notification date:* Continuous.

CONTACT Mr. Curt Martin, Director of Financial Aid, Colorado Mesa University, 1100 North Avenue, Grand Junction, CO 81501-3122, 970-248-1065 or toll-free 800-982-MESA. *Fax:* 970-248-1191. *E-mail:* cumartin@coloradomesa.edu. *Website:* http://www.coloradomesa.edu/.

COLORADO MOUNTAIN COLLEGE
Glenwood Springs, CO

Tuition & fees: N/R	Average undergraduate aid package: N/A

ABOUT THE INSTITUTION District-supported, coed. *Awards:* certificates, associate, and bachelor's degrees. 26 undergraduate majors. *Total enrollment:* 5,847. Undergraduates: 5,847. Freshmen: 686. Both federal and institutional methodology are used as a basis for awarding need-based institutional aid.

UNDERGRADUATE EXPENSES for 2016–2017 *Tuition, area resident:* part-time $62 per credit hour. *Tuition, state resident:* part-time $127 per credit hour. *Tuition, nonresident:* part-time $429 per credit hour.

FRESHMAN FINANCIAL AID (Fall 2015) 15% of all full-time freshmen had no need and received non-need-based gift aid.

UNDERGRADUATE FINANCIAL AID (Fall 2015) 17% of all full-time undergraduates had no need and received non-need-based gift aid.

GIFT AID (NEED-BASED) *Total amount:* $5,045,510 (72% federal, 28% state). *Receiving aid:* Freshmen: 30% (106); all full-time undergraduates: 29% (530). *Average award:* Freshmen: $1677; Undergraduates: $1680. *Scholarships, grants, and awards:* Federal Pell, FSEOG, state, private, college/university gift aid from institutional funds.

GIFT AID (NON-NEED-BASED) *Total amount:* $1,121,890 (73% institutional, 27% external sources). *Average award:* Freshmen: $1179. Undergraduates: $1241. *Scholarships, grants, and awards by category: Special characteristics:* local/state students.

LOANS *Student loans:* $4,603,769 (51% need-based, 49% non-need-based). *Parent loans:* $595,942 (100% non-need-based). *Programs:* Federal Direct (Subsidized and Unsubsidized Stafford, PLUS), Perkins, Federal Nursing, state.

WORK-STUDY *Federal work-study:* jobs available. *State or other work-study/employment:* Total amount: $422,074 (41% need-based, 59% non-need-based). Part-time jobs available.

APPLYING FOR FINANCIAL AID *Required financial aid form:* FAFSA. *Financial aid deadline (priority):* 3/31. *Notification date:* Continuous.

CONTACT Mr. Thomas S. Valles, Director of Financial Aid, Colorado Mountain College, 802 Grand Avenue, Glenwood Springs, CO 81601, 970-947-8338 or toll-free 800-621-8559. *E-mail:* tvalles@coloradomtn.edu. *Website:* http://www.coloradomtn.edu/.

COLORADO MOUNTAIN COLLEGE
Leadville, CO

CONTACT Financial Aid Office, Colorado Mountain College, 901 South Highway 24, Leadville, CO 80461, 719-486-2015 or toll-free 800-621-8559. *Website:* http://www.coloradomtn.edu/.

COLORADO MOUNTAIN COLLEGE
Steamboat Springs, CO

CONTACT Mr. Thomas S. Valles, Director of Financial Aid, Colorado Mountain College, 802 Grand Avenue, Glenwood Springs, CO 81601, 800-621-8559 Ext. 8338 or toll-free 800-621-8559. *Fax:* 970-947-8318. *E-mail:* finaid@coloradomtn.edu. *Website:* http://www.coloradomtn.edu/.

COLORADO SCHOOL OF MINES
Golden, CO

Tuition & fees (CO res): $17,842	Average undergraduate aid package: $14,039

ABOUT THE INSTITUTION State-supported, coed. *Awards:* certificates, bachelor's, master's, and doctoral degrees. 17 undergraduate majors. *Total enrollment:* 5,876. Undergraduates: 4,612. Freshmen: 977. Federal methodology is used as a basis for awarding need-based institutional aid.

UNDERGRADUATE EXPENSES for 2016–2017 *Application fee:* $45. *Tuition, state resident:* full-time $15,690; part-time $523 per credit hour. *Tuition, nonresident:* full-time $34,020; part-time $1134 per credit hour. *Required fees:* full-time $2152. Full-time tuition and fees vary according to course load. *College room and board:* $11,477. Room and board charges vary according to board plan and housing facility.

FRESHMAN FINANCIAL AID (Fall 2015) 803 applied for aid; of those 59% were deemed to have need. 100% of freshmen with need received aid; of those 27% had need fully met. *Average percent of need met:* 64% (excluding resources awarded to replace EFC). *Average financial aid package:* $15,787 (excluding resources awarded to replace EFC). 28% of all full-time freshmen had no need and received non-need-based gift aid.

UNDERGRADUATE FINANCIAL AID (Fall 2015) 2,842 applied for aid; of those 71% were deemed to have need. 99% of undergraduates with need received aid; of those 18% had need fully met. *Average percent of need met:* 56% (excluding resources awarded to replace EFC). *Average financial aid package:* $14,039 (excluding resources awarded to replace EFC). 30% of all full-time undergraduates had no need and received non-need-based gift aid.

GIFT AID (NEED-BASED) *Total amount:* $16,353,550 (20% federal, 6% state, 62% institutional, 12% external sources). *Receiving aid:* Freshmen: 24% (236); all full-time undergraduates: 26% (1,128). *Average award:* Freshmen: $5626; Undergraduates: $5478. *Scholarships, grants, and awards:* Federal Pell, FSEOG, state, private, college/university gift aid from institutional funds.

GIFT AID (NON-NEED-BASED) *Total amount:* $13,032,703 (87% institutional, 13% external sources). *Receiving aid:* Freshmen: 41% (411). Undergraduates: 31% (1,351). *Average award:* Freshmen: $7809. Undergraduates: $8182. *Scholarships, grants, and awards by category: Academic interests/achievement:* business, computer science, engineering/technologies, general academic interests/achievements, mathematics, military science, physical sciences. *Tuition waivers:* Full or partial for employees or children of employees. *ROTC:* Army, Air Force.

LOANS *Student loans:* $27,004,644 (47% need-based, 53% non-need-based). 58% of past graduating class borrowed through all loan programs. *Average indebtedness per student:* $32,901. *Average need-based loan:* Freshmen: $3335. Undergrad-

uates: $4661. *Parent loans:* $12,875,574 (55% need-based, 45% non-need-based). *Programs:* Federal Direct (Subsidized and Unsubsidized Stafford, PLUS), Perkins, college/university.

WORK-STUDY *Federal work-study:* 395 jobs averaging $1787. *State or other work-study/employment:* Total amount: $4,320,545 (56% need-based, 44% non-need-based). 1,719 part-time jobs averaging $2417.

ATHLETIC AWARDS Total amount: $14,430,730 (85% need-based, 15% non-need-based).

APPLYING FOR FINANCIAL AID *Required financial aid form:* FAFSA. *Financial aid deadline (priority):* 3/1. *Notification date:* Continuous beginning 3/1.

CONTACT Jill Robertson, Director of Financial Aid, Colorado School of Mines, 1600 Maple Street, Golden, CO 80401-1887, 303-273-3301 or toll-free 800-446-9488 Ext. 3220. *Fax:* 303-384-2252. *E-mail:* finaid@mines.edu.

Website: http://www.mines.edu/.

COLORADO STATE UNIVERSITY
Fort Collins, CO

Tuition & fees (CO res): $11,052	Average undergraduate aid package: $11,098

ABOUT THE INSTITUTION State-supported, coed. *Awards:* certificates, bachelor's, master's, and doctoral degrees. 114 undergraduate majors. *Total enrollment:* 33,058. Undergraduates: 25,688. Freshmen: 4,956. Both federal and institutional methodology are used as a basis for awarding need-based institutional aid.

UNDERGRADUATE EXPENSES for 2016–2017 *Application fee:* $50. *Tuition, state resident:* full-time $8716; part-time $395.90 per credit hour. *Tuition, nonresident:* full-time $26,010; part-time $1300 per credit hour. *Required fees:* full-time $2336; $56.96 per credit hour or $284.82 per term. Full-time tuition and fees vary according to course level, course load, program, and student level. Part-time tuition and fees vary according to course level, course load, program, and student level. *College room and board:* $11,110; *Room only:* $5416. Room and board charges vary according to board plan, housing facility, and location.

FRESHMAN FINANCIAL AID (Fall 2015) 3,876 applied for aid; of those 63% were deemed to have need. 92% of freshmen with need received aid; of those 35% had need fully met. *Average percent of need met:* 84% (excluding resources awarded to replace EFC). *Average financial aid package:* $10,664 (excluding resources awarded to replace EFC). 17% of all full-time freshmen had no need and received non-need-based gift aid.

UNDERGRADUATE FINANCIAL AID (Fall 2015) 15,237 applied for aid; of those 73% were deemed to have need. 92% of undergraduates with need received aid; of those 24% had need fully met. *Average percent of need met:* 80% (excluding resources awarded to replace EFC). *Average financial aid package:* $11,098 (excluding resources awarded to replace EFC). 12% of all full-time undergraduates had no need and received non-need-based gift aid.

GIFT AID (NEED-BASED) *Total amount:* $76,294,729 (29% federal, 13% state, 50% institutional, 8% external sources). *Receiving aid:* Freshmen: 40% (1,799); all full-time undergraduates: 33% (7,488). *Average award:* Freshmen: $8107; Undergraduates: $7663. *Scholarships, grants, and awards:* Federal Pell, FSEOG, state, private, college/university gift aid from institutional funds.

GIFT AID (NON-NEED-BASED) *Total amount:* $17,495,203 (1% federal, 3% state, 77% institutional, 19% external sources). *Receiving aid:* Freshmen: 14% (631). Undergraduates: 5% (1,216). *Average award:* Freshmen: $5142. Undergraduates: $4616. *Scholarships, grants, and awards by category:* Academic interests/achievement: general academic interests/achievements. Creative arts/performance: art/fine arts, creative writing, dance, music, performing arts, theater/drama. Special achievements/activities: general special achievements/activities. Special characteristics: children of faculty/staff, first-generation college students, international students, members of minority groups, veterans. *Tuition waivers:* Full or partial for employees or children of employees. *ROTC:* Army, Air Force.

LOANS *Student loans:* $88,751,185 (66% need-based, 34% non-need-based). 54% of past graduating class borrowed through all loan programs. *Average indebtedness per student:* $25,155. *Average need-based loan:* Freshmen: $4976. Undergraduates: $6431. *Parent loans:* $50,691,120 (34% need-based, 66% non-need-based). *Programs:* Federal Direct (Subsidized and Unsubsidized Stafford, PLUS), Perkins, alternative loans.

WORK-STUDY *Federal work-study:* jobs available. *State or other work-study/employment:* Total amount: $2,977,931 (65% need-based, 35% non-need-based). Part-time jobs available.

ATHLETIC AWARDS Total amount: $8,468,396 (31% need-based, 69% non-need-based).

APPLYING FOR FINANCIAL AID *Required financial aid forms:* FAFSA, CSS Financial Aid PROFILE, noncustodial (divorced/separated) parent's statement. *Financial aid deadline (priority):* 3/1. *Notification date:* Continuous beginning 3/1.

CONTACT Office of Student Financial Services, Colorado State University, Centennial Hall, 1065 Campus Delivery, Fort Collins, CO 80523-8024, 970-491-6321. *Fax:* 970-491-5010. *E-mail:* financialaid@colostate.edu.

Website: http://www.colostate.edu/.

COLORADO STATE UNIVERSITY– GLOBAL CAMPUS
Greenwood Village, CO

CONTACT Financial Aid Office, Colorado State University–Global Campus, 8000 E. Maplewood Avenue, Greenwood Village, CO 80111, 720-279-0159 or toll-free 800-920-6723.

Website: http://csuglobal.edu/.

COLORADO STATE UNIVERSITY– PUEBLO
Pueblo, CO

ABOUT THE INSTITUTION State-supported, coed. *Awards:* bachelor's and master's degrees. 27 undergraduate majors. *Total enrollment:* 7,563. Undergraduates: 5,006. Freshmen: 793.

GIFT AID (NEED-BASED) *Scholarships, grants, and awards:* Federal Pell, FSEOG, state, private, college/university gift aid from institutional funds, Federal Nursing, TEACH Grants.

GIFT AID (NON-NEED-BASED) *Scholarships, grants, and awards by category:* Academic interests/achievement: biological sciences, business, communication, computer science, education, engineering/technologies, English, foreign languages, general academic interests/achievements, health fields, mathematics, physical sciences, premedicine, social sciences. Creative arts/performance: applied art and design, art/fine arts, cinema/film/broadcasting, journalism/publications, music. Special achievements/activities: community service, general special achievements/activities, leadership. Special characteristics: adult students, children and siblings of alumni, children of current students, children of faculty/staff, ethnic background, first-generation college students, general special characteristics, handicapped students, international students, local/state students, married students, members of minority groups, out-of-state students.

LOANS *Programs:* Federal Direct (Subsidized and Unsubsidized Stafford, PLUS), Perkins, Federal Nursing.

WORK-STUDY *Federal work-study:* 686 jobs averaging $3000. *State or other work-study/employment:* Total amount: $1,131,250 (61% need-based, 39% non-need-based). 1,109 part-time jobs averaging $3000.

APPLYING FOR FINANCIAL AID *Required financial aid forms:* FAFSA, institution's own form.

CONTACT Justin Streater, Associate Director of Financial Aid, Colorado State University–Pueblo, 2200 Bonforte Boulevard, Pueblo, CO 81001-4901, 719-549-2967. *Fax:* 719-549-2088. *E-mail:* justin.streater@csupueblo.edu.

Website: http://www.csupueblo.edu/.

COLORADO TECHNICAL UNIVERSITY AURORA

Aurora, CO

CONTACT Ms. Natalie Dietsch, Financial Aid Manager, Colorado Technical University Aurora, 5775 Denver Tech Center Boulevard, Suite 100, Greenwood Village, CO 80111, 303-694-6600 or toll-free 888-309-6555. *Fax:* 303-694-6673. *Website:* http://www.coloradotech.edu/.

COLORADO TECHNICAL UNIVERSITY COLORADO SPRINGS

Colorado Springs, CO

CONTACT Jacqueline Harris, Senior Director of Student Finance Services, Colorado Technical University Colorado Springs, 4435 North Chestnut Street, Colorado Springs, CO 80907-3896, 719-598-0200 or toll-free 866-942-6555. *Fax:* 719-598-3740. *Website:* http://www.coloradotech.edu/.

COLUMBIA CENTRO UNIVERSITARIO

Caguas, PR

CONTACT Financial Aid Officer, Columbia Centro Universitario, Carr 183, Km 1.7, PO Box 8517, Caguas, PR 00726, 787-743-4041 Ext. 244. *Fax:* 787-744-7031. *Website:* http://www.columbiacentral.edu/.

COLUMBIA CENTRO UNIVERSITARIO

Yauco, PR

CONTACT Financial Aid Office, Columbia Centro Universitario, Calle Betances #3, Box 3062, Yauco, PR 00698, 787-856-0945. *Website:* http://www.columbiacentral.edu/.

COLUMBIA COLLEGE

Columbia, MO

Tuition & fees: $21,936	Average undergraduate aid package: $17,042

ABOUT THE INSTITUTION Independent Christian Church (Disciples of Christ), coed. *Awards:* associate, bachelor's, and master's degrees (offers continuing education program with significant enrollment not reflected in profile). 41 undergraduate majors. *Total enrollment:* 1,093. Undergraduates: 936. Freshmen: 204. Both federal and institutional methodology are used as a basis for awarding need-based institutional aid.
UNDERGRADUATE EXPENSES for 2017–2018 *Application fee:* $35. *Comprehensive fee:* $29,568 includes full-time tuition ($21,936) and room and board ($7632). *College room only:* $4855. Full-time tuition and fees vary according to class time, course load, degree level, program, reciprocity agreements, and student level. Room and board charges vary according to board plan and housing facility. *Part-time tuition:* $471 per credit hour. Part-time tuition and fees vary according to class time, course load, degree level, location, and reciprocity agreements. *Payment plan:* Guaranteed tuition.
FRESHMAN FINANCIAL AID (Fall 2015) 98 applied for aid; of those 88% were deemed to have need. 100% of freshmen with need received aid; of those 19% had need fully met. *Average percent of need met:* 69% (excluding resources awarded to replace EFC). *Average financial aid package:* $17,653 (excluding resources awarded to replace EFC). 18% of all full-time freshmen had no need and received non-need-based gift aid.
UNDERGRADUATE FINANCIAL AID (Fall 2015) 493 applied for aid; of those 90% were deemed to have need. 98% of undergraduates with need received aid; of those 20% had need fully met. *Average percent of need met:* 65% (excluding resources awarded to replace EFC). *Average financial aid package:* $17,042 (excluding resources awarded to replace EFC). 14% of all full-time undergraduates had no need and received non-need-based gift aid.
GIFT AID (NEED-BASED) Total amount: $1,862,234 (63% federal, 19% state, 18% institutional). *Receiving aid:* Freshmen: 53% (66); all full-time undergraduates: 48% (328). *Average award:* Freshmen: $6050; Undergraduates: $5314. *Scholarships, grants, and awards:* Federal Pell, FSEOG, state, private, college/university gift aid from institutional funds.
GIFT AID (NON NEED BASED) Total amount: $4,366,962 (97% institutional, 3% external sources). *Receiving aid:* Freshmen: 69% (86). Undergraduates: 55% (375). *Average award:* Freshmen: $7559. Undergraduates: $10,178. *Scholarships, grants, and awards by category:* Academic interests/achievement: 455 awards ($2,042,333 total): biological sciences, business, communication, computer science, education, English, general academic interests/achievements, humanities, mathematics, physical sciences, religion/biblical studies, social sciences. Creative arts/performance: 28 awards ($27,275 total): art/fine arts, creative writing, music. Special achievements/activities: 162 awards ($1,037,870 total): community service, general special achievements/activities, leadership, religious involvement. Special characteristics: 255 awards ($494,908 total): adult students, children and siblings of alumni, children of current students, children of educators, children of faculty/staff, children of union members/company employees, ethnic background, first-generation college students, general special characteristics, international students, local/state students, members of minority groups, parents of current students, previous college experience, religious affiliation, siblings of current students, spouses of current students, veterans, veterans' children. *Tuition waivers:* Full or partial for children of alumni, employees or children of employees, senior citizens. *ROTC:* Army cooperative, Naval cooperative, Air Force cooperative.
LOANS Student loans: $3,123,245 (39% need-based, 61% non-need-based). 53% of past graduating class borrowed through all loan programs. *Average indebtedness per student:* $21,934. *Average need-based loan:* Freshmen: $3007. Undergraduates: $3516. *Parent loans:* $578,361 (100% non-need-based). *Programs:* Federal Direct (Subsidized and Unsubsidized Stafford, PLUS).
WORK-STUDY Federal work-study: 154 jobs averaging $2313. *State or other work-study/employment:* Total amount: $392,805 (100% need-based). 70 part-time jobs averaging $1650.
ATHLETIC AWARDS Total amount: $1,883,409 (100% non-need-based).
APPLYING FOR FINANCIAL AID *Required financial aid form:* FAFSA. *Financial aid deadline (priority):* 3/1. *Notification date:* Continuous beginning 12/15.
CONTACT Nathan Miller, Senior Director of Student Success and Financial Aid, Columbia College, 1001 Rogers Street, Columbia, MO 65216-0002, 573-875-7860 or toll-free 800-231-2391. *Fax:* 573-875-7452. *E-mail:* nbmiller@ccis.edu. *Website:* http://www.ccis.edu/.

COLUMBIA COLLEGE

Columbia, SC

CONTACT Anita Kaminer Elliott, Director of Financial Aid, Columbia College, 1301 Columbia College Drive, Columbia, SC 29203-5998, 803-786-3612 or toll-free 800-277-1301. *Fax:* 803-786-3560. *Website:* http://www.columbiasc.edu/.

COLUMBIA COLLEGE CHICAGO

Chicago, IL

Tuition & fees: $25,580	Average undergraduate aid package: N/A

ABOUT THE INSTITUTION Independent, coed. *Awards:* certificates, bachelor's, and master's degrees. 53 undergraduate majors. *Total enrollment:* 8,120. Undergraduates: 7,809. Freshmen: 1,555. Federal methodology is used as a basis for awarding need-based institutional aid.
UNDERGRADUATE EXPENSES for 2017–2018 *Application fee:* $35. *Tuition:* full-time $25,580. Full-time tuition and fees vary according to course load. Part-time tuition and fees vary according to course load.
FRESHMAN FINANCIAL AID (Fall 2015) 1,570 applied for aid.
UNDERGRADUATE FINANCIAL AID (Fall 2015) 6,354 applied for aid.

GIFT AID (NEED-BASED) *Total amount:* $61,769,060 (26% federal, 11% state, 61% institutional, 2% external sources). *Scholarships, grants, and awards:* Federal Pell, FSEOG, state, private, college/university gift aid from institutional funds.

GIFT AID (NON-NEED-BASED) *Tuition waivers:* Full or partial for employees or children of employees.

LOANS *Student loans:* $53,576,438 (100% need-based). *Parent loans:* $43,002,547 (100% need-based). *Programs:* Federal Direct (Subsidized and Unsubsidized Stafford, PLUS).

WORK-STUDY *Federal work-study:* jobs available.

APPLYING FOR FINANCIAL AID *Required financial aid form:* FAFSA. *Financial aid deadline:* Continuous. *Notification date:* Continuous beginning 11/1.

CONTACT Financial Aid Office, Columbia College Chicago, 600 South Michigan Avenue, Suite 303, Chicago, IL 60605-1996, 866-705-0200.
Website: http://www.colum.edu/.

COLUMBIA COLLEGE HOLLYWOOD
Tarzana, CA

Tuition & fees: N/R	Average undergraduate aid package: $6000

ABOUT THE INSTITUTION Independent, coed. 5 undergraduate majors. Federal methodology is used as a basis for awarding need-based institutional aid.

UNDERGRADUATE FINANCIAL AID (Fall 2016, est.) 300 applied for aid; of those 67% were deemed to have need. 100% of undergraduates with need received aid. *Average financial aid package:* $6000 (excluding resources awarded to replace EFC).

GIFT AID (NEED-BASED) *Total amount:* $1,095,135 (68% federal, 27% state, 5% external sources). *Receiving aid:* All full-time undergraduates: 29% (100). *Average award:* Undergraduates: $2000. *Scholarships, grants, and awards:* Federal Pell, FSEOG, state, private.

LOANS *Student loans:* $4,568,900 (100% need-based). 75% of past graduating class borrowed through all loan programs. *Average need-based loan:* Undergraduates: $1300. *Parent loans:* $1,285,484 (100% need-based). *Programs:* Federal Direct (Subsidized and Unsubsidized Stafford, PLUS), private loans.

WORK-STUDY *Federal work-study:* Total amount: $17,000; 10 jobs averaging $2000.

APPLYING FOR FINANCIAL AID *Required financial aid forms:* FAFSA, institution's own form. *Financial aid deadline:* Continuous. *Notification date:* Continuous. Students must reply within 2 weeks of notification.

CONTACT Ms. Maricela Guzman, Financial Aid Administrator, Columbia College Hollywood, 18618 Oxnard Street, Tarzana, CA 91356, 818-401-1030 or toll-free 800-785-0585. *Fax:* 818-345-8660. *E-mail:* mguzman@columbiacollege.edu.
Website: http://www.columbiacollege.edu/.

COLUMBIA COLLEGE OF NURSING
Glendale, WI

ABOUT THE INSTITUTION Independent, coed, primarily women. 1 undergraduate major.

GIFT AID (NEED-BASED) *Scholarships, grants, and awards:* Federal Pell, FSEOG, state, private, college/university gift aid from institutional funds.

GIFT AID (NON-NEED-BASED) *Scholarships, grants, and awards by category:* Academic interests/achievement: health fields.

LOANS *Programs:* Federal Direct (Subsidized and Unsubsidized Stafford, PLUS), state.

CONTACT Wendy Hilvo, Financial Aid Director, Columbia College of Nursing, 4425 North Port Washington Road, Suite 302, Glendale, WI 53212, 414-326-2337. *Fax:* 414-326-2362. *E-mail:* financialaid@ccon.edu.
Website: http://www.ccon.edu/.

COLUMBIA INTERNATIONAL UNIVERSITY
Columbia, SC

Tuition & fees: $22,390	Average undergraduate aid package: $17,615

ABOUT THE INSTITUTION Independent nondenominational, coed. *Awards:* certificates, associate, bachelor's, master's, and doctoral degrees. 18 undergraduate majors. *Total enrollment:* 965. Undergraduates: 497. Freshmen: 80. Federal methodology is used as a basis for awarding need-based institutional aid.

UNDERGRADUATE EXPENSES for 2017–2018 *Comprehensive fee:* $30,380 includes full-time tuition ($21,720), mandatory fees ($670), and room and board ($7990). Full-time tuition and fees vary according to course load, program, and reciprocity agreements. Room and board charges vary according to board plan and housing facility. *Part-time tuition:* $905 per semester hour. *Part-time fees:* $10 per semester hour; $185 per term. Part-time tuition and fees vary according to course load, program, and reciprocity agreements.

FRESHMAN FINANCIAL AID (Fall 2015) 89 applied for aid; of those 87% were deemed to have need. 100% of freshmen with need received aid; of those 16% had need fully met. *Average percent of need met:* 68% (excluding resources awarded to replace EFC). *Average financial aid package:* $17,331 (excluding resources awarded to replace EFC). 21% of all full-time freshmen had no need and received non-need-based gift aid.

UNDERGRADUATE FINANCIAL AID (Fall 2015) 417 applied for aid; of those 89% were deemed to have need. 100% of undergraduates with need received aid; of those 14% had need fully met. *Average percent of need met:* 63% (excluding resources awarded to replace EFC). *Average financial aid package:* $17,615 (excluding resources awarded to replace EFC). 25% of all full-time undergraduates had no need and received non-need-based gift aid.

GIFT AID (NEED-BASED) *Total amount:* $4,701,709 (21% federal, 21% state, 54% institutional, 4% external sources). *Receiving aid:* Freshmen: 78% (77); all full-time undergraduates: 74% (368). *Average award:* Freshmen: $14,447; Undergraduates: $13,771. *Scholarships, grants, and awards:* Federal Pell, FSEOG, state, private, college/university gift aid from institutional funds.

GIFT AID (NON-NEED-BASED) *Total amount:* $979,675 (19% state, 76% institutional, 5% external sources). *Receiving aid:* Freshmen: 9% (9). Undergraduates: 7% (33). *Average award:* Freshmen: $8197. Undergraduates: $5306. *Scholarships, grants, and awards by category:* Academic interests/achievement: general academic interests/achievements. Special achievements/activities: general special achievements/activities, leadership, religious involvement. Special characteristics: children and siblings of alumni, children of faculty/staff, ethnic background, international students, local/state students, members of minority groups, spouses of current students, veterans, veterans' children. *Tuition waivers:* Full or partial for employees or children of employees.

LOANS *Student loans:* $3,192,531 (81% need-based, 19% non-need-based). 53% of past graduating class borrowed through all loan programs. *Average indebtedness per student:* $22,405. *Average need-based loan:* Freshmen: $3137. Undergraduates: $4132. *Parent loans:* $589,293 (67% need-based, 33% non-need-based). *Programs:* Federal Direct (Subsidized and Unsubsidized Stafford, PLUS).

WORK-STUDY *Federal work-study:* 95 jobs averaging $1157. *State or other work-study/employment:* 243 part-time jobs averaging $1799.

ATHLETIC AWARDS Total amount: $256,810 (71% need-based, 29% non-need-based).

APPLYING FOR FINANCIAL AID *Required financial aid forms:* FAFSA, institution's own form, state aid form. *Financial aid deadline (priority):* 4/15. *Notification date:* Continuous beginning 3/1. Students must reply within 2 weeks of notification.

CONTACT Mrs. Patty Jean Hix, Director of Financial Aid, Columbia International University, 7435 Monticello Road, Columbia, SC 29203, 800-777-2227 Ext. 5037 or toll-free 800-777-2227 Ext. 5024. *Fax:* 803-223-2505. *E-mail:* phix@ciu.edu.
Website: http://www.ciu.edu/.

COLUMBIA UNIVERSITY
New York, NY

Tuition & fees: $55,056	Average undergraduate aid package: $55,521

ABOUT THE INSTITUTION Independent, coed. **Awards:** bachelor's, master's, and doctoral degrees. 78 undergraduate majors. **Total enrollment:** 6,158. Undergraduates: 6,158. Freshmen: 1,420. Both federal and institutional methodology are used as a basis for awarding need-based institutional aid.
UNDERGRADUATE EXPENSES for 2016–2017 Application fee: $85. **Comprehensive fee:** $68,300 includes full-time tuition ($52,478), mandatory fees ($2578), and room and board ($13,244). Room and board charges vary according to board plan and housing facility. **Payment plan:** Tuition prepayment.
FRESHMAN FINANCIAL AID (Fall 2016, est.) 857 applied for aid; of those 85% were deemed to have need. 100% of freshmen with need received aid; of those 100% had need fully met. **Average percent of need met:** 100% (excluding resources awarded to replace EFC). **Average financial aid package:** $55,687 (excluding resources awarded to replace EFC).
UNDERGRADUATE FINANCIAL AID (Fall 2016, est.) 3,290 applied for aid; of those 91% were deemed to have need. 100% of undergraduates with need received aid; of those 97% had need fully met. **Average percent of need met:** 99% (excluding resources awarded to replace EFC). **Average financial aid package:** $55,521 (excluding resources awarded to replace EFC).
GIFT AID (NEED-BASED) Total amount: $151,554,724 (4% federal, 1% state, 93% institutional, 2% external sources). **Receiving aid:** Freshmen: 51% (721); all full-time undergraduates: 48% (2,973). **Average award:** Freshmen: $52,073; Undergraduates: $50,733. **Scholarships, grants, and awards:** Federal Pell, FSEOG, state, private, college/university gift aid from institutional funds.
GIFT AID (NON-NEED-BASED) Total amount: $572,120 (20% federal, 7% state, 73% external sources). **Receiving aid:** Freshmen: 2% (25). Undergraduates: 1% (83). **Tuition waivers:** Full or partial for employees or children of employees.
ROTC: Army cooperative, Naval, Air Force cooperative.
LOANS Student loans: $7,233,925 (34% need-based, 66% non-need-based). **Average need-based loan:** Freshmen: $2907. Undergraduates: $3451. **Parent loans:** $6,578,137 (1% need-based, 99% non-need-based). **Programs:** Federal Direct (Subsidized and Unsubsidized Stafford, PLUS), Perkins, college/university, alternative loans.
WORK-STUDY Federal work-study: Total amount: $5,171,820; jobs available. **State or other work-study/employment:** Total amount: $2,615,215 (77% need-based, 23% non-need-based). Part-time jobs available.
APPLYING FOR FINANCIAL AID Required financial aid forms: FAFSA, CSS Financial Aid PROFILE, noncustodial (divorced/separated) parent's statement, parent and student income tax form(s). **Financial aid deadline (priority):** 2/15. **Notification date:** 3/30. Students must reply by 5/1 or within 3 weeks of notification.
CONTACT Michael Patrick Hall, Executive Director of Financial Aid and Enrollment Operations, Columbia University, 100 Hamilton Hall, MC 2807, New York, NY 10027, 212-854-3713. E-mail: mh3036@columbia.edu.
Website: http://www.columbia.edu/.

COLUMBIA UNIVERSITY, SCHOOL OF GENERAL STUDIES
New York, NY

Tuition & fees: $53,445	Average undergraduate aid package: $30,819

ABOUT THE INSTITUTION Independent, coed. **Awards:** certificates and bachelor's degrees. 79 undergraduate majors. **Total enrollment:** 2,068. Undergraduates: 2,068. Freshmen: 147. Both federal and institutional methodology are used as a basis for awarding need-based institutional aid.
UNDERGRADUATE EXPENSES for 2016–2017 Application fee: $80. **One-time required fee:** $105. **Comprehensive fee:** $67,031 includes full-time tuition ($50,760), mandatory fees ($2685), and room and board ($13,586). **College room only:** $8320. Full-time tuition and fees vary according to course load and program.

Room and board charges vary according to board plan and housing facility. **Part-time tuition:** $1692 per credit hour. Part-time tuition and fees vary according to course load and program. **Payment plan:** Tuition prepayment.
FRESHMAN FINANCIAL AID (Fall 2015) 33 applied for aid; of those 79% were deemed to have need. 96% of freshmen with need received aid. **Average percent of need met:** 28% (excluding resources awarded to replace EFC). **Average financial aid package:** $18,679 (excluding resources awarded to replace EFC). 10% of all full-time freshmen had no need and received non-need-based gift aid.
UNDERGRADUATE FINANCIAL AID (Fall 2015) 950 applied for aid; of those 92% were deemed to have need. 98% of undergraduates with need received aid; of those 3% had need fully met. **Average percent of need met:** 45% (excluding resources awarded to replace EFC). **Average financial aid package:** $30,819 (excluding resources awarded to replace EFC). 6% of all full-time undergraduates had no need and received non-need-based gift aid.
GIFT AID (NEED-BASED) Total amount: $23,597,193 (19% federal, 2% state, 74% institutional, 5% external sources). **Receiving aid:** Freshmen: 60% (24); all full-time undergraduates: 73% (851). **Average award:** Freshmen: $14,874; Undergraduates: $22,797. **Scholarships, grants, and awards:** Federal Pell, FSEOG, state, private, college/university gift aid from institutional funds.
GIFT AID (NON-NEED-BASED) Total amount: $1,541,121 (95% institutional, 5% external sources). **Receiving aid:** Undergraduates: 2% (25). **Average award:** Freshmen: $7755. Undergraduates: $12,545. **Scholarships, grants, and awards by category:** Academic interests/achievement: general academic interests/achievements. **Tuition waivers:** Full or partial for employees or children of employees.
ROTC: Army cooperative, Naval, Air Force cooperative.
LOANS Student loans: $17,192,486 (95% need-based, 5% non-need-based). **Average need-based loan:** Freshmen: $4000. Undergraduates: $8359. **Parent loans:** $1,291,691 (58% need-based, 42% non-need-based). **Programs:** Federal Direct (Subsidized and Unsubsidized Stafford, PLUS), Perkins, college/university.
WORK-STUDY Federal work-study: jobs available.
APPLYING FOR FINANCIAL AID Required financial aid forms: FAFSA, institution's own form. **Financial aid deadline:** 6/1. **Notification date:** Continuous.
CONTACT Mr. William Skip Bailey, Director of Educational Financing, Columbia University, School of General Studies, 408 Lewisohn Hall, 2970 Broadway, New York, NY 10027, 212-854-5410 or toll-free 800-895-1169. Fax: 212-854-6316. E-mail: gs_financial_aid@columbia.edu.
Website: http://www.gs.columbia.edu/.

COLUMBUS COLLEGE OF ART & DESIGN
Columbus, OH

Tuition & fees: $35,375	Average undergraduate aid package: $21,647

ABOUT THE INSTITUTION Independent, coed. **Awards:** bachelor's and master's degrees. 12 undergraduate majors. **Total enrollment:** 1,095. Undergraduates: 1,060. Freshmen: 240. Federal methodology is used as a basis for awarding need-based institutional aid.
UNDERGRADUATE EXPENSES for 2017–2018 Application fee: $50. **Comprehensive fee:** $44,745 includes full-time tuition ($33,960), mandatory fees ($1415), and room and board ($9370). Full-time tuition and fees vary according to course load. Room and board charges vary according to board plan, housing facility, location, and student level. **Part-time tuition:** $1415 per credit hour. Part-time tuition and fees vary according to course load.
FRESHMAN FINANCIAL AID (Fall 2015) 264 applied for aid; of those 90% were deemed to have need. 100% of freshmen with need received aid; of those 7% had need fully met. **Average percent of need met:** 58% (excluding resources awarded to replace EFC). **Average financial aid package:** $22,951 (excluding resources awarded to replace EFC). 19% of all full-time freshmen had no need and received non-need-based gift aid.
UNDERGRADUATE FINANCIAL AID (Fall 2015) 908 applied for aid; of those 93% were deemed to have need. 99% of undergraduates with need received aid; of those 8% had need fully met. **Average percent of need met:** 55% (excluding resources awarded to replace EFC). **Average financial aid package:** $21,647

(excluding resources awarded to replace EFC). 19% of all full-time undergraduates had no need and received non-need-based gift aid.

GIFT AID (NEED-BASED) Total amount: $13,255,860 (15% federal, 5% state, 77% institutional, 3% external sources). **Receiving aid:** Freshmen: 78% (234); all full-time undergraduates: 79% (840). **Average award:** Freshmen: $17,974; Undergraduates: $15,539. **Scholarships, grants, and awards:** Federal Pell, FSEOG, state, private, college/university gift aid from institutional funds.

GIFT AID (NON-NEED-BASED) Total amount: $2,692,506 (96% institutional, 4% external sources). **Receiving aid:** Freshmen: 4% (13). Undergraduates: 4% (43). **Average award:** Freshmen: $12,070. Undergraduates: $11,029. **Scholarships, grants, and awards by category:** Creative arts/performance: 1,061 awards ($12,839,226 total): art/fine arts. **Special characteristics:** 11 awards ($231,850 total): children of educators, children of faculty/staff, local/state students. **Tuition waivers:** Full or partial for employees or children of employees.

LOANS Student loans: $8,545,812 (86% need-based, 14% non-need-based). 81% of past graduating class borrowed through all loan programs. **Average indebtedness per student:** $32,258. **Average need-based loan:** Freshmen: $5995. Undergraduates: $6895. **Parent loans:** $6,610,650 (64% need-based, 36% non-need-based). **Programs:** Federal Direct (Subsidized and Unsubsidized Stafford, PLUS), Perkins, state.

WORK-STUDY Federal work-study: 137 jobs averaging $3550. **State or other work-study/employment:** 297 part-time jobs averaging $3550.

APPLYING FOR FINANCIAL AID Required financial aid forms: FAFSA, institution's own form, federal income tax form(s), verification worksheet. **Financial aid deadline (priority):** 10/15. **Notification date:** 11/1. Students must reply within 2 weeks of notification.

CONTACT Mrs. Anna Marie Schofield, Director of Financial Aid, Columbus College of Art & Design, 60 Cleveland Avenue, Columbus, OH 43215-1758, 614-224-9101 Ext. 3274 or toll-free 877-997-2223. Fax: 614-222-4034. E-mail: aschofield@ccad.edu. Website: http://www.ccad.edu/.

COLUMBUS STATE UNIVERSITY
Columbus, GA

Tuition & fees (GA res): $7076	Average undergraduate aid package: $9309

ABOUT THE INSTITUTION State-supported, coed. **Awards:** certificates, associate, bachelor's, master's, and doctoral degrees. 40 undergraduate majors. **Total enrollment:** 8,407. Undergraduates: 6,789. Freshmen: 926. Federal methodology is used as a basis for awarding need-based institutional aid.

UNDERGRADUATE EXPENSES for 2016–2017 Application fee: $40. **Tuition, state resident:** full-time $5226; part-time $174.20 per credit hour. **Tuition, nonresident:** full-time $18,444; part-time $614.80 per credit hour. **Required fees:** full-time $1850; $925 per term. Full-time tuition and fees vary according to course load, degree level, and program. Part-time tuition and fees vary according to course load, degree level, and program. **College room and board:** $10,198; **Room only:** $6344. Room and board charges vary according to board plan and housing facility.

FRESHMAN FINANCIAL AID (Fall 2016, est.) 787 applied for aid; of those 81% were deemed to have need. 99% of freshmen with need received aid; of those 19% had need fully met. **Average percent of need met:** 68% (excluding resources awarded to replace EFC). **Average financial aid package:** $9304 (excluding resources awarded to replace EFC). 4% of all full-time freshmen had no need and received non-need-based gift aid.

UNDERGRADUATE FINANCIAL AID (Fall 2016, est.) 4,110 applied for aid; of those 83% were deemed to have need. 99% of undergraduates with need received aid; of those 16% had need fully met. **Average percent of need met:** 69% (excluding resources awarded to replace EFC). **Average financial aid package:** $9309 (excluding resources awarded to replace EFC). 4% of all full-time undergraduates had no need and received non-need-based gift aid.

GIFT AID (NEED-BASED) Total amount: $14,958,809 (100% federal). **Receiving aid:** Freshmen: 50% (421); all full-time undergraduates: 52% (2,472). **Average award:** Freshmen: $5083; Undergraduates: $4915. **Scholarships, grants, and awards:** Federal Pell, FSEOG, state, private, college/university gift aid from institutional funds.

GIFT AID (NON-NEED-BASED) Total amount: $9,653,104 (89% state, 6% institutional, 5% external sources). **Receiving aid:** Freshmen: 45% (382). Undergrad-

uates: 30% (1,400). **Average award:** Freshmen: $1853. Undergraduates: $1695. **Scholarships, grants, and awards by category:** Academic interests/achievement: biological sciences, business, communication, computer science, education, English, general academic interests/achievements, health fields, humanities, international studies, mathematics, military science, physical sciences. Creative arts/performance: art/fine arts, dance, music, performing arts, theater/drama. Special achievements/activities: cheerleading/drum major, community service, general special achievements/activities, leadership. **ROTC:** Army.

LOANS Student loans: $31,055,176 (46% need-based, 54% non-need-based). 71% of past graduating class borrowed through all loan programs. **Average indebtedness per student:** $31,676. **Average need-based loan:** Freshmen: $3485. Undergraduates: $4314. **Parent loans:** $3,201,013 (100% non-need-based). **Programs:** Federal Direct (Subsidized and Unsubsidized Stafford, PLUS), Perkins, Federal Nursing, state, college/university.

WORK-STUDY Federal work-study: Total amount: $614,216; jobs available.

ATHLETIC AWARDS Total amount: $1,098,389 (100% non-need-based).

APPLYING FOR FINANCIAL AID Required financial aid form: FAFSA. **Financial aid deadline (priority):** 5/1. **Notification date:** Continuous beginning 5/15.

CONTACT Ms. Patricia Garrett, Associate Director of Financial Aid, Columbus State University, 4225 University Avenue, Columbus, GA 31907-5645, 706-507-8800 or toll-free 866-264-2035. Fax: 706-568-2230. E-mail: garrett_patricia2@columbusstate.edu. Website: http://www.columbusstate.edu/.

COMPASS COLLEGE OF CINEMATIC ARTS
Grand Rapids, MI

CONTACT Financial Aid Office, Compass College of Cinematic Arts, 41 Sheldon Boulevard SE, Grand Rapids, MI 49503, 616-988-1000. Website: http://www.compass.edu/.

CONCEPTION SEMINARY COLLEGE
Conception, MO

ABOUT THE INSTITUTION Independent Roman Catholic, men only. **Awards:** certificates and bachelor's degrees. 3 undergraduate majors.

GIFT AID (NEED-BASED) Scholarships, grants, and awards: Federal Pell, FSEOG, private, college/university gift aid from institutional funds.

GIFT AID (NON-NEED-BASED) Scholarships, grants, and awards by category: Academic interests/achievement: general academic interests/achievements. Special characteristics: religious affiliation.

LOANS Programs: Federal Direct (Subsidized and Unsubsidized Stafford, PLUS).

APPLYING FOR FINANCIAL AID Required financial aid form: FAFSA.

CONTACT Br. Justin Hernandez, PhD, Financial Aid Director, Conception Seminary College, 37174 State Highway VV, Conception, MO 64433-0502, 660-944-2851. Fax: 660-944-2829. E-mail: justin@conception.edu. Website: http://www.conception.edu/.

CONCORDIA COLLEGE
Moorhead, MN

Tuition & fees: $36,878	Average undergraduate aid package: $28,457

ABOUT THE INSTITUTION Independent Evangelical Lutheran Church in America, coed. **Awards:** bachelor's and master's degrees. 55 undergraduate majors. **Total enrollment:** 2,132. Undergraduates: 2,114. Freshmen: 545. Federal methodology is used as a basis for awarding need-based institutional aid.

UNDERGRADUATE EXPENSES for 2016–2017 Application fee: $20. **Comprehensive fee:** $44,688 includes full-time tuition ($36,650), mandatory fees ($228), and room and board ($7810). **College room only:** $3360. Full-time tuition and fees vary according to course load and degree level. Room and board charges vary according to board plan and housing facility. *Part-time tuition:* $1380 per credit. *Part-time fees:* $114 per term. Part-time tuition and fees vary according to course load and degree level.

FRESHMAN FINANCIAL AID (Fall 2015) 492 applied for aid; of those 79% were deemed to have need. 100% of freshmen with need received aid; of those 26% had need fully met. *Average percent of need met:* 91% (excluding resources awarded to replace EFC). *Average financial aid package:* $29,404 (excluding resources awarded to replace EFC). 24% of all full-time freshmen had no need and received non-need-based gift aid.

UNDERGRADUATE FINANCIAL AID (Fall 2015) 1,788 applied for aid; of those 86% were deemed to have need. 100% of undergraduates with need received aid; of those 21% had need fully met. *Average percent of need met:* 90% (excluding resources awarded to replace EFC). *Average financial aid package:* $28,457 (excluding resources awarded to replace EFC). 26% of all full-time undergraduates had no need and received non-need-based gift aid.

GIFT AID (NEED-BASED) *Total amount:* $31,516,003 (9% federal, 8% state, 81% institutional, 2% external sources). *Receiving aid:* Freshmen: 74% (386); all full-time undergraduates: 71% (1,509). *Average award:* Freshmen: $23,282; Undergraduates: $20,861. *Scholarships, grants, and awards:* Federal Pell, FSEOG, state, private, college/university gift aid from institutional funds.

GIFT AID (NON-NEED-BASED) *Total amount:* $10,008,469 (3% federal, 92% institutional, 5% external sources). *Receiving aid:* Freshmen: 13% (67). Undergraduates: 12% (248). *Average award:* Freshmen: $16,329. Undergraduates: $14,568. *Scholarships, grants, and awards by category:* Academic interests/achievement: general academic interests/achievements. Creative arts/performance: art/fine arts, debating, music, theater/drama. Special characteristics: international students. *Tuition waivers:* Full or partial for employees or children of employees. *ROTC:* Army cooperative, Air Force cooperative.

LOANS *Student loans:* $16,667,591 (57% need-based, 43% non-need-based). 77% of past graduating class borrowed through all loan programs. *Average need-based loan:* Freshmen: $4556. Undergraduates: $5463. *Parent loans:* $1,950,649 (21% need-based, 79% non-need-based). *Programs:* Federal Direct (Subsidized and Unsubsidized Stafford, PLUS), Perkins, state, college/university, private loans.

WORK-STUDY *Federal work-study:* jobs available. *State or other work-study/employment:* Total amount: $1,681,315 (17% need-based, 83% non-need-based). Part-time jobs available.

APPLYING FOR FINANCIAL AID *Required financial aid form:* FAFSA. *Financial aid deadline:* Continuous. *Notification date:* Continuous beginning 12/15. Students must reply within 6 weeks of notification.

CONTACT Mr. Eric Addington, Associate Vice President for Enrollment and Financial Aid, Concordia College, 901 South 8th Street, Moorhead, MN 56562, 218-299-3010 or toll-free 800-699-9897. *Fax:* 218-299-3025. *E-mail:* eaddingt@cord.edu. *Website:* http://www.concordiacollege.edu/.

CONCORDIA COLLEGE ALABAMA
Selma, AL

CONTACT Mrs. T. H. Bridges, Financial Aid Office, Concordia College Alabama, 1804 Green Street, Selma, AL 36701, 334-874-5700. *Fax:* 334-874-3728. *E-mail:* tbridges@concordiaselma.edu. *Website:* http://www.ccal.edu/.

CONCORDIA COLLEGE–NEW YORK
Bronxville, NY

CONTACT Janice Spikereit, Director of Financial Aid, Concordia College–New York, 171 White Plains Road, Bronxville, NY 10708, 914-337-9300 Ext. 2146 or toll-free 800-YES-COLLEGE. *Fax:* 914-395-4500. *E-mail:* financialaid@concordia-ny.edu. *Website:* http://www.concordia-ny.edu/.

CONCORDIA UNIVERSITY
Portland, OR

ABOUT THE INSTITUTION Independent Lutheran Church–Missouri Synod, coed. 33 undergraduate majors.

GIFT AID (NEED-BASED) *Scholarships, grants, and awards:* Federal Pell, FSEOG, state, college/university gift aid from institutional funds.

GIFT AID (NON-NEED-BASED) *Scholarships, grants, and awards by category:* Academic interests/achievement: general academic interests/achievements, religion/biblical studies. Creative arts/performance: music. Special achievements/activities: leadership, religious involvement. Special characteristics: children of faculty/staff, general special characteristics, relatives of clergy, religious affiliation.

LOANS *Programs:* Federal Direct (Subsidized and Unsubsidized Stafford, PLUS), state, alternative loans.

APPLYING FOR FINANCIAL AID *Required financial aid form:* FAFSA.

CONTACT Mr. Robert Clarke, Director of Financial Aid, Concordia University, 2811 Northeast Holman Street, Portland, OR 97211-6099, 503-493-6555 or toll-free 800-321-9371. *Fax:* 503-280-8661. *E-mail:* jcullen@cu-portland.edu. *Website:* http://www.cu-portland.edu/.

CONCORDIA UNIVERSITY ANN ARBOR
Ann Arbor, MI

Tuition & fees: $27,710	Average undergraduate aid package: $22,110

ABOUT THE INSTITUTION Independent Lutheran Church–Missouri Synod, coed. 35 undergraduate majors. Federal methodology is used as a basis for awarding need-based institutional aid.

UNDERGRADUATE EXPENSES for 2016–2017 *Comprehensive fee:* $37,290 includes full-time tuition ($27,640), mandatory fees ($70), and room and board ($9580). *College room only:* $7080. Full-time tuition and fees vary according to course load, degree level, location, and program. Room and board charges vary according to housing facility. Part-time tuition and fees vary according to course load, degree level, location, and program.

FRESHMAN FINANCIAL AID (Fall 2016, est.) 195 applied for aid; of those 91% were deemed to have need. 100% of freshmen with need received aid; of those 22% had need fully met. *Average percent of need met:* 70% (excluding resources awarded to replace EFC). *Average financial aid package:* $22,573 (excluding resources awarded to replace EFC). 5% of all full-time freshmen had no need and received non-need-based gift aid.

UNDERGRADUATE FINANCIAL AID (Fall 2016, est.) 712 applied for aid; of those 92% were deemed to have need. 99% of undergraduates with need received aid; of those 22% had need fully met. *Average percent of need met:* 70% (excluding resources awarded to replace EFC). *Average financial aid package:* $22,110 (excluding resources awarded to replace EFC). 5% of all full-time undergraduates had no need and received non-need-based gift aid.

GIFT AID (NEED-BASED) *Total amount:* $8,097,828 (16% federal, 6% state, 73% institutional, 5% external sources). *Receiving aid:* Freshmen: 86% (172); all full-time undergraduates: 84% (629). *Average award:* Freshmen: $15,627; Undergraduates: $14,781. *Scholarships, grants, and awards:* Federal Pell, FSEOG, state, private, college/university gift aid from institutional funds.

GIFT AID (NON-NEED-BASED) *Total amount:* $1,389,738 (100% institutional). *Receiving aid:* Freshmen: 18% (36). Undergraduates: 17% (125). *Average award:* Freshmen: $10,329. Undergraduates: $10,354. *Scholarships, grants, and awards by category:* Academic interests/achievement: business, education, general academic interests/achievements, religion/biblical studies. Creative arts/performance: art/fine arts, music, performing arts, theater/drama. Special characteristics: children and siblings of alumni, children of faculty/staff, ethnic background, general special characteristics, out-of-state students, religious affiliation, siblings of current students. *Tuition waivers:* Full or partial for employees or children of employees.

LOANS *Student loans:* $4,967,766 (62% need-based, 38% non-need-based). 80% of past graduating class borrowed through all loan programs. *Average indebtedness per student:* $20,641. *Average need-based loan:* Freshmen: $5822. Undergraduates: $6765. *Parent loans:* $1,856,180 (100% non-need-based). *Programs:* Federal Direct (Subsidized and Unsubsidized Stafford, PLUS), Perkins.

WORK-STUDY *Federal work-study:* Total amount: $551,990; jobs available. *State or other work-study/employment:* Part-time jobs available.

ATHLETIC AWARDS Total amount: $1,960,608 (88% need-based, 12% non-need-based).

APPLYING FOR FINANCIAL AID *Required financial aid form:* FAFSA. *Financial aid deadline (priority):* 3/15. *Notification date:* Continuous beginning 2/1. Students must reply by 5/1 or within 3 weeks of notification.

CONTACT Vicki Waschow, Financial Aid Office, Concordia University Ann Arbor, 4090 Geddes Road, Ann Arbor, MI 48105-2797, 734-995-7408 or toll-free 877-995-7520 (in-state), 877-955-7520 (out-of-state). *Fax:* 734-995-4610. *E-mail:* vicki.waschow@cuaa.edu. *Website:* http://www.cuaa.edu/.

CONCORDIA UNIVERSITY CHICAGO
River Forest, IL

Tuition & fees: $31,562	Average undergraduate aid package: $20,605

ABOUT THE INSTITUTION Independent Lutheran Church–Missouri Synod, coed. *Awards:* certificates, associate, bachelor's, master's, and doctoral degrees. 72 undergraduate majors. *Total enrollment:* 5,603. Undergraduates: 1,530. Freshmen: 356. Federal methodology is used as a basis for awarding need-based institutional aid.

UNDERGRADUATE EXPENSES for 2017–2018 *Comprehensive fee:* $41,010 includes full-time tuition ($30,656), mandatory fees ($906), and room and board ($9448). *College room only:* $5948. Full-time tuition and fees vary according to course load, degree level, and reciprocity agreements. Room and board charges vary according to board plan and housing facility. *Part-time tuition:* $924 per credit hour. Part-time tuition and fees vary according to course load, degree level, and reciprocity agreements.

FRESHMAN FINANCIAL AID (Fall 2015) 291 applied for aid; of those 91% were deemed to have need. 100% of freshmen with need received aid; of those 13% had need fully met. *Average percent of need met:* 76% (excluding resources awarded to replace EFC). *Average financial aid package:* $22,448 (excluding resources awarded to replace EFC). 9% of all full-time freshmen had no need and received non-need-based gift aid.

UNDERGRADUATE FINANCIAL AID (Fall 2015) 1,265 applied for aid; of those 92% were deemed to have need. 99% of undergraduates with need received aid; of those 15% had need fully met. *Average percent of need met:* 75% (excluding resources awarded to replace EFC). *Average financial aid package:* $20,605 (excluding resources awarded to replace EFC). 10% of all full-time undergraduates had no need and received non-need-based gift aid.

GIFT AID (NEED-BASED) *Total amount:* $18,842,700 (15% federal, 12% state, 73% institutional). *Receiving aid:* Freshmen: 90% (266); all full-time undergraduates: 84% (1,131). *Average award:* Freshmen: $18,952; Undergraduates: $16,518. *Scholarships, grants, and awards:* Federal Pell, FSEOG, state, private, college/university gift aid from institutional funds.

GIFT AID (NON-NEED-BASED) *Total amount:* $3,409,556 (79% institutional, 21% external sources). *Receiving aid:* Freshmen: 10% (28). Undergraduates: 8% (112). *Average award:* Freshmen: $13,401. Undergraduates: $13,473. *Scholarships, grants, and awards by category:* Academic interests/achievement: biological sciences, business, communication, computer science, education, English, foreign languages, general academic interests/achievements, mathematics, religion/biblical studies. *Creative arts/performance:* music. *Special characteristics:* children and siblings of alumni, children of faculty/staff, international students, religious affiliation. *Tuition waivers:* Full or partial for children of alumni, employees or children of employees, senior citizens.

LOANS *Student loans:* $8,829,058 (45% need-based, 55% non-need-based). 84% of past graduating class borrowed through all loan programs. *Average indebtedness per student:* $32,549. *Average need-based loan:* Freshmen: $3231. Undergraduates: $4264. *Parent loans:* $1,810,214 (100% non-need-based). *Programs:* Federal Direct (Subsidized and Unsubsidized Stafford, PLUS), Perkins.

WORK-STUDY *Federal work-study:* jobs available. *State or other work-study/employment:* Total amount: $604,697 (100% non-need-based). Part-time jobs available.

APPLYING FOR FINANCIAL AID *Required financial aid form:* FAFSA. *Financial aid deadline:* 6/1 (priority: 12/1). *Notification date:* Continuous beginning 1/24.

CONTACT Aida Asencio-Pinto, Director of Financial Aid, Concordia University Chicago, 7400 Augusta Street, River Forest, IL 60305-1499, 708-209-3113 or toll-free 800-285-2668. *Fax:* 708-488-4102. *E-mail:* aida.asenciopinto@cuchicago.edu. *Website:* http://www.cuchicago.edu/.

CONCORDIA UNIVERSITY IRVINE
Irvine, CA

Tuition & fees: $34,100	Average undergraduate aid package: $21,103

ABOUT THE INSTITUTION Independent Lutheran Church–Missouri Synod, coed. *Awards:* associate, bachelor's, master's, and doctoral degrees (associate's degree for international students only). 29 undergraduate majors. *Total enrollment:* 4,299. Undergraduates: 1,925. Freshmen: 407. Federal methodology is used as a basis for awarding need-based institutional aid.

UNDERGRADUATE EXPENSES for 2017–2018 *Application fee:* $50. *Comprehensive fee:* $44,860 includes full-time tuition ($33,400), mandatory fees ($700), and room and board ($10,760). *College room only:* $6200. Full-time tuition and fees vary according to course load. Room and board charges vary according to board plan and housing facility. *Part-time tuition:* $995 per unit. Part-time tuition and fees vary according to course load.

FRESHMAN FINANCIAL AID (Fall 2016, est.) 363 applied for aid; of those 81% were deemed to have need. 100% of freshmen with need received aid; of those 21% had need fully met. *Average percent of need met:* 74% (excluding resources awarded to replace EFC). *Average financial aid package:* $26,341 (excluding resources awarded to replace EFC). 18% of all full-time freshmen had no need and received non-need-based gift aid.

UNDERGRADUATE FINANCIAL AID (Fall 2016, est.) 1,443 applied for aid; of those 88% were deemed to have need. 99% of undergraduates with need received aid; of those 15% had need fully met. *Average percent of need met:* 62% (excluding resources awarded to replace EFC). *Average financial aid package:* $21,103 (excluding resources awarded to replace EFC). 16% of all full-time undergraduates had no need and received non-need-based gift aid.

GIFT AID (NEED-BASED) *Total amount:* $18,482,843 (14% federal, 17% state, 69% institutional). *Receiving aid:* Freshmen: 71% (287); all full-time undergraduates: 63% (1,125). *Average award:* Freshmen: $21,886; Undergraduates: $18,100. *Scholarships, grants, and awards:* Federal Pell, FSEOG, state, private, college/university gift aid from institutional funds.

GIFT AID (NON-NEED-BASED) *Total amount:* $4,556,784 (100% institutional). *Receiving aid:* Freshmen: 12% (48). Undergraduates: 7% (125). *Average award:* Freshmen: $13,868. Undergraduates: $10,880. *Scholarships, grants, and awards by category:* Academic interests/achievement: 1,088 awards ($8,802,284 total): general academic interests/achievements. Creative arts/performance: 263 awards ($1,451,686 total): debating, music, theater/drama. Special characteristics: 318 awards ($1,780,637 total): children of faculty/staff, first-generation college students, religious affiliation. *Tuition waivers:* Full or partial for employees or children of employees.

LOANS *Student loans:* $12,530,933 (35% need-based, 65% non-need-based). 73% of past graduating class borrowed through all loan programs. *Average indebtedness per student:* $31,747. *Average need-based loan:* Freshmen: $3457. Undergraduates: $4513. *Parent loans:* $4,600,449 (100% non-need-based). *Programs:* Federal Direct (Subsidized and Unsubsidized Stafford, PLUS), private loans.

WORK-STUDY *Federal work-study:* Total amount: $128,750; 55 jobs averaging $2320. *State or other work-study/employment:* Part-time jobs available.

ATHLETIC AWARDS Total amount: $3,409,400 (62% need-based, 38% non-need-based).

APPLYING FOR FINANCIAL AID *Required financial aid forms:* FAFSA, state aid form, department scholarship application form. *Financial aid deadline:* 3/2. *Notification date:* Continuous beginning 3/1. Students must reply within 4 weeks of notification.

CONTACT Lori McDonald, Director of Financial Aid, Concordia University Irvine, 1530 Concordia West, Irvine, CA 92612-3299, 949-214-3074 or toll-free 800-229-1200. *Fax:* 949-214-3500. *E-mail:* lori.mcdonald@cui.edu. *Website:* http://www.cui.edu/.

CONCORDIA UNIVERSITY, NEBRASKA
Seward, NE

Tuition & fees: $31,000	Average undergraduate aid package: $23,520

ABOUT THE INSTITUTION Independent Lutheran Church–Missouri Synod, coed. **Awards:** bachelor's and master's degrees. 46 undergraduate majors. **Total enrollment:** 2,757. Undergraduates: 1,794. Freshmen: 323. Federal methodology is used as a basis for awarding need-based institutional aid.

UNDERGRADUATE EXPENSES for 2017–2018 **Comprehensive fee:** $39,100 includes full-time tuition ($30,400), mandatory fees ($600), and room and board ($8100). **College room only:** $3400. Room and board charges vary according to board plan and housing facility. **Part-time tuition:** $890 per credit hour.

FRESHMAN FINANCIAL AID (Fall 2016, est.) 301 applied for aid; of those 87% were deemed to have need. 100% of freshmen with need received aid; of those 31% had need fully met. **Average percent of need met:** 81% (excluding resources awarded to replace EFC). **Average financial aid package:** $23,597 (excluding resources awarded to replace EFC). 7% of all full-time freshmen had no need and received non-need-based gift aid.

UNDERGRADUATE FINANCIAL AID (Fall 2016, est.) 1,023 applied for aid; of those 88% were deemed to have need. 100% of undergraduates with need received aid; of those 29% had need fully met. **Average percent of need met:** 81% (excluding resources awarded to replace EFC). **Average financial aid package:** $23,520 (excluding resources awarded to replace EFC). 10% of all full-time undergraduates had no need and received non-need-based gift aid.

GIFT AID (NEED-BASED) Total amount: $14,520,686 (11% federal, 1% state, 75% institutional, 13% external sources). **Receiving aid:** Freshmen: 81% (261); all full-time undergraduates: 75% (899). **Average award:** Freshmen: $19,343; Undergraduates: $18,466. **Scholarships, grants, and awards:** Federal Pell, FSEOG, state, private, college/university gift aid from institutional funds.

GIFT AID (NON-NEED-BASED) Total amount: $4,981,865 (100% institutional). **Receiving aid:** Freshmen: 22% (70). Undergraduates: 16% (190). **Average award:** Freshmen: $15,082. Undergraduates: $14,690. **Scholarships, grants, and awards by category:** Academic interests/achievement: biological sciences, business, communication, computer science, education, English, general academic interests/achievements, health fields, humanities, mathematics, physical sciences, premedicine, religion/biblical studies, social sciences. Creative arts/performance: applied art and design, art/fine arts, dance, debating, music, theater/drama. Special achievements/activities: cheerleading/drum major. Special characteristics: children and siblings of alumni, children of educators, children of faculty/staff, international students, local/state students, members of minority groups, religious affiliation, veterans, veterans' children. **Tuition waivers:** Full or partial for employees or children of employees. **ROTC:** Army cooperative, Air Force cooperative.

LOANS Student loans: $6,631,867 (43% need-based, 57% non-need-based). 73% of past graduating class borrowed through all loan programs. Average indebtedness per student: $26,328. **Average need-based loan:** Freshmen: $3739. Undergraduates: $4658. **Parent loans:** $1,555,732 (100% non-need-based). **Programs:** Federal Direct (Subsidized and Unsubsidized Stafford, PLUS), Perkins.

WORK-STUDY Federal work-study: Total amount: $101,788; 80 jobs averaging $1400.

ATHLETIC AWARDS Total amount: $3,395,800 (72% need-based, 28% non-need-based).

APPLYING FOR FINANCIAL AID Required financial aid form: FAFSA. **Financial aid deadline (priority):** 3/1. **Notification date:** Continuous beginning 3/1. Students must reply within 4 weeks of notification.

CONTACT Mr. Aaron W. Roberts, Director of Undergraduate Recruitment, Concordia University, Nebraska, 800 North Columbia Avenue, Seward, NE 68434-1556, 800-535-5494. Fax: 402-643-4073. E-mail: admiss@cune.edu. Website: http://www.cune.edu/.

CONCORDIA UNIVERSITY, ST. PAUL
St. Paul, MN

Tuition & fees: $21,750	Average undergraduate aid package: $14,088

ABOUT THE INSTITUTION Independent Lutheran Church–Missouri Synod, coed. **Awards:** certificates, associate, bachelor's, master's, and doctoral degrees. 60 undergraduate majors. **Total enrollment:** 4,380. Undergraduates: 2,659. Freshmen: 248. Federal methodology is used as a basis for awarding need-based institutional aid.

UNDERGRADUATE EXPENSES for 2017–2018 **Application fee:** $30. **Comprehensive fee:** $30,500 includes full-time tuition ($21,750) and room and board ($8750). Full-time tuition and fees vary according to degree level and program. Room and board charges vary according to board plan and housing facility. **Part-time tuition:** $600 per credit. Part-time tuition and fees vary according to course load, degree level, and program.

FRESHMAN FINANCIAL AID (Fall 2016, est.) 232 applied for aid; of those 81% were deemed to have need. 99% of freshmen with need received aid; of those 11% had need fully met. **Average percent of need met:** 66% (excluding resources awarded to replace EFC). **Average financial aid package:** $16,332 (excluding resources awarded to replace EFC). 14% of all full-time freshmen had no need and received non-need-based gift aid.

UNDERGRADUATE FINANCIAL AID (Fall 2016, est.) 1,113 applied for aid; of those 85% were deemed to have need. 98% of undergraduates with need received aid; of those 11% had need fully met. **Average percent of need met:** 59% (excluding resources awarded to replace EFC). **Average financial aid package:** $14,088 (excluding resources awarded to replace EFC). 12% of all full-time undergraduates had no need and received non-need-based gift aid.

GIFT AID (NEED-BASED) Total amount: $10,234,482 (36% federal, 26% state, 37% institutional, 1% external sources). **Receiving aid:** Freshmen: 74% (184); all full-time undergraduates: 67% (884). **Average award:** Freshmen: $12,077; Undergraduates: $9941. **Scholarships, grants, and awards:** Federal Pell, FSEOG, state, private, college/university gift aid from institutional funds.

GIFT AID (NON-NEED-BASED) Total amount: $1,469,196 (2% federal, 1% state, 97% institutional). **Receiving aid:** Freshmen: 6% (14). Undergraduates: 6% (73). **Average award:** Freshmen: $4594. Undergraduates: $4806. **Scholarships, grants, and awards by category:** Academic interests/achievement: 1,065 awards ($3,288,905 total): general academic interests/achievements, religion/biblical studies. Creative arts/performance: 109 awards ($92,500 total): music, theater/drama. Special characteristics: 172 awards ($402,512 total): children of faculty/staff, religious affiliation, veterans, veterans' children. **Tuition waivers:** Full or partial for employees or children of employees. **ROTC:** Army cooperative, Air Force cooperative.

LOANS Student loans: $14,439,633 (38% need-based, 62% non-need-based). 80% of past graduating class borrowed through all loan programs. Average indebtedness per student: $33,183. **Average need-based loan:** Freshmen: $3461. Undergraduates: $4493. **Parent loans:** $912,601 (100% non-need-based). **Programs:** Federal Direct (Subsidized and Unsubsidized Stafford, PLUS), Perkins, state, private loans.

WORK-STUDY Federal work-study: Total amount: $160,555; 110 jobs averaging $2358. **State or other work-study/employment:** Total amount: $547,332 (100% need-based). 282 part-time jobs averaging $2335.

ATHLETIC AWARDS Total amount: $1,822,433 (56% need-based, 44% non-need-based).

APPLYING FOR FINANCIAL AID Required financial aid forms: FAFSA, state aid form. **Financial aid deadline (priority):** 5/1. **Notification date:** Continuous beginning 5/10.

CONTACT Ms. Jeanie Peck, Financial Aid Director, Concordia University, St. Paul, 1282 Concordia Avenue, St. Paul, MN 55104-5494, 651-603-6300 or toll-free 800-333-4705. Fax: 651-603-6298. E-mail: finaid@csp.edu. Website: http://www.csp.edu/.

CONCORDIA UNIVERSITY TEXAS
Austin, TX

Tuition & fees: $29,260	Average undergraduate aid package: $23,364

ABOUT THE INSTITUTION Independent Lutheran Church–Missouri Synod, coed. 24 undergraduate majors. Federal methodology is used as a basis for awarding need-based institutional aid.

UNDERGRADUATE EXPENSES for 2016–2017 Comprehensive fee: $39,096 includes full-time tuition ($28,700), mandatory fees ($560), and room and board ($9836). **College room only:** $7586. Full-time tuition and fees vary according to course load, degree level, and program. Room and board charges vary according to board plan. **Part-time tuition:** $940 per credit hour. **Part-time fees:** $120 per credit hour; $10 per credit hour. Part-time tuition and fees vary according to course load, degree level, and program.

FRESHMAN FINANCIAL AID (Fall 2015) 235 applied for aid; of those 89% were deemed to have need. 100% of freshmen with need received aid; of those 23% had need fully met. **Average percent of need met:** 79% (excluding resources awarded to replace EFC). **Average financial aid package:** $26,347 (excluding resources awarded to replace EFC). 17% of all full-time freshmen had no need and received non-need-based gift aid.

UNDERGRADUATE FINANCIAL AID (Fall 2015) 1,027 applied for aid; of those 89% were deemed to have need. 99% of undergraduates with need received aid; of those 18% had need fully met. **Average percent of need met:** 74% (excluding resources awarded to replace EFC). **Average financial aid package:** $23,364 (excluding resources awarded to replace EFC). 20% of all full-time undergraduates had no need and received non-need-based gift aid.

GIFT AID (NEED-BASED) Total amount: $16,537,191 (20% federal, 16% state, 64% institutional). **Receiving aid:** Freshmen: 78% (199); all full-time undergraduates: 70% (864). **Average award:** Freshmen: $19,676; Undergraduates: $17,402. **Scholarships, grants, and awards:** Federal Pell, FSEOG, state, private, college/university gift aid from institutional funds.

GIFT AID (NON-NEED-BASED) Total amount: $4,075,084 (100% institutional). **Receiving aid:** Freshmen: 18% (46). Undergraduates: 12% (142). **Average award:** Freshmen: $13,843. Undergraduates: $12,263. **Scholarships, grants, and awards by category:** Academic interests/achievement: biological sciences, business, communication, computer science, education, English, foreign languages, general academic interests/achievements, home economics, international studies, mathematics, physical sciences, religion/biblical studies, social sciences. **Creative arts/performance:** music. **Special achievements/activities:** junior miss, leadership, religious involvement. **Special characteristics:** adult students, children and siblings of alumni, children of faculty/staff, international students, religious affiliation, siblings of current students, veterans, veterans' children. **Tuition waivers:** Full or partial for children of alumni, employees or children of employees.

LOANS Student loans: $10,361,686 (55% need-based, 45% non-need-based). 78% of past graduating class borrowed through all loan programs. **Average indebtedness per student:** $30,699. **Average need-based loan:** Freshmen: $7052. Undergraduates: $6476. **Parent loans:** $2,007,236 (100% non-need-based). **Programs:** Federal Direct (Subsidized and Unsubsidized Stafford, PLUS), state.

WORK-STUDY Federal work-study: 133 jobs averaging $2563.

APPLYING FOR FINANCIAL AID Required financial aid forms: FAFSA, state aid form. **Financial aid deadline:** Continuous. **Notification date:** Continuous beginning 2/1. Students must reply within 2 weeks of notification.

CONTACT Mr. Russell Jeffrey, Director of Student Financial Services, Concordia University Texas, 11400 Concordia University Drive, Austin, TX 78726, 512-313-4672 or toll-free 800-865-4282. *Fax:* 512-313-1670. *E-mail:* russell.jeffrey@concordia.edu. *Website:* http://www.concordia.edu/.

CONCORDIA UNIVERSITY WISCONSIN
Mequon, WI

Tuition & fees: $28,600	Average undergraduate aid package: $21,208

ABOUT THE INSTITUTION Independent Lutheran Church–Missouri Synod, coed. **Awards:** certificates, associate, bachelor's, master's, and doctoral degrees. 73 undergraduate majors. **Total enrollment:** 7,721. Undergraduates: 3,830. Freshmen: 478. Federal methodology is used as a basis for awarding need-based institutional aid.

UNDERGRADUATE EXPENSES for 2017–2018 Comprehensive fee: $39,130 includes full-time tuition ($28,330), mandatory fees ($270), and room and board ($10,530). **College room only:** $7970. Full-time tuition and fees vary according to program. Room and board charges vary according to board plan. Part-time tuition and fees vary according to program.

FRESHMAN FINANCIAL AID (Fall 2016, est.) 454 applied for aid; of those 86% were deemed to have need. 100% of freshmen with need received aid; of those 33% had need fully met. **Average percent of need met:** 80% (excluding resources awarded to replace EFC). **Average financial aid package:** $24,318 (excluding resources awarded to replace EFC). 17% of all full-time freshmen had no need and received non-need-based gift aid.

UNDERGRADUATE FINANCIAL AID (Fall 2016, est.) 2,287 applied for aid; of those 88% were deemed to have need. 100% of undergraduates with need received aid; of those 25% had need fully met. **Average percent of need met:** 71% (excluding resources awarded to replace EFC). **Average financial aid package:** $21,208 (excluding resources awarded to replace EFC). 16% of all full-time undergraduates had no need and received non-need-based gift aid.

GIFT AID (NEED-BASED) Total amount: $57,057,087 (17% federal, 8% state, 70% institutional, 5% external sources). **Receiving aid:** Freshmen: 78% (373); all full-time undergraduates: 74% (1,857). **Average award:** Freshmen: $16,404; Undergraduates: $13,500. **Scholarships, grants, and awards:** Federal Pell, FSEOG, state, private, college/university gift aid from institutional funds.

GIFT AID (NON-NEED-BASED) Total amount: $15,884,771 (100% institutional). **Receiving aid:** Freshmen: 24% (116). Undergraduates: 18% (442). **Average award:** Freshmen: $12,481. Undergraduates: $11,364. **Scholarships, grants, and awards by category:** Academic interests/achievement: religion/biblical studies. Creative arts/performance: music. Special characteristics: out-of-state students.

LOANS Student loans: $51,335,881 (60% need-based, 40% non-need-based). 83% of past graduating class borrowed through all loan programs. **Average indebtedness per student:** $33,298. **Average need-based loan:** Freshmen: $7197. Undergraduates: $7753. **Parent loans:** $9,167,308 (100% non-need-based). **Programs:** Federal Direct (Subsidized and Unsubsidized Stafford, PLUS), state.

WORK-STUDY Federal work-study: Total amount: $2,941,564; jobs available.

APPLYING FOR FINANCIAL AID Required financial aid form: FAFSA. **Financial aid deadline:** 4/15 (priority: 3/15). **Notification date:** Continuous beginning 2/15. Students must reply within 3 weeks of notification.

CONTACT Mr. Steven P. Taylor, Director of Financial Aid, Concordia University Wisconsin, 12800 North Lake Shore Drive, Mequon, WI 53097-2402, 262-243-4392 or toll-free 888-628-9472. *Fax:* 262-243-2992. *E-mail:* steve.taylor@cuw.edu. *Website:* http://www.cuw.edu/.

CONCORD UNIVERSITY
Athens, WV

Tuition & fees (WV res): $7080	Average undergraduate aid package: $8425

ABOUT THE INSTITUTION State-supported, coed. **Awards:** certificates, bachelor's, and master's degrees. 31 undergraduate majors. **Total enrollment:** 2,451. Undergraduates: 2,102. Freshmen: 471. Federal methodology is used as a basis for awarding need-based institutional aid.

UNDERGRADUATE EXPENSES for 2016–2017 Tuition, state resident: full-time $7080; part-time $295 per credit hour. **Tuition, nonresident:** full-time $15,564; part-time $649 per credit hour. Full-time tuition and fees vary according to course load and program. Part-time tuition and fees vary according to course load and program. **College room and board:** $8350. Room and board charges vary according to board plan.

FRESHMAN FINANCIAL AID (Fall 2016, est.) 447 applied for aid; of those 82% were deemed to have need. 83% of freshmen with need received aid; of those 43% had need fully met. **Average percent of need met:** 83% (excluding resources awarded to replace EFC). **Average financial aid package:** $7863 (excluding resources awarded to replace EFC). 14% of all full-time freshmen had no need and received non-need-based gift aid.

UNDERGRADUATE FINANCIAL AID (Fall 2016, est.) 1,685 applied for aid; of those 84% were deemed to have need. 88% of undergraduates with need received aid; of those 38% had need fully met. **Average percent of need met:** 80% (excluding resources awarded to replace EFC). **Average financial aid package:** $8425

(excluding resources awarded to replace EFC). 11% of all full-time undergraduates had no need and received non-need-based gift aid.
GIFT AID (NEED-BASED) *Total amount:* $6,539,817 (70% federal, 28% state, 2% external sources). *Receiving aid:* Freshmen: 58% (274); all full-time undergraduates: 58% (1,092). *Average award:* Freshmen: $5113; Undergraduates: $5629. *Scholarships, grants, and awards:* Federal Pell, FSEOG, state, private, college/university gift aid from institutional funds.
GIFT AID (NON-NEED-BASED) *Total amount:* $4,740,844 (1% federal, 33% state, 37% institutional, 29% external sources). *Receiving aid:* Freshmen: 61% (285). Undergraduates: 41% (764). *Average award:* Freshmen: $3473. Undergraduates: $3434. *Scholarships, grants, and awards by category: Academic interests/achievement:* 2,363 awards ($1,383,009 total): business, communication, education, English, general academic interests/achievements, mathematics, physical sciences, premedicine, social sciences. *Creative arts/performance:* 15 awards ($38,483 total): art/fine arts, journalism/publications, music, theater/drama. *Special achievements/activities:* 6 awards ($2350 total): community service, general special achievements/activities, leadership. *Special characteristics:* 26 awards ($144,414 total): children of faculty/staff, veterans, veterans' children. *Tuition waivers:* Full or partial for employees or children of employees.
LOANS *Student loans:* $6,663,818 (42% need-based, 58% non-need-based). 89% of past graduating class borrowed through all loan programs. *Average indebtedness per student:* $21,176. *Average need-based loan:* Freshmen: $2948. Undergraduates: $3569. *Parent loans:* $862,067 (100% non-need-based). *Programs:* Federal Direct (Subsidized and Unsubsidized Stafford, PLUS), Perkins.
WORK-STUDY *Federal work-study:* Total amount: $227,445; 182 jobs averaging $1246.
ATHLETIC AWARDS Total amount: $1,469,266 (100% non-need-based).
APPLYING FOR FINANCIAL AID *Required financial aid forms:* FAFSA, institution's own form, state aid form, verification worksheet. *Financial aid deadline:* 4/15. *Notification date:* Continuous beginning 5/15. Students must reply within 3 weeks of notification.
CONTACT Debra Turner, Director of Financial Aid, Concord University, PO Box 1000, Athens, WV 24712-1000, 304-384-6069 or toll-free 888-384-5249. *Fax:* 304-384-3084. *E-mail:* turner@concord.edu.
Website: http://www.concord.edu/.

CONNECTICUT COLLEGE
New London, CT

Tuition & fees: $50,940	Average undergraduate aid package: $40,891

ABOUT THE INSTITUTION Independent, coed. *Awards:* bachelor's and master's degrees. 42 undergraduate majors. *Total enrollment:* 1,865. Undergraduates: 1,865. Freshmen: 472. Both federal and institutional methodology are used as a basis for awarding need-based institutional aid.
UNDERGRADUATE EXPENSES for 2016–2017 *Application fee:* $60. *Comprehensive fee:* $65,000 includes full-time tuition ($50,620), mandatory fees ($320), and room and board ($14,060). *College room only:* $8115. *Part-time tuition:* $1508 per credit hour.
FRESHMAN FINANCIAL AID (Fall 2016, est.) 328 applied for aid; of those 88% were deemed to have need. 100% of freshmen with need received aid; of those 100% had need fully met. *Average percent of need met:* 100% (excluding resources awarded to replace EFC). *Average financial aid package:* $42,724 (excluding resources awarded to replace EFC).
UNDERGRADUATE FINANCIAL AID (Fall 2016, est.) 1,125 applied for aid; of those 92% were deemed to have need. 100% of undergraduates with need received aid; of those 100% had need fully met. *Average percent of need met:* 100% (excluding resources awarded to replace EFC). *Average financial aid package:* $40,891 (excluding resources awarded to replace EFC).
GIFT AID (NEED-BASED) *Total amount:* $37,333,947 (4% federal, 94% institutional, 2% external sources). *Receiving aid:* Freshmen: 59% (280); all full-time undergraduates: 54% (974). *Average award:* Freshmen: $39,698; Undergraduates: $37,745. *Scholarships, grants, and awards:* Federal Pell, FSEOG, state, college/university gift aid from institutional funds.
GIFT AID (NON-NEED-BASED) *Total amount:* $537,431 (100% external sources). *Tuition waivers:* Full or partial for employees or children of employees.

LOANS *Student loans:* $8,469,531 (45% need-based, 55% non-need-based). 49% of past graduating class borrowed through all loan programs. *Average indebtedness per student:* $27,514. *Average need-based loan:* Freshmen: $3294. Undergraduates: $4497. *Parent loans:* $3,486,179 (100% non-need-based). *Programs:* Federal Direct (Subsidized and Unsubsidized Stafford, PLUS), Perkins.
WORK-STUDY *Federal work-study:* Total amount: $1,691,160; jobs available.
APPLYING FOR FINANCIAL AID *Required financial aid forms:* FAFSA, CSS Financial Aid PROFILE, noncustodial (divorced/separated) parent's statement. *Financial aid deadline (priority):* 2/1. *Notification date:* 4/1. Students must reply by 5/1.
CONTACT Mr. Sean Martin, Director of Financial Aid Services, Connecticut College, 270 Mohegan Avenue, New London, CT 06320-4196, 860-439-2058. *Fax:* 860-439-5357. *E-mail:* finaid@conncoll.edu.
Website: http://www.conncoll.edu/.

CONSERVATORIO DE MUSICA DE PUERTO RICO
San Juan, PR

CONTACT Mr. Michael Rajaballey, Director of Financial Aid, Conservatorio de Musica de Puerto Rico, 951 Ave. Ponce de Leon, Miramar, San Juan, PR 00907, 787-751-0160 Ext. 231. *Fax:* 787-763-3886. *E-mail:* mrajaballey@cmpr.gobierno.pr.
Website: http://www.cmpr.edu/.

CONVERSE COLLEGE
Spartanburg, SC

Tuition & fees: $18,030	Average undergraduate aid package: $14,856

ABOUT THE INSTITUTION Independent, undergraduate: women only; graduate: coed. *Awards:* certificates, bachelor's, and master's degrees. 49 undergraduate majors. *Total enrollment:* 1,319. Undergraduates: 870. Freshmen: 242. Federal methodology is used as a basis for awarding need-based institutional aid.
UNDERGRADUATE EXPENSES for 2017–2018 *Comprehensive fee:* $28,640 includes full-time tuition ($17,680), mandatory fees ($350), and room and board ($10,610). Full-time tuition and fees vary according to course load and program. Room and board charges vary according to board plan. *Part-time tuition:* $875 per credit. Part-time tuition and fees vary according to course load and program.
FRESHMAN FINANCIAL AID (Fall 2015) 200 applied for aid; of those 82% were deemed to have need. 99% of freshmen with need received aid; of those 22% had need fully met. *Average percent of need met:* 66% (excluding resources awarded to replace EFC). *Average financial aid package:* $14,679 (excluding resources awarded to replace EFC). 15% of all full-time freshmen had no need and received non-need-based gift aid.
UNDERGRADUATE FINANCIAL AID (Fall 2015) 703 applied for aid; of those 84% were deemed to have need. 99% of undergraduates with need received aid; of those 19% had need fully met. *Average percent of need met:* 67% (excluding resources awarded to replace EFC). *Average financial aid package:* $14,856 (excluding resources awarded to replace EFC). 14% of all full-time undergraduates had no need and received non-need-based gift aid.
GIFT AID (NEED-BASED) *Total amount:* $6,102,259 (26% federal, 42% state, 29% institutional, 3% external sources). *Receiving aid:* Freshmen: 80% (160); all full-time undergraduates: 82% (577). *Average award:* Freshmen: $12,143; Undergraduates: $11,182. *Scholarships, grants, and awards:* Federal Pell, FSEOG, state, private, college/university gift aid from institutional funds.
GIFT AID (NON-NEED-BASED) *Total amount:* $1,189,778 (49% state, 46% institutional, 5% external sources). *Receiving aid:* Freshmen: 12% (23). Undergraduates: 11% (75). *Average award:* Freshmen: $5767. Undergraduates: $4785. *Scholarships, grants, and awards by category: Academic interests/achievement:* 607 awards ($1,750,520 total): general academic interests/achievements. *Creative arts/performance:* 160 awards ($317,730 total): applied art and design, general creative arts/performance, music, theater/drama. *Special characteristics:* 3 awards ($19,519 total): children and siblings of alumni, children of faculty/staff. *Tuition waivers:* Full or partial for employees or children of employees. *ROTC:* Army cooperative.

LOANS *Student loans:* $16,537,144 (20% need-based, 80% non-need-based). 87% of past graduating class borrowed through all loan programs. *Average indebtedness per student:* $28,036. *Average need-based loan:* Freshmen: $3526. Undergraduates: $4818. *Parent loans:* $1,247,187 (46% need-based, 54% non-need-based). *Programs:* Federal Direct (Subsidized and Unsubsidized Stafford, PLUS), Perkins, state.

WORK-STUDY *Federal work-study:* 65 jobs averaging $1128. *State or other work-study/employment:* Total amount: $114,548 (100% non-need-based). 87 part-time jobs averaging $1316.

ATHLETIC AWARDS Total amount: $568,565 (67% need-based, 33% non-need-based).

APPLYING FOR FINANCIAL AID *Required financial aid form:* FAFSA. *Financial aid deadline (priority):* 1/1. *Notification date:* Continuous beginning 12/1. Students must reply by 5/1 or within 2 weeks of notification.

CONTACT Mr. James W. Kellam, Director of Financial Planning, Converse College, 580 East Main Street, Spartanburg, SC 29302-0006, 864-596-9019 or toll-free 800-766-1125. *Fax:* 864-596-9749. *E-mail:* james.kellam@converse.edu. *Website:* http://www.converse.edu/.

COOPER UNION FOR THE ADVANCEMENT OF SCIENCE AND ART
New York, NY

Tuition & fees: $45,100	Average undergraduate aid package: $38,979

ABOUT THE INSTITUTION Independent, coed. *Awards:* certificates, bachelor's, and master's degrees (also offers master's program primarily made up of currently-enrolled students). 7 undergraduate majors. *Total enrollment:* 964. Undergraduates: 876. Freshmen: 222. Federal methodology is used as a basis for awarding need-based institutional aid.

UNDERGRADUATE EXPENSES for 2017–2018 *Comprehensive fee:* $61,370 includes full-time tuition ($43,250), mandatory fees ($1850), and room and board ($16,270). *College room only:* $12,270. Full-time tuition and fees vary according to degree level. Room and board charges vary according to housing facility. *Part-time tuition:* $1250 per credit hour. *Part-time fees:* $925 per term. Part-time tuition and fees vary according to degree level.

FRESHMAN FINANCIAL AID (Fall 2015) 163 applied for aid; of those 76% were deemed to have need. 100% of freshmen with need received aid; of those 100% had need fully met. *Average percent of need met:* 90% (excluding resources awarded to replace EFC). *Average financial aid package:* $38,432 (excluding resources awarded to replace EFC). 47% of all full-time freshmen had no need and received non-need-based gift aid.

UNDERGRADUATE FINANCIAL AID (Fall 2015) 429 applied for aid; of those 84% were deemed to have need. 100% of undergraduates with need received aid; of those 100% had need fully met. *Average percent of need met:* 89% (excluding resources awarded to replace EFC). *Average financial aid package:* $38,979 (excluding resources awarded to replace EFC). 63% of all full-time undergraduates had no need and received non-need-based gift aid.

GIFT AID (NEED-BASED) *Total amount:* $5,341,237 (18% federal, 7% state, 71% institutional, 4% external sources). *Receiving aid:* Freshmen: 53% (124); all full-time undergraduates: 41% (359). *Average award:* Freshmen: $20,768; Undergraduates: $14,250. *Scholarships, grants, and awards:* Federal Pell, FSEOG, state, private, college/university gift aid from institutional funds.

GIFT AID (NON-NEED-BASED) *Total amount:* $26,935,931 (100% institutional). *Receiving aid:* Freshmen: 53% (124). Undergraduates: 41% (359). *Average award:* Freshmen: $21,056. Undergraduates: $32,488. *Scholarships, grants, and awards by category:* Academic interests/achievement: 567 awards ($19,429,058 total): architecture, engineering/technologies. Creative arts/performance: 280 awards ($9,153,794 total): art/fine arts. *Tuition waivers:* Full or partial for employees or children of employees. *ROTC:* Army cooperative.

LOANS *Student loans:* $1,065,721 (80% need-based, 20% non-need-based). 21% of past graduating class borrowed through all loan programs. *Average indebtedness per student:* $18,303. *Average need-based loan:* Freshmen: $3167. Undergraduates: $4077. *Parent loans:* $337,740 (100% need-based). *Programs:* Federal Direct (Subsidized and Unsubsidized Stafford, PLUS), Perkins.

WORK-STUDY *Federal work-study:* 75 jobs averaging $520. *State or other work-study/employment:* Total amount: $486,478 (22% need-based, 78% non-need-based). 489 part-time jobs averaging $1340.

APPLYING FOR FINANCIAL AID *Required financial aid forms:* FAFSA, CSS Financial Aid PROFILE. *Financial aid deadline:* 5/1 (priority: 3/1). *Notification date:* Continuous beginning 12/1. Students must reply by 12/20 or within 2 weeks of notification.

CONTACT Mr. Charlie Xu, Director of Financial Aid, Cooper Union for the Advancement of Science and Art, 30 Cooper Square, New York, NY 10003-7120, 212-353-4043. *Fax:* 212-353-4343. *E-mail:* cxu@cooper.edu. *Website:* http://www.cooper.edu/.

COPPIN STATE UNIVERSITY
Baltimore, MD

CONTACT Ms. Thelma Ross, Director of Financial Aid, Coppin State University, 2500 West North Avenue, Baltimore, MD 21216-3698, 410-951-3633 or toll-free 800-635-3674. *Fax:* 410-951-3637. *E-mail:* thross@coppin.edu. *Website:* http://www.coppin.edu/.

CORBAN UNIVERSITY
Salem, OR

Tuition & fees: $31,640	Average undergraduate aid package: $21,751

ABOUT THE INSTITUTION Independent Christian, coed. *Awards:* certificates, associate, bachelor's, master's, and doctoral degrees. 49 undergraduate majors. *Total enrollment:* 1,193. Undergraduates: 1,022. Freshmen: 239. Federal methodology is used as a basis for awarding need-based institutional aid.

UNDERGRADUATE EXPENSES for 2017–2018 *Application fee:* $40. *One-time required fee:* $100. *Comprehensive fee:* $41,700 includes full-time tuition ($30,980), mandatory fees ($660), and room and board ($10,060). *College room only:* $5852. Full-time tuition and fees vary according to course load, degree level, program, and reciprocity agreements. Room and board charges vary according to board plan. *Part-time tuition:* $1291 per credit hour. *Part-time fees:* $330 per term. Part-time tuition and fees vary according to course load, degree level, program, and reciprocity agreements.

FRESHMAN FINANCIAL AID (Fall 2015) 221 applied for aid; of those 89% were deemed to have need. 99% of freshmen with need received aid; of those 16% had need fully met. *Average percent of need met:* 70% (excluding resources awarded to replace EFC). *Average financial aid package:* $23,247 (excluding resources awarded to replace EFC). 13% of all full-time freshmen had no need and received non-need-based gift aid.

UNDERGRADUATE FINANCIAL AID (Fall 2015) 820 applied for aid; of those 92% were deemed to have need. 100% of undergraduates with need received aid; of those 16% had need fully met. *Average percent of need met:* 68% (excluding resources awarded to replace EFC). *Average financial aid package:* $21,751 (excluding resources awarded to replace EFC). 10% of all full-time undergraduates had no need and received non-need-based gift aid.

GIFT AID (NEED-BASED) *Total amount:* $8,960,715 (21% federal, 3% state, 66% institutional, 10% external sources). *Receiving aid:* Freshmen: 79% (195); all full-time undergraduates: 80% (746). *Average award:* Freshmen: $20,396; Undergraduates: $17,920. *Scholarships, grants, and awards:* Federal Pell, FSEOG, state, private, college/university gift aid from institutional funds.

GIFT AID (NON-NEED-BASED) *Total amount:* $1,363,018 (2% federal, 76% institutional, 22% external sources). *Receiving aid:* Freshmen: 9% (22). Undergraduates: 9% (82). *Average award:* Freshmen: $10,848. Undergraduates: $9516. *Scholarships, grants, and awards by category:* Academic interests/achievement: 458 awards ($4,252,482 total): general academic interests/achievements. Creative arts/performance: 67 awards ($15,250 total): music, performing arts, theater/drama. Special achievements/activities: 290 awards ($549,198 total): general special achievements/activities, leadership, memberships. Special characteristics: 146 awards ($876,497 total): children and siblings of alumni, children of faculty/staff, international students, relatives of clergy, siblings of current students, veterans, veterans' children. *Tuition*

waivers: Full or partial for children of alumni, employees or children of employees, senior citizens. **ROTC:** Army cooperative, Air Force cooperative.

LOANS Student loans: $7,013,722 (78% need-based, 22% non-need-based). 84% of past graduating class borrowed through all loan programs. *Average indebtedness per student:* $27,325. *Average need-based loan:* Freshmen: $3412. Undergraduates: $4392. **Parent loans:** $1,556,247 (58% need-based, 42% non-need-based). **Programs:** Federal Direct (Subsidized and Unsubsidized Stafford, PLUS), Perkins.

WORK-STUDY Federal work-study: 248 jobs averaging $1159.

ATHLETIC AWARDS Total amount: $5,250,568 (69% need-based, 31% non-need-based).

APPLYING FOR FINANCIAL AID Required financial aid form: FAFSA. **Financial aid deadline:** Continuous. **Notification date:** Continuous beginning 2/20.

CONTACT Ellen Zarfas, Director of Financial Aid, Corban University, 5000 Deer Park Drive, SE, Salem, OR 97317, 503-375-7106 or toll-free 800-845-3005. *Fax:* 503-585-4316. *E-mail:* financialaid@corban.edu.

Website: http://www.corban.edu/.

CORNELL COLLEGE
Mount Vernon, IA

Tuition & fees: $39,900	Average undergraduate aid package: $31,933

ABOUT THE INSTITUTION Independent Methodist, coed. **Awards:** bachelor's degrees. 47 undergraduate majors. **Total enrollment:** 978. Undergraduates: 976. Freshmen: 287. Federal methodology is used as a basis for awarding need-based institutional aid.

UNDERGRADUATE EXPENSES for 2017–2018 Application fee: $30. **Comprehensive fee:** $48,800 includes full-time tuition ($39,675), mandatory fees ($225), and room and board ($8900). **College room only:** $4100. Room and board charges vary according to board plan and housing facility. **Part-time tuition:** $39,375 per year. Part-time tuition and fees vary according to course load.

FRESHMAN FINANCIAL AID (Fall 2016, est.) 234 applied for aid; of those 88% were deemed to have need. 100% of freshmen with need received aid; of those 15% had need fully met. *Average percent of need met:* 81% (excluding resources awarded to replace EFC). *Average financial aid package:* $34,118 (excluding resources awarded to replace EFC). 28% of all full-time freshmen had no need and received non-need-based gift aid.

UNDERGRADUATE FINANCIAL AID (Fall 2016, est.) 771 applied for aid; of those 91% were deemed to have need. 100% of undergraduates with need received aid; of those 16% had need fully met. *Average percent of need met:* 78% (excluding resources awarded to replace EFC). *Average financial aid package:* $31,933 (excluding resources awarded to replace EFC). 26% of all full-time undergraduates had no need and received non-need-based gift aid.

GIFT AID (NEED-BASED) Total amount: $18,292,557 (7% federal, 3% state, 88% institutional, 2% external sources). **Receiving aid:** Freshmen: 72% (207); all full-time undergraduates: 72% (704). *Average award:* Freshmen: $29,444; Undergraduates: $26,642. **Scholarships, grants, and awards:** Federal Pell, FSEOG, state, private, college/university gift aid from institutional funds, TEACH Grants.

GIFT AID (NON-NEED-BASED) Total amount: $5,724,702 (99% institutional, 1% external sources). **Receiving aid:** Freshmen: 8% (23). Undergraduates: 8% (80). *Average award:* Freshmen: $20,224. Undergraduates: $19,876. **Scholarships, grants, and awards by category:** Academic interests/achievement: 868 awards ($15,738,821 total): general academic interests/achievements. Creative arts/performance: 134 awards ($957,000 total): art/fine arts, music, performing arts, theater/drama. Special achievements/activities: 3 awards ($42,000 total). Special characteristics: 93 awards ($1,321,132 total): children and siblings of alumni, children of faculty/staff. **Tuition waivers:** Full or partial for employees or children of employees.

LOANS Student loans: $6,086,339 (74% need-based, 26% non-need-based). 75% of past graduating class borrowed through all loan programs. *Average indebtedness per student:* $31,975. *Average need-based loan:* Freshmen: $3434. Undergraduates: $4502. **Parent loans:** $1,797,922 (49% need-based, 51% non-need-based). **Programs:** Federal Direct (Subsidized and Unsubsidized Stafford, PLUS), college/university, United Methodist Student Loans.

WORK-STUDY Federal work-study: Total amount: $553,195; 355 jobs averaging $1558. **State or other work-study/employment:** Total amount: $76,294 (100% non-need-based). 83 part-time jobs averaging $919.

APPLYING FOR FINANCIAL AID Required financial aid form: FAFSA. **Financial aid deadline (priority):** 3/1. **Notification date:** Continuous beginning 3/1. Students must reply by 5/1 or within 2 weeks of notification.

CONTACT Ms. Pam Perry, Director of Financial Assistance, Cornell College, Old Sem, 600 First Street South West, Mount Vernon, IA 52314-1098, 319-895-4216 or toll-free 800-747-1112. *Fax:* 319-895-4106. *E-mail:* pperry@cornellcollege.edu.

Website: http://www.cornellcollege.edu/.

CORNELL UNIVERSITY
Ithaca, NY

Tuition & fees: $50,953	Average undergraduate aid package: $46,339

ABOUT THE INSTITUTION Independent, coed. **Awards:** bachelor's, master's, and doctoral degrees. 78 undergraduate majors. **Total enrollment:** 22,319. Undergraduates: 14,566. Freshmen: 3,315. Federal methodology is used as a basis for awarding need-based institutional aid.

UNDERGRADUATE EXPENSES for 2016–2017 Application fee: $80. **Comprehensive fee:** $64,903 includes full-time tuition ($50,712), mandatory fees ($241), and room and board ($13,950). **College room only:** $8274. Full-time tuition and fees vary according to degree level. Room and board charges vary according to board plan and housing facility.

FRESHMAN FINANCIAL AID (Fall 2016, est.) 1,826 applied for aid; of those 83% were deemed to have need. 100% of freshmen with need received aid; of those 100% had need fully met. *Average percent of need met:* 100% (excluding resources awarded to replace EFC). *Average financial aid package:* $46,569 (excluding resources awarded to replace EFC).

UNDERGRADUATE FINANCIAL AID (Fall 2016, est.) 7,469 applied for aid; of those 88% were deemed to have need. 100% of undergraduates with need received aid; of those 100% had need fully met. *Average percent of need met:* 100% (excluding resources awarded to replace EFC). *Average financial aid package:* $46,339 (excluding resources awarded to replace EFC).

GIFT AID (NEED-BASED) Total amount: $255,432,224 (6% federal, 2% state, 89% institutional, 3% external sources). **Receiving aid:** Freshmen: 45% (1,484); all full-time undergraduates: 44% (6,390). *Average award:* Freshmen: $40,333; Undergraduates: $39,595. **Scholarships, grants, and awards:** Federal Pell, FSEOG, state, private, college/university gift aid from institutional funds.

GIFT AID (NON-NEED-BASED) Tuition waivers: Full or partial for employees or children of employees. **ROTC:** Army, Naval, Air Force.

LOANS Student loans: $31,069,620 (100% need-based). 41% of past graduating class borrowed through all loan programs. *Average indebtedness per student:* $23,389. *Average need-based loan:* Freshmen: $4775. Undergraduates: $5037. **Parent loans:** $11,292,249 (100% need-based). **Programs:** Federal Direct (Subsidized and Unsubsidized Stafford, PLUS), Perkins, college/university.

WORK-STUDY Federal work-study: Total amount: $11,537,504; 4,970 jobs averaging $2321. **State or other work-study/employment:** Total amount: $2,067,616 (100% need-based). 925 part-time jobs averaging $2235.

APPLYING FOR FINANCIAL AID Required financial aid forms: FAFSA, CSS Financial Aid PROFILE, noncustodial (divorced/separated) parent's statement, business/farm supplement, federal income tax form(s). **Financial aid deadline:** 2/15. **Notification date:** 4/1. Students must reply by 5/1.

CONTACT Ms. Susan Hitchcock, Director of Financial Aid and Student Employment, Cornell University, 203 Day Hall, Ithaca, NY 14853-2488, 607-255-5145.

Website: http://www.cornell.edu/.

CORNERSTONE UNIVERSITY
Grand Rapids, MI

Tuition & fees: $27,520	Average undergraduate aid package: $20,891

ABOUT THE INSTITUTION Independent nondenominational, coed. *Awards:* diplomas, associate, bachelor's, master's, and doctoral degrees. 57 undergraduate majors. *Total enrollment:* 2,447. Undergraduates: 1,856. Freshmen: 283. Federal methodology is used as a basis for awarding need-based institutional aid.

UNDERGRADUATE EXPENSES for 2017–2018 Comprehensive fee: $36,550 includes full-time tuition ($27,150), mandatory fees ($370), and room and board ($9030). Full-time tuition and fees vary according to course load and reciprocity agreements. Room and board charges vary according to board plan and housing facility. *Part-time tuition:* $1030 per credit hour. Part-time tuition and fees vary according to course load.

FRESHMAN FINANCIAL AID (Fall 2016, est.) 252 applied for aid; of those 90% were deemed to have need. 100% of freshmen with need received aid; of those 15% had need fully met. *Average percent of need met:* 72% (excluding resources awarded to replace EFC). *Average financial aid package:* $21,902 (excluding resources awarded to replace EFC). 16% of all full-time freshmen had no need and received non-need-based gift aid.

UNDERGRADUATE FINANCIAL AID (Fall 2016, est.) 972 applied for aid; of those 91% were deemed to have need. 100% of undergraduates with need received aid; of those 16% had need fully met. *Average percent of need met:* 69% (excluding resources awarded to replace EFC). *Average financial aid package:* $20,891 (excluding resources awarded to replace EFC). 19% of all full-time undergraduates had no need and received non-need-based gift aid.

GIFT AID (NEED-BASED) Total amount: $13,643,153 (13% federal, 8% state, 77% institutional, 2% external sources). *Receiving aid:* Freshmen: 83% (227); all full-time undergraduates: 79% (886). *Average award:* Freshmen: $18,283; Undergraduates: $16,455. *Scholarships, grants, and awards:* Federal Pell, FSEOG, state, private, college/university gift aid from institutional funds.

GIFT AID (NON-NEED-BASED) Total amount: $2,624,725 (97% institutional, 3% external sources). *Receiving aid:* Freshmen: 10% (27). Undergraduates: 10% (108). *Average award:* Freshmen: $10,355. Undergraduates: $10,983. *Scholarships, grants, and awards by category: Academic interests/achievement:* business, communication, education, English, foreign languages, general academic interests/achievements, humanities, mathematics, physical sciences, religion/biblical studies, social sciences. *Creative arts/performance:* journalism/publications, music. *Special characteristics:* children of faculty/staff, ethnic background, international students, members of minority groups, relatives of clergy. *Tuition waivers:* Full or partial for employees or children of employees. *ROTC:* Army cooperative.

LOANS Student loans: $6,664,140 (47% need-based, 53% non-need-based). 81% of past graduating class borrowed through all loan programs. *Average indebtedness per student:* $32,191. *Average need-based loan:* Freshmen: $3687. Undergraduates: $4633. *Parent loans:* $1,608,637 (100% non-need-based). *Programs:* Federal Direct (Subsidized and Unsubsidized Stafford, PLUS), Perkins.

WORK-STUDY Federal work-study: Total amount: $249,988; 167 jobs averaging $1365.

ATHLETIC AWARDS Total amount: $1,558,886 (60% need-based, 40% non-need-based).

APPLYING FOR FINANCIAL AID Required financial aid form: FAFSA. *Financial aid deadline:* Continuous. *Notification date:* Continuous beginning 12/1. Students must reply within 4 weeks of notification.

CONTACT Mrs. Carol S. Carpenter, Director of Student Financial Services, Cornerstone University, 1001 East Beltline Avenue, NE, Grand Rapids, MI 49525-5897, 616-222-1424 or toll-free 800-787-9778. *Fax:* 616-222-1400. *E-mail:* carol.carpenter@cornerstone.edu. *Website:* http://www.cornerstone.edu/.

CORNISH COLLEGE OF THE ARTS
Seattle, WA

ABOUT THE INSTITUTION Independent, coed. *Awards:* certificates and bachelor's degrees. 16 undergraduate majors. *Total enrollment:* 724. Undergraduates: 720. Freshmen: 179.

GIFT AID (NEED-BASED) Scholarships, grants, and awards: Federal Pell, FSEOG, state, private, college/university gift aid from institutional funds.

GIFT AID (NON-NEED-BASED) Scholarships, grants, and awards by category: *Academic interests/achievement:* general academic interests/achievements. *Creative arts/performance:* art/fine arts, dance, music, theater/drama.

LOANS Programs: Federal Direct (Subsidized and Unsubsidized Stafford, PLUS), Perkins.

WORK-STUDY Federal work-study: jobs available. *State or other work-study/employment:* Total amount: $610,292 (94% need-based, 6% non-need-based). Part-time jobs available.

APPLYING FOR FINANCIAL AID Required financial aid form: FAFSA.

CONTACT Monique Theriault, Office of Financial Aid, Cornish College of the Arts, 1000 Lenora Street, Seattle, WA 98121, 206-726-5013 or toll-free 800-726-ARTS. *Fax:* 206-720-1011. *E-mail:* mtheriault@cornish.edu. *Website:* http://www.cornish.edu/.

COVENANT COLLEGE
Lookout Mountain, GA

Tuition & fees: $32,230	Average undergraduate aid package: $25,772

ABOUT THE INSTITUTION Independent Presbyterian Church in America, coed. *Awards:* bachelor's and master's degrees (master's degree in education only). 27 undergraduate majors. *Total enrollment:* 1,102. Undergraduates: 1,044. Freshmen: 258. Federal methodology is used as a basis for awarding need-based institutional aid.

UNDERGRADUATE EXPENSES for 2016–2017 Application fee: $35. *Comprehensive fee:* $41,860 includes full-time tuition ($31,320), mandatory fees ($910), and room and board ($9630). Full-time tuition and fees vary according to course load. Room and board charges vary according to board plan and housing facility. *Part-time tuition:* $1340 per credit hour. Part-time tuition and fees vary according to course load.

FRESHMAN FINANCIAL AID (Fall 2015) 233 applied for aid; of those 80% were deemed to have need. 100% of freshmen with need received aid; of those 32% had need fully met. *Average percent of need met:* 78% (excluding resources awarded to replace EFC). *Average financial aid package:* $25,833 (excluding resources awarded to replace EFC). 27% of all full-time freshmen had no need and received non-need-based gift aid.

UNDERGRADUATE FINANCIAL AID (Fall 2015) 776 applied for aid; of those 86% were deemed to have need. 100% of undergraduates with need received aid; of those 31% had need fully met. *Average percent of need met:* 79% (excluding resources awarded to replace EFC). *Average financial aid package:* $25,772 (excluding resources awarded to replace EFC). 31% of all full-time undergraduates had no need and received non-need-based gift aid.

GIFT AID (NEED-BASED) Total amount: $12,803,063 (10% federal, 5% state, 82% institutional, 3% external sources). *Receiving aid:* Freshmen: 71% (182); all full-time undergraduates: 66% (657). *Average award:* Freshmen: $20,786; Undergraduates: $19,425. *Scholarships, grants, and awards:* Federal Pell, FSEOG, state, private, college/university gift aid from institutional funds.

GIFT AID (NON-NEED-BASED) Total amount: $4,691,503 (1% federal, 4% state, 87% institutional, 8% external sources). *Receiving aid:* Freshmen: 12% (31). Undergraduates: 11% (108). *Average award:* Freshmen: $13,035. Undergraduates: $13,013. *Scholarships, grants, and awards by category: Academic interests/achievement:* general academic interests/achievements. *Creative arts/performance:* music. *Special achievements/activities:* leadership. *Special characteristics:* children of faculty/staff, international students, members of minority groups, religious affiliation. *Tuition waivers:* Full or partial for employees or children of employees, senior citizens. *ROTC:* Army cooperative.

LOANS Student loans: $3,883,093 (92% need-based, 8% non-need-based). 64% of past graduating class borrowed through all loan programs. *Average indebtedness per student:* $24,484. *Average need-based loan:* Freshmen: $5767. Undergraduates: $6841. *Parent loans:* $1,130,831 (91% need-based, 9% non-need-based). *Programs:* Perkins, state.

WORK-STUDY Federal work-study: jobs available. *State or other work-study/employment:* Total amount: $900,606 (78% need-based, 22% non-need-based). Part-time jobs available.

APPLYING FOR FINANCIAL AID *Required financial aid forms:* FAFSA, state aid form. *Financial aid deadline (priority):* 2/1. *Notification date:* Continuous beginning 3/15. Students must reply by 5/1.

CONTACT Mrs. Margaret Stewart, Assistant Director of Financial Aid, Covenant College, 14049 Scenic Highway, Lookout Mountain, GA 30750, 706-419-1152 or toll-free 888-451-2683. *Fax:* 706-820-2820. *E-mail:* margaret.stewart@covenant.edu. *Website:* http://www.covenant.edu/.

COX COLLEGE
Springfield, MO

Tuition & fees: $10,270	Average undergraduate aid package: $2626

ABOUT THE INSTITUTION Independent, coed, primarily women. *Awards:* certificates, associate, bachelor's, and master's degrees. 5 undergraduate majors. *Total enrollment:* 899. Undergraduates: 778. Freshmen: 778. Federal methodology is used as a basis for awarding need-based institutional aid.

UNDERGRADUATE EXPENSES for 2016–2017 *Application fee:* $50. *One-time required fee:* $225. *Tuition:* full-time $8800; part-time $400 per credit hour. Full-time tuition and fees vary according to course load, degree level, and program. Part-time tuition and fees vary according to course load, degree level, and program.

FRESHMAN FINANCIAL AID (Fall 2015) 4 applied for aid; of those 100% were deemed to have need. 100% of freshmen with need received aid. *Average financial aid package:* $6700 (excluding resources awarded to replace EFC).

UNDERGRADUATE FINANCIAL AID (Fall 2015) 271 applied for aid; of those 92% were deemed to have need. 100% of undergraduates with need received aid. *Average financial aid package:* $2626 (excluding resources awarded to replace EFC).

GIFT AID (NEED-BASED) *Total amount:* $1,850,054 (69% federal, 13% state, 14% institutional, 4% external sources). *Receiving aid:* Freshmen: 50% (2); all full-time undergraduates: 47% (163). *Average award:* Freshmen: $5775; Undergraduates: $4585. *Scholarships, grants, and awards:* Federal Pell, FSEOG, state, private, college/university gift aid from institutional funds, United Negro College Fund, Federal Nursing.

GIFT AID (NON-NEED-BASED) *Scholarships, grants, and awards by category:* Academic interests/achievement: general academic interests/achievements, home economics.

LOANS *Student loans:* $4,733,368 (41% need-based, 59% non-need-based). *Average need-based loan:* Freshmen: $3350. Undergraduates: $3718. *Parent loans:* $179,587 (100% need-based). *Programs:* Federal Direct (Subsidized and Unsubsidized Stafford, PLUS).

WORK-STUDY *Federal work-study:* 21 jobs averaging $1807. *State or other work-study/employment:* Part-time jobs available.

APPLYING FOR FINANCIAL AID *Required financial aid forms:* FAFSA, institution's own form. *Financial aid deadline (priority):* 4/1. *Notification date:* Continuous beginning 5/20.

CONTACT Leesa Taylor , Financial Aid Counselor, Cox College, 1423 North Jefferson Avenue, Springfield, MO 65802, 417-269-3160 or toll-free 866-898-5355 (in-state). *Fax:* 417-269-3586. *E-mail:* leesa.taylor@coxcollege.edu. *Website:* http://www.coxcollege.edu/.

CREATIVE CENTER
Omaha, NE

CONTACT Financial Aid Office, Creative Center, 10850 Emmet Street, Omaha, NE 68164, 402-898-1000 or toll-free 888-898-1789. *Website:* http://www.creativecenter.edu/.

CREIGHTON UNIVERSITY
Omaha, NE

Tuition & fees: $38,750	Average undergraduate aid package: $27,537

ABOUT THE INSTITUTION Independent Roman Catholic (Jesuit), coed. *Awards:* certificates, associate, bachelor's, master's, and doctoral degrees. 50 undergraduate majors. *Total enrollment:* 8,393. Undergraduates: 4,203. Freshmen: 1,033. Federal methodology is used as a basis for awarding need-based institutional aid.

UNDERGRADUATE EXPENSES for 2017–2018 *Application fee:* $40. *Comprehensive fee:* $49,452 includes full-time tuition ($37,086), mandatory fees ($1664), and room and board ($10,702). Full-time tuition and fees vary according to program. Room and board charges vary according to housing facility. *Part-time tuition:* $1160 per credit hour. *Part-time fees:* $163 per term. Part-time tuition and fees vary according to course load and program.

FRESHMAN FINANCIAL AID (Fall 2016, est.) 822 applied for aid; of those 72% were deemed to have need. 100% of freshmen with need received aid; of those 30% had need fully met. *Average percent of need met:* 82% (excluding resources awarded to replace EFC). *Average financial aid package:* $27,658 (excluding resources awarded to replace EFC). 40% of all full-time freshmen had no need and received non-need-based gift aid.

UNDERGRADUATE FINANCIAL AID (Fall 2016, est.) 2,626 applied for aid; of those 82% were deemed to have need. 100% of undergraduates with need received aid; of those 26% had need fully met. *Average percent of need met:* 79% (excluding resources awarded to replace EFC). *Average financial aid package:* $27,537 (excluding resources awarded to replace EFC). 39% of all full-time undergraduates had no need and received non-need-based gift aid.

GIFT AID (NEED-BASED) *Total amount:* $39,929,847 (8% federal, 1% state, 88% institutional, 3% external sources). *Receiving aid:* Freshmen: 58% (594); all full-time undergraduates: 52% (2,062). *Average award:* Freshmen: $20,201; Undergraduates: $21,068. *Scholarships, grants, and awards:* Federal Pell, FSEOG, state, private, college/university gift aid from institutional funds.

GIFT AID (NON-NEED-BASED) *Total amount:* $26,952,274 (95% institutional, 5% external sources). *Receiving aid:* Freshmen: 14% (143). Undergraduates: 10% (390). *Average award:* Freshmen: $15,661. Undergraduates: $15,136. *Scholarships, grants, and awards by category:* Academic interests/achievement: 3,004 awards ($40,023,430 total): business, education, general academic interests/achievements, military science. *Creative arts/performance:* 21 awards ($74,000 total): art/fine arts, dance, music, performing arts, theater/drama. *Special achievements/activities:* 88 awards ($173,000 total): community service, leadership. *Special characteristics:* 132 awards ($1,425,800 total): first-generation college students, members of minority groups. *Tuition waivers:* Full or partial for employees or children of employees, adult students, senior citizens. *ROTC:* Army, Air Force cooperative.

LOANS *Student loans:* $28,362,156 (62% need-based, 38% non-need-based). 61% of past graduating class borrowed through all loan programs. *Average indebtedness per student:* $35,921. *Average need-based loan:* Freshmen: $5254. Undergraduates: $6062. *Parent loans:* $6,293,834 (27% need-based, 73% non-need-based). *Programs:* Federal Direct (Subsidized and Unsubsidized Stafford, PLUS), Perkins, Federal Nursing.

WORK-STUDY *Federal work-study:* Total amount: $1,758,110; 807 jobs averaging $2179.

ATHLETIC AWARDS Total amount: $4,496,951 (24% need-based, 76% non-need-based).

APPLYING FOR FINANCIAL AID *Required financial aid forms:* FAFSA, institution's own form. *Financial aid deadline (priority):* 1/15. *Notification date:* Continuous beginning 2/15. Students must reply within 4 weeks of notification.

CONTACT Ms. Paula S. Kohles, Director of Financial Aid, Creighton University, 2500 California Plaza, Omaha, NE 68178, 402-280-2731 or toll-free 800-282-5835. *Fax:* 402-280-2895. *E-mail:* paulakohles@creighton.edu. *Website:* http://www.creighton.edu/.

CRISWELL COLLEGE
Dallas, TX

Tuition & fees: $9858	Average undergraduate aid package: N/A

ABOUT THE INSTITUTION Independent Southern Baptist Convention, coed. **Awards:** associate, bachelor's, and master's degrees. 7 undergraduate majors. **Total enrollment:** 284. Undergraduates: 225. Freshmen: 16.

UNDERGRADUATE EXPENSES for 2017–2018 Application fee: $35. **Tuition:** full-time $9120; part-time $380 per credit hour. **Required fees:** full-time $738; $738 per year. Full-time tuition and fees vary according to course load. Part-time tuition and fees vary according to course load.

GIFT AID (NEED-BASED) Scholarships, grants, and awards: Federal Pell, private, college/university gift aid from institutional funds.

GIFT AID (NON-NEED-BASED) Scholarships, grants, and awards by category: Academic interests/achievement: general academic interests/achievements, religion/biblical studies. Special achievements/activities: religious involvement. **Tuition waivers:** Full or partial for employees or children of employees.

LOANS Programs: Federal Direct (Subsidized and Unsubsidized Stafford, PLUS).

WORK-STUDY State or other work-study/employment: Part-time jobs available.

APPLYING FOR FINANCIAL AID Required financial aid forms: FAFSA, institution's own form. **Financial aid deadline (priority):** 4/15. **Notification date:** Continuous. Students must reply within 6 weeks of notification.

CONTACT Jimmy Criswell, Director of Financial Aid, Criswell College, 4010 Gaston Avenue, Dallas, TX 75246, 214-818-1393 or toll-free 800-899-0012. Fax: 214-370-0497. E-mail: jcriswell@criswell.edu. Website: http://www.criswell.edu/.

CROSSROADS BIBLE COLLEGE
Indianapolis, IN

Tuition & fees: N/R	Average undergraduate aid package: $6430

ABOUT THE INSTITUTION Independent Baptist, coed. 8 undergraduate majors. Institutional methodology is used as a basis for awarding need-based institutional aid.

FRESHMAN FINANCIAL AID (Fall 2015) 10 applied for aid; of those 100% were deemed to have need. 100% of freshmen with need received aid; of those 100% had need fully met. **Average percent of need met:** 100% (excluding resources awarded to replace EFC). **Average financial aid package:** $9694 (excluding resources awarded to replace EFC).

UNDERGRADUATE FINANCIAL AID (Fall 2015) 156 applied for aid; of those 100% were deemed to have need. 100% of undergraduates with need received aid; of those 40% had need fully met. **Average percent of need met:** 100% (excluding resources awarded to replace EFC). **Average financial aid package:** $6430 (excluding resources awarded to replace EFC).

GIFT AID (NEED-BASED) Receiving aid: Freshmen: 100% (10); all full-time undergraduates: 96% (156). **Average award:** Freshmen: $4154; Undergraduates: $4032. **Scholarships, grants, and awards:** Federal Pell, FSEOG, state, college/university gift aid from institutional funds.

GIFT AID (NON-NEED-BASED) Scholarships, grants, and awards by category: Academic interests/achievement: religion/biblical studies. Special achievements/activities: religious involvement. Special characteristics: 1 award ($5015 total): children of faculty/staff, married students, siblings of current students, spouses of current students.

LOANS Student loans: 100% of past graduating class borrowed through all loan programs. Average indebtedness per student: $37,497. **Average need-based loan:** Freshmen: $2254. Undergraduates: $2226. **Programs:** Federal Direct (Subsidized and Unsubsidized Stafford, PLUS).

WORK-STUDY Federal work-study: 17 jobs averaging $1652.

APPLYING FOR FINANCIAL AID Required financial aid forms: FAFSA, institution's own form. **Financial aid deadline:** 6/30 (priority: 5/31). **Notification date:** 7/31. Students must reply by 6/30 or within 2 weeks of notification.

CONTACT Mrs. Phyllis Dodson, Senior Director of Financial Aid, Crossroads Bible College, 601 North Shortridge Road, Indianapolis, IN 46219, 317-789-8250 or toll-free 800-822-3119. Fax: 317-789-8253. E-mail: pdodson@crossroads.edu. Website: http://www.crossroads.edu/.

CROWN COLLEGE
St. Bonifacius, MN

Tuition & fees: N/R	Average undergraduate aid package: $17,545

ABOUT THE INSTITUTION Independent The Christian and Missionary Alliance, coed. 34 undergraduate majors. Federal methodology is used as a basis for awarding need-based institutional aid.

FRESHMAN FINANCIAL AID (Fall 2015) 142 applied for aid; of those 88% were deemed to have need. 100% of freshmen with need received aid; of those 10% had need fully met. **Average percent of need met:** 66% (excluding resources awarded to replace EFC). **Average financial aid package:** $18,757 (excluding resources awarded to replace EFC). 14% of all full-time freshmen had no need and received non-need-based gift aid.

UNDERGRADUATE FINANCIAL AID (Fall 2015) 629 applied for aid; of those 92% were deemed to have need. 100% of undergraduates with need received aid; of those 9% had need fully met. **Average percent of need met:** 64% (excluding resources awarded to replace EFC). **Average financial aid package:** $17,545 (excluding resources awarded to replace EFC). 11% of all full-time undergraduates had no need and received non-need-based gift aid.

GIFT AID (NEED-BASED) Receiving aid: Freshmen: 81% (122); all full-time undergraduates: 33% (229). **Average award:** Freshmen: $15,777; Undergraduates: $13,700. **Scholarships, grants, and awards:** Federal Pell, FSEOG, state, private, college/university gift aid from institutional funds.

GIFT AID (NON-NEED-BASED) Receiving aid: Freshmen: 5% (7). Undergraduates: 4% (26). **Average award:** Freshmen: $11,892. Undergraduates: $11,143. **Scholarships, grants, and awards by category:** Academic interests/achievement: general academic interests/achievements. Creative arts/performance: music. Special achievements/activities: leadership. Special characteristics: children and siblings of alumni, children of faculty/staff, international students, members of minority groups, relatives of clergy, siblings of current students.

LOANS Student loans: 78% of past graduating class borrowed through all loan programs. Average indebtedness per student: $31,557. **Average need-based loan:** Freshmen: $3556. Undergraduates: $4590. **Programs:** Federal Direct (Subsidized and Unsubsidized Stafford, PLUS), Perkins, state, SELF Loans, CitiAssist Loans, Sallie Mae Signature Loans, alternative loans.

WORK-STUDY Federal work-study jobs available. **State or other work-study/employment:** Part-time jobs available.

APPLYING FOR FINANCIAL AID Required financial aid form: FAFSA. **Financial aid deadline:** 8/1 (priority: 4/15). **Notification date:** Continuous beginning 3/1. Students must reply by 5/1 or within 3 weeks of notification.

CONTACT Mrs. Judy Bedford, Interim Director of Financial Aid, Crown College, 8700 College View Drive, St. Bonifacius, MN 55375-9001, 952-446-4177 or toll-free 800-68-CROWN. Fax: 952-446-4178. E-mail: finaid@crown.edu. Website: http://www.crown.edu/.

THE CULINARY INSTITUTE OF AMERICA
Hyde Park, NY

Tuition & fees: $31,616	Average undergraduate aid package: $16,541

ABOUT THE INSTITUTION Independent, coed. **Awards:** certificates, associate, and bachelor's degrees. 5 undergraduate majors. **Total enrollment:** 2,793. Undergraduates: 2,774. Freshmen: 512. Federal methodology is used as a basis for awarding need-based institutional aid.

UNDERGRADUATE EXPENSES for 2017–2018 Application fee: $50. **Comprehensive fee:** $42,486 includes full-time tuition ($29,380), mandatory fees ($2236), and room and board ($10,870). **College room only:** $7320. Full-time tuition and fees vary according to location. Room and board charges vary according to board plan, housing facility, and location.

FRESHMAN FINANCIAL AID (Fall 2016, est.) 439 applied for aid; of those 90% were deemed to have need. 100% of freshmen with need received aid; of those 9% had need fully met. *Average percent of need met:* 79% (excluding resources awarded to replace EFC). *Average financial aid package:* $18,382 (excluding resources awarded to replace EFC). 17% of all full-time freshmen had no need and received non-need-based gift aid.

UNDERGRADUATE FINANCIAL AID (Fall 2016, est.) 1,924 applied for aid; of those 93% were deemed to have need. 100% of undergraduates with need received aid; of those 7% had need fully met. *Average percent of need met:* 71% (excluding resources awarded to replace EFC). *Average financial aid package:* $16,541 (excluding resources awarded to replace EFC). 5% of all full-time undergraduates had no need and received non-need-based gift aid.

GIFT AID (NEED-BASED) *Total amount:* $20,438,851 (16% federal, 2% state, 79% institutional, 3% external sources). *Receiving aid:* Freshmen: 73% (375); all full-time undergraduates: 59% (1,649). *Average award:* Freshmen: $13,950; Undergraduates: $12,031. *Scholarships, grants, and awards:* Federal Pell, FSEOG, state, private, college/university gift aid from institutional funds.

GIFT AID (NON-NEED-BASED) *Total amount:* $2,506,423 (1% state, 93% institutional, 6% external sources). *Receiving aid:* Freshmen: 66% (338). Undergraduates: 50% (1,375). *Average award:* Freshmen: $5695. Undergraduates: $6359. *Scholarships, grants, and awards by category:* Academic interests/achievement: 1,284 awards ($6,741,972 total): general academic interests/achievements. *Creative arts/performance:* 143 awards ($426,180 total): general creative arts/performance. *Special achievements/activities:* 73 awards ($62,264 total): general special achievements/activities. *Tuition waivers:* Full or partial for employees or children of employees.

LOANS *Student loans:* $19,984,458 (91% need-based, 9% non-need-based). 63% of past graduating class borrowed through all loan programs. *Average indebtedness per student:* $51,200. *Average need-based loan:* Freshmen: $3047. Undergraduates: $3825. *Parent loans:* $8,300,049 (100% non-need-based). *Programs:* Federal Direct (Subsidized and Unsubsidized Stafford, PLUS), Perkins, alternative loans.

WORK-STUDY *Federal work-study:* Total amount: $2,338,771; 1,045 jobs averaging $2238. *State or other work-study/employment:* Part-time jobs available.

APPLYING FOR FINANCIAL AID *Required financial aid forms:* FAFSA, state aid form. *Financial aid deadline:* Continuous. *Notification date:* Continuous beginning 3/5. Students must reply within 2 weeks of notification.

CONTACT Kathleen Gailor, Director of Financial Aid, The Culinary Institute of America, 1946 Campus Drive, Hyde Park, NY 12538-1499, 845-451-1302 or toll-free 800-CULINARY. *Fax:* 845-905-4030. *E-mail:* finaid@culinary.edu.
Website: http://www.ciachef.edu/.

CULINARY INSTITUTE OF VIRGINIA
Norfolk, VA

CONTACT Ms. Lynn Robinson, Director of Financial Aid, Culinary Institute of Virginia, 8 Abbott Park Place, Providence, RI 02903, 401-598-4648 or toll-free 866-619-CHEF. *Fax:* 401-598-1040. *E-mail:* fp@jwu.edu.
Website: http://www.chefva.com/.

CULVER-STOCKTON COLLEGE
Canton, MO

Tuition & fees: $26,040	Average undergraduate aid package: $19,954

ABOUT THE INSTITUTION Independent Christian Church (Disciples of Christ), coed. *Awards:* bachelor's and master's degrees. 40 undergraduate majors. *Total enrollment:* 1,095. Undergraduates: 1,058. Freshmen: 269. Federal methodology is used as a basis for awarding need-based institutional aid.

UNDERGRADUATE EXPENSES for 2017–2018 *One-time required fee:* $210. *Comprehensive fee:* $34,350 includes full-time tuition ($25,615), mandatory fees ($425), and room and board ($8310). *College room only:* $3720. Room and board charges vary according to board plan and housing facility. *Part-time tuition:* $590 per credit hour. *Part-time fees:* $17.71 per credit hour.

FRESHMAN FINANCIAL AID (Fall 2016, est.) 250 applied for aid; of those 94% were deemed to have need. 100% of freshmen with need received aid; of those 18% had need fully met. *Average percent of need met:* 71% (excluding resources awarded to replace EFC). *Average financial aid package:* $18,715 (excluding resources awarded to replace EFC). 12% of all full-time freshmen had no need and received non-need-based gift aid.

UNDERGRADUATE FINANCIAL AID (Fall 2016, est.) 824 applied for aid; of those 92% were deemed to have need. 100% of undergraduates with need received aid; of those 16% had need fully met. *Average percent of need met:* 73% (excluding resources awarded to replace EFC). *Average financial aid package:* $19,954 (excluding resources awarded to replace EFC). 16% of all full-time undergraduates had no need and received non-need-based gift aid.

GIFT AID (NEED-BASED) *Total amount:* $9,845,711 (20% federal, 6% state, 72% institutional, 2% external sources). *Receiving aid:* Freshmen: 87% (234); all full-time undergraduates: 80% (750). *Average award:* Freshmen: $16,041; Undergraduates: $16,376. *Scholarships, grants, and awards:* Federal Pell, FSEOG, state, private, college/university gift aid from institutional funds.

GIFT AID (NON-NEED-BASED) *Total amount:* $1,808,399 (1% state, 95% institutional, 4% external sources). *Receiving aid:* Freshmen: 13% (35). Undergraduates: 10% (93). *Average award:* Freshmen: $9787. Undergraduates: $9710. *Scholarships, grants, and awards by category:* Academic interests/achievement: 916 awards ($6,328,345 total): general academic interests/achievements. *Creative arts/performance:* 133 awards ($588,200 total): art/fine arts, dance, debating, music, theater/drama. *Special achievements/activities:* 139 awards ($353,444 total): cheerleading/drum major, general special achievements/activities, leadership. *Special characteristics:* 119 awards ($647,267 total): children and siblings of alumni, children of faculty/staff, first-generation college students, international students, local/state students, religious affiliation, siblings of current students, veterans, veterans' children. *Tuition waivers:* Full or partial for employees or children of employees, senior citizens.

LOANS *Student loans:* $7,412,726 (74% need-based, 26% non-need-based). 85% of past graduating class borrowed through all loan programs. *Average indebtedness per student:* $28,605. *Average need-based loan:* Freshmen: $3212. Undergraduates: $4145. *Parent loans:* $1,854,447 (47% need-based, 53% non-need-based). *Programs:* Federal Direct (Subsidized and Unsubsidized Stafford, PLUS), Perkins, Federal Nursing, state, college/university.

WORK-STUDY *Federal work-study:* Total amount: $82,505; 80 jobs averaging $1096. *State or other work-study/employment:* Total amount: $401,546 (54% need-based, 46% non-need-based). 396 part-time jobs averaging $1014.

ATHLETIC AWARDS Total amount: $3,440,067 (69% need-based, 31% non-need-based).

APPLYING FOR FINANCIAL AID *Required financial aid form:* FAFSA. *Financial aid deadline:* 6/1 (priority: 1/1). *Notification date:* Continuous. Students must reply within 2 weeks of notification.

CONTACT Ms. Tina M. Wiseman, Director of Financial Aid, Culver-Stockton College, One College Hill, Canton, MO 63435, 573-288-6307 or toll-free 800-537-1883. *Fax:* 573-288-6308. *E-mail:* twiseman@culver.edu.
Website: http://www.culver.edu/.

CUMBERLAND UNIVERSITY
Lebanon, TN

CONTACT Ms. Beatrice LaChance, Executive Director of Enrollment Services, Cumberland University, 1 Cumberland Square, Lebanon, TN 37087-3554, 615-444-2562 Ext. 1244 or toll-free 800-467-0562. *Fax:* 615-443-8424. *E-mail:* lvaughan@cumberland.edu.
Website: http://www.cumberland.edu/.

CURRY COLLEGE
Milton, MA

Tuition & fees: $38,596	Average undergraduate aid package: $27,281

ABOUT THE INSTITUTION Independent, coed. **Awards:** certificates, bachelor's, and master's degrees. 26 undergraduate majors. **Total enrollment:** 2,925. Undergraduates: 2,688. Freshmen: 678. Federal methodology is used as a basis for awarding need-based institutional aid.

UNDERGRADUATE EXPENSES for 2017–2018 Application fee: $50. **One-time required fee:** $340. **Comprehensive fee:** $54,011 includes full-time tuition ($36,780), mandatory fees ($1816), and room and board ($15,415). Full-time tuition and fees vary according to class time, course load, location, and program. Room and board charges vary according to board plan and housing facility. **Part-time tuition:** $1226 per credit. Part-time tuition and fees vary according to class time, course load, location, and program.

FRESHMAN FINANCIAL AID (Fall 2016, est.) 656 applied for aid; of those 83% were deemed to have need. 100% of freshmen with need received aid; of those 13% had need fully met. **Average percent of need met:** 71% (excluding resources awarded to replace EFC). **Average financial aid package:** $29,025 (excluding resources awarded to replace EFC). 19% of all full-time freshmen had no need and received non-need-based gift aid.

UNDERGRADUATE FINANCIAL AID (Fall 2016, est.) 1,586 applied for aid; of those 100% were deemed to have need. 100% of undergraduates with need received aid; of those 13% had need fully met. **Average percent of need met:** 72% (excluding resources awarded to replace EFC). **Average financial aid package:** $27,281 (excluding resources awarded to replace EFC). 21% of all full-time undergraduates had no need and received non-need-based gift aid.

GIFT AID (NEED-BASED) Total amount: $33,800,021 (10% federal, 2% state, 87% institutional, 1% external sources). **Receiving aid:** Freshmen: 81% (545); all full-time undergraduates: 75% (1,575). **Average award:** Freshmen: $26,000; Undergraduates: $22,927. **Scholarships, grants, and awards:** Federal Pell, FSEOG, state, private, college/university gift aid from institutional funds, TEACH Grants.

GIFT AID (NON-NEED-BASED) Total amount: $7,442,519 (4% federal, 94% institutional, 2% external sources). **Receiving aid:** Freshmen: 8% (55). Undergraduates: 6% (135). **Average award:** Freshmen: $17,433. Undergraduates: $13,962. **Scholarships, grants, and awards by category:** Academic interests/achievement: 2,135 awards ($23,684,250 total): general academic interests/achievements. **Special characteristics:** 34 awards ($969,663 total): children and siblings of alumni, children of current students, children of faculty/staff, siblings of current students, spouses of current students. **Tuition waivers:** Full or partial for children of alumni, employees or children of employees. **ROTC:** Army cooperative.

LOANS Student loans: $19,400,219 (33% need-based, 67% non-need-based). 83% of past graduating class borrowed through all loan programs. **Average indebtedness per student:** $42,191. **Average need-based loan:** Freshmen: $3559. Undergraduates: $4347. **Parent loans:** $10,929,519 (100% non-need-based). **Programs:** Federal Direct (Subsidized and Unsubsidized Stafford, PLUS), Perkins, state.

WORK-STUDY Federal work-study: Total amount: $2,182,523; 932 jobs averaging $2320.

APPLYING FOR FINANCIAL AID Required financial aid form: FAFSA. **Financial aid deadline (priority):** 3/1. **Notification date:** Continuous beginning 12/1. Students must reply by 5/1 or within 2 weeks of notification.

CONTACT Linda Brennan, Director of Financial Aid, Curry College, 1071 Blue Hill Avenue, Milton, MA 02186-2395, 617-333-2354 or toll-free 800-669-0686. Fax: 617-333-2915. E-mail: fin-aid@curry.edu. Website: http://www.curry.edu/.

CURTIS INSTITUTE OF MUSIC
Philadelphia, PA

CONTACT Veronica McAuley, Director of Student Financial Assistance, Curtis Institute of Music, 1726 Locust Street, Philadelphia, PA 19103-6107, 215-717-3188. E-mail: veronica.mcauley@curtis.edu. Website: http://www.curtis.edu/.

DAEMEN COLLEGE
Amherst, NY

Tuition & fees: $26,940	Average undergraduate aid package: $25,911

ABOUT THE INSTITUTION Independent, coed. **Awards:** certificates, bachelor's, master's, and doctoral degrees. 36 undergraduate majors. **Total enrollment:** 2,761. Undergraduates: 1,993. Freshmen: 392. Federal methodology is used as a basis for awarding need-based institutional aid.

UNDERGRADUATE EXPENSES for 2016–2017 Application fee: $25. **Comprehensive fee:** $39,365 includes full-time tuition ($26,400), mandatory fees ($540), and room and board ($12,425). Full-time tuition and fees vary according to location and reciprocity agreements. Room and board charges vary according to board plan and housing facility. **Part-time tuition:** $880 per credit hour. **Part-time fees:** $7 per credit hour; $80 per term. Part-time tuition and fees vary according to course load, location, and reciprocity agreements.

FRESHMAN FINANCIAL AID (Fall 2016, est.) 362 applied for aid; of those 76% were deemed to have need. 100% of freshmen with need received aid; of those 10% had need fully met. **Average percent of need met:** 86% (excluding resources awarded to replace EFC). **Average financial aid package:** $28,340 (excluding resources awarded to replace EFC). 19% of all full-time freshmen had no need and received non-need-based gift aid.

UNDERGRADUATE FINANCIAL AID (Fall 2016, est.) 1,523 applied for aid; of those 67% were deemed to have need. 100% of undergraduates with need received aid; of those 13% had need fully met. **Average percent of need met:** 81% (excluding resources awarded to replace EFC). **Average financial aid package:** $25,911 (excluding resources awarded to replace EFC). 26% of all full-time undergraduates had no need and received non-need-based gift aid.

GIFT AID (NEED-BASED) Total amount: $20,535,562 (14% federal, 11% state, 75% institutional). **Receiving aid:** Freshmen: 69% (270); all full-time undergraduates: 62% (1,005). **Average award:** Freshmen: $13,349; Undergraduates: $11,070. **Scholarships, grants, and awards:** Federal Pell, FSEOG, state, private, college/university gift aid from institutional funds, New York State Nursing Grants.

GIFT AID (NON-NEED-BASED) Total amount: $7,085,818 (1% state, 83% institutional, 16% external sources). **Receiving aid:** Freshmen: 64% (250). Undergraduates: 58% (941). **Average award:** Freshmen: $11,873. Undergraduates: $10,645. **Scholarships, grants, and awards by category:** Academic interests/achievement: 1,715 awards ($14,446,187 total): education, general academic interests/achievements, home economics. **Creative arts/performance:** 16 awards ($47,100 total): art/fine arts. **Special achievements/activities:** 97 awards ($122,070 total): leadership. **Special characteristics:** 64 awards ($778,537 total): children of faculty/staff, international students, veterans. **Tuition waivers:** Full or partial for employees or children of employees, senior citizens. **ROTC:** Army cooperative.

LOANS Student loans: $13,292,590 (68% need-based, 32% non-need-based). 85% of past graduating class borrowed through all loan programs. **Average indebtedness per student:** $31,359. **Average need-based loan:** Freshmen: $3892. Undergraduates: $4671. **Parent loans:** $1,940,126 (70% need-based, 30% non-need-based). **Programs:** Federal Direct (Subsidized and Unsubsidized Stafford, PLUS), Perkins, alternative loans.

WORK-STUDY Federal work-study: Total amount: $1,923,068; 713 jobs averaging $2697. **State or other work-study/employment:** Total amount: $398,549 (48% need-based, 52% non-need-based). 90 part-time jobs averaging $4428.

ATHLETIC AWARDS Total amount: $1,027,468 (38% need-based, 62% non-need-based).

APPLYING FOR FINANCIAL AID Required financial aid forms: FAFSA, state aid form. **Financial aid deadline:** Continuous. **Notification date:** Continuous beginning 11/15. Students must reply within 2 weeks of notification.

CONTACT Mr. Jeffrey Pagano, Director of Financial Aid, Daemen College, 4380 Main Street, Amherst, NY 14226-3592, 716-839-8254 or toll-free 800-462-7652. Fax: 716-839-8378. E-mail: jpagano@daemen.edu. Website: http://www.daemen.edu/.

DAKOTA STATE UNIVERSITY
Madison, SD

Tuition & fees (SD res): $8927	Average undergraduate aid package: $8117

ABOUT THE INSTITUTION State-supported, coed. **Awards:** certificates, associate, bachelor's, master's, and doctoral degrees. 28 undergraduate majors. **Total enrollment:** 3,190. Undergraduates: 2,844. Freshmen: 329. Federal methodology is used as a basis for awarding need-based institutional aid.

UNDERGRADUATE EXPENSES for 2016–2017 Application fee: $20. **Tuition, state resident:** full-time $6984; part-time $233 per credit hour. **Tuition, nonresident:** full-time $9900; part-time $330 per credit hour. **Required fees:** full-time $1943; $38.75 per credit. Full-time tuition and fees vary according to location and reciprocity agreements. Part-time tuition and fees vary according to location and reciprocity agreements. **College room and board:** $6411; **Room only:** $3494. Room and board charges vary according to board plan and housing facility.

FRESHMAN FINANCIAL AID (Fall 2015) 291 applied for aid; of those 77% were deemed to have need. 100% of freshmen with need received aid; of those 13% had need fully met. **Average percent of need met:** 77% (excluding resources awarded to replace EFC). **Average financial aid package:** $7718 (excluding resources awarded to replace EFC). 16% of all full-time freshmen had no need and received non-need-based gift aid.

UNDERGRADUATE FINANCIAL AID (Fall 2015) 1,042 applied for aid; of those 81% were deemed to have need. 100% of undergraduates with need received aid; of those 10% had need fully met. **Average percent of need met:** 74% (excluding resources awarded to replace EFC). **Average financial aid package:** $8117 (excluding resources awarded to replace EFC). 8% of all full-time undergraduates had no need and received non-need-based gift aid.

GIFT AID (NEED-BASED) Total amount: $3,798,075 (77% federal, 4% state, 10% institutional, 9% external sources). **Receiving aid:** Freshmen: 42% (136); all full-time undergraduates: 41% (511). **Average award:** Freshmen: $4187; Undergraduates: $4374. **Scholarships, grants, and awards:** Federal Pell, FSEOG, state, private, college/university gift aid from institutional funds, Agency Assistance (Veterans Benefits/Department of Labor).

GIFT AID (NON-NEED-BASED) Total amount: $374,075 (5% federal, 18% state, 41% institutional, 36% external sources). **Receiving aid:** Freshmen: 49% (158). Undergraduates: 30% (373). **Average award:** Freshmen: $4379. Undergraduates: $5138. **Scholarships, grants, and awards by category:** Academic interests/achievement: 382 awards ($480,400 total): biological sciences, business, communication, computer science, education, English, general academic interests/achievements, home economics, mathematics, physical sciences. Creative arts/performance: 8 awards ($2550 total). Special characteristics: 1 award ($700 total): veterans. **Tuition waivers:** Full or partial for employees or children of employees, senior citizens. **ROTC:** Army cooperative, Air Force cooperative.

LOANS Student loans: $10,963,093 (71% need-based, 29% non-need-based). 79% of past graduating class borrowed through all loan programs. Average indebtedness per student: $24,444. **Average need-based loan:** Freshmen: $3235. Undergraduates: $4108. **Parent loans:** $1,280,725 (71% need-based, 29% non-need-based). **Programs:** Federal Direct (Subsidized and Unsubsidized Stafford, PLUS), Perkins, alternative loans.

WORK-STUDY Federal work-study: 131 jobs averaging $2263. **State or other work-study/employment:** Total amount: $121,712 (100% non-need-based). 19 part-time jobs averaging $6405.

ATHLETIC AWARDS Total amount: $444,041 (71% need-based, 29% non-need-based).

APPLYING FOR FINANCIAL AID Required financial aid forms: FAFSA, institutional scholarship application form. **Financial aid deadline (priority):** 3/1. **Notification date:** Continuous beginning 4/1. Students must reply within 2 weeks of notification.

CONTACT Denise Grayson, Financial Aid Director, Dakota State University, 103 Heston Hall, 820 North Washington Avenue, Madison, SD 57042-1799, 605-256-5158 or toll-free 888-DSU-9988. Fax: 605-256-5020. E-mail: fa@dsu.edu. Website: http://www.dsu.edu/.

DAKOTA WESLEYAN UNIVERSITY
Mitchell, SD

Tuition & fees: $26,065	Average undergraduate aid package: N/A

ABOUT THE INSTITUTION Independent United Methodist, coed. 46 undergraduate majors. Federal methodology is used as a basis for awarding need-based institutional aid.

UNDERGRADUATE EXPENSES for 2016–2017 One-time required fee: $150. **Comprehensive fee:** $32,865 includes full-time tuition ($25,750), mandatory fees ($315), and room and board ($6800). **College room only:** $3200. Full-time tuition and fees vary according to course load and location. Room and board charges vary according to board plan and housing facility. **Part-time tuition:** $530 per credit hour. **Part-time fees:** $75 per term. Part-time tuition and fees vary according to course load.

FRESHMAN FINANCIAL AID (Fall 2015) 164 applied for aid; of those 92% were deemed to have need. 100% of freshmen with need received aid; of those 17% had need fully met. **Average percent of need met:** 76% (excluding resources awarded to replace EFC). **Average financial aid package:** $21,889 (excluding resources awarded to replace EFC). 6% of all full-time freshmen had no need and received non-need-based gift aid.

UNDERGRADUATE FINANCIAL AID (Fall 2015) 823 applied for aid; of those 90% were deemed to have need. 100% of undergraduates with need received aid; of those 7% had need fully met. **Average percent of need met:** 58% (excluding resources awarded to replace EFC). 3% of all full-time undergraduates had no need and received non-need-based gift aid.

GIFT AID (NEED-BASED) Total amount: $8,485,184 (16% federal, 3% state, 77% institutional, 4% external sources). **Receiving aid:** Freshmen: 34% (61); all full-time undergraduates: 26% (237). **Average award:** Freshmen: $19,378; Undergraduates: $13,425. **Scholarships, grants, and awards:** Federal Pell, FSEOG, state, college/university gift aid from institutional funds.

GIFT AID (NON-NEED-BASED) Total amount: $37,100 (100% federal). **Receiving aid:** Undergraduates: 1% (10). **Average award:** Freshmen: $12,227. Undergraduates: $10,158. **Scholarships, grants, and awards by category:** Academic interests/achievement: 31 awards ($67,240 total): biological sciences, business, education, general academic interests/achievements, mathematics, premedicine. Creative arts/performance: 33 awards ($69,700 total): art/fine arts, music, theater/drama. Special achievements/activities: 10 awards ($10,000 total): cheerleading/drum major, general special achievements/activities. Special characteristics: 62 awards ($225,719 total): children of faculty/staff, religious affiliation. **Tuition waivers:** Full or partial for employees or children of employees, senior citizens.

LOANS Student loans: $7,436,586 (35% need-based, 65% non-need-based). 85% of past graduating class borrowed through all loan programs. Average indebtedness per student: $37,564. **Average need-based loan:** Freshmen: $6392. Undergraduates: $9320. **Parent loans:** $640,781 (100% non-need-based). **Programs:** Federal Direct (Subsidized and Unsubsidized Stafford, PLUS), Perkins, private loans, United Methodist Student Loans (for members of Methodist Church).

WORK-STUDY Federal work-study: 109 jobs averaging $1550.

ATHLETIC AWARDS Total amount: $1,657,649 (100% need-based).

APPLYING FOR FINANCIAL AID Financial aid deadline (priority): 4/1. **Notification date:** Continuous beginning 3/1. Students must reply within 2 weeks of notification.

CONTACT Mary Alexander, Director of Financial Aid, Dakota Wesleyan University, 1200 West University Avenue, Mitchell, SD 57301, 605-995-2663 or toll-free 800-333-8506. Fax: 605-995-2122. E-mail: maalexan@dwu.edu. Website: http://www.dwu.edu/.

DALLAS BAPTIST UNIVERSITY
Dallas, TX

Tuition & fees: $26,180	Average undergraduate aid package: $15,416

ABOUT THE INSTITUTION Independent Baptist General Convention of Texas, coed. **Awards:** certificates, associate, bachelor's, master's, and doctoral degrees. 54 undergraduate majors. **Total enrollment:** 5,156. Undergraduates: 3,223. Freshmen: 527. Federal methodology is used as a basis for awarding need-based institutional aid.

UNDERGRADUATE EXPENSES for 2016–2017 *Application fee:* $25. *Comprehensive fee:* $33,713 includes full-time tuition ($25,380), mandatory fees ($800), and room and board ($7533). *College room only:* $3685. Full-time tuition and fees vary according to course load. Room and board charges vary according to board plan and housing facility. *Part-time tuition:* $846 per credit hour. *Part-time fees:* $400 per term. Part-time tuition and fees vary according to course load.

FRESHMAN FINANCIAL AID (Fall 2016, est.) 506 applied for aid; of those 74% were deemed to have need. 99% of freshmen with need received aid; of those 36% had need fully met. *Average percent of need met:* 60% (excluding resources awarded to replace EFC). *Average financial aid package:* $15,619 (excluding resources awarded to replace EFC). 23% of all full-time freshmen had no need and received non-need-based gift aid.

UNDERGRADUATE FINANCIAL AID (Fall 2016, est.) 2,067 applied for aid; of those 77% were deemed to have need. 97% of undergraduates with need received aid; of those 34% had need fully met. *Average percent of need met:* 57% (excluding resources awarded to replace EFC). *Average financial aid package:* $15,416 (excluding resources awarded to replace EFC). 21% of all full-time undergraduates had no need and received non-need-based gift aid.

GIFT AID (NEED-BASED) *Total amount:* $6,719,703 (54% federal, 46% state). *Receiving aid:* Freshmen: 44% (229); all full-time undergraduates: 42% (1,004). *Average award:* Freshmen: $4008; Undergraduates: $3975. *Scholarships, grants, and awards:* Federal Pell, FSEOG, state, private, college/university gift aid from institutional funds.

GIFT AID (NON-NEED-BASED) *Total amount:* $18,755,009 (89% institutional, 11% external sources). *Receiving aid:* Freshmen: 68% (353). Undergraduates: 57% (1,377). *Average award:* Freshmen: $9994. Undergraduates: $9026. *Scholarships, grants, and awards by category:* Academic interests/achievement: 988 awards ($2,867,045 total): biological sciences, business, communication, computer science, education, English, general academic interests/achievements, humanities, mathematics, physical sciences, premedicine, religion/biblical studies, social sciences. Creative arts/performance: 104 awards ($363,646 total): art/fine arts, music. Special achievements/activities: 1,686 awards ($8,243,401 total): community service, general special achievements/activities, leadership, memberships, religious involvement. Special characteristics: 266 awards ($1,097,592 total): children of faculty/staff, general special characteristics, relatives of clergy, religious affiliation, veterans, veterans' children. *Tuition waivers:* Full or partial for employees or children of employees. *ROTC:* Army cooperative, Air Force cooperative.

LOANS *Student loans:* $15,567,895 (32% need-based, 68% non-need-based). 79% of past graduating class borrowed through all loan programs. *Average indebtedness per student:* $22,568. *Average need-based loan:* Freshmen: $3321. Undergraduates: $4126. *Parent loans:* $3,916,239 (100% non-need-based). *Programs:* Federal Direct (Subsidized and Unsubsidized Stafford, PLUS), state.

WORK-STUDY *Federal work-study:* Total amount: $367,968; 118 jobs averaging $2433. *State or other work-study/employment:* Total amount: $33,000 (100% need-based). 11 part-time jobs averaging $2139.

ATHLETIC AWARDS Total amount: $1,970,250 (100% non-need-based).

APPLYING FOR FINANCIAL AID *Required financial aid forms:* FAFSA, institution's own form. *Financial aid deadline:* Continuous. *Notification date:* Continuous beginning 2/1.

CONTACT Mr. Lee Ferguson, Assistant Vice President of Financial Aid, Dallas Baptist University, 3000 Mountain Creek Parkway, Dallas, TX 75211-9299, 214-333-5363 or toll-free 800-460-1328. *Fax:* 214-333-5586. *E-mail:* lee@dbu.edu. *Website:* http://www.dbu.edu/.

DALLAS CHRISTIAN COLLEGE
Dallas, TX

CONTACT Robin L. Walker, Director of Student Financial Aid, Dallas Christian College, 2700 Christian Parkway, Dallas, TX 75234-7299, 972-241-3371 Ext. 105 or toll-free 800-688-1029. *Fax:* 972-241-8021. *E-mail:* finaid@dallas.edu. *Website:* http://www.dallas.edu/.

DALTON STATE COLLEGE
Dalton, GA

ABOUT THE INSTITUTION State-supported, coed. *Awards:* certificates, associate, and bachelor's degrees. 37 undergraduate majors. *Total enrollment:* 5,188. Undergraduates: 5,188. Freshmen: 1,059.

GIFT AID (NEED-BASED) *Scholarships, grants, and awards:* Federal Pell, FSEOG, state, private.

GIFT AID (NON-NEED-BASED) *Scholarships, grants, and awards by category:* Academic interests/achievement: biological sciences, business, computer science, education, engineering/technologies, English, general academic interests/achievements, health fields, humanities, social sciences. Special achievements/activities: community service, hobbies/interests, leadership, memberships. Special characteristics: adult students, children of faculty/staff, local/state students, members of minority groups, out-of-state students.

LOANS *Programs:* state.

APPLYING FOR FINANCIAL AID *Required financial aid form:* FAFSA.

CONTACT Holly Woods, Assistant Director of Financial Aid, Dalton State College, 650 College Drive, Dalton, GA 30720, 706-272-4545 or toll-free 800-829-4436. *Fax:* 706-272-2458. *E-mail:* finaid@daltonstate.edu. *Website:* http://www.daltonstate.edu/.

DARTMOUTH COLLEGE
Hanover, NH

Tuition & fees: $51,438	Average undergraduate aid package: $49,141

ABOUT THE INSTITUTION Independent, coed. *Awards:* bachelor's, master's, and doctoral degrees. 60 undergraduate majors. *Total enrollment:* 6,381. Undergraduates: 4,310. Freshmen: 1,116. Both federal and institutional methodology are used as a basis for awarding need-based institutional aid.

UNDERGRADUATE EXPENSES for 2016–2017 *Application fee:* $80. *One-time required fee:* $405. *Comprehensive fee:* $66,174 includes full-time tuition ($49,998), mandatory fees ($1440), and room and board ($14,736). *College room only:* $8886. Room and board charges vary according to board plan. *Payment plan:* Tuition prepayment.

FRESHMAN FINANCIAL AID (Fall 2016, est.) 651 applied for aid; of those 82% were deemed to have need. 100% of freshmen with need received aid; of those 100% had need fully met. *Average percent of need met:* 100% (excluding resources awarded to replace EFC). *Average financial aid package:* $50,643 (excluding resources awarded to replace EFC).

UNDERGRADUATE FINANCIAL AID (Fall 2016, est.) 2,458 applied for aid; of those 89% were deemed to have need. 100% of undergraduates with need received aid; of those 100% had need fully met. *Average percent of need met:* 100% (excluding resources awarded to replace EFC). *Average financial aid package:* $49,141 (excluding resources awarded to replace EFC).

GIFT AID (NEED-BASED) *Total amount:* $98,111,517 (4% federal, 94% institutional, 2% external sources). *Receiving aid:* Freshmen: 46% (508); all full-time undergraduates: 50% (2,097). *Average award:* Freshmen: $49,025; Undergraduates: $46,770. *Scholarships, grants, and awards:* Federal Pell, FSEOG, state, private, college/university gift aid from institutional funds.

GIFT AID (NON-NEED-BASED) *Total amount:* $934,999 (9% federal, 91% external sources). *ROTC:* Army cooperative.

LOANS *Student loans:* $9,697,923 (50% need-based, 50% non-need-based). 48% of past graduating class borrowed through all loan programs. *Average indebtedness per student:* $17,849. *Average need-based loan:* Freshmen: $4213. Undergraduates: $4579. *Parent loans:* $4,009,084 (100% non-need-based). *Programs:* Federal Direct (Subsidized and Unsubsidized Stafford, PLUS), Perkins, state, college/university.

WORK-STUDY *Federal work-study:* Total amount: $2,774,684; 1,232 jobs averaging $2196. *State or other work-study/employment:* Total amount: $1,400,264 (100% need-based). 567 part-time jobs averaging $2480.

APPLYING FOR FINANCIAL AID *Required financial aid forms:* FAFSA, CSS Financial Aid PROFILE, noncustodial (divorced/separated) parent's statement, business/farm supplement, current W-2 or federal tax returns. *Financial aid deadline:* 2/1. *Notification date:* 4/2. Students must reply by 5/1.

CONTACT Mr. Gordon D. Koff, Director of Financial Aid, Dartmouth College, 6024 McNutt Hall, Hanover, NH 03755, 603-646-2451. *Fax:* 603-646-1414. *E-mail:* gordon.d.koff@dartmouth.edu.
Website: http://www.dartmouth.edu/.

DAVENPORT UNIVERSITY
Grand Rapids, MI

CONTACT David DeBoer, Executive Director of Financial Aid, Davenport University, 6191 Kraft Avenue SE, Grand Rapids, MI 49512, 616-732-1132 or toll-free 800-686-1600 (in-state), 866-686-1600 (out-of-state). *Fax:* 616-732-1167. *E-mail:* david.debore@davenport.edu.
Website: http://www.davenport.edu/.

DAVIDSON COLLEGE
Davidson, NC

Tuition & fees: $50,444	Average undergraduate aid package: $45,001

ABOUT THE INSTITUTION Independent Presbyterian, coed. *Awards:* bachelor's degrees. 27 undergraduate majors. *Total enrollment:* 1,796. Undergraduates: 1,796. Freshmen: 514. Both federal and institutional methodology are used as a basis for awarding need-based institutional aid.
UNDERGRADUATE EXPENSES for 2017–2018 *Application fee:* $50. *Comprehensive fee:* $64,398 includes full-time tuition ($49,949), mandatory fees ($495), and room and board ($13,954). *College room only:* $7102. Room and board charges vary according to board plan.
FRESHMAN FINANCIAL AID (Fall 2016, est.) 338 applied for aid; of those 78% were deemed to have need. 100% of freshmen with need received aid; of those 100% had need fully met. *Average percent of need met:* 100% (excluding resources awarded to replace EFC). *Average financial aid package:* $46,079 (excluding resources awarded to replace EFC). 4% of all full-time freshmen had no need and received non-need-based gift aid.
UNDERGRADUATE FINANCIAL AID (Fall 2016, est.) 1,025 applied for aid; of those 86% were deemed to have need. 100% of undergraduates with need received aid; of those 100% had need fully met. *Average percent of need met:* 100% (excluding resources awarded to replace EFC). *Average financial aid package:* $45,001 (excluding resources awarded to replace EFC). 7% of all full-time undergraduates had no need and received non-need-based gift aid.
GIFT AID (NEED-BASED) *Total amount:* $36,663,748 (4% federal, 1% state, 93% institutional, 2% external sources). *Receiving aid:* Freshmen: 51% (262); all full-time undergraduates: 48% (864). *Average award:* Freshmen: $42,011; Undergraduates: $41,998. *Scholarships, grants, and awards:* Federal Pell, FSEOG, state, private, college/university gift aid from institutional funds, need-linked special talent scholarships.
GIFT AID (NON-NEED-BASED) *Total amount:* $5,016,145 (7% federal, 75% institutional, 18% external sources). *Receiving aid:* Freshmen: 17% (89). Undergraduates: 13% (239). *Average award:* Freshmen: $31,207. Undergraduates: $25,572. *Scholarships, grants, and awards by category: Academic interests/achievement:* biological sciences, business, education, foreign languages, general academic interests/achievements, health fields, international studies, mathematics, physical sciences, premedicine, religion/biblical studies, social sciences. *Creative arts/performance:* art/fine arts, creative writing, music, performing arts, theater/drama. *Special achievements/activities:* community service, general special achievements/activities, leadership, religious involvement. *Special characteristics:* first-generation college students, general special characteristics, local/state students, out-of-state students, relatives of clergy, religious affiliation. *Tuition waivers:* Full or partial for employees or children of employees. *ROTC:* Army, Air Force cooperative.
LOANS *Student loans:* $2,882,427 (27% need-based, 73% non-need-based). 26% of past graduating class borrowed through all loan programs. *Average indebtedness per student:* $20,431. *Average need-based loan:* Freshmen: $2719. Undergraduates: $3525. *Parent loans:* $3,220,180 (100% non-need-based). *Programs:* Federal Direct (Subsidized and Unsubsidized Stafford, PLUS), alternative loans.

WORK-STUDY *Federal work-study:* Total amount: $685,328; jobs available. *State or other work-study/employment:* Total amount: $329,330 (100% need-based). Part-time jobs available.
ATHLETIC AWARDS Total amount: $3,589,319 (9% need-based, 91% non-need-based).
APPLYING FOR FINANCIAL AID *Required financial aid forms:* FAFSA, CSS Financial Aid PROFILE, noncustodial (divorced/separated) parent's statement, business/farm supplement, federal income tax form(s), W-2 forms. *Financial aid deadline:* 2/15. *Notification date:* 4/1. Students must reply by 5/1.
CONTACT Mr. David R. Gelinas, Director of Financial Aid, Davidson College, 413 North Main Street, PO Box 7157, Davidson, NC 28035-7157, 704-894-2232 or toll-free 800-768-0380. *Fax:* 704-894-2845. *E-mail:* dagelinas@davidson.edu.
Website: http://www.davidson.edu/.

DAVIS & ELKINS COLLEGE
Elkins, WV

CONTACT Susan M. George, Director of Financial Planning, Davis & Elkins College, 100 Campus Drive, Elkins, WV 26241-3996, 304-637-1373 or toll-free 800-624-3157. *Fax:* 304-637-1986. *E-mail:* ssw@davisandelkins.edu.
Website: http://www.dewv.edu/.

DAVIS COLLEGE
Johnson City, NY

Tuition & fees: $16,300	Average undergraduate aid package: $7098

ABOUT THE INSTITUTION Independent nondenominational, coed. *Awards:* certificates, diplomas, associate, and bachelor's degrees. 8 undergraduate majors. *Total enrollment:* 216. Undergraduates: 216. Freshmen: 42. Federal methodology is used as a basis for awarding need-based institutional aid.
UNDERGRADUATE EXPENSES for 2017–2018 *Application fee:* $45. *One-time required fee:* $150. *Comprehensive fee:* $24,000 includes full-time tuition ($15,000), mandatory fees ($1300), and room and board ($7700). Full-time tuition and fees vary according to course load and location. Room and board charges vary according to board plan and housing facility. *Part-time tuition:* $500 per credit hour. *Part-time fees:* $650 per year. Part-time tuition and fees vary according to course load and location.
FRESHMAN FINANCIAL AID (Fall 2015) 32 applied for aid; of those 100% were deemed to have need. 100% of freshmen with need received aid; of those 47% had need fully met. *Average percent of need met:* 60% (excluding resources awarded to replace EFC). *Average financial aid package:* $9816 (excluding resources awarded to replace EFC).
UNDERGRADUATE FINANCIAL AID (Fall 2015) 224 applied for aid; of those 100% were deemed to have need. 100% of undergraduates with need received aid; of those 19% had need fully met. *Average percent of need met:* 50% (excluding resources awarded to replace EFC). *Average financial aid package:* $7098 (excluding resources awarded to replace EFC). 3% of all full-time undergraduates had no need and received non-need-based gift aid.
GIFT AID (NEED-BASED) *Total amount:* $1,503,693 (45% federal, 18% state, 37% institutional). *Receiving aid:* Freshmen: 97% (31); all full-time undergraduates: 94% (216). *Average award:* Freshmen: $9816; Undergraduates: $7098. *Scholarships, grants, and awards:* Federal Pell, FSEOG, state, private, college/university gift aid from institutional funds.
GIFT AID (NON-NEED-BASED) *Total amount:* $134,563 (41% institutional, 59% external sources). *Receiving aid:* Freshmen: 97% (31). Undergraduates: 94% (216). *Average award:* Freshmen: $2055. Undergraduates: $3694. *Scholarships, grants, and awards by category: Academic interests/achievement:* general academic interests/achievements, religion/biblical studies. *Creative arts/performance:* music. *Special achievements/activities:* leadership. *Special characteristics:* children and siblings of alumni, children of educators, children of faculty/staff, general special characteristics, international students, married students, out-of-state students, relatives of clergy, siblings of current students, spouses of current students. *Tuition waivers:* Full or partial for employees or children of employees.

LOANS *Student loans:* $959,714 (100% need-based). *Average indebtedness per student:* $5360. *Parent loans:* $71,066 (100% need-based). *Programs:* Federal Direct (Subsidized and Unsubsidized Stafford, PLUS), college/university.

WORK-STUDY *Federal work-study:* jobs available. *State or other work-study/employment:* Part-time jobs available.

APPLYING FOR FINANCIAL AID *Required financial aid forms:* FAFSA, institution's own form, state aid form. *Financial aid deadline (priority):* 7/15. *Notification date:* Continuous beginning 8/1. Students must reply within 2 weeks of notification.

CONTACT Sandra Conklin, Financial Aid Director, Davis College, 400 Riverside Drive, Johnson City, NY 13790, 607-729-1581 Ext. 331 or toll-free 877-949-3248. *Fax:* 607-798-7754. *E-mail:* financialaid@davisny.edu.

Website: http://www.davisny.edu/.

DEAN COLLEGE
Franklin, MA

Tuition & fees: $36,960	Average undergraduate aid package: $26,219

ABOUT THE INSTITUTION Independent, coed. *Awards:* certificates, associate, and bachelor's degrees. 25 undergraduate majors. *Total enrollment:* 1,339. Undergraduates: 1,339. Freshmen: 436. Federal methodology is used as a basis for awarding need-based institutional aid.

UNDERGRADUATE EXPENSES for 2016–2017 *Comprehensive fee:* $52,692 includes full-time tuition ($36,660), mandatory fees ($300), and room and board ($15,732). *College room only:* $9936. Full-time tuition and fees vary according to class time, course load, and program. Room and board charges vary according to housing facility. *Part-time tuition:* $335 per credit. *Part-time fees:* $25 per term. Part-time tuition and fees vary according to class time, course load, and program.

FRESHMAN FINANCIAL AID (Fall 2015) 401 applied for aid; of those 94% were deemed to have need. 100% of freshmen with need received aid; of those 16% had need fully met. *Average percent of need met:* 67% (excluding resources awarded to replace EFC). *Average financial aid package:* $27,118 (excluding resources awarded to replace EFC). 9% of all full-time freshmen had no need and received non-need-based gift aid.

UNDERGRADUATE FINANCIAL AID (Fall 2015) 898 applied for aid; of those 100% were deemed to have need. 100% of undergraduates with need received aid; of those 18% had need fully met. *Average percent of need met:* 69% (excluding resources awarded to replace EFC). *Average financial aid package:* $26,219 (excluding resources awarded to replace EFC). 15% of all full-time undergraduates had no need and received non-need-based gift aid.

GIFT AID (NEED-BASED) *Total amount:* $18,202,193 (11% federal, 3% state, 86% institutional). *Receiving aid:* Freshmen: 67% (333); all full-time undergraduates: 74% (760). *Average award:* Freshmen: $7216; Undergraduates: $6336. *Scholarships, grants, and awards:* Federal Pell, FSEOG, state, private, college/university gift aid from institutional funds.

GIFT AID (NON-NEED-BASED) *Total amount:* $3,738,183 (99% institutional, 1% external sources). *Receiving aid:* Freshmen: 70% (350). Undergraduates: 73% (753). *Average award:* Freshmen: $17,457. Undergraduates: $15,568. *Tuition waivers:* Full or partial for employees or children of employees.

LOANS *Student loans:* $9,817,561 (71% need-based, 29% non-need-based). 59% of past graduating class borrowed through all loan programs. *Average indebtedness per student:* $55,598. *Average need-based loan:* Freshmen: $3319. Undergraduates: $4003. *Parent loans:* $5,525,175 (33% need-based, 67% non-need-based). *Programs:* Federal Direct (Subsidized and Unsubsidized Stafford, PLUS), Perkins, Federal Nursing, state.

WORK-STUDY *Federal work-study:* jobs available.

APPLYING FOR FINANCIAL AID *Required financial aid form:* FAFSA. *Financial aid deadline (priority):* 3/1. *Notification date:* Continuous beginning 3/15.

CONTACT Mr. Frank Dunning Mullen, Dean, Student Financial Planning and Services, Dean College, 99 Main Street, Franklin, MA 02038, 508-541-1574 or toll-free 877-TRY-DEAN. *Fax:* 508-541-1941. *E-mail:* fmullen@dean.edu.

Website: http://www.dean.edu/.

DEFIANCE COLLEGE
Defiance, OH

Tuition & fees: $32,190	Average undergraduate aid package: $22,809

ABOUT THE INSTITUTION Independent United Church of Christ, coed. *Awards:* associate, bachelor's, and master's degrees. 33 undergraduate majors. *Total enrollment:* 622. Undergraduates: 582. Freshmen: 138. Federal methodology is used as a basis for awarding need-based institutional aid.

UNDERGRADUATE EXPENSES for 2017–2018 *Application fee:* $25. *Comprehensive fee:* $42,240 includes full-time tuition ($31,480), mandatory fees ($710), and room and board ($10,050). Full-time tuition and fees vary according to course load. Room and board charges vary according to board plan and housing facility. *Part-time tuition:* $495 per credit hour. *Part-time fees:* $100 per term. Part-time tuition and fees vary according to course load.

FRESHMAN FINANCIAL AID (Fall 2015) 180 applied for aid; of those 96% were deemed to have need. 100% of freshmen with need received aid; of those 9% had need fully met. *Average percent of need met:* 67% (excluding resources awarded to replace EFC). *Average financial aid package:* $23,891 (excluding resources awarded to replace EFC). 5% of all full-time freshmen had no need and received non-need-based gift aid.

UNDERGRADUATE FINANCIAL AID (Fall 2015) 535 applied for aid; of those 95% were deemed to have need. 100% of undergraduates with need received aid; of those 11% had need fully met. *Average percent of need met:* 67% (excluding resources awarded to replace EFC). *Average financial aid package:* $22,809 (excluding resources awarded to replace EFC). 12% of all full-time undergraduates had no need and received non-need-based gift aid.

GIFT AID (NEED-BASED) *Total amount:* $9,251,757 (13% federal, 3% state, 76% institutional, 8% external sources). *Receiving aid:* Freshmen: 95% (172); all full-time undergraduates: 88% (506). *Average award:* Freshmen: $19,448; Undergraduates: $17,895. *Scholarships, grants, and awards:* Federal Pell, FSEOG, state, private, college/university gift aid from institutional funds.

GIFT AID (NON-NEED-BASED) *Receiving aid:* Freshmen: 7% (13). Undergraduates: 7% (40). *Average award:* Freshmen: $11,647. Undergraduates: $14,680. *Scholarships, grants, and awards by category: Academic interests/achievement:* biological sciences, business, communication, education, English, general academic interests/achievements, humanities, international studies, mathematics, physical sciences, premedicine, religion/biblical studies, social sciences. *Creative arts/performance:* applied art and design, music. *Special achievements/activities:* community service, general special achievements/activities, leadership, religious involvement. *Special characteristics:* children and siblings of alumni, children of faculty/staff, international students, members of minority groups, religious affiliation, veterans, veterans' children. *Tuition waivers:* Full or partial for employees or children of employees.

LOANS *Student loans:* $4,487,027 (100% need-based). 82% of past graduating class borrowed through all loan programs. *Average indebtedness per student:* $19,554. *Average need-based loan:* Freshmen: $3984. Undergraduates: $4566. *Parent loans:* $992,712 (100% need-based). *Programs:* Federal Direct (Subsidized and Unsubsidized Stafford, PLUS), Perkins, alternative loans.

WORK-STUDY *Federal work-study:* jobs available. *State or other work-study/employment:* Part-time jobs available.

APPLYING FOR FINANCIAL AID *Required financial aid form:* FAFSA. *Financial aid deadline (priority):* 4/1. *Notification date:* Continuous beginning 12/15. Students must reply by 5/1 or within 2 weeks of notification.

CONTACT Amy Francis, Director of Financial Aid, Defiance College, 701 North Clinton Street, Defiance, OH 43512-1610, 419-783-2376 or toll-free 800-520-4632. *Fax:* 419-783-2579. *E-mail:* afrancis@defiance.edu.

Website: http://www.defiance.edu/.

DELAWARE STATE UNIVERSITY
Dover, DE

ABOUT THE INSTITUTION State-supported, coed. *Awards:* bachelor's, master's, and doctoral degrees. 137 undergraduate majors. *Total enrollment:* 4,288. Undergraduates: 3,943. Freshmen: 897.

GIFT AID (NEED-BASED) *Scholarships, grants, and awards:* Federal Pell, FSEOG, state, college/university gift aid from institutional funds, Federal Nursing.

GIFT AID (NON-NEED-BASED) *Scholarships, grants, and awards by category:* *Academic interests/achievement:* general academic interests/achievements. *Creative arts/performance:* music. *Special achievements/activities:* general special achievements/activities. *Special characteristics:* out-of-state students.

LOANS *Programs:* Federal Direct (Subsidized and Unsubsidized Stafford, PLUS), Perkins, Federal Nursing.

APPLYING FOR FINANCIAL AID *Required financial aid form:* FAFSA.

CONTACT Stephen J. Ampersand, Assistant Vice President for Financial Aid Services, Delaware State University, 1200 North DuPont Highway, Dover, DE 19901-2277, 302-857-6250 or toll-free 800-845-2544. *E-mail:* sampersand@desu.edu. *Website:* http://www.desu.edu/.

DELAWARE VALLEY UNIVERSITY
Doylestown, PA

Tuition & fees: $36,750	Average undergraduate aid package: $24,129

ABOUT THE INSTITUTION Independent, coed. *Awards:* certificates, associate, bachelor's, master's, and doctoral degrees. 25 undergraduate majors. *Total enrollment:* 2,376. Undergraduates: 1,967. Freshmen: 451. Federal methodology is used as a basis for awarding need-based institutional aid.

UNDERGRADUATE EXPENSES for 2016–2017 *Application fee:* $50. *Comprehensive fee:* $50,078 includes full-time tuition ($34,440), mandatory fees ($2310), and room and board ($13,328). *College room only:* $6234. Full-time tuition and fees vary according to class time, degree level, and program. Room and board charges vary according to board plan and housing facility. *Part-time tuition:* $950 per credit hour. *Part-time fees:* $116 per course. Part-time tuition and fees vary according to class time, course load, degree level, and program.

FRESHMAN FINANCIAL AID (Fall 2016, est.) 431 applied for aid; of those 88% were deemed to have need. 100% of freshmen with need received aid; of those 14% had need fully met. *Average percent of need met:* 66% (excluding resources awarded to replace EFC). *Average financial aid package:* $28,389 (excluding resources awarded to replace EFC). 16% of all full-time freshmen had no need and received non-need-based gift aid.

UNDERGRADUATE FINANCIAL AID (Fall 2016, est.) 1,549 applied for aid; of those 90% were deemed to have need. 100% of undergraduates with need received aid; of those 12% had need fully met. *Average percent of need met:* 64% (excluding resources awarded to replace EFC). *Average financial aid package:* $24,129 (excluding resources awarded to replace EFC). 19% of all full-time undergraduates had no need and received non-need-based gift aid.

GIFT AID (NEED-BASED) *Total amount:* $29,469,818 (9% federal, 6% state, 84% institutional, 1% external sources). *Receiving aid:* Freshmen: 84% (381); all full-time undergraduates: 79% (1,391). *Average award:* Freshmen: $22,974; Undergraduates: $21,111. *Scholarships, grants, and awards:* Federal Pell, FSEOG, state, private, college/university gift aid from institutional funds.

GIFT AID (NON-NEED-BASED) *Total amount:* $6,649,000 (1% state, 98% institutional, 1% external sources). *Receiving aid:* Freshmen: 9% (42). Undergraduates: 7% (127). *Average award:* Freshmen: $18,474. Undergraduates: $16,925. *Tuition waivers:* Full or partial for employees or children of employees.

LOANS *Student loans:* $16,262,106 (72% need-based, 28% non-need-based). 84% of past graduating class borrowed through all loan programs. *Average indebtedness per student:* $47,640. *Average need-based loan:* Freshmen: $4460. Undergraduates: $3593. *Parent loans:* $8,638,286 (58% need-based, 42% non-need-based). *Programs:* Federal Direct (Subsidized and Unsubsidized Stafford, PLUS), Perkins.

WORK-STUDY *Federal work-study:* Total amount: $272,074; 154 jobs averaging $1767.

APPLYING FOR FINANCIAL AID *Required financial aid forms:* FAFSA, state aid form. *Financial aid deadline (priority):* 4/15. *Notification date:* Continuous beginning 3/1. Students must reply by 5/1 or within 2 weeks of notification.

CONTACT Ms. Joan Hock, Director of Student Financial Aid, Delaware Valley University, 700 East Butler Avenue, Doylestown, PA 18901-2697, 215-489-2975 or toll-free 800-2DELVAL. *E-mail:* finaid@delval.edu. *Website:* http://www.delval.edu/.

DELTA STATE UNIVERSITY
Cleveland, MS

Tuition & fees (MS res): $6418	Average undergraduate aid package: $8361

ABOUT THE INSTITUTION State-supported, coed. 38 undergraduate majors. Federal methodology is used as a basis for awarding need-based institutional aid.

UNDERGRADUATE EXPENSES for 2016–2017 *Tuition, state resident:* full-time $6298; part-time $262.50 per semester hour. *Tuition, nonresident:* full-time $6298; part-time $262.50 per semester hour. *Required fees:* full-time $120; $5 per semester hour. Full-time tuition and fees vary according to course load. Part-time tuition and fees vary according to course load. *College room and board:* $7374; *Room only:* $4314. Room and board charges vary according to board plan and housing facility.

FRESHMAN FINANCIAL AID (Fall 2015) *Average financial aid package:* $7541 (excluding resources awarded to replace EFC).

UNDERGRADUATE FINANCIAL AID (Fall 2015) *Average financial aid package:* $8361 (excluding resources awarded to replace EFC).

GIFT AID (NEED-BASED) *Total amount:* $6,089,345 (87% federal, 7% state, 6% institutional). *Receiving aid:* Freshmen: 62% (199); all full-time undergraduates: 55% (1,229). *Average award:* Freshmen: $5075; Undergraduates: $4826. *Scholarships, grants, and awards:* Federal Pell, FSEOG, state, private, college/university gift aid from institutional funds.

GIFT AID (NON-NEED-BASED) *Total amount:* $4,045,669 (19% state, 64% institutional, 17% external sources). *Receiving aid:* Freshmen: 61% (195). Undergraduates: 53% (1,194). *Scholarships, grants, and awards by category:* Academic interests/achievement: biological sciences, business, computer science, education, English, foreign languages, general academic interests/achievements, health fields, humanities, mathematics, physical sciences, premedicine, social sciences. Creative arts/performance: art/fine arts, creative writing, journalism/publications, music, performing arts. Special achievements/activities: cheerleading/drum major, general special achievements/activities, leadership, memberships. Special characteristics: children and siblings of alumni, children of faculty/staff, general special characteristics, out-of-state students. *Tuition waivers:* Full or partial for employees or children of employees, senior citizens.

LOANS *Student loans:* $11,104,436 (47% need-based, 53% non-need-based). *Average need-based loan:* Freshmen: $3121. Undergraduates: $4172. *Parent loans:* $1,457,008 (100% non-need-based). *Programs:* Federal Direct (Subsidized and Unsubsidized Stafford, PLUS), Perkins.

WORK-STUDY *Federal work-study:* 268 jobs averaging $1408. *State or other work-study/employment:* Part-time jobs available.

ATHLETIC AWARDS Total amount: $1,210,006 (100% non-need-based).

APPLYING FOR FINANCIAL AID *Required financial aid forms:* FAFSA, institution's own form. *Financial aid deadline (priority):* 3/1. *Notification date:* Continuous beginning 5/1.

CONTACT Ms. Christie Rocconi, Director of Student Financial Assistance, Delta State University, Kent Wyatt Hall 144, Highway 8 West, Cleveland, MS 38733-0001, 662-846-4670 or toll-free 800-468-6378. *Fax:* 662-846-4683. *E-mail:* finaid@deltastate.edu. *Website:* http://www.deltastate.edu/.

DENISON UNIVERSITY
Granville, OH

Tuition & fees: $48,960	Average undergraduate aid package: $40,586

ABOUT THE INSTITUTION Independent, coed. *Awards:* bachelor's degrees. 39 undergraduate majors. *Total enrollment:* 2,277. Undergraduates: 2,277. Freshmen: 637. Federal methodology is used as a basis for awarding need-based institutional aid.

UNDERGRADUATE EXPENSES for 2016–2017 *Comprehensive fee:* $60,930 includes full-time tuition ($47,870), mandatory fees ($1090), and room and board ($11,970). *College room only:* $6590. Room and board charges vary according to board plan and housing facility. *Part-time tuition:* $1495 per credit hour. Part-time tuition and fees vary according to course load.

FRESHMAN FINANCIAL AID (Fall 2016, est.) 444 applied for aid; of those 100% were deemed to have need. 100% of freshmen with need received aid; of those 40% had need fully met. *Average percent of need met:* 89% (excluding resources awarded to replace EFC). *Average financial aid package:* $39,755 (excluding resources awarded to replace EFC). 29% of all full-time freshmen had no need and received non-need-based gift aid.

UNDERGRADUATE FINANCIAL AID (Fall 2016, est.) 1,399 applied for aid; of those 100% were deemed to have need. 100% of undergraduates with need received aid; of those 36% had need fully met. *Average percent of need met:* 89% (excluding resources awarded to replace EFC). *Average financial aid package:* $40,586 (excluding resources awarded to replace EFC). 45% of all full-time undergraduates had no need and received non-need-based gift aid.

GIFT AID (NEED-BASED) *Total amount:* $39,434,176 (5% federal, 1% state, 93% institutional, 1% external sources). *Receiving aid:* Freshmen: 70% (444); all full-time undergraduates: 62% (1,395). *Average award:* Freshmen: $34,624; Undergraduates: $34,576. *Scholarships, grants, and awards:* Federal Pell, FSEOG, state, private, college/university gift aid from institutional funds.

GIFT AID (NON-NEED-BASED) *Total amount:* $26,351,964 (99% institutional, 1% external sources). *Receiving aid:* Freshmen: 68% (436). Undergraduates: 61% (1,369). *Average award:* Freshmen: $23,414. Undergraduates: $20,710. *Scholarships, grants, and awards by category:* Academic interests/achievement: biological sciences, English, foreign languages, mathematics, physical sciences. *Special characteristics:* children of faculty/staff, veterans. *Tuition waivers:* Full or partial for employees or children of employees. *ROTC:* Army cooperative.

LOANS *Student loans:* $10,766,615 (45% need-based, 55% non-need-based). 54% of past graduating class borrowed through all loan programs. *Average indebtedness per student:* $28,833. *Average need-based loan:* Freshmen: $3758. Undergraduates: $5103. *Parent loans:* $3,998,902 (32% need-based, 68% non-need-based). *Programs:* Federal Direct (Subsidized and Unsubsidized Stafford, PLUS), Perkins, college/university.

WORK-STUDY *Federal work-study:* Total amount: $1,416,093; jobs available. *State or other work-study/employment:* Total amount: $3,443,678 (26% need-based, 74% non-need-based). Part-time jobs available.

APPLYING FOR FINANCIAL AID *Required financial aid form:* FAFSA. *Financial aid deadline:* Continuous. *Notification date:* Continuous beginning 3/15. Students must reply within 2 weeks of notification.

CONTACT Ms. Laura Meek, Director of Financial Aid, Denison University, PO Box M, Granville, OH 43023-0613, 740-587-6279 or toll-free 800-DENISON. Fax: 740-587-5706. *E-mail:* meekl@denison.edu. *Website:* http://www.denison.edu/.

DENVER SCHOOL OF NURSING
Denver, CO

CONTACT Financial Aid Office, Denver School of Nursing, 1401 19th Street, Denver, CO 80202, 303-292-0015 or toll-free 888-479-5550. *Website:* http://www.denverschoolofnursing.edu/.

DEPAUL UNIVERSITY
Chicago, IL

Tuition & fees: $37,626	Average undergraduate aid package: $22,627

ABOUT THE INSTITUTION Independent Roman Catholic, coed. *Awards:* certificates, bachelor's, master's, and doctoral degrees. 107 undergraduate majors. *Total enrollment:* 23,539. Undergraduates: 15,961. Freshmen: 2,519. Federal methodology is used as a basis for awarding need-based institutional aid.

UNDERGRADUATE EXPENSES for 2016–2017 *Comprehensive fee:* $51,013 includes full-time tuition ($37,020), mandatory fees ($606), and room and board ($13,387). *College room only:* $9640. Full-time tuition and fees vary according to course load and program. Room and board charges vary according to board plan, housing facility, and location. *Part-time tuition:* $600 per credit hour. Part-time tuition and fees vary according to course load and program.

FRESHMAN FINANCIAL AID (Fall 2015) 2,134 applied for aid; of those 84% were deemed to have need. 100% of freshmen with need received aid; of those 13%

had need fully met. *Average percent of need met:* 65% (excluding resources awarded to replace EFC). *Average financial aid package:* $24,454 (excluding resources awarded to replace EFC). 25% of all full-time freshmen had no need and received non-need-based gift aid.

UNDERGRADUATE FINANCIAL AID (Fall 2015) 10,668 applied for aid; of those 88% were deemed to have need. 99% of undergraduates with need received aid; of those 9% had need fully met. *Average percent of need met:* 61% (excluding resources awarded to replace EFC). *Average financial aid package:* $22,627 (excluding resources awarded to replace EFC). 19% of all full-time undergraduates had no need and received non-need-based gift aid.

GIFT AID (NEED-BASED) *Total amount:* $106,207,000 (23% federal, 17% state, 60% institutional). *Receiving aid:* Freshmen: 61% (1,528); all full-time undergraduates: 58% (8,050). *Average award:* Freshmen: $10,623; Undergraduates: $11,848. *Scholarships, grants, and awards:* Federal Pell, FSEOG, state, private, college/university gift aid from institutional funds, TEACH Grants, veteran awards.

GIFT AID (NON-NEED-BASED) *Total amount:* $103,838,000 (6% federal, 91% institutional, 3% external sources). *Receiving aid:* Freshmen: 61% (1,540). Undergraduates: 45% (6,280). *Average award:* Freshmen: $14,906. Undergraduates: $13,981. *Scholarships, grants, and awards by category:* Academic interests/achievement: general academic interests/achievements. Creative arts/performance: art/fine arts, music, theater/drama. Special achievements/activities: community service, leadership. *Special characteristics:* children of faculty/staff, local/state students, veterans, veterans' children. *Tuition waivers:* Full or partial for employees or children of employees. *ROTC:* Army.

LOANS *Student loans:* $85,020,000 (43% need-based, 57% non-need-based). 67% of past graduating class borrowed through all loan programs. *Average indebtedness per student:* $29,829. *Average need-based loan:* Freshmen: $3238. Undergraduates: $4353. *Parent loans:* $59,446,000 (100% non-need-based). *Programs:* Federal Direct (Subsidized and Unsubsidized Stafford, PLUS), Perkins, private loans.

WORK-STUDY *Federal work-study:* 579 jobs averaging $3499. *State or other work-study/employment:* Total amount: $6,606,000 (100% non-need-based). 2,343 part-time jobs averaging $2868.

ATHLETIC AWARDS Total amount: $5,629,000 (100% non-need-based).

APPLYING FOR FINANCIAL AID *Required financial aid form:* FAFSA. *Financial aid deadline:* Continuous. *Notification date:* Continuous beginning 12/15. Students must reply by 5/1 or within 4 weeks of notification.

CONTACT DePaul Central, Office of Financial Aid, DePaul University, 1 East Jackson Boulevard, Chicago, IL 60604-2287, 312-362-8610 or toll-free 800-4DE-PAUL (out-of-state). Fax: 312-362-5748. *Website:* http://www.depaul.edu/.

DEPAUW UNIVERSITY
Greencastle, IN

Tuition & fees: $47,838	Average undergraduate aid package: $39,790

ABOUT THE INSTITUTION Independent United Methodist Church, coed. *Awards:* bachelor's degrees. 44 undergraduate majors. *Total enrollment:* 2,225. Undergraduates: 2,225. Freshmen: 559. Federal methodology is used as a basis for awarding need-based institutional aid.

UNDERGRADUATE EXPENSES for 2017–2018 *Comprehensive fee:* $60,367 includes full-time tuition ($47,026), mandatory fees ($812), and room and board ($12,529). Room and board charges vary according to board plan. *Part-time tuition:* $1470 per credit hour.

FRESHMAN FINANCIAL AID (Fall 2016, est.) 468 applied for aid; of those 85% were deemed to have need. 100% of freshmen with need received aid; of those 27% had need fully met. *Average percent of need met:* 90% (excluding resources awarded to replace EFC). *Average financial aid package:* $40,923 (excluding resources awarded to replace EFC). 30% of all full-time freshmen had no need and received non-need-based gift aid.

UNDERGRADUATE FINANCIAL AID (Fall 2016, est.) 1,487 applied for aid; of those 88% were deemed to have need. 100% of undergraduates with need received aid; of those 27% had need fully met. *Average percent of need met:* 89% (excluding resources awarded to replace EFC). *Average financial aid package:* $39,790 (excluding resources awarded to replace EFC). 39% of all full-time undergraduates had no need and received non-need-based gift aid.

GIFT AID (NEED-BASED) *Total amount:* $44,480,004 (5% federal, 2% state, 88% institutional, 5% external sources). *Receiving aid:* Freshmen: 71% (397); all full-

time undergraduates: 60% (1,305). *Average award:* Freshmen: $36,721; Undergraduates: $34,859. *Scholarships, grants, and awards:* Federal Pell, FSEOG, state, private, college/university gift aid from institutional funds.

GIFT AID (NON-NEED-BASED) *Total amount:* $18,056,342 (90% institutional, 10% external sources). *Receiving aid:* Freshmen: 15% (82). Undergraduates: 12% (254). *Average award:* Freshmen: $18,481. Undergraduates: $17,350. *Scholarships, grants, and awards by category: Academic interests/achievement:* general academic interests/achievements. *Special achievements/activities:* community service. *Special characteristics:* children and siblings of alumni. *Tuition waivers:* Full or partial for employees or children of employees. *ROTC:* Army cooperative, Air Force cooperative.

LOANS *Student loans:* $12,335,905 (60% need-based, 40% non-need-based). 50% of past graduating class borrowed through all loan programs. *Average indebtedness per student:* $22,770. *Average need-based loan:* Freshmen: $4173. Undergraduates: $4920. *Parent loans:* $4,805,647 (26% need-based, 74% non-need-based). *Programs:* Federal Direct (Subsidized and Unsubsidized Stafford, PLUS), Perkins, college/university.

WORK-STUDY *Federal work-study:* Total amount: $930,361; jobs available. *State or other work-study/employment:* Total amount: $1,147,620 (38% need-based, 62% non-need-based). Part-time jobs available.

APPLYING FOR FINANCIAL AID *Required financial aid forms:* FAFSA, CSS Financial Aid PROFILE. *Financial aid deadline:* 2/1 (priority: 12/15). *Notification date:* 2/1. Students must reply by 5/1.

CONTACT Craig Slaughter, Director of Financial Aid, DePauw University, 200 East Seminary, Greencastle, IN 46135-0037, 765-658-4030 or toll-free 800-447-2495. *Fax:* 765-658-4137. *E-mail:* financialaid@depauw.edu. *Website:* http://www.depauw.edu/.

DESALES UNIVERSITY
Center Valley, PA

Tuition & fees: $35,050	Average undergraduate aid package: $24,563

ABOUT THE INSTITUTION Independent Roman Catholic, coed. *Awards:* certificates, bachelor's, master's, and doctoral degrees. 47 undergraduate majors. *Total enrollment:* 3,309. Undergraduates: 2,388. Freshmen: 500. Federal methodology is used as a basis for awarding need-based institutional aid.

UNDERGRADUATE EXPENSES for 2016–2017 *Comprehensive fee:* $47,450 includes full-time tuition ($33,500), mandatory fees ($1550), and room and board ($12,400). *College room only:* $6400. Full-time tuition and fees vary according to class time and course load. Room and board charges vary according to board plan and housing facility. *Part-time tuition:* $1400 per credit hour. Part-time tuition and fees vary according to class time and course load.

FRESHMAN FINANCIAL AID (Fall 2016, est.) 468 applied for aid; of those 85% were deemed to have need. 100% of freshmen with need received aid; of those 29% had need fully met. *Average percent of need met:* 73% (excluding resources awarded to replace EFC). *Average financial aid package:* $26,214 (excluding resources awarded to replace EFC). 20% of all full-time freshmen had no need and received non-need-based gift aid.

UNDERGRADUATE FINANCIAL AID (Fall 2016, est.) 1,612 applied for aid; of those 89% were deemed to have need. 99% of undergraduates with need received aid; of those 21% had need fully met. *Average percent of need met:* 69% (excluding resources awarded to replace EFC). *Average financial aid package:* $24,563 (excluding resources awarded to replace EFC). 18% of all full-time undergraduates had no need and received non-need-based gift aid.

GIFT AID (NEED-BASED) *Total amount:* $25,794,073 (11% federal, 7% state, 81% institutional, 1% external sources). *Receiving aid:* Freshmen: 79% (397); all full-time undergraduates: 73% (1,347). *Average award:* Freshmen: $20,338; Undergraduates: $19,165. *Scholarships, grants, and awards:* Federal Pell, FSEOG, state, private, college/university gift aid from institutional funds.

GIFT AID (NON-NEED-BASED) *Total amount:* $6,575,987 (1% federal, 98% institutional, 1% external sources). *Receiving aid:* Freshmen: 75% (375). Undergraduates: 63% (1,174). *Average award:* Freshmen: $17,423. Undergraduates: $14,996. *Scholarships, grants, and awards by category: Academic interests/achievement:* 1,831 awards ($12,036,012 total): biological sciences, business, communication, computer science, education, English, foreign languages, general academic interests/achievements, health fields, humanities, mathematics, physical sciences, pre-

medicine, religion/biblical studies, social sciences. *Creative arts/performance:* 211 awards ($391,050 total): cinema/film/broadcasting, dance, performing arts, theater/drama. *Special achievements/activities:* 220 awards ($773,250 total): junior miss, leadership. *Special characteristics:* 65 awards ($372,556 total): ethnic background, international students, siblings of current students, veterans' children. *Tuition waivers:* Full or partial for employees or children of employees, adult students, senior citizens. *ROTC:* Army cooperative.

LOANS *Student loans:* $20,313,567 (70% need-based, 30% non-need-based). 78% of past graduating class borrowed through all loan programs. *Average indebtedness per student:* $40,194. *Average need-based loan:* Freshmen: $3505. Undergraduates: $4579. *Parent loans:* $4,860,091 (47% need-based, 53% non-need-based). *Programs:* Federal Direct (Subsidized and Unsubsidized Stafford, PLUS), Perkins, Federal Nursing.

WORK-STUDY *Federal work-study:* Total amount: $825,319; 468 jobs averaging $1996. *State or other work-study/employment:* Total amount: $569,732 (18% need-based, 82% non-need-based). 355 part-time jobs averaging $1992.

APPLYING FOR FINANCIAL AID *Required financial aid forms:* FAFSA, PHEAA form (PA residents only). *Financial aid deadline (priority):* 11/1. *Notification date:* Continuous beginning 12/15. Students must reply by 5/1.

CONTACT Mrs. Joyce Farmer, Director of Financial Aid, DeSales University, 2755 Station Avenue, Center Valley, PA 18034-9568, 610-282-1100 Ext. 1208. *Fax:* 610-282-0131. *E-mail:* joyce.farmer@desales.edu. *Website:* http://www.desales.edu/.

DESIGN INSTITUTE OF SAN DIEGO
San Diego, CA

CONTACT Financial Aid Office, Design Institute of San Diego, 8555 Commerce Avenue, San Diego, CA 92121, 858-566-1200 or toll-free 800-619-4337. *Website:* http://www.disd.edu/.

DEVRY COLLEGE OF NEW YORK– MIDTOWN MANHATTAN CAMPUS
New York, NY

CONTACT Elvira Senese, Dean of Student Finance, DeVry College of New York–Midtown Manhattan Campus, 30-20 Thomson Avenue, Long Island City, NY 11101, 718-472-2728 or toll-free 866-338-7934. *Fax:* 718-269-4284. *Website:* http://www.devry.edu/.

DEVRY UNIVERSITY–ADDISON CAMPUS
Addison, IL

CONTACT Sejal Amin, Director of Student Finance, DeVry University–Addison Campus, 1221 North Swift Road, Addison, IL 60101-6106, 630-953-1300 or toll-free 866-338-7934. *Website:* http://www.devry.edu/.

DEVRY UNIVERSITY–ALPHARETTA CAMPUS
Alpharetta, GA

CONTACT David Pickett, Assistant Director of Financial Aid, DeVry University–Alpharetta Campus, 2555 Northwinds Parkway, Alpharetta, GA 30004, 770-521-4900 or toll-free 866-338-7934. *Fax:* 770-664-8024. *Website:* http://www.devry.edu/.

DEVRY UNIVERSITY–ARLINGTON CAMPUS
Arlington, VA

CONTACT Roberta McDevitt, Director of Student Finance, DeVry University–Arlington Campus, 2341 Jefferson Davis Highway, Arlington, VA 22202, 866-338-7932 or toll-free 866-338-7934. *Fax:* 703-414-4040.
Website: http://www.devry.edu/.

DEVRY UNIVERSITY–CHARLOTTE CAMPUS
Charlotte, NC

CONTACT Financial Aid Office, DeVry University–Charlotte Campus, 2015 Ayrsley Town Boulevard, Suite 109, Charlotte, NC 28273, 704-697-1020 or toll-free 866-338-7934.
Website: http://www.devry.edu/.

DEVRY UNIVERSITY–CHESAPEAKE CAMPUS
Chesapeake, VA

CONTACT Financial Aid Office, DeVry University–Chesapeake Campus, 1317 Executive Boulevard, Suite 100, Chesapeake, VA 23320, 757-382-5680 or toll-free 866-338-7934.
Website: http://www.devry.edu/.

DEVRY UNIVERSITY–CHICAGO CAMPUS
Chicago, IL

CONTACT Milena Dobrina, Director of Financial Aid, DeVry University–Chicago Campus, 3300 North Campbell Avenue, Chicago, IL 60618-5994, 773-929-8500 or toll-free 866-338-7934. *Fax:* 773-348-1780.
Website: http://www.devry.edu/.

DEVRY UNIVERSITY–CHICAGO LOOP CAMPUS
Chicago, IL

CONTACT Financial Aid Office, DeVry University–Chicago Loop Campus, 225 West Washington Street, Suite 100, Chicago, IL 60606, 312-372-4900 or toll-free 866-338-7934.
Website: http://www.devry.edu/.

DEVRY UNIVERSITY–CINCINNATI CAMPUS
Cincinnati, OH

CONTACT Financial Aid Office, DeVry University–Cincinnati Campus, 8800 Governors Hill Drive, Suite 100, Cincinnati, OH 45249, 513-583-5000 or toll-free 866-338-7934.
Website: http://www.devry.edu/.

DEVRY UNIVERSITY–COLUMBUS CAMPUS
Columbus, OH

CONTACT Student Finance Office, DeVry University–Columbus Campus, 1350 Alum Creek Drive, Columbus, OH 43209-2705, 614-253-7291 or toll-free 866-338-7934. *Fax:* 614-252-4108.
Website: http://www.devry.edu/.

DEVRY UNIVERSITY–DECATUR CAMPUS
Decatur, GA

CONTACT Student Finance Office, DeVry University–Decatur Campus, 1 West Court Square, Suite 100, Decatur, GA 30030-2556, 404-270-2702 or toll-free 866-338-7934.
Website: http://www.devry.edu/.

DEVRY UNIVERSITY–FOLSOM CAMPUS
Folsom, CA

CONTACT Financial Aid Office, DeVry University–Folsom Campus, 950 Iron Point Road, Folsom, CA 95630, 916-351-3700 or toll-free 866-338-7934.
Website: http://www.devry.edu/.

DEVRY UNIVERSITY–FREMONT CAMPUS
Fremont, CA

CONTACT Kim Kane, Director of Student Finance, DeVry University–Fremont Campus, 6600 Dumbarton Circle, Fremont, CA 94555, 510-574-1100 or toll-free 866-338-7934. *Fax:* 510-742-0868.
Website: http://www.devry.edu/.

DEVRY UNIVERSITY–FRESNO CAMPUS
Fresno, CA

CONTACT Financial Aid Office, DeVry University–Fresno Campus, 7575 North Fresno Street, Fresno, CA 93720, 559-439-8595 or toll-free 866-338-7934.
Website: http://www.devry.edu/.

DEVRY UNIVERSITY–FT. WASHINGTON CAMPUS
Fort Washington, PA

CONTACT Financial Aid Office, DeVry University–Ft. Washington Campus, 1140 Virginia Drive, Fort Washington, PA 19034, 215-591-5700 or toll-free 866-338-7934.
Website: http://www.devry.edu/.

DEVRY UNIVERSITY–HENDERSON CAMPUS
Henderson, NV

CONTACT Financial Aid Office, DeVry University–Henderson Campus, 2490 Paseo Verde Parkway, Suite 150, Henderson, NV 89074, 702-933-9700 or toll-free 866-338-7934.
Website: http://www.devry.edu/.

DEVRY UNIVERSITY–IRVING CAMPUS
Irving, TX

CONTACT Student Finance Office, DeVry University–Irving Campus, 4800 Regent Boulevard, Irving, TX 75063-2440, 972-929-9310 or toll-free 866-338-7934.
Website: http://www.devry.edu/.

DEVRY UNIVERSITY–JACKSONVILLE CAMPUS
Jacksonville, FL

CONTACT Financial Aid Office, DeVry University–Jacksonville Campus, 5200 Belfort Road, Suite 175, Jacksonville, FL 32256, 904-367-4942 or toll-free 866-338-7934.
Website: http://www.devry.edu/.

DEVRY UNIVERSITY–KANSAS CITY CAMPUS
Kansas City, MO

CONTACT Maureen Kelly, Senior Associate Director of Financial Aid, DeVry University–Kansas City Campus, 11224 Holmes Street, Kansas City, MO 64131-3698, 816-941-0430 or toll-free 866-338-7934.
Website: http://www.devry.edu/.

DEVRY UNIVERSITY–LONG BEACH CAMPUS
Long Beach, CA

CONTACT Kathy Odom, Director of Financial Aid, DeVry University–Long Beach Campus, 3880 Kilroy Airport Way, Long Beach, CA 90806, 562-427-0861 or toll-free 866-338-7934. *Fax:* 562-989-1578.
Website: http://www.devry.edu/.

DEVRY UNIVERSITY–MIRAMAR CAMPUS
Miramar, FL

CONTACT Office of Financial Aid, DeVry University–Miramar Campus, 2300 Southwest 145th Avenue, Miramar, FL 33027, 954-499-9700 or toll-free 866-338-7934.
Website: http://www.devry.edu/.

DEVRY UNIVERSITY–MORRISVILLE CAMPUS
Morrisville, NC

CONTACT Financial Aid Office, DeVry University–Morrisville Campus, 1600 Perimeter Park Drive, Suite 100, Morrisville, NC 27560, 919-463-1380 or toll-free 866-338-7934.
Website: http://www.devry.edu/.

DEVRY UNIVERSITY–NASHVILLE CAMPUS
Nashville, TN

CONTACT Financial Aid Office, DeVry University–Nashville Campus, 3343 Perimeter Hill Drive, Suite 200, Nashville, TN 37211, 615-445-3456 or toll-free 866-338-7934.
Website: http://www.devry.edu/.

DEVRY UNIVERSITY–NORTH BRUNSWICK CAMPUS
North Brunswick, NJ

CONTACT Student Finance Office, DeVry University–North Brunswick Campus, 630 U.S. Highway 1, North Brunswick, NJ 08902, 732-729-3777 or toll-free 866-338-7934.
Website: http://www.devry.edu/.

DEVRY UNIVERSITY–OKLAHOMA CITY CAMPUS
Oklahoma City, OK

CONTACT Financial Aid Office, DeVry University–Oklahoma City Campus, Lakepointe Towers, 4013 Northwest Expressway Street, Suite 100, Oklahoma City, OK 73116, 405-767-9516 or toll-free 866-338-7934.
Website: http://www.devry.edu/.

DEVRY UNIVERSITY ONLINE
Addison, IL

CONTACT Financial Aid Office, DeVry University Online, 1221 North Swift Road, Addison, IL 60101 or toll-free 866-338-7934.
Website: http://www.devry.edu/.

DEVRY UNIVERSITY–ORLANDO CAMPUS
Orlando, FL

CONTACT Estrella Velazquez-Domenech, Director of Student Finance, DeVry University–Orlando Campus, 4000 Millenia Boulevard, Orlando, FL 32839, 407-345-2816 or toll-free 866-338-7934. *Fax:* 407-355-4855.
Website: http://www.devry.edu/.

DEVRY UNIVERSITY–PHOENIX CAMPUS
Phoenix, AZ

CONTACT Student Finance Office, DeVry University–Phoenix Campus, 2149 West Dunlap Avenue, Phoenix, AZ 85021-2995, 602-749-4545 or toll-free 866-338-7934. *Website:* http://www.devry.edu/.

DEVRY UNIVERSITY–POMONA CAMPUS
Pomona, CA

CONTACT Student Finance Office, DeVry University–Pomona Campus, 901 Corporate Center Drive, Pomona, CA 91768-2642, 909-622-8866 or toll-free 866-338-7934. *Website:* http://www.devry.edu/.

DEVRY UNIVERSITY–SAN ANTONIO CAMPUS
San Antonio, TX

CONTACT Financial Aid Office, DeVry University–San Antonio Campus, 618 NW Loop 410, Suite 202, San Antonio, TX 78216, 210-524-5400 or toll-free 866-338-7934. *Website:* http://www.devry.edu/.

DEVRY UNIVERSITY–SAN DIEGO CAMPUS
San Diego, CA

CONTACT Financial Aid Office, DeVry University–San Diego Campus, 2655 Camino Del Rio North, Suite 360, San Diego, CA 92108, 619-683-2446 or toll-free 866-338-7934. *Website:* http://www.devry.edu/.

DEVRY UNIVERSITY–SEVEN HILLS CAMPUS
Seven Hills, OH

CONTACT Financial Aid Office, DeVry University–Seven Hills Campus, 4141 Rockside Road, Suite 110, Seven Hills, OH 44131, 216-328-8754 or toll-free 866-338-7934. *Website:* http://www.devry.edu/.

DEVRY UNIVERSITY–SHERMAN OAKS CAMPUS
Sherman Oaks, CA

CONTACT Financial Aid Office, DeVry University–Sherman Oaks Campus, 15301 Ventura Boulevard, Building D-100, Sherman Oaks, CA 91403, 818-713-8111 or toll-free 866-338-7934. *Website:* http://www.devry.edu/.

DEVRY UNIVERSITY–TINLEY PARK CAMPUS
Tinley Park, IL

CONTACT Director of Student Finance, DeVry University–Tinley Park Campus, 18624 West Creek Drive, Tinley Park, IL 60477, 708-342-3300 or toll-free 866-338-7934. *Fax:* 708-342-3120. *Website:* http://www.devry.edu/.

DEVRY UNIVERSITY–WESTMINSTER CAMPUS
Westminster, CO

CONTACT Office of Financial Aid, DeVry University–Westminster Campus, 1870 West 122nd Avenue, Westminster, CO 80234-2010, 303-280-7400 or toll-free 866-338-7934. *Website:* http://www.devry.edu/.

DICKINSON COLLEGE
Carlisle, PA

Tuition & fees: $51,180	Average undergraduate aid package: $43,737

ABOUT THE INSTITUTION Independent, coed. *Awards:* bachelor's degrees. 43 undergraduate majors. *Total enrollment:* 2,420. Undergraduates: 2,420. Freshmen: 610. Both federal and institutional methodology are used as a basis for awarding need-based institutional aid.

UNDERGRADUATE EXPENSES for 2016–2017 *Application fee:* $65. *One-time required fee:* $25. *Comprehensive fee:* $63,974 includes full-time tuition ($50,730), mandatory fees ($450), and room and board ($12,794). *College room only:* $6598. Room and board charges vary according to board plan and housing facility. *Part-time tuition:* $6342 per course. *Part-time fees:* $56 per course.

FRESHMAN FINANCIAL AID (Fall 2016, est.) 393 applied for aid; of those 93% were deemed to have need. 100% of freshmen with need received aid; of those 98% had need fully met. *Average percent of need met:* 100% (excluding resources awarded to replace EFC). *Average financial aid package:* $45,673 (excluding resources awarded to replace EFC). 16% of all full-time freshmen had no need and received non-need-based gift aid.

UNDERGRADUATE FINANCIAL AID (Fall 2016, est.) 1,395 applied for aid; of those 93% were deemed to have need. 100% of undergraduates with need received aid; of those 85% had need fully met. *Average percent of need met:* 99% (excluding resources awarded to replace EFC). *Average financial aid package:* $43,737 (excluding resources awarded to replace EFC). 17% of all full-time undergraduates had no need and received non-need-based gift aid.

GIFT AID (NEED-BASED) *Total amount:* $48,109,249 (4% federal, 1% state, 93% institutional, 2% external sources). *Receiving aid:* Freshmen: 59% (358); all full-time undergraduates: 54% (1,264). *Average award:* Freshmen: $40,828; Undergraduates: $37,817. *Scholarships, grants, and awards:* Federal Pell, FSEOG, state, private, college/university gift aid from institutional funds.

GIFT AID (NON-NEED-BASED) *Total amount:* $6,617,895 (23% federal, 71% institutional, 6% external sources). *Receiving aid:* Freshmen: 2% (15). Undergraduates: 3% (73). *Average award:* Freshmen: $9474. Undergraduates: $10,918. *Scholarships, grants, and awards by category:* Academic interests/achievement: 909 awards ($13,181,863 total): general academic interests/achievements, military science. *Special characteristics:* 39 awards ($1,234,550 total): children and siblings of alumni, children of faculty/staff, veterans, veterans' children. *Tuition waivers:* Full or partial for employees or children of employees, senior citizens. *ROTC:* Army.

LOANS *Student loans:* $8,655,931 (75% need-based, 25% non-need-based). 54% of past graduating class borrowed through all loan programs. *Average indebtedness per student:* $26,908. *Average need-based loan:* Freshmen: $3549. Undergraduates: $4834. *Parent loans:* $3,615,171 (20% need-based, 80% non-need-based). *Programs:* Federal Direct (Subsidized and Unsubsidized Stafford, PLUS), Perkins, college/university.

WORK-STUDY *Federal work-study:* Total amount: $2,193,396; 964 jobs averaging $2271. *State or other work-study/employment:* Total amount: $748,906 (63% need-based, 37% non-need-based). 196 part-time jobs averaging $3821.
APPLYING FOR FINANCIAL AID *Required financial aid forms:* FAFSA, CSS Financial Aid PROFILE, state aid form, noncustodial (divorced/separated) parent's statement. *Financial aid deadline:* 2/1 (priority: 11/15). *Notification date:* 3/23. Students must reply by 5/1 or within 2 weeks of notification.
CONTACT Rick A. Heckman, Director of Financial Aid, Dickinson College, PO Box 1773, Carlisle, PA 17013-2896, 717-245-1300 or toll-free 000-611-1773. *Fax:* 717-245-1972. *E-mail:* finaid@dickinson.edu.
Website: http://www.dickinson.edu/.

DICKINSON STATE UNIVERSITY
Dickinson, ND

Tuition & fees (ND res): $6348	Average undergraduate aid package: $10,663

ABOUT THE INSTITUTION State-supported, coed. *Awards:* certificates, associate, and bachelor's degrees. 44 undergraduate majors. *Total enrollment:* 1,386. Undergraduates: 1,381. Freshmen: 190. Institutional methodology is used as a basis for awarding need-based institutional aid.
UNDERGRADUATE EXPENSES for 2017–2018 *Application fee:* $35. *Tuition, state resident:* full-time $5139; part-time $2569 per year. *Tuition, nonresident:* full-time $7709; part-time $3854 per year. *Required fees:* full-time $1209; $50.40 per term or $302.40 per term. Full-time tuition and fees vary according to course load, degree level, program, reciprocity agreements, and student level. Part-time tuition and fees vary according to course load, degree level, program, reciprocity agreements, and student level. *College room and board:* $6750; *Room only:* $2650. Room and board charges vary according to board plan and housing facility.
FRESHMAN FINANCIAL AID (Fall 2015) 160 applied for aid; of those 66% were deemed to have need. 93% of freshmen with need received aid; of those 41% had need fully met. *Average percent of need met:* 46% (excluding resources awarded to replace EFC). *Average financial aid package:* $10,046 (excluding resources awarded to replace EFC). 4% of all full-time freshmen had no need and received non-need-based gift aid.
UNDERGRADUATE FINANCIAL AID (Fall 2015) 645 applied for aid; of those 69% were deemed to have need. 98% of undergraduates with need received aid; of those 37% had need fully met. *Average percent of need met:* 54% (excluding resources awarded to replace EFC). *Average financial aid package:* $10,663 (excluding resources awarded to replace EFC). 3% of all full-time undergraduates had no need and received non-need-based gift aid.
GIFT AID (NEED-BASED) *Total amount:* $1,889,465 (66% federal, 19% state, 6% institutional, 9% external sources). *Receiving aid:* Freshmen: 46% (92); all full-time undergraduates: 44% (390). *Average award:* Freshmen: $4959; Undergraduates: $5358. *Scholarships, grants, and awards:* Federal Pell, FSEOG, state, private, college/university gift aid from institutional funds.
GIFT AID (NON-NEED-BASED) *Total amount:* $251,488 (2% federal, 27% state, 28% institutional, 43% external sources). *Receiving aid:* Freshmen: 5% (10). Undergraduates: 2% (22). *Average award:* Freshmen: $2857. Undergraduates: $2227. *Scholarships, grants, and awards by category:* Academic interests/achievement: agriculture, biological sciences, business, communication, computer science, education, English, foreign languages, general academic interests/achievements, health fields, humanities, mathematics, physical sciences, premedicine, social sciences. *Creative arts/performance:* art/fine arts, creative writing, journalism/publications, music, theater/drama. *Special achievements/activities:* cheerleading/drum major, leadership, rodeo. *Special characteristics:* children of faculty/staff, children with a deceased or disabled parent, ethnic background, general special characteristics, international students, members of minority groups, veterans, veterans' children. *Tuition waivers:* Full or partial for employees or children of employees.
LOANS *Student loans:* $4,204,536 (55% need-based, 45% non-need-based). 58% of past graduating class borrowed through all loan programs. *Average indebtedness per student:* $25,936. *Average need-based loan:* Freshmen: $4837. Undergraduates: $5539. *Parent loans:* $164,401 (30% need-based, 70% non-need-based). *Programs:* Federal Direct (Subsidized and Unsubsidized Stafford, PLUS), Perkins, Federal Nursing, private loans, Alaska Loans.
WORK-STUDY *Federal work-study:* 79 jobs averaging $2153. *State or other work-study/employment:* Part-time jobs available.

ATHLETIC AWARDS Total amount: $396,116 (78% need-based, 22% non-need-based).
APPLYING FOR FINANCIAL AID *Required financial aid form:* FAFSA. *Financial aid deadline (priority):* 4/15. *Notification date:* Continuous beginning 3/15. Students must reply within 4 weeks of notification.
CONTACT Mr. Chris Meek, Director of Financial Aid, Dickinson State University, 291 Campus Drive, Dickinson, ND 58601-4896, 701-483-2565 or toll-free 800-279-4295. *Fax:* 701-483-2720. *E-mail:* christopher.meek@dickinsonstate.edu. *Website:* http://www.dickinsonstate.edu/

DIGIPEN INSTITUTE OF TECHNOLOGY
Redmond, WA

Tuition & fees: $30,000	Average undergraduate aid package: $11,409

ABOUT THE INSTITUTION Proprietary, coed. *Awards:* bachelor's and master's degrees. 7 undergraduate majors. *Total enrollment:* 1,054. Undergraduates: 976. Federal methodology is used as a basis for awarding need-based institutional aid.
UNDERGRADUATE EXPENSES for 2017–2018 *Application fee:* $35. *One-time required fee:* $150. *Tuition:* full-time $29,800; part-time $960 per credit. Full-time tuition and fees vary according to course load, degree level, and program. Part-time tuition and fees vary according to course load, degree level, and program. Room and board charges vary according to board plan and housing facility.
FRESHMAN FINANCIAL AID (Fall 2015) 147 applied for aid; of those 80% were deemed to have need. 88% of freshmen with need received aid; of those 2% had need fully met. *Average percent of need met:* 68% (excluding resources awarded to replace EFC). *Average financial aid package:* $9620 (excluding resources awarded to replace EFC).
UNDERGRADUATE FINANCIAL AID (Fall 2015) 628 applied for aid; of those 88% were deemed to have need. 95% of undergraduates with need received aid; of those 20% had need fully met. *Average percent of need met:* 70% (excluding resources awarded to replace EFC). *Average financial aid package:* $11,409 (excluding resources awarded to replace EFC). 1% of all full-time undergraduates had no need and received non-need-based gift aid.
GIFT AID (NEED-BASED) *Receiving aid:* Freshmen: 33% (61); all full-time undergraduates: 32% (287). *Average award:* Freshmen: $7484; Undergraduates: $8614. *Scholarships, grants, and awards:* Federal Pell, FSEOG, state, private, college/university gift aid from institutional funds.
GIFT AID (NON-NEED-BASED) *Receiving aid:* Freshmen: 7% (13). Undergraduates: 14% (124). *Average award:* Undergraduates: $7200. *Scholarships, grants, and awards by category:* Academic interests/achievement: computer science, engineering/technologies, mathematics. *Creative arts/performance:* art/fine arts. *Special achievements/activities:* general special achievements/activities, leadership. *Tuition waivers:* Full or partial for employees or children of employees.
LOANS *Student loans:* 63% of past graduating class borrowed through all loan programs. *Average indebtedness per student:* $27,403. *Average need-based loan:* Freshmen: $3168. Undergraduates: $4054. *Programs:* Federal Direct (Subsidized and Unsubsidized Stafford, PLUS), private loans.
WORK-STUDY *Federal work-study:* 77 jobs averaging $1098.
APPLYING FOR FINANCIAL AID *Required financial aid form:* FAFSA. *Financial aid deadline (priority):* 2/15. *Notification date:* Continuous beginning 11/15. Students must reply within 2 weeks of notification.
CONTACT Mrs. Trinity Huttner, Director of Financial Aid and Scholarships, DigiPen Institute of Technology, 9931 Willows Road, Redmond, WA 98052, 425-629-5096 or toll-free 866-478-5236. *Fax:* 425-558-0378. *E-mail:* kimking@digipen.edu.
Website: http://www.digipen.edu/.

DILLARD UNIVERSITY
New Orleans, LA

CONTACT Mr. Theodis Wright, Director of Financial Aid and Scholarships, Dillard University, 2601 Gentilly Boulevard, New Orleans, LA 70122-3097, 504-816-4677 or toll-free 800-216-8094. *Fax:* 504-816-5456. *E-mail:* twright@dillard.edu. *Website:* http://www.dillard.edu/.

DIXIE STATE UNIVERSITY
St. George, UT

Tuition & fees (UT res): $5080	Average undergraduate aid package: $10,256

ABOUT THE INSTITUTION State-supported, coed. *Awards:* certificates, diplomas, associate, and bachelor's degrees. 60 undergraduate majors. *Total enrollment:* 8,993. Undergraduates: 8,993. Freshmen: 2,166. Federal methodology is used as a basis for awarding need-based institutional aid.

UNDERGRADUATE EXPENSES for 2017–2018 *Tuition, state resident:* full-time $4308; part-time $179.50 per credit hour. *Tuition, nonresident:* full-time $13,776; part-time $574 per credit hour. *Required fees:* full-time $772; $32 per credit hour or $32 per credit hour. Full-time tuition and fees vary according to course load. Part-time tuition and fees vary according to course load. *College room and board:* $5615. Room and board charges vary according to board plan, housing facility, and location.

FRESHMAN FINANCIAL AID (Fall 2016, est.) 1,559 applied for aid; of those 86% were deemed to have need. 100% of freshmen with need received aid; of those 8% had need fully met. *Average percent of need met:* 55% (excluding resources awarded to replace EFC). *Average financial aid package:* $8997 (excluding resources awarded to replace EFC). 3% of all full-time freshmen had no need and received non-need-based gift aid.

UNDERGRADUATE FINANCIAL AID (Fall 2016, est.) 3,994 applied for aid; of those 91% were deemed to have need. 100% of undergraduates with need received aid; of those 10% had need fully met. *Average percent of need met:* 60% (excluding resources awarded to replace EFC). *Average financial aid package:* $10,256 (excluding resources awarded to replace EFC). 2% of all full-time undergraduates had no need and received non-need-based gift aid.

GIFT AID (NEED-BASED) *Total amount:* $22,999,877 (70% federal, 26% state, 2% institutional, 2% external sources). *Receiving aid:* Freshmen: 55% (1,194); all full-time undergraduates: 59% (3,252). *Average award:* Freshmen: $6206; Undergraduates: $6657. *Scholarships, grants, and awards:* Federal Pell, FSEOG, state, private, college/university gift aid from institutional funds.

GIFT AID (NON-NEED-BASED) *Total amount:* $840,020 (95% state, 3% institutional, 2% external sources). *Receiving aid:* Freshmen: 37% (791). Undergraduates: 34% (1,863). *Average award:* Freshmen: $2146. Undergraduates: $2348. *Scholarships, grants, and awards by category:* Academic interests/achievement: 2,785 awards ($11,220,250 total): general academic interests/achievements. *Tuition waivers:* Full or partial for employees or children of employees, senior citizens. *ROTC:* Army.

LOANS *Student loans:* $16,618,124 (99% need-based, 1% non-need-based). 81% of past graduating class borrowed through all loan programs. *Average indebtedness per student:* $15,882. *Average need-based loan:* Freshmen: $3443. Undergraduates: $4261. *Parent loans:* $2,149,482 (86% need-based, 14% non-need-based). *Programs:* Federal Direct (Subsidized and Unsubsidized Stafford, PLUS), Perkins.

WORK-STUDY *Federal work-study:* Total amount: $483,536; 132 jobs averaging $3678. *State or other work-study/employment:* Total amount: $155,500 (100% need-based). 42 part-time jobs averaging $3702.

ATHLETIC AWARDS Total amount: $1,027,464 (92% need-based, 8% non-need-based).

APPLYING FOR FINANCIAL AID *Required financial aid form:* FAFSA. *Financial aid deadline:* 6/30 (priority: 5/1). *Notification date:* Continuous beginning 3/1. Students must reply within 2 weeks of notification.

CONTACT J. D. Robertson, Director of Financial Aid, Dixie State University, 225 South 700 East, St. George, UT 84770, 435-652-7575. *Fax:* 435-656-4087. *E-mail:* finaid@dixie.edu. *Website:* http://www.dixie.edu/.

DOANE UNIVERSITY
Crete, NE

Tuition & fees: $30,434	Average undergraduate aid package: $23,742

ABOUT THE INSTITUTION Independent United Church of Christ, coed. *Awards:* certificates, bachelor's, master's, and doctoral degrees (non-traditional undergraduate programs and graduate programs offered at Lincoln campus). 45 undergraduate majors. *Total enrollment:* 1,047. Undergraduates: 1,047. Freshmen: 303. Both federal and institutional methodology are used as a basis for awarding need-based institutional aid.

UNDERGRADUATE EXPENSES for 2016–2017 *Comprehensive fee:* $39,184 includes full-time tuition ($29,720), mandatory fees ($714), and room and board ($8750). Full-time tuition and fees vary according to location. Room and board charges vary according to board plan, housing facility, and location. *Part-time tuition:* $990 per credit hour. Part-time tuition and fees vary according to course load and location.

FRESHMAN FINANCIAL AID (Fall 2016, est.) 287 applied for aid; of those 86% were deemed to have need. 100% of freshmen with need received aid; of those 41% had need fully met. *Average percent of need met:* 95% (excluding resources awarded to replace EFC). *Average financial aid package:* $24,581 (excluding resources awarded to replace EFC). 7% of all full-time freshmen had no need and received non-need-based gift aid.

UNDERGRADUATE FINANCIAL AID (Fall 2016, est.) 890 applied for aid; of those 89% were deemed to have need. 100% of undergraduates with need received aid; of those 32% had need fully met. *Average percent of need met:* 87% (excluding resources awarded to replace EFC). *Average financial aid package:* $23,742 (excluding resources awarded to replace EFC). 8% of all full-time undergraduates had no need and received non-need-based gift aid.

GIFT AID (NEED-BASED) *Total amount:* $12,241,385 (13% federal, 3% state, 80% institutional, 4% external sources). *Receiving aid:* Freshmen: 82% (248); all full-time undergraduates: 76% (793). *Average award:* Freshmen: $21,913; Undergraduates: $19,722. *Scholarships, grants, and awards:* Federal Pell, FSEOG, state, private, college/university gift aid from institutional funds.

GIFT AID (NON-NEED-BASED) *Total amount:* $3,315,964 (5% federal, 91% institutional, 4% external sources). *Receiving aid:* Freshmen: 18% (55). Undergraduates: 13% (138). *Average award:* Freshmen: $14,690. Undergraduates: $14,600. *Scholarships, grants, and awards by category:* Academic interests/achievement: general academic interests/achievements. Creative arts/performance: art/fine arts, debating, music, performing arts, theater/drama. Special characteristics: children and siblings of alumni, children of faculty/staff, religious affiliation, siblings of current students. *Tuition waivers:* Full or partial for employees or children of employees, senior citizens. *ROTC:* Army cooperative, Air Force cooperative.

LOANS *Student loans:* $6,651,892 (66% need-based, 34% non-need-based). 78% of past graduating class borrowed through all loan programs. *Average indebtedness per student:* $30,720. *Average need-based loan:* Freshmen: $3520. Undergraduates: $4499. *Parent loans:* $3,341,185 (100% non-need-based). *Programs:* Federal Direct (Subsidized and Unsubsidized Stafford, PLUS), Perkins.

WORK-STUDY *Federal work-study:* Total amount: $426,964; jobs available. *State or other work-study/employment:* Total amount: $389,491 (100% non-need-based). Part-time jobs available.

ATHLETIC AWARDS Total amount: $3,571,532 (71% need-based, 29% non-need-based).

APPLYING FOR FINANCIAL AID *Required financial aid form:* FAFSA. *Financial aid deadline:* Continuous. *Notification date:* Continuous beginning 3/15. Students must reply within 4 weeks of notification.

CONTACT Ms. Peggy Tvrdy, Director of Financial Aid, Doane University, 1014 Boswell Avenue, Crete, NE 68333-2430, 402-826-8260 or toll-free 800-333-6263. *Fax:* 402-826-8600. *E-mail:* peggy.tvrdy@doane.edu. *Website:* http://www.doane.edu/.

DOMINICAN COLLEGE
Orangeburg, NY

Tuition & fees: $28,448	Average undergraduate aid package: $21,434

ABOUT THE INSTITUTION Independent, coed. *Awards:* certificates, diplomas, associate, bachelor's, master's, and doctoral degrees. 31 undergraduate majors. *Total enrollment:* 2,012. Undergraduates: 1,478. Freshmen: 253. Federal methodology is used as a basis for awarding need-based institutional aid.

UNDERGRADUATE EXPENSES for 2017–2018 *Application fee:* $35. *Comprehensive fee:* $41,118 includes full-time tuition ($27,588), mandatory fees ($860), and room and board ($12,670). Full-time tuition and fees vary according to degree level. Room and board charges vary according to board plan and housing facility. *Part-time tuition:* $834 per credit hour. *Part-time fees:* $200 per term. Part-time tuition and fees vary according to degree level and program.

FRESHMAN FINANCIAL AID (Fall 2016, est.) 248 applied for aid; of those 88% were deemed to have need. 100% of freshmen with need received aid; of those 14% had need fully met. *Average percent of need met:* 77% (excluding resources awarded to replace EFC). *Average financial aid package:* $26,276 (excluding resources awarded to replace EFC). 13% of all full-time freshmen had no need and received non-need-based gift aid.

UNDERGRADUATE FINANCIAL AID (Fall 2016, est.) 1,202 applied for aid; of those 90% were deemed to have need. 99% of undergraduates with need received aid; of those 12% had need fully met. *Average percent of need met:* 66% (excluding resources awarded to replace EFC). *Average financial aid package:* $21,434 (excluding resources awarded to replace EFC). 14% of all full-time undergraduates had no need and received non-need-based gift aid.

GIFT AID (NEED-BASED) *Total amount:* $16,649,888 (17% federal, 9% state, 72% institutional, 2% external sources). *Receiving aid:* Freshmen: 83% (209); all full-time undergraduates: 78% (1,037). *Average award:* Freshmen: $22,728; Undergraduates: $17,255. *Scholarships, grants, and awards:* Federal Pell, FSEOG, state, private, college/university gift aid from institutional funds.

GIFT AID (NON-NEED-BASED) *Total amount:* $2,301,166 (3% state, 92% institutional, 5% external sources). *Receiving aid:* Freshmen: 11% (28). Undergraduates: 8% (105). *Average award:* Freshmen: $10,335. Undergraduates: $9422. *Scholarships, grants, and awards by category:* Academic interests/achievement: education, general academic interests/achievements. *Special characteristics:* children of faculty/staff, general special characteristics, relatives of clergy. *Tuition waivers:* Full or partial for employees or children of employees, senior citizens.

LOANS *Student loans:* $10,744,629 (79% need-based, 21% non-need-based). 90% of past graduating class borrowed through all loan programs. *Average indebtedness per student:* $31,976. *Average need-based loan:* Freshmen: $3747. Undergraduates: $5165. *Parent loans:* $3,351,789 (57% need-based, 43% non-need-based). *Programs:* Federal Direct (Subsidized and Unsubsidized Stafford, PLUS), Perkins, Federal Nursing.

WORK-STUDY *Federal work-study:* Total amount: $371,836; 305 jobs averaging $701. *State or other work-study/employment:* Total amount: $316,940 (56% need-based, 44% non-need-based). Part-time jobs available.

ATHLETIC AWARDS Total amount: $2,168,976 (63% need-based, 37% non-need-based).

APPLYING FOR FINANCIAL AID *Required financial aid forms:* FAFSA, state aid form. *Financial aid deadline (priority):* 2/15. *Notification date:* Continuous beginning 11/1. Students must reply within 4 weeks of notification.

CONTACT Ms. Stacy Salinas, Director of Financial Aid, Dominican College, 470 Western Highway, Orangeburg, NY 10962-1210, 845-848-7818 or toll-free 866-432-4636. *Fax:* 845-359-4317. *E-mail:* stacy.salinas@dc.edu.
Website: http://www.dc.edu/.

DOMINICAN UNIVERSITY
River Forest, IL

Tuition & fees: $32,530	Average undergraduate aid package: $23,256

ABOUT THE INSTITUTION Independent Roman Catholic, coed. *Awards:* certificates, bachelor's, master's, and doctoral degrees. 65 undergraduate majors. *Total enrollment:* 3,522. Undergraduates: 2,306. Freshmen: 495. Federal methodology is used as a basis for awarding need-based institutional aid.

UNDERGRADUATE EXPENSES for 2017–2018 *Application fee:* $25. *One-time required fee:* $150. *Comprehensive fee:* $42,472 includes full-time tuition ($32,160), mandatory fees ($370), and room and board ($9942). Full-time tuition and fees vary according to course load, program, and reciprocity agreements. Room and board charges vary according to board plan and housing facility. *Part-time tuition:* $1072 per credit hour. *Part-time fees:* $90 per term. Part-time tuition and fees vary according to course load, program, and reciprocity agreements.

FRESHMAN FINANCIAL AID (Fall 2015) 468 applied for aid; of those 95% were deemed to have need. 100% of freshmen with need received aid; of those 6% had need fully met. *Average percent of need met:* 72% (excluding resources awarded to replace EFC). *Average financial aid package:* $24,562 (excluding resources awarded to replace EFC). 8% of all full-time freshmen had no need and received non-need-based gift aid.

UNDERGRADUATE FINANCIAL AID (Fall 2015) 1,745 applied for aid; of those 94% were deemed to have need. 100% of undergraduates with need received aid; of those 10% had need fully met. *Average percent of need met:* 71% (excluding resources awarded to replace EFC). *Average financial aid package:* $23,256 (excluding resources awarded to replace EFC). 9% of all full-time undergraduates had no need and received non-need-based gift aid.

GIFT AID (NEED-BASED) *Total amount:* $23,666,926 (22% federal, 21% state, 55% institutional, 2% external sources). *Receiving aid:* Freshmen: 89% (443); all full-time undergraduates: 88% (1,627). *Average award:* Freshmen: $20,870; Undergraduates: $19,183. *Scholarships, grants, and awards:* Federal Pell, FSEOG, state, private, college/university gift aid from institutional funds.

GIFT AID (NON-NEED-BASED) *Total amount:* $1,896,899 (87% institutional, 13% external sources). *Receiving aid:* Freshmen: 5% (25). Undergraduates: 7% (137). *Average award:* Freshmen: $9404. Undergraduates: $8321. *Scholarships, grants, and awards by category:* Academic interests/achievement: general academic interests/achievements, home economics. *Creative arts/performance:* applied art and design, art/fine arts. *Special characteristics:* children and siblings of alumni, children of faculty/staff, siblings of current students. *Tuition waivers:* Full or partial for employees or children of employees.

LOANS *Student loans:* $12,805,269 (86% need-based, 14% non-need-based). 88% of past graduating class borrowed through all loan programs. *Average indebtedness per student:* $28,533. *Average need-based loan:* Freshmen: $3265. Undergraduates: $4268. *Parent loans:* $2,762,966 (49% need-based, 51% non-need-based). *Programs:* Federal Direct (Subsidized and Unsubsidized Stafford, PLUS).

WORK-STUDY *Federal work-study:* 196 jobs averaging $2500. *State or other work-study/employment:* Total amount: $330,950 (47% need-based, 53% non-need-based). Part-time jobs available.

APPLYING FOR FINANCIAL AID *Required financial aid form:* FAFSA. *Financial aid deadline (priority):* 2/15. *Notification date:* Continuous beginning 11/15. Students must reply within 2 weeks of notification.

CONTACT Victoria Spivak, Director of Financial Aid, Dominican University, 7900 West Division Street, River Forest, IL 60305-1099, 708-524-6950 or toll-free 800-828-8475. *Fax:* 708-366-6478. *E-mail:* vlamick@dom.edu.
Website: http://www.dom.edu/.

DOMINICAN UNIVERSITY OF CALIFORNIA
San Rafael, CA

Tuition & fees: $44,690	Average undergraduate aid package: $27,874

ABOUT THE INSTITUTION Independent Roman Catholic Church, coed. *Awards:* bachelor's and master's degrees. 24 undergraduate majors. *Total enrollment:* 1,843. Undergraduates: 1,391. Freshmen: 269. Federal methodology is used as a basis for awarding need-based institutional aid.

UNDERGRADUATE EXPENSES for 2017–2018 *Comprehensive fee:* $58,750 includes full-time tuition ($44,240), mandatory fees ($450), and room and board ($14,060). *College room only:* $8280. Full-time tuition and fees vary according to course load. Room and board charges vary according to board plan. *Part-time tuition:* $1850 per credit hour. *Part-time fees:* $150 per term. Part-time tuition and fees vary according to course load.

FRESHMAN FINANCIAL AID (Fall 2015) 228 applied for aid; of those 91% were deemed to have need. 100% of freshmen with need received aid; of those 14% had need fully met. *Average percent of need met:* 70% (excluding resources awarded to replace EFC). *Average financial aid package:* $30,452 (excluding resources awarded to replace EFC). 16% of all full-time freshmen had no need and received non-need-based gift aid.

UNDERGRADUATE FINANCIAL AID (Fall 2015) 973 applied for aid; of those 93% were deemed to have need. 100% of undergraduates with need received aid; of those 12% had need fully met. *Average percent of need met:* 66% (excluding resources awarded to replace EFC). *Average financial aid package:* $27,874 (excluding resources awarded to replace EFC). 18% of all full-time undergraduates had no need and received non-need-based gift aid.

GIFT AID (NEED-BASED) *Total amount:* $20,700,485 (9% federal, 13% state, 74% institutional, 4% external sources). *Receiving aid:* Freshmen: 81% (207); all full-time undergraduates: 76% (899). *Average award:* Freshmen: $26,579; Undergraduates: $22,862. *Scholarships, grants, and awards:* Federal Pell, FSEOG, state, private, college/university gift aid from institutional funds, Scholarships for Disadvantaged Students (SDS).

GIFT AID (NON-NEED-BASED) *Total amount:* $4,173,877 (92% institutional, 8% external sources). *Receiving aid:* Freshmen: 10% (25). Undergraduates: 8% (92). *Average award:* Freshmen: $18,377. Undergraduates: $14,866. *Scholarships, grants, and awards by category:* Academic interests/achievement: general academic interests/achievements, humanities. *Creative arts/performance:* dance, music. *Special achievements/activities:* community service, leadership. *Special characteristics:* adult students, children and siblings of alumni, children of faculty/staff, international students, members of minority groups, veterans, veterans' children. *Tuition waivers:* Full or partial for employees or children of employees.

LOANS *Student loans:* $9,869,473 (65% need-based, 35% non-need-based). 82% of past graduating class borrowed through all loan programs. *Average indebtedness per student:* $35,369. *Average need-based loan:* Freshmen: $3349. Undergraduates: $4692. *Parent loans:* $6,010,729 (53% need-based, 47% non-need-based). *Programs:* Federal Direct (Subsidized and Unsubsidized Stafford, PLUS), Perkins, private loans.

WORK-STUDY *Federal work-study:* 223 jobs averaging $1516. *State or other work-study/employment:* Total amount: $160,560 (81% need-based, 19% non-need-based). 12 part-time jobs averaging $13,380.

ATHLETIC AWARDS Total amount: $930,786 (66% need-based, 34% non-need-based).

APPLYING FOR FINANCIAL AID *Required financial aid forms:* FAFSA, institution's own form. *Financial aid deadline (priority):* 3/1. *Notification date:* Continuous beginning 3/15. Students must reply within 2 weeks of notification.

CONTACT Ms. Shanon Little, Director of Financial Aid, Dominican University of California, 50 Acacia Avenue, San Rafael, CA 94901-2298, 415-257-1302 or toll-free 888-323-6763. *Fax:* 415-485-3294. *E-mail:* shanon.little@dominican.edu. *Website:* http://www.dominican.edu/.

DORDT COLLEGE
Sioux Center, IA

Tuition & fees: $29,130	Average undergraduate aid package: $25,429

ABOUT THE INSTITUTION Independent Christian Reformed, coed. 86 undergraduate majors. Federal methodology is used as a basis for awarding need-based institutional aid.

UNDERGRADUATE EXPENSES for 2016–2017 *Comprehensive fee:* $37,860 includes full-time tuition ($28,630), mandatory fees ($500), and room and board ($8730). Full-time tuition and fees vary according to course load. Room and board charges vary according to board plan and housing facility.

FRESHMAN FINANCIAL AID (Fall 2016, est.) 336 applied for aid; of those 81% were deemed to have need. 100% of freshmen with need received aid; of those 51% had need fully met. *Average percent of need met:* 85% (excluding resources awarded to replace EFC). *Average financial aid package:* $26,826 (excluding resources awarded to replace EFC). 25% of all full-time freshmen had no need and received non-need-based gift aid.

UNDERGRADUATE FINANCIAL AID (Fall 2016, est.) 1,104 applied for aid; of those 83% were deemed to have need. 100% of undergraduates with need received aid; of those 46% had need fully met. *Average percent of need met:* 82% (excluding resources awarded to replace EFC). *Average financial aid package:* $25,429 (excluding resources awarded to replace EFC). 25% of all full-time undergraduates had no need and received non-need-based gift aid.

GIFT AID (NEED-BASED) *Total amount:* $17,155,005 (9% federal, 8% state, 74% institutional, 9% external sources). *Receiving aid:* Freshmen: 70% (272); all full-time undergraduates: 67% (918). *Average award:* Freshmen: $19,236; Undergraduates: $16,954. *Scholarships, grants, and awards:* Federal Pell, FSEOG, state, private, college/university gift aid from institutional funds.

GIFT AID (NON-NEED-BASED) *Total amount:* $3,859,065 (92% institutional, 8% external sources). *Receiving aid:* Freshmen: 16% (64). Undergraduates: 14% (186). *Average award:* Freshmen: $21,131. Undergraduates: $21,074. *Scholarships, grants, and awards by category:* Academic interests/achievement: 1,119 awards ($7,867,873 total): agriculture, biological sciences, business, communication, computer science, education, engineering/technologies, English, foreign languages, general academic interests/achievements, humanities, mathematics, physical sciences, premedicine, religion/biblical studies, social sciences. *Creative arts/performance:* 322 awards ($1,119,125 total): debating, journalism/publications, music, theater/drama. *Special achievements/activities:* 53 awards ($86,800 total): community service, general special achievements/activities, leadership. *Special characteristics:* 1,011 awards ($1,452,373 total): children and siblings of alumni, children of faculty/staff, general special characteristics, handicapped students, international students, local/state students, members of minority groups, out-of-state students, religious affiliation. *Tuition waivers:* Full or partial for employees or children of employees, senior citizens.

LOANS *Student loans:* $10,378,725 (87% need-based, 13% non-need-based). 79% of past graduating class borrowed through all loan programs. *Average indebtedness per student:* $29,175. *Average need-based loan:* Freshmen: $4622. Undergraduates: $4936. *Parent loans:* $4,605,403 (75% need-based, 25% non-need-based). *Programs:* Federal Direct (Subsidized and Unsubsidized Stafford, PLUS), Perkins, state, college/university, alternative loans.

WORK-STUDY *Federal work-study:* Total amount: $1,690,022; 409 jobs averaging $3686. *State or other work-study/employment:* Total amount: $2,286,699 (81% need-based, 19% non-need-based). 549 part-time jobs averaging $3879.

ATHLETIC AWARDS Total amount: $3,083,468 (72% need-based, 28% non-need-based).

APPLYING FOR FINANCIAL AID *Required financial aid forms:* FAFSA, institution's own form. *Notification date:* Continuous beginning 1/1. Students must reply within 3 weeks of notification.

CONTACT Mr. Harlan Harmelink, Director of Financial Aid, Dordt College, 498 4th Avenue NE, Sioux Center, IA 51250-1697, 712-722-6082 or toll-free 800-343-6738. *Fax:* 712-722-6035. *E-mail:* harlan.harmelink@dordt.edu. *Website:* http://www.dordt.edu/.

DRAKE UNIVERSITY
Des Moines, IA

Tuition & fees: $35,206	Average undergraduate aid package: $27,171

ABOUT THE INSTITUTION Independent, coed. *Awards:* certificates, bachelor's, master's, and doctoral degrees. 66 undergraduate majors. *Total enrollment:* 5,001. Undergraduates: 3,267. Freshmen: 767. Federal methodology is used as a basis for awarding need-based institutional aid.

UNDERGRADUATE EXPENSES for 2016–2017 *Comprehensive fee:* $45,056 includes full-time tuition ($35,060), mandatory fees ($146), and room and board ($9850). *College room only:* $5300. Full-time tuition and fees vary according to course load, degree level, program, and student level. Room and board charges vary according to board plan and housing facility. *Part-time tuition:* $695 per credit. Part-time tuition and fees vary according to class time, degree level, and program.

FRESHMAN FINANCIAL AID (Fall 2016, est.) 657 applied for aid; of those 79% were deemed to have need. 100% of freshmen with need received aid; of those 29% had need fully met. *Average percent of need met:* 76% (excluding resources awarded to replace EFC). *Average financial aid package:* $26,153 (excluding resources awarded to replace EFC). 26% of all full-time freshmen had no need and received non-need-based gift aid.

UNDERGRADUATE FINANCIAL AID (Fall 2016, est.) 2,200 applied for aid; of those 83% were deemed to have need. 100% of undergraduates with need received aid; of those 27% had need fully met. *Average percent of need met:* 79% (excluding resources awarded to replace EFC). *Average financial aid package:* $27,171 (excluding resources awarded to replace EFC). 34% of all full-time undergraduates had no need and received non-need-based gift aid.

GIFT AID (NEED-BASED) *Total amount:* $34,220,564 (9% federal, 5% state, 84% institutional, 2% external sources). *Receiving aid:* Freshmen: 67% (510); all full-time undergraduates: 58% (1,781). *Average award:* Freshmen: $20,124; Undergraduates: $18,979. *Scholarships, grants, and awards:* Federal Pell, FSEOG, state, private, college/university gift aid from institutional funds.

GIFT AID (NON-NEED-BASED) *Total amount:* $19,501,684 (2% federal, 95% institutional, 3% external sources). *Receiving aid:* Freshmen: 16% (125). Undergraduates: 11% (332). *Average award:* Freshmen: $16,178. Undergraduates: $14,399. *Scholarships, grants, and awards by category:* Academic interests/achievement: 2,540 awards ($31,889,849 total): general academic interests/achievements. Creative arts/performance: 302 awards ($2,158,191 total): art/fine arts, music, theater/drama. Special characteristics: 212 awards ($312,554 total): children and siblings of alumni, international students. *Tuition waivers:* Full or partial for children of alumni, employees or children of employees, senior citizens. *ROTC:* Army cooperative, Air Force cooperative.

LOANS *Student loans:* $29,920,644 (46% need-based, 54% non-need-based). 63% of past graduating class borrowed through all loan programs. *Average indebtedness per student:* $33,649. *Average need-based loan:* Freshmen: $3094. Undergraduates: $5769. *Parent loans:* $43,164,175 (21% need-based, 79% non-need-based). *Programs:* Federal Direct (Subsidized and Unsubsidized Stafford, PLUS), Perkins, college/university, Health Professions Student Loans (HPSL).

WORK-STUDY *Federal work-study:* Total amount: $2,833,968; 1,478 jobs averaging $1917.

ATHLETIC AWARDS Total amount: $4,425,847 (22% need-based, 78% non-need-based).

APPLYING FOR FINANCIAL AID *Required financial aid form:* FAFSA. *Financial aid deadline:* Continuous. *Notification date:* Continuous beginning 1/1. Students must reply by 5/1 or within 3 weeks of notification.

CONTACT Office of Student Financial Planning, Drake University, 2507 University Avenue, Des Moines, IA 50311-4516, 800-443-7253 Ext. 2905 or toll-free 800-44-DRAKE Ext. 3181. *Fax:* 515-271-4042. *E-mail:* financialaid@drake.edu. *Website:* http://www.drake.edu/.

DREW UNIVERSITY
Madison, NJ

Tuition & fees: $47,752	Average undergraduate aid package: $42,435

ABOUT THE INSTITUTION Independent United Methodist Church, coed. *Awards:* certificates, bachelor's, master's, and doctoral degrees. 30 undergraduate majors. *Total enrollment:* 2,129. Undergraduates: 1,521. Freshmen: 350. Federal methodology is used as a basis for awarding need-based institutional aid.

UNDERGRADUATE EXPENSES for 2016–2017 *Application fee:* $40. *Comprehensive fee:* $61,048 includes full-time tuition ($46,920), mandatory fees ($832), and room and board ($13,296). *College room only:* $8396. Room and board charges vary according to board plan and housing facility. *Part-time tuition:* $1955 per credit. Part-time tuition and fees vary according to course load. *Payment plan:* Tuition prepayment.

FRESHMAN FINANCIAL AID (Fall 2016, est.) 300 applied for aid; of those 91% were deemed to have need. 100% of freshmen with need received aid; of those 15% had need fully met. *Average percent of need met:* 86% (excluding resources awarded to replace EFC). *Average financial aid package:* $43,195 (excluding resources awarded to replace EFC). 22% of all full-time freshmen had no need and received non-need-based gift aid.

UNDERGRADUATE FINANCIAL AID (Fall 2016, est.) 1,058 applied for aid; of those 94% were deemed to have need. 100% of undergraduates with need received aid; of those 16% had need fully met. *Average percent of need met:* 84% (excluding resources awarded to replace EFC). *Average financial aid package:* $42,435 (excluding resources awarded to replace EFC). 28% of all full-time undergraduates had no need and received non-need-based gift aid.

GIFT AID (NEED-BASED) *Total amount:* $35,446,559 (7% federal, 8% state, 84% institutional, 1% external sources). *Receiving aid:* Freshmen: 78% (273); all full-time undergraduates: 72% (996). *Average award:* Freshmen: $37,882; Undergraduates: $36,371. *Scholarships, grants, and awards:* Federal Pell, FSEOG, state, private, college/university gift aid from institutional funds.

GIFT AID (NON-NEED-BASED) *Total amount:* $7,933,437 (99% institutional, 1% external sources). *Receiving aid:* Freshmen: 7% (26). Undergraduates: 7% (92). *Average award:* Freshmen: $22,159. Undergraduates: $21,987. *Scholarships, grants, and awards by category:* Academic interests/achievement: general academic interests/achievements. Creative arts/performance: art/fine arts, music, performing arts, theater/drama. Special achievements/activities: community service. *Tuition waivers:* Full or partial for employees or children of employees. *ROTC:* Army cooperative.

LOANS *Student loans:* $5,575,149 (58% need-based, 42% non-need-based). 67% of past graduating class borrowed through all loan programs. *Average indebtedness per student:* $24,964. *Average need-based loan:* Freshmen: $3438. Undergraduates: $4541. *Parent loans:* $5,033,659 (41% need-based, 59% non-need-based). *Programs:* Federal Direct (Subsidized and Unsubsidized Stafford, PLUS), Perkins, state.

WORK-STUDY *Federal work-study:* Total amount: $1,390,535; 710 jobs averaging $2000. *State or other work-study/employment:* Total amount: $392,320 (94% need-based, 6% non-need-based). Part-time jobs available.

APPLYING FOR FINANCIAL AID *Required financial aid form:* FAFSA. *Financial aid deadline (priority):* 2/15. *Notification date:* 3/25. Students must reply by 5/1.

CONTACT Colby McCarthy, Director of Financial Assistance, Drew University, 36 Madison Avenue, Madison, NJ 07940-1493, 973-408-3112. *Fax:* 973-408-3188. *E-mail:* finaid@drew.edu. *Website:* http://www.drew.edu/.

DREXEL UNIVERSITY
Philadelphia, PA

Tuition & fees: $52,002	Average undergraduate aid package: $36,266

ABOUT THE INSTITUTION Independent, coed. *Awards:* certificates, bachelor's, master's, and doctoral degrees. 81 undergraduate majors. *Total*

enrollment: 24,232. Undergraduates: 15,499. Freshmen: 2,327. Federal methodology is used as a basis for awarding need-based institutional aid.

UNDERGRADUATE EXPENSES for 2017–2018 *Application fee:* $50. *Comprehensive fee:* $65,892 includes full-time tuition ($49,632), mandatory fees ($2370), and room and board ($13,890). Full-time tuition and fees vary according to course load, location, program, and student level. Room and board charges vary according to board plan and housing facility. Part-time tuition and fees vary according to course load and program.

FRESHMAN FINANCIAL AID (Fall 2016, est.) 1,957 applied for aid; of those 82% were deemed to have need. 100% of freshmen with need received aid; of those 31% had need fully met. *Average percent of need met:* 80% (excluding resources awarded to replace EFC). *Average financial aid package:* $42,995 (excluding resources awarded to replace EFC). 29% of all full-time freshmen had no need and received non-need-based gift aid.

UNDERGRADUATE FINANCIAL AID (Fall 2016, est.) 8,503 applied for aid; of those 89% were deemed to have need. 100% of undergraduates with need received aid; of those 20% had need fully met. *Average percent of need met:* 69% (excluding resources awarded to replace EFC). *Average financial aid package:* $36,266 (excluding resources awarded to replace EFC). 34% of all full-time undergraduates had no need and received non-need-based gift aid.

GIFT AID (NEED-BASED) *Total amount:* $185,690,700 (9% federal, 3% state, 86% institutional, 2% external sources). *Receiving aid:* Freshmen: 69% (1,599); all full-time undergraduates: 54% (7,212). *Average award:* Freshmen: $33,006; Undergraduates: $26,121. *Scholarships, grants, and awards:* Federal Pell, FSEOG, state, private, college/university gift aid from institutional funds, United Negro College Fund.

GIFT AID (NON-NEED-BASED) *Total amount:* $74,625,195 (97% institutional, 3% external sources). *Receiving aid:* Freshmen: 11% (260). Undergraduates: 5% (697). *Average award:* Freshmen: $14,649. Undergraduates: $15,597. *Scholarships, grants, and awards by category:* Academic interests/achievement: general academic interests/achievements. Creative arts/performance: dance, music, performing arts, theater/drama. Special achievements/activities: cheerleading/drum major. Special characteristics: children and siblings of alumni, siblings of current students, twins. *Tuition waivers:* Full or partial for children of alumni, employees or children of employees. *ROTC:* Army, Naval cooperative, Air Force cooperative.

LOANS *Student loans:* $97,561,526 (75% need-based, 25% non-need-based). *Average need-based loan:* Freshmen: $8257. Undergraduates: $11,010. *Parent loans:* $45,641,143 (100% non-need-based). *Programs:* Federal Direct (Subsidized and Unsubsidized Stafford, PLUS), Perkins, Federal Nursing, college/university.

WORK-STUDY *Federal work-study:* Total amount: $3,918,474; jobs available.

ATHLETIC AWARDS Total amount: $9,113,020 (29% need-based, 71% non-need-based).

APPLYING FOR FINANCIAL AID *Required financial aid form:* FAFSA. *Financial aid deadline:* 2/15. *Notification date:* Continuous beginning 4/1.

CONTACT Helen Gourousis, Director of Financial Aid, Drexel University, 3141 Chestnut Street, Philadelphia, PA 19104-2875, 215-895-5928 or toll-free 800-2-DREXEL. *Fax:* 215-895-6903. *E-mail:* gouroush@drexel.edu. *Website:* http://www.drexel.edu/.

DRURY UNIVERSITY
Springfield, MO

Tuition & fees: $27,005	Average undergraduate aid package: $19,616

ABOUT THE INSTITUTION Independent, coed. *Awards:* bachelor's and master's degrees (also offers evening program with significant enrollment not reflected in profile). 40 undergraduate majors. *Total enrollment:* 1,611. Undergraduates: 1,370. Freshmen: 393. Federal methodology is used as a basis for awarding need-based institutional aid.

UNDERGRADUATE EXPENSES for 2017–2018 *One-time required fee:* $150. *Comprehensive fee:* $35,041 includes full-time tuition ($25,850), mandatory fees ($1155), and room and board ($8036). Full-time tuition and fees vary according to class time. Room and board charges vary according to board plan and housing facility. Part-time tuition and fees vary according to class time.

FRESHMAN FINANCIAL AID (Fall 2015) 249 applied for aid; of those 82% were deemed to have need. 100% of freshmen with need received aid; of those 21% had need fully met. *Average percent of need met:* 73% (excluding resources awarded to replace EFC). *Average financial aid package:* $19,022 (excluding resources

---

awarded to replace EFC). 28% of all full-time freshmen had no need and received non-need-based gift aid.

UNDERGRADUATE FINANCIAL AID (Fall 2015) 929 applied for aid; of those 87% were deemed to have need. 100% of undergraduates with need received aid; of those 18% had need fully met. *Average percent of need met:* 71% (excluding resources awarded to replace EFC). *Average financial aid package:* $19,616 (excluding resources awarded to replace EFC). 31% of all full-time undergraduates had no need and received non-need-based gift aid.

GIFT AID (NEED-BASED) *Total amount:* $11,751,223 (16% federal, 6% state, 71% institutional, 7% external sources). *Receiving aid:* Freshmen: 68% (205); all full-time undergraduates: 63% (803). *Average award:* Freshmen: $15,353; Undergraduates: $15,600. *Scholarships, grants, and awards:* Federal Pell, FSEOG, state, private, college/university gift aid from institutional funds.

GIFT AID (NON-NEED-BASED) *Total amount:* $4,263,345 (3% state, 90% institutional, 7% external sources). *Receiving aid:* Freshmen: 10% (31). Undergraduates: 9% (109). *Average award:* Freshmen: $7325. Undergraduates: $8552. *Scholarships, grants, and awards by category:* Academic interests/achievement: 1,226 awards ($8,922,966 total): architecture, biological sciences, business, communication, computer science, education, English, foreign languages, general academic interests/achievements, health fields, humanities, international studies, mathematics, physical sciences, premedicine, social sciences. Creative arts/performance: 148 awards ($412,335 total): art/fine arts, creative writing, debating, music, theater/drama. Special achievements/activities: 5 awards ($9500 total): cheerleading/drum major, leadership, religious involvement. Special characteristics: 89 awards ($1,128,853 total): children and siblings of alumni, children of faculty/staff, ethnic background, international students, members of minority groups, relatives of clergy, religious affiliation, veterans. *Tuition waivers:* Full or partial for minority students, children of alumni, employees or children of employees. *ROTC:* Army cooperative.

LOANS *Student loans:* $8,632,978 (61% need-based, 39% non-need-based). 55% of past graduating class borrowed through all loan programs. *Average indebtedness per student:* $31,011. *Average need-based loan:* Freshmen: $4176. Undergraduates: $4524. *Parent loans:* $2,095,135 (43% need-based, 57% non-need-based). *Programs:* Federal Direct (Subsidized and Unsubsidized Stafford, PLUS), Perkins, state.

WORK-STUDY *Federal work-study:* 111 jobs averaging $2892. *State or other work-study/employment:* 280 part-time jobs averaging $2405.

APPLYING FOR FINANCIAL AID *Required financial aid form:* FAFSA. *Financial aid deadline (priority):* 1/10. *Notification date:* Continuous beginning 12/15. Students must reply by 5/1 or within 2 weeks of notification.

CONTACT Ms. Becky Ahrens, Director of Financial Aid, Drury University, 900 North Benton Avenue, Springfield, MO 65802-3791, 417-873-7312 or toll-free 800-922-2274. *Fax:* 417-873-6906. *E-mail:* baherns@drury.edu. *Website:* http://www.drury.edu/.

DUKE UNIVERSITY
Durham, NC

Tuition & fees: $51,265	Average undergraduate aid package: $50,312

ABOUT THE INSTITUTION Independent United Methodist Church, coed. *Awards:* certificates, bachelor's, master's, and doctoral degrees. 45 undergraduate majors. *Total enrollment:* 15,984. Undergraduates: 6,639. Freshmen: 1,745. Both federal and institutional methodology are used as a basis for awarding need-based institutional aid.

UNDERGRADUATE EXPENSES for 2016–2017 *Application fee:* $85. *Comprehensive fee:* $65,703 includes full-time tuition ($49,575), mandatory fees ($1690), and room and board ($14,438). *College room only:* $8286. *Part-time tuition:* $1489 per credit hour.

FRESHMAN FINANCIAL AID (Fall 2016, est.) 948 applied for aid; of those 82% were deemed to have need. 100% of freshmen with need received aid; of those 100% had need fully met. *Average percent of need met:* 100% (excluding resources awarded to replace EFC). *Average financial aid package:* $49,774 (excluding resources awarded to replace EFC). 2% of all full-time freshmen had no need and received non-need-based gift aid.

UNDERGRADUATE FINANCIAL AID (Fall 2016, est.) 3,191 applied for aid; of those 87% were deemed to have need. 100% of undergraduates with need received aid; of those 100% had need fully met. *Average percent of need met:* 100% (excluding resources awarded to replace EFC). *Average financial aid package:*

$50,312 (excluding resources awarded to replace EFC). 3% of all full-time undergraduates had no need and received non-need-based gift aid.

GIFT AID (NEED-BASED) Total amount: $120,449,522 (4% federal, 91% institutional, 5% external sources). **Receiving aid:** Freshmen: 44% (753); all full-time undergraduates: 40% (2,651). **Average award:** Freshmen: $46,370; Undergraduates: $47,133. **Scholarships, grants, and awards:** Federal Pell, FSEOG, state, private, college/university gift aid from institutional funds.

GIFT AID (NON-NEED-BASED) Total amount: $17,274,517 (60% institutional, 10% external sources). **Receiving aid:** Freshmen 6% (105). Undergraduates: 4% (272). **Average award:** Freshmen: $65,459. Undergraduates: $63,649. **Scholarships, grants, and awards by category:** Academic interests/achievement: 123 awards ($8,002,963 total): general academic interests/achievements, mathematics. Special achievements/activities: 77 awards ($5,138,888 total): general special achievements/activities, leadership. Special characteristics: 61 awards ($4,094,979 total): children and siblings of alumni, ethnic background, international students, local/state students. **ROTC:** Army, Naval, Air Force.

LOANS Student loans: $16,207,096 (76% need-based, 24% non-need-based). 35% of past graduating class borrowed through all loan programs. Average indebtedness per student: $22,256. **Average need-based loan:** Freshmen: $3608. Undergraduates: $3953. **Parent loans:** $7,151,204 (74% need-based, 26% non-need-based). **Programs:** Federal Direct (Subsidized and Unsubsidized Stafford, PLUS), Perkins, college/university, alternative loans.

WORK-STUDY Federal work-study: Total amount: $3,528,040; 1,739 jobs averaging $1972. **State or other work-study/employment:** Total amount: $2,034,737 (57% need-based, 43% non-need-based). 896 part-time jobs averaging $2030.

ATHLETIC AWARDS Total amount: $19,520,011 (23% need-based, 77% non-need-based).

APPLYING FOR FINANCIAL AID Required financial aid forms: FAFSA, CSS Financial Aid PROFILE, noncustodial (divorced/separated) parent's statement, business/farm supplement, federal income tax form(s), W-2 forms. **Financial aid deadline:** 2/1. **Notification date:** 4/1. Students must reply by 5/1.

CONTACT Alison Rabil, Director of Financial Aid, Duke University, 2127 Campus Drive Addition, Box 90397, Durham, NC 27708-0397, 919-684-6225. Fax: 919-660-9811. E-mail: finaid@duke.edu. Website: http://www.duke.edu/.

DUNLAP-STONE UNIVERSITY
Phoenix, AZ

Tuition & fees: $8000	Average undergraduate aid package: N/A

ABOUT THE INSTITUTION Proprietary, coed. 1 undergraduate major. Institutional methodology is used as a basis for awarding need-based institutional aid.

UNDERGRADUATE EXPENSES for 2016–2017 Tuition: full-time $8000.

APPLYING FOR FINANCIAL AID Notification date: Continuous.

CONTACT Office of the Bursar, Dunlap-Stone University, 19820 North 7th Street, Suite #100, Phoenix, AZ 85024, 800-474-8013. E-mail: info@expandglobal.com. Website: http://www.dunlap-stone.edu/.

DUQUESNE UNIVERSITY
Pittsburgh, PA

Tuition & fees: $35,062	Average undergraduate aid package: $24,000

ABOUT THE INSTITUTION Independent Roman Catholic, coed. **Awards:** certificates, bachelor's, master's, and doctoral degrees. 71 undergraduate majors. **Total enrollment:** 9,340. Undergraduates: 6,039. Freshmen: 1,556. Federal methodology is used as a basis for awarding need-based institutional aid.

UNDERGRADUATE EXPENSES for 2016–2017 Application fee: $50. **Comprehensive fee:** $46,822 includes full-time tuition ($35,062) and room and board ($11,760). **College room only:** $6412. Full-time tuition and fees vary according to course load and program. Room and board charges vary according to board plan and housing facility. **Part-time tuition:** $1162 per credit hour. Part-time tuition and fees vary according to course load and program.

FRESHMAN FINANCIAL AID (Fall 2015) 1,258 applied for aid; of those 81% were deemed to have need. 100% of freshmen with need received aid; of those 21% had need fully met. **Average percent of need met:** 74% (excluding resources awarded to replace EFC). **Average financial aid package:** $25,358 (excluding resources awarded to replace EFC). 25% of all full-time freshmen had no need and received non-need-based gift aid.

UNDERGRADUATE FINANCIAL AID (Fall 2015) 4,581 applied for aid; of those 84% were deemed to have need. 100% of undergraduates with need received aid; of those 19% had need fully met. **Average percent of need met:** 71% (excluding resources awarded to replace EFC). **Average financial aid package:** $24,000 (excluding resources awarded to replace EFC). 27% of all full-time undergraduates had no need and received non-need-based gift aid.

GIFT AID (NEED-BASED) Total amount: $66,769,349 (8% federal, 8% state, 80% institutional, 4% external sources). **Receiving aid:** Freshmen: 71% (1,018); all full-time undergraduates: 65% (3,737). **Average award:** Freshmen: $20,761; Undergraduates: $19,267. **Scholarships, grants, and awards:** Federal Pell, FSEOG, state, private, college/university gift aid from institutional funds, United Negro College Fund.

GIFT AID (NON-NEED-BASED) Total amount: $20,193,849 (97% institutional, 3% external sources). **Receiving aid:** Freshmen: 71% (1,017). Undergraduates: 64% (3,654). **Average award:** Freshmen: $13,158. Undergraduates: $12,168. **Scholarships, grants, and awards by category:** Academic interests/achievement: 4,899 awards ($54,518,543 total): education, general academic interests/achievements. Creative arts/performance: 223 awards ($1,583,250 total): dance, music. Special characteristics: 1,270 awards ($14,224,815 total): children and siblings of alumni, children of faculty/staff, ethnic background, general special characteristics, international students, members of minority groups, relatives of clergy, religious affiliation, veterans, veterans' children. **Tuition waivers:** Full or partial for employees or children of employees, senior citizens. **ROTC:** Army, Naval cooperative, Air Force cooperative.

LOANS Student loans: $48,202,532 (88% need-based, 12% non-need-based). 59% of past graduating class borrowed through all loan programs. Average indebtedness per student: $41,272. **Average need-based loan:** Freshmen: $3918. Undergraduates: $4802. **Parent loans:** $19,284,505 (92% need-based, 8% non-need-based). **Programs:** Federal Direct (Subsidized and Unsubsidized Stafford, PLUS), Perkins, Federal Nursing, private loans.

WORK-STUDY Federal work-study: jobs available.

ATHLETIC AWARDS Total amount: $6,576,859 (46% need-based, 54% non-need-based).

APPLYING FOR FINANCIAL AID Required financial aid forms: FAFSA, institution's own form. **Financial aid deadline:** 5/1. **Notification date:** Continuous beginning 1/31. Students must reply by 5/1 or within 3 weeks of notification.

CONTACT Mr. Richard C. Esposito, Director of Financial Aid, Duquesne University, 600 Forbes Avenue, Pittsburgh, PA 15282-0299, 412-396-6607 or toll-free 800-456-0590. Fax: 412-396-5284. E-mail: esposito@duq.edu. Website: http://www.duq.edu/.

D'YOUVILLE COLLEGE
Buffalo, NY

Tuition & fees: $25,750	Average undergraduate aid package: $19,004

ABOUT THE INSTITUTION Independent, coed. **Awards:** certificates, bachelor's, master's, and doctoral degrees. 23 undergraduate majors. **Total enrollment:** 2,965. Undergraduates: 1,716. Freshmen: 241. Federal methodology is used as a basis for awarding need-based institutional aid.

UNDERGRADUATE EXPENSES for 2017–2018 Comprehensive fee: $37,558 includes full-time tuition ($25,280), mandatory fees ($470), and room and board ($11,808). Full-time tuition and fees vary according to course load, degree level, and program. Room and board charges vary according to board plan and housing facility. **Part-time tuition:** $788 per credit hour. **Part-time fees:** $3 per credit hour; $55 per credit hour. Part-time tuition and fees vary according to course load, degree level, and program. **Payment plan:** Guaranteed tuition.

FRESHMAN FINANCIAL AID (Fall 2015) 217 applied for aid; of those 89% were deemed to have need. 99% of freshmen with need received aid; of those 21% had need fully met. **Average percent of need met:** 74% (excluding resources awarded to replace EFC). **Average financial aid package:** $18,449 (excluding resources awarded to replace EFC). 14% of all full-time freshmen had no need and received non-need-based gift aid.

UNDERGRADUATE FINANCIAL AID (Fall 2015) 810 applied for aid; of those 89% were deemed to have need. 100% of undergraduates with need received aid; of those 22% had need fully met. *Average percent of need met:* 73% (excluding resources awarded to replace EFC). *Average financial aid package:* $19,004 (excluding resources awarded to replace EFC). 14% of all full-time undergraduates had no need and received non-need-based gift aid.

GIFT AID (NEED-BASED) *Total amount:* $9,471,836 (15% federal, 14% state, 68% institutional, 3% external sources). *Receiving aid:* Freshmen: 83% (191); all full-time undergraduates: 82% (714). *Average award:* Freshmen: $15,282; Undergraduates: $15,177. *Scholarships, grants, and awards:* Federal Pell, FSEOG, state, private, college/university gift aid from institutional funds.

GIFT AID (NON-NEED-BASED) *Total amount:* $1,517,574 (1% state, 95% institutional, 4% external sources). *Receiving aid:* Freshmen: 11% (26). Undergraduates: 11% (93). *Average award:* Freshmen: $9814. Undergraduates: $8739. *Scholarships, grants, and awards by category: Academic interests/achievement:* biological sciences, business, education, English, general academic interests/achievements, health fields, humanities, international studies, mathematics, premedicine, social sciences. *Special characteristics:* children and siblings of alumni, children of faculty/staff, veterans. *Tuition waivers:* Full or partial for children of alumni, employees or children of employees, senior citizens. *ROTC:* Army cooperative.

LOANS *Student loans:* $7,194,730 (67% need-based, 33% non-need-based). 86% of past graduating class borrowed through all loan programs. *Average indebtedness per student:* $34,593. *Average need-based loan:* Freshmen: $3678. Undergraduates: $4353. *Parent loans:* $1,269,814 (51% need-based, 49% non-need-based). *Programs:* Federal Direct (Subsidized and Unsubsidized Stafford, PLUS), Perkins, Federal Nursing.

WORK-STUDY *Federal work-study:* jobs available. *State or other work-study/employment:* Total amount: $8348 (25% need-based, 75% non-need-based). Part-time jobs available.

APPLYING FOR FINANCIAL AID *Required financial aid forms:* FAFSA, state aid form. *Financial aid deadline (priority):* 2/15. *Notification date:* Continuous beginning 3/15. Students must reply within 2 weeks of notification.

CONTACT Mr. Matthew R. Metz, Director of Financial Aid, D'Youville College, 320 Porter Avenue, Buffalo, NY 14201-1084, 716-829-7500 or toll-free 800-777-3921. *Fax:* 716-829-7779. *E-mail:* metzm@dyc.edu. *Website:* http://www.dyc.edu/.

EAGLE GATE COLLEGE
Layton, UT

CONTACT Financial Aid Office, Eagle Gate College, 915 North 400 West, Layton, UT 84041, 801-546-7500 or toll-free 866-29-EAGLE. *Website:* http://eaglegatecollege.edu/.

EAGLE GATE COLLEGE
Murray, UT

CONTACT Financial Aid Office, Eagle Gate College, 5588 South Green Street, Murray, UT 84123, 801-333-8100 or toll-free 866-29-EAGLE. *Website:* http://eaglegatecollege.edu/.

EARLHAM COLLEGE
Richmond, IN

Tuition & fees: $45,300	Average undergraduate aid package: $40,987

ABOUT THE INSTITUTION Independent Society of Friends, coed. *Awards:* bachelor's and master's degrees. 36 undergraduate majors. *Total enrollment:* 1,100. Undergraduates: 1,031. Freshmen: 355. Federal methodology is used as a basis for awarding need-based institutional aid.

UNDERGRADUATE EXPENSES for 2016–2017 *Comprehensive fee:* $54,870 includes full-time tuition ($44,370), mandatory fees ($930), and room and board ($9570). *College room only:* $4950. Room and board charges vary according to board plan. *Part-time tuition:* $1479 per credit hour. *Payment plan:* Tuition prepayment.

FRESHMAN FINANCIAL AID (Fall 2015) 247 applied for aid; of those 89% were deemed to have need. 100% of freshmen with need received aid; of those 28% had need fully met. *Average percent of need met:* 93% (excluding resources awarded to replace EFC). *Average financial aid package:* $41,876 (excluding resources awarded to replace EFC). 11% of all full-time freshmen had no need and received non-need-based gift aid.

UNDERGRADUATE FINANCIAL AID (Fall 2015) 891 applied for aid; of those 87% were deemed to have need. 100% of undergraduates with need received aid; of those 31% had need fully met. *Average percent of need met:* 93% (excluding resources awarded to replace EFC). *Average financial aid package:* $40,987 (excluding resources awarded to replace EFC). 12% of all full-time undergraduates had no need and received non-need-based gift aid.

GIFT AID (NEED-BASED) *Total amount:* $25,815,503 (5% federal, 2% state, 92% institutional, 1% external sources). *Receiving aid:* Freshmen: 86% (219); all full-time undergraduates: 83% (774). *Average award:* Freshmen: $36,206; Undergraduates: $34,097. *Scholarships, grants, and awards:* Federal Pell, FSEOG, state, private, college/university gift aid from institutional funds.

GIFT AID (NON-NEED-BASED) *Receiving aid:* Freshmen: 28% (71). Undergraduates: 32% (298). *Average award:* Freshmen: $17,500. Undergraduates: $17,183. *Scholarships, grants, and awards by category: Academic interests/achievement:* general academic interests/achievements. *Special achievements/activities:* religious involvement. *Special characteristics:* ethnic background. *Tuition waivers:* Full or partial for employees or children of employees.

LOANS *Student loans:* $5,192,040 (100% need-based). 60% of past graduating class borrowed through all loan programs. *Average indebtedness per student:* $25,784. *Average need-based loan:* Freshmen: $4187. Undergraduates: $5230. *Parent loans:* $227,551 (100% need-based). *Programs:* Federal Direct (Subsidized and Unsubsidized Stafford, PLUS), Perkins, college/university.

WORK-STUDY *Federal work-study:* jobs available. *State or other work-study/employment:* Total amount: $384,756 (100% need-based). Part-time jobs available.

APPLYING FOR FINANCIAL AID *Required financial aid form:* FAFSA. *Financial aid deadline:* 3/1. *Notification date:* Continuous beginning 3/1. Students must reply by 5/1 or within 3 weeks of notification.

CONTACT Kathy Gottschalk, Director of Financial Aid, Earlham College, National Road West, Richmond, IN 47374-4095, 765-983-1217 or toll-free 800-327-5426. *Fax:* 765-983-1299. *E-mail:* gottska@earlham.edu. *Website:* http://www.earlham.edu/.

EAST CAROLINA UNIVERSITY
Greenville, NC

Tuition & fees (NC res): $6946	Average undergraduate aid package: $10,549

ABOUT THE INSTITUTION State-supported, coed. *Awards:* certificates, bachelor's, master's, and doctoral degrees. 78 undergraduate majors. *Total enrollment:* 28,962. Undergraduates: 22,969. Freshmen: 4,320. Federal methodology is used as a basis for awarding need-based institutional aid.

UNDERGRADUATE EXPENSES for 2017–2018 *Application fee:* $70. *Tuition, state resident:* full-time $4365; part-time $181 per credit hour. *Tuition, nonresident:* full-time $20,323; part-time $846 per credit hour. *Required fees:* full-time $2581. Full-time tuition and fees vary according to location. Part-time tuition and fees vary according to course load and location. *College room and board:* $9835; *Room only:* $5423. Room and board charges vary according to board plan and housing facility.

FRESHMAN FINANCIAL AID (Fall 2016, est.) 3,600 applied for aid; of those 74% were deemed to have need. 95% of freshmen with need received aid; of those 10% had need fully met. *Average percent of need met:* 60% (excluding resources awarded to replace EFC). *Average financial aid package:* $9803 (excluding resources awarded to replace EFC). 2% of all full-time freshmen had no need and received non-need-based gift aid.

UNDERGRADUATE FINANCIAL AID (Fall 2016, est.) 14,848 applied for aid; of those 80% were deemed to have need. 96% of undergraduates with need received

aid; of those 10% had need fully met. **Average percent of need met:** 63% (excluding resources awarded to replace EFC). **Average financial aid package:** $10,549 (excluding resources awarded to replace EFC). 1% of all full-time undergraduates had no need and received non-need-based gift aid.

GIFT AID (NEED-BASED) Total amount: $82,812,204 (42% federal, 22% state, 32% institutional, 4% external sources). **Receiving aid:** Freshmen: 43% (1,848); all full-time undergraduates: 45% (8,818). **Average award:** Freshmen: $7882; Undergraduates: $7748. **Scholarships, grants, and awards:** Federal Pell, FSEOG, state, private, college/university gift aid from institutional funds, Federal Nursing.

GIFT AID (NON-NEED-BASED) Total amount: $843,006 (3% state, 28% institutional, 69% external sources). **Receiving aid:** Freshmen: 15% (650). Undergraduates: 10% (2,046). **Average award:** Freshmen: $3958. Undergraduates: $4375. **Scholarships, grants, and awards by category:** Academic interests/achievement: biological sciences, business, communication, computer science, education, engineering/technologies, English, foreign languages, general academic interests/achievements, health fields, home economics, humanities, international studies, library science, mathematics, military science, physical sciences, social sciences. Creative arts/performance: applied art and design, art/fine arts, dance, music, performing arts. Special characteristics: adult students, children and siblings of alumni, children of faculty/staff, ethnic background, general special characteristics, handicapped students. **Tuition waivers:** Full or partial for employees or children of employees. **ROTC:** Army, Air Force.

LOANS Student loans: $104,832,055 (96% need-based, 4% non-need-based). 65% of past graduating class borrowed through all loan programs. Average indebtedness per student: $29,391. **Average need-based loan:** Freshmen: $5901. Undergraduates: $6717. **Parent loans:** $23,259,655 (100% need-based). **Programs:** Federal Direct (Subsidized and Unsubsidized Stafford, PLUS), Perkins, Federal Nursing, state.

WORK-STUDY Federal work-study: Total amount: $1,517,653; 414 jobs averaging $3829. **State or other work-study/employment:** 5,369 part-time jobs averaging $2922.

ATHLETIC AWARDS Total amount: $6,670,730 (91% need-based, 9% non-need-based).

APPLYING FOR FINANCIAL AID Required financial aid form: FAFSA. **Financial aid deadline (priority):** 3/1. **Notification date:** 4/1. Students must reply within 3 weeks of notification.

CONTACT Ms. Julie Poorman, Director of Financial Aid, East Carolina University, East 5th Street, Greenville, NC 27858-4353, 252-328-6610. Fax: 252-328-4347. E-mail: poormanj@ecu.edu.
Website: http://www.ecu.edu/.

EAST CENTRAL UNIVERSITY
Ada, OK

Tuition & fees (OK res): $6279	Average undergraduate aid package: $6361

ABOUT THE INSTITUTION State-supported, coed. **Awards:** certificates, bachelor's, and master's degrees. 74 undergraduate majors. **Total enrollment:** 4,161. Undergraduates: 3,455. Freshmen: 596. Federal methodology is used as a basis for awarding need-based institutional aid.

UNDERGRADUATE EXPENSES for 2017–2018 Application fee: $20. **Tuition, state resident:** full-time $4980; part-time $166 per semester hour. **Tuition, nonresident:** full-time $15,010; part-time $470 per semester hour. **Required fees:** full-time $1299; $43.30 per semester hour. **College room and board:** $5350; **Room only:** $2200. Room and board charges vary according to board plan and housing facility. **Payment plan:** Guaranteed tuition.

FRESHMAN FINANCIAL AID (Fall 2015) 532 applied for aid; of those 79% were deemed to have need. 100% of freshmen with need received aid. **Average financial aid package:** $5927 (excluding resources awarded to replace EFC). 1% of all full-time freshmen had no need and received non-need-based gift aid.

UNDERGRADUATE FINANCIAL AID (Fall 2015) 2,251 applied for aid; of those 86% were deemed to have need. 100% of undergraduates with need received aid. **Average financial aid package:** $6361 (excluding resources awarded to replace EFC). 1% of all full-time undergraduates had no need and received non-need-based gift aid.

GIFT AID (NEED-BASED) Total amount: $12,044,852 (59% federal, 27% state, 14% external sources). **Receiving aid:** Freshmen: 40% (293); all full-time undergraduates: 45% (1,385). **Average award:** Freshmen: $4598; Undergraduates: $4712.

Scholarships, grants, and awards: Federal Pell, FSEOG, state, private, college/university gift aid from institutional funds.

GIFT AID (NON-NEED-BASED) Total amount: $1,381,769 (11% state, 67% institutional, 22% external sources). **Average award:** Freshmen: $2676. Undergraduates: $2676. **Scholarships, grants, and awards by category:** Academic interests/achievement: communication, general academic interests/achievements. Creative arts/performance: music, performing arts, theater/drama. Special achievements/activities: cheerleading/drum major. Special characteristics: children of faculty/staff, general special characteristics, international students, members of minority groups, out-of-state students, veterans, veterans' children. **Tuition waivers:** Full or partial for employees or children of employees.

LOANS Student loans: $15,271,301 (100% need-based). 34% of past graduating class borrowed through all loan programs. Average indebtedness per student: $19,170. **Average need-based loan:** Freshmen: $4831. Undergraduates: $5576. **Parent loans:** $160,148 (100% need-based). **Programs:** Federal Direct (Subsidized and Unsubsidized Stafford, PLUS).

WORK-STUDY Federal work-study: jobs available. **State or other work-study/employment:** Part-time jobs available.

ATHLETIC AWARDS Total amount: $1,079,409 (100% non-need-based).

APPLYING FOR FINANCIAL AID Required financial aid form: FAFSA. **Financial aid deadline (priority):** 3/1. **Notification date:** Continuous beginning 4/15. Students must reply within 6 weeks of notification.

CONTACT Becky Isaacs, Director of Financial Aid, East Central University, 1100 East 14th Street, Ada, OK 74820-6999, 580-332-8000 Ext. 242. Fax: 580-436-5612. E-mail: bisaacs@ecok.edu.
Website: http://www.ecok.edu/.

EASTERN CONNECTICUT STATE UNIVERSITY
Willimantic, CT

Tuition & fees (CT res): $10,500	Average undergraduate aid package: $9669

ABOUT THE INSTITUTION State-supported, coed. **Awards:** associate, bachelor's, and master's degrees. 32 undergraduate majors. **Total enrollment:** 5,261. Undergraduates: 5,097. Freshmen: 985. Federal methodology is used as a basis for awarding need-based institutional aid.

UNDERGRADUATE EXPENSES for 2016–2017 Application fee: $50. **Tuition, state resident:** full-time $5216; part-time $490 per credit hour. **Tuition, nonresident:** full-time $16,882; part-time $496 per credit hour. **Required fees:** full-time $5284; $80 per year. Part-time tuition and fees vary according to course load. **College room and board:** $12,559; **Room only:** $7172. Room and board charges vary according to board plan and housing facility.

FRESHMAN FINANCIAL AID (Fall 2015) 903 applied for aid; of those 74% were deemed to have need. 99% of freshmen with need received aid; of those 9% had need fully met. **Average percent of need met:** 63% (excluding resources awarded to replace EFC). **Average financial aid package:** $10,848 (excluding resources awarded to replace EFC). 16% of all full-time freshmen had no need and received non-need-based gift aid.

UNDERGRADUATE FINANCIAL AID (Fall 2015) 3,535 applied for aid; of those 81% were deemed to have need. 92% of undergraduates with need received aid; of those 11% had need fully met. **Average percent of need met:** 61% (excluding resources awarded to replace EFC). **Average financial aid package:** $9669 (excluding resources awarded to replace EFC). 7% of all full-time undergraduates had no need and received non-need-based gift aid.

GIFT AID (NEED-BASED) Total amount: $14,867,772 (47% federal, 6% state, 43% institutional, 4% external sources). **Receiving aid:** Freshmen: 54% (524); all full-time undergraduates: 47% (2,008). **Average award:** Freshmen: $6860; Undergraduates: $5743. **Scholarships, grants, and awards:** Federal Pell, FSEOG, state, private, college/university gift aid from institutional funds.

GIFT AID (NON-NEED-BASED) Total amount: $2,061,116 (5% state, 81% institutional, 14% external sources). **Receiving aid:** Freshmen: 39% (379). Undergraduates: 20% (872). **Average award:** Freshmen: $3382. Undergraduates: $3726. **Scholarships, grants, and awards by category:** Academic interests/achievement: 95 awards ($100,950 total): area/ethnic studies, biological sciences, business, communication, computer science, education, English, foreign languages, general academic interests/achievements, home economics, international studies, mathematics, physical sciences, social sciences. *Creative arts/performance:* 8 awards ($6500 total): art/fine arts, general creative arts/performance, music, performing arts, theater/drama. *Special achievements/activities:* 13 awards ($19,000 total): community service, leadership. *Special characteristics:* 25 awards ($29,994 total): adult students, children of union members/company employees, ethnic background, handicapped students, local/state students, members of minority groups, religious affiliation, veterans. *Tuition waivers:* Full or partial for employees or children of employees. *ROTC:* Army cooperative, Air Force cooperative.

LOANS *Student loans:* $27,071,642 (66% need-based, 34% non-need-based). 80% of past graduating class borrowed through all loan programs. *Average indebtedness per student:* $30,566. *Average need-based loan:* Freshmen: $3342. Undergraduates: $4301. *Parent loans:* $5,670,969 (41% need-based, 59% non-need-based). *Programs:* Federal Direct (Subsidized and Unsubsidized Stafford, PLUS), Perkins, alternative loans.

WORK-STUDY *Federal work-study:* 85 jobs averaging $2198.

APPLYING FOR FINANCIAL AID *Required financial aid form:* FAFSA. *Financial aid deadline (priority):* 3/1. *Notification date:* Continuous beginning 3/1. Students must reply by 5/1.

CONTACT Jennifer Horner, Director of Financial Aid, Eastern Connecticut State University, 83 Windham Street, Wood SSC, Willimantic, CT 06226-2295, 860-465-5775. *E-mail:* hornerje@easternct.edu. *Website:* http://www.easternct.edu/.

EASTERN ILLINOIS UNIVERSITY
Charleston, IL

Tuition & fees (IL res): $11,580	Average undergraduate aid package: $9187

ABOUT THE INSTITUTION State-supported, coed. *Awards:* certificates, bachelor's, and master's degrees. 48 undergraduate majors. *Total enrollment:* 7,415. Undergraduates: 5,957. Freshmen: 772. Federal methodology is used as a basis for awarding need-based institutional aid.

UNDERGRADUATE EXPENSES for 2016–2017 *Application fee:* $30. *Tuition, state resident:* full-time $8670; part-time $289 per credit hour. *Tuition, nonresident:* full-time $10,830; part-time $361 per credit hour. *Required fees:* full-time $2910; $105.52 per credit hour. Full-time tuition and fees vary according to course load and student level. Part-time tuition and fees vary according to course load and student level. *College room and board:* $9546. Room and board charges vary according to board plan and housing facility. *Payment plan:* Guaranteed tuition.

FRESHMAN FINANCIAL AID (Fall 2016, est.) 709 applied for aid; of those 79% were deemed to have need. 99% of freshmen with need received aid; of those 9% had need fully met. *Average percent of need met:* 68% (excluding resources awarded to replace EFC). *Average financial aid package:* $10,546 (excluding resources awarded to replace EFC). 11% of all full-time freshmen had no need and received non-need-based gift aid.

UNDERGRADUATE FINANCIAL AID (Fall 2016, est.) 4,747 applied for aid; of those 72% were deemed to have need. 100% of undergraduates with need received aid; of those 10% had need fully met. *Average percent of need met:* 67% (excluding resources awarded to replace EFC). *Average financial aid package:* $9187 (excluding resources awarded to replace EFC). 12% of all full-time undergraduates had no need and received non-need-based gift aid.

GIFT AID (NEED-BASED) *Total amount:* $24,579,822 (43% federal, 31% state, 21% institutional, 5% external sources). *Receiving aid:* Freshmen: 57% (415); all full-time undergraduates: 51% (2,592). *Average award:* Freshmen: $8743; Undergraduates: $7608. *Scholarships, grants, and awards:* Federal Pell, FSEOG, state, private, college/university gift aid from institutional funds.

GIFT AID (NON-NEED-BASED) *Total amount:* $3,235,831 (4% federal, 14% state, 63% institutional, 19% external sources). *Receiving aid:* Freshmen: 49% (362). Undergraduates: 32% (1,633). *Average award:* Freshmen: $3222. Undergraduates: $2808. *Scholarships, grants, and awards by category:* Academic interests/achievement: 2,270 awards ($4,921,830 total): biological sciences, business, communication, computer science, education, engineering/technologies, English, foreign languages, general academic interests/achievements, health fields, home economics, humanities, international studies, mathematics, physical sciences, premedicine, social sciences. *Creative arts/performance:* 274 awards ($318,440 total): applied art and design, art/fine arts, cinema/film/broadcasting, creative writing, debating, general creative arts/performance, journalism/publications, music, performing arts, theater/drama.

Special achievements/activities: 594 awards ($2,963,432 total): general special achievements/activities, leadership. *Tuition waivers:* Full or partial for employees or children of employees, senior citizens. *ROTC:* Army.

LOANS *Student loans:* $26,503,484 (85% need-based, 15% non-need-based). 79% of past graduating class borrowed through all loan programs. *Average indebtedness per student:* $31,382. *Average need-based loan:* Freshmen: $3731. Undergraduates: $4363. *Parent loans:* $5,408,495 (75% need-based, 25% non-need-based). *Programs:* Federal Direct (Subsidized and Unsubsidized Stafford, PLUS), Perkins.

WORK-STUDY *Federal work-study:* Total amount: $313,827; 204 jobs averaging $889. *State or other work-study/employment:* 1,807 part-time jobs averaging $1633.

ATHLETIC AWARDS Total amount: $3,094,430 (48% need-based, 52% non-need-based).

APPLYING FOR FINANCIAL AID *Required financial aid form:* FAFSA. *Financial aid deadline (priority):* 3/1. *Notification date:* Continuous beginning 3/1. Students must reply within 2 weeks of notification.

CONTACT Mandi Starwalt, Interim Senior Associate Director of Financial Aid and Scholarships, Eastern Illinois University, 600 Lincoln Avenue, Charleston, IL 61920, 217-581-7812 or toll-free 877-581-2348. *Fax:* 217-581-6422. *E-mail:* finaid@eiu.edu. *Website:* http://www.eiu.edu/.

EASTERN KENTUCKY UNIVERSITY
Richmond, KY

Tuition & fees (KY res): $8568	Average undergraduate aid package: $10,962

ABOUT THE INSTITUTION State-supported, coed. *Awards:* certificates, associate, bachelor's, master's, and doctoral degrees. 101 undergraduate majors. *Total enrollment:* 16,844. Undergraduates: 14,327. Freshmen: 2,794. Federal methodology is used as a basis for awarding need-based institutional aid.

UNDERGRADUATE EXPENSES for 2016–2017 *Application fee:* $35. *Tuition, state resident:* full-time $8568; part-time $357 per credit hour. *Tuition, nonresident:* full-time $17,880; part-time $745 per credit hour. Full-time tuition and fees vary according to degree level and location. Part-time tuition and fees vary according to course load. *College room and board:* $8466; *Room only:* $4986. Room and board charges vary according to board plan and housing facility.

FRESHMAN FINANCIAL AID (Fall 2016, est.) 2,371 applied for aid; of those 82% were deemed to have need. 99% of freshmen with need received aid; of those 47% had need fully met. *Average percent of need met:* 85% (excluding resources awarded to replace EFC). *Average financial aid package:* $11,557 (excluding resources awarded to replace EFC). 15% of all full-time freshmen had no need and received non-need-based gift aid.

UNDERGRADUATE FINANCIAL AID (Fall 2016, est.) 9,193 applied for aid; of those 86% were deemed to have need. 99% of undergraduates with need received aid; of those 35% had need fully met. *Average percent of need met:* 80% (excluding resources awarded to replace EFC). *Average financial aid package:* $10,962 (excluding resources awarded to replace EFC). 13% of all full-time undergraduates had no need and received non-need-based gift aid.

GIFT AID (NEED-BASED) *Total amount:* $55,151,475 (45% federal, 26% state, 27% institutional, 2% external sources). *Receiving aid:* Freshmen: 46% (1,171); all full-time undergraduates: 45% (4,953). *Average award:* Freshmen: $6180; Undergraduates: $5857. *Scholarships, grants, and awards:* Federal Pell, FSEOG, state, private, college/university gift aid from institutional funds.

GIFT AID (NON-NEED-BASED) *Total amount:* $11,619,954 (1% federal, 28% state, 68% institutional, 3% external sources). *Receiving aid:* Freshmen: 72% (1,835). Undergraduates: 47% (5,211). *Average award:* Freshmen: $6150. Undergraduates: $5596. *Scholarships, grants, and awards by category:* Academic interests/achievement: 3,966 awards ($19,566,900 total): general academic interests/achievements. *Creative arts/performance:* 127 awards ($376,685 total): music. *Special achievements/activities:* 51 awards ($23,000 total): cheerleading/drum major. *Special characteristics:* 458 awards ($1,967,528 total): children and siblings of alumni, children of faculty/staff, members of minority groups. *Tuition waivers:* Full or partial for employees or children of employees, senior citizens. *ROTC:* Army, Air Force cooperative.

LOANS *Student loans:* $60,739,219 (88% need-based, 12% non-need-based). 70% of past graduating class borrowed through all loan programs. *Average indebtedness per student:* $34,358. *Average need-based loan:* Freshmen: $3056. Undergrad-

uates: $4042. *Parent loans:* $21,928,447 (74% need-based, 26% non-need-based). *Programs:* Federal Direct (Subsidized and Unsubsidized Stafford, PLUS), Perkins, college/university.

WORK-STUDY *Federal work-study:* Total amount: $4,875,311; 1,200 jobs averaging $2400. *State or other work-study/employment:* Total amount: $3,372,813 (100% non-need-based). 1,200 part-time jobs averaging $2400.

ATHLETIC AWARDS Total amount: $4,824,238 (48% need-based, 52% non-need-based).

APPLYING FOR FINANCIAL AID *Required financial aid form:* FAFSA. *Financial aid deadline (priority):* 2/1. *Notification date:* Continuous beginning 4/1.

CONTACT Office of Financial Aid, Eastern Kentucky University, 521 Lancaster Avenue, Whitlock Building, CPO Box 59, Richmond, KY 40475-3102, 859-622-2361 or toll-free 800-465-9191. *Fax:* 859-622-2019. *E-mail:* finaid@eku.edu. *Website:* http://www.eku.edu/.

EASTERN MENNONITE UNIVERSITY
Harrisonburg, VA

Tuition & fees: $34,200	Average undergraduate aid package: $29,377

ABOUT THE INSTITUTION Independent Mennonite, coed. *Awards:* certificates, associate, bachelor's, and master's degrees. 38 undergraduate majors. *Total enrollment:* 1,745. Undergraduates: 1,259. Freshmen: 227. Federal methodology is used as a basis for awarding need-based institutional aid.

UNDERGRADUATE EXPENSES for 2016–2017 *Application fee:* $25. *Comprehensive fee:* $44,860 includes full-time tuition ($34,060), mandatory fees ($140), and room and board ($10,660). Room and board charges vary according to board plan and housing facility. *Part-time tuition:* $1350 per credit hour. *Part-time fees:* $6 per credit hour. Part-time tuition and fees vary according to course load.

FRESHMAN FINANCIAL AID (Fall 2015) 236 applied for aid; of those 92% were deemed to have need. 100% of freshmen with need received aid; of those 12% had need fully met. *Average percent of need met:* 76% (excluding resources awarded to replace EFC). *Average financial aid package:* $31,857 (excluding resources awarded to replace EFC). 14% of all full-time freshmen had no need and received non-need-based gift aid.

UNDERGRADUATE FINANCIAL AID (Fall 2015) 872 applied for aid; of those 90% were deemed to have need. 100% of undergraduates with need received aid; of those 17% had need fully met. *Average percent of need met:* 75% (excluding resources awarded to replace EFC). *Average financial aid package:* $29,377 (excluding resources awarded to replace EFC). 15% of all full-time undergraduates had no need and received non-need-based gift aid.

GIFT AID (NEED-BASED) *Total amount:* $14,538,735 (14% federal, 8% state, 72% institutional, 6% external sources). *Receiving aid:* Freshmen: 85% (216); all full-time undergraduates: 72% (781). *Average award:* Freshmen: $22,117; Undergraduates: $18,344. *Scholarships, grants, and awards:* Federal Pell, FSEOG, state, private, college/university gift aid from institutional funds.

GIFT AID (NON-NEED-BASED) *Total amount:* $3,347,515 (7% state, 81% institutional, 12% external sources). *Receiving aid:* Freshmen: 8% (21). Undergraduates: 8% (89). *Average award:* Freshmen: $16,738. Undergraduates: $14,243. *Scholarships, grants, and awards by category:* Academic interests/achievement: biological sciences, business, education, English, foreign languages, general academic interests/achievements, humanities, mathematics, physical sciences, premedicine, religion/biblical studies, social sciences. *Creative arts/performance:* art/fine arts, music. *Special achievements/activities:* general special achievements/activities, religious involvement. *Special characteristics:* children and siblings of alumni, children of faculty/staff, ethnic background, general special characteristics, international students, religious affiliation. *Tuition waivers:* Full or partial for employees or children of employees.

LOANS *Student loans:* $7,595,758 (84% need-based, 16% non-need-based). 80% of past graduating class borrowed through all loan programs. *Average indebtedness per student:* $36,132. *Average need-based loan:* Freshmen: $6934. Undergraduates: $8011. *Parent loans:* $1,797,052 (80% need-based, 20% non-need-based). *Programs:* Federal Direct (Subsidized and Unsubsidized Stafford, PLUS), Perkins, Federal Nursing.

WORK-STUDY *Federal work-study:* jobs available. *State or other work-study/employment:* Total amount: $53,379 (100% need-based). Part-time jobs available.

APPLYING FOR FINANCIAL AID *Required financial aid forms:* FAFSA, state aid form. *Financial aid deadline (priority):* 4/15. *Notification date:* Continuous beginning 2/1. Students must reply within 5 weeks of notification.

CONTACT Ms. Michele Hensley, Director of Financial Assistance, Eastern Mennonite University, 1200 Park Road, Harrisonburg, VA 22802-2462, 540-432-4138 or toll-free 800-368-2665. *Fax:* 540 432 4081. *E-mail:* michele.hensley@emu.edu. *Website:* http://www.emu.edu/.

EASTERN MICHIGAN UNIVERSITY
Ypsilanti, MI

Tuition & fees (MI res): $13,649	Average undergraduate aid package: $8785

ABOUT THE INSTITUTION State-supported, coed. *Awards:* certificates, bachelor's, master's, and doctoral degrees. 131 undergraduate majors. *Total enrollment:* 21,105. Undergraduates: 17,541. Freshmen: 2,808. Federal methodology is used as a basis for awarding need-based institutional aid.

UNDERGRADUATE EXPENSES for 2017–2018 *Application fee:* $35. *One-time required fee:* $323. *Tuition, state resident:* full-time $12,120; part-time $323 per credit hour. *Tuition, nonresident:* full-time $27,711; part-time $872.75 per credit hour. *Required fees:* full-time $1529; $47.30 per credit hour or $50 per credit hour. Full-time tuition and fees vary according to course level and reciprocity agreements. Part-time tuition and fees vary according to course level and reciprocity agreements. Room and board charges vary according to board plan, housing facility, and location.

FRESHMAN FINANCIAL AID (Fall 2015) 2,616 applied for aid; of those 80% were deemed to have need. 99% of freshmen with need received aid; of those 7% had need fully met. *Average percent of need met:* 46% (excluding resources awarded to replace EFC). *Average financial aid package:* $2068 (excluding resources awarded to replace EFC). 24% of all full-time freshmen had no need and received non-need-based gift aid.

UNDERGRADUATE FINANCIAL AID (Fall 2015) 10,796 applied for aid; of those 83% were deemed to have need. 99% of undergraduates with need received aid; of those 4% had need fully met. *Average percent of need met:* 47% (excluding resources awarded to replace EFC). *Average financial aid package:* $8785 (excluding resources awarded to replace EFC). 17% of all full-time undergraduates had no need and received non-need-based gift aid.

GIFT AID (NEED-BASED) *Total amount:* $40,703,052 (80% federal, 2% state, 18% institutional). *Receiving aid:* Freshmen: 50% (1,431); all full-time undergraduates: 50% (6,504). *Average award:* Freshmen: $6857; Undergraduates: $5423. *Scholarships, grants, and awards:* Federal Pell, FSEOG, state, private, college/university gift aid from institutional funds, Federal Nursing.

GIFT AID (NON-NEED-BASED) *Total amount:* $31,765,887 (95% institutional, 5% external sources). *Receiving aid:* Freshmen: 55% (1,562). Undergraduates: 33% (4,255). *Average award:* Freshmen: $5434. Undergraduates: $5427. *Scholarships, grants, and awards by category:* Academic interests/achievement: 6,233 awards ($23,484,290 total): agriculture, architecture, biological sciences, business, communication, computer science, education, engineering/technologies, English, foreign languages, general academic interests/achievements, health fields, home economics, humanities, mathematics, physical sciences, religion/biblical studies, social sciences. *Creative arts/performance:* 111 awards ($113,830 total): applied art and design, art/fine arts, cinema/film/broadcasting, creative writing, dance, debating, general creative arts/performance, music, performing arts, theater/drama. *Special achievements/activities:* 139 awards ($181,982 total): general special achievements/activities, leadership, memberships, religious involvement. *Special characteristics:* 425 awards ($6,005,381 total): children and siblings of alumni, ethnic background, international students, members of minority groups, out-of-state students, previous college experience, religious affiliation. *Tuition waivers:* Full or partial for employees or children of employees. *ROTC:* Army, Naval cooperative, Air Force cooperative.

LOANS *Student loans:* $87,277,983 (42% need-based, 58% non-need-based). 68% of past graduating class borrowed through all loan programs. *Average indebtedness per student:* $30,588. *Average need-based loan:* Freshmen: $1390. Undergraduates: $6756. *Parent loans:* $17,891,875 (100% non-need-based). *Programs:* Federal Direct (Subsidized and Unsubsidized Stafford, PLUS), Perkins, private loans.

WORK-STUDY *Federal work-study:* 615 jobs averaging $1626.
ATHLETIC AWARDS Total amount: $5,950,311 (100% non-need-based).
APPLYING FOR FINANCIAL AID *Required financial aid form:* FAFSA. *Financial aid deadline:* Continuous. *Notification date:* 12/12.
CONTACT Donna Holubik, Director of Financial Aid, Eastern Michigan University, 403 Pierce Hall, Ypsilanti, MI 48197, 734-487-1048 or toll-free 800-GO TO EMU. *Fax:* 734-487-4281. *E-mail:* dholubik@emich.edu.
Website: http://www.emich.edu/.

EASTERN NAZARENE COLLEGE
Quincy, MA

CONTACT Lisa Seals, Interim Director of Financial Aid, Eastern Nazarene College, 23 East Elm Avenue, Quincy, MA 02170, 617-745-3869 or toll-free 800-88-ENC88. *Fax:* 617-745-3992. *E-mail:* lisa.seals@enc .edu.
Website: http://www.enc.edu/.

EASTERN NEW MEXICO UNIVERSITY
Portales, NM

CONTACT Mr. Brent Small, Director of Financial Aid, Eastern New Mexico University, Station 20, 1500 South Avenue K, Portales, NM 88130, 575-562-2194 or toll-free 800-367-3668. *Fax:* 575-562-2198. *E-mail:* brent.small@enmu.edu.
Website: http://www.enmu.edu/.

EASTERN OREGON UNIVERSITY
La Grande, OR

Tuition & fees (OR res): $8004	Average undergraduate aid package: $9506

ABOUT THE INSTITUTION State-supported, coed. *Awards:* certificates, associate, bachelor's, and master's degrees. 22 undergraduate majors. *Total enrollment:* 3,176. Undergraduates: 2,873. Freshmen: 352. Federal methodology is used as a basis for awarding need-based institutional aid.
UNDERGRADUATE EXPENSES for 2016–2017 *Tuition, state resident:* full-time $6570; part-time $146 per credit hour. *Tuition, nonresident:* full-time $17,212; part-time $382.50 per credit hour. *Required fees:* full-time $1434; $306 per term. Full-time tuition and fees vary according to course load, location, and reciprocity agreements. Part-time tuition and fees vary according to course load, location, and reciprocity agreements. *College room and board:* $8930; *Room only:* $5375. Room and board charges vary according to board plan and housing facility.
FRESHMAN FINANCIAL AID (Fall 2015) 294 applied for aid; of those 77% were deemed to have need. 100% of freshmen with need received aid; of those 20% had need fully met. *Average percent of need met:* 63% (excluding resources awarded to replace EFC). *Average financial aid package:* $10,157 (excluding resources awarded to replace EFC). 17% of all full-time freshmen had no need and received non-need-based gift aid.
UNDERGRADUATE FINANCIAL AID (Fall 2015) 1,535 applied for aid; of those 88% were deemed to have need. 97% of undergraduates with need received aid; of those 10% had need fully met. *Average percent of need met:* 55% (excluding resources awarded to replace EFC). *Average financial aid package:* $9506 (excluding resources awarded to replace EFC). 7% of all full-time undergraduates had no need and received non-need-based gift aid.
GIFT AID (NEED-BASED) *Total amount:* $8,207,337 (76% federal, 16% state, 8% institutional). *Receiving aid:* Freshmen: 70% (218); all full-time undergraduates: 72% (1,254). *Average award:* Freshmen: $7574; Undergraduates: $8241. *Scholarships, grants, and awards:* Federal Pell, FSEOG, state, private, college/university gift aid from institutional funds.
GIFT AID (NON-NEED-BASED) *Total amount:* $2,197,106 (47% institutional, 53% external sources). *Receiving aid:* Freshmen: 57% (177). Undergraduates: 31% (535). *Average award:* Freshmen: $1583. Undergraduates: $2254. *Scholarships, grants, and awards by category:* Academic interests/achievement: general academic interests/achievements. Creative arts/performance: art/fine arts, general creative arts/performance. *Special achievements/activities:* leadership. *Special characteristics:* local/state students, members of minority groups. *Tuition waivers:* Full or partial for employees or children of employees, senior citizens. *ROTC:* Army.
LOANS *Student loans:* $12,725,568 (44% need-based, 56% non-need-based). 68% of past graduating class borrowed through all loan programs. *Average indebtedness per student:* $28,942. *Average need-based loan:* Freshmen: $3223. Undergraduates: $4154. *Parent loans:* $2,229,932 (100% non-need-based). *Programs:* Federal Direct (Subsidized and Unsubsidized Stafford, PLUS), Perkins.
WORK-STUDY *Federal work-study:* 164 jobs averaging $2113.
ATHLETIC AWARDS Total amount: $918,001 (100% non-need-based).
APPLYING FOR FINANCIAL AID *Required financial aid form:* FAFSA. *Financial aid deadline:* Continuous. *Notification date:* Continuous beginning 4/1. Students must reply within 4 weeks of notification.
CONTACT Financial Aid Office, Eastern Oregon University, One University Boulevard, Inlow Hall, Room 201, La Grande, OR 97850-2899, 541-962-3550 or toll-free 800-452-8639. *Fax:* 541-962-3661. *E-mail:* fao@eou.edu.
Website: http://www.eou.edu/.

EASTERN UNIVERSITY
St. Davids, PA

Tuition & fees: $32,080	Average undergraduate aid package: $20,007

ABOUT THE INSTITUTION Independent Christian, coed. *Awards:* certificates, diplomas, associate, bachelor's, master's, and doctoral degrees. 36 undergraduate majors. *Total enrollment:* 3,420. Undergraduates: 2,082. Freshmen: 442. Both federal and institutional methodology are used as a basis for awarding need-based institutional aid.
UNDERGRADUATE EXPENSES for 2017–2018 *Application fee:* $35. *One-time required fee:* $60. *Comprehensive fee:* $43,060 includes full-time tuition ($31,700), mandatory fees ($380), and room and board ($10,980). *College room only:* $5840. Full-time tuition and fees vary according to course load, degree level, and program. Room and board charges vary according to housing facility and location. *Part-time tuition:* $695 per credit. *Part-time fees:* $180 per term. Part-time tuition and fees vary according to course load, degree level, and program.
FRESHMAN FINANCIAL AID (Fall 2015) 350 applied for aid; of those 93% were deemed to have need. 100% of freshmen with need received aid; of those 15% had need fully met. *Average percent of need met:* 74% (excluding resources awarded to replace EFC). *Average financial aid package:* $25,751 (excluding resources awarded to replace EFC). 7% of all full-time freshmen had no need and received non-need-based gift aid.
UNDERGRADUATE FINANCIAL AID (Fall 2015) 1,823 applied for aid; of those 93% were deemed to have need. 99% of undergraduates with need received aid; of those 10% had need fully met. *Average percent of need met:* 66% (excluding resources awarded to replace EFC). *Average financial aid package:* $20,007 (excluding resources awarded to replace EFC). 5% of all full-time undergraduates had no need and received non-need-based gift aid.
GIFT AID (NEED-BASED) *Total amount:* $9,927,133 (43% federal, 22% state, 35% institutional). *Receiving aid:* Freshmen: 72% (269); all full-time undergraduates: 78% (1,442). *Average award:* Freshmen: $8320; Undergraduates: $7241. *Scholarships, grants, and awards:* Federal Pell, FSEOG, state, private, college/university gift aid from institutional funds.
GIFT AID (NON-NEED-BASED) *Total amount:* $19,812,656 (96% institutional, 4% external sources). *Receiving aid:* Freshmen: 85% (319). Undergraduates: 75% (1,386). *Average award:* Freshmen: $14,202. Undergraduates: $11,293. *Scholarships, grants, and awards by category:* Academic interests/achievement: 53 awards ($132,600 total): business, engineering/technologies, general academic interests/achievements, religion/biblical studies. Creative arts/performance: 46 awards ($93,250 total): dance, music. Special achievements/activities: 454 awards ($2,615,289 total): community service, leadership, memberships. Special characteristics: 350 awards ($1,414,436 total): children and siblings of alumni, children of faculty/staff, international students, relatives of clergy, siblings of current students. *Tuition waivers:* Full or partial for children of alumni, employees or children of employees. *ROTC:* Army cooperative, Air Force cooperative.
LOANS *Student loans:* $15,944,555 (37% need-based, 63% non-need-based). 79% of past graduating class borrowed through all loan programs. *Average indebtedness per student:* $38,904. *Average need-based loan:* Freshmen: $3213. Undergrad-

uates: $3941. **Parent loans:** $3,108,386 (100% non-need-based). **Programs:** Federal Direct (Subsidized and Unsubsidized Stafford, PLUS), Perkins.
WORK-STUDY **Federal work-study:** 348 jobs averaging $1037. **State or other work-study/employment:** Part-time jobs available.
APPLYING FOR FINANCIAL AID **Required financial aid form:** FAFSA. **Financial aid deadline:** Continuous. **Notification date:** Continuous beginning 4/1.
CONTACT Christal Jennings, Office of Student Financial Aid, Eastern University, 1300 Eagle Road, St. Davids, PA 19007-3696, 610-225-5102 or toll free 800 452 0996. **Fax:** 610-225-5651. **E-mail:** finaid@eastern.edu.
Website: http://www.eastern.edu/.

EASTERN WASHINGTON UNIVERSITY
Cheney, WA

Tuition & fees (WA res): $6951	Average undergraduate aid package: $13,877

ABOUT THE INSTITUTION State-supported, coed. **Awards:** certificates, bachelor's, master's, and doctoral degrees. 93 undergraduate majors. **Total enrollment:** 12,279. Undergraduates: 11,217. Freshmen: 1,697. Federal methodology is used as a basis for awarding need-based institutional aid.
UNDERGRADUATE EXPENSES for 2016–2017 Tuition, state resident: full-time $6110; part-time $204 per credit hour. **Tuition, nonresident:** full-time $22,502; part-time $750 per credit hour. **Required fees:** full-time $841. Full-time tuition and fees vary according to course level, course load, degree level, program, reciprocity agreements, and student level. Part-time tuition and fees vary according to course level, course load, degree level, program, reciprocity agreements, and student level. **College room and board:** $10,941; **Room only:** $6100. Room and board charges vary according to board plan and housing facility.
FRESHMAN FINANCIAL AID (Fall 2015) 1,515 applied for aid; of those 62% were deemed to have need. 100% of freshmen with need received aid; of those 16% had need fully met. **Average percent of need met:** 84% (excluding resources awarded to replace EFC). **Average financial aid package:** $13,873 (excluding resources awarded to replace EFC). 8% of all full-time freshmen had no need and received non-need-based gift aid.
UNDERGRADUATE FINANCIAL AID (Fall 2015) 7,973 applied for aid; of those 71% were deemed to have need. 100% of undergraduates with need received aid; of those 12% had need fully met. **Average percent of need met:** 58% (excluding resources awarded to replace EFC). **Average financial aid package:** $13,877 (excluding resources awarded to replace EFC). 5% of all full-time undergraduates had no need and received non-need-based gift aid.
GIFT AID (NEED-BASED) Total amount: $44,459,828 (44% federal, 43% state, 8% institutional, 5% external sources). **Receiving aid:** Freshmen: 42% (725); all full-time undergraduates: 46% (4,692). **Average award:** Freshmen: $8734; Undergraduates: $8175. **Scholarships, grants, and awards:** Federal Pell, FSEOG, state, private, college/university gift aid from institutional funds.
GIFT AID (NON-NEED-BASED) Total amount: $6,292,303 (3% institutional, 97% external sources). **Receiving aid:** Freshmen: 25% (433). Undergraduates: 12% (1,226). **Average award:** Freshmen: $3435. Undergraduates: $3824. **Scholarships, grants, and awards by category:** Academic interests/achievement: area/ethnic studies, biological sciences, business, communication, computer science, education, engineering/technologies, English, foreign languages, general academic interests/achievements, health fields, humanities, international studies, mathematics, military science, physical sciences, premedicine, social sciences. Creative arts/performance: art/fine arts, cinema/film/broadcasting, creative writing, journalism/publications, music, theater/drama. Special characteristics: adult students, children and siblings of alumni, children of union members/company employees, ethnic background, first-generation college students, handicapped students, local/state students, married students, spouses of deceased or disabled public servants, veterans, veterans' children. **Tuition waivers:** Full or partial for employees or children of employees. **ROTC:** Army.
LOANS Student loans: $43,847,139 (86% need-based, 14% non-need-based). 53% of past graduating class borrowed through all loan programs. Average indebtedness per student: $24,109. **Average need-based loan:** Freshmen: $3251. Undergraduates: $4210. **Parent loans:** $10,581,440 (68% need-based, 32% non-need-based). **Programs:** Federal Direct (Subsidized and Unsubsidized Stafford, PLUS), Perkins, credit-based education loans from commercial lenders.

WORK-STUDY **Federal work-study:** jobs available. **State or other work-study/employment:** Total amount: $491,885 (100% need-based). Part-time jobs available.
ATHLETIC AWARDS Total amount: $2,914,478 (40% need-based, 60% non-need-based).
APPLYING FOR FINANCIAL AID **Required financial aid forms:** FAFSA, Washington Application for Student Financial Aid (WASFA) for undocumented state residents and DACA students only. **Financial aid deadline (priority):** 2/1. **Notification date:** Continuous beginning 4/1. Students must reply within 4 weeks of notification.
CONTACT Mr. Bruce DeFrates, Director of Financial Aid and Scholarships, Eastern Washington University, 102 Sutton Hall, Cheney, WA 99004-2447, 509-359-6329. **Fax:** 509-359-4330. **E-mail:** bdefrates@ewu.edu.
Website: http://www.ewu.edu/.

EAST STROUDSBURG UNIVERSITY OF PENNSYLVANIA
East Stroudsburg, PA

Tuition & fees (PA res): $9944	Average undergraduate aid package: $8213

ABOUT THE INSTITUTION State-supported, coed. **Awards:** certificates, associate, bachelor's, master's, and doctoral degrees. 46 undergraduate majors. **Total enrollment:** 6,830. Undergraduates: 6,159. Freshmen: 1,307. Federal methodology is used as a basis for awarding need-based institutional aid.
UNDERGRADUATE EXPENSES for 2016–2017 Application fee: $25. **Tuition, state resident:** full-time $7238; part-time $302 per credit hour. **Tuition, nonresident:** full-time $18,096; part-time $754 per credit hour. **Required fees:** full-time $2706; $143 per credit hour or $683 per term. Full-time tuition and fees vary according to course load, location, and program. Part-time tuition and fees vary according to location and program. **College room and board:** $8280; **Room only:** $5680. Room and board charges vary according to board plan and housing facility.
FRESHMAN FINANCIAL AID (Fall 2015) 1,221 applied for aid; of those 82% were deemed to have need. 96% of freshmen with need received aid; of those 47% had need fully met. **Average percent of need met:** 40% (excluding resources awarded to replace EFC). **Average financial aid package:** $7703 (excluding resources awarded to replace EFC). 1% of all full-time freshmen had no need and received non-need-based gift aid.
UNDERGRADUATE FINANCIAL AID (Fall 2015) 3,883 applied for aid; of those 83% were deemed to have need. 96% of undergraduates with need received aid; of those 45% had need fully met. **Average percent of need met:** 43% (excluding resources awarded to replace EFC). **Average financial aid package:** $8213 (excluding resources awarded to replace EFC). 1% of all full-time undergraduates had no need and received non-need-based gift aid.
GIFT AID (NEED-BASED) Total amount: $56,808,975 (88% federal, 10% state, 2% external sources). **Receiving aid:** Freshmen: 53% (685); all full-time undergraduates: 36% (2,149). **Average award:** Freshmen: $6277; Undergraduates: $5814. **Scholarships, grants, and awards:** Federal Pell, FSEOG, state, private, college/university gift aid from institutional funds.
GIFT AID (NON-NEED-BASED) Average award: Freshmen: $1065. Undergraduates: $1272. **Scholarships, grants, and awards by category:** Academic interests/achievement: biological sciences, business, communication, computer science, education, English, foreign languages, general academic interests/achievements, health fields, mathematics, physical sciences, social sciences. Creative arts/performance: applied art and design, art/fine arts, music, theater/drama. Special achievements/activities: general special achievements/activities, leadership. Special characteristics: adult students, children and siblings of alumni, handicapped students, international students, local/state students, members of minority groups. **Tuition waivers:** Full or partial for employees or children of employees, senior citizens. **ROTC:** Army, Air Force cooperative.
LOANS Student loans: $39,289,485 (100% need-based). 70% of past graduating class borrowed through all loan programs. Average indebtedness per student: $28,500. **Average need-based loan:** Freshmen: $3147. Undergraduates: $4123. **Programs:** Federal Direct (Subsidized and Unsubsidized Stafford, PLUS), Perkins.

WORK-STUDY *Federal work-study:* jobs available. *State or other work-study/employment:* Total amount: $1,677,860 (100% need-based). Part-time jobs available.

ATHLETIC AWARDS Total amount: $897,375 (100% need-based).

APPLYING FOR FINANCIAL AID *Required financial aid form:* FAFSA. *Financial aid deadline:* 2/16 (priority: 2/16). *Notification date:* 3/16. Students must reply by 5/1.

CONTACT Aristalia Benitez, Office of Financial Aid, East Stroudsburg University of Pennsylvania, 200 Prospect Street, East Stroudsburg, PA 18301-2999, 570-422-2820 or toll-free 877-230-5547. *Fax:* 570-422-2849. *E-mail:* finaid@esu.edu. *Website:* http://www.esu.edu/.

EAST TENNESSEE STATE UNIVERSITY
Johnson City, TN

ABOUT THE INSTITUTION State-supported, coed. *Awards:* certificates, bachelor's, master's, and doctoral degrees. 49 undergraduate majors. *Total enrollment:* 14,022. Undergraduates: 11,065. Freshmen: 1,886.

GIFT AID (NEED-BASED) *Scholarships, grants, and awards:* Federal Pell, FSEOG, state, private, college/university gift aid from institutional funds, Federal Nursing.

GIFT AID (NON-NEED-BASED) *Scholarships, grants, and awards by category:* Academic interests/achievement: biological sciences, business, computer science, education, engineering/technologies, English, general academic interests/achievements, health fields, mathematics, military science, social sciences. *Creative arts/performance:* art/fine arts, journalism/publications, music, theater/drama. *Special achievements/activities:* leadership, memberships. *Special characteristics:* children of union members/company employees, members of minority groups.

LOANS *Programs:* Federal Direct (Subsidized and Unsubsidized Stafford, PLUS), Perkins, Federal Nursing, state, college/university.

APPLYING FOR FINANCIAL AID *Required financial aid form:* FAFSA.

CONTACT Financial Aid Office, East Tennessee State University, PO Box 70722, 105 Burgin Dossett, Johnson City, TN 37614-1710, 423-439-4300 or toll-free 800-462-3878. *Fax:* 423-439-5855. *E-mail:* finaid@etsu.edu. *Website:* http://www.etsu.edu/.

EAST TEXAS BAPTIST UNIVERSITY
Marshall, TX

Tuition & fees: $24,700	Average undergraduate aid package: $18,227

ABOUT THE INSTITUTION Independent Baptist, coed. *Awards:* certificates, bachelor's, and master's degrees. 45 undergraduate majors. *Total enrollment:* 1,461. Undergraduates: 1,339. Freshmen: 346. Federal methodology is used as a basis for awarding need-based institutional aid.

UNDERGRADUATE EXPENSES for 2016–2017 *Application fee:* $25. *Comprehensive fee:* $33,409 includes full-time tuition ($23,700), mandatory fees ($1000), and room and board ($8709). *College room only:* $4576. Room and board charges vary according to board plan and housing facility. *Part-time tuition:* $790 per credit hour. *Part-time fees:* $43 per credit hour.

FRESHMAN FINANCIAL AID (Fall 2015) 324 applied for aid; of those 89% were deemed to have need. 100% of freshmen with need received aid; of those 10% had need fully met. *Average percent of need met:* 28% (excluding resources awarded to replace EFC). *Average financial aid package:* $18,914 (excluding resources awarded to replace EFC). 15% of all full-time freshmen had no need and received non-need-based gift aid.

UNDERGRADUATE FINANCIAL AID (Fall 2015) 1,038 applied for aid; of those 90% were deemed to have need. 100% of undergraduates with need received aid; of those 11% had need fully met. *Average percent of need met:* 30% (excluding resources awarded to replace EFC). *Average financial aid package:* $18,227 (excluding resources awarded to replace EFC). 14% of all full-time undergraduates had no need and received non-need-based gift aid.

GIFT AID (NEED-BASED) *Total amount:* $4,225,516 (58% federal, 41% state, 1% institutional). *Receiving aid:* Freshmen: 65% (220); all full-time undergraduates: 65% (712). *Average award:* Freshmen: $6319; Undergraduates: $6178. *Scholar-ships, grants, and awards:* Federal Pell, FSEOG, state, private, college/university gift aid from institutional funds.

GIFT AID (NON-NEED-BASED) *Total amount:* $11,210,156 (1% federal, 95% institutional, 4% external sources). *Receiving aid:* Freshmen: 84% (285). Undergraduates: 84% (923). *Average award:* Freshmen: $11,579. Undergraduates: $10,502. *Scholarships, grants, and awards by category:* Academic interests/achievement: 874 awards ($5,754,567 total): biological sciences, business, communication, education, English, general academic interests/achievements, health fields, home economics, humanities, mathematics, physical sciences, religion/biblical studies, social sciences. *Creative arts/performance:* 100 awards ($296,185 total): music, theater/drama. *Special achievements/activities:* 699 awards ($1,841,061 total): cheerleading/drum major, general special achievements/activities, leadership, religious involvement, rodeo. *Special characteristics:* 122 awards ($736,712 total): adult students, children and siblings of alumni, children of faculty/staff, general special characteristics, international students, out-of-state students, previous college experience, religious affiliation, veterans. *Tuition waivers:* Full or partial for employees or children of employees.

LOANS *Student loans:* $4,486,280 (67% need-based, 33% non-need-based). 82% of past graduating class borrowed through all loan programs. *Average indebtedness per student:* $34,048. *Average need-based loan:* Freshmen: $3194. Undergraduates: $4011. *Parent loans:* $2,360,740 (100% non-need-based). *Programs:* Federal Direct (Subsidized and Unsubsidized Stafford, PLUS), Perkins, state.

WORK-STUDY *Federal work-study:* 104 jobs averaging $985. *State or other work-study/employment:* Total amount: $358,689 (3% need-based, 97% non-need-based). 278 part-time jobs averaging $1290.

APPLYING FOR FINANCIAL AID *Required financial aid forms:* FAFSA, institution's own form. *Financial aid deadline (priority):* 6/1. *Notification date:* Continuous beginning 1/1.

CONTACT Mr. Tommy Young, Director of Financial Aid, East Texas Baptist University, One Tiger Drive, Marshall, TX 75670-1498, 903-923-2137 or toll-free 800-804-ETBU. *Fax:* 903-934-8120. *E-mail:* tyoung@etbu.edu. *Website:* http://www.etbu.edu/.

EAST-WEST UNIVERSITY
Chicago, IL

CONTACT Cesar Campos, Director of Financial Aid, East-West University, 816 South Michigan Avenue, Chicago, IL 60605-2103, 312-939-0111 Ext. 1806. *Fax:* 312-939-0083. *E-mail:* cesar@eastwest.edu. *Website:* http://www.eastwest.edu/.

ECCLESIA COLLEGE
Springdale, AR

CONTACT Financial Aid Office, Ecclesia College, 9653 Nations Drive, Springdale, AR 72762, 479-248-7236. *Website:* http://www.ecollege.edu/.

ECKERD COLLEGE
St. Petersburg, FL

Comprehensive fee: $54,750	Average undergraduate aid package: $34,291

ABOUT THE INSTITUTION Independent Presbyterian, coed. *Awards:* bachelor's degrees. 38 undergraduate majors. *Total enrollment:* 1,844. Undergraduates: 1,844. Freshmen: 577. Federal methodology is used as a basis for awarding need-based institutional aid.

UNDERGRADUATE EXPENSES for 2017–2018 *Application fee:* $40. *Comprehensive fee:* $54,750 includes full-time tuition ($42,428), mandatory fees ($356), and room and board ($11,706). *College room only:* $5906. Room and board charges vary according to board plan and housing facility. *Part-time tuition:* $5092 per course.

FRESHMAN FINANCIAL AID (Fall 2016, est.) 461 applied for aid; of those 83% were deemed to have need. 100% of freshmen with need received aid; of those 46%

had need fully met. *Average percent of need met:* 87% (excluding resources awarded to replace EFC). *Average financial aid package:* $34,048 (excluding resources awarded to replace EFC). 19% of all full-time freshmen had no need and received non-need-based gift aid.

UNDERGRADUATE FINANCIAL AID (Fall 2016, est.) 1,253 applied for aid; of those 87% were deemed to have need. 100% of undergraduates with need received aid; of those 45% had need fully met. *Average percent of need met:* 86% (excluding resources awarded to replace EFC). *Average financial aid package:* $34,291 (excluding resources awarded to replace EFC). 29% of all full-time undergraduates had no need and received non-need-based gift aid.

GIFT AID (NEED-BASED) *Total amount:* $25,232,970 (7% federal, 4% state, 87% institutional, 2% external sources). *Receiving aid:* Freshmen: 67% (382); all full-time undergraduates: 60% (1,083). *Average award:* Freshmen: $24,449; Undergraduates: $24,086. *Scholarships, grants, and awards:* Federal Pell, FSEOG, state, private, college/university gift aid from institutional funds.

GIFT AID (NON-NEED-BASED) *Total amount:* $13,072,573 (4% state, 94% institutional, 2% external sources). *Average award:* Freshmen: $17,154. Undergraduates: $16,207. *Scholarships, grants, and awards by category:* Academic interests/achievement: 1,533 awards ($23,847,282 total): general academic interests/achievements. *Creative arts/performance:* 37 awards ($36,500 total): art/fine arts, creative writing, music, theater/drama. *Special characteristics:* children of faculty/staff, international students, local/state students, religious affiliation. *Tuition waivers:* Full or partial for employees or children of employees. *ROTC:* Army cooperative, Air Force cooperative.

LOANS *Student loans:* $11,829,627 (66% need-based, 34% non-need-based). 59% of past graduating class borrowed through all loan programs. *Average indebtedness per student:* $33,979. *Average need-based loan:* Freshmen: $4006. Undergraduates: $4626. *Parent loans:* $5,974,980 (33% need-based, 67% non-need-based). *Programs:* Federal Direct (Subsidized and Unsubsidized Stafford, PLUS), Perkins, college/university.

WORK-STUDY *Federal work-study:* Total amount: $1,541,586; 767 jobs averaging $2000. *State or other work-study/employment:* Total amount: $26,000 (100% non-need-based). 13 part-time jobs averaging $2000.

ATHLETIC AWARDS Total amount: $2,368,123 (32% need-based, 68% non-need-based).

APPLYING FOR FINANCIAL AID *Required financial aid form:* FAFSA. *Financial aid deadline (priority):* 3/1. *Notification date:* Continuous beginning 10/15. Students must reply by 5/1.

CONTACT Dr. Pat Garrett Watkins, Director of Financial Aid, Eckerd College, 4200 54th Avenue, South, St. Petersburg, FL 33711, 727-864-8334 or toll-free 800-456-9009. *Fax:* 727-866-2304. *E-mail:* watkinpe@eckerd.edu. *Website:* http://www.eckerd.edu/.

ECPI UNIVERSITY
Virginia Beach, VA

Tuition & fees: N/R	Average undergraduate aid package: N/A

ABOUT THE INSTITUTION Proprietary, coed. 28 undergraduate majors. Federal methodology is used as a basis for awarding need-based institutional aid.

FRESHMAN FINANCIAL AID (Fall 2015) 1,498 applied for aid.

UNDERGRADUATE FINANCIAL AID (Fall 2015) 8,400 applied for aid.

GIFT AID (NEED-BASED) *Total amount:* $55,709,278 (100% federal). *Scholarships, grants, and awards:* Federal Pell, FSEOG, state, private, college/university gift aid from institutional funds.

GIFT AID (NON-NEED-BASED) *Total amount:* $11,717,939 (3% state, 94% institutional, 3% external sources). *Scholarships, grants, and awards by category:* Academic interests/achievement: business, computer science, engineering/technologies, health fields, home economics. *Special achievements/activities:* community service, general special achievements/activities. *Special characteristics:* adult students, children and siblings of alumni, children of current students, children of faculty/staff, general special characteristics, parents of current students, veterans, veterans' children.

LOANS *Student loans:* $114,701,773 (40% need-based, 60% non-need-based). *Parent loans:* $6,215,488 (100% non-need-based). *Programs:* Federal Direct (Subsidized and Unsubsidized Stafford, PLUS), Perkins, college/university, private loans.

WORK-STUDY *Federal work-study:* jobs available. *State or other work-study/employment:* Part-time jobs available.

APPLYING FOR FINANCIAL AID *Required financial aid forms:* FAFSA, institution's own form. *Financial aid deadline:* Continuous. *Notification date:* Continuous beginning 1/1. Students must reply within 12 weeks of notification.

CONTACT Mrs. Kathi Turner, Director of Financial Aid, ECPI University, 5555 Greenwich Road, Suite 300, Virginia Beach, VA 23462, 757-490-9090 or toll-free 844-611-0766. *Fax:* 757-671-8661. *E-mail:* kturner@ecpi.edu. *Website:* http://www.ecpi.edu/.

EDGEWOOD COLLEGE
Madison, WI

Tuition & fees: $27,530	Average undergraduate aid package: $20,707

ABOUT THE INSTITUTION Independent Roman Catholic, coed. *Awards:* certificates, bachelor's, master's, and doctoral degrees. 55 undergraduate majors. *Total enrollment:* 2,552. Undergraduates: 1,661. Freshmen: 263. Federal methodology is used as a basis for awarding need-based institutional aid.

UNDERGRADUATE EXPENSES for 2016–2017 *Application fee:* $30. *Comprehensive fee:* $37,400 includes full-time tuition ($27,530) and room and board ($9870). Full-time tuition and fees vary according to degree level. Room and board charges vary according to housing facility. *Part-time tuition:* $866 per credit. Part-time tuition and fees vary according to course load and degree level.

FRESHMAN FINANCIAL AID (Fall 2015) 274 applied for aid; of those 89% were deemed to have need. 100% of freshmen with need received aid; of those 10% had need fully met. *Average percent of need met:* 79% (excluding resources awarded to replace EFC). *Average financial aid package:* $22,099 (excluding resources awarded to replace EFC). 16% of all full-time freshmen had no need and received non-need-based gift aid.

UNDERGRADUATE FINANCIAL AID (Fall 2015) 1,277 applied for aid; of those 90% were deemed to have need. 100% of undergraduates with need received aid; of those 13% had need fully met. *Average percent of need met:* 74% (excluding resources awarded to replace EFC). *Average financial aid package:* $20,707 (excluding resources awarded to replace EFC). 18% of all full-time undergraduates had no need and received non-need-based gift aid.

GIFT AID (NEED-BASED) *Total amount:* $16,389,349 (16% federal, 12% state, 59% institutional, 13% external sources). *Receiving aid:* Freshmen: 80% (241); all full-time undergraduates: 75% (1,127). *Average award:* Freshmen: $17,036; Undergraduates: $14,227. *Scholarships, grants, and awards:* Federal Pell, FSEOG, state, private, college/university gift aid from institutional funds.

GIFT AID (NON-NEED-BASED) *Total amount:* $3,148,743 (11% federal, 1% state, 61% institutional, 27% external sources). *Receiving aid:* Freshmen: 6% (17). Undergraduates: 6% (85). *Average award:* Freshmen: $6737. Undergraduates: $6048. *Scholarships, grants, and awards by category:* Academic interests/achievement: 1,159 awards ($6,307,513 total): area/ethnic studies, foreign languages, general academic interests/achievements. *Creative arts/performance:* 134 awards ($175,725 total): art/fine arts, creative writing, music, performing arts, theater/drama. *Special achievements/activities:* 42 awards ($328,085 total): community service, religious involvement. *Special characteristics:* 89 awards ($888,749 total): children and siblings of alumni, children of faculty/staff, international students. *Tuition waivers:* Full or partial for employees or children of employees. *ROTC:* Army cooperative, Naval cooperative, Air Force cooperative.

LOANS *Student loans:* $12,895,552 (71% need-based, 29% non-need-based). 80% of past graduating class borrowed through all loan programs. *Average indebtedness per student:* $33,104. *Average need-based loan:* Freshmen: $3993. Undergraduates: $5558. *Parent loans:* $782,240 (100% need-based). *Programs:* Federal Direct (Subsidized and Unsubsidized Stafford, PLUS), Perkins, state.

WORK-STUDY *Federal work-study:* 546 jobs averaging $1992. *State or other work-study/employment:* Total amount: $1,790,015 (36% need-based, 64% non-need-based). 688 part-time jobs averaging $1930.

APPLYING FOR FINANCIAL AID *Required financial aid form:* FAFSA. *Financial aid deadline (priority):* 3/1. *Notification date:* Continuous beginning 3/15. Students must reply by 5/1.

CONTACT Ms. Kari J. Gribble, Director of Financial Aid and Edgewood Central, Edgewood College, 1000 Edgewood College Drive, Madison, WI 53711-1997, 608-663-4300 or toll-free 800-444-4861 Ext. 2294. *E-mail:* ecentral@edgewood.edu. *Website:* http://www.edgewood.edu/.

EDINBORO UNIVERSITY OF PENNSYLVANIA
Edinboro, PA

ABOUT THE INSTITUTION State-supported, coed. 39 undergraduate majors.

GIFT AID (NEED-BASED) *Scholarships, grants, and awards:* Federal Pell, FSEOG, state, private, college/university gift aid from institutional funds.

GIFT AID (NON-NEED-BASED) *Scholarships, grants, and awards by category: Academic interests/achievement:* biological sciences, business, communication, computer science, education, engineering/technologies, English, foreign languages, general academic interests/achievements, health fields, humanities, mathematics, military science, physical sciences, premedicine, religion/biblical studies, social sciences. *Creative arts/performance:* applied art and design, art/fine arts, cinema/film/broadcasting, creative writing, journalism/publications, music, theater/drama. *Special achievements/activities:* community service, general special achievements/activities, leadership, memberships. *Special characteristics:* adult students, children and siblings of alumni, children of faculty/staff, children of union members/company employees, children with a deceased or disabled parent, first-generation college students, general special characteristics, handicapped students, international students, local/state students, members of minority groups, out-of-state students, religious affiliation, veterans, veterans' children.

LOANS *Programs:* Federal Direct (Subsidized and Unsubsidized Stafford, PLUS), Perkins, Federal Nursing.

WORK-STUDY *Federal work-study:* jobs available. *State or other work-study/employment:* Total amount: $978,448 (100% non-need-based). Part-time jobs available.

APPLYING FOR FINANCIAL AID *Required financial aid forms:* FAFSA, state aid form.

CONTACT Ms. Alyssa Dobson, Director of Financial Aid, Edinboro University of Pennsylvania, Hamilton Hall, Edinboro, PA 16444, 814-732-3500 or toll-free 888-846-2676. *Fax:* 814-732-2129. *E-mail:* finaid@edinboro.edu.
Website: http://www.edinboro.edu/.

EDP UNIVERSITY OF PUERTO RICO
Hato Rey, PR

CONTACT Yaitzaenid Gonzalez, Financial Aid Administrator, EDP University of Puerto Rico, PO Box 192303, San Juan, PR 00919-2303, 787-765-3560 Ext. 253. *Fax:* 787-777-0025. *E-mail:* ygonzalez@edpcollege.edu.
Website: http://www.edpuniversity.edu/.

EDP UNIVERSITY OF PUERTO RICO–SAN SEBASTIAN
San Sebastian, PR

CONTACT Mrs. Yaitzaenid Gonzalez, Financial Aid Administrator, EDP University of Puerto Rico–San Sebastian, PO Box 192303, San Juan , PR 00919, 787-765-3560 Ext. 253. *Fax:* 787-777-0025. *E-mail:* ygonzalez@edpcollege.edu.
Website: http://www.edpuniversity.edu/.

EDWARD WATERS COLLEGE
Jacksonville, FL

CONTACT Gabriel Mbomeh, Director of Financial Aid, Edward Waters College, 1658 Kings Road, Jacksonville, FL 32209-6199, 904-366-2528 or toll-free 888-898-3191.
Website: http://www.ewc.edu/.

ELIZABETH CITY STATE UNIVERSITY
Elizabeth City, NC

Tuition & fees (NC res): $4888	Average undergraduate aid package: $7833

ABOUT THE INSTITUTION State-supported, coed. *Awards:* bachelor's and master's degrees. 35 undergraduate majors. *Total enrollment:* 1,357. Undergraduates: 1,310. Freshmen: 203. Federal methodology is used as a basis for awarding need-based institutional aid.

UNDERGRADUATE EXPENSES for 2016–2017 *Application fee:* $30. *Tuition, state resident:* full-time $2800; part-time $350 per credit hour. *Tuition, nonresident:* full-time $15,771; part-time $1971 per credit hour. *Required fees:* full-time $2088; $272.39 per term. Full-time tuition and fees vary according to degree level. Part-time tuition and fees vary according to degree level. *College room and board:* $7479; *Room only:* $4480. Room and board charges vary according to housing facility.

FRESHMAN FINANCIAL AID (Fall 2016, est.) 263 applied for aid; of those 93% were deemed to have need. 100% of freshmen with need received aid; of those 1% had need fully met. *Average percent of need met:* 64% (excluding resources awarded to replace EFC). *Average financial aid package:* $8641 (excluding resources awarded to replace EFC). 6% of all full-time freshmen had no need and received non-need-based gift aid.

UNDERGRADUATE FINANCIAL AID (Fall 2016, est.) 1,365 applied for aid; of those 94% were deemed to have need. 100% of undergraduates with need received aid; of those 1% had need fully met. *Average percent of need met:* 59% (excluding resources awarded to replace EFC). *Average financial aid package:* $7833 (excluding resources awarded to replace EFC). 3% of all full-time undergraduates had no need and received non-need-based gift aid.

GIFT AID (NEED-BASED) *Total amount:* $9,695,280 (44% federal, 18% state, 36% institutional, 2% external sources). *Receiving aid:* Freshmen: 89% (235); all full-time undergraduates: 84% (1,180). *Average award:* Freshmen: $8201; Undergraduates: $7143. *Scholarships, grants, and awards:* Federal Pell, FSEOG, state, college/university gift aid from institutional funds, Thurgood Marshall College Fund.

GIFT AID (NON-NEED-BASED) *Receiving aid:* Freshmen: 11% (30). Undergraduates: 6% (88). *Average award:* Freshmen: $5206. Undergraduates: $4540. *Scholarships, grants, and awards by category: Academic interests/achievement:* computer science, education, general academic interests/achievements, mathematics, military science. *Creative arts/performance:* music, performing arts. *Special characteristics:* ethnic background, handicapped students, international students, members of minority groups, veterans, veterans' children. *ROTC:* Army.

LOANS *Student loans:* $8,204,007 (54% need-based, 46% non-need-based). 86% of past graduating class borrowed through all loan programs. *Average indebtedness per student:* $19,631. *Average need-based loan:* Freshmen: $2493. Undergraduates: $3949. *Programs:* Federal Direct (Subsidized and Unsubsidized Stafford, PLUS), Perkins, state, college/university.

WORK-STUDY *Federal work-study:* Total amount: $312,814; jobs available. *State or other work-study/employment:* Part-time jobs available.

ATHLETIC AWARDS Total amount: $395,408 (100% need-based).

APPLYING FOR FINANCIAL AID *Required financial aid form:* FAFSA. *Financial aid deadline:* 6/1 (priority: 3/15). *Notification date:* Continuous beginning 6/1. Students must reply by 6/30.

CONTACT Jill Gable, Director of Financial Aid, Elizabeth City State University, 1704 Weeksville Road, Campus Box 914, Elizabeth City, NC 27909-7806, 252-335-3283 or toll-free 800-347-3278. *Fax:* 252-335-3716. *E-mail:* jegable@ecsu.edu.
Website: http://www.ecsu.edu/.

ELIZABETHTOWN COLLEGE
Elizabethtown, PA

Tuition & fees: $45,350	Average undergraduate aid package: $31,084

ABOUT THE INSTITUTION Independent Church of the Brethren, coed. *Awards:* bachelor's and master's degrees. 42 undergraduate majors. *Total enrollment:* 1,784. Undergraduates: 1,737. Freshmen: 442. Both federal and institutional methodology are used as a basis for awarding need-based institutional aid.

UNDERGRADUATE EXPENSES for 2017–2018 *Application fee:* $30. *Comprehensive fee:* $56,340 includes full-time tuition ($45,350) and room and board ($10,990). *College room only:* $5440. Full-time tuition and fees vary according to course load. Room and board charges vary according to board plan and housing facility. *Part-time tuition:* $1100 per credit hour. Part-time tuition and fees vary according to course load.

FRESHMAN FINANCIAL AID (Fall 2016, est.) 409 applied for aid; of those 87% were deemed to have need. 100% of freshmen with need received aid; of those 29% had need fully met. *Average percent of need met:* 83% (excluding resources awarded to replace EFC). *Average financial aid package:* $32,839 (excluding resources awarded to replace EFC). 22% of all full-time freshmen had no need and received non-need-based gift aid.

UNDERGRADUATE FINANCIAL AID (Fall 2016, est.) 1,415 applied for aid; of those 91% were deemed to have need. 100% of undergraduates with need received aid; of those 23% had need fully met. *Average percent of need met:* 79% (excluding resources awarded to replace EFC). *Average financial aid package:* $31,084 (excluding resources awarded to replace EFC). 24% of all full-time undergraduates had no need and received non-need-based gift aid.

GIFT AID (NEED-BASED) *Total amount:* $34,356,325 (5% federal, 4% state, 83% institutional, 8% external sources). *Receiving aid:* Freshmen: 80% (353); all full-time undergraduates: 75% (1,280). *Average award:* Freshmen: $29,302; Undergraduates: $26,790. *Scholarships, grants, and awards:* Federal Pell, FSEOG, state, private, college/university gift aid from institutional funds.

GIFT AID (NON-NEED-BASED) *Total amount:* $12,015,219 (86% institutional, 14% external sources). *Receiving aid:* Freshmen: 18% (79). Undergraduates: 14% (235). *Average award:* Freshmen: $23,182. Undergraduates: $21,239. *Scholarships, grants, and awards by category:* Academic interests/achievement: biological sciences, business, communication, computer science, education, engineering/technologies, English, foreign languages, general academic interests/achievements, health fields, humanities, international studies, mathematics, physical sciences, premedicine, religion/biblical studies, social sciences. *Creative arts/performance:* art/fine arts, music, performing arts, theater/drama. *Special achievements/activities:* religious involvement. *Special characteristics:* children of faculty/staff, international students, local/state students, members of minority groups, religious affiliation, siblings of current students. *Tuition waivers:* Full or partial for employees or children of employees.

LOANS *Student loans:* $13,377,246 (61% need-based, 39% non-need-based). 66% of past graduating class borrowed through all loan programs. *Average indebtedness per student:* $28,106. *Average need-based loan:* Freshmen: $3757. Undergraduates: $4524. *Parent loans:* $5,878,513 (43% need-based, 57% non-need-based). *Programs:* Federal Direct (Subsidized and Unsubsidized Stafford, PLUS), Perkins.

WORK-STUDY *Federal work-study:* Total amount: $922,090; 700 jobs averaging $1272.

APPLYING FOR FINANCIAL AID *Required financial aid forms:* FAFSA, state aid form. *Financial aid deadline (priority):* 3/15. *Notification date:* Continuous beginning 11/1. Students must reply by 5/1 or within 2 weeks of notification.

CONTACT Ms. Melodie R. Jackson, Director of Financial Aid, Elizabethtown College, 1 Alpha Drive, Elizabethtown, PA 17022, 717-361-1404. *Fax:* 717-361-1514. *E-mail:* jacksonmr@etown.edu. *Website:* http://www.etown.edu/.

ELMHURST COLLEGE
Elmhurst, IL

Tuition & fees: $35,500	Average undergraduate aid package: $26,073

ABOUT THE INSTITUTION Independent United Church of Christ, coed. *Awards:* bachelor's and master's degrees. 72 undergraduate majors. *Total enrollment:* 3,298. Undergraduates: 2,840. Freshmen: 478. Federal methodology is used as a basis for awarding need-based institutional aid.

UNDERGRADUATE EXPENSES for 2016–2017 *Comprehensive fee:* $45,578 includes full-time tuition ($35,250), mandatory fees ($250), and room and board ($10,078). *College room only:* $6152. Room and board charges vary according to board plan and housing facility. *Part-time tuition:* $997 per semester hour. Part-time tuition and fees vary according to course load.

FRESHMAN FINANCIAL AID (Fall 2016, est.) 407 applied for aid; of those 87% were deemed to have need. 100% of freshmen with need received aid; of those 18% had need fully met. *Average percent of need met:* 78% (excluding resources awarded to replace EFC). *Average financial aid package:* $27,823 (excluding resources awarded to replace EFC). 19% of all full-time freshmen had no need and received non-need-based gift aid.

UNDERGRADUATE FINANCIAL AID (Fall 2016, est.) 2,290 applied for aid; of those 92% were deemed to have need. 100% of undergraduates with need received aid; of those 20% had need fully met. *Average percent of need met:* 79% (excluding resources awarded to replace EFC). *Average financial aid package:* $26,073 (excluding resources awarded to replace EFC). 19% of all full-time undergraduates had no need and received non-need-based gift aid.

GIFT AID (NEED-BASED) *Total amount:* $44,235,795 (11% federal, 88% institutional, 1% external sources). *Receiving aid:* Freshmen: 74% (354); all full-time undergraduates: 77% (2,095). *Average award:* Freshmen: $24,218; Undergraduates: $22,024. *Scholarships, grants, and awards:* Federal Pell, FSEOG, state, private, college/university gift aid from institutional funds, Federal Nursing.

GIFT AID (NON-NEED-BASED) *Total amount:* $10,220,273 (3% federal, 96% institutional, 1% external sources). *Receiving aid:* Freshmen: 10% (49). Undergraduates: 9% (250). *Average award:* Freshmen: $14,008. Undergraduates: $15,289. *Scholarships, grants, and awards by category:* Academic interests/achievement: 1,452 awards ($22,117,190 total): biological sciences, business, communication, computer science, education, English, foreign languages, general academic interests/achievements, health fields, humanities, international studies, mathematics, physical sciences, premedicine, religion/biblical studies, social sciences. *Creative arts/performance:* 155 awards ($1,892,511 total): art/fine arts, music, theater/drama. *Special characteristics:* 1,284 awards ($5,003,740 total): children and siblings of alumni, children of current students, children with a deceased or disabled parent, ethnic background, members of minority groups, religious affiliation, siblings of current students, spouses of current students, veterans, veterans' children. *Tuition waivers:* Full or partial for employees or children of employees, senior citizens. *ROTC:* Army cooperative, Air Force cooperative.

LOANS *Student loans:* $21,573,614 (39% need-based, 61% non-need-based). 78% of past graduating class borrowed through all loan programs. *Average indebtedness per student:* $28,246. *Average need-based loan:* Freshmen: $3429. Undergraduates: $4492. *Parent loans:* $5,062,546 (85% need-based, 15% non-need-based). *Programs:* Federal Direct (Subsidized and Unsubsidized Stafford, PLUS), Perkins, alternative loans.

WORK-STUDY *Federal work-study:* Total amount: $280,374; 347 jobs averaging $1055. *State or other work-study/employment:* Total amount: $448,193 (100% non-need-based). 246 part-time jobs averaging $1622.

APPLYING FOR FINANCIAL AID *Required financial aid form:* FAFSA. *Financial aid deadline (priority):* 12/15. *Notification date:* Continuous beginning 12/1. Students must reply within 3 weeks of notification.

CONTACT Ruth A. Pusich, Director of Student Financial Services, Elmhurst College, Goebel Hall 106A, 190 Prospect Avenue, Elmhurst, IL 60126-3296, 630-617-3080 or toll-free 800-697-1871. *Fax:* 630-617-3487. *E-mail:* ruthp@elmhurst.edu. *Website:* http://www.elmhurst.edu/.

ELMIRA COLLEGE
Elmira, NY

Comprehensive fee: NR	Average undergraduate aid package: $30,976

ABOUT THE INSTITUTION Independent, coed. *Awards:* certificates, associate, bachelor's, and master's degrees. 48 undergraduate majors. *Total enrollment:* 1,187. Undergraduates: 1,101. Freshmen: 208. Federal methodology is used as a basis for awarding need-based institutional aid.

UNDERGRADUATE EXPENSES for 2017–2018 Room and board charges vary according to board plan and housing facility. Part-time tuition and fees vary according to course load. *Payment plan:* Tuition prepayment.

FRESHMAN FINANCIAL AID (Fall 2016, est.) 188 applied for aid; of those 90% were deemed to have need. 100% of freshmen with need received aid; of those 20% had need fully met. *Average percent of need met:* 73% (excluding resources awarded to replace EFC). *Average financial aid package:* $30,560 (excluding resources awarded to replace EFC). 18% of all full-time freshmen had no need and received non-need-based gift aid.

UNDERGRADUATE FINANCIAL AID (Fall 2016, est.) 835 applied for aid; of those 95% were deemed to have need. 100% of undergraduates with need received aid; of those 19% had need fully met. *Average percent of need met:* 76% (excluding resources awarded to replace EFC). *Average financial aid package:* $30,976 (excluding resources awarded to replace EFC). 16% of all full-time undergraduates had no need and received non-need-based gift aid.

GIFT AID (NEED-BASED) *Total amount:* $20,703,003 (7% federal, 4% state, 86% institutional, 3% external sources). *Receiving aid:* Freshmen: 82% (170); all full-time undergraduates: 83% (790). *Average award:* Freshmen: $27,537; Undergraduates: $26,785. *Scholarships, grants, and awards:* Federal Pell, FSEOG, state, private, college/university gift aid from institutional funds.

GIFT AID (NON-NEED-BASED) *Total amount:* $4,976,944 (93% institutional, 7% external sources). *Receiving aid:* Freshmen: 14% (29). Undergraduates: 12% (114). *Average award:* Freshmen: $21,312. Undergraduates: $22,662. *Scholarships, grants, and awards by category:* Academic interests/achievement: 798 awards ($16,667,183 total): general academic interests/achievements. *Special achievements/activities:* 31 awards ($389,500 total): leadership. *Special characteristics:* 607 awards ($2,582,352 total): children and siblings of alumni, children of faculty/staff, international students, local/state students, out-of-state students, previous college experience, siblings of current students, veterans. *Tuition waivers:* Full or partial for employees or children of employees. *ROTC:* Army, Air Force cooperative.

LOANS *Student loans:* $8,564,847 (70% need-based, 30% non-need-based). 83% of past graduating class borrowed through all loan programs. *Average indebtedness per student:* $27,757. *Average need-based loan:* Freshmen: $3393. Undergraduates: $4798. *Parent loans:* $4,159,150 (55% need-based, 45% non-need-based). *Programs:* Federal Direct (Subsidized and Unsubsidized Stafford, PLUS), Perkins.

WORK-STUDY *Federal work-study:* Total amount: $175,478; 144 jobs averaging $1200. *State or other work-study/employment:* Total amount: $236,800 (37% need-based, 63% non-need-based). 164 part-time jobs averaging $1000.

APPLYING FOR FINANCIAL AID *Required financial aid forms:* FAFSA, state aid form. *Financial aid deadline:* Continuous. *Notification date:* Continuous beginning 11/15. Students must reply by 5/1 or within 3 weeks of notification.

CONTACT Dean Kathleen Lynne Cohen, Dean of Financial Aid, Elmira College, One Park Place, Elmira, NY 14901-2099, 607-735-1728 or toll-free 800-935-6472. *Fax:* 607-735-1718. *E-mail:* kcohen@elmira.edu.
Website: http://www.elmira.edu/.

ELMS COLLEGE
Chicopee, MA

Tuition & fees: $33,412	Average undergraduate aid package: $22,505

ABOUT THE INSTITUTION Independent Roman Catholic, coed. *Awards:* certificates, associate, bachelor's, master's, and doctoral degrees. 33 undergraduate majors. *Total enrollment:* 1,604. Undergraduates: 1,188. Freshmen: 164. Federal methodology is used as a basis for awarding need-based institutional aid.

UNDERGRADUATE EXPENSES for 2016–2017 *Application fee:* $30. *Comprehensive fee:* $45,648 includes full-time tuition ($31,846), mandatory fees ($1566), and room and board ($12,236). Room and board charges vary according to board plan. *Part-time tuition:* $646 per credit hour. Part-time tuition and fees vary according to location and program.

FRESHMAN FINANCIAL AID (Fall 2016, est.) 158 applied for aid; of those 95% were deemed to have need. 100% of freshmen with need received aid; of those 13% had need fully met. *Average percent of need met:* 75% (excluding resources awarded to replace EFC). *Average financial aid package:* $27,701 (excluding resources awarded to replace EFC). 8% of all full-time freshmen had no need and received non-need-based gift aid.

UNDERGRADUATE FINANCIAL AID (Fall 2016, est.) 895 applied for aid; of those 96% were deemed to have need. 100% of undergraduates with need received aid; of those 9% had need fully met. *Average percent of need met:* 62% (excluding resources awarded to replace EFC). *Average financial aid package:* $22,505 (excluding resources awarded to replace EFC). 8% of all full-time undergraduates had no need and received non-need-based gift aid.

GIFT AID (NEED-BASED) *Total amount:* $15,473,008 (15% federal, 5% state, 75% institutional, 5% external sources). *Receiving aid:* Freshmen: 92% (150); all full-time undergraduates: 86% (817). *Average award:* Freshmen: $24,376; Undergrad-

uates: $18,629. *Scholarships, grants, and awards:* Federal Pell, FSEOG, state, private, college/university gift aid from institutional funds.

GIFT AID (NON-NEED-BASED) *Total amount:* $1,506,556 (93% institutional, 7% external sources). *Receiving aid:* Freshmen: 9% (14). Undergraduates: 5% (52). *Average award:* Freshmen: $14,730. Undergraduates: $15,004. *Scholarships, grants, and awards by category:* Academic interests/achievement: 752 awards ($9,070,920 total): general academic interests/achievements. *Special characteristics:* 59 awards ($446,314 total): children of faculty/staff, general special characteristics, religious affiliation, siblings of current students. *Tuition waivers:* Full or partial for employees or children of employees, senior citizens. *ROTC:* Army cooperative, Air Force cooperative.

LOANS *Student loans:* $10,959,253 (84% need-based, 16% non-need-based). 89% of past graduating class borrowed through all loan programs. *Average indebtedness per student:* $37,052. *Average need-based loan:* Freshmen: $3484. Undergraduates: $4768. *Parent loans:* $2,528,821 (57% need-based, 43% non-need-based). *Programs:* Federal Direct (Subsidized and Unsubsidized Stafford, PLUS), Perkins.

WORK-STUDY *Federal work-study:* Total amount: $162,599; 138 jobs averaging $1192. *State or other work-study/employment:* Total amount: $1800 (67% need-based, 33% non-need-based). Part-time jobs available.

APPLYING FOR FINANCIAL AID *Required financial aid form:* FAFSA. *Financial aid deadline (priority):* 3/1. *Notification date:* Continuous beginning 3/15. Students must reply within 2 weeks of notification.

CONTACT Financial Aid Office, Elms College, 291 Springfield Street, Chicopee, MA 01013, 413-265-2249 or toll-free 800-255-ELMS. *E-mail:* finaid@elms.edu. *Website:* http://www.elms.edu/.

ELON UNIVERSITY
Elon, NC

Tuition & fees: $33,104	Average undergraduate aid package: $19,000

ABOUT THE INSTITUTION Independent United Church of Christ, coed. *Awards:* bachelor's, master's, and doctoral degrees. 76 undergraduate majors. *Total enrollment:* 6,739. Undergraduates: 6,008. Freshmen: 1,553. Institutional methodology is used as a basis for awarding need-based institutional aid.

UNDERGRADUATE EXPENSES for 2016–2017 *Application fee:* $50. *Comprehensive fee:* $44,599 includes full-time tuition ($32,685), mandatory fees ($419), and room and board ($11,495). *College room only:* $5728. Room and board charges vary according to board plan and housing facility. Part-time tuition and fees vary according to course load.

FRESHMAN FINANCIAL AID (Fall 2016, est.) 849 applied for aid; of those 61% were deemed to have need. 99% of freshmen with need received aid; of those 14% had need fully met. *Average percent of need met:* 62% (excluding resources awarded to replace EFC). *Average financial aid package:* $19,363 (excluding resources awarded to replace EFC). 22% of all full-time freshmen had no need and received non-need-based gift aid.

UNDERGRADUATE FINANCIAL AID (Fall 2016, est.) 2,583 applied for aid; of those 71% were deemed to have need. 99% of undergraduates with need received aid; of those 17% had need fully met. *Average percent of need met:* 61% (excluding resources awarded to replace EFC). *Average financial aid package:* $19,000 (excluding resources awarded to replace EFC). 22% of all full-time undergraduates had no need and received non-need-based gift aid.

GIFT AID (NEED-BASED) *Total amount:* $21,810,402 (11% federal, 6% state, 81% institutional, 2% external sources). *Receiving aid:* Freshmen: 30% (456); all full-time undergraduates: 28% (1,653). *Average award:* Freshmen: $15,145; Undergraduates: $15,052. *Scholarships, grants, and awards:* Federal Pell, FSEOG, state, private, college/university gift aid from institutional funds.

GIFT AID (NON-NEED-BASED) *Total amount:* $10,603,148 (98% institutional, 2% external sources). *Receiving aid:* Freshmen: 15% (225). Undergraduates: 14% (845). *Average award:* Freshmen: $7301. Undergraduates: $7381. *Scholarships, grants, and awards by category:* Academic interests/achievement: 2,379 awards ($11,790,683 total): biological sciences, business, communication, computer science, education, engineering/technologies, general academic interests/achievements, mathematics, military science, physical sciences, premedicine, religion/biblical studies, social sciences. *Creative arts/performance:* 107 awards ($362,295 total): art/fine arts, journalism/publications, music, performing arts, theater/drama. *Special achievements/activities:* 144 awards ($334,400 total): community service, general special achievements/activities, leadership, religious involvement. *Special characteristics:* 178 awards ($2,771,585 total): adult students, children of faculty/staff, ethnic background, first-generation college students, international students, members of minority groups, relatives of clergy, veterans. *Tuition waivers:* Full or partial for employees or children of employees. *ROTC:* Army, Air Force cooperative.

LOANS *Student loans:* $17,331,010 (66% need-based, 34% non-need-based). 42% of past graduating class borrowed through all loan programs. *Average indebtedness per student:* $30,170. *Average need-based loan:* Freshmen: $3462. Undergraduates: $4527. *Parent loans:* $10,972,589 (59% need-based, 41% non-need-based). *Programs:* Federal Direct (Subsidized and Unsubsidized Stafford, PLUS), Perkins, state, college/university, private loans.

WORK-STUDY *Federal work-study:* Total amount: $2,983,652; 1,239 jobs averaging $2397. *State or other work-study/employment:* Total amount: $1,365,591 (100% need-based). Part-time jobs available.

ATHLETIC AWARDS Total amount: $8,887,327 (38% need-based, 62% non-need-based).

APPLYING FOR FINANCIAL AID *Required financial aid forms:* FAFSA, CSS Financial Aid PROFILE. *Financial aid deadline (priority):* 2/15. *Notification date:* 3/30.

CONTACT Dr. Patrick Murphy, Director of Financial Planning, Elon University, 2725 Campus Box, Elon, NC 27244, 336-278-7640 or toll-free 800-334-8448. *Fax:* 336-278-7639. *E-mail:* finaid@elon.edu. *Website:* http://www.elon.edu/.

EMBRY-RIDDLE AERONAUTICAL UNIVERSITY–DAYTONA
Daytona Beach, FL

Tuition & fees: $34,822	Average undergraduate aid package: $17,938

ABOUT THE INSTITUTION Independent, coed. *Awards:* associate, bachelor's, master's, and doctoral degrees. 23 undergraduate majors. *Total enrollment:* 6,011. Undergraduates: 5,447. Freshmen: 1,273. Federal methodology is used as a basis for awarding need-based institutional aid.

UNDERGRADUATE EXPENSES for 2017–2018 *Application fee:* $50. *Comprehensive fee:* $45,922 includes full-time tuition ($33,408), mandatory fees ($1414), and room and board ($11,100). *College room only:* $6660. Room and board charges vary according to board plan, housing facility, and location. *Part-time tuition:* $1392 per credit hour. *Part-time fees:* $707 per term.

FRESHMAN FINANCIAL AID (Fall 2016, est.) 1,024 applied for aid; of those 85% were deemed to have need. 100% of freshmen with need received aid. *Average financial aid package:* $18,189 (excluding resources awarded to replace EFC). 13% of all full-time freshmen had no need and received non-need-based gift aid.

UNDERGRADUATE FINANCIAL AID (Fall 2016, est.) 3,373 applied for aid; of those 90% were deemed to have need. 100% of undergraduates with need received aid. *Average financial aid package:* $17,938 (excluding resources awarded to replace EFC). 11% of all full-time undergraduates had no need and received non-need-based gift aid.

GIFT AID (NEED-BASED) *Total amount:* $73,547,028 (10% federal, 6% state, 70% institutional, 14% external sources). *Receiving aid:* Freshmen: 68% (852); all full-time undergraduates: 60% (2,998). *Average award:* Freshmen: $16,448; Undergraduates: $14,290. *Scholarships, grants, and awards:* Federal Pell, FSEOG, state, private, college/university gift aid from institutional funds.

GIFT AID (NON-NEED-BASED) *Receiving aid:* Freshmen: 57% (715). Undergraduates: 42% (2,120). *Average award:* Freshmen: $13,503. Undergraduates: $12,930. *Scholarships, grants, and awards by category:* Special achievements/activities: leadership. *Tuition waivers:* Full or partial for employees or children of employees. *ROTC:* Army, Naval, Air Force.

LOANS *Student loans:* $37,564,934 (100% need-based). *Average need-based loan:* Freshmen: $3756. Undergraduates: $4742. *Parent loans:* $28,162,197 (100% need-based). *Programs:* Federal Direct (Subsidized and Unsubsidized Stafford, PLUS), Perkins.

WORK-STUDY *Federal work-study:* Total amount: $316,176; 171 jobs averaging $1849. *State or other work-study/employment:* Total amount: $3,728,386 (100% need-based). 1,243 part-time jobs averaging $2999.

ATHLETIC AWARDS Total amount: $3,562,083 (100% need-based).

APPLYING FOR FINANCIAL AID *Required financial aid form:* FAFSA. *Financial aid deadline (priority):* 3/1. *Notification date:* Continuous beginning 3/1. Students must reply within 4 weeks of notification.

CONTACT Financial Aid Office, Embry-Riddle Aeronautical University–Daytona, 600 South Clyde Morris Boulevard, Daytona Beach, FL 32114-3900, 386-226-6300 or toll-free 800-862-2416. *Fax:* 386-226-6307. *E-mail:* dbfinaid@erau.edu. *Website:* http://www.daytonabeach.erau.edu/.

EMBRY-RIDDLE AERONAUTICAL UNIVERSITY–PRESCOTT
Prescott, AZ

Tuition & fees: $34,662	Average undergraduate aid package: $18,769

ABOUT THE INSTITUTION Independent, coed. *Awards:* bachelor's, master's, and doctoral degrees. 21 undergraduate majors. *Total enrollment:* 2,439. Undergraduates: 2,377. Freshmen: 604. Federal methodology is used as a basis for awarding need-based institutional aid.

UNDERGRADUATE EXPENSES for 2017–2018 *Application fee:* $50. *Comprehensive fee:* $45,130 includes full-time tuition ($33,408), mandatory fees ($1254), and room and board ($10,468). *College room only:* $5860. Full-time tuition and fees vary according to course load. Room and board charges vary according to board plan, housing facility, location, and student level. *Part-time tuition:* $1392 per credit hour. *Part-time fees:* $627 per term. Part-time tuition and fees vary according to course load.

FRESHMAN FINANCIAL AID (Fall 2016, est.) 512 applied for aid; of those 83% were deemed to have need. 100% of freshmen with need received aid. *Average financial aid package:* $19,324 (excluding resources awarded to replace EFC). 15% of all full-time freshmen had no need and received non-need-based gift aid.

UNDERGRADUATE FINANCIAL AID (Fall 2016, est.) 1,552 applied for aid; of those 87% were deemed to have need. 99% of undergraduates with need received aid. *Average financial aid package:* $18,769 (excluding resources awarded to replace EFC). 16% of all full-time undergraduates had no need and received non-need-based gift aid.

GIFT AID (NEED-BASED) *Total amount:* $31,120,749 (9% federal, 79% institutional, 12% external sources). *Receiving aid:* Freshmen: 69% (415); all full-time undergraduates: 58% (1,299). *Average award:* Freshmen: $17,335; Undergraduates: $15,121. *Scholarships, grants, and awards:* Federal Pell, FSEOG, state, private, college/university gift aid from institutional funds.

GIFT AID (NON-NEED-BASED) *Receiving aid:* Freshmen: 66% (397). Undergraduates: 50% (1,127). *Average award:* Freshmen: $14,063. Undergraduates: $13,125. *Tuition waivers:* Full or partial for employees or children of employees. *ROTC:* Army, Air Force.

LOANS *Student loans:* $17,292,702 (100% need-based). *Average need-based loan:* Freshmen: $3563. Undergraduates: $4507. *Parent loans:* $9,099,912 (100% need-based). *Programs:* Federal Direct (Subsidized and Unsubsidized Stafford, PLUS), Perkins.

WORK-STUDY *Federal work-study:* Total amount: $71,176; 40 jobs averaging $1793. *State or other work-study/employment:* Total amount: $1,242,052 (100% need-based). 1,213 part-time jobs averaging $1024.

ATHLETIC AWARDS Total amount: $1,704,040 (100% need-based).

APPLYING FOR FINANCIAL AID *Required financial aid form:* FAFSA. *Financial aid deadline (priority):* 3/1. *Notification date:* Continuous beginning 3/1. Students must reply within 4 weeks of notification.

CONTACT Ms. Debra Hintz, Director of Financial Aid, Prescott Campus, Embry-Riddle Aeronautical University–Prescott, 3700 Willow Creek Road, Prescott, AZ 86301-3720, 800-888-3728. *Fax:* 928-777-3893. *E-mail:* prfinaid@erau.edu. *Website:* http://www.embryriddle.edu/.

EMBRY-RIDDLE AERONAUTICAL UNIVERSITY–WORLDWIDE
Daytona Beach, FL

Tuition & fees: $9076 | **Average undergraduate aid package: $6114**

ABOUT THE INSTITUTION Independent, coed. *Awards:* certificates, associate, bachelor's, master's, and doctoral degrees (programs offered at 100 military bases worldwide). 17 undergraduate majors. *Total enrollment:* 4,320. Undergraduates: 11,137. Freshmen: 397. Federal methodology is used as a basis for awarding need-based institutional aid.

UNDERGRADUATE EXPENSES for 2017–2018 *Application fee:* $50. *Tuition:* full-time $9000; part-time $375 per credit hour. Full-time tuition and fees vary according to program. Part-time tuition and fees vary according to program. Room and board charges vary according to location.

FRESHMAN FINANCIAL AID (Fall 2016, est.) 32 applied for aid; of those 69% were deemed to have need. 100% of freshmen with need received aid. *Average financial aid package:* $8193 (excluding resources awarded to replace EFC).

UNDERGRADUATE FINANCIAL AID (Fall 2016, est.) 1,175 applied for aid; of those 88% were deemed to have need. 100% of undergraduates with need received aid. *Average financial aid package:* $6114 (excluding resources awarded to replace EFC).

GIFT AID (NEED-BASED) *Total amount:* $13,308,721 (96% federal, 2% state, 1% institutional, 1% external sources). *Receiving aid:* Freshmen: 25% (22); all full-time undergraduates: 32% (919). *Average award:* Freshmen: $3826; Undergraduates: $4562. *Scholarships, grants, and awards:* Federal Pell, FSEOG, state, private, college/university gift aid from institutional funds.

GIFT AID (NON-NEED-BASED) *Receiving aid:* Freshmen: 1% (1). Undergraduates: 3% (87). *Scholarships, grants, and awards by category:* Special characteristics: children of faculty/staff. *Tuition waivers:* Full or partial for employees or children of employees.

LOANS *Student loans:* $14,184,893 (100% need-based). *Average need-based loan:* Freshmen: $3683. Undergraduates: $4481. *Parent loans:* $104,146 (100% need-based). *Programs:* Federal Direct (Subsidized and Unsubsidized Stafford, PLUS), Perkins.

APPLYING FOR FINANCIAL AID *Required financial aid form:* FAFSA. *Financial aid deadline (priority):* 3/1. *Notification date:* Continuous. Students must reply within 4 weeks of notification.

CONTACT Ms. Dagmar Bowen, Director of Financial Aid, Worldwide, Embry-Riddle Aeronautical University–Worldwide, 600 South Clyde Morris Boulevard, Daytona Beach, FL 32114-3900, 866-567-7202 or toll-free 800-522-6787. *Fax:* 386-226-6915. *E-mail:* wwfinaid@erau.edu.
Website: http://www.worldwide.erau.edu/.

EMERSON COLLEGE
Boston, MA

Tuition & fees: $42,908 | **Average undergraduate aid package: $21,848**

ABOUT THE INSTITUTION Independent, coed. *Awards:* certificates, bachelor's, master's, and doctoral degrees. 28 undergraduate majors. *Total enrollment:* 4,431. Undergraduates: 3,790. Freshmen: 881. Institutional methodology is used as a basis for awarding need-based institutional aid.

UNDERGRADUATE EXPENSES for 2017–2018 *Application fee:* $65. *Comprehensive fee:* $59,228 includes full-time tuition ($42,144), mandatory fees ($764), and room and board ($16,320). Full-time tuition and fees vary according to student level. Room and board charges vary according to board plan. *Part-time tuition:* $1317 per credit hour. Part-time tuition and fees vary according to student level.

FRESHMAN FINANCIAL AID (Fall 2016, est.) 660 applied for aid; of those 68% were deemed to have need. 99% of freshmen with need received aid; of those 14% had need fully met. *Average percent of need met:* 62% (excluding resources awarded to replace EFC). *Average financial aid package:* $24,576 (excluding resources awarded to replace EFC). 18% of all full-time freshmen had no need and received non-need-based gift aid.

UNDERGRADUATE FINANCIAL AID (Fall 2016, est.) 2,410 applied for aid; of those 85% were deemed to have need. 98% of undergraduates with need received aid;

of those 7% had need fully met. *Average percent of need met:* 52% (excluding resources awarded to replace EFC). *Average financial aid package:* $21,848 (excluding resources awarded to replace EFC). 10% of all full-time undergraduates had no need and received non-need-based gift aid.

GIFT AID (NEED-BASED) *Total amount:* $33,758,825 (8% federal, 1% state, 89% institutional, 2% external sources). *Receiving aid:* Freshmen: 48% (420); all full-time undergraduates: 48% (1,794). *Average award:* Freshmen: $20,708; Undergraduates: $18,820. *Scholarships, grants, and awards:* Federal Pell, FSEOG, state, private, college/university gift aid from institutional funds.

GIFT AID (NON-NEED-BASED) *Total amount:* $6,766,215 (96% institutional, 4% external sources). *Receiving aid:* Freshmen: 8% (67). Undergraduates: 4% (150). *Average award:* Freshmen: $14,880. Undergraduates: $15,402. *Scholarships, grants, and awards by category:* Academic interests/achievement: 903 awards ($13,749,523 total): general academic interests/achievements. Creative arts/performance: 7 awards ($91,000 total): performing arts. *Special characteristics:* parents of current students. *Tuition waivers:* Full or partial for employees or children of employees.

LOANS *Student loans:* $29,092,047 (76% need-based, 24% non-need-based). 63% of past graduating class borrowed through all loan programs. *Average indebtedness per student:* $23,225. *Average need-based loan:* Freshmen: $18,815. Undergraduates: $4788. *Parent loans:* $13,822,771 (50% need-based, 50% non-need-based). *Programs:* Federal Direct (Subsidized and Unsubsidized Stafford, PLUS), Perkins, state.

WORK-STUDY *Federal work-study:* Total amount: $768,213; 383 jobs averaging $1980. *State or other work-study/employment:* Total amount: $1,031,948 (54% need-based, 46% non-need-based). 85 part-time jobs averaging $12,943.

APPLYING FOR FINANCIAL AID *Required financial aid forms:* FAFSA, CSS Financial Aid PROFILE, noncustodial (divorced/separated) parent's statement, business/farm supplement. *Financial aid deadline (priority):* 3/2. *Notification date:* 4/1. Students must reply by 5/1 or within 3 weeks of notification.

CONTACT Angela Grant, Director of Financial Aid, Emerson College, 120 Boylston Street, Boston, MA 02116-4624, 617-824-8655. *Fax:* 617-824-8619. *E-mail:* finaid@emerson.edu.
Website: http://www.emerson.edu/.

EMMANUEL COLLEGE
Franklin Springs, GA

Tuition & fees: $19,330 | **Average undergraduate aid package: $15,574**

ABOUT THE INSTITUTION Independent Pentecostal Holiness Church, coed. *Awards:* associate and bachelor's degrees. 25 undergraduate majors. *Total enrollment:* 920. Undergraduates: 920. Freshmen: 238. Federal methodology is used as a basis for awarding need-based institutional aid.

UNDERGRADUATE EXPENSES for 2016–2017 *Application fee:* $25. *Comprehensive fee:* $26,730 includes full-time tuition ($18,990), mandatory fees ($340), and room and board ($7400). Room and board charges vary according to housing facility. *Part-time tuition:* $795 per credit hour.

FRESHMAN FINANCIAL AID (Fall 2016, est.) 205 applied for aid; of those 86% were deemed to have need. 100% of freshmen with need received aid; of those 14% had need fully met. *Average percent of need met:* 68% (excluding resources awarded to replace EFC). *Average financial aid package:* $15,493 (excluding resources awarded to replace EFC). 11% of all full-time freshmen had no need and received non-need-based gift aid.

UNDERGRADUATE FINANCIAL AID (Fall 2016, est.) 626 applied for aid; of those 87% were deemed to have need. 100% of undergraduates with need received aid; of those 20% had need fully met. *Average percent of need met:* 69% (excluding resources awarded to replace EFC). *Average financial aid package:* $15,574 (excluding resources awarded to replace EFC). 13% of all full-time undergraduates had no need and received non-need-based gift aid.

GIFT AID (NEED-BASED) *Total amount:* $4,622,966 (31% federal, 19% state, 41% institutional, 9% external sources). *Receiving aid:* Freshmen: 76% (176); all full-time undergraduates: 76% (540). *Average award:* Freshmen: $12,576; Undergraduates: $12,270. *Scholarships, grants, and awards:* Federal Pell, FSEOG, state, college/university gift aid from institutional funds.

GIFT AID (NON-NEED-BASED) *Total amount:* $1,057,036 (42% state, 48% institutional, 10% external sources). *Receiving aid:* Freshmen: 8% (19). Undergraduates: 11% (78). **Average award:** Freshmen: $4679. Undergraduates: $4388. **Scholarships, grants, and awards by category:** *Academic interests/achievement:* 399 awards ($1,543,775 total): business, communication, education, English, general academic interests/achievements, health fields, religion/biblical studies. *Creative arts/performance:* 22 awards ($37,000 total): applied art and design, art/fine arts, creative writing, dance, general creative arts/performance, journalism/publications, music, performing arts, theater/drama. *Special achievements/activities:* 16 awards ($54,626 total): cheerleading/drum major, general special achievements/activities, hobbies/interests, leadership, memberships, religious involvement. *Special characteristics:* 242 awards ($624,846 total): adult students, children of current students, children of educators, children of faculty/staff, first-generation college students, general special characteristics, international students, local/state students, married students, parents of current students, relatives of clergy, religious affiliation, siblings of current students, spouses of current students, twins. **Tuition waivers:** Full or partial for employees or children of employees, senior citizens.

LOANS Student loans: $3,583,346 (76% need-based, 24% non-need-based). 68% of past graduating class borrowed through all loan programs. *Average indebtedness per student:* $25,609. **Average need-based loan:** Freshmen: $3195. Undergraduates: $3737. **Parent loans:** $2,031,583 (44% need-based, 56% non-need-based). **Programs:** Federal Direct (Subsidized and Unsubsidized Stafford, PLUS), state.

WORK-STUDY Federal work-study: Total amount: $270,000; 102 jobs averaging $839. **State or other work-study/employment:** 135 part-time jobs averaging $842.

ATHLETIC AWARDS Total amount: $3,612,827 (58% need-based, 42% non-need-based).

APPLYING FOR FINANCIAL AID *Required financial aid forms:* FAFSA, institution's own form, state aid form. **Financial aid deadline:** 6/15 (priority: 5/1). **Notification date:** Continuous beginning 3/1. Students must reply within 2 weeks of notification.

CONTACT Mrs. Niki Stinson, Director of Financial Aid, Emmanuel College, PO Box 129, Franklin Springs, GA 30639-0129, 706-245-2871 or toll-free 800-860-8800. *Fax:* 706-245-2846. *E-mail:* nstinson@ec.edu. *Website:* http://www.ec.edu/.

EMMANUEL COLLEGE
Boston, MA

Tuition & fees: $38,844	Average undergraduate aid package: $26,986

ABOUT THE INSTITUTION Independent Roman Catholic, coed. *Awards:* certificates, bachelor's, and master's degrees. 38 undergraduate majors. **Total enrollment:** 2,190. Undergraduates: 2,012. Freshmen: 596. Federal methodology is used as a basis for awarding need-based institutional aid.

UNDERGRADUATE EXPENSES for 2017–2018 Application fee: $60. **One-time required fee:** $300. **Comprehensive fee:** $53,472 includes full-time tuition ($38,584), mandatory fees ($260), and room and board ($14,628). Room and board charges vary according to board plan and housing facility. **Part-time tuition:** $1205.75 per credit hour.

FRESHMAN FINANCIAL AID (Fall 2016, est.) 546 applied for aid; of those 92% were deemed to have need. 100% of freshmen with need received aid; of those 31% had need fully met. *Average percent of need met:* 75% (excluding resources awarded to replace EFC). *Average financial aid package:* $27,814 (excluding resources awarded to replace EFC). 16% of all full-time freshmen had no need and received non-need-based gift aid.

UNDERGRADUATE FINANCIAL AID (Fall 2016, est.) 1,611 applied for aid; of those 92% were deemed to have need. 100% of undergraduates with need received aid; of those 38% had need fully met. *Average percent of need met:* 73% (excluding resources awarded to replace EFC). *Average financial aid package:* $26,986 (excluding resources awarded to replace EFC). 19% of all full-time undergraduates had no need and received non-need-based gift aid.

GIFT AID (NEED-BASED) Total amount: $33,132,768 (8% federal, 2% state, 87% institutional, 3% external sources). *Receiving aid:* Freshmen: 77% (457); all full-time undergraduates: 81% (1,481). *Average award:* Freshmen: $23,727; Undergraduates: $22,528. **Scholarships, grants, and awards:** Federal Pell, FSEOG, state, private, college/university gift aid from institutional funds.

GIFT AID (NON-NEED-BASED) Total amount: $5,091,300 (99% institutional, 1% external sources). *Receiving aid:* Freshmen: 84% (500). Undergraduates: 79%

(1,449). **Average award:** Freshmen: $15,973. Undergraduates: $14,794. **Scholarships, grants, and awards by category:** *Academic interests/achievement:* general academic interests/achievements. *Special achievements/activities:* general special achievements/activities. *Special characteristics:* children of faculty/staff, spouses of current students, veterans. **Tuition waivers:** Full or partial for employees or children of employees. **ROTC:** Army cooperative.

LOANS Student loans: $14,492,899 (89% need-based, 11% non-need-based). 84% of past graduating class borrowed through all loan programs. *Average indebtedness per student:* $36,010. **Average need-based loan:** Freshmen: $3634. Undergraduates: $4709. **Parent loans:** $8,571,355 (100% non-need-based). **Programs:** Federal Direct (Subsidized and Unsubsidized Stafford, PLUS), Perkins, state.

WORK-STUDY Federal work-study: Total amount: $157,683; 516 jobs averaging $2047. **State or other work-study/employment:** Total amount: $1,347,071 (100% non-need-based). Part-time jobs available.

APPLYING FOR FINANCIAL AID *Required financial aid form:* FAFSA. **Financial aid deadline (priority):** 2/15. **Notification date:** Continuous beginning 1/1.

CONTACT Jennifer Porter, Associate Vice President for Student Financial Services, Emmanuel College, 400 The Fenway, Boston, MA 02115, 617-735-9938. *Fax:* 617-735-9939. *E-mail:* financialservices@emmanuel.edu. *Website:* http://www.emmanuel.edu/.

EMMAUS BIBLE COLLEGE
Dubuque, IA

CONTACT Steve Seeman, Financial Aid Director, Emmaus Bible College, 2570 Asbury Road, Dubuque, IA 52001-3097, 800-397-2425 Ext. 1309 or toll-free 800-397-2425. *Fax:* 563-588-1216. *E-mail:* financialaid@emmaus.edu. *Website:* http://www.emmaus.edu/.

EMORY & HENRY COLLEGE
Emory, VA

Tuition & fees: $33,700	Average undergraduate aid package: $29,365

ABOUT THE INSTITUTION Independent United Methodist, coed. *Awards:* bachelor's, master's, and doctoral degrees. 66 undergraduate majors. **Total enrollment:** 1,167. Undergraduates: 1,024. Freshmen: 284. Federal methodology is used as a basis for awarding need-based institutional aid.

UNDERGRADUATE EXPENSES for 2016–2017 Comprehensive fee: $44,900 includes full-time tuition ($33,500), mandatory fees ($200), and room and board ($11,200). **College room only:** $6000. Full-time tuition and fees vary according to degree level, location, and student level. Room and board charges vary according to board plan and housing facility. **Part-time tuition:** $1250 per credit. Part-time tuition and fees vary according to course load, degree level, location, and student level. **Payment plan:** Guaranteed tuition.

FRESHMAN FINANCIAL AID (Fall 2016, est.) 278 applied for aid; of those 91% were deemed to have need. 100% of freshmen with need received aid; of those 20% had need fully met. *Average percent of need met:* 85% (excluding resources awarded to replace EFC). *Average financial aid package:* $31,237 (excluding resources awarded to replace EFC). 10% of all full-time freshmen had no need and received non-need-based gift aid.

UNDERGRADUATE FINANCIAL AID (Fall 2016, est.) 934 applied for aid; of those 89% were deemed to have need. 100% of undergraduates with need received aid; of those 23% had need fully met. *Average percent of need met:* 84% (excluding resources awarded to replace EFC). *Average financial aid package:* $29,365 (excluding resources awarded to replace EFC). 15% of all full-time undergraduates had no need and received non-need-based gift aid.

GIFT AID (NEED-BASED) Total amount: $20,327,050 (9% federal, 8% state, 81% institutional, 2% external sources). *Receiving aid:* Freshmen: 81% (230); all full-time undergraduates: 75% (751). *Average award:* Freshmen: $27,924; Undergraduates: $25,207. **Scholarships, grants, and awards:** Federal Pell, FSEOG, state, private, college/university gift aid from institutional funds.

GIFT AID (NON-NEED-BASED) *Total amount:* $3,511,039 (11% state, 83% institutional, 6% external sources). *Receiving aid:* Freshmen: 8% (24). Undergraduates: 9% (86). *Average award:* Freshmen: $17,652. Undergraduates: $16,857. *Scholarships, grants, and awards by category:* Academic interests/achievement: 990 awards ($15,213,459 total): general academic interests/achievements. *Creative arts/performance:* 126 awards ($215,125 total): art/fine arts, music, theater/drama. *Special achievements/activities:* 53 awards ($38,750 total): religious involvement. *Special characteristics:* 352 awards ($1,155,842 total): children and siblings of alumni, children of educators, children of faculty/staff, out-of-state students, siblings of current students. *Tuition waivers:* Full or partial for employees or children of employees.

LOANS *Student loans:* $5,894,322 (74% need-based, 26% non-need-based). 80% of past graduating class borrowed through all loan programs. *Average indebtedness per student:* $30,514. *Average need-based loan:* Freshmen: $2273. Undergraduates: $3296. *Parent loans:* $3,473,526 (38% need-based, 62% non-need-based). *Programs:* Federal Direct (Subsidized and Unsubsidized Stafford, PLUS), Perkins.

WORK-STUDY *Federal work-study:* Total amount: $267,805; 149 jobs averaging $1774. *State or other work-study/employment:* Total amount: $499,776 (91% need-based, 9% non-need-based). 147 part-time jobs averaging $1835.

APPLYING FOR FINANCIAL AID *Required financial aid forms:* FAFSA, state aid form. *Financial aid deadline (priority):* 3/1. *Notification date:* Continuous beginning 1/2. Students must reply within 2 weeks of notification.

CONTACT Ms. Scarlett C. Blevins, Director of Financial Aid, Emory & Henry College, PO Box 947, Emory, VA 24327-0010, 276-944-6940 or toll-free 800-848-5493. *Fax:* 276-944-6884. *E-mail:* scblevins@ehc.edu.
Website: http://www.ehc.edu/.

EMORY UNIVERSITY
Atlanta, GA

Tuition & fees: $49,392	Average undergraduate aid package: $44,168

ABOUT THE INSTITUTION Independent Methodist, coed. *Awards:* certificates, bachelor's, master's, and doctoral degrees (enrollment figures include Emory University, Oxford College; application data for main campus only). 73 undergraduate majors. *Total enrollment:* 14,077. Undergraduates: 6,861. Freshmen: 1,358. Both federal and institutional methodology are used as a basis for awarding need-based institutional aid.

UNDERGRADUATE EXPENSES for 2017–2018 *Application fee:* $75. *Comprehensive fee:* $63,286 includes full-time tuition ($48,690), mandatory fees ($702), and room and board ($13,894). *College room only:* $8072. Full-time tuition and fees vary according to degree level and location. Room and board charges vary according to board plan, housing facility, and student level. *Part-time tuition:* $2029 per credit hour.

FRESHMAN FINANCIAL AID (Fall 2016, est.) 795 applied for aid; of those 79% were deemed to have need. 100% of freshmen with need received aid; of those 100% had need fully met. *Average percent of need met:* 100% (excluding resources awarded to replace EFC). *Average financial aid package:* $41,301 (excluding resources awarded to replace EFC). 4% of all full-time freshmen had no need and received non-need-based gift aid.

UNDERGRADUATE FINANCIAL AID (Fall 2016, est.) 2,798 applied for aid; of those 87% were deemed to have need. 100% of undergraduates with need received aid; of those 97% had need fully met. *Average percent of need met:* 100% (excluding resources awarded to replace EFC). *Average financial aid package:* $44,168 (excluding resources awarded to replace EFC). 5% of all full-time undergraduates had no need and received non-need-based gift aid.

GIFT AID (NEED-BASED) *Total amount:* $97,414,082 (7% federal, 2% state, 90% institutional, 1% external sources). *Receiving aid:* Freshmen: 43% (580); all full-time undergraduates: 42% (2,270). *Average award:* Freshmen: $38,834; Undergraduates: $40,816. *Scholarships, grants, and awards:* Federal Pell, FSEOG, private, college/university gift aid from institutional funds.

GIFT AID (NON-NEED-BASED) *Total amount:* $11,467,676 (12% state, 77% institutional, 11% external sources). *Receiving aid:* Freshmen: 17% (227). Undergraduates: 11% (614). *Average award:* Freshmen: $23,424. Undergraduates: $25,962. *Scholarships, grants, and awards by category:* Academic interests/achievement: business, general academic interests/achievements, humanities, physical sciences. *Creative arts/performance:* art/fine arts, cinema/film/broadcasting, debating,

music, theater/drama. *Special achievements/activities:* leadership. *Special characteristics:* children of faculty/staff, local/state students, religious affiliation, veterans, veterans' children. *Tuition waivers:* Full or partial for employees or children of employees. *ROTC:* Army cooperative, Naval cooperative, Air Force cooperative.

LOANS *Student loans:* $18,443,347 (55% need-based, 45% non-need-based). 39% of past graduating class borrowed through all loan programs. *Average indebtedness per student:* $29,217. *Average need-based loan:* Freshmen: $3688. Undergraduates: $4747. *Parent loans:* $4,951,602 (17% need-based, 83% non-need-based). *Programs:* Federal Direct (Subsidized and Unsubsidized Stafford, PLUS), Perkins, Federal Nursing, state, college/university, alternative loans.

WORK-STUDY *Federal work-study:* Total amount: $4,872,481; 1,238 jobs averaging $2378. *State or other work-study/employment:* Total amount: $522,324 (26% need-based, 74% non-need-based). Part-time jobs available.

APPLYING FOR FINANCIAL AID *Required financial aid forms:* FAFSA, CSS Financial Aid PROFILE, noncustodial (divorced/separated) parent's statement. *Financial aid deadline:* 3/1 (priority: 2/15). *Notification date:* 4/1. Students must reply by 5/1.

CONTACT Mr. John Leach, Director of Financial Aid, Emory University, Boisfeuillet Jones Center, Suite 300, 200 Dowman Drive, Atlanta, GA 30322-1960, 404-727-6039 or toll-free 800-727-6036. *Fax:* 404-727-6709.
E-mail: john.blanchard.leach@emory.edu.
Website: http://www.emory.edu/.

EMPORIA STATE UNIVERSITY
Emporia, KS

Tuition & fees (KS res): $6178	Average undergraduate aid package: $9163

ABOUT THE INSTITUTION State-supported, coed. *Awards:* certificates, bachelor's, master's, and doctoral degrees. 34 undergraduate majors. *Total enrollment:* 5,887. Undergraduates: 3,702. Freshmen: 665. Federal methodology is used as a basis for awarding need-based institutional aid.

UNDERGRADUATE EXPENSES for 2016–2017 *Application fee:* $30. *Tuition, state resident:* full-time $4892; part-time $163 per credit hour. *Tuition, nonresident:* full-time $18,106; part-time $603.50 per credit hour. *Required fees:* full-time $1286; $78.50 per credit hour. Full-time tuition and fees vary according to course load, degree level, and location. Part-time tuition and fees vary according to course load, degree level, and location. *College room and board:* $8391; *Room only:* $4836. Room and board charges vary according to board plan, housing facility, and location.

FRESHMAN FINANCIAL AID (Fall 2016, est.) 566 applied for aid; of those 74% were deemed to have need. 99% of freshmen with need received aid; of those 15% had need fully met. *Average percent of need met:* 67% (excluding resources awarded to replace EFC). *Average financial aid package:* $8956 (excluding resources awarded to replace EFC). 23% of all full-time freshmen had no need and received non-need-based gift aid.

UNDERGRADUATE FINANCIAL AID (Fall 2016, est.) 2,618 applied for aid; of those 81% were deemed to have need. 100% of undergraduates with need received aid; of those 14% had need fully met. *Average percent of need met:* 66% (excluding resources awarded to replace EFC). *Average financial aid package:* $9163 (excluding resources awarded to replace EFC). 18% of all full-time undergraduates had no need and received non-need-based gift aid.

GIFT AID (NEED-BASED) *Total amount:* $10,239,703 (59% federal, 6% state, 22% institutional, 13% external sources). *Receiving aid:* Freshmen: 58% (386); all full-time undergraduates: 55% (1,857). *Average award:* Freshmen: $5684; Undergraduates: $5821. *Scholarships, grants, and awards:* Federal Pell, FSEOG, state, private, college/university gift aid from institutional funds, Jones Foundation Grants.

GIFT AID (NON-NEED-BASED) *Total amount:* $3,146,852 (1% federal, 55% institutional, 44% external sources). *Receiving aid:* Freshmen: 5% (33). Undergraduates: 3% (96). *Average award:* Freshmen: $2387. Undergraduates: $2662. *Scholarships, grants, and awards by category:* Academic interests/achievement: 1,492 awards ($3,221,264 total): biological sciences, business, communication, computer science, education, engineering/technologies, English, foreign languages, general academic interests/achievements, health fields, humanities, mathematics, physical sciences, premedicine, social sciences. *Creative arts/performance:* 152 awards ($150,018 total): art/fine arts, creative writing, debating, music, theater/drama. *Special achievements/activities:* 52 awards ($39,673 total): general special achievements/activities, leadership, memberships. *Special characteristics:* 114 awards ($89,864 total): children and siblings of alumni, children of faculty/staff, children of union members/company employees, first-generation college students, general special characteristics, handicapped students, international students, members of minority groups, religious affiliation, veterans, veterans' children. *Tuition waivers:* Full or partial for employees or children of employees, senior citizens.

LOANS *Student loans:* $16,838,747 (73% need-based, 27% non-need-based). 62% of past graduating class borrowed through all loan programs. *Average indebtedness per student:* $20,433. *Average need-based loan:* Freshmen: $5948. Undergraduates: $6693. *Parent loans:* $7,575,125 (24% need-based, 76% non-need-based). *Programs:* Federal Direct (Subsidized and Unsubsidized Stafford, PLUS), Perkins, alternative loans, Alaska Loans.

WORK-STUDY *Federal work-study:* Total amount: $411,769; 185 jobs averaging $2180. *State or other work-study/employment:* Total amount: $39,529 (77% need-based, 23% non-need-based). 16 part-time jobs averaging $2471.

ATHLETIC AWARDS Total amount: $1,389,944 (46% need-based, 54% non-need-based).

APPLYING FOR FINANCIAL AID *Required financial aid forms:* FAFSA, state aid form. *Financial aid deadline (priority):* 3/15. *Notification date:* Continuous beginning 3/15. Students must reply within 2 weeks of notification.

CONTACT Elaine Henrie, Director of Financial Aid, Emporia State University, 1 Kellogg Circle, Emporia, KS 66801-5087, 620-341-5457 or toll-free 877-GOTOESU (in-state), 877-468-6378 (out-of-state). *Fax:* 620-341-6088. *E-mail:* ehenrie@emporia.edu. *Website:* http://www.emporia.edu/.

ENDICOTT COLLEGE
Beverly, MA

Tuition & fees: $31,312	Average undergraduate aid package: $21,634

ABOUT THE INSTITUTION Independent, coed. *Awards:* certificates, associate, bachelor's, master's, and doctoral degrees. 39 undergraduate majors. *Total enrollment:* 5,018. Undergraduates: 3,268. Freshmen: 726. Federal methodology is used as a basis for awarding need-based institutional aid.

UNDERGRADUATE EXPENSES for 2016–2017 *Application fee:* $50. *Comprehensive fee:* $45,812 includes full-time tuition ($30,612), mandatory fees ($700), and room and board ($14,500). *College room only:* $9996. Full-time tuition and fees vary according to location and program. Room and board charges vary according to housing facility. *Part-time tuition:* $940 per credit hour. Part-time tuition and fees vary according to location and program. *Payment plan:* Tuition prepayment.

FRESHMAN FINANCIAL AID (Fall 2016, est.) 688 applied for aid; of those 69% were deemed to have need. 100% of freshmen with need received aid; of those 10% had need fully met. *Average percent of need met:* 62% (excluding resources awarded to replace EFC). *Average financial aid package:* $21,538 (excluding resources awarded to replace EFC). 26% of all full-time freshmen had no need and received non-need-based gift aid.

UNDERGRADUATE FINANCIAL AID (Fall 2016, est.) 2,458 applied for aid; of those 72% were deemed to have need. 99% of undergraduates with need received aid; of those 12% had need fully met. *Average percent of need met:* 64% (excluding resources awarded to replace EFC). *Average financial aid package:* $21,634 (excluding resources awarded to replace EFC). 23% of all full-time undergraduates had no need and received non-need-based gift aid.

GIFT AID (NEED-BASED) *Total amount:* $26,209,510 (8% federal, 2% state, 90% institutional). *Receiving aid:* Freshmen: 55% (395); all full-time undergraduates: 50% (1,439). *Average award:* Freshmen: $10,549; Undergraduates: $10,875. *Scholarships, grants, and awards:* Federal Pell, FSEOG, state, private, college/university gift aid from institutional funds.

GIFT AID (NON-NEED-BASED) *Total amount:* $7,136,430 (93% institutional, 7% external sources). *Receiving aid:* Freshmen: 55% (394). Undergraduates: 44% (1,269). *Average award:* Freshmen: $9359. Undergraduates: $8972. *Scholarships, grants, and awards by category: Academic interests/achievement:* 1,682 awards ($14,876,608 total): business, education, general academic interests/achievements, health fields. *Creative arts/performance:* 2 awards ($3900 total): art/fine arts, music, performing arts. *Special achievements/activities:* 9 awards ($113,150 total): community service, general special achievements/activities, leadership, religious involvement. *Special characteristics:* 115 awards ($573,721 total): children and siblings

of alumni, children of educators, general special characteristics, international students, local/state students, religious affiliation. *Tuition waivers:* Full or partial for employees or children of employees. *ROTC:* Army cooperative.

LOANS *Student loans:* $24,726,081 (28% need-based, 72% non-need-based). 71% of past graduating class borrowed through all loan programs. *Average indebtedness per student:* $41,901. *Average need-based loan:* Freshmen: $3645. Undergraduates: $4550. *Parent loans:* $6,012,033 (100% non-need-based). *Programs:* Federal Direct (Subsidized and Unsubsidized Stafford, PLUS), Perkins.

WORK-STUDY *Federal work-study:* Total amount: $1,364,164; 709 jobs averaging $200.

APPLYING FOR FINANCIAL AID *Required financial aid forms:* FAFSA, institution's own form. *Financial aid deadline (priority):* 3/15. *Notification date:* Continuous beginning 1/15. Students must reply within 2 weeks of notification.

CONTACT Ms. Marcia Toomey, Dean of Financial Aid, Endicott College, 376 Hale Street, Beverly, MA 01915-2096, 978-232-2060 or toll-free 800-325-1114. *Fax:* 978-232-2085. *E-mail:* mtoomey@endicott.edu. *Website:* http://www.endicott.edu/.

EPIC BIBLE COLLEGE
Sacramento, CA

CONTACT Financial Aid Office, Epic Bible College, 4330 Auburn Boulevard, Sacramento, CA 95841, 916-348-4689. *Website:* http://epic.edu/.

ERSKINE COLLEGE
Due West, SC

CONTACT Mrs. Becky Pressley, Director of Financial Aid, Erskine College, PO Box 337, Due West, SC 29639, 864-379-8832 or toll-free 800-241-8721. *Fax:* 864-379-2172. *E-mail:* pressley@erskine.edu. *Website:* http://www.erskine.edu/.

ESCUELA DE ARTES PLASTICAS Y DISE&NNO DE PUERTO RICO
San Juan, PR

CONTACT Mr. Alfred Diaz Melendez, Financial Aid Administrator, Escuela de Artes Plasticas y Dise&nno de Puerto Rico, PO Box 9021112, San Juan, PR 00902-1112, 787-725-8120 Ext. 317. *Fax:* 787-725-3798. *E-mail:* adiaz@eap.edu. *Website:* http://www.eap.edu/.

EUGENE LANG COLLEGE OF LIBERAL ARTS
New York, NY

ABOUT THE INSTITUTION Independent, coed. *Awards:* bachelor's degrees. 29 undergraduate majors. *Total enrollment:* 1,663. Undergraduates: 1,663. Freshmen: 494.

GIFT AID (NEED-BASED) *Scholarships, grants, and awards:* Federal Pell, FSEOG, state, private, college/university gift aid from institutional funds.

GIFT AID (NON-NEED-BASED) *Scholarships, grants, and awards by category: Academic interests/achievement:* general academic interests/achievements. *Special achievements/activities:* general special achievements/activities, leadership. *Special characteristics:* local/state students, members of minority groups.

LOANS *Programs:* Federal Direct (Subsidized and Unsubsidized Stafford, PLUS), Perkins.

APPLYING FOR FINANCIAL AID *Required financial aid forms:* FAFSA, state aid form.

CONTACT Office of Student Financial Services, Eugene Lang College of Liberal Arts, 72 Fifth Avenue, New York, NY 10011, 212-229-8930 or toll-free 800-292-3040. *E-mail:* sfs@newschool.edu. *Website:* http://www.newschool.edu/lang.

EUREKA COLLEGE
Eureka, IL

Tuition & fees: $25,390	Average undergraduate aid package: $18,087

ABOUT THE INSTITUTION Independent Christian Church (Disciples of Christ), coed. *Awards:* bachelor's degrees. 23 undergraduate majors. *Total enrollment:* 672. Undergraduates: 672. Freshmen: 153. Both federal and institutional methodology are used as a basis for awarding need-based institutional aid.

UNDERGRADUATE EXPENSES for 2017–2018 *Comprehensive fee:* $34,760 includes full-time tuition ($25,150), mandatory fees ($240), and room and board ($9370). *College room only:* $4490. Full-time tuition and fees vary according to course load and program. Room and board charges vary according to board plan and housing facility. *Part-time tuition:* $700 per semester hour. *Part-time fees:* $120 per semester hour. Part-time tuition and fees vary according to course load and program.

FRESHMAN FINANCIAL AID (Fall 2016, est.) 152 applied for aid; of those 76% were deemed to have need. 100% of freshmen with need received aid; of those 19% had need fully met. *Average percent of need met:* 72% (excluding resources awarded to replace EFC). *Average financial aid package:* $16,660 (excluding resources awarded to replace EFC). 23% of all full-time freshmen had no need and received non-need-based gift aid.

UNDERGRADUATE FINANCIAL AID (Fall 2016, est.) 462 applied for aid; of those 98% were deemed to have need. 100% of undergraduates with need received aid; of those 9% had need fully met. *Average percent of need met:* 71% (excluding resources awarded to replace EFC). *Average financial aid package:* $18,087 (excluding resources awarded to replace EFC). 25% of all full-time undergraduates had no need and received non-need-based gift aid.

GIFT AID (NEED-BASED) *Total amount:* $5,948,898 (19% federal, 20% state, 59% institutional, 2% external sources). *Receiving aid:* Freshmen: 76% (116); all full-time undergraduates: 71% (455). *Average award:* Freshmen: $13,346; Undergraduates: $11,281. *Scholarships, grants, and awards:* Federal Pell, FSEOG, state, private, college/university gift aid from institutional funds.

GIFT AID (NON-NEED-BASED) *Total amount:* $1,265,260 (99% institutional, 1% external sources). *Average award:* Freshmen: $7825. Undergraduates: $7719. *Scholarships, grants, and awards by category:* Academic interests/achievement: $3,106,419 total: general academic interests/achievements. *Creative arts/performance:* $67,875 total: art/fine arts, music, performing arts, theater/drama. *Special achievements/activities:* $853,763 total: community service, leadership, religious involvement. *Special characteristics:* $965,591 total: children and siblings of alumni, children of faculty/staff, relatives of clergy, religious affiliation, siblings of current students. *Tuition waivers:* Full or partial for employees or children of employees, senior citizens.

LOANS *Student loans:* $4,504,711 (84% need-based, 16% non-need-based). 88% of past graduating class borrowed through all loan programs. *Average indebtedness per student:* $40,681. *Average need-based loan:* Freshmen: $3371. Undergraduates: $4444. *Parent loans:* $786,525 (88% need-based, 12% non-need-based). *Programs:* Federal Direct (Subsidized and Unsubsidized Stafford, PLUS), Perkins, alternative loans.

WORK-STUDY *Federal work-study:* Total amount: $73,907; 107 jobs averaging $1967. *State or other work-study/employment:* Total amount: $130,593 (100% non-need-based). Part-time jobs available.

APPLYING FOR FINANCIAL AID *Required financial aid form:* FAFSA. *Financial aid deadline (priority):* 10/1. *Notification date:* 2/15. Students must reply within 2 weeks of notification.

CONTACT Ms. Erin Bline, Director of Financial Aid, Eureka College, 300 East College Avenue, Eureka, IL 61530, 309-467-6311 or toll-free 888-4-EUREKA. *Fax:* 309-467-6897. *E-mail:* ebline@eureka.edu. *Website:* http://www.eureka.edu/.

EVANGEL UNIVERSITY
Springfield, MO

Tuition & fees: $22,707	Average undergraduate aid package: $16,755

ABOUT THE INSTITUTION Independent Assemblies of God, coed. *Awards:* associate, bachelor's, master's, and doctoral degrees. 48 undergraduate majors. *Total enrollment:* 1,464. Undergraduates: 1,464. Freshmen: 387. Federal methodology is used as a basis for awarding need-based institutional aid.

UNDERGRADUATE EXPENSES for 2017–2018 *Comprehensive fee:* $30,825 includes full-time tuition ($21,500), mandatory fees ($1207), and room and board ($8118). *College room only:* $4210. Full-time tuition and fees vary according to course load. Room and board charges vary according to board plan. *Part-time tuition:* $717 per credit hour. Part-time tuition and fees vary according to course load.

FRESHMAN FINANCIAL AID (Fall 2015) 357 applied for aid; of those 87% were deemed to have need. 100% of freshmen with need received aid; of those 12% had need fully met. *Average percent of need met:* 69% (excluding resources awarded to replace EFC). *Average financial aid package:* $16,900 (excluding resources awarded to replace EFC). 12% of all full-time freshmen had no need and received non-need-based gift aid.

UNDERGRADUATE FINANCIAL AID (Fall 2015) 1,489 applied for aid; of those 87% were deemed to have need. 100% of undergraduates with need received aid; of those 10% had need fully met. *Average percent of need met:* 68% (excluding resources awarded to replace EFC). *Average financial aid package:* $16,755 (excluding resources awarded to replace EFC). 12% of all full-time undergraduates had no need and received non-need-based gift aid.

GIFT AID (NEED-BASED) *Total amount:* $13,045,336 (28% federal, 65% institutional, 7% external sources). *Receiving aid:* Freshmen: 85% (309); all full-time undergraduates: 83% (1,277). *Average award:* Freshmen: $12,992; Undergraduates: $12,159. *Scholarships, grants, and awards:* Federal Pell, FSEOG, state, private, college/university gift aid from institutional funds.

GIFT AID (NON-NEED-BASED) *Total amount:* $1,865,909 (87% institutional, 13% external sources). *Receiving aid:* Freshmen: 10% (36). Undergraduates: 8% (128). *Average award:* Freshmen: $9404. Undergraduates: $6771. *Scholarships, grants, and awards by category:* Academic interests/achievement: 1,055 awards ($5,997,570 total): biological sciences, business, communication, computer science, education, engineering/technologies, English, foreign languages, general academic interests/achievements, home economics, humanities, international studies, mathematics, physical sciences, premedicine, religion/biblical studies, social sciences. *Creative arts/performance:* 142 awards ($113,188 total): art/fine arts, debating, music, theater/drama. *Special achievements/activities:* 207 awards ($93,708 total): cheerleading/drum major, general special achievements/activities, leadership, religious involvement. *Special characteristics:* 368 awards ($1,893,136 total): adult students, children and siblings of alumni, children of educators, children of faculty/staff, general special characteristics, out-of-state students, relatives of clergy, religious affiliation. *Tuition waivers:* Full or partial for employees or children of employees. *ROTC:* Army cooperative.

LOANS *Student loans:* $12,538,213 (77% need-based, 23% non-need-based). 68% of past graduating class borrowed through all loan programs. *Average indebtedness per student:* $32,032. *Average need-based loan:* Freshmen: $3518. Undergraduates: $4427. *Parent loans:* $2,634,210 (54% need-based, 46% non-need-based). *Programs:* Federal Direct (Subsidized and Unsubsidized Stafford, PLUS), Perkins, college/university.

WORK-STUDY *Federal work-study:* 978 jobs averaging $1469. *State or other work-study/employment:* Part-time jobs available.

ATHLETIC AWARDS Total amount: $2,359,742 (68% need-based, 32% non-need-based).

APPLYING FOR FINANCIAL AID *Required financial aid form:* FAFSA. *Financial aid deadline (priority):* 3/1. *Notification date:* Continuous beginning 3/1.

CONTACT Mrs. Valerie Sharp, Director of Student Financial Services, Evangel University, 1111 North Glenstone Avenue, Springfield, MO 65802-2191, 417-865-2811 Ext. 7302 or toll-free 800-382-6435. *Fax:* 417-575-5478. *E-mail:* sharpv@evangel.edu. *Website:* http://www.evangel.edu/.

EVEREST UNIVERSITY
Tampa, FL

CONTACT Mr. Rod Kirkwood, Financial Aid Director, Everest University, 3319 West Hillsborough Avenue, Tampa, FL 33614, 813-879-6000 Ext. 145. *Fax:* 813-871-2483. *E-mail:* rkirkwoo@cci.edu.
Website: http://www.everest.edu/.

EVERGLADES UNIVERSITY
Boca Raton, FL

Tuition & fees: $16,648	Average undergraduate aid package: N/A

ABOUT THE INSTITUTION Independent, coed. *Awards:* bachelor's and master's degrees. 11 undergraduate majors. *Total enrollment:* 1,451. Undergraduates: 1,313. Freshmen: 53.

UNDERGRADUATE EXPENSES for 2016–2017 Application fee: $50. *One-time required fee:* $145. *Tuition:* full-time $15,048; part-time $627 per credit. *Required fees:* full-time $1600; $100 per term.

GIFT AID (NEED-BASED) Scholarships, grants, and awards: Federal Pell, FSEOG, state, private, college/university gift aid from institutional funds.

GIFT AID (NON-NEED-BASED) Scholarships, grants, and awards by category: *Special characteristics:* general special characteristics, local/state students, veterans.

LOANS Programs: Federal Direct (Subsidized and Unsubsidized Stafford, PLUS), Perkins.

WORK-STUDY Federal work-study jobs available.

APPLYING FOR FINANCIAL AID Required financial aid forms: FAFSA, institution's own form. *Financial aid deadline:* Continuous. *Notification date:* Continuous beginning 1/1. Students must reply within 2 weeks of notification.

CONTACT Miss Seeta Singh Moonilall, Regional Director of Financial Aid, Everglades University, 5002 T-Rex Avenue, Suite 100, Boca Raton, FL 33431, 561-912-1211 or toll-free 888-772-6077. *Fax:* 516-912-1191.
E-mail: smoonilall@evergladesuniversity.edu.
Website: http://www.evergladesuniversity.edu/.

THE EVERGREEN STATE COLLEGE
Olympia, WA

Tuition & fees (WA res): $7239	Average undergraduate aid package: $12,646

ABOUT THE INSTITUTION State-supported, coed. *Awards:* bachelor's and master's degrees. 45 undergraduate majors. *Total enrollment:* 4,089. Undergraduates: 3,787. Freshmen: 572. Federal methodology is used as a basis for awarding need-based institutional aid.

UNDERGRADUATE EXPENSES for 2016–2017 Application fee: $50. *Tuition, state resident:* full-time $6534; part-time $217.80 per credit hour. *Tuition, nonresident:* full-time $23,007; part-time $766.90 per credit hour. *Required fees:* full-time $705; $9.25 per credit hour or $5 per term. Full-time tuition and fees vary according to course load, location, and program. Part-time tuition and fees vary according to course load, location, and program. *College room and board:* $9360; *Room only:* $6195. Room and board charges vary according to board plan, housing facility, location, and student level.

FRESHMAN FINANCIAL AID (Fall 2015) 470 applied for aid; of those 80% were deemed to have need. 95% of freshmen with need received aid; of those 9% had need fully met. *Average percent of need met:* 55% (excluding resources awarded to replace EFC). *Average financial aid package:* $10,960 (excluding resources awarded to replace EFC). 1% of all full-time freshmen had no need and received non-need-based gift aid.

UNDERGRADUATE FINANCIAL AID (Fall 2015) 2,727 applied for aid; of those 88% were deemed to have need. 94% of undergraduates with need received aid; of those 7% had need fully met. *Average percent of need met:* 60% (excluding resources awarded to replace EFC). *Average financial aid package:* $12,646

(excluding resources awarded to replace EFC). 1% of all full-time undergraduates had no need and received non-need-based gift aid.

GIFT AID (NEED-BASED) Total amount: $17,120,449 (46% federal, 45% state, 8% institutional, 1% external sources). *Receiving aid:* Freshmen: 59% (341); all full-time undergraduates: 58% (2,087). *Average award:* Freshmen: $9090; Undergraduates: $9826. *Scholarships, grants, and awards:* Federal Pell, FSEOG, state, private, college/university gift aid from institutional funds.

GIFT AID (NON-NEED-BASED) Total amount: $178,483 (36% state, 37% institutional, 27% external sources). *Receiving aid:* Freshmen: 3% (16), Undergraduates: 1% (31). *Average award:* Freshmen: $6586. Undergraduates: $3062. *Scholarships, grants, and awards by category:* Academic interests/achievement: general academic interests/achievements. *Creative arts/performance:* general creative arts/performance. *Special achievements/activities:* general special achievements/activities. *Special characteristics:* adult students, ethnic background, first-generation college students, general special characteristics, local/state students, out-of-state students, veterans, veterans' children. *Tuition waivers:* Full or partial for employees or children of employees, senior citizens.

LOANS Student loans: $14,470,532 (90% need-based, 10% non-need-based). 54% of past graduating class borrowed through all loan programs. *Average indebtedness per student:* $21,215. *Average need-based loan:* Freshmen: $3405. Undergraduates: $4279. *Parent loans:* $4,186,913 (77% need-based, 23% non-need-based). *Programs:* Federal Direct (Subsidized and Unsubsidized Stafford, PLUS), Perkins, college/university.

WORK-STUDY Federal work-study: jobs available. *State or other work-study/employment:* Total amount: $669,231 (100% need-based). Part-time jobs available.

ATHLETIC AWARDS Total amount: $283,393 (65% need-based, 35% non-need-based).

APPLYING FOR FINANCIAL AID Required financial aid form: FAFSA. *Financial aid deadline (priority):* 2/1. *Notification date:* Continuous beginning 4/1. Students must reply within 6 weeks of notification.

CONTACT Tracy Hall, Director of Financial Aid, The Evergreen State College, 2700 Evergreen Parkway NW, Olympia, WA 98505, 360-867-6205. *Fax:* 360-866-6576. *E-mail:* finaid@evergreen.edu.
Website: http://www.evergreen.edu/.

EXCELSIOR COLLEGE
Albany, NY

Tuition & fees: N/R	Average undergraduate aid package: N/A

ABOUT THE INSTITUTION Independent, coed. *Awards:* certificates, associate, bachelor's, and master's degrees (offers only external degree programs). 46 undergraduate majors. *Total enrollment:* 38,309. Undergraduates: 35,161. Federal methodology is used as a basis for awarding need-based institutional aid.

UNDERGRADUATE EXPENSES for 2016–2017 Application fee: $50. *Tuition:* part-time $510 per credit. Part-time tuition and fees vary according to reciprocity agreements.

GIFT AID (NEED-BASED) Total amount: $14,462,559 (72% federal, 8% state, 3% institutional, 17% external sources). *Scholarships, grants, and awards:* Federal Pell, FSEOG, state, private, college/university gift aid from institutional funds, Federal Nursing, Veterans Education Benefits (GI Bill).

GIFT AID (NON-NEED-BASED) Tuition waivers: Full or partial for employees or children of employees.

LOANS Student loans: $28,065,060 (98% need-based, 2% non-need-based). *Programs:* Federal Direct (Subsidized and Unsubsidized Stafford, PLUS), Federal Nursing, college/university.

APPLYING FOR FINANCIAL AID Financial aid deadline: Continuous. *Notification date:* Continuous.

CONTACT Director of Financial Aid, Excelsior College, 7 Columbia Circle, Albany, NY 12203-5159, 518-464-8500 or toll-free 888-647-2388. *Fax:* 518-464-8777.
Website: http://www.excelsior.edu/.

FAIRFIELD UNIVERSITY
Fairfield, CT

Tuition & fees: $46,000	Average undergraduate aid package: $33,012

ABOUT THE INSTITUTION Independent Roman Catholic (Jesuit), coed. *Awards:* certificates, bachelor's, master's, and doctoral degrees. 44 undergraduate majors. *Total enrollment:* 5,137. Undergraduates: 4,032. Freshmen: 1,056. Both federal and institutional methodology are used as a basis for awarding need-based institutional aid.

UNDERGRADUATE EXPENSES for 2016–2017 *Application fee:* $60. *One-time required fee:* $280. *Comprehensive fee:* $59,860 includes full-time tuition ($45,350), mandatory fees ($650), and room and board ($13,860). *College room only:* $8490. Full-time tuition and fees vary according to class time, course level, course load, degree level, and program. Room and board charges vary according to board plan and housing facility. *Part-time tuition:* $725 per credit hour. *Part-time fees:* $60 per term. Part-time tuition and fees vary according to class time, course level, course load, degree level, and program.

FRESHMAN FINANCIAL AID (Fall 2016, est.) 817 applied for aid; of those 66% were deemed to have need. 100% of freshmen with need received aid; of those 29% had need fully met. *Average percent of need met:* 84% (excluding resources awarded to replace EFC). *Average financial aid package:* $34,622 (excluding resources awarded to replace EFC). 38% of all full-time freshmen had no need and received non-need-based gift aid.

UNDERGRADUATE FINANCIAL AID (Fall 2016, est.) 2,470 applied for aid; of those 70% were deemed to have need. 100% of undergraduates with need received aid; of those 32% had need fully met. *Average percent of need met:* 82% (excluding resources awarded to replace EFC). *Average financial aid package:* $33,012 (excluding resources awarded to replace EFC). 28% of all full-time undergraduates had no need and received non-need-based gift aid.

GIFT AID (NEED-BASED) *Total amount:* $45,738,452 (6% federal, 94% institutional). *Receiving aid:* Freshmen: 50% (533); all full-time undergraduates: 39% (1,476). *Average award:* Freshmen: $28,829; Undergraduates: $26,170. *Scholarships, grants, and awards:* Federal Pell, FSEOG, state, private, college/university gift aid from institutional funds, Federal Nursing.

GIFT AID (NON-NEED-BASED) *Total amount:* $23,100,624 (93% institutional, 7% external sources). *Receiving aid:* Freshmen: 47% (496). Undergraduates: 40% (1,521). *Average award:* Freshmen: $14,826. Undergraduates: $14,445. *Scholarships, grants, and awards by category:* Academic interests/achievement: 1,321 awards ($17,391,350 total): general academic interests/achievements. Creative arts/performance: 37 awards ($10,784 total): general creative arts/performance. Special achievements/activities: 8 awards ($36,900 total): general special achievements/activities. Special characteristics: 198 awards ($3,138,267 total): children and siblings of alumni, children of faculty/staff, children with a deceased or disabled parent, ethnic background, first-generation college students, general special characteristics, members of minority groups, veterans, veterans' children. *Tuition waivers:* Full or partial for employees or children of employees. *ROTC:* Army cooperative, Air Force cooperative.

LOANS *Student loans:* $23,587,355 (32% need-based, 68% non-need-based). 66% of past graduating class borrowed through all loan programs. *Average indebtedness per student:* $37,910. *Average need-based loan:* Freshmen: $3431. Undergraduates: $4654. *Parent loans:* $6,657,421 (100% non-need-based). *Programs:* Federal Direct (Subsidized and Unsubsidized Stafford, PLUS), Perkins, Federal Nursing, state, private loans.

WORK-STUDY *Federal work-study:* Total amount: $555,425; 508 jobs averaging $1091.

ATHLETIC AWARDS Total amount: $6,165,024 (100% non-need-based).

APPLYING FOR FINANCIAL AID *Required financial aid forms:* FAFSA, CSS Financial Aid PROFILE, noncustodial (divorced/separated) parent's statement, business/farm supplement. *Financial aid deadline:* 1/15. *Notification date:* 4/1. Students must reply by 5/1.

CONTACT Diana Draper, Director of Financial Aid, Fairfield University, 1073 North Benson Road, Fairfield, CT 06824, 203-254-4125. *Fax:* 203-254-4008. *E-mail:* finaid@fairfield.edu.
Website: http://www.fairfield.edu/.

FAIRLEIGH DICKINSON UNIVERSITY, COLLEGE AT FLORHAM
Madison, NJ

CONTACT Financial Aid Office, Fairleigh Dickinson University, College at Florham, 285 Madison Avenue, Madison, NJ 07940-1099, 973-443-8700 or toll-free 800-338-8803.
Website: http://www.fdu.edu/.

FAIRLEIGH DICKINSON UNIVERSITY, METROPOLITAN CAMPUS
Teaneck, NJ

CONTACT Financial Aid Office, Fairleigh Dickinson University, Metropolitan Campus, 100 River Road, Teaneck, NJ 07666-1914, 201-692-2363 or toll-free 800-338-8803.
Website: http://www.fdu.edu/.

FAIRMONT STATE UNIVERSITY
Fairmont, WV

Tuition & fees (WV res): $8684	Average undergraduate aid package: $8761

ABOUT THE INSTITUTION State-supported, coed. *Awards:* associate, bachelor's, and master's degrees. 42 undergraduate majors. *Total enrollment:* 4,041. Undergraduates: 3,807. Freshmen: 823. Federal methodology is used as a basis for awarding need-based institutional aid.

UNDERGRADUATE EXPENSES for 2016–2017 *Tuition, state resident:* full-time $6950; part-time $281 per credit hour. *Tuition, nonresident:* full-time $14,666; part-time $603 per credit hour. *Required fees:* full-time $1734. Full-time tuition and fees vary according to location. Part-time tuition and fees vary according to course load and location. *College room and board:* $9640; *Room only:* $5096. Room and board charges vary according to board plan and housing facility.

FRESHMAN FINANCIAL AID (Fall 2015) 780 applied for aid; of those 75% were deemed to have need. 99% of freshmen with need received aid; of those 13% had need fully met. *Average percent of need met:* 72% (excluding resources awarded to replace EFC). *Average financial aid package:* $8592 (excluding resources awarded to replace EFC). 9% of all full-time freshmen had no need and received non-need-based gift aid.

UNDERGRADUATE FINANCIAL AID (Fall 2015) 2,925 applied for aid; of those 78% were deemed to have need. 98% of undergraduates with need received aid; of those 8% had need fully met. *Average percent of need met:* 70% (excluding resources awarded to replace EFC). *Average financial aid package:* $8761 (excluding resources awarded to replace EFC). 9% of all full-time undergraduates had no need and received non-need-based gift aid.

GIFT AID (NEED-BASED) *Total amount:* $13,745,504 (51% federal, 41% state, 8% institutional). *Receiving aid:* Freshmen: 63% (511); all full-time undergraduates: 60% (1,938). *Average award:* Freshmen: $6883; Undergraduates: $6377. *Scholarships, grants, and awards:* Federal Pell, FSEOG, state, private, college/university gift aid from institutional funds.

GIFT AID (NON-NEED-BASED) *Total amount:* $1,054,699 (2% state, 44% institutional, 54% external sources). *Receiving aid:* Freshmen: 25% (204). Undergraduates: 17% (558). *Average award:* Freshmen: $8265. Undergraduates: $6614. *Scholarships, grants, and awards by category:* Academic interests/achievement: 592 awards ($2,250,734 total): architecture, biological sciences, business, computer science, education, engineering/technologies, English, general academic interests/achievements, health fields, humanities, international studies, mathematics, physical sciences, social sciences. Creative arts/performance: 715 awards ($3,010,443 total): art/fine arts, creative writing, debating, general creative arts/performance, journalism/publications, music, theater/drama. Special achievements/activities: 77 awards ($81,780 total): cheerleading/drum major, general special achievements/activities, leadership. Special characteristics: 28 awards ($45,700 total): adult students, children and siblings of alumni, children of faculty/staff, ethnic background, first-generation college students, general special characteristics, handicapped students, international students, local/state students, members of minority groups, out-of-state students, previous college experience, veterans, veterans' children. *Tuition waivers:* Full or partial for employees or children of employees. *ROTC:* Army, Air Force cooperative.

LOANS *Student loans:* $15,253,913 (40% need-based, 60% non-need-based). 71% of past graduating class borrowed through all loan programs. *Average indebtedness per student:* $26,314. *Average need-based loan:* Freshmen: $2920. Undergraduates: $3605. *Parent loans:* $1,896,566 (100% non-need-based). *Programs:* Federal Direct (Subsidized and Unsubsidized Stafford, PLUS).

WORK-STUDY *Federal work study:* 124 jobs averaging $1686. *State or other work-study/employment:* 388 part-time jobs averaging $1951.

ATHLETIC AWARDS Total amount: $1,471,697 (60% need-based, 40% non-need-based).

APPLYING FOR FINANCIAL AID *Required financial aid form:* FAFSA. *Financial aid deadline (priority):* 3/1. *Notification date:* Continuous beginning 12/1. Students must reply within 2 weeks of notification.

CONTACT Patricia Wiemer, Director of Financial Aid and Scholarships, Fairmont State University, 1201 Locust Avenue, Fairmont, WV 26554, 304-367-4892 or toll-free 800-641-5678. *Fax:* 304-367-4789. *E-mail:* patricia.weimer@fairmontstate.edu. *Website:* http://www.fairmontstate.edu/.

FAITH BAPTIST BIBLE COLLEGE AND THEOLOGICAL SEMINARY
Ankeny, IA

CONTACT Mr. Breck Appell, Director of Financial Assistance, Faith Baptist Bible College and Theological Seminary, 1900 Northwest 4th Street, Ankeny, IA 50021-2152, 515-964-0601 or toll-free 888-FAITH 4U. *Fax:* 515-964-1638. *Website:* http://www.faith.edu/.

FAITH THEOLOGICAL SEMINARY
Baltimore, MD

CONTACT Financial Aid Office, Faith Theological Seminary, 529 Walker Avenue, Baltimore, MD 21212, 410-323-6211. *Website:* http://www.faiththeological.org/.

FAMILY OF FAITH COLLEGE
Shawnee, OK

CONTACT Financial Aid Office, Family of Faith College, 30 Kinville, Shawnee, OK 74802, 405-273-5331. *Website:* http://www.familyoffaithcollege.edu/.

FARMINGDALE STATE COLLEGE
Farmingdale, NY

Tuition & fees (NY res): $7860	Average undergraduate aid package: $7859

ABOUT THE INSTITUTION State-supported, coed. *Awards:* certificates, associate, bachelor's, and master's degrees. 35 undergraduate majors. *Total enrollment:* 9,235. Undergraduates: 9,235. Freshmen: 1,281. Federal methodology is used as a basis for awarding need-based institutional aid.

UNDERGRADUATE EXPENSES for 2016–2017 *Application fee:* $50. *Tuition, state resident:* full-time $6470; part-time $270 per credit. *Tuition, nonresident:* full-time $16,320; part-time $680 per credit. *Required fees:* full-time $1390; $55.90 per credit or $10 per term. Full-time tuition and fees vary according to program. Part-time tuition and fees vary according to course load and program. *College room and board:* $12,764; *Room only:* $7774. Room and board charges vary according to housing facility.

FRESHMAN FINANCIAL AID (Fall 2015) 817 applied for aid; of those 66% were deemed to have need. 89% of freshmen with need received aid; of those 9% had need fully met. *Average percent of need met:* 60% (excluding resources awarded to replace EFC). *Average financial aid package:* $7802 (excluding resources awarded to replace EFC). 1% of all full-time freshmen had no need and received non-need-based gift aid.

UNDERGRADUATE FINANCIAL AID (Fall 2015) 4,444 applied for aid; of those 76% were deemed to have need. 93% of undergraduates with need received aid; of those 8% had need fully met. *Average percent of need met:* 56% (excluding resources awarded to replace EFC). *Average financial aid package:* $7859 (excluding resources awarded to replace EFC). 1% of all full-time undergraduates had no need and received non-need-based gift aid.

GIFT AID (NEED-BASED) *Total amount:* $18,631,561 (53% federal, 46% state, 1% institutional). *Receiving aid:* Freshmen: 41% (411); all full-time undergraduates: 43% (2,671). *Average award:* Freshmen: $7225; Undergraduates: $6569. *Scholarships, grants, and awards:* Federal Pell, FSEOG, state, private, college/university gift aid from institutional funds.

GIFT AID (NON-NEED-BASED) *Total amount:* $776,801 (24% state, 17% institutional, 59% external sources). *Receiving aid:* Freshmen: 1% (10). Undergraduates: 1% (36). *Average award:* Freshmen: $1583. Undergraduates: $1693. *Tuition waivers:* Full or partial for employees or children of employees. *ROTC:* Army cooperative, Naval cooperative, Air Force.

LOANS *Student loans:* $18,397,746 (60% need-based, 40% non-need-based). *Average need-based loan:* Freshmen: $3004. Undergraduates: $3809. *Parent loans:* $1,493,279 (34% need-based, 66% non-need-based). *Programs:* Federal Direct (Subsidized and Unsubsidized Stafford, PLUS), Perkins, alternative loans.

WORK-STUDY *Federal work-study:* jobs available. *State or other work-study/employment:* Total amount: $348,642 (18% need-based, 82% non-need-based). Part-time jobs available.

APPLYING FOR FINANCIAL AID *Required financial aid form:* FAFSA. *Financial aid deadline (priority):* 4/1. *Notification date:* Continuous beginning 3/1.

CONTACT Office of Financial Aid, Farmingdale State College, 2350 Broadhollow Road, Laffin Hall, Room 324, Farmingdale, NY 11735, 631-420-2578. *Fax:* 631-420-3662. *E-mail:* faoffice@farmingdale.edu. *Website:* http://www.farmingdale.edu/.

FASHION INSTITUTE OF TECHNOLOGY
New York, NY

Tuition & fees (NY res): $7215	Average undergraduate aid package: $11,804

ABOUT THE INSTITUTION State and locally supported, coed, primarily women. *Awards:* certificates, associate, bachelor's, and master's degrees. 23 undergraduate majors. *Total enrollment:* 9,272. Undergraduates: 9,096. Freshmen: 1,273. Federal methodology is used as a basis for awarding need-based institutional aid.

UNDERGRADUATE EXPENSES for 2016–2017 *Application fee:* $50. *Tuition, state resident:* full-time $6470; part-time $270 per credit hour. *Tuition, nonresident:* full-time $19,592; part-time $816 per credit hour. *Required fees:* full-time $745. Full-time tuition and fees vary according to degree level. Part-time tuition and fees vary according to degree level. *College room and board:* $13,386; *Room only:* $8910. Room and board charges vary according to board plan and housing facility.

FRESHMAN FINANCIAL AID (Fall 2015) 849 applied for aid; of those 74% were deemed to have need. 100% of freshmen with need received aid; of those 42% had need fully met. *Average percent of need met:* 71% (excluding resources awarded to replace EFC). *Average financial aid package:* $10,959 (excluding resources awarded to replace EFC). 7% of all full-time freshmen had no need and received non-need-based gift aid.

UNDERGRADUATE FINANCIAL AID (Fall 2015) 4,591 applied for aid; of those 82% were deemed to have need. 100% of undergraduates with need received aid; of those 44% had need fully met. *Average percent of need met:* 67% (excluding resources awarded to replace EFC). *Average financial aid package:* $11,804 (excluding resources awarded to replace EFC). 3% of all full-time undergraduates had no need and received non-need-based gift aid.

GIFT AID (NEED-BASED) *Total amount:* $18,438,075 (61% federal, 30% state, 9% institutional). *Receiving aid:* Freshmen: 37% (466); all full-time undergraduates: 39% (2,864). *Average award:* Freshmen: $6083; Undergraduates: $6078. *Scholarships, grants, and awards:* Federal Pell, FSEOG, state, private, college/university gift aid from institutional funds.

GIFT AID (NON-NEED-BASED) *Total amount:* $404,900 (35% institutional, 65% external sources). *Receiving aid:* Freshmen: 12% (149). Undergraduates: 4% (306). *Average award:* Freshmen: $689. Undergraduates: $773. *Tuition waivers:* Full or partial for employees or children of employees.

LOANS *Student loans:* $30,662,106 (37% need-based, 63% non-need-based). 53% of past graduating class borrowed through all loan programs. *Average indebtedness per student:* $24,850. *Average need-based loan:* Freshmen: $2534. Undergraduates: $3135. *Parent loans:* $11,353,839 (100% non-need-based). *Programs:* Federal Direct (Subsidized and Unsubsidized Stafford, PLUS), Perkins, alternative loans.

WORK-STUDY *Federal work-study:* jobs available.

APPLYING FOR FINANCIAL AID *Required financial aid forms:* FAFSA, state aid form. *Financial aid deadline (priority):* 2/15. *Notification date:* Continuous beginning 4/1. Students must reply within 2 weeks of notification.

CONTACT Financial Aid Office, Fashion Institute of Technology, Seventh Avenue at 27th Street, New York, NY 10001-5992, 212-217-3560.
Website: http://www.fitnyc.edu/.

FAULKNER UNIVERSITY
Montgomery, AL

Tuition & fees: $20,590	Average undergraduate aid package: $14,006

ABOUT THE INSTITUTION Independent Church of Christ, coed. *Awards:* associate, bachelor's, master's, and doctoral degrees. 48 undergraduate majors. *Total enrollment:* 3,319. Undergraduates: 2,583. Freshmen: 314. Federal methodology is used as a basis for awarding need-based institutional aid.

UNDERGRADUATE EXPENSES for 2017–2018 Comprehensive fee: $28,840 includes full-time tuition ($18,780), mandatory fees ($1810), and room and board ($8250). *College room only:* $4300. Full-time tuition and fees vary according to class time, course load, location, and program. Room and board charges vary according to board plan and housing facility. *Part-time tuition:* $635 per semester hour. *Part-time fees:* $320 per term. Part-time tuition and fees vary according to class time, course load, location, and program.

FRESHMAN FINANCIAL AID (Fall 2015) 242 applied for aid; of those 93% were deemed to have need. 100% of freshmen with need received aid; of those 12% had need fully met. *Average percent of need met:* 61% (excluding resources awarded to replace EFC). *Average financial aid package:* $14,144 (excluding resources awarded to replace EFC). 9% of all full-time freshmen had no need and received non-need-based gift aid.

UNDERGRADUATE FINANCIAL AID (Fall 2015) 253 applied for aid; of those 93% were deemed to have need. 100% of undergraduates with need received aid; of those 11% had need fully met. *Average percent of need met:* 61% (excluding resources awarded to replace EFC). *Average financial aid package:* $14,006 (excluding resources awarded to replace EFC). 9% of all full-time undergraduates had no need and received non-need-based gift aid.

GIFT AID (NEED-BASED) *Total amount:* $2,369,694 (31% federal, 5% state, 58% institutional, 6% external sources). *Receiving aid:* Freshmen: 86% (226); all full-time undergraduates: 85% (234). *Average award:* Freshmen: $11,651; Undergraduates: $11,587. *Scholarships, grants, and awards:* Federal Pell, FSEOG, state, private, college/university gift aid from institutional funds.

GIFT AID (NON-NEED-BASED) *Total amount:* $266,404 (10% state, 74% institutional, 16% external sources). *Receiving aid:* Freshmen: 10% (27). Undergraduates: 10% (27). *Average award:* Freshmen: $6113. Undergraduates: $6113. *Scholarships, grants, and awards by category:* Academic interests/achievement: general academic interests/achievements, religion/biblical studies. Creative arts/performance: journalism/publications, music, theater/drama. Special achievements/activities: cheerleading/drum major, leadership, religious involvement. Special characteristics: adult students, children and siblings of alumni, children of faculty/staff, local/state students, out-of-state students, relatives of clergy, religious affiliation, siblings of current students. *Tuition waivers:* Full or partial for employees or children of employees, adult students. *ROTC:* Army cooperative, Air Force cooperative.

LOANS *Student loans:* $1,277,766 (87% need-based, 13% non-need-based). 89% of past graduating class borrowed through all loan programs. *Average indebtedness per student:* $29,000. *Average need-based loan:* Freshmen: $3071. Undergraduates: $3064. *Parent loans:* $528,120 (64% need-based, 36% non-need-based). *Programs:* Federal Direct (Subsidized and Unsubsidized Stafford, PLUS), Perkins.

WORK-STUDY *Federal work-study:* jobs available. *State or other work-study/employment:* Part-time jobs available.

ATHLETIC AWARDS Total amount: $629,287 (63% need-based, 37% non-need-based).

APPLYING FOR FINANCIAL AID *Required financial aid forms:* FAFSA, institution's own form, state aid form. *Financial aid deadline:* 8/1 (priority: 3/15). *Notification date:* 5/1. Students must reply within 3 weeks of notification.

CONTACT Mr. William G. Jackson II, Director of Financial Aid, Faulkner University, 5345 Atlanta Highway, Montgomery, AL 36109-3398, 334-386-7195 or toll-free 800-879-9816. *Fax:* 334-386-7201. *E-mail:* faid@faulkner.edu.
Website: http://www.faulkner.edu/.

FAYETTEVILLE STATE UNIVERSITY
Fayetteville, NC

ABOUT THE INSTITUTION State-supported, coed. *Awards:* bachelor's, master's, and doctoral degrees. 36 undergraduate majors. *Total enrollment:* 6,223. Undergraduates: 5,543. Freshmen: 646.

GIFT AID (NEED-BASED) *Scholarships, grants, and awards:* Federal Pell, FSEOG, state, private, college/university gift aid from institutional funds, United Negro College Fund, Federal Nursing.

GIFT AID (NON-NEED-BASED) *Scholarships, grants, and awards by category:* Academic interests/achievement: general academic interests/achievements. Creative arts/performance: music. Special characteristics: local/state students.

LOANS *Programs:* Federal Direct (Subsidized and Unsubsidized Stafford, PLUS), Perkins.

APPLYING FOR FINANCIAL AID *Required financial aid forms:* FAFSA, federal income tax form(s), W-2 forms.

CONTACT Mr. Keith Townsend, Administrative Assistant, Fayetteville State University, 1200 Murchison Road, Fayetteville, NC 28301-4298, 910-672-1327 or toll-free 800-222-2594. *Fax:* 910-672-1423. *E-mail:* ktownse7@uncfsu.edu.
Website: http://www.uncfsu.edu/.

FELICIAN UNIVERSITY
Lodi, NJ

Tuition & fees: $33,650	Average undergraduate aid package: $25,736

ABOUT THE INSTITUTION Independent Roman Catholic, coed. *Awards:* certificates, associate, bachelor's, master's, and doctoral degrees. 30 undergraduate majors. *Total enrollment:* 2,014. Undergraduates: 1,648. Freshmen: 316. Federal methodology is used as a basis for awarding need-based institutional aid.

UNDERGRADUATE EXPENSES for 2017–2018 Application fee: $30. *Comprehensive fee:* $46,280 includes full-time tuition ($31,290), mandatory fees ($2360), and room and board ($12,630). Full-time tuition and fees vary according to program. Room and board charges vary according to housing facility. *Part-time tuition:* $1035 per credit hour. *Part-time fees:* $465 per term. Part-time tuition and fees vary according to course load and program.

FRESHMAN FINANCIAL AID (Fall 2015) 290 applied for aid; of those 98% were deemed to have need. 99% of freshmen with need received aid; of those 9% had need fully met. *Average percent of need met:* 73% (excluding resources awarded to replace EFC). *Average financial aid package:* $29,766 (excluding resources awarded to replace EFC). 4% of all full-time freshmen had no need and received non-need-based gift aid.

UNDERGRADUATE FINANCIAL AID (Fall 2015) 1,283 applied for aid; of those 97% were deemed to have need. 99% of undergraduates with need received aid; of those 6% had need fully met. *Average percent of need met:* 64% (excluding resources awarded to replace EFC). *Average financial aid package:* $25,736 (excluding resources awarded to replace EFC). 6% of all full-time undergraduates had no need and received non-need-based gift aid.

GIFT AID (NEED-BASED) *Total amount:* $14,485,547 (29% federal, 46% state, 25% institutional). *Receiving aid:* Freshmen: 78% (232); all full-time undergraduates: 74% (1,034). *Average award:* Freshmen: $16,165; Undergraduates: $13,755. *Scholarships, grants, and awards:* Federal Pell, FSEOG, state, private, college/university gift aid from institutional funds.

GIFT AID (NON-NEED-BASED) *Total amount:* $12,781,375 (5% federal, 94% institutional, 1% external sources). *Receiving aid:* Freshmen: 95% (281). Undergraduates: 76% (1,050). *Average award:* Freshmen: $15,500. Undergraduates: $14,498. *Scholarships, grants, and awards by category.* Academic interests/achievement: business, education, English, general academic interests/achievements, health fields, religion/biblical studies. *Special characteristics:* children of faculty/staff, siblings of current students. *Tuition waivers:* Full or partial for employees or children of employees. *ROTC:* Army cooperative, Air Force cooperative.

LOANS *Student loans:* $11,138,090 (41% need-based, 59% non-need-based). 73% of past graduating class borrowed through all loan programs. *Average indebtedness per student:* $32,032. *Average need-based loan:* Freshmen: $3365. Undergraduates: $4246. *Parent loans:* $3,123,441 (100% non-need-based). *Programs:* Federal Direct (Subsidized and Unsubsidized Stafford, PLUS), state.

WORK-STUDY *Federal work-study:* 63 jobs averaging $2583. *State or other work-study/employment:* Total amount: $248,086 (100% non-need-based). Part-time jobs available.

ATHLETIC AWARDS Total amount: $1,675,102 (100% non-need-based).

APPLYING FOR FINANCIAL AID *Required financial aid forms:* FAFSA, state aid form. *Financial aid deadline:* Continuous. *Notification date:* 3/1.

CONTACT Ms. Cynthia Montalvo, Financial Aid Director, Felician University, 262 South Main Street, Lodi, NJ 07644, 201-559-6040. *Fax:* 201-559-6025. *E-mail:* montalvoc@felician.edu.
Website: http://www.felician.edu/.

FERRIS STATE UNIVERSITY
Big Rapids, MI

Tuition & fees (MI res): $11,760	Average undergraduate aid package: $11,350

ABOUT THE INSTITUTION State-supported, coed. *Awards:* certificates, associate, bachelor's, master's, and doctoral degrees. 121 undergraduate majors. *Total enrollment:* 14,187. Undergraduates: 12,866. Freshmen: 1,824. Federal methodology is used as a basis for awarding need-based institutional aid.

UNDERGRADUATE EXPENSES for 2016–2017 *Tuition, state resident:* full-time $11,760; part-time $392 per credit hour. *Tuition, nonresident:* full-time $17,640; part-time $588 per credit hour. Full-time tuition and fees vary according to location, program, and student level. Part-time tuition and fees vary according to location and student level. *College room and board:* $9651. Room and board charges vary according to board plan and housing facility.

FRESHMAN FINANCIAL AID (Fall 2016, est.) 1,678 applied for aid; of those 80% were deemed to have need. 100% of freshmen with need received aid; of those 18% had need fully met. *Average percent of need met:* 72% (excluding resources awarded to replace EFC). *Average financial aid package:* $13,000 (excluding resources awarded to replace EFC). 16% of all full-time freshmen had no need and received non-need-based gift aid.

UNDERGRADUATE FINANCIAL AID (Fall 2016, est.) 8,411 applied for aid; of those 77% were deemed to have need. 99% of undergraduates with need received aid; of those 15% had need fully met. *Average percent of need met:* 66% (excluding resources awarded to replace EFC). *Average financial aid package:* $11,350 (excluding resources awarded to replace EFC). 14% of all full-time undergraduates had no need and received non-need-based gift aid.

GIFT AID (NEED-BASED) *Total amount:* $27,903,180 (80% federal, 2% state, 18% institutional). *Receiving aid:* Freshmen: 63% (1,132); all full-time undergraduates: 53% (4,935). *Average award:* Freshmen: $4760; Undergraduates: $4890. *Scholarships, grants, and awards:* Federal Pell, FSEOG, state, private, college/university gift aid from institutional funds.

GIFT AID (NON-NEED-BASED) *Total amount:* $32,149,970 (2% federal, 32% state, 51% institutional, 15% external sources). *Receiving aid:* Freshmen: 59% (1,060). Undergraduates: 41% (3,811). *Average award:* Freshmen: $5140. Undergraduates: $4420. *Scholarships, grants, and awards by category:* Academic interests/achievement: 3,841 awards ($11,628,822 total): agriculture, architecture, biological sciences, business, communication, computer science, education, engineering/technologies, general academic interests/achievements, health fields, mathematics. *Creative arts/performance:* 482 awards ($1,619,679 total): applied art and design, art/fine arts, debating, general creative arts/performance, journalism/publications, music, theater/drama. *Special achievements/activities:* 119 awards ($46,132 total): general special achievements/activities, memberships. *Special characteristics:* 162 awards ($144,101 total): adult students, children and siblings of alumni, ethnic background, general special characteristics, international students, local/state students, members of minority groups, previous college experience, veterans. *Tuition waivers:* Full or partial for employees or children of employees. *ROTC:* Army cooperative.

LOANS *Student loans:* $65,289,240 (42% need-based, 58% non-need-based). 76% of past graduating class borrowed through all loan programs. *Average indebtedness per student:* $35,710. *Average need-based loan:* Freshmen: $3630. Undergraduates: $4600. *Parent loans:* $8,824,290 (100% non-need-based). *Programs:* Federal Direct (Subsidized and Unsubsidized Stafford, PLUS), Perkins, Federal Nursing, college/university, alternative loans.

WORK-STUDY *Federal work-study:* Total amount: $990,860; 410 jobs averaging $2391. *State or other work-study/employment:* Total amount: $1,464,650 (100% non-need-based). 218 part-time jobs averaging $2031.

ATHLETIC AWARDS Total amount: $2,305,020 (100% non-need-based).

APPLYING FOR FINANCIAL AID *Required financial aid form:* FAFSA. *Financial aid deadline (priority):* 2/15. *Notification date:* Continuous beginning 3/15. Students must reply within 3 weeks of notification.

CONTACT Nancy Wencl, Assistant Director of Financial Aid, Ferris State University, 1201 South State Street, Big Rapids, MI 49307-2020, 231-591-2100 or toll-free 800-433-7747. *Fax:* 231-591-2950. *E-mail:* wencln@ferris.edu.
Website: http://www.ferris.edu/.

FERRUM COLLEGE
Ferrum, VA

CONTACT Heather Hollandsworth, Director of Financial Aid, Ferrum College, PO Box 1000, Ferrum, VA 24088, 540-365-4282 or toll-free 800-868-9797. *Fax:* 540-365-4266. *E-mail:* hhollandsworth@ferrum.edu.
Website: http://www.ferrum.edu/.

FIDM/FASHION INSTITUTE OF DESIGN & MERCHANDISING, LOS ANGELES CAMPUS
Los Angeles, CA

CONTACT Financial Aid Office, FIDM/Fashion Institute of Design & Merchandising, Los Angeles Campus, 919 South Grand Avenue, Los Angeles, CA 90015-1421, 213-624-1200 or toll-free 800-624-1200.
Website: http://www.fidm.edu/.

FIDM/FASHION INSTITUTE OF DESIGN & MERCHANDISING, SAN FRANCISCO CAMPUS
San Francisco, CA

CONTACT Financial Aid Office, FIDM/Fashion Institute of Design & Merchandising, San Francisco Campus, 55 Stockton Street, San Francisco, CA 94108-5829, 415-675-5200 or toll-free 800-422-3436.
Website: http://www.fidm.edu/.

FINLANDIA UNIVERSITY
Hancock, MI

CONTACT Sandra Turnquist, Director of Financial Aid, Finlandia University, 601 Quincy Street, Hancock, MI 49930, 906-487-7240 or toll-free 877-202-5491. *Fax:* 906-487-7383. *E-mail:* sandra.turnquist@finlandia.edu.
Website: http://www.finlandia.edu/.

FISHER COLLEGE
Boston, MA

Tuition & fees: $30,499	Average undergraduate aid package: $20,048

ABOUT THE INSTITUTION Independent, coed. *Awards:* certificates, associate, bachelor's, and master's degrees. 31 undergraduate majors. *Total enrollment:* 2,030. Undergraduates: 1,996. Freshmen: 282. Federal methodology is used as a basis for awarding need-based institutional aid.

UNDERGRADUATE EXPENSES for 2017–2018 *Comprehensive fee:* $46,267 includes full-time tuition ($29,504), mandatory fees ($995), and room and board ($15,768). Room and board charges vary according to housing facility. *Part-time tuition:* $983.47 per course. *Part-time fees:* $995 per term. Part-time tuition and fees vary according to course load.

FRESHMAN FINANCIAL AID (Fall 2015) 254 applied for aid; of those 84% were deemed to have need. 100% of freshmen with need received aid. *Average financial aid package:* $26,205 (excluding resources awarded to replace EFC). 21% of all full-time freshmen had no need and received non-need-based gift aid.

UNDERGRADUATE FINANCIAL AID (Fall 2015) 1,097 applied for aid; of those 74% were deemed to have need. 100% of undergraduates with need received aid. *Average financial aid package:* $20,048 (excluding resources awarded to replace EFC). 6% of all full-time undergraduates had no need and received non-need-based gift aid.

GIFT AID (NEED-BASED) *Total amount:* $13,785,765 (25% federal, 6% state, 69% institutional). *Receiving aid:* Freshmen: 77% (209); all full-time undergraduates: 59% (695). *Average award:* Freshmen: $22,858; Undergraduates: $13,530. *Scholarships, grants, and awards:* Federal Pell, FSEOG, state, private, college/university gift aid from institutional funds.

GIFT AID (NON-NEED-BASED) *Total amount:* $1,138,024 (95% institutional, 5% external sources). *Average award:* Freshmen: $8110. Undergraduates: $6423. *Scholarships, grants, and awards by category:* Academic interests/achievement: general academic interests/achievements. *Tuition waivers:* Full or partial for employees or children of employees. *ROTC:* Army cooperative.

LOANS *Student loans:* $7,600,007 (48% need-based, 52% non-need-based). 49% of past graduating class borrowed through all loan programs. *Average indebtedness per student:* $12,724. *Average need-based loan:* Freshmen: $3875. Undergraduates: $4005. *Parent loans:* $3,173,010 (100% non-need-based). *Programs:* Federal Direct (Subsidized and Unsubsidized Stafford, PLUS), Perkins.

WORK-STUDY *Federal work-study:* 58 jobs averaging $1406.

APPLYING FOR FINANCIAL AID *Required financial aid form:* FAFSA. *Financial aid deadline:* 3/15 (priority: 3/15). *Notification date:* Continuous beginning 3/1.

CONTACT Laura Biechler, Director of Financial Aid, Fisher College, 118 Beacon Street, Boston, MA 02116, 617-236-8821. *E-mail:* lbiechler@fisher.edu.
Website: http://www.fisher.edu/.

FISK UNIVERSITY
Nashville, TN

CONTACT Mary Chambliss, Director of Financial Aid, Fisk University, 1000 17th Avenue North, Nashville, TN 37208-3051, 615-329-8735 or toll-free 888-702-0022. *E-mail:* mchambliss@fisk.edu.
Website: http://www.fisk.edu/.

FITCHBURG STATE UNIVERSITY
Fitchburg, MA

Tuition & fees (MA res): $10,135	Average undergraduate aid package: $10,238

ABOUT THE INSTITUTION State-supported, coed. *Awards:* certificates, bachelor's, and master's degrees. 61 undergraduate majors. *Total enrollment:* 6,763. Undergraduates: 4,162. Freshmen: 763. Federal methodology is used as a basis for awarding need-based institutional aid.

UNDERGRADUATE EXPENSES for 2016–2017 *Application fee:* $50. *Tuition, state resident:* full-time $970; part-time $40.42 per credit hour. *Tuition, nonresident:* full-time $7050; part-time $293.75 per credit hour. *Required fees:* full-time $9165; $381.89 per credit hour. Full-time tuition and fees vary according to class time and reciprocity agreements. Part-time tuition and fees vary according to class time and reciprocity agreements. *College room and board:* $9210. Room and board charges vary according to board plan and housing facility.

FRESHMAN FINANCIAL AID (Fall 2015) 733 applied for aid; of those 72% were deemed to have need. 97% of freshmen with need received aid. *Average percent of need met:* 76% (excluding resources awarded to replace EFC). *Average financial aid package:* $9419 (excluding resources awarded to replace EFC). 8% of all full-time freshmen had no need and received non-need-based gift aid.

UNDERGRADUATE FINANCIAL AID (Fall 2015) 3,003 applied for aid; of those 75% were deemed to have need. 97% of undergraduates with need received aid. *Average percent of need met:* 76% (excluding resources awarded to replace EFC). *Average financial aid package:* $10,238 (excluding resources awarded to replace EFC). 4% of all full-time undergraduates had no need and received non-need-based gift aid.

GIFT AID (NEED-BASED) *Total amount:* $10,887,365 (60% federal, 18% state, 22% institutional). *Receiving aid:* Freshmen: 45% (354); all full-time undergraduates: 46% (1,588). *Average award:* Freshmen: $6317; Undergraduates: $6126. *Scholarships, grants, and awards:* Federal Pell, FSEOG, state, private, college/university gift aid from institutional funds.

GIFT AID (NON-NEED-BASED) *Total amount:* $1,542,951 (21% state, 37% institutional, 42% external sources). *Receiving aid:* Freshmen: 32% (250). Undergraduates: 22% (764). *Average award:* Freshmen: $903. Undergraduates: $1196. *Scholarships, grants, and awards by category:* Academic interests/achievement: biological sciences, business, communication, computer science, education, engineering/technologies, English, foreign languages, general academic interests/achievements, health fields, mathematics, social sciences. *Special achievements/activities:* general special achievements/activities, leadership. *Special characteristics:* adult students, children and siblings of alumni, ethnic background, local/state students, members of minority groups, out-of-state students, previous college experience, veterans. *Tuition waivers:* Full or partial for employees or children of employees, senior citizens. *ROTC:* Army.

LOANS *Student loans:* $22,265,571 (42% need-based, 58% non-need-based). 84% of past graduating class borrowed through all loan programs. *Average indebtedness per student:* $26,684. *Average need-based loan:* Freshmen: $3979. Undergraduates: $4726. *Parent loans:* $3,274,877 (100% non-need-based). *Programs:* Federal Direct (Subsidized and Unsubsidized Stafford, PLUS), Perkins, Federal Nursing, state.

WORK-STUDY *Federal work-study:* 197 jobs averaging $1713.

APPLYING FOR FINANCIAL AID *Required financial aid form:* FAFSA. *Financial aid deadline (priority):* 3/1. *Notification date:* Continuous beginning 2/1. Students must reply within 2 weeks of notification.

CONTACT Office of Financial Aid, Fitchburg State University, 160 Pearl Street, Fitchburg, MA 01420, 978-665-3156 or toll-free 800-705-9692. *Fax:* 978-665-3559. *E-mail:* finaid@fitchburgstate.edu.
Website: http://www.fitchburgstate.edu/.

FIVE TOWNS COLLEGE
Dix Hills, NY

ABOUT THE INSTITUTION Independent, coed. *Awards:* associate, bachelor's, master's, and doctoral degrees. 19 undergraduate majors. *Total enrollment:* 681. Undergraduates: 654. Freshmen: 120.

GIFT AID (NEED-BASED) *Scholarships, grants, and awards:* Federal Pell, FSEOG, state, private, college/university gift aid from institutional funds.

GIFT AID (NON-NEED-BASED) *Scholarships, grants, and awards by category:* *Academic interests/achievement:* business, education, general academic interests/achievements. *Creative arts/performance:* cinema/film/broadcasting, music, theater/drama.

LOANS *Programs:* Federal Direct (Subsidized and Unsubsidized Stafford, PLUS).

APPLYING FOR FINANCIAL AID *Required financial aid forms:* FAFSA, state aid form.

CONTACT Mr. Jason LaBonte, Financial Aid Director, Five Towns College, 305 North Service Road, Dix Hills, NY 11746-5871, 631-656-2113. *Fax:* 631-656-2191. *E-mail:* jason.labonte@ftc.edu. *Website:* http://www.ftc.edu/.

FLAGLER COLLEGE
St. Augustine, FL

Tuition & fees: $18,300	Average undergraduate aid package: $12,151

ABOUT THE INSTITUTION Independent, coed. *Awards:* bachelor's and master's degrees. 33 undergraduate majors. *Total enrollment:* 2,621. Undergraduates: 2,614. Freshmen: 600. Federal methodology is used as a basis for awarding need-based institutional aid.

UNDERGRADUATE EXPENSES for 2017–2018 *Application fee:* $50. *Comprehensive fee:* $28,988 includes full-time tuition ($18,200), mandatory fees ($100), and room and board ($10,688). *College room only:* $5350. Full-time tuition and fees vary according to location. Room and board charges vary according to board plan and housing facility. *Part-time tuition:* $620 per credit hour. Part-time tuition and fees vary according to location.

FRESHMAN FINANCIAL AID (Fall 2016, est.) 516 applied for aid; of those 77% were deemed to have need. 100% of freshmen with need received aid; of those 15% had need fully met. *Average percent of need met:* 56% (excluding resources awarded to replace EFC). *Average financial aid package:* $12,408 (excluding resources awarded to replace EFC). 25% of all full-time freshmen had no need and received non-need-based gift aid.

UNDERGRADUATE FINANCIAL AID (Fall 2016, est.) 1,941 applied for aid; of those 80% were deemed to have need. 100% of undergraduates with need received aid; of those 14% had need fully met. *Average percent of need met:* 57% (excluding resources awarded to replace EFC). *Average financial aid package:* $12,151 (excluding resources awarded to replace EFC). 18% of all full-time undergraduates had no need and received non-need-based gift aid.

GIFT AID (NEED-BASED) *Total amount:* $12,118,851 (26% federal, 29% state, 43% institutional, 2% external sources). *Receiving aid:* Freshmen: 66% (398); all full-time undergraduates: 59% (1,504). *Average award:* Freshmen: $9298; Undergraduates: $8522. *Scholarships, grants, and awards:* Federal Pell, FSEOG, state, private, college/university gift aid from institutional funds.

GIFT AID (NON-NEED-BASED) *Total amount:* $2,864,784 (52% state, 45% institutional, 3% external sources). *Receiving aid:* Freshmen: 6% (36). Undergraduates: 4% (106). *Average award:* Freshmen: $2628. Undergraduates: $2573. *Scholarships, grants, and awards by category:* *Academic interests/achievement:* business, communication, education, English, foreign languages, general academic interests/achievements, humanities, physical sciences, religion/biblical studies, social sciences. *Creative arts/performance:* applied art and design, art/fine arts, cinema/film/broadcasting, creative writing, performing arts, theater/drama. *Special achievements/activities:* community service, general special achievements/activities, leadership, memberships, religious involvement. *Special characteristics:* children of educators, children of faculty/staff, ethnic background, first-generation college students, general special characteristics, international students, local/state students, members of minority groups, out-of-state students. *Tuition waivers:* Full or partial for employees or children of employees.

LOANS *Student loans:* $15,625,360 (65% need-based, 35% non-need-based). 69% of past graduating class borrowed through all loan programs. *Average indebtedness per student:* $29,267. *Average need-based loan:* Freshmen: $3325. Undergraduates: $4047. *Parent loans:* $3,192,578 (46% need-based, 54% non-need-based). *Programs:* Federal Direct (Subsidized and Unsubsidized Stafford, PLUS), Perkins, state.

WORK-STUDY *Federal work-study:* Total amount: $246,261; 261 jobs averaging $1400. *State or other work-study/employment:* Total amount: $62,750 (100% non-need-based). 57 part-time jobs averaging $1400.

ATHLETIC AWARDS Total amount: $1,715,725 (39% need-based, 61% non-need-based).

APPLYING FOR FINANCIAL AID *Required financial aid forms:* FAFSA, state aid form. *Financial aid deadline (priority):* 3/1. *Notification date:* Continuous beginning 11/1. Students must reply by 5/1 or within 2 weeks of notification.

CONTACT Office of Financial Aid, Flagler College, PO Box 1027, St. Augustine, FL 32085-1027, 904-819-6225 or toll-free 800-304-4208. *Fax:* 904-819-6453. *E-mail:* financialaid@flagler.edu. *Website:* http://www.flagler.edu/.

FLAGLER COLLEGE–TALLAHASSEE
Tallahassee, FL

CONTACT Financial Aid Office, Flagler College–Tallahassee, 444 Appleyard Drive, Tallahassee, FL 32304, 850-201-8070. *Website:* http://www.flagler.edu/.

FLORIDA AGRICULTURAL AND MECHANICAL UNIVERSITY
Tallahassee, FL

Tuition & fees (FL res): $5785	Average undergraduate aid package: $13,113

ABOUT THE INSTITUTION State-supported, coed. *Awards:* certificates, associate, bachelor's, master's, and doctoral degrees. 55 undergraduate majors. *Total enrollment:* 9,619. Undergraduates: 7,769. Freshmen: 1,328. Federal methodology is used as a basis for awarding need-based institutional aid.

UNDERGRADUATE EXPENSES for 2017–2018 *Application fee:* $30. *Tuition, state resident:* full-time $5645; part-time $188.16 per credit hour. *Tuition, nonresident:* full-time $17,585; part-time $586.16 per credit hour. *Required fees:* full-time $140. *College room and board:* $10,058; *Room only:* $5780. Room and board charges vary according to board plan and housing facility. *Payment plan:* Tuition prepayment.

FRESHMAN FINANCIAL AID (Fall 2015) 1,572 applied for aid; of those 89% were deemed to have need. 100% of freshmen with need received aid; of those 16% had need fully met. *Average percent of need met:* 71% (excluding resources awarded to replace EFC). *Average financial aid package:* $13,932 (excluding resources awarded to replace EFC). 3% of all full-time freshmen had no need and received non-need-based gift aid.

UNDERGRADUATE FINANCIAL AID (Fall 2015) 6,672 applied for aid; of those 88% were deemed to have need. 100% of undergraduates with need received aid; of those 14% had need fully met. *Average percent of need met:* 70% (excluding resources awarded to replace EFC). *Average financial aid package:* $13,113 (excluding resources awarded to replace EFC). 2% of all full-time undergraduates had no need and received non-need-based gift aid.

GIFT AID (NEED-BASED) *Total amount:* $30,603,283 (80% federal, 9% state, 11% institutional). *Receiving aid:* Freshmen: 77% (1,225); all full-time undergraduates: 73% (5,073). *Average award:* Freshmen: $6303; Undergraduates: $5817. *Scholarships, grants, and awards:* Federal Pell, FSEOG, state, private, college/university gift aid from institutional funds, United Negro College Fund.

GIFT AID (NON-NEED-BASED) *Total amount:* $13,080,293 (31% state, 27% institutional, 42% external sources). *Receiving aid:* Freshmen: 44% (705). Undergraduates: 33% (2,281). *Average award:* Freshmen: $7709. Undergraduates: $6521. *Scholarships, grants, and awards by category:* *Academic interests/achievement:* agriculture, architecture, area/ethnic studies, biological sciences, business, communication, computer science, education, engineering/technologies, English, foreign languages, general academic interests/achievements, health fields, humanities, mathematics, military science, physical sciences, premedicine, social sciences. *Creative arts/performance:* applied art and design, art/fine arts, cinema/film/broadcasting, creative writing, dance, journalism/publications, music, performing arts, theater/drama. *Special achievements/activities:* cheerleading/drum major, community service, general special achievements/activities, leadership. *Special characteristics:* 303 awards ($1,192,432 total): ethnic background, first-generation college students, general special characteristics, local/state students, out-of-state students. *Tuition waivers:*

Full or partial for employees or children of employees, senior citizens. **ROTC:** Army, Naval, Air Force cooperative.
LOANS Student loans: $37,292,760 (48% need-based, 52% non-need-based). 86% of past graduating class borrowed through all loan programs. *Average indebtedness per student:* $33,568. *Average need-based loan:* Freshmen: $3316. Undergraduates: $3902. *Parent loans:* $11,568,058 (100% non-need-based). *Programs:* Federal Direct (Subsidized and Unsubsidized Stafford, PLUS), Perkins, private loans.
WORK-STUDY Federal work-study: 194 jobs averaging $2123.
ATHLETIC AWARDS Total amount: $2,644,962 (100% non-need-based).
APPLYING FOR FINANCIAL AID Required financial aid form: FAFSA. *Financial aid deadline (priority):* 3/1. *Notification date:* Continuous beginning 4/15.
CONTACT Ms. Lisa A. Stewart, Director of Financial Aid, Florida Agricultural and Mechanical University, 101 Foote-Hilyer Administration Center, Tallahassee, FL 32307, 850-599-3730 or toll-free 866-642-1198.
Website: http://www.famu.edu/.

FLORIDA ATLANTIC UNIVERSITY
Boca Raton, FL

Tuition & fees (FL res): $6039	Average undergraduate aid package: $13,345

ABOUT THE INSTITUTION State-supported, coed. *Awards:* certificates, associate, bachelor's, master's, and doctoral degrees. 63 undergraduate majors. *Total enrollment:* 30,538. Undergraduates: 25,400. Freshmen: 3,180. Federal methodology is used as a basis for awarding need-based institutional aid.
UNDERGRADUATE EXPENSES for 2017–2018 Application fee: $30. *Tuition, state resident:* full-time $6039; part-time $105.07 per credit hour. *Tuition, nonresident:* full-time $21,595; part-time $598.93 per credit hour. *Required fees:* $96.22 per credit hour. Full-time tuition and fees vary according to course load. Part-time tuition and fees vary according to course load. *College room and board:* $12,050. Room and board charges vary according to board plan and housing facility. *Payment plan:* Tuition prepayment.
FRESHMAN FINANCIAL AID (Fall 2016, est.) 2,516 applied for aid; of those 75% were deemed to have need. 98% of freshmen with need received aid; of those 17% had need fully met. *Average percent of need met:* 68% (excluding resources awarded to replace EFC). *Average financial aid package:* $13,551 (excluding resources awarded to replace EFC). 4% of all full-time freshmen had no need and received non-need-based gift aid.
UNDERGRADUATE FINANCIAL AID (Fall 2016, est.) 11,501 applied for aid; of those 83% were deemed to have need. 98% of undergraduates with need received aid; of those 13% had need fully met. *Average percent of need met:* 63% (excluding resources awarded to replace EFC). *Average financial aid package:* $13,345 (excluding resources awarded to replace EFC). 1% of all full-time undergraduates had no need and received non-need-based gift aid.
GIFT AID (NEED-BASED) Total amount: $67,535,077 (66% federal, 12% state, 19% institutional, 3% external sources). *Receiving aid:* Freshmen: 51% (1,546); all full-time undergraduates: 48% (7,735). *Average award:* Freshmen: $8472; Undergraduates: $6604. *Scholarships, grants, and awards:* Federal Pell, FSEOG, state, private, college/university gift aid from institutional funds, United Negro College Fund, Federal Nursing.
GIFT AID (NON-NEED-BASED) Total amount: $8,458,455 (46% state, 23% institutional, 31% external sources). *Receiving aid:* Freshmen: 11% (322). Undergraduates: 6% (927). *Average award:* Freshmen: $4023. Undergraduates: $3483. *Scholarships, grants, and awards by category:* Academic interests/achievement: business, engineering/technologies, general academic interests/achievements, physical sciences, social sciences. Creative arts/performance: music, performing arts. *Tuition waivers:* Full or partial for employees or children of employees, senior citizens. **ROTC:** Army, Air Force cooperative.
LOANS Student loans: $136,530,915 (75% need-based, 25% non-need-based). 53% of past graduating class borrowed through all loan programs. *Average indebtedness per student:* $22,648. *Average need-based loan:* Freshmen: $5578. Undergraduates: $7236. *Parent loans:* $9,837,704 (44% need-based, 56% non-need-based). *Programs:* Federal Direct (Subsidized and Unsubsidized Stafford, PLUS), Perkins, Federal Nursing, college/university.

WORK-STUDY Federal work-study: Total amount: $1,020,941; 226 jobs averaging $2230. *State or other work-study/employment:* Total amount: $23,760 (100% need-based). 6 part-time jobs averaging $2329.
ATHLETIC AWARDS Total amount: $5,410,846 (22% need-based, 78% non-need-based).
APPLYING FOR FINANCIAL AID Required financial aid form: FAFSA. *Notification date:* Continuous.
CONTACT Tracy Boulukos, Director of Student Financial Aid, Florida Atlantic University, 777 Glades Road, Boca Raton, FL 33431-0991, 561-297-3528. *E-mail:* tbouluko@fau.edu.
Website: http://www.fau.edu/.

FLORIDA COLLEGE
Temple Terrace, FL

Tuition & fees: $16,550	Average undergraduate aid package: $10,644

ABOUT THE INSTITUTION Independent, coed. *Awards:* associate and bachelor's degrees. 10 undergraduate majors. *Total enrollment:* 533. Undergraduates: 533. Freshmen: 150. Both federal and institutional methodology are used as a basis for awarding need-based institutional aid.
UNDERGRADUATE EXPENSES for 2016–2017 Application fee: $40. *Comprehensive fee:* $24,780 includes full-time tuition ($15,670), mandatory fees ($880), and room and board ($8230). *College room only:* $4180. Room and board charges vary according to board plan and housing facility. *Part-time tuition:* $618 per credit hour. Part-time tuition and fees vary according to course load.
FRESHMAN FINANCIAL AID (Fall 2015) 155 applied for aid; of those 80% were deemed to have need. 100% of freshmen with need received aid; of those 11% had need fully met. *Average percent of need met:* 49% (excluding resources awarded to replace EFC). *Average financial aid package:* $10,026 (excluding resources awarded to replace EFC). 3% of all full-time freshmen had no need and received non-need-based gift aid.
UNDERGRADUATE FINANCIAL AID (Fall 2015) 434 applied for aid; of those 86% were deemed to have need. 100% of undergraduates with need received aid; of those 11% had need fully met. *Average percent of need met:* 56% (excluding resources awarded to replace EFC). *Average financial aid package:* $10,644 (excluding resources awarded to replace EFC). 13% of all full-time undergraduates had no need and received non-need-based gift aid.
GIFT AID (NEED-BASED) Total amount: $2,509,980 (30% federal, 1% state, 69% institutional). *Receiving aid:* Freshmen: 56% (106); all full-time undergraduates: 57% (319). *Average award:* Freshmen: $5779; Undergraduates: $7068. *Scholarships, grants, and awards:* Federal Pell, FSEOG, state, private, college/university gift aid from institutional funds.
GIFT AID (NON-NEED-BASED) Total amount: $1,749,523 (35% state, 35% institutional, 30% external sources). *Receiving aid:* Freshmen: 62% (116). Undergraduates: 61% (341). *Average award:* Freshmen: $3449. Undergraduates: $4048. *Scholarships, grants, and awards by category:* Academic interests/achievement: business, communication, education, English, general academic interests/achievements, religion/biblical studies. Creative arts/performance: music. Special achievements/activities: general special achievements/activities. Special characteristics: 30 awards ($286,609 total): children of faculty/staff. *Tuition waivers:* Full or partial for employees or children of employees. **ROTC:** Army cooperative, Air Force cooperative.
LOANS Student loans: $2,058,056 (71% need-based, 29% non-need-based). *Average need-based loan:* Freshmen: $3501. Undergraduates: $4113. *Parent loans:* $1,820,507 (44% need-based, 56% non-need-based). *Programs:* Federal Direct (Subsidized and Unsubsidized Stafford, PLUS), Perkins.
WORK-STUDY Federal work-study: 35 jobs averaging $665. *State or other work-study/employment:* Part-time jobs available.
ATHLETIC AWARDS Total amount: $244,753 (100% non-need-based).
APPLYING FOR FINANCIAL AID Required financial aid form: FAFSA. *Financial aid deadline (priority):* 1/1. *Notification date:* Continuous beginning 11/1. Students must reply by 9/1.
CONTACT Stephen Blaylock, Director of Financial Aid, Florida College, 119 North Glen Arven Avenue, Temple Terrace, FL 33617, 813-988-5131 Ext. 130. *Fax:* 813-899-6772. *E-mail:* blaylock@floridacollege.edu.
Website: http://www.floridacollege.edu/.

FLORIDA GULF COAST UNIVERSITY
Fort Myers, FL

Tuition & fees: N/R	Average undergraduate aid package: $9585

ABOUT THE INSTITUTION State-supported, coed. *Awards:* certificates, associate, bachelor's, master's, and doctoral degrees. 43 undergraduate majors. *Total enrollment:* 14,840. Undergraduates: 13,711. Freshmen: 2,652. Federal methodology is used as a basis for awarding need-based institutional aid.
FRESHMAN FINANCIAL AID (Fall 2015) 1,926 applied for aid; of those 70% were deemed to have need. 100% of freshmen with need received aid; of those 6% had need fully met. *Average percent of need met:* 41% (excluding resources awarded to replace EFC). *Average financial aid package:* $9123 (excluding resources awarded to replace EFC). 2% of all full-time freshmen had no need and received non-need-based gift aid.
UNDERGRADUATE FINANCIAL AID (Fall 2015) 7,883 applied for aid; of those 67% were deemed to have need. 100% of undergraduates with need received aid; of those 9% had need fully met. *Average percent of need met:* 56% (excluding resources awarded to replace EFC). *Average financial aid package:* $9585 (excluding resources awarded to replace EFC). 3% of all full-time undergraduates had no need and received non-need-based gift aid.
GIFT AID (NEED-BASED) Total amount: $28,837,823 (59% federal, 16% state, 22% institutional, 3% external sources). *Receiving aid:* Freshmen: 33% (854); all full-time undergraduates: 36% (3,865). *Average award:* Freshmen: $4860; Undergraduates: $5299. *Scholarships, grants, and awards:* Federal Pell, FSEOG, state, private, college/university gift aid from institutional funds.
GIFT AID (NON-NEED-BASED) Total amount: $5,038,005 (52% state, 24% institutional, 24% external sources). *Receiving aid:* Freshmen: 19% (507). Undergraduates: 16% (1,699). *Average award:* Freshmen: $4312. Undergraduates: $3888. *Scholarships, grants, and awards by category:* Academic interests/achievement: biological sciences, business, education, engineering/technologies, general academic interests/achievements, health fields, humanities, mathematics, physical sciences, religion/biblical studies, social sciences. *Creative arts/performance:* art/fine arts, music. *Special achievements/activities:* community service, leadership. *Special characteristics:* adult students, ethnic background, handicapped students, international students, local/state students, members of minority groups, out-of-state students.
LOANS Student loans: $42,976,417 (78% need-based, 22% non-need-based). 50% of past graduating class borrowed through all loan programs. *Average indebtedness per student:* $24,763. *Average need-based loan:* Freshmen: $7369. Undergraduates: $7128. *Programs:* Federal Direct (Subsidized and Unsubsidized Stafford, PLUS).
WORK-STUDY Federal work-study: jobs available. *State or other work-study/employment:* Total amount: $9,169,650 (100% need-based). Part-time jobs available.
ATHLETIC AWARDS Total amount: $1,026,352 (100% non-need-based).
APPLYING FOR FINANCIAL AID Required financial aid forms: FAFSA, institution's own form, state aid form. *Financial aid deadline:* 6/30 (priority: 3/1). *Notification date:* Continuous.
CONTACT Jorge Lopez-Rosado, Director of Student Financial Services, Florida Gulf Coast University, 10501 FGCU Boulevard South, Fort Myers, FL 33965, 239-590-1210 or toll-free 888-889-1095. *Fax:* 239-590-7923. *E-mail:* faso@fgcu.edu.
Website: http://www.fgcu.edu/.

FLORIDA INSTITUTE OF TECHNOLOGY
Melbourne, FL

Tuition & fees: $41,240	Average undergraduate aid package: $36,720

ABOUT THE INSTITUTION Independent, coed. *Awards:* certificates, bachelor's, master's, and doctoral degrees. 66 undergraduate majors. *Total enrollment:* 6,451. Undergraduates: 3,629. Freshmen: 761. Federal methodology is used as a basis for awarding need-based institutional aid.

UNDERGRADUATE EXPENSES for 2017–2018 Comprehensive fee: $54,120 includes full-time tuition ($40,490), mandatory fees ($750), and room and board ($12,880). *College room only:* $7000. Full-time tuition and fees vary according to course load and program. Room and board charges vary according to board plan and housing facility. *Part-time tuition:* $1170 per credit hour.
FRESHMAN FINANCIAL AID (Fall 2016, est.) 533 applied for aid; of those 86% were deemed to have need. 100% of freshmen with need received aid; of those 48% had need fully met. *Average percent of need met:* 89% (excluding resources awarded to replace EFC). *Average financial aid package:* $36,771 (excluding resources awarded to replace EFC). 30% of all full-time freshmen had no need and received non-need-based gift aid.
UNDERGRADUATE FINANCIAL AID (Fall 2016, est.) 1,845 applied for aid; of those 90% were deemed to have need. 100% of undergraduates with need received aid; of those 39% had need fully met. *Average percent of need met:* 86% (excluding resources awarded to replace EFC). *Average financial aid package:* $36,720 (excluding resources awarded to replace EFC). 33% of all full-time undergraduates had no need and received non-need-based gift aid.
GIFT AID (NEED-BASED) Total amount: $39,799,000 (15% federal, 9% state, 75% institutional, 1% external sources). *Receiving aid:* Freshmen: 60% (458); all full-time undergraduates: 51% (1,661). *Average award:* Freshmen: $25,931; Undergraduates: $25,435. *Scholarships, grants, and awards:* Federal Pell, FSEOG, state, private, college/university gift aid from institutional funds.
GIFT AID (NON-NEED-BASED) Total amount: $20,721,274 (5% federal, 4% state, 91% institutional). *Receiving aid:* Freshmen: 60% (457). Undergraduates: 49% (1,615). *Average award:* Freshmen: $16,185. Undergraduates: $15,123. *Scholarships, grants, and awards by category:* Academic interests/achievement: 2,258 awards ($32,660,123 total): business, general academic interests/achievements, military science. *Creative arts/performance:* 26 awards ($28,250 total): music. *Special achievements/activities:* 120 awards ($1,484,750 total): cheerleading/drum major, general special achievements/activities, hobbies/interests, leadership, memberships. *Special characteristics:* 1,550 awards ($7,178,563 total): children and siblings of alumni, children of faculty/staff, general special characteristics, international students, previous college experience, siblings of current students. *Tuition waivers:* Full or partial for employees or children of employees, senior citizens. *ROTC:* Army.
LOANS Student loans: $14,173,748 (93% need-based, 7% non-need-based). 52% of past graduating class borrowed through all loan programs. *Average indebtedness per student:* $36,678. *Average need-based loan:* Freshmen: $3673. Undergraduates: $5059. *Parent loans:* $11,797,404 (94% need-based, 6% non-need-based). *Programs:* Federal Direct (Subsidized and Unsubsidized Stafford, PLUS), Perkins, state, college/university.
WORK-STUDY Federal work-study: Total amount: $1,454,411; 634 jobs averaging $2294. *State or other work-study/employment:* 423 part-time jobs averaging $6315.
ATHLETIC AWARDS Total amount: $7,167,526 (50% need-based, 50% non-need-based).
APPLYING FOR FINANCIAL AID Required financial aid forms: FAFSA, state aid form. *Financial aid deadline (priority):* 3/1. *Notification date:* Continuous beginning 11/1. Students must reply by 5/1 or within 4 weeks of notification.
CONTACT Mr. John W. Duncan, Office of Financial Aid, Florida Institute of Technology, 150 West University Boulevard, Melbourne, FL 32901-6975, 321-674-8063 or toll-free 800-888-4348. *Fax:* 321-724-2778. *E-mail:* finaid@fit.edu. *Website:* http://www.fit.edu/.

FLORIDA INTERNATIONAL UNIVERSITY
Miami, FL

Tuition & fees (FL res): $6558	Average undergraduate aid package: $8370

ABOUT THE INSTITUTION State-supported, coed. *Awards:* certificates, bachelor's, master's, and doctoral degrees. 65 undergraduate majors. *Total enrollment:* 55,111. Undergraduates: 45,813. Freshmen: 4,551. Federal methodology is used as a basis for awarding need-based institutional aid.
UNDERGRADUATE EXPENSES for 2017–2018 Application fee: $30. *Tuition, state resident:* full-time $6168; part-time $205.57 per credit hour. *Tuition, nonresident:* full-time $18,566; part-time $618.87 per credit hour.

Required fees: full-time $390. **College room and board:** $10,846; **Room only:** $6487. Room and board charges vary according to board plan and housing facility.
FRESHMAN FINANCIAL AID (Fall 2015) 2,884 applied for aid; of those 100% were deemed to have need. 94% of freshmen with need received aid; of those 6% had need fully met. **Average percent of need met:** 24% (excluding resources awarded to replace EFC). **Average financial aid package:** $7204 (excluding resources awarded to replace EFC). 12% of all full-time freshmen had no need and received non-need-based gift aid.
UNDERGRADUATE FINANCIAL AID (Fall 2015) 18,636 applied for aid; of those 99% were deemed to have need. 96% of undergraduates with need received aid; of those 8% had need fully met. **Average percent of need met:** 23% (excluding resources awarded to replace EFC). **Average financial aid package:** $8370 (excluding resources awarded to replace EFC). 4% of all full-time undergraduates had no need and received non-need-based gift aid.
GIFT AID (NEED-BASED) Total amount: $122,920,099 (72% federal, 10% state, 18% institutional). **Receiving aid:** Freshmen: 49% (2,233); all full-time undergraduates: 55% (14,547). **Average award:** Freshmen: $5293; Undergraduates: $5654. **Scholarships, grants, and awards:** Federal Pell, FSEOG, state, private, college/university gift aid from institutional funds.
GIFT AID (NON-NEED-BASED) Total amount: $46,108,100 (9% federal, 27% state, 56% institutional, 8% external sources). **Receiving aid:** Freshmen: 27% (1,212). Undergraduates: 21% (5,593). **Average award:** Freshmen: $1771. Undergraduates: $2234. **Scholarships, grants, and awards by category:** Academic interests/achievement: architecture, biological sciences, business, communication, computer science, education, engineering/technologies, English, foreign languages, general academic interests/achievements, health fields, humanities, mathematics, physical sciences, social sciences. Creative arts/performance: art/fine arts, dance, journalism/publications, music, performing arts, theater/drama. Special characteristics: first-generation college students, veterans, veterans' children. **Tuition waivers:** Full or partial for employees or children of employees. **ROTC:** Army, Air Force.
LOANS Student loans: $287,769,609 (26% need-based, 74% non-need-based). 50% of past graduating class borrowed through all loan programs. Average indebtedness per student: $19,915. **Average need-based loan:** Freshmen: $3225. Undergraduates: $4666. **Parent loans:** $4,660,426 (1% need-based, 99% non-need-based). **Programs:** Federal Direct (Subsidized and Unsubsidized Stafford, PLUS), Perkins, college/university.
WORK-STUDY Federal work-study: jobs available. **State or other work-study/employment:** Total amount: $126,522 (100% need-based). Part-time jobs available.
ATHLETIC AWARDS Total amount: $5,075,282 (100% non-need-based).
APPLYING FOR FINANCIAL AID Required financial aid form: FAFSA. **Financial aid deadline:** 5/15 (priority: 3/1). **Notification date:** Continuous beginning 2/1. Students must reply by 5/1 or within 4 weeks of notification.
CONTACT Francisco Valines, Director of Financial Aid, Florida International University, 11200 SW 8th Street, PC 125, Miami, FL 33199, 305-348-7272. Fax: 305-348-2346. E-mail: francisco.valines@fiu.edu.
Website: http://www.fiu.edu/.

FLORIDA MEMORIAL UNIVERSITY
Miami-Dade, FL

CONTACT Brian Phillip, Director of Financial Aid, Florida Memorial University, 15800 Northwest 42nd Avenue, Miami, FL 33054, 305-626-3745 or toll-free 800-822-1362. Fax: 305-626-3106.
Website: http://www.fmuniv.edu/.

FLORIDA NATIONAL UNIVERSITY
Hialeah, FL

Tuition & fees: $13,250	Average undergraduate aid package: N/A

ABOUT THE INSTITUTION Proprietary, coed. **Awards:** certificates, diplomas, associate, bachelor's, and master's degrees. 33 undergraduate majors. **Total enrollment:** 3,251. Undergraduates: 3,191. Freshmen: 644. Federal methodology is used as a basis for awarding need-based institutional aid.

UNDERGRADUATE EXPENSES for 2016–2017 Tuition: full-time $12,600; part-time $525 per credit. **Payment plans:** Guaranteed tuition, tuition prepayment.
FRESHMAN FINANCIAL AID (Fall 2015) 360 applied for aid; of those 92% were deemed to have need. 99% of freshmen with need received aid.
UNDERGRADUATE FINANCIAL AID (Fall 2015) 2,376 applied for aid; of those 95% were deemed to have need. 100% of undergraduates with need received aid.
GIFT AID (NEED-BASED) Total amount: $13,533,072 (77% federal, 5% state, 18% institutional). **Receiving aid:** Freshmen: 87% (321); all full-time undergraduates: 88% (2,211). **Average award:** Freshmen: $5750; Undergraduates: $5750. **Scholarships, grants, and awards:** Federal Pell, FSEOG, state, private, college/university gift aid from institutional funds.
GIFT AID (NON-NEED-BASED) Tuition waivers: Full or partial for employees or children of employees.
LOANS Student loans: $17,890,424 (100% need-based). 95% of past graduating class borrowed through all loan programs. **Parent loans:** $598,927 (100% need-based). **Programs:** Federal Direct (Subsidized and Unsubsidized Stafford, PLUS), Perkins.
WORK-STUDY Federal work-study: 42 jobs averaging $8320. **State or other work-study/employment:** Part-time jobs available.
ATHLETIC AWARDS Total amount: $417,092 (100% need-based).
APPLYING FOR FINANCIAL AID Required financial aid form: FAFSA. **Financial aid deadline:** Continuous. **Notification date:** Continuous.
CONTACT Mr. Omar Sanchez, Director of Financial Aid, Florida National University, 4425 West Jose Regueiro (20th) Avenue, Hialeah, FL 33012, 305-821-3333 Ext. 1003. Fax: 305-362-0595. E-mail: omarsnc@fnu.edu.
Website: http://www.fnu.edu/.

FLORIDA SOUTHERN COLLEGE
Lakeland, FL

Tuition & fees: $33,150	Average undergraduate aid package: $26,342

ABOUT THE INSTITUTION Independent United Methodist Church, coed. **Awards:** bachelor's, master's, and doctoral degrees. 62 undergraduate majors. **Total enrollment:** 2,765. Undergraduates: 2,386. Freshmen: 648. Federal methodology is used as a basis for awarding need-based institutional aid.
UNDERGRADUATE EXPENSES for 2016–2017 Application fee: $30. **Comprehensive fee:** $43,830 includes full-time tuition ($32,450), mandatory fees ($700), and room and board ($10,680). **College room only:** $6330. Room and board charges vary according to board plan and housing facility. **Part-time tuition:** $936 per credit hour. Part-time tuition and fees vary according to class time and course load.
FRESHMAN FINANCIAL AID (Fall 2016, est.) 587 applied for aid; of those 82% were deemed to have need. 100% of freshmen with need received aid; of those 28% had need fully met. **Average percent of need met:** 76% (excluding resources awarded to replace EFC). **Average financial aid package:** $27,586 (excluding resources awarded to replace EFC). 25% of all full-time freshmen had no need and received non-need-based gift aid.
UNDERGRADUATE FINANCIAL AID (Fall 2016, est.) 1,830 applied for aid; of those 85% were deemed to have need. 100% of undergraduates with need received aid; of those 25% had need fully met. **Average percent of need met:** 73% (excluding resources awarded to replace EFC). **Average financial aid package:** $26,342 (excluding resources awarded to replace EFC). 32% of all full-time undergraduates had no need and received non-need-based gift aid.
GIFT AID (NEED-BASED) Total amount: $34,075,971 (8% federal, 14% state, 75% institutional, 3% external sources). **Receiving aid:** Freshmen: 75% (481); all full-time undergraduates: 67% (1,543). **Average award:** Freshmen: $22,691; Undergraduates: $20,145. **Scholarships, grants, and awards:** Federal Pell, FSEOG, state, private, college/university gift aid from institutional funds, Federal Nursing.
GIFT AID (NON-NEED-BASED) Total amount: $12,527,048 (13% state, 82% institutional, 5% external sources). **Receiving aid:** Freshmen: 48% (311). Undergraduates: 45% (1,051). **Average award:** Freshmen: $20,580. Undergraduates: $19,947. **Scholarships, grants, and awards by category:** Academic interests/achievement: agriculture, biological sciences, business, communication, education, general academic interests/achievements, health fields, physical sciences, religion/biblical studies, social sciences. Creative arts/performance: art/fine arts, music, theater/drama. Special achievements/activities: community service, general special achieve-

ments/activities, leadership. *Special characteristics:* children and siblings of alumni, children of faculty/staff, general special characteristics, local/state students, out-of-state students, relatives of clergy, religious affiliation, siblings of current students. *Tuition waivers:* Full or partial for children of alumni, employees or children of employees. *ROTC:* Army, Air Force cooperative.

LOANS *Student loans:* $16,325,362 (88% need-based, 12% non-need-based). 81% of past graduating class borrowed through all loan programs. *Average indebtedness per student:* $26,637. *Average need-based loan:* Freshmen: $4303. Undergraduates: $5776. *Parent loans:* $5,849,768 (88% need-based, 12% non-need-based). *Programs:* Federal Direct (Subsidized and Unsubsidized Stafford, PLUS), Perkins.

WORK-STUDY *Federal work-study:* Total amount: $374,404; jobs available. *State or other work-study/employment:* Part-time jobs available.

ATHLETIC AWARDS Total amount: $3,850,428 (40% need-based, 60% non-need-based).

APPLYING FOR FINANCIAL AID *Required financial aid forms:* FAFSA, institution's own form. *Financial aid deadline:* 7/1 (priority: 3/1). *Notification date:* Continuous beginning 3/1. Students must reply within 3 weeks of notification.

CONTACT Mr. William L. Healy, Director of Financial Aid, Florida Southern College, 111 Lake Hollingsworth Drive, Lakeland, FL 33801-5698, 863-680-4140 or toll-free 800-274-4131. *Fax:* 863-680-4567. *E-mail:* whealy@flsouthern.edu. *Website:* http://www.flsouthern.edu/.

FLORIDA STATE UNIVERSITY
Tallahassee, FL

Tuition & fees (FL res): $6507	Average undergraduate aid package: $11,761

ABOUT THE INSTITUTION State-supported, coed. *Awards:* certificates, associate, bachelor's, master's, and doctoral degrees. 51 undergraduate majors. *Total enrollment:* 41,368. Undergraduates: 32,929. Freshmen: 6,277. Federal methodology is used as a basis for awarding need-based institutional aid.

UNDERGRADUATE EXPENSES for 2016–2017 *Application fee:* $30. *Tuition, state resident:* full-time $4640; part-time $215.55 per credit hour. *Tuition, nonresident:* full-time $19,806; part-time $721.10 per credit hour. *Required fees:* full-time $1867. Full-time tuition and fees vary according to course load, degree level, and location. Part-time tuition and fees vary according to course load, degree level, and location. *College room and board:* $10,304; *Room only:* $6256. Room and board charges vary according to board plan and housing facility. *Payment plan:* Tuition prepayment.

FRESHMAN FINANCIAL AID (Fall 2015) 4,969 applied for aid; of those 62% were deemed to have need. 99% of freshmen with need received aid; of those 10% had need fully met. *Average percent of need met:* 66% (excluding resources awarded to replace EFC). *Average financial aid package:* $12,519 (excluding resources awarded to replace EFC). 11% of all full-time freshmen had no need and received non-need-based gift aid.

UNDERGRADUATE FINANCIAL AID (Fall 2015) 20,930 applied for aid; of those 69% were deemed to have need. 89% of undergraduates with need received aid; of those 8% had need fully met. *Average percent of need met:* 62% (excluding resources awarded to replace EFC). *Average financial aid package:* $11,761 (excluding resources awarded to replace EFC). 15% of all full-time undergraduates had no need and received non-need-based gift aid.

GIFT AID (NEED-BASED) *Total amount:* $101,192,170 (39% federal, 30% state, 27% institutional, 4% external sources). *Receiving aid:* Freshmen: 47% (2,867); all full-time undergraduates: 38% (11,097). *Average award:* Freshmen: $10,742; Undergraduates: $9000. *Scholarships, grants, and awards:* Federal Pell, FSEOG, state, private, college/university gift aid from institutional funds, Academic Competitiveness Grants, National SMART Grants.

GIFT AID (NON-NEED-BASED) *Total amount:* $15,452,916 (71% state, 20% institutional, 9% external sources). *Receiving aid:* Freshmen: 37% (2,234). Undergraduates: 30% (8,550). *Average award:* Freshmen: $3992. Undergraduates: $3831. *Scholarships, grants, and awards by category:* Academic interests/achievement: general academic interests/achievements. Creative arts/performance: cinema/film/broadcasting, dance, music, theater/drama. Special characteristics: local/state students. *Tuition waivers:* Full or partial for employees or children of employees, senior citizens. *ROTC:* Army, Naval cooperative, Air Force.

LOANS *Student loans:* $85,763,517 (77% need-based, 23% non-need-based). 50% of past graduating class borrowed through all loan programs. *Average indebtedness per student:* $23,679. *Average need-based loan:* Freshmen: $3341. Undergraduates: $4363. *Parent loans:* $11,826,999 (44% need-based, 56% non-need-based). *Programs:* Federal Direct (Subsidized and Unsubsidized Stafford, PLUS), Perkins, college/university.

WORK-STUDY *Federal work-study:* 780 jobs averaging $2400. *State or other work-study/employment:* 34 part-time jobs averaging $2400.

ATHLETIC AWARDS Total amount: $6,325,259 (90% need-based, 10% non-need-based).

APPLYING FOR FINANCIAL AID *Required financial aid form:* FAFSA. *Financial aid deadline:* Continuous. *Notification date:* Continuous beginning 3/1.

CONTACT Darryl Marshall, Director of Financial Aid, Florida State University, University Center A4400, Tallahassee, FL 32306-2430, 850-644-5716. *Fax:* 850-644-6404. *E-mail:* ofacs@admin.fsu.edu. *Website:* http://www.fsu.edu/.

FONTBONNE UNIVERSITY
St. Louis, MO

ABOUT THE INSTITUTION Independent Roman Catholic, coed. *Awards:* certificates, bachelor's, and master's degrees. 38 undergraduate majors. *Total enrollment:* 1,713. Undergraduates: 1,099. Freshmen: 178.

GIFT AID (NEED-BASED) *Scholarships, grants, and awards:* Federal Pell, FSEOG, state, private, college/university gift aid from institutional funds.

GIFT AID (NON-NEED-BASED) *Scholarships, grants, and awards by category:* Academic interests/achievement: computer science, English, general academic interests/achievements. Creative arts/performance: art/fine arts, creative writing, theater/drama. Special achievements/activities: community service, general special achievements/activities, leadership. Special characteristics: religious affiliation, siblings of current students.

LOANS *Programs:* Federal Direct (Subsidized and Unsubsidized Stafford, PLUS), Perkins, CitiAssist loans.

WORK-STUDY *Federal work-study:* 116 jobs averaging $1546. *State or other work-study/employment:* Total amount: $122,454 (100% non-need-based). 76 part-time jobs averaging $1623.

APPLYING FOR FINANCIAL AID *Required financial aid forms:* FAFSA, institution's own form.

CONTACT Financial Aid Office, Fontbonne University, 6800 Wydown Boulevard, St. Louis, MO 63105-3098, 314-889-1414 or toll-free 800-205-5862. *Fax:* 314-889-1457. *E-mail:* fbufinaid@fontbonne.edu. *Website:* http://www.fontbonne.edu/.

FORDHAM UNIVERSITY
New York, NY

Tuition & fees: $49,073	Average undergraduate aid package: $33,566

ABOUT THE INSTITUTION Independent Roman Catholic (Jesuit), coed. *Awards:* certificates, bachelor's, master's, and doctoral degrees (branch locations at Rose Hill and Lincoln Center). 66 undergraduate majors. *Total enrollment:* 15,582. Undergraduates: 9,258. Freshmen: 2,199. Both federal and institutional methodology are used as a basis for awarding need-based institutional aid.

UNDERGRADUATE EXPENSES for 2016–2017 *Application fee:* $70. *Comprehensive fee:* $65,918 includes full-time tuition ($47,850), mandatory fees ($1223), and room and board ($16,845). Room and board charges vary according to board plan, housing facility, and location. Part-time tuition and fees vary according to class time and course load.

FRESHMAN FINANCIAL AID (Fall 2015) 1,943 applied for aid; of those 71% were deemed to have need. 100% of freshmen with need received aid; of those 31% had need fully met. *Average percent of need met:* 81% (excluding resources awarded to replace EFC). *Average financial aid package:* $34,004 (excluding resources awarded to replace EFC). 27% of all full-time freshmen had no need and received non-need-based gift aid.

UNDERGRADUATE FINANCIAL AID (Fall 2015) 6,960 applied for aid; of those 75% were deemed to have need. 100% of undergraduates with need received aid; of those 29% had need fully met. *Average percent of need met:* 78% (excluding resources awarded to replace EFC). *Average financial aid package:* $33,566 (excluding resources awarded to replace EFC). 21% of all full-time undergraduates had no need and received non-need-based gift aid.

GIFT AID (NEED-BASED) *Total amount:* $121,140,581 (7% federal, 5% state, 83% institutional, 5% external sources). *Receiving aid:* Freshmen: 62% (1,356); all full-time undergraduates: 60% (5,009). *Average award:* Freshmen: $26,779; Undergraduates: $25,493. *Scholarships, grants, and awards:* Federal Pell, FSEOG, state, private, college/university gift aid from institutional funds.

GIFT AID (NON-NEED-BASED) *Total amount:* $37,293,989 (2% state, 87% institutional, 11% external sources). *Receiving aid:* Freshmen: 15% (320). Undergraduates: 12% (979). *Average award:* Freshmen: $16,180. Undergraduates: $15,724. *Scholarships, grants, and awards by category: Academic interests/achievement:* biological sciences, business, communication, foreign languages, general academic interests/achievements. *Creative arts/performance:* dance, music. *Special achievements/activities:* general special achievements/activities. *Special characteristics:* adult students, children and siblings of alumni, children of faculty/staff, children with a deceased or disabled parent, handicapped students. *Tuition waivers:* Full or partial for employees or children of employees. *ROTC:* Army, Naval cooperative, Air Force cooperative.

LOANS *Student loans:* $49,984,641 (59% need-based, 41% non-need-based). 60% of past graduating class borrowed through all loan programs. *Average indebtedness per student:* $25,069. *Average need-based loan:* Freshmen: $5095. Undergraduates: $6396. *Parent loans:* $23,658,431 (44% need-based, 56% non-need-based). *Programs:* Federal Direct (Subsidized and Unsubsidized Stafford, PLUS), Perkins.

WORK-STUDY *Federal work-study:* jobs available. *State or other work-study/employment:* Part-time jobs available.

ATHLETIC AWARDS Total amount: $12,089,165 (64% need-based, 36% non-need-based).

APPLYING FOR FINANCIAL AID *Required financial aid forms:* FAFSA, CSS Financial Aid PROFILE, state aid form, noncustodial (divorced/separated) parent's statement, business/farm supplement. *Financial aid deadline:* 2/1. *Notification date:* Continuous beginning 3/31. Students must reply by 5/1 or within 2 weeks of notification.

CONTACT Angela Van Dekker, Assistant Vice President of Student Financial Services, Fordham University, 441 East Fordham Road, Thebaud Hall, Room 208, New York, NY 10458, 718-817-3804 or toll-free 800-FORDHAM. *Fax:* 718-817-3817. *E-mail:* avandekker@fordham.edu. *Website:* http://www.fordham.edu/.

FORT HAYS STATE UNIVERSITY
Hays, KS

Tuition & fees: N/R	Average undergraduate aid package: $7361

ABOUT THE INSTITUTION State-supported, coed. *Awards:* certificates, associate, bachelor's, and master's degrees. 66 undergraduate majors. *Total enrollment:* 14,210. Undergraduates: 11,831. Freshmen: 962. Federal methodology is used as a basis for awarding need-based institutional aid.

FRESHMAN FINANCIAL AID (Fall 2015) 668 applied for aid; of those 85% were deemed to have need. 95% of freshmen with need received aid; of those 9% had need fully met. *Average percent of need met:* 43% (excluding resources awarded to replace EFC). *Average financial aid package:* $6005 (excluding resources awarded to replace EFC). 13% of all full-time freshmen had no need and received non-need-based gift aid.

UNDERGRADUATE FINANCIAL AID (Fall 2015) 4,647 applied for aid; of those 84% were deemed to have need. 96% of undergraduates with need received aid; of those 9% had need fully met. *Average percent of need met:* 50% (excluding resources awarded to replace EFC). *Average financial aid package:* $7361 (excluding resources awarded to replace EFC). 9% of all full-time undergraduates had no need and received non-need-based gift aid.

GIFT AID (NEED-BASED) *Total amount:* $16,390,692 (78% federal, 5% state, 6% institutional, 11% external sources). *Receiving aid:* Freshmen: 43% (432); all full-time undergraduates: 54% (3,034). *Average award:* Freshmen: $4270; Undergraduates: $4887. *Scholarships, grants, and awards:* Federal Pell, FSEOG, state, private, college/university gift aid from institutional funds.

GIFT AID (NON-NEED-BASED) *Total amount:* $3,068,080 (1% state, 27% institutional, 72% external sources). *Receiving aid:* Freshmen: 2% (18). Undergraduates: 2% (137). *Average award:* Freshmen: $1098. Undergraduates: $1557. *Scholarships, grants, and awards by category: Academic interests/achievement:* agriculture, area/ethnic studies, biological sciences, business, communication, computer science, education, engineering/technologies, English, foreign languages, general academic interests/achievements, health fields, home economics, humanities, international studies, mathematics, military science, physical sciences, premedicine, social sciences. *Creative arts/performance:* applied art and design, art/fine arts, cinema/film/broadcasting, creative writing, dance, general creative arts/performance, journalism/publications, music, performing arts, theater/drama. *Special achievements/activities:* cheerleading/drum major, leadership, rodeo. *Special characteristics:* adult students, children and siblings of alumni, children of faculty/staff, general special characteristics, international students, veterans, veterans' children.

LOANS *Student loans:* $33,573,516 (79% need-based, 21% non-need-based). 68% of past graduating class borrowed through all loan programs. *Average indebtedness per student:* $26,820. *Average need-based loan:* Freshmen: $3002. Undergraduates: $3910. *Parent loans:* $3,548,681 (27% need-based, 73% non-need-based). *Programs:* Federal Direct (Subsidized and Unsubsidized Stafford, PLUS), Perkins, college/university.

WORK-STUDY *Federal work-study:* jobs available. *State or other work-study/employment:* Total amount: $103,219 (38% need-based, 62% non-need-based). Part-time jobs available.

ATHLETIC AWARDS Total amount: $1,935,527 (50% need-based, 50% non-need-based).

APPLYING FOR FINANCIAL AID *Required financial aid forms:* FAFSA, institution's own form. *Financial aid deadline (priority):* 3/1. *Notification date:* Continuous beginning 3/15. Students must reply within 2 weeks of notification.

CONTACT Wendy Rohleder-Sook, Director of Financial Assistance, Fort Hays State University, Picken Hall, Room 202, 600 Park Street, Hays, KS 67601, 785-628-4408 or toll-free 800-628-FHSU. *Fax:* 785-628-4014. *E-mail:* finaid@fhsu.edu. *Website:* http://www.fhsu.edu/.

FORT LEWIS COLLEGE
Durango, CO

Tuition & fees (CO res): $8105	Average undergraduate aid package: $15,959

ABOUT THE INSTITUTION State-supported, coed. *Awards:* certificates, bachelor's, and master's degrees. 55 undergraduate majors. *Total enrollment:* 3,566. Undergraduates: 3,556. Freshmen: 776. Federal methodology is used as a basis for awarding need-based institutional aid.

UNDERGRADUATE EXPENSES for 2016–2017 *Application fee:* $40. *Tuition, state resident:* full-time $6360; part-time $265 per credit hour. *Tuition, nonresident:* full-time $16,072; part-time $670 per credit hour. *Required fees:* full-time $1745; $58.15 per credit hour. Full-time tuition and fees vary according to course load and reciprocity agreements. Part-time tuition and fees vary according to course load and reciprocity agreements. *College room and board:* $9328; *Room only:* $4620. Room and board charges vary according to board plan and housing facility.

FRESHMAN FINANCIAL AID (Fall 2015) 684 applied for aid; of those 80% were deemed to have need. 100% of freshmen with need received aid; of those 16% had need fully met. *Average percent of need met:* 95% (excluding resources awarded to replace EFC). *Average financial aid package:* $15,627 (excluding resources awarded to replace EFC). 23% of all full-time freshmen had no need and received non-need-based gift aid.

UNDERGRADUATE FINANCIAL AID (Fall 2015) 2,572 applied for aid; of those 84% were deemed to have need. 100% of undergraduates with need received aid; of those 16% had need fully met. *Average percent of need met:* 93% (excluding resources awarded to replace EFC). *Average financial aid package:* $15,959 (excluding resources awarded to replace EFC). 18% of all full-time undergraduates had no need and received non-need-based gift aid.

GIFT AID (NEED-BASED) *Total amount:* $13,288,132 (42% federal, 11% state, 30% institutional, 17% external sources). *Receiving aid:* Freshmen: 61% (495); all full-time undergraduates: 54% (1,901). *Average award:* Freshmen: $4833; Undergraduates: $5029. *Scholarships, grants, and awards:* Federal Pell, FSEOG, state, private, college/university gift aid from institutional funds.

GIFT AID (NON-NEED-BASED) *Total amount:* $3,203,991 (1% state, 79% institutional, 20% external sources). *Receiving aid:* Freshmen: 5% (39). Undergraduates: 3% (117). *Average award:* Freshmen: $4564. Undergraduates: $4476. *Scholarships, grants, and awards by category:* Academic interests/achievement: area/ethnic studies, biological sciences, business, communication, education, English, general academic interests/achievements, humanities, mathematics, physical sciences, social sciences. *Creative arts/performance:* art/fine arts, music, performing arts, theater/drama. *Special achievements/activities:* general special achievements/activities, leadership. *Special characteristics:* adult students, children and siblings of alumni, children of faculty/staff, ethnic background, first-generation college students, general special characteristics, handicapped students, international students, local/state students, out-of-state students, veterans' children. *Tuition waivers:* Full or partial for minority students, employees or children of employees.

LOANS *Student loans:* $17,869,429 (52% need-based, 48% non-need-based). 63% of past graduating class borrowed through all loan programs. *Average indebtedness per student:* $22,265. *Average need-based loan:* Freshmen: $3368. Undergraduates: $4113. *Parent loans:* $19,533,449 (12% need-based, 88% non-need-based). *Programs:* Federal Direct (Subsidized and Unsubsidized Stafford, PLUS), Perkins.

WORK-STUDY *Federal work-study:* 147 jobs averaging $1832. *State or other work-study/employment:* Total amount: $513,942 (91% need-based, 9% non-need-based). 257 part-time jobs averaging $1810.

ATHLETIC AWARDS Total amount: $2,121,326 (39% need-based, 61% non-need-based).

APPLYING FOR FINANCIAL AID *Required financial aid form:* FAFSA. *Financial aid deadline (priority):* 11/15. *Notification date:* Continuous beginning 3/6. Students must reply by 9/12.

CONTACT Ms. Tracey Piccoli, Director of Financial Aid, Fort Lewis College, 1000 Rim Drive, 101 Miller Student Services Building, Durango, CO 81301, 800-352-7512 or toll-free 877-FLC-COLO. *Fax:* 970-247-7108. *E-mail:* finaid_off@fortlewis.edu. *Website:* http://www.fortlewis.edu/.

FORT VALLEY STATE UNIVERSITY
Fort Valley, GA

ABOUT THE INSTITUTION State-supported, coed. 35 undergraduate majors.

GIFT AID (NEED-BASED) *Scholarships, grants, and awards:* Federal Pell, FSEOG, state, private, college/university gift aid from institutional funds.

GIFT AID (NON-NEED-BASED) *Scholarships, grants, and awards by category:* Academic interests/achievement: agriculture, business, general academic interests/achievements, home economics, military science, premedicine, social sciences. *Creative arts/performance:* journalism/publications, music. *Special achievements/activities:* general special achievements/activities. *Special characteristics:* handicapped students, international students, out-of-state students.

LOANS *Programs:* Federal Direct (Subsidized and Unsubsidized Stafford, PLUS), Perkins.

WORK-STUDY *Federal work-study:* jobs available. *State or other work-study/employment:* Total amount: $198,897 (98% need-based, 2% non-need-based). Part-time jobs available.

APPLYING FOR FINANCIAL AID *Required financial aid form:* FAFSA.

CONTACT Mr. James Stotts, Office of Financial Aid, Fort Valley State University, 1005 State University Drive, Fort Valley, GA 31030, 478-825-6182 or toll-free 877-462-3878. *Fax:* 478-825-6976. *E-mail:* parksc@tvsu.edu. *Website:* http://www.fvsu.edu/.

FRAMINGHAM STATE UNIVERSITY
Framingham, MA

Tuition & fees (MA res): $9340	Average undergraduate aid package: $9900

ABOUT THE INSTITUTION State-supported, coed. *Awards:* certificates, bachelor's, and master's degrees. 33 undergraduate majors. *Total enrollment:* 5,977. Undergraduates: 4,337. Freshmen: 749. Federal methodology is used as a basis for awarding need-based institutional aid.

UNDERGRADUATE EXPENSES for 2017–2018 *Application fee:* $50. *Tuition, state resident:* full-time $970. *Tuition, nonresident:* full-time $7050.

Required fees: full-time $8370. Full-time tuition and fees vary according to class time and degree level. Part-time tuition and fees vary according to class time, course load, and degree level. *College room and board:* $11,250; *Room only:* $7690. Room and board charges vary according to board plan and housing facility. *Payment plan:* Tuition prepayment.

FRESHMAN FINANCIAL AID (Fall 2015) 731 applied for aid; of those 84% were deemed to have need. 100% of freshmen with need received aid; of those 21% had need fully met. *Average percent of need met:* 60% (excluding resources awarded to replace EFC). *Average financial aid package:* $10,200 (excluding resources awarded to replace EFC). 6% of all full-time freshmen had no need and received non-need-based gift aid.

UNDERGRADUATE FINANCIAL AID (Fall 2015) 3,063 applied for aid; of those 79% were deemed to have need. 100% of undergraduates with need received aid; of those 37% had need fully met. *Average percent of need met:* 60% (excluding resources awarded to replace EFC). *Average financial aid package:* $9900 (excluding resources awarded to replace EFC). 5% of all full-time undergraduates had no need and received non-need-based gift aid.

GIFT AID (NEED-BASED) *Total amount:* $10,420,178 (55% federal, 19% state, 23% institutional, 3% external sources). *Receiving aid:* Freshmen: 60% (504); all full-time undergraduates: 44% (1,966). *Average award:* Freshmen: $4200; Undergraduates: $4400. *Scholarships, grants, and awards:* Federal Pell, FSEOG, state, private, college/university gift aid from institutional funds.

GIFT AID (NON-NEED-BASED) *Total amount:* $468,243 (3% federal, 3% state, 86% institutional, 8% external sources). *Receiving aid:* Freshmen: 3% (27). Undergraduates: 1% (57). *Average award:* Freshmen: $2155. Undergraduates: $2200. *Scholarships, grants, and awards by category:* Academic interests/achievement: biological sciences, education, engineering/technologies, English, general academic interests/achievements, home economics, mathematics, physical sciences. *Special characteristics:* children of faculty/staff, children of public servants, children of union members/company employees, veterans. *Tuition waivers:* Full or partial for employees or children of employees, senior citizens.

LOANS *Student loans:* $22,094,938 (50% need-based, 50% non-need-based). 80% of past graduating class borrowed through all loan programs. *Average indebtedness per student:* $29,493. *Average need-based loan:* Freshmen: $5850. Undergraduates: $5300. *Parent loans:* $4,541,428 (37% need-based, 63% non-need-based). *Programs:* Federal Direct (Subsidized and Unsubsidized Stafford, PLUS), Perkins, state.

WORK-STUDY *Federal work-study:* jobs available. *State or other work-study/employment:* Total amount: $64,000 (100% need-based). Part-time jobs available.

APPLYING FOR FINANCIAL AID *Required financial aid form:* FAFSA. *Financial aid deadline (priority):* 3/1. *Notification date:* Continuous beginning 3/15. Students must reply by 5/1 or within 2 weeks of notification.

CONTACT Office of Financial Aid, Framingham State University, 100 State Street, PO Box 9101, Framingham, MA 01701-9101, 508-626-4534. *Fax:* 508-626-4598. *Website:* http://www.framingham.edu/.

FRANCISCAN UNIVERSITY OF STEUBENVILLE
Steubenville, OH

Tuition & fees: $26,430	Average undergraduate aid package: $15,628

ABOUT THE INSTITUTION Independent Roman Catholic, coed. *Awards:* associate, bachelor's, and master's degrees. 33 undergraduate majors. *Total enrollment:* 2,759. Undergraduates: 2,090. Freshmen: 456. Federal methodology is used as a basis for awarding need-based institutional aid.

UNDERGRADUATE EXPENSES for 2017–2018 *Application fee:* $20. *Comprehensive fee:* $34,830 includes full-time tuition ($25,970), mandatory fees ($460), and room and board ($8400). *College room only:* $4800. Room and board charges vary according to board plan. Part-time tuition and fees vary according to class time and course load.

FRESHMAN FINANCIAL AID (Fall 2016, est.) 376 applied for aid; of those 79% were deemed to have need. 100% of freshmen with need received aid; of those 17% had need fully met. *Average percent of need met:* 67% (excluding resources awarded to replace EFC). *Average financial aid package:* $16,377 (excluding

resources awarded to replace EFC). 30% of all full-time freshmen had no need and received non-need-based gift aid.

UNDERGRADUATE FINANCIAL AID (Fall 2016, est.) 1,501 applied for aid; of those 82% were deemed to have need. 100% of undergraduates with need received aid; of those 16% had need fully met. *Average percent of need met:* 62% (excluding resources awarded to replace EFC). *Average financial aid package:* $15,628 (excluding resources awarded to replace EFC). 32% of all full-time undergraduates had no need and received non-need-based gift aid.

GIFT AID (NEED-BASED) *Total amount:* $13,052,335 (14% federal, 2% state, 69% institutional, 15% external sources). *Receiving aid:* Freshmen: 66% (298); all full-time undergraduates: 63% (1,222). *Average award:* Freshmen: $13,482; Undergraduates: $11,640. *Scholarships, grants, and awards:* Federal Pell, FSEOG, state, private, college/university gift aid from institutional funds.

GIFT AID (NON-NEED-BASED) *Total amount:* $4,912,684 (89% institutional, 11% external sources). *Receiving aid:* Freshmen: 7% (31). Undergraduates: 6% (115). *Average award:* Freshmen: $7184. Undergraduates: $6363. *Scholarships, grants, and awards by category: Academic interests/achievement:* general academic interests/achievements. *Special achievements/activities:* religious involvement. *Special characteristics:* children of faculty/staff, international students, local/state students, religious affiliation, siblings of current students. *Tuition waivers:* Full or partial for employees or children of employees. *ROTC:* Army, Air Force cooperative.

LOANS *Student loans:* $14,648,351 (63% need-based, 37% non-need-based). *Average need-based loan:* Freshmen: $3369. Undergraduates: $4456. *Parent loans:* $3,367,258 (45% need-based, 55% non-need-based). *Programs:* Federal Direct (Subsidized and Unsubsidized Stafford, PLUS), Perkins, Federal Nursing.

WORK-STUDY *Federal work-study:* Total amount: $160,491; jobs available. *State or other work-study/employment:* Total amount: $1,706,826 (68% need-based, 32% non-need-based). Part-time jobs available.

APPLYING FOR FINANCIAL AID *Required financial aid form:* FAFSA. *Financial aid deadline (priority):* 4/1. *Notification date:* Continuous beginning 2/15. Students must reply within 3 weeks of notification.

CONTACT Jody Peeler, Director of Financial Aid, Franciscan University of Steubenville, 1235 University Boulevard, Steubenville, OH 43952-1763, 740-284-5216 or toll-free 800-783-6220. *Fax:* 740-284-5469. *E-mail:* jpeeler@franciscan.edu. *Website:* http://www.franciscan.edu/.

FRANCIS MARION UNIVERSITY
Florence, SC

Tuition & fees (SC res): $10,428	Average undergraduate aid package: $16,226

ABOUT THE INSTITUTION State-supported, coed. *Awards:* certificates, bachelor's, and master's degrees. 33 undergraduate majors. *Total enrollment:* 3,874. Undergraduates: 3,559. Freshmen: 729. Federal methodology is used as a basis for awarding need-based institutional aid.

UNDERGRADUATE EXPENSES for 2016–2017 *Application fee:* $39. *Tuition, state resident:* full-time $9880; part-time $494 per credit hour. *Tuition, nonresident:* full-time $19,760; part-time $988 per credit hour. *Required fees:* full-time $548; $14.80 per credit hour or $73 per term. Full-time tuition and fees vary according to degree level and program. Part-time tuition and fees vary according to course load, degree level, and program. *College room and board:* $7716; *Room only:* $4360. Room and board charges vary according to board plan and housing facility.

FRESHMAN FINANCIAL AID (Fall 2016, est.) 563 applied for aid; of those 88% were deemed to have need. 99% of freshmen with need received aid; of those 28% had need fully met. *Average percent of need met:* 83% (excluding resources awarded to replace EFC). *Average financial aid package:* $16,844 (excluding resources awarded to replace EFC). 4% of all full-time freshmen had no need and received non-need-based gift aid.

UNDERGRADUATE FINANCIAL AID (Fall 2016, est.) 2,129 applied for aid; of those 90% were deemed to have need. 100% of undergraduates with need received aid; of those 11% had need fully met. *Average percent of need met:* 82% (excluding resources awarded to replace EFC). *Average financial aid package:* $16,226 (excluding resources awarded to replace EFC). 2% of all full-time undergraduates had no need and received non-need-based gift aid.

GIFT AID (NEED-BASED) *Total amount:* $14,651,548 (50% federal, 42% state, 6% institutional, 2% external sources). *Receiving aid:* Freshmen: 66% (482); all full-time undergraduates: 58% (1,789). *Average award:* Freshmen: $9736; Undergraduates: $5239. *Scholarships, grants, and awards:* Federal Pell, FSEOG, state, private, college/university gift aid from institutional funds, Federal Nursing.

GIFT AID (NON-NEED-BASED) *Total amount:* $1,785,323 (73% state, 9% institutional, 18% external sources). *Receiving aid:* Freshmen: 4% (28). Undergraduates: 1% (38). *Average award:* Freshmen: $5957. Undergraduates: $4245. *Scholarships, grants, and awards by category: Academic interests/achievement:* biological sciences, business, communication, computer science, education, engineering/technologies, English, foreign languages, general academic interests/achievements, home economics, humanities, mathematics, physical sciences, premedicine, social sciences. *Creative arts/performance:* art/fine arts, journalism/publications, music, performing arts, theater/drama. *Special achievements/activities:* cheerleading/drum major, community service, hobbies/interests, leadership, memberships. *Special characteristics:* adult students, children and siblings of alumni, children of faculty/staff, children of union members/company employees, handicapped students, international students, local/state students, members of minority groups, out-of-state students, public servants, spouses of deceased or disabled public servants, veterans, veterans' children. *Tuition waivers:* Full or partial for employees or children of employees, senior citizens. *ROTC:* Army.

LOANS *Student loans:* $14,156,232 (86% need-based, 14% non-need-based). 80% of past graduating class borrowed through all loan programs. *Average indebtedness per student:* $36,587. *Average need-based loan:* Freshmen: $7901. Undergraduates: $8697. *Parent loans:* $3,624,730 (62% need-based, 38% non-need-based). *Programs:* Federal Direct (Subsidized and Unsubsidized Stafford, PLUS), Perkins, Federal Nursing, college/university.

WORK-STUDY *Federal work-study:* Total amount: $235,020; jobs available. *State or other work-study/employment:* Total amount: $169,950 (100% non-need-based). Part-time jobs available.

ATHLETIC AWARDS Total amount: $768,469 (49% need-based, 51% non-need-based).

APPLYING FOR FINANCIAL AID *Required financial aid form:* FAFSA. *Financial aid deadline (priority):* 3/1. *Notification date:* 11/1.

CONTACT Kim Ellisor, Director of Financial Assistance, Francis Marion University, PO Box 100547, Florence, SC 29502-0547, 843-661-1190 or toll-free 800-368-7551. *Website:* http://www.fmarion.edu/.

FRANKLIN & MARSHALL COLLEGE
Lancaster, PA

Tuition & fees: $52,490	Average undergraduate aid package: $47,144

ABOUT THE INSTITUTION Independent, coed. *Awards:* bachelor's degrees. 40 undergraduate majors. *Total enrollment:* 2,255. Undergraduates: 2,255. Freshmen: 639. Institutional methodology is used as a basis for awarding need-based institutional aid.

UNDERGRADUATE EXPENSES for 2017–2018 *Application fee:* $60. *One-time required fee:* $200. *Comprehensive fee:* $65,610 includes full-time tuition ($52,190), mandatory fees ($300), and room and board ($13,120). *College room only:* $7760. Room and board charges vary according to board plan and housing facility. Part-time tuition and fees vary according to course load.

FRESHMAN FINANCIAL AID (Fall 2016, est.) 417 applied for aid; of those 85% were deemed to have need. 100% of freshmen with need received aid; of those 100% had need fully met. *Average percent of need met:* 100% (excluding resources awarded to replace EFC). *Average financial aid package:* $47,895 (excluding resources awarded to replace EFC). 1% of all full-time freshmen had no need and received non-need-based gift aid.

UNDERGRADUATE FINANCIAL AID (Fall 2016, est.) 1,326 applied for aid; of those 90% were deemed to have need. 100% of undergraduates with need received aid; of those 100% had need fully met. *Average percent of need met:* 100% (excluding resources awarded to replace EFC). *Average financial aid package:* $47,144 (excluding resources awarded to replace EFC). 1% of all full-time undergraduates had no need and received non-need-based gift aid.

GIFT AID (NEED-BASED) *Total amount:* $49,998,543 (4% federal, 1% state, 93% institutional, 2% external sources). *Receiving aid:* Freshmen: 54% (346); all full-time undergraduates: 53% (1,186). *Average award:* Freshmen: $44,761; Undergraduates: $42,719. *Scholarships, grants, and awards:* Federal Pell, FSEOG, state, private, college/university gift aid from institutional funds.

GIFT AID (NON-NEED-BASED) *Total amount:* $1,661,148 (8% federal, 20% institutional, 72% external sources). *Receiving aid:* Freshmen: 14% (92). Undergraduates: 16% (347). *Average award:* Freshmen: $5000. Undergraduates: $6820. *Scholarships, grants, and awards by category: Creative arts/performance:* music. *Tuition waivers:* Full or partial for employees or children of employees. *ROTC:* Army cooperative.

LOANS *Student loans:* $9,637,572 (54% need-based, 46% non-need-based). 60% of past graduating class borrowed through all loan programs. *Average indebtedness per student:* $27,133. *Average need-based loan:* Freshmen: $3030. Undergraduates: $4154. *Parent loans:* $3,388,164 (5% need-based, 95% non-need-based). *Programs:* Federal Direct (Subsidized and Unsubsidized Stafford, PLUS), Perkins, college/university.

WORK-STUDY *Federal work-study:* Total amount: $1,414,964; jobs available. *State or other work-study/employment:* Total amount: $268,645 (100% need-based). Part-time jobs available.

APPLYING FOR FINANCIAL AID *Required financial aid forms:* FAFSA, CSS Financial Aid PROFILE, noncustodial (divorced/separated) parent's statement. *Financial aid deadline:* 2/1 (priority: 2/1). *Notification date:* 4/1. Students must reply by 5/1.

CONTACT Mr. Clarke Paine, Director of Financial Aid, Franklin & Marshall College, PO Box 3003, Lancaster, PA 17604-3003, 717-358-3991 or toll-free 877-678-9111. *Fax:* 717-358-4462. *E-mail:* clarke.paine@fandm.edu.
Website: http://www.fandm.edu/.

FRANKLIN COLLEGE
Franklin, IN

Tuition & fees: $30,771	Average undergraduate aid package: $23,805

ABOUT THE INSTITUTION Independent American Baptist Churches in the U.S.A., coed. *Awards:* bachelor's and master's degrees. 34 undergraduate majors. *Total enrollment:* 1,023. Undergraduates: 1,016. Freshmen: 238. Federal methodology is used as a basis for awarding need-based institutional aid.

UNDERGRADUATE EXPENSES for 2017–2018 *Comprehensive fee:* $39,946 includes full-time tuition ($30,586), mandatory fees ($185), and room and board ($9175). *College room only:* $5463. Full-time tuition and fees vary according to course load and degree level. Room and board charges vary according to board plan. *Part-time fees:* $430 per credit hour. Part-time tuition and fees vary according to course load and degree level.

FRESHMAN FINANCIAL AID (Fall 2016, est.) 232 applied for aid; of those 91% were deemed to have need. 100% of freshmen with need received aid; of those 17% had need fully met. *Average percent of need met:* 78% (excluding resources awarded to replace EFC). *Average financial aid package:* $24,293 (excluding resources awarded to replace EFC). 11% of all full-time freshmen had no need and received non-need-based gift aid.

UNDERGRADUATE FINANCIAL AID (Fall 2016, est.) 904 applied for aid; of those 90% were deemed to have need. 100% of undergraduates with need received aid; of those 16% had need fully met. *Average percent of need met:* 77% (excluding resources awarded to replace EFC). *Average financial aid package:* $23,805 (excluding resources awarded to replace EFC). 15% of all full-time undergraduates had no need and received non-need-based gift aid.

GIFT AID (NEED-BASED) *Total amount:* $15,358,681 (10% federal, 16% state, 71% institutional, 3% external sources). *Receiving aid:* Freshmen: 89% (211); all full-time undergraduates: 84% (811). *Average award:* Freshmen: $20,533; Undergraduates: $19,220. *Scholarships, grants, and awards:* Federal Pell, FSEOG, state, private, college/university gift aid from institutional funds.

GIFT AID (NON-NEED-BASED) *Total amount:* $2,734,969 (92% institutional, 8% external sources). *Receiving aid:* Freshmen: 15% (35). Undergraduates: 12% (118). *Average award:* Freshmen: $13,111. Undergraduates: $13,561. *Scholarships, grants, and awards by category: Academic interests/achievement:* general academic interests/achievements. *Creative arts/performance:* art/fine arts, journalism/publications, music, performing arts, theater/drama. *Special achievements/activities:* general special achievements/activities, leadership, memberships, religious involvement. *Special characteristics:* children and siblings of alumni, children of current students, children of faculty/staff, ethnic background, first-generation college students, handicapped students, local/state students, members of minority groups, out-of-state students, relatives of clergy, religious affiliation, siblings of current students, spouses of current students, veterans, veterans' children. *Tuition waivers:* Full or partial for employees or children of employees, senior citizens. *ROTC:* Army cooperative.

LOANS *Student loans:* $7,608,270 (69% need-based, 31% non-need-based). 86% of past graduating class borrowed through all loan programs. *Average indebtedness per student:* $34,884. *Average need-based loan:* Freshmen: $3242. Undergraduates: $4476. *Parent loans:* $2,682,106 (41% need-based, 59% non-need-based). *Programs:* Federal Direct (Subsidized and Unsubsidized Stafford, PLUS), Perkins, college/university.

WORK-STUDY *Federal work-study:* Total amount: $700,223; jobs available. *State or other work-study/employment:* Total amount: $5200 (30% need-based, 70% non-need-based). Part-time jobs available.

APPLYING FOR FINANCIAL AID *Required financial aid forms:* FAFSA, institution's own form. *Financial aid deadline (priority):* 3/10. *Notification date:* Continuous beginning 12/1. Students must reply by 5/1 or within 4 weeks of notification.

CONTACT Mr. James Vincent-Dunn, Director of Financial Aid, Franklin College, 101 Branigin Boulevard, Franklin, IN 46131-2598, 317-738-8073 or toll-free 800-852-0232. *Fax:* 317-738-8072. *E-mail:* jvincent-dunn@franklincollege.edu.
Website: http://www.franklincollege.edu/.

FRANKLIN PIERCE UNIVERSITY
Rindge, NH

Tuition & fees: N/R	Average undergraduate aid package: $24,607

ABOUT THE INSTITUTION Independent, coed. *Awards:* certificates, associate, bachelor's, master's, and doctoral degrees (profile does not reflect significant enrollment at 6 continuing education sites; master's degree is only offered at these sites). 46 undergraduate majors. *Total enrollment:* 2,377. Undergraduates: 1,752. Freshmen: 653. Federal methodology is used as a basis for awarding need-based institutional aid.

UNDERGRADUATE EXPENSES for 2017–2018 *Application fee:* $40.

FRESHMAN FINANCIAL AID (Fall 2015) 628 applied for aid; of those 93% were deemed to have need. 100% of freshmen with need received aid; of those 22% had need fully met. *Average percent of need met:* 76% (excluding resources awarded to replace EFC). *Average financial aid package:* $26,074 (excluding resources awarded to replace EFC). 12% of all full-time freshmen had no need and received non-need-based gift aid.

UNDERGRADUATE FINANCIAL AID (Fall 2015) 1,418 applied for aid; of those 91% were deemed to have need. 100% of undergraduates with need received aid; of those 20% had need fully met. *Average percent of need met:* 73% (excluding resources awarded to replace EFC). *Average financial aid package:* $24,607 (excluding resources awarded to replace EFC). 15% of all full-time undergraduates had no need and received non-need-based gift aid.

GIFT AID (NEED-BASED) *Total amount:* $24,073,630 (9% federal, 1% state, 90% institutional). *Receiving aid:* Freshmen: 85% (578); all full-time undergraduates: 81% (1,252). *Average award:* Freshmen: $22,501; Undergraduates: $20,919. *Scholarships, grants, and awards:* Federal Pell, FSEOG, state, private, college/university gift aid from institutional funds.

GIFT AID (NON-NEED-BASED) *Total amount:* $5,433,082 (100% institutional). *Receiving aid:* Freshmen: 15% (105). Undergraduates: 13% (199). *Average award:* Freshmen: $17,823. Undergraduates: $16,272. *Scholarships, grants, and awards by category: Academic interests/achievement:* communication, general academic interests/achievements. *Creative arts/performance:* performing arts, theater/drama. *Special achievements/activities:* general special achievements/activities, leadership. *Special characteristics:* adult students, children and siblings of alumni, children of current students, children of educators, children of faculty/staff, general special characteristics, international students, local/state students, married students, parents of current students, siblings of current students, spouses of current students. *Tuition waivers:* Full or partial for employees or children of employees, senior citizens. *ROTC:* Army cooperative, Air Force cooperative.

LOANS *Student loans:* $13,628,704 (67% need-based, 33% non-need-based). 87% of past graduating class borrowed through all loan programs. *Average indebtedness per student:* $36,614. *Average need-based loan:* Freshmen: $3953. Undergraduates: $4545. *Parent loans:* $6,823,348 (46% need-based, 54% non-need-based). *Programs:* Federal Direct (Subsidized and Unsubsidized Stafford, PLUS), Perkins.

WORK-STUDY *Federal work-study:* jobs available. *State or other work-study/employment:* Part-time jobs available.

ATHLETIC AWARDS Total amount: $2,382,352 (47% need-based, 53% non-need-based).

APPLYING FOR FINANCIAL AID *Required financial aid form:* FAFSA. *Financial aid deadline (priority):* 3/1. *Notification date:* Continuous beginning 12/1. Students must reply by 6/1.

CONTACT Kenneth Ferreira, Associate Vice President for Student Financial Services, Franklin Pierce University, 40 University Drive, Rindge, NH 03461-0060, 603-899-4180 or toll-free 800-437-0048. *Fax:* 603-899-4372. *E-mail:* ferreirak@franklinpierce.edu.
Website: http://www.franklinpierce.edu/.

FRANKLIN UNIVERSITY
Columbus, OH

CONTACT Ms. Marlowe Collier, Financial Aid Assistant, Franklin University, 201 South Grant Avenue, Columbus, OH 43215-5399, 614-797-4700 or toll-free 877-341-6300. *Fax:* 614-220-8931. *E-mail:* finaid@franklin.edu.
Website: http://www.franklin.edu/.

FRANKLIN W. OLIN COLLEGE OF ENGINEERING
Needham, MA

Tuition & fees: $49,280	Average undergraduate aid package: $44,286

ABOUT THE INSTITUTION Independent, coed. *Awards:* bachelor's degrees. 3 undergraduate majors. *Total enrollment:* 378. Undergraduates: 378. Freshmen: 79. Federal methodology is used as a basis for awarding need-based institutional aid.

UNDERGRADUATE EXPENSES for 2017–2018 *Application fee:* $85. *One-time required fee:* $2656. *Comprehensive fee:* $65,580 includes full-time tuition ($48,600), mandatory fees ($680), and room and board ($16,300). *Part-time tuition:* $1520 per credit hour.

FRESHMAN FINANCIAL AID (Fall 2016, est.) 59 applied for aid; of those 71% were deemed to have need. 100% of freshmen with need received aid; of those 100% had need fully met. *Average percent of need met:* 100% (excluding resources awarded to replace EFC). *Average financial aid package:* $44,031 (excluding resources awarded to replace EFC). 47% of all full-time freshmen had no need and received non-need-based gift aid.

UNDERGRADUATE FINANCIAL AID (Fall 2016, est.) 184 applied for aid; of those 84% were deemed to have need. 100% of undergraduates with need received aid; of those 97% had need fully met. *Average percent of need met:* 99% (excluding resources awarded to replace EFC). *Average financial aid package:* $44,286 (excluding resources awarded to replace EFC). 55% of all full-time undergraduates had no need and received non-need-based gift aid.

GIFT AID (NEED-BASED) *Total amount:* $6,326,677 (3% federal, 96% institutional, 1% external sources). *Receiving aid:* Freshmen: 53% (42); all full-time undergraduates: 45% (155). *Average award:* Freshmen: $42,683; Undergraduates: $42,535. *Scholarships, grants, and awards:* Federal Pell, FSEOG, college/university gift aid from institutional funds.

GIFT AID (NON-NEED-BASED) *Total amount:* $4,786,533 (96% institutional, 4% external sources). *Receiving aid:* Freshmen: 53% (42). Undergraduates: 45% (155). *Average award:* Freshmen: $24,911. *Scholarships, grants, and awards by category:* Academic interests/achievement: 342 awards ($7,906,550 total): general academic interests/achievements.

LOANS *Student loans:* $692,644 (39% need-based, 61% non-need-based). 32% of past graduating class borrowed through all loan programs. *Average indebtedness per student:* $18,704. *Average need-based loan:* Freshmen: $2981. Undergraduates: $3193. *Parent loans:* $124,087 (100% non-need-based). *Programs:* Federal Direct (Subsidized and Unsubsidized Stafford, PLUS).

APPLYING FOR FINANCIAL AID *Required financial aid form:* FAFSA. *Financial aid deadline:* 2/15. *Notification date:* Continuous beginning 3/24. Students must reply by 5/1 or within 2 weeks of notification.

CONTACT Ms. Jean Ricker, Director of Financial Aid, Franklin W. Olin College of Engineering, 1000 Olin Way, Needham, MA 02492-1200, 781-292-2215. *E-mail:* finaid@olin.edu.
Website: http://www.olin.edu/.

FREED-HARDEMAN UNIVERSITY
Henderson, TN

Tuition & fees: $21,950	Average undergraduate aid package: $18,818

ABOUT THE INSTITUTION Independent Church of Christ, coed. *Awards:* certificates, diplomas, bachelor's, master's, and doctoral degrees. 42 undergraduate majors. *Total enrollment:* 1,906. Undergraduates: 1,402. Freshmen: 325. Federal methodology is used as a basis for awarding need-based institutional aid.

UNDERGRADUATE EXPENSES for 2017–2018 *Comprehensive fee:* $29,900 includes full-time tuition ($21,950) and room and board ($7950). *College room only:* $4320. Full-time tuition and fees vary according to location. Room and board charges vary according to board plan and housing facility. *Part-time tuition:* $725 per credit hour. Part-time tuition and fees vary according to location.

FRESHMAN FINANCIAL AID (Fall 2016, est.) 307 applied for aid; of those 86% were deemed to have need. 100% of freshmen with need received aid; of those 31% had need fully met. *Average percent of need met:* 77% (excluding resources awarded to replace EFC). *Average financial aid package:* $20,151 (excluding resources awarded to replace EFC). 17% of all full-time freshmen had no need and received non-need-based gift aid.

UNDERGRADUATE FINANCIAL AID (Fall 2016, est.) 1,128 applied for aid; of those 84% were deemed to have need. 100% of undergraduates with need received aid; of those 27% had need fully met. *Average percent of need met:* 73% (excluding resources awarded to replace EFC). *Average financial aid package:* $18,818 (excluding resources awarded to replace EFC). 19% of all full-time undergraduates had no need and received non-need-based gift aid.

GIFT AID (NEED-BASED) *Total amount:* $12,318,292 (14% federal, 12% state, 69% institutional, 5% external sources). *Receiving aid:* Freshmen: 80% (259); all full-time undergraduates: 75% (925). *Average award:* Freshmen: $15,537; Undergraduates: $13,949. *Scholarships, grants, and awards:* Federal Pell, FSEOG, state, private, college/university gift aid from institutional funds, Academic Competitiveness Grants, TEACH Grants.

GIFT AID (NON-NEED-BASED) *Total amount:* $3,998,352 (19% state, 75% institutional, 6% external sources). *Receiving aid:* Freshmen: 25% (81). Undergraduates: 21% (252). *Average award:* Freshmen: $12,203. Undergraduates: $11,094. *Tuition waivers:* Full or partial for employees or children of employees.

LOANS *Student loans:* $4,804,854 (80% need-based, 20% non-need-based). 72% of past graduating class borrowed through all loan programs. *Average indebtedness per student:* $32,899. *Average need-based loan:* Freshmen: $2807. Undergraduates: $3829. *Parent loans:* $1,584,371 (64% need-based, 36% non-need-based). *Programs:* Federal Direct (Subsidized and Unsubsidized Stafford, PLUS), Perkins, alternative loans.

WORK-STUDY *Federal work-study:* Total amount: $559,077; jobs available. *State or other work-study/employment:* Part-time jobs available.

ATHLETIC AWARDS Total amount: $1,399,831 (54% need-based, 46% non-need-based).

APPLYING FOR FINANCIAL AID *Required financial aid forms:* FAFSA, institution's own form. *Financial aid deadline:* Continuous. *Notification date:* Continuous beginning 3/1.

CONTACT Mrs. Summer Judd, Director of Financial Aid, Freed-Hardeman University, 158 East Main Street, Henderson, TN 38340-2399, 731-989-6662 or toll-free 800-FHU-FHU-1. *Fax:* 731-989-6775. *E-mail:* sjudd@fhu.edu.
Website: http://www.fhu.edu/.

FRESNO PACIFIC UNIVERSITY
Fresno, CA

Tuition & fees: N/R	Average undergraduate aid package: $21,383

ABOUT THE INSTITUTION Independent Mennonite Brethren Church, coed. *Awards:* certificates, associate, bachelor's, and master's degrees. 23 undergraduate majors. *Total enrollment:* 3,596. Undergraduates: 2,439. Freshmen: 201. Federal methodology is used as a basis for awarding need-based institutional aid.

FRESHMAN FINANCIAL AID (Fall 2016, est.) 182 applied for aid; of those 95% were deemed to have need. 100% of freshmen with need received aid; of those 19% had need fully met. *Average percent of need met:* 49% (excluding resources awarded to replace EFC). *Average financial aid package:* $30,190 (excluding resources awarded to replace EFC). 14% of all full-time freshmen had no need and received non-need-based gift aid.

UNDERGRADUATE FINANCIAL AID (Fall 2016, est.) 1,892 applied for aid; of those 94% were deemed to have need. 99% of undergraduates with need received aid; of those 8% had need fully met. *Average percent of need met:* 50% (excluding resources awarded to replace EFC). *Average financial aid package:* $21,383 (excluding resources awarded to replace EFC). 9% of all full-time undergraduates had no need and received non-need-based gift aid.

GIFT AID (NEED-BASED) *Total amount:* $11,659,695 (52% federal, 47% state, 1% institutional). *Receiving aid:* Freshmen: 69% (137); all full-time undergraduates: 66% (1,381). *Average award:* Freshmen: $11,318; Undergraduates: $8362. *Scholarships, grants, and awards:* Federal Pell, FSEOG, state, private, college/university gift aid from institutional funds.

GIFT AID (NON-NEED-BASED) *Total amount:* $11,550,720 (99% institutional, 1% external sources). *Receiving aid:* Freshmen: 28% (56). Undergraduates: 51% (1,056). *Average award:* Freshmen: $13,121. Undergraduates: $10,883. *Scholarships, grants, and awards by category:* Academic interests/achievement: business, general academic interests/achievements, humanities, social sciences. Creative arts/performance: music, performing arts, theater/drama. Special characteristics: children of faculty/staff, members of minority groups, relatives of clergy, religious affiliation, spouses of current students.

LOANS *Student loans:* $15,491,717 (100% need-based). *Average need-based loan:* Freshmen: $5168. Undergraduates: $8159. *Programs:* Federal Direct (Subsidized and Unsubsidized Stafford, PLUS), Perkins.

WORK-STUDY Federal work-study jobs available. *State or other work-study/employment:* Part-time jobs available.

APPLYING FOR FINANCIAL AID *Required financial aid forms:* FAFSA, institution's own form. *Financial aid deadline (priority):* 3/2. *Notification date:* Continuous beginning 3/2. Students must reply by 7/30 or within 3 weeks of notification.

CONTACT April Powell, Director of Financial Aid, Fresno Pacific University, 1717 South Chestnut Avenue, #2004, Fresno, CA 93702, 559-453-2041 or toll-free 800-660-6089. *Fax:* 559-453-5595. *E-mail:* sfs@fresno.edu.
Website: http://www.fresno.edu/.

FRIENDS UNIVERSITY
Wichita, KS

Tuition & fees: $27,465	Average undergraduate aid package: $16,394

ABOUT THE INSTITUTION Independent Christian non-denominational, coed. *Awards:* bachelor's and master's degrees. 47 undergraduate majors. *Total enrollment:* 1,762. Undergraduates: 1,192. Freshmen: 165. Federal methodology is used as a basis for awarding need-based institutional aid.

UNDERGRADUATE EXPENSES for 2017–2018 *Comprehensive fee:* $35,205 includes full-time tuition ($27,150), mandatory fees ($315), and room and board ($7740). *College room only:* $3680. Full-time tuition and fees vary according to class time, course load, degree level, and location. Room and board charges vary according to board plan and housing facility. *Part-time tuition:* $905 per credit hour. Part-time tuition and fees vary according to class time, course load, degree level, and location.

FRESHMAN FINANCIAL AID (Fall 2015) 153 applied for aid; of those 96% were deemed to have need. 100% of freshmen with need received aid; of those 54% had

need fully met. *Average percent of need met:* 91% (excluding resources awarded to replace EFC). *Average financial aid package:* $18,019 (excluding resources awarded to replace EFC). 10% of all full-time freshmen had no need and received non-need-based gift aid.

UNDERGRADUATE FINANCIAL AID (Fall 2015) 905 applied for aid; of those 89% were deemed to have need. 100% of undergraduates with need received aid; of those 35% had need fully met. *Average percent of need met:* 82% (excluding resources awarded to replace EFC). *Average financial aid package:* $16,394 (excluding resources awarded to replace EFC). 10% of all full-time undergraduates had no need and received non-need-based gift aid.

GIFT AID (NEED-BASED) *Total amount:* $12,111,419 (21% federal, 9% state, 68% institutional, 2% external sources). *Receiving aid:* Freshmen: 79% (130); all full-time undergraduates: 76% (784). *Average award:* Freshmen: $7100; Undergraduates: $8359. *Scholarships, grants, and awards:* Federal Pell, FSEOG, state, private, college/university gift aid from institutional funds.

GIFT AID (NON-NEED-BASED) *Total amount:* $1,145,979 (2% state, 97% institutional, 1% external sources). *Receiving aid:* Freshmen: 86% (141). Undergraduates: 61% (624). *Average award:* Freshmen: $11,635. Undergraduates: $8975. *Scholarships, grants, and awards by category:* Academic interests/achievement: 784 awards ($5,231,394 total): general academic interests/achievements. Creative arts/performance: 255 awards ($780,100 total): art/fine arts, dance, music, performing arts, theater/drama. Special achievements/activities: 102 awards ($136,425 total): cheerleading/drum major, leadership, religious involvement. Special characteristics: 114 awards ($442,268 total): children and siblings of alumni, children of faculty/staff, members of minority groups, relatives of clergy, religious affiliation. *Tuition waivers:* Full or partial for employees or children of employees, senior citizens.

LOANS *Student loans:* $15,291,730 (26% need-based, 74% non-need-based). 79% of past graduating class borrowed through all loan programs. *Average indebtedness per student:* $28,175. *Average need-based loan:* Freshmen: $2969. Undergraduates: $4158. *Parent loans:* $1,123,074 (87% need-based, 13% non-need-based). *Programs:* Federal Direct (Subsidized and Unsubsidized Stafford, PLUS), Perkins.

WORK-STUDY *Federal work-study:* 204 jobs averaging $1091. *State or other work-study/employment:* 252 part-time jobs averaging $1306.

ATHLETIC AWARDS Total amount: $1,890,794 (88% need-based, 12% non-need-based).

APPLYING FOR FINANCIAL AID *Required financial aid form:* FAFSA. *Financial aid deadline (priority):* 4/1. *Notification date:* Continuous beginning 3/1. Students must reply within 3 weeks of notification.

CONTACT Tony Lubbers, Director of Financial Aid, Friends University, 2100 University Street, Wichita, KS 67213, 316-295-5599 or toll-free 800-794-6945. *Fax:* 316-295-5703. *E-mail:* lubberst@friends.edu.
Website: http://www.friends.edu/.

FROSTBURG STATE UNIVERSITY
Frostburg, MD

Tuition & fees (MD res): $8702	Average undergraduate aid package: $9743

ABOUT THE INSTITUTION State-supported, coed. *Awards:* bachelor's, master's, and doctoral degrees. 45 undergraduate majors. *Total enrollment:* 5,676. Undergraduates: 4,884. Freshmen: 830. Federal methodology is used as a basis for awarding need-based institutional aid.

UNDERGRADUATE EXPENSES for 2016–2017 *Application fee:* $30. *Tuition, state resident:* full-time $6340; part-time $262 per credit. *Tuition, non-resident:* full-time $18,864; part-time $530 per credit. *Required fees:* full-time $2362; $111 per credit or $25 per term. Full-time tuition and fees vary according to location. Part-time tuition and fees vary according to course load and location. *College room and board:* $8898; *Room only:* $4316. Room and board charges vary according to board plan and housing facility.

FRESHMAN FINANCIAL AID (Fall 2016, est.) 759 applied for aid; of those 76% were deemed to have need. 100% of freshmen with need received aid; of those 17% had need fully met. *Average percent of need met:* 60% (excluding resources awarded to replace EFC). *Average financial aid package:* $10,044 (excluding resources awarded to replace EFC). 23% of all full-time freshmen had no need and received non-need-based gift aid.

UNDERGRADUATE FINANCIAL AID (Fall 2016, est.) 3,691 applied for aid; of those 77% were deemed to have need. 100% of undergraduates with need received

aid; of those 13% had need fully met. *Average percent of need met:* 58% (excluding resources awarded to replace EFC). *Average financial aid package:* $9743 (excluding resources awarded to replace EFC). 23% of all full-time undergraduates had no need and received non-need-based gift aid.

GIFT AID (NEED-BASED) *Total amount:* $15,569,130 (54% federal, 25% state, 17% institutional, 4% external sources). *Receiving aid:* Freshmen: 46% (390); all full-time undergraduates: 45% (1,940). *Average award:* Freshmen: $8469; Undergraduates: $7452. *Scholarships, grants, and awards:* Federal Pell, FSEOG, state, private, college/university gift aid from institutional funds.

GIFT AID (NON-NEED-BASED) *Total amount:* $5,035,460 (2% federal, 12% state, 66% institutional, 20% external sources). *Receiving aid:* Freshmen: 23% (192). Undergraduates: 23% (976). *Average award:* Freshmen: $3590. Undergraduates: $3432. *Scholarships, grants, and awards by category: Academic interests/achievement:* biological sciences, business, communication, computer science, education, engineering/technologies, English, foreign languages, general academic interests/achievements, health fields, humanities, international studies, mathematics, physical sciences, premedicine, social sciences. *Creative arts/performance:* art/fine arts, creative writing, journalism/publications, music, performing arts, theater/drama. *Special achievements/activities:* community service, leadership. *Special characteristics:* adult students, children of union members/company employees, international students, local/state students, out-of-state students, veterans, veterans' children. *Tuition waivers:* Full or partial for employees or children of employees, senior citizens.

LOANS *Student loans:* $23,227,400 (41% need-based, 59% non-need-based). 76% of past graduating class borrowed through all loan programs. *Average indebtedness per student:* $25,347. *Average need-based loan:* Freshmen: $3356. Undergraduates: $4022. *Parent loans:* $6,149,918 (100% non-need-based). *Programs:* Federal Direct (Subsidized and Unsubsidized Stafford, PLUS), Perkins.

WORK-STUDY *Federal work-study:* Total amount: $11,612; 149 jobs averaging $681. *State or other work-study/employment:* Part-time jobs available.

APPLYING FOR FINANCIAL AID *Required financial aid form:* FAFSA. *Financial aid deadline (priority):* 3/1. *Notification date:* Continuous beginning 3/15. Students must reply within 3 weeks of notification.

CONTACT Mrs. Angela Hovatter, Director of Financial Aid, Frostburg State University, 114 Pullen Hall, Frostburg, MD 21532-1099, 301-687-4301. *Fax:* 301-687-7074. *E-mail:* ahovatter@frostburg.edu. *Website:* http://www.frostburg.edu/.

FULL SAIL UNIVERSITY
Winter Park, FL

CONTACT Financial Aid Office, Full Sail University, 3300 University Boulevard, Winter Park, FL 32792, 800-575-1142 or toll-free 800-226-7625. *Website:* http://www.fullsail.edu/.

FURMAN UNIVERSITY
Greenville, SC

Tuition & fees: $47,164	Average undergraduate aid package: $39,063

ABOUT THE INSTITUTION Independent, coed. *Awards:* bachelor's and master's degrees. 50 undergraduate majors. *Total enrollment:* 3,003. Undergraduates: 2,797. Freshmen: 748. Both federal and institutional methodology are used as a basis for awarding need-based institutional aid.

UNDERGRADUATE EXPENSES for 2016–2017 *Application fee:* $50. *Comprehensive fee:* $59,028 includes full-time tuition ($46,784), mandatory fees ($380), and room and board ($11,864). *College room only:* $6358. Room and board charges vary according to board plan and housing facility. *Part-time tuition:* $1462 per credit. Part-time tuition and fees vary according to course load.

FRESHMAN FINANCIAL AID (Fall 2016, est.) 529 applied for aid; of those 77% were deemed to have need. 100% of freshmen with need received aid; of those 35% had need fully met. *Average percent of need met:* 81% (excluding resources awarded to replace EFC). *Average financial aid package:* $40,141 (excluding resources awarded to replace EFC). 41% of all full-time freshmen had no need and received non-need-based gift aid.

UNDERGRADUATE FINANCIAL AID (Fall 2016, est.) 1,521 applied for aid; of those 83% were deemed to have need. 100% of undergraduates with need received aid; of those 35% had need fully met. *Average percent of need met:* 79% (excluding resources awarded to replace EFC). *Average financial aid package:* $39,063 (excluding resources awarded to replace EFC). 44% of all full-time undergraduates had no need and received non-need-based gift aid.

GIFT AID (NEED-BASED) *Total amount:* $36,567,255 (4% federal, 4% state, 88% institutional, 4% external sources). *Receiving aid:* Freshmen: 54% (406); all full-time undergraduates: 46% (1,250). *Average award:* Freshmen: $37,293; Undergraduates: $35,508. *Scholarships, grants, and awards:* Federal Pell, FSEOG, state, private, college/university gift aid from institutional funds.

GIFT AID (NON-NEED-BASED) *Total amount:* $29,490,616 (11% state, 85% institutional, 4% external sources). *Receiving aid:* Freshmen: 54% (406). Undergraduates: 46% (1,250). *Average award:* Freshmen: $18,327. Undergraduates: $20,472. *Scholarships, grants, and awards by category: Academic interests/achievement:* area/ethnic studies, biological sciences, business, communication, computer science, education, engineering/technologies, English, foreign languages, general academic interests/achievements, health fields, humanities, international studies, mathematics, military science, physical sciences, premedicine, religion/biblical studies, social sciences. *Creative arts/performance:* art/fine arts, creative writing, music, theater/drama. *Special achievements/activities:* community service, leadership, religious involvement. *Special characteristics:* children of faculty/staff, ethnic background, international students, local/state students, relatives of clergy, religious affiliation, veterans. *Tuition waivers:* Full or partial for employees or children of employees. *ROTC:* Army.

LOANS *Student loans:* $8,357,477 (86% need-based, 14% non-need-based). 35% of past graduating class borrowed through all loan programs. *Average indebtedness per student:* $36,846. *Average need-based loan:* Freshmen: $3334. Undergraduates: $4884. *Parent loans:* $4,898,872 (86% need-based, 14% non-need-based). *Programs:* Federal Direct (Subsidized and Unsubsidized Stafford, PLUS), Perkins, state, alternative loans.

WORK-STUDY *Federal work-study:* Total amount: $866,985; 598 jobs averaging $1530.

ATHLETIC AWARDS Total amount: $11,138,163 (43% need-based, 57% non-need-based).

APPLYING FOR FINANCIAL AID *Required financial aid forms:* FAFSA, CSS Financial Aid PROFILE, state aid form. *Financial aid deadline:* 1/15. *Notification date:* 3/15. Students must reply by 5/1 or within 2 weeks of notification.

CONTACT Mr. Forrest Stuart, Associate Vice President of Financial Aid, Furman University, 3300 Poinsett Highway, Greenville, SC 29613, 864-294-2204. *Fax:* 864-294-3127. *E-mail:* forrest.stuart@furman.edu. *Website:* http://www.furman.edu/.

GALEN COLLEGE OF NURSING
Cincinnati, OH

CONTACT Financial Aid Office, Galen College of Nursing, 100 East Business Way, Suite 200, Cincinnati, OH 45241, 513-475-3600 or toll-free 877-223-7040. *Website:* http://www.galencollege.edu/.

GALLAUDET UNIVERSITY
Washington, DC

Tuition & fees: $16,558	Average undergraduate aid package: $21,472

ABOUT THE INSTITUTION Independent, coed. *Awards:* certificates, bachelor's, master's, and doctoral degrees (Undergraduate programs are open primarily to the students with hearing-impairments). 22 undergraduate majors. *Total enrollment:* 1,566. Undergraduates: 2,224. Freshmen: 245. Federal methodology is used as a basis for awarding need-based institutional aid.

UNDERGRADUATE EXPENSES for 2017–2018 *Application fee:* $50. *Comprehensive fee:* $30,596 includes full-time tuition ($16,032), mandatory fees ($526), and room and board ($14,038). *College room only:* $7658. Full-time tuition and fees vary according to course load. Room and board charges vary according to board plan. *Part-time tuition:* $668 per credit hour. Part-time tuition and fees vary according to course load.

FRESHMAN FINANCIAL AID (Fall 2016, est.) 191 applied for aid; of those 91% were deemed to have need. 100% of freshmen with need received aid; of those 25% had need fully met. *Average percent of need met:* 78% (excluding resources awarded to replace EFC). *Average financial aid package:* $23,629 (excluding resources awarded to replace EFC). 8% of all full-time freshmen had no need and received non-need-based gift aid.

UNDERGRADUATE FINANCIAL AID (Fall 2016, est.) 985 applied for aid; of those 93% were deemed to have need. 98% of undergraduates with need received aid; of those 19% had need fully met. *Average percent of need met:* 75% (excluding resources awarded to replace EFC). *Average financial aid package:* $21,472 (excluding resources awarded to replace EFC). 4% of all full-time undergraduates had no need and received non-need-based gift aid.

GIFT AID (NEED-BASED) *Total amount:* $19,536,787 (16% federal, 50% state, 33% institutional, 1% external sources). *Receiving aid:* Freshmen: 82% (174); all full-time undergraduates: 80% (899). *Average award:* Freshmen: $22,197; Undergraduates: $20,580. *Scholarships, grants, and awards:* Federal Pell, FSEOG, state, private, college/university gift aid from institutional funds.

GIFT AID (NON-NEED-BASED) *Total amount:* $1,075,203 (70% state, 29% institutional, 1% external sources). *Receiving aid:* Freshmen: 17% (37). Undergraduates: 12% (137). *Average award:* Freshmen: $8750. Undergraduates: $5812. *Scholarships, grants, and awards by category:* Academic interests/achievement: general academic interests/achievements. Special achievements/activities: leadership. Special characteristics: members of minority groups. *Tuition waivers:* Full or partial for employees or children of employees.

LOANS *Student loans:* $3,562,619 (95% need-based, 5% non-need-based). 61% of past graduating class borrowed through all loan programs. *Average indebtedness per student:* $15,767. *Average need-based loan:* Freshmen: $4887. Undergraduates: $4115. *Parent loans:* $748,443 (86% need-based, 14% non-need-based). *Programs:* Federal Direct (Subsidized and Unsubsidized Stafford, PLUS), Perkins.

WORK-STUDY *Federal work-study:* Total amount: $105,106; jobs available.

APPLYING FOR FINANCIAL AID *Required financial aid forms:* FAFSA, institution's own form. *Financial aid deadline:* Continuous. *Notification date:* Continuous beginning 2/1.

CONTACT Shondra Dickson, Director of Financial Aid, Gallaudet University, Chapel Hall, Room G-02, 800 Florida Avenue, NE, Washington, DC 20002, 202-651-5290 or toll-free 800-995-0550. *Fax:* 202-651-5740. *E-mail:* financial.aid@gallaudet.edu. *Website:* http://www.gallaudet.edu/.

GANNON UNIVERSITY
Erie, PA

Tuition & fees: $30,042	Average undergraduate aid package: $24,832

ABOUT THE INSTITUTION Independent Roman Catholic, coed. *Awards:* certificates, associate, bachelor's, master's, and doctoral degrees. 65 undergraduate majors. *Total enrollment:* 4,343. Undergraduates: 3,098. Freshmen: 631. Federal methodology is used as a basis for awarding need-based institutional aid.

UNDERGRADUATE EXPENSES for 2016–2017 *Application fee:* $25. *Comprehensive fee:* $42,032 includes full-time tuition ($29,300), mandatory fees ($742), and room and board ($11,990). *College room only:* $6370. Full-time tuition and fees vary according to course load and program. Room and board charges vary according to board plan and housing facility. *Part-time tuition:* $710 per credit hour. *Part-time fees:* $25 per credit hour. Part-time tuition and fees vary according to course load and program.

FRESHMAN FINANCIAL AID (Fall 2016, est.) 567 applied for aid; of those 92% were deemed to have need. 100% of freshmen with need received aid; of those 22% had need fully met. *Average percent of need met:* 75% (excluding resources awarded to replace EFC). *Average financial aid package:* $25,699 (excluding resources awarded to replace EFC). 14% of all full-time freshmen had no need and received non-need-based gift aid.

UNDERGRADUATE FINANCIAL AID (Fall 2016, est.) 2,091 applied for aid; of those 92% were deemed to have need. 99% of undergraduates with need received aid; of those 25% had need fully met. *Average percent of need met:* 73% (excluding resources awarded to replace EFC). *Average financial aid package:* $24,832

(excluding resources awarded to replace EFC). 16% of all full-time undergraduates had no need and received non-need-based gift aid.

GIFT AID (NEED-BASED) *Total amount:* $36,563,579 (9% federal, 8% state, 77% institutional, 6% external sources). *Receiving aid:* Freshmen: 82% (515); all full-time undergraduates: 76% (1,874). *Average award:* Freshmen: $22,430; Undergraduates: $20,924. *Scholarships, grants, and awards:* Federal Pell, FSEOG, state, private, college/university gift aid from institutional funds, Federal Nursing.

GIFT AID (NON-NEED-BASED) *Total amount:* $9,769,216 (57% institutional, 43% external sources). *Receiving aid:* Freshmen: 12% (76), Undergraduates: 12% (288). *Average award:* Freshmen: $16,558. Undergraduates: $14,266. *Scholarships, grants, and awards by category:* Academic interests/achievement: biological sciences, business, education, engineering/technologies, English, foreign languages, general academic interests/achievements, humanities, international studies, mathematics, premedicine, religion/biblical studies, social sciences. Creative arts/performance: music, performing arts, theater/drama. Special achievements/activities: community service, leadership. Special characteristics: adult students, ethnic background, international students, members of minority groups, religious affiliation, veterans. *Tuition waivers:* Full or partial for employees or children of employees, senior citizens. *ROTC:* Army.

LOANS *Student loans:* $16,930,554 (57% need-based, 43% non-need-based). *Average need-based loan:* Freshmen: $3404. Undergraduates: $4322. *Parent loans:* $5,338,078 (77% need-based, 23% non-need-based). *Programs:* Federal Direct (Subsidized and Unsubsidized Stafford, PLUS), Federal Nursing.

WORK-STUDY *Federal work-study:* Total amount: $806,333; jobs available. *State or other work-study/employment:* Total amount: $259,246 (100% non-need-based). Part-time jobs available.

ATHLETIC AWARDS Total amount: $4,011,043 (72% need-based, 28% non-need-based).

APPLYING FOR FINANCIAL AID *Required financial aid form:* FAFSA. *Financial aid deadline (priority):* 3/15. *Notification date:* Continuous beginning 11/1.

CONTACT Ms. Sharon Krahe, Director of Financial Aid, Gannon University, 109 University Square, Erie, PA 16541, 814-871-7670 or toll-free 800-GANNONU. *Fax:* 814-871-5826. *E-mail:* krahe001@gannon.edu. *Website:* http://www.gannon.edu/.

GARDNER-WEBB UNIVERSITY
Boiling Springs, NC

Tuition & fees: $29,610	Average undergraduate aid package: $24,191

ABOUT THE INSTITUTION Independent Baptist, coed. *Awards:* certificates, associate, bachelor's, master's, and doctoral degrees. 65 undergraduate majors. *Total enrollment:* 3,884. Undergraduates: 2,343. Freshmen: 444. Federal methodology is used as a basis for awarding need-based institutional aid.

UNDERGRADUATE EXPENSES for 2016–2017 *Application fee:* $40. *Comprehensive fee:* $39,390 includes full-time tuition ($29,420), mandatory fees ($190), and room and board ($9780). *College room only:* $4950. Room and board charges vary according to board plan and housing facility. *Part-time tuition:* $468 per credit hour.

FRESHMAN FINANCIAL AID (Fall 2016, est.) 410 applied for aid; of those 88% were deemed to have need. 100% of freshmen with need received aid; of those 20% had need fully met. *Average percent of need met:* 76% (excluding resources awarded to replace EFC). *Average financial aid package:* $24,926 (excluding resources awarded to replace EFC). 19% of all full-time freshmen had no need and received non-need-based gift aid.

UNDERGRADUATE FINANCIAL AID (Fall 2016, est.) 1,308 applied for aid; of those 90% were deemed to have need. 100% of undergraduates with need received aid; of those 20% had need fully met. *Average percent of need met:* 75% (excluding resources awarded to replace EFC). *Average financial aid package:* $24,191 (excluding resources awarded to replace EFC). 21% of all full-time undergraduates had no need and received non-need-based gift aid.

GIFT AID (NEED-BASED) *Total amount:* $19,739,832 (14% federal, 16% state, 68% institutional, 2% external sources). *Receiving aid:* Freshmen: 64% (286); all full-time undergraduates: 60% (917). *Average award:* Freshmen: $8249; Undergraduates: $7571. *Scholarships, grants, and awards:* Federal Pell, FSEOG, state, private, college/university gift aid from institutional funds.

GIFT AID (NON-NEED-BASED) *Total amount:* $3,793,169 (100% institutional). *Receiving aid:* Freshmen: 78% (346). Undergraduates: 72% (1,105). *Average award:* Freshmen: $14,101. Undergraduates: $11,818. *Scholarships, grants, and awards by category:* Academic interests/achievement: biological sciences, business, communication, computer science, education, English, foreign languages, general academic interests/achievements, health fields, humanities, mathematics, physical sciences, premedicine, religion/biblical studies, social sciences. *Creative arts/performance:* art/fine arts, music, theater/drama. *Special achievements/activities:* cheerleading/drum major, religious involvement. *Special characteristics:* children of faculty/staff, handicapped students, local/state students, members of minority groups, out-of-state students, previous college experience, relatives of clergy. *Tuition waivers:* Full or partial for employees or children of employees. *ROTC:* Army, Air Force cooperative.

LOANS *Student loans:* $8,803,187 (93% need-based, 7% non-need-based). 73% of past graduating class borrowed through all loan programs. *Average indebtedness per student:* $31,901. *Average need-based loan:* Freshmen: $3205. Undergraduates: $4367. *Parent loans:* $5,319,061 (93% need-based, 7% non-need-based). *Programs:* Federal Direct (Subsidized and Unsubsidized Stafford, PLUS), Perkins, state, alternative loans.

WORK-STUDY *Federal work-study:* Total amount: $380,032; 274 jobs averaging $1397. *State or other work-study/employment:* Total amount: $48,572 (67% need-based, 33% non-need-based). 32 part-time jobs averaging $1517.

ATHLETIC AWARDS Total amount: $7,230,836 (55% need-based, 45% non-need-based).

APPLYING FOR FINANCIAL AID *Required financial aid forms:* FAFSA, state aid form. *Financial aid deadline (priority):* 3/15. *Notification date:* 3/1. Students must reply within 2 weeks of notification.

CONTACT Summer Nance, Assistant Vice President of Financial Planning, Gardner-Webb University, PO Box 955, Boiling Springs, NC 28017, 704-406-4243 or toll-free 800-253-6472. *Fax:* 704-406-4102.
Website: http://www.gardner-webb.edu/.

GENEVA COLLEGE
Beaver Falls, PA

Tuition & fees: $26,570	Average undergraduate aid package: $21,000

ABOUT THE INSTITUTION Independent Reformed Presbyterian Church of North America, coed. *Awards:* associate, bachelor's, and master's degrees (also offers non-traditional programs in Philadelphia and western Pennsylvania with significant enrollment not reflected in profile). 36 undergraduate majors. *Total enrollment:* 1,662. Undergraduates: 1,457. Freshmen: 292. Federal methodology is used as a basis for awarding need-based institutional aid.

UNDERGRADUATE EXPENSES for 2017–2018 *Application fee:* $40. *Comprehensive fee:* $36,490 includes full-time tuition ($26,570) and room and board ($9920). Full-time tuition and fees vary according to course load. Room and board charges vary according to board plan. *Part-time tuition:* $880 per credit hour. Part-time tuition and fees vary according to course load.

FRESHMAN FINANCIAL AID (Fall 2016, est.) 275 applied for aid; of those 91% were deemed to have need. 99% of freshmen with need received aid; of those 22% had need fully met. *Average percent of need met:* 78% (excluding resources awarded to replace EFC). *Average financial aid package:* $20,500 (excluding resources awarded to replace EFC). 13% of all full-time freshmen had no need and received non-need-based gift aid.

UNDERGRADUATE FINANCIAL AID (Fall 2016, est.) 1,095 applied for aid; of those 89% were deemed to have need. 100% of undergraduates with need received aid; of those 21% had need fully met. *Average percent of need met:* 79% (excluding resources awarded to replace EFC). *Average financial aid package:* $21,000 (excluding resources awarded to replace EFC). 14% of all full-time undergraduates had no need and received non-need-based gift aid.

GIFT AID (NEED-BASED) *Total amount:* $17,792,790 (11% federal, 10% state, 76% institutional, 3% external sources). *Receiving aid:* Freshmen: 85% (247); all full-time undergraduates: 69% (975). *Average award:* Freshmen: $17,420; Undergraduates: $16,926. *Scholarships, grants, and awards:* Federal Pell, FSEOG, state, private, college/university gift aid from institutional funds.

GIFT AID (NON-NEED-BASED) *Total amount:* $986,590 (98% institutional, 2% external sources). *Receiving aid:* Freshmen: 9% (26). Undergraduates: 9% (130). *Average award:* Freshmen: $12,154. Undergraduates: $10,707. *Scholarships, grants, and awards by category:* Academic interests/achievement: general aca-

demic interests/achievements. *Creative arts/performance:* music. *Special achievements/activities:* leadership. *Special characteristics:* children of faculty/staff, religious affiliation. *Tuition waivers:* Full or partial for employees or children of employees. *ROTC:* Army cooperative.

LOANS *Student loans:* $9,089,172 (83% need-based, 17% non-need-based). 90% of past graduating class borrowed through all loan programs. *Average indebtedness per student:* $10,549. *Average need-based loan:* Freshmen: $3416. Undergraduates: $3795. *Parent loans:* $1,687,484 (69% need-based, 31% non-need-based). *Programs:* Federal Direct (Subsidized and Unsubsidized Stafford, PLUS), Perkins.

WORK-STUDY *Federal work-study:* Total amount: $160,000; 170 jobs averaging $2000.

APPLYING FOR FINANCIAL AID *Required financial aid form:* FAFSA. *Financial aid deadline (priority):* 3/15. *Notification date:* Continuous beginning 11/1. Students must reply within 4 weeks of notification.

CONTACT Ms. Allyson Bentz, Director of Student Financial Services, Geneva College, 3200 College Avenue, Beaver Falls, PA 15010-3599, 724-847-6530 or toll-free 800-847-8255. *Fax:* 724-847-6776. *E-mail:* financialaid@geneva.edu.
Website: http://www.geneva.edu/.

GEORGE FOX UNIVERSITY
Newberg, OR

Tuition & fees: $34,866	Average undergraduate aid package: $22,722

ABOUT THE INSTITUTION Independent Friends, coed. *Awards:* certificates, bachelor's, master's, and doctoral degrees. 46 undergraduate majors. *Total enrollment:* 3,931. Undergraduates: 2,569. Freshmen: 634. Federal methodology is used as a basis for awarding need-based institutional aid.

UNDERGRADUATE EXPENSES for 2017–2018 *Application fee:* $40. *Comprehensive fee:* $45,752 includes full-time tuition ($34,500), mandatory fees ($366), and room and board ($10,886). Full-time tuition and fees vary according to reciprocity agreements. Room and board charges vary according to board plan. Part-time tuition and fees vary according to course load.

FRESHMAN FINANCIAL AID (Fall 2016, est.) 588 applied for aid; of those 83% were deemed to have need. 100% of freshmen with need received aid; of those 44% had need fully met. *Average percent of need met:* 88% (excluding resources awarded to replace EFC). *Average financial aid package:* $24,260 (excluding resources awarded to replace EFC). 24% of all full-time freshmen had no need and received non-need-based gift aid.

UNDERGRADUATE FINANCIAL AID (Fall 2016, est.) 2,135 applied for aid; of those 90% were deemed to have need. 100% of undergraduates with need received aid; of those 39% had need fully met. *Average percent of need met:* 85% (excluding resources awarded to replace EFC). *Average financial aid package:* $22,722 (excluding resources awarded to replace EFC). 22% of all full-time undergraduates had no need and received non-need-based gift aid.

GIFT AID (NEED-BASED) *Total amount:* $32,808,470 (12% federal, 3% state, 80% institutional, 5% external sources). *Receiving aid:* Freshmen: 76% (486); all full-time undergraduates: 74% (1,908). *Average award:* Freshmen: $20,148; Undergraduates: $17,611. *Scholarships, grants, and awards:* Federal Pell, FSEOG, state, private, college/university gift aid from institutional funds, TEACH Grants.

GIFT AID (NON-NEED-BASED) *Total amount:* $8,738,782 (96% institutional, 4% external sources). *Receiving aid:* Freshmen: 10% (64). Undergraduates: 6% (166). *Average award:* Freshmen: $14,413. Undergraduates: $12,945. *Scholarships, grants, and awards by category:* Academic interests/achievement: biological sciences, business, communication, computer science, education, engineering/technologies, English, foreign languages, general academic interests/achievements, health fields, home economics, humanities, international studies, mathematics, physical sciences, religion/biblical studies, social sciences. *Creative arts/performance:* art/fine arts, cinema/film/broadcasting, debating, music, theater/drama. *Special achievements/activities:* leadership, religious involvement. *Special characteristics:* children and siblings of alumni, children of faculty/staff, ethnic background, international students, members of minority groups, out-of-state students, relatives of clergy, religious affiliation. *Tuition waivers:* Full or partial for employees or children of employees, senior citizens. *ROTC:* Air Force cooperative.

LOANS *Student loans:* $18,149,931 (74% need-based, 26% non-need-based). 87% of past graduating class borrowed through all loan programs. *Average indebtedness per student:* $22,799. *Average need-based loan:* Freshmen: $3093. Undergrad-

uates: $4045. **Parent loans:** $6,951,142 (45% need-based, 55% non-need-based). **Programs:** Federal Direct (Subsidized and Unsubsidized Stafford, PLUS), Perkins, alternative loans.

WORK-STUDY *Federal work-study:* Total amount: $2,998,596; 1,364 jobs averaging $2198. *State or other work-study/employment:* Total amount: $869,950 (100% non-need-based). Part-time jobs available.

APPLYING FOR FINANCIAL AID *Required financial aid forms:* FAFSA, state aid form. *Financial aid deadline:* Continuous. *Notification date:* Continuous beginning 12/16. Students must reply by 5/1.

CONTACT Johanna Kaye, Director of Financial Aid, George Fox University, 414 North Meridian Street, Newberg, OR 97132-2697, 503-554-2235 or toll-free 800-765-4369. *Fax:* 503-554-3110. *E-mail:* kayej@georgefox.edu. *Website:* http://www.georgefox.edu/.

GEORGE MASON UNIVERSITY
Fairfax, VA

Tuition & fees (VA res): $11,300	Average undergraduate aid package: $12,890

ABOUT THE INSTITUTION State-supported, coed. *Awards:* certificates, bachelor's, master's, and doctoral degrees. 67 undergraduate majors. *Total enrollment:* 33,925. Undergraduates: 23,062. Freshmen: 3,181. Federal methodology is used as a basis for awarding need-based institutional aid.

UNDERGRADUATE EXPENSES for 2016–2017 *Tuition, state resident:* full-time $8204; part-time $342 per credit hour. *Tuition, nonresident:* full-time $29,486; part-time $1229 per credit hour. *Required fees:* full-time $3096; $129 per credit hour. Full-time tuition and fees vary according to course load. Part-time tuition and fees vary according to course load. *College room and board:* $10,730; *Room only:* $6400. Room and board charges vary according to board plan and housing facility.

FRESHMAN FINANCIAL AID (Fall 2015) 2,611 applied for aid; of those 73% were deemed to have need. 96% of freshmen with need received aid; of those 7% had need fully met. *Average percent of need met:* 65% (excluding resources awarded to replace EFC). *Average financial aid package:* $14,893 (excluding resources awarded to replace EFC). 11% of all full-time freshmen had no need and received non-need-based gift aid.

UNDERGRADUATE FINANCIAL AID (Fall 2015) 12,561 applied for aid; of those 81% were deemed to have need. 95% of undergraduates with need received aid; of those 5% had need fully met. *Average percent of need met:* 57% (excluding resources awarded to replace EFC). *Average financial aid package:* $12,890 (excluding resources awarded to replace EFC). 6% of all full-time undergraduates had no need and received non-need-based gift aid.

GIFT AID (NEED-BASED) *Total amount:* $55,173,628 (48% federal, 33% state, 19% institutional). *Receiving aid:* Freshmen: 48% (1,521); all full-time undergraduates: 44% (7,974). *Average award:* Freshmen: $7258; Undergraduates: $6413. *Scholarships, grants, and awards:* Federal Pell, FSEOG, state, private, college/university gift aid from institutional funds.

GIFT AID (NON-NEED-BASED) *Total amount:* $11,567,258 (72% institutional, 28% external sources). *Receiving aid:* Freshmen: 22% (687). Undergraduates: 10% (1,836). *Average award:* Freshmen: $5700. Undergraduates: $4513. *Scholarships, grants, and awards by category:* Academic interests/achievement: 2,113 awards ($8,008,684 total): general academic interests/achievements. Creative arts/performance: general creative arts/performance. Special characteristics: general special characteristics. *Tuition waivers:* Full or partial for employees or children of employees, senior citizens. *ROTC:* Army, Air Force cooperative.

LOANS *Student loans:* $95,357,069 (75% need-based, 25% non-need-based). 56% of past graduating class borrowed through all loan programs. *Average indebtedness per student:* $30,132. *Average need-based loan:* Freshmen: $3367. Undergraduates: $4450. *Parent loans:* $24,662,033 (51% need-based, 49% non-need-based). *Programs:* Federal Direct (Subsidized and Unsubsidized Stafford, PLUS), Perkins, Federal Nursing.

WORK-STUDY *Federal work-study:* 499 jobs averaging $2162.

ATHLETIC AWARDS Total amount: $5,317,249 (100% non-need-based).

APPLYING FOR FINANCIAL AID *Required financial aid form:* FAFSA. *Financial aid deadline (priority):* 3/1. *Notification date:* Continuous beginning 3/1. Students must reply within 3 weeks of notification.

CONTACT Office of Student Financial Aid, George Mason University, 1111 Student Union Building I, Mail Stop 3B5, Fairfax, VA 22030-4444, 703-993-2353 or toll-free 888-627-6612. *Fax:* 703-993-2350. *E-mail:* finaid@gmu.edu. *Website:* http://www.gmu.edu/.

GEORGETOWN COLLEGE
Georgetown, KY

ABOUT THE INSTITUTION Independent Baptist Church, coed. *Awards:* certificates, bachelor's, and master's degrees. 35 undergraduate majors. *Total enrollment:* 1,526. Undergraduates: 986. Freshmen: 296.

GIFT AID (NEED-BASED) *Scholarships, grants, and awards:* Federal Pell, FSEOG, state, private, college/university gift aid from institutional funds.

GIFT AID (NON-NEED-BASED) *Scholarships, grants, and awards by category:* Academic interests/achievement: general academic interests/achievements, international studies. Creative arts/performance: art/fine arts, music, performing arts, theater/drama. Special achievements/activities: junior miss, religious involvement. Special characteristics: children and siblings of alumni, children of faculty/staff, local/state students, members of minority groups, out-of-state students, relatives of clergy, religious affiliation, veterans, veterans' children.

LOANS *Programs:* Federal Direct (Subsidized and Unsubsidized Stafford, PLUS), Perkins, college/university.

APPLYING FOR FINANCIAL AID *Required financial aid forms:* FAFSA, institution's own form.

CONTACT Mr. Bob Fultz, Director of Student Financial Planning, Georgetown College, 400 East College Street, Georgetown, KY 40324-1696, 502-863-8029 or toll-free 800-788-9985. *Fax:* 502-868-7733. *E-mail:* financialaid@georgetowncollege.edu. *Website:* http://www.georgetowncollege.edu/.

GEORGETOWN UNIVERSITY
Washington, DC

Tuition & fees: $50,547	Average undergraduate aid package: $48,999

ABOUT THE INSTITUTION Independent Roman Catholic (Jesuit), coed. *Awards:* certificates, bachelor's, master's, and doctoral degrees. 48 undergraduate majors. *Total enrollment:* 18,525. Undergraduates: 7,453. Freshmen: 1,574. Both federal and institutional methodology are used as a basis for awarding need-based institutional aid.

UNDERGRADUATE EXPENSES for 2016–2017 *Application fee:* $75. *Comprehensive fee:* $66,115 includes full-time tuition ($49,968), mandatory fees ($579), and room and board ($15,568). *College room only:* $10,726. Full-time tuition and fees vary according to course load and program. Room and board charges vary according to board plan and housing facility. *Part-time tuition:* $2082 per credit hour. Part-time tuition and fees vary according to course load and program.

FRESHMAN FINANCIAL AID (Fall 2016, est.) 1,034 applied for aid; of those 63% were deemed to have need. 100% of freshmen with need received aid; of those 100% had need fully met. *Average percent of need met:* 100% (excluding resources awarded to replace EFC). *Average financial aid package:* $48,620 (excluding resources awarded to replace EFC).

UNDERGRADUATE FINANCIAL AID (Fall 2016, est.) 4,003 applied for aid; of those 68% were deemed to have need. 100% of undergraduates with need received aid; of those 100% had need fully met. *Average percent of need met:* 100% (excluding resources awarded to replace EFC). *Average financial aid package:* $48,999 (excluding resources awarded to replace EFC).

GIFT AID (NEED-BASED) *Total amount:* $108,846,000 (5% federal, 90% institutional, 5% external sources). *Receiving aid:* Freshmen: 37% (576); all full-time undergraduates: 34% (2,400). *Average award:* Freshmen: $41,492; Undergraduates: $40,252. *Scholarships, grants, and awards:* Federal Pell, FSEOG, state, private, college/university gift aid from institutional funds.

GIFT AID (NON-NEED-BASED) *Total amount:* $1,900,000 (92% federal, 8% institutional). *Receiving aid:* Freshmen: 16% (250). Undergraduates: 11% (800). *Scholarships, grants, and awards by category:* Special characteristics: 144 awards ($4,459,254 total): children of faculty/staff. *ROTC:* Army, Naval cooperative, Air Force cooperative.

LOANS *Student loans:* $15,300,000 (47% need-based, 53% non-need-based). 37% of past graduating class borrowed through all loan programs. *Average indebtedness per student:* $23,412. *Average need-based loan:* Freshmen: $2723. Undergraduates: $4076. *Parent loans:* $11,300,000 (100% non-need-based). *Programs:* Federal Direct (Subsidized and Unsubsidized Stafford, PLUS), Perkins, Federal Nursing, alternative loans.

WORK-STUDY *Federal work-study:* Total amount: $7,200,000; 2,520 jobs averaging $2866.

ATHLETIC AWARDS Total amount: $8,000,000 (25% need-based, 75% non-need-based).

APPLYING FOR FINANCIAL AID *Required financial aid forms:* FAFSA, CSS Financial Aid PROFILE, federal income tax form(s). *Financial aid deadline:* 2/1. *Notification date:* 4/1. Students must reply by 5/1 or within 2 weeks of notification.

CONTACT Ms. Patricia A. McWade, Dean of Student Financial Services, Georgetown University, 37th and O Street, NW, Box 1252, Washington, DC 20057, 202-687-4547. *Fax:* 202-687-6542. *E-mail:* mcwadep@georgetown.edu. *Website:* http://www.georgetown.edu/.

THE GEORGE WASHINGTON UNIVERSITY
Washington, DC

Tuition & fees: $53,518	Average undergraduate aid package: $43,674

ABOUT THE INSTITUTION Independent, coed. *Awards:* certificates, associate, bachelor's, master's, and doctoral degrees. 81 undergraduate majors. *Total enrollment:* 27,159. Undergraduates: 11,504. Freshmen: 2,525. Both federal and institutional methodology are used as a basis for awarding need-based institutional aid.

UNDERGRADUATE EXPENSES for 2017–2018 *Application fee:* $75. *Comprehensive fee:* $66,518 includes full-time tuition ($53,435), mandatory fees ($83), and room and board ($13,000). *College room only:* $8900. Full-time tuition and fees vary according to student level. Room and board charges vary according to housing facility. *Part-time tuition:* $1520 per credit hour. Part-time tuition and fees vary according to course load. *Payment plan:* Guaranteed tuition.

FRESHMAN FINANCIAL AID (Fall 2015) 1,699 applied for aid; of those 71% were deemed to have need. 99% of freshmen with need received aid; of those 47% had need fully met. *Average percent of need met:* 87% (excluding resources awarded to replace EFC). *Average financial aid package:* $42,555 (excluding resources awarded to replace EFC). 35% of all full-time freshmen had no need and received non-need-based gift aid.

UNDERGRADUATE FINANCIAL AID (Fall 2015) 5,607 applied for aid; of those 82% were deemed to have need. 99% of undergraduates with need received aid; of those 48% had need fully met. *Average percent of need met:* 87% (excluding resources awarded to replace EFC). *Average financial aid package:* $43,674 (excluding resources awarded to replace EFC). 27% of all full-time undergraduates had no need and received non-need-based gift aid.

GIFT AID (NEED-BASED) *Total amount:* $139,856,830 (6% federal, 94% institutional). *Receiving aid:* Freshmen: 45% (1,158); all full-time undergraduates: 43% (4,330). *Average award:* Freshmen: $28,416; Undergraduates: $29,433. *Scholarships, grants, and awards:* Federal Pell, FSEOG, state, college/university gift aid from institutional funds.

GIFT AID (NON-NEED-BASED) *Total amount:* $43,377,362 (100% institutional). *Receiving aid:* Freshmen: 36% (936). Undergraduates: 21% (2,100). *Average award:* Freshmen: $19,477. Undergraduates: $19,541. *Scholarships, grants, and awards by category:* Academic interests/achievement: general academic interests/achievements. Creative arts/performance: general creative arts/performance. *Tuition waivers:* Full or partial for employees or children of employees. *ROTC:* Army cooperative, Naval, Air Force cooperative.

LOANS *Student loans:* $38,549,085 (72% need-based, 28% non-need-based). 46% of past graduating class borrowed through all loan programs. *Average indebtedness per student:* $33,305. *Average need-based loan:* Freshmen: $4674. Undergraduates: $5809. *Parent loans:* $23,583,131 (27% need-based, 73% non-need-based). *Programs:* Federal Direct (Subsidized and Unsubsidized Stafford, PLUS), Perkins.

WORK-STUDY *Federal work-study:* jobs available.

ATHLETIC AWARDS Total amount: $10,324,210 (38% need-based, 62% non-need-based).

APPLYING FOR FINANCIAL AID *Required financial aid forms:* FAFSA, CSS Financial Aid PROFILE, noncustodial (divorced/separated) parent's statement. *Financial aid deadline:* 2/1 (priority: 2/1). *Notification date:* Continuous beginning 3/24. Students must reply by 5/1.

CONTACT Dan Small, Associate Vice President for Financial Assistance, The George Washington University, 2121 I Street, NW, Rice Hall, Suite 301, Washington, DC 21044, 202-994-6620. *Fax:* 202-994-0906. *E-mail:* finaid@gwu.edu. *Website:* http://www.gwu.edu/.

GEORGIA CHRISTIAN UNIVERSITY
Atlanta, GA

CONTACT Financial Aid Office, Georgia Christian University, 6789 Peachtree Industrial Boulevard, Atlanta, GA 30360, 770-279-0507. *Website:* http://www.gcuniv.edu/.

GEORGIA COLLEGE & STATE UNIVERSITY
Milledgeville, GA

Tuition & fees (GA res): $9202	Average undergraduate aid package: $10,428

ABOUT THE INSTITUTION State-supported, coed. *Awards:* certificates, bachelor's, master's, and doctoral degrees. 36 undergraduate majors. *Total enrollment:* 6,915. Undergraduates: 6,047. Freshmen: 1,381. Federal methodology is used as a basis for awarding need-based institutional aid.

UNDERGRADUATE EXPENSES for 2016–2017 *Application fee:* $40. *Tuition, state resident:* full-time $7180. *Tuition, nonresident:* full-time $25,528. *Required fees:* full-time $2022. Full-time tuition and fees vary according to course load, location, and program. Part-time tuition and fees vary according to course load, location, and program. *College room and board:* $11,946; *Room only:* $6400. Room and board charges vary according to board plan and housing facility.

FRESHMAN FINANCIAL AID (Fall 2016, est.) 1,200 applied for aid; of those 59% were deemed to have need. 98% of freshmen with need received aid; of those 24% had need fully met. *Average percent of need met:* 64% (excluding resources awarded to replace EFC). *Average financial aid package:* $11,211 (excluding resources awarded to replace EFC). 3% of all full-time freshmen had no need and received non-need-based gift aid.

UNDERGRADUATE FINANCIAL AID (Fall 2016, est.) 4,133 applied for aid; of those 66% were deemed to have need. 97% of undergraduates with need received aid; of those 19% had need fully met. *Average percent of need met:* 58% (excluding resources awarded to replace EFC). *Average financial aid package:* $10,428 (excluding resources awarded to replace EFC). 4% of all full-time undergraduates had no need and received non-need-based gift aid.

GIFT AID (NEED-BASED) *Total amount:* $5,350,000 (97% federal, 3% institutional). *Receiving aid:* Freshmen: 20% (273); all full-time undergraduates: 20% (1,099). *Average award:* Freshmen: $4394; Undergraduates: $4309. *Scholarships, grants, and awards:* Federal Pell, FSEOG, state, college/university gift aid from institutional funds.

GIFT AID (NON-NEED-BASED) *Total amount:* $30,300,000 (89% state, 5% institutional, 6% external sources). *Receiving aid:* Freshmen: 47% (654). Undergraduates: 38% (2,124). *Average award:* Freshmen: $2111. Undergraduates: $2069. *Scholarships, grants, and awards by category:* Academic interests/achievement: biological sciences, business, computer science, education, humanities, international studies, physical sciences, social sciences. Creative arts/performance: art/fine arts, journalism/publications, music. Special achievements/activities: general special achievements/activities. Special characteristics: adult students, children of faculty/staff, general special characteristics, local/state students, out-of-state students, public servants. *Tuition waivers:* Full or partial for employees or children of employees, senior citizens. *ROTC:* Army cooperative.

LOANS *Student loans:* $27,900,000 (33% need-based, 67% non-need-based). 54% of past graduating class borrowed through all loan programs. *Average indebtedness per student:* $29,138. *Average need-based loan:* Freshmen: $4233. Undergraduates: $4569. *Parent loans:* $5,000,000 (100% non-need-based). *Programs:* Federal Direct (Subsidized and Unsubsidized Stafford, PLUS), Perkins.

WORK-STUDY *Federal work-study:* Total amount: $200,000; jobs available.

ATHLETIC AWARDS Total amount: $610,000 (100% non-need-based).

APPLYING FOR FINANCIAL AID *Required financial aid form:* FAFSA. *Financial aid deadline (priority):* 3/1. *Notification date:* Continuous beginning 3/1. Students must reply within 2 weeks of notification.

CONTACT Ms. Cathy Crawley, Director of Financial Aid, Georgia College & State University, Campus Box 30, Milledgeville, GA 31061, 478-445-5149 or toll-free 800-342-0471. *Fax:* 478-445-0729. *E-mail:* cathy.crawley@gcsu.edu. *Website:* http://www.gcsu.edu/.

GEORGIA GWINNETT COLLEGE
Lawrenceville, GA

CONTACT Financial Aid Office, Georgia Gwinnett College, 1000 University Center Lane, Lawrenceville, GA 30043, 678-407-5000 or toll-free 877-704-4422. *Website:* http://www.ggc.edu/.

GEORGIA INSTITUTE OF TECHNOLOGY
Atlanta, GA

Tuition & fees (GA res): $12,212	Average undergraduate aid package: $13,171

ABOUT THE INSTITUTION State-supported, coed. *Awards:* bachelor's, master's, and doctoral degrees. 33 undergraduate majors. *Total enrollment:* 26,839. Undergraduates: 15,489. Freshmen: 2,877. Both federal and institutional methodology are used as a basis for awarding need-based institutional aid.

UNDERGRADUATE EXPENSES for 2016–2017 *Application fee:* $75. *Tuition, state resident:* full-time $9812; part-time $2916 per term. *Tuition, non-resident:* full-time $30,004; part-time $8903 per term. *Required fees:* full-time $2400; $1200 per term. Part-time tuition and fees vary according to course load. *College room and board:* $13,640; *Room only:* $8940. Room and board charges vary according to board plan, housing facility, and student level.

FRESHMAN FINANCIAL AID (Fall 2015) 2,459 applied for aid; of those 49% were deemed to have need. 94% of freshmen with need received aid; of those 24% had need fully met. *Average percent of need met:* 58% (excluding resources awarded to replace EFC). *Average financial aid package:* $13,854 (excluding resources awarded to replace EFC). 10% of all full-time freshmen had no need and received non-need-based gift aid.

UNDERGRADUATE FINANCIAL AID (Fall 2015) 8,991 applied for aid; of those 63% were deemed to have need. 96% of undergraduates with need received aid; of those 16% had need fully met. *Average percent of need met:* 52% (excluding resources awarded to replace EFC). *Average financial aid package:* $13,171 (excluding resources awarded to replace EFC). 11% of all full-time undergraduates had no need and received non-need-based gift aid.

GIFT AID (NEED-BASED) *Total amount:* $51,190,679 (21% federal, 47% state, 30% institutional, 2% external sources). *Receiving aid:* Freshmen: 34% (1,039); all full-time undergraduates: 36% (4,926). *Average award:* Freshmen: $12,920; Undergraduates: $11,070. *Scholarships, grants, and awards:* Federal Pell, FSEOG, state, private, college/university gift aid from institutional funds, United Negro College Fund.

GIFT AID (NON-NEED-BASED) *Total amount:* $30,998,289 (83% state, 14% institutional, 3% external sources). *Receiving aid:* Freshmen: 26% (818). Undergraduates: 25% (3,381). *Average award:* Freshmen: $8532. Undergraduates: $11,275. *Scholarships, grants, and awards by category: Academic interests/ achievement:* 2,633 awards ($14,416,348 total): architecture, biological sciences, computer science, engineering/technologies, general academic interests/achievements, physical sciences. *Special achievements/activities:* 229 awards ($456,500 total): cheerleading/drum major, general special achievements/activities, leadership. *Special characteristics:* 6,042 awards ($53,468,266 total): children with a deceased or disabled parent, local/state students, members of minority groups, out-of-state students, veterans, veterans' children. *Tuition waivers:* Full or partial for employees or children of employees, senior citizens. **ROTC:** Army, Naval, Air Force.

GEORGIAN COURT UNIVERSITY
Lakewood, NJ

Tuition & fees: $31,618	Average undergraduate aid package: $28,364

ABOUT THE INSTITUTION Independent Roman Catholic, coed. *Awards:* certificates, bachelor's, and master's degrees. 30 undergraduate majors. *Total enrollment:* 2,302. Undergraduates: 1,591. Freshmen: 221. Federal methodology is used as a basis for awarding need-based institutional aid.

UNDERGRADUATE EXPENSES for 2016–2017 *Application fee:* $40. *Comprehensive fee:* $42,426 includes full-time tuition ($30,158), mandatory fees ($1460), and room and board ($10,808). Full-time tuition and fees vary according to location, program, and reciprocity agreements. *Part-time tuition:* $690 per credit hour. *Part-time fees:* $365 per term. Part-time tuition and fees vary according to location, program, and reciprocity agreements.

FRESHMAN FINANCIAL AID (Fall 2016, est.) 215 applied for aid; of those 97% were deemed to have need. 100% of freshmen with need received aid; of those 27% had need fully met. *Average percent of need met:* 80% (excluding resources awarded to replace EFC). *Average financial aid package:* $29,822 (excluding resources awarded to replace EFC). 6% of all full-time freshmen had no need and received non-need-based gift aid.

UNDERGRADUATE FINANCIAL AID (Fall 2016, est.) 1,193 applied for aid; of those 95% were deemed to have need. 100% of undergraduates with need received aid; of those 21% had need fully met. *Average percent of need met:* 74% (excluding resources awarded to replace EFC). *Average financial aid package:* $28,364 (excluding resources awarded to replace EFC). 11% of all full-time undergraduates had no need and received non-need-based gift aid.

GIFT AID (NEED-BASED) *Total amount:* $21,182,900 (14% federal, 20% state, 66% institutional). *Receiving aid:* Freshmen: 93% (206); all full-time undergraduates: 84% (1,106). *Average award:* Freshmen: $19,904; Undergraduates: $18,406. *Scholarships, grants, and awards:* Federal Pell, FSEOG, state, private, college/university gift aid from institutional funds.

GIFT AID (NON-NEED-BASED) *Total amount:* $2,419,050 (100% institutional). *Receiving aid:* Freshmen: 7% (15). Undergraduates: 4% (56). *Average award:* Freshmen: $12,397. Undergraduates: $13,890. *Scholarships, grants, and awards by category: Academic interests/achievement:* biological sciences, business, computer science, education, English, foreign languages, general academic interests/ achievements, home economics, humanities, international studies, mathematics, physical sciences, premedicine, religion/biblical studies, social sciences. *Creative arts/ performance:* applied art and design, art/fine arts, dance. *Special achievements/activities:* community service, general special achievements/activities, leadership, memberships, religious involvement. *Special characteristics:* adult students, children and siblings of alumni, children of faculty/staff, ethnic background, first-generation college students, local/state students, married students, members of minority groups, out-of-state students, previous college experience, religious affiliation, siblings of current students, veterans. *Tuition waivers:* Full or partial for children of alumni, employees or children of employees, senior citizens.

LOANS *Student loans:* $11,075,803 (81% need-based, 19% non-need-based). 88% of past graduating class borrowed through all loan programs. *Average indebtedness per student:* $40,267. *Average need-based loan:* Freshmen: $5756. Undergrad-

LOANS *Student loans:* $42,090,069 (82% need-based, 18% non-need-based). 39% of past graduating class borrowed through all loan programs. *Average indebtedness per student:* $32,169. *Average need-based loan:* Freshmen: $3945. Undergraduates: $5007. *Parent loans:* $24,221,629 (77% need-based, 23% non-need-based). *Programs:* Federal Direct (Subsidized and Unsubsidized Stafford, PLUS), Perkins, state, college/university.

WORK-STUDY *Federal work-study:* 395 jobs averaging $1831.

ATHLETIC AWARDS Total amount: $6,673,939 (44% need-based, 56% non-need-based).

APPLYING FOR FINANCIAL AID *Required financial aid forms:* FAFSA, institution's own form, CSS Financial Aid PROFILE. *Financial aid deadline:* 1/31. *Notification date:* 4/15. Students must reply by 5/1.

CONTACT Ms. Marie Mons, Director of Student Financial Planning and Services, Georgia Institute of Technology, 225 North Avenue, NW, Atlanta, GA 30332-0460, 404-894-4160. *Fax:* 404-894-7412. *E-mail:* marie.mons@finaid.gatech.edu. *Website:* http://www.gatech.edu/.

uates: $7548. **Parent loans:** $1,752,422 (57% need-based, 43% non-need-based). **Programs:** Federal Direct (Subsidized and Unsubsidized Stafford, PLUS), state. **WORK-STUDY Federal work-study:** Total amount: $237,200; jobs available. **State or other work-study/employment:** Total amount: $24,750 (6% need-based, 94% non-need-based). Part-time jobs available. **ATHLETIC AWARDS** Total amount: $1,818,160 (67% need-based, 33% non-need-based).

APPLYING FOR FINANCIAL AID Required financial aid form: FAFSA. **Financial aid deadline:** 7/1 (priority: 1/15). **Notification date:** Continuous beginning 12/1.

CONTACT Mr. Randy Brown, Director of Financial Aid, Georgian Court University, 900 Lakewood Avenue, Lakewood, NJ 08701-2697, 732-987-2258 or toll-free 800-458-8422. Fax: 732-987-2023. E-mail: rbrown@georgian.edu. Website: http://www.georgian.edu/.

GEORGIA SOUTHERN UNIVERSITY
Statesboro, GA

Tuition & fees (GA res): $6796	Average undergraduate aid package: $9952

ABOUT THE INSTITUTION State-supported, coed. **Awards:** certificates, bachelor's, master's, and doctoral degrees. 81 undergraduate majors. **Total enrollment:** 20,673. Undergraduates: 17,995. Freshmen: 3,600. Federal methodology is used as a basis for awarding need-based institutional aid.

UNDERGRADUATE EXPENSES for 2016–2017 Application fee: $30. **Tuition, state resident:** full-time $4704; part-time $174.20 per credit hour. **Tuition, nonresident:** full-time $16,600; part-time $614.80 per credit hour. **Required fees:** full-time $2092; $1046 per term. Full-time tuition and fees vary according to course load, degree level, location, and program. Part-time tuition and fees vary according to course load, degree level, location, and program. **College room and board:** $9650; **Room only:** $5900. Room and board charges vary according to board plan and housing facility.

FRESHMAN FINANCIAL AID (Fall 2015) 3,231 applied for aid; of those 71% were deemed to have need. 98% of freshmen with need received aid; of those 14% had need fully met. **Average percent of need met:** 57% (excluding resources awarded to replace EFC). **Average financial aid package:** $10,315 (excluding resources awarded to replace EFC). 3% of all full-time freshmen had no need and received non-need-based gift aid.

UNDERGRADUATE FINANCIAL AID (Fall 2015) 14,342 applied for aid; of those 74% were deemed to have need. 98% of undergraduates with need received aid; of those 9% had need fully met. **Average percent of need met:** 51% (excluding resources awarded to replace EFC). **Average financial aid package:** $9952 (excluding resources awarded to replace EFC). 2% of all full-time undergraduates had no need and received non-need-based gift aid.

GIFT AID (NEED-BASED) Total amount: $59,533,819 (53% federal, 43% state, 2% institutional, 2% external sources). **Receiving aid:** Freshmen: 60% (2,065); all full-time undergraduates: 55% (8,740). **Average award:** Freshmen: $7559; Undergraduates: $6864. **Scholarships, grants, and awards:** Federal Pell, FSEOG, state, private, HOPE Scholarships, TEACH Grants, Zell Miller Scholarships.

GIFT AID (NON-NEED-BASED) Total amount: $13,978,270 (92% state, 5% institutional, 3% external sources). **Receiving aid:** Freshmen: 2% (54). Undergraduates: 1% (110). **Average award:** Freshmen: $1652. Undergraduates: $1695. **Scholarships, grants, and awards by category:** Academic interests/achievement: 795 awards ($1,167,070 total): biological sciences, business, communication, computer science, education, engineering/technologies, English, foreign languages, general academic interests/achievements, health fields, home economics, humanities, international studies, mathematics, military science, social sciences. Creative arts/performance: 176 awards ($135,969 total): art/fine arts, cinema/film/broadcasting, general creative arts/performance, music, theater/drama. Special achievements/activities: 169 awards ($231,500 total): cheerleading/drum major, community service, junior miss, leadership, memberships, religious involvement. Special characteristics: 115 awards ($194,329 total): adult students, children and siblings of alumni, children of public servants, first-generation college students, general special characteristics, handicapped students, married students, members of minority groups, religious affiliation. **Tuition waivers:** Full or partial for employees or children of employees, senior citizens. **ROTC:** Army. **LOANS Student loans:** $79,709,333 (81% need-based, 19% non-need-based). 72% of past graduating class borrowed through all loan programs. Average indebtedness per student: $28,098. **Average need-based loan:** Freshmen: $4291. Undergrad-

uates: $4952. **Parent loans:** $15,985,603 (78% need-based, 22% non-need-based). **Programs:** Federal Direct (Subsidized and Unsubsidized Stafford, PLUS), Perkins, state, alternative loans, Student Access Loans (SAL). **WORK-STUDY Federal work-study:** 219 jobs averaging $1814. **ATHLETIC AWARDS** Total amount: $4,456,437 (62% need-based, 38% non-need-based).

APPLYING FOR FINANCIAL AID Required financial aid form: FAFSA. **Financial aid deadline (priority):** 4/20. **Notification date:** Continuous beginning 4/20.

CONTACT Mrs. Tracey Mingo, Director of Financial Aid, Georgia Southern University, PO Box 8065, Statesboro, GA 30460-8065, 912-478-5413. Fax: 912-478-0573. E-mail: tmingo@georgiasouthern.edu. Website: http://www.georgiasouthern.edu/.

GEORGIA SOUTHWESTERN STATE UNIVERSITY
Americus, GA

Tuition & fees (GA res): $6234	Average undergraduate aid package: $9480

ABOUT THE INSTITUTION State-supported, coed. **Awards:** certificates, bachelor's, and master's degrees. 24 undergraduate majors. **Total enrollment:** 2,954. Undergraduates: 2,558. Freshmen: 485. Federal methodology is used as a basis for awarding need-based institutional aid.

UNDERGRADUATE EXPENSES for 2016–2017 Application fee: $25. **Tuition, state resident:** full-time $4858; part-time $161.93 per credit hour. **Tuition, nonresident:** full-time $17,678; part-time $589.27 per credit hour. **Required fees:** full-time $1376; $670 per term. Full-time tuition and fees vary according to course load, location, and program. Part-time tuition and fees vary according to course load, location, and program. **College room and board:** $8952; **Room only:** $5130. Room and board charges vary according to board plan and housing facility.

FRESHMAN FINANCIAL AID (Fall 2016, est.) 447 applied for aid; of those 79% were deemed to have need. 100% of freshmen with need received aid; of those 12% had need fully met. **Average percent of need met:** 64% (excluding resources awarded to replace EFC). **Average financial aid package:** $10,198 (excluding resources awarded to replace EFC). 9% of all full-time freshmen had no need and received non-need-based gift aid.

UNDERGRADUATE FINANCIAL AID (Fall 2016, est.) 1,577 applied for aid; of those 82% were deemed to have need. 98% of undergraduates with need received aid; of those 13% had need fully met. **Average percent of need met:** 60% (excluding resources awarded to replace EFC). **Average financial aid package:** $9480 (excluding resources awarded to replace EFC). 7% of all full-time undergraduates had no need and received non-need-based gift aid.

GIFT AID (NEED-BASED) Total amount: $5,183,792 (100% federal). **Receiving aid:** Freshmen: 51% (241); all full-time undergraduates: 48% (845). **Average award:** Freshmen: $5092; Undergraduates: $4902. **Scholarships, grants, and awards:** Federal Pell, FSEOG, state, private, college/university gift aid from institutional funds.

GIFT AID (NON-NEED-BASED) Total amount: $4,247,399 (77% state, 19% institutional, 4% external sources). **Receiving aid:** Freshmen: 56% (264). Undergraduates: 38% (665). **Average award:** Freshmen: $1807. Undergraduates: $1977. **Scholarships, grants, and awards by category:** Academic interests/achievement: 163 awards ($300,915 total): general academic interests/achievements. Creative arts/performance: 30 awards ($30,975 total): art/fine arts, music, theater/drama. Special achievements/activities: 31 awards ($13,145 total): leadership. Special characteristics: children and siblings of alumni, general special characteristics, local/state students. **Tuition waivers:** Full or partial for senior citizens.

LOANS Student loans: $12,973,504 (44% need-based, 56% non-need-based). 78% of past graduating class borrowed through all loan programs. Average indebtedness per student: $28,469. **Average need-based loan:** Freshmen: $3429. Undergraduates: $3984. **Parent loans:** $670,856 (100% non-need-based). **Programs:** Federal Direct (Subsidized and Unsubsidized Stafford, PLUS), Perkins, state. **WORK-STUDY Federal work-study:** Total amount: $123,565; 56 jobs averaging $2207. **ATHLETIC AWARDS** Total amount: $522,896 (100% non-need-based).

APPLYING FOR FINANCIAL AID *Required financial aid form:* FAFSA. *Financial aid deadline:* 6/15 (priority: 4/15). *Notification date:* Continuous beginning 5/1. Students must reply within 8 weeks of notification.

CONTACT Angela Bryant, Director of Financial Aid, Georgia Southwestern State University, 800 Georgia Southwestern State University Drive, Americus, GA 31709-4693, 229-928-1378 or toll-free 800-338-0082. *Fax:* 229-931-2061. *E-mail:* finaid@gsw.edu.
Website: http://www.gsw.edu/.

GEORGIA STATE UNIVERSITY
Atlanta, GA

Tuition & fees (GA res): $10,686	Average undergraduate aid package: $11,461

ABOUT THE INSTITUTION State-supported, coed. *Awards:* certificates, associate, bachelor's, master's, and doctoral degrees. 49 undergraduate majors. *Total enrollment:* 32,464. Undergraduates: 25,455. Freshmen: 3,975. Federal methodology is used as a basis for awarding need-based institutional aid.

UNDERGRADUATE EXPENSES for 2016–2017 *Application fee:* $60. *Tuition, state resident:* full-time $8558; part-time $285.27 per credit hour. *Tuition, nonresident:* full-time $26,768; part-time $892.27 per credit hour. *Required fees:* full-time $2128; $1064 per term. Part-time tuition and fees vary according to course load. *College room and board:* $14,084; *Room only:* $10,252. Room and board charges vary according to board plan and housing facility.

FRESHMAN FINANCIAL AID (Fall 2015) 3,456 applied for aid; of those 85% were deemed to have need. 98% of freshmen with need received aid; of those 10% had need fully met. *Average percent of need met:* 62% (excluding resources awarded to replace EFC). *Average financial aid package:* $12,561 (excluding resources awarded to replace EFC).

UNDERGRADUATE FINANCIAL AID (Fall 2015) 16,980 applied for aid; of those 87% were deemed to have need. 97% of undergraduates with need received aid; of those 8% had need fully met. *Average percent of need met:* 59% (excluding resources awarded to replace EFC). *Average financial aid package:* $11,461 (excluding resources awarded to replace EFC).

GIFT AID (NEED-BASED) *Total amount:* $63,050,752 (96% federal, 4% institutional). *Receiving aid:* Freshmen: 58% (2,067); all full-time undergraduates: 6% (10,767). *Average award:* Freshmen: $5113; Undergraduates: $4997. *Scholarships, grants, and awards:* Federal Pell, FSEOG, state, private, college/university gift aid from institutional funds, United Negro College Fund.

GIFT AID (NON-NEED-BASED) *Total amount:* $85,291,869 (88% state, 12% institutional). *Receiving aid:* Freshmen: 73% (2,630). Undergraduates: 7% (13,535). *Tuition waivers:* Full or partial for employees or children of employees, senior citizens. *ROTC:* Army, Naval cooperative, Air Force cooperative.

LOANS *Student loans:* $113,250,944 (46% need-based, 54% non-need-based). 70% of past graduating class borrowed through all loan programs. *Average indebtedness per student:* $29,959. *Parent loans:* $16,654,463 (100% non-need-based). *Programs:* Federal Direct (Subsidized and Unsubsidized Stafford, PLUS), Perkins, Federal Nursing, state.

WORK-STUDY *Federal work-study:* jobs available. *State or other work-study/employment:* Part-time jobs available.

ATHLETIC AWARDS *Total amount:* $7,555,066 (100% non-need-based).

APPLYING FOR FINANCIAL AID *Required financial aid form:* FAFSA. *Financial aid deadline:* 4/1. *Notification date:* Continuous beginning 3/1. Students must reply by 4/1 or within 3 weeks of notification.

CONTACT Louis Scott, Director of Student Financial Aid, Georgia State University, PO Box 4040, Atlanta, GA 30302, 404-413-2600. *Fax:* 404-413-2102. *E-mail:* onestopshop@gsu.edu.
Website: http://www.gsu.edu/.

GETTYSBURG COLLEGE
Gettysburg, PA

Tuition & fees: $50,860	Average undergraduate aid package: $41,554

ABOUT THE INSTITUTION Independent Evangelical Lutheran Church in America, coed. *Awards:* bachelor's degrees. 82 undergraduate majors. *Total enrollment:* 2,384. Undergraduates: 2,384. Freshmen: 698. Both federal and institutional methodology are used as a basis for awarding need-based institutional aid.

UNDERGRADUATE EXPENSES for 2016–2017 *Application fee:* $60. *Comprehensive fee:* $63,000 includes full-time tuition ($50,860) and room and board ($12,140). *College room only:* $6510. Room and board charges vary according to board plan and housing facility.

FRESHMAN FINANCIAL AID (Fall 2016, est.) 451 applied for aid; of those 85% were deemed to have need. 99% of freshmen with need received aid; of those 90% had need fully met. *Average percent of need met:* 90% (excluding resources awarded to replace EFC). *Average financial aid package:* $41,630 (excluding resources awarded to replace EFC). 17% of all full-time freshmen had no need and received non-need-based gift aid.

UNDERGRADUATE FINANCIAL AID (Fall 2016, est.) 1,627 applied for aid; of those 89% were deemed to have need. 98% of undergraduates with need received aid; of those 90% had need fully met. *Average percent of need met:* 90% (excluding resources awarded to replace EFC). *Average financial aid package:* $41,554 (excluding resources awarded to replace EFC). 16% of all full-time undergraduates had no need and received non-need-based gift aid.

GIFT AID (NEED-BASED) *Total amount:* $51,526,084 (3% federal, 1% state, 94% institutional, 2% external sources). *Receiving aid:* Freshmen: 53% (367); all full-time undergraduates: 53% (1,376). *Average award:* Freshmen: $35,068; Undergraduates: $34,208. *Scholarships, grants, and awards:* Federal Pell, FSEOG, state, private, college/university gift aid from institutional funds.

GIFT AID (NON-NEED-BASED) *Total amount:* $7,373,901 (13% federal, 81% institutional, 6% external sources). *Receiving aid:* Freshmen: 24% (169). Undergraduates: 21% (534). *Average award:* Freshmen: $11,340. Undergraduates: $12,279. *Scholarships, grants, and awards by category:* Academic interests/achievement: 1,139 awards ($14,331,000 total): general academic interests/achievements. Creative arts/performance: 20 awards ($200,000 total): music. *ROTC:* Army cooperative.

LOANS *Student loans:* $11,712,309 (70% need-based, 30% non-need-based). 63% of past graduating class borrowed through all loan programs. *Average indebtedness per student:* $31,169. *Average need-based loan:* Freshmen: $5602. Undergraduates: $6599. *Parent loans:* $6,066,805 (100% non-need-based). *Programs:* Federal Direct (Subsidized and Unsubsidized Stafford, PLUS), Perkins, college/university.

WORK-STUDY *Federal work-study:* Total amount: $249,956; 366 jobs averaging $903. *State or other work-study/employment:* Total amount: $1,075,641 (100% non-need-based). 1,223 part-time jobs averaging $1084.

APPLYING FOR FINANCIAL AID *Required financial aid forms:* FAFSA, CSS Financial Aid PROFILE, federal income tax form(s), verification worksheet. *Financial aid deadline:* 2/1. *Notification date:* 3/27. Students must reply by 5/1.

CONTACT Christina Gormley, Director of Financial Aid, Gettysburg College, 300 North Washington Street, Gettysburg, PA 17325, 717-337-6620 or toll-free 800-431-0803. *Fax:* 717-337-8555. *E-mail:* finaid@gettysburg.edu.
Website: http://www.gettysburg.edu/.

GLENVILLE STATE COLLEGE
Glenville, WV

Tuition & fees (WV res): $9096	Average undergraduate aid package: $14,500

ABOUT THE INSTITUTION State-supported, coed. *Awards:* associate and bachelor's degrees. 32 undergraduate majors. *Total enrollment:* 1,732. Undergraduates: 1,732. Freshmen: 337. Federal methodology is used as a basis for awarding need-based institutional aid.

UNDERGRADUATE EXPENSES for 2016–2017 *Application fee:* $20. *Tuition, state resident:* full-time $7344; part-time $306 per credit hour. *Tuition, nonresident:* full-time $16,560; part-time $692 per credit hour. *Required fees:*

full-time $1752. Full-time tuition and fees vary according to course load. *College room and board:* $10,042. Room and board charges vary according to board plan and housing facility.

FRESHMAN FINANCIAL AID (Fall 2016, est.) 317 applied for aid; of those 86% were deemed to have need. 98% of freshmen with need received aid; of those 16% had need fully met. *Average percent of need met:* 76% (excluding resources awarded to replace EFC). *Average financial aid package:* $14,552 (excluding resources awarded to replace EFC). 3% of all full-time freshmen had no need and received non-need-based gift aid.

UNDERGRADUATE FINANCIAL AID (Fall 2016, est.) 1,020 applied for aid; of those 87% were deemed to have need. 99% of undergraduates with need received aid; of those 19% had need fully met. *Average percent of need met:* 76% (excluding resources awarded to replace EFC). *Average financial aid package:* $14,500 (excluding resources awarded to replace EFC). 3% of all full-time undergraduates had no need and received non-need-based gift aid.

GIFT AID (NEED-BASED) *Total amount:* $4,508,430 (69% federal, 31% state). *Receiving aid:* Freshmen: 75% (241); all full-time undergraduates: 73% (772). *Average award:* Freshmen: $6696; Undergraduates: $6437. *Scholarships, grants, and awards:* Federal Pell, FSEOG, state, private, college/university gift aid from institutional funds.

GIFT AID (NON-NEED-BASED) *Total amount:* $1,404,672 (44% state, 34% institutional, 22% external sources). *Receiving aid:* Freshmen: 63% (202). Undergraduates: 58% (614). *Average award:* Freshmen: $1833. Undergraduates: $2124. *Scholarships, grants, and awards by category:* Academic interests/achievement: 321 awards ($428,901 total): biological sciences, business, education, English, general academic interests/achievements, international studies, mathematics, social sciences. *Creative arts/performance:* 127 awards ($72,975 total): art/fine arts, journalism/publications, music. *Special achievements/activities:* 1 award ($1000 total): cheerleading/drum major. *Special characteristics:* 319 awards: children of faculty/staff, first-generation college students, out-of-state students, veterans, veterans' children. *Tuition waivers:* Full or partial for employees or children of employees, senior citizens. *ROTC:* Army.

LOANS *Student loans:* $5,467,159 (43% need-based, 57% non-need-based). 74% of past graduating class borrowed through all loan programs. *Average indebtedness per student:* $28,930. *Average need-based loan:* Freshmen: $3064. Undergraduates: $3715. *Parent loans:* $574,890 (100% non-need-based). *Programs:* Federal Direct (Subsidized and Unsubsidized Stafford, PLUS), private loans.

WORK-STUDY *Federal work-study:* Total amount: $77,635; 119 jobs averaging $1152. *State or other work-study/employment:* Total amount: $457,891 (100% non-need-based). 273 part-time jobs averaging $1720.

ATHLETIC AWARDS Total amount: $1,573,776 (100% non-need-based).

APPLYING FOR FINANCIAL AID *Required financial aid form:* FAFSA. *Financial aid deadline (priority):* 2/1. *Notification date:* Continuous beginning 3/1. Students must reply within 3 weeks of notification.

CONTACT Ms. Stephany Harper, Financial Aid Manager, Glenville State College, 200 High Street, Glenville, WV 26351-1200, 304-462-4103 Ext. 5 or toll-free 800-924-2010. *Fax:* 304-462-4407. *E-mail:* stephany.harper@glenville.edu. *Website:* http://www.glenville.edu/.

GLOBE UNIVERSITY–MINNEAPOLIS
Minneapolis, MN

CONTACT Office of Financial Aid, Globe University–Minneapolis, 80 South 8th Street, Suite 51, Minneapolis, MN 55402, 612-455-3000. *Fax:* 612-455-3001. *Website:* http://www.globeuniversity.edu/.

GLOBE UNIVERSITY–WOODBURY
Woodbury, MN

CONTACT Office of Financial Aid, Globe University–Woodbury, 8089 Globe Drive, Woodbury, MN 55125, 651-730-5100 or toll-free 800-231-0660. *Fax:* 651-730-5151. *Website:* http://www.globeuniversity.edu/.

GODDARD COLLEGE
Plainfield, VT

Tuition & fees: N/R	Average undergraduate aid package: $8211

ABOUT THE INSTITUTION Independent, coed. *Awards:* bachelor's and master's degrees. 53 undergraduate majors. *Total enrollment:* 505. Undergraduates: 194. Freshmen: 9. Federal methodology is used as a basis for awarding need-based institutional aid.

FRESHMAN FINANCIAL AID (Fall 2015) 5 applied for aid; of those 100% were deemed to have need. 100% of freshmen with need received aid. *Average percent of need met:* 37% (excluding resources awarded to replace EFC). *Average financial aid package:* $10,090 (excluding resources awarded to replace EFC).

UNDERGRADUATE FINANCIAL AID (Fall 2015) 147 applied for aid; of those 96% were deemed to have need. 99% of undergraduates with need received aid; of those 1% had need fully met. *Average percent of need met:* 35% (excluding resources awarded to replace EFC). *Average financial aid package:* $8211 (excluding resources awarded to replace EFC). 2% of all full-time undergraduates had no need and received non-need-based gift aid.

GIFT AID (NEED-BASED) *Total amount:* $539,115 (87% federal, 7% state, 5% institutional, 1% external sources). *Receiving aid:* Freshmen: 67% (4); all full-time undergraduates: 66% (119). *Average award:* Freshmen: $6925; Undergraduates: $4622. *Scholarships, grants, and awards:* Federal Pell, FSEOG, state, private, college/university gift aid from institutional funds.

GIFT AID (NON-NEED-BASED) *Total amount:* $28,540 (13% federal, 49% state, 17% institutional, 21% external sources). *Average award:* Undergraduates: $1062. *Scholarships, grants, and awards by category:* Creative arts/performance: art/fine arts, creative writing, dance, performing arts, theater/drama.

LOANS *Student loans:* $1,319,773 (94% need-based, 6% non-need-based). *Average need-based loan:* Freshmen: $4550. Undergraduates: $4379. *Parent loans:* $85,611 (75% need-based, 25% non-need-based). *Programs:* Federal Direct (Subsidized and Unsubsidized Stafford, PLUS), Perkins.

APPLYING FOR FINANCIAL AID *Required financial aid form:* FAFSA. *Financial aid deadline:* Continuous. *Notification date:* Continuous. Students must reply within 4 weeks of notification.

CONTACT Shannon Trainor, Associate Director of Financial Aid, Goddard College, 123 Pitkin Road, Plainfield, VT 05667, 802-454-8311 Ext. 303 or toll-free 800-906-8312. *Fax:* 802-322-1000. *E-mail:* shannon.trainor@goddard.edu. *Website:* http://www.goddard.edu/.

GOD'S BIBLE SCHOOL AND COLLEGE
Cincinnati, OH

CONTACT Mrs. Lori Waggoner, Financial Aid Director, God's Bible School and College, 1810 Young Street, Cincinnati, OH 45202-6899, 513-721-7944 Ext. 205 or toll-free 800-486-4637. *Fax:* 513-721-1357. *E-mail:* lwaggoner@gbs.edu. *Website:* http://www.gbs.edu/.

GOLDEN GATE UNIVERSITY
San Francisco, CA

CONTACT Kathleen Kelly, Interim Director of Financial Services, Golden Gate University, 536 Mission Street, San Francisco, CA 94105-2968, 415-442-7297 or toll-free 800-448-3381. *Fax:* 415-442-7819. *E-mail:* kkelly@ggu.edu. *Website:* http://www.ggu.edu/.

GOLDEY-BEACOM COLLEGE
Wilmington, DE

CONTACT Jane H. Lysle, Dean of Enrollment Management, Goldey-Beacom College, 4701 Limestone Road, Wilmington, DE 19808-1999, 302-225-6274 or toll-free 800-833-4877. *Fax:* 302-998-8631. *E-mail:* lyslej@gbc.edu.
Website: http://www.gbc.edu/.

GOLDFARB SCHOOL OF NURSING AT BARNES-JEWISH COLLEGE
St. Louis, MO

Tuition & fees: $20,188	Average undergraduate aid package: N/A

ABOUT THE INSTITUTION Independent, coed, primarily women. *Awards:* certificates, bachelor's, master's, and doctoral degrees. 1 undergraduate major. *Total enrollment:* 688. Undergraduates: 616. Federal methodology is used as a basis for awarding need-based institutional aid.

UNDERGRADUATE EXPENSES for 2017–2018 *Application fee:* $50. *Tuition:* full-time $19,058; part-time $733 per credit hour. *Required fees:* full-time $1130; $615 per term. Full-time tuition and fees vary according to course load and degree level. Part-time tuition and fees vary according to course load and degree level.

GIFT AID (NEED-BASED) *Scholarships, grants, and awards:* Federal Pell, FSEOG, state, private, college/university gift aid from institutional funds.

GIFT AID (NON-NEED-BASED) *Scholarships, grants, and awards by category:* Academic interests/achievement: general academic interests/achievements.

LOANS *Programs:* Federal Direct (Subsidized and Unsubsidized Stafford, PLUS).

WORK-STUDY Federal work-study jobs available.

APPLYING FOR FINANCIAL AID *Required financial aid forms:* FAFSA, institution's own form. *Financial aid deadline (priority):* 4/1. *Notification date:* Continuous beginning 4/1. Students must reply within 2 weeks of notification.

CONTACT Jason Crowe, Director of Financial Aid, Goldfarb School of Nursing at Barnes-Jewish College, 4483 Duncan, St. Louis, MO 63110-1091, 314-454-7770 or toll-free 800-832-9009. *E-mail:* jcrowe@bjc.org.
Website: http://www.barnesjewishcollege.edu/.

GONZAGA UNIVERSITY
Spokane, WA

Tuition & fees: $41,330	Average undergraduate aid package: $29,293

ABOUT THE INSTITUTION Independent Roman Catholic, coed. *Awards:* bachelor's, master's, and doctoral degrees. 64 undergraduate majors. *Total enrollment:* 7,567. Undergraduates: 5,160. Freshmen: 1,271. Federal methodology is used as a basis for awarding need-based institutional aid.

UNDERGRADUATE EXPENSES for 2017–2018 *Application fee:* $50. *Comprehensive fee:* $52,880 includes full-time tuition ($40,540), mandatory fees ($790), and room and board ($11,550). *College room only:* $5900. Full-time tuition and fees vary according to course load, location, program, reciprocity agreements, and student level. Room and board charges vary according to board plan, housing facility, and location. *Part-time tuition:* $1110 per credit. *Part-time fees:* $180 per term. Part-time tuition and fees vary according to course load, location, program, reciprocity agreements, and student level.

FRESHMAN FINANCIAL AID (Fall 2015) 1,157 applied for aid; of those 69% were deemed to have need. 100% of freshmen with need received aid; of those 27% had need fully met. *Average percent of need met:* 80% (excluding resources awarded to replace EFC). *Average financial aid package:* $27,059 (excluding resources awarded to replace EFC). 38% of all full-time freshmen had no need and received non-need-based gift aid.

UNDERGRADUATE FINANCIAL AID (Fall 2015) 3,357 applied for aid; of those 79% were deemed to have need. 100% of undergraduates with need received aid; of those 25% had need fully met. *Average percent of need met:* 79% (excluding resources awarded to replace EFC). *Average financial aid package:*

$29,293 (excluding resources awarded to replace EFC). 42% of all full-time undergraduates had no need and received non-need-based gift aid.

GIFT AID (NEED-BASED) *Total amount:* $30,104,817 (12% federal, 9% state, 73% institutional, 6% external sources). *Receiving aid:* Freshmen: 60% (798); all full-time undergraduates: 55% (2,656). *Average award:* Freshmen: $21,166; Undergraduates: $21,408. *Scholarships, grants, and awards:* Federal Pell, FSEOG, state, private, college/university gift aid from institutional funds, Federal Nursing.

GIFT AID (NON-NEED-BASED) *Total amount:* $54,310,561 (100% institutional). *Receiving aid:* Freshmen: 14% (189). Undergraduates: 12% (563). *Average award:* Freshmen: $14,749. Undergraduates: $14,545. *Scholarships, grants, and awards by category:* Academic interests/achievement: business, engineering/technologies, military science. *Creative arts/performance:* debating, music. *Special achievements/activities:* leadership, memberships. *Special characteristics:* children and siblings of alumni, children of faculty/staff, international students, members of minority groups, siblings of current students. *Tuition waivers:* Full or partial for employees or children of employees, senior citizens. *ROTC:* Army.

LOANS *Student loans:* $27,564,347 (88% need-based, 12% non-need-based). 60% of past graduating class borrowed through all loan programs. *Average indebtedness per student:* $30,700. *Average need-based loan:* Freshmen: $4816. Undergraduates: $5840. *Parent loans:* $9,528,802 (85% need-based, 15% non-need-based). *Programs:* Federal Direct (Subsidized and Unsubsidized Stafford, PLUS), Perkins, Federal Nursing, state, college/university.

WORK-STUDY *Federal work-study:* jobs available. *State or other work-study/employment:* Total amount: $804,687 (100% need-based). Part-time jobs available.

ATHLETIC AWARDS Total amount: $4,447,305 (28% need-based, 72% non-need-based).

APPLYING FOR FINANCIAL AID *Required financial aid form:* FAFSA. *Financial aid deadline (priority):* 2/1. *Notification date:* Continuous beginning 3/1. Students must reply by 5/1 or within 3 weeks of notification.

CONTACT James White, Dean of Student Financial Services, Gonzaga University, 502 East Boone Avenue, Spokane, WA 99258-0072, 509-313-6568 or toll-free 800-322-2584 Ext. 6572. *Fax:* 509-313-5816. *E-mail:* whitej@gonzaga.edu.
Website: http://www.gonzaga.edu/.

GORDON COLLEGE
Wenham, MA

Tuition & fees: $36,740	Average undergraduate aid package: $24,830

ABOUT THE INSTITUTION Independent nondenominational, coed. *Awards:* bachelor's and master's degrees. 37 undergraduate majors. *Total enrollment:* 2,004. Undergraduates: 1,657. Freshmen: 425. Federal methodology is used as a basis for awarding need-based institutional aid.

UNDERGRADUATE EXPENSES for 2017–2018 *Application fee:* $50. *Comprehensive fee:* $47,740 includes full-time tuition ($35,180), mandatory fees ($1560), and room and board ($11,000). *College room only:* $7000. Full-time tuition and fees vary according to course load and program. Room and board charges vary according to board plan and housing facility. *Part-time tuition:* $879 per credit. Part-time tuition and fees vary according to course load and program.

FRESHMAN FINANCIAL AID (Fall 2016, est.) 356 applied for aid; of those 83% were deemed to have need. 100% of freshmen with need received aid; of those 14% had need fully met. *Average percent of need met:* 70% (excluding resources awarded to replace EFC). *Average financial aid package:* $24,811 (excluding resources awarded to replace EFC). 29% of all full-time freshmen had no need and received non-need-based gift aid.

UNDERGRADUATE FINANCIAL AID (Fall 2016, est.) 1,198 applied for aid; of those 86% were deemed to have need. 100% of undergraduates with need received aid; of those 17% had need fully met. *Average percent of need met:* 71% (excluding resources awarded to replace EFC). *Average financial aid package:* $24,830 (excluding resources awarded to replace EFC). 32% of all full-time undergraduates had no need and received non-need-based gift aid.

GIFT AID (NEED-BASED) *Total amount:* $20,829,156 (9% federal, 1% state, 82% institutional, 8% external sources). *Receiving aid:* Freshmen: 69% (296); all full-time undergraduates: 65% (1,035). *Average award:* Freshmen: $20,550; Undergraduates: $19,776. *Scholarships, grants, and awards:* Federal Pell, FSEOG, state, private, college/university gift aid from institutional funds.

GIFT AID (NON-NEED-BASED) *Total amount:* $10,209,309 (84% institutional, 16% external sources). *Receiving aid:* Freshmen: 8% (32). Undergraduates: 8% (122). *Average award:* Freshmen: $15,187. Undergraduates: $15,066. *Scholarships, grants, and awards by category:* Academic interests/achievement: general academic interests/achievements. *Creative arts/performance:* art/fine arts, music, theater/drama. *Special achievements/activities:* leadership. *Special characteristics:* children and siblings of alumni, children of faculty/staff, international students, relatives of clergy, veterans, veterans' children. *Tuition waivers:* Full or partial for employees or children of employees. *ROTC:* Army cooperative.

LOANS *Student loans:* $11,606,998 (70% need-based, 30% non-need-based). 86% of past graduating class borrowed through all loan programs. *Average indebtedness per student:* $36,557. *Average need-based loan:* Freshmen: $3734. Undergraduates: $4788. *Parent loans:* $2,787,530 (51% need-based, 49% non-need-based). *Programs:* Federal Direct (Subsidized and Unsubsidized Stafford, PLUS), Perkins, state.

WORK-STUDY *Federal work-study:* Total amount: $250,711; jobs available.

APPLYING FOR FINANCIAL AID *Required financial aid form:* FAFSA. *Financial aid deadline (priority):* 3/1. *Notification date:* Continuous beginning 2/15. Students must reply by 5/1 or within 2 weeks of notification.

CONTACT Daniel O'Connell, Senior Director of Student Financial Services, Gordon College, 255 Grapevine Road, Wenham, MA 01984-1899, 978-867-4246 or toll-free 866-464-6736. *Fax:* 978-867-4657. *E-mail:* daniel.oconnell@gordon.edu. *Website:* http://www.gordon.edu/.

GOSHEN COLLEGE
Goshen, IN

Tuition & fees: $33,200	Average undergraduate aid package: $25,976

ABOUT THE INSTITUTION Independent Mennonite, coed. *Awards:* bachelor's and master's degrees. 57 undergraduate majors. *Total enrollment:* 870. Undergraduates: 800. Freshmen: 185. Federal methodology is used as a basis for awarding need-based institutional aid.

UNDERGRADUATE EXPENSES for 2017–2018 *Application fee:* $25. *Comprehensive fee:* $43,700 includes full-time tuition ($33,200) and room and board ($10,500). *College room only:* $5675. Full-time tuition and fees vary according to degree level and program. Room and board charges vary according to board plan and housing facility. *Part-time tuition:* $1380 per credit hour. Part-time tuition and fees vary according to course load, degree level, and program.

FRESHMAN FINANCIAL AID (Fall 2016, est.) 167 applied for aid; of those 92% were deemed to have need. 100% of freshmen with need received aid; of those 20% had need fully met. *Average percent of need met:* 84% (excluding resources awarded to replace EFC). *Average financial aid package:* $27,826 (excluding resources awarded to replace EFC). 17% of all full-time freshmen had no need and received non-need-based gift aid.

UNDERGRADUATE FINANCIAL AID (Fall 2016, est.) 616 applied for aid; of those 90% were deemed to have need. 100% of undergraduates with need received aid; of those 18% had need fully met. *Average percent of need met:* 81% (excluding resources awarded to replace EFC). *Average financial aid package:* $25,976 (excluding resources awarded to replace EFC). 22% of all full-time undergraduates had no need and received non-need-based gift aid.

GIFT AID (NEED-BASED) *Total amount:* $10,391,226 (12% federal, 11% state, 67% institutional, 10% external sources). *Receiving aid:* Freshmen: 83% (154); all full-time undergraduates: 73% (541). *Average award:* Freshmen: $24,235; Undergraduates: $21,784. *Scholarships, grants, and awards:* Federal Pell, FSEOG, state, private, college/university gift aid from institutional funds, Federal Nursing.

GIFT AID (NON-NEED-BASED) *Total amount:* $3,562,250 (80% institutional, 20% external sources). *Receiving aid:* Freshmen: 16% (29). Undergraduates: 13% (96). *Average award:* Freshmen: $18,370. Undergraduates: $15,430. *Scholarships, grants, and awards by category:* Academic interests/achievement: business, communication, education, general academic interests/achievements. *Creative arts/performance:* music, theater/drama. *Special achievements/activities:* community service, junior miss. *Special characteristics:* children of educators, children of faculty/staff, ethnic background, international students, members of minority groups. *Tuition waivers:* Full or partial for employees or children of employees.

LOANS *Student loans:* $4,789,342 (71% need-based, 29% non-need-based). 68% of past graduating class borrowed through all loan programs. *Average indebtedness*

---

per student: $27,534. *Average need-based loan:* Freshmen: $3730. Undergraduates: $4965. *Parent loans:* $734,409 (43% need-based, 57% non-need-based). *Programs:* Federal Direct (Subsidized and Unsubsidized Stafford, PLUS), Perkins, Federal Nursing.

WORK-STUDY *Federal work-study:* Total amount: $317,563; jobs available. *State or other work-study/employment:* Total amount: $88,100 (100% non-need-based). Part-time jobs available.

ATHLETIC AWARDS Total amount: $1,384,604 (63% need-based, 37% non-need-based).

APPLYING FOR FINANCIAL AID *Required financial aid form:* FAFSA. *Financial aid deadline:* Continuous. *Notification date:* Continuous beginning 1/10. Students must reply within 2 weeks of notification.

CONTACT Mr. Joel D. Short, Director of Student Financial Aid, Goshen College, 1700 South Main Street, Goshen, IN 46526-4794, 574-535-7525 or toll-free 800-348-7422. *Fax:* 574-535-7654. *E-mail:* joelds@goshen.edu. *Website:* http://www.goshen.edu/.

GOUCHER COLLEGE
Baltimore, MD

Tuition & fees: $43,440	Average undergraduate aid package: $34,502

ABOUT THE INSTITUTION Independent, coed. *Awards:* certificates, bachelor's, and master's degrees. 34 undergraduate majors. *Total enrollment:* 2,172. Undergraduates: 1,473. Freshmen: 441. Both federal and institutional methodology are used as a basis for awarding need-based institutional aid.

UNDERGRADUATE EXPENSES for 2017–2018 *Application fee:* $55. *Comprehensive fee:* $56,110 includes full-time tuition ($42,600), mandatory fees ($840), and room and board ($12,670). Room and board charges vary according to board plan and housing facility. *Part-time tuition:* $1420 per credit hour. *Payment plan:* Tuition prepayment.

FRESHMAN FINANCIAL AID (Fall 2016, est.) 381 applied for aid; of those 86% were deemed to have need. 100% of freshmen with need received aid; of those 25% had need fully met. *Average percent of need met:* 84% (excluding resources awarded to replace EFC). *Average financial aid package:* $36,465 (excluding resources awarded to replace EFC). 25% of all full-time freshmen had no need and received non-need-based gift aid.

UNDERGRADUATE FINANCIAL AID (Fall 2016, est.) 1,080 applied for aid; of those 90% were deemed to have need. 100% of undergraduates with need received aid; of those 23% had need fully met. *Average percent of need met:* 81% (excluding resources awarded to replace EFC). *Average financial aid package:* $34,502 (excluding resources awarded to replace EFC). 30% of all full-time undergraduates had no need and received non-need-based gift aid.

GIFT AID (NEED-BASED) *Total amount:* $29,955,174 (5% federal, 4% state, 87% institutional, 4% external sources). *Receiving aid:* Freshmen: 75% (329); all full-time undergraduates: 68% (971). *Average award:* Freshmen: $33,643; Undergraduates: $30,811. *Scholarships, grants, and awards:* Federal Pell, FSEOG, state, private, college/university gift aid from institutional funds.

GIFT AID (NON-NEED-BASED) *Total amount:* $9,412,298 (88% institutional, 12% external sources). *Receiving aid:* Freshmen: 14% (62). Undergraduates: 10% (149). *Average award:* Freshmen: $17,258. Undergraduates: $17,200. *Scholarships, grants, and awards by category:* Creative arts/performance: 33 awards ($362,750 total): art/fine arts, dance, music, performing arts, theater/drama. *Special achievements/activities:* 12 awards ($134,250 total): leadership. *Tuition waivers:* Full or partial for employees or children of employees. *ROTC:* Army cooperative, Air Force cooperative.

LOANS *Student loans:* $8,407,609 (66% need-based, 34% non-need-based). 62% of past graduating class borrowed through all loan programs. *Average indebtedness per student:* $33,446. *Average need-based loan:* Freshmen: $2794. Undergraduates: $3924. *Parent loans:* $3,364,381 (39% need-based, 61% non-need-based). *Programs:* Federal Direct (Subsidized and Unsubsidized Stafford, PLUS), Perkins.

WORK-STUDY *Federal work-study:* Total amount: $441,080; 365 jobs averaging $1150.

APPLYING FOR FINANCIAL AID *Required financial aid forms:* FAFSA, CSS Financial Aid PROFILE, noncustodial (divorced/separated) parent's statement. *Financial aid deadline (priority):* 2/1. *Notification date:* Continuous beginning 11/1. Students must reply by 5/1.

CONTACT Ms. Stephanie Bender, Director of Student Financial Aid, Goucher College, 1021 Dulaney Valley Road, Baltimore, MD 21204-2794, 410-337-6141 or toll-free 800-468-2437. *Fax:* 410-337-6504. *E-mail:* stephanie.bender@goucher.edu. *Website:* http://www.goucher.edu/.

GOVERNORS STATE UNIVERSITY
University Park, IL

Tuition & fees (IL res): $10,516	Average undergraduate aid package: $10,462

ABOUT THE INSTITUTION State-supported, coed. *Awards:* certificates, bachelor's, master's, and doctoral degrees. 30 undergraduate majors. *Total enrollment:* 5,819. Undergraduates: 3,517. Freshmen: 200. Both federal and institutional methodology are used as a basis for awarding need-based institutional aid.

UNDERGRADUATE EXPENSES for 2016–2017 *Application fee:* $25. *Tuition, state resident:* full-time $8160; part-time $272 per credit hour. *Tuition, nonresident:* full-time $16,320; part-time $544 per credit hour. *Required fees:* full-time $2356; $76 per credit hour or $38 per term. Full-time tuition and fees vary according to course load, degree level, reciprocity agreements, and student level. Part-time tuition and fees vary according to course load, degree level, reciprocity agreements, and student level. *College room and board:* $9868; *Room only:* $7868. Room and board charges vary according to board plan and housing facility. *Payment plan:* Guaranteed tuition.

FRESHMAN FINANCIAL AID (Fall 2016, est.) 195 applied for aid; of those 87% were deemed to have need. 95% of freshmen with need received aid; of those 25% had need fully met. *Average percent of need met:* 55% (excluding resources awarded to replace EFC). *Average financial aid package:* $10,606 (excluding resources awarded to replace EFC). 48% of all full-time freshmen had no need and received non-need-based gift aid.

UNDERGRADUATE FINANCIAL AID (Fall 2016, est.) 1,719 applied for aid; of those 87% were deemed to have need. 95% of undergraduates with need received aid; of those 23% had need fully met. *Average percent of need met:* 51% (excluding resources awarded to replace EFC). *Average financial aid package:* $10,462 (excluding resources awarded to replace EFC). 10% of all full-time undergraduates had no need and received non-need-based gift aid.

GIFT AID (NEED-BASED) *Total amount:* $14,590,956 (61% federal, 38% state, 1% institutional). *Receiving aid:* Freshmen: 72% (143); all full-time undergraduates: 63% (1,212). *Average award:* Freshmen: $4062; Undergraduates: $4348. *Scholarships, grants, and awards:* Federal Pell, FSEOG, state, private, college/university gift aid from institutional funds.

GIFT AID (NON-NEED-BASED) *Total amount:* $454,979 (67% institutional, 33% external sources). *Receiving aid:* Freshmen: 44% (89). Undergraduates: 15% (296). *Average award:* Freshmen: $2903. Undergraduates: $2825. *Scholarships, grants, and awards by category: Academic interests/achievement:* biological sciences, business, communication, education, English, general academic interests/achievements, health fields, mathematics, physical sciences, social sciences. *Creative arts/performance:* general creative arts/performance. *Special achievements/activities:* general special achievements/activities. *Special characteristics:* children of educators, children of public servants, members of minority groups, veterans. *Tuition waivers:* Full or partial for employees or children of employees, senior citizens.

LOANS *Student loans:* $16,949,097 (98% need-based, 2% non-need-based). *Average need-based loan:* Freshmen: $3171. Undergraduates: $4429. *Parent loans:* $623,645 (100% non-need-based). *Programs:* Federal Direct (Subsidized and Unsubsidized Stafford, PLUS), Perkins.

WORK-STUDY *Federal work-study:* Total amount: $184,988; 103 jobs averaging $1827. *State or other work-study/employment:* Part-time jobs available.

ATHLETIC AWARDS Total amount: $266,760 (100% non-need-based).

APPLYING FOR FINANCIAL AID *Required financial aid form:* FAFSA. *Financial aid deadline:* 10/1 (priority: 5/1). *Notification date:* Continuous beginning 3/1. Students must reply within 2 weeks of notification.

CONTACT John Perry, Director of Financial Aid, Governors State University, 1 University Parkway, University Park, IL 60484, 708-534-4483 or toll-free 800-478-8478. *Fax:* 708-534-1172. *E-mail:* jperry@govst.edu. *Website:* http://www.govst.edu/.

GRACE BIBLE COLLEGE
Grand Rapids, MI

CONTACT Mr. Kurt Postma, Director of Financial Aid, Grace Bible College, 1011 Aldon Street, SW, Grand Rapids, MI 49509-1921, 616-538-2330 or toll-free 800-968-1887. *Fax:* 616-538-0599. *E-mail:* kpostma@gbcol.edu. *Website:* http://www.gbcol.edu/.

GRACE COLLEGE
Winona Lake, IN

CONTACT Charlette Sauders, Director of Financial Aid, Grace College, 200 Seminary Drive, Winona Lake, IN 46590-1294, 574-372-5100 Ext. 6161 or toll-free 800-54-GRACE. *Fax:* 574-372-5144. *E-mail:* charlette.sauders@grace.edu. *Website:* http://www.grace.edu/.

GRACE COLLEGE OF DIVINITY
Fayetteville, NC

CONTACT Financial Aid Office, Grace College of Divinity, 5117 Cliffdale Road, Fayetteville, NC 28314, 910-221-2224. *Website:* http://www.gcdivinity.org/.

GRACELAND UNIVERSITY
Lamoni, IA

Tuition & fees: $28,110	Average undergraduate aid package: $22,282

ABOUT THE INSTITUTION Independent Community of Christ, coed. *Awards:* certificates, bachelor's, master's, and doctoral degrees. 47 undergraduate majors. *Total enrollment:* 2,230. Undergraduates: 1,446. Freshmen: 256. Federal methodology is used as a basis for awarding need-based institutional aid.

UNDERGRADUATE EXPENSES for 2017–2018 *Comprehensive fee:* $36,590 includes full-time tuition ($27,500), mandatory fees ($610), and room and board ($8480). *College room only:* $3300. Full-time tuition and fees vary according to course load, location, and program. Room and board charges vary according to board plan, housing facility, and location. *Part-time tuition:* $800 per semester hour. *Part-time fees:* $285 per semester hour. Part-time tuition and fees vary according to course load, location, and program.

FRESHMAN FINANCIAL AID (Fall 2016, est.) 240 applied for aid; of those 90% were deemed to have need. 100% of freshmen with need received aid; of those 19% had need fully met. *Average percent of need met:* 78% (excluding resources awarded to replace EFC). *Average financial aid package:* $24,666 (excluding resources awarded to replace EFC). 13% of all full-time freshmen had no need and received non-need-based gift aid.

UNDERGRADUATE FINANCIAL AID (Fall 2016, est.) 1,081 applied for aid; of those 91% were deemed to have need. 97% of undergraduates with need received aid; of those 16% had need fully met. *Average percent of need met:* 72% (excluding resources awarded to replace EFC). *Average financial aid package:* $22,282 (excluding resources awarded to replace EFC). 15% of all full-time undergraduates had no need and received non-need-based gift aid.

GIFT AID (NEED-BASED) *Total amount:* $14,653,468 (20% federal, 6% state, 72% institutional, 2% external sources). *Receiving aid:* Freshmen: 78% (200); all full-time undergraduates: 74% (921). *Average award:* Freshmen: $20,199; Undergraduates: $18,222. *Scholarships, grants, and awards:* Federal Pell, FSEOG, state, private, college/university gift aid from institutional funds.

GIFT AID (NON-NEED-BASED) *Total amount:* $2,355,906 (1% federal, 95% institutional, 4% external sources). *Receiving aid:* Freshmen: 32% (82). Undergraduates: 22% (277). *Average award:* Freshmen: $14,327. Undergraduates: $12,738. *Scholarships, grants, and awards by category: Academic interests/achievement:* computer science, engineering/technologies, general academic interests/achievements. *Creative arts/performance:* art/fine arts, creative writing, dance, music, theater/drama. *Special achievements/activities:* cheerleading/drum major, general special achievements/activities, hobbies/interests, leadership, religious involvement. *Special characteristics:* adult students, children and siblings of alumni, children of faculty/staff, first-generation college students, general special characteristics, international students, local/state students, members of minority groups, previous college experience, religious affiliation. *Tuition waivers:* Full or partial for employees or children of employees, senior citizens.

LOANS *Student loans:* $8,862,159 (79% need-based, 21% non-need-based). 80% of past graduating class borrowed through all loan programs. *Average indebtedness per student:* $30,676. *Average need-based loan:* Freshmen: $3337. Undergraduates: $4581. *Parent loans:* $1,730,730 (56% need-based, 44% non-need-based). *Programs:* Federal Direct (Subsidized and Unsubsidized Stafford, PLUS), Perkins, college/university.

WORK-STUDY *Federal work-study:* Total amount: $238,820; jobs available. *State or other work-study/employment:* Total amount: $965,203 (60% need-based, 40% non-need-based). Part-time jobs available.

ATHLETIC AWARDS Total amount: $2,857,013 (74% need-based, 26% non-need-based).

APPLYING FOR FINANCIAL AID *Required financial aid form:* FAFSA. *Financial aid deadline:* Continuous. *Notification date:* Continuous beginning 2/1. Students must reply within 2 weeks of notification.

CONTACT Talia Brown, Director of Financial Aid, Graceland University, 1 University Place, Lamoni, IA 50140, 641-784-5117 or toll-free 866-GRACELAND. *Fax:* 641-784-5242. *E-mail:* talia.brown@graceland.edu. *Website:* http://www.graceland.edu/.

GRACE MISSION UNIVERSITY
Fullerton, CA

CONTACT Financial Aid Office, Grace Mission University, 1645 West Valencia Drive, Fullerton, CA 92833, 714-525-0088. *Website:* http://www.gm.edu/.

GRACE SCHOOL OF THEOLOGY
Conroe, TX

CONTACT Financial Aid Office, Grace School of Theology, 3705 College Park Drive Suite 140, Conroe, TX 77384-4894. *Website:* http://www.gsot.edu/.

GRACE UNIVERSITY
Omaha, NE

CONTACT Marcy Pierce, Director of Financial Aid, Grace University, 1311 South Ninth Street, Omaha, NE 68108-3629, 402-449-2810 or toll-free 800-383-1422. *Fax:* 402-449-2921. *E-mail:* gufinaid@graceu.edu. *Website:* http://www.graceuniversity.edu/.

GRAMBLING STATE UNIVERSITY
Grambling, LA

Tuition & fees (LA res): $6256	Average undergraduate aid package: $3731

ABOUT THE INSTITUTION State-supported, coed. *Awards:* certificates, bachelor's, master's, and doctoral degrees. 27 undergraduate majors. *Total enrollment:* 4,863. Undergraduates: 3,883. Freshmen: 865. Federal methodology is used as a basis for awarding need-based institutional aid.

UNDERGRADUATE EXPENSES for 2017–2018 *Application fee:* $20. *Tuition, state resident:* full-time $5140; part-time $215 per credit hour. *Tuition, nonresident:* full-time $14,163; part-time $591 per credit hour. *Required fees:* full-time $1116. Full-time tuition and fees vary according to course load, degree level,

and student level. Part-time tuition and fees vary according to course load, degree level, and student level. *College room and board:* $8954; *Room only:* $5480. Room and board charges vary according to housing facility.

FRESHMAN FINANCIAL AID (Fall 2016, est.) 850 applied for aid; of those 99% were deemed to have need. 100% of freshmen with need received aid. *Average financial aid package:* $3450 (excluding resources awarded to replace EFC). 3% of all full-time freshmen had no need and received non-need-based gift aid.

UNDERGRADUATE FINANCIAL AID (Fall 2016, est.) 3,378 applied for aid; of those 99% were deemed to have need. 100% of undergraduates with need received aid. *Average financial aid package:* $3731 (excluding resources awarded to replace EFC). 3% of all full-time undergraduates had no need and received non-need-based gift aid.

GIFT AID (NEED-BASED) *Total amount:* $16,892,248 (94% federal, 5% state, 1% external sources). *Receiving aid:* Freshmen: 83% (721); all full-time undergraduates: 80% (2,892). *Average award:* Freshmen: $3907; Undergraduates: $4051. *Scholarships, grants, and awards:* Federal Pell, FSEOG, state, private, college/university gift aid from institutional funds.

GIFT AID (NON-NEED-BASED) *Total amount:* $1,593,375 (4% federal, 34% state, 62% institutional). *Receiving aid:* Freshmen: 12% (102). Undergraduates: 10% (350). *Average award:* Freshmen: $2567. Undergraduates: $2313. *Scholarships, grants, and awards by category:* Academic interests/achievement: biological sciences, business, communication, computer science, education, engineering/technologies, English, foreign languages, general academic interests/achievements, health fields, home economics, humanities, mathematics, military science, physical sciences, premedicine, social sciences. *Creative arts/performance:* dance, general creative arts/performance, music, performing arts, theater/drama. *Special achievements/activities:* cheerleading/drum major, junior miss, leadership. *Special characteristics:* children and siblings of alumni, children of faculty/staff, children of public servants, ethnic background, international students, local/state students, members of minority groups, out-of-state students, public servants, veterans, veterans' children. *Tuition waivers:* Full or partial for children of alumni, employees or children of employees, senior citizens. *ROTC:* Army, Air Force cooperative.

LOANS *Student loans:* $44,177,088 (29% need-based, 71% non-need-based). 31% of past graduating class borrowed through all loan programs. *Average indebtedness per student:* $49,648. *Average need-based loan:* Freshmen: $3241. Undergraduates: $3812. *Parent loans:* $11,450,061 (100% non-need-based). *Programs:* Federal Direct (Subsidized and Unsubsidized Stafford, PLUS), alternative loans.

WORK-STUDY *Federal work-study:* Total amount: $808,886; 719 jobs averaging $1127.

ATHLETIC AWARDS Total amount: $2,427,323 (100% non-need-based).

APPLYING FOR FINANCIAL AID *Required financial aid form:* FAFSA. *Financial aid deadline:* 6/1 (priority: 4/1). *Notification date:* Continuous beginning 3/1. Students must reply within 2 weeks of notification.

CONTACT Mr. Gavin Hamms, Director of Student Financial Aid and Scholarships, Grambling State University, PO Box 629, Grambling, LA 71245, 318-274-6328 or toll-free 800-569-4714. *Fax:* 318-274-3358. *E-mail:* hammsg@gram.edu. *Website:* http://www.gram.edu/.

GRAND CANYON UNIVERSITY
Phoenix, AZ

CONTACT Director of Financial Aid, Grand Canyon University, 3300 West Camelback Road, PO Box 11097, Phoenix, AZ 85017-3030, 800-800-9776 Ext. 2885 or toll-free 800-800-9776. *Fax:* 602-589-2044. *Website:* http://www.gcu.edu/.

GRAND VALLEY STATE UNIVERSITY
Allendale, MI

Tuition & fees (MI res): $11,520	Average undergraduate aid package: $9698

ABOUT THE INSTITUTION State-supported, coed. *Awards:* certificates, bachelor's, master's, and doctoral degrees. 105 undergraduate majors. *Total enrollment:* 25,460. Undergraduates: 22,209. Freshmen: 4,306. Federal methodology is used as a basis for awarding need-based institutional aid.

UNDERGRADUATE EXPENSES for 2016–2017 *Application fee:* $30. *Tuition, state resident:* full-time $11,520; part-time $506 per credit hour. *Tuition, nonresident:* full-time $16,392; part-time $709 per credit hour. Full-time tuition and fees vary according to course level, course load, program, and student level. Part-time tuition and fees vary according to course level, course load, program, and student level. *College room and board:* $8400. Room and board charges vary according to board plan and housing facility.

FRESHMAN FINANCIAL AID (Fall 2016, est.) 3,783 applied for aid; of those 69% were deemed to have need. 99% of freshmen with need received aid; of those 15% had need fully met. *Average percent of need met:* 69% (excluding resources awarded to replace EFC). *Average financial aid package:* $10,870 (excluding resources awarded to replace EFC). 18% of all full-time freshmen had no need and received non-need-based gift aid.

UNDERGRADUATE FINANCIAL AID (Fall 2016, est.) 15,826 applied for aid; of those 71% were deemed to have need. 99% of undergraduates with need received aid; of those 18% had need fully met. *Average percent of need met:* 69% (excluding resources awarded to replace EFC). *Average financial aid package:* $9698 (excluding resources awarded to replace EFC). 17% of all full-time undergraduates had no need and received non-need-based gift aid.

GIFT AID (NEED-BASED) *Total amount:* $63,569,591 (45% federal, 4% state, 47% institutional, 4% external sources). *Receiving aid:* Freshmen: 52% (2,247); all full-time undergraduates: 48% (9,494). *Average award:* Freshmen: $8060; Undergraduates: $6699. *Scholarships, grants, and awards:* Federal Pell, FSEOG, state, private, college/university gift aid from institutional funds.

GIFT AID (NON-NEED-BASED) *Total amount:* $11,498,052 (1% state, 87% institutional, 12% external sources). *Receiving aid:* Freshmen: 3% (145). Undergraduates: 2% (436). *Average award:* Freshmen: $3476. Undergraduates: $3256. *Scholarships, grants, and awards by category: Academic interests/achievement:* business, communication, computer science, education, engineering/technologies, English, foreign languages, general academic interests/achievements, health fields, humanities, international studies, mathematics, physical sciences, premedicine, social sciences. *Creative arts/performance:* applied art and design, art/fine arts, cinema/film/broadcasting, dance, journalism/publications, music, theater/drama. *Special characteristics:* adult students, children and siblings of alumni, children of faculty/staff, children of union members/company employees, children of workers in trades, general special characteristics, handicapped students, international students, local/state students, out-of-state students, public servants, spouses of deceased or disabled public servants, veterans, veterans' children. *Tuition waivers:* Full or partial for employees or children of employees.

LOANS *Student loans:* $116,592,964 (39% need-based, 61% non-need-based). 71% of past graduating class borrowed through all loan programs. *Average indebtedness per student:* $29,675. *Average need-based loan:* Freshmen: $3755. Undergraduates: $4055. *Parent loans:* $71,909,743 (100% non-need-based). *Programs:* Federal Direct (Subsidized and Unsubsidized Stafford, PLUS), Perkins, Federal Nursing.

WORK-STUDY *Federal work-study:* Total amount: $3,290,653; 1,302 jobs averaging $2526. *State or other work-study/employment:* Part-time jobs available.

ATHLETIC AWARDS Total amount: $3,442,390 (36% need-based, 64% non-need-based).

APPLYING FOR FINANCIAL AID *Required financial aid form:* FAFSA. *Financial aid deadline (priority):* 3/1. *Notification date:* 3/10. Students must reply by 5/1 or within 4 weeks of notification.

CONTACT Michelle Rhodes, Office of Financial Aid, Grand Valley State University, 100 Student Services Building, Allendale, MI 49401, 616-331-3234 or toll-free 800-748-0246. *Fax:* 616-331-3180. *E-mail:* rhodesmi@gvsu.edu. *Website:* http://www.gvsu.edu/.

board ($8834). Full-time tuition and fees vary according to class time and course load. Room and board charges vary according to board plan and housing facility. *Part-time tuition:* $642 per credit hour. Part-time tuition and fees vary according to class time and course load.

FRESHMAN FINANCIAL AID (Fall 2016, est.) 306 applied for aid; of those 88% were deemed to have need. 100% of freshmen with need received aid; of those 36% had need fully met. *Average percent of need met:* 88% (excluding resources awarded to replace EFC). *Average financial aid package:* $23,261 (excluding resources awarded to replace EFC). 19% of all full-time freshmen had no need and received non-need-based gift aid.

UNDERGRADUATE FINANCIAL AID (Fall 2016, est.) 1,499 applied for aid; of those 90% were deemed to have need. 100% of undergraduates with need received aid; of those 27% had need fully met. *Average percent of need met:* 78% (excluding resources awarded to replace EFC). *Average financial aid package:* $19,738 (excluding resources awarded to replace EFC). 16% of all full-time undergraduates had no need and received non-need-based gift aid.

GIFT AID (NEED-BASED) *Total amount:* $18,240,333 (17% federal, 24% state, 57% institutional, 2% external sources). *Receiving aid:* Freshmen: 72% (240); all full-time undergraduates: 74% (1,215). *Average award:* Freshmen: $21,768; Undergraduates: $17,665. *Scholarships, grants, and awards:* Federal Pell, FSEOG, state, private, college/university gift aid from institutional funds.

GIFT AID (NON-NEED-BASED) *Total amount:* $2,756,506 (3% state, 88% institutional, 9% external sources). *Receiving aid:* Freshmen: 17% (56). Undergraduates: 11% (185). *Average award:* Freshmen: $10,470. Undergraduates: $9015. *Scholarships, grants, and awards by category: Academic interests/achievement:* 1,901 awards ($10,911,835 total): biological sciences, business, communication, education, English, general academic interests/achievements, international studies, mathematics, physical sciences, religion/biblical studies, social sciences. *Creative arts/performance:* 160 awards ($269,365 total): applied art and design, art/fine arts, dance, music, theater/drama. *Special achievements/activities:* 747 awards ($4,451,114 total): cheerleading/drum major, community service, junior miss, memberships, religious involvement. *Special characteristics:* 327 awards ($1,298,178 total): adult students, children and siblings of alumni, children of educators, children of faculty/staff, ethnic background, first-generation college students, general special characteristics, international students, out-of-state students, religious affiliation, veterans. *Tuition waivers:* Full or partial for children of alumni, employees or children of employees, senior citizens. *ROTC:* Army cooperative, Air Force cooperative.

LOANS *Student loans:* $14,416,438 (66% need-based, 34% non-need-based). 86% of past graduating class borrowed through all loan programs. *Average indebtedness per student:* $37,158. *Average need-based loan:* Freshmen: $3894. Undergraduates: $4535. *Parent loans:* $2,506,557 (14% need-based, 86% non-need-based). *Programs:* Federal Direct (Subsidized and Unsubsidized Stafford, PLUS), Perkins, college/university, private loans.

WORK-STUDY *Federal work-study:* Total amount: $501,000; 336 jobs averaging $1354. *State or other work-study/employment:* Part-time jobs available.

ATHLETIC AWARDS Total amount: $4,825,332 (68% need-based, 32% non-need-based).

APPLYING FOR FINANCIAL AID *Financial aid deadline (priority):* 1/15. *Notification date:* Continuous beginning 11/1. Students must reply by 5/1 or within 3 weeks of notification.

CONTACT Ms. Michele Dunne, Director of Financial Aid, Grand View University, 1200 Grandview Avenue, Des Moines, IA 50316-1599, 515-263-2820 or toll-free 800-444-6083. *Fax:* 515-263-6191. *E-mail:* mdunne@grandview.edu. *Website:* http://www.grandview.edu/.

GRAND VIEW UNIVERSITY
Des Moines, IA

Tuition & fees: $26,516	Average undergraduate aid package: $19,738

ABOUT THE INSTITUTION Independent Evangelical Lutheran Church in America, coed. *Awards:* certificates, bachelor's, and master's degrees. 44 undergraduate majors. *Total enrollment:* 1,971. Undergraduates: 1,910. Freshmen: 338. Federal methodology is used as a basis for awarding need-based institutional aid.

UNDERGRADUATE EXPENSES for 2017–2018 *Comprehensive fee:* $35,350 includes full-time tuition ($25,836), mandatory fees ($680), and room and

GRANTHAM UNIVERSITY
Lenexa, KS

CONTACT Financial Aid Office, Grantham University, 16025 West 113th Street, Lenexa, KS 66219 or toll-free 800-955-2527. *Website:* http://www.grantham.edu/.

GREAT LAKES CHRISTIAN COLLEGE
Lansing, MI

CONTACT Financial Aid Officer, Great Lakes Christian College, 6211 West Willow Highway, Lansing, MI 48917-1299, 517-321-0242 or toll-free 800-YES-GLCC. *Website:* http://www.glcc.edu/.

GREEN MOUNTAIN COLLEGE
Poultney, VT

CONTACT Wendy J. Ellis, Director of Student Financial Services, Green Mountain College, One Brennan Circle, Poultney, VT 05764-1199, 800-776-6675 Ext. 8209 or toll-free 800-776-6675. *Fax:* 802-287-8096. *E-mail:* ellisw@greenmtn.edu. *Website:* http://www.greenmtn.edu/.

GREENSBORO COLLEGE
Greensboro, NC

ABOUT THE INSTITUTION Independent United Methodist, coed. *Awards:* certificates, bachelor's, and master's degrees. 53 undergraduate majors. *Total enrollment:* 1,037. Undergraduates: 960. Freshmen: 249.

GIFT AID (NEED-BASED) *Scholarships, grants, and awards:* Federal Pell, FSEOG, state, private, college/university gift aid from institutional funds.

GIFT AID (NON-NEED-BASED) *Scholarships, grants, and awards by category:* Academic interests/achievement: general academic interests/achievements. *Creative arts/performance:* art/fine arts, music, theater/drama. *Special achievements/activities:* community service, leadership, religious involvement. *Special characteristics:* adult students, children and siblings of alumni, children of faculty/staff, international students, relatives of clergy, religious affiliation, siblings of current students, veterans.

LOANS *Programs:* Federal Direct (Subsidized and Unsubsidized Stafford, PLUS), Perkins, college/university.

WORK-STUDY *Federal work-study:* 131 jobs averaging $717.

APPLYING FOR FINANCIAL AID *Required financial aid forms:* FAFSA, institution's own form, state aid form.

CONTACT Lindsay Latham, Director of Financial Aid, Greensboro College, 815 West Market Street, Greensboro, NC 27401-1875, 336-272-7102 Ext. 217 or toll-free 800-346-8226. *Fax:* 336-230-9622. *E-mail:* dvanarsdale@greensborocollege.edu. *Website:* http://www.greensboro.edu/.

GREENVILLE COLLEGE
Greenville, IL

Tuition & fees: $26,356	Average undergraduate aid package: $20,443

ABOUT THE INSTITUTION Independent Free Methodist, coed. *Awards:* bachelor's and master's degrees. 52 undergraduate majors. *Total enrollment:* 1,211. Undergraduates: 994. Freshmen: 200. Federal methodology is used as a basis for awarding need-based institutional aid.

UNDERGRADUATE EXPENSES for 2017–2018 *Comprehensive fee:* $35,678 includes full-time tuition ($26,124), mandatory fees ($232), and room and board ($9322). *College room only:* $4918. Full-time tuition and fees vary according to degree level. Room and board charges vary according to housing facility. Part-time tuition and fees vary according to course load and degree level.

FRESHMAN FINANCIAL AID (Fall 2015) 247 applied for aid; of those 89% were deemed to have need. 100% of freshmen with need received aid; of those 15% had need fully met. *Average percent of need met:* 77% (excluding resources awarded to replace EFC). *Average financial aid package:* $20,851 (excluding resources awarded to replace EFC). 16% of all full-time freshmen had no need and received non-need-based gift aid.

UNDERGRADUATE FINANCIAL AID (Fall 2015) 925 applied for aid; of those 90% were deemed to have need. 99% of undergraduates with need received aid; of those 15% had need fully met. *Average percent of need met:* 76% (excluding resources awarded to replace EFC). *Average financial aid package:* $20,443

(excluding resources awarded to replace EFC). 15% of all full-time undergraduates had no need and received non-need-based gift aid.

GIFT AID (NEED-BASED) *Total amount:* $13,860,622 (15% federal, 9% state, 73% institutional, 3% external sources). *Receiving aid:* Freshmen: 84% (220); all full-time undergraduates: 84% (825). *Average award:* Freshmen: $18,029; Undergraduates: $16,716. *Scholarships, grants, and awards:* Federal Pell, FSEOG, state, private, college/university gift aid from institutional funds.

GIFT AID (NON-NEED-BASED) *Total amount:* $1,963,612 (1% federal, 90% institutional, 9% external sources). *Receiving aid:* Freshmen: 11% (29). Undergraduates: 9% (84). *Average award:* Freshmen: $10,780. Undergraduates: $9594. *Scholarships, grants, and awards by category:* Academic interests/achievement: biological sciences, engineering/technologies, mathematics, physical sciences. *Creative arts/performance:* applied art and design, art/fine arts, music, performing arts. *Special achievements/activities:* cheerleading/drum major, leadership, memberships, religious involvement. *Special characteristics:* children and siblings of alumni, children of faculty/staff, international students, local/state students, out-of-state students, religious affiliation, siblings of current students. *Tuition waivers:* Full or partial for employees or children of employees, senior citizens.

LOANS *Student loans:* $6,998,121 (78% need-based, 22% non-need-based). 82% of past graduating class borrowed through all loan programs. *Average indebtedness per student:* $32,860. *Average need-based loan:* Freshmen: $3260. Undergraduates: $4337. *Parent loans:* $2,385,193 (30% need-based, 70% non-need-based). *Programs:* Federal Direct (Subsidized and Unsubsidized Stafford, PLUS), Perkins, college/university.

WORK-STUDY *Federal work-study:* jobs available. *State or other work-study/employment:* Part-time jobs available.

APPLYING FOR FINANCIAL AID *Required financial aid form:* FAFSA. *Financial aid deadline (priority):* 11/1. *Notification date:* Continuous beginning 11/1. Students must reply within 3 weeks of notification.

CONTACT David Kessinger, Director of Financial Aid, Greenville College, 315 East College Avenue, Greenville, IL 62246-0159, 618-664-7108 or toll-free 800-345-4440. *Fax:* 618-664-7198. *E-mail:* david.kessinger@greenville.edu. *Website:* http://www.greenville.edu/.

GRINNELL COLLEGE
Grinnell, IA

Tuition & fees: $50,464	Average undergraduate aid package: $45,717

ABOUT THE INSTITUTION Independent, coed. *Awards:* bachelor's degrees. 27 undergraduate majors. *Total enrollment:* 1,699. Undergraduates: 1,699. Freshmen: 407. Both federal and institutional methodology are used as a basis for awarding need-based institutional aid.

UNDERGRADUATE EXPENSES for 2017–2018 *Comprehensive fee:* $62,864 includes full-time tuition ($50,014), mandatory fees ($450), and room and board ($12,400). *College room only:* $5856. Room and board charges vary according to board plan and housing facility. *Part-time tuition:* $1563 per credit hour.

FRESHMAN FINANCIAL AID (Fall 2016, est.) 324 applied for aid; of those 84% were deemed to have need. 100% of freshmen with need received aid; of those 100% had need fully met. *Average percent of need met:* 100% (excluding resources awarded to replace EFC). *Average financial aid package:* $46,431 (excluding resources awarded to replace EFC). 16% of all full-time freshmen had no need and received non-need-based gift aid.

UNDERGRADUATE FINANCIAL AID (Fall 2016, est.) 1,218 applied for aid; of those 92% were deemed to have need. 100% of undergraduates with need received aid; of those 100% had need fully met. *Average percent of need met:* 100% (excluding resources awarded to replace EFC). *Average financial aid package:* $45,717 (excluding resources awarded to replace EFC). 18% of all full-time undergraduates had no need and received non-need-based gift aid.

GIFT AID (NEED-BASED) *Total amount:* $44,287,448 (4% federal, 1% state, 93% institutional, 2% external sources). *Receiving aid:* Freshmen: 66% (272); all full-time undergraduates: 68% (1,122). *Average award:* Freshmen: $41,090; Undergraduates: $39,444. *Scholarships, grants, and awards:* Federal Pell, FSEOG, state, private, college/university gift aid from institutional funds, National Merit Scholarships, Dollars for Scholars Matching Funds.

GIFT AID (NON-NEED-BASED) *Total amount:* $5,810,328 (89% institutional, 11% external sources). *Receiving aid:* Freshmen: 9% (38). Undergraduates: 8% (125). *Average award:* Freshmen: $17,329. Undergraduates: $17,026. *Scholarships, grants, and awards by category:* Academic interests/achievement: general academic interests/achievements. *Tuition waivers:* Full or partial for employees or children of employees.

LOANS *Student loans:* $4,327,500 (94% need-based, 6% non-need-based). 50% of past graduating class borrowed through all loan programs. *Average indebtedness per student:* $18,780. *Average need-based loan:* Freshmen: $2924. Undergraduates: $4078. *Programs:* Federal Direct (Subsidized and Unsubsidized Stafford, PLUS), Perkins, college/university.

WORK-STUDY *Federal work-study:* Total amount: $216,435; 551 jobs averaging $2032. *State or other work-study/employment:* Total amount: $2,477,465 (94% need-based, 6% non-need-based). 575 part-time jobs averaging $2149.

APPLYING FOR FINANCIAL AID *Required financial aid forms:* FAFSA, CSS Financial Aid PROFILE, noncustodial (divorced/separated) parent's statement. *Financial aid deadline:* 1/15. *Notification date:* 4/1. Students must reply by 5/1.

CONTACT Mr. Brad Lindberg, Assistant Vice President of Enrollment/Director of Financial Aid, Grinnell College, 1103 Park Street, Grinnell, IA 50112-1690, 641-269-3250 or toll-free 800-247-0113. *Fax:* 641-269-4937. *E-mail:* lindbergb@grinnell.edu. *Website:* http://www.grinnell.edu/.

GROVE CITY COLLEGE
Grove City, PA

Tuition & fees: $16,630	Average undergraduate aid package: $7206

ABOUT THE INSTITUTION Independent Presbyterian, coed. *Awards:* bachelor's degrees. 48 undergraduate majors. *Total enrollment:* 2,392. Undergraduates: 2,392. Freshmen: 583. Institutional methodology is used as a basis for awarding need-based institutional aid.

UNDERGRADUATE EXPENSES for 2016–2017 *Application fee:* $50. *Comprehensive fee:* $25,692 includes full-time tuition ($16,630) and room and board ($9062). Room and board charges vary according to housing facility. *Part-time tuition:* $540 per credit hour.

FRESHMAN FINANCIAL AID (Fall 2016, est.) 398 applied for aid; of those 76% were deemed to have need. 100% of freshmen with need received aid; of those 12% had need fully met. *Average percent of need met:* 53% (excluding resources awarded to replace EFC). *Average financial aid package:* $7804 (excluding resources awarded to replace EFC). 7% of all full-time freshmen had no need and received non-need-based gift aid.

UNDERGRADUATE FINANCIAL AID (Fall 2016, est.) 1,292 applied for aid; of those 82% were deemed to have need. 99% of undergraduates with need received aid; of those 9% had need fully met. *Average percent of need met:* 51% (excluding resources awarded to replace EFC). *Average financial aid package:* $7206 (excluding resources awarded to replace EFC). 17% of all full-time undergraduates had no need and received non-need-based gift aid.

GIFT AID (NEED-BASED) *Total amount:* $7,459,145 (13% state, 78% institutional, 9% external sources). *Receiving aid:* Freshmen: 51% (299); all full-time undergraduates: 44% (1,033). *Average award:* Freshmen: $7804; Undergraduates: $7206. *Scholarships, grants, and awards:* state, private, college/university gift aid from institutional funds.

GIFT AID (NON-NEED-BASED) *Total amount:* $1,992,973 (2% state, 52% institutional, 46% external sources). *Receiving aid:* Freshmen: 6% (36). Undergraduates: 4% (90). *Average award:* Freshmen: $7203. Undergraduates: $2247. *Scholarships, grants, and awards by category:* Academic interests/achievement: 724 awards ($1,400,823 total): biological sciences, business, communication, education, engineering/technologies, English, foreign languages, general academic interests/achievements, international studies, mathematics, physical sciences, religion/biblical studies, social sciences. *Creative arts/performance:* 5 awards ($7100 total): creative writing, music. *Special achievements/activities:* 30 awards ($105,708 total): community service, general special achievements/activities, leadership, memberships, religious involvement. *Special characteristics:* 21 awards ($159,765 total): ethnic background, first-generation college students, general special characteristics, handicapped students, members of minority groups. *Tuition waivers:* Full or partial for employees or children of employees.

LOANS *Student loans:* $13,828,792 (36% need-based, 64% non-need-based). 54% of past graduating class borrowed through all loan programs. *Average indebtedness per student:* $37,655. *Programs:* state, private loans.

APPLYING FOR FINANCIAL AID *Financial aid deadline:* 4/15. *Notification date:* Continuous beginning 3/15. Students must reply by 5/1.

CONTACT Mr. Thomas G. Ball, Director of Financial Aid, Grove City College, 100 Campus Drive, Grove City, PA 16127-2104, 724-458-3300. *Fax:* 724-450-4040. *E-mail:* financialaid@gcc.edu. *Website:* http://www.gcc.edu/.

GUILFORD COLLEGE
Greensboro, NC

Tuition & fees: $34,215	Average undergraduate aid package: $22,816

ABOUT THE INSTITUTION Independent Society of Friends, coed. *Awards:* certificates and bachelor's degrees. 36 undergraduate majors. *Total enrollment:* 1,809. Undergraduates: 1,809. Freshmen: 428. Federal methodology is used as a basis for awarding need-based institutional aid.

UNDERGRADUATE EXPENSES for 2017–2018 *Comprehensive fee:* $44,437 includes full-time tuition ($33,710), mandatory fees ($505), and room and board ($10,222). *College room only:* $5000. Full-time tuition and fees vary according to program. Room and board charges vary according to board plan and housing facility. *Part-time tuition:* $1032 per credit hour. *Part-time fees:* $205 per term. Part-time tuition and fees vary according to course load and program.

FRESHMAN FINANCIAL AID (Fall 2015) 288 applied for aid; of those 98% were deemed to have need. 100% of freshmen with need received aid; of those 10% had need fully met. *Average percent of need met:* 68% (excluding resources awarded to replace EFC). *Average financial aid package:* $26,190 (excluding resources awarded to replace EFC). 11% of all full-time freshmen had no need and received non-need-based gift aid.

UNDERGRADUATE FINANCIAL AID (Fall 2015) 1,183 applied for aid; of those 91% were deemed to have need. 100% of undergraduates with need received aid; of those 8% had need fully met. *Average percent of need met:* 67% (excluding resources awarded to replace EFC). *Average financial aid package:* $22,816 (excluding resources awarded to replace EFC). 7% of all full-time undergraduates had no need and received non-need-based gift aid.

GIFT AID (NEED-BASED) *Total amount:* $9,636,999 (33% federal, 22% state, 45% institutional). *Receiving aid:* Freshmen: 70% (231); all full-time undergraduates: 64% (929). *Average award:* Freshmen: $9242; Undergraduates: $5023. *Scholarships, grants, and awards:* Federal Pell, FSEOG, state, private, college/university gift aid from institutional funds.

GIFT AID (NON-NEED-BASED) *Total amount:* $16,490,702 (92% institutional, 8% external sources). *Receiving aid:* Freshmen: 85% (279). Undergraduates: 53% (775). *Average award:* Freshmen: $9119. Undergraduates: $8653. *Scholarships, grants, and awards by category:* Academic interests/achievement: biological sciences, general academic interests/achievements. *Creative arts/performance:* music, theater/drama. *Special characteristics:* children of faculty/staff, first-generation college students, local/state students. *Tuition waivers:* Full or partial for employees or children of employees. *ROTC:* Army cooperative, Air Force cooperative.

LOANS *Student loans:* $12,461,955 (37% need-based, 63% non-need-based). 89% of past graduating class borrowed through all loan programs. *Average indebtedness per student:* $20,682. *Average need-based loan:* Freshmen: $2844. Undergraduates: $3819. *Parent loans:* $2,250,157 (100% need-based). *Programs:* Federal Direct (Subsidized and Unsubsidized Stafford, PLUS), Perkins, college/university.

WORK-STUDY *Federal work-study:* jobs available. *State or other work-study/employment:* Total amount: $160,172 (100% need-based). Part-time jobs available.

APPLYING FOR FINANCIAL AID *Required financial aid form:* FAFSA. *Financial aid deadline (priority):* 2/15. *Notification date:* Continuous beginning 3/1. Students must reply within 2 weeks of notification.

CONTACT Mr. Brian DeYoung, Director of Financial Aid, Guilford College, 5800 West Friendly Avenue, Greensboro, NC 27410, 336-316-2410 or toll-free 800-992-7759. *Fax:* 336-316-2942. *E-mail:* deyoungbk@guilford.edu. *Website:* http://www.guilford.edu/.

GUSTAVUS ADOLPHUS COLLEGE
St. Peter, MN

Tuition & fees: $42,550	Average undergraduate aid package: $34,694

ABOUT THE INSTITUTION Independent Evangelical Lutheran Church in America, coed. *Awards:* bachelor's degrees. 67 undergraduate majors. *Total enrollment:* 2,386. Undergraduates: 2,386. Freshmen: 614. Both federal and institutional methodology are used as a basis for awarding need-based institutional aid.

UNDERGRADUATE EXPENSES for 2016–2017 *One-time required fee:* $480. *Comprehensive fee:* $51,950 includes full-time tuition ($42,360), mandatory fees ($190), and room and board ($9400). *College room only:* $5990. Room and board charges vary according to board plan and housing facility. *Part-time tuition:* $7290 per course. *Payment plan:* Tuition prepayment.

FRESHMAN FINANCIAL AID (Fall 2015) 530 applied for aid; of those 87% were deemed to have need. 100% of freshmen with need received aid; of those 38% had need fully met. *Average percent of need met:* 93% (excluding resources awarded to replace EFC). *Average financial aid package:* $37,682 (excluding resources awarded to replace EFC). 25% of all full-time freshmen had no need and received non-need-based gift aid.

UNDERGRADUATE FINANCIAL AID (Fall 2015) 1,847 applied for aid; of those 89% were deemed to have need. 100% of undergraduates with need received aid; of those 32% had need fully met. *Average percent of need met:* 90% (excluding resources awarded to replace EFC). *Average financial aid package:* $34,694 (excluding resources awarded to replace EFC). 29% of all full-time undergraduates had no need and received non-need-based gift aid.

GIFT AID (NEED-BASED) *Total amount:* $44,569,530 (6% federal, 8% state, 84% institutional, 2% external sources). *Receiving aid:* Freshmen: 74% (460); all full-time undergraduates: 70% (1,642). *Average award:* Freshmen: $32,194; Undergraduates: $29,745. *Scholarships, grants, and awards:* Federal Pell, FSEOG, state, private, college/university gift aid from institutional funds.

GIFT AID (NON-NEED-BASED) *Total amount:* $15,537,470 (95% institutional, 5% external sources). *Receiving aid:* Freshmen: 11% (69). Undergraduates: 10% (224). *Average award:* Freshmen: $23,279. Undergraduates: $20,598. *Scholarships, grants, and awards by category:* Academic interests/achievement: general academic interests/achievements. Creative arts/performance: art/fine arts, dance, debating, music, theater/drama. Special achievements/activities: junior miss. Special characteristics: children and siblings of alumni, ethnic background, first-generation college students, international students, members of minority groups, out-of-state students, siblings of current students. *Tuition waivers:* Full or partial for employees or children of employees. *ROTC:* Army cooperative.

LOANS *Student loans:* $16,284,970 (35% need-based, 65% non-need-based). 85% of past graduating class borrowed through all loan programs. *Average indebtedness per student:* $34,773. *Average need-based loan:* Freshmen: $3176. Undergraduates: $3489. *Parent loans:* $2,206,859 (100% non-need-based). *Programs:* Federal Direct (Subsidized and Unsubsidized Stafford, PLUS), Perkins, state.

WORK-STUDY *Federal work-study:* jobs available. *State or other work-study/employment:* Total amount: $922,520 (74% need-based, 26% non-need-based). Part-time jobs available.

APPLYING FOR FINANCIAL AID *Required financial aid form:* FAFSA. *Financial aid deadline:* 4/15 (priority: 3/15). *Notification date:* Continuous beginning 12/15. Students must reply by 5/1 or within 2 weeks of notification.

CONTACT Mr. Doug Minter, Dean of Financial Aid, Gustavus Adolphus College, 800 West College Avenue, St. Peter, MN 56082-1498, 507-933-7527 or toll-free 800-GUSTAVU(S). *Fax:* 507-933-7727. *E-mail:* finaid@gustavus.edu. *Website:* http://www.gustavus.edu/.

GUTENBERG COLLEGE
Eugene, OR

CONTACT Financial Aid Office, Gutenberg College, 1883 University Street, Eugene, OR 97403, 541-683-5141. *Website:* http://www.gutenberg.edu/.

GWYNEDD MERCY UNIVERSITY
Gwynedd Valley, PA

Tuition & fees: $33,520	Average undergraduate aid package: $20,302

ABOUT THE INSTITUTION Independent Roman Catholic, coed. *Awards:* certificates, bachelor's, master's, and doctoral degrees. 31 undergraduate majors. *Total enrollment:* 2,667. Undergraduates: 2,035. Freshmen: 225. Federal methodology is used as a basis for awarding need-based institutional aid.

UNDERGRADUATE EXPENSES for 2017–2018 *Comprehensive fee:* $45,150 includes full-time tuition ($32,820), mandatory fees ($700), and room and board ($11,630). *College room only:* $5360. Full-time tuition and fees vary according to location and program. Room and board charges vary according to board plan and housing facility. *Part-time tuition:* $725 per credit hour. Part-time tuition and fees vary according to location and program.

FRESHMAN FINANCIAL AID (Fall 2016, est.) 217 applied for aid; of those 91% were deemed to have need. 100% of freshmen with need received aid; of those 13% had need fully met. *Average percent of need met:* 72% (excluding resources awarded to replace EFC). *Average financial aid package:* $25,666 (excluding resources awarded to replace EFC). 10% of all full-time freshmen had no need and received non-need-based gift aid.

UNDERGRADUATE FINANCIAL AID (Fall 2016, est.) 1,504 applied for aid; of those 92% were deemed to have need. 99% of undergraduates with need received aid; of those 12% had need fully met. *Average percent of need met:* 60% (excluding resources awarded to replace EFC). *Average financial aid package:* $20,302 (excluding resources awarded to replace EFC). 9% of all full-time undergraduates had no need and received non-need-based gift aid.

GIFT AID (NEED-BASED) *Total amount:* $22,256,587 (13% federal, 10% state, 70% institutional, 7% external sources). *Receiving aid:* Freshmen: 90% (198); all full-time undergraduates: 72% (1,215). *Average award:* Freshmen: $21,708; Undergraduates: $18,273. *Scholarships, grants, and awards:* Federal Pell, FSEOG, state, private, college/university gift aid from institutional funds.

GIFT AID (NON-NEED-BASED) *Total amount:* $2,889,266 (1% federal, 1% state, 87% institutional, 11% external sources). *Receiving aid:* Freshmen: 7% (16). Undergraduates: 7% (110). *Average award:* Freshmen: $16,095. Undergraduates: $12,507. *Scholarships, grants, and awards by category:* Academic interests/achievement: general academic interests/achievements. Special achievements/activities: general special achievements/activities. Special characteristics: children and siblings of alumni, children of faculty/staff, siblings of current students, veterans, veterans' children. *Tuition waivers:* Full or partial for employees or children of employees.

LOANS *Student loans:* $17,712,523 (75% need-based, 25% non-need-based). 88% of past graduating class borrowed through all loan programs. *Average indebtedness per student:* $43,789. *Average need-based loan:* Freshmen: $3417. Undergraduates: $4134. *Parent loans:* $3,037,166 (53% need-based, 47% non-need-based). *Programs:* Federal Direct (Subsidized and Unsubsidized Stafford, PLUS), Perkins, Federal Nursing, alternative loans.

WORK-STUDY *Federal work-study:* Total amount: $584,820; jobs available. *State or other work-study/employment:* Part-time jobs available.

APPLYING FOR FINANCIAL AID *Required financial aid forms:* FAFSA, institution's own form. *Financial aid deadline:* 5/1 (priority: 3/15). *Notification date:* Continuous beginning 2/15. Students must reply by 5/1 or within 2 weeks of notification.

CONTACT Mrs. Elizabeth R. Howard, Director of Student Financial Aid, Gwynedd Mercy University, PO Box 901, Gwynedd Valley, PA 19437-0901, 215-646-7300 Ext. 483 or toll-free 800-342-5462. *Fax:* 215-641-5556. *E-mail:* howard.e@gmercyu.edu. *Website:* http://www.gmercyu.edu/.

HALLMARK UNIVERSITY
San Antonio, TX

CONTACT Financial Aid Office, Hallmark University, 10401 IH 10 West, San Antonio, TX 78230, 210-690-9000 or toll-free 800-880-6600. *Website:* http://www.hallmarkuniversity.edu/.

HAMILTON COLLEGE
Clinton, NY

Tuition & fees: $51,240	Average undergraduate aid package: $47,003

ABOUT THE INSTITUTION Independent, coed. *Awards:* bachelor's degrees. 43 undergraduate majors. *Total enrollment:* 1,879. Undergraduates: 1,879. Freshmen: 472. Both federal and institutional methodology are used as a basis for awarding need-based institutional aid.

UNDERGRADUATE EXPENSES for 2016–2017 *Application fee:* $50. *Comprehensive fee:* $64,250 includes full-time tuition ($50,730), mandatory fees ($510), and room and board ($13,010). *College room only:* $7110. Room and board charges vary according to board plan. *Part-time tuition:* $6341 per course.

FRESHMAN FINANCIAL AID (Fall 2016, est.) 267 applied for aid; of those 93% were deemed to have need. 100% of freshmen with need received aid; of those 100% had need fully met. *Average percent of need met:* 100% (excluding resources awarded to replace EFC). *Average financial aid package:* $48,371 (excluding resources awarded to replace EFC).

UNDERGRADUATE FINANCIAL AID (Fall 2016, est.) 938 applied for aid; of those 95% were deemed to have need. 100% of undergraduates with need received aid; of those 100% had need fully met. *Average percent of need met:* 100% (excluding resources awarded to replace EFC). *Average financial aid package:* $47,003 (excluding resources awarded to replace EFC).

GIFT AID (NEED-BASED) *Total amount:* $38,193,143 (3% federal, 2% state, 93% institutional, 2% external sources). *Receiving aid:* Freshmen: 52% (247); all full-time undergraduates: 48% (892). *Average award:* Freshmen: $43,936; Undergraduates: $41,825. *Scholarships, grants, and awards:* Federal Pell, FSEOG, state, private, college/university gift aid from institutional funds.

GIFT AID (NON-NEED-BASED) *Total amount:* $456,508 (1% state, 17% institutional, 82% external sources). *Tuition waivers:* Full or partial for employees or children of employees. *ROTC:* Army cooperative, Air Force cooperative.

LOANS *Student loans:* $2,872,057 (100% need-based). 45% of past graduating class borrowed through all loan programs. *Average indebtedness per student:* $21,491. *Average need-based loan:* Freshmen: $3291. Undergraduates: $4292. *Programs:* Federal Direct (Subsidized and Unsubsidized Stafford, PLUS), Perkins, state, college/university.

WORK-STUDY *Federal work-study:* Total amount: $1,034,180; 563 jobs averaging $1837. *State or other work-study/employment:* Total amount: $101,000 (100% need-based). 52 part-time jobs averaging $1942.

APPLYING FOR FINANCIAL AID *Required financial aid forms:* FAFSA, institution's own form, CSS Financial Aid PROFILE, state aid form, noncustodial (divorced/separated) parent's statement, business/farm supplement. *Financial aid deadline:* 2/15. *Notification date:* 4/1. Students must reply by 5/1.

CONTACT Office of Financial Aid, Hamilton College, 198 College Hill Road, Clinton, NY 13323, 315-859-4434 or toll-free 800-843-2655. *Fax:* 315-859-4962. *E-mail:* finaid@hamilton.edu.
Website: http://www.hamilton.edu/.

HAMILTON TECHNICAL COLLEGE
Davenport, IA

CONTACT Ms. Lisa Boyd, Executive Vice President/Director of Financial Aid, Hamilton Technical College, 1011 East 53rd Street, Davenport, IA 52807-2653, 563-386-3570 Ext. 33 or toll-free 866-966-4825. *Fax:* 563-386-6756.
Website: http://www.hamiltontechcollege.edu/.

HAMLINE UNIVERSITY
St. Paul, MN

Tuition & fees: $40,332	Average undergraduate aid package: $29,877

ABOUT THE INSTITUTION Independent United Methodist Church, coed. *Awards:* certificates, bachelor's, master's, and doctoral degrees. 56 undergraduate majors. *Total enrollment:* 3,852. Undergraduates: 2,184. Freshmen: 548. Federal methodology is used as a basis for awarding need-based institutional aid.

UNDERGRADUATE EXPENSES for 2017–2018 *Comprehensive fee:* $50,488 includes full-time tuition ($39,206), mandatory fees ($1126), and room and board ($10,156). *College room only:* $5076. Room and board charges vary according to board plan and housing facility. *Part-time tuition:* $1225 per credit hour. *Part-time fees:* $767 per year. Part-time tuition and fees vary according to course load.

FRESHMAN FINANCIAL AID (Fall 2016, est.) 522 applied for aid; of those 93% were deemed to have need. 100% of freshmen with need received aid; of those 22% had need fully met. *Average percent of need met:* 85% (excluding resources awarded to replace EFC). *Average financial aid package:* $32,000 (excluding resources awarded to replace EFC). 10% of all full-time freshmen had no need and received non-need-based gift aid.

UNDERGRADUATE FINANCIAL AID (Fall 2016, est.) 1,861 applied for aid; of those 93% were deemed to have need. 100% of undergraduates with need received aid; of those 17% had need fully met. *Average percent of need met:* 79% (excluding resources awarded to replace EFC). *Average financial aid package:* $29,877 (excluding resources awarded to replace EFC). 15% of all full-time undergraduates had no need and received non-need-based gift aid.

GIFT AID (NEED-BASED) *Total amount:* $40,095,007 (9% federal, 11% state, 79% institutional, 1% external sources). *Receiving aid:* Freshmen: 89% (485); all full-time undergraduates: 83% (1,725). *Average award:* Freshmen: $25,648; Undergraduates: $23,426. *Scholarships, grants, and awards:* Federal Pell, FSEOG, state, private, college/university gift aid from institutional funds, Academic Competitiveness Grants, National SMART Grants, TEACH Grants, United Methodist Scholarships.

GIFT AID (NON-NEED-BASED) *Total amount:* $7,365,322 (1% federal, 97% institutional, 2% external sources). *Receiving aid:* Freshmen: 16% (86). Undergraduates: 10% (211). *Average award:* Freshmen: $19,965. Undergraduates: $16,630. *Scholarships, grants, and awards by category: Academic interests/achievement:* 1,944 awards ($29,689,420 total): biological sciences, business, communication, education, English, foreign languages, general academic interests/achievements, humanities, mathematics, physical sciences, premedicine, religion/biblical studies, social sciences. *Creative arts/performance:* 209 awards ($522,034 total): applied art and design, art/fine arts, creative writing, general creative arts/performance, journalism/publications, music, theater/drama. *Special achievements/activities:* 167 awards ($415,212 total): community service, general special achievements/activities, leadership, memberships. *Special characteristics:* 572 awards ($1,959,946 total): children and siblings of alumni, first-generation college students, general special characteristics, international students, local/state students, members of minority groups, out-of-state students, previous college experience, relatives of clergy, religious affiliation, veterans. *Tuition waivers:* Full or partial for employees or children of employees. *ROTC:* Army cooperative, Air Force cooperative.

LOANS *Student loans:* $15,332,958 (72% need-based, 28% non-need-based). 80% of past graduating class borrowed through all loan programs. *Average indebtedness per student:* $34,935. *Average need-based loan:* Freshmen: $3484. Undergraduates: $4748. *Parent loans:* $5,545,772 (45% need-based, 55% non-need-based). *Programs:* Federal Direct (Subsidized and Unsubsidized Stafford, PLUS), Perkins, state, alternative loans, United Methodist Student Loans.

WORK-STUDY *Federal work-study:* Total amount: $727,760; 323 jobs averaging $2261. *State or other work-study/employment:* Total amount: $2,612,026 (66% need-based, 34% non-need-based). 1,009 part-time jobs averaging $2589.

APPLYING FOR FINANCIAL AID *Required financial aid form:* FAFSA. *Financial aid deadline (priority):* 3/15. *Notification date:* Continuous beginning 3/15. Students must reply by 5/1 or within 2 weeks of notification.

CONTACT Ms. Lynette Wahl, Office of Financial Aid, Hamline University, 1536 Hewitt Avenue, MS C1915, St. Paul, MN 55104, 651-523-3000 or toll-free 800-753-9753. *Fax:* 651-523-2585. *E-mail:* finaid@hamline.edu.
Website: http://www.hamline.edu/.

HAMPDEN-SYDNEY COLLEGE
Hampden-Sydney, VA

Tuition & fees: $43,940	Average undergraduate aid package: $32,430

ABOUT THE INSTITUTION Independent Presbyterian Church (U.S.A.), men only. *Awards:* bachelor's degrees. 25 undergraduate majors. *Total enrollment:*

1,027. Undergraduates: 1,027. Freshmen: 283. Federal methodology is used as a basis for awarding need-based institutional aid.

UNDERGRADUATE EXPENSES for 2017–2018 *Application fee:* $30. *Comprehensive fee:* $57,360 includes full-time tuition ($42,470), mandatory fees ($1470), and room and board ($13,420). *College room only:* $6012. Full-time tuition and fees vary according to course load and student level. Room and board charges vary according to board plan and housing facility. *Part-time tuition:* $1330 per credit hour. Part-time tuition and fees vary according to course load and student level.

FRESHMAN FINANCIAL AID (Fall 2016, est.) 241 applied for aid; of those 82% were deemed to have need. 100% of freshmen with need received aid; of those 30% had need fully met. *Average percent of need met:* 81% (excluding resources awarded to replace EFC). *Average financial aid package:* $31,743 (excluding resources awarded to replace EFC). 29% of all full-time freshmen had no need and received non-need-based gift aid.

UNDERGRADUATE FINANCIAL AID (Fall 2016, est.) 754 applied for aid; of those 87% were deemed to have need. 100% of undergraduates with need received aid; of those 22% had need fully met. *Average percent of need met:* 79% (excluding resources awarded to replace EFC). *Average financial aid package:* $32,430 (excluding resources awarded to replace EFC). 34% of all full-time undergraduates had no need and received non-need-based gift aid.

GIFT AID (NEED-BASED) *Total amount:* $18,708,691 (5% federal, 7% state, 86% institutional, 2% external sources). *Receiving aid:* Freshmen: 70% (197); all full-time undergraduates: 64% (658). *Average award:* Freshmen: $28,603; Undergraduates: $28,432. *Scholarships, grants, and awards:* Federal Pell, FSEOG, state, private, college/university gift aid from institutional funds.

GIFT AID (NON-NEED-BASED) *Total amount:* $8,092,838 (10% state, 84% institutional, 6% external sources). *Receiving aid:* Freshmen: 18% (52). Undergraduates: 11% (117). *Average award:* Freshmen: $20,519. Undergraduates: $17,333. *Scholarships, grants, and awards by category: Academic interests/achievement:* biological sciences, education, general academic interests/achievements, home economics, international studies, premedicine. *Creative arts/performance:* music. *Special achievements/activities:* general special achievements/activities, leadership. *Special characteristics:* children of educators, children of faculty/staff, ethnic background, international students, members of minority groups, out-of-state students, veterans, veterans' children. *Tuition waivers:* Full or partial for employees or children of employees. *ROTC:* Army cooperative.

LOANS *Student loans:* $6,395,247 (57% need-based, 43% non-need-based). 68% of past graduating class borrowed through all loan programs. *Average indebtedness per student:* $34,344. *Average need-based loan:* Freshmen: $3837. Undergraduates: $4837. *Parent loans:* $4,233,466 (31% need-based, 69% non-need-based). *Programs:* Federal Direct (Subsidized and Unsubsidized Stafford, PLUS), Perkins, college/university.

WORK-STUDY *Federal work-study:* Total amount: $263,765; 227 jobs averaging $1272.

APPLYING FOR FINANCIAL AID *Required financial aid forms:* FAFSA, state aid form. *Financial aid deadline (priority):* 3/1. *Notification date:* 3/15. Students must reply by 5/1 or within 2 weeks of notification.

CONTACT Ms. Zita Marie Barree, Director of Financial Aid, Hampden-Sydney College, PO Box 726, Hampden-Sydney, VA 23943-0726, 434-223-6119 or toll-free 800-755-0733. *Fax:* 434-223-6075. *E-mail:* hsfinaid@hsc.edu. *Website:* http://www.hsc.edu/.

HAMPSHIRE COLLEGE
Amherst, MA

Tuition & fees: $50,030	Average undergraduate aid package: $42,326

ABOUT THE INSTITUTION Independent, coed. *Awards:* bachelor's degrees. 57 undergraduate majors. *Total enrollment:* 1,321. Undergraduates: 1,321. Freshmen: 327. Both federal and institutional methodology are used as a basis for awarding need-based institutional aid.

UNDERGRADUATE EXPENSES for 2017–2018 *Comprehensive fee:* $63,636 includes full-time tuition ($50,030) and room and board ($13,606). *College room only:* $8520. Room and board charges vary according to board plan.

FRESHMAN FINANCIAL AID (Fall 2016, est.) 271 applied for aid; of those 89% were deemed to have need. 100% of freshmen with need received aid; of those 10% had need fully met. *Average percent of need met:* 95% (excluding resources

awarded to replace EFC). *Average financial aid package:* $45,654 (excluding resources awarded to replace EFC). 20% of all full-time freshmen had no need and received non-need-based gift aid.

UNDERGRADUATE FINANCIAL AID (Fall 2016, est.) 997 applied for aid; of those 86% were deemed to have need. 100% of undergraduates with need received aid; of those 13% had need fully met. *Average percent of need met:* 93% (excluding resources awarded to replace EFC). *Average financial aid package:* $42,326 (excluding resources awarded to replace EFC). 27% of all full-time undergraduates had no need and received non-need-based gift aid.

GIFT AID (NEED-BASED) *Total amount:* $28,844,519 (7% federal, 1% state, 90% institutional, 2% external sources). *Receiving aid:* Freshmen: 74% (241); all full-time undergraduates: 64% (838). *Average award:* Freshmen: $38,891; Undergraduates: $35,237. *Scholarships, grants, and awards:* Federal Pell, FSEOG, state, private, college/university gift aid from institutional funds.

GIFT AID (NON-NEED-BASED) *Total amount:* $5,714,799 (1% federal, 86% institutional, 13% external sources). *Receiving aid:* Freshmen: 6% (20). Undergraduates: 8% (100). *Average award:* Freshmen: $7989. Undergraduates: $12,652. *Scholarships, grants, and awards by category: Academic interests/achievement:* biological sciences, English, general academic interests/achievements, humanities, international studies, mathematics, physical sciences, social sciences. *Creative arts/performance:* creative writing. *Special achievements/activities:* community service, leadership. *Special characteristics:* children of faculty/staff. *Tuition waivers:* Full or partial for employees or children of employees. *ROTC:* Army cooperative.

LOANS *Student loans:* $7,317,632 (75% need-based, 25% non-need-based). 55% of past graduating class borrowed through all loan programs. *Average indebtedness per student:* $21,758. *Average need-based loan:* Freshmen: $3405. Undergraduates: $4354. *Parent loans:* $2,827,683 (34% need-based, 66% non-need-based). *Programs:* Federal Direct (Subsidized and Unsubsidized Stafford, PLUS), Perkins.

WORK-STUDY *Federal work-study:* Total amount: $1,170,736; 575 jobs averaging $2900. *State or other work-study/employment:* Total amount: $487,351 (23% need-based, 77% non-need-based). 253 part-time jobs averaging $2900.

APPLYING FOR FINANCIAL AID *Required financial aid forms:* FAFSA, CSS Financial Aid PROFILE, noncustodial (divorced/separated) parent's statement. *Financial aid deadline (priority):* 2/1. *Notification date:* 4/1. Students must reply by 5/1.

CONTACT Ms. Jennifer Garratt Lawton, Director of Financial Aid, Hampshire College, 893 West Street, Amherst, MA 01002, 413-559-5484 or toll-free 877-937-4267. *Fax:* 413-559-5585. *E-mail:* financialaid@hampshire.edu. *Website:* http://www.hampshire.edu/.

HAMPTON UNIVERSITY
Hampton, VA

Tuition & fees: $24,242	Average undergraduate aid package: $5613

ABOUT THE INSTITUTION Independent, coed. *Awards:* certificates, associate, bachelor's, master's, and doctoral degrees. 76 undergraduate majors. *Total enrollment:* 4,646. Undergraduates: 3,836. Freshmen: 1,278. Federal methodology is used as a basis for awarding need-based institutional aid.

UNDERGRADUATE EXPENSES for 2016–2017 *Application fee:* $35. *Comprehensive fee:* $34,926 includes full-time tuition ($21,552), mandatory fees ($2690), and room and board ($10,684). *College room only:* $5556. Full-time tuition and fees vary according to course load, degree level, location, program, and reciprocity agreements. Room and board charges vary according to board plan, housing facility, and location. *Part-time tuition:* $548 per credit hour. Part-time tuition and fees vary according to class time, course load, location, and reciprocity agreements.

FRESHMAN FINANCIAL AID (Fall 2015) 705 applied for aid; of those 82% were deemed to have need. 97% of freshmen with need received aid; of those 40% had need fully met. *Average percent of need met:* 40% (excluding resources awarded to replace EFC). *Average financial aid package:* $5641 (excluding resources awarded to replace EFC). 4% of all full-time freshmen had no need and received non-need-based gift aid.

UNDERGRADUATE FINANCIAL AID (Fall 2015) 2,131 applied for aid; of those 79% were deemed to have need. 96% of undergraduates with need received aid; of those 41% had need fully met. *Average percent of need met:* 41% (excluding resources awarded to replace EFC). *Average financial aid package:* $5613

(excluding resources awarded to replace EFC). 21% of all full-time undergraduates had no need and received non-need-based gift aid.

GIFT AID (NEED-BASED) *Total amount:* $11,823,986 (57% federal, 11% state, 5% institutional, 27% external sources). *Receiving aid:* Freshmen: 67% (562); all full-time undergraduates: 54% (1,588). *Average award:* Freshmen: $5206; Undergraduates: $5145. *Scholarships, grants, and awards:* Federal Pell, FSEOG, state, private, college/university gift aid from institutional funds, United Negro College Fund.

GIFT AID (NON-NEED-BASED) *Total amount:* $17,038,659 (6% federal, 4% state, 87% institutional, 3% external sources). *Receiving aid:* Freshmen: 61% (510). Undergraduates: 38% (1,121). *Average award:* Freshmen: $2742. Undergraduates: $10,956. *Scholarships, grants, and awards by category: Academic interests/achievement:* 147 awards ($2,053,966 total): architecture, biological sciences, business, communication, computer science, education, engineering/technologies, general academic interests/achievements, health fields, physical sciences. *Creative arts/performance:* 4 awards ($26,500 total): music. *Special achievements/activities:* 12 awards ($30,000 total): leadership. *Special characteristics:* 706 awards ($2,466,472 total): adult students, children of faculty/staff, international students, members of minority groups, veterans, veterans' children. *Tuition waivers:* Full or partial for employees or children of employees. *ROTC:* Army, Naval.

LOANS *Student loans:* $19,552,262 (93% need-based, 7% non-need-based). 73% of past graduating class borrowed through all loan programs. *Average indebtedness per student:* $34,367. *Average need-based loan:* Freshmen: $5770. Undergraduates: $5707. *Parent loans:* $26,860,005 (89% need-based, 11% non-need-based). *Programs:* Federal Direct (Subsidized and Unsubsidized Stafford, PLUS), Perkins, Federal Nursing.

WORK-STUDY *Federal work-study:* 226 jobs averaging $1452. *State or other work-study/employment:* Total amount: $94,257 (84% need-based, 16% non-need-based). Part-time jobs available.

ATHLETIC AWARDS Total amount: $2,044,364 (92% need-based, 8% non-need-based).

APPLYING FOR FINANCIAL AID *Required financial aid forms:* FAFSA, state aid form (VA residents only). *Financial aid deadline:* 4/15 (priority: 2/15). *Notification date:* Continuous beginning 4/15. Students must reply within 2 weeks of notification.

CONTACT Mr. Martin Miles, Director of Financial Aid, Hampton University, Whipple Barn, 2nd Floor, Hampton, VA 23668, 757-727-5332 or toll-free 800-624-3328. *Fax:* 757-728-6567. *E-mail:* martin.miles@hamptonu.edu. *Website:* http://www.hamptonu.edu/.

HANNIBAL-LAGRANGE UNIVERSITY
Hannibal, MO

CONTACT Brice Baumgardner, Director of Financial Aid, Hannibal-LaGrange University, 2800 Palmyra Road, Hannibal, MO 63401-1940, 573-629-3279 Ext. 3279 or toll-free 800-HLG-1119. *Fax:* 573-248-0954. *E-mail:* bbaumgardner@hlg.edu. *Website:* http://www.hlg.edu/.

HANOVER COLLEGE
Hanover, IN

Tuition & fees: $36,520	Average undergraduate aid package: $28,284

ABOUT THE INSTITUTION Independent Presbyterian, coed. *Awards:* bachelor's degrees. 38 undergraduate majors. *Total enrollment:* 1,090. Undergraduates: 1,090. Freshmen: 308. Federal methodology is used as a basis for awarding need-based institutional aid.

UNDERGRADUATE EXPENSES for 2017–2018 *One-time required fee:* $350. *Comprehensive fee:* $47,750 includes full-time tuition ($35,750), mandatory fees ($770), and room and board ($11,230). *College room only:* $5600. Full-time tuition and fees vary according to reciprocity agreements. Room and board charges vary according to housing facility. *Part-time tuition:* $3972 per unit. Part-time tuition and fees vary according to course load and reciprocity agreements.

FRESHMAN FINANCIAL AID (Fall 2015) 302 applied for aid; of those 64% were deemed to have need. 100% of freshmen with need received aid; of those 28% had

need fully met. *Average percent of need met:* 82% (excluding resources awarded to replace EFC). *Average financial aid package:* $28,162 (excluding resources awarded to replace EFC). 16% of all full-time freshmen had no need and received non-need-based gift aid.

UNDERGRADUATE FINANCIAL AID (Fall 2015) 975 applied for aid; of those 88% were deemed to have need. 100% of undergraduates with need received aid; of those 22% had need fully met. *Average percent of need met:* 79% (excluding resources awarded to replace EFC). *Average financial aid package:* $28,284 (excluding resources awarded to replace EFC). 23% of all full-time undergraduates had no need and received non-need-based gift aid.

GIFT AID (NEED-BASED) *Total amount:* $20,529,662 (8% federal, 8% state, 80% institutional, 4% external sources). *Receiving aid:* Freshmen: 60% (194); all full-time undergraduates: 76% (856). *Average award:* Freshmen: $25,651; Undergraduates: $24,741. *Scholarships, grants, and awards:* Federal Pell, FSEOG, state, private, college/university gift aid from institutional funds.

GIFT AID (NON-NEED-BASED) *Total amount:* $6,224,379 (96% institutional, 4% external sources). *Receiving aid:* Freshmen: 13% (41). Undergraduates: 12% (137). *Average award:* Freshmen: $20,772. Undergraduates: $19,305. *Scholarships, grants, and awards by category: Academic interests/achievement:* general academic interests/achievements. *Special characteristics:* children and siblings of alumni, children of faculty/staff, international students, members of minority groups, out-of-state students, religious affiliation, siblings of current students. *Tuition waivers:* Full or partial for employees or children of employees, senior citizens.

LOANS *Student loans:* $6,535,113 (70% need-based, 30% non-need-based). 76% of past graduating class borrowed through all loan programs. *Average indebtedness per student:* $29,745. *Average need-based loan:* Freshmen: $3548. Undergraduates: $4290. *Parent loans:* $3,638,508 (39% need-based, 61% non-need-based). *Programs:* Federal Direct (Subsidized and Unsubsidized Stafford, PLUS), college/university.

WORK-STUDY *Federal work-study:* 384 jobs averaging $457.

APPLYING FOR FINANCIAL AID *Required financial aid form:* FAFSA. *Financial aid deadline (priority):* 3/1. *Notification date:* Continuous beginning 3/1. Students must reply by 5/1.

CONTACT Mr. Richard A. Nash, Director of Financial Aid, Hanover College, 517 Ball Drive, Hanover, IN 47243-0108, 800-213-2178 Ext. 7029 or toll-free 800-213-2178. *Fax:* 812-866-7284. *E-mail:* finaid@hanover.edu. *Website:* http://www.hanover.edu/.

HARDING UNIVERSITY
Searcy, AR

Tuition & fees: $18,440	Average undergraduate aid package: $17,723

ABOUT THE INSTITUTION Independent Church of Christ, coed. *Awards:* certificates, bachelor's, master's, and doctoral degrees. 85 undergraduate majors. *Total enrollment:* 5,904. Undergraduates: 4,419. Freshmen: 1,019. Federal methodology is used as a basis for awarding need-based institutional aid.

UNDERGRADUATE EXPENSES for 2016–2017 *Application fee:* $50. *Comprehensive fee:* $25,196 includes full-time tuition ($17,940), mandatory fees ($500), and room and board ($6756). *College room only:* $3266. Full-time tuition and fees vary according to course load. Room and board charges vary according to board plan and housing facility. *Part-time tuition:* $598 per credit hour. *Part-time fees:* $25 per credit hour. Part-time tuition and fees vary according to course load. *Payment plan:* Tuition prepayment.

FRESHMAN FINANCIAL AID (Fall 2015) 873 applied for aid; of those 74% were deemed to have need. 100% of freshmen with need received aid; of those 39% had need fully met. *Average percent of need met:* 82% (excluding resources awarded to replace EFC). *Average financial aid package:* $16,994 (excluding resources awarded to replace EFC). 22% of all full-time freshmen had no need and received non-need-based gift aid.

UNDERGRADUATE FINANCIAL AID (Fall 2015) 3,163 applied for aid; of those 80% were deemed to have need. 99% of undergraduates with need received aid; of those 37% had need fully met. *Average percent of need met:* 78% (excluding resources awarded to replace EFC). *Average financial aid package:* $17,723 (excluding resources awarded to replace EFC). 13% of all full-time undergraduates had no need and received non-need-based gift aid.

GIFT AID (NEED-BASED) *Total amount:* $21,255,105 (24% federal, 9% state, 62% institutional, 5% external sources). *Receiving aid:* Freshmen: 62% (616); all full-time undergraduates: 57% (2,335). *Average award:* Freshmen: $8475; Undergraduates: $7147. *Scholarships, grants, and awards:* Federal Pell, FSEOG, state, private, college/university gift aid from institutional funds.

GIFT AID (NON-NEED-BASED) *Total amount:* $12,105,018 (1% federal, 6% state, 91% institutional, 2% external sources). *Receiving aid:* Freshmen: 14% (135). Undergraduates: 10% (419). *Average award:* Freshmen: $7309. Undergraduates: $6574. *Scholarships, grants, and awards by category:* Academic interests/achievement: 3,636 awards ($23,288,609 total): communication, computer science, engineering/technologies, English, general academic interests/achievements, health fields, religion/biblical studies. Creative arts/performance: art/fine arts, cinema/film/broadcasting, debating, general creative arts/performance, journalism/publications, music. Special achievements/activities: cheerleading/drum major, general special achievements/activities, leadership, religious involvement. Special characteristics: children of faculty/staff, children with a deceased or disabled parent, general special characteristics, international students, relatives of clergy, siblings of current students. *Tuition waivers:* Full or partial for employees or children of employees, senior citizens.

LOANS *Student loans:* $21,973,264 (81% need-based, 19% non-need-based). 66% of past graduating class borrowed through all loan programs. *Average indebtedness per student:* $30,570. *Average need-based loan:* Freshmen: $6682. Undergraduates: $8010. *Parent loans:* $7,373,098 (71% need-based, 29% non-need-based). *Programs:* Federal Direct (Subsidized and Unsubsidized Stafford, PLUS), Perkins, Federal Nursing, state, college/university.

WORK-STUDY *Federal work-study:* 544 jobs averaging $1069. *State or other work-study/employment:* Total amount: $1,797,355 (57% need-based, 43% non-need-based). 1,488 part-time jobs averaging $1201.

ATHLETIC AWARDS Total amount: $2,549,628 (50% need-based, 50% non-need-based).

APPLYING FOR FINANCIAL AID *Required financial aid form:* FAFSA. *Financial aid deadline (priority):* 4/15. *Notification date:* Continuous. Students must reply within 2 weeks of notification.

CONTACT Dr. Jonathan C. Roberts, Director of Student Financial Services, Harding University, PO Box 12282, Searcy, AR 72149-2282, 501-279-4257 or toll-free 800-477-4407. *Fax:* 501-279-4129. *E-mail:* jroberts@harding.edu.
Website: http://www.harding.edu/.

HARDIN-SIMMONS UNIVERSITY
Abilene, TX

Tuition & fees: $27,440	Average undergraduate aid package: $25,683

ABOUT THE INSTITUTION Independent Baptist, coed. *Awards:* certificates, bachelor's, master's, and doctoral degrees. 64 undergraduate majors. *Total enrollment:* 2,205. Undergraduates: 1,721. Freshmen: 393. Federal methodology is used as a basis for awarding need-based institutional aid.

UNDERGRADUATE EXPENSES for 2017–2018 *Comprehensive fee:* $35,860 includes full-time tuition ($26,240), mandatory fees ($1200), and room and board ($8420). *College room only:* $3900. Full-time tuition and fees vary according to program. Room and board charges vary according to board plan and housing facility. *Part-time tuition:* $800 per credit hour. *Part-time fees:* $545 per term. Part-time tuition and fees vary according to course load and program. *Payment plan:* Guaranteed tuition.

FRESHMAN FINANCIAL AID (Fall 2016, est.) 392 applied for aid; of those 77% were deemed to have need. 100% of freshmen with need received aid; of those 36% had need fully met. *Average percent of need met:* 92% (excluding resources awarded to replace EFC). *Average financial aid package:* $28,600 (excluding resources awarded to replace EFC). 23% of all full-time freshmen had no need and received non-need-based gift aid.

UNDERGRADUATE FINANCIAL AID (Fall 2016, est.) 1,490 applied for aid; of those 74% were deemed to have need. 100% of undergraduates with need received aid; of those 24% had need fully met. *Average percent of need met:* 80% (excluding resources awarded to replace EFC). *Average financial aid package:* $25,683 (excluding resources awarded to replace EFC). 26% of all full-time undergraduates had no need and received non-need-based gift aid.

GIFT AID (NEED-BASED) *Total amount:* $6,345,225 (45% federal, 43% state, 12% institutional). *Receiving aid:* Freshmen: 55% (217); all full-time undergraduates:

55% (837). *Average award:* Freshmen: $8882; Undergraduates: $7318. *Scholarships, grants, and awards:* Federal Pell, FSEOG, state, private, college/university gift aid from institutional funds.

GIFT AID (NON-NEED-BASED) *Total amount:* $20,710,030 (97% institutional, 3% external sources). *Receiving aid:* Freshmen: 77% (301). Undergraduates: 70% (1,058). *Average award:* Freshmen: $14,115. Undergraduates: $11,983. *Scholarships, grants, and awards by category:* Academic interests/achievement: biological sciences, business, communication, computer science, education, English, foreign languages, general academic interests/achievements, health fields, humanities, mathematics, physical sciences, premedicine, religion/biblical studies, social sciences. Creative arts/performance: applied art and design, art/fine arts, creative writing, journalism/publications, music, performing arts, theater/drama. Special achievements/activities: general special achievements/activities. Special characteristics: children and siblings of alumni, children of educators, children of faculty/staff, ethnic background, general special characteristics, handicapped students, out-of-state students, public servants, relatives of clergy, religious affiliation, siblings of current students, veterans, veterans' children. *Tuition waivers:* Full or partial for employees or children of employees.

LOANS *Student loans:* $18,610,543 (26% need-based, 74% non-need-based). 66% of past graduating class borrowed through all loan programs. *Average indebtedness per student:* $39,597. *Average need-based loan:* Freshmen: $2981. Undergraduates: $4170. *Parent loans:* $2,675,830 (100% non-need-based). *Programs:* Federal Direct (Subsidized and Unsubsidized Stafford, PLUS), Perkins, Federal Nursing, state, college/university.

WORK-STUDY *Federal work-study:* Total amount: $150,000; jobs available. *State or other work-study/employment:* Total amount: $17,000 (100% need-based). Part-time jobs available.

APPLYING FOR FINANCIAL AID *Required financial aid form:* FAFSA. *Financial aid deadline (priority):* 3/1. *Notification date:* Continuous beginning 2/1. Students must reply by 6/1 or within 2 weeks of notification.

CONTACT Mrs. Bridget Moore, Director of Financial Aid and Scholarships, Hardin-Simmons University, Box 16050, Abilene, TX 79698, 325-670-1482 or toll-free 877-464-7889. *Fax:* 325-670-5822. *E-mail:* bnmoore@hsutx.edu.
Website: http://www.hsutx.edu/.

HARRISBURG UNIVERSITY OF SCIENCE AND TECHNOLOGY
Harrisburg, PA

Tuition & fees: N/R	Average undergraduate aid package: $19,814

ABOUT THE INSTITUTION Independent, coed. *Awards:* bachelor's and master's degrees. 8 undergraduate majors. *Total enrollment:* 1,842. Undergraduates: 387. Freshmen: 153. Federal methodology is used as a basis for awarding need-based institutional aid.

UNDERGRADUATE EXPENSES for 2017–2018 *Tuition:* part-time $1000 per semester hour. Full-time tuition and fees vary according to class time, course level, course load, degree level, location, program, reciprocity agreements, and student level. Part-time tuition and fees vary according to class time, course level, course load, degree level, location, program, reciprocity agreements, and student level. Room and board charges vary according to housing facility.

FRESHMAN FINANCIAL AID (Fall 2016, est.) 150 applied for aid; of those 95% were deemed to have need. 100% of freshmen with need received aid; of those 18% had need fully met. *Average percent of need met:* 65% (excluding resources awarded to replace EFC). *Average financial aid package:* $20,188 (excluding resources awarded to replace EFC). 9% of all full-time freshmen had no need and received non-need-based gift aid.

UNDERGRADUATE FINANCIAL AID (Fall 2016, est.) 335 applied for aid; of those 96% were deemed to have need. 100% of undergraduates with need received aid; of those 18% had need fully met. *Average percent of need met:* 65% (excluding resources awarded to replace EFC). *Average financial aid package:* $19,814 (excluding resources awarded to replace EFC). 6% of all full-time undergraduates had no need and received non-need-based gift aid.

GIFT AID (NEED-BASED) *Total amount:* $7,551,650 (13% federal, 6% state, 50% institutional, 31% external sources). *Receiving aid:* Freshmen: 89% (140); all full-time undergraduates: 92% (317). *Average award:* Freshmen: $18,149; Undergraduates: $16,857. *Scholarships, grants, and awards:* Federal Pell, FSEOG, state, private, college/university gift aid from institutional funds.

GIFT AID (NON-NEED-BASED) *Total amount:* $727,359 (1% state, 94% institutional, 5% external sources). *Receiving aid:* Freshmen: 16% (25). Undergraduates: 14% (47). *Average award:* Freshmen: $19,442. Undergraduates: $15,789. *Scholarships, grants, and awards by category:* Academic interests/achievement: biological sciences, business, computer science, physical sciences.

LOANS *Student loans:* $2,122,385 (83% need-based, 17% non-need-based). 94% of past graduating class borrowed through all loan programs. *Average indebtedness per student:* $34,547. *Average need-based loan:* Freshmen: $3164. Undergraduates: $3923. *Parent loans:* $602,030 (70% need-based, 22% non-need based). *Programs:* Federal Direct (Subsidized and Unsubsidized Stafford, PLUS).

WORK-STUDY *Federal work-study:* Total amount: $15,800; 15 jobs averaging $2000.

APPLYING FOR FINANCIAL AID *Required financial aid form:* FAFSA. *Financial aid deadline:* Continuous. *Notification date:* Continuous. Students must reply within 2 weeks of notification.

CONTACT Mr. Vince P. Frank, Director of Financial Aid Services, Harrisburg University of Science and Technology, 326 Market Street, Harrisburg, PA 17101-2208, 717-901-5115 or toll-free 866-HBG-UNIV. *Fax:* 717-901-3115. *E-mail:* vfrank@harrisburgu.edu.
Website: http://www.HarrisburgU.edu/.

HARRISON COLLEGE
Indianapolis, IN

CONTACT Financial Aid Office, Harrison College, 550 East Washington Street, Indianapolis, IN 46204, 317-447-6200 or toll-free 888-544-4422.
Website: http://www.harrison.edu/.

HARRISON COLLEGE
Grove City, OH

CONTACT Financial Aid Office, Harrison College, 3880 Jackpot Road, Grove City, OH 43123, 614-539-8800 or toll-free 888-544-4422.
Website: http://www.harrison.edu/.

HARRIS-STOWE STATE UNIVERSITY
St. Louis, MO

Tuition & fees (MO res): $5220	Average undergraduate aid package: $10,140

ABOUT THE INSTITUTION State-supported, coed. *Awards:* certificates and bachelor's degrees. 22 undergraduate majors. *Total enrollment:* 1,464. Undergraduates: 1,464. Freshmen: 379. Federal methodology is used as a basis for awarding need-based institutional aid.

UNDERGRADUATE EXPENSES for 2017–2018 *Application fee:* $20. *Tuition, state resident:* full-time $4776; part-time $199 per credit hour. *Tuition, nonresident:* full-time $9409; part-time $392 per credit hour. *Required fees:* full-time $444. Full-time tuition and fees vary according to course load. *Room only:* $6500. Room and board charges vary according to housing facility.

FRESHMAN FINANCIAL AID (Fall 2015) 261 applied for aid; of those 93% were deemed to have need. 100% of freshmen with need received aid; of those 77% had need fully met. *Average percent of need met:* 83% (excluding resources awarded to replace EFC). *Average financial aid package:* $12,836 (excluding resources awarded to replace EFC). 9% of all full-time freshmen had no need and received non-need-based gift aid.

UNDERGRADUATE FINANCIAL AID (Fall 2015) 1,022 applied for aid; of those 99% were deemed to have need. 100% of undergraduates with need received aid; of those 56% had need fully met. *Average percent of need met:* 78% (excluding resources awarded to replace EFC). *Average financial aid package:* $10,140 (excluding resources awarded to replace EFC). 6% of all full-time undergraduates had no need and received non-need-based gift aid.

GIFT AID (NEED-BASED) *Total amount:* $5,306,039 (89% federal, 10% state, 1% external sources). *Receiving aid:* Freshmen: 75% (199); all full-time undergrad-

uates: 82% (846). *Average award:* Freshmen: $6956; Undergraduates: $5210. *Scholarships, grants, and awards:* Federal Pell, FSEOG, state, private, college/university gift aid from institutional funds.

GIFT AID (NON-NEED-BASED) *Total amount:* $871,001 (9% federal, 91% institutional). *Receiving aid:* Freshmen: 21% (56). Undergraduates: 33% (346). *Average award:* Freshmen: $2532. Undergraduates: $2267. *Scholarships, grants, and awards by category:* Academic interests/achievement: general academic interests/achievements. Creative arts/performance: music, theater/drama. *Tuition waivers:* Full or partial for employees or children of employees. *ROTC:* Army cooperative.

LOANS *Student loans:* $8,509,891 (40% need-based, 60% non-need-based). *Average need-based loan:* Freshmen: $2701. Undergraduates: $2859. *Parent loans:* $605,346 (100% need-based). *Programs:* Federal Direct (Subsidized and Unsubsidized Stafford, PLUS), college/university.

WORK-STUDY *Federal work-study:* jobs available. *State or other work-study/employment:* Total amount: $52,571 (100% need-based). Part-time jobs available.

APPLYING FOR FINANCIAL AID *Required financial aid forms:* FAFSA, institution's own form. *Financial aid deadline:* Continuous. *Notification date:* Continuous beginning 4/1.

CONTACT Regina Blackshear, Director of Financial Aid, Harris-Stowe State University, 3026 Laclede Avenue, St. Louis, MO 63103-2136, 314-340-3502. *Fax:* 314-340-3503.
Website: http://www.hssu.edu/.

HARTWICK COLLEGE
Oneonta, NY

Tuition & fees: $44,134	Average undergraduate aid package: $33,725

ABOUT THE INSTITUTION Independent, coed. *Awards:* bachelor's degrees. 37 undergraduate majors. *Total enrollment:* 1,396. Undergraduates: 1,396. Freshmen: 402. Federal methodology is used as a basis for awarding need-based institutional aid.

UNDERGRADUATE EXPENSES for 2017–2018 *One-time required fee:* $400. *Comprehensive fee:* $56,227 includes full-time tuition ($43,312), mandatory fees ($822), and room and board ($12,093). *College room only:* $6268. Full-time tuition and fees vary according to course load. Room and board charges vary according to board plan and housing facility. *Part-time tuition:* $1390 per credit hour. Part-time tuition and fees vary according to course load.

FRESHMAN FINANCIAL AID (Fall 2016, est.) 370 applied for aid; of those 95% were deemed to have need. 100% of freshmen with need received aid; of those 19% had need fully met. *Average percent of need met:* 81% (excluding resources awarded to replace EFC). *Average financial aid package:* $35,640 (excluding resources awarded to replace EFC). 12% of all full-time freshmen had no need and received non-need-based gift aid.

UNDERGRADUATE FINANCIAL AID (Fall 2016, est.) 1,198 applied for aid; of those 95% were deemed to have need. 100% of undergraduates with need received aid; of those 14% had need fully met. *Average percent of need met:* 79% (excluding resources awarded to replace EFC). *Average financial aid package:* $33,725 (excluding resources awarded to replace EFC). 15% of all full-time undergraduates had no need and received non-need-based gift aid.

GIFT AID (NEED-BASED) *Total amount:* $30,431,649 (8% federal, 5% state, 85% institutional, 2% external sources). *Receiving aid:* Freshmen: 86% (352); all full-time undergraduates: 83% (1,132). *Average award:* Freshmen: $28,810; Undergraduates: $27,125. *Scholarships, grants, and awards:* Federal Pell, FSEOG, state, private, college/university gift aid from institutional funds.

GIFT AID (NON-NEED-BASED) *Total amount:* $5,758,437 (98% institutional, 2% external sources). *Receiving aid:* Freshmen: 13% (51). Undergraduates: 10% (138). *Average award:* Freshmen: $25,005. Undergraduates: $22,312. *Scholarships, grants, and awards by category:* Academic interests/achievement: 138 awards ($5,758,437 total): general academic interests/achievements. Creative arts/performance: art/fine arts, music. *Special characteristics:* children and siblings of alumni, children of faculty/staff, international students, siblings of current students, veterans. *Tuition waivers:* Full or partial for employees or children of employees.

LOANS *Student loans:* $13,581,442 (70% need-based, 30% non-need-based). 71% of past graduating class borrowed through all loan programs. *Average indebtedness per student:* $27,653. *Average need-based loan:* Freshmen: $4716. Undergrad-

uates: $4965. **Parent loans:** $16,169,348 (42% need-based, 58% non-need-based). **Programs:** Federal Direct (Subsidized and Unsubsidized Stafford, PLUS), Perkins, Federal Nursing, college/university, alternative loans.

WORK-STUDY **Federal work-study:** Total amount: $1,768,016; 890 jobs averaging $2000.

ATHLETIC AWARDS Total amount: $874,223 (6% need-based, 94% non-need-based).

APPLYING FOR FINANCIAL AID **Required financial aid form:** FAFSA. **Financial aid deadline:** Continuous. **Notification date:** Continuous beginning 12/22. Students must reply by 5/1 or within 2 weeks of notification.

CONTACT Mrs. Melissa Allen, Director of Financial Aid, Hartwick College, One Hartwick Drive, Oneonta, NY 13820, 607-431-4130 or toll-free 888-HARTWICK. Fax: 607-431-4006. E-mail: finaid@hartwick.edu. Website: http://www.hartwick.edu/.

HARVARD UNIVERSITY
Cambridge, MA

Tuition & fees: $47,074	Average undergraduate aid package: $51,308

ABOUT THE INSTITUTION Independent, coed. **Awards:** bachelor's, master's, and doctoral degrees. 47 undergraduate majors. **Total enrollment:** 11,038. Undergraduates: 6,712. Freshmen: 1,661. Institutional methodology is used as a basis for awarding need-based institutional aid.

UNDERGRADUATE EXPENSES for 2016–2017 Application fee: $75. **Comprehensive fee:** $63,025 includes full-time tuition ($43,280), mandatory fees ($3794), and room and board ($15,951). **College room only:** $9894. **Payment plan:** Tuition prepayment.

FRESHMAN FINANCIAL AID (Fall 2015) 1,058 applied for aid; of those 86% were deemed to have need. 100% of freshmen with need received aid; of those 100% had need fully met. **Average percent of need met:** 100% (excluding resources awarded to replace EFC). **Average financial aid package:** $53,071 (excluding resources awarded to replace EFC). 1% of all full-time freshmen had no need and received non-need-based gift aid.

UNDERGRADUATE FINANCIAL AID (Fall 2015) 3,985 applied for aid; of those 93% were deemed to have need. 100% of undergraduates with need received aid; of those 100% had need fully met. **Average percent of need met:** 100% (excluding resources awarded to replace EFC). **Average financial aid package:** $51,308 (excluding resources awarded to replace EFC). 1% of all full-time undergraduates had no need and received non-need-based gift aid.

GIFT AID (NEED-BASED) Total amount: $179,179,012 (5% federal, 92% institutional, 3% external sources). **Receiving aid:** Freshmen: 55% (907); all full-time undergraduates: 55% (3,687). **Average award:** Freshmen: $51,314; Undergraduates: $48,598. **Scholarships, grants, and awards:** Federal Pell, FSEOG, state, private, college/university gift aid from institutional funds.

GIFT AID (NON-NEED-BASED) Total amount: $6,503,393 (12% federal, 1% state, 7% institutional, 80% external sources). **Average award:** Freshmen: $33,400. Undergraduates: $23,954. **ROTC:** Army, Naval, Air Force.

LOANS Student loans: $4,973,621 (68% need-based, 32% non-need-based). 23% of past graduating class borrowed through all loan programs. **Average indebtedness per student:** $16,702. **Average need-based loan:** Freshmen: $2617. Undergraduates: $2901. **Parent loans:** $6,338,566 (100% non-need-based). **Programs:** Federal Direct (Subsidized and Unsubsidized Stafford, PLUS), state, college/university.

WORK-STUDY **Federal work-study:** jobs available. **State or other work-study/employment:** Total amount: $6,044,922 (89% need-based, 11% non-need-based). Part-time jobs available.

APPLYING FOR FINANCIAL AID **Required financial aid forms:** FAFSA, CSS Financial Aid PROFILE, noncustodial (divorced/separated) parent's statement, business/farm supplement, federal income tax form(s). **Financial aid deadline (priority):** 3/1. **Notification date:** 4/1. Students must reply by 5/1 or within 2 weeks of notification.

CONTACT Financial Aid Office, Harvard University, 86 Brattle Street, Cambridge, MA 02138, 617-495-1581. Website: http://www.harvard.edu/.

HARVEY MUDD COLLEGE
Claremont, CA

Tuition & fees: $52,666	Average undergraduate aid package: $42,799

ABOUT THE INSTITUTION Independent, coed. **Awards:** bachelor's degrees. 7 undergraduate majors. **Total enrollment:** 829. Undergraduates: 829. Freshmen: 214. Both federal and institutional methodology are used as a basis for awarding need-based institutional aid.

UNDERGRADUATE EXPENSES for 2016–2017 Application fee: $70. **One-time required fee:** $250. **Comprehensive fee:** $69,717 includes full-time tuition ($52,383), mandatory fees ($283), and room and board ($17,051). **College room only:** $9209. Room and board charges vary according to board plan. **Part-time tuition:** $1637 per unit. Part-time tuition and fees vary according to course load.

FRESHMAN FINANCIAL AID (Fall 2015) 152 applied for aid; of those 76% were deemed to have need. 100% of freshmen with need received aid; of those 100% had need fully met. **Average percent of need met:** 100% (excluding resources awarded to replace EFC). **Average financial aid package:** $46,466 (excluding resources awarded to replace EFC). 20% of all full-time freshmen had no need and received non-need-based gift aid.

UNDERGRADUATE FINANCIAL AID (Fall 2015) 478 applied for aid; of those 87% were deemed to have need. 100% of undergraduates with need received aid; of those 100% had need fully met. **Average percent of need met:** 100% (excluding resources awarded to replace EFC). **Average financial aid package:** $42,799 (excluding resources awarded to replace EFC). 21% of all full-time undergraduates had no need and received non-need-based gift aid.

GIFT AID (NEED-BASED) Total amount: $15,785,819 (4% federal, 4% state, 89% institutional, 3% external sources). **Receiving aid:** Freshmen: 52% (112); all full-time undergraduates: 49% (395). **Average award:** Freshmen: $44,042; Undergraduates: $39,799. **Scholarships, grants, and awards:** Federal Pell, FSEOG, state, private, college/university gift aid from institutional funds.

GIFT AID (NON-NEED-BASED) Total amount: $2,212,331 (90% institutional, 10% external sources). **Receiving aid:** Freshmen: 14% (30). Undergraduates: 8% (68). **Average award:** Freshmen: $10,533. Undergraduates: $11,822. **Scholarships, grants, and awards by category:** Academic interests/achievement: 290 awards ($3,783,854 total): general academic interests/achievements. **Special characteristics:** 2 awards ($75,000 total): international students. **Tuition waivers:** Full or partial for employees or children of employees. **ROTC:** Army cooperative, Air Force.

LOANS Student loans: $2,639,163 (93% need-based, 7% non-need-based). 42% of past graduating class borrowed through all loan programs. **Average indebtedness per student:** $25,412. **Average need-based loan:** Freshmen: $3673. Undergraduates: $5259. **Parent loans:** $1,636,278 (75% need-based, 25% non-need-based). **Programs:** Federal Direct (Subsidized and Unsubsidized Stafford, PLUS), Perkins, college/university, private loans.

WORK-STUDY **Federal work-study:** 133 jobs averaging $652. **State or other work-study/employment:** Total amount: $191,950 (39% need-based, 61% non-need-based). 25 part-time jobs averaging $7678.

APPLYING FOR FINANCIAL AID **Required financial aid forms:** FAFSA, CSS Financial Aid PROFILE, state aid form, noncustodial (divorced/separated) parent's statement, business/farm supplement. **Financial aid deadline:** 2/1. **Notification date:** 4/1. Students must reply by 5/1.

CONTACT Mrs. Gilma Lopez, Director of Financial Aid, Harvey Mudd College, 301 Platt Boulevard, Claremont, CA 91711-5994, 909-621-8055. Fax: 909-607-4494. E-mail: financial_aid@hmc.edu. Website: http://www.hmc.edu/.

HASKELL INDIAN NATIONS UNIVERSITY
Lawrence, KS

CONTACT Reta Brewer, Director of Financial Aid, Haskell Indian Nations University, 155 Indian Avenue, Box 5027, Lawrence, KS 66046-4800, 785-749-8468. Fax: 785-832-6617. Website: http://www.haskell.edu/.

HASTINGS COLLEGE
Hastings, NE

ABOUT THE INSTITUTION Independent Presbyterian, coed. *Awards:* bachelor's and master's degrees. 83 undergraduate majors. *Total enrollment:* 1,212. Undergraduates: 1,183. Freshmen: 345.

GIFT AID (NEED-BASED) *Scholarships, grants, and awards:* Federal Pell, FSEOG, state, private, college/university gift aid from institutional funds.

GIFT AID (NON-NEED-BASED) *Scholarships, grants, and awards by category:* *Academic interests/achievement:* business, communication, general academic interests/achievements, religion/biblical studies. *Creative arts/performance:* art/fine arts, cinema/film/broadcasting, dance, debating, journalism/publications, music, performing arts, theater/drama. *Special achievements/activities:* cheerleading/drum major, memberships, rodeo. *Special characteristics:* adult students, children and siblings of alumni, children of educators, children of faculty/staff, international students, previous college experience, religious affiliation, siblings of current students, spouses of current students.

LOANS *Programs:* Federal Direct (Subsidized and Unsubsidized Stafford, PLUS), Perkins, college/university.

WORK-STUDY *Federal work-study:* 62 jobs averaging $1736. *State or other work-study/employment:* Total amount: $37,769 (42% need-based, 58% non-need-based). Part-time jobs available.

APPLYING FOR FINANCIAL AID *Required financial aid forms:* FAFSA, institution's own form.

CONTACT Mrs. Traci Noelle Boeve, Director of Student Financial Aid, Hastings College, 710 North Turner Avenue, Hastings, NE 68901, 402-461-7431 or toll-free 800-532-7642. *Fax:* 402-461-7714. *E-mail:* tboeve@hastings.edu.
Website: http://www.hastings.edu/.

HAVERFORD COLLEGE
Haverford, PA

Tuition & fees: $51,024	Average undergraduate aid package: $49,186

ABOUT THE INSTITUTION Independent, coed. *Awards:* bachelor's degrees. 38 undergraduate majors. *Total enrollment:* 1,268. Undergraduates: 1,268. Freshmen: 349. Institutional methodology is used as a basis for awarding need-based institutional aid.

UNDERGRADUATE EXPENSES for 2016-2017 *Application fee:* $65. *One-time required fee:* $235. *Comprehensive fee:* $66,490 includes full-time tuition ($50,564), mandatory fees ($460), and room and board ($15,466). *College room only:* $8826. *Payment plan:* Tuition prepayment.

FRESHMAN FINANCIAL AID (Fall 2016, est.) 197 applied for aid; of those 81% were deemed to have need. 100% of freshmen with need received aid; of those 100% had need fully met. *Average percent of need met:* 100% (excluding resources awarded to replace EFC). *Average financial aid package:* $49,928 (excluding resources awarded to replace EFC).

UNDERGRADUATE FINANCIAL AID (Fall 2016, est.) 694 applied for aid; of those 91% were deemed to have need. 100% of undergraduates with need received aid; of those 100% had need fully met. *Average percent of need met:* 100% (excluding resources awarded to replace EFC). *Average financial aid package:* $49,186 (excluding resources awarded to replace EFC).

GIFT AID (NEED-BASED) *Total amount:* $29,590,922 (3% federal, 1% state, 94% institutional, 2% external sources). *Receiving aid:* Freshmen: 45% (158); all full-time undergraduates: 50% (629). *Average award:* Freshmen: $46,398; Undergraduates: $46,009. *Scholarships, grants, and awards:* Federal Pell, FSEOG, state, college/university gift aid from institutional funds.

GIFT AID (NON-NEED-BASED) *Receiving aid:* Undergraduates: 1% (8). *Tuition waivers:* Full or partial for employees or children of employees.

LOANS *Student loans:* $1,681,841 (30% need-based, 70% non-need-based). 29% of past graduating class borrowed through all loan programs. *Average indebtedness per student:* $13,000. *Average need-based loan:* Freshmen: $2764. Undergraduates: $3433. *Parent loans:* $1,490,243 (100% non-need-based). *Programs:* Federal Direct (Subsidized and Unsubsidized Stafford, PLUS).

WORK-STUDY *Federal work-study:* Total amount: $308,831; jobs available. *State or other work-study/employment:* Total amount: $699,387 (28% need-based, 72% non-need-based). Part-time jobs available.

APPLYING FOR FINANCIAL AID *Required financial aid forms:* FAFSA, CSS Financial Aid PROFILE, noncustodial (divorced/separated) parent's statement, business/farm supplement. *Financial aid deadline (priority):* 2/1. *Notification date:* 4/1. Students must reply by 5/1.

CONTACT Mr. Michael Colahan, Director of Financial Aid, Haverford College, 370 Lancaster Avenue, Haverford, PA 19041-1392, 610-896-1350. *Fax:* 610-896-1338. *E-mail:* finaid@haverford.edu.
Website: http://www.haverford.edu/.

HAWAII PACIFIC UNIVERSITY
Honolulu, HI

Tuition & fees: $24,500	Average undergraduate aid package: $15,142

ABOUT THE INSTITUTION Independent, coed. *Awards:* certificates, associate, bachelor's, and master's degrees. 36 undergraduate majors. *Total enrollment:* 4,081. Undergraduates: 3,436. Freshmen: 478. Federal methodology is used as a basis for awarding need-based institutional aid.

UNDERGRADUATE EXPENSES for 2017-2018 *Application fee:* $50. *Comprehensive fee:* $38,704 includes full-time tuition ($24,200), mandatory fees ($300), and room and board ($14,204). *College room only:* $7830. Full-time tuition and fees vary according to course level, course load, degree level, location, program, and student level. Room and board charges vary according to board plan, housing facility, and location. *Part-time tuition:* $810 per credit. *Part-time fees:* $25 per term. Part-time tuition and fees vary according to course level, course load, degree level, location, program, and student level.

FRESHMAN FINANCIAL AID (Fall 2016, est.) 391 applied for aid; of those 86% were deemed to have need. 99% of freshmen with need received aid; of those 23% had need fully met. *Average percent of need met:* 63% (excluding resources awarded to replace EFC). *Average financial aid package:* $16,446 (excluding resources awarded to replace EFC). 23% of all full-time freshmen had no need and received non-need-based gift aid.

UNDERGRADUATE FINANCIAL AID (Fall 2016, est.) 1,602 applied for aid; of those 88% were deemed to have need. 98% of undergraduates with need received aid; of those 17% had need fully met. *Average percent of need met:* 48% (excluding resources awarded to replace EFC). *Average financial aid package:* $15,142 (excluding resources awarded to replace EFC). 24% of all full-time undergraduates had no need and received non-need-based gift aid.

GIFT AID (NEED-BASED) *Total amount:* $5,683,562 (81% federal, 19% institutional). *Receiving aid:* Freshmen: 68% (317); all full-time undergraduates: 43% (1,093). *Average award:* Freshmen: $3949; Undergraduates: $4549. *Scholarships, grants, and awards:* Federal Pell, FSEOG, private, college/university gift aid from institutional funds, Federal Nursing.

GIFT AID (NON-NEED-BASED) *Total amount:* $13,909,701 (92% institutional, 8% external sources). *Receiving aid:* Freshmen: 59% (273). Undergraduates: 40% (1,016). *Average award:* Freshmen: $10,268. Undergraduates: $9260. *Scholarships, grants, and awards by category:* *Academic interests/achievement:* 15 awards ($318,464 total): business, education, general academic interests/achievements. *Creative arts/performance:* 41 awards ($154,250 total): dance, debating, journalism/publications, music, performing arts. *Special achievements/activities:* 14 awards ($98,820 total): cheerleading/drum major, community service, hobbies/interests, leadership, memberships, religious involvement. *Special characteristics:* 325 awards ($1,525,003 total): ethnic background, international students, local/state students, out-of-state students, previous college experience, relatives of clergy, religious affiliation. *Tuition waivers:* Full or partial for employees or children of employees. *ROTC:* Army cooperative, Air Force cooperative.

LOANS *Student loans:* $16,914,728 (40% need-based, 60% non-need-based). 57% of past graduating class borrowed through all loan programs. *Average indebtedness per student:* $28,893. *Average need-based loan:* Freshmen: $2978. Undergraduates: $4345. *Parent loans:* $9,395,078 (100% non-need-based). *Programs:* Federal Direct (Subsidized and Unsubsidized Stafford, PLUS), Perkins, Federal Nursing.

WORK-STUDY *Federal work-study:* Total amount: $1,358,386; 455 jobs averaging $2834.

ATHLETIC AWARDS Total amount: $2,987,372 (100% non-need-based).

APPLYING FOR FINANCIAL AID *Required financial aid form:* FAFSA. *Financial aid deadline (priority):* 3/1. *Notification date:* Continuous beginning 3/15. Students must reply within 3 weeks of notification.

CONTACT James M. Oshiro, Executive Director of Financial Aid, Hawaii Pacific University, 1164 Bishop Street, Suite 201, Honolulu, HI 96813-2785, 808-544-0253 or toll-free 866-225-5478. *Fax:* 808-544-0884. *E-mail:* financialaid@hpu.edu. *Website:* http://www.hpu.edu/.

HEBREW THEOLOGICAL COLLEGE
Skokie, IL

CONTACT Ms. Rhoda Morris, Financial Aid Administrator , Hebrew Theological College, 7135 Carpenter Road, Skokie, IL 60077-3263, 847-982-2500. *Fax:* 847-674-6381. *Website:* http://www.htc.edu/.

HEIDELBERG UNIVERSITY
Tiffin, OH

Tuition & fees: $30,200	Average undergraduate aid package: $22,421

ABOUT THE INSTITUTION Independent United Church of Christ, coed. *Awards:* bachelor's and master's degrees. 44 undergraduate majors. *Total enrollment:* 1,314. Undergraduates: 1,123. Freshmen: 371. Federal methodology is used as a basis for awarding need-based institutional aid.

UNDERGRADUATE EXPENSES for 2017–2018 *Comprehensive fee:* $40,400 includes full-time tuition ($29,600), mandatory fees ($600), and room and board ($10,200). *College room only:* $5300. Full-time tuition and fees vary according to course load and degree level. Room and board charges vary according to housing facility. *Part-time tuition:* $822 per contact hour. Part-time tuition and fees vary according to course load and degree level.

FRESHMAN FINANCIAL AID (Fall 2016, est.) 364 applied for aid; of those 91% were deemed to have need. 100% of freshmen with need received aid; of those 22% had need fully met. *Average percent of need met:* 81% (excluding resources awarded to replace EFC). *Average financial aid package:* $24,888 (excluding resources awarded to replace EFC). 8% of all full-time freshmen had no need and received non-need-based gift aid.

UNDERGRADUATE FINANCIAL AID (Fall 2016, est.) 1,035 applied for aid; of those 92% were deemed to have need. 100% of undergraduates with need received aid; of those 30% had need fully met. *Average percent of need met:* 79% (excluding resources awarded to replace EFC). *Average financial aid package:* $22,421 (excluding resources awarded to replace EFC). 14% of all full-time undergraduates had no need and received non-need-based gift aid.

GIFT AID (NEED-BASED) *Total amount:* $24,830,752 (8% federal, 3% state, 87% institutional, 2% external sources). *Receiving aid:* Freshmen: 90% (333); all full-time undergraduates: 89% (948). *Average award:* Freshmen: $19,650; Undergraduates: $19,536. *Scholarships, grants, and awards:* Federal Pell, FSEOG, state, private, college/university gift aid from institutional funds.

GIFT AID (NON-NEED-BASED) *Total amount:* $2,778,131 (98% institutional, 2% external sources). *Receiving aid:* Freshmen: 9% (32). Undergraduates: 14% (147). *Average award:* Freshmen: $14,166. Undergraduates: $13,998. *Scholarships, grants, and awards by category: Academic interests/achievement:* 799 awards ($9,856,692 total): general academic interests/achievements. *Creative arts/performance:* 29 awards ($59,100 total): music, performing arts. *Special characteristics:* 234 awards ($1,488,588 total): children and siblings of alumni, children of faculty/staff, out-of-state students, relatives of clergy, religious affiliation. *Tuition waivers:* Full or partial for employees or children of employees. *ROTC:* Army cooperative, Air Force cooperative.

LOANS *Student loans:* $9,010,985 (95% need-based, 5% non-need-based). 86% of past graduating class borrowed through all loan programs. *Average indebtedness per student:* $35,872. *Average need-based loan:* Freshmen: $3950. Undergraduates: $4854. *Parent loans:* $4,513,137 (97% need-based, 3% non-need-based). *Programs:* Federal Direct (Subsidized and Unsubsidized Stafford, PLUS), Perkins.

WORK-STUDY *Federal work-study:* Total amount: $1,348,065; 703 jobs averaging $2000. *State or other work-study/employment:* Total amount: $82,045 (100% non-need-based). 61 part-time jobs averaging $1000.

APPLYING FOR FINANCIAL AID *Required financial aid form:* FAFSA. *Financial aid deadline:* Continuous. *Notification date:* Continuous beginning 12/15. Students must reply by 5/1.

CONTACT Ms. Juli L. Weininger, Director of Financial Aid, Heidelberg University, 310 East Market Street, Tiffin, OH 44883-2462, 419-448-2293 or toll-free 800-434-3352. *Fax:* 419-448-2296. *Website:* http://www.heidelberg.edu/.

HELLENIC COLLEGE
Brookline, MA

Tuition & fees: $22,490	Average undergraduate aid package: N/A

ABOUT THE INSTITUTION Independent Greek Orthodox, coed. *Awards:* bachelor's and master's degrees (also offers graduate degree programs through Holy Cross Greek Orthodox School of Theology). 6 undergraduate majors. *Total enrollment:* 193. Undergraduates: 92. Freshmen: 31. Both federal and institutional methodology are used as a basis for awarding need-based institutional aid.

UNDERGRADUATE EXPENSES for 2016–2017 *Application fee:* $50. *Tuition:* full-time $21,940; part-time $950 per credit hour. *Required fees:* full-time $550; $450 per year. Room and board charges vary according to board plan and housing facility.

GIFT AID (NEED-BASED) *Total amount:* $2,018,141 (8% federal, 73% institutional, 19% external sources). *Scholarships, grants, and awards:* Federal Pell, FSEOG, state, private, college/university gift aid from institutional funds.

GIFT AID (NON-NEED-BASED) *Scholarships, grants, and awards by category: Academic interests/achievement:* religion/biblical studies. *Special achievements/activities:* religious involvement.

LOANS *Student loans:* $771,553 (100% need-based). *Parent loans:* $143,976 (100% need-based). *Programs:* Federal Direct (Subsidized and Unsubsidized Stafford, PLUS), state.

WORK-STUDY *Federal work-study:* 12 jobs averaging $2500. *State or other work-study/employment:* Total amount: $50,600 (69% need-based, 31% non-need-based). Part-time jobs available.

APPLYING FOR FINANCIAL AID *Required financial aid forms:* FAFSA, institution's own form. *Notification date:* Continuous.

CONTACT Michael Kirchmaier, Director of Financial Aid, Hellenic College, 50 Goddard Avenue, Brookline, MA 02146-7496, 617-850-1239 or toll-free 866-424-2338. *Fax:* 617-850-1240. *E-mail:* mkirchmaier@hchc.edu. *Website:* http://www.hchc.edu/.

HENDERSON STATE UNIVERSITY
Arkadelphia, AR

CONTACT Ms. Vicki Taylor, Director of Financial Aid, Henderson State University, 1100 Henderson Street, HSU Box 7812, Arkadelphia, AR 71999-0001, 870-230-5138 or toll-free 800-228-7333. *Fax:* 870-230-5481. *E-mail:* taylorv@hsu.edu. *Website:* http://www.hsu.edu/.

HENDRIX COLLEGE
Conway, AR

Tuition & fees: $44,070	Average undergraduate aid package: $35,223

ABOUT THE INSTITUTION Independent United Methodist, coed. *Awards:* bachelor's and master's degrees. 30 undergraduate majors. *Total enrollment:* 1,328. Undergraduates: 1,321. Freshmen: 351. Federal methodology is used as a basis for awarding need-based institutional aid.

UNDERGRADUATE EXPENSES for 2017–2018 *Application fee:* $40. *Comprehensive fee:* $55,996 includes full-time tuition ($43,720), mandatory fees ($350), and room and board ($11,926). **College room only:** $6140. Full-time tuition and fees vary according to course load. Room and board charges vary according to board plan and housing facility. **Part-time tuition:** $5261 per course. Part-time tuition and fees vary according to course load.

FRESHMAN FINANCIAL AID (Fall 2016, est.) 339 applied for aid; of those 85% were deemed to have need. 100% of freshmen with need received aid; of those 42% had need fully met. **Average percent of need met:** 89% (excluding resources awarded to replace EFC). **Average financial aid package:** $38,093 (excluding resources awarded to replace EFC). 17% of all full-time freshmen had no need and received non-need-based gift aid.

UNDERGRADUATE FINANCIAL AID (Fall 2016, est.) 1,099 applied for aid; of those 82% were deemed to have need. 100% of undergraduates with need received aid; of those 39% had need fully met. **Average percent of need met:** 85% (excluding resources awarded to replace EFC). **Average financial aid package:** $35,223 (excluding resources awarded to replace EFC). 29% of all full-time undergraduates had no need and received non-need-based gift aid.

GIFT AID (NEED-BASED) Total amount: $27,242,584 (6% federal, 5% state, 88% institutional, 1% external sources). **Receiving aid:** Freshmen: 82% (288); all full-time undergraduates: 69% (902). **Average award:** Freshmen: $24,350; Undergraduates: $31,309. **Scholarships, grants, and awards:** Federal Pell, FSEOG, state, private, college/university gift aid from institutional funds.

GIFT AID (NON-NEED-BASED) Total amount: $13,965,356 (12% state, 86% institutional, 2% external sources). **Receiving aid:** Freshmen: 26% (90). Undergraduates: 20% (267). **Average award:** Freshmen: $27,435. Undergraduates: $25,907. **Scholarships, grants, and awards by category:** Academic interests/achievement: 1,254 awards ($21,402,074 total): general academic interests/achievements. Creative arts/performance: 92 awards ($206,423 total): art/fine arts, dance, music, theater/drama. Special achievements/activities: 1,234 awards ($4,671,000 total): community service, general special achievements/activities, leadership, religious involvement. Special characteristics: 46 awards ($1,724,645 total): children of faculty/staff, international students, previous college experience, relatives of clergy. **Tuition waivers:** Full or partial for employees or children of employees. **ROTC:** Army cooperative.

LOANS Student loans: $5,207,386 (60% need-based, 40% non-need-based). 47% of past graduating class borrowed through all loan programs. **Average indebtedness per student:** $30,213. **Average need-based loan:** Freshmen: $3331. Undergraduates: $3675. **Parent loans:** $2,255,740 (33% need-based, 67% non-need-based). **Programs:** Federal Direct (Subsidized and Unsubsidized Stafford, PLUS), Perkins, United Methodist Student Loans.

WORK-STUDY Federal work-study: Total amount: $1,131,750; 579 jobs averaging $1911. **State or other work-study/employment:** Total amount: $458,658 (19% need-based, 81% non-need-based). 328 part-time jobs averaging $1684.

APPLYING FOR FINANCIAL AID Required financial aid forms: FAFSA, state aid form. **Financial aid deadline (priority):** 3/1. **Notification date:** Continuous beginning 12/1. Students must reply by 5/1 or within 4 weeks of notification.

CONTACT Ms. Kristina Burford, Associate Vice President for Enrollment/Director of Financial Aid, Hendrix College, 1600 Washington Avenue, Conway, AR 72032, 501-450-1368 or toll-free 800-277-9017. Fax: 501-450-3871. E-mail: burford@hendrix.edu.
Website: http://www.hendrix.edu/.

HENLEY-PUTNAM UNIVERSITY
San Jose, CA

CONTACT Financial Aid Office, Henley-Putnam University, 2107 N. First Street, Suite 210, San Jose, CA 95131, 408-453-9900 or toll-free 888-852-8746.
Website: http://www.henley-putnam.edu/.

HERITAGE BIBLE COLLEGE
Dunn, NC

Tuition & fees: N/R	Average undergraduate aid package: $2739

ABOUT THE INSTITUTION Independent Pentecostal Free Will Baptist, coed. **Awards:** associate and bachelor's degrees. 2 undergraduate majors. **Total**

enrollment: 69. Undergraduates: 69. Freshmen: 10. Federal methodology is used as a basis for awarding need-based institutional aid.

FRESHMAN FINANCIAL AID (Fall 2015) 1 applied for aid; of those 100% were deemed to have need. % of freshmen with need received aid.

UNDERGRADUATE FINANCIAL AID (Fall 2015) 36 applied for aid; of those 100% were deemed to have need. 100% of undergraduates with need received aid; of those 8% had need fully met. **Average percent of need met:** 54% (excluding resources awarded to replace EFC). **Average financial aid package:** $2739 (excluding resources awarded to replace EFC).

GIFT AID (NEED-BASED) Total amount: $412,098 (94% federal, 2% state, 4% institutional). **Receiving aid:** All full-time undergraduates: 100% (36). **Average award:** Undergraduates: $200. **Scholarships, grants, and awards:** Federal Pell, FSEOG, private, college/university gift aid from institutional funds.

GIFT AID (NON-NEED-BASED) Total amount: $2000 (100% institutional). **Scholarships, grants, and awards by category:** Academic interests/achievement: religion/biblical studies. Special achievements/activities: leadership, religious involvement.

LOANS Student loans: $309,493 (100% need-based). 100% of past graduating class borrowed through all loan programs. **Average indebtedness per student:** $15,000. **Average need-based loan:** Undergraduates: $1712. **Programs:** Federal Direct (Subsidized and Unsubsidized Stafford, PLUS).

WORK-STUDY Federal work-study: 3 jobs averaging $1872.

APPLYING FOR FINANCIAL AID Required financial aid forms: FAFSA, institution's own form, verification worksheet. **Financial aid deadline:** 7/1 (priority: 4/30). **Notification date:** Continuous. Students must reply within 8 weeks of notification.

CONTACT Ms. Kayla Bullard, Director of Financial Aid, Heritage Bible College, PO Box 1628, Dunn, NC 28335, 910-892-3178 Ext. 232 or toll-free 800-297-6351. Fax: 910-891-1660. E-mail: ksutton@heritagebiblecollege.edu.
Website: http://www.heritagebiblecollege.edu/.

HERITAGE CHRISTIAN UNIVERSITY
Florence, AL

CONTACT Mechelle R. Thompson, Associate Director of Financial Aid, Heritage Christian University, PO Box HCU, Florence, AL 35630, 800-367-3565 Ext. 303 or toll-free 800-367-3565. Fax: 256-716-8021. E-mail: mthompson@hcu.edu.
Website: http://www.hcu.edu/.

HERITAGE UNIVERSITY
Toppenish, WA

CONTACT Mr. Norberto Espindola, Director of Enrollment Management Services, Heritage University, 3240 Fort Road, Toppenish, WA 98948-9599, 509-865-8500 or toll-free 888-272-6190. Fax: 509-865-8659. E-mail: financial_aid@heritage.edu.
Website: http://www.heritage.edu/.

HERZING UNIVERSITY
Birmingham, AL

CONTACT Financial Aid Office, Herzing University, 280 West Valley Avenue, Birmingham, AL 35209, 205-916-2800 or toll-free 800-596-0724.
Website: http://www.herzing.edu/birmingham/.

HERZING UNIVERSITY
Winter Park, FL

CONTACT Financial Aid Office, Herzing University, 1865 SR 436, Winter Park, FL 32792, 407-641-5227 or toll-free 800-596-0724.
Website: http://www.herzing.edu/orlando.

HERZING UNIVERSITY
Atlanta, GA

CONTACT Financial Aid Office, Herzing University, 3393 Peachtree Road, Suite 1003, Atlanta, GA 30326, 404-816-4533 or toll-free 800-596-0724. *Website:* http://www.herzing.edu/atlanta/.

HERZING UNIVERSITY
Kenner, LA

CONTACT Financial Aid Office, Herzing University, 2500 Williams Boulevard, Kenner, LA 70062, 504-733-0074 or toll-free 800-596-0724. *Website:* http://www.herzing.edu/new-orleans.

HERZING UNIVERSITY
Brookfield, WI

CONTACT Financial Aid Office, Herzing University, 555 South Executive Drive, Brookfield, WI 53005, 262-649-1710 or toll-free 800-596-0724. *Website:* http://www.herzing.edu/brookfield.

HERZING UNIVERSITY
Kenosha, WI

CONTACT Financial Aid Office, Herzing University, 4006 Washington Road, Kenosha, WI 53144, 262-671-0675 or toll-free 800-596-0724. *Website:* http://www.herzing.edu/kenosha.

HERZING UNIVERSITY
Madison, WI

CONTACT Financial Aid Office, Herzing University, 5218 East Terrace Drive, Madison, WI 53718, 608-249-6611 or toll-free 800-596-0724. *Website:* http://www.herzing.edu/madison/.

HERZING UNIVERSITY ONLINE
Menomonee Falls, WI

CONTACT Financial Aid Office, Herzing University Online, W140N8917 Lilly Road, Menomonee Falls, WI 53051, 866-508-0748. *Website:* http://www.herzingonline.edu/.

HICKEY COLLEGE
St. Louis, MO

CONTACT Financial Aid Office, Hickey College, 2700 North Lindbergh Boulevard, St. Louis, MO 63114, 314-434-2212 or toll-free 800-777-1544. *Website:* http://www.hickeycollege.edu/.

HIGH POINT UNIVERSITY
High Point, NC

Tuition & fees: $34,005	Average undergraduate aid package: $17,929

ABOUT THE INSTITUTION Independent United Methodist, coed. *Awards:* certificates, bachelor's, master's, and doctoral degrees. 47 undergraduate majors. *Total enrollment:* 4,837. Undergraduates: 4,546. Freshmen: 1,382. Institutional methodology is used as a basis for awarding need-based institutional aid.

UNDERGRADUATE EXPENSES for 2017–2018 *Application fee:* $50. *Comprehensive fee:* $47,355 includes full-time tuition ($29,800), mandatory fees ($4205), and room and board ($13,350). Full-time tuition and fees vary according to course load and reciprocity agreements. Room and board charges vary according to board plan and housing facility. *Part-time tuition:* $955 per credit hour. *Part-time fees:* $200 per term. Part-time tuition and fees vary according to course load and reciprocity agreements.

FRESHMAN FINANCIAL AID (Fall 2015) 834 applied for aid; of those 71% were deemed to have need. 100% of freshmen with need received aid; of those 18% had need fully met. *Average percent of need met:* 55% (excluding resources awarded to replace EFC). *Average financial aid package:* $16,330 (excluding resources awarded to replace EFC). 14% of all full-time freshmen had no need and received non-need-based gift aid.

UNDERGRADUATE FINANCIAL AID (Fall 2015) 2,342 applied for aid; of those 76% were deemed to have need. 100% of undergraduates with need received aid; of those 17% had need fully met. *Average percent of need met:* 57% (excluding resources awarded to replace EFC). *Average financial aid package:* $17,929 (excluding resources awarded to replace EFC). 9% of all full-time undergraduates had no need and received non-need-based gift aid.

GIFT AID (NEED-BASED) *Total amount:* $6,436,051 (34% federal, 19% state, 46% institutional, 1% external sources). *Receiving aid:* Freshmen: 30% (410); all full-time undergraduates: 29% (1,237). *Average award:* Freshmen: $5308; Undergraduates: $5126. *Scholarships, grants, and awards:* Federal Pell, FSEOG, state, private, college/university gift aid from institutional funds.

GIFT AID (NON-NEED-BASED) *Total amount:* $23,533,345 (83% institutional, 17% external sources). *Receiving aid:* Freshmen: 36% (489). Undergraduates: 32% (1,401). *Average award:* Freshmen: $7236. Undergraduates: $7245. *Scholarships, grants, and awards by category:* Academic interests/achievement: biological sciences, business, education, English, foreign languages, general academic interests/achievements, humanities, international studies, mathematics, physical sciences, premedicine, religion/biblical studies. *Creative arts/performance:* art/fine arts, music. *Special achievements/activities:* general special achievements/activities. *Special characteristics:* relatives of clergy. *Tuition waivers:* Full or partial for employees or children of employees. *ROTC:* Army cooperative, Air Force cooperative.

LOANS *Student loans:* $24,957,544 (23% need-based, 77% non-need-based). 58% of past graduating class borrowed through all loan programs. *Average indebtedness per student:* $35,897. *Average need-based loan:* Freshmen: $3182. Undergraduates: $4239. *Parent loans:* $16,489,873 (100% non-need-based). *Programs:* Federal Direct (Subsidized and Unsubsidized Stafford, PLUS), Perkins, state.

WORK-STUDY *Federal work-study:* 281 jobs averaging $1500. *State or other work-study/employment:* Part-time jobs available.

ATHLETIC AWARDS Total amount: $5,831,214 (100% non-need-based).

APPLYING FOR FINANCIAL AID *Required financial aid forms:* FAFSA, state aid form. *Financial aid deadline (priority):* 3/1. *Notification date:* Continuous beginning 2/1. Students must reply within 3 weeks of notification.

CONTACT Mr. Ron Elmore, Director of Student Financial Planning, High Point University, Box 3232, University Station, One University Parkway, High Point, NC 27268, 336-841-9128 or toll-free 800-345-6993. *Fax:* 336-884-0221. *E-mail:* relmore@highpoint.edu. *Website:* http://www.highpoint.edu/.

HILBERT COLLEGE
Hamburg, NY

Tuition & fees: $22,350	Average undergraduate aid package: $15,037

ABOUT THE INSTITUTION Independent Roman Catholic, coed. *Awards:* associate, bachelor's, and master's degrees. 23 undergraduate majors. *Total enrollment:* 866. Undergraduates: 809. Freshmen: 148. Federal methodology is used as a basis for awarding need-based institutional aid.

UNDERGRADUATE EXPENSES for 2017–2018 *Application fee:* $25. *Comprehensive fee:* $31,350 includes full-time tuition ($21,750), mandatory fees ($600), and room and board ($9000). Room and board charges vary according to board plan and housing facility. *Part-time tuition:* $545 per credit hour. *Part-time fees:* $13 per credit hour; $55 per term.

FRESHMAN FINANCIAL AID (Fall 2016, est.) 85 applied for aid; of those 89% were deemed to have need. 100% of freshmen with need received aid; of those 16% had need fully met. *Average percent of need met:* 70% (excluding resources awarded to replace EFC). *Average financial aid package:* $16,676 (excluding resources awarded to replace EFC). 10% of all full-time freshmen had no need and received non-need-based gift aid.

UNDERGRADUATE FINANCIAL AID (Fall 2016, est.) 710 applied for aid; of those 92% were deemed to have need. 100% of undergraduates with need received aid; of those 22% had need fully met. *Average percent of need met:* 70% (excluding resources awarded to replace EFC). *Average financial aid package:* $15,037 (excluding resources awarded to replace EFC). 9% of all full-time undergraduates had no need and received non-need-based gift aid.

GIFT AID (NEED-BASED) *Total amount:* $6,879,394 (25% federal, 16% state, 50% institutional, 9% external sources). *Receiving aid:* Freshmen: 88% (76); all full-time undergraduates: 87% (629). *Average award:* Freshmen: $12,901; Undergraduates: $10,857. *Scholarships, grants, and awards:* Federal Pell, FSEOG, state, private, college/university gift aid from institutional funds.

GIFT AID (NON-NEED-BASED) *Total amount:* $659,049 (79% institutional, 21% external sources). *Receiving aid:* Freshmen: 5% (4). Undergraduates: 7% (50). *Average award:* Freshmen: $7194. Undergraduates: $6091. *Scholarships, grants, and awards by category:* Academic interests/achievement: general academic interests/achievements. *Special achievements/activities:* leadership. *Special characteristics:* children and siblings of alumni, members of minority groups, siblings of current students. *Tuition waivers:* Full or partial for minority students, children of alumni, employees or children of employees, adult students, senior citizens. *ROTC:* Army cooperative.

LOANS *Student loans:* $5,851,122 (73% need-based, 27% non-need-based). 89% of past graduating class borrowed through all loan programs. *Average indebtedness per student:* $19,233. *Average need-based loan:* Freshmen: $4228. Undergraduates: $5171. *Parent loans:* $1,260,016 (55% need-based, 45% non-need-based). *Programs:* Federal Direct (Subsidized and Unsubsidized Stafford, PLUS), Perkins.

WORK-STUDY *Federal work-study:* Total amount: $148,802; 80 jobs averaging $1860.

APPLYING FOR FINANCIAL AID *Required financial aid forms:* FAFSA, state aid form. *Financial aid deadline (priority):* 3/1. *Notification date:* Continuous beginning 3/1. Students must reply within 2 weeks of notification.

CONTACT Beverly Chudy-Szczur, Director of Financial Aid, Hilbert College, 5200 South Park Avenue, Hamburg, NY 14075-1597, 716-649-7900 Ext. 207 or toll-free 800-649-8003. *Fax:* 716-649-1152. *E-mail:* bchudy@hilbert.edu.
Website: http://www.hilbert.edu/.

HILLSDALE COLLEGE
Hillsdale, MI

Tuition & fees: $25,522	Average undergraduate aid package: $15,776

ABOUT THE INSTITUTION Independent, coed. *Awards:* bachelor's, master's, and doctoral degrees. 38 undergraduate majors. *Total enrollment:* 1,526. Undergraduates: 1,486. Freshmen: 364. Both federal and institutional methodology are used as a basis for awarding need-based institutional aid.

UNDERGRADUATE EXPENSES for 2016–2017 *Application fee:* $35. *One-time required fee:* $300. *Comprehensive fee:* $35,722 includes full-time tuition ($24,670), mandatory fees ($852), and room and board ($10,200). *College room only:* $5040. Full-time tuition and fees vary according to degree level. Room and board charges vary according to board plan. *Part-time tuition:* $985 per credit hour. *Part-time fees:* $85 per credit hour; $852 per year. Part-time tuition and fees vary according to degree level.

FRESHMAN FINANCIAL AID (Fall 2016, est.) 219 applied for aid; of those 89% were deemed to have need. 97% of freshmen with need received aid; of those 40% had need fully met. *Average percent of need met:* 60% (excluding resources awarded to replace EFC). *Average financial aid package:* $15,323 (excluding resources awarded to replace EFC). 45% of all full-time freshmen had no need and received non-need-based gift aid.

UNDERGRADUATE FINANCIAL AID (Fall 2016, est.) 817 applied for aid; of those 95% were deemed to have need. 96% of undergraduates with need received aid; of those 43% had need fully met. *Average percent of need met:* 65% (excluding resources awarded to replace EFC). *Average financial aid package:* $15,776 (excluding resources awarded to replace EFC). 46% of all full-time undergraduates had no need and received non-need-based gift aid.

GIFT AID (NEED-BASED) *Total amount:* $4,216,700 (100% institutional). *Receiving aid:* Freshmen: 33% (121); all full-time undergraduates: 33% (495). *Average award:* Freshmen: $6969; Undergraduates: $7275. *Scholarships, grants, and awards:* private, college/university gift aid from institutional funds.

GIFT AID (NON-NEED-BASED) *Total amount:* $16,636,377 (97% institutional, 3% external sources). *Receiving aid:* Freshmen: 47% (172). Undergraduates: 47% (697). *Average award:* Freshmen: $15,192. Undergraduates: $13,159. *Scholarships, grants, and awards by category:* Academic interests/achievement: 958 awards ($13,860,823 total): biological sciences, business, communication, education, engineering/technologies, English, foreign languages, general academic interests/achievements, mathematics, physical sciences, premedicine, social sciences. *Creative arts/performance:* 172 awards ($628,585 total): art/fine arts, debating, journalism/publications, music, theater/drama. *Special achievements/activities:* 37 awards ($198,000 total): community service, leadership. *Special characteristics:* 102 awards ($1,973,146 total): children of educators, children of faculty/staff, international students, veterans. *Tuition waivers:* Full or partial for children of alumni, employees or children of employees.

LOANS *Student loans:* $5,419,652 (41% need-based, 59% non-need-based). 54% of past graduating class borrowed through all loan programs. *Average indebtedness per student:* $26,941. *Average need-based loan:* Freshmen: $5214. Undergraduates: $5701. *Programs:* college/university.

ATHLETIC AWARDS Total amount: $3,055,170 (100% non-need-based).

APPLYING FOR FINANCIAL AID *Required financial aid form:* institution's own form. *Financial aid deadline (priority):* 5/1. *Notification date:* Continuous beginning 12/1. Students must reply within 4 weeks of notification.

CONTACT Mr. Rich Moeggengberg, Director of Student Financial Aid, Hillsdale College, 33 East College Street, Hillsdale, MI 49242-1298, 517-607-2350. *Fax:* 517-607-2298. *E-mail:* rmoeggenberg@hillsdale.edu.
Website: http://www.hillsdale.edu/.

HIRAM COLLEGE
Hiram, OH

CONTACT Ann Marie Gruber, Associate Director of Financial Aid, Hiram College, Box 67, Hiram, OH 44234-0067, 330-569-5107 or toll-free 800-362-5280. *Fax:* 330-569-5499.
Website: http://www.hiram.edu/.

HOBART AND WILLIAM SMITH COLLEGES
Geneva, NY

Tuition & fees: $53,525	Average undergraduate aid package: $35,123

ABOUT THE INSTITUTION Independent, coed. **Awards:** certificates, bachelor's, and master's degrees. 47 undergraduate majors. **Total enrollment:** 2,271. Undergraduates: 2,262. Freshmen: 581. Both federal and institutional methodology are used as a basis for awarding need-based institutional aid.

UNDERGRADUATE EXPENSES for 2017–2018 **Comprehensive fee:** $67,050 includes full-time tuition ($52,345), mandatory fees ($1180), and room and board ($13,525). Room and board charges vary according to board plan. **Payment plan:** Tuition prepayment.

FRESHMAN FINANCIAL AID (Fall 2015) 475 applied for aid; of those 82% were deemed to have need. 100% of freshmen with need received aid; of those 60% had need fully met. **Average percent of need met:** 82% (excluding resources awarded to replace EFC). **Average financial aid package:** $35,738 (excluding resources awarded to replace EFC). 33% of all full-time freshmen had no need and received non-need-based gift aid.

UNDERGRADUATE FINANCIAL AID (Fall 2015) 1,493 applied for aid; of those 85% were deemed to have need. 100% of undergraduates with need received aid; of those 68% had need fully met. **Average percent of need met:** 79% (excluding resources awarded to replace EFC). **Average financial aid package:** $35,123 (excluding resources awarded to replace EFC). 34% of all full-time undergraduates had no need and received non-need-based gift aid.

GIFT AID (NEED-BASED) Total amount: $39,514,527 (5% federal, 3% state, 87% institutional, 5% external sources). **Receiving aid:** Freshmen: 66% (390); all full-time undergraduates: 64% (1,266). **Average award:** Freshmen: $32,453; Undergraduates: $31,175. **Scholarships, grants, and awards:** Federal Pell, FSEOG, state, private, college/university gift aid from institutional funds.

GIFT AID (NON-NEED-BASED) Total amount: $13,167,490 (89% institutional, 11% external sources). **Receiving aid:** Freshmen: 13% (75). Undergraduates: 11% (226). **Average award:** Freshmen: $13,688. Undergraduates: $14,853. **Scholarships, grants, and awards by category:** Academic interests/achievement: 535 awards ($10,771,003 total): general academic interests/achievements, premedicine. Creative arts/performance: 90 awards ($805,697 total): art/fine arts, creative writing, dance, music, performing arts. Special achievements/activities: 224 awards ($3,248,537 total): community service, leadership. Special characteristics: 191 awards ($1,026,343 total): children and siblings of alumni, relatives of clergy, veterans' children. **Tuition waivers:** Full or partial for employees or children of employees. **ROTC:** Army cooperative, Air Force cooperative.

LOANS Student loans: $11,773,420 (59% need-based, 41% non-need-based). 73% of past graduating class borrowed through all loan programs. **Average indebtedness per student:** $35,935. **Average need-based loan:** Freshmen: $3219. Undergraduates: $3906. **Parent loans:** $5,967,622 (44% need-based, 56% non-need-based). **Programs:** Federal Direct (Subsidized and Unsubsidized Stafford, PLUS), Perkins, college/university.

WORK-STUDY Federal work-study: 834 jobs averaging $1836. **State or other work-study/employment:** Total amount: $1,197,850 (14% need-based, 86% non-need-based). 490 part-time jobs averaging $1865.

APPLYING FOR FINANCIAL AID Required financial aid forms: FAFSA, CSS Financial Aid PROFILE, state aid form, noncustodial (divorced/separated) parent's statement. **Financial aid deadline:** 2/1 (priority: 2/1). **Notification date:** 4/1. Students must reply by 5/1.

CONTACT Beth Nepa, Director of Financial Aid, Hobart and William Smith Colleges, Demarest Hall, 300 Pulteney Street, Geneva, NY 14456-3397, 315-781-3315 or toll-free 800-852-2256. Fax: 315-781-4048. E-mail: nepa@hws.edu. Website: http://www.hws.edu/.

HOBE SOUND BIBLE COLLEGE
Hobe Sound, FL

CONTACT Director of Financial Aid, Hobe Sound Bible College, PO Box 1065, Hobe Sound, FL 33475-1065, 561-546-5534. Fax: 561-545-1422. Website: http://www.hsbc.edu/.

HODGES UNIVERSITY
Naples, FL

ABOUT THE INSTITUTION Independent, coed. **Awards:** certificates, associate, bachelor's, and master's degrees. 8 undergraduate majors. **Total enrollment:** 1,724. Undergraduates: 1,487. Freshmen: 146.

GIFT AID (NEED-BASED) Scholarships, grants, and awards: Federal Pell, FSEOG, state, private, college/university gift aid from institutional funds.

GIFT AID (NON-NEED-BASED) Scholarships, grants, and awards by category: Special achievements/activities: general special achievements/activities. Special characteristics: children of current students, first-generation college students, general special characteristics, spouses of current students, veterans.

LOANS Programs: Federal Direct (Subsidized and Unsubsidized Stafford, PLUS).

WORK-STUDY Federal work-study: 60 jobs averaging $4370.

APPLYING FOR FINANCIAL AID Required financial aid form: FAFSA.

CONTACT Mr. Joe Gilchrist, Vice President of Financial Aid, Hodges University, 2655 Northbrooke Drive, Naples, FL 34119, 239-598-6116 or toll-free 800-466-8017. Fax: 239-598-6257. E-mail: jgilchrist@hodges.edu. Website: http://www.hodges.edu/.

HOFSTRA UNIVERSITY
Hempstead, NY

Tuition & fees: $42,160	Average undergraduate aid package: $29,000

ABOUT THE INSTITUTION Independent, coed. **Awards:** certificates, bachelor's, master's, and doctoral degrees. 132 undergraduate majors. **Total enrollment:** 11,145. Undergraduates: 6,899. Freshmen: 1,647. Federal methodology is used as a basis for awarding need-based institutional aid.

UNDERGRADUATE EXPENSES for 2016–2017 **Application fee:** $70. **Comprehensive fee:** $56,620 includes full-time tuition ($41,100), mandatory fees ($1060), and room and board ($14,460). **College room only:** $9700. Full-time tuition and fees vary according to course load. Room and board charges vary according to board plan and housing facility. **Part-time tuition:** $1380 per credit hour. **Part-time fees:** $155 per term. Part-time tuition and fees vary according to course load. **Payment plan:** Guaranteed tuition.

FRESHMAN FINANCIAL AID (Fall 2016, est.) 1,438 applied for aid; of those 82% were deemed to have need. 100% of freshmen with need received aid; of those 26% had need fully met. **Average percent of need met:** 70% (excluding resources awarded to replace EFC). **Average financial aid package:** $31,000 (excluding resources awarded to replace EFC). 22% of all full-time freshmen had no need and received non-need-based gift aid.

UNDERGRADUATE FINANCIAL AID (Fall 2016, est.) 4,945 applied for aid; of those 84% were deemed to have need. 100% of undergraduates with need received aid; of those 25% had need fully met. **Average percent of need met:** 65% (excluding resources awarded to replace EFC). **Average financial aid package:** $29,000 (excluding resources awarded to replace EFC). 25% of all full-time undergraduates had no need and received non-need-based gift aid.

GIFT AID (NEED-BASED) Total amount: $77,510,000 (10% federal, 5% state, 84% institutional, 1% external sources). **Receiving aid:** Freshmen: 71% (1,161); all full-time undergraduates: 61% (3,947). **Average award:** Freshmen: $22,000; Undergraduates: $20,000. **Scholarships, grants, and awards:** Federal Pell, FSEOG, state, private, college/university gift aid from institutional funds, United Negro College Fund.

GIFT AID (NON-NEED-BASED) Total amount: $35,640,000 (1% federal, 1% state, 96% institutional, 2% external sources). **Receiving aid:** Freshmen: 16% (256). Undergraduates: 10% (653). **Average award:** Freshmen: $20,000. Undergraduates: $17,000. **Scholarships, grants, and awards by category:** Academic interests/achievement: 6,196 awards ($87,116,658 total): communication, engineering/technologies, general academic interests/achievements. Creative arts/performance: 241 awards ($766,067 total): applied art and design, art/fine arts, cinema/film/broadcasting, dance, journalism/publications, music, performing arts, theater/drama. Special achievements/activities: 261 awards ($6,013,350 total): cheerleading/drum major, general special achievements/activities, leadership. Special characteristics: 406 awards ($9,356,936 total): children and siblings of alumni, children of faculty/staff, children of union members/company employees, general special characteristics, handicapped students, local/state students, members of minority groups, public servants, veterans, veterans' children. **Tuition waivers:** Full or partial for employees or children of employees. **ROTC:** Army.

LOANS Student loans: $45,300,000 (69% need-based, 31% non-need-based). 69% of past graduating class borrowed through all loan programs. **Average need-based loan:** Freshmen: $4000. Undergraduates: $5000. **Parent loans:** $34,900,000 (58% need-based, 42% non-need-based). **Programs:** Federal Direct (Subsidized and Unsubsidized Stafford, PLUS), Perkins, state, college/university.

WORK-STUDY Federal work-study: Total amount: $5,300,000; 1,749 jobs averaging $3009. **State or other work-study/employment:** Total amount: $4,700,000 (21% need-based, 79% non-need-based). 1,513 part-time jobs averaging $3074.

ATHLETIC AWARDS Total amount: $6,050,000 (49% need-based, 51% non-need-based).

APPLYING FOR FINANCIAL AID Required financial aid forms: FAFSA, state aid form. **Financial aid deadline (priority):** 2/1. **Notification date:** Continuous beginning 3/1. Students must reply by 5/1 or within 2 weeks of notification.

CONTACT Sandra Mervius, Director of Financial Aid, Hofstra University, 126 Hofstra University, Hempstead, NY 11549, 516-463-4335 or toll-free 800-HOFSTRA. *Fax:* 516-463-4936. *E-mail:* sandra.a.filbry@hofstra.edu. *Website:* http://www.hofstra.edu/.

HOLLINS UNIVERSITY
Roanoke, VA

Tuition & fees: $36,835	Average undergraduate aid package: $35,508

ABOUT THE INSTITUTION Independent, undergraduate: women only; graduate: coed. **Awards:** certificates, bachelor's, and master's degrees. 28 undergraduate majors. **Total enrollment:** 827. Undergraduates: 654. Freshmen: 224. Federal methodology is used as a basis for awarding need-based institutional aid.

UNDERGRADUATE EXPENSES for 2016–2017 Comprehensive fee: $49,635 includes full-time tuition ($36,200), mandatory fees ($635), and room and board ($12,800). **Part-time tuition:** $1132 per credit hour. **Part-time fees:** $322.50 per year. Part-time tuition and fees vary according to course load. **Payment plan:** Tuition prepayment.

FRESHMAN FINANCIAL AID (Fall 2016, est.) 212 applied for aid; of those 89% were deemed to have need. 100% of freshmen with need received aid; of those 26% had need fully met. **Average percent of need met:** 85% (excluding resources awarded to replace EFC). **Average financial aid package:** $36,183 (excluding resources awarded to replace EFC). 16% of all full-time freshmen had no need and received non-need-based gift aid.

UNDERGRADUATE FINANCIAL AID (Fall 2016, est.) 568 applied for aid; of those 92% were deemed to have need. 100% of undergraduates with need received aid; of those 23% had need fully met. **Average percent of need met:** 84% (excluding resources awarded to replace EFC). **Average financial aid package:** $35,508 (excluding resources awarded to replace EFC). 18% of all full-time undergraduates had no need and received non-need-based gift aid.

GIFT AID (NEED-BASED) Total amount: $16,122,785 (9% federal, 5% state, 85% institutional, 1% external sources). **Receiving aid:** Freshmen: 84% (189); all full-time undergraduates: 82% (525). **Average award:** Freshmen: $30,186; Undergraduates: $29,001. **Scholarships, grants, and awards:** Federal Pell, FSEOG, state, private, college/university gift aid from institutional funds.

GIFT AID (NON-NEED-BASED) Total amount: $3,225,600 (4% state, 95% institutional, 1% external sources). **Receiving aid:** Freshmen: 84% (189). Undergraduates: 82% (525). **Average award:** Freshmen: $29,647. Undergraduates: $26,663. **Scholarships, grants, and awards by category:** Academic interests/achievement: general academic interests/achievements. Creative arts/performance: creative writing, dance, music, theater/drama. Special achievements/activities: community service, general special achievements/activities, hobbies/interests, leadership. Special characteristics: adult students, children and siblings of alumni, children of faculty/staff, international students, local/state students, out-of-state students, previous college experience, veterans. **Tuition waivers:** Full or partial for employees or children of employees.

LOANS Student loans: $4,241,524 (82% need-based, 18% non-need-based). 76% of past graduating class borrowed through all loan programs. *Average indebtedness per student:* $34,414. **Average need-based loan:** Freshmen: $4128. Undergraduates: $5026. **Parent loans:** $1,658,974 (51% need-based, 49% non-need-based).

Programs: Federal Direct (Subsidized and Unsubsidized Stafford, PLUS), Perkins, college/university.

WORK-STUDY Federal work-study: Total amount: $184,800; jobs available. **State or other work-study/employment:** Total amount: $333,775 (42% need-based, 58% non-need-based). Part-time jobs available.

APPLYING FOR FINANCIAL AID Required financial aid forms: FAFSA, state aid form. **Financial aid deadline (priority):** 1/1. **Notification date:** Continuous beginning 12/1. Students must reply by 5/1.

CONTACT Mrs. MaryJoan Sullivan, Director of Scholarships and Financial Assistance, Hollins University, 7916 Williamson Road, Box 9718, Roanoke, VA 24020, 540-362-6332 or toll-free 800-456-9595. *Fax:* 540-362-6093. *E-mail:* sfa@hollins.edu. *Website:* http://www.hollins.edu/.

HOLY CROSS COLLEGE
Notre Dame, IN

CONTACT Robert Benjamin, Director of Financial Aid, Holy Cross College, PO Box 308, Notre Dame, IN 46556, 574-239-8362. *E-mail:* rbenjamin@hcc-nd.edu. *Website:* http://www.hcc-nd.edu/.

HOLY FAMILY UNIVERSITY
Philadelphia, PA

Tuition & fees: $29,338	Average undergraduate aid package: $22,642

ABOUT THE INSTITUTION Independent Roman Catholic, coed. **Awards:** certificates, associate, bachelor's, master's, and doctoral degrees. 43 undergraduate majors. **Total enrollment:** 2,737. Undergraduates: 1,950. Freshmen: 328. Federal methodology is used as a basis for awarding need-based institutional aid.

UNDERGRADUATE EXPENSES for 2017–2018 Application fee: $25. **Comprehensive fee:** $42,914 includes full-time tuition ($28,350), mandatory fees ($988), and room and board ($13,576). **College room only:** $7140. Full-time tuition and fees vary according to class time, course level, course load, degree level, program, and reciprocity agreements. Room and board charges vary according to board plan and housing facility. **Part-time tuition:** $615 per credit hour. **Part-time fees:** $110 per term. Part-time tuition and fees vary according to class time, course level, course load, degree level, program, and reciprocity agreements.

FRESHMAN FINANCIAL AID (Fall 2016, est.) 315 applied for aid; of those 95% were deemed to have need. 100% of freshmen with need received aid; of those 20% had need fully met. **Average percent of need met:** 85% (excluding resources awarded to replace EFC). **Average financial aid package:** $26,244 (excluding resources awarded to replace EFC). 9% of all full-time freshmen had no need and received non-need-based gift aid.

UNDERGRADUATE FINANCIAL AID (Fall 2016, est.) 1,308 applied for aid; of those 93% were deemed to have need. 100% of undergraduates with need received aid; of those 17% had need fully met. **Average percent of need met:** 77% (excluding resources awarded to replace EFC). **Average financial aid package:** $22,642 (excluding resources awarded to replace EFC). 11% of all full-time undergraduates had no need and received non-need-based gift aid.

GIFT AID (NEED-BASED) Total amount: $20,649,162 (14% federal, 12% state, 72% institutional, 2% external sources). **Receiving aid:** Freshmen: 91% (298); all full-time undergraduates: 80% (1,145). **Average award:** Freshmen: $19,313; Undergraduates: $14,458. **Scholarships, grants, and awards:** Federal Pell, FSEOG, state, private, college/university gift aid from institutional funds.

GIFT AID (NON-NEED-BASED) Total amount: $2,019,827 (98% institutional, 2% external sources). **Receiving aid:** Freshmen: 91% (298). Undergraduates: 78% (1,117). **Average award:** Freshmen: $15,929. Undergraduates: $13,021. **Scholarships, grants, and awards by category:** Academic interests/achievement: 1,287 awards ($17,974,534 total): general academic interests/achievements. **Tuition waivers:** Full or partial for employees or children of employees, senior citizens. **ROTC:** Army cooperative.

LOANS Student loans: $13,044,049 (92% need-based, 8% non-need-based). 86% of past graduating class borrowed through all loan programs. *Average indebtedness per student:* $39,664. **Average need-based loan:** Freshmen: $3665. Undergraduates: $4440. **Parent loans:** $2,133,887 (94% need-based, 6% non-need-based). **Pro-**

grams: Federal Direct (Subsidized and Unsubsidized Stafford, PLUS), Perkins, Federal Nursing.

WORK-STUDY *Federal work-study:* Total amount: $477,308; 414 jobs averaging $1143.

ATHLETIC AWARDS Total amount: $1,264,778 (81% need-based, 19% non-need-based).

APPLYING FOR FINANCIAL AID *Required financial aid form:* FAFSA. *Financial aid deadline (priority):* 3/1. *Notification date:* Continuous beginning 3/15.

CONTACT Ms. Janice Hetrick, Director of Financial Aid, Holy Family University, 9801 Frankford Avenue, Philadelphia, PA 19114-2094, 215-637-7700 Ext. 3233. *Fax:* 215-599-1694. *E-mail:* finaid@holyfamily.edu. *Website:* http://www.holyfamily.edu/.

HOLY NAMES UNIVERSITY
Oakland, CA

CONTACT Christina Miller, Director of Financial Aid, Holy Names University, 3500 Mountain Boulevard, Oakland, CA 94619-1699, 510-436-1327 or toll-free 800-430-1321. *Fax:* 510-436-1199. *E-mail:* miller@hnu.edu. *Website:* http://www.hnu.edu/.

HOOD COLLEGE
Frederick, MD

Tuition & fees: $37,960	Average undergraduate aid package: $29,186

ABOUT THE INSTITUTION Independent, coed. *Awards:* certificates, bachelor's, master's, and doctoral degrees (also offers adult program with significant enrollment not reflected in profile). 33 undergraduate majors. *Total enrollment:* 2,144. Undergraduates: 1,174. Freshmen: 219. Federal methodology is used as a basis for awarding need-based institutional aid.

UNDERGRADUATE EXPENSES for 2017–2018 *Comprehensive fee:* $50,540 includes full-time tuition ($37,400), mandatory fees ($560), and room and board ($12,580). *College room only:* $6600. Room and board charges vary according to board plan. *Part-time tuition:* $1090 per credit hour. *Part-time fees:* $280 per term.

FRESHMAN FINANCIAL AID (Fall 2016, est.) 210 applied for aid; of those 92% were deemed to have need. 100% of freshmen with need received aid; of those 16% had need fully met. *Average percent of need met:* 79% (excluding resources awarded to replace EFC). *Average financial aid package:* $32,632 (excluding resources awarded to replace EFC). 11% of all full-time freshmen had no need and received non-need-based gift aid.

UNDERGRADUATE FINANCIAL AID (Fall 2016, est.) 957 applied for aid; of those 91% were deemed to have need. 100% of undergraduates with need received aid; of those 20% had need fully met. *Average percent of need met:* 75% (excluding resources awarded to replace EFC). *Average financial aid package:* $29,186 (excluding resources awarded to replace EFC). 17% of all full-time undergraduates had no need and received non-need-based gift aid.

GIFT AID (NEED-BASED) *Total amount:* $21,701,114 (9% federal, 7% state, 79% institutional, 5% external sources). *Receiving aid:* Freshmen: 88% (193); all full-time undergraduates: 80% (869). *Average award:* Freshmen: $28,791; Undergraduates: $25,391. *Scholarships, grants, and awards:* Federal Pell, FSEOG, state, private, college/university gift aid from institutional funds.

GIFT AID (NON-NEED-BASED) *Total amount:* $5,126,529 (1% state, 81% institutional, 18% external sources). *Receiving aid:* Freshmen: 13% (28). Undergraduates: 14% (149). *Average award:* Freshmen: $20,903. Undergraduates: $16,993. *Scholarships, grants, and awards by category:* Academic interests/achievement: 38 awards ($196,772 total): biological sciences, business, communication, computer science, education, English, foreign languages, general academic interests/achievements, humanities, mathematics, religion/biblical studies, social sciences. *Creative arts/performance:* 21 awards ($17,519 total): art/fine arts, music. *Special achievements/activities:* 21 awards ($20,500 total): leadership. *Special characteristics:* 277 awards ($983,475 total): children and siblings of alumni, children of faculty/staff, ethnic background, first-generation college students, international students, local/state students, out-of-state students, previous college experience, religious

affiliation, siblings of current students, veterans, veterans' children. *Tuition waivers:* Full or partial for employees or children of employees, senior citizens. *ROTC:* Army.

LOANS *Student loans:* $7,661,719 (74% need-based, 26% non-need-based). 71% of past graduating class borrowed through all loan programs. *Average indebtedness per student:* $30,554. *Average need-based loan:* Freshmen: $4406. Undergraduates: $4553. *Parent loans:* $2,933,281 (42% need-based, 58% non-need-based). *Programs:* Federal Direct (Subsidized and Unsubsidized Stafford, PLUS), Perkins.

WORK-STUDY *Federal work-study:* Total amount: $169,418; 205 jobs averaging $2000. *State or other work-study/employment:* Total amount: $247,575 (50% need-based, 50% non-need-based). 132 part-time jobs averaging $2000.

APPLYING FOR FINANCIAL AID *Required financial aid forms:* FAFSA, institution's own form. *Financial aid deadline (priority):* 2/15. *Notification date:* 3/1. Students must reply by 5/1 or within 4 weeks of notification.

CONTACT Ms. Brenda DiSorbo, Director of Financial Aid, Hood College, 401 Rosemont Avenue, Frederick, MD 21701-8575, 301-696-3411 or toll-free 800-922-1599. *Fax:* 301-696-3812. *E-mail:* disorbo@hood.edu. *Website:* http://www.hood.edu/.

HOPE COLLEGE
Holland, MI

Tuition & fees: $31,560	Average undergraduate aid package: $25,792

ABOUT THE INSTITUTION Independent Reformed Church in America, coed. *Awards:* bachelor's degrees. 63 undergraduate majors. *Total enrollment:* 3,234. Undergraduates: 3,234. Freshmen: 727. Federal methodology is used as a basis for awarding need-based institutional aid.

UNDERGRADUATE EXPENSES for 2016–2017 *Application fee:* $35. *Comprehensive fee:* $41,250 includes full-time tuition ($31,380), mandatory fees ($180), and room and board ($9690). *College room only:* $4450. Room and board charges vary according to board plan. *Part-time tuition:* $1207 per semester hour. Part-time tuition and fees vary according to course load and program.

FRESHMAN FINANCIAL AID (Fall 2016, est.) 600 applied for aid; of those 76% were deemed to have need. 100% of freshmen with need received aid; of those 26% had need fully met. *Average percent of need met:* 81% (excluding resources awarded to replace EFC). *Average financial aid package:* $26,468 (excluding resources awarded to replace EFC). 27% of all full-time freshmen had no need and received non-need-based gift aid.

UNDERGRADUATE FINANCIAL AID (Fall 2016, est.) 2,084 applied for aid; of those 82% were deemed to have need. 99% of undergraduates with need received aid; of those 25% had need fully met. *Average percent of need met:* 80% (excluding resources awarded to replace EFC). *Average financial aid package:* $25,792 (excluding resources awarded to replace EFC). 31% of all full-time undergraduates had no need and received non-need-based gift aid.

GIFT AID (NEED-BASED) *Total amount:* $26,897,828 (10% federal, 6% state, 83% institutional, 1% external sources). *Receiving aid:* Freshmen: 59% (415); all full-time undergraduates: 52% (1,486). *Average award:* Freshmen: $21,105; Undergraduates: $19,244. *Scholarships, grants, and awards:* Federal Pell, FSEOG, state, private, college/university gift aid from institutional funds.

GIFT AID (NON-NEED-BASED) *Total amount:* $9,507,343 (4% federal, 88% institutional, 8% external sources). *Receiving aid:* Freshmen: 52% (362). Undergraduates: 45% (1,281). *Average award:* Freshmen: $8714. Undergraduates: $8527. *Scholarships, grants, and awards by category:* Academic interests/achievement: 1,987 awards ($13,698,164 total): general academic interests/achievements. *Creative arts/performance:* 136 awards ($341,000 total): art/fine arts, creative writing, dance, music, theater/drama. *Special characteristics:* 220 awards ($1,851,333 total): ethnic background. *Tuition waivers:* Full or partial for employees or children of employees. *ROTC:* Army cooperative.

LOANS *Student loans:* $14,268,838 (46% need-based, 54% non-need-based). 64% of past graduating class borrowed through all loan programs. *Average indebtedness per student:* $33,969. *Average need-based loan:* Freshmen: $4085. Undergraduates: $5134. *Parent loans:* $4,824,451 (100% non-need-based). *Programs:* Federal Direct (Subsidized and Unsubsidized Stafford, PLUS), Perkins.

WORK-STUDY *Federal work-study:* Total amount: $321,491; 145 jobs averaging $2111. *State or other work-study/employment:* Total amount: $2,600,000 (62% need-based, 38% non-need-based). 567 part-time jobs averaging $1152.

APPLYING FOR FINANCIAL AID *Required financial aid forms:* FAFSA, institution's own form. *Financial aid deadline (priority):* 3/1. *Notification date:* Continuous beginning 3/15. Students must reply within 2 weeks of notification.

CONTACT Ms. Jill Nutt, Director of Financial Aid, Hope College, 141 East 12th Street, Holland, MI 49422-9000, 616-395-7765 or toll-free 800-968-7850. *Fax:* 616-395-7160. *E-mail:* nutt@hope.edu.
Website: http://www.hope.edu/.

HOPE INTERNATIONAL UNIVERSITY
Fullerton, CA

Tuition & fees: $31,800	Average undergraduate aid package: $20,029

ABOUT THE INSTITUTION Independent Christian Churches and Churches of Christ, coed. *Awards:* certificates, associate, bachelor's, and master's degrees. 17 undergraduate majors. *Total enrollment:* 1,346. Undergraduates: 853. Freshmen: 105. Federal methodology is used as a basis for awarding need-based institutional aid.

UNDERGRADUATE EXPENSES for 2017–2018 *Application fee:* $40. *Comprehensive fee:* $41,730 includes full-time tuition ($30,700), mandatory fees ($1100), and room and board ($9930). *College room only:* $4900. Full-time tuition and fees vary according to course level, course load, degree level, location, program, and reciprocity agreements. Room and board charges vary according to board plan. *Part-time tuition:* $1395 per credit hour. Part-time tuition and fees vary according to course level, course load, degree level, location, program, and reciprocity agreements.

FRESHMAN FINANCIAL AID (Fall 2015) 104 applied for aid; of those 86% were deemed to have need. 100% of freshmen with need received aid; of those 19% had need fully met. *Average percent of need met:* 33% (excluding resources awarded to replace EFC). *Average financial aid package:* $20,526 (excluding resources awarded to replace EFC). 6% of all full-time freshmen had no need and received non-need-based gift aid.

UNDERGRADUATE FINANCIAL AID (Fall 2015) 355 applied for aid; of those 91% were deemed to have need. 100% of undergraduates with need received aid; of those 2% had need fully met. *Average percent of need met:* 42% (excluding resources awarded to replace EFC). *Average financial aid package:* $20,029 (excluding resources awarded to replace EFC). 3% of all full-time undergraduates had no need and received non-need-based gift aid.

GIFT AID (NEED-BASED) *Total amount:* $3,685,575 (48% federal, 36% state, 16% institutional). *Receiving aid:* Freshmen: 56% (61); all full-time undergraduates: 40% (202). *Average award:* Freshmen: $13,194; Undergraduates: $15,971. *Scholarships, grants, and awards:* Federal Pell, FSEOG, state, private, college/university gift aid from institutional funds.

GIFT AID (NON-NEED-BASED) *Total amount:* $2,532,804 (94% institutional, 6% external sources). *Receiving aid:* Freshmen: 73% (79). Undergraduates: 23% (118). *Average award:* Freshmen: $15,250. Undergraduates: $9407. *Scholarships, grants, and awards by category: Academic interests/achievement:* 168 awards ($1,635,108 total): general academic interests/achievements. *Creative arts/performance:* 6 awards ($72,000 total): music. *Special achievements/activities:* 51 awards ($431,250 total): cheerleading/drum major, leadership. *Special characteristics:* 27 awards ($312,777 total): children of faculty/staff, veterans. *Tuition waivers:* Full or partial for employees or children of employees. *ROTC:* Army cooperative.

LOANS *Student loans:* $5,196,302 (49% need-based, 51% non-need-based). 91% of past graduating class borrowed through all loan programs. *Average indebtedness per student:* $28,438. *Average need-based loan:* Freshmen: $2582. Undergraduates: $4819. *Parent loans:* $1,415,556 (88% need-based, 12% non-need-based). *Programs:* Federal Direct (Subsidized and Unsubsidized Stafford, PLUS).

WORK-STUDY *Federal work-study:* 61 jobs averaging $2000. *State or other work-study/employment:* Total amount: $419,301 (100% non-need-based). 97 part-time jobs averaging $2000.

ATHLETIC AWARDS Total amount: $3,038,188 (100% non-need-based).

APPLYING FOR FINANCIAL AID *Required financial aid forms:* FAFSA, institution's own form. *Financial aid deadline (priority):* 3/2. *Notification date:* Continuous beginning 3/1. Students must reply within 2 weeks of notification.

CONTACT Ms. Shannon O'Shields, Director of Student Financial Services, Hope International University, 2500 East Nutwood Avenue, Fullerton, CA 92831, 714-879-3901 Ext. 2207 or toll-free 866-722-HOPE. *Fax:* 714-681-7421. *E-mail:* soshields@hiu.edu.
Website: http://www.hiu.edu/.

HORIZON UNIVERSITY
San Diego, CA

CONTACT Financial Aid Office, Horizon University, 5331 Mt. Alifan Drive, San Diego, CA 92111, 858-695-8587 or toll-free 800-553-HORIZON.
Website: http://www.horizonuniversity.edu/.

HOUGHTON COLLEGE
Houghton, NY

Tuition & fees: N/R	Average undergraduate aid package: $25,309

ABOUT THE INSTITUTION Independent Wesleyan, coed. *Awards:* associate, bachelor's, and master's degrees. 66 undergraduate majors. *Total enrollment:* 1,059. Undergraduates: 1,043. Freshmen: 257. Federal methodology is used as a basis for awarding need-based institutional aid.

UNDERGRADUATE EXPENSES for 2017–2018 *Application fee:* $40.

FRESHMAN FINANCIAL AID (Fall 2016, est.) 244 applied for aid; of those 89% were deemed to have need. 100% of freshmen with need received aid; of those 22% had need fully met. *Average percent of need met:* 80% (excluding resources awarded to replace EFC). *Average financial aid package:* $24,589 (excluding resources awarded to replace EFC). 16% of all full-time freshmen had no need and received non-need-based gift aid.

UNDERGRADUATE FINANCIAL AID (Fall 2016, est.) 873 applied for aid; of those 92% were deemed to have need. 100% of undergraduates with need received aid; of those 17% had need fully met. *Average percent of need met:* 80% (excluding resources awarded to replace EFC). *Average financial aid package:* $25,309 (excluding resources awarded to replace EFC). 19% of all full-time undergraduates had no need and received non-need-based gift aid.

GIFT AID (NEED-BASED) *Total amount:* $14,552,422 (13% federal, 8% state, 75% institutional, 4% external sources). *Receiving aid:* Freshmen: 82% (217); all full-time undergraduates: 79% (798). *Average award:* Freshmen: $19,693; Undergraduates: $19,457. *Scholarships, grants, and awards:* Federal Pell, FSEOG, state, private, college/university gift aid from institutional funds.

GIFT AID (NON-NEED-BASED) *Total amount:* $3,761,638 (2% state, 92% institutional, 6% external sources). *Receiving aid:* Freshmen: 16% (43). Undergraduates: 11% (110). *Average award:* Freshmen: $18,443. Undergraduates: $15,099. *Scholarships, grants, and awards by category: Academic interests/achievement:* biological sciences, business, communication, education, English, general academic interests/achievements, international studies, mathematics, physical sciences, religion/biblical studies. *Creative arts/performance:* art/fine arts, music, performing arts. *Special achievements/activities:* community service, general special achievements/activities, leadership, memberships, religious involvement. *Special characteristics:* adult students, children and siblings of alumni, children of faculty/staff, general special characteristics, handicapped students, international students, local/state students, relatives of clergy, religious affiliation, siblings of current students, veterans. *Tuition waivers:* Full or partial for employees or children of employees, senior citizens. *ROTC:* Army cooperative.

LOANS *Student loans:* $7,257,491 (71% need-based, 29% non-need-based). 67% of past graduating class borrowed through all loan programs. *Average indebtedness per student:* $23,277. *Average need-based loan:* Freshmen: $4172. Undergraduates: $5480. *Parent loans:* $1,749,418 (56% need-based, 44% non-need-based). *Programs:* Federal Direct (Subsidized and Unsubsidized Stafford, PLUS), Perkins, state.

WORK-STUDY *Federal work-study:* Total amount: $889,704; 477 jobs averaging $1861. *State or other work-study/employment:* Total amount: $236,132 (36% need-based, 64% non-need-based). 123 part-time jobs averaging $1945.

APPLYING FOR FINANCIAL AID *Required financial aid forms:* FAFSA, noncustodial (divorced/separated) parent's statement. *Financial aid deadline (priority):* 3/1. *Notification date:* Continuous beginning 3/1.

CONTACT Mrs. Marianne Loper, Director of Financial Aid, Houghton College, One Willard Avenue, Houghton, NY 14744, 585-567-9328 or toll-free 800-777-2556. *Fax:* 585-567-9610. *E-mail:* sfso@houghton.edu.
Website: http://www.houghton.edu/.

HOUSTON BAPTIST UNIVERSITY
Houston, TX

Tuition & fees: $30,800	Average undergraduate aid package: $30,060

ABOUT THE INSTITUTION Independent Baptist, coed. *Awards:* bachelor's, master's, and doctoral degrees. 57 undergraduate majors. *Total enrollment:* 3,270. Undergraduates: 2,332. Freshmen: 577. Federal methodology is used as a basis for awarding need-based institutional aid.

UNDERGRADUATE EXPENSES for 2016–2017 *Application fee:* $25. *Comprehensive fee:* $38,658 includes full-time tuition ($28,850), mandatory fees ($1950), and room and board ($7858). *College room only:* $4770. Room and board charges vary according to board plan and housing facility. *Part-time tuition:* $1200 per credit hour. *Part-time fees:* $975 per term. Part-time tuition and fees vary according to course load.

FRESHMAN FINANCIAL AID (Fall 2016, est.) 507 applied for aid; of those 92% were deemed to have need. 100% of freshmen with need received aid; of those 26% had need fully met. *Average percent of need met:* 78% (excluding resources awarded to replace EFC). *Average financial aid package:* $30,077 (excluding resources awarded to replace EFC). 19% of all full-time freshmen had no need and received non-need-based gift aid.

UNDERGRADUATE FINANCIAL AID (Fall 2016, est.) 1,680 applied for aid; of those 95% were deemed to have need. 100% of undergraduates with need received aid; of those 28% had need fully met. *Average percent of need met:* 74% (excluding resources awarded to replace EFC). *Average financial aid package:* $30,060 (excluding resources awarded to replace EFC). 24% of all full-time undergraduates had no need and received non-need-based gift aid.

GIFT AID (NEED-BASED) *Total amount:* $26,833,983 (18% federal, 10% state, 71% institutional, 1% external sources). *Receiving aid:* Freshmen: 81% (466); all full-time undergraduates: 73% (1,571). *Average award:* Freshmen: $20,660; Undergraduates: $19,431. *Scholarships, grants, and awards:* Federal Pell, FSEOG, state.

GIFT AID (NON-NEED-BASED) *Total amount:* $8,117,897 (99% institutional, 1% external sources). *Receiving aid:* Freshmen: 81% (465). Undergraduates: 68% (1,476). *Average award:* Freshmen: $14,160. Undergraduates: $14,164. *Scholarships, grants, and awards by category:* Academic interests/achievement: 2,733 awards ($24,460,307 total): education, general academic interests/achievements. *Creative arts/performance:* 63 awards ($277,356 total): art/fine arts, music. *Special achievements/activities:* 149 awards ($184,929 total): cheerleading/drum major, religious involvement. *Special characteristics:* 157 awards ($862,756 total): children of faculty/staff, relatives of clergy, religious affiliation. *Tuition waivers:* Full or partial for employees or children of employees, senior citizens. *ROTC:* Army cooperative, Naval cooperative, Air Force cooperative.

LOANS *Student loans:* $17,111,274 (76% need-based, 24% non-need-based). 66% of past graduating class borrowed through all loan programs. *Average indebtedness per student:* $32,027. *Average need-based loan:* Freshmen: $5293. Undergraduates: $5934. *Parent loans:* $4,881,272 (5% need-based, 95% non-need-based). *Programs:* Federal Direct (Subsidized and Unsubsidized Stafford, PLUS), state.

WORK-STUDY *Federal work-study:* Total amount: $2,000,930; 1,029 jobs averaging $1944.

ATHLETIC AWARDS Total amount: $8,265,774 (48% need-based, 52% non-need-based).

APPLYING FOR FINANCIAL AID *Required financial aid form:* FAFSA. *Financial aid deadline (priority):* 3/1. *Notification date:* Continuous beginning 11/15.

CONTACT Ms. Veronica Jene Gabbard, Senior Director of Financial Aid and Scholarships, Houston Baptist University, 7502 Fondren Road, Houston, TX 77074-3298, 281-649-3747 or toll-free 800-696-3210. *Fax:* 281-649-3298. *E-mail:* financialaid@hbu.edu.
Website: http://www.hbu.edu/.

HOWARD PAYNE UNIVERSITY
Brownwood, TX

Tuition & fees: $27,690	Average undergraduate aid package: $20,390

ABOUT THE INSTITUTION Independent Baptist General Convention of Texas, coed. *Awards:* certificates, bachelor's, and master's degrees. 69 undergraduate majors. *Total enrollment:* 1,189. Undergraduates: 1,098. Freshmen: 330. Federal methodology is used as a basis for awarding need-based institutional aid.

UNDERGRADUATE EXPENSES for 2017–2018 *Comprehensive fee:* $35,994 includes full-time tuition ($25,290), mandatory fees ($2400), and room and board ($8304). Full-time tuition and fees vary according to course load, location, and program. Room and board charges vary according to board plan and housing facility. *Part-time tuition:* $820 per credit hour. Part-time tuition and fees vary according to location and program.

FRESHMAN FINANCIAL AID (Fall 2016, est.) 311 applied for aid; of those 93% were deemed to have need. 100% of freshmen with need received aid; of those 18% had need fully met. *Average percent of need met:* 78% (excluding resources awarded to replace EFC). *Average financial aid package:* $19,362 (excluding resources awarded to replace EFC). 8% of all full-time freshmen had no need and received non-need-based gift aid.

UNDERGRADUATE FINANCIAL AID (Fall 2016, est.) 871 applied for aid; of those 93% were deemed to have need. 100% of undergraduates with need received aid; of those 20% had need fully met. *Average percent of need met:* 78% (excluding resources awarded to replace EFC). *Average financial aid package:* $20,390 (excluding resources awarded to replace EFC). 15% of all full-time undergraduates had no need and received non-need-based gift aid.

GIFT AID (NEED-BASED) *Total amount:* $13,003,297 (16% federal, 11% state, 70% institutional, 3% external sources). *Receiving aid:* Freshmen: 88% (286); all full-time undergraduates: 84% (801). *Average award:* Freshmen: $15,777; Undergraduates: $16,195. *Scholarships, grants, and awards:* Federal Pell, FSEOG, state, private, college/university gift aid from institutional funds.

GIFT AID (NON-NEED-BASED) *Total amount:* $2,569,614 (96% institutional, 4% external sources). *Receiving aid:* Freshmen: 12% (39). Undergraduates: 11% (103). *Average award:* Freshmen: $11,327. Undergraduates: $12,984. *Scholarships, grants, and awards by category:* Academic interests/achievement: biological sciences, business, communication, education, English, general academic interests/achievements, mathematics, physical sciences, premedicine, religion/biblical studies, social sciences. *Creative arts/performance:* art/fine arts, music, theater/drama. *Special achievements/activities:* community service, leadership, religious involvement. *Special characteristics:* children and siblings of alumni, children of faculty/staff, local/state students, relatives of clergy, religious affiliation, siblings of current students. *Tuition waivers:* Full or partial for employees or children of employees.

LOANS *Student loans:* $7,645,088 (67% need-based, 33% non-need-based). 73% of past graduating class borrowed through all loan programs. *Average indebtedness per student:* $34,875. *Average need-based loan:* Freshmen: $4476. Undergraduates: $5129. *Parent loans:* $1,189,522 (55% need-based, 45% non-need-based). *Programs:* Federal Direct (Subsidized and Unsubsidized Stafford, PLUS), Perkins, state.

WORK-STUDY *Federal work-study:* Total amount: $125,034; jobs available. *State or other work-study/employment:* Total amount: $9047 (100% need-based). Part-time jobs available.

APPLYING FOR FINANCIAL AID *Required financial aid forms:* FAFSA, institution's own form, Core Residency Form. *Financial aid deadline (priority):* 3/15. *Notification date:* Continuous beginning 2/1. Students must reply within 2 weeks of notification.

CONTACT Mrs. Glenda Huff, Director of Financial Aid, Howard Payne University, 1000 Fisk Avenue, Brownwood, TX 76801, 325-649-8014 or toll-free 800-880-4478. *Fax:* 325-649-8973. *E-mail:* ghuff@hputx.edu.
Website: http://www.hputx.edu/.

HOWARD UNIVERSITY
Washington, DC

Tuition & fees: N/R	Average undergraduate aid package: $14,601

ABOUT THE INSTITUTION Independent, coed. *Awards:* certificates, bachelor's, master's, and doctoral degrees. 65 undergraduate majors. *Total enrollment:* 10,002. Undergraduates: 6,883. Freshmen: 1,676. Federal methodology is used as a basis for awarding need-based institutional aid.
FRESHMAN FINANCIAL AID (Fall 2015) 1,445 applied for aid; of those 90% were deemed to have need. 96% of freshmen with need received aid; of those 6% had need fully met. *Average percent of need met:* 63% (excluding resources awarded to replace EFC). *Average financial aid package:* $14,968 (excluding resources awarded to replace EFC). 10% of all full-time freshmen had no need and received non-need-based gift aid.
UNDERGRADUATE FINANCIAL AID (Fall 2015) 5,440 applied for aid; of those 91% were deemed to have need. 97% of undergraduates with need received aid; of those 7% had need fully met. *Average percent of need met:* 62% (excluding resources awarded to replace EFC). *Average financial aid package:* $14,601 (excluding resources awarded to replace EFC). 8% of all full-time undergraduates had no need and received non-need-based gift aid.
GIFT AID (NEED-BASED) *Total amount:* $29,136,293 (52% federal, 48% institutional). *Receiving aid:* Freshmen: 50% (796); all full-time undergraduates: 50% (3,107). *Average award:* Freshmen $8793; Undergraduates: $8264. *Scholarships, grants, and awards:* Federal Pell, FSEOG, state, private, college/university gift aid from institutional funds, Federal Nursing.
GIFT AID (NON-NEED-BASED) *Total amount:* $50,579,202 (1% federal, 99% institutional). *Receiving aid:* Freshmen: 34% (537). Undergraduates: 32% (1,994). *Average award:* Freshmen: $28,263. Undergraduates: $27,095. *Scholarships, grants, and awards by category: Academic interests/achievement:* architecture, biological sciences, business, communication, computer science, education, engineering/technologies, English, foreign languages, health fields, humanities, international studies, mathematics, military science, physical sciences, premedicine, religion/biblical studies, social sciences. *Creative arts/performance:* applied art and design, art/fine arts, cinema/film/broadcasting, dance, journalism/publications, music, performing arts, theater/drama. *Special achievements/activities:* cheerleading/drum major, general special achievements/activities, leadership, memberships, religious involvement. *Special characteristics:* adult students, ethnic background, first-generation college students, handicapped students, international students, local/state students, married students, members of minority groups, previous college experience, religious affiliation. *ROTC:* Army, Air Force.
LOANS *Student loans:* $40,543,482 (38% need-based, 62% non-need-based). 79% of past graduating class borrowed through all loan programs. *Average indebtedness per student:* $26,181. *Average need-based loan:* Freshmen: $3377. Undergraduates: $4184. *Parent loans:* $44,243,025 (100% non-need-based). *Programs:* Federal Direct (Subsidized and Unsubsidized Stafford, PLUS), Perkins, Federal Nursing, district, college/university.
WORK-STUDY *Federal work-study:* jobs available. *State or other work-study/employment:* Total amount: $815,521 (100% non-need-based). Part-time jobs available.
ATHLETIC AWARDS Total amount: $6,620,728 (100% non-need-based).
APPLYING FOR FINANCIAL AID *Required financial aid form:* FAFSA. *Financial aid deadline:* 5/1 (priority: 2/1). *Notification date:* Continuous beginning 4/1. Students must reply by 2/16 or within 3 weeks of notification.
CONTACT Office of Financial Aid, Howard University, 2400 Sixth Street, NW, Washington, DC 20059, 202-806-2864 or toll-free 800-822-6363. *Fax:* 202-806-2818. *Website:* http://www.howard.edu/.

HULT INTERNATIONAL BUSINESS SCHOOL
Cambridge, MA

Tuition & fees: N/R	Average undergraduate aid package: $14,476

ABOUT THE INSTITUTION Independent, coed. 1 undergraduate major. Institutional methodology is used as a basis for awarding need-based institutional aid.
FRESHMAN FINANCIAL AID (Fall 2016, est.) 112 applied for aid; of those 100% were deemed to have need. 100% of freshmen with need received aid. *Average financial aid package:* $14,470 (excluding resources awarded to replace EFC). 16% of all full-time freshmen had no need and received non-need-based gift aid.
UNDERGRADUATE FINANCIAL AID (Fall 2016, est.) 352 applied for aid; of those 100% were deemed to have need. 100% of undergraduates with need received aid. *Average financial aid package:* $14,476 (excluding resources awarded to replace EFC). 9% of all full-time undergraduates had no need and received non-need-based gift aid.
GIFT AID (NEED-BASED) *Total amount:* $5,195,994 (2% federal, 98% institutional). *Receiving aid:* Freshmen: 65% (94); all full-time undergraduates: 76% (316). *Average award:* Freshmen: $12,143; Undergraduates: $11,717. *Scholarships, grants, and awards:* college/university gift aid from institutional funds.
GIFT AID (NON-NEED-BASED) *Receiving aid:* Freshmen: 69% (99). Undergraduates: 54% (225). *Average award:* Freshmen: $6221. Undergraduates: $5736. *Scholarships, grants, and awards by category: Academic interests/achievement:* general academic interests/achievements.
LOANS *Student loans:* $608,443 (15% need-based, 85% non-need-based). 89% of past graduating class borrowed through all loan programs. *Average indebtedness per student:* $16,053. *Parent loans:* $185,795 (100% non-need-based).
APPLYING FOR FINANCIAL AID *Required financial aid form:* institution's own form. *Financial aid deadline:* Continuous. *Notification date:* Continuous beginning 11/15. Students must reply by 5/1.
CONTACT Karen Van Dyne, Director of Financial Aid, Hult International Business School, 1 Education Street, Cambridge, MA 02141, 617-619-1097. *E-mail:* karen.vandyne@hult.edu.
Website: http://www.hult.edu/.

HUMBOLDT STATE UNIVERSITY
Arcata, CA

Tuition & fees (CA res): $7212	Average undergraduate aid package: $13,650

ABOUT THE INSTITUTION State-supported, coed. *Awards:* certificates, bachelor's, and master's degrees. 67 undergraduate majors. *Total enrollment:* 8,503. Undergraduates: 7,968. Freshmen: 1,295. Federal methodology is used as a basis for awarding need-based institutional aid.
UNDERGRADUATE EXPENSES for 2017–2018 *Application fee:* $55. *Tuition, state resident:* full-time $5472; part-time $3174 per year. *Tuition, non-resident:* full-time $16,632; part-time $372 per credit hour. *Required fees:* full-time $1740; $1306 per year. Full-time tuition and fees vary according to degree level. Part-time tuition and fees vary according to course load and degree level. *College room and board:* $12,638; *Room only:* $7726. Room and board charges vary according to board plan and housing facility.
FRESHMAN FINANCIAL AID (Fall 2016, est.) 1,167 applied for aid; of those 80% were deemed to have need. 98% of freshmen with need received aid; of those 9% had need fully met. *Average percent of need met:* 69% (excluding resources awarded to replace EFC). *Average financial aid package:* $13,687 (excluding resources awarded to replace EFC). 6% of all full-time freshmen had no need and received non-need-based gift aid.
UNDERGRADUATE FINANCIAL AID (Fall 2016, est.) 6,547 applied for aid; of those 89% were deemed to have need. 98% of undergraduates with need received aid; of those 7% had need fully met. *Average percent of need met:* 68% (excluding resources awarded to replace EFC). *Average financial aid package:* $13,650 (excluding resources awarded to replace EFC). 4% of all full-time undergraduates had no need and received non-need-based gift aid.

GIFT AID (NEED-BASED) *Total amount:* $51,043,717 (43% federal, 29% state, 25% institutional, 3% external sources). *Receiving aid:* Freshmen: 68% (869); all full-time undergraduates: 73% (5,450). *Average award:* Freshmen: $9186; Undergraduates: $8692. *Scholarships, grants, and awards:* Federal Pell, FSEOG, state, private, college/university gift aid from institutional funds.

GIFT AID (NON-NEED-BASED) *Total amount:* $607,423 (27% state, 12% institutional, 61% external sources). *Receiving aid:* Freshmen: 1% (16). Undergraduates: 1% (84). *Average award:* Freshmen: $650. Undergraduates: $722. *Scholarships, grants, and awards by category:* Academic interests/achievement: 354 awards ($617,022 total): general academic interests/achievements. *Tuition waivers:* Full or partial for employees or children of employees.

LOANS *Student loans:* $31,971,459 (86% need-based, 14% non-need-based). 74% of past graduating class borrowed through all loan programs. *Average indebtedness per student:* $24,337. *Average need-based loan:* Freshmen: $5945. Undergraduates: $7074. *Parent loans:* $3,570,626 (30% need-based, 70% non-need-based). *Programs:* Federal Direct (Subsidized and Unsubsidized Stafford, PLUS), Perkins, college/university.

WORK-STUDY *Federal work-study:* Total amount: $630,357; 309 jobs averaging $2040.

ATHLETIC AWARDS Total amount: $876,697 (64% need-based, 36% non-need-based).

APPLYING FOR FINANCIAL AID *Required financial aid form:* FAFSA. *Financial aid deadline (priority):* 3/2. *Notification date:* Continuous beginning 4/1. Students must reply within 4 weeks of notification.

CONTACT Peggy Metzger, Director of Financial Aid, Humboldt State University, 1 Harpst Street, Arcata, CA 95521-8299, 707-826-4321 or toll-free 866-850-9556. *E-mail:* pmetzger@humboldt.edu.
Website: http://www.humboldt.edu/.

HUMPHREYS COLLEGE
Stockton, CA

CONTACT Rita Franco, Director of Financial Aid, Humphreys College, 6650 Inglewood Avenue, Stockton, CA 95207-3896, 209-478-0800. *Fax:* 209-235-2983. *Website:* http://www.humphreys.edu/.

HUNTER COLLEGE OF THE CITY UNIVERSITY OF NEW YORK
New York, NY

CONTACT Aristalia Cortorreal Diaz, Director of Financial Aid, Hunter College of the City University of New York, 695 Park Avenue, New York, NY 10065-5085, 212-772-4400. *Fax:* 212-650-3666. *E-mail:* aristalia@hunter.cuny.edu. *Website:* http://www.hunter.cuny.edu/.

HUNTINGDON COLLEGE
Montgomery, AL

Tuition & fees: $26,400	Average undergraduate aid package: $18,551

ABOUT THE INSTITUTION Independent United Methodist, coed. *Awards:* bachelor's degrees. 33 undergraduate majors. *Total enrollment:* 1,148. Undergraduates: 1,148. Freshmen: 277. Both federal and institutional methodology are used as a basis for awarding need-based institutional aid.

UNDERGRADUATE EXPENSES for 2017–2018 *Comprehensive fee:* $35,900 includes full-time tuition ($24,900), mandatory fees ($1500), and room and board ($9500). Full-time tuition and fees vary according to course load, program, and student level. Room and board charges vary according to housing facility. *Part-time tuition:* $1040 per credit hour. Part-time tuition and fees vary according to course load and program. *Payment plan:* Guaranteed tuition.

FRESHMAN FINANCIAL AID (Fall 2016, est.) 249 applied for aid; of those 89% were deemed to have need. 100% of freshmen with need received aid; of those 12%

had need fully met. *Average percent of need met:* 68% (excluding resources awarded to replace EFC). *Average financial aid package:* $19,204 (excluding resources awarded to replace EFC). 18% of all full-time freshmen had no need and received non-need-based gift aid.

UNDERGRADUATE FINANCIAL AID (Fall 2016, est.) 757 applied for aid; of those 89% were deemed to have need. 100% of undergraduates with need received aid; of those 14% had need fully met. *Average percent of need met:* 68% (excluding resources awarded to replace EFC). *Average financial aid package:* $18,551 (excluding resources awarded to replace EFC). 23% of all full-time undergraduates had no need and received non-need-based gift aid.

GIFT AID (NEED-BASED) *Total amount:* $10,696,245 (23% federal, 3% state, 68% institutional, 6% external sources). *Receiving aid:* Freshmen: 82% (222); all full-time undergraduates: 76% (670). *Average award:* Freshmen: $16,346; Undergraduates: $15,171. *Scholarships, grants, and awards:* Federal Pell, FSEOG, state, private, college/university gift aid from institutional funds.

GIFT AID (NON-NEED-BASED) *Total amount:* $3,132,055 (3% state, 82% institutional, 15% external sources). *Receiving aid:* Freshmen: 9% (25). Undergraduates: 8% (73). *Average award:* Freshmen: $12,253. Undergraduates: $11,209. *Scholarships, grants, and awards by category:* Academic interests/achievement: 111 awards ($1,164,118 total): biological sciences, computer science, general academic interests/achievements, mathematics. *Creative arts/performance:* 118 awards ($834,027 total): dance, music, performing arts. *Special achievements/activities:* 16 awards ($176,500 total): cheerleading/drum major, community service, junior miss. *Special characteristics:* 276 awards ($2,728,970 total): children and siblings of alumni, children of faculty/staff, children of workers in trades, international students, local/state students, religious affiliation, spouses of current students, veterans, veterans' children. *Tuition waivers:* Full or partial for children of alumni, employees or children of employees. *ROTC:* Army cooperative, Air Force cooperative.

LOANS *Student loans:* $6,983,555 (77% need-based, 23% non-need-based). 81% of past graduating class borrowed through all loan programs. *Average indebtedness per student:* $33,503. *Average need-based loan:* Freshmen: $3264. Undergraduates: $4023. *Parent loans:* $2,104,503 (58% need-based, 42% non-need-based). *Programs:* Federal Direct (Subsidized and Unsubsidized Stafford, PLUS), Perkins.

WORK-STUDY *Federal work-study:* Total amount: $94,170; 147 jobs averaging $901.

APPLYING FOR FINANCIAL AID *Required financial aid form:* FAFSA. *Financial aid deadline (priority):* 3/1. *Notification date:* Continuous beginning 3/1. Students must reply by 5/1 or within 2 weeks of notification.

CONTACT Ms. Brittany Nicole Davis, Director of Financial Aid, Huntingdon College, 1500 East Fairview Avenue, Montgomery, AL 36106-2148, 334-833-4428 or toll-free 800-763-0313. *Fax:* 334-833-4235. *E-mail:* finaid@hawks.huntingdon.edu. *Website:* http://www.huntingdon.edu/.

HUNTINGTON UNIVERSITY
Huntington, IN

Comprehensive fee: $33,996	Average undergraduate aid package: $22,123

ABOUT THE INSTITUTION Independent Church of the United Brethren in Christ, coed. *Awards:* associate, bachelor's, master's, and doctoral degrees. 87 undergraduate majors. *Total enrollment:* 1,295. Undergraduates: 996. Freshmen: 196. Federal methodology is used as a basis for awarding need-based institutional aid.

UNDERGRADUATE EXPENSES for 2017–2018 *Application fee:* $20. *Comprehensive fee:* $33,996 includes full-time tuition ($24,694), mandatory fees ($846), and room and board ($8456). *College room only:* $3980.

FRESHMAN FINANCIAL AID (Fall 2016, est.) 172 applied for aid; of those 90% were deemed to have need. 100% of freshmen with need received aid; of those 2% had need fully met. *Average percent of need met:* 85% (excluding resources awarded to replace EFC). *Average financial aid package:* $19,592 (excluding resources awarded to replace EFC). 21% of all full-time freshmen had no need and received non-need-based gift aid.

UNDERGRADUATE FINANCIAL AID (Fall 2016, est.) 743 applied for aid; of those 87% were deemed to have need. 100% of undergraduates with need received aid; of those .2% had need fully met. *Average percent of need met:* 82% (excluding resources awarded to replace EFC). *Average financial aid package:* $22,123 (excluding resources awarded to replace EFC). 18% of all full-time undergraduates had no need and received non-need-based gift aid.

GIFT AID (NEED-BASED) *Total amount:* $10,726,665 (12% federal, 11% state, 71% institutional, 6% external sources). *Receiving aid:* Freshmen: 60% (118); all full-time undergraduates: 60% (495). *Average award:* Freshmen: $8834; Undergraduates: $9657. *Scholarships, grants, and awards:* Federal Pell, FSEOG, state, private, college/university gift aid from institutional funds.

GIFT AID (NON-NEED-BASED) *Receiving aid:* Freshmen: 78% (152). Undergraduates: 70% (581). *Scholarships, grants, and awards by category: Academic interests/achievement:* communication, general academic interests/achievements. *Creative arts/performance:* applied art and design, art/fine arts, cinema/film/broadcasting, creative writing, journalism/publications, music, performing arts, theater/drama. *Special achievements/activities:* cheerleading/drum major. *Special characteristics:* children and siblings of alumni, children of faculty/staff, ethnic background, international students, local/state students, relatives of clergy, religious affiliation, veterans, veterans' children.

LOANS *Student loans:* $5,303,275 (100% need-based). 78% of past graduating class borrowed through all loan programs. *Average indebtedness per student:* $32,509. *Average need-based loan:* Freshmen: $3318. Undergraduates: $4538. *Parent loans:* $1,404,748 (100% need-based). *Programs:* Federal Direct (Subsidized and Unsubsidized Stafford, PLUS), Perkins.

WORK-STUDY *Federal work-study:* Total amount: $85,984; jobs available.

ATHLETIC AWARDS Total amount: $1,286,000 (100% need-based).

APPLYING FOR FINANCIAL AID *Required financial aid form:* FAFSA. *Financial aid deadline (priority):* 3/10. *Notification date:* Continuous beginning 3/15. Students must reply by 5/1 or within 2 weeks of notification.

CONTACT Lisa Montany, Director of Financial Aid, Huntington University, 2303 College Avenue, Huntington, IN 46750, 260-359-4014 or toll-free 800-642-6493. *Fax:* 260-358-3699. *E-mail:* finaid@huntington.edu.

Website: http://www.huntington.edu/.

HUNTSVILLE BIBLE COLLEGE
Huntsville, AL

CONTACT Financial Aid Office, Huntsville Bible College, 904 Oakwood Avenue, Huntsville, AL 35811-1632, 256-539-0834.

Website: http://www.hbc1.edu/.

HUSSIAN COLLEGE, SCHOOL OF ART
Philadelphia, PA

CONTACT Financial Aid Office, Hussian College, School of Art, The Bourse - Suite 300, 111 South Independence Mall East, Philadelphia, PA 19106, 215-981-0900. *Website:* http://www.hussiancollege.edu/.

HUSSON UNIVERSITY
Bangor, ME

Tuition & fees: $17,561	Average undergraduate aid package: $12,592

ABOUT THE INSTITUTION Independent, coed. *Awards:* certificates, associate, bachelor's, master's, and doctoral degrees. 46 undergraduate majors. *Total enrollment:* 3,669. Undergraduates: 2,834. Freshmen: 626. Federal methodology is used as a basis for awarding need-based institutional aid.

UNDERGRADUATE EXPENSES for 2017–2018 *Application fee:* $40. *One-time required fee:* $125. *Comprehensive fee:* $27,059 includes full-time tuition ($17,081), mandatory fees ($480), and room and board ($9498). *College room only:* $4760. Full-time tuition and fees vary according to class time and location. Room and board charges vary according to board plan and housing facility. *Part-time tuition:* $551 per credit. *Part-time fees:* $110 per year. Part-time tuition and fees vary according to class time, course load, and location. *Payment plan:* Tuition prepayment.

FRESHMAN FINANCIAL AID (Fall 2016, est.) 576 applied for aid; of those 86% were deemed to have need. 100% of freshmen with need received aid; of those 27%

had need fully met. *Average percent of need met:* 72% (excluding resources awarded to replace EFC). *Average financial aid package:* $13,131 (excluding resources awarded to replace EFC). 11% of all full-time freshmen had no need and received non-need-based gift aid.

UNDERGRADUATE FINANCIAL AID (Fall 2016, est.) 2,208 applied for aid; of those 90% were deemed to have need. 100% of undergraduates with need received aid; of those 20% had need fully met. *Average percent of need met:* 65% (excluding resources awarded to replace EFC). *Average financial aid package:* $12,592 (excluding resources awarded to replace EFC). 8% of all full-time undergraduates had no need and received non-need-based gift aid.

GIFT AID (NEED-BASED) *Total amount:* $17,953,698 (31% federal, 7% state, 56% institutional, 6% external sources). *Receiving aid:* Freshmen: 72% (444); all full-time undergraduates: 71% (1,671). *Average award:* Freshmen: $9452; Undergraduates: $8302. *Scholarships, grants, and awards:* Federal Pell, FSEOG, state, private, college/university gift aid from institutional funds.

GIFT AID (NON-NEED-BASED) *Total amount:* $1,311,816 (85% institutional, 15% external sources). *Receiving aid:* Freshmen: 79% (486). Undergraduates: 67% (1,562). *Average award:* Freshmen: $3346. Undergraduates: $2666. *Scholarships, grants, and awards by category: Academic interests/achievement:* biological sciences, business, communication, computer science, education, English, general academic interests/achievements, health fields, home economics, humanities, physical sciences, premedicine, social sciences. *Creative arts/performance:* cinema/film/broadcasting, journalism/publications, theater/drama. *Special achievements/activities:* leadership. *Special characteristics:* children and siblings of alumni, children of faculty/staff, children of union members/company employees, ethnic background, international students, members of minority groups, out-of-state students. *Tuition waivers:* Full or partial for employees or children of employees, senior citizens. *ROTC:* Army, Naval cooperative.

LOANS *Student loans:* $19,352,985 (75% need-based, 25% non-need-based). 88% of past graduating class borrowed through all loan programs. *Average indebtedness per student:* $33,412. *Average need-based loan:* Freshmen: $3300. Undergraduates: $4248. *Parent loans:* $3,533,563 (46% need-based, 54% non-need-based). *Programs:* Federal Direct (Subsidized and Unsubsidized Stafford, PLUS), Perkins, state, alternative loans.

WORK-STUDY *Federal work-study:* Total amount: $1,533,573; 425 jobs averaging $1600.

APPLYING FOR FINANCIAL AID *Required financial aid form:* FAFSA. *Financial aid deadline:* 4/15. *Notification date:* Continuous beginning 12/1. Students must reply by 5/1 or within 2 weeks of notification.

CONTACT Anne Tabor, Director of Financial Aid, Husson University, 1 College Circle, Bangor, ME 04401, 207-941-7156 or toll-free 800-4-HUSSON. *Fax:* 207-941-7932. *E-mail:* tabora@husson.edu.

Website: http://www.husson.edu/.

HUSTON-TILLOTSON UNIVERSITY
Austin, TX

Tuition & fees: $14,346	Average undergraduate aid package: N/A

ABOUT THE INSTITUTION Independent interdenominational, coed. *Awards:* associate, bachelor's, and master's degrees. 26 undergraduate majors. *Total enrollment:* 1,012. Undergraduates: 965. Freshmen: 145. Both federal and institutional methodology are used as a basis for awarding need-based institutional aid.

UNDERGRADUATE EXPENSES for 2016–2017 *Application fee:* $25. *Comprehensive fee:* $21,914 includes full-time tuition ($12,262), mandatory fees ($2084), and room and board ($7568). *College room only:* $3642. Full-time tuition and fees vary according to course load. Room and board charges vary according to housing facility. *Part-time tuition:* $410 per credit hour. Part-time tuition and fees vary according to course load.

GIFT AID (NEED-BASED) *Scholarships, grants, and awards:* Federal Pell, FSEOG, state, private, college/university gift aid from institutional funds, United Negro College Fund.

GIFT AID (NON-NEED-BASED) *Scholarships, grants, and awards by category: Academic interests/achievement:* general academic interests/achievements. *Creative arts/performance:* music. *Special characteristics:* general special characteristics. *Tuition waivers:* Full or partial for employees or children of employees.

LOANS *Programs:* Federal Direct (Subsidized and Unsubsidized Stafford, PLUS), state, private loans.
WORK-STUDY Federal work-study jobs available. *State or other work-study/ employment:* Part-time jobs available.
APPLYING FOR FINANCIAL AID *Required financial aid forms:* FAFSA, institution's own form. *Financial aid deadline (priority):* 3/15. *Notification date:* Continuous. Students must reply within 2 weeks of notification.
CONTACT Office of Financial Aid, Huston-Tillotson University, 900 Chicon Street, Austin, TX 78702, 512-505-3031. *Fax:* 512-505-3192.
Website: http://www.htu.edu/.

IDAHO STATE UNIVERSITY
Pocatello, ID

Tuition & fees (ID res): $6956	Average undergraduate aid package: $8494

ABOUT THE INSTITUTION State-supported, coed. *Awards:* certificates, bachelor's, master's, and doctoral degrees. 98 undergraduate majors. *Total enrollment:* 13,062. Undergraduates: 11,087. Freshmen: 1,342. Federal methodology is used as a basis for awarding need-based institutional aid.
UNDERGRADUATE EXPENSES for 2017–2018 *Application fee:* $50. *Tuition, state resident:* full-time $5243; part-time $348 per credit hour. *Tuition, nonresident:* full-time $19,310; part-time $576 per credit hour. *Required fees:* full-time $1713. Full-time tuition and fees vary according to course load, program, and reciprocity agreements. Part-time tuition and fees vary according to course load. *College room and board:* $6663; *Room only:* $2875. Room and board charges vary according to board plan, housing facility, and location. *Payment plan:* Guaranteed tuition.
FRESHMAN FINANCIAL AID (Fall 2015) 1,084 applied for aid; of those 80% were deemed to have need. 98% of freshmen with need received aid; of those 6% had need fully met. *Average percent of need met:* 46% (excluding resources awarded to replace EFC). *Average financial aid package:* $8065 (excluding resources awarded to replace EFC). 12% of all full-time freshmen had no need and received non-need-based gift aid.
UNDERGRADUATE FINANCIAL AID (Fall 2015) 4,967 applied for aid; of those 87% were deemed to have need. 98% of undergraduates with need received aid; of those 5% had need fully met. *Average percent of need met:* 46% (excluding resources awarded to replace EFC). *Average financial aid package:* $8494 (excluding resources awarded to replace EFC). 8% of all full-time undergraduates had no need and received non-need-based gift aid.
GIFT AID (NEED-BASED) *Total amount:* $20,218,002 (78% federal, 4% state, 14% institutional, 4% external sources). *Receiving aid:* Freshmen: 49% (645); all full-time undergraduates: 47% (3,233). *Average award:* Freshmen: $4955; Undergraduates: $4686. *Scholarships, grants, and awards:* Federal Pell, FSEOG, state, private, college/university gift aid from institutional funds, Federal Nursing.
GIFT AID (NON-NEED-BASED) *Total amount:* $2,418,827 (1% federal, 4% state, 71% institutional, 24% external sources). *Receiving aid:* Freshmen: 34% (446). Undergraduates: 21% (1,458). *Average award:* Freshmen: $2324. Undergraduates: $2251. *Scholarships, grants, and awards by category:* Academic interests/ achievement: architecture, biological sciences, business, communication, computer science, education, engineering/technologies, English, foreign languages, general academic interests/achievements, home economics, humanities, international studies, mathematics, military science, physical sciences, premedicine, social sciences. *Creative arts/performance:* art/fine arts, dance, debating, journalism/publications, music, performing arts, theater/drama. *Special achievements/activities:* cheerleading/drum major, general special achievements/activities. *Special characteristics:* children of faculty/staff, children with a deceased or disabled parent, ethnic background, first-generation college students, general special characteristics, handicapped students, international students, local/state students, members of minority groups, out-of-state students. *Tuition waivers:* Full or partial for employees or children of employees, senior citizens. *ROTC:* Army.
LOANS *Student loans:* $32,823,642 (95% need-based, 5% non-need-based). 66% of past graduating class borrowed through all loan programs. *Average indebtedness per student:* $30,617. *Average need-based loan:* Freshmen: $3067. Undergraduates: $3834. *Parent loans:* $1,223,875 (81% need-based, 19% non-need-based). *Programs:* Federal Direct (Subsidized and Unsubsidized Stafford, PLUS), Perkins, Federal Nursing.

WORK-STUDY *Federal work-study:* jobs available. *State or other work-study/employment:* Total amount: $314,843 (100% need-based). Part-time jobs available.
ATHLETIC AWARDS Total amount: $2,181,294 (28% need-based, 72% non-need-based).
APPLYING FOR FINANCIAL AID *Required financial aid form:* FAFSA. *Financial aid deadline (priority):* 3/1. *Notification date:* Continuous beginning 4/1.
CONTACT Mr. James R. Martin, Director of Financial Aid, Idaho State University, 921 South 8th Avenue, Museum Building 337, Stop 8077, Pocatello, ID 83209-8077, 208-282-2756. *Fax:* 208-282-4755. *E-mail:* finaidem@isu.edu.
Website: http://www.isu.edu/.

IGLOBAL UNIVERSITY
Vienna, VA

CONTACT Financial Aid Office, IGlobal University, 8133 Leesburg Pike, #230, Vienna, VA 22182, 703-941-2020.
Website: http://www.iglobal.edu/.

ILLINOIS COLLEGE
Jacksonville, IL

Tuition & fees: $32,140	Average undergraduate aid package: $27,778

ABOUT THE INSTITUTION Independent interdenominational, coed. *Awards:* bachelor's and master's degrees. 44 undergraduate majors. *Total enrollment:* 960. Undergraduates: 955. Freshmen: 293. Federal methodology is used as a basis for awarding need-based institutional aid.
UNDERGRADUATE EXPENSES for 2017–2018 *Comprehensive fee:* $41,330 includes full-time tuition ($31,590), mandatory fees ($550), and room and board ($9190). Room and board charges vary according to board plan and housing facility. *Part-time tuition:* $970 per credit hour. Part-time tuition and fees vary according to course load.
FRESHMAN FINANCIAL AID (Fall 2015) 220 applied for aid; of those 94% were deemed to have need. 100% of freshmen with need received aid; of those 15% had need fully met. *Average percent of need met:* 88% (excluding resources awarded to replace EFC). *Average financial aid package:* $29,911 (excluding resources awarded to replace EFC). 14% of all full-time freshmen had no need and received non-need-based gift aid.
UNDERGRADUATE FINANCIAL AID (Fall 2015) 849 applied for aid; of those 93% were deemed to have need. 100% of undergraduates with need received aid; of those 20% had need fully met. *Average percent of need met:* 87% (excluding resources awarded to replace EFC). *Average financial aid package:* $27,778 (excluding resources awarded to replace EFC). 15% of all full-time undergraduates had no need and received non-need-based gift aid.
GIFT AID (NEED-BASED) *Total amount:* $17,584,289 (11% federal, 10% state, 77% institutional, 2% external sources). *Receiving aid:* Freshmen: 86% (206); all full-time undergraduates: 85% (792). *Average award:* Freshmen: $24,615; Undergraduates: $22,176. *Scholarships, grants, and awards:* Federal Pell, FSEOG, state, private, college/university gift aid from institutional funds.
GIFT AID (NON-NEED-BASED) *Total amount:* $3,268,946 (96% institutional, 4% external sources). *Receiving aid:* Freshmen: 9% (22). Undergraduates: 10% (98). *Average award:* Freshmen: $19,913. Undergraduates: $17,939. *Scholarships, grants, and awards by category:* Academic interests/achievement: general academic interests/achievements. *Creative arts/performance:* art/fine arts, music, theater/drama. *Special characteristics:* children of faculty/staff, international students, previous college experience. *Tuition waivers:* Full or partial for employees or children of employees.
LOANS *Student loans:* $7,342,005 (70% need-based, 30% non-need-based). 78% of past graduating class borrowed through all loan programs. *Average indebtedness per student:* $32,000. *Average need-based loan:* Freshmen: $4641. Undergraduates: $5289. *Parent loans:* $1,882,064 (39% need-based, 61% non-need-based). *Programs:* Federal Direct (Subsidized and Unsubsidized Stafford, PLUS), Perkins.
WORK-STUDY *Federal work-study:* jobs available.

APPLYING FOR FINANCIAL AID *Required financial aid form:* FAFSA. *Financial aid deadline (priority):* 10/31. **Notification date:** Continuous beginning 3/1. Students must reply within 2 weeks of notification.

CONTACT Office of Financial Aid, Illinois College, 1101 West College Avenue, Jacksonville, IL 62650-2299, 217-245-3035 or toll-free 866-464-5265. *Fax:* 217-245-3274. *E-mail:* sfs@mail.ic.edu.

Website: http://www.ic.edu/.

THE ILLINOIS INSTITUTE OF ART–CHICAGO
Chicago, IL

Financial Aid Office, The Illinois Institute of Art–Chicago, 350 North Orleans Street, Suite 136, Chicago, IL 60654-1593, 800-351-3450.

THE ILLINOIS INSTITUTE OF ART–SCHAUMBURG
Schaumburg, IL

CONTACT Financial Aid Office, The Illinois Institute of Art–Schaumburg, 1000 North Plaza Drive, Suite 100, Schaumburg, IL 60173, 847-619-3450 or toll-free 800-314-3450.

Website: http://www.artinstitutes.edu/schaumburg/.

ILLINOIS INSTITUTE OF TECHNOLOGY
Chicago, IL

Tuition & fees: $46,323	Average undergraduate aid package: $36,732

ABOUT THE INSTITUTION Independent, coed. *Awards:* certificates, bachelor's, master's, and doctoral degrees. 38 undergraduate majors. *Total enrollment:* 7,792. Undergraduates: 2,991. Freshmen: 479. Federal methodology is used as a basis for awarding need-based institutional aid.

UNDERGRADUATE EXPENSES for 2016–2017 *One-time required fee:* $330. *Comprehensive fee:* $59,141 includes full-time tuition ($43,500), mandatory fees ($2823), and room and board ($12,818). *College room only:* $6062. Full-time tuition and fees vary according to student level. Room and board charges vary according to board plan and housing facility. *Part-time tuition:* $1359 per credit hour. *Part-time fees:* $40 per course; $155 per term. Part-time tuition and fees vary according to course load and student level.

FRESHMAN FINANCIAL AID (Fall 2015) 350 applied for aid; of those 92% were deemed to have need. 100% of freshmen with need received aid; of those 18% had need fully met. *Average percent of need met:* 82% (excluding resources awarded to replace EFC). *Average financial aid package:* $39,070 (excluding resources awarded to replace EFC). 33% of all full-time freshmen had no need and received non-need-based gift aid.

UNDERGRADUATE FINANCIAL AID (Fall 2015) 1,685 applied for aid; of those 96% were deemed to have need. 100% of undergraduates with need received aid; of those 12% had need fully met. *Average percent of need met:* 76% (excluding resources awarded to replace EFC). *Average financial aid package:* $36,732 (excluding resources awarded to replace EFC). 38% of all full-time undergraduates had no need and received non-need-based gift aid.

GIFT AID (NEED-BASED) *Total amount:* $50,515,040 (11% federal, 5% state, 83% institutional, 1% external sources). *Receiving aid:* Freshmen: 67% (320); all full-time undergraduates: 57% (1,601). *Average award:* Freshmen: $33,676; Undergraduates: $31,201. *Scholarships, grants, and awards:* Federal Pell, FSEOG, state, private, college/university gift aid from institutional funds.

GIFT AID (NON-NEED-BASED) *Total amount:* $26,547,287 (1% federal, 98% institutional, 1% external sources). *Receiving aid:* Freshmen: 10% (47). Undergraduates: 5% (141). *Average award:* Freshmen: $25,552. Undergraduates: $23,056.

Scholarships, grants, and awards by category: Academic interests/achievement: architecture, biological sciences, business, communication, computer science, engineering/technologies, general academic interests/achievements, humanities, mathematics, premedicine, social sciences. *Creative arts/performance:* applied art and design. *Special achievements/activities:* community service, general special achievements/activities, hobbies/interests, leadership, memberships. *Special characteristics:* children and siblings of alumni, children of faculty/staff, children of public servants, general special characteristics, international students, local/state students, previous college experience, veterans, veterans' children. *Tuition waivers:* Full or partial for employees or children of employees. *ROTC:* Army, Naval, Air Force.

LOANS *Student loans:* $12,247,038 (84% need-based, 16% non-need-based). 59% of past graduating class borrowed through all loan programs. *Average indebtedness per student:* $30,569. *Average need-based loan:* Freshmen: $3861. Undergraduates: $5011. *Parent loans:* $5,892,160 (51% need-based, 49% non-need-based).

WORK-STUDY *Federal work-study:* jobs available. *State or other work-study/employment:* Part-time jobs available.

APPLYING FOR FINANCIAL AID *Required financial aid form:* FAFSA. *Financial aid deadline (priority):* 1/15. **Notification date:** Continuous beginning 3/1.

CONTACT Abby McGrath, Director of Financial Aid, Illinois Institute of Technology, 3300 South Federal Street, Chicago, IL 60616, 312-567-5730 or toll-free 800-448-2329. *Fax:* 312-567-3982. *E-mail:* finaid@iit.edu.

Website: http://www.iit.edu/.

ILLINOIS STATE UNIVERSITY
Normal, IL

CONTACT Mr. David Krueger, Associate Director of Financial Aid, Illinois State University, Campus Box 2320, Normal, IL 61790-2320, 309-438-2231 or toll-free 800-366-2478. *Fax:* 309-438-3755. *E-mail:* financialaid@illinoisitate.edu.

Website: http://www.illinoisstate.edu/.

ILLINOIS WESLEYAN UNIVERSITY
Bloomington, IL

Tuition & fees: $45,856	Average undergraduate aid package: $32,607

ABOUT THE INSTITUTION Independent, coed. *Awards:* bachelor's degrees. 48 undergraduate majors. *Total enrollment:* 1,771. Undergraduates: 1,771. Freshmen: 425. Both federal and institutional methodology are used as a basis for awarding need-based institutional aid.

UNDERGRADUATE EXPENSES for 2017–2018 *Comprehensive fee:* $56,430 includes full-time tuition ($45,654), mandatory fees ($202), and room and board ($10,574). *College room only:* $6622. Room and board charges vary according to housing facility. *Part-time tuition:* $1427 per credit hour.

FRESHMAN FINANCIAL AID (Fall 2016, est.) 373 applied for aid; of those 77% were deemed to have need. 100% of freshmen with need received aid; of those 53% had need fully met. *Average percent of need met:* 89% (excluding resources awarded to replace EFC). *Average financial aid package:* $34,845 (excluding resources awarded to replace EFC). 31% of all full-time freshmen had no need and received non-need-based gift aid.

UNDERGRADUATE FINANCIAL AID (Fall 2016, est.) 1,342 applied for aid; of those 82% were deemed to have need. 100% of undergraduates with need received aid; of those 42% had need fully met. *Average percent of need met:* 86% (excluding resources awarded to replace EFC). *Average financial aid package:* $32,607 (excluding resources awarded to replace EFC). 35% of all full-time undergraduates had no need and received non-need-based gift aid.

GIFT AID (NEED-BASED) *Total amount:* $28,099,189 (6% federal, 7% state, 86% institutional, 1% external sources). *Receiving aid:* Freshmen: 67% (289); all full-time undergraduates: 62% (1,100). *Average award:* Freshmen: $28,592; Undergraduates: $25,892. *Scholarships, grants, and awards:* Federal Pell, FSEOG, state, private, college/university gift aid from institutional funds.

GIFT AID (NON-NEED-BASED) *Total amount:* $12,575,036 (100% institutional). *Receiving aid:* Freshmen: 13% (55). Undergraduates: 8% (135). *Average* *award:* Freshmen: $21,219. Undergraduates: $18,240. *Scholarships, grants, and awards by category: Academic interests/achievement:* general academic interests/achievements. *Creative arts/performance:* art/fine arts, general creative arts/performance, music, theater/drama. *Special characteristics:* children of faculty/staff, general special characteristics, international students. *Tuition waivers:* Full or partial for employees or children of employees. *ROTC:* Army cooperative.

LOANS *Student loans:* $10,336,529 (46% need-based, 54% non-need-based). 73% of past graduating class borrowed through all loan programs. *Average indebtedness per student:* $34,999. *Average need-based loan:* Freshmen: $4620. Undergraduates: $5616. *Parent loans:* $4,408,551 (100% non-need-based). *Programs:* Federal Direct (Subsidized and Unsubsidized Stafford, PLUS), Perkins, Federal Nursing, college/university.

WORK-STUDY *Federal work-study:* Total amount: $339,200; jobs available. *State or other work-study/employment:* Total amount: $1,686,550 (80% need-based, 20% non-need-based). Part-time jobs available.

APPLYING FOR FINANCIAL AID *Required financial aid forms:* FAFSA, institution's own form. *Financial aid deadline (priority):* 3/1. *Notification date:* Continuous beginning 3/1. Students must reply by 5/1.

CONTACT Mr. Scott Seibring, Director of Financial Aid, Illinois Wesleyan University, 1312 North Park Street, PO Box 2900, Bloomington, IL 61702-2900, 309-556-3393 or toll-free 800-332-2498. *Fax:* 309-556-3833. *E-mail:* seibring@iwu.edu. *Website:* http://www.iwu.edu/.

IMMACULATA UNIVERSITY
Immaculata, PA

ABOUT THE INSTITUTION Independent Roman Catholic, coed. *Awards:* certificates, associate, bachelor's, master's, and doctoral degrees. 44 undergraduate majors. *Total enrollment:* 2,610. Undergraduates: 1,555. Freshmen: 219.

GIFT AID (NEED-BASED) *Scholarships, grants, and awards:* Federal Pell, FSEOG, state, private, college/university gift aid from institutional funds.

GIFT AID (NON-NEED-BASED) *Scholarships, grants, and awards by category: Academic interests/achievement:* general academic interests/achievements, military science. *Creative arts/performance:* general creative arts/performance, music, theater/drama. *Special achievements/activities:* leadership, religious involvement. *Special characteristics:* children and siblings of alumni, local/state students, religious affiliation.

LOANS *Programs:* Perkins.

APPLYING FOR FINANCIAL AID *Required financial aid form:* FAFSA.

CONTACT Mr. Robert Forest, Director of Student Financial Aid, Immaculata University, 1145 King Road, Box 500, Immaculata, PA 19345, 610-647-4400 Ext. 3026 or toll-free 877-428-6329. *Fax:* 610-640-0836. *E-mail:* rforest@immaculata.edu. *Website:* http://www.immaculata.edu/.

INDEPENDENCE UNIVERSITY
Salt Lake City, UT

CONTACT Financial Aid Director, Independence University, 2423 Hoover Avenue, National City, CA 91950-6605, 619-477-4800 or toll-free 800-917-6391. *Fax:* 619-477-5202. *Website:* http://www.independence.edu/.

INDIANA STATE UNIVERSITY
Terre Haute, IN

Tuition & fees (IN res): $8746	Average undergraduate aid package: $10,813

ABOUT THE INSTITUTION State-supported, coed. *Awards:* certificates, bachelor's, master's, and doctoral degrees. 74 undergraduate majors. *Total enrollment:* 13,565. Undergraduates: 11,202. Freshmen: 2,447. Federal methodology is used as a basis for awarding need-based institutional aid.

UNDERGRADUATE EXPENSES for 2016–2017 *Application fee:* $25. *Tuition, state resident:* full-time $8546; part-time $310 per credit hour. *Tuition, nonresident:* full-time $18,876; part-time $669 per credit hour. *Required fees:* full-time $200; $100 per term. Full-time tuition and fees vary according to reciprocity agreements. Part-time tuition and fees vary according to course load and reciprocity agreements. *College room and board:* $9696. Room and board charges vary according to board plan, housing facility, and student level.

FRESHMAN FINANCIAL AID (Fall 2015) 2,636 applied for aid; of those 86% were deemed to have need. 96% of freshmen with need received aid; of those 18% had need fully met. *Average percent of need met:* 83% (excluding resources awarded to replace EFC). *Average financial aid package:* $11,170 (excluding resources awarded to replace EFC). 9% of all full-time freshmen had no need and received non-need-based gift aid.

UNDERGRADUATE FINANCIAL AID (Fall 2015) 8,312 applied for aid; of those 86% were deemed to have need. 96% of undergraduates with need received aid; of those 15% had need fully met. *Average percent of need met:* 82% (excluding resources awarded to replace EFC). *Average financial aid package:* $10,813 (excluding resources awarded to replace EFC). 9% of all full-time undergraduates had no need and received non-need-based gift aid.

GIFT AID (NEED-BASED) *Total amount:* $27,399,431 (76% federal, 16% state, 7% institutional, 1% external sources). *Receiving aid:* Freshmen: 53% (1,483); all full-time undergraduates: 47% (4,548). *Average award:* Freshmen: $5817; Undergraduates: $5792. *Scholarships, grants, and awards:* Federal Pell, FSEOG, state, private, college/university gift aid from institutional funds.

GIFT AID (NON-NEED-BASED) *Total amount:* $29,384,720 (58% state, 33% institutional, 9% external sources). *Receiving aid:* Freshmen: 55% (1,514). Undergraduates: 40% (3,823). *Average award:* Freshmen: $4372. Undergraduates: $4153. *Scholarships, grants, and awards by category: Academic interests/achievement:* 4,379 awards ($7,434,182 total): area/ethnic studies, biological sciences, business, communication, computer science, education, engineering/technologies, English, foreign languages, general academic interests/achievements, health fields, humanities, mathematics, physical sciences, premedicine, social sciences. *Creative arts/performance:* 86 awards ($317,000 total): applied art and design, art/fine arts, music, performing arts, theater/drama. *Special characteristics:* 361 awards ($924,519 total): children and siblings of alumni, children of faculty/staff, members of minority groups, previous college experience, veterans. *Tuition waivers:* Full or partial for employees or children of employees, senior citizens. *ROTC:* Army, Air Force.

LOANS *Student loans:* $48,009,051 (44% need-based, 56% non-need-based). 71% of past graduating class borrowed through all loan programs. *Average indebtedness per student:* $27,705. *Average need-based loan:* Freshmen: $3069. Undergraduates: $3898. *Parent loans:* $11,976,052 (100% non-need-based). *Programs:* Federal Direct (Subsidized and Unsubsidized Stafford, PLUS), Perkins.

WORK-STUDY *Federal work-study:* jobs available.

ATHLETIC AWARDS Total amount: $4,473,162 (100% non-need-based).

APPLYING FOR FINANCIAL AID *Required financial aid form:* FAFSA. *Financial aid deadline:* 7/1 (priority: 3/1). *Notification date:* Continuous beginning 3/15.

CONTACT Crystal Baker, Director of Student Financial Aid, Indiana State University, 150 Tirey Hall, Terre Haute, IN 47809-1401, 812-237-2215 or toll-free 800-468-6478. *Fax:* 812-237-4330. *E-mail:* isu-finaid@mail.indstate.edu. *Website:* http://www.indstate.edu/.

INDIANA TECH
Fort Wayne, IN

Tuition & fees: $26,370	Average undergraduate aid package: $18,880

ABOUT THE INSTITUTION Independent, coed. 31 undergraduate majors. Federal methodology is used as a basis for awarding need-based institutional aid.

UNDERGRADUATE EXPENSES for 2016–2017 *Comprehensive fee:* $35,950 includes full-time tuition ($25,940), mandatory fees ($430), and room and board ($9580). *College room only:* $5800. Full-time tuition and fees vary according to class time, course load, and program. Room and board charges vary according to board plan and housing facility. *Part-time tuition:* $510 per credit hour. Part-time tuition and fees vary according to class time, course load, and program. *Payment plan:* Guaranteed tuition.

FRESHMAN FINANCIAL AID (Fall 2015) 693 applied for aid; of those 96% were deemed to have need. 100% of freshmen with need received aid. *Average percent* *of need met:* 26% (excluding resources awarded to replace EFC). *Average financial aid package:* $21,084 (excluding resources awarded to replace EFC). 2% of all full-time freshmen had no need and received non-need-based gift aid.

UNDERGRADUATE FINANCIAL AID (Fall 2015) 3,737 applied for aid; of those 96% were deemed to have need. 100% of undergraduates with need received aid. *Average percent of need met:* 37% (excluding resources awarded to replace EFC). *Average financial aid package:* $18,880 (excluding resources awarded to replace EFC). 2% of all full-time undergraduates had no need and received non-need-based gift aid.

GIFT AID (NEED-BASED) *Total amount:* $39,267,038 (50% federal, 25% state, 24% institutional, 1% external sources). *Receiving aid:* Freshmen: 77% (576); all full-time undergraduates: 75% (3,090). *Average award:* Freshmen: $6383; Undergraduates: $8883. *Scholarships, grants, and awards:* Federal Pell, FSEOG, state, private, college/university gift aid from institutional funds.

GIFT AID (NON-NEED-BASED) *Receiving aid:* Freshmen: 35% (263). Undergraduates: 19% (773). *Average award:* Freshmen: $8766. Undergraduates: $8944. *Scholarships, grants, and awards by category: Academic interests/achievement:* 953 awards ($7,583,948 total): computer science, education, engineering/technologies, general academic interests/achievements. *Special characteristics:* 142 awards ($743,918 total): children of current students, children of faculty/staff, local/state students, married students, siblings of current students, spouses of current students, veterans, veterans' children. *Tuition waivers:* Full or partial for employees or children of employees.

LOANS *Student loans:* $44,651,923 (41% need-based, 59% non-need-based). 74% of past graduating class borrowed through all loan programs. *Average indebtedness per student:* $41,844. *Average need-based loan:* Freshmen: $3139. Undergraduates: $3485. *Parent loans:* $2,827,640 (100% non-need-based). *Programs:* Federal Direct (Subsidized and Unsubsidized Stafford, PLUS), Perkins.

WORK-STUDY *Federal work-study:* 93 jobs averaging $1379.

ATHLETIC AWARDS Total amount: $5,329,161 (100% non-need-based).

APPLYING FOR FINANCIAL AID *Required financial aid form:* FAFSA. *Financial aid deadline (priority):* 3/10. *Notification date:* Continuous beginning 2/20. Students must reply within 2 weeks of notification.

CONTACT Mrs. Lisa Claudette Green, Financial Aid Systems Analyst, Indiana Tech, 1600 East Washington Boulevard, Fort Wayne, IN 46803-1297, 800-937-2448 Ext. 2334 or toll-free 800-937-2448. *Fax:* 219-422-1578. *E-mail:* financialaid@indianatech.edu.
Website: https://www.indianatech.edu/.

INDIANA UNIVERSITY BLOOMINGTON
Bloomington, IN

Tuition & fees (IN res): $10,388	Average undergraduate aid package: $12,864

ABOUT THE INSTITUTION State-supported, coed. *Awards:* certificates, associate, bachelor's, master's, and doctoral degrees. 107 undergraduate majors. *Total enrollment:* 49,695. Undergraduates: 39,184. Freshmen: 6,971. Federal methodology is used as a basis for awarding need-based institutional aid.

UNDERGRADUATE EXPENSES for 2016–2017 *Application fee:* $60. *Tuition, state resident:* full-time $9087; part-time $283.92 per credit hour. *Tuition, nonresident:* full-time $32,945; part-time $1029.54 per credit hour. *Required fees:* full-time $1301. Full-time tuition and fees vary according to location and program. Part-time tuition and fees vary according to course load, location, and program. *College room and board:* $10,041. Room and board charges vary according to board plan and housing facility.

FRESHMAN FINANCIAL AID (Fall 2015) 5,624 applied for aid; of those 64% were deemed to have need. 95% of freshmen with need received aid; of those 30% had need fully met. *Average percent of need met:* 69% (excluding resources awarded to replace EFC). *Average financial aid package:* $13,666 (excluding resources awarded to replace EFC). 25% of all full-time freshmen had no need and received non-need-based gift aid.

UNDERGRADUATE FINANCIAL AID (Fall 2015) 18,554 applied for aid; of those 71% were deemed to have need. 96% of undergraduates with need received aid; of those 28% had need fully met. *Average percent of need met:* 67% (excluding resources awarded to replace EFC). *Average financial aid package:* $12,864

(excluding resources awarded to replace EFC). 29% of all full-time undergraduates had no need and received non-need-based gift aid.

GIFT AID (NEED-BASED) *Total amount:* $112,269,340 (25% federal, 31% state, 39% institutional, 5% external sources). *Receiving aid:* Freshmen: 37% (2,892); all full-time undergraduates: 33% (10,497). *Average award:* Freshmen: $12,495; Undergraduates: $10,983. *Scholarships, grants, and awards:* Federal Pell, FSEOG, state, private, college/university gift aid from institutional funds.

GIFT AID (NON-NEED-BASED) *Total amount:* $73,043,521 (2% federal, 3% state, 82% institutional, 13% external sources). *Receiving aid:* Freshmen: 8% (632). Undergraduates: 6% (2,041). *Average award:* Freshmen: $7182. Undergraduates: $5776. *Tuition waivers:* Full or partial for employees or children of employees. *ROTC:* Army, Air Force.

LOANS *Student loans:* $104,730,790 (57% need-based, 43% non-need-based). 44% of past graduating class borrowed through all loan programs. *Average indebtedness per student:* $28,039. *Average need-based loan:* Freshmen: $3029. Undergraduates: $4302. *Parent loans:* $39,569,988 (35% need-based, 65% non-need-based). *Programs:* Federal Direct (Subsidized and Unsubsidized Stafford, PLUS), Perkins, Federal Nursing, college/university.

WORK-STUDY *Federal work-study:* jobs available. *State or other work-study/employment:* Total amount: $50,323 (47% need-based, 53% non-need-based). Part-time jobs available.

ATHLETIC AWARDS Total amount: $12,520,997 (32% need-based, 68% non-need-based).

APPLYING FOR FINANCIAL AID *Required financial aid form:* FAFSA. *Financial aid deadline (priority):* 3/10. *Notification date:* Continuous beginning 4/1.

CONTACT Jackie Kennedy-Fletcher, Director of Student Financial Assistance, Indiana University Bloomington, 408 North Union Street, Bloomington, IN 47405, 812-855-6500. *Fax:* 812-855-7615. *E-mail:* rsvposfa@indiana.edu.
Website: http://www.iub.edu/.

INDIANA UNIVERSITY EAST
Richmond, IN

Tuition & fees (IN res): $7073	Average undergraduate aid package: $8844

ABOUT THE INSTITUTION State-supported, coed. *Awards:* certificates, bachelor's, and master's degrees. 26 undergraduate majors. *Total enrollment:* 4,479. Undergraduates: 4,287. Freshmen: 357. Federal methodology is used as a basis for awarding need-based institutional aid.

UNDERGRADUATE EXPENSES for 2016–2017 *Application fee:* $35. *Tuition, state resident:* full-time $6478; part-time $215.92 per credit hour. *Tuition, nonresident:* full-time $18,088; part-time $602.93 per credit hour. *Required fees:* full-time $595. Full-time tuition and fees vary according to course load, location, program, and reciprocity agreements. Part-time tuition and fees vary according to course load, location, program, and reciprocity agreements.

FRESHMAN FINANCIAL AID (Fall 2015) 324 applied for aid; of those 87% were deemed to have need. 96% of freshmen with need received aid; of those 25% had need fully met. *Average percent of need met:* 70% (excluding resources awarded to replace EFC). *Average financial aid package:* $8589 (excluding resources awarded to replace EFC). 6% of all full-time freshmen had no need and received non-need-based gift aid.

UNDERGRADUATE FINANCIAL AID (Fall 2015) 1,785 applied for aid; of those 88% were deemed to have need. 96% of undergraduates with need received aid; of those 15% had need fully met. *Average percent of need met:* 63% (excluding resources awarded to replace EFC). *Average financial aid package:* $8844 (excluding resources awarded to replace EFC). 6% of all full-time undergraduates had no need and received non-need-based gift aid.

GIFT AID (NEED-BASED) *Total amount:* $10,327,301 (57% federal, 31% state, 8% institutional, 4% external sources). *Receiving aid:* Freshmen: 74% (251); all full-time undergraduates: 68% (1,320). *Average award:* Freshmen: $7627; Undergraduates: $6931. *Scholarships, grants, and awards:* Federal Pell, FSEOG, state, private, college/university gift aid from institutional funds.

GIFT AID (NON-NEED-BASED) *Total amount:* $794,853 (15% federal, 10% state, 40% institutional, 35% external sources). *Receiving aid:* Freshmen: 14% (49). Undergraduates: 7% (142). *Average award:* Freshmen: $1611. Undergraduates: $1955. *Tuition waivers:* Full or partial for employees or children of employees.

LOANS *Student loans:* $12,299,557 (78% need-based, 22% non-need-based). 78% of past graduating class borrowed through all loan programs. *Average indebtedness per student:* $27,379. *Average need-based loan:* Freshmen: $2568. Undergraduates: $3811. *Parent loans:* $227,239 (29% need-based, 71% non-need-based). *Programs:* Federal Direct (Subsidized and Unsubsidized Stafford, PLUS), Perkins, college/university.

WORK-STUDY *Federal work-study:* jobs available. *State or other work-study/employment:* Part-time jobs available.

ATHLETIC AWARDS Total amount: $377,488 (57% need-based, 43% non-need-based).

APPLYING FOR FINANCIAL AID *Required financial aid forms:* FAFSA, institution's own form. *Financial aid deadline (priority):* 3/10. *Notification date:* Continuous beginning 5/1. Students must reply within 2 weeks of notification.

CONTACT Sarah Soper, Director of Financial Aid and Scholarships, Indiana University East, Whitewater Hall 112, 2325 Chester Boulevard, Richmond, IN 47374-1289, 765-973-8206 or toll-free 800-959-EAST. *Fax:* 765-973-8288. *E-mail:* eaosfa@iue.edu.
Website: http://www.iue.edu/.

INDIANA UNIVERSITY KOKOMO
Kokomo, IN

Tuition & fees (IN res): $7073	Average undergraduate aid package: $8568

ABOUT THE INSTITUTION State-supported, coed. *Awards:* certificates, associate, bachelor's, and master's degrees. 32 undergraduate majors. *Total enrollment:* 4,106. Undergraduates: 3,977. Freshmen: 499. Federal methodology is used as a basis for awarding need-based institutional aid.

UNDERGRADUATE EXPENSES for 2016–2017 *Application fee:* $35. *Tuition, state resident:* full-time $6478; part-time $215.92 per credit hour. *Tuition, nonresident:* full-time $18,088; part-time $602.93 per credit hour. *Required fees:* full-time $595. Full-time tuition and fees vary according to course load, location, and program. Part-time tuition and fees vary according to course load, location, and program.

FRESHMAN FINANCIAL AID (Fall 2015) 517 applied for aid; of those 80% were deemed to have need. 97% of freshmen with need received aid; of those 15% had need fully met. *Average percent of need met:* 67% (excluding resources awarded to replace EFC). *Average financial aid package:* $8473 (excluding resources awarded to replace EFC). 8% of all full-time freshmen had no need and received non-need-based gift aid.

UNDERGRADUATE FINANCIAL AID (Fall 2015) 1,920 applied for aid; of those 82% were deemed to have need. 96% of undergraduates with need received aid; of those 11% had need fully met. *Average percent of need met:* 64% (excluding resources awarded to replace EFC). *Average financial aid package:* $8568 (excluding resources awarded to replace EFC). 6% of all full-time undergraduates had no need and received non-need-based gift aid.

GIFT AID (NEED-BASED) *Total amount:* $10,070,052 (54% federal, 38% state, 5% institutional, 3% external sources). *Receiving aid:* Freshmen: 65% (357); all full-time undergraduates: 60% (1,288). *Average award:* Freshmen: $7762; Undergraduates: $7104. *Scholarships, grants, and awards:* Federal Pell, FSEOG, state, private, college/university gift aid from institutional funds.

GIFT AID (NON-NEED-BASED) *Total amount:* $910,620 (12% federal, 23% state, 27% institutional, 38% external sources). *Receiving aid:* Freshmen: 6% (34). Undergraduates: 4% (81). *Average award:* Freshmen: $1807. Undergraduates: $1494. *Tuition waivers:* Full or partial for employees or children of employees. *ROTC:* Army.

LOANS *Student loans:* $9,695,333 (73% need-based, 27% non-need-based). 74% of past graduating class borrowed through all loan programs. *Average indebtedness per student:* $25,675. *Average need-based loan:* Freshmen: $2619. Undergraduates: $3527. *Parent loans:* $253,701 (21% need-based, 79% non-need-based). *Programs:* Federal Direct (Subsidized and Unsubsidized Stafford, PLUS), Perkins, Federal Nursing, college/university.

WORK-STUDY *Federal work-study:* jobs available. *State or other work-study/employment:* Total amount: $3145 (100% need-based). Part-time jobs available.

ATHLETIC AWARDS Total amount: $79,300 (53% need-based, 47% non-need-based).

APPLYING FOR FINANCIAL AID *Required financial aid form:* FAFSA. *Financial aid deadline:* 6/30 (priority: 3/10). *Notification date:* Continuous beginning 3/30.

CONTACT Karen Shaw, Director of Scholarships and Financial Aid, Indiana University Kokomo, Kelley Student Center, Room 230, 2300 South Washington Street, Kokomo, IN 46904-9003, 765-455-9216 or toll-free 888-875-4485. *Fax:* 765-455-9537. *E-mail:* finaidko@iuk.edu.
Website: http://www.iuk.edu/.

INDIANA UNIVERSITY NORTHWEST
Gary, IN

Tuition & fees (IN res): $7073	Average undergraduate aid package: $8109

ABOUT THE INSTITUTION State-supported, coed. *Awards:* certificates, associate, bachelor's, and master's degrees. 44 undergraduate majors. *Total enrollment:* 5,591. Undergraduates: 5,244. Freshmen: 585. Federal methodology is used as a basis for awarding need-based institutional aid.

UNDERGRADUATE EXPENSES for 2016–2017 *Application fee:* $35. *Tuition, state resident:* full-time $6478; part-time $215.92 per credit hour. *Tuition, nonresident:* full-time $18,088; part-time $602.93 per credit hour. *Required fees:* full-time $595. Full-time tuition and fees vary according to course load, location, and program. Part-time tuition and fees vary according to course load, location, and program.

FRESHMAN FINANCIAL AID (Fall 2015) 542 applied for aid; of those 74% were deemed to have need. 92% of freshmen with need received aid; of those 14% had need fully met. *Average percent of need met:* 67% (excluding resources awarded to replace EFC). *Average financial aid package:* $7420 (excluding resources awarded to replace EFC). 9% of all full-time freshmen had no need and received non-need-based gift aid.

UNDERGRADUATE FINANCIAL AID (Fall 2015) 2,544 applied for aid; of those 79% were deemed to have need. 94% of undergraduates with need received aid; of those 13% had need fully met. *Average percent of need met:* 65% (excluding resources awarded to replace EFC). *Average financial aid package:* $8109 (excluding resources awarded to replace EFC). 7% of all full-time undergraduates had no need and received non-need-based gift aid.

GIFT AID (NEED-BASED) *Total amount:* $12,116,204 (60% federal, 31% state, 6% institutional, 3% external sources). *Receiving aid:* Freshmen: 55% (321); all full-time undergraduates: 53% (1,565). *Average award:* Freshmen: $6759; Undergraduates: $6785. *Scholarships, grants, and awards:* Federal Pell, FSEOG, state, private, college/university gift aid from institutional funds, United Negro College Fund, Federal Nursing.

GIFT AID (NON-NEED-BASED) *Total amount:* $1,332,291 (7% federal, 7% state, 71% institutional, 15% external sources). *Receiving aid:* Freshmen: 5% (27). Undergraduates: 3% (79). *Average award:* Freshmen: $4511. Undergraduates: $3976. *Tuition waivers:* Full or partial for employees or children of employees. *ROTC:* Army.

LOANS *Student loans:* $13,564,362 (71% need-based, 29% non-need-based). 68% of past graduating class borrowed through all loan programs. *Average indebtedness per student:* $29,701. *Average need-based loan:* Freshmen: $2793. Undergraduates: $3562. *Parent loans:* $507,891 (19% need-based, 81% non-need-based). *Programs:* Federal Direct (Subsidized and Unsubsidized Stafford, PLUS), Perkins, college/university.

WORK-STUDY *Federal work-study:* jobs available. *State or other work-study/employment:* Part-time jobs available.

ATHLETIC AWARDS Total amount: $51,550 (46% need-based, 54% non-need-based).

APPLYING FOR FINANCIAL AID *Required financial aid form:* FAFSA. *Financial aid deadline (priority):* 3/10. *Notification date:* Continuous beginning 4/15. Students must reply by 6/30.

CONTACT Harold Burtley, Director of Scholarships and Financial Aid, Indiana University Northwest, 3400 Broadway, Hawthorn Hall, Room 111, Gary, IN 46408, 219-980-6778 or toll-free 800-968-7486. *Fax:* 219-981-5622. *E-mail:* finaidnw@iun.edu.
Website: http://www.iun.edu/.

INDIANA UNIVERSITY OF PENNSYLVANIA
Indiana, PA

Tuition & fees (PA res): $11,368	Average undergraduate aid package: $9845

ABOUT THE INSTITUTION State-supported, coed. *Awards:* certificates, associate, bachelor's, master's, and doctoral degrees. 62 undergraduate majors. *Total enrollment:* 12,853. Undergraduates: 10,618. Freshmen: 2,203. Federal methodology is used as a basis for awarding need-based institutional aid.

UNDERGRADUATE EXPENSES for 2016–2017 *Application fee:* $25. *Tuition, state resident:* full-time $8430; part-time $281 per credit hour. *Tuition, nonresident:* full-time $18,096; part-time $754 per credit hour. *Required fees:* full-time $2938; $108.60 per credit hour or $50 per term. Full-time tuition and fees vary according to course load and reciprocity agreements. Part-time tuition and fees vary according to course load and reciprocity agreements. *College room and board:* $12,402; *Room only:* $8950. Room and board charges vary according to board plan, housing facility, and location.

FRESHMAN FINANCIAL AID (Fall 2015) 2,325 applied for aid; of those 80% were deemed to have need. 99% of freshmen with need received aid; of those 10% had need fully met. *Average percent of need met:* 63% (excluding resources awarded to replace EFC). *Average financial aid package:* $11,192 (excluding resources awarded to replace EFC). 5% of all full-time freshmen had no need and received non-need-based gift aid.

UNDERGRADUATE FINANCIAL AID (Fall 2015) 9,198 applied for aid; of those 82% were deemed to have need. 99% of undergraduates with need received aid; of those 9% had need fully met. *Average percent of need met:* 58% (excluding resources awarded to replace EFC). *Average financial aid package:* $9845 (excluding resources awarded to replace EFC). 3% of all full-time undergraduates had no need and received non-need-based gift aid.

GIFT AID (NEED-BASED) *Total amount:* $31,042,615 (63% federal, 37% state). *Receiving aid:* Freshmen: 52% (1,277); all full-time undergraduates: 47% (5,064). *Average award:* Freshmen: $6693; Undergraduates: $6004. *Scholarships, grants, and awards:* Federal Pell, FSEOG, state, private, college/university gift aid from institutional funds, United Negro College Fund.

GIFT AID (NON-NEED-BASED) *Total amount:* $8,132,199 (11% state, 52% institutional, 37% external sources). *Receiving aid:* Freshmen: 38% (937). Undergraduates: 19% (2,055). *Average award:* Freshmen: $2021. Undergraduates: $1880. *Scholarships, grants, and awards by category:* Academic interests/achievement: 2,536 awards ($6,181,860 total): area/ethnic studies, biological sciences, business, communication, computer science, education, engineering/technologies, English, foreign languages, general academic interests/achievements, health fields, home economics, humanities, international studies, mathematics, military science, physical sciences, premedicine, religion/biblical studies, social sciences. *Creative arts/performance:* applied art and design, art/fine arts, dance, general creative arts/performance, journalism/publications, music, performing arts, theater/drama. *Special achievements/activities:* community service, general special achievements/activities, hobbies/interests, leadership. *Special characteristics:* adult students, children of faculty/staff, ethnic background, international students. *Tuition waivers:* Full or partial for employees or children of employees, senior citizens. *ROTC:* Army.

LOANS *Student loans:* $77,907,926 (37% need-based, 63% non-need-based). 83% of past graduating class borrowed through all loan programs. *Average indebtedness per student:* $36,514. *Average need-based loan:* Freshmen: $3635. Undergraduates: $4196. *Parent loans:* $21,048,932 (100% non-need-based). *Programs:* Federal Direct (Subsidized and Unsubsidized Stafford, PLUS), Perkins.

WORK-STUDY *Federal work-study:* 1,534 jobs averaging $2763. *State or other work-study/employment:* Total amount: $1,233,933 (100% non-need-based). 881 part-time jobs averaging $1881.

ATHLETIC AWARDS Total amount: $1,539,273 (100% non-need-based).

APPLYING FOR FINANCIAL AID *Required financial aid forms:* FAFSA, state aid form. *Financial aid deadline (priority):* 4/15. *Notification date:* Continuous beginning 12/15.

CONTACT Ms. Ragan Griffin, Director of Financial Aid, Indiana University of Pennsylvania, 1090 South Drive, 213 Clark Hall, Indiana, PA 15705, 724-357-2218 or toll-free 800-442-6830. *Fax:* 724-357-2094. *E-mail:* financial-aid@iup.edu. *Website:* http://www.iup.edu/.

INDIANA UNIVERSITY–PURDUE UNIVERSITY FORT WAYNE
Fort Wayne, IN

Tuition & fees (IN res): $8212	Average undergraduate aid package: $9786

ABOUT THE INSTITUTION State-supported, coed. 103 undergraduate majors. Federal methodology is used as a basis for awarding need-based institutional aid.

UNDERGRADUATE EXPENSES for 2016–2017 *Tuition, state resident:* full-time $7138; part-time $237.95 per credit hour. *Tuition, nonresident:* full-time $18,652; part-time $621.75 per credit hour. *Required fees:* full-time $1074; $35.80 per credit hour. Full-time tuition and fees vary according to course load. Part-time tuition and fees vary according to course load. *Room only:* $6844. Room and board charges vary according to housing facility.

FRESHMAN FINANCIAL AID (Fall 2015) 1,407 applied for aid; of those 78% were deemed to have need. 93% of freshmen with need received aid; of those 7% had need fully met. *Average percent of need met:* 57% (excluding resources awarded to replace EFC). *Average financial aid package:* $9480 (excluding resources awarded to replace EFC). 1% of all full-time freshmen had no need and received non-need-based gift aid.

UNDERGRADUATE FINANCIAL AID (Fall 2015) 5,658 applied for aid; of those 81% were deemed to have need. 94% of undergraduates with need received aid; of those 5% had need fully met. *Average percent of need met:* 56% (excluding resources awarded to replace EFC). *Average financial aid package:* $9786 (excluding resources awarded to replace EFC). 2% of all full-time undergraduates had no need and received non-need-based gift aid.

GIFT AID (NEED-BASED) *Total amount:* $25,936,449 (53% federal, 39% state, 5% institutional, 3% external sources). *Receiving aid:* Freshmen: 43% (669); all full-time undergraduates: 45% (2,963). *Average award:* Freshmen: $5090; Undergraduates: $5401. *Scholarships, grants, and awards:* Federal Pell, FSEOG, state, private, college/university gift aid from institutional funds.

GIFT AID (NON-NEED-BASED) *Total amount:* $2,124,778 (41% state, 29% institutional, 30% external sources). *Receiving aid:* Freshmen: 32% (501). Undergraduates: 21% (1,363). *Average award:* Freshmen: $8198. Undergraduates: $3710. *Scholarships, grants, and awards by category:* Academic interests/achievement: biological sciences, engineering/technologies, general academic interests/achievements, premedicine. *Creative arts/performance:* art/fine arts, music, theater/drama. *Special achievements/activities:* leadership. *Special characteristics:* children and siblings of alumni, general special characteristics, local/state students. *Tuition waivers:* Full or partial for employees or children of employees, senior citizens.

LOANS *Student loans:* $29,962,034 (96% need-based, 4% non-need-based). 11% of past graduating class borrowed through all loan programs. *Average indebtedness per student:* $29,419. *Average need-based loan:* Freshmen: $2961. Undergraduates: $3751. *Parent loans:* $1,626,028 (97% need-based, 3% non-need-based). *Programs:* Federal Direct (Subsidized and Unsubsidized Stafford, PLUS), Perkins.

WORK-STUDY *Federal work-study:* jobs available.

ATHLETIC AWARDS Total amount: $2,159,736 (26% need-based, 74% non-need-based).

APPLYING FOR FINANCIAL AID *Required financial aid forms:* FAFSA, general scholarship application form. *Financial aid deadline (priority):* 3/10. *Notification date:* 4/26.

CONTACT Mr. David Peterson, Director of Financial Aid, Indiana University–Purdue University Fort Wayne, 2101 East Coliseum Boulevard, Fort Wayne, IN 46805-1499, 260-481-6240 or toll-free 800-324-4739. *E-mail:* finaid@ipfw.edu. *Website:* http://www.ipfw.edu/.

INDIANA UNIVERSITY–PURDUE UNIVERSITY INDIANAPOLIS
Indianapolis, IN

Tuition & fees (IN res): $9205	Average undergraduate aid package: $10,391

ABOUT THE INSTITUTION State-supported, coed. *Awards:* certificates, associate, bachelor's, master's, and doctoral degrees. 86 undergraduate majors. *Total*

enrollment: 29,804. Undergraduates: 21,748. Freshmen: 3,737. Federal methodology is used as a basis for awarding need-based institutional aid.

UNDERGRADUATE EXPENSES for 2016–2017 *Application fee:* $55. *Tuition, state resident:* full-time $8141; part-time $271.37 per credit hour. *Tuition, nonresident:* full-time $28,727; part-time $957.58 per credit hour. *Required fees:* full-time $1064. Full-time tuition and fees vary according to course load, location, and program. Part-time tuition and fees vary according to course load, location, and program. *College room and board:* $8462. Room and board charges vary according to board plan and housing facility.

FRESHMAN FINANCIAL AID (Fall 2015) 3,393 applied for aid; of those 77% were deemed to have need. 95% of freshmen with need received aid; of those 25% had need fully met. *Average percent of need met:* 69% (excluding resources awarded to replace EFC). *Average financial aid package:* $10,900 (excluding resources awarded to replace EFC). 10% of all full-time freshmen had no need and received non-need-based gift aid.

UNDERGRADUATE FINANCIAL AID (Fall 2015) 14,147 applied for aid; of those 81% were deemed to have need. 97% of undergraduates with need received aid; of those 17% had need fully met. *Average percent of need met:* 65% (excluding resources awarded to replace EFC). *Average financial aid package:* $10,391 (excluding resources awarded to replace EFC). 10% of all full-time undergraduates had no need and received non-need-based gift aid.

GIFT AID (NEED-BASED) *Total amount:* $84,367,471 (43% federal, 37% state, 17% institutional, 3% external sources). *Receiving aid:* Freshmen: 58% (2,170); all full-time undergraduates: 54% (9,211). *Average award:* Freshmen: $9706; Undergraduates: $8662. *Scholarships, grants, and awards:* Federal Pell, FSEOG, state, private, college/university gift aid from institutional funds.

GIFT AID (NON-NEED-BASED) *Total amount:* $26,522,462 (4% federal, 6% state, 41% institutional, 49% external sources). *Receiving aid:* Freshmen: 10% (357). Undergraduates: 7% (1,136). *Average award:* Freshmen: $5702. Undergraduates: $4862. *Tuition waivers:* Full or partial for employees or children of employees. *ROTC:* Army, Air Force cooperative.

LOANS *Student loans:* $82,487,723 (71% need-based, 29% non-need-based). 70% of past graduating class borrowed through all loan programs. *Average indebtedness per student:* $28,951. *Average need-based loan:* Freshmen: $3209. Undergraduates: $4009. *Parent loans:* $9,699,171 (29% need-based, 71% non-need-based). *Programs:* Federal Direct (Subsidized and Unsubsidized Stafford, PLUS), Perkins, Federal Nursing, college/university.

WORK-STUDY *Federal work-study:* jobs available. *State or other work-study/employment:* Total amount: $45,526 (69% need-based, 31% non-need-based). Part-time jobs available.

ATHLETIC AWARDS Total amount: $2,421,716 (39% need-based, 61% non-need-based).

APPLYING FOR FINANCIAL AID *Required financial aid form:* FAFSA. *Financial aid deadline (priority):* 3/10. *Notification date:* Continuous beginning 4/1.

CONTACT Marvin Smith, Director of Student Financial Services, Indiana University–Purdue University Indianapolis, 420 University Boulevard, CE 250, Indianapolis, IN 46202-5145, 317-274-4162. *Fax:* 317-274-3664. *E-mail:* finaid@iupui.edu. *Website:* http://www.iupui.edu/.

INDIANA UNIVERSITY SOUTH BEND
South Bend, IN

Tuition & fees (IN res): $7073	Average undergraduate aid package: $8524

ABOUT THE INSTITUTION State-supported, coed. *Awards:* certificates, diplomas, associate, bachelor's, and master's degrees. 60 undergraduate majors. *Total enrollment:* 7,185. Undergraduates: 6,653. Freshmen: 894. Federal methodology is used as a basis for awarding need-based institutional aid.

UNDERGRADUATE EXPENSES for 2016–2017 *Application fee:* $35. *Tuition, state resident:* full-time $6478; part-time $215.92 per credit hour. *Tuition, nonresident:* full-time $18,088; part-time $602.93 per credit hour. *Required fees:* full-time $595. Full-time tuition and fees vary according to course load, location, and program. Part-time tuition and fees vary according to course load, location, and program. *Room only:* $7222. Room and board charges vary according to housing facility.

FRESHMAN FINANCIAL AID (Fall 2015) 771 applied for aid; of those 81% were deemed to have need. 94% of freshmen with need received aid; of those 10% had need

---

fully met. *Average percent of need met:* 62% (excluding resources awarded to replace EFC). *Average financial aid package:* $8243 (excluding resources awarded to replace EFC). 10% of all full-time freshmen had no need and received non-need-based gift aid.

UNDERGRADUATE FINANCIAL AID (Fall 2015) 3,311 applied for aid; of those 86% were deemed to have need. 95% of undergraduates with need received aid; of those 10% had need fully met. *Average percent of need met:* 61% (excluding resources awarded to replace EFC). *Average financial aid package:* $8524 (excluding resources awarded to replace EFC). 7% of all full-time undergraduates had no need and received non-need-based gift aid.

GIFT AID (NEED-BASED) *Total amount:* $17,884,849 (55% federal, 34% state, 8% institutional, 3% external sources). *Receiving aid:* Freshmen: 64% (541); all full-time undergraduates: 62% (2,348). *Average award:* Freshmen: $7206; Undergraduates: $6933. *Scholarships, grants, and awards:* Federal Pell, FSEOG, state, private, college/university gift aid from institutional funds.

GIFT AID (NON-NEED-BASED) *Total amount:* $1,788,997 (8% federal, 7% state, 37% institutional, 48% external sources). *Receiving aid:* Freshmen: 4% (36). Undergraduates: 4% (169). *Average award:* Freshmen: $1427. Undergraduates: $1761. *Tuition waivers:* Full or partial for employees or children of employees. *ROTC:* Army cooperative, Naval cooperative, Air Force cooperative.

LOANS *Student loans:* $16,699,190 (78% need-based, 22% non-need-based). 76% of past graduating class borrowed through all loan programs. *Average indebtedness per student:* $27,306. *Average need-based loan:* Freshmen: $2787. Undergraduates: $3576. *Parent loans:* $607,361 (38% need-based, 62% non-need-based). *Programs:* Federal Direct (Subsidized and Unsubsidized Stafford, PLUS), Perkins, state.

WORK-STUDY *Federal work-study:* jobs available. *State or other work-study/employment:* Total amount: $5674 (65% need-based, 35% non-need-based). Part-time jobs available.

ATHLETIC AWARDS Total amount: $295,063 (70% need-based, 30% non-need-based).

APPLYING FOR FINANCIAL AID *Required financial aid forms:* FAFSA, institution's own form. *Financial aid deadline (priority):* 3/10. *Notification date:* Continuous beginning 5/1.

CONTACT Jill Bertrand, Director of Financial Aid and Scholarships, Indiana University South Bend, 1002 South Esther Street, PO Box 7111, South Bend, IN 46634-7111, 574-520-4357 or toll-free 877-GO-2-IUSB. *Fax:* 574-520-5561. *E-mail:* sbfinaid@iusb.edu. *Website:* http://www.iusb.edu/.

INDIANA UNIVERSITY SOUTHEAST
New Albany, IN

Tuition & fees (IN res): $7073	Average undergraduate aid package: $7993

ABOUT THE INSTITUTION State-supported, coed. *Awards:* certificates, associate, bachelor's, and master's degrees. 38 undergraduate majors. *Total enrollment:* 5,874. Undergraduates: 5,486. Freshmen: 862. Federal methodology is used as a basis for awarding need-based institutional aid.

UNDERGRADUATE EXPENSES for 2016–2017 *Application fee:* $35. *Tuition, state resident:* full-time $6478; part-time $215.92 per credit hour. *Tuition, nonresident:* full-time $18,088; part-time $602.93 per credit hour. *Required fees:* full-time $595. Full-time tuition and fees vary according to course load, location, program, and reciprocity agreements. Part-time tuition and fees vary according to course load, location, program, and reciprocity agreements. *Room only:* $6520. Room and board charges vary according to board plan and housing facility.

FRESHMAN FINANCIAL AID (Fall 2015) 757 applied for aid; of those 78% were deemed to have need. 94% of freshmen with need received aid; of those 9% had need fully met. *Average percent of need met:* 59% (excluding resources awarded to replace EFC). *Average financial aid package:* $7724 (excluding resources awarded to replace EFC). 8% of all full-time freshmen had no need and received non-need-based gift aid.

UNDERGRADUATE FINANCIAL AID (Fall 2015) 2,904 applied for aid; of those 81% were deemed to have need. 95% of undergraduates with need received aid; of those 10% had need fully met. *Average percent of need met:* 59% (excluding resources awarded to replace EFC). *Average financial aid package:* $7993 (excluding resources awarded to replace EFC). 6% of all full-time undergraduates had no need and received non-need-based gift aid.

GIFT AID (NEED-BASED) *Total amount:* $14,019,694 (59% federal, 30% state, 6% institutional, 5% external sources). *Receiving aid:* Freshmen: 61% (506); all full-time undergraduates: 56% (1,916). *Average award:* Freshmen: $6775; Undergraduates: $6336. *Scholarships, grants, and awards:* Federal Pell, FSEOG, state, private, college/university gift aid from institutional funds.

GIFT AID (NON-NEED-BASED) *Total amount:* $1,551,974 (16% federal, 17% state, 29% institutional, 38% external sources). *Receiving aid:* Freshmen: 4% (35). Undergraduates: 3% (106). *Average award:* Freshmen: $1234. Undergraduates: $1568. *Tuition waivers:* Full or partial for employees or children of employees. *ROTC:* Army cooperative, Air Force cooperative.

LOANS *Student loans:* $15,774,942 (74% need-based, 26% non-need-based). 71% of past graduating class borrowed through all loan programs. *Average indebtedness per student:* $22,612. *Average need-based loan:* Freshmen: $2789. Undergraduates: $3772. *Parent loans:* $723,931 (34% need-based, 66% non-need-based). *Programs:* Federal Direct (Subsidized and Unsubsidized Stafford, PLUS), Perkins, college/university.

WORK-STUDY *Federal work-study:* jobs available. *State or other work-study/employment:* Total amount: $10,323 (42% need-based, 58% non-need-based). Part-time jobs available.

ATHLETIC AWARDS Total amount: $137,200 (70% need-based, 30% non-need-based).

APPLYING FOR FINANCIAL AID *Required financial aid form:* FAFSA. *Financial aid deadline (priority):* 3/10. *Notification date:* Continuous beginning 5/1.

CONTACT Traci Armes, Director of Financial Aid, Indiana University Southeast, University Center, South Room 105, New Albany, IN 47150, 812-941-2246 or toll-free 800-852-8835. *Fax:* 812-941-2546. *E-mail:* financialaid@ius.edu. *Website:* http://www.ius.edu/.

INDIANA WESLEYAN UNIVERSITY
Marion, IN

Tuition & fees: $25,346	Average undergraduate aid package: $27,709

ABOUT THE INSTITUTION Independent Wesleyan, coed. *Awards:* certificates, associate, bachelor's, master's, and doctoral degrees (also offers adult program with significant enrollment not reflected in profile). 86 undergraduate majors. *Total enrollment:* 3,186. Undergraduates: 2,933. Freshmen: 684. Both federal and institutional methodology are used as a basis for awarding need-based institutional aid.

UNDERGRADUATE EXPENSES for 2016–2017 *Comprehensive fee:* $33,494 includes full-time tuition ($25,346) and room and board ($8148). *College room only:* $4074. Full-time tuition and fees vary according to course load and degree level. Room and board charges vary according to board plan. *Part-time tuition:* $538 per credit hour. Part-time tuition and fees vary according to course load and degree level.

FRESHMAN FINANCIAL AID (Fall 2016, est.) 638 applied for aid; of those 85% were deemed to have need. 100% of freshmen with need received aid; of those 52% had need fully met. *Average percent of need met:* 92% (excluding resources awarded to replace EFC). *Average financial aid package:* $27,960 (excluding resources awarded to replace EFC). 14% of all full-time freshmen had no need and received non-need-based gift aid.

UNDERGRADUATE FINANCIAL AID (Fall 2016, est.) 2,297 applied for aid; of those 87% were deemed to have need. 100% of undergraduates with need received aid; of those 54% had need fully met. *Average percent of need met:* 92% (excluding resources awarded to replace EFC). *Average financial aid package:* $27,709 (excluding resources awarded to replace EFC). 11% of all full-time undergraduates had no need and received non-need-based gift aid.

GIFT AID (NEED-BASED) *Total amount:* $24,337,786 (13% federal, 12% state, 69% institutional, 6% external sources). *Receiving aid:* Freshmen: 68% (463); all full-time undergraduates: 63% (1,653). *Average award:* Undergraduates: $17,155. *Scholarships, grants, and awards:* Federal Pell, FSEOG, state, private, college/university gift aid from institutional funds.

GIFT AID (NON-NEED-BASED) *Total amount:* $10,111,596 (3% state, 86% institutional, 11% external sources). *Receiving aid:* Freshmen: 73% (499). Undergraduates: 67% (1,759). *Average award:* Freshmen: $9196. Undergraduates: $8682. *Scholarships, grants, and awards by category:* *Academic interests/achievement:* biological sciences, business, communication, computer science, education, English, foreign languages, general academic interests/achievements, health fields, international studies, mathematics, physical sciences, premedicine, religion/biblical studies, social sciences. *Creative arts/performance:* art/fine arts, music, theater/drama. *Special achievements/activities:* cheerleading/drum major, community service, hobbies/interests, religious involvement. *Special characteristics:* children and siblings of alumni, children of faculty/staff, relatives of clergy, religious affiliation, siblings of current students, veterans. *Tuition waivers:* Full or partial for employees or children of employees. *ROTC:* Army.

LOANS *Student loans:* $19,247,909 (63% need-based, 37% non-need-based). 73% of past graduating class borrowed through all loan programs. *Average indebtedness per student:* $28,907. *Average need-based loan:* Freshmen: $3209. Undergraduates: $4077. *Parent loans:* $21,293,189 (45% need-based, 55% non-need-based). *Programs:* Federal Direct (Subsidized and Unsubsidized Stafford, PLUS), Perkins, college/university.

WORK-STUDY *Federal work-study:* Total amount: $2,837,884; jobs available.

ATHLETIC AWARDS Total amount: $1,648,099 (56% need-based, 44% non-need-based).

APPLYING FOR FINANCIAL AID *Required financial aid forms:* FAFSA, institution's own form. *Financial aid deadline (priority):* 3/1. *Notification date:* Continuous beginning 9/1.

CONTACT Lisa Montany, Financial Aid Office, Indiana Wesleyan University, 4201 South Washington Street, Marion, IN 46953-4999, 765-677-2116 or toll-free 866-468-6498. *Fax:* 765-677-2809. *E-mail:* finaid@indwes.edu. *Website:* http://www.indwes.edu/.

INDIAN RIVER STATE COLLEGE
Fort Pierce, FL

Tuition & fees: N/R	Average undergraduate aid package: N/A

ABOUT THE INSTITUTION State-supported, coed. 92 undergraduate majors.

GIFT AID (NEED-BASED) *Scholarships, grants, and awards:* Federal Pell, FSEOG, state, private, college/university gift aid from institutional funds.

LOANS *Programs:* Federal Direct (Subsidized and Unsubsidized Stafford, PLUS).

WORK-STUDY Federal work-study jobs available.

APPLYING FOR FINANCIAL AID *Required financial aid forms:* FAFSA, institution's own form. *Financial aid deadline (priority):* 7/16. *Notification date:* Continuous.

CONTACT Mary Lewis, Director of Financial Aid, Indian River State College, W Building, Main Campus, Fort Pierce, FL 34981, 772-462-7450 or toll-free 866-792-4772. *E-mail:* financialaid-info@irsc.edu. *Website:* http://www.irsc.edu/.

INSTE BIBLE COLLEGE
Ankeny, IA

CONTACT Financial Aid Office, INSTE Bible College, 2302 SW 3rd Street, Ankeny, IA 50023, 515-289-9200. *Website:* http://www.inste.edu/.

INSTITUTE OF AMERICAN INDIAN ARTS
Santa Fe, NM

CONTACT Lala M. Gallegos, Director of Financial Aid, Institute of American Indian Arts, 83 Avan Nu Po Road, Santa Fe, NM 87508, 505-424-5724. *Fax:* 505-424-0909. *E-mail:* lgallegos@iaia.edu. *Website:* http://www.iaia.edu/.

INTER AMERICAN UNIVERSITY OF PUERTO RICO, AGUADILLA CAMPUS
Aguadilla, PR

CONTACT Mr. Juan Gonzalez, Director of Financial Aid , Inter American University of Puerto Rico, Aguadilla Campus, PO Box 20000, Aguadilla, PR 00605, 787-891-0925 Ext. 2108. *Fax:* 787-882-3020.
Website: http://www.aguadilla.inter.edu/.

INTER AMERICAN UNIVERSITY OF PUERTO RICO, ARECIBO CAMPUS
Arecibo, PR

CONTACT Ramón O. de Jesús, Financial Aid Director, Inter American University of Puerto Rico, Arecibo Campus, PO Box 4050, Arecibo, PR 00614-4050, 787-878-5475 Ext. 2275. *Fax:* 787-880-1624.
Website: http://www.arecibo.inter.edu/.

INTER AMERICAN UNIVERSITY OF PUERTO RICO, BARRANQUITAS CAMPUS
Barranquitas, PR

CONTACT Mr. Eduardo Fontanez Colon, Financial Aid Officer, Inter American University of Puerto Rico, Barranquitas Campus, Box 517, Barranquitas, PR 00794, 787-857-3600 Ext. 2049. *Fax:* 787-857-2244.
Website: http://www.br.inter.edu/.

INTER AMERICAN UNIVERSITY OF PUERTO RICO, BAYAMÓN CAMPUS
Bayamón, PR

Tuition & fees: $5178	Average undergraduate aid package: $3755

ABOUT THE INSTITUTION Independent, coed. *Awards:* certificates, associate, bachelor's, and master's degrees. 36 undergraduate majors. *Total enrollment:* 4,450. Undergraduates: 4,328. Freshmen: 910. Both federal and institutional methodology are used as a basis for awarding need-based institutional aid.
UNDERGRADUATE EXPENSES for 2017–2018 *Comprehensive fee:* $11,292 includes full-time tuition ($4488), mandatory fees ($690), and room and board ($6114). *College room only:* $3113. Full-time tuition and fees vary according to course load and program. *Part-time tuition:* $1122 per credit hour. *Part-time fees:* $187 per credit; $305 per semester hour. Part-time tuition and fees vary according to course load and program.
FRESHMAN FINANCIAL AID (Fall 2016, est.) 1,012 applied for aid; of those 99% were deemed to have need. 96% of freshmen with need received aid; of those .1% had need fully met. *Average percent of need met:* 10% (excluding resources awarded to replace EFC). *Average financial aid package:* $1311 (excluding resources awarded to replace EFC).
UNDERGRADUATE FINANCIAL AID (Fall 2016, est.) 2,592 applied for aid; of those 99% were deemed to have need. 98% of undergraduates with need received aid; of those .3% had need fully met. *Average percent of need met:* 28% (excluding resources awarded to replace EFC). *Average financial aid package:* $3755 (excluding resources awarded to replace EFC).
GIFT AID (NEED-BASED) *Total amount:* $1,097,378 (15% federal, 30% state, 55% institutional). *Receiving aid:* Freshmen: 93% (950); all full-time undergraduates: 89% (2,409). *Average award:* Freshmen: $1322; Undergraduates: $3231. *Scholarships, grants, and awards:* Federal Pell, state, college/university gift aid from institutional funds.

GIFT AID (NON-NEED-BASED) *ROTC:* Army cooperative.
LOANS *Student loans:* $3,027,063 (100% need-based). *Average need-based loan:* Freshmen: $237. Undergraduates: $2904. *Parent loans:* $384,706 (100% need-based). *Programs:* Perkins.
WORK-STUDY *Federal work-study:* Total amount: $142,368; jobs available.
APPLYING FOR FINANCIAL AID *Required financial aid form:* FAFSA. *Notification date:* Continuous.
CONTACT Mrs. Aurelis Baez, Director of Student Services, Inter American University of Puerto Rico, Bayamón Campus, 500 Dr. John Will Harris Road, Bayamon, PR 00957, 787-279-1912 Ext. 2017. *E-mail:* abaez@bayamon.inter.edu.
Website: http://bayamon.inter.edu/.

INTER AMERICAN UNIVERSITY OF PUERTO RICO, FAJARDO CAMPUS
Fajardo, PR

CONTACT Financial Aid Director, Inter American University of Puerto Rico, Fajardo Campus, Call Box 700003, Fajardo, PR 00738-7003, 787-863-2390 Ext. 2208.
Website: http://www.fajardo.inter.edu/.

INTER AMERICAN UNIVERSITY OF PUERTO RICO, GUAYAMA CAMPUS
Guayama, PR

Tuition & fees: $6425	Average undergraduate aid package: $4163

ABOUT THE INSTITUTION Independent, coed. *Awards:* certificates, associate, bachelor's, and master's degrees. 18 undergraduate majors. *Total enrollment:* 1,927. Undergraduates: 1,815. Freshmen: 245. Both federal and institutional methodology are used as a basis for awarding need-based institutional aid.
UNDERGRADUATE EXPENSES for 2017–2018 *One-time required fee:* $55. *Tuition:* full-time $5610.
FRESHMAN FINANCIAL AID (Fall 2015) 380 applied for aid; of those 98% were deemed to have need. 96% of freshmen with need received aid. *Average percent of need met:* 8% (excluding resources awarded to replace EFC). *Average financial aid package:* $1399 (excluding resources awarded to replace EFC).
UNDERGRADUATE FINANCIAL AID (Fall 2015) 1,039 applied for aid; of those 100% were deemed to have need. 99% of undergraduates with need received aid; of those .1% had need fully met. *Average percent of need met:* 29% (excluding resources awarded to replace EFC). *Average financial aid package:* $4163 (excluding resources awarded to replace EFC).
GIFT AID (NEED-BASED) *Total amount:* $8,468,438 (95% federal, 2% state, 3% institutional). *Receiving aid:* Freshmen: 93% (356); all full-time undergraduates: 91% (960). *Average award:* Freshmen: $1198; Undergraduates: $3301. *Scholarships, grants, and awards:* Federal Pell, FSEOG, state, college/university gift aid from institutional funds.
GIFT AID (NON-NEED-BASED) *Tuition waivers:* Full or partial for employees or children of employees. *ROTC:* Army cooperative.
LOANS *Average need-based loan:* Freshmen: $240. Undergraduates: $2279. *Parent loans:* $35,532 (100% need-based). *Programs:* Federal Direct (Subsidized and Unsubsidized Stafford, PLUS).
WORK-STUDY *Federal work-study:* jobs available.
APPLYING FOR FINANCIAL AID *Required financial aid form:* FAFSA. *Financial aid deadline:* Continuous. *Notification date:* Continuous beginning 3/1. Students must reply by 8/15 or within 5 weeks of notification.
CONTACT Mr. Jose A. Vechini, Director of Financial Aid, Inter American University of Puerto Rico, Guayama Campus, Call Box 10004, Guayama, PR 00785, 787-864-2222 Ext. 2206. *Fax:* 787-864-8232. *E-mail:* jose.vechini@guayama.inter.edu.
Website: http://www.guayama.inter.edu/.

INTER AMERICAN UNIVERSITY OF PUERTO RICO, METROPOLITAN CAMPUS
San Juan, PR

CONTACT Mrs. Luz M. Medina, Acting Director of Financial Aid, Inter American University of Puerto Rico, Metropolitan Campus, PO Box 191293, San Juan, PR 00919-1293, 787-758-2891. *Fax:* 787-250-0782.
Website: http://metro.inter.edu/.

INTER AMERICAN UNIVERSITY OF PUERTO RICO, PONCE CAMPUS
Mercedita, PR

CONTACT Debra Martinez, Financial Aid Officer, Inter American University of Puerto Rico, Ponce Campus, 104 Turpeaux Industrial Park, Mercedita, PR 00715-2201, 787-284-1912 Ext. 2161. *Fax:* 787-841-0103. *E-mail:* dmartinez@ponce.inter.edu.
Website: http://www.ponce.inter.edu/.

INTER AMERICAN UNIVERSITY OF PUERTO RICO, SAN GERMÁN CAMPUS
San Germán, PR

CONTACT Ms. Maria I. Lugo, Financial Aid Director, Inter American University of Puerto Rico, San Germán Campus, PO Box 5100, San German, PR 00683-5008, 787-264-1912 Ext. 7252 or toll-free 800-981-8075 (in-state). *Fax:* 787-892-6350.
Website: http://www.sg.inter.edu/.

INTERIOR DESIGNERS INSTITUTE
Newport Beach, CA

CONTACT Office of Financial Aid, Interior Designers Institute, 1061 Camelback Road, Newport Beach, CA 92660, 949-675-4451.
Website: http://www.idi.edu/.

INTERNATIONAL BAPTIST COLLEGE AND SEMINARY
Chandler, AZ

CONTACT Financial Aid Office, International Baptist College and Seminary, 2211 West Germann Road, Chandler, AZ 85286, 480-838-7070 Ext. 268 or toll-free 800-422-4858. *Fax:* 480-838-5432. *E-mail:* financialaid@ibconline.edu.
Website: http://www.ibcs.edu/.

INTERNATIONAL BUSINESS COLLEGE
Fort Wayne, IN

CONTACT Financial Aid Office, International Business College, 5699 Coventry Lane, Fort Wayne, IN 46804, 260-459-4500 or toll-free 800-589-6363.
Website: http://www.ibcfortwayne.edu/.

IONA COLLEGE
New Rochelle, NY

Tuition & fees: $37,682	Average undergraduate aid package: $25,451

ABOUT THE INSTITUTION Independent Roman Catholic Church, coed. *Awards:* certificates, bachelor's, and master's degrees. 50 undergraduate majors. *Total enrollment:* 4,019. Undergraduates: 3,329. Freshmen: 935. Federal methodology is used as a basis for awarding need-based institutional aid.

UNDERGRADUATE EXPENSES for 2017–2018 *Application fee:* $50. *Comprehensive fee:* $52,514 includes full-time tuition ($35,482), mandatory fees ($2200), and room and board ($14,832). Room and board charges vary according to board plan. *Part-time tuition:* $1176 per credit hour. *Part-time fees:* $540 per term. Part-time tuition and fees vary according to course load.

FRESHMAN FINANCIAL AID (Fall 2016, est.) 933 applied for aid; of those 89% were deemed to have need. 100% of freshmen with need received aid; of those 19% had need fully met. *Average percent of need met:* 14% (excluding resources awarded to replace EFC). *Average financial aid package:* $26,835 (excluding resources awarded to replace EFC). 11% of all full-time freshmen had no need and received non-need-based gift aid.

UNDERGRADUATE FINANCIAL AID (Fall 2016, est.) 3,004 applied for aid; of those 85% were deemed to have need. 99% of undergraduates with need received aid; of those 20% had need fully met. *Average percent of need met:* 16% (excluding resources awarded to replace EFC). *Average financial aid package:* $25,451 (excluding resources awarded to replace EFC). 14% of all full-time undergraduates had no need and received non-need-based gift aid.

GIFT AID (NEED-BASED) *Total amount:* $49,876,587 (10% federal, 6% state, 81% institutional, 3% external sources). *Receiving aid:* Freshmen: 39% (360); all full-time undergraduates: 34% (1,043). *Average award:* Freshmen: $5374; Undergraduates: $5626. *Scholarships, grants, and awards:* Federal Pell, FSEOG, state, private, college/university gift aid from institutional funds.

GIFT AID (NON-NEED-BASED) *Total amount:* $9,819,021 (2% state, 95% institutional, 3% external sources). *Receiving aid:* Freshmen: 89% (829). Undergraduates: 83% (2,535). *Average award:* Freshmen: $19,672. Undergraduates: $17,647. *Scholarships, grants, and awards by category: Academic interests/achievement:* 1,946 awards ($16,238,332 total): general academic interests/achievements. *Creative arts/performance:* 23 awards ($85,500 total): music. *Special achievements/activities:* 6 awards ($85,980 total): community service. *Special characteristics:* 311 awards ($1,185,869 total): children and siblings of alumni, religious affiliation, siblings of current students, veterans, veterans' children. *Tuition waivers:* Full or partial for children of alumni, employees or children of employees. *ROTC:* Army cooperative, Air Force cooperative.

LOANS *Student loans:* $18,948,565 (72% need-based, 28% non-need-based). 76% of past graduating class borrowed through all loan programs. *Average indebtedness per student:* $34,199. *Average need-based loan:* Freshmen: $3242. Undergraduates: $3629. *Parent loans:* $13,184,764 (56% need-based, 44% non-need-based). *Programs:* Federal Direct (Subsidized and Unsubsidized Stafford, PLUS), Perkins.

WORK-STUDY *Federal work-study:* Total amount: $533,264; 352 jobs averaging $1482. *State or other work-study/employment:* Part-time jobs available.

ATHLETIC AWARDS Total amount: $4,130,373 (60% need-based, 40% non-need-based).

APPLYING FOR FINANCIAL AID *Required financial aid forms:* FAFSA, state aid form. *Financial aid deadline:* 4/15. *Notification date:* 1/1. Students must reply by 5/1 or within 2 weeks of notification.

CONTACT Mary Grant, Director of Financial Aid, Iona College, 715 North Avenue, New Rochelle, NY 10801-1890, 914-633-2676 or toll-free 800-231-IONA. *Fax:* 914-633-2486. *E-mail:* mgrant@iona.edu.
Website: http://www.iona.edu/.

IOWA STATE UNIVERSITY OF SCIENCE AND TECHNOLOGY
Ames, IA

Tuition & fees (IA res): $8420	Average undergraduate aid package: $11,923

ABOUT THE INSTITUTION State-supported, coed. *Awards:* certificates, bachelor's, master's, and doctoral degrees. 133 undergraduate majors. *Total enrollment:* 35,767. Undergraduates: 30,671. Freshmen: 6,325. Federal methodology is used as a basis for awarding need-based institutional aid.

UNDERGRADUATE EXPENSES for 2017–2018 *Application fee:* $40. *Tuition, state resident:* full-time $7240; part-time $296 per credit hour. *Tuition, nonresident:* full-time $21,076; part-time $853 per credit hour. *Required fees:* full-time $1180. Full-time tuition and fees vary according to class time, degree level, program, and student level. Part-time tuition and fees vary according to class time, course load, degree level, program, and student level. *College room and board:* $8356; *Room only:* $4429. Room and board charges vary according to board plan and housing facility.

FRESHMAN FINANCIAL AID (Fall 2015) 5,122 applied for aid; of those 61% were deemed to have need. 99% of freshmen with need received aid; of those 37% had need fully met. *Average percent of need met:* 82% (excluding resources awarded to replace EFC). *Average financial aid package:* $12,176 (excluding resources awarded to replace EFC). 38% of all full-time freshmen had no need and received non-need-based gift aid.

UNDERGRADUATE FINANCIAL AID (Fall 2015) 21,462 applied for aid; of those 65% were deemed to have need. 98% of undergraduates with need received aid; of those 35% had need fully met. *Average percent of need met:* 79% (excluding resources awarded to replace EFC). *Average financial aid package:* $11,923 (excluding resources awarded to replace EFC). 34% of all full-time undergraduates had no need and received non-need-based gift aid.

GIFT AID (NEED-BASED) *Total amount:* $96,896,145 (30% federal, 1% state, 64% institutional, 5% external sources). *Receiving aid:* Freshmen: 51% (3,053); all full-time undergraduates: 49% (13,650). *Average award:* Freshmen: $8333; Undergraduates: $7125. *Scholarships, grants, and awards:* Federal Pell, FSEOG, state, college/university gift aid from institutional funds.

GIFT AID (NON-NEED-BASED) *Total amount:* $44,715,131 (6% federal, 1% state, 71% institutional, 22% external sources). *Receiving aid:* Freshmen: 24% (1,466). Undergraduates: 22% (6,266). *Average award:* Freshmen: $4261. Undergraduates: $3164. *Scholarships, grants, and awards by category: Academic interests/achievement:* agriculture, architecture, area/ethnic studies, biological sciences, business, communication, computer science, education, engineering/technologies, English, foreign languages, general academic interests/achievements, health fields, home economics, humanities, international studies, library science, mathematics, military science, physical sciences, premedicine, social sciences. *Creative arts/performance:* applied art and design, art/fine arts, journalism/publications, music, theater/drama. *Special achievements/activities:* community service, general special achievements/activities, leadership. *Special characteristics:* adult students, children and siblings of alumni, ethnic background, first-generation college students, general special characteristics, international students, local/state students, members of minority groups, out-of-state students, veterans, veterans' children. *ROTC:* Army, Naval, Air Force.

LOANS *Student loans:* $124,999,470 (58% need-based, 42% non-need-based). 60% of past graduating class borrowed through all loan programs. *Average indebtedness per student:* $28,617. *Average need-based loan:* Freshmen: $3385. Undergraduates: $4429. *Parent loans:* $32,361,889 (24% need-based, 76% non-need-based). *Programs:* Federal Direct (Subsidized and Unsubsidized Stafford, PLUS), Perkins, state, college/university, private loans.

WORK-STUDY *Federal work-study:* 1,579 jobs averaging $915. *State or other work-study/employment:* Total amount: $1,109,136 (100% need-based). Part-time jobs available.

ATHLETIC AWARDS Total amount: $7,686,219 (42% need-based, 58% non-need-based).

APPLYING FOR FINANCIAL AID *Required financial aid form:* FAFSA. *Financial aid deadline (priority):* 3/1. *Notification date:* Continuous beginning 4/1. Students must reply by 5/1.

CONTACT Ms. Roberta Johnson, Director of Financial Aid, Iowa State University of Science and Technology, 0210 Beardshear Hall, 515 Morrill Road, Ames, IA 50011-2103, 515-294-2223 or toll-free 800-262-3810. *Fax:* 515-294-3622. *E-mail:* rljohns@iastate.edu.
Website: http://www.iastate.edu/.

IOWA WESLEYAN UNIVERSITY
Mount Pleasant, IA

Tuition & fees: $29,146	Average undergraduate aid package: $14,130

ABOUT THE INSTITUTION Independent United Methodist, coed. *Awards:* bachelor's degrees. 25 undergraduate majors. *Total enrollment:* 473. Undergraduates: 473. Freshmen: 75. Federal methodology is used as a basis for awarding need-based institutional aid.

UNDERGRADUATE EXPENSES for 2016–2017 *Application fee:* $20. *Comprehensive fee:* $39,200 includes full-time tuition ($28,146), mandatory fees ($1000), and room and board ($10,054). *College room only:* $3826. Room and board charges vary according to housing facility. *Part-time tuition:* $710 per credit hour. *Part-time fees:* $20 per credit hour. Part-time tuition and fees vary according to class time, course load, and location.

FRESHMAN FINANCIAL AID (Fall 2015) 118 applied for aid; of those 100% were deemed to have need. 100% of freshmen with need received aid; of those 8% had need fully met. *Average percent of need met:* 69% (excluding resources awarded to replace EFC). *Average financial aid package:* $20,098 (excluding resources awarded to replace EFC). 8% of all full-time freshmen had no need and received non-need-based gift aid.

UNDERGRADUATE FINANCIAL AID (Fall 2015) 381 applied for aid; of those 100% were deemed to have need. 100% of undergraduates with need received aid; of those 10% had need fully met. *Average percent of need met:* 66% (excluding resources awarded to replace EFC). *Average financial aid package:* $14,130 (excluding resources awarded to replace EFC). 10% of all full-time undergraduates had no need and received non-need-based gift aid.

GIFT AID (NEED-BASED) *Total amount:* $6,785,587 (15% federal, 10% state, 73% institutional, 2% external sources). *Receiving aid:* Freshmen: 70% (83); all full-time undergraduates: 69% (266). *Average award:* Freshmen: $19,949; Undergraduates: $9521. *Scholarships, grants, and awards:* Federal Pell, FSEOG, state, private, college/university gift aid from institutional funds.

GIFT AID (NON-NEED-BASED) *Receiving aid:* Freshmen: 100% (118). Undergraduates: 96% (370). *Average award:* Freshmen: $22,598. Undergraduates: $21,500. *Scholarships, grants, and awards by category: Academic interests/achievement:* 427 awards ($2,768,456 total): business, education, English, general academic interests/achievements, health fields, social sciences. *Creative arts/performance:* 34 awards ($52,034 total): art/fine arts, music. *Special characteristics:* 66 awards ($336,438 total): children and siblings of alumni, children of faculty/staff, international students, out-of-state students, siblings of current students. *Tuition waivers:* Full or partial for employees or children of employees.

LOANS *Student loans:* $2,792,511 (44% need-based, 56% non-need-based). 75% of past graduating class borrowed through all loan programs. *Average indebtedness per student:* $33,152. *Average need-based loan:* Freshmen: $3076. Undergraduates: $3190. *Parent loans:* $663,553 (100% non-need-based). *Programs:* Federal Direct (Subsidized and Unsubsidized Stafford, PLUS), alternative loans.

WORK-STUDY *Federal work-study:* 100 jobs averaging $661. *State or other work-study/employment:* Total amount: $1000 (100% need-based). Part-time jobs available.

APPLYING FOR FINANCIAL AID *Required financial aid form:* FAFSA. *Financial aid deadline:* Continuous. *Notification date:* Continuous beginning 3/15.

CONTACT Kristy J. Johnson, Director of Financial Aid, Iowa Wesleyan University, 601 North Main Street, Mount Pleasant, IA 52641-1398, 319-385-6241 or toll-free 800-582-2383. *Fax:* 319-385-6203. *E-mail:* kristy.johnson@iw.edu.
Website: http://www.iw.edu/.

ITHACA COLLEGE
Ithaca, NY

Tuition & fees: $42,884	Average undergraduate aid package: $35,707

ABOUT THE INSTITUTION Independent, coed. *Awards:* certificates, bachelor's, master's, and doctoral degrees. 102 undergraduate majors. *Total enrollment:* 6,678. Undergraduates: 6,221. Freshmen: 1,634. Institutional methodology is used as a basis for awarding need-based institutional aid.

UNDERGRADUATE EXPENSES for 2017–2018 *Application fee:* $60. *Tuition:* full-time $42,884; part-time $1429 per credit hour. Room and board charges vary according to board plan and housing facility.
FRESHMAN FINANCIAL AID (Fall 2016, est.) 1,410 applied for aid; of those 81% were deemed to have need. 100% of freshmen with need received aid; of those 56% had need fully met. *Average percent of need met:* 90% (excluding resources awarded to replace EFC). *Average financial aid package:* $36,465 (excluding resources awarded to replace EFC). 24% of all full-time freshmen had no need and received non-need-based gift aid.
UNDERGRADUATE FINANCIAL AID (Fall 2016, est.) 4,757 applied for aid; of those 86% were deemed to have need. 100% of undergraduates with need received aid; of those 41% had need fully met. *Average percent of need met:* 85% (excluding resources awarded to replace EFC). *Average financial aid package:* $35,707 (excluding resources awarded to replace EFC). 25% of all full-time undergraduates had no need and received non-need-based gift aid.
GIFT AID (NEED-BASED) *Total amount:* $104,724,218 (6% federal, 4% state, 88% institutional, 2% external sources). *Receiving aid:* Freshmen: 68% (1,106); all full-time undergraduates: 66% (4,045). *Average award:* Freshmen: $26,477; Undergraduates: $25,787. *Scholarships, grants, and awards:* Federal Pell, FSEOG, state, private, college/university gift aid from institutional funds.
GIFT AID (NON-NEED-BASED) *Total amount:* $29,421,571 (4% federal, 91% institutional, 5% external sources). *Receiving aid:* Freshmen: 23% (380). Undergraduates: 11% (649). *Average award:* Freshmen: $15,358. Undergraduates: $14,882. *Scholarships, grants, and awards by category:* Academic interests/achievement: 4,504 awards ($64,228,653 total): communication, general academic interests/achievements. *Creative arts/performance:* 188 awards ($683,144 total): cinema/film/broadcasting, dance, journalism/publications, music, performing arts, theater/drama. *Special achievements/activities:* 284 awards ($1,381,000 total): leadership. *Special characteristics:* 790 awards ($4,355,798 total): children and siblings of alumni, children of faculty/staff, general special characteristics, members of minority groups, siblings of current students. *Tuition waivers:* Full or partial for children of alumni, employees or children of employees. *ROTC:* Army cooperative, Air Force cooperative.
LOANS *Student loans:* $31,706,556 (75% need-based, 25% non-need-based). 70% of past graduating class borrowed through all loan programs. *Average indebtedness per student:* $40,595. *Average need-based loan:* Freshmen: $5469. Undergraduates: $6569. *Parent loans:* $33,346,996 (40% need-based, 60% non-need-based). *Programs:* Federal Direct (Subsidized and Unsubsidized Stafford, PLUS), Perkins, alternative loans.
WORK-STUDY *Federal work-study:* Total amount: $1,500,000; jobs available. *State or other work-study/employment:* Total amount: $9,595,725 (63% need-based, 37% non-need-based). 1,802 part-time jobs averaging $2402.
APPLYING FOR FINANCIAL AID *Required financial aid forms:* FAFSA, CSS Financial Aid PROFILE. *Financial aid deadline (priority):* 2/1. *Notification date:* Continuous beginning 2/15. Students must reply by 5/1.
CONTACT Ms. Lisa Hoskey, Director of Student Financial Services, Ithaca College, 953 Danby Road, Ithaca, NY 14850-7002, 800-429-4275 or toll-free 800-429-4274. *Fax:* 607-274-1895. *E-mail:* finaid@ithaca.edu. *Website:* http://www.ithaca.edu/.

JACKSON STATE UNIVERSITY
Jackson, MS

Tuition & fees (MS res): $7261	Average undergraduate aid package: $12,324

ABOUT THE INSTITUTION State-supported, coed. *Awards:* certificates, bachelor's, master's, and doctoral degrees. 43 undergraduate majors. *Total enrollment:* 9,811. Undergraduates: 7,492. Freshmen: 1,292. Federal methodology is used as a basis for awarding need-based institutional aid.
UNDERGRADUATE EXPENSES for 2016–2017 *Tuition, state resident:* full-time $7141; part-time $298 per credit hour. *Tuition, nonresident:* full-time $17,494; part-time $432 per credit hour. *Required fees:* full-time $120. Full-time tuition and fees vary according to course level, course load, degree level, location, program, and student level. Part-time tuition and fees vary according to course level, degree level, location, program, and student level. *College room and board:* $8708; *Room only:* $5258. Room and board charges vary according to housing facility.

FRESHMAN FINANCIAL AID (Fall 2016, est.) 1,226 applied for aid; of those 90% were deemed to have need. 94% of freshmen with need received aid; of those 7% had need fully met. *Average percent of need met:* 55% (excluding resources awarded to replace EFC). *Average financial aid package:* $13,483 (excluding resources awarded to replace EFC). 1% of all full-time freshmen had no need and received non-need-based gift aid.
UNDERGRADUATE FINANCIAL AID (Fall 2016, est.) 6,143 applied for aid; of those 91% were deemed to have need. 97% of undergraduates with need received aid; of those 5% had need fully met. *Average percent of need met:* 53% (excluding resources awarded to replace EFC). *Average financial aid package:* $12,324 (excluding resources awarded to replace EFC). 1% of all full-time undergraduates had no need and received non-need-based gift aid.
GIFT AID (NEED-BASED) *Total amount:* $23,994,205 (100% federal). *Receiving aid:* Freshmen: 67% (855); all full-time undergraduates: 66% (4,287). *Average award:* Freshmen: $8102; Undergraduates: $7543. *Scholarships, grants, and awards:* Federal Pell, FSEOG, state, college/university gift aid from institutional funds.
GIFT AID (NON-NEED-BASED) *Total amount:* $18,266,889 (10% state, 83% institutional, 7% external sources). *Receiving aid:* Freshmen: 32% (408). Undergraduates: 27% (1,775). *Average award:* Freshmen: $11,875. Undergraduates: $12,373. *Scholarships, grants, and awards by category:* Academic interests/achievement: 1,023 awards ($10,889,925 total): general academic interests/achievements. *Creative arts/performance:* 199 awards ($649,921 total): music. *Special achievements/activities:* 96 awards ($95,500 total): leadership. *Special characteristics:* 101 awards ($1,009,418 total): children and siblings of alumni, children of faculty/staff. *Tuition waivers:* Full or partial for children of alumni, employees or children of employees. *ROTC:* Army, Air Force.
LOANS *Student loans:* $44,113,839 (45% need-based, 55% non-need-based). 86% of past graduating class borrowed through all loan programs. *Average indebtedness per student:* $28,311. *Average need-based loan:* Freshmen: $3543. Undergraduates: $4163. *Parent loans:* $9,167,371 (100% non-need-based). *Programs:* Federal Direct (Subsidized and Unsubsidized Stafford, PLUS), Perkins.
WORK-STUDY *Federal work-study:* Total amount: $2,501,804; 1,184 jobs averaging $2341.
ATHLETIC AWARDS Total amount: $2,802,223 (100% non-need-based).
APPLYING FOR FINANCIAL AID *Required financial aid form:* FAFSA. *Financial aid deadline (priority):* 4/15. *Notification date:* Continuous beginning 5/1.
CONTACT Mrs. Betty Moncure, Director of Financial Aid, Jackson State University, 1400 J.R. Lynch Street, PO Box 17065, Jackson, MS 39217, 601-979-2227 or toll-free 800-848-6817. *Fax:* 601-979-2237. *E-mail:* betty.j.moncure@jsums.edu. *Website:* http://www.jsums.edu/.

JACKSONVILLE STATE UNIVERSITY
Jacksonville, AL

Tuition & fees (AL res): $9660	Average undergraduate aid package: $9592

ABOUT THE INSTITUTION State-supported, coed. *Awards:* certificates, bachelor's, master's, and doctoral degrees. 63 undergraduate majors. *Total enrollment:* 8,514. Undergraduates: 7,561. Freshmen: 1,320. Federal methodology is used as a basis for awarding need-based institutional aid.
UNDERGRADUATE EXPENSES for 2016–2017 *Application fee:* $35. *Tuition, state resident:* full-time $9135; part-time $300 per credit hour. *Tuition, nonresident:* full-time $18,270; part-time $600 per credit hour. *Required fees:* full-time $525; $525 per year or $525 per year. *College room and board:* $7128. Room and board charges vary according to board plan and housing facility.
FRESHMAN FINANCIAL AID (Fall 2015) 961 applied for aid; of those 98% were deemed to have need. 100% of freshmen with need received aid. *Average financial aid package:* $9970 (excluding resources awarded to replace EFC).
UNDERGRADUATE FINANCIAL AID (Fall 2015) 4,849 applied for aid; of those 98% were deemed to have need. 100% of undergraduates with need received aid. *Average financial aid package:* $9592 (excluding resources awarded to replace EFC).
GIFT AID (NEED-BASED) *Total amount:* $31,220,540 (41% federal, 1% state, 55% institutional, 3% external sources). *Receiving aid:* Freshmen: 44% (452); all full-time undergraduates: 46% (2,502). *Average award:* Freshmen: $4756; Undergrad-

uates: $4558. **Scholarships, grants, and awards:** Federal Pell, FSEOG, state, private, college/university gift aid from institutional funds.

GIFT AID (NON-NEED-BASED) Receiving aid: Freshmen: 67% (679). Undergraduates: 45% (2,469). **Scholarships, grants, and awards by category:** Academic interests/achievement: biological sciences, business, communication, computer science, education, English, general academic interests/achievements, health fields, home economics, humanities, mathematics, military science, physical sciences, social sciences. Creative arts/performance: art/fine arts, journalism/publications, music, theater/drama. Special achievements/activities: general special achievements/activities, leadership. Special characteristics: children and siblings of alumni, local/state students. **Tuition waivers:** Full or partial for employees or children of employees. **ROTC:** Army.

LOANS Student loans: $36,277,475 (39% need-based, 61% non-need-based). **Average need-based loan:** Freshmen: $1000. Undergraduates: $992. **Parent loans:** $3,248,657 (100% non-need-based). **Programs:** Federal Direct (Subsidized and Unsubsidized Stafford, PLUS), state, college/university.

WORK-STUDY Federal work-study: jobs available. **State or other work-study/employment:** Total amount: $2,707,181 (100% non-need-based). Part-time jobs available.

ATHLETIC AWARDS Total amount: $4,806,442 (100% non-need-based).

APPLYING FOR FINANCIAL AID Required financial aid forms: FAFSA, institution's own form. **Financial aid deadline (priority):** 3/15. **Notification date:** Continuous beginning 4/16. Students must reply within 2 weeks of notification.

CONTACT Ms. Vickie Adams, Director of Financial Aid, Jacksonville State University, 700 Pelham Road North, Jacksonville, AL 36265-9982, 256-782-5006 Ext. 8399 or toll-free 800-231-5291. Fax: 256-782-5476. E-mail: finaid@jsu.edu. Website: http://www.jsu.edu/.

JACKSONVILLE UNIVERSITY
Jacksonville, FL

Tuition & fees: $33,930	Average undergraduate aid package: $22,584

ABOUT THE INSTITUTION Independent, coed. **Awards:** certificates, bachelor's, master's, and doctoral degrees. 94 undergraduate majors. **Total enrollment:** 4,060. Undergraduates: 2,889. Freshmen: 504. Federal methodology is used as a basis for awarding need-based institutional aid.

UNDERGRADUATE EXPENSES for 2016–2017 Application fee: $30. **Comprehensive fee:** $47,480 includes full-time tuition ($33,930) and room and board ($13,550). **College room only:** $9150. Full-time tuition and fees vary according to course level, course load, degree level, and program. Room and board charges vary according to board plan and housing facility. **Part-time tuition:** $1130 per credit hour. **Part-time fees:** $560 per credit hour. Part-time tuition and fees vary according to course level, course load, degree level, and program.

FRESHMAN FINANCIAL AID (Fall 2016, est.) 482 applied for aid; of those 98% were deemed to have need. 100% of freshmen with need received aid; of those 28% had need fully met. **Average percent of need met:** 88% (excluding resources awarded to replace EFC). **Average financial aid package:** $25,336 (excluding resources awarded to replace EFC). 9% of all full-time freshmen had no need and received non-need-based gift aid.

UNDERGRADUATE FINANCIAL AID (Fall 2016, est.) 2,087 applied for aid; of those 87% were deemed to have need. 100% of undergraduates with need received aid; of those 28% had need fully met. **Average percent of need met:** 87% (excluding resources awarded to replace EFC). **Average financial aid package:** $22,584 (excluding resources awarded to replace EFC). 8% of all full-time undergraduates had no need and received non-need-based gift aid.

GIFT AID (NEED-BASED) Total amount: $28,513,365 (14% federal, 13% state, 73% institutional). **Receiving aid:** Freshmen: 94% (471); all full-time undergraduates: 86% (1,810). **Average award:** Freshmen: $20,431; Undergraduates: $16,212. **Scholarships, grants, and awards:** Federal Pell, FSEOG, state, private, college/university gift aid from institutional funds.

GIFT AID (NON-NEED-BASED) Total amount: $2,835,540 (20% state, 80% institutional). **Receiving aid:** Freshmen: 12% (61). Undergraduates: 13% (274). **Average award:** Freshmen: $14,936. Undergraduates: $12,264. **Scholarships, grants, and awards by category:** Academic interests/achievement: general academic interests/achievements. Creative arts/performance: art/fine arts, general creative arts/performance, music, theater/drama. Special achievements/activities: general

special achievements/activities, leadership. Special characteristics: children of educators, children of faculty/staff, international students. **Tuition waivers:** Full or partial for employees or children of employees. **ROTC:** Army, Naval.

LOANS Student loans: $16,129,573 (85% need-based, 15% non-need-based). **Average need-based loan:** Freshmen: $2468. Undergraduates: $3015. **Parent loans:** $5,044,698 (94% need-based, 6% non-need-based). **Programs:** Federal Direct (Subsidized and Unsubsidized Stafford, PLUS), Perkins.

WORK-STUDY Federal work-study: Total amount: $278,476; 158 jobs averaging $1763. **State or other work-study/employment:** Total amount: $75,307 (92% need-based, 8% non-need-based). 164 part-time jobs averaging $425.

ATHLETIC AWARDS Total amount: $4,968,420 (87% need-based, 13% non-need-based).

APPLYING FOR FINANCIAL AID Required financial aid forms: FAFSA, institution's own form, proof of medical insurance coverage and waiver form. **Financial aid deadline (priority):** 3/31. **Notification date:** Continuous beginning 2/20.

CONTACT Chip Moore, Director of Financial Aid, Jacksonville University, 2800 University Boulevard North, Jacksonville, FL 32211, 904-256-7062 or toll-free 800-225-2027. Fax: 904-256-7148. E-mail: cmoore@ju.edu. Website: http://www.ju.edu/.

JAMES MADISON UNIVERSITY
Harrisonburg, VA

Tuition & fees (VA res): $10,342	Average undergraduate aid package: $8528

ABOUT THE INSTITUTION State-supported, coed. **Awards:** bachelor's, master's, and doctoral degrees (also offers specialist in education degree). 46 undergraduate majors. **Total enrollment:** 1,722. Undergraduates: 19,548. Freshmen: 4,505. Federal methodology is used as a basis for awarding need-based institutional aid.

UNDERGRADUATE EXPENSES for 2016–2017 Application fee: $70. **Tuition, state resident:** full-time $5896; part-time $196 per credit hour. **Tuition, nonresident:** full-time $21,670; part-time $703 per credit hour. **Required fees:** full-time $4446. **College room and board:** $9334; **Room only:** $4786. Room and board charges vary according to board plan.

FRESHMAN FINANCIAL AID (Fall 2016, est.) 3,183 applied for aid; of those 65% were deemed to have need. 87% of freshmen with need received aid; of those 88% had need fully met. **Average percent of need met:** 39% (excluding resources awarded to replace EFC). **Average financial aid package:** $9593 (excluding resources awarded to replace EFC). 2% of all full-time freshmen had no need and received non-need-based gift aid.

UNDERGRADUATE FINANCIAL AID (Fall 2016, est.) 10,856 applied for aid; of those 69% were deemed to have need. 91% of undergraduates with need received aid; of those 74% had need fully met. **Average percent of need met:** 43% (excluding resources awarded to replace EFC). **Average financial aid package:** $8528 (excluding resources awarded to replace EFC). 1% of all full-time undergraduates had no need and received non-need-based gift aid.

GIFT AID (NEED-BASED) Total amount: $32,404,417 (38% federal, 24% state, 29% institutional, 9% external sources). **Receiving aid:** Freshmen: 24% (1,070); all full-time undergraduates: 21% (3,808). **Average award:** Freshmen: $8376; Undergraduates: $7300. **Scholarships, grants, and awards:** Federal Pell, FSEOG, state, private, college/university gift aid from institutional funds.

GIFT AID (NON-NEED-BASED) Total amount: $5,187,747 (2% state, 93% institutional, 5% external sources). **Receiving aid:** Freshmen: 3% (140). Undergraduates: 3% (642). **Average award:** Freshmen: $6094. Undergraduates: $4418. **Scholarships, grants, and awards by category:** Academic interests/achievement: architecture, biological sciences, business, computer science, education, engineering/technologies, English, general academic interests/achievements, health fields, humanities, international studies, mathematics, military science, physical sciences, premedicine, religion/biblical studies, social sciences. Creative arts/performance: art/fine arts, cinema/film/broadcasting, dance, journalism/publications, music, theater/drama. Special achievements/activities: cheerleading/drum major, general special achievements/activities, leadership. Special characteristics: children and siblings of alumni, children of faculty/staff, handicapped students, international students, local/state students, members of minority groups, out-of-state students, siblings of current students. **Tuition waivers:** Full or partial for employees or children of employees. **ROTC:** Army, Air Force cooperative.

LOANS *Student loans:* $66,950,962 (34% need-based, 66% non-need-based). 52% of past graduating class borrowed through all loan programs. *Average indebtedness per student:* $28,407. *Average need-based loan:* Freshmen: $3490. Undergraduates: $3767. *Parent loans:* $50,076,570 (100% non-need-based). *Programs:* Federal Direct (Subsidized and Unsubsidized Stafford, PLUS), Perkins.

WORK-STUDY *Federal work-study:* Total amount: $601,090; jobs available. *State or other work-study/employment:* Total amount: $5,838,221 (100% non-need-based). Part-time jobs available.

ATHLETIC AWARDS Total amount: $7,111,009 (100% non-need-based).

APPLYING FOR FINANCIAL AID *Required financial aid form:* FAFSA. *Financial aid deadline (priority):* 3/1. *Notification date:* Continuous beginning 4/1. Students must reply within 4 weeks of notification.

CONTACT Lisa L. Tumer, Director of Financial Aid and Scholarships, James Madison University, 800 South Main Street, MSC 3519, Harrisonburg, VA 22807, 540-568-7820. *Fax:* 540-568-7994. *E-mail:* fin_aid@jmu.edu.
Website: http://www.jmu.edu/.

JARVIS CHRISTIAN COLLEGE
Hawkins, TX

CONTACT Alice Copeland, Director of Financial Aid, Jarvis Christian College, PO Box 1470, Hawkins, TX 75765, 903-730-4890 Ext. 2402. *Fax:* 903-730-4891. *E-mail:* alice.copeland@jarvis.edu.
Website: http://www.jarvis.edu/.

JEFFERSON COLLEGE OF HEALTH SCIENCES
Roanoke, VA

ABOUT THE INSTITUTION Independent, coed. *Awards:* certificates, associate, bachelor's, and master's degrees. 11 undergraduate majors. *Total enrollment:* 1,062. Undergraduates: 800. Freshmen: 133.

GIFT AID (NEED-BASED) *Scholarships, grants, and awards:* Federal Pell, FSEOG, state, private, college/university gift aid from institutional funds.

GIFT AID (NON-NEED-BASED) *Scholarships, grants, and awards by category:* Academic interests/achievement: biological sciences, health fields. *Special characteristics:* local/state students.

LOANS *Programs:* Federal Direct (Subsidized and Unsubsidized Stafford, PLUS), alternative loans.

APPLYING FOR FINANCIAL AID *Required financial aid forms:* FAFSA, state aid form.

CONTACT Debra A. Johnson, Director of Financial Aid, Jefferson College of Health Sciences, 101 Elm Avenue SE, Roanoke, VA 24013-2222, 540-985-8492 or toll-free 888-985-8483. *Fax:* 540-224-6916. *E-mail:* djjohnson@jchs.edu.
Website: http://www.jchs.edu/.

THE JEWISH THEOLOGICAL SEMINARY
New York, NY

CONTACT Linda Levine, Registrar/Director of Financial Aid, The Jewish Theological Seminary, 3080 Broadway, New York, NY 10027-4649, 212-678-8007. *Fax:* 212-678-8947. *E-mail:* financialaid@jtsa.edu.
Website: http://www.jtsa.edu/.

JOHN BROWN UNIVERSITY
Siloam Springs, AR

Tuition & fees: $25,324	Average undergraduate aid package: $18,587

ABOUT THE INSTITUTION Independent interdenominational, coed. *Awards:* certificates, associate, bachelor's, and master's degrees. 39 undergraduate majors. *Total enrollment:* 2,708. Undergraduates: 2,017. Freshmen: 322. Federal methodology is used as a basis for awarding need-based institutional aid.

UNDERGRADUATE EXPENSES for 2016–2017 *Application fee:* $25. *Comprehensive fee:* $34,164 includes full-time tuition ($24,218), mandatory fees ($1106), and room and board ($8840). Full-time tuition and fees vary according to course load. Room and board charges vary according to board plan and housing facility. *Part-time tuition:* $807 per credit hour. *Part-time fees:* $277 per term. Part-time tuition and fees vary according to course load.

FRESHMAN FINANCIAL AID (Fall 2015) 321 applied for aid; of those 52% were deemed to have need. 100% of freshmen with need received aid; of those 1% had need fully met. *Average percent of need met:* 71% (excluding resources awarded to replace EFC). *Average financial aid package:* $22,106 (excluding resources awarded to replace EFC). 52% of all full-time freshmen had no need and received non-need-based gift aid.

UNDERGRADUATE FINANCIAL AID (Fall 2015) 1,227 applied for aid; of those 67% were deemed to have need. 100% of undergraduates with need received aid; of those 1% had need fully met. *Average percent of need met:* 59% (excluding resources awarded to replace EFC). *Average financial aid package:* $18,587 (excluding resources awarded to replace EFC). 41% of all full-time undergraduates had no need and received non-need-based gift aid.

GIFT AID (NEED-BASED) *Total amount:* $12,158,284 (20% federal, 9% state, 68% institutional, 3% external sources). *Receiving aid:* Freshmen: 46% (165); all full-time undergraduates: 48% (741). *Average award:* Freshmen: $17,775; Undergraduates: $13,803. *Scholarships, grants, and awards:* Federal Pell, FSEOG, state, private, college/university gift aid from institutional funds.

GIFT AID (NON-NEED-BASED) *Total amount:* $7,369,980 (5% state, 65% institutional, 30% external sources). *Receiving aid:* Freshmen: 42% (150). Undergraduates: 37% (561). *Average award:* Freshmen: $16,142. Undergraduates: $15,006. *Scholarships, grants, and awards by category:* Academic interests/achievement: general academic interests/achievements. *Creative arts/performance:* art/fine arts, journalism/publications, music, theater/drama. *Tuition waivers:* Full or partial for employees or children of employees. *ROTC:* Army cooperative, Air Force cooperative.

LOANS *Student loans:* $7,278,446 (70% need-based, 30% non-need-based). 59% of past graduating class borrowed through all loan programs. *Average indebtedness per student:* $26,651. *Average need-based loan:* Freshmen: $4750. Undergraduates: $4523. *Parent loans:* $1,752,757 (17% need-based, 83% non-need-based). *Programs:* Federal Direct (Subsidized and Unsubsidized Stafford, PLUS), Perkins, college/university.

WORK-STUDY *Federal work-study:* jobs available. *State or other work-study/employment:* Total amount: $630,926 (84% need-based, 16% non-need-based). Part-time jobs available.

ATHLETIC AWARDS Total amount: $1,625,666 (35% need-based, 65% non-need-based).

APPLYING FOR FINANCIAL AID *Required financial aid forms:* FAFSA, institution's own form, state aid form. *Financial aid deadline (priority):* 3/1. *Notification date:* Continuous beginning 3/1. Students must reply by 5/1.

CONTACT Mr. Kim Eldridge, Director of Student Financial Aid, John Brown University, 2000 West University Street, Siloam Springs, AR 72761-2121, 479-524-7424 or toll-free 877-JBU-INFO. *Fax:* 479-524-7405. *E-mail:* keldridg@jbu.edu.
Website: http://www.jbu.edu/.

JOHN CARROLL UNIVERSITY
University Heights, OH

Tuition & fees: $39,790	Average undergraduate aid package: $30,799

ABOUT THE INSTITUTION Independent Roman Catholic (Jesuit), coed. *Awards:* certificates, bachelor's, and master's degrees. 53 undergraduate majors. *Total enrollment:* 3,525. Undergraduates: 3,026. Freshmen: 717. Federal methodology is used as a basis for awarding need-based institutional aid.

UNDERGRADUATE EXPENSES for 2017–2018 *One-time required fee:* $325. *Tuition:* full-time $38,490; part-time $1275 per credit hour. Full-time tuition and fees vary according to degree level. Part-time tuition and fees vary according to course load and degree level. Room and board charges vary according to board plan and housing facility.

FRESHMAN FINANCIAL AID (Fall 2016, est.) 649 applied for aid; of those 84% were deemed to have need. 100% of freshmen with need received aid; of those 29% had need fully met. *Average percent of need met:* 84% (excluding resources awarded to replace EFC). *Average financial aid package:* $31,492 (excluding resources awarded to replace EFC). 24% of all full-time freshmen had no need and received non-need-based gift aid.

UNDERGRADUATE FINANCIAL AID (Fall 2016, est.) 2,441 applied for aid; of those 84% were deemed to have need. 100% of undergraduates with need received aid; of those 27% had need fully met. *Average percent of need met:* 82% (excluding resources awarded to replace EFC). *Average financial aid package:* $30,799 (excluding resources awarded to replace EFC). 26% of all full-time undergraduates had no need and received non-need-based gift aid.

GIFT AID (NEED-BASED) *Total amount:* $49,035,336 (8% federal, 2% state, 89% institutional, 1% external sources). *Receiving aid:* Freshmen: 74% (529); all full-time undergraduates: 70% (2,022). *Average award:* Freshmen: $25,319; Undergraduates: $24,502. *Scholarships, grants, and awards:* Federal Pell, FSEOG, state, private, college/university gift aid from institutional funds.

GIFT AID (NON-NEED-BASED) *Total amount:* $19,376,042 (100% institutional). *Receiving aid:* Freshmen: 75% (533). Undergraduates: 70% (2,027). *Average award:* Freshmen: $21,195. Undergraduates: $19,475. *Scholarships, grants, and awards by category:* Academic interests/achievement: biological sciences, business, communication, computer science, education, English, foreign languages, health fields, mathematics, military science, physical sciences, premedicine, religion/biblical studies, social sciences. *Special achievements/activities:* community service, leadership. *Special characteristics:* children of educators, children of faculty/staff, local/state students, veterans, veterans' children. *Tuition waivers:* Full or partial for employees or children of employees, senior citizens. *ROTC:* Army.

LOANS *Student loans:* $17,582,292 (86% need-based, 14% non-need-based). 73% of past graduating class borrowed through all loan programs. *Average indebtedness per student:* $31,993. *Average need-based loan:* Freshmen: $2739. Undergraduates: $3981. *Parent loans:* $6,256,133 (79% need-based, 21% non-need-based). *Programs:* Federal Direct (Subsidized and Unsubsidized Stafford, PLUS), Perkins.

WORK-STUDY *Federal work-study:* Total amount: $1,258,480; jobs available.

APPLYING FOR FINANCIAL AID *Required financial aid form:* FAFSA. *Financial aid deadline:* 3/15 (priority: 12/1). *Notification date:* Continuous beginning 1/15. Students must reply by 5/1 or within 4 weeks of notification.

CONTACT Ms. Claudia A. Wenzel, Director of Financial Assistance, John Carroll University, 20700 North Park Boulevard, University Heights, OH 44118-4581, 216-397-4248 or toll-free 888-335-6800. *Fax:* 216-397-3098. *E-mail:* jcuofa@jcu.edu. *Website:* http://www.jcu.edu/.

JOHN F. KENNEDY UNIVERSITY
Pleasant Hill, CA

CONTACT Mindy Bergeron, Director of Financial Aid, John F. Kennedy University, 100 Ellinwood Way, Pleasant Hill, CA 94523, 925-969-3385 or toll-free 800-696-JFKU. *Fax:* 925-969-3390. *E-mail:* bergeron@jfku.edu. *Website:* http://www.jfku.edu/.

JOHN JAY COLLEGE OF CRIMINAL JUSTICE OF THE CITY UNIVERSITY OF NEW YORK
New York, NY

Tuition & fees: N/R	Average undergraduate aid package: $8437

ABOUT THE INSTITUTION State and locally supported, coed. *Awards:* certificates, bachelor's, and master's degrees. 28 undergraduate majors. *Total enrollment:* 14,430. Undergraduates: 12,674. Freshmen: 1,523. Federal methodology is used as a basis for awarding need-based institutional aid.

FRESHMAN FINANCIAL AID (Fall 2015) 2,931 applied for aid; of those 92% were deemed to have need. 92% of freshmen with need received aid. *Average percent of need met:* 85% (excluding resources awarded to replace EFC). *Average financial aid package:* $8437 (excluding resources awarded to replace EFC).

UNDERGRADUATE FINANCIAL AID (Fall 2015) 9,810 applied for aid; of those 96% were deemed to have need. 85% of undergraduates with need received aid. *Average percent of need met:* 85% (excluding resources awarded to replace EFC). *Average financial aid package:* $8437 (excluding resources awarded to replace EFC).

GIFT AID (NEED-BASED) *Total amount:* $64,918,517 (54% federal, 43% state, 1% institutional, 2% external sources). *Receiving aid:* Freshmen: 61% (2,290); all full-time undergraduates: 61% (7,386). *Average award:* Freshmen: $2639; Undergraduates: $2639. *Scholarships, grants, and awards:* Federal Pell, FSEOG, state, college/university gift aid from institutional funds.

GIFT AID (NON-NEED-BASED) *Receiving aid:* Freshmen: 5% (205). Undergraduates: 2% (217). *Scholarships, grants, and awards by category:* Academic interests/achievement: general academic interests/achievements.

LOANS *Student loans:* $21,845,119 (33% need-based, 67% non-need-based). 31% of past graduating class borrowed through all loan programs. *Average need-based loan:* Freshmen: $3825. Undergraduates: $3825. *Parent loans:* $1,127,861 (100% non-need-based). *Programs:* Federal Direct (Subsidized and Unsubsidized Stafford, PLUS), Perkins, college/university.

WORK-STUDY *Federal work-study:* jobs available. *State or other work-study/employment:* Part-time jobs available.

APPLYING FOR FINANCIAL AID *Required financial aid forms:* FAFSA, state aid form. *Financial aid deadline:* Continuous. *Notification date:* Continuous beginning 4/1. Students must reply within 2 weeks of notification.

CONTACT Sylvia C. Lopez-Crespo, Director of Financial Aid, John Jay College of Criminal Justice of the City University of New York, 524 West 59th Street, New York, NY 10019-1093, 212-237-8897 or toll-free 877-JOHNJAY. *Fax:* 212-237-8936. *E-mail:* sylopez@jjay.cuny.edu. *Website:* http://www.jjay.cuny.edu/.

JOHN PAUL THE GREAT CATHOLIC UNIVERSITY
Escondido, CA

Tuition & fees: $24,900	Average undergraduate aid package: $13,005

ABOUT THE INSTITUTION Independent Roman Catholic Church, coed. *Awards:* certificates, bachelor's, and master's degrees. 2 undergraduate majors. *Total enrollment:* 343. Undergraduates: 227. Freshmen: 74. Both federal and institutional methodology are used as a basis for awarding need-based institutional aid.

UNDERGRADUATE EXPENSES for 2016–2017 *Application fee:* $50. *Tuition:* full-time $24,000; part-time $667 per credit. Full-time tuition and fees vary according to degree level. Part-time tuition and fees vary according to degree level. Room and board charges vary according to housing facility. *Payment plan:* Guaranteed tuition.

FRESHMAN FINANCIAL AID (Fall 2015) 60 applied for aid; of those 78% were deemed to have need. 100% of freshmen with need received aid; of those 2% had need fully met. *Average percent of need met:* 43% (excluding resources awarded to replace EFC). *Average financial aid package:* $18,914 (excluding resources awarded to replace EFC). 2% of all full-time freshmen had no need and received non-need-based gift aid.

UNDERGRADUATE FINANCIAL AID (Fall 2015) 172 applied for aid; of those 83% were deemed to have need. 100% of undergraduates with need received aid; of those 8% had need fully met. *Average percent of need met:* 34% (excluding resources awarded to replace EFC). *Average financial aid package:* $13,005 (excluding resources awarded to replace EFC). 8% of all full-time undergraduates had no need and received non-need-based gift aid.

GIFT AID (NEED-BASED) *Total amount:* $1,859,726 (13% federal, 4% state, 81% institutional, 2% external sources). *Receiving aid:* Freshmen: 75% (47); all full-time undergraduates: 74% (143). *Average award:* Freshmen: $14,645; Undergraduates: $12,678. *Scholarships, grants, and awards:* Federal Pell, FSEOG, state, private, college/university gift aid from institutional funds.

GIFT AID (NON-NEED-BASED) *Total amount:* $216,051 (98% institutional, 2% external sources). *Receiving aid:* Freshmen: 17% (11). Undergraduates: 5% (9). *Average award:* Freshmen: $5000. Undergraduates: $8564.

LOANS *Student loans:* $1,020,926 (79% need-based, 21% non-need-based). *Average need-based loan:* Freshmen: $3280. Undergraduates: $7115. *Parent loans:* $762,885 (35% need-based, 65% non-need-based). *Programs:* Federal Direct (Subsidized and Unsubsidized Stafford, PLUS).

WORK-STUDY *Federal work-study:* jobs available.

APPLYING FOR FINANCIAL AID *Required financial aid forms:* FAFSA, institution's own form. *Financial aid deadline:* 4/15. *Notification date:* Continuous beginning 11/1. Students must reply by 5/1 or within 2 weeks of notification.

CONTACT Lisa Williams, Director of Financial Aid, John Paul the Great Catholic University, 220 West Grand Avenue, Escondido, CA 92025, 858-653-6740 Ext. 1303. *Fax:* 858-653-3791. *E-mail:* lwilliams@jpcatholic.com.

Website: http://www.jpcatholic.com/.

JOHNS HOPKINS UNIVERSITY
Baltimore, MD

ABOUT THE INSTITUTION Independent, coed. *Awards:* certificates, diplomas, bachelor's, master's, and doctoral degrees. 66 undergraduate majors. *Total enrollment:* 23,992. Undergraduates: 6,117. Freshmen: 1,369.

GIFT AID (NEED-BASED) *Scholarships, grants, and awards:* Federal Pell, FSEOG, state, private, college/university gift aid from institutional funds.

GIFT AID (NON-NEED-BASED) *Scholarships, grants, and awards by category:* Academic interests/achievement: engineering/technologies, general academic interests/achievements. *Special characteristics:* children of faculty/staff, local/state students.

LOANS *Programs:* Federal Direct (Subsidized and Unsubsidized Stafford, PLUS), Perkins, college/university.

WORK-STUDY *Federal work-study:* 1,696 jobs averaging $2428. *State or other work-study/employment:* Total amount: $525,624 (100% need-based). Part-time jobs available.

APPLYING FOR FINANCIAL AID *Required financial aid forms:* FAFSA, CSS Financial Aid PROFILE, noncustodial (divorced/separated) parent's statement, federal income tax form(s).

CONTACT Mr. Tom McDermott, Director of Student Financial Services, Johns Hopkins University, 146 Garland Hall, Baltimore, MD 21218, 410-516-8028. *Fax:* 410-516-6015. *E-mail:* tmcderm1@jhu.edu.

Website: http://www.jhu.edu/.

JOHNSON & WALES UNIVERSITY
Denver, CO

ABOUT THE INSTITUTION Independent, coed. *Awards:* associate, bachelor's, and master's degrees. 16 undergraduate majors. *Total enrollment:* 1,388. Undergraduates: 1,356. Freshmen: 351.

GIFT AID (NEED-BASED) *Scholarships, grants, and awards:* Federal Pell, FSEOG, state, private, college/university gift aid from institutional funds.

GIFT AID (NON-NEED-BASED) *Scholarships, grants, and awards by category:* Academic interests/achievement: general academic interests/achievements. *Special achievements/activities:* leadership, memberships. *Special characteristics:* children and siblings of alumni, children of faculty/staff, local/state students.

LOANS *Programs:* Federal Direct (Subsidized and Unsubsidized Stafford, PLUS), Perkins, state.

WORK-STUDY *Federal work-study:* jobs available.

APPLYING FOR FINANCIAL AID *Required financial aid form:* FAFSA.

CONTACT Ms. Lynn Robinson, Executive Director of Student Financial Services, Johnson & Wales University, 8 Abbott Park Place, Providence, RI 02903, 401-598-4648 or toll-free 877-598-3368. *Fax:* 401-598-1040. *E-mail:* fp@jwu.edu.

Website: http://www.jwu.edu/denver/.

JOHNSON & WALES UNIVERSITY
North Miami, FL

ABOUT THE INSTITUTION Independent, coed. *Awards:* associate and bachelor's degrees. 14 undergraduate majors. *Total enrollment:* 1,752. Undergraduates: 1,752. Freshmen: 453.

GIFT AID (NEED-BASED) *Scholarships, grants, and awards:* Federal Pell, FSEOG, state, private, college/university gift aid from institutional funds.

GIFT AID (NON-NEED-BASED) *Scholarships, grants, and awards by category:* Academic interests/achievement: general academic interests/achievements. *Special achievements/activities:* leadership, memberships. *Special characteristics:* children and siblings of alumni, children of faculty/staff, local/state students.

LOANS *Programs:* Federal Direct (Subsidized and Unsubsidized Stafford, PLUS), Perkins.

WORK-STUDY *Federal work-study:* jobs available. *State or other work-study/employment:* Part-time jobs available.

APPLYING FOR FINANCIAL AID *Required financial aid form:* FAFSA.

CONTACT Ms. Lynn Robinson, Executive Director of Student Financial Services, Johnson & Wales University, 8 Abbott Park Place, Providence, RI 02903, 401-598-4648 or toll-free 866-598-3567. *Fax:* 401-598-1040. *E-mail:* fp@jwu.edu.

Website: http://www.jwu.edu/northmiami/.

JOHNSON & WALES UNIVERSITY
Charlotte, NC

ABOUT THE INSTITUTION Independent, coed. 13 undergraduate majors.

GIFT AID (NEED-BASED) *Scholarships, grants, and awards:* Federal Pell, FSEOG, state, private, college/university gift aid from institutional funds.

GIFT AID (NON-NEED-BASED) *Scholarships, grants, and awards by category:* Academic interests/achievement: general academic interests/achievements. *Special achievements/activities:* leadership, memberships. *Special characteristics:* children and siblings of alumni, children of faculty/staff, local/state students.

LOANS *Programs:* Federal Direct (Subsidized and Unsubsidized Stafford, PLUS), Perkins.

WORK-STUDY *Federal work-study:* jobs available.

APPLYING FOR FINANCIAL AID *Required financial aid form:* FAFSA.

CONTACT Ms. Lynn Robinson, Executive Director of Student Financial Services, Johnson & Wales University, 8 Abbott Park Place, Providence, RI 02903, 401-598-1648 or toll-free 866-598-2427. *Fax:* 401-598-4751. *E-mail:* fp@jwu.edu.

Website: http://www.jwu.edu/charlotte/.

JOHNSON & WALES UNIVERSITY
Providence, RI

ABOUT THE INSTITUTION Independent, coed. *Awards:* certificates, diplomas, associate, bachelor's, master's, and doctoral degrees (branch locations in Charlotte, NC; Denver, CO; North Miami, FL). 38 undergraduate majors. *Total enrollment:* 9,454. Undergraduates: 8,718. Freshmen: 2,065.

GIFT AID (NEED-BASED) *Scholarships, grants, and awards:* Federal Pell, FSEOG, state, private, college/university gift aid from institutional funds.

GIFT AID (NON-NEED-BASED) *Scholarships, grants, and awards by category:* Academic interests/achievement: general academic interests/achievements. *Special achievements/activities:* leadership, memberships. *Special characteristics:* children and siblings of alumni, children of faculty/staff, local/state students.

LOANS *Programs:* Federal Direct (Subsidized and Unsubsidized Stafford, PLUS), Perkins.
WORK-STUDY *Federal work-study:* jobs available.
APPLYING FOR FINANCIAL AID *Required financial aid form:* FAFSA.
CONTACT Ms. Lynn Robinson, Executive Director of Student Financial Services, Johnson & Wales University, 8 Abbott Park Place, Providence, RI 02903, 401-598-4648 or toll-free 800-342-5598. *Fax:* 401-598-1040. *E-mail:* fp@jwu.edu.
Website: http://www.jwu.edu/providence/.

JOHNSON C. SMITH UNIVERSITY
Charlotte, NC

Tuition & fees: $18,236	Average undergraduate aid package: $15,853

ABOUT THE INSTITUTION Independent, coed. *Awards:* bachelor's and master's degrees. 26 undergraduate majors. *Total enrollment:* 1,428. Undergraduates: 1,326. Freshmen: 302. Federal methodology is used as a basis for awarding need-based institutional aid.
UNDERGRADUATE EXPENSES for 2017–2018 *Application fee:* $25. *Comprehensive fee:* $25,336 includes full-time tuition ($18,236) and room and board ($7100). *College room only:* $4086. Full-time tuition and fees vary according to course load. Room and board charges vary according to board plan and housing facility. *Part-time tuition:* $418 per credit hour. Part-time tuition and fees vary according to course load.
FRESHMAN FINANCIAL AID (Fall 2016, est.) 293 applied for aid; of those 95% were deemed to have need. 99% of freshmen with need received aid; of those 4% had need fully met. *Average percent of need met:* 57% (excluding resources awarded to replace EFC). *Average financial aid package:* $16,194 (excluding resources awarded to replace EFC). 5% of all full-time freshmen had no need and received non-need-based gift aid.
UNDERGRADUATE FINANCIAL AID (Fall 2016, est.) 1,222 applied for aid; of those 96% were deemed to have need. 99% of undergraduates with need received aid; of those 6% had need fully met. *Average percent of need met:* 57% (excluding resources awarded to replace EFC). *Average financial aid package:* $15,853 (excluding resources awarded to replace EFC). 6% of all full-time undergraduates had no need and received non-need-based gift aid.
GIFT AID (NEED-BASED) *Total amount:* $12,400,554 (42% federal, 22% state, 34% institutional, 2% external sources). *Receiving aid:* Freshmen: 87% (262); all full-time undergraduates: 87% (1,121). *Average award:* Freshmen: $13,498; Undergraduates: $12,023. *Scholarships, grants, and awards:* Federal Pell, FSEOG, state, private, college/university gift aid from institutional funds, United Negro College Fund.
GIFT AID (NON-NEED-BASED) *Total amount:* $1,252,802 (4% state, 93% institutional, 3% external sources). *Receiving aid:* Freshmen: 4% (12). Undergraduates: 3% (43). *Average award:* Freshmen: $13,498. Undergraduates: $14,345. *Scholarships, grants, and awards by category: Academic interests/achievement:* biological sciences, computer science, engineering/technologies, general academic interests/achievements, mathematics. *Creative arts/performance:* music. *Special achievements/activities:* general special achievements/activities. *Special characteristics:* children of faculty/staff, ethnic background, general special characteristics, international students, out-of-state students, siblings of current students. *Tuition waivers:* Full or partial for employees or children of employees.
LOANS *Student loans:* $9,403,160 (94% need-based, 6% non-need-based). 79% of past graduating class borrowed through all loan programs. *Average indebtedness per student:* $38,732. *Average need-based loan:* Freshmen: $3478. Undergraduates: $4036. *Parent loans:* $1,738,741 (24% need-based, 76% non-need-based). *Programs:* Federal Direct (Subsidized and Unsubsidized Stafford, PLUS).
WORK-STUDY *Federal work-study:* Total amount: $446,679; 195 jobs averaging $2521. *State or other work-study/employment:* Total amount: $273,003 (66% need-based, 34% non-need-based). Part-time jobs available.
ATHLETIC AWARDS Total amount: $1,776,356 (65% need-based, 35% non-need-based).
APPLYING FOR FINANCIAL AID *Required financial aid forms:* FAFSA, state aid form. *Financial aid deadline:* 4/1 (priority: 3/1). *Notification date:* 3/15.

CONTACT Shelline Warren, Office of Financial Aid, Johnson C. Smith University, 100 Beatties Ford Road, Charlotte, NC 28216, 704-378-1498 or toll-free 800-782-7303. *Fax:* 704-378-1292.
Website: http://www.jcsu.edu/.

JOHNSON STATE COLLEGE
Johnson, VT

CONTACT Ms. Kimberly Goodell, Financial Aid Officer, Johnson State College, 337 College Hill, Johnson, VT 05656-9405, 802-635-2356 or toll-free 800-635-2356. *Fax:* 802-635-1463. *E-mail:* goodellk@badger.jsc.vsc.edu.
Website: http://www.jsc.edu/.

JOHNSON UNIVERSITY
Knoxville, TN

CONTACT Mr. Lawrence Rector, CPA, Financial Aid Director, Johnson University, 7900 Johnson Drive, Knoxville, TN 37998, 865-251-2303 Ext. 2316 or toll-free 800-827-2122. *Fax:* 865-251-2337. *E-mail:* lrector@jbc.edu.
Website: http://www.johnsonu.edu/.

JOHNSON UNIVERSITY FLORIDA
Kissimmee, FL

CONTACT Ms. Sandra Peppard, Director of Student Financial Aid, Johnson University Florida, 1011 Bill Beck Boulevard, Kissimmee, FL 34744-5301, 407-847-8966 Ext. 365 or toll-free 888-468-6322. *Fax:* 407-847-3925. *E-mail:* sandi.peppard@fcc.edu.
Website: http://www.johnsonu.edu/.

JOHN WESLEY UNIVERSITY
High Point, NC

Tuition & fees: $11,230	Average undergraduate aid package: $8343

ABOUT THE INSTITUTION Independent interdenominational, coed. *Awards:* certificates, associate, bachelor's, master's, and doctoral degrees. 7 undergraduate majors. *Total enrollment:* 150. Undergraduates: 126. Freshmen: 33. Federal methodology is used as a basis for awarding need-based institutional aid.
UNDERGRADUATE EXPENSES for 2016–2017 *Application fee:* $20. *Tuition:* full-time $10,500; part-time $5250 per year. *Required fees:* full-time $730; $730 per year. Full-time tuition and fees vary according to program. Part-time tuition and fees vary according to program.
FRESHMAN FINANCIAL AID (Fall 2016, est.) 48 applied for aid; of those 100% were deemed to have need. 100% of freshmen with need received aid; of those 4% had need fully met. *Average percent of need met:* 52% (excluding resources awarded to replace EFC). *Average financial aid package:* $8102 (excluding resources awarded to replace EFC).
UNDERGRADUATE FINANCIAL AID (Fall 2016, est.) 117 applied for aid; of those 100% were deemed to have need. 100% of undergraduates with need received aid; of those 3% had need fully met. *Average percent of need met:* 51% (excluding resources awarded to replace EFC). *Average financial aid package:* $8343 (excluding resources awarded to replace EFC). 2% of all full-time undergraduates had no need and received non-need-based gift aid.
GIFT AID (NEED-BASED) *Total amount:* $492,454 (63% federal, 3% state, 34% institutional). *Receiving aid:* Freshmen: 94% (45); all full-time undergraduates: 91% (107). *Average award:* Freshmen: $6152; Undergraduates: $5781. *Scholarships, grants, and awards:* Federal Pell, FSEOG, state, private, college/university gift aid from institutional funds.
GIFT AID (NON-NEED-BASED) *Receiving aid:* Freshmen: 4% (2). Undergraduates: 5% (6). *Average award:* Undergraduates: $1125. *Scholarships, grants,*

and awards by category: *Academic interests/achievement:* 29 awards: business, education, general academic interests/achievements, religion/biblical studies. *Creative arts/performance:* 11 awards: music. *Special achievements/activities:* 36 awards: leadership. *Special characteristics:* 1 award: children of faculty/staff, general special characteristics, married students, spouses of current students. **Tuition waivers:** Full or partial for employees or children of employees.

LOANS *Student loans:* $1,096,241 (35% need-based, 65% non-need-based). 100% of past graduating class borrowed through all loan programs. *Average indebtedness per student:* $28,217. *Average need-based loan:* Freshmen: $3042. Undergraduates: $4106. *Parent loans:* $129,860 (100% non-need-based). *Programs:* Federal Direct (Subsidized and Unsubsidized Stafford, PLUS).

WORK-STUDY *Federal work-study:* Total amount: $11,691; 7 jobs averaging $1671. **State or other work-study/employment:** Total amount: $20,936 (100% need-based). 13 part-time jobs averaging $1610.

ATHLETIC AWARDS Total amount: $239,000 (100% need-based).

APPLYING FOR FINANCIAL AID *Required financial aid form:* FAFSA. *Financial aid deadline:* 8/1 (priority: 4/1). *Notification date:* 5/15. Students must reply by 8/1 or within 2 weeks of notification.

CONTACT Mrs. Mary Emily Kennon, Assistant Director of Business Affairs, John Wesley University, 1215 Eastchester Drive, High Point, NC 27265, 336-887-3000 or toll-free 855-528-7358. *Fax:* 336-889-2261. *E-mail:* mkennon@johnwesley.edu. *Website:* http://www.johnwesley.edu/.

JONES COLLEGE
Jacksonville, FL

CONTACT Mrs. Becky Davis, Director of Financial Assistance, Jones College, 5353 Arlington Expressway, Jacksonville, FL 32211-5540, 904-743-1122 or toll-free 800-331-0176. *Fax:* 904-743-4446. *Website:* http://www.jones.edu/.

JOSE MARIA VARGAS UNIVERSITY
Pembroke Pines, FL

CONTACT Financial Aid Office, Jose Maria Vargas University, 10131 Pines Boulevard, Pembroke Pines, FL 33026, 954-322-4446. *Website:* http://www.jmvu.edu/.

JUDSON COLLEGE
Marion, AL

Tuition & fees: $17,376	Average undergraduate aid package: N/A

ABOUT THE INSTITUTION Independent Baptist, coed, primarily women. *Awards:* associate and bachelor's degrees. 22 undergraduate majors. **Total enrollment:** 374. Undergraduates: 374. Freshmen: 65. Federal methodology is used as a basis for awarding need-based institutional aid.

UNDERGRADUATE EXPENSES for 2016–2017 *Application fee:* $42. *Comprehensive fee:* $27,354 includes full-time tuition ($16,248), mandatory fees ($1128), and room and board ($9978). *College room only:* $5616. Full-time tuition and fees vary according to course load, degree level, and program. Room and board charges vary according to board plan. *Part-time tuition:* $550 per credit hour. *Part-time fees:* $564 per term. Part-time tuition and fees vary according to course load, degree level, and program.

GIFT AID (NEED-BASED) *Scholarships, grants, and awards:* Federal Pell, FSEOG, state, private, college/university gift aid from institutional funds, Academic Competitiveness Grants, National SMART Grants, TEACH Grants.

GIFT AID (NON-NEED-BASED) *Scholarships, grants, and awards by category:* *Academic interests/achievement:* biological sciences, general academic interests/achievements, premedicine. *Creative arts/performance:* art/fine arts, music. *Special achievements/activities:* general special achievements/activities. *Special characteristics:* children of educators, children of faculty/staff, relatives of clergy, religious

affiliation. **Tuition waivers:** Full or partial for employees or children of employees. **ROTC:** Army cooperative.

LOANS *Programs:* Perkins, college/university.

WORK-STUDY Federal work-study jobs available. **State or other work-study/employment:** Part-time jobs available.

APPLYING FOR FINANCIAL AID *Required financial aid forms:* FAFSA, state aid form. *Financial aid deadline (priority):* 3/1. *Notification date:* Continuous beginning 3/15. Students must reply within 2 weeks of notification.

CONTACT Mrs. Melena Verity, Acting Director of Financial Aid, Judson College, 302 Bibb Street, Marion, AL 36756, 334-683-5170 or toll-free 800-447-9472. *Fax:* 334-683-5282. *E-mail:* mverity@judson.edu. *Website:* http://www.judson.edu/.

JUDSON UNIVERSITY
Elgin, IL

Tuition & fees: $29,434	Average undergraduate aid package: $18,502

ABOUT THE INSTITUTION Independent Baptist, coed. *Awards:* certificates, associate, bachelor's, master's, and doctoral degrees. 42 undergraduate majors. **Total enrollment:** 1,285. Undergraduates: 1,123. Freshmen: 192. Federal methodology is used as a basis for awarding need-based institutional aid.

UNDERGRADUATE EXPENSES for 2017–2018 *Application fee:* $50. *One-time required fee:* $100. *Comprehensive fee:* $39,274 includes full-time tuition ($28,408), mandatory fees ($1026), and room and board ($9840). Full-time tuition and fees vary according to course load and program. Room and board charges vary according to board plan. *Part-time tuition:* $1145 per credit. Part-time tuition and fees vary according to course load and program.

FRESHMAN FINANCIAL AID (Fall 2015) 171 applied for aid; of those 94% were deemed to have need. 100% of freshmen with need received aid; of those 11% had need fully met. *Average percent of need met:* 68% (excluding resources awarded to replace EFC). *Average financial aid package:* $20,435 (excluding resources awarded to replace EFC). 8% of all full-time freshmen had no need and received non-need-based gift aid.

UNDERGRADUATE FINANCIAL AID (Fall 2015) 729 applied for aid; of those 93% were deemed to have need. 100% of undergraduates with need received aid; of those 79% had need fully met. *Average percent of need met:* 62% (excluding resources awarded to replace EFC). *Average financial aid package:* $18,502 (excluding resources awarded to replace EFC). 9% of all full-time undergraduates had no need and received non-need-based gift aid.

GIFT AID (NEED-BASED) *Total amount:* $10,483,568 (2% federal, 10% state, 32% institutional, 56% external sources). *Receiving aid:* Freshmen: 34% (70); all full-time undergraduates: 22% (230). *Average award:* Freshmen: $10,414; Undergraduates: $9762. *Scholarships, grants, and awards:* Federal Pell, FSEOG, state, private, college/university gift aid from institutional funds.

GIFT AID (NON-NEED-BASED) *Total amount:* $2,355,021 (96% institutional, 4% external sources). *Receiving aid:* Freshmen: 52% (107). Undergraduates: 38% (407). *Average award:* Freshmen: $8558. Undergraduates: $7582. *Scholarships, grants, and awards by category:* *Academic interests/achievement:* general academic interests/achievements. *Creative arts/performance:* art/fine arts, music, theater/drama. *Special achievements/activities:* 5 awards ($50,000 total): leadership. **Tuition waivers:** Full or partial for employees or children of employees, adult students, senior citizens. **ROTC:** Army cooperative.

LOANS *Student loans:* $5,911,146 (41% need-based, 59% non-need-based). *Average need-based loan:* Freshmen: $4317. Undergraduates: $4719. *Parent loans:* $1,012,248 (100% non-need-based). *Programs:* Federal Direct (Subsidized and Unsubsidized Stafford, PLUS), Perkins.

WORK-STUDY *Federal work-study:* 271 jobs averaging $1610. **State or other work-study/employment:** Part-time jobs available.

ATHLETIC AWARDS Total amount: $2,717,879 (40% need-based, 60% non-need-based).

APPLYING FOR FINANCIAL AID *Required financial aid form:* FAFSA. *Financial aid deadline:* 8/1 (priority: 3/1). *Notification date:* Continuous beginning 3/1. Students must reply by 5/1 or within 4 weeks of notification.

CONTACT Diana Winton, Director of Financial Aid, Judson University, 1151 North State Street, Elgin, IL 60123-1498, 847-628-2532 or toll-free 800-879-5376. *Fax:* 847-628-2533. *E-mail:* diana.winton@judsonu.edu. *Website:* http://www.judsonu.edu/.

THE JUILLIARD SCHOOL
New York, NY

Tuition & fees: $41,660	Average undergraduate aid package: $32,644

ABOUT THE INSTITUTION Independent, coed. *Awards:* certificates, diplomas, bachelor's, master's, and doctoral degrees. 4 undergraduate majors. *Total enrollment:* 939. Undergraduates: 580. Freshmen: 114. Federal methodology is used as a basis for awarding need-based institutional aid.

UNDERGRADUATE EXPENSES for 2016–2017 *Application fee:* $110. *Comprehensive fee:* $57,040 includes full-time tuition ($41,310), mandatory fees ($350), and room and board ($15,380).

FRESHMAN FINANCIAL AID (Fall 2016, est.) 109 applied for aid; of those 83% were deemed to have need. 100% of freshmen with need received aid; of those 26% had need fully met. *Average percent of need met:* 77% (excluding resources awarded to replace EFC). *Average financial aid package:* $32,580 (excluding resources awarded to replace EFC). 11% of all full-time freshmen had no need and received non-need-based gift aid.

UNDERGRADUATE FINANCIAL AID (Fall 2016, est.) 433 applied for aid; of those 85% were deemed to have need. 100% of undergraduates with need received aid; of those 24% had need fully met. *Average percent of need met:* 74% (excluding resources awarded to replace EFC). *Average financial aid package:* $32,644 (excluding resources awarded to replace EFC). 10% of all full-time undergraduates had no need and received non-need-based gift aid.

GIFT AID (NEED-BASED) *Total amount:* $10,786,136 (5% federal, 92% institutional, 3% external sources). *Receiving aid:* Freshmen: 80% (90); all full-time undergraduates: 72% (359). *Average award:* Freshmen: $28,696; Undergraduates: $27,980. *Scholarships, grants, and awards:* Federal Pell, FSEOG, state, private, college/university gift aid from institutional funds.

GIFT AID (NON-NEED-BASED) *Total amount:* $2,417,518 (99% institutional, 1% external sources). *Receiving aid:* Freshmen: 5% (6). Undergraduates: 2% (8). *Average award:* Freshmen: $23,052. Undergraduates: $20,950. *Scholarships, grants, and awards by category:* Creative arts/performance: dance, music, performing arts, theater/drama. *Tuition waivers:* Full or partial for employees or children of employees.

LOANS *Student loans:* $2,494,772 (83% need-based, 17% non-need-based). 48% of past graduating class borrowed through all loan programs. *Average indebtedness per student:* $32,493. *Average need-based loan:* Freshmen: $3604. Undergraduates: $5046. *Parent loans:* $650,244 (89% need-based, 11% non-need-based). *Programs:* Federal Direct (Subsidized and Unsubsidized Stafford, PLUS), Perkins.

WORK-STUDY *Federal work-study:* Total amount: $331,041; 168 jobs averaging $1970. *State or other work-study/employment:* Total amount: $607,500 (66% need-based, 34% non-need-based). 202 part-time jobs averaging $1988.

APPLYING FOR FINANCIAL AID *Required financial aid forms:* FAFSA, CSS Financial Aid PROFILE. *Financial aid deadline:* 3/1. *Notification date:* 4/1. Students must reply by 5/1.

CONTACT Ms. Tina Gonzalez, Director of Financial Aid, The Juilliard School, 60 Lincoln Center Plaza, New York, NY 10023, 212-799-5000 Ext. 211. *Fax:* 212-358-2594. *E-mail:* financialaid@juilliard.edu. *Website:* http://www.juilliard.edu/.

JUNIATA COLLEGE
Huntingdon, PA

Tuition & fees: $43,875	Average undergraduate aid package: $35,585

ABOUT THE INSTITUTION Independent Church of the Brethren, coed. *Awards:* bachelor's and master's degrees. 61 undergraduate majors. *Total enrollment:* 3,935. Undergraduates: 3,796. Federal methodology is used as a basis for awarding need-based institutional aid.

UNDERGRADUATE EXPENSES for 2017–2018 *Comprehensive fee:* $55,915 includes full-time tuition ($43,050), mandatory fees ($825), and room and board ($12,040). *College room only:* $6410. Full-time tuition and fees vary according to course load, degree level, and program. Room and board charges vary according to board plan and housing facility. *Part-time tuition:* $1765 per credit. Part-time tuition and fees vary according to course load and degree level.

FRESHMAN FINANCIAL AID (Fall 2016, est.) 350 applied for aid; of those 89% were deemed to have need. 100% of freshmen with need received aid; of those 26% had need fully met. *Average percent of need met:* 85% (excluding resources awarded to replace EFC). *Average financial aid package:* $32,797 (excluding resources awarded to replace EFC). 21% of all full-time freshmen had no need and received non-need-based gift aid.

UNDERGRADUATE FINANCIAL AID (Fall 2016, est.) 1,197 applied for aid; of those 93% were deemed to have need. 98% of undergraduates with need received aid; of those 25% had need fully met. *Average percent of need met:* 82% (excluding resources awarded to replace EFC). *Average financial aid package:* $35,585 (excluding resources awarded to replace EFC). 22% of all full-time undergraduates had no need and received non-need-based gift aid.

GIFT AID (NEED-BASED) *Total amount:* $29,631,725 (6% federal, 5% state, 88% institutional, 1% external sources). *Receiving aid:* Freshmen: 77% (304); all full-time undergraduates: 69% (1,085). *Average award:* Freshmen: $37,797; Undergraduates: $29,430. *Scholarships, grants, and awards:* Federal Pell, FSEOG, state, private, college/university gift aid from institutional funds.

GIFT AID (NON-NEED-BASED) *Total amount:* $8,354,353 (1% federal, 98% institutional, 1% external sources). *Receiving aid:* Freshmen: 77% (304). Undergraduates: 69% (1,085). *Average award:* Freshmen: $23,221. Undergraduates: $19,992. *Scholarships, grants, and awards by category:* Academic interests/achievement: biological sciences, business, communication, computer science, education, foreign languages, general academic interests/achievements, home economics, humanities, international studies, mathematics, physical sciences, premedicine, social sciences. *Creative arts/performance:* art/fine arts, music, performing arts, theater/drama. *Special achievements/activities:* community service, general special achievements/activities, leadership. *Special characteristics:* children and siblings of alumni, children of faculty/staff, ethnic background, first-generation college students, international students, local/state students, siblings of current students. *Tuition waivers:* Full or partial for employees or children of employees, senior citizens.

LOANS *Student loans:* $10,635,090 (64% need-based, 36% non-need-based). 73% of past graduating class borrowed through all loan programs. *Average indebtedness per student:* $36,338. *Average need-based loan:* Freshmen: $3467. Undergraduates: $4534. *Parent loans:* $3,136,925 (40% need-based, 60% non-need-based). *Programs:* Federal Direct (Subsidized and Unsubsidized Stafford, PLUS), Perkins, college/university.

WORK-STUDY *Federal work-study:* Total amount: $1,073,064; 310 jobs averaging $435. *State or other work-study/employment:* Total amount: $960,060 (4% need-based, 96% non-need-based). 720 part-time jobs averaging $837.

APPLYING FOR FINANCIAL AID *Required financial aid form:* FAFSA. *Financial aid deadline (priority):* 2/15. *Notification date:* Continuous beginning 3/1. Students must reply by 5/1 or within 2 weeks of notification.

CONTACT Tracie Patrick, Director of Student Financial Planning, Juniata College, 1700 Moore Street, Huntingdon, PA 16652-2119, 814-641-3140 or toll-free 877-JUNIATA. *Fax:* 814-641-5311. *E-mail:* patrict@juniata.edu. *Website:* http://www.juniata.edu/.

KALAMAZOO COLLEGE
Kalamazoo, MI

Tuition & fees: $46,692	Average undergraduate aid package: $37,979

ABOUT THE INSTITUTION Independent American Baptist Churches in the U.S.A., coed. *Awards:* bachelor's degrees. 28 undergraduate majors. *Total enrollment:* 1,443. Undergraduates: 1,443. Freshmen: 347. Both federal and institutional methodology are used as a basis for awarding need-based institutional aid.

UNDERGRADUATE EXPENSES for 2017–2018 *Comprehensive fee:* $56,082 includes full-time tuition ($46,350), mandatory fees ($342), and room and board ($9390). *College room only:* $4680. Full-time tuition and fees vary according to course load. Room and board charges vary according to board plan and housing facility. Part-time tuition and fees vary according to course load.

FRESHMAN FINANCIAL AID (Fall 2016, est.) 310 applied for aid; of those 85% were deemed to have need. 100% of freshmen with need received aid; of those 50% had need fully met. *Average percent of need met:* 95% (excluding resources awarded to replace EFC). *Average financial aid package:* $39,792 (excluding resources awarded to replace EFC). 22% of all full-time freshmen had no need and received non-need-based gift aid.

UNDERGRADUATE FINANCIAL AID (Fall 2016, est.) 1,083 applied for aid; of those 90% were deemed to have need. 100% of undergraduates with need received aid; of those 41% had need fully met. *Average percent of need met:* 92% (excluding resources awarded to replace EFC). *Average financial aid package:* $37,979 (excluding resources awarded to replace EFC). 28% of all full-time undergraduates had no need and received non-need-based gift aid.

GIFT AID (NEED-BASED) *Total amount:* $28,754,283 (6% federal, 3% state, 89% institutional, 2% external sources). *Receiving aid:* Freshmen: 75% (260); all full-time undergraduates: 67% (956). *Average award:* Freshmen: $31,667; Undergraduates: $29,998. *Scholarships, grants, and awards:* Federal Pell, FSEOG, state, private, college/university gift aid from institutional funds.

GIFT AID (NON-NEED-BASED) *Total amount:* $10,605,980 (85% institutional, 15% external sources). *Receiving aid:* Freshmen: 18% (62). Undergraduates: 12% (169). *Average award:* Freshmen: $20,728. Undergraduates: $19,558. *Scholarships, grants, and awards by category: Academic interests/achievement:* general academic interests/achievements. *Creative arts/performance:* art/fine arts, music, performing arts. *Special achievements/activities:* leadership. *Special characteristics:* children and siblings of alumni. *Tuition waivers:* Full or partial for employees or children of employees. *ROTC:* Army cooperative.

LOANS *Student loans:* $8,791,280 (68% need-based, 32% non-need-based). 61% of past graduating class borrowed through all loan programs. *Average indebtedness per student:* $27,653. *Average need-based loan:* Freshmen: $5409. Undergraduates: $6214. *Parent loans:* $2,030,646 (100% non-need-based). *Programs:* Federal Direct (Subsidized and Unsubsidized Stafford, PLUS), Perkins.

WORK-STUDY *Federal work-study:* Total amount: $1,430,371; jobs available. *State or other work-study/employment:* Total amount: $193,000 (100% need-based). Part-time jobs available.

APPLYING FOR FINANCIAL AID *Required financial aid forms:* FAFSA, institution's own form. *Financial aid deadline (priority):* 11/15. *Notification date:* Continuous beginning 3/15. Students must reply by 5/1.

CONTACT Marian Stowers, Director of Financial Aid, Kalamazoo College, 1200 Academy Street, Kalamazoo, MI 49006-3295, 269-337-7192 or toll-free 800-253-3602. *Fax:* 269-337-7390.

Website: http://www.kzoo.edu/.

KANSAS CITY ART INSTITUTE
Kansas City, MO

Tuition & fees: $37,550	Average undergraduate aid package: $25,758

ABOUT THE INSTITUTION Independent, coed. *Awards:* certificates, diplomas, and bachelor's degrees. 12 undergraduate majors. *Total enrollment:* 635. Undergraduates: 635. Freshmen: 163. Federal methodology is used as a basis for awarding need-based institutional aid.

UNDERGRADUATE EXPENSES for 2017–2018 *Application fee:* $45. *Comprehensive fee:* $47,950 includes full-time tuition ($37,400), mandatory fees ($150), and room and board ($10,400). Full-time tuition and fees vary according to program. *Part-time tuition:* $1510 per credit hour. Part-time tuition and fees vary according to program.

FRESHMAN FINANCIAL AID (Fall 2016, est.) 159 applied for aid; of those 92% were deemed to have need. 99% of freshmen with need received aid; of those 10% had need fully met. *Average percent of need met:* 60% (excluding resources awarded to replace EFC). *Average financial aid package:* $25,957 (excluding resources awarded to replace EFC). 11% of all full-time freshmen had no need and received non-need-based gift aid.

UNDERGRADUATE FINANCIAL AID (Fall 2016, est.) 587 applied for aid; of those 92% were deemed to have need. 100% of undergraduates with need received aid; of those 12% had need fully met. *Average percent of need met:* 62% (excluding resources awarded to replace EFC). *Average financial aid package:*

$25,758 (excluding resources awarded to replace EFC). 14% of all full-time undergraduates had no need and received non-need-based gift aid.

GIFT AID (NEED-BASED) *Total amount:* $11,559,167 (12% federal, 2% state, 80% institutional, 6% external sources). *Receiving aid:* Freshmen: 88% (146); all full-time undergraduates: 86% (541). *Average award:* Freshmen: $22,992; Undergraduates: $21,321. *Scholarships, grants, and awards:* Federal Pell, FSEOG, state, private, college/university gift aid from institutional funds.

GIFT AID (NON-NEED-BASED) *Total amount:* $2,040,936 (1% state, 88% institutional, 11% external sources). *Receiving aid:* Freshmen: 7% (12). Undergraduates: 7% (45). *Average award:* Freshmen: $18,855. Undergraduates: $17,330. *Scholarships, grants, and awards by category: Creative arts/performance:* art/fine arts. *Tuition waivers:* Full or partial for employees or children of employees.

LOANS *Student loans:* $4,910,956 (83% need-based, 17% non-need-based). 85% of past graduating class borrowed through all loan programs. *Average indebtedness per student:* $25,000. *Average need-based loan:* Freshmen: $3384. Undergraduates: $4606. *Parent loans:* $1,657,280 (72% need-based, 28% non-need-based). *Programs:* Federal Direct (Subsidized and Unsubsidized Stafford, PLUS), Perkins, alternative loans.

WORK-STUDY *Federal work-study:* Total amount: $113,066; 109 jobs averaging $1037. *State or other work-study/employment:* Total amount: $234,789 (56% need-based, 44% non-need-based). 193 part-time jobs averaging $1216.

APPLYING FOR FINANCIAL AID *Required financial aid form:* FAFSA. *Financial aid deadline (priority):* 3/15. *Notification date:* Continuous beginning 3/15. Students must reply within 2 weeks of notification.

CONTACT Mrs. Lori Lynn Baer, Financial Aid Director, Kansas City Art Institute, 4415 Warwick Boulevard, Kansas City, MO 64111-1874, 816-802-3337 or toll-free 800-522-5224. *Fax:* 816-802-3453. *E-mail:* financialaid@kcai.edu. *Website:* http://www.kcai.edu/.

KANSAS STATE UNIVERSITY
Manhattan, KS

Tuition & fees (KS res): $9874	Average undergraduate aid package: $12,646

ABOUT THE INSTITUTION State-supported, coed. *Awards:* certificates, associate, bachelor's, master's, and doctoral degrees. 87 undergraduate majors. *Total enrollment:* 23,779. Undergraduates: 19,472. Freshmen: 3,581. Federal methodology is used as a basis for awarding need-based institutional aid.

UNDERGRADUATE EXPENSES for 2016–2017 *Application fee:* $30. *Tuition, state resident:* full-time $9012. *Tuition, nonresident:* full-time $23,913. *Required fees:* full-time $862. Full-time tuition and fees vary according to course level, course load, degree level, location, program, and reciprocity agreements. Part-time tuition and fees vary according to course level, course load, degree level, location, program, and reciprocity agreements. *College room and board:* $9150. Room and board charges vary according to board plan, housing facility, and location.

FRESHMAN FINANCIAL AID (Fall 2015) 2,774 applied for aid; of those 69% were deemed to have need. 98% of freshmen with need received aid; of those 23% had need fully met. *Average percent of need met:* 80% (excluding resources awarded to replace EFC). *Average financial aid package:* $12,682 (excluding resources awarded to replace EFC). 18% of all full-time freshmen had no need and received non-need-based gift aid.

UNDERGRADUATE FINANCIAL AID (Fall 2015) 12,011 applied for aid; of those 74% were deemed to have need. 98% of undergraduates with need received aid; of those 19% had need fully met. *Average percent of need met:* 78% (excluding resources awarded to replace EFC). *Average financial aid package:* $12,646 (excluding resources awarded to replace EFC). 9% of all full-time undergraduates had no need and received non-need-based gift aid.

GIFT AID (NEED-BASED) *Total amount:* $49,647,703 (38% federal, 5% state, 48% institutional, 9% external sources). *Receiving aid:* Freshmen: 28% (1,007); all full-time undergraduates: 28% (5,008). *Average award:* Freshmen: $4468; Undergraduates: $4329. *Scholarships, grants, and awards:* Federal Pell, FSEOG, state, private, college/university gift aid from institutional funds.

GIFT AID (NON-NEED-BASED) *Total amount:* $10,447,263 (1% state, 83% institutional, 16% external sources). *Receiving aid:* Freshmen: 40% (1,438). Undergraduates: 26% (4,574). *Average award:* Freshmen: $5152. Undergraduates: $4250. *Tuition waivers:* Full or partial for employees or children of employees. *ROTC:* Army, Air Force.

LOANS *Student loans:* $73,380,002 (69% need-based, 31% non-need-based). 57% of past graduating class borrowed through all loan programs. *Average indebtedness per student:* $27,198. *Average need-based loan:* Freshmen: $3694. Undergraduates: $4501. *Parent loans:* $31,438,053 (31% need-based, 69% non-need-based). *Programs:* Federal Direct (Subsidized and Unsubsidized Stafford, PLUS), Perkins, college/university.

WORK-STUDY *Federal work-study:* jobs available. *State or other work-study/employment:* Total amount: $12,814,874 (80% need-based, 20% non-need-based). Part-time jobs available.

ATHLETIC AWARDS Total amount: $6,623,317 (86% need-based, 14% non-need-based).

APPLYING FOR FINANCIAL AID *Required financial aid form:* FAFSA. *Financial aid deadline (priority):* 3/1. *Notification date:* Continuous beginning 4/1. Students must reply within 2 weeks of notification.

CONTACT Mr. Larry Moeder, Executive Director of Undergraduate Admissions and Student Financial Assistance, Kansas State University, 104 Fairchild Hall, Manhattan, KS 66506, 785-532-6420 or toll-free 800-432-8270. *E-mail:* larrym@ksu.edu. *Website:* http://www.k-state.edu/.

KANSAS WESLEYAN UNIVERSITY
Salina, KS

Tuition & fees: $28,980	Average undergraduate aid package: N/A

ABOUT THE INSTITUTION Independent United Methodist, coed. *Awards:* associate, bachelor's, and master's degrees. 63 undergraduate majors. *Total enrollment:* 764. Undergraduates: 693. Freshmen: 162. Federal methodology is used as a basis for awarding need-based institutional aid.

UNDERGRADUATE EXPENSES for 2017–2018 *Application fee:* $20. *One-time required fee:* $300. *Comprehensive fee:* $37,930 includes full-time tuition ($28,980) and room and board ($8950). Room and board charges vary according to housing facility. *Part-time tuition:* $2600 per term. Part-time tuition and fees vary according to course load.

FRESHMAN FINANCIAL AID (Fall 2016, est.) 162 applied for aid; of those 86% were deemed to have need. 100% of freshmen with need received aid; of those 12% had need fully met. 13% of all full-time freshmen had no need and received non-need-based gift aid.

UNDERGRADUATE FINANCIAL AID (Fall 2016, est.) 658 applied for aid; of those 85% were deemed to have need. 100% of undergraduates with need received aid; of those 18% had need fully met. 12% of all full-time undergraduates had no need and received non-need-based gift aid.

GIFT AID (NEED-BASED) *Total amount:* $3,377,122 (44% federal, 14% state, 42% institutional). *Receiving aid:* Freshmen: 76% (123); all full-time undergraduates: 78% (513). *Average award:* Freshmen: $7081; Undergraduates: $7609. *Scholarships, grants, and awards:* Federal Pell, FSEOG, state, private, college/university gift aid from institutional funds, United Negro College Fund.

GIFT AID (NON-NEED-BASED) *Total amount:* $6,807,037 (97% institutional, 3% external sources). *Receiving aid:* Freshmen: 80% (129). Undergraduates: 78% (515). *Average award:* Freshmen: $12,214. Undergraduates: $11,422. *Scholarships, grants, and awards by category: Academic interests/achievement:* 686 awards ($4,178,014 total): biological sciences, business, communication, computer science, education, English, foreign languages, general academic interests/achievements, home economics, humanities, mathematics, physical sciences, premedicine, religion/biblical studies, social sciences. *Creative arts/performance:* 60 awards ($196,280 total): applied art and design, art/fine arts, cinema/film/broadcasting, dance, debating, journalism/publications, music, performing arts, theater/drama. *Special achievements/activities:* 8 awards ($21,500 total): cheerleading/drum major, junior miss. *Special characteristics:* 159 awards ($542,894 total): children and siblings of alumni, children of current students, children of educators, children of faculty/staff, general special characteristics, international students, local/state students, previous college experience, religious affiliation, siblings of current students, spouses of current students, veterans, veterans' children. *Tuition waivers:* Full or partial for children of alumni, employees or children of employees, senior citizens.

LOANS *Student loans:* $4,987,049 (47% need-based, 53% non-need-based). 87% of past graduating class borrowed through all loan programs. *Average indebtedness per student:* $34,526. *Average need-based loan:* Freshmen: $3204. Undergraduates: $4296. *Parent loans:* $2,583,079 (100% non-need-based). *Programs:* Federal Direct (Subsidized and Unsubsidized Stafford, PLUS), Perkins, private loans.

WORK-STUDY *Federal work-study:* Total amount: $140,587; 92 jobs averaging $1560. *State or other work-study/employment:* Total amount: $17,050 (100% non-need-based). 13 part-time jobs averaging $1377.

ATHLETIC AWARDS Total amount: $588,296 (100% non-need-based).

APPLYING FOR FINANCIAL AID *Required financial aid form:* FAFSA. *Financial aid deadline (priority):* 3/15. *Notification date:* Continuous beginning 10/15.

CONTACT Mrs. Lois Elizabeth Madsen, Director of Student Financial Planning, Kansas Wesleyan University, 100 East Claflin, Hall of the Pioneers, Room 285, Salina, KS 67401-6196, 785-833-4315 or toll-free 800-874-1154 Ext. 1285. *Fax:* 785-827-0927. *E-mail:* lois.madsen@kwu.edu. *Website:* http://www.kwu.edu/.

KAPLAN UNIVERSITY, AUGUSTA
Augusta, ME

CONTACT Financial Aid Office, Kaplan University, Augusta, 14 Marketplace Drive, Augusta, ME 04330, 207-213-2500 or toll-free 888-561-4343. *Website:* http://www.kaplanuniversity.edu/.

KAPLAN UNIVERSITY, DAVENPORT CAMPUS
Davenport, IA

CONTACT Financial Aid Office, Kaplan University, Davenport Campus, 1801 East Kimberly Road, Suite 1, Davenport, IA 52807, 563-355-3500 or toll-free 800-987-7734. *Website:* http://www.kaplanuniversity.edu/.

KAPLAN UNIVERSITY, MASON CITY CAMPUS
Mason City, IA

CONTACT Financial Aid Office, Kaplan University, Mason City Campus, 2570 4th Street, SW, Mason City, IA 50401, 641-423-2530 or toll-free 800-987-7734. *Website:* http://www.kaplanuniversity.edu/.

KEAN UNIVERSITY
Union, NJ

Tuition & fees (NJ res): $11,870	Average undergraduate aid package: $10,497

ABOUT THE INSTITUTION State-supported, coed. *Awards:* certificates, bachelor's, master's, and doctoral degrees. 48 undergraduate majors. *Total enrollment:* 14,070. Undergraduates: 11,812. Freshmen: 1,526. Federal methodology is used as a basis for awarding need-based institutional aid.

UNDERGRADUATE EXPENSES for 2016–2017 *Application fee:* $75. *Tuition, state resident:* full-time $7754; part-time $302 per credit. *Tuition, non-resident:* full-time $14,521; part-time $513 per credit. *Required fees:* full-time $4116; $151 per credit. Part-time tuition and fees vary according to course load. *College room and board:* $12,780. Room and board charges vary according to board plan, housing facility, and student level.

FRESHMAN FINANCIAL AID (Fall 2016, est.) 1,373 applied for aid; of those 84% were deemed to have need. 93% of freshmen with need received aid; of those 1% had need fully met. *Average percent of need met:* 77% (excluding resources awarded to replace EFC). *Average financial aid package:* $10,100 (excluding resources awarded to replace EFC). 3% of all full-time freshmen had no need and received non-need-based gift aid.

UNDERGRADUATE FINANCIAL AID (Fall 2016, est.) 7,574 applied for aid; of those 86% were deemed to have need. 96% of undergraduates with need received aid;

of those 1% had need fully met. *Average percent of need met:* 82% (excluding resources awarded to replace EFC). *Average financial aid package:* $10,497 (excluding resources awarded to replace EFC). 1% of all full-time undergraduates had no need and received non-need-based gift aid.
GIFT AID (NEED-BASED) *Total amount:* $40,389,964 (59% federal, 35% state, 5% institutional, 1% external sources). *Receiving aid:* Freshmen: 51% (767); all full-time undergraduates: 50% (4,566). *Average award:* Freshmen: $8910; Undergraduates: $8204. *Scholarships, grants, and awards:* Federal Pell, FSEOG, state, private, college/university gift aid from institutional funds.
GIFT AID (NON-NEED-BASED) *Total amount:* $47,705 (100% state). *Receiving aid:* Freshmen: 12% (178). Undergraduates: 8% (710). *Average award:* Freshmen: $3798. Undergraduates: $3814. *Scholarships, grants, and awards by category: Academic interests/achievement:* architecture, area/ethnic studies, biological sciences, business, communication, computer science, education, engineering/technologies, English, foreign languages, general academic interests/achievements, health fields, home economics, humanities, international studies, mathematics, physical sciences, premedicine, social sciences. *Creative arts/performance:* applied art and design, art/fine arts, cinema/film/broadcasting, dance, general creative arts/performance, music, performing arts, theater/drama. *Special achievements/activities:* community service, general special achievements/activities, leadership, memberships. *Special characteristics:* adult students, first-generation college students, general special characteristics, local/state students, previous college experience, veterans. *Tuition waivers:* Full or partial for employees or children of employees, senior citizens. *ROTC:* Army cooperative, Air Force cooperative.
LOANS *Student loans:* $64,107,441 (42% need-based, 58% non-need-based). 75% of past graduating class borrowed through all loan programs. *Average indebtedness per student:* $33,693. *Average need-based loan:* Freshmen: $3438. Undergraduates: $4450. *Parent loans:* $9,136,936 (100% non-need-based). *Programs:* Federal Direct (Subsidized and Unsubsidized Stafford, PLUS), Perkins.
WORK-STUDY *Federal work-study:* Total amount: $699,296; 252 jobs averaging $2455.
APPLYING FOR FINANCIAL AID *Required financial aid form:* FAFSA. *Financial aid deadline (priority):* 4/17. *Notification date:* Continuous beginning 3/1. Students must reply by 5/1.
CONTACT Ms. Sherrell Watson Hall, Director of Financial Aid, Kean University, 1000 Morris Avenue, Union, NJ 07083, 908-737-3190. *Fax:* 908-737-3200. *E-mail:* finaid@kean.edu.
Website: http://www.kean.edu/.

KEENE STATE COLLEGE
Keene, NH

Tuition & fees (NH res): $13,613	Average undergraduate aid package: $12,285

ABOUT THE INSTITUTION State-supported, coed. *Awards:* certificates, bachelor's, and master's degrees. 62 undergraduate majors. *Total enrollment:* 4,282. Undergraduates: 4,165. Freshmen: 1,049. Federal methodology is used as a basis for awarding need-based institutional aid.
UNDERGRADUATE EXPENSES for 2016–2017 *Application fee:* $50. *Tuition, state resident:* full-time $10,968; part-time $458 per credit hour. *Tuition, nonresident:* full-time $19,352; part-time $806 per credit hour. *Required fees:* full-time $2645; $106 per credit hour. Part-time tuition and fees vary according to course load. *College room and board:* $10,390. Room and board charges vary according to board plan and housing facility.
FRESHMAN FINANCIAL AID (Fall 2015) 837 applied for aid; of those 80% were deemed to have need. 97% of freshmen with need received aid; of those 10% had need fully met. *Average percent of need met:* 67% (excluding resources awarded to replace EFC). *Average financial aid package:* $13,279 (excluding resources awarded to replace EFC). 17% of all full-time freshmen had no need and received non-need-based gift aid.
UNDERGRADUATE FINANCIAL AID (Fall 2015) 3,420 applied for aid; of those 78% were deemed to have need. 99% of undergraduates with need received aid; of those 11% had need fully met. *Average percent of need met:* 65% (excluding resources awarded to replace EFC). *Average financial aid package:* $12,285 (excluding resources awarded to replace EFC). 14% of all full-time undergraduates had no need and received non-need-based gift aid.

GIFT AID (NEED-BASED) *Total amount:* $13,913,734 (33% federal, 2% state, 56% institutional, 9% external sources). *Receiving aid:* Freshmen: 53% (491); all full-time undergraduates: 46% (1,883). *Average award:* Freshmen: $8277; Undergraduates: $7227. *Scholarships, grants, and awards:* Federal Pell, FSEOG, state, private, college/university gift aid from institutional funds.
GIFT AID (NON-NEED-BASED) *Total amount:* $7,538,032 (92% institutional, 8% external sources). *Receiving aid:* Freshmen: 46% (422). Undergraduates: 32% (1,317). *Average award:* Freshmen: $3963. Undergraduates: $3548. *Scholarships, grants, and awards by category: Academic interests/achievement:* 1,639 awards ($5,584,558 total): general academic interests/achievements. *Creative arts/performance:* 19 awards ($65,625 total): applied art and design, art/fine arts, cinema/film/broadcasting, dance, general creative arts/performance, music, theater/drama. *Special achievements/activities:* 37 awards ($68,000 total): general special achievements/activities, leadership. *Special characteristics:* children and siblings of alumni. *Tuition waivers:* Full or partial for employees or children of employees, senior citizens. *ROTC:* Army cooperative, Air Force cooperative.
LOANS *Student loans:* $34,638,553 (30% need-based, 70% non-need-based). 84% of past graduating class borrowed through all loan programs. *Average indebtedness per student:* $41,016. *Average need-based loan:* Freshmen: $3461. Undergraduates: $4334. *Parent loans:* $8,919,542 (100% non-need-based). *Programs:* Federal Direct (Subsidized and Unsubsidized Stafford, PLUS), Perkins, college/university.
WORK-STUDY *Federal work-study:* 1,375 jobs averaging $2304. *State or other work-study/employment:* Total amount: $879,472 (100% non-need-based). 661 part-time jobs averaging $1318.
APPLYING FOR FINANCIAL AID *Required financial aid form:* FAFSA. *Financial aid deadline:* 3/1. *Notification date:* Continuous. Students must reply within 4 weeks of notification.
CONTACT Mr. Steven Goetsch, Associate Vice President for Enrollment Management, Keene State College, 229 Main Street, Keene, NH 03435-2606, 603-358-2058 or toll-free 800-KSC-1909. *Fax:* 603-358-2794. *E-mail:* steven.goetsch@keene.edu.
Website: http://www.keene.edu/.

KEHILATH YAKOV RABBINICAL SEMINARY
Ossining, NY

CONTACT Financial Aid Office, Kehilath Yakov Rabbinical Seminary, 206 Wilson Street, Brooklyn, NY 11211-7207, 718-963-1212.
Website: http://kehilathyakov.com/.

KEISER UNIVERSITY
Fort Lauderdale, FL

Tuition & fees: $15,498	Average undergraduate aid package: $5512

ABOUT THE INSTITUTION Independent, coed. 57 undergraduate majors. Federal methodology is used as a basis for awarding need-based institutional aid.
UNDERGRADUATE EXPENSES for 2016–2017 *Tuition:* full-time $14,585. Full-time tuition and fees vary according to course load and program. Part-time tuition and fees vary according to course load and program.
FRESHMAN FINANCIAL AID (Fall 2015) 5,198 applied for aid; of those 100% were deemed to have need. 100% of freshmen with need received aid; of those 100% had need fully met. *Average financial aid package:* $3965 (excluding resources awarded to replace EFC).
UNDERGRADUATE FINANCIAL AID (Fall 2015) 17,735 applied for aid; of those 100% were deemed to have need. 100% of undergraduates with need received aid; of those 100% had need fully met. *Average financial aid package:* $5512 (excluding resources awarded to replace EFC).
GIFT AID (NEED-BASED) *Total amount:* $118,031,258 (53% federal, 17% state, 30% institutional). *Receiving aid:* Freshmen: 96% (5,047); all full-time undergraduates: 93% (17,735). *Average award:* Freshmen: $6086; Undergraduates: $5512. *Scholarships, grants, and awards:* Federal Pell, FSEOG, state, private, college/university gift aid from institutional funds.

LOANS *Student loans:* $202,787,263 (100% need-based). *Average need-based loan:* Freshmen: $8665. Undergraduates: $10,068. *Parent loans:* $13,748,650 (100% need-based). *Programs:* Federal Direct (Subsidized and Unsubsidized Stafford, PLUS), Perkins.

WORK-STUDY *Federal work-study:* 47 jobs averaging $2890.

ATHLETIC AWARDS Total amount: $1,948,467 (100% need-based).

APPLYING FOR FINANCIAL AID *Required financial aid form:* FAFSA. *Financial aid deadline:* Continuous. *Notification date:* Continuous. Students must reply within 2 weeks of notification.

CONTACT Mr. Fred Pfeffer, Associate Vice Chancellor for Student Financial Services, Keiser University, 1500 West Commercial Boulevard, Fort Lauderdale, FL 33309, 954-776-4456 or toll-free 888-534-7379. *Fax:* 954-749-4456. *E-mail:* fredp@keiseruniversity.edu.

Website: http://www.keiseruniversity.edu/.

KENDALL COLLEGE
Chicago, IL

CONTACT Lauren Walker, Director of Financial Aid, Kendall College, 900 N. North Branch Street, Chicago, IL 60642, 312-752-2267 or toll-free 888-90-KENDALL. *E-mail:* financial_aid@kendall.edu.

Website: http://www.kendall.edu/.

KENNESAW STATE UNIVERSITY
Kennesaw, GA

Tuition & fees (GA res): $8276	Average undergraduate aid package: $8426

ABOUT THE INSTITUTION State-supported, coed. *Awards:* certificates, bachelor's, master's, and doctoral degrees. 87 undergraduate majors. *Total enrollment:* 35,018. Undergraduates: 32,166. Freshmen: 5,347. Federal methodology is used as a basis for awarding need-based institutional aid.

UNDERGRADUATE EXPENSES for 2016–2017 *Application fee:* $40. *Tuition, state resident:* full-time $5320; part-time $177 per credit hour. *Tuition, nonresident:* full-time $18,776; part-time $626 per credit hour. *Required fees:* full-time $2956; $1478 per term. Full-time tuition and fees vary according to course load, degree level, location, program, and student level. Part-time tuition and fees vary according to course load, degree level, location, program, and student level. *College room and board:* $11,467. Room and board charges vary according to board plan, housing facility, and student level.

FRESHMAN FINANCIAL AID (Fall 2016, est.) 4,998 applied for aid; of those 80% were deemed to have need. 97% of freshmen with need received aid; of those 6% had need fully met. *Average percent of need met:* 38% (excluding resources awarded to replace EFC). *Average financial aid package:* $9249 (excluding resources awarded to replace EFC). 1% of all full-time freshmen had no need and received non-need-based gift aid.

UNDERGRADUATE FINANCIAL AID (Fall 2016, est.) 21,674 applied for aid; of those 82% were deemed to have need. 97% of undergraduates with need received aid; of those 4% had need fully met. *Average percent of need met:* 38% (excluding resources awarded to replace EFC). *Average financial aid package:* $8426 (excluding resources awarded to replace EFC). 1% of all full-time undergraduates had no need and received non-need-based gift aid.

GIFT AID (NEED-BASED) *Total amount:* $55,080,027 (99% federal, 1% institutional). *Receiving aid:* Freshmen: 33% (1,731); all full-time undergraduates: 39% (9,345). *Average award:* Freshmen: $4704; Undergraduates: $4654. *Scholarships, grants, and awards:* Federal Pell, FSEOG, state, private, college/university gift aid from institutional funds.

GIFT AID (NON-NEED-BASED) *Total amount:* $76,463,604 (97% state, 3% institutional). *Receiving aid:* Freshmen: 59% (3,076). Undergraduates: 38% (9,228). *Average award:* Freshmen: $1294. Undergraduates: $1229. *Scholarships, grants, and awards by category:* Academic interests/achievement: biological sciences, business, communication, computer science, education, engineering/technologies, English, foreign languages, general academic interests/achievements, health fields, humanities, international studies, mathematics, physical sciences, premedicine, social sciences. Creative arts/performance: art/fine arts, dance, music, performing arts, theater/drama. Special achievements/activities: community service, leadership, mem-

berships. Special characteristics: children and siblings of alumni, children of union members/company employees, children of workers in trades, ethnic background, general special characteristics, handicapped students, international students, local/state students, members of minority groups, religious affiliation, veterans, veterans' children. *Tuition waivers:* Full or partial for employees or children of employees, senior citizens. *ROTC:* Army cooperative, Air Force cooperative.

LOANS *Student loans:* $140,064,610 (39% need-based, 61% non-need-based). 61% of past graduating class borrowed through all loan programs. *Average indebtedness per student:* $25,613. *Average need-based loan:* Freshmen: $2710. Undergraduates: $3475. *Parent loans:* $19,119,997 (100% non-need-based). *Programs:* Federal Direct (Subsidized and Unsubsidized Stafford, PLUS), Perkins.

WORK-STUDY *Federal work-study:* Total amount: $793,217; jobs available.

ATHLETIC AWARDS Total amount: $3,721,905 (100% non-need-based).

APPLYING FOR FINANCIAL AID *Required financial aid form:* FAFSA. *Financial aid deadline (priority):* 4/1. *Notification date:* Continuous beginning 4/1.

CONTACT Mr. Ron H. Day, Director of Student Financial Aid, Kennesaw State University, 585 Cobb Avenue, NW, Mail Drop #0119, Kennesaw, GA 30144-5591, 770-423-6074. *Fax:* 470-578-9096. *E-mail:* finaid@kennesaw.edu. *Website:* http://www.kennesaw.edu/.

KENT STATE UNIVERSITY
Kent, OH

Tuition & fees (OH res): $10,012	Average undergraduate aid package: $10,292

ABOUT THE INSTITUTION State-supported, coed. *Awards:* certificates, bachelor's, master's, and doctoral degrees. 88 undergraduate majors. *Total enrollment:* 29,911. Undergraduates: 23,684. Freshmen: 4,347. Federal methodology is used as a basis for awarding need-based institutional aid.

UNDERGRADUATE EXPENSES for 2016–2017 *Application fee:* $45. *One-time required fee:* $150. *Tuition, state resident:* full-time $10,012; part-time $456 per credit hour. *Tuition, nonresident:* full-time $18,376; part-time $818 per credit hour. Full-time tuition and fees vary according to course load. Part-time tuition and fees vary according to course load. *College room and board:* $10,720; *Room only:* $6760. Room and board charges vary according to board plan and housing facility.

FRESHMAN FINANCIAL AID (Fall 2016, est.) 3,911 applied for aid; of those 76% were deemed to have need. 100% of freshmen with need received aid; of those 13% had need fully met. *Average percent of need met:* 62% (excluding resources awarded to replace EFC). *Average financial aid package:* $11,097 (excluding resources awarded to replace EFC). 22% of all full-time freshmen had no need and received non-need-based gift aid.

UNDERGRADUATE FINANCIAL AID (Fall 2016, est.) 15,408 applied for aid; of those 82% were deemed to have need. 99% of undergraduates with need received aid; of those 11% had need fully met. *Average percent of need met:* 57% (excluding resources awarded to replace EFC). *Average financial aid package:* $10,292 (excluding resources awarded to replace EFC). 18% of all full-time undergraduates had no need and received non-need-based gift aid.

GIFT AID (NEED-BASED) *Total amount:* $75,590,302 (40% federal, 10% state, 46% institutional, 4% external sources). *Receiving aid:* Freshmen: 36% (1,581); all full-time undergraduates: 35% (6,843). *Average award:* Freshmen: $6105; Undergraduates: $5437. *Scholarships, grants, and awards:* Federal Pell, FSEOG, state, private, college/university gift aid from institutional funds.

GIFT AID (NON-NEED-BASED) *Total amount:* $25,036,182 (1% federal, 4% state, 83% institutional, 12% external sources). *Receiving aid:* Freshmen: 51% (2,223). Undergraduates: 35% (6,938). *Average award:* Freshmen: $5269. Undergraduates: $5064. *Scholarships, grants, and awards by category:* Academic interests/achievement: architecture, area/ethnic studies, biological sciences, business, communication, computer science, education, engineering/technologies, English, foreign languages, general academic interests/achievements, health fields, humanities, international studies, library science, mathematics, military science, physical sciences, premedicine, religion/biblical studies, social sciences. Creative arts/performance: applied art and design, art/fine arts, cinema/film/broadcasting, creative writing, dance, general creative arts/performance, journalism/publications, music, performing arts, theater/drama. Special achievements/activities: community service, general special achievements/activities, leadership. Special characteristics: adult students, children and siblings of alumni, children of faculty/staff, children of union members/company employees, ethnic background, first-generation college students, handicapped students, international students, local/state students, members of minority groups, out-of-state students, previous college experience, veterans, veterans' children. *Tuition waivers:* Full or partial for employees or children of employees, senior citizens. *ROTC:* Army, Air Force.

LOANS *Student loans:* $113,790,655 (74% need-based, 26% non-need-based). 76% of past graduating class borrowed through all loan programs. *Average indebtedness per student:* $33,234. *Average need-based loan:* Freshmen: $4021. Undergraduates: $1516. *Parent loans* $11,882,363 (46% need based, 54% non need based). *Programs:* Federal Direct (Subsidized and Unsubsidized Stafford, PLUS), Perkins, Federal Nursing, state, college/university, alternative loans.

WORK-STUDY *Federal work-study:* Total amount: $1,568,617; 329 jobs averaging $3191.

ATHLETIC AWARDS Total amount: $6,575,340 (36% need-based, 64% non-need-based).

APPLYING FOR FINANCIAL AID *Required financial aid form:* FAFSA. *Financial aid deadline (priority):* 3/1. *Notification date:* 3/15. Students must reply within 2 weeks of notification.

CONTACT Mark A. Evans, Director of Student Financial Aid, Kent State University, 103 Schwartz Center, Kent, OH 44242-0001, 330-672-2972 or toll-free 800-988-KENT. *Fax:* 330-672-4014. *E-mail:* mevans@kent.edu.

Website: http://www.kent.edu/.

KENT STATE UNIVERSITY AT GEAUGA
Burton, OH

Tuition & fees (OH res): $5664	Average undergraduate aid package: $6815

ABOUT THE INSTITUTION State-supported, coed. *Awards:* certificates, associate, bachelor's, and master's degrees. 10 undergraduate majors. *Total enrollment:* 2,415. Undergraduates: 2,415. Freshmen: 339. Federal methodology is used as a basis for awarding need-based institutional aid.

UNDERGRADUATE EXPENSES for 2016–2017 *Application fee:* $40. *One-time required fee:* $150. *Tuition, state resident:* full-time $5664; part-time $258 per credit hour. *Tuition, nonresident:* full-time $14,028; part-time $620 per credit hour. Full-time tuition and fees vary according to course level and course load. Part-time tuition and fees vary according to course level and course load.

FRESHMAN FINANCIAL AID (Fall 2016, est.) 230 applied for aid; of those 77% were deemed to have need. 100% of freshmen with need received aid; of those 5% had need fully met. *Average percent of need met:* 53% (excluding resources awarded to replace EFC). *Average financial aid package:* $6535 (excluding resources awarded to replace EFC). 1% of all full-time freshmen had no need and received non-need-based gift aid.

UNDERGRADUATE FINANCIAL AID (Fall 2016, est.) 567 applied for aid; of those 80% were deemed to have need. 98% of undergraduates with need received aid; of those 6% had need fully met. *Average percent of need met:* 54% (excluding resources awarded to replace EFC). *Average financial aid package:* $6815 (excluding resources awarded to replace EFC). 1% of all full-time undergraduates had no need and received non-need-based gift aid.

GIFT AID (NEED-BASED) *Total amount:* $2,376,562 (94% federal, 3% state, 2% institutional, 1% external sources). *Receiving aid:* Freshmen: 46% (131); all full-time undergraduates: 42% (311). *Average award:* Freshmen: $4884; Undergraduates: $4778. *Scholarships, grants, and awards:* Federal Pell, FSEOG, state, private, college/university gift aid from institutional funds.

GIFT AID (NON-NEED-BASED) *Total amount:* $47,168 (8% federal, 4% state, 24% institutional, 64% external sources). *Receiving aid:* Freshmen: 1% (4). Undergraduates: 4% (26). *Average award:* Freshmen: $1375. Undergraduates: $773. *Scholarships, grants, and awards by category:* Academic interests/achievement: business, education, general academic interests/achievements, home economics, humanities. *Special characteristics:* children of faculty/staff, out-of-state students. *Tuition waivers:* Full or partial for employees or children of employees, senior citizens.

LOANS *Student loans:* $5,267,350 (78% need-based, 22% non-need-based). *Average need-based loan:* Freshmen: $3377. Undergraduates: $3751. *Parent loans:* $225,982 (42% need-based, 58% non-need-based). *Programs:* Federal Direct

(Subsidized and Unsubsidized Stafford, PLUS), Perkins, Federal Nursing, state, college/university, alternative loans.

APPLYING FOR FINANCIAL AID *Required financial aid form:* FAFSA. *Financial aid deadline (priority):* 3/1. *Notification date:* 3/15. Students must reply within 2 weeks of notification.

CONTACT Donna Holcomb, Financial Aid Advisor, Kent State University at Geauga, 14111 Claridon-Troy Road, Burton, OH 44021, 440-834-3737. *Fax:* 440-834-8846. *E-mail:* dholcomb@kent.edu.

Website: http://www.geauga.kent.edu/.

KENT STATE UNIVERSITY AT STARK
Canton, OH

Tuition & fees (OH res): $5664	Average undergraduate aid package: $6840

ABOUT THE INSTITUTION State-supported, coed. *Awards:* associate, bachelor's, and master's degrees. 17 undergraduate majors. *Total enrollment:* 5,031. Undergraduates: 4,998. Freshmen: 747. Federal methodology is used as a basis for awarding need-based institutional aid.

UNDERGRADUATE EXPENSES for 2016–2017 *Application fee:* $40. *One-time required fee:* $150. *Tuition, state resident:* full-time $5664; part-time $258 per credit hour. *Tuition, nonresident:* full-time $14,028; part-time $620 per credit hour. Full-time tuition and fees vary according to course level and course load. Part-time tuition and fees vary according to course level and course load.

FRESHMAN FINANCIAL AID (Fall 2016, est.) 554 applied for aid; of those 78% were deemed to have need. 100% of freshmen with need received aid; of those 11% had need fully met. *Average percent of need met:* 63% (excluding resources awarded to replace EFC). *Average financial aid package:* $6368 (excluding resources awarded to replace EFC). 10% of all full-time freshmen had no need and received non-need-based gift aid.

UNDERGRADUATE FINANCIAL AID (Fall 2016, est.) 1,924 applied for aid; of those 82% were deemed to have need. 99% of undergraduates with need received aid; of those 9% had need fully met. *Average percent of need met:* 59% (excluding resources awarded to replace EFC). *Average financial aid package:* $6840 (excluding resources awarded to replace EFC). 5% of all full-time undergraduates had no need and received non-need-based gift aid.

GIFT AID (NEED-BASED) *Total amount:* $7,341,914 (87% federal, 2% state, 8% institutional, 3% external sources). *Receiving aid:* Freshmen: 47% (298); all full-time undergraduates: 50% (1,152). *Average award:* Freshmen: $4429; Undergraduates: $4228. *Scholarships, grants, and awards:* Federal Pell, FSEOG, state, private, college/university gift aid from institutional funds.

GIFT AID (NON-NEED-BASED) *Total amount:* $518,521 (1% federal, 16% state, 57% institutional, 26% external sources). *Receiving aid:* Freshmen: 21% (132). Undergraduates: 12% (272). *Average award:* Freshmen: $1935. Undergraduates: $1843. *Scholarships, grants, and awards by category:* Academic interests/achievement: business, communication, education, foreign languages, general academic interests/achievements, home economics, social sciences. *Creative arts/performance:* journalism/publications, music, performing arts, theater/drama. *Special achievements/activities:* community service. *Special characteristics:* adult students, children and siblings of alumni, children of faculty/staff, first-generation college students, general special characteristics, members of minority groups, out-of-state students, public servants, veterans. *Tuition waivers:* Full or partial for employees or children of employees, senior citizens. *ROTC:* Army cooperative, Air Force cooperative.

LOANS *Student loans:* $14,339,541 (79% need-based, 21% non-need-based). *Average need-based loan:* Freshmen: $3212. Undergraduates: $3823. *Parent loans:* $467,238 (29% need-based, 71% non-need-based). *Programs:* Federal Direct (Subsidized and Unsubsidized Stafford, PLUS), Perkins, Federal Nursing, state, college/university, alternative loans.

WORK-STUDY *Federal work-study:* Total amount: $84,557; jobs available.

APPLYING FOR FINANCIAL AID *Required financial aid form:* FAFSA. *Financial aid deadline (priority):* 3/1. *Notification date:* 3/15. Students must reply within 2 weeks of notification.

CONTACT Amber Wallace, Assistant Director for Financial Aid, Kent State University at Stark, 134 Main Hall, North Canton, OH 44720, 330-244-3257. *Fax:* 330-499-0301. *E-mail:* gpukys@kent.edu.

Website: http://www.stark.kent.edu/.

KENTUCKY CHRISTIAN UNIVERSITY
Grayson, KY

CONTACT Mrs. Jennie M. Bender, Director of Financial Aid, Kentucky Christian University, 100 Academic Parkway, Grayson, KY 41143-2205, 606-474-3226 or toll-free 800-522-3181. *Fax:* 606-474-3268. *E-mail:* jbender@kcu.edu. *Website:* http://www.kcu.edu/.

KENTUCKY MOUNTAIN BIBLE COLLEGE
Jackson, KY

Tuition & fees: $8070	Average undergraduate aid package: $9336

ABOUT THE INSTITUTION Independent interdenominational, coed. *Awards:* associate and bachelor's degrees. 9 undergraduate majors. *Total enrollment:* 85. Undergraduates: 85. Freshmen: 20. Both federal and institutional methodology are used as a basis for awarding need-based institutional aid.

UNDERGRADUATE EXPENSES for 2016–2017 *Application fee:* $25. *One-time required fee:* $640. *Comprehensive fee:* $12,920 includes full-time tuition ($7360), mandatory fees ($710), and room and board ($4850). *College room only:* $1750. Full-time tuition and fees vary according to program. *Part-time tuition:* $230 per credit hour. *Part-time fees:* $250 per semester hour. Part-time tuition and fees vary according to program.

FRESHMAN FINANCIAL AID (Fall 2015) 14 applied for aid; of those 100% were deemed to have need. 100% of freshmen with need received aid; of those 29% had need fully met. *Average percent of need met:* 66% (excluding resources awarded to replace EFC). *Average financial aid package:* $8941 (excluding resources awarded to replace EFC). 18% of all full-time freshmen had no need and received non-need-based gift aid.

UNDERGRADUATE FINANCIAL AID (Fall 2015) 54 applied for aid; of those 98% were deemed to have need. 100% of undergraduates with need received aid; of those 9% had need fully met. *Average percent of need met:* 66% (excluding resources awarded to replace EFC). *Average financial aid package:* $9336 (excluding resources awarded to replace EFC). 12% of all full-time undergraduates had no need and received non-need-based gift aid.

GIFT AID (NEED-BASED) *Total amount:* $304,355 (71% federal, 2% state, 25% institutional, 2% external sources). *Receiving aid:* Freshmen: 82% (14); all full-time undergraduates: 87% (52). *Average award:* Freshmen: $5393; Undergraduates: $5889. *Scholarships, grants, and awards:* Federal Pell, FSEOG, state, private, college/university gift aid from institutional funds.

GIFT AID (NON-NEED-BASED) *Total amount:* $33,990 (71% institutional, 29% external sources). *Receiving aid:* Freshmen: 71% (12). Undergraduates: 37% (22). *Average award:* Freshmen: $3090. Undergraduates: $2808. *Scholarships, grants, and awards by category:* Academic interests/achievement: general academic interests/achievements. *Creative arts/performance:* music, theater/drama. *Special characteristics:* children of faculty/staff. *Tuition waivers:* Full or partial for employees or children of employees.

LOANS *Student loans:* $163,573 (81% need-based, 19% non-need-based). 75% of past graduating class borrowed through all loan programs. *Average indebtedness per student:* $7370. *Average need-based loan:* Freshmen: $6625. Undergraduates: $3707. *Programs:* college/university.

WORK-STUDY *Federal work-study:* jobs available. *State or other work-study/employment:* Total amount: $54,781 (100% non-need-based). Part-time jobs available.

APPLYING FOR FINANCIAL AID *Required financial aid forms:* FAFSA, institution's own form. *Financial aid deadline (priority):* 4/1. *Notification date:* Continuous.

CONTACT Mrs. Adelle Semrow, Director of Financial Aid, Kentucky Mountain Bible College, 855 Highway 541, Jackson, KY 41339, 800-879-KMBC Ext. 175 or toll-free 800-879-KMBC. *Fax:* 800-659-4324. *E-mail:* finaid@kmbc.edu. *Website:* http://www.kmbc.edu/.

KENTUCKY STATE UNIVERSITY
Frankfort, KY

Tuition & fees (KY res): $7796	Average undergraduate aid package: $11,792

ABOUT THE INSTITUTION State-related, coed. *Awards:* certificates, associate, bachelor's, master's, and doctoral degrees. 28 undergraduate majors. *Total enrollment:* 1,736. Undergraduates: 1,568. Freshmen: 204. Federal methodology is used as a basis for awarding need-based institutional aid.

UNDERGRADUATE EXPENSES for 2016–2017 *Tuition, state resident:* full-time $7406; part-time $309 per credit hour. *Tuition, nonresident:* full-time $18,314; part-time $763 per credit hour. *Required fees:* full-time $390. Full-time tuition and fees vary according to course load. Part-time tuition and fees vary according to course load. *College room and board:* $6690; *Room only:* $3340. Room and board charges vary according to board plan and housing facility.

FRESHMAN FINANCIAL AID (Fall 2016, est.) 186 applied for aid; of those 99% were deemed to have need. 100% of freshmen with need received aid; of those 2% had need fully met. *Average percent of need met:* 73% (excluding resources awarded to replace EFC). *Average financial aid package:* $12,795 (excluding resources awarded to replace EFC). 7% of all full-time freshmen had no need and received non-need-based gift aid.

UNDERGRADUATE FINANCIAL AID (Fall 2016, est.) 1,004 applied for aid; of those 52% were deemed to have need. 100% of undergraduates with need received aid; of those 3% had need fully met. *Average percent of need met:* 83% (excluding resources awarded to replace EFC). *Average financial aid package:* $11,792 (excluding resources awarded to replace EFC). 12% of all full-time undergraduates had no need and received non-need-based gift aid.

GIFT AID (NEED-BASED) *Total amount:* $8,558,472 (48% federal, 11% state, 37% institutional, 4% external sources). *Receiving aid:* Freshmen: 89% (173); all full-time undergraduates: 50% (518). *Average award:* Freshmen: $8967; Undergraduates: $7697. *Scholarships, grants, and awards:* Federal Pell, FSEOG, state, private, college/university gift aid from institutional funds.

GIFT AID (NON-NEED-BASED) *Total amount:* $793,828 (9% state, 77% institutional, 14% external sources). *Receiving aid:* Undergraduates: 5. *Average award:* Freshmen: $4880. Undergraduates: $4822. *Scholarships, grants, and awards by category:* Academic interests/achievement: 13 awards ($279,443 total): general academic interests/achievements. *Creative arts/performance:* 5 awards ($46,976 total): art/fine arts, music, performing arts. *Special achievements/activities:* 8 awards ($180,354 total): cheerleading/drum major, general special achievements/activities. *Special characteristics:* 14 awards ($274,899 total): adult students, children of faculty/staff, children of union members/company employees, children with a deceased or disabled parent, ethnic background, local/state students, public servants, veterans. *Tuition waivers:* Full or partial for employees or children of employees, senior citizens. *ROTC:* Army cooperative, Air Force cooperative.

LOANS *Student loans:* $6,973,500 (91% need-based, 9% non-need-based). 87% of past graduating class borrowed through all loan programs. *Average indebtedness per student:* $36,323. *Average need-based loan:* Freshmen: $3384. Undergraduates: $4078. *Parent loans:* $2,093,203 (83% need-based, 17% non-need-based). *Programs:* Federal Direct (Subsidized and Unsubsidized Stafford, PLUS), private loans.

WORK-STUDY *Federal work-study:* Total amount: $484,700; 115 jobs averaging $4215. *State or other work-study/employment:* Total amount: $108,962 (67% need-based, 33% non-need-based). 25 part-time jobs averaging $469.

ATHLETIC AWARDS Total amount: $906,511 (80% need-based, 20% non-need-based).

APPLYING FOR FINANCIAL AID *Required financial aid form:* FAFSA. *Financial aid deadline (priority):* 4/15. *Notification date:* Continuous beginning 3/15. Students must reply within 4 weeks of notification.

CONTACT Ms. Qiana Hall, Director of Financial Aid, Kentucky State University, 400 East Main Street, Frankfort, KY 40601, 502-597-5759 or toll-free 877-367-5978. *Fax:* 502-597-5950. *E-mail:* qiana.hall@kysu.edu. *Website:* http://www.kysu.edu/.

KENTUCKY WESLEYAN COLLEGE
Owensboro, KY

Tuition & fees: $3209	Average undergraduate aid package: N/A

ABOUT THE INSTITUTION Independent Methodist, coed. *Awards:* bachelor's degrees. 31 undergraduate majors. *Total enrollment:* 785. Undergraduates: 785. Freshmen: 194. Federal methodology is used as a basis for awarding need-based institutional aid.

UNDERGRADUATE EXPENSES for 2017–2018 *Comprehensive fee:* $11,959 includes full-time tuition ($2429), mandatory fees ($780), and room and board ($8750). Full-time tuition and fees vary according to course load. Room and board charges vary according to board plan and housing facility. *Part-time tuition:* $700 per credit hour. *Part-time fees:* $650 per term. Part-time tuition and fees vary according to course load.

GIFT AID (NEED-BASED) *Total amount:* $9,989,658 (40% federal, 12% state, 45% institutional, 3% external sources). *Scholarships, grants, and awards:* Federal Pell, FSEOG, state, private, college/university gift aid from institutional funds.

GIFT AID (NON-NEED-BASED) *Total amount:* $1,565,708 (37% state, 61% institutional, 2% external sources). *Scholarships, grants, and awards by category: Academic interests/achievement:* general academic interests/achievements. *Creative arts/performance:* art/fine arts, creative writing, general creative arts/performance, music, performing arts. *Special achievements/activities:* general special achievements/activities, junior miss, leadership. *Special characteristics:* children and siblings of alumni, children of faculty/staff, general special characteristics, local/state students, out-of-state students, relatives of clergy, religious affiliation, veterans. *Tuition waivers:* Full or partial for children of alumni, employees or children of employees, senior citizens. *ROTC:* Army cooperative.

LOANS *Student loans:* $3,304,424 (51% need-based, 49% non-need-based). 83% of past graduating class borrowed through all loan programs. *Average indebtedness per student:* $24,150. *Parent loans:* $1,032,620 (100% non-need-based). *Programs:* Federal Direct (Subsidized and Unsubsidized Stafford, PLUS), Perkins.

WORK-STUDY *Federal work-study:* jobs available. *State or other work-study/employment:* Part-time jobs available.

ATHLETIC AWARDS Total amount: $1,037,120 (100% non-need-based).

APPLYING FOR FINANCIAL AID *Required financial aid form:* FAFSA. *Financial aid deadline:* 3/15. *Notification date:* Continuous. Students must reply within 2 weeks of notification.

CONTACT Mrs. Crystal Hamilton, Director of Financial Aid, Kentucky Wesleyan College, 3000 Frederica Street, Owensboro, KY 42301, 270-852-3130 or toll-free 800-999-0592 (in-state), 800-990-0592 (out-of-state). *Fax:* 270-852-3133. *E-mail:* cLhamilton@kwc.edu.
Website: http://www.kwc.edu/.

KENYON COLLEGE
Gambier, OH

Tuition & fees: $51,200	Average undergraduate aid package: $43,532

ABOUT THE INSTITUTION Independent, coed. *Awards:* bachelor's degrees. 35 undergraduate majors. *Total enrollment:* 1,708. Undergraduates: 1,708. Freshmen: 487. Institutional methodology is used as a basis for awarding need-based institutional aid.

UNDERGRADUATE EXPENSES for 2016–2017 *Comprehensive fee:* $63,330 includes full-time tuition ($49,220), mandatory fees ($1980), and room and board ($12,130). *College room only:* $5340. Full-time tuition and fees vary according to reciprocity agreements. Room and board charges vary according to housing facility and student level. Part-time tuition and fees vary according to reciprocity agreements.

FRESHMAN FINANCIAL AID (Fall 2016, est.) 265 applied for aid; of those 76% were deemed to have need. 100% of freshmen with need received aid; of those 100% had need fully met. *Average percent of need met:* 100% (excluding resources awarded to replace EFC). *Average financial aid package:* $41,728 (excluding resources awarded to replace EFC). 14% of all full-time freshmen had no need and received non-need-based gift aid.

UNDERGRADUATE FINANCIAL AID (Fall 2016, est.) 831 applied for aid; of those 89% were deemed to have need. 100% of undergraduates with need received aid; of those 100% had need fully met. *Average percent of need met:* 100% (excluding resources awarded to replace EFC). *Average financial aid package:* $43,532 (excluding resources awarded to replace EFC). 11% of all full-time undergraduates had no need and received non-need-based gift aid.

GIFT AID (NEED-BASED) *Total amount:* $29,669,865 (3% federal, 94% institutional, 3% external sources). *Receiving aid:* Freshmen: 41% (198); all full-time undergraduates: 41% (735). *Average award:* Freshmen: $38,811; Undergraduates: $39,612. *Scholarships, grants, and awards:* Federal Pell, FSEOG, state, private, college/university gift aid from institutional funds.

GIFT AID (NON-NEED-BASED) *Total amount:* $6,312,582 (73% institutional, 27% external sources). *Receiving aid:* Freshmen: 13% (63). Undergraduates: 9% (156). *Average award:* Freshmen: $14,320. Undergraduates: $16,488. *Scholarships, grants, and awards by category: Academic interests/achievement:* 292 awards ($4,697,075 total): biological sciences, computer science, general academic interests/achievements, humanities, mathematics, physical sciences. *Creative arts/performance:* 36 awards ($439,710 total): art/fine arts, creative writing, music. *Special characteristics:* 92 awards ($1,180,132 total): ethnic background, first-generation college students. *Tuition waivers:* Full or partial for employees or children of employees.

LOANS *Student loans:* $5,929,684 (57% need-based, 43% non-need-based). 36% of past graduating class borrowed through all loan programs. *Average indebtedness per student:* $27,000. *Average need-based loan:* Freshmen: $2465. Undergraduates: $4103. *Parent loans:* $2,460,667 (7% need-based, 93% non-need-based). *Programs:* Federal Direct (Subsidized and Unsubsidized Stafford, PLUS), Perkins, college/university.

WORK-STUDY *Federal work-study:* Total amount: $453,082; 213 jobs averaging $2861. *State or other work-study/employment:* Total amount: $366,024 (99% need-based, 1% non-need-based). 120 part-time jobs averaging $2516.

APPLYING FOR FINANCIAL AID *Required financial aid forms:* FAFSA, CSS Financial Aid PROFILE, noncustodial (divorced/separated) parent's statement, federal income tax and W-2 forms. *Financial aid deadline (priority):* 1/15. *Notification date:* 4/1. Students must reply by 5/1.

CONTACT Mr. Craig Alan Slaughter, Director of Financial Aid, Kenyon College, Edelstein House, Gambier, OH 43022-9623, 740-427-5430 or toll-free 800-848-2468. *Fax:* 740-427-5240. *E-mail:* slaughterc@kenyon.edu.
Website: http://www.kenyon.edu/.

KETTERING COLLEGE
Kettering, OH

CONTACT Financial Aid Office, Kettering College, 3737 Southern Boulevard, Kettering, OH 45429-1299, 937-395-8601 or toll-free 800-433-5262.
Website: http://www.kc.edu/.

KETTERING UNIVERSITY
Flint, MI

ABOUT THE INSTITUTION Independent, coed. *Awards:* bachelor's and master's degrees. 15 undergraduate majors. *Total enrollment:* 2,327. Undergraduates: 1,905. Freshmen: 418.

GIFT AID (NEED-BASED) *Scholarships, grants, and awards:* Federal Pell, FSEOG, state, private, college/university gift aid from institutional funds, United Negro College Fund.

GIFT AID (NON-NEED-BASED) *Scholarships, grants, and awards by category: Academic interests/achievement:* business, computer science, engineering/technologies, general academic interests/achievements, mathematics, physical sciences. *Special achievements/activities:* general special achievements/activities, leadership, memberships. *Special characteristics:* children of faculty/staff, siblings of current students.

LOANS *Programs:* Federal Direct (Subsidized and Unsubsidized Stafford, PLUS).

WORK-STUDY Federal work-study jobs available.

APPLYING FOR FINANCIAL AID *Required financial aid form:* FAFSA.

CONTACT Diane Bice, Director of Financial Aid, Kettering University, 1700 University Avenue, Flint, MI 48504, 800-955-4464 Ext. 7859 or toll-free 800-955-4464 Ext. 7865 (in-state), 800-955-4464 (out-of-state). *Fax:* 810-762-9807. *E-mail:* finaid@kettering.edu.
Website: http://www.kettering.edu/.

KEUKA COLLEGE
Keuka Park, NY

Tuition & fees: $30,946	Average undergraduate aid package: $20,979

ABOUT THE INSTITUTION Independent American Baptist Churches in the U.S.A., coed. *Awards:* bachelor's and master's degrees. 35 undergraduate majors. *Total enrollment:* 2,003. Undergraduates: 1,730. Freshmen: 365. Federal methodology is used as a basis for awarding need-based institutional aid.

UNDERGRADUATE EXPENSES for 2017–2018 *One-time required fee:* $225. *Comprehensive fee:* $42,398 includes full-time tuition ($29,926), mandatory fees ($1020), and room and board ($11,452). *College room only:* $5520. Full-time tuition and fees vary according to course load, degree level, program, and reciprocity agreements. Room and board charges vary according to board plan and housing facility. *Part-time tuition:* $999 per credit hour. Part-time tuition and fees vary according to course load, degree level, program, and reciprocity agreements.

FRESHMAN FINANCIAL AID (Fall 2015) 312 applied for aid; of those 94% were deemed to have need. 100% of freshmen with need received aid; of those 10% had need fully met. *Average financial aid package:* $26,408 (excluding resources awarded to replace EFC). 7% of all full-time freshmen had no need and received non-need-based gift aid.

UNDERGRADUATE FINANCIAL AID (Fall 2015) 1,206 applied for aid; of those 93% were deemed to have need. 100% of undergraduates with need received aid; of those 9% had need fully met. *Average financial aid package:* $20,979 (excluding resources awarded to replace EFC). 3% of all full-time undergraduates had no need and received non-need-based gift aid.

GIFT AID (NEED-BASED) *Total amount:* $15,593,357 (22% federal, 12% state, 60% institutional, 6% external sources). *Receiving aid:* Freshmen: 77% (247); all full-time undergraduates: 70% (928). *Average award:* Freshmen: $9280; Undergraduates: $8769. *Scholarships, grants, and awards:* Federal Pell, FSEOG, state, college/university gift aid from institutional funds.

GIFT AID (NON-NEED-BASED) *Total amount:* $3,991,643 (3% federal, 6% state, 85% institutional, 6% external sources). *Receiving aid:* Freshmen: 88% (281). Undergraduates: 57% (758). *Average award:* Freshmen: $13,303. Undergraduates: $11,602. *Scholarships, grants, and awards by category:* Academic interests/achievement: 725 awards ($8,005,051 total): education, general academic interests/achievements. *Special achievements/activities:* 11 awards ($199,542 total): community service, leadership. *Special characteristics:* 217 awards ($1,923,209 total): children and siblings of alumni, children of faculty/staff, first-generation college students, international students, members of minority groups, religious affiliation, siblings of current students, veterans, veterans' children. *Tuition waivers:* Full or partial for employees or children of employees.

LOANS *Student loans:* $11,406,323 (80% need-based, 20% non-need-based). *Average need-based loan:* Freshmen: $3502. Undergraduates: $4288. *Parent loans:* $2,847,636 (80% need-based, 20% non-need-based). *Programs:* Federal Direct (Subsidized and Unsubsidized Stafford, PLUS), Perkins.

WORK-STUDY *Federal work-study:* jobs available. *State or other work-study/employment:* Total amount: $181,819 (80% need-based, 20% non-need-based). Part-time jobs available.

APPLYING FOR FINANCIAL AID *Required financial aid form:* FAFSA. *Financial aid deadline:* Continuous. *Notification date:* 11/1. Students must reply by 5/1 or within 2 weeks of notification.

CONTACT Jennifer Bates, Executive Director of Financial Aid, Keuka College, 141 Central Avenue, Keuka Park, NY 14478-0098, 315-279-5232 or toll-free 800-33-KEUKA. *Fax:* 315-536-5327. *E-mail:* jbates@keuka.edu.
Website: http://www.keuka.edu/.

KEYSTONE COLLEGE
La Plume, PA

CONTACT Director of Financial Assistance and Planning, Keystone College, One College Green, La Plume, PA 18440, 570-945-8134 or toll-free 877-4-COLLEGE. *Fax:* 570-945-8134. *E-mail:* financialaid@keystone.edu.
Website: http://www.keystone.edu/.

THE KING'S COLLEGE
New York, NY

Tuition & fees: $34,720	Average undergraduate aid package: $26,187

ABOUT THE INSTITUTION Independent nondenominational, coed. *Awards:* bachelor's degrees. 6 undergraduate majors. *Total enrollment:* 534. Undergraduates: 534. Freshmen: 161. Federal methodology is used as a basis for awarding need-based institutional aid.

UNDERGRADUATE EXPENSES for 2016–2017 *Application fee:* $30. *Tuition:* full-time $34,320; part-time $1410 per credit. *Required fees:* full-time $400; $200 per term. Full-time tuition and fees vary according to course load. Part-time tuition and fees vary according to course load. Room and board charges vary according to location.

FRESHMAN FINANCIAL AID (Fall 2015) 138 applied for aid; of those 86% were deemed to have need. 100% of freshmen with need received aid; of those 10% had need fully met. *Average percent of need met:* 65% (excluding resources awarded to replace EFC). *Average financial aid package:* $26,863 (excluding resources awarded to replace EFC). 20% of all full-time freshmen had no need and received non-need-based gift aid.

UNDERGRADUATE FINANCIAL AID (Fall 2015) 394 applied for aid; of those 89% were deemed to have need. 99% of undergraduates with need received aid; of those 14% had need fully met. *Average percent of need met:* 68% (excluding resources awarded to replace EFC). *Average financial aid package:* $26,187 (excluding resources awarded to replace EFC). 27% of all full-time undergraduates had no need and received non-need-based gift aid.

GIFT AID (NEED-BASED) *Total amount:* $7,685,261 (9% federal, 1% state, 88% institutional, 2% external sources). *Receiving aid:* Freshmen: 80% (119); all full-time undergraduates: 72% (347). *Average award:* Freshmen: $22,725; Undergraduates: $21,913. *Scholarships, grants, and awards:* Federal Pell, FSEOG, state, private, college/university gift aid from institutional funds.

GIFT AID (NON-NEED-BASED) *Total amount:* $2,084,850 (99% institutional, 1% external sources). *Average award:* Freshmen: $14,626. Undergraduates: $16,036. *Scholarships, grants, and awards by category:* Academic interests/achievement: 101 awards ($1,244,597 total): general academic interests/achievements. *Special achievements/activities:* 64 awards ($146,000 total): general special achievements/activities, leadership. *Special characteristics:* 10 awards ($69,740 total): children and siblings of alumni. *Tuition waivers:* Full or partial for employees or children of employees. *ROTC:* Army cooperative.

LOANS *Student loans:* $2,969,545 (95% need-based, 5% non-need-based). 70% of past graduating class borrowed through all loan programs. *Average indebtedness per student:* $32,934. *Average need-based loan:* Freshmen: $3375. Undergraduates: $4204. *Parent loans:* $787,319 (99% need-based, 1% non-need-based). *Programs:* Federal Direct (Subsidized and Unsubsidized Stafford, PLUS), private loans.

APPLYING FOR FINANCIAL AID *Required financial aid form:* FAFSA. *Financial aid deadline:* Continuous. *Notification date:* Continuous beginning 11/15.

CONTACT Noah Hunter, Director of New Student Financial Aid, The King's College, 56 Broadway, New York, NY 10004, 212-659-3610 or toll-free 888-969-7200 Ext. 3610. *E-mail:* financialservices@tkc.edu.
Website: http://www.tkc.edu/.

KING'S COLLEGE
Wilkes-Barre, PA

Tuition & fees: $34,720	Average undergraduate aid package: $24,694

ABOUT THE INSTITUTION Independent Roman Catholic, coed. *Awards:* certificates, bachelor's, and master's degrees. 42 undergraduate majors. *Total enrollment:* 2,421. Undergraduates: 2,082. Freshmen: 573. Federal methodology is used as a basis for awarding need-based institutional aid.

UNDERGRADUATE EXPENSES for 2016–2017 *Application fee:* $30. *Comprehensive fee:* $46,858 includes full-time tuition ($33,620), mandatory fees ($1100), and room and board ($12,138). *College room only:* $6060. Room and board charges vary according to board plan. *Part-time tuition:* $550 per credit hour.

FRESHMAN FINANCIAL AID (Fall 2016, est.) 501 applied for aid; of those 91% were deemed to have need. 100% of freshmen with need received aid; of those 18% had need fully met. *Average percent of need met:* 76% (excluding resources awarded to replace EFC). *Average financial aid package:* $25,853 (excluding resources awarded to replace EFC). 11% of all full-time freshmen had no need and received non-need-based gift aid.

UNDERGRADUATE FINANCIAL AID (Fall 2016, est.) 1,645 applied for aid; of those 91% were deemed to have need. 100% of undergraduates with need received aid; of those 18% had need fully met. *Average percent of need met:* 73% (excluding resources awarded to replace EFC). *Average financial aid package:* $24,694 (excluding resources awarded to replace EFC). 14% of all full-time undergraduates had no need and received non-need-based gift aid.

GIFT AID (NEED-BASED) *Total amount:* $27,937,402 (10% federal, 8% state, 81% institutional, 1% external sources). *Receiving aid:* Freshmen: 80% (455); all full-time undergraduates: 79% (1,498). *Average award:* Freshmen: $21,094; Undergraduates: $19,407. *Scholarships, grants, and awards:* Federal Pell, FSEOG, state, private, college/university gift aid from institutional funds.

GIFT AID (NON-NEED-BASED) *Total amount:* $5,495,913 (2% federal, 95% institutional, 3% external sources). *Receiving aid:* Freshmen: 12% (66). Undergraduates: 11% (203). *Average award:* Freshmen: $15,926. Undergraduates: $14,708. *Scholarships, grants, and awards by category:* Academic interests/achievement: 1,541 awards ($17,475,094 total): biological sciences, business, communication, computer science, education, engineering/technologies, English, foreign languages, general academic interests/achievements, health fields, humanities, mathematics, physical sciences, premedicine, religion/biblical studies, social sciences. Special achievements/activities: 1,164 awards ($4,086,064 total): community service, general special achievements/activities, leadership. Special characteristics: 348 awards ($3,051,564 total): children and siblings of alumni, children of educators, children of faculty/staff, international students, relatives of clergy, siblings of current students, veterans. *Tuition waivers:* Full or partial for employees or children of employees, senior citizens. *ROTC:* Army, Air Force cooperative.

LOANS *Student loans:* $16,460,622 (72% need-based, 28% non-need-based). 86% of past graduating class borrowed through all loan programs. *Average indebtedness per student:* $37,874. *Average need-based loan:* Freshmen: $3733. Undergraduates: $4760. *Parent loans:* $4,596,685 (49% need-based, 51% non-need-based). *Programs:* Federal Direct (Subsidized and Unsubsidized Stafford, PLUS), Perkins, private loans.

WORK-STUDY *Federal work-study:* Total amount: $345,000; 313 jobs averaging $1542. *State or other work-study/employment:* Total amount: $255,000 (100% non-need-based). 284 part-time jobs averaging $1122.

APPLYING FOR FINANCIAL AID *Required financial aid form:* FAFSA. *Financial aid deadline (priority):* 2/15. *Notification date:* Continuous beginning 3/1. Students must reply by 5/1 or within 2 weeks of notification.

CONTACT Ms. Donna Cerza, Director of Financial Aid, King's College, 133 North River Street, Wilkes-Barre, PA 18711-0801, 570-208-5868 or toll-free 888-KINGSPA. *Fax:* 570-208-6015. *E-mail:* finaid@kings.edu. *Website:* http://www.kings.edu/.

THE KING'S UNIVERSITY
Southlake, TX

CONTACT Mr. Norman V. Stoppenbrink Jr., Financial Aid Officer, The King's University, 14800 Sherman Way, Los Angeles, CA 91405, 818-779-8040 Ext. 8278 or toll-free 888-779-8040. *Fax:* 818-779-8251. *E-mail:* financialaid@kingsuniversity.edu. *Website:* http://www.tku.edu/.

KING UNIVERSITY
Bristol, TN

Tuition & fees: $27,276	Average undergraduate aid package: $14,306

ABOUT THE INSTITUTION Independent Presbyterian Church (U.S.A.), coed. *Awards:* certificates, associate, bachelor's, master's, and doctoral degrees. 60 undergraduate majors. *Total enrollment:* 2,804. Undergraduates: 2,343. Freshmen: 159. Federal methodology is used as a basis for awarding need-based institutional aid.

UNDERGRADUATE EXPENSES for 2016–2017 *Application fee:* $25. *One-time required fee:* $125. *Comprehensive fee:* $35,456 includes full-time tuition ($25,798), mandatory fees ($1478), and room and board ($8180). *College room only:* $4108. Full-time tuition and fees vary according to class time, course load, degree level, location, and program. Room and board charges vary according to board plan and housing facility. *Part-time tuition:* $600 per credit. *Part-time fees:* $120 per term. Part-time tuition and fees vary according to class time, course load, degree level, location, and program.

FRESHMAN FINANCIAL AID (Fall 2016, est.) 160 applied for aid; of those 94% were deemed to have need. 99% of freshmen with need received aid; of those 18% had need fully met. *Average percent of need met:* 79% (excluding resources awarded to replace EFC). *Average financial aid package:* $23,738 (excluding resources awarded to replace EFC). 12% of all full-time freshmen had no need and received non-need-based gift aid.

UNDERGRADUATE FINANCIAL AID (Fall 2016, est.) 1,877 applied for aid; of those 91% were deemed to have need. 99% of undergraduates with need received aid; of those 13% had need fully met. *Average percent of need met:* 63% (excluding resources awarded to replace EFC). *Average financial aid package:* $14,306 (excluding resources awarded to replace EFC). 5% of all full-time undergraduates had no need and received non-need-based gift aid.

GIFT AID (NEED-BASED) *Total amount:* $14,568,168 (31% federal, 16% state, 50% institutional, 3% external sources). *Receiving aid:* Freshmen: 82% (148); all full-time undergraduates: 68% (1,358). *Average award:* Freshmen: $19,422; Undergraduates: $12,095. *Scholarships, grants, and awards:* Federal Pell, FSEOG, state, private, college/university gift aid from institutional funds.

GIFT AID (NON-NEED-BASED) *Total amount:* $1,702,172 (14% state, 77% institutional, 9% external sources). *Receiving aid:* Freshmen: 11% (20). Undergraduates: 6% (115). *Average award:* Freshmen: $10,636. Undergraduates: $10,036. *Scholarships, grants, and awards by category:* Academic interests/achievement: 685 awards ($6,023,568 total): general academic interests/achievements. Creative arts/performance: 73 awards ($271,500 total): art/fine arts, music, performing arts, theater/drama. Special achievements/activities: 82 awards ($79,000 total): general special achievements/activities. Special characteristics: 241 awards ($1,853,495 total): children of faculty/staff, out-of-state students, veterans, veterans' children. *Tuition waivers:* Full or partial for employees or children of employees, senior citizens.

LOANS *Student loans:* $17,902,362 (80% need-based, 20% non-need-based). 83% of past graduating class borrowed through all loan programs. *Average indebtedness per student:* $23,950. *Average need-based loan:* Freshmen: $3901. Undergraduates: $4509. *Parent loans:* $764,605 (48% need-based, 52% non-need-based). *Programs:* Federal Direct (Subsidized and Unsubsidized Stafford, PLUS), Perkins.

WORK-STUDY *Federal work-study:* Total amount: $142,857; 138 jobs averaging $1123. *State or other work-study/employment:* Total amount: $195,654 (100% non-need-based). 105 part-time jobs averaging $1268.

ATHLETIC AWARDS *Total amount:* $3,039,346 (61% need-based, 39% non-need-based).

APPLYING FOR FINANCIAL AID *Required financial aid form:* FAFSA. *Financial aid deadline (priority):* 3/1. *Notification date:* Continuous beginning 12/15. Students must reply within 4 weeks of notification.

CONTACT Richard J. Brand, Director of Financial Aid, King University, 1350 King College Road, Bristol, TN 37620-2699, 423-652-4728 or toll-free 800-362-0014. *Fax:* 423-652-6039. *E-mail:* rjbrand@king.edu. *Website:* http://www.king.edu/.

KNOX COLLEGE
Galesburg, IL

Tuition & fees: $44,958	Average undergraduate aid package: $36,532

ABOUT THE INSTITUTION Independent, coed. *Awards:* bachelor's degrees. 42 undergraduate majors. *Total enrollment:* 1,357. Undergraduates: 1,357. Freshmen: 347. Both federal and institutional methodology are used as a basis for awarding need-based institutional aid.

UNDERGRADUATE EXPENSES for 2017–2018 *Application fee:* $50. *Comprehensive fee:* $54,624 includes full-time tuition ($44,191), mandatory fees ($767), and room and board ($9666). *College room only:* $4854. Full-time tuition and fees vary according to course load. Room and board charges vary according to housing facility. Part-time tuition and fees vary according to course load.

FRESHMAN FINANCIAL AID (Fall 2016, est.) 317 applied for aid; of those 91% were deemed to have need. 100% of freshmen with need received aid; of those 34% had need fully met. *Average percent of need met:* 91% (excluding resources awarded to replace EFC). *Average financial aid package:* $38,463 (excluding resources awarded to replace EFC). 17% of all full-time freshmen had no need and received non-need-based gift aid.

UNDERGRADUATE FINANCIAL AID (Fall 2016, est.) 1,122 applied for aid; of those 93% were deemed to have need. 100% of undergraduates with need received aid; of those 26% had need fully met. *Average percent of need met:* 87% (excluding resources awarded to replace EFC). *Average financial aid package:* $36,532 (excluding resources awarded to replace EFC). 20% of all full-time undergraduates had no need and received non-need-based gift aid.

GIFT AID (NEED-BASED) *Total amount:* $32,181,419 (6% federal, 5% state, 87% institutional, 2% external sources). *Receiving aid:* Freshmen: 81% (280); all full-time undergraduates: 75% (1,021). *Average award:* Freshmen: $33,547; Undergraduates: $31,006. *Scholarships, grants, and awards:* Federal Pell, FSEOG, state, private, college/university gift aid from institutional funds.

GIFT AID (NON-NEED-BASED) *Total amount:* $5,350,547 (98% institutional, 2% external sources). *Receiving aid:* Freshmen: 9% (31). Undergraduates: 7% (89). *Average award:* Freshmen: $20,991. Undergraduates: $19,121. *Scholarships, grants, and awards by category:* Academic interests/achievement: general academic interests/achievements, mathematics. *Creative arts/performance:* art/fine arts, creative writing, dance, music, theater/drama. *Special achievements/activities:* community service. *Special characteristics:* children of faculty/staff, veterans. *Tuition waivers:* Full or partial for employees or children of employees.

LOANS *Student loans:* $7,788,982 (63% need-based, 37% non-need-based). 64% of past graduating class borrowed through all loan programs. *Average indebtedness per student:* $30,368. *Average need-based loan:* Freshmen: $4899. Undergraduates: $5250. *Parent loans:* $1,831,690 (100% non-need-based). *Programs:* Federal Direct (Subsidized and Unsubsidized Stafford, PLUS), Perkins, college/university, private loans.

WORK-STUDY *Federal work-study:* Total amount: $1,471,050; jobs available. *State or other work-study/employment:* Total amount: $312,075 (100% need-based). Part-time jobs available.

APPLYING FOR FINANCIAL AID *Required financial aid forms:* FAFSA, institution's own form. *Financial aid deadline (priority):* 10/1. *Notification date:* Continuous beginning 12/15. Students must reply by 5/1 or within 2 weeks of notification.

CONTACT Ms. Ann M. Brill, Director of Financial Aid, Knox College, 2 East South Street, Galesburg, IL 61401, 309-341-7149 or toll-free 800-678-KNOX. *Fax:* 309-341-7453. *E-mail:* abrill@knox.edu. *Website:* http://www.knox.edu/.

KUTZTOWN UNIVERSITY OF PENNSYLVANIA
Kutztown, PA

Tuition & fees (PA res): $9618	Average undergraduate aid package: $8699

ABOUT THE INSTITUTION State-supported, coed. *Awards:* certificates, bachelor's, master's, and doctoral degrees. 42 undergraduate majors. *Total enrollment:* 8,513. Undergraduates: 7,718. Freshmen: 1,695. Federal methodology is used as a basis for awarding need-based institutional aid.

UNDERGRADUATE EXPENSES for 2016–2017 *Application fee:* $35. *One-time required fee:* $238. *Tuition, state resident:* full-time $7238; part-time $302 per credit hour. *Tuition, nonresident:* full-time $18,096; part-time $754 per credit hour. *Required fees:* full-time $2380; $99.54 per credit hour. Full-time tuition and fees vary according to course load. Part-time tuition and fees vary according to course load. *College room and board:* $9438; *Room only:* $5720. Room and board charges vary according to board plan and housing facility.

FRESHMAN FINANCIAL AID (Fall 2015) 1,741 applied for aid; of those 81% were deemed to have need. 98% of freshmen with need received aid; of those 6% had need fully met. *Average percent of need met:* 41% (excluding resources awarded to replace EFC). *Average financial aid package:* $8375 (excluding resources awarded to replace EFC). 11% of all full-time freshmen had no need and received non-need-based gift aid.

UNDERGRADUATE FINANCIAL AID (Fall 2015) 6,724 applied for aid; of those 83% were deemed to have need. 98% of undergraduates with need received aid; of those 7% had need fully met. *Average percent of need met:* 47% (excluding resources awarded to replace EFC). *Average financial aid package:* $8699 (excluding resources awarded to replace EFC). 4% of all full-time undergraduates had no need and received non-need-based gift aid.

GIFT AID (NEED-BASED) *Total amount:* $24,391,452 (51% federal, 35% state, 7% institutional, 7% external sources). *Receiving aid:* Freshmen: 46% (864); all full-time undergraduates: 44% (3,432). *Average award:* Freshmen: $6118; Undergraduates: $5726. *Scholarships, grants, and awards:* Federal Pell, FSEOG, state, private, college/university gift aid from institutional funds.

GIFT AID (NON-NEED-BASED) *Total amount:* $753,202 (1% federal, 16% state, 31% institutional, 52% external sources). *Receiving aid:* Freshmen: 50% (922). Undergraduates: 19% (1,485). *Average award:* Freshmen: $543. Undergraduates: $776. *Scholarships, grants, and awards by category:* Academic interests/achievement: 381 awards ($1,236,933 total): biological sciences, business, communication, computer science, education, English, foreign languages, general academic interests/achievements, humanities, international studies, library science, mathematics, physical sciences. *Creative arts/performance:* 31 awards ($33,433 total): applied art and design, art/fine arts, dance, music. *Special achievements/activities:* 252 awards ($579,232 total): community service, general special achievements/activities, leadership, religious involvement. *Special characteristics:* 130 awards ($873,758 total): children of faculty/staff, children of union members/company employees, first-generation college students, handicapped students, local/state students. *Tuition waivers:* Full or partial for employees or children of employees, senior citizens. *ROTC:* Army cooperative.

LOANS *Student loans:* $60,612,071 (82% need-based, 18% non-need-based). 80% of past graduating class borrowed through all loan programs. *Average indebtedness per student:* $39,230. *Average need-based loan:* Freshmen: $3364. Undergraduates: $4172. *Parent loans:* $15,533,451 (84% need-based, 16% non-need-based). *Programs:* Federal Direct (Subsidized and Unsubsidized Stafford, PLUS), Perkins.

WORK-STUDY *Federal work-study:* 447 jobs averaging $2587.

ATHLETIC AWARDS Total amount: $641,834 (69% need-based, 31% non-need-based).

APPLYING FOR FINANCIAL AID *Required financial aid form:* FAFSA. *Financial aid deadline (priority):* 3/1. *Notification date:* Continuous beginning 3/30. Students must reply by 5/1 or within 4 weeks of notification.

CONTACT Mr. Bernard McCree, Director of Financial Aid, Kutztown University of Pennsylvania, 209 Stratton Administration Center, Kutztown, PA 19530-0730, 610-683-4032 or toll-free 877-628-1915. *Fax:* 610-683-1380. *E-mail:* mccree@kutztown.edu. *Website:* http://www.kutztown.edu/.

KUYPER COLLEGE
Grand Rapids, MI

Tuition & fees: $20,302	Average undergraduate aid package: $15,300

ABOUT THE INSTITUTION Independent Christian, coed. **Awards:** certificates, associate, and bachelor's degrees. 25 undergraduate majors. **Total enrollment:** 208. Undergraduates: 208. Freshmen: 38. Federal methodology is used as a basis for awarding need-based institutional aid.

UNDERGRADUATE EXPENSES for 2016–2017 One-time required fee: $554. **Comprehensive fee:** $27,102 includes full-time tuition ($19,718), mandatory fees ($584), and room and board ($6800). Full-time tuition and fees vary according to course load and reciprocity agreements. Room and board charges vary according to board plan, housing facility, and student level. **Part-time tuition:** $945 per credit hour. **Part-time fees:** $295 per year. Part-time tuition and fees vary according to course load and reciprocity agreements.

FRESHMAN FINANCIAL AID (Fall 2016, est.) 34 applied for aid; of those 97% were deemed to have need. 100% of freshmen with need received aid; of those 12% had need fully met. **Average percent of need met:** 73% (excluding resources awarded to replace EFC). **Average financial aid package:** $17,306 (excluding resources awarded to replace EFC). 3% of all full-time freshmen had no need and received non-need-based gift aid.

UNDERGRADUATE FINANCIAL AID (Fall 2016, est.) 156 applied for aid; of those 90% were deemed to have need. 100% of undergraduates with need received aid; of those 4% had need fully met. **Average percent of need met:** 69% (excluding resources awarded to replace EFC). **Average financial aid package:** $15,300 (excluding resources awarded to replace EFC). 15% of all full-time undergraduates had no need and received non-need-based gift aid.

GIFT AID (NEED-BASED) Total amount: $1,731,913 (19% federal, 13% state, 67% institutional, 1% external sources). **Receiving aid:** Freshmen: 94% (32); all full-time undergraduates: 83% (140). **Average award:** Freshmen: $14,639; Undergraduates: $11,984. **Scholarships, grants, and awards:** Federal Pell, FSEOG, state, private, college/university gift aid from institutional funds.

GIFT AID (NON-NEED-BASED) Total amount: $158,636 (99% institutional, 1% external sources). **Receiving aid:** Freshmen: 18% (6). Undergraduates: 4% (7). **Average award:** Freshmen: $8500. Undergraduates: $6574. **Scholarships, grants, and awards by category:** Academic interests/achievement: 110 awards ($439,250 total): general academic interests/achievements. Creative arts/performance: 8 awards ($3173 total): music. Special achievements/activities: 8 awards ($14,000 total): leadership. Special characteristics: 37 awards ($171,050 total): children and siblings of alumni, children of faculty/staff, handicapped students, international students, relatives of clergy, siblings of current students. **Tuition waivers:** Full or partial for employees or children of employees. **ROTC:** Army cooperative.

LOANS Student loans: $964,016 (88% need-based, 12% non-need-based). 63% of past graduating class borrowed through all loan programs. Average indebtedness per student: $25,906. **Average need-based loan:** Freshmen: $4956. Undergraduates: $4661. **Parent loans:** $60,908 (100% need-based). **Programs:** Federal Direct (Subsidized and Unsubsidized Stafford, PLUS), alternative loans.

WORK-STUDY Federal work-study: Total amount: $33,382; 19 jobs averaging $1737. **State or other work-study/employment:** Total amount: $332,619 (100% non-need-based). 100 part-time jobs averaging $3226.

APPLYING FOR FINANCIAL AID Required financial aid form: FAFSA. **Financial aid deadline (priority):** 3/1. **Notification date:** Continuous beginning 3/20. Students must reply within 2 weeks of notification.

CONTACT Ms. Agnes Russell, Director of Financial Aid, Kuyper College, 3333 East Beltline NE, Grand Rapids, MI 49525-9749, 616-222-3000 Ext. 656. Fax: 616-222-3045. E-mail: arussell@kuyper.edu. Website: http://www.kuyper.edu/.

LAFAYETTE COLLEGE
Easton, PA

Comprehensive fee: $65,890	Average undergraduate aid package: $45,615

ABOUT THE INSTITUTION Independent Presbyterian Church (U.S.A.), coed. **Awards:** bachelor's degrees. 35 undergraduate majors. **Total enrollment:** 2,550. Undergraduates: 2,550. Freshmen: 649. Both federal and institutional methodology are used as a basis for awarding need-based institutional aid.

UNDERGRADUATE EXPENSES for 2017–2018 One-time required fee: $450. **Comprehensive fee:** $65,890. **Payment plan:** Guaranteed tuition.

FRESHMAN FINANCIAL AID (Fall 2016, est.) 411 applied for aid; of those 59% were deemed to have need. 100% of freshmen with need received aid; of those 100% had need fully met. **Average percent of need met:** 100% (excluding resources awarded to replace EFC). **Average financial aid package:** $45,502 (excluding resources awarded to replace EFC). 5% of all full-time freshmen had no need and received non-need-based gift aid.

UNDERGRADUATE FINANCIAL AID (Fall 2016, est.) 1,299 applied for aid; of those 59% were deemed to have need. 100% of undergraduates with need received aid; of those 100% had need fully met. **Average percent of need met:** 100% (excluding resources awarded to replace EFC). **Average financial aid package:** $45,615 (excluding resources awarded to replace EFC). 9% of all full-time undergraduates had no need and received non-need-based gift aid.

GIFT AID (NEED-BASED) Total amount: $29,241,096 (5% federal, 1% state, 93% institutional, 1% external sources). **Receiving aid:** Freshmen: 35% (228); all full-time undergraduates: 29% (721). **Average award:** Freshmen: $41,091; Undergraduates: $40,285. **Scholarships, grants, and awards:** Federal Pell, FSEOG, state, private, college/university gift aid from institutional funds.

GIFT AID (NON-NEED-BASED) Total amount: $7,702,606 (84% institutional, 16% external sources). **Receiving aid:** Freshmen: 10% (62). Undergraduates: 6% (162). **Average award:** Freshmen: $27,738. Undergraduates: $27,358. **Scholarships, grants, and awards by category:** Academic interests/achievement: general academic interests/achievements. Creative arts/performance: applied art and design, art/fine arts, cinema/film/broadcasting, creative writing, dance, general creative arts/performance, music, performing arts, theater/drama. **ROTC:** Army cooperative.

LOANS Student loans: $9,796,338 (37% need-based, 63% non-need-based). 48% of past graduating class borrowed through all loan programs. Average indebtedness per student: $29,324. **Average need-based loan:** Freshmen: $3458. Undergraduates: $4417. **Parent loans:** $3,269,378 (100% non-need-based). **Programs:** Federal Direct (Subsidized and Unsubsidized Stafford, PLUS), Perkins, college/university.

WORK-STUDY Federal work-study: Total amount: $576,768; 448 jobs averaging $1287. **State or other work-study/employment:** Total amount: $1,254,020 (32% need-based, 68% non-need-based). Part-time jobs available.

ATHLETIC AWARDS Total amount: $9,264,008 (4% need-based, 96% non-need-based).

APPLYING FOR FINANCIAL AID Required financial aid forms: FAFSA, CSS Financial Aid PROFILE, noncustodial (divorced/separated) parent's statement, federal income tax form(s). **Financial aid deadline:** 1/15 (priority: 1/15). **Notification date:** 4/1. Students must reply by 5/1.

CONTACT Ms. Ashley Bianchi, Director of Financial Aid, Lafayette College, 730 High Street, 107 Markle Hall, Easton, PA 18042-1777, 610-330-5055. Fax: 610-330-5758. E-mail: bianchia@lafayette.edu. Website: http://www.lafayette.edu/.

LAGRANGE COLLEGE
LaGrange, GA

Tuition & fees: $28,490	Average undergraduate aid package: $24,242

ABOUT THE INSTITUTION Independent United Methodist, coed. **Awards:** bachelor's and master's degrees. 29 undergraduate majors. **Total enrollment:** 1,026. Undergraduates: 906. Freshmen: 240. Federal methodology is used as a basis for awarding need-based institutional aid.

UNDERGRADUATE EXPENSES for 2016–2017 One-time required fee: $150. **Comprehensive fee:** $39,930 includes full-time tuition ($28,160), mandatory fees ($330), and room and board ($11,440). **College room only:** $6310. Full-time tuition and fees vary according to class time, course load, and program. Room and board charges vary according to board plan and housing facility. **Part-time tuition:** $1160 per credit hour. Part-time tuition and fees vary according to class time, course load, and program.

FRESHMAN FINANCIAL AID (Fall 2015) 258 applied for aid; of those 90% were deemed to have need. 100% of freshmen with need received aid; of those 18% had need fully met. **Average percent of need met:** 73% (excluding resources awarded to replace EFC). **Average financial aid package:** $23,680 (excluding resources awarded to replace EFC). 5% of all full-time freshmen had no need and received non-need-based gift aid.

UNDERGRADUATE FINANCIAL AID (Fall 2015) 815 applied for aid; of those 91% were deemed to have need. 100% of undergraduates with need received aid; of those 19% had need fully met. **Average percent of need met:** 71% (excluding resources awarded to replace EFC). **Average financial aid package:** $24,242 (excluding resources awarded to replace EFC). 8% of all full-time undergraduates had no need and received non-need-based gift aid.

GIFT AID (NEED-BASED) Total amount: $4,609,424 (40% federal, 60% institutional). **Receiving aid:** Freshmen: 80% (210); all full-time undergraduates: 73% (628). **Average award:** Freshmen: $6772; Undergraduates: $6878. **Scholarships, grants, and awards:** Federal Pell, FSEOG, private, college/university gift aid from institutional funds.

GIFT AID (NON-NEED-BASED) Total amount: $13,097,272 (16% state, 83% institutional, 1% external sources). **Receiving aid:** Freshmen: 87% (228). Undergraduates: 85% (730). **Average award:** Freshmen: $10,067. Undergraduates: $11,088. **Scholarships, grants, and awards by category:** Academic interests/achievement: education, general academic interests/achievements. Creative arts/performance: art/fine arts, music, theater/drama. Special achievements/activities: leadership. Special characteristics: children of faculty/staff, ethnic background, first-generation college students, relatives of clergy, religious affiliation. **Tuition waivers:** Full or partial for employees or children of employees, senior citizens.

LOANS Student loans: $8,680,420 (36% need-based, 64% non-need-based). 82% of past graduating class borrowed through all loan programs. Average indebtedness per student: $29,301. **Average need-based loan:** Freshmen: $3591. Undergraduates: $4218. **Parent loans:** $1,488,636 (100% non-need-based). **Programs:** Federal Direct (Subsidized and Unsubsidized Stafford, PLUS), state.

WORK-STUDY Federal work-study: jobs available. **State or other work-study/employment:** Total amount: $379,362 (100% non-need-based). Part-time jobs available.

APPLYING FOR FINANCIAL AID Required financial aid forms: FAFSA, state aid form. **Financial aid deadline (priority):** 3/1. **Notification date:** Continuous beginning 3/15. Students must reply within 4 weeks of notification.

CONTACT Michelle Reeves, Assistant Director, LaGrange College, 601 Broad Street, LaGrange, GA 30240-2999, 888-253-9918 or toll-free 800-593-2885. Fax: 706-880-8348. E-mail: mreeves@lagrange.edu.
Website: http://www.lagrange.edu/.

LAGUNA COLLEGE OF ART & DESIGN
Laguna Beach, CA

Tuition & fees: $29,800	Average undergraduate aid package: N/A

ABOUT THE INSTITUTION Independent, coed. **Awards:** certificates, bachelor's, and master's degrees. 14 undergraduate majors. **Total enrollment:** 612. Undergraduates: 567. Freshmen: 88. Federal methodology is used as a basis for awarding need-based institutional aid.

UNDERGRADUATE EXPENSES for 2017–2018 Application fee: $45. **Tuition:** full-time $29,800; part-time $1242 per unit. Full-time tuition and fees vary according to course load and degree level. Part-time tuition and fees vary according to course load and degree level.

GIFT AID (NEED-BASED) Total amount: $1,488,355 (60% federal, 37% state, 3% external sources). **Scholarships, grants, and awards:** Federal Pell, FSEOG, state, private, college/university gift aid from institutional funds.

GIFT AID (NON-NEED-BASED) Scholarships, grants, and awards by category: Academic interests/achievement: general academic interests/achievements. Creative arts/performance: 573 awards: applied art and design, art/fine arts. **Tuition waivers:** Full or partial for employees or children of employees.

LOANS Student loans: $2,652,945 (44% need-based, 56% non-need-based). 90% of past graduating class borrowed through all loan programs. Average indebtedness per student: $38,000. **Parent loans:** $2,566,166 (100% need-based). **Programs:** Federal Direct (Subsidized and Unsubsidized Stafford, PLUS).

WORK-STUDY Federal work-study: Total amount: $49,066; 28 jobs averaging $1752.

APPLYING FOR FINANCIAL AID Required financial aid form: FAFSA. **Financial aid deadline:** Continuous. **Notification date:** Continuous beginning 2/1.

CONTACT Christopher Brown, Director of Admissions and Financial Aid, Laguna College of Art & Design, 2825 Laguna Canyon Road, Laguna Beach, CA 92651-1136, 949-376-6000 or toll-free 800-255-0762. Fax: 949-715-4084. E-mail: cbrown@lcad.edu.
Website: http://www.lcad.edu/.

LAKE ERIE COLLEGE
Painesville, OH

Tuition & fees: $30,862	Average undergraduate aid package: $23,882

ABOUT THE INSTITUTION Independent, coed. **Awards:** certificates, bachelor's, and master's degrees. 35 undergraduate majors. **Total enrollment:** 1,201. Undergraduates: 955. Freshmen: 219. Federal methodology is used as a basis for awarding need-based institutional aid.

UNDERGRADUATE EXPENSES for 2017–2018 Application fee: $30. **One-time required fee:** $350. **Comprehensive fee:** $39,994 includes full-time tuition ($29,426), mandatory fees ($1436), and room and board ($9132). **College room only:** $4508. Full-time tuition and fees vary according to course load, degree level, and program. Room and board charges vary according to board plan and housing facility. **Part-time tuition:** $780 per credit hour. **Part-time fees:** $51 per credit hour. Part-time tuition and fees vary according to course load, degree level, and program.

FRESHMAN FINANCIAL AID (Fall 2016, est.) 206 applied for aid; of those 94% were deemed to have need. 99% of freshmen with need received aid; of those 21% had need fully met. **Average percent of need met:** 79% (excluding resources awarded to replace EFC). **Average financial aid package:** $25,607 (excluding resources awarded to replace EFC). 7% of all full-time freshmen had no need and received non-need-based gift aid.

UNDERGRADUATE FINANCIAL AID (Fall 2016, est.) 633 applied for aid; of those 92% were deemed to have need. 100% of undergraduates with need received aid; of those 19% had need fully met. **Average percent of need met:** 75% (excluding resources awarded to replace EFC). **Average financial aid package:** $23,882 (excluding resources awarded to replace EFC). 13% of all full-time undergraduates had no need and received non-need-based gift aid.

GIFT AID (NEED-BASED) Total amount: $9,339,000 (13% federal, 4% state, 82% institutional, 1% external sources). **Receiving aid:** Freshmen: 88% (192); all full-time undergraduates: 82% (583). **Average award:** Freshmen: $22,391; Undergraduates: $19,849. **Scholarships, grants, and awards:** Federal Pell, FSEOG, state, private, college/university gift aid from institutional funds.

GIFT AID (NON-NEED-BASED) Total amount: $1,631,438 (97% institutional, 3% external sources). **Receiving aid:** Freshmen: 15% (32). Undergraduates: 11% (78). **Average award:** Freshmen: $15,649. Undergraduates: $13,855. **Scholarships, grants, and awards by category:** Academic interests/achievement: biological sciences, business, communication, education, English, foreign languages, general academic interests/achievements, humanities, international studies, mathematics, physical sciences, social sciences. Creative arts/performance: art/fine arts, dance, general creative arts/performance, music, performing arts, theater/drama. Special achievements/activities: community service, general special achievements/activities, hobbies/interests. Special characteristics: children of faculty/staff, twins, veterans, veterans' children. **Tuition waivers:** Full or partial for employees or children of employees, senior citizens.

LOANS Student loans: $5,252,785 (74% need-based, 26% non-need-based). 77% of past graduating class borrowed through all loan programs. Average indebtedness per student: $38,234. **Average need-based loan:** Freshmen: $3452. Undergraduates: $4342. **Parent loans:** $1,475,562 (47% need-based, 53% non-need-based). **Programs:** Federal Direct (Subsidized and Unsubsidized Stafford, PLUS), Perkins.

WORK-STUDY Federal work-study: Total amount: $107,143; jobs available.

ATHLETIC AWARDS Total amount: $3,455,021 (62% need-based, 38% non-need-based).

APPLYING FOR FINANCIAL AID *Required financial aid form:* FAFSA. *Financial aid deadline:* Continuous. *Notification date:* Continuous beginning 2/15. Students must reply by 5/1 or within 4 weeks of notification.

CONTACT Tricia Pangonis, Director of Financial Aid, Lake Erie College, 391 West Washington Street, Painesville, OH 44077-3389, 440-375-7102 or toll-free 800-916-0904. *Fax:* 440-375-7103. *E-mail:* finaid@lec.edu.
Website: http://www.lec.edu/.

LAKE FOREST COLLEGE
Lake Forest, IL

CONTACT Mr. Jerry Cebrzynski, Director of Financial Aid, Lake Forest College, 555 North Sheridan Road, Lake Forest, IL 60045-2399, 847-735-5104 or toll-free 800-828-4751. *Fax:* 847-735-6271. *E-mail:* cebrzynski@lakeforest.edu.
Website: http://www.lakeforest.edu/.

LAKELAND UNIVERSITY
Plymouth, WI

CONTACT Ms. Patty Taylor, Director of Financial Aid, Lakeland University, PO Box 359, Sheboygan, WI 53082-0359, 920-565-1214 or toll-free 800-569-2166. *Fax:* 920-565-1470.
Website: http://www.lakeland.edu/.

LAKE SUPERIOR STATE UNIVERSITY
Sault Sainte Marie, MI

ABOUT THE INSTITUTION State-supported, coed. 70 undergraduate majors.
GIFT AID (NEED-BASED) *Scholarships, grants, and awards:* Federal Pell, FSEOG, state, private, college/university gift aid from institutional funds, Federal Nursing, Academic Competitiveness Grants, National SMART Grants.
GIFT AID (NON-NEED-BASED) *Scholarships, grants, and awards by category:* Academic interests/achievement: general academic interests/achievements.
LOANS *Programs:* Federal Direct (Subsidized and Unsubsidized Stafford, PLUS), Perkins, Federal Nursing, alternative loans.
APPLYING FOR FINANCIAL AID *Required financial aid form:* FAFSA.

CONTACT Deborah Faust, Director of Financial Aid, Lake Superior State University, 650 West Easterday Avenue, Sault Sainte Marie, MI 49783, 906-635-2678 or toll-free 888-800-LSSU Ext. 2231. *Fax:* 906-635-6669. *E-mail:* finaid@lssu.edu.
Website: http://www.lssu.edu/.

LAKEVIEW COLLEGE OF NURSING
Danville, IL

ABOUT THE INSTITUTION Independent, coed, primarily women. *Awards:* bachelor's degrees. 1 undergraduate major. *Total enrollment:* 236. Undergraduates: 236.
GIFT AID (NEED-BASED) *Scholarships, grants, and awards:* Federal Pell, state, private, college/university gift aid from institutional funds.
GIFT AID (NON-NEED-BASED) *Scholarships, grants, and awards by category:* Academic interests/achievement: health fields.
LOANS *Programs:* Federal Direct (Subsidized and Unsubsidized Stafford, PLUS).
CONTACT Ms. Tammy Garza, Assistant Director of Financial Aid, Lakeview College of Nursing, 903 North Logan Avenue, Danville, IL 61832, 217-709-0928. *Fax:* 217-709-0956. *E-mail:* tgarza@lakeviewcol.edu.
Website: http://www.lakeviewcol.edu/.

LAMAR UNIVERSITY
Beaumont, TX

Tuition & fees (TX res): $9901	Average undergraduate aid package: $5009

ABOUT THE INSTITUTION State-supported, coed. *Awards:* certificates, bachelor's, master's, and doctoral degrees. 52 undergraduate majors. *Total enrollment:* 15,001. Undergraduates: 9,326. Freshmen: 1,467. Federal methodology is used as a basis for awarding need-based institutional aid.
UNDERGRADUATE EXPENSES for 2017–2018 *Application fee:* $25. *One-time required fee:* $10. *Tuition, state resident:* full-time $7080; part-time $336 per credit hour. *Tuition, nonresident:* full-time $19,320; part-time $744 per credit hour. *Required fees:* full-time $2821; $382 per credit hour. Full-time tuition and fees vary according to course load, location, and program. Part-time tuition and fees vary according to course load, location, and program. *College room and board:* $8450; *Room only:* $5350. Room and board charges vary according to board plan. *Payment plan:* Guaranteed tuition.
FRESHMAN FINANCIAL AID (Fall 2015) 1,264 applied for aid; of those 75% were deemed to have need. 97% of freshmen with need received aid; of those 14% had need fully met. *Average percent of need met:* 49% (excluding resources awarded to replace EFC). *Average financial aid package:* $9982 (excluding resources awarded to replace EFC). 12% of all full-time freshmen had no need and received non-need-based gift aid.
UNDERGRADUATE FINANCIAL AID (Fall 2015) 5,289 applied for aid; of those 81% were deemed to have need. 98% of undergraduates with need received aid; of those 13% had need fully met. *Average percent of need met:* 49% (excluding resources awarded to replace EFC). *Average financial aid package:* $5009 (excluding resources awarded to replace EFC). 11% of all full-time undergraduates had no need and received non-need-based gift aid.
GIFT AID (NEED-BASED) *Total amount:* $23,700,913 (68% federal, 32% state). *Receiving aid:* Freshmen: 49% (742); all full-time undergraduates: 49% (3,385). *Average award:* Freshmen: $7618; Undergraduates: $6657. *Scholarships, grants, and awards:* Federal Pell, FSEOG, state, private, college/university gift aid from institutional funds, United Negro College Fund.
GIFT AID (NON-NEED-BASED) *Total amount:* $7,515,905 (1% state, 78% institutional, 21% external sources). *Receiving aid:* Freshmen: 20% (299). Undergraduates: 14% (983). *Average award:* Freshmen: $3993. Undergraduates: $4090. *Scholarships, grants, and awards by category:* Academic interests/achievement: general academic interests/achievements. Creative arts/performance: general creative arts/performance. Special achievements/activities: general special achievements/activities. *Tuition waivers:* Full or partial for employees or children of employees, senior citizens. ROTC: Air Force cooperative.
LOANS *Student loans:* $35,081,835 (42% need-based, 58% non-need-based). 39% of past graduating class borrowed through all loan programs. *Average indebtedness per student:* $11,878. *Average need-based loan:* Freshmen: $3176. Undergraduates: $3930. *Parent loans:* $3,924,134 (100% non-need-based). *Programs:* Federal Direct (Subsidized and Unsubsidized Stafford, PLUS), Perkins, Federal Nursing, state.
WORK-STUDY *Federal work-study:* 230 jobs averaging $3140. *State or other work-study/employment:* Total amount: $120,223 (100% need-based). 64 part-time jobs averaging $1878.
APPLYING FOR FINANCIAL AID *Required financial aid forms:* FAFSA, institution's own form. *Financial aid deadline (priority):* 3/31. *Notification date:* Continuous beginning 5/15. Students must reply within 2 weeks of notification.
CONTACT Student Financial Assistance Office, Lamar University, PO Box 10042, Beaumont, TX 77710, 409-880-8450. *Fax:* 409-880-8934. *E-mail:* financialaid@lamar.edu.
Website: http://www.lamar.edu/.

LANCASTER BIBLE COLLEGE
Lancaster, PA

Tuition & fees: N/R	Average undergraduate aid package: $17,736

ABOUT THE INSTITUTION Independent nondenominational, coed. 17 undergraduate majors. Federal methodology is used as a basis for awarding need-based institutional aid.

FRESHMAN FINANCIAL AID (Fall 2016, est.) 198 applied for aid; of those 86% were deemed to have need. 100% of freshmen with need received aid; of those 26% had need fully met. *Average percent of need met:* 78% (excluding resources awarded to replace EFC). *Average financial aid package:* $17,408 (excluding resources awarded to replace EFC). 18% of all full-time freshmen had no need and received non-need-based gift aid.

UNDERGRADUATE FINANCIAL AID (Fall 2016, est.) 672 applied for aid; of those 88% were deemed to have need. 100% of undergraduates with need received aid; of those 29% had need fully met. *Average percent of need met:* 76% (excluding resources awarded to replace EFC). *Average financial aid package:* $17,736 (excluding resources awarded to replace EFC). 20% of all full-time undergraduates had no need and received non-need-based gift aid.

GIFT AID (NEED-BASED) *Total amount:* $6,872,948 (21% federal, 14% state, 61% institutional, 4% external sources). *Receiving aid:* Freshmen: 82% (170); all full-time undergraduates: 79% (587). *Average award:* Freshmen: $14,765; Undergraduates: $14,542. *Scholarships, grants, and awards:* Federal Pell, FSEOG, state, private, college/university gift aid from institutional funds, Office of Vocational Rehabilitation Awards, Blindness and Visual Services Awards.

GIFT AID (NON-NEED-BASED) *Total amount:* $1,225,977 (97% institutional, 3% external sources). *Receiving aid:* Freshmen: 81% (168). Undergraduates: 76% (561). *Average award:* Freshmen: $5843. Undergraduates: $6507. *Scholarships, grants, and awards by category:* Academic interests/achievement: 429 awards ($1,386,162 total): general academic interests/achievements. Creative arts/performance: 54 awards ($124,400 total): general creative arts/performance, music. Special achievements/activities: 122 awards ($155,787 total): general special achievements/activities, leadership, religious involvement. Special characteristics: 262 awards ($1,241,377 total): children and siblings of alumni, children of current students, children of faculty/staff, international students, relatives of clergy, siblings of current students.

LOANS *Student loans:* $4,983,715 (71% need-based, 29% non-need-based). 77% of past graduating class borrowed through all loan programs. *Average indebtedness per student:* $30,511. *Average need-based loan:* Freshmen: $3270. Undergraduates: $4004. *Parent loans:* $632,534 (59% need-based, 41% non-need-based). *Programs:* Federal Direct (Subsidized and Unsubsidized Stafford, PLUS), Perkins, state, college/university, alternative loans.

WORK-STUDY *Federal work-study:* Total amount: $120,000; 138 jobs averaging $1500.

APPLYING FOR FINANCIAL AID *Required financial aid forms:* FAFSA, state aid form. *Financial aid deadline (priority):* 5/1. *Notification date:* Continuous beginning 3/1. Students must reply within 3 weeks of notification.

CONTACT Mrs. Karen Fox, Director of Financial Aid, Lancaster Bible College, 901 Eden Road, Lancaster, PA 17601, 717-560-8254 Ext. 5352 or toll-free 800-544-7335. *Fax:* 717-560-8216. *E-mail:* kfox@lbc.edu.
Website: http://www.lbc.edu/.

LANDER UNIVERSITY
Greenwood, SC

CONTACT Director of Financial Aid, Lander University, 320 Stanley Avenue, Greenwood, SC 29649, 864-388-8340 or toll-free 888-452-6337. *Fax:* 864-388-8811. *E-mail:* fhardin@lander.edu.
Website: http://www.lander.edu/.

LANE COLLEGE
Jackson, TN

Tuition & fees: $10,690	Average undergraduate aid package: $12,240

ABOUT THE INSTITUTION Independent Christian Methodist Episcopal Church, coed. *Awards:* bachelor's degrees. 16 undergraduate majors. *Total enrollment:* 1,427. Undergraduates: 1,427. Freshmen: 403. Both federal and institutional methodology are used as a basis for awarding need-based institutional aid.

UNDERGRADUATE EXPENSES for 2017–2018 *Tuition:* full-time $9000; part-time $375 per credit hour. Full-time tuition and fees vary according to course load. Part-time tuition and fees vary according to course load.

FRESHMAN FINANCIAL AID (Fall 2016, est.) 397 applied for aid; of those 100% were deemed to have need. 98% of freshmen with need received aid. *Average financial aid package:* $12,591 (excluding resources awarded to replace EFC).

UNDERGRADUATE FINANCIAL AID (Fall 2016, est.) 1,365 applied for aid; of those 100% were deemed to have need. 95% of undergraduates with need received aid. *Average financial aid package:* $12,240 (excluding resources awarded to replace EFC). 1% of all full-time undergraduates had no need and received non-need-based gift aid.

GIFT AID (NEED-BASED) *Total amount:* $18,055,157 (83% federal, 11% state, 6% institutional). *Receiving aid:* Freshmen: 98% (388); all full-time undergraduates: 94% (1,286). *Average award:* Freshmen: $13,759; Undergraduates: $13,527. *Scholarships, grants, and awards:* Federal Pell, FSEOG, state, private, college/university gift aid from institutional funds, United Negro College Fund.

GIFT AID (NON-NEED-BASED) *Receiving aid:* Freshmen: 85% (339). Undergraduates: 81% (1,104). *Average award:* Undergraduates: $4761. *Tuition waivers:* Full or partial for employees or children of employees, adult students. *ROTC:* Army.

LOANS *Student loans:* $9,532,897 (65% need-based, 35% non-need-based). *Average need-based loan:* Freshmen: $3190. Undergraduates: $3568. *Parent loans:* $1,088,111 (100% need-based). *Programs:* Federal Direct (Subsidized and Unsubsidized Stafford, PLUS).

WORK-STUDY *Federal work-study:* Total amount: $449,000; jobs available.

ATHLETIC AWARDS Total amount: $676,657 (100% non-need-based).

APPLYING FOR FINANCIAL AID *Required financial aid form:* FAFSA. *Financial aid deadline (priority):* 3/1. *Notification date:* Continuous beginning 3/1. Students must reply within 2 weeks of notification.

CONTACT Mr. Tony Calhoun, Director of Financial Aid, Lane College, 545 Lane Avenue, Jackson, TN 38301, 731-426-7558 or toll-free 800-960-7533. *Fax:* 731-426-7652. *E-mail:* tcalhoun@lanecollege.edu.
Website: http://www.lanecollege.edu/.

LANGSTON UNIVERSITY
Langston, OK

Tuition & fees (OK res): $5388	Average undergraduate aid package: $10,893

ABOUT THE INSTITUTION State-supported, coed. *Awards:* associate, bachelor's, master's, and doctoral degrees. 27 undergraduate majors. *Total enrollment:* 2,495. Undergraduates: 2,160. Freshmen: 645. Federal methodology is used as a basis for awarding need-based institutional aid.

UNDERGRADUATE EXPENSES for 2016–2017 *Tuition, state resident:* full-time $3707; part-time $124 per credit hour. *Tuition, nonresident:* full-time $11,046; part-time $368 per credit hour. *Required fees:* full-time $1681; $420 per term or $420 per term. Full-time tuition and fees vary according to degree level, location, and program. Part-time tuition and fees vary according to degree level, location, and program. *College room and board:* $10,050; *Room only:* $6800. Room and board charges vary according to board plan and housing facility. *Payment plans:* Guaranteed tuition, tuition prepayment.

FRESHMAN FINANCIAL AID (Fall 2015) 590 applied for aid; of those 95% were deemed to have need. 94% of freshmen with need received aid; of those 12% had need fully met. *Average percent of need met:* 48% (excluding resources awarded to replace EFC). *Average financial aid package:* $10,170 (excluding resources awarded to replace EFC). 7% of all full-time freshmen had no need and received non-need-based gift aid.

UNDERGRADUATE FINANCIAL AID (Fall 2015) 1,939 applied for aid; of those 94% were deemed to have need. 94% of undergraduates with need received aid; of those 20% had need fully met. *Average percent of need met:* 54% (excluding resources awarded to replace EFC). *Average financial aid package:* $10,893 (excluding resources awarded to replace EFC). 10% of all full-time undergraduates had no need and received non-need-based gift aid.

GIFT AID (NEED-BASED) *Total amount:* $7,946,749 (94% federal, 4% state, 2% institutional). *Receiving aid:* Freshmen: 82% (498); all full-time undergraduates: 75% (1,503). *Average award:* Freshmen: $5161; Undergraduates: $5109. *Scholarships, grants, and awards:* Federal Pell, FSEOG, state.

GIFT AID (NON-NEED-BASED) *Total amount:* $3,313,928 (2% federal, 75% state, 23% institutional). *Receiving aid:* Freshmen: 22% (130). Undergraduates: 26% (513). *Average award:* Freshmen: $7879. Undergraduates: $6138. **Scholarships, grants, and awards by category:** *Academic interests/achievement:* agriculture, business, education, engineering/technologies, general academic interests/achievements, health fields. *Creative arts/performance:* music. *Special achievements/activities:* cheerleading/drum major, leadership. *Special characteristics:* ethnic background. *Tuition waivers:* Full or partial for children of alumni, employees or children of employees. *ROTC:* Army cooperative.

LOANS *Student loans:* $12,435,511 (100% need-based). 85% of past graduating class borrowed through all loan programs. *Average indebtedness per student:* $39,681. *Parent loans:* $3,518,871 (100% need-based). *Programs:* Federal Direct (Subsidized and Unsubsidized Stafford, PLUS).

WORK-STUDY *Federal work-study:* jobs available. *State or other work-study/employment:* Part-time jobs available.

ATHLETIC AWARDS Total amount: $626,951 (100% need-based).

APPLYING FOR FINANCIAL AID *Required financial aid forms:* FAFSA, institution's own form. *Financial aid deadline (priority):* 3/15. *Notification date:* 6/30.

CONTACT Sheila Mcgill, Director of Financial Aid, Langston University, Success Center, Langston, OK 73050, 405-466-3287. *Fax:* 405-466-2986. *E-mail:* smcgill@langston.edu.
Website: http://www.langston.edu/.

LA ROCHE COLLEGE
Pittsburgh, PA

Tuition & fees: $27,000	Average undergraduate aid package: $29,356

ABOUT THE INSTITUTION Independent Roman Catholic Church, coed. *Awards:* certificates, associate, bachelor's, and master's degrees. 35 undergraduate majors. *Total enrollment:* 1,555. Undergraduates: 1,406. Freshmen: 265. Federal methodology is used as a basis for awarding need-based institutional aid.

UNDERGRADUATE EXPENSES for 2016–2017 *Application fee:* $50. *Comprehensive fee:* $37,924 includes full-time tuition ($26,200), mandatory fees ($800), and room and board ($10,924). *College room only:* $6916. Room and board charges vary according to board plan and housing facility. *Part-time tuition:* $665 per credit hour.

FRESHMAN FINANCIAL AID (Fall 2016, est.) 206 applied for aid; of those 91% were deemed to have need. 100% of freshmen with need received aid; of those 33% had need fully met. *Average percent of need met:* 93% (excluding resources awarded to replace EFC). *Average financial aid package:* $32,150 (excluding resources awarded to replace EFC). 7% of all full-time freshmen had no need and received non-need-based gift aid.

UNDERGRADUATE FINANCIAL AID (Fall 2016, est.) 835 applied for aid; of those 93% were deemed to have need. 100% of undergraduates with need received aid; of those 67% had need fully met. *Average percent of need met:* 92% (excluding resources awarded to replace EFC). *Average financial aid package:* $29,356 (excluding resources awarded to replace EFC). 5% of all full-time undergraduates had no need and received non-need-based gift aid.

GIFT AID (NEED-BASED) *Total amount:* $5,503,771 (40% federal, 29% state, 31% institutional). *Receiving aid:* Freshmen: 66% (170); all full-time undergraduates: 54% (616). *Average award:* Freshmen: $9370; Undergraduates: $8538. **Scholarships, grants, and awards:** Federal Pell, FSEOG, state, private, college/university gift aid from institutional funds.

GIFT AID (NON-NEED-BASED) *Total amount:* $12,103,074 (92% institutional, 8% external sources). *Receiving aid:* Freshmen: 73% (188). Undergraduates:

62% (710). *Average award:* Freshmen: $21,890. Undergraduates: $23,179. *Scholarships, grants, and awards by category:* Academic interests/achievement: 908 awards ($8,606,600 total): general academic interests/achievements. *Tuition waivers:* Full or partial for employees or children of employees, senior citizens. *ROTC:* Army cooperative, Air Force cooperative.

LOANS *Student loans:* $7,670,430 (41% need-based, 59% non-need-based). 79% of past graduating class borrowed through all loan programs. *Average indebtedness per student:* $34,992. *Average need-based loan:* Freshmen: $3498. Undergraduates: $5791. *Parent loans:* $23,047,091 (100% non-need-based). *Programs:* Federal Direct (Subsidized and Unsubsidized Stafford, PLUS), Perkins, state.

WORK-STUDY *Federal work-study:* Total amount: $245,750; 132 jobs averaging $1573.

APPLYING FOR FINANCIAL AID *Required financial aid form:* FAFSA. *Financial aid deadline (priority):* 5/1. *Notification date:* Continuous beginning 2/15. Students must reply within 2 weeks of notification.

CONTACT Mrs. Sharon E. Platt, Director of Financial Aid, La Roche College, 9000 Babcock Boulevard, Pittsburgh, PA 15237-5898, 412-536-1125 or toll-free 800-838-4LRC. *Fax:* 412-536-1072. *E-mail:* sharon.platt@laroche.edu.
Website: http://www.laroche.edu/.

LA SALLE UNIVERSITY
Philadelphia, PA

Tuition & fees: $29,500	Average undergraduate aid package: $31,356

ABOUT THE INSTITUTION Independent Roman Catholic, coed. *Awards:* certificates, associate, bachelor's, master's, and doctoral degrees. 58 undergraduate majors. *Total enrollment:* 5,197. Undergraduates: 3,652. Freshmen: 869. Federal methodology is used as a basis for awarding need-based institutional aid.

UNDERGRADUATE EXPENSES for 2017–2018 *Application fee:* $35. *One-time required fee:* $150. *Comprehensive fee:* $44,580 includes full-time tuition ($28,800), mandatory fees ($700), and room and board ($15,080). *College room only:* $7530. Full-time tuition and fees vary according to course load and program. Room and board charges vary according to board plan and housing facility. *Part-time tuition:* $570 per credit hour. *Part-time fees:* $175 per term. Part-time tuition and fees vary according to course load and program.

FRESHMAN FINANCIAL AID (Fall 2015) 739 applied for aid; of those 94% were deemed to have need. 100% of freshmen with need received aid; of those 12% had need fully met. *Average percent of need met:* 73% (excluding resources awarded to replace EFC). *Average financial aid package:* $31,471 (excluding resources awarded to replace EFC). 12% of all full-time freshmen had no need and received non-need-based gift aid.

UNDERGRADUATE FINANCIAL AID (Fall 2015) 2,912 applied for aid; of those 94% were deemed to have need. 100% of undergraduates with need received aid; of those 13% had need fully met. *Average percent of need met:* 74% (excluding resources awarded to replace EFC). *Average financial aid package:* $31,356 (excluding resources awarded to replace EFC). 15% of all full-time undergraduates had no need and received non-need-based gift aid.

GIFT AID (NEED-BASED) *Total amount:* $68,572,169 (13% federal, 6% state, 80% institutional, 1% external sources). *Receiving aid:* Freshmen: 85% (678); all full-time undergraduates: 80% (2,662). *Average award:* Freshmen: $25,952; Undergraduates: $25,297. *Scholarships, grants, and awards:* Federal Pell, FSEOG, state, private, college/university gift aid from institutional funds.

GIFT AID (NON-NEED-BASED) *Total amount:* $11,289,857 (97% institutional, 3% external sources). *Receiving aid:* Freshmen: 6% (49). Undergraduates: 5% (180). *Average award:* Freshmen: $18,091. Undergraduates: $18,533. **Scholarships, grants, and awards by category:** *Academic interests/achievement:* 2,988 awards ($48,419,442 total): general academic interests/achievements. *Special achievements/activities:* 16 awards ($155,000 total): community service. *Special characteristics:* 105 awards ($3,464,300 total): children of faculty/staff, relatives of clergy, veterans. *Tuition waivers:* Full or partial for employees or children of employees. *ROTC:* Army cooperative, Air Force cooperative.

LOANS *Student loans:* $31,746,238 (72% need-based, 28% non-need-based). 77% of past graduating class borrowed through all loan programs. *Average indebtedness per student:* $36,907. *Average need-based loan:* Freshmen: $3656. Undergrad-

uates: $4720. **Parent loans:** $10,451,669 (56% need-based, 44% non-need-based).
Programs: Federal Direct (Subsidized and Unsubsidized Stafford, PLUS), Perkins.
WORK-STUDY *Federal work-study:* 394 jobs averaging $1807.
ATHLETIC AWARDS Total amount: $6,057,906 (43% need-based, 57% non-need-based).
APPLYING FOR FINANCIAL AID *Required financial aid form:* FAFSA. *Financial aid deadline (priority):* 2/15. *Notification date:* Continuous beginning 3/15. Students must reply by 5/1 or within 2 weeks of notification.
CONTACT Joseph Alaimo, Financial Aid Director, La Salle University, 1900 West Olney Avenue, Philadelphia, PA 19141-1199, 215-951-1070 or toll-free 800-328-1910. *Fax:* 215-951-5098.
Website: http://www.lasalle.edu/.

LASELL COLLEGE
Newton, MA

Tuition & fees: $34,600	Average undergraduate aid package: $26,531

ABOUT THE INSTITUTION Independent, coed. **Awards:** bachelor's and master's degrees. 39 undergraduate majors. **Total enrollment:** 2,104. Undergraduates: 1,788. Freshmen: 439. Federal methodology is used as a basis for awarding need-based institutional aid.
UNDERGRADUATE EXPENSES for 2017–2018 Application fee: $40. **Comprehensive fee:** $49,400 includes full-time tuition ($33,300), mandatory fees ($1300), and room and board ($14,800). Room and board charges vary according to housing facility. **Part-time tuition:** $1075 per credit hour. **Part-time fees:** $325 per term. Part-time tuition and fees vary according to course load.
FRESHMAN FINANCIAL AID (Fall 2016, est.) 406 applied for aid; of those 93% were deemed to have need. 100% of freshmen with need received aid; of those 15% had need fully met. **Average percent of need met:** 76% (excluding resources awarded to replace EFC). **Average financial aid package:** $27,698 (excluding resources awarded to replace EFC). 13% of all full-time freshmen had no need and received non-need-based gift aid.
UNDERGRADUATE FINANCIAL AID (Fall 2016, est.) 1,455 applied for aid; of those 93% were deemed to have need. 100% of undergraduates with need received aid; of those 17% had need fully met. **Average percent of need met:** 74% (excluding resources awarded to replace EFC). **Average financial aid package:** $26,531 (excluding resources awarded to replace EFC). 15% of all full-time undergraduates had no need and received non-need-based gift aid.
GIFT AID (NEED-BASED) Total amount: $29,878,314 (8% federal, 2% state, 86% institutional, 4% external sources). **Receiving aid:** Freshmen: 86% (376); all full-time undergraduates: 77% (1,352). **Average award:** Freshmen: $23,983; Undergraduates: $22,074. **Scholarships, grants, and awards:** Federal Pell, FSEOG, state, private, college/university gift aid from institutional funds.
GIFT AID (NON-NEED-BASED) Total amount: $5,988,586 (65% institutional, 35% external sources). **Receiving aid:** Freshmen: 8% (36). Undergraduates: 9% (149). **Average award:** Freshmen: $10,365. Undergraduates: $12,019. **Scholarships, grants, and awards by category:** Academic interests/achievement: general academic interests/achievements. Special achievements/activities: general special achievements/activities. Special characteristics: children and siblings of alumni, children of faculty/staff, siblings of current students, veterans, veterans' children. **Tuition waivers:** Full or partial for children of alumni, employees or children of employees.
LOANS Student loans: $14,879,664 (67% need-based, 33% non-need-based). 88% of past graduating class borrowed through all loan programs. Average indebtedness per student: $41,100. Average need-based loan: Freshmen: $3230. Undergraduates: $4133. **Parent loans:** $6,645,615 (50% need-based, 50% non-need-based). **Programs:** Federal Direct (Subsidized and Unsubsidized Stafford, PLUS).
WORK-STUDY *Federal work-study:* Total amount: $210,500; 120 jobs averaging $1800.
APPLYING FOR FINANCIAL AID *Required financial aid form:* FAFSA. *Financial aid deadline (priority):* 11/20. *Notification date:* Continuous beginning 11/30. Students must reply by 5/1 or within 2 weeks of notification.
CONTACT Michele R. Kosboth, Director of Student Financial Planning, Lasell College, 1844 Commonwealth Avenue, Newton, MA 02466-2709, 617-243-2227 or toll-free 888-LASELL-4. *Fax:* 617-243-2326. *E-mail:* finaid@lasell.edu.
Website: http://www.lasell.edu/.

LA SIERRA UNIVERSITY
Riverside, CA

CONTACT Mrs. Elina Bascomb, Director of Financial Aid, La Sierra University, 4500 Riverwalk Parkway, Riverside, CA 92515, 951-785-2359 or toll-free 800-874-5587. *Fax:* 951-785-2942. *E-mail:* sfs@lasierra.edu.
Website: http://www.lasierra.edu/.

LAWRENCE TECHNOLOGICAL UNIVERSITY
Southfield, MI

Tuition & fees: $31,140	Average undergraduate aid package: $24,577

ABOUT THE INSTITUTION Independent, coed. **Awards:** certificates, associate, bachelor's, master's, and doctoral degrees. 43 undergraduate majors. **Total enrollment:** 3,309. Undergraduates: 2,164. Freshmen: 375. Federal methodology is used as a basis for awarding need-based institutional aid.
UNDERGRADUATE EXPENSES for 2016–2017 Application fee: $30. **Comprehensive fee:** $41,247 includes full-time tuition ($30,420), mandatory fees ($720), and room and board ($10,107). **College room only:** $5907. Full-time tuition and fees vary according to course level, degree level, location, program, and student level. Room and board charges vary according to board plan and housing facility. **Part-time tuition:** $1014 per credit hour. **Part-time fees:** $360 per term. Part-time tuition and fees vary according to course level, degree level, location, program, and student level.
FRESHMAN FINANCIAL AID (Fall 2015) 324 applied for aid; of those 79% were deemed to have need. 100% of freshmen with need received aid; of those 23% had need fully met. **Average percent of need met:** 73% (excluding resources awarded to replace EFC). **Average financial aid package:** $24,465 (excluding resources awarded to replace EFC). 17% of all full-time freshmen had no need and received non-need-based gift aid.
UNDERGRADUATE FINANCIAL AID (Fall 2015) 1,323 applied for aid; of those 75% were deemed to have need. 99% of undergraduates with need received aid; of those 17% had need fully met. **Average percent of need met:** 69% (excluding resources awarded to replace EFC). **Average financial aid package:** $24,577 (excluding resources awarded to replace EFC). 18% of all full-time undergraduates had no need and received non-need-based gift aid.
GIFT AID (NEED-BASED) Total amount: $14,888,893 (14% federal, 9% state, 75% institutional, 2% external sources). **Receiving aid:** Freshmen: 75% (254); all full-time undergraduates: 59% (962). **Average award:** Freshmen: $15,820; Undergraduates: $14,835. **Scholarships, grants, and awards:** Federal Pell, FSEOG, state, private, college/university gift aid from institutional funds, Michigan National Guard and ROTC Scholarships.
GIFT AID (NON-NEED-BASED) Total amount: $4,433,954 (99% institutional, 1% external sources). **Receiving aid:** Freshmen: 69% (233). Undergraduates: 50% (812). **Average award:** Freshmen: $15,755. Undergraduates: $14,871. **Scholarships, grants, and awards by category:** Academic interests/achievement: 2,451 awards ($16,004,937 total): architecture, biological sciences, business, communication, computer science, education, engineering/technologies, general academic interests/achievements, humanities, international studies, mathematics, military science, physical sciences, premedicine. Special achievements/activities: 44 awards ($23,606 total): cheerleading/drum major, junior miss, leadership. Special characteristics: 296 awards ($1,689,427 total): adult students, children and siblings of alumni, children of faculty/staff, international students, local/state students, married students, members of minority groups, previous college experience, veterans. **Tuition waivers:** Full or partial for employees or children of employees. **ROTC:** Air Force cooperative.
LOANS Student loans: $6,924,619 (96% need-based, 4% non-need-based). 69% of past graduating class borrowed through all loan programs. Average indebtedness per student: $40,976. Average need-based loan: Freshmen: $5891. Undergraduates: $7299. **Parent loans:** $7,669,759 (94% need-based, 6% non-need-based). **Programs:** Federal Direct (Subsidized and Unsubsidized Stafford, PLUS), Perkins, state, college/university, alternative loans.
WORK-STUDY *Federal work-study:* 101 jobs averaging $1213. **State or other work-study/employment:** Part-time jobs available.
ATHLETIC AWARDS Total amount: $2,348,238 (100% non-need-based).

APPLYING FOR FINANCIAL AID *Required financial aid form:* FAFSA. *Financial aid deadline (priority):* 4/1. *Notification date:* Continuous beginning 4/1. Students must reply within 2 weeks of notification.

CONTACT Susie Poli Smith, Director of Financial Aid, Lawrence Technological University, 21000 West Ten Mile Road, Southfield, MI 48075-1058, 248-204-2126 or toll-free 800-225-5588. *Fax:* 248-204-2228. *E-mail:* spolismit@ltu.edu. *Website:* http://www.ltu.edu/.

LAWRENCE UNIVERSITY
Appleton, WI

Tuition & fees: $46,101	Average undergraduate aid package: $38,487

ABOUT THE INSTITUTION Independent, coed. *Awards:* bachelor's degrees. 59 undergraduate majors. *Total enrollment:* 1,532. Undergraduates: 1,532. Freshmen: 374. Institutional methodology is used as a basis for awarding need-based institutional aid.

UNDERGRADUATE EXPENSES for 2017–2018 *Comprehensive fee:* $56,133 includes full-time tuition ($45,801), mandatory fees ($300), and room and board ($10,032). *College room only:* $4989.

FRESHMAN FINANCIAL AID (Fall 2016, est.) 301 applied for aid; of those 81% were deemed to have need. 100% of freshmen with need received aid; of those 55% had need fully met. *Average percent of need met:* 95% (excluding resources awarded to replace EFC). *Average financial aid package:* $38,758 (excluding resources awarded to replace EFC). 33% of all full-time freshmen had no need and received non-need-based gift aid.

UNDERGRADUATE FINANCIAL AID (Fall 2016, est.) 1,056 applied for aid; of those 84% were deemed to have need. 100% of undergraduates with need received aid; of those 51% had need fully met. *Average percent of need met:* 93% (excluding resources awarded to replace EFC). *Average financial aid package:* $38,487 (excluding resources awarded to replace EFC). 37% of all full-time undergraduates had no need and received non-need-based gift aid.

GIFT AID (NEED-BASED) *Total amount:* $27,890,719 (6% federal, 2% state, 89% institutional, 3% external sources). *Receiving aid:* Freshmen: 64% (238); all full-time undergraduates: 59% (877). *Average award:* Freshmen: $33,637; Undergraduates: $31,617. *Scholarships, grants, and awards:* Federal Pell, FSEOG, state, private, college/university gift aid from institutional funds.

GIFT AID (NON-NEED-BASED) *Total amount:* $12,353,455 (97% institutional, 3% external sources). *Average award:* Freshmen: $22,716. Undergraduates: $21,124. *Scholarships, grants, and awards by category: Academic interests/achievement:* general academic interests/achievements. *Creative arts/performance:* music, performing arts, theater/drama. *Special achievements/activities:* community service, general special achievements/activities, leadership. *Special characteristics:* children and siblings of alumni, ethnic background, general special characteristics, international students, siblings of current students, veterans, veterans' children. *Tuition waivers:* Full or partial for employees or children of employees.

LOANS *Student loans:* $7,553,901 (53% need-based, 47% non-need-based). 64% of past graduating class borrowed through all loan programs. *Average indebtedness per student:* $34,750. *Average need-based loan:* Freshmen: $5023. Undergraduates: $5658. *Parent loans:* $1,516,872 (100% non-need-based). *Programs:* Federal Direct (Subsidized and Unsubsidized Stafford, PLUS), Perkins, private loans.

WORK-STUDY *Federal work-study:* Total amount: $1,200,845; jobs available. *State or other work-study/employment:* Total amount: $860,795 (100% non-need-based). Part-time jobs available.

APPLYING FOR FINANCIAL AID *Required financial aid forms:* FAFSA, CSS Financial Aid PROFILE, noncustodial (divorced/separated) parent's statement, federal income tax form(s). *Financial aid deadline (priority):* 2/1. *Notification date:* Continuous beginning 2/5. Students must reply by 5/1.

CONTACT Mrs. Sara Beth Holman, Director of Financial Aid, Lawrence University, 711 East Boldt Way, SPC 32, Appleton, WI 54911, 920-832-6583 or toll-free 800-227-0982. *Fax:* 920-832-6582. *E-mail:* sara.b.holman@lawrence.edu. *Website:* http://www.lawrence.edu/.

LEBANON VALLEY COLLEGE
Annville, PA

Tuition & fees: $42,180	Average undergraduate aid package: $31,829

ABOUT THE INSTITUTION Independent United Methodist, coed. *Awards:* certificates, bachelor's, master's, and doctoral degrees. 42 undergraduate majors. *Total enrollment:* 1,916. Undergraduates: 1,712. Freshmen: 423. Federal methodology is used as a basis for awarding need-based institutional aid.

UNDERGRADUATE EXPENSES for 2017–2018 *Comprehensive fee:* $53,590 includes full-time tuition ($40,990), mandatory fees ($1190), and room and board ($11,410). *College room only:* $5520. Room and board charges vary according to board plan and housing facility. *Part-time tuition:* $650 per credit hour. Part-time tuition and fees vary according to class time and degree level.

FRESHMAN FINANCIAL AID (Fall 2016, est.) 410 applied for aid; of those 90% were deemed to have need. 100% of freshmen with need received aid; of those 29% had need fully met. *Average percent of need met:* 83% (excluding resources awarded to replace EFC). *Average financial aid package:* $33,464 (excluding resources awarded to replace EFC). 14% of all full-time freshmen had no need and received non-need-based gift aid.

UNDERGRADUATE FINANCIAL AID (Fall 2016, est.) 1,486 applied for aid; of those 92% were deemed to have need. 100% of undergraduates with need received aid; of those 24% had need fully met. *Average percent of need met:* 79% (excluding resources awarded to replace EFC). *Average financial aid package:* $31,829 (excluding resources awarded to replace EFC). 14% of all full-time undergraduates had no need and received non-need-based gift aid.

GIFT AID (NEED-BASED) *Total amount:* $32,883,840 (6% federal, 7% state, 87% institutional). *Receiving aid:* Freshmen: 85% (365); all full-time undergraduates: 85% (1,351). *Average award:* Freshmen: $26,695; Undergraduates: $25,805. *Scholarships, grants, and awards:* Federal Pell, FSEOG, state, private, college/university gift aid from institutional funds, TEACH Grants.

GIFT AID (NON-NEED-BASED) *Total amount:* $6,471,048 (1% federal, 84% institutional, 15% external sources). *Receiving aid:* Freshmen: 10% (43). Undergraduates: 9% (147). *Average award:* Freshmen: $21,089. Undergraduates: $19,319. *Scholarships, grants, and awards by category: Academic interests/achievement:* 1,429 awards ($24,725,358 total): biological sciences, English, general academic interests/achievements, mathematics, physical sciences, religion/biblical studies, social sciences. *Creative arts/performance:* 62 awards ($115,505 total): music. *Special achievements/activities:* 2 awards ($4140 total): general special achievements/activities. *Special characteristics:* 109 awards ($1,089,824 total): children and siblings of alumni, children of faculty/staff, general special characteristics, international students, veterans. *Tuition waivers:* Full or partial for employees or children of employees, senior citizens.

LOANS *Student loans:* $14,507,830 (36% need-based, 64% non-need-based). 79% of past graduating class borrowed through all loan programs. *Average indebtedness per student:* $46,346. *Average need-based loan:* Freshmen: $3965. Undergraduates: $4466. *Parent loans:* $6,185,743 (100% non-need-based). *Programs:* Federal Direct (Subsidized and Unsubsidized Stafford, PLUS), Perkins.

WORK-STUDY *Federal work-study:* Total amount: $1,475,280; 986 jobs averaging $1475.

APPLYING FOR FINANCIAL AID *Required financial aid form:* FAFSA. *Financial aid deadline (priority):* 2/15. *Notification date:* Continuous beginning 3/1. Students must reply by 5/1 or within 2 weeks of notification.

CONTACT Mrs. Kendra M. Feigert, Director of Financial Aid, Lebanon Valley College, 101 North College Avenue, Annville, PA 17003, 866-582-4236 or toll-free 866-LVC-4ADM. *Fax:* 717-867-6027. *E-mail:* feigert@lvc.edu. *Website:* http://www.lvc.edu/.

LEES-MCRAE COLLEGE
Banner Elk, NC

Tuition & fees: $26,198	Average undergraduate aid package: $24,611

ABOUT THE INSTITUTION Independent Presbyterian Church (U.S.A.), coed. *Awards:* bachelor's degrees. 24 undergraduate majors. *Total enrollment:* 991.

Undergraduates: 991. Freshmen: 187. Both federal and institutional methodology are used as a basis for awarding need-based institutional aid.

UNDERGRADUATE EXPENSES for 2017–2018 *Application fee:* $35. *Comprehensive fee:* $36,956 includes full-time tuition ($24,878), mandatory fees ($1320), and room and board ($10,758). *College room only:* $5142. Full-time tuition and fees vary according to course load, location, and reciprocity agreements. Room and board charges vary according to housing facility. *Part-time tuition:* $710 per credit hour. Part-time tuition and fees vary according to course load, location, and reciprocity agreements. *Payment plan:* Guaranteed tuition.

FRESHMAN FINANCIAL AID (Fall 2016, est.) 171 applied for aid; of those 89% were deemed to have need. 100% of freshmen with need received aid; of those 2% had need fully met. *Average percent of need met:* 69% (excluding resources awarded to replace EFC). *Average financial aid package:* $23,931 (excluding resources awarded to replace EFC). 8% of all full-time freshmen had no need and received non-need-based gift aid.

UNDERGRADUATE FINANCIAL AID (Fall 2016, est.) 836 applied for aid; of those 94% were deemed to have need. 100% of undergraduates with need received aid; of those 1% had need fully met. *Average percent of need met:* 70% (excluding resources awarded to replace EFC). *Average financial aid package:* $24,611 (excluding resources awarded to replace EFC). 9% of all full-time undergraduates had no need and received non-need-based gift aid.

GIFT AID (NEED-BASED) *Total amount:* $15,966,290 (12% federal, 11% state, 75% institutional, 2% external sources). *Receiving aid:* Freshmen: 67% (126); all full-time undergraduates: 66% (642). *Average award:* Freshmen: $9539; Undergraduates: $9137. *Scholarships, grants, and awards:* Federal Pell, FSEOG, state, private, college/university gift aid from institutional funds.

GIFT AID (NON-NEED-BASED) *Receiving aid:* Freshmen: 82% (153). Undergraduates: 80% (787). *Average award:* Freshmen: $12,723. Undergraduates: $12,371. *Scholarships, grants, and awards by category: Academic interests/ achievement:* biological sciences, education, general academic interests/achievements, humanities, mathematics. *Creative arts/performance:* dance, journalism/publications, performing arts, theater/drama. *Special achievements/activities:* cheerleading/drum major, general special achievements/activities. *Special characteristics:* children of faculty/staff, children with a deceased or disabled parent, international students, local/ state students, previous college experience, relatives of clergy, religious affiliation, siblings of current students, veterans, veterans' children. *Tuition waivers:* Full or partial for employees or children of employees.

LOANS *Student loans:* $5,943,635 (100% need-based). *Average need-based loan:* Freshmen: $3500. Undergraduates: $5492. *Parent loans:* $2,126,702 (100% need-based). *Programs:* Federal Direct (Subsidized and Unsubsidized Stafford, PLUS), Perkins, state.

WORK-STUDY *Federal work-study:* Total amount: $154,740; jobs available.

ATHLETIC AWARDS Total amount: $1,793,181 (100% need-based).

APPLYING FOR FINANCIAL AID *Required financial aid forms:* FAFSA, state aid form. *Financial aid deadline (priority):* 4/15. *Notification date:* Continuous beginning 12/15. Students must reply within 2 weeks of notification.

CONTACT Cathy Shell, Director of Financial Aid, Lees-McRae College, PO Box 128, Banner Elk, NC 28604-0128, 828-898-8740 or toll-free 800-280-4562. *Fax:* 828-898-8746. *E-mail:* shell@lmc.edu. *Website:* http://www.lmc.edu/.

LEE UNIVERSITY
Cleveland, TN

Tuition & fees: $16,730	Average undergraduate aid package: $11,437

ABOUT THE INSTITUTION Independent Church of God, coed. *Awards:* certificates, bachelor's, and master's degrees. 72 undergraduate majors. *Total enrollment:* 5,302. Undergraduates: 4,821. Freshmen: 889. Federal methodology is used as a basis for awarding need-based institutional aid.

UNDERGRADUATE EXPENSES for 2017–2018 *Comprehensive fee:* $24,810 includes full-time tuition ($16,080), mandatory fees ($650), and room and board ($8080). *College room only:* $4420. Full-time tuition and fees vary according to course load, location, and program. Room and board charges vary according to board plan and housing facility. *Part-time tuition:* $670 per credit hour. *Part-time fees:* $35 per term. Part-time tuition and fees vary according to course load, location, and program.

FRESHMAN FINANCIAL AID (Fall 2016, est.) 813 applied for aid; of those 66% were deemed to have need. 100% of freshmen with need received aid; of those 52% had need fully met. *Average percent of need met:* 76% (excluding resources awarded to replace EFC). *Average financial aid package:* $11,130 (excluding resources awarded to replace EFC). 27% of all full-time freshmen had no need and received non-need-based gift aid.

UNDERGRADUATE FINANCIAL AID (Fall 2016, est.) 3,326 applied for aid; of those 79% were deemed to have need. 99% of undergraduates with need received aid; of those 22% had need fully met. *Average percent of need met:* 54% (excluding resources awarded to replace EFC). *Average financial aid package:* $11,437 (excluding resources awarded to replace EFC). 18% of all full-time undergraduates had no need and received non-need-based gift aid.

GIFT AID (NEED-BASED) *Total amount:* $19,334,178 (39% federal, 19% state, 40% institutional, 2% external sources). *Receiving aid:* Freshmen: 58% (516); all full-time undergraduates: 61% (2,336). *Average award:* Freshmen: $9738; Undergraduates: $8732. *Scholarships, grants, and awards:* Federal Pell, FSEOG, state, private, college/university gift aid from institutional funds.

GIFT AID (NON-NEED-BASED) *Total amount:* $8,483,874 (1% federal, 24% state, 71% institutional, 4% external sources). *Receiving aid:* Freshmen: 24% (214). Undergraduates: 10% (367). *Average award:* Freshmen: $9345. Undergraduates: $7425. *Scholarships, grants, and awards by category: Academic interests/ achievement:* biological sciences, business, communication, education, general academic interests/achievements, religion/biblical studies. *Creative arts/performance:* music, theater/drama. *Special achievements/activities:* cheerleading/drum major, leadership, religious involvement. *Special characteristics:* children of faculty/staff, local/ state students, siblings of current students, spouses of current students. *Tuition waivers:* Full or partial for employees or children of employees, senior citizens.

LOANS *Student loans:* $26,067,189 (68% need-based, 32% non-need-based). 60% of past graduating class borrowed through all loan programs. *Average indebtedness per student:* $31,630. *Average need-based loan:* Freshmen: $3031. Undergraduates: $4286. *Parent loans:* $5,467,125 (46% need-based, 54% non-need-based). *Programs:* Federal Direct (Subsidized and Unsubsidized Stafford, PLUS), Perkins.

WORK-STUDY *Federal work-study:* Total amount: $362,715; 240 jobs averaging $1643. *State or other work-study/employment:* Total amount: $8697 (51% need-based, 49% non-need-based). 714 part-time jobs averaging $1410.

ATHLETIC AWARDS Total amount: $2,306,223 (40% need-based, 60% non-need-based).

APPLYING FOR FINANCIAL AID *Required financial aid form:* FAFSA. *Financial aid deadline (priority):* 3/15. *Notification date:* Continuous beginning 2/1.

CONTACT Mrs. Marian Dill, Director of Student Financial Aid, Lee University, 1120 North Ocoee Street, Cleveland, TN 37311, 423-614-8300 or toll-free 800-533-9930. *Fax:* 423-614-8308. *E-mail:* finaid@leeuniversity.edu. *Website:* http://www.leeuniversity.edu/.

LEHIGH UNIVERSITY
Bethlehem, PA

Tuition & fees: $48,320	Average undergraduate aid package: $43,376

ABOUT THE INSTITUTION Independent, coed. *Awards:* certificates, bachelor's, master's, and doctoral degrees. 68 undergraduate majors. *Total enrollment:* 7,059. Undergraduates: 5,080. Freshmen: 1,249. Both federal and institutional methodology are used as a basis for awarding need-based institutional aid.

UNDERGRADUATE EXPENSES for 2016–2017 *Application fee:* $70. *Comprehensive fee:* $61,010 includes full-time tuition ($47,920), mandatory fees ($400), and room and board ($12,690). *College room only:* $7320. Room and board charges vary according to board plan and housing facility. *Part-time tuition:* $2000 per credit hour. *Payment plan:* Tuition prepayment.

FRESHMAN FINANCIAL AID (Fall 2016, est.) 791 applied for aid; of those 62% were deemed to have need. 100% of freshmen with need received aid; of those 80% had need fully met. *Average percent of need met:* 98% (excluding resources awarded to replace EFC). *Average financial aid package:* $42,844 (excluding resources awarded to replace EFC). 4% of all full-time freshmen had no need and received non-need-based gift aid.

UNDERGRADUATE FINANCIAL AID (Fall 2016, est.) 2,640 applied for aid; of those 73% were deemed to have need. 100% of undergraduates with need received

aid; of those 82% had need fully met. **Average percent of need met:** 97% (excluding resources awarded to replace EFC). **Average financial aid package:** $43,376 (excluding resources awarded to replace EFC). 5% of all full-time undergraduates had no need and received non-need-based gift aid.

GIFT AID (NEED-BASED) Total amount: $69,390,520 (5% federal, 2% state, 93% institutional). **Receiving aid:** Freshmen: 38% (476); all full-time undergraduates: 38% (1,887). **Average award:** Freshmen: $38,851; Undergraduates: $37,699. **Scholarships, grants, and awards:** Federal Pell, FSEOG, state, private, college/university gift aid from institutional funds.

GIFT AID (NON-NEED-BASED) Total amount: $7,746,407 (53% institutional, 47% external sources). **Receiving aid:** Freshmen: 8% (97). Undergraduates: 7% (333). **Average award:** Freshmen: $8921. Undergraduates: $12,914. **Scholarships, grants, and awards by category:** Academic interests/achievement: 194 awards ($1,734,435 total): business, communication, engineering/technologies, general academic interests/achievements, international studies, military science. Creative arts/performance: 82 awards ($154,060 total): general creative arts/performance, journalism/publications, music, performing arts, theater/drama. Special achievements/activities: 11 awards ($18,750 total): general special achievements/activities. Special characteristics: 98 awards ($4,491,480 total): children of faculty/staff, members of minority groups. Tuition waivers: Full or partial for employees or children of employees. **ROTC:** Army.

LOANS Student loans: $24,539,198 (35% need-based, 65% non-need-based). 53% of past graduating class borrowed through all loan programs. Average indebtedness per student: $34,215. **Average need-based loan:** Freshmen: $3462. Undergraduates: $4320. **Parent loans:** $5,343,481 (100% non-need-based). **Programs:** Federal Direct (Subsidized and Unsubsidized Stafford, PLUS), Perkins, college/university.

WORK-STUDY Federal work-study: Total amount: $2,521,854; 1,107 jobs averaging $1893. **State or other work-study/employment:** Total amount: $949,640 (16% need-based, 84% non-need-based). 75 part-time jobs averaging $1713.

ATHLETIC AWARDS Total amount: $11,098,692 (2% need-based, 98% non-need-based).

APPLYING FOR FINANCIAL AID Required financial aid forms: FAFSA, CSS Financial Aid PROFILE, noncustodial (divorced/separated) parent's statement, business/farm supplement. **Financial aid deadline:** 2/15. **Notification date:** 3/30. Students must reply by 5/1 or within 3 weeks of notification.

CONTACT Jennifer Mertz, Director of Financial Aid, Lehigh University, 27 Memorial Drive West, Bethlehem, PA 18015-3094, 610-758-3181. Fax: 610-758-6211. E-mail: jlm207@lehigh.edu.
Website: http://www.lehigh.edu/.

LEHMAN COLLEGE OF THE CITY UNIVERSITY OF NEW YORK
Bronx, NY

Tuition & fees (NY res): $7010	Average undergraduate aid package: $7344

ABOUT THE INSTITUTION State and locally supported, coed. **Awards:** certificates, bachelor's, and master's degrees. 52 undergraduate majors. **Total enrollment:** 13,486. Undergraduates: 11,477. Freshmen: 690. Federal methodology is used as a basis for awarding need-based institutional aid.

UNDERGRADUATE EXPENSES for 2017–2018 Application fee: $65. **Tuition, state resident:** full-time $6330. **Tuition, nonresident:** full-time $13,440. **Required fees:** full-time $680.

FRESHMAN FINANCIAL AID (Fall 2016, est.) 426 applied for aid; of those 100% were deemed to have need. 84% of freshmen with need received aid; of those 93% had need fully met. **Average percent of need met:** 85% (excluding resources awarded to replace EFC). **Average financial aid package:** $7330 (excluding resources awarded to replace EFC). 37% of all full-time freshmen had no need and received non-need-based gift aid.

UNDERGRADUATE FINANCIAL AID (Fall 2016, est.) 6,168 applied for aid; of those 100% were deemed to have need. 97% of undergraduates with need received aid; of those 93% had need fully met. **Average percent of need met:** 90% (excluding resources awarded to replace EFC). **Average financial aid package:** $7344 (excluding resources awarded to replace EFC). 37% of all full-time undergraduates had no need and received non-need-based gift aid.

GIFT AID (NEED-BASED) Total amount: $48,442,244 (61% federal, 37% state, 2% external sources). **Receiving aid:** Freshmen: 50% (334); all full-time undergraduates: 84% (5,565). **Average award:** Freshmen: $7155; Undergraduates: $7169. **Scholarships, grants, and awards:** Federal Pell, FSEOG, state, college/university gift aid from institutional funds.

GIFT AID (NON-NEED-BASED) Total amount: $905,581 (12% state, 88% institutional). **Receiving aid:** Freshmen: 11% (76). Undergraduates: 19% (1,262). **Average award:** Freshmen: $1409. Undergraduates: $1450. **ROTC:** Army cooperative.

LOANS Student loans: $13,066,669 (58% need-based, 42% non-need-based). 25% of past graduating class borrowed through all loan programs. Average indebtedness per student: $8525. **Average need-based loan:** Freshmen: $2079. Undergraduates: $2083. **Parent loans:** $33,357 (100% non-need-based). **Programs:** Federal Direct (Subsidized and Unsubsidized Stafford, PLUS), Perkins.

WORK-STUDY Federal work-study: Total amount: $555,193; jobs available. **State or other work-study/employment:** Part-time jobs available.

APPLYING FOR FINANCIAL AID Required financial aid forms: FAFSA, state aid form. **Financial aid deadline:** Continuous. **Notification date:** Continuous beginning 3/1.

CONTACT David Martinez, Director of Financial Aid, Lehman College of the City University of New York, 250 Bedford Park Boulevard West, Bronx, NY 10468-1589, 718-960-8545 or toll-free 877-LEHMAN1. Fax: 718-960-8328. E-mail: idmlc@cunyvm.cuny.edu.
Website: http://www.lehman.cuny.edu/.

LE MOYNE COLLEGE
Syracuse, NY

Tuition & fees: $33,030	Average undergraduate aid package: $25,276

ABOUT THE INSTITUTION Independent Roman Catholic (Jesuit), coed. **Awards:** certificates, bachelor's, and master's degrees. 53 undergraduate majors. **Total enrollment:** 3,549. Undergraduates: 2,897. Freshmen: 631. Both federal and institutional methodology are used as a basis for awarding need-based institutional aid.

UNDERGRADUATE EXPENSES for 2016–2017 Application fee: $35. **Comprehensive fee:** $46,000 includes full-time tuition ($32,040), mandatory fees ($990), and room and board ($12,970). **College room only:** $8120. Room and board charges vary according to board plan and housing facility. **Part-time tuition:** $672 per credit hour. Part-time tuition and fees vary according to class time and course load.

FRESHMAN FINANCIAL AID (Fall 2015) 602 applied for aid; of those 89% were deemed to have need. 100% of freshmen with need received aid; of those 25% had need fully met. **Average percent of need met:** 80% (excluding resources awarded to replace EFC). **Average financial aid package:** $26,507 (excluding resources awarded to replace EFC). 13% of all full-time freshmen had no need and received non-need-based gift aid.

UNDERGRADUATE FINANCIAL AID (Fall 2015) 2,247 applied for aid; of those 91% were deemed to have need. 100% of undergraduates with need received aid; of those 24% had need fully met. **Average percent of need met:** 77% (excluding resources awarded to replace EFC). **Average financial aid package:** $25,276 (excluding resources awarded to replace EFC). 13% of all full-time undergraduates had no need and received non-need-based gift aid.

GIFT AID (NEED-BASED) Total amount: $41,154,721 (9% federal, 8% state, 80% institutional, 3% external sources). **Receiving aid:** Freshmen: 84% (534); all full-time undergraduates: 82% (2,040). **Average award:** Freshmen: $22,529; Undergraduates: $20,514. **Scholarships, grants, and awards:** Federal Pell, FSEOG, state, private, college/university gift aid from institutional funds.

GIFT AID (NON-NEED-BASED) Total amount: $5,669,348 (1% federal, 93% institutional, 6% external sources). **Receiving aid:** Freshmen: 14% (86). Undergraduates: 11% (285). **Average award:** Freshmen: $16,196. Undergraduates: $13,829. **Scholarships, grants, and awards by category:** Academic interests/achievement: 873 awards ($14,914,685 total): general academic interests/achievements. Creative arts/performance: 31 awards ($8365 total): music. Special achievements/activities: 430 awards ($5,156,684 total): leadership. Special characteristics: 176 awards ($743,150 total): children and siblings of alumni, members of minority groups. Tuition waivers: Full or partial for employees or children of employees. **ROTC:** Army cooperative, Air Force cooperative.

LOANS *Student loans:* $21,253,290 (93% need-based, 7% non-need-based). 84% of past graduating class borrowed through all loan programs. *Average indebtedness per student:* $37,337. *Average need-based loan:* Freshmen: $3726. Undergraduates: $4676. *Parent loans:* $5,413,373 (97% need-based, 3% non-need-based). *Programs:* Federal Direct (Subsidized and Unsubsidized Stafford, PLUS), Perkins.
WORK-STUDY *Federal work-study:* 294 jobs averaging $1091. *State or other work-study/employment:* 464 part-time jobs averaging $1800.
ATHLETIC AWARDS Total amount: $2,462,307 (55% need-based, 45% non-need-based).
APPLYING FOR FINANCIAL AID *Required financial aid forms:* FAFSA, state aid form. *Financial aid deadline (priority):* 2/15. *Notification date:* 2/15. Students must reply by 5/1 or within 2 weeks of notification.
CONTACT Mrs. Sharon J. Halpin, Director of Financial Aid, Le Moyne College, 1419 Salt Springs Road, Syracuse, NY 13214-1301, 315-445-4400 or toll-free 800-333-4733. *Fax:* 315-445-4182. *E-mail:* halpins@lemoyne.edu.
Website: http://www.lemoyne.edu/.

LEMOYNE-OWEN COLLEGE
Memphis, TN

ABOUT THE INSTITUTION Independent United Church of Christ, coed. *Awards:* certificates and bachelor's degrees. 25 undergraduate majors. *Total enrollment:* 945. Undergraduates: 945. Freshmen: 183.
GIFT AID (NEED-BASED) *Scholarships, grants, and awards:* Federal Pell, FSEOG, state, private, college/university gift aid from institutional funds, United Negro College Fund.
GIFT AID (NON-NEED-BASED) *Scholarships, grants, and awards by category:* Academic interests/achievement: general academic interests/achievements. Creative arts/performance: journalism/publications, music. Special characteristics: children of faculty/staff.
LOANS *Programs:* Federal Direct (Subsidized and Unsubsidized Stafford, PLUS).
APPLYING FOR FINANCIAL AID *Required financial aid forms:* FAFSA, institution's own form.
CONTACT Office of Student Financial Services, LeMoyne-Owen College, 807 Walker Avenue, Memphis, TN 38126-6595, 901-435-1552 or toll-free 800-737-7778. *Fax:* 901-435-1574.
Website: http://www.loc.edu/.

LENOIR-RHYNE UNIVERSITY
Hickory, NC

Tuition & fees: $35,350	Average undergraduate aid package: $27,008

ABOUT THE INSTITUTION Independent Lutheran, coed. *Awards:* bachelor's and master's degrees. 50 undergraduate majors. *Total enrollment:* 2,523. Undergraduates: 1,710. Freshmen: 491. Federal methodology is used as a basis for awarding need-based institutional aid.
UNDERGRADUATE EXPENSES for 2017–2018 *Application fee:* $35. *Comprehensive fee:* $47,500 includes full-time tuition ($35,350) and room and board ($12,150). Room and board charges vary according to board plan. *Part-time tuition:* $1460 per credit.
FRESHMAN FINANCIAL AID (Fall 2015) 426 applied for aid; of those 91% were deemed to have need. 100% of freshmen with need received aid; of those 20% had need fully met. *Average percent of need met:* 78% (excluding resources awarded to replace EFC). *Average financial aid package:* $29,154 (excluding resources awarded to replace EFC). 13% of all full-time freshmen had no need and received non-need-based gift aid.
UNDERGRADUATE FINANCIAL AID (Fall 2015) 1,261 applied for aid; of those 94% were deemed to have need. 100% of undergraduates with need received aid; of those 15% had need fully met. *Average percent of need met:* 71% (excluding resources awarded to replace EFC). *Average financial aid package:* $27,008 (excluding resources awarded to replace EFC). 13% of all full-time undergraduates had no need and received non-need-based gift aid.
GIFT AID (NEED-BASED) *Total amount:* $23,828,218 (13% federal, 14% state, 70% institutional, 3% external sources). *Receiving aid:* Freshmen: 87% (388); all full-

time undergraduates: 86% (1,169). *Average award:* Freshmen: $25,436; Undergraduates: $22,559. *Scholarships, grants, and awards:* Federal Pell, FSEOG, state, private, college/university gift aid from institutional funds.
GIFT AID (NON-NEED-BASED) *Total amount:* $3,634,240 (96% institutional, 4% external sources). *Receiving aid:* Freshmen: 14% (61). Undergraduates: 10% (141). *Average award:* Freshmen: $19,466. Undergraduates: $15,825. *Scholarships, grants, and awards by category:* Academic interests/achievement: general academic interests/achievements. Creative arts/performance: music. Special achievements/activities: cheerleading/drum major, leadership. Special characteristics: children and siblings of alumni, children of faculty/staff, ethnic background, local/state students, members of minority groups, relatives of clergy, religious affiliation, siblings of current students. *Tuition waivers:* Full or partial for employees or children of employees, senior citizens.
LOANS *Student loans:* $8,200,258 (86% need-based, 14% non-need-based). 81% of past graduating class borrowed through all loan programs. *Average indebtedness per student:* $28,294. *Average need-based loan:* Freshmen: $3296. Undergraduates: $4282. *Parent loans:* $4,985,434 (60% need-based, 40% non-need-based). *Programs:* Federal Direct (Subsidized and Unsubsidized Stafford, PLUS), Perkins, state.
WORK-STUDY *Federal work-study:* jobs available. *State or other work-study/employment:* Part-time jobs available.
ATHLETIC AWARDS Total amount: $4,341,668 (61% need-based, 39% non-need-based).
APPLYING FOR FINANCIAL AID *Required financial aid form:* FAFSA. *Financial aid deadline:* Continuous. *Notification date:* Continuous beginning 3/1. Students must reply within 3 weeks of notification.
CONTACT Nick Jenkins, Financial Aid Counselor, Lenoir-Rhyne University, PO Box 7227, Hickory, NC 28603, 828-328-7301 or toll-free 800-277-5721. *Fax:* 828-328-7039. *E-mail:* finaid@lr.edu.
Website: http://www.lr.edu/.

LESLEY UNIVERSITY
Cambridge, MA

Tuition & fees: $26,300	Average undergraduate aid package: $16,470

ABOUT THE INSTITUTION Independent, coed, primarily women. *Awards:* certificates, associate, bachelor's, master's, and doctoral degrees. 22 undergraduate majors. *Total enrollment:* 4,826. Undergraduates: 1,929. Freshmen: 372. Both federal and institutional methodology are used as a basis for awarding need-based institutional aid.
UNDERGRADUATE EXPENSES for 2017–2018 *Comprehensive fee:* $42,050 includes full-time tuition ($26,300) and room and board ($15,750). *College room only:* $9750. Full-time tuition and fees vary according to class time, course level, course load, degree level, location, program, and reciprocity agreements. Room and board charges vary according to board plan. *Part-time tuition:* $877 per credit hour.
FRESHMAN FINANCIAL AID (Fall 2015) 333 applied for aid; of those 85% were deemed to have need. 100% of freshmen with need received aid; of those 13% had need fully met. *Average percent of need met:* 80% (excluding resources awarded to replace EFC). *Average financial aid package:* $16,718 (excluding resources awarded to replace EFC). 22% of all full-time freshmen had no need and received non-need-based gift aid.
UNDERGRADUATE FINANCIAL AID (Fall 2015) 1,217 applied for aid; of those 86% were deemed to have need. 100% of undergraduates with need received aid; of those 7% had need fully met. *Average percent of need met:* 70% (excluding resources awarded to replace EFC). *Average financial aid package:* $16,470 (excluding resources awarded to replace EFC). 26% of all full-time undergraduates had no need and received non-need-based gift aid.
GIFT AID (NEED-BASED) *Total amount:* $12,815,280 (19% federal, 4% state, 70% institutional, 7% external sources). *Receiving aid:* Freshmen: 76% (282); all full-time undergraduates: 63% (973). *Average award:* Freshmen: $12,259; Undergraduates: $8278. *Scholarships, grants, and awards:* Federal Pell, FSEOG, state, private, college/university gift aid from institutional funds.
GIFT AID (NON-NEED-BASED) *Total amount:* $3,413,972 (100% institutional). *Receiving aid:* Freshmen: 5% (17). Undergraduates: 5% (76). *Average award:* Freshmen: $10,034. Undergraduates: $8278. *Scholarships, grants, and*

awards by category: Special achievements/activities: general special achievements/activities. *Special characteristics:* ethnic background. *Tuition waivers:* Full or partial for employees or children of employees.

LOANS *Student loans:* $12,760,565 (58% need-based, 42% non-need-based). 80% of past graduating class borrowed through all loan programs. *Average indebtedness per student:* $23,000. *Average need-based loan:* Freshmen: $3865. *Parent loans:* $5,031,734 (100% non-need-based). *Programs:* Federal Direct (Subsidized and Unsubsidized Stafford, PLUS), Perkins.

WORK-STUDY *Federal work-study:* Jobs available. *State or other work study/employment:* Part-time jobs available.

APPLYING FOR FINANCIAL AID *Required financial aid form:* FAFSA. *Financial aid deadline (priority):* 2/15. *Notification date:* Continuous beginning 2/1.

CONTACT Scott A. Jewell, Director of Student Financial Services, Lesley University, 29 Everett Street, Cambridge, MA 02138-2790, 617-349-8714 or toll-free 800-999-1959 Ext. 8800. *Fax:* 617-349-8667. *E-mail:* sjewell@lesley.edu.
Website: http://www.lesley.edu/.

LETOURNEAU UNIVERSITY
Longview, TX

Tuition & fees: $29,320	Average undergraduate aid package: $22,747

ABOUT THE INSTITUTION Independent nondenominational, coed. *Awards:* associate, bachelor's, and master's degrees. 77 undergraduate majors. *Total enrollment:* 2,721. Undergraduates: 2,253. Freshmen: 280. Federal methodology is used as a basis for awarding need-based institutional aid.

UNDERGRADUATE EXPENSES for 2017–2018 *Comprehensive fee:* $39,190 includes full-time tuition ($28,770), mandatory fees ($550), and room and board ($9870). Full-time tuition and fees vary according to course level, course load, location, and program. Room and board charges vary according to board plan and housing facility. Part-time tuition and fees vary according to course level, course load, location, and program.

FRESHMAN FINANCIAL AID (Fall 2016, est.) 237 applied for aid; of those 87% were deemed to have need. 100% of freshmen with need received aid; of those 23% had need fully met. *Average percent of need met:* 79% (excluding resources awarded to replace EFC). *Average financial aid package:* $25,035 (excluding resources awarded to replace EFC). 20% of all full-time freshmen had no need and received non-need-based gift aid.

UNDERGRADUATE FINANCIAL AID (Fall 2016, est.) 995 applied for aid; of those 91% were deemed to have need. 100% of undergraduates with need received aid; of those 16% had need fully met. *Average percent of need met:* 70% (excluding resources awarded to replace EFC). *Average financial aid package:* $22,747 (excluding resources awarded to replace EFC). 23% of all full-time undergraduates had no need and received non-need-based gift aid.

GIFT AID (NEED-BASED) *Total amount:* $17,838,730 (19% federal, 11% state, 68% institutional, 2% external sources). *Receiving aid:* Freshmen: 78% (203); all full-time undergraduates: 70% (872). *Average award:* Freshmen: $20,002; Undergraduates: $17,265. *Scholarships, grants, and awards:* Federal Pell, FSEOG, state, private, college/university gift aid from institutional funds.

GIFT AID (NON-NEED-BASED) *Total amount:* $2,563,200 (4% federal, 88% institutional, 8% external sources). *Receiving aid:* Freshmen: 15% (38). Undergraduates: 7% (85). *Average award:* Freshmen: $15,640. Undergraduates: $13,316. *Tuition waivers:* Full or partial for employees or children of employees.

LOANS *Student loans:* $14,968,012 (81% need-based, 19% non-need-based). 69% of past graduating class borrowed through all loan programs. *Average indebtedness per student:* $38,988. *Average need-based loan:* Freshmen: $4663. Undergraduates: $5335. *Parent loans:* $1,781,574 (52% need-based, 48% non-need-based). *Programs:* Federal Direct (Subsidized and Unsubsidized Stafford, PLUS), Perkins, state.

WORK-STUDY *Federal work-study:* Total amount: $419,071; jobs available. *State or other work-study/employment:* Total amount: $11,810 (100% need-based). Part-time jobs available.

APPLYING FOR FINANCIAL AID *Required financial aid form:* FAFSA. *Financial aid deadline (priority):* 8/1. *Notification date:* Continuous beginning 11/30. Students must reply within 2 weeks of notification.

CONTACT Financial Aid Office, LeTourneau University, PO Box 7001, Longview, TX 75607, 903-233-4312 or toll-free 800-759-8811. *Fax:* 903-233-4302. *E-mail:* financialaid@letu.edu.
Website: http://www.letu.edu/.

LEWIS & CLARK COLLEGE
Portland, OR

Tuition & fees: $46,894	Average undergraduate aid package: $42,109

ABOUT THE INSTITUTION Independent, coed. *Awards:* certificates, bachelor's, master's, and doctoral degrees. 35 undergraduate majors. *Total enrollment:* 3,419. Undergraduates: 2,134. Freshmen: 506. Both federal and institutional methodology are used as a basis for awarding need-based institutional aid.

UNDERGRADUATE EXPENSES for 2016–2017 *Comprehensive fee:* $58,434 includes full-time tuition ($46,534), mandatory fees ($360), and room and board ($11,540). *College room only:* $6376. Room and board charges vary according to board plan and housing facility. *Part-time tuition:* $2327 per credit hour. *Part-time fees:* $18 per credit hour. Part-time tuition and fees vary according to course load.

FRESHMAN FINANCIAL AID (Fall 2016, est.) 401 applied for aid; of those 68% were deemed to have need. 100% of freshmen with need received aid; of those 53% had need fully met. *Average percent of need met:* 92% (excluding resources awarded to replace EFC). *Average financial aid package:* $41,197 (excluding resources awarded to replace EFC). 38% of all full-time freshmen had no need and received non-need-based gift aid.

UNDERGRADUATE FINANCIAL AID (Fall 2016, est.) 1,407 applied for aid; of those 82% were deemed to have need. 100% of undergraduates with need received aid; of those 54% had need fully met. *Average percent of need met:* 91% (excluding resources awarded to replace EFC). *Average financial aid package:* $42,109 (excluding resources awarded to replace EFC). 35% of all full-time undergraduates had no need and received non-need-based gift aid.

GIFT AID (NEED-BASED) *Total amount:* $36,219,754 (6% federal, 89% institutional, 5% external sources). *Receiving aid:* Freshmen: 54% (271); all full-time undergraduates: 56% (1,138). *Average award:* Freshmen: $32,589; Undergraduates: $31,828. *Scholarships, grants, and awards:* Federal Pell, FSEOG, state, private, college/university gift aid from institutional funds.

GIFT AID (NON-NEED-BASED) *Total amount:* $11,881,039 (98% institutional, 2% external sources). *Receiving aid:* Freshmen: 9% (45). Undergraduates: 5% (96). *Average award:* Freshmen: $16,420. Undergraduates: $15,538. *Scholarships, grants, and awards by category: Academic interests/achievement:* general academic interests/achievements. *Creative arts/performance:* debating, music. *Special achievements/activities:* community service, leadership. *Special characteristics:* children of faculty/staff. *Tuition waivers:* Full or partial for employees or children of employees. *ROTC:* Army cooperative.

LOANS *Student loans:* $10,855,436 (67% need-based, 33% non-need-based). 55% of past graduating class borrowed through all loan programs. *Average indebtedness per student:* $29,913. *Average need-based loan:* Freshmen: $5443. Undergraduates: $7597. *Parent loans:* $3,079,359 (56% need-based, 44% non-need-based). *Programs:* Federal Direct (Subsidized and Unsubsidized Stafford, PLUS), Perkins.

WORK-STUDY *Federal work-study:* Total amount: $2,284,528; 935 jobs averaging $2443. *State or other work-study/employment:* Total amount: $901,064 (57% need-based, 43% non-need-based). 190 part-time jobs averaging $4742.

APPLYING FOR FINANCIAL AID *Required financial aid forms:* FAFSA, CSS Financial Aid PROFILE. *Financial aid deadline (priority):* 1/15. *Notification date:* Continuous beginning 1/30. Students must reply by 7/1 or within 2 weeks of notification.

CONTACT Anastacia Dillon, Director of Financial Aid, Lewis & Clark College, Templeton Campus Center, MSC 56, Portland, OR 97219-7899, 503-768-7090 or toll-free 800-444-4111. *Fax:* 503-768-7074. *E-mail:* fao@lclark.edu.
Website: http://www.lclark.edu/.

LEWIS-CLARK STATE COLLEGE
Lewiston, ID

Tuition & fees (ID res): $7224	Average undergraduate aid package: $10,773

ABOUT THE INSTITUTION State-supported, coed. *Awards:* certificates, associate, and bachelor's degrees. 50 undergraduate majors. *Total enrollment:* 3,633. Undergraduates: 3,633. Freshmen: 543. Federal methodology is used as a basis for awarding need-based institutional aid.

UNDERGRADUATE EXPENSES for 2016–2017 *Tuition, state resident:* full-time $6000; part-time $307 per credit hour. *Tuition, nonresident:* full-time $17,000; part-time $307 per credit hour. *Required fees:* full-time $1224. Full-time tuition and fees vary according to course load and reciprocity agreements. *College room and board:* $6570; *Room only:* $3570. Room and board charges vary according to board plan and housing facility.

FRESHMAN FINANCIAL AID (Fall 2015) 491 applied for aid; of those 76% were deemed to have need. 99% of freshmen with need received aid; of those 10% had need fully met. *Average percent of need met:* 68% (excluding resources awarded to replace EFC). *Average financial aid package:* $8033 (excluding resources awarded to replace EFC). 18% of all full-time freshmen had no need and received non-need-based gift aid.

UNDERGRADUATE FINANCIAL AID (Fall 2015) 2,265 applied for aid; of those 83% were deemed to have need. 98% of undergraduates with need received aid; of those 29% had need fully met. *Average percent of need met:* 77% (excluding resources awarded to replace EFC). *Average financial aid package:* $10,773 (excluding resources awarded to replace EFC). 13% of all full-time undergraduates had no need and received non-need-based gift aid.

GIFT AID (NEED-BASED) *Total amount:* $6,727,897 (90% federal, 8% state, 2% institutional). *Receiving aid:* Freshmen: 55% (275); all full-time undergraduates: 49% (1,356). *Average award:* Freshmen: $4275; Undergraduates: $4386. *Scholarships, grants, and awards:* Federal Pell, FSEOG, state, private, college/university gift aid from institutional funds.

GIFT AID (NON-NEED-BASED) *Total amount:* $2,226,289 (4% federal, 16% state, 55% institutional, 25% external sources). *Receiving aid:* Freshmen: 51% (256). Undergraduates: 29% (796). *Average award:* Freshmen: $3603. Undergraduates: $4350. *Scholarships, grants, and awards by category:* Academic interests/achievement: 40 awards ($38,500 total): biological sciences, business, communication, education, engineering/technologies, English, general academic interests/achievements, health fields, home economics, humanities, mathematics, physical sciences, social sciences. *Creative arts/performance:* 6 awards ($29,000 total): art/fine arts, creative writing, debating, music, theater/drama. *Special achievements/activities:* 113 awards ($157,389 total): community service, general special achievements/activities, junior miss, leadership, memberships, rodeo. *Special characteristics:* adult students, children and siblings of alumni, children of faculty/staff, ethnic background, first-generation college students, general special characteristics, members of minority groups, out-of-state students, previous college experience. *Tuition waivers:* Full or partial for employees or children of employees, senior citizens. *ROTC:* Army cooperative, Naval cooperative, Air Force cooperative.

LOANS *Student loans:* $13,881,591 (43% need-based, 57% non-need-based). 77% of past graduating class borrowed through all loan programs. *Average indebtedness per student:* $27,370. *Average need-based loan:* Freshmen: $2856. Undergraduates: $3671. *Parent loans:* $384,249 (100% non-need-based). *Programs:* Federal Direct (Subsidized and Unsubsidized Stafford, PLUS), Perkins, Federal Nursing.

WORK-STUDY *Federal work-study:* 66 jobs averaging $1584. *State or other work-study/employment:* Total amount: $119,064 (58% need-based, 42% non-need-based). 98 part-time jobs averaging $1306.

ATHLETIC AWARDS Total amount: $2,145,222 (100% non-need-based).

APPLYING FOR FINANCIAL AID *Required financial aid form:* FAFSA. *Financial aid deadline (priority):* 3/1. *Notification date:* Continuous beginning 4/15. Students must reply within 2 weeks of notification.

CONTACT Ms. Laura Hughes, Director of Financial Aid, Lewis-Clark State College, 500 8th Avenue, Lewiston, ID 83501-2698, 208-792-2224 or toll-free 800-933-5272. *Fax:* 208-792-2063. *E-mail:* lhughes@lcsc.edu. *Website:* http://www.lcsc.edu/.

LEWIS UNIVERSITY
Romeoville, IL

Tuition & fees: $31,250	Average undergraduate aid package: $24,080

ABOUT THE INSTITUTION Independent Roman Catholic Church, coed. *Awards:* certificates, associate, bachelor's, master's, and doctoral degrees. 78 undergraduate majors. *Total enrollment:* 6,544. Undergraduates: 4,553. Freshmen: 642. Federal methodology is used as a basis for awarding need-based institutional aid.

UNDERGRADUATE EXPENSES for 2017–2018 *Application fee:* $40. *Comprehensive fee:* $41,710 includes full-time tuition ($31,100), mandatory fees ($150), and room and board ($10,460). *College room only:* $6560. Full-time tuition and fees vary according to course load, location, and program. Room and board charges vary according to board plan and housing facility. *Part-time tuition:* $913 per credit. *Part-time fees:* $75 per term. Part-time tuition and fees vary according to course load, location, and program.

FRESHMAN FINANCIAL AID (Fall 2016, est.) 605 applied for aid; of those 88% were deemed to have need. 100% of freshmen with need received aid; of those 21% had need fully met. *Average percent of need met:* 88% (excluding resources awarded to replace EFC). *Average financial aid package:* $26,765 (excluding resources awarded to replace EFC). 16% of all full-time freshmen had no need and received non-need-based gift aid.

UNDERGRADUATE FINANCIAL AID (Fall 2016, est.) 3,212 applied for aid; of those 89% were deemed to have need. 100% of undergraduates with need received aid; of those 19% had need fully met. *Average percent of need met:* 85% (excluding resources awarded to replace EFC). *Average financial aid package:* $24,080 (excluding resources awarded to replace EFC). 16% of all full-time undergraduates had no need and received non-need-based gift aid.

GIFT AID (NEED-BASED) *Total amount:* $40,009,717 (17% federal, 13% state, 69% institutional, 1% external sources). *Receiving aid:* Freshmen: 83% (530); all full-time undergraduates: 73% (2,717). *Average award:* Freshmen: $18,633; Undergraduates: $14,923. *Scholarships, grants, and awards:* Federal Pell, FSEOG, state, private, college/university gift aid from institutional funds, Federal Nursing.

GIFT AID (NON-NEED-BASED) *Total amount:* $7,854,438 (99% institutional, 1% external sources). *Receiving aid:* Freshmen: 13% (81). Undergraduates: 9% (325). *Average award:* Freshmen: $12,773. Undergraduates: $10,919. *Scholarships, grants, and awards by category:* Academic interests/achievement: general academic interests/achievements. *Creative arts/performance:* art/fine arts, music, theater/drama. *Special achievements/activities:* cheerleading/drum major, community service, general special achievements/activities, leadership, memberships, religious involvement. *Special characteristics:* children and siblings of alumni, children of faculty/staff, religious affiliation, veterans, veterans' children. *Tuition waivers:* Full or partial for children of alumni, employees or children of employees, adult students. *ROTC:* Army cooperative, Air Force cooperative.

LOANS *Student loans:* $33,143,975 (72% need-based, 28% non-need-based). 81% of past graduating class borrowed through all loan programs. *Average indebtedness per student:* $36,073. *Average need-based loan:* Freshmen: $3400. Undergraduates: $4430. *Parent loans:* $9,028,110 (45% need-based, 55% non-need-based). *Programs:* Federal Direct (Subsidized and Unsubsidized Stafford, PLUS), Perkins.

WORK-STUDY *Federal work-study:* Total amount: $4,107,385; jobs available. *State or other work-study/employment:* Total amount: $1,263,821 (40% need-based, 60% non-need-based). Part-time jobs available.

ATHLETIC AWARDS Total amount: $3,512,402 (45% need-based, 55% non-need-based).

APPLYING FOR FINANCIAL AID *Required financial aid form:* FAFSA. *Financial aid deadline:* 5/1 (priority: 10/31). *Notification date:* Continuous beginning 11/1. Students must reply by 5/1 or within 2 weeks of notification.

CONTACT Ms. Janeen Decharinte, Director of Financial Aid Services, Lewis University, One University Parkway, Romeoville, IL 60446, 815-836-5263 or toll-free 800-897-9000. *Fax:* 815-836-5135. *E-mail:* decharja@lewisu.edu. *Website:* http://www.lewisu.edu/.

LIBERTY UNIVERSITY
Lynchburg, VA

Tuition & fees: $23,020	Average undergraduate aid package: $15,118

ABOUT THE INSTITUTION Independent nondenominational, coed. *Awards:* certificates, associate, bachelor's, master's, and doctoral degrees (also offers external degree program with significant enrollment not reflected in profile). 87 undergraduate majors. *Total enrollment:* 15,175. Undergraduates: 13,646. Freshmen: 2,917. Federal methodology is used as a basis for awarding need-based institutional aid.

UNDERGRADUATE EXPENSES for 2016–2017 *Application fee:* $50. *Comprehensive fee:* $32,326 includes full-time tuition ($22,000), mandatory fees ($1020), and room and board ($9306). *College room only:* $5806. Full-time tuition and fees vary according to course load. Room and board charges vary according to housing facility. *Part-time tuition:* $917 per credit hour. Part-time tuition and fees vary according to course load.

FRESHMAN FINANCIAL AID (Fall 2016, est.) 2,760 applied for aid; of those 76% were deemed to have need. 100% of freshmen with need received aid; of those 14% had need fully met. *Average percent of need met:* 58% (excluding resources awarded to replace EFC). *Average financial aid package:* $14,427 (excluding resources awarded to replace EFC). 22% of all full-time freshmen had no need and received non-need-based gift aid.

UNDERGRADUATE FINANCIAL AID (Fall 2016, est.) 12,050 applied for aid; of those 79% were deemed to have need. 100% of undergraduates with need received aid; of those 13% had need fully met. *Average percent of need met:* 60% (excluding resources awarded to replace EFC). *Average financial aid package:* $15,118 (excluding resources awarded to replace EFC). 19% of all full-time undergraduates had no need and received non-need-based gift aid.

GIFT AID (NEED-BASED) *Total amount:* $102,494,816 (16% federal, 7% state, 73% institutional, 4% external sources). *Receiving aid:* Freshmen: 71% (2,073); all full-time undergraduates: 71% (9,347). *Average award:* Freshmen: $10,702; Undergraduates: $10,831. *Scholarships, grants, and awards:* Federal Pell, FSEOG, state, private, college/university gift aid from institutional funds.

GIFT AID (NON-NEED-BASED) *Total amount:* $37,354,035 (8% state, 88% institutional, 4% external sources). *Receiving aid:* Freshmen: 16% (470). Undergraduates: 15% (1,939). *Average award:* Freshmen: $8080. Undergraduates: $8343. *Scholarships, grants, and awards by category: Academic interests/achievement:* biological sciences, business, communication, computer science, education, engineering/technologies, English, general academic interests/achievements, mathematics, premedicine, religion/biblical studies. *Creative arts/performance:* cinema/film/broadcasting, debating, journalism/publications, music, performing arts. *Special achievements/activities:* cheerleading/drum major, leadership. *Special characteristics:* children of faculty/staff, international students, local/state students, religious affiliation, veterans. *Tuition waivers:* Full or partial for employees or children of employees.

ROTC: Army, Air Force cooperative.

LOANS *Student loans:* $69,822,816 (80% need-based, 20% non-need-based). 59% of past graduating class borrowed through all loan programs. *Average indebtedness per student:* $21,474. *Average need-based loan:* Freshmen: $3443. Undergraduates: $4219. *Parent loans:* $27,934,585 (78% need-based, 22% non-need-based). *Programs:* Federal Direct (Subsidized and Unsubsidized Stafford, PLUS), state, college/university, Canadian federal and provincial loans.

WORK-STUDY *Federal work-study:* Total amount: $2,754,509; jobs available. *State or other work-study/employment:* Part-time jobs available.

ATHLETIC AWARDS Total amount: $7,480,935 (62% need-based, 38% non-need-based).

APPLYING FOR FINANCIAL AID *Required financial aid forms:* FAFSA, state aid form. *Financial aid deadline:* 3/1. *Notification date:* Continuous beginning 3/15. Students must reply within 3 weeks of notification.

CONTACT Robert Ritz, Office of Financial Aid, Liberty University, 1971 University Boulevard, Lynchburg, VA 24515, 434-582-2270 or toll-free 800-543-5317. *Fax:* 434-582-2053. *E-mail:* financialaid@liberty.edu.
Website: http://www.liberty.edu/.

LIFE PACIFIC COLLEGE
San Dimas, CA

CONTACT Mrs. Luci Perez, Director of Financial Aid, Life Pacific College, 1100 Covina Boulevard, San Dimas, CA 91773-3298, 909-599-5433 Ext. 322 or toll-free 877-886-5433 Ext. 314. *Fax:* 909-706-3031. *E-mail:* lperez@lifepacific.edu.
Website: http://www.lifepacific.edu/.

LIFE UNIVERSITY
Marietta, GA

Tuition & fees: $11,220	Average undergraduate aid package: $10,000

ABOUT THE INSTITUTION Independent, coed. *Awards:* certificates, associate, bachelor's, master's, and doctoral degrees. 11 undergraduate majors. *Total enrollment:* 2,672. Undergraduates: 718. Freshmen: 128. Federal methodology is used as a basis for awarding need-based institutional aid.

UNDERGRADUATE EXPENSES for 2017–2018 *Application fee:* $50. *Comprehensive fee:* $25,620 includes full-time tuition ($10,170), mandatory fees ($1050), and room and board ($14,400). *College room only:* $5100. Full-time tuition and fees vary according to course load. Room and board charges vary according to housing facility. *Part-time tuition:* $226 per credit hour.

FRESHMAN FINANCIAL AID (Fall 2016, est.) 95 applied for aid; of those 89% were deemed to have need. 100% of freshmen with need received aid. *Average percent of need met:* 27% (excluding resources awarded to replace EFC). *Average financial aid package:* $10,000 (excluding resources awarded to replace EFC).

UNDERGRADUATE FINANCIAL AID (Fall 2016, est.) 475 applied for aid; of those 92% were deemed to have need. 100% of undergraduates with need received aid; of those 1% had need fully met. *Average percent of need met:* 27% (excluding resources awarded to replace EFC). *Average financial aid package:* $10,000 (excluding resources awarded to replace EFC).

GIFT AID (NEED-BASED) *Total amount:* $1,745,000 (100% federal). *Receiving aid:* Freshmen: 42% (47); all full-time undergraduates: 45% (267). *Average award:* Freshmen: $5300; Undergraduates: $5400. *Scholarships, grants, and awards:* Federal Pell, FSEOG.

GIFT AID (NON-NEED-BASED) *Total amount:* $487,500 (67% state, 27% institutional, 6% external sources). *Receiving aid:* Freshmen: 76% (85). Undergraduates: 58% (343). *Scholarships, grants, and awards by category: Academic interests/achievement:* general academic interests/achievements. *Special achievements/activities:* general special achievements/activities, leadership. *Special characteristics:* children and siblings of alumni, general special characteristics, international students, local/state students, members of minority groups. *Tuition waivers:* Full or partial for employees or children of employees.

LOANS *Student loans:* $2,440,000 (43% need-based, 57% non-need-based). 72% of past graduating class borrowed through all loan programs. *Average indebtedness per student:* $38,800. *Average need-based loan:* Freshmen: $3700. Undergraduates: $4600. *Parent loans:* $455,000 (100% need-based). *Programs:* Federal Direct (Subsidized and Unsubsidized Stafford, PLUS), Perkins, state, college/university, alternative loans.

WORK-STUDY *Federal work-study:* Total amount: $154,000; jobs available. *State or other work-study/employment:* Total amount: $13,000 (100% non-need-based). Part-time jobs available.

ATHLETIC AWARDS Total amount: $443,000 (100% non-need-based).

APPLYING FOR FINANCIAL AID *Required financial aid form:* FAFSA. *Financial aid deadline (priority):* 3/1. *Notification date:* Continuous beginning 4/1.

CONTACT Melissa Waters, Director of Financial Aid, Life University, 1269 Barclay Circle, Marietta, GA 30060, 770-426-2901 or toll-free 800-543-3202. *Fax:* 770-426-2926. *E-mail:* finaid@life.edu.
Website: http://www.life.edu/.

LIM COLLEGE
New York, NY

Tuition & fees: $26,350	Average undergraduate aid package: $10,246

ABOUT THE INSTITUTION Proprietary, coed, primarily women. *Awards:* certificates, associate, bachelor's, and master's degrees. 5 undergraduate majors. *Total enrollment:* 221. Undergraduates: 1,499. Freshmen: 260. Both federal and institutional methodology are used as a basis for awarding need-based institutional aid.

UNDERGRADUATE EXPENSES for 2017–2018 Comprehensive fee: $46,700 includes full-time tuition ($25,575), mandatory fees ($775), and room and board ($20,350). *College room only:* $16,350. Room and board charges vary according to housing facility. *Part-time tuition:* $850 per credit. *Part-time fees:* $388 per term.

FRESHMAN FINANCIAL AID (Fall 2015) 258 applied for aid; of those 72% were deemed to have need. 98% of freshmen with need received aid; of those 7% had need fully met. *Average percent of need met:* 54% (excluding resources awarded to replace EFC). *Average financial aid package:* $10,954 (excluding resources awarded to replace EFC). 16% of all full-time freshmen had no need and received non-need-based gift aid.

UNDERGRADUATE FINANCIAL AID (Fall 2015) 1,363 applied for aid; of those 71% were deemed to have need. 98% of undergraduates with need received aid; of those 3% had need fully met. *Average percent of need met:* 42% (excluding resources awarded to replace EFC). *Average financial aid package:* $10,246 (excluding resources awarded to replace EFC). 11% of all full-time undergraduates had no need and received non-need-based gift aid.

GIFT AID (NEED-BASED) Total amount: $6,286,186 (37% federal, 9% state, 52% institutional, 2% external sources). *Receiving aid:* Freshmen: 51% (136); all full-time undergraduates: 48% (686). *Average award:* Freshmen: $9697; Undergraduates: $8338. *Scholarships, grants, and awards:* Federal Pell, FSEOG, state, private, college/university gift aid from institutional funds.

GIFT AID (NON-NEED-BASED) Total amount: $1,169,434 (12% federal, 1% state, 83% institutional, 4% external sources). *Receiving aid:* Freshmen: 46% (125). Undergraduates: 31% (444). *Average award:* Freshmen: $5446. Undergraduates: $4975. *Scholarships, grants, and awards by category:* Academic interests/achievement: general academic interests/achievements. *Special achievements/activities:* leadership, memberships. *Special characteristics:* children of faculty/staff, local/state students, siblings of current students. *Tuition waivers:* Full or partial for employees or children of employees.

LOANS Student loans: $10,955,964 (33% need-based, 67% non-need-based). 75% of past graduating class borrowed through all loan programs. *Average indebtedness per student:* $34,717. *Average need-based loan:* Freshmen: $3309. Undergraduates: $4425. *Parent loans:* $9,280,323 (100% non-need-based). *Programs:* Federal Direct (Subsidized and Unsubsidized Stafford, PLUS).

WORK-STUDY Federal work-study jobs available.

APPLYING FOR FINANCIAL AID Required financial aid forms: FAFSA, state aid form. *Financial aid deadline:* 11/15 (priority: 3/1). *Notification date:* Continuous beginning 2/25. Students must reply by 7/31 or within 2 weeks of notification.

CONTACT Office of Student Financial Services, LIM College, 12 East 53rd Street, New York, NY 10022-5268, 212-310-0632 Ext. 389 or toll-free 800-677-1323. *Fax:* 212-750-3452. *E-mail:* sfs@limcollege.edu.
Website: http://www.limcollege.edu/.

LIMESTONE COLLEGE
Gaffney, SC

ABOUT THE INSTITUTION Independent, coed. *Awards:* associate, bachelor's, and master's degrees. 61 undergraduate majors. *Total enrollment:* 1,280. Undergraduates: 1,227. Freshmen: 416.

GIFT AID (NEED-BASED) Scholarships, grants, and awards: Federal Pell, FSEOG, state, private, college/university gift aid from institutional funds.

GIFT AID (NON-NEED-BASED) Scholarships, grants, and awards by category: Academic interests/achievement: biological sciences, business, communication, computer science, education, English, general academic interests/achievements, health fields, humanities, mathematics, physical sciences, premedicine, religion/biblical studies, social sciences. *Creative arts/performance:* art/fine arts, music, performing arts, theater/drama. *Special achievements/activities:* cheerleading/drum major, general special achievements/activities, leadership, religious involvement. *Special characteristics:* children of faculty/staff, local/state students, out-of-state students, previous college experience, siblings of current students.

LOANS Programs: Federal Direct (Subsidized and Unsubsidized Stafford, PLUS), Perkins.

WORK-STUDY Federal work-study: 105 jobs averaging $1101. *State or other work-study/employment:* Total amount: $5000 (40% need-based, 60% non-need-based). 90 part-time jobs averaging $673.

APPLYING FOR FINANCIAL AID Required financial aid form: FAFSA.

CONTACT Mr. Bobby Greer, Director of Financial Aid, Limestone College, 1115 College Drive, Gaffney, SC 29340-3799, 864-488-4567 or toll-free 800-795-7151. *Fax:* 864-487-8706. *E-mail:* bgreer@limestone.edu.
Website: http://www.limestone.edu/.

LINCOLN CHRISTIAN UNIVERSITY
Lincoln, IL

Tuition & fees: $13,020	Average undergraduate aid package: $10,199

ABOUT THE INSTITUTION Independent Christian Churches and Churches of Christ, coed. *Awards:* associate, bachelor's, master's, and doctoral degrees. 13 undergraduate majors. *Total enrollment:* 886. Undergraduates: 528. Freshmen: 91. Federal methodology is used as a basis for awarding need-based institutional aid.

UNDERGRADUATE EXPENSES for 2017–2018 Comprehensive fee: $20,584 includes full-time tuition ($13,020) and room and board ($7564). *College room only:* $3600. *Part-time tuition:* $434 per credit hour.

FRESHMAN FINANCIAL AID (Fall 2015) 80 applied for aid; of those 86% were deemed to have need. 100% of freshmen with need received aid; of those 6% had need fully met. *Average percent of need met:* 52% (excluding resources awarded to replace EFC). *Average financial aid package:* $9973 (excluding resources awarded to replace EFC). 19% of all full-time freshmen had no need and received non-need-based gift aid.

UNDERGRADUATE FINANCIAL AID (Fall 2015) 392 applied for aid; of those 89% were deemed to have need. 98% of undergraduates with need received aid; of those 6% had need fully met. *Average percent of need met:* 52% (excluding resources awarded to replace EFC). *Average financial aid package:* $10,199 (excluding resources awarded to replace EFC). 15% of all full-time undergraduates had no need and received non-need-based gift aid.

GIFT AID (NEED-BASED) Total amount: $2,654,684 (37% federal, 20% state, 35% institutional, 8% external sources). *Receiving aid:* Freshmen: 78% (69); all full-time undergraduates: 80% (335). *Average award:* Freshmen: $6886; Undergraduates: $7018. *Scholarships, grants, and awards:* Federal Pell, FSEOG, state, private, college/university gift aid from institutional funds.

GIFT AID (NON-NEED-BASED) Total amount: $313,087 (69% institutional, 31% external sources). *Receiving aid:* Freshmen: 1% (1). Undergraduates: 2% (9). *Average award:* Freshmen: $3624. Undergraduates: $2866. *Scholarships, grants, and awards by category:* Academic interests/achievement: 150 awards ($394,511 total): general academic interests/achievements. *Special characteristics:* 47 awards ($115,314 total): children of faculty/staff, international students, relatives of clergy. *Tuition waivers:* Full or partial for employees or children of employees, senior citizens.

LOANS Student loans: $2,826,757 (76% need-based, 24% non-need-based). 84% of past graduating class borrowed through all loan programs. *Average indebtedness per student:* $32,138. *Average need-based loan:* Freshmen: $3516. Undergraduates: $3805. *Parent loans:* $329,823 (48% need-based, 52% non-need-based). *Programs:* Federal Direct (Subsidized and Unsubsidized Stafford, PLUS), Perkins, alternative loans.

WORK-STUDY Federal work-study: 60 jobs averaging $1945. *State or other work-study/employment:* Total amount: $229,140 (100% non-need-based). 120 part-time jobs averaging $1910.

ATHLETIC AWARDS Total amount: $116,200 (79% need-based, 21% non-need-based).

APPLYING FOR FINANCIAL AID Required financial aid form: FAFSA. *Financial aid deadline (priority):* 3/1. *Notification date:* Continuous beginning 11/1. Students must reply within 4 weeks of notification.

CONTACT Nancy Siddens, Director of Financial Aid, Lincoln Christian University, 100 Campus View Drive, Lincoln, IL 62656, 217-732-3168 Ext. 2250 or toll-free 888-522-5228. *Fax:* 217-732-4199. *E-mail:* finaid@lincolnchristian.edu. *Website:* http://www.lincolnchristian.edu/.

LINCOLN COLLEGE–NORMAL
Normal, IL

ABOUT THE INSTITUTION Independent, coed. *Awards:* certificates, associate, and bachelor's degrees. 9 undergraduate majors. *Total enrollment:* 527. Undergraduates: 527.

GIFT AID (NEED-BASED) *Scholarships, grants, and awards:* Federal Pell, FSEOG, state, private, college/university gift aid from institutional funds.

GIFT AID (NON-NEED-BASED) *Scholarships, grants, and awards by category:* Academic interests/achievement: premedicine, social sciences.

LOANS *Programs:* Federal Direct (Subsidized and Unsubsidized Stafford, PLUS).

APPLYING FOR FINANCIAL AID *Required financial aid form:* FAFSA.

CONTACT Financial Aid Office, Lincoln College–Normal, 300 Keokuk Street, Lincoln , IL 62656, 217-735-7231 or toll-free 800-569-0558. *Fax:* 217-735-6016. *E-mail:* lclfinancialaid@linoclncollege.edu.
Website: http://www.lincolncollege.edu/normal/.

LINCOLN COLLEGE OF NEW ENGLAND
Southington, CT

CONTACT Financial Aid Office, Lincoln College of New England, 2279 Mount Vernon Road, Southington, CT 06489-1057, 860-628-4751 or toll-free 800-825-0087. *Website:* http://www.lincolncollegene.edu/.

LINCOLN CULINARY INSTITUTE
West Palm Beach, FL

CONTACT Financial Aid Office, Lincoln Culinary Institute, 2410 Metrocentre Boulevard, West Palm Beach, FL 33407, 561-842-8324.
Website: http://www.lincolnedu.com/campus/west-palm-beach-culinary-fl.

LINCOLN MEMORIAL UNIVERSITY
Harrogate, TN

Tuition & fees: N/R	Average undergraduate aid package: N/A

ABOUT THE INSTITUTION Independent, coed. 43 undergraduate majors. Federal methodology is used as a basis for awarding need-based institutional aid.

GIFT AID (NEED-BASED) *Scholarships, grants, and awards:* Federal Pell, FSEOG, state, private, college/university gift aid from institutional funds.

GIFT AID (NON-NEED-BASED) *Scholarships, grants, and awards by category:* Academic interests/achievement: general academic interests/achievements. Creative arts/performance: music. Special achievements/activities: cheerleading/drum major. Special characteristics: children and siblings of alumni, children of faculty/staff, local/state students, members of minority groups.

LOANS *Student loans:* 57% of past graduating class borrowed through all loan programs. Average indebtedness per student: $19,987. *Programs:* Federal Direct (Subsidized and Unsubsidized Stafford, PLUS), Perkins, Federal Nursing.

WORK-STUDY Federal work-study jobs available. *State or other work-study/employment:* Part-time jobs available.

APPLYING FOR FINANCIAL AID *Required financial aid form:* FAFSA. *Financial aid deadline (priority):* 2/15. *Notification date:* 3/15.

CONTACT Tammy Tomfohrde, Executive Director of Financial Aid, Lincoln Memorial University, 6965 Cumberland Gap Parkway, Harrogate, TN 37752-1901, 423-869-6465 or toll-free 800-325-0900. *Fax:* 423-869-6347. *E-mail:* tammy.tomfohrde@lmunet.edu.
Website: http://www.lmunet.edu/.

LINCOLN UNIVERSITY
Oakland, CA

CONTACT Financial Aid Office, Lincoln University, 401 15th Street, Oakland, CA 94612, 510-628-8010 or toll-free 888-810-9998.
Website: http://www.lincolnuca.edu/.

LINCOLN UNIVERSITY
Jefferson City, MO

Tuition & fees (MO res): $7042	Average undergraduate aid package: $11,908

ABOUT THE INSTITUTION State-supported, coed. *Awards:* certificates, associate, bachelor's, and master's degrees. 41 undergraduate majors. *Total enrollment:* 2,738. Undergraduates: 2,618. Freshmen: 460. Federal methodology is used as a basis for awarding need-based institutional aid.

UNDERGRADUATE EXPENSES for 2016–2017 *Tuition, state resident:* full-time $6150; part-time $205 per credit hour. *Tuition, nonresident:* full-time $12,540; part-time $418 per credit hour. *Required fees:* full-time $892; $6.75 per credit hour or $345 per term. Full-time tuition and fees vary according to course load, location, and reciprocity agreements. Part-time tuition and fees vary according to course load, location, and reciprocity agreements. *College room and board:* $6560; *Room only:* $3400. Room and board charges vary according to board plan and housing facility.

FRESHMAN FINANCIAL AID (Fall 2016, est.) 432 applied for aid; of those 92% were deemed to have need. 98% of freshmen with need received aid; of those 7% had need fully met. *Average percent of need met:* 59% (excluding resources awarded to replace EFC). *Average financial aid package:* $12,542 (excluding resources awarded to replace EFC). 1% of all full-time freshmen had no need and received non-need-based gift aid.

UNDERGRADUATE FINANCIAL AID (Fall 2016, est.) 1,692 applied for aid; of those 88% were deemed to have need. 99% of undergraduates with need received aid; of those 5% had need fully met. *Average percent of need met:* 62% (excluding resources awarded to replace EFC). *Average financial aid package:* $11,908 (excluding resources awarded to replace EFC). 1% of all full-time undergraduates had no need and received non-need-based gift aid.

GIFT AID (NEED-BASED) *Total amount:* $9,247,864 (71% federal, 9% state, 13% institutional, 7% external sources). *Receiving aid:* Freshmen: 78% (352); all full-time undergraduates: 72% (1,319). *Average award:* Freshmen: $6340; Undergraduates: $6014. *Scholarships, grants, and awards:* Federal Pell, FSEOG, state, private, college/university gift aid from institutional funds.

GIFT AID (NON-NEED-BASED) *Total amount:* $683,108 (5% federal, 2% state, 17% institutional, 76% external sources). *Receiving aid:* Freshmen: 41% (186). Undergraduates: 32% (587). *Average award:* Freshmen: $3000. Undergraduates: $5288. *Scholarships, grants, and awards by category:* Academic interests/achievement: 129 awards ($862,889 total): agriculture, general academic interests/achievements, military science. Creative arts/performance: 86 awards ($149,307 total): art/fine arts, journalism/publications, music, performing arts, theater/drama. Special achievements/activities: 12 awards ($6054 total): cheerleading/drum major. Special characteristics: 423 awards ($2,393,585 total): adult students, children of faculty/staff, international students, out-of-state students. Tuition waivers: Full or partial for employees or children of employees, senior citizens. ROTC: Army.

LOANS *Student loans:* $13,797,010 (45% need-based, 55% non-need-based). 75% of past graduating class borrowed through all loan programs. Average indebtedness per student: $32,691. *Average need-based loan:* Freshmen: $3440. Undergraduates: $4092. *Parent loans:* $2,693,644 (100% non-need-based). *Programs:* Federal Direct (Subsidized and Unsubsidized Stafford, PLUS), private loans.

WORK-STUDY *Federal work-study:* Total amount: $214,400; 178 jobs averaging $602. *State or other work-study/employment:* Total amount: $71,364 (100% non-need-based). 49 part-time jobs averaging $1456.
ATHLETIC AWARDS Total amount: $1,010,100 (100% need-based).
APPLYING FOR FINANCIAL AID *Required financial aid forms:* FAFSA, institution's own form. *Financial aid deadline (priority):* 3/1. *Notification date:* Continuous beginning 3/15. Students must reply within 2 weeks of notification.
CONTACT Mr. Alfred Robinson, Director of Student Financial Aid, Lincoln University, 820 Chestnut Street, Jefferson City, MO 65102-0029, 573-681-6156. *Fax:* 573-681-5871. *E-mail:* robinsona@lincolnu.edu.
Website: http://www.lincolnu.edu/.

LINCOLN UNIVERSITY
Lincoln University, PA

Tuition & fees (PA res): $11,102	Average undergraduate aid package: $12,451

ABOUT THE INSTITUTION State-related, coed. *Awards:* certificates, bachelor's, and master's degrees. 35 undergraduate majors. *Total enrollment:* 2,092. Undergraduates: 1,824. Freshmen: 526. Federal methodology is used as a basis for awarding need-based institutional aid.
UNDERGRADUATE EXPENSES for 2016–2017 *Application fee:* $20. *One-time required fee:* $100. *Tuition, state resident:* full-time $7487; part-time $315 per credit hour. *Tuition, nonresident:* full-time $12,375; part-time $519 per credit hour. *Required fees:* full-time $3615; $135 per credit hour. Full-time tuition and fees vary according to course load, degree level, location, program, and student level. Part-time tuition and fees vary according to course load, degree level, location, program, and student level. *College room and board:* $9268; *Room only:* $5010. Room and board charges vary according to board plan and housing facility. *Payment plan:* Guaranteed tuition.
FRESHMAN FINANCIAL AID (Fall 2015) 441 applied for aid; of those 96% were deemed to have need. 100% of freshmen with need received aid; of those 5% had need fully met. *Average percent of need met:* 42% (excluding resources awarded to replace EFC). *Average financial aid package:* $11,351 (excluding resources awarded to replace EFC). 2% of all full-time freshmen had no need and received non-need-based gift aid.
UNDERGRADUATE FINANCIAL AID (Fall 2015) 1,489 applied for aid; of those 94% were deemed to have need. 99% of undergraduates with need received aid; of those 7% had need fully met. *Average percent of need met:* 47% (excluding resources awarded to replace EFC). *Average financial aid package:* $12,451 (excluding resources awarded to replace EFC). 3% of all full-time undergraduates had no need and received non-need-based gift aid.
GIFT AID (NEED-BASED) *Total amount:* $14,121,752 (40% federal, 10% state, 35% institutional, 15% external sources). *Receiving aid:* Freshmen: 93% (421); all full-time undergraduates: 89% (1,385). *Average award:* Freshmen: $7026; Undergraduates: $7112. *Scholarships, grants, and awards:* Federal Pell, FSEOG, state, private, college/university gift aid from institutional funds, United Negro College Fund.
GIFT AID (NON-NEED-BASED) *Receiving aid:* Freshmen: 61% (276). Undergraduates: 53% (829). *Average award:* Freshmen: $3466. Undergraduates: $6045. *Scholarships, grants, and awards by category:* Academic interests/achievement: general academic interests/achievements. Creative arts/performance: music. Special achievements/activities: general special achievements/activities. Special characteristics: children and siblings of alumni, children of faculty/staff, international students. *Tuition waivers:* Full or partial for children of alumni, employees or children of employees. *ROTC:* Army cooperative.
LOANS *Student loans:* $11,672,744 (100% need-based). 85% of past graduating class borrowed through all loan programs. *Average indebtedness per student:* $31,555. *Average need-based loan:* Freshmen: $3433. Undergraduates: $4249. *Parent loans:* $7,132,462 (100% need-based). *Programs:* Federal Direct (Subsidized and Unsubsidized Stafford, PLUS), Perkins, private loans.
WORK-STUDY *Federal work-study:* jobs available.
ATHLETIC AWARDS Total amount: $512,392 (100% need-based).
APPLYING FOR FINANCIAL AID *Required financial aid form:* FAFSA. *Financial aid deadline (priority):* 4/1. *Notification date:* 2/1. Students must reply within 2 weeks of notification.

CONTACT Ms. Kim Anderson, Director of Financial Aid, Lincoln University, 1570 Baltimore Pike, Lincoln University, PA 19352, 484-365-7810 or toll-free 800-790-0191. *Fax:* 484-365-8198. *E-mail:* kanderson@lincoln.edu.
Website: http://www.lincoln.edu/.

LINDENWOOD UNIVERSITY
St. Charles, MO

Tuition & fees: $16,332	Average undergraduate aid package: $9635

ABOUT THE INSTITUTION Independent Presbyterian, coed. *Awards:* certificates, bachelor's, master's, and doctoral degrees. 88 undergraduate majors. *Total enrollment:* 10,750. Undergraduates: 7,549. Freshmen: 1,008. Federal methodology is used as a basis for awarding need-based institutional aid.
UNDERGRADUATE EXPENSES for 2016–2017 *Application fee:* $30. *Comprehensive fee:* $25,132 includes full-time tuition ($15,672), mandatory fees ($660), and room and board ($8800). Full-time tuition and fees vary according to class time. Room and board charges vary according to board plan. *Part-time tuition:* $453 per credit hour. *Part-time fees:* $255 per term. Part-time tuition and fees vary according to course load.
FRESHMAN FINANCIAL AID (Fall 2016, est.) 687 applied for aid; of those 75% were deemed to have need. 100% of freshmen with need received aid; of those 25% had need fully met. *Average percent of need met:* 80% (excluding resources awarded to replace EFC). *Average financial aid package:* $11,533 (excluding resources awarded to replace EFC). 40% of all full-time freshmen had no need and received non-need-based gift aid.
UNDERGRADUATE FINANCIAL AID (Fall 2016, est.) 4,603 applied for aid; of those 82% were deemed to have need. 100% of undergraduates with need received aid; of those 20% had need fully met. *Average percent of need met:* 76% (excluding resources awarded to replace EFC). *Average financial aid package:* $9635 (excluding resources awarded to replace EFC). 31% of all full-time undergraduates had no need and received non-need-based gift aid.
GIFT AID (NEED-BASED) *Receiving aid:* Freshmen: 47% (461); all full-time undergraduates: 46% (3,130). *Average award:* Freshmen: $7712; Undergraduates: $5986. *Scholarships, grants, and awards:* Federal Pell, FSEOG, state, private, college/university gift aid from institutional funds.
GIFT AID (NON-NEED-BASED) *Receiving aid:* Freshmen: 44% (432). Undergraduates: 30% (2,015). *Average award:* Freshmen: $6915. Undergraduates: $5628. *Scholarships, grants, and awards by category:* Academic interests/achievement: biological sciences, business, communication, computer science, education, engineering/technologies, English, foreign languages, general academic interests/achievements, health fields, humanities, international studies, library science, mathematics, military science, physical sciences, premedicine, religion/biblical studies, social sciences. Creative arts/performance: applied art and design, art/fine arts, cinema/film/broadcasting, dance, debating, general creative arts/performance, journalism/publications, music, performing arts, theater/drama. Special achievements/activities: cheerleading/drum major, community service, general special achievements/activities, junior miss, leadership. Special characteristics: children and siblings of alumni, children of faculty/staff, children of union members/company employees, public servants, veterans, veterans' children. *Tuition waivers:* Full or partial for employees or children of employees, senior citizens. *ROTC:* Army cooperative, Air Force cooperative.
LOANS *Student loans:* $46,200,000 (43% need-based, 57% non-need-based). 66% of past graduating class borrowed through all loan programs. *Average indebtedness per student:* $31,488. *Average need-based loan:* Freshmen: $3293. Undergraduates: $4023. *Parent loans:* $6,806,000 (100% non-need-based). *Programs:* Federal Direct (Subsidized and Unsubsidized Stafford, PLUS), Perkins.
WORK-STUDY *Federal work-study:* Total amount: $648,274; 311 jobs averaging $2358. *State or other work-study/employment:* Total amount: $6,300,000 (100% non-need-based). Part-time jobs available.
ATHLETIC AWARDS Total amount: $4,230,000 (100% non-need-based).
APPLYING FOR FINANCIAL AID *Required financial aid form:* FAFSA. *Financial aid deadline (priority):* 4/1. *Notification date:* Continuous. Students must reply within 2 weeks of notification.
CONTACT Ms. Lori Bode, Director, Financial Aid, Lindenwood University, 209 South Kingshighway, St. Charles, MO 63301-1695, 636-949-4925. *Fax:* 636-949-4924. *E-mail:* lbode@lindenwood.edu.
Website: http://www.lindenwood.edu/.

LINDSEY WILSON COLLEGE
Columbia, KY

Tuition & fees: $24,246	Average undergraduate aid package: N/A

ABOUT THE INSTITUTION Independent United Methodist, coed. **Awards:** associate, bachelor's, master's, and doctoral degrees. 34 undergraduate majors. **Total enrollment:** 2,500. Undergraduates: 2,143. Freshmen: 493. Federal methodology is used as a basis for awarding need-based institutional aid.

UNDERGRADUATE EXPENSES for 2017–2018 **Comprehensive fee:** $33,546 includes full-time tuition ($24,000), mandatory fees ($246), and room and board ($9300). **College room only:** $3370. Full-time tuition and fees vary according to class time, degree level, and location. **Part-time tuition:** $1000 per credit hour. **Part-time fees:** $48 per term. Part-time tuition and fees vary according to class time, degree level, and location.

FRESHMAN FINANCIAL AID (Fall 2016, est.) 484 applied for aid; of those 95% were deemed to have need. 100% of freshmen with need received aid; of those 25% had need fully met.

UNDERGRADUATE FINANCIAL AID (Fall 2016, est.) 2,059 applied for aid; of those 94% were deemed to have need. 99% of undergraduates with need received aid; of those 22% had need fully met.

GIFT AID (NEED-BASED) Total amount: $32,550,680 (18% federal, 19% state, 60% institutional, 3% external sources). **Receiving aid:** Freshmen: 94% (457); all full-time undergraduates: 91% (1,894). **Average award:** Freshmen: $20,364; Undergraduates: $18,556. **Scholarships, grants, and awards:** Federal Pell, FSEOG, state, private, college/university gift aid from institutional funds.

GIFT AID (NON-NEED-BASED) Scholarships, grants, and awards by category: Academic interests/achievement: biological sciences, business, education, English, general academic interests/achievements, mathematics, premedicine, religion/biblical studies. Creative arts/performance: applied art and design, music. Special achievements/activities: cheerleading/drum major, general special achievements/activities, junior miss, leadership, religious involvement. Special characteristics: children and siblings of alumni, children of faculty/staff, relatives of clergy, religious affiliation. **Tuition waivers:** Full or partial for employees or children of employees, senior citizens.

LOANS Student loans: $10,670,577 (100% need-based). 72% of past graduating class borrowed through all loan programs. Average indebtedness per student: $26,869. **Average need-based loan:** Freshmen: $7752. Undergraduates: $4176. **Parent loans:** $987,766 (100% need-based). **Programs:** Federal Direct (Subsidized and Unsubsidized Stafford, PLUS), Perkins, college/university.

WORK-STUDY Federal work-study: Total amount: $487,423; 252 jobs averaging $2158. **State or other work-study/employment:** Total amount: $45,500 (100% need-based). 16 part-time jobs averaging $2344.

ATHLETIC AWARDS Total amount: $2,538,061 (100% need-based).

APPLYING FOR FINANCIAL AID Required financial aid form: FAFSA. **Financial aid deadline (priority):** 4/1. **Notification date:** Continuous beginning 4/15. Students must reply within 2 weeks of notification.

CONTACT Ms. Marilyn D. Radford, Director of Student Financial Services, Lindsey Wilson College, 210 Lindsey Wilson Street, Columbia, KY 42728, 270-384-8022 or toll-free 800-264-0138. Fax: 270-384-8591. E-mail: radfordm@lindsey.edu. Website: http://www.lindsey.edu/.

LINFIELD COLLEGE
McMinnville, OR

Tuition & fees: $41,576	Average undergraduate aid package: $32,663

ABOUT THE INSTITUTION Independent American Baptist Churches in the USA, coed. **Awards:** certificates and bachelor's degrees (Linfield College includes the Linfield College McMinnville Campus in McMinnville, Oregon; the Linfield-Good Samaritan School of Nursing in Portland, Oregon(Portland Campus) and the Linfield College Adult Degree Program online). 49 undergraduate majors. **Total enrollment:** 1,632. Undergraduates: 1,632. Freshmen: 393. Federal methodology is used as a basis for awarding need-based institutional aid.

UNDERGRADUATE EXPENSES for 2017–2018 **Comprehensive fee:** $53,346 includes full-time tuition ($41,100), mandatory fees ($476), and room and board ($11,770). **College room only:** $6400. Full-time tuition and fees vary according to course load, location, and program. Room and board charges vary according to board plan, housing facility, and location. **Part-time tuition:** $1285 per semester hour. **Part-time fees:** $132 per term. Part-time tuition and fees vary according to course load, location, and program.

FRESHMAN FINANCIAL AID (Fall 2016, est.) 355 applied for aid; of those 89% were deemed to have need. 100% of freshmen with need received aid; of those 20% had need fully met. **Average percent of need met:** 84% (excluding resources awarded to replace EFC). **Average financial aid package:** $34,943 (excluding resources awarded to replace EFC). 18% of all full-time freshmen had no need and received non-need-based gift aid.

UNDERGRADUATE FINANCIAL AID (Fall 2016, est.) 1,360 applied for aid; of those 89% were deemed to have need. 100% of undergraduates with need received aid; of those 21% had need fully met. **Average percent of need met:** 82% (excluding resources awarded to replace EFC). **Average financial aid package:** $32,663 (excluding resources awarded to replace EFC). 22% of all full-time undergraduates had no need and received non-need-based gift aid.

GIFT AID (NEED-BASED) Total amount: $31,471,661 (7% federal, 2% state, 88% institutional, 3% external sources). **Receiving aid:** Freshmen: 67% (265); all full-time undergraduates: 61% (969). **Average award:** Freshmen: $28,872; Undergraduates: $26,818. **Scholarships, grants, and awards:** Federal Pell, FSEOG, state, private, college/university gift aid from institutional funds.

GIFT AID (NON-NEED-BASED) Total amount: $5,695,377 (97% institutional, 3% external sources). **Receiving aid:** Freshmen: 77% (303). Undergraduates: 72% (1,141). **Average award:** Freshmen: $19,324. Undergraduates: $18,275. **Scholarships, grants, and awards by category:** Academic interests/achievement: 1,264 awards ($20,462,141 total): biological sciences, business, communication, computer science, education, English, foreign languages, general academic interests/achievements, humanities, international studies, mathematics, physical sciences, religion/biblical studies, social sciences. Creative arts/performance: 69 awards ($176,520 total): debating, music, theater/drama. Special achievements/activities: 63 awards ($123,500 total): community service, leadership. Special characteristics: 591 awards ($6,417,621 total): children of faculty/staff, international students, members of minority groups, previous college experience, veterans. **Tuition waivers:** Full or partial for employees or children of employees, senior citizens. **ROTC:** Air Force cooperative.

LOANS Student loans: $10,358,354 (70% need-based, 30% non-need-based). 70% of past graduating class borrowed through all loan programs. Average indebtedness per student: $34,320. **Average need-based loan:** Freshmen: $4590. Undergraduates: $4896. **Parent loans:** $4,788,266 (40% need-based, 60% non-need-based). **Programs:** Federal Direct (Subsidized and Unsubsidized Stafford, PLUS), Perkins, private loans.

WORK-STUDY Federal work-study: Total amount: $2,275,478; 584 jobs averaging $1153. **State or other work-study/employment:** Total amount: $1,721,055 (6% need-based, 94% non-need-based). 544 part-time jobs averaging $1328.

APPLYING FOR FINANCIAL AID Required financial aid form: FAFSA. **Financial aid deadline (priority):** 2/1. **Notification date:** 4/1. Students must reply by 5/1 or within 2 weeks of notification.

CONTACT Ms. Keri Burke, Director of Financial Aid, Linfield College, 900 Southeast Baker Street, A484, McMinnville, OR 97128-6894, 503-883-2269 or toll-free 800-640-2287. Fax: 503-883-2486. E-mail: finaid@linfield.edu. Website: http://www.linfield.edu/.

LIPSCOMB UNIVERSITY
Nashville, TN

Tuition & fees: $30,932	Average undergraduate aid package: $24,556

ABOUT THE INSTITUTION Independent Church of Christ, coed. **Awards:** certificates, associate, bachelor's, master's, and doctoral degrees. 102 undergraduate majors. **Total enrollment:** 4,632. Undergraduates: 2,986. Freshmen: 637. Federal methodology is used as a basis for awarding need-based institutional aid.

UNDERGRADUATE EXPENSES for 2017–2018 **Application fee:** $50. **Comprehensive fee:** $42,966 includes full-time tuition ($28,556), mandatory fees ($2376), and room and board ($12,034). **College room only:** $6834. Room and board charges vary according to board plan and housing facility. **Part-time tuition:** $1194 per credit hour.

FRESHMAN FINANCIAL AID (Fall 2016, est.) 632 applied for aid; of those 67% were deemed to have need. 100% of freshmen with need received aid; of those 25% had need fully met. *Average percent of need met:* 68% (excluding resources awarded to replace EFC). *Average financial aid package:* $23,179 (excluding resources awarded to replace EFC). 32% of all full-time freshmen had no need and received non-need-based gift aid.

UNDERGRADUATE FINANCIAL AID (Fall 2016, est.) 2,565 applied for aid; of those 65% were deemed to have need. 100% of undergraduates with need received aid; of those 28% had need fully met. *Average percent of need met:* 65% (excluding resources awarded to replace EFC). *Average financial aid package:* $24,556 (excluding resources awarded to replace EFC). 32% of all full-time undergraduates had no need and received non-need-based gift aid.

GIFT AID (NEED-BASED) *Total amount:* $27,748,953 (12% federal, 15% state, 65% institutional, 8% external sources). *Receiving aid:* Freshmen: 67% (425); all full-time undergraduates: 61% (1,626). *Average award:* Freshmen: $4239; Undergraduates: $4195. *Scholarships, grants, and awards:* Federal Pell, FSEOG, state, private, college/university gift aid from institutional funds.

GIFT AID (NON-NEED-BASED) *Total amount:* $12,245,841 (13% state, 81% institutional, 6% external sources). *Receiving aid:* Freshmen: 67% (423). Undergraduates: 54% (1,439). *Average award:* Freshmen: $12,865. Undergraduates: $15,231. *Scholarships, grants, and awards by category:* Academic interests/achievement: 2,078 awards: biological sciences, business, communication, education, engineering/technologies, English, general academic interests/achievements, home economics, mathematics, premedicine, religion/biblical studies. Creative arts/performance: 111 awards ($802,400 total): art/fine arts, journalism/publications, music, theater/drama. Special achievements/activities: 152 awards ($656,799 total): cheerleading/drum major, community service, general special achievements/activities, leadership, religious involvement. Special characteristics: 1,009 awards: adult students, children of educators, children of faculty/staff, children with a deceased or disabled parent, international students, local/state students, members of minority groups, out-of-state students, relatives of clergy, religious affiliation. *Tuition waivers:* Full or partial for employees or children of employees. *ROTC:* Army cooperative, Air Force cooperative.

LOANS *Student loans:* $12,590,126 (86% need-based, 14% non-need-based). 56% of past graduating class borrowed through all loan programs. *Average indebtedness per student:* $31,082. *Average need-based loan:* Freshmen: $3636. Undergraduates: $5436. *Parent loans:* $5,657,620 (89% need-based, 11% non-need-based). *Programs:* Federal Direct (Subsidized and Unsubsidized Stafford, PLUS), Perkins.

WORK-STUDY *Federal work-study:* Total amount: $530,572; 239 jobs averaging $2320.

ATHLETIC AWARDS Total amount: $4,848,450 (59% need-based, 41% non-need-based).

APPLYING FOR FINANCIAL AID *Required financial aid form:* FAFSA. *Financial aid deadline (priority):* 3/1. *Notification date:* Continuous beginning 3/1.

CONTACT Ms. Tiffany Summers, Director of Financial Aid, Lipscomb University, One University Park Drive, Nashville, TN 37204-3951, 615-966-1791 or toll-free 877-582-4766. *Fax:* 615-966-7640. *E-mail:* tiffany.summers@lipscomb.edu. *Website:* http://www.lipscomb.edu/.

LIVINGSTONE COLLEGE
Salisbury, NC

CONTACT Mrs. Terry Jefferies, Financial Aid Director, Livingstone College, 701 West Monroe Street, Price Building, Salisbury, NC 28144-5298, 704-216-6069 or toll-free 800-835-3435. *Fax:* 704-216-6319. *E-mail:* tjefferies@livingstone.edu. *Website:* http://www.livingstone.edu/.

LOCK HAVEN UNIVERSITY OF PENNSYLVANIA
Lock Haven, PA

Tuition & fees (PA res): $10,229	Average undergraduate aid package: $8046

ABOUT THE INSTITUTION State-supported, coed. *Awards:* associate, bachelor's, and master's degrees. 40 undergraduate majors. *Total enrollment:* 4,220. Undergraduates: 3,845. Freshmen: 828. Federal methodology is used as a basis for awarding need-based institutional aid.

UNDERGRADUATE EXPENSES for 2016–2017 *Application fee:* $25. *Tuition, state resident:* full-time $7238; part-time $302 per credit hour. *Tuition, nonresident:* full-time $16,096; part-time $671 per credit hour. *Required fees:* full-time $2991; $156.35 per credit hour. Full-time tuition and fees vary according to course load, location, and program. Part-time tuition and fees vary according to course load, location, and program. *College room and board:* $9588; *Room only:* $6144. Room and board charges vary according to board plan and housing facility.

FRESHMAN FINANCIAL AID (Fall 2016, est.) 779 applied for aid; of those 86% were deemed to have need. 99% of freshmen with need received aid; of those 96% had need fully met. *Average percent of need met:* 70% (excluding resources awarded to replace EFC). *Average financial aid package:* $5916 (excluding resources awarded to replace EFC). 2% of all full-time freshmen had no need and received non-need-based gift aid.

UNDERGRADUATE FINANCIAL AID (Fall 2016, est.) 3,095 applied for aid; of those 85% were deemed to have need. 98% of undergraduates with need received aid; of those 94% had need fully met. *Average percent of need met:* 73% (excluding resources awarded to replace EFC). *Average financial aid package:* $8046 (excluding resources awarded to replace EFC). 1% of all full-time undergraduates had no need and received non-need-based gift aid.

GIFT AID (NEED-BASED) *Total amount:* $12,756,091 (53% federal, 40% state, 7% institutional). *Receiving aid:* Freshmen: 57% (470); all full-time undergraduates: 52% (1,827). *Average award:* Freshmen: $3027; Undergraduates: $6187. *Scholarships, grants, and awards:* Federal Pell, FSEOG, state, private, college/university gift aid from institutional funds.

GIFT AID (NON-NEED-BASED) *Total amount:* $1,261,870 (3% federal, 44% institutional, 53% external sources). *Receiving aid:* Freshmen: 20% (165). Undergraduates: 9% (317). *Average award:* Freshmen: $1852. Undergraduates: $1486. *Scholarships, grants, and awards by category:* Academic interests/achievement: 455 awards ($507,635 total): biological sciences, business, communication, computer science, education, English, foreign languages, general academic interests/achievements, health fields, international studies, library science, mathematics, physical sciences, premedicine, social sciences. Creative arts/performance: 14 awards ($5250 total): art/fine arts, journalism/publications, music, performing arts. Special achievements/activities: 50 awards ($71,125 total): community service, general special achievements/activities, leadership, memberships. Special characteristics: 53 awards ($50,925 total): adult students, ethnic background, handicapped students, international students, local/state students, married students, members of minority groups, previous college experience. *Tuition waivers:* Full or partial for minority students, employees or children of employees, senior citizens. *ROTC:* Army.

LOANS *Student loans:* $38,073,909 (29% need-based, 71% non-need-based). 93% of past graduating class borrowed through all loan programs. *Average indebtedness per student:* $34,192. *Average need-based loan:* Freshmen: $3332. Undergraduates: $4258. *Parent loans:* $6,009,231 (100% non-need-based). *Programs:* Federal Direct (Subsidized and Unsubsidized Stafford, PLUS), Perkins, college/university, alternative loans.

WORK-STUDY *Federal work-study:* Total amount: $201,746; 244 jobs averaging $649. *State or other work-study/employment:* Total amount: $250,000 (100% non-need-based). 330 part-time jobs averaging $1350.

ATHLETIC AWARDS Total amount: $598,518 (100% non-need-based).

APPLYING FOR FINANCIAL AID *Required financial aid forms:* FAFSA, state aid form. *Financial aid deadline (priority):* 3/15. *Notification date:* Continuous beginning 3/20. Students must reply within 2 weeks of notification.

CONTACT Robert Fryer, Director of Financial Aid, Lock Haven University of Pennsylvania, 401 North Fairview Street, 223 Ulmer Hall, Lock Haven, PA 17745-2390, 570-484-2452 or toll-free 800-332-8900 (in-state), 800-233-8978 (out-of-state). *Fax:* 570-484-2918. *E-mail:* rcf138@lhup.edu. *Website:* http://www.lhup.edu/.

LOGAN UNIVERSITY
Chesterfield, MO

Tuition & fees: $6760	Average undergraduate aid package: $10,203

ABOUT THE INSTITUTION Independent, coed. *Awards:* bachelor's, master's, and doctoral degrees. 2 undergraduate majors. *Total enrollment:* 1,136. Undergraduates: 131. Federal methodology is used as a basis for awarding need-based institutional aid.

UNDERGRADUATE EXPENSES for 2016–2017 *Application fee:* $25. *Tuition:* full-time $6600; part-time $275 per credit hour. *Required fees:* full-time $160; $80 per term. Full-time tuition and fees vary according to course load, degree level, and program. Part-time tuition and fees vary according to course load, degree level, and program.

UNDERGRADUATE FINANCIAL AID (Fall 2016, est.) 45 applied for aid; of those 98% were deemed to have need. 100% of undergraduates with need received aid; of those 5% had need fully met. *Average percent of need met:* 28% (excluding resources awarded to replace EFC). *Average financial aid package:* $10,203 (excluding resources awarded to replace EFC).

GIFT AID (NEED-BASED) *Total amount:* $178,832 (97% federal, 3% state). *Receiving aid:* All full-time undergraduates: 60% (27). *Average award:* Undergraduates: $4616. *Scholarships, grants, and awards:* Federal Pell, FSEOG, state, private.

GIFT AID (NON-NEED-BASED) *Tuition waivers:* Full or partial for employees or children of employees.

LOANS *Student loans:* $886,347 (88% need-based, 12% non-need-based). *Average need-based loan:* Undergraduates: $7216. *Parent loans:* $3439 (100% need-based). *Programs:* Federal Direct (Subsidized and Unsubsidized Stafford, PLUS), Perkins.

WORK-STUDY *Federal work-study:* Total amount: $18,219; 7 jobs averaging $2603.

APPLYING FOR FINANCIAL AID *Required financial aid form:* FAFSA. *Financial aid deadline:* Continuous. *Notification date:* Continuous beginning 3/1. Students must reply within 2 weeks of notification.

CONTACT Kerry R. Hallahan, Director of Financial Aid, Logan University, 1851 Schoettler Road, Chesterfield, MO 63017, 636-230-1741 or toll-free 800-533-9210. *E-mail:* kerry.hallahan@logan.edu.
Website: http://www.logan.edu/.

LOMA LINDA UNIVERSITY
Loma Linda, CA

CONTACT Verdell Schaefer, Director of Financial Aid, Loma Linda University, 11139 Anderson Street, Loma Linda, CA 92350, 909-558-4509 or toll-free 800-422-4558. *Fax:* 909-558-4879. *E-mail:* finaid@univ.llu.edu.
Website: http://www.llu.edu/.

LONG ISLAND UNIVERSITY–LIU BROOKLYN
Brooklyn, NY

Tuition & fees: $36,256	Average undergraduate aid package: $20,506

ABOUT THE INSTITUTION Independent, coed. *Awards:* certificates, associate, bachelor's, master's, and doctoral degrees. 57 undergraduate majors. *Total enrollment:* 8,170. Undergraduates: 4,661. Freshmen: 834. Both federal and institutional methodology are used as a basis for awarding need-based institutional aid.

UNDERGRADUATE EXPENSES for 2016–2017 *Application fee:* $50. *Comprehensive fee:* $49,682 includes full-time tuition ($34,352), mandatory fees ($1904), and room and board ($13,426). Full-time tuition and fees vary according to program. Room and board charges vary according to board plan and housing facility.

Part-time tuition: $1072 per credit. *Part-time fees:* $451 per term. Part-time tuition and fees vary according to program.

FRESHMAN FINANCIAL AID (Fall 2016, est.) 667 applied for aid; of those 94% were deemed to have need. 98% of freshmen with need received aid; of those 5% had need fully met. *Average percent of need met:* 55% (excluding resources awarded to replace EFC). *Average financial aid package:* $22,880 (excluding resources awarded to replace EFC). 6% of all full-time freshmen had no need and received non-need-based gift aid.

UNDERGRADUATE FINANCIAL AID (Fall 2016, est.) 3,578 applied for aid; of those 96% were deemed to have need. 94% of undergraduates with need received aid, of those 5% had need fully met. *Average percent of need met:* 50% (excluding resources awarded to replace EFC). *Average financial aid package:* $20,506 (excluding resources awarded to replace EFC). 4% of all full-time undergraduates had no need and received non-need-based gift aid.

GIFT AID (NEED-BASED) *Total amount:* $33,852,416 (35% federal, 26% state, 39% institutional). *Receiving aid:* Freshmen: 73% (516); all full-time undergraduates: 74% (2,785). *Average award:* Freshmen: $13,701; Undergraduates: $11,883. *Scholarships, grants, and awards:* Federal Pell, FSEOG, state, private, college/university gift aid from institutional funds, United Negro College Fund, Scholarships for Disadvantaged Students (SDS).

GIFT AID (NON-NEED-BASED) *Total amount:* $19,727,256 (3% federal, 95% institutional, 2% external sources). *Receiving aid:* Freshmen: 54% (382). Undergraduates: 51% (1,908). *Average award:* Freshmen: $14,659. Undergraduates: $12,577. *Scholarships, grants, and awards by category:* Academic interests/achievement: general academic interests/achievements, home economics, international studies. Creative arts/performance: art/fine arts, cinema/film/broadcasting, creative writing, dance, journalism/publications, music, performing arts, theater/drama. Special achievements/activities: cheerleading/drum major, general special achievements/activities. Special characteristics: children and siblings of alumni, children of current students, children of educators, children of faculty/staff, general special characteristics, international students, siblings of current students, spouses of current students, twins, veterans, veterans' children. *Tuition waivers:* Full or partial for employees or children of employees. *ROTC:* Army cooperative.

LOANS *Student loans:* $27,617,184 (39% need-based, 61% non-need-based). 84% of past graduating class borrowed through all loan programs. *Average indebtedness per student:* $43,243. *Average need-based loan:* Freshmen: $3591. Undergraduates: $4561. *Parent loans:* $17,504,525 (100% non-need-based). *Programs:* Federal Direct (Subsidized and Unsubsidized Stafford, PLUS), Perkins, Health Professions Student Loans (HPSL).

WORK-STUDY *Federal work-study:* Total amount: $883,265; 437 jobs averaging $2168.

ATHLETIC AWARDS Total amount: $7,058,624 (100% non-need-based).

APPLYING FOR FINANCIAL AID *Required financial aid forms:* FAFSA, state aid form. *Financial aid deadline:* Continuous. *Notification date:* Continuous beginning 2/15. Students must reply by 5/1 or within 2 weeks of notification.

CONTACT Ms. Margaret Nelson, Executive Director of Enrollment Services, Long Island University–LIU Brooklyn, 1 University Plaza, Brooklyn, NY 11201-8423, 718-488-1037 or toll-free 800-LIU-PLAN. *Fax:* 718-488-3343. *E-mail:* brooklyn-enrollmentservices@liu.edu.
Website: http://www.liu.edu/.

LONG ISLAND UNIVERSITY–LIU POST
Brookville, NY

Tuition & fees: $36,256	Average undergraduate aid package: $21,316

ABOUT THE INSTITUTION Independent, coed. *Awards:* certificates, associate, bachelor's, master's, and doctoral degrees. 77 undergraduate majors. *Total enrollment:* 8,623. Undergraduates: 6,224. Freshmen: 530. Federal methodology is used as a basis for awarding need-based institutional aid.

UNDERGRADUATE EXPENSES for 2016–2017 *Application fee:* $50. *Comprehensive fee:* $49,682 includes full-time tuition ($34,352), mandatory fees ($1904), and room and board ($13,426). Full-time tuition and fees vary according to program. Room and board charges vary according to board plan and housing facility. *Part-time tuition:* $1072 per credit. *Part-time fees:* $451 per term. Part-time tuition and fees vary according to program.

FRESHMAN FINANCIAL AID (Fall 2016, est.) 487 applied for aid; of those 84% were deemed to have need. 98% of freshmen with need received aid; of those 19% had need fully met. *Average percent of need met:* 58% (excluding resources awarded to replace EFC). *Average financial aid package:* $23,466 (excluding resources awarded to replace EFC). 16% of all full-time freshmen had no need and received non-need-based gift aid.

UNDERGRADUATE FINANCIAL AID (Fall 2016, est.) 2,490 applied for aid; of those 86% were deemed to have need. 94% of undergraduates with need received aid; of those 13% had need fully met. *Average percent of need met:* 55% (excluding resources awarded to replace EFC). *Average financial aid package:* $21,316 (excluding resources awarded to replace EFC). 12% of all full-time undergraduates had no need and received non-need-based gift aid.

GIFT AID (NEED-BASED) *Total amount:* $13,591,996 (38% federal, 26% state, 36% institutional). *Receiving aid:* Freshmen: 46% (244); all full-time undergraduates: 48% (1,377). *Average award:* Freshmen: $9190; Undergraduates: $9647. *Scholarships, grants, and awards:* Federal Pell, FSEOG, state, private, college/university gift aid from institutional funds, Scholarships for Disadvantaged Students (SDS).

GIFT AID (NON-NEED-BASED) *Total amount:* $22,393,088 (1% state, 98% institutional, 1% external sources). *Receiving aid:* Freshmen: 66% (350). Undergraduates: 51% (1,460). *Average award:* Freshmen: $14,635. Undergraduates: $13,089. *Scholarships, grants, and awards by category:* Academic interests/achievement: business, general academic interests/achievements, home economics, international studies. Creative arts/performance: art/fine arts, cinema/film/broadcasting, creative writing, dance, journalism/publications, music, performing arts, theater/drama. Special achievements/activities: cheerleading/drum major, general special achievements/activities. Special characteristics: children and siblings of alumni, children of current students, children of educators, children of faculty/staff, general special characteristics, international students, siblings of current students, spouses of current students, twins, veterans, veterans' children. *Tuition waivers:* Full or partial for employees or children of employees. *ROTC:* Army cooperative.

LOANS *Student loans:* $17,026,338 (38% need-based, 62% non-need-based). 62% of past graduating class borrowed through all loan programs. *Average indebtedness per student:* $35,102. *Average need-based loan:* Freshmen: $3435. Undergraduates: $4751. *Parent loans:* $14,663,865 (100% non-need-based). *Programs:* Federal Direct (Subsidized and Unsubsidized Stafford, PLUS), Perkins.

WORK-STUDY *Federal work-study:* Total amount: $933,816; 489 jobs averaging $2029.

ATHLETIC AWARDS Total amount: $6,208,422 (100% non-need-based).

APPLYING FOR FINANCIAL AID *Required financial aid forms:* FAFSA, state aid form. *Financial aid deadline:* Continuous. *Notification date:* Continuous beginning 2/15. Students must reply by 5/1 or within 2 weeks of notification.

CONTACT Ms. Joanne Graziano, Executive Director of Enrollment Services, Long Island University–LIU Post, 720 Northern Boulevard, Brookville, NY 11548-1300, 516-299-2553 or toll-free 800-LIU-PLAN. *Fax:* 516-299-3833. *E-mail:* post-enrollmentservices@liu.edu. *Website:* http://www.liu.edu/.

LONGWOOD UNIVERSITY
Farmville, VA

Tuition & fees (VA res): $12,240	Average undergraduate aid package: $14,059

ABOUT THE INSTITUTION State-supported, coed. *Awards:* certificates, bachelor's, and master's degrees. 25 undergraduate majors. *Total enrollment:* 4,883. Undergraduates: 4,386. Freshmen: 929. Federal methodology is used as a basis for awarding need-based institutional aid.

UNDERGRADUATE EXPENSES for 2016–2017 *Application fee:* $50. *Tuition, state resident:* full-time $7350; part-time $245 per credit. *Tuition, nonresident:* full-time $21,780; part-time $706 per credit. *Required fees:* full-time $4890; $163 per credit hour. Full-time tuition and fees vary according to course load and program. Part-time tuition and fees vary according to course load and program. *College room and board:* $10,685; *Room only:* $6650. Room and board charges vary according to board plan, housing facility, and location.

FRESHMAN FINANCIAL AID (Fall 2015) 872 applied for aid; of those 70% were deemed to have need. 96% of freshmen with need received aid; of those 41% had need fully met. *Average percent of need met:* 77% (excluding resources awarded to replace EFC). *Average financial aid package:* $13,539 (excluding resources

awarded to replace EFC). 7% of all full-time freshmen had no need and received non-need-based gift aid.

UNDERGRADUATE FINANCIAL AID (Fall 2015) 3,102 applied for aid; of those 76% were deemed to have need. 97% of undergraduates with need received aid; of those 44% had need fully met. *Average percent of need met:* 80% (excluding resources awarded to replace EFC). *Average financial aid package:* $14,059 (excluding resources awarded to replace EFC). 6% of all full-time undergraduates had no need and received non-need-based gift aid.

GIFT AID (NEED-BASED) *Total amount:* $12,972,463 (36% federal, 34% state, 24% institutional, 6% external sources). *Receiving aid:* Freshmen: 49% (507); all full-time undergraduates: 42% (1,791). *Average award:* Freshmen: $7235; Undergraduates: $7045. *Scholarships, grants, and awards:* Federal Pell, FSEOG, state, private, college/university gift aid from institutional funds.

GIFT AID (NON-NEED-BASED) *Total amount:* $2,094,506 (1% state, 71% institutional, 28% external sources). *Receiving aid:* Freshmen: 3% (33). Undergraduates: 2% (95). *Average award:* Freshmen: $3958. Undergraduates: $4283. *Scholarships, grants, and awards by category:* Academic interests/achievement: biological sciences, business, computer science, education, English, general academic interests/achievements, humanities, international studies, mathematics, military science, social sciences. Creative arts/performance: art/fine arts, music, theater/drama. Special achievements/activities: community service, leadership, memberships. Special characteristics: children and siblings of alumni, general special characteristics, local/state students. *Tuition waivers:* Full or partial for employees or children of employees, senior citizens. *ROTC:* Army.

LOANS *Student loans:* $21,113,936 (66% need-based, 34% non-need-based). 66% of past graduating class borrowed through all loan programs. *Average indebtedness per student:* $28,047. *Average need-based loan:* Freshmen: $3436. Undergraduates: $4380. *Parent loans:* $14,097,889 (32% need-based, 68% non-need-based). *Programs:* Federal Direct (Subsidized and Unsubsidized Stafford, PLUS), Perkins, private loans.

WORK-STUDY *Federal work-study:* 384 jobs averaging $1896. *State or other work-study/employment:* Part-time jobs available.

ATHLETIC AWARDS Total amount: $2,588,852 (41% need-based, 59% non-need-based).

APPLYING FOR FINANCIAL AID *Required financial aid form:* FAFSA. *Financial aid deadline (priority):* 3/1. *Notification date:* Continuous beginning 4/1. Students must reply within 4 weeks of notification.

CONTACT Ms. Terry Harris, Financial Aid Counselor, Longwood University, 201 High Street, Farmville, VA 23909, 434-395-2171 or toll-free 800-281-4677. *Fax:* 434-395-2829. *E-mail:* harristt@longwood.edu. *Website:* http://www.longwood.edu/.

LORAS COLLEGE
Dubuque, IA

Tuition & fees: $32,886	Average undergraduate aid package: $26,390

ABOUT THE INSTITUTION Independent Roman Catholic, coed. *Awards:* certificates, bachelor's, and master's degrees. 35 undergraduate majors. *Total enrollment:* 1,524. Undergraduates: 1,463. Freshmen: 328. Federal methodology is used as a basis for awarding need-based institutional aid.

UNDERGRADUATE EXPENSES for 2017–2018 *Comprehensive fee:* $40,726 includes full-time tuition ($31,418), mandatory fees ($1468), and room and board ($7840). *College room only:* $4000. Full-time tuition and fees vary according to course load and degree level. Room and board charges vary according to board plan and housing facility. *Part-time tuition:* $610 per credit. *Part-time fees:* $35 per credit.

FRESHMAN FINANCIAL AID (Fall 2016, est.) 305 applied for aid; of those 84% were deemed to have need. 100% of freshmen with need received aid; of those 34% had need fully met. *Average percent of need met:* 90% (excluding resources awarded to replace EFC). *Average financial aid package:* $27,644 (excluding resources awarded to replace EFC). 22% of all full-time freshmen had no need and received non-need-based gift aid.

UNDERGRADUATE FINANCIAL AID (Fall 2016, est.) 1,190 applied for aid; of those 86% were deemed to have need. 100% of undergraduates with need received aid; of those 35% had need fully met. *Average percent of need met:* 89% (excluding resources awarded to replace EFC). *Average financial aid package:*

$26,390 (excluding resources awarded to replace EFC). 27% of all full-time undergraduates had no need and received non-need-based gift aid.

GIFT AID (NEED-BASED) *Total amount:* $20,586,226 (8% federal, 8% state, 84% institutional). *Receiving aid:* Freshmen: 78% (255); all full-time undergraduates: 73% (1,026). *Average award:* Freshmen: $21,464; Undergraduates: $20,037. *Scholarships, grants, and awards:* Federal Pell, FSEOG, state, private, college/university gift aid from institutional funds.

GIFT AID (NON-NEED-BASED) *Total amount:* $8,402,479 (98% institutional, 2% external sources). *Receiving aid:* Freshmen: 20% (66). Undergraduates: 16% (218). *Average award:* Freshmen: $18,877. Undergraduates: $17,841. *Scholarships, grants, and awards by category:* Academic interests/achievement: 1,275 awards ($20,476,338 total): biological sciences, business, communication, computer science, education, engineering/technologies, English, general academic interests/ achievements, home economics, mathematics, physical sciences, premedicine, religion/ biblical studies. *Creative arts/performance:* 87 awards ($91,350 total): music. *Tuition waivers:* Full or partial for employees or children of employees. *ROTC:* Army cooperative.

LOANS *Student loans:* $8,147,524 (45% need-based, 55% non-need-based). 80% of past graduating class borrowed through all loan programs. *Average indebtedness per student:* $34,775. *Average need-based loan:* Freshmen: $4528. Undergraduates: $5261. *Parent loans:* $1,559,963 (100% non-need-based). *Programs:* Federal Direct (Subsidized and Unsubsidized Stafford, PLUS), Perkins, college/university.

WORK-STUDY *Federal work-study:* Total amount: $1,227,970; 507 jobs averaging $2422. *State or other work-study/employment:* Total amount: $5000 (40% need-based, 60% non-need-based). Part-time jobs available.

APPLYING FOR FINANCIAL AID *Required financial aid form:* FAFSA. *Financial aid deadline (priority):* 3/1. *Notification date:* Continuous beginning 3/1. Students must reply within 3 weeks of notification.

CONTACT Ms. Julie A. Dunn, Director of Financial Planning, Loras College, 1450 Alta Vista Street, Dubuque, IA 52001-4327, 563-588-7136 or toll-free 800-245-6727. *Fax:* 563-588-7119. *E-mail:* julie.dunn@loras.edu.
Website: http://www.loras.edu/.

LOS ANGELES FILM SCHOOL
Hollywood, CA

CONTACT Financial Aid Office, Los Angeles Film School, 6363 Sunset Boulevard, Hollywood, CA 90028, 323-860-0789 or toll-free 877-952-3456.
Website: http://www.lafilm.edu/.

LOUISIANA COLLEGE
Pineville, LA

ABOUT THE INSTITUTION Independent Southern Baptist, coed. *Awards:* associate, bachelor's, and master's degrees. 64 undergraduate majors. *Total enrollment:* 1,093. Undergraduates: 909. Freshmen: 248.

GIFT AID (NEED-BASED) *Scholarships, grants, and awards:* Federal Pell, FSEOG, state, private, college/university gift aid from institutional funds.

GIFT AID (NON-NEED-BASED) *Scholarships, grants, and awards by category:* Academic interests/achievement: business, general academic interests/achievements, health fields, religion/biblical studies. *Creative arts/performance:* music, performing arts, theater/drama. *Special achievements/activities:* leadership. *Special characteristics:* children of faculty/staff.

LOANS *Programs:* Federal Direct (Subsidized and Unsubsidized Stafford, PLUS).

WORK-STUDY *Federal work-study:* jobs available.

APPLYING FOR FINANCIAL AID *Required financial aid forms:* FAFSA, institution's own form.

CONTACT David Barnard, Director of Financial Aid, Louisiana College, 1140 College Drive, Pineville, LA 71359-0001, 318-487-7387 or toll-free 800-487-1906. *Fax:* 318-487-7449. *E-mail:* david.barnard@lacollege.edu.
Website: http://www.lacollege.edu/.

LOUISIANA STATE UNIVERSITY AND AGRICULTURAL & MECHANICAL COLLEGE
Baton Rouge, LA

Tuition & fees (LA res): $10,814   Average undergraduate aid package: $16,020

ABOUT THE INSTITUTION State-supported, coed. *Awards:* certificates, bachelor's, master's, and doctoral degrees. 69 undergraduate majors. *Total enrollment:* 31,409. Undergraduates: 26,118. Freshmen: 5,475. Federal methodology is used as a basis for awarding need-based institutional aid.

UNDERGRADUATE EXPENSES for 2016–2017 *Application fee:* $40. *Tuition, state resident:* full-time $8038. *Tuition, nonresident:* full-time $24,715. *Required fees:* full-time $2776. Full-time tuition and fees vary according to course load. Part-time tuition and fees vary according to course load. *College room and board:* $11,540; *Room only:* $7530. Room and board charges vary according to board plan and housing facility.

FRESHMAN FINANCIAL AID (Fall 2015) 4,135 applied for aid; of those 70% were deemed to have need. 99% of freshmen with need received aid; of those 24% had need fully met. *Average percent of need met:* 71% (excluding resources awarded to replace EFC). *Average financial aid package:* $16,340 (excluding resources awarded to replace EFC). 17% of all full-time freshmen had no need and received non-need-based gift aid.

UNDERGRADUATE FINANCIAL AID (Fall 2015) 14,289 applied for aid; of those 76% were deemed to have need. 98% of undergraduates with need received aid; of those 21% had need fully met. *Average percent of need met:* 66% (excluding resources awarded to replace EFC). *Average financial aid package:* $16,020 (excluding resources awarded to replace EFC). 15% of all full-time undergraduates had no need and received non-need-based gift aid.

GIFT AID (NEED-BASED) *Total amount:* $105,231,669 (24% federal, 43% state, 31% institutional, 2% external sources). *Receiving aid:* Freshmen: 49% (2,768); all full-time undergraduates: 40% (9,308). *Average award:* Freshmen: $11,465; Undergraduates: $11,020. *Scholarships, grants, and awards:* Federal Pell, FSEOG, state, private, college/university gift aid from institutional funds.

GIFT AID (NON-NEED-BASED) *Total amount:* $73,334,579 (2% federal, 67% state, 23% institutional, 8% external sources). *Receiving aid:* Freshmen: 2% (113). Undergraduates: 1% (281). *Average award:* Freshmen: $4824. Undergraduates: $4299. *Scholarships, grants, and awards by category:* Academic interests/ achievement: 1,083 awards ($1,207,247 total): agriculture, architecture, biological sciences, business, computer science, education, engineering/technologies, English, foreign languages, general academic interests/achievements, health fields, humanities, mathematics, physical sciences. *Creative arts/performance:* 99 awards ($216,916 total): applied art and design, art/fine arts, journalism/publications, music, performing arts, theater/drama. *Special characteristics:* 944 awards ($10,085,183 total): children with a deceased or disabled parent, general special characteristics, out-of-state students, veterans. *Tuition waivers:* Full or partial for employees or children of employees. *ROTC:* Army, Naval cooperative, Air Force.

LOANS *Student loans:* $81,405,534 (70% need-based, 30% non-need-based). 42% of past graduating class borrowed through all loan programs. *Average indebtedness per student:* $24,699. *Average need-based loan:* Freshmen: $5513. Undergraduates: $6725. *Parent loans:* $42,111,125 (46% need-based, 54% non-need-based). *Programs:* Federal Direct (Subsidized and Unsubsidized Stafford, PLUS), Perkins, college/university.

WORK-STUDY *Federal work-study:* 786 jobs averaging $2000. *State or other work-study/employment:* Total amount: $13,178,608 (34% need-based, 66% non-need-based). 4,918 part-time jobs averaging $2300.

ATHLETIC AWARDS Total amount: $12,546,486 (36% need-based, 64% non-need-based).

APPLYING FOR FINANCIAL AID *Required financial aid forms:* FAFSA, institution's own form. *Financial aid deadline (priority):* 4/1. *Notification date:* Continuous beginning 12/15. Students must reply by 5/1.

CONTACT Ms. Amy Marix, Director of Financial Aid and Scholarships, Louisiana State University and Agricultural & Mechanical College, 1146 Pleasant Hall, Baton Rouge, LA 70803, 225-578-3103. *Fax:* 225-578-6300. *E-mail:* financialaid@lsu.edu. *Website:* http://www.lsu.edu/.

LOUISIANA STATE UNIVERSITY AT ALEXANDRIA
Alexandria, LA

CONTACT Financial Aid Office, Louisiana State University at Alexandria, 8100 Highway 71 South, Alexandria, LA 71302-9121, 318-445-3672 or toll-free 888-473-6417.
Website: http://www.lsua.edu/.

LOUISIANA STATE UNIVERSITY HEALTH SCIENCES CENTER
New Orleans, LA

CONTACT Mr. Patrick Gorman, Director of Financial Aid, Louisiana State University Health Sciences Center, 433 Bolivar Street, New Orleans, LA 70112, 504-568-4821. *Fax:* 504-599-1390.
Website: http://www.lsuhsc.edu/.

LOUISIANA STATE UNIVERSITY IN SHREVEPORT
Shreveport, LA

Tuition & fees (LA res): $7339 — **Average undergraduate aid package: N/A**

ABOUT THE INSTITUTION State-supported, coed. *Awards:* certificates, bachelor's, master's, and doctoral degrees. 32 undergraduate majors. *Total enrollment:* 4,428. Undergraduates: 2,776. Freshmen: 357. Federal methodology is used as a basis for awarding need-based institutional aid.

UNDERGRADUATE EXPENSES for 2016–2017 *Application fee:* $20. *Tuition, state resident:* full-time $5806; part-time $235.67 per credit hour. *Tuition, nonresident:* full-time $9480; part-time $783.73 per credit hour. *Required fees:* full-time $1533; $62.11 per credit hour. Full-time tuition and fees vary according to course load. Part-time tuition and fees vary according to course load.

GIFT AID (NEED-BASED) *Total amount:* $7,120,635 (61% federal, 13% state, 23% institutional, 3% external sources). *Receiving aid:* Freshmen: 48% (170); all full-time undergraduates: 43% (1,048). *Average award:* Freshmen: $4559; Undergraduates: $4174. *Scholarships, grants, and awards:* Federal Pell, FSEOG, state, private, college/university gift aid from institutional funds.

GIFT AID (NON-NEED-BASED) *Total amount:* $3,513,951 (100% state). *Receiving aid:* Freshmen: 77% (276). Undergraduates: 37% (909). *Scholarships, grants, and awards by category: Academic interests/achievement:* biological sciences, business, computer science, education, English, general academic interests/achievements, humanities, physical sciences, premedicine, social sciences. *Tuition waivers:* Full or partial for employees or children of employees. *ROTC:* Army.

LOANS *Student loans:* $7,792,323 (52% need-based, 48% non-need-based). *Parent loans:* $212,542 (100% need-based). *Programs:* Federal Direct (Subsidized and Unsubsidized Stafford, PLUS).

WORK-STUDY *Federal work-study:* 38 jobs averaging $2804.

ATHLETIC AWARDS Total amount: $208,684 (100% need-based).

APPLYING FOR FINANCIAL AID *Required financial aid form:* FAFSA. *Financial aid deadline (priority):* 5/1. *Notification date:* Continuous beginning 7/15.

CONTACT Office of Student Financial Aid, Louisiana State University in Shreveport, One University Place, Shreveport, LA 71115-2399, 318-797-5363 or toll-free 800-229-5957. *Fax:* 318-797-5366. *E-mail:* finaid@lsus.edu.
Website: http://www.lsus.edu/.

LOUISIANA TECH UNIVERSITY
Ruston, LA

Tuition & fees (LA res): $9117 — **Average undergraduate aid package: $11,606**

ABOUT THE INSTITUTION State-supported, coed. *Awards:* certificates, associate, bachelor's, master's, and doctoral degrees. 79 undergraduate majors. *Total enrollment:* 12,672. Undergraduates: 11,281. Freshmen: 2,018. Federal methodology is used as a basis for awarding need-based institutional aid.

UNDERGRADUATE EXPENSES for 2016–2017 *Application fee:* $20. *Tuition, state resident:* full-time $6401; part-time $380 per credit hour. *Tuition, nonresident:* full-time $23,135; part-time $1077 per credit hour. *Required fees:* full-time $2716. Full-time tuition and fees vary according to course load, location, and program. Part-time tuition and fees vary according to course load, location, and program. *College room and board:* $5925. Room and board charges vary according to board plan and housing facility.

FRESHMAN FINANCIAL AID (Fall 2015) 1,828 applied for aid; of those 65% were deemed to have need. 99% of freshmen with need received aid; of those 27% had need fully met. *Average percent of need met:* 86% (excluding resources awarded to replace EFC). *Average financial aid package:* $12,283 (excluding resources awarded to replace EFC). 28% of all full-time freshmen had no need and received non-need-based gift aid.

UNDERGRADUATE FINANCIAL AID (Fall 2015) 5,887 applied for aid; of those 68% were deemed to have need. 98% of undergraduates with need received aid; of those 22% had need fully met. *Average percent of need met:* 81% (excluding resources awarded to replace EFC). *Average financial aid package:* $11,606 (excluding resources awarded to replace EFC). 24% of all full-time undergraduates had no need and received non-need-based gift aid.

GIFT AID (NEED-BASED) *Total amount:* $28,272,895 (33% federal, 43% state, 21% institutional, 3% external sources). *Receiving aid:* Freshmen: 60% (1,155); all full-time undergraduates: 53% (3,697). *Average award:* Freshmen: $10,983; Undergraduates: $10,040. *Scholarships, grants, and awards:* Federal Pell, FSEOG, state, private, college/university gift aid from institutional funds.

GIFT AID (NON-NEED-BASED) *Total amount:* $20,572,695 (57% state, 39% institutional, 4% external sources). *Receiving aid:* Freshmen: 15% (298). Undergraduates: 12% (823). *Average award:* Freshmen: $3966. Undergraduates: $4030. *Scholarships, grants, and awards by category: Academic interests/achievement:* agriculture, architecture, biological sciences, business, computer science, education, engineering/technologies, English, foreign languages, general academic interests/achievements, health fields, home economics, international studies, mathematics, military science, physical sciences, social sciences. *Creative arts/performance:* applied art and design, art/fine arts, creative writing, debating, general creative arts/performance, journalism/publications, music, performing arts, theater/drama. *Special achievements/activities:* cheerleading/drum major, junior miss. *Special characteristics:* children and siblings of alumni, children of faculty/staff, children of public servants, handicapped students, international students, members of minority groups, out-of-state students, spouses of deceased or disabled public servants, veterans, veterans' children. *Tuition waivers:* Full or partial for children of alumni, employees or children of employees, senior citizens. *ROTC:* Army cooperative, Air Force.

LOANS *Student loans:* $21,290,492 (67% need-based, 33% non-need-based). 49% of past graduating class borrowed through all loan programs. *Average indebtedness per student:* $23,001. *Average need-based loan:* Freshmen: $2787. Undergraduates: $3506. *Parent loans:* $6,476,860 (34% need-based, 66% non-need-based). *Programs:* Federal Direct (Subsidized and Unsubsidized Stafford, PLUS), Perkins, private loans.

WORK-STUDY *Federal work-study:* 297 jobs averaging $1753. *State or other work-study/employment:* Total amount: $2,588,288 (100% non-need-based). 1,172 part-time jobs averaging $2159.

ATHLETIC AWARDS Total amount: $4,857,112 (49% need-based, 51% non-need-based).

APPLYING FOR FINANCIAL AID *Required financial aid forms:* FAFSA, institution's own form. *Financial aid deadline (priority):* 4/15. *Notification date:* Continuous beginning 3/1. Students must reply within 3 weeks of notification.

CONTACT Aimee D. Baxter, Office of Financial Aid, Louisiana Tech University, PO Box 7925, Ruston, LA 71272, 318-257-2641 or toll-free 800-528-3241. *Fax:* 318-257-2628. *E-mail:* techaid@latech.edu.
Website: http://www.latech.edu/.

LOURDES UNIVERSITY
Sylvania, OH

CONTACT Deb LaJeunesse, Director of Financial Aid, Lourdes University, 6832 Convent Boulevard, Sylvania, OH 43560-2898, 419-824-3732 or toll-free 800-878-3210. *Fax:* 419-517-8866. *E-mail:* finaid@lourdes.edu. *Website:* http://www.lourdes.edu/.

LOYOLA MARYMOUNT UNIVERSITY
Los Angeles, CA

Tuition & fees: $44,230	Average undergraduate aid package: $29,049

ABOUT THE INSTITUTION Independent Roman Catholic, coed. *Awards:* certificates, bachelor's, master's, and doctoral degrees. 50 undergraduate majors. *Total enrollment:* 9,330. Undergraduates: 6,261. Freshmen: 1,331. Both federal and institutional methodology are used as a basis for awarding need-based institutional aid.

UNDERGRADUATE EXPENSES for 2016–2017 One-time required fee: $250. *Comprehensive fee:* $58,715 includes full-time tuition ($43,526), mandatory fees ($704), and room and board ($14,485). *College room only:* $10,085. Full-time tuition and fees vary according to reciprocity agreements. Room and board charges vary according to board plan and housing facility. *Part-time tuition:* $1816 per credit hour. *Part-time fees:* $8 per unit; $64 per term. Part-time tuition and fees vary according to course load.

FRESHMAN FINANCIAL AID (Fall 2015) 1,059 applied for aid; of those 70% were deemed to have need. 99% of freshmen with need received aid; of those 20% had need fully met. *Average percent of need met:* 65% (excluding resources awarded to replace EFC). *Average financial aid package:* $27,843 (excluding resources awarded to replace EFC). 31% of all full-time freshmen had no need and received non-need-based gift aid.

UNDERGRADUATE FINANCIAL AID (Fall 2015) 4,462 applied for aid; of those 74% were deemed to have need. 99% of undergraduates with need received aid; of those 20% had need fully met. *Average percent of need met:* 66% (excluding resources awarded to replace EFC). *Average financial aid package:* $29,049 (excluding resources awarded to replace EFC). 25% of all full-time undergraduates had no need and received non-need-based gift aid.

GIFT AID (NEED-BASED) Total amount: $64,939,786 (10% federal, 13% state, 76% institutional, 1% external sources). *Receiving aid:* Freshmen: 53% (715); all full-time undergraduates: 53% (3,167). *Average award:* Freshmen: $20,509; Undergraduates: $20,440. *Scholarships, grants, and awards:* Federal Pell, FSEOG, state, private, college/university gift aid from institutional funds.

GIFT AID (NON-NEED-BASED) Total amount: $19,477,321 (90% institutional, 10% external sources). *Receiving aid:* Freshmen: 7% (101). Undergraduates: 6% (374). *Average award:* Freshmen: $10,832. Undergraduates: $10,085. *Scholarships, grants, and awards by category: Academic interests/achievement:* 2,813 awards ($29,170,682 total): area/ethnic studies, biological sciences, business, communication, education, engineering/technologies, English, foreign languages, general academic interests/achievements, health fields, humanities, international studies, mathematics, physical sciences, religion/biblical studies, social sciences. *Creative arts/performance:* 68 awards ($319,866 total): applied art and design, art/fine arts, cinema/film/broadcasting, creative writing, dance, general creative arts/performance, journalism/publications, music, performing arts, theater/drama. *Special achievements/activities:* 237 awards ($2,122,919 total): community service, general special achievements/activities, leadership, memberships, religious involvement. *Special characteristics:* 449 awards ($7,561,426 total): adult students, children and siblings of alumni, children of faculty/staff, ethnic background, first-generation college students, general special characteristics, handicapped students, international students, local/state students, members of minority groups, out-of-state students, previous college experience, religious affiliation, veterans, veterans' children. *Tuition waivers:* Full or partial for employees or children of employees. *ROTC:* Army cooperative, Air Force.

LOANS Student loans: $26,666,651 (76% need-based, 24% non-need-based). 54% of past graduating class borrowed through all loan programs. *Average indebtedness per student:* $30,698. *Average need-based loan:* Freshmen: $5109. Undergraduates: $6041. *Parent loans:* $23,711,935 (49% need-based, 51% non-need-based). *Programs:* Federal Direct (Subsidized and Unsubsidized Stafford, PLUS), Perkins, college/university.

WORK-STUDY *Federal work-study:* 1,426 jobs averaging $1848. *State or other work-study/employment:* Total amount: $5,612,515 (27% need-based, 73% non-need-based). 2,300 part-time jobs averaging $2440.

ATHLETIC AWARDS Total amount: $8,167,782 (47% need-based, 53% non-need-based).

APPLYING FOR FINANCIAL AID *Required financial aid form:* FAFSA. *Financial aid deadline (priority):* 2/1. *Notification date:* Continuous beginning 12/15. Students must reply by 5/1 or within 4 weeks of notification.

CONTACT Dr. Maureen Weatherall, Vice Provost for Enrollment Management, Loyola Marymount University, One LMU Drive, Suite 270, Los Angeles, CA 90045-2659, 310-338-2753 or toll-free 800-LMU-INFO. *Fax:* 310-338-2793. *E-mail:* finaid@lmu.edu. *Website:* http://www.lmu.edu/.

LOYOLA UNIVERSITY CHICAGO
Chicago, IL

Tuition & fees: $42,828	Average undergraduate aid package: $33,514

ABOUT THE INSTITUTION Independent Roman Catholic (Jesuit), coed. *Awards:* certificates, associate, bachelor's, master's, and doctoral degrees (also offers adult part-time program with significant enrollment not reflected in profile). 84 undergraduate majors. *Total enrollment:* 16,422. Undergraduates: 11,129. Freshmen: 2,622. Federal methodology is used as a basis for awarding need-based institutional aid.

UNDERGRADUATE EXPENSES for 2017–2018 Comprehensive fee: $56,908 includes full-time tuition ($41,470), mandatory fees ($1358), and room and board ($14,080). *College room only:* $8800. Full-time tuition and fees vary according to degree level, location, program, and student level. Room and board charges vary according to board plan, housing facility, and location. *Part-time tuition:* $770 per credit. *Part-time fees:* $350 per year. Part-time tuition and fees vary according to course load.

FRESHMAN FINANCIAL AID (Fall 2016, est.) 2,219 applied for aid; of those 83% were deemed to have need. 100% of freshmen with need received aid; of those 16% had need fully met. *Average percent of need met:* 82% (excluding resources awarded to replace EFC). *Average financial aid package:* $36,209 (excluding resources awarded to replace EFC). 27% of all full-time freshmen had no need and received non-need-based gift aid.

UNDERGRADUATE FINANCIAL AID (Fall 2016, est.) 7,715 applied for aid; of those 88% were deemed to have need. 100% of undergraduates with need received aid; of those 14% had need fully met. *Average percent of need met:* 80% (excluding resources awarded to replace EFC). *Average financial aid package:* $33,514 (excluding resources awarded to replace EFC). 27% of all full-time undergraduates had no need and received non-need-based gift aid.

GIFT AID (NEED-BASED) Total amount: $132,290,319 (12% federal, 8% state, 78% institutional, 2% external sources). *Receiving aid:* Freshmen: 70% (1,829); all full-time undergraduates: 64% (6,519). *Average award:* Freshmen: $23,366; Undergraduates: $20,311. *Scholarships, grants, and awards:* Federal Pell, FSEOG, state, private, college/university gift aid from institutional funds.

GIFT AID (NON-NEED-BASED) Total amount: $49,974,677 (4% federal, 93% institutional, 3% external sources). *Receiving aid:* Freshmen: 9% (229). Undergraduates: 6% (650). *Average award:* Freshmen: $17,499. Undergraduates: $15,184. *Scholarships, grants, and awards by category: Academic interests/achievement:* 7,306 awards ($115,850,735 total): general academic interests/achievements. *Creative arts/performance:* 45 awards ($123,054 total): art/fine arts, debating, journalism/publications, music, theater/drama. *Special achievements/activities:* 371 awards ($2,872,428 total): community service, general special achievements/activities, leadership, memberships. *Special characteristics:* 1,416 awards ($3,877,157 total): adult students, general special characteristics, religious affiliation. *Tuition waivers:* Full or partial for employees or children of employees, senior citizens. *ROTC:* Army, Naval cooperative, Air Force cooperative.

LOANS Student loans: $67,766,731 (74% need-based, 26% non-need-based). 68% of past graduating class borrowed through all loan programs. *Average indebtedness per student:* $33,319. *Average need-based loan:* Freshmen: $3822. Undergraduates: $4521. *Parent loans:* $48,780,990 (55% need-based, 45% non-need-based). *Programs:* Federal Direct (Subsidized and Unsubsidized Stafford, PLUS), Perkins, Federal Nursing.

WORK-STUDY *Federal work-study:* Total amount: $14,481,780; 5,014 jobs averaging $2780.

ATHLETIC AWARDS Total amount: $4,319,660 (37% need-based, 63% non-need-based).

APPLYING FOR FINANCIAL AID *Required financial aid form:* FAFSA. *Financial aid deadline:* Continuous. *Notification date:* Continuous beginning 2/15. Students must reply within 3 weeks of notification.

CONTACT Mr. Tobyn Friar, Director of Financial Aid, Loyola University Chicago, 6525 North Sheridan Road, Chicago, IL 60660, 773-508-7704 or toll-free 800-262-2373. *Fax:* 773-508-3397. *E-mail:* nmerz@luc.edu. *Website:* http://www.luc.edu/.

LOYOLA UNIVERSITY MARYLAND
Baltimore, MD

Tuition & fees: $46,595	Average undergraduate aid package: $32,100

ABOUT THE INSTITUTION Independent Roman Catholic (Jesuit), coed. *Awards:* certificates, bachelor's, master's, and doctoral degrees. 35 undergraduate majors. *Total enrollment:* 6,084. Undergraduates: 4,104. Freshmen: 1,095. Institutional methodology is used as a basis for awarding need-based institutional aid.

UNDERGRADUATE EXPENSES for 2016–2017 *Application fee:* $60. *Comprehensive fee:* $60,465 includes full-time tuition ($45,030), mandatory fees ($1565), and room and board ($13,870). Full-time tuition and fees vary according to course load. Room and board charges vary according to board plan and housing facility. *Part-time tuition:* $730 per credit. Part-time tuition and fees vary according to course load.

FRESHMAN FINANCIAL AID (Fall 2015) 817 applied for aid; of those 80% were deemed to have need. 100% of freshmen with need received aid; of those 92% had need fully met. *Average percent of need met:* 89% (excluding resources awarded to replace EFC). *Average financial aid package:* $33,250 (excluding resources awarded to replace EFC). 21% of all full-time freshmen had no need and received non-need-based gift aid.

UNDERGRADUATE FINANCIAL AID (Fall 2015) 2,614 applied for aid; of those 85% were deemed to have need. 100% of undergraduates with need received aid; of those 93% had need fully met. *Average percent of need met:* 91% (excluding resources awarded to replace EFC). *Average financial aid package:* $32,100 (excluding resources awarded to replace EFC). 15% of all full-time undergraduates had no need and received non-need-based gift aid.

GIFT AID (NEED-BASED) *Total amount:* $57,004,467 (7% federal, 1% state, 90% institutional, 2% external sources). *Receiving aid:* Freshmen: 47% (481); all full-time undergraduates: 42% (1,695). *Average award:* Freshmen: $25,990; Undergraduates: $24,200. *Scholarships, grants, and awards:* Federal Pell, FSEOG, state, private, college/university gift aid from institutional funds.

GIFT AID (NON-NEED-BASED) *Total amount:* $14,944,059 (10% federal, 85% institutional, 5% external sources). *Receiving aid:* Freshmen: 40% (408). Undergraduates: 27% (1,088). *Average award:* Freshmen: $17,165. Undergraduates: $14,960. *Scholarships, grants, and awards by category:* Academic interests/achievement: general academic interests/achievements. *Tuition waivers:* Full or partial for employees or children of employees. *ROTC:* Army, Air Force cooperative.

LOANS *Student loans:* $24,062,249 (81% need-based, 19% non-need-based). 62% of past graduating class borrowed through all loan programs. *Average indebtedness per student:* $36,208. *Average need-based loan:* Freshmen: $6010. Undergraduates: $6750. *Parent loans:* $17,861,296 (100% non-need-based). *Programs:* Federal Direct (Subsidized and Unsubsidized Stafford, PLUS), Perkins, college/university.

WORK-STUDY *Federal work-study:* jobs available. *State or other work-study/employment:* Total amount: $1,111,000 (69% need-based, 31% non-need-based). Part-time jobs available.

ATHLETIC AWARDS Total amount: $5,472,626 (27% need-based, 73% non-need-based).

APPLYING FOR FINANCIAL AID *Required financial aid forms:* FAFSA, CSS Financial Aid PROFILE, noncustodial (divorced/separated) parent's statement. *Financial aid deadline:* 1/15. *Notification date:* 3/15. Students must reply by 5/1.

CONTACT Office of Financial Aid, Loyola University Maryland, Knott Humanities Center 211A, Baltimore, MD 21210, 410-617-2576 or toll-free 800-221-9107. *Fax:* 410-617-5149. *E-mail:* financialaid@loyola.edu. *Website:* http://www.loyola.edu/.

LOYOLA UNIVERSITY NEW ORLEANS
New Orleans, LA

Tuition & fees: $39,242	Average undergraduate aid package: $32,315

ABOUT THE INSTITUTION Independent Roman Catholic (Jesuit), coed. *Awards:* certificates, bachelor's, master's, and doctoral degrees. 56 undergraduate majors. *Total enrollment:* 3,679. Undergraduates: 2,483. Freshmen: 615. Federal methodology is used as a basis for awarding need-based institutional aid.

UNDERGRADUATE EXPENSES for 2017–2018 *One-time required fee:* $250. *Comprehensive fee:* $52,456 includes full-time tuition ($37,676), mandatory fees ($1566), and room and board ($13,214). *College room only:* $7430. Full-time tuition and fees vary according to class time, course load, and degree level. Room and board charges vary according to board plan and housing facility. *Part-time tuition:* $1073 per credit hour. *Part-time fees:* $402 per term. Part-time tuition and fees vary according to class time and degree level.

FRESHMAN FINANCIAL AID (Fall 2016, est.) 575 applied for aid; of those 85% were deemed to have need. 100% of freshmen with need received aid; of those 14% had need fully met. *Average percent of need met:* 82% (excluding resources awarded to replace EFC). *Average financial aid package:* $34,087 (excluding resources awarded to replace EFC). 19% of all full-time freshmen had no need and received non-need-based gift aid.

UNDERGRADUATE FINANCIAL AID (Fall 2016, est.) 1,837 applied for aid; of those 89% were deemed to have need. 100% of undergraduates with need received aid; of those 14% had need fully met. *Average percent of need met:* 77% (excluding resources awarded to replace EFC). *Average financial aid package:* $32,315 (excluding resources awarded to replace EFC). 23% of all full-time undergraduates had no need and received non-need-based gift aid.

GIFT AID (NEED-BASED) *Total amount:* $43,777,265 (9% federal, 7% state, 82% institutional, 2% external sources). *Receiving aid:* Freshmen: 80% (490); all full-time undergraduates: 71% (1,623). *Average award:* Freshmen: $30,311; Undergraduates: $27,988. *Scholarships, grants, and awards:* Federal Pell, FSEOG, state, private, college/university gift aid from institutional funds, United Negro College Fund.

GIFT AID (NON-NEED-BASED) *Total amount:* $11,083,269 (1% federal, 7% state, 89% institutional, 3% external sources). *Receiving aid:* Freshmen: 11% (65). Undergraduates: 8% (184). *Average award:* Freshmen: $17,357. Undergraduates: $16,161. *Scholarships, grants, and awards by category:* Academic interests/achievement: general academic interests/achievements. Creative arts/performance: art/fine arts, general creative arts/performance. Special achievements/activities: leadership. Special characteristics: children and siblings of alumni, children of faculty/staff, veterans' children. *Tuition waivers:* Full or partial for employees or children of employees, senior citizens. *ROTC:* Army cooperative, Naval cooperative, Air Force cooperative.

LOANS *Student loans:* $13,015,058 (75% need-based, 25% non-need-based). 69% of past graduating class borrowed through all loan programs. *Average indebtedness per student:* $30,524. *Average need-based loan:* Freshmen: $3308. Undergraduates: $4555. *Parent loans:* $5,092,076 (46% need-based, 54% non-need-based). *Programs:* Federal Direct (Subsidized and Unsubsidized Stafford, PLUS), Perkins.

WORK-STUDY *Federal work-study:* Total amount: $1,039,215; 692 jobs averaging $1600.

ATHLETIC AWARDS Total amount: $1,862,480 (59% need-based, 41% non-need-based).

APPLYING FOR FINANCIAL AID *Required financial aid form:* FAFSA. *Financial aid deadline (priority):* 3/1. *Notification date:* Continuous beginning 3/1.

CONTACT Ms. Carrie E. Glass, Director of Scholarships and Financial Aid, Loyola University New Orleans, 6363 St. Charles Avenue, New Orleans, LA 70118-6195, 504-865-3231 or toll-free 800-4-LOYOLA. *Fax:* 504-865-3233. *E-mail:* finaid@loyno.edu. *Website:* http://www.loyno.edu/.

LUBBOCK CHRISTIAN UNIVERSITY
Lubbock, TX

Tuition & fees: $21,166	Average undergraduate aid package: $15,385

ABOUT THE INSTITUTION Independent Church of Christ, coed. *Awards:* bachelor's and master's degrees. 61 undergraduate majors. *Total enrollment:* 1,912. Undergraduates: 1,471. Freshmen: 320. Federal methodology is used as a basis for awarding need-based institutional aid.

UNDERGRADUATE EXPENSES for 2016–2017 *Application fee:* $25. *Comprehensive fee:* $28,426 includes full-time tuition ($21,166) and room and board ($7260). Full-time tuition and fees vary according to degree level and program. Room and board charges vary according to board plan and housing facility. *Part-time tuition:* $685 per credit hour. *Part-time fees:* $60 per term. Part-time tuition and fees vary according to course load, degree level, and program.

FRESHMAN FINANCIAL AID (Fall 2016, est.) 262 applied for aid; of those 84% were deemed to have need. 100% of freshmen with need received aid; of those 11% had need fully met. *Average percent of need met:* 66% (excluding resources awarded to replace EFC). *Average financial aid package:* $15,219 (excluding resources awarded to replace EFC). 18% of all full-time freshmen had no need and received non-need-based gift aid.

UNDERGRADUATE FINANCIAL AID (Fall 2016, est.) 1,087 applied for aid; of those 87% were deemed to have need. 100% of undergraduates with need received aid; of those 9% had need fully met. *Average percent of need met:* 65% (excluding resources awarded to replace EFC). *Average financial aid package:* $15,385 (excluding resources awarded to replace EFC). 16% of all full-time undergraduates had no need and received non-need-based gift aid.

GIFT AID (NEED-BASED) *Total amount:* $7,473,142 (30% federal, 24% state, 35% institutional, 11% external sources). *Receiving aid:* Freshmen: 68% (217); all full-time undergraduates: 72% (908). *Average award:* Freshmen: $11,296; Undergraduates: $10,846. *Scholarships, grants, and awards:* Federal Pell, FSEOG, state, college/university gift aid from institutional funds.

GIFT AID (NON-NEED-BASED) *Total amount:* $1,796,473 (76% institutional, 24% external sources). *Receiving aid:* Freshmen: 7% (23). Undergraduates: 6% (74). *Average award:* Freshmen: $6528. Undergraduates: $5813. *Scholarships, grants, and awards by category:* Academic interests/achievement: 826 awards ($3,458,799 total): agriculture, business, communication, computer science, education, English, foreign languages, general academic interests/achievements, humanities, physical sciences, religion/biblical studies, social sciences. *Creative arts/performance:* 61 awards ($80,500 total): art/fine arts, journalism/publications, music, performing arts, theater/drama. *Special achievements/activities:* 49 awards ($89,094 total): leadership. *Special characteristics:* 45 awards ($767,604 total): children of faculty/staff. *Tuition waivers:* Full or partial for employees or children of employees. *ROTC:* Army cooperative, Air Force cooperative.

LOANS *Student loans:* $11,128,308 (72% need-based, 28% non-need-based). 61% of past graduating class borrowed through all loan programs. *Average indebtedness per student:* $31,089. *Average need-based loan:* Freshmen: $3538. Undergraduates: $4512. *Parent loans:* $3,855,610 (43% need-based, 57% non-need-based). *Programs:* Federal Direct (Subsidized and Unsubsidized Stafford, PLUS), Perkins, state.

WORK-STUDY *Federal work-study:* Total amount: $917,615; 642 jobs averaging $1716. *State or other work-study/employment:* Total amount: $10,090 (83% need-based, 17% non-need-based). 13 part-time jobs averaging $781.

ATHLETIC AWARDS Total amount: $2,243,129 (52% need-based, 48% non-need-based).

APPLYING FOR FINANCIAL AID *Required financial aid forms:* FAFSA, institution's own form. *Financial aid deadline (priority):* 6/1. *Notification date:* Continuous beginning 3/1.

CONTACT Mrs. Amy Hardesty, Director of Financial Aid, Lubbock Christian University, 5601 19th Street, Lubbock, TX 79407, 806-720-7176 or toll-free 800-933-7601. *Fax:* 806-720-7185. *E-mail:* amy.hardesty@lcu.edu.
Website: http://www.lcu.edu/.

LUTHER COLLEGE
Decorah, IA

Tuition & fees: $41,020	Average undergraduate aid package: $33,407

ABOUT THE INSTITUTION Independent Evangelical Lutheran Church in America, coed. *Awards:* bachelor's degrees. 42 undergraduate majors. *Total enrollment:* 2,169. Undergraduates: 2,169. Freshmen: 520. Federal methodology is used as a basis for awarding need-based institutional aid.

UNDERGRADUATE EXPENSES for 2017–2018 *Comprehensive fee:* $49,990 includes full-time tuition ($40,710), mandatory fees ($310), and room and board ($8970). *College room only:* $4170. Full-time tuition and fees vary according to course load. Room and board charges vary according to board plan and housing facility. *Part-time tuition:* $1454 per credit hour. Part-time tuition and fees vary according to course load.

FRESHMAN FINANCIAL AID (Fall 2016, est.) 488 applied for aid; of those 89% were deemed to have need. 100% of freshmen with need received aid; of those 44% had need fully met. *Average percent of need met:* 92% (excluding resources awarded to replace EFC). *Average financial aid package:* $35,228 (excluding resources awarded to replace EFC). 16% of all full-time freshmen had no need and received non-need-based gift aid.

UNDERGRADUATE FINANCIAL AID (Fall 2016, est.) 1,827 applied for aid; of those 89% were deemed to have need. 100% of undergraduates with need received aid; of those 38% had need fully met. *Average percent of need met:* 88% (excluding resources awarded to replace EFC). *Average financial aid package:* $33,407 (excluding resources awarded to replace EFC). 20% of all full-time undergraduates had no need and received non-need-based gift aid.

GIFT AID (NEED-BASED) *Total amount:* $44,978,708 (5% federal, 3% state, 85% institutional, 7% external sources). *Receiving aid:* Freshmen: 83% (432); all full-time undergraduates: 77% (1,614). *Average award:* Freshmen: $26,547; Undergraduates: $23,960. *Scholarships, grants, and awards:* Federal Pell, FSEOG, state, private, college/university gift aid from institutional funds.

GIFT AID (NON-NEED-BASED) *Total amount:* $11,432,493 (1% federal, 94% institutional, 5% external sources). *Receiving aid:* Freshmen: 22% (112). Undergraduates: 14% (295). *Average award:* Freshmen: $20,486. Undergraduates: $19,184. *Scholarships, grants, and awards by category:* Academic interests/achievement: 1,799 awards ($29,509,845 total): general academic interests/achievements. *Creative arts/performance:* 739 awards ($2,923,735 total): music. *Special characteristics:* 637 awards ($1,049,635 total): children and siblings of alumni, members of minority groups, religious affiliation. *Tuition waivers:* Full or partial for employees or children of employees.

LOANS *Student loans:* $10,181,884 (75% need-based, 25% non-need-based). 69% of past graduating class borrowed through all loan programs. *Average indebtedness per student:* $35,642. *Average need-based loan:* Freshmen: $5436. Undergraduates: $5815. *Parent loans:* $5,648,900 (32% need-based, 68% non-need-based). *Programs:* Federal Direct (Subsidized and Unsubsidized Stafford, PLUS), Perkins, college/university.

WORK-STUDY *Federal work-study:* Total amount: $1,736,828; 832 jobs averaging $2086. *State or other work-study/employment:* Total amount: $1,550,701 (16% need-based, 84% non-need-based). 989 part-time jobs averaging $2051.

APPLYING FOR FINANCIAL AID *Required financial aid forms:* FAFSA, institution's own form. *Financial aid deadline (priority):* 3/1. *Notification date:* Continuous beginning 3/15. Students must reply by 5/1.

CONTACT Ms. Janice Cordell, Director of Financial Aid, Luther College, 700 College Drive, Decorah, IA 52101-1045, 563-387-1018 or toll-free 800-458-8437. *Fax:* 563-387-2241. *E-mail:* cordellj@luther.edu.
Website: http://www.luther.edu/.

LUTHER RICE COLLEGE & SEMINARY
Lithonia, GA

ABOUT THE INSTITUTION Independent Baptist, coed. *Awards:* bachelor's, master's, and doctoral degrees. 1 undergraduate major. *Total enrollment:* 1,079. Undergraduates: 351. Freshmen: 17.

GIFT AID (NEED-BASED) *Scholarships, grants, and awards:* Federal Pell, FSEOG, college/university gift aid from institutional funds.

LOANS *Programs:* Federal Direct (Subsidized and Unsubsidized Stafford), private loans.
APPLYING FOR FINANCIAL AID *Required financial aid form:* FAFSA.
CONTACT Mr. Casey Kuffrey, Financial Aid Director, Luther Rice College & Seminary, 3038 Evans Mill Road, Lithonia, GA 30038-2418, 770-484-1204 Ext. 5284 or toll-free 800-442-1577. *Fax:* 678-990-5388. *E-mail:* casey.kuffrey@lutherrice.edu. *Website:* http://www.lutherrice.edu/.

LYCOMING COLLEGE
Williamsport, PA

Tuition & fees: $37,162	Average undergraduate aid package: $35,046

ABOUT THE INSTITUTION Independent United Methodist, coed. *Awards:* bachelor's degrees. 38 undergraduate majors. *Total enrollment:* 1,272. Undergraduates: 1,272. Freshmen: 343. Federal methodology is used as a basis for awarding need-based institutional aid.
UNDERGRADUATE EXPENSES for 2016–2017 *One-time required fee:* $225. *Comprehensive fee:* $48,580 includes full-time tuition ($36,432), mandatory fees ($730), and room and board ($11,418). Room and board charges vary according to board plan and housing facility. *Part-time tuition:* $1138 per credit hour. Part-time tuition and fees vary according to course load.
FRESHMAN FINANCIAL AID (Fall 2016, est.) 317 applied for aid; of those 96% were deemed to have need. 100% of freshmen with need received aid; of those 16% had need fully met. *Average percent of need met:* 85% (excluding resources awarded to replace EFC). *Average financial aid package:* $36,681 (excluding resources awarded to replace EFC). 11% of all full-time freshmen had no need and received non-need-based gift aid.
UNDERGRADUATE FINANCIAL AID (Fall 2016, est.) 1,106 applied for aid; of those 95% were deemed to have need. 100% of undergraduates with need received aid; of those 28% had need fully met. *Average percent of need met:* 85% (excluding resources awarded to replace EFC). *Average financial aid package:* $35,046 (excluding resources awarded to replace EFC). 15% of all full-time undergraduates had no need and received non-need-based gift aid.
GIFT AID (NEED-BASED) *Total amount:* $31,714,701 (7% federal, 5% state, 86% institutional, 2% external sources). *Receiving aid:* Freshmen: 89% (304); all full-time undergraduates: 84% (1,048). *Average award:* Freshmen: $31,764; Undergraduates: $29,394. *Scholarships, grants, and awards:* Federal Pell, FSEOG, state, private, college/university gift aid from institutional funds.
GIFT AID (NON-NEED-BASED) *Receiving aid:* Freshmen: 10% (33). Undergraduates: 11% (141). *Average award:* Freshmen: $25,412. Undergraduates: $22,873. *Scholarships, grants, and awards by category:* Academic interests/achievement: biological sciences, business, communication, computer science, education, English, foreign languages, general academic interests/achievements, health fields, humanities, international studies, mathematics, physical sciences, premedicine, religion/biblical studies, social sciences. *Creative arts/performance:* applied art and design, art/fine arts, creative writing, music, theater/drama. *Special achievements/activities:* community service, general special achievements/activities, leadership. *Special characteristics:* children of educators, children of faculty/staff, local/state students, relatives of clergy. *Tuition waivers:* Full or partial for employees or children of employees. *ROTC:* Army cooperative.
LOANS *Student loans:* $9,875,244 (69% need-based, 31% non-need-based). *Average need-based loan:* Freshmen: $3605. Undergraduates: $4630. *Parent loans:* $3,067,043 (36% need-based, 64% non-need-based). *Programs:* Federal Direct (Subsidized and Unsubsidized Stafford, PLUS), Perkins, college/university.
WORK-STUDY *Federal work-study:* Total amount: $216,417; jobs available.
APPLYING FOR FINANCIAL AID *Required financial aid form:* FAFSA. *Financial aid deadline (priority):* 5/1. *Notification date:* Continuous beginning 3/1. Students must reply by 5/1.
CONTACT Mr. James S. Lakis, Director of Financial Aid, Lycoming College, 700 College Place, Williamsport, PA 17701-5192, 570-321-4040 or toll-free 800-345-3920 Ext. 4026. *Fax:* 570-321-4993. *E-mail:* lakis@lycoming.edu. *Website:* http://www.lycoming.edu/.

LYNCHBURG COLLEGE
Lynchburg, VA

Tuition & fees: $36,620	Average undergraduate aid package: $27,341

ABOUT THE INSTITUTION Independent Christian Church (Disciples of Christ), coed. *Awards:* certificates, bachelor's, master's, and doctoral degrees. 38 undergraduate majors. *Total enrollment:* 2,720. Undergraduates: 2,079. Freshmen: 521. Federal methodology is used as a basis for awarding need-based institutional aid.
UNDERGRADUATE EXPENSES for 2016–2017 *Application fee:* $30. *Comprehensive fee:* $46,740 includes full-time tuition ($35,650), mandatory fees ($970), and room and board ($10,120). *College room only:* $5160. Room and board charges vary according to board plan and housing facility. *Part-time tuition:* $490 per credit hour. *Part-time fees:* $5.10 per credit hour. Part-time tuition and fees vary according to course load. *Payment plan:* Tuition prepayment.
FRESHMAN FINANCIAL AID (Fall 2016, est.) 474 applied for aid; of those 88% were deemed to have need. 100% of freshmen with need received aid; of those 27% had need fully met. *Average percent of need met:* 81% (excluding resources awarded to replace EFC). *Average financial aid package:* $28,414 (excluding resources awarded to replace EFC). 20% of all full-time freshmen had no need and received non-need-based gift aid.
UNDERGRADUATE FINANCIAL AID (Fall 2016, est.) 1,611 applied for aid; of those 92% were deemed to have need. 99% of undergraduates with need received aid; of those 21% had need fully met. *Average percent of need met:* 76% (excluding resources awarded to replace EFC). *Average financial aid package:* $27,341 (excluding resources awarded to replace EFC). 20% of all full-time undergraduates had no need and received non-need-based gift aid.
GIFT AID (NEED-BASED) *Total amount:* $34,264,249 (9% federal, 8% state, 81% institutional, 2% external sources). *Receiving aid:* Freshmen: 80% (418); all full-time undergraduates: 75% (1,461). *Average award:* Freshmen: $25,614; Undergraduates: $23,781. *Scholarships, grants, and awards:* Federal Pell, FSEOG, state, private, college/university gift aid from institutional funds.
GIFT AID (NON-NEED-BASED) *Total amount:* $9,689,918 (12% state, 82% institutional, 6% external sources). *Receiving aid:* Freshmen: 15% (79). Undergraduates: 11% (209). *Average award:* Freshmen: $19,222. Undergraduates: $17,162. *Scholarships, grants, and awards by category:* Academic interests/achievement: general academic interests/achievements. *Creative arts/performance:* art/fine arts, music, theater/drama. *Tuition waivers:* Full or partial for employees or children of employees, adult students, senior citizens.
LOANS *Student loans:* $14,965,619 (60% need-based, 40% non-need-based). 77% of past graduating class borrowed through all loan programs. *Average indebtedness per student:* $35,614. *Average need-based loan:* Freshmen: $2445. Undergraduates: $3578. *Parent loans:* $4,943,094 (62% need-based, 38% non-need-based). *Programs:* Federal Direct (Subsidized and Unsubsidized Stafford, PLUS), Perkins, alternative loans.
WORK-STUDY *Federal work-study:* Total amount: $251,929; jobs available. *State or other work-study/employment:* Total amount: $303,040 (22% need-based, 78% non-need-based). Part-time jobs available.
APPLYING FOR FINANCIAL AID *Required financial aid forms:* FAFSA, state aid form. *Financial aid deadline (priority):* 11/1. *Notification date:* Continuous beginning 12/1. Students must reply by 5/1 or within 2 weeks of notification.
CONTACT Mrs. Michelle G. Davis, Associate Director of Financial Aid, Lynchburg College, 1501 Lakeside Drive, Lynchburg, VA 24501, 434-544-8228 or toll-free 800-426-8101. *Fax:* 434-544-8653. *E-mail:* davis@lynchburg.edu. *Website:* http://www.lynchburg.edu/.

LYNDON STATE COLLEGE
Lyndonville, VT

CONTACT Student Services Consultant, Lyndon State College, 1001 College Road, Lyndonville, VT 05851, 802-626-6396 or toll-free 800-225-1998. *Fax:* 802-626-9770. *E-mail:* financialaid@lyndonstate.edu. *Website:* http://www.lyndonstate.edu/.

LYNN UNIVERSITY
Boca Raton, FL

Tuition & fees: $37,510	Average undergraduate aid package: $22,404

ABOUT THE INSTITUTION Independent, coed. *Awards:* certificates, bachelor's, master's, and doctoral degrees. 28 undergraduate majors. *Total enrollment:* 2,842. Undergraduates: 2,095. Freshmen: 566. Both federal and institutional methodology are used as a basis for awarding need-based institutional aid.

UNDERGRADUATE EXPENSES for 2017–2018 *Application fee:* $45. *One-time required fee:* $1000. *Comprehensive fee:* $49,480 includes full-time tuition ($35,260), mandatory fees ($2250), and room and board ($11,970). Full-time tuition and fees vary according to class time, degree level, and program. Room and board charges vary according to board plan and housing facility. *Part-time tuition:* $1020 per credit hour. Part-time tuition and fees vary according to class time, course load, and program.

FRESHMAN FINANCIAL AID (Fall 2016, est.) 521 applied for aid; of those 51% were deemed to have need. 100% of freshmen with need received aid; of those 100% had need fully met. *Average percent of need met:* 59% (excluding resources awarded to replace EFC). *Average financial aid package:* $24,185 (excluding resources awarded to replace EFC). 36% of all full-time freshmen had no need and received non-need-based gift aid.

UNDERGRADUATE FINANCIAL AID (Fall 2016, est.) 1,613 applied for aid; of those 52% were deemed to have need. 100% of undergraduates with need received aid; of those 100% had need fully met. *Average percent of need met:* 55% (excluding resources awarded to replace EFC). *Average financial aid package:* $22,404 (excluding resources awarded to replace EFC). 26% of all full-time undergraduates had no need and received non-need-based gift aid.

GIFT AID (NEED-BASED) *Total amount:* $11,495,340 (20% federal, 11% state, 66% institutional, 3% external sources). *Receiving aid:* Freshmen: 41% (230); all full-time undergraduates: 36% (700). *Average award:* Freshmen: $11,150; Undergraduates: $9991. *Scholarships, grants, and awards:* Federal Pell, FSEOG, state, private, college/university gift aid from institutional funds.

GIFT AID (NON-NEED-BASED) *Total amount:* $6,205,867 (8% state, 90% institutional, 2% external sources). *Receiving aid:* Freshmen: 46% (255). Undergraduates: 38% (733). *Average award:* Freshmen: $10,022. Undergraduates: $10,739. *Scholarships, grants, and awards by category: Academic interests/achievement:* 461 awards ($4,047,330 total): biological sciences, business, communication, general academic interests/achievements, international studies. *Creative arts/performance:* 46 awards ($1,418,733 total): music. *Special achievements/activities:* 1 award ($5000 total): leadership. *Special characteristics:* 369 awards ($2,497,405 total): children and siblings of alumni, children of educators, children of faculty/staff, out-of-state students, siblings of current students, veterans. *Tuition waivers:* Full or partial for employees or children of employees. *ROTC:* Air Force cooperative.

LOANS *Student loans:* $6,613,728 (86% need-based, 14% non-need-based). 30% of past graduating class borrowed through all loan programs. *Average indebtedness per student:* $33,689. *Average need-based loan:* Freshmen: $4068. Undergraduates: $4572. *Parent loans:* $8,376,917 (91% need-based, 9% non-need-based). *Programs:* Federal Direct (Subsidized and Unsubsidized Stafford, PLUS), Perkins.

WORK-STUDY *Federal work-study:* Total amount: $373,163; 183 jobs averaging $2039. *State or other work-study/employment:* Total amount: $252,790 (66% need-based, 34% non-need-based). 34 part-time jobs averaging $7435.

ATHLETIC AWARDS Total amount: $3,234,554 (54% need-based, 46% non-need-based).

APPLYING FOR FINANCIAL AID *Required financial aid form:* FAFSA. *Financial aid deadline (priority):* 3/1. *Notification date:* Continuous beginning 11/1. Students must reply within 2 weeks of notification.

CONTACT Mr. John Chambers, Director of Student Financial Assistance, Lynn University, 3601 North Military Trail, Boca Raton, FL 33431-5598, 561-237-7973 or toll-free 800-888-5966. *Fax:* 561-237-7189. *E-mail:* jchambers@lynn.edu. *Website:* http://www.lynn.edu/.

LYON COLLEGE
Batesville, AR

Tuition & fees: $26,290	Average undergraduate aid package: $21,210

ABOUT THE INSTITUTION Independent Presbyterian, coed. *Awards:* bachelor's degrees. 14 undergraduate majors. *Total enrollment:* 690. Undergraduates: 690. Freshmen: 200. Federal methodology is used as a basis for awarding need-based institutional aid.

UNDERGRADUATE EXPENSES for 2016–2017 *Application fee:* $25. *Comprehensive fee:* $34,730 includes full-time tuition ($26,050), mandatory fees ($240), and room and board ($8440). Full-time tuition and fees vary according to course load. Room and board charges vary according to board plan and housing facility. *Part-time tuition:* $860 per credit hour.

FRESHMAN FINANCIAL AID (Fall 2016, est.) 198 applied for aid; of those 85% were deemed to have need. 100% of freshmen with need received aid; of those 29% had need fully met. *Average percent of need met:* 68% (excluding resources awarded to replace EFC). *Average financial aid package:* $18,887 (excluding resources awarded to replace EFC). 15% of all full-time freshmen had no need and received non-need-based gift aid.

UNDERGRADUATE FINANCIAL AID (Fall 2016, est.) 569 applied for aid; of those 89% were deemed to have need. 100% of undergraduates with need received aid; of those 23% had need fully met. *Average percent of need met:* 71% (excluding resources awarded to replace EFC). *Average financial aid package:* $21,210 (excluding resources awarded to replace EFC). 15% of all full-time undergraduates had no need and received non-need-based gift aid.

GIFT AID (NEED-BASED) *Total amount:* $6,466,833 (17% federal, 11% state, 67% institutional, 5% external sources). *Receiving aid:* Freshmen: 80% (168); all full-time undergraduates: 75% (507). *Average award:* Freshmen: $16,922; Undergraduates: $18,345. *Scholarships, grants, and awards:* Federal Pell, FSEOG, state, private, college/university gift aid from institutional funds.

GIFT AID (NON-NEED-BASED) *Total amount:* $2,413,846 (1% federal, 24% state, 71% institutional, 4% external sources). *Receiving aid:* Freshmen: 18% (37). Undergraduates: 13% (91). *Average award:* Freshmen: $12,680. Undergraduates: $14,205. *Scholarships, grants, and awards by category: Academic interests/achievement:* 325 awards ($5,064,545 total): business, general academic interests/achievements. *Creative arts/performance:* 47 awards ($220,860 total): art/fine arts, music, theater/drama. *Special achievements/activities:* 14 awards ($53,554 total): cheerleading/drum major, general special achievements/activities. *Special characteristics:* 27 awards ($295,871 total): children and siblings of alumni, children of faculty/staff, ethnic background, first-generation college students, local/state students, members of minority groups, religious affiliation. *Tuition waivers:* Full or partial for employees or children of employees.

LOANS *Student loans:* $3,332,421 (70% need-based, 30% non-need-based). 78% of past graduating class borrowed through all loan programs. *Average indebtedness per student:* $22,321. *Average need-based loan:* Freshmen: $2928. Undergraduates: $3992. *Parent loans:* $875,160 (47% need-based, 53% non-need-based). *Programs:* Federal Direct (Subsidized and Unsubsidized Stafford, PLUS), Perkins.

WORK-STUDY *Federal work-study:* Total amount: $103,520; 142 jobs averaging $963. *State or other work-study/employment:* 7 part-time jobs averaging $857.

ATHLETIC AWARDS Total amount: $4,225,824 (63% need-based, 37% non-need-based).

APPLYING FOR FINANCIAL AID *Required financial aid form:* FAFSA. *Financial aid deadline (priority):* 3/15. *Notification date:* Continuous beginning 9/1. Students must reply by 8/15.

CONTACT Mr. Tommy Tucker, Director of Student Assistance, Lyon College, 2300 Highland Road, Batesville, AR 72501, 870-307-7257 or toll-free 800-423-2542. *Fax:* 870-307-7542. *E-mail:* financialaid@lyon.edu. *Website:* http://www.lyon.edu/.

MACALESTER COLLEGE
St. Paul, MN

Tuition & fees: $52,464	Average undergraduate aid package: $43,969

ABOUT THE INSTITUTION Independent, coed. *Awards:* bachelor's degrees. 37 undergraduate majors. *Total enrollment:* 2,146. Undergraduates: 2,146. Freshmen: 506. Both federal and institutional methodology are used as a basis for awarding need-based institutional aid.

UNDERGRADUATE EXPENSES for 2017–2018 *Application fee:* $40. *Comprehensive fee:* $64,136 includes full-time tuition ($52,234), mandatory fees ($230), and room and board ($11,672). *College room only:* $6238. Full-time tuition and fees vary according to course load. Room and board charges vary according to board plan and housing facility. *Part-time tuition:* $1632 per credit. Part-time tuition and fees vary according to course load.

FRESHMAN FINANCIAL AID (Fall 2016, est.) 392 applied for aid; of those 89% were deemed to have need. 100% of freshmen with need received aid; of those 100% had need fully met. *Average percent of need met:* 100% (excluding resources awarded to replace EFC). *Average financial aid package:* $43,701 (excluding resources awarded to replace EFC). 15% of all full-time freshmen had no need and received non-need-based gift aid.

UNDERGRADUATE FINANCIAL AID (Fall 2016, est.) 1,587 applied for aid; of those 90% were deemed to have need. 100% of undergraduates with need received aid; of those 100% had need fully met. *Average percent of need met:* 100% (excluding resources awarded to replace EFC). *Average financial aid package:* $43,969 (excluding resources awarded to replace EFC). 12% of all full-time undergraduates had no need and received non-need-based gift aid.

GIFT AID (NEED-BASED) *Total amount:* $53,481,987 (2% federal, 1% state, 95% institutional, 2% external sources). *Receiving aid:* Freshmen: 69% (348); all full-time undergraduates: 68% (1,420). *Average award:* Freshmen: $38,178; Undergraduates: $37,392. *Scholarships, grants, and awards:* Federal Pell, FSEOG, state, private, college/university gift aid from institutional funds.

GIFT AID (NON-NEED-BASED) *Total amount:* $3,935,272 (92% institutional, 8% external sources). *Receiving aid:* Freshmen: 4% (21). Undergraduates: 3% (56). *Average award:* Freshmen: $14,973. Undergraduates: $13,752. *Scholarships, grants, and awards by category:* Academic interests/achievement: general academic interests/achievements. *Special characteristics:* ethnic background. *Tuition waivers:* Full or partial for employees or children of employees. *ROTC:* Army cooperative, Naval cooperative, Air Force cooperative.

LOANS *Student loans:* $8,025,622 (92% need-based, 8% non-need-based). 63% of past graduating class borrowed through all loan programs. *Average indebtedness per student:* $23,875. *Average need-based loan:* Freshmen: $3947. Undergraduates: $5065. *Parent loans:* $1,510,148 (100% non-need-based). *Programs:* Federal Direct (Subsidized and Unsubsidized Stafford, PLUS), Perkins, state, college/university.

WORK-STUDY *Federal work-study:* Total amount: $500,972; jobs available. *State or other work-study/employment:* Total amount: $3,083,752 (96% need-based, 4% non-need-based). Part-time jobs available.

APPLYING FOR FINANCIAL AID *Required financial aid forms:* FAFSA, CSS Financial Aid PROFILE, noncustodial (divorced/separated) parent's statement, federal income tax form(s). *Financial aid deadline (priority):* 2/1. *Notification date:* 4/1. Students must reply by 5/1.

CONTACT Financial Aid Office, Macalester College, 1600 Grand Avenue, St. Paul, MN 55105, 651-696-6214 or toll-free 800-231-7974. *Fax:* 651-696-6866. *E-mail:* financialaid@macalester.edu.
Website: http://www.macalester.edu/.

MACMURRAY COLLEGE
Jacksonville, IL

Tuition & fees: $26,100	Average undergraduate aid package: $21,509

ABOUT THE INSTITUTION Independent United Methodist, coed. *Awards:* associate and bachelor's degrees. 19 undergraduate majors. *Total enrollment:* 552. Undergraduates: 552. Freshmen: 147. Federal methodology is used as a basis for awarding need-based institutional aid.

UNDERGRADUATE EXPENSES for 2017–2018 *Comprehensive fee:* $35,025 includes full-time tuition ($25,340), mandatory fees ($760), and room and board ($8925). Full-time tuition and fees vary according to course load and location. Room and board charges vary according to housing facility. *Part-time tuition:* $780 per credit hour. *Part-time fees:* $40 per credit hour; $10 per term. Part-time tuition and fees vary according to course load and location.

FRESHMAN FINANCIAL AID (Fall 2016, est.) 133 applied for aid; of those 95% were deemed to have need. 100% of freshmen with need received aid; of those 23% had need fully met. *Average percent of need met:* 83% (excluding resources awarded to replace EFC). *Average financial aid package:* $23,570 (excluding resources awarded to replace EFC). 3% of all full-time freshmen had no need and received non-need-based gift aid.

UNDERGRADUATE FINANCIAL AID (Fall 2016, est.) 512 applied for aid; of those 94% were deemed to have need. 100% of undergraduates with need received aid; of those 20% had need fully met. *Average percent of need met:* 80% (excluding resources awarded to replace EFC). *Average financial aid package:* $21,509 (excluding resources awarded to replace EFC). 8% of all full-time undergraduates had no need and received non-need-based gift aid.

GIFT AID (NEED-BASED) *Total amount:* $7,818,661 (18% federal, 13% state, 67% institutional, 2% external sources). *Receiving aid:* Freshmen: 93% (127); all full-time undergraduates: 91% (480). *Average award:* Freshmen: $19,118; Undergraduates: $16,287. *Scholarships, grants, and awards:* Federal Pell, FSEOG, state, private, college/university gift aid from institutional funds.

GIFT AID (NON-NEED-BASED) *Total amount:* $931,913 (1% federal, 89% institutional, 10% external sources). *Receiving aid:* Freshmen: 14% (19). Undergraduates: 11% (59). *Average award:* Freshmen: $13,833. Undergraduates: $11,288. *Scholarships, grants, and awards by category:* Academic interests/achievement: 533 awards ($5,432,812 total): general academic interests/achievements. *Special achievements/activities:* 26 awards ($52,650 total): leadership, religious involvement. *Special characteristics:* 91 awards ($191,729 total): children and siblings of alumni, children of faculty/staff, first-generation college students, general special characteristics, out-of-state students, veterans. *Tuition waivers:* Full or partial for children of alumni, employees or children of employees, senior citizens.

LOANS *Student loans:* $4,722,970 (75% need-based, 25% non-need-based). 88% of past graduating class borrowed through all loan programs. *Average indebtedness per student:* $36,877. *Average need-based loan:* Freshmen: $4319. Undergraduates: $5134. *Parent loans:* $1,187,470 (41% need-based, 59% non-need-based). *Programs:* Federal Direct (Subsidized and Unsubsidized Stafford, PLUS), Perkins.

WORK-STUDY *Federal work-study:* Total amount: $383,949; 313 jobs averaging $1510.

APPLYING FOR FINANCIAL AID *Required financial aid form:* FAFSA. *Financial aid deadline (priority):* 11/1. *Notification date:* Continuous beginning 12/1. Students must reply within 2 weeks of notification.

CONTACT Mrs. Laci N. Engelbrecht, Director of One-Stop Student Services, MacMurray College, 447 East College Avenue, Jacksonville, IL 62650, 217-479-7041 or toll-free 800-252-7485. *Fax:* 217-479-7013. *E-mail:* one-stop@mac.edu.
Website: http://www.mac.edu/.

MACHZIKEI HADATH RABBINICAL COLLEGE
Brooklyn, NY

CONTACT Rabbi Baruch Rozmarin, Director of Financial Aid, Machzikei Hadath Rabbinical College, 5407 16th Avenue, Brooklyn, NY 11204-1805, 718-854-8777.

MADONNA UNIVERSITY
Livonia, MI

CONTACT Cathy Durham, Financial Aid Secretary, Madonna University, 36600 Schoolcraft Road, Livonia, MI 48150-1173, 734-432-5663 or toll-free 800-852-4951. *Fax:* 734-432-5344. *E-mail:* finaid@madonna.edu.
Website: http://www.madonna.edu/.

MAHARISHI UNIVERSITY OF MANAGEMENT
Fairfield, IA

CONTACT Mr. Bill Christensen, Director of Financial Aid, Maharishi University of Management, 1000 North 4th Street, DB 1127, Fairfield, IA 52557-1127, 641-472-1156 or toll-free 800-369-6480. *Fax:* 641-472-1133. *E-mail:* bchrist@mum.edu. *Website:* http://www.mum.edu/.

MAINE COLLEGE OF ART
Portland, ME

CONTACT Adrienne J. Amari, Director of Financial Aid, Maine College of Art, 522 Congress Street, Portland, ME 04101-3987, 207-775-3052 Ext. 5073 or toll-free 800-699-1509. *Fax:* 207-772-5069. *E-mail:* aamari@meca.edu. *Website:* http://www.meca.edu/.

MAINE MARITIME ACADEMY
Castine, ME

CONTACT Mrs. Kathy S. Heath, Director of Financial Aid, Maine Maritime Academy, Pleasant Street, Castine, ME 04420, 207-326-2205 or toll-free 800-464-6565 (in-state), 800-227-8465 (out-of-state). *Fax:* 207-326-2515. *E-mail:* bbayle@mma.edu. *Website:* http://www.mainemaritime.edu/.

MALONE UNIVERSITY
Canton, OH

Tuition & fees: $29,900	Average undergraduate aid package: $22,939

ABOUT THE INSTITUTION Independent Evangelical Friends Church–Eastern Region, coed. *Awards:* bachelor's and master's degrees. 48 undergraduate majors. *Total enrollment:* 1,689. Undergraduates: 1,311. Freshmen: 311. Institutional methodology is used as a basis for awarding need-based institutional aid.

UNDERGRADUATE EXPENSES for 2017–2018 *Application fee:* $20. *Comprehensive fee:* $39,200 includes full-time tuition ($29,000), mandatory fees ($900), and room and board ($9300). *College room only:* $4500. Room and board charges vary according to board plan. *Part-time tuition:* $500 per credit hour. *Part-time fees:* $225 per term. Part-time tuition and fees vary according to course load.

FRESHMAN FINANCIAL AID (Fall 2016, est.) 295 applied for aid; of those 93% were deemed to have need. 100% of freshmen with need received aid; of those 13% had need fully met. *Average percent of need met:* 79% (excluding resources awarded to replace EFC). *Average financial aid package:* $25,125 (excluding resources awarded to replace EFC). 10% of all full-time freshmen had no need and received non-need-based gift aid.

UNDERGRADUATE FINANCIAL AID (Fall 2016, est.) 1,025 applied for aid; of those 94% were deemed to have need. 100% of undergraduates with need received aid; of those 15% had need fully met. *Average percent of need met:* 76% (excluding resources awarded to replace EFC). *Average financial aid package:* $22,939 (excluding resources awarded to replace EFC). 10% of all full-time undergraduates had no need and received non-need-based gift aid.

GIFT AID (NEED-BASED) *Total amount:* $15,163,468 (15% federal, 5% state, 76% institutional, 4% external sources). *Receiving aid:* Freshmen: 89% (275); all full-time undergraduates: 84% (953). *Average award:* Freshmen: $21,480; Undergraduates: $19,293. *Scholarships, grants, and awards:* Federal Pell, FSEOG, state, private, college/university gift aid from institutional funds.

GIFT AID (NON-NEED-BASED) *Total amount:* $1,494,332 (91% institutional, 9% external sources). *Receiving aid:* Freshmen: 9% (28). Undergraduates: 8% (93). *Average award:* Freshmen: $7766. Undergraduates: $10,038. *Scholarships, grants, and awards by category:* Academic interests/achievement: biological sciences, business, communication, education, general academic interests/achievements,

health fields, mathematics, premedicine, religion/biblical studies, social sciences. *Creative arts/performance:* creative writing, debating, journalism/publications, music, theater/drama. *Special achievements/activities:* cheerleading/drum major, general special achievements/activities, leadership, religious involvement. *Special characteristics:* children and siblings of alumni, handicapped students, international students, local/state students, members of minority groups, relatives of clergy, religious affiliation, veterans. *Tuition waivers:* Full or partial for employees or children of employees, senior citizens.

LOANS *Student loans:* $7,955,035 (77% need-based, 23% non-need-based). 86% of past graduating class borrowed through all loan programs. *Average indebtedness per student:* $31,225. *Average need-based loan:* Freshmen: $3380. Undergraduates: $4072. *Parent loans:* $2,764,977 (50% need-based, 50% non-need-based). *Programs:* Federal Direct (Subsidized and Unsubsidized Stafford, PLUS), Perkins, state, college/university, private loans.

WORK-STUDY *Federal work-study:* Total amount: $458,698; jobs available.

ATHLETIC AWARDS Total amount: $3,669,486 (72% need-based, 28% non-need-based).

APPLYING FOR FINANCIAL AID *Required financial aid form:* FAFSA. *Financial aid deadline:* 7/31 (priority: 3/1). *Notification date:* Continuous beginning 3/1. Students must reply within 2 weeks of notification.

CONTACT Mrs. Pamela Pustay, Director of Financial Aid, Malone University, 2600 Cleveland Avenue NW, Canton, OH 44709, 330-471-8161 or toll-free 800-521-1146. *Fax:* 330-471-8652. *E-mail:* ppustay@malone.edu. *Website:* http://www.malone.edu/.

MANCHESTER UNIVERSITY
North Manchester, IN

Tuition & fees: $31,660	Average undergraduate aid package: $28,495

ABOUT THE INSTITUTION Independent Church of the Brethren, coed. *Awards:* associate, bachelor's, master's, and doctoral degrees. 86 undergraduate majors. *Total enrollment:* 1,598. Undergraduates: 1,272. Freshmen: 389. Federal methodology is used as a basis for awarding need-based institutional aid.

UNDERGRADUATE EXPENSES for 2017–2018 *Application fee:* $25. *One-time required fee:* $250. *Comprehensive fee:* $41,540 includes full-time tuition ($30,450), mandatory fees ($1210), and room and board ($9880). *College room only:* $5750. Room and board charges vary according to board plan and housing facility. *Part-time tuition:* $700 per credit hour. *Part-time fees:* $30 per credit hour. Part-time tuition and fees vary according to course load.

FRESHMAN FINANCIAL AID (Fall 2016, est.) 352 applied for aid; of those 94% were deemed to have need. 100% of freshmen with need received aid; of those 24% had need fully met. *Average percent of need met:* 86% (excluding resources awarded to replace EFC). *Average financial aid package:* $30,084 (excluding resources awarded to replace EFC). 12% of all full-time freshmen had no need and received non-need-based gift aid.

UNDERGRADUATE FINANCIAL AID (Fall 2016, est.) 1,131 applied for aid; of those 93% were deemed to have need. 99% of undergraduates with need received aid; of those 26% had need fully met. *Average percent of need met:* 86% (excluding resources awarded to replace EFC). *Average financial aid package:* $28,495 (excluding resources awarded to replace EFC). 14% of all full-time undergraduates had no need and received non-need-based gift aid.

GIFT AID (NEED-BASED) *Total amount:* $22,524,004 (9% federal, 13% state, 76% institutional, 2% external sources). *Receiving aid:* Freshmen: 88% (332); all full-time undergraduates: 85% (1,042). *Average award:* Freshmen: $24,878; Undergraduates: $22,528. *Scholarships, grants, and awards:* Federal Pell, FSEOG, state, private, college/university gift aid from institutional funds.

GIFT AID (NON-NEED-BASED) *Total amount:* $5,038,703 (98% institutional, 2% external sources). *Receiving aid:* Freshmen: 10% (36). Undergraduates: 10% (126). *Average award:* Freshmen: $18,616. Undergraduates: $18,192. *Scholarships, grants, and awards by category:* Academic interests/achievement: general academic interests/achievements. *Creative arts/performance:* music. *Special characteristics:* children and siblings of alumni, children of faculty/staff, international students, members of minority groups, out-of-state students, parents of current students, religious affiliation, siblings of current students, spouses of current students. *Tuition waivers:* Full or partial for employees or children of employees.

LOANS *Student loans:* $7,144,222 (79% need-based, 21% non-need-based). 87% of past graduating class borrowed through all loan programs. *Average indebtedness per student:* $33,011. *Average need-based loan:* Freshmen: $3403. Undergraduates: $4304. *Parent loans:* $3,608,180 (42% need-based, 58% non-need-based). *Programs:* Federal Direct (Subsidized and Unsubsidized Stafford, PLUS), Perkins.

WORK-STUDY *Federal work-study:* Total amount: $1,117,844; jobs available.

APPLYING FOR FINANCIAL AID *Required financial aid form:* FAFSA. *Financial aid deadline (priority):* 3/1. *Notification date:* Continuous beginning 3/18. Students must reply by 5/1 or within 3 weeks of notification.

CONTACT Mrs. Sherri Shockey, Director of Student Financial Services, Manchester University, 604 East College Avenue, North Manchester, IN 46962-1225, 260-982-5066 or toll-free 800-852-3648. *Fax:* 260-982-5043. *E-mail:* slshockey@manchester.edu.

Website: http://www.manchester.edu/.

MANHATTAN CHRISTIAN COLLEGE
Manhattan, KS

CONTACT Mrs. Margaret Carlisle, Director of Financial Aid, Manhattan Christian College, 1415 Anderson Avenue, Manhattan, KS 66502-4081, 785-539-3571 or toll-free 877-246-4622. *E-mail:* carlisle@mccks.edu.

Website: http://www.mccks.edu/.

MANHATTAN COLLEGE
Riverdale, NY

Tuition & fees: $40,639	Average undergraduate aid package: $23,453

ABOUT THE INSTITUTION Independent Roman Catholic Church, coed. *Awards:* certificates, bachelor's, and master's degrees. 44 undergraduate majors. *Total enrollment:* 4,214. Undergraduates: 3,637. Freshmen: 816. Both federal and institutional methodology are used as a basis for awarding need-based institutional aid.

UNDERGRADUATE EXPENSES for 2016–2017 *Application fee:* $60. *Comprehensive fee:* $55,649 includes full-time tuition ($36,900), mandatory fees ($3739), and room and board ($15,010). Full-time tuition and fees vary according to course load, program, and student level. Room and board charges vary according to board plan. *Part-time tuition:* $945 per credit. Part-time tuition and fees vary according to course load.

FRESHMAN FINANCIAL AID (Fall 2015) 599 applied for aid; of those 100% were deemed to have need. 97% of freshmen with need received aid; of those 51% had need fully met. *Average percent of need met:* 88% (excluding resources awarded to replace EFC). *Average financial aid package:* $23,453 (excluding resources awarded to replace EFC). 21% of all full-time freshmen had no need and received non-need-based gift aid.

UNDERGRADUATE FINANCIAL AID (Fall 2015) 3,080 applied for aid; of those 100% were deemed to have need. 100% of undergraduates with need received aid; of those 12% had need fully met. *Average percent of need met:* 70% (excluding resources awarded to replace EFC). *Average financial aid package:* $23,453 (excluding resources awarded to replace EFC). 24% of all full-time undergraduates had no need and received non-need-based gift aid.

GIFT AID (NEED-BASED) *Total amount:* $56,177,254 (8% federal, 6% state, 84% institutional, 2% external sources). *Receiving aid:* Freshmen: 63% (565); all full-time undergraduates: 74% (2,494). *Average award:* Freshmen: $23,453; Undergraduates: $15,542. *Scholarships, grants, and awards:* Federal Pell, FSEOG, state, private, college/university gift aid from institutional funds.

GIFT AID (NON-NEED-BASED) *Total amount:* $2,906,373 (9% state, 91% institutional). *Receiving aid:* Freshmen: 13% (120). Undergraduates: 11% (373). *Average award:* Freshmen: $8898. Undergraduates: $4877. *Scholarships, grants, and awards by category: Academic interests/achievement:* biological sciences, business, computer science, engineering/technologies, foreign languages, general academic interests/achievements, mathematics, military science. *Creative arts/performance:* music. *Special achievements/activities:* community service, leadership. *Special characteristics:* children of faculty/staff. *Tuition waivers:* Full or partial for employees or children of employees. *ROTC:* Army cooperative, Air Force.

LOANS *Student loans:* $18,489,000 (92% need-based, 8% non-need-based). 76% of past graduating class borrowed through all loan programs. *Average indebtedness per student:* $39,443. *Parent loans:* $12,715,681 (88% need-based, 12% non-need-based). *Programs:* Federal Direct (Subsidized and Unsubsidized Stafford, PLUS), Perkins.

WORK-STUDY *Federal work-study:* jobs available. *State or other work-study/employment:* Part-time jobs available.

ATHLETIC AWARDS Total amount: $5,553,260 (91% need-based, 9% non-need-based).

APPLYING FOR FINANCIAL AID *Required financial aid forms:* FAFSA, institution's own form, state aid form. *Financial aid deadline (priority):* 3/1. *Notification date:* 4/1. Students must reply by 5/1.

CONTACT Mr. Denise Scalzo, Director of Financial Aid, Manhattan College, 4513 Manhattan College Parkway, Riverdale, NY 10471, 718-862-7100 or toll-free 800-622-9235. *Fax:* 718-862-8027. *E-mail:* dcsalzo01@manhattan.edu.

Website: http://www.manhattan.edu/.

MANHATTAN SCHOOL OF MUSIC
New York, NY

ABOUT THE INSTITUTION Independent, coed. 7 undergraduate majors.

GIFT AID (NEED-BASED) *Scholarships, grants, and awards:* Federal Pell, FSEOG, state, private, college/university gift aid from institutional funds.

GIFT AID (NON-NEED-BASED) *Scholarships, grants, and awards by category: Creative arts/performance:* music.

LOANS *Programs:* Federal Direct (Subsidized and Unsubsidized Stafford, PLUS), Perkins.

WORK-STUDY *Federal work-study:* jobs available.

APPLYING FOR FINANCIAL AID *Required financial aid forms:* FAFSA, CSS Financial Aid PROFILE.

CONTACT Ms. Amy Anderson, Assistant Dean for Enrollment Management, Manhattan School of Music, 120 Claremont Avenue, New York, NY 10027-4698, 212-749-2802 Ext. 4501. *Fax:* 212-749-3025. *E-mail:* aanderson@msmnyc.edu.

Website: http://www.msmnyc.edu/.

MANHATTANVILLE COLLEGE
Purchase, NY

Tuition & fees: $37,910	Average undergraduate aid package: $27,769

ABOUT THE INSTITUTION Independent, coed. *Awards:* certificates, bachelor's, master's, and doctoral degrees. 47 undergraduate majors. *Total enrollment:* 2,834. Undergraduates: 1,794. Freshmen: 483. Federal methodology is used as a basis for awarding need-based institutional aid.

UNDERGRADUATE EXPENSES for 2017–2018 *Application fee:* $50. *Comprehensive fee:* $52,430 includes full-time tuition ($36,460), mandatory fees ($1450), and room and board ($14,520). *College room only:* $8680. Full-time tuition and fees vary according to course load. Room and board charges vary according to board plan. *Part-time tuition:* $825 per credit. *Part-time fees:* $60 per term. Part-time tuition and fees vary according to course load and program.

FRESHMAN FINANCIAL AID (Fall 2016, est.) 426 applied for aid; of those 89% were deemed to have need. 100% of freshmen with need received aid; of those 12% had need fully met. *Average percent of need met:* 77% (excluding resources awarded to replace EFC). *Average financial aid package:* $28,549 (excluding resources awarded to replace EFC). 20% of all full-time freshmen had no need and received non-need-based gift aid.

UNDERGRADUATE FINANCIAL AID (Fall 2016, est.) 1,415 applied for aid; of those 83% were deemed to have need. 100% of undergraduates with need received aid; of those 16% had need fully met. *Average percent of need met:* 75% (excluding resources awarded to replace EFC). *Average financial aid package:* $27,769 (excluding resources awarded to replace EFC). 23% of all full-time undergraduates had no need and received non-need-based gift aid.

GIFT AID (NEED-BASED) *Total amount:* $31,693,471 (9% federal, 5% state, 86% institutional). *Receiving aid:* Freshmen: 59% (284); all full-time undergraduates: 59% (999). *Average award:* Freshmen: $6761; Undergraduates: $5609. *Scholar-

ships, grants, and awards: Federal Pell, FSEOG, state, private, college/university gift aid from institutional funds.

GIFT AID (NON-NEED-BASED) Total amount: $8,548,404 (96% institutional, 4% external sources). **Receiving aid:** Freshmen: 78% (375). Undergraduates: 61% (1,046). **Average award:** Freshmen: $20,039. Undergraduates: $18,604. **Scholarships, grants, and awards by category:** *Academic interests/achievement:* general academic interests/achievements. *Creative arts/performance:* art/fine arts, creative writing, dance, music, performing arts, theater/drama. *Special achievements/activities:* community service. *Special characteristics:* children of faculty/staff, general special characteristics, previous college experience, veterans. **Tuition waivers:** Full or partial for children of alumni, employees or children of employees.

LOANS Student loans: $10,293,160 (38% need-based, 62% non-need-based). 69% of past graduating class borrowed through all loan programs. *Average indebtedness per student:* $32,212. **Average need-based loan:** Freshmen: $3641. Undergraduates: $4549. **Parent loans:** $4,561,978 (100% non-need-based). **Programs:** Federal Direct (Subsidized and Unsubsidized Stafford, PLUS), Perkins.

WORK-STUDY Federal work-study: Total amount: $225,834; 507 jobs averaging $1530. **State or other work-study/employment:** Part-time jobs available.

APPLYING FOR FINANCIAL AID Required financial aid forms: FAFSA, state aid form. **Financial aid deadline (priority):** 3/1. **Notification date:** 3/15. Students must reply by 5/1 or within 2 weeks of notification.

CONTACT Mr. Robert Gilmore, Director of Financial Aid, Manhattanville College, 2900 Purchase Street, Purchase, NY 10577-2132, 914-323-5357 or toll-free 800-328-4553. *Fax:* 914-323-5382. *E-mail:* robert.gilmore@mville.edu.
Website: http://www.mville.edu/.

MANSFIELD UNIVERSITY OF PENNSYLVANIA
Mansfield, PA

Tuition & fees (PA res): $11,908	Average undergraduate aid package: $10,187

ABOUT THE INSTITUTION State-supported, coed. **Awards:** associate, bachelor's, and master's degrees. 51 undergraduate majors. **Total enrollment:** 2,198. Undergraduates: 2,112. Freshmen: 450. Federal methodology is used as a basis for awarding need-based institutional aid.

UNDERGRADUATE EXPENSES for 2017–2018 Tuition, state resident: full-time $9150; part-time $305 per credit hour. **Tuition, nonresident:** full-time $15,090; part-time $610 per credit hour. **Required fees:** full-time $2758. Part-time tuition and fees vary according to course load. **College room and board:** $11,468; **Room only:** $8142. Room and board charges vary according to board plan and housing facility.

FRESHMAN FINANCIAL AID (Fall 2015) 455 applied for aid; of those 90% were deemed to have need. 100% of freshmen with need received aid; of those 6% had need fully met. **Average percent of need met:** 55% (excluding resources awarded to replace EFC). **Average financial aid package:** $9957 (excluding resources awarded to replace EFC). 3% of all full-time freshmen had no need and received non-need-based gift aid.

UNDERGRADUATE FINANCIAL AID (Fall 2015) 1,950 applied for aid; of those 89% were deemed to have need. 100% of undergraduates with need received aid; of those 9% had need fully met. **Average percent of need met:** 63% (excluding resources awarded to replace EFC). **Average financial aid package:** $10,187 (excluding resources awarded to replace EFC). 3% of all full-time undergraduates had no need and received non-need-based gift aid.

GIFT AID (NEED-BASED) Total amount: $6,991,069 (62% federal, 33% state, 5% institutional). **Receiving aid:** Freshmen: 61% (284); all full-time undergraduates: 57% (1,199). **Average award:** Freshmen: $2868; Undergraduates: $2952. **Scholarships, grants, and awards:** Federal Pell, FSEOG, state, private, college/university gift aid from institutional funds.

GIFT AID (NON-NEED-BASED) Total amount: $1,399,838 (1% federal, 3% state, 64% institutional, 32% external sources). **Receiving aid:** Freshmen: 40% (188). Undergraduates: 30% (631). **Average award:** Freshmen: $2436. Undergraduates: $2069. **Scholarships, grants, and awards by category:** *Academic interests/achievement:* biological sciences, communication, education, general academic interests/achievements, health fields, mathematics, physical sciences. *Creative arts/performance:* art/fine arts, journalism/publications, music. *Special achievements/activities:*

leadership. *Special characteristics:* children and siblings of alumni, local/state students, members of minority groups, religious affiliation. **Tuition waivers:** Full or partial for employees or children of employees, senior citizens. **ROTC:** Army cooperative.

LOANS Student loans: $17,836,597 (38% need-based, 62% non-need-based). 80% of past graduating class borrowed through all loan programs. *Average indebtedness per student:* $41,816. **Average need-based loan:** Freshmen: $2402. Undergraduates: $3097. **Parent loans:** $4,347,386 (100% non-need-based). **Programs:** Federal Direct (Subsidized and Unsubsidized Stafford, PLUS), Perkins.

WORK-STUDY Federal work-study: jobs available. **State or other work-study/employment:** Total amount: $310,417 (100% non-need-based). Part-time jobs available.

ATHLETIC AWARDS Total amount: $487,272 (100% non-need-based).

APPLYING FOR FINANCIAL AID Required financial aid forms: FAFSA, state aid form. **Financial aid deadline:** 6/30 (priority: 2/15). **Notification date:** Continuous beginning 2/17. Students must reply within 4 weeks of notification.

CONTACT Mr. Charles M. Scheetz, Director of Financial Aid, Mansfield University of Pennsylvania, 224 South Hall, 71 South Academy Street, Mansfield, PA 16933, 570-662-4129 or toll-free 800-577-6826. *Fax:* 570-662-4136.
Website: http://www.mansfield.edu/.

MAPLE SPRINGS BAPTIST BIBLE COLLEGE AND SEMINARY
Capitol Heights, MD

CONTACT Ms. Fannie G. Thompson, Director of Business Affairs, Maple Springs Baptist Bible College and Seminary, 4130 Belt Road, Capitol Heights, MD 20743, 301-736-3631. *Fax:* 301-735-6507.
Website: http://www.msbbcs.edu/.

MARANATHA BAPTIST UNIVERSITY
Watertown, WI

Tuition & fees: $14,260	Average undergraduate aid package: $10,139

ABOUT THE INSTITUTION Independent Baptist, coed. **Awards:** certificates, associate, bachelor's, master's, and doctoral degrees. 31 undergraduate majors. **Total enrollment:** 1,118. Undergraduates: 953. Freshmen: 186. Federal methodology is used as a basis for awarding need-based institutional aid.

UNDERGRADUATE EXPENSES for 2017–2018 Application fee: $50. **Comprehensive fee:** $20,980 includes full-time tuition ($13,100), mandatory fees ($1160), and room and board ($6720). Full-time tuition and fees vary according to location and program. **Part-time tuition:** $546 per credit hour. Part-time tuition and fees vary according to course load.

FRESHMAN FINANCIAL AID (Fall 2015) 126 applied for aid; of those 94% were deemed to have need. 100% of freshmen with need received aid; of those 11% had need fully met. **Average percent of need met:** 51% (excluding resources awarded to replace EFC). **Average financial aid package:** $10,213 (excluding resources awarded to replace EFC). 10% of all full-time freshmen had no need and received non-need-based gift aid.

UNDERGRADUATE FINANCIAL AID (Fall 2015) 523 applied for aid; of those 91% were deemed to have need. 100% of undergraduates with need received aid; of those 11% had need fully met. **Average percent of need met:** 52% (excluding resources awarded to replace EFC). **Average financial aid package:** $10,139 (excluding resources awarded to replace EFC). 10% of all full-time undergraduates had no need and received non-need-based gift aid.

GIFT AID (NEED-BASED) Total amount: $3,179,339 (40% federal, 7% state, 40% institutional, 13% external sources). **Receiving aid:** Freshmen: 89% (117); all full-time undergraduates: 82% (453). **Average award:** Freshmen: $7232; Undergraduates: $6718. **Scholarships, grants, and awards:** Federal Pell, FSEOG, state, private, college/university gift aid from institutional funds.

GIFT AID (NON-NEED-BASED) Total amount: $447,280 (1% state, 58% institutional, 41% external sources). **Receiving aid:** Freshmen: 5% (6). Undergraduates: 4% (22). **Average award:** Freshmen: $3961. Undergraduates: $3962. **Scholarships, grants, and awards by category:** *Academic interests/achievement:* business, general academic interests/achievements, religion/biblical studies. *Creative arts/performance:* music. *Special characteristics:* children and siblings of alumni, children of educators, children of faculty/staff, relatives of clergy, spouses of current students. *Tuition waivers:* Full or partial for employees or children of employees. *ROTC:* Army, Air Force cooperative.

LOANS *Student loans:* $4,367,535 (81% need-based, 19% non-need-based). 69% of past graduating class borrowed through all loan programs. *Average indebtedness per student:* $20,965. *Average need-based loan:* Freshmen: $3205. Undergraduates: $4129. *Parent loans:* $135,685 (49% need-based, 51% non-need-based). *Programs:* Federal Direct (Subsidized and Unsubsidized Stafford, PLUS), state, alternative loans.

WORK-STUDY *State or other work-study/employment:* Part-time jobs available.

APPLYING FOR FINANCIAL AID *Required financial aid form:* FAFSA. *Financial aid deadline (priority):* 3/1. *Notification date:* Continuous. Students must reply within 2 weeks of notification.

CONTACT Mr. Bruce Roth, Associate Director of Financial Aid, Maranatha Baptist University, 745 West Main Street, Watertown, WI 53094, 920-206-2318 or toll-free 800-622-2947. *Fax:* 920-261-9109. *E-mail:* financialaid@mbu.edu. *Website:* http://www.mbu.edu/.

MARCONI INTERNATIONAL UNIVERSITY
Pembroke Pines, FL

CONTACT Financial Aid Office, Marconi International University, 1806 Flamingo Road, Suite 120, Pembroke Pines, FL 33028, 954-374-4701. *Website:* http://www.marconiinternationaluniversity.edu/.

MARIA COLLEGE
Albany, NY

Tuition & fees: $14,210	Average undergraduate aid package: $7789

ABOUT THE INSTITUTION Independent, coed. *Awards:* certificates, associate, and bachelor's degrees. 8 undergraduate majors. *Total enrollment:* 779. Undergraduates: 779. Freshmen: 48. Federal methodology is used as a basis for awarding need-based institutional aid.

UNDERGRADUATE EXPENSES for 2016–2017 *Application fee:* $35. *Comprehensive fee:* $21,710 includes full-time tuition ($13,800), mandatory fees ($410), and room and board ($7500). Full-time tuition and fees vary according to course load, program, and reciprocity agreements. *Part-time tuition:* $595 per credit hour. Part-time tuition and fees vary according to course load, program, and reciprocity agreements.

FRESHMAN FINANCIAL AID (Fall 2016, est.) 35 applied for aid; of those 94% were deemed to have need. 91% of freshmen with need received aid; of those 7% had need fully met. *Average percent of need met:* 61% (excluding resources awarded to replace EFC). *Average financial aid package:* $12,127 (excluding resources awarded to replace EFC). 3% of all full-time freshmen had no need and received non-need-based gift aid.

UNDERGRADUATE FINANCIAL AID (Fall 2016, est.) 242 applied for aid; of those 83% were deemed to have need. 68% of undergraduates with need received aid; of those 4% had need fully met. *Average percent of need met:* 43% (excluding resources awarded to replace EFC). *Average financial aid package:* $7789 (excluding resources awarded to replace EFC). 1% of all full-time undergraduates had no need and received non-need-based gift aid.

GIFT AID (NEED-BASED) *Total amount:* $6,769,918 (19% federal, 81% state). *Receiving aid:* Freshmen: 67% (24); all full-time undergraduates: 44% (108). *Average award:* Freshmen: $3687; Undergraduates: $6531. *Scholarships, grants, and awards:* Federal Pell, FSEOG, state, private, college/university gift aid from institutional funds.

GIFT AID (NON-NEED-BASED) *Total amount:* $344,751 (43% federal, 26% institutional, 31% external sources). *Receiving aid:* Freshmen: 11% (4). Undergraduates: 7% (18). *Average award:* Freshmen: $6900. Undergraduates: $6900. *Scholarships, grants, and awards by category:* Academic interests/achievement:

communication, general academic interests/achievements, home economics. *Tuition waivers:* Full or partial for employees or children of employees. *ROTC:* Air Force cooperative.

LOANS *Student loans:* $4,835,189 (38% need-based, 62% non-need-based). *Average need-based loan:* Freshmen: $3385. Undergraduates: $3472. *Parent loans:* $167,057 (100% non-need-based). *Programs:* Federal Direct (Subsidized and Unsubsidized Stafford, PLUS), Perkins.

WORK-STUDY *Federal work-study:* Total amount: $39,829; 36 jobs averaging $1198.

APPLYING FOR FINANCIAL AID *Required financial aid forms:* FAFSA, state aid form. *Financial aid deadline:* Continuous. *Notification date:* Continuous beginning 4/1. Students must reply within 4 weeks of notification.

CONTACT Ms. Donna Myers, Director of Financial Aid, Maria College, 700 New Scotland, Albany, NY 12208, 518-438-3111. *E-mail:* dmyers01@mariacollege.edu. *Website:* http://www.mariacollege.edu/.

MARIAN UNIVERSITY
Indianapolis, IN

CONTACT Mr. John E. Shelton, Dean of Financial Aid, Marian University, 3200 Cold Spring Road, Indianapolis, IN 46222-1997, 317-955-6040 or toll-free 800-772-7264 (in-state). *Fax:* 317-955-6424. *E-mail:* jshelton@marian.edu. *Website:* http://www.marian.edu/.

MARIAN UNIVERSITY
Fond du Lac, WI

Tuition & fees: $27,370	Average undergraduate aid package: $16,769

ABOUT THE INSTITUTION Independent Roman Catholic, coed. *Awards:* certificates, bachelor's, master's, and doctoral degrees. 43 undergraduate majors. *Total enrollment:* 1,974. Undergraduates: 1,487. Freshmen: 267. Both federal and institutional methodology are used as a basis for awarding need-based institutional aid.

UNDERGRADUATE EXPENSES for 2017–2018 *Application fee:* $20. *One-time required fee:* $100. *Comprehensive fee:* $34,370 includes full-time tuition ($26,950), mandatory fees ($420), and room and board ($7000). *College room only:* $4220. Full-time tuition and fees vary according to course load and program. Room and board charges vary according to board plan. *Part-time tuition:* $450 per credit hour. Part-time tuition and fees vary according to course load and program.

FRESHMAN FINANCIAL AID (Fall 2015) 280 applied for aid; of those 93% were deemed to have need. 100% of freshmen with need received aid; of those 8% had need fully met. *Average percent of need met:* 64% (excluding resources awarded to replace EFC). *Average financial aid package:* $18,740 (excluding resources awarded to replace EFC). 7% of all full-time freshmen had no need and received non-need-based gift aid.

UNDERGRADUATE FINANCIAL AID (Fall 2015) 1,271 applied for aid; of those 93% were deemed to have need. 100% of undergraduates with need received aid; of those 6% had need fully met. *Average percent of need met:* 60% (excluding resources awarded to replace EFC). *Average financial aid package:* $16,769 (excluding resources awarded to replace EFC). 7% of all full-time undergraduates had no need and received non-need-based gift aid.

GIFT AID (NEED-BASED) *Total amount:* $15,542,475 (16% federal, 11% state, 68% institutional, 5% external sources). *Receiving aid:* Freshmen: 92% (260); all full-time undergraduates: 90% (1,157). *Average award:* Freshmen: $15,501; Undergraduates: $12,996. *Scholarships, grants, and awards:* Federal Pell, FSEOG, state, private, college/university gift aid from institutional funds, endowed and restricted scholarships and grants.

GIFT AID (NON-NEED-BASED) *Total amount:* $1,070,499 (1% state, 97% institutional, 2% external sources). *Receiving aid:* Freshmen: 15% (41). Undergraduates: 12% (152). *Average award:* Freshmen: $11,838. Undergraduates: $6038. *Scholarships, grants, and awards by category:* Academic interests/achievement: general academic interests/achievements. *Creative arts/performance:* music. *Special characteristics:* children of faculty/staff, children of union members/company employees, children with a deceased or disabled parent, local/state students, out-of-state students, siblings of current students, veterans. *Tuition waivers:* Full or partial for employees or children of employees, senior citizens. **ROTC:** Army cooperative.

LOANS *Student loans:* $8,340,300 (87% need-based, 13% non-need-based). 87% of past graduating class borrowed through all loan programs. *Average indebtedness per student:* $30,565. *Average need-based loan:* Freshmen: $2712. Undergraduates: $3444. *Parent loans:* $2,312,710 (52% need-based, 48% non-need-based). *Programs:* Federal Direct (Subsidized and Unsubsidized Stafford, PLUS), Perkins, Federal Nursing.

WORK-STUDY *Federal work-study:* 146 jobs averaging $443. *State or other work-study/employment:* Total amount: $436,255 (100% non-need-based). 342 part-time jobs averaging $1465.

APPLYING FOR FINANCIAL AID *Required financial aid forms:* FAFSA, institution's own form. *Financial aid deadline (priority):* 3/1. *Notification date:* Continuous beginning 3/1. Students must reply within 4 weeks of notification.

CONTACT Mr. John Smith, Interim Director of Financial Aid, Marian University, 45 South National Avenue, Fond du Lac, WI 54935-4699, 920-923-7614 or toll-free 800-2-MARIAN. *Fax:* 920-923-8767. *E-mail:* jrsmith49@marianuniversity.edu. *Website:* http://www.marianuniversity.edu/.

MARIETTA COLLEGE
Marietta, OH

Tuition & fees: $36,060	Average undergraduate aid package: $29,627

ABOUT THE INSTITUTION Independent, coed. *Awards:* certificates, associate, bachelor's, and master's degrees. 44 undergraduate majors. *Total enrollment:* 1,224. Undergraduates: 1,144. Freshmen: 245. Federal methodology is used as a basis for awarding need-based institutional aid.

UNDERGRADUATE EXPENSES for 2017–2018 *Comprehensive fee:* $47,380 includes full-time tuition ($35,050), mandatory fees ($1010), and room and board ($11,320). Full-time tuition and fees vary according to course load. Room and board charges vary according to board plan and housing facility. *Part-time tuition:* $1170 per credit hour. Part-time tuition and fees vary according to course load.

FRESHMAN FINANCIAL AID (Fall 2016, est.) 208 applied for aid; of those 91% were deemed to have need. 100% of freshmen with need received aid; of those 22% had need fully met. *Average percent of need met:* 72% (excluding resources awarded to replace EFC). *Average financial aid package:* $30,481 (excluding resources awarded to replace EFC). 7% of all full-time freshmen had no need and received non-need-based gift aid.

UNDERGRADUATE FINANCIAL AID (Fall 2016, est.) 804 applied for aid; of those 90% were deemed to have need. 100% of undergraduates with need received aid; of those 26% had need fully met. *Average percent of need met:* 75% (excluding resources awarded to replace EFC). *Average financial aid package:* $29,627 (excluding resources awarded to replace EFC). 11% of all full-time undergraduates had no need and received non-need-based gift aid.

GIFT AID (NEED-BASED) *Total amount:* $9,114,346 (17% federal, 4% state, 79% institutional). *Receiving aid:* Freshmen: 75% (183); all full-time undergraduates: 64% (678). *Average award:* Freshmen: $16,588; Undergraduates: $18,393. *Scholarships, grants, and awards:* Federal Pell, FSEOG, state, private, college/university gift aid from institutional funds.

GIFT AID (NON-NEED-BASED) *Total amount:* $9,160,213 (90% institutional, 10% external sources). *Receiving aid:* Freshmen: 74% (179). Undergraduates: 60% (627). *Average award:* Freshmen: $19,903. Undergraduates: $15,236. *Scholarships, grants, and awards by category: Academic interests/achievement:* 901 awards ($9,676,540 total): general academic interests/achievements. *Creative arts/performance:* 35 awards ($102,798 total): art/fine arts, music, performing arts, theater/drama. *Special characteristics:* 88 awards ($391,750 total): children and siblings of alumni, members of minority groups. *Tuition waivers:* Full or partial for employees or children of employees.

LOANS *Student loans:* $9,064,926 (32% need-based, 68% non-need-based). 78% of past graduating class borrowed through all loan programs. *Average indebtedness per student:* $40,196. *Average need-based loan:* Freshmen: $3335. Undergraduates: $4733. *Parent loans:* $2,603,826 (100% non-need-based). *Programs:* Federal Direct (Subsidized and Unsubsidized Stafford, PLUS), Perkins.

WORK-STUDY *Federal work-study:* Total amount: $1,194,505; 605 jobs averaging $1909.

APPLYING FOR FINANCIAL AID *Required financial aid form:* FAFSA. *Financial aid deadline (priority):* 2/15. *Notification date:* 1/1. Students must reply by 5/1 or within 2 weeks of notification.

CONTACT Mrs. Emily Schuck, Director of Financial Aid, Marietta College, 215 Fifth Street, Marietta, OH 45750-4000, 740-376-4712 or toll-free 800-331-7896. *Fax:* 740-376-4990. *E-mail:* finaid@marietta.edu. *Website:* http://www.marietta.edu/.

MARIST COLLEGE
Poughkeepsie, NY

Tuition & fees: $35,110	Average undergraduate aid package: $20,750

ABOUT THE INSTITUTION Independent, coed. *Awards:* certificates, bachelor's, and master's degrees. 45 undergraduate majors. *Total enrollment:* 6,569. Undergraduates: 5,616. Freshmen: 1,225. Federal methodology is used as a basis for awarding need-based institutional aid.

UNDERGRADUATE EXPENSES for 2016–2017 *Application fee:* $50. *One-time required fee:* $100. *Comprehensive fee:* $51,273 includes full-time tuition ($34,550), mandatory fees ($560), and room and board ($16,163). Full-time tuition and fees vary according to course load and location. Room and board charges vary according to board plan, housing facility, and location. *Part-time tuition:* $650 per credit. *Part-time fees:* $40 per term. Part-time tuition and fees vary according to course load.

FRESHMAN FINANCIAL AID (Fall 2016, est.) 960 applied for aid; of those 72% were deemed to have need. 100% of freshmen with need received aid; of those 18% had need fully met. *Average percent of need met:* 65% (excluding resources awarded to replace EFC). *Average financial aid package:* $20,812 (excluding resources awarded to replace EFC). 30% of all full-time freshmen had no need and received non-need-based gift aid.

UNDERGRADUATE FINANCIAL AID (Fall 2016, est.) 3,461 applied for aid; of those 80% were deemed to have need. 100% of undergraduates with need received aid; of those 17% had need fully met. *Average percent of need met:* 62% (excluding resources awarded to replace EFC). *Average financial aid package:* $20,750 (excluding resources awarded to replace EFC). 28% of all full-time undergraduates had no need and received non-need-based gift aid.

GIFT AID (NEED-BASED) *Total amount:* $38,096,785 (9% federal, 5% state, 84% institutional, 2% external sources). *Receiving aid:* Freshmen: 41% (502); all full-time undergraduates: 39% (1,949). *Average award:* Freshmen: $18,378; Undergraduates: $17,371. *Scholarships, grants, and awards:* Federal Pell, FSEOG, state, private, college/university gift aid from institutional funds.

GIFT AID (NON-NEED-BASED) *Total amount:* $13,684,342 (3% state, 94% institutional, 3% external sources). *Receiving aid:* Freshmen: 43% (521). Undergraduates: 38% (1,876). *Average award:* Freshmen: $9264. Undergraduates: $8440. *Scholarships, grants, and awards by category: Academic interests/achievement:* 3,368 awards ($29,295,624 total): general academic interests/achievements. *Creative arts/performance:* 100 awards ($196,000 total): debating, music, theater/drama. *Special characteristics:* 70 awards ($350,000 total): local/state students. *Tuition waivers:* Full or partial for employees or children of employees, adult students. *ROTC:* Army.

LOANS *Student loans:* $31,246,579 (74% need-based, 26% non-need-based). 66% of past graduating class borrowed through all loan programs. *Average indebtedness per student:* $39,584. *Average need-based loan:* Freshmen: $4280. Undergraduates: $5065. *Parent loans:* $12,084,088 (69% need-based, 31% non-need-based). *Programs:* Federal Direct (Subsidized and Unsubsidized Stafford, PLUS), Perkins, college/university, alternative loans.

WORK-STUDY *Federal work-study:* Total amount: $3,456,668; 1,414 jobs averaging $2598. *State or other work-study/employment:* Total amount: $1,190,000 (25% need-based, 75% non-need-based). 576 part-time jobs averaging $2004.

ATHLETIC AWARDS Total amount: $4,803,792 (44% need-based, 56% non-need-based).

APPLYING FOR FINANCIAL AID *Required financial aid forms:* FAFSA, institution's own form. *Financial aid deadline:* 5/1 (priority: 2/15). *Notification date:* Continuous beginning 4/1. Students must reply by 5/1 or within 2 weeks of notification.

CONTACT Joseph R. Weglarz, Executive Director of Student Financial Services, Marist College, 3399 North Road, Poughkeepsie, NY 12601, 845-575-3230 or toll-free 800-436-5483. *Fax:* 845-575-3099. *E-mail:* joseph.weglarz@marist.edu. *Website:* http://www.marist.edu/.

MARLBORO COLLEGE
Marlboro, VT

Tuition & fees: $40,425	Average undergraduate aid package: $36,348

ABOUT THE INSTITUTION Independent, coed. *Awards:* bachelor's and master's degrees. 138 undergraduate majors. *Total enrollment:* 280. Undergraduates: 196. Freshmen: 55. Federal methodology is used as a basis for awarding need-based institutional aid.

UNDERGRADUATE EXPENSES for 2017–2018 *Application fee:* $50. *Comprehensive fee:* $52,355 includes full-time tuition ($39,481), mandatory fees ($944), and room and board ($11,930). *College room only:* $6900. Full-time tuition and fees vary according to reciprocity agreements. *Part-time tuition:* $1316 per credit hour. Part-time tuition and fees vary according to course load.

FRESHMAN FINANCIAL AID (Fall 2016, est.) 51 applied for aid; of those 90% were deemed to have need. 100% of freshmen with need received aid; of those 98% had need fully met. *Average percent of need met:* 77% (excluding resources awarded to replace EFC). *Average financial aid package:* $39,972 (excluding resources awarded to replace EFC). 5% of all full-time freshmen had no need and received non-need-based gift aid.

UNDERGRADUATE FINANCIAL AID (Fall 2016, est.) 169 applied for aid; of those 94% were deemed to have need. 100% of undergraduates with need received aid; of those 100% had need fully met. *Average percent of need met:* 79% (excluding resources awarded to replace EFC). *Average financial aid package:* $36,348 (excluding resources awarded to replace EFC). 14% of all full-time undergraduates had no need and received non-need-based gift aid.

GIFT AID (NEED-BASED) *Total amount:* $5,227,997 (9% federal, 1% state, 88% institutional, 2% external sources). *Receiving aid:* Freshmen: 80% (44); all full-time undergraduates: 83% (156). *Average award:* Freshmen: $36,494; Undergraduates: $30,266. *Scholarships, grants, and awards:* Federal Pell, FSEOG, state, private, college/university gift aid from institutional funds.

GIFT AID (NON-NEED-BASED) *Receiving aid:* Freshmen: 60% (33). Undergraduates: 65% (123). *Average award:* Freshmen: $13,000. Undergraduates: $17,937. *Scholarships, grants, and awards by category:* Academic interests/achievement: general academic interests/achievements. Creative arts/performance: art/fine arts, general creative arts/performance. Special achievements/activities: leadership. *Tuition waivers:* Full or partial for employees or children of employees.

LOANS *Student loans:* $1,570,616 (61% need-based, 39% non-need-based). 77% of past graduating class borrowed through all loan programs. *Average indebtedness per student:* $31,747. *Average need-based loan:* Freshmen: $3294. Undergraduates: $4387. *Parent loans:* $241,523 (100% need-based). *Programs:* Federal Direct (Subsidized and Unsubsidized Stafford, PLUS).

WORK-STUDY *Federal work-study:* Total amount: $293,460; jobs available. *State or other work-study/employment:* Part-time jobs available.

APPLYING FOR FINANCIAL AID *Required financial aid form:* FAFSA. *Financial aid deadline:* 3/1. *Notification date:* Continuous beginning 3/1. Students must reply by 5/1 or within 2 weeks of notification.

CONTACT Financial Aid Office, Marlboro College, PO Box A, 2582 South Road, Marlboro, VT 05344-0300, 802-258-9237 or toll-free 800-343-0049. *Fax:* 802-258-9300. *E-mail:* finaid@marlboro.edu. *Website:* http://www.marlboro.edu/.

MARQUETTE UNIVERSITY
Milwaukee, WI

Tuition & fees: $39,800	Average undergraduate aid package: $27,906

ABOUT THE INSTITUTION Independent Roman Catholic (Jesuit), coed. *Awards:* certificates, bachelor's, master's, and doctoral degrees. 78 undergraduate majors. *Total enrollment:* 11,294. Undergraduates: 8,238. Freshmen: 2,005. Federal methodology is used as a basis for awarding need-based institutional aid.

UNDERGRADUATE EXPENSES for 2017–2018 *Tuition:* full-time $39,330; part-time $1025 per credit hour. Full-time tuition and fees vary according to course load and program. Part-time tuition and fees vary according to program. Room and board charges vary according to housing facility.

FRESHMAN FINANCIAL AID (Fall 2016, est.) 1,647 applied for aid; of those 75% were deemed to have need. 100% of freshmen with need received aid; of those 27% had need fully met. *Average percent of need met:* 82% (excluding resources awarded to replace EFC). *Average financial aid package:* $29,842 (excluding resources awarded to replace EFC). 37% of all full-time freshmen had no need and received non-need-based gift aid.

UNDERGRADUATE FINANCIAL AID (Fall 2016, est.) 5,641 applied for aid; of those 79% were deemed to have need. 100% of undergraduates with need received aid; of those 27% had need fully met. *Average percent of need met:* 80% (excluding resources awarded to replace EFC). *Average financial aid package:* $27,906 (excluding resources awarded to replace EFC). 40% of all full-time undergraduates had no need and received non-need-based gift aid.

GIFT AID (NEED-BASED) *Total amount:* $87,482,694 (8% federal, 3% state, 83% institutional, 6% external sources). *Receiving aid:* Freshmen: 61% (1,223); all full-time undergraduates: 55% (4,381). *Average award:* Freshmen: $23,771; Undergraduates: $20,324. *Scholarships, grants, and awards:* Federal Pell, FSEOG, state, private, college/university gift aid from institutional funds, Federal Nursing, Veterans Education Benefits (GI Bill).

GIFT AID (NON-NEED-BASED) *Total amount:* $45,179,825 (91% institutional, 9% external sources). *Receiving aid:* Freshmen: 9% (175). Undergraduates: 7% (525). *Average award:* Freshmen: $14,756. Undergraduates: $11,877. *Scholarships, grants, and awards by category:* Academic interests/achievement: 7,019 awards ($77,779,834 total): biological sciences, business, communication, education, engineering/technologies, English, foreign languages, general academic interests/achievements, home economics, mathematics, physical sciences. Creative arts/performance: 10 awards ($7250 total): theater/drama. Special characteristics: 149 awards ($5,378,016 total): children of faculty/staff. *Tuition waivers:* Full or partial for employees or children of employees, senior citizens. *ROTC:* Army, Naval, Air Force.

LOANS *Student loans:* $49,648,893 (63% need-based, 37% non-need-based). 56% of past graduating class borrowed through all loan programs. *Average indebtedness per student:* $35,421. *Average need-based loan:* Freshmen: $5249. Undergraduates: $7646. *Parent loans:* $17,184,216 (30% need-based, 70% non-need-based). *Programs:* Federal Direct (Subsidized and Unsubsidized Stafford, PLUS), Perkins, Federal Nursing, state, college/university, private loans.

WORK-STUDY *Federal work-study:* Total amount: $3,796,827; jobs available. *State or other work-study/employment:* Part-time jobs available.

ATHLETIC AWARDS Total amount: $5,904,911 (30% need-based, 70% non-need-based).

APPLYING FOR FINANCIAL AID *Required financial aid form:* FAFSA. *Financial aid deadline:* Continuous. *Notification date:* Continuous beginning 3/3.

CONTACT Susan Teerink, Director of Financial Aid, Marquette University, Zilber Hall, 1250 West Wisconsin Avenue, Milwaukee, WI 53201-1881, 414-288-4000 or toll-free 800-222-6544. *Fax:* 414-288-1718. *E-mail:* financialaid@marquette.edu. *Website:* http://www.marquette.edu/.

MARSHALL UNIVERSITY
Huntington, WV

Tuition & fees (WV res): $7154	Average undergraduate aid package: $10,625

ABOUT THE INSTITUTION State-supported, coed. *Awards:* certificates, associate, bachelor's, master's, and doctoral degrees. 55 undergraduate majors. *Total enrollment:* 13,647. Undergraduates: 9,615. Freshmen: 1,888. Federal methodology is used as a basis for awarding need-based institutional aid.

UNDERGRADUATE EXPENSES for 2016–2017 *Application fee:* $30. *Tuition, state resident:* full-time $6032; part-time $251.50 per credit hour. *Tuition, nonresident:* full-time $15,260; part-time $636 per credit hour. *Required fees:* full-time $1122; $47 per credit hour or $47 per credit hour. Full-time tuition and fees vary according to degree level, location, program, and reciprocity agreements. Part-time tuition and fees vary according to course load, degree level, location, program, and reciprocity agreements. *College room and board:* $10,126; *Room* only: $6266. Room and board charges vary according to board plan and housing facility.

FRESHMAN FINANCIAL AID (Fall 2016, est.) 1,824 applied for aid; of those 77% were deemed to have need. 99% of freshmen with need received aid; of those 33% had need fully met. *Average percent of need met:* 50% (excluding resources awarded to replace EFC). *Average financial aid package:* $11,418 (excluding resources awarded to replace EFC). 16% of all full-time freshmen had no need and received non-need-based gift aid.

UNDERGRADUATE FINANCIAL AID (Fall 2016, est.) 7,039 applied for aid; of those 79% were deemed to have need. 99% of undergraduates with need received aid; of those 28% had need fully met. *Average percent of need met:* 49% (excluding resources awarded to replace EFC). *Average financial aid package:* $10,625 (excluding resources awarded to replace EFC). 13% of all full-time undergraduates had no need and received non-need-based gift aid.

GIFT AID (NEED-BASED) *Total amount:* $27,992,871 (63% federal, 32% state, 5% institutional). *Receiving aid:* Freshmen: 58% (1,092); all full-time undergraduates: 53% (4,227). *Average award:* Freshmen: $7050; Undergraduates: $6326. *Scholarships, grants, and awards:* Federal Pell, FSEOG, state, private, college/university gift aid from institutional funds, Federal Nursing.

GIFT AID (NON-NEED-BASED) *Total amount:* $18,963,065 (49% state, 34% institutional, 17% external sources). *Receiving aid:* Freshmen: 45% (856). Undergraduates: 33% (2,586). *Average award:* Freshmen: $2523. Undergraduates: $2230. *Scholarships, grants, and awards by category: Academic interests/ achievement:* general academic interests/achievements. *Creative arts/performance:* art/fine arts, general creative arts/performance. *Special characteristics:* children and siblings of alumni, children of faculty/staff, local/state students, members of minority groups. *Tuition waivers:* Full or partial for children of alumni, employees or children of employees, senior citizens. *ROTC:* Army.

LOANS *Student loans:* $38,694,576 (90% need-based, 10% non-need-based). 69% of past graduating class borrowed through all loan programs. *Average indebtedness per student:* $27,121. *Average need-based loan:* Freshmen: $5535. Undergraduates: $6843. *Parent loans:* $7,123,979 (100% non-need-based). *Programs:* Federal Direct (Subsidized and Unsubsidized Stafford, PLUS), Perkins, Federal Nursing.

WORK-STUDY *Federal work-study:* Total amount: $634,539; jobs available. *State or other work-study/employment:* Part-time jobs available.

ATHLETIC AWARDS Total amount: $5,645,224 (100% non-need-based).

APPLYING FOR FINANCIAL AID *Required financial aid forms:* FAFSA, state aid form. *Financial aid deadline (priority):* 3/1. *Notification date:* 4/1.

CONTACT Ms. Kathy Bialk, Director of Student Financial Aid, Marshall University, One John Marshall Drive, Huntington, WV 25755, 304-696-2280 or toll-free 800-642-3499. *Fax:* 304-696-3242. *E-mail:* bialkk@marshall.edu. *Website:* http://www.marshall.edu/.

MARS HILL UNIVERSITY
Mars Hill, NC

CONTACT Amanda Randolph, Director of Financial Aid, Mars Hill University, PO Box 370, Mars Hill, NC 28754, 828-689-1123 or toll-free 866-648-4968. *Fax:* 828-689-1300. *E-mail:* arandolph@mhc.edu. *Website:* http://www.mhu.edu/.

MARTIN LUTHER COLLEGE
New Ulm, MN

Tuition & fees: $14,680	Average undergraduate aid package: $11,797

ABOUT THE INSTITUTION Independent Wisconsin Evangelical Lutheran Synod, coed. *Awards:* certificates, diplomas, bachelor's, and master's degrees. 6 undergraduate majors. *Total enrollment:* 937. Undergraduates: 859. Freshmen: 196. Federal methodology is used as a basis for awarding need-based institutional aid.

UNDERGRADUATE EXPENSES for 2017–2018 *Comprehensive fee:* $20,470 includes full-time tuition ($14,680) and room and board ($5790). Room and board charges vary according to housing facility.

FRESHMAN FINANCIAL AID (Fall 2015) 149 applied for aid; of those 87% were deemed to have need. 100% of freshmen with need received aid; of those 10% had

need fully met. *Average percent of need met:* 69% (excluding resources awarded to replace EFC). *Average financial aid package:* $11,379 (excluding resources awarded to replace EFC). 13% of all full-time freshmen had no need and received non-need-based gift aid.

UNDERGRADUATE FINANCIAL AID (Fall 2015) 571 applied for aid; of those 87% were deemed to have need. 100% of undergraduates with need received aid; of those 13% had need fully met. *Average percent of need met:* 70% (excluding resources awarded to replace EFC). *Average financial aid package:* $11,797 (excluding resources awarded to replace EFC). 16% of all full-time undergraduates had no need and received non-need-based gift aid.

GIFT AID (NEED-BASED) *Total amount:* $3,702,884 (24% federal, 7% state, 54% institutional, 15% external sources). *Receiving aid:* Freshmen: 80% (128); all full-time undergraduates: 77% (488). *Average award:* Freshmen: $7906; Undergraduates: $7554. *Scholarships, grants, and awards:* Federal Pell, FSEOG, state, private, college/university gift aid from institutional funds.

GIFT AID (NON-NEED-BASED) *Total amount:* $583,964 (51% institutional, 49% external sources). *Receiving aid:* Freshmen: 4% (7). Undergraduates: 4% (24). *Average award:* Freshmen: $2928. Undergraduates: $2746. *Scholarships, grants, and awards by category: Academic interests/achievement:* general academic interests/achievements. *Creative arts/performance:* music.

LOANS *Student loans:* $4,190,389 (72% need-based, 28% non-need-based). 75% of past graduating class borrowed through all loan programs. *Average indebtedness per student:* $22,582. *Average need-based loan:* Freshmen: $3836. Undergraduates: $4554. *Parent loans:* $145,735 (44% need-based, 56% non-need-based). *Programs:* Federal Direct (Subsidized and Unsubsidized Stafford, PLUS), Perkins, state, college/university, alternative loans.

WORK-STUDY *Federal work-study:* jobs available. *State or other work-study/employment:* Total amount: $21,003 (100% need-based). Part-time jobs available.

APPLYING FOR FINANCIAL AID *Required financial aid forms:* FAFSA, institution's own form. *Financial aid deadline:* 4/15. *Notification date:* Continuous beginning 3/15. Students must reply by 9/1.

CONTACT Mr. Mark Bauer, Director of Financial Aid, Martin Luther College, 1995 Luther Court, New Ulm, MN 56073, 507-354-8221 or toll-free 877-MLC-1995. *Fax:* 507-354-8225. *E-mail:* bauermd@mlc-wels.edu. *Website:* http://www.mlc-wels.edu/.

MARTIN METHODIST COLLEGE
Pulaski, TN

CONTACT Ms. Anita Beecham, Financial Aid Assistant, Martin Methodist College, 433 West Madison Street, Pulaski, TN 38478-2716, 931-363-9808 or toll-free 800-467-1273. *Fax:* 931-363-9818. *E-mail:* abeecham@martinmethodist.edu. *Website:* http://www.martinmethodist.edu/.

MARTIN UNIVERSITY
Indianapolis, IN

CONTACT Berdia Marshall, Director of Financial Aid, Martin University, 2171 Avondale Place, Indianapolis, IN 46218-3867, 317-543-3670. *Fax:* 317-543-4790. *E-mail:* bmarshall@martin.edu. *Website:* http://www.martin.edu/.

MARY BALDWIN UNIVERSITY
Staunton, VA

Tuition & fees: $31,085	Average undergraduate aid package: $24,347

ABOUT THE INSTITUTION Independent, coed, primarily women. *Awards:* certificates, bachelor's, master's, and doctoral degrees. 27 undergraduate majors. *Total enrollment:* 1,748. Undergraduates: 1,310. Freshmen: 227. Federal methodology is used as a basis for awarding need-based institutional aid.

UNDERGRADUATE EXPENSES for 2017–2018 *Comprehensive fee:* $40,495 includes full-time tuition ($30,690), mandatory fees ($395), and room and board ($9410). Full-time tuition and fees vary according to degree level. Room and board charges vary according to housing facility and student level. *Part-time tuition:* $460 per semester hour. *Part-time fees:* $58 per term. Part-time tuition and fees vary according to degree level.

FRESHMAN FINANCIAL AID (Fall 2016, est.) 223 applied for aid; of those 97% were deemed to have need. 100% of freshmen with need received aid; of those 17% had need fully met. *Average percent of need met:* 80% (excluding resources awarded to replace EFC). *Average financial aid package:* $28,645 (excluding resources awarded to replace EFC). 4% of all full-time freshmen had no need and received non-need-based gift aid.

UNDERGRADUATE FINANCIAL AID (Fall 2016, est.) 786 applied for aid; of those 96% were deemed to have need. 100% of undergraduates with need received aid; of those 14% had need fully met. *Average percent of need met:* 70% (excluding resources awarded to replace EFC). *Average financial aid package:* $24,347 (excluding resources awarded to replace EFC). 7% of all full-time undergraduates had no need and received non-need-based gift aid.

GIFT AID (NEED-BASED) Total amount: $15,702,951 (22% federal, 9% state, 68% institutional, 1% external sources). *Receiving aid:* Freshmen: 96% (217); all full-time undergraduates: 91% (752). *Average award:* Freshmen: $25,259; Undergraduates: $20,360. *Scholarships, grants, and awards:* Federal Pell, FSEOG, state, private, college/university gift aid from institutional funds.

GIFT AID (NON-NEED-BASED) Total amount: $1,117,377 (5% federal, 8% state, 85% institutional, 2% external sources). *Average award:* Freshmen: $16,475. Undergraduates: $16,960. *Scholarships, grants, and awards by category:* Academic interests/achievement: 626 awards ($9,038,612 total): general academic interests/achievements. *Special characteristics:* 13 awards ($253,290 total): children of educators, children of faculty/staff. *Tuition waivers:* Full or partial for employees or children of employees. *ROTC:* Army cooperative, Naval cooperative, Air Force cooperative.

LOANS Student loans: $7,896,918 (96% need-based, 4% non-need-based). 84% of past graduating class borrowed through all loan programs. *Average indebtedness per student:* $35,169. *Average need-based loan:* Freshmen: $3248. Undergraduates: $4317. *Parent loans:* $1,113,315 (95% need-based, 5% non-need-based). *Programs:* Federal Direct (Subsidized and Unsubsidized Stafford, PLUS), Perkins, alternative loans.

WORK-STUDY Federal work-study: Total amount: $313,113; 214 jobs averaging $1463. *State or other work-study/employment:* Total amount: $162,284 (87% need-based, 13% non-need-based). 104 part-time jobs averaging $1553.

APPLYING FOR FINANCIAL AID Required financial aid forms: FAFSA, state aid form. *Financial aid deadline (priority):* 3/1. *Notification date:* Continuous beginning 12/1.

CONTACT Mrs. Robin Dietrich, Director of Financial Aid, Mary Baldwin University, PO Box 1500, Staunton, VA 24402, 540-887-7025 or toll-free 800-468-2262. *Fax:* 540-887-7229. *E-mail:* rdietric@marybaldwin.edu.
Website: http://www.marybaldwin.edu/.

MARYGROVE COLLEGE
Detroit, MI

Tuition & fees: $22,064	Average undergraduate aid package: N/A

ABOUT THE INSTITUTION Independent Roman Catholic, coed, primarily women. 32 undergraduate majors.

UNDERGRADUATE EXPENSES for 2016–2017 *Comprehensive fee:* $29,164 includes full-time tuition ($21,526), mandatory fees ($538), and room and board ($7100). Room and board charges vary according to board plan. *Part-time tuition:* $620 per credit hour. *Part-time fees:* $228 per term. Part-time tuition and fees vary according to location.

GIFT AID (NEED-BASED) Scholarships, grants, and awards: Federal Pell, FSEOG, state, private, college/university gift aid from institutional funds.

GIFT AID (NON-NEED-BASED) Scholarships, grants, and awards by category: Academic interests/achievement: general academic interests/achievements. Creative arts/performance: art/fine arts, dance, music. Special achievements/activities: leadership. Special characteristics: children of faculty/staff, out-of-state students, parents of current students, siblings of current students, spouses of current students, veterans, veterans' children.

LOANS Programs: Perkins, state.
WORK-STUDY Federal work-study jobs available.
APPLYING FOR FINANCIAL AID Required financial aid forms: FAFSA, institution's own form, nontaxable income verification, independent student verification. *Notification date:* 8/15.
CONTACT Office of Scholarships and Financial Aid, Marygrove College, 8425 West McNichols Road, Detroit, MI 48221-2599, 313-927-1692 or toll-free 866-313-1297. *Fax:* 313-927-1533. *E-mail:* mfao@marygrove.edu.
Website: http://www.marygrove.edu/.

MARYLAND INSTITUTE COLLEGE OF ART
Baltimore, MD

CONTACT Ms. Diane Prengaman, Associate Vice President for Financial Aid, Maryland Institute College of Art, 1300 Mount Royal Avenue, Baltimore, MD 21217, 410-225-2285. *Fax:* 410-225-2337. *E-mail:* dprengam@mica.edu.
Website: http://www.mica.edu/.

MARYLHURST UNIVERSITY
Marylhurst, OR

Tuition & fees: $20,835	Average undergraduate aid package: $17,455

ABOUT THE INSTITUTION Independent Roman Catholic, coed. *Awards:* certificates, bachelor's, and master's degrees. 12 undergraduate majors. *Total enrollment:* 410. Undergraduates: 398. Freshmen: 2. Federal methodology is used as a basis for awarding need-based institutional aid.

UNDERGRADUATE EXPENSES for 2016–2017 *Application fee:* $50. *Tuition:* full-time $20,835; part-time $463 per credit hour. Full-time tuition and fees vary according to program. Part-time tuition and fees vary according to program.

FRESHMAN FINANCIAL AID (Fall 2016, est.) 1 applied for aid; of those 100% were deemed to have need. 100% of freshmen with need received aid. *Average percent of need met:* 42% (excluding resources awarded to replace EFC). *Average financial aid package:* $8266 (excluding resources awarded to replace EFC).

UNDERGRADUATE FINANCIAL AID (Fall 2016, est.) 123 applied for aid; of those 95% were deemed to have need. 100% of undergraduates with need received aid; of those 2% had need fully met. *Average percent of need met:* 52% (excluding resources awarded to replace EFC). *Average financial aid package:* $17,455 (excluding resources awarded to replace EFC). 19% of all full-time undergraduates had no need and received non-need-based gift aid.

GIFT AID (NEED-BASED) Total amount: $2,253,876 (33% federal, 8% state, 54% institutional, 5% external sources). *Receiving aid:* Freshmen: 100% (1); all full-time undergraduates: 86% (116). *Average award:* Freshmen: $4766; Undergraduates: $11,607. *Scholarships, grants, and awards:* Federal Pell, FSEOG, state, private, college/university gift aid from institutional funds, United Negro College Fund.

GIFT AID (NON-NEED-BASED) Total amount: $209,743 (3% federal, 1% state, 95% institutional, 1% external sources). *Average award:* Undergraduates: $4553. *Tuition waivers:* Full or partial for employees or children of employees.

LOANS Student loans: $2,389,279 (89% need-based, 11% non-need-based). 100% of past graduating class borrowed through all loan programs. *Average indebtedness per student:* $51,833. *Average need-based loan:* Freshmen: $3500. Undergraduates: $4030. *Parent loans:* $72,225 (80% need-based, 20% non-need-based). *Programs:* Federal Direct (Subsidized and Unsubsidized Stafford, PLUS), Perkins.

WORK-STUDY Federal work-study: Total amount: $512,611; 111 jobs averaging $5728.

APPLYING FOR FINANCIAL AID Required financial aid forms: FAFSA, institution's own form. *Financial aid deadline:* Continuous. *Notification date:* Continuous beginning 4/1. Students must reply within 8 weeks of notification.

CONTACT Tracy Reisinger, Office of Financial Aid, Marylhurst University, 17600 Pacific Highway, PO Box 261, Marylhurst, OR 97036, 503-699-6253 Ext. 7025 or toll-free 800-634-9982. *Fax:* 503-635-6585. *E-mail:* treisinger@marylhurst.edu.
Website: http://www.marylhurst.edu/.

MARYMOUNT CALIFORNIA UNIVERSITY
Rancho Palos Verdes, CA

Tuition & fees: $35,884   **Average undergraduate aid package: $34,529**

ABOUT THE INSTITUTION Independent Roman Catholic, coed. *Awards:* associate, bachelor's, and master's degrees. 7 undergraduate majors. *Total enrollment:* 985. Undergraduates: 942. Freshmen: 219. Federal methodology is used as a basis for awarding need-based institutional aid.

UNDERGRADUATE EXPENSES for 2017–2018 *Application fee:* $50. *One-time required fee:* $300. *Comprehensive fee:* $50,296 includes full-time tuition ($34,134), mandatory fees ($1750), and room and board ($14,412). *College room only:* $9004. Full-time tuition and fees vary according to location. Room and board charges vary according to board plan and housing facility. *Part-time tuition:* $1475 per credit hour. *Part-time fees:* $600 per year. Part-time tuition and fees vary according to location.

FRESHMAN FINANCIAL AID (Fall 2016, est.) 158 applied for aid; of those 99% were deemed to have need. 100% of freshmen with need received aid; of those 33% had need fully met. *Average percent of need met:* 94% (excluding resources awarded to replace EFC). *Average financial aid package:* $34,769 (excluding resources awarded to replace EFC). 11% of all full-time freshmen had no need and received non-need-based gift aid.

UNDERGRADUATE FINANCIAL AID (Fall 2016, est.) 607 applied for aid; of those 99% were deemed to have need. 100% of undergraduates with need received aid; of those 24% had need fully met. *Average percent of need met:* 91% (excluding resources awarded to replace EFC). *Average financial aid package:* $34,529 (excluding resources awarded to replace EFC). 10% of all full-time undergraduates had no need and received non-need-based gift aid.

GIFT AID (NEED-BASED) *Total amount:* $7,711,553 (25% federal, 25% state, 48% institutional, 2% external sources). *Receiving aid:* Freshmen: 71% (156); all full-time undergraduates: 68% (598). *Average award:* Freshmen: $23,201; Undergraduates: $22,320. *Scholarships, grants, and awards:* Federal Pell, FSEOG, state, private, college/university gift aid from institutional funds.

GIFT AID (NON-NEED-BASED) *Total amount:* $7,768,586 (1% state, 91% institutional, 8% external sources). *Receiving aid:* Freshmen: 58% (128). Undergraduates: 57% (504). *Average award:* Freshmen: $10,959. Undergraduates: $14,914. *Scholarships, grants, and awards by category:* Creative arts/performance: 9 awards ($49,000 total): applied art and design. *Tuition waivers:* Full or partial for employees or children of employees, senior citizens.

LOANS *Student loans:* $4,899,180 (43% need-based, 57% non-need-based). 78% of past graduating class borrowed through all loan programs. *Average indebtedness per student:* $32,470. *Average need-based loan:* Freshmen: $3500. Undergraduates: $4351. *Parent loans:* $2,932,436 (100% non-need-based). *Programs:* Federal Direct (Subsidized and Unsubsidized Stafford, PLUS), alternative loans.

WORK-STUDY *Federal work-study:* Total amount: $24,000; 7 jobs averaging $4000. *State or other work-study/employment:* Total amount: $1,195,284 (100% non-need-based). Part-time jobs available.

ATHLETIC AWARDS Total amount: $2,912,143 (100% non-need-based).

APPLYING FOR FINANCIAL AID *Required financial aid form:* FAFSA. *Financial aid deadline:* 2/15 (priority: 3/2). *Notification date:* Continuous beginning 3/1. Students must reply by 8/1 or within 3 weeks of notification.

CONTACT Mr. Pedro Ladino, Director of Financial Aid, Marymount California University, 30800 Palos Verdes Drive East, Rancho Palos Verdes, CA 90275, 310-303-7217. Fax: 310-303-7270. E-mail: pladino@marymountcalifornia.edu. *Website:* http://www.marymountcalifornia.edu/.

MARYMOUNT MANHATTAN COLLEGE
New York, NY

Tuition & fees: $31,950   **Average undergraduate aid package: $17,046**

ABOUT THE INSTITUTION Independent, coed. *Awards:* associate and bachelor's degrees. 53 undergraduate majors. *Total enrollment:* 2,069. Undergraduates: 2,069. Freshmen: 552. Both federal and institutional methodology are used as a basis for awarding need-based institutional aid.

UNDERGRADUATE EXPENSES for 2017–2018 *Application fee:* $60. *Comprehensive fee:* $48,350 includes full-time tuition ($30,458), mandatory fees ($1492), and room and board ($16,400). *College room only:* $14,400. Full-time tuition and fees vary according to course load and program. Room and board charges vary according to board plan. *Part-time tuition:* $1018 per credit hour. *Part-time fees:* $684 per term. Part-time tuition and fees vary according to course load and program.

FRESHMAN FINANCIAL AID (Fall 2015) 431 applied for aid; of those 81% were deemed to have need. 99% of freshmen with need received aid; of those 7% had need fully met. *Average percent of need met:* 51% (excluding resources awarded to replace EFC). *Average financial aid package:* $17,274 (excluding resources awarded to replace EFC). 15% of all full-time freshmen had no need and received non-need-based gift aid.

UNDERGRADUATE FINANCIAL AID (Fall 2015) 1,330 applied for aid; of those 86% were deemed to have need. 99% of undergraduates with need received aid; of those 8% had need fully met. *Average percent of need met:* 51% (excluding resources awarded to replace EFC). *Average financial aid package:* $17,046 (excluding resources awarded to replace EFC). 9% of all full-time undergraduates had no need and received non-need-based gift aid.

GIFT AID (NEED-BASED) *Total amount:* $15,873,015 (15% federal, 7% state, 76% institutional, 2% external sources). *Receiving aid:* Freshmen: 68% (345); all full-time undergraduates: 66% (1,129). *Average award:* Freshmen: $14,781; Undergraduates: $13,396. *Scholarships, grants, and awards:* Federal Pell, FSEOG, state, private, college/university gift aid from institutional funds.

GIFT AID (NON-NEED-BASED) *Total amount:* $3,750,957 (8% federal, 89% institutional, 3% external sources). *Average award:* Freshmen: $9202. Undergraduates: $8889. *Scholarships, grants, and awards by category:* Academic interests/achievement: 1,121 awards ($8,865,013 total): biological sciences, general academic interests/achievements. Creative arts/performance: 373 awards ($1,119,972 total): art/fine arts, dance, performing arts. Special achievements/activities: 47 awards ($88,162 total): leadership. Special characteristics: 77 awards ($474,245 total): general special characteristics, international students, local/state students, out-of-state students, veterans, veterans' children. *Tuition waivers:* Full or partial for employees or children of employees, senior citizens.

LOANS *Student loans:* $10,356,873 (37% need-based, 63% non-need-based). 71% of past graduating class borrowed through all loan programs. *Average indebtedness per student:* $31,606. *Average need-based loan:* Freshmen: $3293. Undergraduates: $4219. *Parent loans:* $11,882,370 (100% non-need-based). *Programs:* Federal Direct (Subsidized and Unsubsidized Stafford, PLUS).

WORK-STUDY *Federal work-study:* 139 jobs averaging $3181.

APPLYING FOR FINANCIAL AID *Required financial aid forms:* FAFSA, state aid form. *Financial aid deadline:* Continuous. *Notification date:* Continuous beginning 2/15. Students must reply by 5/1 or within 2 weeks of notification.

CONTACT Christina Bennett, Director of Financial Aid, Marymount Manhattan College, 221 East 71st Street, New York, NY 10021, 212-517-0556 or toll-free 800-627-9668. E-mail: cbennett@mmm.edu. *Website:* http://www.mmm.edu/.

MARYMOUNT UNIVERSITY
Arlington, VA

Tuition & fees: $30,426	Average undergraduate aid package: $19,015

ABOUT THE INSTITUTION Independent Roman Catholic Church, coed. *Awards:* certificates, bachelor's, master's, and doctoral degrees. 26 undergraduate majors. *Total enrollment:* 3,369. Undergraduates: 2,323. Freshmen: 442. Both federal and institutional methodology are used as a basis for awarding need-based institutional aid.

UNDERGRADUATE EXPENSES for 2017–2018 *Application fee:* $40. *One-time required fee:* $450. *Comprehensive fee:* $43,231 includes full-time tuition ($29,950), mandatory fees ($476), and room and board ($12,805). Room and board charges vary according to housing facility. *Part-time tuition:* $975 per credit hour. *Part-time fees:* $11 per credit hour.

FRESHMAN FINANCIAL AID (Fall 2016, est.) 353 applied for aid; of those 88% were deemed to have need. 100% of freshmen with need received aid; of those 17% had need fully met. *Average percent of need met:* 68% (excluding resources awarded to replace EFC). *Average financial aid package:* $24,041 (excluding resources awarded to replace EFC). 23% of all full-time freshmen had no need and received non-need-based gift aid.

UNDERGRADUATE FINANCIAL AID (Fall 2016, est.) 1,447 applied for aid; of those 91% were deemed to have need. 100% of undergraduates with need received aid; of those 13% had need fully met. *Average percent of need met:* 55% (excluding resources awarded to replace EFC). *Average financial aid package:* $19,015 (excluding resources awarded to replace EFC). 20% of all full-time undergraduates had no need and received non-need-based gift aid.

GIFT AID (NEED-BASED) *Total amount:* $5,870,729 (49% federal, 1% state, 50% institutional). *Receiving aid:* Freshmen: 46% (202); all full-time undergraduates: 40% (839). *Average award:* Freshmen: $6527; Undergraduates: $6568. *Scholarships, grants, and awards:* Federal Pell, FSEOG, state, private, college/university gift aid from institutional funds.

GIFT AID (NON-NEED-BASED) *Total amount:* $19,701,347 (13% state, 86% institutional, 1% external sources). *Receiving aid:* Freshmen: 70% (307). Undergraduates: 52% (1,106). *Average award:* Freshmen: $14,374. Undergraduates: $12,782. *Scholarships, grants, and awards by category:* Academic interests/achievement: 1,426 awards ($15,160,131 total): biological sciences, business, communication, English, general academic interests/achievements, health fields, mathematics, religion/biblical studies, social sciences. *Special achievements/activities:* 379 awards ($1,016,161 total): community service, general special achievements/activities, leadership, memberships. *Special characteristics:* 1,300 awards ($3,449,017 total): children of current students, children of faculty/staff, general special characteristics, international students, local/state students, out-of-state students, religious affiliation, siblings of current students, veterans, veterans' children. *Tuition waivers:* Full or partial for employees or children of employees, senior citizens. *ROTC:* Army cooperative.

LOANS *Student loans:* $14,271,313 (33% need-based, 67% non-need-based). 73% of past graduating class borrowed through all loan programs. *Average indebtedness per student:* $35,545. *Average need-based loan:* Freshmen: $3458. Undergraduates: $4459. *Parent loans:* $8,244,524 (100% non-need-based). *Programs:* Federal Direct (Subsidized and Unsubsidized Stafford, PLUS), Perkins.

WORK-STUDY *Federal work-study:* Total amount: $1,113,356; 574 jobs averaging $1940. *State or other work-study/employment:* Part-time jobs available.

APPLYING FOR FINANCIAL AID *Required financial aid form:* FAFSA. *Financial aid deadline (priority):* 3/1. *Notification date:* Continuous beginning 3/15. Students must reply within 3 weeks of notification.

CONTACT Mrs. Debbie A. Raines, Director of Financial Aid, Marymount University, 2807 North Glebe Road, Arlington, VA 22207-4299, 703-284-1530 or toll-free 800-548-7638. *Fax:* 703-516-4771. *E-mail:* debbie.raines@marymount.edu. *Website:* http://www.marymount.edu/.

MARYVILLE COLLEGE
Maryville, TN

Tuition & fees: $33,524	Average undergraduate aid package: $33,152

ABOUT THE INSTITUTION Independent Presbyterian, coed. *Awards:* bachelor's degrees. 59 undergraduate majors. *Total enrollment:* 1,213. Undergraduates: 1,213. Freshmen: 338. Federal methodology is used as a basis for awarding need-based institutional aid.

UNDERGRADUATE EXPENSES for 2016–2017 *Comprehensive fee:* $44,392 includes full-time tuition ($32,746), mandatory fees ($778), and room and board ($10,868). *College room only:* $5450. Full-time tuition and fees vary according to course load. Room and board charges vary according to board plan and housing facility. Part-time tuition and fees vary according to course load.

FRESHMAN FINANCIAL AID (Fall 2016, est.) 323 applied for aid; of those 89% were deemed to have need. 100% of freshmen with need received aid; of those 26% had need fully met. *Average percent of need met:* 84% (excluding resources awarded to replace EFC). *Average financial aid package:* $32,660 (excluding resources awarded to replace EFC). 11% of all full-time freshmen had no need and received non-need-based gift aid.

UNDERGRADUATE FINANCIAL AID (Fall 2016, est.) 1,177 applied for aid; of those 84% were deemed to have need. 100% of undergraduates with need received aid; of those 25% had need fully met. *Average percent of need met:* 85% (excluding resources awarded to replace EFC). *Average financial aid package:* $33,152 (excluding resources awarded to replace EFC). 16% of all full-time undergraduates had no need and received non-need-based gift aid.

GIFT AID (NEED-BASED) *Total amount:* $26,100,256 (11% federal, 10% state, 78% institutional, 1% external sources). *Receiving aid:* Freshmen: 89% (286); all full-time undergraduates: 84% (988). *Average award:* Freshmen: $27,557; Undergraduates: $26,305. *Scholarships, grants, and awards:* Federal Pell, FSEOG, state, private, college/university gift aid from institutional funds.

GIFT AID (NON-NEED-BASED) *Total amount:* $5,865,400 (4% federal, 10% state, 85% institutional, 1% external sources). *Receiving aid:* Freshmen: 36% (116). Undergraduates: 33% (386). *Average award:* Freshmen: $22,190. Undergraduates: $21,614. *Scholarships, grants, and awards by category:* Academic interests/achievement: general academic interests/achievements. *Creative arts/performance:* art/fine arts, music, theater/drama. *Special achievements/activities:* community service, leadership. *Special characteristics:* children and siblings of alumni, children of faculty/staff, members of minority groups, religious affiliation, veterans. *Tuition waivers:* Full or partial for employees or children of employees.

LOANS *Student loans:* $8,903,971 (94% need-based, 6% non-need-based). *Average need-based loan:* Freshmen: $3809. Undergraduates: $4972. *Parent loans:* $2,435,492 (100% non-need-based). *Programs:* Federal Direct (Subsidized and Unsubsidized Stafford, PLUS), Perkins.

WORK-STUDY *Federal work-study:* Total amount: $1,059,134; jobs available. *State or other work-study/employment:* Total amount: $72,850 (65% need-based, 35% non-need-based). Part-time jobs available.

APPLYING FOR FINANCIAL AID *Required financial aid form:* FAFSA. *Financial aid deadline (priority):* 3/1. *Notification date:* Continuous beginning 3/15. Students must reply within 4 weeks of notification.

CONTACT Ms. Alayne Bowman, Director of Financial Aid, Maryville College, 502 East Lamar Alexander Parkway, Maryville, TN 37804-5907, 865-981-8087 or toll-free 800-597-2687. *Fax:* 865-981-8084. *E-mail:* alayne.bowman@maryvillecollege.edu. *Website:* http://www.maryvillecollege.edu/.

MARYVILLE UNIVERSITY OF SAINT LOUIS
St. Louis, MO

Tuition & fees: $27,958	Average undergraduate aid package: $19,215

ABOUT THE INSTITUTION Independent, coed. *Awards:* certificates, bachelor's, master's, and doctoral degrees. 56 undergraduate majors. *Total enrollment:* 6,828. Undergraduates: 2,967. Freshmen: 554. Both federal and institutional methodology are used as a basis for awarding need-based institutional aid.

UNDERGRADUATE EXPENSES for 2017–2018 *Comprehensive fee:* $38,046 includes full-time tuition ($25,558), mandatory fees ($2400), and room and board ($10,088). Full-time tuition and fees vary according to course load, degree level, and program. Room and board charges vary according to board plan and housing facility. *Part-time tuition:* $766 per credit hour. *Part-time fees:* $450 per term. Part-time tuition and fees vary according to class time, degree level, and program.

FRESHMAN FINANCIAL AID (Fall 2016, est.) 446 applied for aid; of those 89% were deemed to have need. 100% of freshmen with need received aid; of those 16% had need fully met. *Average percent of need met:* 60% (excluding resources awarded to replace EFC). *Average financial aid package:* $21,739 (excluding resources awarded to replace EFC). 28% of all full-time freshmen had no need and received non-need-based gift aid.

UNDERGRADUATE FINANCIAL AID (Fall 2016, est.) 1,609 applied for aid; of those 91% were deemed to have need. 100% of undergraduates with need received aid; of those 12% had need fully met. *Average percent of need met:* 52% (excluding resources awarded to replace EFC). *Average financial aid package:* $19,215 (excluding resources awarded to replace EFC). 27% of all full-time undergraduates had no need and received non-need-based gift aid.

GIFT AID (NEED-BASED) *Total amount:* $21,625,123 (15% federal, 4% state, 80% institutional, 1% external sources). *Receiving aid:* Freshmen: 71% (395); all full-time undergraduates: 66% (1,412). *Average award:* Freshmen: $18,465; Undergraduates: $15,556. *Scholarships, grants, and awards:* Federal Pell, FSEOG, state, private, college/university gift aid from institutional funds, United Negro College Fund, Academic Competitiveness Grants, National SMART Grants, TEACH Grants.

GIFT AID (NON-NEED-BASED) *Total amount:* $8,159,576 (1% state, 97% institutional, 2% external sources). *Receiving aid:* Freshmen: 11% (59). Undergraduates: 6% (137). *Average award:* Freshmen: $14,015. Undergraduates: $17,414. *Scholarships, grants, and awards by category:* Academic interests/achievement: 2,265 awards ($20,141,964 total): biological sciences, business, computer science, education, English, general academic interests/achievements, health fields, home economics, international studies, mathematics, social sciences. *Creative arts/performance:* 83 awards ($192,912 total): applied art and design, art/fine arts, music. *Special achievements/activities:* 501 awards ($3,739,665 total): cheerleading/drum major, community service, general special achievements/activities, leadership, religious involvement. *Special characteristics:* 467 awards ($2,532,007 total): adult students, children and siblings of alumni, ethnic background, general special characteristics, international students, members of minority groups, out-of-state students, parents of current students. *Tuition waivers:* Full or partial for employees or children of employees, senior citizens. *ROTC:* Army cooperative.

LOANS *Student loans:* $13,319,185 (78% need-based, 22% non-need-based). 84% of past graduating class borrowed through all loan programs. *Average indebtedness per student:* $19,266. *Average need-based loan:* Freshmen: $2767. Undergraduates: $3964. *Parent loans:* $5,601,862 (55% need-based, 45% non-need-based). *Programs:* Federal Direct (Subsidized and Unsubsidized Stafford, PLUS), Perkins, private loans.

WORK-STUDY *Federal work-study:* Total amount: $455,653; 350 jobs averaging $959. *State or other work-study/employment:* Total amount: $444,513 (69% need-based, 31% non-need-based). 334 part-time jobs averaging $316.

ATHLETIC AWARDS Total amount: $2,686,271 (39% need-based, 61% non-need-based).

APPLYING FOR FINANCIAL AID *Required financial aid form:* FAFSA. *Financial aid deadline (priority):* 3/1. *Notification date:* Continuous beginning 3/15. Students must reply by 5/1 or within 2 weeks of notification.

CONTACT Ms. Martha Harbaugh, Director of Financial Aid, Maryville University of Saint Louis, 650 Maryville University Drive, St. Louis, MO 63141-7299, 800-627-9855 Ext. 9361 or toll-free 800-627-9855. *Fax:* 314-529-9199. *E-mail:* mharbaugh@maryville.edu.
Website: http://www.maryville.edu/.

MARYWOOD UNIVERSITY
Scranton, PA

Tuition & fees: $33,000	Average undergraduate aid package: $24,643

ABOUT THE INSTITUTION Independent Roman Catholic, coed. *Awards:* certificates, bachelor's, master's, and doctoral degrees. 67 undergraduate majors. *Total enrollment:* 3,008. Undergraduates: 1,931. Freshmen: 325. Federal methodology is used as a basis for awarding need-based institutional aid.

UNDERGRADUATE EXPENSES for 2016–2017 *Application fee:* $35. *Comprehensive fee:* $46,900 includes full-time tuition ($31,250), mandatory fees ($1750), and room and board ($13,900). *College room only:* $7822. Full-time tuition and fees vary according to course load. Room and board charges vary according to board plan and housing facility. *Part-time tuition:* $630 per credit. *Part-time fees:* $450 per term. Part-time tuition and fees vary according to course load.

FRESHMAN FINANCIAL AID (Fall 2016, est.) 308 applied for aid; of those 90% were deemed to have need. 100% of freshmen with need received aid; of those 20% had need fully met. *Average percent of need met:* 75% (excluding resources awarded to replace EFC). *Average financial aid package:* $25,698 (excluding resources awarded to replace EFC). 14% of all full-time freshmen had no need and received non-need-based gift aid.

UNDERGRADUATE FINANCIAL AID (Fall 2016, est.) 1,561 applied for aid; of those 91% were deemed to have need. 100% of undergraduates with need received aid; of those 16% had need fully met. *Average percent of need met:* 69% (excluding resources awarded to replace EFC). *Average financial aid package:* $24,643 (excluding resources awarded to replace EFC). 15% of all full-time undergraduates had no need and received non-need-based gift aid.

GIFT AID (NEED-BASED) *Total amount:* $27,313,395 (10% federal, 8% state, 80% institutional, 2% external sources). *Receiving aid:* Freshmen: 85% (276); all full-time undergraduates: 82% (1,426). *Average award:* Freshmen: $20,946; Undergraduates: $19,504. *Scholarships, grants, and awards:* Federal Pell, FSEOG, state, private, college/university gift aid from institutional funds.

GIFT AID (NON-NEED-BASED) *Total amount:* $4,783,325 (1% federal, 95% institutional, 4% external sources). *Receiving aid:* Freshmen: 15% (47). Undergraduates: 8% (144). *Average award:* Freshmen: $15,609. Undergraduates: $13,963. *Scholarships, grants, and awards by category:* Academic interests/achievement: architecture, biological sciences, business, communication, computer science, education, English, foreign languages, general academic interests/achievements, health fields, home economics, mathematics, religion/biblical studies, social sciences. *Creative arts/performance:* art/fine arts, music. *Special achievements/activities:* community service, general special achievements/activities, leadership. *Tuition waivers:* Full or partial for employees or children of employees, senior citizens. *ROTC:* Army cooperative, Air Force cooperative.

LOANS *Student loans:* $15,120,676 (70% need-based, 30% non-need-based). 86% of past graduating class borrowed through all loan programs. *Average indebtedness per student:* $42,603. *Average need-based loan:* Freshmen: $3537. Undergraduates: $4509. *Parent loans:* $4,747,371 (52% need-based, 48% non-need-based). *Programs:* Federal Direct (Subsidized and Unsubsidized Stafford, PLUS), Perkins.

WORK-STUDY *Federal work-study:* Total amount: $1,132,364; 584 jobs averaging $1917.

APPLYING FOR FINANCIAL AID *Required financial aid forms:* FAFSA, state aid form. *Financial aid deadline (priority):* 2/15. *Notification date:* Continuous beginning 3/15. Students must reply by 5/1 or within 3 weeks of notification.

CONTACT Barbara Schmitt, Director of Financial Aid, Marywood University, 2300 Adams Avenue, Scranton, PA 18509-1598, 570-348-6225 or toll-free 866-279-9663. *Fax:* 570-961-4739. *E-mail:* schmitt@marywood.edu.
Website: http://www.marywood.edu/.

MASSACHUSETTS COLLEGE OF ART AND DESIGN
Boston, MA

Tuition & fees (MA res): $12,200	Average undergraduate aid package: $10,741

ABOUT THE INSTITUTION State-supported, coed. *Awards:* certificates, bachelor's, and master's degrees. 18 undergraduate majors. *Total enrollment:* 1,982. Undergraduates: 1,835. Freshmen: 374. Federal methodology is used as a basis for awarding need-based institutional aid.

UNDERGRADUATE EXPENSES for 2016–2017 *Application fee:* $70. *Tuition, state resident:* full-time $12,200. *Tuition, nonresident:* full-time $32,800. Part-time tuition and fees vary according to course load. *College room*

and board: $13,100. Room and board charges vary according to board plan and housing facility.

FRESHMAN FINANCIAL AID (Fall 2015) 254 applied for aid; of those 78% were deemed to have need. 100% of freshmen with need received aid. **Average financial aid package:** $11,838 (excluding resources awarded to replace EFC). 13% of all full-time freshmen had no need and received non-need-based gift aid.

UNDERGRADUATE FINANCIAL AID (Fall 2015) 1,080 applied for aid; of those 74% were deemed to have need. 100% of undergraduates with need received aid. **Average financial aid package:** $10,741 (excluding resources awarded to replace EFC). 13% of all full-time undergraduates had no need and received non-need-based gift aid.

GIFT AID (NEED-BASED) Total amount: $6,127,679 (31% federal, 9% state, 60% institutional). **Receiving aid:** Freshmen: 67% (195); all full-time undergraduates: 41% (640). **Average award:** Freshmen: $9005; Undergraduates: $9310. **Scholarships, grants, and awards:** Federal Pell, FSEOG, state, private, college/university gift aid from institutional funds.

GIFT AID (NON-NEED-BASED) Total amount: $2,183,632 (4% federal, 80% institutional, 16% external sources). **Receiving aid:** Freshmen: 2% (5). Undergraduates: 1% (8). **Average award:** Freshmen: $8066. Undergraduates: $6373. **Scholarships, grants, and awards by category:** Special characteristics: children of faculty/staff, children of union members/company employees, veterans. **Tuition waivers:** Full or partial for employees or children of employees, senior citizens.

LOANS Student loans: $8,555,838 (36% need-based, 64% non-need-based). 76% of past graduating class borrowed through all loan programs. **Average indebtedness per student:** $26,792. **Average need-based loan:** Freshmen: $3425. Undergraduates: $4277. **Parent loans:** $2,477,240 (100% non-need-based). **Programs:** Federal Direct (Subsidized and Unsubsidized Stafford, PLUS), Perkins, state, alternative loans.

WORK-STUDY Federal work-study: 154 jobs averaging $1258. **State or other work-study/employment:** Part-time jobs available.

APPLYING FOR FINANCIAL AID Required financial aid form: FAFSA. **Financial aid deadline (priority):** 3/1. **Notification date:** Continuous beginning 3/15. Students must reply within 3 weeks of notification.

CONTACT Auelio Ramirez, Director of Student Financial Assistance, Massachusetts College of Art and Design, 621 Huntington Avenue, Boston, MA 02115-5882, 617-879-7850. Fax: 617-879-7880. E-mail: aurelio.ramirez@massart.edu. Website: http://www.massart.edu/.

MASSACHUSETTS COLLEGE OF LIBERAL ARTS
North Adams, MA

Tuition & fees (MA res): $10,050	Average undergraduate aid package: $15,633

ABOUT THE INSTITUTION State-supported, coed. **Awards:** certificates, bachelor's, and master's degrees. 41 undergraduate majors. **Total enrollment:** 1,644. Undergraduates: 1,444. Freshmen: 327. Federal methodology is used as a basis for awarding need-based institutional aid.

UNDERGRADUATE EXPENSES for 2016–2017 Tuition, state resident: full-time $1030; part-time $42.92 per credit. **Tuition, nonresident:** full-time $9975; part-time $415.63 per credit. **Required fees:** full-time $9020; $300.08 per credit. Full-time tuition and fees vary according to reciprocity agreements. Part-time tuition and fees vary according to course load and reciprocity agreements. **College room and board:** $10,078. Room and board charges vary according to board plan and housing facility.

FRESHMAN FINANCIAL AID (Fall 2016, est.) 318 applied for aid; of those 81% were deemed to have need. 100% of freshmen with need received aid; of those 79% had need fully met. **Average percent of need met:** 79% (excluding resources awarded to replace EFC). **Average financial aid package:** $15,549 (excluding resources awarded to replace EFC). 11% of all full-time freshmen had no need and received non-need-based gift aid.

UNDERGRADUATE FINANCIAL AID (Fall 2016, est.) 1,154 applied for aid; of those 82% were deemed to have need. 99% of undergraduates with need received aid; of those 77% had need fully met. **Average percent of need met:** 80% (excluding resources awarded to replace EFC). **Average financial aid package:** $15,633 (excluding resources awarded to replace EFC). 7% of all full-time undergraduates had no need and received non-need-based gift aid.

GIFT AID (NEED-BASED) Total amount: $6,603,558 (46% federal, 16% state, 30% institutional, 8% external sources). **Receiving aid:** Freshmen: 69% (223); all full-time undergraduates: 63% (794). **Average award:** Freshmen: $6942; Undergraduates: $6517. **Scholarships, grants, and awards:** Federal Pell, FSEOG, state, private, college/university gift aid from institutional funds.

GIFT AID (NON-NEED-BASED) Total amount: $315,954 (5% state, 76% institutional, 19% external sources). **Receiving aid:** Freshmen: 47% (152). Undergraduates: 27% (334). **Average award:** Freshmen: $3455. Undergraduates: $3212. **Scholarships, grants, and awards by category:** Academic interests/achievement: biological sciences, business, communication, computer science, education, English, general academic interests/achievements, health fields, humanities, mathematics, physical sciences, social sciences. Creative arts/performance: applied art and design, art/fine arts, cinema/film/broadcasting, journalism/publications, music, performing arts, theater/drama. Special achievements/activities: general special achievements/activities, leadership, memberships. **Tuition waivers:** Full or partial for employees or children of employees, senior citizens.

LOANS Student loans: $8,752,791 (86% need-based, 14% non-need-based). 83% of past graduating class borrowed through all loan programs. **Average indebtedness per student:** $29,933. **Average need-based loan:** Freshmen: $3188. Undergraduates: $4138. **Parent loans:** $1,088,115 (86% need-based, 14% non-need-based). **Programs:** Federal Direct (Subsidized and Unsubsidized Stafford, PLUS), Perkins, state.

WORK-STUDY Federal work-study: Total amount: $403,366; jobs available. **State or other work-study/employment:** Part-time jobs available.

APPLYING FOR FINANCIAL AID Required financial aid form: FAFSA. **Financial aid deadline (priority):** 3/1. **Notification date:** Continuous beginning 3/1. Students must reply by 5/1 or within 2 weeks of notification.

CONTACT Mrs. Elizabeth M. Petri, Director of Financial Aid, Massachusetts College of Liberal Arts, 375 Church Street, North Adams, MA 01247, 413-662-5219 or toll-free 800-989-MCLA. Fax: 413-662-5105. E-mail: e.petri@mcla.edu. Website: http://www.mcla.edu/.

MASSACHUSETTS INSTITUTE OF TECHNOLOGY
Cambridge, MA

Tuition & fees: $49,892	Average undergraduate aid package: $44,056

ABOUT THE INSTITUTION Independent, coed. **Awards:** bachelor's, master's, and doctoral degrees. 39 undergraduate majors. **Total enrollment:** 11,376. Undergraduates: 4,524. Freshmen: 1,110. Institutional methodology is used as a basis for awarding need-based institutional aid.

UNDERGRADUATE EXPENSES for 2017–2018 Application fee: $75. **Comprehensive fee:** $64,612 includes full-time tuition ($49,580), mandatory fees ($312), and room and board ($14,720). **College room only:** $9420. Room and board charges vary according to board plan and housing facility. Part-time tuition and fees vary according to course load.

FRESHMAN FINANCIAL AID (Fall 2015) 850 applied for aid; of those 74% were deemed to have need. 100% of freshmen with need received aid; of those 100% had need fully met. **Average percent of need met:** 100% (excluding resources awarded to replace EFC). **Average financial aid package:** $44,934 (excluding resources awarded to replace EFC).

UNDERGRADUATE FINANCIAL AID (Fall 2015) 2,967 applied for aid; of those 86% were deemed to have need. 100% of undergraduates with need received aid; of those 100% had need fully met. **Average percent of need met:** 100% (excluding resources awarded to replace EFC). **Average financial aid package:** $44,056 (excluding resources awarded to replace EFC).

GIFT AID (NEED-BASED) Total amount: $106,737,095 (5% federal, 91% institutional, 4% external sources). **Receiving aid:** Freshmen: 55% (615); all full-time undergraduates: 55% (2,472). **Average award:** Freshmen: $42,351; Undergraduates: $41,767. **Scholarships, grants, and awards:** Federal Pell, FSEOG, state, private, college/university gift aid from institutional funds, United Negro College Fund.

GIFT AID (NON-NEED-BASED) Total amount: $8,783,735 (9% federal, 91% external sources). **Receiving aid:** Freshmen: 3% (29). Undergraduates: 1% (59). **Tuition waivers:** Full or partial for employees or children of employees. **ROTC:** Army, Naval, Air Force.

LOANS *Student loans:* $10,332,990 (52% need-based, 48% non-need-based). 27% of past graduating class borrowed through all loan programs. *Average indebtedness per student:* $24,954. *Average need-based loan:* Freshmen: $2608. Undergraduates: $2679. *Parent loans:* $4,098,483 (5% need-based, 95% non-need-based). *Programs:* Federal Direct (Subsidized and Unsubsidized Stafford, PLUS), Perkins, college/university.

WORK-STUDY *Federal work-study:* 734 jobs averaging $2417. *State or other work-study/employment:* Total amount: $2,964,101 (72% need-based, 28% non-need-based). 1,093 part-time jobs averaging $2712.

APPLYING FOR FINANCIAL AID *Required financial aid forms:* FAFSA, CSS Financial Aid PROFILE, noncustodial (divorced/separated) parent's statement, business/farm supplement, federal income tax form(s), W-2 forms. *Financial aid deadline:* 2/15 (priority: 2/15). *Notification date:* 3/17. Students must reply by 5/1.

CONTACT Stuart Schmill, Dean of Admissions and Student Financial Services, Massachusetts Institute of Technology, 77 Massachusetts Avenue, Room 11-120, Cambridge, MA 02139-4307, 617-258-5529. *Fax:* 617-648-9968. *E-mail:* sfs@mit.edu. *Website:* http://www.mit.edu/.

MASSACHUSETTS MARITIME ACADEMY
Buzzards Bay, MA

Tuition & fees (MA res): $8004	Average undergraduate aid package: $12,188

ABOUT THE INSTITUTION State-supported, coed. *Awards:* bachelor's and master's degrees. 7 undergraduate majors. *Total enrollment:* 1,751. Undergraduates: 1,677. Freshmen: 402. Federal methodology is used as a basis for awarding need-based institutional aid.

UNDERGRADUATE EXPENSES for 2016–2017 *Application fee:* $50. *Tuition, state resident:* full-time $1632; part-time $322.38 per credit. *Tuition, nonresident:* full-time $18,228; part-time $1013.88 per credit. *Required fees:* full-time $6372. Full-time tuition and fees vary according to degree level and program. Part-time tuition and fees vary according to degree level and program. *College room and board:* $11,978; *Room only:* $7134.

FRESHMAN FINANCIAL AID (Fall 2016, est.) 364 applied for aid; of those 69% were deemed to have need. 100% of freshmen with need received aid; of those 27% had need fully met. *Average percent of need met:* 66% (excluding resources awarded to replace EFC). *Average financial aid package:* $12,533 (excluding resources awarded to replace EFC). 8% of all full-time freshmen had no need and received non-need-based gift aid.

UNDERGRADUATE FINANCIAL AID (Fall 2016, est.) 1,260 applied for aid; of those 71% were deemed to have need. 100% of undergraduates with need received aid; of those 33% had need fully met. *Average percent of need met:* 72% (excluding resources awarded to replace EFC). *Average financial aid package:* $12,188 (excluding resources awarded to replace EFC). 7% of all full-time undergraduates had no need and received non-need-based gift aid.

GIFT AID (NEED-BASED) *Total amount:* $5,505,369 (21% federal, 10% state, 69% institutional). *Receiving aid:* Freshmen: 42% (167); all full-time undergraduates: 40% (641). *Average award:* Freshmen: $12,373; Undergraduates: $10,061. *Scholarships, grants, and awards:* Federal Pell, FSEOG, state, private, college/university gift aid from institutional funds.

GIFT AID (NON-NEED-BASED) *Total amount:* $1,448,368 (15% state, 25% institutional, 60% external sources). *Receiving aid:* Freshmen: 1% (3). Undergraduates: 1% (24). *Average award:* Freshmen: $3586. Undergraduates: $3131. *Scholarships, grants, and awards by category:* Academic interests/achievement: 15 awards ($150,000 total): general academic interests/achievements. *Special achievements/activities:* leadership. *Special characteristics:* ethnic background, members of minority groups. *Tuition waivers:* Full or partial for employees or children of employees. *ROTC:* Army cooperative.

LOANS *Student loans:* $12,281,576 (26% need-based, 74% non-need-based). 79% of past graduating class borrowed through all loan programs. *Average indebtedness per student:* $37,414. *Average need-based loan:* Freshmen: $3363. Undergraduates: $4087. *Parent loans:* $2,257,325 (100% non-need-based). *Programs:* Federal Direct (Subsidized and Unsubsidized Stafford, PLUS).

WORK-STUDY *Federal work-study:* Total amount: $200,000; 190 jobs averaging $1467.

APPLYING FOR FINANCIAL AID *Required financial aid form:* FAFSA. *Financial aid deadline (priority):* 3/1. *Notification date:* Continuous beginning 2/15.

CONTACT Ms. Catherine Kedski, Director of Financial Aid, Massachusetts Maritime Academy, 101 Academy Drive, Buzzards Bay, MA 02532, 508-830-5042 or toll-free 800-544-3411. *Fax:* 508-830-5077. *E-mail:* ckedski@maritime.edu. *Website:* http://www.maritime.edu/.

THE MASTER'S UNIVERSITY
Santa Clarita, CA

Tuition & fees: $33,020	Average undergraduate aid package: $22,088

ABOUT THE INSTITUTION Independent nondenominational, coed. *Awards:* bachelor's, master's, and doctoral degrees. 45 undergraduate majors. *Total enrollment:* 1,936. Undergraduates: 1,390. Freshmen: 173. Federal methodology is used as a basis for awarding need-based institutional aid.

UNDERGRADUATE EXPENSES for 2017–2018 *Application fee:* $40. *Comprehensive fee:* $43,870 includes full-time tuition ($32,600), mandatory fees ($420), and room and board ($10,850). *College room only:* $5950. Full-time tuition and fees vary according to class time, course load, location, and program. Room and board charges vary according to board plan. *Part-time tuition:* $1370 per credit hour. Part-time tuition and fees vary according to class time, course load, location, and program.

FRESHMAN FINANCIAL AID (Fall 2015) 200 applied for aid; of those 84% were deemed to have need. 98% of freshmen with need received aid; of those 14% had need fully met. *Average percent of need met:* 68% (excluding resources awarded to replace EFC). *Average financial aid package:* $22,869 (excluding resources awarded to replace EFC). 17% of all full-time freshmen had no need and received non-need-based gift aid.

UNDERGRADUATE FINANCIAL AID (Fall 2015) 878 applied for aid; of those 86% were deemed to have need. 98% of undergraduates with need received aid; of those 14% had need fully met. *Average percent of need met:* 66% (excluding resources awarded to replace EFC). *Average financial aid package:* $22,088 (excluding resources awarded to replace EFC). 15% of all full-time undergraduates had no need and received non-need-based gift aid.

GIFT AID (NEED-BASED) *Total amount:* $12,369,000 (12% federal, 14% state, 58% institutional, 16% external sources). *Receiving aid:* Freshmen: 72% (163); all full-time undergraduates: 76% (736). *Average award:* Freshmen: $19,224; Undergraduates: $18,112. *Scholarships, grants, and awards:* Federal Pell, FSEOG, state, private, college/university gift aid from institutional funds.

GIFT AID (NON-NEED-BASED) *Total amount:* $2,397,832 (68% institutional, 32% external sources). *Receiving aid:* Freshmen: 10% (22). Undergraduates: 8% (79). *Average award:* Freshmen: $11,652. Undergraduates: $9865. *Scholarships, grants, and awards by category:* Academic interests/achievement: 546 awards ($3,601,474 total): biological sciences, business, communication, computer science, education, general academic interests/achievements, mathematics, physical sciences, religion/biblical studies, social sciences. *Creative arts/performance:* 71 awards ($209,243 total): music. *Special achievements/activities:* 21 awards ($287,000 total): leadership. *Special characteristics:* 298 awards ($2,341,049 total): children and siblings of alumni, children of faculty/staff, general special characteristics, international students, relatives of clergy, veterans, veterans' children. *Tuition waivers:* Full or partial for employees or children of employees. *ROTC:* Army cooperative, Air Force cooperative.

LOANS *Student loans:* $7,088,942 (76% need-based, 24% non-need-based). 84% of past graduating class borrowed through all loan programs. *Average indebtedness per student:* $29,133. *Average need-based loan:* Freshmen: $3312. Undergraduates: $4249. *Parent loans:* $1,799,049 (58% need-based, 42% non-need-based). *Programs:* Federal Direct (Subsidized and Unsubsidized Stafford, PLUS), alternative loans.

WORK-STUDY *Federal work-study:* 60 jobs averaging $2577. *State or other work-study/employment:* Total amount: $471,250 (65% need-based, 35% non-need-based). 174 part-time jobs averaging $1904.

ATHLETIC AWARDS *Total amount:* $2,028,267 (61% need-based, 39% non-need-based).

APPLYING FOR FINANCIAL AID *Required financial aid forms:* FAFSA, institution's own form, state aid form. *Financial aid deadline (priority):* 3/2. *Notification date:* Continuous beginning 2/1. Students must reply by 5/1 or within 2 weeks of notification.

CONTACT Mr. Gary Edwards, Director of Financial Aid, The Master's University, 21726 Placerita Canyon Road, Santa Clarita, CA 91321-1200, 661-362-2291 or toll-free 800-568-6248. *Fax:* 661-362-2693. *E-mail:* gedwards@masters.edu.
Website: http://www.masters.edu/.

MAYVILLE STATE UNIVERSITY
Mayville, ND

Tuition & fees (ND res): $6254	Average undergraduate aid package: $11,355

ABOUT THE INSTITUTION State-supported, coed. *Awards:* associate and bachelor's degrees. 36 undergraduate majors. *Total enrollment:* 1,081. Undergraduates: 1,056. Freshmen: 174. Federal methodology is used as a basis for awarding need-based institutional aid.

UNDERGRADUATE EXPENSES for 2016–2017 *Application fee:* $35. *One-time required fee:* $35. *Tuition, state resident:* full-time $5053; part-time $210.55 per credit hour. *Tuition, nonresident:* full-time $7580; part-time $315.83 per credit hour. *Required fees:* full-time $1201; $50.06 per credit hour. Full-time tuition and fees vary according to course load, location, and reciprocity agreements. Part-time tuition and fees vary according to course load, location, and reciprocity agreements. *College room and board:* $7107; *Room only:* $3300. Room and board charges vary according to board plan and housing facility.

FRESHMAN FINANCIAL AID (Fall 2015) 116 applied for aid; of those 77% were deemed to have need. 97% of freshmen with need received aid; of those 35% had need fully met. *Average percent of need met:* 67% (excluding resources awarded to replace EFC). *Average financial aid package:* $10,710 (excluding resources awarded to replace EFC). 17% of all full-time freshmen had no need and received non-need-based gift aid.

UNDERGRADUATE FINANCIAL AID (Fall 2015) 514 applied for aid; of those 78% were deemed to have need. 99% of undergraduates with need received aid; of those 33% had need fully met. *Average percent of need met:* 74% (excluding resources awarded to replace EFC). *Average financial aid package:* $11,355 (excluding resources awarded to replace EFC). 15% of all full-time undergraduates had no need and received non-need-based gift aid.

GIFT AID (NEED-BASED) *Total amount:* $1,892,893 (70% federal, 16% state, 9% institutional, 5% external sources). *Receiving aid:* Freshmen: 62% (83); all full-time undergraduates: 61% (369). *Average award:* Freshmen: $5666; Undergraduates: $5497. *Scholarships, grants, and awards:* Federal Pell, FSEOG, state, private, college/university gift aid from institutional funds.

GIFT AID (NON-NEED-BASED) *Total amount:* $350,278 (5% federal, 22% state, 42% institutional, 31% external sources). *Receiving aid:* Freshmen: 7% (9). Undergraduates: 3% (20). *Average award:* Freshmen: $2097. Undergraduates: $1387. *Scholarships, grants, and awards by category:* Academic interests/achievement: biological sciences, business, communication, computer science, education, English, general academic interests/achievements, health fields, library science, mathematics, physical sciences, premedicine, social sciences. *Creative arts/performance:* music, theater/drama. *Special characteristics:* children of faculty/staff, international students, local/state students, members of minority groups, out-of-state students, veterans' children. *Tuition waivers:* Full or partial for minority students, employees or children of employees, senior citizens. *ROTC:* Army cooperative, Air Force cooperative.

LOANS *Student loans:* $3,714,925 (61% need-based, 39% non-need-based). 71% of past graduating class borrowed through all loan programs. *Average indebtedness per student:* $32,424. *Average need-based loan:* Freshmen: $5666. Undergraduates: $5497. *Parent loans:* $288,926 (37% need-based, 63% non-need-based). *Programs:* Federal Direct (Subsidized and Unsubsidized Stafford, PLUS), Perkins, Federal Nursing, college/university.

WORK-STUDY *Federal work-study:* jobs available.

ATHLETIC AWARDS Total amount: $293,063 (62% need-based, 38% non-need-based).

APPLYING FOR FINANCIAL AID *Required financial aid form:* FAFSA. *Financial aid deadline (priority):* 2/15. *Notification date:* Continuous beginning 5/1. Students must reply within 2 weeks of notification.

CONTACT Ms. Shirley Hanson, Director of Financial Aid, Mayville State University, 330 3rd Street NE, Mayville, ND 58257-1299, 701-788-4767 or toll-free 800-437-4104. *Fax:* 701-788-4818. *E-mail:* shirley.m.hanson@mayvillestate.edu. *Website:* http://www.mayvillestate.edu/.

MCDANIEL COLLEGE
Westminster, MD

Tuition & fees: $41,800	Average undergraduate aid package: $35,192

ABOUT THE INSTITUTION Independent, coed. *Awards:* certificates, bachelor's, and master's degrees. 34 undergraduate majors. *Total enrollment:* 2,903. Undergraduates: 1,559. Freshmen: 388. Federal methodology is used as a basis for awarding need-based institutional aid.

UNDERGRADUATE EXPENSES for 2017–2018 *Application fee:* $50. *Comprehensive fee:* $52,910 includes full-time tuition ($41,800) and room and board ($11,110). *College room only:* $5100. Full-time tuition and fees vary according to course load. Room and board charges vary according to board plan and housing facility. *Part-time tuition:* $1306 per credit hour. Part-time tuition and fees vary according to course load and reciprocity agreements.

FRESHMAN FINANCIAL AID (Fall 2016, est.) 347 applied for aid; of those 91% were deemed to have need. 100% of freshmen with need received aid; of those 30% had need fully met. *Average percent of need met:* 90% (excluding resources awarded to replace EFC). *Average financial aid package:* $38,381 (excluding resources awarded to replace EFC). 18% of all full-time freshmen had no need and received non-need-based gift aid.

UNDERGRADUATE FINANCIAL AID (Fall 2016, est.) 1,278 applied for aid; of those 91% were deemed to have need. 100% of undergraduates with need received aid; of those 25% had need fully met. *Average percent of need met:* 86% (excluding resources awarded to replace EFC). *Average financial aid package:* $35,192 (excluding resources awarded to replace EFC). 22% of all full-time undergraduates had no need and received non-need-based gift aid.

GIFT AID (NEED-BASED) *Total amount:* $32,691,624 (8% federal, 7% state, 83% institutional, 2% external sources). *Receiving aid:* Freshmen: 81% (314); all full-time undergraduates: 75% (1,164). *Average award:* Freshmen: $35,159; Undergraduates: $31,289. *Scholarships, grants, and awards:* Federal Pell, FSEOG, state, private, college/university gift aid from institutional funds, TEACH Grants.

GIFT AID (NON-NEED-BASED) *Total amount:* $9,937,258 (6% federal, 93% institutional, 1% external sources). *Receiving aid:* Freshmen: 18% (69). Undergraduates: 12% (190). *Average award:* Freshmen: $23,009. Undergraduates: $19,544. *Scholarships, grants, and awards by category:* Academic interests/achievement: general academic interests/achievements. *Special achievements/activities:* junior miss, leadership. *Special characteristics:* children of educators, general special characteristics, local/state students, previous college experience, siblings of current students, veterans. *Tuition waivers:* Full or partial for employees or children of employees. *ROTC:* Army.

LOANS *Student loans:* $9,186,420 (67% need-based, 33% non-need-based). 71% of past graduating class borrowed through all loan programs. *Average indebtedness per student:* $35,397. *Average need-based loan:* Freshmen: $4025. Undergraduates: $4583. *Parent loans:* $2,900,883 (36% need-based, 64% non-need-based). *Programs:* Federal Direct (Subsidized and Unsubsidized Stafford, PLUS), Perkins.

WORK-STUDY *Federal work-study:* Total amount: $691,330; jobs available. *State or other work-study/employment:* Part-time jobs available.

APPLYING FOR FINANCIAL AID *Required financial aid form:* FAFSA. *Financial aid deadline (priority):* 3/1. *Notification date:* Continuous beginning 3/15. Students must reply by 5/1 or within 2 weeks of notification.

CONTACT Financial Aid Office, McDaniel College, 2 College Hill, Westminster, MD 21157-4390, 410-857-2233 or toll-free 800-638-5005. *Fax:* 410-857-2729. *E-mail:* finaid@mcdaniel.edu.
Website: http://www.mcdaniel.edu/.

MCKENDREE UNIVERSITY
Lebanon, IL

Tuition & fees: $29,640	Average undergraduate aid package: $21,543

ABOUT THE INSTITUTION Independent United Methodist Church, coed. *Awards:* certificates, associate, bachelor's, master's, and doctoral degrees. 45 undergraduate majors. *Total enrollment:* 2,937. Undergraduates: 2,290. Freshmen: 458. Federal methodology is used as a basis for awarding need-based institutional aid.

UNDERGRADUATE EXPENSES for 2017–2018 *Comprehensive fee:* $38,990 includes full-time tuition ($28,560), mandatory fees ($1080), and room and board ($9350). *College room only:* $5020. Full-time tuition and fees vary according to course load, degree level, and location. Room and board charges vary according to board plan and housing facility. *Part-time tuition:* $935 per credit hour. Part-time tuition and fees vary according to course load, degree level, and location.

FRESHMAN FINANCIAL AID (Fall 2016, est.) 410 applied for aid; of those 90% were deemed to have need. 99% of freshmen with need received aid; of those 26% had need fully met. *Average percent of need met:* 77% (excluding resources awarded to replace EFC). *Average financial aid package:* $22,693 (excluding resources awarded to replace EFC). 16% of all full-time freshmen had no need and received non-need-based gift aid.

UNDERGRADUATE FINANCIAL AID (Fall 2016, est.) 1,577 applied for aid; of those 91% were deemed to have need. 97% of undergraduates with need received aid; of those 20% had need fully met. *Average percent of need met:* 73% (excluding resources awarded to replace EFC). *Average financial aid package:* $21,543 (excluding resources awarded to replace EFC). 18% of all full-time undergraduates had no need and received non-need-based gift aid.

GIFT AID (NEED-BASED) *Total amount:* $22,144,066 (16% federal, 11% state, 70% institutional, 3% external sources). *Receiving aid:* Freshmen: 81% (366); all full-time undergraduates: 75% (1,361). *Average award:* Freshmen: $19,238; Undergraduates: $17,864. *Scholarships, grants, and awards:* Federal Pell, FSEOG, state, private, college/university gift aid from institutional funds.

GIFT AID (NON-NEED-BASED) *Total amount:* $4,752,007 (91% institutional, 9% external sources). *Receiving aid:* Freshmen: 15% (69). Undergraduates: 10% (187). *Average award:* Freshmen: $14,221. Undergraduates: $11,556. *Scholarships, grants, and awards by category: Academic interests/achievement:* 1,177 awards ($9,542,854 total): biological sciences, business, general academic interests/achievements, religion/biblical studies. *Creative arts/performance:* 119 awards ($428,713 total): dance, debating, music. *Special achievements/activities:* 538 awards ($2,258,395 total): cheerleading/drum major, community service, leadership. *Special characteristics:* 254 awards ($1,066,523 total): children and siblings of alumni, children of faculty/staff, general special characteristics, international students, religious affiliation, veterans, veterans' children. *Tuition waivers:* Full or partial for children of alumni, employees or children of employees. *ROTC:* Army cooperative, Air Force cooperative.

LOANS *Student loans:* $11,034,771 (68% need-based, 32% non-need-based). 72% of past graduating class borrowed through all loan programs. *Average indebtedness per student:* $30,029. *Average need-based loan:* Freshmen: $3363. Undergraduates: $4027. *Parent loans:* $5,699,381 (38% need-based, 62% non-need-based). *Programs:* Federal Direct (Subsidized and Unsubsidized Stafford, PLUS), Perkins.

WORK-STUDY *Federal work-study:* Total amount: $1,056,798; 881 jobs averaging $1785. *State or other work-study/employment:* Total amount: $76,238 (2% need-based, 98% non-need-based). 67 part-time jobs averaging $1138.

ATHLETIC AWARDS Total amount: $5,167,265 (45% need-based, 55% non-need-based).

APPLYING FOR FINANCIAL AID *Required financial aid form:* FAFSA. *Financial aid deadline (priority):* 5/31. *Notification date:* Continuous beginning 3/1.

CONTACT Elizabeth L. Juehne, Director of Financial Aid, McKendree University, 701 College Road, Lebanon, IL 62254-1299, 618-537-6532 or toll-free 800-232-7228. *Fax:* 618-537-6530. *E-mail:* bjuehne@mckendree.edu. *Website:* http://www.mckendree.edu/.

MCMURRY UNIVERSITY
Abilene, TX

ABOUT THE INSTITUTION Independent United Methodist, coed. *Awards:* bachelor's and master's degrees. 45 undergraduate majors. *Total enrollment:* 1,074. Undergraduates: 1,073. Freshmen: 284.

GIFT AID (NEED-BASED) *Scholarships, grants, and awards:* Federal Pell, FSEOG, state, private, college/university gift aid from institutional funds.

GIFT AID (NON-NEED-BASED) *Scholarships, grants, and awards by category: Academic interests/achievement:* biological sciences, business, computer science, education, English, foreign languages, general academic interests/achievements, mathematics, physical sciences, premedicine, religion/biblical studies, social sciences. *Creative arts/performance:* art/fine arts, music, theater/drama. *Special achievements/activities:* general special achievements/activities, religious involvement. *Special characteristics:* adult students, children of faculty/staff, ethnic background, first-generation college students, general special characteristics, international students, local/state students, members of minority groups, out-of-state students, previous college experience, relatives of clergy, religious affiliation, veterans, veterans' children.

LOANS *Programs:* Federal Direct (Subsidized and Unsubsidized Stafford, PLUS), Perkins, state, private loans, United Methodist Student Loans.

WORK-STUDY *Federal work-study:* Total amount: $1,526,120; 164 jobs averaging $1440. *State or other work-study/employment:* Total amount: $80,628 (18% need-based, 82% non-need-based). 58 part-time jobs averaging $1321.

APPLYING FOR FINANCIAL AID *Required financial aid forms:* FAFSA, institution's own form.

CONTACT Mr. Tim Sechrist, Director of Student Financial Services, McMurry University, #1 McMurry University Box 908, Abilene, TX 79697, 325-793-4978 or toll-free 800-460-2392. *Fax:* 325-793-4718. *E-mail:* financialaid@mcm.edu. *Website:* http://www.mcm.edu/.

MCNALLY SMITH COLLEGE OF MUSIC
Saint Paul, MN

Tuition & fees: N/R	Average undergraduate aid package: $15,793

ABOUT THE INSTITUTION Proprietary, coed. 9 undergraduate majors. Federal methodology is used as a basis for awarding need-based institutional aid.

FRESHMAN FINANCIAL AID (Fall 2015) 65 applied for aid; of those 86% were deemed to have need. 98% of freshmen with need received aid. *Average percent of need met:* 40% (excluding resources awarded to replace EFC). *Average financial aid package:* $14,729 (excluding resources awarded to replace EFC). 11% of all full-time freshmen had no need and received non-need-based gift aid.

UNDERGRADUATE FINANCIAL AID (Fall 2015) 287 applied for aid; of those 92% were deemed to have need. 99% of undergraduates with need received aid. *Average percent of need met:* 50% (excluding resources awarded to replace EFC). *Average financial aid package:* $15,793 (excluding resources awarded to replace EFC). 13% of all full-time undergraduates had no need and received non-need-based gift aid.

GIFT AID (NEED-BASED) *Total amount:* $4,223,966 (40% federal, 19% state, 41% institutional). *Receiving aid:* Freshmen: 49% (39); all full-time undergraduates: 48% (179). *Average award:* Freshmen: $11,197; Undergraduates: $10,370. *Scholarships, grants, and awards:* Federal Pell, FSEOG, state, private, college/university gift aid from institutional funds.

GIFT AID (NON-NEED-BASED) *Total amount:* $3,571,681 (17% federal, 1% state, 73% institutional, 9% external sources). *Receiving aid:* Freshmen: 25% (20). Undergraduates: 27% (100). *Average award:* Freshmen: $9468. Undergraduates: $12,829. *Scholarships, grants, and awards by category: Creative arts/performance:* 167 awards ($1,350,416 total): music. *Special characteristics:* 14 awards ($330,520 total): children of faculty/staff, veterans, veterans' children.

LOANS *Student loans:* $8,444,710 (100% need-based). 83% of past graduating class borrowed through all loan programs. *Average indebtedness per student:* $58,458. *Average need-based loan:* Freshmen: $3672. Undergraduates: $4523. *Parent loans:* $5,181,722 (100% non-need-based). *Programs:* Federal Direct (Subsidized and Unsubsidized Stafford, PLUS), state, private loans.

WORK-STUDY *Federal work-study:* 39 jobs averaging $1530. *State or other work-study/employment:* Part-time jobs available.

APPLYING FOR FINANCIAL AID *Required financial aid form:* FAFSA. *Financial aid deadline:* 8/1 (priority: 5/1). *Notification date:* Continuous beginning 3/15. Students must reply by 5/1 or within 2 weeks of notification.

CONTACT Tony Palermo, Financial Aid Administrator, McNally Smith College of Music, 19 Exchange Street East, St. Paul, MN 55101-2220, 651-361-3321 or toll-free 800-594-9500. *Fax:* 651-291-0366. *E-mail:* tony.palermo@mcnallysmith.edu. *Website:* http://www.mcnallysmith.edu/.

MCNEESE STATE UNIVERSITY
Lake Charles, LA

ABOUT THE INSTITUTION State-supported, coed. *Awards:* certificates, associate, bachelor's, and master's degrees. 36 undergraduate majors. *Total enrollment:* 7,626. Undergraduates: 6,961. Freshmen: 1,244.

GIFT AID (NEED-BASED) *Scholarships, grants, and awards:* Federal Pell, FSEOG, state, private.

LOANS *Programs:* Federal Direct (Subsidized and Unsubsidized Stafford, PLUS), Perkins.

APPLYING FOR FINANCIAL AID *Required financial aid forms:* FAFSA, institution's own form.

CONTACT Ms. Taina J. Savoit, Director of Financial Aid, McNeese State University, PO Box 93260, Lake Charles, LA 70609-3260, 337-475-5065 or toll-free 800-622-3352. *Fax:* 337-475-5068. *E-mail:* financialaid@mcneese.edu. *Website:* http://www.mcneese.edu/.

MCPHERSON COLLEGE
McPherson, KS

Tuition & fees: $26,498	Average undergraduate aid package: $24,898

ABOUT THE INSTITUTION Independent Church of the Brethren, coed. 28 undergraduate majors. Both federal and institutional methodology are used as a basis for awarding need-based institutional aid.

UNDERGRADUATE EXPENSES for 2016–2017 *Comprehensive fee:* $34,909 includes full-time tuition ($25,788), mandatory fees ($710), and room and board ($8411). *College room only:* $3528. Full-time tuition and fees vary according to course load. Room and board charges vary according to board plan and housing facility. *Part-time tuition:* $590 per credit hour. *Part-time fees:* $10 per credit hour.

FRESHMAN FINANCIAL AID (Fall 2016, est.) 171 applied for aid; of those 100% were deemed to have need. 100% of freshmen with need received aid; of those 25% had need fully met. *Average percent of need met:* 86% (excluding resources awarded to replace EFC). *Average financial aid package:* $25,862 (excluding resources awarded to replace EFC). 9% of all full-time freshmen had no need and received non-need-based gift aid.

UNDERGRADUATE FINANCIAL AID (Fall 2016, est.) 558 applied for aid; of those 100% were deemed to have need. 100% of undergraduates with need received aid; of those 23% had need fully met. *Average percent of need met:* 82% (excluding resources awarded to replace EFC). *Average financial aid package:* $24,898 (excluding resources awarded to replace EFC). 8% of all full-time undergraduates had no need and received non-need-based gift aid.

GIFT AID (NEED-BASED) *Total amount:* $2,014,432 (65% federal, 19% state, 16% institutional). *Receiving aid:* Freshmen: 61% (122); all full-time undergraduates: 57% (372). *Average award:* Freshmen: $5842; Undergraduates: $5722. *Scholarships, grants, and awards:* Federal Pell, FSEOG, state, private, college/university gift aid from institutional funds.

GIFT AID (NON-NEED-BASED) *Total amount:* $9,296,079 (98% institutional, 2% external sources). *Receiving aid:* Freshmen: 86% (171). Undergraduates: 85% (558). *Average award:* Freshmen: $14,933. Undergraduates: $14,626. *Scholarships, grants, and awards by category:* Academic interests/achievement: general academic interests/achievements. Creative arts/performance: art/fine arts, music, performing arts, theater/drama. Special achievements/activities: cheerleading/drum major. Special characteristics: children and siblings of alumni, children of faculty/staff, international students, religious affiliation. *Tuition waivers:* Full or partial for children of alumni, employees or children of employees.

LOANS *Student loans:* $4,090,764 (100% need-based). 86% of past graduating class borrowed through all loan programs. *Average indebtedness per student:* $28,615. *Average need-based loan:* Freshmen: $7740. Undergraduates: $8592. *Parent loans:* $1,446,023 (100% non-need-based). *Programs:* Federal Direct (Subsidized and Unsubsidized Stafford, PLUS), Perkins.

WORK-STUDY *Federal work-study:* Total amount: $274,450; jobs available. *State or other work-study/employment:* Part-time jobs available.

ATHLETIC AWARDS Total amount: $1,908,278 (100% non-need-based).

APPLYING FOR FINANCIAL AID *Required financial aid form:* FAFSA. *Financial aid deadline (priority):* 3/1. *Notification date:* Continuous beginning 3/1. Students must reply within 3 weeks of notification.

CONTACT Ms. Sara Brubaker, Director of Financial Aid and Admissions Operations, McPherson College, 1600 East Euclid, McPherson, KS 67460-1402, 620-242-0400 or toll-free 800-365-7402. *Fax:* 620-241-8443. *E-mail:* krehbieb2@mcpherson.edu. *Website:* http://www.mcpherson.edu/.

MCPHS UNIVERSITY
Boston, MA

Tuition & fees: $31,670	Average undergraduate aid package: $8724

ABOUT THE INSTITUTION Independent, coed. *Awards:* certificates, bachelor's, master's, and doctoral degrees. 12 undergraduate majors. *Total enrollment:* 7,095. Undergraduates: 3,843. Freshmen: 798. Federal methodology is used as a basis for awarding need-based institutional aid.

UNDERGRADUATE EXPENSES for 2017–2018 *Comprehensive fee:* $47,504 includes full-time tuition ($30,600), mandatory fees ($1070), and room and board ($15,834). *College room only:* $12,600. Full-time tuition and fees vary according to course load, degree level, location, program, and student level. Room and board charges vary according to board plan, housing facility, and location. *Part-time tuition:* $1125 per credit. *Part-time fees:* $253 per term.

FRESHMAN FINANCIAL AID (Fall 2016, est.) 643 applied for aid; of those 92% were deemed to have need. 100% of freshmen with need received aid; of those 46% had need fully met. *Average percent of need met:* 26% (excluding resources awarded to replace EFC). *Average financial aid package:* $10,459 (excluding resources awarded to replace EFC). 24% of all full-time freshmen had no need and received non-need-based gift aid.

UNDERGRADUATE FINANCIAL AID (Fall 2016, est.) 2,722 applied for aid; of those 93% were deemed to have need. 100% of undergraduates with need received aid; of those 38% had need fully met. *Average percent of need met:* 23% (excluding resources awarded to replace EFC). *Average financial aid package:* $8724 (excluding resources awarded to replace EFC). 23% of all full-time undergraduates had no need and received non-need-based gift aid.

GIFT AID (NEED-BASED) *Total amount:* $9,305,562 (58% federal, 6% state, 36% institutional). *Receiving aid:* Freshmen: 76% (590); all full-time undergraduates: 71% (2,353). *Average award:* Freshmen: $7984; Undergraduates: $6408. *Scholarships, grants, and awards:* Federal Pell, FSEOG, state, college/university gift aid from institutional funds.

GIFT AID (NON-NEED-BASED) *Total amount:* $9,780,601 (93% institutional, 7% external sources). *Average award:* Freshmen: $6693. Undergraduates: $6116. *Scholarships, grants, and awards by category:* Academic interests/achievement: general academic interests/achievements. *Tuition waivers:* Full or partial for employees or children of employees.

LOANS *Student loans:* $28,115,189 (26% need-based, 74% non-need-based). *Average need-based loan:* Freshmen: $2534. Undergraduates: $2952. *Parent loans:* $10,414,220 (100% non-need-based). *Programs:* Federal Direct (Subsidized and Unsubsidized Stafford, PLUS), Perkins, state, college/university.

WORK-STUDY *Federal work-study:* Total amount: $359,474; jobs available.

APPLYING FOR FINANCIAL AID *Required financial aid form:* FAFSA. *Financial aid deadline (priority):* 3/15. *Notification date:* Continuous beginning 2/15.

CONTACT Elizabeth Goreham, Director of Student Financial Services, MCPHS University, 179 Longwood Avenue, Boston, MA 02115-5896, 617-879-5986. *E-mail:* elizabeth.goreham@mcphs.edu. *Website:* http://www.mcphs.edu/.

MEDAILLE COLLEGE
Buffalo, NY

CONTACT Ms. Catherine Buzanski, Director of Financial Aid, Medaille College, 18 Agassiz Circle, Buffalo, NY 14214-2695, 716-880-2179 or toll-free 800-292-1582. *Fax:* 716-884-0291. *E-mail:* cbuzanski@medaille.edu. *Website:* http://www.medaille.edu/.

MEDGAR EVERS COLLEGE OF THE CITY UNIVERSITY OF NEW YORK
Brooklyn, NY

Tuition & fees (NY res): $6650	Average undergraduate aid package: $9212

ABOUT THE INSTITUTION State and locally supported, coed. *Awards:* certificates, associate, and bachelor's degrees. 15 undergraduate majors. *Total enrollment:* 6,819. Undergraduates: 6,819. Federal methodology is used as a basis for awarding need-based institutional aid.

UNDERGRADUATE EXPENSES for 2016–2017 *Application fee:* $65. *Tuition, state resident:* full-time $6330; part-time $275 per credit. *Tuition, nonresident:* full-time $16,800; part-time $560 per credit. *Required fees:* full-time $320; $100.85 per term. Full-time tuition and fees vary according to course load. Part-time tuition and fees vary according to course load.

FRESHMAN FINANCIAL AID (Fall 2016, est.) 954 applied for aid; of those 100% were deemed to have need. 93% of freshmen with need received aid. *Average financial aid package:* $8729 (excluding resources awarded to replace EFC).

UNDERGRADUATE FINANCIAL AID (Fall 2016, est.) 4,072 applied for aid; of those 100% were deemed to have need. 96% of undergraduates with need received aid. *Average financial aid package:* $9212 (excluding resources awarded to replace EFC).

GIFT AID (NEED-BASED) Total amount: $30,956,973 (58% federal, 42% state). *Receiving aid:* Freshmen: 85% (857); all full-time undergraduates: 84% (3,671). *Average award:* Freshmen: $8266; Undergraduates: $7867. *Scholarships, grants, and awards:* Federal Pell, FSEOG, state, private, college/university gift aid from institutional funds, Thurgood Marshall Scholarship Fund.

GIFT AID (NON-NEED-BASED) Total amount: $1,098,354 (100% external sources). *Receiving aid:* Freshmen: 10% (105). Undergraduates: 19% (835). *Average award:* Freshmen: $2167. Undergraduates: $3034. *Scholarships, grants, and awards by category:* Academic interests/achievement: general academic interests/achievements.

LOANS Student loans: $5,819,003 (100% need-based). *Programs:* Federal Direct (Subsidized and Unsubsidized Stafford, PLUS), Perkins.

WORK-STUDY Federal work-study: Total amount: $1,124,156; jobs available. *State or other work-study/employment:* Part-time jobs available.

APPLYING FOR FINANCIAL AID Required financial aid forms: FAFSA, state aid form, University Financial Aid Information Supplemental Request (FASIR). *Financial aid deadline (priority):* 1/2. *Notification date:* Continuous beginning 4/1. Students must reply within 3 weeks of notification.

CONTACT Nigel Thompson, Director of Financial Aid, Medgar Evers College of the City University of New York, 1650 Bedford Avenue, Brooklyn, NY 11225, 718-270-6038. *Fax:* 718-270-6194. *E-mail:* nigel.thompson@mec.cuny.edu. *Website:* http://www.mec.cuny.edu/.

MEDICAL UNIVERSITY OF SOUTH CAROLINA
Charleston, SC

Tuition & fees: N/R	Average undergraduate aid package: $10,666

ABOUT THE INSTITUTION State-supported, coed. 2 undergraduate majors. Federal methodology is used as a basis for awarding need-based institutional aid.

UNDERGRADUATE FINANCIAL AID (Fall 2015) 275 applied for aid; of those 89% were deemed to have need. 98% of undergraduates with need received aid; of those 1% had need fully met. *Average percent of need met:* 32% (excluding resources awarded to replace EFC). *Average financial aid package:* $10,666 (excluding resources awarded to replace EFC). 2% of all full-time undergraduates had no need and received non-need-based gift aid.

GIFT AID (NEED-BASED) Total amount: $507,133 (35% federal, 57% state, 1% institutional, 7% external sources). *Receiving aid:* All full-time undergraduates: 29% (93). *Average award:* Undergraduates: $5237. *Scholarships, grants, and awards:* Federal Pell, FSEOG, state, private, college/university gift aid from institutional funds, Federal Nursing, Scholarships for Disadvantaged Students (SDS).

GIFT AID (NON-NEED-BASED) Total amount: $570,488 (7% federal, 48% state, 13% institutional, 32% external sources). *Receiving aid:* Undergraduates: 17% (55). *Average award:* Undergraduates: $10,000. *Scholarships, grants, and awards by category:* Academic interests/achievement: general academic interests/achievements, home economics. Special characteristics: ethnic background, general special characteristics, local/state students, members of minority groups.

LOANS Student loans: $4,913,322 (31% need-based, 69% non-need-based). *Average need-based loan:* Undergraduates: $7365. *Parent loans:* $18,700 (100% non-need-based). *Programs:* Federal Direct (Subsidized and Unsubsidized Stafford, PLUS), Perkins, Federal Nursing, state, alternative loans, Health Professions Student Loans (HPSL), Loans for Disadvantaged Students program, Primary Care Loans.

WORK-STUDY Federal work-study: jobs available.

APPLYING FOR FINANCIAL AID Required financial aid form: FAFSA. *Notification date:* Continuous.

CONTACT Mr. Joseph M. DuRant, Director for Student Financial Aid Services, Medical University of South Carolina, 45 Courtenay Drive, MSC 203, Charleston, SC 29425, 843-792-2252. *Fax:* 843-792-6356. *E-mail:* durantjm@musc.edu. *Website:* http://www.musc.edu/.

MEMPHIS COLLEGE OF ART
Memphis, TN

Tuition & fees: $31,700	Average undergraduate aid package: $22,858

ABOUT THE INSTITUTION Independent, coed. *Awards:* bachelor's and master's degrees. 10 undergraduate majors. *Total enrollment:* 435. Undergraduates: 366. Freshmen: 100. Both federal and institutional methodology are used as a basis for awarding need-based institutional aid.

UNDERGRADUATE EXPENSES for 2016–2017 *Comprehensive fee:* $40,450 includes full-time tuition ($31,000), mandatory fees ($700), and room and board ($8750). *College room only:* $6750. Full-time tuition and fees vary according to degree level and reciprocity agreements. Room and board charges vary according to housing facility. *Part-time tuition:* $3875 per course. *Part-time fees:* $350 per term. Part-time tuition and fees vary according to course load and degree level. *Payment plan:* Tuition prepayment.

FRESHMAN FINANCIAL AID (Fall 2015) 79 applied for aid; of those 90% were deemed to have need. 100% of freshmen with need received aid; of those 3% had need fully met. *Average percent of need met:* 61% (excluding resources awarded to replace EFC). *Average financial aid package:* $23,909 (excluding resources awarded to replace EFC). 11% of all full-time freshmen had no need and received non-need-based gift aid.

UNDERGRADUATE FINANCIAL AID (Fall 2015) 290 applied for aid; of those 92% were deemed to have need. 100% of undergraduates with need received aid; of those 11% had need fully met. *Average percent of need met:* 61% (excluding resources awarded to replace EFC). *Average financial aid package:* $22,858 (excluding resources awarded to replace EFC). 14% of all full-time undergraduates had no need and received non-need-based gift aid.

GIFT AID (NEED-BASED) Total amount: $5,566,297 (18% federal, 11% state, 68% institutional, 3% external sources). *Receiving aid:* Freshmen: 89% (71); all full-time undergraduates: 86% (267). *Average award:* Freshmen: $21,093; Undergraduates: $19,009. *Scholarships, grants, and awards:* Federal Pell, FSEOG, state, private, college/university gift aid from institutional funds.

GIFT AID (NON-NEED-BASED) Total amount: $922,596 (9% state, 81% institutional, 10% external sources). *Receiving aid:* Freshmen: 2% (2). Undergraduates: 8% (24). *Average award:* Freshmen: $13,513. Undergraduates: $14,439. *Scholar-*

ships, grants, and awards by category: *Creative arts/performance:* applied art and design, art/fine arts. *Special characteristics:* children of faculty/staff, previous college experience. *Tuition waivers:* Full or partial for employees or children of employees.

LOANS *Student loans:* $2,404,218 (89% need-based, 11% non-need-based). 80% of past graduating class borrowed through all loan programs. *Average indebtedness per student:* $34,828. *Average need-based loan:* Freshmen: $3097. Undergraduates: $4484. *Parent loans:* $1,275,739 (72% need-based, 28% non-need-based). *Programs:* Federal Direct (Subsidized and Unsubsidized Stafford, PLUS), college/university.

WORK-STUDY *Federal work-study:* 95 jobs averaging $520. *State or other work-study/employment:* Total amount: $11,392 (5% need-based, 95% non-need-based). 22 part-time jobs averaging $539.

APPLYING FOR FINANCIAL AID *Required financial aid form:* FAFSA. *Financial aid deadline (priority):* 3/1. *Notification date:* Continuous beginning 1/15. Students must reply within 4 weeks of notification.

CONTACT Aaron White, Director of Financial Aid, Memphis College of Art, 1930 Poplar Avenue, Overton Park, Memphis, TN 38104, 901-272-5136 or toll-free 800-727-1088. *Fax:* 901-272-5134. *E-mail:* awhite@mca.edu. *Website:* http://www.mca.edu/.

MENLO COLLEGE
Atherton, CA

CONTACT Jessica Ayers, Director of Financial Aid, Menlo College, 1000 El Camino Real, Atherton, CA 94027-4301, 650-543-3880 or toll-free 800-556-3656. *Fax:* 650-543-4103. *E-mail:* financialaid@menlo.edu. *Website:* http://www.menlo.edu/.

MERCER UNIVERSITY
Macon, GA

Tuition & fees: $35,130	Average undergraduate aid package: $34,952

ABOUT THE INSTITUTION Independent Baptist, coed. *Awards:* certificates, bachelor's, master's, and doctoral degrees. 59 undergraduate majors. *Total enrollment:* 6,955. Undergraduates: 3,046. Freshmen: 828. Federal methodology is used as a basis for awarding need-based institutional aid.

UNDERGRADUATE EXPENSES for 2016–2017 *Application fee:* $50. *Comprehensive fee:* $47,046 includes full-time tuition ($34,830), mandatory fees ($300), and room and board ($11,916). *College room only:* $5978. Full-time tuition and fees vary according to location. Room and board charges vary according to board plan, housing facility, location, and student level. *Part-time tuition:* $1161 per credit hour. *Part-time fees:* $10 per credit hour. Part-time tuition and fees vary according to course load and location.

FRESHMAN FINANCIAL AID (Fall 2015) 825 applied for aid; of those 72% were deemed to have need. 100% of freshmen with need received aid; of those 46% had need fully met. *Average percent of need met:* 91% (excluding resources awarded to replace EFC). *Average financial aid package:* $36,478 (excluding resources awarded to replace EFC). 25% of all full-time freshmen had no need and received non-need-based gift aid.

UNDERGRADUATE FINANCIAL AID (Fall 2015) 2,940 applied for aid; of those 69% were deemed to have need. 100% of undergraduates with need received aid; of those 42% had need fully met. *Average percent of need met:* 86% (excluding resources awarded to replace EFC). *Average financial aid package:* $34,952 (excluding resources awarded to replace EFC). 28% of all full-time undergraduates had no need and received non-need-based gift aid.

GIFT AID (NEED-BASED) *Total amount:* $46,673,133 (10% federal, 11% state, 77% institutional, 2% external sources). *Receiving aid:* Freshmen: 71% (589); all full-time undergraduates: 67% (1,998). *Average award:* Freshmen: $25,244; Undergraduates: $24,409. *Scholarships, grants, and awards:* Federal Pell, FSEOG, state, college/university gift aid from institutional funds, Federal Nursing.

GIFT AID (NON-NEED-BASED) *Total amount:* $24,412,464 (16% state, 81% institutional, 3% external sources). *Receiving aid:* Freshmen: 22% (181). Undergraduates: 19% (563). *Average award:* Freshmen: $19,796. Undergraduates: $19,813.

Scholarships, grants, and awards by category: *Academic interests/achievement:* biological sciences, business, education, engineering/technologies, English, foreign languages, general academic interests/achievements, international studies, military science, religion/biblical studies. *Creative arts/performance:* art/fine arts, debating, music, theater/drama. *Special achievements/activities:* community service, general special achievements/activities, leadership. *Special characteristics:* adult students, children of faculty/staff, children of public servants, general special characteristics, international students, relatives of clergy, siblings of current students. *Tuition waivers:* Full or partial for employees or children of employees. *ROTC:* Army.

LOANS *Student loans:* $13,478,765 (71% need-based, 29% non-need-based). 64% of past graduating class borrowed through all loan programs. *Average indebtedness per student:* $28,194. *Average need-based loan:* Freshmen: $9769. Undergraduates: $10,046. *Parent loans:* $3,301,587 (41% need-based, 59% non-need-based). *Programs:* Federal Direct (Subsidized and Unsubsidized Stafford, PLUS), Perkins, Federal Nursing, college/university.

WORK-STUDY *Federal work-study:* jobs available.

ATHLETIC AWARDS *Total amount:* $7,746,691 (42% need-based, 58% non-need-based).

APPLYING FOR FINANCIAL AID *Required financial aid forms:* FAFSA, institution's own form, state aid form (GA residents only). *Financial aid deadline (priority):* 4/1. *Notification date:* Continuous. Students must reply within 2 weeks of notification.

CONTACT Ms. Maria Hammett, Associate Vice President, Mercer University, Office of Financial Planning, Macon, GA 31207-0003, 478-301-2226 or toll-free 800-MERCER-U. *Fax:* 478-301-2671. *E-mail:* hammett_ma@mercer.edu. *Website:* http://www.mercer.edu/.

MERCY COLLEGE
Dobbs Ferry, NY

Tuition & fees: $18,392	Average undergraduate aid package: $13,223

ABOUT THE INSTITUTION Independent, coed. *Awards:* certificates, associate, bachelor's, master's, and doctoral degrees. 36 undergraduate majors. *Total enrollment:* 10,099. Undergraduates: 7,157. Freshmen: 948. Federal methodology is used as a basis for awarding need-based institutional aid.

UNDERGRADUATE EXPENSES for 2016–2017 *Application fee:* $40. *Comprehensive fee:* $31,892 includes full-time tuition ($17,772), mandatory fees ($620), and room and board ($13,500). *College room only:* $9150. Full-time tuition and fees vary according to course load. Room and board charges vary according to board plan. *Part-time tuition:* $748 per credit. *Part-time fees:* $155 per term. Part-time tuition and fees vary according to course load.

FRESHMAN FINANCIAL AID (Fall 2015) 898 applied for aid; of those 93% were deemed to have need. 96% of freshmen with need received aid; of those 3% had need fully met. *Average percent of need met:* 56% (excluding resources awarded to replace EFC). *Average financial aid package:* $14,650 (excluding resources awarded to replace EFC). 3% of all full-time freshmen had no need and received non-need-based gift aid.

UNDERGRADUATE FINANCIAL AID (Fall 2015) 4,821 applied for aid; of those 95% were deemed to have need. 96% of undergraduates with need received aid; of those 3% had need fully met. *Average percent of need met:* 51% (excluding resources awarded to replace EFC). *Average financial aid package:* $13,223 (excluding resources awarded to replace EFC). 2% of all full-time undergraduates had no need and received non-need-based gift aid.

GIFT AID (NEED-BASED) *Total amount:* $39,196,449 (42% federal, 23% state, 35% institutional). *Receiving aid:* Freshmen: 77% (713); all full-time undergraduates: 76% (3,972). *Average award:* Freshmen: $11,869; Undergraduates: $9597. *Scholarships, grants, and awards:* Federal Pell, FSEOG, state, private, college/university gift aid from institutional funds, Federal Nursing.

GIFT AID (NON-NEED-BASED) *Total amount:* $5,195,210 (7% state, 89% institutional, 4% external sources). *Receiving aid:* Freshmen: 39% (365). Undergraduates: 25% (1,301). *Average award:* Freshmen: $4500. Undergraduates: $4139. *Scholarships, grants, and awards by category:* *Academic interests/achievement:* business, general academic interests/achievements. *Special characteristics:* children of faculty/staff. *Tuition waivers:* Full or partial for employees or children of employees, senior citizens. **ROTC:** Army cooperative, Air Force cooperative.

LOANS *Student loans:* $35,452,106 (43% need-based, 57% non-need-based). 88% of past graduating class borrowed through all loan programs. *Average indebtedness per student:* $29,197. *Average need-based loan:* Freshmen: $3179. Undergraduates: $4076. *Parent loans:* $6,178,190 (100% non-need-based). *Programs:* Federal Direct (Subsidized and Unsubsidized Stafford, PLUS), Federal Nursing.

WORK-STUDY *Federal work-study:* jobs available.

ATHLETIC AWARDS Total amount: $1,177,973 (100% non-need-based).

APPLYING FOR FINANCIAL AID *Required financial aid forms:* FAFSA, state aid form. *Financial aid deadline (priority):* 2/15. *Notification date:* Continuous beginning 2/20. Students must reply by 5/1 or within 2 weeks of notification.

CONTACT Margaret M. McGrail, Vice President of Enrollment Services, Mercy College, 555 Broadway, Dobbs Ferry, NY 10522, 877-637-2946 or toll-free 877-MERCY-GO (out-of-state). *Fax:* 914-674-7382. *E-mail:* admissions@mercy.edu. *Website:* http://www.mercy.edu/.

MERCY COLLEGE OF HEALTH SCIENCES
Des Moines, IA

CONTACT Lisa Croat, Financial Aid Director, Mercy College of Health Sciences, 921 Sixth Avenue, Des Moines, IA 50309, 515-643-6636 or toll-free 800-637-2994. *Fax:* 515-643-6747. *E-mail:* financialaid@mchs.edu. *Website:* http://www.mchs.edu/.

MERCY COLLEGE OF OHIO
Toledo, OH

Tuition & fees: $14,610	Average undergraduate aid package: N/A

ABOUT THE INSTITUTION Independent Roman Catholic Church, coed, primarily women. *Awards:* certificates, associate, and bachelor's degrees. 8 undergraduate majors. *Total enrollment:* 1,351. Undergraduates: 1,351. Freshmen: 62. Federal methodology is used as a basis for awarding need-based institutional aid.

UNDERGRADUATE EXPENSES for 2017–2018 *Application fee:* $25. *One-time required fee:* $250. *Tuition:* full-time $12,360; part-time $454 per credit hour. *Required fees:* full-time $2250; $55 per credit hour or $300 per term. Full-time tuition and fees vary according to course load, location, and program. Part-time tuition and fees vary according to course load, location, and program. Room and board charges vary according to housing facility.

GIFT AID (NEED-BASED) *Total amount:* $2,756,143 (76% federal, 21% state, 3% institutional). *Scholarships, grants, and awards:* Federal Pell, FSEOG, state, private, college/university gift aid from institutional funds, Federal Nursing.

GIFT AID (NON-NEED-BASED) *Total amount:* $678,086 (1% state, 37% institutional, 62% external sources). *Scholarships, grants, and awards by category:* Academic interests/achievement: general academic interests/achievements, home economics, premedicine. *Special characteristics:* first-generation college students. *Tuition waivers:* Full or partial for employees or children of employees.

LOANS *Student loans:* $8,548,646 (39% need-based, 61% non-need-based). *Parent loans:* $737,592 (100% non-need-based). *Programs:* Federal Direct (Subsidized and Unsubsidized Stafford, PLUS), state, college/university.

WORK-STUDY *Federal work-study:* 24 jobs averaging $1744.

APPLYING FOR FINANCIAL AID *Required financial aid form:* FAFSA. *Financial aid deadline:* Continuous. *Notification date:* Continuous beginning 3/1. Students must reply by 8/15.

CONTACT Julie Leslie, Director of Financial Aid, Mercy College of Ohio, 2221 Madison Avenue, Toledo, OH 43604, 419-251-1598 or toll-free 888-80-MERCY. *Fax:* 419-251-0969. *E-mail:* julie.leslie@mercycollege.edu. *Website:* http://www.mercycollege.edu/.

MERCYHURST UNIVERSITY
Erie, PA

ABOUT THE INSTITUTION Independent Roman Catholic, coed. *Awards:* certificates, bachelor's, and master's degrees. 69 undergraduate majors. *Total enrollment:* 2,822. Undergraduates: 2,494. Freshmen: 718.

GIFT AID (NEED-BASED) *Scholarships, grants, and awards:* Federal Pell, FSEOG, state, private, college/university gift aid from institutional funds.

GIFT AID (NON-NEED-BASED) *Scholarships, grants, and awards by category:* Academic interests/achievement: general academic interests/achievements. Creative arts/performance: applied art and design, art/fine arts, dance, music. *Special characteristics:* children and siblings of alumni, children of faculty/staff.

LOANS *Programs:* Federal Direct (Subsidized and Unsubsidized Stafford, PLUS), Perkins, college/university.

WORK-STUDY *Federal work-study:* jobs available. *State or other work-study/employment:* Total amount: $297,000 (37% need-based, 63% non-need-based). Part-time jobs available.

APPLYING FOR FINANCIAL AID *Required financial aid form:* FAFSA.

CONTACT Carrie Newman, Director of Student Financial Services, Mercyhurst University, 501 East 38th Street, Erie, PA 16546, 814-824-2288 or toll-free 800-825-1926. *Fax:* 814-824-2300. *E-mail:* sfs@mercyhurst.edu. *Website:* http://www.mercyhurst.edu/.

MEREDITH COLLEGE
Raleigh, NC

Tuition & fees: $34,907	Average undergraduate aid package: $24,977

ABOUT THE INSTITUTION Independent, undergraduate: women only; graduate: coed. *Awards:* certificates, bachelor's, and master's degrees. 40 undergraduate majors. *Total enrollment:* 1,949. Undergraduates: 1,685. Freshmen: 423. Federal methodology is used as a basis for awarding need-based institutional aid.

UNDERGRADUATE EXPENSES for 2016–2017 *Application fee:* $40. *Comprehensive fee:* $45,297 includes full-time tuition ($34,807), mandatory fees ($100), and room and board ($10,390). Full-time tuition and fees vary according to course load. Room and board charges vary according to board plan and housing facility. *Part-time tuition:* $864 per credit hour. *Part-time fees:* $100 per year. Part-time tuition and fees vary according to course load.

FRESHMAN FINANCIAL AID (Fall 2016, est.) 394 applied for aid; of those 88% were deemed to have need. 100% of freshmen with need received aid; of those 19% had need fully met. *Average percent of need met:* 76% (excluding resources awarded to replace EFC). *Average financial aid package:* $25,635 (excluding resources awarded to replace EFC). 11% of all full-time freshmen had no need and received non-need-based gift aid.

UNDERGRADUATE FINANCIAL AID (Fall 2016, est.) 1,347 applied for aid; of those 89% were deemed to have need. 100% of undergraduates with need received aid; of those 16% had need fully met. *Average percent of need met:* 72% (excluding resources awarded to replace EFC). *Average financial aid package:* $24,977 (excluding resources awarded to replace EFC). 8% of all full-time undergraduates had no need and received non-need-based gift aid.

GIFT AID (NEED-BASED) *Total amount:* $25,173,121 (13% federal, 15% state, 65% institutional, 7% external sources). *Receiving aid:* Freshmen: 79% (345); all full-time undergraduates: 74% (1,199). *Average award:* Freshmen: $22,218; Undergraduates: $20,935. *Scholarships, grants, and awards:* Federal Pell, FSEOG, state, private, college/university gift aid from institutional funds.

GIFT AID (NON-NEED-BASED) *Total amount:* $5,904,349 (1% federal, 86% institutional, 13% external sources). *Average award:* Freshmen: $14,853. Undergraduates: $13,427. *Scholarships, grants, and awards by category:* Academic interests/achievement: biological sciences, business, computer science, education, English, foreign languages, general academic interests/achievements, mathematics, physical sciences, religion/biblical studies. *Creative arts/performance:* applied art and design, art/fine arts, creative writing, music. *Special achievements/activities:* community service, leadership. *Special characteristics:* adult students, children of faculty/staff, ethnic background, first-generation college students, international students, members of minority groups, out-of-state students, previous college experience, religious affiliation. *Tuition waivers:* Full or partial for employees or children of employees. *ROTC:* Army cooperative, Air Force cooperative.

LOANS *Student loans:* $16,250,418 (93% need-based, 7% non-need-based). 69% of past graduating class borrowed through all loan programs. *Average indebtedness per student:* $33,993. *Average need-based loan:* Freshmen: $3391. Undergraduates: $4348. *Parent loans:* $3,207,563 (91% need-based, 9% non-need-based). *Programs:* Federal Direct (Subsidized and Unsubsidized Stafford, PLUS), Perkins, college/university.

WORK-STUDY *Federal work-study:* Total amount: $578,156; jobs available. *State or other work-study/employment:* Part-time jobs available.

APPLYING FOR FINANCIAL AID *Required financial aid form:* FAFSA. *Financial aid deadline (priority):* 2/15. *Notification date:* Continuous beginning 3/15. Students must reply by 5/1 or within 2 weeks of notification.

CONTACT Mr. Kevin Michaelsen, Director of Financial Assistance, Meredith College, 3800 Hillsborough Street, Raleigh, NC 27607-5298, 919-760-8565 or toll-free 800-MEREDITH. *Fax:* 919-760-2375. *E-mail:* michaelsen@meredith.edu. *Website:* http://www.meredith.edu/.

MERRIMACK COLLEGE
North Andover, MA

Tuition & fees: $38,825	Average undergraduate aid package: $23,143

ABOUT THE INSTITUTION Independent Roman Catholic, coed. *Awards:* certificates, bachelor's, and master's degrees. 62 undergraduate majors. *Total enrollment:* 4,029. Undergraduates: 3,448. Freshmen: 1,005. Federal methodology is used as a basis for awarding need-based institutional aid.

UNDERGRADUATE EXPENSES for 2016–2017 *Comprehensive fee:* $53,170 includes full-time tuition ($36,625), mandatory fees ($2200), and room and board ($14,345). Full-time tuition and fees vary according to degree level. Room and board charges vary according to board plan and housing facility. *Part-time tuition:* $1310 per credit. Part-time tuition and fees vary according to class time, course load, and degree level.

FRESHMAN FINANCIAL AID (Fall 2016, est.) 870 applied for aid; of those 89% were deemed to have need. 100% of freshmen with need received aid; of those 12% had need fully met. *Average percent of need met:* 65% (excluding resources awarded to replace EFC). *Average financial aid package:* $23,779 (excluding resources awarded to replace EFC). 18% of all full-time freshmen had no need and received non-need-based gift aid.

UNDERGRADUATE FINANCIAL AID (Fall 2016, est.) 2,656 applied for aid; of those 89% were deemed to have need. 100% of undergraduates with need received aid; of those 13% had need fully met. *Average percent of need met:* 65% (excluding resources awarded to replace EFC). *Average financial aid package:* $23,143 (excluding resources awarded to replace EFC). 21% of all full-time undergraduates had no need and received non-need-based gift aid.

GIFT AID (NEED-BASED) *Total amount:* $40,967,527 (7% federal, 3% state, 89% institutional, 1% external sources). *Receiving aid:* Freshmen: 77% (775); all full-time undergraduates: 70% (2,334). *Average award:* Freshmen: $20,834; Undergraduates: $19,409. *Scholarships, grants, and awards:* Federal Pell, FSEOG, state, private, college/university gift aid from institutional funds.

GIFT AID (NON-NEED-BASED) *Total amount:* $9,949,947 (1% state, 99% institutional). *Receiving aid:* Freshmen: 8% (78). Undergraduates: 8% (263). *Average award:* Freshmen: $12,715. Undergraduates: $12,017. *Scholarships, grants, and awards by category: Academic interests/achievement:* general academic interests/achievements. *Special achievements/activities:* leadership. *Special characteristics:* children of faculty/staff, international students, relatives of clergy, religious affiliation, siblings of current students, veterans. *Tuition waivers:* Full or partial for employees or children of employees, senior citizens. *ROTC:* Air Force cooperative.

LOANS *Student loans:* $32,046,724 (63% need-based, 37% non-need-based). *Average need-based loan:* Freshmen: $3401. Undergraduates: $4527. *Parent loans:* $9,309,886 (48% need-based, 52% non-need-based). *Programs:* Federal Direct (Subsidized and Unsubsidized Stafford, PLUS), Perkins, state, college/university.

WORK-STUDY *Federal work-study:* Total amount: $177,190; jobs available. *State or other work-study/employment:* Part-time jobs available.

ATHLETIC AWARDS Total amount: $8,781,943 (42% need-based, 58% non-need-based).

APPLYING FOR FINANCIAL AID *Required financial aid form:* FAFSA. *Financial aid deadline (priority):* 2/15. *Notification date:* Continuous beginning 3/15.

CONTACT Adrienne Montgomery, Director of Financial Aid, Merrimack College, 315 Turnpike Street, North Andover, MA 01845, 978-837-5186. *Fax:* 978-837-5067. *E-mail:* montgomerya@merrimack.edu. *Website:* http://www.merrimack.edu/.

MESIVTA OF EASTERN PARKWAY– YESHIVA ZICHRON MEILECH
Brooklyn, NY

CONTACT Rabbi Joseph Halberstadt, Dean, Mesivta of Eastern Parkway–Yeshiva Zichron Meilech, 510 Dahill Road, Brooklyn, NY 11218-5559, 718-438-1002.

MESIVTA TORAH VODAATH RABBINICAL SEMINARY
Brooklyn, NY

CONTACT Mrs. Kayla Goldring, Director of Financial Aid, Mesivta Torah Vodaath Rabbinical Seminary, 425 East Ninth Street, Brooklyn, NY 11218-5209, 718-941-8000. *Website:* http://www.torahvodaath.org/.

MESIVTHA TIFERETH JERUSALEM OF AMERICA
New York, NY

CONTACT Rabbi Dickstein, Director of Financial Aid, Mesivtha Tifereth Jerusalem of America, 141 East Broadway, New York, NY 10002-6301, 212-964-2830.

MESSENGER COLLEGE
Euless, TX

CONTACT Patricia J. Pentecost, Director of Financial Aid, Messenger College, 300 East 50th Street, Joplin, MO 64804, 417-624-7070 Ext. 104 or toll-free 800-385-8940. *Fax:* 417-624-5070. *E-mail:* ppentecost@messengercollege.edu. *Website:* http://www.messengercollege.edu/.

MESSIAH COLLEGE
Mechanicsburg, PA

Tuition & fees: $33,180	Average undergraduate aid package: $23,627

ABOUT THE INSTITUTION Independent interdenominational, coed. *Awards:* certificates, bachelor's, master's, and doctoral degrees. 77 undergraduate majors. *Total enrollment:* 3,305. Undergraduates: 2,788. Freshmen: 685. Federal methodology is used as a basis for awarding need-based institutional aid.

UNDERGRADUATE EXPENSES for 2016–2017 *Application fee:* $50. *Comprehensive fee:* $43,100 includes full-time tuition ($32,350), mandatory fees ($830), and room and board ($9920). *College room only:* $5250. Room and board charges vary according to board plan and housing facility. *Part-time tuition:* $1350 per credit hour.

FRESHMAN FINANCIAL AID (Fall 2016, est.) 594 applied for aid; of those 87% were deemed to have need. 100% of freshmen with need received aid; of those 21% had need fully met. *Average percent of need met:* 74% (excluding resources awarded to replace EFC). *Average financial aid package:* $24,666 (excluding

resources awarded to replace EFC). 24% of all full-time freshmen had no need and received non-need-based gift aid.

UNDERGRADUATE FINANCIAL AID (Fall 2016, est.) 2,134 applied for aid; of those 90% were deemed to have need. 100% of undergraduates with need received aid; of those 19% had need fully met. *Average percent of need met:* 72% (excluding resources awarded to replace EFC). *Average financial aid package:* $23,627 (excluding resources awarded to replace EFC). 26% of all full-time undergraduates had no need and received non-need-based gift aid.

GIFT AID (NEED-BASED) *Total amount:* $33,427,336 (8% federal, 7% state, 82% institutional, 3% external sources). *Receiving aid:* Freshmen: 75% (515); all full-time undergraduates: 72% (1,894). *Average award:* Freshmen: $18,821; Undergraduates: $17,599. *Scholarships, grants, and awards:* Federal Pell, FSEOG, state, private, college/university gift aid from institutional funds, Federal Nursing.

GIFT AID (NON-NEED-BASED) *Total amount:* $12,314,238 (3% federal, 93% institutional, 4% external sources). *Receiving aid:* Freshmen: 11% (73). Undergraduates: 9% (233). *Average award:* Freshmen: $15,583. Undergraduates: $14,515. *Scholarships, grants, and awards by category: Academic interests/achievement:* 2,031 awards ($22,716,720 total): general academic interests/achievements, humanities. *Creative arts/performance:* 121 awards ($921,069 total): art/fine arts, dance, music, theater/drama. *Special achievements/activities:* 437 awards ($7,961,317 total): leadership. *Special characteristics:* 150 awards ($2,048,576 total): adult students, children of faculty/staff, local/state students, religious affiliation. *Tuition waivers:* Full or partial for employees or children of employees, adult students, senior citizens.

LOANS *Student loans:* $19,176,649 (68% need-based, 32% non-need-based). 70% of past graduating class borrowed through all loan programs. *Average indebtedness per student:* $39,617. *Average need-based loan:* Freshmen: $3934. Undergraduates: $4861. *Parent loans:* $4,524,312 (47% need-based, 53% non-need-based). *Programs:* Federal Direct (Subsidized and Unsubsidized Stafford, PLUS), Perkins, Federal Nursing.

WORK-STUDY *Federal work-study:* Total amount: $1,787,888; 851 jobs averaging $2131. *State or other work-study/employment:* Total amount: $2,524,340 (20% need-based, 80% non-need-based). 821 part-time jobs averaging $2046.

APPLYING FOR FINANCIAL AID *Required financial aid form:* FAFSA. *Financial aid deadline (priority):* 4/1. *Notification date:* Continuous beginning 12/1. Students must reply by 5/1 or within 4 weeks of notification.

CONTACT Mr. Michael Strite, Assistant Director of Financial Aid, Messiah College, One College Avenue, Suite 3006, Mechanicsburg, PA 17055, 717-691-6007 or toll-free 800-233-4220. *Fax:* 717-796-4791. *E-mail:* mstrite@messiah.edu. *Website:* http://www.messiah.edu/.

METHODIST COLLEGE
Peoria, IL

CONTACT Financial Aid Office, Methodist College, 415 St. Mark Court, Peoria, IL 61603, 309-672-5513.
Website: http://www.methodistcol.edu/.

METHODIST UNIVERSITY
Fayetteville, NC

Tuition & fees: N/R	Average undergraduate aid package: $20,854

ABOUT THE INSTITUTION Independent United Methodist, coed. 57 undergraduate majors. Federal methodology is used as a basis for awarding need-based institutional aid.

FRESHMAN FINANCIAL AID (Fall 2015) 448 applied for aid; of those 94% were deemed to have need. 100% of freshmen with need received aid; of those 8% had need fully met. *Average percent of need met:* 68% (excluding resources awarded to replace EFC). *Average financial aid package:* $23,494 (excluding resources awarded to replace EFC). 16% of all full-time freshmen had no need and received non-need-based gift aid.

UNDERGRADUATE FINANCIAL AID (Fall 2015) 1,618 applied for aid; of those 94% were deemed to have need. 99% of undergraduates with need received aid; of those 7% had need fully met. *Average percent of need met:* 61% (excluding

resources awarded to replace EFC). *Average financial aid package:* $20,854 (excluding resources awarded to replace EFC). 16% of all full-time undergraduates had no need and received non-need-based gift aid.

GIFT AID (NEED-BASED) *Receiving aid:* Freshmen: 70% (355); all full-time undergraduates: 68% (1,328). *Average award:* Freshmen: $12,375; Undergraduates: $10,020. *Scholarships, grants, and awards:* Federal Pell, FSEOG, state, private, college/university gift aid from institutional funds.

GIFT AID (NON-NEED-BASED) *Receiving aid:* Freshmen: 75% (381). Undergraduates: 66% (1,301). *Average award:* Freshmen: $20,404. Undergraduates: $16,882. *Scholarships, grants, and awards by category: Academic interests/achievement:* 1,397 awards ($12,475,448 total): business, education, English, foreign languages, general academic interests/achievements, international studies, military science, religion/biblical studies. *Creative arts/performance:* 58 awards ($397,986 total): dance, debating, music, theater/drama. *Special achievements/activities:* 105 awards ($438,229 total): cheerleading/drum major, leadership, religious involvement. *Special characteristics:* 215 awards ($3,565,372 total): children and siblings of alumni, children of faculty/staff, ethnic background, general special characteristics, local/state students, members of minority groups, relatives of clergy, religious affiliation, siblings of current students, veterans.

LOANS *Student loans:* 74% of past graduating class borrowed through all loan programs. *Average indebtedness per student:* $27,863. *Average need-based loan:* Freshmen: $3259. Undergraduates: $4207. *Programs:* Federal Direct (Subsidized and Unsubsidized Stafford, PLUS), Perkins.

WORK-STUDY *Federal work-study:* 470 jobs averaging $570. *State or other work-study/employment:* 141 part-time jobs averaging $1248.

APPLYING FOR FINANCIAL AID *Required financial aid form:* FAFSA. *Financial aid deadline (priority):* 8/1. *Notification date:* Continuous beginning 3/6. Students must reply within 2 weeks of notification.

CONTACT Bonnie Adamson, Financial Aid Office, Methodist University, 5400 Ramsey Street, Fayetteville, NC 28311-1420, 910-630-7307 or toll-free 800-488-7110 Ext. 7027. *Fax:* 910-630-7285. *E-mail:* adamson@methodist.edu. *Website:* http://www.methodist.edu/.

METROPOLITAN COLLEGE OF NEW YORK
New York, NY

Tuition & fees: $19,180	Average undergraduate aid package: $16,577

ABOUT THE INSTITUTION Independent, coed. *Awards:* certificates, associate, bachelor's, and master's degrees. 7 undergraduate majors. *Total enrollment:* 1,059. Undergraduates: 697. Freshmen: 75. Federal methodology is used as a basis for awarding need-based institutional aid.

UNDERGRADUATE EXPENSES for 2017–2018 *Application fee:* $30. *Tuition:* full-time $18,330; part-time $766 per credit. Full-time tuition and fees vary according to degree level and program. Part-time tuition and fees vary according to degree level and program. *Payment plan:* Guaranteed tuition.

FRESHMAN FINANCIAL AID (Fall 2016, est.) 71 applied for aid; of those 97% were deemed to have need. 99% of freshmen with need received aid. *Average percent of need met:* 48% (excluding resources awarded to replace EFC). *Average financial aid package:* $14,593 (excluding resources awarded to replace EFC). 1% of all full-time freshmen had no need and received non-need-based gift aid.

UNDERGRADUATE FINANCIAL AID (Fall 2016, est.) 588 applied for aid; of those 99% were deemed to have need. 100% of undergraduates with need received aid; of those .3% had need fully met. *Average percent of need met:* 44% (excluding resources awarded to replace EFC). *Average financial aid package:* $16,577 (excluding resources awarded to replace EFC). 2% of all full-time undergraduates had no need and received non-need-based gift aid.

GIFT AID (NEED-BASED) *Total amount:* $7,005,757 (42% federal, 25% state, 25% institutional, 8% external sources). *Receiving aid:* Freshmen: 93% (68); all full-time undergraduates: 94% (582). *Average award:* Freshmen: $11,818; Undergraduates: $11,596. *Scholarships, grants, and awards:* Federal Pell, FSEOG, state, private, college/university gift aid from institutional funds.

GIFT AID (NON-NEED-BASED) *Total amount:* $281,561 (27% institutional, 73% external sources). *Receiving aid:* Undergraduates: 1. *Average award:* Freshmen: $2000. Undergraduates: $2430. *Scholarships, grants, and awards by*

category: Academic interests/achievement: general academic interests/achievements. **Tuition waivers:** Full or partial for employees or children of employees.
LOANS Student loans: $7,424,182 (99% need-based, 1% non-need-based). 95% of past graduating class borrowed through all loan programs. *Average indebtedness per student:* $49,357. **Average need-based loan:** Freshmen: $3530. Undergraduates: $5264. **Parent loans:** $28,610 (34% need-based, 66% non-need-based). **Programs:** Federal Direct (Subsidized and Unsubsidized Stafford, PLUS).
WORK-STUDY Federal work-study: Total amount: $83,400; jobs available. **State or other work-study/employment:** Part-time jobs available.
APPLYING FOR FINANCIAL AID Required financial aid forms: FAFSA, state aid form. **Financial aid deadline:** Continuous. **Notification date:** Continuous.
CONTACT Mr. Douane Campbell, Acting Director of Financial Aid, Metropolitan College of New York, 60 West Street, New York, NY 10006, 212-343-1234 Ext. 5004 or toll-free 800-33-THINK Ext. 5001. *Fax:* 212-343-7399.
Website: http://www.metropolitan.edu/.

METROPOLITAN STATE UNIVERSITY
St. Paul, MN

ABOUT THE INSTITUTION State-supported, coed. 49 undergraduate majors.
GIFT AID (NEED-BASED) Scholarships, grants, and awards: Federal Pell, FSEOG, state, private, college/university gift aid from institutional funds.
GIFT AID (NON-NEED-BASED) Scholarships, grants, and awards by category: Academic interests/achievement: education, general academic interests/achievements.
LOANS Programs: Federal Direct (Subsidized and Unsubsidized Stafford, PLUS), state.
APPLYING FOR FINANCIAL AID Required financial aid form: FAFSA.
CONTACT Dr. Lois J. Larson, Director of Financial Aid, Metropolitan State University, 700 East 7th Street, St. Paul, MN 55106-5000, 651-793-1411. *Fax:* 651-642-0636. *E-mail:* financial.aid@metrostate.edu.
Website: http://www.metrostate.edu/.

METROPOLITAN STATE UNIVERSITY OF DENVER
Denver, CO

Tuition & fees (CO res): $6929	Average undergraduate aid package: $8590

ABOUT THE INSTITUTION State-supported, coed. **Awards:** certificates, bachelor's, and master's degrees. 69 undergraduate majors. **Total enrollment:** 20,474. Undergraduates: 19,940. Freshmen: 2,255. Federal methodology is used as a basis for awarding need-based institutional aid.
UNDERGRADUATE EXPENSES for 2016–2017 Application fee: $25. **Tuition, state resident:** full-time $5693. **Tuition, nonresident:** full-time $18,859. **Required fees:** full-time $1236. Full-time tuition and fees vary according to course load and location. Part-time tuition and fees vary according to course load and location.
FRESHMAN FINANCIAL AID (Fall 2015) 1,368 applied for aid; of those 79% were deemed to have need. 86% of freshmen with need received aid; of those 3% had need fully met. **Average percent of need met:** 54% (excluding resources awarded to replace EFC). **Average financial aid package:** $7181 (excluding resources awarded to replace EFC). 16% of all full-time freshmen had no need and received non-need-based gift aid.
UNDERGRADUATE FINANCIAL AID (Fall 2015) 9,425 applied for aid; of those 85% were deemed to have need. 91% of undergraduates with need received aid; of those 3% had need fully met. **Average percent of need met:** 57% (excluding resources awarded to replace EFC). **Average financial aid package:** $8590 (excluding resources awarded to replace EFC). 21% of all full-time undergraduates had no need and received non-need-based gift aid.
GIFT AID (NEED-BASED) Total amount: $50,379,383 (53% federal, 30% state, 14% institutional, 3% external sources). **Receiving aid:** Freshmen: 41% (664); all full-time undergraduates: 44% (5,355). **Average award:** Freshmen: $6129; Undergrad-

uates: $6515. **Scholarships, grants, and awards:** Federal Pell, FSEOG, state, private, college/university gift aid from institutional funds.
GIFT AID (NON-NEED-BASED) Total amount: $996,536 (8% state, 58% institutional, 34% external sources). **Receiving aid:** Freshmen: 1. Undergraduates: 1% (115). **Average award:** Freshmen: $1921. Undergraduates: $2380. **Scholarships, grants, and awards by category:** Academic interests/achievement: biological sciences, business, communication, computer science, education, engineering/technologies, English, foreign languages, general academic interests/achievements, home economics, humanities, mathematics, physical sciences, social sciences. *Creative arts/performance:* music, performing arts, theater/drama. *Special achievements/activities:* leadership. *Special characteristics:* adult students, first-generation college students, local/state students, veterans. **Tuition waivers:** Full or partial for senior citizens.
ROTC: Army, Air Force cooperative.
LOANS Student loans: $66,414,268 (86% need-based, 14% non-need-based). 63% of past graduating class borrowed through all loan programs. *Average indebtedness per student:* $28,380. **Average need-based loan:** Freshmen: $3182. Undergraduates: $4013. **Parent loans:** $2,384,487 (54% need-based, 46% non-need-based). **Programs:** Federal Direct (Subsidized and Unsubsidized Stafford, PLUS), Perkins.
WORK-STUDY Federal work-study: 153 jobs averaging $3585. **State or other work-study/employment:** Total amount: $2,221,086 (83% need-based, 17% non-need-based). 687 part-time jobs averaging $3388.
ATHLETIC AWARDS Total amount: $1,726,700 (54% need-based, 46% non-need-based).
APPLYING FOR FINANCIAL AID Required financial aid form: FAFSA. **Financial aid deadline:** Continuous. **Notification date:** Continuous beginning 12/1.
CONTACT Office of Financial Aid, Metropolitan State University of Denver, PO Box 173362, Denver, CO 80217-3362, 303-556-8593. *Fax:* 303-556-4927.
Website: http://www.msudenver.edu/.

MIAMI INTERNATIONAL UNIVERSITY OF ART & DESIGN
Miami, FL

Financial Aid Office, Miami International University of Art & Design, 1737 Bayshore Drive, Miami, FL 33132, 800-225-9023 Ext. 125 or toll-free 800-225-9023. *Fax:* 305-374-7946.

MIAMI REGIONAL UNIVERSITY
Miami Springs, FL

CONTACT Financial Aid Office, Miami Regional University, 700 South Royal Poinciana Boulevard, Miami Springs, FL 33166, 305-442-9223.
Website: http://www.mru.edu/.

MIAMI UNIVERSITY
Oxford, OH

Tuition & fees (OH res): $14,288	Average undergraduate aid package: $13,240

ABOUT THE INSTITUTION State-related, coed. **Awards:** certificates, associate, bachelor's, master's, and doctoral degrees. 106 undergraduate majors. **Total enrollment:** 19,697. Undergraduates: 16,981. Freshmen: 3,799. Federal methodology is used as a basis for awarding need-based institutional aid.
UNDERGRADUATE EXPENSES for 2016–2017 Application fee: $50. **Tuition, state resident:** full-time $13,534; part-time $563.88 per credit hour. **Tuition, nonresident:** full-time $30,838; part-time $1284.92 per credit hour. **Required fees:** full-time $754; $29.16 per credit hour. Full-time tuition and fees vary according to location, program, and student level. Part-time tuition and fees vary according to course load, location, program, and student level. **College room and board:** $12,014; **Room only:** $7314. Room and board charges vary according to board plan, housing facility, and student level. **Payment plan:** Guaranteed tuition.

FRESHMAN FINANCIAL AID (Fall 2015) 2,667 applied for aid; of those 56% were deemed to have need. 97% of freshmen with need received aid; of those 27% had need fully met. *Average percent of need met:* 59% (excluding resources awarded to replace EFC). *Average financial aid package:* $13,219 (excluding resources awarded to replace EFC). 34% of all full-time freshmen had no need and received non-need-based gift aid.

UNDERGRADUATE FINANCIAL AID (Fall 2015) 8,309 applied for aid; of those 65% were deemed to have need. 98% of undergraduates with need received aid; of those 20% had need fully met. *Average percent of need met:* 59% (excluding resources awarded to replace EFC). *Average financial aid package:* $13,240 (excluding resources awarded to replace EFC). 30% of all full-time undergraduates had no need and received non-need-based gift aid.

GIFT AID (NEED-BASED) *Total amount:* $39,865,102 (24% federal, 3% state, 73% institutional). *Receiving aid:* Freshmen: 33% (1,253); all full-time undergraduates: 30% (4,631). *Average award:* Freshmen: $10,287; Undergraduates: $9543. *Scholarships, grants, and awards:* Federal Pell, FSEOG, state, private, college/university gift aid from institutional funds.

GIFT AID (NON-NEED-BASED) *Total amount:* $47,847,613 (93% institutional, 7% external sources). *Receiving aid:* Freshmen: 8% (308). Undergraduates: 5% (723). *Average award:* Freshmen: $9337. Undergraduates: $8001. *Scholarships, grants, and awards by category:* Academic interests/achievement: architecture, education, engineering/technologies, general academic interests/achievements. Creative arts/performance: art/fine arts, music, theater/drama. Special achievements/activities: general special achievements/activities, leadership. Special characteristics: children of faculty/staff, local/state students, members of minority groups, out-of-state students. *Tuition waivers:* Full or partial for employees or children of employees. *ROTC:* Army cooperative, Naval, Air Force.

LOANS *Student loans:* $57,866,437 (30% need-based, 70% non-need-based). 53% of past graduating class borrowed through all loan programs. *Average indebtedness per student:* $30,015. *Average need-based loan:* Freshmen: $3622. Undergraduates: $4580. *Parent loans:* $26,299,133 (100% non-need-based). *Programs:* Federal Direct (Subsidized and Unsubsidized Stafford, PLUS), Perkins, college/university, private loans.

WORK-STUDY *Federal work-study:* 3,293 jobs averaging $710.

ATHLETIC AWARDS Total amount: $9,047,172 (100% non-need-based).

APPLYING FOR FINANCIAL AID *Required financial aid form:* FAFSA. *Financial aid deadline (priority):* 2/15. *Notification date:* Continuous beginning 3/20. Students must reply by 5/1 or within 3 weeks of notification.

CONTACT Mr. Brent Shock, Office of Student Financial Aid, Miami University, Campus Avenue Building, Oxford, OH 45056-3427, 513-529-0001. *Fax:* 513-529-8713. *E-mail:* financialaid@miamioh.edu. *Website:* http://miamioh.edu/.

MIAMI UNIVERSITY HAMILTON
Hamilton, OH

CONTACT Financial Aid Office, Miami University Hamilton, 1601 Peck Boulevard, Hamilton, OH 45011-3399, 513-785-3000. *Website:* http://regionals.miamioh.edu/.

MICHIGAN STATE UNIVERSITY
East Lansing, MI

Tuition & fees (MI res): $14,062	Average undergraduate aid package: $13,202

ABOUT THE INSTITUTION State-supported, coed. *Awards:* certificates, bachelor's, master's, and doctoral degrees. 147 undergraduate majors. *Total enrollment:* 50,344. Undergraduates: 39,090. Freshmen: 8,190. Federal methodology is used as a basis for awarding need-based institutional aid.

UNDERGRADUATE EXPENSES for 2016–2017 *Application fee:* $65. *Tuition, state resident:* full-time $14,062; part-time $468.75 per credit hour. *Tuition, nonresident:* full-time $37,890; part-time $1263 per credit hour. Full-time tuition and fees vary according to course load, program, and student level. Part-time tuition and fees vary according to course load, program, and student level. *College*

---

room and board: $9734; *Room only:* $4020. Room and board charges vary according to board plan and housing facility.

FRESHMAN FINANCIAL AID (Fall 2016, est.) 5,525 applied for aid; of those 68% were deemed to have need. 96% of freshmen with need received aid; of those 18% had need fully met. *Average percent of need met:* 60% (excluding resources awarded to replace EFC). *Average financial aid package:* $13,208 (excluding resources awarded to replace EFC). 1% of all full-time freshmen had no need and received non-need-based gift aid.

UNDERGRADUATE FINANCIAL AID (Fall 2016, est.) 21,594 applied for aid; of those 77% were deemed to have need. 97% of undergraduates with need received aid; of those 14% had need fully met. *Average percent of need met:* 60% (excluding resources awarded to replace EFC). *Average financial aid package:* $13,202 (excluding resources awarded to replace EFC). 9% of all full-time undergraduates had no need and received non-need-based gift aid.

GIFT AID (NEED-BASED) *Total amount:* $132,362,457 (31% federal, 3% state, 66% institutional). *Receiving aid:* Freshmen: 3% (2,640); all full-time undergraduates: 35% (12,293). *Average award:* Freshmen: $10,138; Undergraduates: $10,183. *Scholarships, grants, and awards:* Federal Pell, FSEOG, state, private, college/university gift aid from institutional funds, United Negro College Fund.

GIFT AID (NON-NEED-BASED) *Total amount:* $78,126,563 (2% federal, 69% institutional, 29% external sources). *Receiving aid:* Freshmen: 2% (1,565). Undergraduates: 13% (4,615). *Average award:* Freshmen: $9915. Undergraduates: $9960. *Scholarships, grants, and awards by category:* Academic interests/achievement: agriculture, biological sciences, business, communication, computer science, education, engineering/technologies, English, foreign languages, general academic interests/achievements, health fields, home economics, international studies, mathematics, military science, physical sciences, social sciences. Creative arts/performance: art/fine arts, creative writing, debating, journalism/publications, music, performing arts, theater/drama. Special achievements/activities: community service, general special achievements/activities, hobbies/interests, leadership, memberships, rodeo. Special characteristics: children and siblings of alumni, children of faculty/staff, children of union members/company employees, first-generation college students, handicapped students, international students, local/state students, out-of-state students, spouses of deceased or disabled public servants, veterans. *Tuition waivers:* Full or partial for employees or children of employees. *ROTC:* Army, Air Force.

LOANS *Student loans:* $127,694,010 (41% need-based, 59% non-need-based). *Average need-based loan:* Freshmen: $3080. Undergraduates: $4003. *Parent loans:* $87,748,797 (100% non-need-based). *Programs:* Federal Direct (Subsidized and Unsubsidized Stafford, PLUS), college/university.

WORK-STUDY *Federal work-study:* Total amount: $3,084,950; 1,690 jobs averaging $1825.

ATHLETIC AWARDS Total amount: $13,602,539 (46% need-based, 54% non-need-based).

APPLYING FOR FINANCIAL AID *Required financial aid form:* FAFSA. *Financial aid deadline:* Continuous. *Notification date:* Continuous beginning 3/15. Students must reply within 4 weeks of notification.

CONTACT Mr. Keith Williams, Associate Director of Financial Aid, Michigan State University, 252 Student Services Building, East Lansing, MI 48824-1113, 517-353-5940. *Fax:* 517-432-1155. *E-mail:* willi398@msu.edu. *Website:* http://www.msu.edu/.

MICHIGAN TECHNOLOGICAL UNIVERSITY
Houghton, MI

Tuition & fees (MI res): $14,634	Average undergraduate aid package: $14,423

ABOUT THE INSTITUTION State-supported, coed. *Awards:* certificates, associate, bachelor's, master's, and doctoral degrees. 55 undergraduate majors. *Total enrollment:* 7,270. Undergraduates: 5,829. Freshmen: 1,381. Federal methodology is used as a basis for awarding need-based institutional aid.

UNDERGRADUATE EXPENSES for 2016–2017 *Tuition, state resident:* full-time $14,334; part-time $542 per credit hour. *Tuition, nonresident:* full-time $30,668; part-time $1136 per credit hour. *Required fees:* full-time $300; $150 per term. Full-time tuition and fees vary according to program and student level. Part-time tuition and fees vary according to course load, program, and student level. *College*

---

room and board: $10,105; *Room only:* $5610. Room and board charges vary according to board plan and housing facility.

FRESHMAN FINANCIAL AID (Fall 2016, est.) 1,239 applied for aid; of those 71% were deemed to have need. 100% of freshmen with need received aid; of those 23% had need fully met. *Average percent of need met:* 81% (excluding resources awarded to replace EFC). *Average financial aid package:* $15,282 (excluding resources awarded to replace EFC). 30% of all full-time freshmen had no need and received non-need-based gift aid.

UNDERGRADUATE FINANCIAL AID (Fall 2016, est.) 4,317 applied for aid; of those 80% were deemed to have need. 100% of undergraduates with need received aid; of those 18% had need fully met. *Average percent of need met:* 73% (excluding resources awarded to replace EFC). *Average financial aid package:* $14,423 (excluding resources awarded to replace EFC). 26% of all full-time undergraduates had no need and received non-need-based gift aid.

GIFT AID (NEED-BASED) *Total amount:* $40,389,147 (20% federal, 8% state, 66% institutional, 6% external sources). *Receiving aid:* Freshmen: 51% (703); all full-time undergraduates: 50% (2,749). *Average award:* Freshmen: $9425; Undergraduates: $7785. *Scholarships, grants, and awards:* Federal Pell, FSEOG, state, private, college/university gift aid from institutional funds.

GIFT AID (NON-NEED-BASED) *Total amount:* $9,435,367 (87% institutional, 13% external sources). *Receiving aid:* Freshmen: 53% (725). Undergraduates: 47% (2,560). *Average award:* Freshmen: $5437. Undergraduates: $5468. *Scholarships, grants, and awards by category: Academic interests/achievement:* 22 awards ($99,137 total): business. *Creative arts/performance:* 23 awards ($43,500 total): art/fine arts, performing arts, theater/drama. *Special achievements/activities:* 21 awards ($195,000 total): general special achievements/activities. *Special characteristics:* 989 awards ($4,322,318 total): children and siblings of alumni, children of faculty/staff, veterans, veterans' children. *Tuition waivers:* Full or partial for children of alumni, employees or children of employees, senior citizens. *ROTC:* Army, Air Force.

LOANS *Student loans:* $38,781,771 (82% need-based, 18% non-need-based). 68% of past graduating class borrowed through all loan programs. *Average indebtedness per student:* $34,942. *Average need-based loan:* Freshmen: $3256. Undergraduates: $4693. *Parent loans:* $7,332,748 (82% need-based, 18% non-need-based). *Programs:* Federal Direct (Subsidized and Unsubsidized Stafford, PLUS), Perkins, college/university.

WORK-STUDY *Federal work-study:* Total amount: $393,064; 227 jobs averaging $1477.

ATHLETIC AWARDS Total amount: $3,354,605 (35% need-based, 65% non-need-based).

APPLYING FOR FINANCIAL AID *Required financial aid form:* FAFSA. *Financial aid deadline (priority):* 3/1. *Notification date:* Continuous beginning 2/1. Students must reply by 5/1.

CONTACT Mr. Joseph Cooper, Director of Student Financial Services, Michigan Technological University, 1400 Townsend Drive, Houghton, MI 49931-1295, 906-487-2622 or toll-free 888-MTU-1885. *Fax:* 906-487-3042. *E-mail:* jjcooper@mtu.edu. *Website:* http://www.mtu.edu/.

MID-AMERICA CHRISTIAN UNIVERSITY
Oklahoma City, OK

CONTACT Mr. Todd Martin, Director of Financial Aid, Mid-America Christian University, 3500 Southwest 119th Street, Oklahoma City, OK 73170-4504, 405-691-3800 or toll-free 888-436-3035. *Fax:* 405-692-3165. *E-mail:* tmartin@mabc.edu. *Website:* http://www.macu.edu/.

MIDAMERICA NAZARENE UNIVERSITY
Olathe, KS

CONTACT Rhonda L. Cole, Director of Student Financial Services, MidAmerica Nazarene University, 2030 East College Way, Olathe, KS 66062-1899, 913-791-3298 or toll-free 800-800-8887. *Fax:* 913-791-3482. *E-mail:* rcole@mnu.edu. *Website:* http://www.mnu.edu/.

MID-ATLANTIC CHRISTIAN UNIVERSITY
Elizabeth City, NC

Tuition & fees: $13,600	Average undergraduate aid package: $11,333

ABOUT THE INSTITUTION Independent Christian, coed. *Awards:* certificates, associate, and bachelor's degrees. 12 undergraduate majors. *Total enrollment:* 186. Undergraduates: 186. Freshmen: 50. Both federal and institutional methodology are used as a basis for awarding need-based institutional aid.

UNDERGRADUATE EXPENSES for 2016–2017 *Application fee:* $50. *Comprehensive fee:* $21,800 includes full-time tuition ($13,600) and room and board ($8200). Full-time tuition and fees vary according to program. Room and board charges vary according to housing facility. *Part-time tuition:* $425 per credit. Part-time tuition and fees vary according to program.

FRESHMAN FINANCIAL AID (Fall 2015) 59 applied for aid; of those 88% were deemed to have need. 100% of freshmen with need received aid; of those 10% had need fully met. *Average percent of need met:* 66% (excluding resources awarded to replace EFC). *Average financial aid package:* $8414 (excluding resources awarded to replace EFC). 12% of all full-time freshmen had no need and received non-need-based gift aid.

UNDERGRADUATE FINANCIAL AID (Fall 2015) 170 applied for aid; of those 92% were deemed to have need. 100% of undergraduates with need received aid; of those 6% had need fully met. *Average percent of need met:* 55% (excluding resources awarded to replace EFC). *Average financial aid package:* $11,333 (excluding resources awarded to replace EFC). 9% of all full-time undergraduates had no need and received non-need-based gift aid.

GIFT AID (NEED-BASED) *Total amount:* $1,018,035 (55% federal, 42% state, 3% institutional). *Receiving aid:* Freshmen: 64% (38); all full-time undergraduates: 80% (143). *Average award:* Freshmen: $6227; Undergraduates: $6671. *Scholarships, grants, and awards:* Federal Pell, FSEOG, state, private, college/university gift aid from institutional funds.

GIFT AID (NON-NEED-BASED) *Total amount:* $642,085 (96% institutional, 4% external sources). *Receiving aid:* Freshmen: 12% (7). Undergraduates: 7% (13). *Average award:* Freshmen: $3155. Undergraduates: $3478. *Scholarships, grants, and awards by category: Academic interests/achievement:* general academic interests/achievements, religion/biblical studies. *Special achievements/activities:* general special achievements/activities, religious involvement. *Special characteristics:* children and siblings of alumni, children of faculty/staff, general special characteristics, handicapped students, international students, married students, spouses of current students. *Tuition waivers:* Full or partial for children of alumni, employees or children of employees, senior citizens. *ROTC:* Army cooperative.

LOANS *Student loans:* $1,090,516 (93% need-based, 7% non-need-based). 90% of past graduating class borrowed through all loan programs. *Average indebtedness per student:* $26,414. *Average need-based loan:* Freshmen: $3113. Undergraduates: $3758. *Parent loans:* $121,068 (73% need-based, 27% non-need-based). *Programs:* Federal Direct (Subsidized and Unsubsidized Stafford, PLUS), private loans.

WORK-STUDY *Federal work-study:* jobs available. *State or other work-study/employment:* Part-time jobs available.

APPLYING FOR FINANCIAL AID *Required financial aid forms:* FAFSA, institution's own form. *Financial aid deadline:* 3/1 (priority: 2/1). *Notification date:* Continuous beginning 4/1. Students must reply by 5/1 or within 2 weeks of notification.

CONTACT Jenny Rowland, Financial Aid Administrator, Mid-Atlantic Christian University, 715 North Poindexter Street, Elizabeth City, NC 27909, 252-334-2020 or toll-free 866-996-MACU. *Fax:* 252-334-2064. *E-mail:* jenny.rowland@macuniversity.edu. *Website:* http://www.macuniversity.edu/.

MIDDLEBURY COLLEGE
Middlebury, VT

Tuition & fees: $50,063	Average undergraduate aid package: $48,000

ABOUT THE INSTITUTION Independent, coed. *Awards:* bachelor's, master's, and doctoral degrees. 48 undergraduate majors. *Total enrollment:* 2,558. Undergraduates: 2,532. Freshmen: 606. Both federal and institutional methodology are used as a basis for awarding need-based institutional aid.

UNDERGRADUATE EXPENSES for 2016–2017 *Application fee:* $65. *Comprehensive fee:* $64,332 includes full-time tuition ($49,648), mandatory fees ($415), and room and board ($14,269). *Payment plan:* Tuition prepayment.

FRESHMAN FINANCIAL AID (Fall 2016, est.) 313 applied for aid; of those 82% were deemed to have need. 100% of freshmen with need received aid; of those 100% had need fully met. *Average percent of need met:* 100% (excluding resources awarded to replace EFC). *Average financial aid package:* $47,554 (excluding resources awarded to replace EFC). 1% of all full-time freshmen had no need and received non-need-based gift aid.

UNDERGRADUATE FINANCIAL AID (Fall 2016, est.) 1,291 applied for aid; of those 86% were deemed to have need. 100% of undergraduates with need received aid; of those 100% had need fully met. *Average percent of need met:* 100% (excluding resources awarded to replace EFC). *Average financial aid package:* $48,000 (excluding resources awarded to replace EFC). 1% of all full-time undergraduates had no need and received non-need-based gift aid.

GIFT AID (NEED-BASED) *Total amount:* $51,006,638 (4% federal, 94% institutional, 2% external sources). *Receiving aid:* Freshmen: 42% (253); all full-time undergraduates: 43% (1,085). *Average award:* Freshmen: $44,843; Undergraduates: $45,035. *Scholarships, grants, and awards:* Federal Pell, FSEOG, state, private, college/university gift aid from institutional funds.

GIFT AID (NON-NEED-BASED) *Total amount:* $20,000 (100% institutional). *Average award:* Freshmen: $5000. Undergraduates: $5000. *Tuition waivers:* Full or partial for employees or children of employees. *ROTC:* Army cooperative.

LOANS *Student loans:* $5,197,095 (40% need-based, 60% non-need-based). 45% of past graduating class borrowed through all loan programs. *Average indebtedness per student:* $18,736. *Average need-based loan:* Freshmen: $3095. Undergraduates: $3509. *Parent loans:* $2,200,000 (100% non-need-based). *Programs:* Federal Direct (Subsidized and Unsubsidized Stafford, PLUS), college/university.

WORK-STUDY *Federal work-study:* Total amount: $398,771; jobs available. *State or other work-study/employment:* Total amount: $2,190,409 (33% need-based, 67% non-need-based). Part-time jobs available.

APPLYING FOR FINANCIAL AID *Required financial aid forms:* FAFSA, institution's own form, CSS Financial Aid PROFILE, noncustodial (divorced/separated) parent's statement. *Financial aid deadline:* 2/1 (priority: 11/15). *Notification date:* 4/1. Students must reply by 5/1.

CONTACT Ms. Marguerite Corbin, Student Financial Services Counselor, Middlebury College, Service Building 104, Middlebury, VT 05753, 802-443-5158. *Fax:* 802-443-2065. *E-mail:* studentfinancialservices@middlebury.edu. *Website:* http://www.middlebury.edu/.

MIDDLE GEORGIA STATE UNIVERSITY
Macon, GA

Tuition & fees (GA res): $4542	Average undergraduate aid package: $4309

ABOUT THE INSTITUTION State-supported, coed. *Awards:* certificates, associate, bachelor's, and master's degrees. 35 undergraduate majors. *Total enrollment:* 7,676. Undergraduates: 7,676. Freshmen: 1,535. Federal methodology is used as a basis for awarding need-based institutional aid.

UNDERGRADUATE EXPENSES for 2016–2017 *Application fee:* $30. *Tuition, state resident:* full-time $3260; part-time $108.67 per hour. *Tuition, nonresident:* full-time $12,046; part-time $401.53 per hour. *Required fees:* full-time $1282. *College room and board:* $7870. Room and board charges vary according to board plan, housing facility, and location.

FRESHMAN FINANCIAL AID (Fall 2015) 1,300 applied for aid; of those 100% were deemed to have need. 88% of freshmen with need received aid. *Average financial aid package:* $4309 (excluding resources awarded to replace EFC).

UNDERGRADUATE FINANCIAL AID (Fall 2015) 7,540 applied for aid; of those 100% were deemed to have need. 67% of undergraduates with need received aid. *Average financial aid package:* $4309 (excluding resources awarded to replace EFC).

GIFT AID (NEED-BASED) *Total amount:* $16,824,160 (100% federal). *Receiving aid:* Freshmen: 76% (1,090); all full-time undergraduates: 49% (3,729). *Average award:* Freshmen: $4091; Undergraduates: $4091. *Scholarships, grants, and awards:* Federal Pell, FSEOG, state, private, college/university gift aid from institutional funds, Zell Miller Scholarships, HOPE Scholarships.

GIFT AID (NON-NEED-BASED) *Total amount:* $3,914,451 (100% state). *Receiving aid:* Freshmen: 1% (21). *Average award:* Freshmen: $1000. Undergraduates: $1000. *Scholarships, grants, and awards by category:* Academic interests/achievement: biological sciences, business, communication, education, engineering/technologies, general academic interests/achievements, health fields, social sciences. *Creative arts/performance:* journalism/publications. *Special characteristics:* local/state students. *Tuition waivers:* Full or partial for employees or children of employees, senior citizens. *ROTC:* Army cooperative.

LOANS *Student loans:* $28,478,684 (49% need-based, 51% non-need-based). *Average need-based loan:* Freshmen: $3520. Undergraduates: $3520. *Parent loans:* $4,957,900 (100% non-need-based). *Programs:* Federal Direct (Subsidized and Unsubsidized Stafford, PLUS), state, college/university.

WORK-STUDY *Federal work-study:* 87 jobs averaging $2385. *State or other work-study/employment:* Part-time jobs available.

ATHLETIC AWARDS Total amount: $578,841 (100% non-need-based).

APPLYING FOR FINANCIAL AID *Required financial aid forms:* FAFSA, state aid form. *Financial aid deadline (priority):* 3/15. *Notification date:* 4/20. Students must reply within 2 weeks of notification.

CONTACT Office of Financial Aid, Middle Georgia State University, 100 University Parkway, Macon, GA 31206, 877-238-8664 or toll-free 800-272-7619. *Fax:* 478-471-2790. *E-mail:* fainfo@mga.edu. *Website:* http://www.mga.edu/.

MIDDLE TENNESSEE STATE UNIVERSITY
Murfreesboro, TN

Tuition & fees (TN res): $8610	Average undergraduate aid package: $9552

ABOUT THE INSTITUTION State-supported, coed. *Awards:* certificates, bachelor's, master's, and doctoral degrees. 61 undergraduate majors. *Total enrollment:* 22,511. Undergraduates: 20,140. Freshmen: 2,839. Federal methodology is used as a basis for awarding need-based institutional aid.

UNDERGRADUATE EXPENSES for 2016–2017 *Application fee:* $25. *Tuition, state resident:* full-time $6930; part-time $275 per credit hour. *Tuition, nonresident:* full-time $24,930; part-time $989 per credit hour. *Required fees:* full-time $1680; $70 per credit hour. Full-time tuition and fees vary according to course load. Part-time tuition and fees vary according to course load. *College room and board:* $8850. Room and board charges vary according to board plan and housing facility.

FRESHMAN FINANCIAL AID (Fall 2016, est.) 2,468 applied for aid; of those 78% were deemed to have need. 99% of freshmen with need received aid; of those 12% had need fully met. *Average percent of need met:* 65% (excluding resources awarded to replace EFC). *Average financial aid package:* $10,478 (excluding resources awarded to replace EFC). 17% of all full-time freshmen had no need and received non-need-based gift aid.

UNDERGRADUATE FINANCIAL AID (Fall 2016, est.) 13,665 applied for aid; of those 80% were deemed to have need. 99% of undergraduates with need received aid; of those 10% had need fully met. *Average percent of need met:* 62% (excluding resources awarded to replace EFC). *Average financial aid package:* $9552 (excluding resources awarded to replace EFC). 12% of all full-time undergraduates had no need and received non-need-based gift aid.

GIFT AID (NEED-BASED) *Total amount:* $42,707,841 (77% federal, 23% state). *Receiving aid:* Freshmen: 44% (1,239); all full-time undergraduates: 45% (7,133).

Average award: Freshmen: $6478; Undergraduates: $5667. **Scholarships, grants, and awards:** Federal Pell, FSEOG, state, private, college/university gift aid from institutional funds.

GIFT AID (NON-NEED-BASED) *Total amount:* $52,292,289 (10% federal, 46% state, 22% institutional, 22% external sources). *Receiving aid:* Freshmen: 59% (1,668). Undergraduates: 40% (6,372). *Average award:* Freshmen: $8033. Undergraduates: $8032. *Scholarships, grants, and awards by category:* Academic interests/achievement: 1,960 awards ($1,883,217 total): agriculture, area/ethnic studies, biological sciences, business, communication, computer science, education, engineering/technologies, English, foreign languages, general academic interests/achievements, health fields, home economics, humanities, international studies, mathematics, military science, physical sciences, premedicine, social sciences. Creative arts/performance: 527 awards ($728,315 total): creative writing, dance, debating, journalism/publications, music, performing arts, theater/drama. Special achievements/activities: 2,134 awards ($6,592,940 total): cheerleading/drum major, general special achievements/activities, hobbies/interests, leadership, memberships. Special characteristics: 456 awards ($1,736,474 total): adult students, children and siblings of alumni, ethnic background, first-generation college students, general special characteristics, handicapped students, international students, local/state students, members of minority groups. **Tuition waivers:** Full or partial for employees or children of employees. **ROTC:** Army, Air Force cooperative.

LOANS *Student loans:* $68,794,900 (46% need-based, 54% non-need-based). 64% of past graduating class borrowed through all loan programs. *Average indebtedness per student:* $25,456. *Average need-based loan:* Freshmen: $3267. Undergraduates: $4027. *Parent loans:* $10,772,664 (100% non-need-based). **Programs:** Federal Direct (Subsidized and Unsubsidized Stafford, PLUS), Perkins, state, college/university.

WORK-STUDY *Federal work-study:* Total amount: $581,944; 249 jobs averaging $2339.

ATHLETIC AWARDS Total amount: $7,104,445 (100% non-need-based).

APPLYING FOR FINANCIAL AID *Required financial aid form:* FAFSA. *Financial aid deadline (priority):* 1/17. *Notification date:* Continuous beginning 2/15. Students must reply by 6/1.

CONTACT Stephen White, Director of Financial Aid, Middle Tennessee State University, SSAC 260, 1301 East Main Street, Murfreesboro, TN 37132, 615-898-2830 or toll-free 800-331-MTSU. *Fax:* 615-898-5167. *E-mail:* stephen.white@mtsu.edu. *Website:* http://www.mtsu.edu/.

MIDLAND COLLEGE
Midland, TX

Tuition & fees (area res): $2064	Average undergraduate aid package: N/A

ABOUT THE INSTITUTION State and locally supported, coed. *Awards:* certificates, associate, and bachelor's degrees. 26 undergraduate majors. *Total enrollment:* 4,618. Undergraduates: 4,618. Freshmen: 810. Federal methodology is used as a basis for awarding need-based institutional aid.

UNDERGRADUATE EXPENSES for 2017–2018 *Tuition, area resident:* full-time $2064. *Tuition, state resident:* full-time $3264. *Tuition, nonresident:* full-time $4224. Full-time tuition and fees vary according to class time, course level, course load, degree level, location, program, reciprocity agreements, and student level. Part-time tuition and fees vary according to class time, course level, course load, degree level, location, program, reciprocity agreements, and student level. *College room and board:* $5014. Room and board charges vary according to board plan and housing facility.

GIFT AID (NEED-BASED) *Scholarships, grants, and awards:* Federal Pell, FSEOG, state, private, college/university gift aid from institutional funds.

GIFT AID (NON-NEED-BASED) *Tuition waivers:* Full or partial for employees or children of employees, senior citizens.

WORK-STUDY *Federal work-study* jobs available. *State or other work-study/employment:* Part-time jobs available.

APPLYING FOR FINANCIAL AID *Required financial aid form:* FAFSA. *Financial aid deadline (priority):* 5/1. *Notification date:* Continuous.

CONTACT Yolanda Ramos, Director of Financial Aid, Midland College, 3600 North Garfield, Midland, TX 79705, 432-685-5511. *Fax:* 432-685-6451. *E-mail:* finaid@midland.edu. *Website:* http://www.midland.edu/.

MIDLAND UNIVERSITY
Fremont, NE

CONTACT Penny James, Director of Financial Aid, Midland University, 900 North Clarkson Street, Fremont, NE 68025-4200, 402-721-5480 Ext. 6520 or toll-free 800-642-8382 Ext. 6501. *Fax:* 402-721-0250. *E-mail:* finaid@mlc.edu. *Website:* http://www.midlandu.edu/.

MID-SOUTH CHRISTIAN COLLEGE
Memphis, TN

CONTACT Financial Aid Office, Mid-South Christian College, 3097 Knight Road, Memphis, TN 38118-3151. *Website:* http://www.midsouthchristian.edu/.

MIDSTATE COLLEGE
Peoria, IL

CONTACT Financial Aid Office, Midstate College, 411 West Northmoor Road, Peoria, IL 61614, 309-692-4092 or toll-free 800-251-4299. *Website:* http://www.midstate.edu/.

MIDWAY UNIVERSITY
Midway, KY

Tuition & fees: N/R	Average undergraduate aid package: N/A

ABOUT THE INSTITUTION Independent Christian Church (Disciples of Christ), coed. 26 undergraduate majors. Federal methodology is used as a basis for awarding need-based institutional aid.

GIFT AID (NEED-BASED) *Scholarships, grants, and awards:* Federal Pell, FSEOG, state, private, college/university gift aid from institutional funds.

GIFT AID (NON-NEED-BASED) *Scholarships, grants, and awards by category:* Academic interests/achievement: agriculture, business, general academic interests/achievements, premedicine. Creative arts/performance: music. Special achievements/activities: cheerleading/drum major, general special achievements/activities, junior miss, leadership, religious involvement. Special characteristics: adult students, children and siblings of alumni, children of faculty/staff, members of minority groups, previous college experience, relatives of clergy, religious affiliation, veterans.

LOANS *Programs:* Federal Direct (Subsidized and Unsubsidized Stafford, PLUS), Perkins.

WORK-STUDY *Federal work-study* jobs available. *State or other work-study/employment:* Part-time jobs available.

APPLYING FOR FINANCIAL AID *Required financial aid forms:* FAFSA, institution's own form. *Financial aid deadline (priority):* 3/15. *Notification date:* Continuous. Students must reply within 4 weeks of notification.

CONTACT Justin Cristello, Director of Student Financial Planning, Midway University, 512 East Stephens Street, Midway, KY 40347-1120, 859-846-5340 or toll-free 800-755-0031. *Fax:* 859-846-5751. *E-mail:* faid@midway.edu. *Website:* http://www.midway.edu/.

MIDWESTERN STATE UNIVERSITY
Wichita Falls, TX

Tuition & fees: N/R	Average undergraduate aid package: $10,027

ABOUT THE INSTITUTION State-supported, coed. *Awards:* certificates, associate, bachelor's, and master's degrees. 73 undergraduate majors. *Total enrollment:* 6,043. Undergraduates: 5,287. Freshmen: 826. Federal methodology is used as a basis for awarding need-based institutional aid.

FRESHMAN FINANCIAL AID (Fall 2016, est.) 666 applied for aid; of those 74% were deemed to have need. 100% of freshmen with need received aid; of those 53% had need fully met. *Average percent of need met:* 70% (excluding resources awarded to replace EFC). *Average financial aid package:* $10,955 (excluding resources awarded to replace EFC). 16% of all full-time freshmen had no need and received non-need-based gift aid.

UNDERGRADUATE FINANCIAL AID (Fall 2016, est.) 3,619 applied for aid; of those 70% were deemed to have need. 99% of undergraduates with need received aid; of those 57% had need fully met. *Average percent of need met:* 65% (excluding resources awarded to replace EFC). *Average financial aid package:* $10,027 (excluding resources awarded to replace EFC). 18% of all full-time undergraduates had no need and received non-need-based gift aid.

GIFT AID (NEED-BASED) *Total amount:* $17,223,568 (49% federal, 26% state, 22% institutional, 3% external sources). *Receiving aid:* Freshmen: 62% (453); all full-time undergraduates: 54% (2,228). *Average award:* Freshmen: $8728; Undergraduates: $7005. *Scholarships, grants, and awards:* Federal Pell, FSEOG, state, private, college/university gift aid from institutional funds, state nursing scholarships.

GIFT AID (NON-NEED-BASED) *Total amount:* $2,191,569 (1% federal, 1% state, 85% institutional, 13% external sources). *Receiving aid:* Freshmen: 7% (51). Undergraduates: 5% (226). *Average award:* Freshmen: $2250. Undergraduates: $2085. *Scholarships, grants, and awards by category: Academic interests/ achievement:* biological sciences, business, communication, computer science, education, engineering/technologies, English, foreign languages, general academic interests/ achievements, health fields, humanities, international studies, mathematics, physical sciences, premedicine, social sciences. *Creative arts/performance:* art/fine arts, creative writing, general creative arts/performance, journalism/publications, music, theater/ drama. *Special achievements/activities:* cheerleading/drum major, general special achievements/activities, leadership. *Special characteristics:* children and siblings of alumni, children of faculty/staff, children of union members/company employees, children of workers in trades, children with a deceased or disabled parent, first-generation college students, handicapped students, international students, members of minority groups, veterans, veterans' children. *ROTC:* Air Force cooperative.

LOANS *Student loans:* $23,573,975 (81% need-based, 19% non-need-based). 66% of past graduating class borrowed through all loan programs. *Average indebtedness per student:* $28,468. *Average need-based loan:* Freshmen: $5191. Undergraduates: $6768. *Parent loans:* $6,289,779 (50% need-based, 50% non-need-based). *Programs:* Federal Direct (Subsidized and Unsubsidized Stafford, PLUS), state, college/university, private loans.

WORK-STUDY *Federal work-study:* Total amount: $117,269; jobs available. *State or other work-study/employment:* Total amount: $39,636 (100% need-based). Part-time jobs available.

ATHLETIC AWARDS Total amount: $1,692,068 (46% need-based, 54% non-need-based).

APPLYING FOR FINANCIAL AID *Required financial aid forms:* FAFSA, institution's own form, verification documents including tax transcript and verification worksheet. *Financial aid deadline (priority):* 3/1. *Notification date:* Continuous beginning 4/15. Students must reply within 4 weeks of notification.

CONTACT Ms. Kathy Browning, Director of Financial Aid, Midwestern State University, 3410 Taft Boulevard, Wichita Falls, TX 76308, 940-397-4214 or toll-free 800-842-1922. *Fax:* 940-397-4852. *E-mail:* financial-aid@mwsu.edu. *Website:* http://www.mwsu.edu/.

MIDWEST UNIVERSITY
Wentzville, MO

CONTACT Financial Aid Office, Midwest University, 851 Parr Road, Wentzville, MO 63385, 636-327-4645. *Website:* http://www.midwest.edu/.

MIDWIVES COLLEGE OF UTAH
Salt Lake City, UT

CONTACT Financial Aid Office, Midwives College of Utah, 1174 East 2700 South, Suite 2, Salt Lake City, UT 84106, 801-764-9068 or toll-free 866-680-2756. *Website:* http://www.midwifery.edu/.

MILES COLLEGE
Fairfield, AL

CONTACT P. N. Lanier, Financial Aid Administrator, Miles College, PO Box 3800, Birmingham, AL 35208, 205-929-1663 or toll-free 800-445-0708 (out-of-state). *Fax:* 205-929-1668. *E-mail:* pnlani@netscape.net. *Website:* http://www.miles.edu/.

MILLENNIA ATLANTIC UNIVERSITY
Doral, FL

Tuition & fees: N/R	Average undergraduate aid package: $26,841

ABOUT THE INSTITUTION Proprietary, coed. 8 undergraduate majors. Federal methodology is used as a basis for awarding need-based institutional aid.

UNDERGRADUATE FINANCIAL AID (Fall 2016, est.) 2 applied for aid; of those 100% were deemed to have need. 100% of undergraduates with need received aid. *Average percent of need met:* 100% (excluding resources awarded to replace EFC). *Average financial aid package:* $26,841 (excluding resources awarded to replace EFC).

GIFT AID (NEED-BASED) *Total amount:* $11,813 (63% federal, 23% state, 14% institutional). *Receiving aid:* All full-time undergraduates: 50% (1). *Average award:* Undergraduates: $9244. *Scholarships, grants, and awards:* Federal Pell, FSEOG, state, college/university gift aid from institutional funds.

LOANS *Student loans:* $62,652 (100% need-based). 100% of past graduating class borrowed through all loan programs. *Average indebtedness per student:* $10,500. *Average need-based loan:* Undergraduates: $3572. *Parent loans:* $2969 (100% need-based). *Programs:* Federal Direct (Subsidized and Unsubsidized Stafford, PLUS), private loans.

WORK-STUDY *Federal work-study:* Total amount: $7213; 1 job averaging $7212.

APPLYING FOR FINANCIAL AID *Required financial aid forms:* FAFSA, institution's own form. *Financial aid deadline:* Continuous. *Notification date:* Continuous beginning 7/1. Students must reply by 8/1 or within 2 weeks of notification.

CONTACT Mrs. Maria C. Velar, Financial Aid Manager, Millennia Atlantic University, 3801 NW 97th Avenue, Suite 100, Doral, FL 33178, 785-331-1000 Ext. 202. *E-mail:* mvelar@maufl.edu. *Website:* http://www.maufl.edu/.

MILLERSVILLE UNIVERSITY OF PENNSYLVANIA
Millersville, PA

Tuition & fees (PA res): $11,494	Average undergraduate aid package: $8501

ABOUT THE INSTITUTION State-supported, coed. *Awards:* certificates, associate, bachelor's, master's, and doctoral degrees. 37 undergraduate majors. *Total enrollment:* 7,927. Undergraduates: 6,980. Freshmen: 1,327. Federal methodology is used as a basis for awarding need-based institutional aid.

UNDERGRADUATE EXPENSES for 2016–2017 *Application fee:* $50. *Tuition, state resident:* full-time $8970; part-time $299 per credit. *Tuition, non-resident:* full-time $18,096; part-time $754 per credit. *Required fees:* full-time $2524; $86.50 per credit or $19 per credit. Full-time tuition and fees vary according to course load and program. Part-time tuition and fees vary according to course load and program. *College room and board:* $12,228; *Room only:* $8274. Room and board charges vary according to board plan and housing facility.

FRESHMAN FINANCIAL AID (Fall 2015) 1,235 applied for aid; of those 76% were deemed to have need. 96% of freshmen with need received aid; of those 5% had need fully met. *Average percent of need met:* 59% (excluding resources awarded to replace EFC). *Average financial aid package:* $7350 (excluding resources awarded to replace EFC). 4% of all full-time freshmen had no need and received non-need-based gift aid.

UNDERGRADUATE FINANCIAL AID (Fall 2015) 5,151 applied for aid; of those 82% were deemed to have need. 96% of undergraduates with need received aid;

of those 5% had need fully met. *Average percent of need met:* 63% (excluding resources awarded to replace EFC). *Average financial aid package:* $8501 (excluding resources awarded to replace EFC). 3% of all full-time undergraduates had no need and received non-need-based gift aid.
GIFT AID (NEED-BASED) *Total amount:* $18,636,445 (51% federal, 35% state, 9% institutional, 5% external sources). *Receiving aid:* Freshmen: 48% (640); all full-time undergraduates: 49% (3,017). *Average award:* Freshmen: $5438; Undergraduates: $5823. *Scholarships, grants, and awards:* Federal Pell, FSEOG, state, private, college/university gift aid from institutional funds, Schock Scholarships.
GIFT AID (NON-NEED-BASED) *Total amount:* $2,800,280 (9% state, 45% institutional, 46% external sources). *Receiving aid:* Freshmen: 10% (130). Undergraduates: 7% (433). *Average award:* Freshmen: $2598. Undergraduates: $3238. *Scholarships, grants, and awards by category: Academic interests/achievement:* 539 awards ($1,761,338 total): biological sciences, business, communication, computer science, education, English, foreign languages, general academic interests/achievements, home economics, humanities, mathematics, physical sciences, social sciences. *Creative arts/performance:* 50 awards ($47,831 total): art/fine arts, music. *Special achievements/activities:* 4 awards ($9883 total): community service. *Special characteristics:* 117 awards ($843,536 total): children of union members/company employees, international students. *Tuition waivers:* Full or partial for employees or children of employees, senior citizens. *ROTC:* Army.
LOANS *Student loans:* $34,452,364 (44% need-based, 56% non-need-based). 74% of past graduating class borrowed through all loan programs. *Average indebtedness per student:* $29,481. *Average need-based loan:* Freshmen: $3207. Undergraduates: $4072. *Parent loans:* $11,925,792 (100% non-need-based). *Programs:* Federal Direct (Subsidized and Unsubsidized Stafford, PLUS), college/university, private loans.
WORK-STUDY *Federal work-study:* 198 jobs averaging $1494. *State or other work-study/employment:* Total amount: $2,430,153 (100% non-need-based). 1,601 part-time jobs averaging $1518.
ATHLETIC AWARDS Total amount: $686,799 (32% need-based, 68% non-need-based).
APPLYING FOR FINANCIAL AID *Required financial aid form:* FAFSA. *Financial aid deadline (priority):* 3/15. *Notification date:* Continuous beginning 3/19. Students must reply within 2 weeks of notification.
CONTACT Mr. Dwight G. Horsey, Director of Financial Aid/Assistant Vice President for Enrollment Management, Millersville University of Pennsylvania, PO Box 1002, Millersville, PA 17551-0302, 717-871-5100 or toll-free 800-MU-ADMIT. *Fax:* 717-871-7980. *E-mail:* dwight.horsey@millersville.edu.
Website: http://www.millersville.edu/.

MILLIGAN COLLEGE
Milligan College, TN

Tuition & fees: $31,450	Average undergraduate aid package: $23,410

ABOUT THE INSTITUTION Independent Christian, coed. *Awards:* bachelor's, master's, and doctoral degrees. 37 undergraduate majors. *Total enrollment:* 1,194. Undergraduates: 892. Freshmen: 187. Federal methodology is used as a basis for awarding need-based institutional aid.
UNDERGRADUATE EXPENSES for 2016–2017 *Application fee:* $30. *One-time required fee:* $75. *Comprehensive fee:* $38,150 includes full-time tuition ($30,250), mandatory fees ($1200), and room and board ($6700). Full-time tuition and fees vary according to course load and degree level. Room and board charges vary according to housing facility. *Part-time tuition:* $840 per credit. *Part-time fees:* $375 per term. Part-time tuition and fees vary according to course load and degree level.
FRESHMAN FINANCIAL AID (Fall 2016, est.) 177 applied for aid; of those 88% were deemed to have need. 100% of freshmen with need received aid; of those 31% had need fully met. *Average percent of need met:* 78% (excluding resources awarded to replace EFC). *Average financial aid package:* $23,603 (excluding resources awarded to replace EFC). 14% of all full-time freshmen had no need and received non-need-based gift aid.
UNDERGRADUATE FINANCIAL AID (Fall 2016, est.) 710 applied for aid; of those 88% were deemed to have need. 100% of undergraduates with need received aid; of those 27% had need fully met. *Average percent of need met:* 77% (excluding resources awarded to replace EFC). *Average financial aid package:*

$23,410 (excluding resources awarded to replace EFC). 1% of all full-time undergraduates had no need and received non-need-based gift aid.
GIFT AID (NEED-BASED) *Total amount:* $9,014,880 (13% federal, 13% state, 67% institutional, 7% external sources). *Receiving aid:* Freshmen: 85% (155); all full-time undergraduates: 82% (620). *Average award:* Freshmen: $21,012; Undergraduates: $19,771. *Scholarships, grants, and awards:* Federal Pell, FSEOG, state, private, college/university gift aid from institutional funds.
GIFT AID (NON-NEED-BASED) *Total amount:* $2,228,859 (20% state, 68% institutional, 12% external sources). *Receiving aid:* Freshmen: 22% (40). Undergraduates: 18% (135). *Average award:* Freshmen: $11,271. Undergraduates: $10,939. *Scholarships, grants, and awards by category: Academic interests/achievement:* 589 awards ($6,392,488 total): general academic interests/achievements. *Creative arts/performance:* 49 awards ($238,950 total): art/fine arts, cinema/film/broadcasting, dance, music, theater/drama. *Special achievements/activities:* 61 awards ($245,000 total): cheerleading/drum major, community service. *Special characteristics:* 25 awards ($630,823 total): children of faculty/staff. *Tuition waivers:* Full or partial for employees or children of employees.
LOANS *Student loans:* $4,325,400 (73% need-based, 27% non-need-based). 63% of past graduating class borrowed through all loan programs. *Average indebtedness per student:* $28,510. *Average need-based loan:* Freshmen: $3624. Undergraduates: $4895. *Parent loans:* $1,240,690 (44% need-based, 56% non-need-based). *Programs:* Federal Direct (Subsidized and Unsubsidized Stafford, PLUS), Perkins, alternative loans.
WORK-STUDY *Federal work-study:* Total amount: $120,590; 100 jobs averaging $1200. *State or other work-study/employment:* Total amount: $237,498 (20% need-based, 80% non-need-based). 149 part-time jobs averaging $1594.
ATHLETIC AWARDS Total amount: $4,243,313 (66% need-based, 34% non-need-based).
APPLYING FOR FINANCIAL AID *Required financial aid form:* FAFSA. *Financial aid deadline (priority):* 12/1. *Notification date:* Continuous beginning 12/1. Students must reply within 2 weeks of notification.
CONTACT Diane Keasling, Coordinator of Financial Aid, Milligan College, PO Box 250, Milligan College, TN 37682, 423-461-8968 or toll-free 800-262-8337. *Fax:* 423-929-2368. *E-mail:* dlkeasling@milligan.edu.
Website: http://www.milligan.edu/.

MILLIKIN UNIVERSITY
Decatur, IL

Tuition & fees: $31,824	Average undergraduate aid package: $23,593

ABOUT THE INSTITUTION Independent Presbyterian Church (U.S.A.), coed. *Awards:* certificates, bachelor's, master's, and doctoral degrees. 56 undergraduate majors. *Total enrollment:* 2,056. Undergraduates: 1,971. Freshmen: 448. Federal methodology is used as a basis for awarding need-based institutional aid.
UNDERGRADUATE EXPENSES for 2016–2017 *Comprehensive fee:* $42,159 includes full-time tuition ($31,032), mandatory fees ($792), and room and board ($10,335). *College room only:* $8035. Room and board charges vary according to board plan, housing facility, and student level. *Part-time tuition:* $449 per credit hour. *Part-time fees:* $22 per credit hour.
FRESHMAN FINANCIAL AID (Fall 2015) 409 applied for aid; of those 90% were deemed to have need. 100% of freshmen with need received aid; of those 23% had need fully met. *Average percent of need met:* 84% (excluding resources awarded to replace EFC). *Average financial aid package:* $25,400 (excluding resources awarded to replace EFC). 10% of all full-time freshmen had no need and received non-need-based gift aid.
UNDERGRADUATE FINANCIAL AID (Fall 2015) 1,815 applied for aid; of those 88% were deemed to have need. 100% of undergraduates with need received aid; of those 46% had need fully met. *Average percent of need met:* 89% (excluding resources awarded to replace EFC). *Average financial aid package:* $23,593 (excluding resources awarded to replace EFC). 9% of all full-time undergraduates had no need and received non-need-based gift aid.
GIFT AID (NEED-BASED) *Total amount:* $12,536,665 (29% federal, 26% state, 45% institutional). *Receiving aid:* Freshmen: 78% (329); all full-time undergraduates: 72% (1,417). *Average award:* Freshmen: $9359; Undergraduates: $8748. *Scholarships, grants, and awards:* Federal Pell, FSEOG, state, private, college/university gift aid from institutional funds.

GIFT AID (NON-NEED-BASED) *Total amount:* $23,089,833 (98% institutional, 2% external sources). *Receiving aid:* Freshmen: 88% (369). Undergraduates: 75% (1,466). *Average award:* Freshmen: $15,575. Undergraduates: $14,219. *Scholarships, grants, and awards by category:* Academic interests/achievement: 1,902 awards ($20,643,303 total): biological sciences, business, communication, education, English, foreign languages, general academic interests/achievements, home economics, humanities, international studies, mathematics, physical sciences, premedicine. *Creative arts/performance:* 468 awards ($1,160,150 total): art/fine arts, creative writing, dance, music, theater/drama. *Special achievements/activities:* 62 awards ($114,444 total): community service, general special achievements/activities, leadership. *Special characteristics:* 212 awards ($894,968 total): children and siblings of alumni, children of faculty/staff, children of union members/company employees, children with a deceased or disabled parent, general special characteristics, international students, parents of current students, previous college experience, relatives of clergy, siblings of current students, veterans. *Tuition waivers:* Full or partial for employees or children of employees.

LOANS *Student loans:* $13,109,226 (45% need-based, 55% non-need-based). 81% of past graduating class borrowed through all loan programs. *Average indebtedness per student:* $32,924. *Average need-based loan:* Freshmen: $4387. Undergraduates: $4626. *Parent loans:* $4,301,399 (100% non-need-based). *Programs:* Federal Direct (Subsidized and Unsubsidized Stafford, PLUS), Perkins, private loans.

WORK-STUDY *Federal work-study:* 458 jobs averaging $957. *State or other work-study/employment:* Total amount: $317,695 (100% non-need-based). 420 part-time jobs averaging $756.

APPLYING FOR FINANCIAL AID *Required financial aid form:* FAFSA. *Financial aid deadline (priority):* 1/6. *Notification date:* Continuous beginning 1/6. Students must reply by 5/1 or within 4 weeks of notification.

CONTACT Cheryl Howerton, Director of Financial Aid, Millikin University, 1184 West Main Street, Decatur, IL 62522-2084, 217-424-6317 or toll-free 800-373-7733. *Fax:* 217-424-5070. *E-mail:* studentservicecenter@millikin.edu. *Website:* http://www.millikin.edu/.

MILLSAPS COLLEGE
Jackson, MS

Tuition & fees: $39,380	Average undergraduate aid package: $33,569

ABOUT THE INSTITUTION Independent United Methodist, coed. *Awards:* bachelor's and master's degrees. 31 undergraduate majors. *Total enrollment:* 873. Undergraduates: 809. Freshmen: 259. Federal methodology is used as a basis for awarding need-based institutional aid.

UNDERGRADUATE EXPENSES for 2017–2018 *Comprehensive fee:* $52,780 includes full-time tuition ($36,830), mandatory fees ($2550), and room and board ($13,400). *College room only:* $7500. Room and board charges vary according to board plan and housing facility. *Part-time tuition:* $1120 per semester hour. *Part-time fees:* $36 per semester hour.

FRESHMAN FINANCIAL AID (Fall 2015) 224 applied for aid; of those 86% were deemed to have need. 100% of freshmen with need received aid; of those 20% had need fully met. *Average percent of need met:* 80% (excluding resources awarded to replace EFC). *Average financial aid package:* $35,439 (excluding resources awarded to replace EFC). 25% of all full-time freshmen had no need and received non-need-based gift aid.

UNDERGRADUATE FINANCIAL AID (Fall 2015) 561 applied for aid; of those 88% were deemed to have need. 100% of undergraduates with need received aid; of those 24% had need fully met. *Average percent of need met:* 79% (excluding resources awarded to replace EFC). *Average financial aid package:* $33,569 (excluding resources awarded to replace EFC). 36% of all full-time undergraduates had no need and received non-need-based gift aid.

GIFT AID (NEED-BASED) *Total amount:* $13,340,323 (7% federal, 3% state, 88% institutional, 2% external sources). *Receiving aid:* Freshmen: 74% (192); all full-time undergraduates: 62% (494). *Average award:* Freshmen: $29,331; Undergraduates: $26,997. *Scholarships, grants, and awards:* Federal Pell, FSEOG, state, private, college/university gift aid from institutional funds.

GIFT AID (NON-NEED-BASED) *Total amount:* $7,772,759 (3% state, 95% institutional, 2% external sources). *Receiving aid:* Freshmen: 13% (33). Undergraduates: 10% (82). *Average award:* Freshmen: $24,326. Undergraduates: $22,981. *Scholarships, grants, and awards by category:* Academic interests/achievement: business, general academic interests/achievements. *Creative arts/performance:* art/fine arts, music, theater/drama. *Special achievements/activities:* community service, general special achievements/activities, hobbies/interests, leadership, religious involvement. *Special characteristics:* adult students, children of faculty/staff, ethnic background, first-generation college students, local/state students, religious affiliation. *Tuition waivers:* Full or partial for employees or children of employees. **ROTC:** Army cooperative, Air Force cooperative.

LOANS *Student loans:* $4,290,792 (67% need-based, 33% non-need-based). 64% of past graduating class borrowed through all loan programs. *Average indebtedness per student:* $31,419. *Average need-based loan:* Freshmen: $3841. Undergraduates: $4809. *Parent loans:* $2,391,668 (43% need-based, 57% non-need-based). *Programs:* Federal Direct (Subsidized and Unsubsidized Stafford, PLUS), Perkins.

WORK-STUDY *Federal work-study:* jobs available.

APPLYING FOR FINANCIAL AID *Required financial aid form:* FAFSA. *Financial aid deadline (priority):* 3/1. *Notification date:* Continuous beginning 3/15. Students must reply by 5/1 or within 2 weeks of notification.

CONTACT Office of Financial Aid, Millsaps College, 1701 North State Street, Jackson, MS 39210-0001, 601-974-1220 or toll-free 800-352-1050. *Fax:* 601-974-1224. *E-mail:* financialaid@millsaps.edu. *Website:* http://www.millsaps.edu/.

MILLS COLLEGE
Oakland, CA

Tuition & fees: $45,635	Average undergraduate aid package: $42,502

ABOUT THE INSTITUTION Independent, undergraduate: women only; graduate: coed. *Awards:* certificates, bachelor's, master's, and doctoral degrees. 31 undergraduate majors. *Total enrollment:* 1,367. Undergraduates: 819. Freshmen: 170. Federal methodology is used as a basis for awarding need-based institutional aid.

UNDERGRADUATE EXPENSES for 2016–2017 *Application fee:* $50. *Comprehensive fee:* $59,163 includes full-time tuition ($44,322), mandatory fees ($1313), and room and board ($13,528). *College room only:* $6926. Full-time tuition and fees vary according to course load. Room and board charges vary according to board plan and housing facility. *Part-time tuition:* $1847 per credit. Part-time tuition and fees vary according to course load.

FRESHMAN FINANCIAL AID (Fall 2016, est.) 162 applied for aid; of those 93% were deemed to have need. 100% of freshmen with need received aid; of those 19% had need fully met. *Average percent of need met:* 87% (excluding resources awarded to replace EFC). *Average financial aid package:* $45,649 (excluding resources awarded to replace EFC). 9% of all full-time freshmen had no need and received non-need-based gift aid.

UNDERGRADUATE FINANCIAL AID (Fall 2016, est.) 697 applied for aid; of those 94% were deemed to have need. 100% of undergraduates with need received aid; of those 15% had need fully met. *Average percent of need met:* 81% (excluding resources awarded to replace EFC). *Average financial aid package:* $42,502 (excluding resources awarded to replace EFC). 4% of all full-time undergraduates had no need and received non-need-based gift aid.

GIFT AID (NEED-BASED) *Total amount:* $21,361,396 (10% federal, 12% state, 77% institutional, 1% external sources). *Receiving aid:* Freshmen: 79% (133); all full-time undergraduates: 78% (602). *Average award:* Freshmen: $42,147; Undergraduates: $35,497. *Scholarships, grants, and awards:* Federal Pell, FSEOG, state, private, college/university gift aid from institutional funds.

GIFT AID (NON-NEED-BASED) *Total amount:* $688,440 (100% institutional). *Receiving aid:* Freshmen: 88% (149). Undergraduates: 82% (637). *Average award:* Freshmen: $22,600. Undergraduates: $20,894. *Scholarships, grants, and awards by category:* Academic interests/achievement: biological sciences, computer science, general academic interests/achievements, mathematics, physical sciences, premedicine. *Creative arts/performance:* music. *Special achievements/activities:* leadership. *Tuition waivers:* Full or partial for employees or children of employees. **ROTC:** Army cooperative.

LOANS *Student loans:* $5,062,945 (96% need-based, 4% non-need-based). 76% of past graduating class borrowed through all loan programs. *Average indebtedness per student:* $33,327. *Average need-based loan:* Freshmen: $5454. Undergraduates: $7141. *Parent loans:* $1,488,513 (100% need-based). *Programs:* Federal Direct (Subsidized and Unsubsidized Stafford, PLUS), Perkins, college/university.

WORK-STUDY *Federal work-study:* Total amount: $684,262; 318 jobs averaging $2667. *State or other work-study/employment:* Total amount: $460,057 (96% need-based, 4% non-need-based). 315 part-time jobs averaging $3376.

APPLYING FOR FINANCIAL AID *Required financial aid forms:* FAFSA, state aid form. *Financial aid deadline:* 2/15 (priority: 2/1). *Notification date:* Continuous beginning 3/1. Students must reply by 5/1 or within 4 weeks of notification.

CONTACT Mr. Dustin Smith-Salinas, Director of Financial Aid, Mills College, 5000 MacArthur Boulevard, Oakland, CA 94613, 510-430-2039 or toll-free 800-87-MILLS. *Fax:* 510-430-2003. *E-mail:* dsmithsalinas@mills.edu.
Website: http://www.mills.edu/.

MILWAUKEE INSTITUTE OF ART AND DESIGN
Milwaukee, WI

CONTACT Carol Masse, Director of Financial Aid, Milwaukee Institute of Art and Design, 273 East Erie Street, Milwaukee, WI 53202-6003, 414-291-3272 or toll-free 888-749-MIAD. *Fax:* 414-291-8077. *E-mail:* carolmasse@miad.edu.
Website: http://www.miad.edu/.

MILWAUKEE SCHOOL OF ENGINEERING
Milwaukee, WI

Tuition & fees: $39,429	Average undergraduate aid package: $27,296

ABOUT THE INSTITUTION Independent, coed, primarily men. *Awards:* bachelor's and master's degrees. 15 undergraduate majors. *Total enrollment:* 2,880. Undergraduates: 2,675. Freshmen: 555. Federal methodology is used as a basis for awarding need-based institutional aid.

UNDERGRADUATE EXPENSES for 2017–2018 *Comprehensive fee:* $48,531 includes full-time tuition ($37,719), mandatory fees ($1710), and room and board ($9102). *College room only:* $5718. Full-time tuition and fees vary according to course load. Room and board charges vary according to board plan and housing facility. *Part-time tuition:* $655 per credit hour. *Part-time fees:* $420 per credit hour. Part-time tuition and fees vary according to course load.

FRESHMAN FINANCIAL AID (Fall 2015) 475 applied for aid; of those 89% were deemed to have need. 100% of freshmen with need received aid; of those 25% had need fully met. *Average percent of need met:* 82% (excluding resources awarded to replace EFC). *Average financial aid package:* $28,091 (excluding resources awarded to replace EFC). 18% of all full-time freshmen had no need and received non-need-based gift aid.

UNDERGRADUATE FINANCIAL AID (Fall 2015) 2,123 applied for aid; of those 90% were deemed to have need. 100% of undergraduates with need received aid; of those 22% had need fully met. *Average percent of need met:* 76% (excluding resources awarded to replace EFC). *Average financial aid package:* $27,296 (excluding resources awarded to replace EFC). 16% of all full-time undergraduates had no need and received non-need-based gift aid.

GIFT AID (NEED-BASED) *Total amount:* $45,426,037 (6% federal, 5% state, 83% institutional, 6% external sources). *Receiving aid:* Freshmen: 85% (422); all full-time undergraduates: 75% (1,919). *Average award:* Freshmen: $25,627; Undergraduates: $23,666. *Scholarships, grants, and awards:* Federal Pell, FSEOG, state, private, college/university gift aid from institutional funds.

GIFT AID (NON-NEED-BASED) *Total amount:* $8,777,481 (1% federal, 91% institutional, 8% external sources). *Receiving aid:* Freshmen: 15% (76). Undergraduates: 12% (296). *Average award:* Freshmen: $12,435. Undergraduates: $14,232. *Scholarships, grants, and awards by category: Academic interests/ achievement:* 2,414 awards ($31,547,828 total): business, communication, computer science, engineering/technologies, home economics, mathematics. *Special characteristics:* 33 awards ($829,072 total): children of faculty/staff. *Tuition waivers:* Full or partial for employees or children of employees. *ROTC:* Army cooperative, Naval cooperative, Air Force cooperative.

LOANS *Student loans:* $19,914,896 (68% need-based, 32% non-need-based). 76% of past graduating class borrowed through all loan programs. *Average indebtedness*

per student: $38,745. *Average need-based loan:* Freshmen: $3129. Undergraduates: $4279. *Parent loans:* $3,340,745 (43% need-based, 57% non-need-based). *Programs:* Federal Direct (Subsidized and Unsubsidized Stafford, PLUS), Perkins, state, college/university.

WORK-STUDY *Federal work-study:* 269 jobs averaging $1120.

APPLYING FOR FINANCIAL AID *Required financial aid form:* FAFSA. *Financial aid deadline (priority):* 1/1. *Notification date:* Continuous beginning 1/15. Students must reply within 2 weeks of notification.

CONTACT Steve Midthun, Associate Director of Financial Aid, Milwaukee School of Engineering, 1025 North Broadway, Milwaukee, WI 53202-3109, 414-277-7223 or toll-free 800-332-6763. *Fax:* 414-277-6952. *E-mail:* finaid@msoe.edu.
Website: http://www.msoe.edu/.

MINNEAPOLIS COLLEGE OF ART AND DESIGN
Minneapolis, MN

CONTACT Ms. Laura Link, Director of Financial Aid, Minneapolis College of Art and Design, 2501 Stevens Avenue South, Minneapolis, MN 55404-4347, 612-874-3733 or toll-free 800-874-6223. *Fax:* 612-874-3701. *E-mail:* laura_link@mead.edu.
Website: http://www.mcad.edu/.

MINNESOTA STATE UNIVERSITY MANKATO
Mankato, MN

Tuition & fees (MN res): $8812	Average undergraduate aid package: $9396

ABOUT THE INSTITUTION State-supported, coed. *Awards:* certificates, associate, bachelor's, master's, and doctoral degrees. 108 undergraduate majors. *Total enrollment:* 15,407. Undergraduates: 13,459. Freshmen: 2,456. Federal methodology is used as a basis for awarding need-based institutional aid.

UNDERGRADUATE EXPENSES for 2016–2017 *Tuition, area resident:* part-time $407.50 per credit hour. *Tuition, state resident:* full-time $7858; part-time $271.66 per credit hour. *Tuition, nonresident:* full-time $15,602; part-time $584.05 per credit hour. *Required fees:* full-time $954; $39.65 per credit hour. Full-time tuition and fees vary according to course load, location, program, and reciprocity agreements. Part-time tuition and fees vary according to course load, location, program, and reciprocity agreements. *College room and board:* $8716; *Room only:* $5314. Room and board charges vary according to board plan and housing facility.

FRESHMAN FINANCIAL AID (Fall 2016, est.) 2,059 applied for aid; of those 65% were deemed to have need. 98% of freshmen with need received aid; of those 24% had need fully met. *Average percent of need met:* 77% (excluding resources awarded to replace EFC). *Average financial aid package:* $9580 (excluding resources awarded to replace EFC). 6% of all full-time freshmen had no need and received non-need-based gift aid.

UNDERGRADUATE FINANCIAL AID (Fall 2016, est.) 8,380 applied for aid; of those 70% were deemed to have need. 98% of undergraduates with need received aid; of those 22% had need fully met. *Average percent of need met:* 74% (excluding resources awarded to replace EFC). *Average financial aid package:* $9396 (excluding resources awarded to replace EFC). 7% of all full-time undergraduates had no need and received non-need-based gift aid.

GIFT AID (NEED-BASED) *Total amount:* $25,442,258 (58% federal, 32% state, 4% institutional, 6% external sources). *Receiving aid:* Freshmen: 43% (1,030); all full-time undergraduates: 41% (4,403). *Average award:* Freshmen: $5693; Undergraduates: $5508. *Scholarships, grants, and awards:* Federal Pell, FSEOG, state, private, college/university gift aid from institutional funds.

GIFT AID (NON-NEED-BASED) *Total amount:* $7,965,496 (4% federal, 1% state, 55% institutional, 40% external sources). *Receiving aid:* Freshmen: 8% (189). Undergraduates: 4% (412). *Average award:* Freshmen: $2481. Undergraduates: $4907. *Scholarships, grants, and awards by category: Academic interests/ achievement:* general academic interests/achievements. *Creative arts/performance:* art/fine arts, general creative arts/performance. *Special achievements/activities:* lead-

ership. *Special characteristics:* members of minority groups. *Tuition waivers:* Full or partial for employees or children of employees, senior citizens. *ROTC:* Army.
LOANS *Student loans:* $73,724,249 (54% need-based, 46% non-need-based). 76% of past graduating class borrowed through all loan programs. *Average indebtedness per student:* $31,453. *Average need-based loan:* Freshmen: $3788. Undergraduates: $4294. *Parent loans:* $5,249,887 (12% need-based, 88% non-need-based). *Programs:* Federal Direct (Subsidized and Unsubsidized Stafford, PLUS), Perkins, state, college/university, alternative loans.
WORK-STUDY *Federal work-study:* Total amount: $1,702,511; 373 jobs averaging $4316. *State or other work-study/employment:* Total amount: $2,006,852 (100% need-based). 483 part-time jobs averaging $4093.
ATHLETIC AWARDS Total amount: $2,765,380 (23% need-based, 77% non-need-based).
APPLYING FOR FINANCIAL AID *Required financial aid form:* FAFSA. *Financial aid deadline (priority):* 3/15. *Notification date:* Continuous beginning 3/30.
CONTACT Sandra Loerts, Director of Financial Aid, Minnesota State University Mankato, 120 Wigley Administration Center, Mankato, MN 56001, 507-389-1866 or toll-free 800-722-0544. *Fax:* 507-389-2227. *E-mail:* campushub@mnsu.edu. *Website:* http://www.mnsu.edu/.

MINNESOTA STATE UNIVERSITY MOORHEAD
Moorhead, MN

Tuition & fees (MN res): $7136	Average undergraduate aid package: $3208

ABOUT THE INSTITUTION State-supported, coed. *Awards:* certificates, associate, bachelor's, and master's degrees. 71 undergraduate majors. *Total enrollment:* 5,924. Undergraduates: 5,205. Freshmen: 869. Federal methodology is used as a basis for awarding need-based institutional aid.
UNDERGRADUATE EXPENSES for 2017–2018 *Application fee:* $20. *Tuition, state resident:* full-time $7136; part-time $230.25 per credit hour. *Tuition, nonresident:* full-time $14,272; part-time $460.50 per credit hour. *Required fees:* $40.13 per credit or $490.07 per term. Full-time tuition and fees vary according to course load. Part-time tuition and fees vary according to reciprocity agreements. *College room and board:* $8076; *Room only:* $5072.
FRESHMAN FINANCIAL AID (Fall 2016, est.) 720 applied for aid; of those 71% were deemed to have need. 99% of freshmen with need received aid. *Average financial aid package:* $2635 (excluding resources awarded to replace EFC).
UNDERGRADUATE FINANCIAL AID (Fall 2016, est.) 3,303 applied for aid; of those 76% were deemed to have need. 98% of undergraduates with need received aid. *Average financial aid package:* $3208 (excluding resources awarded to replace EFC).
GIFT AID (NEED-BASED) *Total amount:* $8,766,280 (67% federal, 30% state, 1% institutional, 2% external sources). *Receiving aid:* Freshmen: 38% (325); all full-time undergraduates: 37% (1,564). *Average award:* Freshmen: $2380; Undergraduates: $2637. *Scholarships, grants, and awards:* Federal Pell, FSEOG, state, private, college/university gift aid from institutional funds, TEACH Grants.
GIFT AID (NON-NEED-BASED) *Total amount:* $3,920,393 (17% federal, 3% state, 55% institutional, 25% external sources). *Receiving aid:* Freshmen: 43% (369). Undergraduates: 24% (1,014). *Scholarships, grants, and awards by category: Academic interests/achievement:* biological sciences, business, communication, computer science, education, engineering/technologies, English, general academic interests/achievements, home economics, international studies, mathematics, physical sciences, premedicine, social sciences. *Creative arts/performance:* art/fine arts, cinema/film/broadcasting, creative writing, music, theater/drama. *Special achievements/activities:* community service, general special achievements/activities. *Special characteristics:* adult students, children of faculty/staff, first-generation college students, members of minority groups, out-of-state students. *Tuition waivers:* Full or partial for employees or children of employees. *ROTC:* Army cooperative, Air Force cooperative.
LOANS *Student loans:* $25,710,977 (35% need-based, 65% non-need-based). 86% of past graduating class borrowed through all loan programs. *Average indebtedness per student:* $34,697. *Average need-based loan:* Freshmen: $3274. Undergraduates: $3935. *Parent loans:* $436,433 (100% non-need-based). *Programs:* Federal Direct (Subsidized and Unsubsidized Stafford, PLUS), Perkins, state, private loans.

WORK-STUDY *Federal work-study:* Total amount: $332,866; 181 jobs averaging $2260. *State or other work-study/employment:* Total amount: $3,741,451 (15% need-based, 85% non-need-based). 246 part-time jobs averaging $2391.
ATHLETIC AWARDS Total amount: $990,820 (100% non-need-based).
APPLYING FOR FINANCIAL AID *Required financial aid form:* FAFSA. *Financial aid deadline:* Continuous. *Notification date:* Continuous beginning 6/1. Students must reply within 2 weeks of notification.
CONTACT Ms. Carolyn Zehren, Director of Financial Aid, Minnesota State University Moorhead, 1104 7th Avenue South, Moorhead, MN 56563, 218-477-2251 or toll-free 800-593-7246. *Fax:* 218-477-2058. *E-mail:* finaid@mnstate.edu. *Website:* http://www.mnstate.edu/.

MINOT STATE UNIVERSITY
Minot, ND

Tuition & fees (ND res): $6568	Average undergraduate aid package: $10,048

ABOUT THE INSTITUTION State-supported, coed. *Awards:* certificates, associate, bachelor's, and master's degrees. 58 undergraduate majors. *Total enrollment:* 3,412. Undergraduates: 3,136. Freshmen: 357. Federal methodology is used as a basis for awarding need-based institutional aid.
UNDERGRADUATE EXPENSES for 2016–2017 *Application fee:* $35. *Tuition, state resident:* full-time $5193; part-time $216.36 per credit hour. *Tuition, nonresident:* full-time $5193; part-time $216.36 per credit hour. *Required fees:* full-time $1375; $57.31 per credit hour. Full-time tuition and fees vary according to class time, course load, degree level, location, program, and reciprocity agreements. Part-time tuition and fees vary according to class time, course load, degree level, location, program, and reciprocity agreements. Room and board charges vary according to board plan and housing facility.
FRESHMAN FINANCIAL AID (Fall 2015) 207 applied for aid; of those 55% were deemed to have need. 97% of freshmen with need received aid; of those 55% had need fully met. *Average percent of need met:* 72% (excluding resources awarded to replace EFC). *Average financial aid package:* $9531 (excluding resources awarded to replace EFC). 25% of all full-time freshmen had no need and received non-need-based gift aid.
UNDERGRADUATE FINANCIAL AID (Fall 2015) 1,322 applied for aid; of those 68% were deemed to have need. 96% of undergraduates with need received aid; of those 37% had need fully met. *Average percent of need met:* 68% (excluding resources awarded to replace EFC). *Average financial aid package:* $10,048 (excluding resources awarded to replace EFC). 16% of all full-time undergraduates had no need and received non-need-based gift aid.
GIFT AID (NEED-BASED) *Total amount:* $3,898,215 (63% federal, 19% state, 9% institutional, 9% external sources). *Receiving aid:* Freshmen: 33% (105); all full-time undergraduates: 38% (771). *Average award:* Freshmen: $5572; Undergraduates: $5106. *Scholarships, grants, and awards:* Federal Pell, FSEOG, state, private, college/university gift aid from institutional funds.
GIFT AID (NON-NEED-BASED) *Total amount:* $1,226,083 (1% federal, 23% state, 36% institutional, 40% external sources). *Receiving aid:* Freshmen: 5% (17). Undergraduates: 2% (46). *Average award:* Freshmen: $1178. Undergraduates: $1348. *Scholarships, grants, and awards by category: Academic interests/achievement:* biological sciences, business, communication, computer science, education, English, foreign languages, general academic interests/achievements, health fields, home economics, humanities, mathematics, social sciences. *Creative arts/performance:* art/fine arts, cinema/film/broadcasting, music, performing arts, theater/drama. *Special characteristics:* children and siblings of alumni, children of faculty/staff, ethnic background, international students, local/state students, members of minority groups, out-of-state students, veterans, veterans' children. *Tuition waivers:* Full or partial for minority students, children of alumni, employees or children of employees, senior citizens.
LOANS *Student loans:* $7,862,302 (58% need-based, 42% non-need-based). 48% of past graduating class borrowed through all loan programs. *Average indebtedness per student:* $25,110. *Average need-based loan:* Freshmen: $3830. Undergraduates: $5778. *Parent loans:* $66,272 (9% need-based, 91% non-need-based). *Programs:* Federal Direct (Subsidized and Unsubsidized Stafford, PLUS), Perkins, Federal Nursing.
WORK-STUDY *Federal work-study:* 92 jobs averaging $1581.

ATHLETIC AWARDS Total amount: $1,011,694 (75% need-based, 25% non-need-based).

APPLYING FOR FINANCIAL AID *Required financial aid forms:* FAFSA, institutional scholarship application form. *Financial aid deadline (priority):* 4/15. *Notification date:* Continuous beginning 4/15. Students must reply within 4 weeks of notification.

CONTACT Ms. Laurie Weber, Director of Financial Aid, Minot State University, 500 University Avenue, West, Minot, ND 58707-0002, 701-858-3875 or toll-free 800-777-0750 Ext. 3350. *Fax:* 701-858-4310. *E-mail:* laurie.weber@minotstateu.edu. *Website:* http://www.minotstateu.edu/.

MIRRER YESHIVA
Brooklyn, NY

CONTACT Financial Aid Office, Mirrer Yeshiva, 1795 Ocean Parkway, Brooklyn, NY 11223-2010, 718-645-0536.

MISERICORDIA UNIVERSITY
Dallas, PA

Tuition & fees: $31,660	Average undergraduate aid package: $22,829

ABOUT THE INSTITUTION Independent Roman Catholic, coed. *Awards:* certificates, bachelor's, master's, and doctoral degrees. 35 undergraduate majors. *Total enrollment:* 2,879. Undergraduates: 2,195. Freshmen: 430. Federal methodology is used as a basis for awarding need-based institutional aid.

UNDERGRADUATE EXPENSES for 2017–2018 *Application fee:* $35. *Comprehensive fee:* $45,210 includes full-time tuition ($30,030), mandatory fees ($1630), and room and board ($13,550). *College room only:* $7380. Full-time tuition and fees vary according to degree level. Room and board charges vary according to board plan and housing facility. *Part-time tuition:* $595 per credit. Part-time tuition and fees vary according to class time and location.

FRESHMAN FINANCIAL AID (Fall 2016, est.) 411 applied for aid; of those 87% were deemed to have need. 100% of freshmen with need received aid; of those 21% had need fully met. *Average percent of need met:* 80% (excluding resources awarded to replace EFC). *Average financial aid package:* $23,823 (excluding resources awarded to replace EFC). 13% of all full-time freshmen had no need and received non-need-based gift aid.

UNDERGRADUATE FINANCIAL AID (Fall 2016, est.) 1,508 applied for aid; of those 89% were deemed to have need. 100% of undergraduates with need received aid; of those 23% had need fully met. *Average percent of need met:* 79% (excluding resources awarded to replace EFC). *Average financial aid package:* $22,829 (excluding resources awarded to replace EFC). 11% of all full-time undergraduates had no need and received non-need-based gift aid.

GIFT AID (NEED-BASED) *Total amount:* $22,814,456 (13% federal, 8% state, 78% institutional, 1% external sources). *Receiving aid:* Freshmen: 84% (357); all full-time undergraduates: 81% (1,329). *Average award:* Freshmen: $18,448; Undergraduates: $16,553. *Scholarships, grants, and awards:* Federal Pell, FSEOG, state, private, college/university gift aid from institutional funds.

GIFT AID (NON-NEED-BASED) *Total amount:* $5,267,967 (98% institutional, 2% external sources). *Receiving aid:* Freshmen: 15% (63). Undergraduates: 14% (232). *Average award:* Freshmen: $14,047. Undergraduates: $12,739. *Scholarships, grants, and awards by category:* Academic interests/achievement: general academic interests/achievements. Special achievements/activities: community service, general special achievements/activities, leadership. Special characteristics: children and siblings of alumni, children of current students, children of faculty/staff, general special characteristics, members of minority groups, out-of-state students, previous college experience, relatives of clergy, siblings of current students. *Tuition waivers:* Full or partial for employees or children of employees. *ROTC:* Army cooperative, Air Force cooperative.

LOANS *Student loans:* $16,946,560 (65% need-based, 35% non-need-based). 84% of past graduating class borrowed through all loan programs. *Average indebtedness per student:* $42,686. *Average need-based loan:* Freshmen: $7657. Undergraduates: $8709. *Parent loans:* $4,575,577 (38% need-based, 62% non-need-based).

Programs: Federal Direct (Subsidized and Unsubsidized Stafford, PLUS), Perkins, Federal Nursing, state.

WORK-STUDY Federal work-study jobs available.

APPLYING FOR FINANCIAL AID *Required financial aid form:* FAFSA. *Financial aid deadline:* 5/1 (priority: 3/1). *Notification date:* 3/15. Students must reply within 2 weeks of notification.

CONTACT Jane Dessoye, Executive Director of Enrollment Management, Misericordia University, 301 Lake Street, Dallas, PA 18612-1098, 570-674-6280 or toll-free 866-262-6363. *Fax:* 570-675-2441. *E-mail:* finaid@misericordia.edu. *Website:* http://www.misericordia.edu/.

MISSISSIPPI COLLEGE
Clinton, MS

ABOUT THE INSTITUTION Independent Southern Baptist, coed. *Awards:* certificates, bachelor's, master's, and doctoral degrees. 59 undergraduate majors. *Total enrollment:* 5,036. Undergraduates: 3,004. Freshmen: 604.

GIFT AID (NEED-BASED) *Scholarships, grants, and awards:* Federal Pell, FSEOG, state, private, college/university gift aid from institutional funds, Federal Nursing.

GIFT AID (NON-NEED-BASED) *Scholarships, grants, and awards by category:* Academic interests/achievement: general academic interests/achievements. Creative arts/performance: applied art and design, art/fine arts, music. Special achievements/activities: general special achievements/activities, leadership, religious involvement. Special characteristics: children and siblings of alumni, children of faculty/staff, general special characteristics, relatives of clergy.

LOANS *Programs:* Federal Direct (Subsidized and Unsubsidized Stafford, PLUS), Perkins, Federal Nursing, college/university.

WORK-STUDY *Federal work-study:* Total amount: $171,890; 185 jobs averaging $929.

APPLYING FOR FINANCIAL AID *Required financial aid forms:* FAFSA, state aid form.

CONTACT Mrs. Karon Q. McMillan, Director of Financial Aid, Mississippi College, Box 4035, 200 South Capitol Street, Clinton, MS 39058-0001, 601-925-3249 or toll-free 800-738-1236. *Fax:* 601-925-3950. *E-mail:* kmcmilla@mc.edu. *Website:* http://www.mc.edu/.

MISSISSIPPI STATE UNIVERSITY
Mississippi State, MS

Tuition & fees (MS res): $7780	Average undergraduate aid package: $14,105

ABOUT THE INSTITUTION State-supported, coed. *Awards:* certificates, associate, bachelor's, master's, and doctoral degrees. 74 undergraduate majors. *Total enrollment:* 21,622. Undergraduates: 18,090. Freshmen: 3,624. Federal methodology is used as a basis for awarding need-based institutional aid.

UNDERGRADUATE EXPENSES for 2016–2017 *Application fee:* $40. *One-time required fee:* $55. *Tuition, state resident:* full-time $7780; part-time $324.34 per credit hour. *Tuition, nonresident:* full-time $20,900; part-time $871.09 per credit hour. Full-time tuition and fees vary according to degree level and location. Part-time tuition and fees vary according to course load, degree level, and location. *College room and board:* $9418; *Room only:* $5848. Room and board charges vary according to board plan, housing facility, and student level. *Payment plan:* Tuition prepayment.

FRESHMAN FINANCIAL AID (Fall 2015) 2,880 applied for aid; of those 84% were deemed to have need. 99% of freshmen with need received aid; of those 30% had need fully met. *Average percent of need met:* 61% (excluding resources awarded to replace EFC). *Average financial aid package:* $16,024 (excluding resources awarded to replace EFC). 29% of all full-time freshmen had no need and received non-need-based gift aid.

UNDERGRADUATE FINANCIAL AID (Fall 2015) 11,640 applied for aid; of those 86% were deemed to have need. 98% of undergraduates with need received aid; of those 23% had need fully met. *Average percent of need met:* 59% (excluding resources awarded to replace EFC). *Average financial aid package:* $14,105 (excluding resources awarded to replace EFC). 21% of all full-time undergraduates had no need and received non-need-based gift aid.

GIFT AID (NEED-BASED) *Total amount:* $57,257,260 (46% federal, 13% state, 32% institutional, 9% external sources). *Receiving aid:* Freshmen: 67% (2,312); all full-time undergraduates: 54% (8,732). *Average award:* Freshmen: $6319; Undergraduates: $6000. *Scholarships, grants, and awards:* Federal Pell, FSEOG, state, private, college/university gift aid from institutional funds, United Negro College Fund.

GIFT AID (NON-NEED-BASED) *Total amount:* $22,058,592 (13% state, 80% institutional, 7% external sources). *Receiving aid:* Freshmen: 10% (334). Undergraduates: 5% (761). *Average award:* Freshmen: $3872. Undergraduates: $4553. *Scholarships, grants, and awards by category: Academic interests/achievement:* agriculture, architecture, area/ethnic studies, biological sciences, business, communication, computer science, education, engineering/technologies, English, foreign languages, general academic interests/achievements, health fields, home economics, humanities, international studies, library science, mathematics, military science, physical sciences, premedicine, religion/biblical studies, social sciences. *Creative arts/performance:* applied art and design, art/fine arts, cinema/film/broadcasting, creative writing, dance, debating, general creative arts/performance, journalism/publications, music, performing arts, theater/drama. *Special achievements/activities:* cheerleading/drum major, general special achievements/activities, junior miss, leadership, memberships. *Special characteristics:* adult students, children and siblings of alumni, children of educators, children of faculty/staff, children of public servants, first-generation college students, handicapped students, local/state students, out-of-state students, previous college experience, spouses of deceased or disabled public servants. *Tuition waivers:* Full or partial for children of alumni, employees or children of employees, senior citizens. *ROTC:* Army, Air Force.

LOANS *Student loans:* $101,209,306 (83% need-based, 17% non-need-based). 57% of past graduating class borrowed through all loan programs. *Average indebtedness per student:* $30,659. *Average need-based loan:* Freshmen: $3293. Undergraduates: $3896. *Parent loans:* $19,481,486 (68% need-based, 32% non-need-based). *Programs:* Federal Direct (Subsidized and Unsubsidized Stafford, PLUS), Perkins, college/university.

WORK-STUDY *Federal work-study:* 832 jobs averaging $3126.

ATHLETIC AWARDS Total amount: $8,377,362 (100% non-need-based).

APPLYING FOR FINANCIAL AID *Required financial aid forms:* FAFSA, state aid form, state grant/scholarship application. *Financial aid deadline (priority):* 3/1. *Notification date:* Continuous beginning 12/1. Students must reply by 5/1.

CONTACT Mr. Kenneth Paul McKinney, Director of Financial Aid, Mississippi State University, PO Box 6035, Mississippi State, MS 39762, 662-325-7428. *Fax:* 662-325-0702. *E-mail:* financialaid@saffairs.msstate.edu.
Website: http://www.msstate.edu/.

MISSISSIPPI UNIVERSITY FOR WOMEN
Columbus, MS

ABOUT THE INSTITUTION State-supported, coed. *Awards:* certificates, associate, bachelor's, master's, and doctoral degrees. 29 undergraduate majors. *Total enrollment:* 2,673. Undergraduates: 2,470. Freshmen: 246.

GIFT AID (NEED-BASED) *Scholarships, grants, and awards:* Federal Pell, FSEOG, state, private, college/university gift aid from institutional funds.

GIFT AID (NON-NEED-BASED) *Scholarships, grants, and awards by category: Academic interests/achievement:* biological sciences, business, communication, computer science, education, English, general academic interests/achievements, health fields, home economics, humanities, mathematics, physical sciences. *Creative arts/performance:* art/fine arts, journalism/publications, music, performing arts, theater/drama. *Special achievements/activities:* junior miss, leadership. *Special characteristics:* adult students, children and siblings of alumni, children of faculty/staff, ethnic background, international students, members of minority groups, out-of-state students, parents of current students.

LOANS *Programs:* Federal Direct (Subsidized and Unsubsidized Stafford, PLUS), Perkins.

APPLYING FOR FINANCIAL AID *Required financial aid forms:* FAFSA, institution's own form, state aid form.

CONTACT Ms. Nicole Patrick, Director of Financial Aid, Mississippi University for Women, 1100 College Street, MUW 1614, Columbus, MS 39701-4044, 662-329-7114 or toll-free 877-GO 2 THE W. *Fax:* 662-329-7325. *E-mail:* jnpatrick@muw.edu.
Website: http://www.muw.edu/.

MISSISSIPPI VALLEY STATE UNIVERSITY
Itta Bena, MS

CONTACT Margaret Sherrer, Director of Student Financial Aid, Mississippi Valley State University, 14000 Highway 82W #7268, Itta Bena, MS 38941-1400, 662-254-3335 or toll-free 800-844-6885 (in-state). *Fax:* 662-254-7900. *E-mail:* margaret.sherrer@mvsu.edu.
Website: http://www.mvsu.edu/.

MISSOURI BAPTIST UNIVERSITY
St. Louis, MO

Tuition & fees: $26,020	Average undergraduate aid package: $18,734

ABOUT THE INSTITUTION Independent Southern Baptist, coed. *Awards:* certificates, associate, bachelor's, master's, and doctoral degrees. 54 undergraduate majors. *Total enrollment:* 5,732. Undergraduates: 4,631. Freshmen: 287. Federal methodology is used as a basis for awarding need-based institutional aid.

UNDERGRADUATE EXPENSES for 2017–2018 *Application fee:* $35. *Comprehensive fee:* $36,400 includes full-time tuition ($24,764), mandatory fees ($1256), and room and board ($10,380). Full-time tuition and fees vary according to course load and location. Room and board charges vary according to board plan and housing facility. *Part-time tuition:* $857 per credit hour. *Part-time fees:* $27 per credit hour. Part-time tuition and fees vary according to course load and location.

FRESHMAN FINANCIAL AID (Fall 2016, est.) 263 applied for aid; of those 83% were deemed to have need. 100% of freshmen with need received aid; of those 35% had need fully met. *Average financial aid package:* $22,262 (excluding resources awarded to replace EFC). 5% of all full-time freshmen had no need and received non-need-based gift aid.

UNDERGRADUATE FINANCIAL AID (Fall 2016, est.) 1,254 applied for aid; of those 89% were deemed to have need. 100% of undergraduates with need received aid; of those 24% had need fully met. *Average financial aid package:* $18,734 (excluding resources awarded to replace EFC). 3% of all full-time undergraduates had no need and received non-need-based gift aid.

GIFT AID (NEED-BASED) *Total amount:* $14,602,592 (47% federal, 10% state, 42% institutional, 1% external sources). *Receiving aid:* Freshmen: 66% (183); all full-time undergraduates: 62% (892). *Average award:* Freshmen: $5524; Undergraduates: $5288. *Scholarships, grants, and awards:* Federal Pell, FSEOG, state, private, college/university gift aid from institutional funds.

GIFT AID (NON-NEED-BASED) *Total amount:* $803,255 (2% federal, 2% state, 85% institutional, 11% external sources). *Receiving aid:* Freshmen: 78% (216). Undergraduates: 64% (916). *Average award:* Freshmen: $9980. Undergraduates: $10,573. *Scholarships, grants, and awards by category: Academic interests/achievement:* general academic interests/achievements, religion/biblical studies. *Creative arts/performance:* music, theater/drama. *Special achievements/activities:* cheerleading/drum major, memberships, religious involvement. *Special characteristics:* adult students, children and siblings of alumni, children of current students, children of faculty/staff, first-generation college students, parents of current students, public servants, relatives of clergy, religious affiliation, siblings of current students, spouses of current students, veterans, veterans' children. *Tuition waivers:* Full or partial for children of alumni, employees or children of employees, senior citizens. *ROTC:* Army cooperative.

LOANS *Student loans:* $21,905,709 (95% need-based, 5% non-need-based). 91% of past graduating class borrowed through all loan programs. *Average indebtedness per student:* $26,015. *Average need-based loan:* Freshmen: $3786. Undergraduates: $4546. *Parent loans:* $4,098,056 (93% need-based, 7% non-need-based). *Programs:* Federal Direct (Subsidized and Unsubsidized Stafford, PLUS).

WORK-STUDY *Federal work-study:* Total amount: $2,225,554; 553 jobs averaging $1711. *State or other work-study/employment:* Part-time jobs available.

ATHLETIC AWARDS Total amount: $16,304,600 (89% need-based, 11% non-need-based).

APPLYING FOR FINANCIAL AID *Required financial aid forms:* FAFSA, institution's own form. *Financial aid deadline (priority):* 4/1. *Notification date:* Continuous beginning 4/15. Students must reply within 2 weeks of notification.

CONTACT Mr. Zach Greenlee, Director of Student Financial Services, Missouri Baptist University, One College Park Drive, St. Louis, MO 63141, 314-392-2398 or toll-free 877-434-1115 Ext. 2290. *Fax:* 314-744-5320. *E-mail:* greenleez@mobap.edu. *Website:* http://www.mobap.edu/.

MISSOURI SOUTHERN STATE UNIVERSITY
Joplin, MO

ABOUT THE INSTITUTION State-supported, coed. *Awards:* certificates, associate, bachelor's, and master's degrees. 51 undergraduate majors. *Total enrollment:* 5,783. Undergraduates: 5,732. Freshmen: 925.

GIFT AID (NEED-BASED) Scholarships, grants, and awards: Federal Pell, FSEOG, state, private, college/university gift aid from institutional funds, TEACH Grants.

GIFT AID (NON-NEED-BASED) Scholarships, grants, and awards by category: *Academic interests/achievement:* general academic interests/achievements. *Creative arts/performance:* art/fine arts, journalism/publications, music, theater/drama. *Special achievements/activities:* cheerleading/drum major, general special achievements/activities, leadership. *Special characteristics:* veterans.

LOANS Programs: Federal Direct (Subsidized and Unsubsidized Stafford, PLUS), Perkins.

APPLYING FOR FINANCIAL AID Required financial aid form: FAFSA.

CONTACT Becca L. Diskin, Director of Financial Aid, Missouri Southern State University, 3950 Newman Road, Joplin, MO 64801-1595, 417-659-5422 or toll-free 866-818-MSSU. *Fax:* 417-659-4474. *E-mail:* diskin-b@mssu.edu. *Website:* http://www.mssu.edu/.

MISSOURI STATE UNIVERSITY
Springfield, MO

Tuition & fees (MO res): $7060	Average undergraduate aid package: $9171

ABOUT THE INSTITUTION State-supported, coed. *Awards:* certificates, bachelor's, master's, and doctoral degrees. 97 undergraduate majors. *Total enrollment:* 23,538. Undergraduates: 20,316. Freshmen: 3,194. Federal methodology is used as a basis for awarding need-based institutional aid.

UNDERGRADUATE EXPENSES for 2016–2017 Application fee: $35. *Tuition, state resident:* full-time $6150; part-time $258 per credit hour. *Tuition, nonresident:* full-time $13,020; part-time $518 per credit hour. *Required fees:* full-time $910. Full-time tuition and fees vary according to course level, course load, and program. Part-time tuition and fees vary according to course level, course load, and program. *College room and board:* $8288. Room and board charges vary according to board plan, housing facility, and location.

FRESHMAN FINANCIAL AID (Fall 2016, est.) 2,744 applied for aid; of those 69% were deemed to have need. 98% of freshmen with need received aid; of those 19% had need fully met. *Average percent of need met:* 64% (excluding resources awarded to replace EFC). *Average financial aid package:* $9620 (excluding resources awarded to replace EFC). 19% of all full-time freshmen had no need and received non-need-based gift aid.

UNDERGRADUATE FINANCIAL AID (Fall 2016, est.) 11,741 applied for aid; of those 77% were deemed to have need. 96% of undergraduates with need received aid; of those 15% had need fully met. *Average percent of need met:* 60% (excluding resources awarded to replace EFC). *Average financial aid package:* $9171 (excluding resources awarded to replace EFC). 12% of all full-time undergraduates had no need and received non-need-based gift aid.

GIFT AID (NEED-BASED) Total amount: $46,952,925 (56% federal, 23% state, 17% institutional, 4% external sources). *Receiving aid:* Freshmen: 53% (1,679); all full-time undergraduates: 48% (7,234). *Average award:* Freshmen: $6452; Undergraduates: $6017. *Scholarships, grants, and awards:* Federal Pell, FSEOG, state, private, college/university gift aid from institutional funds.

GIFT AID (NON-NEED-BASED) Total amount: $12,117,260 (7% federal, 13% state, 53% institutional, 27% external sources). *Receiving aid:* Freshmen: 5% (159). Undergraduates: 3% (431). *Average award:* Freshmen: $3039. Undergraduates: $3332. *Scholarships, grants, and awards by category:* Academic interests/

achievement: general academic interests/achievements. *Creative arts/performance:* general creative arts/performance. *Special achievements/activities:* leadership. *Special characteristics:* children and siblings of alumni, local/state students, members of minority groups. *Tuition waivers:* Full or partial for children of alumni, employees or children of employees, senior citizens. *ROTC:* Army.

LOANS Student loans: $78,177,852 (66% need-based, 34% non-need-based). 63% of past graduating class borrowed through all loan programs. *Average indebtedness per student:* $24,734. *Average need-based loan:* Freshmen: $3440. Undergraduates: $4198. *Parent loans:* $9,692,295 (23% need-based, 77% non-need-based). *Programs:* Federal Direct (Subsidized and Unsubsidized Stafford, PLUS), Perkins.

WORK-STUDY Federal work-study: Total amount: $809,933; jobs available.

ATHLETIC AWARDS Total amount: $3,502,421 (25% need-based, 75% non-need-based).

APPLYING FOR FINANCIAL AID Required financial aid form: FAFSA. *Financial aid deadline (priority):* 3/31. *Notification date:* Continuous beginning 3/31.

CONTACT Vicki Mattocks, Director of Financial Aid, Missouri State University, 901 South National Avenue, Springfield, MO 65804, 417-836-5262 or toll-free 800-492-7900. *E-mail:* financialaid@missouristate.edu. *Website:* http://www.missouristate.edu/.

MISSOURI UNIVERSITY OF SCIENCE AND TECHNOLOGY
Rolla, MO

Tuition & fees (MO res): $9637	Average undergraduate aid package: $14,980

ABOUT THE INSTITUTION State-supported, coed. *Awards:* certificates, bachelor's, master's, and doctoral degrees. 36 undergraduate majors. *Total enrollment:* 8,838. Undergraduates: 6,909. Federal methodology is used as a basis for awarding need-based institutional aid.

UNDERGRADUATE EXPENSES for 2017–2018 Application fee: $50. *Tuition, state resident:* full-time $8286; part-time $276.20 per credit hour. *Tuition, nonresident:* full-time $25,554; part-time $841.80 per credit hour. *Required fees:* full-time $1351; $49.38 per credit hour. Full-time tuition and fees vary according to course load, degree level, program, and student level. Part-time tuition and fees vary according to course load, degree level, program, and student level. *College room and board:* $9780. Room and board charges vary according to board plan, housing facility, and location.

FRESHMAN FINANCIAL AID (Fall 2015) 836 applied for aid; of those 94% were deemed to have need. 100% of freshmen with need received aid; of those 19% had need fully met. *Average percent of need met:* 29% (excluding resources awarded to replace EFC). *Average financial aid package:* $17,252 (excluding resources awarded to replace EFC). 20% of all full-time freshmen had no need and received non-need-based gift aid.

UNDERGRADUATE FINANCIAL AID (Fall 2015) 3,545 applied for aid; of those 95% were deemed to have need. 100% of undergraduates with need received aid; of those 29% had need fully met. *Average percent of need met:* 35% (excluding resources awarded to replace EFC). *Average financial aid package:* $14,980 (excluding resources awarded to replace EFC). 12% of all full-time undergraduates had no need and received non-need-based gift aid.

GIFT AID (NEED-BASED) Total amount: $26,563,298 (27% federal, 16% state, 50% institutional, 7% external sources). *Receiving aid:* Freshmen: 51% (749); all full-time undergraduates: 51% (3,096). *Average award:* Freshmen: $10,282; Undergraduates: $7931. *Scholarships, grants, and awards:* Federal Pell, FSEOG, state, private, college/university gift aid from institutional funds, ROTC (Army and Air Force) Scholarships.

GIFT AID (NON-NEED-BASED) Total amount: $16,808,847 (10% state, 72% institutional, 18% external sources). *Receiving aid:* Freshmen: 18% (261). Undergraduates: 20% (1,231). *Average award:* Freshmen: $6492. Undergraduates: $5583. *Scholarships, grants, and awards by category:* Academic interests/achievement: 3,946 awards ($18,710,486 total): biological sciences, business, communication, computer science, education, engineering/technologies, English, general academic interests/achievements, humanities, international studies, mathematics, military science, physical sciences, premedicine, social sciences. *Creative arts/performance:* 1 award ($1000 total): music, theater/drama. *Special characteristics:* 995 awards ($5,986,371 total): children and siblings of alumni, children of faculty/staff, children of union members/company employees, members of minority groups, out-of-state students. *Tuition waivers:* Full or partial for employees or children of employees. **ROTC:** Army, Air Force.

LOANS *Student loans:* $37,987,364 (80% need-based, 20% non-need-based). 76% of past graduating class borrowed through all loan programs. *Average indebtedness per student:* $28,259. *Average need-based loan:* Freshmen: $7108. Undergraduates: $7472. *Parent loans:* $11,119,526 (75% need-based, 25% non-need-based). *Programs:* Perkins, state, college/university, alternative loans.

WORK-STUDY *Federal work-study:* 156 jobs averaging $1675. *State or other work-study/employment:* Total amount: $10,867 (100% need-based). 17 part-time jobs averaging $639.

ATHLETIC AWARDS Total amount: $2,787,985 (49% need-based, 51% non-need-based).

APPLYING FOR FINANCIAL AID *Required financial aid form:* FAFSA. *Financial aid deadline (priority):* 3/1. *Notification date:* Continuous beginning 4/1. Students must reply within 3 weeks of notification.

CONTACT Ms. Bridgette Betz, Director of Student Financial Assistance, Missouri University of Science and Technology, G1 Parker Hall, Rolla, MO 65409, 573-341-4282 or toll-free 800-522-0938. *Fax:* 573-341-4274. *E-mail:* berry@mst.edu. *Website:* http://www.mst.edu/.

MISSOURI VALLEY COLLEGE
Marshall, MO

CONTACT Mrs. Rachel Kimberly Robinson, Director of Financial Aid, Missouri Valley College, 500 East College, Marshall, MO 65340-3197, 660-831-4176. *Fax:* 660-831-4003. *E-mail:* robinsonr@moval.edu. *Website:* http://www.moval.edu/.

MISSOURI WESTERN STATE UNIVERSITY
St. Joseph, MO

Tuition & fees (MO res): $6652	Average undergraduate aid package: N/A

ABOUT THE INSTITUTION State-supported, coed. *Awards:* certificates, associate, bachelor's, and master's degrees. 53 undergraduate majors. *Total enrollment:* 5,363. Undergraduates: 5,120. Freshmen: 844. Federal methodology is used as a basis for awarding need-based institutional aid.

UNDERGRADUATE EXPENSES for 2016–2017 *Tuition, state resident:* full-time $5934; part-time $197.79 per credit hour. *Tuition, nonresident:* full-time $12,362; part-time $412.05 per credit hour. *Required fees:* full-time $718; $99.10 per credit hour. Full-time tuition and fees vary according to course load, location, and program. Part-time tuition and fees vary according to course load, location, and program. *College room and board:* $7834; *Room only:* $4508. Room and board charges vary according to board plan and housing facility.

GIFT AID (NEED-BASED) *Scholarships, grants, and awards:* Federal Pell, FSEOG, state, private, college/university gift aid from institutional funds.

GIFT AID (NON-NEED-BASED) *Scholarships, grants, and awards by category:* Academic interests/achievement: architecture, biological sciences, business, communication, computer science, education, engineering/technologies, English, foreign languages, general academic interests/achievements, home economics, humanities, mathematics, military science, physical sciences, premedicine, religion/biblical studies, social sciences. *Creative arts/performance:* art/fine arts, cinema/film/broadcasting, creative writing, dance, journalism/publications, music, performing arts, theater/drama. *Special achievements/activities:* cheerleading/drum major, community service, general special achievements/activities, leadership, memberships, religious involvement. *Special characteristics:* adult students, children and siblings of alumni, children of public servants, children of union members/company employees, children of workers in trades, first-generation college students, general special characteristics, international students, local/state students, out-of-state students, previous college experience, public servants, religious affiliation. *Tuition waivers:* Full or partial for employees or children of employees, senior citizens. **ROTC:** Army.

LOANS *Programs:* Federal Direct (Subsidized and Unsubsidized Stafford, PLUS), Perkins.

WORK-STUDY *Federal work-study:* 311 jobs averaging $1495. *State or other work-study/employment:* 665 part-time jobs averaging $1912.

APPLYING FOR FINANCIAL AID *Required financial aid forms:* FAFSA, institutional scholarship application form. *Financial aid deadline:* Continuous. *Notification date:* Continuous beginning 4/15. Students must reply within 2 weeks of notification.

CONTACT Marilyn Baker, Director of Financial Aid, Missouri Western State University, 4525 Downs Drive, Saint Joseph, MO 64507-2294, 816-271-5986 or toll-free 800-662-7041. *Fax:* 016-271-5079. *E-mail:* mbaker3@missouriwestern.edu *Website:* http://www.missouriwestern.edu/.

MITCHELL COLLEGE
New London, CT

CONTACT Jacklyn Stoltz, Director of Financial Aid, Mitchell College, 437 Pequot Avenue, New London, CT 06320-4498, 800-443-2811. *Fax:* 860-444-1209. *E-mail:* stoltz_j@mitchell.edu. *Website:* http://www.mitchell.edu/.

MOLLOY COLLEGE
Rockville Centre, NY

Tuition & fees: $29,100	Average undergraduate aid package: $15,825

ABOUT THE INSTITUTION Independent, coed. *Awards:* certificates, associate, bachelor's, master's, and doctoral degrees. 42 undergraduate majors. *Total enrollment:* 5,069. Undergraduates: 3,598. Freshmen: 565. Federal methodology is used as a basis for awarding need-based institutional aid.

UNDERGRADUATE EXPENSES for 2016–2017 *Application fee:* $40. *Comprehensive fee:* $43,350 includes full-time tuition ($28,000), mandatory fees ($1100), and room and board ($14,250). Full-time tuition and fees vary according to degree level. Room and board charges vary according to board plan. *Part-time tuition:* $925 per credit hour. Part-time tuition and fees vary according to degree level.

FRESHMAN FINANCIAL AID (Fall 2015) 527 applied for aid; of those 87% were deemed to have need. 100% of freshmen with need received aid; of those 8% had need fully met. *Average percent of need met:* 56% (excluding resources awarded to replace EFC). *Average financial aid package:* $18,731 (excluding resources awarded to replace EFC). 11% of all full-time freshmen had no need and received non-need-based gift aid.

UNDERGRADUATE FINANCIAL AID (Fall 2015) 2,561 applied for aid; of those 89% were deemed to have need. 100% of undergraduates with need received aid; of those 9% had need fully met. *Average percent of need met:* 47% (excluding resources awarded to replace EFC). *Average financial aid package:* $15,825 (excluding resources awarded to replace EFC). 8% of all full-time undergraduates had no need and received non-need-based gift aid.

GIFT AID (NEED-BASED) *Total amount:* $23,868,310 (19% federal, 14% state, 66% institutional, 1% external sources). *Receiving aid:* Freshmen: 83% (449); all full-time undergraduates: 77% (2,109). *Average award:* Freshmen: $14,182; Undergraduates: $12,044. *Scholarships, grants, and awards:* Federal Pell, FSEOG, state, private, college/university gift aid from institutional funds, Federal Nursing, TEACH Grants, TRiO Grants.

GIFT AID (NON-NEED-BASED) *Total amount:* $3,212,740 (1% federal, 4% state, 94% institutional, 1% external sources). *Receiving aid:* Freshmen: 6% (31). Undergraduates: 5% (142). *Average award:* Freshmen: $11,780. Undergraduates: $9280. *Scholarships, grants, and awards by category:* Academic interests/achievement: 1,359 awards ($11,309,364 total): biological sciences, business, communication, education, English, general academic interests/achievements, humanities, international studies, mathematics, social sciences. *Creative arts/performance:* 68 awards ($154,750 total): art/fine arts, creative writing, music, performing arts, theater/drama. *Special achievements/activities:* 475 awards ($2,403,634 total): community service, general special achievements/activities, leadership, memberships, religious involvement. *Special characteristics:* 81 awards ($107,576 total): ethnic background, members of minority groups, religious affiliation, siblings of current students, veterans.

Tuition waivers: Full or partial for employees or children of employees, senior citizens. **ROTC:** Army cooperative, Naval cooperative.

LOANS Student loans: $26,072,414 (85% need-based, 15% non-need-based). 72% of past graduating class borrowed through all loan programs. *Average indebtedness per student:* $33,826. **Average need-based loan:** Freshmen: $3142. Undergraduates: $4183. **Parent loans:** $11,050,351 (65% need-based, 35% non-need-based). **Programs:** Federal Direct (Subsidized and Unsubsidized Stafford, PLUS), Perkins, Federal Nursing, private loans.

WORK-STUDY Federal work-study: 204 jobs averaging $1389.

ATHLETIC AWARDS Total amount: $1,817,489 (79% need-based, 21% non-need-based).

APPLYING FOR FINANCIAL AID Required financial aid forms: FAFSA, state aid form. **Financial aid deadline:** 5/1 (priority: 4/15). **Notification date:** Continuous beginning 2/1. Students must reply within 5 weeks of notification.

CONTACT Ana C. Lockward, Director of Financial Aid, Molloy College, 1000 Hempstead Avenue, Rockville Centre, NY 11571, 516-323-4200 or toll-free 888-4MOLLOY. *Fax:* 516-323-4213. *E-mail:* alockward@molloy.edu. *Website:* http://www.molloy.edu/.

MONMOUTH COLLEGE
Monmouth, IL

Tuition & fees: $36,400	Average undergraduate aid package: $31,972

ABOUT THE INSTITUTION Independent Presbyterian Church, coed. **Awards:** bachelor's degrees. 36 undergraduate majors. **Total enrollment:** 1,147. Undergraduates: 1,147. Freshmen: 285. Both federal and institutional methodology are used as a basis for awarding need-based institutional aid.

UNDERGRADUATE EXPENSES for 2017–2018 Comprehensive fee: $45,020 includes full-time tuition ($36,400) and room and board ($8620). **College room only:** $4860. Full-time tuition and fees vary according to course load. Room and board charges vary according to housing facility. **Part-time tuition:** $4552 per course.

FRESHMAN FINANCIAL AID (Fall 2016, est.) 263 applied for aid; of those 93% were deemed to have need. 100% of freshmen with need received aid; of those 26% had need fully met. **Average percent of need met:** 89% (excluding resources awarded to replace EFC). **Average financial aid package:** $32,985 (excluding resources awarded to replace EFC). 16% of all full-time freshmen had no need and received non-need-based gift aid.

UNDERGRADUATE FINANCIAL AID (Fall 2016, est.) 991 applied for aid; of those 94% were deemed to have need. 100% of undergraduates with need received aid; of those 22% had need fully met. **Average percent of need met:** 87% (excluding resources awarded to replace EFC). **Average financial aid package:** $31,972 (excluding resources awarded to replace EFC). 17% of all full-time undergraduates had no need and received non-need-based gift aid.

GIFT AID (NEED-BASED) Total amount: $24,549,864 (9% federal, 9% state, 80% institutional, 2% external sources). **Receiving aid:** Freshmen: 84% (245); all full-time undergraduates: 82% (930). **Average award:** Freshmen: $27,630; Undergraduates: $26,314. **Scholarships, grants, and awards:** Federal Pell, FSEOG, state, private, college/university gift aid from institutional funds.

GIFT AID (NON-NEED-BASED) Total amount: $4,836,312 (96% institutional, 4% external sources). **Receiving aid:** Freshmen: 17% (49). Undergraduates: 13% (148). **Average award:** Freshmen: $21,501. Undergraduates: $21,021. **Scholarships, grants, and awards by category:** *Academic interests/achievement:* foreign languages, general academic interests/achievements. *Creative arts/performance:* art/fine arts, debating, music, theater/drama. *Special achievements/activities:* general special achievements/activities, religious involvement. *Special characteristics:* international students, veterans. **Tuition waivers:** Full or partial for employees or children of employees. **ROTC:** Army cooperative.

LOANS Student loans: $6,961,913 (48% need-based, 52% non-need-based). 85% of past graduating class borrowed through all loan programs. *Average indebtedness per student:* $31,037. **Average need-based loan:** Freshmen: $3870. Undergraduates: $4802. **Parent loans:** $3,637,697 (100% non-need-based). **Programs:** Federal Direct (Subsidized and Unsubsidized Stafford, PLUS), Perkins.

WORK-STUDY Federal work-study: Total amount: $713,148; 496 jobs averaging $1442. **State or other work-study/employment:** Part-time jobs available.

APPLYING FOR FINANCIAL AID Required financial aid form: FAFSA. **Financial aid deadline (priority):** 10/15. **Notification date:** Continuous beginning 11/15. Students must reply by 5/1.

CONTACT Mrs. Jayne A. Schreck, Associate Vice President for Financial Aid, Monmouth College, 700 East Broadway, Monmouth, IL 61462-1998, 309-457-2129 or toll-free 800-747-2687. *Fax:* 309-457-2373. *E-mail:* jayne@monmouthcollege.edu. *Website:* http://www.monmouthcollege.edu/.

MONMOUTH UNIVERSITY
West Long Branch, NJ

Tuition & fees: $36,732	Average undergraduate aid package: $24,121

ABOUT THE INSTITUTION Independent, coed. **Awards:** certificates, bachelor's, master's, and doctoral degrees. 34 undergraduate majors. **Total enrollment:** 6,371. Undergraduates: 4,828. Freshmen: 1,089. Federal methodology is used as a basis for awarding need-based institutional aid.

UNDERGRADUATE EXPENSES for 2017–2018 Application fee: $50. **One-time required fee:** $200. **Comprehensive fee:** $50,284 includes full-time tuition ($36,032), mandatory fees ($700), and room and board ($13,552). **College room only:** $7784. Room and board charges vary according to board plan and housing facility. **Part-time tuition:** $1043 per credit hour. **Part-time fees:** $175 per term. Part-time tuition and fees vary according to course load.

FRESHMAN FINANCIAL AID (Fall 2016, est.) 998 applied for aid; of those 87% were deemed to have need. 100% of freshmen with need received aid; of those 13% had need fully met. **Average percent of need met:** 66% (excluding resources awarded to replace EFC). **Average financial aid package:** $25,579 (excluding resources awarded to replace EFC). 18% of all full-time freshmen had no need and received non-need-based gift aid.

UNDERGRADUATE FINANCIAL AID (Fall 2016, est.) 3,680 applied for aid; of those 88% were deemed to have need. 100% of undergraduates with need received aid; of those 14% had need fully met. **Average percent of need met:** 64% (excluding resources awarded to replace EFC). **Average financial aid package:** $24,121 (excluding resources awarded to replace EFC). 26% of all full-time undergraduates had no need and received non-need-based gift aid.

GIFT AID (NEED-BASED) Total amount: $48,820,715 (14% federal, 21% state, 12% institutional, 53% external sources). **Receiving aid:** Freshmen: 59% (640); all full-time undergraduates: 41% (1,849). **Average award:** Freshmen: $12,513; Undergraduates: $12,285. **Scholarships, grants, and awards:** Federal Pell, FSEOG, state, private, college/university gift aid from institutional funds, Federal Nursing.

GIFT AID (NON-NEED-BASED) Total amount: $40,290,838 (100% institutional). **Receiving aid:** Freshmen: 77% (842). Undergraduates: 68% (3,045). **Average award:** Freshmen: $10,146. Undergraduates: $9131. **Scholarships, grants, and awards by category:** *Academic interests/achievement:* 4,345 awards ($41,791,232 total): biological sciences, business, communication, computer science, education, English, foreign languages, general academic interests/achievements, health fields, home economics, humanities, mathematics, physical sciences, social sciences. *Special achievements/activities:* 1 award ($2500 total): leadership. *Special characteristics:* 755 awards ($6,204,747 total): adult students, children and siblings of alumni, children of faculty/staff, children of public servants, first-generation college students, general special characteristics, international students, local/state students, members of minority groups, out-of-state students, previous college experience, veterans, veterans' children. **Tuition waivers:** Full or partial for employees or children of employees, senior citizens. **ROTC:** Army cooperative, Air Force cooperative.

LOANS Student loans: $25,855,391 (48% need-based, 52% non-need-based). 75% of past graduating class borrowed through all loan programs. *Average indebtedness per student:* $29,483. **Average need-based loan:** Freshmen: $3703. Undergraduates: $4656. **Parent loans:** $15,732,961 (100% non-need-based). **Programs:** Federal Direct (Subsidized and Unsubsidized Stafford, PLUS), Perkins, state, college/university, private loans.

WORK-STUDY Federal work-study: Total amount: $1,887,762; 1,032 jobs averaging $2040.

ATHLETIC AWARDS Total amount: $9,046,566 (100% non-need-based).

APPLYING FOR FINANCIAL AID Required financial aid form: FAFSA. **Financial aid deadline:** Continuous. **Notification date:** Continuous beginning 12/15. Students must reply within 2 weeks of notification.

CONTACT Ms. Claire Alasio, Associate Vice President and Director of Financial Aid, Monmouth University, 400 Cedar Avenue, West Long Branch, NJ 07764-1898, 732-571-3463 or toll-free 800-543-9671. *Fax:* 732-923-4791. *E-mail:* finaid@monmouth.edu.
Website: http://www.monmouth.edu/.

MONROE COLLEGE
Bronx, NY

ABOUT THE INSTITUTION Proprietary, coed. *Awards:* certificates, associate, bachelor's, and master's degrees. 15 undergraduate majors. *Total enrollment:* 6,862. Undergraduates: 6,137. Freshmen: 1,112.
GIFT AID (NEED-BASED) *Scholarships, grants, and awards:* Federal Pell, FSEOG, state, private, college/university gift aid from institutional funds.
LOANS *Programs:* Federal Direct (Subsidized and Unsubsidized Stafford, PLUS), state, college/university.
WORK-STUDY *Federal work-study:* 173 jobs averaging $4335.
APPLYING FOR FINANCIAL AID *Required financial aid forms:* FAFSA, state aid form.
CONTACT Mr. Daniel Sharon, Director of Student Financial Services, Monroe College, 2501 Jerome Avenue, Bronx, NY 10468, 646-393-8257 or toll-free 800-55MONROE. *Fax:* 718-817-8401. *E-mail:* dsharon@monroecollege.edu.
Website: http://www.monroecollege.edu/.

MONTANA BIBLE COLLEGE
Bozeman, MT

CONTACT Financial Aid Office, Montana Bible College, 3625 South 19th Avenue, Bozeman, MT 59718, 406-586-3585 or toll-free 888-462-2463.
Website: http://www.montanabiblecollege.edu/.

MONTANA STATE UNIVERSITY
Bozeman, MT

Tuition & fees: N/R	Average undergraduate aid package: $11,297

ABOUT THE INSTITUTION State-supported, coed. *Awards:* certificates, associate, bachelor's, master's, and doctoral degrees. 59 undergraduate majors. *Total enrollment:* 16,440. Undergraduates: 14,400. Freshmen: 3,503. Federal methodology is used as a basis for awarding need-based institutional aid.
UNDERGRADUATE EXPENSES for 2017–2018 *Application fee:* $30. *Tuition, state resident:* part-time $222 per credit hour. *Tuition, nonresident:* part-time $889 per credit hour. Full-time tuition and fees vary according to course load, degree level, location, and program. Part-time tuition and fees vary according to course load, degree level, location, and program. Room and board charges vary according to board plan and housing facility.
FRESHMAN FINANCIAL AID (Fall 2015) 1,744 applied for aid; of those 62% were deemed to have need. 94% of freshmen with need received aid; of those 40% had need fully met. *Average percent of need met:* 75% (excluding resources awarded to replace EFC). *Average financial aid package:* $11,418 (excluding resources awarded to replace EFC). 16% of all full-time freshmen had no need and received non-need-based gift aid.
UNDERGRADUATE FINANCIAL AID (Fall 2015) 7,337 applied for aid; of those 72% were deemed to have need. 96% of undergraduates with need received aid; of those 32% had need fully met. *Average percent of need met:* 74% (excluding resources awarded to replace EFC). *Average financial aid package:* $11,297 (excluding resources awarded to replace EFC). 10% of all full-time undergraduates had no need and received non-need-based gift aid.
GIFT AID (NEED-BASED) *Total amount:* $19,975,399 (73% federal, 2% state, 12% institutional, 13% external sources). *Receiving aid:* Freshmen: 36% (816); all full-time undergraduates: 32% (3,637). *Average award:* Freshmen: $5214; Undergraduates: $4878. *Scholarships, grants, and awards:* Federal Pell, FSEOG, state, private, college/university gift aid from institutional funds, Federal Nursing.

GIFT AID (NON-NEED-BASED) *Total amount:* $4,760,788 (8% state, 46% institutional, 46% external sources). *Receiving aid:* Freshmen: 4% (82). Undergraduates: 1% (161). *Average award:* Freshmen: $1868. Undergraduates: $1849. *Scholarships, grants, and awards by category: Academic interests/achievement:* agriculture, architecture, area/ethnic studies, biological sciences, business, communication, computer science, education, engineering/technologies, English, foreign languages, general academic interests/achievements, health fields, home economics, humanities, mathematics, military science, physical sciences, social sciences. *Creative arts/performance:* art/fine arts, cinema/film/broadcasting, dance, music, theater/drama. *Special achievements/activities:* general special achievements/activities, leadership. *Special characteristics:* children and siblings of alumni, general special characteristics, local/state students, members of minority groups. *Tuition waivers:* Full or partial for minority students, employees or children of employees, senior citizens. *ROTC:* Army, Air Force.
LOANS *Student loans:* $47,346,265 (73% need-based, 27% non-need-based). 55% of past graduating class borrowed through all loan programs. *Average indebtedness per student:* $28,463. *Average need-based loan:* Freshmen: $6124. Undergraduates: $7293. *Parent loans:* $23,717,356 (35% need-based, 65% non-need-based). *Programs:* Federal Direct (Subsidized and Unsubsidized Stafford, PLUS), Perkins, Federal Nursing, college/university.
WORK-STUDY *Federal work-study:* jobs available. *State or other work-study/employment:* Total amount: $465,764 (100% need-based). Part-time jobs available.
ATHLETIC AWARDS Total amount: $1,737,688 (20% need-based, 80% non-need-based).
APPLYING FOR FINANCIAL AID *Required financial aid form:* FAFSA. *Financial aid deadline (priority):* 3/1. *Notification date:* Continuous beginning 4/1.
CONTACT Brandi Payne, Director of Financial Aid, Montana State University, PO Box 174160, Bozeman, MT 59717-4160, 406-994-2845 or toll-free 888-MSU-CATS. *Fax:* 406-994-6962. *E-mail:* bpayne@montana.edu.
Website: http://www.montana.edu/.

MONTANA STATE UNIVERSITY BILLINGS
Billings, MT

Tuition & fees (MT res): $5826	Average undergraduate aid package: $6981

ABOUT THE INSTITUTION State-supported, coed. *Awards:* certificates, associate, bachelor's, and master's degrees. 70 undergraduate majors. *Total enrollment:* 4,388. Undergraduates: 3,972. Federal methodology is used as a basis for awarding need-based institutional aid.
UNDERGRADUATE EXPENSES for 2017–2018 *Application fee:* $30. *Tuition, state resident:* full-time $4397; part-time $183.20 per credit hour. *Tuition, nonresident:* full-time $16,662; part-time $694.25 per credit hour. *Required fees:* full-time $1429. Full-time tuition and fees vary according to course load and location. Part-time tuition and fees vary according to course load and location. *College room and board:* $7510. Room and board charges vary according to board plan and housing facility.
FRESHMAN FINANCIAL AID (Fall 2015) 502 applied for aid; of those 72% were deemed to have need. 98% of freshmen with need received aid; of those 25% had need fully met. *Average percent of need met:* 67% (excluding resources awarded to replace EFC). *Average financial aid package:* $8740 (excluding resources awarded to replace EFC). 9% of all full-time freshmen had no need and received non-need-based gift aid.
UNDERGRADUATE FINANCIAL AID (Fall 2015) 1,570 applied for aid; of those 100% were deemed to have need. 98% of undergraduates with need received aid; of those 29% had need fully met. *Average percent of need met:* 72% (excluding resources awarded to replace EFC). *Average financial aid package:* $6981 (excluding resources awarded to replace EFC). 6% of all full-time undergraduates had no need and received non-need-based gift aid.
GIFT AID (NEED-BASED) *Total amount:* $6,864,979 (79% federal, 2% state, 14% institutional, 5% external sources). *Receiving aid:* Freshmen: 50% (298); all full-time undergraduates: 47% (1,252). *Average award:* Freshmen: $4492; Undergrad-

uates: $4513. **Scholarships, grants, and awards:** Federal Pell, FSEOG, private, college/university gift aid from institutional funds, Montana Tuition Waiver Awards.

GIFT AID (NON-NEED-BASED) Total amount: $773,043 (4% state, 68% institutional, 28% external sources). **Receiving aid:** Freshmen: 3% (17). Undergraduates: 1% (34). **Average award:** Freshmen: $1752. Undergraduates: $2671. **Scholarships, grants, and awards by category:** Academic interests/achievement: biological sciences, business, communication, computer science, education, engineering/technologies, English, foreign languages, general academic interests/achievements, health fields, humanities, mathematics, physical sciences, premedicine, social sciences. Creative arts/performance: art/fine arts, music, theater/drama. Special achievements/activities: cheerleading/drum major, general special achievements/activities. Special characteristics: adult students, children and siblings of alumni, children of faculty/staff, children of union members/company employees, ethnic background, first-generation college students, local/state students, members of minority groups, out-of-state students, veterans. **Tuition waivers:** Full or partial for employees or children of employees, senior citizens. **ROTC:** Army.

LOANS Student loans: $13,485,431 (76% need-based, 24% non-need-based). 65% of past graduating class borrowed through all loan programs. Average indebtedness per student: $28,337. **Average need-based loan:** Freshmen: $4987. Undergraduates: $6241. **Parent loans:** $2,554,498 (23% need-based, 77% non-need-based). **Programs:** Federal Direct (Subsidized and Unsubsidized Stafford, PLUS), college/university.

WORK-STUDY Federal work-study: jobs available. **State or other work-study/employment:** Total amount: $221,863 (85% need-based, 15% non-need-based). Part-time jobs available.

ATHLETIC AWARDS Total amount: $751,930 (46% need-based, 54% non-need-based).

APPLYING FOR FINANCIAL AID Required financial aid form: FAFSA. **Financial aid deadline:** Continuous. **Notification date:** Continuous beginning 3/15.

CONTACT Emily Williamson, Director of Financial Aid and Scholarships, Montana State University Billings, 1500 University Drive, Billings, MT 59101, 406-657-1617 or toll-free 800-565-6782. Fax: 406-657-1789. E-mail: finaid@msubillings.edu. Website: http://www.msubillings.edu/.

MONTANA STATE UNIVERSITY–NORTHERN
Havre, MT

CONTACT Cindy Small, Director of Financial Aid, Montana State University–Northern, PO Box 7751, Havre, MT 59501, 406-265-3787 or toll-free 800-662-6132. Website: http://www.msun.edu/.

MONTANA TECH OF THE UNIVERSITY OF MONTANA
Butte, MT

Tuition & fees (MT res): $6881	Average undergraduate aid package: $11,159

ABOUT THE INSTITUTION State-supported, coed. **Awards:** certificates, diplomas, associate, bachelor's, master's, and doctoral degrees. 40 undergraduate majors. **Total enrollment:** 2,809. Undergraduates: 2,594. Freshmen: 346. Federal methodology is used as a basis for awarding need-based institutional aid.

UNDERGRADUATE EXPENSES for 2016–2017 Application fee: $30. **Tuition, state resident:** full-time $5177; part-time $216 per credit. **Tuition, non-resident:** full-time $19,303; part-time $801 per credit. **Required fees:** full-time $1704; $69 per credit. Full-time tuition and fees vary according to course load, degree level, location, program, and student level. Part-time tuition and fees vary according to course load, degree level, location, program, and student level. **College room and board:** $8932; **Room only:** $3978. Room and board charges vary according to board plan.

FRESHMAN FINANCIAL AID (Fall 2015) 332 applied for aid; of those 65% were deemed to have need. 100% of freshmen with need received aid; of those 21% had need fully met. **Average percent of need met:** 67% (excluding resources awarded

to replace EFC). **Average financial aid package:** $9696 (excluding resources awarded to replace EFC). 18% of all full-time freshmen had no need and received non-need-based gift aid.

UNDERGRADUATE FINANCIAL AID (Fall 2015) 1,515 applied for aid; of those 78% were deemed to have need. 100% of undergraduates with need received aid; of those 13% had need fully met. **Average percent of need met:** 63% (excluding resources awarded to replace EFC). **Average financial aid package:** $11,159 (excluding resources awarded to replace EFC). 13% of all full-time undergraduates had no need and received non-need-based gift aid.

GIFT AID (NEED-BASED) Total amount: $6,071,235 (64% federal, 2% state, 27% institutional, 7% external sources). **Receiving aid:** Freshmen: 47% (192); all full-time undergraduates: 45% (1,007). **Average award:** Freshmen: $5807; Undergraduates: $5646. **Scholarships, grants, and awards:** Federal Pell, FSEOG, state, private, college/university gift aid from institutional funds.

GIFT AID (NON-NEED-BASED) Total amount: $2,058,892 (6% state, 69% institutional, 25% external sources). **Receiving aid:** Freshmen: 7% (29). Undergraduates: 3% (73). **Average award:** Freshmen: $3839. Undergraduates: $4085. **Scholarships, grants, and awards by category:** Academic interests/achievement: business, computer science, engineering/technologies, general academic interests/achievements, health fields, mathematics, physical sciences. Special achievements/activities: community service, general special achievements/activities, hobbies/interests, leadership, memberships. Special characteristics: children and siblings of alumni, children of faculty/staff, first-generation college students, general special characteristics, local/state students, married students, out-of-state students, veterans. **Tuition waivers:** Full or partial for minority students, employees or children of employees, senior citizens.

LOANS Student loans: $8,268,268 (77% need-based, 23% non-need-based). 56% of past graduating class borrowed through all loan programs. Average indebtedness per student: $27,193. **Average need-based loan:** Freshmen: $3003. Undergraduates: $3826. **Parent loans:** $1,898,852 (37% need-based, 63% non-need-based). **Programs:** Federal Direct (Subsidized and Unsubsidized Stafford, PLUS), Perkins, college/university.

WORK-STUDY Federal work-study: jobs available. **State or other work-study/employment:** Total amount: $37,611 (100% need-based). Part-time jobs available.

ATHLETIC AWARDS Total amount: $927,153 (50% need-based, 50% non-need-based).

APPLYING FOR FINANCIAL AID Required financial aid form: FAFSA. **Financial aid deadline (priority):** 3/1. **Notification date:** Continuous beginning 3/15. Students must reply within 2 weeks of notification.

CONTACT Mike Richardson, Director of Financial Aid, Montana Tech of The University of Montana, 1300 West Park Street, Butte, MT 59701-8997, 406-496-4256 or toll-free 800-445-TECH. Fax: 406-496-4710. E-mail: financialaid@mtech.edu. Website: http://www.mtech.edu/.

MONTCLAIR STATE UNIVERSITY
Montclair, NJ

Tuition & fees (NJ res): $12,116	Average undergraduate aid package: $9734

ABOUT THE INSTITUTION State-supported, coed. **Awards:** certificates, bachelor's, master's, and doctoral degrees. 63 undergraduate majors. **Total enrollment:** 20,987. Undergraduates: 16,810. Freshmen: 2,984. Federal methodology is used as a basis for awarding need-based institutional aid.

UNDERGRADUATE EXPENSES for 2016–2017 Application fee: $65. **Tuition, state resident:** full-time $8768; part-time $292 per credit. **Tuition, non-resident:** full-time $16,659; part-time $555 per credit. **Required fees:** full-time $3348; $112 per credit. **College room and board:** $14,094. Room and board charges vary according to board plan and housing facility.

FRESHMAN FINANCIAL AID (Fall 2015) 2,822 applied for aid; of those 85% were deemed to have need. 91% of freshmen with need received aid; of those 2% had need fully met. **Average percent of need met:** 66% (excluding resources awarded to replace EFC). **Average financial aid package:** $9149 (excluding resources awarded to replace EFC). 6% of all full-time freshmen had no need and received non-need-based gift aid.

UNDERGRADUATE FINANCIAL AID (Fall 2015) 11,805 applied for aid; of those 86% were deemed to have need. 93% of undergraduates with need received aid; of those 3% had need fully met. **Average percent of need met:** 67% (excluding resources awarded to replace EFC). *Average financial aid package:* $9734 (excluding resources awarded to replace EFC). 5% of all full-time undergraduates had no need and received non-need-based gift aid.

GIFT AID (NEED-BASED) *Total amount:* $55,341,053 (55% federal, 45% state). *Receiving aid:* Freshmen: 49% (1,505); all full-time undergraduates: 45% (6,425). *Average award:* Freshmen: $10,145; Undergraduates: $8862. *Scholarships, grants, and awards:* Federal Pell, FSEOG, state, private, college/university gift aid from institutional funds.

GIFT AID (NON-NEED-BASED) *Total amount:* $9,884,955 (3% state, 79% institutional, 18% external sources). *Receiving aid:* Freshmen: 6% (181). Undergraduates: 5% (673). *Average award:* Freshmen: $5354. Undergraduates: $5571. *Scholarships, grants, and awards by category:* Academic interests/achievement: biological sciences, business, communication, education, English, foreign languages, general academic interests/achievements, home economics, humanities, international studies, mathematics, physical sciences, religion/biblical studies, social sciences. Creative arts/performance: art/fine arts, cinema/film/broadcasting, dance, music, performing arts, theater/drama. Special achievements/activities: community service, general special achievements/activities, leadership. Special characteristics: children and siblings of alumni, international students. *Tuition waivers:* Full or partial for employees or children of employees, senior citizens.

LOANS *Student loans:* $91,137,566 (39% need-based, 61% non-need-based). 71% of past graduating class borrowed through all loan programs. *Average indebtedness per student:* $28,070. *Average need-based loan:* Freshmen: $3321. Undergraduates: $4399. *Parent loans:* $20,777,054 (100% non-need-based). *Programs:* Federal Direct (Subsidized and Unsubsidized Stafford, PLUS), Perkins, state, private loans.

WORK-STUDY *Federal work-study:* 475 jobs averaging $1275. *State or other work-study/employment:* Total amount: $5,871,237 (100% non-need-based). Part-time jobs available.

APPLYING FOR FINANCIAL AID *Required financial aid form:* FAFSA. *Financial aid deadline (priority):* 2/1. *Notification date:* Continuous beginning 3/15. Students must reply within 2 weeks of notification.

CONTACT Mr. James T. Anderson, Director of Financial Aid, Montclair State University, College Hall, Room 222, Montclair, NJ 07043, 973-655-7022. *Fax:* 973-655-7712. *E-mail:* financialaid@montclair.edu.

Website: http://www.montclair.edu/.

MONTREAT COLLEGE
Montreat, NC

Tuition & fees: $24,940	Average undergraduate aid package: $19,762

ABOUT THE INSTITUTION Independent Presbyterian Church (U.S.A.), coed. *Awards:* certificates, associate, bachelor's, and master's degrees. 19 undergraduate majors. *Total enrollment:* 1,008. Undergraduates: 808. Freshmen: 158. Federal methodology is used as a basis for awarding need-based institutional aid.

UNDERGRADUATE EXPENSES for 2016–2017 *Comprehensive fee:* $33,310 includes full-time tuition ($24,740), mandatory fees ($200), and room and board ($8370). *College room only:* $4196. Full-time tuition and fees vary according to course load and degree level. Room and board charges vary according to board plan and housing facility. *Part-time tuition:* $640 per semester hour. Part-time tuition and fees vary according to course load and degree level.

FRESHMAN FINANCIAL AID (Fall 2015) 155 applied for aid; of those 92% were deemed to have need. 100% of freshmen with need received aid; of those 19% had need fully met. *Average percent of need met:* 70% (excluding resources awarded to replace EFC). *Average financial aid package:* $20,724 (excluding resources awarded to replace EFC). 10% of all full-time freshmen had no need and received non-need-based gift aid.

UNDERGRADUATE FINANCIAL AID (Fall 2015) 439 applied for aid; of those 92% were deemed to have need. 100% of undergraduates with need received aid; of those 16% had need fully met. *Average percent of need met:* 68% (excluding resources awarded to replace EFC). *Average financial aid package:* $19,762 (excluding resources awarded to replace EFC). 14% of all full-time undergraduates had no need and received non-need-based gift aid.

GIFT AID (NEED-BASED) *Total amount:* $5,674,110 (25% federal, 16% state, 48% institutional, 11% external sources). *Receiving aid:* Freshmen: 84% (141); all full-time undergraduates: 81% (393). *Average award:* Freshmen: $17,851; Under-

graduates: $15,916. *Scholarships, grants, and awards:* Federal Pell, FSEOG, state, private, college/university gift aid from institutional funds.

GIFT AID (NON-NEED-BASED) *Total amount:* $956,019 (88% institutional, 12% external sources). *Receiving aid:* Freshmen: 11% (19). Undergraduates: 10% (48). *Average award:* Freshmen: $10,909. Undergraduates: $10,845. *Scholarships, grants, and awards by category:* Academic interests/achievement: computer science, general academic interests/achievements. Creative arts/performance: music. Special achievements/activities: leadership. Special characteristics: children and siblings of alumni, children of faculty/staff, first-generation college students, international students, local/state students, relatives of clergy, religious affiliation, veterans, veterans' children. *Tuition waivers:* Full or partial for employees or children of employees, adult students.

LOANS *Student loans:* $4,413,335 (84% need-based, 16% non-need-based). 67% of past graduating class borrowed through all loan programs. *Average indebtedness per student:* $24,512. *Average need-based loan:* Freshmen: $3448. Undergraduates: $4135. *Parent loans:* $743,754 (64% need-based, 36% non-need-based). *Programs:* Federal Direct (Subsidized and Unsubsidized Stafford, PLUS), Perkins.

WORK-STUDY *Federal work-study:* jobs available. *State or other work-study/employment:* Total amount: $278,664 (18% need-based, 82% non-need-based). Part-time jobs available.

ATHLETIC AWARDS Total amount: $1,286,086 (77% need-based, 23% non-need-based).

APPLYING FOR FINANCIAL AID *Required financial aid form:* FAFSA. *Financial aid deadline (priority):* 3/1. *Notification date:* Continuous beginning 1/15. Students must reply within 2 weeks of notification.

CONTACT MacKenzie May, Financial Aid Counselor, Montreat College, PO Box 1267, Montreat, NC 28757, 828-669-8012 or toll-free 800-622-6968. *Fax:* 828-412-0257. *E-mail:* financialaid@montreat.edu.

Website: http://www.montreat.edu/.

MONTSERRAT COLLEGE OF ART
Beverly, MA

CONTACT Emma Puglisi, Director of Financial Aid, Montserrat College of Art, 23 Essex Street, PO Box 26, Beverly, MA 01915, 978-922-8222 Ext. 1155 or toll-free 800-836-0487. *Fax:* 978-922-4268. *E-mail:* finaid@montserrat.edu.

Website: http://www.montserrat.edu/.

MOODY BIBLE INSTITUTE
Chicago, IL

ABOUT THE INSTITUTION Independent nondenominational, coed. 8 undergraduate majors.

GIFT AID (NEED-BASED) *Scholarships, grants, and awards:* Federal Pell, FSEOG, private, college/university gift aid from institutional funds.

LOANS *Programs:* alternative loans.

APPLYING FOR FINANCIAL AID *Required financial aid forms:* FAFSA, institution's own form.

CONTACT Moody Central, Moody Bible Institute, 820 North LaSalle Boulevard, Chicago, IL 60610-3284, 312-329-4184 or toll-free 800-967-4MBI. *Fax:* 312-329-4274. *E-mail:* financial.aid@moody.edu.

Website: http://www.moody.edu/.

MOORE COLLEGE OF ART & DESIGN
Philadelphia, PA

CONTACT MIchelle Shonleber, Director of Financial Aid, Moore College of Art & Design, 20th and the Parkway, Philadelphia, PA 19103-1179, 215-965-4042 or toll-free 800-523-2025. *Fax:* 215-568-1773. *E-mail:* mshonleber@moore.edu.

Website: http://www.moore.edu/.

MORAVIAN COLLEGE
Bethlehem, PA

Tuition & fees: $42,024	Average undergraduate aid package: $29,554

ABOUT THE INSTITUTION Independent Moravian Church, coed. **Awards:** certificates, bachelor's, and master's degrees. 32 undergraduate majors. **Total enrollment:** 2,448. Undergraduates: 2,006. Freshmen: 488. Federal methodology is used as a basis for awarding need-based institutional aid.

UNDERGRADUATE EXPENSES for 2017–2018 One-time required fee: $140. **Comprehensive fee:** $54,718 includes full-time tuition ($40,293), mandatory fees ($1731), and room and board ($12,694). **College room only:** $7132. Room and board charges vary according to board plan and housing facility. **Part-time tuition:** $1120 per credit. Part-time tuition and fees vary according to class time.

FRESHMAN FINANCIAL AID (Fall 2016, est.) 437 applied for aid; of those 93% were deemed to have need. 100% of freshmen with need received aid; of those 16% had need fully met. **Average percent of need met:** 80% (excluding resources awarded to replace EFC). **Average financial aid package:** $32,775 (excluding resources awarded to replace EFC). 16% of all full-time freshmen had no need and received non-need-based gift aid.

UNDERGRADUATE FINANCIAL AID (Fall 2016, est.) 1,553 applied for aid; of those 93% were deemed to have need. 100% of undergraduates with need received aid; of those 14% had need fully met. **Average percent of need met:** 74% (excluding resources awarded to replace EFC). **Average financial aid package:** $29,554 (excluding resources awarded to replace EFC). 19% of all full-time undergraduates had no need and received non-need-based gift aid.

GIFT AID (NEED-BASED) Total amount: $33,878,145 (8% federal, 6% state, 84% institutional, 2% external sources). **Receiving aid:** Freshmen: 84% (407); all full-time undergraduates: 80% (1,438). **Average award:** Freshmen: $27,649; Undergraduates: $23,904. **Scholarships, grants, and awards:** Federal Pell, FSEOG, state, private, college/university gift aid from institutional funds, United Negro College Fund, Federal Nursing.

GIFT AID (NON-NEED-BASED) Total amount: $5,254,620 (96% institutional, 4% external sources). **Receiving aid:** Freshmen: 10% (49). Undergraduates: 8% (145). **Average award:** Freshmen: $17,056. Undergraduates: $12,336. **Scholarships, grants, and awards by category:** Academic interests/achievement: area/ethnic studies, biological sciences, business, communication, computer science, education, engineering/technologies, English, foreign languages, general academic interests/achievements, health fields, home economics, humanities, international studies, library science, mathematics, military science, physical sciences, premedicine, religion/biblical studies, social sciences. Creative arts/performance: art/fine arts, music. Special achievements/activities: community service, leadership, religious involvement. Special characteristics: adult students, children and siblings of alumni, children of educators, children of faculty/staff, children of union members/company employees, first-generation college students, international students, out-of-state students, relatives of clergy, religious affiliation, siblings of current students, veterans, veterans' children. **Tuition waivers:** Full or partial for employees or children of employees. **ROTC:** Army cooperative.

LOANS Student loans: $16,642,551 (70% need-based, 30% non-need-based). 87% of past graduating class borrowed through all loan programs. Average indebtedness per student: $33,377. **Average need-based loan:** Freshmen: $3654. Undergraduates: $4448. **Parent loans:** $7,125,575 (48% need-based, 52% non-need-based). **Programs:** Federal Direct (Subsidized and Unsubsidized Stafford, PLUS), Perkins, private loans.

WORK-STUDY Federal work-study: Total amount: $2,445,937; 1,200 jobs averaging $2400. **State or other work-study/employment:** Total amount: $178,100 (15% need-based, 85% non-need-based). 140 part-time jobs averaging $1100.

APPLYING FOR FINANCIAL AID Required financial aid form: FAFSA. **Financial aid deadline (priority):** 3/1. **Notification date:** 2/16. Students must reply by 5/1.

CONTACT Dr. Dennis P. Levy, Director of Financial Aid Services, Moravian College, 1200 Main Street, Bethlehem, PA 18018-6650, 610-861-1330 or toll-free 800-441-3191. Fax: 610-861-1346. E-mail: levyd@moravian.edu. Website: http://www.moravian.edu/.

MOREHEAD STATE UNIVERSITY
Morehead, KY

Tuition & fees (KY res): $7031	Average undergraduate aid package: $11,197

ABOUT THE INSTITUTION State-supported, coed. **Awards:** certificates, associate, bachelor's, master's, and doctoral degrees. 56 undergraduate majors. **Total enrollment:** 16,440. Undergraduates: 14,400. Freshmen: 3,503. Federal methodology is used as a basis for awarding need-based institutional aid.

UNDERGRADUATE EXPENSES for 2017–2018 Application fee: $30. **Tuition, state resident:** full-time $5330; part-time $222 per credit hour. **Tuition, nonresident:** full-time $21,341; part-time $889 per credit hour. **Required fees:** full-time $1701. Full-time tuition and fees vary according to course load, degree level, location, reciprocity agreements, and student level. Part-time tuition and fees vary according to course load, degree level, location, reciprocity agreements, and student level. **College room and board:** $8900. Room and board charges vary according to board plan and housing facility.

FRESHMAN FINANCIAL AID (Fall 2016, est.) 1,209 applied for aid; of those 84% were deemed to have need. 99% of freshmen with need received aid; of those 20% had need fully met. **Average percent of need met:** 64% (excluding resources awarded to replace EFC). **Average financial aid package:** $11,553 (excluding resources awarded to replace EFC). 14% of all full-time freshmen had no need and received non-need-based gift aid.

UNDERGRADUATE FINANCIAL AID (Fall 2016, est.) 4,964 applied for aid; of those 86% were deemed to have need. 99% of undergraduates with need received aid; of those 19% had need fully met. **Average percent of need met:** 62% (excluding resources awarded to replace EFC). **Average financial aid package:** $11,197 (excluding resources awarded to replace EFC). 14% of all full-time undergraduates had no need and received non-need-based gift aid.

GIFT AID (NEED-BASED) Total amount: $18,027,332 (77% federal, 21% state, 2% institutional). **Receiving aid:** Freshmen: 50% (653); all full-time undergraduates: 49% (2,857). **Average award:** Freshmen: $5940; Undergraduates: $5742. **Scholarships, grants, and awards:** Federal Pell, FSEOG, state, private, college/university gift aid from institutional funds.

GIFT AID (NON-NEED-BASED) Total amount: $21,682,329 (28% state, 63% institutional, 9% external sources). **Receiving aid:** Freshmen: 73% (950). Undergraduates: 50% (2,870). **Average award:** Freshmen: $6411. Undergraduates: $6212. **Scholarships, grants, and awards by category:** Academic interests/achievement: 2,053 awards ($9,576,526 total): agriculture, biological sciences, business, communication, education, engineering/technologies, general academic interests/achievements, health fields, international studies, military science, physical sciences, social sciences. Creative arts/performance: 104 awards ($211,949 total): applied art and design, art/fine arts, journalism/publications, music, theater/drama. Special achievements/activities: 144 awards ($478,983 total): cheerleading/drum major, community service, general special achievements/activities, junior miss, leadership. Special characteristics: 990 awards ($2,518,020 total): adult students, children and siblings of alumni, ethnic background, general special characteristics, handicapped students, international students, local/state students, members of minority groups, out-of-state students, previous college experience, veterans, veterans' children. **Tuition waivers:** Full or partial for minority students, children of alumni, employees or children of employees, senior citizens. **ROTC:** Army, Air Force.

LOANS Student loans: $30,923,269 (43% need-based, 57% non-need-based). 70% of past graduating class borrowed through all loan programs. Average indebtedness per student: $28,125. **Average need-based loan:** Freshmen: $3250. Undergraduates: $3839. **Parent loans:** $3,329,750 (100% non-need-based). **Programs:** Federal Direct (Subsidized and Unsubsidized Stafford, PLUS), Perkins, college/university.

WORK-STUDY Federal work-study: Total amount: $914,033; 374 jobs averaging $2381. **State or other work-study/employment:** Total amount: $2,100,070 (100% non-need-based). 733 part-time jobs averaging $2805.

ATHLETIC AWARDS Total amount: $2,397,069 (100% non-need-based).

APPLYING FOR FINANCIAL AID Required financial aid form: FAFSA. **Financial aid deadline (priority):** 3/15. **Notification date:** Continuous.

CONTACT Denise Trusty, Director of Financial Aid, Morehead State University, 205 Enrollment Services Center, Morehead, KY 40351, 606-783-2011 or toll-free 800-585-6781. Fax: 606-783-2293. E-mail: dmtrusty@moreheadstate.edu. Website: http://www.moreheadstate.edu/.

MOREHOUSE COLLEGE
Atlanta, GA

Tuition & fees: $27,278	Average undergraduate aid package: $21,187

ABOUT THE INSTITUTION Independent, men only. *Awards:* bachelor's degrees. 26 undergraduate majors. *Total enrollment:* 2,108. Undergraduates: 2,108. Freshmen: 611. Both federal and institutional methodology are used as a basis for awarding need-based institutional aid.

UNDERGRADUATE EXPENSES for 2017–2018 *Application fee:* $50. *One-time required fee:* $1013. *Comprehensive fee:* $40,835 includes full-time tuition ($25,055), mandatory fees ($2223), and room and board ($13,557). *College room only:* $7510. Full-time tuition and fees vary according to course load. Room and board charges vary according to board plan and housing facility. *Part-time tuition:* $1013 per credit hour. Part-time tuition and fees vary according to course load.

FRESHMAN FINANCIAL AID (Fall 2016, est.) 595 applied for aid; of those 85% were deemed to have need. 100% of freshmen with need received aid; of those 11% had need fully met. *Average percent of need met:* 50% (excluding resources awarded to replace EFC). *Average financial aid package:* $19,948 (excluding resources awarded to replace EFC). 7% of all full-time freshmen had no need and received non-need-based gift aid.

UNDERGRADUATE FINANCIAL AID (Fall 2016, est.) 1,912 applied for aid; of those 87% were deemed to have need. 100% of undergraduates with need received aid; of those 14% had need fully met. *Average percent of need met:* 53% (excluding resources awarded to replace EFC). *Average financial aid package:* $21,187 (excluding resources awarded to replace EFC). 5% of all full-time undergraduates had no need and received non-need-based gift aid.

GIFT AID (NEED-BASED) *Total amount:* $28,029,093 (22% federal, 3% state, 56% institutional, 19% external sources). *Receiving aid:* Freshmen: 68% (417); all full-time undergraduates: 68% (1,380). *Average award:* Freshmen: $19,192; Undergraduates: $19,607. *Scholarships, grants, and awards:* Federal Pell, FSEOG, state, private, college/university gift aid from institutional funds, United Negro College Fund.

GIFT AID (NON-NEED-BASED) *Total amount:* $1,005,840 (25% institutional, 75% external sources). *Receiving aid:* Freshmen: 2% (14). Undergraduates: 2% (44). *Average award:* Freshmen: $20,037. Undergraduates: $21,075. *Scholarships, grants, and awards by category: Academic interests/achievement:* biological sciences, business, computer science, engineering/technologies, general academic interests/achievements, mathematics, military science. *Creative arts/performance:* art/fine arts, music. *Special achievements/activities:* cheerleading/drum major, community service, leadership, religious involvement. *Special characteristics:* children and siblings of alumni, children of faculty/staff, local/state students. *Tuition waivers:* Full or partial for employees or children of employees. *ROTC:* Army, Naval, Air Force cooperative.

LOANS *Student loans:* $15,026,329 (46% need-based, 54% non-need-based). 79% of past graduating class borrowed through all loan programs. *Average indebtedness per student:* $30,485. *Average need-based loan:* Freshmen: $4295. Undergraduates: $5178. *Parent loans:* $30,553,154 (100% non-need-based). *Programs:* Federal Direct (Subsidized and Unsubsidized Stafford, PLUS), Perkins, state.

WORK-STUDY *Federal work-study:* Total amount: $689,061; 201 jobs averaging $3334. *State or other work-study/employment:* Total amount: $305,175 (55% need-based, 45% non-need-based). 100 part-time jobs averaging $3012.

ATHLETIC AWARDS Total amount: $2,108,295 (100% need-based).

APPLYING FOR FINANCIAL AID *Required financial aid forms:* FAFSA, institution's own form, CSS Financial Aid PROFILE, state aid form. *Financial aid deadline:* 4/1 (priority: 2/15). *Notification date:* 4/1. Students must reply by 5/1 or within 2 weeks of notification.

CONTACT Sheryl T. Spivey, Director of Financial Aid, Morehouse College, 830 Westview Drive, SW, Atlanta, GA 30314, 404-653-7750 or toll-free 800-851-1254. *Fax:* 404-215-2711. *E-mail:* sheryl.spivey@morehouse.edu. *Website:* http://www.morehouse.edu/.

MORGAN STATE UNIVERSITY
Baltimore, MD

Tuition & fees (MD res): $7636	Average undergraduate aid package: $9817

ABOUT THE INSTITUTION State-supported, coed. 55 undergraduate majors. Federal methodology is used as a basis for awarding need-based institutional aid.

UNDERGRADUATE EXPENSES for 2016–2017 *Tuition, state resident:* full-time $5161; part-time $235 per credit. *Tuition, nonresident:* full-time $15,029; part-time $592 per credit. *Required fees:* full-time $2475; $78 per credit. *College room and board:* $10,490; *Room only:* $6340. Room and board charges vary according to board plan and housing facility.

FRESHMAN FINANCIAL AID (Fall 2015) 1,137 applied for aid; of those 90% were deemed to have need. 100% of freshmen with need received aid; of those 11% had need fully met. *Average percent of need met:* 37% (excluding resources awarded to replace EFC). *Average financial aid package:* $9542 (excluding resources awarded to replace EFC). 7% of all full-time freshmen had no need and received non-need-based gift aid.

UNDERGRADUATE FINANCIAL AID (Fall 2015) 5,116 applied for aid; of those 96% were deemed to have need. 100% of undergraduates with need received aid; of those 12% had need fully met. *Average percent of need met:* 40% (excluding resources awarded to replace EFC). *Average financial aid package:* $9817 (excluding resources awarded to replace EFC). 7% of all full-time undergraduates had no need and received non-need-based gift aid.

GIFT AID (NEED-BASED) *Total amount:* $26,956,002 (71% federal, 14% state, 11% institutional, 4% external sources). *Receiving aid:* Freshmen: 69% (796); all full-time undergraduates: 69% (3,838). *Average award:* Freshmen: $6798; Undergraduates: $6492. *Scholarships, grants, and awards:* Federal Pell, FSEOG, state, private, college/university gift aid from institutional funds.

GIFT AID (NON-NEED-BASED) *Total amount:* $4,696,332 (7% federal, 14% state, 66% institutional, 13% external sources). *Receiving aid:* Freshmen: 19% (225). Undergraduates: 15% (861). *Average award:* Freshmen: $7514. Undergraduates: $7292. *Scholarships, grants, and awards by category: Academic interests/achievement:* 478 awards ($6,821,012 total): general academic interests/achievements. *Tuition waivers:* Full or partial for employees or children of employees.

LOANS *Student loans:* $37,636,046 (53% need-based, 47% non-need-based). 81% of past graduating class borrowed through all loan programs. *Average indebtedness per student:* $52,622. *Average need-based loan:* Freshmen: $2941. Undergraduates: $3391. *Parent loans:* $13,787,601 (100% need-based). *Programs:* Federal Direct (Subsidized and Unsubsidized Stafford, PLUS), Perkins.

WORK-STUDY *Federal work-study:* 299 jobs averaging $2102. *State or other work-study/employment:* Part-time jobs available.

ATHLETIC AWARDS Total amount: $3,261,258 (100% non-need-based).

APPLYING FOR FINANCIAL AID *Required financial aid forms:* FAFSA, institution's own form, federal income tax form(s). *Financial aid deadline (priority):* 4/1. *Notification date:* Continuous beginning 6/1. Students must reply within 2 weeks of notification.

CONTACT Tanya Wilkerson, Director of Financial Aid, Morgan State University, 1700 East Cold Spring Lane, Baltimore, MD 21251, 443-885-3170 or toll-free 800-332-6674. *Fax:* 443-885-8272. *Website:* http://www.morgan.edu/.

MORNINGSIDE COLLEGE
Sioux City, IA

Tuition & fees: $29,094	Average undergraduate aid package: $23,298

ABOUT THE INSTITUTION Independent United Methodist Church, coed. *Awards:* certificates, bachelor's, and master's degrees. 44 undergraduate majors. *Total enrollment:* 2,902. Undergraduates: 1,321. Freshmen: 341. Federal methodology is used as a basis for awarding need-based institutional aid.

UNDERGRADUATE EXPENSES for 2016–2017 *Comprehensive fee:* $37,684 includes full-time tuition ($27,620), mandatory fees ($1474), and room and board ($8590). *College room only:* $4390. Full-time tuition and fees vary according to program. Room and board charges vary according to housing facility. *Part-time* *tuition:* $880 per credit hour. Part-time tuition and fees vary according to course load and program.

FRESHMAN FINANCIAL AID (Fall 2016, est.) 307 applied for aid; of those 92% were deemed to have need. 100% of freshmen with need received aid; of those 38% had need fully met. *Average percent of need met:* 79% (excluding resources awarded to replace EFC). *Average financial aid package:* $24,316 (excluding resources awarded to replace EFC). 17% of all full-time freshmen had no need and received non-need-based gift aid.

UNDERGRADUATE FINANCIAL AID (Fall 2016, est.) 1,149 applied for aid; of those 90% were deemed to have need. 100% of undergraduates with need received aid; of those 37% had need fully met. *Average percent of need met:* 78% (excluding resources awarded to replace EFC). *Average financial aid package:* $23,298 (excluding resources awarded to replace EFC). 20% of all full-time undergraduates had no need and received non-need-based gift aid.

GIFT AID (NEED-BASED) *Total amount:* $4,396,722 (41% federal, 48% state, 11% institutional). *Receiving aid:* Freshmen: 54% (184); all full-time undergraduates: 51% (663). *Average award:* Freshmen: $6193; Undergraduates: $6471. *Scholarships, grants, and awards:* Federal Pell, FSEOG, state, private, college/university gift aid from institutional funds.

GIFT AID (NON-NEED-BASED) *Total amount:* $16,574,038 (6% federal, 2% state, 88% institutional, 4% external sources). *Receiving aid:* Freshmen: 83% (281). Undergraduates: 79% (1,029). *Average award:* Freshmen: $16,908. Undergraduates: $14,978. *Scholarships, grants, and awards by category: Academic interests/ achievement:* 1,541 awards ($10,825,218 total): computer science, general academic interests/achievements. *Creative arts/performance:* 228 awards ($797,410 total): art/ fine arts, cinema/film/broadcasting, creative writing, dance, journalism/publications, music, theater/drama. *Special achievements/activities:* 3 awards ($1250 total): cheer-leading/drum major, leadership. *Special characteristics:* 137 awards ($2,416,331 total): children and siblings of alumni, children of faculty/staff, international students, local/ state students, out-of-state students. *Tuition waivers:* Full or partial for children of alumni, employees or children of employees, senior citizens. *ROTC:* Army cooperative.

LOANS *Student loans:* $9,214,147 (41% need-based, 59% non-need-based). 78% of past graduating class borrowed through all loan programs. *Average indebtedness per student:* $36,233. *Average need-based loan:* Freshmen: $4072. Undergraduates: $4684. *Parent loans:* $2,095,251 (100% non-need-based). *Programs:* Federal Direct (Subsidized and Unsubsidized Stafford, PLUS), Perkins, college/university, private loans.

WORK-STUDY *Federal work-study:* Total amount: $628,986; 526 jobs averaging $1184. *State or other work-study/employment:* Total amount: $520,285 (100% non-need-based). 251 part-time jobs averaging $2027.

ATHLETIC AWARDS Total amount: $2,751,191 (100% non-need-based).

APPLYING FOR FINANCIAL AID *Required financial aid form:* FAFSA. *Financial aid deadline:* Continuous. *Notification date:* 11/24.

CONTACT Karen Gagnon, Director of Student Financial Planning, Morningside College, 1501 Morningside Avenue, Sioux City, IA 51106, 712-274-5272 or toll-free 800-831-0806 Ext. 5111. *Fax:* 712-274-5605. *E-mail:* gagnon@morningside.edu. *Website:* http://www.morningside.edu/.

Undergraduates: 3,003. Freshmen: 912. Federal methodology is used as a basis for awarding need-based institutional aid.

UNDERGRADUATE EXPENSES for 2017–2018 *Application fee:* $50. *Tuition, state resident:* full-time $6470; part-time $270 per credit hour. *Tuition, nonresident:* full-time $11,300; part-time $458 per credit hour. *Required fees:* full-time $1553; $66.10 per credit hour. Full-time tuition and fees vary according to course level, degree level, location, and program. Part-time tuition and fees vary according to class time, course level, course load, degree level, location, and program. *College room and board:* $13,837; *Room only:* $8448. Room and board charges vary according to board plan, housing facility, and location.

FRESHMAN FINANCIAL AID (Fall 2015) 776 applied for aid; of those 89% were deemed to have need. 99% of freshmen with need received aid; of those .4% had need fully met. *Average percent of need met:* 47% (excluding resources awarded to replace EFC). *Average financial aid package:* $9793 (excluding resources awarded to replace EFC). 15% of all full-time freshmen had no need and received non-need-based gift aid.

UNDERGRADUATE FINANCIAL AID (Fall 2015) 2,335 applied for aid; of those 93% were deemed to have need. 97% of undergraduates with need received aid; of those 1% had need fully met. *Average percent of need met:* 49% (excluding resources awarded to replace EFC). *Average financial aid package:* $9758 (excluding resources awarded to replace EFC). 11% of all full-time undergraduates had no need and received non-need-based gift aid.

GIFT AID (NEED-BASED) *Total amount:* $13,461,468 (54% federal, 46% state). *Receiving aid:* Freshmen: 74% (600); all full-time undergraduates: 73% (1,825). *Average award:* Freshmen: $7325; Undergraduates: $6963. *Scholarships, grants, and awards:* Federal Pell, FSEOG, state, college/university gift aid from institutional funds.

GIFT AID (NON-NEED-BASED) *Total amount:* $1,807,023 (9% state, 49% institutional, 42% external sources). *Receiving aid:* Freshmen: 27% (220). Undergraduates: 20% (493). *Average award:* Freshmen: $1711. Undergraduates: $1761. *Scholarships, grants, and awards by category: Academic interests/ achievement:* general academic interests/achievements. *Special achievements/activities:* leadership, memberships. *Special characteristics:* children of faculty/staff, local/ state students, members of minority groups, out-of-state students. *Tuition waivers:* Full or partial for minority students, children of alumni, employees or children of employees, senior citizens. *ROTC:* Army cooperative, Air Force cooperative.

LOANS *Student loans:* $17,106,214 (44% need-based, 56% non-need-based). 90% of past graduating class borrowed through all loan programs. *Average indebtedness per student:* $28,106. *Average need-based loan:* Freshmen: $3363. Undergraduates: $3874. *Parent loans:* $7,672,379 (100% non-need-based). *Programs:* Federal Direct (Subsidized and Unsubsidized Stafford, PLUS), Perkins, Federal Nursing.

WORK-STUDY *Federal work-study:* jobs available.

APPLYING FOR FINANCIAL AID *Required financial aid forms:* FAFSA, state aid form. *Financial aid deadline (priority):* 3/1. *Notification date:* Continuous beginning 3/15. Students must reply by 5/1.

CONTACT Financial Aid Office, Morrisville State College, PO Box 901, Morrisville, NY 13408-0901, 315-684-6289 or toll-free 800-258-0111. *Fax:* 315-684-6628. *E-mail:* finaid@morrisville.edu. *Website:* http://www.morrisville.edu/.

MORRIS COLLEGE
Sumter, SC

CONTACT Ms. Sandra S. Gibson, Director of Financial Aid, Morris College, 100 West College Street, Sumter, SC 29150-3599, 803-934-3238 or toll-free 866-853-1345. *Fax:* 803-773-3687. *Website:* http://www.morris.edu/.

MORTHLAND COLLEGE
West Frankfort, IL

CONTACT Financial Aid Office, Morthland College, 202 East Oak Street, West Frankfort, IL 62896, 618-937-2127. *Website:* http://www.morthland.edu/.

MORRISVILLE STATE COLLEGE
Morrisville, NY

Tuition & fees (NY res): $8023	Average undergraduate aid package: $9758

ABOUT THE INSTITUTION State-supported, coed. *Awards:* certificates, associate, and bachelor's degrees. 94 undergraduate majors. *Total enrollment:* 3,003.

MOUNT ALOYSIUS COLLEGE
Cresson, PA

Tuition & fees: $21,850	Average undergraduate aid package: $14,140

ABOUT THE INSTITUTION Independent Roman Catholic, coed. *Awards:* certificates, associate, bachelor's, and master's degrees. 25 undergraduate majors. *Total*

enrollment: 1,785. Undergraduates: 1,720. Freshmen: 275. Federal methodology is used as a basis for awarding need-based institutional aid.

UNDERGRADUATE EXPENSES for 2016–2017 *Application fee:* $30. *Comprehensive fee:* $31,790 includes full-time tuition ($20,710), mandatory fees ($1140), and room and board ($9940). *College room only:* $5000. *Part-time tuition:* $770 per credit hour.

FRESHMAN FINANCIAL AID (Fall 2016, est.) 272 applied for aid; of those 77% were deemed to have need. 100% of freshmen with need received aid. *Average percent of need met:* 35% (excluding resources awarded to replace EFC). *Average financial aid package:* $13,800 (excluding resources awarded to replace EFC). 23% of all full-time freshmen had no need and received non-need-based gift aid.

UNDERGRADUATE FINANCIAL AID (Fall 2016, est.) 1,075 applied for aid; of those 84% were deemed to have need. 100% of undergraduates with need received aid. *Average percent of need met:* 38% (excluding resources awarded to replace EFC). *Average financial aid package:* $14,140 (excluding resources awarded to replace EFC). 17% of all full-time undergraduates had no need and received non-need-based gift aid.

GIFT AID (NEED-BASED) *Total amount:* $11,763,554 (21% federal, 16% state, 61% institutional, 2% external sources). *Receiving aid:* Freshmen: 77% (209); all full-time undergraduates: 83% (898). *Average award:* Freshmen: $2880; Undergraduates: $2650. *Scholarships, grants, and awards:* Federal Pell, FSEOG, state, private, college/university gift aid from institutional funds.

GIFT AID (NON-NEED-BASED) *Receiving aid:* Freshmen: 23% (63). Undergraduates: 17% (178). *Average award:* Freshmen: $5000. Undergraduates: $5200. *Scholarships, grants, and awards by category:* Academic interests/achievement: general academic interests/achievements. Creative arts/performance: music, performing arts. Special achievements/activities: leadership. Special characteristics: children of current students, parents of current students, religious affiliation, siblings of current students, spouses of current students, twins.

LOANS *Student loans:* $8,114,751 (100% need-based). *Average need-based loan:* Freshmen: $3800. Undergraduates: $4260. *Parent loans:* $3,822,648 (100% need-based). *Programs:* Federal Direct (Subsidized and Unsubsidized Stafford, PLUS), Perkins, Federal Nursing, alternative loans.

WORK-STUDY *Federal work-study:* Total amount: $287,949; jobs available.

APPLYING FOR FINANCIAL AID *Required financial aid form:* FAFSA. *Financial aid deadline (priority):* 4/1. *Notification date:* Continuous beginning 2/15. Students must reply within 2 weeks of notification.

CONTACT Mrs. Stacy L. Schenk, Director of Financial Aid, Mount Aloysius College, 7373 Admiral Peary Highway, Cresson, PA 16630-1900, 814-886-6357 or toll-free 888-823-2220. *Fax:* 814-886-6463. *E-mail:* sschenk@mtaloy.edu. *Website:* http://www.mtaloy.edu/.

MOUNT ANGEL SEMINARY
Saint Benedict, OR

CONTACT Dorene Preis, Director of Student Financial Aid/Registrar, Mount Angel Seminary, 1 Abbey Drive, Saint Benedict, OR 97373, 503-845-3951. *Fax:* 503-845-3126. *E-mail:* dpreis@mtangel.edu. *Website:* http://www.mountangelabbey.org/seminary/.

MOUNT CARMEL COLLEGE OF NURSING
Columbus, OH

Tuition & fees: $13,107	Average undergraduate aid package: $11,070

ABOUT THE INSTITUTION Independent, coed, primarily women. *Awards:* certificates, bachelor's, master's, and doctoral degrees. 1 undergraduate major. *Total enrollment:* 179. Undergraduates: 926. Freshmen: 111. Federal methodology is used as a basis for awarding need-based institutional aid.

UNDERGRADUATE EXPENSES for 2017–2018 *Application fee:* $30. *One-time required fee:* $225. *Tuition:* full-time $12,927; part-time $417 per credit hour. Full-time tuition and fees vary according to course level, course load, program,

and student level. Part-time tuition and fees vary according to course level, course load, program, and student level.

FRESHMAN FINANCIAL AID (Fall 2016, est.) 86 applied for aid; of those 95% were deemed to have need. 100% of freshmen with need received aid; of those 9% had need fully met. *Average percent of need met:* 35% (excluding resources awarded to replace EFC). *Average financial aid package:* $6516 (excluding resources awarded to replace EFC). 11% of all full-time freshmen had no need and received non-need-based gift aid.

UNDERGRADUATE FINANCIAL AID (Fall 2016, est.) 458 applied for aid; of those 90% were deemed to have need. 97% of undergraduates with need received aid, of those 8% had need fully met. *Average percent of need met:* 40% (excluding resources awarded to replace EFC). *Average financial aid package:* $11,070 (excluding resources awarded to replace EFC). 5% of all full-time undergraduates had no need and received non-need-based gift aid.

GIFT AID (NEED-BASED) *Total amount:* $3,402,919 (30% federal, 12% state, 15% institutional, 43% external sources). *Receiving aid:* Freshmen: 65% (64); all full-time undergraduates: 49% (311). *Average award:* Freshmen: $4998; Undergraduates: $9230. *Scholarships, grants, and awards:* Federal Pell, FSEOG, state, private, Federal Nursing.

GIFT AID (NON-NEED-BASED) *Total amount:* $1,814,428 (6% institutional, 94% external sources). *Receiving aid:* Freshmen: 2% (2). Undergraduates: 2% (15). *Average award:* Freshmen: $1752. Undergraduates: $2950. *Scholarships, grants, and awards by category:* Academic interests/achievement: general academic interests/achievements. Special achievements/activities: community service. Special characteristics: children of faculty/staff, members of minority groups. *Tuition waivers:* Full or partial for employees or children of employees. *ROTC:* Army cooperative, Naval cooperative, Air Force cooperative.

LOANS *Student loans:* $5,533,052 (79% need-based, 21% non-need-based). 63% of past graduating class borrowed through all loan programs. *Average indebtedness per student:* $35,713. *Average need-based loan:* Freshmen: $3241. Undergraduates: $4584. *Parent loans:* $1,279,027 (55% need-based, 45% non-need-based). *Programs:* Federal Direct (Subsidized and Unsubsidized Stafford, PLUS), Federal Nursing, state, college/university.

WORK-STUDY *State or other work-study/employment:* Total amount: $7812 (66% need-based, 34% non-need-based). Part-time jobs available.

APPLYING FOR FINANCIAL AID *Required financial aid form:* FAFSA. *Financial aid deadline (priority):* 3/1. *Notification date:* Continuous beginning 3/1. Students must reply within 2 weeks of notification.

CONTACT Todd Everett, Director of Financial Aid, Mount Carmel College of Nursing, 127 South Davis Avenue, Columbus, OH 43222, 614-234-5800 Ext. 5177 or toll-free 800-556-6942. *Fax:* 614-234-5427. *E-mail:* teverett@mccn.edu. *Website:* http://www.mccn.edu/.

MOUNT HOLYOKE COLLEGE
South Hadley, MA

Tuition & fees: $45,866	Average undergraduate aid package: $37,763

ABOUT THE INSTITUTION Independent, women only. *Awards:* certificates, bachelor's, and master's degrees. 50 undergraduate majors. *Total enrollment:* 2,330. Undergraduates: 2,202. Freshmen: 569. Both federal and institutional methodology are used as a basis for awarding need-based institutional aid.

UNDERGRADUATE EXPENSES for 2016–2017 *Application fee:* $60. *Comprehensive fee:* $59,306 includes full-time tuition ($45,680), mandatory fees ($186), and room and board ($13,440). *College room only:* $6560. *Part-time tuition:* $1430 per credit hour.

FRESHMAN FINANCIAL AID (Fall 2016, est.) 429 applied for aid; of those 78% were deemed to have need. 100% of freshmen with need received aid; of those 100% had need fully met. *Average percent of need met:* 100% (excluding resources awarded to replace EFC). *Average financial aid package:* $37,581 (excluding resources awarded to replace EFC). 14% of all full-time freshmen had no need and received non-need-based gift aid.

UNDERGRADUATE FINANCIAL AID (Fall 2016, est.) 1,620 applied for aid; of those 71% were deemed to have need. 100% of undergraduates with need received aid; of those 100% had need fully met. *Average percent of need met:* 100% (excluding resources awarded to replace EFC). *Average financial aid package:*

$37,763 (excluding resources awarded to replace EFC). 18% of all full-time undergraduates had no need and received non-need-based gift aid.

GIFT AID (NEED-BASED) *Total amount:* $36,732,113 (7% federal, 1% state, 90% institutional, 2% external sources). *Receiving aid:* Freshmen: 59% (334); all full-time undergraduates: 52% (1,144). *Average award:* Freshmen: $33,647; Undergraduates: $32,773. *Scholarships, grants, and awards:* Federal Pell, FSEOG, state, private, college/university gift aid from institutional funds.

GIFT AID (NON-NEED-BASED) *Total amount:* $17,791,436 (95% institutional, 5% external sources). *Receiving aid:* Freshmen: 14% (78). Undergraduates: 11% (240). *Average award:* Freshmen: $17,926. Undergraduates: $24,244. *Scholarships, grants, and awards by category: Academic interests/achievement:* general academic interests/achievements. *Special characteristics:* general special characteristics. *Tuition waivers:* Full or partial for employees or children of employees. *ROTC:* Army cooperative, Air Force cooperative.

LOANS *Student loans:* $8,980,826 (56% need-based, 44% non-need-based). 60% of past graduating class borrowed through all loan programs. *Average indebtedness per student:* $23,872. *Average need-based loan:* Freshmen: $2898. Undergraduates: $4371. *Parent loans:* $3,317,762 (100% non-need-based). *Programs:* Federal Direct (Subsidized and Unsubsidized Stafford, PLUS), Perkins, state, college/university.

WORK-STUDY *Federal work-study:* Total amount: $1,637,366; 773 jobs averaging $2115. *State or other work-study/employment:* Total amount: $824,863 (100% need-based). 346 part-time jobs averaging $2167.

APPLYING FOR FINANCIAL AID *Required financial aid forms:* FAFSA, CSS Financial Aid PROFILE, noncustodial (divorced/separated) parent's statement, federal income tax form(s), W-2 forms. *Financial aid deadline:* 3/1 (priority: 2/1). *Notification date:* 4/1. Students must reply by 5/1.

CONTACT Ms. Kathryn Blaisdell, Director of Student Financial Services, Mount Holyoke College, 50 College Street, South Hadley, MA 01075-1492, 413-538-2291. *Fax:* 413-538-2512. *E-mail:* kblaisde@mtholyoke.edu. *Website:* http://www.mtholyoke.edu/.

MOUNT IDA COLLEGE
Newton, MA

Tuition & fees: $35,720	Average undergraduate aid package: $24,176

ABOUT THE INSTITUTION Independent, coed. *Awards:* certificates, associate, bachelor's, and master's degrees. 25 undergraduate majors. *Total enrollment:* 1,337. Undergraduates: 1,320. Freshmen: 433. Federal methodology is used as a basis for awarding need-based institutional aid.

UNDERGRADUATE EXPENSES for 2017–2018 *Comprehensive fee:* $49,400 includes full-time tuition ($34,200), mandatory fees ($1520), and room and board ($13,680). Full-time tuition and fees vary according to program. Room and board charges vary according to board plan. *Part-time tuition:* $1075 per credit. Part-time tuition and fees vary according to program.

FRESHMAN FINANCIAL AID (Fall 2015) 400 applied for aid; of those 94% were deemed to have need. 100% of freshmen with need received aid; of those 10% had need fully met. *Average percent of need met:* 66% (excluding resources awarded to replace EFC). *Average financial aid package:* $25,304 (excluding resources awarded to replace EFC). 13% of all full-time freshmen had no need and received non-need-based gift aid.

UNDERGRADUATE FINANCIAL AID (Fall 2015) 1,071 applied for aid; of those 94% were deemed to have need. 100% of undergraduates with need received aid; of those 10% had need fully met. *Average percent of need met:* 64% (excluding resources awarded to replace EFC). *Average financial aid package:* $24,176 (excluding resources awarded to replace EFC). 19% of all full-time undergraduates had no need and received non-need-based gift aid.

GIFT AID (NEED-BASED) *Total amount:* $19,987,151 (12% federal, 4% state, 78% institutional, 6% external sources). *Receiving aid:* Freshmen: 87% (376); all full-time undergraduates: 81% (1,011). *Average award:* Freshmen: $21,506; Undergraduates: $19,682. *Scholarships, grants, and awards:* Federal Pell, FSEOG, state, private, college/university gift aid from institutional funds.

GIFT AID (NON-NEED-BASED) *Total amount:* $3,277,635 (11% state, 73% institutional, 16% external sources). *Receiving aid:* Freshmen: 6% (27). Undergraduates: 6% (70). *Average award:* Freshmen: $13,581. Undergraduates: $8930. *Scholarships, grants, and awards by category: Creative arts/performance:* 177 awards ($349,875 total): applied art and design, art/fine arts, general creative arts/per-

formance. *Special achievements/activities:* 1,232 awards ($14,670,923 total): community service, general special achievements/activities, leadership.

LOANS *Student loans:* $11,579,957 (77% need-based, 23% non-need-based). 78% of past graduating class borrowed through all loan programs. *Average indebtedness per student:* $44,963. *Average need-based loan:* Freshmen: $3277. Undergraduates: $4078. *Parent loans:* $4,776,930 (60% need-based, 40% non-need-based). *Programs:* Federal Direct (Subsidized and Unsubsidized Stafford, PLUS), state, private loans.

WORK-STUDY *Federal work-study:* 158 jobs averaging $1439. *State or other work-study/employment:* Total amount: $39,936 (71% need-based, 29% non-need-based). 21 part-time jobs averaging $1902.

APPLYING FOR FINANCIAL AID *Required financial aid form:* FAFSA. *Financial aid deadline (priority):* 5/1. *Notification date:* Continuous beginning 1/1. Students must reply by 8/15.

CONTACT Ms. Dyan Teehan , Director of Student Financial Services, Mount Ida College, 777 Dedham Street, Newton, MA 02459-3310, 617-928-4780. *Fax:* 617-332-7869. *E-mail:* finaid@mountida.edu. *Website:* http://www.mountida.edu/.

MOUNT MARTY COLLEGE
Yankton, SD

Tuition & fees: $26,310	Average undergraduate aid package: $24,755

ABOUT THE INSTITUTION Independent Roman Catholic, coed. *Awards:* certificates, associate, bachelor's, master's, and doctoral degrees. 31 undergraduate majors. *Total enrollment:* 1,162. Undergraduates: 1,006. Freshmen: 117. Federal methodology is used as a basis for awarding need-based institutional aid.

UNDERGRADUATE EXPENSES for 2017–2018 *Application fee:* $35. *Comprehensive fee:* $34,156 includes full-time tuition ($24,160), mandatory fees ($2150), and room and board ($7846). Full-time tuition and fees vary according to degree level, location, and program. Room and board charges vary according to board plan. *Part-time tuition:* $530 per credit hour. *Part-time fees:* $45 per credit hour. Part-time tuition and fees vary according to course load, degree level, location, and program.

FRESHMAN FINANCIAL AID (Fall 2016, est.) 100 applied for aid; of those 89% were deemed to have need. 100% of freshmen with need received aid; of those 42% had need fully met. *Average percent of need met:* 89% (excluding resources awarded to replace EFC). *Average financial aid package:* $28,743 (excluding resources awarded to replace EFC). 9% of all full-time freshmen had no need and received non-need-based gift aid.

UNDERGRADUATE FINANCIAL AID (Fall 2016, est.) 429 applied for aid; of those 85% were deemed to have need. 99% of undergraduates with need received aid; of those 43% had need fully met. *Average percent of need met:* 83% (excluding resources awarded to replace EFC). *Average financial aid package:* $24,755 (excluding resources awarded to replace EFC). 12% of all full-time undergraduates had no need and received non-need-based gift aid.

GIFT AID (NEED-BASED) *Total amount:* $4,757,701 (19% federal, 2% state, 76% institutional, 3% external sources). *Receiving aid:* Freshmen: 80% (83); all full-time undergraduates: 73% (336). *Average award:* Freshmen: $19,650; Undergraduates: $14,929. *Scholarships, grants, and awards:* Federal Pell, FSEOG, state, private, college/university gift aid from institutional funds.

GIFT AID (NON-NEED-BASED) *Total amount:* $602,887 (4% state, 85% institutional, 11% external sources). *Average award:* Freshmen: $11,944. Undergraduates: $9298. *Scholarships, grants, and awards by category: Academic interests/achievement:* 359 awards ($3,305,534 total): general academic interests/achievements. *Creative arts/performance:* 41 awards ($57,095 total): art/fine arts, music, performing arts, theater/drama. *Special achievements/activities:* community service, general special achievements/activities, leadership, religious involvement. *Special characteristics:* children of current students, children of faculty/staff, international students, parents of current students, religious affiliation, siblings of current students, spouses of current students. *Tuition waivers:* Full or partial for employees or children of employees. *ROTC:* Army cooperative.

LOANS *Student loans:* $1,985,723 (95% need-based, 5% non-need-based). 70% of past graduating class borrowed through all loan programs. *Average indebtedness per student:* $30,083. *Average need-based loan:* Freshmen: $4258. Undergraduates: $4888. *Parent loans:* $624,176 (90% need-based, 10% non-need-based). *Programs:*

Federal Direct (Subsidized and Unsubsidized Stafford, PLUS), Perkins, Federal Nursing, state, college/university.

WORK-STUDY *Federal work-study:* Total amount: $215,196; 119 jobs averaging $1771. *State or other work-study/employment:* Total amount: $108,000 (65% need-based, 35% non-need-based). 60 part-time jobs averaging $1800.

ATHLETIC AWARDS Total amount: $872,779 (83% need-based, 17% non-need-based).

APPLYING FOR FINANCIAL AID *Required financial aid forms:* FAFSA, institution's own form. *Financial aid deadline (priority):* 3/1. *Notification date:* Continuous beginning 3/15. Students must reply within 2 weeks of notification.

CONTACT Mr. Ken Kocer, Director of Financial Assistance, Mount Marty College, 1105 West 8th Street, Yankton, SD 57078-3724, 605-668-1589 or toll-free 800-658-4552. *Fax:* 605-668-1585. *E-mail:* kkocer@mtmc.edu. *Website:* http://www.mtmc.edu/.

MOUNT MARY UNIVERSITY
Milwaukee, WI

Tuition & fees: $29,510	Average undergraduate aid package: $23,785

ABOUT THE INSTITUTION Independent Roman Catholic, undergraduate: women only; graduate: coed. *Awards:* certificates, bachelor's, master's, and doctoral degrees. 44 undergraduate majors. *Total enrollment:* 1,404. Undergraduates: 807. Freshmen: 118. Federal methodology is used as a basis for awarding need-based institutional aid.

UNDERGRADUATE EXPENSES for 2017–2018 *Comprehensive fee:* $38,040 includes full-time tuition ($28,940), mandatory fees ($570), and room and board ($8530). Full-time tuition and fees vary according to degree level and program. Room and board charges vary according to board plan. *Part-time tuition:* $860 per credit. *Part-time fees:* $350 per year. Part-time tuition and fees vary according to course load, degree level, and program.

FRESHMAN FINANCIAL AID (Fall 2016, est.) 127 applied for aid; of those 94% were deemed to have need. 100% of freshmen with need received aid; of those 13% had need fully met. *Average percent of need met:* 81% (excluding resources awarded to replace EFC). *Average financial aid package:* $27,107 (excluding resources awarded to replace EFC). 6% of all full-time freshmen had no need and received non-need-based gift aid.

UNDERGRADUATE FINANCIAL AID (Fall 2016, est.) 677 applied for aid; of those 94% were deemed to have need. 100% of undergraduates with need received aid; of those 9% had need fully met. *Average percent of need met:* 71% (excluding resources awarded to replace EFC). *Average financial aid package:* $23,785 (excluding resources awarded to replace EFC). 7% of all full-time undergraduates had no need and received non-need-based gift aid.

GIFT AID (NEED-BASED) *Total amount:* $12,244,120 (16% federal, 12% state, 70% institutional, 2% external sources). *Receiving aid:* Freshmen: 93% (120); all full-time undergraduates: 93% (638). *Average award:* Freshmen: $22,742; Undergraduates: $18,915. *Scholarships, grants, and awards:* Federal Pell, FSEOG, state, private, college/university gift aid from institutional funds.

GIFT AID (NON-NEED-BASED) *Total amount:* $959,948 (1% state, 95% institutional, 4% external sources). *Receiving aid:* Freshmen: 11% (14). Undergraduates: 7% (51). *Average award:* Freshmen: $10,690. Undergraduates: $12,425. *Scholarships, grants, and awards by category: Academic interests/achievement:* 622 awards ($5,302,531 total): business, communication, education, English, general academic interests/achievements, humanities, mathematics, social sciences. *Creative arts/performance:* 41 awards ($45,394 total): applied art and design, art/fine arts, music. *Special achievements/activities:* 6 awards ($55,200 total): general special achievements/activities, leadership. *Special characteristics:* 29 awards ($140,260 total): children and siblings of alumni, children of faculty/staff, siblings of current students, veterans. *Tuition waivers:* Full or partial for employees or children of employees, senior citizens.

LOANS *Student loans:* $5,596,785 (87% need-based, 13% non-need-based). 88% of past graduating class borrowed through all loan programs. *Average indebtedness per student:* $27,811. *Average need-based loan:* Freshmen: $3437. Undergraduates: $4532. *Parent loans:* $494,966 (62% need-based, 38% non-need-based). *Programs:* Federal Direct (Subsidized and Unsubsidized Stafford, PLUS), Perkins, state.

WORK-STUDY *Federal work-study:* Total amount: $139,882; 97 jobs averaging $1442. *State or other work-study/employment:* Total amount: $200,220 (100% non-need-based). 114 part-time jobs averaging $1756.

APPLYING FOR FINANCIAL AID *Required financial aid form:* FAFSA. *Financial aid deadline (priority):* 12/1. *Notification date:* Continuous beginning 12/15. Students must reply within 2 weeks of notification.

CONTACT Debra Duff, Director of Financial Aid, Mount Mary University, 2900 North Menomonee River Parkway, Milwaukee, WI 53222-4597, 414-930-3163 or toll-free 800-321-6265. *Fax:* 414-930-3709. *E-mail:* finaid@mtmary.edu. *Website:* http://www.mtmary.edu/.

MOUNT MERCY UNIVERSITY
Cedar Rapids, IA

Tuition & fees: $30,582	Average undergraduate aid package: $23,169

ABOUT THE INSTITUTION Independent Roman Catholic, coed. *Awards:* bachelor's and master's degrees. 49 undergraduate majors. *Total enrollment:* 1,886. Undergraduates: 1,580. Freshmen: 241. Federal methodology is used as a basis for awarding need-based institutional aid.

UNDERGRADUATE EXPENSES for 2017–2018 *Comprehensive fee:* $39,748 includes full-time tuition ($30,382), mandatory fees ($200), and room and board ($9166). Full-time tuition and fees vary according to course load and degree level. Room and board charges vary according to board plan and housing facility. *Part-time tuition:* $920 per credit hour. *Part-time fees:* $200 per year. Part-time tuition and fees vary according to course load and degree level.

FRESHMAN FINANCIAL AID (Fall 2016, est.) 222 applied for aid; of those 93% were deemed to have need. 99% of freshmen with need received aid; of those 24% had need fully met. *Average percent of need met:* 78% (excluding resources awarded to replace EFC). *Average financial aid package:* $25,028 (excluding resources awarded to replace EFC). 14% of all full-time freshmen had no need and received non-need-based gift aid.

UNDERGRADUATE FINANCIAL AID (Fall 2016, est.) 955 applied for aid; of those 92% were deemed to have need. 98% of undergraduates with need received aid; of those 20% had need fully met. *Average percent of need met:* 74% (excluding resources awarded to replace EFC). *Average financial aid package:* $23,169 (excluding resources awarded to replace EFC). 15% of all full-time undergraduates had no need and received non-need-based gift aid.

GIFT AID (NEED-BASED) *Total amount:* $17,884,843 (12% federal, 18% state, 65% institutional, 5% external sources). *Receiving aid:* Freshmen: 84% (203); all full-time undergraduates: 74% (861). *Average award:* Freshmen: $22,203; Undergraduates: $19,697. *Scholarships, grants, and awards:* Federal Pell, FSEOG, state, private, college/university gift aid from institutional funds.

GIFT AID (NON-NEED-BASED) *Total amount:* $3,231,998 (2% state, 92% institutional, 6% external sources). *Receiving aid:* Freshmen: 16% (38). Undergraduates: 11% (128). *Average award:* Freshmen: $15,040. Undergraduates: $13,254. *Scholarships, grants, and awards by category: Academic interests/achievement:* general academic interests/achievements. *Creative arts/performance:* 93 awards ($235,155 total): art/fine arts, creative writing, music, theater/drama. *Special characteristics:* 30 awards ($24,000 total): previous college experience. *Tuition waivers:* Full or partial for employees or children of employees.

LOANS *Student loans:* $9,067,540 (71% need-based, 29% non-need-based). 88% of past graduating class borrowed through all loan programs. *Average indebtedness per student:* $26,603. *Average need-based loan:* Freshmen: $3047. Undergraduates: $3852. *Parent loans:* $2,286,624 (46% need-based, 54% non-need-based). *Programs:* Federal Direct (Subsidized and Unsubsidized Stafford, PLUS), Perkins, state, college/university.

WORK-STUDY *Federal work-study:* Total amount: $321,408; 254 jobs averaging $1552. *State or other work-study/employment:* Total amount: $200,744 (42% need-based, 58% non-need-based). 419 part-time jobs averaging $915.

APPLYING FOR FINANCIAL AID *Required financial aid form:* FAFSA. *Financial aid deadline (priority):* 3/1. *Notification date:* Continuous beginning 3/15. Students must reply by 5/1 or within 3 weeks of notification.

CONTACT Bethany Rinderknecht, Director of Financial Aid, Mount Mercy University, 1330 Elmhurst Drive NE, Cedar Rapids, IA 52402-4797, 319-368-6467 Ext. 1545 or toll-free 800-248-4504. *Fax:* 319-364-3546. *E-mail:* brinderknecht@ mtmercy.edu.
Website: http://www.mtmercy.edu/.

MOUNT ST. JOSEPH UNIVERSITY
Cincinnati, OH

Tuition & fees: $29,100	Average undergraduate aid package: $18,827

ABOUT THE INSTITUTION Independent Roman Catholic, coed. *Awards:* certificates, associate, bachelor's, master's, and doctoral degrees. 48 undergraduate majors. *Total enrollment:* 2,045. Undergraduates: 1,336. Freshmen: 249. Federal methodology is used as a basis for awarding need-based institutional aid.

UNDERGRADUATE EXPENSES for 2017–2018 *Application fee:* $25. *One-time required fee:* $125. *Comprehensive fee:* $38,366 includes full-time tuition ($28,100), mandatory fees ($1000), and room and board ($9266). Full-time tuition and fees vary according to course load and reciprocity agreements. Room and board charges vary according to board plan and housing facility. *Part-time tuition:* $525 per credit hour. *Part-time fees:* $500 per year. Part-time tuition and fees vary according to course load and reciprocity agreements.

FRESHMAN FINANCIAL AID (Fall 2016, est.) 236 applied for aid; of those 92% were deemed to have need. 100% of freshmen with need received aid; of those 17% had need fully met. *Average percent of need met:* 75% (excluding resources awarded to replace EFC). *Average financial aid package:* $20,897 (excluding resources awarded to replace EFC). 10% of all full-time freshmen had no need and received non-need-based gift aid.

UNDERGRADUATE FINANCIAL AID (Fall 2016, est.) 905 applied for aid; of those 88% were deemed to have need. 100% of undergraduates with need received aid; of those 16% had need fully met. *Average percent of need met:* 72% (excluding resources awarded to replace EFC). *Average financial aid package:* $18,827 (excluding resources awarded to replace EFC). 19% of all full-time undergraduates had no need and received non-need-based gift aid.

GIFT AID (NEED-BASED) *Total amount:* $12,842,592 (20% federal, 6% state, 72% institutional, 2% external sources). *Receiving aid:* Freshmen: 89% (215); all full-time undergraduates: 79% (784). *Average award:* Freshmen: $17,845; Undergraduates: $15,762. *Scholarships, grants, and awards:* Federal Pell, FSEOG, state, private, college/university gift aid from institutional funds.

GIFT AID (NON-NEED-BASED) *Total amount:* $2,156,127 (9% federal, 89% institutional, 2% external sources). *Receiving aid:* Freshmen: 9% (21). Undergraduates: 9% (85). *Average award:* Freshmen: $11,770. Undergraduates: $11,234. *Scholarships, grants, and awards by category:* Academic interests/ achievement: 103 awards ($1,059,200 total): general academic interests/achievements. Creative arts/performance: 5 awards ($9500 total): art/fine arts, music. Special achievements/activities: community service, leadership. Special characteristics: 6 awards ($169,980 total): adult students, children and siblings of alumni, children of faculty/staff. *Tuition waivers:* Full or partial for employees or children of employees, senior citizens. *ROTC:* Army cooperative.

LOANS *Student loans:* $7,925,152 (91% need-based, 9% non-need-based). *Average need-based loan:* Freshmen: $3504. Undergraduates: $3775. *Parent loans:* $2,745,847 (92% need-based, 8% non-need-based). *Programs:* Federal Direct (Subsidized and Unsubsidized Stafford, PLUS), Perkins, Federal Nursing, state.

WORK-STUDY *Federal work-study:* Total amount: $301,200; 187 jobs averaging $1611. *State or other work-study/employment:* Total amount: $280,600 (98% need-based, 2% non-need-based). 192 part-time jobs averaging $1461.

APPLYING FOR FINANCIAL AID *Required financial aid form:* FAFSA. *Financial aid deadline (priority):* 3/1. *Notification date:* Continuous beginning 1/31. Students must reply by 5/1 or within 4 weeks of notification.

CONTACT Ms. Kathryn Kelly, Director of Student Administrative Services, Mount St. Joseph University, 5701 Delhi Road, Cincinnati, OH 45233-1670, 513-244-4418 or toll-free 800-654-9314. *Fax:* 513-244-4201. *E-mail:* kathryn.kelly@msj.edu.
Website: http://www.msj.edu/.

MOUNT SAINT MARY COLLEGE
Newburgh, NY

Tuition & fees: $29,920	Average undergraduate aid package: $19,472

ABOUT THE INSTITUTION Independent, coed. *Awards:* certificates, bachelor's, and master's degrees. 25 undergraduate majors. *Total enrollment:* 2,468. Undergraduates: 2,128. Freshmen: 387. Federal methodology is used as a basis for awarding need-based institutional aid.

UNDERGRADUATE EXPENSES for 2017–2018 *Application fee:* $45. *Comprehensive fee:* $44,448 includes full-time tuition ($28,890), mandatory fees ($1030), and room and board ($14,528). *College room only:* $8416. Full-time tuition and fees vary according to class time, course load, location, and program. Room and board charges vary according to board plan and housing facility. *Part-time tuition:* $963 per credit. *Part-time fees:* $82 per term. Part-time tuition and fees vary according to class time, course load, location, and program.

FRESHMAN FINANCIAL AID (Fall 2016, est.) 375 applied for aid; of those 86% were deemed to have need. 100% of freshmen with need received aid; of those 17% had need fully met. *Average percent of need met:* 70% (excluding resources awarded to replace EFC). *Average financial aid package:* $22,653 (excluding resources awarded to replace EFC). 15% of all full-time freshmen had no need and received non-need-based gift aid.

UNDERGRADUATE FINANCIAL AID (Fall 2016, est.) 1,594 applied for aid; of those 88% were deemed to have need. 99% of undergraduates with need received aid; of those 16% had need fully met. *Average percent of need met:* 62% (excluding resources awarded to replace EFC). *Average financial aid package:* $19,472 (excluding resources awarded to replace EFC). 15% of all full-time undergraduates had no need and received non-need-based gift aid.

GIFT AID (NEED-BASED) *Total amount:* $21,521,052 (15% federal, 10% state, 73% institutional, 2% external sources). *Receiving aid:* Freshmen: 84% (323); all full-time undergraduates: 79% (1,373). *Average award:* Freshmen: $18,817; Undergraduates: $15,486. *Scholarships, grants, and awards:* Federal Pell, FSEOG, state, private, college/university gift aid from institutional funds, Federal Nursing, Academic Competitiveness Grants, National SMART Grants.

GIFT AID (NON-NEED-BASED) *Total amount:* $3,999,397 (1% federal, 4% state, 92% institutional, 3% external sources). *Receiving aid:* Freshmen: 12% (45). Undergraduates: 8% (144). *Average award:* Freshmen: $12,120. Undergraduates: $10,356. *Scholarships, grants, and awards by category:* Academic interests/ achievement: 1,566 awards ($15,877,488 total): general academic interests/achievements. Special achievements/activities: 19 awards ($62,500 total): leadership. Special characteristics: 35 awards ($933,736 total): children of faculty/staff. *Tuition waivers:* Full or partial for employees or children of employees. *ROTC:* Army cooperative.

LOANS *Student loans:* $17,833,211 (71% need-based, 29% non-need-based). 80% of past graduating class borrowed through all loan programs. *Average indebtedness per student:* $26,773. *Average need-based loan:* Freshmen: $3404. Undergraduates: $4354. *Parent loans:* $22,750,945 (37% need-based, 63% non-need-based). *Programs:* Federal Direct (Subsidized and Unsubsidized Stafford, PLUS), Perkins, Federal Nursing.

WORK-STUDY *Federal work-study:* Total amount: $593,070; 394 jobs averaging $1449. *State or other work-study/employment:* Part-time jobs available.

APPLYING FOR FINANCIAL AID *Required financial aid form:* FAFSA. *Financial aid deadline:* 3/1 (priority: 2/15). *Notification date:* Continuous beginning 3/15. Students must reply by 5/1.

CONTACT Jason Franky, Interim Director of Financial Aid, Mount Saint Mary College, 330 Powell Avenue, Newburgh, NY 12550-3494, 845-561-3394 or toll-free 888-937-6762. *Fax:* 845-569-3302. *E-mail:* jason.franky@msmc.edu.
Website: http://www.msmc.edu/.

MOUNT SAINT MARY'S UNIVERSITY
Los Angeles, CA

Tuition & fees: $37,722	Average undergraduate aid package: $27,165

ABOUT THE INSTITUTION Independent Roman Catholic, coed, primarily women. *Awards:* certificates, associate, bachelor's, master's, and doctoral degrees. 47 undergraduate majors. *Total enrollment:* 3,541. Undergraduates: 2,831. Freshmen:

572. Both federal and institutional methodology are used as a basis for awarding need-based institutional aid.

UNDERGRADUATE EXPENSES for 2016–2017 *Comprehensive fee:* $49,173 includes full-time tuition ($36,682), mandatory fees ($1040), and room and board ($11,451). *College room only:* $6870. Full-time tuition and fees vary according to course load, degree level, and program. Room and board charges vary according to board plan and housing facility. *Part-time tuition:* $1528 per unit. Part-time tuition and fees vary according to course load, degree level, and program.

FRESHMAN FINANCIAL AID (Fall 2016, est.) 521 applied for aid; of those 95% were deemed to have need. 100% of freshmen with need received aid; of those 2% had need fully met. *Average percent of need met:* 64% (excluding resources awarded to replace EFC). *Average financial aid package:* $30,636 (excluding resources awarded to replace EFC). 3% of all full-time freshmen had no need and received non-need-based gift aid.

UNDERGRADUATE FINANCIAL AID (Fall 2016, est.) 2,002 applied for aid; of those 91% were deemed to have need. 99% of undergraduates with need received aid; of those 3% had need fully met. *Average percent of need met:* 53% (excluding resources awarded to replace EFC). *Average financial aid package:* $27,165 (excluding resources awarded to replace EFC). 12% of all full-time undergraduates had no need and received non-need-based gift aid.

GIFT AID (NEED-BASED) *Total amount:* $47,086,827 (16% federal, 20% state, 64% institutional). *Receiving aid:* Freshmen: 80% (435); all full-time undergraduates: 69% (1,461). *Average award:* Freshmen: $19,743; Undergraduates: $17,115. *Scholarships, grants, and awards:* Federal Pell, FSEOG, state, private, college/university gift aid from institutional funds.

GIFT AID (NON-NEED-BASED) *Total amount:* $3,300,574 (98% institutional, 2% external sources). *Receiving aid:* Freshmen: 90% (485). Undergraduates: 82% (1,742). *Average award:* Freshmen: $15,605. Undergraduates: $9786. *Scholarships, grants, and awards by category:* Academic interests/achievement: general academic interests/achievements. *Creative arts/performance:* music. *Special achievements/activities:* community service, leadership. *Special characteristics:* children and siblings of alumni. *Tuition waivers:* Full or partial for employees or children of employees.

LOANS *Student loans:* $13,190,709 (93% need-based, 7% non-need-based). 86% of past graduating class borrowed through all loan programs. *Average indebtedness per student:* $32,805. *Average need-based loan:* Freshmen: $3504. Undergraduates: $4634. *Parent loans:* $6,490,146 (94% need-based, 6% non-need-based). *Programs:* Federal Direct (Subsidized and Unsubsidized Stafford, PLUS), Federal Nursing, college/university.

WORK-STUDY *Federal work-study:* Total amount: $1,475,457; jobs available. *State or other work-study/employment:* Part-time jobs available.

APPLYING FOR FINANCIAL AID *Required financial aid form:* FAFSA. *Financial aid deadline (priority):* 3/1. *Notification date:* Continuous beginning 3/1. Students must reply by 5/1.

CONTACT La Royce Housley, Director of Financial Aid, Mount Saint Mary's University, 12001 Chalon Road, Los Angeles, CA 90049, 310-954-4192 or toll-free 800-999-9893.
Website: http://www.msmu.edu/.

MOUNT ST. MARY'S UNIVERSITY
Emmitsburg, MD

Tuition & fees: $40,550	Average undergraduate aid package: $26,219

ABOUT THE INSTITUTION Independent Roman Catholic, coed. *Awards:* certificates, bachelor's, and master's degrees. 33 undergraduate majors. *Total enrollment:* 2,186. Undergraduates: 1,729. Freshmen: 417. Federal methodology is used as a basis for awarding need-based institutional aid.

UNDERGRADUATE EXPENSES for 2017–2018 *Application fee:* $45. *Comprehensive fee:* $53,380 includes full-time tuition ($39,200), mandatory fees ($1350), and room and board ($12,830). *College room only:* $6500. Full-time tuition and fees vary according to location and program. Room and board charges vary according to housing facility. *Part-time tuition:* $1275 per credit hour. Part-time tuition and fees vary according to location and program.

FRESHMAN FINANCIAL AID (Fall 2016, est.) 372 applied for aid; of those 87% were deemed to have need. 100% of freshmen with need received aid; of those 26% had need fully met. *Average percent of need met:* 75% (excluding resources

awarded to replace EFC). *Average financial aid package:* $28,795 (excluding resources awarded to replace EFC). 21% of all full-time freshmen had no need and received non-need-based gift aid.

UNDERGRADUATE FINANCIAL AID (Fall 2016, est.) 1,311 applied for aid; of those 88% were deemed to have need. 100% of undergraduates with need received aid; of those 24% had need fully met. *Average percent of need met:* 71% (excluding resources awarded to replace EFC). *Average financial aid package:* $26,219 (excluding resources awarded to replace EFC). 25% of all full-time undergraduates had no need and received non-need-based gift aid.

GIFT AID (NEED-BASED) *Total amount:* $23,531,603 (8% federal, 5% state, 84% institutional, 3% external sources). *Receiving aid:* Freshmen: 77% (323); all full-time undergraduates: 70% (1,145). *Average award:* Freshmen: $24,533; Undergraduates: $21,936. *Scholarships, grants, and awards:* Federal Pell, FSEOG, state, private, college/university gift aid from institutional funds.

GIFT AID (NON-NEED-BASED) *Total amount:* $9,701,001 (3% federal, 1% state, 87% institutional, 9% external sources). *Receiving aid:* Freshmen: 18% (76). Undergraduates: 13% (214). *Average award:* Freshmen: $19,615. Undergraduates: $17,586. *Scholarships, grants, and awards by category:* Academic interests/achievement: 1,377 awards ($23,617,741 total): general academic interests/achievements. *Creative arts/performance:* 11 awards ($40,000 total): art/fine arts. *Special achievements/activities:* 29 awards ($144,000 total): religious involvement. *Special characteristics:* 81 awards ($915,595 total): children of educators, children of faculty/staff, members of minority groups, siblings of current students. *Tuition waivers:* Full or partial for employees or children of employees. *ROTC:* Army cooperative.

LOANS *Student loans:* $11,921,999 (62% need-based, 38% non-need-based). 77% of past graduating class borrowed through all loan programs. *Average indebtedness per student:* $33,894. *Average need-based loan:* Freshmen: $4248. Undergraduates: $4636. *Parent loans:* $6,883,184 (46% need-based, 54% non-need-based). *Programs:* Federal Direct (Subsidized and Unsubsidized Stafford, PLUS), Perkins.

WORK-STUDY *Federal work-study:* Total amount: $210,000; 105 jobs averaging $1862. *State or other work-study/employment:* Total amount: $926,006 (83% need-based, 17% non-need-based). 665 part-time jobs averaging $1320.

ATHLETIC AWARDS Total amount: $3,556,100 (39% need-based, 61% non-need-based).

APPLYING FOR FINANCIAL AID *Required financial aid form:* FAFSA. *Financial aid deadline:* 3/1. *Notification date:* Continuous beginning 2/15. Students must reply by 5/1.

CONTACT Mr. David C. Reeder, Director of Financial Aid, Mount St. Mary's University, 16300 Old Emmitsburg Road, Emmitsburg, MD 21727-7799, 301-447-5207 or toll-free 800-448-4347. *Fax:* 301-447-5915. *E-mail:* reeder@msmary.edu.
Website: http://www.msmary.edu/.

MT. SIERRA COLLEGE
Monrovia, CA

Tuition & fees: N/R	Average undergraduate aid package: $12,320

ABOUT THE INSTITUTION Proprietary, coed. 10 undergraduate majors. Both federal and institutional methodology are used as a basis for awarding need-based institutional aid.

FRESHMAN FINANCIAL AID (Fall 2016, est.) 9 applied for aid; of those 100% were deemed to have need. 100% of freshmen with need received aid. *Average percent of need met:* 83% (excluding resources awarded to replace EFC). *Average financial aid package:* $12,100 (excluding resources awarded to replace EFC).

UNDERGRADUATE FINANCIAL AID (Fall 2016, est.) 173 applied for aid; of those 100% were deemed to have need. 100% of undergraduates with need received aid. *Average percent of need met:* 83% (excluding resources awarded to replace EFC). *Average financial aid package:* $12,320 (excluding resources awarded to replace EFC). 5% of all full-time undergraduates had no need and received non-need-based gift aid.

GIFT AID (NEED-BASED) *Total amount:* $981,219 (77% federal, 13% state, 10% institutional). *Receiving aid:* Freshmen: 64% (9); all full-time undergraduates: 73% (160). *Average award:* Freshmen: $9100; Undergraduates: $9100. *Scholarships, grants, and awards:* Federal Pell, FSEOG, private, college/university gift aid from institutional funds.

GIFT AID (NON-NEED-BASED) *Total amount:* $135,250 (100% institutional). *Receiving aid:* Undergraduates: 27% (60). *Average award:* Undergraduates: $3000.

LOANS *Student loans:* $1,379,912 (49% need-based, 51% non-need-based). 100% of past graduating class borrowed through all loan programs. *Average indebtedness per student:* $28,000. *Average need-based loan:* Freshmen: $5000. Undergraduates: $5000. *Parent loans:* $154,365 (100% non-need-based). *Programs:* Federal Direct (Subsidized and Unsubsidized Stafford, PLUS).

WORK-STUDY *Federal work-study:* Total amount: $35,320; 13 jobs averaging $2700.

APPLYING FOR FINANCIAL AID *Required financial aid forms:* FAFSA, institution's own form. *Financial aid deadline:* Continuous. *Notification date:* Continuous. Students must reply within 2 weeks of notification.

CONTACT Financial Aid Office, Mt. Sierra College, 800 Royal Oaks Drive, Suite 101, Monrovia, CA 91016, 888-828-8800 or toll-free 888-828-8000. *Website:* http://www.mtsierra.edu/.

MOUNT VERNON NAZARENE UNIVERSITY
Mount Vernon, OH

Tuition & fees: $28,090	Average undergraduate aid package: $18,251

ABOUT THE INSTITUTION Independent Nazarene, coed. *Awards:* associate, bachelor's, and master's degrees. 73 undergraduate majors. *Total enrollment:* 2,245. Undergraduates: 1,831. Freshmen: 387. Federal methodology is used as a basis for awarding need-based institutional aid.

UNDERGRADUATE EXPENSES for 2017–2018 *Application fee:* $25. *Comprehensive fee:* $35,944 includes full-time tuition ($27,840), mandatory fees ($250), and room and board ($7854). *College room only:* $4388. Full-time tuition and fees vary according to program. *Part-time tuition:* $773 per credit hour. Part-time tuition and fees vary according to course load and program.

FRESHMAN FINANCIAL AID (Fall 2016, est.) 346 applied for aid; of those 92% were deemed to have need. 100% of freshmen with need received aid; of those 35% had need fully met. *Average percent of need met:* 66% (excluding resources awarded to replace EFC). *Average financial aid package:* $23,264 (excluding resources awarded to replace EFC). 11% of all full-time freshmen had no need and received non-need-based gift aid.

UNDERGRADUATE FINANCIAL AID (Fall 2016, est.) 1,456 applied for aid; of those 87% were deemed to have need. 99% of undergraduates with need received aid; of those 42% had need fully met. *Average percent of need met:* 63% (excluding resources awarded to replace EFC). *Average financial aid package:* $18,251 (excluding resources awarded to replace EFC). 25% of all full-time undergraduates had no need and received non-need-based gift aid.

GIFT AID (NEED-BASED) *Total amount:* $18,300,434 (13% federal, 5% state, 78% institutional, 4% external sources). *Receiving aid:* Freshmen: 89% (319); all full-time undergraduates: 74% (1,254). *Average award:* Freshmen: $20,276; Undergraduates: $16,247. *Scholarships, grants, and awards:* Federal Pell, FSEOG, state, private, college/university gift aid from institutional funds.

GIFT AID (NON-NEED-BASED) *Total amount:* $2,836,850 (4% state, 93% institutional, 3% external sources). *Receiving aid:* Freshmen: 31% (112). Undergraduates: 31% (530). *Average award:* Freshmen: $13,799. Undergraduates: $12,652. *Scholarships, grants, and awards by category:* Academic interests/achievement: general academic interests/achievements. Creative arts/performance: art/fine arts, music. Special achievements/activities: general special achievements/activities, religious involvement. Special characteristics: children of faculty/staff, international students, members of minority groups, relatives of clergy, religious affiliation. *Tuition waivers:* Full or partial for employees or children of employees, senior citizens.

LOANS *Student loans:* $8,679,819 (92% need-based, 8% non-need-based). 82% of past graduating class borrowed through all loan programs. *Average indebtedness per student:* $21,564. *Average need-based loan:* Freshmen: $3241. Undergraduates: $3783. *Parent loans:* $2,133,555 (93% need-based, 7% non-need-based). *Programs:* Federal Direct (Subsidized and Unsubsidized Stafford, PLUS), Perkins, Federal Nursing, state, college/university, Charles E. Schell Foundation loans.

WORK-STUDY *Federal work-study:* Total amount: $126,029; jobs available. *State or other work-study/employment:* Total amount: $22,250 (100% non-need-based). Part-time jobs available.

ATHLETIC AWARDS Total amount: $966,448 (69% need-based, 31% non-need-based).

APPLYING FOR FINANCIAL AID *Required financial aid form:* FAFSA. *Financial aid deadline (priority):* 3/1. *Notification date:* Continuous beginning 3/1.

CONTACT Jared M. Sponseller, Director of Student Financial Services, Mount Vernon Nazarene University, 800 Martinsburg Road, Mount Vernon, OH 43050-9500, 866-686-8243 or toll-free 866-462-6868. *Fax:* 740-399-8682. *E-mail:* finaid@mvnu.edu. *Website:* http://www.mvnu.edu/.

MUHLENBERG COLLEGE
Allentown, PA

Tuition & fees: $48,310	Average undergraduate aid package: $33,371

ABOUT THE INSTITUTION Independent Lutheran Church, coed. *Awards:* certificates, associate, and bachelor's degrees. 37 undergraduate majors. *Total enrollment:* 2,408. Undergraduates: 2,408. Freshmen: 593. Institutional methodology is used as a basis for awarding need-based institutional aid.

UNDERGRADUATE EXPENSES for 2016–2017 *Application fee:* $50. *Comprehensive fee:* $59,400 includes full-time tuition ($47,825), mandatory fees ($485), and room and board ($11,090). *College room only:* $6025. Room and board charges vary according to board plan, housing facility, and location. Part-time tuition and fees vary according to program.

FRESHMAN FINANCIAL AID (Fall 2016, est.) 454 applied for aid; of those 77% were deemed to have need. 100% of freshmen with need received aid; of those 31% had need fully met. *Average percent of need met:* 87% (excluding resources awarded to replace EFC). *Average financial aid package:* $34,265 (excluding resources awarded to replace EFC). 34% of all full-time freshmen had no need and received non-need-based gift aid.

UNDERGRADUATE FINANCIAL AID (Fall 2016, est.) 1,491 applied for aid; of those 85% were deemed to have need. 99% of undergraduates with need received aid; of those 29% had need fully met. *Average percent of need met:* 87% (excluding resources awarded to replace EFC). *Average financial aid package:* $33,371 (excluding resources awarded to replace EFC). 36% of all full-time undergraduates had no need and received non-need-based gift aid.

GIFT AID (NEED-BASED) *Total amount:* $35,493,000 (5% federal, 2% state, 93% institutional). *Receiving aid:* Freshmen: 58% (346); all full-time undergraduates: 53% (1,233). *Average award:* Freshmen: $31,115; Undergraduates: $29,760. *Scholarships, grants, and awards:* Federal Pell, FSEOG, state, private, college/university gift aid from institutional funds, United Negro College Fund.

GIFT AID (NON-NEED-BASED) *Total amount:* $12,472,000 (97% institutional, 3% external sources). *Receiving aid:* Freshmen: 14% (83). Undergraduates: 9% (218). *Average award:* Freshmen: $12,645. Undergraduates: $12,817. *Scholarships, grants, and awards by category:* Academic interests/achievement: general academic interests/achievements. Creative arts/performance: art/fine arts, cinema/film/broadcasting, dance, music, performing arts, theater/drama. *Tuition waivers:* Full or partial for employees or children of employees. *ROTC:* Army cooperative.

LOANS *Student loans:* $10,912,000 (72% need-based, 28% non-need-based). 58% of past graduating class borrowed through all loan programs. *Average indebtedness per student:* $31,063. *Average need-based loan:* Freshmen: $3444. Undergraduates: $4514. *Programs:* Federal Direct (Subsidized and Unsubsidized Stafford, PLUS), Perkins.

WORK-STUDY *Federal work-study:* Total amount: $250,000; jobs available. *State or other work-study/employment:* Total amount: $300,000 (33% need-based, 67% non-need-based). Part-time jobs available.

APPLYING FOR FINANCIAL AID *Required financial aid forms:* FAFSA, institution's own form, CSS Financial Aid PROFILE, noncustodial (divorced/separated) parent's statement, business/farm supplement. *Financial aid deadline:* 3/1. *Notification date:* 4/1. Students must reply by 5/1.

CONTACT Mr. Greg Mitton, Director of Financial Aid, Muhlenberg College, 2400 Chew Street, Allentown, PA 18104-5586, 484-664-3175. *Fax:* 484-664-3234. *E-mail:* gregmitton@muhlenberg.edu.
Website: http://www.muhlenberg.edu/.

MULTNOMAH UNIVERSITY
Portland, OR

CONTACT Mrs. Mary J. McGlothlan, Director of Financial Aid, Multnomah University, 8435 NE Glisan Street, Portland, OR 97220-5898, 503-251-5337 or toll-free 877-251-6560. *Fax:* 503-445-5199. *E-mail:* mmcglothlan@multnomah.edu.
Website: http://www.multnomah.edu/.

MURRAY STATE UNIVERSITY
Murray, KY

Tuition & fees (KY res): $8400	Average undergraduate aid package: $12,577

ABOUT THE INSTITUTION State-supported, coed. *Awards:* certificates, associate, bachelor's, master's, and doctoral degrees. 65 undergraduate majors. *Total enrollment:* 10,495. Undergraduates: 8,886. Freshmen: 1,502. Federal methodology is used as a basis for awarding need-based institutional aid.
UNDERGRADUATE EXPENSES for 2016–2017 *Application fee:* $40. *Tuition, state resident:* full-time $8400; part-time $350 per credit hour. *Tuition, nonresident:* full-time $22,680; part-time $945 per credit hour. Full-time tuition and fees vary according to course load. *College room and board:* $8588; *Room only:* $5044. Room and board charges vary according to board plan and housing facility.
FRESHMAN FINANCIAL AID (Fall 2015) 1,252 applied for aid; of those 79% were deemed to have need. 100% of freshmen with need received aid; of those 26% had need fully met. *Average percent of need met:* 35% (excluding resources awarded to replace EFC). *Average financial aid package:* $12,919 (excluding resources awarded to replace EFC). 11% of all full-time freshmen had no need and received non-need-based gift aid.
UNDERGRADUATE FINANCIAL AID (Fall 2015) 5,353 applied for aid; of those 82% were deemed to have need. 100% of undergraduates with need received aid; of those 26% had need fully met. *Average percent of need met:* 31% (excluding resources awarded to replace EFC). *Average financial aid package:* $12,577 (excluding resources awarded to replace EFC). 7% of all full-time undergraduates had no need and received non-need-based gift aid.
GIFT AID (NEED-BASED) *Total amount:* $24,478,664 (51% federal, 21% state, 22% institutional, 6% external sources). *Receiving aid:* Freshmen: 62% (910); all full-time undergraduates: 53% (3,774). *Average award:* Freshmen: $6658; Undergraduates: $6089. *Scholarships, grants, and awards:* Federal Pell, FSEOG, state, private, college/university gift aid from institutional funds.
GIFT AID (NON-NEED-BASED) *Total amount:* $11,777,123 (1% federal, 20% state, 49% institutional, 30% external sources). *Receiving aid:* Freshmen: 9% (125). Undergraduates: 5% (333). *Average award:* Freshmen: $5927. Undergraduates: $5056. *Scholarships, grants, and awards by category: Academic interests/ achievement:* 2,033 awards ($3,807,313 total): agriculture, biological sciences, business, communication, computer science, education, engineering/technologies, English, general academic interests/achievements, health fields, home economics, humanities, international studies, mathematics, military science, physical sciences, pre-medicine, social sciences. *Creative arts/performance:* 155 awards ($241,967 total): art/ fine arts, dance, journalism/publications, music, theater/drama. *Special achievements/ activities:* 263 awards ($1,091,936 total): memberships, rodeo. *Special characteristics:* 612 awards ($1,889,754 total): adult students, children of faculty/staff, general special characteristics, local/state students, members of minority groups, out-of-state students. *Tuition waivers:* Full or partial for children of alumni, employees or children of employees, senior citizens. *ROTC:* Army.
LOANS *Student loans:* $31,393,490 (77% need-based, 23% non-need-based). 49% of past graduating class borrowed through all loan programs. *Average indebtedness per student:* $27,564. *Average need-based loan:* Freshmen: $4954. Undergraduates: $6265. *Parent loans:* $5,013,580 (41% need-based, 59% non-need-based). *Programs:* Federal Direct (Subsidized and Unsubsidized Stafford, PLUS), Perkins, Federal Nursing, college/university.

WORK-STUDY *Federal work-study:* 343 jobs averaging $1584. *State or other work-study/employment:* Total amount: $3,864,662 (38% need-based, 62% non-need-based). 1,993 part-time jobs averaging $2122.
ATHLETIC AWARDS Total amount: $3,972,710 (46% need-based, 54% non-need-based).
APPLYING FOR FINANCIAL AID *Required financial aid forms:* FAFSA, general scholarship application form, application for summer term institutional loans. *Financial aid deadline (priority):* 10/1. *Notification date:* Continuous beginning 3/15. Students must reply by 5/1.
CONTACT Janet Balok, Director of Financial Aid, Murray State University, 500 Sparks Hall, Murray, KY 42071-0009, 270-809-2546 or toll-free 800-272-4678. *Fax:* 270-809-3116. *E-mail:* jbalok@murraystate.edu.
Website: http://www.murraystate.edu/.

MUSICIANS INSTITUTE
Hollywood, CA

CONTACT Director of Financial Aid, Musicians Institute, 1655 North McCadden Place, Hollywood, CA 90028, 323-462-1384 or toll-free 800-255-PLAY.
Website: http://www.mi.edu/.

MUSKINGUM UNIVERSITY
New Concord, OH

Tuition & fees: $27,812	Average undergraduate aid package: $24,239

ABOUT THE INSTITUTION Independent Presbyterian Church (U.S.A.), coed. *Awards:* bachelor's and master's degrees. 73 undergraduate majors. *Total enrollment:* 2,121. Undergraduates: 1,549. Freshmen: 319. Federal methodology is used as a basis for awarding need-based institutional aid.
UNDERGRADUATE EXPENSES for 2017–2018 *One-time required fee:* $250. *Comprehensive fee:* $38,852 includes full-time tuition ($26,900), mandatory fees ($912), and room and board ($11,040). *College room only:* $5720. Room and board charges vary according to board plan. *Part-time tuition:* $595 per credit hour. Part-time tuition and fees vary according to course load.
FRESHMAN FINANCIAL AID (Fall 2016, est.) 300 applied for aid; of those 95% were deemed to have need. 100% of freshmen with need received aid; of those 26% had need fully met. *Average percent of need met:* 79% (excluding resources awarded to replace EFC). *Average financial aid package:* $25,880 (excluding resources awarded to replace EFC). 10% of all full-time freshmen had no need and received non-need-based gift aid.
UNDERGRADUATE FINANCIAL AID (Fall 2016, est.) 1,156 applied for aid; of those 95% were deemed to have need. 100% of undergraduates with need received aid; of those 17% had need fully met. *Average percent of need met:* 77% (excluding resources awarded to replace EFC). *Average financial aid package:* $24,239 (excluding resources awarded to replace EFC). 14% of all full-time undergraduates had no need and received non-need-based gift aid.
GIFT AID (NEED-BASED) *Total amount:* $20,804,862 (15% federal, 6% state, 77% institutional, 2% external sources). *Receiving aid:* Freshmen: 89% (284); all full-time undergraduates: 85% (1,093). *Average award:* Freshmen: $20,701; Undergraduates: $19,222. *Scholarships, grants, and awards:* Federal Pell, FSEOG, state, private, college/university gift aid from institutional funds.
GIFT AID (NON-NEED-BASED) *Total amount:* $2,843,381 (1% state, 97% institutional, 2% external sources). *Receiving aid:* Freshmen: 83% (265). Undergraduates: 77% (994). *Average award:* Freshmen: $14,490. Undergraduates: $13,018. *Scholarships, grants, and awards by category: Academic interests/ achievement:* 658 awards ($8,784,425 total): biological sciences, computer science, engineering/technologies, general academic interests/achievements, mathematics, physical sciences, premedicine. *Creative arts/performance:* 121 awards ($187,570 total): applied art and design, art/fine arts, debating, journalism/publications, music, theater/drama. *Special achievements/activities:* 240 awards ($222,950 total): community service, junior miss, leadership. *Special characteristics:* 861 awards ($1,838,401 total): children and siblings of alumni, ethnic background, international students, local/ state students, members of minority groups, previous college experience, relatives of

clergy, religious affiliation, siblings of current students. *Tuition waivers:* Full or partial for children of alumni, employees or children of employees.

LOANS *Student loans:* $12,586,238 (76% need-based, 24% non-need-based). 78% of past graduating class borrowed through all loan programs. *Average indebtedness per student:* $33,490. *Average need-based loan:* Freshmen: $4584. Undergraduates: $5331. *Parent loans:* $3,444,710 (46% need-based, 54% non-need-based). *Programs:* Federal Direct (Subsidized and Unsubsidized Stafford, PLUS), Perkins, Federal Nursing, college/university.

WORK-STUDY *Federal work-study:* Total amount: $149,639; 394 jobs averaging $1000. *State or other work-study/employment:* Total amount: $500,000 (60% need-based, 40% non-need-based). Part-time jobs available.

APPLYING FOR FINANCIAL AID *Required financial aid form:* FAFSA. *Financial aid deadline (priority):* 3/1. *Notification date:* Continuous beginning 12/1. Students must reply by 5/1 or within 2 weeks of notification.

CONTACT Mrs. Beth DaLonzo, Senior Director of Admission and Student Financial Services, Muskingum University, 163 Stormont Street, New Concord, OH 43762, 740-826-8139 or toll-free 800-752-6082. *Fax:* 740-826-8100. *E-mail:* bdalonzo@muskingum.edu.
Website: http://www.muskingum.edu/.

NAROPA UNIVERSITY
Boulder, CO

ABOUT THE INSTITUTION Independent, coed. *Awards:* bachelor's and master's degrees. 14 undergraduate majors. *Total enrollment:* 942. Undergraduates: 397. Freshmen: 45.

GIFT AID (NEED-BASED) *Scholarships, grants, and awards:* Federal Pell, FSEOG, state, private, college/university gift aid from institutional funds.

LOANS *Programs:* Federal Direct (Subsidized and Unsubsidized Stafford, PLUS), Perkins.

WORK-STUDY *Federal work-study:* 168 jobs averaging $3077. *State or other work-study/employment:* Total amount: $40,500 (100% need-based). 11 part-time jobs averaging $2455.

APPLYING FOR FINANCIAL AID *Required financial aid form:* FAFSA.

CONTACT Ms. Nancy Morrell, Director of Student Financial Services, Naropa University, 2130 Arapahoe Avenue, Boulder, CO 80302-6697, 303-546-3534 or toll-free 800-772-6951. *Fax:* 303-546-3536. *E-mail:* finaid@naropa.edu.
Website: http://www.naropa.edu/.

NATIONAL AMERICAN UNIVERSITY
Centennial, CO

CONTACT Financial Aid Office, National American University, 8242 South University Boulevard, Suite 100, Centennial, CO 80122, 303-542-7000 or toll-free 877-628-5211.
Website: http://www.national.edu/.

NATIONAL AMERICAN UNIVERSITY
Colorado Springs, CO

CONTACT Financial Aid Office, National American University, 1079 Space Center Drive, Suite 140, Colorado Springs, CO 80915, 719-208-3800 or toll-free 855-369-9397.
Website: http://www.national.edu/.

NATIONAL AMERICAN UNIVERSITY
Colorado Springs, CO

CONTACT Financial Aid Coordinator, National American University, 2577 North Chelton Road, Colorado Springs, CO 80909, 719-471-4205 or toll-free 855-369-9397.
Website: http://www.national.edu/.

NATIONAL AMERICAN UNIVERSITY
Overland Park, KS

CONTACT Financial Aid Office, National American University, 10310 Mastin Street, Overland Park, KS 66212, 913-981-8700 or toll-free 866-628-1288.
Website: http://www.national.edu/.

NATIONAL AMERICAN UNIVERSITY
Bloomington, MN

CONTACT Financial Aid Office, National American University, 7801 Metro Parkway, Suite 200, Bloomington, MN 55425, 952-356-3600 or toll-free 866-628-6387.
Website: http://www.national.edu/.

NATIONAL AMERICAN UNIVERSITY
Burnsville, MN

CONTACT Financial Aid Office, National American University, 513 West Travelers Trail, Burnsville, MN 55337, 952-563-1250 or toll-free 866-628-6387.
Website: http://www.national.edu/.

NATIONAL AMERICAN UNIVERSITY
Roseville, MN

CONTACT Financial Aid Office, National American University, 1550 West Highway 36, Roseville, MN 55113, 651-855-6300 or toll-free 866-628-6387.
Website: http://www.national.edu/.

NATIONAL AMERICAN UNIVERSITY
Kansas City, MO

CONTACT Mary Anderson, Coordinator of Financial Aid, National American University, 4200 Blue Ridge, Kansas City, MO 64133, 816-353-4554 or toll-free 866-628-1288. *Fax:* 816-353-1176.
Website: http://www.national.edu/.

NATIONAL AMERICAN UNIVERSITY
Lee's Summit, MO

CONTACT Financial Aid Office, National American University, 401 NW Murray Road, Lee's Summit, MO 64081, 816-600-3900 or toll-free 866-628-1288.
Website: http://www.national.edu/.

NATIONAL AMERICAN UNIVERSITY
Bellevue, NE

CONTACT Financial Aid Office, National American University, 3604 Summit Plaza Drive, Bellevue, NE 68123, 402-972-4250.
Website: http://www.national.edu/.

NATIONAL AMERICAN UNIVERSITY
Albuquerque, NM

CONTACT Financial Aid Office, National American University, 10131 Coors Boulevard NW, Suite 1-01, Albuquerque, NM 87114, 505-348-3750 or toll-free 800-895-9904.
Website: http://www.national.edu/.

NATIONAL AMERICAN UNIVERSITY
Albuquerque, NM

CONTACT Director of Financial Aid, National American University, 321 Kansas City Street, Rapid City, SD 57701, 605-394-4800 or toll-free 800-895-9904.
Website: http://www.national.edu/.

NATIONAL AMERICAN UNIVERSITY
Tulsa, OK

CONTACT Financial Aid Office, National American University, 8040 South Sheridan Road, Tulsa, OK 74133, 918-879-8400 or toll-free 800-209-0338.
Website: http://www.national.edu/.

NATIONAL AMERICAN UNIVERSITY
Ellsworth AFB, SD

CONTACT Financial Aid Office, National American University, 1000 Ellsworth Street, Rushmore Center, Suite 2400B, Ellsworth AFB, SD 57706, 605-718-6550.
Website: http://www.national.edu/.

NATIONAL AMERICAN UNIVERSITY
Rapid City, SD

CONTACT Financial Aid Director, National American University, PO Box 1780, Rapid City, SD 57709-1780, 605-721-5213 or toll-free 800-209-0490.
Website: http://www.national.edu/.

NATIONAL AMERICAN UNIVERSITY
Sioux Falls, SD

CONTACT Ms. Rhonda Kohnen, Financial Aid Coordinator, National American University, 2801 South Kiwanis Avenue, Suite 100, Sioux Falls, SD 57105-4293, 605-334-5430 or toll-free 800-388-5430. *Fax:* 605-334-1575. *E-mail:* rkohnen@national.edu.
Website: http://www.national.edu/.

NATIONAL AMERICAN UNIVERSITY
Mesquite, TX

CONTACT Financial Aid Office, National American University, 18600 LBJ Freeway, Mesquite, TX 75150, 972-773-8800 or toll-free 800-548-0605.
Website: http://www.national.edu/.

NATIONAL LOUIS UNIVERSITY
Chicago, IL

CONTACT Janet Jazwiec, Assistant Director of Student Finance, National Louis University, 1000 Capitol Drive, Wheeling, IL 60090, 847-947-5453 or toll-free 888-658-8632. *Fax:* 847-947-5453. *E-mail:* jjazwiec@nl.edu.
Website: http://www.nl.edu/.

NATIONAL PARALEGAL COLLEGE
Phoenix, AZ

CONTACT Financial Aid Office, National Paralegal College, 717 East Maryland Avenue, Suite 115, Phoenix, AZ 85014, 845-371-9101 or toll-free 800-371-6105.
Website: http://nationalparalegal.edu/.

NATIONAL UNIVERSITY
La Jolla, CA

Tuition & fees: $13,032	Average undergraduate aid package: $7768

ABOUT THE INSTITUTION Independent, coed. *Awards:* certificates, associate, bachelor's, and master's degrees. 54 undergraduate majors. *Total enrollment:* 17,173. Undergraduates: 8,314. Freshmen: 117. Both federal and institutional methodology are used as a basis for awarding need-based institutional aid.

UNDERGRADUATE EXPENSES for 2017–2018 *Application fee:* $60. *One-time required fee:* $60. *Tuition:* full-time $13,032; part-time $362 per unit.

FRESHMAN FINANCIAL AID (Fall 2015) 10 applied for aid; of those 70% were deemed to have need. 86% of freshmen with need received aid. *Average percent of need met:* 44% (excluding resources awarded to replace EFC). *Average financial aid package:* $4936 (excluding resources awarded to replace EFC).

UNDERGRADUATE FINANCIAL AID (Fall 2015) 4,546 applied for aid; of those 85% were deemed to have need. 94% of undergraduates with need received aid; of those 6% had need fully met. *Average percent of need met:* 48% (excluding resources awarded to replace EFC). *Average financial aid package:* $7768 (excluding resources awarded to replace EFC). 1% of all full-time undergraduates had no need and received non-need-based gift aid.

GIFT AID (NEED-BASED) *Total amount:* $2,985,079 (32% federal, 65% state, 2% institutional, 1% external sources). *Receiving aid:* Freshmen: 17% (4); all full-time undergraduates: 31% (2,501). *Average award:* Freshmen: $1632; Undergraduates: $3240. *Scholarships, grants, and awards:* Federal Pell, FSEOG, state, college/university gift aid from institutional funds.

GIFT AID (NON-NEED-BASED) *Total amount:* $1,706,829 (23% federal, 77% institutional). *Receiving aid:* Freshmen: 4% (1). Undergraduates: 8% (621). *Average award:* Undergraduates: $2076. *Scholarships, grants, and awards by category:* Academic interests/achievement: 685 awards ($1,319,740 total): general academic interests/achievements. Special achievements/activities: leadership. *Tuition waivers:* Full or partial for employees or children of employees. *ROTC:* Army cooperative, Air Force cooperative.

LOANS *Student loans:* $38,368,176 (40% need-based, 60% non-need-based). 74% of past graduating class borrowed through all loan programs. *Average indebtedness per student:* $52,986. *Average need-based loan:* Freshmen: $3500. Undergraduates: $5505. *Parent loans:* $776,221 (100% non-need-based). *Programs:* Federal Direct (Subsidized and Unsubsidized Stafford, PLUS), Perkins, college/university.

WORK-STUDY *Federal work-study:* jobs available.

APPLYING FOR FINANCIAL AID *Required financial aid forms:* FAFSA, institution's own form. *Financial aid deadline:* Continuous. *Notification date:* Continuous beginning 6/30.

CONTACT Valerie Ryan, Director of Financial Aid, National University, 9980 Carroll Canyon, San Diego, CA 92131, 858-642-8500 or toll-free 800-628-8648. *Fax:* 858-642-8720. *E-mail:* vryan@nu.edu.
Website: http://www.nu.edu/.

NATIONAL UNIVERSITY COLLEGE
Bayamón, PR

CONTACT Ms. Elizabeth Cruz, Institutional Director of Financial Aid, National University College, PO Box 2036, Bayamon, PR 00961, 787-780-5134 Ext. 4021 or toll-free 800-780-5134. *E-mail:* ecruz@nuc.edu. *Website:* http://www.nuc.edu/.

NATIONAL UNIVERSITY COLLEGE
Caguas, PR

CONTACT Financial Aid Office, National University College, 190 Avenida Gautier Benitez Esquina Avenida Federico Degatau, Caguas, PR 00725, 787-653-4733 or toll-free 800-780-5134. *Website:* http://www.nuc.edu/.

NATIONAL UNIVERSITY COLLEGE
Ponce, PR

CONTACT Financial Aid Office, National University College, PO Box 801243, Ponce, PR 00716, 787-840-4474. *Website:* http://www.nuc.edu/.

NATIONAL UNIVERSITY COLLEGE
Rio Grande, PR

CONTACT Financial Aid Office, National University College, Carretera #3 Km. 22.1, Bo. Ciénaga Baja, Rio Grande, PR 00745, 787-809-5100 or toll-free 800-981-0812. *Website:* http://www.nuc.edu/.

NAVAJO TECHNICAL UNIVERSITY
Crownpoint, NM

ABOUT THE INSTITUTION Independent, coed. 13 undergraduate majors.
GIFT AID (NEED-BASED) *Scholarships, grants, and awards:* Federal Pell, FSEOG, tribal scholarships, American Indian College Fund, Academic Competitiveness Grants.
APPLYING FOR FINANCIAL AID *Required financial aid forms:* FAFSA, institution's own form.
CONTACT Office of Financial Aid, Navajo Technical University, PO Box 849, Crownpoint, NM 87313, 505-786-4309. *Website:* http://www.navajotech.edu/.

NAZARENE BIBLE COLLEGE
Colorado Springs, CO

CONTACT Miss Jenny Madsen, Director of Financial Aid, Nazarene Bible College, 1111 Academy Park Loop, Colorado Springs, CO 80910-3717, 719-884-5051 or toll-free 800-873-3873. *Fax:* 719-884-5199. *Website:* http://www.nbc.edu/.

NAZARETH COLLEGE OF ROCHESTER
Rochester, NY

Tuition & fees: $32,424	Average undergraduate aid package: $26,668

ABOUT THE INSTITUTION Independent, coed. *Awards:* certificates, bachelor's, master's, and doctoral degrees. 75 undergraduate majors. *Total enrollment:* 2,883. Undergraduates: 2,159. Freshmen: 517. Federal methodology is used as a basis for awarding need-based institutional aid.
UNDERGRADUATE EXPENSES for 2017–2018 *Application fee:* $45. *Comprehensive fee:* $45,574 includes full-time tuition ($31,024), mandatory fees ($1400), and room and board ($13,150). Full-time tuition and fees vary according to course load, program, and reciprocity agreements. Room and board charges vary according to board plan and housing facility. *Part-time tuition:* $740 per credit hour. *Part-time fees:* $80 per term.
FRESHMAN FINANCIAL AID (Fall 2016, est.) 498 applied for aid; of those 90% were deemed to have need. 100% of freshmen with need received aid; of those 42% had need fully met. *Average percent of need met:* 85% (excluding resources awarded to replace EFC). *Average financial aid package:* $26,585 (excluding resources awarded to replace EFC). 13% of all full-time freshmen had no need and received non-need-based gift aid.
UNDERGRADUATE FINANCIAL AID (Fall 2016, est.) 1,852 applied for aid; of those 90% were deemed to have need. 100% of undergraduates with need received aid; of those 32% had need fully met. *Average percent of need met:* 80% (excluding resources awarded to replace EFC). *Average financial aid package:* $26,668 (excluding resources awarded to replace EFC). 18% of all full-time undergraduates had no need and received non-need-based gift aid.
GIFT AID (NEED-BASED) *Total amount:* $28,184,635 (10% federal, 9% state, 78% institutional, 3% external sources). *Receiving aid:* Freshmen: 87% (449); all full-time undergraduates: 82% (1,667). *Average award:* Freshmen: $18,244; Undergraduates: $16,818. *Scholarships, grants, and awards:* Federal Pell, FSEOG, state, private, college/university gift aid from institutional funds, Federal Nursing.
GIFT AID (NON-NEED-BASED) *Total amount:* $5,577,483 (1% state, 93% institutional, 6% external sources). *Receiving aid:* Freshmen: 43% (221). Undergraduates: 29% (585). *Average award:* Freshmen: $18,512. Undergraduates: $16,510. *Scholarships, grants, and awards by category:* Academic interests/achievement: $17,732,469 total: general academic interests/achievements. *Creative arts/performance:* $870,475 total: art/fine arts, music, theater/drama. *Special achievements/activities:* $41,250 total: leadership. *Special characteristics:* $3,457,790 total: children and siblings of alumni, children of faculty/staff, ethnic background, out-of-state students, siblings of current students, veterans. *Tuition waivers:* Full or partial for minority students, children of alumni, employees or children of employees. *ROTC:* Army cooperative, Air Force cooperative.
LOANS *Student loans:* $18,359,812 (80% need-based, 20% non-need-based). 82% of past graduating class borrowed through all loan programs. *Average indebtedness per student:* $40,567. *Average need-based loan:* Freshmen: $3389. Undergraduates: $4493. *Parent loans:* $6,884,509 (54% need-based, 46% non-need-based). *Programs:* Federal Direct (Subsidized and Unsubsidized Stafford, PLUS), Perkins, Federal Nursing.
WORK-STUDY *Federal work-study:* Total amount: $2,290,353; 1,054 jobs averaging $2070.
APPLYING FOR FINANCIAL AID *Required financial aid forms:* FAFSA, state aid form. *Financial aid deadline (priority):* 2/1. *Notification date:* Continuous beginning 1/15. Students must reply by 5/1 or within 2 weeks of notification.
CONTACT Janice Scheutzow, Director of Financial Aid, Nazareth College of Rochester, 4245 East Avenue, Rochester, NY 14618-3790, 585-389-2310 or toll-free 800-462-3944. *Fax:* 585-389-2317. *E-mail:* jscheut1@naz.edu. *Website:* http://www.naz.edu/.

NEBRASKA CHRISTIAN COLLEGE OF HOPE INTERNATIONAL UNIVERSITY
Papillion, NE

CONTACT Mrs. Sarah Nigro, Director of Financial Aid, Nebraska Christian College of Hope International University, 12550 South 114th Street, Papillion, NE 68046, 402-935-9400. *Fax:* 402-935-9500. *E-mail:* snigro@nechristian.edu. *Website:* http://www.nechristian.edu/.

NEBRASKA METHODIST COLLEGE
Omaha, NE

Tuition & fees: $16,088	Average undergraduate aid package: $9043

ABOUT THE INSTITUTION Independent United Methodist Church, coed. *Awards:* certificates, associate, bachelor's, master's, and doctoral degrees. 11 undergraduate majors. *Total enrollment:* 1,088. Undergraduates: 865. Freshmen: 44. Federal methodology is used as a basis for awarding need-based institutional aid.

UNDERGRADUATE EXPENSES for 2017–2018 Application fee: $25. *Tuition:* full-time $15,768; part-time $584 per credit hour. *Required fees:* full-time $320; $160 per term. Full-time tuition and fees vary according to course load, degree level, and program. Part-time tuition and fees vary according to course load, degree level, and program.

FRESHMAN FINANCIAL AID (Fall 2016, est.) 44 applied for aid; of those 61% were deemed to have need. 100% of freshmen with need received aid; of those 11% had need fully met. *Average percent of need met:* 46% (excluding resources awarded to replace EFC). *Average financial aid package:* $8748 (excluding resources awarded to replace EFC). 39% of all full-time freshmen had no need and received non-need-based gift aid.

UNDERGRADUATE FINANCIAL AID (Fall 2016, est.) 430 applied for aid; of those 88% were deemed to have need. 99% of undergraduates with need received aid; of those 3% had need fully met. *Average percent of need met:* 32% (excluding resources awarded to replace EFC). *Average financial aid package:* $9043 (excluding resources awarded to replace EFC). 15% of all full-time undergraduates had no need and received non-need-based gift aid.

GIFT AID (NEED-BASED) Total amount: $2,816,451 (40% federal, 7% state, 42% institutional, 11% external sources). *Receiving aid:* Freshmen: 59% (26); all full-time undergraduates: 66% (309). *Average award:* Freshmen: $5588; Undergraduates: $6101. *Scholarships, grants, and awards:* Federal Pell, FSEOG, state, private, college/university gift aid from institutional funds, Federal Nursing.

GIFT AID (NON-NEED-BASED) Total amount: $459,268 (1% state, 79% institutional, 20% external sources). *Receiving aid:* Freshmen: 2% (1). Undergraduates: 1% (5). *Average award:* Freshmen: $3482. Undergraduates: $3980. *Scholarships, grants, and awards by category:* Academic interests/achievement: general academic interests/achievements, home economics. *Special achievements/activities:* general special achievements/activities, leadership, memberships. *Special characteristics:* children of faculty/staff, religious affiliation. *Tuition waivers:* Full or partial for employees or children of employees. *ROTC:* Air Force cooperative.

LOANS Student loans: $7,045,546 (86% need-based, 14% non-need-based). 100% of past graduating class borrowed through all loan programs. *Average indebtedness per student:* $28,461. *Average need-based loan:* Freshmen: $3449. Undergraduates: $4342. *Parent loans:* $1,092,171 (51% need-based, 49% non-need-based). *Programs:* Federal Direct (Subsidized and Unsubsidized Stafford, PLUS), Perkins, Federal Nursing, private loans.

WORK-STUDY Federal work-study: Total amount: $26,734; 27 jobs averaging $1500.

APPLYING FOR FINANCIAL AID Required financial aid forms: FAFSA, institution's own form. *Financial aid deadline (priority):* 3/1. *Notification date:* Continuous beginning 3/15. Students must reply within 3 weeks of notification.

CONTACT Ms. Penny James, Director of Financial Aid, Nebraska Methodist College, The Josie Harper Campus, 720 North 87th Street, Omaha, NE 68114-3426, 402-354-7225 or toll-free 800-335-5510. *Fax:* 402-354-7020. *E-mail:* penny.james@methodistcollege.edu. *Website:* http://www.methodistcollege.edu/.

NEBRASKA WESLEYAN UNIVERSITY
Lincoln, NE

CONTACT Mr. Thomas J. Ochsner, Director of Scholarships and Financial Aid, Nebraska Wesleyan University, 5000 Saint Paul Avenue, Lincoln, NE 68504, 402-465-2212 or toll-free 800-541-3818. *Fax:* 402-465-2194. *E-mail:* tjo@nebrwesleyan.edu. *Website:* http://www.nebrwesleyan.edu/.

NER ISRAEL RABBINICAL COLLEGE
Baltimore, MD

CONTACT Mr. Moshe Pelberg, Financial Aid Administrator, Ner Israel Rabbinical College, 400 Mount Wilson Lane, Baltimore, MD 21208, 410-484-7200.

NEUMANN UNIVERSITY
Aston, PA

Tuition & fees: $28,580	Average undergraduate aid package: $16,971

ABOUT THE INSTITUTION Independent Roman Catholic, coed. *Awards:* certificates, associate, bachelor's, master's, and doctoral degrees. 22 undergraduate majors. *Total enrollment:* 3,011. Undergraduates: 2,278. Freshmen: 375. Institutional methodology is used as a basis for awarding need-based institutional aid.

UNDERGRADUATE EXPENSES for 2016–2017 Application fee: $35. *Comprehensive fee:* $40,738 includes full-time tuition ($27,340), mandatory fees ($1240), and room and board ($12,158). *College room only:* $7314. Full-time tuition and fees vary according to degree level. Room and board charges vary according to board plan and housing facility. *Part-time tuition:* $625 per credit hour. *Part-time fees:* $80 per term. Part-time tuition and fees vary according to degree level.

FRESHMAN FINANCIAL AID (Fall 2016, est.) 360 applied for aid; of those 91% were deemed to have need. 100% of freshmen with need received aid. *Average percent of need met:* 70% (excluding resources awarded to replace EFC). *Average financial aid package:* $23,340 (excluding resources awarded to replace EFC). 12% of all full-time freshmen had no need and received non-need-based gift aid.

UNDERGRADUATE FINANCIAL AID (Fall 2016, est.) 1,495 applied for aid; of those 89% were deemed to have need. 100% of undergraduates with need received aid. *Average percent of need met:* 70% (excluding resources awarded to replace EFC). *Average financial aid package:* $16,971 (excluding resources awarded to replace EFC). 15% of all full-time undergraduates had no need and received non-need-based gift aid.

GIFT AID (NEED-BASED) Total amount: $21,817,259 (18% federal, 10% state, 71% institutional, 1% external sources). *Receiving aid:* Freshmen: 70% (262); all full-time undergraduates: 69% (1,109). *Average award:* Freshmen: $10,145; Undergraduates: $7460. *Scholarships, grants, and awards:* Federal Pell, FSEOG, state, private, college/university gift aid from institutional funds.

GIFT AID (NON-NEED-BASED) Total amount: $2,490,311 (99% institutional, 1% external sources). *Receiving aid:* Freshmen: 87% (328). Undergraduates: 80% (1,279). *Average award:* Freshmen: $10,120. Undergraduates: $9707. *Scholarships, grants, and awards by category:* Academic interests/achievement: general academic interests/achievements. *Tuition waivers:* Full or partial for employees or children of employees. *ROTC:* Army cooperative, Air Force cooperative.

LOANS Student loans: $15,963,226 (98% need-based, 2% non-need-based). 90% of past graduating class borrowed through all loan programs. *Average need-based loan:* Freshmen: $3406. Undergraduates: $4462. *Parent loans:* $4,855,757 (89% need-based, 11% non-need-based). *Programs:* Federal Direct (Subsidized and Unsubsidized Stafford, PLUS), Federal Nursing.

WORK-STUDY Federal work-study: Total amount: $2,052,465; jobs available. *State or other work-study/employment:* Part-time jobs available.

APPLYING FOR FINANCIAL AID Required financial aid forms: FAFSA, state aid form. *Financial aid deadline:* Continuous. *Notification date:* Continuous beginning 3/1. Students must reply by 5/1 or within 2 weeks of notification.

CONTACT Ms. Andrea Del Vacchio, Director of Financial Assistance, Neumann University, One Neumann Drive, Aston, PA 19014-1298, 610-558-5532 or toll-free 800-963-8626. *Fax:* 610-558-5521. *E-mail:* vanhorna@neumann.edu. *Website:* http://www.neumann.edu/.

NEUMONT UNIVERSITY
Salt Lake City, UT

ABOUT THE INSTITUTION Proprietary, coed. *Awards:* bachelor's degrees. 15 undergraduate majors. *Total enrollment:* 429. Undergraduates: 429. Freshmen: 170.

GIFT AID (NEED-BASED) *Scholarships, grants, and awards:* Federal Pell, FSEOG, private, college/university gift aid from institutional funds.

GIFT AID (NON-NEED-BASED) *Scholarships, grants, and awards by category:* Academic interests/achievement: computer science, general academic interests/achievements. *Special achievements/activities:* community service, religious involvement. *Special characteristics:* children of faculty/staff, international students, local/state students, veterans.

LOANS *Programs:* Federal Direct (Subsidized and Unsubsidized Stafford, PLUS), college/university.

APPLYING FOR FINANCIAL AID *Required financial aid forms:* FAFSA, institution's own form.

CONTACT Mr. Nate Blanchard, Director of Financial Aid, Neumont University, 143 South Main Street, Salt Lake City, UT 84111, 801-302-2873 or toll-free 888-NEUMONT. *Fax:* 801-302-2834. *E-mail:* nate.blanchard@neumont.edu. *Website:* http://www.neumont.edu/.

NEVADA STATE COLLEGE
Henderson, NV

ABOUT THE INSTITUTION State-supported, coed. *Awards:* bachelor's degrees. 35 undergraduate majors. *Total enrollment:* 3,747. Undergraduates: 3,747. Freshmen: 282.

GIFT AID (NEED-BASED) *Scholarships, grants, and awards:* Federal Pell, FSEOG, state.

CONTACT Anthony Morrone, Director of Financial Aid, Nevada State College, 1124 Nevada State Drive, Henderson, NV 89002, 702-992-2150. *Fax:* 702-992-2151. *E-mail:* finaid@nsc.edu. *Website:* http://www.nsc.edu/.

NEWBERRY COLLEGE
Newberry, SC

Tuition & fees: $25,600	Average undergraduate aid package: $21,976

ABOUT THE INSTITUTION Independent Evangelical Lutheran, coed. *Awards:* bachelor's degrees. 34 undergraduate majors. *Total enrollment:* 1,070. Undergraduates: 1,070. Freshmen: 285. Federal methodology is used as a basis for awarding need-based institutional aid.

UNDERGRADUATE EXPENSES for 2016–2017 *Application fee:* $30. *Comprehensive fee:* $35,444 includes full-time tuition ($23,500), mandatory fees ($2100), and room and board ($9844). Full-time tuition and fees vary according to course load and student level. Room and board charges vary according to board plan and housing facility. *Part-time tuition:* $735 per credit hour. *Part-time fees:* $67.50 per credit hour. Part-time tuition and fees vary according to course load and student level. *Payment plan:* Guaranteed tuition.

FRESHMAN FINANCIAL AID (Fall 2015) 256 applied for aid; of those 94% were deemed to have need. 100% of freshmen with need received aid; of those 13% had need fully met. *Average percent of need met:* 67% (excluding resources awarded to replace EFC). *Average financial aid package:* $22,048 (excluding resources awarded to replace EFC). 9% of all full-time freshmen had no need and received non-need-based gift aid.

UNDERGRADUATE FINANCIAL AID (Fall 2015) 974 applied for aid; of those 93% were deemed to have need. 100% of undergraduates with need received aid; of those 14% had need fully met. *Average percent of need met:* 66% (excluding resources awarded to replace EFC). *Average financial aid package:* $21,976 (excluding resources awarded to replace EFC). 12% of all full-time undergraduates had no need and received non-need-based gift aid.

GIFT AID (NEED-BASED) *Total amount:* $15,264,920 (14% federal, 20% state, 61% institutional, 5% external sources). *Receiving aid:* Freshmen: 90% (240); all full-time undergraduates: 87% (904). *Average award:* Freshmen: $19,607; Undergraduates: $18,730. *Scholarships, grants, and awards:* Federal Pell, FSEOG, state, private, college/university gift aid from institutional funds.

GIFT AID (NON-NEED-BASED) *Total amount:* $2,324,762 (23% state, 71% institutional, 6% external sources). *Receiving aid:* Freshmen: 12% (32). Undergraduates: 11% (117). *Average award:* Freshmen: $10,674. Undergraduates: $9928. *Scholarships, grants, and awards by category:* Academic interests/achievement: biological sciences, business, communication, education, foreign languages, general academic interests/achievements, humanities, mathematics, physical sciences, religion/biblical studies, social sciences. *Creative arts/performance:* music, theater/drama. *Special achievements/activities:* cheerleading/drum major, religious involvement. *Special characteristics:* children and siblings of alumni, children of faculty/staff, international students, local/state students, relatives of clergy, religious affiliation, siblings of current students. *Tuition waivers:* Full or partial for employees or children of employees. *ROTC:* Army.

LOANS *Student loans:* $6,709,611 (76% need-based, 24% non-need-based). 76% of past graduating class borrowed through all loan programs. *Average indebtedness per student:* $18,566. *Average need-based loan:* Freshmen: $3001. Undergraduates: $3935. *Parent loans:* $2,404,839 (81% need-based, 19% non-need-based). *Programs:* Federal Direct (Subsidized and Unsubsidized Stafford, PLUS), Perkins.

WORK-STUDY *Federal work-study:* 120 jobs averaging $1100.

ATHLETIC AWARDS Total amount: $2,984,701 (58% need-based, 42% non-need-based).

APPLYING FOR FINANCIAL AID *Required financial aid form:* FAFSA. *Financial aid deadline (priority):* 3/15. *Notification date:* Continuous beginning 3/15. Students must reply by 8/20.

CONTACT Danielle Bell, Director of Financial Aid, Newberry College, 2100 College Street, Newberry, SC 29108, 803-321-5128 or toll-free 800-845-4955. *Fax:* 803-321-5627. *E-mail:* danielle.bell@newberry.edu. *Website:* http://www.newberry.edu/.

NEWBURY COLLEGE
Brookline, MA

CONTACT Elreo Campbell, Executive Director of Student Financial Services, Newbury College, 129 Fisher Avenue, Brookline, MA 02445-5796, 617-730-7100 or toll-free 800-NEWBURY. *Fax:* 617-730-7108. *Website:* http://www.newbury.edu/.

NEW COLLEGE OF FLORIDA
Sarasota, FL

Tuition & fees (FL res): $6916	Average undergraduate aid package: $13,458

ABOUT THE INSTITUTION State-supported, coed. *Awards:* bachelor's and master's degrees. 46 undergraduate majors. *Total enrollment:* 875. Undergraduates: 861. Freshmen: 231. Federal methodology is used as a basis for awarding need-based institutional aid.

UNDERGRADUATE EXPENSES for 2017–2018 *Application fee:* $30. *Tuition, state resident:* full-time $6916. *Tuition, nonresident:* full-time $29,944. *College room and board:* $9264; *Room only:* $6602. Room and board charges vary according to board plan and housing facility.

FRESHMAN FINANCIAL AID (Fall 2016, est.) 208 applied for aid; of those 64% were deemed to have need. 100% of freshmen with need received aid; of those 40% had need fully met. *Average percent of need met:* 83% (excluding resources awarded to replace EFC). *Average financial aid package:* $14,369 (excluding resources awarded to replace EFC). 35% of all full-time freshmen had no need and received non-need-based gift aid.

UNDERGRADUATE FINANCIAL AID (Fall 2016, est.) 689 applied for aid; of those 69% were deemed to have need. 98% of undergraduates with need received aid;

of those 36% had need fully met. **Average percent of need met:** 81% (excluding resources awarded to replace EFC). **Average financial aid package:** $13,458 (excluding resources awarded to replace EFC). 36% of all full-time undergraduates had no need and received non-need-based gift aid.

GIFT AID (NEED-BASED) Total amount: $3,826,553 (31% federal, 25% state, 42% institutional, 2% external sources). **Receiving aid:** Freshmen: 54% (125); all full-time undergraduates: 50% (433). **Average award:** Freshmen: $9728; Undergraduates: $8832. **Scholarships, grants, and awards:** Federal Pell, FSEOG, state, private, college/university gift aid from institutional funds.

GIFT AID (NON-NEED-BASED) Total amount: $1,864,987 (1% federal, 54% state, 42% institutional, 3% external sources). **Receiving aid:** Freshmen: 10% (22). Undergraduates: 8% (68). **Average award:** Freshmen: $2286. Undergraduates: $2454. **Scholarships, grants, and awards by category:** Academic interests/achievement: 908 awards ($3,326,974 total): general academic interests/achievements. Special achievements/activities: 39 awards ($86,421 total): general special achievements/activities. Special characteristics: 170 awards ($2,039,257 total): out-of-state students.

LOANS Student loans: $3,539,066 (54% need-based, 46% non-need-based). 48% of past graduating class borrowed through all loan programs. Average indebtedness per student: $15,173. **Average need-based loan:** Freshmen: $2754. Undergraduates: $3714. **Parent loans:** $277,392 (38% need-based, 62% non-need-based). **Programs:** Federal Direct (Subsidized and Unsubsidized Stafford, PLUS), alternative loans.

WORK-STUDY Federal work-study: Total amount: $22,732; 29 jobs averaging $1071. **State or other work-study/employment:** Part-time jobs available.

APPLYING FOR FINANCIAL AID Required financial aid form: FAFSA. **Financial aid deadline (priority):** 11/1. **Notification date:** Continuous beginning 2/1. Students must reply by 5/1 or within 2 weeks of notification.

CONTACT Tara Karas, Director of Financial Aid, New College of Florida, 5800 Bay Shore Road, Sarasota, FL 34243-2109, 941-487-5000. *Fax:* 941-487-5010. *E-mail:* tkaras@ncf.edu.
Website: http://www.ncf.edu/.

NEW ENGLAND COLLEGE
Henniker, NH

Tuition & fees: $36,954	Average undergraduate aid package: $21,673

ABOUT THE INSTITUTION Independent, coed. **Awards:** associate, bachelor's, master's, and doctoral degrees. 35 undergraduate majors. **Total enrollment:** 2,625. Undergraduates: 1,756. Freshmen: 353. Both federal and institutional methodology are used as a basis for awarding need-based institutional aid.

UNDERGRADUATE EXPENSES for 2017–2018 Application fee: $35. **Comprehensive fee:** $50,828 includes full-time tuition ($35,858), mandatory fees ($1096), and room and board ($13,874). **College room only:** $6274. Full-time tuition and fees vary according to class time, course load, location, program, and reciprocity agreements. Room and board charges vary according to board plan and housing facility. **Part-time tuition:** $439 per credit hour. Part-time tuition and fees vary according to class time, course load, location, and program.

FRESHMAN FINANCIAL AID (Fall 2016, est.) 319 applied for aid; of those 97% were deemed to have need. 92% of freshmen with need received aid; of those 12% had need fully met. **Average percent of need met:** 74% (excluding resources awarded to replace EFC). **Average financial aid package:** $34,662 (excluding resources awarded to replace EFC). 9% of all full-time freshmen had no need and received non-need-based gift aid.

UNDERGRADUATE FINANCIAL AID (Fall 2016, est.) 1,511 applied for aid; of those 96% were deemed to have need. 92% of undergraduates with need received aid; of those 11% had need fully met. **Average percent of need met:** 74% (excluding resources awarded to replace EFC). **Average financial aid package:** $21,673 (excluding resources awarded to replace EFC). 1% of all full-time undergraduates had no need and received non-need-based gift aid.

GIFT AID (NEED-BASED) Total amount: $20,662,886 (21% federal, 1% state, 78% institutional). **Receiving aid:** Freshmen: 81% (281); all full-time undergraduates: 7% (1,219). **Average award:** Freshmen: $25,226; Undergraduates: $17,062. **Scholarships, grants, and awards:** Federal Pell, FSEOG, state, private, college/university gift aid from institutional funds.

GIFT AID (NON-NEED-BASED) Total amount: $2,290,486 (1% state, 99% institutional). **Receiving aid:** Freshmen: 4% (14). Undergraduates: 60. **Average**

award: Freshmen: $21,601. Undergraduates: $19,073. **Scholarships, grants, and awards by category:** Academic interests/achievement: 150 awards ($2,401,444 total): biological sciences, business, communication, computer science, education, general academic interests/achievements, humanities, international studies, social sciences. Creative arts/performance: 1 award ($20,000 total): applied art and design, art/fine arts, creative writing, theater/drama. Special achievements/activities: 216 awards ($3,202,100 total): community service, leadership. Special characteristics: 134 awards ($1,680,359 total): children and siblings of alumni, children of educators, children of faculty/staff, ethnic background, international students, local/state students, parents of current students, siblings of current students, veterans, veterans' children. **Tuition waivers:** Full or partial for children of alumni, employees or children of employees, adult students, senior citizens. **ROTC:** Army cooperative, Air Force cooperative.

LOANS Student loans: $7,948,311 (70% need-based, 30% non-need-based). 88% of past graduating class borrowed through all loan programs. Average indebtedness per student: $35,230. **Average need-based loan:** Freshmen: $4128. Undergraduates: $2824. **Parent loans:** $4,394,353 (99% need-based, 1% non-need-based). **Programs:** Federal Direct (Subsidized and Unsubsidized Stafford, PLUS), Perkins, state.

WORK-STUDY Federal work-study: Total amount: $682,970; 357 jobs averaging $1913. **State or other work-study/employment:** 39 part-time jobs averaging $1121.

APPLYING FOR FINANCIAL AID Required financial aid form: FAFSA. **Financial aid deadline (priority):** 4/1. **Notification date:** Continuous beginning 2/1. Students must reply by 9/7 or within 4 weeks of notification.

CONTACT Kristen Blase, Student Financial Services Director, New England College, 15 Main Street, Henniker, NH 03242-3293, 603-428-2226 or toll-free 800-521-7642. *Fax:* 603-428-2404. *E-mail:* rstein@nec.edu.
Website: http://www.nec.edu/.

NEW ENGLAND COLLEGE OF BUSINESS AND FINANCE
Boston, MA

CONTACT Financial Aid Office, New England College of Business and Finance, 10 High Street, Suite 204, Boston, MA 02111-2645, 617-951-2350 or toll-free 800-997-1673.
Website: http://necb.edu/.

NEW ENGLAND CONSERVATORY OF MUSIC
Boston, MA

Tuition & fees: $44,755	Average undergraduate aid package: $28,008

ABOUT THE INSTITUTION Independent, coed. **Awards:** certificates, diplomas, bachelor's, master's, and doctoral degrees. 9 undergraduate majors. **Total enrollment:** 788. Undergraduates: 409. Freshmen: 90. Federal methodology is used as a basis for awarding need-based institutional aid.

UNDERGRADUATE EXPENSES for 2016–2017 Application fee: $115. **Comprehensive fee:** $58,655 includes full-time tuition ($44,300), mandatory fees ($455), and room and board ($13,900). Room and board charges vary according to board plan. **Part-time tuition:** $1420 per credit. **Part-time fees:** $455 per year.

FRESHMAN FINANCIAL AID (Fall 2015) 52 applied for aid; of those 75% were deemed to have need. 100% of freshmen with need received aid; of those 26% had need fully met. **Average percent of need met:** 73% (excluding resources awarded to replace EFC). **Average financial aid package:** $29,114 (excluding resources awarded to replace EFC). 50% of all full-time freshmen had no need and received non-need-based gift aid.

UNDERGRADUATE FINANCIAL AID (Fall 2015) 221 applied for aid; of those 77% were deemed to have need. 100% of undergraduates with need received aid; of those 20% had need fully met. **Average percent of need met:** 67% (excluding resources awarded to replace EFC). **Average financial aid package:** $28,008 (excluding resources awarded to replace EFC). 49% of all full-time undergraduates had no need and received non-need-based gift aid.

GIFT AID (NEED-BASED) *Total amount:* $3,624,358 (11% federal, 77% institutional, 12% external sources). *Receiving aid:* Freshmen: 45% (39); all full-time undergraduates: 46% (170). *Average award:* Freshmen: $24,149; Undergraduates: $21,634. *Scholarships, grants, and awards:* Federal Pell, FSEOG, state, private, college/university gift aid from institutional funds.

GIFT AID (NON-NEED-BASED) *Total amount:* $3,476,783 (84% institutional, 16% external sources). *Receiving aid:* Freshmen: 10% (9). Undergraduates: 9% (33). *Average award:* Freshmen: $15,501. Undergraduates: $15,027. *Scholarships, grants, and awards by category: Creative arts/performance:* 354 awards ($5,776,265 total): music. *Tuition waivers:* Full or partial for employees or children of employees.

LOANS *Student loans:* $1,969,085 (71% need-based, 29% non-need-based). 48% of past graduating class borrowed through all loan programs. *Average indebtedness per student:* $31,039. *Average need-based loan:* Freshmen $6914. Undergraduates: $6891. *Parent loans:* $587,890 (71% need-based, 29% non-need-based). *Programs:* Federal Direct (Subsidized and Unsubsidized Stafford, PLUS), state.

WORK-STUDY *Federal work-study:* 212 jobs averaging $1732.

APPLYING FOR FINANCIAL AID *Required financial aid forms:* FAFSA, institution's own form. *Financial aid deadline (priority):* 2/15. *Notification date:* 4/1. Students must reply by 5/1.

CONTACT Ms. Lauren Gayle Urbanek, Director of Financial Aid, New England Conservatory of Music, 290 Huntington Avenue, Boston, MA 02115, 617-585-1110. *Fax:* 617-585-1115. *E-mail:* finaid@necmusic.edu. *Website:* http://necmusic.edu/.

NEW ENGLAND INSTITUTE OF TECHNOLOGY
East Greenwich, RI

CONTACT Financial Aid Office, New England Institute of Technology, One New England Tech Boulevard, East Greenwich, RI 02818, 401-467-7744 or toll-free 800-736-7744. *Website:* http://www.neit.edu/.

NEW HAMPSHIRE INSTITUTE OF ART
Manchester, NH

CONTACT Linda Lavallee, Director of Financial Aid, New Hampshire Institute of Art, 148 Concord Street, Manchester, NH 03104-4858, 603-623-0313 Ext. 577 or toll-free 866-241-4918. *Fax:* 603-647-0658. *E-mail:* llavallee@nhia.edu. *Website:* http://www.nhia.edu/.

NEW HOPE CHRISTIAN COLLEGE
Eugene, OR

CONTACT Nathan Icenhower, Financial Aid Administrator, New Hope Christian College, 2155 Bailey Hill Road, Eugene, OR 97405-1194, 541-485-1780 Ext. 3106 or toll-free 800-322-2638. *Fax:* 541-343-5801. *E-mail:* finaid@newhope.edu. *Website:* http://www.newhope.edu/.

NEW JERSEY CITY UNIVERSITY
Jersey City, NJ

Tuition & fees (NJ res): $11,431	Average undergraduate aid package: $10,213

ABOUT THE INSTITUTION State-supported, coed. *Awards:* certificates, bachelor's, master's, and doctoral degrees. 31 undergraduate majors. *Total enrollment:* 8,505. Undergraduates: 6,663. Freshmen: 988. Federal methodology is used as a basis for awarding need-based institutional aid.

UNDERGRADUATE EXPENSES for 2017–2018 *Application fee:* $50. *Tuition, state resident:* full-time $8115; part-time $270.45 per credit hour. *Tuition, nonresident:* full-time $17,142; part-time $571.40 per credit hour. *Required fees:* full-time $3316. Part-time tuition and fees vary according to course load. *College room and board:* $12,446. Room and board charges vary according to board plan and housing facility.

FRESHMAN FINANCIAL AID (Fall 2015) 764 applied for aid; of those 95% were deemed to have need. 97% of freshmen with need received aid; of those 2% had need fully met. *Average percent of need met:* 54% (excluding resources awarded to replace EFC). *Average financial aid package:* $11,020 (excluding resources awarded to replace EFC). 2% of all full-time freshmen had no need and received non-need-based gift aid.

UNDERGRADUATE FINANCIAL AID (Fall 2015) 4,408 applied for aid; of those 95% were deemed to have need. 97% of undergraduates with need received aid; of those 3% had need fully met. *Average percent of need met:* 50% (excluding resources awarded to replace EFC). *Average financial aid package:* $10,213 (excluding resources awarded to replace EFC). 1% of all full-time undergraduates had no need and received non-need-based gift aid.

GIFT AID (NEED-BASED) *Total amount:* $28,287,263 (58% federal, 42% state). *Receiving aid:* Freshmen: 77% (608); all full-time undergraduates: 69% (3,316). *Average award:* Freshmen: $9884; Undergraduates: $8191. *Scholarships, grants, and awards:* Federal Pell, FSEOG, state, college/university gift aid from institutional funds.

GIFT AID (NON-NEED-BASED) *Total amount:* $3,444,228 (4% state, 87% institutional, 9% external sources). *Receiving aid:* Freshmen: 20% (154). Undergraduates: 13% (642). *Average award:* Freshmen: $7254. Undergraduates: $7464. *Scholarships, grants, and awards by category: Academic interests/achievement:* general academic interests/achievements. *Tuition waivers:* Full or partial for employees or children of employees, senior citizens.

LOANS *Student loans:* $24,208,491 (50% need-based, 50% non-need-based). 69% of past graduating class borrowed through all loan programs. *Average indebtedness per student:* $26,093. *Average need-based loan:* Freshmen: $3150. Undergraduates: $4178. *Parent loans:* $1,555,276 (100% non-need-based). *Programs:* Federal Direct (Subsidized and Unsubsidized Stafford, PLUS), Perkins, state.

WORK-STUDY *Federal work-study:* jobs available.

APPLYING FOR FINANCIAL AID *Required financial aid form:* FAFSA. *Financial aid deadline (priority):* 3/15. *Notification date:* 5/15.

CONTACT Mr. Frank Cuozzo, Director of Financial Aid, New Jersey City University, 2039 Kennedy Boulevard, Jersey City, NJ 07305-1597, 201-200-3173 or toll-free 888-441-NJCU. *Website:* http://www.njcu.edu/.

NEW JERSEY INSTITUTE OF TECHNOLOGY
Newark, NJ

Tuition & fees (NJ res): $16,430	Average undergraduate aid package: $13,200

ABOUT THE INSTITUTION State-supported, coed. *Awards:* certificates, bachelor's, master's, and doctoral degrees. 41 undergraduate majors. *Total enrollment:* 11,325. Undergraduates: 8,008. Freshmen: 1,108. Federal methodology is used as a basis for awarding need-based institutional aid.

UNDERGRADUATE EXPENSES for 2016–2017 *Application fee:* $75. *Tuition, state resident:* full-time $13,602; part-time $517 per credit. *Tuition, nonresident:* full-time $28,206; part-time $1206 per credit. *Required fees:* full-time $2828; $166 per credit. Full-time tuition and fees vary according to course load and degree level. Part-time tuition and fees vary according to course load and degree level. *College room and board:* $13,400; *Room only:* $9026. Room and board charges vary according to board plan and housing facility.

FRESHMAN FINANCIAL AID (Fall 2015) 899 applied for aid; of those 81% were deemed to have need. 96% of freshmen with need received aid; of those 16% had need fully met. *Average percent of need met:* 58% (excluding resources awarded to replace EFC). *Average financial aid package:* $14,168 (excluding resources awarded to replace EFC). 15% of all full-time freshmen had no need and received non-need-based gift aid.

UNDERGRADUATE FINANCIAL AID (Fall 2015) 4,929 applied for aid; of those 89% were deemed to have need. 96% of undergraduates with need received aid;

of those 9% had need fully met. *Average percent of need met:* 52% (excluding resources awarded to replace EFC). *Average financial aid package:* $13,200 (excluding resources awarded to replace EFC). 9% of all full-time undergraduates had no need and received non-need-based gift aid.

GIFT AID (NEED-BASED) *Total amount:* $42,328,825 (30% federal, 43% state, 26% institutional, 1% external sources). *Receiving aid:* Freshmen: 70% (700); all full-time undergraduates: 70% (4,255). *Average award:* Freshmen: $13,482; Undergraduates: $12,789. *Scholarships, grants, and awards:* Federal Pell, FSEOG, state, private, college/university gift aid from institutional funds, United Negro College Fund.

GIFT AID (NON-NEED-BASED) *Total amount:* $10,738,968 (99% institutional, 1% external sources). *Receiving aid:* Freshmen: 43% (428). Undergraduates: 24% (1,475). *Average award:* Freshmen: $16,035. Undergraduates: $14,346. *Scholarships, grants, and awards by category:* Academic interests/achievement: 599 awards ($10,086,741 total): architecture, area/ethnic studies, biological sciences, business, communication, computer science, education, engineering/technologies, general academic interests/achievements, humanities, international studies, mathematics, physical sciences, premedicine. *Creative arts/performance:* 147 awards ($421,685 total): applied art and design, art/fine arts, journalism/publications, performing arts, theater/drama. *Special achievements/activities:* community service, general special achievements/activities, hobbies/interests, leadership, religious involvement. *Special characteristics:* adult students, children of faculty/staff, children of union members/company employees, ethnic background, first-generation college students, general special characteristics, handicapped students, international students, local/state students, members of minority groups, out-of-state students, relatives of clergy, religious affiliation, siblings of current students, veterans, veterans' children. *Tuition waivers:* Full or partial for employees or children of employees. *ROTC:* Army cooperative, Air Force.

LOANS *Student loans:* $36,685,524 (37% need-based, 63% non-need-based). 64% of past graduating class borrowed through all loan programs. *Average indebtedness per student:* $40,967. *Average need-based loan:* Freshmen: $3284. Undergraduates: $4420. *Parent loans:* $4,098,284 (100% non-need-based). *Programs:* Federal Direct (Subsidized and Unsubsidized Stafford, PLUS), state, alternative loans.

WORK-STUDY *Federal work-study:* 278 jobs averaging $1405. *State or other work-study/employment:* Total amount: $1,977,892 (100% non-need-based). 1,260 part-time jobs averaging $1247.

ATHLETIC AWARDS Total amount: $3,849,545 (37% need-based, 63% non-need-based).

APPLYING FOR FINANCIAL AID *Required financial aid forms:* FAFSA, institution's own form. *Financial aid deadline:* 5/15 (priority: 3/15). *Notification date:* 11/19. Students must reply by 5/1 or within 2 weeks of notification.

CONTACT Ivon Nunez, Director of Financial Aid Services, New Jersey Institute of Technology, Student Mall, University Heights, Newark, NJ 07102, 973-596-3476 or toll-free 800-925-NJIT. *Fax:* 973-596-6471. *E-mail:* ivon.nunez@njit.edu. *Website:* http://www.njit.edu/.

NEWMAN UNIVERSITY
Wichita, KS

CONTACT Charly Smith, Director of Financial Aid, Newman University, 3100 McCormick Avenue, Wichita, KS 67213, 316-942-4291 Ext. 2132 or toll-free 877-NEWMANU. *Fax:* 316-942-4483. *E-mail:* smithc@newmanu.edu. *Website:* http://www.newmanu.edu/.

NEW MEXICO HIGHLANDS UNIVERSITY
Las Vegas, NM

Tuition & fees (NM res): $5550	Average undergraduate aid package: $1811

ABOUT THE INSTITUTION State-supported, coed. *Awards:* certificates, bachelor's, and master's degrees. 44 undergraduate majors. *Total enrollment:* 3,471. Undergraduates: 2,181. Freshmen: 316. Both federal and institutional methodology are used as a basis for awarding need-based institutional aid.

UNDERGRADUATE EXPENSES for 2017–2018 *Tuition, state resident:* full-time $3952; part-time $165 per credit hour. *Tuition, nonresident:* full-time $7052; part-time $294 per credit hour. *Required fees:* full-time $1598. Full-time tuition and fees vary according to course load and location. Part-time tuition and fees vary according to course load and location. *College room and board:* $7235; *Room only:* $3635. Room and board charges vary according to board plan and housing facility.

FRESHMAN FINANCIAL AID (Fall 2015) 275 applied for aid; of those 84% were deemed to have need. 100% of freshmen with need received aid; of those 10% had need fully met. *Average percent of need met:* 19% (excluding resources awarded to replace EFC). *Average financial aid package:* $1553 (excluding resources awarded to replace EFC). 55% of all full-time freshmen had no need and received non-need-based gift aid.

UNDERGRADUATE FINANCIAL AID (Fall 2015) 1,299 applied for aid; of those 87% were deemed to have need. 97% of undergraduates with need received aid; of those 9% had need fully met. *Average percent of need met:* 19% (excluding resources awarded to replace EFC). *Average financial aid package:* $1811 (excluding resources awarded to replace EFC). 34% of all full-time undergraduates had no need and received non-need-based gift aid.

GIFT AID (NEED-BASED) *Total amount:* $6,037,037 (88% federal, 8% state, 4% external sources). *Receiving aid:* Freshmen: 60% (180); all full-time undergraduates: 63% (928). *Average award:* Freshmen: $1838; Undergraduates: $1945. *Scholarships, grants, and awards:* Federal Pell, FSEOG, state, private, college/university gift aid from institutional funds.

GIFT AID (NON-NEED-BASED) *Total amount:* $2,311,502 (4% federal, 50% state, 33% institutional, 13% external sources). *Receiving aid:* Freshmen: 69% (206). Undergraduates: 45% (666). *Average award:* Freshmen: $1871. Undergraduates: $2229. *Scholarships, grants, and awards by category:* Academic interests/achievement: biological sciences, business, communication, computer science, education, engineering/technologies, English, foreign languages, general academic interests/achievements, health fields, humanities, mathematics, physical sciences, social sciences. *Creative arts/performance:* art/fine arts, music, performing arts. *Tuition waivers:* Full or partial for employees or children of employees, senior citizens.

LOANS *Student loans:* $1,721,966 (36% need-based, 64% non-need-based). 51% of past graduating class borrowed through all loan programs. *Average indebtedness per student:* $17,312. *Average need-based loan:* Freshmen: $2138. Undergraduates: $2531. *Parent loans:* $66,092 (100% non-need-based). *Programs:* Federal Direct (Subsidized and Unsubsidized Stafford, PLUS), Perkins.

WORK-STUDY *Federal work-study:* jobs available. *State or other work-study/employment:* Total amount: $155,195 (84% need-based, 16% non-need-based). Part-time jobs available.

ATHLETIC AWARDS Total amount: $618,793 (100% non-need-based).

APPLYING FOR FINANCIAL AID *Required financial aid form:* FAFSA. *Financial aid deadline:* Continuous. *Notification date:* Continuous beginning 3/15. Students must reply within 2 weeks of notification.

CONTACT Eileen Sedillo, Director of Financial Aid, New Mexico Highlands University, PO Box 9000, Las Vegas, NM 87701, 505-454-3430 or toll-free 800-338-6648. *Fax:* 505-454-3398. *E-mail:* sedillo_e@nmhu.edu. *Website:* http://www.nmhu.edu/.

NEW MEXICO INSTITUTE OF MINING AND TECHNOLOGY
Socorro, NM

Tuition & fees (NM res): $6891	Average undergraduate aid package: $13,264

ABOUT THE INSTITUTION State-supported, coed. *Awards:* associate, bachelor's, master's, and doctoral degrees. 22 undergraduate majors. *Total enrollment:* 2,135. Undergraduates: 1,569. Freshmen: 302. Federal methodology is used as a basis for awarding need-based institutional aid.

UNDERGRADUATE EXPENSES for 2016–2017 *Application fee:* $15. *Tuition, state resident:* full-time $5841; part-time $243.37 per credit hour. *Tuition, nonresident:* full-time $18,991; part-time $791.31 per credit hour. *Required fees:* full-time $1050; $64.50 per credit hour or $216 per term. Full-time tuition and fees vary according to reciprocity agreements. Part-time tuition and fees vary according to course load. **College room and board:** $7942. Room and board charges vary according to board plan and housing facility.

FRESHMAN FINANCIAL AID (Fall 2016, est.) 297 applied for aid; of those 61% were deemed to have need. 99% of freshmen with need received aid; of those 15% had need fully met. **Average percent of need met:** 84% (excluding resources awarded to replace EFC). **Average financial aid package:** $12,388 (excluding resources awarded to replace EFC). 34% of all full-time freshmen had no need and received non-need-based gift aid.

UNDERGRADUATE FINANCIAL AID (Fall 2016, est.) 1,247 applied for aid; of those 61% were deemed to have need. 97% of undergraduates with need received aid; of those 23% had need fully met. **Average percent of need met:** 82% (excluding resources awarded to replace EFC). **Average financial aid package:** $13,264 (excluding resources awarded to replace EFC). 31% of all full-time undergraduates had no need and received non-need-based gift aid.

GIFT AID (NEED-BASED) Total amount: $2,965,798 (83% federal, 13% state, 4% external sources). **Receiving aid:** Freshmen: 45% (147); all full-time undergraduates: 37% (513). **Average award:** Freshmen: $4635; Undergraduates: $5662. **Scholarships, grants, and awards:** Federal Pell, FSEOG, state, private, college/university gift aid from institutional funds.

GIFT AID (NON-NEED-BASED) Total amount: $6,037,549 (49% state, 44% institutional, 7% external sources). **Receiving aid:** Freshmen: 52% (171). Undergraduates: 38% (530). **Average award:** Freshmen: $6623. Undergraduates: $6659. **Scholarships, grants, and awards by category:** Academic interests/achievement: general academic interests/achievements. **Tuition waivers:** Full or partial for employees or children of employees, senior citizens.

LOANS Student loans: $3,908,051 (45% need-based, 55% non-need-based). 45% of past graduating class borrowed through all loan programs. **Average indebtedness per student:** $22,355. **Average need-based loan:** Freshmen: $3350. Undergraduates: $4399. **Parent loans:** $243,677 (100% non-need-based). **Programs:** Federal Direct (Subsidized and Unsubsidized Stafford, PLUS), Perkins.

WORK-STUDY Federal work-study: Total amount: $573,324; jobs available. **State or other work-study/employment:** Total amount: $159,431 (38% need-based, 62% non-need-based). Part-time jobs available.

APPLYING FOR FINANCIAL AID Required financial aid form: FAFSA. **Financial aid deadline (priority):** 5/1. **Notification date:** Continuous beginning 5/1. Students must reply within 2 weeks of notification.

CONTACT Mr. Kenneth Aerts, Assistant Director of Financial Aid, New Mexico Institute of Mining and Technology, 801 Leroy Place, Socorro, NM 87801, 575-835-5333 or toll-free 800-428-TECH. *Fax:* 575-835-5959. *E-mail:* kenneth.aerts@nmt.edu. *Website:* http://www.nmt.edu/.

NEW MEXICO STATE UNIVERSITY
Las Cruces, NM

Tuition & fees (NM res): $6094	Average undergraduate aid package: $11,817

ABOUT THE INSTITUTION State-supported, coed. **Awards:** certificates, master's, and doctoral degrees. 86 undergraduate majors. **Total enrollment:** 14,852. Undergraduates: 12,027. Freshmen: 1,842. Federal methodology is used as a basis for awarding need-based institutional aid.

UNDERGRADUATE EXPENSES for 2016–2017 **Application fee:** $20. **One-time required fee:** $40. **Tuition, state resident:** full-time $4956; part-time $206.50 per credit hour. **Tuition, nonresident:** full-time $18,514; part-time $771.40 per credit hour. **Required fees:** full-time $1138; $47.40 per credit hour. Full-time tuition and fees vary according to course load and reciprocity agreements. **College room and board:** $7988; **Room only:** $4296. Room and board charges vary according to board plan and housing facility.

FRESHMAN FINANCIAL AID (Fall 2015) 1,667 applied for aid; of those 82% were deemed to have need. 100% of freshmen with need received aid; of those 12% had need fully met. **Average percent of need met:** 65% (excluding resources awarded to replace EFC). **Average financial aid package:** $11,360 (excluding resources awarded to replace EFC). 18% of all full-time freshmen had no need and received non-need-based gift aid.

UNDERGRADUATE FINANCIAL AID (Fall 2015) 7,483 applied for aid; of those 87% were deemed to have need. 100% of undergraduates with need received aid; of those 9% had need fully met. **Average percent of need met:** 65% (excluding resources awarded to replace EFC). **Average financial aid package:** $11,817

(excluding resources awarded to replace EFC). 12% of all full-time undergraduates had no need and received non-need-based gift aid.

GIFT AID (NEED-BASED) Total amount: $40,477,392 (55% federal, 26% state, 14% institutional, 5% external sources). **Receiving aid:** Freshmen: 68% (1,351); all full-time undergraduates: 60% (6,227). **Average award:** Freshmen: $10,052; Undergraduates: $9998. **Scholarships, grants, and awards:** Federal Pell, FSEOG, state, private, college/university gift aid from institutional funds.

GIFT AID (NON-NEED-BASED) Total amount: $11,769,473 (2% federal, 55% state, 33% institutional, 10% external sources). **Receiving aid:** Freshmen: 6% (119). Undergraduates: 4% (420). **Average award:** Freshmen: $3188. Undergraduates: $2571. **Scholarships, grants, and awards by category:** Academic interests/achievement: 602 awards ($573,434 total): agriculture, area/ethnic studies, biological sciences, business, communication, computer science, education, engineering/technologies, English, foreign languages, general academic interests/achievements, health fields, home economics, humanities, mathematics, military science, physical sciences, social sciences. Creative arts/performance: 57 awards ($42,100 total): applied art and design, art/fine arts, cinema/film/broadcasting, creative writing, dance, general creative arts/performance, journalism/publications, music, performing arts, theater/drama. Special achievements/activities: 38 awards ($40,405 total): cheerleading/drum major, general special achievements/activities, hobbies/interests, junior miss, leadership, memberships, rodeo. Special characteristics: 608 awards ($875,816 total): adult students, children and siblings of alumni, children of current students, children of faculty/staff, children of public servants, children of union members/company employees, children of workers in trades, children with a deceased or disabled parent, ethnic background, handicapped students, international students, local/state students, married students, members of minority groups, out-of-state students, previous college experience, public servants, spouses of current students, spouses of deceased or disabled public servants, veterans, veterans' children. **Tuition waivers:** Full or partial for employees or children of employees, senior citizens. **ROTC:** Army, Air Force.

LOANS Student loans: $32,913,049 (82% need-based, 18% non-need-based). 56% of past graduating class borrowed through all loan programs. **Average indebtedness per student:** $21,402. **Average need-based loan:** Freshmen: $2555. Undergraduates: $3557. **Parent loans:** $1,086,359 (48% need-based, 52% non-need-based). **Programs:** Federal Direct (Subsidized and Unsubsidized Stafford, PLUS), Perkins, state.

WORK-STUDY Federal work-study: 308 jobs averaging $2652. **State or other work-study/employment:** Total amount: $1,880,443 (77% need-based, 23% non-need-based). 337 part-time jobs averaging $5609.

ATHLETIC AWARDS Total amount: $4,078,020 (23% need-based, 77% non-need-based).

APPLYING FOR FINANCIAL AID Required financial aid form: FAFSA. **Financial aid deadline:** 6/30 (priority: 3/1). **Notification date:** Continuous beginning 1/1.

CONTACT Ms. McKenzie Vandeen, Director of Financial Aid, New Mexico State University, Box 30001, Department 5100, Las Cruces, NM 88003-8001, 575-646-4105 or toll-free 800-662-6678. *Fax:* 575-646-7381. *E-mail:* financialaid@nmsu.edu. *Website:* http://www.nmsu.edu/.

NEW ORLEANS BAPTIST THEOLOGICAL SEMINARY
New Orleans, LA

CONTACT Owen Nease, Financial Aid Office, New Orleans Baptist Theological Seminary, 3939 Gentilly Boulevard, New Orleans, LA 70126-4858, 504-282-4455 Ext. 3348 or toll-free 800-662-8701. *Fax:* 504-816-8437. *E-mail:* financialaid@nobts.edu. *Website:* http://www.nobts.edu/.

NEW SAINT ANDREWS COLLEGE
Moscow, ID

CONTACT Brenda Schlect, College Bursars Office, New Saint Andrews College, 405 South Main Street, PO Box 9025, Moscow, ID 83843, 208-882-1566 Ext. 113. *Fax:* 208-882-4297. *E-mail:* bschlect@nsa.edu. *Website:* http://www.nsa.edu/.

THE NEW SCHOOL COLLEGE OF PERFORMING ARTS
New York, NY

ABOUT THE INSTITUTION Independent, coed. *Awards:* diplomas, bachelor's, and master's degrees. 8 undergraduate majors. *Total enrollment:* 865. Undergraduates: 564. Freshmen: 144.

GIFT AID (NEED-BASED) *Scholarships, grants, and awards:* Federal Pell, FSEOG, state, private, college/university gift aid from institutional funds.

GIFT AID (NON-NEED-BASED) *Scholarships, grants, and awards by category: Academic interests/achievement:* general academic interests/achievements. *Creative arts/performance:* general creative arts/performance. *Special achievements/ activities:* leadership. *Special characteristics:* members of minority groups.

LOANS *Programs:* Federal Direct (Subsidized and Unsubsidized Stafford, PLUS), Perkins.

APPLYING FOR FINANCIAL AID *Required financial aid forms:* FAFSA, state aid form.

CONTACT Office of Student Financial Services, The New School College of Performing Arts, 72 Fifth Avenue, New York, NY 10011, 212-229-8930 or toll-free 800-292-3040. *E-mail:* sfs@newschool.edu.
Website: http://www.newschool.edu/performing-arts/.

THE NEW SCHOOL FOR PUBLIC ENGAGEMENT
New York, NY

ABOUT THE INSTITUTION Independent, coed. *Awards:* certificates, bachelor's, master's, and doctoral degrees. 8 undergraduate majors. *Total enrollment:* 1,622. Undergraduates: 486. Freshmen: 15.

GIFT AID (NEED-BASED) *Scholarships, grants, and awards:* Federal Pell, FSEOG, state, private, college/university gift aid from institutional funds.

GIFT AID (NON-NEED-BASED) *Scholarships, grants, and awards by category: Academic interests/achievement:* general academic interests/achievements.

LOANS *Programs:* Federal Direct (Subsidized and Unsubsidized Stafford, PLUS), Perkins.

APPLYING FOR FINANCIAL AID *Required financial aid forms:* FAFSA, state aid form.

CONTACT Eileen F. Doyle, Assistant Vice President for Student Financial Services, The New School for Public Engagement, 65 Fifth Avenue, New York, NY 10003, 212-229-8930 or toll-free 800-292-3040. *Fax:* 212-229-5919. *E-mail:* sfs@newschool.edu.
Website: http://www.newschool.edu/public-engagement/.

NEWSCHOOL OF ARCHITECTURE AND DESIGN
San Diego, CA

Tuition & fees: N/R	Average undergraduate aid package: $23,256

ABOUT THE INSTITUTION Proprietary, coed, primarily men. *Awards:* bachelor's and master's degrees. 9 undergraduate majors. *Total enrollment:* 515. Undergraduates: 408. Freshmen: 56. Federal methodology is used as a basis for awarding need-based institutional aid.

FRESHMAN FINANCIAL AID (Fall 2015) 42 applied for aid; of those 81% were deemed to have need. 100% of freshmen with need received aid; of those 3% had need fully met. *Average percent of need met:* 54% (excluding resources awarded to replace EFC). *Average financial aid package:* $21,644 (excluding resources awarded to replace EFC). 9% of all full-time freshmen had no need and received non-need-based gift aid.

UNDERGRADUATE FINANCIAL AID (Fall 2015) 282 applied for aid; of those 88% were deemed to have need. 96% of undergraduates with need received aid; of those 3% had need fully met. *Average percent of need met:* 56% (excluding resources awarded to replace EFC). *Average financial aid package:* $23,256

(excluding resources awarded to replace EFC). 6% of all full-time undergraduates had no need and received non-need-based gift aid.

GIFT AID (NEED-BASED) *Total amount:* $2,658,943 (40% federal, 13% state, 46% institutional, 1% external sources). *Receiving aid:* Freshmen: 60% (33); all full-time undergraduates: 63% (229). *Average award:* Freshmen: $11,125; Undergraduates: $10,065. *Scholarships, grants, and awards:* Federal Pell, FSEOG, state, private, college/university gift aid from institutional funds.

GIFT AID (NON-NEED-BASED) *Total amount:* $35,720 (100% institutional). *Receiving aid:* Freshmen: 2% (1), Undergraduates: 1% (2). *Average award:* Freshmen: $2750. Undergraduates: $8610. *Scholarships, grants, and awards by category: Academic interests/achievement:* architecture, general academic interests/ achievements. *Creative arts/performance:* general creative arts/performance. *Special characteristics:* children of faculty/staff, international students, veterans.

LOANS *Student loans:* $3,173,333 (93% need-based, 7% non-need-based). 80% of past graduating class borrowed through all loan programs. *Average indebtedness per student:* $40,000. *Average need-based loan:* Freshmen: $3094. Undergraduates: $4400. *Parent loans:* $842,292 (76% need-based, 24% non-need-based). *Programs:* Federal Direct (Subsidized and Unsubsidized Stafford, PLUS), alternative loans.

WORK-STUDY *Federal work-study:* 19 jobs averaging $3428. *State or other work-study/employment:* 1 part-time job averaging $6000.

APPLYING FOR FINANCIAL AID *Required financial aid forms:* FAFSA, institution's own form. *Financial aid deadline:* Continuous. *Notification date:* Continuous beginning 7/1. Students must reply within 4 weeks of notification.

CONTACT Bryan Charbonneau, Director of Financial Aid, NewSchool of Architecture and Design, 1249 F Street, San Diego, CA 92101-6634, 619-684-8774 or toll-free 800-490-7081. *Fax:* 619-684-8880. *E-mail:* bcharbonneau@ newschoolarch.edu.
Website: http://www.newschoolarch.edu/.

NEW WORLD SCHOOL OF THE ARTS
Miami, FL

CONTACT Financial Aid Office, New World School of the Arts, 300 NE 2nd Avenue, Miami, FL 33132, 305-237-3135.
Website: http://www.mdc.edu/nwsa/.

NEW YORK CITY COLLEGE OF TECHNOLOGY OF THE CITY UNIVERSITY OF NEW YORK
Brooklyn, NY

CONTACT Sandra Higgins, Director of Financial Aid, New York City College of Technology of the City University of New York, 300 Jay Street, Namm Hall, Room G-13, Brooklyn, NY 11201, 718-260-5700. *Fax:* 718-254-8525. *E-mail:* financialaid@ citytech.cuny.edu.
Website: http://www.citytech.cuny.edu/.

NEW YORK COLLEGE OF HEALTH PROFESSIONS
Syosset, NY

CONTACT Financial Aid Office, New York College of Health Professions, 6801 Jericho Turnpike, Syosset, NY 11791-4413, 516-364-0808 or toll-free 800-922-7337 Ext. 351.
Website: http://www.nycollege.edu/.

NEW YORK FILM ACADEMY
Burbank, CA

CONTACT Financial Aid Office, New York Film Academy, 3300 Riverside Drive, Burbank, CA 91505, 818-333-3558.
Website: https://www.nyfa.edu/.

NEW YORK INSTITUTE OF TECHNOLOGY
Old Westbury, NY

Tuition & fees: $35,160	Average undergraduate aid package: $21,916

ABOUT THE INSTITUTION Independent, coed. *Awards:* certificates, associate, bachelor's, master's, and doctoral degrees. 39 undergraduate majors. *Total enrollment:* 7,662. Undergraduates: 3,609. Freshmen: 713. Federal methodology is used as a basis for awarding need-based institutional aid.

UNDERGRADUATE EXPENSES for 2016–2017 *Application fee:* $50. *Comprehensive fee:* $48,730 includes full-time tuition ($33,920), mandatory fees ($1240), and room and board ($13,570). *College room only:* $8790. Full-time tuition and fees vary according to program. Room and board charges vary according to location. *Part-time tuition:* $1150 per credit. *Part-time fees:* $515 per term. Part-time tuition and fees vary according to course load and program.

FRESHMAN FINANCIAL AID (Fall 2016, est.) 618 applied for aid; of those 91% were deemed to have need. 100% of freshmen with need received aid. *Average financial aid package:* $24,827 (excluding resources awarded to replace EFC). 14% of all full-time freshmen had no need and received non-need-based gift aid.

UNDERGRADUATE FINANCIAL AID (Fall 2016, est.) 2,590 applied for aid; of those 91% were deemed to have need. 100% of undergraduates with need received aid. *Average financial aid package:* $21,916 (excluding resources awarded to replace EFC). 13% of all full-time undergraduates had no need and received non-need-based gift aid.

GIFT AID (NEED-BASED) *Total amount:* $16,987,663 (37% federal, 23% state, 40% institutional). *Receiving aid:* Freshmen: 66% (447); all full-time undergraduates: 64% (2,026). *Average award:* Freshmen: $9056; Undergraduates: $8131. *Scholarships, grants, and awards:* Federal Pell, FSEOG, state, private, college/university gift aid from institutional funds.

GIFT AID (NON-NEED-BASED) *Total amount:* $30,760,874 (4% federal, 1% state, 92% institutional, 3% external sources). *Receiving aid:* Freshmen: 79% (541). Undergraduates: 64% (2,018). *Average award:* Freshmen: $15,308. Undergraduates: $12,606. *Scholarships, grants, and awards by category:* Academic interests/achievement: general academic interests/achievements. *Special characteristics:* children of faculty/staff, previous college experience, veterans. *Tuition waivers:* Full or partial for employees or children of employees, senior citizens. *ROTC:* Army cooperative, Air Force cooperative.

LOANS *Student loans:* $17,460,974 (40% need-based, 60% non-need-based). *Average need-based loan:* Freshmen: $3508. Undergraduates: $4298. *Parent loans:* $14,576,652 (100% non-need-based). *Programs:* Federal Direct (Subsidized and Unsubsidized Stafford, PLUS), Perkins, alternative loans.

WORK-STUDY *Federal work-study:* Total amount: $696,627; jobs available. *State or other work-study/employment:* Total amount: $622,371 (100% non-need-based). Part-time jobs available.

ATHLETIC AWARDS Total amount: $3,348,257 (100% non-need-based).

APPLYING FOR FINANCIAL AID *Required financial aid form:* FAFSA. *Financial aid deadline (priority):* 3/1. *Notification date:* Continuous beginning 3/1. Students must reply within 4 weeks of notification.

CONTACT Ms. Doreen Meyer, Director of Financial Aid, New York Institute of Technology, PO Box 8000, Old Westbury, NY 11568-8000, 516-686-1083 or toll-free 800-345-NYIT. *Fax:* 516-686-7997. *E-mail:* dmeyer@nyit.edu.
Website: http://www.nyit.edu/.

NEW YORK SCHOOL OF INTERIOR DESIGN
New York, NY

Tuition & fees: $30,945	Average undergraduate aid package: $12,753

ABOUT THE INSTITUTION Independent, coed, primarily women. *Awards:* certificates, associate, bachelor's, and master's degrees. 1 undergraduate major. *Total enrollment:* 538. Undergraduates: 381. Freshmen: 12. Federal methodology is used as a basis for awarding need-based institutional aid.

UNDERGRADUATE EXPENSES for 2016–2017 *Application fee:* $60. *Tuition:* full-time $30,195; part-time $915 per credit. Full-time tuition and fees vary according to course load. Part-time tuition and fees vary according to course load.

FRESHMAN FINANCIAL AID (Fall 2016, est.) 9 applied for aid; of those 67% were deemed to have need. 83% of freshmen with need received aid. *Average percent of need met:* 24% (excluding resources awarded to replace EFC). *Average financial aid package:* $11,311 (excluding resources awarded to replace EFC). 10% of all full-time freshmen had no need and received non-need-based gift aid.

UNDERGRADUATE FINANCIAL AID (Fall 2016, est.) 65 applied for aid; of those 88% were deemed to have need. 93% of undergraduates with need received aid. *Average percent of need met:* 25% (excluding resources awarded to replace EFC). *Average financial aid package:* $12,753 (excluding resources awarded to replace EFC). 19% of all full-time undergraduates had no need and received non-need-based gift aid.

GIFT AID (NEED-BASED) *Total amount:* $556,426 (38% federal, 8% state, 53% institutional, 1% external sources). *Receiving aid:* Freshmen: 40% (4); all full-time undergraduates: 55% (42). *Average award:* Freshmen: $10,638; Undergraduates: $10,346. *Scholarships, grants, and awards:* Federal Pell, FSEOG, state, private, college/university gift aid from institutional funds.

GIFT AID (NON-NEED-BASED) *Total amount:* $151,900 (90% institutional, 10% external sources). *Average award:* Freshmen: $10,000. Undergraduates: $8633. *Tuition waivers:* Full or partial for employees or children of employees.

LOANS *Student loans:* $1,235,204 (82% need-based, 18% non-need-based). 73% of past graduating class borrowed through all loan programs. *Average indebtedness per student:* $26,458. *Average need-based loan:* Freshmen: $3500. Undergraduates: $4372. *Parent loans:* $602,997 (65% need-based, 35% non-need-based). *Programs:* Federal Direct (Subsidized and Unsubsidized Stafford, PLUS).

WORK-STUDY *Federal work-study:* Total amount: $28,431; 14 jobs averaging $3019.

APPLYING FOR FINANCIAL AID *Required financial aid forms:* FAFSA, state aid form. *Financial aid deadline (priority):* 8/1. *Notification date:* Continuous beginning 4/15. Students must reply within 2 weeks of notification.

CONTACT Mrs. Rashmi H. Wadhvani, Financial Aid Consultant, New York School of Interior Design, 170 East 70th Street, New York, NY 10021-5110, 212-472-1500 Ext. 204 or toll-free 800-336-9743 Ext. 205. *Fax:* 212-472-1867. *E-mail:* rwadhvani@nysid.edu.
Website: http://www.nysid.edu/.

NEW YORK UNIVERSITY
New York, NY

Tuition & fees: $49,062	Average undergraduate aid package: $34,532

ABOUT THE INSTITUTION Independent, coed. 116 undergraduate majors. Both federal and institutional methodology are used as a basis for awarding need-based institutional aid.

UNDERGRADUATE EXPENSES for 2016–2017 *Comprehensive fee:* $66,640 includes full-time tuition ($46,590), mandatory fees ($2472), and room and board ($17,578). *College room only:* $12,476. Full-time tuition and fees vary according to course load and program. Room and board charges vary according to board plan and housing facility. *Part-time tuition:* $1373 per credit hour. *Part-time fees:* $470 per term. Part-time tuition and fees vary according to program. *Payment plan:* Tuition prepayment.

FRESHMAN FINANCIAL AID (Fall 2015) 3,880 applied for aid; of those 75% were deemed to have need. 98% of freshmen with need received aid; of those 9% had need fully met. **Average percent of need met:** 67% (excluding resources awarded to replace EFC). **Average financial aid package:** $37,805 (excluding resources awarded to replace EFC). 3% of all full-time freshmen had no need and received non-need-based gift aid.

UNDERGRADUATE FINANCIAL AID (Fall 2015) 15,702 applied for aid; of those 80% were deemed to have need. 96% of undergraduates with need received aid; of those 7% had need fully met. **Average percent of need met:** 60% (excluding resources awarded to replace EFC). **Average financial aid package:** $34,532 (excluding resources awarded to replace EFC). 5% of all full-time undergraduates had no need and received non-need-based gift aid.

GIFT AID (NEED-BASED) Total amount: $341,120,938 (8% federal, 4% state, 86% institutional, 2% external sources). **Receiving aid:** Freshmen: 45% (2,630); all full-time undergraduates: 46% (11,104). **Average award:** Freshmen: $34,462; Undergraduates: $29,971. **Scholarships, grants, and awards:** Federal Pell, FSEOG, state, private, college/university gift aid from institutional funds, Federal Nursing.

GIFT AID (NON-NEED-BASED) Total amount: $18,042,209 (1% federal, 2% state, 59% institutional, 38% external sources). **Receiving aid:** Freshmen: 2. Undergraduates: 9. **Average award:** Freshmen: $4476. Undergraduates: $6167. **Scholarships, grants, and awards by category:** Academic interests/achievement: general academic interests/achievements. Creative arts/performance: general creative arts/performance. **Tuition waivers:** Full or partial for employees or children of employees.

LOANS Student loans: $100,726,522 (79% need-based, 21% non-need-based). 46% of past graduating class borrowed through all loan programs. Average indebtedness per student: $31,210. **Average need-based loan:** Freshmen: $3823. Undergraduates: $5233. **Parent loans:** $135,998,405 (51% need-based, 49% non-need-based). **Programs:** Federal Direct (Subsidized and Unsubsidized Stafford, PLUS), Perkins, Federal Nursing, college/university.

WORK-STUDY Federal work-study: jobs available.

APPLYING FOR FINANCIAL AID Required financial aid forms: FAFSA, CSS Financial Aid PROFILE, state aid form, noncustodial (divorced/separated) parent's statement. **Financial aid deadline:** 2/15. **Notification date:** 4/1. Students must reply by 5/1.

CONTACT Office of Financial Aid, New York University, 25 West Fourth Street, New York, NY 10012-1199, 212-998-4444. *Fax:* 212-995-4661. *E-mail:* financial.aid@nyu.edu.
Website: http://www.nyu.edu/.

NIAGARA UNIVERSITY
Niagara Falls, NY

Tuition & fees: $30,950	Average undergraduate aid package: $25,326

ABOUT THE INSTITUTION Independent Roman Catholic Church, coed. *Awards:* certificates, associate, bachelor's, master's, and doctoral degrees. 53 undergraduate majors. **Total enrollment:** 4,017. Undergraduates: 3,136. Freshmen: 625. Federal methodology is used as a basis for awarding need-based institutional aid.

UNDERGRADUATE EXPENSES for 2016–2017 Comprehensive fee: $43,650 includes full-time tuition ($29,500), mandatory fees ($1450), and room and board ($12,700). Full-time tuition and fees vary according to program. Room and board charges vary according to housing facility. **Part-time tuition:** $985 per credit hour. Part-time tuition and fees vary according to program.

FRESHMAN FINANCIAL AID (Fall 2016, est.) 553 applied for aid; of those 93% were deemed to have need. 100% of freshmen with need received aid; of those 52% had need fully met. **Average percent of need met:** 86% (excluding resources awarded to replace EFC). **Average financial aid package:** $27,638 (excluding resources awarded to replace EFC). 15% of all full-time freshmen had no need and received non-need-based gift aid.

UNDERGRADUATE FINANCIAL AID (Fall 2016, est.) 2,302 applied for aid; of those 92% were deemed to have need. 100% of undergraduates with need received aid; of those 53% had need fully met. **Average percent of need met:** 83% (excluding resources awarded to replace EFC). **Average financial aid package:** $25,326 (excluding resources awarded to replace EFC). 17% of all full-time undergraduates had no need and received non-need-based gift aid.

GIFT AID (NEED-BASED) Total amount: $44,144,613 (12% federal, 7% state, 80% institutional, 1% external sources). **Receiving aid:** Freshmen: 81% (496); all full-time undergraduates: 71% (2,064). **Average award:** Freshmen: $23,519; Undergrad-

uates: $20,970. **Scholarships, grants, and awards:** Federal Pell, FSEOG, state, private, college/university gift aid from institutional funds.

GIFT AID (NON-NEED-BASED) Total amount: $7,917,122 (5% federal, 94% institutional, 1% external sources). **Receiving aid:** Freshmen: 70% (428). Undergraduates: 57% (1,677). **Average award:** Freshmen: $15,699. Undergraduates: $14,868. **Scholarships, grants, and awards by category:** Academic interests/achievement: 2,536 awards ($32,685,981 total): general academic interests/achievements. Creative arts/performance: 57 awards ($280,706 total): theater/drama. Special achievements/activities: 16 awards ($80,000 total): community service. Special characteristics: 91 awards ($2,361,669 total): children of faculty/staff, relatives of clergy. **Tuition waivers:** Full or partial for employees or children of employees. **ROTC:** Army.

LOANS Student loans: $19,590,958 (94% need-based, 6% non-need-based). 74% of past graduating class borrowed through all loan programs. Average indebtedness per student: $32,251. **Average need-based loan:** Freshmen: $4649. Undergraduates: $4984. **Parent loans:** $7,645,188 (61% need-based, 39% non-need-based). **Programs:** Federal Direct (Subsidized and Unsubsidized Stafford, PLUS), Perkins, Federal Nursing, college/university.

WORK-STUDY Federal work-study: Total amount: $1,342,263; 424 jobs averaging $3380. **State or other work-study/employment:** Total amount: $233,364 (100% non-need-based). 46 part-time jobs averaging $5335.

ATHLETIC AWARDS Total amount: $4,499,279 (41% need-based, 59% non-need-based).

APPLYING FOR FINANCIAL AID Required financial aid forms: FAFSA, state aid form. **Financial aid deadline (priority):** 2/15. **Notification date:** Continuous beginning 2/15. Students must reply within 3 weeks of notification.

CONTACT Ms. Katie L. Kocsis, Director of Financial Aid, Niagara University, PO Box 2010, Niagara University, NY 14109, 716-286-8686 or toll-free 800-462-2111. *Fax:* 716-286-8678. *E-mail:* kkocsis@niagara.edu.
Website: http://www.niagara.edu/.

NICHOLLS STATE UNIVERSITY
Thibodaux, LA

Tuition & fees (LA res): $7641	Average undergraduate aid package: $10,110

ABOUT THE INSTITUTION State-supported, coed. 37 undergraduate majors. Federal methodology is used as a basis for awarding need-based institutional aid.

UNDERGRADUATE EXPENSES for 2016–2017 Tuition, state resident: full-time $4922. **Tuition, nonresident:** full-time $15,853. **Required fees:** full-time $2719. Full-time tuition and fees vary according to location and program. Part-time tuition and fees vary according to course load, location, and program. **College room and board:** $9676. Room and board charges vary according to board plan, housing facility, and location.

FRESHMAN FINANCIAL AID (Fall 2015) 1,136 applied for aid; of those 68% were deemed to have need. 98% of freshmen with need received aid; of those 20% had need fully met. **Average percent of need met:** 70% (excluding resources awarded to replace EFC). **Average financial aid package:** $11,512 (excluding resources awarded to replace EFC). 11% of all full-time freshmen had no need and received non-need-based gift aid.

UNDERGRADUATE FINANCIAL AID (Fall 2015) 4,099 applied for aid; of those 73% were deemed to have need. 98% of undergraduates with need received aid; of those 16% had need fully met. **Average percent of need met:** 62% (excluding resources awarded to replace EFC). **Average financial aid package:** $10,110 (excluding resources awarded to replace EFC). 8% of all full-time undergraduates had no need and received non-need-based gift aid.

GIFT AID (NEED-BASED) Total amount: $18,958,488 (47% federal, 35% state, 10% institutional, 8% external sources). **Receiving aid:** Freshmen: 61% (731); all full-time undergraduates: 57% (2,614). **Average award:** Freshmen: $8557; Undergraduates: $7472. **Scholarships, grants, and awards:** Federal Pell, FSEOG, state, private, college/university gift aid from institutional funds.

GIFT AID (NON-NEED-BASED) Total amount: $7,896,324 (4% federal, 67% state, 22% institutional, 7% external sources). **Receiving aid:** Freshmen: 10% (114). Undergraduates: 8% (360). **Average award:** Freshmen: $3580. Undergraduates: $3796. **Scholarships, grants, and awards by category:** Academic interests/achievement: general academic interests/achievements. Creative arts/performance: dance, music. Special achievements/activities: cheerleading/drum major, leadership.

Special characteristics: children of faculty/staff, general special characteristics, local/state students, members of minority groups, out-of-state students, previous college experience, public servants, veterans. *Tuition waivers:* Full or partial for employees or children of employees, senior citizens.

LOANS *Student loans:* $9,688,561 (51% need-based, 49% non-need-based). *Average need-based loan:* Freshmen: $2683. Undergraduates: $3160. *Parent loans:* $2,503,856 (59% need-based, 41% non-need-based). *Programs:* Federal Direct (Subsidized and Unsubsidized Stafford, PLUS).

WORK-STUDY *Federal work-study:* 11 jobs averaging $1470. *State or other work-study/employment:* Total amount: $369,790 (69% need-based, 31% non-need-based). 77 part-time jobs averaging $4802.

ATHLETIC AWARDS Total amount: $2,152,937 (61% need-based, 39% non-need-based).

APPLYING FOR FINANCIAL AID *Required financial aid forms:* FAFSA, institution's own form, state aid form, noncustodial (divorced/separated) parent's statement. *Financial aid deadline:* 6/30 (priority: 4/15). *Notification date:* Continuous.

CONTACT Casie Triche, Director of Financial Aid, Nicholls State University, PO Box 2005, Thibodaux, LA 70310, 985-448-4077 or toll-free 877-NICHOLLS. *Fax:* 985-448-4124. *E-mail:* finaid@nicholls.edu.
Website: http://www.nicholls.edu/.

NICHOLS COLLEGE
Dudley, MA

Tuition & fees: $34,000	Average undergraduate aid package: $28,590

ABOUT THE INSTITUTION Independent, coed. *Awards:* certificates, associate, bachelor's, and master's degrees. 16 undergraduate majors. *Total enrollment:* 1,479. Undergraduates: 1,272. Freshmen: 353. Federal methodology is used as a basis for awarding need-based institutional aid.

UNDERGRADUATE EXPENSES for 2017–2018 *Comprehensive fee:* $47,800 includes full-time tuition ($33,600), mandatory fees ($400), and room and board ($13,800). Room and board charges vary according to board plan and housing facility. *Part-time tuition:* $1120 per credit. *Part-time fees:* $200 per term. Part-time tuition and fees vary according to course load.

FRESHMAN FINANCIAL AID (Fall 2016, est.) 326 applied for aid; of those 90% were deemed to have need. 100% of freshmen with need received aid; of those 21% had need fully met. *Average percent of need met:* 81% (excluding resources awarded to replace EFC). *Average financial aid package:* $28,773 (excluding resources awarded to replace EFC). 15% of all full-time freshmen had no need and received non-need-based gift aid.

UNDERGRADUATE FINANCIAL AID (Fall 2016, est.) 1,047 applied for aid; of those 91% were deemed to have need. 100% of undergraduates with need received aid; of those 21% had need fully met. *Average percent of need met:* 84% (excluding resources awarded to replace EFC). *Average financial aid package:* $28,590 (excluding resources awarded to replace EFC). 19% of all full-time undergraduates had no need and received non-need-based gift aid.

GIFT AID (NEED-BASED) *Total amount:* $20,836,023 (9% federal, 2% state, 88% institutional, 1% external sources). *Receiving aid:* Freshmen: 84% (294); all full-time undergraduates: 82% (954). *Average award:* Freshmen: $21,521; Undergraduates: $20,349. *Scholarships, grants, and awards:* Federal Pell, FSEOG, state, private, college/university gift aid from institutional funds.

GIFT AID (NON-NEED-BASED) *Total amount:* $1,881,000 (100% institutional). *Receiving aid:* Freshmen: 7% (23). Undergraduates: 11% (126). *Average award:* Freshmen: $17,221. Undergraduates: $15,404. *Scholarships, grants, and awards by category: Academic interests/achievement:* general academic interests/achievements. *Special achievements/activities:* community service, general special achievements/activities, leadership. *Special characteristics:* children and siblings of alumni, children of faculty/staff, siblings of current students. *Tuition waivers:* Full or partial for employees or children of employees.

LOANS *Student loans:* $8,565,370 (92% need-based, 8% non-need-based). 88% of past graduating class borrowed through all loan programs. *Average indebtedness per student:* $35,392. *Average need-based loan:* Freshmen: $3332. Undergraduates: $4214. *Parent loans:* $5,063,372 (95% need-based, 5% non-need-based). *Programs:* Federal Direct (Subsidized and Unsubsidized Stafford, PLUS).

WORK-STUDY *Federal work-study:* Total amount: $351,931; jobs available.

APPLYING FOR FINANCIAL AID *Required financial aid form:* FAFSA. *Financial aid deadline (priority):* 3/1. *Notification date:* Continuous beginning 12/1. Students must reply within 2 weeks of notification.

CONTACT Mrs. Jennifer Bianco, Director of Financial Assistance, Nichols College, PO Box 5000, Dudley, MA 01571, 508-213-2340 or toll-free 800-470-3379. *Fax:* 508-213-2118. *E-mail:* jennifer.bianco@nichols.edu.
Website: http://www.nichols.edu/.

NORFOLK STATE UNIVERSITY
Norfolk, VA

CONTACT Mr. Kevin Burns, Director of Financial Aid, Norfolk State University, 700 Park Avenue, Norfolk, VA 23504-3907, 757-823-8381 or toll-free 800-274-1821. *Fax:* 757-823-9059. *E-mail:* kburns@nsu.edu.
Website: http://www.nsu.edu/.

NORTH AMERICAN UNIVERSITY
Stafford, TX

CONTACT Financial Aid Office, North American University, 11929 West Airport Boulevard, Stafford, TX 77477, 832-230-5555.
Website: http://www.na.edu/.

NORTH CAROLINA AGRICULTURAL AND TECHNICAL STATE UNIVERSITY
Greensboro, NC

Tuition & fees (NC res): $6372	Average undergraduate aid package: $10,989

ABOUT THE INSTITUTION State-supported, coed. 92 undergraduate majors. Both federal and institutional methodology are used as a basis for awarding need-based institutional aid.

UNDERGRADUATE EXPENSES for 2016–2017 *Tuition, state resident:* full-time $3470. *Tuition, nonresident:* full-time $16,230. *Required fees:* full-time $2902. Full-time tuition and fees vary according to course load, degree level, and program. Part-time tuition and fees vary according to course load, degree level, and program. *College room and board:* $7153; *Room only:* $3859. Room and board charges vary according to board plan and housing facility.

FRESHMAN FINANCIAL AID (Fall 2016, est.) 1,884 applied for aid; of those 90% were deemed to have need. 99% of freshmen with need received aid; of those 9% had need fully met. *Average percent of need met:* 64% (excluding resources awarded to replace EFC). *Average financial aid package:* $11,393 (excluding resources awarded to replace EFC). 2% of all full-time freshmen had no need and received non-need-based gift aid.

UNDERGRADUATE FINANCIAL AID (Fall 2016, est.) 8,219 applied for aid; of those 91% were deemed to have need. 98% of undergraduates with need received aid; of those 8% had need fully met. *Average percent of need met:* 65% (excluding resources awarded to replace EFC). *Average financial aid package:* $10,989 (excluding resources awarded to replace EFC). 2% of all full-time undergraduates had no need and received non-need-based gift aid.

GIFT AID (NEED-BASED) *Total amount:* $51,932,499 (51% federal, 39% state, 10% institutional). *Receiving aid:* Freshmen: 77% (1,480); all full-time undergraduates: 71% (6,157). *Average award:* Freshmen: $7701; Undergraduates: $7258. *Scholarships, grants, and awards:* Federal Pell, FSEOG, state, private, college/university gift aid from institutional funds.

GIFT AID (NON-NEED-BASED) *Total amount:* $520,830 (1% federal, 23% state, 76% institutional). *Receiving aid:* Freshmen: 33% (643). Undergraduates: 22% (1,919). *Average award:* Freshmen: $5021. Undergraduates: $5597. *Scholarships, grants, and awards by category: Academic interests/achievement:* agriculture, business, engineering/technologies, general academic interests/achievements. *Creative arts/performance:* music.

LOANS *Student loans:* $55,621,839 (94% need-based, 6% non-need-based). 65% of past graduating class borrowed through all loan programs. *Average indebtedness*

per student: $31,010. *Average need-based loan:* Freshmen: $3332. Undergraduates: $4001. *Parent loans:* $17,460,855 (71% need-based, 29% non-need-based). *Programs:* Federal Direct (Subsidized and Unsubsidized Stafford, PLUS), Perkins.

WORK-STUDY *Federal work-study:* Total amount: $489,081; jobs available.

ATHLETIC AWARDS Total amount: $3,085,959 (92% need-based, 8% non-need-based).

APPLYING FOR FINANCIAL AID *Required financial aid form:* FAFSA. *Financial aid deadline (priority):* 3/1. *Notification date:* 4/15. Students must reply within 2 weeks of notification.

CONTACT Mrs. Sherri Avent, Director of Student Financial Aid, North Carolina Agricultural and Technical State University, Dowdy Administration Building, Room 100, 1601 East Market Street, Greensboro, NC 27411, 336-334-7973 or toll-free 800-443-8964 (in-state). *Fax:* 336-334-7954. *E-mail:* avent@ncat.edu.

Website: http://www.ncat.edu/.

NORTH CAROLINA CENTRAL UNIVERSITY
Durham, NC

ABOUT THE INSTITUTION State-supported, coed. *Awards:* bachelor's, master's, and doctoral degrees. 30 undergraduate majors. *Total enrollment:* 8,096. Undergraduates: 6,285. Freshmen: 1,151.

GIFT AID (NEED-BASED) *Scholarships, grants, and awards:* Federal Pell, FSEOG, state, private, college/university gift aid from institutional funds, Federal Nursing.

GIFT AID (NON-NEED-BASED) *Scholarships, grants, and awards by category:* *Academic interests/achievement:* biological sciences, business, computer science, education, English, general academic interests/achievements, library science, physical sciences, social sciences. *Creative arts/performance:* art/fine arts, music, theater/drama. *Special achievements/activities:* leadership. *Special characteristics:* children and siblings of alumni, general special characteristics.

LOANS *Programs:* Federal Direct (Subsidized and Unsubsidized Stafford, PLUS), Perkins, Federal Nursing.

APPLYING FOR FINANCIAL AID *Required financial aid form:* FAFSA.

CONTACT Mrs. Sharon J. Oliver, Director of Financial Aid, North Carolina Central University, 106 Student Services Building, Durham, NC 27707-3129, 919-530-5313 or toll-free 877-667-7533. *Fax:* 919-530-7959. *E-mail:* soliver@nccu.edu.

Website: http://www.nccu.edu/.

NORTH CAROLINA STATE UNIVERSITY
Raleigh, NC

Tuition & fees (NC res): $9058	Average undergraduate aid package: $13,082

ABOUT THE INSTITUTION State-supported, coed. *Awards:* certificates, associate, bachelor's, master's, and doctoral degrees. 93 undergraduate majors. *Total enrollment:* 33,755. Undergraduates: 23,847. Freshmen: 4,388. Federal methodology is used as a basis for awarding need-based institutional aid.

UNDERGRADUATE EXPENSES for 2017-2018 *Application fee:* $85. *Tuition, state resident:* full-time $6535. *Tuition, nonresident:* full-time $24,883. *Required fees:* full-time $2523. Full-time tuition and fees vary according to degree level, location, program, and reciprocity agreements. Part-time tuition and fees vary according to course load, degree level, location, program, and reciprocity agreements. *College room and board:* $10,854; *Room only:* $6618. Room and board charges vary according to board plan and housing facility. *Payment plan:* Guaranteed tuition.

FRESHMAN FINANCIAL AID (Fall 2016, est.) 3,408 applied for aid; of those 60% were deemed to have need. 98% of freshmen with need received aid; of those 25% had need fully met. *Average percent of need met:* 79% (excluding resources awarded to replace EFC). *Average financial aid package:* $13,394 (excluding resources awarded to replace EFC). 4% of all full-time freshmen had no need and received non-need-based gift aid.

UNDERGRADUATE FINANCIAL AID (Fall 2016, est.) 13,940 applied for aid; of those 73% were deemed to have need. 98% of undergraduates with need received

aid; of those 23% had need fully met. *Average percent of need met:* 77% (excluding resources awarded to replace EFC). *Average financial aid package:* $13,082 (excluding resources awarded to replace EFC). 5% of all full-time undergraduates had no need and received non-need-based gift aid.

GIFT AID (NEED-BASED) *Total amount:* $94,095,598 (22% federal, 18% state, 56% institutional, 4% external sources). *Receiving aid:* Freshmen: 43% (1,897); all full-time undergraduates: 44% (9,148). *Average award:* Freshmen: $10,526; Undergraduates: $10,004. *Scholarships, grants, and awards:* Federal Pell, FSEOG, state, private, college/university gift aid from institutional funds, United Negro College Fund.

GIFT AID (NON-NEED-BASED) *Total amount:* $18,114,193 (5% state, 54% institutional, 41% external sources). *Receiving aid:* Freshmen: 9% (412). Undergraduates: 6% (1,334). *Average award:* Freshmen: $6552. Undergraduates: $5995. *Scholarships, grants, and awards by category:* *Academic interests/achievement:* 3,949 awards ($15,289,770 total): agriculture, architecture, biological sciences, business, computer science, education, engineering/technologies, general academic interests/achievements, humanities, mathematics, military science, physical sciences, social sciences. *Special achievements/activities:* cheerleading/drum major, general special achievements/activities, leadership. *Special characteristics:* children and siblings of alumni, children of faculty/staff, general special characteristics, local/state students. *Tuition waivers:* Full or partial for employees or children of employees. *ROTC:* Army, Naval, Air Force.

LOANS *Student loans:* $68,859,763 (62% need-based, 38% non-need-based). 54% of past graduating class borrowed through all loan programs. *Average indebtedness per student:* $21,507. *Average need-based loan:* Freshmen: $3130. Undergraduates: $3944. *Parent loans:* $13,805,386 (15% need-based, 85% non-need-based). *Programs:* Federal Direct (Subsidized and Unsubsidized Stafford, PLUS), Perkins, state, college/university.

WORK-STUDY *Federal work-study:* Total amount: $1,318,381; 876 jobs averaging $1645. *State or other work-study/employment:* Total amount: $2,276,643 (31% need-based, 69% non-need-based). 1,385 part-time jobs averaging $1910.

ATHLETIC AWARDS Total amount: $9,872,768 (46% need-based, 54% non-need-based).

APPLYING FOR FINANCIAL AID *Required financial aid form:* FAFSA. *Financial aid deadline (priority):* 3/1. *Notification date:* Continuous beginning 4/1.

CONTACT Ms. Krista Ringler, Director of Scholarships and Financial Aid, North Carolina State University, 2016 Harris Hall, Box 7302, Raleigh, NC 27695-7302, 919-515-2421. *Fax:* 919-515-8422. *E-mail:* krista_ringler@ncsu.edu.

Website: http://www.ncsu.edu/.

NORTH CAROLINA WESLEYAN COLLEGE
Rocky Mount, NC

CONTACT Leah Hill, Director of Financial Aid, North Carolina Wesleyan College, 3400 North Wesleyan Boulevard, Rocky Mount, NC 27804, 252-985-5200 or toll-free 800-488-6292. *Fax:* 252-985-5295. *E-mail:* lhill@ncwc.edu.

Website: http://www.ncwc.edu/.

NORTH CENTRAL COLLEGE
Naperville, IL

Tuition & fees: $36,654	Average undergraduate aid package: $24,522

ABOUT THE INSTITUTION Independent United Methodist, coed. *Awards:* certificates, bachelor's, and master's degrees. 70 undergraduate majors. *Total enrollment:* 2,949. Undergraduates: 2,716. Freshmen: 589. Federal methodology is used as a basis for awarding need-based institutional aid.

UNDERGRADUATE EXPENSES for 2016-2017 *Application fee:* $25. *Comprehensive fee:* $47,010 includes full-time tuition ($36,474), mandatory fees ($180), and room and board ($10,356). *College room only:* $7173. Room and board charges vary according to housing facility. *Part-time tuition:* $1013 per credit hour.

Part-time fees: $20 per term. Part-time tuition and fees vary according to course load.
FRESHMAN FINANCIAL AID (Fall 2016, est.) 545 applied for aid; of those 88% were deemed to have need. 100% of freshmen with need received aid; of those 23% had need fully met. *Average percent of need met:* 82% (excluding resources awarded to replace EFC). *Average financial aid package:* $25,507 (excluding resources awarded to replace EFC). 18% of all full-time freshmen had no need and received non-need-based gift aid.
UNDERGRADUATE FINANCIAL AID (Fall 2016, est.) 2,207 applied for aid; of those 90% were deemed to have need. 100% of undergraduates with need received aid; of those 18% had need fully met. *Average percent of need met:* 78% (excluding resources awarded to replace EFC). *Average financial aid package:* $24,522 (excluding resources awarded to replace EFC). 21% of all full-time undergraduates had no need and received non-need-based gift aid.
GIFT AID (NEED-BASED) Total amount: $42,246,689 (7% federal, 8% state, 83% institutional, 2% external sources). *Receiving aid:* Freshmen: 82% (482); all full-time undergraduates: 78% (1,989). *Average award:* Freshmen: $23,024; Undergraduates: $20,954. *Scholarships, grants, and awards:* Federal Pell, FSEOG, state, private, college/university gift aid from institutional funds.
GIFT AID (NON-NEED-BASED) Total amount: $11,187,297 (96% institutional, 4% external sources). *Receiving aid:* Freshmen: 16% (92). Undergraduates: 11% (279). *Average award:* Freshmen: $17,875. Undergraduates: $17,057. *Scholarships, grants, and awards by category: Academic interests/achievement:* biological sciences, business, communication, computer science, education, English, foreign languages, general academic interests/achievements, humanities, international studies, mathematics, physical sciences, premedicine, religion/biblical studies, social sciences. *Creative arts/performance:* art/fine arts, cinema/film/broadcasting, debating, journalism/publications, music, theater/drama. *Special achievements/activities:* community service, religious involvement. *Special characteristics:* adult students, children of faculty/staff, general special characteristics, international students, relatives of clergy. *Tuition waivers:* Full or partial for employees or children of employees, senior citizens. *ROTC:* Army cooperative, Air Force cooperative.
LOANS Student loans: $19,101,926 (68% need-based, 32% non-need-based). 79% of past graduating class borrowed through all loan programs. *Average indebtedness per student:* $34,911. *Average need-based loan:* Freshmen: $3297. Undergraduates: $4481. *Parent loans:* $6,267,982 (40% need-based, 60% non-need-based). *Programs:* Federal Direct (Subsidized and Unsubsidized Stafford, PLUS), Perkins, college/university.
WORK-STUDY Federal work-study: Total amount: $352,925; 1,423 jobs averaging $248. *State or other work-study/employment:* Part-time jobs available.
APPLYING FOR FINANCIAL AID Required financial aid forms: FAFSA, federal income tax form(s). *Financial aid deadline:* Continuous. *Notification date:* Continuous beginning 2/1. Students must reply within 4 weeks of notification.
CONTACT Kristina Bonn, Director of Financial Aid, North Central College, 30 North Brainard Street, Naperville, IL 60540, 630-637-5600 or toll-free 800-411-1861. *Fax:* 630-637-5608. *E-mail:* klbonn@noctrl.edu.
Website: http://www.northcentralcollege.edu/.

NORTH CENTRAL UNIVERSITY
Minneapolis, MN

CONTACT Mrs. Donna Jager, Director of Financial Aid, North Central University, 910 Elliot Avenue, Minneapolis, MN 55404-1322, 612-343-4485 or toll-free 800-289-6222. *Fax:* 612-343-8067. *E-mail:* finaid@northcentral.edu.
Website: http://www.northcentral.edu/.

NORTH DAKOTA STATE UNIVERSITY
Fargo, ND

CONTACT Jeanne Enebo, Director of Financial Aid, North Dakota State University, PO Box 5315, Fargo, ND 58105, 701-231-7537 or toll-free 800-488-6378. *Fax:* 701-231-6126. *E-mail:* j.enebo@ndsu.edu.
Website: http://www.ndsu.edu/.

NORTHEAST CATHOLIC COLLEGE
Warner, NH

Tuition & fees: N/R	Average undergraduate aid package: $18,976

ABOUT THE INSTITUTION Independent Roman Catholic, coed. 1 undergraduate major. Institutional methodology is used as a basis for awarding need-based institutional aid.
FRESHMAN FINANCIAL AID (Fall 2015) 23 applied for aid; of those 100% were deemed to have need. 100% of freshmen with need received aid; of those 100% had need fully met. *Average percent of need met:* 100% (excluding resources awarded to replace EFC). *Average financial aid package:* $24,638 (excluding resources awarded to replace EFC).
UNDERGRADUATE FINANCIAL AID (Fall 2015) 65 applied for aid; of those 100% were deemed to have need. 100% of undergraduates with need received aid; of those 100% had need fully met. *Average percent of need met:* 100% (excluding resources awarded to replace EFC). *Average financial aid package:* $18,976 (excluding resources awarded to replace EFC).
GIFT AID (NEED-BASED) Total amount: $632,626 (27% federal, 73% institutional). *Receiving aid:* Freshmen: 70% (23); all full-time undergraduates: 76% (65). *Average award:* Freshmen: $12,312; Undergraduates: $18,686. *Scholarships, grants, and awards:* Federal Pell, state, private, college/university gift aid from institutional funds.
GIFT AID (NON-NEED-BASED) Total amount: $914,420 (99% institutional, 1% external sources). *Receiving aid:* Freshmen: 70% (23). Undergraduates: 56% (48). *Scholarships, grants, and awards by category: Academic interests/achievement:* English, general academic interests/achievements, humanities, religion/biblical studies.
LOANS Student loans: $364,305 (52% need-based, 48% non-need-based). 71% of past graduating class borrowed through all loan programs. *Average indebtedness per student:* $18,186. *Parent loans:* $29,868 (100% need-based). *Programs:* Federal Direct (Subsidized and Unsubsidized Stafford, PLUS), alternative loans.
WORK-STUDY State or other work-study/employment: Total amount: $102,463 (100% need-based). Part-time jobs available.
APPLYING FOR FINANCIAL AID Required financial aid forms: institution's own form, business/farm supplement, federal income tax form(s). *Financial aid deadline:* Continuous. *Notification date:* Continuous beginning 2/1. Students must reply within 4 weeks of notification.
CONTACT Marie A. Lasher, Financial Aid Director, Northeast Catholic College, 511 Kearsarge Mountain Road, Warner, NH 03278, 603-456-2656 Ext. 136 or toll-free 877-498-1723. *Fax:* 603-456-2660. *E-mail:* mlasher@northeastcatholic.edu.
Website: http://www.magdalen.edu/.

NORTHEASTERN ILLINOIS UNIVERSITY
Chicago, IL

Tuition & fees (IL res): $13,001	Average undergraduate aid package: $8549

ABOUT THE INSTITUTION State-supported, coed. *Awards:* certificates, bachelor's, and master's degrees. 41 undergraduate majors. *Total enrollment:* 9,538. Undergraduates: 7,665. Freshmen: 801. Federal methodology is used as a basis for awarding need-based institutional aid.
UNDERGRADUATE EXPENSES for 2017-2018 Application fee: $30. *Tuition, state resident:* full-time $11,320; part-time $377 per credit hour. *Tuition, nonresident:* full-time $22,639; part-time $755 per credit hour. *Required fees:* full-time $1681. Full-time tuition and fees vary according to course load and degree level. Part-time tuition and fees vary according to course load and degree level. *College room and board:* $11,424; *Room only:* $8424. Room and board charges vary according to housing facility. *Payment plan:* Guaranteed tuition.
FRESHMAN FINANCIAL AID (Fall 2016, est.) 694 applied for aid; of those 77% were deemed to have need. 85% of freshmen with need received aid; of those 4% had need fully met. *Average percent of need met:* 18% (excluding resources awarded to replace EFC). *Average financial aid package:* $9090 (excluding resources awarded to replace EFC). 1% of all full-time freshmen had no need and received non-need-based gift aid.

UNDERGRADUATE FINANCIAL AID (Fall 2016, est.) 3,473 applied for aid; of those 83% were deemed to have need. 91% of undergraduates with need received aid; of those 4% had need fully met. *Average percent of need met:* 17% (excluding resources awarded to replace EFC). *Average financial aid package:* $8549 (excluding resources awarded to replace EFC). 2% of all full-time undergraduates had no need and received non-need-based gift aid.
GIFT AID (NEED-BASED) *Total amount:* $28,636,990 (64% federal, 29% state, 3% institutional, 4% external sources). *Receiving aid:* Freshmen: 60% (457); all full-time undergraduates: 52% (2,237). *Average award:* Freshmen: $7774; Undergraduates: $6882. *Scholarships, grants, and awards:* Federal Pell, FSEOG, state, private, college/university gift aid from institutional funds.
GIFT AID (NON-NEED-BASED) *Total amount:* $816,683 (42% state, 26% institutional, 32% external sources). *Receiving aid:* Freshmen: 9% (66). Undergraduates: 10% (445). *Average award:* Freshmen: $11,524. Undergraduates: $1936. *Scholarships, grants, and awards by category: Academic interests/achievement:* biological sciences, business, communication, computer science, education, English, foreign languages, general academic interests/achievements, mathematics, physical sciences, social sciences. *Creative arts/performance:* art/fine arts, creative writing, dance, journalism/publications, music, performing arts, theater/drama. *Special achievements/activities:* leadership. *Special characteristics:* adult students, children of faculty/staff, children of union members/company employees, general special characteristics. *Tuition waivers:* Full or partial for employees or children of employees, senior citizens. *ROTC:* Army cooperative, Air Force cooperative.
LOANS *Student loans:* $17,914,676 (43% need-based, 57% non-need-based). 55% of past graduating class borrowed through all loan programs. *Average indebtedness per student:* $16,247. *Average need-based loan:* Freshmen: $3314. Undergraduates: $4277. *Parent loans:* $695,142 (100% non-need-based). *Programs:* Federal Direct (Subsidized and Unsubsidized Stafford, PLUS), Perkins.
WORK-STUDY *Federal work-study:* Total amount: $131,996; jobs available. *State or other work-study/employment:* Total amount: $400,737 (100% non-need-based). Part-time jobs available.
APPLYING FOR FINANCIAL AID *Required financial aid form:* FAFSA. *Financial aid deadline (priority):* 2/28. *Notification date:* Continuous beginning 3/15. Students must reply within 2 weeks of notification.
CONTACT Ms. Maureen T. Amos, Director of Financial Aid, Northeastern Illinois University, 5500 North St. Louis Avenue, Chicago, IL 60625, 773-442-5010. Fax: 773-442-5040. *E-mail:* financial-aid@neiu.edu.
Website: http://www.neiu.edu/.

(excluding resources awarded to replace EFC). 4% of all full-time undergraduates had no need and received non-need-based gift aid.
GIFT AID (NEED-BASED) *Total amount:* $21,461,753 (70% federal, 23% state, 1% institutional, 6% external sources). *Receiving aid:* Freshmen: 59% (522); all full-time undergraduates: 59% (2,853). *Average award:* Freshmen: $7035; Undergraduates: $6898. *Scholarships, grants, and awards:* Federal Pell, FSEOG, state, private, college/university gift aid from institutional funds, United Negro College Fund.
GIFT AID (NON-NEED-BASED) *Total amount:* $1,758,673 (1% federal, 3% state, 39% institutional, 57% external sources). *Receiving aid:* Freshmen: 18% (157). Undergraduates: 10% (504). *Average award:* Freshmen: $2710. Undergraduates: $2703. *Scholarships, grants, and awards by category: Academic interests/achievement:* biological sciences, business, communication, computer science, education, English, foreign languages, general academic interests/achievements, health fields, home economics, humanities, library science, mathematics, physical sciences, premedicine, social sciences. *Creative arts/performance:* applied art and design, art/fine arts, dance, debating, journalism/publications, music, performing arts, theater/drama. *Special achievements/activities:* cheerleading/drum major, community service, junior miss, leadership. *Special characteristics:* children and siblings of alumni, children of faculty/staff, children with a deceased or disabled parent, local/state students, members of minority groups, out-of-state students, religious affiliation, spouses of deceased or disabled public servants. *Tuition waivers:* Full or partial for employees or children of employees. *ROTC:* Army.
LOANS *Student loans:* $33,155,954 (75% need-based, 25% non-need-based). 65% of past graduating class borrowed through all loan programs. *Average indebtedness per student:* $23,840. *Average need-based loan:* Freshmen: $5127. Undergraduates: $6920. *Parent loans:* $8,016,598 (19% need-based, 81% non-need-based). *Programs:* Federal Direct (Subsidized and Unsubsidized Stafford, PLUS), Perkins.
WORK-STUDY *Federal work-study:* Total amount: $396,793; 210 jobs averaging $1133. *State or other work-study/employment:* Total amount: $2,205,189 (100% non-need-based). 776 part-time jobs averaging $1786.
ATHLETIC AWARDS Total amount: $1,031,406 (12% need-based, 88% non-need-based).
APPLYING FOR FINANCIAL AID *Required financial aid form:* FAFSA. *Financial aid deadline:* Continuous. *Notification date:* Continuous beginning 11/1.
CONTACT Dr. Teri Cochran, Director of Student Financial Services, Northeastern State University, 715 North Grand Avenue, Tahlequah, OK 74464-2399, 918-444-3410 or toll-free 800-722-9614. Fax: 918-458-2510. *E-mail:* cochrant@nsuok.edu.
Website: http://www.nsuok.edu/.

NORTHEASTERN STATE UNIVERSITY
Tahlequah, OK

Tuition & fees (OK res): $6207	Average undergraduate aid package: $12,453

ABOUT THE INSTITUTION State-supported, coed. *Awards:* certificates, bachelor's, master's, and doctoral degrees. 59 undergraduate majors. *Total enrollment:* 8,100. Undergraduates: 6,923. Freshmen: 878. Federal methodology is used as a basis for awarding need-based institutional aid.
UNDERGRADUATE EXPENSES for 2016–2017 *Application fee:* $25. *Tuition, state resident:* full-time $5085; part-time $169.50 per credit hour. *Tuition, nonresident:* full-time $12,585; part-time $419.50 per credit hour. *Required fees:* full-time $1122; $37.40 per credit hour. Full-time tuition and fees vary according to course load and program. Part-time tuition and fees vary according to course load and program. *College room and board:* $6650; *Room only:* $2900. Room and board charges vary according to board plan and housing facility. *Payment plan:* Guaranteed tuition.
FRESHMAN FINANCIAL AID (Fall 2016, est.) 828 applied for aid; of those 68% were deemed to have need. 100% of freshmen with need received aid; of those 86% had need fully met. *Average percent of need met:* 99% (excluding resources awarded to replace EFC). *Average financial aid package:* $11,045 (excluding resources awarded to replace EFC). 8% of all full-time freshmen had no need and received non-need-based gift aid.
UNDERGRADUATE FINANCIAL AID (Fall 2016, est.) 4,180 applied for aid; of those 78% were deemed to have need. 99% of undergraduates with need received aid; of those 70% had need fully met. *Average percent of need met:* 95% (excluding resources awarded to replace EFC). *Average financial aid package:* $12,453

NORTHEASTERN UNIVERSITY
Boston, MA

Tuition & fees: $47,653	Average undergraduate aid package: $31,140

ABOUT THE INSTITUTION Independent, coed. *Awards:* certificates, bachelor's, master's, and doctoral degrees. 65 undergraduate majors. *Total enrollment:* 25,466. Undergraduates: 17,923. Freshmen: 2,676. Institutional methodology is used as a basis for awarding need-based institutional aid.
UNDERGRADUATE EXPENSES for 2016–2017 *Application fee:* $75. *Comprehensive fee:* $63,253 includes full-time tuition ($46,720), mandatory fees ($933), and room and board ($15,600). *College room only:* $8400. Room and board charges vary according to board plan and housing facility.
FRESHMAN FINANCIAL AID (Fall 2016, est.) 1,832 applied for aid; of those 69% were deemed to have need. 100% of freshmen with need received aid; of those 100% had need fully met. *Average percent of need met:* 100% (excluding resources awarded to replace EFC). *Average financial aid package:* $39,320 (excluding resources awarded to replace EFC). 22% of all full-time freshmen had no need and received non-need-based gift aid.
UNDERGRADUATE FINANCIAL AID (Fall 2016, est.) 8,632 applied for aid; of those 78% were deemed to have need. 98% of undergraduates with need received aid; of those 38% had need fully met. *Average percent of need met:* 86% (excluding resources awarded to replace EFC). *Average financial aid package:* $31,140 (excluding resources awarded to replace EFC). 23% of all full-time undergraduates had no need and received non-need-based gift aid.
GIFT AID (NEED-BASED) *Total amount:* $167,231,512 (7% federal, 1% state, 90% institutional, 2% external sources). *Receiving aid:* Freshmen: 47% (1,251); all

full-time undergraduates: 34% (6,129). *Average award:* Freshmen: $34,803; Undergraduates: $27,534. *Scholarships, grants, and awards:* Federal Pell, FSEOG, state, private, college/university gift aid from institutional funds.

GIFT AID (NON-NEED-BASED) *Total amount:* $86,516,887 (1% federal, 93% institutional, 6% external sources). *Receiving aid:* Freshmen: 21% (575). Undergraduates: 13% (2,434). *Average award:* Freshmen: $19,869. Undergraduates: $15,579. *Tuition waivers:* Full or partial for employees or children of employees. *ROTC:* Army, Naval cooperative, Air Force cooperative.

LOANS *Student loans:* $79,818,280 (53% need-based, 47% non-need-based). *Average need-based loan:* Freshmen: $4281. Undergraduates: $4958. *Parent loans:* $12,120,651 (22% need-based, 78% non-need-based). *Programs:* Federal Direct (Subsidized and Unsubsidized Stafford, PLUS), Perkins, Federal Nursing, state.

WORK-STUDY *Federal work-study:* Total amount: $8,386,769; jobs available.

ATHLETIC AWARDS Total amount: $11,295,487 (19% need-based, 81% non-need-based).

APPLYING FOR FINANCIAL AID *Required financial aid forms:* FAFSA, CSS Financial Aid PROFILE, noncustodial (divorced/separated) parent's statement. *Financial aid deadline (priority):* 2/15. *Notification date:* 4/1. Students must reply by 5/1.

CONTACT Mr. Anthony Erwin, Dean of Financial Aid, Northeastern University, 360 Huntington Avenue, Boston, MA 02115, 617-373-3190. *Fax:* 617-373-8735. *E-mail:* sfs@northeastern.edu.
Website: http://www.northeastern.edu/.

NORTHERN ARIZONA UNIVERSITY
Flagstaff, AZ

Tuition & fees (AZ res): $10,764	Average undergraduate aid package: $11,505

ABOUT THE INSTITUTION State-supported, coed. *Awards:* certificates, bachelor's, master's, and doctoral degrees. 65 undergraduate majors. *Total enrollment:* 30,368. Undergraduates: 26,506. Freshmen: 5,607. Federal methodology is used as a basis for awarding need-based institutional aid.

UNDERGRADUATE EXPENSES for 2016–2017 *Application fee:* $25. *Tuition, state resident:* full-time $9746; part-time $696 per credit hour. *Tuition, nonresident:* full-time $23,126; part-time $964 per credit hour. *Required fees:* full-time $1018; $336 per credit hour. Full-time tuition and fees vary according to course load, location, and reciprocity agreements. Part-time tuition and fees vary according to course load, location, and reciprocity agreements. *College room and board:* $9482; *Room only:* $5128. Room and board charges vary according to board plan and housing facility. *Payment plan:* Guaranteed tuition.

FRESHMAN FINANCIAL AID (Fall 2016, est.) 4,141 applied for aid; of those 78% were deemed to have need. 98% of freshmen with need received aid; of those 13% had need fully met. *Average percent of need met:* 63% (excluding resources awarded to replace EFC). *Average financial aid package:* $12,205 (excluding resources awarded to replace EFC). 22% of all full-time freshmen had no need and received non-need-based gift aid.

UNDERGRADUATE FINANCIAL AID (Fall 2016, est.) 15,323 applied for aid; of those 83% were deemed to have need. 97% of undergraduates with need received aid; of those 10% had need fully met. *Average percent of need met:* 60% (excluding resources awarded to replace EFC). *Average financial aid package:* $11,505 (excluding resources awarded to replace EFC). 14% of all full-time undergraduates had no need and received non-need-based gift aid.

GIFT AID (NEED-BASED) *Total amount:* $114,949,140 (38% federal, 2% state, 55% institutional, 5% external sources). *Receiving aid:* Freshmen: 45% (2,119); all full-time undergraduates: 43% (8,768). *Average award:* Freshmen: $7010; Undergraduates: $6784. *Scholarships, grants, and awards:* Federal Pell, private, TEACH Grants, tribal grants, LEAP Grants.

GIFT AID (NON-NEED-BASED) *Total amount:* $16,789,473 (1% federal, 93% institutional, 6% external sources). *Receiving aid:* Freshmen: 52% (2,443). Undergraduates: 33% (6,648). *Average award:* Freshmen: $5897. Undergraduates: $6483. *Scholarships, grants, and awards by category:* Academic interests/achievement: general academic interests/achievements. *Creative arts/performance:* art/fine arts, music, theater/drama. *Special achievements/activities:* leadership. *Special characteristics:* children and siblings of alumni, local/state students, members of minority groups. *Tuition waivers:* Full or partial for employees or children of employees. *ROTC:* Army, Air Force.

LOANS *Student loans:* $102,501,051 (85% need-based, 15% non-need-based). 64% of past graduating class borrowed through all loan programs. *Average indebtedness per student:* $26,279. *Average need-based loan:* Freshmen: $3373. Undergraduates: $4253. *Parent loans:* $75,406,789 (41% need-based, 59% non-need-based). *Programs:* Federal Direct (Subsidized and Unsubsidized Stafford, PLUS), Perkins, Federal Nursing, state, college/university.

WORK-STUDY *Federal work-study:* Total amount: $903,989; jobs available. *State or other work-study/employment:* Total amount: $11,759,744 (67% need-based, 33% non-need-based). Part-time jobs available.

ATHLETIC AWARDS Total amount: $5,006,840 (48% need-based, 52% non-need-based).

APPLYING FOR FINANCIAL AID *Required financial aid form:* FAFSA. *Financial aid deadline (priority):* 2/1. *Notification date:* Continuous beginning 2/1.

CONTACT Office of Financial Aid, Northern Arizona University, PO Box 4108, Flagstaff, AZ 86011-4108, 928-523-4951 or toll-free 888-628-2968. *Fax:* 928-523-1551. *E-mail:* financial.aid@nau.edu.
Website: http://www.nau.edu/.

NORTHERN ILLINOIS UNIVERSITY
De Kalb, IL

Tuition & fees (IL res): $12,212	Average undergraduate aid package: $12,366

ABOUT THE INSTITUTION State-supported, coed. *Awards:* bachelor's, master's, and doctoral degrees. 66 undergraduate majors. *Total enrollment:* 19,015. Undergraduates: 14,079. Freshmen: 1,802. Federal methodology is used as a basis for awarding need-based institutional aid.

UNDERGRADUATE EXPENSES for 2016–2017 *Application fee:* $40. *Tuition, state resident:* full-time $9466. *Tuition, nonresident:* full-time $18,931. *Required fees:* full-time $2746; $94 per credit hour or $125 per term. Part-time tuition and fees vary according to course load and location. *College room and board:* $10,776. Room and board charges vary according to student level.

FRESHMAN FINANCIAL AID (Fall 2015) 2,084 applied for aid; of those 85% were deemed to have need. 100% of freshmen with need received aid; of those 9% had need fully met. *Average percent of need met:* 65% (excluding resources awarded to replace EFC). *Average financial aid package:* $13,947 (excluding resources awarded to replace EFC). 15% of all full-time freshmen had no need and received non-need-based gift aid.

UNDERGRADUATE FINANCIAL AID (Fall 2015) 11,615 applied for aid; of those 87% were deemed to have need. 99% of undergraduates with need received aid; of those 7% had need fully met. *Average percent of need met:* 59% (excluding resources awarded to replace EFC). *Average financial aid package:* $12,366 (excluding resources awarded to replace EFC). 9% of all full-time undergraduates had no need and received non-need-based gift aid.

GIFT AID (NEED-BASED) *Total amount:* $67,312,286 (46% federal, 30% state, 21% institutional, 3% external sources). *Receiving aid:* Freshmen: 75% (1,708); all full-time undergraduates: 61% (8,414). *Average award:* Freshmen: $9519; Undergraduates: $7955. *Scholarships, grants, and awards:* Federal Pell, FSEOG, state, private, college/university gift aid from institutional funds, TEACH Grants.

GIFT AID (NON-NEED-BASED) *Total amount:* $8,347,819 (12% federal, 9% state, 70% institutional, 9% external sources). *Receiving aid:* Freshmen: 5% (111). Undergraduates: 2% (260). *Average award:* Freshmen: $4512. Undergraduates: $4207. *Scholarships, grants, and awards by category:* Academic interests/achievement: area/ethnic studies, biological sciences, business, communication, computer science, education, engineering/technologies, English, foreign languages, general academic interests/achievements, health fields, humanities, international studies, library science, mathematics, military science, physical sciences, social sciences. *Creative arts/performance:* applied art and design, art/fine arts, creative writing, dance, debating, journalism/publications, music, performing arts, theater/drama. *Special achievements/activities:* cheerleading/drum major, community service, general special achievements/activities, leadership, memberships. *Special characteristics:* adult students, children and siblings of alumni, children of faculty/staff, children with a deceased or disabled parent, ethnic background, first-generation college students, handicapped students, international students, members of minority groups, veterans, veterans' children. *Tuition waivers:* Full or partial for employees or children of employees, senior citizens. *ROTC:* Army, Air Force cooperative.

LOANS *Student loans:* $87,837,589 (80% need-based, 20% non-need-based). 78% of past graduating class borrowed through all loan programs. *Average indebtedness per student:* $34,714. *Average need-based loan:* Freshmen: $3417. Undergraduates: $4455. *Parent loans:* $21,269,588 (54% need-based, 46% non-need-based). *Programs:* Federal Direct (Subsidized and Unsubsidized Stafford, PLUS).
WORK-STUDY *Federal work-study:* 6,183 jobs averaging $2644.
ATHLETIC AWARDS Total amount: $7,310,648 (33% need-based, 67% non-need-based).
APPLYING FOR FINANCIAL AID *Required financial aid form:* FAFSA. *Notification date:* Continuous beginning 3/1.
CONTACT Ms. Rebecca A. Babel, Director of Student Financial Aid, Northern Illinois University, Swen Parson Hall, Room 245, De Kalb, IL 60115, 815-753-1395 or toll-free 800-892-3050. *Fax:* 815-753-9475. *E-mail:* finaid@niu.edu. *Website:* http://www.niu.edu/.

NORTHERN KENTUCKY UNIVERSITY
Highland Heights, KY

Tuition & fees (KY res): $9384	Average undergraduate aid package: $10,940

ABOUT THE INSTITUTION State-supported, coed. *Awards:* certificates, bachelor's, master's, and doctoral degrees. 65 undergraduate majors. *Total enrollment:* 14,551. Undergraduates: 12,389. Freshmen: 2,148. Federal methodology is used as a basis for awarding need-based institutional aid.
UNDERGRADUATE EXPENSES for 2016–2017 *Application fee:* $40. *Tuition, state resident:* full-time $9000; part-time $375 per credit hour. *Tuition, nonresident:* full-time $18,000; part-time $750 per credit hour. *Required fees:* full-time $384; $16 per credit hour. Full-time tuition and fees vary according to course load and reciprocity agreements. Part-time tuition and fees vary according to course load and reciprocity agreements. *College room and board:* $6549. Room and board charges vary according to board plan and housing facility.
FRESHMAN FINANCIAL AID (Fall 2015) 1,877 applied for aid; of those 79% were deemed to have need. 100% of freshmen with need received aid; of those 27% had need fully met. *Average percent of need met:* 70% (excluding resources awarded to replace EFC). *Average financial aid package:* $11,586 (excluding resources awarded to replace EFC). 17% of all full-time freshmen had no need and received non-need-based gift aid.
UNDERGRADUATE FINANCIAL AID (Fall 2015) 7,400 applied for aid; of those 82% were deemed to have need. 99% of undergraduates with need received aid; of those 20% had need fully met. *Average percent of need met:* 64% (excluding resources awarded to replace EFC). *Average financial aid package:* $10,940 (excluding resources awarded to replace EFC). 12% of all full-time undergraduates had no need and received non-need-based gift aid.
GIFT AID (NEED-BASED) *Total amount:* $23,904,230 (80% federal, 17% state, 3% institutional). *Receiving aid:* Freshmen: 40% (855); all full-time undergraduates: 39% (3,611). *Average award:* Freshmen: $6141; Undergraduates: $5687. *Scholarships, grants, and awards:* Federal Pell, FSEOG, state, private, college/university gift aid from institutional funds.
GIFT AID (NON-NEED-BASED) *Total amount:* $29,743,369 (3% federal, 21% state, 63% institutional, 13% external sources). *Receiving aid:* Freshmen: 54% (1,152). Undergraduates: 35% (3,299). *Average award:* Freshmen: $5607. Undergraduates: $6162. *Scholarships, grants, and awards by category:* Academic interests/achievement: biological sciences, business, communication, computer science, education, engineering/technologies, English, foreign languages, general academic interests/achievements, health fields, home economics, international studies, mathematics, physical sciences, premedicine, social sciences. *Creative arts/performance:* art/fine arts, music, theater/drama. *Special achievements/activities:* cheerleading/drum major, community service, general special achievements/activities, leadership. *Special characteristics:* adult students, children and siblings of alumni, children of faculty/staff, children of public servants, children with a deceased or disabled parent, general special characteristics, handicapped students, local/state students, members of minority groups, spouses of deceased or disabled public servants, veterans, veterans' children. *Tuition waivers:* Full or partial for employees or children of employees, senior citizens. *ROTC:* Army cooperative, Air Force cooperative.
LOANS *Student loans:* $72,362,292 (39% need-based, 61% non-need-based). 67% of past graduating class borrowed through all loan programs. *Average indebtedness per student:* $28,355. *Average need-based loan:* Freshmen: $3548. Undergrad-

uates: $4475. *Parent loans:* $57,763,665 (100% non-need-based). *Programs:* Federal Direct (Subsidized and Unsubsidized Stafford, PLUS), Perkins, Federal Nursing, college/university.
WORK-STUDY *Federal work-study:* jobs available. *State or other work-study/employment:* Total amount: $3,149,854 (100% non-need-based). Part-time jobs available.
ATHLETIC AWARDS Total amount: $3,246,197 (100% non-need-based).
APPLYING FOR FINANCIAL AID *Required financial aid form:* FAFSA. *Financial aid deadline:* Continuous. *Notification date:* Continuous beginning 3/15.
CONTACT Leah Stewart, Director of Student Financial Assistance, Northern Kentucky University, 416 Administrative Center, Highland Heights, KY 41099, 859-572-5144 or toll-free 800-637-9948. *Fax:* 859-572-6997. *E-mail:* ofa@nku.edu. *Website:* http://www.nku.edu/.

NORTHERN MICHIGAN UNIVERSITY
Marquette, MI

Tuition & fees: N/R	Average undergraduate aid package: $9962

ABOUT THE INSTITUTION State-supported, coed. 146 undergraduate majors. Federal methodology is used as a basis for awarding need-based institutional aid.
FRESHMAN FINANCIAL AID (Fall 2015) 1,266 applied for aid; of those 78% were deemed to have need. 99% of freshmen with need received aid; of those 22% had need fully met. *Average percent of need met:* 71% (excluding resources awarded to replace EFC). *Average financial aid package:* $10,070 (excluding resources awarded to replace EFC). 15% of all full-time freshmen had no need and received non-need-based gift aid.
UNDERGRADUATE FINANCIAL AID (Fall 2015) 5,403 applied for aid; of those 81% were deemed to have need. 98% of undergraduates with need received aid; of those 16% had need fully met. *Average percent of need met:* 66% (excluding resources awarded to replace EFC). *Average financial aid package:* $9962 (excluding resources awarded to replace EFC). 9% of all full-time undergraduates had no need and received non-need-based gift aid.
GIFT AID (NEED-BASED) *Total amount:* $15,176,471 (76% federal, 2% state, 20% institutional, 2% external sources). *Receiving aid:* Freshmen: 48% (684); all full-time undergraduates: 45% (2,956). *Average award:* Freshmen: $4651; Undergraduates: $4881. *Scholarships, grants, and awards:* Federal Pell, FSEOG, state, private, college/university gift aid from institutional funds.
GIFT AID (NON-NEED-BASED) *Total amount:* $16,253,646 (25% state, 65% institutional, 10% external sources). *Receiving aid:* Freshmen: 55% (772). Undergraduates: 40% (2,681). *Average award:* Freshmen: $3155. Undergraduates: $3121. *Scholarships, grants, and awards by category:* Academic interests/achievement: biological sciences, business, communication, computer science, education, engineering/technologies, English, foreign languages, general academic interests/achievements, health fields, home economics, humanities, international studies, mathematics, military science, physical sciences, premedicine, social sciences. *Creative arts/performance:* applied art and design, music, theater/drama. *Special achievements/activities:* cheerleading/drum major, leadership, memberships. *Special characteristics:* children and siblings of alumni, children of faculty/staff, children of union members/company employees, international students, local/state students, members of minority groups, out-of-state students.
LOANS *Student loans:* $36,881,481 (42% need-based, 58% non-need-based). 76% of past graduating class borrowed through all loan programs. *Average indebtedness per student:* $31,257. *Average need-based loan:* Freshmen: $3408. Undergraduates: $4229. *Parent loans:* $5,175,554 (100% non-need-based). *Programs:* Federal Direct (Subsidized and Unsubsidized Stafford, PLUS), Perkins, state, alternative loans.
WORK-STUDY *Federal work-study:* 522 jobs averaging $1852.
ATHLETIC AWARDS Total amount: $3,102,012 (100% non-need-based).
APPLYING FOR FINANCIAL AID *Required financial aid form:* FAFSA. *Financial aid deadline (priority):* 3/1. *Notification date:* Continuous beginning 12/15.
CONTACT Michael Rotundo, Director of Financial Aid, Northern Michigan University, 1401 Presque Isle Avenue, Marquette, MI 49855, 906-227-2327 or toll-free 800-682-9797. *Fax:* 906-227-2321. *E-mail:* fao@nmu.edu. *Website:* http://www.nmu.edu/.

NORTHERN NEW MEXICO COLLEGE
Espa&nnola, NM

CONTACT Financial Aid Office, Northern New Mexico College, 921 Paseo de O&nnate, Espa&nnola, NM 87532, 505-747-2100.
Website: http://www.nnmc.edu/.

NORTHERN STATE UNIVERSITY
Aberdeen, SD

Tuition & fees (SD res): $8280	Average undergraduate aid package: $10,128

ABOUT THE INSTITUTION State-supported, coed. *Awards:* certificates, associate, bachelor's, and master's degrees. 45 undergraduate majors. *Total enrollment:* 3,587. Undergraduates: 3,075. Freshmen: 323. Federal methodology is used as a basis for awarding need-based institutional aid.

UNDERGRADUATE EXPENSES for 2017–2018 *Application fee:* $20. *Tuition, area resident:* part-time $239.70 per credit hour. *Tuition, state resident:* full-time $7191; part-time $239.70 per credit hour. *Tuition, nonresident:* full-time $10,120; part-time $337.35 per credit hour. *Required fees:* full-time $1089; $36.30 per credit hour. *College room and board:* $7850; *Room only:* $3640. Room and board charges vary according to board plan and housing facility.

FRESHMAN FINANCIAL AID (Fall 2016, est.) 274 applied for aid; of those 68% were deemed to have need. 100% of freshmen with need received aid; of those 27% had need fully met. *Average percent of need met:* 77% (excluding resources awarded to replace EFC). *Average financial aid package:* $10,752 (excluding resources awarded to replace EFC). 21% of all full-time freshmen had no need and received non-need-based gift aid.

UNDERGRADUATE FINANCIAL AID (Fall 2016, est.) 988 applied for aid; of those 76% were deemed to have need. 100% of undergraduates with need received aid; of those 31% had need fully met. *Average percent of need met:* 77% (excluding resources awarded to replace EFC). *Average financial aid package:* $10,128 (excluding resources awarded to replace EFC). 10% of all full-time undergraduates had no need and received non-need-based gift aid.

GIFT AID (NEED-BASED) *Total amount:* $3,418,991 (71% federal, 3% state, 13% institutional, 13% external sources). *Receiving aid:* Freshmen: 54% (166); all full-time undergraduates: 51% (623). *Average award:* Freshmen: $5563; Undergraduates: $4730. *Scholarships, grants, and awards:* Federal Pell, FSEOG, state, private, college/university gift aid from institutional funds, South Dakota Education Access Foundation Grants.

GIFT AID (NON-NEED-BASED) *Total amount:* $836,463 (7% federal, 11% state, 58% institutional, 24% external sources). *Receiving aid:* Freshmen: 4% (11). Undergraduates: 3% (38). *Average award:* Freshmen: $1246. Undergraduates: $1702. *Scholarships, grants, and awards by category: Academic interests/achievement:* 503 awards ($784,588 total): agriculture, biological sciences, business, communication, computer science, education, English, foreign languages, general academic interests/achievements, humanities, international studies, mathematics, physical sciences, social sciences. *Creative arts/performance:* 95 awards ($99,911 total): art/fine arts, music, theater/drama. *Special achievements/activities:* 2 awards ($1422 total): leadership. *Special characteristics:* 54 awards ($53,664 total): adult students, ethnic background, handicapped students, international students, local/state students, members of minority groups. *Tuition waivers:* Full or partial for children of alumni, employees or children of employees, senior citizens.

LOANS *Student loans:* $7,028,404 (65% need-based, 35% non-need-based). 78% of past graduating class borrowed through all loan programs. *Average indebtedness per student:* $28,142. *Average need-based loan:* Freshmen: $4455. Undergraduates: $5346. *Parent loans:* $438,411 (27% need-based, 73% non-need-based). *Programs:* Federal Direct (Subsidized and Unsubsidized Stafford, PLUS), Perkins, college/university, alternative loans.

WORK-STUDY *Federal work-study:* Total amount: $821,220; 334 jobs averaging $2504. *State or other work-study/employment:* Total amount: $372,407 (100% non-need-based). 369 part-time jobs averaging $1009.

ATHLETIC AWARDS Total amount: $1,286,329 (43% need-based, 57% non-need-based).

APPLYING FOR FINANCIAL AID *Required financial aid form:* FAFSA. *Financial aid deadline (priority):* 3/1. *Notification date:* 4/15. Students must reply within 2 weeks of notification.

CONTACT Sharon Kienow, Director of Financial Aid, Northern State University, 1200 South Jay Street, Aberdeen, SD 57401-7198, 605-626-2640 or toll-free 800-678-5330. *Fax:* 605-626-2587. *E-mail:* finaid@northern.edu. *Website:* http://www.northern.edu/.

NORTH GREENVILLE UNIVERSITY
Tigerville, SC

ABOUT THE INSTITUTION Independent Southern Baptist, coed. *Awards:* bachelor's, master's, and doctoral degrees. 38 undergraduate majors. *Total enrollment:* 2,691. Undergraduates: 2,481. Freshmen: 531.

GIFT AID (NEED-BASED) *Scholarships, grants, and awards:* Federal Pell, FSEOG, state, private, college/university gift aid from institutional funds.

GIFT AID (NON-NEED-BASED) *Scholarships, grants, and awards by category: Academic interests/achievement:* biological sciences, communication, education, general academic interests/achievements, military science, religion/biblical studies. *Creative arts/performance:* journalism/publications, music, theater/drama. *Special characteristics:* children of faculty/staff.

LOANS *Programs:* Perkins, state.

WORK-STUDY *Federal work-study:* jobs available. *State or other work-study/employment:* Total amount: $301,532 (100% non-need-based). Part-time jobs available.

APPLYING FOR FINANCIAL AID *Required financial aid form:* FAFSA.

CONTACT Mike Jordan, Director of Financial Aid, North Greenville University, PO Box 1892, Tigerville, SC 29688, 864-977-7058 or toll-free 800-468-6642 Ext. 7001. *Fax:* 864-977-7177. *E-mail:* mjordan@ngu.edu. *Website:* http://www.ngu.edu/.

NORTHLAND COLLEGE
Ashland, WI

Tuition & fees: $35,157	Average undergraduate aid package: $37,720

ABOUT THE INSTITUTION Independent United Church of Christ, coed. *Awards:* bachelor's degrees. 31 undergraduate majors. *Total enrollment:* 582. Undergraduates: 582. Freshmen: 168. Federal methodology is used as a basis for awarding need-based institutional aid.

UNDERGRADUATE EXPENSES for 2017–2018 *Comprehensive fee:* $44,043 includes full-time tuition ($33,640), mandatory fees ($1517), and room and board ($8886). *College room only:* $4069. Full-time tuition and fees vary according to course load. Room and board charges vary according to board plan and housing facility. *Part-time tuition:* $650 per credit. Part-time tuition and fees vary according to course load.

FRESHMAN FINANCIAL AID (Fall 2016, est.) 164 applied for aid; of those 90% were deemed to have need. 100% of freshmen with need received aid; of those 19% had need fully met. *Average percent of need met:* 85% (excluding resources awarded to replace EFC). *Average financial aid package:* $38,069 (excluding resources awarded to replace EFC). 13% of all full-time freshmen had no need and received non-need-based gift aid.

UNDERGRADUATE FINANCIAL AID (Fall 2016, est.) 517 applied for aid; of those 90% were deemed to have need. 100% of undergraduates with need received aid; of those 24% had need fully met. *Average percent of need met:* 85% (excluding resources awarded to replace EFC). *Average financial aid package:* $37,720 (excluding resources awarded to replace EFC). 15% of all full-time undergraduates had no need and received non-need-based gift aid.

GIFT AID (NEED-BASED) *Total amount:* $10,999,401 (10% federal, 4% state, 85% institutional, 1% external sources). *Receiving aid:* Freshmen: 81% (136); all full-time undergraduates: 81% (449). *Average award:* Freshmen: $24,697; Undergraduates: $23,487. *Scholarships, grants, and awards:* Federal Pell, FSEOG, state, private, college/university gift aid from institutional funds.

GIFT AID (NON-NEED-BASED) *Total amount:* $1,536,723 (1% state, 99% institutional). *Receiving aid:* Freshmen: 13% (22). Undergraduates: 11% (64). *Average award:* Freshmen: $19,541. Undergraduates: $18,605. *Scholarships, grants, and awards by category: Academic interests/achievement:* $5,382,030 total: general academic interests/achievements. *Creative arts/performance:* $40,500 total: art/fine arts, creative writing, music. *Special achievements/activities:* $654,750 total: leadership. *Special characteristics:* $338,355 total: children and siblings of alumni, ethnic background, general special characteristics, members of minority groups, out-of-state students. *Tuition waivers:* Full or partial for employees or children of employees.

LOANS *Student loans:* $3,637,795 (43% need-based, 57% non-need-based). 83% of past graduating class borrowed through all loan programs. *Average indebtedness per student:* $34,144. *Average need-based loan:* Freshmen: $3831. Undergraduates: $4773. *Parent loans:* $437,051 (98% need-based, 2% non-need-based). *Programs:* Federal Direct (Subsidized and Unsubsidized Stafford, PLUS), Perkins, state.

WORK-STUDY *Federal work-study:* Total amount: $438,578; 266 jobs averaging $1649. *State or other work-study/employment:* Total amount: $370,946 (100% non-need-based). 236 part-time jobs averaging $1572.

APPLYING FOR FINANCIAL AID *Required financial aid form:* FAFSA. *Financial aid deadline:* Continuous. *Notification date:* Continuous beginning 3/1. Students must reply by 5/1 or within 4 weeks of notification.

CONTACT Kelly Dunn, Director of Financial Aid, Northland College, 1411 Ellis Avenue, Ashland, WI 54806, 715-682-1255 or toll-free 800-753-1840 (in-state), 800-753-1040 (out-of-state). *Fax:* 715-682-1368. *E-mail:* finaid@northland.edu. *Website:* http://www.northland.edu/.

NORTH PARK UNIVERSITY
Chicago, IL

CONTACT Dr. Lucy Shaker, Director of Financial Aid , North Park University, 3225 West Foster Avenue, Chicago, IL 60625-4895, 773-244-5526 or toll-free 800-888-NPC8. *Fax:* 773-244-4953.
Website: http://www.northpark.edu/.

NORTHPOINT BIBLE COLLEGE
Haverhill, MA

CONTACT Financial Aid Office, Northpoint Bible College, 320 South Main Street, Haverhill, MA 01835, 978-478-3400 or toll-free 800-356-4014.
Website: http://northpoint.edu/.

NORTHWEST CHRISTIAN UNIVERSITY
Eugene, OR

Tuition & fees: $28,680	Average undergraduate aid package: $21,401

ABOUT THE INSTITUTION Independent Christian, coed. *Awards:* certificates, associate, bachelor's, and master's degrees. 26 undergraduate majors. *Total enrollment:* 766. Undergraduates: 566. Freshmen: 81. Federal methodology is used as a basis for awarding need-based institutional aid.

UNDERGRADUATE EXPENSES for 2017–2018 *Comprehensive fee:* $37,480 includes full-time tuition ($28,500), mandatory fees ($180), and room and board ($8800). Full-time tuition and fees vary according to course load. Room and board charges vary according to housing facility. *Part-time tuition:* $950 per credit hour. Part-time tuition and fees vary according to course load.

FRESHMAN FINANCIAL AID (Fall 2016, est.) 79 applied for aid; of those 92% were deemed to have need. 100% of freshmen with need received aid; of those 21% had need fully met. *Average percent of need met:* 77% (excluding resources awarded to replace EFC). *Average financial aid package:* $22,454 (excluding resources awarded to replace EFC). 10% of all full-time freshmen had no need and received non-need-based gift aid.

UNDERGRADUATE FINANCIAL AID (Fall 2016, est.) 371 applied for aid; of those 91% were deemed to have need. 100% of undergraduates with need received aid; of those 16% had need fully met. *Average percent of need met:* 70% (excluding resources awarded to replace EFC). *Average financial aid package:* $21,401 (excluding resources awarded to replace EFC). 15% of all full-time undergraduates had no need and received non-need-based gift aid.

GIFT AID (NEED-BASED) *Total amount:* $5,280,876 (23% federal, 5% state, 67% institutional, 5% external sources). *Receiving aid:* Freshmen: 90% (73); all full-time undergraduates: 78% (329). *Average award:* Freshmen: $19,094; Undergraduates: $17,468. *Scholarships, grants, and awards:* Federal Pell, FSEOG, state, private, college/university gift aid from institutional funds.

GIFT AID (NON-NEED-BASED) *Total amount:* $847,683 (3% federal, 78% institutional, 19% external sources). *Receiving aid:* Freshmen: 12% (10). Undergraduates: 8% (35). *Average award:* Freshmen: $10,587. Undergraduates: $8803. *Scholarships, grants, and awards by category:* Academic interests/achievement: 262 awards ($1,960,115 total): general academic interests/achievements, religion/biblical studies. Creative arts/performance: 63 awards ($123,065 total): music. *Special achievements/activities:* 271 awards ($229,269 total): community service, leadership, religious involvement. *Special characteristics:* 151 awards ($353,148 total): children of faculty/staff, international students, relatives of clergy, religious affiliation, siblings of current students. *Tuition waivers:* Full or partial for employees or children of employees.

LOANS *Student loans:* $3,368,626 (79% need-based, 21% non-need-based). 92% of past graduating class borrowed through all loan programs. *Average indebtedness per student:* $23,279. *Average need-based loan:* Freshmen: $3089. Undergraduates: $4631. *Parent loans:* $716,967 (61% need-based, 39% non-need-based). *Programs:* Federal Direct (Subsidized and Unsubsidized Stafford, PLUS), Perkins.

WORK-STUDY *Federal work-study:* Total amount: $244,464; 108 jobs averaging $2750. *State or other work-study/employment:* Total amount: $9625 (29% need-based, 71% non-need-based). 8 part-time jobs averaging $2750.

ATHLETIC AWARDS Total amount: $1,110,350 (73% need-based, 27% non-need-based).

APPLYING FOR FINANCIAL AID *Required financial aid form:* FAFSA. *Financial aid deadline (priority):* 3/1. *Notification date:* Continuous beginning 1/1. Students must reply within 2 weeks of notification.

CONTACT Jocelyn Hubbs, Director of Financial Aid, Northwest Christian University, 828 East 11th Avenue, Eugene, OR 97401-3745, 541-684-7291 or toll-free 877-463-6622. *Fax:* 541-684-7300. *E-mail:* jhubbs@nwcu.edu.
Website: http://www.nwcu.edu/.

NORTHWEST COLLEGE OF ART & DESIGN
Poulsbo, WA

Tuition & fees: $19,075	Average undergraduate aid package: $11,429

ABOUT THE INSTITUTION Proprietary, coed. *Awards:* bachelor's degrees. 1 undergraduate major. *Total enrollment:* 114. Undergraduates: 114. Federal methodology is used as a basis for awarding need-based institutional aid.

UNDERGRADUATE EXPENSES for 2017–2018 *Tuition:* full-time $18,975; part-time $825 per credit hour. *Required fees:* full-time $100; $100 per year. Part-time tuition and fees vary according to course load.

UNDERGRADUATE FINANCIAL AID (Fall 2015) 75 applied for aid; of those 100% were deemed to have need. 100% of undergraduates with need received aid; of those 80% had need fully met. *Average percent of need met:* 55% (excluding resources awarded to replace EFC). *Average financial aid package:* $11,429 (excluding resources awarded to replace EFC). 1% of all full-time undergraduates had no need and received non-need-based gift aid.

GIFT AID (NEED-BASED) *Total amount:* $455,053 (42% federal, 58% state). *Receiving aid:* All full-time undergraduates: 54% (46). *Average award:* Undergraduates: $9892. *Scholarships, grants, and awards:* Federal Pell, state, private, college/university gift aid from institutional funds.

GIFT AID (NON-NEED-BASED) *Total amount:* $77,352 (23% institutional, 77% external sources). *Receiving aid:* Undergraduates: 14% (12). *Average award:* Undergraduates: $1111. *Scholarships, grants, and awards by category:* Creative arts/performance: applied art and design, art/fine arts. *Tuition waivers:* Full or partial for children of alumni, employees or children of employees.

LOANS *Student loans:* $1,436,791 (36% need-based, 64% non-need-based). 100% of past graduating class borrowed through all loan programs. *Average indebtedness per student:* $20,426. *Parent loans:* $422,058 (100% non-need-based). *Programs:* Federal Direct (Subsidized and Unsubsidized Stafford, PLUS), Sallie Mae Smart Option Loans.

APPLYING FOR FINANCIAL AID *Required financial aid form:* FAFSA. *Financial aid deadline:* Continuous. *Notification date:* Continuous.
CONTACT Julie Perigard, Financial Aid Officer, Northwest College of Art & Design, 16301 Creative Drive NE, Poulsbo, WA 98370, 360-779-9993 or toll-free 800-769-ARTS. *Fax:* 360-779-9933. *E-mail:* jperigard@ncad.edu. *Website:* http://www.ncad.edu/.

NORTHWESTERN COLLEGE
Orange City, IA

Tuition & fees: $30,300	Average undergraduate aid package: $24,640

ABOUT THE INSTITUTION Independent Reformed Church in America, coed. *Awards:* certificates, bachelor's, and master's degrees. 49 undergraduate majors. *Total enrollment:* 1,260. Undergraduates: 1,099. Freshmen: 282. Federal methodology is used as a basis for awarding need-based institutional aid.
UNDERGRADUATE EXPENSES for 2017–2018 *Comprehensive fee:* $39,300 includes full-time tuition ($30,000), mandatory fees ($300), and room and board ($9000). Room and board charges vary according to board plan and housing facility. *Part-time tuition:* $650 per credit hour. *Part-time fees:* $75 per term. Part-time tuition and fees vary according to course load. *Payment plan:* Tuition prepayment.
FRESHMAN FINANCIAL AID (Fall 2015) 231 applied for aid; of those 78% were deemed to have need. 100% of freshmen with need received aid; of those 62% had need fully met. *Average percent of need met:* 93% (excluding resources awarded to replace EFC). *Average financial aid package:* $24,357 (excluding resources awarded to replace EFC). 30% of all full-time freshmen had no need and received non-need-based gift aid.
UNDERGRADUATE FINANCIAL AID (Fall 2015) 916 applied for aid; of those 84% were deemed to have need. 100% of undergraduates with need received aid; of those 59% had need fully met. *Average percent of need met:* 92% (excluding resources awarded to replace EFC). *Average financial aid package:* $24,640 (excluding resources awarded to replace EFC). 25% of all full-time undergraduates had no need and received non-need-based gift aid.
GIFT AID (NEED-BASED) *Total amount:* $6,584,890 (20% federal, 22% state, 58% institutional). *Receiving aid:* Freshmen: 70% (181); all full-time undergraduates: 70% (738). *Average award:* Freshmen: $6370; Undergraduates: $7490. *Scholarships, grants, and awards:* Federal Pell, FSEOG, state, private, college/university gift aid from institutional funds.
GIFT AID (NON-NEED-BASED) *Total amount:* $9,741,699 (1% federal, 94% institutional, 5% external sources). *Receiving aid:* Freshmen: 68% (176). Undergraduates: 72% (756). *Average award:* Freshmen: $12,514. Undergraduates: $10,699. *Scholarships, grants, and awards by category:* Academic interests/achievement: 948 awards ($8,678,129 total): biological sciences, business, communication, computer science, education, English, foreign languages, general academic interests/achievements, humanities, mathematics, physical sciences, premedicine, religion/biblical studies, social sciences. *Creative arts/performance:* 154 awards ($454,449 total): art/fine arts, dance, music, performing arts, theater/drama. *Special characteristics:* 558 awards ($1,657,134 total): children and siblings of alumni, children of faculty/staff, ethnic background, first-generation college students, handicapped students, international students, religious affiliation, siblings of current students, veterans. *Tuition waivers:* Full or partial for employees or children of employees.
LOANS *Student loans:* $6,376,592 (47% need-based, 53% non-need-based). 78% of past graduating class borrowed through all loan programs. *Average indebtedness per student:* $28,501. *Average need-based loan:* Freshmen: $4322. Undergraduates: $5187. *Parent loans:* $1,392,645 (100% non-need-based). *Programs:* Federal Direct (Subsidized and Unsubsidized Stafford, PLUS), Perkins, college/university, alternative loans.
WORK-STUDY *Federal work-study:* 217 jobs averaging $987. *State or other work-study/employment:* Total amount: $670,153 (100% non-need-based). 676 part-time jobs averaging $991.
ATHLETIC AWARDS Total amount: $2,986,125 (100% non-need-based).
APPLYING FOR FINANCIAL AID *Required financial aid form:* FAFSA. *Financial aid deadline (priority):* 4/15. *Notification date:* Continuous beginning 12/1. Students must reply within 3 weeks of notification.

CONTACT Mr. Eric Anderson, Director of Financial Aid, Northwestern College, 101 Seventh Street, SW, Orange City, IA 51041-1996, 712-707-7131 or toll-free 800-747-4757. *Fax:* 712-707-7164. *E-mail:* finaid@nwciowa.edu. *Website:* http://www.nwciowa.edu/.

NORTHWESTERN OKLAHOMA STATE UNIVERSITY
Alva, OK

CONTACT Rita J. Castleberry, Director of Financial Aid, Northwestern Oklahoma State University, 709 Oklahoma Boulevard, Alva, OK 73717-2799, 580-327-8542. *Fax:* 580-327-8177. *E-mail:* rjcastleberry@nwosu.edu. *Website:* http://www.nwosu.edu/.

NORTHWESTERN STATE UNIVERSITY OF LOUISIANA
Natchitoches, LA

Tuition & fees: N/R	Average undergraduate aid package: $13,863

ABOUT THE INSTITUTION State-supported, coed. *Awards:* certificates, associate, bachelor's, master's, and doctoral degrees. 35 undergraduate majors. *Total enrollment:* 9,819. Undergraduates: 8,700. Freshmen: 1,420. Federal methodology is used as a basis for awarding need-based institutional aid.
FRESHMAN FINANCIAL AID (Fall 2015) 1,152 applied for aid; of those 82% were deemed to have need. 98% of freshmen with need received aid; of those 14% had need fully met. *Average percent of need met:* 20% (excluding resources awarded to replace EFC). *Average financial aid package:* $13,729 (excluding resources awarded to replace EFC). 9% of all full-time freshmen had no need and received non-need-based gift aid.
UNDERGRADUATE FINANCIAL AID (Fall 2015) 4,388 applied for aid; of those 83% were deemed to have need. 99% of undergraduates with need received aid; of those 11% had need fully met. *Average percent of need met:* 21% (excluding resources awarded to replace EFC). *Average financial aid package:* $13,863 (excluding resources awarded to replace EFC). 7% of all full-time undergraduates had no need and received non-need-based gift aid.
GIFT AID (NEED-BASED) *Total amount:* $32,040,112 (46% federal, 26% state, 15% institutional, 13% external sources). *Receiving aid:* Freshmen: 72% (881); all full-time undergraduates: 65% (3,248). *Average award:* Freshmen: $7672; Undergraduates: $7342. *Scholarships, grants, and awards:* Federal Pell, FSEOG, state, private, college/university gift aid from institutional funds.
GIFT AID (NON-NEED-BASED) *Total amount:* $6,385,982 (63% state, 27% institutional, 10% external sources). *Receiving aid:* Freshmen: 11% (129). Undergraduates: 7% (346). *Average award:* Freshmen: $3665. Undergraduates: $3962. *Scholarships, grants, and awards by category:* Academic interests/achievement: biological sciences, business, communication, education, engineering/technologies, English, general academic interests/achievements, health fields, humanities, mathematics, military science, social sciences. *Creative arts/performance:* art/fine arts, cinema/film/broadcasting, creative writing, dance, general creative arts/performance, music, performing arts, theater/drama. *Special achievements/activities:* cheerleading/drum major, general special achievements/activities, leadership, memberships. *Special characteristics:* adult students, children of faculty/staff, children of public servants, general special characteristics, international students, married students, out-of-state students, public servants, veterans, veterans' children. *ROTC:* Army, Air Force cooperative.
LOANS *Student loans:* $41,317,305 (86% need-based, 14% non-need-based). 64% of past graduating class borrowed through all loan programs. *Average indebtedness per student:* $41,500. *Average need-based loan:* Freshmen: $5616. Undergraduates: $6915. *Parent loans:* $2,305,216 (69% need-based, 31% non-need-based). *Programs:* Federal Direct (Subsidized and Unsubsidized Stafford, PLUS), Perkins, Federal Nursing, state, college/university, alternative loans.
WORK-STUDY *Federal work-study:* jobs available. *State or other work-study/employment:* Total amount: $330,210 (57% need-based, 43% non-need-based). Part-time jobs available.

ATHLETIC AWARDS Total amount: $3,929,200 (88% need-based, 12% non-need-based).

APPLYING FOR FINANCIAL AID *Required financial aid forms:* FAFSA, institution's own form. *Financial aid deadline (priority):* 5/1. *Notification date:* Continuous beginning 5/1. Students must reply within 4 weeks of notification.

CONTACT Ms. Lauren Jackson, Director of Financial Aid, Northwestern State University of Louisiana, 212 Student Services Center, Natchitoches, LA 71497, 318-357-5961 or toll-free 800-327-1903. *Fax:* 318-357-5488. *E-mail:* nsufinaid@nsula.edu. *Website:* http://www.nsula.edu/

NORTHWESTERN UNIVERSITY
Evanston, IL

Tuition & fees: $50,855	Average undergraduate aid package: $45,505

ABOUT THE INSTITUTION Independent, coed. *Awards:* certificates, bachelor's, master's, and doctoral degrees. 112 undergraduate majors. *Total enrollment:* 21,208. Undergraduates: 8,353. Freshmen: 1,985. Both federal and institutional methodology are used as a basis for awarding need-based institutional aid.

UNDERGRADUATE EXPENSES for 2016–2017 *Application fee:* $75. *Comprehensive fee:* $66,344 includes full-time tuition ($50,424), mandatory fees ($431), and room and board ($15,489). Room and board charges vary according to board plan and housing facility.

FRESHMAN FINANCIAL AID (Fall 2016, est.) 1,064 applied for aid; of those 85% were deemed to have need. 100% of freshmen with need received aid; of those 100% had need fully met. *Average percent of need met:* 100% (excluding resources awarded to replace EFC). *Average financial aid package:* $48,603 (excluding resources awarded to replace EFC). 4% of all full-time freshmen had no need and received non-need-based gift aid.

UNDERGRADUATE FINANCIAL AID (Fall 2016, est.) 3,997 applied for aid; of those 90% were deemed to have need. 100% of undergraduates with need received aid; of those 100% had need fully met. *Average percent of need met:* 100% (excluding resources awarded to replace EFC). *Average financial aid package:* $45,505 (excluding resources awarded to replace EFC). 4% of all full-time undergraduates had no need and received non-need-based gift aid.

GIFT AID (NEED-BASED) *Total amount:* $157,829,229 (5% federal, 2% state, 90% institutional, 3% external sources). *Receiving aid:* Freshmen: 45% (889); all full-time undergraduates: 43% (3,547). *Average award:* Freshmen: $42,976; Undergraduates: $39,409. *Scholarships, grants, and awards:* Federal Pell, FSEOG, state, college/university gift aid from institutional funds.

GIFT AID (NON-NEED-BASED) *Total amount:* $2,428,140 (57% institutional, 43% external sources). *Average award:* Freshmen: $8034. Undergraduates: $4006. *Scholarships, grants, and awards by category: Creative arts/performance:* music. *Special characteristics:* international students. *ROTC:* Army cooperative, Naval, Air Force cooperative.

LOANS *Student loans:* $14,843,359 (48% need-based, 52% non-need-based). 42% of past graduating class borrowed through all loan programs. *Average indebtedness per student:* $20,308. *Average need-based loan:* Freshmen: $2983. Undergraduates: $4652. *Parent loans:* $9,957,035 (100% non-need-based). *Programs:* Federal Direct (Subsidized and Unsubsidized Stafford, PLUS), Perkins, college/university.

WORK-STUDY *Federal work-study:* Total amount: $4,594,425; jobs available. *State or other work-study/employment:* Part-time jobs available.

ATHLETIC AWARDS Total amount: $17,217,134 (100% non-need-based).

APPLYING FOR FINANCIAL AID *Required financial aid forms:* FAFSA, CSS Financial Aid PROFILE, noncustodial (divorced/separated) parent's statement, parent and student tax forms. *Financial aid deadline:* 3/5. *Notification date:* 4/15. Students must reply by 5/1 or within 2 weeks of notification.

CONTACT Office of Financial Aid, Northwestern University, 1801 Hinman Avenue, Evanston, IL 60204-1270, 847-491-7400. *E-mail:* undergradaid@u.northwestern.edu. *Website:* http://www.northwestern.edu/.

NORTHWEST MISSOURI STATE UNIVERSITY
Maryville, MO

Tuition & fees (MO res): $9178	Average undergraduate aid package: $9731

ABOUT THE INSTITUTION State-supported, coed. *Awards:* certificates, bachelor's, and master's degrees. 71 undergraduate majors. *Total enrollment:* 6,530. Undergraduates: 5,628. Freshmen: 1,405. Federal methodology is used as a basis for awarding need-based institutional aid.

UNDERGRADUATE EXPENSES for 2016–2017 *Tuition, state resident:* full-time $5418; part-time $180.61 per credit hour. *Tuition, nonresident:* full-time $11,739; part-time $391.29 per credit hour. *Required fees:* full-time $3760; $125.35 per credit hour. Full-time tuition and fees vary according to course load, location, and reciprocity agreements. Part-time tuition and fees vary according to course load and location. *College room and board:* $9612; *Room only:* $6138. Room and board charges vary according to board plan and housing facility.

FRESHMAN FINANCIAL AID (Fall 2015) 1,266 applied for aid; of those 75% were deemed to have need. 100% of freshmen with need received aid; of those 60% had need fully met. *Average percent of need met:* 71% (excluding resources awarded to replace EFC). *Average financial aid package:* $11,074 (excluding resources awarded to replace EFC). 13% of all full-time freshmen had no need and received non-need-based gift aid.

UNDERGRADUATE FINANCIAL AID (Fall 2015) 4,147 applied for aid; of those 80% were deemed to have need. 99% of undergraduates with need received aid; of those 39% had need fully met. *Average percent of need met:* 57% (excluding resources awarded to replace EFC). *Average financial aid package:* $9731 (excluding resources awarded to replace EFC). 9% of all full-time undergraduates had no need and received non-need-based gift aid.

GIFT AID (NEED-BASED) *Total amount:* $14,644,415 (51% federal, 17% state, 28% institutional, 4% external sources). *Receiving aid:* Freshmen: 63% (842); all full-time undergraduates: 57% (2,769). *Average award:* Freshmen: $7375; Undergraduates: $6243. *Scholarships, grants, and awards:* Federal Pell, FSEOG, state, private, college/university gift aid from institutional funds.

GIFT AID (NON-NEED-BASED) *Total amount:* $4,213,734 (2% federal, 5% state, 85% institutional, 8% external sources). *Receiving aid:* Freshmen: 35% (473). Undergraduates: 18% (884). *Average award:* Freshmen: $3467. Undergraduates: $2808. *Scholarships, grants, and awards by category: Academic interests/achievement:* agriculture, biological sciences, business, communication, computer science, education, English, foreign languages, general academic interests/achievements, health fields, home economics, humanities, mathematics, physical sciences, social sciences. *Creative arts/performance:* art/fine arts, cinema/film/broadcasting, dance, debating, journalism/publications, music, theater/drama. *Special achievements/activities:* cheerleading/drum major, general special achievements/activities, leadership, memberships. *Special characteristics:* children and siblings of alumni, children of faculty/staff, general special characteristics, members of minority groups, out-of-state students, previous college experience. *Tuition waivers:* Full or partial for employees or children of employees, senior citizens. *ROTC:* Army cooperative.

LOANS *Student loans:* $26,731,663 (55% need-based, 45% non-need-based). 71% of past graduating class borrowed through all loan programs. *Average indebtedness per student:* $28,332. *Average need-based loan:* Freshmen: $3343. Undergraduates: $3917. *Parent loans:* $6,603,683 (19% need-based, 81% non-need-based). *Programs:* Federal Direct (Subsidized and Unsubsidized Stafford, PLUS), Perkins.

WORK-STUDY *Federal work-study:* 388 jobs averaging $1263. *State or other work-study/employment:* Total amount: $1,495,169 (23% need-based, 77% non-need-based). 1,058 part-time jobs averaging $1772.

ATHLETIC AWARDS Total amount: $2,145,778 (40% need-based, 60% non-need-based).

APPLYING FOR FINANCIAL AID *Required financial aid form:* FAFSA. *Financial aid deadline:* Continuous. *Notification date:* Continuous beginning 3/15.

CONTACT Mr. Charles Mayfield, Director of Financial Assistance, Northwest Missouri State University, 800 University Drive, Maryville, MO 64468-6001, 660-562-1138 or toll-free 800-633-1175. *Website:* http://www.nwmissouri.edu/.

NORTHWEST NAZARENE UNIVERSITY
Nampa, ID

Tuition & fees: $28,650	Average undergraduate aid package: $21,877

ABOUT THE INSTITUTION Independent Church of the Nazarene, coed. *Awards:* certificates, associate, bachelor's, master's, and doctoral degrees. 72 undergraduate majors. *Total enrollment:* 2,229. Undergraduates: 1,517. Freshmen: 267. Federal methodology is used as a basis for awarding need-based institutional aid.

UNDERGRADUATE EXPENSES for 2016–2017 *Application fee:* $40. *Comprehensive fee:* $35,450 includes full-time tuition ($28,150), mandatory fees ($500), and room and board ($6800). *College room only:* $3200. Full-time tuition and fees vary according to class time, course load, degree level, location, program, and reciprocity agreements. Room and board charges vary according to board plan. *Part-time tuition:* $1200 per credit hour. Part-time tuition and fees vary according to class time, location, and program.

FRESHMAN FINANCIAL AID (Fall 2016, est.) 201 applied for aid; of those 86% were deemed to have need. 100% of freshmen with need received aid; of those 20% had need fully met. *Average percent of need met:* 78% (excluding resources awarded to replace EFC). *Average financial aid package:* $23,388 (excluding resources awarded to replace EFC). 15% of all full-time freshmen had no need and received non-need-based gift aid.

UNDERGRADUATE FINANCIAL AID (Fall 2016, est.) 985 applied for aid; of those 91% were deemed to have need. 99% of undergraduates with need received aid; of those 21% had need fully met. *Average percent of need met:* 73% (excluding resources awarded to replace EFC). *Average financial aid package:* $21,877 (excluding resources awarded to replace EFC). 16% of all full-time undergraduates had no need and received non-need-based gift aid.

GIFT AID (NEED-BASED) *Total amount:* $14,017,397 (16% federal, 1% state, 76% institutional, 7% external sources). *Receiving aid:* Freshmen: 76% (173); all full-time undergraduates: 37% (431). *Average award:* Freshmen: $5158; Undergraduates: $5014. *Scholarships, grants, and awards:* Federal Pell, FSEOG, state, private, college/university gift aid from institutional funds.

GIFT AID (NON-NEED-BASED) *Total amount:* $3,303,967 (92% institutional, 8% external sources). *Receiving aid:* Freshmen: 10% (24). Undergraduates: 8% (93). *Average award:* Freshmen: $13,493. Undergraduates: $10,815. *Scholarships, grants, and awards by category:* Academic interests/achievement: 932 awards ($7,680,663 total): biological sciences, business, communication, computer science, education, engineering/technologies, English, general academic interests/achievements, home economics, mathematics, military science, physical sciences, premedicine, religion/biblical studies, social sciences. *Creative arts/performance:* 130 awards ($363,540 total): debating, music, theater/drama. *Special achievements/activities:* 40 awards ($71,525 total): leadership, religious involvement. *Special characteristics:* 534 awards ($3,336,582 total): children and siblings of alumni, children of faculty/staff, international students, relatives of clergy, religious affiliation. *Tuition waivers:* Full or partial for employees or children of employees. *ROTC:* Army.

LOANS *Student loans:* $7,333,312 (81% need-based, 19% non-need-based). 82% of past graduating class borrowed through all loan programs. *Average indebtedness per student:* $31,318. *Average need-based loan:* Freshmen: $7206. Undergraduates: $8199. *Parent loans:* $1,255,706 (38% need-based, 62% non-need-based). *Programs:* Federal Direct (Subsidized and Unsubsidized Stafford, PLUS), Perkins, college/university.

WORK-STUDY *Federal work-study:* Total amount: $69,428; 95 jobs averaging $731.

ATHLETIC AWARDS Total amount: $2,058,233 (37% need-based, 63% non-need-based).

APPLYING FOR FINANCIAL AID *Required financial aid form:* FAFSA. *Financial aid deadline (priority):* 2/1. *Notification date:* Continuous beginning 12/1.

CONTACT Mrs. Ann Crabb, Director of Financial Aid, Northwest Nazarene University, 623 South University Boulevard, Nampa, ID 83686, 208-467-8638 or toll-free 877-668-4968. *Fax:* 208-467-8375. *E-mail:* atcrabb@nnu.edu. *Website:* http://www.nnu.edu/.

NORTHWEST UNIVERSITY
Kirkland, WA

Tuition & fees: $29,187	Average undergraduate aid package: $17,538

ABOUT THE INSTITUTION Independent Assemblies of God, coed. *Awards:* certificates, diplomas, associate, bachelor's, master's, and doctoral degrees. 67 undergraduate majors. *Total enrollment:* 2,636. Undergraduates: 1,820. Freshmen: 186. Federal methodology is used as a basis for awarding need-based institutional aid.

UNDERGRADUATE EXPENSES for 2017–2018 *Application fee:* $30. *Comprehensive fee:* $36,977 includes full-time tuition ($28,800), mandatory fees ($387), and room and board ($7790). *College room only:* $4660. Full-time tuition and fees vary according to class time, course load, location, program, and reciprocity agreements. Room and board charges vary according to housing facility and student level. *Part-time tuition:* $1200 per credit hour. Part-time tuition and fees vary according to class time, course load, and location.

FRESHMAN FINANCIAL AID (Fall 2015) 299 applied for aid; of those 84% were deemed to have need. 100% of freshmen with need received aid; of those 13% had need fully met. *Average percent of need met:* 71% (excluding resources awarded to replace EFC). *Average financial aid package:* $17,809 (excluding resources awarded to replace EFC). 15% of all full-time freshmen had no need and received non-need-based gift aid.

UNDERGRADUATE FINANCIAL AID (Fall 2015) 1,116 applied for aid; of those 86% were deemed to have need. 100% of undergraduates with need received aid; of those 11% had need fully met. *Average percent of need met:* 69% (excluding resources awarded to replace EFC). *Average financial aid package:* $17,538 (excluding resources awarded to replace EFC). 14% of all full-time undergraduates had no need and received non-need-based gift aid.

GIFT AID (NEED-BASED) *Total amount:* $12,389,625 (20% federal, 14% state, 62% institutional, 4% external sources). *Receiving aid:* Freshmen: 74% (240); all full-time undergraduates: 75% (913). *Average award:* Freshmen: $14,819; Undergraduates: $14,107. *Scholarships, grants, and awards:* Federal Pell, FSEOG, state, private, college/university gift aid from institutional funds.

GIFT AID (NON-NEED-BASED) *Total amount:* $2,197,484 (1% state, 94% institutional, 5% external sources). *Receiving aid:* Freshmen: 7% (22). Undergraduates: 7% (83). *Average award:* Freshmen: $7441. Undergraduates: $9290. *Scholarships, grants, and awards by category:* Academic interests/achievement: 561 awards ($4,540,370 total): general academic interests/achievements. *Creative arts/performance:* 126 awards ($391,500 total): debating, music. *Special achievements/activities:* 55 awards ($922,534 total): leadership, religious involvement. *Special characteristics:* 75 awards ($1,796,744 total): children of current students, children of educators, children of faculty/staff, general special characteristics, international students, married students, parents of current students, relatives of clergy, religious affiliation, siblings of current students, spouses of current students. *Tuition waivers:* Full or partial for employees or children of employees. *ROTC:* Army cooperative, Air Force cooperative.

LOANS *Student loans:* $8,286,780 (75% need-based, 25% non-need-based). 80% of past graduating class borrowed through all loan programs. *Average indebtedness per student:* $23,516. *Average need-based loan:* Freshmen: $3176. Undergraduates: $3831. *Parent loans:* $1,600,457 (45% need-based, 55% non-need-based). *Programs:* Federal Direct (Subsidized and Unsubsidized Stafford, PLUS), Perkins, state, alternative loans.

WORK-STUDY *Federal work-study:* jobs available. *State or other work-study/employment:* Total amount: $8700 (100% need-based). 5 part-time jobs averaging $2611.

ATHLETIC AWARDS Total amount: $1,078,562 (58% need-based, 42% non-need-based).

APPLYING FOR FINANCIAL AID *Required financial aid form:* FAFSA. *Financial aid deadline:* Continuous. *Notification date:* Continuous beginning 12/1. Students must reply within 4 weeks of notification.

CONTACT Mr. Roger Wilson, Director of Financial Aid, Northwest University, PO Box 579, Kirkland, WA 98083-0579, 425-889-5336 or toll-free 800-669-3781. *Fax:* 425-889-5224. *E-mail:* roger.wilson@northwestu.edu. *Website:* http://www.northwestu.edu/.

NORTHWOOD UNIVERSITY, MICHIGAN CAMPUS
Midland, MI

CONTACT Terri Mieler, Director of Financial Aid, Northwood University, Michigan Campus, 4000 Whiting Drive, Midland, MI 48640-2398, 989-837-4301 or toll-free 800-457-7878. *Fax:* 989-837-4130. *E-mail:* mieler@northwood.edu. *Website:* http://www.northwood.edu/.

NORWICH UNIVERSITY
Northfield, VT

CONTACT Ms. Jana Cox, Director of Student Financial Planning, Norwich University, 158 Harmon Drive, Northfield, VT 05663, 802-485-2015 or toll-free 800-468-6679. *Fax:* 802-485-2024. *E-mail:* jcox1@norwich.edu. *Website:* http://www.norwich.edu/.

NOSSI COLLEGE OF ART
Nashville, TN

CONTACT Ms. Mary P. Kidd, Director of Financial Aid, Nossi College of Art, 590 Cheron Road, Nashville, TN 37115, 615-514-2787 or toll-free 888-986-ARTS. *Fax:* 615-514-2788. *E-mail:* financialaid@nossi.edu. *Website:* http://www.nossi.edu/.

NOTRE DAME COLLEGE
South Euclid, OH

CONTACT Ms. Dianna Roberts, Assistant Director of Financial Aid, Notre Dame College, 4545 College Road, South Euclid, OH 44118, 216-373-5213 or toll-free 877-NDC-OHIO. *Fax:* 216-373-5243. *E-mail:* droberts@ndc.edu. *Website:* http://www.notredamecollege.edu/.

NOTRE DAME DE NAMUR UNIVERSITY
Belmont, CA

CONTACT Wilbert Lleses, Director of Financial Aid, Notre Dame de Namur University, 1500 Ralston Avenue, Belmont, CA 94002, 650-508-3441 or toll-free 800-263-0545. *Fax:* 650-508-3635. *E-mail:* wlleses@ndnu.edu. *Website:* http://www.ndnu.edu/.

NOTRE DAME OF MARYLAND UNIVERSITY
Baltimore, MD

CONTACT Audrey Brooks, Director of Financial Aid, Notre Dame of Maryland University, 4701 North Charles Street, Baltimore, MD 21210-2404, 410-532-5369 or toll-free 800-435-0200. *Fax:* 410-532-6287. *E-mail:* finaid@ndm.edu. *Website:* http://www.ndm.edu/.

NOVA SOUTHEASTERN UNIVERSITY
Fort Lauderdale, FL

Tuition & fees: $28,736	Average undergraduate aid package: $28,480

ABOUT THE INSTITUTION Independent, coed. *Awards:* certificates, associate, bachelor's, master's, and doctoral degrees. 49 undergraduate majors. *Total enrollment:* 17,330. Undergraduates: 4,295. Freshmen: 659. Federal methodology is used as a basis for awarding need-based institutional aid.

UNDERGRADUATE EXPENSES for 2016–2017 Application fee: $50. *Comprehensive fee:* $40,276 includes full-time tuition ($27,986), mandatory fees ($750), and room and board ($11,540). *College room only:* $8550. Full-time tuition and fees vary according to class time and program. Room and board charges vary according to board plan and housing facility. *Part-time tuition:* $933 per credit hour. Part-time tuition and fees vary according to class time, course load, and program.

FRESHMAN FINANCIAL AID (Fall 2016, est.) 583 applied for aid; of those 85% were deemed to have need. 100% of freshmen with need received aid; of those 19% had need fully met. *Average percent of need met:* 86% (excluding resources awarded to replace EFC). *Average financial aid package:* $30,160 (excluding resources awarded to replace EFC). 23% of all full-time freshmen had no need and received non-need-based gift aid.

UNDERGRADUATE FINANCIAL AID (Fall 2016, est.) 2,566 applied for aid; of those 88% were deemed to have need. 100% of undergraduates with need received aid; of those 14% had need fully met. *Average percent of need met:* 68% (excluding resources awarded to replace EFC). *Average financial aid package:* $28,480 (excluding resources awarded to replace EFC). 19% of all full-time undergraduates had no need and received non-need-based gift aid.

GIFT AID (NEED-BASED) Total amount: $40,229,855 (23% federal, 22% state, 47% institutional, 8% external sources). *Receiving aid:* Freshmen: 76% (493); all full-time undergraduates: 71% (2,172). *Average award:* Freshmen: $18,553; Undergraduates: $15,156. *Scholarships, grants, and awards:* Federal Pell, FSEOG, state, private, college/university gift aid from institutional funds, United Negro College Fund.

GIFT AID (NON-NEED-BASED) Total amount: $9,460,362 (1% federal, 11% state, 83% institutional, 5% external sources). *Receiving aid:* Freshmen: 9% (55). Undergraduates: 5% (148). *Average award:* Freshmen: $12,779. Undergraduates: $10,813. *Scholarships, grants, and awards by category:* Academic interests/achievement: 2,221 awards ($27,627,037 total): general academic interests/achievements. Creative arts/performance: 41 awards ($73,000 total): general creative arts/performance. Special achievements/activities: 222 awards ($1,528,501 total): general special achievements/activities. Special characteristics: 75 awards ($402,061 total): children of faculty/staff, veterans. *Tuition waivers:* Full or partial for employees or children of employees.

LOANS Student loans: $28,845,500 (93% need-based, 7% non-need-based). 51% of past graduating class borrowed through all loan programs. *Average indebtedness per student:* $34,763. *Average need-based loan:* Freshmen: $2803. Undergraduates: $3873. *Parent loans:* $8,231,784 (89% need-based, 11% non-need-based). *Programs:* Federal Direct (Subsidized and Unsubsidized Stafford, PLUS), Perkins.

WORK-STUDY Federal work-study: Total amount: $7,741,470; 1,198 jobs averaging $6462. *State or other work-study/employment:* Total amount: $507,600 (71% need-based, 29% non-need-based). 412 part-time jobs averaging $1232.

ATHLETIC AWARDS Total amount: $4,581,509 (39% need-based, 61% non-need-based).

APPLYING FOR FINANCIAL AID Required financial aid forms: FAFSA, state aid form. *Financial aid deadline (priority):* 4/15. *Notification date:* Continuous beginning 3/1.

CONTACT Dr. Stephanie G. Brown, Vice President for Enrollment and Student Services, Nova Southeastern University, 3301 College Avenue, Fort Lauderdale, FL 33314, 954-262-7456 or toll-free 800-541-NOVA. *Fax:* 954-262-3967. *E-mail:* browstep@nova.edu. *Website:* http://www.nova.edu/.

NYACK COLLEGE
Nyack, NY

ABOUT THE INSTITUTION Independent The Christian and Missionary Alliance, coed. **Awards:** associate, bachelor's, master's, and doctoral degrees. 36 undergraduate majors. **Total enrollment:** 2,502. Undergraduates: 1,451. Freshmen: 233.

GIFT AID (NEED-BASED) Scholarships, grants, and awards: Federal Pell, FSEOG, state, private, college/university gift aid from institutional funds.

GIFT AID (NON-NEED-BASED) Scholarships, grants, and awards by category: Academic interests/achievement: general academic interests/achievements. Creative arts/performance: journalism/publications, music, performing arts, theater/drama. Special achievements/activities: cheerleading/drum major, community service, general special achievements/activities, leadership, religious involvement. Special characteristics: children and siblings of alumni, children of educators, children of faculty/staff, general special characteristics, international students, local/state students, out-of-state students, relatives of clergy, religious affiliation, siblings of current students, spouses of current students.

LOANS Programs: Federal Direct (Subsidized and Unsubsidized Stafford, PLUS), Perkins.

APPLYING FOR FINANCIAL AID Required financial aid forms: FAFSA, state aid form.

CONTACT Steve Phillips, Director of Student Financial Services, Nyack College, 1 South Boulevard, Nyack, NY 10960-3698, 845-675-4747 or toll-free 800-33-NYACK. Fax: 845-358-7016. E-mail: nyacksfs@nyack.edu. Website: http://www.nyack.edu/.

OAK HILLS CHRISTIAN COLLEGE
Bemidji, MN

CONTACT Daniel Hovestol, Financial Aid Director, Oak Hills Christian College, 1600 Oak Hills Road, SW, Bemidji, MN 56601-8832, 218-751-8671 Ext. 1220 or toll-free 888-751-8670 Ext. 1285. Fax: 218-444-1311. E-mail: ohfinaid@oakhills.edu. Website: http://www.oakhills.edu/.

OAKLAND CITY UNIVERSITY
Oakland City, IN

Tuition & fees: $23,700	Average undergraduate aid package: $21,000

ABOUT THE INSTITUTION Independent General Baptist, coed. **Awards:** certificates, associate, bachelor's, master's, and doctoral degrees. 28 undergraduate majors. **Total enrollment:** 1,470. Undergraduates: 1,270. Freshmen: 93. Both federal and institutional methodology are used as a basis for awarding need-based institutional aid.

UNDERGRADUATE EXPENSES for 2017–2018 Application fee: $35. **Comprehensive fee:** $33,150 includes full-time tuition ($23,700) and room and board ($9450). **College room only:** $3200. Full-time tuition and fees vary according to degree level. Room and board charges vary according to board plan and housing facility. **Part-time tuition:** $790 per credit hour.

FRESHMAN FINANCIAL AID (Fall 2015) 81 applied for aid; of those 100% were deemed to have need. 100% of freshmen with need received aid. **Average percent of need met:** 96% (excluding resources awarded to replace EFC). **Average financial aid package:** $17,862 (excluding resources awarded to replace EFC).

UNDERGRADUATE FINANCIAL AID (Fall 2015) 462 applied for aid; of those 100% were deemed to have need. 100% of undergraduates with need received aid. **Average percent of need met:** 37% (excluding resources awarded to replace EFC). **Average financial aid package:** $21,000 (excluding resources awarded to replace EFC).

GIFT AID (NEED-BASED) Total amount: $5,848,919 (23% federal, 15% state, 61% institutional, 1% external sources). **Receiving aid:** Freshmen: 77% (65); all full-time undergraduates: 27% (331). **Average award:** Freshmen: $4811; Undergraduates: $4189. **Scholarships, grants, and awards:** Federal Pell, FSEOG, state, private, college/university gift aid from institutional funds.

GIFT AID (NON-NEED-BASED) Scholarships, grants, and awards by category: Academic interests/achievement: general academic interests/achievements. Creative arts/performance: art/fine arts, music. Special achievements/activities: reli-

gious involvement. Special characteristics: children and siblings of alumni, children of faculty/staff, ethnic background, international students, members of minority groups, religious affiliation. **Tuition waivers:** Full or partial for employees or children of employees.

LOANS Student loans: $2,375,422 (100% need-based). **Parent loans:** $151,081 (100% need-based). **Programs:** Federal Direct (Subsidized and Unsubsidized Stafford, PLUS), Perkins, college/university.

WORK-STUDY Federal work-study: jobs available. **State or other work-study/employment:** Part-time jobs available.

ATHLETIC AWARDS Total amount: $1,230,784 (100% need-based).

APPLYING FOR FINANCIAL AID Required financial aid form: FAFSA. **Financial aid deadline (priority):** 3/10. **Notification date:** Continuous beginning 5/15.

CONTACT Nicole Sharp, Director of Financial Aid, Oakland City University, 138 North Lucretia Street, Oakland City, IN 47660-1099, 812-749-1225 or toll-free 800-737-5125. Fax: 812-749-1438. E-mail: nsharp@oak.edu. Website: http://www.oak.edu/.

OAKLAND UNIVERSITY
Rochester, MI

Tuition & fees (MI res): $11,970	Average undergraduate aid package: $13,766

ABOUT THE INSTITUTION State-supported, coed. **Awards:** certificates, bachelor's, master's, and doctoral degrees. 90 undergraduate majors. **Total enrollment:** 20,261. Undergraduates: 16,793. Freshmen: 2,658. Federal methodology is used as a basis for awarding need-based institutional aid.

UNDERGRADUATE EXPENSES for 2016–2017 Tuition, state resident: full-time $11,970; part-time $399 per credit hour. **Tuition, nonresident:** full-time $23,873; part-time $795.75 per credit hour. Full-time tuition and fees vary according to program and student level. Part-time tuition and fees vary according to program and student level. **College room and board:** $9620. Room and board charges vary according to housing facility.

FRESHMAN FINANCIAL AID (Fall 2015) 2,201 applied for aid; of those 76% were deemed to have need. 96% of freshmen with need received aid; of those 10% had need fully met. **Average percent of need met:** 77% (excluding resources awarded to replace EFC). **Average financial aid package:** $14,475 (excluding resources awarded to replace EFC). 16% of all full-time freshmen had no need and received non-need-based gift aid.

UNDERGRADUATE FINANCIAL AID (Fall 2015) 9,774 applied for aid; of those 83% were deemed to have need. 98% of undergraduates with need received aid; of those 8% had need fully met. **Average percent of need met:** 72% (excluding resources awarded to replace EFC). **Average financial aid package:** $13,766 (excluding resources awarded to replace EFC). 18% of all full-time undergraduates had no need and received non-need-based gift aid.

GIFT AID (NEED-BASED) Total amount: $35,951,269 (58% federal, 2% state, 40% institutional). **Receiving aid:** Freshmen: 49% (1,307); all full-time undergraduates: 44% (5,612). **Average award:** Freshmen: $8102; Undergraduates: $5996. **Scholarships, grants, and awards:** Federal Pell, FSEOG, state, private, college/university gift aid from institutional funds.

GIFT AID (NON-NEED-BASED) Total amount: $30,323,246 (72% institutional, 28% external sources). **Receiving aid:** Freshmen: 30% (804). Undergraduates: 34% (4,419). **Average award:** Freshmen: $5174. Undergraduates: $3885. **Scholarships, grants, and awards by category:** Academic interests/achievement: humanities. **Tuition waivers:** Full or partial for employees or children of employees, senior citizens. **ROTC:** Air Force cooperative.

LOANS Student loans: $62,084,922 (45% need-based, 55% non-need-based). 65% of past graduating class borrowed through all loan programs. **Average indebtedness per student:** $27,669. **Average need-based loan:** Freshmen: $2828. Undergraduates: $4069. **Parent loans:** $13,474,199 (100% non-need-based). **Programs:** Federal Direct (Subsidized and Unsubsidized Stafford, PLUS), Perkins, private loans.

WORK-STUDY Federal work-study: jobs available. **State or other work-study/employment:** Part-time jobs available.

ATHLETIC AWARDS Total amount: $4,064,403 (100% non-need-based).

APPLYING FOR FINANCIAL AID Required financial aid form: FAFSA. **Financial aid deadline:** Continuous. **Notification date:** Continuous beginning 3/8.

CONTACT Ms. Cindy Hermsen, Director of Financial Aid, Oakland University, 120 North Foundation Hall, Rochester, MI 48309-4401, 248-370-2550 or toll-free 800-OAK-UNIV. *E-mail:* finaid@oakland.edu. *Website:* http://www.oakland.edu/.

OAKWOOD UNIVERSITY
Huntsville, AL

CONTACT Financial Aid Director, Oakwood University, 7000 Adventist Boulevard, Huntsville, AL 35896, 256-726-7210 or toll-free 800-824-5312. *Website:* http://www.oakwood.edu/.

OBERLIN COLLEGE
Oberlin, OH

Tuition & fees: $52,052	Average undergraduate aid package: $41,836

ABOUT THE INSTITUTION Independent, coed. *Awards:* certificates, diplomas, bachelor's, and master's degrees. 55 undergraduate majors. *Total enrollment:* 2,912. Undergraduates: 2,895. Freshmen: 762. Both federal and institutional methodology are used as a basis for awarding need-based institutional aid.

UNDERGRADUATE EXPENSES for 2016–2017 Comprehensive fee: $66,062 includes full-time tuition ($51,324), mandatory fees ($728), and room and board ($14,010). *College room only:* $7278. Room and board charges vary according to board plan and housing facility. *Part-time tuition:* $2120 per credit.

FRESHMAN FINANCIAL AID (Fall 2016, est.) 493 applied for aid; of those 83% were deemed to have need. 100% of freshmen with need received aid; of those 100% had need fully met. *Average percent of need met:* 100% (excluding resources awarded to replace EFC). *Average financial aid package:* $42,479 (excluding resources awarded to replace EFC). 36% of all full-time freshmen had no need and received non-need-based gift aid.

UNDERGRADUATE FINANCIAL AID (Fall 2016, est.) 1,596 applied for aid; of those 85% were deemed to have need. 100% of undergraduates with need received aid; of those 100% had need fully met. *Average percent of need met:* 100% (excluding resources awarded to replace EFC). *Average financial aid package:* $41,836 (excluding resources awarded to replace EFC). 41% of all full-time undergraduates had no need and received non-need-based gift aid.

GIFT AID (NEED-BASED) Total amount: $49,919,887 (3% federal, 93% institutional, 4% external sources). *Receiving aid:* Freshmen: 53% (407); all full-time undergraduates: 47% (1,339). *Average award:* Freshmen: $38,361; Undergraduates: $37,059. *Scholarships, grants, and awards:* Federal Pell, FSEOG, state, private, college/university gift aid from institutional funds.

GIFT AID (NON-NEED-BASED) Total amount: $17,577,070 (88% institutional, 12% external sources). *Receiving aid:* Freshmen: 43% (331). Undergraduates: 37% (1,072). *Average award:* Freshmen: $13,130. Undergraduates: $14,434. *Scholarships, grants, and awards by category:* Academic interests/achievement: 1,753 awards ($24,252,629 total): general academic interests/achievements, physical sciences. *Creative arts/performance:* 539 awards ($9,851,046 total): music. *Tuition waivers:* Full or partial for employees or children of employees.

LOANS Student loans: $1,803,813 (40% need-based, 60% non-need-based). 47% of past graduating class borrowed through all loan programs. *Average indebtedness per student:* $27,114. *Average need-based loan:* Freshmen: $4113. Undergraduates: $5102. *Parent loans:* $2,759,730 (78% need-based, 22% non-need-based). *Programs:* Federal Direct (Subsidized and Unsubsidized Stafford, PLUS), Perkins.

WORK-STUDY Federal work-study: Total amount: $1,725,558; jobs available. *State or other work-study/employment:* Total amount: $1,064,087 (80% need-based, 20% non-need-based). 600 part-time jobs averaging $2400.

APPLYING FOR FINANCIAL AID Required financial aid forms: FAFSA, CSS Financial Aid PROFILE, institution's own non-custodial form. *Financial aid deadline (priority):* 2/15. *Notification date:* 3/25. Students must reply by 5/1.

CONTACT Mr. Robert A. Reddy Jr., Director of Financial Aid, Oberlin College, Carnegie Building #123, 52 West Lorain Street, Oberlin, OH 44074, 440-775-8142 or toll-free 800-622-OBIE. *Fax:* 440-775-8249. *E-mail:* financial.aid@oberlin.edu. *Website:* http://www.oberlin.edu/.

OCCIDENTAL COLLEGE
Los Angeles, CA

Tuition & fees: $51,070	Average undergraduate aid package: $46,791

ABOUT THE INSTITUTION Independent, coed. *Awards:* diplomas, bachelor's, and master's degrees. 31 undergraduate majors. *Total enrollment:* 2,062. Undergraduates: 2,062. Freshmen: 502. Institutional methodology is used as a basis for awarding need-based institutional aid.

UNDERGRADUATE EXPENSES for 2016–2017 Application fee: $65. *Comprehensive fee:* $65,530 includes full-time tuition ($50,492), mandatory fees ($578), and room and board ($14,460). *College room only:* $8230. Room and board charges vary according to board plan. *Part-time tuition:* $2104 per unit. *Part-time fees:* $578 per year. Part-time tuition and fees vary according to course load. *Payment plan:* Tuition prepayment.

FRESHMAN FINANCIAL AID (Fall 2015) 372 applied for aid; of those 82% were deemed to have need. 100% of freshmen with need received aid; of those 100% had need fully met. *Average percent of need met:* 100% (excluding resources awarded to replace EFC). *Average financial aid package:* $46,151 (excluding resources awarded to replace EFC). 10% of all full-time freshmen had no need and received non-need-based gift aid.

UNDERGRADUATE FINANCIAL AID (Fall 2015) 1,331 applied for aid; of those 86% were deemed to have need. 100% of undergraduates with need received aid; of those 100% had need fully met. *Average percent of need met:* 100% (excluding resources awarded to replace EFC). *Average financial aid package:* $46,791 (excluding resources awarded to replace EFC). 12% of all full-time undergraduates had no need and received non-need-based gift aid.

GIFT AID (NEED-BASED) Total amount: $43,016,029 (5% federal, 5% state, 87% institutional, 3% external sources). *Receiving aid:* Freshmen: 58% (300); all full-time undergraduates: 54% (1,137). *Average award:* Freshmen: $38,734; Undergraduates: $36,889. *Scholarships, grants, and awards:* Federal Pell, FSEOG, state, private, college/university gift aid from institutional funds.

GIFT AID (NON-NEED-BASED) Total amount: $4,600,136 (90% institutional, 10% external sources). *Receiving aid:* Freshmen: 33% (171). Undergraduates: 27% (575). *Average award:* Freshmen: $11,808. Undergraduates: $11,219. *Scholarships, grants, and awards by category:* Academic interests/achievement: 488 awards ($5,749,874 total): general academic interests/achievements. *Creative arts/performance:* 28 awards ($18,576 total): music. *Special achievements/activities:* 22 awards ($330,000 total): leadership. *Special characteristics:* 54 awards ($1,346,944 total): children of educators, children of faculty/staff, veterans, veterans' children. *Tuition waivers:* Full or partial for employees or children of employees. *ROTC:* Army cooperative, Air Force cooperative.

LOANS Student loans: $9,762,615 (60% need-based, 40% non-need-based). 53% of past graduating class borrowed through all loan programs. *Average indebtedness per student:* $29,940. *Average need-based loan:* Freshmen: $4592. Undergraduates: $6124. *Parent loans:* $2,934,061 (100% non-need-based). *Programs:* Federal Direct (Subsidized and Unsubsidized Stafford, PLUS), Perkins, college/university, alternative loans.

WORK-STUDY Federal work-study: 800 jobs averaging $2713. *State or other work-study/employment:* Total amount: $912,712 (83% need-based, 17% non-need-based). 181 part-time jobs averaging $1481.

APPLYING FOR FINANCIAL AID Required financial aid forms: FAFSA, CSS Financial Aid PROFILE, state aid form, noncustodial (divorced/separated) parent's statement. *Financial aid deadline:* 1/15. *Notification date:* 3/25. Students must reply by 5/1.

CONTACT Gina Becerril, Director of Financial Aid, Occidental College, 1600 Campus Road, Los Angeles, CA 90041, 323-259-2548 or toll-free 800-825-5262. *Fax:* 323-341-4961. *E-mail:* finaid@oxy.edu. *Website:* http://www.oxy.edu/.

OGLALA LAKOTA COLLEGE
Kyle, SD

CONTACT Financial Aid Director, Oglala Lakota College, 490 Piya Wiconi Road, Kyle, SD 57752-0490, 605-455-6000. *Website:* http://www.olc.edu/.

OGLETHORPE UNIVERSITY
Atlanta, GA

Tuition & fees: $35,425	Average undergraduate aid package: $30,022

ABOUT THE INSTITUTION Independent, coed. **Awards:** bachelor's degrees. 32 undergraduate majors. **Total enrollment:** 1,147. Undergraduates: 1,147. Freshmen: 323. Federal methodology is used as a basis for awarding need-based institutional aid.

UNDERGRADUATE EXPENSES for 2016–2017 Application fee: $50. **Comprehensive fee:** $48,135 includes full-time tuition ($35,000), mandatory fees ($425), and room and board ($12,710). **College room only:** $4050. Full-time tuition and fees vary according to degree level. Room and board charges vary according to housing facility and location. **Part-time tuition:** $1467 per credit hour. Part-time tuition and fees vary according to class time, course load, and degree level. **Payment plan:** Tuition prepayment.

FRESHMAN FINANCIAL AID (Fall 2016, est.) 284 applied for aid; of those 89% were deemed to have need. 100% of freshmen with need received aid; of those 23% had need fully met. **Average percent of need met:** 78% (excluding resources awarded to replace EFC). **Average financial aid package:** $31,827 (excluding resources awarded to replace EFC). 24% of all full-time freshmen had no need and received non-need-based gift aid.

UNDERGRADUATE FINANCIAL AID (Fall 2016, est.) 840 applied for aid; of those 91% were deemed to have need. 100% of undergraduates with need received aid; of those 19% had need fully met. **Average percent of need met:** 75% (excluding resources awarded to replace EFC). **Average financial aid package:** $30,022 (excluding resources awarded to replace EFC). 31% of all full-time undergraduates had no need and received non-need-based gift aid.

GIFT AID (NEED-BASED) Total amount: $19,094,410 (11% federal, 10% state, 79% institutional). **Receiving aid:** Freshmen: 76% (252); all full-time undergraduates: 69% (762). **Average award:** Freshmen: $26,930; Undergraduates: $24,906. **Scholarships, grants, and awards:** Federal Pell, FSEOG, state, private, college/university gift aid from institutional funds.

GIFT AID (NON-NEED-BASED) Total amount: $8,173,319 (5% state, 95% institutional). **Receiving aid:** Freshmen: 16% (54). Undergraduates: 11% (119). **Average award:** Freshmen: $20,989. Undergraduates: $18,916. **Scholarships, grants, and awards by category:** Academic interests/achievement: general academic interests/achievements. Creative arts/performance: art/fine arts, journalism/publications, music, performing arts, theater/drama. Special achievements/activities: community service, religious involvement. Special characteristics: children of faculty/staff, siblings of current students. **Tuition waivers:** Full or partial for employees or children of employees. **ROTC:** Army cooperative, Naval cooperative, Air Force cooperative.

LOANS Student loans: $7,279,809 (72% need-based, 28% non-need-based). 65% of past graduating class borrowed through all loan programs. Average indebtedness per student: $26,660. **Average need-based loan:** Freshmen: $3381. Undergraduates: $3407. **Parent loans:** $2,155,150 (59% need-based, 41% non-need-based). **Programs:** Federal Direct (Subsidized and Unsubsidized Stafford, PLUS), Perkins, state.

WORK-STUDY Federal work-study: Total amount: $148,969; 86 jobs averaging $1819.

APPLYING FOR FINANCIAL AID Required financial aid form: FAFSA. **Financial aid deadline (priority):** 2/15. **Notification date:** Continuous beginning 12/1. Students must reply by 5/1.

CONTACT Mr. Chris Summers, Director of Financial Aid, Oglethorpe University, 4484 Peachtree Road NE, Atlanta, GA 30319, 404-364-8355 or toll-free 800-428-4484. E-mail: csummers@oglethorpe.edu. Website: http://www.oglethorpe.edu/.

OHIO CHRISTIAN UNIVERSITY
Circleville, OH

CONTACT Michael Fracassa, Assistant Vice President of Finance, Ohio Christian University, 1476 Lancaster Pike, PO Box 458, Circleville, OH 43113-9487, 740-477-7758 or toll-free 877-762-8669. Fax: 740-477-5921. E-mail: mfracassa@ohiochristian.edu. Website: http://www.ohiochristian.edu/.

OHIO DOMINICAN UNIVERSITY
Columbus, OH

CONTACT Ms. Cynthia A. Hahn, Director of Financial Aid, Ohio Dominican University, 1216 Sunbury Road, Columbus, OH 43219, 614-251-4778 or toll-free 800-955-6446. Fax: 614-251-4456. E-mail: fin-aid@ohiodominican.edu. Website: http://www.ohiodominican.edu/.

OHIO NORTHERN UNIVERSITY
Ada, OH

Tuition & fees: $29,820	Average undergraduate aid package: $26,452

ABOUT THE INSTITUTION Independent United Methodist Church, coed. **Awards:** certificates, bachelor's, master's, and doctoral degrees. 124 undergraduate majors. **Total enrollment:** 3,238. Undergraduates: 2,259. Freshmen: 585. Federal methodology is used as a basis for awarding need-based institutional aid.

UNDERGRADUATE EXPENSES for 2016–2017 Comprehensive fee: $40,870 includes full-time tuition ($29,240), mandatory fees ($580), and room and board ($11,050). Full-time tuition and fees vary according to course load, degree level, and program. Room and board charges vary according to board plan, housing facility, and student level. **Part-time tuition:** $1220 per credit hour. **Part-time fees:** $125 per term. Part-time tuition and fees vary according to course load, degree level, and program.

FRESHMAN FINANCIAL AID (Fall 2016, est.) 561 applied for aid; of those 86% were deemed to have need. 100% of freshmen with need received aid; of those 23% had need fully met. **Average percent of need met:** 23% (excluding resources awarded to replace EFC). **Average financial aid package:** $27,557 (excluding resources awarded to replace EFC). 19% of all full-time freshmen had no need and received non-need-based gift aid.

UNDERGRADUATE FINANCIAL AID (Fall 2016, est.) 1,824 applied for aid; of those 89% were deemed to have need. 100% of undergraduates with need received aid; of those 23% had need fully met. **Average percent of need met:** 23% (excluding resources awarded to replace EFC). **Average financial aid package:** $26,452 (excluding resources awarded to replace EFC). 18% of all full-time undergraduates had no need and received non-need-based gift aid.

GIFT AID (NEED-BASED) Total amount: $34,257,948 (6% federal, 3% state, 87% institutional, 4% external sources). **Receiving aid:** Freshmen: 80% (481); all full-time undergraduates: 79% (1,619). **Average award:** Freshmen: $23,487; Undergraduates: $2020. **Scholarships, grants, and awards:** Federal Pell, FSEOG, state, private, college/university gift aid from institutional funds.

GIFT AID (NON-NEED-BASED) Total amount: $5,314,929 (98% institutional, 2% external sources). **Average award:** Freshmen: $16,160. Undergraduates: $14,006. **Scholarships, grants, and awards by category:** Academic interests/achievement: biological sciences, business, communication, computer science, education, engineering/technologies, English, foreign languages, general academic interests/achievements, health fields, humanities, international studies, mathematics, physical sciences, premedicine, religion/biblical studies, social sciences. Creative arts/performance: applied art and design, art/fine arts, creative writing, dance, journalism/publications, music, performing arts, theater/drama. Special achievements/activities: community service, general special achievements/activities, junior miss, leadership. Special characteristics: children and siblings of alumni, children of faculty/staff, ethnic background, international students, out-of-state students, relatives of clergy, religious affiliation, siblings of current students, veterans. **Tuition waivers:** Full or partial for minority students, children of alumni, employees or children of employees. **ROTC:** Army cooperative, Air Force cooperative.

LOANS Student loans: $16,022,085 (41% need-based, 59% non-need-based). 78% of past graduating class borrowed through all loan programs. **Average need-based loan:** Freshmen: $5342. Undergraduates: $5646. **Parent loans:** $4,309,629 (100% non-need-based). **Programs:** Federal Direct (Subsidized and Unsubsidized Stafford, PLUS), Perkins, state, college/university, Health Profession Student Loans (HPSL).

WORK-STUDY Federal work-study: Total amount: $341,514; jobs available. **State or other work-study/employment:** Total amount: $179,195 (100% need-based). Part-time jobs available.

APPLYING FOR FINANCIAL AID Required financial aid form: FAFSA. **Financial aid deadline (priority):** 3/1. **Notification date:** Continuous beginning 12/1. Students must reply within 2 weeks of notification.

CONTACT Melanie Weaver, Director of Financial Aid, Ohio Northern University, 525 South Main Street, Ada, OH 45810, 419-772-2272 or toll-free 888-408-4ONU. *Fax:* 419-772-2313. *E-mail:* m-weaver.2@onu.edu. *Website:* http://www.onu.edu/.

CONTACT Ms. Diane Corbett, Executive Director of Student Financial Aid, The Ohio State University, 281 West Lane Avenue, 4th Floor, Columbus, OH 43210, 614-292-8595. *E-mail:* buckeyelink@osu.edu. *Website:* http://www.osu.edu/.

THE OHIO STATE UNIVERSITY
Columbus, OH

Tuition & fees (OH res): $10,037	Average undergraduate aid package: $13,354

ABOUT THE INSTITUTION State-supported, coed. *Awards:* certificates, diplomas, bachelor's, master's, and doctoral degrees. 187 undergraduate majors. *Total enrollment:* 58,663. Undergraduates: 45,831. Freshmen: 7,938. Federal methodology is used as a basis for awarding need-based institutional aid.

UNDERGRADUATE EXPENSES for 2016–2017 *Tuition, state resident:* full-time $10,037; part-time $454.70 per credit hour. *Tuition, nonresident:* full-time $28,229; part-time $1213 per credit hour. Full-time tuition and fees vary according to course load, location, program, and reciprocity agreements. Part-time tuition and fees vary according to course load, location, program, and reciprocity agreements. *College room and board:* $11,666. Room and board charges vary according to board plan, housing facility, and location.

FRESHMAN FINANCIAL AID (Fall 2016, est.) 6,127 applied for aid; of those 59% were deemed to have need. 99% of freshmen with need received aid; of those 28% had need fully met. *Average percent of need met:* 75% (excluding resources awarded to replace EFC). *Average financial aid package:* $14,399 (excluding resources awarded to replace EFC). 28% of all full-time freshmen had no need and received non-need-based gift aid.

UNDERGRADUATE FINANCIAL AID (Fall 2016, est.) 27,556 applied for aid; of those 71% were deemed to have need. 98% of undergraduates with need received aid; of those 19% had need fully met. *Average percent of need met:* 69% (excluding resources awarded to replace EFC). *Average financial aid package:* $13,354 (excluding resources awarded to replace EFC). 20% of all full-time undergraduates had no need and received non-need-based gift aid.

GIFT AID (NEED-BASED) *Total amount:* $158,025,649 (26% federal, 6% state, 64% institutional, 4% external sources). *Receiving aid:* Freshmen: 41% (3,256); all full-time undergraduates: 40% (16,716). *Average award:* Freshmen: $10,699; Undergraduates: $9548. *Scholarships, grants, and awards:* Federal Pell, FSEOG, state, private, college/university gift aid from institutional funds.

GIFT AID (NON-NEED-BASED) *Total amount:* $86,435,602 (2% state, 88% institutional, 10% external sources). *Receiving aid:* Freshmen: 4% (302). Undergraduates: 2% (824). *Average award:* Freshmen: $7166. Undergraduates: $7034. *Scholarships, grants, and awards by category:* Academic interests/achievement: agriculture, architecture, area/ethnic studies, biological sciences, business, communication, computer science, education, engineering/technologies, English, foreign languages, general academic interests/achievements, health fields, home economics, humanities, international studies, mathematics, military science, physical sciences, premedicine, social sciences. *Creative arts/performance:* creative writing, dance, journalism/publications, music, performing arts, theater/drama. *Special achievements/activities:* cheerleading/drum major, hobbies/interests, leadership, memberships. *Special characteristics:* adult students, children and siblings of alumni, children of faculty/staff, children of public servants, children of union members/company employees, children of workers in trades, ethnic background, handicapped students, members of minority groups, out-of-state students, previous college experience. *Tuition waivers:* Full or partial for employees or children of employees, senior citizens. *ROTC:* Army, Naval, Air Force.

LOANS *Student loans:* $201,334,424 (61% need-based, 39% non-need-based). 54% of past graduating class borrowed through all loan programs. *Average indebtedness per student:* $27,930. *Average need-based loan:* Freshmen: $3960. Undergraduates: $4742. *Parent loans:* $46,328,801 (100% non-need-based). *Programs:* Federal Direct (Subsidized and Unsubsidized Stafford, PLUS), Perkins, Federal Nursing, state, college/university.

WORK-STUDY *Federal work-study:* Total amount: $5,595,720; 1,926 jobs averaging $2908. *State or other work-study/employment:* Total amount: $5000 (100% non-need-based). 3 part-time jobs averaging $1667.

ATHLETIC AWARDS Total amount: $18,927,683 (100% non-need-based).

APPLYING FOR FINANCIAL AID *Required financial aid form:* FAFSA. *Financial aid deadline (priority):* 2/1. *Notification date:* 3/15. Students must reply by 5/1 or within 4 weeks of notification.

OHIO UNIVERSITY
Athens, OH

Tuition & fees (OH res): $11,744	Average undergraduate aid package: $9240

ABOUT THE INSTITUTION State-supported, coed. *Awards:* certificates, associate, bachelor's, master's, and doctoral degrees. 124 undergraduate majors. *Total enrollment:* 29,712. Undergraduates: 23,788. Freshmen: 4,331. Federal methodology is used as a basis for awarding need-based institutional aid.

UNDERGRADUATE EXPENSES for 2016–2017 *Application fee:* $50. *Tuition, state resident:* full-time $11,744; part-time $556 per semester hour. *Tuition, nonresident:* full-time $21,208; part-time $1022 per semester hour. Full-time tuition and fees vary according to degree level, location, program, and reciprocity agreements. Part-time tuition and fees vary according to course load, degree level, location, program, and reciprocity agreements. *College room and board:* $11,176. Room and board charges vary according to board plan. *Payment plan:* Guaranteed tuition.

FRESHMAN FINANCIAL AID (Fall 2016, est.) 3,623 applied for aid; of those 75% were deemed to have need. 100% of freshmen with need received aid; of those 42% had need fully met. *Average percent of need met:* 52% (excluding resources awarded to replace EFC). *Average financial aid package:* $10,034 (excluding resources awarded to replace EFC). 8% of all full-time freshmen had no need and received non-need-based gift aid.

UNDERGRADUATE FINANCIAL AID (Fall 2016, est.) 12,709 applied for aid; of those 79% were deemed to have need. 100% of undergraduates with need received aid; of those 36% had need fully met. *Average percent of need met:* 47% (excluding resources awarded to replace EFC). *Average financial aid package:* $9240 (excluding resources awarded to replace EFC). 9% of all full-time undergraduates had no need and received non-need-based gift aid.

GIFT AID (NEED-BASED) *Total amount:* $64,433,400 (39% federal, 7% state, 49% institutional, 5% external sources). *Receiving aid:* Freshmen: 58% (2,485); all full-time undergraduates: 45% (7,767). *Average award:* Freshmen: $6960; Undergraduates: $6510. *Scholarships, grants, and awards:* Federal Pell, FSEOG, state, private, college/university gift aid from institutional funds.

GIFT AID (NON-NEED-BASED) *Total amount:* $10,445,845 (1% federal, 4% state, 90% institutional, 5% external sources). *Receiving aid:* Freshmen: 8% (350). Undergraduates: 10% (1,691). *Average award:* Freshmen: $3757. Undergraduates: $4231. *Scholarships, grants, and awards by category:* Academic interests/achievement: area/ethnic studies, biological sciences, business, communication, computer science, education, engineering/technologies, English, foreign languages, general academic interests/achievements, health fields, home economics, humanities, international studies, mathematics, military science, physical sciences, premedicine, social sciences. *Creative arts/performance:* applied art and design, art/fine arts, cinema/film/broadcasting, creative writing, dance, debating, journalism/publications, music, performing arts, theater/drama. *Special characteristics:* children and siblings of alumni, children of faculty/staff, first-generation college students. *Tuition waivers:* Full or partial for employees or children of employees, senior citizens. *ROTC:* Army, Air Force.

LOANS *Student loans:* $120,180,368 (90% need-based, 10% non-need-based). 67% of past graduating class borrowed through all loan programs. *Average indebtedness per student:* $27,879. *Average need-based loan:* Freshmen: $2867. Undergraduates: $3751. *Parent loans:* $38,862,121 (51% need-based, 49% non-need-based). *Programs:* Federal Direct (Subsidized and Unsubsidized Stafford, PLUS), Perkins, state, college/university.

WORK-STUDY *Federal work-study:* Total amount: $1,574,918; 724 jobs averaging $1684. *State or other work-study/employment:* Total amount: $21,818,174 (100% non-need-based). Part-time jobs available.

ATHLETIC AWARDS Total amount: $7,933,332 (26% need-based, 74% non-need-based).

APPLYING FOR FINANCIAL AID *Required financial aid form:* FAFSA. *Financial aid deadline (priority):* 1/15. *Notification date:* 2/1.

CONTACT Ms. Valerie K. Miller, Director of Financial Aid, Ohio University, 020 Chubb Hall, Athens, OH 45701-2979, 740-593-9853. *Fax:* 740-593-4140. *E-mail:* millerv@ohio.edu.
Website: http://www.ohio.edu/.

OHIO UNIVERSITY–CHILLICOTHE
Chillicothe, OH

Tuition & fees: N/R	Average undergraduate aid package: $7323

ABOUT THE INSTITUTION State-supported, coed. *Awards:* associate, bachelor's, and master's degrees (offers first 2 years of most bachelor's degree programs available at the main campus in Athens; also offers several bachelor's degree programs that can be completed at this campus and several programs exclusive to this campus; also offers some graduate programs). 22 undergraduate majors. *Total enrollment:* 2,200. Undergraduates: 2,200. Federal methodology is used as a basis for awarding need-based institutional aid.

FRESHMAN FINANCIAL AID (Fall 2016, est.) 266 applied for aid; of those 74% were deemed to have need. 100% of freshmen with need received aid; of those 15% had need fully met. *Average percent of need met:* 60% (excluding resources awarded to replace EFC). *Average financial aid package:* $6473 (excluding resources awarded to replace EFC). 1% of all full-time freshmen had no need and received non-need-based gift aid.

UNDERGRADUATE FINANCIAL AID (Fall 2016, est.) 824 applied for aid; of those 83% were deemed to have need. 100% of undergraduates with need received aid; of those 13% had need fully met. *Average percent of need met:* 54% (excluding resources awarded to replace EFC). *Average financial aid package:* $7323 (excluding resources awarded to replace EFC). 1% of all full-time undergraduates had no need and received non-need-based gift aid.

GIFT AID (NEED-BASED) *Total amount:* $4,655,057 (80% federal, 2% state, 15% institutional, 3% external sources). *Receiving aid:* Freshmen: 50% (168); all full-time undergraduates: 60% (563). *Average award:* Freshmen: $5233; Undergraduates: $5439. *Scholarships, grants, and awards:* Federal Pell, FSEOG, state, private, college/university gift aid from institutional funds.

GIFT AID (NON-NEED-BASED) *Total amount:* $105,761 (13% federal, 2% state, 58% institutional, 27% external sources). *Receiving aid:* Freshmen: 1% (2). Undergraduates: 1% (14). *Average award:* Freshmen: $6060. Undergraduates: $4111. *Scholarships, grants, and awards by category:* Academic interests/achievement: area/ethnic studies, biological sciences, business, communication, computer science, education, engineering/technologies, English, foreign languages, general academic interests/achievements, health fields, home economics, humanities, international studies, mathematics, military science, physical sciences, premedicine, social sciences. *Creative arts/performance:* applied art and design, art/fine arts, cinema/film/broadcasting, creative writing, dance, debating, journalism/publications, music, performing arts, theater/drama. *Special characteristics:* children and siblings of alumni, children of faculty/staff, first-generation college students.

LOANS *Student loans:* $4,852,821 (96% need-based, 4% non-need-based). 67% of past graduating class borrowed through all loan programs. *Average indebtedness per student:* $27,879. *Average need-based loan:* Freshmen: $1749. Undergraduates: $2675. *Parent loans:* $88,718 (36% need-based, 64% non-need-based). *Programs:* Federal Direct (Subsidized and Unsubsidized Stafford, PLUS), Perkins, state, college/university.

WORK-STUDY *Federal work-study:* Total amount: $35,712; 18 jobs averaging $1504.

APPLYING FOR FINANCIAL AID *Required financial aid form:* FAFSA. *Financial aid deadline (priority):* 1/15. *Notification date:* 2/1.

CONTACT Ms. Valerie K. Miller, Director of Financial Aid, Ohio University–Chillicothe, 020 Chubb Hall, Athens, OH 45701-2979, 740-593-4141 or toll-free 877-462-6824. *Fax:* 740-593-4140. *E-mail:* millerv@ohio.edu.
Website: http://www.chillicothe.ohiou.edu/.

OHIO UNIVERSITY–EASTERN
St. Clairsville, OH

Tuition & fees (area res): $5150	Average undergraduate aid package: $6256

ABOUT THE INSTITUTION State-supported, coed. *Awards:* associate, bachelor's, and master's degrees (also offers some graduate courses). 11 undergraduate majors. *Total enrollment:* 751. Undergraduates: 751. Federal methodology is used as a basis for awarding need-based institutional aid.

UNDERGRADUATE EXPENSES for 2017–2018 *Application fee:* $20. *Tuition, area resident:* full-time $5084. *Tuition, state resident:* part-time $219 per credit hour. *Tuition, nonresident:* part-time $305 per credit hour. *Required fees:* full-time $66; $3 per credit hour. Full-time tuition and fees vary according to course load, location, program, reciprocity agreements, and student level. Part-time tuition and fees vary according to course load, location, program, reciprocity agreements, and student level.

FRESHMAN FINANCIAL AID (Fall 2016, est.) 105 applied for aid; of those 72% were deemed to have need. 100% of freshmen with need received aid; of those 12% had need fully met. *Average percent of need met:* 59% (excluding resources awarded to replace EFC). *Average financial aid package:* $5698 (excluding resources awarded to replace EFC). 1% of all full-time freshmen had no need and received non-need-based gift aid.

UNDERGRADUATE FINANCIAL AID (Fall 2016, est.) 275 applied for aid; of those 76% were deemed to have need. 100% of undergraduates with need received aid; of those 14% had need fully met. *Average percent of need met:* 56% (excluding resources awarded to replace EFC). *Average financial aid package:* $6256 (excluding resources awarded to replace EFC). 2% of all full-time undergraduates had no need and received non-need-based gift aid.

GIFT AID (NEED-BASED) *Total amount:* $1,193,096 (72% federal, 1% state, 24% institutional, 3% external sources). *Receiving aid:* Freshmen: 50% (64); all full-time undergraduates: 52% (168). *Average award:* Freshmen: $5282; Undergraduates: $5032. *Scholarships, grants, and awards:* Federal Pell, FSEOG, state, college/university gift aid from institutional funds.

GIFT AID (NON-NEED-BASED) *Total amount:* $30,997 (11% federal, 74% institutional, 15% external sources). *Receiving aid:* Freshmen: 1% (1). Undergraduates: 2% (5). *Average award:* Freshmen: $4968. Undergraduates: $3482. *Scholarships, grants, and awards by category:* Academic interests/achievement: area/ethnic studies, biological sciences, business, communication, computer science, education, engineering/technologies, English, foreign languages, general academic interests/achievements, health fields, home economics, humanities, international studies, mathematics, military science, physical sciences, premedicine, social sciences. *Creative arts/performance:* applied art and design, art/fine arts, cinema/film/broadcasting, creative writing, dance, debating, journalism/publications, music, performing arts, theater/drama. *Special characteristics:* children and siblings of alumni, children of faculty/staff, first-generation college students. *Tuition waivers:* Full or partial for employees or children of employees, senior citizens.

LOANS *Student loans:* $1,114,940 (97% need-based, 3% non-need-based). 67% of past graduating class borrowed through all loan programs. *Average indebtedness per student:* $27,879. *Average need-based loan:* Freshmen: $1182. Undergraduates: $2207. *Parent loans:* $18,259 (100% need-based). *Programs:* Federal Direct (Subsidized and Unsubsidized Stafford, PLUS), Perkins, state, college/university.

WORK-STUDY *Federal work-study:* Total amount: $14,110; 7 jobs averaging $1781.

APPLYING FOR FINANCIAL AID *Required financial aid form:* FAFSA. *Financial aid deadline (priority):* 1/15. *Notification date:* 2/1.

CONTACT Ms. Valerie K. Miller, Director of Financial Aid, Ohio University–Eastern, 020 Chubb Hall, Athens, OH 45701-2979, 740-593-4141 or toll-free 800-648-3331. *Fax:* 740-593-4140. *E-mail:* millerv@ohio.edu.
Website: http://www.eastern.ohiou.edu/.

OHIO UNIVERSITY–LANCASTER
Lancaster, OH

Tuition & fees: N/R	Average undergraduate aid package: $6654

ABOUT THE INSTITUTION State-supported, coed. 14 undergraduate majors. Federal methodology is used as a basis for awarding need-based institutional aid.
FRESHMAN FINANCIAL AID (Fall 2016, est.) 277 applied for aid; of those 76% were deemed to have need. 100% of freshmen with need received aid; of those 15% had need fully met. *Average percent of need met:* 62% (excluding resources awarded to replace EFC). *Average financial aid package:* $6296 (excluding resources awarded to replace EFC). 3% of all full-time freshmen had no need and received non-need-based gift aid.
UNDERGRADUATE FINANCIAL AID (Fall 2016, est.) 755 applied for aid; of those 80% were deemed to have need. 100% of undergraduates with need received aid; of those 13% had need fully met. *Average percent of need met:* 56% (excluding resources awarded to replace EFC). *Average financial aid package:* $6654 (excluding resources awarded to replace EFC). 3% of all full-time undergraduates had no need and received non-need-based gift aid.
GIFT AID (NEED-BASED) Total amount: $3,705,449 (80% federal, 1% state, 16% institutional, 3% external sources). *Receiving aid:* Freshmen: 50% (167); all full-time undergraduates: 54% (459). *Average award:* Freshmen: $5326; Undergraduates: $5232. *Scholarships, grants, and awards:* Federal Pell, FSEOG, state, private, college/university gift aid from institutional funds.
GIFT AID (NON-NEED-BASED) Total amount: $127,058 (8% federal, 84% institutional, 8% external sources). *Receiving aid:* Freshmen: 3% (11). Undergraduates: 3% (26). *Average award:* Freshmen: $2676. Undergraduates: $4008. *Scholarships, grants, and awards by category:* Academic interests/achievement: area/ethnic studies, biological sciences, business, communication, computer science, education, engineering/technologies, English, foreign languages, general academic interests/achievements, health fields, home economics, humanities, international studies, mathematics, military science, physical sciences, premedicine, social sciences. Creative arts/performance: applied art and design, art/fine arts, cinema/film/broadcasting, creative writing, dance, debating, journalism/publications, music, performing arts, theater/drama. Special characteristics: children and siblings of alumni, children of faculty/staff, first-generation college students.
LOANS Student loans: $3,938,291 (97% need-based, 3% non-need-based). 67% of past graduating class borrowed through all loan programs. *Average indebtedness per student:* $27,879. *Average need-based loan:* Freshmen: $1661. Undergraduates: $2470. *Parent loans:* $98,879 (39% need-based, 61% non-need-based). *Programs:* Federal Direct (Subsidized and Unsubsidized Stafford, PLUS), Perkins, state, college/university.
WORK-STUDY Federal work-study: Total amount: $25,522; 15 jobs averaging $1421.
APPLYING FOR FINANCIAL AID Required financial aid form: FAFSA. *Financial aid deadline (priority):* 1/15. *Notification date:* 2/1.
CONTACT Ms. Valerie K. Miller, Director of Financial Aid, Ohio University–Lancaster, 020 Chubb Hall, Athens, OH 45701-2979, 740-593-4141 or toll-free 888-446-4468. *Fax:* 740-593-4140. *E-mail:* millerv@ohio.edu. *Website:* http://www.ohiou.edu/lancaster/.

OHIO UNIVERSITY–SOUTHERN CAMPUS
Ironton, OH

Tuition & fees: N/R	Average undergraduate aid package: $7752

ABOUT THE INSTITUTION State-supported, coed. 17 undergraduate majors. Federal methodology is used as a basis for awarding need-based institutional aid.
FRESHMAN FINANCIAL AID (Fall 2016, est.) 189 applied for aid; of those 92% were deemed to have need. 100% of freshmen with need received aid; of those 13% had need fully met. *Average percent of need met:* 57% (excluding resources awarded to replace EFC). *Average financial aid package:* $6840 (excluding resources awarded to replace EFC). 2% of all full-time freshmen had no need and received non-need-based gift aid.

UNDERGRADUATE FINANCIAL AID (Fall 2016, est.) 734 applied for aid; of those 91% were deemed to have need. 100% of undergraduates with need received aid; of those 16% had need fully met. *Average percent of need met:* 56% (excluding resources awarded to replace EFC). *Average financial aid package:* $7752 (excluding resources awarded to replace EFC). 2% of all full-time undergraduates had no need and received non-need-based gift aid.
GIFT AID (NEED-BASED) Total amount: $4,111,949 (81% federal, 1% state, 17% institutional, 1% external sources). *Receiving aid:* Freshmen: 76% (150); all full-time undergraduates: 80% (584). *Average award:* Freshmen: $5233; Undergraduates: $5444. *Scholarships, grants, and awards:* Federal Pell, FSEOG, state, private, college/university gift aid from institutional funds.
GIFT AID (NON-NEED-BASED) Total amount: $74,352 (17% federal, 6% state, 71% institutional, 6% external sources). *Receiving aid:* Freshmen: 2% (4). Undergraduates: 2% (13). *Average award:* Freshmen: $1245. Undergraduates: $2125. *Scholarships, grants, and awards by category:* Academic interests/achievement: area/ethnic studies, biological sciences, business, communication, computer science, education, engineering/technologies, English, foreign languages, general academic interests/achievements, health fields, home economics, humanities, international studies, mathematics, military science, physical sciences, premedicine, social sciences. Creative arts/performance: applied art and design, art/fine arts, cinema/film/broadcasting, creative writing, dance, debating, journalism/publications, music, performing arts, theater/drama. Special characteristics: children and siblings of alumni, children of faculty/staff, first-generation college students.
LOANS Student loans: $4,173,746 (95% need-based, 5% non-need-based). 67% of past graduating class borrowed through all loan programs. *Average indebtedness per student:* $27,879. *Average need-based loan:* Freshmen: $2005. Undergraduates: $2891. *Parent loans:* $61,461 (50% need-based, 50% non-need-based). *Programs:* Federal Direct (Subsidized and Unsubsidized Stafford, PLUS), Perkins, state, college/university.
WORK-STUDY Federal work-study: Total amount: $40,825; 20 jobs averaging $1759.
APPLYING FOR FINANCIAL AID Required financial aid form: FAFSA. *Financial aid deadline (priority):* 1/15. *Notification date:* 2/1.
CONTACT Ms. Valerie K. Miller, Director of Financial Aid, Ohio University–Southern Campus, 020 Chubb Hall, Athens, OH 45701-2979, 740-593-4141 or toll-free 800-626-0513. *Fax:* 740-593-4140. *E-mail:* millerv@ohio.edu. *Website:* http://www.ohiou.edu/.

OHIO UNIVERSITY–ZANESVILLE
Zanesville, OH

Tuition & fees (OH res): $5076	Average undergraduate aid package: $6619

ABOUT THE INSTITUTION State-supported, coed. *Awards:* associate and bachelor's degrees (offers first 2 years of most bachelor's degree programs available at the main campus in Athens; also offers several bachelor's degree programs that can be completed at this campus; also offers some graduate courses). 7 undergraduate majors. *Total enrollment:* 1,968. Undergraduates: 1,968. Freshmen: 300. Federal methodology is used as a basis for awarding need-based institutional aid.
UNDERGRADUATE EXPENSES for 2016–2017 Application fee: $20. *Tuition, state resident:* full-time $4984; part-time $234 per semester hour. *Tuition, nonresident:* full-time $8624; part-time $413 per semester hour. *Required fees:* full-time $92; $6 per semester hour or $8 per term. Full-time tuition and fees vary according to course load and student level. Part-time tuition and fees vary according to course load and student level.
FRESHMAN FINANCIAL AID (Fall 2016, est.) 239 applied for aid; of those 76% were deemed to have need. 100% of freshmen with need received aid; of those 10% had need fully met. *Average percent of need met:* 57% (excluding resources awarded to replace EFC). *Average financial aid package:* $6206 (excluding resources awarded to replace EFC). 1% of all full-time freshmen had no need and received non-need-based gift aid.
UNDERGRADUATE FINANCIAL AID (Fall 2016, est.) 702 applied for aid; of those 78% were deemed to have need. 100% of undergraduates with need received aid; of those 14% had need fully met. *Average percent of need met:* 55% (excluding resources awarded to replace EFC). *Average financial aid package:* $6619 (excluding resources awarded to replace EFC). 1% of all full-time undergraduates had no need and received non-need-based gift aid.

GIFT AID (NEED-BASED) *Total amount:* $3,242,860 (74% federal, 1% state, 19% institutional, 6% external sources). *Receiving aid:* Freshmen: 59% (156); all full-time undergraduates: 57% (447). *Average award:* Freshmen: $4907; Undergraduates: $5229. *Scholarships, grants, and awards:* Federal Pell, FSEOG, state, private, college/university gift aid from institutional funds.

GIFT AID (NON-NEED-BASED) *Total amount:* $40,052 (12% state, 74% institutional, 14% external sources). *Receiving aid:* Freshmen: 1. Undergraduates: 1% (10). *Average award:* Freshmen: $2538. Undergraduates: $2778. *Scholarships, grants, and awards by category:* Academic interests/achievement: area/ethnic studies, biological sciences, business, communication, computer science, education, engineering/technologies, English, foreign languages, general academic interests/achievements, health fields, home economics, humanities, international studies, mathematics, military science, physical sciences, premedicine, social sciences. *Creative arts/performance:* applied art and design, art/fine arts, cinema/film/broadcasting, creative writing, dance, debating, journalism/publications, music, performing arts, theater/drama. *Special characteristics:* children and siblings of alumni, children of faculty/staff, first-generation college students. *Tuition waivers:* Full or partial for employees or children of employees, senior citizens.

LOANS *Student loans:* $3,235,645 (98% need-based, 2% non-need-based). 67% of past graduating class borrowed through all loan programs. *Average indebtedness per student:* $27,879. *Average need-based loan:* Freshmen: $1671. Undergraduates: $2259. *Parent loans:* $136,223 (62% need-based, 38% non-need-based). *Programs:* Federal Direct (Subsidized and Unsubsidized Stafford, PLUS), Perkins, state, college/university.

WORK-STUDY *Federal work-study:* Total amount: $10,004; 3 jobs averaging $1282.

APPLYING FOR FINANCIAL AID *Required financial aid form:* FAFSA. *Financial aid deadline (priority):* 1/15. *Notification date:* 2/1.

CONTACT Ms. Valerie K. Miller, Director of Financial Aid, Ohio University–Zanesville, 020 Chubb Hall, Athens, OH 45701-2979, 740-593-4141. *Fax:* 740-593-4140. *E-mail:* millerv@ohio.edu.
Website: http://www.ohio.edu/zanesville/.

OHIO VALLEY UNIVERSITY
Vienna, WV

Tuition & fees: $21,100	Average undergraduate aid package: $14,912

ABOUT THE INSTITUTION Independent Church of Christ, coed. *Awards:* certificates, associate, bachelor's, and master's degrees. 16 undergraduate majors. *Total enrollment:* 432. Undergraduates: 403. Freshmen: 116. Federal methodology is used as a basis for awarding need-based institutional aid.

UNDERGRADUATE EXPENSES for 2017–2018 *Comprehensive fee:* $28,800 includes full-time tuition ($21,100) and room and board ($7700). *College room only:* $3850. Full-time tuition and fees vary according to course load. Room and board charges vary according to board plan. *Part-time tuition:* $700 per credit hour. Part-time tuition and fees vary according to course load.

FRESHMAN FINANCIAL AID (Fall 2015) 122 applied for aid; of those 89% were deemed to have need. 94% of freshmen with need received aid; of those 14% had need fully met. *Average percent of need met:* 64% (excluding resources awarded to replace EFC). *Average financial aid package:* $16,026 (excluding resources awarded to replace EFC). 10% of all full-time freshmen had no need and received non-need-based gift aid.

UNDERGRADUATE FINANCIAL AID (Fall 2015) 337 applied for aid; of those 93% were deemed to have need. 96% of undergraduates with need received aid; of those 20% had need fully met. *Average percent of need met:* 65% (excluding resources awarded to replace EFC). *Average financial aid package:* $14,912 (excluding resources awarded to replace EFC). 14% of all full-time undergraduates had no need and received non-need-based gift aid.

GIFT AID (NEED-BASED) *Total amount:* $2,385,722 (35% federal, 7% state, 54% institutional, 4% external sources). *Receiving aid:* Freshmen: 70% (102); all full-time undergraduates: 69% (293). *Average award:* Freshmen: $13,468; Undergraduates: $12,093. *Scholarships, grants, and awards:* Federal Pell, FSEOG, state, private, college/university gift aid from institutional funds.

GIFT AID (NON-NEED-BASED) *Total amount:* $627,531 (8% state, 83% institutional, 9% external sources). *Receiving aid:* Freshmen: 10% (14). Undergraduates: 14% (60). *Average award:* Freshmen: $4543. Undergraduates: $5588. *Scholar-ships, grants, and awards by category:* Academic interests/achievement: business, computer science, education, English, general academic interests/achievements, mathematics, religion/biblical studies. *Creative arts/performance:* general creative arts/performance, journalism/publications, music, performing arts, theater/drama. *Special achievements/activities:* community service, general special achievements/activities, leadership, religious involvement. *Special characteristics:* adult students, children of faculty/staff, ethnic background, general special characteristics, international students, local/state students, relatives of clergy, religious affiliation. *Tuition waivers:* Full or partial for employees or children of employees.

LOANS *Student loans:* $1,719,167 (84% need-based, 16% non-need-based). 70% of past graduating class borrowed through all loan programs. *Average indebtedness per student:* $23,841. *Average need-based loan:* Freshmen: $2832. Undergraduates: $3471. *Parent loans:* $673,303 (51% need-based, 49% non-need-based). *Programs:* Federal Direct (Subsidized and Unsubsidized Stafford, PLUS), Perkins.

WORK-STUDY *Federal work-study:* jobs available. *State or other work-study/employment:* Part-time jobs available.

ATHLETIC AWARDS Total amount: $1,981,643 (100% need-based).

APPLYING FOR FINANCIAL AID *Required financial aid form:* FAFSA. *Financial aid deadline (priority):* 5/1. *Notification date:* Continuous beginning 3/1. Students must reply within 4 weeks of notification.

CONTACT Lindsay Cole, Director of Financial Aid, Ohio Valley University, 1 Campus View Drive, Vienna, WV 26105-8000, 304-865-6077 or toll-free 877-446-8668. *Fax:* 304-865-6001. *E-mail:* lindsay.cole@ovu.edu.
Website: http://www.ovu.edu/.

OHIO WESLEYAN UNIVERSITY
Delaware, OH

Tuition & fees: $44,090	Average undergraduate aid package: $34,662

ABOUT THE INSTITUTION Independent United Methodist, coed. *Awards:* bachelor's degrees. 87 undergraduate majors. *Total enrollment:* 1,639. Undergraduates: 1,639. Freshmen: 489. Federal methodology is used as a basis for awarding need-based institutional aid.

UNDERGRADUATE EXPENSES for 2016–2017 *Comprehensive fee:* $55,860 includes full-time tuition ($43,770), mandatory fees ($320), and room and board ($11,770). Full-time tuition and fees vary according to course load. Room and board charges vary according to board plan and housing facility. *Part-time tuition:* $1267 per credit hour. Part-time tuition and fees vary according to course load.

FRESHMAN FINANCIAL AID (Fall 2015) 396 applied for aid; of those 87% were deemed to have need. 100% of freshmen with need received aid; of those 17% had need fully met. *Average percent of need met:* 79% (excluding resources awarded to replace EFC). *Average financial aid package:* $35,757 (excluding resources awarded to replace EFC). 26% of all full-time freshmen had no need and received non-need-based gift aid.

UNDERGRADUATE FINANCIAL AID (Fall 2015) 1,269 applied for aid; of those 90% were deemed to have need. 100% of undergraduates with need received aid; of those 21% had need fully met. *Average percent of need met:* 79% (excluding resources awarded to replace EFC). *Average financial aid package:* $34,662 (excluding resources awarded to replace EFC). 31% of all full-time undergraduates had no need and received non-need-based gift aid.

GIFT AID (NEED-BASED) *Total amount:* $33,232,876 (7% federal, 1% state, 91% institutional, 1% external sources). *Receiving aid:* Freshmen: 74% (344); all full-time undergraduates: 69% (1,138). *Average award:* Freshmen: $31,114; Undergraduates: $29,200. *Scholarships, grants, and awards:* Federal Pell, FSEOG, state, private, college/university gift aid from institutional funds.

GIFT AID (NON-NEED-BASED) *Total amount:* $13,538,497 (99% institutional, 1% external sources). *Receiving aid:* Freshmen: 11% (53). Undergraduates: 13% (220). *Average award:* Freshmen: $22,477. Undergraduates: $22,895. *Scholarships, grants, and awards by category:* Academic interests/achievement: business, education, general academic interests/achievements. *Creative arts/performance:* applied art and design, art/fine arts, dance, music, performing arts, theater/drama. *Special achievements/activities:* general special achievements/activities, leadership. *Special characteristics:* children and siblings of alumni, international students, local/state students, members of minority groups, relatives of clergy, religious affiliation, twins. *Tuition waivers:* Full or partial for employees or children of employees. *ROTC:* Army cooperative, Air Force cooperative.

LOANS *Student loans:* $11,755,915 (69% need-based, 31% non-need-based). 65% of past graduating class borrowed through all loan programs. *Average indebtedness per student:* $34,666. *Average need-based loan:* Freshmen: $3493. Undergraduates: $4766. *Parent loans:* $4,805,009 (45% need-based, 55% non-need-based). *Programs:* Federal Direct (Subsidized and Unsubsidized Stafford, PLUS), Perkins, college/university.

WORK-STUDY *Federal work-study:* jobs available. *State or other work-study/employment:* Total amount: $676,054 (14% need-based, 86% non-need-based). Part-time jobs available.

APPLYING FOR FINANCIAL AID *Required financial aid form:* FAFSA. *Financial aid deadline (priority):* 12/1. *Notification date:* Continuous beginning 2/15. Students must reply by 5/1 or within 2 weeks of notification.

CONTACT Mr. Kevin Paskvan, Director of Financial Aid, Ohio Wesleyan University, 61 South Sandusky Street, Delaware, OH 43015, 740-368-3050 or toll-free 800-922-8953. *Fax:* 740-368-3066. *E-mail:* financialaid@owu.edu. *Website:* http://www.owu.edu/.

OHR HAMEIR THEOLOGICAL SEMINARY
Cortlandt Manor, NY

CONTACT Financial Aid Office, Ohr Hameir Theological Seminary, Furnace Woods Road, Peekskill, NY 10566, 914-736-1500.

OHR SOMAYACH/JOSEPH TANENBAUM EDUCATIONAL CENTER
Monsey, NY

CONTACT Financial Aid Office, Ohr Somayach/Joseph Tanenbaum Educational Center, PO Box 334244, Route 306, Monsey, NY 10952-0334, 914-425-1370. *Website:* http://ohr.edu/.

OKLAHOMA BAPTIST UNIVERSITY
Shawnee, OK

Tuition & fees: $26,840	Average undergraduate aid package: $21,800

ABOUT THE INSTITUTION Independent Southern Baptist, coed. *Awards:* associate, bachelor's, and master's degrees. 68 undergraduate majors. *Total enrollment:* 2,016. Undergraduates: 1,904. Freshmen: 582. Federal methodology is used as a basis for awarding need-based institutional aid.

UNDERGRADUATE EXPENSES for 2017–2018 *Comprehensive fee:* $33,990 includes full-time tuition ($23,940), mandatory fees ($2900), and room and board ($7150). Room and board charges vary according to housing facility. *Part-time tuition:* $778 per credit hour. *Part-time fees:* $2900 per term. Part-time tuition and fees vary according to course load.

FRESHMAN FINANCIAL AID (Fall 2015) 494 applied for aid; of those 90% were deemed to have need. 100% of freshmen with need received aid; of those 30% had need fully met. *Average percent of need met:* 91% (excluding resources awarded to replace EFC). *Average financial aid package:* $22,070 (excluding resources awarded to replace EFC). 19% of all full-time freshmen had no need and received non-need-based institutional aid.

UNDERGRADUATE FINANCIAL AID (Fall 2015) 1,442 applied for aid; of those 91% were deemed to have need. 100% of undergraduates with need received aid; of those 31% had need fully met. *Average percent of need met:* 89% (excluding resources awarded to replace EFC). *Average financial aid package:* $21,800 (excluding resources awarded to replace EFC). 25% of all full-time undergraduates had no need and received non-need-based gift aid.

GIFT AID (NEED-BASED) *Total amount:* $11,004,755 (27% federal, 18% state, 48% institutional, 7% external sources). *Receiving aid:* Freshmen: 68% (378); all full-time undergraduates: 67% (1,204). *Average award:* Freshmen: $9131; Undergrad-

uates: $8275. *Scholarships, grants, and awards:* Federal Pell, FSEOG, state, private, college/university gift aid from institutional funds, TEACH Grants.

GIFT AID (NON-NEED-BASED) *Total amount:* $20,127,021 (3% federal, 95% institutional, 2% external sources). *Receiving aid:* Freshmen: 79% (442). Undergraduates: 70% (1,262). *Average award:* Freshmen: $8320. Undergraduates: $9477. *Scholarships, grants, and awards by category: Academic interests/achievement:* 1,840 awards ($11,586,045 total): biological sciences, business, computer science, education, English, foreign languages, general academic interests/achievements, health fields, humanities, mathematics, physical sciences, premedicine, religion/biblical studies, social sciences. *Creative arts/performance:* 368 awards ($563,039 total): applied art and design, art/fine arts, music, performing arts, theater/drama. *Special achievements/activities:* 411 awards ($601,170 total): cheerleading/drum major, leadership, religious involvement. *Special characteristics:* 829 awards ($2,066,684 total): adult students, children and siblings of alumni, children of faculty/staff, general special characteristics, international students, local/state students, members of minority groups, out-of-state students, relatives of clergy, religious affiliation, veterans. *Tuition waivers:* Full or partial for employees or children of employees, senior citizens. *ROTC:* Air Force cooperative.

LOANS *Student loans:* $3,942,379 (89% need-based, 11% non-need-based). 58% of past graduating class borrowed through all loan programs. *Average indebtedness per student:* $24,451. *Average need-based loan:* Freshmen: $3282. Undergraduates: $4154. *Parent loans:* $2,126,241 (40% need-based, 60% non-need-based). *Programs:* Federal Direct (Subsidized and Unsubsidized Stafford, PLUS), Perkins.

WORK-STUDY *Federal work-study:* jobs available. *State or other work-study/employment:* Total amount: $2,010,919 (97% need-based, 3% non-need-based). Part-time jobs available.

ATHLETIC AWARDS Total amount: $2,689,889 (12% need-based, 88% non-need-based).

APPLYING FOR FINANCIAL AID *Required financial aid form:* FAFSA. *Financial aid deadline:* Continuous. *Notification date:* Continuous beginning 10/31. Students must reply within 2 weeks of notification.

CONTACT Jonna Raney, Director of Student Financial Services, Oklahoma Baptist University, 500 West University, Shawnee, OK 74804, 405-585-5020 or toll-free 800-654-3285. *Fax:* 405-585-5030. *E-mail:* jonna.raney@okbu.edu. *Website:* http://www.okbu.edu/.

OKLAHOMA CHRISTIAN UNIVERSITY
Oklahoma City, OK

Tuition & fees: $21,670	Average undergraduate aid package: $22,287

ABOUT THE INSTITUTION Independent Church of Christ, coed. *Awards:* certificates, bachelor's, and master's degrees. 60 undergraduate majors. *Total enrollment:* 2,570. Undergraduates: 1,974. Freshmen: 458. Federal methodology is used as a basis for awarding need-based institutional aid.

UNDERGRADUATE EXPENSES for 2017–2018 *Application fee:* $25. *Comprehensive fee:* $29,260 includes full-time tuition ($21,600), mandatory fees ($70), and room and board ($7590). Full-time tuition and fees vary according to course load, program, and reciprocity agreements. Room and board charges vary according to board plan and housing facility. *Part-time tuition:* $900 per credit hour. Part-time tuition and fees vary according to course load, program, and reciprocity agreements. *Payment plan:* Tuition prepayment.

FRESHMAN FINANCIAL AID (Fall 2015) 376 applied for aid; of those 81% were deemed to have need. 100% of freshmen with need received aid; of those 43% had need fully met. *Average percent of need met:* 67% (excluding resources awarded to replace EFC). *Average financial aid package:* $22,667 (excluding resources awarded to replace EFC). 29% of all full-time freshmen had no need and received non-need-based gift aid.

UNDERGRADUATE FINANCIAL AID (Fall 2015) 1,421 applied for aid; of those 85% were deemed to have need. 100% of undergraduates with need received aid; of those 39% had need fully met. *Average percent of need met:* 73% (excluding resources awarded to replace EFC). *Average financial aid package:* $22,287 (excluding resources awarded to replace EFC). 30% of all full-time undergraduates had no need and received non-need-based gift aid.

GIFT AID (NEED-BASED) *Total amount:* $14,159,110 (18% federal, 4% state, 71% institutional, 7% external sources). *Receiving aid:* Freshmen: 44% (198); all full-time undergraduates: 40% (764). *Average award:* Freshmen: $3138; Undergrad-

uates: $3217. **Scholarships, grants, and awards:** Federal Pell, FSEOG, state, private, college/university gift aid from institutional funds.

GIFT AID (NON-NEED-BASED) Total amount: $7,347,975 (1% federal, 2% state, 85% institutional, 12% external sources). **Receiving aid:** Freshmen: 61% (276). Undergraduates: 51% (971). **Average award:** Freshmen: $6458. Undergraduates: $7609. **Scholarships, grants, and awards by category:** Academic interests/achievement: engineering/technologies, general academic interests/achievements, religion/biblical studies. Creative arts/performance: applied art and design, journalism/publications, music, theater/drama. Special achievements/activities: cheerleading/drum major. Special characteristics: children of faculty/staff, international students. **Tuition waivers:** Full or partial for employees or children of employees. **ROTC:** Army cooperative, Air Force cooperative.

LOANS Student loans: $8,339,134 (74% need-based, 26% non-need-based). 58% of past graduating class borrowed through all loan programs. Average indebtedness per student: $27,793. **Average need-based loan:** Freshmen: $2309. Undergraduates: $2349. **Parent loans:** $2,983,114 (33% need-based, 67% non-need-based). **Programs:** Federal Direct (Subsidized and Unsubsidized Stafford, PLUS), Perkins, alternative loans.

WORK-STUDY Federal work-study: jobs available.

ATHLETIC AWARDS Total amount: $2,179,976 (34% need-based, 66% non-need-based).

APPLYING FOR FINANCIAL AID Required financial aid form: FAFSA. **Financial aid deadline:** 8/31 (priority: 4/1). **Notification date:** Continuous beginning 2/15. Students must reply within 4 weeks of notification.

CONTACT Clint LaRue, Director of Financial Services, Oklahoma Christian University, Box 11000, Oklahoma City, OK 73136-1100, 405-425-5190 or toll-free 800-877-5010. Fax: 405-425-5197. E-mail: clint.larue@oc.edu. Website: http://www.oc.edu/.

OKLAHOMA CITY UNIVERSITY
Oklahoma City, OK

Tuition & fees: $30,726	Average undergraduate aid package: $21,048

ABOUT THE INSTITUTION Independent United Methodist, coed. **Awards:** bachelor's, master's, and doctoral degrees. 69 undergraduate majors. **Total enrollment:** 2,939. Undergraduates: 1,764. Freshmen: 329. Federal methodology is used as a basis for awarding need-based institutional aid.

UNDERGRADUATE EXPENSES for 2017–2018 One-time required fee: $300. **Comprehensive fee:** $39,350 includes full-time tuition ($27,276), mandatory fees ($3450), and room and board ($8624). **College room only:** $4100. Full-time tuition and fees vary according to course level, course load, degree level, program, and student level. Room and board charges vary according to board plan and housing facility. **Part-time tuition:** $925 per credit hour. **Part-time fees:** $115 per credit hour. Part-time tuition and fees vary according to course level, degree level, program, and student level.

FRESHMAN FINANCIAL AID (Fall 2016, est.) 282 applied for aid; of those 77% were deemed to have need. 98% of freshmen with need received aid; of those 82% had need fully met. **Average percent of need met:** 66% (excluding resources awarded to replace EFC). **Average financial aid package:** $22,440 (excluding resources awarded to replace EFC). 19% of all full-time freshmen had no need and received non-need-based gift aid.

UNDERGRADUATE FINANCIAL AID (Fall 2016, est.) 1,139 applied for aid; of those 86% were deemed to have need. 98% of undergraduates with need received aid; of those 85% had need fully met. **Average percent of need met:** 60% (excluding resources awarded to replace EFC). **Average financial aid package:** $21,048 (excluding resources awarded to replace EFC). 9% of all full-time undergraduates had no need and received non-need-based gift aid.

GIFT AID (NEED-BASED) Total amount: $3,378,576 (45% federal, 9% state, 29% institutional, 17% external sources). **Receiving aid:** Freshmen: 64% (212); all full-time undergraduates: 56% (912). **Average award:** Freshmen: $18,836; Undergraduates: $17,061. **Scholarships, grants, and awards:** Federal Pell, FSEOG, state, private, college/university gift aid from institutional funds, United Negro College Fund, Federal Nursing, Native American Grants.

GIFT AID (NON-NEED-BASED) Total amount: $257,700 (1% federal, 2% state, 22% institutional, 75% external sources). **Receiving aid:** Freshmen: 12% (38). Undergraduates: 9% (145). **Average award:** Freshmen: $16,236. Undergraduates:

$14,594. **Scholarships, grants, and awards by category:** Academic interests/achievement: 962 awards: business, communication, education, general academic interests/achievements, home economics, religion/biblical studies. Creative arts/performance: 541 awards: applied art and design, art/fine arts, dance, debating, music, performing arts, theater/drama. Special achievements/activities: 98 awards: general special achievements/activities, junior miss, leadership, religious involvement. Special characteristics: 73 awards: children of faculty/staff, relatives of clergy, religious affiliation. **Tuition waivers:** Full or partial for employees or children of employees. **ROTC:** Army cooperative, Air Force cooperative.

LOANS Student loans: $6,431,984 (82% need-based, 18% non-need-based). 57% of past graduating class borrowed through all loan programs. Average indebtedness per student: $26,329. **Average need-based loan:** Freshmen: $3098. Undergraduates: $4527. **Parent loans:** $6,861,590 (49% need-based, 51% non-need-based). **Programs:** Federal Direct (Subsidized and Unsubsidized Stafford, PLUS), Perkins, Federal Nursing.

WORK-STUDY Federal work-study: Total amount: $279,436; 239 jobs averaging $1259. **State or other work-study/employment:** Total amount: $325,986 (100% non-need-based). 351 part-time jobs averaging $1217.

ATHLETIC AWARDS Total amount: $4,734,844 (89% need-based, 11% non-need-based).

APPLYING FOR FINANCIAL AID Required financial aid form: FAFSA. **Financial aid deadline (priority):** 3/1. **Notification date:** Continuous beginning 3/25. Students must reply within 4 weeks of notification.

CONTACT Denise Flis, Senior Director of Student Financial Services, Oklahoma City University, 2501 North Blackwelder, Oklahoma City, OK 73106-1493, 405-208-5848 or toll-free 800-633-7242. Fax: 405-208-5466. E-mail: dflis@okcu.edu. Website: http://www.okcu.edu/.

OKLAHOMA PANHANDLE STATE UNIVERSITY
Goodwell, OK

Tuition & fees (OK res): $7294	Average undergraduate aid package: N/A

ABOUT THE INSTITUTION State-supported, coed. 28 undergraduate majors. Federal methodology is used as a basis for awarding need-based institutional aid.

UNDERGRADUATE EXPENSES for 2016–2017 Tuition, state resident: full-time $4620; part-time $154 per credit hour. **Tuition, nonresident:** full-time $5559; part-time $185 per credit hour. **Required fees:** full-time $2674; $98 per credit hour or $42 per term. Full-time tuition and fees vary according to course level, program, and student level. Part-time tuition and fees vary according to course level, program, and student level. **College room and board:** $5344; **Room only:** $1306. Room and board charges vary according to board plan and housing facility. **Payment plan:** Guaranteed tuition.

GIFT AID (NEED-BASED) Scholarships, grants, and awards: Federal Pell, FSEOG, state, private, college/university gift aid from institutional funds.

GIFT AID (NON-NEED-BASED) Scholarships, grants, and awards by category: Academic interests/achievement: agriculture, biological sciences, business, computer science, education, English, general academic interests/achievements, health fields, home economics, mathematics, physical sciences. Creative arts/performance: art/fine arts, debating, music, performing arts, theater/drama. Special achievements/activities: cheerleading/drum major, general special achievements/activities, rodeo. Special characteristics: children and siblings of alumni, children of faculty/staff, general special characteristics, local/state students, out-of-state students, veterans, veterans' children. **Tuition waivers:** Full or partial for employees or children of employees, senior citizens.

LOANS Programs: Perkins.

WORK-STUDY Federal work-study jobs available. **State or other work-study/employment:** Part-time jobs available.

APPLYING FOR FINANCIAL AID Required financial aid form: FAFSA. **Financial aid deadline (priority):** 3/15. **Notification date:** 5/1. Students must reply by 8/1.

CONTACT Ms. Lori Ferguson, Director of Financial Aid, Oklahoma Panhandle State University, PO Box 430, Goodwell, OK 73939-0430, 580-349-1582 or toll-free 800-664-6778. E-mail: lorif@opsu.edu. Website: http://www.opsu.edu/.

OKLAHOMA STATE UNIVERSITY
Stillwater, OK

Tuition & fees (OK res): $8320	Average undergraduate aid package: $14,155

ABOUT THE INSTITUTION State-supported, coed. *Awards:* certificates, bachelor's, master's, and doctoral degrees. 81 undergraduate majors. *Total enrollment:* 25,594. Undergraduates: 21,093. Freshmen: 4,096. Federal methodology is used as a basis for awarding need-based institutional aid.

UNDERGRADUATE EXPENSES for 2016–2017 *Application fee:* $40. *One-time required fee:* $95. *Tuition, state resident:* full-time $4942; part-time $164.75 per credit hour. *Tuition, nonresident:* full-time $19,065; part-time $635.50 per credit hour. *Required fees:* full-time $3378; $112.60 per credit hour. Full-time tuition and fees vary according to program. Part-time tuition and fees vary according to course load and program. *College room and board:* $8443; *Room only:* $4743. Room and board charges vary according to board plan and housing facility. *Payment plan:* Guaranteed tuition.

FRESHMAN FINANCIAL AID (Fall 2015) 3,234 applied for aid; of those 67% were deemed to have need. 98% of freshmen with need received aid; of those 18% had need fully met. *Average percent of need met:* 79% (excluding resources awarded to replace EFC). *Average financial aid package:* $14,732 (excluding resources awarded to replace EFC). 28% of all full-time freshmen had no need and received non-need-based gift aid.

UNDERGRADUATE FINANCIAL AID (Fall 2015) 12,120 applied for aid; of those 76% were deemed to have need. 98% of undergraduates with need received aid; of those 14% had need fully met. *Average percent of need met:* 77% (excluding resources awarded to replace EFC). *Average financial aid package:* $14,155 (excluding resources awarded to replace EFC). 29% of all full-time undergraduates had no need and received non-need-based gift aid.

GIFT AID (NEED-BASED) *Total amount:* $56,568,554 (43% federal, 25% state, 21% institutional, 11% external sources). *Receiving aid:* Freshmen: 43% (1,709); all full-time undergraduates: 38% (7,009). *Average award:* Freshmen: $8337; Undergraduates: $7293. *Scholarships, grants, and awards:* Federal Pell, FSEOG, state, private, college/university gift aid from institutional funds, TEACH Grants.

GIFT AID (NON-NEED-BASED) *Total amount:* $17,799,795 (3% federal, 8% state, 38% institutional, 51% external sources). *Receiving aid:* Freshmen: 5% (216). Undergraduates: 3% (546). *Average award:* Freshmen: $6662. Undergraduates: $5617. *Scholarships, grants, and awards by category:* Academic interests/achievement: agriculture, architecture, area/ethnic studies, biological sciences, business, communication, computer science, education, engineering/technologies, English, foreign languages, general academic interests/achievements, home economics, humanities, international studies, mathematics, military science, physical sciences, pre-medicine, social sciences. *Creative arts/performance:* art/fine arts, creative writing, general creative arts/performance, journalism/publications, music, theater/drama. *Special achievements/activities:* cheerleading/drum major, community service, general special achievements/activities, leadership, memberships, rodeo. *Special characteristics:* adult students, children and siblings of alumni, ethnic background, first-generation college students, general special characteristics, handicapped students, international students, local/state students, out-of-state students, previous college experience. *Tuition waivers:* Full or partial for children of alumni, employees or children of employees, senior citizens. *ROTC:* Army, Air Force.

LOANS *Student loans:* $64,190,241 (71% need-based, 29% non-need-based). 50% of past graduating class borrowed through all loan programs. *Average indebtedness per student:* $24,252. *Average need-based loan:* Freshmen: $3181. Undergraduates: $4128. *Parent loans:* $37,488,315 (34% need-based, 66% non-need-based). *Programs:* Federal Direct (Subsidized and Unsubsidized Stafford, PLUS), Perkins.

WORK-STUDY *Federal work-study:* 397 jobs averaging $2112. *State or other work-study/employment:* Total amount: $13,055,747 (100% non-need-based). 4,553 part-time jobs averaging $2868.

ATHLETIC AWARDS Total amount: $5,978,261 (24% need-based, 76% non-need-based).

APPLYING FOR FINANCIAL AID *Required financial aid form:* FAFSA. *Financial aid deadline:* Continuous. *Notification date:* Continuous beginning 4/1. Students must reply by 5/1 or within 2 weeks of notification.

CONTACT Office of Scholarships and Financial Aid, Oklahoma State University, 119 Student Union, Stillwater, OK 74078-5061, 405-744-6604 or toll-free 800-233-5019. *Fax:* 405-744-6438. *E-mail:* finaid@okstate.edu. *Website:* http://www.okstate.edu/.

OKLAHOMA WESLEYAN UNIVERSITY
Bartlesville, OK

Tuition & fees: N/R	Average undergraduate aid package: $17,022

ABOUT THE INSTITUTION Independent Wesleyan Church, coed. *Awards:* associate, bachelor's, and master's degrees. 39 undergraduate majors. *Total enrollment:* 1,527. Undergraduates: 1,229. Freshmen: 198. Both federal and institutional methodology are used as a basis for awarding need-based institutional aid.

FRESHMAN FINANCIAL AID (Fall 2016, est.) 204 applied for aid; of those 92% were deemed to have need. 100% of freshmen with need received aid; of those 13% had need fully met. *Average percent of need met:* 57% (excluding resources awarded to replace EFC). *Average financial aid package:* $15,663 (excluding resources awarded to replace EFC). 13% of all full-time freshmen had no need and received non-need-based gift aid.

UNDERGRADUATE FINANCIAL AID (Fall 2016, est.) 553 applied for aid; of those 89% were deemed to have need. 100% of undergraduates with need received aid; of those 13% had need fully met. *Average percent of need met:* 61% (excluding resources awarded to replace EFC). *Average financial aid package:* $17,022 (excluding resources awarded to replace EFC). 18% of all full-time undergraduates had no need and received non-need-based gift aid.

GIFT AID (NEED-BASED) *Total amount:* $5,568,344 (37% federal, 8% state, 46% institutional, 9% external sources). *Receiving aid:* Freshmen: 85% (188); all full-time undergraduates: 78% (486). *Average award:* Freshmen: $12,215; Undergraduates: $12,875. *Scholarships, grants, and awards:* Federal Pell, FSEOG, state, private, college/university gift aid from institutional funds.

GIFT AID (NON-NEED-BASED) *Total amount:* $1,140,255 (2% federal, 77% institutional, 21% external sources). *Receiving aid:* Freshmen: 10% (22). Undergraduates: 7% (43). *Average award:* Freshmen: $6803. Undergraduates: $6515. *Scholarships, grants, and awards by category:* Academic interests/achievement: biological sciences, business, computer science, education, general academic interests/achievements, health fields, religion/biblical studies. *Creative arts/performance:* music. *Special achievements/activities:* leadership, religious involvement. *Special characteristics:* children and siblings of alumni, children of educators, children of faculty/staff, international students, relatives of clergy, religious affiliation, siblings of current students.

LOANS *Student loans:* $6,539,994 (82% need-based, 18% non-need-based). 66% of past graduating class borrowed through all loan programs. *Average indebtedness per student:* $25,234. *Average need-based loan:* Freshmen: $3420. Undergraduates: $4459. *Parent loans:* $4,510,845 (53% need-based, 47% non-need-based). *Programs:* Federal Direct (Subsidized and Unsubsidized Stafford, PLUS), Perkins, college/university.

WORK-STUDY *Federal work-study:* Total amount: $211,120; 129 jobs averaging $1633. *State or other work-study/employment:* Total amount: $44,960 (66% need-based, 34% non-need-based). 30 part-time jobs averaging $1489.

ATHLETIC AWARDS Total amount: $2,794,202 (56% need-based, 44% non-need-based).

APPLYING FOR FINANCIAL AID *Required financial aid forms:* FAFSA, institution's own form. *Financial aid deadline (priority):* 3/1. *Notification date:* Continuous beginning 1/15.

CONTACT Mrs. Kandi Lyn Molder, Director of Student Financial Services, Oklahoma Wesleyan University, 2201 Silver Lake Road, Bartlesville, OK 74006, 918-335-6282 or toll-free 866-222-8226. *Fax:* 918-335-6811. *E-mail:* financialaid@okwu.edu. *Website:* http://www.okwu.edu/.

OLD DOMINION UNIVERSITY
Norfolk, VA

Tuition & fees (VA res): $10,046	Average undergraduate aid package: $10,584

ABOUT THE INSTITUTION State-supported, coed. *Awards:* certificates, bachelor's, master's, and doctoral degrees. 49 undergraduate majors. *Total enrollment:* 24,322. Undergraduates: 19,793. Freshmen: 2,757. Federal methodology is used as a basis for awarding need-based institutional aid.

UNDERGRADUATE EXPENSES for 2016–2017 *Application fee:* $50. *Tuition, state resident:* full-time $9750; part-time $325 per credit hour. *Tuition, nonresident:* full-time $26,730; part-time $891 per credit hour. *Required fees:* full-time $296; $66 per term. *College room and board:* $10,864; *Room only:* $6094. Room and board charges vary according to board plan and housing facility.

FRESHMAN FINANCIAL AID (Fall 2016, est.) 2,464 applied for aid; of those 83% were deemed to have need. 97% of freshmen with need received aid; of those 18% had need fully met. *Average percent of need met:* 49% (excluding resources awarded to replace EFC). *Average financial aid package:* $11,895 (excluding resources awarded to replace EFC). 9% of all full-time freshmen had no need and received non-need-based gift aid.

UNDERGRADUATE FINANCIAL AID (Fall 2016, est.) 12,174 applied for aid; of those 84% were deemed to have need. 97% of undergraduates with need received aid; of those 14% had need fully met. *Average percent of need met:* 46% (excluding resources awarded to replace EFC). *Average financial aid package:* $10,584 (excluding resources awarded to replace EFC). 6% of all full-time undergraduates had no need and received non-need-based gift aid.

GIFT AID (NEED-BASED) *Total amount:* $60,076,781 (57% federal, 35% state, 8% institutional). *Receiving aid:* Freshmen: 59% (1,599); all full-time undergraduates: 51% (7,810). *Average award:* Freshmen: $8273; Undergraduates: $7011. *Scholarships, grants, and awards:* Federal Pell, FSEOG, state, private, college/university gift aid from institutional funds, United Negro College Fund, Federal Nursing.

GIFT AID (NON-NEED-BASED) *Total amount:* $12,497,559 (11% state, 73% institutional, 16% external sources). *Receiving aid:* Freshmen: 28% (754). Undergraduates: 13% (2,048). *Average award:* Freshmen: $5344. Undergraduates: $4842. *Scholarships, grants, and awards by category:* Academic interests/achievement: 2,836 awards ($10,407,852 total): area/ethnic studies, biological sciences, business, communication, computer science, education, engineering/technologies, English, foreign languages, general academic interests/achievements, health fields, humanities, international studies, library science, mathematics, military science, physical sciences, social sciences. *Creative arts/performance:* 180 awards ($176,591 total): applied art and design, art/fine arts, cinema/film/broadcasting, creative writing, dance, general creative arts/performance, journalism/publications, music, performing arts, theater/drama. *Special achievements/activities:* 26 awards ($35,500 total): cheerleading/drum major, community service, leadership, memberships. *Special characteristics:* 195 awards ($536,402 total): children of faculty/staff, international students, local/state students, previous college experience, veterans' children. *Tuition waivers:* Full or partial for employees or children of employees, senior citizens. *ROTC:* Army, Naval.

LOANS *Student loans:* $93,784,882 (42% need-based, 58% non-need-based). 70% of past graduating class borrowed through all loan programs. *Average indebtedness per student:* $30,410. *Average need-based loan:* Freshmen: $3427. Undergraduates: $4315. *Parent loans:* $17,699,023 (100% non-need-based). *Programs:* Federal Direct (Subsidized and Unsubsidized Stafford, PLUS), Perkins, Federal Nursing, college/university.

WORK-STUDY *Federal work-study:* Total amount: $3,140,776; 200 jobs averaging $2400.

ATHLETIC AWARDS Total amount: $6,649,395 (100% non-need-based).

APPLYING FOR FINANCIAL AID *Required financial aid form:* FAFSA. *Financial aid deadline:* 3/15 (priority: 2/15). *Notification date:* Continuous beginning 3/1. Students must reply within 2 weeks of notification.

CONTACT Office of Financial Aid, Old Dominion University, 2000 Rollins Hall, Norfolk, VA 23529, 757-683-3683 or toll-free 800-348-7926. *Fax:* 757-683-5920. *E-mail:* finaid@odu.edu. *Website:* http://www.odu.edu/.

OLIVET COLLEGE
Olivet, MI

Tuition & fees: $25,520	Average undergraduate aid package: $18,560

ABOUT THE INSTITUTION Independent Congregational Christian Church, coed. *Awards:* bachelor's and master's degrees. 34 undergraduate majors. *Total enrollment:* 1,078. Undergraduates: 1,045. Freshmen: 351. Federal methodology is used as a basis for awarding need-based institutional aid.

UNDERGRADUATE EXPENSES for 2016–2017 *Application fee:* $25. *Comprehensive fee:* $34,470 includes full-time tuition ($24,670), mandatory fees ($850), and room and board ($8950). Full-time tuition and fees vary according to course load.

Room and board charges vary according to board plan and housing facility. *Part-time tuition:* $824 per semester hour. Part-time tuition and fees vary according to course load.

FRESHMAN FINANCIAL AID (Fall 2015) 237 applied for aid; of those 86% were deemed to have need. 100% of freshmen with need received aid; of those 24% had need fully met. *Average percent of need met:* 81% (excluding resources awarded to replace EFC). *Average financial aid package:* $18,990 (excluding resources awarded to replace EFC). 17% of all full-time freshmen had no need and received non-need-based gift aid.

UNDERGRADUATE FINANCIAL AID (Fall 2015) 951 applied for aid; of those 86% were deemed to have need. 100% of undergraduates with need received aid; of those 19% had need fully met. *Average percent of need met:* 80% (excluding resources awarded to replace EFC). *Average financial aid package:* $18,560 (excluding resources awarded to replace EFC). 10% of all full-time undergraduates had no need and received non-need-based gift aid.

GIFT AID (NEED-BASED) *Total amount:* $11,884,005 (19% federal, 9% state, 70% institutional, 2% external sources). *Receiving aid:* Freshmen: 73% (174); all full-time undergraduates: 77% (763). *Average award:* Freshmen: $15,100; Undergraduates: $13,720. *Scholarships, grants, and awards:* Federal Pell, FSEOG, state, private, college/university gift aid from institutional funds.

GIFT AID (NON-NEED-BASED) *Total amount:* $1,443,100 (97% institutional, 3% external sources). *Receiving aid:* Freshmen: 13% (31). Undergraduates: 7% (70). *Average award:* Freshmen: $13,330. Undergraduates: $13,112. *Scholarships, grants, and awards by category:* Academic interests/achievement: 566 awards ($4,929,495 total): business, communication, education, English, foreign languages, general academic interests/achievements. *Creative arts/performance:* 25 awards ($30,225 total): art/fine arts, journalism/publications, music. *Special achievements/activities:* 197 awards ($390,550 total): community service, leadership, memberships. *Special characteristics:* 47 awards ($744,332 total): children and siblings of alumni, children of faculty/staff, international students, religious affiliation, siblings of current students. *ROTC:* Air Force cooperative.

LOANS *Student loans:* $8,250,158 (61% need-based, 39% non-need-based). 87% of past graduating class borrowed through all loan programs. *Average indebtedness per student:* $26,872. *Average need-based loan:* Freshmen: $3422. Undergraduates: $5035. *Parent loans:* $2,064,285 (40% need-based, 60% non-need-based). *Programs:* Federal Direct (Subsidized and Unsubsidized Stafford, PLUS), Perkins, alternative loans, CitiAssist Loans, Sallie Mae Smart Option Loans.

WORK-STUDY *Federal work-study:* 187 jobs averaging $952.

APPLYING FOR FINANCIAL AID *Required financial aid form:* FAFSA. *Financial aid deadline:* Continuous. *Notification date:* Continuous beginning 3/1.

CONTACT Ms. Libby M. Jean, Director of Student Services, Olivet College, 320 South Main Street, Olivet, MI 49076-9701, 269-749-7655 or toll-free 800-456-7189. *Fax:* 269-749-3821. *E-mail:* ljean@olivetcollege.edu. *Website:* http://www.olivetcollege.edu/.

OLIVET NAZARENE UNIVERSITY
Bourbonnais, IL

Tuition & fees: $34,480	Average undergraduate aid package: $25,369

ABOUT THE INSTITUTION Independent Church of the Nazarene, coed. *Awards:* associate, bachelor's, master's, and doctoral degrees. 60 undergraduate majors. *Total enrollment:* 4,907. Undergraduates: 3,358. Freshmen: 704. Federal methodology is used as a basis for awarding need-based institutional aid.

UNDERGRADUATE EXPENSES for 2016–2017 *Application fee:* $25. *Comprehensive fee:* $42,380 includes full-time tuition ($33,490), mandatory fees ($990), and room and board ($7900). Full-time tuition and fees vary according to course load. Room and board charges vary according to board plan. *Part-time tuition:* $1373 per semester hour. Part-time tuition and fees vary according to course load.

FRESHMAN FINANCIAL AID (Fall 2015) 700 applied for aid; of those 90% were deemed to have need. 100% of freshmen with need received aid; of those 26% had need fully met. *Average percent of need met:* 80% (excluding resources awarded to replace EFC). *Average financial aid package:* $25,886 (excluding resources awarded to replace EFC). 14% of all full-time freshmen had no need and received non-need-based gift aid.

UNDERGRADUATE FINANCIAL AID (Fall 2015) 2,666 applied for aid; of those 92% were deemed to have need. 100% of undergraduates with need received

aid; of those 25% had need fully met. **Average percent of need met:** 80% (excluding resources awarded to replace EFC). **Average financial aid package:** $25,369 (excluding resources awarded to replace EFC). 19% of all full-time undergraduates had no need and received non-need-based gift aid.

GIFT AID (NEED-BASED) Total amount: $46,179,000 (11% federal, 7% state, 81% institutional, 1% external sources). **Receiving aid:** Freshmen: 86% (631); all full-time undergraduates: 81% (2,432). **Average award:** Freshmen: $21,424; Undergraduates: $20,623. **Scholarships, grants, and awards:** Federal Pell, FSEOG, state, private, college/university gift aid from institutional funds.

GIFT AID (NON-NEED-BASED) Total amount: $10,716,890 (7% federal, 91% institutional, 2% external sources). **Receiving aid:** Freshmen: 17% (127). Undergraduates: 15% (439). **Average award:** Freshmen: $15,790. Undergraduates: $13,320. **Scholarships, grants, and awards by category:** Academic interests/achievement: 2,884 awards ($34,140,303 total): general academic interests/achievements, military science. **Creative arts/performance:** 315 awards ($970,244 total): art/fine arts, music, performing arts, theater/drama. **Special achievements/activities:** 24 awards ($28,125 total): cheerleading/drum major. **Special characteristics:** 889 awards ($9,717,443 total): children of faculty/staff, general special characteristics, relatives of clergy, religious affiliation, veterans. **Tuition waivers:** Full or partial for employees or children of employees. **ROTC:** Army.

LOANS Student loans: $19,122,715 (68% need-based, 32% non-need-based). 74% of past graduating class borrowed through all loan programs. **Average indebtedness per student:** $32,754. **Average need-based loan:** Freshmen: $2465. Undergraduates: $3203. **Parent loans:** $6,004,851 (40% need-based, 60% non-need-based). **Programs:** Federal Direct (Subsidized and Unsubsidized Stafford, PLUS), Perkins, private loans.

WORK-STUDY Federal work-study: 350 jobs averaging $845. **State or other work-study/employment:** Total amount: $1,065,580 (27% need-based, 73% non-need-based). 1,032 part-time jobs averaging $1657.

ATHLETIC AWARDS Total amount: $5,045,630 (53% need-based, 47% non-need-based).

APPLYING FOR FINANCIAL AID Financial aid deadline (priority): 3/1. **Notification date:** Continuous beginning 11/1. Students must reply within 2 weeks of notification.

CONTACT Mr. Greg Bruner, Director of Financial Aid, Olivet Nazarene University, One University Avenue, Bourbonnais, IL 60914, 815-939-5249 or toll-free 800-648-1463. Fax: 815-939-5074. E-mail: gbruner@olivet.edu. Website: http://www.olivet.edu/.

O'MORE COLLEGE OF DESIGN
Franklin, TN

Tuition & fees: $28,176	Average undergraduate aid package: $16,617

ABOUT THE INSTITUTION Independent, coed. **Awards:** bachelor's degrees. 6 undergraduate majors. **Total enrollment:** 170. Undergraduates: 170. Freshmen: 34. Both federal and institutional methodology are used as a basis for awarding need-based institutional aid.

UNDERGRADUATE EXPENSES for 2016–2017 Application fee: $50. **Tuition:** full-time $28,176; part-time $1174 per credit hour. Full-time tuition and fees vary according to course load.

FRESHMAN FINANCIAL AID (Fall 2015) 31 applied for aid; of those 97% were deemed to have need. 100% of freshmen with need received aid; of those 20% had need fully met. **Average percent of need met:** 75% (excluding resources awarded to replace EFC). **Average financial aid package:** $18,902 (excluding resources awarded to replace EFC). 3% of all full-time freshmen had no need and received non-need-based gift aid.

UNDERGRADUATE FINANCIAL AID (Fall 2015) 147 applied for aid; of those 88% were deemed to have need. 100% of undergraduates with need received aid; of those 14% had need fully met. **Average percent of need met:** 76% (excluding resources awarded to replace EFC). **Average financial aid package:** $16,617 (excluding resources awarded to replace EFC). 19% of all full-time undergraduates had no need and received non-need-based gift aid.

GIFT AID (NEED-BASED) Total amount: $1,576,415 (19% federal, 17% state, 64% institutional). **Receiving aid:** Freshmen: 91% (30); all full-time undergraduates: 73% (128). **Average award:** Freshmen: $16,865; Undergraduates: $13,756. **Schol-**

arships, grants, and awards: Federal Pell, FSEOG, state, college/university gift aid from institutional funds.

GIFT AID (NON-NEED-BASED) Total amount: $370,058 (10% state, 83% institutional, 7% external sources). **Receiving aid:** Freshmen: 12% (4). Undergraduates: 6% (10). **Average award:** Freshmen: $6158. Undergraduates: $5934. **Scholarships, grants, and awards by category:** Academic interests/achievement: 156 awards ($534,841 total): general academic interests/achievements. **Creative arts/performance:** 122 awards ($419,412 total): art/fine arts, general creative arts/performance. **Special achievements/activities:** 31 awards ($24,874 total): general special achievements/activities, leadership, memberships. **Special characteristics:** 9 awards ($47,114 total): children of faculty/staff, international students. **Tuition waivers:** Full or partial for employees or children of employees.

LOANS Student loans: $813,664 (76% need-based, 24% non-need-based). 55% of past graduating class borrowed through all loan programs. **Average indebtedness per student:** $31,773. **Average need-based loan:** Freshmen: $3500. Undergraduates: $4762. **Parent loans:** $286,259 (75% need-based, 25% non-need-based). **Programs:** Federal Direct (Subsidized and Unsubsidized Stafford, PLUS).

WORK-STUDY Federal work-study: 13 jobs averaging $1285. **State or other work-study/employment:** Total amount: $22,685 (100% non-need-based). 17 part-time jobs averaging $2130.

APPLYING FOR FINANCIAL AID Required financial aid form: FAFSA. **Financial aid deadline:** Continuous. **Notification date:** Continuous beginning 3/15.

CONTACT Sara Martin, Financial Aid Director, O'More College of Design, 423 South Margin Street, Franklin, TN 37064-2816, 615-794-4254 Ext. 226 or toll-free 888-662-1970. Fax: 615-790-1662. E-mail: financialaid@omorecollege.edu. Website: http://www.omorecollege.edu/.

ORAL ROBERTS UNIVERSITY
Tulsa, OK

Tuition & fees: $26,792	Average undergraduate aid package: $24,085

ABOUT THE INSTITUTION Independent interdenominational, coed. **Awards:** certificates, diplomas, bachelor's, master's, and doctoral degrees. 75 undergraduate majors. **Total enrollment:** 3,852. Undergraduates: 3,288. Freshmen: 486. Federal methodology is used as a basis for awarding need-based institutional aid.

UNDERGRADUATE EXPENSES for 2017–2018 Application fee: $35. **Comprehensive fee:** $35,542 includes full-time tuition ($25,800), mandatory fees ($992), and room and board ($8750). **College room only:** $3860. Full-time tuition and fees vary according to course load, degree level, and location. Room and board charges vary according to board plan and housing facility. **Part-time tuition:** $1078 per contact hour. Part-time tuition and fees vary according to course load, degree level, and location.

FRESHMAN FINANCIAL AID (Fall 2016, est.) 556 applied for aid; of those 100% were deemed to have need. 100% of freshmen with need received aid; of those 56% had need fully met. **Average percent of need met:** 91% (excluding resources awarded to replace EFC). **Average financial aid package:** $28,341 (excluding resources awarded to replace EFC). 23% of all full-time freshmen had no need and received non-need-based gift aid.

UNDERGRADUATE FINANCIAL AID (Fall 2016, est.) 2,192 applied for aid; of those 91% were deemed to have need. 100% of undergraduates with need received aid; of those 46% had need fully met. **Average percent of need met:** 90% (excluding resources awarded to replace EFC). **Average financial aid package:** $24,085 (excluding resources awarded to replace EFC). 23% of all full-time undergraduates had no need and received non-need-based gift aid.

GIFT AID (NEED-BASED) Total amount: $30,869,569 (19% federal, 4% state, 75% institutional, 2% external sources). **Receiving aid:** Freshmen: 90% (552); all full-time undergraduates: 70% (1,955). **Average award:** Freshmen: $20,980; Undergraduates: $16,966. **Scholarships, grants, and awards:** Federal Pell, FSEOG, state, private, college/university gift aid from institutional funds.

GIFT AID (NON-NEED-BASED) Total amount: $8,094,921 (97% institutional, 3% external sources). **Receiving aid:** Freshmen: 25% (156). Undergraduates: 26% (733). **Average award:** Freshmen: $14,338. Undergraduates: $12,373. **Scholarships, grants, and awards by category:** Academic interests/achievement: biological sciences, business, communication, education, engineering/technologies, general academic interests/achievements, health fields, religion/biblical studies. **Creative arts/**

performance: applied art and design, art/fine arts, cinema/film/broadcasting, journalism/publications, music. *Special achievements/activities:* cheerleading/drum major, community service, general special achievements/activities, leadership, memberships, religious involvement. *Special characteristics:* children and siblings of alumni, children of faculty/staff, general special characteristics, international students, local/state students, relatives of clergy, siblings of current students. *Tuition waivers:* Full or partial for employees or children of employees. *ROTC:* Air Force cooperative.

LOANS *Student loans:* $15,766,376 (63% need-based, 37% non-need-based). *Average indebtedness per student:* $32,970. *Average need-based loan:* Freshmen: $7287. Undergraduates: $7337. *Parent loans:* $6,597,545 (58% need-based, 42% non-need-based). *Programs:* Federal Direct (Subsidized and Unsubsidized Stafford, PLUS), Perkins.

WORK-STUDY *Federal work-study:* Total amount: $639,160; jobs available. *State or other work-study/employment:* Total amount: $978,277 (52% need-based, 48% non-need-based). Part-time jobs available.

ATHLETIC AWARDS Total amount: $4,010,837 (33% need-based, 67% non-need-based).

APPLYING FOR FINANCIAL AID *Required financial aid form:* FAFSA. *Financial aid deadline (priority):* 3/1. *Notification date:* Continuous beginning 3/5. Students must reply by 5/1 or within 3 weeks of notification.

CONTACT Office of Financial Aid, Oral Roberts University, 7777 South Lewis Avenue, Tulsa, OK 74171, 918-495-6510 or toll-free 800-678-8876. *Fax:* 918-495-6803.
Website: http://www.oru.edu/.

OREGON COLLEGE OF ART AND CRAFT
Portland, OR

Tuition & fees: $33,160	Average undergraduate aid package: $19,960

ABOUT THE INSTITUTION Independent, coed. *Awards:* certificates, bachelor's, and master's degrees. 2 undergraduate majors. *Total enrollment:* 163. Undergraduates: 123. Freshmen: 27. Both federal and institutional methodology are used as a basis for awarding need-based institutional aid.

UNDERGRADUATE EXPENSES for 2017–2018 *Application fee:* $45. *One-time required fee:* $40. *Comprehensive fee:* $43,060 includes full-time tuition ($31,500), mandatory fees ($1660), and room and board ($9900). *College room only:* $6400. Full-time tuition and fees vary according to course load and degree level. Room and board charges vary according to board plan and housing facility. *Part-time tuition:* $1315 per credit hour. *Part-time fees:* $46.50 per credit hour; $365 per term. Part-time tuition and fees vary according to course load and degree level.

FRESHMAN FINANCIAL AID (Fall 2015) 14 applied for aid; of those 79% were deemed to have need. 100% of freshmen with need received aid; of those 27% had need fully met. *Average percent of need met:* 60% (excluding resources awarded to replace EFC). *Average financial aid package:* $15,902 (excluding resources awarded to replace EFC). 31% of all full-time freshmen had no need and received non-need-based gift aid.

UNDERGRADUATE FINANCIAL AID (Fall 2015) 83 applied for aid; of those 83% were deemed to have need. 100% of undergraduates with need received aid; of those 9% had need fully met. *Average percent of need met:* 58% (excluding resources awarded to replace EFC). *Average financial aid package:* $19,960 (excluding resources awarded to replace EFC). 27% of all full-time undergraduates had no need and received non-need-based gift aid.

GIFT AID (NEED-BASED) *Total amount:* $1,230,311 (26% federal, 2% state, 68% institutional, 4% external sources). *Receiving aid:* Freshmen: 69% (11); all full-time undergraduates: 73% (69). *Average award:* Freshmen: $13,471; Undergraduates: $15,856. *Scholarships, grants, and awards:* Federal Pell, FSEOG, state, private, college/university gift aid from institutional funds.

GIFT AID (NON-NEED-BASED) *Total amount:* $260,189 (100% institutional). *Receiving aid:* Freshmen: 19% (3). Undergraduates: 4% (4). *Average award:* Freshmen: $12,925. Undergraduates: $9639. *Scholarships, grants, and awards by category:* Academic interests/achievement: general academic interests/achievements. Creative arts/performance: art/fine arts. *Tuition waivers:* Full or partial for employees or children of employees.

LOANS *Student loans:* $861,918 (79% need-based, 21% non-need-based). 80% of past graduating class borrowed through all loan programs. *Average indebtedness per*

student: $20,793. *Average need-based loan:* Freshmen: $3000. Undergraduates: $3891. *Parent loans:* $152,536 (47% need-based, 53% non-need-based). *Programs:* Federal Direct (Subsidized and Unsubsidized Stafford, PLUS), private loans.

WORK-STUDY *Federal work-study:* jobs available. *State or other work-study/employment:* Total amount: $56,208 (65% need-based, 35% non-need-based). Part-time jobs available.

APPLYING FOR FINANCIAL AID *Required financial aid forms:* FAFSA, scholarship application. *Financial aid deadline:* Continuous. *Notification date:* Continuous beginning 1/15. Students must reply by 5/1.

CONTACT Ms. Linda L. Anderson, Director of Financial Aid, Oregon College of Art and Craft, 8245 Southwest Barnes Road, Portland, OR 97225, 971-255-4224 or toll-free 800-390-0632. *Fax:* 503-297-9651. *E-mail:* landerson@ocac.edu.
Website: http://www.ocac.edu/.

OREGON HEALTH & SCIENCE UNIVERSITY
Portland, OR

Tuition & fees: N/R	Average undergraduate aid package: $14,386

ABOUT THE INSTITUTION State-related, coed. *Awards:* certificates, bachelor's, master's, and doctoral degrees. 2 undergraduate majors. *Total enrollment:* 2,895. Undergraduates: 827. Federal methodology is used as a basis for awarding need-based institutional aid.

UNDERGRADUATE FINANCIAL AID (Fall 2016, est.) 287 applied for aid; of those 94% were deemed to have need. 96% of undergraduates with need received aid; of those 5% had need fully met. *Average percent of need met:* 38% (excluding resources awarded to replace EFC). *Average financial aid package:* $14,386 (excluding resources awarded to replace EFC).

GIFT AID (NEED-BASED) *Total amount:* $3,268,459 (42% federal, 11% state, 31% institutional, 16% external sources). *Receiving aid:* All full-time undergraduates: 52% (163). *Average award:* Undergraduates: $9563. *Scholarships, grants, and awards:* Federal Pell, FSEOG, state, private, college/university gift aid from institutional funds.

GIFT AID (NON-NEED-BASED) *Total amount:* $29,095 (2% federal, 3% institutional, 95% external sources). *Receiving aid:* Undergraduates: 1. *Scholarships, grants, and awards by category:* Academic interests/achievement: 107 awards ($950,066 total): home economics.

LOANS *Student loans:* $13,028,401 (87% need-based, 13% non-need-based). *Average need-based loan:* Undergraduates: $6369. *Parent loans:* $670,427 (54% need-based, 46% non-need-based). *Programs:* Federal Direct (Subsidized and Unsubsidized Stafford, PLUS), Perkins, Federal Nursing, college/university, alternative loans.

WORK-STUDY *Federal work-study:* Total amount: $22,754; 23 jobs averaging $1000.

APPLYING FOR FINANCIAL AID *Notification date:* Continuous.

CONTACT Becca Moore, Administrative Coordinator, Oregon Health & Science University, 3181 SW Sam Jackson Park Road, Mail Code L109, Portland, OR 97239-3089, 503-494-7800. *Fax:* 503-494-4629. *E-mail:* glawatz@ohsu.edu.
Website: http://www.ohsu.edu/.

OREGON INSTITUTE OF TECHNOLOGY
Klamath Falls, OR

CONTACT Tracey Lehman, Director of Financial Aid, Oregon Institute of Technology, 3201 Campus Drive, Klamath Falls, OR 97601, 541-885-1280 or toll-free 800-422-2017. *Fax:* 541-885-1024. *E-mail:* tracey.lehman@oit.edu.
Website: http://www.oit.edu/.

OREGON STATE UNIVERSITY
Corvallis, OR

Tuition & fees (OR res): $10,366	Average undergraduate aid package: $13,267

ABOUT THE INSTITUTION State-supported, coed. *Awards:* certificates, bachelor's, master's, and doctoral degrees. 81 undergraduate majors. *Total enrollment:* 30,354. Undergraduates: 25,327. Freshmen: 3,814. Federal methodology is used as a basis for awarding need-based institutional aid.

UNDERGRADUATE EXPENSES for 2016–2017 *Application fee:* $60. *One-time required fee:* $350. *Tuition, state resident:* full-time $8715; part-time $187 per credit hour. *Tuition, nonresident:* full-time $27,195; part-time $582 per credit hour. *Required fees:* full-time $1651; $505.31 per term. Full-time tuition and fees vary according to course load, location, and program. Part-time tuition and fees vary according to course load, location, and program. *College room and board:* $12,153; *Room only:* $8340. Room and board charges vary according to board plan and housing facility.

FRESHMAN FINANCIAL AID (Fall 2015) 2,872 applied for aid; of those 68% were deemed to have need. 99% of freshmen with need received aid; of those 10% had need fully met. *Average percent of need met:* 65% (excluding resources awarded to replace EFC). *Average financial aid package:* $11,816 (excluding resources awarded to replace EFC). 20% of all full-time freshmen had no need and received non-need-based gift aid.

UNDERGRADUATE FINANCIAL AID (Fall 2015) 12,585 applied for aid; of those 79% were deemed to have need. 99% of undergraduates with need received aid; of those 8% had need fully met. *Average percent of need met:* 65% (excluding resources awarded to replace EFC). *Average financial aid package:* $13,267 (excluding resources awarded to replace EFC). 14% of all full-time undergraduates had no need and received non-need-based gift aid.

GIFT AID (NEED-BASED) *Total amount:* $75,319,690 (41% federal, 12% state, 38% institutional, 9% external sources). *Receiving aid:* Freshmen: 50% (1,672); all full-time undergraduates: 44% (7,995). *Average award:* Freshmen: $7563; Undergraduates: $7295. *Scholarships, grants, and awards:* Federal Pell, FSEOG, state, private, college/university gift aid from institutional funds.

GIFT AID (NON-NEED-BASED) *Total amount:* $14,464,020 (10% federal, 75% institutional, 15% external sources). *Receiving aid:* Freshmen: 1% (19). Undergraduates: 72. *Average award:* Freshmen: $4203. Undergraduates: $4660. *Scholarships, grants, and awards by category: Academic interests/achievement:* general academic interests/achievements. *Special achievements/activities:* leadership. *Special characteristics:* children and siblings of alumni, local/state students, members of minority groups. *Tuition waivers:* Full or partial for employees or children of employees. *ROTC:* Army, Naval, Air Force.

LOANS *Student loans:* $112,419,365 (84% need-based, 16% non-need-based). 60% of past graduating class borrowed through all loan programs. *Average indebtedness per student:* $26,453. *Average need-based loan:* Freshmen: $3583. Undergraduates: $4642. *Parent loans:* $33,189,320 (78% need-based, 22% non-need-based). *Programs:* Federal Direct (Subsidized and Unsubsidized Stafford, PLUS), Perkins, college/university.

WORK-STUDY *Federal work-study:* 1,164 jobs averaging $2983.

ATHLETIC AWARDS *Total amount:* $6,967,248 (14% need-based, 86% non-need-based).

APPLYING FOR FINANCIAL AID *Required financial aid form:* FAFSA. *Financial aid deadline (priority):* 2/28. *Notification date:* Continuous beginning 4/1. Students must reply within 4 weeks of notification.

CONTACT Doug Severs, Director of Financial Aid and Scholarships, Oregon State University, 218 Kerr Administration Building, Corvallis, OR 97331-2120, 541-737-2241 or toll-free 800-291-4192. *Fax:* 541-737-4494. *E-mail:* financial.aid@oregonstate.edu. *Website:* http://www.oregonstate.edu/.

OREGON STATE UNIVERSITY–CASCADES
Bend, OR

CONTACT Financial Aid Office, Oregon State University–Cascades, 2600 Northwest College Way, Bend, OR 97701, 541-322-3100. *Website:* http://www.osucascades.edu/.

OTIS COLLEGE OF ART AND DESIGN
Los Angeles, CA

CONTACT Jessika Huerta, Director of Financial Aid, Otis College of Art and Design, 9045 Lincoln Boulevard, Los Angeles, CA 90045-9785, 310-665-6898 or toll-free 800-527-OTIS. *Fax:* 310-665-6884. *E-mail:* jhuerta@otis.edu. *Website:* http://www.otis.edu/.

OTTAWA UNIVERSITY
Ottawa, KS

CONTACT Financial Aid Coordinator, Ottawa University, 1001 South Cedar, Ottawa, KS 66067-3399, 785-242-5200 or toll-free 800-755-5200. *E-mail:* finaid@ottawa.edu. *Website:* http://www.ottawa.edu/.

OTTERBEIN UNIVERSITY
Westerville, OH

Tuition & fees: $31,874	Average undergraduate aid package: $23,544

ABOUT THE INSTITUTION Independent United Methodist, coed. *Awards:* certificates, bachelor's, master's, and doctoral degrees. 48 undergraduate majors. *Total enrollment:* 2,943. Undergraduates: 2,485. Freshmen: 647. Both federal and institutional methodology are used as a basis for awarding need-based institutional aid.

UNDERGRADUATE EXPENSES for 2017–2018 *Application fee:* $25. *Comprehensive fee:* $42,702 includes full-time tuition ($31,424), mandatory fees ($450), and room and board ($10,828). *College room only:* $6256. Room and board charges vary according to board plan and housing facility. *Part-time tuition:* $564 per credit hour.

FRESHMAN FINANCIAL AID (Fall 2015) 528 applied for aid; of those 88% were deemed to have need. 100% of freshmen with need received aid; of those 23% had need fully met. *Average percent of need met:* 79% (excluding resources awarded to replace EFC). *Average financial aid package:* $25,048 (excluding resources awarded to replace EFC). 16% of all full-time freshmen had no need and received non-need-based gift aid.

UNDERGRADUATE FINANCIAL AID (Fall 2015) 1,803 applied for aid; of those 89% were deemed to have need. 100% of undergraduates with need received aid; of those 19% had need fully met. *Average percent of need met:* 75% (excluding resources awarded to replace EFC). *Average financial aid package:* $23,544 (excluding resources awarded to replace EFC). 21% of all full-time undergraduates had no need and received non-need-based gift aid.

GIFT AID (NEED-BASED) *Total amount:* $28,518,407 (9% federal, 4% state, 85% institutional, 2% external sources). *Receiving aid:* Freshmen: 81% (456); all full-time undergraduates: 74% (1,576). *Average award:* Freshmen: $19,539; Undergraduates: $17,851. *Scholarships, grants, and awards:* Federal Pell, FSEOG, state, private, college/university gift aid from institutional funds, Federal Nursing.

GIFT AID (NON-NEED-BASED) *Total amount:* $8,588,060 (95% institutional, 5% external sources). *Receiving aid:* Freshmen: 15% (82). Undergraduates: 11% (242). *Average award:* Freshmen: $18,123. Undergraduates: $17,222. *Scholarships, grants, and awards by category: Academic interests/achievement:* 1,932 awards ($24,443,041 total): general academic interests/achievements. *Creative arts/performance:* 303 awards ($1,963,917 total): art/fine arts, music, theater/drama.

Special achievements/activities: 22 awards ($33,000 total): community service, leadership. *Special characteristics:* 325 awards ($1,470,882 total): children and siblings of alumni, children of faculty/staff, general special characteristics, international students, members of minority groups, previous college experience, relatives of clergy, siblings of current students, veterans. *Tuition waivers:* Full or partial for employees or children of employees. *ROTC:* Army cooperative, Air Force cooperative.

LOANS *Student loans:* $5,510,165 (99% need-based, 1% non-need-based). 77% of past graduating class borrowed through all loan programs. *Average indebtedness per student:* $40,397. *Average need-based loan:* Freshmen: $3188. Undergraduates: $4177. *Parent loans:* $6,164,001 (44% need-based, 56% non-need-based). *Programs:* Federal Direct (Subsidized and Unsubsidized Stafford, PLUS), Perkins, Federal Nursing, state, college/university.

WORK-STUDY *Federal work-study:* 868 jobs averaging $1511. *State or other work-study/employment:* Total amount: $210,625 (100% non-need-based). Part-time jobs available.

APPLYING FOR FINANCIAL AID *Required financial aid form:* FAFSA. *Financial aid deadline (priority):* 2/15. *Notification date:* Continuous beginning 1/10.

CONTACT Mr. Thomas V. Yarnell, Director of Student Financial Services, Otterbein University, One Otterbein College, Westerville, OH 43081-2006, 614-823-1502 or toll-free 800-488-8144. *Fax:* 614-823-1588. *E-mail:* tyarnell@otterbein.edu. *Website:* http://www.otterbein.edu/.

OUACHITA BAPTIST UNIVERSITY
Arkadelphia, AR

Tuition & fees: $25,870	Average undergraduate aid package: $22,754

ABOUT THE INSTITUTION Independent Baptist, coed. *Awards:* associate and bachelor's degrees. 54 undergraduate majors. *Total enrollment:* 1,494. Undergraduates: 1,494. Freshmen: 396. Both federal and institutional methodology are used as a basis for awarding need-based institutional aid.

UNDERGRADUATE EXPENSES for 2017–2018 *Comprehensive fee:* $33,500 includes full-time tuition ($25,300), mandatory fees ($570), and room and board ($7630). Full-time tuition and fees vary according to degree level. Room and board charges vary according to housing facility. *Part-time tuition:* $700 per semester hour. Part-time tuition and fees vary according to degree level.

FRESHMAN FINANCIAL AID (Fall 2016, est.) 366 applied for aid; of those 77% were deemed to have need. 100% of freshmen with need received aid; of those 29% had need fully met. *Average percent of need met:* 83% (excluding resources awarded to replace EFC). *Average financial aid package:* $22,721 (excluding resources awarded to replace EFC). 27% of all full-time freshmen had no need and received non-need-based gift aid.

UNDERGRADUATE FINANCIAL AID (Fall 2016, est.) 1,136 applied for aid; of those 79% were deemed to have need. 100% of undergraduates with need received aid; of those 36% had need fully met. *Average percent of need met:* 84% (excluding resources awarded to replace EFC). *Average financial aid package:* $22,754 (excluding resources awarded to replace EFC). 36% of all full-time undergraduates had no need and received non-need-based gift aid.

GIFT AID (NEED-BASED) *Total amount:* $13,901,581 (13% federal, 9% state, 74% institutional, 4% external sources). *Receiving aid:* Freshmen: 69% (274); all full-time undergraduates: 60% (892). *Average award:* Freshmen: $18,055; Undergraduates: $17,433. *Scholarships, grants, and awards:* Federal Pell, FSEOG, state, private, college/university gift aid from institutional funds.

GIFT AID (NON-NEED-BASED) *Total amount:* $8,091,124 (22% state, 72% institutional, 6% external sources). *Receiving aid:* Freshmen: 12% (48). Undergraduates: 13% (197). *Average award:* Freshmen: $11,498. Undergraduates: $10,861. *Scholarships, grants, and awards by category:* Academic interests/achievement: area/ethnic studies, biological sciences, business, communication, computer science, education, engineering/technologies, English, foreign languages, general academic interests/achievements, health fields, home economics, humanities, international studies, mathematics, physical sciences, premedicine, religion/biblical studies, social sciences. *Creative arts/performance:* art/fine arts, journalism/publications, music, performing arts, theater/drama. *Special achievements/activities:* cheerleading/drum major, general special achievements/activities. *Special characteristics:* children and siblings of alumni, children of faculty/staff, ethnic background, first-generation college students, general special characteristics, handicapped students, international students, local/state students, married students, members of minority groups, out-of-

state students, previous college experience, relatives of clergy, religious affiliation, twins. *Tuition waivers:* Full or partial for employees or children of employees. *ROTC:* Army.

LOANS *Student loans:* $6,943,778 (55% need-based, 45% non-need-based). 50% of past graduating class borrowed through all loan programs. *Average indebtedness per student:* $29,298. *Average need-based loan:* Freshmen: $3275. Undergraduates: $3872. *Parent loans:* $1,882,587 (33% need-based, 67% non-need-based). *Programs:* Federal Direct (Subsidized and Unsubsidized Stafford, PLUS), Perkins, college/university.

WORK-STUDY *Federal work-study:* Total amount: $458,240; jobs available. *State or other work-study/employment:* Total amount: $271,876 (26% need-based, 74% non-need-based). Part-time jobs available.

ATHLETIC AWARDS Total amount: $2,646,143 (46% need-based, 54% non-need-based).

APPLYING FOR FINANCIAL AID *Required financial aid forms:* FAFSA, state aid form. *Financial aid deadline:* 5/1 (priority: 12/1). *Notification date:* Continuous beginning 10/1.

CONTACT Ms. Susan Hurst, Director of Financial Aid, Ouachita Baptist University, PO Box 3774, Arkadelphia, AR 71998-0001, 870-245-5570 or toll-free 800-342-5628. *Fax:* 870-245-5318. *E-mail:* hursts@obu.edu. *Website:* http://www.obu.edu/.

OUR LADY OF THE LAKE COLLEGE
Baton Rouge, LA

CONTACT Tiffany D. Magee, Director of Financial Aid, Our Lady of the Lake College, 7434 Perkins Road, Baton Rouge, LA 70808, 225-768-1701. *Fax:* 225-490-1632. *E-mail:* tiffany.magee@ololcollege.edu. *Website:* http://www.ololcollege.edu/.

OUR LADY OF THE LAKE UNIVERSITY
San Antonio, TX

Tuition & fees: $28,192	Average undergraduate aid package: $21,000

ABOUT THE INSTITUTION Independent Roman Catholic, coed. *Awards:* bachelor's, master's, and doctoral degrees. 32 undergraduate majors. *Total enrollment:* 3,130. Undergraduates: 1,347. Freshmen: 216. Both federal and institutional methodology are used as a basis for awarding need-based institutional aid.

UNDERGRADUATE EXPENSES for 2017–2018 *Comprehensive fee:* $37,580 includes full-time tuition ($27,364), mandatory fees ($828), and room and board ($9388). *College room only:* $5600. Full-time tuition and fees vary according to course load and location. Room and board charges vary according to board plan and housing facility. *Part-time tuition:* $877 per credit hour. Part-time tuition and fees vary according to course load and location.

FRESHMAN FINANCIAL AID (Fall 2015) 292 applied for aid; of those 93% were deemed to have need. 100% of freshmen with need received aid; of those 15% had need fully met. *Average percent of need met:* 75% (excluding resources awarded to replace EFC). *Average financial aid package:* $21,794 (excluding resources awarded to replace EFC). 10% of all full-time freshmen had no need and received non-need-based gift aid.

UNDERGRADUATE FINANCIAL AID (Fall 2015) 1,247 applied for aid; of those 93% were deemed to have need. 100% of undergraduates with need received aid; of those 23% had need fully met. *Average percent of need met:* 77% (excluding resources awarded to replace EFC). *Average financial aid package:* $21,000 (excluding resources awarded to replace EFC). 8% of all full-time undergraduates had no need and received non-need-based gift aid.

GIFT AID (NEED-BASED) *Total amount:* $16,776,616 (25% federal, 18% state, 55% institutional, 2% external sources). *Receiving aid:* Freshmen: 89% (271); all full-time undergraduates: 85% (1,137). *Average award:* Freshmen: $17,627; Undergraduates: $15,658. *Scholarships, grants, and awards:* Federal Pell, FSEOG, state, private, college/university gift aid from institutional funds.

GIFT AID (NON-NEED-BASED) *Total amount:* $1,464,044 (100% institutional). *Receiving aid:* Freshmen: 10% (30). Undergraduates: 14% (193). *Average award:* Freshmen: $8565. Undergraduates: $8743. *Scholarships, grants, and* *awards by category: Academic interests/achievement:* general academic interests/achievements. *Special characteristics:* children of faculty/staff, religious affiliation. *Tuition waivers:* Full or partial for employees or children of employees. *ROTC:* Army cooperative.

LOANS *Student loans:* $10,213,229 (76% need-based, 24% non-need-based). 87% of past graduating class borrowed through all loan programs. *Average indebtedness per student:* $31,438. *Average need-based loan:* Freshmen: $3687. Undergraduates: $4716. *Parent loans:* $1,851,411 (40% need-based, 60% non-need-based). *Programs:* Federal Direct (Subsidized and Unsubsidized Stafford, PLUS), Perkins, state, private loans.

WORK-STUDY *Federal work-study:* jobs available. *State or other work-study/employment:* Total amount: $23,170 (100% need-based). Part-time jobs available.

ATHLETIC AWARDS Total amount: $1,321,973 (58% need-based, 42% non-need-based).

APPLYING FOR FINANCIAL AID *Required financial aid forms:* FAFSA, institution's own form. *Financial aid deadline (priority):* 5/1. *Notification date:* Continuous beginning 3/1.

CONTACT Esmeralda Flores, Director of Financial Aid, Our Lady of the Lake University, 411 Southwest 24th Street, San Antonio, TX 78207-4689, 210-434-6711 Ext. 2558 or toll-free 800-436-6558. *Fax:* 210-431-3958. *E-mail:* emflores@lake.ollusa.edu.
Website: http://www.ollusa.edu/.

OZARK CHRISTIAN COLLEGE
Joplin, MO

CONTACT Jill Kaminsky, Application Processor, Ozark Christian College, 1111 North Main Street, Joplin, MO 64801-4804, 417-624-2518 Ext. 2017 or toll-free 800-299-4622. *Fax:* 417-624-0090. *E-mail:* finaid@occ.edu.
Website: http://www.occ.edu/.

PACE UNIVERSITY
New York, NY

CONTACT Financial Aid Office, Pace University, 1 Pace Plaza, New York, NY 10038, 877-672-1830 or toll-free 800-874-7223. *Fax:* 212-346-1750. *E-mail:* financialaid@pace.edu.
Website: http://www.pace.edu/nyc.

PACE UNIVERSITY, PLEASANTVILLE CAMPUS
Pleasantville, NY

CONTACT Financial Aid Office, Pace University, Pleasantville Campus, 861 Bedford Road, Pleasantville, NY 10570, 914-773-3200 or toll-free 800-874-PACE.
Website: http://www.pace.edu/westchester.

PACIFIC COLLEGE
Costa Mesa, CA

CONTACT Financial Aid Office, Pacific College, 3160 Red Hill Avenue, Costa Mesa, CA 92626, 714-662-4402.
Website: http://www.pacific-college.edu/.

PACIFIC ISLANDS UNIVERSITY
Mangilao, GU

CONTACT Financial Aid Office, Pacific Islands University, 172 Kinney's Road, Mangilao, GU 96913, 671-734-1812.
Website: http://www.piu.edu/.

PACIFIC LUTHERAN UNIVERSITY
Tacoma, WA

ABOUT THE INSTITUTION Independent Evangelical Lutheran Church in America, coed. *Awards:* certificates, bachelor's, master's, and doctoral degrees. 40 undergraduate majors. *Total enrollment:* 3,077. Undergraduates: 2,782. Freshmen: 678.

GIFT AID (NEED-BASED) *Scholarships, grants, and awards:* Federal Pell, FSEOG, state, private, college/university gift aid from institutional funds, Federal Nursing.

GIFT AID (NON-NEED-BASED) *Scholarships, grants, and awards by category: Academic interests/achievement:* general academic interests/achievements. *Creative arts/performance:* art/fine arts, dance, debating, music, theater/drama. *Special achievements/activities:* leadership. *Special characteristics:* children and siblings of alumni, children of faculty/staff, international students, out-of-state students, relatives of clergy, religious affiliation.

LOANS *Programs:* Federal Direct (Subsidized and Unsubsidized Stafford, PLUS), Perkins, Federal Nursing, state.

WORK-STUDY *Federal work-study:* 675 jobs averaging $3189. *State or other work-study/employment:* Total amount: $1,839,424 (100% need-based). 477 part-time jobs averaging $3808.

APPLYING FOR FINANCIAL AID *Required financial aid form:* FAFSA.

CONTACT Kay W. Soltis, Office of Financial Aid, Pacific Lutheran University, Hauge Administration Building, Room 130, Tacoma, WA 98447, 253-535-7134 or toll-free 800-274-6758. *Fax:* 253-535-8406. *E-mail:* finaid@plu.edu.
Website: http://www.plu.edu/.

PACIFIC NORTHWEST COLLEGE OF ART
Portland, OR

CONTACT Peggy Burgus, Director of Financial Aid, Pacific Northwest College of Art, 1241 Northwest Johnson Street, Portland, OR 97209, 503-821-8976. *Fax:* 503-821-8978.
Website: http://www.pnca.edu/.

PACIFIC OAKS COLLEGE
Pasadena, CA

CONTACT Rosie Tristan, Financial Aid Specialist, Pacific Oaks College, 5 Westmoreland Place, Pasadena, CA 91103, 626-397-1350 or toll-free 877-314-2380. *Fax:* 626-577-6144. *E-mail:* financial@pacificoaks.edu.
Website: http://www.pacificoaks.edu/.

PACIFIC RIM CHRISTIAN UNIVERSITY
Honolulu, HI

CONTACT Financial Aid Office, Pacific Rim Christian University, 2223 Ho'one'e Place, Honolulu, HI 96819, 808-518-4791.
Website: http://www.pacrim.edu/.

PACIFIC UNION COLLEGE
Angwin, CA

Tuition & fees: $28,629	Average undergraduate aid package: $25,507

ABOUT THE INSTITUTION Independent Seventh-day Adventist, coed. *Awards:* certificates, associate, bachelor's, and master's degrees. 40 undergraduate majors. *Total enrollment:* 1,555. Undergraduates: 1,550. Freshmen: 251. Federal methodology is used as a basis for awarding need-based institutional aid.

UNDERGRADUATE EXPENSES for 2016–2017 *Application fee:* $30. *Comprehensive fee:* $36,456 includes full-time tuition ($27,999), mandatory fees ($630), and room and board ($7827). *College room only:* $4632. *Part-time tuition:* $810 per unit.

FRESHMAN FINANCIAL AID (Fall 2016, est.) 251 applied for aid; of those 80% were deemed to have need. 100% of freshmen with need received aid; of those 5% had need fully met. *Average percent of need met:* 65% (excluding resources awarded to replace EFC). *Average financial aid package:* $26,516 (excluding resources awarded to replace EFC). 20% of all full-time freshmen had no need and received non-need-based gift aid.

UNDERGRADUATE FINANCIAL AID (Fall 2016, est.) 1,282 applied for aid; of those 82% were deemed to have need. 100% of undergraduates with need received aid; of those 4% had need fully met. *Average percent of need met:* 57% (excluding resources awarded to replace EFC). *Average financial aid package:* $25,507 (excluding resources awarded to replace EFC). 19% of all full-time undergraduates had no need and received non-need-based gift aid.

GIFT AID (NEED-BASED) *Total amount:* $24,430,025 (14% federal, 13% state, 63% institutional, 10% external sources). *Receiving aid:* Freshmen: 80% (202); all full-time undergraduates: 81% (1,049). *Average award:* Freshmen: $19,614; Undergraduates: $17,219. *Scholarships, grants, and awards:* Federal Pell, FSEOG, state, private, college/university gift aid from institutional funds.

GIFT AID (NON-NEED-BASED) *Total amount:* $4,288,065 (63% institutional, 37% external sources). *Receiving aid:* Freshmen: 24% (60). Undergraduates: 27% (344). *Average award:* Freshmen: $13,045. Undergraduates: $12,335. *Scholarships, grants, and awards by category:* Academic interests/achievement: 110 awards ($305,419 total): education, religion/biblical studies. Creative arts/performance: 24 awards ($71,750 total): art/fine arts, music, theater/drama. Special achievements/activities: 83 awards ($183,333 total): community service, leadership, religious involvement. Special characteristics: 278 awards ($300,944 total): children and siblings of alumni, siblings of current students, spouses of current students, veterans.

LOANS *Student loans:* $11,681,692 (44% need-based, 56% non-need-based). 80% of past graduating class borrowed through all loan programs. *Average indebtedness per student:* $40,263. *Average need-based loan:* Freshmen: $3509. Undergraduates: $4745. *Parent loans:* $2,101,573 (60% need-based, 40% non-need-based). *Programs:* Federal Direct (Subsidized and Unsubsidized Stafford, PLUS), Perkins, college/university.

WORK-STUDY *Federal work-study:* Total amount: $662,889; jobs available.

ATHLETIC AWARDS Total amount: $213,466 (60% need-based, 40% non-need-based).

APPLYING FOR FINANCIAL AID *Required financial aid forms:* FAFSA, institution's own form. *Financial aid deadline (priority):* 3/2. *Notification date:* Continuous beginning 4/1. Students must reply within 3 weeks of notification.

CONTACT Laurie Wheeler, Director of Student Financial Services, Pacific Union College, One Angwin Avenue, Angwin, CA 94508, 707-965-7321 or toll-free 800-862-7080. *Fax:* 707-965-6595. *E-mail:* llwheeler@puc.edu.
Website: http://www.puc.edu/.

PACIFIC UNIVERSITY
Forest Grove, OR

Tuition & fees: $41,054	Average undergraduate aid package: $30,945

ABOUT THE INSTITUTION Independent, coed. *Awards:* certificates, bachelor's, master's, and doctoral degrees. 50 undergraduate majors. *Total enrollment:* 3,810. Undergraduates: 1,924. Freshmen: 479. Federal methodology is used as a basis for awarding need-based institutional aid.

UNDERGRADUATE EXPENSES for 2016–2017 *Application fee:* $40. *Comprehensive fee:* $52,876 includes full-time tuition ($40,120), mandatory fees ($934), and room and board ($11,822). *College room only:* $6528. Room and board charges vary according to board plan and housing facility. *Part-time tuition:* $1672 per credit hour. Part-time tuition and fees vary according to course load.

FRESHMAN FINANCIAL AID (Fall 2016, est.) 411 applied for aid; of those 91% were deemed to have need. 100% of freshmen with need received aid; of those 17% had need fully met. *Average percent of need met:* 76% (excluding resources awarded to replace EFC). *Average financial aid package:* $33,197 (excluding resources awarded to replace EFC). 13% of all full-time freshmen had no need and received non-need-based gift aid.

UNDERGRADUATE FINANCIAL AID (Fall 2016, est.) 1,597 applied for aid; of those 92% were deemed to have need. 100% of undergraduates with need received aid; of those 16% had need fully met. *Average percent of need met:* 72% (excluding resources awarded to replace EFC). *Average financial aid package:* $30,945 (excluding resources awarded to replace EFC). 16% of all full-time undergraduates had no need and received non-need-based gift aid.

GIFT AID (NEED-BASED) *Total amount:* $35,834,350 (7% federal, 2% state, 88% institutional, 3% external sources). *Receiving aid:* Freshmen: 63% (270); all full-time undergraduates: 59% (1,064). *Average award:* Freshmen: $10,695; Undergraduates: $10,383. *Scholarships, grants, and awards:* Federal Pell, FSEOG, state, private, college/university gift aid from institutional funds.

GIFT AID (NON-NEED-BASED) *Total amount:* $7,313,644 (98% institutional, 2% external sources). *Receiving aid:* Freshmen: 84% (361). Undergraduates: 77% (1,372). *Average award:* Freshmen: $20,244. Undergraduates: $19,350. *Scholarships, grants, and awards by category:* Academic interests/achievement: biological sciences, business, communication, education, English, foreign languages, general academic interests/achievements, health fields, humanities, mathematics, physical sciences, premedicine, social sciences. Creative arts/performance: art/fine arts, debating, journalism/publications, music, theater/drama. Special achievements/activities: community service, memberships, religious involvement. Special characteristics: children and siblings of alumni, children of faculty/staff, ethnic background, first-generation college students, general special characteristics, international students, relatives of clergy, veterans. *Tuition waivers:* Full or partial for employees or children of employees. *ROTC:* Army cooperative, Air Force cooperative.

LOANS *Student loans:* $13,393,571 (85% need-based, 15% non-need-based). 76% of past graduating class borrowed through all loan programs. *Average indebtedness per student:* $34,282. *Average need-based loan:* Freshmen: $3748. Undergraduates: $4991. *Parent loans:* $5,684,703 (63% need-based, 37% non-need-based). *Programs:* Federal Direct (Subsidized and Unsubsidized Stafford, PLUS), Perkins, private loans.

WORK-STUDY *Federal work-study:* Total amount: $1,577,901; jobs available. *State or other work-study/employment:* Total amount: $2500 (40% need-based, 60% non-need-based). Part-time jobs available.

APPLYING FOR FINANCIAL AID *Required financial aid form:* FAFSA. *Financial aid deadline (priority):* 3/1. *Notification date:* Continuous beginning 3/1.

CONTACT Office of Financial Aid, Pacific University, 2043 College Way, Forest Grove, OR 97116-1797, 503-352-2222 or toll-free 877-722-8648. *E-mail:* financialaid@pacificu.edu.
Website: http://www.pacificu.edu/.

PAIER COLLEGE OF ART, INC.
Hamden, CT

CONTACT Mr. John DeRose, Director of Financial Aid, Paier College of Art, Inc., 20 Gorham Avenue, Hamden, CT 06514-3902, 203-287-3034. *Fax:* 203-287-3021. *E-mail:* paier.art@snet.net.
Website: http://www.paiercollegeofart.edu/.

PAINE COLLEGE
Augusta, GA

CONTACT Ms. Gerri Bogan, Director of Financial Aid, Paine College, 1235 15th Street, Augusta, GA 30901, 706-821-8262 or toll-free 800-476-7703. *Fax:* 706-821-8691. *E-mail:* bogang@mail.paine.edu.
Website: http://www.paine.edu/.

PALM BEACH ATLANTIC UNIVERSITY
West Palm Beach, FL

Tuition & fees: $29,950	Average undergraduate aid package: $20,358

ABOUT THE INSTITUTION Independent nondenominational, coed. *Awards:* bachelor's, master's, and doctoral degrees. 50 undergraduate majors. *Total enrollment:* 3,764. Undergraduates: 2,926. Freshmen: 505. Federal methodology is used as a basis for awarding need-based institutional aid.

UNDERGRADUATE EXPENSES for 2017–2018 *Application fee:* $50. *Comprehensive fee:* $39,490 includes full-time tuition ($29,510), mandatory fees ($440), and room and board ($9540). *College room only:* $5030. Full-time tuition and fees vary according to course load, location, and program. Room and board charges vary according to board plan and housing facility. Part-time tuition and fees vary according to course load, location, and program.

FRESHMAN FINANCIAL AID (Fall 2016, est.) 447 applied for aid; of those 84% were deemed to have need. 100% of freshmen with need received aid; of those 23% had need fully met. *Average percent of need met:* 67% (excluding resources awarded to replace EFC). *Average financial aid package:* $21,274 (excluding resources awarded to replace EFC). 25% of all full-time freshmen had no need and received non-need-based gift aid.

UNDERGRADUATE FINANCIAL AID (Fall 2016, est.) 1,883 applied for aid; of those 87% were deemed to have need. 100% of undergraduates with need received aid; of those 19% had need fully met. *Average percent of need met:* 63% (excluding resources awarded to replace EFC). *Average financial aid package:* $20,358 (excluding resources awarded to replace EFC). 27% of all full-time undergraduates had no need and received non-need-based gift aid.

GIFT AID (NEED-BASED) *Total amount:* $27,233,806 (14% federal, 14% state, 62% institutional, 10% external sources). *Receiving aid:* Freshmen: 75% (374); all full-time undergraduates: 70% (1,621). *Average award:* Freshmen: $19,109; Undergraduates: $17,448. *Scholarships, grants, and awards:* Federal Pell, FSEOG, state, private, college/university gift aid from institutional funds.

GIFT AID (NON-NEED-BASED) *Total amount:* $11,106,710 (15% state, 77% institutional, 8% external sources). *Receiving aid:* Freshmen: 15% (75). Undergraduates: 11% (244). *Average award:* Freshmen: $13,696. Undergraduates: $11,954. *Scholarships, grants, and awards by category: Academic interests/achievement:* general academic interests/achievements. *Creative arts/performance:* dance, music, theater/drama. *Special achievements/activities:* leadership. *Special characteristics:* adult students, children and siblings of alumni, children of current students, children of educators, children of faculty/staff, previous college experience. *Tuition waivers:* Full or partial for children of alumni, employees or children of employees. *ROTC:* Army cooperative.

LOANS *Student loans:* $11,070,965 (77% need-based, 23% non-need-based). 63% of past graduating class borrowed through all loan programs. *Average indebtedness per student:* $28,862. *Average need-based loan:* Freshmen: $3273. Undergraduates: $3940. *Parent loans:* $4,126,812 (57% need-based, 43% non-need-based). *Programs:* Federal Direct (Subsidized and Unsubsidized Stafford, PLUS).

WORK-STUDY *Federal work-study:* Total amount: $473,432; 194 jobs averaging $2898. *State or other work-study/employment:* Total amount: $12,682 (100% need-based). 8 part-time jobs averaging $2335.

ATHLETIC AWARDS Total amount: $2,004,449 (35% need-based, 65% non-need-based).

APPLYING FOR FINANCIAL AID *Required financial aid forms:* FAFSA, state aid form. *Financial aid deadline (priority):* 5/1. *Notification date:* Continuous beginning 10/15. Students must reply by 5/1.

CONTACT Mrs. Jennifer McMahon, Director of Financial Aid, Palm Beach Atlantic University, PO Box 24708, West Palm Beach, FL 33416-4708, 561-803-2000 or toll-free 888-GO-TO-PBA. *Fax:* 561-803-2130. *E-mail:* finaid@pba.edu.
Website: http://www.pba.edu/.

PALM BEACH STATE COLLEGE
Lake Worth, FL

CONTACT Financial Aid Office, Palm Beach State College, 4200 Congress Avenue, Lake Worth, FL 33461-4796, 561-967-7222.
Website: http://www.palmbeachstate.edu/.

PARK UNIVERSITY
Parkville, MO

CONTACT Cathy Colapietro, Executive Director of Student Financial Services, Park University, 8700 NW River Park Drive, Parkville, MO 64152, 816-584-6728 or toll-free 800-745-7275. *E-mail:* cathy.colapietro@park.edu.
Website: http://www.park.edu/.

PARSONS SCHOOL OF DESIGN
New York, NY

ABOUT THE INSTITUTION Independent, coed. *Awards:* certificates, associate, bachelor's, and master's degrees. 15 undergraduate majors. *Total enrollment:* 5,231. Undergraduates: 4,301. Freshmen: 953.

GIFT AID (NEED-BASED) *Scholarships, grants, and awards:* Federal Pell, FSEOG, state, private, college/university gift aid from institutional funds.

GIFT AID (NON-NEED-BASED) *Scholarships, grants, and awards by category: Academic interests/achievement:* general academic interests/achievements. *Creative arts/performance:* general creative arts/performance. *Special achievements/activities:* leadership. *Special characteristics:* members of minority groups.

LOANS *Programs:* Federal Direct (Subsidized and Unsubsidized Stafford, PLUS), Perkins.

APPLYING FOR FINANCIAL AID *Required financial aid forms:* FAFSA, state aid form.

CONTACT Office of Student Financial Services, Parsons School of Design, 72 Fifth Avenue, New York, NY 10011, 212-229-8930 or toll-free 800-292-3040. *E-mail:* sfs@newschool.edu.
Website: http://www.newschool.edu/parsons/.

PATRICK HENRY COLLEGE
Purcellville, VA

Tuition & fees: $28,172	Average undergraduate aid package: $14,600

ABOUT THE INSTITUTION Independent nondenominational, coed. *Awards:* bachelor's degrees. 7 undergraduate majors. *Total enrollment:* 277. Undergraduates: 277. Freshmen: 51. Institutional methodology is used as a basis for awarding need-based institutional aid.

UNDERGRADUATE EXPENSES for 2017–2018 *Application fee:* $20. *Comprehensive fee:* $38,900 includes full-time tuition ($27,922), mandatory fees ($250), and room and board ($10,728). Full-time tuition and fees vary according to course load. Room and board charges vary according to board plan and housing facility. *Part-time tuition:* $1163 per credit hour. Part-time tuition and fees vary according to course level and course load.

FRESHMAN FINANCIAL AID (Fall 2016, est.) 29 applied for aid; of those 52% were deemed to have need. 100% of freshmen with need received aid. *Average percent of need met:* 35% (excluding resources awarded to replace EFC).

Average financial aid package: $14,200 (excluding resources awarded to replace EFC). 57% of all full-time freshmen had no need and received non-need-based gift aid.
UNDERGRADUATE FINANCIAL AID (Fall 2016, est.) 94 applied for aid; of those 74% were deemed to have need. 100% of undergraduates with need received aid. **Average percent of need met:** 35% (excluding resources awarded to replace EFC). **Average financial aid package:** $14,600 (excluding resources awarded to replace EFC). 57% of all full-time undergraduates had no need and received non-need-based gift aid.
GIFT AID (NEED-BASED) Total amount: $561,848 (100% institutional). **Receiving aid:** Freshmen: 29% (15); all full-time undergraduates: 29% (70). **Average award:** Freshmen: $7000; Undergraduates: $7000. **Scholarships, grants, and awards:** private, college/university gift aid from institutional funds.
GIFT AID (NON-NEED-BASED) Total amount: $2,187,707 (97% institutional, 3% external sources). **Receiving aid:** Freshmen: 25% (13). Undergraduates: 24% (60). **Average award:** Freshmen: $9100. Undergraduates: $9100. **Scholarships, grants, and awards by category:** Academic interests/achievement: general academic interests/achievements. Creative arts/performance: debating, journalism/publications, music. Special achievements/activities: community service, leadership, memberships, religious involvement. Special characteristics: children of faculty/staff, children of public servants, public servants, relatives of clergy, veterans. **Tuition waivers:** Full or partial for employees or children of employees.
LOANS Student loans: $1,392,461 (100% need-based). 35% of past graduating class borrowed through all loan programs. **Average indebtedness per student:** $44,000. **Programs:** private loans.
APPLYING FOR FINANCIAL AID Required financial aid form: CSS Financial Aid PROFILE. **Financial aid deadline:** 6/15 (priority: 3/15). **Notification date:** Continuous beginning 3/1. Students must reply within 4 weeks of notification.
CONTACT Mr. William K. Kellaris, Director of Financial Aid, Patrick Henry College, 10 Patrick Henry Circle, Purcellville, VA 20132, 540-441-8140 or toll-free 888-338-1776. Fax: 540-441-8149. E-mail: financialaid@phc.edu.
Website: http://www.phc.edu/.

PATTEN UNIVERSITY
Oakland, CA

CONTACT Mr. Robert A. Olivera, Dean of Enrollment Services, Patten University, 2433 Coolidge Avenue, Oakland, CA 94601-2699, 510-261-8500 Ext. 783 or toll-free 877-4PATTEN. Fax: 510-534-8969. E-mail: oliverob@patten.edu.
Website: http://patten.edu/.

PAUL QUINN COLLEGE
Dallas, TX

Tuition & fees: N/R	Average undergraduate aid package: $7988

ABOUT THE INSTITUTION Independent African Methodist Episcopal, coed. 9 undergraduate majors. Federal methodology is used as a basis for awarding need-based institutional aid.
FRESHMAN FINANCIAL AID (Fall 2016, est.) 150 applied for aid; of those 100% were deemed to have need. 100% of freshmen with need received aid; of those 100% had need fully met. **Average percent of need met:** 97% (excluding resources awarded to replace EFC). **Average financial aid package:** $7988 (excluding resources awarded to replace EFC).
UNDERGRADUATE FINANCIAL AID (Fall 2016, est.) 435 applied for aid; of those 100% were deemed to have need. 100% of undergraduates with need received aid; of those 100% had need fully met. **Average percent of need met:** 86% (excluding resources awarded to replace EFC). **Average financial aid package:** $7988 (excluding resources awarded to replace EFC).
GIFT AID (NEED-BASED) Total amount: $2,402,271 (85% federal, 13% state, 2% external sources). **Receiving aid:** Freshmen: 100% (150); all full-time undergraduates: 74% (435). **Average award:** Freshmen: $4515; Undergraduates: $4515. **Scholarships, grants, and awards:** Federal Pell, FSEOG, state, private, college/university gift aid from institutional funds, United Negro College Fund.
GIFT AID (NON-NEED-BASED) Total amount: $1,236,098 (95% institutional, 5% external sources). **Receiving aid:** Freshmen: 15% (22). Undergraduates: 3% (20).

Scholarships, grants, and awards by category: Creative arts/performance: music, performing arts. Special characteristics: first-generation college students, local/state students.
LOANS Student loans: $2,123,581 (57% need-based, 43% non-need-based). 37% of past graduating class borrowed through all loan programs. **Average indebtedness per student:** $6102. **Average need-based loan:** Freshmen: $3473. Undergraduates: $3473. **Parent loans:** $53,206 (100% non-need-based). **Programs:** Federal Direct (Subsidized and Unsubsidized Stafford, PLUS), alternative loans.
WORK-STUDY Federal work-study: Total amount: $200,000; 100 jobs averaging $2000. **State or other work-study/employment:** 204 part-time jobs averaging $5000.
ATHLETIC AWARDS Total amount: $33,465 (100% non-need-based).
APPLYING FOR FINANCIAL AID Required financial aid form: FAFSA. **Financial aid deadline:** 6/15 (priority: 4/1). **Notification date:** 2/1. Students must reply within 4 weeks of notification.
CONTACT Mildred Martinez, Financial Aid Officer I, Paul Quinn College, 3837 Simpson Stuart Road, Dallas, TX 75241, 214-379-5438 or toll-free 877-346-1063. Fax: 214-379-5448. E-mail: mmartinez@pqc.edu.
Website: http://www.pqc.edu/.

PAUL SMITH'S COLLEGE
Paul Smiths, NY

Tuition & fees: $25,210	Average undergraduate aid package: N/A

ABOUT THE INSTITUTION Independent, coed. 12 undergraduate majors. Federal methodology is used as a basis for awarding need-based institutional aid.
UNDERGRADUATE EXPENSES for 2016–2017 Comprehensive fee: $36,500 includes full-time tuition ($24,210), mandatory fees ($1000), and room and board ($11,290). **College room only:** $6020.
FRESHMAN FINANCIAL AID (Fall 2016, est.) 239 applied for aid; of those 100% were deemed to have need. 100% of freshmen with need received aid.
UNDERGRADUATE FINANCIAL AID (Fall 2016, est.) 848 applied for aid; of those 100% were deemed to have need. 100% of undergraduates with need received aid.
GIFT AID (NEED-BASED) Total amount: $14,814,947 (18% federal, 9% state, 70% institutional, 3% external sources). **Receiving aid:** Freshmen: 95% (228); all full-time undergraduates: 50% (428). **Scholarships, grants, and awards:** Federal Pell, FSEOG, state, private, college/university gift aid from institutional funds.
GIFT AID (NON-NEED-BASED) Scholarships, grants, and awards by category: Academic interests/achievement: 843 awards ($10,488,402 total): general academic interests/achievements, social sciences. Special achievements/activities: leadership, memberships. Special characteristics: 17 awards ($48,720 total): veterans, veterans' children.
LOANS Student loans: $7,458,742 (100% need-based). 91% of past graduating class borrowed through all loan programs. **Average indebtedness per student:** $16,175. **Parent loans:** $2,891,570 (100% need-based). **Programs:** Federal Direct (Subsidized and Unsubsidized Stafford, PLUS), Perkins.
WORK-STUDY Federal work-study: Total amount: $101,282; jobs available. **State or other work-study/employment:** Total amount: $1,595,101 (100% need-based). Part-time jobs available.
APPLYING FOR FINANCIAL AID Required financial aid forms: FAFSA, state aid form. **Financial aid deadline (priority):** 3/15. **Notification date:** Continuous. Students must reply within 4 weeks of notification.
CONTACT Mary Ellen Chamberlain, Director of Financial Aid, Paul Smith's College, Routes 86 and 30, Paul Smiths, NY 12970, 518-327-6119 or toll-free 800-421-2605. Fax: 518-327-6055. E-mail: mchamberlain@paulsmiths.edu.
Website: http://www.paulsmiths.edu/.

PEABODY CONSERVATORY OF THE JOHNS HOPKINS UNIVERSITY
Baltimore, MD

Tuition & fees: $44,872	Average undergraduate aid package: $7933

ABOUT THE INSTITUTION Independent, coed. 10 undergraduate majors. Federal methodology is used as a basis for awarding need-based institutional aid.

UNDERGRADUATE EXPENSES for 2016–2017 *One-time required fee:* $700. *Comprehensive fee:* $59,994 includes full-time tuition ($44,122), mandatory fees ($750), and room and board ($15,122). Full-time tuition and fees vary according to program. Room and board charges vary according to board plan. *Part-time tuition:* $1258 per semester hour. Part-time tuition and fees vary according to course load.

FRESHMAN FINANCIAL AID (Fall 2016, est.) 36 applied for aid; of those 78% were deemed to have need. 100% of freshmen with need received aid; of those 46% had need fully met. *Average percent of need met:* 46% (excluding resources awarded to replace EFC). *Average financial aid package:* $8164 (excluding resources awarded to replace EFC). 13% of all full-time freshmen had no need and received non-need-based gift aid.

UNDERGRADUATE FINANCIAL AID (Fall 2016, est.) 246 applied for aid; of those 50% were deemed to have need. 100% of undergraduates with need received aid; of those 59% had need fully met. *Average percent of need met:* 59% (excluding resources awarded to replace EFC). *Average financial aid package:* $7933 (excluding resources awarded to replace EFC). 6% of all full-time undergraduates had no need and received non-need-based gift aid.

GIFT AID (NEED-BASED) *Receiving aid:* Freshmen: 28% (18); all full-time undergraduates: 29% (85). *Average award:* Freshmen: $9963; Undergraduates: $8586. *Scholarships, grants, and awards:* Federal Pell, FSEOG, state, private, college/university gift aid from institutional funds.

GIFT AID (NON-NEED-BASED) *Receiving aid:* Freshmen: 36% (23). Undergraduates: 30% (88). *Average award:* Freshmen: $16,426. Undergraduates: $12,846. *Scholarships, grants, and awards by category:* Creative arts/performance: music.

LOANS *Student loans:* 32% of past graduating class borrowed through all loan programs. *Average indebtedness per student:* $20,730. *Average need-based loan:* Freshmen: $4618. Undergraduates: $6631. *Programs:* Federal Direct (Subsidized and Unsubsidized Stafford, PLUS), Perkins, college/university.

WORK-STUDY Federal work-study jobs available.

APPLYING FOR FINANCIAL AID *Required financial aid form:* FAFSA. *Financial aid deadline (priority):* 3/1. *Notification date:* 4/1. Students must reply by 5/1.

CONTACT Rebecca Polgar, Director of Financial Aid, Peabody Conservatory of The Johns Hopkins University, 1 East Mount Vernon Place, Baltimore, MD 21202-2397, 667-208-6590 or toll-free 800-368-2521 (out-of-state). *Fax:* 410-659-8102. *E-mail:* finaid@peabody.jhu.edu. *Website:* http://www.peabody.jhu.edu/.

PEIRCE COLLEGE
Philadelphia, PA

Tuition & fees: $14,472	Average undergraduate aid package: $12,116

ABOUT THE INSTITUTION Independent, coed, primarily women. *Awards:* certificates, associate, bachelor's, and master's degrees. 10 undergraduate majors. *Total enrollment:* 1,563. Undergraduates: 1,491. Freshmen: 64. Federal methodology is used as a basis for awarding need-based institutional aid.

UNDERGRADUATE EXPENSES for 2016–2017 *Application fee:* $50. *Tuition:* full-time $13,872; part-time $578 per credit. Full-time tuition and fees vary according to course load and reciprocity agreements. Part-time tuition and fees vary according to course load and reciprocity agreements.

FRESHMAN FINANCIAL AID (Fall 2015) 18 applied for aid; of those 100% were deemed to have need. 100% of freshmen with need received aid. *Average percent of need met:* 56% (excluding resources awarded to replace EFC). *Average financial aid package:* $11,202 (excluding resources awarded to replace EFC).

UNDERGRADUATE FINANCIAL AID (Fall 2015) 286 applied for aid; of those 98% were deemed to have need. 99% of undergraduates with need received aid; of those 4% had need fully met. *Average percent of need met:* 63% (excluding resources awarded to replace EFC). *Average financial aid package:* $12,116 (excluding resources awarded to replace EFC). 3% of all full-time undergraduates had no need and received non-need-based gift aid.

GIFT AID (NEED-BASED) *Total amount:* $6,677,650 (50% federal, 21% state, 28% institutional, 1% external sources). *Receiving aid:* Freshmen: 94% (17); all full-time undergraduates: 88% (266). *Average award:* Freshmen: $10,193; Undergraduates: $7911. *Scholarships, grants, and awards:* Federal Pell, FSEOG, state, private, college/university gift aid from institutional funds.

GIFT AID (NON-NEED-BASED) *Total amount:* $164,445 (100% institutional). *Receiving aid:* Freshmen: 39% (7). Undergraduates: 44% (135). *Average award:* Undergraduates: $4457. *Scholarships, grants, and awards by category:* Academic interests/achievement: business, computer science, general academic interests/achievements, health fields. *Special achievements/activities:* leadership, memberships. *Special characteristics:* children and siblings of alumni, children of faculty/staff, children of public servants, international students, public servants, siblings of current students, veterans, veterans' children. *Tuition waivers:* Full or partial for children of alumni, employees or children of employees.

LOANS *Student loans:* $11,257,722 (92% need-based, 8% non-need-based). *Average need-based loan:* Freshmen: $2350. Undergraduates: $4250. *Parent loans:* $245,735 (100% need-based). *Programs:* Federal Direct (Subsidized and Unsubsidized Stafford, PLUS).

WORK-STUDY *Federal work-study:* jobs available.

APPLYING FOR FINANCIAL AID *Required financial aid form:* FAFSA. *Financial aid deadline:* Continuous. *Notification date:* Continuous beginning 5/1.

CONTACT Chanel Greene, Manager of Financial Aid, Peirce College, 1420 Pine Street, Philadelphia, PA 19102, 215-670-9330 or toll-free 888-467-3472. *Fax:* 215-545-3671. *E-mail:* cgreen1@peirce.edu. *Website:* http://www.peirce.edu/.

PENN STATE ABINGTON
Abington, PA

Tuition & fees (PA res): $14,172	Average undergraduate aid package: $10,520

ABOUT THE INSTITUTION State-related, coed. *Awards:* certificates, associate, and bachelor's degrees (enrollment figures include students enrolled at The Graduate School at Penn State who are taking courses at this location). 118 undergraduate majors. *Total enrollment:* 3,951. Undergraduates: 3,950. Freshmen: 892. Federal methodology is used as a basis for awarding need-based institutional aid.

UNDERGRADUATE EXPENSES for 2016–2017 *Application fee:* $65. *Tuition, state resident:* full-time $13,212; part-time $543 per credit hour. *Tuition, nonresident:* full-time $20,782; part-time $866 per credit hour. *Required fees:* full-time $960. Full-time tuition and fees vary according to course level, degree level, location, program, and student level. Part-time tuition and fees vary according to course level, course load, degree level, location, program, and student level.

FRESHMAN FINANCIAL AID (Fall 2015) 725 applied for aid; of those 84% were deemed to have need. 98% of freshmen with need received aid; of those 4% had need fully met. *Average percent of need met:* 60% (excluding resources awarded to replace EFC). *Average financial aid package:* $10,608 (excluding resources awarded to replace EFC). 7% of all full-time freshmen had no need and received non-need-based gift aid.

UNDERGRADUATE FINANCIAL AID (Fall 2015) 2,526 applied for aid; of those 87% were deemed to have need. 98% of undergraduates with need received aid; of those 3% had need fully met. *Average percent of need met:* 59% (excluding resources awarded to replace EFC). *Average financial aid package:* $10,520 (excluding resources awarded to replace EFC). 5% of all full-time undergraduates had no need and received non-need-based gift aid.

GIFT AID (NEED-BASED) *Total amount:* $15,735,060 (50% federal, 29% state, 19% institutional, 2% external sources). *Receiving aid:* Freshmen: 56% (480); all full-time undergraduates: 55% (1,695). *Average award:* Freshmen: $8148; Undergraduates: $7588. *Scholarships, grants, and awards:* Federal Pell, FSEOG, state, private, college/university gift aid from institutional funds.

GIFT AID (NON-NEED-BASED) *Total amount:* $1,152,377 (30% federal, 1% state, 51% institutional, 18% external sources). *Receiving aid:* Freshmen: 27% (231). Undergraduates: 18% (544). *Average award:* Freshmen: $4288. Undergraduates: $3591. *Scholarships, grants, and awards by category:* Academic interests/achievement: general academic interests/achievements. *Special characteristics:* children and siblings of alumni, general special characteristics. *Tuition waivers:* Full or partial for employees or children of employees, senior citizens. *ROTC:* Army cooperative, Air Force cooperative.

LOANS *Student loans:* $17,617,655 (86% need-based, 14% non-need-based). 76% of past graduating class borrowed through all loan programs. *Average indebtedness per student:* $35,758. *Average need-based loan:* Freshmen: $3259. Undergraduates: $4125. *Parent loans:* $2,466,923 (80% need-based, 20% non-need-based). *Programs:* Federal Direct (Subsidized and Unsubsidized Stafford, PLUS), Perkins, college/university, private loans.

WORK-STUDY *Federal work-study:* jobs available.

APPLYING FOR FINANCIAL AID *Required financial aid form:* FAFSA. *Financial aid deadline (priority):* 2/15. *Notification date:* Continuous.

CONTACT Student Aid Office, Penn State Abington, 1600 Woodland Road, Abington, PA 19001-3990, 215-881-7348. *Fax:* 215-881-7655. *Website:* http://www.abington.psu.edu/.

PENN STATE ALTOONA
Altoona, PA

Tuition & fees (PA res): $14,828	Average undergraduate aid package: $10,460

ABOUT THE INSTITUTION State-related, coed. *Awards:* certificates, associate, and bachelor's degrees (enrollment figures include students enrolled at The Graduate School at Penn State who are taking courses at this location). 125 undergraduate majors. *Total enrollment:* 3,491. Undergraduates: 3,491. Freshmen: 1,203. Federal methodology is used as a basis for awarding need-based institutional aid.

UNDERGRADUATE EXPENSES for 2016–2017 *Application fee:* $65. *Tuition, state resident:* full-time $13,868; part-time $578 per credit hour. *Tuition, nonresident:* full-time $21,874; part-time $911 per credit hour. *Required fees:* full-time $960. Full-time tuition and fees vary according to course level, degree level, location, program, and student level. Part-time tuition and fees vary according to course level, course load, degree level, location, program, and student level. *College room and board:* $11,860; *Room only:* $5940. Room and board charges vary according to board plan, housing facility, and location.

FRESHMAN FINANCIAL AID (Fall 2015) 1,143 applied for aid; of those 80% were deemed to have need. 97% of freshmen with need received aid; of those 4% had need fully met. *Average percent of need met:* 58% (excluding resources awarded to replace EFC). *Average financial aid package:* $9690 (excluding resources awarded to replace EFC). 7% of all full-time freshmen had no need and received non-need-based gift aid.

UNDERGRADUATE FINANCIAL AID (Fall 2015) 2,910 applied for aid; of those 84% were deemed to have need. 98% of undergraduates with need received aid; of those 5% had need fully met. *Average percent of need met:* 59% (excluding resources awarded to replace EFC). *Average financial aid package:* $10,460 (excluding resources awarded to replace EFC). 8% of all full-time undergraduates had no need and received non-need-based gift aid.

GIFT AID (NEED-BASED) *Total amount:* $14,396,384 (43% federal, 25% state, 26% institutional, 6% external sources). *Receiving aid:* Freshmen: 40% (546); all full-time undergraduates: 41% (1,512). *Average award:* Freshmen: $6906; Undergraduates: $6704. *Scholarships, grants, and awards:* Federal Pell, FSEOG, state, private, college/university gift aid from institutional funds.

GIFT AID (NON-NEED-BASED) *Total amount:* $1,867,585 (23% federal, 1% state, 46% institutional, 30% external sources). *Receiving aid:* Freshmen: 27% (376). Undergraduates: 26% (956). *Average award:* Freshmen: $3251. Undergraduates: $3096. *Scholarships, grants, and awards by category:* Academic interests/achievement: general academic interests/achievements. *Special characteristics:* children and siblings of alumni, general special characteristics. *Tuition waivers:* Full or partial for employees or children of employees, senior citizens. *ROTC:* Army, Air Force.

LOANS *Student loans:* $25,747,211 (85% need-based, 15% non-need-based). 78% of past graduating class borrowed through all loan programs. *Average indebtedness per student:* $41,435. *Average need-based loan:* Freshmen: $3403. Undergrad-

uates: $4042. *Parent loans:* $8,666,525 (89% need-based, 11% non-need-based). *Programs:* Federal Direct (Subsidized and Unsubsidized Stafford, PLUS), Perkins, college/university, private loans.

WORK-STUDY *Federal work-study:* jobs available.

APPLYING FOR FINANCIAL AID *Required financial aid form:* FAFSA. *Financial aid deadline (priority):* 2/15. *Notification date:* Continuous beginning 3/1.

CONTACT Mr. David Pearlman, Director of Student Aid, Penn State Altoona, W113 Smith Building, Altoona, PA 16601-3760, 814-949-5055 or toll-free 800-848-9843. *Fax:* 814-949-5536. *E-mail:* dpp1@psu.edu. *Website:* http://www.altoona.psu.edu/.

PENN STATE BEAVER
Monaca, PA

Tuition & fees (PA res): $13,678	Average undergraduate aid package: $11,692

ABOUT THE INSTITUTION State-related, coed. *Awards:* certificates and bachelor's degrees. 118 undergraduate majors. *Total enrollment:* 726. Undergraduates: 726. Freshmen: 231. Federal methodology is used as a basis for awarding need-based institutional aid.

UNDERGRADUATE EXPENSES for 2016–2017 *Application fee:* $65. *Tuition, state resident:* full-time $12,718; part-time $524 per credit hour. *Tuition, nonresident:* full-time $19,598; part-time $817 per credit hour. *Required fees:* full-time $960. Full-time tuition and fees vary according to course level, degree level, location, program, and student level. Part-time tuition and fees vary according to course level, course load, degree level, location, program, and student level. *College room and board:* $11,860; *Room only:* $5940. Room and board charges vary according to board plan, housing facility, and location.

FRESHMAN FINANCIAL AID (Fall 2015) 190 applied for aid; of those 76% were deemed to have need. 99% of freshmen with need received aid; of those 6% had need fully met. *Average percent of need met:* 65% (excluding resources awarded to replace EFC). *Average financial aid package:* $11,002 (excluding resources awarded to replace EFC). 18% of all full-time freshmen had no need and received non-need-based gift aid.

UNDERGRADUATE FINANCIAL AID (Fall 2015) 534 applied for aid; of those 82% were deemed to have need. 100% of undergraduates with need received aid; of those 5% had need fully met. *Average percent of need met:* 66% (excluding resources awarded to replace EFC). *Average financial aid package:* $11,692 (excluding resources awarded to replace EFC). 12% of all full-time undergraduates had no need and received non-need-based gift aid.

GIFT AID (NEED-BASED) *Total amount:* $3,353,881 (39% federal, 26% state, 28% institutional, 7% external sources). *Receiving aid:* Freshmen: 47% (99); all full-time undergraduates: 51% (313). *Average award:* Freshmen: $7497; Undergraduates: $7378. *Scholarships, grants, and awards:* Federal Pell, FSEOG, state, private, college/university gift aid from institutional funds.

GIFT AID (NON-NEED-BASED) *Total amount:* $322,606 (24% federal, 1% state, 67% institutional, 8% external sources). *Receiving aid:* Freshmen: 41% (85). Undergraduates: 37% (225). *Average award:* Freshmen: $3476. Undergraduates: $2886. *Scholarships, grants, and awards by category:* Academic interests/achievement: general academic interests/achievements. *Special characteristics:* children and siblings of alumni. *Tuition waivers:* Full or partial for employees or children of employees, senior citizens.

LOANS *Student loans:* $3,615,592 (88% need-based, 12% non-need-based). 81% of past graduating class borrowed through all loan programs. *Average indebtedness per student:* $32,739. *Average need-based loan:* Freshmen: $3483. Undergraduates: $4201. *Parent loans:* $1,338,113 (80% need-based, 20% non-need-based). *Programs:* Federal Direct (Subsidized and Unsubsidized Stafford, PLUS), Perkins, college/university, private loans.

WORK-STUDY *Federal work-study:* jobs available. *State or other work-study/employment:* Part-time jobs available.

APPLYING FOR FINANCIAL AID *Required financial aid form:* FAFSA. *Financial aid deadline (priority):* 2/15. *Notification date:* Continuous beginning 3/1.

CONTACT Gail Gray, Student Aid and Veterans Coordinator, Penn State Beaver, 113 Student Union Building, 100 University Drive, Monaca, PA 15061, 724-773-3803. *E-mail:* gailgray@psu.edu.
Website: http://www.br.psu.edu/.

PENN STATE BERKS
Reading, PA

Tuition & fees (PA res): $14,828	Average undergraduate aid package: $10,537

ABOUT THE INSTITUTION State-related, coed. *Awards:* certificates, associate, and bachelor's degrees (enrollment figures include students enrolled at The Graduate School at Penn State who are taking courses at this location). 129 undergraduate majors. *Total enrollment:* 2,888. Undergraduates: 2,888. Freshmen: 738. Federal methodology is used as a basis for awarding need-based institutional aid.

UNDERGRADUATE EXPENSES for 2016–2017 *Application fee:* $65. *Tuition, state resident:* full-time $13,868; part-time $578 per credit hour. *Tuition, nonresident:* full-time $21,874; part-time $911 per credit hour. *Required fees:* full-time $960. Full-time tuition and fees vary according to course level, degree level, location, program, and student level. Part-time tuition and fees vary according to course level, course load, degree level, location, program, and student level. *College room and board:* $12,940; *Room only:* $7020. Room and board charges vary according to board plan, housing facility, and location.

FRESHMAN FINANCIAL AID (Fall 2015) 699 applied for aid; of those 80% were deemed to have need. 98% of freshmen with need received aid; of those 4% had need fully met. *Average percent of need met:* 58% (excluding resources awarded to replace EFC). *Average financial aid package:* $9828 (excluding resources awarded to replace EFC). 6% of all full-time freshmen had no need and received non-need-based gift aid.

UNDERGRADUATE FINANCIAL AID (Fall 2015) 2,173 applied for aid; of those 83% were deemed to have need. 98% of undergraduates with need received aid; of those 5% had need fully met. *Average percent of need met:* 60% (excluding resources awarded to replace EFC). *Average financial aid package:* $10,537 (excluding resources awarded to replace EFC). 6% of all full-time undergraduates had no need and received non-need-based gift aid.

GIFT AID (NEED-BASED) *Total amount:* $11,702,127 (44% federal, 28% state, 23% institutional, 5% external sources). *Receiving aid:* Freshmen: 46% (358); all full-time undergraduates: 48% (1,229). *Average award:* Freshmen: $7280; Undergraduates: $7087. *Scholarships, grants, and awards:* Federal Pell, FSEOG, state, private, college/university gift aid from institutional funds.

GIFT AID (NON-NEED-BASED) *Total amount:* $932,239 (44% federal, 2% state, 41% institutional, 13% external sources). *Receiving aid:* Freshmen: 27% (212). Undergraduates: 22% (563). *Average award:* Freshmen: $2826. Undergraduates: $2378. *Scholarships, grants, and awards by category: Academic interests/achievement:* general academic interests/achievements. *Special characteristics:* children and siblings of alumni. *Tuition waivers:* Full or partial for employees or children of employees, senior citizens. *ROTC:* Army cooperative.

LOANS *Student loans:* $18,426,378 (85% need-based, 15% non-need-based). 76% of past graduating class borrowed through all loan programs. *Average indebtedness per student:* $38,227. *Average need-based loan:* Freshmen: $3390. Undergraduates: $4241. *Parent loans:* $6,320,585 (89% need-based, 11% non-need-based). *Programs:* Federal Direct (Subsidized and Unsubsidized Stafford, PLUS), Perkins, college/university, private loans.

WORK-STUDY *Federal work-study:* jobs available.

APPLYING FOR FINANCIAL AID *Required financial aid form:* FAFSA. *Financial aid deadline (priority):* 2/15. *Notification date:* Continuous beginning 3/1.

CONTACT Judith A. Rile, Financial Aid Coordinator, Penn State Berks, Perkins Student Center, Room 6, Reading, PA 19610-6009, 610-396-6070. *Fax:* 610-396-6316. *E-mail:* jar38@psu.edu.
Website: http://www.bk.psu.edu/.

PENN STATE BRANDYWINE
Media, PA

Tuition & fees (PA res): $14,134	Average undergraduate aid package: $10,682

ABOUT THE INSTITUTION State-related, coed. *Awards:* certificates, associate, and bachelor's degrees. 120 undergraduate majors. *Total enrollment:* 1,379. Undergraduates: 1,379. Freshmen: 331. Federal methodology is used as a basis for awarding need-based institutional aid.

UNDERGRADUATE EXPENSES for 2016–2017 *Application fee:* $65. *Tuition, state resident:* full-time $13,174; part-time $542 per credit hour. *Tuition, nonresident:* full-time $20,608; part-time $859 per credit hour. *Required fees:* full-time $960. Full-time tuition and fees vary according to course level, degree level, location, program, and student level. Part-time tuition and fees vary according to course level, course load, degree level, location, program, and student level.

FRESHMAN FINANCIAL AID (Fall 2015) 330 applied for aid; of those 75% were deemed to have need. 97% of freshmen with need received aid; of those 5% had need fully met. *Average percent of need met:* 62% (excluding resources awarded to replace EFC). *Average financial aid package:* $10,170 (excluding resources awarded to replace EFC). 15% of all full-time freshmen had no need and received non-need-based gift aid.

UNDERGRADUATE FINANCIAL AID (Fall 2015) 984 applied for aid; of those 77% were deemed to have need. 98% of undergraduates with need received aid; of those 6% had need fully met. *Average percent of need met:* 63% (excluding resources awarded to replace EFC). *Average financial aid package:* $10,682 (excluding resources awarded to replace EFC). 10% of all full-time undergraduates had no need and received non-need-based gift aid.

GIFT AID (NEED-BASED) *Total amount:* $5,646,851 (44% federal, 27% state, 26% institutional, 3% external sources). *Receiving aid:* Freshmen: 48% (176); all full-time undergraduates: 48% (567). *Average award:* Freshmen: $7384; Undergraduates: $7185. *Scholarships, grants, and awards:* Federal Pell, FSEOG, state, private, college/university gift aid from institutional funds.

GIFT AID (NON-NEED-BASED) *Total amount:* $829,313 (23% federal, 1% state, 56% institutional, 20% external sources). *Receiving aid:* Freshmen: 28% (103). Undergraduates: 22% (254). *Average award:* Freshmen: $4095. Undergraduates: $3796. *Scholarships, grants, and awards by category: Academic interests/achievement:* general academic interests/achievements. *Special characteristics:* children and siblings of alumni. *Tuition waivers:* Full or partial for employees or children of employees, senior citizens. *ROTC:* Army cooperative, Air Force cooperative.

LOANS *Student loans:* $6,408,026 (82% need-based, 18% non-need-based). 78% of past graduating class borrowed through all loan programs. *Average indebtedness per student:* $32,742. *Average need-based loan:* Freshmen: $3104. Undergraduates: $3961. *Parent loans:* $1,265,079 (70% need-based, 30% non-need-based). *Programs:* Federal Direct (Subsidized and Unsubsidized Stafford, PLUS), Perkins, college/university, private loans.

WORK-STUDY *Federal work-study:* jobs available. *State or other work-study/employment:* Part-time jobs available.

APPLYING FOR FINANCIAL AID *Required financial aid form:* FAFSA. *Financial aid deadline (priority):* 2/15. *Notification date:* Continuous beginning 3/1.

CONTACT Student Financial Aid Office, Penn State Brandywine, 105 Main Building, 25 Yearsley Mill Road, Media, PA 19063, 610-892-1260. *E-mail:* bw-financial@psu.edu.
Website: http://www.brandywine.psu.edu/.

PENN STATE ERIE, THE BEHREND COLLEGE
Erie, PA

Tuition & fees (PA res): $14,828	Average undergraduate aid package: $11,015

ABOUT THE INSTITUTION State-related, coed. *Awards:* certificates, associate, bachelor's, and master's degrees. 129 undergraduate majors. *Total enrollment:*

4,566. Undergraduates: 4,420. Freshmen: 1,166. Federal methodology is used as a basis for awarding need-based institutional aid.

UNDERGRADUATE EXPENSES for 2016–2017 *Application fee:* $65. *Tuition, state resident:* full-time $13,868; part-time $578 per credit hour. *Tuition, nonresident:* full-time $21,874; part-time $911 per credit hour. *Required fees:* full-time $960. Full-time tuition and fees vary according to course level, degree level, location, program, and student level. Part-time tuition and fees vary according to course level, course load, degree level, location, program, and student level. *College room and board:* $11,860; *Room only:* $5940. Room and board charges vary according to board plan, housing facility, and location.

FRESHMAN FINANCIAL AID (Fall 2015) 972 applied for aid; of those 82% were deemed to have need. 97% of freshmen with need received aid; of those 4% had need fully met. *Average percent of need met:* 62% (excluding resources awarded to replace EFC). *Average financial aid package:* $10,712 (excluding resources awarded to replace EFC). 4% of all full-time freshmen had no need and received non-need-based gift aid.

UNDERGRADUATE FINANCIAL AID (Fall 2015) 3,132 applied for aid; of those 85% were deemed to have need. 98% of undergraduates with need received aid; of those 5% had need fully met. *Average percent of need met:* 61% (excluding resources awarded to replace EFC). *Average financial aid package:* $11,015 (excluding resources awarded to replace EFC). 6% of all full-time undergraduates had no need and received non-need-based gift aid.

GIFT AID (NEED-BASED) *Total amount:* $17,844,496 (36% federal, 25% state, 30% institutional, 9% external sources). *Receiving aid:* Freshmen: 44% (511); all full-time undergraduates: 43% (1,683). *Average award:* Freshmen: $7493; Undergraduates: $7241. *Scholarships, grants, and awards:* Federal Pell, FSEOG, state, private, college/university gift aid from institutional funds.

GIFT AID (NON-NEED-BASED) *Total amount:* $2,000,763 (12% federal, 40% institutional, 48% external sources). *Receiving aid:* Freshmen: 33% (390). Undergraduates: 27% (1,056). *Average award:* Freshmen: $3408. Undergraduates: $3368. *Scholarships, grants, and awards by category:* Academic interests/achievement: general academic interests/achievements. *Special characteristics:* children and siblings of alumni. *Tuition waivers:* Full or partial for employees or children of employees, senior citizens. *ROTC:* Army.

LOANS *Student loans:* $28,219,997 (89% need-based, 11% non-need-based). 75% of past graduating class borrowed through all loan programs. *Average indebtedness per student:* $39,209. *Average need-based loan:* Freshmen: $3518. Undergraduates: $4381. *Parent loans:* $8,655,861 (90% need-based, 10% non-need-based). *Programs:* Federal Direct (Subsidized and Unsubsidized Stafford, PLUS), Perkins, college/university, private loans.

WORK-STUDY *Federal work-study:* jobs available.

APPLYING FOR FINANCIAL AID *Required financial aid form:* FAFSA. *Financial aid deadline (priority):* 2/15. *Notification date:* Continuous beginning 3/1.

CONTACT Ms. Jane Brady, Associate Director of Financial Aid, Penn State Erie, The Behrend College, 4851 College Drive, Metzgar Admissions and Alumni Center, Erie, PA 16563, 814-898-6162 or toll-free 866-374-3378. *Fax:* 814-898-7595. *E-mail:* jub9@psu.edu.
Website: http://www.psbehrend.psu.edu/.

PENN STATE GREATER ALLEGHENY
McKeesport, PA

Tuition & fees (PA res): $13,666	Average undergraduate aid package: $12,576

ABOUT THE INSTITUTION State-related, coed. *Awards:* certificates, associate, bachelor's, and master's degrees. 119 undergraduate majors. *Total enrollment:* 550. Undergraduates: 550. Freshmen: 158. Federal methodology is used as a basis for awarding need-based institutional aid.

UNDERGRADUATE EXPENSES for 2016–2017 *Application fee:* $65. *Tuition, state resident:* full-time $12,718; part-time $524 per credit hour. *Tuition, nonresident:* full-time $19,598; part-time $817 per credit hour. *Required fees:* full-time $948. Full-time tuition and fees vary according to course level, degree level, location, program, and student level. Part-time tuition and fees vary according to course level, course load, degree level, location, program, and student level. *College room and board:* $11,860; *Room only:* $5940. Room and board charges vary according to board plan, housing facility, and location.

FRESHMAN FINANCIAL AID (Fall 2015) 148 applied for aid; of those 83% were deemed to have need. 100% of freshmen with need received aid; of those 5% had need fully met. *Average percent of need met:* 68% (excluding resources awarded to replace EFC). *Average financial aid package:* $13,390 (excluding resources awarded to replace EFC). 9% of all full-time freshmen had no need and received non-need-based gift aid.

UNDERGRADUATE FINANCIAL AID (Fall 2015) 447 applied for aid; of those 88% were deemed to have need. 99% of undergraduates with need received aid; of those 6% had need fully met. *Average percent of need met:* 67% (excluding resources awarded to replace EFC). *Average financial aid package:* $12,576 (excluding resources awarded to replace EFC). 6% of all full-time undergraduates had no need and received non-need-based gift aid.

GIFT AID (NEED-BASED) *Total amount:* $3,558,419 (38% federal, 26% state, 21% institutional, 15% external sources). *Receiving aid:* Freshmen: 68% (108); all full-time undergraduates: 65% (318). *Average award:* Freshmen: $8142; Undergraduates: $7570. *Scholarships, grants, and awards:* Federal Pell, FSEOG, state, private, college/university gift aid from institutional funds.

GIFT AID (NON-NEED-BASED) *Total amount:* $171,299 (13% federal, 60% institutional, 27% external sources). *Receiving aid:* Freshmen: 43% (68). Undergraduates: 37% (180). *Average award:* Freshmen: $3408. Undergraduates: $3332. *Tuition waivers:* Full or partial for employees or children of employees, senior citizens.

LOANS *Student loans:* $3,139,739 (91% need-based, 9% non-need-based). 80% of past graduating class borrowed through all loan programs. *Average indebtedness per student:* $42,291. *Average need-based loan:* Freshmen: $3274. Undergraduates: $3983. *Parent loans:* $773,778 (87% need-based, 13% non-need-based). *Programs:* Federal Direct (Subsidized and Unsubsidized Stafford, PLUS), Perkins, college/university, private loans.

WORK-STUDY *Federal work-study:* jobs available. *State or other work-study/employment:* Part-time jobs available.

APPLYING FOR FINANCIAL AID *Required financial aid form:* FAFSA. *Financial aid deadline (priority):* 2/15. *Notification date:* Continuous beginning 3/1.

CONTACT Student Aid Office, Penn State Greater Allegheny, 4000 University Drive, McKeesport, PA 15132-7698, 412-675-9160. *Fax:* 412-675-9036. *Website:* http://www.ga.psu.edu/.

PENN STATE HARRISBURG
Middletown, PA

Tuition & fees (PA res): $14,828	Average undergraduate aid package: $11,083

ABOUT THE INSTITUTION State-related, coed. *Awards:* certificates, associate, bachelor's, master's, and doctoral degrees. 29 undergraduate majors. *Total enrollment:* 5,046. Undergraduates: 4,200. Freshmen: 1,023. Federal methodology is used as a basis for awarding need-based institutional aid.

UNDERGRADUATE EXPENSES for 2016–2017 *Application fee:* $65. *Tuition, state resident:* full-time $13,868; part-time $578 per credit hour. *Tuition, nonresident:* full-time $21,874; part-time $911 per credit hour. *Required fees:* full-time $960. Full-time tuition and fees vary according to course level, degree level, location, program, and student level. Part-time tuition and fees vary according to course level, course load, degree level, location, program, and student level. *College room and board:* $13,460; *Room only:* $7540. Room and board charges vary according to board plan, housing facility, and location.

FRESHMAN FINANCIAL AID (Fall 2015) 642 applied for aid; of those 83% were deemed to have need. 97% of freshmen with need received aid; of those 6% had need fully met. *Average percent of need met:* 59% (excluding resources awarded to replace EFC). *Average financial aid package:* $10,740 (excluding resources awarded to replace EFC). 10% of all full-time freshmen had no need and received non-need-based gift aid.

UNDERGRADUATE FINANCIAL AID (Fall 2015) 2,592 applied for aid; of those 87% were deemed to have need. 98% of undergraduates with need received aid; of those 6% had need fully met. *Average percent of need met:* 57% (excluding resources awarded to replace EFC). *Average financial aid package:* $11,083 (excluding resources awarded to replace EFC). 9% of all full-time undergraduates had no need and received non-need-based gift aid.

GIFT AID (NEED-BASED) *Total amount:* $15,538,032 (47% federal, 24% state, 24% institutional, 5% external sources). *Receiving aid:* Freshmen: 41% (346); all full-

time undergraduates: 44% (1,486). *Average award:* Freshmen: $7395; Undergraduates: $6886. *Scholarships, grants, and awards:* Federal Pell, FSEOG, state, private, college/university gift aid from institutional funds.

GIFT AID (NON-NEED-BASED) *Total amount:* $2,497,303 (26% federal, 1% state, 27% institutional, 46% external sources). *Receiving aid:* Freshmen: 35% (296). Undergraduates: 29% (994). *Average award:* Freshmen: $2255. Undergraduates: $1997. *Scholarships, grants, and awards by category:* Academic interests/ achievement: general academic interests/achievements. *Special characteristics:* children and siblings of alumni, general special characteristics. *Tuition waivers:* Full or partial for employees or children of employees, senior citizens. *ROTC:* Army cooperative.

LOANS *Student loans:* $23,517,660 (88% need-based, 12% non-need-based). 65% of past graduating class borrowed through all loan programs. *Average indebtedness per student:* $42,149. *Average need-based loan:* Freshmen: $3503. Undergraduates: $4433. *Parent loans:* $7,027,923 (88% need-based, 12% non-need-based). *Programs:* Federal Direct (Subsidized and Unsubsidized Stafford, PLUS), Perkins, college/university, private loans.

WORK-STUDY *Federal work-study:* jobs available.

APPLYING FOR FINANCIAL AID *Required financial aid form:* FAFSA. *Financial aid deadline (priority):* 2/15. *Notification date:* Continuous beginning 3/1.

CONTACT Student Aid Office, Penn State Harrisburg, 777 West Harrisburg Pike, Middletown, PA 17057-4898, 717-948-6307 or toll-free 800-222-2056. *Fax:* 717-948-6008. *E-mail:* hbgfinaid@psu.edu.
Website: http://www.hbg.psu.edu/.

PENN STATE HAZLETON
Hazleton, PA

Tuition & fees (PA res): $14,072	Average undergraduate aid package: $11,533

ABOUT THE INSTITUTION State-related, coed. *Awards:* certificates, associate, and bachelor's degrees. 125 undergraduate majors. *Total enrollment:* 863. Undergraduates: 863. Freshmen: 306. Federal methodology is used as a basis for awarding need-based institutional aid.

UNDERGRADUATE EXPENSES for 2016–2017 *Application fee:* $65. *Tuition, state resident:* full-time $13,174; part-time $542 per credit hour. *Tuition, nonresident:* full-time $20,608; part-time $859 per credit hour. *Required fees:* full-time $898. Full-time tuition and fees vary according to course level, degree level, location, program, and student level. Part-time tuition and fees vary according to course level, course load, degree level, location, program, and student level. *College room and board:* $11,860; *Room only:* $5940. Room and board charges vary according to board plan, housing facility, and location.

FRESHMAN FINANCIAL AID (Fall 2015) 247 applied for aid; of those 88% were deemed to have need. 99% of freshmen with need received aid; of those 3% had need fully met. *Average percent of need met:* 64% (excluding resources awarded to replace EFC). *Average financial aid package:* $11,406 (excluding resources awarded to replace EFC). 9% of all full-time freshmen had no need and received non-need-based gift aid.

UNDERGRADUATE FINANCIAL AID (Fall 2015) 643 applied for aid; of those 90% were deemed to have need. 99% of undergraduates with need received aid; of those 3% had need fully met. *Average percent of need met:* 62% (excluding resources awarded to replace EFC). *Average financial aid package:* $11,533 (excluding resources awarded to replace EFC). 10% of all full-time undergraduates had no need and received non-need-based gift aid.

GIFT AID (NEED-BASED) *Total amount:* $4,620,938 (41% federal, 22% state, 34% institutional, 3% external sources). *Receiving aid:* Freshmen: 64% (168); all full-time undergraduates: 61% (441). *Average award:* Freshmen: $7387; Undergraduates: $7452. *Scholarships, grants, and awards:* Federal Pell, FSEOG, state, private, college/university gift aid from institutional funds.

GIFT AID (NON-NEED-BASED) *Total amount:* $360,661 (24% federal, 63% institutional, 13% external sources). *Receiving aid:* Freshmen: 54% (141). Undergraduates: 41% (293). *Average award:* Freshmen: $3083. Undergraduates: $3241. *Scholarships, grants, and awards by category:* Academic interests/ achievement: general academic interests/achievements. *Special characteristics:*

children and siblings of alumni. *Tuition waivers:* Full or partial for employees or children of employees, senior citizens. *ROTC:* Air Force cooperative.

LOANS *Student loans:* $4,910,151 (90% need-based, 10% non-need-based). 86% of past graduating class borrowed through all loan programs. *Average indebtedness per student:* $43,579. *Average need-based loan:* Freshmen: $3441. Undergraduates: $4032. *Parent loans:* $2,192,074 (93% need-based, 7% non-need-based). *Programs:* Federal Direct (Subsidized and Unsubsidized Stafford, PLUS), Perkins, college/ university, private loans.

WORK-STUDY *Federal work-study:* jobs available. *State or other work-study/employment:* Part-time jobs available.

APPLYING FOR FINANCIAL AID *Required financial aid form:* FAFSA. *Financial aid deadline (priority):* 2/15. *Notification date:* Continuous beginning 3/1.

CONTACT Mrs. Sarah Evancho, Student Aid Coordinator, Penn State Hazleton, Administration Building, Room 222, Hazleton, PA 18201-1291, 570-450-3163 or toll-free 800-279-8495. *E-mail:* sjw37@psu.edu.
Website: http://www.hn.psu.edu/.

PENN STATE LEHIGH VALLEY
Center Valley, PA

Tuition & fees (PA res): $14,134	Average undergraduate aid package: $10,792

ABOUT THE INSTITUTION State-related, coed. *Awards:* certificates, associate, and bachelor's degrees (enrollment figures include students enrolled at The Graduate School at Penn State who are taking courses at this location). 119 undergraduate majors. *Total enrollment:* 877. Undergraduates: 868. Freshmen: 228. Federal methodology is used as a basis for awarding need-based institutional aid.

UNDERGRADUATE EXPENSES for 2016–2017 *Application fee:* $65. *Tuition, state resident:* full-time $13,174; part-time $542 per credit hour. *Tuition, nonresident:* full-time $20,608; part-time $859 per credit hour. *Required fees:* full-time $960. Full-time tuition and fees vary according to course level, degree level, location, program, and student level. Part-time tuition and fees vary according to course level, course load, degree level, location, program, and student level.

FRESHMAN FINANCIAL AID (Fall 2015) 177 applied for aid; of those 74% were deemed to have need. 99% of freshmen with need received aid; of those 4% had need fully met. *Average percent of need met:* 63% (excluding resources awarded to replace EFC). *Average financial aid package:* $10,604 (excluding resources awarded to replace EFC). 11% of all full-time freshmen had no need and received non-need-based gift aid.

UNDERGRADUATE FINANCIAL AID (Fall 2015) 566 applied for aid; of those 79% were deemed to have need. 98% of undergraduates with need received aid; of those 3% had need fully met. *Average percent of need met:* 61% (excluding resources awarded to replace EFC). *Average financial aid package:* $10,792 (excluding resources awarded to replace EFC). 11% of all full-time undergraduates had no need and received non-need-based gift aid.

GIFT AID (NEED-BASED) *Total amount:* $3,283,862 (49% federal, 31% state, 19% institutional, 1% external sources). *Receiving aid:* Freshmen: 50% (102); all full-time undergraduates: 52% (357). *Average award:* Freshmen: $8429; Undergraduates: $7528. *Scholarships, grants, and awards:* Federal Pell, FSEOG, state, private, college/university gift aid from institutional funds.

GIFT AID (NON-NEED-BASED) *Total amount:* $347,311 (39% federal, 2% state, 41% institutional, 18% external sources). *Receiving aid:* Freshmen: 27% (56). Undergraduates: 19% (128). *Average award:* Freshmen: $1933. Undergraduates: $1814. *Scholarships, grants, and awards by category:* Academic interests/ achievement: general academic interests/achievements. *Special characteristics:* general special characteristics. *Tuition waivers:* Full or partial for employees or children of employees, senior citizens. *ROTC:* Army cooperative.

LOANS *Student loans:* $3,766,995 (82% need-based, 18% non-need-based). 82% of past graduating class borrowed through all loan programs. *Average indebtedness per student:* $34,713. *Average need-based loan:* Freshmen: $3396. Undergraduates: $4203. *Parent loans:* $507,861 (69% need-based, 31% non-need-based). *Programs:* Federal Direct (Subsidized and Unsubsidized Stafford, PLUS), Perkins, college/ university, private loans.

WORK-STUDY *Federal work-study:* jobs available. *State or other work-study/employment:* Part-time jobs available.

APPLYING FOR FINANCIAL AID *Required financial aid form:* FAFSA. *Financial aid deadline:* Continuous. *Notification date:* Continuous beginning 3/1.

CONTACT Maryann Hubick, Student Aid Coordinator, Penn State Lehigh Valley, 8380 Mohr Lane, Fogelsville, PA 18051, 610-285-5033. *Fax:* 610-285-5220. *E-mail:* mxh61@psu.edu.

Website: http://www.lv.psu.edu/.

PENN STATE NEW KENSINGTON
New Kensington, PA

Tuition & fees (PA res): $13,616	Average undergraduate aid package: $10,679

ABOUT THE INSTITUTION State-related, coed. *Awards:* certificates, associate, and bachelor's degrees. 124 undergraduate majors. *Total enrollment:* 686. Undergraduates: 686. Freshmen: 199. Federal methodology is used as a basis for awarding need-based institutional aid.

UNDERGRADUATE EXPENSES for 2016–2017 *Application fee:* $65. *Tuition, state resident:* full-time $12,718; part-time $524 per credit hour. *Tuition, nonresident:* full-time $19,598; part-time $817 per credit hour. *Required fees:* full-time $898. Full-time tuition and fees vary according to course level, degree level, location, program, and student level. Part-time tuition and fees vary according to course level, course load, degree level, location, program, and student level.

FRESHMAN FINANCIAL AID (Fall 2015) 159 applied for aid; of those 78% were deemed to have need. 95% of freshmen with need received aid; of those 15% had need fully met. *Average percent of need met:* 69% (excluding resources awarded to replace EFC). *Average financial aid package:* $10,771 (excluding resources awarded to replace EFC). 13% of all full-time freshmen had no need and received non-need-based gift aid.

UNDERGRADUATE FINANCIAL AID (Fall 2015) 423 applied for aid; of those 83% were deemed to have need. 97% of undergraduates with need received aid; of those 10% had need fully met. *Average percent of need met:* 67% (excluding resources awarded to replace EFC). *Average financial aid package:* $10,679 (excluding resources awarded to replace EFC). 12% of all full-time undergraduates had no need and received non-need-based gift aid.

GIFT AID (NEED-BASED) *Total amount:* $2,528,529 (39% federal, 29% state, 23% institutional, 9% external sources). *Receiving aid:* Freshmen: 59% (103); all full-time undergraduates: 53% (264). *Average award:* Freshmen: $6376; Undergraduates: $6292. *Scholarships, grants, and awards:* Federal Pell, FSEOG, state, private, college/university gift aid from institutional funds.

GIFT AID (NON-NEED-BASED) *Total amount:* $419,802 (46% federal, 2% state, 40% institutional, 12% external sources). *Receiving aid:* Freshmen: 34% (60). Undergraduates: 28% (139). *Average award:* Freshmen: $3416. Undergraduates: $2862. *Scholarships, grants, and awards by category:* Academic interests/achievement: general academic interests/achievements. *Special characteristics:* children and siblings of alumni. *Tuition waivers:* Full or partial for employees or children of employees, senior citizens. *ROTC:* Air Force cooperative.

LOANS *Student loans:* $2,942,065 (84% need-based, 16% non-need-based). 79% of past graduating class borrowed through all loan programs. *Average indebtedness per student:* $34,024. *Average need-based loan:* Freshmen: $3259. Undergraduates: $4020. *Parent loans:* $447,336 (78% need-based, 22% non-need-based). *Programs:* Federal Direct (Subsidized and Unsubsidized Stafford, PLUS), Perkins, college/university, private loans.

WORK-STUDY *Federal work-study:* jobs available. *State or other work-study/employment:* Part-time jobs available.

APPLYING FOR FINANCIAL AID *Required financial aid form:* FAFSA. *Financial aid deadline (priority):* 2/15. *Notification date:* Continuous beginning 3/1.

CONTACT Office of Student Aid, Penn State New Kensington, Administrative Building, 3550 Seventh Street Road, New Kensington, PA 15068, 724-334-6047 or toll-free 888-968-7297. *Fax:* 724-334-6111. *E-mail:* nk-finaid@psu.edu.

Website: http://www.nk.psu.edu/.

PENN STATE SCHUYLKILL
Schuylkill Haven, PA

Tuition & fees (PA res): $14,072	Average undergraduate aid package: $12,117

ABOUT THE INSTITUTION State-related, coed. *Awards:* certificates, associate, and bachelor's degrees (bachelor's degree programs completed at the Harrisburg campus). 124 undergraduate majors. *Total enrollment:* 759. Undergraduates: 759. Freshmen: 205. Federal methodology is used as a basis for awarding need-based institutional aid.

UNDERGRADUATE EXPENSES for 2016–2017 *Application fee:* $65. *Tuition, state resident:* full-time $13,174; part-time $542 per credit hour. *Tuition, nonresident:* full-time $20,608; part-time $859 per credit hour. *Required fees:* full-time $898. Full-time tuition and fees vary according to course level, degree level, location, program, and student level. Part-time tuition and fees vary according to course level, course load, degree level, location, program, and student level. *College room and board:* $8240; *Room only:* $6240. Room and board charges vary according to board plan, housing facility, and location.

FRESHMAN FINANCIAL AID (Fall 2015) 201 applied for aid; of those 92% were deemed to have need. 100% of freshmen with need received aid; of those 6% had need fully met. *Average percent of need met:* 66% (excluding resources awarded to replace EFC). *Average financial aid package:* $12,159 (excluding resources awarded to replace EFC). 7% of all full-time freshmen had no need and received non-need-based gift aid.

UNDERGRADUATE FINANCIAL AID (Fall 2015) 571 applied for aid; of those 91% were deemed to have need. 99% of undergraduates with need received aid; of those 7% had need fully met. *Average percent of need met:* 66% (excluding resources awarded to replace EFC). *Average financial aid package:* $12,117 (excluding resources awarded to replace EFC). 6% of all full-time undergraduates had no need and received non-need-based gift aid.

GIFT AID (NEED-BASED) *Total amount:* $4,504,086 (40% federal, 23% state, 33% institutional, 4% external sources). *Receiving aid:* Freshmen: 70% (150); all full-time undergraduates: 69% (417). *Average award:* Freshmen: $7488; Undergraduates: $7340. *Scholarships, grants, and awards:* Federal Pell, FSEOG, state, private, college/university gift aid from institutional funds.

GIFT AID (NON-NEED-BASED) *Total amount:* $212,562 (34% federal, 2% state, 51% institutional, 13% external sources). *Receiving aid:* Freshmen: 64% (138). Undergraduates: 47% (286). *Average award:* Freshmen: $3434. Undergraduates: $2760. *Scholarships, grants, and awards by category:* Academic interests/achievement: general academic interests/achievements. *Special characteristics:* general special characteristics. *Tuition waivers:* Full or partial for employees or children of employees, senior citizens.

LOANS *Student loans:* $4,602,972 (93% need-based, 7% non-need-based). 88% of past graduating class borrowed through all loan programs. *Average indebtedness per student:* $41,345. *Average need-based loan:* Freshmen: $3412. Undergraduates: $4022. *Parent loans:* $1,328,742 (95% need-based, 5% non-need-based). *Programs:* Federal Direct (Subsidized and Unsubsidized Stafford, PLUS), Perkins, college/university, private loans.

WORK-STUDY *Federal work-study:* jobs available. *State or other work-study/employment:* Part-time jobs available.

APPLYING FOR FINANCIAL AID *Required financial aid form:* FAFSA. *Financial aid deadline (priority):* 2/15. *Notification date:* Continuous beginning 3/1.

CONTACT Student Aid and Admissions Office, Penn State Schuylkill, 200 University Drive, Schuylkill Haven, PA 17972-2208, 570-385-6244. *Fax:* 570-385-6272. *E-mail:* sl-financialaid@psu.edu.

Website: http://www.sl.psu.edu/.

PENN STATE UNIVERSITY PARK
State College, PA

Tuition & fees (PA res): $17,900	Average undergraduate aid package: $11,498

ABOUT THE INSTITUTION State-related, coed. *Awards:* certificates, associate, bachelor's, master's, and doctoral degrees. 126 undergraduate majors. *Total*

enrollment: 47,789. Undergraduates: 41,359. Freshmen: 8,499. Federal methodology is used as a basis for awarding need-based institutional aid.

UNDERGRADUATE EXPENSES for 2016–2017 Application fee: $65. **Tuition, state resident:** full-time $16,952; part-time $706 per credit hour. **Tuition, nonresident:** full-time $31,434; part-time $1310 per credit hour. **Required fees:** full-time $948. Full-time tuition and fees vary according to course level, degree level, location, program, and student level. Part-time tuition and fees vary according to course level, course load, degree level, location, program, and student level. **College room and board:** $11,860; **Room only:** $5940. Room and board charges vary according to board plan, housing facility, and location.

FRESHMAN FINANCIAL AID (Fall 2015) 5,468 applied for aid; of those 64% were deemed to have need. 92% of freshmen with need received aid; of those 9% had need fully met. **Average percent of need met:** 58% (excluding resources awarded to replace EFC). **Average financial aid package:** $10,524 (excluding resources awarded to replace EFC). 8% of all full-time freshmen had no need and received non-need-based gift aid.

UNDERGRADUATE FINANCIAL AID (Fall 2015) 23,999 applied for aid; of those 77% were deemed to have need. 96% of undergraduates with need received aid; of those 8% had need fully met. **Average percent of need met:** 59% (excluding resources awarded to replace EFC). **Average financial aid package:** $11,498 (excluding resources awarded to replace EFC). 10% of all full-time undergraduates had no need and received non-need-based gift aid.

GIFT AID (NEED-BASED) Total amount: $113,574,012 (34% federal, 18% state, 40% institutional, 8% external sources). **Receiving aid:** Freshmen: 18% (1,398); all full-time undergraduates: 23% (9,122). **Average award:** Freshmen: $7155; Undergraduates: $7685. **Scholarships, grants, and awards:** Federal Pell, FSEOG, state, private, college/university gift aid from institutional funds.

GIFT AID (NON-NEED-BASED) Total amount: $52,006,812 (16% federal, 30% institutional, 54% external sources). **Receiving aid:** Freshmen: 23% (1,761). Undergraduates: 18% (7,016). **Average award:** Freshmen: $4185. Undergraduates: $3933. **Scholarships, grants, and awards by category:** *Academic interests/achievement:* general academic interests/achievements. **Tuition waivers:** Full or partial for employees or children of employees, senior citizens. **ROTC:** Army, Naval, Air Force.

LOANS Student loans: $225,476,235 (81% need-based, 19% non-need-based). 54% of past graduating class borrowed through all loan programs. *Average indebtedness per student:* $37,213. **Average need-based loan:** Freshmen: $3495. Undergraduates: $4712. **Parent loans:** $113,319,043 (85% need-based, 15% non-need-based). **Programs:** Federal Direct (Subsidized and Unsubsidized Stafford, PLUS), Perkins, college/university, private loans.

WORK-STUDY Federal work-study: 994 jobs averaging $3144.

ATHLETIC AWARDS Total amount: $18,661,221 (31% need-based, 69% non-need-based).

APPLYING FOR FINANCIAL AID Required financial aid form: FAFSA. **Financial aid deadline (priority):** 2/15. **Notification date:** Continuous.

CONTACT Ms. Anna M. Griswold, Executive Director for Student Aid, Penn State University Park, 311 Shields Building, University Park, PA 16802, 814-863-0507. *Fax:* 814-863-0322.

Website: http://www.psu.edu/.

PENN STATE WILKES-BARRE
Lehman, PA

Tuition & fees (PA res): $13,540	Average undergraduate aid package: $11,107

ABOUT THE INSTITUTION State-related, coed. **Awards:** certificates, associate, and bachelor's degrees (enrollment figures include students enrolled at The Graduate School at Penn State who are taking courses at this location). 122 undergraduate majors. **Total enrollment:** 487. Undergraduates: 477. Freshmen: 125. Federal methodology is used as a basis for awarding need-based institutional aid.

UNDERGRADUATE EXPENSES for 2016–2017 Application fee: $65. **Tuition, state resident:** full-time $12,718; part-time $524 per credit hour. **Tuition, nonresident:** full-time $19,598; part-time $817 per credit hour. **Required fees:** full-time $822. Full-time tuition and fees vary according to course level, degree level, location, program, and student level. Part-time tuition and fees vary according to course level, course load, degree level, location, program, and student level.

FRESHMAN FINANCIAL AID (Fall 2015) 136 applied for aid; of those 71% were deemed to have need. 97% of freshmen with need received aid; of those 8% had need fully met. **Average percent of need met:** 64% (excluding resources awarded to replace EFC). **Average financial aid package:** $10,737 (excluding resources awarded to replace EFC). 17% of all full-time freshmen had no need and received non-need-based gift aid.

UNDERGRADUATE FINANCIAL AID (Fall 2015) 400 applied for aid; of those 78% were deemed to have need. 98% of undergraduates with need received aid; of those 7% had need fully met. **Average percent of need met:** 66% (excluding resources awarded to replace EFC). **Average financial aid package:** $11,107 (excluding resources awarded to replace EFC). 10% of all full-time undergraduates had no need and received non-need-based gift aid.

GIFT AID (NEED-BASED) Total amount: $2,374,874 (42% federal, 28% state, 29% institutional, 1% external sources). **Receiving aid:** Freshmen: 53% (75); all full-time undergraduates: 56% (244). **Average award:** Freshmen: $7044; Undergraduates: $7239. **Scholarships, grants, and awards:** Federal Pell, FSEOG, state, private, college/university gift aid from institutional funds.

GIFT AID (NON-NEED-BASED) Total amount: $186,963 (30% federal, 63% institutional, 7% external sources). **Receiving aid:** Freshmen: 39% (55). Undergraduates: 31% (135). **Average award:** Freshmen: $3073. Undergraduates: $2626. **Tuition waivers:** Full or partial for employees or children of employees, senior citizens. **ROTC:** Army cooperative, Air Force cooperative.

LOANS Student loans: $2,595,986 (84% need-based, 16% non-need-based). 79% of past graduating class borrowed through all loan programs. *Average indebtedness per student:* $35,984. **Average need-based loan:** Freshmen: $3374. Undergraduates: $4224. **Parent loans:** $559,648 (73% need-based, 27% non-need-based). **Programs:** Federal Direct (Subsidized and Unsubsidized Stafford, PLUS), Perkins, college/university, private loans.

WORK-STUDY Federal work-study: jobs available. **State or other work-study/employment:** Part-time jobs available.

APPLYING FOR FINANCIAL AID Required financial aid form: FAFSA. **Financial aid deadline (priority):** 2/15. **Notification date:** Continuous beginning 3/1.

CONTACT Stacey Zelinka, Financial Aid Coordinator, Penn State Wilkes-Barre, Old Route 115, PO Box PSU, Lehman, PA 18627, 570-675-9238. *Fax:* 570-675-9113. *E-mail:* saz3@psu.edu.

Website: http://www.wb.psu.edu/.

PENN STATE WORTHINGTON SCRANTON
Dunmore, PA

Tuition & fees (PA res): $14,072	Average undergraduate aid package: $10,523

ABOUT THE INSTITUTION State-related, coed. **Awards:** certificates, associate, and bachelor's degrees. 119 undergraduate majors. **Total enrollment:** 1,019. Undergraduates: 1,019. Freshmen: 250. Federal methodology is used as a basis for awarding need-based institutional aid.

UNDERGRADUATE EXPENSES for 2016–2017 Application fee: $65. **Tuition, state resident:** full-time $13,174; part-time $542 per credit hour. **Tuition, nonresident:** full-time $20,608; part-time $859 per credit hour. **Required fees:** full-time $898. Full-time tuition and fees vary according to course level, degree level, location, program, and student level. Part-time tuition and fees vary according to course level, course load, degree level, location, program, and student level.

FRESHMAN FINANCIAL AID (Fall 2015) 213 applied for aid; of those 83% were deemed to have need. 98% of freshmen with need received aid; of those 4% had need fully met. **Average percent of need met:** 62% (excluding resources awarded to replace EFC). **Average financial aid package:** $10,263 (excluding resources awarded to replace EFC). 7% of all full-time freshmen had no need and received non-need-based gift aid.

UNDERGRADUATE FINANCIAL AID (Fall 2015) 778 applied for aid; of those 87% were deemed to have need. 98% of undergraduates with need received aid; of those 5% had need fully met. **Average percent of need met:** 61% (excluding resources awarded to replace EFC). **Average financial aid package:** $10,523 (excluding resources awarded to replace EFC). 5% of all full-time undergraduates had no need and received non-need-based gift aid.

GIFT AID (NEED-BASED) *Total amount:* $4,926,506 (47% federal, 32% state, 19% institutional, 2% external sources). *Receiving aid:* Freshmen: 69% (155); all full-time undergraduates: 65% (556). *Average award:* Freshmen: $7212; Undergraduates: $7043. *Scholarships, grants, and awards:* Federal Pell, FSEOG, state, private, college/university gift aid from institutional funds.

GIFT AID (NON-NEED-BASED) *Total amount:* $181,666 (7% federal, 1% state, 73% institutional, 19% external sources). *Receiving aid:* Freshmen: 24% (54). Undergraduates: 20% (174). *Average award:* Freshmen: $3960. Undergraduates: $3412. *Tuition waivers:* Full or partial for employees or children of employees, senior citizens. **ROTC:** Army cooperative, Air Force cooperative.

LOANS *Student loans:* $5,961,677 (89% need-based, 11% non-need-based). 87% of past graduating class borrowed through all loan programs. *Average indebtedness per student:* $37,098. *Average need-based loan:* Freshmen: $3277. Undergraduates: $3918. *Parent loans:* $641,349 (72% need-based, 28% non-need-based). *Programs:* Federal Direct (Subsidized and Unsubsidized Stafford, PLUS), Perkins, college/university, private loans.

WORK-STUDY *Federal work-study:* jobs available. *State or other work-study/employment:* Part-time jobs available.

APPLYING FOR FINANCIAL AID *Required financial aid form:* FAFSA. *Financial aid deadline:* Continuous. *Notification date:* Continuous beginning 3/1.

CONTACT Financial Aid Office, Penn State Worthington Scranton, Room 21, Study Learning Center, 120 Ridge View Drive, Dunmore, PA 18512, 570-963-2690. *Fax:* 570-963-2683.
Website: http://www.sn.psu.edu/.

PENN STATE YORK
York, PA

Tuition & fees (PA res): $14,134	Average undergraduate aid package: $10,704

ABOUT THE INSTITUTION State-related, coed. *Awards:* certificates, associate, bachelor's, and master's degrees (also offers up to 2 years of most bachelor's degree programs offered at University Park campus). 126 undergraduate majors. *Total enrollment:* 1,066. Undergraduates: 1,060. Freshmen: 303. Federal methodology is used as a basis for awarding need-based institutional aid.

UNDERGRADUATE EXPENSES for 2016–2017 *Application fee:* $65. *Tuition, state resident:* full-time $13,174; part-time $542 per credit hour. *Tuition, nonresident:* full-time $20,608; part-time $859 per credit hour. *Required fees:* full-time $960. Full-time tuition and fees vary according to course level, degree level, location, program, and student level. Part-time tuition and fees vary according to course level, course load, degree level, location, program, and student level.

FRESHMAN FINANCIAL AID (Fall 2015) 202 applied for aid; of those 73% were deemed to have need. 99% of freshmen with need received aid; of those 8% had need fully met. *Average percent of need met:* 63% (excluding resources awarded to replace EFC). *Average financial aid package:* $10,832 (excluding resources awarded to replace EFC). 15% of all full-time freshmen had no need and received non-need-based gift aid.

UNDERGRADUATE FINANCIAL AID (Fall 2015) 570 applied for aid; of those 79% were deemed to have need. 99% of undergraduates with need received aid; of those 8% had need fully met. *Average percent of need met:* 62% (excluding resources awarded to replace EFC). *Average financial aid package:* $10,704 (excluding resources awarded to replace EFC). 14% of all full-time undergraduates had no need and received non-need-based gift aid.

GIFT AID (NEED-BASED) *Total amount:* $3,369,675 (45% federal, 25% state, 26% institutional, 4% external sources). *Receiving aid:* Freshmen: 37% (113); all full-time undergraduates: 44% (350). *Average award:* Freshmen: $6663; Undergraduates: $6597. *Scholarships, grants, and awards:* Federal Pell, FSEOG, state, private, college/university gift aid from institutional funds.

GIFT AID (NON-NEED-BASED) *Total amount:* $618,869 (33% federal, 1% state, 46% institutional, 20% external sources). *Receiving aid:* Freshmen: 27% (84). Undergraduates: 26% (204). *Average award:* Freshmen: $3171. Undergraduates: $2381. *Scholarships, grants, and awards by category:* Academic interests/achievement: general academic interests/achievements. *Special characteristics:* children and siblings of alumni. *Tuition waivers:* Full or partial for employees or children of employees, senior citizens.

LOANS *Student loans:* $4,488,160 (78% need-based, 22% non-need-based). 80% of past graduating class borrowed through all loan programs. *Average indebtedness per student:* $36,176. *Average need-based loan:* Freshmen: $3395. Undergraduates: $4008. *Parent loans:* $735,079 (77% need-based, 23% non-need-based). *Programs:* Federal Direct (Subsidized and Unsubsidized Stafford, PLUS), Perkins, college/university, private loans.

WORK-STUDY *Federal work-study:* jobs available. *State or other work-study/employment:* Part-time jobs available.

APPLYING FOR FINANCIAL AID *Required financial aid form:* FAFSA. *Financial aid deadline (priority):* 2/15. *Notification date:* Continuous beginning 3/1.

CONTACT Financial Aid Office, Penn State York, 1031 Edgecomb Avenue, York, PA 17403-3326, 717-771-4045 or toll-free 800-778-6227. *E-mail:* yorkfinaid@yk.psu.edu. *Website:* http://www.yk.psu.edu/.

PENNSYLVANIA ACADEMY OF THE FINE ARTS
Philadelphia, PA

ABOUT THE INSTITUTION Independent, coed. 1 undergraduate major.

GIFT AID (NEED-BASED) *Scholarships, grants, and awards:* Federal Pell, FSEOG, state.

LOANS *Programs:* Federal Direct (Subsidized and Unsubsidized Stafford, PLUS).

WORK-STUDY *Federal work-study:* jobs available.

CONTACT Dana Moore, Director of Financial Aid, Pennsylvania Academy of the Fine Arts, 128 North Broad Street, Philadelphia, PA 19102, 215-972-2019. *Fax:* 215-972-0839. *E-mail:* dmoore@pafa.edu. *Website:* http://www.pafa.edu/.

PENNSYLVANIA COLLEGE OF ART & DESIGN
Lancaster, PA

CONTACT J. David Hershey, Registrar/Director of Financial Aid, Pennsylvania College of Art & Design, 204 North Prince Street, PO Box 59, Lancaster, PA 17608-0059, 717-396-7833 Ext. 13 or toll-free 800-689-0379 Ext. 1001. *Fax:* 717-396-1339. *E-mail:* finaid@pcad.edu. *Website:* http://www.pcad.edu/.

PENNSYLVANIA COLLEGE OF HEALTH SCIENCES
Lancaster, PA

CONTACT Financial Aid Office, Pennsylvania College of Health Sciences, 850 Greenfield Road, Lancaster, PA 17601, 717-544-4912 or toll-free 800-622-5443. *Website:* http://www.pacollege.edu/.

PENNSYLVANIA COLLEGE OF TECHNOLOGY
Williamsport, PA

Tuition & fees (PA res): $18,570	Average undergraduate aid package: $13,124

ABOUT THE INSTITUTION State-related, coed. *Awards:* certificates, associate, and bachelor's degrees. 76 undergraduate majors. *Total enrollment:* 5,432. Undergraduates: 5,432. Freshmen: 1,227. Federal methodology is used as a basis for awarding need-based institutional aid.

UNDERGRADUATE EXPENSES for 2017–2018 *Application fee:* $50. *Tuition, state resident:* full-time $16,080; part-time $536 per credit hour. *Tuition, nonresident:* full-time $22,890; part-time $763 per credit hour. *Required fees:* full-time $2490. Full-time tuition and fees vary according to course load and program. Part-time tuition and fees vary according to course load and program. *College room and board:* $11,244; *Room only:* $6456. Room and board charges vary according to board plan and housing facility.
FRESHMAN FINANCIAL AID (Fall 2015) 1,181 applied for aid; of those 93% were deemed to have need. 100% of freshmen with need received aid. *Average percent of need met:* 24% (excluding resources awarded to replace EFC). *Average financial aid package:* $12,327 (excluding resources awarded to replace EFC).
UNDERGRADUATE FINANCIAL AID (Fall 2015) 4,434 applied for aid; of those 96% were deemed to have need. 100% of undergraduates with need received aid. *Average percent of need met:* 24% (excluding resources awarded to replace EFC). *Average financial aid package:* $13,124 (excluding resources awarded to replace EFC).
GIFT AID (NEED-BASED) *Total amount:* $31,861,846 (30% federal, 21% state, 5% institutional, 44% external sources). *Receiving aid:* Freshmen: 71% (854); all full-time undergraduates: 69% (3,175). *Average award:* Freshmen: $7186; Undergraduates: $8247. *Scholarships, grants, and awards:* Federal Pell, FSEOG, state, private, college/university gift aid from institutional funds.
GIFT AID (NON-NEED-BASED) *Tuition waivers:* Full or partial for employees or children of employees. *ROTC:* Army.
LOANS *Student loans:* $45,379,921 (100% need-based). *Average need-based loan:* Freshmen: $3354. Undergraduates: $4146. *Parent loans:* $16,922,384 (100% need-based). *Programs:* Federal Direct (Subsidized and Unsubsidized Stafford, PLUS).
WORK-STUDY *Federal work-study:* 120 jobs averaging $1638.
APPLYING FOR FINANCIAL AID *Required financial aid forms:* FAFSA, institution's own form. *Financial aid deadline (priority):* 3/1. *Notification date:* Continuous beginning 12/1. Students must reply within 2 weeks of notification.
CONTACT Mr. Dennis Correll, Associate Dean for Enrollment Management, Pennsylvania College of Technology, One College Avenue, Williamsport, PA 17701, 570-326-4766 or toll-free 800-367-9222. *Fax:* 570-321-5552. *E-mail:* dcorrell@pct.edu.
Website: http://www.pct.edu/.

PENSACOLA CHRISTIAN COLLEGE
Pensacola, FL

CONTACT Financial Aid Office, Pensacola Christian College, 250 Brent Lane, Pensacola, FL 32503-2267, 850-478-8496 or toll-free 800-722-4636.
Website: http://www.pcci.edu/.

PEPPERDINE UNIVERSITY
Malibu, CA

Tuition & fees: $50,022	Average undergraduate aid package: $39,927

ABOUT THE INSTITUTION Independent Church of Christ, coed. *Awards:* bachelor's, master's, and doctoral degrees. 60 undergraduate majors. *Total enrollment:* 7,826. Undergraduates: 3,542. Freshmen: 743. Federal methodology is used as a basis for awarding need-based institutional aid.
UNDERGRADUATE EXPENSES for 2016–2017 *Application fee:* $65. *Comprehensive fee:* $64,352 includes full-time tuition ($49,770), mandatory fees ($252), and room and board ($14,330). Room and board charges vary according to board plan and housing facility. *Part-time tuition:* $1565 per credit hour.
FRESHMAN FINANCIAL AID (Fall 2016, est.) 740 applied for aid; of those 59% were deemed to have need. 99% of freshmen with need received aid; of those 17% had need fully met. *Average percent of need met:* 75% (excluding resources awarded to replace EFC). *Average financial aid package:* $38,688 (excluding resources awarded to replace EFC). 22% of all full-time freshmen had no need and received non-need-based gift aid.
UNDERGRADUATE FINANCIAL AID (Fall 2016, est.) 3,176 applied for aid; of those 52% were deemed to have need. 99% of undergraduates with need received aid;

of those 19% had need fully met. *Average percent of need met:* 75% (excluding resources awarded to replace EFC). *Average financial aid package:* $39,927 (excluding resources awarded to replace EFC). 26% of all full-time undergraduates had no need and received non-need-based gift aid.
GIFT AID (NEED-BASED) *Total amount:* $56,506,942 (6% federal, 6% state, 85% institutional, 3% external sources). *Receiving aid:* Freshmen: 58% (431); all full-time undergraduates: 51% (1,617). *Average award:* Freshmen: $35,827; Undergraduates: $36,283. *Scholarships, grants, and awards:* Federal Pell, FSEOG, state, private, college/university gift aid from institutional funds, United Negro College Fund.
GIFT AID (NON-NEED-BASED) *Total amount:* $16,543,538 (3% federal, 93% institutional, 4% external sources). *Average award:* Freshmen: $21,773. Undergraduates: $18,084. *Tuition waivers:* Full or partial for employees or children of employees. *ROTC:* Army cooperative, Air Force cooperative.
LOANS *Student loans:* $13,539,409 (86% need-based, 14% non-need-based). 60% of past graduating class borrowed through all loan programs. *Average indebtedness per student:* $29,640. *Average need-based loan:* Freshmen: $4343. Undergraduates: $5877. *Parent loans:* $16,434,964 (86% need-based, 14% non-need-based). *Programs:* Federal Direct (Subsidized and Unsubsidized Stafford, PLUS), Perkins, college/university.
WORK-STUDY *Federal work-study:* Total amount: $189,261; 901 jobs averaging $1217. *State or other work-study/employment:* Total amount: $65,938 (52% need-based, 48% non-need-based). 230 part-time jobs averaging $1029.
ATHLETIC AWARDS Total amount: $6,560,855 (32% need-based, 68% non-need-based).
APPLYING FOR FINANCIAL AID *Required financial aid form:* FAFSA. *Financial aid deadline (priority):* 2/15. *Notification date:* 4/15. Students must reply by 5/1.
CONTACT Ms. Janet Lockhart, Director of Financial Assistance, Pepperdine University, 24255 Pacific Coast Highway, Malibu, CA 90263-4301, 310-506-4301. *Fax:* 310-506-4746. *E-mail:* janet.lockhart@pepperdine.edu.
Website: http://www.pepperdine.edu/.

PERU STATE COLLEGE
Peru, NE

CONTACT Diana Lind, Director of Financial Aid, Peru State College, PO Box 10, Peru, NE 68421, 402-872-2228 or toll-free 800-742-4412 (in-state), 800-741-4412 (out-of-state). *Fax:* 402-872-2419. *E-mail:* finaid@oakmail.peru.edu.
Website: http://www.peru.edu/.

PFEIFFER UNIVERSITY
Misenheimer, NC

CONTACT Amy Brown, Director of Financial Aid, Pfeiffer University, PO Box 960, Misenheimer, NC 28109, 704-463-1360 Ext. 3046 or toll-free 800-338-2060. *Fax:* 704-463-1363. *E-mail:* amy.brown@pfeiffer.edu.
Website: http://www.pfeiffer.edu/.

PHILADELPHIA UNIVERSITY
Philadelphia, PA

Tuition & fees: $37,800	Average undergraduate aid package: $27,325

ABOUT THE INSTITUTION Independent, coed. *Awards:* certificates, associate, bachelor's, master's, and doctoral degrees. 32 undergraduate majors. *Total enrollment:* 3,757. Undergraduates: 2,906. Freshmen: 661. Federal methodology is used as a basis for awarding need-based institutional aid.
UNDERGRADUATE EXPENSES for 2016–2017 *Application fee:* $40. *Comprehensive fee:* $50,370 includes full-time tuition ($36,870), mandatory fees ($930), and room and board ($12,570). *College room only:* $5870. Full-time tuition and fees vary according to course load, degree level, program, and student level. Room and board charges vary according to board plan and housing facility. *Part-time tuition:*

$605 per credit hour. *Part-time fees:* $25 per credit hour. Part-time tuition and fees vary according to class time, course load, degree level, program, and reciprocity agreements.

FRESHMAN FINANCIAL AID (Fall 2016, est.) 456 applied for aid; of those 89% were deemed to have need. 100% of freshmen with need received aid; of those 9% had need fully met. *Average percent of need met:* 80% (excluding resources awarded to replace EFC). *Average financial aid package:* $33,094 (excluding resources awarded to replace EFC). 15% of all full-time freshmen had no need and received non-need-based gift aid.

UNDERGRADUATE FINANCIAL AID (Fall 2016, est.) 2,095 applied for aid; of those 90% were deemed to have need. 100% of undergraduates with need received aid; of those 11% had need fully met. *Average percent of need met:* 70% (excluding resources awarded to replace EFC). *Average financial aid package:* $27,325 (excluding resources awarded to replace EFC). 15% of all full-time undergraduates had no need and received non-need-based gift aid.

GIFT AID (NEED-BASED) *Total amount:* $39,247,510 (11% federal, 5% state, 83% institutional, 1% external sources). *Receiving aid:* Freshmen: 83% (404); all full-time undergraduates: 78% (1,851). *Average award:* Freshmen: $28,603; Undergraduates: $23,340. *Scholarships, grants, and awards:* Federal Pell, FSEOG, state, private, college/university gift aid from institutional funds, university-chosen non-endowed scholarships from outside sources.

GIFT AID (NON-NEED-BASED) *Total amount:* $5,562,974 (2% federal, 97% institutional, 1% external sources). *Receiving aid:* Freshmen: 7% (33). Undergraduates: 8% (180). *Average award:* Freshmen: $13,211. Undergraduates: $11,952. *Scholarships, grants, and awards by category:* Academic interests/achievement: engineering/technologies, general academic interests/achievements. *Tuition waivers:* Full or partial for employees or children of employees.

LOANS *Student loans:* $19,375,283 (72% need-based, 28% non-need-based). 80% of past graduating class borrowed through all loan programs. *Average indebtedness per student:* $40,227. *Average need-based loan:* Freshmen: $4101. Undergraduates: $4449. *Parent loans:* $10,105,080 (45% need-based, 55% non-need-based). *Programs:* Federal Direct (Subsidized and Unsubsidized Stafford, PLUS), Perkins, private loans.

WORK-STUDY *Federal work-study:* Total amount: $2,129,067; jobs available. *State or other work-study/employment:* Total amount: $564,302 (80% need-based, 20% non-need-based). Part-time jobs available.

ATHLETIC AWARDS Total amount: $2,876,782 (51% need-based, 49% non-need-based).

APPLYING FOR FINANCIAL AID *Required financial aid form:* FAFSA. *Financial aid deadline:* 4/15 (priority: 3/1). *Notification date:* Continuous beginning 3/11. Students must reply by 5/1.

CONTACT Ms. Lisa J. Cooper, Director of Financial Aid, Philadelphia University, School House Lane and Henry Avenue, Philadelphia, PA 19144, 215-951-2940. *Fax:* 215-951-2941. *E-mail:* cooperl@philau.edu. *Website:* http://www.philau.edu/.

PHILANDER SMITH COLLEGE
Little Rock, AR

Tuition & fees: N/R	Average undergraduate aid package: $12,847

ABOUT THE INSTITUTION Independent United Methodist, coed. *Awards:* bachelor's degrees. 19 undergraduate majors. *Total enrollment:* 765. Undergraduates: 765. Freshmen: 289. Federal methodology is used as a basis for awarding need-based institutional aid.

FRESHMAN FINANCIAL AID (Fall 2015) 170 applied for aid; of those 98% were deemed to have need. 98% of freshmen with need received aid; of those 5% had need fully met. *Average percent of need met:* 50% (excluding resources awarded to replace EFC). *Average financial aid package:* $12,280 (excluding resources awarded to replace EFC). 3% of all full-time freshmen had no need and received non-need-based gift aid.

UNDERGRADUATE FINANCIAL AID (Fall 2015) 536 applied for aid; of those 97% were deemed to have need. 98% of undergraduates with need received aid; of those 8% had need fully met. *Average percent of need met:* 51% (excluding resources awarded to replace EFC). *Average financial aid package:* $12,847 (excluding resources awarded to replace EFC). 6% of all full-time undergraduates had no need and received non-need-based gift aid.

GIFT AID (NEED-BASED) *Total amount:* $4,649,403 (47% federal, 4% state, 41% institutional, 8% external sources). *Receiving aid:* Freshmen: 86% (159); all full-time undergraduates: 83% (488). *Average award:* Freshmen: $9589; Undergraduates: $9808. *Scholarships, grants, and awards:* Federal Pell, FSEOG, state, private, college/university gift aid from institutional funds, United Negro College Fund.

GIFT AID (NON-NEED-BASED) *Receiving aid:* Freshmen: 4% (7). Undergraduates: 3% (19). *Average award:* Freshmen: $7536. Undergraduates: $15,616. *Scholarships, grants, and awards by category:* Academic interests/achievement: 197 awards ($2,104,267 total): general academic interests/achievements. *Creative arts/performance:* 22 awards ($43,750 total): music. *Special achievements/activities:* 73 awards ($130,850 total): community service, general special achievements/activities, leadership, religious involvement. *Special characteristics:* 2 awards ($13,100 total): children of faculty/staff. *ROTC:* Army cooperative.

LOANS *Student loans:* $5,372,128 (65% need-based, 35% non-need-based). 78% of past graduating class borrowed through all loan programs. *Average indebtedness per student:* $46,965. *Average need-based loan:* Freshmen: $3119. Undergraduates: $3562. *Parent loans:* $970,450 (100% need-based). *Programs:* Federal Direct (Subsidized and Unsubsidized Stafford, PLUS).

WORK-STUDY *Federal work-study:* 117 jobs averaging $2600.

ATHLETIC AWARDS Total amount: $239,830 (100% need-based).

APPLYING FOR FINANCIAL AID *Required financial aid forms:* FAFSA, institution's own form. *Financial aid deadline (priority):* 3/1. *Notification date:* Continuous beginning 3/1.

CONTACT K Michael Francois, Director of Financial Aid, Philander Smith College, 900 Daisy Bates Drive, Little Rock, AR 72202-3799, 501-370-5350 or toll-free 800-446-6772. *Fax:* 501-370-5357. *E-mail:* kmfrancois@philander.edu. *Website:* http://www.philander.edu/.

PIEDMONT COLLEGE
Demorest, GA

Tuition & fees: $24,468	Average undergraduate aid package: $19,224

ABOUT THE INSTITUTION Independent United Church of Christ, coed. *Awards:* certificates, bachelor's, master's, and doctoral degrees. 50 undergraduate majors. *Total enrollment:* 2,266. Undergraduates: 1,295. Freshmen: 274. Both federal and institutional methodology are used as a basis for awarding need-based institutional aid.

UNDERGRADUATE EXPENSES for 2017–2018 *Comprehensive fee:* $34,338 includes full-time tuition ($24,268), mandatory fees ($200), and room and board ($9870). *College room only:* $5502. Full-time tuition and fees vary according to course load, degree level, location, and program. Room and board charges vary according to board plan. *Part-time tuition:* $1011 per credit hour. Part-time tuition and fees vary according to course load, degree level, location, and program.

FRESHMAN FINANCIAL AID (Fall 2016, est.) 259 applied for aid; of those 89% were deemed to have need. 100% of freshmen with need received aid; of those 26% had need fully met. *Average percent of need met:* 78% (excluding resources awarded to replace EFC). *Average financial aid package:* $20,504 (excluding resources awarded to replace EFC). 16% of all full-time freshmen had no need and received non-need-based gift aid.

UNDERGRADUATE FINANCIAL AID (Fall 2016, est.) 1,047 applied for aid; of those 91% were deemed to have need. 100% of undergraduates with need received aid; of those 19% had need fully met. *Average percent of need met:* 70% (excluding resources awarded to replace EFC). *Average financial aid package:* $19,224 (excluding resources awarded to replace EFC). 16% of all full-time undergraduates had no need and received non-need-based gift aid.

GIFT AID (NEED-BASED) *Total amount:* $14,870,371 (18% federal, 17% state, 64% institutional, 1% external sources). *Receiving aid:* Freshmen: 84% (230); all full-time undergraduates: 82% (949). *Average award:* Freshmen: $16,946; Undergraduates: $15,294. *Scholarships, grants, and awards:* Federal Pell, FSEOG, state, private, college/university gift aid from institutional funds.

GIFT AID (NON-NEED-BASED) *Total amount:* $3,506,226 (15% state, 84% institutional, 1% external sources). *Receiving aid:* Freshmen: 16% (44). Undergraduates: 10% (117). *Average award:* Freshmen: $11,899. Undergraduates: $11,511. *Scholarships, grants, and awards by category:* Academic interests/achievement: 1,382 awards ($8,979,602 total): biological sciences, business, communication, education, English, foreign languages, general academic interests/achievements, health fields, humanities, mathematics, physical sciences, premedicine, religion/biblical studies, social sciences. *Creative arts/performance:* 142 awards ($170,392 total): applied art and design, art/fine arts, debating, journalism/publications, music, performing arts, theater/drama. *Special achievements/activities:* 23 awards ($218,642 total): community service, leadership, religious involvement. *Special characteristics:* 155 awards ($1,438,972 total): adult students, children of faculty/staff, international students, out-of-state students, siblings of current students, veterans, veterans' children. *Tuition waivers:* Full or partial for employees or children of employees, adult students.

LOANS *Student loans:* $7,349,810 (80% need-based, 20% non-need-based). 84% of past graduating class borrowed through all loan programs. *Average indebtedness per student:* $30,187. *Average need-based loan:* Freshmen: $3195. Undergraduates: $4064. *Parent loans:* $1,512,714 (37% need-based, 63% non-need-based). *Programs:* Federal Direct (Subsidized and Unsubsidized Stafford, PLUS), state.

WORK-STUDY *Federal work-study:* Total amount: $159,813; 76 jobs averaging $2103. *State or other work-study/employment:* Total amount: $658,873 (45% need-based, 55% non-need-based). 324 part-time jobs averaging $2033.

APPLYING FOR FINANCIAL AID *Required financial aid forms:* FAFSA, institution's own form, state aid form. *Financial aid deadline (priority):* 3/1. *Notification date:* Continuous beginning 1/1. Students must reply within 4 weeks of notification.

CONTACT Mr. David Richmond McMillion, Director of Financial Aid, Piedmont College, PO Box 10, Demorest, GA 30535-0010, 706-778-3000 Ext. 1191 or toll-free 800-277-7020. *Fax:* 706-778-0708. *E-mail:* dmcmillion@piedmont.edu. *Website:* http://www.piedmont.edu/.

PIEDMONT INTERNATIONAL UNIVERSITY
Winston-Salem, NC

Tuition & fees: $10,100	Average undergraduate aid package: $9317

ABOUT THE INSTITUTION Independent Baptist, coed. *Awards:* certificates, associate, bachelor's, master's, and doctoral degrees. 15 undergraduate majors. *Total enrollment:* 384. Undergraduates: 197. Freshmen: 33. Federal methodology is used as a basis for awarding need-based institutional aid.

UNDERGRADUATE EXPENSES for 2017–2018 *Application fee:* $55. *Comprehensive fee:* $17,285 includes full-time tuition ($9300), mandatory fees ($800), and room and board ($7185). Full-time tuition and fees vary according to program. Room and board charges vary according to board plan. *Part-time tuition:* $325 per credit hour. *Part-time fees:* $60 per course; $100 per term. Part-time tuition and fees vary according to program.

FRESHMAN FINANCIAL AID (Fall 2016, est.) 24 applied for aid; of those 96% were deemed to have need. 100% of freshmen with need received aid; of those 9% had need fully met. *Average percent of need met:* 43% (excluding resources awarded to replace EFC). *Average financial aid package:* $8102 (excluding resources awarded to replace EFC). 8% of all full-time freshmen had no need and received non-need-based gift aid.

UNDERGRADUATE FINANCIAL AID (Fall 2016, est.) 174 applied for aid; of those 93% were deemed to have need. 99% of undergraduates with need received aid; of those 4% had need fully met. *Average percent of need met:* 42% (excluding resources awarded to replace EFC). *Average financial aid package:* $9317 (excluding resources awarded to replace EFC). 7% of all full-time undergraduates had no need and received non-need-based gift aid.

GIFT AID (NEED-BASED) *Total amount:* $1,924,161 (40% federal, 59% institutional, 1% external sources). *Receiving aid:* Freshmen: 88% (23); all full-time undergraduates: 88% (159). *Average award:* Freshmen: $6124; Undergraduates: $6843. *Scholarships, grants, and awards:* Federal Pell, FSEOG, college/university gift aid from institutional funds.

GIFT AID (NON-NEED-BASED) *Total amount:* $151,783 (93% institutional, 7% external sources). *Receiving aid:* Freshmen: 8% (2). Undergraduates: 2% (4). *Average award:* Freshmen: $6765. Undergraduates: $4605. *Scholarships, grants, and awards by category:* Academic interests/achievement: 39 awards ($97,656 total): general academic interests/achievements. Special characteristics: 223 awards ($325,633 total): children of faculty/staff, ethnic background, international students,

relatives of clergy, spouses of current students, veterans. *Tuition waivers:* Full or partial for employees or children of employees.

LOANS *Student loans:* $2,597,106 (25% need-based, 75% non-need-based). 69% of past graduating class borrowed through all loan programs. *Average indebtedness per student:* $19,784. *Average need-based loan:* Freshmen: $3500. Undergraduates: $4283. *Parent loans:* $85,496 (100% need-based). *Programs:* Federal Direct (Subsidized and Unsubsidized Stafford, PLUS).

WORK-STUDY Federal work-study jobs available.

APPLYING FOR FINANCIAL AID *Required financial aid forms:* FAFSA, institution's own form. *Financial aid deadline (priority):* 3/1. *Notification date:* Continuous beginning 3/15. Students must reply within 2 weeks of notification.

CONTACT Mandy McLain, Director of Financial Aid, Piedmont International University, 420 South Broad Street, Winston-Salem, NC 27101-5197, 336-714-7878 or toll-free 800-937-5097. *Fax:* 336-714-7820. *E-mail:* finaid@piedmontu.edu. *Website:* http://www.piedmontu.edu/.

PILLAR COLLEGE
Newark, NJ

CONTACT Financial Aid Office, Pillar College, 60 Park Place, Suite 701, Newark, NJ 07102, 973-803-5000 or toll-free 800-234-9305. *Website:* http://www.pillar.edu/.

PINE MANOR COLLEGE
Chestnut Hill, MA

ABOUT THE INSTITUTION Independent, coed. *Awards:* associate, bachelor's, and master's degrees. 12 undergraduate majors. *Total enrollment:* 486. Undergraduates: 447. Freshmen: 97.

GIFT AID (NEED-BASED) *Scholarships, grants, and awards:* Federal Pell, FSEOG, state, private, college/university gift aid from institutional funds.

GIFT AID (NON-NEED-BASED) *Scholarships, grants, and awards by category:* Academic interests/achievement: biological sciences, education, general academic interests/achievements. *Special achievements/activities:* general special achievements/activities, leadership. *Special characteristics:* children and siblings of alumni, members of minority groups, siblings of current students.

LOANS *Programs:* Federal Direct (Subsidized and Unsubsidized Stafford, PLUS), state, alternative loans.

WORK-STUDY *Federal work-study:* jobs available.

APPLYING FOR FINANCIAL AID *Required financial aid form:* FAFSA.

CONTACT Deborah A. Gravel, Director of Financial Aid, Pine Manor College, 400 Heath Street, Chestnut Hill, MA 02467, 617-731-7628 or toll-free 800-762-1357. *Fax:* 617-731-7102. *E-mail:* egorra@pmc.edu. *Website:* http://www.pmc.edu/.

PIONEER PACIFIC COLLEGE
Wilsonville, OR

CONTACT Financial Aid Office, Pioneer Pacific College, 27501 Southwest Parkway Avenue, Wilsonville, OR 97070, 503-682-3903 or toll-free 866-PPC-INFO. *Website:* http://www.pioneerpacific.edu/.

PITTSBURG STATE UNIVERSITY
Pittsburg, KS

Tuition & fees: N/R	Average undergraduate aid package: $6926

ABOUT THE INSTITUTION State-supported, coed. *Awards:* certificates, associate, bachelor's, master's, and doctoral degrees. 62 undergraduate majors. *Total*

enrollment: 7,102. Undergraduates: 5,905. Freshmen: 973. Federal methodology is used as a basis for awarding need-based institutional aid.

FRESHMAN FINANCIAL AID (Fall 2015) *Average financial aid package:* $6091 (excluding resources awarded to replace EFC).

UNDERGRADUATE FINANCIAL AID (Fall 2015) *Average financial aid package:* $6926 (excluding resources awarded to replace EFC).

GIFT AID (NEED-BASED) *Total amount:* $10,741,306 (91% federal, 6% state, 3% institutional). *Receiving aid:* Freshmen: 39% (408); all full-time undergraduates: 42% (2,231). *Average award:* Freshmen: $4710; Undergraduates: $4498. *Scholarships, grants, and awards:* Federal Pell, FSEOG, state, private, college/university gift aid from institutional funds.

GIFT AID (NON-NEED-BASED) *Total amount:* $12,095,687 (12% federal, 3% state, 46% institutional, 39% external sources). *Receiving aid:* Freshmen: 67% (702). Undergraduates: 50% (2,689). *Average award:* Freshmen: $3019. Undergraduates: $2334. *Scholarships, grants, and awards by category:* Academic interests/achievement: biological sciences, business, communication, computer science, education, engineering/technologies, English, foreign languages, general academic interests/achievements, health fields, home economics, mathematics, military science, physical sciences, social sciences. *Creative arts/performance:* music. *Special characteristics:* children and siblings of alumni, general special characteristics. *ROTC:* Army.

LOANS *Student loans:* $28,906,995 (39% need-based, 61% non-need-based). 70% of past graduating class borrowed through all loan programs. *Average indebtedness per student:* $24,384. *Average need-based loan:* Freshmen: $3312. Undergraduates: $4030. *Programs:* Federal Direct (Subsidized and Unsubsidized Stafford, PLUS), Perkins, Federal Nursing, college/university.

WORK-STUDY *Federal work-study:* jobs available. *State or other work-study/employment:* Total amount: $5000 (100% non-need-based). Part-time jobs available.

APPLYING FOR FINANCIAL AID *Required financial aid forms:* FAFSA, state aid form. *Financial aid deadline (priority):* 3/1. *Notification date:* Continuous beginning 3/1. Students must reply within 2 weeks of notification.

CONTACT Tammy Higgins, Director of Student Financial Assistance, Pittsburg State University, 1701 South Broadway Street, Pittsburg, KS 66762-7534, 620-235-4238 or toll-free 800-854-7488. *Fax:* 620-235-4078. *E-mail:* thiggins@pittstate.edu. *Website:* http://www.pittstate.edu/.

PITZER COLLEGE
Claremont, CA

Tuition & fees: N/R	Average undergraduate aid package: $45,338

ABOUT THE INSTITUTION Independent, coed. *Awards:* bachelor's degrees. 37 undergraduate majors. *Total enrollment:* 1,089. Undergraduates: 1,089. Freshmen: 268. Both federal and institutional methodology are used as a basis for awarding need-based institutional aid.

FRESHMAN FINANCIAL AID (Fall 2016, est.) 147 applied for aid; of those 75% were deemed to have need. 100% of freshmen with need received aid; of those 100% had need fully met. *Average percent of need met:* 100% (excluding resources awarded to replace EFC). *Average financial aid package:* $47,280 (excluding resources awarded to replace EFC). 1% of all full-time freshmen had no need and received non-need-based gift aid.

UNDERGRADUATE FINANCIAL AID (Fall 2016, est.) 492 applied for aid; of those 84% were deemed to have need. 99% of undergraduates with need received aid; of those 99% had need fully met. *Average percent of need met:* 100% (excluding resources awarded to replace EFC). *Average financial aid package:* $45,338 (excluding resources awarded to replace EFC). 1% of all full-time undergraduates had no need and received non-need-based gift aid.

GIFT AID (NEED-BASED) *Total amount:* $17,419,912 (6% federal, 4% state, 88% institutional, 2% external sources). *Receiving aid:* Freshmen: 41% (110); all full-time undergraduates: 38% (406). *Average award:* Freshmen: $42,956; Undergraduates: $40,447. *Scholarships, grants, and awards:* Federal Pell, FSEOG, state, private, college/university gift aid from institutional funds, United World College Scholarships.

GIFT AID (NON-NEED-BASED) *Total amount:* $152,690 (52% institutional, 48% external sources). *Receiving aid:* Freshmen: 2% (5). Undergraduates: 2% (23). *Average award:* Freshmen: $8561. Undergraduates: $6187. *Scholarships, grants, and awards by category:* Academic interests/achievement: 37 awards ($172,500

total): general academic interests/achievements. *ROTC:* Army cooperative, Air Force cooperative.

LOANS *Student loans:* $2,283,148 (53% need-based, 47% non-need-based). 38% of past graduating class borrowed through all loan programs. *Average indebtedness per student:* $21,569. *Average need-based loan:* Freshmen: $3242. Undergraduates: $4101. *Parent loans:* $1,528,774 (2% need-based, 98% non-need-based). *Programs:* Federal Direct (Subsidized and Unsubsidized Stafford, PLUS), Perkins, college/university.

WORK-STUDY *Federal work-study:* Total amount: $795,369; jobs available. *State or other work-study/employment:* Total amount: $26,910 (100% need-based). Part-time jobs available.

APPLYING FOR FINANCIAL AID *Required financial aid forms:* FAFSA, institution's own form, CSS Financial Aid PROFILE, state aid form, noncustodial (divorced/separated) parent's statement, business/farm supplement. *Financial aid deadline:* 2/1. *Notification date:* 4/1. Students must reply by 5/1.

CONTACT Robin Thompson, Director of Financial Aid, Pitzer College, 1050 North Mills Avenue, Claremont, CA 91711-6101, 909-621-8208 or toll-free 800-748-9371. *Fax:* 909-607-1205. *E-mail:* robin_thompson@pitzer.edu. *Website:* http://www.pitzer.edu/.

PLATT COLLEGE
Riverside, CA

CONTACT Financial Aid Office, Platt College, 6465 Sycamore Canyon Boulevard, Suite 100, Riverside, CA 92507, 951-572-4300 or toll-free 888-807-5288. *Website:* http://www.plattcollege.edu/.

PLATT COLLEGE
Aurora, CO

Tuition & fees: N/R	Average undergraduate aid package: $7500

ABOUT THE INSTITUTION Proprietary, coed. 2 undergraduate majors. Federal methodology is used as a basis for awarding need-based institutional aid.

FRESHMAN FINANCIAL AID (Fall 2015) 2 applied for aid; of those 100% were deemed to have need. 100% of freshmen with need received aid. *Average percent of need met:* 50% (excluding resources awarded to replace EFC). *Average financial aid package:* $7500 (excluding resources awarded to replace EFC).

UNDERGRADUATE FINANCIAL AID (Fall 2015) 125 applied for aid; of those 100% were deemed to have need. 100% of undergraduates with need received aid. *Average percent of need met:* 75% (excluding resources awarded to replace EFC). *Average financial aid package:* $7500 (excluding resources awarded to replace EFC).

GIFT AID (NEED-BASED) *Total amount:* $1,480,173 (96% federal, 4% external sources). *Receiving aid:* Freshmen: 50% (1); all full-time undergraduates: 40% (55). *Average award:* Freshmen: $2000; Undergraduates: $3500. *Scholarships, grants, and awards:* Federal Pell, FSEOG.

GIFT AID (NON-NEED-BASED) *Total amount:* $1,387,343 (100% federal).

LOANS *Student loans:* $2,194,201 (40% need-based, 60% non-need-based). 96% of past graduating class borrowed through all loan programs. *Average indebtedness per student:* $43,477. *Average need-based loan:* Freshmen: $3100. Undergraduates: $3500. *Parent loans:* $65,171 (100% non-need-based). *Programs:* Federal Direct (Subsidized and Unsubsidized Stafford, PLUS), Perkins.

APPLYING FOR FINANCIAL AID *Required financial aid forms:* FAFSA, institution's own form. *Financial aid deadline:* Continuous. *Notification date:* Continuous beginning 1/1.

CONTACT Ms. Margie Rose, Director of Financial Aid, Platt College, 3100 South Parker Road, #200, Aurora, CO 80014, 303-369-5151 Ext. 233. *Fax:* 303-745-1433. *E-mail:* margie.rose@plattcolorado.edu. *Website:* http://www.plattcolorado.edu/.

PLATT COLLEGE SAN DIEGO
San Diego, CA

CONTACT Matilde Aguilar, Student Accounts Coordinator, Platt College San Diego, 6250 El Cajon Boulevard, San Diego, CA 92115, 619-265-0107 Ext. 12 or toll-free 866-752-8826. *Fax:* 619-265-8655. *E-mail:* maguilar@platt.edu. *Website:* http://www.platt.edu/.

PLYMOUTH STATE UNIVERSITY
Plymouth, NH

Tuition & fees (NH res): $13,472	Average undergraduate aid package: $11,792

ABOUT THE INSTITUTION State-supported, coed. *Awards:* certificates, bachelor's, master's, and doctoral degrees. 54 undergraduate majors. *Total enrollment:* 5,050. Undergraduates: 4,125. Freshmen: 1,144. Federal methodology is used as a basis for awarding need-based institutional aid.

UNDERGRADUATE EXPENSES for 2016–2017 *Application fee:* $50. *Tuition, state resident:* full-time $11,020; part-time $459 per credit hour. *Tuition, nonresident:* full-time $19,280; part-time $803 per credit hour. *Required fees:* full-time $2452; $102 per credit hour. Full-time tuition and fees vary according to reciprocity agreements. Part-time tuition and fees vary according to reciprocity agreements. *College room and board:* $11,008; *Room only:* $6850. Room and board charges vary according to board plan, housing facility, and student level.

FRESHMAN FINANCIAL AID (Fall 2015) 1,241 applied for aid; of those 79% were deemed to have need. 100% of freshmen with need received aid; of those 22% had need fully met. *Average percent of need met:* 64% (excluding resources awarded to replace EFC). *Average financial aid package:* $10,951 (excluding resources awarded to replace EFC). 25% of all full-time freshmen had no need and received non-need-based gift aid.

UNDERGRADUATE FINANCIAL AID (Fall 2015) 3,338 applied for aid; of those 79% were deemed to have need. 100% of undergraduates with need received aid; of those 17% had need fully met. *Average percent of need met:* 60% (excluding resources awarded to replace EFC). *Average financial aid package:* $11,792 (excluding resources awarded to replace EFC). 20% of all full-time undergraduates had no need and received non-need-based gift aid.

GIFT AID (NEED-BASED) *Total amount:* $9,072,557 (59% federal, 6% state, 35% institutional). *Receiving aid:* Freshmen: 48% (641); all full-time undergraduates: 44% (1,683). *Average award:* Freshmen: $5054; Undergraduates: $5229. *Scholarships, grants, and awards:* Federal Pell, FSEOG, state, private, college/university gift aid from institutional funds.

GIFT AID (NON-NEED-BASED) *Total amount:* $12,356,481 (87% institutional, 13% external sources). *Receiving aid:* Freshmen: 70% (939). Undergraduates: 49% (1,879). *Average award:* Freshmen: $4266. Undergraduates: $3788. *Scholarships, grants, and awards by category:* Academic interests/achievement: 2,281 awards ($9,573,005 total): biological sciences, computer science, engineering/technologies, general academic interests/achievements, mathematics, premedicine. *Creative arts/performance:* 57 awards ($92,100 total): creative writing, dance, music, theater/drama. *Special characteristics:* 58 awards ($199,428 total): children of faculty/staff, international students. *Tuition waivers:* Full or partial for employees or children of employees, senior citizens. *ROTC:* Army cooperative, Air Force cooperative.

LOANS *Student loans:* $30,866,641 (34% need-based, 66% non-need-based). 85% of past graduating class borrowed through all loan programs. *Average indebtedness per student:* $37,801. *Average need-based loan:* Freshmen: $3394. Undergraduates: $4101. *Parent loans:* $7,862,982 (100% non-need-based). *Programs:* Federal Direct (Subsidized and Unsubsidized Stafford, PLUS), Perkins.

WORK-STUDY *Federal work-study:* 1,960 jobs averaging $2257.

APPLYING FOR FINANCIAL AID *Required financial aid form:* FAFSA. *Financial aid deadline (priority):* 3/1. *Notification date:* Continuous beginning 3/1. Students must reply by 5/1.

CONTACT Crystal Gaff, Director of Financial Aid, Plymouth State University, 17 High Street, Plymouth, NH 03264-1595, 603-535-2338 or toll-free 800-842-6900. *Fax:* 603-535-2627. *E-mail:* clgaff@plymouth.edu. *Website:* http://www.plymouth.edu/.

POINT LOMA NAZARENE UNIVERSITY
San Diego, CA

Tuition & fees: $34,600	Average undergraduate aid package: $22,624

ABOUT THE INSTITUTION Independent Nazarene, coed. *Awards:* certificates, bachelor's, and master's degrees. 65 undergraduate majors. *Total enrollment:* 4,156. Undergraduates: 3,053. Freshmen: 594. Federal methodology is used as a basis for awarding need-based institutional aid.

UNDERGRADUATE EXPENSES for 2017–2018 *Application fee:* $55. *Comprehensive fee:* $44,750 includes full-time tuition ($34,000), mandatory fees ($600), and room and board ($10,150). Full-time tuition and fees vary according to course load and program. Room and board charges vary according to board plan. *Part-time tuition:* $1417 per credit hour. Part-time tuition and fees vary according to course load and program.

FRESHMAN FINANCIAL AID (Fall 2015) 519 applied for aid; of those 78% were deemed to have need. 99% of freshmen with need received aid; of those 16% had need fully met. *Average percent of need met:* 65% (excluding resources awarded to replace EFC). *Average financial aid package:* $23,119 (excluding resources awarded to replace EFC). 21% of all full-time freshmen had no need and received non-need-based gift aid.

UNDERGRADUATE FINANCIAL AID (Fall 2015) 2,022 applied for aid; of those 85% were deemed to have need. 100% of undergraduates with need received aid; of those 14% had need fully met. *Average percent of need met:* 61% (excluding resources awarded to replace EFC). *Average financial aid package:* $22,624 (excluding resources awarded to replace EFC). 19% of all full-time undergraduates had no need and received non-need-based gift aid.

GIFT AID (NEED-BASED) *Total amount:* $26,282,677 (13% federal, 19% state, 54% institutional, 14% external sources). *Receiving aid:* Freshmen: 64% (385); all full-time undergraduates: 62% (1,607). *Average award:* Freshmen: $18,825; Undergraduates: $17,325. *Scholarships, grants, and awards:* Federal Pell, FSEOG, state, private, college/university gift aid from institutional funds, Federal Nursing.

GIFT AID (NON-NEED-BASED) *Total amount:* $7,106,488 (79% institutional, 21% external sources). *Receiving aid:* Freshmen: 6% (38). Undergraduates: 6% (144). *Average award:* Freshmen: $11,038. Undergraduates: $10,270. *Scholarships, grants, and awards by category:* Academic interests/achievement: biological sciences, business, communication, education, engineering/technologies, general academic interests/achievements, health fields, home economics, humanities, mathematics, religion/biblical studies, social sciences. *Creative arts/performance:* art/fine arts, debating, music, theater/drama. *Tuition waivers:* Full or partial for employees or children of employees, senior citizens. *ROTC:* Army cooperative, Naval cooperative, Air Force cooperative.

LOANS *Student loans:* $17,086,034 (71% need-based, 29% non-need-based). 69% of past graduating class borrowed through all loan programs. *Average indebtedness per student:* $34,844. *Average need-based loan:* Freshmen: $3367. Undergraduates: $4792. *Parent loans:* $9,216,774 (52% need-based, 48% non-need-based). *Programs:* Federal Direct (Subsidized and Unsubsidized Stafford, PLUS), Perkins, Federal Nursing.

WORK-STUDY *Federal work-study:* jobs available.

ATHLETIC AWARDS Total amount: $2,525,090 (52% need-based, 48% non-need-based).

APPLYING FOR FINANCIAL AID *Required financial aid form:* FAFSA. *Financial aid deadline (priority):* 3/2. *Notification date:* Continuous beginning 12/15. Students must reply by 5/15.

CONTACT Pam Macias, Director of Financial Aid, Point Loma Nazarene University, 3900 Lomaland Drive, San Diego, CA 92106, 619-849-2538 or toll-free 800-733-7770. *Fax:* 619-849-7078. *E-mail:* sfs@pointloma.edu. *Website:* http://www.pointloma.edu/.

POINT PARK UNIVERSITY
Pittsburgh, PA

Tuition & fees: $30,130	Average undergraduate aid package: $23,782

ABOUT THE INSTITUTION Independent, coed. *Awards:* certificates, associate, bachelor's, and master's degrees. 51 undergraduate majors. *Total enrollment:* 4,093. Undergraduates: 3,276. Freshmen: 611. Federal methodology is used as a basis for awarding need-based institutional aid.

UNDERGRADUATE EXPENSES for 2017–2018 *Application fee:* $40. *Comprehensive fee:* $42,090 includes full-time tuition ($28,860), mandatory fees ($1270), and room and board ($11,960). *College room only:* $5220. Full-time tuition and fees vary according to program. Room and board charges vary according to board plan and housing facility. *Part-time tuition:* $819 per credit. *Part-time fees:* $55 per credit. Part-time tuition and fees vary according to program.

FRESHMAN FINANCIAL AID (Fall 2016, est.) 580 applied for aid; of those 91% were deemed to have need. 100% of freshmen with need received aid; of those 16% had need fully met. *Average percent of need met:* 75% (excluding resources awarded to replace EFC). *Average financial aid package:* $26,242 (excluding resources awarded to replace EFC). 9% of all full-time freshmen had no need and received non-need-based gift aid.

UNDERGRADUATE FINANCIAL AID (Fall 2016, est.) 2,367 applied for aid; of those 93% were deemed to have need. 100% of undergraduates with need received aid; of those 14% had need fully met. *Average percent of need met:* 69% (excluding resources awarded to replace EFC). *Average financial aid package:* $23,782 (excluding resources awarded to replace EFC). 7% of all full-time undergraduates had no need and received non-need-based gift aid.

GIFT AID (NEED-BASED) *Total amount:* $39,138,619 (12% federal, 9% state, 71% institutional, 8% external sources). *Receiving aid:* Freshmen: 90% (523); all full-time undergraduates: 92% (2,182). *Average award:* Freshmen: $21,465; Undergraduates: $18,277. *Scholarships, grants, and awards:* Federal Pell, FSEOG, state, private, college/university gift aid from institutional funds.

GIFT AID (NON-NEED-BASED) *Total amount:* $3,202,696 (82% institutional, 18% external sources). *Receiving aid:* Freshmen: 10% (58). Undergraduates: 9% (202). *Average award:* Freshmen: $13,340. Undergraduates: $11,847. *Scholarships, grants, and awards by category: Academic interests/achievement:* biological sciences, business, communication, computer science, education, engineering/technologies, English, general academic interests/achievements, health fields, humanities, international studies, mathematics, physical sciences, premedicine, social sciences. *Creative arts/performance:* cinema/film/broadcasting, dance, performing arts, theater/drama. *Special achievements/activities:* community service, memberships. *Special characteristics:* children of faculty/staff, international students, previous college experience, siblings of current students. *Tuition waivers:* Full or partial for employees or children of employees. *ROTC:* Army cooperative, Air Force cooperative.

LOANS *Student loans:* $20,941,032 (76% need-based, 24% non-need-based). 80% of past graduating class borrowed through all loan programs. *Average indebtedness per student:* $26,729. *Average need-based loan:* Freshmen: $4495. Undergraduates: $5235. *Parent loans:* $7,720,750 (59% need-based, 41% non-need-based). *Programs:* Federal Direct (Subsidized and Unsubsidized Stafford, PLUS), Perkins.

WORK-STUDY *Federal work-study:* Total amount: $551,508; jobs available. *State or other work-study/employment:* Total amount: $1,289,935 (53% need-based, 47% non-need-based). Part-time jobs available.

ATHLETIC AWARDS Total amount: $1,881,469 (82% need-based, 18% non-need-based).

APPLYING FOR FINANCIAL AID *Required financial aid form:* FAFSA. *Financial aid deadline (priority):* 3/15. *Notification date:* Continuous beginning 2/15.

CONTACT Director of Financial Aid, Point Park University, 201 Wood Street, Pittsburgh, PA 15222-1984, 412-392-3930 or toll-free 800-321-0129. *E-mail:* financialaid@pointpark.edu.
Website: http://www.pointpark.edu/.

POINT UNIVERSITY
West Point, GA

CONTACT Blair Walker, Director of Financial Aid, Point University, 2605 Ben Hill Road, East Point, GA 30344, 404-761-8861 or toll-free 855-37-POINT. *Fax:* 404-669-2024. *E-mail:* blairw@acc.edu.
Website: http://point.edu/.

POLK STATE COLLEGE
Winter Haven, FL

CONTACT Lenora Burnett, Financial Aid Supervisor, Polk State College, 999 Avenue H, NE, Winter Haven, FL 33881, 863-297-5269. *E-mail:* lburnett@polk.edu.
Website: http://www.polk.edu/.

POLYTECHNIC UNIVERSITY OF PUERTO RICO
Hato Rey, PR

Tuition & fees: $8328	Average undergraduate aid package: $7698

ABOUT THE INSTITUTION Independent, coed. *Awards:* associate, bachelor's, master's, and doctoral degrees. 21 undergraduate majors. *Total enrollment:* 4,291. Undergraduates: 3,493. Freshmen: 361. Federal methodology is used as a basis for awarding need-based institutional aid.

UNDERGRADUATE EXPENSES for 2017–2018 *Application fee:* $30. *Comprehensive fee:* $20,165 includes full-time tuition ($7488), mandatory fees ($840), and room and board ($11,837). Full-time tuition and fees vary according to course level, course load, degree level, and program. Part-time tuition and fees vary according to course level, course load, degree level, and program.

FRESHMAN FINANCIAL AID (Fall 2015) 327 applied for aid; of those 96% were deemed to have need. 97% of freshmen with need received aid; of those .3% had need fully met. *Average percent of need met:* 29% (excluding resources awarded to replace EFC). *Average financial aid package:* $5339 (excluding resources awarded to replace EFC).

UNDERGRADUATE FINANCIAL AID (Fall 2015) 1,918 applied for aid; of those 97% were deemed to have need. 95% of undergraduates with need received aid; of those .5% had need fully met. *Average percent of need met:* 45% (excluding resources awarded to replace EFC). *Average financial aid package:* $7698 (excluding resources awarded to replace EFC).

GIFT AID (NEED-BASED) *Total amount:* $11,060,429 (96% federal, 4% state). *Receiving aid:* Freshmen: 88% (303); all full-time undergraduates: 81% (1,774). *Average award:* Freshmen: $2904; Undergraduates: $2535. *Scholarships, grants, and awards:* Federal Pell, FSEOG, state, private, college/university gift aid from institutional funds.

GIFT AID (NON-NEED-BASED) *Total amount:* $227,950 (100% institutional). *Receiving aid:* Freshmen: 50% (172). Undergraduates: 20% (441). *Average award:* Freshmen: $208. Undergraduates: $245. *Tuition waivers:* Full or partial for employees or children of employees. *ROTC:* Army cooperative.

LOANS *Student loans:* $16,352,130 (47% need-based, 53% non-need-based). *Average need-based loan:* Freshmen: $1752. Undergraduates: $2665. *Parent loans:* $23,731 (100% need-based). *Programs:* Federal Direct (Subsidized and Unsubsidized Stafford, PLUS).

WORK-STUDY Federal work-study jobs available.

ATHLETIC AWARDS Total amount: $168,580 (100% non-need-based).

APPLYING FOR FINANCIAL AID *Required financial aid form:* FAFSA. *Financial aid deadline:* Continuous. *Notification date:* 7/15. Students must reply within 2 weeks of notification.

CONTACT Sergio E. Villoldo, Financial Aid Director, Polytechnic University of Puerto Rico, 377 Ponce de Leon Avenue, Hato Rey, PR 00918, 787-754-8000 Ext. 253. *Fax:* 787-766-1163. *E-mail:* svilloldo@pupr.edu.
Website: http://www.pupr.edu/.

POLYTECHNIC UNIVERSITY OF PUERTO RICO, MIAMI CAMPUS
Miami, FL

CONTACT Maria Victoria Shehadeh, Administrative Affairs Coordinator/Financial Aid Officer, Polytechnic University of Puerto Rico, Miami Campus, 8180 Northwest 36th Street, Suite 401, Miami, FL 33166, 305-418-8000 Ext. 204 or toll-free 888-729-7659. *E-mail:* mshehadeh@pupr.edu.
Website: http://www.pupr.edu/miami/.

POLYTECHNIC UNIVERSITY OF PUERTO RICO, ORLANDO CAMPUS
Orlando, FL

CONTACT Mrs. Ileana Diaz, Financial Aid Officer, Polytechnic University of Puerto Rico, Orlando Campus, 550 North Econlockhatchee Trail, Orlando, FL 32825, 407-677-7000 Ext. 806 or toll-free 888-577-POLY. *Fax:* 407-677-5082. *E-mail:* idiaz@pupr.edu.
Website: http://www.pupr.edu/orlando/.

POMONA COLLEGE
Claremont, CA

Tuition & fees: $49,352	Average undergraduate aid package: $48,034

ABOUT THE INSTITUTION Independent, coed. *Awards:* bachelor's degrees. 49 undergraduate majors. *Total enrollment:* 1,660. Undergraduates: 1,660. Freshmen: 411. Both federal and institutional methodology are used as a basis for awarding need-based institutional aid.
UNDERGRADUATE EXPENSES for 2016–2017 *Application fee:* $70. *Comprehensive fee:* $64,957 includes full-time tuition ($49,005), mandatory fees ($347), and room and board ($15,605). Room and board charges vary according to board plan.
FRESHMAN FINANCIAL AID (Fall 2015) 259 applied for aid; of those 85% were deemed to have need. 100% of freshmen with need received aid; of those 100% had need fully met. *Average percent of need met:* 100% (excluding resources awarded to replace EFC). *Average financial aid package:* $51,284 (excluding resources awarded to replace EFC). 1% of all full-time freshmen had no need and received non-need-based gift aid.
UNDERGRADUATE FINANCIAL AID (Fall 2015) 1,148 applied for aid; of those 80% were deemed to have need. 100% of undergraduates with need received aid; of those 100% had need fully met. *Average percent of need met:* 100% (excluding resources awarded to replace EFC). *Average financial aid package:* $48,034 (excluding resources awarded to replace EFC). 1% of all full-time undergraduates had no need and received non-need-based gift aid.
GIFT AID (NEED-BASED) *Total amount:* $42,139,154 (5% federal, 3% state, 90% institutional, 2% external sources). *Receiving aid:* Freshmen: 55% (220); all full-time undergraduates: 56% (917). *Average award:* Freshmen: $49,433; Undergraduates: $46,039. *Scholarships, grants, and awards:* Federal Pell, FSEOG, state, private, college/university gift aid from institutional funds.
GIFT AID (NON-NEED-BASED) *Total amount:* $852,749 (14% federal, 2% institutional, 84% external sources). *Receiving aid:* Freshmen: 2. Undergraduates: 2. *Average award:* Freshmen: $5000. Undergraduates: $5000. *Tuition waivers:* Full or partial for employees or children of employees. *ROTC:* Army cooperative, Air Force cooperative.
LOANS *Student loans:* $1,851,571 (100% non-need-based). 36% of past graduating class borrowed through all loan programs. *Average indebtedness per student:* $18,738. *Parent loans:* $1,162,724 (100% non-need-based). *Programs:* Federal Direct (Subsidized and Unsubsidized Stafford, PLUS), Perkins, college/university.
WORK-STUDY *Federal work-study:* 153 jobs averaging $1566. *State or other work-study/employment:* Total amount: $1,615,959 (63% need-based, 37% non-need-based). 676 part-time jobs averaging $2300.
APPLYING FOR FINANCIAL AID *Required financial aid forms:* FAFSA, CSS Financial Aid PROFILE, state aid form, noncustodial (divorced/separated) parent's statement, business/farm supplement. *Financial aid deadline:* 3/1. *Notification date:* 4/1. Students must reply by 5/1.
CONTACT Robin Thompson, Director of Financial Aid, Pomona College, 333 North College Way, Sumner Hall, Claremont, CA 91711, 909-621-8205. *Fax:* 909-607-7941. *E-mail:* financial_aid@pomadm.pomona.edu.
Website: http://www.pomona.edu/.

PONTIFICAL CATHOLIC UNIVERSITY OF PUERTO RICO
Ponce, PR

CONTACT Mrs. Rosalia Martinez, Director of Financial Aid, Pontifical Catholic University of Puerto Rico, 2250 Las Americas Avenue, Suite 549, Ponce, PR 00717-9777, 787-841-2000 Ext. 1065 or toll-free 800-961-7696. *Fax:* 787-651-2041. *E-mail:* rosalia.martinez@email.pucpr.edu.
Website: http://www.pucpr.edu/.

PONTIFICAL CATHOLIC UNIVERSITY OF PUERTO RICO–ARECIBO CAMPUS
Arecibo, PR

CONTACT Financial Aid Office, Pontifical Catholic University of Puerto Rico–Arecibo Campus, PO Box 144045, Arecibo, PR 00614-4045, 787-881-1212 Ext.6000.
Website: http://www.pucpr.edu/arecibo/.

PONTIFICAL CATHOLIC UNIVERSITY OF PUERTO RICO–MAYAGUEZ CAMPUS
Mayaguez, PR

CONTACT Financial Aid Office, Pontifical Catholic University of Puerto Rico–Mayaguez Campus, 482 Sur Calle Ramon Emerito Betances, Mayaguez, PR 00680.
Website: http://www.pucpr.edu/mayaguez/.

PONTIFICAL COLLEGE JOSEPHINUM
Columbus, OH

CONTACT Marky Leichtnam, Financial Aid Director, Pontifical College Josephinum, 7625 North High Street, Columbus, OH 43235-1498, 614-985-2212 or toll-free 888-252-5812. *Fax:* 614-885-2307. *E-mail:* mleichtnam@pcj.edu.
Website: http://www.pcj.edu/.

PORTLAND STATE UNIVERSITY
Portland, OR

Tuition & fees (OR res): $6933	Average undergraduate aid package: $9293

ABOUT THE INSTITUTION State-supported, coed. *Awards:* certificates, bachelor's, master's, and doctoral degrees. 80 undergraduate majors. *Total enrollment:* 27,229. Undergraduates: 21,633. Freshmen: 1,758. Federal methodology is used as a basis for awarding need-based institutional aid.
UNDERGRADUATE EXPENSES for 2016–2017 *Application fee:* $50. *Tuition, state resident:* full-time $5616; part-time $156 per credit hour. *Tuition, nonresident:* full-time $18,828; part-time $523 per credit hour. *Required fees:* full-time $1317; $17 per credit hour or $106 per term. Full-time tuition and fees vary

according to program and reciprocity agreements. Part-time tuition and fees vary according to program and reciprocity agreements. **College room and board:** $12,822; **Room only:** $9204. Room and board charges vary according to board plan and housing facility.

FRESHMAN FINANCIAL AID (Fall 2015) 1,358 applied for aid; of those 78% were deemed to have need. 97% of freshmen with need received aid; of those 8% had need fully met. **Average percent of need met:** 59% (excluding resources awarded to replace EFC). **Average financial aid package:** $9943 (excluding resources awarded to replace EFC). 1% of all full-time freshmen had no need and received non-need-based gift aid.

UNDERGRADUATE FINANCIAL AID (Fall 2015) 10,901 applied for aid; of those 89% were deemed to have need. 97% of undergraduates with need received aid; of those 4% had need fully met. **Average percent of need met:** 52% (excluding resources awarded to replace EFC). **Average financial aid package:** $9293 (excluding resources awarded to replace EFC). 1% of all full-time undergraduates had no need and received non-need-based gift aid.

GIFT AID (NEED-BASED) Total amount: $50,924,664 (72% federal, 19% state, 3% institutional, 6% external sources). **Receiving aid:** Freshmen: 48% (761); all full-time undergraduates: 52% (7,525). **Average award:** Freshmen: $6195; Undergraduates: $5798. **Scholarships, grants, and awards:** Federal Pell, FSEOG, state, private, college/university gift aid from institutional funds, United Negro College Fund.

GIFT AID (NON-NEED-BASED) Total amount: $931,938 (11% federal, 1% state, 37% institutional, 51% external sources). **Receiving aid:** Freshmen: 1% (16). Undergraduates: 57. **Average award:** Freshmen: $2090. Undergraduates: $2652. **Scholarships, grants, and awards by category:** Academic interests/achievement: architecture, area/ethnic studies, business, computer science, education, engineering/technologies, foreign languages, general academic interests/achievements, humanities, international studies, physical sciences, social sciences. Creative arts/performance: art/fine arts, general creative arts/performance, music, theater/drama. Special achievements/activities: community service, general special achievements/activities, leadership, memberships. Special characteristics: adult students, ethnic background, handicapped students, international students, members of minority groups, out-of-state students, veterans. **Tuition waivers:** Full or partial for employees or children of employees, senior citizens. **ROTC:** Army cooperative, Air Force cooperative.

LOANS Student loans: $88,206,797 (88% need-based, 12% non-need-based). 64% of past graduating class borrowed through all loan programs. Average indebtedness per student: $27,213. **Average need-based loan:** Freshmen: $3120. Undergraduates: $4188. **Parent loans:** $8,683,400 (54% need-based, 46% non-need-based). **Programs:** Federal Direct (Subsidized and Unsubsidized Stafford, PLUS), Perkins.

WORK-STUDY Federal work-study: jobs available. **State or other work-study/employment:** Part-time jobs available.

ATHLETIC AWARDS Total amount: $1,323,404 (43% need-based, 57% non-need-based).

APPLYING FOR FINANCIAL AID Required financial aid form: FAFSA. **Financial aid deadline:** Continuous. **Notification date:** Continuous beginning 3/15.

CONTACT G. Michael Johnson, Director of Financial Aid, Portland State University, PO Box 851, Portland, OR 97207, 800-547-8887. Fax: 503-725-5965. E-mail: askfa@pdx.edu.
Website: http://www.pdx.edu/.

POST UNIVERSITY
Waterbury, CT

ABOUT THE INSTITUTION Independent, coed. **Awards:** certificates, associate, bachelor's, and master's degrees. 20 undergraduate majors. **Total enrollment:** 828. Undergraduates: 828. Freshmen: 194.

GIFT AID (NEED-BASED) Scholarships, grants, and awards: Federal Pell, FSEOG, state, private, college/university gift aid from institutional funds.

GIFT AID (NON-NEED-BASED) Scholarships, grants, and awards by category: Academic interests/achievement: agriculture, biological sciences, business, communication, computer science, education, general academic interests/achievements, humanities, international studies, social sciences. Special characteristics: children and siblings of alumni, local/state students, siblings of current students.

LOANS Programs: Federal Direct (Subsidized and Unsubsidized Stafford, PLUS), college/university.

APPLYING FOR FINANCIAL AID Required financial aid form: FAFSA.

CONTACT Ms. Michelle Gambacini, Director of Financial Aid, Post University, 800 Country Club Road, Waterbury, CT 06723-2540, 203-591-5615 or toll-free 800-345-2562. Fax: 203-596-4599. E-mail: mgambacini@post.edu.
Website: http://www.post.edu/.

PRAIRIE VIEW A&M UNIVERSITY
Prairie View, TX

Tuition & fees (TX res): $10,059	Average undergraduate aid package: $15,280

ABOUT THE INSTITUTION State-supported, coed. **Awards:** certificates, bachelor's, master's, and doctoral degrees. 40 undergraduate majors. **Total enrollment:** 8,762. Undergraduates: 7,455. Freshmen: 1,839. Federal methodology is used as a basis for awarding need-based institutional aid.

UNDERGRADUATE EXPENSES for 2016–2017 Application fee: $40. **Tuition, state resident:** full-time $6216; part-time $241 per credit hour. **Tuition, nonresident:** full-time $19,535; part-time $684 per credit hour. **Required fees:** full-time $3843. Full-time tuition and fees vary according to course load, degree level, program, and reciprocity agreements. Part-time tuition and fees vary according to course load, degree level, program, and reciprocity agreements. **College room and board:** $8626; **Room only:** $5922. Room and board charges vary according to board plan, housing facility, and student level. **Payment plan:** Guaranteed tuition.

FRESHMAN FINANCIAL AID (Fall 2015) 1,552 applied for aid; of those 93% were deemed to have need. 97% of freshmen with need received aid; of those 7% had need fully met. **Average percent of need met:** 75% (excluding resources awarded to replace EFC). **Average financial aid package:** $16,160 (excluding resources awarded to replace EFC). 3% of all full-time freshmen had no need and received non-need-based gift aid.

UNDERGRADUATE FINANCIAL AID (Fall 2015) 5,923 applied for aid; of those 94% were deemed to have need. 98% of undergraduates with need received aid; of those 12% had need fully met. **Average percent of need met:** 74% (excluding resources awarded to replace EFC). **Average financial aid package:** $15,280 (excluding resources awarded to replace EFC). 2% of all full-time undergraduates had no need and received non-need-based gift aid.

GIFT AID (NEED-BASED) Total amount: $37,085,703 (60% federal, 31% state, 9% institutional). **Receiving aid:** Freshmen: 77% (1,232); all full-time undergraduates: 73% (4,621). **Average award:** Freshmen: $10,485; Undergraduates: $7742. **Scholarships, grants, and awards:** Federal Pell, FSEOG, state, private, college/university gift aid from institutional funds, United Negro College Fund, Federal Nursing.

GIFT AID (NON-NEED-BASED) Total amount: $12,042,245 (87% institutional, 13% external sources). **Receiving aid:** Freshmen: 33% (523). Undergraduates: 35% (2,224). **Average award:** Freshmen: $6374. Undergraduates: $5649. **Tuition waivers:** Full or partial for employees or children of employees, senior citizens. **ROTC:** Army, Naval, Air Force cooperative.

LOANS Student loans: $39,490,395 (77% need-based, 23% non-need-based). 87% of past graduating class borrowed through all loan programs. Average indebtedness per student: $34,752. **Average need-based loan:** Freshmen: $5993. Undergraduates: $7695. **Parent loans:** $10,256,926 (100% non-need-based). **Programs:** Federal Direct (Subsidized and Unsubsidized Stafford, PLUS), state, alternative loans.

WORK-STUDY Federal work-study: 453 jobs averaging $2796. **State or other work-study/employment:** Total amount: $69,097 (100% need-based). 18 part-time jobs averaging $3217.

ATHLETIC AWARDS Total amount: $2,718,508 (100% non-need-based).

APPLYING FOR FINANCIAL AID Required financial aid form: FAFSA. **Financial aid deadline:** 3/15. **Notification date:** 6/1. Students must reply by 8/1.

CONTACT Mr. Ralph Perri, Director of Student Financial Aid and Scholarships, Prairie View A&M University, PO Box 519, Mail Stop 1005, Prairie View, TX 77446, 936-261-1000. E-mail: finaidscholarships@pvamu.edu.
Website: http://www.pvamu.edu/.

PRATT INSTITUTE
Brooklyn, NY

ABOUT THE INSTITUTION Independent, coed. *Awards:* certificates, associate, bachelor's, and master's degrees. 25 undergraduate majors. *Total enrollment:* 4,659. Undergraduates: 3,310. Freshmen: 709.

GIFT AID (NEED-BASED) *Scholarships, grants, and awards:* Federal Pell, FSEOG, state, college/university gift aid from institutional funds.

GIFT AID (NON-NEED-BASED) *Scholarships, grants, and awards by category:* Academic interests/achievement: general academic interests/achievements.

LOANS *Programs:* Federal Direct (Subsidized and Unsubsidized Stafford, PLUS), Perkins.

WORK-STUDY *Federal work-study:* jobs available. *State or other work-study/employment:* Part-time jobs available.

APPLYING FOR FINANCIAL AID *Required financial aid forms:* FAFSA, state aid form.

CONTACT Nedzad Goga, Director of Financial Aid, Pratt Institute, 200 Willoughby Avenue, Myrtle Hall, Room 6E-9, Brooklyn, NY 11205-3899, 718-636-3563 or toll-free 800-331-0834. *Fax:* 718-636-3739. *E-mail:* finaid@pratt.edu.
Website: http://www.pratt.edu/.

PRESBYTERIAN COLLEGE
Clinton, SC

Tuition & fees: $37,842	Average undergraduate aid package: $33,431

ABOUT THE INSTITUTION Independent Presbyterian Church (U.S.A.), coed. *Awards:* bachelor's and doctoral degrees. 29 undergraduate majors. *Total enrollment:* 1,352. Undergraduates: 1,063. Freshmen: 287. Federal methodology is used as a basis for awarding need-based institutional aid.

UNDERGRADUATE EXPENSES for 2017–2018 *Comprehensive fee:* $48,140 includes full-time tuition ($34,982), mandatory fees ($2860), and room and board ($10,298). *College room only:* $4992. Full-time tuition and fees vary according to course load and reciprocity agreements. Room and board charges vary according to board plan and housing facility. *Part-time tuition:* $1457 per credit hour. *Part-time fees:* $27 per credit hour. Part-time tuition and fees vary according to course load and program.

FRESHMAN FINANCIAL AID (Fall 2016, est.) 270 applied for aid; of those 85% were deemed to have need. 100% of freshmen with need received aid; of those 32% had need fully met. *Average percent of need met:* 83% (excluding resources awarded to replace EFC). *Average financial aid package:* $34,989 (excluding resources awarded to replace EFC). 20% of all full-time freshmen had no need and received non-need-based gift aid.

UNDERGRADUATE FINANCIAL AID (Fall 2016, est.) 822 applied for aid; of those 85% were deemed to have need. 100% of undergraduates with need received aid; of those 34% had need fully met. *Average percent of need met:* 81% (excluding resources awarded to replace EFC). *Average financial aid package:* $33,431 (excluding resources awarded to replace EFC). 26% of all full-time undergraduates had no need and received non-need-based gift aid.

GIFT AID (NEED-BASED) *Total amount:* $17,168,689 (7% federal, 21% state, 70% institutional, 2% external sources). *Receiving aid:* Freshmen: 80% (229); all full-time undergraduates: 74% (699). *Average award:* Freshmen: $27,139; Undergraduates: $24,657. *Scholarships, grants, and awards:* Federal Pell, FSEOG, state, private, college/university gift aid from institutional funds.

GIFT AID (NON-NEED-BASED) *Total amount:* $6,305,158 (8% state, 86% institutional, 6% external sources). *Receiving aid:* Freshmen: 17% (50). Undergraduates: 18% (169). *Average award:* Freshmen: $15,705. Undergraduates: $15,972. *Scholarships, grants, and awards by category:* Academic interests/achievement: general academic interests/achievements. *Creative arts/performance:* music. *Special achievements/activities:* leadership, religious involvement. *Special characteristics:* children of faculty/staff, relatives of clergy, religious affiliation. *Tuition waivers:* Full or partial for employees or children of employees, senior citizens. **ROTC:** Army.

LOANS *Student loans:* $4,327,572 (63% need-based, 37% non-need-based). 62% of past graduating class borrowed through all loan programs. *Average indebtedness per student:* $24,930. *Average need-based loan:* Freshmen: $3500. Undergrad-

uates: $4873. *Parent loans:* $2,083,608 (39% need-based, 61% non-need-based). *Programs:* Federal Direct (Subsidized and Unsubsidized Stafford, PLUS), Perkins, state.

WORK-STUDY *Federal work-study:* Total amount: $355,931; 180 jobs averaging $1977. *State or other work-study/employment:* Total amount: $253,988 (12% need-based, 88% non-need-based). 168 part-time jobs averaging $1511.

ATHLETIC AWARDS Total amount: $6,455,954 (51% need-based, 49% non-need-based).

APPLYING FOR FINANCIAL AID *Required financial aid form:* FAFSA *Financial aid deadline (priority):* 11/1. *Notification date:* 3/1. Students must reply by 5/1.

CONTACT Mr. Brian J Fortman, Director of Financial Aid, Presbyterian College, 503 South Broad Street, Clinton, SC 29325, 864-833-8287 or toll-free 800-476-7272. *E-mail:* bjfortman@presby.edu.
Website: http://www.presby.edu/.

PRESCOTT COLLEGE
Prescott, AZ

Tuition & fees: $29,566	Average undergraduate aid package: $20,132

ABOUT THE INSTITUTION Independent, coed. *Awards:* certificates, bachelor's, master's, and doctoral degrees. 30 undergraduate majors. *Total enrollment:* 703. Undergraduates: 356. Freshmen: 47. Federal methodology is used as a basis for awarding need-based institutional aid.

UNDERGRADUATE EXPENSES for 2017–2018 *Comprehensive fee:* $37,266 includes full-time tuition ($28,976), mandatory fees ($590), and room and board ($7700). *College room only:* $6900. Room and board charges vary according to board plan.

FRESHMAN FINANCIAL AID (Fall 2016, est.) 38 applied for aid; of those 68% were deemed to have need. 100% of freshmen with need received aid; of those 4% had need fully met. *Average percent of need met:* 70% (excluding resources awarded to replace EFC). *Average financial aid package:* $23,691 (excluding resources awarded to replace EFC). 40% of all full-time freshmen had no need and received non-need-based gift aid.

UNDERGRADUATE FINANCIAL AID (Fall 2016, est.) 218 applied for aid; of those 86% were deemed to have need. 100% of undergraduates with need received aid; of those 9% had need fully met. *Average percent of need met:* 64% (excluding resources awarded to replace EFC). *Average financial aid package:* $20,132 (excluding resources awarded to replace EFC). 28% of all full-time undergraduates had no need and received non-need-based gift aid.

GIFT AID (NEED-BASED) *Total amount:* $3,127,144 (24% federal, 73% institutional, 3% external sources). *Receiving aid:* Freshmen: 55% (26); all full-time undergraduates: 68% (187). *Average award:* Freshmen: $19,534; Undergraduates: $15,202. *Scholarships, grants, and awards:* Federal Pell, FSEOG, state, private, college/university gift aid from institutional funds.

GIFT AID (NON-NEED-BASED) *Total amount:* $601,400 (1% federal, 96% institutional, 3% external sources). *Receiving aid:* Freshmen: 2% (1). Undergraduates: 3% (9). *Average award:* Freshmen: $10,346. Undergraduates: $6575. *Scholarships, grants, and awards by category:* Academic interests/achievement: general academic interests/achievements. *Special achievements/activities:* general special achievements/activities, leadership. *Tuition waivers:* Full or partial for employees or children of employees.

LOANS *Student loans:* $2,275,235 (82% need-based, 18% non-need-based). 72% of past graduating class borrowed through all loan programs. *Average indebtedness per student:* $27,130. *Average need-based loan:* Freshmen: $3262. Undergraduates: $4576. *Parent loans:* $361,988 (42% need-based, 58% non-need-based). *Programs:* Federal Direct (Subsidized and Unsubsidized Stafford, PLUS).

WORK-STUDY *Federal work-study:* Total amount: $116,975; jobs available. *State or other work-study/employment:* Part-time jobs available.

APPLYING FOR FINANCIAL AID *Required financial aid form:* FAFSA. *Financial aid deadline:* Continuous. *Notification date:* Continuous beginning 11/1.

CONTACT Mary Frances Causey, Director of Financial Aid, Prescott College, 220 Grove Avenue, Prescott, AZ 86301, 928-350-1111 or toll-free 877-350-2100. *Fax:* 928-350-1120. *E-mail:* finaid@prescott.edu.
Website: http://www.prescott.edu/.

PRESENTATION COLLEGE
Aberdeen, SD

CONTACT Ms. Janel Wagner, Director of Financial Aid, Presentation College, 1500 North Main Street, Aberdeen, SD 57401-1299, 605-229-8427 or toll-free 800-437-6060. *Fax:* 605-229-8537. *E-mail:* janel.wagner@presentation.edu.
Website: http://www.presentation.edu/.

PRINCETON UNIVERSITY
Princeton, NJ

Tuition & fees: $45,320	Average undergraduate aid package: $49,502

ABOUT THE INSTITUTION Independent, coed. *Awards:* bachelor's, master's, and doctoral degrees. 38 undergraduate majors. *Total enrollment:* 8,181. Undergraduates: 5,400. Freshmen: 1,305. Both federal and institutional methodology are used as a basis for awarding need-based institutional aid.

UNDERGRADUATE EXPENSES for 2017–2018 *Application fee:* $65. *Comprehensive fee:* $60,090 includes full-time tuition ($45,320) and room and board ($14,770). *College room only:* $8335. Room and board charges vary according to board plan.

FRESHMAN FINANCIAL AID (Fall 2016, est.) 929 applied for aid; of those 84% were deemed to have need. 100% of freshmen with need received aid; of those 100% had need fully met. *Average percent of need met:* 100% (excluding resources awarded to replace EFC). *Average financial aid package:* $51,390 (excluding resources awarded to replace EFC).

UNDERGRADUATE FINANCIAL AID (Fall 2016, est.) 3,433 applied for aid; of those 91% were deemed to have need. 100% of undergraduates with need received aid; of those 100% had need fully met. *Average percent of need met:* 100% (excluding resources awarded to replace EFC). *Average financial aid package:* $49,502 (excluding resources awarded to replace EFC).

GIFT AID (NEED-BASED) *Total amount:* $148,300,000 (3% federal, 94% institutional, 3% external sources). *Receiving aid:* Freshmen: 60% (782); all full-time undergraduates: 60% (3,126). *Average award:* Freshmen: $49,870; Undergraduates: $47,497. *Scholarships, grants, and awards:* Federal Pell, FSEOG, state, private, college/university gift aid from institutional funds.

GIFT AID (NON-NEED-BASED) *Tuition waivers:* Full or partial for employees or children of employees. *ROTC:* Army, Naval cooperative, Air Force cooperative.

LOANS *Student loans:* 18% of past graduating class borrowed through all loan programs. *Average indebtedness per student:* $8908. *Parent loans:* $675,000 (100% non-need-based). *Programs:* Federal Direct (Subsidized and Unsubsidized Stafford, PLUS), Perkins, college/university.

WORK-STUDY *Federal work-study:* Total amount: $800,000; jobs available. *State or other work-study/employment:* Total amount: $2,100,000 (100% need-based). Part-time jobs available.

APPLYING FOR FINANCIAL AID *Required financial aid forms:* FAFSA, institution's own form. *Financial aid deadline (priority):* 2/1. *Notification date:* 4/1. Students must reply by 5/1.

CONTACT Robin Moscato, Director of Financial Aid, Princeton University, PO Box 591, Princeton, NJ 08542, 609-258-3330. *Fax:* 609-258-3558. *E-mail:* pfaa@princeton.edu.
Website: http://www.princeton.edu/.

PRINCIPIA COLLEGE
Elsah, IL

Tuition & fees: $28,920	Average undergraduate aid package: $31,415

ABOUT THE INSTITUTION Independent Christian Science, coed. *Awards:* bachelor's degrees. 22 undergraduate majors. *Total enrollment:* 479. Undergraduates: 479. Freshmen: 112. Institutional methodology is used as a basis for awarding need-based institutional aid.

UNDERGRADUATE EXPENSES for 2017–2018 *Comprehensive fee:* $40,350 includes full-time tuition ($28,320), mandatory fees ($600), and room and board ($11,430). *College room only:* $5430. Full-time tuition and fees vary according to course load. Room and board charges vary according to board plan. *Part-time tuition:* $916 per credit hour. *Part-time fees:* $300 per term. Part-time tuition and fees vary according to course load.

FRESHMAN FINANCIAL AID (Fall 2016, est.) 73 applied for aid; of those 99% were deemed to have need. 100% of freshmen with need received aid; of those 56% had need fully met. *Average percent of need met:* 96% (excluding resources awarded to replace EFC). *Average financial aid package:* $31,528 (excluding resources awarded to replace EFC). 34% of all full-time freshmen had no need and received non-need-based gift aid.

UNDERGRADUATE FINANCIAL AID (Fall 2016, est.) 345 applied for aid; of those 97% were deemed to have need. 100% of undergraduates with need received aid; of those 55% had need fully met. *Average percent of need met:* 95% (excluding resources awarded to replace EFC). *Average financial aid package:* $31,415 (excluding resources awarded to replace EFC). 28% of all full-time undergraduates had no need and received non-need-based gift aid.

GIFT AID (NEED-BASED) *Total amount:* $9,425,855 (100% institutional). *Receiving aid:* Freshmen: 64% (72); all full-time undergraduates: 70% (335). *Average award:* Freshmen: $26,806; Undergraduates: $27,447. *Scholarships, grants, and awards:* private, college/university gift aid from institutional funds.

GIFT AID (NON-NEED-BASED) *Total amount:* $3,006,017 (100% institutional). *Receiving aid:* Freshmen: 56% (63). Undergraduates: 45% (215). *Average award:* Freshmen: $23,648. Undergraduates: $23,301. *Scholarships, grants, and awards by category: Academic interests/achievement:* 160 awards ($1,957,291 total): general academic interests/achievements. *Special achievements/activities:* 273 awards ($3,185,125 total): community service, general special achievements/activities, leadership, religious involvement. *Special characteristics:* 433 awards ($5,142,416 total): children and siblings of alumni, children of faculty/staff. *Tuition waivers:* Full or partial for employees or children of employees.

LOANS *Student loans:* $1,416,000 (94% need-based, 6% non-need-based). 63% of past graduating class borrowed through all loan programs. *Average indebtedness per student:* $21,260. *Average need-based loan:* Freshmen: $5762. Undergraduates: $5580. *Programs:* college/university.

APPLYING FOR FINANCIAL AID *Required financial aid forms:* CSS Financial Aid PROFILE, noncustodial (divorced/separated) parent's statement, federal income tax form(s). *Financial aid deadline (priority):* 3/1. *Notification date:* Continuous beginning 3/1. Students must reply by 5/1 or within 4 weeks of notification.

CONTACT Katie Schiele, Assistant Director of Financial Aid, Principia College, 1 Maybeck Place, Elsah, IL 62028-9799, 618-374-5628 or toll-free 800-277-4648 Ext. 2804. *Fax:* 618-374-4000. *E-mail:* kaite.schiele@principia.edu.
Website: http://www.principiacollege.edu/.

PROVIDENCE CHRISTIAN COLLEGE
Pasadena, CA

CONTACT Financial Aid Office, Providence Christian College, 1539 East Howard Street, Pasadena, CA 91124, 626-696-4000.
Website: http://www.providencecc.edu/.

PROVIDENCE COLLEGE
Providence, RI

Tuition & fees: $46,970	Average undergraduate aid package: $32,024

ABOUT THE INSTITUTION Independent Roman Catholic, coed. *Awards:* certificates, bachelor's, and master's degrees. 67 undergraduate majors. *Total enrollment:* 4,804. Undergraduates: 4,270. Freshmen: 1,058. Both federal and institutional methodology are used as a basis for awarding need-based institutional aid.

UNDERGRADUATE EXPENSES for 2016–2017 *Comprehensive fee:* $60,760 includes full-time tuition ($46,080), mandatory fees ($890), and room and board ($13,790). *College room only:* $7950. Full-time tuition and fees vary according to class time and degree level. Room and board charges vary according to board plan and housing facility. *Part-time tuition:* $1645.71 per credit hour. Part-time tuition and fees vary according to class time and degree level.

FRESHMAN FINANCIAL AID (Fall 2016, est.) 782 applied for aid; of those 69% were deemed to have need. 100% of freshmen with need received aid; of those 30% had need fully met. *Average percent of need met:* 87% (excluding resources awarded to replace EFC). *Average financial aid package:* $32,374 (excluding resources awarded to replace EFC). 14% of all full-time freshmen had no need and received non-need-based gift aid.

UNDERGRADUATE FINANCIAL AID (Fall 2016, est.) 2,582 applied for aid; of those 74% were deemed to have need. 100% of undergraduates with need received aid; of those 26% had need fully met. *Average percent of need met:* 84% (excluding resources awarded to replace EFC). *Average financial aid package:* $32,024 (excluding resources awarded to replace EFC). 16% of all full-time undergraduates had no need and received non-need-based gift aid.

GIFT AID (NEED-BASED) *Total amount:* $52,847,999 (6% federal, 92% institutional, 2% external sources). *Receiving aid:* Freshmen: 50% (524); all full-time undergraduates: 47% (1,871). *Average award:* Freshmen: $26,741; Undergraduates: $26,410. *Scholarships, grants, and awards:* Federal Pell, FSEOG, state, private, college/university gift aid from institutional funds, Academic Competitiveness Grants, National SMART Grants.

GIFT AID (NON-NEED-BASED) *Total amount:* $14,493,853 (83% institutional, 17% external sources). *Receiving aid:* Freshmen: 5% (54). Undergraduates: 4% (149). *Average award:* Freshmen: $20,837. Undergraduates: $18,351. *Scholarships, grants, and awards by category:* Academic interests/achievement: business, general academic interests/achievements, military science, premedicine. Creative arts/performance: theater/drama. Special achievements/activities: community service. Special characteristics: siblings of current students. *Tuition waivers:* Full or partial for employees or children of employees. *ROTC:* Army.

LOANS *Student loans:* $25,987,556 (50% need-based, 50% non-need-based). 70% of past graduating class borrowed through all loan programs. *Average indebtedness per student:* $39,775. *Average need-based loan:* Freshmen: $4821. Undergraduates: $5171. *Parent loans:* $8,376,490 (24% need-based, 76% non-need-based). *Programs:* Federal Direct (Subsidized and Unsubsidized Stafford, PLUS), Perkins.

WORK-STUDY *Federal work-study:* Total amount: $1,540,000; jobs available. *State or other work-study/employment:* Total amount: $1,200,000 (100% non-need-based). Part-time jobs available.

ATHLETIC AWARDS Total amount: $9,117,614 (9% need-based, 91% non-need-based).

APPLYING FOR FINANCIAL AID *Required financial aid forms:* FAFSA, CSS Financial Aid PROFILE, federal income tax form(s). *Financial aid deadline:* 2/1. *Notification date:* 3/17. Students must reply by 5/1.

CONTACT Ms. Sandra J. Oliveira, Executive Director of Financial Aid, Providence College, One Cunningham Square, Providence, RI 02918, 401-865-2286 or toll-free 800-721-6444. *Fax:* 401-865-1186. *E-mail:* solivei6@providence.edu. *Website:* http://www.providence.edu/.

PURCHASE COLLEGE, STATE UNIVERSITY OF NEW YORK
Purchase, NY

Tuition & fees (NY res): $8298	Average undergraduate aid package: $10,029

ABOUT THE INSTITUTION State-supported, coed. *Awards:* certificates, bachelor's, and master's degrees. 43 undergraduate majors. *Total enrollment:* 4,224. Undergraduates: 4,121. Freshmen: 732. Federal methodology is used as a basis for awarding need-based institutional aid.

UNDERGRADUATE EXPENSES for 2017–2018 *Application fee:* $50. *One-time required fee:* $210. *Tuition, state resident:* full-time $6470; part-time $270 per credit. *Tuition, nonresident:* full-time $16,320; part-time $680 per credit. *Required fees:* full-time $1828; $74.72 per credit. Full-time tuition and fees vary according to program. Part-time tuition and fees vary according to course load and program. *College room and board:* $12,952; *Room only:* $8442. Room and board charges vary according to board plan and housing facility.

FRESHMAN FINANCIAL AID (Fall 2016, est.) 657 applied for aid; of those 72% were deemed to have need. 100% of freshmen with need received aid; of those .4% had need fully met. *Average percent of need met:* 44% (excluding resources awarded to replace EFC). *Average financial aid package:* $9087 (excluding resources awarded to replace EFC). 10% of all full-time freshmen had no need and received non-need-based gift aid.

UNDERGRADUATE FINANCIAL AID (Fall 2016, est.) 2,879 applied for aid; of those 77% were deemed to have need. 100% of undergraduates with need received aid; of those 1% had need fully met. *Average percent of need met:* 49% (excluding resources awarded to replace EFC). *Average financial aid package:* $10,029 (excluding resources awarded to replace EFC). 11% of all full-time undergraduates had no need and received non-need-based gift aid.

GIFT AID (NEED-BASED) *Total amount:* $13,713,595 (49% federal, 35% state, 16% institutional). *Receiving aid:* Freshmen: 63% (460); all full-time undergraduates: 59% (2,171). *Average award:* Freshmen: $8807; Undergraduates: $9724. *Scholarships, grants, and awards:* Federal Pell, FSEOG, state, private, college/university gift aid from institutional funds.

GIFT AID (NON-NEED-BASED) *Total amount:* $807,807 (4% federal, 14% state, 82% institutional). *Receiving aid:* Freshmen: 9% (68). Undergraduates: 10% (384). *Average award:* Freshmen: $2465. Undergraduates: $2174. *Scholarships, grants, and awards by category:* Academic interests/achievement: area/ethnic studies, biological sciences, computer science, English, general academic interests/achievements, humanities, mathematics, social sciences. Creative arts/performance: art/fine arts, cinema/film/broadcasting, creative writing, dance, general creative arts/performance, music, performing arts, theater/drama. *Tuition waivers:* Full or partial for employees or children of employees.

LOANS *Student loans:* $21,560,850 (74% need-based, 26% non-need-based). 68% of past graduating class borrowed through all loan programs. *Average indebtedness per student:* $31,188. *Average need-based loan:* Freshmen: $3468. Undergraduates: $4453. *Parent loans:* $32,743,886 (36% need-based, 64% non-need-based). *Programs:* Federal Direct (Subsidized and Unsubsidized Stafford, PLUS), Perkins.

WORK-STUDY *Federal work-study:* Total amount: $270,406; jobs available. *State or other work-study/employment:* Total amount: $666,135 (4% need-based, 96% non-need-based). Part-time jobs available.

APPLYING FOR FINANCIAL AID *Required financial aid forms:* FAFSA, state aid form. *Financial aid deadline (priority):* 2/1. *Notification date:* Continuous beginning 3/1.

CONTACT Ms. Corey York, Director of Student Financial Services, Purchase College, State University of New York, 735 Anderson Hill Road, Purchase, NY 10577-1400, 914-251-6085. *Fax:* 914-251-6099. *E-mail:* corey.york@purchase.edu. *Website:* http://www.purchase.edu/.

PURDUE UNIVERSITY
West Lafayette, IN

Tuition & fees (IN res): $10,002	Average undergraduate aid package: $13,849

ABOUT THE INSTITUTION State-supported, coed. **Awards:** certificates, associate, bachelor's, master's, and doctoral degrees. 140 undergraduate majors. **Total enrollment:** 40,451. Undergraduates: 30,043. Freshmen: 7,243. Federal methodology is used as a basis for awarding need-based institutional aid.

UNDERGRADUATE EXPENSES for 2016–2017 Application fee: $60. **Tuition, state resident:** full-time $9208; part-time $330 per credit hour. **Tuition, nonresident:** full-time $28,010; part-time $930 per credit hour. **Required fees:** full-time $794; $18 per credit hour. Full-time tuition and fees vary according to course load and program. Part-time tuition and fees vary according to course load. **College room and board:** $10,030; **Room only:** $4860. Room and board charges vary according to board plan and housing facility.

FRESHMAN FINANCIAL AID (Fall 2016, est.) 5,339 applied for aid; of those 68% were deemed to have need. 100% of freshmen with need received aid; of those 52% had need fully met. **Average percent of need met:** 82% (excluding resources awarded to replace EFC). **Average financial aid package:** $13,088 (excluding resources awarded to replace EFC). 14% of all full-time freshmen had no need and received non-need-based gift aid.

UNDERGRADUATE FINANCIAL AID (Fall 2016, est.) 16,737 applied for aid; of those 72% were deemed to have need. 100% of undergraduates with need received aid; of those 47% had need fully met. **Average percent of need met:** 85% (excluding resources awarded to replace EFC). **Average financial aid package:** $13,849 (excluding resources awarded to replace EFC). 13% of all full-time undergraduates had no need and received non-need-based gift aid.

GIFT AID (NEED-BASED) Total amount: $85,860,898 (25% federal, 27% state, 45% institutional, 3% external sources). **Receiving aid:** Freshmen: 30% (2,141); all full-time undergraduates: 27% (7,648). **Average award:** Freshmen: $14,008; Undergraduates: $13,404. **Scholarships, grants, and awards:** Federal Pell, FSEOG, state, private, college/university gift aid from institutional funds.

GIFT AID (NON-NEED-BASED) Total amount: $49,895,480 (11% federal, 5% state, 66% institutional, 18% external sources). **Receiving aid:** Freshmen: 25% (1,798). Undergraduates: 18% (5,212). **Average award:** Freshmen: $4966. Undergraduates: $5959. **Scholarships, grants, and awards by category:** Academic interests/achievement: agriculture, computer science, education, engineering/technologies, general academic interests/achievements, health fields, humanities, mathematics, military science, physical sciences. Creative arts/performance: music. Special achievements/activities: leadership. Special characteristics: children of faculty/staff. **Tuition waivers:** Full or partial for employees or children of employees, senior citizens. **ROTC:** Army, Naval, Air Force.

LOANS Student loans: $119,545,376 (55% need-based, 45% non-need-based). 46% of past graduating class borrowed through all loan programs. Average indebtedness per student: $27,530. **Average need-based loan:** Freshmen: $4318. Undergraduates: $5117. **Parent loans:** $102,937,192 (17% need-based, 83% non-need-based). **Programs:** Federal Direct (Subsidized and Unsubsidized Stafford, PLUS), Perkins, college/university.

WORK-STUDY Federal work-study: Total amount: $4,296,960; 1,772 jobs averaging $2229. **State or other work-study/employment:** Total amount: $2,919,313 (25% need-based, 75% non-need-based). Part-time jobs available.

ATHLETIC AWARDS Total amount: $8,978,587 (26% need-based, 74% non-need-based).

APPLYING FOR FINANCIAL AID Required financial aid form: FAFSA. **Financial aid deadline (priority):** 3/1. **Notification date:** 3/15.

CONTACT Theodore E. Malone, Division of Financial Aid, Purdue University, Schleman Hall of Student Services, Room 305, West Lafayette, IN 47907-2050, 765-494-5056. Fax: 765-496-3918.
Website: http://www.purdue.edu/.

PURDUE UNIVERSITY NORTHWEST
Hammond, IN

ABOUT THE INSTITUTION State-supported, coed. **Awards:** certificates, associate, bachelor's, master's, and doctoral degrees. 48 undergraduate majors. **Total enrollment:** 15,286. Undergraduates: 14,385. Freshmen: 1,301.

GIFT AID (NEED-BASED) Scholarships, grants, and awards: Federal Pell, FSEOG, state, private, college/university gift aid from institutional funds.
GIFT AID (NON-NEED-BASED) Scholarships, grants, and awards by category: Academic interests/achievement: general academic interests/achievements.
LOANS Programs: Federal Direct (Subsidized and Unsubsidized Stafford, PLUS), Perkins.
APPLYING FOR FINANCIAL AID Required financial aid form: FAFSA.
CONTACT Ms. Mary Ann Bishel, Executive Director of Financial Aid, Purdue University Northwest, 2200 169th Street, Hammond, IN 46323-2094, 219-989-2301 or toll-free 800-447-8738. Fax: 219-989-2141. E-mail: finaid2@purduecal.edu.
Website: http://www.pnw.edu/.

QUEENS COLLEGE OF THE CITY UNIVERSITY OF NEW YORK
Queens, NY

Tuition & fees (NY res): $6938	Average undergraduate aid package: $7990

ABOUT THE INSTITUTION State and locally supported, coed. **Awards:** certificates, bachelor's, and master's degrees. 69 undergraduate majors. **Total enrollment:** 19,632. Undergraduates: 16,326. Freshmen: 1,481. Federal methodology is used as a basis for awarding need-based institutional aid.

UNDERGRADUATE EXPENSES for 2017–2018 Application fee: $65. **Tuition, state resident:** full-time $6330; part-time $275 per credit. **Tuition, nonresident:** full-time $16,800; part-time $560 per credit. **Required fees:** full-time $608; $208.85 per term. Full-time tuition and fees vary according to course load. Part-time tuition and fees vary according to course load. **College room and board:** $14,370; **Room only:** $12,020. Room and board charges vary according to board plan and housing facility.

FRESHMAN FINANCIAL AID (Fall 2015) 1,259 applied for aid; of those 86% were deemed to have need. 94% of freshmen with need received aid; of those 5% had need fully met. **Average percent of need met:** 62% (excluding resources awarded to replace EFC). **Average financial aid package:** $8780 (excluding resources awarded to replace EFC). 2% of all full-time freshmen had no need and received non-need-based gift aid.

UNDERGRADUATE FINANCIAL AID (Fall 2015) 8,618 applied for aid; of those 92% were deemed to have need. 92% of undergraduates with need received aid; of those 5% had need fully met. **Average percent of need met:** 53% (excluding resources awarded to replace EFC). **Average financial aid package:** $7990 (excluding resources awarded to replace EFC). 1% of all full-time undergraduates had no need and received non-need-based gift aid.

GIFT AID (NEED-BASED) Total amount: $56,397,473 (54% federal, 45% state, 1% institutional). **Receiving aid:** Freshmen: 64% (983); all full-time undergraduates: 60% (6,853). **Average award:** Freshmen: $9227; Undergraduates: $7787. **Scholarships, grants, and awards:** Federal Pell, FSEOG, state, private, college/university gift aid from institutional funds.

GIFT AID (NON-NEED-BASED) Total amount: $3,823,270 (10% state, 46% institutional, 44% external sources). **Receiving aid:** Freshmen: 10% (148). Undergraduates: 6% (696). **Average award:** Freshmen: $6021. Undergraduates: $7255. **Scholarships, grants, and awards by category:** Academic interests/achievement: general academic interests/achievements. Creative arts/performance: music, theater/drama. Special characteristics: local/state students. **Tuition waivers:** Full or partial for employees or children of employees, senior citizens. **ROTC:** Army cooperative, Air Force cooperative.

LOANS Student loans: $14,102,313 (50% need-based, 50% non-need-based). 16% of past graduating class borrowed through all loan programs. Average indebtedness per student: $14,225. **Average need-based loan:** Freshmen: $3152. Undergraduates: $4191. **Parent loans:** $670,528 (100% non-need-based). **Programs:** Federal Direct (Subsidized and Unsubsidized Stafford, PLUS), Perkins.

WORK-STUDY Federal work-study: 860 jobs averaging $2106. **State or other work-study/employment:** Part-time jobs available.

ATHLETIC AWARDS Total amount: $1,014,798 (100% non-need-based).

APPLYING FOR FINANCIAL AID Required financial aid forms: FAFSA, institution's own form, state aid form. **Notification date:** Continuous beginning 3/1. Students must reply within 3 weeks of notification.

CONTACT Mr. Clifford Couloute, Director of Financial Aid, Queens College of the City University of New York, 65-30 Kissena Boulevard, Queens, NY 11367-1597, 718-997-5109. *Fax:* 718-997-5122. *E-mail:* qc.finaid@qc.cuny.edu.
Website: http://www.qc.cuny.edu/.

QUEENS UNIVERSITY OF CHARLOTTE
Charlotte, NC

Tuition & fees: $32,560	Average undergraduate aid package: $21,349

ABOUT THE INSTITUTION Independent Presbyterian, coed. *Awards:* certificates, bachelor's, and master's degrees. 40 undergraduate majors. *Total enrollment:* 2,286. Undergraduates: 1,641. Freshmen: 284. Federal methodology is used as a basis for awarding need-based institutional aid.

UNDERGRADUATE EXPENSES for 2016–2017 *Comprehensive fee:* $44,046 includes full-time tuition ($31,360), mandatory fees ($1200), and room and board ($11,486). Full-time tuition and fees vary according to course load, program, and student level. Room and board charges vary according to board plan and housing facility. Part-time tuition and fees vary according to course load and program.

FRESHMAN FINANCIAL AID (Fall 2015) 224 applied for aid; of those 76% were deemed to have need. 100% of freshmen with need received aid; of those 25% had need fully met. *Average percent of need met:* 69% (excluding resources awarded to replace EFC). *Average financial aid package:* $22,842 (excluding resources awarded to replace EFC). 37% of all full-time freshmen had no need and received non-need-based gift aid.

UNDERGRADUATE FINANCIAL AID (Fall 2015) 1,012 applied for aid; of those 86% were deemed to have need. 100% of undergraduates with need received aid; of those 20% had need fully met. *Average percent of need met:* 66% (excluding resources awarded to replace EFC). *Average financial aid package:* $21,349 (excluding resources awarded to replace EFC). 30% of all full-time undergraduates had no need and received non-need-based gift aid.

GIFT AID (NEED-BASED) *Total amount:* $13,711,486 (14% federal, 12% state, 72% institutional, 2% external sources). *Receiving aid:* Freshmen: 61% (171); all full-time undergraduates: 65% (857). *Average award:* Freshmen: $19,788; Undergraduates: $17,769. *Scholarships, grants, and awards:* Federal Pell, FSEOG, state, private, college/university gift aid from institutional funds.

GIFT AID (NON-NEED-BASED) *Total amount:* $5,573,608 (1% state, 96% institutional, 3% external sources). *Receiving aid:* Freshmen: 14% (40). Undergraduates: 11% (148). *Average award:* Freshmen: $12,563. Undergraduates: $12,303. *Scholarships, grants, and awards by category: Academic interests/achievement:* business, communication, education, general academic interests/achievements, home economics, humanities, social sciences. *Creative arts/performance:* art/fine arts, music, theater/drama. *Special achievements/activities:* cheerleading/drum major, community service, general special achievements/activities, leadership, memberships, religious involvement. *Special characteristics:* adult students, children and siblings of alumni, children of current students, children of faculty/staff, first-generation college students, international students, relatives of clergy, religious affiliation, siblings of current students, veterans, veterans' children. *Tuition waivers:* Full or partial for employees or children of employees.

LOANS *Student loans:* $10,260,321 (74% need-based, 26% non-need-based). *Average need-based loan:* Freshmen: $3215. Undergraduates: $4267. *Parent loans:* $3,962,175 (47% need-based, 53% non-need-based). *Programs:* Federal Direct (Subsidized and Unsubsidized Stafford, PLUS), state.

WORK-STUDY *Federal work-study:* jobs available. *State or other work-study/employment:* Total amount: $3750 (100% non-need-based). Part-time jobs available.

ATHLETIC AWARDS Total amount: $4,351,282 (40% need-based, 60% non-need-based).

APPLYING FOR FINANCIAL AID *Required financial aid form:* FAFSA. *Financial aid deadline:* Continuous. *Notification date:* Continuous beginning 2/15.

CONTACT Nancy Buchanan, Senior Director of Financial Aid, Queens University of Charlotte, 1900 Selwyn Avenue, Charlotte, NC 28274-0002, 704-337-2713 or toll-free 800-849-0202. *Fax:* 704-337-2416. *E-mail:* buchanann@queens.edu.
Website: http://www.queens.edu/.

QUINCY UNIVERSITY
Quincy, IL

ABOUT THE INSTITUTION Independent Roman Catholic, coed. *Awards:* associate, bachelor's, and master's degrees. 40 undergraduate majors. *Total enrollment:* 1,293. Undergraduates: 1,140. Freshmen: 278.

GIFT AID (NEED-BASED) *Scholarships, grants, and awards:* Federal Pell, FSEOG, state, private, college/university gift aid from institutional funds.

GIFT AID (NON-NEED-BASED) *Scholarships, grants, and awards by category: Academic interests/achievement:* biological sciences, business, communication, computer science, education, English, general academic interests/achievements, health fields, humanities, international studies, mathematics, physical sciences, premedicine, religion/biblical studies, social sciences. *Creative arts/performance:* art/fine arts, cinema/film/broadcasting, music. *Special achievements/activities:* cheerleading/drum major, community service, general special achievements/activities, hobbies/interests, leadership, memberships. *Special characteristics:* adult students, children and siblings of alumni, children of faculty/staff, first-generation college students, general special characteristics, local/state students, members of minority groups.

LOANS *Programs:* Federal Direct (Subsidized and Unsubsidized Stafford, PLUS), Perkins.

WORK-STUDY *Federal work-study:* 250 jobs averaging $1794. *State or other work-study/employment:* Total amount: $112,763 (79% need-based, 21% non-need-based). 107 part-time jobs averaging $1580.

APPLYING FOR FINANCIAL AID *Required financial aid form:* FAFSA.

CONTACT Lisa Flack, Director of Financial Aid, Quincy University, 1800 College Avenue, Quincy, IL 62301-2699, 217-228-5260 or toll-free 800-688-4295. *Fax:* 217-228-5635. *E-mail:* financialaid@quincy.edu.
Website: http://www.quincy.edu/.

QUINNIPIAC UNIVERSITY
Hamden, CT

Tuition & fees: $46,100	Average undergraduate aid package: $27,228

ABOUT THE INSTITUTION Independent, coed. *Awards:* certificates, bachelor's, master's, and doctoral degrees. 67 undergraduate majors. *Total enrollment:* 9,900. Undergraduates: 7,099. Freshmen: 1,910. Both federal and institutional methodology are used as a basis for awarding need-based institutional aid.

UNDERGRADUATE EXPENSES for 2017–2018 *Application fee:* $65. *Comprehensive fee:* $60,290 includes full-time tuition ($44,420), mandatory fees ($1680), and room and board ($14,190). Room and board charges vary according to housing facility. *Part-time tuition:* $1020 per credit. *Part-time fees:* $40 per credit. Part-time tuition and fees vary according to class time and course load.

FRESHMAN FINANCIAL AID (Fall 2016, est.) 1,609 applied for aid; of those 83% were deemed to have need. 100% of freshmen with need received aid; of those 18% had need fully met. *Average percent of need met:* 67% (excluding resources awarded to replace EFC). *Average financial aid package:* $27,621 (excluding resources awarded to replace EFC). 24% of all full-time freshmen had no need and received non-need-based gift aid.

UNDERGRADUATE FINANCIAL AID (Fall 2016, est.) 4,968 applied for aid; of those 86% were deemed to have need. 100% of undergraduates with need received aid; of those 16% had need fully met. *Average percent of need met:* 65% (excluding resources awarded to replace EFC). *Average financial aid package:* $27,228 (excluding resources awarded to replace EFC). 25% of all full-time undergraduates had no need and received non-need-based gift aid.

GIFT AID (NEED-BASED) *Total amount:* $81,927,270 (6% federal, 1% state, 88% institutional, 5% external sources). *Receiving aid:* Freshmen: 69% (1,307); all full-time undergraduates: 61% (4,124). *Average award:* Freshmen: $22,466; Undergraduates: $21,612. *Scholarships, grants, and awards:* Federal Pell, FSEOG, state, private, college/university gift aid from institutional funds.

GIFT AID (NON-NEED-BASED) *Total amount:* $37,861,853 (97% institutional, 3% external sources). *Receiving aid:* Freshmen: 54% (1,019). Undergraduates: 42% (2,849). *Average award:* Freshmen: $17,609. Undergraduates: $16,502. *Scholarships, grants, and awards by category: Academic interests/achievement:* 4,285 awards ($70,732,198 total): general academic interests/achievements. *Special characteristics:* 330 awards ($4,206,552 total): children of faculty/staff, international students, siblings of current students. *Tuition waivers:* Full or partial for employees or children of employees. *ROTC:* Army cooperative, Air Force cooperative.

LOANS *Student loans:* $56,837,687 (71% need-based, 29% non-need-based). 71% of past graduating class borrowed through all loan programs. *Average indebtedness per student:* $47,217. *Average need-based loan:* Freshmen: $3453. Undergraduates: $4438. *Parent loans:* $27,076,346 (100% non-need-based). *Programs:* Federal Direct (Subsidized and Unsubsidized Stafford, PLUS).

WORK-STUDY *Federal work-study:* Total amount: $3,043,282; 1,448 jobs averaging $2053.

ATHLETIC AWARDS Total amount: $11,554,053 (100% non-need-based).

APPLYING FOR FINANCIAL AID *Required financial aid forms:* FAFSA, CSS Financial Aid PROFILE, noncustodial (divorced/separated) parent's statement. *Financial aid deadline (priority):* 3/1. *Notification date:* Continuous beginning 2/15. Students must reply by 5/1 or within 2 weeks of notification.

CONTACT Mr. Dominic Yoia, Associate Vice President and University Director of Financial Aid, Quinnipiac University, 275 Mount Carmel Avenue, Hamden, CT 06518, 203-582-5224 or toll-free 800-462-1944. *Fax:* 203-582-5238. *E-mail:* finaid@ quinnipiac.edu.

Website: http://www.qu.edu/.

RABBI JACOB JOSEPH SCHOOL
Edison, NJ

CONTACT Financial Aid Office, Rabbi Jacob Joseph School, One Plainfield Ave, Edison, NJ 08817, 732-985-6533.

RABBINICAL ACADEMY MESIVTA RABBI CHAIM BERLIN
Brooklyn, NY

CONTACT Office of Financial Aid, Rabbinical Academy Mesivta Rabbi Chaim Berlin, 1605 Coney Island Avenue, Brooklyn, NY 11230-4715, 718-377-0777.

RABBINICAL COLLEGE BETH SHRAGA
Monsey, NY

CONTACT Financial Aid Office, Rabbinical College Beth Shraga, 28 Saddle River Road, Monsey, NY 10952-3035, 914-356-1980.

RABBINICAL COLLEGE BOBOVER YESHIVA B'NEI ZION
Brooklyn, NY

CONTACT Financial Aid Office, Rabbinical College Bobover Yeshiva B'nei Zion, 1577 48th Street, Brooklyn, NY 11219, 718-438-2018.

RABBINICAL COLLEGE OF AMERICA
Morristown, NJ

CONTACT Financial Aid Office , Rabbinical College of America, 226 Sussex Avenue, Morristown, NJ 07960, 973-267-9404. *Fax:* 973-267-5208.

Website: http://www.rca.edu/.

RABBINICAL COLLEGE OF LONG ISLAND
Long Beach, NY

CONTACT Rabbi Cone, Financial Aid Administrator, Rabbinical College of Long Island, 201 Magnolia Boulevard, Long Beach, NY 11561-3305, 516-431-7414.

RABBINICAL COLLEGE OF OHR SHIMON YISROEL
Brooklyn, NY

CONTACT Financial Aid Office, Rabbinical College of Ohr Shimon Yisroel, 215-217 Hewes Street, Brooklyn, NY 11211, 718-855-4092.

RABBINICAL COLLEGE OF TELSHE
Wickliffe, OH

CONTACT Financial Aid Office, Rabbinical College of Telshe, 28400 Euclid Avenue, Wickliffe, OH 44092-2523, 216-943-5300.

RABBINICAL SEMINARY OF AMERICA
Flushing, NY

CONTACT Ms. Leah Eisenstein, Director of Financial Aid, Rabbinical Seminary of America, 92-15 69th Avenue, Forest Hills, NY 11375, 718-268-4700. *Fax:* 718-268-4684.

RADFORD UNIVERSITY
Radford, VA

Tuition & fees (VA res): $10,081	Average undergraduate aid package: $10,116

ABOUT THE INSTITUTION State-supported, coed. *Awards:* certificates, bachelor's, master's, and doctoral degrees. 38 undergraduate majors. *Total enrollment:* 9,401. Undergraduates: 8,453. Freshmen: 1,751. Federal methodology is used as a basis for awarding need-based institutional aid.

UNDERGRADUATE EXPENSES for 2016–2017 *Tuition, state resident:* full-time $6991; part-time $291 per credit hour. *Tuition, nonresident:* full-time $18,626; part-time $776 per credit hour. *Required fees:* full-time $3090; $130 per credit hour. Part-time tuition and fees vary according to course load. *College room and board:* $8946; *Room only:* $4962. Room and board charges vary according to board plan and housing facility.

FRESHMAN FINANCIAL AID (Fall 2016, est.) 1,504 applied for aid; of those 76% were deemed to have need. 94% of freshmen with need received aid; of those 24% had need fully met. *Average percent of need met:* 80% (excluding resources awarded to replace EFC). *Average financial aid package:* $10,394 (excluding resources awarded to replace EFC). 4% of all full-time freshmen had no need and received non-need-based gift aid.

UNDERGRADUATE FINANCIAL AID (Fall 2016, est.) 6,144 applied for aid; of those 79% were deemed to have need. 96% of undergraduates with need received aid; of those 28% had need fully met. *Average percent of need met:* 80% (excluding resources awarded to replace EFC). *Average financial aid package:* $10,116 (excluding resources awarded to replace EFC). 4% of all full-time undergraduates had no need and received non-need-based gift aid.

GIFT AID (NEED-BASED) *Total amount:* $27,154,336 (46% federal, 36% state, 15% institutional, 3% external sources). *Receiving aid:* Freshmen: 41% (712); all full-time undergraduates: 36% (2,933). *Average award:* Freshmen: $8754; Undergraduates: $8110. *Scholarships, grants, and awards:* Federal Pell, FSEOG, state, private, college/university gift aid from institutional funds.

GIFT AID (NON-NEED-BASED) *Total amount:* $2,359,523 (25% federal, 3% state, 57% institutional, 15% external sources). *Receiving aid:* Freshmen: 17% (296). Undergraduates: 12% (993). *Average award:* Freshmen: $5149. Undergraduates: $4230. *Scholarships, grants, and awards by category: Academic interests/ achievement:* 741 awards ($2,450,954 total): general academic interests/achievements. *Tuition waivers:* Full or partial for employees or children of employees, senior citizens. *ROTC:* Army.

LOANS *Student loans:* $45,832,423 (81% need-based, 19% non-need-based). 69% of past graduating class borrowed through all loan programs. *Average indebtedness per student:* $29,103. *Average need-based loan:* Freshmen: $3385. Undergraduates: $4221. *Parent loans:* $12,189,961 (75% need-based, 25% non-need-based). *Programs:* Federal Direct (Subsidized and Unsubsidized Stafford, PLUS), Perkins, Federal Nursing, state, college/university.

WORK-STUDY *Federal work-study:* Total amount: $916,751; 377 jobs averaging $2432. *State or other work-study/employment:* Total amount: $948,262 (61% need-based, 39% non-need-based). 407 part-time jobs averaging $2330.

ATHLETIC AWARDS Total amount: $2,869,940 (84% need-based, 16% non-need-based).

APPLYING FOR FINANCIAL AID *Required financial aid form:* FAFSA. *Financial aid deadline (priority):* 2/15. *Notification date:* 4/15. Students must reply within 2 weeks of notification.

CONTACT Mrs. Barbara Porter, Director of Financial Aid, Radford University, PO Box 6905, Radford, VA 24142, 540-831-5408. *Fax:* 540-831-5138. *E-mail:* finaid@radford.edu.
Website: http://www.radford.edu/.

RAMAPO COLLEGE OF NEW JERSEY
Mahwah, NJ

Tuition & fees (NJ res): $13,870	Average undergraduate aid package: $17,215

ABOUT THE INSTITUTION State-supported, coed. *Awards:* certificates, bachelor's, and master's degrees. 36 undergraduate majors. *Total enrollment:* 6,234. Undergraduates: 5,762. Freshmen: 931. Federal methodology is used as a basis for awarding need-based institutional aid.

UNDERGRADUATE EXPENSES for 2016–2017 *Application fee:* $60. *Tuition, state resident:* full-time $8998; part-time $281.20 per credit hour. *Tuition, nonresident:* full-time $17,998; part-time $562.45 per credit hour. *Required fees:* full-time $4872; $152.25 per credit hour. Full-time tuition and fees vary according to reciprocity agreements. Part-time tuition and fees vary according to reciprocity agreements. *College room and board:* $12,030; *Room only:* $8340. Room and board charges vary according to board plan and housing facility.

FRESHMAN FINANCIAL AID (Fall 2015) 835 applied for aid; of those 69% were deemed to have need. 94% of freshmen with need received aid; of those 14% had need fully met. *Average percent of need met:* 65% (excluding resources awarded to replace EFC). *Average financial aid package:* $17,874 (excluding resources awarded to replace EFC). 11% of all full-time freshmen had no need and received non-need-based gift aid.

UNDERGRADUATE FINANCIAL AID (Fall 2015) 3,912 applied for aid; of those 71% were deemed to have need. 96% of undergraduates with need received aid; of those 14% had need fully met. *Average percent of need met:* 65% (excluding resources awarded to replace EFC). *Average financial aid package:* $17,215 (excluding resources awarded to replace EFC). 9% of all full-time undergraduates had no need and received non-need-based gift aid.

GIFT AID (NEED-BASED) *Total amount:* $12,903,037 (49% federal, 43% state, 8% institutional). *Receiving aid:* Freshmen: 24% (225); all full-time undergraduates: 27% (1,322). *Average award:* Freshmen: $13,210; Undergraduates: $9545. *Scholarships, grants, and awards:* Federal Pell, FSEOG, state, private, college/university gift aid from institutional funds, Federal Nursing.

GIFT AID (NON-NEED-BASED) *Total amount:* $9,925,957 (3% state, 89% institutional, 8% external sources). *Receiving aid:* Freshmen: 21% (196). Undergraduates: 13% (629). *Average award:* Freshmen: $12,149. Undergraduates: $11,002. *Scholarships, grants, and awards by category: Academic interests/ achievement:* 884 awards ($8,857,147 total): general academic interests/achievements. *Special characteristics:* 233 awards ($817,836 total): children of faculty/staff, international students, out-of-state students. *Tuition waivers:* Full or partial for employees

or children of employees, senior citizens. *ROTC:* Army cooperative, Air Force cooperative.

LOANS *Student loans:* $33,936,556 (30% need-based, 70% non-need-based). 69% of past graduating class borrowed through all loan programs. *Average indebtedness per student:* $33,300. *Average need-based loan:* Freshmen: $3305. Undergraduates: $4295. *Parent loans:* $6,495,897 (100% non-need-based). *Programs:* Federal Direct (Subsidized and Unsubsidized Stafford, PLUS), state.

WORK-STUDY *Federal work-study:* 171 jobs averaging $2347. *State or other work-study/employment:* Total amount: $1,700,615 (100% non-need-based). 926 part-time jobs averaging $1845.

APPLYING FOR FINANCIAL AID *Required financial aid form:* FAFSA. *Financial aid deadline (priority):* 3/1. *Notification date:* Continuous beginning 4/1. Students must reply by 5/1 or within 2 weeks of notification.

CONTACT F. Shawn O Neill, Director of Financial Aid, Ramapo College of New Jersey, 505 Ramapo Valley Road, Mahwah, NJ 07430-1680, 201-684-7550 or toll-free 800-9RAMAPO. *Fax:* 201-684-7085. *E-mail:* finaid@ramapo.edu.
Website: http://www.ramapo.edu/.

RANDALL UNIVERSITY
Moore, OK

Tuition & fees: $13,040	Average undergraduate aid package: $12,926

ABOUT THE INSTITUTION Independent Free Will Baptist, coed. 24 undergraduate majors. Both federal and institutional methodology are used as a basis for awarding need-based institutional aid.

UNDERGRADUATE EXPENSES for 2016–2017 *Comprehensive fee:* $20,400 includes full-time tuition ($9980), mandatory fees ($3060), and room and board ($7360). *College room only:* $2860. Full-time tuition and fees vary according to course load. Room and board charges vary according to board plan and housing facility. *Part-time tuition:* $420 per credit hour. *Part-time fees:* $50 per credit hour; $280 per term. Part-time tuition and fees vary according to course load.

FRESHMAN FINANCIAL AID (Fall 2016, est.) 74 applied for aid; of those 89% were deemed to have need. 100% of freshmen with need received aid; of those 6% had need fully met. *Average percent of need met:* 50% (excluding resources awarded to replace EFC). *Average financial aid package:* $10,336 (excluding resources awarded to replace EFC). 7% of all full-time freshmen had no need and received non-need-based gift aid.

UNDERGRADUATE FINANCIAL AID (Fall 2016, est.) 232 applied for aid; of those 90% were deemed to have need. 100% of undergraduates with need received aid; of those 12% had need fully met. *Average percent of need met:* 60% (excluding resources awarded to replace EFC). *Average financial aid package:* $12,926 (excluding resources awarded to replace EFC). 9% of all full-time undergraduates had no need and received non-need-based gift aid.

GIFT AID (NEED-BASED) *Total amount:* $1,147,752 (72% federal, 26% state, 2% institutional). *Receiving aid:* Freshmen: 58% (44); all full-time undergraduates: 65% (155). *Average award:* Freshmen: $5994; Undergraduates: $5583. *Scholarships, grants, and awards:* Federal Pell, FSEOG, state, private, college/university gift aid from institutional funds, Bureau of Indian Affairs Grants.

GIFT AID (NON-NEED-BASED) *Total amount:* $899,478 (92% institutional, 8% external sources). *Receiving aid:* Freshmen: 70% (53). Undergraduates: 79% (190). *Average award:* Freshmen: $5474. Undergraduates: $6025. *Scholarships, grants, and awards by category: Academic interests/achievement:* 132 awards ($505,999 total): business, education, English, general academic interests/achievements, health fields, religion/biblical studies. *Creative arts/performance:* 18 awards ($20,320 total): music, theater/drama. *Special achievements/activities:* 15 awards ($25,070 total): religious involvement. *Special characteristics:* 71 awards ($148,961 total): children and siblings of alumni, children of faculty/staff, general special characteristics, local/state students, relatives of clergy, religious affiliation, veterans, veterans' children. *Tuition waivers:* Full or partial for children of alumni, employees or children of employees, senior citizens.

LOANS *Student loans:* $1,658,368 (43% need-based, 57% non-need-based). 75% of past graduating class borrowed through all loan programs. *Average indebtedness per student:* $25,813. *Average need-based loan:* Freshmen: $3238. Undergraduates: $3696. *Parent loans:* $294,293 (100% non-need-based). *Programs:* Federal Direct (Subsidized and Unsubsidized Stafford, PLUS).

WORK-STUDY *Federal work-study:* Total amount: $38,000; 23 jobs averaging $1935.
APPLYING FOR FINANCIAL AID *Required financial aid forms:* FAFSA, institution's own form. *Financial aid deadline (priority):* 6/30. *Notification date:* Continuous beginning 4/1. Students must reply within 4 weeks of notification.
CONTACT Denise Conklin, Director of Financial Aid, Randall University, PO Box 7208, Moore, OK 73153-1208, 405-912-9012. *Fax:* 405-912-9050. *E-mail:* dconklin@hc.edu.
Website: http://www.hc.edu/.

RANDOLPH COLLEGE
Lynchburg, VA

Tuition & fees: $36,770	Average undergraduate aid package: $30,377

ABOUT THE INSTITUTION Independent Methodist, coed. *Awards:* bachelor's and master's degrees. 37 undergraduate majors. *Total enrollment:* 679. Undergraduates: 663. Freshmen: 187. Federal methodology is used as a basis for awarding need-based institutional aid.
UNDERGRADUATE EXPENSES for 2016–2017 *Comprehensive fee:* $49,350 includes full-time tuition ($36,160), mandatory fees ($610), and room and board ($12,580). *Part-time tuition:* $1500 per credit hour. *Part-time fees:* $52.50 per term. Part-time tuition and fees vary according to course load.
FRESHMAN FINANCIAL AID (Fall 2016, est.) 163 applied for aid; of those 90% were deemed to have need. 100% of freshmen with need received aid; of those 21% had need fully met. *Average percent of need met:* 79% (excluding resources awarded to replace EFC). *Average financial aid package:* $31,340 (excluding resources awarded to replace EFC). 21% of all full-time freshmen had no need and received non-need-based gift aid.
UNDERGRADUATE FINANCIAL AID (Fall 2016, est.) 531 applied for aid; of those 90% were deemed to have need. 100% of undergraduates with need received aid; of those 22% had need fully met. *Average percent of need met:* 77% (excluding resources awarded to replace EFC). *Average financial aid package:* $30,377 (excluding resources awarded to replace EFC). 25% of all full-time undergraduates had no need and received non-need-based gift aid.
GIFT AID (NEED-BASED) *Total amount:* $12,160,311 (9% federal, 8% state, 82% institutional, 1% external sources). *Receiving aid:* Freshmen: 77% (146); all full-time undergraduates: 74% (476). *Average award:* Freshmen: $27,667; Undergraduates: $25,987. *Scholarships, grants, and awards:* Federal Pell, FSEOG, state, private, college/university gift aid from institutional funds.
GIFT AID (NON-NEED-BASED) *Total amount:* $4,463,163 (1% federal, 9% state, 90% institutional). *Receiving aid:* Freshmen: 13% (25). Undergraduates: 12% (80). *Average award:* Freshmen: $23,791. Undergraduates: $21,877. *Scholarships, grants, and awards by category:* Academic interests/achievement: biological sciences, education, English, general academic interests/achievements, mathematics, physical sciences, premedicine, social sciences. *Special achievements/activities:* community service, general special achievements/activities, leadership. *Special characteristics:* adult students, children of faculty/staff, international students, local/state students, relatives of clergy, religious affiliation, twins. *Tuition waivers:* Full or partial for employees or children of employees, adult students.
LOANS *Student loans:* $5,291,899 (63% need-based, 37% non-need-based). 67% of past graduating class borrowed through all loan programs. *Average indebtedness per student:* $35,199. *Average need-based loan:* Freshmen: $3869. Undergraduates: $4687. *Parent loans:* $2,111,850 (49% need-based, 51% non-need-based). *Programs:* Federal Direct (Subsidized and Unsubsidized Stafford, PLUS), Perkins, college/university.
WORK-STUDY *Federal work-study:* Total amount: $248,067; jobs available. *State or other work-study/employment:* Total amount: $137,143 (3% need-based, 97% non-need-based). Part-time jobs available.
APPLYING FOR FINANCIAL AID *Required financial aid forms:* FAFSA, noncustodial (divorced/separated) parent's statement. *Financial aid deadline (priority):* 3/1. *Notification date:* Continuous beginning 10/1. Students must reply within 2 weeks of notification.
CONTACT Debi Woodall-Stevens, Director of Student Financial Services, Randolph College, 2500 Rivermont Avenue, Lynchburg, VA 24503, 434-947-8128 or toll-free 800-745-7692. *Fax:* 434-947-8996. *E-mail:* dwstevens@randolphcollege.edu.
Website: http://www.randolphcollege.edu/.

RANDOLPH-MACON COLLEGE
Ashland, VA

Tuition & fees: $40,000	Average undergraduate aid package: $28,588

ABOUT THE INSTITUTION Independent United Methodist, coed. *Awards:* bachelor's degrees. 32 undergraduate majors. *Total enrollment:* 1,446. Undergraduates: 1,446. Freshmen: 396. Both federal and institutional methodology are used as a basis for awarding need-based institutional aid.
UNDERGRADUATE EXPENSES for 2017–2018 *Application fee:* $30. *One-time required fee:* $100. *Comprehensive fee:* $51,480 includes full-time tuition ($38,750), mandatory fees ($1250), and room and board ($11,480). *College room only:* $6390. Full-time tuition and fees vary according to reciprocity agreements. Room and board charges vary according to board plan and housing facility.
FRESHMAN FINANCIAL AID (Fall 2016, est.) 373 applied for aid; of those 83% were deemed to have need. 100% of freshmen with need received aid; of those 33% had need fully met. *Average percent of need met:* 83% (excluding resources awarded to replace EFC). *Average financial aid package:* $28,332 (excluding resources awarded to replace EFC). 22% of all full-time freshmen had no need and received non-need-based gift aid.
UNDERGRADUATE FINANCIAL AID (Fall 2016, est.) 1,234 applied for aid; of those 84% were deemed to have need. 100% of undergraduates with need received aid; of those 31% had need fully met. *Average percent of need met:* 82% (excluding resources awarded to replace EFC). *Average financial aid package:* $28,588 (excluding resources awarded to replace EFC). 26% of all full-time undergraduates had no need and received non-need-based gift aid.
GIFT AID (NEED-BASED) *Total amount:* $25,067,416 (6% federal, 8% state, 82% institutional, 4% external sources). *Receiving aid:* Freshmen: 78% (308); all full-time undergraduates: 74% (1,036). *Average award:* Freshmen: $24,778; Undergraduates: $24,444. *Scholarships, grants, and awards:* Federal Pell, FSEOG, state, private, college/university gift aid from institutional funds.
GIFT AID (NON-NEED-BASED) *Total amount:* $11,056,828 (12% state, 76% institutional, 12% external sources). *Receiving aid:* Freshmen: 23% (93). Undergraduates: 20% (277). *Average award:* Freshmen: $20,207. Undergraduates: $17,939. *Scholarships, grants, and awards by category:* Academic interests/achievement: general academic interests/achievements, religion/biblical studies. *Special achievements/activities:* general special achievements/activities, religious involvement. *Special characteristics:* children and siblings of alumni, children of faculty/staff, ethnic background, out-of-state students, relatives of clergy, siblings of current students, veterans, veterans' children. *Tuition waivers:* Full or partial for employees or children of employees. *ROTC:* Army cooperative.
LOANS *Student loans:* $10,609,951 (59% need-based, 41% non-need-based). 70% of past graduating class borrowed through all loan programs. *Average indebtedness per student:* $33,015. *Average need-based loan:* Freshmen: $4659. Undergraduates: $5271. *Parent loans:* $5,392,316 (32% need-based, 68% non-need-based). *Programs:* Federal Direct (Subsidized and Unsubsidized Stafford, PLUS), Perkins, college/university.
WORK-STUDY *Federal work-study:* Total amount: $347,034; jobs available.
APPLYING FOR FINANCIAL AID *Required financial aid forms:* FAFSA, state aid form. *Financial aid deadline (priority):* 2/15. *Notification date:* 3/1. Students must reply by 5/1 or within 2 weeks of notification.
CONTACT Ms. Mary Neal, Director of Financial Aid, Randolph-Macon College, PO Box 5005, Ashland, VA 23005-5505, 804-752-7259 or toll-free 800-888-1762. *Fax:* 804-752-3719. *E-mail:* mneal@rmc.edu.
Website: http://www.rmc.edu/.

RASMUSSEN COLLEGE AURORA
Aurora, IL

CONTACT Financial Aid Office, Rasmussen College Aurora, 2363 Sequoia Drive, Aurora, IL 60506, 630-888-3500 or toll-free 888-549-6755.
Website: http://www.rasmussen.edu/.

RASMUSSEN COLLEGE BLAINE
Blaine, MN

CONTACT Financial Aid Office, Rasmussen College Blaine, 3629 95th Avenue NE, Blaine, MN 55014, 763-795-4720 or toll-free 888-549-6755.
Website: http://www.rasmussen.edu/.

RASMUSSEN COLLEGE BLOOMINGTON
Bloomington, MN

CONTACT Financial Aid Office, Rasmussen College Bloomington, 4400 West 78th Street, Bloomington, MN 55435, 952-545-2000 or toll-free 888-549-6755.
Website: http://www.rasmussen.edu/.

RASMUSSEN COLLEGE EAGAN
Eagan, MN

CONTACT Financial Aid Office, Rasmussen College Eagan, 3500 Federal Drive, Eagan, MN 55122, 651-687-9000 or toll-free 888-549-6755.
Website: http://www.rasmussen.edu/.

RASMUSSEN COLLEGE FARGO
Fargo, ND

CONTACT Financial Aid Office, Rasmussen College Fargo, 4012 19th Avenue South, Fargo, ND 58103, 701-277-3889 or toll-free 888-549-6755.
Website: http://www.rasmussen.edu/.

RASMUSSEN COLLEGE FORT MYERS
Fort Myers, FL

CONTACT Financial Aid Office, Rasmussen College Fort Myers, 9160 Forum Corporate Parkway, Suite 100, Fort Myers, FL 33905, 239-477-2100 or toll-free 888-549-6755.
Website: http://www.rasmussen.edu/.

RASMUSSEN COLLEGE GREEN BAY
Green Bay, WI

CONTACT Financial Aid Office, Rasmussen College Green Bay, 904 South Taylor Street, Suite 100, Green Bay, WI 54303, 920-593-8400 or toll-free 888-549-6755.
Website: http://www.rasmussen.edu/.

RASMUSSEN COLLEGE KANSAS CITY/ OVERLAND PARK
Overland Park, KS

CONTACT Financial Aid Office, Rasmussen College Kansas City/Overland Park, 11600 College Boulevard, Overland Park, KS 66210, 913-491-7870 or toll-free 888-549-6755.
Website: http://www.rasmussen.edu/.

RASMUSSEN COLLEGE LAKE ELMO/ WOODBURY
Lake Elmo, MN

CONTACT Financial Aid Office, Rasmussen College Lake Elmo/Woodbury, 8565 Eagle Point Circle, Lake Elmo, MN 55042, 651-259-6600 or toll-free 888-549-6755.
Website: http://www.rasmussen.edu/.

RASMUSSEN COLLEGE LAND O' LAKES
Land O' Lakes, FL

CONTACT Financial Aid Office, Rasmussen College Land O' Lakes, 18600 Fernview Street, Land O' Lakes, FL 34638, 813-435-3601 or toll-free 888-549-6755.
Website: http://www.rasmussen.edu/.

RASMUSSEN COLLEGE MANKATO
Mankato, MN

CONTACT Financial Aid Office, Rasmussen College Mankato, 130 Saint Andrews Drive, Mankato, MN 56001, 507-625-6556 or toll-free 888-549-6755.
Website: http://www.rasmussen.edu/.

RASMUSSEN COLLEGE MOKENA/ TINLEY PARK
Mokena, IL

CONTACT Financial Aid Office, Rasmussen College Mokena/Tinley Park, 8650 West Spring Lake Road, Mokena, IL 60448, 815-534-3300 or toll-free 888-549-6755.
Website: http://www.rasmussen.edu/.

RASMUSSEN COLLEGE MOORHEAD
Moorhead, MN

CONTACT Financial Aid Office, Rasmussen College Moorhead, 1250 29th Avenue South, Moorhead, MN 56560, 218-304-6200 or toll-free 888-549-6755.
Website: http://www.rasmussen.edu/.

RASMUSSEN COLLEGE NEW PORT RICHEY
New Port Richey, FL

CONTACT Financial Aid Office, Rasmussen College New Port Richey, 8661 Citizens Drive, New Port Richey, FL 34654, 727-942-0069 or toll-free 888-549-6755.
Website: http://www.rasmussen.edu/.

RASMUSSEN COLLEGE OCALA
Ocala, FL

CONTACT Financial Aid Office, Rasmussen College Ocala, 4755 SW 46th Court, Ocala, FL 34474, 352-629-1941 or toll-free 888-549-6755.
Website: http://www.rasmussen.edu/.

RASMUSSEN COLLEGE OCALA SCHOOL OF NURSING

Ocala, FL

CONTACT Financial Aid Office, Rasmussen College Ocala School of Nursing, 2100 SW 22nd Place, Ocala, FL 34471, 352-291-8560 or toll-free 888-549-6755. *Website:* http://www.rasmussen.edu/.

RASMUSSEN COLLEGE ROMEOVILLE/JOLIET

Romeoville, IL

CONTACT Financial Aid Office, Rasmussen College Romeoville/Joliet, 1400 West Normantown Road, Romeoville, IL 60446, 815-306-2600 or toll-free 888-549-6755. *Website:* http://www.rasmussen.edu/.

RASMUSSEN COLLEGE ST. CLOUD

St. Cloud, MN

CONTACT Financial Aid Office, Rasmussen College St. Cloud, 226 Park Avenue South, St. Cloud, MN 56301, 320-251-5600 or toll-free 888-549-6755. *Website:* http://www.rasmussen.edu/.

RASMUSSEN COLLEGE TAMPA/BRANDON

Tampa, FL

CONTACT Financial Aid Office, Rasmussen College Tampa/Brandon, 4042 Park Oaks Boulevard, Suite 100, Tampa, FL 33610, 813-246-7600 or toll-free 888-549-6755. *Website:* http://www.rasmussen.edu/.

RASMUSSEN COLLEGE TOPEKA

Topeka, KS

CONTACT Financial Aid Office, Rasmussen College Topeka, 620 SW Governor View, Topeka, KS 66606, 785-228-7320 or toll-free 888-549-6755. *Website:* http://www.rasmussen.edu/.

RASMUSSEN COLLEGE WAUSAU

Wausau, WI

CONTACT Financial Aid Office, Rasmussen College Wausau, 1101 Westwood Drive, Wausau, WI 54401, 715-841-8000 or toll-free 888-549-6755. *Website:* http://www.rasmussen.edu/.

REED COLLEGE

Portland, OR

Tuition & fees: $52,150	Average undergraduate aid package: $45,050

ABOUT THE INSTITUTION Independent, coed. *Awards:* bachelor's and master's degrees. 33 undergraduate majors. *Total enrollment:* 1,427. Undergraduates: 1,410. Freshmen: 354. Both federal and institutional methodology are used as a basis for awarding need-based institutional aid.

UNDERGRADUATE EXPENSES for 2016–2017 *Comprehensive fee:* $65,300 includes full-time tuition ($51,850), mandatory fees ($300), and room and board ($13,150). *College room only:* $6890. Full-time tuition and fees vary according to degree level. Room and board charges vary according to board plan and housing facility. *Part-time tuition:* $8790 per unit. *Part-time fees:* $150 per term. Part-time tuition and fees vary according to course load and degree level.

FRESHMAN FINANCIAL AID (Fall 2016, est.) 228 applied for aid; of those 81% were deemed to have need. 96% of freshmen with need received aid; of those 89% had need fully met. *Average percent of need met:* 100% (excluding resources awarded to replace EFC). *Average financial aid package:* $41,643 (excluding resources awarded to replace EFC).

UNDERGRADUATE FINANCIAL AID (Fall 2016, est.) 799 applied for aid; of those 93% were deemed to have need. 98% of undergraduates with need received aid; of those 84% had need fully met. *Average percent of need met:* 100% (excluding resources awarded to replace EFC). *Average financial aid package:* $45,050 (excluding resources awarded to replace EFC).

GIFT AID (NEED-BASED) *Total amount:* $29,618,153 (5% federal, 94% institutional, 1% external sources). *Receiving aid:* Freshmen: 50% (177); all full-time undergraduates: 52% (725). *Average award:* Freshmen: $37,665; Undergraduates: $39,915. *Scholarships, grants, and awards:* Federal Pell, FSEOG, state, private, college/university gift aid from institutional funds.

GIFT AID (NON-NEED-BASED) *Total amount:* $35,280 (100% external sources). *Tuition waivers:* Full or partial for employees or children of employees.

LOANS *Student loans:* $4,123,902 (88% need-based, 12% non-need-based). 44% of past graduating class borrowed through all loan programs. *Average indebtedness per student:* $19,627. *Average need-based loan:* Freshmen: $2215. Undergraduates: $3298. *Parent loans:* $1,555,300 (100% non-need-based). *Programs:* Federal Direct (Subsidized and Unsubsidized Stafford, PLUS), Perkins, college/university.

WORK-STUDY *Federal work-study:* Total amount: $631,772; jobs available. *State or other work-study/employment:* Total amount: $411,300 (100% need-based). Part-time jobs available.

APPLYING FOR FINANCIAL AID *Required financial aid forms:* FAFSA, CSS Financial Aid PROFILE, noncustodial (divorced/separated) parent's statement. *Financial aid deadline:* 2/1. *Notification date:* 4/1. Students must reply by 5/1 or within 2 weeks of notification.

CONTACT Leslie Limper, Director of Financial Aid, Reed College, 3203 Southeast Woodstock Boulevard, Portland, OR 97202-8199, 503-777-7223 or toll-free 800-547-4750. *Fax:* 503-788-6682. *E-mail:* financial.aid@reed.edu. *Website:* http://www.reed.edu/.

REGENT UNIVERSITY

Virginia Beach, VA

Tuition & fees: $16,700	Average undergraduate aid package: $10,870

ABOUT THE INSTITUTION Independent Christian, coed. *Awards:* certificates, associate, bachelor's, master's, and doctoral degrees. 27 undergraduate majors. *Total enrollment:* 8,868. Undergraduates: 3,806. Freshmen: 453. Federal methodology is used as a basis for awarding need-based institutional aid.

UNDERGRADUATE EXPENSES for 2016–2017 *Application fee:* $50. *Comprehensive fee:* $25,180 includes full-time tuition ($15,900), mandatory fees ($800), and room and board ($8480). *College room only:* $5960. Full-time tuition and fees vary according to course load. Room and board charges vary according to board plan and housing facility. *Part-time tuition:* $530 per credit hour. *Part-time fees:* $489 per term. Part-time tuition and fees vary according to course load.

FRESHMAN FINANCIAL AID (Fall 2016, est.) 300 applied for aid; of those 82% were deemed to have need. 100% of freshmen with need received aid; of those 17% had need fully met. *Average percent of need met:* 55% (excluding resources awarded to replace EFC). *Average financial aid package:* $12,457 (excluding resources awarded to replace EFC). 26% of all full-time freshmen had no need and received non-need-based gift aid.

UNDERGRADUATE FINANCIAL AID (Fall 2016, est.) 1,879 applied for aid; of those 90% were deemed to have need. 100% of undergraduates with need received aid; of those 10% had need fully met. *Average percent of need met:* 54% (excluding resources awarded to replace EFC). *Average financial aid package:* $10,870 (excluding resources awarded to replace EFC). 16% of all full-time undergraduates had no need and received non-need-based gift aid.

GIFT AID (NEED-BASED) *Total amount:* $15,040,587 (57% federal, 12% state, 30% institutional, 1% external sources). *Receiving aid:* Freshmen: 70% (234); all full-time undergraduates: 74% (1,542). *Average award:* Freshmen: $9877; Undergraduates: $7610. *Scholarships, grants, and awards:* Federal Pell, state, private, college/university gift aid from institutional funds.

GIFT AID (NON-NEED-BASED) *Total amount:* $2,869,898 (25% state, 71% institutional, 4% external sources). *Receiving aid:* Freshmen: 11% (38). Undergraduates: 6% (125) *Average award:* Freshmen: $7974. Undergraduates: $6596. *Scholarships, grants, and awards by category:* Special achievements/activities: 162 awards ($217,150 total): leadership, memberships, religious involvement. *Special characteristics:* 267 awards ($347,984 total): children and siblings of alumni, children of faculty/staff, children of public servants, public servants, religious affiliation, siblings of current students, spouses of current students, veterans, veterans' children. *Tuition waivers:* Full or partial for employees or children of employees. *ROTC:* Army cooperative, Naval cooperative.

LOANS *Student loans:* $34,720,624 (29% need-based, 71% non-need-based). 71% of past graduating class borrowed through all loan programs. *Average indebtedness per student:* $28,780. *Average need-based loan:* Freshmen: $3125. Undergraduates: $3886. *Parent loans:* $10,641,687 (37% need-based, 63% non-need-based). *Programs:* Federal Direct (Subsidized and Unsubsidized Stafford, PLUS).

APPLYING FOR FINANCIAL AID *Required financial aid forms:* FAFSA, institution's own form, state aid form. *Financial aid deadline:* Continuous. *Notification date:* Continuous beginning 3/15. Students must reply within 2 weeks of notification.

CONTACT Mrs. Rachael Moser, Assistant Director, Regent University, 1000 Regent University Drive, Virginia Beach, VA 23464, 757-352-4125 or toll-free 800-373-5504. *Fax:* 757-352-4118. *E-mail:* finaid@regent.edu.

Website: http://www.regent.edu/.

REGIS COLLEGE
Weston, MA

ABOUT THE INSTITUTION Independent Roman Catholic, coed. *Awards:* certificates, associate, bachelor's, master's, and doctoral degrees. 16 undergraduate majors. *Total enrollment:* 1,954. Undergraduates: 1,235. Freshmen: 267.

GIFT AID (NEED-BASED) *Scholarships, grants, and awards:* Federal Pell, FSEOG, state, private, college/university gift aid from institutional funds.

GIFT AID (NON-NEED-BASED) *Scholarships, grants, and awards by category:* Academic interests/achievement: general academic interests/achievements. Special achievements/activities: community service, leadership. Special characteristics: adult students, children of faculty/staff, international students, relatives of clergy, religious affiliation, siblings of current students.

LOANS *Programs:* Federal Direct (Subsidized and Unsubsidized Stafford, PLUS), Perkins, state.

APPLYING FOR FINANCIAL AID *Required financial aid forms:* FAFSA, institution's own form.

CONTACT Bonnie L. Quinn, Director of Financial Aid, Regis College, Box 81, Weston, MA 02493, 781-768-7270 or toll-free 866-438-7344. *Fax:* 781-768-7225. *E-mail:* finaid@regiscollege.edu.

Website: http://www.regiscollege.edu/.

REGIS UNIVERSITY
Denver, CO

Tuition & fees: $34,675	Average undergraduate aid package: $27,284

ABOUT THE INSTITUTION Independent Roman Catholic (Jesuit), coed. *Awards:* certificates, bachelor's, master's, and doctoral degrees. 44 undergraduate majors. *Total enrollment:* 8,368. Undergraduates: 4,070. Freshmen: 486. Federal methodology is used as a basis for awarding need-based institutional aid.

UNDERGRADUATE EXPENSES for 2017–2018 *Comprehensive fee:* $45,095 includes full-time tuition ($34,100), mandatory fees ($575), and room and board ($10,420). *College room only:* $5600. Full-time tuition and fees vary according to class time, course level, course load, degree level, location, program, rec-

iprocity agreements, and student level. Room and board charges vary according to board plan and housing facility. *Part-time tuition:* $1066 per credit hour. Part-time tuition and fees vary according to class time, course level, course load, degree level, location, program, reciprocity agreements, and student level.

FRESHMAN FINANCIAL AID (Fall 2015) 457 applied for aid; of those 83% were deemed to have need. 100% of freshmen with need received aid; of those 14% had need fully met. *Average percent of need met:* 82% (excluding resources awarded to replace EFC). *Average financial aid package:* $30,885 (excluding resources awarded to replace EFC). 28% of all full-time freshmen had no need and received non-need-based gift aid.

UNDERGRADUATE FINANCIAL AID (Fall 2015) 1,871 applied for aid; of those 89% were deemed to have need. 99% of undergraduates with need received aid; of those 16% had need fully met. *Average percent of need met:* 76% (excluding resources awarded to replace EFC). *Average financial aid package:* $27,284 (excluding resources awarded to replace EFC). 21% of all full-time undergraduates had no need and received non-need-based gift aid.

GIFT AID (NEED-BASED) *Total amount:* $27,169,545 (18% federal, 9% state, 69% institutional, 4% external sources). *Receiving aid:* Freshmen: 69% (378); all full-time undergraduates: 59% (1,433). *Average award:* Freshmen: $21,539; Undergraduates: $17,582. *Scholarships, grants, and awards:* Federal Pell, FSEOG, state, private, college/university gift aid from institutional funds.

GIFT AID (NON-NEED-BASED) *Total amount:* $7,936,819 (97% institutional, 3% external sources). *Receiving aid:* Freshmen: 8% (44). Undergraduates: 6% (138). *Average award:* Freshmen: $13,188. Undergraduates: $12,827. *Scholarships, grants, and awards by category:* Academic interests/achievement: 870 awards ($10,666,209 total): biological sciences, general academic interests/achievements, mathematics, physical sciences. Creative arts/performance: 36 awards ($143,130 total): debating, music. Special achievements/activities: 54 awards ($436,520 total): leadership. Special characteristics: 33 awards ($321,260 total): adult students, children of faculty/staff, local/state students, public servants. *Tuition waivers:* Full or partial for employees or children of employees. *ROTC:* Army cooperative, Naval cooperative, Air Force cooperative.

LOANS *Student loans:* $24,628,104 (81% need-based, 19% non-need-based). 62% of past graduating class borrowed through all loan programs. *Average indebtedness per student:* $28,153. *Average need-based loan:* Freshmen: $3723. Undergraduates: $4437. *Parent loans:* $4,596,425 (35% need-based, 65% non-need-based). *Programs:* Federal Direct (Subsidized and Unsubsidized Stafford, PLUS), Perkins, Federal Nursing.

WORK-STUDY *Federal work-study:* 366 jobs averaging $1726. *State or other work-study/employment:* Total amount: $1,081,016 (44% need-based, 56% non-need-based). 508 part-time jobs averaging $1785.

ATHLETIC AWARDS Total amount: $2,449,424 (34% need-based, 66% non-need-based).

APPLYING FOR FINANCIAL AID *Required financial aid form:* FAFSA. *Financial aid deadline (priority):* 5/31. *Notification date:* Continuous beginning 3/15.

CONTACT Ellie Miller, Director of Financial Aid, Regis University, 3333 Regis Boulevard, Denver, CO 80221-1099, 303-964-5758 or toll-free 800-388-2366 Ext. 4900. *Fax:* 303-964-5449. *E-mail:* emiller@regis.edu.

Website: http://www.regis.edu/.

REINHARDT UNIVERSITY
Waleska, GA

CONTACT Angela D. Harlow, Director of Financial Aid, Reinhardt University, 7300 Reinhardt College Circle, Waleska, GA 30183-2981, 770-720-5603. *Fax:* 770-720-9126.

Website: http://www.reinhardt.edu/.

RENSSELAER POLYTECHNIC INSTITUTE
Troy, NY

Tuition & fees: $52,305 | **Average undergraduate aid package: $38,742**

ABOUT THE INSTITUTION Independent, coed. *Awards:* bachelor's, master's, and doctoral degrees. 40 undergraduate majors. *Total enrollment:* 7,442. Undergraduates: 6,265. Freshmen: 1,691. Both federal and institutional methodology are used as a basis for awarding need-based institutional aid.

UNDERGRADUATE EXPENSES for 2017–2018 *Application fee:* $70. *Comprehensive fee:* $67,265 includes full-time tuition ($51,000), mandatory fees ($1305), and room and board ($14,960). *College room only:* $8480. Room and board charges vary according to board plan and location. *Part-time tuition:* $1595 per credit hour.

FRESHMAN FINANCIAL AID (Fall 2016, est.) 1,337 applied for aid; of those 83% were deemed to have need. 100% of freshmen with need received aid; of those 22% had need fully met. *Average percent of need met:* 86% (excluding resources awarded to replace EFC). *Average financial aid package:* $41,926 (excluding resources awarded to replace EFC). 22% of all full-time freshmen had no need and received non-need-based gift aid.

UNDERGRADUATE FINANCIAL AID (Fall 2016, est.) 4,239 applied for aid; of those 89% were deemed to have need. 100% of undergraduates with need received aid; of those 19% had need fully met. *Average percent of need met:* 80% (excluding resources awarded to replace EFC). *Average financial aid package:* $38,742 (excluding resources awarded to replace EFC). 26% of all full-time undergraduates had no need and received non-need-based gift aid.

GIFT AID (NEED-BASED) *Total amount:* $124,411,678 (10% federal, 2% state, 86% institutional, 2% external sources). *Receiving aid:* Freshmen: 66% (1,110); all full-time undergraduates: 61% (3,760). *Average award:* Freshmen: $36,325; Undergraduates: $33,119. *Scholarships, grants, and awards:* Federal Pell, FSEOG, state, private, college/university gift aid from institutional funds, Academic Competitiveness Grants, National SMART Grants, Gates Millennium Scholarships.

GIFT AID (NON-NEED-BASED) *Total amount:* $38,299,759 (4% federal, 1% state, 93% institutional, 2% external sources). *Receiving aid:* Freshmen: 12% (199). Undergraduates: 8% (492). *Average award:* Freshmen: $20,910. Undergraduates: $17,920. *Scholarships, grants, and awards by category:* Academic interests/achievement: general academic interests/achievements, humanities, mathematics, military science. *Creative arts/performance:* general creative arts/performance. *Special achievements/activities:* general special achievements/activities. *Special characteristics:* children and siblings of alumni, children of faculty/staff, ethnic background, general special characteristics, members of minority groups. *Tuition waivers:* Full or partial for employees or children of employees. *ROTC:* Army, Naval, Air Force.

LOANS *Student loans:* $41,947,469 (60% need-based, 40% non-need-based). 64% of past graduating class borrowed through all loan programs. *Average need-based loan:* Freshmen: $4929. Undergraduates: $5398. *Parent loans:* $10,608,749 (24% need-based, 76% non-need-based). *Programs:* Federal Direct (Subsidized and Unsubsidized Stafford, PLUS), Perkins, college/university.

WORK-STUDY *Federal work-study:* Total amount: $1,395,526; 795 jobs averaging $1983.

ATHLETIC AWARDS Total amount: $2,379,984 (100% non-need-based).

APPLYING FOR FINANCIAL AID *Required financial aid forms:* FAFSA, CSS Financial Aid PROFILE. *Financial aid deadline (priority):* 2/1. *Notification date:* 3/15.

CONTACT Mr. Martin Daniels, Director of Financial Aid, Rensselaer Polytechnic Institute, Academy Hall, Troy, NY 12180-3590, 518-276-6813. *Fax:* 518-276-4797. *E-mail:* financial_aid@rpi.edu. *Website:* http://www.rpi.edu/.

RESEARCH COLLEGE OF NURSING
Kansas City, MO

Tuition & fees: $35,700 | **Average undergraduate aid package: $28,500**

ABOUT THE INSTITUTION Independent, coed, primarily women. *Awards:* certificates, bachelor's, and master's degrees (bachelor's degree offered jointly with Rockhurst College). 1 undergraduate major. *Total enrollment:* 474. Undergraduates: 340. Freshmen: 78. Federal methodology is used as a basis for awarding need-based institutional aid.

UNDERGRADUATE EXPENSES for 2016–2017 *Comprehensive fee:* $45,050 includes full-time tuition ($34,880), mandatory fees ($820), and room and board ($9350). *College room only:* $5850. Room and board charges vary according to board plan, housing facility, and location. *Part-time tuition:* $1164 per credit hour. Part-time tuition and fees vary according to class time.

UNDERGRADUATE FINANCIAL AID (Fall 2015) 138 applied for aid; of those 74% were deemed to have need. 100% of undergraduates with need received aid; of those 51% had need fully met. *Average percent of need met:* 78% (excluding resources awarded to replace EFC). *Average financial aid package:* $28,500 (excluding resources awarded to replace EFC). 100% of all full-time undergraduates had no need and received non-need-based gift aid.

GIFT AID (NEED-BASED) *Total amount:* $116,793 (82% federal, 18% state). *Receiving aid:* All full-time undergraduates: 57% (92). *Average award:* Undergraduates: $9200. *Scholarships, grants, and awards:* Federal Pell, FSEOG, state, private, college/university gift aid from institutional funds.

GIFT AID (NON-NEED-BASED) *Total amount:* $4,037,652 (100% institutional). *Receiving aid:* Undergraduates: 63% (102). *Average award:* Undergraduates: $34,800. *Scholarships, grants, and awards by category:* Academic interests/achievement: general academic interests/achievements, health fields. *Special characteristics:* children and siblings of alumni, children of educators, children of faculty/staff, siblings of current students. *Tuition waivers:* Full or partial for employees or children of employees, senior citizens. *ROTC:* Army cooperative.

LOANS *Student loans:* $1,840,812 (31% need-based, 69% non-need-based). *Average need-based loan:* Undergraduates: $5500. *Parent loans:* $136,053 (100% non-need-based). *Programs:* Federal Direct (Subsidized and Unsubsidized Stafford, PLUS), Federal Nursing.

APPLYING FOR FINANCIAL AID *Required financial aid form:* FAFSA. *Financial aid deadline (priority):* 3/15. *Notification date:* Continuous. Students must reply within 2 weeks of notification.

CONTACT Ms. Stacie Withers, Director of Financial Aid, Research College of Nursing, 2525 East Meyer Boulevard, Kansas City, MO 64132, 816-995-2832. *Fax:* 816-995-2833. *E-mail:* stacie.withers@researchcollege.edu. *Website:* http://www.researchcollege.edu/.

RESURRECTION UNIVERSITY
Chicago, IL

Tuition & fees: N/R | **Average undergraduate aid package: $18,775**

ABOUT THE INSTITUTION Independent, coed. *Awards:* certificates, bachelor's, and master's degrees. 2 undergraduate majors. *Total enrollment:* 678. Undergraduates: 609. Both federal and institutional methodology are used as a basis for awarding need-based institutional aid.

UNDERGRADUATE FINANCIAL AID (Fall 2016, est.) 434 applied for aid; of those 100% were deemed to have need. 100% of undergraduates with need received aid; of those 23% had need fully met. *Average percent of need met:* 80% (excluding resources awarded to replace EFC). *Average financial aid package:* $18,775 (excluding resources awarded to replace EFC). 1% of all full-time undergraduates had no need and received non-need-based gift aid.

GIFT AID (NEED-BASED) *Total amount:* $8,427,054 (13% federal, 84% state, 3% institutional). *Receiving aid:* All full-time undergraduates: 52% (288). *Average award:* Undergraduates: $5000. *Scholarships, grants, and awards:* Federal Pell, FSEOG, state, private, college/university gift aid from institutional funds.

GIFT AID (NON-NEED-BASED) *Total amount:* $348,802 (90% institutional, 10% external sources). *Receiving aid:* Undergraduates: 16% (90). *Average award:* Undergraduates: $2000.

LOANS *Student loans:* $7,464,472 (31% need-based, 69% non-need-based). *Average need-based loan:* Undergraduates: $5500. *Parent loans:* $997,015 (100% non-need-based). *Programs:* Federal Direct (Subsidized and Unsubsidized Stafford, PLUS).

WORK-STUDY *Federal work-study:* Total amount: $251,641; jobs available.

APPLYING FOR FINANCIAL AID *Notification date:* Continuous.

CONTACT Ms. Shirley Howell, Financial Aid Officer, Resurrection University, 1431 North Claremont Avenue, Chicago, IL 60622, 773-252-5125. *Fax:* 773-227-5134. *E-mail:* shirley.howell@resu.edu. *Website:* http://www.resu.edu/.

RHODE ISLAND COLLEGE
Providence, RI

Tuition & fees (RI res): $8206	Average undergraduate aid package: $9027

ABOUT THE INSTITUTION State-supported, coed. *Awards:* certificates, bachelor's, master's, and doctoral degrees. 103 undergraduate majors. *Total enrollment:* 8,446. Undergraduates: 7,398. Freshmen: 1,170. Institutional methodology is used as a basis for awarding need-based institutional aid.

UNDERGRADUATE EXPENSES for 2017–2018 *Application fee:* $50. *Tuition, state resident:* full-time $7118; part-time $280 per credit. *Tuition, nonresident:* full-time $18,779; part-time $690 per credit. *Required fees:* full-time $1088; $32 per credit or $74 per term. Part-time tuition and fees vary according to course load. *College room and board:* $10,794; *Room only:* $6180. Room and board charges vary according to housing facility.

FRESHMAN FINANCIAL AID (Fall 2016, est.) 1,082 applied for aid; of those 80% were deemed to have need. 95% of freshmen with need received aid; of those 12% had need fully met. *Average percent of need met:* 71% (excluding resources awarded to replace EFC). *Average financial aid package:* $10,242 (excluding resources awarded to replace EFC). 3% of all full-time freshmen had no need and received non-need-based gift aid.

UNDERGRADUATE FINANCIAL AID (Fall 2016, est.) 4,693 applied for aid; of those 81% were deemed to have need. 94% of undergraduates with need received aid; of those 21% had need fully met. *Average percent of need met:* 68% (excluding resources awarded to replace EFC). *Average financial aid package:* $9027 (excluding resources awarded to replace EFC). 2% of all full-time undergraduates had no need and received non-need-based gift aid.

GIFT AID (NEED-BASED) *Total amount:* $22,742,349 (61% federal, 8% state, 26% institutional, 5% external sources). *Receiving aid:* Freshmen: 62% (711); all full-time undergraduates: 55% (3,064). *Average award:* Freshmen: $7802; Undergraduates: $6532. *Scholarships, grants, and awards:* Federal Pell, FSEOG, state, private, college/university gift aid from institutional funds.

GIFT AID (NON-NEED-BASED) *Total amount:* $665,800 (61% institutional, 39% external sources). *Receiving aid:* Freshmen: 1% (16). Undergraduates: 2% (91). *Average award:* Freshmen: $2406. Undergraduates: $2342. *Scholarships, grants, and awards by category:* Academic interests/achievement: general academic interests/achievements. Creative arts/performance: art/fine arts, cinema/film/broadcasting, dance, journalism/publications, music, theater/drama. *Special characteristics:* children and siblings of alumni. *Tuition waivers:* Full or partial for employees or children of employees. *ROTC:* Army cooperative.

LOANS *Student loans:* $30,523,288 (69% need-based, 31% non-need-based). 72% of past graduating class borrowed through all loan programs. *Average indebtedness per student:* $26,519. *Average need-based loan:* Freshmen: $3343. Undergraduates: $3856. *Parent loans:* $1,661,190 (37% need-based, 63% non-need-based). *Programs:* Federal Direct (Subsidized and Unsubsidized Stafford, PLUS), Perkins, state, alternative loans.

WORK-STUDY *Federal work-study:* Total amount: $1,858,596; jobs available.

APPLYING FOR FINANCIAL AID *Required financial aid forms:* FAFSA, institution's own form. *Financial aid deadline (priority):* 3/1. *Notification date:* Continuous beginning 3/15. Students must reply by 5/1 or within 3 weeks of notification.

CONTACT Mr. Kenneth Ferus, Director of Financial Aid, Rhode Island College, 600 Mount Pleasant Avenue, Providence, RI 02908, 401-456-8033 or toll-free 800-669-5760. *Fax:* 401-456-8686. *E-mail:* kferus@ric.edu. *Website:* http://www.ric.edu/.

RHODE ISLAND SCHOOL OF DESIGN
Providence, RI

Tuition & fees: $47,110	Average undergraduate aid package: $29,371

ABOUT THE INSTITUTION Independent, coed. *Awards:* bachelor's and master's degrees 16 undergraduate majors. *Total enrollment:* 2,478. Undergraduates: 2,000. Freshmen: 456. Both federal and institutional methodology are used as a basis for awarding need-based institutional aid.

UNDERGRADUATE EXPENSES for 2016–2017 *Comprehensive fee:* $59,960 includes full-time tuition ($46,800), mandatory fees ($310), and room and board ($12,850). *College room only:* $7350. Room and board charges vary according to board plan and housing facility.

FRESHMAN FINANCIAL AID (Fall 2016, est.) 240 applied for aid; of those 73% were deemed to have need. 100% of freshmen with need received aid; of those 3% had need fully met. *Average percent of need met:* 67% (excluding resources awarded to replace EFC). *Average financial aid package:* $27,614 (excluding resources awarded to replace EFC).

UNDERGRADUATE FINANCIAL AID (Fall 2016, est.) 900 applied for aid; of those 86% were deemed to have need. 100% of undergraduates with need received aid; of those 1% had need fully met. *Average percent of need met:* 65% (excluding resources awarded to replace EFC). *Average financial aid package:* $29,371 (excluding resources awarded to replace EFC). 1% of all full-time undergraduates had no need and received non-need-based gift aid.

GIFT AID (NEED-BASED) *Total amount:* $19,020,000 (9% federal, 87% institutional, 4% external sources). *Receiving aid:* Freshmen: 33% (150); all full-time undergraduates: 35% (705). *Average award:* Freshmen: $23,864; Undergraduates: $22,934. *Scholarships, grants, and awards:* Federal Pell, FSEOG, state, private, college/university gift aid from institutional funds.

GIFT AID (NON-NEED-BASED) *Receiving aid:* Undergraduates: 1% (20). *Average award:* Undergraduates: $7500. *Scholarships, grants, and awards by category:* Creative arts/performance: applied art and design, art/fine arts. *Special characteristics:* children of faculty/staff. *Tuition waivers:* Full or partial for employees or children of employees. *ROTC:* Army cooperative.

LOANS *Student loans:* $5,400,000 (100% need-based). 41% of past graduating class borrowed through all loan programs. *Average indebtedness per student:* $31,037. *Average need-based loan:* Freshmen: $3598. Undergraduates: $5216. *Parent loans:* $6,000,000 (100% need-based). *Programs:* Federal Direct (Subsidized and Unsubsidized Stafford, PLUS), Perkins.

WORK-STUDY *Federal work-study:* Total amount: $273,000; jobs available. *State or other work-study/employment:* Total amount: $1,500,000 (100% need-based). Part-time jobs available.

APPLYING FOR FINANCIAL AID *Required financial aid forms:* FAFSA, CSS Financial Aid PROFILE. *Financial aid deadline:* 2/15. *Notification date:* 4/1. Students must reply by 5/1 or within 4 weeks of notification.

CONTACT Anthony Gallonio, Assistant Vice President of Enrollment Services, Rhode Island School of Design, 2 College Street, Providence, RI 02903-2784, 401-454-6661 or toll-free 800-364-7473. *Fax:* 401-454-6412. *E-mail:* financialaid@risd.edu. *Website:* http://www.risd.edu/.

RHODES COLLEGE
Memphis, TN

Tuition & fees: $44,942	Average undergraduate aid package: $37,616

ABOUT THE INSTITUTION Independent, coed. *Awards:* bachelor's and master's degrees (master's degree in accounting only). 34 undergraduate majors. *Total enrollment:* 2,029. Undergraduates: 1,999. Freshmen: 507. Both federal and institutional methodology are used as a basis for awarding need-based institutional aid.

UNDERGRADUATE EXPENSES for 2017–2018 *Comprehensive fee:* $56,010 includes full-time tuition ($44,632), mandatory fees ($310), and room and board ($11,068). *College room only:* $5534. Room and board charges vary according to board plan and housing facility.

FRESHMAN FINANCIAL AID (Fall 2016, est.) 425 applied for aid; of those 72% were deemed to have need. 100% of freshmen with need received aid; of those 60%

had need fully met. **Average percent of need met:** 93% (excluding resources awarded to replace EFC). **Average financial aid package:** $37,546 (excluding resources awarded to replace EFC). 34% of all full-time freshmen had no need and received non-need-based gift aid.

UNDERGRADUATE FINANCIAL AID (Fall 2016, est.) 1,286 applied for aid; of those 55% were deemed to have need. 100% of undergraduates with need received aid; of those 42% had need fully met. **Average percent of need met:** 88% (excluding resources awarded to replace EFC). **Average financial aid package:** $37,616 (excluding resources awarded to replace EFC). 58% of all full-time undergraduates had no need and received non-need-based gift aid.

GIFT AID (NEED-BASED) Total amount: $21,650,343 (6% federal, 5% state, 88% institutional, 1% external sources). **Receiving aid:** Freshmen: 61% (307); all full-time undergraduates: 35% (699). **Average award:** Freshmen: $29,756; Undergraduates: $31,002. **Scholarships, grants, and awards:** Federal Pell, FSEOG, state, private, college/university gift aid from institutional funds.

GIFT AID (NON-NEED-BASED) Total amount: $30,023,595 (4% state, 92% institutional, 4% external sources). **Receiving aid:** Freshmen: 29% (149). Undergraduates: 11% (226). **Average award:** Freshmen: $22,297. Undergraduates: $22,703. **Scholarships, grants, and awards by category:** Academic interests/achievement: general academic interests/achievements, physical sciences. Creative arts/performance: art/fine arts, general creative arts/performance, music, theater/drama. Special characteristics: children of faculty/staff, members of minority groups, relatives of clergy, religious affiliation. **Tuition waivers:** Full or partial for employees or children of employees. **ROTC:** Army cooperative, Naval cooperative, Air Force cooperative.

LOANS Student loans: $6,829,576 (31% need-based, 69% non-need-based). 49% of past graduating class borrowed through all loan programs. Average indebtedness per student: $25,859. **Average need-based loan:** Freshmen: $3275. Undergraduates: $4534. **Parent loans:** $2,168,393 (14% need-based, 86% non-need-based). **Programs:** Federal Direct (Subsidized and Unsubsidized Stafford, PLUS), Perkins.

WORK-STUDY Federal work-study: Total amount: $568,215; jobs available. **State or other work-study/employment:** Total amount: $934,162 (25% need-based, 75% non-need-based). Part-time jobs available.

APPLYING FOR FINANCIAL AID Required financial aid forms: FAFSA, CSS Financial Aid PROFILE, noncustodial (divorced/separated) parent's statement. **Financial aid deadline:** 3/1 (priority: 3/1). **Notification date:** 4/15. Students must reply by 5/1.

CONTACT Mr. Michael Morgan, Director of Financial Aid, Rhodes College, 2000 North Parkway, Memphis, TN 38112-1690, 901-843-3808 or toll-free 800-844-5969. Fax: 901-843-3435. E-mail: morganm@rhodes.edu. Website: http://www.rhodes.edu/.

RICE UNIVERSITY
Houston, TX

Tuition & fees: $43,918	Average undergraduate aid package: $41,888

ABOUT THE INSTITUTION Independent, coed. **Awards:** bachelor's, master's, and doctoral degrees. 58 undergraduate majors. **Total enrollment:** 6,855. Undergraduates: 3,893. Freshmen: 978. Both federal and institutional methodology are used as a basis for awarding need-based institutional aid.

UNDERGRADUATE EXPENSES for 2016–2017 Application fee: $75. **One-time required fee:** $635. **Comprehensive fee:** $57,668 includes full-time tuition ($43,220), mandatory fees ($698), and room and board ($13,750). **College room only:** $9415. Room and board charges vary according to board plan. **Part-time tuition:** $1801 per credit hour.

FRESHMAN FINANCIAL AID (Fall 2016, est.) 762 applied for aid; of those 55% were deemed to have need. 100% of freshmen with need received aid; of those 100% had need fully met. **Average percent of need met:** 100% (excluding resources awarded to replace EFC). **Average financial aid package:** $42,573 (excluding resources awarded to replace EFC). 9% of all full-time freshmen had no need and received non-need-based gift aid.

UNDERGRADUATE FINANCIAL AID (Fall 2016, est.) 2,701 applied for aid; of those 55% were deemed to have need. 99% of undergraduates with need received aid; of those 100% had need fully met. **Average percent of need met:** 100% (excluding resources awarded to replace EFC). **Average financial aid package:** $41,888

(excluding resources awarded to replace EFC). 10% of all full-time undergraduates had no need and received non-need-based gift aid.

GIFT AID (NEED-BASED) Total amount: $53,612,198 (4% federal, 3% state, 93% institutional). **Receiving aid:** Freshmen: 41% (402); all full-time undergraduates: 37% (1,456). **Average award:** Freshmen: $37,253; Undergraduates: $36,772. **Scholarships, grants, and awards:** Federal Pell, FSEOG, state, private, college/university gift aid from institutional funds.

GIFT AID (NON-NEED-BASED) Total amount: $11,642,624 (3% federal, 72% institutional, 25% external sources). **Receiving aid:** Freshmen: 3% (27). Undergraduates: 1% (55). **Average award:** Freshmen: $23,037. Undergraduates: $19,019. **Scholarships, grants, and awards by category:** Academic interests/achievement: engineering/technologies, general academic interests/achievements. Creative arts/performance: art/fine arts, music. Special achievements/activities: general special achievements/activities, leadership. Special characteristics: local/state students, members of minority groups. **Tuition waivers:** Full or partial for employees or children of employees. **ROTC:** Army cooperative, Naval, Air Force cooperative.

LOANS Student loans: $6,046,663 (34% need-based, 66% non-need-based). 27% of past graduating class borrowed through all loan programs. Average indebtedness per student: $22,497. **Average need-based loan:** Freshmen: $2892. Undergraduates: $3643. **Parent loans:** $2,186,048 (100% non-need-based). **Programs:** Federal Direct (Subsidized and Unsubsidized Stafford, PLUS), Perkins, state.

WORK-STUDY Federal work-study: Total amount: $2,330,922; jobs available. **State or other work-study/employment:** Part-time jobs available.

ATHLETIC AWARDS Total amount: $12,595,897 (9% need-based, 91% non-need-based).

APPLYING FOR FINANCIAL AID Required financial aid forms: FAFSA, CSS Financial Aid PROFILE, noncustodial (divorced/separated) parent's statement, business/farm supplement, federal income tax form(s), W-2 forms. **Financial aid deadline:** 4/15 (priority: 3/1). **Notification date:** Continuous beginning 4/1. Students must reply by 5/1.

CONTACT Office of Student Financial Services, Rice University, 116 Allen Center, MS 12, Houston, TX 77005, 713-348-4958. Fax: 713-348-2139. E-mail: fina@rice.edu. Website: http://www.rice.edu/.

RIDER UNIVERSITY
Lawrenceville, NJ

Tuition & fees: $39,820	Average undergraduate aid package: $28,684

ABOUT THE INSTITUTION Independent, coed. **Awards:** certificates, associate, bachelor's, and master's degrees. 65 undergraduate majors. **Total enrollment:** 5,075. Undergraduates: 4,128. Freshmen: 862. Federal methodology is used as a basis for awarding need-based institutional aid.

UNDERGRADUATE EXPENSES for 2016–2017 Application fee: $50. **Comprehensive fee:** $54,050 includes full-time tuition ($39,080), mandatory fees ($740), and room and board ($14,230). **College room only:** $9270. Full-time tuition and fees vary according to program. Room and board charges vary according to board plan and housing facility. **Part-time tuition:** $1140 per credit hour. **Part-time fees:** $16.67 per credit; $50 per course.

FRESHMAN FINANCIAL AID (Fall 2016, est.) 781 applied for aid; of those 90% were deemed to have need. 100% of freshmen with need received aid; of those 14% had need fully met. **Average percent of need met:** 75% (excluding resources awarded to replace EFC). **Average financial aid package:** $31,784 (excluding resources awarded to replace EFC). 17% of all full-time freshmen had no need and received non-need-based gift aid.

UNDERGRADUATE FINANCIAL AID (Fall 2016, est.) 2,976 applied for aid; of those 91% were deemed to have need. 100% of undergraduates with need received aid; of those 15% had need fully met. **Average percent of need met:** 73% (excluding resources awarded to replace EFC). **Average financial aid package:** $28,684 (excluding resources awarded to replace EFC). 19% of all full-time undergraduates had no need and received non-need-based gift aid.

GIFT AID (NEED-BASED) Total amount: $61,127,861 (10% federal, 13% state, 76% institutional, 1% external sources). **Receiving aid:** Freshmen: 80% (697); all full-time undergraduates: 73% (2,662). **Average award:** Freshmen: $27,328; Undergraduates: $24,578. **Scholarships, grants, and awards:** Federal Pell, FSEOG, state, private, college/university gift aid from institutional funds.

GIFT AID (NON-NEED-BASED) *Total amount:* $15,534,460 (2% federal, 97% institutional, 1% external sources). *Receiving aid:* Freshmen: 11% (99). Undergraduates: 11% (398). *Average award:* Freshmen: $17,423. Undergraduates: $16,998. *Scholarships, grants, and awards by category:* Academic interests/achievement: general academic interests/achievements. *Creative arts/performance:* theater/drama. *Special characteristics:* members of minority groups. *Tuition waivers:* Full or partial for employees or children of employees. *ROTC:* Army cooperative.
LOANS *Student loans:* $33,805,853 (68% need-based, 32% non-need-based). 77% of past graduating class borrowed through all loan programs. *Average indebtedness per student:* $36,032. *Average need-based loan:* Freshmen: $3147. Undergraduates: $3785. *Parent loans:* $12,352,353 (57% need-based, 43% non-need-based). *Programs:* Federal Direct (Subsidized and Unsubsidized Stafford, PLUS), Perkins.
WORK-STUDY *Federal work-study:* Total amount: $3,777,533; jobs available.
ATHLETIC AWARDS Total amount: $4,581,472 (38% need-based, 62% non-need-based).
APPLYING FOR FINANCIAL AID *Required financial aid form:* FAFSA. *Financial aid deadline (priority):* 2/1. *Notification date:* Continuous beginning 2/1.
CONTACT Mr. Drew Aromando, Office of Financial Aid, Rider University, 2083 Lawrenceville Road, Lawrenceville, NJ 08648-3001, 609-896-5360 or toll-free 800-257-9026. *Fax:* 609-219-4487. *E-mail:* finaid@rider.edu. *Website:* http://www.rider.edu/.

RINGLING COLLEGE OF ART AND DESIGN
Sarasota, FL

Tuition & fees: $43,040	Average undergraduate aid package: $24,503

ABOUT THE INSTITUTION Independent, coed. *Awards:* bachelor's degrees. 11 undergraduate majors. *Total enrollment:* 1,341. Undergraduates: 1,341. Freshmen: 355. Federal methodology is used as a basis for awarding need-based institutional aid.
UNDERGRADUATE EXPENSES for 2016–2017 *Application fee:* $70. *Comprehensive fee:* $57,430 includes full-time tuition ($39,510), mandatory fees ($3530), and room and board ($14,390). *College room only:* $7750. Full-time tuition and fees vary according to course load, program, and student level. Room and board charges vary according to board plan and housing facility. *Part-time tuition:* $1840 per credit hour. Part-time tuition and fees vary according to program and student level.
FRESHMAN FINANCIAL AID (Fall 2016, est.) 266 applied for aid; of those 89% were deemed to have need. 100% of freshmen with need received aid; of those 8% had need fully met. *Average percent of need met:* 49% (excluding resources awarded to replace EFC). *Average financial aid package:* $23,925 (excluding resources awarded to replace EFC). 6% of all full-time freshmen had no need and received non-need-based gift aid.
UNDERGRADUATE FINANCIAL AID (Fall 2016, est.) 935 applied for aid; of those 92% were deemed to have need. 100% of undergraduates with need received aid; of those 5% had need fully met. *Average percent of need met:* 48% (excluding resources awarded to replace EFC). *Average financial aid package:* $24,503 (excluding resources awarded to replace EFC). 24% of all full-time undergraduates had no need and received non-need-based gift aid.
GIFT AID (NEED-BASED) *Total amount:* $13,952,884 (15% federal, 10% state, 70% institutional, 5% external sources). *Receiving aid:* Freshmen: 67% (237); all full-time undergraduates: 67% (859). *Average award:* Freshmen: $16,106; Undergraduates: $15,839. *Scholarships, grants, and awards:* Federal Pell, FSEOG, state, private, college/university gift aid from institutional funds.
GIFT AID (NON-NEED-BASED) *Total amount:* $4,162,816 (4% state, 92% institutional, 4% external sources). *Receiving aid:* Freshmen: 4% (13). Undergraduates: 2% (29). *Average award:* Freshmen: $8500. Undergraduates: $11,663. *Scholarships, grants, and awards by category:* Academic interests/achievement: general academic interests/achievements. *Creative arts/performance:* applied art and design, art/fine arts, cinema/film/broadcasting. *Special achievements/activities:* community service. *Tuition waivers:* Full or partial for employees or children of employees.

LOANS *Student loans:* $10,129,958 (86% need-based, 14% non-need-based). 63% of past graduating class borrowed through all loan programs. *Average indebtedness per student:* $44,384. *Average need-based loan:* Freshmen: $7191. Undergraduates: $7807. *Parent loans:* $11,275,665 (83% need-based, 17% non-need-based). *Programs:* Federal Direct (Subsidized and Unsubsidized Stafford, PLUS).
WORK-STUDY *Federal work-study:* Total amount: $132,830; jobs available. *State or other work-study/employment:* Total amount: $242,000 (7% need-based, 93% non-need-based). Part-time jobs available.
APPLYING FOR FINANCIAL AID *Required financial aid form:* FAFSA. *Financial aid deadline (priority):* 3/1. *Notification date:* Continuous beginning 2/1.
CONTACT Mr. Lee Harrell, Director of Financial Aid, Ringling College of Art and Design, 2700 North Tamiami Trail, Sarasota, FL 34243, 941-359-7532 or toll-free 800-255-7695. *Fax:* 941-359-6107. *E-mail:* lharrell@ringling.edu. *Website:* http://www.ringling.edu/.

RIO GRANDE BIBLE INSTITUTE
Edinburg, TX

CONTACT Financial Aid Office, Rio Grande Bible Institute, 4300 S US Hwy 281, Edinburg, TX 78539, 956-380-8100. *Website:* http://www.riogrande.edu/.

RIPON COLLEGE
Ripon, WI

CONTACT Mr. Leigh D. Mlodzik, Dean of Admission and Financial Aid, Ripon College, 300 Seward Street, Ripon, WI 54971, 920-748-8704 or toll-free 800-947-4766. *Fax:* 920-748-8335. *E-mail:* financialaid@ripon.edu. *Website:* http://www.ripon.edu/.

RIVIER UNIVERSITY
Nashua, NH

CONTACT Valerie Patnaude, Director of Financial Aid, Rivier University, 420 Main Street, Nashua, NH 03060-5086, 603-897-8533 or toll-free 800-44RIVIER. *Fax:* 603-897-8810. *E-mail:* vpatnaude@rivier.edu. *Website:* http://www.rivier.edu/.

ROANOKE COLLEGE
Salem, VA

Tuition & fees: $42,694	Average undergraduate aid package: $32,685

ABOUT THE INSTITUTION Independent Evangelical Lutheran Church in America, coed. *Awards:* bachelor's degrees. 34 undergraduate majors. *Total enrollment:* 1,992. Undergraduates: 1,992. Freshmen: 508. Federal methodology is used as a basis for awarding need-based institutional aid.
UNDERGRADUATE EXPENSES for 2017–2018 *Application fee:* $30. *One-time required fee:* $125. *Comprehensive fee:* $55,952 includes full-time tuition ($41,110), mandatory fees ($1584), and room and board ($13,258). *College room only:* $6156. Room and board charges vary according to board plan and housing facility. *Part-time tuition:* $1964 per course. *Part-time fees:* $60 per term. Part-time tuition and fees vary according to course load and reciprocity agreements.
FRESHMAN FINANCIAL AID (Fall 2016, est.) 456 applied for aid; of those 85% were deemed to have need. 100% of freshmen with need received aid; of those 28% had need fully met. *Average percent of need met:* 82% (excluding resources awarded to replace EFC). *Average financial aid package:* $33,990 (excluding resources awarded to replace EFC). 23% of all full-time freshmen had no need and received non-need-based gift aid.

UNDERGRADUATE FINANCIAL AID (Fall 2016, est.) 1,611 applied for aid; of those 89% were deemed to have need. 100% of undergraduates with need received aid; of those 24% had need fully met. *Average percent of need met:* 81% (excluding resources awarded to replace EFC). *Average financial aid package:* $32,685 (excluding resources awarded to replace EFC). 24% of all full-time undergraduates had no need and received non-need-based gift aid.

GIFT AID (NEED-BASED) *Total amount:* $39,632,375 (6% federal, 6% state, 85% institutional, 3% external sources). *Receiving aid:* Freshmen: 76% (387); all full-time undergraduates: 73% (1,414). *Average award:* Freshmen: $29,600; Undergraduates: $27,005. *Scholarships, grants, and awards:* Federal Pell, FSEOG, state, private, college/university gift aid from institutional funds.

GIFT AID (NON-NEED-BASED) *Total amount:* $10,263,974 (6% state, 89% institutional, 5% external sources). *Receiving aid:* Freshmen: 76% (387). Undergraduates: 72% (1,388). *Average award:* Freshmen: $21,328. Undergraduates: $18,442. *Scholarships, grants, and awards by category:* Academic interests/achievement: general academic interests/achievements. Creative arts/performance: art/fine arts, music. *Tuition waivers:* Full or partial for employees or children of employees, adult students, senior citizens.

LOANS *Student loans:* $14,358,130 (91% need-based, 9% non-need-based). 77% of past graduating class borrowed through all loan programs. *Average indebtedness per student:* $39,175. *Average need-based loan:* Freshmen: $4212. Undergraduates: $4930. *Parent loans:* $4,502,996 (94% need-based, 6% non-need-based). *Programs:* Federal Direct (Subsidized and Unsubsidized Stafford, PLUS), Perkins, college/university, alternative loans.

WORK-STUDY *Federal work-study:* Total amount: $1,478,884; jobs available.

APPLYING FOR FINANCIAL AID *Required financial aid forms:* FAFSA, state aid form. *Financial aid deadline (priority):* 3/1. *Notification date:* Continuous beginning 10/1. Students must reply within 2 weeks of notification.

CONTACT Mr. Thomas S. Blair Jr., Director of Financial Aid, Roanoke College, 221 College Lane, Salem, VA 24153-3794, 540-375-2235 or toll-free 800-388-2276. *E-mail:* finaid@roanoke.edu.
Website: http://www.roanoke.edu/.

ROBERT MORRIS UNIVERSITY
Moon Township, PA

Tuition & fees: $28,250	Average undergraduate aid package: $21,873

ABOUT THE INSTITUTION Independent, coed. *Awards:* certificates, bachelor's, master's, and doctoral degrees. 32 undergraduate majors. *Total enrollment:* 5,199. Undergraduates: 4,384. Freshmen: 880. Federal methodology is used as a basis for awarding need-based institutional aid.

UNDERGRADUATE EXPENSES for 2016–2017 *Application fee:* $30. *Comprehensive fee:* $39,160 includes full-time tuition ($27,320), mandatory fees ($930), and room and board ($10,910). *College room only:* $6070. Full-time tuition and fees vary according to degree level and program. Room and board charges vary according to board plan and housing facility. *Part-time tuition:* $875 per credit hour. *Part-time fees:* $75 per credit hour. Part-time tuition and fees vary according to course load, degree level, and program.

FRESHMAN FINANCIAL AID (Fall 2016, est.) 767 applied for aid; of those 89% were deemed to have need. 100% of freshmen with need received aid; of those 13% had need fully met. *Average percent of need met:* 74% (excluding resources awarded to replace EFC). *Average financial aid package:* $24,242 (excluding resources awarded to replace EFC). 17% of all full-time freshmen had no need and received non-need-based gift aid.

UNDERGRADUATE FINANCIAL AID (Fall 2016, est.) 3,096 applied for aid; of those 89% were deemed to have need. 100% of undergraduates with need received aid; of those 14% had need fully met. *Average percent of need met:* 71% (excluding resources awarded to replace EFC). *Average financial aid package:* $21,873 (excluding resources awarded to replace EFC). 18% of all full-time undergraduates had no need and received non-need-based gift aid.

GIFT AID (NEED-BASED) *Total amount:* $40,969,083 (16% federal, 13% state, 67% institutional, 4% external sources). *Receiving aid:* Freshmen: 78% (685); all full-time undergraduates: 69% (2,703). *Average award:* Freshmen: $18,623; Undergraduates: $15,789. *Scholarships, grants, and awards:* Federal Pell, FSEOG, state, private, college/university gift aid from institutional funds.

GIFT AID (NON-NEED-BASED) *Total amount:* $10,874,336 (10% federal, 1% state, 85% institutional, 4% external sources). *Receiving aid:* Freshmen: 8% (69). Undergraduates: 7% (272). *Average award:* Freshmen: $13,372. Undergraduates: $11,540. *Scholarships, grants, and awards by category:* Academic interests/achievement: general academic interests/achievements. *Special characteristics:* children of faculty/staff, veterans. *Tuition waivers:* Full or partial for employees or children of employees. *ROTC:* Army, Naval cooperative, Air Force cooperative.

LOANS *Student loans:* $32,594,951 (70% need-based, 30% non-need-based). 82% of past graduating class borrowed through all loan programs. *Average indebtedness per student:* $39,431. *Average need-based loan:* Freshmen: $4989. Undergraduates: $6302. *Parent loans:* $13,107,421 (52% need-based, 48% non-need-based). *Programs:* Federal Direct (Subsidized and Unsubsidized Stafford, PLUS), Perkins, private loans.

WORK-STUDY *Federal work-study:* Total amount: $2,642,635; jobs available. *State or other work-study/employment:* Part-time jobs available.

ATHLETIC AWARDS Total amount: $3,574,490 (43% need-based, 57% non-need-based).

APPLYING FOR FINANCIAL AID *Required financial aid form:* FAFSA. *Financial aid deadline:* Continuous. *Notification date:* Continuous beginning 2/15. Students must reply within 2 weeks of notification.

CONTACT Ms. Stephanie Hendershot, Director of Financial Aid, Robert Morris University, 6001 University Boulevard, Moon Township, PA 15108-1189, 412-397-6250 or toll-free 800-762-0097. *Fax:* 412-397-2200. *E-mail:* finaid@rmu.edu.
Website: http://www.rmu.edu/.

ROBERT MORRIS UNIVERSITY ILLINOIS
Chicago, IL

Tuition & fees: $27,180	Average undergraduate aid package: $17,131

ABOUT THE INSTITUTION Independent, coed. *Awards:* associate, bachelor's, and master's degrees. 16 undergraduate majors. *Total enrollment:* 2,703. Undergraduates: 2,352. Freshmen: 551. Federal methodology is used as a basis for awarding need-based institutional aid.

UNDERGRADUATE EXPENSES for 2017–2018 *Application fee:* $20. *Comprehensive fee:* $40,380 includes full-time tuition ($26,700), mandatory fees ($480), and room and board ($13,200). *Part-time tuition:* $742 per quarter hour. Part-time tuition and fees vary according to course load.

FRESHMAN FINANCIAL AID (Fall 2016, est.) 682 applied for aid; of those 96% were deemed to have need. 97% of freshmen with need received aid; of those 4% had need fully met. *Average percent of need met:* 50% (excluding resources awarded to replace EFC). *Average financial aid package:* $17,285 (excluding resources awarded to replace EFC). 5% of all full-time freshmen had no need and received non-need-based gift aid.

UNDERGRADUATE FINANCIAL AID (Fall 2016, est.) 2,081 applied for aid; of those 95% were deemed to have need. 92% of undergraduates with need received aid; of those 6% had need fully met. *Average percent of need met:* 48% (excluding resources awarded to replace EFC). *Average financial aid package:* $17,131 (excluding resources awarded to replace EFC). 3% of all full-time undergraduates had no need and received non-need-based gift aid.

GIFT AID (NEED-BASED) *Total amount:* $18,432,001 (47% federal, 24% state, 29% institutional). *Receiving aid:* Freshmen: 90% (631); all full-time undergraduates: 61% (1,794). *Average award:* Freshmen: $13,218; Undergraduates: $13,701. *Scholarships, grants, and awards:* Federal Pell, FSEOG, state, private, college/university gift aid from institutional funds.

GIFT AID (NON-NEED-BASED) *Total amount:* $12,756,005 (100% institutional). *Receiving aid:* Freshmen: 72% (505). Undergraduates: 54% (1,588). *Average award:* Freshmen: $12,824. Undergraduates: $13,002. *Scholarships, grants, and awards by category:* Academic interests/achievement: architecture, business, computer science, general academic interests/achievements, health fields. Creative arts/performance: applied art and design, dance, journalism/publications, music, performing arts, theater/drama. *Special achievements/activities:* cheerleading/drum major, community service, general special achievements/activities, leadership. *Special characteristics:* adult students, children of faculty/staff, children of public servants, general special characteristics, local/state students, out-of-state students, veterans. *Tuition waivers:* Full or partial for employees or children of employees. *ROTC:* Army cooperative.

LOANS *Student loans:* $17,632,821 (96% need-based, 4% non-need-based). 98% of past graduating class borrowed through all loan programs. *Average indebtedness per student:* $30,985. *Average need-based loan:* Freshmen: $3955. Undergraduates: $4303. *Parent loans:* $5,407,608 (89% need-based, 11% non-need-based). *Programs:* Federal Direct (Subsidized and Unsubsidized Stafford, PLUS), Perkins.

WORK-STUDY *Federal work-study:* Total amount: $237,664; 114 jobs averaging $1099.

ATHLETIC AWARDS Total amount: $8,067,017 (88% need-based, 12% non-need-based).

APPLYING FOR FINANCIAL AID *Required financial aid form:* FAFSA. *Financial aid deadline:* Continuous. *Notification date:* Continuous.

CONTACT Leigh Brinson, Vice President of Financial Services, Robert Morris University Illinois, 401 South State Street, Suite 122, Chicago, IL 60605, 312-935-4106 or toll-free 800-762-5960. *Fax:* 312-935-4043. *E-mail:* lbrinson@robertmorris.edu. *Website:* http://www.robertmorris.edu/.

ROBERTS WESLEYAN COLLEGE
Rochester, NY

Tuition & fees: $30,686	Average undergraduate aid package: $21,746

ABOUT THE INSTITUTION Independent Free Methodist Church of North America, coed. *Awards:* bachelor's and master's degrees. 62 undergraduate majors. *Total enrollment:* 1,698. Undergraduates: 1,316. Freshmen: 227. Federal methodology is used as a basis for awarding need-based institutional aid.

UNDERGRADUATE EXPENSES for 2017–2018 *Comprehensive fee:* $41,116 includes full-time tuition ($29,600), mandatory fees ($1086), and room and board ($10,430). *College room only:* $6548. Room and board charges vary according to board plan and housing facility. Part-time tuition and fees vary according to course load.

FRESHMAN FINANCIAL AID (Fall 2016, est.) 201 applied for aid; of those 92% were deemed to have need. 100% of freshmen with need received aid; of those 12% had need fully met. *Average percent of need met:* 80% (excluding resources awarded to replace EFC). *Average financial aid package:* $26,551 (excluding resources awarded to replace EFC). 19% of all full-time freshmen had no need and received non-need-based gift aid.

UNDERGRADUATE FINANCIAL AID (Fall 2016, est.) 1,082 applied for aid; of those 95% were deemed to have need. 100% of undergraduates with need received aid; of those 13% had need fully met. *Average percent of need met:* 70% (excluding resources awarded to replace EFC). *Average financial aid package:* $21,746 (excluding resources awarded to replace EFC). 14% of all full-time undergraduates had no need and received non-need-based gift aid.

GIFT AID (NEED-BASED) *Total amount:* $15,705,349 (14% federal, 8% state, 66% institutional, 12% external sources). *Receiving aid:* Freshmen: 80% (184); all full-time undergraduates: 81% (980). *Average award:* Freshmen: $21,398; Undergraduates: $16,755. *Scholarships, grants, and awards:* Federal Pell, FSEOG, state, private, college/university gift aid from institutional funds, Academic Competitiveness Grants, National SMART Grants, TEACH Grants.

GIFT AID (NON-NEED-BASED) *Total amount:* $3,107,596 (1% state, 74% institutional, 25% external sources). *Receiving aid:* Freshmen: 8% (18). Undergraduates: 8% (92). *Average award:* Freshmen: $13,968. Undergraduates: $10,221. *Scholarships, grants, and awards by category:* Academic interests/achievement: 540 awards ($4,837,381 total): general academic interests/achievements. Creative arts/performance: 96 awards ($399,416 total): art/fine arts, music. Special achievements/activities: 250 awards ($799,375 total): general special achievements/activities, junior miss, religious involvement. Special characteristics: 378 awards ($1,251,011 total): children and siblings of alumni, children of faculty/staff, international students, out-of-state students, relatives of clergy, religious affiliation. *Tuition waivers:* Full or partial for employees or children of employees, senior citizens. *ROTC:* Army cooperative, Air Force cooperative.

LOANS *Student loans:* $9,087,050 (83% need-based, 17% non-need-based). 84% of past graduating class borrowed through all loan programs. *Average indebtedness per student:* $34,679. *Average need-based loan:* Freshmen: $4702. Undergraduates: $5387. *Parent loans:* $2,237,834 (57% need-based, 43% non-need-based). *Programs:* Federal Direct (Subsidized and Unsubsidized Stafford, PLUS), Perkins.

WORK-STUDY *Federal work-study:* Total amount: $288,816; 646 jobs averaging $447. *State or other work-study/employment:* Total amount: $78,000 (100% non-need-based). 41 part-time jobs averaging $1878.

ATHLETIC AWARDS Total amount: $1,298,832 (60% need-based, 40% non-need-based).

APPLYING FOR FINANCIAL AID *Required financial aid forms:* FAFSA, state aid form. *Financial aid deadline (priority):* 3/15. *Notification date:* Continuous beginning 11/1. Students must reply by 5/1 or within 2 weeks of notification.

CONTACT Student Financial Services Office, Roberts Wesleyan College, 2301 Westside Drive, Rochester, NY 14624-1997, 585-594-6150 or toll-free 800-777-4RWC. *Fax:* 585-594-6036. *E-mail:* finaid@roberts.edu. *Website:* http://www.roberts.edu/.

ROCHESTER COLLEGE
Rochester Hills, MI

CONTACT Student Financial Services, Rochester College, 800 West Avon Road, Rochester Hills, MI 48307, 248-218-2038 or toll-free 800-521-6010. *Fax:* 248-218-2065. *Website:* http://www.rc.edu/.

ROCHESTER INSTITUTE OF TECHNOLOGY
Rochester, NY

Tuition & fees: $38,568	Average undergraduate aid package: $24,700

ABOUT THE INSTITUTION Independent, coed. *Awards:* certificates, associate, bachelor's, master's, and doctoral degrees. 114 undergraduate majors. *Total enrollment:* 16,507. Undergraduates: 13,384. Both federal and institutional methodology are used as a basis for awarding need-based institutional aid.

UNDERGRADUATE EXPENSES for 2016–2017 *Application fee:* $60. *Comprehensive fee:* $50,842 includes full-time tuition ($38,024), mandatory fees ($544), and room and board ($12,274). *College room only:* $7162. Full-time tuition and fees vary according to course load. Room and board charges vary according to board plan and housing facility. *Part-time tuition:* $1408 per credit hour. *Part-time fees:* $69 per term. Part-time tuition and fees vary according to class time and course load. *Payment plan:* Tuition prepayment.

FRESHMAN FINANCIAL AID (Fall 2015) 2,574 applied for aid; of those 87% were deemed to have need. 100% of freshmen with need received aid; of those 82% had need fully met. *Average percent of need met:* 87% (excluding resources awarded to replace EFC). *Average financial aid package:* $25,200 (excluding resources awarded to replace EFC). 19% of all full-time freshmen had no need and received non-need-based gift aid.

UNDERGRADUATE FINANCIAL AID (Fall 2015) 10,265 applied for aid; of those 90% were deemed to have need. 100% of undergraduates with need received aid; of those 81% had need fully met. *Average percent of need met:* 86% (excluding resources awarded to replace EFC). *Average financial aid package:* $24,700 (excluding resources awarded to replace EFC). 18% of all full-time undergraduates had no need and received non-need-based gift aid.

GIFT AID (NEED-BASED) *Total amount:* $160,840,048 (11% federal, 5% state, 84% institutional). *Receiving aid:* Freshmen: 73% (2,131); all full-time undergraduates: 70% (8,757). *Average award:* Freshmen: $22,000; Undergraduates: $20,000. *Scholarships, grants, and awards:* Federal Pell, FSEOG, state, private, college/university gift aid from institutional funds, United Negro College Fund, National Science Foundation Grants.

GIFT AID (NON-NEED-BASED) *Total amount:* $50,505,318 (16% federal, 26% state, 48% institutional, 10% external sources). *Receiving aid:* Freshmen: 23% (661). Undergraduates: 25% (3,096). *Average award:* Freshmen: $11,792. Undergraduates: $10,800. *Scholarships, grants, and awards by category:* Academic interests/achievement: biological sciences, business, communication, computer science, engineering/technologies, general academic interests/achievements, home economics, humanities, international studies, mathematics, military science, physical sciences, premedicine, social sciences. *Creative arts/performance:* applied art and design, art/fine arts, cinema/film/broadcasting. *Special achievements/activities:* community service, leadership. *Special characteristics:* children of faculty/staff, veterans. **Tuition waivers:** Full or partial for employees or children of employees. **ROTC:** Army, Naval cooperative, Air Force.

LOANS *Student loans:* $78,822,132 (51% need-based, 49% non-need-based). 76% of past graduating class borrowed through all loan programs. *Average indebtedness per student:* $38,198. **Average need-based loan:** Freshmen: $4600. Undergraduates: $6500. **Parent loans:** $26,186,069 (41% need-based, 59% non-need-based). **Programs:** Federal Direct (Subsidized and Unsubsidized Stafford, PLUS), Perkins.

WORK-STUDY *Federal work-study:* jobs available. **State or other work-study/employment:** Total amount: $11,000,000 (100% non-need-based). Part-time jobs available.

APPLYING FOR FINANCIAL AID *Required financial aid forms:* FAFSA, state aid form. *Financial aid deadline (priority):* 3/1. *Notification date:* Continuous beginning 3/15. Students must reply by 5/1.

CONTACT Mr. Larry Chambers, Associate Vice President for Financial Aid and Scholarships, Rochester Institute of Technology, 56 Lomb Memorial Drive, Rochester, NY 14623-5604, 585-475-2186. *Fax:* 585-475-7270. *E-mail:* larry.chambers@rit.edu. *Website:* http://www.rit.edu/.

ROCKFORD UNIVERSITY
Rockford, IL

Tuition & fees: $30,050	Average undergraduate aid package: $18,757

ABOUT THE INSTITUTION Independent, coed. *Awards:* certificates, bachelor's, and master's degrees. 52 undergraduate majors. *Total enrollment:* 1,298. Undergraduates: 1,086. Freshmen: 162. Federal methodology is used as a basis for awarding need-based institutional aid.

UNDERGRADUATE EXPENSES for 2017–2018 *Comprehensive fee:* $38,470 includes full-time tuition ($29,920), mandatory fees ($130), and room and board ($8420). *College room only:* $4570. Full-time tuition and fees vary according to course load. Room and board charges vary according to board plan and housing facility. *Part-time tuition:* $785 per credit hour. Part-time tuition and fees vary according to course load.

FRESHMAN FINANCIAL AID (Fall 2015) 163 applied for aid; of those 93% were deemed to have need. 100% of freshmen with need received aid; of those 13% had need fully met. *Average percent of need met:* 68% (excluding resources awarded to replace EFC). *Average financial aid package:* $19,125 (excluding resources awarded to replace EFC). 10% of all full-time freshmen had no need and received non-need-based gift aid.

UNDERGRADUATE FINANCIAL AID (Fall 2015) 851 applied for aid; of those 95% were deemed to have need. 100% of undergraduates with need received aid; of those 12% had need fully met. *Average percent of need met:* 64% (excluding resources awarded to replace EFC). *Average financial aid package:* $18,757 (excluding resources awarded to replace EFC). 9% of all full-time undergraduates had no need and received non-need-based gift aid.

GIFT AID (NEED-BASED) *Total amount:* $11,646,061 (19% federal, 14% state, 65% institutional, 2% external sources). *Receiving aid:* Freshmen: 90% (151); all full-time undergraduates: 89% (795). *Average award:* Freshmen: $15,643; Undergraduates: $14,176. *Scholarships, grants, and awards:* Federal Pell, FSEOG, state, private, college/university gift aid from institutional funds.

GIFT AID (NON-NEED-BASED) *Total amount:* $1,629,904 (89% institutional, 11% external sources). *Receiving aid:* Freshmen: 11% (18). Undergraduates: 11% (96). *Average award:* Freshmen: $12,246. Undergraduates: $10,221. *Scholarships, grants, and awards by category:* Academic interests/achievement: 848 awards ($6,400,463 total): biological sciences, business, computer science, education, English, foreign languages, general academic interests/achievements, mathematics, physical sciences, premedicine, social sciences. *Creative arts/performance:* 39 awards ($100,935 total): art/fine arts, dance, music, performing arts, theater/drama. *Special achievements/activities:* 4 awards ($7183 total): community service, leadership. *Special characteristics:* 147 awards ($876,108 total): children and siblings of alumni, children of current students, children of educators, children of faculty/staff, general special characteristics, international students, out-of-state students, parents of current students, siblings of current students. **Tuition waivers:** Full or partial for employees or children of employees.

LOANS *Student loans:* $8,384,648 (85% need-based, 15% non-need-based). 84% of past graduating class borrowed through all loan programs. *Average indebtedness per student:* $40,313. *Average need-based loan:* Freshmen: $3680. Undergraduates: $5046. **Parent loans:** $1,813,748 (47% need-based, 53% non-need-based). **Programs:** Federal Direct (Subsidized and Unsubsidized Stafford, PLUS), Perkins, college/university, alternative loans.

WORK-STUDY *Federal work-study:* 130 jobs averaging $727. **State or other work-study/employment:** Total amount: $353,820 (13% need-based, 87% non-need-based). 164 part-time jobs averaging $859.

APPLYING FOR FINANCIAL AID *Required financial aid form:* FAFSA. *Financial aid deadline (priority):* 3/1. *Notification date:* Continuous beginning 3/15. Students must reply within 4 weeks of notification.

CONTACT Todd M. Fischer-Free, Assistant Vice President of Student Administrative Services, Rockford University, 5050 East State Street, Rockford, IL 61108, 815-226-3385 or toll-free 800-892-2984. *Fax:* 815-394-5174. *E-mail:* tfree@rockford.edu. *Website:* http://www.rockford.edu/.

ROCKHURST UNIVERSITY
Kansas City, MO

Tuition & fees: $35,670	Average undergraduate aid package: $29,123

ABOUT THE INSTITUTION Independent Roman Catholic (Jesuit), coed. *Awards:* certificates, bachelor's, master's, and doctoral degrees. 30 undergraduate majors. *Total enrollment:* 2,854. Undergraduates: 2,042. Freshmen: 403. Federal methodology is used as a basis for awarding need-based institutional aid.

UNDERGRADUATE EXPENSES for 2016–2017 *Application fee:* $25. *Comprehensive fee:* $45,350 includes full-time tuition ($34,880), mandatory fees ($790), and room and board ($9680). *College room only:* $5880. Full-time tuition and fees vary according to class time and course load. Room and board charges vary according to board plan and housing facility. *Part-time tuition:* $582 per semester hour. *Part-time fees:* $25 per credit hour. Part-time tuition and fees vary according to class time and course load.

FRESHMAN FINANCIAL AID (Fall 2015) 316 applied for aid; of those 79% were deemed to have need. 100% of freshmen with need received aid; of those 27% had need fully met. *Average percent of need met:* 90% (excluding resources awarded to replace EFC). *Average financial aid package:* $29,298 (excluding resources awarded to replace EFC). 20% of all full-time freshmen had no need and received non-need-based gift aid.

UNDERGRADUATE FINANCIAL AID (Fall 2015) 1,431 applied for aid; of those 72% were deemed to have need. 100% of undergraduates with need received aid; of those 26% had need fully met. *Average percent of need met:* 87% (excluding resources awarded to replace EFC). *Average financial aid package:* $29,123 (excluding resources awarded to replace EFC). 27% of all full-time undergraduates had no need and received non-need-based gift aid.

GIFT AID (NEED-BASED) *Total amount:* $21,797,148 (7% federal, 3% state, 89% institutional, 1% external sources). *Receiving aid:* Freshmen: 79% (251); all full-time undergraduates: 71% (1,026). *Average award:* Freshmen: $21,393; Undergraduates: $21,074. *Scholarships, grants, and awards:* Federal Pell, FSEOG, state, private, college/university gift aid from institutional funds, United Negro College Fund.

GIFT AID (NON-NEED-BASED) *Total amount:* $9,358,089 (1% state, 98% institutional, 1% external sources). *Receiving aid:* Freshmen: 41% (130). Undergraduates: 32% (465). *Average award:* Freshmen: $19,356. Undergraduates: $19,287. *Scholarships, grants, and awards by category:* Academic interests/achievement: biological sciences, business, communication, computer science, education, engineering/technologies, English, foreign languages, general academic interests/achievements, health fields, humanities, international studies, mathematics, physical sciences, premedicine, religion/biblical studies, social sciences. *Creative arts/performance:* creative writing, music, performing arts, theater/drama. *Special achievements/activities:* community service, leadership. *Special characteristics:* children of faculty/staff, siblings of current students. **Tuition waivers:** Full or partial for employees or children of employees, senior citizens. **ROTC:** Army cooperative.

LOANS *Student loans:* $10,391,847 (65% need-based, 35% non-need-based). 78% of past graduating class borrowed through all loan programs. *Average indebtedness per student:* $23,753. *Average need-based loan:* Freshmen: $3679. Undergraduates: $4521. **Parent loans:** $2,491,040 (8% need-based, 92% non-need-based). **Programs:** Federal Direct (Subsidized and Unsubsidized Stafford, PLUS), Perkins.

WORK-STUDY *Federal work-study:* jobs available. *State or other work-study/employment:* Part-time jobs available.
ATHLETIC AWARDS Total amount: $2,746,894 (25% need-based, 75% non-need-based).
APPLYING FOR FINANCIAL AID *Required financial aid form:* FAFSA. *Financial aid deadline (priority):* 3/1. *Notification date:* Continuous beginning 3/1. Students must reply by 6/1 or within 4 weeks of notification.
CONTACT Maureen McKinnon, Director of Financial Aid, Rockhurst University, 1100 Rockhurst Road, Kansas City, MO 64110-2561, 816-501-4831 or toll-free 800-842-6776. *Fax:* 816-501-3139. *E-mail:* maureen.mckinnon@rockhurst.edu.
Website: http://www.rockhurst.edu/.

ROCKY MOUNTAIN COLLEGE
Billings, MT

Tuition & fees: $27,566	Average undergraduate aid package: $23,133

ABOUT THE INSTITUTION Independent interdenominational, coed. *Awards:* associate, bachelor's, and master's degrees. 48 undergraduate majors. *Total enrollment:* 1,000. Undergraduates: 908. Freshmen: 217. Federal methodology is used as a basis for awarding need-based institutional aid.
UNDERGRADUATE EXPENSES for 2017–2018 *Application fee:* $35. *Comprehensive fee:* $35,776 includes full-time tuition ($27,036), mandatory fees ($530), and room and board ($8210). *College room only:* $3898. Full-time tuition and fees vary according to course load, degree level, and program. Room and board charges vary according to board plan and housing facility. *Part-time tuition:* $1127 per credit. *Part-time fees:* $160 per term. Part-time tuition and fees vary according to course load, degree level, and program.
FRESHMAN FINANCIAL AID (Fall 2016, est.) 203 applied for aid; of those 92% were deemed to have need. 100% of freshmen with need received aid; of those 23% had need fully met. *Average percent of need met:* 76% (excluding resources awarded to replace EFC). *Average financial aid package:* $22,601 (excluding resources awarded to replace EFC). 5% of all full-time freshmen had no need and received non-need-based gift aid.
UNDERGRADUATE FINANCIAL AID (Fall 2016, est.) 712 applied for aid; of those 89% were deemed to have need. 100% of undergraduates with need received aid; of those 19% had need fully met. *Average percent of need met:* 76% (excluding resources awarded to replace EFC). *Average financial aid package:* $23,133 (excluding resources awarded to replace EFC). 6% of all full-time undergraduates had no need and received non-need-based gift aid.
GIFT AID (NEED-BASED) *Total amount:* $11,647,762 (12% federal, 76% institutional, 12% external sources). *Receiving aid:* Freshmen: 86% (186); all full-time undergraduates: 73% (628). *Average award:* Freshmen: $18,300; Undergraduates: $18,115. *Scholarships, grants, and awards:* Federal Pell, FSEOG, state, private, college/university gift aid from institutional funds.
GIFT AID (NON-NEED-BASED) *Total amount:* $1,463,947 (85% institutional, 15% external sources). *Receiving aid:* Freshmen: 19% (40). Undergraduates: 13% (113). *Average award:* Freshmen: $13,091. Undergraduates: $11,271. *Scholarships, grants, and awards by category:* Academic interests/achievement: 728 awards ($8,090,386 total): general academic interests/achievements. *Creative arts/performance:* music. *Special achievements/activities:* 9 awards ($13,000 total): cheerleading/drum major. *Tuition waivers:* Full or partial for employees or children of employees. *ROTC:* Army cooperative.
LOANS *Student loans:* $4,782,687 (74% need-based, 26% non-need-based). 83% of past graduating class borrowed through all loan programs. *Average indebtedness per student:* $30,035. *Average need-based loan:* Freshmen: $3217. Undergraduates: $4273. *Parent loans:* $1,023,214 (45% need-based, 55% non-need-based). *Programs:* Federal Direct (Subsidized and Unsubsidized Stafford, PLUS), Perkins.
WORK-STUDY *Federal work-study:* Total amount: $137,788; 298 jobs averaging $466. *State or other work-study/employment:* Total amount: $131,029 (66% need-based, 34% non-need-based). 170 part-time jobs averaging $771.
ATHLETIC AWARDS Total amount: $2,732,543 (87% need-based, 13% non-need-based).
APPLYING FOR FINANCIAL AID *Required financial aid form:* FAFSA. *Financial aid deadline:* Continuous. *Notification date:* Continuous beginning 2/15. Students must reply within 4 weeks of notification.

CONTACT Jessica Francischetti, Director of Financial Assistance, Rocky Mountain College, 1511 Poly Drive, Billings, MT 59102-1796, 406-657-1031 or toll-free 800-877-6259. *Fax:* 406-657-1169. *E-mail:* finaid@rocky.edu.
Website: http://www.rocky.edu/.

ROCKY MOUNTAIN COLLEGE OF ART + DESIGN
Lakewood, CO

ABOUT THE INSTITUTION Proprietary, coed. *Awards:* certificates, bachelor's, and master's degrees. 10 undergraduate majors. *Total enrollment:* 1,096. Undergraduates: 1,079. Freshmen: 102.
GIFT AID (NEED-BASED) *Scholarships, grants, and awards:* Federal Pell, FSEOG, state, college/university gift aid from institutional funds.
GIFT AID (NON-NEED-BASED) *Scholarships, grants, and awards by category:* Academic interests/achievement: general academic interests/achievements. *Creative arts/performance:* applied art and design, art/fine arts. *Special characteristics:* children of faculty/staff.
LOANS *Programs:* Federal Direct (Subsidized and Unsubsidized Stafford, PLUS), alternative loans.
APPLYING FOR FINANCIAL AID *Required financial aid form:* FAFSA.
CONTACT Michael Dulay, Director of Financial Aid, Rocky Mountain College of Art + Design, 1600 Pierce Street, Lakewood, CO 80214, 303-753-6046 or toll-free 800-888-ARTS. *Fax:* 303-567-7280. *E-mail:* mdulay@rmcad.edu.
Website: http://www.rmcad.edu/.

ROGERS STATE UNIVERSITY
Claremore, OK

Tuition & fees (OK res): $7000	Average undergraduate aid package: $9679

ABOUT THE INSTITUTION State-supported, coed. *Awards:* associate, bachelor's, and master's degrees. 25 undergraduate majors. *Total enrollment:* 3,917. Undergraduates: 3,889. Freshmen: 639. Federal methodology is used as a basis for awarding need-based institutional aid.
UNDERGRADUATE EXPENSES for 2017–2018 *Application fee:* $20. *Tuition, state resident:* full-time $4170. *Tuition, nonresident:* full-time $12,480. *Required fees:* full-time $2830. Full-time tuition and fees vary according to course level, course load, location, program, and student level. Part-time tuition and fees vary according to course level, course load, location, program, and student level. *College room and board:* $9512; *Room only:* $5354. Room and board charges vary according to housing facility.
FRESHMAN FINANCIAL AID (Fall 2016, est.) 552 applied for aid; of those 81% were deemed to have need. 99% of freshmen with need received aid; of those 10% had need fully met. *Average percent of need met:* 55% (excluding resources awarded to replace EFC). *Average financial aid package:* $9200 (excluding resources awarded to replace EFC). 3% of all full-time freshmen had no need and received non-need-based gift aid.
UNDERGRADUATE FINANCIAL AID (Fall 2016, est.) 2,041 applied for aid; of those 85% were deemed to have need. 99% of undergraduates with need received aid; of those 11% had need fully met. *Average percent of need met:* 54% (excluding resources awarded to replace EFC). *Average financial aid package:* $9679 (excluding resources awarded to replace EFC). 3% of all full-time undergraduates had no need and received non-need-based gift aid.
GIFT AID (NEED-BASED) *Total amount:* $11,999,440 (63% federal, 16% state, 13% institutional, 8% external sources). *Receiving aid:* Freshmen: 54% (393); all full-time undergraduates: 62% (1,509). *Average award:* Freshmen: $7177; Undergraduates: $7037. *Scholarships, grants, and awards:* Federal Pell, FSEOG, state, private, college/university gift aid from institutional funds.
GIFT AID (NON-NEED-BASED) *Total amount:* $1,750,625 (1% federal, 12% state, 67% institutional, 20% external sources). *Receiving aid:* Freshmen: 3% (24). Undergraduates: 4% (108). *Average award:* Freshmen: $8898. Undergraduates: $7137. *Scholarships, grants, and awards by category:* Academic interests/achievement: 52 awards ($41,090 total): business, general academic interests/achieve-

ments, military science, premedicine. *Creative arts/performance:* 41 awards ($42,650 total): art/fine arts, dance, music, theater/drama. *Special achievements/activities:* 50 awards ($299,376 total): cheerleading/drum major, junior miss, leadership. *Special characteristics:* 164 awards ($1,125,884 total): adult students, out-of-state students, veterans. *Tuition waivers:* Full or partial for employees or children of employees, senior citizens.

LOANS *Student loans:* $20,209,043 (84% need-based, 16% non-need-based). 51% of past graduating class borrowed through all loan programs. *Average indebtedness per student:* $16,164. *Average need-based loan:* Freshmen: $3254. Undergraduates: $3832. *Parent loans:* $521,795 (37% need-based, 63% non-need-based). *Programs:* Federal Direct (Subsidized and Unsubsidized Stafford, PLUS), alternative loans.

WORK-STUDY *Federal work-study:* Total amount: $115,584; 54 jobs averaging $2035. *State or other work-study/employment:* Total amount: $945,000 (33% need-based, 67% non-need-based). 208 part-time jobs averaging $2027.

ATHLETIC AWARDS Total amount: $1,449,726 (45% need-based, 55% non-need-based).

APPLYING FOR FINANCIAL AID *Required financial aid form:* FAFSA. *Financial aid deadline (priority):* 5/1. *Notification date:* Continuous beginning 3/15. Students must reply within 2 weeks of notification.

CONTACT Ms. Kelly Hicks, Director of Financial Aid, Rogers State University, 1701 West Will Rogers Boulevard, Claremore, OK 74017-3252, 918-343-7553 or toll-free 800-256-7511. *Fax:* 918-343-7598. *E-mail:* finaid@rsu.edu. *Website:* http://www.rsu.edu/.

ROGER WILLIAMS UNIVERSITY
Bristol, RI

Tuition & fees: $31,850	Average undergraduate aid package: $21,104

ABOUT THE INSTITUTION Independent, coed. *Awards:* certificates, associate, bachelor's, master's, and doctoral degrees. 69 undergraduate majors. *Total enrollment:* 5,193. Undergraduates: 4,902. Freshmen: 1,211. Both federal and institutional methodology are used as a basis for awarding need-based institutional aid.

UNDERGRADUATE EXPENSES for 2017–2018 *Application fee:* $50. *One-time required fee:* $250. *Comprehensive fee:* $47,262 includes full-time tuition ($29,976), mandatory fees ($1874), and room and board ($15,412). *College room only:* $8230. Full-time tuition and fees vary according to class time, course load, degree level, and program. Room and board charges vary according to board plan and housing facility. *Part-time tuition:* $1249 per credit hour. Part-time tuition and fees vary according to class time, course load, degree level, and program. *Payment plan:* Guaranteed tuition.

FRESHMAN FINANCIAL AID (Fall 2016, est.) 1,049 applied for aid; of those 80% were deemed to have need. 100% of freshmen with need received aid; of those 7% had need fully met. *Average percent of need met:* 81% (excluding resources awarded to replace EFC). *Average financial aid package:* $19,829 (excluding resources awarded to replace EFC). 30% of all full-time freshmen had no need and received non-need-based gift aid.

UNDERGRADUATE FINANCIAL AID (Fall 2016, est.) 3,124 applied for aid; of those 82% were deemed to have need. 99% of undergraduates with need received aid; of those 11% had need fully met. *Average percent of need met:* 81% (excluding resources awarded to replace EFC). *Average financial aid package:* $21,104 (excluding resources awarded to replace EFC). 13% of all full-time undergraduates had no need and received non-need-based gift aid.

GIFT AID (NEED-BASED) *Total amount:* $39,175,021 (6% federal, 1% state, 91% institutional, 2% external sources). *Receiving aid:* Freshmen: 32% (389); all full-time undergraduates: 43% (1,760). *Average award:* Freshmen: $13,809; Undergraduates: $14,200. *Scholarships, grants, and awards:* Federal Pell, FSEOG, state, private, college/university gift aid from institutional funds.

GIFT AID (NON-NEED-BASED) *Total amount:* $6,746,746 (99% institutional, 1% external sources). *Receiving aid:* Freshmen: 68% (819). Undergraduates: 53% (2,202). *Average award:* Freshmen: $11,813. Undergraduates: $12,612. *Scholarships, grants, and awards by category:* Academic interests/achievement: 3,514 awards ($37,469,342 total): general academic interests/achievements. *Tuition waivers:* Full or partial for employees or children of employees. *ROTC:* Army.

LOANS *Student loans:* $16,283,509 (86% need-based, 14% non-need-based). 58% of past graduating class borrowed through all loan programs. *Average indebtedness per student:* $41,632. *Average need-based loan:* Freshmen: $3326. Undergrad-

uates: $3730. *Parent loans:* $11,430,160 (93% need-based, 7% non-need-based). *Programs:* Federal Direct (Subsidized and Unsubsidized Stafford, PLUS), Perkins.

WORK-STUDY *Federal work-study:* Total amount: $522,307; jobs available. *State or other work-study/employment:* Part-time jobs available.

APPLYING FOR FINANCIAL AID *Required financial aid forms:* FAFSA, CSS Financial Aid PROFILE. *Financial aid deadline:* 2/1 (priority: 1/1). *Notification date:* Continuous beginning 12/15. Students must reply by 5/1 or within 2 weeks of notification.

CONTACT Diane Usher, Associate Director of Student Financial Aid and Planning, Roger Williams University, One Old Ferry Road, Bristol, RI 02809, 800-458-7144 Ext. 3100 or toll-free 800-458-7144. *Fax:* 401-254-3356. *E-mail:* finaid@rwu.edu. *Website:* http://www.rwu.edu/.

ROLLINS COLLEGE
Winter Park, FL

Tuition & fees: $48,335	Average undergraduate aid package: $39,204

ABOUT THE INSTITUTION Independent, coed. *Awards:* bachelor's, master's, and doctoral degrees. 36 undergraduate majors. *Total enrollment:* 3,240. Undergraduates: 1,942. Freshmen: 538. Federal methodology is used as a basis for awarding need-based institutional aid.

UNDERGRADUATE EXPENSES for 2017–2018 *Application fee:* $50. *Comprehensive fee:* $63,065 includes full-time tuition ($48,335) and room and board ($14,730). *College room only:* $8715. Room and board charges vary according to housing facility.

FRESHMAN FINANCIAL AID (Fall 2016, est.) 356 applied for aid; of those 87% were deemed to have need. 100% of freshmen with need received aid; of those 30% had need fully met. *Average percent of need met:* 80% (excluding resources awarded to replace EFC). *Average financial aid package:* $40,560 (excluding resources awarded to replace EFC). 27% of all full-time freshmen had no need and received non-need-based gift aid.

UNDERGRADUATE FINANCIAL AID (Fall 2016, est.) 1,104 applied for aid; of those 89% were deemed to have need. 100% of undergraduates with need received aid; of those 27% had need fully met. *Average percent of need met:* 78% (excluding resources awarded to replace EFC). *Average financial aid package:* $39,204 (excluding resources awarded to replace EFC). 29% of all full-time undergraduates had no need and received non-need-based gift aid.

GIFT AID (NEED-BASED) *Total amount:* $28,786,902 (7% federal, 10% state, 82% institutional, 1% external sources). *Receiving aid:* Freshmen: 58% (311); all full-time undergraduates: 51% (982). *Average award:* Freshmen: $32,953; Undergraduates: $31,145. *Scholarships, grants, and awards:* Federal Pell, FSEOG, state, private, college/university gift aid from institutional funds.

GIFT AID (NON-NEED-BASED) *Total amount:* $13,991,203 (14% state, 85% institutional, 1% external sources). *Receiving aid:* Freshmen: 9% (48). Undergraduates: 8% (149). *Average award:* Freshmen: $20,948. Undergraduates: $20,042. *Scholarships, grants, and awards by category:* Academic interests/achievement: 146 awards ($587,708 total): computer science, engineering/technologies, general academic interests/achievements, mathematics, physical sciences. *Creative arts/performance:* 45 awards ($334,419 total): art/fine arts, music, theater/drama. *Tuition waivers:* Full or partial for employees or children of employees.

LOANS *Student loans:* $6,924,697 (72% need-based, 28% non-need-based). 48% of past graduating class borrowed through all loan programs. *Average indebtedness per student:* $32,208. *Average need-based loan:* Freshmen: $3499. Undergraduates: $4557. *Parent loans:* $5,050,452 (50% need-based, 50% non-need-based). *Programs:* Federal Direct (Subsidized and Unsubsidized Stafford, PLUS).

WORK-STUDY *Federal work-study:* Total amount: $506,127; 232 jobs averaging $1251. *State or other work-study/employment:* Total amount: $3500 (100% need-based). 3 part-time jobs averaging $4000.

ATHLETIC AWARDS Total amount: $3,954,730 (35% need-based, 65% non-need-based).

APPLYING FOR FINANCIAL AID *Required financial aid form:* FAFSA. *Financial aid deadline (priority):* 3/1. *Notification date:* Continuous beginning 1/1. Students must reply by 5/1.

CONTACT Mr. Steve Booker, Director of Financial Aid, Rollins College, 1000 Holt Avenue, #2721, Winter Park, FL 32789-4499, 407-646-2395. *Fax:* 407-646-2173. *E-mail:* sbooker@rollins.edu.
Website: http://www.rollins.edu/.

ROOSEVELT UNIVERSITY
Chicago, IL

ABOUT THE INSTITUTION Independent, coed. *Awards:* certificates, bachelor's, master's, and doctoral degrees. 59 undergraduate majors. *Total enrollment:* 5,352. Undergraduates: 3,239. Freshmen: 361.
GIFT AID (NEED-BASED) *Scholarships, grants, and awards:* Federal Pell, FSEOG, state, private, college/university gift aid from institutional funds.
GIFT AID (NON-NEED-BASED) *Scholarships, grants, and awards by category: Academic interests/achievement:* general academic interests/achievements. *Creative arts/performance:* music, theater/drama. *Special achievements/activities:* general special achievements/activities. *Special characteristics:* general special characteristics.
APPLYING FOR FINANCIAL AID *Required financial aid forms:* FAFSA, institution's own form.
CONTACT Office of Financial Aid, Roosevelt University, 430 South Michigan Avenue, Chicago, IL 60605-1394, 866-421-0935 or toll-free 877-APPLYRU. *Fax:* 312-341-3545. *E-mail:* fao@roosevelt.edu.
Website: http://www.roosevelt.edu/.

ROSE-HULMAN INSTITUTE OF TECHNOLOGY
Terre Haute, IN

Tuition & fees: $44,010	Average undergraduate aid package: $29,940

ABOUT THE INSTITUTION Independent, coed, primarily men. *Awards:* bachelor's and master's degrees. 16 undergraduate majors. *Total enrollment:* 2,278. Undergraduates: 2,202. Freshmen: 543. Federal methodology is used as a basis for awarding need-based institutional aid.
UNDERGRADUATE EXPENSES for 2016–2017 *Application fee:* $40. *One-time required fee:* $2200. *Comprehensive fee:* $57,303 includes full-time tuition ($43,122), mandatory fees ($888), and room and board ($13,293). *College room only:* $8151. Full-time tuition and fees vary according to course load. Room and board charges vary according to board plan. *Part-time tuition:* $1259 per credit hour. Part-time tuition and fees vary according to course load. *Payment plan:* Tuition prepayment.
FRESHMAN FINANCIAL AID (Fall 2016, est.) 421 applied for aid; of those 81% were deemed to have need. 100% of freshmen with need received aid; of those 21% had need fully met. *Average percent of need met:* 75% (excluding resources awarded to replace EFC). *Average financial aid package:* $31,060 (excluding resources awarded to replace EFC). 36% of all full-time freshmen had no need and received non-need-based gift aid.
UNDERGRADUATE FINANCIAL AID (Fall 2016, est.) 1,502 applied for aid; of those 87% were deemed to have need. 100% of undergraduates with need received aid; of those 19% had need fully met. *Average percent of need met:* 73% (excluding resources awarded to replace EFC). *Average financial aid package:* $29,940 (excluding resources awarded to replace EFC). 39% of all full-time undergraduates had no need and received non-need-based gift aid.
GIFT AID (NEED-BASED) *Total amount:* $34,024,967 (4% federal, 2% state, 86% institutional, 8% external sources). *Receiving aid:* Freshmen: 54% (292); all full-time undergraduates: 51% (1,100). *Average award:* Freshmen: $27,812; Undergraduates: $25,299. *Scholarships, grants, and awards:* Federal Pell, FSEOG, state, college/university gift aid from institutional funds.
GIFT AID (NON-NEED-BASED) *Total amount:* $12,152,127 (83% institutional, 17% external sources). *Receiving aid:* Freshmen: 63% (340). Undergraduates: 60% (1,293). *Average award:* Freshmen: $11,758. Undergraduates: $11,938. *Tuition waivers:* Full or partial for employees or children of employees. *ROTC:* Army, Air Force.

LOANS *Student loans:* $14,103,996 (92% need-based, 8% non-need-based). 65% of past graduating class borrowed through all loan programs. *Average indebtedness per student:* $59,113. *Average need-based loan:* Freshmen: $3571. Undergraduates: $5366. *Parent loans:* $6,592,315 (93% need-based, 7% non-need-based). *Programs:* Federal Direct (Subsidized and Unsubsidized Stafford, PLUS), Perkins.
WORK-STUDY *Federal work-study:* Total amount: $387,818; 307 jobs averaging $1230. *State or other work-study/employment:* Total amount: $631,079 (100% need-based). 500 part-time jobs averaging $1238.
APPLYING FOR FINANCIAL AID *Required financial aid form:* FAFSA. *Financial aid deadline (priority):* 3/1. *Notification date:* 12/15. Students must reply by 5/1.
CONTACT Mrs. Melinda L. Middleton, Director of Financial Aid, Rose-Hulman Institute of Technology, 5500 Wabash Avenue, CM 5, Terre Haute, IN 47803, 812-877-8259 or toll-free 800-248-7448. *Fax:* 812-877-8746. *E-mail:* melinda.middleton@rose-hulman.edu.
Website: http://www.rose-hulman.edu/.

ROSEMONT COLLEGE
Rosemont, PA

Tuition & fees: $19,480	Average undergraduate aid package: $18,171

ABOUT THE INSTITUTION Independent Roman Catholic, coed. *Awards:* certificates, bachelor's, and master's degrees. 24 undergraduate majors. *Total enrollment:* 1,038. Undergraduates: 646. Freshmen: 158. Federal methodology is used as a basis for awarding need-based institutional aid.
UNDERGRADUATE EXPENSES for 2017–2018 *Tuition:* full-time $18,500. Room and board charges vary according to board plan and housing facility.
FRESHMAN FINANCIAL AID (Fall 2016, est.) 201 applied for aid; of those 100% were deemed to have need. 100% of freshmen with need received aid; of those 12% had need fully met. *Average percent of need met:* 85% (excluding resources awarded to replace EFC). *Average financial aid package:* $14,549 (excluding resources awarded to replace EFC). 5% of all full-time freshmen had no need and received non-need-based gift aid.
UNDERGRADUATE FINANCIAL AID (Fall 2016, est.) 275 applied for aid; of those 100% were deemed to have need. 100% of undergraduates with need received aid; of those 17% had need fully met. *Average percent of need met:* 84% (excluding resources awarded to replace EFC). *Average financial aid package:* $18,171 (excluding resources awarded to replace EFC). 9% of all full-time undergraduates had no need and received non-need-based gift aid.
GIFT AID (NEED-BASED) *Total amount:* $3,190,586 (43% federal, 25% state, 30% institutional, 2% external sources). *Receiving aid:* Freshmen: 96% (201); all full-time undergraduates: 91% (275). *Average award:* Freshmen: $11,253; Undergraduates: $16,152. *Scholarships, grants, and awards:* Federal Pell, FSEOG, state, private, college/university gift aid from institutional funds, Academic Competitiveness Grants, National SMART Grants.
GIFT AID (NON-NEED-BASED) *Total amount:* $3,417,578 (100% institutional). *Receiving aid:* Freshmen: 96% (201). Undergraduates: 91% (275). *Average award:* Freshmen: $6000. Undergraduates: $8000. *Scholarships, grants, and awards by category: Academic interests/achievement:* 512 awards ($2,018,496 total): general academic interests/achievements. *Creative arts/performance:* 1 award ($500 total): art/fine arts. *Tuition waivers:* Full or partial for employees or children of employees.
LOANS *Student loans:* $3,948,374 (100% need-based). 90% of past graduating class borrowed through all loan programs. *Average indebtedness per student:* $40,792. *Average need-based loan:* Freshmen: $3500. Undergraduates: $4500. *Parent loans:* $1,142,589 (86% need-based, 14% non-need-based). *Programs:* Federal Direct (Subsidized and Unsubsidized Stafford, PLUS), Perkins, alternative loans.
WORK-STUDY *Federal work-study:* Total amount: $102,732; 130 jobs averaging $910. *State or other work-study/employment:* Total amount: $12,353 (100% need-based). 6 part-time jobs averaging $2000.
APPLYING FOR FINANCIAL AID *Required financial aid form:* FAFSA. *Financial aid deadline:* Continuous. *Notification date:* Continuous beginning 3/15. Students must reply by 5/1 or within 4 weeks of notification.

CONTACT Mrs. Deborah A. Cawley, Director of Enrollment Services and Financial Aid Compliance, Rosemont College, 1400 Montgomery Avenue, Rosemont, PA 19010, 610-527-0200 Ext. 2214 or toll-free 888-2-ROSEMONT. *Fax:* 610-526-2971. *E-mail:* deborah.cawley@rosemont.edu.
Website: http://www.rosemont.edu/.

ROWAN UNIVERSITY
Glassboro, NJ

Tuition & fees (NJ res): $13,108	Average undergraduate aid package: $9084

ABOUT THE INSTITUTION State-supported, coed. *Awards:* certificates, bachelor's, master's, and doctoral degrees. 62 undergraduate majors. *Total enrollment:* 17,355. Undergraduates: 14,363. Freshmen: 2,199. Both federal and institutional methodology are used as a basis for awarding need-based institutional aid.
UNDERGRADUATE EXPENSES for 2017–2018 *Application fee:* $65. *Tuition, state resident:* full-time $9434; part-time $362 per credit hour. *Tuition, nonresident:* full-time $17,704; part-time $682 per credit hour. *Required fees:* full-time $3674; $157 per credit hour. Full-time tuition and fees vary according to course load, degree level, location, and program. Part-time tuition and fees vary according to course load, degree level, location, and program. *College room and board:* $11,688; *Room only:* $7608. Room and board charges vary according to board plan and housing facility.
FRESHMAN FINANCIAL AID (Fall 2015) 2,043 applied for aid; of those 71% were deemed to have need. 94% of freshmen with need received aid; of those 4% had need fully met. *Average percent of need met:* 72% (excluding resources awarded to replace EFC). *Average financial aid package:* $8834 (excluding resources awarded to replace EFC). 13% of all full-time freshmen had no need and received non-need-based gift aid.
UNDERGRADUATE FINANCIAL AID (Fall 2015) 9,578 applied for aid; of those 78% were deemed to have need. 95% of undergraduates with need received aid; of those 6% had need fully met. *Average percent of need met:* 69% (excluding resources awarded to replace EFC). *Average financial aid package:* $9084 (excluding resources awarded to replace EFC). 10% of all full-time undergraduates had no need and received non-need-based gift aid.
GIFT AID (NEED-BASED) *Total amount:* $48,237,024 (39% federal, 36% state, 23% institutional, 2% external sources). *Receiving aid:* Freshmen: 33% (725); all full-time undergraduates: 35% (4,088). *Average award:* Freshmen: $9557; Undergraduates: $8437. *Scholarships, grants, and awards:* Federal Pell, FSEOG, state, private, college/university gift aid from institutional funds.
GIFT AID (NON-NEED-BASED) *Total amount:* $10,334,138 (94% institutional, 6% external sources). *Receiving aid:* Freshmen: 28% (613). Undergraduates: 18% (2,093). *Average award:* Freshmen: $6712. Undergraduates: $8324. *Scholarships, grants, and awards by category:* Academic interests/achievement: general academic interests/achievements. Creative arts/performance: general creative arts/performance, music. *Tuition waivers:* Full or partial for employees or children of employees. *ROTC:* Army cooperative.
LOANS *Student loans:* $77,762,090 (92% need-based, 8% non-need-based). 69% of past graduating class borrowed through all loan programs. *Average indebtedness per student:* $30,899. *Average need-based loan:* Freshmen: $3271. Undergraduates: $4264. *Parent loans:* $20,059,949 (100% need-based). *Programs:* Federal Direct (Subsidized and Unsubsidized Stafford, PLUS), state.
WORK-STUDY *Federal work-study:* 465 jobs averaging $1467. *State or other work-study/employment:* Total amount: $1,596,875 (59% need-based, 41% non-need-based). Part-time jobs available.
APPLYING FOR FINANCIAL AID *Required financial aid form:* FAFSA. *Financial aid deadline (priority):* 3/16. *Notification date:* Continuous beginning 3/16. Students must reply by 5/1.
CONTACT Jeff Hand, Vice President for Strategic Enrollment Management, Rowan University, 201 Mullica Hill Road, Glassboro, NJ 08028-1701, 856-256-5186 or toll-free 800-447-1165 (in-state), 800-447-1165N (out-of-state). *Fax:* 856-256-4413. *E-mail:* handj@rowan.edu.
Website: http://www.rowan.edu/.

RUSH UNIVERSITY
Chicago, IL

CONTACT Mike Frechette, Director of Student Financial Aid, Rush University, 600 South Paulina Street, Suite 440, Chicago, IL 60612-3832, 312-942-6256. *Fax:* 312-942-2732. *E-mail:* michael_frechette@rush.edu.
Website: http://www.rushu.rush.edu/.

RUST COLLEGE
Holly Springs, MS

CONTACT Mrs. Helen L. Street, Director of Financial Aid, Rust College, 150 Rust Avenue, Holly Springs, MS 38635, 662-252-8000 Ext. 4061 or toll-free 888-886-8492 Ext. 4065. *Fax:* 662-252-8895.
Website: http://www.rustcollege.edu/.

RUTGERS UNIVERSITY–CAMDEN
Camden, NJ

Tuition & fees (NJ res): $14,238	Average undergraduate aid package: $11,704

ABOUT THE INSTITUTION State-supported, coed. *Awards:* bachelor's, master's, and doctoral degrees. 33 undergraduate majors. *Total enrollment:* 6,475. Undergraduates: 5,021. Freshmen: 675. Both federal and institutional methodology are used as a basis for awarding need-based institutional aid.
UNDERGRADUATE EXPENSES for 2016–2017 *Application fee:* $70. *Tuition, state resident:* full-time $11,408; part-time $367 per credit hour. *Tuition, nonresident:* full-time $26,551; part-time $862 per credit hour. *Required fees:* full-time $2830. Part-time tuition and fees vary according to course load. *College room and board:* $11,908; *Room only:* $8298. Room and board charges vary according to board plan and housing facility.
FRESHMAN FINANCIAL AID (Fall 2015) 377 applied for aid; of those 91% were deemed to have need. 100% of freshmen with need received aid; of those 2% had need fully met. *Average percent of need met:* 52% (excluding resources awarded to replace EFC). *Average financial aid package:* $14,016 (excluding resources awarded to replace EFC). 5% of all full-time freshmen had no need and received non-need-based gift aid.
UNDERGRADUATE FINANCIAL AID (Fall 2015) 3,748 applied for aid; of those 93% were deemed to have need. 100% of undergraduates with need received aid; of those 1% had need fully met. *Average percent of need met:* 47% (excluding resources awarded to replace EFC). *Average financial aid package:* $11,704 (excluding resources awarded to replace EFC). 1% of all full-time undergraduates had no need and received non-need-based gift aid.
GIFT AID (NEED-BASED) *Total amount:* $25,560,719 (38% federal, 41% state, 21% institutional). *Receiving aid:* Freshmen: 62% (261); all full-time undergraduates: 67% (2,649). *Average award:* Freshmen: $11,710; Undergraduates: $9207. *Scholarships, grants, and awards:* Federal Pell, FSEOG, state, private, college/university gift aid from institutional funds, Federal Nursing.
GIFT AID (NON-NEED-BASED) *Total amount:* $3,244,255 (92% institutional, 8% external sources). *Receiving aid:* Freshmen: 30% (127). Undergraduates: 12% (480). *Average award:* Freshmen: $5064. Undergraduates: $3956. *Tuition waivers:* Full or partial for employees or children of employees. *ROTC:* Army cooperative, Air Force cooperative.
LOANS *Student loans:* $37,464,612 (37% need-based, 63% non-need-based). 71% of past graduating class borrowed through all loan programs. *Average indebtedness per student:* $29,624. *Average need-based loan:* Freshmen: $3757. Undergraduates: $4463. *Parent loans:* $3,518,441 (100% non-need-based). *Programs:* Federal Direct (Subsidized and Unsubsidized Stafford, PLUS), Perkins, Federal Nursing, state, college/university, alternative loans.
WORK-STUDY *Federal work-study:* 198 jobs averaging $2195. *State or other work-study/employment:* Total amount: $1,640,887 (100% non-need-based). 584 part-time jobs averaging $2810.
APPLYING FOR FINANCIAL AID *Required financial aid form:* FAFSA. *Financial aid deadline (priority):* 3/15. *Notification date:* Continuous beginning 3/1. Students must reply within 2 weeks of notification.

CONTACT Ms. Carolann Pierre, Senior Funds Management Specialist, Rutgers University–Camden, 620 George Street, New Brunswick, NJ 08901, 848-932-2603. *Fax:* 732-932-0516. *E-mail:* carolann.pierre@ofa.rutgers.edu. *Website:* http://www.camden.rutgers.edu/.

RUTGERS UNIVERSITY–NEWARK
Newark, NJ

Tuition & fees (NJ res): $13,829	Average undergraduate aid package: $13,082

ABOUT THE INSTITUTION State-supported, coed. *Awards:* associate, bachelor's, master's, and doctoral degrees. 59 undergraduate majors. *Total enrollment:* 12,321. Undergraduates: 8,170. Freshmen: 1,344. Federal methodology is used as a basis for awarding need-based institutional aid.

UNDERGRADUATE EXPENSES for 2016–2017 Application fee: $65. **Tuition, state resident:** full-time $11,408; part-time $367 per credit hour. **Tuition, nonresident:** full-time $27,059; part-time $878 per credit hour. **Required fees:** full-time $2421. Part-time tuition and fees vary according to course load. **College room and board:** $13,459; **Room only:** $8095. Room and board charges vary according to board plan and housing facility.

FRESHMAN FINANCIAL AID (Fall 2015) 945 applied for aid; of those 92% were deemed to have need. 100% of freshmen with need received aid; of those 2% had need fully met. *Average percent of need met:* 53% (excluding resources awarded to replace EFC). *Average financial aid package:* $14,424 (excluding resources awarded to replace EFC). 3% of all full-time freshmen had no need and received non-need-based gift aid.

UNDERGRADUATE FINANCIAL AID (Fall 2015) 5,400 applied for aid; of those 95% were deemed to have need. 100% of undergraduates with need received aid; of those 1% had need fully met. *Average percent of need met:* 50% (excluding resources awarded to replace EFC). *Average financial aid package:* $13,082 (excluding resources awarded to replace EFC). 1% of all full-time undergraduates had no need and received non-need-based gift aid.

GIFT AID (NEED-BASED) Total amount: $47,078,576 (37% federal, 47% state, 16% institutional). *Receiving aid:* Freshmen: 62% (738); all full-time undergraduates: 70% (4,330). *Average award:* Freshmen: $11,909; Undergraduates: $10,557. *Scholarships, grants, and awards:* Federal Pell, FSEOG, state, private, college/university gift aid from institutional funds.

GIFT AID (NON-NEED-BASED) Total amount: $4,841,735 (88% institutional, 12% external sources). *Receiving aid:* Freshmen: 13% (160). Undergraduates: 7% (460). *Average award:* Freshmen: $10,613. Undergraduates: $9427. *Tuition waivers:* Full or partial for employees or children of employees. *ROTC:* Army, Naval, Air Force.

LOANS Student loans: $39,937,109 (44% need-based, 56% non-need-based). 49% of past graduating class borrowed through all loan programs. *Average indebtedness per student:* $27,881. *Average need-based loan:* Freshmen: $3928. Undergraduates: $4518. *Parent loans:* $3,935,455 (100% non-need-based). *Programs:* Federal Direct (Subsidized and Unsubsidized Stafford, PLUS), Perkins, state, college/university, alternative loans.

WORK-STUDY Federal work-study: 610 jobs averaging $1917. *State or other work-study/employment:* Total amount: $1,933,471 (100% non-need-based). 868 part-time jobs averaging $2228.

APPLYING FOR FINANCIAL AID Required financial aid form: FAFSA. **Financial aid deadline (priority):** 3/15. **Notification date:** Continuous beginning 3/1. Students must reply within 4 weeks of notification.

CONTACT Ms. Carolann Pierre, Senior Funds Management Specialist, Rutgers University–Newark, 620 George Street, New Brunswick, NJ 08901, 848-932-2603. *Fax:* 732-932-0516. *E-mail:* carolann.pierre@ofa.rutgers.edu. *Website:* http://www.newark.rutgers.edu/.

RUTGERS UNIVERSITY–NEW BRUNSWICK
Piscataway, NJ

Tuition & fees (NJ res): $14,372	Average undergraduate aid package: $13,444

ABOUT THE INSTITUTION State-supported, coed. *Awards:* certificates, associate, bachelor's, master's, and doctoral degrees. 137 undergraduate majors. *Total enrollment:* 50,146. Undergraduates: 36,168. Freshmen: 6,466. Federal methodology is used as a basis for awarding need-based institutional aid.

UNDERGRADUATE EXPENSES for 2016–2017 Application fee: $65. **Tuition, state resident:** full-time $11,408; part-time $367 per credit hour. **Tuition, nonresident:** full-time $27,059; part-time $878 per credit hour. **Required fees:** full-time $2964. Part-time tuition and fees vary according to course load. **College room and board:** $12,260; **Room only:** $7490. Room and board charges vary according to board plan and housing facility.

FRESHMAN FINANCIAL AID (Fall 2015) 4,494 applied for aid; of those 80% were deemed to have need. 100% of freshmen with need received aid; of those 6% had need fully met. *Average percent of need met:* 51% (excluding resources awarded to replace EFC). *Average financial aid package:* $14,740 (excluding resources awarded to replace EFC). 7% of all full-time freshmen had no need and received non-need-based gift aid.

UNDERGRADUATE FINANCIAL AID (Fall 2015) 21,739 applied for aid; of those 86% were deemed to have need. 100% of undergraduates with need received aid; of those 4% had need fully met. *Average percent of need met:* 48% (excluding resources awarded to replace EFC). *Average financial aid package:* $13,444 (excluding resources awarded to replace EFC). 2% of all full-time undergraduates had no need and received non-need-based gift aid.

GIFT AID (NEED-BASED) Total amount: $147,431,425 (35% federal, 45% state, 20% institutional). *Receiving aid:* Freshmen: 54% (3,539); all full-time undergraduates: 40% (13,169). *Average award:* Freshmen: $19,765; Undergraduates: $10,883. *Scholarships, grants, and awards:* Federal Pell, FSEOG, state, private, college/university gift aid from institutional funds, Federal Nursing.

GIFT AID (NON-NEED-BASED) Total amount: $62,990,963 (91% institutional, 9% external sources). *Receiving aid:* Freshmen: 16% (1,042). Undergraduates: 10% (3,270). *Average award:* Freshmen: $12,865. Undergraduates: $9759. *Tuition waivers:* Full or partial for employees or children of employees. *ROTC:* Army, Naval, Air Force.

LOANS Student loans: $228,463,552 (32% need-based, 68% non-need-based). 56% of past graduating class borrowed through all loan programs. *Average indebtedness per student:* $25,974. *Average need-based loan:* Freshmen: $3866. Undergraduates: $4581. *Parent loans:* $41,228,163 (100% non-need-based). *Programs:* Federal Direct (Subsidized and Unsubsidized Stafford, PLUS), Perkins, Federal Nursing, state, college/university, alternative loans.

WORK-STUDY Federal work-study: 2,495 jobs averaging $2111. *State or other work-study/employment:* Total amount: $13,764,131 (100% non-need-based). Part-time jobs available.

ATHLETIC AWARDS Total amount: $12,431,356 (100% non-need-based).

APPLYING FOR FINANCIAL AID Required financial aid form: FAFSA. **Financial aid deadline (priority):** 3/15. **Notification date:** Continuous beginning 3/1. Students must reply within 2 weeks of notification.

CONTACT Ms. Carolann Pierre, Senior Funds Management Specialist, Rutgers University–New Brunswick, 620 George Street, New Brunswick, NJ 08901, 848-932-2603. *Fax:* 732-932-0516. *E-mail:* carolann.pierre@ofa.rutgers.edu. *Website:* http://newbrunswick.rutgers.edu/.

SACRED HEART MAJOR SEMINARY
Detroit, MI

CONTACT Financial Aid Office, Sacred Heart Major Seminary, 2701 Chicago Boulevard, Detroit, MI 48206-1799, 313-883-8534. *Fax:* 313-868-7025. *E-mail:* financialaid@shms.edu. *Website:* http://www.shms.edu/.

SACRED HEART UNIVERSITY
Fairfield, CT

Tuition & fees: $38,300	Average undergraduate aid package: $20,275

ABOUT THE INSTITUTION Independent Roman Catholic, coed. **Awards:** certificates, bachelor's, master's, and doctoral degrees (also offers part-time program with significant enrollment not reflected in profile). 33 undergraduate majors. **Total enrollment:** 8,532. Undergraduates: 5,428. Freshmen: 1,322. Both federal and institutional methodology are used as a basis for awarding need-based institutional aid.

UNDERGRADUATE EXPENSES for 2016–2017 Application fee: $50. **Comprehensive fee:** $52,750 includes full-time tuition ($38,050), mandatory fees ($250), and room and board ($14,450). **College room only:** $10,000. Room and board charges vary according to board plan and housing facility. **Part-time tuition:** $600 per credit hour. **Part-time fees:** $115 per term. Part-time tuition and fees vary according to course load.

FRESHMAN FINANCIAL AID (Fall 2016, est.) 1,163 applied for aid; of those 81% were deemed to have need. 100% of freshmen with need received aid; of those 18% had need fully met. **Average percent of need met:** 56% (excluding resources awarded to replace EFC). **Average financial aid package:** $19,822 (excluding resources awarded to replace EFC). 28% of all full-time freshmen had no need and received non-need-based gift aid.

UNDERGRADUATE FINANCIAL AID (Fall 2016, est.) 3,895 applied for aid; of those 83% were deemed to have need. 100% of undergraduates with need received aid; of those 18% had need fully met. **Average percent of need met:** 58% (excluding resources awarded to replace EFC). **Average financial aid package:** $20,275 (excluding resources awarded to replace EFC). 30% of all full-time undergraduates had no need and received non-need-based gift aid.

GIFT AID (NEED-BASED) Total amount: $48,490,156 (9% federal, 1% state, 82% institutional, 8% external sources). **Receiving aid:** Freshmen: 71% (941); all full-time undergraduates: 66% (3,187). **Average award:** Freshmen: $15,890; Undergraduates: $16,046. **Scholarships, grants, and awards:** Federal Pell, FSEOG, state, private, college/university gift aid from institutional funds.

GIFT AID (NON-NEED-BASED) Total amount: $23,358,340 (5% federal, 85% institutional, 10% external sources). **Receiving aid:** Freshmen: 11% (151). Undergraduates: 10% (474). **Average award:** Freshmen: $12,778. Undergraduates: $12,067. **Scholarships, grants, and awards by category:** Academic interests/achievement: 1,490 awards ($19,196,304 total): biological sciences, business, computer science, education, English, general academic interests/achievements, health fields, humanities, mathematics, physical sciences, premedicine. Creative arts/performance: 627 awards ($1,682,500 total): applied art and design, art/fine arts, cinema/film/broadcasting, creative writing, dance, music, performing arts, theater/drama. Special achievements/activities: 607 awards ($876,396 total): community service, general special achievements/activities, hobbies/interests, leadership, memberships, religious involvement. Special characteristics: 264 awards ($2,722,820 total): adult students, children and siblings of alumni, children of current students, children of faculty/staff, children of union members/company employees, ethnic background, general special characteristics, handicapped students, international students, local/state students, members of minority groups, out-of-state students, religious affiliation, siblings of current students, twins, veterans, veterans' children. **Tuition waivers:** Full or partial for employees or children of employees. **ROTC:** Air Force cooperative.

LOANS Student loans: $39,212,883 (64% need-based, 36% non-need-based). 76% of past graduating class borrowed through all loan programs. **Average indebtedness per student:** $40,240. **Average need-based loan:** Freshmen: $4121. Undergraduates: $4953. **Parent loans:** $20,880,779 (54% need-based, 46% non-need-based). **Programs:** Federal Direct (Subsidized and Unsubsidized Stafford, PLUS), Perkins, state.

WORK-STUDY Federal work-study: Total amount: $1,138,755; 888 jobs averaging $1450. **State or other work-study/employment:** Total amount: $891,326 (15% need-based, 85% non-need-based). 514 part-time jobs averaging $1141.

ATHLETIC AWARDS Total amount: $8,195,708 (39% need-based, 61% non-need-based).

APPLYING FOR FINANCIAL AID Required financial aid forms: FAFSA, CSS Financial Aid PROFILE, noncustodial (divorced/separated) parent's statement. **Financial aid deadline (priority):** 2/15. **Notification date:** Continuous beginning 3/1. Students must reply within 2 weeks of notification.

CONTACT Ms. Julie B. Savino, Executive Director of University Financial Assistance, Sacred Heart University, 5151 Park Avenue, Fairfield, CT 06825, 203-371-7980. *Fax:* 203-365-7608. *E-mail:* savinoj@sacredheart.edu. *Website:* http://www.sacredheart.edu/.

SAE EXPRESSION COLLEGE
Emeryville, CA

CONTACT Financial Aid Office, SAE Expression College, 6601 Shellmound Street, Emeryville, CA 94608, 510-654-2934 or toll-free 877-833-8800. *Website:* http://www.sae.edu/.

THE SAGE COLLEGES
Troy, NY

Tuition & fees: $28,805	Average undergraduate aid package: N/A

ABOUT THE INSTITUTION Independent, coed. **Awards:** certificates, bachelor's, master's, and doctoral degrees. 29 undergraduate majors. **Total enrollment:** 2,732. Undergraduates: 1,473. Freshmen: 206. Both federal and institutional methodology are used as a basis for awarding need-based institutional aid.

UNDERGRADUATE EXPENSES for 2016–2017 Application fee: $30. **Comprehensive fee:** $41,213 includes full-time tuition ($27,405), mandatory fees ($1400), and room and board ($12,408). **College room only:** $6430. Room and board charges vary according to board plan. **Part-time tuition:** $914 per credit hour.

FRESHMAN FINANCIAL AID (Fall 2016, est.) 200 applied for aid; of those 96% were deemed to have need. 100% of freshmen with need received aid. 2% of all full-time freshmen had no need and received non-need-based gift aid.

UNDERGRADUATE FINANCIAL AID (Fall 2016, est.) 1,243 applied for aid; of those 94% were deemed to have need. 100% of undergraduates with need received aid. 6% of all full-time undergraduates had no need and received non-need-based gift aid.

GIFT AID (NEED-BASED) Total amount: $20,844,106 (14% federal, 10% state, 75% institutional, 1% external sources). **Receiving aid:** Freshmen: 62% (127); all full-time undergraduates: 68% (866). **Average award:** Freshmen: $13,492; Undergraduates: $13,925. **Scholarships, grants, and awards:** Federal Pell, FSEOG, state, private, college/university gift aid from institutional funds, Federal Nursing.

GIFT AID (NON-NEED-BASED) Total amount: $2,303,099 (93% institutional, 7% external sources). **Receiving aid:** Freshmen: 87% (179). Undergraduates: 77% (988). **Average award:** Freshmen: $13,400. Undergraduates: $11,274. **Scholarships, grants, and awards by category:** Academic interests/achievement: business, education, English, general academic interests/achievements, home economics. Creative arts/performance: art/fine arts, performing arts, theater/drama. Special achievements/activities: community service, general special achievements/activities, leadership. Special characteristics: adult students, children and siblings of alumni, ethnic background, first-generation college students, general special characteristics, members of minority groups, veterans. **Tuition waivers:** Full or partial for employees or children of employees. **ROTC:** Army cooperative, Air Force cooperative.

LOANS Student loans: $9,350,996 (51% need-based, 49% non-need-based). 92% of past graduating class borrowed through all loan programs. **Average indebtedness per student:** $31,699. **Average need-based loan:** Freshmen: $3010. Undergraduates: $4573. **Parent loans:** $2,654,336 (12% need-based, 88% non-need-based). **Programs:** Federal Direct (Subsidized and Unsubsidized Stafford, PLUS), Perkins.

WORK-STUDY Federal work-study: Total amount: $722,101; jobs available. **State or other work-study/employment:** Total amount: $143,035 (100% non-need-based). Part-time jobs available.

APPLYING FOR FINANCIAL AID Required financial aid forms: FAFSA, state aid form. **Financial aid deadline (priority):** 2/15. **Notification date:** Continuous beginning 1/20. Students must reply by 5/1 or within 2 weeks of notification.

CONTACT Financial Aid Office, The Sage Colleges, 65 First Street, Troy, NY 12180, 518-244-4525. *Fax:* 518-244-2460. *E-mail:* finaid@sage.edu. *Website:* http://www.sage.edu/.

SAGINAW VALLEY STATE UNIVERSITY
University Center, MI

Tuition & fees (MI res): $9345	Average undergraduate aid package: N/A

ABOUT THE INSTITUTION State-supported, coed. *Awards:* certificates, bachelor's, master's, and doctoral degrees. 83 undergraduate majors. *Total enrollment:* 9,165. Undergraduates: 8,397. Freshmen: 1,353. Federal methodology is used as a basis for awarding need-based institutional aid.

UNDERGRADUATE EXPENSES for 2016–2017 *Application fee:* $30. *Tuition, state resident:* full-time $8907; part-time $296.90 per credit hour. *Tuition, nonresident:* full-time $21,508; part-time $716.95 per credit hour. *Required fees:* full-time $438; $14.60 per credit hour. Full-time tuition and fees vary according to course level, degree level, location, and program. Part-time tuition and fees vary according to course level, degree level, location, and program. *College room and board:* $7950; *Room only:* $4300. Room and board charges vary according to board plan and housing facility.

FRESHMAN FINANCIAL AID (Fall 2016, est.) 1,170 applied for aid; of those 80% were deemed to have need. 100% of freshmen with need received aid. 19% of all full-time freshmen had no need and received non-need-based gift aid.

UNDERGRADUATE FINANCIAL AID (Fall 2016, est.) 5,287 applied for aid; of those 84% were deemed to have need. 100% of undergraduates with need received aid. 14% of all full-time undergraduates had no need and received non-need-based gift aid.

GIFT AID (NEED-BASED) *Total amount:* $23,600,862 (54% federal, 5% state, 31% institutional, 10% external sources). *Receiving aid:* Freshmen: 64% (863); all full-time undergraduates: 55% (3,723). *Average award:* Freshmen: $7368; Undergraduates: $5960. *Scholarships, grants, and awards:* Federal Pell, FSEOG, state, private, college/university gift aid from institutional funds.

GIFT AID (NON-NEED-BASED) *Total amount:* $11,638,311 (2% state, 50% institutional, 48% external sources). *Receiving aid:* Freshmen: 3% (35). Undergraduates: 2% (108). *Average award:* Freshmen: $5051. Undergraduates: $5737. *Scholarships, grants, and awards by category:* Academic interests/achievement: biological sciences, business, computer science, education, engineering/technologies, general academic interests/achievements, health fields, mathematics, physical sciences. *Creative arts/performance:* art/fine arts, music, theater/drama. *Special achievements/activities:* community service, leadership. *Special characteristics:* adult students, local/state students, members of minority groups, veterans, veterans' children. *Tuition waivers:* Full or partial for employees or children of employees.

LOANS *Student loans:* $38,680,936 (81% need-based, 19% non-need-based). 73% of past graduating class borrowed through all loan programs. *Average indebtedness per student:* $31,695. *Parent loans:* $7,416,232 (66% need-based, 34% non-need-based). *Programs:* Federal Direct (Subsidized and Unsubsidized Stafford, PLUS), Citi-Assist Loans, Chase Select loans, Charter One TruFit Student Loans, Discover Private Educational Loans.

WORK-STUDY Federal work-study jobs available. *State or other work-study/employment:* Total amount: $368,809 (56% need-based, 44% non-need-based). Part-time jobs available.

ATHLETIC AWARDS Total amount: $2,319,071 (53% need-based, 47% non-need-based).

APPLYING FOR FINANCIAL AID *Required financial aid forms:* FAFSA, institution's own form, CSS Financial Aid PROFILE. *Financial aid deadline:* Continuous. *Notification date:* Continuous beginning 3/1.

CONTACT Robert Lemuel, Director of Scholarships and Financial Aid, Saginaw Valley State University, 7400 Bay Road, University Center, MI 48710, 989-964-4900 or toll-free 800-968-9500. *Fax:* 989-790-0180. *E-mail:* cfsc@svsu.edu. *Website:* http://www.svsu.edu/.

ST. AMBROSE UNIVERSITY
Davenport, IA

Tuition & fees: $30,016	Average undergraduate aid package: $22,153

ABOUT THE INSTITUTION Independent Roman Catholic, coed. *Awards:* certificates, bachelor's, master's, and doctoral degrees. 48 undergraduate majors. *Total enrollment:* 3,178. Undergraduates: 2,398. Freshmen: 454. Federal methodology is used as a basis for awarding need-based institutional aid.

UNDERGRADUATE EXPENSES for 2017–2018 *Comprehensive fee:* $40,180 includes full-time tuition ($29,736), mandatory fees ($280), and room and board ($10,164). Full-time tuition and fees vary according to course load and location. Room and board charges vary according to board plan and housing facility. *Part-time tuition:* $915 per credit hour. *Part-time fees:* $280 per term. Part-time tuition and fees vary according to course load and location.

FRESHMAN FINANCIAL AID (Fall 2016, est.) 423 applied for aid; of those 90% were deemed to have need. 100% of freshmen with need received aid; of those 23% had need fully met. *Average percent of need met:* 70% (excluding resources awarded to replace EFC). *Average financial aid package:* $22,362 (excluding resources awarded to replace EFC). 16% of all full-time freshmen had no need and received non-need-based gift aid.

UNDERGRADUATE FINANCIAL AID (Fall 2016, est.) 1,877 applied for aid; of those 86% were deemed to have need. 100% of undergraduates with need received aid; of those 24% had need fully met. *Average percent of need met:* 70% (excluding resources awarded to replace EFC). *Average financial aid package:* $22,153 (excluding resources awarded to replace EFC). 19% of all full-time undergraduates had no need and received non-need-based gift aid.

GIFT AID (NEED-BASED) *Total amount:* $25,644,147 (10% federal, 8% state, 78% institutional, 4% external sources). *Receiving aid:* Freshmen: 83% (379); all full-time undergraduates: 67% (1,590). *Average award:* Freshmen: $16,618; Undergraduates: $16,958. *Scholarships, grants, and awards:* Federal Pell, FSEOG, state, private, college/university gift aid from institutional funds.

GIFT AID (NON-NEED-BASED) *Total amount:* $5,740,157 (100% institutional). *Receiving aid:* Freshmen: 35% (157). Undergraduates: 18% (418). *Average award:* Freshmen: $14,774. Undergraduates: $12,731. *Scholarships, grants, and awards by category:* Academic interests/achievement: biological sciences, communication, engineering/technologies, foreign languages, general academic interests/achievements, health fields, international studies, religion/biblical studies. *Creative arts/performance:* art/fine arts, dance, journalism/publications, music, theater/drama. *Special achievements/activities:* cheerleading/drum major, leadership. *Special characteristics:* adult students, children and siblings of alumni, children of educators, children of faculty/staff, international students, members of minority groups, out-of-state students, previous college experience, religious affiliation, veterans. *Tuition waivers:* Full or partial for employees or children of employees.

LOANS *Student loans:* $18,126,034 (90% need-based, 10% non-need-based). 75% of past graduating class borrowed through all loan programs. *Average indebtedness per student:* $27,929. *Average need-based loan:* Freshmen: $3544. Undergraduates: $4724. *Parent loans:* $5,112,469 (92% need-based, 8% non-need-based). *Programs:* Federal Direct (Subsidized and Unsubsidized Stafford, PLUS), Perkins, private loans.

WORK-STUDY *Federal work-study:* Total amount: $972,425; jobs available. *State or other work-study/employment:* Total amount: $350,715 (84% need-based, 16% non-need-based). Part-time jobs available.

ATHLETIC AWARDS Total amount: $2,702,743 (70% need-based, 30% non-need-based).

APPLYING FOR FINANCIAL AID *Required financial aid form:* FAFSA. *Financial aid deadline:* Continuous. *Notification date:* Continuous beginning 2/15. Students must reply within 2 weeks of notification.

CONTACT Ms. Julie Haack, Director of Financial Aid, St. Ambrose University, 518 West Locust Street, Davenport, IA 52803, 563-333-5775 or toll-free 800-383-2627. *Fax:* 563-333-6243. *E-mail:* haackjuliea@sau.edu. *Website:* http://www.sau.edu/.

ST. ANDREWS UNIVERSITY
Laurinburg, NC

Tuition & fees: $24,874	Average undergraduate aid package: $21,033

ABOUT THE INSTITUTION Independent Presbyterian, coed. **Awards:** diplomas, bachelor's, and master's degrees. 16 undergraduate majors. **Total enrollment:** 722. Undergraduates: 688. Freshmen: 224. Federal methodology is used as a basis for awarding need-based institutional aid.

UNDERGRADUATE EXPENSES for 2016–2017 **Application fee:** $35. **Comprehensive fee:** $35,270 includes full-time tuition ($24,874) and room and board ($10,396). Full-time tuition and fees vary according to course load and location. Room and board charges vary according to housing facility. **Part-time tuition:** $280 per credit hour. Part-time tuition and fees vary according to location.

FRESHMAN FINANCIAL AID (Fall 2016, est.) 195 applied for aid; of those 97% were deemed to have need. 99% of freshmen with need received aid; of those 8% had need fully met. **Average percent of need met:** 67% (excluding resources awarded to replace EFC). **Average financial aid package:** $21,099 (excluding resources awarded to replace EFC). 8% of all full-time freshmen had no need and received non-need-based gift aid.

UNDERGRADUATE FINANCIAL AID (Fall 2016, est.) 482 applied for aid; of those 94% were deemed to have need. 99% of undergraduates with need received aid; of those 10% had need fully met. **Average percent of need met:** 71% (excluding resources awarded to replace EFC). **Average financial aid package:** $21,033 (excluding resources awarded to replace EFC). 14% of all full-time undergraduates had no need and received non-need-based gift aid.

GIFT AID (NEED-BASED) Total amount: $4,935,103 (23% federal, 17% state, 55% institutional, 5% external sources). **Receiving aid:** Freshmen: 83% (188); all full-time undergraduates: 73% (448). **Average award:** Freshmen: $17,909; Undergraduates: $17,118. **Scholarships, grants, and awards:** Federal Pell, FSEOG, state, private, college/university gift aid from institutional funds.

GIFT AID (NON-NEED-BASED) Total amount: $1,015,355 (97% institutional, 3% external sources). **Receiving aid:** Freshmen: 7% (15). Undergraduates: 6% (37). **Average award:** Freshmen: $10,005. Undergraduates: $10,580. **Scholarships, grants, and awards by category:** Academic interests/achievement: business, general academic interests/achievements. Creative arts/performance: general creative arts/performance, performing arts, theater/drama. Special achievements/activities: community service, general special achievements/activities, leadership. **Tuition waivers:** Full or partial for employees or children of employees, adult students, senior citizens.

LOANS Student loans: $3,348,486 (81% need-based, 19% non-need-based). 72% of past graduating class borrowed through all loan programs. **Average indebtedness per student:** $25,327. **Average need-based loan:** Freshmen: $3554. Undergraduates: $4456. **Parent loans:** $2,202,820 (53% need-based, 47% non-need-based). **Programs:** Federal Direct (Subsidized and Unsubsidized Stafford, PLUS), state.

WORK-STUDY Federal work-study: Total amount: $71,245; jobs available. **State or other work-study/employment:** Part-time jobs available.

ATHLETIC AWARDS Total amount: $3,239,902 (82% need-based, 18% non-need-based).

APPLYING FOR FINANCIAL AID Required financial aid forms: FAFSA, state aid form. **Financial aid deadline:** Continuous. **Notification date:** Continuous beginning 2/1. Students must reply within 2 weeks of notification.

CONTACT Shawn Caulder, Director of Financial Aid, St. Andrews University, 1700 Dogwood Mile, Laurinburg, NC 28352, 910-277-5562 or toll-free 800-763-0198. *Fax:* 910-277-5206.
Website: http://www.sa.edu/.

SAINT ANSELM COLLEGE
Manchester, NH

Tuition & fees: $39,990	Average undergraduate aid package: $26,687

ABOUT THE INSTITUTION Independent Roman Catholic, coed. **Awards:** bachelor's degrees. 42 undergraduate majors. **Total enrollment:** 1,930. Undergraduates: 1,930. Freshmen: 518. Both federal and institutional methodology are used as a basis for awarding need-based institutional aid.

UNDERGRADUATE EXPENSES for 2017–2018 Application fee: $50. **Comprehensive fee:** $54,136 includes full-time tuition ($38,960), mandatory fees ($1030), and room and board ($14,146). **College room only:** $8676. Full-time tuition and fees vary according to program. Room and board charges vary according to housing facility.

FRESHMAN FINANCIAL AID (Fall 2016, est.) 467 applied for aid; of those 80% were deemed to have need. 100% of freshmen with need received aid; of those 30% had need fully met. **Average percent of need met:** 81% (excluding resources awarded to replace EFC). **Average financial aid package:** $26,931 (excluding resources awarded to replace EFC). 25% of all full-time freshmen had no need and received non-need-based gift aid.

UNDERGRADUATE FINANCIAL AID (Fall 2016, est.) 1,564 applied for aid; of those 84% were deemed to have need. 100% of undergraduates with need received aid; of those 28% had need fully met. **Average percent of need met:** 81% (excluding resources awarded to replace EFC). **Average financial aid package:** $26,687 (excluding resources awarded to replace EFC). 26% of all full-time undergraduates had no need and received non-need-based gift aid.

GIFT AID (NEED-BASED) Total amount: $28,030,386 (5% federal, 93% institutional, 2% external sources). **Receiving aid:** Freshmen: 73% (375); all full-time undergraduates: 69% (1,305). **Average award:** Freshmen: $23,638; Undergraduates: $22,330. **Scholarships, grants, and awards:** Federal Pell, FSEOG, state, private, college/university gift aid from institutional funds.

GIFT AID (NON-NEED-BASED) Total amount: $8,196,690 (96% institutional, 4% external sources). **Receiving aid:** Freshmen: 18% (92). Undergraduates: 15% (276). **Average award:** Freshmen: $16,408. Undergraduates: $14,323. **Scholarships, grants, and awards by category:** Academic interests/achievement: 1,203 awards ($15,651,465 total): general academic interests/achievements. Creative arts/performance: 375 awards ($5,591,000 total): general creative arts/performance. Special characteristics: 296 awards ($3,420,482 total): children of educators, children of faculty/staff, siblings of current students. **Tuition waivers:** Full or partial for employees or children of employees. **ROTC:** Army cooperative.

LOANS Student loans: $15,179,639 (53% need-based, 47% non-need-based). 81% of past graduating class borrowed through all loan programs. **Average indebtedness per student:** $35,601. **Average need-based loan:** Freshmen: $2692. Undergraduates: $3970. **Parent loans:** $5,831,474 (30% need-based, 70% non-need-based). **Programs:** Federal Direct (Subsidized and Unsubsidized Stafford, PLUS), Perkins.

WORK-STUDY Federal work-study: Total amount: $1,518,336; 1,030 jobs averaging $1474. **State or other work-study/employment:** Total amount: $15,500 (100% need-based). 8 part-time jobs averaging $1938.

ATHLETIC AWARDS Total amount: $1,949,591 (37% need-based, 63% non-need-based).

APPLYING FOR FINANCIAL AID Required financial aid forms: FAFSA, CSS Financial Aid PROFILE, noncustodial (divorced/separated) parent's statement, parent and student federal tax returns and W-2 forms. **Financial aid deadline:** 2/15. **Notification date:** Continuous beginning 2/1. Students must reply by 5/1 or within 2 weeks of notification.

CONTACT Elizabeth Keuffel, Director of Financial Aid, Saint Anselm College, 100 Saint Anselm Drive, Manchester, NH 03102-1310, 603-641-7110 or toll-free 888-4ANSELM. *Fax:* 603-656-6015. *E-mail:* financial_aid@anselm.edu.
Website: http://www.anselm.edu/.

SAINT ANTHONY COLLEGE OF NURSING
Rockford, IL

Tuition & fees: N/R	Average undergraduate aid package: $9203

ABOUT THE INSTITUTION Independent Roman Catholic, coed, primarily women. **Awards:** certificates, bachelor's, master's, and doctoral degrees. 1 undergraduate major. **Total enrollment:** 321. Undergraduates: 238. Federal methodology is used as a basis for awarding need-based institutional aid.

UNDERGRADUATE FINANCIAL AID (Fall 2015) 154 applied for aid; of those 94% were deemed to have need. 98% of undergraduates with need received aid; of those 2% had need fully met. **Average percent of need met:** 38% (excluding resources awarded to replace EFC). **Average financial aid package:** $9203 (excluding resources awarded to replace EFC). 1% of all full-time undergraduates had no need and received non-need-based gift aid.

GIFT AID (NEED-BASED) *Total amount:* $894,594 (47% federal, 37% state, 10% institutional, 6% external sources). *Receiving aid:* Entering class: 100% (1); all full-time undergraduates: 60% (98). *Average award:* Freshmen: $10,191; Undergraduates: $7100. *Scholarships, grants, and awards:* Federal Pell, state, private, college/university gift aid from institutional funds.

GIFT AID (NON-NEED-BASED) *Total amount:* $6016 (1% federal, 99% external sources). *Receiving aid:* Freshmen: 100% (1). Undergraduates: 1% (2). *Average award:* Undergraduates: $4000.

LOANS *Student loans:* $2,233,654 (88% need-based, 12% non-need-based). *Average need-based loan:* Undergraduates: $4268. *Parent loans:* $361,614 (63% need-based, 37% non-need-based). *Programs:* Federal Direct (Subsidized and Unsubsidized Stafford, PLUS), alternative loans.

WORK-STUDY *State or other work-study/employment:* Total amount: $175,141 (90% need-based, 10% non-need-based). Part-time jobs available.

APPLYING FOR FINANCIAL AID *Required financial aid form:* FAFSA. *Financial aid deadline (priority):* 4/15. *Notification date:* Continuous beginning 4/17.

CONTACT Serrita Woods, Financial Aid Coordinator, Saint Anthony College of Nursing, 5658 East State Street, Rockford, IL 61108, 815-395-5089. *Fax:* 815-227-2730. *E-mail:* serritawoods@sacn.edu. *Website:* http://www.sacn.edu/.

ST. AUGUSTINE COLLEGE
Chicago, IL

CONTACT Mrs. Maria Zambonino, Director of Financial Aid, St. Augustine College, 1345 W Angyle, Chicago, IL 60640, 773-878-3813. *Fax:* 773-878-9032. *E-mail:* mzambonino@hotmail.com. *Website:* http://www.staugustine.edu/.

SAINT AUGUSTINE'S UNIVERSITY
Raleigh, NC

Tuition & fees: $17,890	Average undergraduate aid package: N/A

ABOUT THE INSTITUTION Independent Episcopal, coed. *Awards:* bachelor's degrees. 25 undergraduate majors. *Total enrollment:* 944. Undergraduates: 944. Freshmen: 347. Federal methodology is used as a basis for awarding need-based institutional aid.

UNDERGRADUATE EXPENSES for 2017–2018 *Application fee:* $50. *Comprehensive fee:* $25,582 includes full-time tuition ($12,890), mandatory fees ($5000), and room and board ($7692). *College room only:* $3182. Full-time tuition and fees vary according to course load. Room and board charges vary according to housing facility. *Part-time tuition:* $537 per credit hour. *Part-time fees:* $208 per credit hour. Part-time tuition and fees vary according to course load.

GIFT AID (NEED-BASED) *Scholarships, grants, and awards:* Federal Pell, FSEOG, state, private, college/university gift aid from institutional funds, United Negro College Fund.

GIFT AID (NON-NEED-BASED) *Scholarships, grants, and awards by category:* Academic interests/achievement: 801 awards ($9,792,407 total): biological sciences, general academic interests/achievements, military science. *Creative arts/performance:* music, performing arts. *Special characteristics:* 801 awards ($9,793,407 total): children of faculty/staff, local/state students. *Tuition waivers:* Full or partial for children of alumni, employees or children of employees. *ROTC:* Army, Air Force cooperative.

LOANS *Student loans:* 93% of past graduating class borrowed through all loan programs. *Average indebtedness per student:* $19,500. *Programs:* Federal Direct (Subsidized and Unsubsidized Stafford, PLUS), Perkins.

WORK-STUDY Federal work-study jobs available. *State or other work-study/employment:* Part-time jobs available.

APPLYING FOR FINANCIAL AID *Required financial aid forms:* FAFSA, institution's own form. *Financial aid deadline (priority):* 3/15. *Notification date:* Continuous beginning 3/15. Students must reply within 2 weeks of notification.

CONTACT Ms. Carmela D. Cohen-Perry, Director of Financial Aid, Saint Augustine's University, 1315 Oakwood Avenue, Raleigh, NC 27610-2298, 919-516-4128 or toll-free 800-948-1126. *Fax:* 919-516-4431. *E-mail:* cdcohen-perry@st-aug.edu. *Website:* http://www.st-aug.edu/.

ST. BONAVENTURE UNIVERSITY
St. Bonaventure, NY

Tuition & fees: $32,331	Average undergraduate aid package: $24,764

ABOUT THE INSTITUTION Independent Roman Catholic Church, coed. *Awards:* certificates, associate, bachelor's, and master's degrees. 38 undergraduate majors. *Total enrollment:* 2,052. Undergraduates: 1,660. Freshmen: 433. Federal methodology is used as a basis for awarding need-based institutional aid.

UNDERGRADUATE EXPENSES for 2016–2017 *One-time required fee:* $100. *Comprehensive fee:* $43,804 includes full-time tuition ($31,366), mandatory fees ($965), and room and board ($11,473). *College room only:* $6048. Room and board charges vary according to board plan and housing facility. *Part-time fees:* $934 per credit hour. Part-time tuition and fees vary according to course load.

FRESHMAN FINANCIAL AID (Fall 2015) 363 applied for aid; of those 84% were deemed to have need. 100% of freshmen with need received aid; of those 23% had need fully met. *Average percent of need met:* 90% (excluding resources awarded to replace EFC). *Average financial aid package:* $27,649 (excluding resources awarded to replace EFC). 21% of all full-time freshmen had no need and received non-need-based gift aid.

UNDERGRADUATE FINANCIAL AID (Fall 2015) 1,402 applied for aid; of those 87% were deemed to have need. 100% of undergraduates with need received aid; of those 22% had need fully met. *Average percent of need met:* 87% (excluding resources awarded to replace EFC). *Average financial aid package:* $24,764 (excluding resources awarded to replace EFC). 25% of all full-time undergraduates had no need and received non-need-based gift aid.

GIFT AID (NEED-BASED) *Total amount:* $22,060,545 (13% federal, 7% state, 78% institutional, 2% external sources). *Receiving aid:* Freshmen: 78% (306); all full-time undergraduates: 72% (1,216). *Average award:* Freshmen: $23,396; Undergraduates: $20,750. *Scholarships, grants, and awards:* Federal Pell, FSEOG, state, private, college/university gift aid from institutional funds.

GIFT AID (NON-NEED-BASED) *Total amount:* $5,959,883 (8% federal, 1% state, 89% institutional, 2% external sources). *Receiving aid:* Freshmen: 70% (272). Undergraduates: 62% (1,051). *Average award:* Freshmen: $14,942. Undergraduates: $12,440. *Scholarships, grants, and awards by category:* Academic interests/achievement: 1,401 awards ($16,700,374 total): business, education, general academic interests/achievements. *Creative arts/performance:* 82 awards ($115,433 total): journalism/publications, music, performing arts. *Special characteristics:* 492 awards ($3,139,084 total): children of faculty/staff, local/state students, members of minority groups, out-of-state students, relatives of clergy, religious affiliation, siblings of current students. *Tuition waivers:* Full or partial for employees or children of employees, senior citizens. *ROTC:* Army.

LOANS *Student loans:* $11,620,922 (90% need-based, 10% non-need-based). 76% of past graduating class borrowed through all loan programs. *Average indebtedness per student:* $36,649. *Average need-based loan:* Freshmen: $3963. Undergraduates: $4598. *Parent loans:* $4,980,585 (92% need-based, 8% non-need-based). *Programs:* Federal Direct (Subsidized and Unsubsidized Stafford, PLUS), Perkins, college/university.

WORK-STUDY *Federal work-study:* 305 jobs averaging $898. *State or other work-study/employment:* Total amount: $327,649 (100% non-need-based). 362 part-time jobs averaging $904.

ATHLETIC AWARDS Total amount: $3,136,565 (58% need-based, 42% non-need-based).

APPLYING FOR FINANCIAL AID *Required financial aid forms:* FAFSA, state aid form. *Financial aid deadline (priority):* 2/15. *Notification date:* Continuous beginning 3/1. Students must reply by 5/1 or within 2 weeks of notification.

CONTACT Mr. Troy R. Martin, Director of Financial Aid, St. Bonaventure University, 3261 West State Road, St. Bonaventure, NY 14778-2284, 716-375-2373 or toll-free 800-462-5050. *Fax:* 716-375-2087. *E-mail:* tmartin@sbu.edu. *Website:* http://www.sbu.edu/.

ST. CATHERINE UNIVERSITY
St. Paul, MN

ABOUT THE INSTITUTION Independent Roman Catholic, undergraduate: women only; graduate: coed. *Awards:* certificates, associate, bachelor's, master's, and doctoral degrees. 80 undergraduate majors. *Total enrollment:* 4,686. Undergraduates: 3,176. Freshmen: 430.

GIFT AID (NEED-BASED) *Scholarships, grants, and awards:* Federal Pell, FSEOG, state, private, college/university gift aid from institutional funds.

GIFT AID (NON-NEED-BASED) *Scholarships, grants, and awards by category: Academic interests/achievement:* business, education, English, foreign languages, general academic interests/achievements, health fields, home economics, humanities, mathematics, physical sciences, premedicine, social sciences. *Creative arts/performance:* art/fine arts, music. *Special achievements/activities:* community service, general special achievements/activities, leadership, memberships. *Special characteristics:* adult students, children and siblings of alumni, children of current students, children of educators, children of faculty/staff, ethnic background, general special characteristics, international students, local/state students, out-of-state students, religious affiliation, siblings of current students, spouses of current students.

LOANS *Programs:* Federal Direct (Subsidized and Unsubsidized Stafford, PLUS), Perkins, Federal Nursing, state, alternative loans.

WORK-STUDY *Federal work-study:* Total amount: $305,772; jobs available. *State or other work-study/employment:* Total amount: $384,001 (100% need-based). Part-time jobs available.

APPLYING FOR FINANCIAL AID *Required financial aid forms:* FAFSA, institution's own form.

CONTACT Beth Stevens, Director of Financial Aid, St. Catherine University, 2004 Randolph Avenue, Derham Hall, Suite 208, St. Paul, MN 55105, 651-690-6540 or toll-free 800-945-4599. *Fax:* 651-690-6765. *E-mail:* finaid@stkate.edu. *Website:* http://www.stkate.edu/.

SAINT CHARLES BORROMEO SEMINARY, OVERBROOK
Wynnewood, PA

CONTACT Ms. Nora M. Downey, Coordinator of Financial Aid, Saint Charles Borromeo Seminary, Overbrook, 100 East Wynnewood Road, Wynnewood, PA 19096-3099, 610-785-6582. *Fax:* 610-667-3971. *E-mail:* ndowney@scs.edu. *Website:* http://www.scs.edu/.

ST. CLOUD STATE UNIVERSITY
St. Cloud, MN

ABOUT THE INSTITUTION State-supported, coed. *Awards:* certificates, diplomas, associate, bachelor's, master's, and doctoral degrees. 98 undergraduate majors. *Total enrollment:* 15,092. Undergraduates: 13,236. Freshmen: 1,800.

GIFT AID (NEED-BASED) *Scholarships, grants, and awards:* Federal Pell, FSEOG, state, private, college/university gift aid from institutional funds.

GIFT AID (NON-NEED-BASED) *Scholarships, grants, and awards by category: Academic interests/achievement:* biological sciences, business, communication, computer science, education, engineering/technologies, English, general academic interests/achievements, health fields, international studies, mathematics, physical sciences, social sciences. *Creative arts/performance:* applied art and design, art/fine arts, cinema/film/broadcasting, creative writing, journalism/publications, music, performing arts, theater/drama. *Special achievements/activities:* community service, general special achievements/activities, leadership. *Special characteristics:* children of faculty/staff, children of union members/company employees, out-of-state students.

LOANS *Programs:* Federal Direct (Subsidized and Unsubsidized Stafford, PLUS), Perkins, state.

WORK-STUDY *Federal work-study:* jobs available. *State or other work-study/employment:* Total amount: $2,064,012 (100% need-based). Part-time jobs available.

APPLYING FOR FINANCIAL AID *Required financial aid forms:* FAFSA, institution's own form.

CONTACT Financial Aid Office, St. Cloud State University, 720 4th Avenue South, AS106, St. Cloud, MN 56301-4498, 320-308-2047 or toll-free 877-654-7278. *Fax:* 320-308-5424. *E-mail:* financialaid@stcloudstate.edu. *Website:* http://www.stcloudstate.edu/.

ST. EDWARD'S UNIVERSITY
Austin, TX

Tuition & fees: $43,050	Average undergraduate aid package: $32,523

ABOUT THE INSTITUTION Independent Roman Catholic, coed. *Awards:* certificates, bachelor's, and master's degrees. 56 undergraduate majors. *Total enrollment:* 4,601. Undergraduates: 4,056. Freshmen: 864. Federal methodology is used as a basis for awarding need-based institutional aid.

UNDERGRADUATE EXPENSES for 2017–2018 *Application fee:* $50. *Comprehensive fee:* $55,990 includes full-time tuition ($42,550), mandatory fees ($500), and room and board ($12,940). Full-time tuition and fees vary according to degree level. Room and board charges vary according to board plan and housing facility. *Part-time tuition:* $1419 per credit hour. *Part-time fees:* $150 per year. Part-time tuition and fees vary according to course load and degree level.

FRESHMAN FINANCIAL AID (Fall 2016, est.) 760 applied for aid; of those 86% were deemed to have need. 100% of freshmen with need received aid; of those 13% had need fully met. *Average percent of need met:* 75% (excluding resources awarded to replace EFC). *Average financial aid package:* $35,885 (excluding resources awarded to replace EFC). 9% of all full-time freshmen had no need and received non-need-based gift aid.

UNDERGRADUATE FINANCIAL AID (Fall 2016, est.) 2,714 applied for aid; of those 91% were deemed to have need. 99% of undergraduates with need received aid; of those 11% had need fully met. *Average percent of need met:* 68% (excluding resources awarded to replace EFC). *Average financial aid package:* $32,523 (excluding resources awarded to replace EFC). 4% of all full-time undergraduates had no need and received non-need-based gift aid.

GIFT AID (NEED-BASED) *Total amount:* $47,694,701 (14% federal, 10% state, 76% institutional). *Receiving aid:* Freshmen: 67% (582); all full-time undergraduates: 62% (2,233). *Average award:* Freshmen: $23,009; Undergraduates: $20,681. *Scholarships, grants, and awards:* Federal Pell, FSEOG, state, private, college/university gift aid from institutional funds.

GIFT AID (NON-NEED-BASED) *Total amount:* $32,665,989 (6% federal, 89% institutional, 5% external sources). *Receiving aid:* Freshmen: 53% (460). Undergraduates: 46% (1,666). *Average award:* Freshmen: $17,959. Undergraduates: $16,563. *Scholarships, grants, and awards by category: Academic interests/achievement:* 1,965 awards ($26,625,347 total): biological sciences, business, communication, computer science, education, English, foreign languages, general academic interests/achievements, home economics, humanities, international studies, mathematics, military science, physical sciences, premedicine, religion/biblical studies, social sciences. *Creative arts/performance:* 43 awards ($110,091 total): art/fine arts, journalism/publications, theater/drama. *Special achievements/activities:* 36 awards ($91,227 total): cheerleading/drum major, community service, general special achievements/activities, leadership. *Special characteristics:* 215 awards ($2,410,093 total): adult students, children of faculty/staff, local/state students, out-of-state students, religious affiliation, veterans, veterans' children. *Tuition waivers:* Full or partial for employees or children of employees. *ROTC:* Army cooperative, Air Force cooperative.

LOANS *Student loans:* $23,357,563 (37% need-based, 63% non-need-based). 67% of past graduating class borrowed through all loan programs. *Average indebtedness per student:* $37,377. *Average need-based loan:* Freshmen: $3696. Undergraduates: $4517. *Parent loans:* $4,898,911 (100% non-need-based). *Programs:* Federal Direct (Subsidized and Unsubsidized Stafford, PLUS), Perkins, state, private loans.

WORK-STUDY *Federal work-study:* Total amount: $459,918; 233 jobs averaging $1974. *State or other work-study/employment:* Total amount: $36,000 (100% need-based). 18 part-time jobs averaging $2000.

ATHLETIC AWARDS Total amount: $3,882,252 (100% non-need-based).

APPLYING FOR FINANCIAL AID *Required financial aid form:* FAFSA. *Financial aid deadline (priority):* 2/1. *Notification date:* Continuous beginning 11/1. Students must reply by 5/1 or within 2 weeks of notification.

CONTACT Office of Student Financial Services, St. Edward's University, 3001 South Congress Avenue, Austin, TX 78704-6489, 512-448-8523 or toll-free 800-555-0164. *Fax:* 512-416-5837. *E-mail:* seu.finaid@stedwards.edu. *Website:* http://www.stedwards.edu/.

ST. FRANCIS COLLEGE
Brooklyn Heights, NY

CONTACT Ms. Hellitz Lopez, Director of Student Financial Services, St. Francis College, 180 Remsen Street, Brooklyn Heights, NY 11201-4398, 718-489-5346. *Fax:* 718-643-0076. *E-mail:* hlopez@sfc.edu. *Website:* http://www.sfc.edu/.

SAINT FRANCIS MEDICAL CENTER COLLEGE OF NURSING
Peoria, IL

Tuition & fees: $20,854	Average undergraduate aid package: $9152

ABOUT THE INSTITUTION Independent Roman Catholic, coed, primarily women. *Awards:* certificates, bachelor's, master's, and doctoral degrees. 1 undergraduate major. *Total enrollment:* 638. Undergraduates: 392. Federal methodology is used as a basis for awarding need-based institutional aid.

UNDERGRADUATE EXPENSES for 2017–2018 *Application fee:* $50. *Tuition:* full-time $19,734; part-time $598 per semester hour. *Required fees:* full-time $1120; $90 per course. Full-time tuition and fees vary according to course load, degree level, program, and student level. Part-time tuition and fees vary according to course load, degree level, program, and student level.

UNDERGRADUATE FINANCIAL AID (Fall 2016, est.) 249 applied for aid; of those 88% were deemed to have need. 100% of undergraduates with need received aid; of those 6% had need fully met. *Average percent of need met:* 40% (excluding resources awarded to replace EFC). *Average financial aid package:* $9152 (excluding resources awarded to replace EFC). 7% of all full-time undergraduates had no need and received non-need-based gift aid.

GIFT AID (NEED-BASED) *Total amount:* $1,131,116 (34% federal, 46% state, 11% institutional, 9% external sources). *Receiving aid:* All full-time undergraduates: 50% (149). *Average award:* Undergraduates: $6840. *Scholarships, grants, and awards:* Federal Pell, state, private, college/university gift aid from institutional funds.

GIFT AID (NON-NEED-BASED) *Total amount:* $115,213 (1% federal, 7% state, 44% institutional, 48% external sources). *Receiving aid:* Undergraduates: 1% (2). *Average award:* Undergraduates: $2123. *Scholarships, grants, and awards by category:* Academic interests/achievement: 24 awards ($24,000 total): general academic interests/achievements, health fields. *Tuition waivers:* Full or partial for employees or children of employees.

LOANS *Student loans:* $2,999,211 (69% need-based, 31% non-need-based). *Average need-based loan:* Undergraduates: $5450. *Parent loans:* $523,964 (38% need-based, 62% non-need-based). *Programs:* Federal Direct (Subsidized and Unsubsidized Stafford, PLUS), college/university.

APPLYING FOR FINANCIAL AID *Required financial aid forms:* FAFSA, institution's own form. *Financial aid deadline (priority):* 3/1. *Notification date:* Continuous beginning 5/1.

CONTACT Ms. Nancy Perryman, Coordinator for Student Financial Assistance, Saint Francis Medical Center College of Nursing, 511 Northeast Greenleaf Street, Peoria, IL 61603-3783, 309-655-4119. *Fax:* 309-655-3962. *E-mail:* nancy.s.perryman@osfhealthcare.org. *Website:* http://www.sfmccon.edu/.

SAINT FRANCIS UNIVERSITY
Loretto, PA

ABOUT THE INSTITUTION Independent Roman Catholic, coed. *Awards:* certificates, associate, bachelor's, master's, and doctoral degrees. 68 undergraduate majors. *Total enrollment:* 2,329. Undergraduates: 1,707. Freshmen: 352.

GIFT AID (NEED-BASED) *Scholarships, grants, and awards:* Federal Pell, FSEOG, state, private, college/university gift aid from institutional funds.

GIFT AID (NON-NEED-BASED) *Scholarships, grants, and awards by category:* Academic interests/achievement: biological sciences, business, communication, computer science, education, engineering/technologies, English, general academic interests/achievements, health fields, humanities, international studies, mathematics, religion/biblical studies, social sciences. *Creative arts/performance:* art/fine arts. *Special achievements/activities:* cheerleading/drum major, leadership, religious involvement. *Special characteristics:* adult students, children and siblings of alumni, children of current students, children of educators, children of faculty/staff, international students, out-of-state students, previous college experience, religious affiliation, siblings of current students, spouses of current students.

LOANS *Programs:* Federal Direct (Subsidized and Unsubsidized Stafford, PLUS), Perkins, private loans.

WORK-STUDY *Federal work-study:* 285 jobs averaging $1000. *State or other work-study/employment:* Total amount: $489,697 (93% need-based, 7% non-need-based). 780 part-time jobs averaging $1000.

APPLYING FOR FINANCIAL AID *Required financial aid form:* FAFSA.

CONTACT Mr. Jamie Kosh, Director of Financial Aid, Saint Francis University, PO Box 600, Loretto, PA 15931, 814-472-3010 or toll-free 866-DIAL-SFU. *Fax:* 814-472-3999. *E-mail:* jkosh@francis.edu. *Website:* http://www.francis.edu/.

ST. GREGORY'S UNIVERSITY
Shawnee, OK

Tuition & fees: N/R	Average undergraduate aid package: $19,328

ABOUT THE INSTITUTION Independent Roman Catholic, coed. *Awards:* certificates, associate, bachelor's, and master's degrees. 33 undergraduate majors. *Total enrollment:* 702. Undergraduates: 636. Freshmen: 102. Federal methodology is used as a basis for awarding need-based institutional aid.

UNDERGRADUATE EXPENSES for 2016–2017 *Payment plans:* Guaranteed tuition, tuition prepayment.

FRESHMAN FINANCIAL AID (Fall 2015) 86 applied for aid; of those 98% were deemed to have need. 100% of freshmen with need received aid; of those 36% had need fully met. *Average percent of need met:* 72% (excluding resources awarded to replace EFC). *Average financial aid package:* $19,328 (excluding resources awarded to replace EFC). 12% of all full-time freshmen had no need and received non-need-based gift aid.

UNDERGRADUATE FINANCIAL AID (Fall 2015) 519 applied for aid; of those 84% were deemed to have need. 100% of undergraduates with need received aid; of those 12% had need fully met. *Average percent of need met:* 72% (excluding resources awarded to replace EFC). *Average financial aid package:* $19,328 (excluding resources awarded to replace EFC). 13% of all full-time undergraduates had no need and received non-need-based gift aid.

GIFT AID (NEED-BASED) *Total amount:* $3,804,847 (32% federal, 11% state, 51% institutional, 6% external sources). *Receiving aid:* Freshmen: 48% (41); all full-time undergraduates: 54% (325). *Average award:* Freshmen: $14,540; Undergraduates: $12,603. *Scholarships, grants, and awards:* Federal Pell, FSEOG, state, private, college/university gift aid from institutional funds.

GIFT AID (NON-NEED-BASED) *Receiving aid:* Freshmen: 70% (60). Undergraduates: 59% (354). *Average award:* Freshmen: $3000. Undergraduates: $3000. *Scholarships, grants, and awards by category:* Academic interests/achievement: 280 awards ($569,198 total): general academic interests/achievements. *Creative arts/performance:* 59 awards ($71,777 total): art/fine arts, dance, music, theater/drama. *Special achievements/activities:* 237 awards ($341,782 total): religious involvement. *Special characteristics:* 128 awards ($311,633 total): children of union members/company employees, international students. *Tuition waivers:* Full or partial for employees or children of employees.

LOANS *Student loans:* $4,591,711 (96% need-based, 4% non-need-based). 80% of past graduating class borrowed through all loan programs. *Average indebtedness per student:* $35,000. *Average need-based loan:* Freshmen: $4500. Undergraduates: $3500. *Parent loans:* $372,799 (86% need-based, 14% non-need-based). *Programs:* Perkins, alternative loans.

WORK-STUDY *Federal work-study:* 34 jobs averaging $900. *State or other work-study/employment:* Total amount: $7250 (100% non-need-based). 30 part-time jobs averaging $2000.

ATHLETIC AWARDS Total amount: $2,352,157 (100% need-based).

APPLYING FOR FINANCIAL AID *Required financial aid forms:* FAFSA, institution's own form. *Financial aid deadline:* Continuous. *Notification date:* Continuous beginning 2/15. Students must reply within 2 weeks of notification.

CONTACT Lori K. Deardorff, Director of Financial Aid, St. Gregory's University, 1900 West MacArthur Drive, Shawnee, OK 74804, 405-878-5448 or toll-free 888-STGREGS. *Fax:* 405-878-5403. *E-mail:* lkdeardorff@stgregorys.edu. *Website:* http://www.stgregorys.edu/.

ST. GREGORY THE GREAT SEMINARY
Seward, NE

CONTACT Financial Aid Office, St. Gregory the Great Seminary, 800 Fletcher Road, Seward, NE 67434, 402-643-4052.
Website: http://www.stgregoryseminary.edu/.

ST. JOHN FISHER COLLEGE
Rochester, NY

Tuition & fees: $33,120	Average undergraduate aid package: $22,202

ABOUT THE INSTITUTION Independent Roman Catholic Church, coed. *Awards:* certificates, bachelor's, master's, and doctoral degrees. 40 undergraduate majors. *Total enrollment:* 3,787. Undergraduates: 2,786. Freshmen: 576. Federal methodology is used as a basis for awarding need-based institutional aid.

UNDERGRADUATE EXPENSES for 2017–2018 *Comprehensive fee:* $45,270 includes full-time tuition ($32,540), mandatory fees ($580), and room and board ($12,150). *College room only:* $7780. Full-time tuition and fees vary according to program. Room and board charges vary according to board plan. *Part-time tuition:* $885 per credit hour. *Part-time fees:* $10 per credit hour. Part-time tuition and fees vary according to course load and program.

FRESHMAN FINANCIAL AID (Fall 2016, est.) 553 applied for aid; of those 87% were deemed to have need. 100% of freshmen with need received aid; of those 44% had need fully met. *Average percent of need met:* 74% (excluding resources awarded to replace EFC). *Average financial aid package:* $23,070 (excluding resources awarded to replace EFC). 17% of all full-time freshmen had no need and received non-need-based gift aid.

UNDERGRADUATE FINANCIAL AID (Fall 2016, est.) 2,331 applied for aid; of those 91% were deemed to have need. 100% of undergraduates with need received aid; of those 37% had need fully met. *Average percent of need met:* 70% (excluding resources awarded to replace EFC). *Average financial aid package:* $22,202 (excluding resources awarded to replace EFC). 18% of all full-time undergraduates had no need and received non-need-based gift aid.

GIFT AID (NEED-BASED) *Total amount:* $35,944,533 (13% federal, 8% state, 77% institutional, 2% external sources). *Receiving aid:* Freshmen: 83% (479); all full-time undergraduates: 81% (2,118). *Average award:* Freshmen: $19,076; Undergraduates: $17,370. *Scholarships, grants, and awards:* Federal Pell, FSEOG, state, private, college/university gift aid from institutional funds, Federal Nursing.

GIFT AID (NON-NEED-BASED) *Total amount:* $5,520,722 (1% federal, 96% institutional, 3% external sources). *Receiving aid:* Freshmen: 61% (351). Undergraduates: 59% (1,544). *Average award:* Freshmen: $13,272. Undergraduates: $11,112. *Scholarships, grants, and awards by category:* Academic interests/achievement: 1,372 awards ($16,124,000 total): biological sciences, business, English, foreign languages, general academic interests/achievements, humanities, mathematics, physical sciences, social sciences. *Special achievements/activities:* 90 awards ($1,823,230 total): community service. *Special characteristics:* 223 awards ($2,627,214 total): children and siblings of alumni, children of faculty/staff, ethnic background, first-generation college students, local/state students, members of minority groups.

Tuition waivers: Full or partial for employees or children of employees. **ROTC:** Army cooperative, Naval cooperative, Air Force cooperative.

LOANS *Student loans:* $23,255,284 (93% need-based, 7% non-need-based). 85% of past graduating class borrowed through all loan programs. *Average indebtedness per student:* $35,925. *Average need-based loan:* Freshmen: $4241. Undergraduates: $4925. *Parent loans:* $13,269,059 (88% need-based, 12% non-need-based). *Programs:* Federal Direct (Subsidized and Unsubsidized Stafford, PLUS), Perkins.

WORK-STUDY *Federal work-study:* Total amount: $1,595,184; 1,238 jobs averaging $1283.

APPLYING FOR FINANCIAL AID *Required financial aid forms:* FAFSA, state aid form. *Financial aid deadline (priority):* 1/15. *Notification date:* Continuous beginning 2/21. Students must reply by 5/1 or within 3 weeks of notification.

CONTACT Mrs. Angela Monnat, Director of Financial Aid, St. John Fisher College, 3690 East Avenue, Rochester, NY 14618-3597, 585-385-8042 or toll-free 800-444-4640. *Fax:* 585-385-8044. *E-mail:* amonnat@sjfc.edu. *Website:* http://www.sjfc.edu/.

ST. JOHN'S COLLEGE
Springfield, IL

CONTACT Mary M. Deatherage, Financial Aid Officer, St. John's College, 421 North Ninth Street, Springfield, IL 62702, 217-544-6464 Ext. 44705. *Fax:* 217-757-6870. *E-mail:* mdeather@st-johns.org.
Website: http://www.stjohnscollegespringfield.edu/.

ST. JOHN'S COLLEGE
Annapolis, MD

Tuition & fees: $51,670	Average undergraduate aid package: $41,636

ABOUT THE INSTITUTION Independent, coed. *Awards:* bachelor's and master's degrees. 1 undergraduate major. *Total enrollment:* 484. Undergraduates: 434. Freshmen: 127. Both federal and institutional methodology are used as a basis for awarding need-based institutional aid.

UNDERGRADUATE EXPENSES for 2017–2018 *One-time required fee:* $125. *Comprehensive fee:* $63,904 includes full-time tuition ($51,200), mandatory fees ($470), and room and board ($12,234). *College room only:* $5984. Room and board charges vary according to board plan and housing facility. *Payment plan:* Tuition prepayment.

FRESHMAN FINANCIAL AID (Fall 2016, est.) 104 applied for aid; of those 88% were deemed to have need. 100% of freshmen with need received aid; of those 25% had need fully met. *Average percent of need met:* 91% (excluding resources awarded to replace EFC). *Average financial aid package:* $42,952 (excluding resources awarded to replace EFC). 24% of all full-time freshmen had no need and received non-need-based gift aid.

UNDERGRADUATE FINANCIAL AID (Fall 2016, est.) 359 applied for aid; of those 88% were deemed to have need. 100% of undergraduates with need received aid; of those 25% had need fully met. *Average percent of need met:* 88% (excluding resources awarded to replace EFC). *Average financial aid package:* $41,636 (excluding resources awarded to replace EFC). 25% of all full-time undergraduates had no need and received non-need-based gift aid.

GIFT AID (NEED-BASED) *Total amount:* $11,306,483 (3% federal, 1% state, 93% institutional, 3% external sources). *Receiving aid:* Freshmen: 72% (89); all full-time undergraduates: 72% (311). *Average award:* Freshmen: $39,178; Undergraduates: $36,355. *Scholarships, grants, and awards:* Federal Pell, FSEOG, state, private, college/university gift aid from institutional funds.

GIFT AID (NON-NEED-BASED) *Total amount:* $2,966,624 (86% institutional, 14% external sources). *Receiving aid:* Freshmen: 14% (17). Undergraduates: 15% (66). *Average award:* Freshmen: $21,720. Undergraduates: $19,112. *Scholarships, grants, and awards by category:* Academic interests/achievement: general academic interests/achievements. *Tuition waivers:* Full or partial for employees or children of employees.

LOANS *Student loans:* $2,804,375 (74% need-based, 26% non-need-based). 74% of past graduating class borrowed through all loan programs. *Average indebtedness*

per student: $34,212. **Average need-based loan:** Freshmen: $3856. Undergraduates: $4823. **Parent loans:** $895,420 (16% need-based, 84% non-need-based). **Programs:** Federal Direct (Subsidized and Unsubsidized Stafford, PLUS), Perkins, college/university.

WORK-STUDY *Federal work-study:* Total amount: $130,000; 52 jobs averaging $2700. **State or other work-study/employment:** Total amount: $239,690 (69% need-based, 31% non-need-based). 130 part-time jobs averaging $2700.

APPLYING FOR FINANCIAL AID *Required financial aid forms:* FAFSA, CSS Financial Aid PROFILE, state aid form. *Financial aid deadline (priority):* 2/1. **Notification date:** Continuous beginning 12/15. Students must reply by 5/1 or within 2 weeks of notification.

CONTACT Mr. Steven Bell, Director of Financial Aid, St. John's College, 60 College Avenue, Annapolis, MD 21401, 410-626-2502 or toll-free 800-727-9238. *Fax:* 410-626-2885. *E-mail:* skbell@sjc.edu.
Website: http://www.sjc.edu/.

ST. JOHN'S COLLEGE
Santa Fe, NM

Tuition & fees: $52,320	Average undergraduate aid package: $40,988

ABOUT THE INSTITUTION Independent, coed. *Awards:* bachelor's and master's degrees. 3 undergraduate majors. *Total enrollment:* 400. Undergraduates: 326. Freshmen: 67. Both federal and institutional methodology are used as a basis for awarding need-based institutional aid.

UNDERGRADUATE EXPENSES for 2017–2018 *Comprehensive fee:* $63,806 includes full-time tuition ($51,200), mandatory fees ($1120), and room and board ($11,486). Room and board charges vary according to board plan and housing facility. *Part-time tuition:* $1506 per credit.

FRESHMAN FINANCIAL AID (Fall 2016, est.) 83 applied for aid; of those 98% were deemed to have need. 100% of freshmen with need received aid; of those 58% had need fully met. *Average percent of need met:* 86% (excluding resources awarded to replace EFC). *Average financial aid package:* $44,225 (excluding resources awarded to replace EFC). 14% of all full-time freshmen had no need and received non-need-based gift aid.

UNDERGRADUATE FINANCIAL AID (Fall 2016, est.) 294 applied for aid; of those 98% were deemed to have need. 100% of undergraduates with need received aid; of those 56% had need fully met. *Average percent of need met:* 88% (excluding resources awarded to replace EFC). *Average financial aid package:* $40,988 (excluding resources awarded to replace EFC). 12% of all full-time undergraduates had no need and received non-need-based gift aid.

GIFT AID (NEED-BASED) *Total amount:* $6,952,211 (10% federal, 90% institutional). *Receiving aid:* Freshmen: 86% (81); all full-time undergraduates: 88% (288). *Average award:* Freshmen: $31,750; Undergraduates: $32,455. *Scholarships, grants, and awards:* Federal Pell, FSEOG, state, private, college/university gift aid from institutional funds.

GIFT AID (NON-NEED-BASED) *Total amount:* $5,301,888 (3% federal, 95% institutional, 2% external sources). *Receiving aid:* Freshmen: 86% (81). Undergraduates: 71% (232). *Average award:* Freshmen: $20,666. Undergraduates: $16,250. *Scholarships, grants, and awards by category:* Special characteristics: 2 awards ($99,516 total): children of faculty/staff, veterans. *Tuition waivers:* Full or partial for employees or children of employees.

LOANS *Student loans:* $2,307,164 (74% need-based, 26% non-need-based). 71% of past graduating class borrowed through all loan programs. *Average indebtedness per student:* $27,790. *Average need-based loan:* Freshmen: $4500. Undergraduates: $7280. *Parent loans:* $335,888 (100% non-need-based). *Programs:* Federal Direct (Subsidized and Unsubsidized Stafford, PLUS), Perkins, college/university.

WORK-STUDY *Federal work-study:* Total amount: $193,477; 74 jobs averaging $2720. *State or other work-study/employment:* Total amount: $368,530 (3% need-based, 97% non-need-based). 120 part-time jobs averaging $3040.

APPLYING FOR FINANCIAL AID *Required financial aid forms:* FAFSA, CSS Financial Aid PROFILE. *Financial aid deadline (priority):* 2/15. **Notification date:** Continuous beginning 12/15. Students must reply by 5/1 or within 2 weeks of notification.

CONTACT Michael R. Rodriguez, Director of Financial Aid, St. John's College, 1160 Camino Cruz Blanca, Santa Fe, NM 87505, 505-984-6058 or toll-free 800-331-5232. *Fax:* 505-984-6164. *E-mail:* mrodriguez@sjc.edu.
Website: http://www.sjc.edu/.

SAINT JOHN'S UNIVERSITY
Collegeville, MN

Tuition & fees: $41,732	Average undergraduate aid package: $32,178

ABOUT THE INSTITUTION Independent Roman Catholic, undergraduate: men only; graduate: coed. *Awards:* bachelor's and master's degrees (coordinate with College of Saint Benedict for women). 50 undergraduate majors. *Total enrollment:* 1,849. Undergraduates: 1,754. Freshmen: 461. Federal methodology is used as a basis for awarding need-based institutional aid.

UNDERGRADUATE EXPENSES for 2016–2017 *Comprehensive fee:* $51,624 includes full-time tuition ($41,016), mandatory fees ($716), and room and board ($9892). *College room only:* $4946. Room and board charges vary according to board plan and housing facility. *Part-time tuition:* $1709 per credit. Part-time tuition and fees vary according to course load.

FRESHMAN FINANCIAL AID (Fall 2016, est.) 399 applied for aid; of those 88% were deemed to have need. 100% of freshmen with need received aid; of those 40% had need fully met. *Average percent of need met:* 93% (excluding resources awarded to replace EFC). *Average financial aid package:* $33,080 (excluding resources awarded to replace EFC). 20% of all full-time freshmen had no need and received non-need-based gift aid.

UNDERGRADUATE FINANCIAL AID (Fall 2016, est.) 1,379 applied for aid; of those 86% were deemed to have need. 100% of undergraduates with need received aid; of those 37% had need fully met. *Average percent of need met:* 90% (excluding resources awarded to replace EFC). *Average financial aid package:* $32,178 (excluding resources awarded to replace EFC). 25% of all full-time undergraduates had no need and received non-need-based gift aid.

GIFT AID (NEED-BASED) *Total amount:* $33,659,785 (6% federal, 6% state, 86% institutional, 2% external sources). *Receiving aid:* Freshmen: 74% (340); all full-time undergraduates: 67% (1,162). *Average award:* Freshmen: $29,853; Undergraduates: $28,255. *Scholarships, grants, and awards:* Federal Pell, FSEOG, state, private, college/university gift aid from institutional funds.

GIFT AID (NON-NEED-BASED) *Total amount:* $11,150,751 (83% institutional, 17% external sources). *Receiving aid:* Freshmen: 73% (335). Undergraduates: 64% (1,107). *Average award:* Freshmen: $17,609. Undergraduates: $16,453. *Scholarships, grants, and awards by category:* Academic interests/achievement: 1,650 awards ($21,803,473 total): general academic interests/achievements. *Creative arts/performance:* 106 awards ($310,645 total): art/fine arts, music, theater/drama. *Special characteristics:* 399 awards ($2,201,225 total): international students, out-of-state students. *Tuition waivers:* Full or partial for employees or children of employees. *ROTC:* Army.

LOANS *Student loans:* $12,526,656 (89% need-based, 11% non-need-based). 66% of past graduating class borrowed through all loan programs. *Average indebtedness per student:* $40,272. *Average need-based loan:* Freshmen: $2295. Undergraduates: $3245. *Parent loans:* $1,479,967 (94% need-based, 6% non-need-based). *Programs:* Federal Direct (Subsidized and Unsubsidized Stafford, PLUS), Perkins, state, alternative loans.

WORK-STUDY *Federal work-study:* Total amount: $634,576; 205 jobs averaging $3345. *State or other work-study/employment:* Total amount: $2,637,796 (75% need-based, 25% non-need-based). 721 part-time jobs averaging $3345.

APPLYING FOR FINANCIAL AID *Required financial aid forms:* FAFSA, institution's own form, federal income tax form(s). *Financial aid deadline (priority):* 3/15. *Notification date:* Continuous beginning 3/15. Students must reply by 5/1 or within 3 weeks of notification.

CONTACT Mrs. Kari Vogt, Financial Aid Counselor, Saint John's University, PO Box 5000, Collegeville, MN 56321-5000, 320-363-3664 or toll-free 800-544-1489. *Fax:* 320-363-3102. *E-mail:* kvogt@csbsju.edu.
Website: http://www.csbsju.edu/.

ST. JOHN'S UNIVERSITY
Queens, NY

Tuition & fees: $39,460	Average undergraduate aid package: $26,295

ABOUT THE INSTITUTION Independent Roman Catholic Church, coed. *Awards:* certificates, bachelor's, master's, and doctoral degrees. 66 undergraduate majors. *Total enrollment:* 21,087. Undergraduates: 16,440. Freshmen: 3,248. Institutional methodology is used as a basis for awarding need-based institutional aid.

UNDERGRADUATE EXPENSES for 2016–2017 *One-time required fee:* $250. *Comprehensive fee:* $55,850 includes full-time tuition ($38,630), mandatory fees ($830), and room and board ($16,390). *College room only:* $10,510. Full-time tuition and fees vary according to course load, location, and program. Room and board charges vary according to board plan, housing facility, and location. *Part-time tuition:* $1288 per credit. *Part-time fees:* $312.50 per term. Part-time tuition and fees vary according to course load, location, and program.

FRESHMAN FINANCIAL AID (Fall 2015) 2,971 applied for aid; of those 92% were deemed to have need. 100% of freshmen with need received aid; of those 15% had need fully met. *Average percent of need met:* 70% (excluding resources awarded to replace EFC). *Average financial aid package:* $28,216 (excluding resources awarded to replace EFC). 7% of all full-time freshmen had no need and received non-need-based gift aid.

UNDERGRADUATE FINANCIAL AID (Fall 2015) 9,419 applied for aid; of those 93% were deemed to have need. 100% of undergraduates with need received aid; of those 13% had need fully met. *Average percent of need met:* 64% (excluding resources awarded to replace EFC). *Average financial aid package:* $26,295 (excluding resources awarded to replace EFC). 6% of all full-time undergraduates had no need and received non-need-based gift aid.

GIFT AID (NEED-BASED) *Total amount:* $62,996,328 (35% federal, 19% state, 46% institutional). *Receiving aid:* Freshmen: 63% (2,055); all full-time undergraduates: 62% (6,796). *Average award:* Freshmen: $9204; Undergraduates: $9951. *Scholarships, grants, and awards:* Federal Pell, FSEOG, state, private, college/university gift aid from institutional funds.

GIFT AID (NON-NEED-BASED) *Total amount:* $162,472,652 (1% state, 93% institutional, 6% external sources). *Receiving aid:* Freshmen: 84% (2,721). Undergraduates: 74% (8,089). *Average award:* Freshmen: $19,847. Undergraduates: $17,343. *Scholarships, grants, and awards by category:* Academic interests/achievement: 6,661 awards ($101,943,113 total): biological sciences, business, communication, computer science, education, English, foreign languages, general academic interests/achievements, health fields, humanities, mathematics, military science, physical sciences, premedicine, social sciences. *Creative arts/performance:* 114 awards ($527,236 total): art/fine arts, cinema/film/broadcasting, creative writing, dance, debating, journalism/publications, music. *Special achievements/activities:* 421 awards ($1,341,111 total): cheerleading/drum major, community service, general special achievements/activities, hobbies/interests, leadership, religious involvement. *Special characteristics:* 2,773 awards ($11,956,579 total): children of faculty/staff, general special characteristics, local/state students, previous college experience, public servants, relatives of clergy, religious affiliation, veterans, veterans' children. *Tuition waivers:* Full or partial for employees or children of employees, adult students, senior citizens. *ROTC:* Army.

LOANS *Student loans:* $61,950,794 (44% need-based, 56% non-need-based). 74% of past graduating class borrowed through all loan programs. *Average indebtedness per student:* $34,234. *Average need-based loan:* Freshmen: $3618. Undergraduates: $4602. *Parent loans:* $67,959,917 (100% non-need-based). *Programs:* Federal Direct (Subsidized and Unsubsidized Stafford, PLUS), Perkins, Health Professions Student Loans (HPSL).

WORK-STUDY *Federal work-study:* 816 jobs averaging $2309. *State or other work-study/employment:* Part-time jobs available.

ATHLETIC AWARDS Total amount: $5,884,464 (100% non-need-based).

APPLYING FOR FINANCIAL AID *Required financial aid form:* FAFSA. *Financial aid deadline (priority):* 12/15. *Notification date:* Continuous beginning 1/25. Students must reply by 5/1 or within 2 weeks of notification.

CONTACT Mrs. Maryanne Twomey, Director for Institutional Programs and Research, St. John's University, 8000 Utopia Parkway, Queens, NY 11439, 718-990-2000 or toll-free 888-9STJOHNS. *Fax:* 718-990-5945. *E-mail:* studentfinancialserv@stjohns.edu. *Website:* http://www.stjohns.edu/.

ST. JOHN VIANNEY COLLEGE SEMINARY
Miami, FL

CONTACT Ms. Bonnie DeAngulo, Director of Financial Aid, St. John Vianney College Seminary, 2900 Southwest 87th Avenue, Miami, FL 33165-3244, 305-223-4561 Ext. 10. *Website:* http://www.sjvcs.edu/.

ST. JOSEPH'S COLLEGE, LONG ISLAND CAMPUS
Patchogue, NY

Tuition & fees: $25,930	Average undergraduate aid package: $13,213

ABOUT THE INSTITUTION Independent, coed. *Awards:* certificates, bachelor's, and master's degrees. 38 undergraduate majors. *Total enrollment:* 3,914. Undergraduates: 3,075. Freshmen: 431. Federal methodology is used as a basis for awarding need-based institutional aid.

UNDERGRADUATE EXPENSES for 2017–2018 *Application fee:* $25. *Tuition:* full-time $25,930; part-time $840 per credit. Full-time tuition and fees vary according to course load, location, and program. Part-time tuition and fees vary according to course load, location, and program.

FRESHMAN FINANCIAL AID (Fall 2015) 348 applied for aid; of those 79% were deemed to have need. 100% of freshmen with need received aid; of those 37% had need fully met. *Average percent of need met:* 74% (excluding resources awarded to replace EFC). *Average financial aid package:* $17,511 (excluding resources awarded to replace EFC). 18% of all full-time freshmen had no need and received non-need-based gift aid.

UNDERGRADUATE FINANCIAL AID (Fall 2015) 2,251 applied for aid; of those 80% were deemed to have need. 99% of undergraduates with need received aid; of those 34% had need fully met. *Average percent of need met:* 63% (excluding resources awarded to replace EFC). *Average financial aid package:* $13,213 (excluding resources awarded to replace EFC). 16% of all full-time undergraduates had no need and received non-need-based gift aid.

GIFT AID (NEED-BASED) *Total amount:* $19,744,088 (22% federal, 12% state, 66% institutional). *Receiving aid:* Freshmen: 77% (275); all full-time undergraduates: 73% (1,728). *Average award:* Freshmen: $13,006; Undergraduates: $10,945. *Scholarships, grants, and awards:* Federal Pell, FSEOG, state, private, college/university gift aid from institutional funds.

GIFT AID (NON-NEED-BASED) *Total amount:* $3,873,273 (2% state, 95% institutional, 3% external sources). *Receiving aid:* Freshmen: 76% (270). Undergraduates: 65% (1,557). *Average award:* Freshmen: $9903. Undergraduates: $8984. *Scholarships, grants, and awards by category:* Academic interests/achievement: 1,715 awards ($14,066,280 total): general academic interests/achievements. *Special achievements/activities:* 3 awards ($6250 total): community service, leadership. *Special characteristics:* 192 awards ($656,343 total): children and siblings of alumni, children of faculty/staff, parents of current students, public servants, siblings of current students, spouses of current students, twins. *Tuition waivers:* Full or partial for employees or children of employees.

LOANS *Student loans:* $15,086,904 (85% need-based, 15% non-need-based). 66% of past graduating class borrowed through all loan programs. *Average indebtedness per student:* $27,364. *Average need-based loan:* Freshmen: $3032. Undergraduates: $4285. *Parent loans:* $3,582,266 (79% need-based, 21% non-need-based). *Programs:* Federal Direct (Subsidized and Unsubsidized Stafford, PLUS), Perkins, state.

WORK-STUDY *Federal work-study:* 105 jobs averaging $2951. *State or other work-study/employment:* Total amount: $232,522 (71% need-based, 29% non-need-based). 81 part-time jobs averaging $2884.

APPLYING FOR FINANCIAL AID *Required financial aid forms:* FAFSA, state aid form. *Financial aid deadline (priority):* 2/25. *Notification date:* Continuous beginning 3/15. Students must reply by 5/1 or within 2 weeks of notification.

CONTACT Amy Thompson, Director of Financial Aid, St. Joseph's College, Long Island Campus, 155 West Roe Boulevard, Patchogue, NY 11772-2399, 631-687-2600. *Fax:* 631-650-2525. *E-mail:* financialaid.li@sjcny.edu. *Website:* http://www.sjcny.edu/.

ST. JOSEPH'S COLLEGE, NEW YORK
Brooklyn, NY

Tuition & fees: $25,930	Average undergraduate aid package: $16,186

ABOUT THE INSTITUTION Independent, coed. *Awards:* certificates, bachelor's, and master's degrees. 39 undergraduate majors. *Total enrollment:* 1,205. Undergraduates: 965. Freshmen: 198. Federal methodology is used as a basis for awarding need-based institutional aid.

UNDERGRADUATE EXPENSES for 2017–2018 *Application fee:* $25. *Tuition:* full-time $25,930; part-time $840 per credit. Full-time tuition and fees vary according to course load and program. Part-time tuition and fees vary according to course load and program.

FRESHMAN FINANCIAL AID (Fall 2015) 149 applied for aid; of those 83% were deemed to have need. 100% of freshmen with need received aid; of those 20% had need fully met. *Average percent of need met:* 68% (excluding resources awarded to replace EFC). *Average financial aid package:* $19,674 (excluding resources awarded to replace EFC). 17% of all full-time freshmen had no need and received non-need-based gift aid.

UNDERGRADUATE FINANCIAL AID (Fall 2015) 722 applied for aid; of those 84% were deemed to have need. 100% of undergraduates with need received aid; of those 22% had need fully met. *Average percent of need met:* 65% (excluding resources awarded to replace EFC). *Average financial aid package:* $16,186 (excluding resources awarded to replace EFC). 14% of all full-time undergraduates had no need and received non-need-based gift aid.

GIFT AID (NEED-BASED) *Total amount:* $9,250,685 (28% federal, 14% state, 58% institutional). *Receiving aid:* Freshmen: 82% (123); all full-time undergraduates: 80% (597). *Average award:* Freshmen: $15,580; Undergraduates: $14,636. *Scholarships, grants, and awards:* Federal Pell, FSEOG, state, private, college/university gift aid from institutional funds.

GIFT AID (NON-NEED-BASED) *Total amount:* $1,445,114 (3% state, 85% institutional, 12% external sources). *Receiving aid:* Freshmen: 81% (122). Undergraduates: 72% (537). *Average award:* Freshmen: $10,489. Undergraduates: $10,377. *Scholarships, grants, and awards by category: Academic interests/achievement:* 430 awards ($3,903,320 total): general academic interests/achievements. *Special achievements/activities:* 4 awards ($10,000 total): community service, leadership. *Special characteristics:* 62 awards ($227,326 total): children and siblings of alumni, children of faculty/staff, parents of current students, public servants, siblings of current students, spouses of current students, twins. *Tuition waivers:* Full or partial for employees or children of employees.

LOANS *Student loans:* $3,641,128 (87% need-based, 13% non-need-based). 45% of past graduating class borrowed through all loan programs. *Average indebtedness per student:* $23,124. *Average need-based loan:* Freshmen: $2936. Undergraduates: $3747. *Parent loans:* $913,504 (86% need-based, 14% non-need-based). *Programs:* Federal Direct (Subsidized and Unsubsidized Stafford, PLUS), Perkins, state.

WORK-STUDY *Federal work-study:* 93 jobs averaging $2244. *State or other work-study/employment:* Total amount: $40,823 (83% need-based, 17% non-need-based). 17 part-time jobs averaging $2401.

APPLYING FOR FINANCIAL AID *Required financial aid forms:* FAFSA, state aid form. *Financial aid deadline (priority):* 2/25. *Notification date:* Continuous beginning 3/15. Students must reply by 5/1 or within 2 weeks of notification.

CONTACT Ms. Amy Thompson, Director of Financial Aid, St. Joseph's College, New York, 245 Clinton Avenue, Brooklyn, NY 11205-3688, 718-940-5700. *Fax:* 718-636-6827. *E-mail:* financialaid.bk@sjcny.edu.
Website: http://www.sjcny.edu/.

SAINT JOSEPH'S COLLEGE OF MAINE
Standish, ME

CONTACT Office of Financial Aid, Saint Joseph's College of Maine, 278 Whites Bridge Road, Standish, ME 04084-5263, 800-752-1266 or toll-free 800-338-7057. *Fax:* 207-893-6699. *E-mail:* finaid@sjcme.edu.
Website: http://www.sjcme.edu/.

SAINT JOSEPH SEMINARY COLLEGE
Saint Benedict, LA

ABOUT THE INSTITUTION Independent Roman Catholic, men only. 1 undergraduate major.

GIFT AID (NEED-BASED) *Scholarships, grants, and awards:* Federal Pell, state, private, college/university gift aid from institutional funds.

LOANS *Programs:* Federal Direct (Subsidized and Unsubsidized Stafford, PLUS).

APPLYING FOR FINANCIAL AID *Required financial aid form:* FAFSA.

CONTACT Katie F. Plude, Director of Student Financial Aid, Saint Joseph Seminary College, 75376 River Road, Saint Benedict, LA 70457, 985-867-2248. *Fax:* 985-867-2270. *E-mail:* kplude@sjasc.edu.
Website: http://www.sjasc.edu/.

SAINT JOSEPH'S UNIVERSITY
Philadelphia, PA

Tuition & fees: $43,020	Average undergraduate aid package: $27,253

ABOUT THE INSTITUTION Independent Roman Catholic (Jesuit), coed. *Awards:* certificates, associate, bachelor's, master's, and doctoral degrees. 70 undergraduate majors. *Total enrollment:* 8,415. Undergraduates: 5,377. Freshmen: 1,271. Federal methodology is used as a basis for awarding need-based institutional aid.

UNDERGRADUATE EXPENSES for 2016–2017 *Application fee:* $50. *Comprehensive fee:* $57,544 includes full-time tuition ($42,840), mandatory fees ($180), and room and board ($14,524). *College room only:* $9240. Full-time tuition and fees vary according to course load. Room and board charges vary according to board plan and housing facility. *Part-time tuition:* $573 per credit. Part-time tuition and fees vary according to course load.

FRESHMAN FINANCIAL AID (Fall 2016, est.) 1,068 applied for aid; of those 78% were deemed to have need. 100% of freshmen with need received aid; of those 23% had need fully met. *Average percent of need met:* 79% (excluding resources awarded to replace EFC). *Average financial aid package:* $30,163 (excluding resources awarded to replace EFC). 28% of all full-time freshmen had no need and received non-need-based gift aid.

UNDERGRADUATE FINANCIAL AID (Fall 2016, est.) 3,404 applied for aid; of those 82% were deemed to have need. 100% of undergraduates with need received aid; of those 23% had need fully met. *Average percent of need met:* 72% (excluding resources awarded to replace EFC). *Average financial aid package:* $27,253 (excluding resources awarded to replace EFC). 32% of all full-time undergraduates had no need and received non-need-based gift aid.

GIFT AID (NEED-BASED) *Total amount:* $64,019,250 (5% federal, 3% state, 91% institutional, 1% external sources). *Receiving aid:* Freshmen: 64% (807); all full-time undergraduates: 50% (2,577). *Average award:* Freshmen: $24,541; Undergraduates: $22,112. *Scholarships, grants, and awards:* Federal Pell, FSEOG, state, private, college/university gift aid from institutional funds, United Negro College Fund.

GIFT AID (NON-NEED-BASED) *Total amount:* $26,243,445 (97% institutional, 3% external sources). *Receiving aid:* Freshmen: 9% (118). Undergraduates: 7% (373). *Average award:* Freshmen: $15,393. Undergraduates: $12,083. *Scholarships, grants, and awards by category: Academic interests/achievement:* biological sciences, computer science, general academic interests/achievements, mathematics, physical sciences, premedicine. *Creative arts/performance:* debating, general creative arts/performance, theater/drama. *Special achievements/activities:* community service, general special achievements/activities. *Special characteristics:* children and siblings of alumni, children of faculty/staff, members of minority groups, siblings of current students, veterans, veterans' children. *Tuition waivers:* Full or partial for employees or children of employees. *ROTC:* Army cooperative, Naval cooperative, Air Force.

LOANS *Student loans:* $56,091,158 (68% need-based, 32% non-need-based). *Average need-based loan:* Freshmen: $3312. Undergraduates: $4317. *Parent loans:* $15,800,408 (40% need-based, 60% non-need-based). *Programs:* Federal Direct (Subsidized and Unsubsidized Stafford, PLUS).

WORK-STUDY *Federal work-study:* Total amount: $2,037,543; jobs available.

ATHLETIC AWARDS Total amount: $7,276,849 (39% need-based, 61% non-need-based).

APPLYING FOR FINANCIAL AID *Required financial aid form:* FAFSA. *Financial aid deadline (priority):* 2/15. *Notification date:* Continuous beginning 3/31. Students must reply by 5/1.

CONTACT Susan M. Wendling, Interim Director of Financial Aid, Saint Joseph's University, 5600 City Avenue, Philadelphia, PA 19131-1395, 610-660-2000 or toll-free 888-BE-A-HAWK (in-state), 800-BE-A-HAWK (out-of-state). *Fax:* 610-660-1342. *E-mail:* hawkcentral@sju.edu. *Website:* http://www.sju.edu/.

SAINT KATHERINE COLLEGE
San Marcos, CA

CONTACT Financial Aid Office, Saint Katherine College, 1637 Capalina Road, San Marcos, CA 92069, 760-471-1316.
Website: http://www.stkath.org/.

ST. LAWRENCE UNIVERSITY
Canton, NY

Tuition & fees: $51,200	Average undergraduate aid package: $41,517

ABOUT THE INSTITUTION Independent, coed. *Awards:* certificates, bachelor's, and master's degrees. 38 undergraduate majors. *Total enrollment:* 2,534. Undergraduates: 2,435. Freshmen: 679. Both federal and institutional methodology are used as a basis for awarding need-based institutional aid.

UNDERGRADUATE EXPENSES for 2016–2017 *Application fee:* $60. *Comprehensive fee:* $64,390 includes full-time tuition ($50,830), mandatory fees ($370), and room and board ($13,190). *College room only:* $7104. Room and board charges vary according to board plan. *Part-time tuition:* $1765 per credit hour. *Payment plan:* Tuition prepayment.

FRESHMAN FINANCIAL AID (Fall 2016, est.) 421 applied for aid; of those 89% were deemed to have need. 100% of freshmen with need received aid; of those 26% had need fully met. *Average percent of need met:* 85% (excluding resources awarded to replace EFC). *Average financial aid package:* $45,406 (excluding resources awarded to replace EFC). 32% of all full-time freshmen had no need and received non-need-based gift aid.

UNDERGRADUATE FINANCIAL AID (Fall 2016, est.) 1,719 applied for aid; of those 83% were deemed to have need. 100% of undergraduates with need received aid; of those 28% had need fully met. *Average percent of need met:* 84% (excluding resources awarded to replace EFC). *Average financial aid package:* $41,517 (excluding resources awarded to replace EFC). 34% of all full-time undergraduates had no need and received non-need-based gift aid.

GIFT AID (NEED-BASED) *Total amount:* $47,377,368 (5% federal, 3% state, 92% institutional). *Receiving aid:* Freshmen: 66% (371); all full-time undergraduates: 61% (1,431). *Average award:* Freshmen: $35,470; Undergraduates: $34,115. *Scholarships, grants, and awards:* Federal Pell, FSEOG, state, private, college/university gift aid from institutional funds.

GIFT AID (NON-NEED-BASED) *Total amount:* $20,385,421 (90% institutional, 10% external sources). *Receiving aid:* Freshmen: 49% (275). Undergraduates: 43% (999). *Average award:* Freshmen: $17,494. Undergraduates: $19,174. *Scholarships, grants, and awards by category:* Academic interests/achievement: general academic interests/achievements. *Special achievements/activities:* community service, leadership. *Special characteristics:* children and siblings of alumni, siblings of current students, veterans' children. *Tuition waivers:* Full or partial for employees or children of employees. *ROTC:* Army cooperative, Air Force cooperative.

LOANS *Student loans:* $11,445,481 (40% need-based, 60% non-need-based). 58% of past graduating class borrowed through all loan programs. *Average indebtedness per student:* $37,919. *Average need-based loan:* Freshmen: $3411. Undergraduates: $4625. *Parent loans:* $4,209,553 (100% non-need-based). *Programs:* Federal Direct (Subsidized and Unsubsidized Stafford, PLUS), Perkins, college/university.

WORK-STUDY *Federal work-study:* Total amount: $1,280,670; 811 jobs averaging $1579. *State or other work-study/employment:* Total amount: $511,278 (100% non-need-based). 318 part-time jobs averaging $1608.

ATHLETIC AWARDS Total amount: $2,236,336 (100% non-need-based).

APPLYING FOR FINANCIAL AID *Required financial aid forms:* FAFSA, noncustodial (divorced/separated) parent's statement. *Financial aid deadline:* 2/1 (priority: 2/1). *Notification date:* 3/20. Students must reply by 5/1 or within 2 weeks of notification.

CONTACT Mrs. Patricia J.B. Farmer, Director of Financial Aid, St. Lawrence University, Payson Hall, 23 Romoda Drive, Canton, NY 13617-1455, 315-229-5265 or toll-free 800-285-1856. *Fax:* 315-229-7418. *E-mail:* pfarmer@stlawu.edu. *Website:* http://www.stlawu.edu/.

SAINT LEO UNIVERSITY
Saint Leo, FL

Tuition & fees: $21,970	Average undergraduate aid package: $20,298

ABOUT THE INSTITUTION Independent Roman Catholic, coed. *Awards:* certificates, associate, bachelor's, master's, and doctoral degrees. 34 undergraduate majors. *Total enrollment:* 5,898. Undergraduates: 2,264. Freshmen: 610. Federal methodology is used as a basis for awarding need-based institutional aid.

UNDERGRADUATE EXPENSES for 2017–2018 *Application fee:* $40. *Comprehensive fee:* $32,540 includes full-time tuition ($21,600), mandatory fees ($370), and room and board ($10,570). *College room only:* $5620. Room and board charges vary according to board plan and housing facility.

FRESHMAN FINANCIAL AID (Fall 2016, est.) 514 applied for aid; of those 87% were deemed to have need. 100% of freshmen with need received aid; of those 13% had need fully met. *Average percent of need met:* 71% (excluding resources awarded to replace EFC). *Average financial aid package:* $20,841 (excluding resources awarded to replace EFC). 26% of all full-time freshmen had no need and received non-need-based gift aid.

UNDERGRADUATE FINANCIAL AID (Fall 2016, est.) 1,804 applied for aid; of those 86% were deemed to have need. 100% of undergraduates with need received aid; of those 16% had need fully met. *Average percent of need met:* 70% (excluding resources awarded to replace EFC). *Average financial aid package:* $20,298 (excluding resources awarded to replace EFC). 26% of all full-time undergraduates had no need and received non-need-based gift aid.

GIFT AID (NEED-BASED) *Total amount:* $22,813,285 (22% federal, 18% state, 58% institutional, 2% external sources). *Receiving aid:* Freshmen: 73% (445); all full-time undergraduates: 71% (1,555). *Average award:* Freshmen: $16,208; Undergraduates: $15,376. *Scholarships, grants, and awards:* Federal Pell, FSEOG, state, private, college/university gift aid from institutional funds, United Negro College Fund.

GIFT AID (NON-NEED-BASED) *Total amount:* $5,315,080 (17% state, 80% institutional, 3% external sources). *Receiving aid:* Freshmen: 4% (26). Undergraduates: 5% (109). *Average award:* Freshmen: $8586. Undergraduates: $7073. *Scholarships, grants, and awards by category:* Academic interests/achievement: 2,603 awards ($3,435,061 total): general academic interests/achievements. *Special characteristics:* 67 awards ($588,081 total): children of faculty/staff, general special characteristics, local/state students, veterans' children. *Tuition waivers:* Full or partial for employees or children of employees. *ROTC:* Army, Air Force.

LOANS *Student loans:* $13,703,281 (77% need-based, 23% non-need-based). 65% of past graduating class borrowed through all loan programs. *Average indebtedness per student:* $28,542. *Average need-based loan:* Freshmen: $3378. Undergraduates: $4088. *Parent loans:* $4,392,097 (77% need-based, 23% non-need-based). *Programs:* Federal Direct (Subsidized and Unsubsidized Stafford, PLUS).

WORK-STUDY *Federal work-study:* Total amount: $1,440,477; 334 jobs averaging $4313. *State or other work-study/employment:* Total amount: $23,417 (100% need-based). 6 part-time jobs averaging $3903.

ATHLETIC AWARDS Total amount: $3,086,830 (37% need-based, 63% non-need-based).

APPLYING FOR FINANCIAL AID *Required financial aid form:* FAFSA. *Financial aid deadline (priority):* 3/1. *Notification date:* Continuous beginning 1/1.

CONTACT Ms. Melinda Clark, Associate Vice President of Financial Aid, Saint Leo University, PO Box 6665, MC 2228, Saint Leo, FL 33574-6665, 800-240-7658 or toll-free 800-334-5532. *Fax:* 866-708-7770. *E-mail:* finaid@saintleo.edu. *Website:* http://www.saintleo.edu/.

SAINT LOUIS CHRISTIAN COLLEGE
Florissant, MO

CONTACT Mrs. Catherine Wilhoit, Director of Financial Aid, Saint Louis Christian College, 1360 Grandview Drive, Florissant, MO 63033-6499, 314-837-6777 Ext. 1101 or toll-free 800-887-SLCC. *Fax:* 314-837-8291.
Website: http://www.stlchristian.edu/.

ST. LOUIS COLLEGE OF PHARMACY
St. Louis, MO

Tuition & fees: $28,620	Average undergraduate aid package: $16,526

ABOUT THE INSTITUTION Independent, coed. *Awards:* bachelor's and doctoral degrees. 2 undergraduate majors. *Total enrollment:* 1,384. Undergraduates: 539. Freshmen: 120. Federal methodology is used as a basis for awarding need-based institutional aid.

UNDERGRADUATE EXPENSES for 2016–2017 *Application fee:* $55. *Comprehensive fee:* $38,711 includes full-time tuition ($27,400), mandatory fees ($1220), and room and board ($10,091). *College room only:* $5880. Full-time tuition and fees vary according to student level. Room and board charges vary according to board plan and housing facility. *Part-time tuition:* $914 per credit hour. *Part-time fees:* $1220 per year.

FRESHMAN FINANCIAL AID (Fall 2015) 165 applied for aid; of those 89% were deemed to have need. 100% of freshmen with need received aid; of those 16% had need fully met. *Average percent of need met:* 63% (excluding resources awarded to replace EFC). *Average financial aid package:* $20,446 (excluding resources awarded to replace EFC). 21% of all full-time freshmen had no need and received non-need-based gift aid.

UNDERGRADUATE FINANCIAL AID (Fall 2015) 587 applied for aid; of those 91% were deemed to have need. 99% of undergraduates with need received aid; of those 9% had need fully met. *Average percent of need met:* 48% (excluding resources awarded to replace EFC). *Average financial aid package:* $16,526 (excluding resources awarded to replace EFC). 18% of all full-time undergraduates had no need and received non-need-based gift aid.

GIFT AID (NEED-BASED) *Total amount:* $5,839,425 (16% federal, 5% state, 73% institutional, 6% external sources). *Receiving aid:* Freshmen: 77% (147); all full-time undergraduates: 71% (489). *Average award:* Freshmen: $16,388; Undergraduates: $12,168. *Scholarships, grants, and awards:* Federal Pell, FSEOG, state, private, college/university gift aid from institutional funds.

GIFT AID (NON-NEED-BASED) *Total amount:* $1,499,573 (1% state, 87% institutional, 12% external sources). *Receiving aid:* Freshmen: 10% (19). Undergraduates: 4% (31). *Average award:* Freshmen: $12,672. Undergraduates: $9403. *Scholarships, grants, and awards by category: Academic interests/achievement:* 611 awards ($5,762,909 total): general academic interests/achievements. *Special achievements/activities:* 31 awards ($118,000 total): community service, general special achievements/activities, leadership. *Special characteristics:* children of faculty/staff. *Tuition waivers:* Full or partial for employees or children of employees. *ROTC:* Army cooperative, Naval cooperative, Air Force cooperative.

LOANS *Student loans:* $7,278,799 (80% need-based, 20% non-need-based). 84% of past graduating class borrowed through all loan programs. *Average indebtedness per student:* $112,161. *Average need-based loan:* Freshmen: $5174. Undergraduates: $5789. *Parent loans:* $3,221,884 (58% need-based, 42% non-need-based). *Programs:* Federal Direct (Subsidized and Unsubsidized Stafford, PLUS), Perkins, Health Professions Student Loans (HPSL).

WORK-STUDY *Federal work-study:* 138 jobs averaging $854. *State or other work-study/employment:* Total amount: $4500 (44% need-based, 56% non-need-based). Part-time jobs available.

ATHLETIC AWARDS Total amount: $176,277 (82% need-based, 18% non-need-based).

APPLYING FOR FINANCIAL AID *Required financial aid form:* FAFSA. *Financial aid deadline (priority):* 3/15. *Notification date:* Continuous beginning 3/15. Students must reply within 2 weeks of notification.

CONTACT Mr. Dan Stiffler, Director of Financial Aid, St. Louis College of Pharmacy, 4588 Parkview Place, St. Louis, MO 63110, 314-367-8700 Ext. 4001 or toll-free 800-278-5267. *Fax:* 314-446-8310. *E-mail:* financialaid@stlcop.edu. *Website:* http://www.stlcop.edu/.

SAINT LOUIS UNIVERSITY
St. Louis, MO

Tuition & fees: $40,726	Average undergraduate aid package: $26,841

ABOUT THE INSTITUTION Independent Roman Catholic (Jesuit), coed. *Awards:* certificates, bachelor's, master's, and doctoral degrees. 84 undergraduate majors. *Total enrollment:* 12,280. Undergraduates: 7,454. Freshmen: 1,559. Federal methodology is used as a basis for awarding need-based institutional aid.

UNDERGRADUATE EXPENSES for 2016–2017 *Comprehensive fee:* $51,366 includes full-time tuition ($40,100), mandatory fees ($626), and room and board ($10,640). *College room only:* $5974. Full-time tuition and fees vary according to course level, course load, degree level, location, program, and reciprocity agreements. Room and board charges vary according to board plan, housing facility, and location. *Part-time tuition:* $1400 per credit hour. *Part-time fees:* $197.50 per term. Part-time tuition and fees vary according to course level, course load, degree level, location, program, and reciprocity agreements.

FRESHMAN FINANCIAL AID (Fall 2015) 1,341 applied for aid; of those 81% were deemed to have need. 100% of freshmen with need received aid; of those 29% had need fully met. *Average percent of need met:* 78% (excluding resources awarded to replace EFC). *Average financial aid package:* $29,211 (excluding resources awarded to replace EFC). 29% of all full-time freshmen had no need and received non-need-based gift aid.

UNDERGRADUATE FINANCIAL AID (Fall 2015) 4,768 applied for aid; of those 86% were deemed to have need. 100% of undergraduates with need received aid; of those 23% had need fully met. *Average percent of need met:* 72% (excluding resources awarded to replace EFC). *Average financial aid package:* $26,841 (excluding resources awarded to replace EFC). 33% of all full-time undergraduates had no need and received non-need-based gift aid.

GIFT AID (NEED-BASED) *Total amount:* $90,539,196 (9% federal, 2% state, 86% institutional, 3% external sources). *Receiving aid:* Freshmen: 64% (1,028); all full-time undergraduates: 52% (3,875). *Average award:* Freshmen: $24,456; Undergraduates: $22,446. *Scholarships, grants, and awards:* Federal Pell, FSEOG, state, private, college/university gift aid from institutional funds, Federal Nursing.

GIFT AID (NON-NEED-BASED) *Total amount:* $40,597,073 (2% federal, 2% state, 73% institutional, 23% external sources). *Receiving aid:* Freshmen: 12% (192). Undergraduates: 7% (524). *Average award:* Freshmen: $17,750. Undergraduates: $16,283. *Scholarships, grants, and awards by category: Academic interests/achievement:* 5,669 awards ($80,739,908 total): area/ethnic studies, biological sciences, business, communication, computer science, education, engineering/technologies, English, foreign languages, general academic interests/achievements, home economics, humanities, international studies, mathematics, military science, physical sciences, premedicine, religion/biblical studies, social sciences. *Creative arts/performance:* 134 awards ($245,922 total): art/fine arts, music, performing arts, theater/drama. *Special achievements/activities:* 387 awards ($6,211,860 total): cheerleading/drum major, community service, general special achievements/activities, leadership, memberships, religious involvement. *Special characteristics:* 1,201 awards ($18,584,801 total): children of faculty/staff, first-generation college students, general special characteristics, international students, members of minority groups, previous college experience, religious affiliation, siblings of current students, spouses of current students, veterans. *Tuition waivers:* Full or partial for children of alumni, employees or children of employees. *ROTC:* Army cooperative, Air Force.

LOANS *Student loans:* $40,495,802 (37% need-based, 63% non-need-based). 58% of past graduating class borrowed through all loan programs. *Average indebtedness per student:* $33,299. *Average need-based loan:* Freshmen: $3379. Undergraduates: $4793. *Parent loans:* $13,719,742 (100% non-need-based). *Programs:* Federal Direct (Subsidized and Unsubsidized Stafford, PLUS), Federal Nursing, state, college/university.

WORK-STUDY *Federal work-study:* 623 jobs averaging $1794. *State or other work-study/employment:* Total amount: $359,553 (100% non-need-based). 203 part-time jobs averaging $1771.

ATHLETIC AWARDS Total amount: $5,471,036 (30% need-based, 70% non-need-based).

APPLYING FOR FINANCIAL AID *Required financial aid form:* FAFSA. *Financial aid deadline (priority):* 2/1. *Notification date:* Continuous beginning 2/1. Students must reply by 5/1 or within 4 weeks of notification.

CONTACT Cari S. Wickliffe, Director of Student Financial Services, Saint Louis University, One Grand Boulevard, DuBourg Hall, Room 121, St. Louis, MO 63103, 314-977-2350 or toll-free 800-758-3678. *Fax:* 314-977-3437. *E-mail:* sfs@slu.edu. *Website:* http://www.slu.edu/.

SAINT LUKE'S COLLEGE OF HEALTH SCIENCES
Kansas City, MO

ABOUT THE INSTITUTION Independent Episcopal, coed, primarily women. 1 undergraduate major.

GIFT AID (NEED-BASED) *Scholarships, grants, and awards:* Federal Pell, FSEOG, state, private, college/university gift aid from institutional funds.

LOANS *Programs:* Federal Direct (Subsidized and Unsubsidized Stafford, PLUS), Perkins, Federal Nursing, college/university.

WORK-STUDY *Federal work-study:* 8 jobs averaging $2200.

CONTACT Jennifer Wright, Financial Aid Administrator, Saint Luke's College of Health Sciences, 624 Westport Road, Kansas City, MO 64111, 816-932-6749. *Fax:* 816-932-6760. *E-mail:* jrwright@saintlukescollege.edu. *Website:* http://www.saintlukescollege.edu/.

SAINT MARTIN'S UNIVERSITY
Lacey, WA

Tuition & fees: $35,656	Average undergraduate aid package: $25,969

ABOUT THE INSTITUTION Independent Roman Catholic, coed. *Awards:* certificates, bachelor's, and master's degrees. 24 undergraduate majors. *Total enrollment:* 1,585. Undergraduates: 1,281. Freshmen: 241. Federal methodology is used as a basis for awarding need-based institutional aid.

UNDERGRADUATE EXPENSES for 2017–2018 *Comprehensive fee:* $46,686 includes full-time tuition ($35,250), mandatory fees ($406), and room and board ($11,030). *College room only:* $5410. Full-time tuition and fees vary according to course load, degree level, location, and program. Room and board charges vary according to board plan and housing facility. *Part-time tuition:* $1190 per credit. Part-time tuition and fees vary according to degree level, location, and program.

FRESHMAN FINANCIAL AID (Fall 2015) 137 applied for aid; of those 93% were deemed to have need. 100% of freshmen with need received aid; of those 28% had need fully met. *Average percent of need met:* 81% (excluding resources awarded to replace EFC). *Average financial aid package:* $25,672 (excluding resources awarded to replace EFC). 13% of all full-time freshmen had no need and received non-need-based gift aid.

UNDERGRADUATE FINANCIAL AID (Fall 2015) 808 applied for aid; of those 92% were deemed to have need. 99% of undergraduates with need received aid; of those 23% had need fully met. *Average percent of need met:* 76% (excluding resources awarded to replace EFC). *Average financial aid package:* $25,969 (excluding resources awarded to replace EFC). 14% of all full-time undergraduates had no need and received non-need-based gift aid.

GIFT AID (NEED-BASED) *Total amount:* $15,781,229 (13% federal, 15% state, 59% institutional, 13% external sources). *Receiving aid:* Freshmen: 85% (127); all full-time undergraduates: 81% (730). *Average award:* Freshmen: $23,613; Undergraduates: $22,929. *Scholarships, grants, and awards:* Federal Pell, FSEOG, state, private, college/university gift aid from institutional funds.

GIFT AID (NON-NEED-BASED) *Total amount:* $2,577,862 (2% state, 84% institutional, 14% external sources). *Receiving aid:* Freshmen: 22% (33). Undergraduates: 15% (137). *Average award:* Freshmen: $13,526. Undergraduates: $12,771. *Scholarships, grants, and awards by category:* Academic interests/achievement: business, education, engineering/technologies, general academic interests/achievements, international studies, premedicine. *Creative arts/performance:* music, theater/drama. *Special achievements/activities:* community service, general special achievements/activities, hobbies/interests, leadership, religious involvement.

Special characteristics: children and siblings of alumni, children of faculty/staff, ethnic background, general special characteristics, international students, local/state students, members of minority groups, out-of-state students, siblings of current students, veterans, veterans' children. *Tuition waivers:* Full or partial for children of alumni, employees or children of employees. *ROTC:* Army cooperative, Air Force cooperative.

LOANS *Student loans:* $5,919,697 (73% need-based, 27% non-need-based). 78% of past graduating class borrowed through all loan programs. *Average indebtedness per student:* $27,807. *Average need-based loan:* Freshmen: $3126. Undergraduates: $4191. *Parent loans:* $1,478,043 (38% need-based, 62% non-need-based). *Programs:* Federal Direct (Subsidized and Unsubsidized Stafford, PLUS), Perkins, state, alternative loans.

WORK-STUDY *Federal work-study:* 120 jobs averaging $1667. *State or other work-study/employment:* Total amount: $50,042 (100% need-based). 26 part-time jobs averaging $7110.

ATHLETIC AWARDS Total amount: $1,646,613 (57% need-based, 43% non-need-based).

APPLYING FOR FINANCIAL AID *Required financial aid form:* FAFSA. *Financial aid deadline (priority):* 1/15. *Notification date:* Continuous beginning 11/21. Students must reply within 3 weeks of notification.

CONTACT Mr. Michael Grosso, Director of Financial Aid, Saint Martin's University, 5000 Abbey Way SE, Lacey, WA 98503-7500, 360-438-4389 or toll-free 800-368-8803. *Fax:* 360-412-6190. *E-mail:* finaid@stmartin.edu. *Website:* http://www.stmartin.edu/.

SAINT MARY-OF-THE-WOODS COLLEGE
Saint Mary of the Woods, IN

Tuition & fees: $28,932	Average undergraduate aid package: $21,115

ABOUT THE INSTITUTION Independent Roman Catholic, coed, primarily women. *Awards:* certificates, associate, bachelor's, and master's degrees (also offers external degree program with significant enrollment not reflected in profile). 37 undergraduate majors. *Total enrollment:* 883. Undergraduates: 886. Freshmen: 80. Federal methodology is used as a basis for awarding need-based institutional aid.

UNDERGRADUATE EXPENSES for 2016–2017 *Comprehensive fee:* $39,632 includes full-time tuition ($28,932) and room and board ($10,700). *College room only:* $5350. Full-time tuition and fees vary according to student level. Room and board charges vary according to housing facility. *Part-time tuition:* $496 per credit hour. Part-time tuition and fees vary according to course load and student level. *Payment plan:* Guaranteed tuition.

FRESHMAN FINANCIAL AID (Fall 2016, est.) 77 applied for aid; of those 100% were deemed to have need. 100% of freshmen with need received aid. *Average financial aid package:* $25,188 (excluding resources awarded to replace EFC).

UNDERGRADUATE FINANCIAL AID (Fall 2016, est.) 398 applied for aid; of those 100% were deemed to have need. 100% of undergraduates with need received aid. *Average financial aid package:* $21,115 (excluding resources awarded to replace EFC).

GIFT AID (NEED-BASED) *Total amount:* $7,040,779 (18% federal, 17% state, 65% institutional). *Receiving aid:* Freshmen: 97% (77); all full-time undergraduates: 96% (392). *Average award:* Freshmen: $22,824; Undergraduates: $18,631. *Scholarships, grants, and awards:* Federal Pell, FSEOG, state, private, college/university gift aid from institutional funds.

GIFT AID (NON-NEED-BASED) *Total amount:* $8202 (100% external sources). *Scholarships, grants, and awards by category:* Academic interests/achievement: general academic interests/achievements. *Creative arts/performance:* applied art and design, art/fine arts, creative writing, dance, general creative arts/performance, journalism/publications, music, performing arts, theater/drama. *Special achievements/activities:* community service, general special achievements/activities, leadership, memberships, religious involvement. *Special characteristics:* adult students, children and siblings of alumni, children of current students, children of faculty/staff, ethnic background, first-generation college students, general special characteristics, international students, local/state students, members of minority groups, out-of-state students, parents of current students, religious affiliation, siblings of current students, spouses of current students. *Tuition waivers:* Full or partial for employees or children of employees.

LOANS *Student loans:* $2,642,540 (50% need-based, 50% non-need-based). *Average need-based loan:* Freshmen: $3072. Undergraduates: $3987. *Parent loans:* $564,314 (100% non-need-based). *Programs:* Federal Direct (Subsidized and Unsubsidized Stafford, PLUS), Perkins, college/university, private loans.

WORK-STUDY *Federal work-study:* Total amount: $2500; jobs available.

ATHLETIC AWARDS Total amount: $644,399 (100% need-based).

APPLYING FOR FINANCIAL AID *Required financial aid form:* FAFSA. *Financial aid deadline:* 3/10 (priority: 3/10). *Notification date:* Continuous beginning 3/1. Students must reply by 5/1.

CONTACT Ms. Darla Hopper, Director of Financial Aid, Saint Mary-of-the-Woods College, 226 Guerin Hall, Saint Mary-of-the-Woods, IN 47876, 812-535-5110 or toll-free 800-926-SMWC. *Fax:* 812-535-4900. *E-mail:* dhopper@smwc.edu. *Website:* http://www.smwc.edu/.

SAINT MARY'S COLLEGE
Notre Dame, IN

Tuition & fees: $40,800	Average undergraduate aid package: $33,468

ABOUT THE INSTITUTION Independent Roman Catholic, women only. *Awards:* bachelor's, master's, and doctoral degrees. 37 undergraduate majors. *Total enrollment:* 1,701. Undergraduates: 1,625. Freshmen: 427. Federal methodology is used as a basis for awarding need-based institutional aid.

UNDERGRADUATE EXPENSES for 2017–2018 *One-time required fee:* $150. *Comprehensive fee:* $52,900 includes full-time tuition ($39,980), mandatory fees ($820), and room and board ($12,100). *College room only:* $7500. Full-time tuition and fees vary according to course load. Room and board charges vary according to board plan and housing facility. *Part-time tuition:* $1500 per credit hour. Part-time tuition and fees vary according to course load.

FRESHMAN FINANCIAL AID (Fall 2016, est.) 382 applied for aid; of those 83% were deemed to have need. 100% of freshmen with need received aid; of those 22% had need fully met. *Average percent of need met:* 87% (excluding resources awarded to replace EFC). *Average financial aid package:* $33,250 (excluding resources awarded to replace EFC). 26% of all full-time freshmen had no need and received non-need-based gift aid.

UNDERGRADUATE FINANCIAL AID (Fall 2016, est.) 1,259 applied for aid; of those 86% were deemed to have need. 100% of undergraduates with need received aid; of those 22% had need fully met. *Average percent of need met:* 84% (excluding resources awarded to replace EFC). *Average financial aid package:* $33,468 (excluding resources awarded to replace EFC). 29% of all full-time undergraduates had no need and received non-need-based gift aid.

GIFT AID (NEED-BASED) *Total amount:* $27,755,677 (6% federal, 3% state, 89% institutional, 2% external sources). *Receiving aid:* Freshmen: 74% (316); all full-time undergraduates: 68% (1,081). *Average award:* Freshmen: $29,989; Undergraduates: $28,661. *Scholarships, grants, and awards:* Federal Pell, FSEOG, state, private, college/university gift aid from institutional funds.

GIFT AID (NON-NEED-BASED) *Total amount:* $7,310,621 (98% institutional, 2% external sources). *Receiving aid:* Freshmen: 70% (301). Undergraduates: 63% (993). *Average award:* Freshmen: $15,766. Undergraduates: $14,460. *Tuition waivers:* Full or partial for employees or children of employees. *ROTC:* Army cooperative, Naval cooperative, Air Force cooperative.

LOANS *Student loans:* $9,108,937 (66% need-based, 34% non-need-based). 68% of past graduating class borrowed through all loan programs. *Average indebtedness per student:* $31,036. *Average need-based loan:* Freshmen: $3287. Undergraduates: $4687. *Parent loans:* $3,771,461 (100% non-need-based). *Programs:* Federal Direct (Subsidized and Unsubsidized Stafford, PLUS), Perkins.

WORK-STUDY *Federal work-study:* Total amount: $533,650; jobs available. *State or other work-study/employment:* Part-time jobs available.

APPLYING FOR FINANCIAL AID *Required financial aid form:* FAFSA. *Financial aid deadline:* 3/1. *Notification date:* Continuous beginning 3/15. Students must reply within 3 weeks of notification.

CONTACT Kathleen M. Brown, Director of Financial Aid, Saint Mary's College, 141 Le Mans Hall, Notre Dame, IN 46556, 574-284-4557 or toll-free 800-551-7621. *Fax:* 574-284-4818. *E-mail:* kbrown@saintmarys.edu. *Website:* http://www.saintmarys.edu/.

SAINT MARY'S COLLEGE OF CALIFORNIA
Moraga, CA

ABOUT THE INSTITUTION Independent Roman Catholic, coed. *Awards:* bachelor's, master's, and doctoral degrees. 64 undergraduate majors. *Total enrollment:* 3,908. Undergraduates: 2,802. Entering class: 89.

GIFT AID (NEED-BASED) *Scholarships, grants, and awards:* Federal Pell, FSEOG, state, private, college/university gift aid from institutional funds.

GIFT AID (NON-NEED-BASED) *Scholarships, grants, and awards by category: Academic interests/achievement:* English, general academic interests/achievements, humanities, international studies, mathematics, physical sciences, religion/biblical studies. *Creative arts/performance:* cinema/film/broadcasting, dance, debating, music, performing arts, theater/drama. *Special achievements/activities:* leadership, memberships. *Special characteristics:* children and siblings of alumni, children of educators, children of faculty/staff, general special characteristics, relatives of clergy, veterans, veterans' children.

LOANS *Programs:* Federal Direct (Subsidized and Unsubsidized Stafford, PLUS), Perkins.

WORK-STUDY *Federal work-study:* jobs available.

APPLYING FOR FINANCIAL AID *Required financial aid form:* FAFSA.

CONTACT Priscilla Muha, Director of Financial Aid, Saint Mary's College of California, 1928 St. Mary's Road, PMB 4530, Moraga, CA 94575, 925-631-4370 or toll-free 800-800-4SMC. *Fax:* 925-376-2965. *E-mail:* finaid@stmarys-ca.edu. *Website:* http://www.stmarys-ca.edu/.

ST. MARY'S COLLEGE OF MARYLAND
St. Mary's City, MD

Tuition & fees (MD res): $14,192	Average undergraduate aid package: $12,632

ABOUT THE INSTITUTION State-supported, coed. *Awards:* bachelor's and master's degrees. 26 undergraduate majors. *Total enrollment:* 1,674. Undergraduates: 1,643. Freshmen: 334. Federal methodology is used as a basis for awarding need-based institutional aid.

UNDERGRADUATE EXPENSES for 2016–2017 *Application fee:* $50. *Tuition, state resident:* full-time $11,418; part-time $200 per credit hour. *Tuition, nonresident:* full-time $26,566; part-time $200 per credit hour. *Required fees:* full-time $2774. Full-time tuition and fees vary according to course load. Part-time tuition and fees vary according to course load. *College room and board:* $12,442; *Room only:* $7184. Room and board charges vary according to board plan and housing facility.

FRESHMAN FINANCIAL AID (Fall 2015) 327 applied for aid; of those 65% were deemed to have need. 99% of freshmen with need received aid; of those 7% had need fully met. *Average percent of need met:* 72% (excluding resources awarded to replace EFC). *Average financial aid package:* $13,772 (excluding resources awarded to replace EFC). 31% of all full-time freshmen had no need and received non-need-based gift aid.

UNDERGRADUATE FINANCIAL AID (Fall 2015) 1,202 applied for aid; of those 69% were deemed to have need. 98% of undergraduates with need received aid; of those 4% had need fully met. *Average percent of need met:* 67% (excluding resources awarded to replace EFC). *Average financial aid package:* $12,632 (excluding resources awarded to replace EFC). 23% of all full-time undergraduates had no need and received non-need-based gift aid.

GIFT AID (NEED-BASED) *Total amount:* $7,527,737 (18% federal, 19% state, 59% institutional, 4% external sources). *Receiving aid:* Freshmen: 48% (190); all full-time undergraduates: 35% (604). *Average award:* Freshmen: $10,408; Undergraduates: $9707. *Scholarships, grants, and awards:* Federal Pell, FSEOG, state, private, college/university gift aid from institutional funds.

GIFT AID (NON-NEED-BASED) *Total amount:* $1,726,928 (8% state, 85% institutional, 7% external sources). *Receiving aid:* Freshmen: 29% (116). Undergraduates: 29% (492). *Average award:* Freshmen: $3807. Undergraduates: $3717. *Scholarships, grants, and awards by category: Academic interests/achievement:* 778 awards ($2,860,281 total): education, general academic interests/achievements. *Special characteristics:* 9 awards ($76,668 total): children of faculty/staff.

Tuition waivers: Full or partial for employees or children of employees, senior citizens.
LOANS Student loans: $5,861,199 (74% need-based, 26% non-need-based). 53% of past graduating class borrowed through all loan programs. *Average indebtedness per student:* $24,213. *Average need-based loan:* Freshmen: $3222. Undergraduates: $4107. *Parent loans:* $4,950,939 (65% need-based, 35% non-need-based).
Programs: Federal Direct (Subsidized and Unsubsidized Stafford, PLUS), Perkins.
WORK-STUDY Federal work-study: 229 jobs averaging $960.
APPLYING FOR FINANCIAL AID Required financial aid form: FAFSA. *Financial aid deadline (priority):* 2/15. *Notification date:* Continuous beginning 1/15. Students must reply by 5/1.
CONTACT Ms. Nadine Hutton, Director of Financial Aid, St. Mary's College of Maryland, 18952 East Fisher Road, St. Mary's City, MD 20686-3001, 240-895-3000 or toll-free 800-492-7181. *Fax:* 240-895-4959. *E-mail:* nlhutton@smcm.edu.
Website: http://www.smcm.edu/.

ST. MARY'S UNIVERSITY
San Antonio, TX

Tuition & fees: N/R	Average undergraduate aid package: $24,223

ABOUT THE INSTITUTION Independent Roman Catholic, coed. *Awards:* bachelor's, master's, and doctoral degrees. 41 undergraduate majors. *Total enrollment:* 3,625. Undergraduates: 2,309. Freshmen: 593. Federal methodology is used as a basis for awarding need-based institutional aid.
FRESHMAN FINANCIAL AID (Fall 2015) 497 applied for aid; of those 92% were deemed to have need. 100% of freshmen with need received aid; of those 13% had need fully met. *Average percent of need met:* 75% (excluding resources awarded to replace EFC). *Average financial aid package:* $25,269 (excluding resources awarded to replace EFC). 17% of all full-time freshmen had no need and received non-need-based gift aid.
UNDERGRADUATE FINANCIAL AID (Fall 2015) 1,708 applied for aid; of those 93% were deemed to have need. 100% of undergraduates with need received aid; of those 13% had need fully met. *Average percent of need met:* 71% (excluding resources awarded to replace EFC). *Average financial aid package:* $24,223 (excluding resources awarded to replace EFC). 18% of all full-time undergraduates had no need and received non-need-based gift aid.
GIFT AID (NEED-BASED) Total amount: $28,748,948 (19% federal, 16% state, 63% institutional, 2% external sources). *Receiving aid:* Freshmen: 77% (455); all full-time undergraduates: 71% (1,556). *Average award:* Freshmen: $20,303; Undergraduates: $18,310. *Scholarships, grants, and awards:* Federal Pell, FSEOG, state, private, college/university gift aid from institutional funds.
GIFT AID (NON-NEED-BASED) Total amount: $7,921,420 (98% institutional, 2% external sources). *Receiving aid:* Freshmen: 7% (42). Undergraduates: 5% (112). *Average award:* Freshmen: $19,334. Undergraduates: $17,244. *Scholarships, grants, and awards by category: Academic interests/achievement:* 2,400 awards ($18,300,156 total): general academic interests/achievements, military science. *Creative arts/performance:* 60 awards ($195,175 total): music. *Special achievements/ activities:* 25 awards ($42,400 total): cheerleading/drum major. *Special characteristics:* 128 awards ($2,910,908 total): children of faculty/staff, veterans, veterans' children. *ROTC:* Army, Air Force cooperative.
LOANS Student loans: $14,325,684 (83% need-based, 17% non-need-based). 77% of past graduating class borrowed through all loan programs. *Average indebtedness per student:* $39,883. *Average need-based loan:* Freshmen: $3500. Undergraduates: $5016. *Parent loans:* $1,912,278 (63% need-based, 37% non-need-based).
Programs: Federal Direct (Subsidized and Unsubsidized Stafford, PLUS), state.
WORK-STUDY Federal work-study: 436 jobs averaging $2127. *State or other work-study/employment:* Total amount: $217,864 (21% need-based, 79% non-need-based). 48 part-time jobs averaging $2033.
ATHLETIC AWARDS Total amount: $2,469,002 (30% need-based, 70% non-need-based).
APPLYING FOR FINANCIAL AID Required financial aid form: FAFSA. *Financial aid deadline:* 6/1 (priority: 3/1). *Notification date:* Continuous beginning 10/1. Students must reply within 2 weeks of notification.

CONTACT Mr. David R. Krause, Director of Financial Assistance, St. Mary's University, One Camino Santa Maria, San Antonio, TX 78228-8541, 210-436-3141 or toll-free 800-367-7868. *Fax:* 210-431-2221. *E-mail:* dkrause@stmarytx.edu.
Website: http://www.stmarytx.edu/.

SAINT MARY'S UNIVERSITY OF MINNESOTA
Winona, MN

Tuition & fees: $33,560	Average undergraduate aid package: $25,847

ABOUT THE INSTITUTION Independent Roman Catholic, coed. *Awards:* certificates, diplomas, bachelor's, master's, and doctoral degrees. 54 undergraduate majors. *Total enrollment:* 5,640. Undergraduates: 1,590. Freshmen: 283. Federal methodology is used as a basis for awarding need-based institutional aid.
UNDERGRADUATE EXPENSES for 2017–2018 Application fee: $25. *Comprehensive fee:* $42,440 includes full-time tuition ($33,020), mandatory fees ($540), and room and board ($8880). *College room only:* $5000. Full-time tuition and fees vary according to course load and location. Room and board charges vary according to board plan and housing facility. *Part-time tuition:* $1110 per credit. Part-time tuition and fees vary according to course load and location.
FRESHMAN FINANCIAL AID (Fall 2016, est.) 276 applied for aid; of those 88% were deemed to have need. 85% of freshmen with need received aid; of those 27% had need fully met. *Average percent of need met:* 82% (excluding resources awarded to replace EFC). *Average financial aid package:* $26,439 (excluding resources awarded to replace EFC). 26% of all full-time freshmen had no need and received non-need-based gift aid.
UNDERGRADUATE FINANCIAL AID (Fall 2016, est.) 925 applied for aid; of those 89% were deemed to have need. 99% of undergraduates with need received aid; of those 23% had need fully met. *Average percent of need met:* 76% (excluding resources awarded to replace EFC). *Average financial aid package:* $25,847 (excluding resources awarded to replace EFC). 23% of all full-time undergraduates had no need and received non-need-based gift aid.
GIFT AID (NEED-BASED) Total amount: $20,995,573 (9% federal, 7% state, 82% institutional, 2% external sources). *Receiving aid:* Freshmen: 73% (206); all full-time undergraduates: 69% (799). *Average award:* Freshmen: $23,582; Undergraduates: $20,523. *Scholarships, grants, and awards:* Federal Pell, FSEOG, state, college/university gift aid from institutional funds.
GIFT AID (NON-NEED-BASED) Average award: Freshmen: $16,821. Undergraduates: $17,903. *Scholarships, grants, and awards by category: Academic interests/achievement:* 859 awards ($11,685,700 total): general academic interests/ achievements. *Creative arts/performance:* 121 awards ($269,750 total): art/fine arts, music, theater/drama. *Special achievements/activities:* 101 awards ($255,750 total): leadership. *Special characteristics:* 596 awards ($1,537,821 total): children and siblings of alumni, children of faculty/staff, ethnic background, international students, local/state students, members of minority groups. *Tuition waivers:* Full or partial for employees or children of employees. *ROTC:* Army cooperative.
LOANS Student loans: $8,783,752 (100% need-based). 80% of past graduating class borrowed through all loan programs. *Average indebtedness per student:* $39,196. *Average need-based loan:* Freshmen: $3675. Undergraduates: $4747. *Parent loans:* $1,664,455 (100% need-based). *Programs:* Federal Direct (Subsidized and Unsubsidized Stafford, PLUS), Perkins, state.
WORK-STUDY Federal work-study: Total amount: $270,318; 130 jobs averaging $1932. *State or other work-study/employment:* Total amount: $519,446 (100% need-based). 228 part-time jobs averaging $3784.
APPLYING FOR FINANCIAL AID Required financial aid form: FAFSA. *Financial aid deadline (priority):* 3/15. *Notification date:* Continuous beginning 2/1. Students must reply within 3 weeks of notification.
CONTACT Ms. Joy Rockwell, Associate Director of Financial Aid, Saint Mary's University of Minnesota, 700 Terrace Heights, #5, Winona, MN 55987-1399, 507-457-1472 or toll-free 800-635-5987. *Fax:* 507-457-6698. *E-mail:* jrockwel@smumn.edu.
Website: http://www.smumn.edu/.

SAINT MICHAEL'S COLLEGE
Colchester, VT

Tuition & fees: $41,975	Average undergraduate aid package: $30,235

ABOUT THE INSTITUTION Independent Roman Catholic, coed. *Awards:* certificates, bachelor's, and master's degrees. 39 undergraduate majors. *Total enrollment:* 2,226. Undergraduates: 1,902. Freshmen: 461. Federal methodology is used as a basis for awarding need-based institutional aid.

UNDERGRADUATE EXPENSES for 2016–2017 *Application fee:* $50. *Comprehensive fee:* $53,275 includes full-time tuition ($41,650), mandatory fees ($325), and room and board ($11,300). Full-time tuition and fees vary according to course load. Room and board charges vary according to board plan and housing facility. *Part-time tuition:* $1340 per credit hour. Part-time tuition and fees vary according to course load.

FRESHMAN FINANCIAL AID (Fall 2016, est.) 386 applied for aid; of those 85% were deemed to have need. 100% of freshmen with need received aid; of those 36% had need fully met. *Average percent of need met:* 83% (excluding resources awarded to replace EFC). *Average financial aid package:* $32,135 (excluding resources awarded to replace EFC). 27% of all full-time freshmen had no need and received non-need-based gift aid.

UNDERGRADUATE FINANCIAL AID (Fall 2016, est.) 1,369 applied for aid; of those 85% were deemed to have need. 100% of undergraduates with need received aid; of those 29% had need fully met. *Average percent of need met:* 77% (excluding resources awarded to replace EFC). *Average financial aid package:* $30,235 (excluding resources awarded to replace EFC). 35% of all full-time undergraduates had no need and received non-need-based gift aid.

GIFT AID (NEED-BASED) *Total amount:* $26,873,866 (6% federal, 1% state, 91% institutional, 2% external sources). *Receiving aid:* Freshmen: 72% (328); all full-time undergraduates: 63% (1,156). *Average award:* Freshmen: $24,168; Undergraduates: $24,498. *Scholarships, grants, and awards:* Federal Pell, FSEOG, state, private, college/university gift aid from institutional funds.

GIFT AID (NON-NEED-BASED) *Total amount:* $13,382,592 (98% institutional, 2% external sources). *Receiving aid:* Freshmen: 19% (85). Undergraduates: 13% (237). *Average award:* Freshmen: $17,100. Undergraduates: $17,355. *Scholarships, grants, and awards by category: Academic interests/achievement:* general academic interests/achievements, mathematics. *Creative arts/performance:* art/fine arts, performing arts, theater/drama. *Special characteristics:* members of minority groups, out-of-state students, siblings of current students, veterans, veterans' children. *Tuition waivers:* Full or partial for employees or children of employees. *ROTC:* Army cooperative, Air Force cooperative.

LOANS *Student loans:* $14,211,772 (58% need-based, 42% non-need-based). 72% of past graduating class borrowed through all loan programs. *Average indebtedness per student:* $38,226. *Average need-based loan:* Freshmen: $4965. Undergraduates: $5563. *Parent loans:* $3,579,751 (37% need-based, 63% non-need-based). *Programs:* Federal Direct (Subsidized and Unsubsidized Stafford, PLUS), Perkins.

WORK-STUDY *Federal work-study:* Total amount: $492,950; 250 jobs averaging $1750. *State or other work-study/employment:* Total amount: $569,350 (100% need-based). 280 part-time jobs averaging $1750.

ATHLETIC AWARDS Total amount: $1,077,380 (100% non-need-based).

APPLYING FOR FINANCIAL AID *Required financial aid form:* FAFSA. *Financial aid deadline (priority):* 2/1. *Notification date:* 4/1. Students must reply by 5/1 or within 2 weeks of notification.

CONTACT Daniel Couture, Director of Student Financial Services, Saint Michael's College, One Winooski Park, Colchester, VT 05439, 802-654-3243 or toll-free 800-762-8000. *Fax:* 802-654-2591. *E-mail:* finaid@smcvt.edu.
Website: http://www.smcvt.edu/.

ST. NORBERT COLLEGE
De Pere, WI

Tuition & fees: $36,593	Average undergraduate aid package: $25,511

ABOUT THE INSTITUTION Independent Roman Catholic, coed. *Awards:* bachelor's and master's degrees. 35 undergraduate majors. *Total enrollment:* 2,211.

Undergraduates: 2,102. Freshmen: 584. Federal methodology is used as a basis for awarding need-based institutional aid.

UNDERGRADUATE EXPENSES for 2017–2018 *Application fee:* $10. *Comprehensive fee:* $46,060 includes full-time tuition ($35,878), mandatory fees ($715), and room and board ($9467). *College room only:* $5077. Full-time tuition and fees vary according to course load. Room and board charges vary according to board plan and housing facility. *Part-time tuition:* $1121 per credit hour. Part-time tuition and fees vary according to course load.

FRESHMAN FINANCIAL AID (Fall 2015) 537 applied for aid; of those 86% were deemed to have need. 100% of freshmen with need received aid; of those 22% had need fully met. *Average percent of need met:* 82% (excluding resources awarded to replace EFC). *Average financial aid package:* $25,870 (excluding resources awarded to replace EFC). 18% of all full-time freshmen had no need and received non-need-based gift aid.

UNDERGRADUATE FINANCIAL AID (Fall 2015) 1,741 applied for aid; of those 88% were deemed to have need. 100% of undergraduates with need received aid; of those 25% had need fully met. *Average percent of need met:* 83% (excluding resources awarded to replace EFC). *Average financial aid package:* $25,511 (excluding resources awarded to replace EFC). 22% of all full-time undergraduates had no need and received non-need-based gift aid.

GIFT AID (NEED-BASED) *Total amount:* $30,703,857 (7% federal, 7% state, 81% institutional, 5% external sources). *Receiving aid:* Freshmen: 75% (449); all full-time undergraduates: 74% (1,494). *Average award:* Freshmen: $20,925; Undergraduates: $19,617. *Scholarships, grants, and awards:* Federal Pell, FSEOG, state, private, college/university gift aid from institutional funds.

GIFT AID (NON-NEED-BASED) *Total amount:* $6,389,425 (1% federal, 86% institutional, 13% external sources). *Receiving aid:* Freshmen: 2% (10). Undergraduates: 2% (50). *Average award:* Freshmen: $14,163. Undergraduates: $12,234. *Scholarships, grants, and awards by category: Academic interests/achievement:* general academic interests/achievements. *Creative arts/performance:* art/fine arts, music, theater/drama. *Special characteristics:* children of faculty/staff, international students. *Tuition waivers:* Full or partial for employees or children of employees. *ROTC:* Army.

LOANS *Student loans:* $15,782,310 (96% need-based, 4% non-need-based). 74% of past graduating class borrowed through all loan programs. *Average indebtedness per student:* $33,948. *Average need-based loan:* Freshmen: $4005. Undergraduates: $4938. *Parent loans:* $3,658,454 (92% need-based, 8% non-need-based). *Programs:* Federal Direct (Subsidized and Unsubsidized Stafford, PLUS), Perkins, state, college/university.

WORK-STUDY *Federal work-study:* 377 jobs averaging $1227. *State or other work-study/employment:* Total amount: $762,712 (67% need-based, 33% non-need-based). Part-time jobs available.

APPLYING FOR FINANCIAL AID *Required financial aid form:* FAFSA. *Financial aid deadline (priority):* 1/1. *Notification date:* Continuous beginning 1/1. Students must reply within 2 weeks of notification.

CONTACT Ms. Jessica Rafeld, Director of Financial Aid, St. Norbert College, 100 Grant Street, De Pere, WI 54115-2099, 920-403-3071 or toll-free 800-236-4878. *Fax:* 920-403-3062. *E-mail:* financialaid@snc.edu.
Website: http://www.snc.edu/.

ST. OLAF COLLEGE
Northfield, MN

Tuition & fees: $46,000	Average undergraduate aid package: $37,224

ABOUT THE INSTITUTION Independent Lutheran, coed. *Awards:* bachelor's degrees. 44 undergraduate majors. *Total enrollment:* 3,040. Undergraduates: 3,040. Freshmen: 824. Both federal and institutional methodology are used as a basis for awarding need-based institutional aid.

UNDERGRADUATE EXPENSES for 2017–2018 *Comprehensive fee:* $56,430 includes full-time tuition ($46,000) and room and board ($10,430). *College room only:* $5000. Room and board charges vary according to board plan. *Part-time tuition:* $5750 per course. Part-time tuition and fees vary according to course load.

FRESHMAN FINANCIAL AID (Fall 2016, est.) 669 applied for aid; of those 85% were deemed to have need. 100% of freshmen with need received aid; of those 97% had need fully met. *Average percent of need met:* 99% (excluding resources awarded to replace EFC). *Average financial aid package:* $38,733 (excluding resources awarded to replace EFC). 24% of all full-time freshmen had no need and received non-need-based gift aid.

UNDERGRADUATE FINANCIAL AID (Fall 2016, est.) 2,078 applied for aid; of those 92% were deemed to have need. 100% of undergraduates with need received aid; of those 89% had need fully met. *Average percent of need met:* 98% (excluding resources awarded to replace EFC). *Average financial aid package:* $37,224 (excluding resources awarded to replace EFC). 23% of all full-time undergraduates had no need and received non-need-based gift aid.

GIFT AID (NEED-BASED) *Total amount:* $63,499,351 (4% federal, 3% state, 93% institutional). *Receiving aid:* Freshmen: 69% (569); all full-time undergraduates: 64% (1,907). *Average award:* Freshmen: $32,991; Undergraduates: $30,463. *Scholarships, grants, and awards:* Federal Pell, FSEOG, state, private, college/university gift aid from institutional funds.

GIFT AID (NON-NEED-BASED) *Total amount:* $12,577,789 (79% institutional, 21% external sources). *Receiving aid:* Freshmen: 37% (302). Undergraduates: 24% (708). *Average award:* Freshmen: $15,496. Undergraduates: $14,942. *Scholarships, grants, and awards by category:* Academic interests/achievement: 584 awards ($8,049,703 total): general academic interests/achievements. *Creative arts/performance:* 119 awards ($829,574 total): art/fine arts, dance, music, theater/drama. *Special achievements/activities:* 91 awards ($457,312 total): community service, religious involvement. *Tuition waivers:* Full or partial for employees or children of employees, senior citizens.

LOANS *Student loans:* $16,558,182 (41% need-based, 59% non-need-based). 60% of past graduating class borrowed through all loan programs. *Average indebtedness per student:* $27,945. *Average need-based loan:* Freshmen: $2254. Undergraduates: $3548. *Parent loans:* $2,612,869 (100% non-need-based). *Programs:* Federal Direct (Subsidized and Unsubsidized Stafford, PLUS), Perkins, Federal Nursing, state, college/university.

WORK-STUDY *Federal work-study:* Total amount: $1,248,686; 440 jobs averaging $2161. *State or other work-study/employment:* Total amount: $3,476,669 (90% need-based, 10% non-need-based). 1,662 part-time jobs averaging $1976.

APPLYING FOR FINANCIAL AID *Required financial aid forms:* FAFSA, CSS Financial Aid PROFILE, noncustodial (divorced/separated) parent's statement. *Financial aid deadline:* 3/1 (priority: 2/1). *Notification date:* 4/1. Students must reply by 5/1.

CONTACT Ms. Carly Eichhorst, Director of Student Financial Aid, St. Olaf College, 1520 Saint Olaf Avenue, Northfield, MN 55057-1098, 507-786-3019 or toll-free 800-800-3025. *Fax:* 507-786-6688. *E-mail:* eichho1@stolaf.edu. *Website:* http://www.stolaf.edu/.

ST. PETERSBURG COLLEGE
St. Petersburg, FL

Comprehensive fee: $14,214 **Average undergraduate aid package: N/A**

ABOUT THE INSTITUTION State and locally supported, coed. *Awards:* certificates, diplomas, associate, and bachelor's degrees. 48 undergraduate majors. *Total enrollment:* 29,835. Undergraduates: 29,835. Freshmen: 2,827. Federal methodology is used as a basis for awarding need-based institutional aid.

UNDERGRADUATE EXPENSES for 2017–2018 *Application fee:* $30. *Comprehensive fee:* $14,214 includes mandatory fees ($957).

GIFT AID (NEED-BASED) *Scholarships, grants, and awards:* Federal Pell, FSEOG, state, college/university gift aid from institutional funds, Federal Nursing.

GIFT AID (NON-NEED-BASED) *ROTC:* Army cooperative.

LOANS *Programs:* Federal Direct (Subsidized and Unsubsidized Stafford, PLUS), college/university.

WORK-STUDY Federal work-study jobs available.

APPLYING FOR FINANCIAL AID *Required financial aid form:* FAFSA. *Financial aid deadline (priority):* 5/1. *Notification date:* Continuous.

CONTACT Office of Financial Aid, St. Petersburg College, 6605 Fifth Avenue N, St. Petersburg, FL 33710, 727-341-7907. *Website:* http://www.spcollege.edu/.

SAINT PETER'S UNIVERSITY
Jersey City, NJ

Tuition & fees: N/R **Average undergraduate aid package: $31,003**

ABOUT THE INSTITUTION Independent Roman Catholic (Jesuit), coed. *Awards:* certificates, associate, bachelor's, master's, and doctoral degrees. 45 undergraduate majors. *Total enrollment:* 3,544. Undergraduates: 2,707. Freshmen: 626. Federal methodology is used as a basis for awarding need-based institutional aid.

FRESHMAN FINANCIAL AID (Fall 2016, est.) 625 applied for aid; of those 95% were deemed to have need. 100% of freshmen with need received aid; of those 11% had need fully met. *Average percent of need met:* 84% (excluding resources awarded to replace EFC). *Average financial aid package:* $33,205 (excluding resources awarded to replace EFC). 5% of all full-time freshmen had no need and received non-need-based gift aid.

UNDERGRADUATE FINANCIAL AID (Fall 2016, est.) 2,357 applied for aid; of those 92% were deemed to have need. 100% of undergraduates with need received aid; of those 16% had need fully met. *Average percent of need met:* 80% (excluding resources awarded to replace EFC). *Average financial aid package:* $31,003 (excluding resources awarded to replace EFC). 8% of all full-time undergraduates had no need and received non-need-based gift aid.

GIFT AID (NEED-BASED) *Total amount:* $60,471,356 (14% federal, 24% state, 62% institutional). *Receiving aid:* Freshmen: 94% (591); all full-time undergraduates: 90% (2,144). *Average award:* Freshmen: $31,066; Undergraduates: $27,665. *Scholarships, grants, and awards:* Federal Pell, FSEOG, state, private, college/university gift aid from institutional funds, Federal Nursing.

GIFT AID (NON-NEED-BASED) *Total amount:* $5,136,415 (1% federal, 99% institutional). *Receiving aid:* Freshmen: 8% (50). Undergraduates: 5% (129). *Average award:* Freshmen: $22,169. Undergraduates: $18,761. *Scholarships, grants, and awards by category:* Academic interests/achievement: general academic interests/achievements. *Special achievements/activities:* leadership. *Special characteristics:* children of faculty/staff, general special characteristics, relatives of clergy, religious affiliation. *ROTC:* Army cooperative, Air Force cooperative.

LOANS *Student loans:* $18,930,333 (82% need-based, 18% non-need-based). 76% of past graduating class borrowed through all loan programs. *Average indebtedness per student:* $29,724. *Average need-based loan:* Freshmen: $3332. Undergraduates: $4200. *Parent loans:* $4,951,609 (55% need-based, 45% non-need-based). *Programs:* Federal Direct (Subsidized and Unsubsidized Stafford, PLUS).

WORK-STUDY *Federal work-study:* Total amount: $428,293; jobs available.

ATHLETIC AWARDS Total amount: $3,181,674 (59% need-based, 41% non-need-based).

APPLYING FOR FINANCIAL AID *Required financial aid forms:* FAFSA, noncustodial (divorced/separated) parent's statement. *Financial aid deadline (priority):* 3/15. *Notification date:* Continuous beginning 2/15. Students must reply within 2 weeks of notification.

CONTACT Jennifer Ragsdale, Acting Director of Financial Aid, Saint Peter's University, 2641 Kennedy Boulevard, Jersey City, NJ 07306, 201-761-6071 or toll-free 888-SPC-9933. *Fax:* 201-761-6073. *E-mail:* jragsdale@spc.edu. *Website:* http://www.saintpeters.edu/.

ST. THOMAS AQUINAS COLLEGE
Sparkill, NY

Tuition & fees: $29,800 **Average undergraduate aid package: $17,100**

ABOUT THE INSTITUTION Independent, coed. *Awards:* certificates, associate, bachelor's, and master's degrees. 43 undergraduate majors. *Total enrollment:* 1,851. Undergraduates: 1,721. Freshmen: 256. Federal methodology is used as a basis for awarding need-based institutional aid.

UNDERGRADUATE EXPENSES for 2016–2017 *Application fee:* $30. *Comprehensive fee:* $42,190 includes full-time tuition ($28,800), mandatory fees ($1000), and room and board ($12,390). *College room only:* $6690. Room and board charges vary according to board plan and housing facility. *Part-time tuition:* $920 per credit. *Part-time fees:* $200 per term.

FRESHMAN FINANCIAL AID (Fall 2016, est.) 229 applied for aid; of those 90% were deemed to have need. 99% of freshmen with need received aid; of those 20% had need fully met. *Average percent of need met:* 34% (excluding resources awarded to replace EFC). *Average financial aid package:* $16,016 (excluding resources awarded to replace EFC). 23% of all full-time freshmen had no need and received non-need-based gift aid.

UNDERGRADUATE FINANCIAL AID (Fall 2016, est.) 1,093 applied for aid; of those 78% were deemed to have need. 96% of undergraduates with need received aid; of those 16% had need fully met. *Average percent of need met:* 38% (excluding resources awarded to replace EFC). *Average financial aid package:* $17,100 (excluding resources awarded to replace EFC). 20% of all full-time undergraduates had no need and received non-need-based gift aid.

GIFT AID (NEED-BASED) *Total amount:* $5,383,170 (34% federal, 24% state, 37% institutional, 5% external sources). *Receiving aid:* Freshmen: 81% (205); all full-time undergraduates: 69% (779). *Average award:* Freshmen: $10,815; Undergraduates: $10,815. *Scholarships, grants, and awards:* Federal Pell, FSEOG, state, private, college/university gift aid from institutional funds.

GIFT AID (NON-NEED-BASED) *Total amount:* $9,326,545 (1% state, 98% institutional, 1% external sources). *Receiving aid:* Freshmen: 51% (129). Undergraduates: 51% (575). *Average award:* Freshmen: $13,690. Undergraduates: $12,375. *Scholarships, grants, and awards by category: Academic interests/achievement:* business, communication, computer science, education, engineering/technologies, English, foreign languages, general academic interests/achievements, humanities, mathematics, religion/biblical studies, social sciences. *Creative arts/performance:* creative writing. *Special achievements/activities:* community service, leadership. *Special characteristics:* siblings of current students, spouses of current students, twins, veterans. *Tuition waivers:* Full or partial for employees or children of employees. *ROTC:* Air Force cooperative.

LOANS *Student loans:* $5,439,000 (42% need-based, 58% non-need-based). 78% of past graduating class borrowed through all loan programs. *Average indebtedness per student:* $28,750. *Average need-based loan:* Freshmen: $3500. Undergraduates: $4800. *Parent loans:* $3,884,293 (85% need-based, 15% non-need-based). *Programs:* Federal Direct (Subsidized and Unsubsidized Stafford, PLUS), Perkins, state, alternative loans.

WORK-STUDY *Federal work-study:* Total amount: $159,268; 124 jobs averaging $1284.

ATHLETIC AWARDS Total amount: $2,138,914 (100% non-need-based).

APPLYING FOR FINANCIAL AID *Required financial aid forms:* FAFSA, state aid form. *Financial aid deadline (priority):* 2/15. *Notification date:* Continuous beginning 3/1. Students must reply by 5/1 or within 2 weeks of notification.

CONTACT Mrs. Jean Marie Mohr, Director of Financial Aid, St. Thomas Aquinas College, 125 Route 340, Sparkill, NY 10976, 845-398-4098. *Fax:* 845-398-4114. *E-mail:* jmohr@stac.edu.
Website: http://www.stac.edu/.

ST. THOMAS UNIVERSITY
Miami Gardens, FL

Tuition & fees: $28,800	Average undergraduate aid package: N/A

ABOUT THE INSTITUTION Independent Roman Catholic, coed. *Awards:* certificates, bachelor's, master's, and doctoral degrees. 49 undergraduate majors. *Total enrollment:* 4,674. Undergraduates: 2,752. Freshmen: 195. Both federal and institutional methodology are used as a basis for awarding need-based institutional aid.

UNDERGRADUATE EXPENSES for 2016–2017 *Comprehensive fee:* $40,500 includes full-time tuition ($28,800) and room and board ($11,700). *College room only:* $7200. Full-time tuition and fees vary according to course load. Room and board charges vary according to board plan and housing facility. *Part-time tuition:* $576 per credit hour. Part-time tuition and fees vary according to course load.

FRESHMAN FINANCIAL AID (Fall 2015) 189 applied for aid; of those 100% were deemed to have need. 100% of freshmen with need received aid.

UNDERGRADUATE FINANCIAL AID (Fall 2015) 806 applied for aid; of those 98% were deemed to have need. 100% of undergraduates with need received aid.

GIFT AID (NEED-BASED) *Total amount:* $2,472,595 (83% federal, 17% state). *Scholarships, grants, and awards:* Federal Pell, FSEOG, state, private, college/university gift aid from institutional funds.

GIFT AID (NON-NEED-BASED) *Total amount:* $11,409,604 (14% state, 83% institutional, 3% external sources). *Scholarships, grants, and awards by cat-*

egory: *Academic interests/achievement:* general academic interests/achievements. *Special achievements/activities:* leadership. *Tuition waivers:* Full or partial for employees or children of employees.

LOANS *Student loans:* $2,708,317 (100% need-based). *Parent loans:* $1,187,715 (100% non-need-based). *Programs:* Federal Direct (Subsidized and Unsubsidized Stafford, PLUS), Perkins.

WORK-STUDY *Federal work-study:* jobs available.

ATHLETIC AWARDS Total amount: $1,538,554 (100% non-need-based).

APPLYING FOR FINANCIAL AID *Required financial aid form:* FAFSA. *Financial aid deadline (priority):* 4/1. *Notification date:* Continuous beginning 3/1.

CONTACT Mr. Luis Betancourt, Director of Financial Aid, St. Thomas University, 16401 Northwest 37th Avenue, Miami Gardens, FL 33054, 305-474-6965 or toll-free 800-367-9010. *Fax:* 305-474-6930.
Website: http://www.stu.edu/.

SAINT VINCENT COLLEGE
Latrobe, PA

Tuition & fees: $33,814	Average undergraduate aid package: $29,677

ABOUT THE INSTITUTION Independent Roman Catholic, coed. *Awards:* certificates, bachelor's, master's, and doctoral degrees. 50 undergraduate majors. *Total enrollment:* 1,833. Undergraduates: 1,646. Freshmen: 393. Federal methodology is used as a basis for awarding need-based institutional aid.

UNDERGRADUATE EXPENSES for 2016–2017 *Application fee:* $25. *Comprehensive fee:* $44,919 includes full-time tuition ($32,540), mandatory fees ($1274), and room and board ($11,105). *College room only:* $5973. Full-time tuition and fees vary according to course load and degree level. Room and board charges vary according to board plan and housing facility. *Part-time tuition:* $1018 per credit hour. Part-time tuition and fees vary according to course load and degree level.

FRESHMAN FINANCIAL AID (Fall 2016, est.) 361 applied for aid; of those 89% were deemed to have need. 100% of freshmen with need received aid; of those 31% had need fully met. *Average percent of need met:* 83% (excluding resources awarded to replace EFC). *Average financial aid package:* $30,476 (excluding resources awarded to replace EFC). 17% of all full-time freshmen had no need and received non-need-based gift aid.

UNDERGRADUATE FINANCIAL AID (Fall 2016, est.) 1,341 applied for aid; of those 92% were deemed to have need. 100% of undergraduates with need received aid; of those 28% had need fully met. *Average percent of need met:* 82% (excluding resources awarded to replace EFC). *Average financial aid package:* $29,677 (excluding resources awarded to replace EFC). 21% of all full-time undergraduates had no need and received non-need-based gift aid.

GIFT AID (NEED-BASED) *Total amount:* $28,134,653 (8% federal, 8% state, 83% institutional, 1% external sources). *Receiving aid:* Freshmen: 70% (274); all full-time undergraduates: 63% (994). *Average award:* Freshmen: $7071; Undergraduates: $6405. *Scholarships, grants, and awards:* Federal Pell, FSEOG, state, private, college/university gift aid from institutional funds, United Negro College Fund.

GIFT AID (NON-NEED-BASED) *Total amount:* $1,460,667 (96% institutional, 4% external sources). *Receiving aid:* Freshmen: 77% (301). Undergraduates: 78% (1,232). *Average award:* Freshmen: $22,539. Undergraduates: $19,530. *Scholarships, grants, and awards by category: Academic interests/achievement:* biological sciences, business, general academic interests/achievements, home economics, mathematics, physical sciences. *Special characteristics:* children of faculty/staff, first-generation college students, general special characteristics, out-of-state students, previous college experience, religious affiliation. *Tuition waivers:* Full or partial for employees or children of employees. *ROTC:* Army cooperative, Air Force cooperative.

LOANS *Student loans:* $10,721,054 (46% need-based, 54% non-need-based). 76% of past graduating class borrowed through all loan programs. *Average indebtedness per student:* $38,493. *Average need-based loan:* Freshmen: $3660. Undergraduates: $4296. *Parent loans:* $3,662,194 (10% need-based, 90% non-need-based). *Programs:* Federal Direct (Subsidized and Unsubsidized Stafford, PLUS), Perkins, private loans.

WORK-STUDY *Federal work-study:* Total amount: $193,027; jobs available. *State or other work-study/employment:* Total amount: $322,069 (100% need-based). Part-time jobs available.

APPLYING FOR FINANCIAL AID *Required financial aid forms:* FAFSA, state aid form. *Financial aid deadline (priority):* 5/1. *Notification date:* Continuous beginning 12/1.

CONTACT Mrs. Mary Gazal, Director of Financial Aid, Saint Vincent College, 300 Fraser Purchase Road, Latrobe, PA 15650, 724-805-2627 or toll-free 800-782-5549. *Fax:* 724-805-2953. *E-mail:* mary.gazal@stvincent.edu. *Website:* http://www.stvincent.edu/.

SAINT XAVIER UNIVERSITY
Chicago, IL

ABOUT THE INSTITUTION Independent Roman Catholic, coed. 39 undergraduate majors.

GIFT AID (NEED-BASED) *Scholarships, grants, and awards:* Federal Pell, FSEOG, state, private, college/university gift aid from institutional funds, United Negro College Fund, Federal Nursing.

GIFT AID (NON-NEED-BASED) *Scholarships, grants, and awards by category:* Academic interests/achievement: general academic interests/achievements. Creative arts/performance: art/fine arts, music. Special achievements/activities: religious involvement. Special characteristics: children of faculty/staff.

LOANS *Programs:* Federal Direct (Subsidized and Unsubsidized Stafford, PLUS), Perkins.

WORK-STUDY *Federal work-study:* jobs available. *State or other work-study/employment:* Part-time jobs available.

APPLYING FOR FINANCIAL AID *Required financial aid form:* FAFSA.

CONTACT Ms. Susan Swisher, Director of Financial Aid, Saint Xavier University, 3700 West 103rd Street, Chicago, IL 60655-3105, 773-298-3073 or toll-free 800-462-9288. *Fax:* 773-298-3033. *E-mail:* swisher@sxu.edu. *Website:* http://www.sxu.edu/.

SALEM COLLEGE
Winston-Salem, NC

Tuition & fees: $27,406	Average undergraduate aid package: N/A

ABOUT THE INSTITUTION Independent Moravian, coed, primarily women. *Awards:* certificates, bachelor's, and master's degrees (only students age 23 or over are eligible to enroll part-time). 30 undergraduate majors. **Total enrollment:** 1,087. Undergraduates: 938. Freshmen: 186. Federal methodology is used as a basis for awarding need-based institutional aid.

UNDERGRADUATE EXPENSES for 2016–2017 *Application fee:* $30. **Comprehensive fee:** $38,906 includes full-time tuition ($27,040), mandatory fees ($366), and room and board ($11,500). **College room only:** $5900. Room and board charges vary according to housing facility. **Part-time tuition:** $390 per semester hour. **Part-time fees:** $150 per year.

GIFT AID (NEED-BASED) *Total amount:* $2,634,539 (19% federal, 15% state, 66% institutional). *Scholarships, grants, and awards:* Federal Pell, FSEOG, state, private, college/university gift aid from institutional funds.

GIFT AID (NON-NEED-BASED) *Total amount:* $2,063,628 (95% institutional, 5% external sources). *Scholarships, grants, and awards by category:* Academic interests/achievement: general academic interests/achievements. Creative arts/performance: music. Special achievements/activities: leadership. Special characteristics: children of educators, children of faculty/staff, relatives of clergy. **ROTC:** Army cooperative, Air Force cooperative.

LOANS *Student loans:* $792,325 (57% need-based, 43% non-need-based). 76% of past graduating class borrowed through all loan programs. *Parent loans:* $182,993 (100% non-need-based). *Programs:* Federal Direct (Subsidized and Unsubsidized Stafford, PLUS).

WORK-STUDY *Federal work-study:* jobs available. *State or other work-study/employment:* Total amount: $171,200 (100% need-based). Part-time jobs available.

APPLYING FOR FINANCIAL AID *Required financial aid forms:* FAFSA, state aid form. *Financial aid deadline (priority):* 3/1. *Notification date:* Continuous beginning 3/1. Students must reply by 5/1 or within 2 weeks of notification.

CONTACT Paul J. Coscia, Assistant Vice President for Financial Aid, Salem College, 601 South Church Street, Winston-Salem, NC 27101, 336-917-5577 or toll-free 800-327-2536. *Fax:* 336-917-5584. *E-mail:* paul.coscia@salem.edu. *Website:* http://www.salem.edu/.

SALEM INTERNATIONAL UNIVERSITY
Salem, WV

Tuition & fees: N/R	Average undergraduate aid package: N/A

ABOUT THE INSTITUTION Independent, coed. 9 undergraduate majors. Both federal and institutional methodology are used as a basis for awarding need-based institutional aid.

GIFT AID (NEED-BASED) *Scholarships, grants, and awards:* Federal Pell, FSEOG, state, private, college/university gift aid from institutional funds.

GIFT AID (NON-NEED-BASED) *Scholarships, grants, and awards by category:* Academic interests/achievement: business, education, general academic interests/achievements, humanities. Special characteristics: out-of-state students, religious affiliation.

LOANS *Programs:* Perkins, alternative loans.

WORK-STUDY Federal work-study jobs available. *State or other work-study/employment:* Part-time jobs available.

APPLYING FOR FINANCIAL AID *Required financial aid form:* FAFSA. *Financial aid deadline:* Continuous. *Notification date:* Continuous beginning 2/15. Students must reply within 4 weeks of notification.

CONTACT Donald Ronan, Director of Financial Aid and Compliance , Salem International University, 615 West Carmel Drive, Suite 140, Carmel, IN 46032, 317-805-1793 or toll-free 888-235-5024. *Fax:* 317-573-8997. *E-mail:* dronan@salemu.edu. *Website:* http://www.salemu.edu/.

SALEM STATE UNIVERSITY
Salem, MA

CONTACT Mary Benda, Director of Financial Aid, Salem State University, 352 Lafayette Street, Salem, MA 01970-5353, 978-542-6139. *Fax:* 978-542-6876. *Website:* http://www.salemstate.edu/.

SALISBURY UNIVERSITY
Salisbury, MD

Tuition & fees (MD res): $9364	Average undergraduate aid package: $8246

ABOUT THE INSTITUTION State-supported, coed. *Awards:* certificates, bachelor's, master's, and doctoral degrees. 48 undergraduate majors. **Total enrollment:** 8,748. Undergraduates: 7,861. Freshmen: 1,329. Federal methodology is used as a basis for awarding need-based institutional aid.

UNDERGRADUATE EXPENSES for 2016–2017 *Application fee:* $50. *Tuition, state resident:* full-time $6846; part-time $281 per credit hour. *Tuition, nonresident:* full-time $15,258; part-time $631 per credit hour. *Required fees:* full-time $2518; $84 per credit hour. *College room and board:* $11,350; *Room only:* $6550. Room and board charges vary according to board plan and housing facility.

FRESHMAN FINANCIAL AID (Fall 2015) 938 applied for aid; of those 66% were deemed to have need. 100% of freshmen with need received aid; of those 17% had need fully met. *Average percent of need met:* 51% (excluding resources awarded to replace EFC). *Average financial aid package:* $8395 (excluding resources awarded to replace EFC). 21% of all full-time freshmen had no need and received non-need-based gift aid.

UNDERGRADUATE FINANCIAL AID (Fall 2015) 5,263 applied for aid; of those 72% were deemed to have need. 99% of undergraduates with need received aid;

of those 12% had need fully met. *Average percent of need met:* 48% (excluding resources awarded to replace EFC). *Average financial aid package:* $8246 (excluding resources awarded to replace EFC). 12% of all full-time undergraduates had no need and received non-need-based gift aid.

GIFT AID (NEED-BASED) *Total amount:* $17,696,062 (43% federal, 25% state, 27% institutional, 5% external sources). *Receiving aid:* Freshmen: 44% (525); all full-time undergraduates: 42% (2,983). *Average award:* Freshmen: $7197; Undergraduates: $6043. *Scholarships, grants, and awards:* Federal Pell, FSEOG, state, private, college/university gift aid from institutional funds.

GIFT AID (NON-NEED-BASED) *Total amount:* $3,188,964 (11% state, 78% institutional, 11% external sources). *Average award:* Freshmen: $2824. Undergraduates: $2569. *Scholarships, grants, and awards by category: Academic interests/achievement:* 1,885 awards ($4,730,692 total): business, communication, computer science, education, general academic interests/achievements, home economics, humanities, international studies, physical sciences, social sciences. *Creative arts/performance:* 25 awards ($15,900 total): art/fine arts, music, theater/drama. *Special achievements/activities:* 3 awards ($2500 total): leadership. *Special characteristics:* 33 awards ($52,500 total): adult students, children and siblings of alumni, first-generation college students, previous college experience. *Tuition waivers:* Full or partial for employees or children of employees, senior citizens. *ROTC:* Army, Air Force cooperative.

LOANS *Student loans:* $34,200,057 (74% need-based, 26% non-need-based). 59% of past graduating class borrowed through all loan programs. *Average indebtedness per student:* $26,940. *Average need-based loan:* Freshmen: $3212. Undergraduates: $4252. *Parent loans:* $18,850,673 (67% need-based, 33% non-need-based). *Programs:* Federal Direct (Subsidized and Unsubsidized Stafford, PLUS), Perkins.

WORK-STUDY *Federal work-study:* 73 jobs averaging $1779.

APPLYING FOR FINANCIAL AID *Required financial aid form:* FAFSA. *Financial aid deadline (priority):* 3/1. *Notification date:* Continuous beginning 3/15. Students must reply by 5/1.

CONTACT Ms. Elizabeth Zimmerman, Director of Financial Aid, Salisbury University, 1101 Camden Avenue, Salisbury, MD 21801, 410-543-6165 or toll-free 888-543-0148. *Fax:* 410-543-6138. *E-mail:* finaid@salisbury.edu. *Website:* http://www.salisbury.edu/.

SALVE REGINA UNIVERSITY
Newport, RI

Tuition & fees: $37,820	Average undergraduate aid package: $26,402

ABOUT THE INSTITUTION Independent Roman Catholic, coed. *Awards:* certificates, associate, bachelor's, master's, and doctoral degrees. 51 undergraduate majors. *Total enrollment:* 2,746. Undergraduates: 2,124. Freshmen: 548. Federal methodology is used as a basis for awarding need-based institutional aid.

UNDERGRADUATE EXPENSES for 2016–2017 *Application fee:* $50. *Comprehensive fee:* $51,470 includes full-time tuition ($37,270), mandatory fees ($550), and room and board ($13,650). Full-time tuition and fees vary according to location. Room and board charges vary according to board plan and housing facility. *Part-time tuition:* $1242 per credit. *Part-time fees:* $50 per term. Part-time tuition and fees vary according to course load and location.

FRESHMAN FINANCIAL AID (Fall 2016, est.) 501 applied for aid; of those 86% were deemed to have need. 100% of freshmen with need received aid; of those 12% had need fully met. *Average percent of need met:* 69% (excluding resources awarded to replace EFC). *Average financial aid package:* $27,009 (excluding resources awarded to replace EFC). 18% of all full-time freshmen had no need and received non-need-based gift aid.

UNDERGRADUATE FINANCIAL AID (Fall 2016, est.) 1,698 applied for aid; of those 90% were deemed to have need. 100% of undergraduates with need received aid; of those 12% had need fully met. *Average percent of need met:* 68% (excluding resources awarded to replace EFC). *Average financial aid package:* $26,402 (excluding resources awarded to replace EFC). 19% of all full-time undergraduates had no need and received non-need-based gift aid.

GIFT AID (NEED-BASED) *Total amount:* $12,280,730 (17% federal, 2% state, 77% institutional, 4% external sources). *Receiving aid:* Freshmen: 78% (430); all full-time undergraduates: 77% (1,522). *Average award:* Freshmen: $22,871; Undergraduates: $21,395. *Scholarships, grants, and awards:* Federal Pell, FSEOG, state, private, college/university gift aid from institutional funds.

GIFT AID (NON-NEED-BASED) *Total amount:* $25,712,833 (98% institutional, 2% external sources). *Receiving aid:* Freshmen: 6% (34). Undergraduates: 7% (132). *Average award:* Freshmen: $15,628. Undergraduates: $14,506. *Scholarships, grants, and awards by category: Academic interests/achievement:* 1,810 awards ($24,414,201 total): general academic interests/achievements. *Creative arts/performance:* 17 awards ($62,500 total): art/fine arts. *Special characteristics:* 16 awards ($7950 total): children and siblings of alumni. *Tuition waivers:* Full or partial for employees or children of employees. *ROTC:* Army cooperative.

LOANS *Student loans:* $10,507,958 (59% need-based, 41% non-need-based). 69% of past graduating class borrowed through all loan programs. *Average indebtedness per student:* $29,192. *Average need-based loan:* Freshmen: $3357. Undergraduates: $4498. *Parent loans:* $5,478,720 (100% non-need-based). *Programs:* Federal Direct (Subsidized and Unsubsidized Stafford, PLUS), Perkins, Federal Nursing, alternative loans.

WORK-STUDY *Federal work-study:* Total amount: $2,401,708; jobs available. *State or other work-study/employment:* Part-time jobs available.

APPLYING FOR FINANCIAL AID *Required financial aid form:* FAFSA. *Financial aid deadline (priority):* 3/1. *Notification date:* Continuous beginning 1/1. Students must reply by 5/1 or within 2 weeks of notification.

CONTACT Mrs. Anne McDermott, Director of Financial Aid, Salve Regina University, 100 Ochre Point Avenue, Newport, RI 02840-4192, 401-341-2901 or toll-free 888-GO SALVE. *Fax:* 401-341-2928. *E-mail:* financial_aid@salve.edu. *Website:* http://www.salve.edu/.

SAMFORD UNIVERSITY
Birmingham, AL

Tuition & fees: $30,490	Average undergraduate aid package: $19,005

ABOUT THE INSTITUTION Independent Baptist, coed. *Awards:* certificates, bachelor's, master's, and doctoral degrees. 73 undergraduate majors. *Total enrollment:* 5,471. Undergraduates: 3,341. Freshmen: 916. Federal methodology is used as a basis for awarding need-based institutional aid.

UNDERGRADUATE EXPENSES for 2017–2018 *Application fee:* $40. *Comprehensive fee:* $40,770 includes full-time tuition ($29,640), mandatory fees ($850), and room and board ($10,280). *College room only:* $5416. Full-time tuition and fees vary according to course load and program. Room and board charges vary according to board plan and housing facility. Part-time tuition and fees vary according to course load and program.

FRESHMAN FINANCIAL AID (Fall 2015) 605 applied for aid; of those 63% were deemed to have need. 100% of freshmen with need received aid; of those 26% had need fully met. *Average percent of need met:* 72% (excluding resources awarded to replace EFC). *Average financial aid package:* $18,690 (excluding resources awarded to replace EFC). 45% of all full-time freshmen had no need and received non-need-based gift aid.

UNDERGRADUATE FINANCIAL AID (Fall 2015) 1,762 applied for aid; of those 72% were deemed to have need. 100% of undergraduates with need received aid; of those 22% had need fully met. *Average percent of need met:* 70% (excluding resources awarded to replace EFC). *Average financial aid package:* $19,005 (excluding resources awarded to replace EFC). 45% of all full-time undergraduates had no need and received non-need-based gift aid.

GIFT AID (NEED-BASED) *Total amount:* $15,028,794 (11% federal, 2% state, 83% institutional, 4% external sources). *Receiving aid:* Freshmen: 46% (377); all full-time undergraduates: 40% (1,207). *Average award:* Freshmen: $14,824; Undergraduates: $15,072. *Scholarships, grants, and awards:* Federal Pell, FSEOG, state, private, college/university gift aid from institutional funds, United Negro College Fund, Federal Nursing.

GIFT AID (NON-NEED-BASED) *Total amount:* $15,828,667 (1% state, 93% institutional, 6% external sources). *Receiving aid:* Freshmen: 11% (90). Undergraduates: 8% (246). *Average award:* Freshmen: $10,896. Undergraduates: $10,222. *Scholarships, grants, and awards by category: Academic interests/achievement:* 2,291 awards ($19,347,433 total): biological sciences, business, computer science, education, English, foreign languages, general academic interests/achievements, health fields, home economics, humanities, international studies, mathematics, physical sciences, premedicine, religion/biblical studies, social sciences. *Creative arts/performance:* 246 awards ($1,447,278 total): debating, journalism/publications, music, performing arts, theater/drama. *Special achievements/activities:* 988 awards

($1,771,092 total): cheerleading/drum major, leadership. *Special characteristics:* 171 awards ($2,368,432 total): children of faculty/staff, members of minority groups, relatives of clergy, siblings of current students, spouses of current students, veterans. *Tuition waivers:* Full or partial for employees or children of employees. *ROTC:* Army cooperative, Air Force.

LOANS *Student loans:* $15,090,400 (61% need-based, 39% non-need-based). 36% of past graduating class borrowed through all loan programs. *Average indebtedness per student:* $29,292. *Average need-based loan:* Freshmen: $3212. Undergraduates: $3843. *Parent loans:* $14,401,267 (32% need-based, 68% non-need-based). *Programs:* Federal Direct (Subsidized and Unsubsidized Stafford, PLUS), Perkins, Federal Nursing, college/university.

WORK-STUDY *Federal work-study:* 433 jobs averaging $1964. *State or other work-study/employment:* Total amount: $1,142,006 (19% need-based, 81% non-need-based). 717 part-time jobs averaging $1648.

ATHLETIC AWARDS Total amount: $7,579,355 (44% need-based, 56% non-need-based).

APPLYING FOR FINANCIAL AID *Required financial aid forms:* FAFSA, state aid form. *Financial aid deadline (priority):* 3/1. *Notification date:* 4/1. Students must reply by 5/1.

CONTACT Lane Smith, Director of Financial Aid, Samford University, 800 Lakeshore Drive, Birmingham, AL 35229, 205-726-2905 or toll-free 800-888-7218. *Fax:* 205-726-2738. *E-mail:* lsmith1@samford.edu.
Website: http://www.samford.edu/.

SAM HOUSTON STATE UNIVERSITY
Huntsville, TX

Tuition & fees (TX res): $9516	Average undergraduate aid package: $11,140

ABOUT THE INSTITUTION State-supported, coed. *Awards:* certificates, bachelor's, master's, and doctoral degrees. 104 undergraduate majors. *Total enrollment:* 20,477. Undergraduates: 17,902. Freshmen: 2,758. Federal methodology is used as a basis for awarding need-based institutional aid.

UNDERGRADUATE EXPENSES for 2017–2018 *Application fee:* $45. *Tuition, state resident:* full-time $6465; part-time $215.50 per credit hour. *Tuition, nonresident:* full-time $18,705; part-time $623.50 per credit hour. *Required fees:* full-time $3051. Full-time tuition and fees vary according to course load and location. Part-time tuition and fees vary according to course load and location. *College room and board:* $8780; *Room only:* $4920. Room and board charges vary according to board plan and housing facility. *Payment plan:* Guaranteed tuition.

FRESHMAN FINANCIAL AID (Fall 2015) 2,095 applied for aid; of those 80% were deemed to have need. 98% of freshmen with need received aid; of those 17% had need fully met. *Average percent of need met:* 82% (excluding resources awarded to replace EFC). *Average financial aid package:* $12,150 (excluding resources awarded to replace EFC). 10% of all full-time freshmen had no need and received non-need-based gift aid.

UNDERGRADUATE FINANCIAL AID (Fall 2015) 10,811 applied for aid; of those 86% were deemed to have need. 97% of undergraduates with need received aid; of those 11% had need fully met. *Average percent of need met:* 79% (excluding resources awarded to replace EFC). *Average financial aid package:* $11,140 (excluding resources awarded to replace EFC). 8% of all full-time undergraduates had no need and received non-need-based gift aid.

GIFT AID (NEED-BASED) *Total amount:* $60,697,067 (49% federal, 40% state, 5% institutional, 6% external sources). *Receiving aid:* Freshmen: 61% (1,436); all full-time undergraduates: 55% (7,705). *Average award:* Freshmen: $9271; Undergraduates: $7387. *Scholarships, grants, and awards:* Federal Pell, FSEOG, state, college/university gift aid from institutional funds.

GIFT AID (NON-NEED-BASED) *Total amount:* $4,516,180 (48% institutional, 52% external sources). *Receiving aid:* Freshmen: 7% (176). Undergraduates: 3% (441). *Average award:* Freshmen: $2990. Undergraduates: $2530. *Scholarships, grants, and awards by category: Academic interests/achievement:* agriculture, biological sciences, business, communication, computer science, education, engineering/technologies, English, foreign languages, general academic interests/achievements, health fields, home economics, humanities, library science, mathematics, military science, physical sciences, social sciences. *Creative arts/performance:* art/fine arts, cinema/film/broadcasting, dance, journalism/publications, music, performing arts, theater/drama. *Special achievements/activities:* general special achievements/activities,

leadership, rodeo. *Special characteristics:* children of union members/company employees, ethnic background, first-generation college students, members of minority groups, veterans. *Tuition waivers:* Full or partial for employees or children of employees. *ROTC:* Army.

LOANS *Student loans:* $101,944,864 (76% need-based, 24% non-need-based). 66% of past graduating class borrowed through all loan programs. *Average indebtedness per student:* $26,135. *Average need-based loan:* Freshmen: $5713. Undergraduates: $7610. *Parent loans:* $51,055,031 (54% need-based, 46% non-need-based). *Programs:* Federal Direct (Subsidized and Unsubsidized Stafford, PLUS), Perkins, state.

WORK-STUDY *Federal work-study:* jobs available. *State or other work-study/employment:* Total amount: $156,330 (100% need-based). Part-time jobs available.

ATHLETIC AWARDS Total amount: $3,947,201 (40% need-based, 60% non-need-based).

APPLYING FOR FINANCIAL AID *Required financial aid form:* FAFSA. *Financial aid deadline (priority):* 3/15. *Notification date:* Continuous beginning 4/1. Students must reply within 4 weeks of notification.

CONTACT Lydia Hall, Director of Financial Aid, Sam Houston State University, 1903 University, Estill 201, Box 2328, Huntsville, TX 77341-2328, 936-294-1750 or toll-free 866-232-7528 Ext. 1828. *Fax:* 936-294-3668. *E-mail:* lth003@shsu.edu. *Website:* http://www.shsu.edu/.

SAMUEL MERRITT UNIVERSITY
Oakland, CA

Tuition & fees: N/R	Average undergraduate aid package: $11,358

ABOUT THE INSTITUTION Independent, coed, primarily women. *Awards:* certificates, bachelor's, master's, and doctoral degrees (bachelor's degree offered jointly with Saint Mary's College of California). 1 undergraduate major. *Total enrollment:* 1,907. Undergraduates: 738. Entering class: 215. Federal methodology is used as a basis for awarding need-based institutional aid.

UNDERGRADUATE FINANCIAL AID (Fall 2015) 714 applied for aid; of those 98% were deemed to have need. 100% of undergraduates with need received aid. *Average percent of need met:* 18% (excluding resources awarded to replace EFC). *Average financial aid package:* $11,358 (excluding resources awarded to replace EFC).

GIFT AID (NEED-BASED) *Total amount:* $4,190,347 (18% federal, 16% state, 64% institutional, 2% external sources). *Receiving aid:* All full-time undergraduates: 44% (328). *Average award:* Undergraduates: $12,120. *Scholarships, grants, and awards:* Federal Pell, FSEOG, state, private, college/university gift aid from institutional funds, Federal Nursing.

LOANS *Student loans:* $17,239,953 (19% need-based, 81% non-need-based). *Average need-based loan:* Undergraduates: $5534. *Parent loans:* $1,875,006 (100% non-need-based). *Programs:* Federal Direct (Subsidized and Unsubsidized Stafford, PLUS), Perkins, Federal Nursing.

WORK-STUDY *Federal work-study:* 147 jobs averaging $1354. *State or other work-study/employment:* Part-time jobs available.

APPLYING FOR FINANCIAL AID *Required financial aid form:* FAFSA. *Financial aid deadline (priority):* 3/2. *Notification date:* Continuous beginning 4/15. Students must reply within 2 weeks of notification.

CONTACT Saeng Saephanh, Financial Aid Technician, Samuel Merritt University, 3100 Telegraph Avenue, Peralta Medical Office Building, Oakland, CA 94609, 510-869-1527 or toll-free 800-607-6377. *Fax:* 510-869-1529. *E-mail:* ssaephanh@samuelmerritt.edu.
Website: http://www.samuelmerritt.edu/.

SAN DIEGO CHRISTIAN COLLEGE
Santee, CA

Tuition & fees: $29,550	Average undergraduate aid package: $24,561

ABOUT THE INSTITUTION Independent nondenominational, coed. *Awards:* certificates, associate, bachelor's, and master's degrees. 28 undergraduate majors. *Total enrollment:* 916. Undergraduates: 880. Freshmen: 110. Federal methodology is used as a basis for awarding need-based institutional aid.

UNDERGRADUATE EXPENSES for 2016–2017 *Application fee:* $25. *Comprehensive fee:* $40,524 includes full-time tuition ($28,100), mandatory fees ($1450), and room and board ($10,974). Full-time tuition and fees vary according to course load, location, and program. Room and board charges vary according to board plan and student level. *Part-time tuition:* $1210 per credit. *Part-time fees:* $290 per term. Part-time tuition and fees vary according to course load, location, and program.

FRESHMAN FINANCIAL AID (Fall 2016, est.) 56 applied for aid; of those 86% were deemed to have need. 100% of freshmen with need received aid; of those 25% had need fully met. *Average financial aid package:* $24,097 (excluding resources awarded to replace EFC). 5% of all full-time freshmen had no need and received non-need-based gift aid.

UNDERGRADUATE FINANCIAL AID (Fall 2016, est.) 650 applied for aid; of those 95% were deemed to have need. 100% of undergraduates with need received aid; of those 24% had need fully met. *Average financial aid package:* $24,561 (excluding resources awarded to replace EFC). 2% of all full-time undergraduates had no need and received non-need-based gift aid.

GIFT AID (NEED-BASED) *Total amount:* $4,496,657 (36% federal, 23% state, 41% institutional). *Receiving aid:* Freshmen: 63% (36); all full-time undergraduates: 62% (460). *Average award:* Freshmen: $4094; Undergraduates: $4516. *Scholarships, grants, and awards:* Federal Pell, FSEOG, state, private, college/university gift aid from institutional funds.

GIFT AID (NON-NEED-BASED) *Total amount:* $139,867 (100% external sources). *Receiving aid:* Freshmen: 67% (38). Undergraduates: 68% (505). *Average award:* Freshmen: $14,166. Undergraduates: $10,369. *Scholarships, grants, and awards by category:* Academic interests/achievement: 129 awards ($626,941 total): general academic interests/achievements. Creative arts/performance: 19 awards ($71,784 total): music, performing arts, theater/drama. Special achievements/activities: 107 awards ($578,608 total): general special achievements/activities, leadership, memberships, religious involvement. Special characteristics: 120 awards ($517,273 total): children and siblings of alumni, children of faculty/staff, out-of-state students, relatives of clergy, religious affiliation, siblings of current students, veterans, veterans' children. *Tuition waivers:* Full or partial for employees or children of employees. *ROTC:* Army cooperative, Air Force cooperative.

LOANS *Student loans:* $5,510,238 (39% need-based, 61% non-need-based). 58% of past graduating class borrowed through all loan programs. *Average indebtedness per student:* $19,212. *Average need-based loan:* Freshmen: $2828. Undergraduates: $3505. *Parent loans:* $1,959,644 (100% non-need-based). *Programs:* Federal Direct (Subsidized and Unsubsidized Stafford, PLUS), Perkins.

WORK-STUDY *Federal work-study:* Total amount: $298,880; 65 jobs averaging $2400. *State or other work-study/employment:* Total amount: $65,000 (100% need-based). 29 part-time jobs averaging $2400.

ATHLETIC AWARDS Total amount: $2,444,868 (100% non-need-based).

APPLYING FOR FINANCIAL AID *Required financial aid form:* FAFSA. *Financial aid deadline:* 7/1 (priority: 3/2). *Notification date:* 12/1. Students must reply by 7/1 or within 4 weeks of notification.

CONTACT Mr. Daniel Reed, Director of Financial Aid, San Diego Christian College, 200 Riverview Parkway, Santee, CA 92071, 619-201-8730 or toll-free 800-676-2242. *Fax:* 619-201-8797. *E-mail:* daniel.reed@sdcc.edu. *Website:* http://www.sdcc.edu/.

SAN DIEGO STATE UNIVERSITY
San Diego, CA

Tuition & fees (CA res): $7084	Average undergraduate aid package: $11,400

ABOUT THE INSTITUTION State-supported, coed. *Awards:* certificates, bachelor's, master's, and doctoral degrees. 104 undergraduate majors. *Total enrollment:* 34,688. Undergraduates: 29,853. Freshmen: 5,077. Federal methodology is used as a basis for awarding need-based institutional aid.

UNDERGRADUATE EXPENSES for 2016–2017 *Application fee:* $55. *Tuition, state resident:* full-time $5472. *Tuition, nonresident:* full-time $16,632. *Required fees:* full-time $1612. Full-time tuition and fees vary according to course load, degree level, and location. Part-time tuition and fees vary according to course load, degree level, and location. *College room and board:* $14,812. Room and board charges vary according to board plan and housing facility.

FRESHMAN FINANCIAL AID (Fall 2016, est.) 3,800 applied for aid; of those 71% were deemed to have need. 96% of freshmen with need received aid; of those 8% had need fully met. *Average percent of need met:* 63% (excluding resources awarded to replace EFC). *Average financial aid package:* $9200 (excluding resources awarded to replace EFC). 3% of all full-time freshmen had no need and received non-need-based gift aid.

UNDERGRADUATE FINANCIAL AID (Fall 2016, est.) 18,000 applied for aid; of those 82% were deemed to have need. 97% of undergraduates with need received aid; of those 31% had need fully met. *Average percent of need met:* 69% (excluding resources awarded to replace EFC). *Average financial aid package:* $11,400 (excluding resources awarded to replace EFC). 4% of all full-time undergraduates had no need and received non-need-based gift aid.

GIFT AID (NEED-BASED) *Total amount:* $113,500,000 (44% federal, 29% state, 27% institutional). *Receiving aid:* Freshmen: 33% (1,600); all full-time undergraduates: 44% (11,800). *Average award:* Freshmen: $9600; Undergraduates: $9600. *Scholarships, grants, and awards:* Federal Pell, FSEOG, state, private, college/university gift aid from institutional funds.

GIFT AID (NON-NEED-BASED) *Total amount:* $9,021,000 (25% state, 37% institutional, 38% external sources). *Receiving aid:* Freshmen: 29% (1,400). Undergraduates: 22% (5,800). *Average award:* Freshmen: $3800. Undergraduates: $2500. *Scholarships, grants, and awards by category:* Academic interests/achievement: area/ethnic studies, biological sciences, business, communication, computer science, education, engineering/technologies, English, foreign languages, general academic interests/achievements, health fields, home economics, humanities, international studies, mathematics, military science, physical sciences, religion/biblical studies, social sciences. Creative arts/performance: applied art and design, art/fine arts, cinema/film/broadcasting, creative writing, dance, debating, journalism/publications, music, performing arts, theater/drama. Special achievements/activities: cheerleading/drum major, hobbies/interests, leadership, memberships. Special characteristics: adult students, children and siblings of alumni, children of faculty/staff, children of workers in trades, first-generation college students, handicapped students, local/state students, previous college experience, veterans, veterans' children. *Tuition waivers:* Full or partial for employees or children of employees. *ROTC:* Army, Naval, Air Force.

LOANS *Student loans:* $126,000,000 (71% need-based, 29% non-need-based). 49% of past graduating class borrowed through all loan programs. *Average indebtedness per student:* $19,969. *Average need-based loan:* Freshmen: $3200. Undergraduates: $4300. *Parent loans:* $92,500,000 (27% need-based, 73% non-need-based). *Programs:* Federal Direct (Subsidized and Unsubsidized Stafford, PLUS), college/university.

WORK-STUDY *Federal work-study:* Total amount: $1,400,000; 660 jobs averaging $2200.

ATHLETIC AWARDS Total amount: $7,600,000 (100% non-need-based).

APPLYING FOR FINANCIAL AID *Required financial aid forms:* FAFSA, state aid form. *Financial aid deadline:* 3/2 (priority: 4/1). *Notification date:* Continuous beginning 3/15.

CONTACT Mrs. Rose Pasenelli, Director of Financial Aid and Scholarships, San Diego State University, 5500 Campanile Drive, SSW-3605, San Diego, CA 92182-7436, 619-594-6323 or toll-free 855-594-6336 (in-state), 855-594-3983 (out-of-state). *E-mail:* rpasenel@mail.sdsu.edu. *Website:* http://www.sdsu.edu/.

SAN FRANCISCO ART INSTITUTE
San Francisco, CA

Tuition & fees: $43,090	Average undergraduate aid package: $15,441

ABOUT THE INSTITUTION Independent, coed. *Awards:* certificates, bachelor's, and master's degrees. 8 undergraduate majors. *Total enrollment:* 506. Undergraduates: 338. Freshmen: 62. Both federal and institutional methodology are used as a basis for awarding need-based institutional aid.

UNDERGRADUATE EXPENSES for 2016–2017 *Application fee:* $75. *Comprehensive fee:* $58,505 includes full-time tuition ($42,220), mandatory fees ($870), and room and board ($15,415). *College room only:* $11,500. Full-time tuition and fees vary according to degree level. Room and board charges vary according to housing facility. *Part-time tuition:* $1849 per unit. Part-time tuition and fees vary according to degree level.

FRESHMAN FINANCIAL AID (Fall 2016, est.) 40 applied for aid; of those 78% were deemed to have need. 100% of freshmen with need received aid; of those 6% had need fully met. *Average percent of need met:* 43% (excluding resources awarded to replace EFC). *Average financial aid package:* $13,935 (excluding resources awarded to replace EFC). 46% of all full-time freshmen had no need and received non-need-based gift aid.

UNDERGRADUATE FINANCIAL AID (Fall 2016, est.) 200 applied for aid; of those 86% were deemed to have need. 100% of undergraduates with need received aid; of those 10% had need fully met. *Average percent of need met:* 53% (excluding resources awarded to replace EFC). *Average financial aid package:* $15,441 (excluding resources awarded to replace EFC). 41% of all full-time undergraduates had no need and received non-need-based gift aid.

GIFT AID (NEED-BASED) *Total amount:* $2,987,789 (11% federal, 4% state, 79% institutional, 6% external sources). *Receiving aid:* Freshmen: 46% (28); all full-time undergraduates: 47% (146). *Average award:* Freshmen: $5372; Undergraduates: $5918. *Scholarships, grants, and awards:* Federal Pell, FSEOG, state, private, college/university gift aid from institutional funds.

GIFT AID (NON-NEED-BASED) *Receiving aid:* Freshmen: 49% (30). Undergraduates: 54% (166). *Average award:* Freshmen: $6052. Undergraduates: $5583. *Scholarships, grants, and awards by category:* Academic interests/achievement: general academic interests/achievements. Creative arts/performance: art/fine arts. Special characteristics: children and siblings of alumni, first-generation college students. *Tuition waivers:* Full or partial for employees or children of employees.

LOANS *Student loans:* $759,186 (100% need-based). 59% of past graduating class borrowed through all loan programs. *Average indebtedness per student:* $32,515. *Average need-based loan:* Freshmen: $1750. Undergraduates: $2318. *Parent loans:* $807,929 (100% need-based). *Programs:* Federal Direct (Subsidized and Unsubsidized Stafford, PLUS).

WORK-STUDY *Federal work-study:* Total amount: $145,333; jobs available. *State or other work-study/employment:* Part-time jobs available.

APPLYING FOR FINANCIAL AID *Required financial aid form:* FAFSA. *Financial aid deadline (priority):* 3/1. *Notification date:* Continuous beginning 3/1. Students must reply within 2 weeks of notification.

CONTACT Annita Alldredge, Director of Financial Aid, San Francisco Art Institute, 800 Chestnut Street, San Francisco, CA 94133, 415-749-4560 or toll-free 800-345-SFAI. *Fax:* 415-351-3503. *E-mail:* aalldredge@sfai.edu. *Website:* http://www.sfai.edu/.

SAN FRANCISCO CONSERVATORY OF MUSIC
San Francisco, CA

Tuition & fees: $43,410	Average undergraduate aid package: $35,305

ABOUT THE INSTITUTION Independent, coed. *Awards:* certificates, diplomas, bachelor's, and master's degrees. 8 undergraduate majors. *Total enrollment:* 401. Undergraduates: 188. Freshmen: 54. Both federal and institutional methodology are used as a basis for awarding need-based institutional aid.

UNDERGRADUATE EXPENSES for 2016–2017 *One-time required fee:* $50. *Comprehensive fee:* $59,110 includes full-time tuition ($42,400), mandatory fees ($1010), and room and board ($15,700). *College room only:* $12,100. Room and board charges vary according to board plan and housing facility. *Part-time tuition:* $1868 per credit. *Part-time fees:* $1010 per year. Part-time tuition and fees vary according to course load.

FRESHMAN FINANCIAL AID (Fall 2016, est.) 38 applied for aid; of those 97% were deemed to have need. 100% of freshmen with need received aid; of those 8% had need fully met. *Average percent of need met:* 77% (excluding resources awarded to replace EFC). *Average financial aid package:* $45,000 (excluding resources awarded to replace EFC). 42% of all full-time freshmen had no need and received non-need-based gift aid.

UNDERGRADUATE FINANCIAL AID (Fall 2016, est.) 157 applied for aid; of those 80% were deemed to have need. 100% of undergraduates with need received aid; of those 78% had need fully met. *Average percent of need met:* 46% (excluding resources awarded to replace EFC). *Average financial aid package:* $35,305 (excluding resources awarded to replace EFC). 19% of all full-time undergraduates had no need and received non-need-based gift aid.

GIFT AID (NEED-BASED) *Total amount:* $3,798,948 (7% federal, 6% state, 86% institutional, 1% external sources). *Receiving aid:* Freshmen: 62% (37); all full-time undergraduates: 69% (126). *Average award:* Freshmen: $15,220; Undergraduates: $17,754. *Scholarships, grants, and awards:* Federal Pell, FSEOG, state, college/university gift aid from institutional funds.

GIFT AID (NON-NEED-BASED) *Total amount:* $775,320 (100% institutional). *Receiving aid:* Freshmen: 62% (37). Undergraduates: 69% (126). *Average award:* Freshmen: $14,700. Undergraduates: $15,900. *Scholarships, grants, and awards by category:* Creative arts/performance: 34 awards ($540,500 total): music. *Tuition waivers:* Full or partial for employees or children of employees.

LOANS *Student loans:* $740,000 (89% need-based, 11% non-need-based). 50% of past graduating class borrowed through all loan programs. *Average indebtedness per student:* $36,113. *Average need-based loan:* Freshmen: $3750. Undergraduates: $5200. *Parent loans:* $847,250 (100% need-based). *Programs:* Federal Direct (Subsidized and Unsubsidized Stafford, PLUS), Perkins.

WORK-STUDY *Federal work-study:* Total amount: $19,500; 25 jobs averaging $2500. *State or other work-study/employment:* 4 part-time jobs averaging $2500.

APPLYING FOR FINANCIAL AID *Required financial aid forms:* FAFSA, institution's own form, CSS Financial Aid PROFILE, state aid form, noncustodial (divorced/separated) parent's statement. *Financial aid deadline:* 3/1 (priority: 2/15). *Notification date:* Continuous beginning 4/1. Students must reply within 2 weeks of notification.

CONTACT Doris Howard, Director of Financial Aid, San Francisco Conservatory of Music, 50 Oak Street, San Francisco, CA 94102-6011, 415-503-6214. *Fax:* 415-503-6299. *E-mail:* finaid@sfcm.edu. *Website:* http://www.sfcm.edu/.

SAN FRANCISCO STATE UNIVERSITY
San Francisco, CA

Tuition & fees (CA res): $6484	Average undergraduate aid package: $15,082

ABOUT THE INSTITUTION State-supported, coed. *Awards:* certificates, bachelor's, master's, and doctoral degrees. 90 undergraduate majors. *Total enrollment:* 29,045. Undergraduates: 25,945. Freshmen: 3,642. Federal methodology is used as a basis for awarding need-based institutional aid.

UNDERGRADUATE EXPENSES for 2016–2017 *Application fee:* $55. *Tuition, state resident:* full-time $5472; part-time $1587 per term. *Tuition, nonresident:* full-time $16,632; part-time $3819 per term. *Required fees:* full-time $1012; $506 per term. Full-time tuition and fees vary according to course load. Part-time tuition and fees vary according to course load. *College room and board:* $12,698; *Room only:* $8330. Room and board charges vary according to board plan and housing facility.

FRESHMAN FINANCIAL AID (Fall 2016, est.) 2,730 applied for aid; of those 83% were deemed to have need. 95% of freshmen with need received aid; of those 34% had need fully met. *Average percent of need met:* 75% (excluding resources awarded to replace EFC). *Average financial aid package:* $15,973 (excluding

resources awarded to replace EFC). 1% of all full-time freshmen had no need and received non-need-based gift aid.

UNDERGRADUATE FINANCIAL AID (Fall 2016, est.) 16,565 applied for aid; of those 90% were deemed to have need. 95% of undergraduates with need received aid; of those 25% had need fully met. *Average percent of need met:* 70% (excluding resources awarded to replace EFC). *Average financial aid package:* $15,082 (excluding resources awarded to replace EFC). 1% of all full-time undergraduates had no need and received non-need-based gift aid.

GIFT AID (NEED-BASED) *Total amount:* $138,171,839 (41% federal, 58% state, 1% external sources). *Receiving aid:* Freshmen: 65% (2,040); all full-time undergraduates: 62% (13,201). *Average award:* Freshmen: $9109; Undergraduates: $9103. *Scholarships, grants, and awards:* Federal Pell, FSEOG, state, private, college/university gift aid from institutional funds.

GIFT AID (NON-NEED-BASED) *Total amount:* $51,301 (29% institutional, 71% external sources). *Receiving aid:* Freshmen: 16% (508). Undergraduates: 4% (868). *Average award:* Freshmen: $1340. Undergraduates: $1850. *Tuition waivers:* Full or partial for employees or children of employees, senior citizens. *ROTC:* Army cooperative, Air Force cooperative.

LOANS *Student loans:* $62,951,898 (95% need-based, 5% non-need-based). 50% of past graduating class borrowed through all loan programs. *Average indebtedness per student:* $20,716. *Average need-based loan:* Freshmen: $3409. Undergraduates: $4495. *Parent loans:* $27,265,625 (100% need-based). *Programs:* Federal Direct (Subsidized and Unsubsidized Stafford, PLUS), Perkins.

WORK-STUDY *Federal work-study:* Total amount: $1,675,000; jobs available.

ATHLETIC AWARDS Total amount: $553,005 (100% need-based).

APPLYING FOR FINANCIAL AID *Required financial aid form:* FAFSA. *Financial aid deadline (priority):* 3/2. *Notification date:* Continuous beginning 4/15. Students must reply within 2 weeks of notification.

CONTACT Barbara Hubler, Director of Financial Aid, San Francisco State University, 1600 Holloway Avenue, San Francisco, CA 94132-1722, 415-338-7000. *Fax:* 415-338-0949. *E-mail:* finaid@sfsu.edu. *Website:* http://www.sfsu.edu/.

SAN JOSE STATE UNIVERSITY
San Jose, CA

Tuition & fees (CA res): $7417	Average undergraduate aid package: $18,142

ABOUT THE INSTITUTION State-supported, coed. *Awards:* bachelor's and master's degrees. 88 undergraduate majors. *Total enrollment:* 32,773. Undergraduates: 26,831. Freshmen: 3,461. Federal methodology is used as a basis for awarding need-based institutional aid.

UNDERGRADUATE EXPENSES for 2016–2017 *Application fee:* $55. *Tuition, state resident:* full-time $5472; part-time $1587 per term. *Tuition, nonresident:* full-time $14,400; part-time $3819 per term. *Required fees:* full-time $1945; $1945 per year. *College room and board:* $14,867; *Room only:* $9467. Room and board charges vary according to board plan, housing facility, and location.

FRESHMAN FINANCIAL AID (Fall 2016, est.) 2,473 applied for aid; of those 78% were deemed to have need. 98% of freshmen with need received aid; of those 55% had need fully met. *Average percent of need met:* 85% (excluding resources awarded to replace EFC). *Average financial aid package:* $17,379 (excluding resources awarded to replace EFC). 1% of all full-time freshmen had no need and received non-need-based gift aid.

UNDERGRADUATE FINANCIAL AID (Fall 2016, est.) 15,319 applied for aid; of those 88% were deemed to have need. 98% of undergraduates with need received aid; of those 74% had need fully met. *Average percent of need met:* 86% (excluding resources awarded to replace EFC). *Average financial aid package:* $18,142 (excluding resources awarded to replace EFC). 1% of all full-time undergraduates had no need and received non-need-based gift aid.

GIFT AID (NEED-BASED) *Total amount:* $112,990,304 (44% federal, 54% state, 1% institutional, 1% external sources). *Receiving aid:* Freshmen: 58% (1,783); all full-time undergraduates: 58% (12,600). *Average award:* Freshmen: $11,596; Undergraduates: $10,957. *Scholarships, grants, and awards:* Federal Pell, FSEOG, state, private, college/university gift aid from institutional funds.

GIFT AID (NON-NEED-BASED) *Total amount:* $132,078 (40% institutional, 60% external sources). *Receiving aid:* Freshmen: 4% (125). Undergraduates: 3% (547). *Average award:* Freshmen: $757. Undergraduates: $1519. *Scholarships,*

grants, and awards by category: Academic interests/achievement: general academic interests/achievements. *Creative arts/performance:* art/fine arts, general creative arts/performance, music, theater/drama. *Special achievements/activities:* leadership. *Special characteristics:* local/state students. *Tuition waivers:* Full or partial for employees or children of employees. *ROTC:* Army cooperative, Air Force.

LOANS *Student loans:* $46,763,125 (88% need-based, 12% non-need-based). 43% of past graduating class borrowed through all loan programs. *Average indebtedness per student:* $19,797. *Average need-based loan:* Freshmen: $3366. Undergraduates: $4229. *Parent loans:* $13,100,386 (70% need-based, 30% non-need-based). *Programs:* Federal Direct (Subsidized and Unsubsidized Stafford, PLUS), Perkins, state.

WORK-STUDY *Federal work-study:* Total amount: $1,722,217; jobs available.

ATHLETIC AWARDS Total amount: $6,543,577 (85% need-based, 15% non-need-based).

APPLYING FOR FINANCIAL AID *Required financial aid forms:* FAFSA, state aid form. *Financial aid deadline:* 4/28 (priority: 3/2). *Notification date:* Continuous beginning 3/1.

CONTACT Coleetta McElroy, Director of Financial Aid and Scholarship Office, San Jose State University, One Washington Square, San Jose, CA 95192-0036, 408-924-6086. *E-mail:* coleetta.mcelroy@sjsu.edu. *Website:* http://www.sjsu.edu/.

SANTA BARBARA BUSINESS COLLEGE
Ventura, CA

CONTACT Financial Aid Office, Santa Barbara Business College, 4839 Market Street, Ventura, CA 93003, 805-339-2999. *Website:* http://www.sbbcollege.edu/.

SANTA CLARA UNIVERSITY
Santa Clara, CA

Tuition & fees: $47,112	Average undergraduate aid package: $34,298

ABOUT THE INSTITUTION Independent Roman Catholic (Jesuit), coed. *Awards:* certificates, bachelor's, master's, and doctoral degrees. 48 undergraduate majors. *Total enrollment:* 8,422. Undergraduates: 5,438. Freshmen: 1,317. Both federal and institutional methodology are used as a basis for awarding need-based institutional aid.

UNDERGRADUATE EXPENSES for 2016–2017 *Application fee:* $60. *Comprehensive fee:* $61,077 includes full-time tuition ($47,112) and room and board ($13,965). Room and board charges vary according to board plan and housing facility. *Part-time tuition:* $1309 per unit. Part-time tuition and fees vary according to course load.

FRESHMAN FINANCIAL AID (Fall 2016, est.) 778 applied for aid; of those 70% were deemed to have need. 97% of freshmen with need received aid; of those 46% had need fully met. *Average percent of need met:* 86% (excluding resources awarded to replace EFC). *Average financial aid package:* $36,762 (excluding resources awarded to replace EFC). 25% of all full-time freshmen had no need and received non-need-based gift aid.

UNDERGRADUATE FINANCIAL AID (Fall 2016, est.) 3,103 applied for aid; of those 78% were deemed to have need. 80% of undergraduates with need received aid; of those 39% had need fully met. *Average percent of need met:* 76% (excluding resources awarded to replace EFC). *Average financial aid package:* $34,298 (excluding resources awarded to replace EFC). 26% of all full-time undergraduates had no need and received non-need-based gift aid.

GIFT AID (NEED-BASED) *Total amount:* $58,690,250 (5% federal, 7% state, 86% institutional, 2% external sources). *Receiving aid:* Freshmen: 36% (474); all full-time undergraduates: 32% (1,736). *Average award:* Freshmen: $28,790; Undergraduates: $27,281. *Scholarships, grants, and awards:* Federal Pell, FSEOG, state, private, college/university gift aid from institutional funds.

GIFT AID (NON-NEED-BASED) *Total amount:* $24,726,401 (96% institutional, 4% external sources). *Receiving aid:* Freshmen: 21% (281). Undergraduates: 15% (803). *Average award:* Freshmen: $11,456. Undergraduates: $14,378. *Scholarships, grants, and awards by category:* Academic interests/achievement:

2,365 awards ($35,621,970 total): business, engineering/technologies, general academic interests/achievements, military science. *Creative arts/performance:* 97 awards ($291,134 total): dance, debating, music, theater/drama. *Special characteristics:* 88 awards ($3,552,270 total): children and siblings of alumni, children of faculty/staff, children with a deceased or disabled parent, handicapped students. *Tuition waivers:* Full or partial for employees or children of employees. *ROTC:* Army, Air Force cooperative.

LOANS *Student loans:* $9,121,381 (87% need-based, 13% non-need-based). 44% of past graduating class borrowed through all loan programs. *Average indebtedness per student:* $27,385. *Average need-based loan:* Freshmen: $3333. Undergraduates: $4976. *Parent loans:* $9,277,293 (86% need-based, 14% non-need-based). *Programs:* Federal Direct (Subsidized and Unsubsidized Stafford, PLUS), Perkins, private loans.

WORK-STUDY *Federal work-study:* Total amount: $514,975; 306 jobs averaging $2965. *State or other work-study/employment:* Total amount: $223,458 (23% need-based, 77% non-need-based). Part-time jobs available.

ATHLETIC AWARDS Total amount: $5,952,133 (22% need-based, 78% non-need-based).

APPLYING FOR FINANCIAL AID *Financial aid deadline (priority):* 2/1. *Notification date:* 4/1. Students must reply by 5/1 or within 4 weeks of notification.

CONTACT Mrs. Nancy Merz, Dean of Financial Aid, Santa Clara University, 500 El Camino Real, Santa Clara, CA 95053, 408-551-1000. *Fax:* 408-554-2154. *E-mail:* nmerz@scu.edu.
Website: http://www.scu.edu/.

SANTA FE COLLEGE
Gainesville, FL

CONTACT Financial Aid Office, Santa Fe College, 3000 Northwest 83rd Street, Gainesville, FL 32606, 352-395-5000.
Website: http://www.sfcollege.edu/.

SARAH LAWRENCE COLLEGE
Bronxville, NY

Tuition & fees: $52,350	Average undergraduate aid package: $37,319

ABOUT THE INSTITUTION Independent, coed. *Awards:* bachelor's and master's degrees. 60 undergraduate majors. *Total enrollment:* 1,736. Undergraduates: 1,438. Freshmen: 377. Both federal and institutional methodology are used as a basis for awarding need-based institutional aid.

UNDERGRADUATE EXPENSES for 2016–2017 *Application fee:* $60. *Comprehensive fee:* $67,186 includes full-time tuition ($51,196), mandatory fees ($1154), and room and board ($14,836). *College room only:* $9640. Full-time tuition and fees vary according to course load. Room and board charges vary according to board plan. *Part-time tuition:* $1706.53 per credit hour. *Part-time fees:* $276 per term. Part-time tuition and fees vary according to course load.

FRESHMAN FINANCIAL AID (Fall 2016, est.) 270 applied for aid; of those 81% were deemed to have need. 100% of freshmen with need received aid; of those 17% had need fully met. *Average percent of need met:* 77% (excluding resources awarded to replace EFC). *Average financial aid package:* $35,892 (excluding resources awarded to replace EFC). 20% of all full-time freshmen had no need and received non-need-based gift aid.

UNDERGRADUATE FINANCIAL AID (Fall 2016, est.) 958 applied for aid; of those 86% were deemed to have need. 99% of undergraduates with need received aid; of those 16% had need fully met. *Average percent of need met:* 76% (excluding resources awarded to replace EFC). *Average financial aid package:* $37,319 (excluding resources awarded to replace EFC). 21% of all full-time undergraduates had no need and received non-need-based gift aid.

GIFT AID (NEED-BASED) *Total amount:* $27,992,772 (4% federal, 1% state, 93% institutional, 2% external sources). *Receiving aid:* Freshmen: 57% (215); all full-time undergraduates: 59% (800). *Average award:* Freshmen: $33,546; Undergraduates: $34,799. *Scholarships, grants, and awards:* Federal Pell, FSEOG, state, private, college/university gift aid from institutional funds.

GIFT AID (NON-NEED-BASED) *Total amount:* $5,856,184 (93% institutional, 7% external sources). *Receiving aid:* Freshmen: 9% (35). Undergraduates: 8% (114). *Average award:* Freshmen: $14,964. Undergraduates: $15,178. *Scholarships, grants, and awards by category:* Academic interests/achievement: 375 awards ($5,081,635 total): general academic interests/achievements. *Tuition waivers:* Full or partial for employees or children of employees. *ROTC:* Air Force cooperative.

LOANS *Student loans:* $5,228,222 (60% need-based, 40% non-need-based). 35% of past graduating class borrowed through all loan programs. *Average indebtedness per student:* $19,772. *Average need-based loan:* Freshmen: $2244. Undergraduates: $2690. *Parent loans:* $3,508,302 (45% need-based, 55% non-need-based). *Programs:* Federal Direct (Subsidized and Unsubsidized Stafford, PLUS), Perkins, private loans.

WORK-STUDY *Federal work-study:* Total amount: $800,852; 604 jobs averaging $1663. *State or other work-study/employment:* Total amount: $149,700 (39% need-based, 61% non-need-based). 43 part-time jobs averaging $1724.

APPLYING FOR FINANCIAL AID *Required financial aid forms:* FAFSA, CSS Financial Aid PROFILE, state aid form, noncustodial (divorced/separated) parent's statement. *Financial aid deadline:* 2/1. *Notification date:* 4/1. Students must reply by 5/1.

CONTACT Mr. Nicholas Salinas, Director of Financial Aid, Sarah Lawrence College, One Mead Way, Bronxville, NY 10708, 914-395-2570 or toll-free 800-888-2858. *Fax:* 914-395-2676. *E-mail:* nsalinas@sarahlawrence.edu.
Website: http://www.sarahlawrence.edu/.

SAVANNAH COLLEGE OF ART AND DESIGN
Savannah, GA

Tuition & fees: N/R	Average undergraduate aid package: $17,818

ABOUT THE INSTITUTION Independent, coed. *Awards:* certificates, bachelor's, and master's degrees. 30 undergraduate majors. *Total enrollment:* 12,951. Undergraduates: 10,573. Freshmen: 2,345. Federal methodology is used as a basis for awarding need-based institutional aid.

UNDERGRADUATE EXPENSES for 2017–2018 *Application fee:* $70.

FRESHMAN FINANCIAL AID (Fall 2016, est.) 1,511 applied for aid; of those 82% were deemed to have need. 100% of freshmen with need received aid; of those 11% had need fully met. *Average percent of need met:* 43% (excluding resources awarded to replace EFC). *Average financial aid package:* $17,428 (excluding resources awarded to replace EFC). 41% of all full-time freshmen had no need and received non-need-based gift aid.

UNDERGRADUATE FINANCIAL AID (Fall 2016, est.) 5,105 applied for aid; of those 86% were deemed to have need. 99% of undergraduates with need received aid; of those 10% had need fully met. *Average percent of need met:* 41% (excluding resources awarded to replace EFC). *Average financial aid package:* $17,818 (excluding resources awarded to replace EFC). 41% of all full-time undergraduates had no need and received non-need-based gift aid.

GIFT AID (NEED-BASED) *Total amount:* $64,507,072 (17% federal, 6% state, 75% institutional, 2% external sources). *Receiving aid:* Freshmen: 55% (1,223); all full-time undergraduates: 48% (4,192). *Average award:* Freshmen: $14,041; Undergraduates: $13,801. *Scholarships, grants, and awards:* Federal Pell, FSEOG, state, private, college/university gift aid from institutional funds, United Negro College Fund.

GIFT AID (NON-NEED-BASED) *Total amount:* $45,620,050 (3% state, 92% institutional, 5% external sources). *Receiving aid:* Freshmen: 6% (133). Undergraduates: 4% (377). *Average award:* Freshmen: $9569. Undergraduates: $9351. *Scholarships, grants, and awards by category:* Academic interests/achievement: architecture, general academic interests/achievements. *Creative arts/performance:* applied art and design, art/fine arts, cinema/film/broadcasting, creative writing, dance, debating, general creative arts/performance, journalism/publications, music, performing arts, theater/drama. *Special achievements/activities:* general special achievements/activities. *Special characteristics:* general special characteristics, veterans, veterans' children. *Tuition waivers:* Full or partial for employees or children of employees.

LOANS *Student loans:* $59,471,611 (74% need-based, 26% non-need-based). 56% of past graduating class borrowed through all loan programs. *Average indebtedness per student:* $37,390. *Average need-based loan:* Freshmen: $3444. Undergrad-

uates: $4417. *Parent loans:* $61,789,149 (63% need-based, 37% non-need-based). *Programs:* Federal Direct (Subsidized and Unsubsidized Stafford, PLUS), state, private loans.

WORK-STUDY *Federal work-study:* Total amount: $763,187; jobs available. *State or other work-study/employment:* Total amount: $1,681,436 (100% need-based). Part-time jobs available.

ATHLETIC AWARDS Total amount: $6,040,749 (34% need-based, 66% non-need-based).

APPLYING FOR FINANCIAL AID *Required financial aid forms:* FAFSA, state aid form. *Financial aid deadline:* Continuous. *Notification date:* Continuous beginning 3/1. Students must reply within 4 weeks of notification.

CONTACT Ms. Kim Beveridge, Director of Financial Aid, Savannah College of Art and Design, PO Box 3146, Savannah, GA 31402-3146, 800-859-7223 or toll-free 800-869-7223. *E-mail:* admission@scad.edu. *Website:* http://www.scad.edu/.

SAVANNAH STATE UNIVERSITY
Savannah, GA

Tuition & fees (GA res): $6616	Average undergraduate aid package: N/A

ABOUT THE INSTITUTION State-supported, coed. *Awards:* certificates, associate, bachelor's, and master's degrees. 29 undergraduate majors. *Total enrollment:* 4,800. Undergraduates: 4,645. Freshmen: 1,186. Federal methodology is used as a basis for awarding need-based institutional aid.

UNDERGRADUATE EXPENSES for 2016–2017 *Tuition, state resident:* full-time $4858; part-time $161.93 per credit hour. *Tuition, nonresident:* full-time $17,678; part-time $589.27 per credit hour. *Required fees:* full-time $1758; $879 per term. Full-time tuition and fees vary according to course load, program, and reciprocity agreements. Part-time tuition and fees vary according to course load, program, and reciprocity agreements. Room and board charges vary according to board plan and housing facility.

GIFT AID (NEED-BASED) *Total amount:* $17,337,095 (100% federal). *Scholarships, grants, and awards:* Federal Pell, FSEOG, state, private, college/university gift aid from institutional funds.

GIFT AID (NON-NEED-BASED) *Total amount:* $4,547,499 (71% state, 11% institutional, 18% external sources). *Scholarships, grants, and awards by category:* Academic interests/achievement: biological sciences, business, computer science, engineering/technologies, English, general academic interests/achievements, humanities, mathematics, military science, physical sciences, social sciences. *Tuition waivers:* Full or partial for employees or children of employees, senior citizens. *ROTC:* Army, Naval.

LOANS *Student loans:* $39,795,141 (35% need-based, 65% non-need-based). *Parent loans:* $9,843,953 (100% non-need-based). *Programs:* Federal Direct (Subsidized and Unsubsidized Stafford, PLUS), Perkins, state, college/university.

WORK-STUDY *Federal work-study:* jobs available. *State or other work-study/employment:* Total amount: $14,748 (100% non-need-based). Part-time jobs available.

ATHLETIC AWARDS Total amount: $2,056,880 (100% non-need-based).

APPLYING FOR FINANCIAL AID *Required financial aid form:* FAFSA. *Financial aid deadline:* 7/31. *Notification date:* Continuous beginning 4/1. Students must reply within 8 weeks of notification.

CONTACT Mr. Kenneth Wilson, Director of Financial Aid, Savannah State University, PO Box 20523, Savannah, GA 31404, 912-358-4162 or toll-free 800-788-0478. *Fax:* 912-358-3167. *E-mail:* finaid@savannahstate.edu. *Website:* http://www.savannahstate.edu/.

SCHILLER INTERNATIONAL UNIVERSITY
Largo, FL

CONTACT Financial Aid Office, Schiller International University, 8560 Ulmerton Road, Largo, FL 33771, 727-736-5082 or toll-free 800-261-9571 (in-state), 800-261-9751 (out-of-state). *Website:* http://www.schiller.edu/.

SCHOOL OF THE ART INSTITUTE OF CHICAGO
Chicago, IL

Tuition & fees: $45,750	Average undergraduate aid package: $34,730

ABOUT THE INSTITUTION Independent, coed. *Awards:* certificates, bachelor's, and master's degrees. 33 undergraduate majors. *Total enrollment:* 3,570. Undergraduates: 2,849. Freshmen: 634. Federal methodology is used as a basis for awarding need-based institutional aid.

UNDERGRADUATE EXPENSES for 2016–2017 *Application fee:* $65. *Comprehensive fee:* $60,940 includes full-time tuition ($44,910), mandatory fees ($840), and room and board ($15,190). *College room only:* $11,600. Full-time tuition and fees vary according to course load, degree level, and program. Room and board charges vary according to board plan and housing facility. *Part-time tuition:* $1497 per credit hour. *Part-time fees:* $285 per term. Part-time tuition and fees vary according to course load, degree level, and program.

FRESHMAN FINANCIAL AID (Fall 2015) 325 applied for aid; of those 85% were deemed to have need. 100% of freshmen with need received aid; of those 10% had need fully met. *Average percent of need met:* 63% (excluding resources awarded to replace EFC). *Average financial aid package:* $35,464 (excluding resources awarded to replace EFC). 36% of all full-time freshmen had no need and received non-need-based gift aid.

UNDERGRADUATE FINANCIAL AID (Fall 2015) 1,320 applied for aid; of those 88% were deemed to have need. 100% of undergraduates with need received aid; of those 9% had need fully met. *Average percent of need met:* 60% (excluding resources awarded to replace EFC). *Average financial aid package:* $34,730 (excluding resources awarded to replace EFC). 47% of all full-time undergraduates had no need and received non-need-based gift aid.

GIFT AID (NEED-BASED) *Receiving aid:* Freshmen: 48% (276); all full-time undergraduates: 44% (1,149). *Average award:* Freshmen: $20,318; Undergraduates: $18,949. *Scholarships, grants, and awards:* Federal Pell, FSEOG, state, private, college/university gift aid from institutional funds.

GIFT AID (NON-NEED-BASED) *Receiving aid:* Freshmen: 4% (25). Undergraduates: 3% (85). *Average award:* Freshmen: $11,499. Undergraduates: $9363. *Scholarships, grants, and awards by category:* Academic interests/achievement: general academic interests/achievements. Creative arts/performance: art/fine arts. *Tuition waivers:* Full or partial for employees or children of employees.

LOANS *Student loans:* 48% of past graduating class borrowed through all loan programs. *Average indebtedness per student:* $35,455. *Average need-based loan:* Freshmen: $4116. Undergraduates: $5178. *Programs:* Federal Direct (Subsidized and Unsubsidized Stafford, PLUS), Perkins.

WORK-STUDY Federal work-study jobs available. *State or other work-study/employment:* Part-time jobs available.

APPLYING FOR FINANCIAL AID *Required financial aid form:* FAFSA. *Financial aid deadline (priority):* 3/1. *Notification date:* Continuous beginning 4/1.

CONTACT Mr. Patrick James, Student Financial Services Office, School of the Art Institute of Chicago, 36 South Wabash, Suite 1218, Chicago, IL 60603-3103, 312-629-6600 or toll-free 800-232-SAIC. *Fax:* 312-629-6601. *E-mail:* finaid@saic.edu. *Website:* http://www.saic.edu/.

SCHOOL OF VISUAL ARTS
New York, NY

Tuition & fees: $36,500	Average undergraduate aid package: $17,121

ABOUT THE INSTITUTION Proprietary, coed. *Awards:* bachelor's and master's degrees. 15 undergraduate majors. *Total enrollment:* 4,407. Undergraduates: 3,707. Freshmen: 698. Federal methodology is used as a basis for awarding need-based institutional aid.

UNDERGRADUATE EXPENSES for 2016–2017 *Application fee:* $50. *Comprehensive fee:* $54,800 includes full-time tuition ($36,500) and room and board

($18,300). *College room only:* $15,400. *Part-time tuition:* $1270 per credit hour.

FRESHMAN FINANCIAL AID (Fall 2016, est.) 366 applied for aid; of those 90% were deemed to have need. 98% of freshmen with need received aid; of those 3% had need fully met. *Average percent of need met:* 4% (excluding resources awarded to replace EFC). *Average financial aid package:* $17,143 (excluding resources awarded to replace EFC). 10% of all full-time freshmen had no need and received non-need-based gift aid.

UNDERGRADUATE FINANCIAL AID (Fall 2016, est.) 1,581 applied for aid; of those 93% were deemed to have need. 97% of undergraduates with need received aid; of those 1% had need fully met. *Average percent of need met:* 36% (excluding resources awarded to replace EFC). *Average financial aid package:* $17,121 (excluding resources awarded to replace EFC). 8% of all full-time undergraduates had no need and received non-need-based gift aid.

GIFT AID (NEED-BASED) *Total amount:* $16,758,555 (24% federal, 7% state, 66% institutional, 3% external sources). *Receiving aid:* Freshmen: 38% (282); all full-time undergraduates: 33% (1,163). *Average award:* Freshmen: $14,668; Undergraduates: $13,772. *Scholarships, grants, and awards:* Federal Pell, FSEOG, state, private, college/university gift aid from institutional funds.

GIFT AID (NON-NEED-BASED) *Total amount:* $2,610,891 (9% federal, 80% institutional, 11% external sources). *Receiving aid:* Freshmen: 22% (164). Undergraduates: 15% (534). *Average award:* Freshmen: $11,290. Undergraduates: $12,192. *Scholarships, grants, and awards by category:* Creative arts/performance: art/fine arts.

LOANS *Student loans:* $16,377,670 (94% need-based, 6% non-need-based). 58% of past graduating class borrowed through all loan programs. *Average indebtedness per student:* $46,328. *Average need-based loan:* Freshmen: $3022. Undergraduates: $4253. *Parent loans:* $13,702,062 (94% need-based, 6% non-need-based). *Programs:* Federal Direct (Subsidized and Unsubsidized Stafford, PLUS), Perkins, alternative loans.

WORK-STUDY *Federal work-study:* Total amount: $697,692; jobs available. *State or other work-study/employment:* Total amount: $668,700 (63% need-based, 37% non-need-based). Part-time jobs available.

APPLYING FOR FINANCIAL AID *Required financial aid forms:* FAFSA, state aid form. *Financial aid deadline:* 3/1 (priority: 2/1). *Notification date:* Continuous beginning 2/15. Students must reply within 4 weeks of notification.

CONTACT Mr. William Berrios, Financial Aid Office, School of Visual Arts, 209 East 23rd Street, New York, NY 10010, 212-592-2030 or toll-free 800-436-4204. *Fax:* 212-592-2029. *E-mail:* fa@sva.edu.
Website: http://www.sva.edu/.

SCHREINER UNIVERSITY
Kerrville, TX

Tuition & fees: $26,750	Average undergraduate aid package: $19,712

ABOUT THE INSTITUTION Independent Presbyterian, coed. *Awards:* certificates, associate, bachelor's, and master's degrees. 36 undergraduate majors. *Total enrollment:* 1,308. Undergraduates: 1,237. Freshmen: 302. Federal methodology is used as a basis for awarding need-based institutional aid.

UNDERGRADUATE EXPENSES for 2017–2018 *Application fee:* $25. *Comprehensive fee:* $37,662 includes full-time tuition ($24,990), mandatory fees ($1760), and room and board ($10,912). *College room only:* $5740. Full-time tuition and fees vary according to course load, location, program, and student level. Room and board charges vary according to board plan and housing facility. *Part-time tuition:* $1069 per credit hour. *Part-time fees:* $830 per year. Part-time tuition and fees vary according to course load and program.

FRESHMAN FINANCIAL AID (Fall 2015) 263 applied for aid; of those 84% were deemed to have need. 100% of freshmen with need received aid; of those 19% had need fully met. *Average percent of need met:* 71% (excluding resources awarded to replace EFC). *Average financial aid package:* $18,806 (excluding resources awarded to replace EFC). 25% of all full-time freshmen had no need and received non-need-based gift aid.

UNDERGRADUATE FINANCIAL AID (Fall 2015) 869 applied for aid; of those 88% were deemed to have need. 100% of undergraduates with need received aid; of those 14% had need fully met. *Average percent of need met:* 71% (excluding resources awarded to replace EFC). *Average financial aid package:* $19,712

(excluding resources awarded to replace EFC). 23% of all full-time undergraduates had no need and received non-need-based gift aid.

GIFT AID (NEED-BASED) *Total amount:* $12,589,830 (15% federal, 13% state, 55% institutional, 17% external sources). *Receiving aid:* Freshmen: 75% (220); all full-time undergraduates: 79% (761). *Average award:* Freshmen: $16,171; Undergraduates: $16,250. *Scholarships, grants, and awards:* Federal Pell, FSEOG, state, private, college/university gift aid from institutional funds.

GIFT AID (NON-NEED-BASED) *Total amount:* $3,342,799 (1% state, 72% institutional, 27% external sources). *Receiving aid:* Freshmen: 13% (37). Undergraduates: 9% (84). *Average award:* Freshmen: $10,014. Undergraduates: $9654. *Scholarships, grants, and awards by category:* Academic interests/achievement: biological sciences, business, communication, education, English, general academic interests/achievements, mathematics, physical sciences, premedicine, religion/biblical studies, social sciences. *Creative arts/performance:* applied art and design, art/fine arts, journalism/publications, music, theater/drama. *Special achievements/activities:* community service, leadership, memberships, religious involvement. *Special characteristics:* children of faculty/staff, general special characteristics, international students, local/state students, relatives of clergy, religious affiliation, siblings of current students, veterans. *Tuition waivers:* Full or partial for employees or children of employees.

LOANS *Student loans:* $8,544,101 (68% need-based, 32% non-need-based). 75% of past graduating class borrowed through all loan programs. *Average indebtedness per student:* $29,020. *Average need-based loan:* Freshmen: $3051. Undergraduates: $3892. *Parent loans:* $1,732,609 (45% need-based, 55% non-need-based). *Programs:* Federal Direct (Subsidized and Unsubsidized Stafford, PLUS), state, alternative loans.

WORK-STUDY *Federal work-study:* jobs available. *State or other work-study/employment:* Total amount: $17,763 (48% need-based, 52% non-need-based). Part-time jobs available.

APPLYING FOR FINANCIAL AID *Required financial aid form:* FAFSA. *Financial aid deadline (priority):* 5/1. *Notification date:* Continuous beginning 2/15. Students must reply within 2 weeks of notification.

CONTACT Ms. Toni Bryant, Director of Financial Aid, Schreiner University, 2100 Memorial Boulevard, Kerrville, TX 78028, 830-792-7217 or toll-free 800-343-4919. *Fax:* 830-792-7226. *E-mail:* tlbryant@schreiner.edu.
Website: http://www.schreiner.edu/.

SCRIPPS COLLEGE
Claremont, CA

Tuition & fees: $50,982	Average undergraduate aid package: $42,513

ABOUT THE INSTITUTION Independent, women only. *Awards:* certificates and bachelor's degrees. 62 undergraduate majors. *Total enrollment:* 1,057. Undergraduates: 1,039. Freshmen: 270. Both federal and institutional methodology are used as a basis for awarding need-based institutional aid.

UNDERGRADUATE EXPENSES for 2016–2017 *Application fee:* $60. *Comprehensive fee:* $66,664 includes full-time tuition ($50,766), mandatory fees ($216), and room and board ($15,682). *College room only:* $8538. Full-time tuition and fees vary according to course load and degree level. Room and board charges vary according to board plan. *Part-time tuition:* $6346 per course. Part-time tuition and fees vary according to course load and degree level. *Payment plan:* Tuition prepayment.

FRESHMAN FINANCIAL AID (Fall 2015) 154 applied for aid; of those 60% were deemed to have need. 100% of freshmen with need received aid; of those 100% had need fully met. *Average percent of need met:* 100% (excluding resources awarded to replace EFC). *Average financial aid package:* $40,005 (excluding resources awarded to replace EFC). 4% of all full-time freshmen had no need and received non-need-based gift aid.

UNDERGRADUATE FINANCIAL AID (Fall 2015) 472 applied for aid; of those 79% were deemed to have need. 100% of undergraduates with need received aid; of those 100% had need fully met. *Average percent of need met:* 100% (excluding resources awarded to replace EFC). *Average financial aid package:* $42,513 (excluding resources awarded to replace EFC). 4% of all full-time undergraduates had no need and received non-need-based gift aid.

GIFT AID (NEED-BASED) *Total amount:* $14,044,269 (4% federal, 3% state, 91% institutional, 2% external sources). *Receiving aid:* Freshmen: 34% (93); all full-time undergraduates: 38% (371). *Average award:* Freshmen: $35,730; Undergrad-

uates: $37,361. *Scholarships, grants, and awards:* Federal Pell, FSEOG, state, private, college/university gift aid from institutional funds.
GIFT AID (NON-NEED-BASED) *Total amount:* $3,555,065 (87% institutional, 13% external sources). *Average award:* Freshmen: $16,757. Undergraduates: $10,993. *Scholarships, grants, and awards by category:* Academic interests/achievement: general academic interests/achievements. *Tuition waivers:* Full or partial for employees or children of employees. *ROTC:* Army cooperative, Air Force cooperative.
LOANS *Student loans:* $2,040,678 (84% need-based, 16% non-need-based). 39% of past graduating class borrowed through all loan programs. *Average indebtedness per student:* $20,205. *Average need-based loan:* Freshmen: $3731. Undergraduates: $4329. *Parent loans:* $1,029,865 (71% need-based, 29% non-need-based). *Programs:* Federal Direct (Subsidized and Unsubsidized Stafford, PLUS), Perkins, college/university.
WORK-STUDY *Federal work-study:* jobs available. *State or other work-study/employment:* Total amount: $13,883 (84% need-based, 16% non-need-based). Part-time jobs available.
APPLYING FOR FINANCIAL AID *Required financial aid forms:* FAFSA, CSS Financial Aid PROFILE, state aid form, noncustodial (divorced/separated) parent's statement, business/farm supplement. *Financial aid deadline:* 2/1 (priority: 2/1). *Notification date:* 4/1. Students must reply by 5/1.
CONTACT Patrick Moore, Director of Financial Aid, Scripps College, 1030 Columbia Avenue, Claremont, CA 91711-3948, 909-621-8275 or toll-free 800-770-1333. *Fax:* 909-607-7742. *E-mail:* finaid@scrippscollege.edu.
Website: http://www.scrippscollege.edu/.

SEATTLE PACIFIC UNIVERSITY
Seattle, WA

Tuition & fees: $38,940	Average undergraduate aid package: $32,869

ABOUT THE INSTITUTION Independent Free Methodist, coed. *Awards:* certificates, bachelor's, master's, and doctoral degrees. 51 undergraduate majors. *Total enrollment:* 4,061. Undergraduates: 3,095. Freshmen: 685. Federal methodology is used as a basis for awarding need-based institutional aid.
UNDERGRADUATE EXPENSES for 2016–2017 *Application fee:* $50. *Comprehensive fee:* $49,764 includes full-time tuition ($38,520), mandatory fees ($420), and room and board ($10,824). *College room only:* $5883. Room and board charges vary according to board plan and housing facility. *Part-time tuition:* $1070 per credit hour. Part-time tuition and fees vary according to course load.
FRESHMAN FINANCIAL AID (Fall 2016, est.) 616 applied for aid; of those 79% were deemed to have need. 100% of freshmen with need received aid; of those 9% had need fully met. *Average percent of need met:* 79% (excluding resources awarded to replace EFC). *Average financial aid package:* $31,816 (excluding resources awarded to replace EFC). 23% of all full-time freshmen had no need and received non-need-based gift aid.
UNDERGRADUATE FINANCIAL AID (Fall 2016, est.) 2,422 applied for aid; of those 86% were deemed to have need. 100% of undergraduates with need received aid; of those 7% had need fully met. *Average percent of need met:* 79% (excluding resources awarded to replace EFC). *Average financial aid package:* $32,869 (excluding resources awarded to replace EFC). 24% of all full-time undergraduates had no need and received non-need-based gift aid.
GIFT AID (NEED-BASED) *Total amount:* $54,150,177 (8% federal, 6% state, 80% institutional, 6% external sources). *Receiving aid:* Freshmen: 73% (488); all full-time undergraduates: 70% (2,075). *Average award:* Freshmen: $30,822; Undergraduates: $30,163. *Scholarships, grants, and awards:* Federal Pell, FSEOG, state, private, college/university gift aid from institutional funds.
GIFT AID (NON-NEED-BASED) *Total amount:* $16,273,763 (81% institutional, 19% external sources). *Average award:* Freshmen: $24,277. Undergraduates: $22,062. *Scholarships, grants, and awards by category:* Academic interests/achievement: 584 awards ($8,566,692 total): engineering/technologies, general academic interests/achievements. *Creative arts/performance:* 40 awards ($59,500 total): art/fine arts, performing arts. *Special characteristics:* 263 awards ($1,226,296 total): children and siblings of alumni, children of faculty/staff, general special characteristics, international students, relatives of clergy, religious affiliation, veterans, veterans' children. *Tuition waivers:* Full or partial for employees or children of employees, senior citizens. *ROTC:* Army cooperative, Naval cooperative, Air Force cooperative.

LOANS *Student loans:* $16,270,620 (92% need-based, 8% non-need-based). 69% of past graduating class borrowed through all loan programs. *Average indebtedness per student:* $28,880. *Average need-based loan:* Freshmen: $4378. Undergraduates: $5088. *Parent loans:* $8,687,460 (87% need-based, 13% non-need-based). *Programs:* Federal Direct (Subsidized and Unsubsidized Stafford, PLUS), Perkins, Federal Nursing, state, college/university.
WORK-STUDY *Federal work-study:* Total amount: $1,018,209; 425 jobs averaging $2396. *State or other work-study/employment:* Total amount: $301,879 (100% need-based). 140 part-time jobs averaging $2156.
ATHLETIC AWARDS Total amount: $2,147,072 (45% need-based, 55% non-need-based).
APPLYING FOR FINANCIAL AID *Required financial aid form:* FAFSA. *Financial aid deadline (priority):* 3/15. *Notification date:* Continuous beginning 3/15. Students must reply by 5/1 or within 4 weeks of notification.
CONTACT Mr. Jordan Grant, Director of Student Financial Services, Seattle Pacific University, 3307 Third Avenue West, Seattle, WA 98119-1997, 206-281-2469 or toll-free 800-366-3344. *E-mail:* grantj@spu.edu.
Website: http://www.spu.edu/.

SEATTLE UNIVERSITY
Seattle, WA

Tuition & fees: $41,265	Average undergraduate aid package: $33,772

ABOUT THE INSTITUTION Independent Roman Catholic, coed. *Awards:* certificates, bachelor's, master's, and doctoral degrees. 71 undergraduate majors. *Total enrollment:* 7,477. Undergraduates: 4,776. Freshmen: 982. Federal methodology is used as a basis for awarding need-based institutional aid.
UNDERGRADUATE EXPENSES for 2016–2017 *Application fee:* $50. *Comprehensive fee:* $52,764 includes full-time tuition ($40,500), mandatory fees ($765), and room and board ($11,499). *College room only:* $7059. Full-time tuition and fees vary according to course load. Room and board charges vary according to board plan and housing facility. *Part-time tuition:* $900 per credit hour. Part-time tuition and fees vary according to course load.
FRESHMAN FINANCIAL AID (Fall 2016, est.) 829 applied for aid; of those 76% were deemed to have need. 100% of freshmen with need received aid; of those 12% had need fully met. *Average percent of need met:* 73% (excluding resources awarded to replace EFC). *Average financial aid package:* $32,663 (excluding resources awarded to replace EFC). 11% of all full-time freshmen had no need and received non-need-based gift aid.
UNDERGRADUATE FINANCIAL AID (Fall 2016, est.) 3,093 applied for aid; of those 81% were deemed to have need. 100% of undergraduates with need received aid; of those 12% had need fully met. *Average percent of need met:* 70% (excluding resources awarded to replace EFC). *Average financial aid package:* $33,772 (excluding resources awarded to replace EFC). 4% of all full-time undergraduates had no need and received non-need-based gift aid.
GIFT AID (NEED-BASED) *Total amount:* $72,283,516 (9% federal, 5% state, 82% institutional, 4% external sources). *Receiving aid:* Freshmen: 56% (552); all full-time undergraduates: 50% (2,272). *Average award:* Freshmen: $25,004; Undergraduates: $23,620. *Scholarships, grants, and awards:* Federal Pell, FSEOG, state, private, college/university gift aid from institutional funds, Federal Nursing.
GIFT AID (NON-NEED-BASED) *Total amount:* $17,988,798 (15% federal, 70% institutional, 15% external sources). *Receiving aid:* Freshmen: 37% (367). Undergraduates: 25% (1,127). *Average award:* Freshmen: $15,357. Undergraduates: $13,344. *Scholarships, grants, and awards by category:* Academic interests/achievement: general academic interests/achievements. *Creative arts/performance:* art/fine arts, music, theater/drama. *Special achievements/activities:* leadership. *Special characteristics:* children and siblings of alumni, children of educators, children of faculty/staff, members of minority groups, religious affiliation. *Tuition waivers:* Full or partial for employees or children of employees. *ROTC:* Army, Naval cooperative, Air Force cooperative.
LOANS *Student loans:* $21,858,620 (67% need-based, 33% non-need-based). 67% of past graduating class borrowed through all loan programs. *Average indebtedness per student:* $28,297. *Average need-based loan:* Freshmen: $3739. Undergraduates: $5659. *Parent loans:* $8,642,104 (5% need-based, 95% non-need-based). *Programs:* Federal Direct (Subsidized and Unsubsidized Stafford, PLUS), Perkins, Federal Nursing.

WORK-STUDY *Federal work-study:* Total amount: $1,617,704; 484 jobs averaging $3893. *State or other work-study/employment:* Total amount: $2,258,628 (100% need-based). 599 part-time jobs averaging $5179.

ATHLETIC AWARDS Total amount: $5,535,095 (100% non-need-based).

APPLYING FOR FINANCIAL AID *Required financial aid form:* FAFSA. *Financial aid deadline (priority):* 2/1. *Notification date:* 3/1. Students must reply by 5/1 or within 2 weeks of notification.

CONTACT Mr. Jeff Scofield, Director of Student Financial Services, Seattle University, 901 12th Avenue, PO Box 222000, Seattle, WA 98122-1090, 206-296-2000 or toll-free 800-542-0833 (in-state), 800-426-7123 (out-of-state). *Fax:* 206-296-5755. *E-mail:* financial-aid@seattleu.edu. *Website:* http://www.seattleu.edu/.

SELMA UNIVERSITY
Selma, AL

CONTACT Financial Aid Office, Selma University, 1501 Lapsley Street, Selma, AL 36701-5299, 334-872-2533. *Website:* http://www.selmauniversity.edu/.

SENTARA COLLEGE OF HEALTH SCIENCES
Chesapeake, VA

CONTACT Financial Aid Office, Sentara College of Health Sciences, 1441 Crossways Boulevard, Crossways I, Suite 105, Chesapeake, VA 23320, 757-388-2900. *Website:* http://www.sentara.edu/.

SETON HALL UNIVERSITY
South Orange, NJ

CONTACT Office of Enrollment Services, Seton Hall University, 400 South Orange Avenue, South Orange, NJ 07079, 973-761-9350 or toll-free 800-THE HALL. *Fax:* 973-275-2040. *E-mail:* thehall@shu.edu. *Website:* http://www.shu.edu/.

SETON HILL UNIVERSITY
Greensburg, PA

Tuition & fees: $33,520	Average undergraduate aid package: $24,866

ABOUT THE INSTITUTION Independent Roman Catholic, coed. *Awards:* certificates, bachelor's, and master's degrees. 74 undergraduate majors. *Total enrollment:* 1,942. Undergraduates: 1,606. Freshmen: 367. Federal methodology is used as a basis for awarding need-based institutional aid.

UNDERGRADUATE EXPENSES for 2016–2017 *Application fee:* $35. *Comprehensive fee:* $44,520 includes full-time tuition ($32,520), mandatory fees ($1000), and room and board ($11,000). Full-time tuition and fees vary according to course load, degree level, and program. Room and board charges vary according to board plan and housing facility. *Part-time tuition:* $872 per credit. *Part-time fees:* $25 per credit. Part-time tuition and fees vary according to course load, degree level, and program.

FRESHMAN FINANCIAL AID (Fall 2015) 371 applied for aid; of those 91% were deemed to have need. 100% of freshmen with need received aid; of those 22% had need fully met. *Average percent of need met:* 76% (excluding resources awarded to replace EFC). *Average financial aid package:* $25,298 (excluding resources awarded to replace EFC). 17% of all full-time freshmen had no need and received non-need-based gift aid.

UNDERGRADUATE FINANCIAL AID (Fall 2015) 1,354 applied for aid; of those 92% were deemed to have need. 100% of undergraduates with need received aid; of those 17% had need fully met. *Average percent of need met:* 73%

(excluding resources awarded to replace EFC). *Average financial aid package:* $24,866 (excluding resources awarded to replace EFC). 15% of all full-time undergraduates had no need and received non-need-based gift aid.

GIFT AID (NEED-BASED) *Total amount:* $21,901,253 (11% federal, 10% state, 77% institutional, 2% external sources). *Receiving aid:* Freshmen: 86% (336); all full-time undergraduates: 84% (1,243). *Average award:* Freshmen: $20,878; Undergraduates: $19,244. *Scholarships, grants, and awards:* Federal Pell, FSEOG, state, private, college/university gift aid from institutional funds.

GIFT AID (NON-NEED-BASED) *Total amount:* $3,848,048 (97% institutional, 3% external sources). *Receiving aid:* Freshmen: 15% (60). Undergraduates: 10% (152). *Average award:* Freshmen: $15,028. Undergraduates: $13,432. *Scholarships, grants, and awards by category: Academic interests/achievement:* 1,012 awards ($13,353,790 total): general academic interests/achievements. *Creative arts/performance:* 61 awards ($79,750 total): applied art and design, art/fine arts, dance, music, performing arts, theater/drama. *Special achievements/activities:* 68 awards ($42,000 total): cheerleading/drum major, general special achievements/activities. *Special characteristics:* 93 awards ($503,380 total): children and siblings of alumni, children of faculty/staff, international students, siblings of current students. *Tuition waivers:* Full or partial for employees or children of employees. *ROTC:* Army cooperative.

LOANS *Student loans:* $12,485,734 (74% need-based, 26% non-need-based). 86% of past graduating class borrowed through all loan programs. *Average indebtedness per student:* $38,414. *Average need-based loan:* Freshmen: $5534. Undergraduates: $6309. *Parent loans:* $3,984,925 (59% need-based, 41% non-need-based). *Programs:* Federal Direct (Subsidized and Unsubsidized Stafford, PLUS), Perkins, college/university.

WORK-STUDY *Federal work-study:* 602 jobs averaging $1500. *State or other work-study/employment:* Total amount: $240,754 (27% need-based, 73% non-need-based). 107 part-time jobs averaging $303.

ATHLETIC AWARDS Total amount: $4,256,901 (54% need-based, 46% non-need-based).

APPLYING FOR FINANCIAL AID *Required financial aid forms:* FAFSA, institution's own form. *Financial aid deadline:* Continuous. *Notification date:* 11/1. Students must reply by 5/1.

CONTACT Tracey Snyder de Baez, Director of Financial Aid, Seton Hill University, 1 Seton Hill Drive, Greensburg, PA 15601, 724-830-1010 or toll-free 800-826-6234. *Fax:* 724-830-1194. *E-mail:* snyderdebaez@setonhill.edu. *Website:* http://www.setonhill.edu/.

SEWANEE: THE UNIVERSITY OF THE SOUTH
Sewanee, TN

Tuition & fees: $45,120	Average undergraduate aid package: $33,055

ABOUT THE INSTITUTION Independent Episcopal, coed. *Awards:* certificates, bachelor's, master's, and doctoral degrees. 37 undergraduate majors. *Total enrollment:* 1,815. Undergraduates: 1,731. Freshmen: 514. Both federal and institutional methodology are used as a basis for awarding need-based institutional aid.

UNDERGRADUATE EXPENSES for 2017–2018 *Comprehensive fee:* $58,000 includes full-time tuition ($44,848), mandatory fees ($272), and room and board ($12,880). *College room only:* $6675. *Part-time tuition:* $1425 per credit hour. *Payment plan:* Guaranteed tuition.

FRESHMAN FINANCIAL AID (Fall 2016, est.) 351 applied for aid; of those 71% were deemed to have need. 100% of freshmen with need received aid; of those 29% had need fully met. *Average percent of need met:* 91% (excluding resources awarded to replace EFC). *Average financial aid package:* $34,638 (excluding resources awarded to replace EFC). 39% of all full-time freshmen had no need and received non-need-based gift aid.

UNDERGRADUATE FINANCIAL AID (Fall 2016, est.) 1,042 applied for aid; of those 77% were deemed to have need. 100% of undergraduates with need received aid; of those 38% had need fully met. *Average percent of need met:* 93% (excluding resources awarded to replace EFC). *Average financial aid package:* $33,055 (excluding resources awarded to replace EFC). 35% of all full-time undergraduates had no need and received non-need-based gift aid.

GIFT AID (NEED-BASED) *Total amount:* $21,734,330 (7% federal, 4% state, 88% institutional, 1% external sources). *Receiving aid:* Freshmen: 47% (243); all full-

time undergraduates: 46% (785). **Average award:** Freshmen: $28,705; Undergraduates: $27,341. **Scholarships, grants, and awards:** Federal Pell, FSEOG, state, private, college/university gift aid from institutional funds.

GIFT AID (NON-NEED-BASED) Total amount: $8,957,442 (5% state, 91% institutional, 4% external sources). **Receiving aid:** Freshmen: 11% (54). Undergraduates: 12% (204). **Average award:** Freshmen: $13,395. Undergraduates: $12,275. **Scholarships, grants, and awards by category:** Academic interests/ achievement: general academic interests/achievements. Creative arts/performance: general creative arts/performance. Special achievements/activities: general special achievements/activities. Special characteristics: general special characteristics. **Tuition waivers:** Full or partial for employees or children of employees.

LOANS Student loans: $3,660,498 (71% need-based, 29% non-need-based). 43% of past graduating class borrowed through all loan programs. **Average indebtedness per student:** $24,431. **Average need-based loan:** Freshmen: $3476. Undergraduates: $4290. **Parent loans:** $3,198,070 (15% need-based, 85% non-need-based). **Programs:** Federal Direct (Subsidized and Unsubsidized Stafford, PLUS), Perkins, private loans.

WORK-STUDY Federal work-study: Total amount: $682,631; 426 jobs averaging $1602. **State or other work-study/employment:** Total amount: $456,726 (31% need-based, 69% non-need-based). 153 part-time jobs averaging $2985.

APPLYING FOR FINANCIAL AID Required financial aid forms: FAFSA, CSS Financial Aid PROFILE. **Financial aid deadline:** 12/1. **Notification date:** Continuous beginning 2/1. Students must reply by 5/1 or within 2 weeks of notification.

CONTACT Ms. Beth A. Cragar, Associate Dean of Admission for Financial Aid, Sewanee: The University of the South, 735 University Avenue, Sewanee, TN 37383-1000, 931-598-1312 or toll-free 800-522-2234. Fax: 931-598-3273. E-mail: finaid@sewanee.edu.

Website: http://www.sewanee.edu/.

SHASTA BIBLE COLLEGE
Redding, CA

Tuition & fees: $9280	Average undergraduate aid package: N/A

ABOUT THE INSTITUTION Independent nondenominational, coed. 3 undergraduate majors. Federal methodology is used as a basis for awarding need-based institutional aid.

UNDERGRADUATE EXPENSES for 2016–2017 Tuition: full-time $8400; part-time $4100 per year. **Required fees:** full-time $880; $350 per unit or $880 per year.

GIFT AID (NEED-BASED) Scholarships, grants, and awards: Federal Pell, FSEOG, state, private, college/university gift aid from institutional funds.

GIFT AID (NON-NEED-BASED) Scholarships, grants, and awards by category: Academic interests/achievement: education. Creative arts/performance: music. Special achievements/activities: general special achievements/activities. Special characteristics: relatives of clergy, veterans. **Tuition waivers:** Full or partial for employees or children of employees.

LOANS Programs: Federal Direct (Subsidized and Unsubsidized Stafford, PLUS).

WORK-STUDY Federal work-study jobs available. **State or other work-study/ employment:** Part-time jobs available.

APPLYING FOR FINANCIAL AID Required financial aid forms: FAFSA, institution's own form, state aid form. **Financial aid deadline:** Continuous. **Notification date:** Continuous beginning 7/15. Students must reply within 3 weeks of notification.

CONTACT Linda Iles, Financial Aid Administrator, Shasta Bible College, 2951 Goodwater Avenue, Redding, CA 96002, 530-221-4275 Ext. 32 or toll-free 800-800-4SBC. Fax: 530-221-6929. E-mail: finaid@shasta.edu.

Website: http://www.shasta.edu/.

SHAWNEE STATE UNIVERSITY
Portsmouth, OH

Tuition & fees (OH res): $11,296	Average undergraduate aid package: $8972

ABOUT THE INSTITUTION State-supported, coed. **Awards:** certificates, associate, bachelor's, and master's degrees. 49 undergraduate majors. **Total enrollment:** 3,772. Undergraduates: 3,603. Freshmen: 864. Federal methodology is used as a basis for awarding need-based institutional aid.

UNDERGRADUATE EXPENSES for 2017–2018 Tuition, state resident: full-time $7614; part-time $297.34 per credit hour. **Tuition, nonresident:** full-time $13,396; part-time $530.45 per credit hour. **Required fees:** full-time $3682; $46.39 per credit hour. Full-time tuition and fees vary according to course load, program, and reciprocity agreements. Part-time tuition and fees vary according to course load, program, and reciprocity agreements. **College room and board:** $10,116; **Room only:** $5645. Room and board charges vary according to board plan and housing facility.

FRESHMAN FINANCIAL AID (Fall 2016, est.) 817 applied for aid; of those 72% were deemed to have need. 100% of freshmen with need received aid; of those 5% had need fully met. **Average percent of need met:** 44% (excluding resources awarded to replace EFC). **Average financial aid package:** $8662 (excluding resources awarded to replace EFC). 14% of all full-time freshmen had no need and received non-need-based gift aid.

UNDERGRADUATE FINANCIAL AID (Fall 2016, est.) 2,874 applied for aid; of those 66% were deemed to have need. 100% of undergraduates with need received aid; of those 5% had need fully met. **Average percent of need met:** 45% (excluding resources awarded to replace EFC). **Average financial aid package:** $8972 (excluding resources awarded to replace EFC). 13% of all full-time undergraduates had no need and received non-need-based gift aid.

GIFT AID (NEED-BASED) Total amount: $13,163,279 (61% federal, 14% state, 18% institutional, 7% external sources). **Receiving aid:** Freshmen: 50% (425); all full-time undergraduates: 46% (1,417). **Average award:** Freshmen: $5954; Undergraduates: $5855. **Scholarships, grants, and awards:** Federal Pell, FSEOG, state, private, college/university gift aid from institutional funds.

GIFT AID (NON-NEED-BASED) Total amount: $736,498 (3% state, 75% institutional, 22% external sources). **Receiving aid:** Freshmen: 37% (310). Undergraduates: 22% (665). **Average award:** Freshmen: $3522. Undergraduates: $3875. **Scholarships, grants, and awards by category:** Academic interests/ achievement: general academic interests/achievements. Special characteristics: children of faculty/staff, out-of-state students, veterans. **Tuition waivers:** Full or partial for employees or children of employees, senior citizens.

LOANS Student loans: $16,844,770 (79% need-based, 21% non-need-based). 79% of past graduating class borrowed through all loan programs. **Average indebtedness per student:** $30,554. **Average need-based loan:** Freshmen: $3360. Undergraduates: $3964. **Parent loans:** $3,564,890 (66% need-based, 34% non-need-based). **Programs:** Federal Direct (Subsidized and Unsubsidized Stafford, PLUS), state, private loans.

WORK-STUDY Federal work-study: Total amount: $130,703; jobs available.

ATHLETIC AWARDS Total amount: $562,288 (48% need-based, 52% non-need-based).

APPLYING FOR FINANCIAL AID Required financial aid form: FAFSA. **Financial aid deadline:** Continuous. **Notification date:** Continuous beginning 12/15.

CONTACT Ms. Charlotte Hardy, Assistant Director of Financial Aid, Shawnee State University, 940 Second Street, Portsmouth, OH 45662-4344, 740-351-3548 or toll-free 800-959-2778. E-mail: chardy@shawnee.edu.

Website: http://www.shawnee.edu/.

SHAW UNIVERSITY
Raleigh, NC

CONTACT Rochelle King, Director of Financial Aid, Shaw University, 118 East South Street, Raleigh, NC 27601-2399, 919-546-8565 or toll-free 800-214-6683. Fax: 919-546-8356. E-mail: rking@shawu.edu.

Website: http://www.shawu.edu/.

SHENANDOAH UNIVERSITY
Winchester, VA

Tuition & fees: $31,920	Average undergraduate aid package: $19,949

ABOUT THE INSTITUTION Independent United Methodist, coed. *Awards:* certificates, bachelor's, master's, and doctoral degrees. 39 undergraduate majors. *Total enrollment:* 3,918. Undergraduates: 2,099. Freshmen: 460. Federal methodology is used as a basis for awarding need-based institutional aid.

UNDERGRADUATE EXPENSES for 2017–2018 *Comprehensive fee:* $42,100 includes full-time tuition ($30,700), mandatory fees ($1220), and room and board ($10,180). Full-time tuition and fees vary according to course load and program. Room and board charges vary according to board plan and housing facility. *Part-time tuition:* $895 per credit hour. *Part-time fees:* $370 per term. Part-time tuition and fees vary according to course load and program.

FRESHMAN FINANCIAL AID (Fall 2016, est.) 413 applied for aid; of those 85% were deemed to have need. 100% of freshmen with need received aid; of those 8% had need fully met. *Average percent of need met:* 51% (excluding resources awarded to replace EFC). *Average financial aid package:* $16,640 (excluding resources awarded to replace EFC). 14% of all full-time freshmen had no need and received non-need-based gift aid.

UNDERGRADUATE FINANCIAL AID (Fall 2016, est.) 1,697 applied for aid; of those 88% were deemed to have need. 100% of undergraduates with need received aid; of those 8% had need fully met. *Average percent of need met:* 22% (excluding resources awarded to replace EFC). *Average financial aid package:* $19,949 (excluding resources awarded to replace EFC). 10% of all full-time undergraduates had no need and received non-need-based gift aid.

GIFT AID (NEED-BASED) *Total amount:* $7,859,782 (31% federal, 69% institutional). *Receiving aid:* Freshmen: 54% (248); all full-time undergraduates: 54% (1,082). *Average award:* Freshmen: $6638; Undergraduates: $6758. *Scholarships, grants, and awards:* Federal Pell, FSEOG, state, college/university gift aid from institutional funds.

GIFT AID (NON-NEED-BASED) *Total amount:* $18,511,875 (15% state, 85% institutional). *Receiving aid:* Freshmen: 76% (350). Undergraduates: 73% (1,462). *Average award:* Freshmen: $9406. Undergraduates: $7916. *Scholarships, grants, and awards by category:* Academic interests/achievement: business, general academic interests/achievements. Creative arts/performance: dance, music, performing arts, theater/drama. Special achievements/activities: religious involvement. Special characteristics: children of faculty/staff, local/state students, relatives of clergy, religious affiliation. *Tuition waivers:* Full or partial for employees or children of employees.

LOANS *Student loans:* $15,741,734 (33% need-based, 67% non-need-based). 72% of past graduating class borrowed through all loan programs. *Average indebtedness per student:* $22,392. *Average need-based loan:* Freshmen: $3136. Undergraduates: $4061. *Parent loans:* $6,816,527 (100% non-need-based). *Programs:* Federal Direct (Subsidized and Unsubsidized Stafford, PLUS), Perkins, Federal Nursing.

WORK-STUDY *Federal work-study:* Total amount: $327,571; jobs available. *State or other work-study/employment:* Total amount: $2,889,876 (100% non-need-based). Part-time jobs available.

APPLYING FOR FINANCIAL AID *Required financial aid forms:* FAFSA, state aid form. *Financial aid deadline:* Continuous. *Notification date:* Continuous beginning 3/15. Students must reply within 4 weeks of notification.

CONTACT Ms. Karen Bucher, Director of Financial Aid, Shenandoah University, 1460 University Drive, Winchester, VA 22601-5195, 540-665-4538 or toll-free 800-432-2266. *Fax:* 540-665-4939. *E-mail:* kbucher@su.edu.
Website: http://www.su.edu/.

SHEPHERD UNIVERSITY
Los Angeles, CA

CONTACT Financial Aid Office, Shepherd University, 3200 North San Fernando Road, Los Angeles, CA 90065, 323-550-8888.
Website: http://www.shepherduniversity.edu/.

SHEPHERD UNIVERSITY
Shepherdstown, WV

Tuition & fees (WV res): $7170	Average undergraduate aid package: $12,398

ABOUT THE INSTITUTION State-supported, coed. *Awards:* bachelor's and master's degrees. 25 undergraduate majors. *Total enrollment:* 3,779. Undergraduates: 3,436. Freshmen: 564. Federal methodology is used as a basis for awarding need-based institutional aid.

UNDERGRADUATE EXPENSES for 2016–2017 *Application fee:* $45. *Tuition, state resident:* full-time $7170; part-time $293 per credit hour. *Tuition, nonresident:* full-time $17,482; part-time $722 per credit hour. Full-time tuition and fees vary according to program and reciprocity agreements. Part-time tuition and fees vary according to program. *College room and board:* $10,054. Room and board charges vary according to board plan and housing facility.

FRESHMAN FINANCIAL AID (Fall 2016, est.) 541 applied for aid; of those 69% were deemed to have need. 98% of freshmen with need received aid; of those 33% had need fully met. *Average percent of need met:* 82% (excluding resources awarded to replace EFC). *Average financial aid package:* $12,241 (excluding resources awarded to replace EFC). 25% of all full-time freshmen had no need and received non-need-based gift aid.

UNDERGRADUATE FINANCIAL AID (Fall 2016, est.) 2,573 applied for aid; of those 68% were deemed to have need. 97% of undergraduates with need received aid; of those 29% had need fully met. *Average percent of need met:* 77% (excluding resources awarded to replace EFC). *Average financial aid package:* $12,398 (excluding resources awarded to replace EFC). 22% of all full-time undergraduates had no need and received non-need-based gift aid.

GIFT AID (NEED-BASED) *Total amount:* $6,646,452 (72% federal, 23% state, 5% institutional). *Receiving aid:* Freshmen: 48% (271); all full-time undergraduates: 44% (1,184). *Average award:* Freshmen: $5381; Undergraduates: $5100. *Scholarships, grants, and awards:* Federal Pell, FSEOG, state, private, college/university gift aid from institutional funds.

GIFT AID (NON-NEED-BASED) *Total amount:* $6,323,535 (37% state, 55% institutional, 8% external sources). *Receiving aid:* Freshmen: 33% (185). Undergraduates: 23% (639). *Average award:* Freshmen: $10,039. Undergraduates: $10,451. *Scholarships, grants, and awards by category:* Academic interests/achievement: biological sciences, business, communication, computer science, education, engineering/technologies, English, general academic interests/achievements, health fields, home economics, humanities, mathematics, physical sciences, premedicine, social sciences. Creative arts/performance: applied art and design, art/fine arts, music, performing arts, theater/drama. Special achievements/activities: leadership. Special characteristics: ethnic background, handicapped students, local/state students, members of minority groups, out-of-state students, previous college experience. *Tuition waivers:* Full or partial for minority students, employees or children of employees, senior citizens. *ROTC:* Air Force cooperative.

LOANS *Student loans:* $12,235,612 (42% need-based, 58% non-need-based). 72% of past graduating class borrowed through all loan programs. *Average indebtedness per student:* $30,526. *Average need-based loan:* Freshmen: $3114. Undergraduates: $3859. *Parent loans:* $4,429,146 (100% non-need-based). *Programs:* Federal Direct (Subsidized and Unsubsidized Stafford, PLUS), Perkins.

WORK-STUDY *Federal work-study:* Total amount: $207,811; 47 jobs averaging $205. *State or other work-study/employment:* Total amount: $683,843 (100% non-need-based). 455 part-time jobs averaging $1503.

ATHLETIC AWARDS Total amount: $1,402,788 (100% non-need-based).

APPLYING FOR FINANCIAL AID *Required financial aid forms:* FAFSA, state aid form. *Financial aid deadline (priority):* 3/1. *Notification date:* 2/1. Students must reply within 2 weeks of notification.

CONTACT Ms. Joyce Cabral, Director of Financial Aid, Shepherd University, PO Box 5000, Shepherdstown, WV 25443-5000, 304-876-5470 or toll-free 800-344-5231. *Fax:* 304-876-5238. *E-mail:* faoweb@shepherd.edu.
Website: http://www.shepherd.edu/.

SHILOH UNIVERSITY
Kalona, IA

CONTACT Financial Aid Office, Shiloh University, 100 Shiloh Drive, Kalona, IA 52247, 319-656-2447.
Website: http://www.shilohuniversity.edu/.

SHIPPENSBURG UNIVERSITY OF PENNSYLVANIA
Shippensburg, PA

Tuition & fees (PA res): $11,452	Average undergraduate aid package: $8971

ABOUT THE INSTITUTION State-supported, coed. **Awards:** certificates, bachelor's, master's, and doctoral degrees. 39 undergraduate majors. **Total enrollment:** 6,989. Undergraduates: 5,912. Freshmen: 1,381. Federal methodology is used as a basis for awarding need-based institutional aid.

UNDERGRADUATE EXPENSES for 2016–2017 **Application fee:** $45. **Tuition, state resident:** full-time $8430; part-time $281 per credit hour. **Tuition, nonresident:** full-time $16,286; part-time $679 per credit hour. **Required fees:** full-time $3022; $126 per credit hour. Full-time tuition and fees vary according to course load and location. Part-time tuition and fees vary according to course load and location. **College room and board:** $11,756; **Room only:** $7706. Room and board charges vary according to board plan and housing facility.

FRESHMAN FINANCIAL AID (Fall 2016, est.) 1,292 applied for aid; of those 81% were deemed to have need. 99% of freshmen with need received aid; of those 5% had need fully met. **Average percent of need met:** 48% (excluding resources awarded to replace EFC). **Average financial aid package:** $8766 (excluding resources awarded to replace EFC). 7% of all full-time freshmen had no need and received non-need-based gift aid.

UNDERGRADUATE FINANCIAL AID (Fall 2016, est.) 4,789 applied for aid; of those 80% were deemed to have need. 99% of undergraduates with need received aid; of those 9% had need fully met. **Average percent of need met:** 53% (excluding resources awarded to replace EFC). **Average financial aid package:** $8971 (excluding resources awarded to replace EFC). 7% of all full-time undergraduates had no need and received non-need-based gift aid.

GIFT AID (NEED-BASED) Total amount: $17,578,664 (46% federal, 36% state, 9% institutional, 9% external sources). **Receiving aid:** Freshmen: 58% (800); all full-time undergraduates: 51% (2,841). **Average award:** Freshmen: $6894; Undergraduates: $6554. **Scholarships, grants, and awards:** Federal Pell, FSEOG, state, private, college/university gift aid from institutional funds.

GIFT AID (NON-NEED-BASED) Total amount: $1,424,750 (17% state, 10% institutional, 73% external sources). **Receiving aid:** Freshmen: 2% (33). Undergraduates: 3% (147). **Average award:** Freshmen: $4946. Undergraduates: $5565. **Scholarships, grants, and awards by category:** *Academic interests/achievement:* biological sciences, business, communication, computer science, education, English, foreign languages, general academic interests/achievements, humanities, mathematics, physical sciences, social sciences. *Creative arts/performance:* art/fine arts, music, theater/drama. *Special achievements/activities:* community service, general special achievements/activities, leadership. *Special characteristics:* children and siblings of alumni, general special characteristics, handicapped students, local/state students. **Tuition waivers:** Full or partial for employees or children of employees, senior citizens. **ROTC:** Army.

LOANS Student loans: $44,335,977 (66% need-based, 34% non-need-based). 80% of past graduating class borrowed through all loan programs. *Average indebtedness per student:* $33,673. **Average need-based loan:** Freshmen: $3466. Undergraduates: $4003. **Parent loans:** $12,894,467 (48% need-based, 52% non-need-based). **Programs:** Federal Direct (Subsidized and Unsubsidized Stafford, PLUS), Perkins, alternative loans.

WORK-STUDY Federal work-study: Total amount: $148,756; 125 jobs averaging $1190. **State or other work-study/employment:** Total amount: $1,222,497 (32% need-based, 68% non-need-based). 602 part-time jobs averaging $2031.

ATHLETIC AWARDS Total amount: $1,091,453 (60% need-based, 40% non-need-based).

APPLYING FOR FINANCIAL AID *Required financial aid form:* FAFSA. *Financial aid deadline (priority):* 3/15. **Notification date:** Continuous. Students must reply within 2 weeks of notification.
CONTACT Mrs. Trina M. Snyder, Director of Financial Aid and Scholarships, Shippensburg University of Pennsylvania, 1871 Old Main Drive, Shippensburg, PA 17257-2299, 717-477-1131 or toll-free 800-822-8028 (in-state). *Fax:* 717-477-4028. *E-mail:* finaid@ship.edu.
Website: http://www.ship.edu/.

SHORTER UNIVERSITY
Rome, GA

CONTACT Ms. Tara Jones, Director of Financial Aid, Shorter University, 315 Shorter Avenue, Rome, GA 30165, 706-233-7227 or toll-free 800-868-6980. *Fax:* 706-233-7314. *E-mail:* tjones@shorter.edu.
Website: http://www.shorter.edu/.

SH'OR YOSHUV RABBINICAL COLLEGE
Lawrence, NY

CONTACT Office of Financial Aid, Sh'or Yoshuv Rabbinical College, 1526 Central Avenue, Far Rockaway, NY 11691-4002, 718-327-2048.
Website: http://www.shoryoshuv.org/.

SIENA COLLEGE
Loudonville, NY

Tuition & fees: $35,735	Average undergraduate aid package: $28,167

ABOUT THE INSTITUTION Independent Roman Catholic, coed. **Awards:** certificates, bachelor's, and master's degrees. 33 undergraduate majors. **Total enrollment:** 3,247. Undergraduates: 3,186. Freshmen: 764. Federal methodology is used as a basis for awarding need-based institutional aid.

UNDERGRADUATE EXPENSES for 2017–2018 **Application fee:** $50. **Comprehensive fee:** $50,285 includes full-time tuition ($35,435), mandatory fees ($300), and room and board ($14,550). **College room only:** $8580. Full-time tuition and fees vary according to course load. Room and board charges vary according to board plan and housing facility. **Part-time tuition:** $675 per credit. **Part-time fees:** $100 per term. Part-time tuition and fees vary according to course load.

FRESHMAN FINANCIAL AID (Fall 2015) 702 applied for aid; of those 86% were deemed to have need. 100% of freshmen with need received aid; of those 25% had need fully met. **Average percent of need met:** 82% (excluding resources awarded to replace EFC). **Average financial aid package:** $29,503 (excluding resources awarded to replace EFC). 17% of all full-time freshmen had no need and received non-need-based gift aid.

UNDERGRADUATE FINANCIAL AID (Fall 2015) 2,481 applied for aid; of those 88% were deemed to have need. 100% of undergraduates with need received aid; of those 29% had need fully met. **Average percent of need met:** 82% (excluding resources awarded to replace EFC). **Average financial aid package:** $28,167 (excluding resources awarded to replace EFC). 18% of all full-time undergraduates had no need and received non-need-based gift aid.

GIFT AID (NEED-BASED) Total amount: $48,281,241 (8% federal, 6% state, 86% institutional). **Receiving aid:** Freshmen: 80% (603); all full-time undergraduates: 72% (2,173). **Average award:** Freshmen: $23,046; Undergraduates: $21,101. **Scholarships, grants, and awards:** Federal Pell, FSEOG, state, private, college/university gift aid from institutional funds, Siena Grants, Franciscan Community Grants.

GIFT AID (NON-NEED-BASED) Total amount: $8,231,374 (1% federal, 1% state, 84% institutional, 14% external sources). **Receiving aid:** Freshmen: 76% (575). Undergraduates: 67% (2,028). **Average award:** Freshmen: $13,296. Undergraduates: $10,554. **Scholarships, grants, and awards by category:** *Academic interests/achievement:* biological sciences, business, communication, computer science, education, English, foreign languages, general academic interests/achievements, health fields, humanities, international studies, mathematics, military science, physical sciences, premedicine, religion/biblical studies, social sciences. *Creative arts/performance:* creative writing, general creative arts/performance, journalism/publications, music, performing arts, theater/drama. *Special achievements/activities:* community service, general special achievements/activities, hobbies/interests, leadership, memberships, religious involvement. *Special characteristics:* adult students, children and siblings of alumni, children of faculty/staff, children of public servants, children of union members/company employees, children of workers in trades, children with a deceased or disabled parent, ethnic background, general special characteristics, local/state students, out-of-state students, previous college experience, relatives of clergy, religious affiliation, veterans' children. *Tuition waivers:* Full or partial for employees or children of employees. *ROTC:* Army, Air Force cooperative.

LOANS *Student loans:* $21,267,486 (82% need-based, 18% non-need-based). 77% of past graduating class borrowed through all loan programs. *Average indebtedness per student:* $35,874. *Average need-based loan:* Freshmen: $3112. Undergraduates: $4346. *Parent loans:* $7,618,806 (77% need-based, 23% non-need-based). *Programs:* Federal Direct (Subsidized and Unsubsidized Stafford, PLUS), Perkins.

WORK-STUDY *Federal work-study:* jobs available.

ATHLETIC AWARDS Total amount: $4,978,879 (40% need-based, 60% non-need-based).

APPLYING FOR FINANCIAL AID *Required financial aid forms:* FAFSA, state aid form. *Financial aid deadline:* 5/1 (priority: 2/15). *Notification date:* 4/1. Students must reply by 5/1.

CONTACT Mary Lawyer, Associate Vice President for Enrollment Management, Siena College, 515 Loudon Road, Loudonville, NY 12211-1462, 518-783-2427 or toll-free 888-AT-SIENA. *Fax:* 518-783-2410. *E-mail:* aid@siena.edu. *Website:* http://www.siena.edu/.

SIENA HEIGHTS UNIVERSITY
Adrian, MI

CONTACT Office of Financial Aid, Siena Heights University, 1247 East Siena Heights Drive, Adrian, MI 49221, 517-264-7130 or toll-free 800-521-0009. *Website:* http://www.sienaheights.edu/.

SIERRA NEVADA COLLEGE
Incline Village, NV

CONTACT Nicole D. Ferguson, Director of Financial Aid, Sierra Nevada College, 999 Tahoe Boulevard, Incline Village, NV 89451, 775-831-1314 Ext. 7404. *Fax:* 775-832-1678 . *E-mail:* nferguson@sierranevada.edu. *Website:* http://www.sierranevada.edu/.

SILICON VALLEY UNIVERSITY
San Jose, CA

CONTACT Financial Aid Office, Silicon Valley University, 2010 Fortune Drive, San Jose, CA 95131, 408-435-8989. *Website:* http://www.svuca.edu/.

SILVER LAKE COLLEGE OF THE HOLY FAMILY
Manitowoc, WI

CONTACT Ms. Michelle Leider, Associate Director of Financial Aid, Silver Lake College of the Holy Family, 2406 South Alverno Road, Manitowoc, WI 54220-9319, 920-686-6122 or toll-free 800-236-4752 Ext. 175. *Fax:* 920-684-7082. *E-mail:* financialaid@sl.edu. *Website:* http://www.sl.edu/.

SIMMONS COLLEGE
Boston, MA

Tuition & fees: $39,610	Average undergraduate aid package: $30,318

ABOUT THE INSTITUTION Independent, undergraduate: women only; graduate: coed. *Awards:* certificates, bachelor's, master's, and doctoral degrees. 55 undergraduate majors. *Total enrollment:* 6,213. Undergraduates: 1,802. Freshmen: 452. Federal methodology is used as a basis for awarding need-based institutional aid.

UNDERGRADUATE EXPENSES for 2017–2018 *Application fee:* $55. *Comprehensive fee:* $54,410 includes full-time tuition ($38,500), mandatory fees ($1110), and room and board ($14,800). Full-time tuition and fees vary according to course load and program. Room and board charges vary according to board plan and location. *Part-time tuition:* $1200 per credit hour. *Part-time fees:* $260 per term. Part-time tuition and fees vary according to course load and program.

FRESHMAN FINANCIAL AID (Fall 2016, est.) 409 applied for aid; of those 87% were deemed to have need. 100% of freshmen with need received aid; of those 17% had need fully met. *Average percent of need met:* 80% (excluding resources awarded to replace EFC). *Average financial aid package:* $31,648 (excluding resources awarded to replace EFC). 21% of all full-time freshmen had no need and received non-need-based gift aid.

UNDERGRADUATE FINANCIAL AID (Fall 2016, est.) 1,349 applied for aid; of those 91% were deemed to have need. 100% of undergraduates with need received aid; of those 13% had need fully met. *Average percent of need met:* 75% (excluding resources awarded to replace EFC). *Average financial aid package:* $30,318 (excluding resources awarded to replace EFC). 20% of all full-time undergraduates had no need and received non-need-based gift aid.

GIFT AID (NEED-BASED) *Total amount:* $33,793,227 (8% federal, 1% state, 88% institutional, 3% external sources). *Receiving aid:* Freshmen: 78% (354); all full-time undergraduates: 77% (1,225). *Average award:* Freshmen: $28,172; Undergraduates: $26,528. *Scholarships, grants, and awards:* Federal Pell, FSEOG, state, private, college/university gift aid from institutional funds.

GIFT AID (NON-NEED-BASED) *Total amount:* $6,392,603 (96% institutional, 4% external sources). *Receiving aid:* Freshmen: 10% (45). Undergraduates: 6% (93). *Average award:* Freshmen: $19,238. Undergraduates: $17,279. *Scholarships, grants, and awards by category:* Academic interests/achievement: general academic interests/achievements. *Special achievements/activities:* community service, general special achievements/activities. *Special characteristics:* children and siblings of alumni, general special characteristics. *Tuition waivers:* Full or partial for employees or children of employees. *ROTC:* Army cooperative.

LOANS *Student loans:* $13,402,294 (35% need-based, 65% non-need-based). *Average need-based loan:* Freshmen: $3020. Undergraduates: $4096. *Parent loans:* $4,085,168 (100% non-need-based). *Programs:* Federal Direct (Subsidized and Unsubsidized Stafford, PLUS), Perkins, college/university.

WORK-STUDY *Federal work-study:* Total amount: $1,971,860; 841 jobs averaging $2345.

APPLYING FOR FINANCIAL AID *Required financial aid forms:* FAFSA, institution's own form. *Financial aid deadline (priority):* 3/1. *Notification date:* Continuous beginning 3/15.

CONTACT Amanda Galban, Senior Associate Director of Financial Aid, Simmons College, 300 The Fenway, Boston, MA 02115, 617-521-2001 or toll-free 800-345-8468. *Fax:* 617-521-3195. *E-mail:* amanda.galban@simmons.edu. *Website:* http://www.simmons.edu/.

SIMMONS COLLEGE OF KENTUCKY
Louisville, KY

CONTACT Financial Aid Office, Simmons College of Kentucky, 1018 South 7th Street, Louisville, KY 40203, 502-776-1443. *Website:* http://www.simmonscollegeky.edu/.

SIMPSON COLLEGE
Indianola, IA

Tuition & fees: $37,663	Average undergraduate aid package: $27,950

ABOUT THE INSTITUTION Independent United Methodist, coed. *Awards:* certificates, bachelor's, and master's degrees. 60 undergraduate majors. *Total enrollment:* 1,608. Undergraduates: 1,543. Freshmen: 348. Federal methodology is used as a basis for awarding need-based institutional aid.

UNDERGRADUATE EXPENSES for 2017–2018 *One-time required fee:* $200. *Comprehensive fee:* $45,626 includes full-time tuition ($36,969), mandatory fees ($694), and room and board ($7963). *College room only:* $3860. Full-time tuition and fees vary according to class time, course load, degree level, and program. Room and board charges vary according to board plan and housing facility. *Part-time tuition:* $415 per credit hour. *Part-time fees:* $6 per credit hour. Part-time tuition and fees vary according to class time, course load, degree level, and program.

FRESHMAN FINANCIAL AID (Fall 2016, est.) 348 applied for aid; of those 85% were deemed to have need. 100% of freshmen with need received aid; of those 28% had need fully met. *Average percent of need met:* 86% (excluding resources awarded to replace EFC). *Average financial aid package:* $32,435 (excluding resources awarded to replace EFC). 15% of all full-time freshmen had no need and received non-need-based gift aid.

UNDERGRADUATE FINANCIAL AID (Fall 2016, est.) 1,371 applied for aid; of those 82% were deemed to have need. 100% of undergraduates with need received aid; of those 23% had need fully met. *Average percent of need met:* 79% (excluding resources awarded to replace EFC). *Average financial aid package:* $27,950 (excluding resources awarded to replace EFC). 16% of all full-time undergraduates had no need and received non-need-based gift aid.

GIFT AID (NEED-BASED) *Total amount:* $25,134,043 (8% federal, 13% state, 76% institutional, 3% external sources). *Receiving aid:* Freshmen: 84% (291); all full-time undergraduates: 80% (1,105). *Average award:* Freshmen: $26,776; Undergraduates: $22,580. *Scholarships, grants, and awards:* Federal Pell, FSEOG, state, private, college/university gift aid from institutional funds.

GIFT AID (NON-NEED-BASED) *Total amount:* $6,075,675 (2% federal, 92% institutional, 6% external sources). *Receiving aid:* Freshmen: 17% (59). Undergraduates: 12% (163). *Average award:* Freshmen: $22,431. Undergraduates: $20,338. *Scholarships, grants, and awards by category:* Academic interests/achievement: $14,717,949 total: general academic interests/achievements. *Creative arts/performance:* $573,005 total: art/fine arts, debating, music, theater/drama. *Special achievements/activities:* $189,300 total: community service, leadership, religious involvement. *Special characteristics:* $3,811,045 total: adult students, children and siblings of alumni, children of educators, children of faculty/staff, ethnic background, international students, members of minority groups, relatives of clergy, religious affiliation, siblings of current students, twins, veterans, veterans' children. *Tuition waivers:* Full or partial for children of alumni, employees or children of employees, senior citizens.

LOANS *Student loans:* $10,768,749 (70% need-based, 30% non-need-based). 83% of past graduating class borrowed through all loan programs. *Average indebtedness per student:* $37,228. *Average need-based loan:* Freshmen: $4947. Undergraduates: $4981. *Parent loans:* $2,213,899 (42% need-based, 58% non-need-based). *Programs:* Federal Direct (Subsidized and Unsubsidized Stafford, PLUS), Perkins, state, college/university, alternative loans.

WORK-STUDY *Federal work-study:* Total amount: $391,509; 335 jobs averaging $1158. *State or other work-study/employment:* Total amount: $670,990 (31% need-based, 69% non-need-based). 451 part-time jobs averaging $1545.

APPLYING FOR FINANCIAL AID *Required financial aid form:* FAFSA. *Financial aid deadline (priority):* 2/1. *Notification date:* Continuous beginning 12/15. Students must reply by 5/1 or within 3 weeks of notification.

CONTACT Tracie Lynn Pavon, Assistant Vice President for Enrollment and Financial Assistance, Simpson College, 701 North C Street, Indianola, IA 50125-1297, 515-961-1630 Ext. 1596 or toll-free 800-362-2454. *Fax:* 515-961-1300. *E-mail:* tracie.pavon@simpson.edu.
Website: http://www.simpson.edu/.

SIMPSON UNIVERSITY
Redding, CA

Tuition & fees: $27,350	Average undergraduate aid package: $17,174

ABOUT THE INSTITUTION Independent The Christian and Missionary Alliance, coed. *Awards:* certificates, associate, bachelor's, and master's degrees. 31 undergraduate majors. *Total enrollment:* 1,012. Undergraduates: 790. Freshmen: 118. Federal methodology is used as a basis for awarding need-based institutional aid.

UNDERGRADUATE EXPENSES for 2017–2018 *Application fee:* $35. *Comprehensive fee:* $35,700 includes full-time tuition ($27,250), mandatory fees ($100), and room and board ($8350). Full-time tuition and fees vary according to course load. Room and board charges vary according to board plan and housing facility. *Part-time tuition:* $1150 per credit hour. Part-time tuition and fees vary according to course load.

FRESHMAN FINANCIAL AID (Fall 2016, est.) 114 applied for aid; of those 83% were deemed to have need. 100% of freshmen with need received aid; of those 14% had need fully met. *Average percent of need met:* 69% (excluding resources awarded to replace EFC). *Average financial aid package:* $22,370 (excluding resources awarded to replace EFC). 16% of all full-time freshmen had no need and received non-need-based gift aid.

UNDERGRADUATE FINANCIAL AID (Fall 2016, est.) 702 applied for aid; of those 89% were deemed to have need. 100% of undergraduates with need received aid; of those 11% had need fully met. *Average percent of need met:* 59% (excluding resources awarded to replace EFC). *Average financial aid package:* $17,174 (excluding resources awarded to replace EFC). 4% of all full-time undergraduates had no need and received non-need-based gift aid.

GIFT AID (NEED-BASED) *Total amount:* $10,508,555 (17% federal, 18% state, 63% institutional, 2% external sources). *Receiving aid:* Freshmen: 81% (95); all full-time undergraduates: 73% (542). *Average award:* Freshmen: $16,658; Undergraduates: $11,606. *Scholarships, grants, and awards:* Federal Pell, FSEOG, state, private, college/university gift aid from institutional funds.

GIFT AID (NON-NEED-BASED) *Total amount:* $557,112 (94% institutional, 6% external sources). *Receiving aid:* Freshmen: 52% (61). Undergraduates: 11% (83). *Average award:* Freshmen: $11,624. Undergraduates: $10,039. *Scholarships, grants, and awards by category:* Academic interests/achievement: 302 awards ($1,135,936 total): business, communication, general academic interests/achievements. *Creative arts/performance:* 39 awards ($84,709 total): music. *Special achievements/activities:* 125 awards ($257,037 total): community service, leadership, religious involvement. *Special characteristics:* 161 awards ($461,428 total): children and siblings of alumni, children of faculty/staff, ethnic background, general special characteristics, members of minority groups, out-of-state students, relatives of clergy, religious affiliation, siblings of current students, spouses of current students, veterans, veterans' children. *Tuition waivers:* Full or partial for employees or children of employees.

LOANS *Student loans:* $4,981,168 (85% need-based, 15% non-need-based). 86% of past graduating class borrowed through all loan programs. *Average indebtedness per student:* $26,938. *Average need-based loan:* Freshmen: $2730. Undergraduates: $4556. *Parent loans:* $1,010,358 (47% need-based, 53% non-need-based). *Programs:* Federal Direct (Subsidized and Unsubsidized Stafford, PLUS), Perkins, private loans.

WORK-STUDY *Federal work-study:* Total amount: $52,204; 58 jobs averaging $1229.

ATHLETIC AWARDS Total amount: $2,118,163 (19% need-based, 81% non-need-based).

APPLYING FOR FINANCIAL AID *Required financial aid forms:* FAFSA, state aid form. *Financial aid deadline (priority):* 3/2. *Notification date:* 3/2. Students must reply within 3 weeks of notification.

CONTACT Miss Kari Meyers, Associate Director of Financial Aid, Simpson University, 2211 College View Drive, Redding, CA 96003-8606, 530-226-4621 or toll-free 888-9-SIMPSON. *Fax:* 530-226-4855. *E-mail:* financialaid@simpsonu.edu.
Website: http://www.simpsonu.edu/.

SINTE GLESKA UNIVERSITY
Mission, SD

CONTACT Office of Financial Aid, Sinte Gleska University, PO Box 105, Mission, SD 5755504105, 605-856-8197 Ext. 8477. *Fax:* 605-856-5874. *E-mail:* bhay@sintegleska.edu.
Website: http://www.sintegleska.edu/.

SITTING BULL COLLEGE
Fort Yates, ND

CONTACT Donna M. Seaboy, Financial Aid Director, Sitting Bull College, 9299 Highway 24, Fort Yates, ND 58538, 701-854-8013. *Fax:* 701-854-3403. *E-mail:* donnas@sbci.edu.
Website: http://www.sittingbull.edu/.

SKIDMORE COLLEGE
Saratoga Springs, NY

Tuition & fees: $50,684	Average undergraduate aid package: $45,900

ABOUT THE INSTITUTION Independent, coed. *Awards:* bachelor's degrees. 41 undergraduate majors. *Total enrollment:* 2,686. Undergraduates: 2,680. Freshmen: 714. Both federal and institutional methodology are used as a basis for awarding need-based institutional aid.
UNDERGRADUATE EXPENSES for 2016–2017 *Application fee:* $65. *One-time required fee:* $150. *Comprehensive fee:* $64,214 includes full-time tuition ($49,716), mandatory fees ($968), and room and board ($13,530). *College room only:* $7998. Full-time tuition and fees vary according to course load. Room and board charges vary according to board plan and housing facility. *Part-time tuition:* $1657 per credit. *Part-time fees:* $25 per term. Part-time tuition and fees vary according to course load. *Payment plan:* Tuition prepayment.
FRESHMAN FINANCIAL AID (Fall 2016, est.) 340 applied for aid; of those 81% were deemed to have need. 100% of freshmen with need received aid; of those 100% had need fully met. *Average percent of need met:* 100% (excluding resources awarded to replace EFC). *Average financial aid package:* $43,000 (excluding resources awarded to replace EFC). 1% of all full-time freshmen had no need and received non-need-based gift aid.
UNDERGRADUATE FINANCIAL AID (Fall 2016, est.) 1,365 applied for aid; of those 78% were deemed to have need. 100% of undergraduates with need received aid; of those 93% had need fully met. *Average percent of need met:* 94% (excluding resources awarded to replace EFC). *Average financial aid package:* $45,900 (excluding resources awarded to replace EFC). 1% of all full-time undergraduates had no need and received non-need-based gift aid.
GIFT AID (NEED-BASED) *Total amount:* $44,650,000 (5% federal, 3% state, 92% institutional). *Receiving aid:* Freshmen: 39% (277); all full-time undergraduates: 41% (1,070). *Average award:* Freshmen: $41,900; Undergraduates: $40,300. *Scholarships, grants, and awards:* Federal Pell, FSEOG, state, private, college/university gift aid from institutional funds.
GIFT AID (NON-NEED-BASED) *Total amount:* $1,410,000 (9% state, 45% institutional, 46% external sources). *Receiving aid:* Freshmen: 2% (17). Undergraduates: 3% (84). *Average award:* Freshmen: $12,000. Undergraduates: $12,800. *Scholarships, grants, and awards by category:* Academic interests/achievement: biological sciences, computer science, mathematics, physical sciences. Creative arts/performance: music. Special characteristics: children of faculty/staff. *Tuition waivers:* Full or partial for employees or children of employees, senior citizens. *ROTC:* Army cooperative, Air Force cooperative.
LOANS *Student loans:* $4,300,000 (51% need-based, 49% non-need-based). 39% of past graduating class borrowed through all loan programs. *Average indebtedness per student:* $25,001. *Average need-based loan:* Freshmen: $2975. Undergraduates: $4200. *Parent loans:* $2,600,000 (100% non-need-based). *Programs:* Federal Direct (Subsidized and Unsubsidized Stafford, PLUS), Perkins, state.

WORK-STUDY *Federal work-study:* Total amount: $825,000; jobs available. *State or other work-study/employment:* Total amount: $875,000 (100% non-need-based). Part-time jobs available.
APPLYING FOR FINANCIAL AID *Required financial aid forms:* CSS Financial Aid PROFILE, noncustodial (divorced/separated) parent's statement. *Financial aid deadline:* 2/1. *Notification date:* 4/1. Students must reply by 5/1.
CONTACT Ms. Beth A. Post Lundquist, Director of Financial Aid, Skidmore College, 815 North Broadway, Saratoga Springs, NY 12866-1632, 518-580-5750 or toll-free 800-867-6007. *Fax:* 518-580-5752. *E-mail:* finaid@skidmore.edu.
Website: http://www.skidmore.edu/.

SLIPPERY ROCK UNIVERSITY OF PENNSYLVANIA
Slippery Rock, PA

Tuition & fees (PA res): $9862	Average undergraduate aid package: $9251

ABOUT THE INSTITUTION State-supported, coed. *Awards:* certificates, bachelor's, master's, and doctoral degrees. 50 undergraduate majors. *Total enrollment:* 8,881. Undergraduates: 7,664. Freshmen: 1,564. Federal methodology is used as a basis for awarding need-based institutional aid.
UNDERGRADUATE EXPENSES for 2016–2017 *Application fee:* $30. *Tuition, state resident:* full-time $7238; part-time $302 per credit hour. *Tuition, nonresident:* full-time $10,858; part-time $452 per credit hour. *Required fees:* full-time $2624; $109.75 per credit hour. Full-time tuition and fees vary according to course load. Part-time tuition and fees vary according to course load. *College room and board:* $10,110; *Room only:* $6620. Room and board charges vary according to board plan and housing facility.
FRESHMAN FINANCIAL AID (Fall 2016, est.) 1,484 applied for aid; of those 77% were deemed to have need. 100% of freshmen with need received aid; of those 10% had need fully met. *Average percent of need met:* 59% (excluding resources awarded to replace EFC). *Average financial aid package:* $9282 (excluding resources awarded to replace EFC). 13% of all full-time freshmen had no need and received non-need-based gift aid.
UNDERGRADUATE FINANCIAL AID (Fall 2016, est.) 6,142 applied for aid; of those 79% were deemed to have need. 98% of undergraduates with need received aid; of those 9% had need fully met. *Average percent of need met:* 60% (excluding resources awarded to replace EFC). *Average financial aid package:* $9251 (excluding resources awarded to replace EFC). 8% of all full-time undergraduates had no need and received non-need-based gift aid.
GIFT AID (NEED-BASED) *Total amount:* $18,993,785 (53% federal, 40% state, 6% institutional, 1% external sources). *Receiving aid:* Freshmen: 49% (759); all full-time undergraduates: 44% (3,118). *Average award:* Freshmen: $6386; Undergraduates: $5945. *Scholarships, grants, and awards:* Federal Pell, FSEOG, state, private, college/university gift aid from institutional funds.
GIFT AID (NON-NEED-BASED) *Total amount:* $6,332,048 (11% state, 49% institutional, 40% external sources). *Receiving aid:* Freshmen: 37% (571). Undergraduates: 19% (1,340). *Average award:* Freshmen: $2635. Undergraduates: $2749. *Scholarships, grants, and awards by category:* Academic interests/achievement: biological sciences, business, communication, computer science, education, engineering/technologies, English, foreign languages, general academic interests/achievements, home economics, mathematics, military science, physical sciences, social sciences. Creative arts/performance: applied art and design, art/fine arts, dance, music, performing arts, theater/drama. Special achievements/activities: community service, general special achievements/activities, leadership. Special characteristics: children and siblings of alumni, children of faculty/staff, children of union members/company employees, ethnic background, general special characteristics, local/state students, members of minority groups, out-of-state students, previous college experience. *Tuition waivers:* Full or partial for minority students, employees or children of employees, senior citizens. *ROTC:* Army.
LOANS *Student loans:* $51,768,201 (37% need-based, 63% non-need-based). 87% of past graduating class borrowed through all loan programs. *Average indebtedness per student:* $33,303. *Average need-based loan:* Freshmen: $3708. Undergraduates: $4383. *Parent loans:* $11,584,697 (100% non-need-based). *Programs:* Federal Direct (Subsidized and Unsubsidized Stafford, PLUS), Perkins.

WORK-STUDY *Federal work-study:* Total amount: $769,858; 554 jobs averaging $1572. *State or other work-study/employment:* Total amount: $1,695,460 (100% non-need-based). 906 part-time jobs averaging $1960.
ATHLETIC AWARDS Total amount: $1,130,467 (100% non-need-based).
APPLYING FOR FINANCIAL AID *Required financial aid form:* FAFSA. *Financial aid deadline (priority):* 5/1. *Notification date:* Continuous beginning 12/15.
CONTACT Ms. Alyssa Dobson, Director of Financial Aid and Scholarships, Slippery Rock University of Pennsylvania, 108 Maltby Center, Suite 107, Slippery Rock, PA 16057, 724-738-2044 or toll-free 800-SRU-9111. *Fax:* 724-738-2922. *E-mail:* alyssa.dobson@sru.edu.
Website: http://www.sru.edu/.

SMITH COLLEGE
Northampton, MA

Tuition & fees: $50,044	Average undergraduate aid package: $48,115

ABOUT THE INSTITUTION Independent, undergraduate: women only; graduate: coed. *Awards:* certificates, bachelor's, master's, and doctoral degrees. 53 undergraduate majors. *Total enrollment:* 2,896. Undergraduates: 2,514. Freshmen: 654. Both federal and institutional methodology are used as a basis for awarding need-based institutional aid.
UNDERGRADUATE EXPENSES for 2017–2018 *Comprehensive fee:* $66,774 includes full-time tuition ($49,760), mandatory fees ($284), and room and board ($16,730). *Part-time tuition:* $1560 per credit hour. *Payment plan:* Tuition prepayment.
FRESHMAN FINANCIAL AID (Fall 2016, est.) 487 applied for aid; of those 84% were deemed to have need. 100% of freshmen with need received aid; of those 100% had need fully met. *Average percent of need met:* 100% (excluding resources awarded to replace EFC). *Average financial aid package:* $48,887 (excluding resources awarded to replace EFC). 9% of all full-time freshmen had no need and received non-need-based gift aid.
UNDERGRADUATE FINANCIAL AID (Fall 2016, est.) 1,723 applied for aid; of those 87% were deemed to have need. 100% of undergraduates with need received aid; of those 100% had need fully met. *Average percent of need met:* 100% (excluding resources awarded to replace EFC). *Average financial aid package:* $48,115 (excluding resources awarded to replace EFC). 6% of all full-time undergraduates had no need and received non-need-based gift aid.
GIFT AID (NEED-BASED) *Total amount:* $64,077,867 (4% federal, 1% state, 93% institutional, 2% external sources). *Receiving aid:* Freshmen: 60% (392); all full-time undergraduates: 58% (1,459). *Average award:* Freshmen: $43,839; Undergraduates: $41,786. *Scholarships, grants, and awards:* Federal Pell, FSEOG, state, private, college/university gift aid from institutional funds.
GIFT AID (NON-NEED-BASED) *Total amount:* $3,187,143 (1% federal, 79% institutional, 20% external sources). *Receiving aid:* Freshmen: 2% (10). Undergraduates: 1% (18). *Average award:* Freshmen: $15,484. Undergraduates: $16,473. *Scholarships, grants, and awards by category:* Academic interests/achievement: general academic interests/achievements. *Special characteristics:* local/state students. *Tuition waivers:* Full or partial for employees or children of employees. *ROTC:* Army cooperative, Air Force cooperative.
LOANS *Student loans:* $7,715,832 (67% need-based, 33% non-need-based). 62% of past graduating class borrowed through all loan programs. *Average indebtedness per student:* $23,857. *Average need-based loan:* Freshmen: $3011. Undergraduates: $4323. *Parent loans:* $3,234,925 (84% need-based, 16% non-need-based). *Programs:* Federal Direct (Subsidized and Unsubsidized Stafford, PLUS), Perkins, college/university.
WORK-STUDY *Federal work-study:* Total amount: $2,288,347; jobs available. *State or other work-study/employment:* Total amount: $1,414,574 (84% need-based, 16% non-need-based). Part-time jobs available.
APPLYING FOR FINANCIAL AID *Required financial aid forms:* FAFSA, institution's own form, CSS Financial Aid PROFILE, noncustodial (divorced/separated) parent's statement, student/parent tax returns. *Financial aid deadline:* 2/15. *Notification date:* 4/1. Students must reply by 5/1.

CONTACT David Belanger, Director of Student Financial Services, Smith College, College Hall 106, 10 Elm Street, Northampton, MA 01063, 413-585-2530 or toll-free 800-383-3232. *Fax:* 413-585-2566. *E-mail:* sfs@smith.edu.
Website: http://www.smith.edu/.

SOKA UNIVERSITY OF AMERICA
Aliso Viejo, CA

Tuition & fees: $31,776	Average undergraduate aid package: $34,969

ABOUT THE INSTITUTION Independent, coed. *Awards:* bachelor's and master's degrees. 1 undergraduate major. *Total enrollment:* 431. Undergraduates: 419. Freshmen: 104. Both federal and institutional methodology are used as a basis for awarding need-based institutional aid.
UNDERGRADUATE EXPENSES for 2017–2018 *Application fee:* $45. *Comprehensive fee:* $43,942 includes full-time tuition ($30,106), mandatory fees ($1670), and room and board ($12,166). Full-time tuition and fees vary according to class time, course level, course load, and program. Room and board charges vary according to board plan. *Part-time tuition:* $1255 per credit hour. Part-time tuition and fees vary according to class time, course level, course load, and program.
FRESHMAN FINANCIAL AID (Fall 2016, est.) 104 applied for aid; of those 86% were deemed to have need. 100% of freshmen with need received aid; of those 89% had need fully met. *Average percent of need met:* 73% (excluding resources awarded to replace EFC). *Average financial aid package:* $33,399 (excluding resources awarded to replace EFC). 7% of all full-time freshmen had no need and received non-need-based gift aid.
UNDERGRADUATE FINANCIAL AID (Fall 2016, est.) 417 applied for aid; of those 87% were deemed to have need. 100% of undergraduates with need received aid; of those 89% had need fully met. *Average percent of need met:* 72% (excluding resources awarded to replace EFC). *Average financial aid package:* $34,969 (excluding resources awarded to replace EFC). 5% of all full-time undergraduates had no need and received non-need-based gift aid.
GIFT AID (NEED-BASED) *Total amount:* $9,471,050 (6% federal, 4% state, 90% institutional). *Receiving aid:* Freshmen: 86% (89); all full-time undergraduates: 87% (361). *Average award:* Freshmen: $24,472; Undergraduates: $26,236. *Scholarships, grants, and awards:* Federal Pell, FSEOG, state, private, college/university gift aid from institutional funds.
GIFT AID (NON-NEED-BASED) *Total amount:* $3,973,952 (99% institutional, 1% external sources). *Receiving aid:* Freshmen: 86% (89). Undergraduates: 87% (361). *Average award:* Freshmen: $13,785. Undergraduates: $11,409. *Scholarships, grants, and awards by category:* Academic interests/achievement: general academic interests/achievements. *Special achievements/activities:* leadership. *Special characteristics:* children of faculty/staff. *Tuition waivers:* Full or partial for employees or children of employees.
LOANS *Student loans:* $1,189,390 (81% need-based, 19% non-need-based). 57% of past graduating class borrowed through all loan programs. *Average indebtedness per student:* $22,409. *Average need-based loan:* Freshmen: $8584. Undergraduates: $6959. *Parent loans:* $362,139 (100% non-need-based). *Programs:* Federal Direct (Subsidized and Unsubsidized Stafford, PLUS), college/university.
WORK-STUDY *Federal work-study:* Total amount: $77,880; 77 jobs averaging $2000. *State or other work-study/employment:* Part-time jobs available.
ATHLETIC AWARDS Total amount: $452,883 (100% non-need-based).
APPLYING FOR FINANCIAL AID *Required financial aid forms:* FAFSA, state aid form. *Financial aid deadline:* 3/2 (priority: 2/15). *Notification date:* 3/15. Students must reply by 5/1 or within 4 weeks of notification.

CONTACT Dr. Andrew Woolsey, Director of Enrollment Services, Soka University of America, 1 University Drive, Aliso Viejo, CA 92656, 949-480-4112 or toll-free 888-600-SOKA. *Fax:* 949-480-4151. *E-mail:* awoolsey@soka.edu.
Website: http://www.soka.edu/.

SONOMA STATE UNIVERSITY
Rohnert Park, CA

Tuition & fees (CA res): $7330	Average undergraduate aid package: $10,085

ABOUT THE INSTITUTION State-supported, coed. **Awards:** bachelor's and master's degrees. 63 undergraduate majors. **Total enrollment:** 9,323. Undergraduates: 8,606. Freshmen: 1,806. Federal methodology is used as a basis for awarding need-based institutional aid.

UNDERGRADUATE EXPENSES for 2017–2018 Application fee: $55. **Tuition, state resident:** full-time $5472. **Tuition, nonresident:** full-time $16,632. **Required fees:** full-time $1858. Full-time tuition and fees vary according to course load and degree level. Part-time tuition and fees vary according to course load and degree level. **College room and board:** $13,146. Room and board charges vary according to board plan and housing facility.

FRESHMAN FINANCIAL AID (Fall 2015) 1,087 applied for aid; of those 76% were deemed to have need. 82% of freshmen with need received aid; of those 4% had need fully met. **Average percent of need met:** 53% (excluding resources awarded to replace EFC). **Average financial aid package:** $10,004 (excluding resources awarded to replace EFC). 3% of all full-time freshmen had no need and received non-need-based gift aid.

UNDERGRADUATE FINANCIAL AID (Fall 2015) 5,589 applied for aid; of those 81% were deemed to have need. 93% of undergraduates with need received aid; of those 5% had need fully met. **Average percent of need met:** 54% (excluding resources awarded to replace EFC). **Average financial aid package:** $10,085 (excluding resources awarded to replace EFC). 3% of all full-time undergraduates had no need and received non-need-based gift aid.

GIFT AID (NEED-BASED) Total amount: $31,326,136 (41% federal, 59% state). **Receiving aid:** Freshmen: 31% (458); all full-time undergraduates: 40% (2,926). **Average award:** Freshmen: $10,498; Undergraduates: $9968. **Scholarships, grants, and awards:** Federal Pell, FSEOG, state, private, college/university gift aid from institutional funds.

GIFT AID (NON-NEED-BASED) Total amount: $2,896,685 (1% federal, 33% state, 26% institutional, 40% external sources). **Receiving aid:** Freshmen: 19% (273). Undergraduates: 20% (1,463). **Average award:** Freshmen: $645. Undergraduates: $936. **Scholarships, grants, and awards by category:** Academic interests/achievement: area/ethnic studies, biological sciences, business, communication, computer science, education, engineering/technologies, English, foreign languages, general academic interests/achievements, health fields, humanities, mathematics, physical sciences, premedicine, social sciences. Creative arts/performance: applied art and design, art/fine arts, cinema/film/broadcasting, creative writing, dance, journalism/publications, music, performing arts, theater/drama. Special achievements/activities: community service, leadership, memberships. Special characteristics: adult students, children and siblings of alumni, children of educators, children of faculty/staff, children of public servants, children of union members/company employees, children of workers in trades, ethnic background, first-generation college students, general special characteristics, handicapped students, international students, local/state students, married students, members of minority groups, out-of-state students, previous college experience, veterans. **Tuition waivers:** Full or partial for employees or children of employees. **ROTC:** Army cooperative, Air Force cooperative.

LOANS Student loans: $23,342,117 (49% need-based, 51% non-need-based). 59% of past graduating class borrowed through all loan programs. **Average indebtedness per student:** $20,797. **Average need-based loan:** Freshmen: $3212. Undergraduates: $4056. **Parent loans:** $10,328,522 (100% non-need-based). **Programs:** Federal Direct (Subsidized and Unsubsidized Stafford, PLUS), Perkins.

WORK-STUDY Federal work-study: 212 jobs averaging $2214. **State or other work-study/employment:** Total amount: $1,600,000 (100% non-need-based). Part-time jobs available.

ATHLETIC AWARDS Total amount: $526,047 (100% non-need-based).

APPLYING FOR FINANCIAL AID Required financial aid form: FAFSA. **Financial aid deadline (priority):** 1/31. **Notification date:** Continuous beginning 3/15. Students must reply within 2 weeks of notification.

CONTACT Susan Gutierrez, Director of Financial Aid, Sonoma State University, 1801 East Cotati Avenue, Rohnert Park, CA 94928-3609, 707-664-2287. Fax: 707-664-4242. E-mail: susan.gutierrez@sonoma.edu. Website: http://www.sonoma.edu/.

SOUTH CAROLINA STATE UNIVERSITY
Orangeburg, SC

ABOUT THE INSTITUTION State-supported, coed. **Awards:** certificates, bachelor's, master's, and doctoral degrees. 44 undergraduate majors. **Total enrollment:** 2,905. Undergraduates: 2,529. Freshmen: 628.

GIFT AID (NEED-BASED) Scholarships, grants, and awards: Federal Pell, FSEOG, state, private, college/university gift aid from institutional funds.

GIFT AID (NON-NEED-BASED) Scholarships, grants, and awards by category: Academic interests/achievement: general academic interests/achievements. Creative arts/performance: music.

LOANS Programs: Federal Direct (Subsidized and Unsubsidized Stafford, PLUS).

APPLYING FOR FINANCIAL AID Required financial aid forms: FAFSA, institution's own form, state aid form.

CONTACT Sandra S. Davis, Director of Financial Aid, South Carolina State University, 300 College Street Northeast, Orangeburg, SC 29117, 803-536-7067 or toll-free 800-260-5956. Fax: 803-536-8420. E-mail: sdavis@scsu.edu. Website: http://www.scsu.edu/.

SOUTH COLLEGE
Knoxville, TN

CONTACT Financial Aid Office, South College, 720 North Fifth Avenue, Knoxville, TN 37917, 865-524-3043. Website: http://www.southcollegetn.edu/.

SOUTH DAKOTA SCHOOL OF MINES AND TECHNOLOGY
Rapid City, SD

Tuition & fees (SD res): $11,170	Average undergraduate aid package: $14,262

ABOUT THE INSTITUTION State-supported, coed. **Awards:** certificates, associate, bachelor's, master's, and doctoral degrees. 17 undergraduate majors. **Total enrollment:** 2,859. Undergraduates: 2,485. Freshmen: 497. Both federal and institutional methodology are used as a basis for awarding need-based institutional aid.

UNDERGRADUATE EXPENSES for 2016–2017 Application fee: $20. **Tuition, state resident:** full-time $4530; part-time $244.80 per credit hour. **Tuition, nonresident:** full-time $7590; part-time $383.40 per credit hour. **Required fees:** full-time $6640; $127.33 per credit hour. Full-time tuition and fees vary according to course level, course load, program, and reciprocity agreements. Part-time tuition and fees vary according to course level, course load, program, and reciprocity agreements. **College room and board:** $7300; **Room only:** $3800. Room and board charges vary according to board plan and housing facility.

FRESHMAN FINANCIAL AID (Fall 2015) 481 applied for aid; of those 53% were deemed to have need. 100% of freshmen with need received aid; of those 39% had need fully met. **Average percent of need met:** 74% (excluding resources awarded to replace EFC). **Average financial aid package:** $14,379 (excluding resources awarded to replace EFC). 38% of all full-time freshmen had no need and received non-need-based gift aid.

UNDERGRADUATE FINANCIAL AID (Fall 2015) 1,812 applied for aid; of those 60% were deemed to have need. 100% of undergraduates with need received aid; of those 31% had need fully met. **Average percent of need met:** 71% (excluding resources awarded to replace EFC). **Average financial aid package:** $14,262 (excluding resources awarded to replace EFC). 20% of all full-time undergraduates had no need and received non-need-based gift aid.

GIFT AID (NEED-BASED) Total amount: $4,876,747 (57% federal, 4% state, 20% institutional, 19% external sources). **Receiving aid:** Freshmen: 35% (176); all full-time undergraduates: 34% (693). **Average award:** Freshmen: $4517; Undergraduates: $4616. **Scholarships, grants, and awards:** Federal Pell, FSEOG, state, private, college/university gift aid from institutional funds.

GIFT AID (NON-NEED-BASED) *Total amount:* $716,137 (10% state, 52% institutional, 38% external sources). *Receiving aid:* Freshmen: 31% (153). Undergraduates: 20% (411). *Average award:* Freshmen: $3544. Undergraduates: $3360. *Scholarships, grants, and awards by category:* *Academic interests/achievement:* 505 awards ($368,695 total): biological sciences, computer science, engineering/technologies, mathematics, military science, physical sciences. *Special characteristics:* 505 awards ($368,695 total): adult students, ethnic background, international students, local/state students, married students, members of minority groups, out-of-state students. *Tuition waivers:* Full or partial for children of alumni, employees or children of employees, senior citizens. *ROTC:* Army.

LOANS *Student loans:* $11,370,027 (82% need-based, 18% non-need-based). 71% of past graduating class borrowed through all loan programs. *Average indebtedness per student:* $32,995. *Average need-based loan:* Freshmen: $2878. Undergraduates: $4106. *Parent loans:* $3,493,691 (75% need-based, 25% non-need-based). *Programs:* Federal Direct (Subsidized and Unsubsidized Stafford, PLUS), Perkins.

WORK-STUDY *Federal work-study:* 148 jobs averaging $1718.

ATHLETIC AWARDS Total amount: $1,104,580 (54% need-based, 46% non-need-based).

APPLYING FOR FINANCIAL AID *Required financial aid form:* FAFSA. *Financial aid deadline:* Continuous. *Notification date:* Continuous beginning 4/15. Students must reply within 3 weeks of notification.

CONTACT David W. Martin, Director of Financial Aid, South Dakota School of Mines and Technology, 501 East Saint Joseph Street, Rapid City, SD 57701-3995, 605-394-2274 or toll-free 800-544-8162. *Fax:* 605-394-1979. *E-mail:* david.martin@sdsmt.edu. *Website:* http://www.sdsmt.edu/.

SOUTH DAKOTA STATE UNIVERSITY
Brookings, SD

ABOUT THE INSTITUTION State-supported, coed. *Awards:* certificates, associate, bachelor's, master's, and doctoral degrees. 81 undergraduate majors. *Total enrollment:* 12,613. Undergraduates: 10,959. Freshmen: 2,273.

GIFT AID (NEED-BASED) *Scholarships, grants, and awards:* Federal Pell, FSEOG, state, private, college/university gift aid from institutional funds, United Negro College Fund, Federal Nursing.

GIFT AID (NON-NEED-BASED) *Scholarships, grants, and awards by category:* *Academic interests/achievement:* agriculture, area/ethnic studies, biological sciences, business, communication, computer science, education, engineering/technologies, English, foreign languages, general academic interests/achievements, health fields, home economics, humanities, international studies, mathematics, military science, physical sciences, premedicine, social sciences. *Creative arts/performance:* art/fine arts, debating, general creative arts/performance, journalism/publications, music, performing arts, theater/drama. *Special achievements/activities:* community service, general special achievements/activities, hobbies/interests, junior miss, leadership, memberships, rodeo. *Special characteristics:* adult students, children of faculty/staff, children of workers in trades, ethnic background, first-generation college students, general special characteristics, handicapped students, international students, members of minority groups, veterans, veterans' children.

LOANS *Programs:* Federal Direct (Subsidized and Unsubsidized Stafford, PLUS), Perkins, Federal Nursing.

APPLYING FOR FINANCIAL AID *Required financial aid form:* FAFSA.

CONTACT Carolyn Halgerson, Director of Financial Aid, South Dakota State University, Administration 100, PO Box 2201, Brookings, SD 57007, 605-688-4695 or toll-free 800-952-3541. *Fax:* 605-688-5882. *E-mail:* carolyn.halgerson@sdstate.edu. *Website:* http://www.sdstate.edu/.

SOUTHEASTERN BAPTIST COLLEGE
Laurel, MS

CONTACT Financial Aid Officer, Southeastern Baptist College, 4229 Highway 15 North, Laurel, MS 39440-1096, 601-426-6346. *Website:* http://www.southeasternbaptist.edu/.

SOUTHEASTERN BAPTIST THEOLOGICAL SEMINARY
Wake Forest, NC

CONTACT Financial Aid Office, Southeastern Baptist Theological Seminary, PO Box 1889, Wake Forest, NC 27588-1889, 919-761-2100 or toll-free 800-284-6317. *Website:* http://www.sebts.edu/.

SOUTHEASTERN LOUISIANA UNIVERSITY
Hammond, LA

Tuition & fees (LA res): $7773	Average undergraduate aid package: $9745

ABOUT THE INSTITUTION State-supported, coed. *Awards:* certificates, associate, bachelor's, master's, and doctoral degrees. 37 undergraduate majors. *Total enrollment:* 14,499. Undergraduates: 13,559. Freshmen: 2,618. Federal methodology is used as a basis for awarding need-based institutional aid.

UNDERGRADUATE EXPENSES for 2016–2017 *Application fee:* $20. *Tuition, state resident:* full-time $5652; part-time $324 per credit hour. *Tuition, nonresident:* full-time $18,130; part-time $844 per credit hour. *Required fees:* full-time $2121. Full-time tuition and fees vary according to course load. Part-time tuition and fees vary according to course load. *College room and board:* $7510; *Room only:* $4800. Room and board charges vary according to board plan and housing facility.

FRESHMAN FINANCIAL AID (Fall 2015) 2,074 applied for aid; of those 79% were deemed to have need. 98% of freshmen with need received aid; of those 14% had need fully met. *Average financial aid package:* $9379 (excluding resources awarded to replace EFC). 10% of all full-time freshmen had no need and received non-need-based gift aid.

UNDERGRADUATE FINANCIAL AID (Fall 2015) 7,539 applied for aid; of those 80% were deemed to have need. 99% of undergraduates with need received aid; of those 13% had need fully met. *Average financial aid package:* $9745 (excluding resources awarded to replace EFC). 15% of all full-time undergraduates had no need and received non-need-based gift aid.

GIFT AID (NEED-BASED) *Total amount:* $22,138,678 (85% federal, 14% state, 1% institutional). *Receiving aid:* Freshmen: 49% (1,053); all full-time undergraduates: 47% (4,005). *Average award:* Freshmen: $5103; Undergraduates: $5178. *Scholarships, grants, and awards:* Federal Pell, FSEOG, state, private, college/university gift aid from institutional funds.

GIFT AID (NON-NEED-BASED) *Total amount:* $31,599,345 (70% state, 21% institutional, 9% external sources). *Receiving aid:* Freshmen: 51% (1,090). Undergraduates: 36% (3,090). *Average award:* Freshmen: $1720. Undergraduates: $2443. *Scholarships, grants, and awards by category:* *Academic interests/achievement:* business, communication, computer science, education, English, foreign languages, general academic interests/achievements, humanities, mathematics, premedicine, social sciences. *Creative arts/performance:* art/fine arts, music, theater/drama. *Special achievements/activities:* cheerleading/drum major, leadership, memberships. *Special characteristics:* adult students, children and siblings of alumni, children of faculty/staff, first-generation college students, out-of-state students, veterans, veterans' children. *Tuition waivers:* Full or partial for employees or children of employees. *ROTC:* Army.

LOANS *Student loans:* $33,520,421 (45% need-based, 55% non-need-based). 54% of past graduating class borrowed through all loan programs. *Average indebtedness per student:* $23,536. *Average need-based loan:* Freshmen: $2997. Undergraduates: $3701. *Parent loans:* $2,162,958 (100% non-need-based). *Programs:* Federal Direct (Subsidized and Unsubsidized Stafford, PLUS), Perkins, college/university.

WORK-STUDY *Federal work-study:* 151 jobs averaging $2119. *State or other work-study/employment:* Total amount: $2,312,225 (100% non-need-based). 973 part-time jobs averaging $2268.

ATHLETIC AWARDS Total amount: $3,099,364 (100% non-need-based).

APPLYING FOR FINANCIAL AID *Required financial aid form:* FAFSA. *Financial aid deadline (priority):* 5/1. *Notification date:* Continuous beginning 4/1. Students must reply within 2 weeks of notification.

CONTACT Mr. Charles Cambre, Director of Financial Aid, Southeastern Louisiana University, SLU 10768, Hammond, LA 70402, 985-549-2244 or toll-free 800-222-7358. *Fax:* 985-549-5077. *E-mail:* finaid@selu.edu. *Website:* http://www.southeastern.edu/.

CONTACT Tony Lehrling, Director of Student Financial Aid, Southeastern Oklahoma State University, 1405 North 4th Avenue, Durant, OK 74701-0609, 580-745-2186 or toll-free 800-435-1327. *Fax:* 580-745-7469. *E-mail:* shudson@se.edu. *Website:* http://www.se.edu/.

SOUTHEASTERN OKLAHOMA STATE UNIVERSITY
Durant, OK

Tuition & fees (OK res): $6450	Average undergraduate aid package: $11,195

ABOUT THE INSTITUTION State-supported, coed. *Awards:* certificates, bachelor's, and master's degrees. 41 undergraduate majors. *Total enrollment:* 3,724. Undergraduates: 3,132. Freshmen: 517. Federal methodology is used as a basis for awarding need-based institutional aid.

UNDERGRADUATE EXPENSES for 2016–2017 *Application fee:* $20. *Tuition, state resident:* full-time $5940; part-time $198 per credit hour. *Tuition, nonresident:* full-time $15,210; part-time $507 per credit hour. *Required fees:* full-time $510; $17 per credit hour. Full-time tuition and fees vary according to course level, course load, degree level, location, and program. Part-time tuition and fees vary according to course level, course load, degree level, location, and program. *College room and board:* $6535; *Room only:* $3435. Room and board charges vary according to board plan, housing facility, and student level. *Payment plan:* Guaranteed tuition.

FRESHMAN FINANCIAL AID (Fall 2015) 343 applied for aid; of those 83% were deemed to have need. 98% of freshmen with need received aid; of those 10% had need fully met. *Average percent of need met:* 7% (excluding resources awarded to replace EFC). *Average financial aid package:* $11,434 (excluding resources awarded to replace EFC). 4% of all full-time freshmen had no need and received non-need-based gift aid.

UNDERGRADUATE FINANCIAL AID (Fall 2015) 1,747 applied for aid; of those 90% were deemed to have need. 97% of undergraduates with need received aid; of those 7% had need fully met. *Average percent of need met:* 8% (excluding resources awarded to replace EFC). *Average financial aid package:* $11,195 (excluding resources awarded to replace EFC). 1% of all full-time undergraduates had no need and received non-need-based gift aid.

GIFT AID (NEED-BASED) Total amount: $9,502,286 (70% federal, 30% state). *Receiving aid:* Freshmen: 51% (196); all full-time undergraduates: 51% (1,125). *Average award:* Freshmen: $1899; Undergraduates: $1915. *Scholarships, grants, and awards:* Federal Pell, FSEOG, state, private, college/university gift aid from institutional funds.

GIFT AID (NON-NEED-BASED) Total amount: $3,365,809 (3% state, 19% institutional, 78% external sources). *Receiving aid:* Freshmen: 32% (123). Undergraduates: 23% (502). *Average award:* Freshmen: $1008. Undergraduates: $1013. *Scholarships, grants, and awards by category: Academic interests/achievement:* biological sciences, business, communication, computer science, education, engineering/technologies, English, general academic interests/achievements, mathematics, physical sciences, social sciences. *Creative arts/performance:* art/fine arts, dance, debating, music, performing arts, theater/drama. *Special achievements/activities:* cheerleading/drum major, leadership, rodeo. *Special characteristics:* children and siblings of alumni, out-of-state students. *Tuition waivers:* Full or partial for minority students, children of alumni, employees or children of employees, adult students, senior citizens.

LOANS Student loans: $4,281,601 (100% non-need-based). 53% of past graduating class borrowed through all loan programs. *Average indebtedness per student:* $20,983. *Average need-based loan:* Freshmen: $1369. Undergraduates: $2084. *Parent loans:* $812,429 (100% non-need-based). *Programs:* Federal Direct (Subsidized and Unsubsidized Stafford, PLUS).

WORK-STUDY Federal work-study: jobs available. *State or other work-study/employment:* Part-time jobs available.

ATHLETIC AWARDS Total amount: $1,807,032 (100% non-need-based).

APPLYING FOR FINANCIAL AID Required financial aid forms: FAFSA, institution's own form. *Financial aid deadline (priority):* 3/1. *Notification date:* Continuous beginning 4/15. Students must reply within 2 weeks of notification.

SOUTHEASTERN UNIVERSITY
Lakeland, FL

Tuition & fees: $24,160	Average undergraduate aid package: $15,184

ABOUT THE INSTITUTION Independent Assemblies of God, coed. *Awards:* certificates, associate, bachelor's, master's, and doctoral degrees. 50 undergraduate majors. *Total enrollment:* 5,804. Undergraduates: 5,055. Freshmen: 1,071. Federal methodology is used as a basis for awarding need-based institutional aid.

UNDERGRADUATE EXPENSES for 2017–2018 *Application fee:* $40. *Comprehensive fee:* $33,610 includes full-time tuition ($23,160), mandatory fees ($1000), and room and board ($9450). Full-time tuition and fees vary according to class time, degree level, location, and reciprocity agreements. Room and board charges vary according to board plan and housing facility. *Part-time tuition:* $965 per hour. Part-time tuition and fees vary according to class time, course load, degree level, location, and reciprocity agreements.

FRESHMAN FINANCIAL AID (Fall 2016, est.) 951 applied for aid; of those 87% were deemed to have need. 100% of freshmen with need received aid; of those 11% had need fully met. *Average percent of need met:* 61% (excluding resources awarded to replace EFC). *Average financial aid package:* $15,337 (excluding resources awarded to replace EFC). 18% of all full-time freshmen had no need and received non-need-based gift aid.

UNDERGRADUATE FINANCIAL AID (Fall 2016, est.) 3,458 applied for aid; of those 88% were deemed to have need. 100% of undergraduates with need received aid; of those 12% had need fully met. *Average percent of need met:* 63% (excluding resources awarded to replace EFC). *Average financial aid package:* $15,184 (excluding resources awarded to replace EFC). 18% of all full-time undergraduates had no need and received non-need-based gift aid.

GIFT AID (NEED-BASED) Total amount: $34,029,521 (26% federal, 16% state, 56% institutional, 2% external sources). *Receiving aid:* Freshmen: 65% (664); all full-time undergraduates: 63% (2,425). *Average award:* Freshmen: $6106; Undergraduates: $6089. *Scholarships, grants, and awards:* Federal Pell, FSEOG, state, private, college/university gift aid from institutional funds.

GIFT AID (NON-NEED-BASED) Total amount: $4,916,465 (22% state, 73% institutional, 5% external sources). *Receiving aid:* Freshmen: 81% (826). Undergraduates: 79% (3,033). *Average award:* Freshmen: $9816. Undergraduates: $9400. *Scholarships, grants, and awards by category: Academic interests/achievement:* communication, education, general academic interests/achievements, religion/biblical studies. *Creative arts/performance:* art/fine arts, cinema/film/broadcasting, journalism/publications, music, performing arts. *Special achievements/activities:* cheerleading/drum major, general special achievements/activities, leadership, religious involvement. *Special characteristics:* children of educators, children of faculty/staff, international students, religious affiliation. *Tuition waivers:* Full or partial for employees or children of employees. *ROTC:* Army cooperative.

LOANS Student loans: $20,784,300 (91% need-based, 9% non-need-based). 89% of past graduating class borrowed through all loan programs. *Average indebtedness per student:* $29,224. *Average need-based loan:* Freshmen: $3159. Undergraduates: $3935. *Parent loans:* $13,225,102 (87% need-based, 13% non-need-based). *Programs:* Federal Direct (Subsidized and Unsubsidized Stafford, PLUS), Perkins.

WORK-STUDY Federal work-study: Total amount: $165,629; 75 jobs averaging $2208.

ATHLETIC AWARDS Total amount: $2,584,995 (70% need-based, 30% non-need-based).

APPLYING FOR FINANCIAL AID Required financial aid form: FAFSA. *Financial aid deadline (priority):* 2/15. *Notification date:* Continuous beginning 3/15. Students must reply by 5/1 or within 6 weeks of notification.

CONTACT Mr. Michael E. Yohe, Executive Director of Student Financial Services, Southeastern University, 1000 Longfellow Boulevard, Lakeland, FL 33801-6099, 863-667-5000 or toll-free 800-500-8760. *Fax:* 863-667-5200. *E-mail:* meyohe@seu.edu. *Website:* http://www.seu.edu/.

SOUTHEAST MISSOURI STATE UNIVERSITY
Cape Girardeau, MO

Tuition & fees (MO res): $6990	Average undergraduate aid package: $8995

ABOUT THE INSTITUTION State-supported, coed. *Awards:* certificates, associate, bachelor's, and master's degrees. 64 undergraduate majors. *Total enrollment:* 11,978. Undergraduates: 10,693. Freshmen: 1,858. Both federal and institutional methodology are used as a basis for awarding need-based institutional aid.

UNDERGRADUATE EXPENSES for 2016–2017 *Application fee:* $30. *Tuition, state resident:* full-time $5979; part-time $199.30 per credit hour. *Tuition, nonresident:* full-time $11,364; part-time $378.80 per credit hour. *Required fees:* full-time $1011; $33.70 per credit hour. Full-time tuition and fees vary according to course load and location. Part-time tuition and fees vary according to course load and location. *College room and board:* $8508. Room and board charges vary according to board plan and housing facility.

FRESHMAN FINANCIAL AID (Fall 2015) 1,391 applied for aid; of those 76% were deemed to have need. 99% of freshmen with need received aid; of those 18% had need fully met. *Average percent of need met:* 63% (excluding resources awarded to replace EFC). *Average financial aid package:* $9797 (excluding resources awarded to replace EFC). 22% of all full-time freshmen had no need and received non-need-based gift aid.

UNDERGRADUATE FINANCIAL AID (Fall 2015) 6,073 applied for aid; of those 79% were deemed to have need. 98% of undergraduates with need received aid; of those 13% had need fully met. *Average percent of need met:* 58% (excluding resources awarded to replace EFC). *Average financial aid package:* $8995 (excluding resources awarded to replace EFC). 18% of all full-time undergraduates had no need and received non-need-based gift aid.

GIFT AID (NEED-BASED) *Total amount:* $27,457,514 (52% federal, 17% state, 28% institutional, 3% external sources). *Receiving aid:* Freshmen: 65% (1,017); all full-time undergraduates: 54% (4,207). *Average award:* Freshmen $7034; Undergraduates: $5990. *Scholarships, grants, and awards:* Federal Pell, FSEOG, state, private, college/university gift aid from institutional funds.

GIFT AID (NON-NEED-BASED) *Total amount:* $9,649,156 (6% federal, 20% state, 69% institutional, 5% external sources). *Receiving aid:* Freshmen: 9% (134). Undergraduates: 4% (330). *Average award:* Freshmen: $4221. Undergraduates: $3934. *Scholarships, grants, and awards by category: Academic interests/achievement:* 3,116 awards ($9,633,903 total): agriculture, biological sciences, business, communication, computer science, education, engineering/technologies, English, foreign languages, general academic interests/achievements, health fields, home economics, humanities, international studies, mathematics, military science, physical sciences, premedicine, religion/biblical studies, social sciences. *Creative arts/performance:* 304 awards ($326,375 total): dance, music, performing arts, theater/drama. *Special achievements/activities:* 1,658 awards ($4,406,575 total): cheerleading/drum major, general special achievements/activities, leadership, memberships. *Special characteristics:* 1,145 awards ($3,189,212 total): children of faculty/staff, first-generation college students, general special characteristics, international students, members of minority groups, out-of-state students, previous college experience, veterans. *Tuition waivers:* Full or partial for employees or children of employees, senior citizens. *ROTC:* Air Force.

LOANS *Student loans:* $33,844,870 (72% need-based, 28% non-need-based). 64% of past graduating class borrowed through all loan programs. *Average indebtedness per student:* $27,991. *Average need-based loan:* Freshmen: $3535. Undergraduates: $4154. *Parent loans:* $5,924,338 (33% need-based, 67% non-need-based). *Programs:* Federal Direct (Subsidized and Unsubsidized Stafford, PLUS), Perkins.

WORK-STUDY *Federal work-study:* 217 jobs averaging $1583. *State or other work-study/employment:* Total amount: $3,147,223 (100% non-need-based). 1,565 part-time jobs averaging $2172.

ATHLETIC AWARDS Total amount: $3,159,035 (45% need-based, 55% non-need-based).

APPLYING FOR FINANCIAL AID *Required financial aid form:* FAFSA. *Financial aid deadline (priority):* 3/1. *Notification date:* Continuous beginning 4/1. Students must reply within 3 weeks of notification.

CONTACT Ms. Karen Walker, Director of Financial Aid, Southeast Missouri State University, One University Plaza, Cape Girardeau, MO 63701, 573-651-2253. *Fax:* 573-986-6431. *E-mail:* sfs@semo.edu.
Website: http://www.semo.edu/.

SOUTHERN ADVENTIST UNIVERSITY
Collegedale, TN

Tuition & fees: $21,150	Average undergraduate aid package: $16,232

ABOUT THE INSTITUTION Independent Seventh-day Adventist, coed. *Awards:* certificates, associate, bachelor's, master's, and doctoral degrees. 82 undergraduate majors. *Total enrollment:* 3,125. Undergraduates: 2,673. Freshmen: 539. Federal methodology is used as a basis for awarding need-based institutional aid.

UNDERGRADUATE EXPENSES for 2016–2017 *Application fee:* $25. *Comprehensive fee:* $27,600 includes full-time tuition ($20,300), mandatory fees ($850), and room and board ($6450). *College room only:* $4050. Full-time tuition and fees vary according to course load. Room and board charges vary according to board plan. *Part-time tuition:* $850 per credit hour. *Part-time fees:* $850 per term. Part-time tuition and fees vary according to course load.

FRESHMAN FINANCIAL AID (Fall 2016, est.) 415 applied for aid; of those 83% were deemed to have need. 100% of freshmen with need received aid; of those 2% had need fully met. *Average percent of need met:* 69% (excluding resources awarded to replace EFC). *Average financial aid package:* $16,647 (excluding resources awarded to replace EFC). 30% of all full-time freshmen had no need and received non-need-based gift aid.

UNDERGRADUATE FINANCIAL AID (Fall 2016, est.) 1,671 applied for aid; of those 86% were deemed to have need. 100% of undergraduates with need received aid; of those 1% had need fully met. *Average percent of need met:* 67% (excluding resources awarded to replace EFC). *Average financial aid package:* $16,232 (excluding resources awarded to replace EFC). 25% of all full-time undergraduates had no need and received non-need-based gift aid.

GIFT AID (NEED-BASED) *Total amount:* $5,871,576 (7% federal, 7% state, 86% institutional). *Receiving aid:* Freshmen: 65% (321); all full-time undergraduates: 63% (1,331). *Average award:* Freshmen: $10,958; Undergraduates: $10,431. *Scholarships, grants, and awards:* Federal Pell, FSEOG, state, private, college/university gift aid from institutional funds.

GIFT AID (NON-NEED-BASED) *Total amount:* $10,527,164 (9% state, 85% institutional, 6% external sources). *Receiving aid:* Freshmen: 3% (13). Undergraduates: 1% (28). *Average award:* Freshmen: $8137. Undergraduates: $6926. *Scholarships, grants, and awards by category: Academic interests/achievement:* biological sciences, business, communication, computer science, education, English, foreign languages, general academic interests/achievements, health fields, home economics, humanities, mathematics, physical sciences, premedicine, religion/biblical studies. *Creative arts/performance:* art/fine arts, journalism/publications, music, theater/drama. *Special achievements/activities:* community service, general special achievements/activities, leadership, religious involvement. *Special characteristics:* children and siblings of alumni, general special characteristics, international students, local/state students, members of minority groups, out-of-state students, siblings of current students, spouses of current students. *Tuition waivers:* Full or partial for senior citizens.

LOANS *Student loans:* $14,430,477 (36% need-based, 64% non-need-based). 64% of past graduating class borrowed through all loan programs. *Average indebtedness per student:* $33,320. *Average need-based loan:* Freshmen: $4003. Undergraduates: $4521. *Parent loans:* $1,685,828 (100% non-need-based). *Programs:* Federal Direct (Subsidized and Unsubsidized Stafford, PLUS), Perkins, Federal Nursing, college/university.

WORK-STUDY *Federal work-study:* Total amount: $388,035; jobs available. *State or other work-study/employment:* Part-time jobs available.

APPLYING FOR FINANCIAL AID *Required financial aid form:* FAFSA. *Financial aid deadline (priority):* 11/30. *Notification date:* Continuous. Students must reply within 2 weeks of notification.

CONTACT Mr. Glenn Carter, Associate Vice President of Student Finance, Southern Adventist University, PO Box 370, Collegedale, TN 37315-0370, 423-236-2535 or toll-free 800-768-8437. *Fax:* 423-236-1894.
Website: http://www.southern.edu/.

SOUTHERN ARKANSAS UNIVERSITY–MAGNOLIA
Magnolia, AR

Tuition & fees: N/R	Average undergraduate aid package: $11,880

ABOUT THE INSTITUTION State-supported, coed. *Awards:* certificates, associate, bachelor's, and master's degrees. 40 undergraduate majors. *Total enrollment:* 4,771. Undergraduates: 3,286. Freshmen: 854. Federal methodology is used as a basis for awarding need-based institutional aid.

FRESHMAN FINANCIAL AID (Fall 2015) 756 applied for aid; of those 88% were deemed to have need. 99% of freshmen with need received aid; of those 34% had need fully met. *Average percent of need met:* 83% (excluding resources awarded to replace EFC). *Average financial aid package:* $12,025 (excluding resources awarded to replace EFC). 13% of all full-time freshmen had no need and received non-need-based gift aid.

UNDERGRADUATE FINANCIAL AID (Fall 2015) 2,368 applied for aid; of those 89% were deemed to have need. 99% of undergraduates with need received aid; of those 35% had need fully met. *Average percent of need met:* 78% (excluding resources awarded to replace EFC). *Average financial aid package:* $11,880 (excluding resources awarded to replace EFC). 16% of all full-time undergraduates had no need and received non-need-based gift aid.

GIFT AID (NEED-BASED) Total amount: $7,746,161 (97% federal, 3% state). *Receiving aid:* Freshmen: 61% (481); all full-time undergraduates: 57% (1,512). *Average award:* Freshmen: $4831; Undergraduates: $4713. *Scholarships, grants, and awards:* Federal Pell, FSEOG, state, private, college/university gift aid from institutional funds.

GIFT AID (NON-NEED-BASED) Total amount: $12,354,541 (27% state, 55% institutional, 18% external sources). *Receiving aid:* Freshmen: 70% (549). Undergraduates: 53% (1,405). *Average award:* Freshmen: $5250. Undergraduates: $5066. *Scholarships, grants, and awards by category: Academic interests/achievement:* 1,217 awards ($6,072,024 total): agriculture, biological sciences, business, computer science, education, English, foreign languages, general academic interests/achievements, health fields, library science, mathematics, physical sciences, social sciences. *Creative arts/performance:* 200 awards ($562,930 total): art/fine arts, dance, music, theater/drama. *Special achievements/activities:* 54 awards ($198,516 total): cheerleading/drum major, leadership, rodeo. *Special characteristics:* 809 awards ($2,574,229 total): adult students, children and siblings of alumni, children of faculty/staff, out-of-state students.

LOANS Student loans: $10,448,685 (49% need-based, 51% non-need-based). 51% of past graduating class borrowed through all loan programs. *Average indebtedness per student:* $21,092. *Average need-based loan:* Freshmen: $3056. Undergraduates: $3790. *Parent loans:* $1,297,703 (100% non-need-based). *Programs:* Federal Direct (Subsidized and Unsubsidized Stafford, PLUS), Perkins.

WORK-STUDY Federal work-study: 529 jobs averaging $1749. *State or other work-study/employment:* Total amount: $719,341 (100% non-need-based). 481 part-time jobs averaging $2626.

ATHLETIC AWARDS Total amount: $1,202,136 (100% non-need-based).

APPLYING FOR FINANCIAL AID *Required financial aid forms:* FAFSA, state aid form. *Financial aid deadline (priority):* 6/1. *Notification date:* Continuous beginning 2/1.

CONTACT Ms. Marcela D. Brunson, Director of Student Aid, Southern Arkansas University–Magnolia, MSC 9344, Magnolia, AR 71753, 870-235-4023 or toll-free 800-332-7286. *Fax:* 870-235-4913. *E-mail:* mdbrunson@saumag.edu. *Website:* http://www.saumag.edu/.

THE SOUTHERN BAPTIST THEOLOGICAL SEMINARY
Louisville, KY

CONTACT Mrs. Erin Joiner, Manager of Financial Aid, The Southern Baptist Theological Seminary, 2825 Lexington Road, Louisville, KY 40280, 502-897-4206. *Fax:* 502-897-4031. *E-mail:* financialaid@sbts.edu. *Website:* http://www.sbts.edu/.

SOUTHERN CALIFORNIA INSTITUTE OF ARCHITECTURE
Los Angeles, CA

Tuition & fees: $42,900	Average undergraduate aid package: $19,661

ABOUT THE INSTITUTION Independent, coed. *Awards:* bachelor's and master's degrees. 1 undergraduate major. *Total enrollment:* 502. Undergraduates: 255. Freshmen: 31. Federal methodology is used as a basis for awarding need-based institutional aid.

UNDERGRADUATE EXPENSES for 2016–2017 *Application fee:* $85. *Tuition:* full-time $41,800. Full-time tuition and fees vary according to course load.

FRESHMAN FINANCIAL AID (Fall 2016, est.) 3 applied for aid; of those 100% were deemed to have need. 100% of freshmen with need received aid. *Average percent of need met:* 64% (excluding resources awarded to replace EFC). *Average financial aid package:* $27,752 (excluding resources awarded to replace EFC). 13% of all full-time freshmen had no need and received non-need-based gift aid.

UNDERGRADUATE FINANCIAL AID (Fall 2016, est.) 78 applied for aid; of those 96% were deemed to have need. 100% of undergraduates with need received aid; of those 1% had need fully met. *Average percent of need met:* 31% (excluding resources awarded to replace EFC). *Average financial aid package:* $19,661 (excluding resources awarded to replace EFC). 19% of all full-time undergraduates had no need and received non-need-based gift aid.

GIFT AID (NEED-BASED) Total amount: $1,177,742 (23% federal, 17% state, 59% institutional, 1% external sources). *Receiving aid:* Freshmen: 19% (3); all full-time undergraduates: 68% (65). *Average award:* Freshmen: $25,419; Undergraduates: $17,745. *Scholarships, grants, and awards:* Federal Pell, FSEOG, state, private, college/university gift aid from institutional funds.

GIFT AID (NON-NEED-BASED) Total amount: $394,181 (1% federal, 98% institutional, 1% external sources). *Receiving aid:* Undergraduates: 1% (1). *Average award:* Freshmen: $24,700. Undergraduates: $20,452. *Scholarships, grants, and awards by category: Academic interests/achievement:* architecture.

LOANS Student loans: $1,436,374 (93% need-based, 7% non-need-based). 87% of past graduating class borrowed through all loan programs. *Average indebtedness per student:* $39,287. *Average need-based loan:* Freshmen: $3500. Undergraduates: $4553. *Parent loans:* $1,465,116 (93% need-based, 7% non-need-based). *Programs:* Federal Direct (Subsidized and Unsubsidized Stafford, PLUS), alternative loans.

WORK-STUDY Federal work-study: Total amount: $28,742; jobs available.

APPLYING FOR FINANCIAL AID *Required financial aid forms:* FAFSA, institution's own form. *Financial aid deadline (priority):* 3/2. *Notification date:* 4/1. Students must reply within 4 weeks of notification.

CONTACT Marisela De La Torre, Financial Aid Counselor, Southern California Institute of Architecture, 960 East 3rd Street, Los Angeles, CA 90013, 213-613-2200 Ext. 376. *Fax:* 213-613-2260. *E-mail:* financialaid@sciarc.edu. *Website:* http://www.sciarc.edu/.

SOUTHERN CALIFORNIA INSTITUTE OF TECHNOLOGY
Anaheim, CA

CONTACT Financial Aid Office, Southern California Institute of Technology, 525 North Muller Street, Anaheim, CA 92801, 714-520-5552. *Website:* http://www.scitech.edu/.

SOUTHERN CALIFORNIA SEMINARY
El Cajon, CA

CONTACT Financial Aid Office, Southern California Seminary, 2075 East Madison Avenue, El Cajon, CA 92019, 619-201-8999 or toll-free 888-389-7244 (out-of-state). *Website:* http://www.socalsem.edu/.

SOUTHERN CONNECTICUT STATE UNIVERSITY
New Haven, CT

Tuition & fees (CT res): $10,054	Average undergraduate aid package: $14,501

ABOUT THE INSTITUTION State-supported, coed. **Awards:** certificates, bachelor's, master's, and doctoral degrees. 43 undergraduate majors. **Total enrollment:** 10,320. Undergraduates: 7,963. Freshmen: 1,404. Federal methodology is used as a basis for awarding need-based institutional aid.

UNDERGRADUATE EXPENSES for 2016–2017 Application fee: $50. **Tuition, state resident:** full-time $5216; part-time $519 per credit hour. **Tuition, nonresident:** full-time $16,882; part-time $535 per credit hour. **Required fees:** full-time $4838; $55 per term. Full-time tuition and fees vary according to course load and reciprocity agreements. Part-time tuition and fees vary according to course load. **College room and board:** $11,870; **Room only:** $6594. Room and board charges vary according to board plan and housing facility.

FRESHMAN FINANCIAL AID (Fall 2016, est.) 1,124 applied for aid; of those 83% were deemed to have need. 100% of freshmen with need received aid; of those 21% had need fully met. **Average percent of need met:** 68% (excluding resources awarded to replace EFC). **Average financial aid package:** $15,069 (excluding resources awarded to replace EFC). 5% of all full-time freshmen had no need and received non-need-based gift aid.

UNDERGRADUATE FINANCIAL AID (Fall 2016, est.) 5,412 applied for aid; of those 85% were deemed to have need. 100% of undergraduates with need received aid; of those 25% had need fully met. **Average percent of need met:** 68% (excluding resources awarded to replace EFC). **Average financial aid package:** $14,501 (excluding resources awarded to replace EFC). 3% of all full-time undergraduates had no need and received non-need-based gift aid.

GIFT AID (NEED-BASED) Total amount: $21,109,477 (64% federal, 13% state, 23% institutional). **Receiving aid:** Freshmen: 44% (610); all full-time undergraduates: 44% (3,036). **Average award:** Freshmen: $6522; Undergraduates: $6639. **Scholarships, grants, and awards:** Federal Pell, FSEOG, state, private, college/university gift aid from institutional funds.

GIFT AID (NON-NEED-BASED) Total amount: $4,390,438 (1% federal, 19% state, 45% institutional, 35% external sources). **Receiving aid:** Freshmen: 22% (303). Undergraduates: 14% (953). **Average award:** Freshmen: $3877. Undergraduates: $4636. **Scholarships, grants, and awards by category:** Special characteristics: children of faculty/staff, veterans. **Tuition waivers:** Full or partial for employees or children of employees, senior citizens. **ROTC:** Army cooperative, Air Force cooperative.

LOANS Student loans: $38,283,635 (46% need-based, 54% non-need-based). 75% of past graduating class borrowed through all loan programs. **Average indebtedness per student:** $28,370. **Average need-based loan:** Freshmen: $3374. Undergraduates: $4359. **Parent loans:** $17,075,911 (100% non-need-based). **Programs:** Federal Direct (Subsidized and Unsubsidized Stafford, PLUS), Perkins.

WORK-STUDY Federal work-study: Total amount: $398,609; 96 jobs averaging $4196. **State or other work-study/employment:** Total amount: $92,000 (100% non-need-based). Part-time jobs available.

ATHLETIC AWARDS Total amount: $1,580,395 (100% non-need-based).

APPLYING FOR FINANCIAL AID Required financial aid form: FAFSA. **Financial aid deadline:** 3/9 (priority: 3/5). **Notification date:** Continuous beginning 4/11. Students must reply within 2 weeks of notification.

CONTACT Mrs. Gloria Lee, Director of Financial Aid, Southern Connecticut State University, Wintergreen Building, New Haven, CT 06515-1355, 203-392-5445. *Fax:* 203-392-5229. *E-mail:* leeg1@southernct.edu. *Website:* http://www.southernct.edu/.

SOUTHERN ILLINOIS UNIVERSITY CARBONDALE
Carbondale, IL

Tuition & fees (IL res): $13,481	Average undergraduate aid package: $14,946

ABOUT THE INSTITUTION State-supported, coed. **Awards:** certificates, associate, bachelor's, master's, and doctoral degrees. 81 undergraduate majors. **Total enrollment:** 15,987. Undergraduates: 12,182. Freshmen: 1,611. Federal methodology is used as a basis for awarding need-based institutional aid.

UNDERGRADUATE EXPENSES for 2016–2017 Application fee: $40. **Tuition, state resident:** full-time $9099; part-time $303.30 per credit hour. **Tuition, nonresident:** full-time $22,748; part-time $758.25 per credit hour. **Required fees:** full-time $4382; $951.33 per credit hour. Full-time tuition and fees vary according to course load, location, program, reciprocity agreements, and student level. Part-time tuition and fees vary according to course load, location, program, reciprocity agreements, and student level. **College room and board:** $10,186. Room and board charges vary according to board plan and housing facility. **Payment plan:** Guaranteed tuition.

FRESHMAN FINANCIAL AID (Fall 2016, est.) 1,469 applied for aid; of those 85% were deemed to have need. 99% of freshmen with need received aid; of those 10% had need fully met. **Average percent of need met:** 63% (excluding resources awarded to replace EFC). **Average financial aid package:** $16,329 (excluding resources awarded to replace EFC). 7% of all full-time freshmen had no need and received non-need-based gift aid.

UNDERGRADUATE FINANCIAL AID (Fall 2016, est.) 8,475 applied for aid; of those 87% were deemed to have need. 99% of undergraduates with need received aid; of those 9% had need fully met. **Average percent of need met:** 60% (excluding resources awarded to replace EFC). **Average financial aid package:** $14,946 (excluding resources awarded to replace EFC). 5% of all full-time undergraduates had no need and received non-need-based gift aid.

GIFT AID (NEED-BASED) Total amount: $49,220,505 (48% federal, 26% state, 22% institutional, 4% external sources). **Receiving aid:** Freshmen: 50% (793); all full-time undergraduates: 45% (4,751). **Average award:** Freshmen: $8605; Undergraduates: $7533. **Scholarships, grants, and awards:** Federal Pell, FSEOG, state, private, college/university gift aid from institutional funds.

GIFT AID (NON-NEED-BASED) Total amount: $12,026,464 (8% federal, 50% institutional, 42% external sources). **Receiving aid:** Freshmen: 28% (450). Undergraduates: 22% (2,349). **Average award:** Freshmen: $7224. Undergraduates: $6788. **Scholarships, grants, and awards by category:** Academic interests/achievement: agriculture, architecture, area/ethnic studies, biological sciences, business, communication, computer science, education, engineering/technologies, English, foreign languages, general academic interests/achievements, health fields, home economics, humanities, international studies, mathematics, military science, physical sciences, premedicine, social sciences. Creative arts/performance: applied art and design, art/fine arts, cinema/film/broadcasting, creative writing, dance, debating, general creative arts/performance, journalism/publications, music, performing arts, theater/drama. Special achievements/activities: cheerleading/drum major, community service, general special achievements/activities, leadership. Special characteristics: children and siblings of alumni, children of educators, children of faculty/staff, children of public servants, children with a deceased or disabled parent, first-generation college students, general special characteristics, handicapped students, international students, local/state students, members of minority groups, public servants, spouses of deceased or disabled public servants, veterans, veterans' children. **Tuition waivers:** Full or partial for children of alumni, employees or children of employees, senior citizens. **ROTC:** Army, Air Force.

LOANS Student loans: $64,650,055 (76% need-based, 24% non-need-based). 72% of past graduating class borrowed through all loan programs. **Average indebtedness per student:** $33,218. **Average need-based loan:** Freshmen: $3373. Undergraduates: $4439. **Parent loans:** $10,811,257 (37% need-based, 63% non-need-based). **Programs:** Federal Direct (Subsidized and Unsubsidized Stafford, PLUS), Perkins.

WORK-STUDY Federal work-study: Total amount: $11,763,968; 1,495 jobs averaging $1039.

ATHLETIC AWARDS Total amount: $3,169,967 (36% need-based, 64% non-need-based).

APPLYING FOR FINANCIAL AID Required financial aid form: FAFSA. **Financial aid deadline (priority):** 3/1. **Notification date:** Continuous beginning 3/15.

CONTACT Terri R. Harfst, Director of Financial Aid, Southern Illinois University Carbondale, Student Services Building, 1263 Lincoln Drive, 2nd Floor, Carbondale, IL 62901-4702, 618-453-3102. *Fax:* 618-453-4606. *E-mail:* fao@siu.edu. *Website:* http://www.siu.edu/.

SOUTHERN ILLINOIS UNIVERSITY EDWARDSVILLE
Edwardsville, IL

Tuition & fees (IL res): $11,493	Average undergraduate aid package: $11,223

ABOUT THE INSTITUTION State-supported, coed. *Awards:* certificates, bachelor's, master's, and doctoral degrees. 48 undergraduate majors. *Total enrollment:* 14,142. Undergraduates: 11,720. Freshmen: 1,932. Federal methodology is used as a basis for awarding need-based institutional aid.

UNDERGRADUATE EXPENSES for 2017–2018 *Application fee:* $40. *Tuition, state resident:* full-time $8772; part-time $292.40 per credit hour. *Tuition, nonresident:* full-time $8772; part-time $731 per credit hour. *Required fees:* full-time $2721. Full-time tuition and fees vary according to course load, degree level, location, and program. Part-time tuition and fees vary according to course load, degree level, location, and program. *College room and board:* $9481. Room and board charges vary according to board plan, housing facility, and student level. *Payment plan:* Guaranteed tuition.

FRESHMAN FINANCIAL AID (Fall 2015) 1,874 applied for aid; of those 74% were deemed to have need. 97% of freshmen with need received aid; of those 44% had need fully met. *Average percent of need met:* 64% (excluding resources awarded to replace EFC). *Average financial aid package:* $11,553 (excluding resources awarded to replace EFC). 4% of all full-time freshmen had no need and received non-need-based gift aid.

UNDERGRADUATE FINANCIAL AID (Fall 2015) 8,167 applied for aid; of those 80% were deemed to have need. 97% of undergraduates with need received aid; of those 39% had need fully met. *Average percent of need met:* 60% (excluding resources awarded to replace EFC). *Average financial aid package:* $11,223 (excluding resources awarded to replace EFC). 5% of all full-time undergraduates had no need and received non-need-based gift aid.

GIFT AID (NEED-BASED) *Total amount:* $34,391,334 (57% federal, 24% state, 15% institutional, 4% external sources). *Receiving aid:* Freshmen: 54% (1,111); all full-time undergraduates: 49% (4,871). *Average award:* Freshmen: $8070; Undergraduates: $7760. *Scholarships, grants, and awards:* Federal Pell, FSEOG, state, private, college/university gift aid from institutional funds, Federal Nursing.

GIFT AID (NON-NEED-BASED) *Total amount:* $7,856,657 (16% federal, 15% state, 58% institutional, 11% external sources). *Receiving aid:* Freshmen: 29% (601). Undergraduates: 23% (2,270). *Average award:* Freshmen: $5674. Undergraduates: $5113. *Scholarships, grants, and awards by category:* Academic interests/achievement: business, education, general academic interests/achievements, home economics. *Creative arts/performance:* art/fine arts, dance, music, theater/drama. *Special characteristics:* children of faculty/staff. *Tuition waivers:* Full or partial for employees or children of employees, senior citizens. *ROTC:* Army, Air Force cooperative.

LOANS *Student loans:* $45,441,272 (76% need-based, 24% non-need-based). 59% of past graduating class borrowed through all loan programs. *Average indebtedness per student:* $22,277. *Average need-based loan:* Freshmen: $3523. Undergraduates: $4496. *Parent loans:* $23,310,641 (25% need-based, 75% non-need-based). *Programs:* Federal Direct (Subsidized and Unsubsidized Stafford, PLUS), Perkins, Federal Nursing, college/university, alternative loans.

WORK-STUDY *Federal work-study:* jobs available. *State or other work-study/employment:* Part-time jobs available.

ATHLETIC AWARDS Total amount: $1,003,243 (30% need-based, 70% non-need-based).

APPLYING FOR FINANCIAL AID *Required financial aid form:* FAFSA. *Financial aid deadline (priority):* 3/1. *Notification date:* Continuous beginning 3/15. Students must reply within 2 weeks of notification.

CONTACT Sally Mullen, Director of Financial Aid, Southern Illinois University Edwardsville, Campus Box 1060, Edwardsville, IL 62026-1060, 618-650-3834 or toll-free 800-447-SIUE. *Fax:* 618-650-3885. *E-mail:* smullen@siue.edu. *Website:* http://www.siue.edu/.

SOUTHERN METHODIST UNIVERSITY
Dallas, TX

Tuition & fees: $52,498	Average undergraduate aid package: $41,761

ABOUT THE INSTITUTION Independent United Methodist Church, coed. *Awards:* certificates, bachelor's, master's, and doctoral degrees. 68 undergraduate majors. *Total enrollment:* 11,739. Undergraduates: 6,521. Freshmen: 1,522. Both federal and institutional methodology are used as a basis for awarding need-based institutional aid.

UNDERGRADUATE EXPENSES for 2017–2018 *Application fee:* $60. *Comprehensive fee:* $69,408 includes full-time tuition ($46,594), mandatory fees ($5904), and room and board ($16,910). Room and board charges vary according to board plan and housing facility. *Part-time tuition:* $1946 per credit hour. Part-time tuition and fees vary according to course load. *Payment plan:* Tuition prepayment.

FRESHMAN FINANCIAL AID (Fall 2016, est.) 823 applied for aid; of those 72% were deemed to have need. 100% of freshmen with need received aid; of those 40% had need fully met. *Average percent of need met:* 90% (excluding resources awarded to replace EFC). *Average financial aid package:* $43,984 (excluding resources awarded to replace EFC). 40% of all full-time freshmen had no need and received non-need-based gift aid.

UNDERGRADUATE FINANCIAL AID (Fall 2016, est.) 2,497 applied for aid; of those 83% were deemed to have need. 99% of undergraduates with need received aid; of those 30% had need fully met. *Average percent of need met:* 85% (excluding resources awarded to replace EFC). *Average financial aid package:* $41,761 (excluding resources awarded to replace EFC). 36% of all full-time undergraduates had no need and received non-need-based gift aid.

GIFT AID (NEED-BASED) *Total amount:* $64,566,890 (6% federal, 5% state, 87% institutional, 2% external sources). *Receiving aid:* Freshmen: 27% (404); all full-time undergraduates: 24% (1,499). *Average award:* Freshmen: $21,971; Undergraduates: $22,210. *Scholarships, grants, and awards:* Federal Pell, FSEOG, state, private, college/university gift aid from institutional funds.

GIFT AID (NON-NEED-BASED) *Total amount:* $49,162,175 (96% institutional, 4% external sources). *Receiving aid:* Freshmen: 30% (463). Undergraduates: 22% (1,382). *Average award:* Freshmen: $23,315. Undergraduates: $23,323. *Tuition waivers:* Full or partial for employees or children of employees. *ROTC:* Army, Air Force cooperative.

LOANS *Student loans:* $21,711,128 (54% need-based, 46% non-need-based). 35% of past graduating class borrowed through all loan programs. *Average indebtedness per student:* $29,601. *Average need-based loan:* Freshmen: $3249. Undergraduates: $4278. *Parent loans:* $10,748,339 (26% need-based, 74% non-need-based). *Programs:* Federal Direct (Subsidized and Unsubsidized Stafford, PLUS), Perkins, state, college/university.

WORK-STUDY *Federal work-study:* Total amount: $5,141,721; jobs available. *State or other work-study/employment:* Total amount: $191,158 (40% need-based, 60% non-need-based). Part-time jobs available.

ATHLETIC AWARDS Total amount: $15,845,158 (38% need-based, 62% non-need-based).

APPLYING FOR FINANCIAL AID *Required financial aid forms:* FAFSA, CSS Financial Aid PROFILE, noncustodial (divorced/separated) parent's statement. *Financial aid deadline (priority):* 11/1. *Notification date:* 1/20. Students must reply by 5/1.

CONTACT Marc Peterson, Director of Financial Aid, Southern Methodist University, PO Box 750181, Dallas, TX 75275, 214-768-3417 or toll-free 800-323-0672. *Fax:* 214-768-3878. *E-mail:* enrol_serv@smu.edu. *Website:* http://www.smu.edu/.

SOUTHERN NAZARENE UNIVERSITY
Bethany, OK

CONTACT Diana Lee, Director of Financial Assistance, Southern Nazarene University, 6729 Northwest 39th Expressway, Bethany, OK 73008, 405-491-6310 or toll-free 800-648-9899. *Fax:* 405-717-6271. *E-mail:* dlee@snu.edu. *Website:* http://www.snu.edu/.

SOUTHERN NEW HAMPSHIRE UNIVERSITY
Manchester, NH

Tuition & fees: $31,136	Average undergraduate aid package: $23,425

ABOUT THE INSTITUTION Independent, coed. *Awards:* certificates, associate, bachelor's, master's, and doctoral degrees. 47 undergraduate majors. *Total enrollment:* 4,092. Undergraduates: 3,020. Freshmen: 768. Federal methodology is used as a basis for awarding need-based institutional aid.

UNDERGRADUATE EXPENSES for 2017–2018 *Application fee:* $40. *Comprehensive fee:* $43,198 includes full-time tuition ($30,756), mandatory fees ($380), and room and board ($12,062). *College room only:* $8583. Full-time tuition and fees vary according to course load. Room and board charges vary according to board plan and housing facility. *Part-time tuition:* $1282 per credit hour.

FRESHMAN FINANCIAL AID (Fall 2016, est.) 699 applied for aid; of those 89% were deemed to have need. 100% of freshmen with need received aid; of those 15% had need fully met. *Average percent of need met:* 66% (excluding resources awarded to replace EFC). *Average financial aid package:* $23,900 (excluding resources awarded to replace EFC). 17% of all full-time freshmen had no need and received non-need-based gift aid.

UNDERGRADUATE FINANCIAL AID (Fall 2016, est.) 2,294 applied for aid; of those 91% were deemed to have need. 100% of undergraduates with need received aid; of those 17% had need fully met. *Average percent of need met:* 66% (excluding resources awarded to replace EFC). *Average financial aid package:* $23,425 (excluding resources awarded to replace EFC). 20% of all full-time undergraduates had no need and received non-need-based gift aid.

GIFT AID (NEED-BASED) *Total amount:* $40,921,090 (9% federal, 1% state, 88% institutional, 2% external sources). *Receiving aid:* Freshmen: 49% (377); all full-time undergraduates: 42% (1,231). *Average award:* Freshmen: $6178; Undergraduates: $6558. *Scholarships, grants, and awards:* Federal Pell, FSEOG, state, private, college/university gift aid from institutional funds.

GIFT AID (NON-NEED-BASED) *Total amount:* $2,773,310 (99% institutional, 1% external sources). *Receiving aid:* Freshmen: 80% (616). Undergraduates: 68% (1,992). *Average award:* Freshmen: $13,028. Undergraduates: $13,342. *Scholarships, grants, and awards by category:* Academic interests/achievement: business, computer science, education, general academic interests/achievements, social sciences. Creative arts/performance: music. Special achievements/activities: community service, general special achievements/activities, hobbies/interests, leadership, memberships. Special characteristics: children and siblings of alumni, children of educators, handicapped students, international students, local/state students, previous college experience, siblings of current students, twins, veterans. *Tuition waivers:* Full or partial for employees or children of employees, senior citizens. *ROTC:* Army cooperative, Air Force cooperative.

LOANS *Student loans:* $26,432,672 (94% need-based, 6% non-need-based). 67% of past graduating class borrowed through all loan programs. *Average indebtedness per student:* $41,028. *Average need-based loan:* Freshmen: $3434. Undergraduates: $4330. *Parent loans:* $9,171,640 (96% need-based, 4% non-need-based). *Programs:* Federal Direct (Subsidized and Unsubsidized Stafford, PLUS).

WORK-STUDY *Federal work-study:* Total amount: $3,514,154; 1,258 jobs averaging $3033.

ATHLETIC AWARDS Total amount: $2,926,336 (94% need-based, 6% non-need-based).

APPLYING FOR FINANCIAL AID *Required financial aid form:* FAFSA. *Financial aid deadline:* 6/30 (priority: 3/15). *Notification date:* Continuous beginning 3/15.

CONTACT Student Financial Services, Southern New Hampshire University, 2500 North River Road, Manchester, NH 03106, 603-645-9645 or toll-free 888-327-7648. *Fax:* 603-645-9639. *E-mail:* sfscampus@snhu.edu. *Website:* http://www.snhu.edu/.

SOUTHERN OREGON UNIVERSITY
Ashland, OR

Tuition & fees (OR res): $8523	Average undergraduate aid package: $11,131

ABOUT THE INSTITUTION State-supported, coed. *Awards:* certificates, bachelor's, and master's degrees. 39 undergraduate majors. *Total enrollment:* 5,916. Undergraduates: 5,314. Freshmen: 675. Federal methodology is used as a basis for awarding need-based institutional aid.

UNDERGRADUATE EXPENSES for 2016–2017 *Application fee:* $60. *Tuition, state resident:* full-time $6813; part-time $151 per credit hour. *Tuition, nonresident:* full-time $21,460; part-time $477 per credit hour. *Required fees:* full-time $1710; $61 per credit hour. Full-time tuition and fees vary according to course load, program, and reciprocity agreements. Part-time tuition and fees vary according to course load, program, and reciprocity agreements. *College room and board:* $12,756; *Room only:* $7065. Room and board charges vary according to board plan and housing facility.

FRESHMAN FINANCIAL AID (Fall 2016, est.) 580 applied for aid; of those 64% were deemed to have need. 95% of freshmen with need received aid; of those 29% had need fully met. *Average percent of need met:* 70% (excluding resources awarded to replace EFC). *Average financial aid package:* $9406 (excluding resources awarded to replace EFC).

UNDERGRADUATE FINANCIAL AID (Fall 2016, est.) 2,729 applied for aid; of those 78% were deemed to have need. 97% of undergraduates with need received aid; of those 24% had need fully met. *Average percent of need met:* 77% (excluding resources awarded to replace EFC). *Average financial aid package:* $11,131 (excluding resources awarded to replace EFC).

GIFT AID (NEED-BASED) *Total amount:* $12,705,828 (65% federal, 16% state, 19% institutional). *Receiving aid:* Freshmen: 44% (292); all full-time undergraduates: 49% (1,646). *Average award:* Freshmen: $7043; Undergraduates: $6825. *Scholarships, grants, and awards:* Federal Pell, FSEOG, state, private, college/university gift aid from institutional funds.

GIFT AID (NON-NEED-BASED) *Total amount:* $1,281,326 (66% institutional, 34% external sources). *Receiving aid:* Freshmen: 31% (206). Undergraduates: 21% (704). *Scholarships, grants, and awards by category:* Academic interests/achievement: 1,252 awards ($2,725,722 total): biological sciences, business, education, English, foreign languages, general academic interests/achievements, health fields, mathematics, physical sciences, social sciences. Creative arts/performance: 55 awards ($96,086 total): art/fine arts, creative writing, journalism/publications, music, theater/drama. Special achievements/activities: 11 awards ($21,500 total): community service, general special achievements/activities, hobbies/interests, leadership, memberships. Special characteristics: 251 awards ($633,974 total): adult students, international students, members of minority groups, out-of-state students, previous college experience, veterans, veterans' children. *Tuition waivers:* Full or partial for employees or children of employees, senior citizens. *ROTC:* Army.

LOANS *Student loans:* $16,718,331 (82% need-based, 18% non-need-based). 68% of past graduating class borrowed through all loan programs. *Average indebtedness per student:* $27,375. *Average need-based loan:* Freshmen: $5497. Undergraduates: $7371. *Parent loans:* $5,710,042 (19% need-based, 81% non-need-based). *Programs:* Federal Direct (Subsidized and Unsubsidized Stafford, PLUS), Perkins.

WORK-STUDY *Federal work-study:* Total amount: $263,219; 195 jobs averaging $2977.

ATHLETIC AWARDS Total amount: $382,350 (65% need-based, 35% non-need-based).

APPLYING FOR FINANCIAL AID *Financial aid deadline (priority):* 3/1. *Notification date:* Continuous beginning 3/2.

CONTACT Enrollment Services Center, Southern Oregon University, 1250 Siskiyou Boulevard, Ashland, OR 97520, 541-552-6600 or toll-free 855-470-3377 (out-of-state). *Fax:* 541-552-6614. *E-mail:* esc@sou.edu. *Website:* http://www.sou.edu/.

SOUTHERN TECHNICAL COLLEGE
Fort Myers, FL

CONTACT Financial Aid Office, Southern Technical College, 1685 Medical Lane, Fort Myers, FL 33907, 239-939-4766 or toll-free 877-347-5492. *Website:* http://www.southerntech.edu/locations/ft-myers/.

SOUTHERN UNIVERSITY AND AGRICULTURAL AND MECHANICAL COLLEGE
Baton Rouge, LA

CONTACT Mr. Phillip Rodgers Sr., Director of Financial Aid, Southern University and Agricultural and Mechanical College, PO Box 9961, Baton Rouge, LA 70813, 225-771-2790. *Fax:* 225-771-5898. *E-mail:* phillip_rodgers@cxs.subr.edu. *Website:* http://www.subr.edu/.

SOUTHERN UNIVERSITY AT NEW ORLEANS
New Orleans, LA

CONTACT La'Charlotte C. Garrett, Director of Financial Aid, Southern University at New Orleans, 6400 Press Drive, New Orleans, LA 70126, 504-286-5435. *Fax:* 504-286-5213. *E-mail:* lgarrett@suno.edu. *Website:* http://www.suno.edu/.

SOUTHERN UTAH UNIVERSITY
Cedar City, UT

Tuition & fees (UT res): $6530	Average undergraduate aid package: $8958

ABOUT THE INSTITUTION State-supported, coed. *Awards:* certificates, diplomas, associate, bachelor's, and master's degrees. 73 undergraduate majors. *Total enrollment:* 9,299. Undergraduates: 8,407. Freshmen: 1,526. Federal methodology is used as a basis for awarding need-based institutional aid.
UNDERGRADUATE EXPENSES for 2016–2017 *Application fee:* $50. *Tuition, state resident:* full-time $5774; part-time $271 per credit. *Tuition, non-resident:* full-time $19,054; part-time $897 per credit. *Required fees:* full-time $756; $378 per term. Full-time tuition and fees vary according to program. Part-time tuition and fees vary according to course load and program. *College room and board:* $7067; *Room only:* $3167. Room and board charges vary according to board plan and housing facility.
FRESHMAN FINANCIAL AID (Fall 2015) 1,031 applied for aid; of those 77% were deemed to have need. 100% of freshmen with need received aid; of those 14% had need fully met. *Average percent of need met:* 61% (excluding resources awarded to replace EFC). *Average financial aid package:* $9641 (excluding resources awarded to replace EFC). 49% of all full-time freshmen had no need and received non-need-based gift aid.
UNDERGRADUATE FINANCIAL AID (Fall 2015) 3,849 applied for aid; of those 87% were deemed to have need. 100% of undergraduates with need received aid; of those 8% had need fully met. *Average percent of need met:* 56% (excluding resources awarded to replace EFC). *Average financial aid package:* $8958 (excluding resources awarded to replace EFC). 23% of all full-time undergraduates had no need and received non-need-based gift aid.
GIFT AID (NEED-BASED) *Total amount:* $12,774,438 (100% federal). *Receiving aid:* Freshmen: 44% (460); all full-time undergraduates: 44% (2,391). *Average award:* Freshmen: $4218; Undergraduates: $4469. *Scholarships, grants, and awards:* Federal Pell, FSEOG, state, private, college/university gift aid from institutional funds.
GIFT AID (NON-NEED-BASED) *Total amount:* $18,843,774 (3% state, 92% institutional, 5% external sources). *Receiving aid:* Freshmen: 46% (475). Undergrad-uates: 20% (1,079). *Average award:* Freshmen: $6503. Undergraduates: $6146. *Scholarships, grants, and awards by category:* Academic interests/achievement: general academic interests/achievements. Creative arts/performance: art/fine arts, music, theater/drama. *Special achievements/activities:* general special achievements/activities, leadership. *Special characteristics:* children and siblings of alumni, local/state students, members of minority groups. *Tuition waivers:* Full or partial for children of alumni, employees or children of employees, senior citizens. *ROTC:* Army.
LOANS *Student loans:* $17,596,005 (46% need-based, 54% non-need-based). 51% of past graduating class borrowed through all loan programs. *Average indebtedness per student:* $16,892. *Average need-based loan:* Freshmen: $2904. Undergraduates: $3746. *Parent loans:* $685,552 (100% non-need-based). *Programs:* Federal Direct (Subsidized and Unsubsidized Stafford, PLUS), Perkins, college/university.
WORK-STUDY *Federal work-study:* jobs available. *State or other work-study/employment:* Total amount: $79,730 (100% need-based). Part-time jobs available.
ATHLETIC AWARDS Total amount: $2,895,520 (100% non-need-based).
APPLYING FOR FINANCIAL AID *Required financial aid forms:* FAFSA, institution's own form. *Financial aid deadline:* Continuous. *Notification date:* Continuous beginning 3/1.
CONTACT David Hughes, Director of Financial Aid and Scholarships, Southern Utah University, 351 West University Boulevard, Cedar City, UT 84720-2498, 435-586-7735. *Fax:* 435-586-7736. *E-mail:* hughes@suu.edu. *Website:* http://www.suu.edu/.

SOUTHERN VERMONT COLLEGE
Bennington, VT

Tuition & fees: N/R	Average undergraduate aid package: N/A

ABOUT THE INSTITUTION Independent, coed. *Awards:* certificates, associate, and bachelor's degrees. 14 undergraduate majors. *Total enrollment:* 475. Undergraduates: 475. Freshmen: 105. Federal methodology is used as a basis for awarding need-based institutional aid.
GIFT AID (NEED-BASED) *Total amount:* $3,655,146 (23% federal, 9% state, 68% institutional). *Scholarships, grants, and awards:* Federal Pell, FSEOG, state, private, college/university gift aid from institutional funds.
GIFT AID (NON-NEED-BASED) *Total amount:* $1,040,542 (96% institutional, 4% external sources). *Scholarships, grants, and awards by category:* Academic interests/achievement: general academic interests/achievements. *Special achievements/activities:* 67 awards ($134,000 total): community service, leadership. *Special characteristics:* 10 awards ($96,134 total): children of faculty/staff.
LOANS *Student loans:* $3,668,152 (100% need-based). *Parent loans:* $957,579 (100% need-based). *Programs:* Federal Direct (Subsidized and Unsubsidized Stafford, PLUS).
WORK-STUDY *Federal work-study:* Total amount: $102,944; 98 jobs averaging $1000. *State or other work-study/employment:* Total amount: $23,245 (100% non-need-based). 8 part-time jobs averaging $2000.
APPLYING FOR FINANCIAL AID *Required financial aid form:* FAFSA. *Financial aid deadline (priority):* 1/1. *Notification date:* Continuous beginning 12/15. Students must reply by 5/1.
CONTACT Susan Rochette, Director of Student Financial Services, Southern Vermont College, 982 Mansion Drive, Bennington, VT 05201, 802-447-6339. *Fax:* 802-447-6329. *E-mail:* financialaid@svc.edu. *Website:* http://www.svc.edu/.

SOUTHERN VIRGINIA UNIVERSITY
Buena Vista, VA

CONTACT Darin Hassell, Financial Aid Specialist, Southern Virginia University, One University Hill Drive, Buena Vista, VA 24416, 540-261-4351 or toll-free 800-229-8420. *Fax:* 540-261-8559. *E-mail:* finaid@svu.edu. *Website:* http://www.svu.edu/.

SOUTHERN WESLEYAN UNIVERSITY
Central, SC

ABOUT THE INSTITUTION Independent Wesleyan Church, coed. 35 undergraduate majors.

GIFT AID (NEED-BASED) *Scholarships, grants, and awards:* Federal Pell, FSEOG, state, private, college/university gift aid from institutional funds.

GIFT AID (NON-NEED-BASED) *Scholarships, grants, and awards by category: Academic interests/achievement:* biological sciences, business, computer science, education, English, general academic interests/achievements, humanities, mathematics, physical sciences, premedicine, religion/biblical studies, social sciences. *Creative arts/performance:* journalism/publications, music. *Special achievements/activities:* community service, leadership, religious involvement. *Special characteristics:* children of faculty/staff, relatives of clergy, religious affiliation, veterans.

LOANS *Programs:* Federal Direct (Subsidized and Unsubsidized Stafford, PLUS), Perkins, state.

APPLYING FOR FINANCIAL AID *Required financial aid forms:* FAFSA, state aid form.

CONTACT Mrs. Laura Hedden, Financial Aid Associate, Southern Wesleyan University, 907 Wesleyan Drive, Central, SC 29630-1020, 800-282-8798 Ext. 5517 or toll-free 800-CU-AT-SWU. *Fax:* 864-644-5970. *E-mail:* finaid@swu.edu. *Website:* http://www.swu.edu/.

SOUTH FLORIDA BIBLE COLLEGE AND THEOLOGICAL SEMINARY
Deerfield Beach, FL

CONTACT Financial Aid Office, South Florida Bible College and Theological Seminary, 1100 South Federal Highway, Deerfield Beach, FL 33441, 954-428-8980. *Website:* http://www.sfbc.edu/.

SOUTH UNIVERSITY
Montgomery, AL

CONTACT Financial Aid Office, South University, 5355 Vaughn Road, Montgomery, AL 36116-1120, 334-395-8800 or toll-free 866-629-2962. *Website:* http://www.southuniversity.edu/montgomery/.

SOUTH UNIVERSITY
Royal Palm Beach, FL

Financial Aid Office, South University, University Centre, 9801 Belvedere Road, Royal Palm Beach, FL 33411, 561-697-9200 or toll-free 866-629-2902.

SOUTH UNIVERSITY
Tampa, FL

CONTACT Financial Aid Office, South University, 4401 North Himes Avenue, Suite 175, Tampa, FL 33614, 813-393-3800 or toll-free 800-846-1472. *Website:* http://www.southuniversity.edu/tampa/.

SOUTH UNIVERSITY
Savannah, GA

CONTACT Financial Aid Office, South University, 709 Mall Boulevard, Savannah, GA 31406, 912-201-8000 or toll-free 866-629-2901. *Website:* http://www.southuniversity.edu/savannah/.

SOUTH UNIVERSITY
Novi, MI

CONTACT Financial Aid Office, South University, 41555 Twelve Mile Road, Novi, MI 48377, 248-675-0200 or toll-free 877-693-2085. *Website:* http://www.southuniversity.edu/novi.aspx.

SOUTH UNIVERSITY
High Point, NC

CONTACT Financial Aid Office, South University, 3975 Premier Drive, High Point, NC 27265, 336-812-7200 or toll-free 855-268-2187. *Website:* http://www.southuniversity.edu/high-point.aspx.

SOUTH UNIVERSITY
Cleveland, OH

CONTACT Financial Aid Office, South University, 4743 Richmond Road, Cleveland, OH 44128, 216-755-5000 or toll-free 855-398-9280. *Website:* http://www.southuniversity.edu/cleveland.aspx.

SOUTH UNIVERSITY
Columbia, SC

CONTACT Financial Aid Office, South University, 9 Science Court, Columbia, SC 29203, 803-799-9082 or toll-free 866-629-3031. *Website:* http://www.southuniversity.edu/columbia/.

SOUTH UNIVERSITY
Round Rock, TX

CONTACT Financial Aid Office, South University, 1220 West Louis Henna Boulevard, Round Rock, TX 78681, 512-516-8800 or toll-free 877-659-5706. *Website:* http://www.southuniversity.edu/austin.aspx.

SOUTH UNIVERSITY
Glen Allen, VA

CONTACT Financial Aid Office, South University, 2151 Old Brick Road, Glen Allen, VA 23060, 804-727-6800 or toll-free 888-422-5076. *Website:* http://www.southuniversity.edu/richmond.

SOUTH UNIVERSITY
Virginia Beach, VA

CONTACT Financial Aid Office, South University, 301 Bendix Road, Suite 100, Virginia Beach, VA 23452, 757-493-6900 or toll-free 877-206-1845. *Website:* http://www.southuniversity.edu/virginia-beach.

SOUTHWEST BAPTIST UNIVERSITY
Bolivar, MO

Tuition & fees: $22,440	Average undergraduate aid package: $17,297

ABOUT THE INSTITUTION Independent Southern Baptist, coed. **Awards:** certificates, associate, bachelor's, master's, and doctoral degrees. 56 undergraduate majors. **Total enrollment:** 3,615. Undergraduates: 2,881. Federal methodology is used as a basis for awarding need-based institutional aid.

UNDERGRADUATE EXPENSES for 2016–2017 Application fee: $30. **Comprehensive fee:** $29,900 includes full-time tuition ($21,600), mandatory fees ($840), and room and board ($7460). **College room only:** $3400. Full-time tuition and fees vary according to course load and location. Room and board charges vary according to board plan and housing facility. **Part-time tuition:** $840 per credit hour. **Part-time fees:** $180 per term. Part-time tuition and fees vary according to course load and location.

FRESHMAN FINANCIAL AID (Fall 2016, est.) 353 applied for aid; of those 91% were deemed to have need. 99% of freshmen with need received aid; of those 18% had need fully met. **Average percent of need met:** 70% (excluding resources awarded to replace EFC). **Average financial aid package:** $19,867 (excluding resources awarded to replace EFC). 3% of all full-time freshmen had no need and received non-need-based gift aid.

UNDERGRADUATE FINANCIAL AID (Fall 2016, est.) 1,592 applied for aid; of those 92% were deemed to have need. 99% of undergraduates with need received aid; of those 16% had need fully met. **Average percent of need met:** 67% (excluding resources awarded to replace EFC). **Average financial aid package:** $17,297 (excluding resources awarded to replace EFC). 5% of all full-time undergraduates had no need and received non-need-based gift aid.

GIFT AID (NEED-BASED) Total amount: $19,196,242 (24% federal, 7% state, 69% institutional). **Receiving aid:** Freshmen: 65% (242); all full-time undergraduates: 56% (1,052). **Average award:** Freshmen: $5206; Undergraduates: $5295. **Scholarships, grants, and awards:** Federal Pell, FSEOG, state, private, college/university gift aid from institutional funds, Federal Nursing.

GIFT AID (NON-NEED-BASED) Total amount: $3,590,708 (14% state, 62% institutional, 24% external sources). **Receiving aid:** Freshmen: 41% (151). Undergraduates: 34% (628). **Average award:** Freshmen: $1847. Undergraduates: $7267. **Scholarships, grants, and awards by category:** Academic interests/achievement: $9,835,669 total: general academic interests/achievements. Creative arts/performance: $338,965 total: art/fine arts, debating, music, theater/drama. Special achievements/activities: $252,000 total: religious involvement. Special characteristics: $474,457 total: general special characteristics, handicapped students, international students, local/state students, relatives of clergy, religious affiliation. **Tuition waivers:** Full or partial for employees or children of employees. **ROTC:** Army cooperative.

LOANS Student loans: $13,814,926 (44% need-based, 56% non-need-based). 77% of past graduating class borrowed through all loan programs. **Average indebtedness per student:** $26,615. **Average need-based loan:** Freshmen: $2884. Undergraduates: $3982. **Parent loans:** $1,219,805 (100% non-need-based). **Programs:** Federal Direct (Subsidized and Unsubsidized Stafford, PLUS), Perkins, Federal Nursing, state, alternative loans.

WORK-STUDY Federal work-study: Total amount: $628,263; 341 jobs averaging $1842.

ATHLETIC AWARDS Total amount: $3,131,795 (100% non-need-based).

APPLYING FOR FINANCIAL AID Required financial aid form: FAFSA. **Financial aid deadline (priority):** 2/1. **Notification date:** Continuous beginning 12/1. Students must reply within 2 weeks of notification.

CONTACT Mr. Brad Gamble, Director of Financial Aid, Southwest Baptist University, 1600 University Avenue, Bolivar, MO 65613-2597, 417-328-1823 or toll-free 800-526-5859. Fax: 417-328-1514. E-mail: bgamble@sbuniv.edu. Website: http://www.sbuniv.edu/.

SOUTHWESTERN ADVENTIST UNIVERSITY
Keene, TX

CONTACT Student Financial Services, Southwestern Adventist University, PO Box 567, Keene, TX 76059, 817-645-3921 Ext. 262 or toll-free 800-433-2240. Fax: 817-556-4744. Website: http://www.swau.edu/.

SOUTHWESTERN ASSEMBLIES OF GOD UNIVERSITY
Waxahachie, TX

CONTACT Financial Aid Office, Southwestern Assemblies of God University, 1200 Sycamore Street, Waxahachie, TX 75165-2397, 972-825-4730 or toll-free 888-937-7248. Fax: 972-937-4001. E-mail: finaid@sagu.edu. Website: http://www.sagu.edu/.

SOUTHWESTERN CHRISTIAN COLLEGE
Terrell, TX

ABOUT THE INSTITUTION Independent Church of Christ, coed. 2 undergraduate majors.

GIFT AID (NEED-BASED) Scholarships, grants, and awards: Federal Pell, FSEOG, state, college/university gift aid from institutional funds.

GIFT AID (NON-NEED-BASED) Scholarships, grants, and awards by category: Academic interests/achievement: general academic interests/achievements. Creative arts/performance: music. Special characteristics: children of faculty/staff, local/state students.

LOANS Programs: Federal Direct (Subsidized and Unsubsidized Stafford, PLUS).

APPLYING FOR FINANCIAL AID Required financial aid form: FAFSA.

CONTACT Ms. Kim Smith, Financial Aid Counselor, Southwestern Christian College, PO Box 10, 200 Bowser Circle, Terrell, TX 75160, 972-524-3341 Ext. 124. Fax: 972-563-7133. E-mail: ksmit@swcc.edu. Website: http://www.swcc.edu/.

SOUTHWESTERN CHRISTIAN UNIVERSITY
Bethany, OK

CONTACT Mrs. Billie Stewart, Financial Aid Director, Southwestern Christian University, PO Box 340, Bethany, OK 73008, 405-789-7661 Ext. 3456. Fax: 405-495-0078. E-mail: billie.stewart@swcu.edu. Website: http://www.swcu.edu/.

SOUTHWESTERN COLLEGE
Winfield, KS

Tuition & fees: $28,750	Average undergraduate aid package: $21,780

ABOUT THE INSTITUTION Independent United Methodist, coed. **Awards:** certificates, bachelor's, master's, and doctoral degrees. 56 undergraduate majors. **Total enrollment:** 1,467. Undergraduates: 1,226. Freshmen: 181. Federal methodology is used as a basis for awarding need-based institutional aid.

UNDERGRADUATE EXPENSES for 2017–2018 Application fee: $25. **Comprehensive fee:** $36,270 includes full-time tuition ($28,600), mandatory fees ($150), and room and board ($7520). **College room only:** $3500. Full-time tuition and fees vary according to course load, degree level, location, and program. Room and board charges vary according to board plan and housing facility. **Part-time tuition:** $1192 per credit hour. Part-time tuition and fees vary according to course load, degree level, location, and program.

FRESHMAN FINANCIAL AID (Fall 2015) 79 applied for aid; of those 89% were deemed to have need. 100% of freshmen with need received aid; of those 16% had need fully met. **Average percent of need met:** 81% (excluding resources awarded to replace EFC). **Average financial aid package:** $23,041 (excluding resources awarded to replace EFC). 12% of all full-time freshmen had no need and received non-need-based gift aid.

UNDERGRADUATE FINANCIAL AID (Fall 2015) 396 applied for aid; of those 93% were deemed to have need. 100% of undergraduates with need received aid; of those 14% had need fully met. **Average percent of need met:** 74% (excluding resources awarded to replace EFC). **Average financial aid package:** $21,780 (excluding resources awarded to replace EFC). 14% of all full-time undergraduates had no need and received non-need-based gift aid.

GIFT AID (NEED-BASED) Total amount: $5,695,826 (31% federal, 7% state, 56% institutional, 6% external sources). **Receiving aid:** Freshmen: 78% (70); all full-time undergraduates: 77% (363). **Average award:** Freshmen: $17,958; Undergraduates: $15,224. **Scholarships, grants, and awards:** Federal Pell, FSEOG, state, private, college/university gift aid from institutional funds.

GIFT AID (NON-NEED-BASED) Total amount: $636,021 (1% state, 90% institutional, 9% external sources). **Receiving aid:** Freshmen: 7% (6). Undergraduates: 5% (23). **Average award:** Freshmen: $7273. Undergraduates: $7618. **Scholarships, grants, and awards by category:** Academic interests/achievement: 423 awards ($2,190,364 total): biological sciences, business, communication, computer science, education, general academic interests/achievements, health fields, physical sciences, religion/biblical studies, social sciences. Creative arts/performance: 47 awards ($191,588 total): cinema/film/broadcasting, dance, journalism/publications, music, performing arts, theater/drama. Special achievements/activities: 73 awards ($303,635 total): cheerleading/drum major, community service, general special achievements/activities, leadership, memberships, religious involvement. Special characteristics: 173 awards ($329,462 total): children of faculty/staff, international students, members of minority groups, religious affiliation, veterans. **Tuition waivers:** Full or partial for employees or children of employees, senior citizens.

LOANS Student loans: $5,389,961 (90% need-based, 10% non-need-based). 75% of past graduating class borrowed through all loan programs. Average indebtedness per student: $38,318. **Average need-based loan:** Freshmen: $4933. Undergraduates: $6170. **Parent loans:** $1,701,988 (33% need-based, 67% non-need-based). **Programs:** Federal Direct (Subsidized and Unsubsidized Stafford, PLUS), Perkins.

WORK-STUDY Federal work-study: 164 jobs averaging $1492. **State or other work-study/employment:** Total amount: $101,585 (36% need-based, 64% non-need-based). 127 part-time jobs averaging $1472.

ATHLETIC AWARDS Total amount: $1,039,200 (82% need-based, 18% non-need-based).

APPLYING FOR FINANCIAL AID Required financial aid form: FAFSA. **Financial aid deadline (priority):** 4/1. **Notification date:** Continuous beginning 2/1. Students must reply within 4 weeks of notification.

CONTACT Mrs. Brenda D. Hicks, Director of Financial Aid, Southwestern College, 100 College Street, Winfield, KS 67156-2499, 620-229-6215 or toll-free 800-846-1543. Fax: 620-229-6363. E-mail: finaid@sckans.edu. Website: http://www.sckans.edu/.

SOUTHWESTERN OKLAHOMA STATE UNIVERSITY
Weatherford, OK

Tuition & fees (OK res): $6690	Average undergraduate aid package: $5622

ABOUT THE INSTITUTION State-supported, coed. **Awards:** certificates, associate, bachelor's, master's, and doctoral degrees. 43 undergraduate majors. **Total enrollment:** 5,320. Undergraduates: 4,510. Freshmen: 990. Both federal and institutional methodology are used as a basis for awarding need-based institutional aid.

UNDERGRADUATE EXPENSES for 2016–2017 Application fee: $15. **One-time required fee:** $100. **Tuition, state resident:** full-time $5295; part-time $176.50 per credit hour. **Tuition, nonresident:** full-time $12,045; part-time $401.50 per credit hour. **Required fees:** full-time $1395; $46.50 per credit hour or $46.50 per credit hour. Full-time tuition and fees vary according to degree level, location, and program. Part-time tuition and fees vary according to degree level, location, and program. **College room and board:** $5400; **Room only:** $2200. Room and board charges vary according to board plan and housing facility.

FRESHMAN FINANCIAL AID (Fall 2015) 488 applied for aid; of those 76% were deemed to have need. 99% of freshmen with need received aid; of those 17% had need fully met. **Average percent of need met:** 96% (excluding resources awarded to replace EFC). **Average financial aid package:** $5780 (excluding resources awarded to replace EFC). 14% of all full-time freshmen had no need and received non-need-based gift aid.

UNDERGRADUATE FINANCIAL AID (Fall 2015) 1,748 applied for aid; of those 83% were deemed to have need. 98% of undergraduates with need received aid; of those 20% had need fully met. **Average percent of need met:** 96% (excluding resources awarded to replace EFC). **Average financial aid package:** $5622 (excluding resources awarded to replace EFC). 36% of all full-time undergraduates had no need and received non-need-based gift aid.

GIFT AID (NEED-BASED) Total amount: $9,775,927 (59% federal, 7% state, 34% external sources). **Receiving aid:** Freshmen: 35% (318); all full-time undergraduates: 35% (1,231). **Average award:** Freshmen: $1491; Undergraduates: $1658. **Scholarships, grants, and awards:** Federal Pell, FSEOG, state, private, college/university gift aid from institutional funds.

GIFT AID (NON-NEED-BASED) Total amount: $3,217,355 (18% federal, 17% state, 31% institutional, 34% external sources). **Receiving aid:** Freshmen: 24% (214). Undergraduates: 15% (531). **Average award:** Freshmen: $516. Undergraduates: $585. **Scholarships, grants, and awards by category:** Academic interests/achievement: biological sciences, business, communication, computer science, education, engineering/technologies, English, foreign languages, general academic interests/achievements, mathematics, physical sciences, social sciences. Creative arts/performance: applied art and design, art/fine arts, music, theater/drama. Special achievements/activities: cheerleading/drum major, leadership, rodeo. Special characteristics: children and siblings of alumni, children of faculty/staff, local/state students, out-of-state students. **Tuition waivers:** Full or partial for children of alumni, employees or children of employees, senior citizens.

LOANS Student loans: $13,390,012 (40% need-based, 60% non-need-based). 46% of past graduating class borrowed through all loan programs. Average indebtedness per student: $18,809. **Average need-based loan:** Freshmen: $1140. Undergraduates: $1599. **Parent loans:** $7,814,644 (100% non-need-based). **Programs:** Federal Direct (Subsidized and Unsubsidized Stafford, PLUS).

WORK-STUDY Federal work-study: jobs available.

ATHLETIC AWARDS Total amount: $1,754,003 (100% non-need-based).

APPLYING FOR FINANCIAL AID Required financial aid forms: FAFSA, institution's own form. **Financial aid deadline:** 3/1. **Notification date:** Continuous beginning 3/15.

CONTACT Mr. Jerome Wichert, Director of Student Financial Services, Southwestern Oklahoma State University, 100 Campus Drive, Weatherford, OK 73096, 580-774-3786. Fax: 580-774-7066. E-mail: jerome.wichert@swosu.edu. Website: http://www.swosu.edu/.

SOUTHWESTERN UNIVERSITY
Georgetown, TX

Tuition & fees: $40,560	Average undergraduate aid package: $34,758

ABOUT THE INSTITUTION Independent Methodist, coed. **Awards:** bachelor's degrees. 35 undergraduate majors. **Total enrollment:** 1,486. Undergraduates: 1,486. Freshmen: 381. Federal methodology is used as a basis for awarding need-based institutional aid.

UNDERGRADUATE EXPENSES for 2017–2018 Comprehensive fee: $52,370 includes full-time tuition ($40,560) and room and board ($11,810). **College room only:** $6290. Room and board charges vary according to board plan and housing facility. **Part-time tuition:** $1690 per credit hour. Part-time tuition and fees vary according to course load.

FRESHMAN FINANCIAL AID (Fall 2016, est.) 314 applied for aid; of those 81% were deemed to have need. 100% of freshmen with need received aid; of those 36% had need fully met. **Average percent of need met:** 96% (excluding resources awarded to replace EFC). *Average financial aid package:* $34,827 (excluding resources awarded to replace EFC). 33% of all full-time freshmen had no need and received non-need-based gift aid.

UNDERGRADUATE FINANCIAL AID (Fall 2016, est.) 1,053 applied for aid; of those 87% were deemed to have need. 100% of undergraduates with need received aid; of those 28% had need fully met. *Average percent of need met:* 89% (excluding resources awarded to replace EFC). *Average financial aid package:* $34,758 (excluding resources awarded to replace EFC). 36% of all full-time undergraduates had no need and received non-need-based gift aid.

GIFT AID (NEED-BASED) *Total amount:* $26,030,305 (8% federal, 6% state, 81% institutional, 5% external sources). *Receiving aid:* Freshmen: 65% (249); all full-time undergraduates: 62% (909). *Average award:* Freshmen: $30,013; Undergraduates: $28,975. *Scholarships, grants, and awards:* Federal Pell, FSEOG, state, private, college/university gift aid from institutional funds.

GIFT AID (NON-NEED-BASED) *Total amount:* $11,112,939 (96% institutional, 4% external sources). *Receiving aid:* Freshmen: 64% (244). Undergraduates: 61% (886). *Average award:* Freshmen: $22,126. Undergraduates: $20,622. *Scholarships, grants, and awards by category: Academic interests/achievement:* 1,689 awards ($28,049,729 total): business, general academic interests/achievements, humanities, international studies, mathematics, premedicine, social sciences. *Creative arts/performance:* 122 awards ($1,660,989 total): art/fine arts, music, theater/drama. *Special achievements/activities:* 5 awards ($5000 total): leadership. *Special characteristics:* 69 awards ($1,230,447 total): children of faculty/staff, ethnic background, general special characteristics, relatives of clergy, religious affiliation. *Tuition waivers:* Full or partial for employees or children of employees. *ROTC:* Air Force cooperative.

LOANS *Student loans:* $7,884,347 (91% need-based, 9% non-need-based). 56% of past graduating class borrowed through all loan programs. *Average indebtedness per student:* $32,801. *Average need-based loan:* Freshmen: $4133. Undergraduates: $5263. *Parent loans:* $4,790,953 (92% need-based, 8% non-need-based). *Programs:* Federal Direct (Subsidized and Unsubsidized Stafford, PLUS), Perkins, state, college/university.

WORK-STUDY *Federal work-study:* Total amount: $233,009; 112 jobs averaging $2134. *State or other work-study/employment:* Total amount: $1,274,250 (68% need-based, 32% non-need-based). 601 part-time jobs averaging $2392.

APPLYING FOR FINANCIAL AID *Required financial aid form:* FAFSA. *Financial aid deadline (priority):* 3/1. *Notification date:* Continuous beginning 12/1. Students must reply by 5/1 or within 2 weeks of notification.

CONTACT Mr. James P. Gaeta, Director of Financial Aid, Southwestern University, PO Box 770, Georgetown, TX 78627-0770, 512-863-1259 or toll-free 800-252-3166. *Fax:* 512-863-1507. *E-mail:* gaetaj@southwestern.edu. *Website:* http://www.southwestern.edu/.

SOUTHWEST MINNESOTA STATE UNIVERSITY
Marshall, MN

ABOUT THE INSTITUTION State-supported, coed. 56 undergraduate majors.

GIFT AID (NEED-BASED) *Scholarships, grants, and awards:* Federal Pell, FSEOG, state, private, college/university gift aid from institutional funds.

GIFT AID (NON-NEED-BASED) *Scholarships, grants, and awards by category: Academic interests/achievement:* agriculture, biological sciences, business, communication, computer science, education, English, foreign languages, general academic interests/achievements, mathematics, physical sciences, premedicine, social sciences. *Creative arts/performance:* art/fine arts, creative writing, debating, journalism/publications, music, performing arts, theater/drama. *Special achievements/activities:* general special achievements/activities, hobbies/interests, leadership. *Special characteristics:* children and siblings of alumni, children of union members/company employees, ethnic background, first-generation college students, general special characteristics, handicapped students, international students, local/state students, members of minority groups, previous college experience, veterans, veterans' children.

LOANS *Programs:* Federal Direct (Subsidized and Unsubsidized Stafford, PLUS), Perkins, state, private loans.

WORK-STUDY *Federal work-study:* 112 jobs averaging $2258. *State or other work-study/employment:* Total amount: $836,253 (39% need-based, 61% non-need-based). 141 part-time jobs averaging $2262.

APPLYING FOR FINANCIAL AID *Required financial aid form:* FAFSA.

CONTACT Mr. David Vikander, Director of Financial Aid, Southwest Minnesota State University, 1501 State Street, Marshall, MN 56258, 507-537-6281 or toll-free 800-642-0684. *Fax:* 507-537-6275. *E-mail:* vikander@smsu.edu. *Website:* http://www.smsu.edu/.

SOUTHWEST UNIVERSITY
Kenner, LA

CONTACT Financial Aid Office, Southwest University, 2200 Veterans Memorial Boulevard, Kenner, LA 70062, 504-468-2900 or toll-free 800-433-5923. *Website:* http://www.southwest.edu/.

SOUTHWEST UNIVERSITY AT EL PASO
El Paso, TX

CONTACT Financial Aid Office, Southwest University at El Paso, 1414 Geronimo Drive, El Paso, TX 79925, 915-778-4001. *Website:* http://southwestuniversity.edu/.

SOUTHWEST UNIVERSITY OF VISUAL ARTS
Tucson, AZ

CONTACT Financial Aid Office, Southwest University of Visual Arts, 2525 North Country Club Road, Tucson, AZ 85716-2505, 520-325-0123 or toll-free 800-825-8753. *Website:* http://www.suva.edu/.

SPALDING UNIVERSITY
Louisville, KY

CONTACT Director of Student Financial Services, Spalding University, 851 South Fourth Street, Louisville, KY 40203, 502-588-7185 or toll-free 800-896-8941. *Fax:* 502-585-7128. *E-mail:* onestop@spalding.edu. *Website:* http://www.spalding.edu/.

SPELMAN COLLEGE
Atlanta, GA

Tuition & fees: $26,638	Average undergraduate aid package: $16,900

ABOUT THE INSTITUTION Independent, women only. *Awards:* bachelor's degrees. 31 undergraduate majors. *Total enrollment:* 2,125. Undergraduates: 2,125. Freshmen: 533. Federal methodology is used as a basis for awarding need-based institutional aid.

UNDERGRADUATE EXPENSES for 2016–2017 *Application fee:* $35. *Comprehensive fee:* $39,001 includes full-time tuition ($22,827), mandatory fees ($3811), and room and board ($12,363). Full-time tuition and fees vary according to course load. Room and board charges vary according to board plan and housing facility. *Part-time fees:* $950 per credit hour. Part-time tuition and fees vary according to course load.

FRESHMAN FINANCIAL AID (Fall 2016, est.) 513 applied for aid; of those 89% were deemed to have need. 100% of freshmen with need received aid; of those .4% had need fully met. *Average percent of need met:* 33% (excluding resources awarded to replace EFC). *Average financial aid package:* $15,771 (excluding resources awarded to replace EFC). 1% of all full-time freshmen had no need and received non-need-based gift aid.

UNDERGRADUATE FINANCIAL AID (Fall 2016, est.) 1,853 applied for aid; of those 92% were deemed to have need. 99% of undergraduates with need received aid; of those 1% had need fully met. *Average percent of need met:* 33% (excluding resources awarded to replace EFC). *Average financial aid package:* $16,900 (excluding resources awarded to replace EFC). 1% of all full-time undergraduates had no need and received non-need-based gift aid.

GIFT AID (NEED-BASED) *Total amount:* $23,585,775 (22% federal, 6% state, 56% institutional, 16% external sources). *Receiving aid:* Freshmen: 65% (345); all full-time undergraduates: 65% (1,344). *Average award:* Freshmen: $12,459; Undergraduates: $12,410. *Scholarships, grants, and awards:* FSEOG, state, college/university gift aid from institutional funds, United Negro College Fund.

GIFT AID (NON-NEED-BASED) *Total amount:* $537,206 (100% institutional). *Receiving aid:* Undergraduates: 2. *Average award:* Freshmen: $42,292. Undergraduates: $35,697. *Scholarships, grants, and awards by category:* Creative arts/performance: music, theater/drama. *Tuition waivers:* Full or partial for employees or children of employees. *ROTC:* Army cooperative, Naval cooperative, Air Force cooperative.

LOANS *Student loans:* $10,698,187 (60% need-based, 40% non-need-based). 73% of past graduating class borrowed through all loan programs. *Average indebtedness per student:* $38,430. *Average need-based loan:* Freshmen: $3914. Undergraduates: $5013. *Parent loans:* $30,113,192 (100% need-based). *Programs:* Federal Direct (Subsidized and Unsubsidized Stafford, PLUS), Perkins, state.

WORK-STUDY *Federal work-study:* Total amount: $301,498; jobs available.

APPLYING FOR FINANCIAL AID *Required financial aid forms:* FAFSA, state aid form. *Financial aid deadline (priority):* 2/1. *Notification date:* Continuous beginning 2/15. Students must reply within 2 weeks of notification.

CONTACT Ms. Lenora Jackson, Director of Financial Aid, Spelman College, 350 Spelman Lane, SW, Atlanta, GA 30314-4399, 404-270-5212 or toll-free 800-982-2411. *Fax:* 404-270-5220. *E-mail:* lenoraj@spelman.edu. *Website:* http://www.spelman.edu/.

SPRING ARBOR UNIVERSITY
Spring Arbor, MI

Tuition & fees: $26,730	Average undergraduate aid package: $23,256

ABOUT THE INSTITUTION Independent Free Methodist, coed. *Awards:* certificates, associate, bachelor's, and master's degrees. 62 undergraduate majors. *Total enrollment:* 3,404. Undergraduates: 2,435. Freshmen: 291. Federal methodology is used as a basis for awarding need-based institutional aid.

UNDERGRADUATE EXPENSES for 2016–2017 *Application fee:* $30. *Comprehensive fee:* $36,000 includes full-time tuition ($26,130), mandatory fees ($600), and room and board ($9270). *College room only:* $4320. Full-time tuition and fees vary according to course load, degree level, and program. Room and board charges vary according to board plan and housing facility. *Part-time tuition:* $635 per credit hour. *Part-time fees:* $285 per term. Part-time tuition and fees vary according to course load, degree level, program, and reciprocity agreements.

FRESHMAN FINANCIAL AID (Fall 2016, est.) 282 applied for aid; of those 90% were deemed to have need. 100% of freshmen with need received aid; of those 27% had need fully met. *Average percent of need met:* 84% (excluding resources awarded to replace EFC). *Average financial aid package:* $24,198 (excluding resources awarded to replace EFC).

UNDERGRADUATE FINANCIAL AID (Fall 2016, est.) 1,106 applied for aid; of those 91% were deemed to have need. 100% of undergraduates with need received aid; of those 21% had need fully met. *Average percent of need met:* 79% (excluding resources awarded to replace EFC). *Average financial aid package:* $23,256 (excluding resources awarded to replace EFC). 1% of all full-time undergraduates had no need and received non-need-based gift aid.

GIFT AID (NEED-BASED) *Total amount:* $18,846,512 (20% federal, 8% state, 72% institutional). *Receiving aid:* Freshmen: 86% (255); all full-time undergraduates: 82% (994). *Average award:* Freshmen: $17,396; Undergraduates: $15,712. *Scholarships, grants, and awards:* Federal Pell, FSEOG, private, college/university gift aid from institutional funds.

GIFT AID (NON-NEED-BASED) *Total amount:* $293,422 (43% state, 57% external sources). *Receiving aid:* Freshmen: 8% (23). Undergraduates: 9% (113). *Average award:* Undergraduates: $4578. *Scholarships, grants, and awards by category:* Academic interests/achievement: general academic interests/achieve-

---

ments. *Creative arts/performance:* art/fine arts. *Special achievements/activities:* junior miss. *Special characteristics:* adult students, children of faculty/staff, general special characteristics, international students, members of minority groups, relatives of clergy, religious affiliation. *Tuition waivers:* Full or partial for employees or children of employees. *ROTC:* Army, Air Force cooperative.

LOANS *Student loans:* $31,585,138 (21% need-based, 79% non-need-based). 79% of past graduating class borrowed through all loan programs. *Average indebtedness per student:* $32,602. *Average need-based loan:* Freshmen: $4094. Undergraduates: $4845. *Parent loans:* $2,299,999 (100% need-based). *Programs:* Federal Direct (Subsidized and Unsubsidized Stafford, PLUS), Perkins.

WORK-STUDY *Federal work-study:* Total amount: $176,111; jobs available.

ATHLETIC AWARDS Total amount: $2,487,600 (100% need-based).

APPLYING FOR FINANCIAL AID *Required financial aid form:* FAFSA. *Financial aid deadline (priority):* 3/1. *Notification date:* Continuous. Students must reply within 2 weeks of notification.

CONTACT Herbert Rotich, Director of Financial Aid, Spring Arbor University, 106 East Main Street, Spring Arbor, MI 49283-9799, 517-750-6463 or toll-free 800-968-0011. *Fax:* 517-750-6620. *E-mail:* hrotich@arbor.edu. *Website:* http://www.arbor.edu/.

SPRINGFIELD COLLEGE
Springfield, MA

Tuition & fees: N/R	Average undergraduate aid package: $26,866

ABOUT THE INSTITUTION Independent, coed. *Awards:* certificates, bachelor's, master's, and doctoral degrees. 38 undergraduate majors. *Total enrollment:* 3,254. Undergraduates: 2,160. Freshmen: 546. Federal methodology is used as a basis for awarding need-based institutional aid.

FRESHMAN FINANCIAL AID (Fall 2016, est.) 519 applied for aid; of those 92% were deemed to have need. 100% of freshmen with need received aid; of those 9% had need fully met. *Average percent of need met:* 79% (excluding resources awarded to replace EFC). *Average financial aid package:* $27,824 (excluding resources awarded to replace EFC). 10% of all full-time freshmen had no need and received non-need-based gift aid.

UNDERGRADUATE FINANCIAL AID (Fall 2016, est.) 1,861 applied for aid; of those 91% were deemed to have need. 100% of undergraduates with need received aid; of those 9% had need fully met. *Average percent of need met:* 76% (excluding resources awarded to replace EFC). *Average financial aid package:* $26,866 (excluding resources awarded to replace EFC). 13% of all full-time undergraduates had no need and received non-need-based gift aid.

GIFT AID (NEED-BASED) *Total amount:* $35,679,832 (7% federal, 1% state, 88% institutional, 4% external sources). *Receiving aid:* Freshmen: 88% (476); all full-time undergraduates: 82% (1,697). *Average award:* Freshmen: $23,269; Undergraduates: $21,379. *Scholarships, grants, and awards:* Federal Pell, FSEOG, state, private, college/university gift aid from institutional funds.

GIFT AID (NON-NEED-BASED) *Total amount:* $3,959,518 (91% institutional, 9% external sources). *Receiving aid:* Freshmen: 7% (36). Undergraduates: 6% (115). *Average award:* Freshmen: $11,937. Undergraduates: $11,161. *Scholarships, grants, and awards by category:* Academic interests/achievement: 1,270 awards ($15,064,365 total): general academic interests/achievements. *Special characteristics:* 72 awards ($1,408,140 total): children and siblings of alumni, children of current students, children of faculty/staff, siblings of current students. *ROTC:* Army cooperative, Air Force cooperative.

LOANS *Student loans:* $20,396,460 (68% need-based, 32% non-need-based). 86% of past graduating class borrowed through all loan programs. *Average indebtedness per student:* $42,650. *Average need-based loan:* Freshmen: $3820. Undergraduates: $4421. *Parent loans:* $6,473,169 (41% need-based, 59% non-need-based). *Programs:* Federal Direct (Subsidized and Unsubsidized Stafford, PLUS), private loans.

WORK-STUDY *Federal work-study:* Total amount: $1,639,452; 1,399 jobs averaging $1830. *State or other work-study/employment:* Total amount: $803,342 (92% need-based, 8% non-need-based). 97 part-time jobs averaging $8391.

APPLYING FOR FINANCIAL AID *Required financial aid forms:* FAFSA, state aid form. *Financial aid deadline (priority):* 3/15. *Notification date:* Continuous beginning 11/15. Students must reply within 2 weeks of notification.

CONTACT Ms. Kinser Cancelmo, Assistant Director of Financial Aid, Springfield College, 263 Alden Street, Springfield, MA 01109-3797, 413-748-3108 or toll-free 800-343-1257. *Fax:* 413-748-3462. *E-mail:* financialaid@springfieldcollege.edu. *Website:* http://www.springfield.edu/.

SPRING HILL COLLEGE
Mobile, AL

Tuition & fees: $35,798	Average undergraduate aid package: $32,092

ABOUT THE INSTITUTION Independent Roman Catholic (Jesuit), coed. *Awards:* certificates, bachelor's, and master's degrees. 48 undergraduate majors. *Total enrollment:* 1,491. Undergraduates: 1,396. Freshmen: 392. Federal methodology is used as a basis for awarding need-based institutional aid.

UNDERGRADUATE EXPENSES for 2016–2017 *Application fee:* $25. *Comprehensive fee:* $48,488 includes full-time tuition ($33,634), mandatory fees ($2164), and room and board ($12,690). *College room only:* $6700. Full-time tuition and fees vary according to course load. Room and board charges vary according to board plan and housing facility. *Part-time tuition:* $1024 per credit hour. *Part-time fees:* $53 per credit hour. Part-time tuition and fees vary according to course load.

FRESHMAN FINANCIAL AID (Fall 2016, est.) 356 applied for aid; of those 86% were deemed to have need. 100% of freshmen with need received aid; of those 25% had need fully met. *Average percent of need met:* 80% (excluding resources awarded to replace EFC). *Average financial aid package:* $33,531 (excluding resources awarded to replace EFC). 22% of all full-time freshmen had no need and received non-need-based gift aid.

UNDERGRADUATE FINANCIAL AID (Fall 2016, est.) 1,088 applied for aid; of those 89% were deemed to have need. 100% of undergraduates with need received aid; of those 24% had need fully met. *Average percent of need met:* 79% (excluding resources awarded to replace EFC). *Average financial aid package:* $32,092 (excluding resources awarded to replace EFC). 26% of all full-time undergraduates had no need and received non-need-based gift aid.

GIFT AID (NEED-BASED) *Total amount:* $24,656,544 (8% federal, 1% state, 90% institutional, 1% external sources). *Receiving aid:* Freshmen: 77% (301); all full-time undergraduates: 69% (951). *Average award:* Freshmen: $27,459; Undergraduates: $25,089. *Scholarships, grants, and awards:* Federal Pell, FSEOG, state, private, college/university gift aid from institutional funds, TEACH Grants.

GIFT AID (NON-NEED-BASED) *Total amount:* $9,582,066 (1% state, 99% institutional). *Receiving aid:* Freshmen: 76% (296). Undergraduates: 55% (754). *Average award:* Freshmen: $22,880. Undergraduates: $21,065. *Scholarships, grants, and awards by category:* Academic interests/achievement: general academic interests/achievements. *Special achievements/activities:* community service. *Special characteristics:* children of faculty/staff, siblings of current students. *Tuition waivers:* Full or partial for employees or children of employees. *ROTC:* Army cooperative, Air Force cooperative.

LOANS *Student loans:* $6,709,098 (74% need-based, 26% non-need-based). *Average need-based loan:* Freshmen: $3428. Undergraduates: $4530. *Parent loans:* $3,668,116 (54% need-based, 46% non-need-based). *Programs:* Federal Direct (Subsidized and Unsubsidized Stafford, PLUS), Perkins, alternative loans.

WORK-STUDY *Federal work-study:* Total amount: $405,271; jobs available. *State or other work-study/employment:* Total amount: $146,400 (100% non-need-based). Part-time jobs available.

ATHLETIC AWARDS Total amount: $1,584,059 (48% need-based, 52% non-need-based).

APPLYING FOR FINANCIAL AID *Required financial aid forms:* FAFSA, state aid form. *Financial aid deadline (priority):* 3/1. *Notification date:* Continuous beginning 2/15. Students must reply by 5/1 or within 2 weeks of notification.

CONTACT Mrs. Melinda N. McCall, Interim Director of Financial Aid, Spring Hill College, 4000 Dauphin Street, Mobile, AL 36608, 251-380-2253 or toll-free 800-SHC-6704. *Fax:* 251-460-2176. *E-mail:* mmccall@shc.edu. *Website:* http://www.shc.edu/.

STANBRIDGE UNIVERSITY
Irvine, CA

CONTACT Financial Aid Office, Stanbridge University, 2041 Business Center Drive, Irvine, CA 92612, 949-794-9090. *Website:* http://www.stanbridge.edu/.

STANFORD UNIVERSITY
Stanford, CA

Tuition & fees: $47,940	Average undergraduate aid package: $49,124

ABOUT THE INSTITUTION Independent, coed. *Awards:* certificates, bachelor's, master's, and doctoral degrees. 72 undergraduate majors. *Total enrollment:* 16,914. Undergraduates: 7,034. Freshmen: 1,738. Both federal and institutional methodology are used as a basis for awarding need-based institutional aid.

UNDERGRADUATE EXPENSES for 2017–2018 *Application fee:* $90. *Comprehensive fee:* $62,541 includes full-time tuition ($47,331), mandatory fees ($609), and room and board ($14,601). *College room only:* $8712. Room and board charges vary according to board plan.

FRESHMAN FINANCIAL AID (Fall 2015) 960 applied for aid; of those 79% were deemed to have need. 100% of freshmen with need received aid; of those 94% had need fully met. *Average percent of need met:* 100% (excluding resources awarded to replace EFC). *Average financial aid package:* $50,547 (excluding resources awarded to replace EFC). 1% of all full-time freshmen had no need and received non-need-based gift aid.

UNDERGRADUATE FINANCIAL AID (Fall 2015) 3,730 applied for aid; of those 89% were deemed to have need. 100% of undergraduates with need received aid; of those 90% had need fully met. *Average percent of need met:* 100% (excluding resources awarded to replace EFC). *Average financial aid package:* $49,124 (excluding resources awarded to replace EFC). 1% of all full-time undergraduates had no need and received non-need-based gift aid.

GIFT AID (NEED-BASED) *Total amount:* $147,395,183 (4% federal, 2% state, 91% institutional, 3% external sources). *Receiving aid:* Freshmen: 43% (747); all full-time undergraduates: 47% (3,255). *Average award:* Freshmen: $47,664; Undergraduates: $45,318. *Scholarships, grants, and awards:* Federal Pell, FSEOG, state, private, college/university gift aid from institutional funds.

GIFT AID (NON-NEED-BASED) *Total amount:* $7,401,984 (7% federal, 18% institutional, 75% external sources). *Receiving aid:* Freshmen: 1% (20). Undergraduates: 2% (121). *Average award:* Freshmen: $6883. Undergraduates: $13,697. *Tuition waivers:* Full or partial for employees or children of employees. *ROTC:* Army cooperative, Naval cooperative, Air Force cooperative.

LOANS *Student loans:* $6,882,277 (26% need-based, 74% non-need-based). 21% of past graduating class borrowed through all loan programs. *Average indebtedness per student:* $21,987. *Average need-based loan:* Freshmen: $2646. Undergraduates: $3231. *Parent loans:* $4,321,491 (100% non-need-based). *Programs:* Federal Direct (Subsidized and Unsubsidized Stafford, PLUS), Perkins.

WORK-STUDY *Federal work-study:* 558 jobs averaging $2360. *State or other work-study/employment:* Total amount: $4,011,301 (85% need-based, 15% non-need-based). 1,776 part-time jobs averaging $2249.

ATHLETIC AWARDS Total amount: $22,299,303 (13% need-based, 87% non-need-based).

APPLYING FOR FINANCIAL AID *Required financial aid forms:* FAFSA, CSS Financial Aid PROFILE. *Financial aid deadline (priority):* 2/15. *Notification date:* Continuous beginning 4/1. Students must reply by 5/1.

CONTACT Financial Aid Office, Stanford University, Montag Hall, 355 Galvez Street, Stanford, CA 94305-3021, 650-723-3058. *Fax:* 650-725-0540. *E-mail:* financialaid@stanford.edu. *Website:* http://www.stanford.edu/.

STATE COLLEGE OF FLORIDA MANATEE-SARASOTA
Bradenton, FL

CONTACT Financial Aid Office, State College of Florida Manatee-Sarasota, 5840 26th Street West, PO Box 1849, Bradenton, FL 34206-7046, 941-752-5000. *Website:* http://www.scf.edu/.

STATE UNIVERSITY OF NEW YORK AT FREDONIA
Fredonia, NY

Tuition & fees (NY res): $8089	Average undergraduate aid package: $10,936

ABOUT THE INSTITUTION State-supported, coed. *Awards:* certificates, bachelor's, and master's degrees. 71 undergraduate majors. *Total enrollment:* 4,612. Undergraduates: 4,386. Freshmen: 935. Federal methodology is used as a basis for awarding need-based institutional aid.

UNDERGRADUATE EXPENSES for 2017–2018 *Application fee:* $50. *Tuition, state resident:* full-time $6470; part-time $270 per credit hour. *Tuition, nonresident:* full-time $16,320; part-time $680 per credit hour. *Required fees:* full-time $1619; $67.30 per credit hour or $67.30 per credit hour. *College room and board:* $12,730; *Room only:* $7600. Room and board charges vary according to board plan and housing facility.

FRESHMAN FINANCIAL AID (Fall 2016, est.) 869 applied for aid; of those 81% were deemed to have need. 99% of freshmen with need received aid; of those 15% had need fully met. *Average percent of need met:* 65% (excluding resources awarded to replace EFC). *Average financial aid package:* $12,060 (excluding resources awarded to replace EFC). 15% of all full-time freshmen had no need and received non-need-based gift aid.

UNDERGRADUATE FINANCIAL AID (Fall 2016, est.) 3,658 applied for aid; of those 82% were deemed to have need. 98% of undergraduates with need received aid; of those 15% had need fully met. *Average percent of need met:* 60% (excluding resources awarded to replace EFC). *Average financial aid package:* $10,936 (excluding resources awarded to replace EFC). 8% of all full-time undergraduates had no need and received non-need-based gift aid.

GIFT AID (NEED-BASED) *Total amount:* $18,481,212 (42% federal, 39% state, 16% institutional, 3% external sources). *Receiving aid:* Freshmen: 60% (552); all full-time undergraduates: 52% (2,219). *Average award:* Freshmen: $6062; Undergraduates: $5682. *Scholarships, grants, and awards:* Federal Pell, FSEOG, state, private, college/university gift aid from institutional funds, TEACH Grants.

GIFT AID (NON-NEED-BASED) *Total amount:* $286,470 (100% federal). *Receiving aid:* Freshmen: 48% (438). Undergraduates: 23% (965). *Average award:* Freshmen: $3833. Undergraduates: $3117. *Scholarships, grants, and awards by category:* Academic interests/achievement: 333 awards ($449,534 total): biological sciences, business, communication, computer science, education, English, foreign languages, general academic interests/achievements, humanities, international studies, mathematics, physical sciences, social sciences. *Creative arts/performance:* 139 awards ($128,600 total): applied art and design, art/fine arts, dance, music, performing arts, theater/drama. *Special achievements/activities:* 20 awards ($63,950 total): general special achievements/activities, leadership. *Special characteristics:* 123 awards ($339,700 total): children and siblings of alumni, ethnic background, general special characteristics, international students, local/state students, members of minority groups, out-of-state students, parents of current students, previous college experience.

LOANS *Student loans:* $31,283,363 (42% need-based, 58% non-need-based). 82% of past graduating class borrowed through all loan programs. *Average indebtedness per student:* $32,083. *Average need-based loan:* Freshmen: $5482. Undergraduates: $5276. *Parent loans:* $4,531,827 (100% non-need-based). *Programs:* Federal Direct (Subsidized and Unsubsidized Stafford, PLUS), Perkins, alternative loans.

WORK-STUDY *Federal work-study:* Total amount: $330,562; 201 jobs averaging $1778.

APPLYING FOR FINANCIAL AID *Required financial aid forms:* FAFSA, state aid form. *Financial aid deadline:* Continuous. *Notification date:* Continuous beginning 12/1. Students must reply by 5/1.

CONTACT Mark Zaffalon, Financial Aid Counselor, State University of New York at Fredonia, 209 Maytum Hall, Fredonia, NY 14063, 716-673-3253 or toll-free 800-252-1212. *Fax:* 716-673-3785. *E-mail:* mark.zaffalon@fredonia.edu. *Website:* http://www.fredonia.edu/.

STATE UNIVERSITY OF NEW YORK AT NEW PALTZ
New Paltz, NY

Tuition & fees (NY res): $7754	Average undergraduate aid package: $11,074

ABOUT THE INSTITUTION State-supported, coed. *Awards:* certificates, bachelor's, and master's degrees. 67 undergraduate majors. *Total enrollment:* 7,628. Undergraduates: 6,717. Freshmen: 1,092. Federal methodology is used as a basis for awarding need-based institutional aid.

UNDERGRADUATE EXPENSES for 2016–2017 *Application fee:* $50. *Tuition, state resident:* full-time $6470; part-time $270 per credit hour. *Tuition, nonresident:* full-time $16,320; part-time $680 per credit hour. *Required fees:* full-time $1284; $36.64 per credit hour or $200 per term. *College room and board:* $12,000; *Room only:* $8040. Room and board charges vary according to board plan.

FRESHMAN FINANCIAL AID (Fall 2016, est.) 980 applied for aid; of those 69% were deemed to have need. 99% of freshmen with need received aid; of those 7% had need fully met. *Average percent of need met:* 57% (excluding resources awarded to replace EFC). *Average financial aid package:* $11,489 (excluding resources awarded to replace EFC). 1% of all full-time freshmen had no need and received non-need-based gift aid.

UNDERGRADUATE FINANCIAL AID (Fall 2016, est.) 4,748 applied for aid; of those 74% were deemed to have need. 99% of undergraduates with need received aid; of those 7% had need fully met. *Average percent of need met:* 56% (excluding resources awarded to replace EFC). *Average financial aid package:* $11,074 (excluding resources awarded to replace EFC). 1% of all full-time undergraduates had no need and received non-need-based gift aid.

GIFT AID (NEED-BASED) *Total amount:* $19,643,227 (55% federal, 45% state). *Receiving aid:* Freshmen: 35% (380); all full-time undergraduates: 33% (2,069). *Average award:* Freshmen: $5256; Undergraduates: $5016. *Scholarships, grants, and awards:* Federal Pell, FSEOG, state, private, college/university gift aid from institutional funds.

GIFT AID (NON-NEED-BASED) *Total amount:* $1,440,226 (29% state, 23% institutional, 48% external sources). *Receiving aid:* Freshmen: 6% (67). Undergraduates: 5% (281). *Average award:* Freshmen: $3800. Undergraduates: $2504. *Scholarships, grants, and awards by category:* Academic interests/achievement: area/ethnic studies, biological sciences, business, communication, education, engineering/technologies, English, foreign languages, general academic interests/achievements, international studies, mathematics, physical sciences. *Creative arts/performance:* art/fine arts, music, theater/drama. *Special characteristics:* children of faculty/staff, ethnic background, first-generation college students, local/state students, members of minority groups.

LOANS *Student loans:* $27,415,679 (49% need-based, 51% non-need-based). 62% of past graduating class borrowed through all loan programs. *Average indebtedness per student:* $26,283. *Average need-based loan:* Freshmen: $3348. Undergraduates: $4293. *Parent loans:* $22,483,084 (100% non-need-based). *Programs:* Federal Direct (Subsidized and Unsubsidized Stafford, PLUS), Perkins.

WORK-STUDY *Federal work-study:* Total amount: $1,622,351; jobs available. *State or other work-study/employment:* Total amount: $973,088 (100% non-need-based). Part-time jobs available.

APPLYING FOR FINANCIAL AID *Required financial aid forms:* FAFSA, state aid form. *Financial aid deadline (priority):* 3/1. *Notification date:* Continuous beginning 2/15.

CONTACT Mrs. Maureen Lohan-Bremer, Director of Financial Aid, State University of New York at New Paltz, 200 Hawk Drive, New Paltz, NY 12561-2437, 845-257-3250 or toll-free 877-MY-NP-411 (in-state). *Fax:* 845-257-3568. *E-mail:* fao@newpaltz.edu. *Website:* http://www.newpaltz.edu/.

STATE UNIVERSITY OF NEW YORK AT OSWEGO
Oswego, NY

Tuition & fees (NY res): $7961	Average undergraduate aid package: $11,290

ABOUT THE INSTITUTION State-supported, coed. *Awards:* certificates, bachelor's, and master's degrees. 68 undergraduate majors. *Total enrollment:* 8,004. Undergraduates: 7,150. Freshmen: 1,441. Federal methodology is used as a basis for awarding need-based institutional aid.

UNDERGRADUATE EXPENSES for 2016–2017 *Application fee:* $50. *Tuition, state resident:* full-time $6470; part-time $270 per credit hour. *Tuition, nonresident:* full-time $16,320; part-time $680 per credit hour. *Required fees:* full-time $1491; $47.09 per credit hour. Part-time tuition and fees vary according to course load. *College room and board:* $13,390; *Room only:* $8390. Room and board charges vary according to board plan and housing facility.

FRESHMAN FINANCIAL AID (Fall 2016, est.) 1,305 applied for aid; of those 77% were deemed to have need. 99% of freshmen with need received aid; of those 6% had need fully met. *Average percent of need met:* 83% (excluding resources awarded to replace EFC). *Average financial aid package:* $12,366 (excluding resources awarded to replace EFC). 20% of all full-time freshmen had no need and received non-need-based gift aid.

UNDERGRADUATE FINANCIAL AID (Fall 2016, est.) 5,670 applied for aid; of those 80% were deemed to have need. 99% of undergraduates with need received aid; of those 9% had need fully met. *Average percent of need met:* 80% (excluding resources awarded to replace EFC). *Average financial aid package:* $11,290 (excluding resources awarded to replace EFC). 12% of all full-time undergraduates had no need and received non-need-based gift aid.

GIFT AID (NEED-BASED) *Total amount:* $30,110,149 (45% federal, 41% state, 12% institutional, 2% external sources). *Receiving aid:* Freshmen: 66% (955); all full-time undergraduates: 57% (3,913). *Average award:* Freshmen: $8317; Undergraduates: $7538. *Scholarships, grants, and awards:* Federal Pell, FSEOG, state, private, college/university gift aid from institutional funds.

GIFT AID (NON-NEED-BASED) *Total amount:* $2,407,771 (1% federal, 4% state, 84% institutional, 11% external sources). *Receiving aid:* Freshmen: 48% (684). Undergraduates: 23% (1,612). *Average award:* Freshmen: $2237. Undergraduates: $2529. *Scholarships, grants, and awards by category:* Academic interests/achievement: area/ethnic studies, biological sciences, business, communication, computer science, education, English, foreign languages, general academic interests/achievements, humanities, international studies, mathematics, physical sciences, premedicine, social sciences. ROTC: Army cooperative, Air Force cooperative.

LOANS *Student loans:* $41,120,362 (82% need-based, 18% non-need-based). 81% of past graduating class borrowed through all loan programs. *Average indebtedness per student:* $28,676. *Average need-based loan:* Freshmen: $4321. Undergraduates: $4602. *Parent loans:* $16,288,620 (73% need-based, 27% non-need-based). *Programs:* Federal Direct (Subsidized and Unsubsidized Stafford, PLUS), Perkins.

WORK-STUDY *Federal work-study:* Total amount: $825,878; 457 jobs averaging $1250. *State or other work-study/employment:* Total amount: $930,650 (57% need-based, 43% non-need-based). Part-time jobs available.

APPLYING FOR FINANCIAL AID *Required financial aid forms:* FAFSA, state aid form. *Financial aid deadline (priority):* 2/15. *Notification date:* Continuous beginning 1/15. Students must reply by 5/1 or within 3 weeks of notification.

CONTACT Dr. Mark C. Humbert, Director of Financial Aid, State University of New York at Oswego, 206 Culkin Hall, Oswego, NY 13126, 315-312-2248. *Fax:* 315-312-3696. *E-mail:* finaid@oswego.edu. *Website:* http://www.oswego.edu/.

STATE UNIVERSITY OF NEW YORK AT PLATTSBURGH
Plattsburgh, NY

Tuition & fees (NY res): $7906	Average undergraduate aid package: $13,278

ABOUT THE INSTITUTION State-supported, coed. *Awards:* certificates, bachelor's, and master's degrees. 58 undergraduate majors. *Total enrollment:* 5,520. Undergraduates: 5,215. Freshmen: 1,021. Federal methodology is used as a basis for awarding need-based institutional aid.

UNDERGRADUATE EXPENSES for 2016–2017 *Application fee:* $50. *Tuition, state resident:* full-time $6470; part-time $270 per contact hour. *Tuition, nonresident:* full-time $16,320; part-time $680 per contact hour. *Required fees:* full-time $1436; $60.77 per contact hour. Full-time tuition and fees vary according to course load and location. Part-time tuition and fees vary according to course load and location. *College room and board:* $12,150; *Room only:* $7750. Room and board charges vary according to board plan and housing facility.

FRESHMAN FINANCIAL AID (Fall 2015) 857 applied for aid; of those 77% were deemed to have need. 99% of freshmen with need received aid; of those 18% had need fully met. *Average percent of need met:* 78% (excluding resources awarded to replace EFC). *Average financial aid package:* $13,814 (excluding resources awarded to replace EFC). 18% of all full-time freshmen had no need and received non-need-based gift aid.

UNDERGRADUATE FINANCIAL AID (Fall 2015) 3,976 applied for aid; of those 80% were deemed to have need. 98% of undergraduates with need received aid; of those 17% had need fully met. *Average percent of need met:* 76% (excluding resources awarded to replace EFC). *Average financial aid package:* $13,278 (excluding resources awarded to replace EFC). 13% of all full-time undergraduates had no need and received non-need-based gift aid.

GIFT AID (NEED-BASED) *Total amount:* $20,879,371 (44% federal, 34% state, 19% institutional, 3% external sources). *Receiving aid:* Freshmen: 61% (588); all full-time undergraduates: 55% (2,716). *Average award:* Freshmen: $8751; Undergraduates: $7606. *Scholarships, grants, and awards:* Federal Pell, FSEOG, state, private, college/university gift aid from institutional funds.

GIFT AID (NON-NEED-BASED) *Total amount:* $3,297,105 (3% federal, 6% state, 86% institutional, 5% external sources). *Receiving aid:* Freshmen: 19% (187). Undergraduates: 14% (716). *Average award:* Freshmen: $4613. Undergraduates: $4235. *Scholarships, grants, and awards by category:* Academic interests/achievement: 4,480 awards ($6,649,301 total): area/ethnic studies, biological sciences, business, communication, computer science, education, engineering/technologies, English, general academic interests/achievements, health fields, home economics, humanities, international studies, mathematics, physical sciences, premedicine, social sciences. Creative arts/performance: 321 awards ($430,685 total): art/fine arts, journalism/publications, music, theater/drama. Special achievements/activities: 10 awards ($15,500 total): community service, general special achievements/activities, leadership. Special characteristics: 863 awards ($2,438,578 total): international students, out-of-state students.

LOANS *Student loans:* $26,753,213 (79% need-based, 21% non-need-based). 75% of past graduating class borrowed through all loan programs. *Average indebtedness per student:* $28,779. *Average need-based loan:* Freshmen: $6688. Undergraduates: $7806. *Parent loans:* $5,482,561 (71% need-based, 29% non-need-based). *Programs:* Federal Direct (Subsidized and Unsubsidized Stafford, PLUS), Perkins, Federal Nursing, private loans.

WORK-STUDY *Federal work-study:* 385 jobs averaging $2556. *State or other work-study/employment:* Part-time jobs available.

APPLYING FOR FINANCIAL AID *Required financial aid forms:* FAFSA, state aid form. *Financial aid deadline (priority):* 12/15. *Notification date:* Continuous beginning 12/15. Students must reply by 5/1.

CONTACT Mr. Todd Moravec, Director of Financial Aid, State University of New York at Plattsburgh, 101 Broad Street, Plattsburgh, NY 12901-2681, 518-564-2072 or toll-free 888-673-0012. *Fax:* 518-564-4079. *E-mail:* todd.moravec@plattsburgh.edu. *Website:* http://www.plattsburgh.edu/.

STATE UNIVERSITY OF NEW YORK COLLEGE AT CORTLAND
Cortland, NY

Tuition & fees (NY res): $8106	Average undergraduate aid package: $14,563

ABOUT THE INSTITUTION State-supported, coed. **Awards:** certificates, bachelor's, and master's degrees. 57 undergraduate majors. **Total enrollment:** 6,900. Undergraduates: 6,304. Freshmen: 1,238. Federal methodology is used as a basis for awarding need-based institutional aid.

UNDERGRADUATE EXPENSES for 2016–2017 **Application fee:** $50. **Tuition, state resident:** full-time $6470; part-time $270 per credit hour. **Tuition, nonresident:** full-time $16,320; part-time $680 per credit hour. **Required fees:** full-time $1636. Full-time tuition and fees vary according to course load and degree level. Part-time tuition and fees vary according to course load and degree level. **College room and board:** $12,600; **Room only:** $7820. Room and board charges vary according to board plan and housing facility.

FRESHMAN FINANCIAL AID (Fall 2015) 942 applied for aid; of those 72% were deemed to have need. 96% of freshmen with need received aid; of those 9% had need fully met. **Average percent of need met:** 67% (excluding resources awarded to replace EFC). **Average financial aid package:** $14,839 (excluding resources awarded to replace EFC). 5% of all full-time freshmen had no need and received non-need-based gift aid.

UNDERGRADUATE FINANCIAL AID (Fall 2015) 4,859 applied for aid; of those 77% were deemed to have need. 97% of undergraduates with need received aid; of those 9% had need fully met. **Average percent of need met:** 66% (excluding resources awarded to replace EFC). **Average financial aid package:** $14,563 (excluding resources awarded to replace EFC). 5% of all full-time undergraduates had no need and received non-need-based gift aid.

GIFT AID (NEED-BASED) Total amount: $13,695,035 (56% federal, 43% state, 1% institutional). **Receiving aid:** Freshmen: 48% (486); all full-time undergraduates: 46% (2,686). **Average award:** Freshmen: $5369; Undergraduates: $5865. **Scholarships, grants, and awards:** Federal Pell, FSEOG, state, private, college/university gift aid from institutional funds.

GIFT AID (NON-NEED-BASED) Total amount: $5,519,632 (20% federal, 44% institutional, 36% external sources). **Receiving aid:** Freshmen: 26% (260). Undergraduates: 18% (1,076). **Average award:** Freshmen: $3674. Undergraduates: $3533. **Scholarships, grants, and awards by category:** Academic interests/achievement: education, general academic interests/achievements, international studies, mathematics, physical sciences. Creative arts/performance: art/fine arts, music. Special achievements/activities: community service, general special achievements/activities, hobbies/interests, leadership. Special characteristics: adult students, local/state students, members of minority groups. **Tuition waivers:** Full or partial for employees or children of employees. **ROTC:** Army cooperative, Air Force cooperative.

LOANS Student loans: $34,271,459 (39% need-based, 61% non-need-based). 75% of past graduating class borrowed through all loan programs. **Average indebtedness per student:** $29,674. **Average need-based loan:** Freshmen: $3542. Undergraduates: $4222. **Parent loans:** $8,868,079 (100% non-need-based). **Programs:** Federal Direct (Subsidized and Unsubsidized Stafford, PLUS), Perkins.

WORK-STUDY Federal work-study: jobs available. **State or other work-study/employment:** Total amount: $942,256 (100% non-need-based). Part-time jobs available.

APPLYING FOR FINANCIAL AID Required financial aid forms: FAFSA, state aid form. **Financial aid deadline (priority):** 3/1. **Notification date:** Continuous beginning 3/15. Students must reply by 5/1 or within 4 weeks of notification.

CONTACT Karen Gallagher, Director of Financial Advisement, State University of New York College at Cortland, PO Box 2000, Cortland, NY 13045, 607-753-4717. Fax: 607-753-5990. E-mail: finaid@cortland.edu. Website: http://www.cortland.edu/.

STATE UNIVERSITY OF NEW YORK COLLEGE AT GENESEO
Geneseo, NY

Tuition & fees (NY res): $8176	Average undergraduate aid package: $9487

ABOUT THE INSTITUTION State-supported, coed. **Awards:** bachelor's and master's degrees. 43 undergraduate majors. **Total enrollment:** 5,521. Undergraduates: 5,431. Freshmen: 1,238. Federal methodology is used as a basis for awarding need-based institutional aid.

UNDERGRADUATE EXPENSES for 2016–2017 **Application fee:** $50. **Tuition, state resident:** full-time $6470; part-time $270 per credit hour. **Tuition, nonresident:** full-time $16,320; part-time $680 per credit hour. **Required fees:** full-time $1706; $70.85 per credit hour. Part-time tuition and fees vary according to course load. **College room and board:** $12,264; **Room only:** $7660. Room and board charges vary according to board plan and housing facility.

FRESHMAN FINANCIAL AID (Fall 2016, est.) 1,075 applied for aid; of those 56% were deemed to have need. 100% of freshmen with need received aid; of those 10% had need fully met. **Average percent of need met:** 40% (excluding resources awarded to replace EFC). **Average financial aid package:** $9147 (excluding resources awarded to replace EFC). 11% of all full-time freshmen had no need and received non-need-based gift aid.

UNDERGRADUATE FINANCIAL AID (Fall 2016, est.) 3,947 applied for aid; of those 65% were deemed to have need. 100% of undergraduates with need received aid; of those 10% had need fully met. **Average percent of need met:** 41% (excluding resources awarded to replace EFC). **Average financial aid package:** $9487 (excluding resources awarded to replace EFC). 7% of all full-time undergraduates had no need and received non-need-based gift aid.

GIFT AID (NEED-BASED) Total amount: $11,731,593 (50% federal, 50% state). **Receiving aid:** Freshmen: 38% (472); all full-time undergraduates: 37% (2,011). **Average award:** Freshmen: $2348; Undergraduates: $2242. **Scholarships, grants, and awards:** Federal Pell, FSEOG, state.

GIFT AID (NON-NEED-BASED) Total amount: $6,078,234 (1% federal, 21% state, 58% institutional, 20% external sources). **Receiving aid:** Freshmen: 14% (174). Undergraduates: 11% (601). **Average award:** Freshmen: $3545. Undergraduates: $2774. **Scholarships, grants, and awards by category:** Academic interests/achievement: 140 awards ($202,097 total): area/ethnic studies, biological sciences, business, communication, computer science, education, English, foreign languages, general academic interests/achievements, humanities, international studies, mathematics, physical sciences, premedicine, social sciences. Creative arts/performance: 40 awards ($31,840 total): applied art and design, art/fine arts, creative writing, dance, general creative arts/performance, journalism/publications, music, performing arts, theater/drama. Special achievements/activities: 93 awards ($150,550 total): community service, general special achievements/activities, leadership, memberships. Special characteristics: 40 awards ($136,320 total): adult students, ethnic background, first-generation college students, general special characteristics, handicapped students, international students, local/state students, members of minority groups, religious affiliation, veterans. **ROTC:** Army cooperative, Air Force cooperative.

LOANS Student loans: $20,815,187 (46% need-based, 54% non-need-based). 55% of past graduating class borrowed through all loan programs. **Average indebtedness per student:** $24,784. **Average need-based loan:** Freshmen: $2832. Undergraduates: $3624. **Parent loans:** $9,274,530 (100% non-need-based). **Programs:** Federal Direct (Subsidized and Unsubsidized Stafford, PLUS), Perkins.

WORK-STUDY Federal work-study: Total amount: $657,223; 430 jobs averaging $1517.

APPLYING FOR FINANCIAL AID Required financial aid forms: FAFSA, state aid form. **Financial aid deadline (priority):** 2/15. **Notification date:** Continuous beginning 3/15. Students must reply by 5/1.

CONTACT Susan Romano, Director of Financial Aid, State University of New York College at Geneseo, 1 College Circle, Erwin Hall 104, Geneseo, NY 14454, 585-245-5731 or toll-free 866-245-5211. Fax: 585-245-5717. E-mail: finaid@geneseo.edu. Website: http://www.geneseo.edu/.

STATE UNIVERSITY OF NEW YORK COLLEGE AT OLD WESTBURY
Old Westbury, NY

ABOUT THE INSTITUTION State-supported, coed. *Awards:* certificates, bachelor's, and master's degrees. 43 undergraduate majors. *Total enrollment:* 4,461. Undergraduates: 4,242. Freshmen: 501.

GIFT AID (NEED-BASED) *Scholarships, grants, and awards:* Federal Pell, FSEOG, state, private, college/university gift aid from institutional funds.

GIFT AID (NON-NEED-BASED) *Scholarships, grants, and awards by category:* Academic interests/achievement: biological sciences, health fields, physical sciences.

LOANS *Programs:* Federal Direct (Subsidized and Unsubsidized Stafford, PLUS), Perkins.

WORK-STUDY *Federal work-study:* 245 jobs averaging $975. *State or other work-study/employment:* Total amount: $238,816 (100% need-based). Part-time jobs available.

APPLYING FOR FINANCIAL AID *Required financial aid forms:* FAFSA, institution's own form, state aid form, verification worksheet.

CONTACT Ms. Vivian Mendonis, Financial Aid Assistant, State University of New York College at Old Westbury, PO Box 210, Old Westbury, NY 11568-0210, 516-876-3223. *Fax:* 516-876-3008. *E-mail:* finaid@oldwestbury.edu. *Website:* http://www.oldwestbury.edu/.

STATE UNIVERSITY OF NEW YORK COLLEGE AT ONEONTA
Oneonta, NY

CONTACT Mr. Bill Goodhue, Director of Financial Aid, State University of New York College at Oneonta, 108 Ravine Parkway, Oneonta, NY 13820, 607-436-2992 or toll-free 800-SUNY-123. *Fax:* 607-436-2659. *E-mail:* bill.goodhue@oneonta.edu. *Website:* http://www.oneonta.edu/.

STATE UNIVERSITY OF NEW YORK COLLEGE AT POTSDAM
Potsdam, NY

Tuition & fees (NY res): $7984	Average undergraduate aid package: $16,045

ABOUT THE INSTITUTION State-supported, coed. *Awards:* certificates, bachelor's, and master's degrees. 53 undergraduate majors. *Total enrollment:* 3,696. Undergraduates: 3,416. Freshmen: 788. Federal methodology is used as a basis for awarding need-based institutional aid.

UNDERGRADUATE EXPENSES for 2016–2017 *Application fee:* $50. *Tuition, state resident:* full-time $6470; part-time $270 per credit hour. *Tuition, nonresident:* full-time $16,320; part-time $680 per credit hour. *Required fees:* full-time $1514; $81.30 per credit hour. *College room and board:* $12,420; *Room only:* $7120. Room and board charges vary according to board plan and housing facility.

FRESHMAN FINANCIAL AID (Fall 2016, est.) 762 applied for aid; of those 84% were deemed to have need. 100% of freshmen with need received aid; of those 6% had need fully met. *Average percent of need met:* 96% (excluding resources awarded to replace EFC). *Average financial aid package:* $17,571 (excluding resources awarded to replace EFC). 8% of all full-time freshmen had no need and received non-need-based gift aid.

UNDERGRADUATE FINANCIAL AID (Fall 2016, est.) 3,063 applied for aid; of those 80% were deemed to have need. 100% of undergraduates with need received aid; of those 9% had need fully met. *Average percent of need met:* 95% (excluding resources awarded to replace EFC). *Average financial aid package:* $16,045 (excluding resources awarded to replace EFC). 8% of all full-time undergraduates had no need and received non-need-based gift aid.

GIFT AID (NEED-BASED) *Total amount:* $19,979,208 (42% federal, 41% state, 15% institutional, 2% external sources). *Receiving aid:* Freshmen: 70% (547); all full-time undergraduates: 61% (2,033). *Average award:* Freshmen: $9812; Undergraduates: $8044. *Scholarships, grants, and awards:* Federal Pell, FSEOG, state, private, college/university gift aid from institutional funds, TEACH Grants.

GIFT AID (NON-NEED-BASED) *Total amount:* $1,142,272 (9% state, 91% institutional). *Receiving aid:* Freshmen: 33% (255). Undergraduates: 27% (883). *Average award:* Freshmen: $2905. Undergraduates: $3129. *Scholarships, grants, and awards by category:* Academic interests/achievement: 321 awards ($388,161 total): biological sciences, business, communication, computer science, education, engineering/technologies, English, foreign languages, general academic interests/achievements, humanities, mathematics, physical sciences, social sciences. *Creative arts/performance:* 171 awards ($261,725 total): art/fine arts, dance, music, performing arts, theater/drama. *Special achievements/activities:* 853 awards ($2,235,101 total): community service, general special achievements/activities, leadership. *Special characteristics:* 93 awards ($120,175 total): adult students, children and siblings of alumni, children of faculty/staff, ethnic background, handicapped students, local/state students, members of minority groups, previous college experience. *Tuition waivers:* Full or partial for employees or children of employees. *ROTC:* Army cooperative, Air Force cooperative.

LOANS *Student loans:* $20,577,915 (73% need-based, 27% non-need-based). 79% of past graduating class borrowed through all loan programs. *Average indebtedness per student:* $28,582. *Average need-based loan:* Freshmen: $3904. Undergraduates: $4571. *Parent loans:* $18,543,435 (32% need-based, 68% non-need-based). *Programs:* Federal Direct (Subsidized and Unsubsidized Stafford, PLUS), Perkins, alternative loans.

WORK-STUDY *Federal work-study:* Total amount: $238,829; 206 jobs averaging $1123.

APPLYING FOR FINANCIAL AID *Required financial aid forms:* FAFSA, state aid form. *Financial aid deadline:* 5/1 (priority: 3/1). *Notification date:* Continuous beginning 2/1. Students must reply by 5/1 or within 4 weeks of notification.

CONTACT Susan E. Godreau, Director of Financial Aid, State University of New York College at Potsdam, 44 Pierrepont Avenue, Potsdam, NY 13676, 315-267-2162 or toll-free 877-POTSDAM. *Fax:* 315-267-3067. *E-mail:* finaid@potsdam.edu. *Website:* http://www.potsdam.edu/.

STATE UNIVERSITY OF NEW YORK COLLEGE OF AGRICULTURE AND TECHNOLOGY AT COBLESKILL
Cobleskill, NY

Tuition & fees (NY res): $7929	Average undergraduate aid package: $7513

ABOUT THE INSTITUTION State-supported, coed. *Awards:* certificates, associate, and bachelor's degrees. 51 undergraduate majors. *Total enrollment:* 2,304. Undergraduates: 2,304. Freshmen: 656. Federal methodology is used as a basis for awarding need-based institutional aid.

UNDERGRADUATE EXPENSES for 2016–2017 *Application fee:* $50. *Tuition, state resident:* full-time $6470; part-time $269.58 per credit hour. *Tuition, nonresident:* full-time $16,320; part-time $680 per credit hour. *Required fees:* full-time $1459; $58.11 per credit hour. Full-time tuition and fees vary according to degree level and program. Part-time tuition and fees vary according to degree level and program. *College room and board:* $13,018; *Room only:* $7800. Room and board charges vary according to board plan and housing facility.

FRESHMAN FINANCIAL AID (Fall 2015) 711 applied for aid; of those 88% were deemed to have need. 99% of freshmen with need received aid; of those 1% had need fully met. *Average percent of need met:* 66% (excluding resources awarded to replace EFC). *Average financial aid package:* $7607 (excluding resources awarded to replace EFC). 4% of all full-time freshmen had no need and received non-need-based gift aid.

UNDERGRADUATE FINANCIAL AID (Fall 2015) 2,176 applied for aid; of those 91% were deemed to have need. 99% of undergraduates with need received aid; of those 1% had need fully met. *Average percent of need met:* 64% (excluding resources awarded to replace EFC). *Average financial aid package:* $7513 (excluding resources awarded to replace EFC). 2% of all full-time undergraduates had no need and received non-need-based gift aid.

GIFT AID (NEED-BASED) *Total amount:* $11,008,252 (51% federal, 49% state). *Receiving aid:* Freshmen: 68% (516); all full-time undergraduates: 64% (1,601).

Average award: Freshmen: $4671; Undergraduates: $4432. **Scholarships, grants, and awards:** Federal Pell, FSEOG, state, private, college/university gift aid from institutional funds.

GIFT AID (NON-NEED-BASED) Total amount: $1,415,986 (25% federal, 36% institutional, 39% external sources). **Receiving aid:** Freshmen: 25% (187). Undergraduates: 17% (434). **Average award:** Freshmen: $2935. Undergraduates: $2453. **Scholarships, grants, and awards by category:** Academic interests/achievement: general academic interests/achievements. Special achievements/activities: leadership. Special characteristics: children and siblings of alumni, local/state students, members of minority groups. **Tuition waivers:** Full or partial for employees or children of employees, senior citizens.

LOANS Student loans: $12,950,537 (44% need-based, 56% non-need-based). 73% of past graduating class borrowed through all loan programs. Average indebtedness per student: $26,520. **Average need-based loan:** Freshmen: $2054. Undergraduates: $225. **Parent loans:** $5,522,859 (100% non-need-based). **Programs:** Federal Direct (Subsidized and Unsubsidized Stafford, PLUS), Perkins.

WORK-STUDY Federal work-study: 136 jobs averaging $622. **State or other work-study/employment:** 460 part-time jobs averaging $1404.

APPLYING FOR FINANCIAL AID Required financial aid forms: FAFSA, institution's own form, state aid form. **Financial aid deadline (priority):** 2/15. **Notification date:** Continuous beginning 3/10. Students must reply within 2 weeks of notification.

CONTACT Office of Financial Aid, State University of New York College of Agriculture and Technology at Cobleskill, 118B Knapp Hall, Cobleskill, NY 12043, 518-255-5623 or toll-free 800-295-8988. Fax: 518-255-5844. E-mail: financialaid@cobleskill.edu.
Website: http://www.cobleskill.edu/.

STATE UNIVERSITY OF NEW YORK COLLEGE OF ENVIRONMENTAL SCIENCE AND FORESTRY
Syracuse, NY

Tuition & fees (NY res): $8103	Average undergraduate aid package: $15,400

ABOUT THE INSTITUTION State-supported, coed. **Awards:** certificates, associate, bachelor's, master's, and doctoral degrees. 27 undergraduate majors. **Total enrollment:** 2,716. Undergraduates: 2,271. Freshmen: 327. Federal methodology is used as a basis for awarding need-based institutional aid.

UNDERGRADUATE EXPENSES for 2016–2017 Application fee: $50. **Tuition, state resident:** full-time $6470; part-time $270 per credit hour. **Tuition, nonresident:** full-time $16,320; part-time $680 per credit hour. **Required fees:** full-time $1633. Full-time tuition and fees vary according to location. Part-time tuition and fees vary according to course load and location. **College room and board:** $15,040; **Room only:** $8060. Room and board charges vary according to board plan, housing facility, and location.

FRESHMAN FINANCIAL AID (Fall 2015) 295 applied for aid; of those 89% were deemed to have need. 100% of freshmen with need received aid; of those 48% had need fully met. **Average percent of need met:** 82% (excluding resources awarded to replace EFC). **Average financial aid package:** $14,200 (excluding resources awarded to replace EFC). 18% of all full-time freshmen had no need and received non-need-based gift aid.

UNDERGRADUATE FINANCIAL AID (Fall 2015) 1,412 applied for aid; of those 76% were deemed to have need. 100% of undergraduates with need received aid; of those 70% had need fully met. **Average percent of need met:** 87% (excluding resources awarded to replace EFC). **Average financial aid package:** $15,400 (excluding resources awarded to replace EFC). 14% of all full-time undergraduates had no need and received non-need-based gift aid.

GIFT AID (NEED-BASED) Total amount: $7,276,056 (31% federal, 24% state, 41% institutional, 4% external sources). **Receiving aid:** Freshmen: 76% (243); all full-time undergraduates: 60% (1,058). **Average award:** Freshmen: $6000; Undergraduates: $4700. **Scholarships, grants, and awards:** Federal Pell, FSEOG, state, private, college/university gift aid from institutional funds.

GIFT AID (NON-NEED-BASED) Total amount: $1,146,844 (2% federal, 30% state, 45% institutional, 23% external sources). **Receiving aid:** Freshmen: 55% (175).

Undergraduates: 35% (610). **Average award:** Freshmen: $3384. Undergraduates: $3075. **Scholarships, grants, and awards by category:** Academic interests/achievement: agriculture, architecture, biological sciences, engineering/technologies, general academic interests/achievements, physical sciences, premedicine. Special achievements/activities: community service, general special achievements/activities, leadership, memberships. Special characteristics: children and siblings of alumni, general special characteristics, international students, local/state students, members of minority groups, out-of-state students. **ROTC:** Army cooperative, Air Force cooperative.

LOANS Student loans: $7,334,478 (43% need-based, 57% non-need-based). 64% of past graduating class borrowed through all loan programs. Average indebtedness per student: $24,269. **Average need-based loan:** Freshmen: $4100. Undergraduates: $4400. **Parent loans:** $2,487,982 (32% need-based, 68% non-need-based). **Programs:** Federal Direct (Subsidized and Unsubsidized Stafford, PLUS), Perkins.

WORK-STUDY Federal work-study: 170 jobs averaging $1788. **State or other work-study/employment:** Total amount: $353,939 (47% need-based, 53% non-need-based). 333 part-time jobs averaging $1063.

APPLYING FOR FINANCIAL AID Required financial aid forms: FAFSA, state aid form. **Financial aid deadline (priority):** 3/1. **Notification date:** Continuous beginning 3/15. Students must reply by 5/1 or within 2 weeks of notification.

CONTACT Mr. Mark J. Hill, Director of Financial Aid, State University of New York College of Environmental Science and Forestry, One Forestry Drive, Syracuse, NY 13210-2779, 315-470-6673. Fax: 315-470-4734. E-mail: mjhill@esf.edu.
Website: http://www.esf.edu/.

STATE UNIVERSITY OF NEW YORK COLLEGE OF TECHNOLOGY AT CANTON
Canton, NY

Tuition & fees (NY res): $7881	Average undergraduate aid package: $10,876

ABOUT THE INSTITUTION State-supported, coed. **Awards:** certificates, associate, and bachelor's degrees. 35 undergraduate majors. **Total enrollment:** 3,241. Undergraduates: 3,241. Freshmen: 699. Federal methodology is used as a basis for awarding need-based institutional aid.

UNDERGRADUATE EXPENSES for 2016–2017 Application fee: $50. **One-time required fee:** $100. **Tuition, state resident:** full-time $6470; part-time $270 per credit hour. **Tuition, nonresident:** full-time $16,320; part-time $680 per credit hour. **Required fees:** full-time $1411; $56.95 per credit hour or $5 per term. Full-time tuition and fees vary according to degree level. Part-time tuition and fees vary according to degree level. **College room and board:** $12,150; **Room only:** $7100. Room and board charges vary according to board plan and housing facility.

FRESHMAN FINANCIAL AID (Fall 2015) 618 applied for aid; of those 90% were deemed to have need. 99% of freshmen with need received aid; of those 21% had need fully met. **Average percent of need met:** 21% (excluding resources awarded to replace EFC). **Average financial aid package:** $11,458 (excluding resources awarded to replace EFC). 1% of all full-time freshmen had no need and received non-need-based gift aid.

UNDERGRADUATE FINANCIAL AID (Fall 2015) 2,454 applied for aid; of those 91% were deemed to have need. 99% of undergraduates with need received aid; of those 18% had need fully met. **Average percent of need met:** 18% (excluding resources awarded to replace EFC). **Average financial aid package:** $10,876 (excluding resources awarded to replace EFC). 1% of all full-time undergraduates had no need and received non-need-based gift aid.

GIFT AID (NEED-BASED) Total amount: $16,833,527 (52% federal, 45% state, 3% institutional). **Receiving aid:** Freshmen: 77% (499); all full-time undergraduates: 73% (1,917). **Average award:** Freshmen: $8722; Undergraduates: $8015. **Scholarships, grants, and awards:** Federal Pell, FSEOG, state, college/university gift aid from institutional funds, Bureau of Indian Affairs Grants.

GIFT AID (NON-NEED-BASED) Receiving aid: Freshmen: 10% (64). Undergraduates: 8% (206). **Average award:** Freshmen: $2667. Undergraduates: $2350. **Tuition waivers:** Full or partial for employees or children of employees. **ROTC:** Army cooperative, Air Force cooperative.

LOANS *Student loans:* $8,085,279 (100% need-based). 89% of past graduating class borrowed through all loan programs. *Average indebtedness per student:* $31,665. *Average need-based loan:* Freshmen: $3511. Undergraduates: $3958. *Parent loans:* $4,890,794 (100% need-based). *Programs:* Federal Direct (Subsidized and Unsubsidized Stafford, PLUS), Perkins.

WORK-STUDY *Federal work-study:* 178 jobs averaging $1123. *State or other work-study/employment:* Total amount: $204,728 (100% need-based). 13 part-time jobs averaging $1206.

APPLYING FOR FINANCIAL AID *Required financial aid forms:* FAFSA, state aid form. *Financial aid deadline (priority):* 3/1. *Notification date:* Continuous beginning 12/1. Students must reply within 4 weeks of notification.

CONTACT Ms. Kerrie Cooper, Director of Financial Aid, State University of New York College of Technology at Canton, Student Service Center, Canton, NY 13617, 315-386-7616 or toll-free 800-388-7123. *Fax:* 315-386-7930. *E-mail:* cooper@canton.edu.

Website: http://www.canton.edu/.

STATE UNIVERSITY OF NEW YORK COLLEGE OF TECHNOLOGY AT DELHI
Delhi, NY

Tuition & fees (NY res): $8095	Average undergraduate aid package: N/A

ABOUT THE INSTITUTION State-supported, coed. *Awards:* certificates, associate, bachelor's, and master's degrees. 36 undergraduate majors. *Total enrollment:* 3,450. Undergraduates: 3,424. Freshmen: 828. Federal methodology is used as a basis for awarding need-based institutional aid.

UNDERGRADUATE EXPENSES for 2016–2017 *Application fee:* $50. *Tuition, state resident:* full-time $6470; part-time $270 per credit hour. *Tuition, nonresident:* full-time $10,840; part-time $452 per credit hour. *Required fees:* full-time $1625; $55.93 per credit hour or $5 per term. Full-time tuition and fees vary according to degree level and location. Part-time tuition and fees vary according to course load, degree level, and location. *College room and board:* $11,680; *Room only:* $6700. Room and board charges vary according to board plan and housing facility.

GIFT AID (NEED-BASED) *Scholarships, grants, and awards:* Federal Pell, FSEOG, state, private, college/university gift aid from institutional funds.

GIFT AID (NON-NEED-BASED) *Scholarships, grants, and awards by category:* Academic interests/achievement: general academic interests/achievements. Special achievements/activities: community service.

LOANS *Student loans:* 81% of past graduating class borrowed through all loan programs. *Average indebtedness per student:* $28,367. *Programs:* Federal Direct (Subsidized and Unsubsidized Stafford, PLUS), Perkins.

WORK-STUDY *Federal work-study:* 72 jobs averaging $1188. *State or other work-study/employment:* Part-time jobs available.

APPLYING FOR FINANCIAL AID *Required financial aid forms:* FAFSA, state aid form. *Financial aid deadline (priority):* 2/15. *Notification date:* Continuous beginning 3/15.

CONTACT Nancy B. Hughes, Director of Financial Aid, State University of New York College of Technology at Delhi, 158 Bush Hall, Delhi, NY 13753, 607-746-4570 or toll-free 800-96-DELHI. *Fax:* 607-746-4104.

Website: http://www.delhi.edu/.

STATE UNIVERSITY OF NEW YORK DOWNSTATE MEDICAL CENTER
Brooklyn, NY

CONTACT Financial Aid Office, State University of New York Downstate Medical Center, 450 Clarkson Avenue, Brooklyn, NY 11203-2098, 718-270-2488. *Fax:* 718-270-7592. *E-mail:* finaid1@downstate.edu.

Website: http://www.downstate.edu/.

STATE UNIVERSITY OF NEW YORK MARITIME COLLEGE
Throggs Neck, NY

Tuition & fees (NY res): $7834	Average undergraduate aid package: $4446

ABOUT THE INSTITUTION State-supported, coed. *Awards:* associate, bachelor's, and master's degrees. 9 undergraduate majors. *Total enrollment:* 1,832. Undergraduates: 1,635. Freshmen: 309. Federal methodology is used as a basis for awarding need-based institutional aid.

UNDERGRADUATE EXPENSES for 2016–2017 *Application fee:* $50. *Tuition, state resident:* full-time $6470; part-time $270 per credit hour. *Tuition, nonresident:* full-time $16,320; part-time $680 per credit hour. *Required fees:* full-time $1364. Full-time tuition and fees vary according to course load. Part-time tuition and fees vary according to course load. *College room and board:* $11,948; *Room only:* $7714. Room and board charges vary according to board plan and housing facility.

FRESHMAN FINANCIAL AID (Fall 2015) 298 applied for aid; of those 65% were deemed to have need. 99% of freshmen with need received aid; of those 28% had need fully met. *Average percent of need met:* 41% (excluding resources awarded to replace EFC). *Average financial aid package:* $4479 (excluding resources awarded to replace EFC). 16% of all full-time freshmen had no need and received non-need-based gift aid.

UNDERGRADUATE FINANCIAL AID (Fall 2015) 1,261 applied for aid; of those 71% were deemed to have need. 99% of undergraduates with need received aid; of those 14% had need fully met. *Average percent of need met:* 20% (excluding resources awarded to replace EFC). *Average financial aid package:* $4446 (excluding resources awarded to replace EFC). 6% of all full-time undergraduates had no need and received non-need-based gift aid.

GIFT AID (NEED-BASED) *Total amount:* $5,298,276 (33% federal, 40% state, 17% institutional, 10% external sources). *Receiving aid:* Freshmen: 39% (131); all full-time undergraduates: 38% (611). *Average award:* Freshmen: $4072; Undergraduates: $3553. *Scholarships, grants, and awards:* Federal Pell, FSEOG, state, private, college/university gift aid from institutional funds, Educational Opportunity Program (EOP).

GIFT AID (NON-NEED-BASED) *Total amount:* $717,124 (37% institutional, 63% external sources). *Average award:* Freshmen: $1433. Undergraduates: $1399. *Scholarships, grants, and awards by category:* Academic interests/achievement: general academic interests/achievements. Special achievements/activities: leadership. *ROTC:* Army cooperative, Naval.

LOANS *Student loans:* $9,986,096 (34% need-based, 66% non-need-based). 33% of past graduating class borrowed through all loan programs. *Average need-based loan:* Freshmen: $1816. Undergraduates: $2160. *Parent loans:* $14,180,819 (100% non-need-based). *Programs:* Federal Direct (Subsidized and Unsubsidized Stafford, PLUS), Perkins, alternative loans.

WORK-STUDY *Federal work-study:* 101 jobs averaging $352. *State or other work-study/employment:* Total amount: $394,831 (100% non-need-based). 235 part-time jobs averaging $1600.

APPLYING FOR FINANCIAL AID *Required financial aid form:* FAFSA. *Financial aid deadline (priority):* 2/1. *Notification date:* 2/15. Students must reply by 5/1.

CONTACT Ms. Andrea Damar, Director of Financial Aid, State University of New York Maritime College, 6 Pennyfield Avenue, Throgs Neck, NY 10465-4198, 718-409-7227. *Fax:* 718-409-7275. *E-mail:* adamar@sunymaritime.edu.

Website: http://www.sunymaritime.edu/.

STATE UNIVERSITY OF NEW YORK POLYTECHNIC INSTITUTE
Utica, NY

Tuition & fees (NY res): $7890	Average undergraduate aid package: $10,449

ABOUT THE INSTITUTION State-supported, coed. *Awards:* certificates, bachelor's, master's, and doctoral degrees. 23 undergraduate majors. *Total*

enrollment: 2,705. Undergraduates: 2,012. Freshmen: 314. Federal methodology is used as a basis for awarding need-based institutional aid.

UNDERGRADUATE EXPENSES for 2017–2018 *Application fee:* $50. *Tuition, state resident:* full-time $6470; part-time $270 per credit hour. *Tuition, nonresident:* full-time $16,320; part-time $680 per credit hour. *Required fees:* full-time $1420; $54.35 per credit hour. Full-time tuition and fees vary according to course load and location. Part-time tuition and fees vary according to course load and location. *College room and board:* $12,068. Room and board charges vary according to board plan and location.

FRESHMAN FINANCIAL AID (Fall 2016, est.) 288 applied for aid; of those 76% were deemed to have need. 100% of freshmen with need received aid; of those 100% had need fully met. *Average percent of need met:* 100% (excluding resources awarded to replace EFC). *Average financial aid package:* $6215 (excluding resources awarded to replace EFC). 24% of all full-time freshmen had no need and received non-need-based gift aid.

UNDERGRADUATE FINANCIAL AID (Fall 2016, est.) 1,402 applied for aid; of those 81% were deemed to have need. 100% of undergraduates with need received aid; of those 99% had need fully met. *Average percent of need met:* 99% (excluding resources awarded to replace EFC). *Average financial aid package:* $10,449 (excluding resources awarded to replace EFC). 14% of all full-time undergraduates had no need and received non-need-based gift aid.

GIFT AID (NEED-BASED) *Total amount:* $7,619,925 (41% federal, 32% state, 24% institutional, 3% external sources). *Receiving aid:* Freshmen: 65% (204); all full-time undergraduates: 59% (999). *Average award:* Freshmen: $4899; Undergraduates: $7506. *Scholarships, grants, and awards:* Federal Pell, FSEOG, state, private, college/university gift aid from institutional funds.

GIFT AID (NON-NEED-BASED) *Total amount:* $1,387,537 (18% state, 70% institutional, 12% external sources). *Receiving aid:* Freshmen: 51% (161). Undergraduates: 26% (442). *Average award:* Freshmen: $2085. Undergraduates: $4137. *Scholarships, grants, and awards by category: Special characteristics:* local/state students, members of minority groups, previous college experience. *ROTC:* Army cooperative, Air Force cooperative.

LOANS *Student loans:* $10,114,590 (82% need-based, 18% non-need-based). *Average need-based loan:* Freshmen: $1784. Undergraduates: $4309. *Parent loans:* $5,137,786 (67% need-based, 33% non-need-based). *Programs:* Federal Direct (Subsidized and Unsubsidized Stafford, PLUS), Perkins, Federal Nursing.

WORK-STUDY *Federal work-study:* Total amount: $365,472; 126 jobs averaging $1500. *State or other work-study/employment:* Total amount: $342,116 (68% need-based, 32% non-need-based). Part-time jobs available.

APPLYING FOR FINANCIAL AID *Required financial aid forms:* FAFSA, state aid form. *Financial aid deadline (priority):* 3/1. *Notification date:* Continuous beginning 3/15. Students must reply within 2 weeks of notification.

CONTACT Financial Aid Office, State University of New York Polytechnic Institute, 100 Seymour Road, Utica, NY 13502, 315-792-7210 or toll-free 866-278-6948. *Fax:* 315-792-7220. *E-mail:* finaid@sunyit.edu. *Website:* http://www.sunypoly.edu/.

STATE UNIVERSITY OF NEW YORK UPSTATE MEDICAL UNIVERSITY
Syracuse, NY

CONTACT Michael Pede, Office of Financial Aid, State University of New York Upstate Medical University, Weiskotten Hall, Room 1213, 766 Irving Avenue, Syracuse, NY 13210-2375, 315-464-4329 or toll-free 800-736-2171. *E-mail:* finaid@upstate.edu. *Website:* http://www.upstate.edu/.

STEPHEN F. AUSTIN STATE UNIVERSITY
Nacogdoches, TX

Tuition & fees (TX res): $9537	Average undergraduate aid package: $11,866

ABOUT THE INSTITUTION State supported, coed. *Awards:* bachelor's, master's, and doctoral degrees. 68 undergraduate majors. *Total enrollment:* 12,742. Undergraduates: 11,140. Freshmen: 2,173. Federal methodology is used as a basis for awarding need-based institutional aid.

UNDERGRADUATE EXPENSES for 2016–2017 *Application fee:* $45. *Tuition, state resident:* full-time $7260; part-time $242 per credit hour. *Tuition, nonresident:* full-time $19,500; part-time $650 per credit hour. *Required fees:* full-time $2277; $157.50 per credit hour. Full-time tuition and fees vary according to course load, degree level, and location. Part-time tuition and fees vary according to course load, degree level, and location. *College room and board:* $8868. Room and board charges vary according to board plan and housing facility. *Payment plan:* Guaranteed tuition.

FRESHMAN FINANCIAL AID (Fall 2015) 1,820 applied for aid; of those 76% were deemed to have need. 100% of freshmen with need received aid; of those 12% had need fully met. *Average percent of need met:* 60% (excluding resources awarded to replace EFC). *Average financial aid package:* $12,414 (excluding resources awarded to replace EFC). 15% of all full-time freshmen had no need and received non-need-based gift aid.

UNDERGRADUATE FINANCIAL AID (Fall 2015) 8,036 applied for aid; of those 81% were deemed to have need. 100% of undergraduates with need received aid; of those 15% had need fully met. *Average percent of need met:* 60% (excluding resources awarded to replace EFC). *Average financial aid package:* $11,866 (excluding resources awarded to replace EFC). 9% of all full-time undergraduates had no need and received non-need-based gift aid.

GIFT AID (NEED-BASED) *Total amount:* $35,065,240 (56% federal, 24% state, 20% institutional). *Receiving aid:* Freshmen: 47% (996); all full-time undergraduates: 50% (5,079). *Average award:* Freshmen: $9758; Undergraduates: $7373. *Scholarships, grants, and awards:* Federal Pell, FSEOG, state, private, college/university gift aid from institutional funds, TEACH Grants.

GIFT AID (NON-NEED-BASED) *Total amount:* $13,307,265 (2% federal, 2% state, 69% institutional, 27% external sources). *Receiving aid:* Freshmen: 36% (761). Undergraduates: 24% (2,384). *Average award:* Freshmen: $2332. Undergraduates: $2445. *Scholarships, grants, and awards by category: Academic interests/achievement:* agriculture, biological sciences, business, communication, computer science, education, general academic interests/achievements, health fields, home economics, mathematics, military science, physical sciences, premedicine. *Creative arts/performance:* journalism/publications, music, theater/drama. *Special achievements/activities:* cheerleading/drum major, general special achievements/activities, hobbies/interests, leadership, rodeo. *Special characteristics:* adult students, children and siblings of alumni, children of faculty/staff, children of union members/company employees, first-generation college students, general special characteristics, local/state students, previous college experience, veterans, veterans' children. *Tuition waivers:* Full or partial for employees or children of employees, senior citizens. *ROTC:* Army.

LOANS *Student loans:* $65,452,836 (35% need-based, 65% non-need-based). 68% of past graduating class borrowed through all loan programs. *Average indebtedness per student:* $29,574. *Average need-based loan:* Freshmen: $3644. Undergraduates: $4764. *Parent loans:* $22,760,423 (100% non-need-based). *Programs:* Federal Direct (Subsidized and Unsubsidized Stafford, PLUS), Perkins, college/university.

WORK-STUDY *Federal work-study:* jobs available. *State or other work-study/employment:* Total amount: $82,136 (100% need-based). Part-time jobs available.

ATHLETIC AWARDS Total amount: $4,036,445 (100% non-need-based).

APPLYING FOR FINANCIAL AID *Required financial aid form:* FAFSA. *Financial aid deadline:* Continuous. *Notification date:* Continuous beginning 3/15.

CONTACT H. Rachele Garrett, Office of Financial Aid, Stephen F. Austin State University, PO Box 13052, Nacogdoches, TX 75962, 936-468-2403 or toll-free 800-731-2902. *Fax:* 936-468-1048. *E-mail:* finaid@sfasu.edu. *Website:* http://www.sfasu.edu/.

STEPHENS COLLEGE
Columbia, MO

Tuition & fees: N/R	Average undergraduate aid package: $10,000

ABOUT THE INSTITUTION Independent, undergraduate: women only; graduate: coed. *Awards:* certificates, associate, bachelor's, and master's degrees. 23 undergraduate majors. *Total enrollment:* 706. Undergraduates: 706. Freshmen: 191. Federal methodology is used as a basis for awarding need-based institutional aid.

FRESHMAN FINANCIAL AID (Fall 2015) 227 applied for aid; of those 100% were deemed to have need. 100% of freshmen with need received aid. *Average percent of need met:* 80% (excluding resources awarded to replace EFC). *Average financial aid package:* $12,000 (excluding resources awarded to replace EFC). 1% of all full-time freshmen had no need and received non-need-based gift aid.

UNDERGRADUATE FINANCIAL AID (Fall 2015) 521 applied for aid; of those 100% were deemed to have need. 100% of undergraduates with need received aid. *Average percent of need met:* 70% (excluding resources awarded to replace EFC). *Average financial aid package:* $10,000 (excluding resources awarded to replace EFC). 8% of all full-time undergraduates had no need and received non-need-based gift aid.

GIFT AID (NEED-BASED) *Total amount:* $4,429,364 (33% federal, 8% state, 59% institutional). *Receiving aid:* Freshmen: 227; all full-time undergraduates: 76% (521). *Average award:* Freshmen: $16,000; Undergraduates: $14,000. *Scholarships, grants, and awards:* Federal Pell, FSEOG, state, private, college/university gift aid from institutional funds, Academic Competitiveness Grants, National SMART Grants.

GIFT AID (NON-NEED-BASED) *Total amount:* $5,262,245 (1% state, 97% institutional, 2% external sources). *Receiving aid:* Freshmen: 190. Undergraduates: 70% (485). *Average award:* Freshmen: $10,000. Undergraduates: $8000. *Scholarships, grants, and awards by category:* Academic interests/achievement: English, general academic interests/achievements. Creative arts/performance: dance, music, performing arts, theater/drama. Special achievements/activities: leadership, memberships. Special characteristics: children of faculty/staff, children of union members/company employees, parents of current students, siblings of current students, veterans, veterans' children. *ROTC:* Army cooperative, Naval cooperative, Air Force cooperative.

LOANS *Student loans:* $3,995,609 (51% need-based, 49% non-need-based). 93% of past graduating class borrowed through all loan programs. *Parent loans:* $1,148,705 (100% non-need-based). *Programs:* Federal Direct (Subsidized and Unsubsidized Stafford, PLUS), Perkins, alternative loans.

WORK-STUDY *Federal work-study:* jobs available. *State or other work-study/employment:* Total amount: $137,798 (100% non-need-based). Part-time jobs available.

ATHLETIC AWARDS Total amount: $796,840 (100% non-need-based).

APPLYING FOR FINANCIAL AID *Required financial aid form:* FAFSA. *Financial aid deadline (priority):* 3/15. *Notification date:* Continuous beginning 3/1.

CONTACT Mrs. Kim Stonecipher-Fisher, Director of Financial Aid, Stephens College, 1200 East Broadway, Columbia, MO 65215-0002, 800-876-7207. *Fax:* 573-876-2320. *E-mail:* finaid@stephens.edu.
Website: http://www.stephens.edu/.

STERLING COLLEGE
Sterling, KS

Tuition & fees: $24,485	Average undergraduate aid package: $22,213

ABOUT THE INSTITUTION Independent Presbyterian, coed. *Awards:* bachelor's degrees. 20 undergraduate majors. *Total enrollment:* 650. Undergraduates: 650. Freshmen: 128. Federal methodology is used as a basis for awarding need-based institutional aid.

UNDERGRADUATE EXPENSES for 2017-2018 *Application fee:* $25. *One-time required fee:* $100. *Comprehensive fee:* $33,065 includes full-time tuition ($23,985), mandatory fees ($500), and room and board ($8580). Full-time tuition and fees vary according to course load. Room and board charges vary according to board plan and housing facility. *Part-time tuition:* $448 per credit hour. Part-time tuition and fees vary according to course load.

FRESHMAN FINANCIAL AID (Fall 2016, est.) 108 applied for aid; of those 90% were deemed to have need. 100% of freshmen with need received aid; of those 15% had need fully met. *Average percent of need met:* 72% (excluding resources awarded to replace EFC). *Average financial aid package:* $20,318 (excluding resources awarded to replace EFC). 10% of all full-time freshmen had no need and received non-need-based gift aid.

UNDERGRADUATE FINANCIAL AID (Fall 2016, est.) 546 applied for aid; of those 86% were deemed to have need. 100% of undergraduates with need received aid; of those 24% had need fully met. *Average percent of need met:* 82% (excluding resources awarded to replace EFC). *Average financial aid package:* $22,213 (excluding resources awarded to replace EFC). 13% of all full-time undergraduates had no need and received non-need-based gift aid.

GIFT AID (NEED-BASED) *Total amount:* $4,938,237 (26% federal, 10% state, 64% institutional). *Receiving aid:* Freshmen: 85% (92); all full-time undergraduates: 82% (449). *Average award:* Freshmen: $9495; Undergraduates: $11,049. *Scholarships, grants, and awards:* Federal Pell, FSEOG, state, private, college/university gift aid from institutional funds.

GIFT AID (NON-NEED-BASED) *Total amount:* $756,774 (73% institutional, 27% external sources). *Average award:* Freshmen: $9853. Undergraduates: $10,084. *Scholarships, grants, and awards by category:* Academic interests/achievement: 450 awards ($2,695,014 total): general academic interests/achievements. Creative arts/performance: 122 awards ($272,144 total): art/fine arts, cinema/film/broadcasting, creative writing, debating, general creative arts/performance, journalism/publications, music, performing arts, theater/drama. Special achievements/activities: 26 awards ($71,000 total): cheerleading/drum major, religious involvement. Special characteristics: 86 awards ($480,454 total): children and siblings of alumni, children of faculty/staff, public servants, siblings of current students, twins, veterans' children. *Tuition waivers:* Full or partial for employees or children of employees, senior citizens.

LOANS *Student loans:* $3,927,446 (64% need-based, 36% non-need-based). 81% of past graduating class borrowed through all loan programs. *Average indebtedness per student:* $28,221. *Average need-based loan:* Freshmen: $4804. Undergraduates: $5696. *Parent loans:* $1,410,216 (100% non-need-based). *Programs:* Federal Direct (Subsidized and Unsubsidized Stafford, PLUS), Perkins, college/university.

WORK-STUDY *Federal work-study:* Total amount: $271,560; jobs available.

ATHLETIC AWARDS Total amount: $2,064,522 (87% need-based, 13% non-need-based).

APPLYING FOR FINANCIAL AID *Required financial aid form:* FAFSA. *Financial aid deadline (priority):* 3/15. *Notification date:* Continuous beginning 2/1. Students must reply within 2 weeks of notification.

CONTACT Ms. Mitzi Suhler, Director of Financial Aid, Sterling College, 125 West Cooper, Sterling, KS 67579, 620-278-4226 or toll-free 800-346-1017. *Fax:* 620-869-9033. *E-mail:* msuhler@sterling.edu.
Website: http://www.sterling.edu/.

STERLING COLLEGE
Craftsbury Common, VT

ABOUT THE INSTITUTION Independent, coed. *Awards:* bachelor's degrees. 11 undergraduate majors. *Total enrollment:* 119. Undergraduates: 119. Freshmen: 20.

GIFT AID (NEED-BASED) *Scholarships, grants, and awards:* Federal Pell, FSEOG, state, private, college/university gift aid from institutional funds, Veterans Education Benefits (GI Bill), Yellow Ribbon Grant Program.

GIFT AID (NON-NEED-BASED) *Scholarships, grants, and awards by category:* Academic interests/achievement: general academic interests/achievements. Special achievements/activities: general special achievements/activities, leadership. Special characteristics: general special characteristics, previous college experience.

LOANS *Programs:* Federal Direct (Subsidized and Unsubsidized Stafford, PLUS).

APPLYING FOR FINANCIAL AID *Required financial aid forms:* FAFSA, institution's own form.

CONTACT Barbara Stuart, Director of Financial Aid, Sterling College, PO Box 72, Craftsbury Common, VT 05827, 800-648-3591 Ext. 3 or toll-free 800-648-3591 Ext. 100. *Fax:* 802-586-2596. *E-mail:* bstuart@sterlingcollege.edu.
Website: http://www.sterlingcollege.edu/.

STETSON UNIVERSITY
DeLand, FL

Tuition & fees: $43,240	Average undergraduate aid package: $34,778

ABOUT THE INSTITUTION Independent, coed. *Awards:* certificates, bachelor's, master's, and doctoral degrees. 55 undergraduate majors. *Total enrollment:* 4,330. Undergraduates: 3,084. Freshmen: 983. Federal methodology is used as a basis for awarding need-based institutional aid.

UNDERGRADUATE EXPENSES for 2016–2017 *Application fee:* $50. *Comprehensive fee:* $55,566 includes full-time tuition ($42,890), mandatory fees ($350), and room and board ($12,326). *College room only:* $7094. Room and board charges vary according to board plan and housing facility. *Part-time tuition:* $4445 per course. Part-time tuition and fees vary according to course load.

FRESHMAN FINANCIAL AID (Fall 2016, est.) 704 applied for aid; of those 88% were deemed to have need. 100% of freshmen with need received aid; of those 22% had need fully met. *Average percent of need met:* 77% (excluding resources awarded to replace EFC). *Average financial aid package:* $35,646 (excluding resources awarded to replace EFC). 21% of all full-time freshmen had no need and received non-need-based gift aid.

UNDERGRADUATE FINANCIAL AID (Fall 2016, est.) 2,338 applied for aid; of those 90% were deemed to have need. 100% of undergraduates with need received aid; of those 19% had need fully met. *Average percent of need met:* 74% (excluding resources awarded to replace EFC). *Average financial aid package:* $34,778 (excluding resources awarded to replace EFC). 25% of all full-time undergraduates had no need and received non-need-based gift aid.

GIFT AID (NEED-BASED) *Total amount:* $56,753,256 (9% federal, 10% state, 81% institutional). *Receiving aid:* Freshmen: 76% (614); all full-time undergraduates: 69% (2,084). *Average award:* Freshmen: $28,933; Undergraduates: $28,073. *Scholarships, grants, and awards:* Federal Pell, FSEOG, state, private, college/university gift aid from institutional funds.

GIFT AID (NON-NEED-BASED) *Total amount:* $24,554,649 (11% state, 88% institutional, 1% external sources). *Receiving aid:* Freshmen: 15% (120). Undergraduates: 11% (332). *Average award:* Freshmen: $24,027. Undergraduates: $22,185. *Scholarships, grants, and awards by category: Academic interests/achievement:* area/ethnic studies, biological sciences, business, communication, computer science, education, English, foreign languages, general academic interests/achievements, humanities, mathematics, military science, physical sciences, premedicine, religion/biblical studies, social sciences. *Creative arts/performance:* applied art and design, art/fine arts, music, theater/drama. *Special achievements/activities:* cheerleading/drum major, community service, general special achievements/activities, junior miss, leadership, religious involvement. *Special characteristics:* children and siblings of alumni, children of faculty/staff, ethnic background, first-generation college students, general special characteristics, international students, local/state students, members of minority groups, out-of-state students, veterans, veterans' children. *Tuition waivers:* Full or partial for children of alumni, employees or children of employees. *ROTC:* Army cooperative.

LOANS *Student loans:* $17,044,279 (78% need-based, 22% non-need-based). 70% of past graduating class borrowed through all loan programs. *Average indebtedness per student:* $31,457. *Average need-based loan:* Freshmen: $3575. Undergraduates: $4899. *Parent loans:* $8,562,907 (65% need-based, 35% non-need-based). *Programs:* Federal Direct (Subsidized and Unsubsidized Stafford, PLUS), Perkins.

WORK-STUDY *Federal work-study:* Total amount: $1,371,867; 558 jobs averaging $2459. *State or other work-study/employment:* Total amount: $254,411 (52% need-based, 48% non-need-based). 69 part-time jobs averaging $3687.

ATHLETIC AWARDS Total amount: $5,730,164 (33% need-based, 67% non-need-based).

APPLYING FOR FINANCIAL AID *Required financial aid form:* FAFSA. *Financial aid deadline (priority):* 12/1. *Notification date:* 3/1. Students must reply within 2 weeks of notification.

CONTACT Beth Kieft, Director of Financial Aid, Stetson University, 421 North Woodland Boulevard, DeLand, FL 32723, 386-822-7120 or toll-free 800-688-0101. *Fax:* 386-822-7126. *E-mail:* finaid@stetson.edu. *Website:* http://www.stetson.edu/.

STEVENS-HENAGER COLLEGE
Boise, ID

CONTACT Ms. Jaime L. Davis, Training and Project Development, Stevens-Henager College, 1444 South Entertainment Avenue, Boise, ID 83709, 208-383-4540 Ext. 1875 or toll-free 800-622-2640. *Fax:* 208-345-6999. *E-mail:* jaime.davis@stevenshenager.edu. *Website:* http://www.stevenshenager.edu/.

STEVENS-HENAGER COLLEGE
Idaho Falls, ID

CONTACT Financial Aid Office, Stevens-Henager College, 901 Pier View Drive, Suite 105, Idaho Falls, ID 83402, 208-522-0887 or toll-free 800-622-2640. *Website:* http://www.stevenshenager.edu/.

STEVENS-HENAGER COLLEGE
Logan, UT

CONTACT Financial Aid Office, Stevens-Henager College, 755 South Main Street, Logan, UT 84321, 435-752-0903 or toll-free 800-622-2640. *Website:* http://www.stevenshenager.edu/.

STEVENS-HENAGER COLLEGE
Orem, UT

CONTACT Financial Aid Office, Stevens-Henager College, 1476 South Sandhill Road, Orem, UT 84058, 801-373-0285 or toll-free 800-622-2640. *Website:* http://www.stevenshenager.edu/.

STEVENS-HENAGER COLLEGE
St. George, UT

CONTACT Financial Aid Office, Stevens-Henager College, 720 South River Road, Suite C-130, St. George, UT 84790, 435-628-9150 or toll-free 800-622-2640. *Website:* http://www.stevenshenager.edu/.

STEVENS-HENAGER COLLEGE
Salt Lake City, UT

CONTACT Financial Aid Office, Stevens-Henager College, 383 West Vine Street, Salt Lake City, UT 84123, 801-531-1180 or toll-free 800-622-2640. *Website:* http://www.stevenshenager.edu/.

STEVENS-HENAGER COLLEGE
West Haven, UT

CONTACT Financial Aid Office, Stevens-Henager College, 1890 South 1350 West, West Haven, UT 84401, 801-392-1471 or toll-free 800-622-2640. *Website:* http://www.stevenshenager.edu/.

STEVENS INSTITUTE OF TECHNOLOGY
Hoboken, NJ

Tuition & fees: $50,554	Average undergraduate aid package: $29,633

ABOUT THE INSTITUTION Independent, coed. *Awards:* certificates, bachelor's, master's, and doctoral degrees. 42 undergraduate majors. *Total enrollment:* 6,617. Undergraduates: 3,115. Freshmen: 737. Both federal and institutional methodology are used as a basis for awarding need-based institutional aid.

UNDERGRADUATE EXPENSES for 2017–2018 *Application fee:* $65. *Comprehensive fee:* $64,954 includes full-time tuition ($48,784), mandatory fees ($1770), and room and board ($14,400). *College room only:* $8000. Full-time tuition and fees vary according to course load. Room and board charges vary according to board plan and housing facility. *Part-time tuition:* $1626 per credit. *Part-time fees:* $885 per term. Part-time tuition and fees vary according to course load.

UNDERGRADUATE FINANCIAL AID (Fall 2015) 1,653 applied for aid; of those 83% were deemed to have need. 99% of undergraduates with need received aid; of those 20% had need fully met. *Average percent of need met:* 73% (excluding resources awarded to replace EFC). *Average financial aid package:* $29,633 (excluding resources awarded to replace EFC). 25% of all full-time undergraduates had no need and received non-need-based gift aid.

GIFT AID (NEED-BASED) *Total amount:* $11,538,211 (17% federal, 16% state, 67% institutional). *Receiving aid:* All full-time undergraduates: 30% (882). *Average award:* Undergraduates: $12,955. *Scholarships, grants, and awards:* Federal Pell, FSEOG, state, private, college/university gift aid from institutional funds, United Negro College Fund.

GIFT AID (NON-NEED-BASED) *Total amount:* $35,016,545 (98% institutional, 2% external sources). *Receiving aid:* Undergraduates: 43% (1,260). *Average award:* Undergraduates: $17,730. *Scholarships, grants, and awards by category: Academic interests/achievement:* business, computer science, engineering/technologies, general academic interests/achievements, humanities, mathematics, physical sciences, premedicine. *Creative arts/performance:* art/fine arts, journalism/publications, music, performing arts, theater/drama. *Special characteristics:* children and siblings of alumni, children of educators, children of faculty/staff, international students, local/state students, members of minority groups. *Tuition waivers:* Full or partial for employees or children of employees. *ROTC:* Army cooperative, Air Force cooperative.

LOANS *Student loans:* $8,964,847 (60% need-based, 40% non-need-based). 73% of past graduating class borrowed through all loan programs. *Average need-based loan:* Undergraduates: $4971. *Parent loans:* $3,327,266 (100% non-need-based). *Programs:* Federal Direct (Subsidized and Unsubsidized Stafford, PLUS), Perkins.

WORK-STUDY *Federal work-study:* jobs available.

APPLYING FOR FINANCIAL AID *Required financial aid forms:* FAFSA, CSS Financial Aid PROFILE. *Financial aid deadline (priority):* 2/15. *Notification date:* Continuous beginning 4/1. Students must reply by 5/1 or within 2 weeks of notification.

CONTACT Ms. Susan Gross, Director of Financial Aid, Stevens Institute of Technology, Castle Point on Hudson, Hoboken, NJ 07030, 201-216-8142 or toll-free 800-458-5323. *Fax:* 201-216-8050. *E-mail:* susan.gross@stevens.edu. *Website:* http://www.stevens.edu/.

STEVENSON UNIVERSITY
Stevenson, MD

Tuition & fees: $30,884	Average undergraduate aid package: $21,222

ABOUT THE INSTITUTION Independent, coed. *Awards:* bachelor's and master's degrees. 34 undergraduate majors. *Total enrollment:* 4,122. Undergraduates: 3,621. Freshmen: 778. Federal methodology is used as a basis for awarding need-based institutional aid.

UNDERGRADUATE EXPENSES for 2017–2018 *Application fee:* $40. *One-time required fee:* $780. *Tuition:* full-time $30,884. Room and board charges vary according to board plan.

FRESHMAN FINANCIAL AID (Fall 2016, est.) 740 applied for aid; of those 96% were deemed to have need. 100% of freshmen with need received aid; of those 16% had need fully met. *Average percent of need met:* 61% (excluding resources awarded to replace EFC). *Average financial aid package:* $24,074 (excluding resources awarded to replace EFC). 15% of all full-time freshmen had no need and received non-need-based gift aid.

UNDERGRADUATE FINANCIAL AID (Fall 2016, est.) 2,691 applied for aid; of those 90% were deemed to have need. 97% of undergraduates with need received aid; of those 15% had need fully met. *Average percent of need met:* 59% (excluding resources awarded to replace EFC). *Average financial aid package:* $21,222 (excluding resources awarded to replace EFC). 18% of all full-time undergraduates had no need and received non-need-based gift aid.

GIFT AID (NEED-BASED) *Total amount:* $42,831,309 (11% federal, 10% state, 77% institutional, 2% external sources). *Receiving aid:* Freshmen: 81% (636); all full-time undergraduates: 73% (2,244). *Average award:* Freshmen: $20,230; Undergraduates: $18,721. *Scholarships, grants, and awards:* Federal Pell, FSEOG, state, private, college/university gift aid from institutional funds.

GIFT AID (NON-NEED-BASED) *Total amount:* $9,484,611 (1% state, 94% institutional, 5% external sources). *Receiving aid:* Freshmen: 10% (75). Undergraduates: 8% (249). *Average award:* Freshmen: $16,010. Undergraduates: $12,969. *Scholarships, grants, and awards by category: Academic interests/achievement:* 2,714 awards ($36,817,259 total): general academic interests/achievements. *Creative arts/performance:* 13 awards ($34,750 total): art/fine arts. *Tuition waivers:* Full or partial for employees or children of employees. *ROTC:* Army cooperative, Air Force cooperative.

LOANS *Student loans:* $22,827,472 (63% need-based, 37% non-need-based). 78% of past graduating class borrowed through all loan programs. *Average indebtedness per student:* $34,324. *Average need-based loan:* Freshmen: $3308. Undergraduates: $4256. *Parent loans:* $17,898,674 (52% need-based, 48% non-need-based). *Programs:* Federal Direct (Subsidized and Unsubsidized Stafford, PLUS), Perkins.

WORK-STUDY *Federal work-study:* Total amount: $259,807; 157 jobs averaging $1655.

APPLYING FOR FINANCIAL AID *Required financial aid form:* FAFSA. *Financial aid deadline (priority):* 2/15. *Notification date:* Continuous beginning 3/15. Students must reply by 5/1 or within 2 weeks of notification.

CONTACT Ms. Barbara L. Miller, Office of Financial Aid, Stevenson University, 100 Campus Circle, Owings Mills, MD 21117, 443-352-4369 or toll-free 877-468-6852 (in-state), 877-468-3852 (out-of-state). *Fax:* 443-352-4370. *E-mail:* blmiller@stevenson.edu. *Website:* http://www.stevenson.edu/.

STEVENS–THE INSTITUTE OF BUSINESS & ARTS
St. Louis, MO

CONTACT Financial Aid Office, Stevens–The Institute of Business & Arts, 1521 Washington Avenue, St. Louis, MO 63102, 314-421-0949 or toll-free 800-871-0949. *Website:* http://www.siba.edu/.

STILLMAN COLLEGE
Tuscaloosa, AL

CONTACT Jacqueline S. Morris, Director of Financial Aid, Stillman College, PO Box 1430, Tuscaloosa, AL 35403, 205-366-8950 or toll-free 800-841-5722. *Fax:* 205-247-8106. *E-mail:* jmorris@stillman.edu. *Website:* http://www.stillman.edu/.

STOCKTON UNIVERSITY
Galloway, NJ

Tuition & fees (NJ res): $13,077	Average undergraduate aid package: $16,344

ABOUT THE INSTITUTION State-supported, coed. *Awards:* certificates, bachelor's, master's, and doctoral degrees 31 undergraduate majors. *Total enrollment:* 8,728. Undergraduates: 7,854. Freshmen: 1,190. Federal methodology is used as a basis for awarding need-based institutional aid.

UNDERGRADUATE EXPENSES for 2016–2017 *Application fee:* $50. *Tuition, state resident:* full-time $8435; part-time $324.41 per credit. *Tuition, nonresident:* full-time $15,209; part-time $585.35 per credit. *Required fees:* full-time $4642; $178.53 per credit or $100 per term. Part-time tuition and fees vary according to course load. *College room and board:* $11,942; *Room only:* $7912. Room and board charges vary according to board plan and housing facility.

FRESHMAN FINANCIAL AID (Fall 2016, est.) 1,132 applied for aid; of those 77% were deemed to have need. 97% of freshmen with need received aid; of those 34% had need fully met. *Average percent of need met:* 76% (excluding resources awarded to replace EFC). *Average financial aid package:* $17,669 (excluding resources awarded to replace EFC). 9% of all full-time freshmen had no need and received non-need-based gift aid.

UNDERGRADUATE FINANCIAL AID (Fall 2016, est.) 6,391 applied for aid; of those 83% were deemed to have need. 97% of undergraduates with need received aid; of those 28% had need fully met. *Average percent of need met:* 67% (excluding resources awarded to replace EFC). *Average financial aid package:* $16,344 (excluding resources awarded to replace EFC). 7% of all full-time undergraduates had no need and received non-need-based gift aid.

GIFT AID (NEED-BASED) *Total amount:* $36,774,137 (37% federal, 31% state, 30% institutional, 2% external sources). *Receiving aid:* Freshmen: 46% (544); all full-time undergraduates: 42% (3,119). *Average award:* Freshmen: $9491; Undergraduates: $8710. *Scholarships, grants, and awards:* Federal Pell, FSEOG, state, private, college/university gift aid from institutional funds.

GIFT AID (NON-NEED-BASED) *Total amount:* $3,289,815 (3% state, 85% institutional, 12% external sources). *Receiving aid:* Freshmen: 23% (278). Undergraduates: 20% (1,498). *Average award:* Freshmen: $6487. Undergraduates: $5319. *Scholarships, grants, and awards by category:* Academic interests/achievement: area/ethnic studies, biological sciences, business, communication, computer science, education, general academic interests/achievements, health fields, home economics, humanities, mathematics, physical sciences, social sciences. *Creative arts/performance:* applied art and design, art/fine arts, creative writing, dance, journalism/publications, music, performing arts, theater/drama. *Special achievements/activities:* community service, general special achievements/activities, leadership. *Special characteristics:* adult students, children of faculty/staff, children of union members/company employees, ethnic background, first-generation college students, general special characteristics, international students, local/state students, members of minority groups, previous college experience. *Tuition waivers:* Full or partial for employees or children of employees, senior citizens. *ROTC:* Army cooperative.

LOANS *Student loans:* $58,156,706 (76% need-based, 24% non-need-based). 76% of past graduating class borrowed through all loan programs. *Average indebtedness per student:* $33,201. *Average need-based loan:* Freshmen: $3338. Undergraduates: $4575. *Parent loans:* $8,515,996 (72% need-based, 28% non-need-based). *Programs:* Federal Direct (Subsidized and Unsubsidized Stafford, PLUS), Perkins, state.

WORK-STUDY *Federal work-study:* Total amount: $433,930; 230 jobs averaging $1908. *State or other work-study/employment:* Total amount: $1,199,058 (100% non-need-based). 872 part-time jobs averaging $1375.

APPLYING FOR FINANCIAL AID *Required financial aid forms:* FAFSA, state aid form. *Financial aid deadline (priority):* 3/1. *Notification date:* Continuous beginning 4/1. Students must reply within 2 weeks of notification.

CONTACT Mrs. Jeanne S. Lewis, Director of Financial Aid, Stockton University, 101 Vera King Farris Drive, Galloway, NJ 08205-9441, 609-652-4203. *Fax:* 609-626-5517. *E-mail:* jeanne.lewis@stockton.edu. *Website:* http://www.stockton.edu/.

STONEHILL COLLEGE
Easton, MA

Tuition & fees: $39,900	Average undergraduate aid package: $30,606

ABOUT THE INSTITUTION Independent Roman Catholic, coed. *Awards:* bachelor's degrees. 44 undergraduate majors. *Total enrollment:* 2,481. Undergraduates: 2,481. Freshmen: 734. Institutional methodology is used as a basis for awarding need-based institutional aid.

UNDERGRADUATE EXPENSES for 2016–2017 *Application fee:* $60. *Comprehensive fee:* $55,130 includes full-time tuition ($39,900) and room and board ($15,230). Room and board charges vary according to board plan. *Part-time tuition:* $1330 per credit. Part-time tuition and fees vary according to course load. *Payment plan:* Tuition prepayment.

FRESHMAN FINANCIAL AID (Fall 2016, est.) 650 applied for aid; of those 72% were deemed to have need. 100% of freshmen with need received aid; of those 43% had need fully met. *Average percent of need met:* 87% (excluding resources awarded to replace EFC). *Average financial aid package:* $28,147 (excluding resources awarded to replace EFC). 34% of all full-time freshmen had no need and received non-need-based gift aid.

UNDERGRADUATE FINANCIAL AID (Fall 2016, est.) 1,891 applied for aid; of those 85% were deemed to have need. 100% of undergraduates with need received aid; of those 46% had need fully met. *Average percent of need met:* 91% (excluding resources awarded to replace EFC). *Average financial aid package:* $30,606 (excluding resources awarded to replace EFC). 28% of all full-time undergraduates had no need and received non-need-based gift aid.

GIFT AID (NEED-BASED) *Total amount:* $36,771,183 (6% federal, 3% state, 89% institutional, 2% external sources). *Receiving aid:* Freshmen: 63% (461); all full-time undergraduates: 64% (1,559). *Average award:* Freshmen: $23,248; Undergraduates: $25,017. *Scholarships, grants, and awards:* Federal Pell, FSEOG, state, private, college/university gift aid from institutional funds.

GIFT AID (NON-NEED-BASED) *Total amount:* $15,046,803 (1% federal, 98% institutional, 1% external sources). *Receiving aid:* Freshmen: 18% (129). Undergraduates: 14% (341). *Average award:* Freshmen: $18,770. Undergraduates: $17,418. *Scholarships, grants, and awards by category:* Academic interests/achievement: general academic interests/achievements. *Special characteristics:* children of faculty/staff, children of union members/company employees, relatives of clergy, siblings of current students, veterans, veterans' children. *Tuition waivers:* Full or partial for employees or children of employees. *ROTC:* Army.

LOANS *Student loans:* $16,916,852 (46% need-based, 54% non-need-based). 74% of past graduating class borrowed through all loan programs. *Average indebtedness per student:* $35,462. *Average need-based loan:* Freshmen: $3779. Undergraduates: $4660. *Parent loans:* $7,812,625 (15% need-based, 85% non-need-based). *Programs:* Federal Direct (Subsidized and Unsubsidized Stafford, PLUS), Perkins, state.

WORK-STUDY *Federal work-study:* Total amount: $1,288,540; jobs available. *State or other work-study/employment:* Total amount: $309,500 (2% need-based, 98% non-need-based). Part-time jobs available.

ATHLETIC AWARDS Total amount: $2,806,679 (26% need-based, 74% non-need-based).

APPLYING FOR FINANCIAL AID *Required financial aid forms:* FAFSA, CSS Financial Aid PROFILE, noncustodial (divorced/separated) parent's statement. *Financial aid deadline (priority):* 12/1. *Notification date:* 4/1. Students must reply by 5/1.

CONTACT Rhonda Nickley, Office Manager, Stonehill College, 320 Washington Street, Easton, MA 02357, 508-565-1088. *Fax:* 508-565-1426. *E-mail:* finaid@stonehill.edu. *Website:* http://www.stonehill.edu/.

STONY BROOK UNIVERSITY, STATE UNIVERSITY OF NEW YORK
Stony Brook, NY

Tuition & fees (NY res): $8999	Average undergraduate aid package: $12,521

ABOUT THE INSTITUTION State-supported, coed. *Awards:* certificates, bachelor's, master's, and doctoral degrees. 63 undergraduate majors. *Total enrollment:* 25,734. Undergraduates: 17,026. Freshmen: 2,934. Federal methodology is used as a basis for awarding need-based institutional aid.

UNDERGRADUATE EXPENSES for 2016–2017 *Application fee:* $50. *Tuition, state resident:* full-time $6470; part-time $270 per credit hour. *Tuition, nonresident:* full-time $23,710; part-time $988 per credit hour. *Required fees:* full-time $2529; $125.40 per credit hour. Full-time tuition and fees vary according to course load and program. Part-time tuition and fees vary according to course load and program. *College room and board:* $12,882; *Room only:* $8082. Room and board charges vary according to board plan, housing facility, and location.

FRESHMAN FINANCIAL AID (Fall 2015) 2,139 applied for aid; of those 70% were deemed to have need. 99% of freshmen with need received aid; of those 17% had need fully met. *Average percent of need met:* 71% (excluding resources awarded to replace EFC). *Average financial aid package:* $13,687 (excluding resources awarded to replace EFC). 19% of all full-time freshmen had no need and received non-need-based gift aid.

UNDERGRADUATE FINANCIAL AID (Fall 2015) 10,506 applied for aid; of those 82% were deemed to have need. 98% of undergraduates with need received aid; of those 16% had need fully met. *Average percent of need met:* 66% (excluding resources awarded to replace EFC). *Average financial aid package:* $12,521 (excluding resources awarded to replace EFC). 10% of all full-time undergraduates had no need and received non-need-based gift aid.

GIFT AID (NEED-BASED) *Total amount:* $60,556,839 (42% federal, 34% state, 23% institutional, 1% external sources). *Receiving aid:* Freshmen: 48% (1,357); all full-time undergraduates: 47% (7,223). *Average award:* Freshmen: $10,195; Undergraduates: $8227. *Scholarships, grants, and awards:* Federal Pell, FSEOG, state, private, college/university gift aid from institutional funds.

GIFT AID (NON-NEED-BASED) *Total amount:* $11,201,417 (2% federal, 9% state, 75% institutional, 14% external sources). *Receiving aid:* Freshmen: 6% (180). Undergraduates: 3% (413). *Average award:* Freshmen: $5727. Undergraduates: $5073. *Scholarships, grants, and awards by category: Academic interests/achievement:* area/ethnic studies, biological sciences, business, computer science, engineering/technologies, English, foreign languages, general academic interests/achievements, health fields, international studies, mathematics, physical sciences, social sciences. *Creative arts/performance:* cinema/film/broadcasting, journalism/publications, music. *Special achievements/activities:* community service, leadership. *Special characteristics:* ethnic background, general special characteristics. *ROTC:* Army, Air Force cooperative.

LOANS *Student loans:* $82,479,718 (70% need-based, 30% non-need-based). 55% of past graduating class borrowed through all loan programs. *Average indebtedness per student:* $24,656. *Average need-based loan:* Freshmen: $3442. Undergraduates: $4554. *Parent loans:* $7,188,084 (39% need-based, 61% non-need-based). *Programs:* Federal Direct (Subsidized and Unsubsidized Stafford, PLUS), Perkins.

WORK-STUDY *Federal work-study:* 391 jobs averaging $1967. *State or other work-study/employment:* Total amount: $9,137,635 (32% need-based, 68% non-need-based). 2,594 part-time jobs averaging $3523.

ATHLETIC AWARDS Total amount: $5,989,204 (42% need-based, 58% non-need-based).

APPLYING FOR FINANCIAL AID *Required financial aid forms:* FAFSA, state aid form. *Financial aid deadline (priority):* 3/1. *Notification date:* Continuous beginning 4/1. Students must reply by 5/1.

CONTACT Office of Student Financial Aid and Scholarship Services, Stony Brook University, State University of New York, Administration Building, Room 180, Stony Brook, NY 11794, 631-632-6840. *Fax:* 631-632-9525. *E-mail:* finaid@stonybrook.edu. *Website:* http://www.stonybrook.edu/.

STRATFORD UNIVERSITY
Baltimore, MD

CONTACT Lesley Otterbein, Student Accounts Manager, Stratford University, 17 Commerce Street, Baltimore, MD 21202, 410-752-0490 or toll-free 800-624-9926 (in-state), 800-624-9926 Ext. 120 (out-of-state). *Fax:* 410-752-3730. *E-mail:* studentaccounts@stratford.edu. *Website:* http://www.stratford.edu/.

STRATFORD UNIVERSITY
Alexandria, VA

CONTACT Financial Aid Office, Stratford University, 2900 Eisenhower Avenue, Alexandria, VA 22314, 571-699-3200 or toll-free 800-444-0804. *Website:* http://www.stratford.edu/.

STRATFORD UNIVERSITY
Falls Church, VA

CONTACT Imane Babsiri, Student Account Manager, Stratford University, 7777 Leesburg Pike, Falls Church, VA 22043, 703-821-8570 Ext. 3401 or toll-free 800-444-0804. *E-mail:* ibabsiri@stratford.edu. *Website:* http://www.stratford.edu/.

STRATFORD UNIVERSITY
Glen Allen, VA

CONTACT Noshuo Rivers, Student Account Manager, Stratford University, 11104 West Broad Street, Glen Allen, VA 23060, 804-290-4231 or toll-free 877-373-5173. *E-mail:* studentaccounts@stratford.edu. *Website:* http://www.stratford.edu/.

STRATFORD UNIVERSITY
Newport News, VA

CONTACT Sheryl Kimberly, Student Accounts Manager, Stratford University, 836 J. Clyde Morris Boulevard, Newport News, VA 23601, 757-873-4235 or toll-free 855-873-4235. *E-mail:* skimberly@stratford.edu. *Website:* http://www.stratford.edu/.

STRATFORD UNIVERSITY
Virginia Beach, VA

CONTACT Financial Aid Office, Stratford University, 555 South Independence Boulevard, Virginia Beach, VA 23452, 757-497-4466 or toll-free 866-528-8363. *Website:* http://www.stratford.edu/.

STRATFORD UNIVERSITY
Woodbridge, VA

CONTACT Sherrese Whiting, Student Account Manager, Stratford University, 14349 Gideon Drive, Woodbridge, VA 22192, 703-897-1982 or toll-free 888-546-1250. *E-mail:* studentaccounts@stratford.edu. *Website:* http://www.stratford.edu/.

STRAYER UNIVERSITY–ALEXANDRIA CAMPUS
Alexandria, VA

CONTACT Financial Aid Office, Strayer University–Alexandria Campus, 2730 Eisenhower Avenue, Alexandria, VA 22314, 703-317-2626.
Website: http://www.strayer.edu/virginia/alexandria/.

STRAYER UNIVERSITY–ALLENTOWN CAMPUS
Center Valley, PA

CONTACT Financial Aid Office, Strayer University–Allentown Campus, 3800 Sierra Circle, Suite 300, Center Valley, PA 18034, 484-809-7770.
Website: http://www.strayer.edu/pennsylvania/allentown/.

STRAYER UNIVERSITY–ANNE ARUNDEL CAMPUS
Millersville, MD

CONTACT Financial Aid Office, Strayer University–Anne Arundel Campus, 1520 Jabez Run, Millersville, MD 21108, 410-923-4500.
Website: http://www.strayer.edu/maryland/anne-arundel/.

STRAYER UNIVERSITY–ARLINGTON CAMPUS
Arlington, VA

CONTACT Financial Aid Office, Strayer University–Arlington Campus, 2121 15th Street North, Arlington, VA 22201, 703-892-5100.
Website: http://www.strayer.edu/virginia/arlington/.

STRAYER UNIVERSITY–AUGUSTA CAMPUS
Augusta, GA

CONTACT Financial Aid Office, Strayer University–Augusta Campus, 1330 Augusta West Parkway, Augusta, GA 30909, 706-855-8233.
Website: http://www.strayer.edu/georgia/augusta/.

STRAYER UNIVERSITY–BAYMEADOWS CAMPUS
Jacksonville, FL

CONTACT Financial Aid Office, Strayer University–Baymeadows Campus, 8375 Dix Ellis Trail, Suite 200, Jacksonville, FL 32256, 904-538-1000.
Website: http://www.strayer.edu/florida/baymeadows/.

STRAYER UNIVERSITY–BIRMINGHAM CAMPUS
Birmingham, AL

CONTACT Financial Aid Office, Strayer University–Birmingham Campus, 3570 Grandview Parkway, Suite 200, Birmingham, AL 35243, 205-453-6300.
Website: http://www.strayer.edu/alabama/birmingham/.

STRAYER UNIVERSITY–BRICKELL CAMPUS
Miami, FL

CONTACT Financial Aid Office, Strayer University–Brickell Campus, 1201 Brickell Avenue, Suite 700, Miami, FL 33131, 305-507-5800.
Website: http://www.strayer.edu/florida/brickell/.

STRAYER UNIVERSITY–CENTER CITY CAMPUS
Philadelphia, PA

CONTACT Financial Aid Office, Strayer University–Center City Campus, 1601 Cherry Street, Suite 100, Philadelphia, PA 19102, 267-256-0200.
Website: http://www.strayer.edu/pennsylvania/center-city/.

STRAYER UNIVERSITY–CHAMBLEE CAMPUS
Atlanta, GA

CONTACT Financial Aid Office, Strayer University–Chamblee Campus, 3355 Northeast Expressway, Suite 100, Atlanta, GA 30341, 770-454-9270.
Website: http://www.strayer.edu/georgia/chamblee/.

STRAYER UNIVERSITY–CHARLESTON CAMPUS
North Charleston, SC

CONTACT Financial Aid Office, Strayer University–Charleston Campus, 5010 Wetland Crossing, North Charleston, SC 29418, 843-746-5100.
Website: http://www.strayer.edu/south-carolina/charleston/.

STRAYER UNIVERSITY–CHERRY HILL CAMPUS
Cherry Hill, NJ

CONTACT Financial Aid Office, Strayer University–Cherry Hill Campus, 2201 Route 38, Suite 100, Cherry Hill, NJ 08002, 856-482-4200.
Website: http://www.strayer.edu/new-jersey/cherry-hill/.

STRAYER UNIVERSITY–CHESAPEAKE CAMPUS
Chesapeake, VA

CONTACT Financial Aid Office, Strayer University–Chesapeake Campus, 676 Independence Parkway, Suite 300, Chesapeake, VA 23320, 757-382-9900. *Website:* http://www.strayer.edu/virginia/chesapeake/.

STRAYER UNIVERSITY–CHESTERFIELD CAMPUS
Midlothian, VA

CONTACT Financial Aid Office, Strayer University–Chesterfield Campus, 2820 Waterford Lake Drive, Suite 100, Midlothian, VA 23112, 804-763-6300. *Website:* http://www.strayer.edu/virginia/chesterfield/.

STRAYER UNIVERSITY–CHRISTIANA CAMPUS
Newark, DE

CONTACT Financial Aid Office, Strayer University–Christiana Campus, 240 Continental Drive, Suite 108, Newark, DE 19713, 302-292-6100. *Website:* http://www.strayer.edu/delaware/christiana/.

STRAYER UNIVERSITY–COBB COUNTY CAMPUS
Atlanta, GA

CONTACT Financial Aid Office, Strayer University–Cobb County Campus, 3101 Towercreek Parkway, SE, Suite 700, Atlanta, GA 30339-3256, 770-612-2170. *Website:* http://www.strayer.edu/georgia/cobb-county/.

STRAYER UNIVERSITY–COLUMBIA CAMPUS
Columbia, SC

CONTACT Financial Aid Office, Strayer University–Columbia Campus, 200 Center Point Circle, Suite 300, Columbia, SC 29210, 803-750-2500. *Website:* http://www.strayer.edu/south-carolina/columbia/.

STRAYER UNIVERSITY–CORAL SPRINGS CAMPUS
Pompano Beach, FL

CONTACT Financial Aid Office, Strayer University–Coral Springs Campus, 5830 Coral Ridge Drive, Suite 300, Pompano Beach, FL 33076, 954-369-0700. *Website:* http://www.strayer.edu/florida/coral-springs/.

STRAYER UNIVERSITY–DELAWARE COUNTY CAMPUS
Springfield, PA

CONTACT Financial Aid Office, Strayer University–Delaware County Campus, 760 West Sproul Road, Suite 200, Springfield, PA 19064-1215, 610-604-7700. *Website:* http://www.strayer.edu/pennsylvania/delaware-county/.

STRAYER UNIVERSITY–DORAL CAMPUS
Miami, FL

CONTACT Financial Aid Office, Strayer University–Doral Campus, 11430 Northwest 20th Street, Suite 150, Miami, FL 33172, 305-507-5700. *Website:* http://www.strayer.edu/florida/doral/.

STRAYER UNIVERSITY–DOUGLASVILLE CAMPUS
Douglasville, GA

CONTACT Financial Aid Office, Strayer University–Douglasville Campus, 4655 Timber Ridge Drive, Douglasville, GA 30135, 678-715-2200. *Website:* http://www.strayer.edu/georgia/douglasville/.

STRAYER UNIVERSITY–FORT LAUDERDALE CAMPUS
Fort Lauderdale, FL

CONTACT Financial Aid Office, Strayer University–Fort Lauderdale Campus, 2307 West Broward Boulevard, Suite 100, Fort Lauderdale, FL 33312, 954-745-6960. *Website:* http://www.strayer.edu/florida/fort-lauderdale/.

STRAYER UNIVERSITY–FREDERICKSBURG CAMPUS
Fredericksburg, VA

CONTACT Financial Aid Office, Strayer University–Fredericksburg Campus, 150 Riverside Parkway, Suite 100, Fredericksburg, VA 22406, 540-374-4300. *Website:* http://www.strayer.edu/virginia/fredericksburg/.

STRAYER UNIVERSITY–GREENSBORO CAMPUS
Greensboro, NC

CONTACT Financial Aid Office, Strayer University–Greensboro Campus, 4900 Koger Boulevard, Suite 400, Greensboro, NC 27407, 336-315-7800. *Website:* http://www.strayer.edu/north-carolina/greensboro/.

STRAYER UNIVERSITY–GREENVILLE CAMPUS

Greenville, SC

CONTACT Financial Aid Office, Strayer University–Greenville Campus, 555 North Pleasantburg Drive, Suite 300, Greenville, SC 29607, 864-250-7000.
Website: http://www.strayer.edu/south-carolina/greenville/.

STRAYER UNIVERSITY–HENRICO CAMPUS

Glen Allen, VA

CONTACT Financial Aid Office, Strayer University–Henrico Campus, 11501 Nuckols Road, Glen Allen, VA 23059, 804-527-1000.
Website: http://www.strayer.edu/virginia/henrico/.

STRAYER UNIVERSITY–HUNTERSVILLE CAMPUS

Huntersville, NC

CONTACT Financial Aid Office, Strayer University–Huntersville Campus, 13620 Reese Boulevard, Suite 310, Huntersville, NC 28078, 704-379-6800.
Website: http://www.strayer.edu/north-carolina/huntersville/.

STRAYER UNIVERSITY–HUNTSVILLE CAMPUS

Huntsville, AL

CONTACT Financial Aid Office, Strayer University–Huntsville Campus, 4955 Corporate Drive, NW, Suite 200, Huntsville, AL 35805, 256-665-9800.
Website: http://www.strayer.edu/alabama/huntsville/.

STRAYER UNIVERSITY–IRVING CAMPUS

Irving, TX

CONTACT Financial Aid Office, Strayer University–Irving Campus, 7701 Las Colinas Ridge, Suite 450, Irving, TX 75063, 214-429-3900.
Website: http://www.strayer.edu/texas/irving/.

STRAYER UNIVERSITY–JACKSON CAMPUS

Jackson, MS

CONTACT Financial Aid Office, Strayer University–Jackson Campus, 460 Briarwood Drive, Suite 200, Jackson, MS 39206, 601-718-5900.
Website: http://www.strayer.edu/mississippi/jackson/.

STRAYER UNIVERSITY–KING OF PRUSSIA CAMPUS

King of Prussia, PA

CONTACT Financial Aid Office, Strayer University–King of Prussia Campus, 234 Mall Boulevard, Suite G-50, King of Prussia, PA 19406, 610-992-1700.
Website: http://www.strayer.edu/pennsylvania/king-prussia/.

STRAYER UNIVERSITY–KNOXVILLE CAMPUS

Knoxville, TN

CONTACT Financial Aid Office, Strayer University–Knoxville Campus, 10118 Parkside Drive, Suite 200, Knoxville, TN 37922, 865-288-6000.
Website: http://www.strayer.edu/tennessee/knoxville/.

STRAYER UNIVERSITY–LAWRENCEVILLE CAMPUS

Lawrenceville, NJ

CONTACT Financial Aid Office, Strayer University–Lawrenceville Campus, 3150 Brunswick Pike, Suite 100, Lawrenceville, NJ 08648, 609-406-7600.
Website: http://www.strayer.edu/new-jersey/lawrenceville/.

STRAYER UNIVERSITY–LITHONIA CAMPUS

Lithonia, GA

CONTACT Financial Aid Office, Strayer University–Lithonia Campus, 3120 Stonecrest Boulevard, Suite 200, Lithonia, GA 30038, 678-323-7700.
Website: http://www.strayer.edu/georgia/lithonia/.

STRAYER UNIVERSITY–LITTLE ROCK CAMPUS

Little Rock, AR

CONTACT Financial Aid Office, Strayer University–Little Rock Campus, 10825 Financial Centre Parkway, Suite 131, Little Rock, AR 72211.
Website: http://www.strayer.edu/arkansas/little-rock/.

STRAYER UNIVERSITY–LOUDOUN CAMPUS

Ashburn, VA

CONTACT Financial Aid Office, Strayer University–Loudoun Campus, 45150 Russell Branch Parkway, Suite 200, Ashburn, VA 20147, 703-729-8800.
Website: http://www.strayer.edu/virginia/loudoun/.

STRAYER UNIVERSITY–LOWER BUCKS COUNTY CAMPUS

Trevose, PA

CONTACT Financial Aid Office, Strayer University–Lower Bucks County Campus, 3800 Horizon Boulevard, Suite 100, Trevose, PA 19053, 215-953-5999.
Website: http://www.strayer.edu/pennsylvania/lower-bucks-county/.

STRAYER UNIVERSITY–MAITLAND CAMPUS

Maitland, FL

CONTACT Financial Aid Office, Strayer University–Maitland Campus, 850 Trafalgar Court, Suite 360, Maitland, FL 32751, 407-618-5900.
Website: http://www.strayer.edu/florida/maitland/.

STRAYER UNIVERSITY–MANASSAS CAMPUS

Manassas, VA

CONTACT Financial Aid Office, Strayer University–Manassas Campus, 9990 Battleview Parkway, Manassas, VA 20109, 703-330-8400.
Website: http://www.strayer.edu/virginia/manassas/.

STRAYER UNIVERSITY–MIRAMAR CAMPUS

Miramar, FL

CONTACT Financial Aid Office, Strayer University–Miramar Campus, 15620 Southwest 29th Street, Miramar, FL 33027, 954-378-2400.
Website: http://www.strayer.edu/florida/miramar/.

STRAYER UNIVERSITY–MORROW CAMPUS

Morrow, GA

CONTACT Financial Aid Office, Strayer University–Morrow Campus, 3000 Corporate Center Drive, Suite 100, Morrow, GA 30260, 678-422-4100.
Website: http://www.strayer.edu/georgia/morrow/.

STRAYER UNIVERSITY–NASHVILLE CAMPUS

Nashville, TN

CONTACT Financial Aid Office, Strayer University–Nashville Campus, 1809 Dabbs Avenue, Nashville, TN 37210, 615-871-2260.
Website: http://www.strayer.edu/tennessee/nashville/.

STRAYER UNIVERSITY–NEWPORT NEWS CAMPUS

Newport News, VA

CONTACT Financial Aid Office, Strayer University–Newport News Campus, 99 Old Oyster Point Road, Unit 1, Newport News, VA 23602, 757-873-3100.
Website: http://www.strayer.edu/virginia/newport-news/.

STRAYER UNIVERSITY–NORTH AUSTIN CAMPUS

Austin, TX

CONTACT Financial Aid Office, Strayer University–North Austin Campus, 8501 North Mopac Expressway, Suite 100, Austin, TX 78759, 512-568-3300.
Website: http://www.strayer.edu/texas/north-austin/.

STRAYER UNIVERSITY–NORTH CHARLOTTE CAMPUS

Concord, NC

CONTACT Financial Aid Office, Strayer University–North Charlotte Campus, 7870 Commons Park Circle NW, Concord, NC 28027, 704-886-6500.
Website: http://www.strayer.edu/north-carolina/north-charlotte/.

STRAYER UNIVERSITY–NORTH RALEIGH CAMPUS

Raleigh, NC

CONTACT Financial Aid Office, Strayer University–North Raleigh Campus, 8701 Wadford Drive, Raleigh, NC 27616, 919-878-9900.
Website: http://www.strayer.edu/north-carolina/north-raleigh/.

STRAYER UNIVERSITY–NORTHWEST HOUSTON CAMPUS

Houston, TX

CONTACT Financial Aid Office, Strayer University–Northwest Houston Campus, 10940 West Sam Houston Parkway North, Suite 200, Houston, TX 77064, 281-949-1800.
Website: http://www.strayer.edu/texas/northwest-houston/.

STRAYER UNIVERSITY–ORLANDO EAST CAMPUS

Orlando, FL

CONTACT Financial Aid Office, Strayer University–Orlando East Campus, 2200 North Alafaya Trail, Suite 500, Orlando, FL 32826, 407-926-2000.
Website: http://www.strayer.edu/florida/orlando-east/.

STRAYER UNIVERSITY–OWINGS MILLS CAMPUS

Owings Mills, MD

CONTACT Financial Aid Office, Strayer University–Owings Mills Campus, 500 Redland Court, Suite 100, Owings Mills, MD 21117, 443-394-3339.
Website: http://www.strayer.edu/maryland/owings-mills/.

STRAYER UNIVERSITY–PALM BEACH GARDENS CAMPUS

West Palm Beach, FL

CONTACT Financial Aid Office, Strayer University–Palm Beach Gardens Campus, 11025 RCA Center Drive, Suite 200, West Palm Beach, FL 33410, 561-904-3000.
Website: http://www.strayer.edu/florida/palm-beach-gardens/.

STRAYER UNIVERSITY–PISCATAWAY CAMPUS

Piscataway, NJ

CONTACT Financial Aid Office, Strayer University–Piscataway Campus, 242 Old New Brunswick Road, Suite 220, Piscataway, NJ 08854, 732-743-3800.
Website: http://www.strayer.edu/new-jersey/piscataway/.

STRAYER UNIVERSITY–PLANO CAMPUS

Plano, TX

CONTACT Financial Aid Office, Strayer University–Plano Campus, 2701 North Dallas Parkway, Suite 300, Plano, TX 75093, 972-535-3700.
Website: http://www.strayer.edu/texas/plano/.

STRAYER UNIVERSITY–PRINCE GEORGE'S CAMPUS

Suitland, MD

CONTACT Financial Aid Office, Strayer University–Prince George's Campus, 4710 Auth Place, First Floor, Suitland, MD 20746, 301-423-3600.
Website: http://www.strayer.edu/maryland/prince-georges/.

STRAYER UNIVERSITY–ROCKVILLE CAMPUS

Rockville, MD

CONTACT Financial Aid Office, Strayer University–Rockville Campus, 4 Research Place, Suite 100, Rockville, MD 20850, 301-548-5500.
Website: http://www.strayer.edu/maryland/rockville/.

STRAYER UNIVERSITY–ROSWELL CAMPUS

Roswell, GA

CONTACT Financial Aid Office, Strayer University–Roswell Campus, 100 Mansell Court East, Suite 100, Roswell, GA 30076, 770-650-3000.
Website: http://www.strayer.edu/georgia/roswell/.

STRAYER UNIVERSITY–RTP CAMPUS

Morrisville, NC

CONTACT Financial Aid Office, Strayer University–RTP Campus, 4 Copley Parkway, Morrisville, NC 27560, 919-466-4400.
Website: http://www.strayer.edu/north-carolina/rtp/.

STRAYER UNIVERSITY–SAND LAKE CAMPUS

Orlando, FL

CONTACT Financial Aid Office, Strayer University–Sand Lake Campus, 8541 South Park Circle, Building 900, Orlando, FL 32819, 407-264-9400.
Website: http://www.strayer.edu/florida/sand-lake/.

STRAYER UNIVERSITY–SAVANNAH CAMPUS

Savannah, GA

CONTACT Financial Aid Office, Strayer University–Savannah Campus, 20 Martin Court, Savannah, GA 31419, 912-921-2900.
Website: http://www.strayer.edu/georgia/savannah/.

STRAYER UNIVERSITY–SHELBY CAMPUS

Memphis, TN

CONTACT Financial Aid Office, Strayer University–Shelby Campus, 7275 Appling Farms Parkway, Memphis, TN 38133, 901-383-6750.
Website: http://www.strayer.edu/tennessee/shelby/.

STRAYER UNIVERSITY–SOUTH CHARLOTTE CAMPUS

Charlotte, NC

CONTACT Financial Aid Office, Strayer University–South Charlotte Campus, 9101 Kings Parade Boulevard, Suite 200, Charlotte, NC 28273, 704-499-9200.
Website: http://www.strayer.edu/north-carolina/south-charlotte/.

STRAYER UNIVERSITY–SOUTH RALEIGH CAMPUS
Raleigh, NC

CONTACT Financial Aid Office, Strayer University–South Raleigh Campus, 3421 Olympia Drive, Raleigh, NC 27603, 919-890-7500.
Website: http://www.strayer.edu/north-carolina/south-raleigh/.

STRAYER UNIVERSITY–TAKOMA PARK CAMPUS
Washington, DC

CONTACT Financial Aid Office, Strayer University–Takoma Park Campus, 6830 Laurel Street, NW, Washington, DC 20012, 202-722-8100.
Website: http://www.strayer.edu/district-columbia/takoma-park/.

STRAYER UNIVERSITY–TAMPA EAST CAMPUS
Tampa, FL

CONTACT Financial Aid Office, Strayer University–Tampa East Campus, 5650 Breckenridge Park Drive, Suite 300, Tampa, FL 33610, 813-663-0100.
Website: http://www.strayer.edu/florida/tampa-east/.

STRAYER UNIVERSITY–TAMPA WESTSHORE CAMPUS
Tampa, FL

CONTACT Financial Aid Office, Strayer University–Tampa Westshore Campus, 4902 Eisenhower Boulevard, Suite 100, Tampa, FL 33634, 813-882-0100.
Website: http://www.strayer.edu/florida/tampa-westshore/.

STRAYER UNIVERSITY–TEAYS VALLEY CAMPUS
Scott Depot, WV

CONTACT Financial Aid Office, Strayer University–Teays Valley Campus, 3 Corporate Center Drive, Scott Depot, WV 25560, 304-760-1700.
Website: http://www.strayer.edu/west-virginia/teays-valley/.

STRAYER UNIVERSITY–THOUSAND OAKS CAMPUS
Memphis, TN

CONTACT Financial Aid Office, Strayer University–Thousand Oaks Campus, 2620 Thousand Oaks Boulevard, Suite 1100, Memphis, TN 38118, 901-369-0835.
Website: http://www.strayer.edu/tennessee/thousand-oaks/.

STRAYER UNIVERSITY–VIRGINIA BEACH CAMPUS
Virginia Beach, VA

CONTACT Financial Aid Office, Strayer University–Virginia Beach Campus, 249 Central Park Avenue, Suite 350, Virginia Beach, VA 23462, 757-493-6000.
Website: http://www.strayer.edu/virginia/virginia-beach/.

STRAYER UNIVERSITY–WARRENDALE CAMPUS
Warrendale, PA

CONTACT Financial Aid Office, Strayer University–Warrendale Campus, 802 Warrendale Village Drive, Warrendale, PA 15086, 724-799-2900.
Website: http://www.strayer.edu/pennsylvania/warrendale/.

STRAYER UNIVERSITY–WASHINGTON CAMPUS
Washington, DC

CONTACT Financial Aid Office, Strayer University–Washington Campus, 1133 15th Street, NW, Washington, DC 20025, 202-408-2400.
Website: http://www.strayer.edu/district-columbia/washington/.

STRAYER UNIVERSITY–WHITE MARSH CAMPUS
Nottingham, MD

CONTACT Financial Aid Office, Strayer University–White Marsh Campus, 9920 Franklin Square Drive, Suite 200, Nottingham, MD 21236, 410-238-9000.
Website: http://www.strayer.edu/maryland/white-marsh/.

STRAYER UNIVERSITY–WILLINGBORO CAMPUS
Willingboro, NJ

CONTACT Financial Aid Office, Strayer University–Willingboro Campus, 300 Willingboro Parkway, Willingboro Town Center, Suite 125, Willingboro, NJ 08046, 609-835-6000.
Website: http://www.strayer.edu/new-jersey/willingboro/.

STRAYER UNIVERSITY–WOODBRIDGE CAMPUS
Woodbridge, VA

CONTACT Financial Aid Office, Strayer University–Woodbridge Campus, 13385 Minnieville Road, Woodbridge, VA 22192, 703-878-2800.
Website: http://www.strayer.edu/virginia/woodbridge/.

SUFFOLK UNIVERSITY
Boston, MA

Tuition & fees: $37,266	Average undergraduate aid package: $31,105

ABOUT THE INSTITUTION Independent, coed. *Awards:* certificates, diplomas, associate, bachelor's, master's, and doctoral degrees (doctoral degree in law). 46 undergraduate majors. *Total enrollment:* 7,560. Undergraduates: 5,290. Freshmen: 1,205. Federal methodology is used as a basis for awarding need-based institutional aid.

UNDERGRADUATE EXPENSES for 2017–2018 *Application fee:* $50. *One-time required fee:* $220. *Comprehensive fee:* $53,842 includes full-time tuition ($37,128), mandatory fees ($138), and room and board ($16,576). *College room only:* $13,928. Full-time tuition and fees vary according to course level and reciprocity agreements. Room and board charges vary according to board plan and housing facility. *Part-time tuition:* $1092 per credit hour. *Part-time fees:* $17 per term. Part-time tuition and fees vary according to course level, course load, and reciprocity agreements.

FRESHMAN FINANCIAL AID (Fall 2016, est.) 905 applied for aid; of those 91% were deemed to have need. 100% of freshmen with need received aid; of those 25% had need fully met. *Average percent of need met:* 78% (excluding resources awarded to replace EFC). *Average financial aid package:* $32,233 (excluding resources awarded to replace EFC). 24% of all full-time freshmen had no need and received non-need-based gift aid.

UNDERGRADUATE FINANCIAL AID (Fall 2016, est.) 3,100 applied for aid; of those 92% were deemed to have need. 100% of undergraduates with need received aid; of those 24% had need fully met. *Average percent of need met:* 76% (excluding resources awarded to replace EFC). *Average financial aid package:* $31,105 (excluding resources awarded to replace EFC). 27% of all full-time undergraduates had no need and received non-need-based gift aid.

GIFT AID (NEED-BASED) *Total amount:* $23,268,143 (29% federal, 7% state, 60% institutional, 4% external sources). *Receiving aid:* Freshmen: 60% (715); all full-time undergraduates: 46% (2,303). *Average award:* Freshmen: $12,505; Undergraduates: $13,578. *Scholarships, grants, and awards:* Federal Pell, FSEOG, state, private, college/university gift aid from institutional funds.

GIFT AID (NON-NEED-BASED) *Total amount:* $51,795,168 (100% institutional). *Receiving aid:* Freshmen: 65% (780). Undergraduates: 47% (2,363). *Average award:* Freshmen: $14,735. Undergraduates: $13,834. *Scholarships, grants, and awards by category:* Academic interests/achievement: 2,820 awards ($30,690,358 total): business, engineering/technologies, foreign languages, general academic interests/achievements, mathematics. Creative arts/performance: 2 awards ($2730 total): general creative arts/performance, journalism/publications. Special achievements/activities: 202 awards ($619,144 total): community service, general special achievements/activities, leadership. Special characteristics: 114 awards ($111,000 total): children and siblings of alumni, children of faculty/staff, general special characteristics, siblings of current students, veterans. *Tuition waivers:* Full or partial for children of alumni, employees or children of employees, senior citizens. *ROTC:* Army cooperative.

LOANS *Student loans:* $29,376,945 (41% need-based, 59% non-need-based). 75% of past graduating class borrowed through all loan programs. *Average indebtedness per student:* $39,091. *Average need-based loan:* Freshmen: $4689. Undergraduates: $5266. *Parent loans:* $9,217,253 (100% non-need-based). *Programs:* Federal Direct (Subsidized and Unsubsidized Stafford, PLUS), Perkins, state, college/university.

WORK-STUDY *Federal work-study:* Total amount: $2,216,176; 925 jobs averaging $2396. *State or other work-study/employment:* Total amount: $1,744,368 (100% non-need-based). 565 part-time jobs averaging $3643.

APPLYING FOR FINANCIAL AID *Required financial aid form:* FAFSA. *Financial aid deadline:* 3/1. *Notification date:* Continuous beginning 2/5. Students must reply by 5/1 or within 2 weeks of notification.

CONTACT Ms. Christine A. Perry, Director of Student Financial Services, Suffolk University, 8 Ashburton Place, Boston, MA 02108, 617-573-8470 or toll-free 800-6-SUFFOLK. *Fax:* 617-720-3579. *E-mail:* finaid@suffolk.edu. *Website:* http://www.suffolk.edu/.

SULLIVAN UNIVERSITY
Louisville, KY

CONTACT Charlene Geiser, Financial Planning Office, Sullivan University, 3101 Bardstown Road, Louisville, KY 40205, 502-456-6504 Ext. 311 or toll-free 800-844-1354. *Fax:* 502-456-0040. *E-mail:* cgeiser@sullivan.edu. *Website:* http://www.sullivan.edu/.

SUL ROSS STATE UNIVERSITY
Alpine, TX

ABOUT THE INSTITUTION State-supported, coed. *Awards:* bachelor's and master's degrees. 22 undergraduate majors. *Total enrollment:* 1,973. Undergraduates: 1,359. Freshmen: 351.

GIFT AID (NEED-BASED) *Scholarships, grants, and awards:* Federal Pell, FSEOG, state, private, college/university gift aid from institutional funds.

GIFT AID (NON-NEED-BASED) *Scholarships, grants, and awards by category:* Academic interests/achievement: agriculture, biological sciences, business, education, English, foreign languages, general academic interests/achievements, health fields. Creative arts/performance: art/fine arts, cinema/film/broadcasting, journalism/publications, music, theater/drama. Special achievements/activities: leadership. Special characteristics: children and siblings of alumni, local/state students.

LOANS *Programs:* Federal Direct (Subsidized and Unsubsidized Stafford, PLUS), state, college/university.

APPLYING FOR FINANCIAL AID *Required financial aid forms:* FAFSA, institution's own form, business/farm supplement.

CONTACT Mickey Corbett, Director of Financial Aid, Sul Ross State University, Box C-2, Lawrence Hall, Alpine, TX 79832, 432-837-8055 or toll-free 888-722-7778. *Fax:* 432-837-8411. *E-mail:* fa@sulross.edu. *Website:* http://www.sulross.edu/.

SUM BIBLE COLLEGE & THEOLOGICAL SEMINARY
Oakland, CA

CONTACT Financial Aid Office, SUM Bible College & Theological Seminary, 735 105th Avenue, Oakland, CA 94603, 510-567-6174 or toll-free 888-567-6174. *Website:* http://www.sum.edu/.

SUSQUEHANNA UNIVERSITY
Selinsgrove, PA

Tuition & fees: $45,470	Average undergraduate aid package: $34,622

ABOUT THE INSTITUTION Independent Evangelical Lutheran Church in America, coed. *Awards:* bachelor's degrees (also offers evening associate degree program limited to local adult students). 53 undergraduate majors. *Total enrollment:* 2,195. Undergraduates: 2,195. Freshmen: 637. Both federal and institutional methodology are used as a basis for awarding need-based institutional aid.

UNDERGRADUATE EXPENSES for 2017–2018 *Comprehensive fee:* $57,560 includes full-time tuition ($44,890), mandatory fees ($580), and room and board ($12,090). *College room only:* $6320. Room and board charges vary according to board plan. *Part-time tuition:* $1430 per credit hour. *Payment plan:* Tuition prepayment.

FRESHMAN FINANCIAL AID (Fall 2016, est.) 593 applied for aid; of those 86% were deemed to have need. 100% of freshmen with need received aid; of those 24% had need fully met. *Average percent of need met:* 83% (excluding resources awarded to replace EFC). *Average financial aid package:* $35,083 (excluding resources awarded to replace EFC). 19% of all full-time freshmen had no need and received non-need-based gift aid.

UNDERGRADUATE FINANCIAL AID (Fall 2016, est.) 1,877 applied for aid; of those 90% were deemed to have need. 100% of undergraduates with need received aid; of those 20% had need fully met. *Average percent of need met:* 81% (excluding resources awarded to replace EFC). *Average financial aid package:* $34,622 (excluding resources awarded to replace EFC). 23% of all full-time undergraduates had no need and received non-need-based gift aid.

GIFT AID (NEED-BASED) *Total amount:* $49,073,096 (6% federal, 4% state, 88% institutional, 2% external sources). *Receiving aid:* Freshmen: 80% (511); all full-time undergraduates: 84% (1,691). *Average award:* Freshmen: $31,727; Undergraduates: $29,983. *Scholarships, grants, and awards:* Federal Pell, FSEOG, state, private, college/university gift aid from institutional funds.

GIFT AID (NON-NEED-BASED) *Total amount:* $12,504,211 (1% federal, 92% institutional, 7% external sources). *Receiving aid:* Freshmen: 15% (98). Undergraduates: 13% (255). *Average award:* Freshmen: $24,566. Undergraduates: $20,454. *Scholarships, grants, and awards by category:* Academic interests/achievement: business, general academic interests/achievements. *Creative arts/performance:* creative writing, music, theater/drama. *Special achievements/activities:* general special achievements/activities, leadership. *Special characteristics:* children and siblings of alumni, children of faculty/staff, relatives of clergy, veterans. *Tuition waivers:* Full or partial for employees or children of employees. *ROTC:* Army cooperative.

LOANS *Student loans:* $15,919,440 (68% need-based, 32% non-need-based). 80% of past graduating class borrowed through all loan programs. *Average indebtedness per student:* $36,882. *Average need-based loan:* Freshmen: $3033. Undergraduates: $4246. *Parent loans:* $7,212,254 (44% need-based, 56% non-need-based). *Programs:* Federal Direct (Subsidized and Unsubsidized Stafford, PLUS), Perkins, college/university.

WORK-STUDY *Federal work-study:* Total amount: $1,605,608; jobs available. *State or other work-study/employment:* Total amount: $637,466 (51% need-based, 49% non-need-based). Part-time jobs available.

APPLYING FOR FINANCIAL AID *Required financial aid forms:* FAFSA, federal income tax form(s). *Financial aid deadline (priority):* 11/1. *Notification date:* 12/1. Students must reply by 5/1.

CONTACT Ms. Erin M. Wolfe, Director of Financial Aid, Susquehanna University, 514 University Avenue, Selinsgrove, PA 17870, 570-372-4450 or toll-free 800-326-9672. *Fax:* 570-372-2722. *E-mail:* wolfeerin@susqu.edu.
Website: http://www.susqu.edu/.

SWARTHMORE COLLEGE
Swarthmore, PA

Tuition & fees: $50,822	Average undergraduate aid package: $47,255

ABOUT THE INSTITUTION Independent, coed. *Awards:* bachelor's degrees. 48 undergraduate majors. *Total enrollment:* 1,620. Undergraduates: 1,620. Freshmen: 415. Institutional methodology is used as a basis for awarding need-based institutional aid.

UNDERGRADUATE EXPENSES for 2017–2018 *Comprehensive fee:* $65,774 includes full-time tuition ($50,424), mandatory fees ($398), and room and board ($14,952). *College room only:* $7670. Room and board charges vary according to board plan.

FRESHMAN FINANCIAL AID (Fall 2016, est.) 290 applied for aid; of those 84% were deemed to have need. 100% of freshmen with need received aid; of those 100% had need fully met. *Average percent of need met:* 100% (excluding resources awarded to replace EFC). *Average financial aid package:* $48,573 (excluding resources awarded to replace EFC). 1% of all full-time freshmen had no need and received non-need-based gift aid.

UNDERGRADUATE FINANCIAL AID (Fall 2016, est.) 985 applied for aid; of those 88% were deemed to have need. 100% of undergraduates with need received aid; of those 100% had need fully met. *Average percent of need met:* 100% (excluding resources awarded to replace EFC). *Average financial aid package:* $47,255 (excluding resources awarded to replace EFC). 1% of all full-time undergraduates had no need and received non-need-based gift aid.

GIFT AID (NEED-BASED) *Total amount:* $39,294,411 (4% federal, 94% institutional, 2% external sources). *Receiving aid:* Freshmen: 59% (243); all full-time undergraduates: 54% (867). *Average award:* Freshmen: $46,897; Undergraduates: $45,536. *Scholarships, grants, and awards:* Federal Pell, FSEOG, state, private, college/university gift aid from institutional funds.

GIFT AID (NON-NEED-BASED) *Total amount:* $725,149 (81% institutional, 19% external sources). *Average award:* Freshmen: $48,720. Undergraduates: $48,720. *Scholarships, grants, and awards by category:* Special characteristics: 13 awards ($584,840 total): local/state students. *ROTC:* Army cooperative, Naval cooperative, Air Force cooperative.

LOANS *Student loans:* $1,468,650 (100% non-need-based). 31% of past graduating class borrowed through all loan programs. *Average indebtedness per student:* $22,957. *Parent loans:* $1,738,590 (100% non-need-based). *Programs:* Federal Direct (Subsidized and Unsubsidized Stafford, PLUS), Perkins, college/university.

WORK-STUDY *Federal work-study:* Total amount: $975,562; 765 jobs averaging $1949. *State or other work-study/employment:* Total amount: $797,994 (88% need-based, 12% non-need-based). Part-time jobs available.

APPLYING FOR FINANCIAL AID *Required financial aid forms:* FAFSA, CSS Financial Aid PROFILE, noncustodial (divorced/separated) parent's statement, federal income tax form(s), W-2 forms. *Financial aid deadline:* 1/1. *Notification date:* 4/1. Students must reply by 5/1.

CONTACT Varo L. Duffins, Director of Financial Aid, Swarthmore College, 500 College Avenue, Swarthmore, PA 19081-1397, 610-328-8358 or toll-free 800-667-3110. *Fax:* 610-690-5751. *E-mail:* finaid@swarthmore.edu.
Website: http://www.swarthmore.edu/.

SWEDISH INSTITUTE, COLLEGE OF HEALTH SCIENCES
New York, NY

CONTACT Financial Aid Office, Swedish Institute, College of Health Sciences, 226 West 26th Street, New York, NY 10001-6700, 212-924-5900.
Website: http://www.swedishinstitute.edu/.

SWEET BRIAR COLLEGE
Sweet Briar, VA

Tuition & fees: $37,160	Average undergraduate aid package: $33,548

ABOUT THE INSTITUTION Independent, women only. *Awards:* bachelor's and master's degrees. 32 undergraduate majors. *Total enrollment:* 376. Undergraduates: 365. Freshmen: 134. Federal methodology is used as a basis for awarding need-based institutional aid.

UNDERGRADUATE EXPENSES for 2017–2018 *Comprehensive fee:* $50,060 includes full-time tuition ($36,520), mandatory fees ($640), and room and board ($12,900). Room and board charges vary according to board plan. *Part-time tuition:* $1070 per credit hour.

FRESHMAN FINANCIAL AID (Fall 2015) 23 applied for aid; of those 100% were deemed to have need. 100% of freshmen with need received aid; of those 17% had need fully met. *Average percent of need met:* 68% (excluding resources awarded to replace EFC). *Average financial aid package:* $12,981 (excluding resources awarded to replace EFC).

UNDERGRADUATE FINANCIAL AID (Fall 2015) 199 applied for aid; of those 90% were deemed to have need. 100% of undergraduates with need received aid; of those 24% had need fully met. *Average percent of need met:* 83% (excluding resources awarded to replace EFC). *Average financial aid package:* $33,548 (excluding resources awarded to replace EFC). 22% of all full-time undergraduates had no need and received non-need-based gift aid.

GIFT AID (NEED-BASED) *Total amount:* $5,083,230 (8% federal, 4% state, 86% institutional, 2% external sources). *Receiving aid:* Freshmen: 92% (22); all full-time undergraduates: 77% (179). *Average award:* Freshmen: $25,949; Undergraduates: $28,394. *Scholarships, grants, and awards:* Federal Pell, FSEOG, state, private, college/university gift aid from institutional funds, United Negro College Fund.

GIFT AID (NON-NEED-BASED) *Total amount:* $1,441,711 (8% state, 90% institutional, 2% external sources). *Receiving aid:* Freshmen: 21% (5). Undergraduates: 20% (47). *Average award:* Undergraduates: $20,074. *Scholarships, grants, and awards by category:* Academic interests/achievement: premedicine. *Creative arts/performance:* music. *Tuition waivers:* Full or partial for employees or children of employees, adult students, senior citizens.

LOANS *Student loans:* $1,111,708 (81% need-based, 19% non-need-based). 70% of past graduating class borrowed through all loan programs. *Average indebtedness per student:* $33,026. *Average need-based loan:* Freshmen: $3463. Undergraduates: $4973. *Parent loans:* $750,453 (33% need-based, 67% non-need-based). *Programs:* Federal Direct (Subsidized and Unsubsidized Stafford, PLUS), Perkins, college/university.

WORK-STUDY *Federal work-study:* jobs available. *State or other work-study/employment:* Total amount: $6000 (100% need-based). Part-time jobs available.

APPLYING FOR FINANCIAL AID *Required financial aid forms:* FAFSA, noncustodial (divorced/separated) parent's statement. *Notification date:* Continuous.

CONTACT Wanda Spradley, Director of Financial Aid, Sweet Briar College, Box 1095, Sweet Briar, VA 24595, 800-381-6156 or toll-free 800-381-6142. *Fax:* 434-381-6450. *E-mail:* spradley@sbc.edu.
Website: http://www.sbc.edu/.

SYRACUSE UNIVERSITY
Syracuse, NY

Tuition & fees: $45,022	Average undergraduate aid package: $37,600

ABOUT THE INSTITUTION Independent, coed. *Awards:* certificates, bachelor's, master's, and doctoral degrees. 145 undergraduate majors. *Total enrollment:* 21,970. Undergraduates: 15,218. Freshmen: 3,712. Both federal and institutional methodology are used as a basis for awarding need-based institutional aid.

UNDERGRADUATE EXPENSES for 2016–2017 *Application fee:* $75. *Comprehensive fee:* $60,239 includes full-time tuition ($43,440), mandatory fees ($1582), and room and board ($15,217). *College room only:* $8067. Full-time tuition and fees vary according to course load. Room and board charges vary according to board plan and housing facility. *Part-time tuition:* $1891 per credit hour. Part-time tuition and fees vary according to course load. *Payment plan:* Tuition prepayment.

FRESHMAN FINANCIAL AID (Fall 2016, est.) 2,513 applied for aid; of those 71% were deemed to have need. 100% of freshmen with need received aid; of those 51% had need fully met. *Average percent of need met:* 96% (excluding resources awarded to replace EFC). *Average financial aid package:* $36,040 (excluding resources awarded to replace EFC). 19% of all full-time freshmen had no need and received non-need-based gift aid.

UNDERGRADUATE FINANCIAL AID (Fall 2016, est.) 9,053 applied for aid; of those 83% were deemed to have need. 100% of undergraduates with need received aid; of those 42% had need fully met. *Average percent of need met:* 93% (excluding resources awarded to replace EFC). *Average financial aid package:* $37,600 (excluding resources awarded to replace EFC). 14% of all full-time undergraduates had no need and received non-need-based gift aid.

GIFT AID (NEED-BASED) *Total amount:* $237,698,777 (9% federal, 4% state, 86% institutional, 1% external sources). *Receiving aid:* Freshmen: 45% (1,664); all full-time undergraduates: 48% (6,910). *Average award:* Freshmen: $28,517; Undergraduates: $29,432. *Scholarships, grants, and awards:* Federal Pell, FSEOG, state, private, college/university gift aid from institutional funds.

GIFT AID (NON-NEED-BASED) *Total amount:* $28,616,189 (9% federal, 1% state, 86% institutional, 4% external sources). *Receiving aid:* Freshmen: 6% (229). Undergraduates: 4% (561). *Average award:* Freshmen: $15,340. Undergraduates: $12,835. *Scholarships, grants, and awards by category:* Academic interests/achievement: general academic interests/achievements. Creative arts/performance: art/fine arts, music, theater/drama. *Tuition waivers:* Full or partial for employees or children of employees. *ROTC:* Army, Air Force.

LOANS *Student loans:* $77,319,814 (89% need-based, 11% non-need-based). 63% of past graduating class borrowed through all loan programs. *Average indebtedness per student:* $37,753. *Average need-based loan:* Freshmen: $4400. Undergraduates: $5400. *Parent loans:* $38,995,323 (86% need-based, 14% non-need-based). *Programs:* Federal Direct (Subsidized and Unsubsidized Stafford, PLUS), Perkins.

WORK-STUDY *Federal work-study:* Total amount: $15,418,756; 6,149 jobs averaging $2554.

ATHLETIC AWARDS Total amount: $16,659,592 (43% need-based, 57% non-need-based).

APPLYING FOR FINANCIAL AID *Required financial aid forms:* FAFSA, CSS Financial Aid PROFILE, noncustodial (divorced/separated) parent's statement. *Financial aid deadline:* 2/1. *Notification date:* 3/15. Students must reply by 5/1.

CONTACT Office of Financial Aid, Syracuse University, 200 Archbold North, Syracuse, NY 13244-1140, 315-443-1513. *E-mail:* finmail@syr.edu.
Website: http://www.syr.edu/.

TABOR COLLEGE
Hillsboro, KS

ABOUT THE INSTITUTION Independent Mennonite Brethren, coed. *Awards:* associate, bachelor's, and master's degrees. 29 undergraduate majors. *Total enrollment:* 727. Undergraduates: 670. Freshmen: 136.

GIFT AID (NEED-BASED) *Scholarships, grants, and awards:* Federal Pell, FSEOG, state, private, college/university gift aid from institutional funds.

GIFT AID (NON-NEED-BASED) *Scholarships, grants, and awards by category:* Academic interests/achievement: biological sciences, communication, general academic interests/achievements, humanities. Creative arts/performance: journalism/publications, music, performing arts, theater/drama. Special achievements/activities: cheerleading/drum major, general special achievements/activities, religious involvement. Special characteristics: children and siblings of alumni, children of faculty/staff, general special characteristics, international students, local/state students, out-of-state students, religious affiliation.

LOANS *Programs:* Federal Direct (Subsidized and Unsubsidized Stafford, PLUS), Perkins.

APPLYING FOR FINANCIAL AID *Required financial aid forms:* FAFSA, state aid form.

CONTACT Sommer Smith, Director of Student Financial Assistance, Tabor College, 400 South Jefferson, Hillsboro, KS 67063, 620-947-3121 Ext. 1726 or toll-free 800-822-6799. *Fax:* 620-947-6276. *E-mail:* sommersmith@tabor.edu.
Website: http://www.tabor.edu/.

TALLADEGA COLLEGE
Talladega, AL

CONTACT K. Michael Francois, Director of Financial Aid, Talladega College, 627 West Battle Street, Talladega, AL 35160, 256-761-6341 or toll-free 866-540-3956. *Fax:* 256-761-6462.
Website: http://www.talladega.edu/.

TALMUDICAL ACADEMY OF NEW JERSEY
Adelphia, NJ

CONTACT Office of Financial Aid, Talmudical Academy of New Jersey, Route 524, Adelphia, NJ 07710, 732-431-1600.

TALMUDICAL INSTITUTE OF UPSTATE NEW YORK
Rochester, NY

CONTACT Mrs. Ella Berenstein, Financial Aid Administrator, Talmudical Institute of Upstate New York, 769 Park Avenue, Rochester, NY 14607-3046, 585-473-2810.
Website: http://www.tiuny.org/.

Peterson's® How to Get Money for College 2018

TALMUDICAL SEMINARY OF BOBOV
Brooklyn, NY

CONTACT Financial Aid Office, Talmudical Seminary of Bobov, 5120 New Utrecht Avenue, Brooklyn, NY 11219, 718-436-2122.

TALMUDICAL SEMINARY OHOLEI TORAH
Brooklyn, NY

CONTACT Financial Aid Administrator, Talmudical Seminary Oholei Torah, 667 Eastern Parkway, Brooklyn, NY 11213-3310, 718-774-5050.

TALMUDICAL YESHIVA OF PHILADELPHIA
Philadelphia, PA

CONTACT Director of Student Financial Aid/Registrar, Talmudical Yeshiva of Philadelphia, 6063 Drexel Road, Philadelphia, PA 19131-1296, 215-473-1212.

TALMUDIC UNIVERSITY
Miami Beach, FL

CONTACT Rabbi Ira Hill, Director of Financial Aid, Talmudic University, 1910 Alton Road, Miami Beach, FL 33139, 305-534-7050. *Fax:* 305-534-8444. *Website:* http://www.talmudicu.edu/.

TARLETON STATE UNIVERSITY
Stephenville, TX

Tuition & fees (TX res): $8703	Average undergraduate aid package: $9221

ABOUT THE INSTITUTION State-supported, coed. *Awards:* associate, bachelor's, master's, and doctoral degrees. 112 undergraduate majors. *Total enrollment:* 13,052. Undergraduates: 11,463. Freshmen: 2,032. Both federal and institutional methodology are used as a basis for awarding need-based institutional aid.
UNDERGRADUATE EXPENSES for 2017–2018 *Application fee:* $45. *Tuition, state resident:* full-time $4876; part-time $154 per credit hour. *Tuition, nonresident:* full-time $16,858; part-time $562 per credit hour. *Required fees:* full-time $3827. Full-time tuition and fees vary according to course load, degree level, program, and student level. Part-time tuition and fees vary according to course load, degree level, program, and student level. *College room and board:* $9970; *Room only:* $6220. Room and board charges vary according to board plan and housing facility. *Payment plan:* Guaranteed tuition.
FRESHMAN FINANCIAL AID (Fall 2015) 1,689 applied for aid; of those 75% were deemed to have need. 99% of freshmen with need received aid; of those 6% had need fully met. *Average percent of need met:* 64% (excluding resources awarded to replace EFC). *Average financial aid package:* $10,538 (excluding resources awarded to replace EFC).
UNDERGRADUATE FINANCIAL AID (Fall 2015) 6,524 applied for aid; of those 82% were deemed to have need. 99% of undergraduates with need received aid; of those 4% had need fully met. *Average percent of need met:* 53% (excluding resources awarded to replace EFC). *Average financial aid package:* $9221 (excluding resources awarded to replace EFC).
GIFT AID (NEED-BASED) *Total amount:* $37,944,297 (51% federal, 22% state, 19% institutional, 8% external sources). *Receiving aid:* Freshmen: 59% (1,144); all full-time undergraduates: 56% (4,669). *Average award:* Freshmen: $8929; Undergraduates: $6874. *Scholarships, grants, and awards:* Federal Pell, FSEOG, state, college/university gift aid from institutional funds.

GIFT AID (NON-NEED-BASED) *Total amount:* $60,856 (100% state). *Receiving aid:* Undergraduates: 33. *Scholarships, grants, and awards by category:* Academic interests/achievement: general academic interests/achievements. Creative arts/performance: music, theater/drama. Special achievements/activities: general special achievements/activities. Special characteristics: children of educators, children of faculty/staff, veterans, veterans' children. ROTC: Army.
LOANS *Student loans:* $57,530,330 (37% need-based, 63% non-need-based). 72% of past graduating class borrowed through all loan programs. *Average indebtedness per student:* $25,725. *Average need-based loan:* Freshmen: $3122. Undergraduates: $3940. *Parent loans:* $8,301,126 (100% non-need-based). *Programs:* Federal Direct (Subsidized and Unsubsidized Stafford, PLUS), state.
WORK-STUDY *Federal work-study:* jobs available. *State or other work-study/employment:* Total amount: $265,890 (100% need-based). Part-time jobs available.
ATHLETIC AWARDS Total amount: $2,040,356 (100% need-based).
APPLYING FOR FINANCIAL AID *Required financial aid form:* FAFSA. *Financial aid deadline:* 11/1 (priority: 3/15). *Notification date:* Continuous beginning 5/1. Students must reply within 2 weeks of notification.
CONTACT Ms. Kathy Purvis, Executive Director, Tarleton State University, Box T-0310, Stephenville, TX 76402, 254-968-9070 or toll-free 800-687-8236. *Fax:* 254-968-9600. *E-mail:* finaid@tarleton.edu. *Website:* http://www.tarleton.edu/.

TAYLOR UNIVERSITY
Upland, IN

Tuition & fees: $31,472	Average undergraduate aid package: $21,985

ABOUT THE INSTITUTION Independent interdenominational, coed. *Awards:* diplomas, bachelor's, and master's degrees. 62 undergraduate majors. *Total enrollment:* 2,170. Undergraduates: 2,131. Freshmen: 473. Federal methodology is used as a basis for awarding need-based institutional aid.
UNDERGRADUATE EXPENSES for 2016–2017 *Application fee:* $25. *Comprehensive fee:* $40,317 includes full-time tuition ($31,232), mandatory fees ($240), and room and board ($8845). *College room only:* $4649. Full-time tuition and fees vary according to course load. Room and board charges vary according to board plan and housing facility. *Part-time tuition:* $1100 per credit hour. *Part-time fees:* $37.50 per term. Part-time tuition and fees vary according to course load.
FRESHMAN FINANCIAL AID (Fall 2016, est.) 380 applied for aid; of those 77% were deemed to have need. 100% of freshmen with need received aid; of those 29% had need fully met. *Average percent of need met:* 78% (excluding resources awarded to replace EFC). *Average financial aid package:* $22,588 (excluding resources awarded to replace EFC). 31% of all full-time freshmen had no need and received non-need-based gift aid.
UNDERGRADUATE FINANCIAL AID (Fall 2016, est.) 1,288 applied for aid; of those 82% were deemed to have need. 100% of undergraduates with need received aid; of those 27% had need fully met. *Average percent of need met:* 76% (excluding resources awarded to replace EFC). *Average financial aid package:* $21,985 (excluding resources awarded to replace EFC). 32% of all full-time undergraduates had no need and received non-need-based gift aid.
GIFT AID (NEED-BASED) *Total amount:* $16,153,937 (11% federal, 6% state, 78% institutional, 5% external sources). *Receiving aid:* Freshmen: 62% (291); all full-time undergraduates: 58% (1,052). *Average award:* Freshmen: $18,748; Undergraduates: $17,757. *Scholarships, grants, and awards:* Federal Pell, FSEOG, state, private, college/university gift aid from institutional funds.
GIFT AID (NON-NEED-BASED) *Total amount:* $9,491,949 (92% institutional, 8% external sources). *Receiving aid:* Freshmen: 11% (54). Undergraduates: 10% (186). *Average award:* Freshmen: $13,079. Undergraduates: $11,652. *Scholarships, grants, and awards by category:* Academic interests/achievement: 1,454 awards ($12,805,822 total): general academic interests/achievements. Creative arts/performance: 113 awards ($285,057 total): music, theater/drama. Special achievements/activities: 438 awards ($1,139,250 total): leadership. Special characteristics: 873 awards ($3,995,397 total): children and siblings of alumni, children of faculty/staff, ethnic background, international students, religious affiliation. *Tuition waivers:* Full or partial for employees or children of employees, senior citizens.
LOANS *Student loans:* $10,197,858 (62% need-based, 38% non-need-based). 53% of past graduating class borrowed through all loan programs. *Average indebtedness*

per student: $29,263. **Average need-based loan:** Freshmen: $4226. Undergraduates: $4771. **Parent loans:** $19,688,743 (25% need-based, 75% non-need-based). **Programs:** Federal Direct (Subsidized and Unsubsidized Stafford, PLUS), Perkins, college/university.

WORK-STUDY Federal work-study: Total amount: $434,056; 774 jobs averaging $561.

ATHLETIC AWARDS Total amount: $2,600,739 (52% need-based, 48% non-need-based).

APPLYING FOR FINANCIAL AID *Required financial aid form:* FAFSA. *Financial aid deadline:* 3/10. *Notification date:* Continuous beginning 11/1. Students must reply by 5/1.

CONTACT Mr. Timothy A. Nace, Director of Financial Aid, Taylor University, 236 West Reade Avenue, Upland, IN 46989-1001, 765-998-5358 or toll-free 800-882-3456. *Fax:* 765-998-4910. *E-mail:* tmnace@taylor.edu. *Website:* http://www.taylor.edu/.

TELSHE YESHIVA–CHICAGO
Chicago, IL

CONTACT Office of Financial Aid, Telshe Yeshiva–Chicago, 3535 West Foster Avenue, Chicago, IL 60625-5598, 773-463-7738.

TEMPLE UNIVERSITY
Philadelphia, PA

Tuition & fees (PA res): $16,274	Average undergraduate aid package: $17,767

ABOUT THE INSTITUTION State-related, coed. *Awards:* certificates, diplomas, associate, bachelor's, master's, and doctoral degrees. 117 undergraduate majors. *Total enrollment:* 39,308. Undergraduates: 29,275. Freshmen: 5,162. Federal methodology is used as a basis for awarding need-based institutional aid.

UNDERGRADUATE EXPENSES for 2016–2017 *Application fee:* $55. *Tuition, state resident:* full-time $15,384; part-time $641 per credit hour. *Tuition, nonresident:* full-time $26,376; part-time $1099 per credit hour. *Required fees:* full-time $890. Full-time tuition and fees vary according to course load, degree level, location, program, reciprocity agreements, and student level. Part-time tuition and fees vary according to course load, degree level, location, program, reciprocity agreements, and student level. *College room and board:* $11,298; *Room only:* $7540. Room and board charges vary according to board plan and housing facility.

FRESHMAN FINANCIAL AID (Fall 2015) 4,264 applied for aid; of those 82% were deemed to have need. 99% of freshmen with need received aid; of those 28% had need fully met. *Average percent of need met:* 69% (excluding resources awarded to replace EFC). *Average financial aid package:* $18,780 (excluding resources awarded to replace EFC). 16% of all full-time freshmen had no need and received non-need-based gift aid.

UNDERGRADUATE FINANCIAL AID (Fall 2015) 19,887 applied for aid; of those 87% were deemed to have need. 99% of undergraduates with need received aid; of those 25% had need fully met. *Average percent of need met:* 66% (excluding resources awarded to replace EFC). *Average financial aid package:* $17,767 (excluding resources awarded to replace EFC). 12% of all full-time undergraduates had no need and received non-need-based gift aid.

GIFT AID (NEED-BASED) *Total amount:* $101,364,354 (40% federal, 26% state, 34% institutional). *Receiving aid:* Freshmen: 60% (2,947); all full-time undergraduates: 58% (14,526). *Average award:* Freshmen: $8129; Undergraduates: $6812. *Scholarships, grants, and awards:* Federal Pell, FSEOG, state, private, college/university gift aid from institutional funds, Federal Nursing.

GIFT AID (NON-NEED-BASED) *Total amount:* $80,269,912 (77% institutional, 23% external sources). *Receiving aid:* Freshmen: 41% (1,999). Undergraduates: 30% (7,638). *Average award:* Freshmen: $8655. Undergraduates: $7109. *Scholarships, grants, and awards by category: Academic interests/achievement:* 8,551 awards ($48,327,009 total): general academic interests/achievements. *Creative arts/performance:* 266 awards ($793,523 total): art/fine arts, dance, general creative arts/performance, music, performing arts, theater/drama. *Special achievements/activities:* 199 awards ($242,343 total): cheerleading/drum major. *Special characteristics:* 364 awards ($3,944,893 total): children of faculty/staff. *Tuition*

waivers: Full or partial for employees or children of employees. **ROTC:** Army, Naval cooperative, Air Force cooperative.

LOANS Student loans: $188,662,087 (75% need-based, 25% non-need-based). 77% of past graduating class borrowed through all loan programs. *Average indebtedness per student:* $37,708. **Average need-based loan:** Freshmen: $3356. Undergraduates: $4497. **Parent loans:** $54,082,502 (100% non-need-based). **Programs:** Federal Direct (Subsidized and Unsubsidized Stafford, PLUS), Perkins, Federal Nursing, state, college/university.

WORK-STUDY Federal work-study: 1,377 jobs averaging $1438.

ATHLETIC AWARDS Total amount: $9,382,734 (100% non-need-based).

APPLYING FOR FINANCIAL AID *Required financial aid form:* FAFSA. *Financial aid deadline (priority):* 3/1. *Notification date:* Continuous beginning 2/15. Students must reply by 5/1 or within 3 weeks of notification.

CONTACT Emilie Van Trieste, Interim Director of Student Financial Services, Temple University, Conwell Hall, Ground Floor, Philadelphia, PA 19122-6096, 215-204-8760 or toll-free 888-340-2222. *Fax:* 215-204-5897. *E-mail:* emilie.vantrieste@temple.edu. *Website:* http://www.temple.edu/.

TENNESSEE STATE UNIVERSITY
Nashville, TN

Tuition & fees: N/R	Average undergraduate aid package: $10,539

ABOUT THE INSTITUTION State-supported, coed. *Awards:* certificates, associate, bachelor's, master's, and doctoral degrees. 58 undergraduate majors. *Total enrollment:* 8,753. Undergraduates: 7,007. Freshmen: 1,300. Federal methodology is used as a basis for awarding need-based institutional aid.

FRESHMAN FINANCIAL AID (Fall 2015) 1,199 applied for aid; of those 95% were deemed to have need. 99% of freshmen with need received aid; of those 67% had need fully met. *Average percent of need met:* 56% (excluding resources awarded to replace EFC). *Average financial aid package:* $11,175 (excluding resources awarded to replace EFC). 4% of all full-time freshmen had no need and received non-need-based gift aid.

UNDERGRADUATE FINANCIAL AID (Fall 2015) 5,534 applied for aid; of those 95% were deemed to have need. 99% of undergraduates with need received aid; of those 5% had need fully met. *Average percent of need met:* 53% (excluding resources awarded to replace EFC). *Average financial aid package:* $10,539 (excluding resources awarded to replace EFC). 4% of all full-time undergraduates had no need and received non-need-based gift aid.

GIFT AID (NEED-BASED) *Total amount:* $24,694,873 (89% federal, 11% state). *Receiving aid:* Freshmen: 75% (961); all full-time undergraduates: 68% (4,185). *Average award:* Freshmen: $5746; Undergraduates: $5332. *Scholarships, grants, and awards:* Federal Pell, FSEOG, state, private, college/university gift aid from institutional funds.

GIFT AID (NON-NEED-BASED) *Total amount:* $25,908,601 (12% state, 52% institutional, 36% external sources). *Receiving aid:* Freshmen: 49% (622). Undergraduates: 37% (2,240). *Average award:* Freshmen: $14,913. Undergraduates: $14,290. *Scholarships, grants, and awards by category: Academic interests/achievement:* general academic interests/achievements. *Creative arts/performance:* music. *Special achievements/activities:* general special achievements/activities. *Special characteristics:* local/state students, members of minority groups. **ROTC:** Army cooperative, Naval cooperative, Air Force.

LOANS Student loans: $39,912,978 (44% need-based, 56% non-need-based). 87% of past graduating class borrowed through all loan programs. *Average indebtedness per student:* $35,214. **Average need-based loan:** Freshmen: $3506. Undergraduates: $4060. **Parent loans:** $5,549,998 (100% non-need-based). **Programs:** Federal Direct (Subsidized and Unsubsidized Stafford, PLUS), Perkins.

WORK-STUDY Federal work-study: jobs available. *State or other work-study/employment:* Total amount: $1,050,489 (100% need-based). Part-time jobs available.

ATHLETIC AWARDS Total amount: $3,220,424 (100% non-need-based).

APPLYING FOR FINANCIAL AID *Required financial aid form:* FAFSA. *Financial aid deadline (priority):* 4/1. *Notification date:* Continuous beginning 4/25. Students must reply within 3 weeks of notification.

CONTACT Amy Wood, Director of Financial Aid, Tennessee State University, 3500 John A. Merritt Boulevard, Nashville, TN 37209-1561, 615-963-7548. *Fax:* 615-963-7540. *E-mail:* awood7@tnstate.edu. *Website:* http://www.tnstate.edu/.

TENNESSEE TECHNOLOGICAL UNIVERSITY
Cookeville, TN

Tuition & fees: N/R	Average undergraduate aid package: $9915

ABOUT THE INSTITUTION State-supported, coed. 67 undergraduate majors. Federal methodology is used as a basis for awarding need-based institutional aid.

FRESHMAN FINANCIAL AID (Fall 2015) 1,428 applied for aid; of those 78% were deemed to have need. 100% of freshmen with need received aid; of those 12% had need fully met. *Average percent of need met:* 65% (excluding resources awarded to replace EFC). *Average financial aid package:* $11,219 (excluding resources awarded to replace EFC). 24% of all full-time freshmen had no need and received non-need-based gift aid.

UNDERGRADUATE FINANCIAL AID (Fall 2015) 7,344 applied for aid; of those 80% were deemed to have need. 99% of undergraduates with need received aid; of those 9% had need fully met. *Average percent of need met:* 60% (excluding resources awarded to replace EFC). *Average financial aid package:* $9915 (excluding resources awarded to replace EFC). 25% of all full-time undergraduates had no need and received non-need-based gift aid.

GIFT AID (NEED-BASED) *Total amount:* $18,327,346 (77% federal, 22% state, 1% institutional). *Receiving aid:* Freshmen: 38% (569); all full-time undergraduates: 39% (3,201). *Average award:* Freshmen: $6212; Undergraduates: $5488. *Scholarships, grants, and awards:* Federal Pell, FSEOG, state, private, college/university gift aid from institutional funds, United Negro College Fund.

GIFT AID (NON-NEED-BASED) *Total amount:* $47,289,154 (45% state, 21% institutional, 34% external sources). *Receiving aid:* Freshmen: 71% (1,051). Undergraduates: 51% (4,221). *Average award:* Freshmen: $9030. Undergraduates: $13,053. *Scholarships, grants, and awards by category:* Academic interests/achievement: 2,972 awards ($6,522,050 total): agriculture, biological sciences, business, communication, computer science, education, engineering/technologies, English, foreign languages, general academic interests/achievements, health fields, home economics, humanities, international studies, mathematics, military science, physical sciences, premedicine, social sciences. *Creative arts/performance:* 241 awards ($546,540 total): art/fine arts, debating, music. *Special achievements/activities:* 1,140 awards ($4,499,735 total): cheerleading/drum major, general special achievements/activities. *Special characteristics:* 334 awards ($1,113,144 total): children and siblings of alumni, children of educators, children of faculty/staff, children of public servants, ethnic background, first-generation college students, local/state students, members of minority groups, out-of-state students, public servants.

LOANS *Student loans:* $26,849,723 (52% need-based, 48% non-need-based). 56% of past graduating class borrowed through all loan programs. *Average indebtedness per student:* $19,363. *Average need-based loan:* Freshmen: $2984. Undergraduates: $3919. *Parent loans:* $2,926,712 (100% non-need-based). *Programs:* Federal Direct (Subsidized and Unsubsidized Stafford, PLUS), Perkins, state, college/university.

WORK-STUDY *Federal work-study:* 491 jobs averaging $1002. *State or other work-study/employment:* Part-time jobs available.

ATHLETIC AWARDS *Total amount:* $5,065,237 (100% non-need-based).

APPLYING FOR FINANCIAL AID *Required financial aid form:* FAFSA. *Financial aid deadline (priority):* 3/15. *Notification date:* Continuous beginning 4/1. Students must reply within 2 weeks of notification.

CONTACT Mr. Lester Clyde McKenzie III, Director of Financial Aid, Tennessee Technological University, PO Box 5076, 1000 North Dixie Avenue, Cookeville, TN 38501, 931-372-3073 or toll-free 800-255-8881. *Fax:* 931-372-6309. *E-mail:* lmckenzie@tntech.edu. *Website:* http://www.tntech.edu/.

TENNESSEE WESLEYAN UNIVERSITY
Athens, TN

Tuition & fees: $23,800	Average undergraduate aid package: $18,069

ABOUT THE INSTITUTION Independent United Methodist, coed. *Awards:* bachelor's and master's degrees (profile includes information for both the main and branch campuses). 43 undergraduate majors. *Total enrollment:* 1,037. Undergraduates: 1,015. Freshmen: 199. Federal methodology is used as a basis for awarding need-based institutional aid.

UNDERGRADUATE EXPENSES for 2017–2018 *Application fee:* $30. *Comprehensive fee:* $31,550 includes full-time tuition ($22,800), mandatory fees ($1000), and room and board ($7750). Full-time tuition and fees vary according to class time and degree level. Room and board charges vary according to board plan and housing facility. *Part-time tuition:* $570 per credit hour. *Part-time fees:* $10 per contact hour. Part-time tuition and fees vary according to class time, course load, degree level, location, and program.

FRESHMAN FINANCIAL AID (Fall 2015) 219 applied for aid; of those 90% were deemed to have need. 98% of freshmen with need received aid; of those 20% had need fully met. *Average percent of need met:* 71% (excluding resources awarded to replace EFC). *Average financial aid package:* $19,231 (excluding resources awarded to replace EFC). 9% of all full-time freshmen had no need and received non-need-based gift aid.

UNDERGRADUATE FINANCIAL AID (Fall 2015) 894 applied for aid; of those 91% were deemed to have need. 97% of undergraduates with need received aid; of those 19% had need fully met. *Average percent of need met:* 68% (excluding resources awarded to replace EFC). *Average financial aid package:* $18,069 (excluding resources awarded to replace EFC). 8% of all full-time undergraduates had no need and received non-need-based gift aid.

GIFT AID (NEED-BASED) *Total amount:* $9,643,482 (21% federal, 22% state, 45% institutional, 12% external sources). *Receiving aid:* Freshmen: 75% (192); all full-time undergraduates: 79% (767). *Average award:* Freshmen: $17,262; Undergraduates: $15,926. *Scholarships, grants, and awards:* Federal Pell, FSEOG, state, private, college/university gift aid from institutional funds.

GIFT AID (NON-NEED-BASED) *Total amount:* $1,762,102 (25% state, 60% institutional, 15% external sources). *Receiving aid:* Freshmen: 14% (35). Undergraduates: 14% (133). *Average award:* Freshmen: $9063. Undergraduates: $9653. *Scholarships, grants, and awards by category:* Academic interests/achievement: 39 awards ($809,205 total): general academic interests/achievements. *Creative arts/performance:* 35 awards ($112,500 total): music. *Special achievements/activities:* 101 awards ($140,958 total): cheerleading/drum major, general special achievements/activities, junior miss, memberships. *Special characteristics:* 173 awards ($356,444 total): children and siblings of alumni, children of faculty/staff, general special characteristics, out-of-state students, relatives of clergy, religious affiliation, siblings of current students. *Tuition waivers:* Full or partial for employees or children of employees.

LOANS *Student loans:* $4,991,252 (79% need-based, 21% non-need-based). 77% of past graduating class borrowed through all loan programs. *Average indebtedness per student:* $20,649. *Average need-based loan:* Freshmen: $3062. Undergraduates: $3835. *Parent loans:* $860,638 (52% need-based, 48% non-need-based). *Programs:* Federal Direct (Subsidized and Unsubsidized Stafford, PLUS).

WORK-STUDY *Federal work-study:* 78 jobs averaging $1199. *State or other work-study/employment:* Total amount: $23,179 (3% need-based, 97% non-need-based). 10 part-time jobs averaging $2318.

ATHLETIC AWARDS *Total amount:* $3,990,146 (66% need-based, 34% non-need-based).

APPLYING FOR FINANCIAL AID *Required financial aid forms:* FAFSA, institution's own form. *Financial aid deadline:* Continuous. *Notification date:* Continuous beginning 2/15. Students must reply within 2 weeks of notification.

CONTACT Mrs. Lacey Weese, Director of Financial Aid, Tennessee Wesleyan University, 204 East College Street, Athens, TN 37303, 423-746-5209 or toll-free 800-PICK-TWU. *Fax:* 423-744-9968. *E-mail:* lweese@tnwesleyan.edu. *Website:* http://www.tnwesleyan.edu/.

TEXAS A&M INTERNATIONAL UNIVERSITY
Laredo, TX

Tuition & fees (TX res): $11,456	Average undergraduate aid package: $11,567

ABOUT THE INSTITUTION State-supported, coed. **Awards:** bachelor's, master's, and doctoral degrees. 24 undergraduate majors. **Total enrollment:** 7,390. Undergraduates: 6,591. Freshmen: 1,026. Federal methodology is used as a basis for awarding need-based institutional aid.

UNDERGRADUATE EXPENSES for 2017–2018 Tuition, state resident: full-time $8320. **Tuition, nonresident:** full-time $20,704. **Required fees:** full-time $3136. Full-time tuition and fees vary according to course load. Part-time tuition and fees vary according to course load and reciprocity agreements. **College room and board:** $7882; **Room only:** $5126. Room and board charges vary according to board plan and housing facility.

FRESHMAN FINANCIAL AID (Fall 2015) 851 applied for aid; of those 95% were deemed to have need. 100% of freshmen with need received aid; of those 5% had need fully met. **Average percent of need met:** 68% (excluding resources awarded to replace EFC). **Average financial aid package:** $11,898 (excluding resources awarded to replace EFC). 6% of all full-time freshmen had no need and received non-need-based gift aid.

UNDERGRADUATE FINANCIAL AID (Fall 2015) 4,374 applied for aid; of those 89% were deemed to have need. 100% of undergraduates with need received aid; of those .1% had need fully met. **Average percent of need met:** 66% (excluding resources awarded to replace EFC). **Average financial aid package:** $11,567 (excluding resources awarded to replace EFC). 3% of all full-time undergraduates had no need and received non-need-based gift aid.

GIFT AID (NEED-BASED) Total amount: $26,892,342 (63% federal, 28% state, 9% institutional). **Receiving aid:** Freshmen: 87% (788); all full-time undergraduates: 68% (3,854). **Average award:** Freshmen: $7741; Undergraduates: $6891. **Scholarships, grants, and awards:** Federal Pell, FSEOG, state, college/university gift aid from institutional funds, Federal Nursing.

GIFT AID (NON-NEED-BASED) Total amount: $3,071,329 (7% state, 84% institutional, 9% external sources). **Receiving aid:** Freshmen: 25% (224). Undergraduates: 21% (1,164). **Average award:** Freshmen: $2902. Undergraduates: $3467. **Scholarships, grants, and awards by category:** Academic interests/achievement: business, communication, education, engineering/technologies, English, foreign languages, general academic interests/achievements, health fields, international studies, mathematics, physical sciences, premedicine, social sciences. Creative arts/performance: art/fine arts, dance, music, performing arts. **Tuition waivers:** Full or partial for senior citizens. **ROTC:** Army.

LOANS Student loans: $10,188,793 (95% need-based, 5% non-need-based). 74% of past graduating class borrowed through all loan programs. Average indebtedness per student: $17,394. **Average need-based loan:** Freshmen: $3087. Undergraduates: $3937. **Parent loans:** $133,467 (100% non-need-based). **Programs:** Federal Direct (Subsidized and Unsubsidized Stafford, PLUS), state, college/university, Hinson-Hazelwood Loan Program.

WORK-STUDY Federal work-study: 100 jobs averaging $2400. **State or other work-study/employment:** Total amount: $62,689 (100% need-based). 25 part-time jobs averaging $2507.

ATHLETIC AWARDS Total amount: $752,679 (100% non-need-based).

APPLYING FOR FINANCIAL AID Required financial aid form: FAFSA. **Financial aid deadline:** 7/30 (priority: 3/15). **Notification date:** Continuous beginning 3/2. Students must reply within 6 weeks of notification.

CONTACT Mrs. Laura Elizondo, Director of Financial Aid, Texas A&M International University, 5201 University Boulevard, Laredo, TX 78041, 956-326-2225 or toll-free 888-489-2648. Fax: 956-326-2224. E-mail: laura@tamiu.edu. Website: http://www.tamiu.edu/.

TEXAS A&M UNIVERSITY
College Station, TX

Tuition & fees (TX res): $10,030	Average undergraduate aid package: $16,491

ABOUT THE INSTITUTION State-supported, coed. **Awards:** certificates, bachelor's, master's, and doctoral degrees. 109 undergraduate majors. **Total enrollment:** 65,302. Undergraduates: 50,735. Freshmen: 10,145. Both federal and institutional methodology are used as a basis for awarding need-based institutional aid.

UNDERGRADUATE EXPENSES for 2017–2018 Application fee: $75. **Tuition, state resident:** full-time $6679; part-time $222.63 per credit hour. **Tuition, nonresident:** full-time $26,857; part-time $895.23 per credit hour. **Required fees:** full-time $3351. Full-time tuition and fees vary according to program. Part-time tuition and fees vary according to program. **College room and board:** $10,368. Room and board charges vary according to board plan, housing facility, and location. **Payment plan:** Guaranteed tuition.

FRESHMAN FINANCIAL AID (Fall 2016, est.) 6,718 applied for aid; of those 63% were deemed to have need. 95% of freshmen with need received aid; of those 27% had need fully met. **Average percent of need met:** 76% (excluding resources awarded to replace EFC). **Average financial aid package:** $18,348 (excluding resources awarded to replace EFC). 16% of all full-time freshmen had no need and received non-need-based gift aid.

UNDERGRADUATE FINANCIAL AID (Fall 2016, est.) 27,389 applied for aid; of those 74% were deemed to have need. 94% of undergraduates with need received aid; of those 23% had need fully met. **Average percent of need met:** 72% (excluding resources awarded to replace EFC). **Average financial aid package:** $16,491 (excluding resources awarded to replace EFC). 12% of all full-time undergraduates had no need and received non-need-based gift aid.

GIFT AID (NEED-BASED) Total amount: $158,900,585 (29% federal, 25% state, 36% institutional, 10% external sources). **Receiving aid:** Freshmen: 43% (3,757); all full-time undergraduates: 37% (16,606). **Average award:** Freshmen: $11,549; Undergraduates: $10,237. **Scholarships, grants, and awards:** Federal Pell, FSEOG, state, private, college/university gift aid from institutional funds.

GIFT AID (NON-NEED-BASED) Total amount: $40,611,113 (1% federal, 8% state, 62% institutional, 29% external sources). **Receiving aid:** Freshmen: 5% (474). Undergraduates: 3% (1,356). **Average award:** Freshmen: $4157. Undergraduates: $4134. **Scholarships, grants, and awards by category:** Academic interests/achievement: agriculture, architecture, biological sciences, business, computer science, education, engineering/technologies, general academic interests/achievements, health fields, mathematics, physical sciences, premedicine. Creative arts/performance: journalism/publications, performing arts, theater/drama. Special achievements/activities: community service, general special achievements/activities, leadership, memberships, rodeo. Special characteristics: children of faculty/staff, first-generation college students, general special characteristics, international students, local/state students, veterans, veterans' children. **ROTC:** Army, Naval, Air Force.

LOANS Student loans: $130,752,308 (62% need-based, 38% non-need-based). 45% of past graduating class borrowed through all loan programs. Average indebtedness per student: $24,072. **Average need-based loan:** Freshmen: $7685. Undergraduates: $8101. **Parent loans:** $67,005,377 (28% need-based, 72% non-need-based). **Programs:** Federal Direct (Subsidized and Unsubsidized Stafford, PLUS), Perkins, Federal Nursing, state, college/university.

WORK-STUDY Federal work-study: Total amount: $2,119,645; 755 jobs averaging $2807. **State or other work-study/employment:** Total amount: $206,436 (100% need-based). 74 part-time jobs averaging $2790.

ATHLETIC AWARDS Total amount: $3,726,546 (27% need-based, 73% non-need-based).

APPLYING FOR FINANCIAL AID Required financial aid forms: FAFSA, scholarships section of the ApplyTexas application. **Financial aid deadline (priority):** 3/15. **Notification date:** Continuous beginning 1/25. Students must reply by 5/1.

CONTACT Scholarships and Financial Aid Office, Texas A&M University, The Pavilion 200, Spence Street, 1252 TAMU, College Station, TX 77842-3016, 979-845-3236. Fax: 979-847-9061. E-mail: financialaid@tamu.edu. Website: http://www.tamu.edu/.

TEXAS A&M UNIVERSITY–COMMERCE
Commerce, TX

Tuition & fees (TX res): $7888	Average undergraduate aid package: $10,155

ABOUT THE INSTITUTION State-supported, coed. **Awards:** certificates, bachelor's, master's, and doctoral degrees. 41 undergraduate majors. **Total enrollment:** 12,385. Undergraduates: 7,605. Freshmen: 917. Federal methodology is used as a basis for awarding need-based institutional aid.

UNDERGRADUATE EXPENSES for 2017–2018 Tuition, state resident: full-time $4790; part-time $50 per credit hour. **Tuition, nonresident:** full-time $20,129; part-time $458 per credit hour. **Required fees:** full-time $3098. Full-time tuition and fees vary according to course load, location, program, and reciprocity agreements. Part-time tuition and fees vary according to course load, location, program, and reciprocity agreements. **College room and board:** $8326. Room and board charges vary according to board plan and housing facility. **Payment plan:** Guaranteed tuition.

FRESHMAN FINANCIAL AID (Fall 2016, est.) 890 applied for aid; of those 82% were deemed to have need. 97% of freshmen with need received aid; of those 8% had need fully met. **Average percent of need met:** 67% (excluding resources awarded to replace EFC). **Average financial aid package:** $11,756 (excluding resources awarded to replace EFC). 6% of all full-time freshmen had no need and received non-need-based gift aid.

UNDERGRADUATE FINANCIAL AID (Fall 2016, est.) 4,840 applied for aid; of those 88% were deemed to have need. 97% of undergraduates with need received aid; of those 7% had need fully met. **Average percent of need met:** 58% (excluding resources awarded to replace EFC). **Average financial aid package:** $10,155 (excluding resources awarded to replace EFC). 4% of all full-time undergraduates had no need and received non-need-based gift aid.

GIFT AID (NEED-BASED) Total amount: $31,274,694 (54% federal, 29% state, 15% institutional, 2% external sources). **Receiving aid:** Freshmen: 69% (679); all full-time undergraduates: 67% (3,830). **Average award:** Freshmen: $11,201; Undergraduates: $8593. **Scholarships, grants, and awards:** Federal Pell, FSEOG, state, private, college/university gift aid from institutional funds.

GIFT AID (NON-NEED-BASED) Total amount: $2,803,967 (3% federal, 88% institutional, 9% external sources). **Average award:** Freshmen: $1989. Undergraduates: $1986. **Scholarships, grants, and awards by category:** Academic interests/achievement: agriculture, biological sciences, business, communication, computer science, education, engineering/technologies, English, foreign languages, general academic interests/achievements, health fields, humanities, international studies, mathematics, physical sciences, premedicine, social sciences. Creative arts/performance: applied art and design, art/fine arts, journalism/publications, music, performing arts, theater/drama. Special achievements/activities: cheerleading/drum major, general special achievements/activities, junior miss, leadership, rodeo. Special characteristics: adult students, children and siblings of alumni, first-generation college students, out-of-state students, previous college experience, veterans, veterans' children. **Tuition waivers:** Full or partial for employees or children of employees, senior citizens. **ROTC:** Air Force cooperative.

LOANS Student loans: $33,758,082 (92% need-based, 8% non-need-based). 63% of past graduating class borrowed through all loan programs. **Average indebtedness per student:** $28,054. **Average need-based loan:** Freshmen: $3029. Undergraduates: $3686. **Parent loans:** $5,008,130 (77% need-based, 23% non-need-based). **Programs:** Federal Direct (Subsidized and Unsubsidized Stafford, PLUS), Perkins, state.

WORK-STUDY Federal work-study: Total amount: $385,401; 122 jobs averaging $1850. **State or other work-study/employment:** Total amount: $91,582 (100% need-based). 15 part-time jobs averaging $1952.

ATHLETIC AWARDS Total amount: $865,489 (58% need-based, 42% non-need-based).

APPLYING FOR FINANCIAL AID Required financial aid form: FAFSA. **Financial aid deadline (priority):** 4/1. **Notification date:** Continuous beginning 5/1. Students must reply within 4 weeks of notification.

CONTACT Ms. Maria Ramos, Director of Financial Aid and Scholarships, Texas A&M University–Commerce, PO Box 3011, Commerce, TX 75429, 903-886-5091 or toll-free 888-868-2682. Fax: 903-886-5098. E-mail: maria.ramos@tamuc.edu. Website: http://www.tamuc.edu/.

TEXAS A&M UNIVERSITY–CORPUS CHRISTI
Corpus Christi, TX

Tuition & fees (TX res): $8620	Average undergraduate aid package: $9234

ABOUT THE INSTITUTION State-supported, coed. **Awards:** bachelor's, master's, and doctoral degrees. 25 undergraduate majors. **Total enrollment:** 12,202. Undergraduates: 10,212. Freshmen: 2,267. Federal methodology is used as a basis for awarding need-based institutional aid.

UNDERGRADUATE EXPENSES for 2016–2017 Application fee: $50. **Tuition, state resident:** full-time $4979; part-time $175.69 per credit. **Tuition, nonresident:** full-time $16,567; part-time $578.24 per credit. **Required fees:** full-time $3641; $402.43 per credit. Full-time tuition and fees vary according to course load, degree level, location, program, and student level. Part-time tuition and fees vary according to course load, degree level, location, program, and student level. **College room and board:** $9195; **Room only:** $5484. Room and board charges vary according to board plan and housing facility. **Payment plan:** Guaranteed tuition.

FRESHMAN FINANCIAL AID (Fall 2016, est.) 1,995 applied for aid; of those 77% were deemed to have need. 96% of freshmen with need received aid; of those 3% had need fully met. **Average percent of need met:** 57% (excluding resources awarded to replace EFC). **Average financial aid package:** $9965 (excluding resources awarded to replace EFC). 3% of all full-time freshmen had no need and received non-need-based gift aid.

UNDERGRADUATE FINANCIAL AID (Fall 2016, est.) 6,457 applied for aid; of those 82% were deemed to have need. 97% of undergraduates with need received aid; of those 3% had need fully met. **Average percent of need met:** 53% (excluding resources awarded to replace EFC). **Average financial aid package:** $9234 (excluding resources awarded to replace EFC). 5% of all full-time undergraduates had no need and received non-need-based gift aid.

GIFT AID (NEED-BASED) Total amount: $29,300,192 (60% federal, 34% state, 6% institutional). **Receiving aid:** Freshmen: 54% (1,257); all full-time undergraduates: 49% (4,099). **Average award:** Freshmen: $7734; Undergraduates: $6540. **Scholarships, grants, and awards:** Federal Pell, FSEOG, state, private, college/university gift aid from institutional funds.

GIFT AID (NON-NEED-BASED) Total amount: $4,920,930 (69% institutional, 31% external sources). **Receiving aid:** Freshmen: 4% (99). Undergraduates: 8% (658). **Average award:** Freshmen: $2950. Undergraduates: $2517. **Scholarships, grants, and awards by category:** Academic interests/achievement: 247 awards ($806,460 total): general academic interests/achievements. Creative arts/performance: 37 awards ($64,750 total): art/fine arts, general creative arts/performance. Special achievements/activities: 7 awards ($2700 total). Special characteristics: 116 awards ($110,225 total): first-generation college students, international students. **Tuition waivers:** Full or partial for senior citizens. **ROTC:** Army.

LOANS Student loans: $46,708,010 (40% need-based, 60% non-need-based). 64% of past graduating class borrowed through all loan programs. **Average indebtedness per student:** $17,804. **Average need-based loan:** Freshmen: $3239. Undergraduates: $3756. **Parent loans:** $19,945,182 (100% non-need-based). **Programs:** Federal Direct (Subsidized and Unsubsidized Stafford, PLUS), Perkins, state, college/university.

WORK-STUDY Federal work-study: Total amount: $314,754; 303 jobs averaging $3121. **State or other work-study/employment:** Total amount: $732,869 (100% need-based). 248 part-time jobs averaging $2742.

ATHLETIC AWARDS Total amount: $2,170,245 (100% non-need-based).

APPLYING FOR FINANCIAL AID Required financial aid form: FAFSA. **Financial aid deadline (priority):** 3/31. **Notification date:** 4/1. Students must reply by 4/30 or within 2 weeks of notification.

CONTACT Jeannie Gage, Director of Financial Assistance, Texas A&M University–Corpus Christi, 6300 Ocean Drive, Corpus Christi, TX 78412-5503, 361-825-2332 or toll-free 800-482-6822. Fax: 361-825-6095. E-mail: faoweb@tamucc.edu. Website: http://www.tamucc.edu/.

TEXAS A&M UNIVERSITY–KINGSVILLE
Kingsville, TX

Tuition & fees (TX res): $8050	Average undergraduate aid package: $10,871

ABOUT THE INSTITUTION State-supported, coed. *Awards:* certificates, bachelor's, master's, and doctoral degrees. 52 undergraduate majors. *Total enrollment:* 9,278. Undergraduates: 6,512. Freshmen: 1,257. Federal methodology is used as a basis for awarding need-based institutional aid.

UNDERGRADUATE EXPENSES for 2016–2017 *Application fee:* $25. *Tuition, area resident:* part-time $3851 per year. *Tuition, state resident:* full-time $8050; part-time $120 per credit hour. *Tuition, nonresident:* full-time $21,356; part-time $458 per credit hour. Full-time tuition and fees vary according to course load and degree level. Part-time tuition and fees vary according to course load and degree level. *College room and board:* $8530. Room and board charges vary according to board plan and housing facility. *Payment plan:* Guaranteed tuition.

FRESHMAN FINANCIAL AID (Fall 2015) 1,109 applied for aid; of those 88% were deemed to have need. 100% of freshmen with need received aid; of those 94% had need fully met. *Average percent of need met:* 75% (excluding resources awarded to replace EFC). *Average financial aid package:* $13,529 (excluding resources awarded to replace EFC). 1% of all full-time freshmen had no need and received non-need-based gift aid.

UNDERGRADUATE FINANCIAL AID (Fall 2015) 5,306 applied for aid; of those 92% were deemed to have need. 100% of undergraduates with need received aid; of those 97% had need fully met. *Average percent of need met:* 65% (excluding resources awarded to replace EFC). *Average financial aid package:* $10,871 (excluding resources awarded to replace EFC). 1% of all full-time undergraduates had no need and received non-need-based gift aid.

GIFT AID (NEED-BASED) *Total amount:* $26,888,107 (74% federal, 26% state). *Receiving aid:* Freshmen: 63% (798); all full-time undergraduates: 58% (3,842). *Average award:* Freshmen: $9207; Undergraduates: $6503. *Scholarships, grants, and awards:* Federal Pell, FSEOG, state, private, college/university gift aid from institutional funds.

GIFT AID (NON-NEED-BASED) *Total amount:* $5,661,108 (99% institutional, 1% external sources). *Receiving aid:* Freshmen: 5. Undergraduates: 1% (35). *Average award:* Freshmen: $3900. Undergraduates: $1897. *Scholarships, grants, and awards by category: Special achievements/activities:* rodeo. *Special characteristics:* general special characteristics. *Tuition waivers:* Full or partial for employees or children of employees, senior citizens. *ROTC:* Army.

LOANS *Student loans:* $37,232,892 (52% need-based, 48% non-need-based). 76% of past graduating class borrowed through all loan programs. *Average indebtedness per student:* $29,307. *Average need-based loan:* Freshmen: $3151. Undergraduates: $4064. *Parent loans:* $2,553,173 (100% non-need-based). *Programs:* Federal Direct (Subsidized and Unsubsidized Stafford, PLUS), state, alternative loans.

WORK-STUDY *Federal work-study:* jobs available. *State or other work-study/employment:* Total amount: $50,040 (100% need-based). Part-time jobs available.

ATHLETIC AWARDS *Total amount:* $1,695,082 (100% non-need-based).

APPLYING FOR FINANCIAL AID *Required financial aid form:* FAFSA. *Financial aid deadline (priority):* 3/15. *Notification date:* Continuous beginning 4/15. Students must reply within 2 weeks of notification.

CONTACT Office of Financial Aid, Texas A&M University–Kingsville, 700 University Boulevard, Kingsville, TX 78363, 361-593-2883 or toll-free 800-687-6000. *Fax:* 361-593-3036. *E-mail:* financial.aid@tamuk.edu.
Website: http://www.tamuk.edu/.

TEXAS A&M UNIVERSITY–SAN ANTONIO
San Antonio, TX

CONTACT Financial Aid Office, Texas A&M University–San Antonio, One University Way, San Antonio, TX 78224, 210-784-1000.
Website: http://www.tamusa.tamus.edu/.

TEXAS A&M UNIVERSITY– TEXARKANA
Texarkana, TX

Tuition & fees: N/R	Average undergraduate aid package: $13,389

ABOUT THE INSTITUTION State-supported, coed. 20 undergraduate majors. Federal methodology is used as a basis for awarding need-based institutional aid.

UNDERGRADUATE FINANCIAL AID (Fall 2015) 815 applied for aid; of those 86% were deemed to have need. 100% of undergraduates with need received aid; of those 12% had need fully met. *Average percent of need met:* 86% (excluding resources awarded to replace EFC). *Average financial aid package:* $13,389 (excluding resources awarded to replace EFC). 12% of all full-time undergraduates had no need and received non-need-based gift aid.

GIFT AID (NEED-BASED) *Total amount:* $4,910,724 (61% federal, 27% state, 10% institutional, 2% external sources). *Receiving aid:* Entering class: 65% (95); all full-time undergraduates: 67% (673). *Average award:* Freshmen: $11,337; Undergraduates: $11,312. *Scholarships, grants, and awards:* Federal Pell, FSEOG, state, private, college/university gift aid from institutional funds.

GIFT AID (NON-NEED-BASED) *Total amount:* $357,185 (1% state, 86% institutional, 13% external sources). *Average award:* Freshmen: $1976. Undergraduates: $2177. *Scholarships, grants, and awards by category: Academic interests/achievement:* business, education, engineering/technologies, English, general academic interests/achievements, mathematics, social sciences. *Special achievements/activities:* community service, general special achievements/activities, leadership, memberships. *Special characteristics:* veterans, veterans' children.

LOANS *Student loans:* $7,018,585 (89% need-based, 11% non-need-based). 57% of past graduating class borrowed through all loan programs. *Average indebtedness per student:* $19,207. *Average need-based loan:* Freshmen: $2807. Undergraduates: $3515. *Parent loans:* $451,762 (67% need-based, 33% non-need-based). *Programs:* Federal Direct (Subsidized and Unsubsidized Stafford, PLUS), state, college/university.

WORK-STUDY *Federal work-study:* 26 jobs averaging $1393. *State or other work-study/employment:* Total amount: $8147 (100% need-based). 7 part-time jobs averaging $1145.

ATHLETIC AWARDS *Total amount:* $88,375 (64% need-based, 36% non-need-based).

APPLYING FOR FINANCIAL AID *Required financial aid form:* FAFSA. *Financial aid deadline (priority):* 3/15. *Notification date:* Continuous beginning 2/15. Students must reply within 2 weeks of notification.

CONTACT Michael G. Fuller, Director of Financial Aid and Veteran Services, Texas A&M University–Texarkana, 7101 University Avenue, Texarkana, TX 75503, 903-223-3060. *Fax:* 903-223-3140. *E-mail:* mfuller@tamut.edu.
Website: http://www.tamut.edu/.

TEXAS CHRISTIAN UNIVERSITY
Fort Worth, TX

Tuition & fees: $42,670	Average undergraduate aid package: $29,456

ABOUT THE INSTITUTION Independent Christian Church (Disciples of Christ), coed. *Awards:* certificates, diplomas, bachelor's, master's, and doctoral degrees. 98 undergraduate majors. *Total enrollment:* 10,394. Undergraduates: 8,891. Freshmen: 1,888. Both federal and institutional methodology are used as a basis for awarding need-based institutional aid.

UNDERGRADUATE EXPENSES for 2016–2017 *Application fee:* $40. *Comprehensive fee:* $54,670 includes full-time tuition ($42,580), mandatory fees ($90), and room and board ($12,000). *College room only:* $7300. Room and board charges vary according to board plan and housing facility. *Part-time tuition:* $1800 per credit hour. *Part-time fees:* $45 per term. Part-time tuition and fees vary according to course load.

FRESHMAN FINANCIAL AID (Fall 2016, est.) 1,066 applied for aid; of those 66% were deemed to have need. 99% of freshmen with need received aid; of those 40% had need fully met. *Average percent of need met:* 71% (excluding resources awarded to replace EFC). *Average financial aid package:* $29,339 (excluding

resources awarded to replace EFC). 30% of all full-time freshmen had no need and received non-need-based gift aid.

UNDERGRADUATE FINANCIAL AID (Fall 2016, est.) 4,115 applied for aid; of those 79% were deemed to have need. 98% of undergraduates with need received aid; of those 28% had need fully met. *Average percent of need met:* 66% (excluding resources awarded to replace EFC). *Average financial aid package:* $29,456 (excluding resources awarded to replace EFC). 28% of all full-time undergraduates had no need and received non-need-based gift aid.

GIFT AID (NEED-BASED) *Total amount:* $75,484,841 (7% federal, 5% state, 86% institutional, 2% external sources). *Receiving aid:* Freshmen: 35% (658); all full-time undergraduates: 35% (3,032). *Average award:* Freshmen: $27,163; Undergraduates: $26,467. *Scholarships, grants, and awards:* Federal Pell, FSEOG, state, private, college/university gift aid from institutional funds.

GIFT AID (NON-NEED-BASED) *Total amount:* $46,608,885 (98% institutional, 2% external sources). *Receiving aid:* Freshmen: 25% (478). Undergraduates: 23% (1,980). *Average award:* Freshmen: $17,976. Undergraduates: $16,838. *Scholarships, grants, and awards by category: Academic interests/achievement:* 3,800 awards ($52,228,006 total): agriculture, biological sciences, business, communication, education, engineering/technologies, English, foreign languages, general academic interests/achievements, health fields, humanities, international studies, mathematics, military science, physical sciences, premedicine, religion/biblical studies, social sciences. *Creative arts/performance:* 648 awards ($4,903,201 total): applied art and design, art/fine arts, cinema/film/broadcasting, creative writing, dance, general creative arts/performance, journalism/publications, music, performing arts, theater/drama. *Special achievements/activities:* 890 awards ($8,958,770 total): community service, general special achievements/activities, leadership, memberships, religious involvement. *Special characteristics:* 805 awards ($17,141,945 total): adult students, children of educators, children of faculty/staff, children of union members/company employees, children of workers in trades, ethnic background, general special characteristics, handicapped students, international students, local/state students, members of minority groups, previous college experience, relatives of clergy, religious affiliation, veterans, veterans' children. *Tuition waivers:* Full or partial for employees or children of employees. *ROTC:* Army, Air Force.

LOANS *Student loans:* $48,209,228 (51% need-based, 49% non-need-based). 37% of past graduating class borrowed through all loan programs. *Average indebtedness per student:* $36,550. *Average need-based loan:* Freshmen: $3228. Undergraduates: $4537. *Parent loans:* $14,123,012 (3% need-based, 97% non-need-based). *Programs:* Federal Direct (Subsidized and Unsubsidized Stafford, PLUS), Perkins, Federal Nursing, state.

WORK-STUDY *Federal work-study:* Total amount: $2,943,355; 1,244 jobs averaging $2076. *State or other work-study/employment:* Part-time jobs available.

ATHLETIC AWARDS Total amount: $16,378,275 (36% need-based, 64% non-need-based).

APPLYING FOR FINANCIAL AID *Required financial aid forms:* FAFSA, CSS Financial Aid PROFILE, noncustodial (divorced/separated) parent's statement. *Financial aid deadline:* 5/1 (priority: 2/15). *Notification date:* Continuous beginning 12/15.

CONTACT Michael Scott, Director of Scholarships and Student Financial Aid, Texas Christian University, PO Box 297012, Fort Worth, TX 76129-0002, 817-257-7858 or toll-free 800-828-3764. *Fax:* 817-257-7462. *E-mail:* m.scott@tcu.edu. *Website:* http://www.tcu.edu/.

TEXAS COLLEGE
Tyler, TX

CONTACT Ms. Cecelia K. Jones, Director of Financial Aid, Texas College, 2404 North Grand Avenue, Tyler, TX 75702, 903-593-8311 Ext. 2241 or toll-free 800-306-6299. *Fax:* 903-593-9607. *E-mail:* ckjones@texascollege.edu. *Website:* http://www.texascollege.edu/.

TEXAS LUTHERAN UNIVERSITY
Seguin, TX

Tuition & fees: $29,000	Average undergraduate aid package: $25,676

ABOUT THE INSTITUTION Independent Evangelical Lutheran Church, coed. *Awards:* bachelor's and master's degrees. 39 undergraduate majors. *Total enrollment:* 1,299. Undergraduates: 1,283. Freshmen: 377. Federal methodology is used as a basis for awarding need-based institutional aid.

UNDERGRADUATE EXPENSES for 2017–2018 *Comprehensive fee:* $38,720 includes full-time tuition ($28,600), mandatory fees ($400), and room and board ($9720). *College room only:* $5600. Full-time tuition and fees vary according to course load. Room and board charges vary according to board plan and housing facility. *Part-time tuition:* $945 per semester hour. *Part-time fees:* $155 per term.

FRESHMAN FINANCIAL AID (Fall 2016, est.) 350 applied for aid; of those 88% were deemed to have need. 100% of freshmen with need received aid. *Average financial aid package:* $27,403 (excluding resources awarded to replace EFC). 1% of all full-time freshmen had no need and received non-need-based gift aid.

UNDERGRADUATE FINANCIAL AID (Fall 2016, est.) 1,115 applied for aid; of those 88% were deemed to have need. 100% of undergraduates with need received aid. *Average financial aid package:* $25,676 (excluding resources awarded to replace EFC). 1% of all full-time undergraduates had no need and received non-need-based gift aid.

GIFT AID (NEED-BASED) *Total amount:* $24,098,778 (9% federal, 7% state, 82% institutional, 2% external sources). *Receiving aid:* Freshmen: 82% (308); all full-time undergraduates: 80% (971). *Average award:* Freshmen: $22,872; Undergraduates: $20,868. *Scholarships, grants, and awards:* Federal Pell, FSEOG, state, private, college/university gift aid from institutional funds, TEACH Grants.

GIFT AID (NON-NEED-BASED) *Total amount:* $23,724 (16% federal, 84% institutional). *Receiving aid:* Freshmen: 4% (15). Undergraduates: 2% (21). *Average award:* Freshmen: $14,293. Undergraduates: $14,746. *Scholarships, grants, and awards by category: Academic interests/achievement:* biological sciences, business, communication, computer science, education, English, foreign languages, general academic interests/achievements, health fields, international studies, mathematics, physical sciences, premedicine, religion/biblical studies, social sciences. *Creative arts/performance:* art/fine arts, cinema/film/broadcasting, journalism/publications, music, performing arts, theater/drama. *Special achievements/activities:* general special achievements/activities, junior miss, leadership, memberships, religious involvement. *Special characteristics:* children and siblings of alumni, children of faculty/staff, first-generation college students, religious affiliation, veterans, veterans' children. *Tuition waivers:* Full or partial for children of alumni, employees or children of employees. *ROTC:* Army cooperative, Air Force cooperative.

LOANS *Student loans:* $8,867,841 (37% need-based, 63% non-need-based). 73% of past graduating class borrowed through all loan programs. *Average indebtedness per student:* $37,337. *Average need-based loan:* Freshmen: $3731. Undergraduates: $4232. *Parent loans:* $2,323,735 (100% non-need-based). *Programs:* Federal Direct (Subsidized and Unsubsidized Stafford, PLUS), Perkins, state, private loans.

WORK-STUDY *Federal work-study:* Total amount: $894,007; jobs available. *State or other work-study/employment:* Total amount: $9655 (100% need-based). Part-time jobs available.

APPLYING FOR FINANCIAL AID *Required financial aid forms:* FAFSA, TASFA. *Financial aid deadline (priority):* 3/1. *Notification date:* Continuous beginning 3/1. Students must reply by 8/15.

CONTACT Bonnie Trevino, Director of Financial Aid, Texas Lutheran University, 1000 West Court Street, Seguin, TX 78155-5999, 830-372-8078 or toll-free 800-771-8521. *Fax:* 830-372-8179. *E-mail:* btrevino@tlu.edu. *Website:* http://www.tlu.edu/.

TEXAS SOUTHERN UNIVERSITY
Houston, TX

Tuition & fees: N/R	Average undergraduate aid package: $15,818

ABOUT THE INSTITUTION State-supported, coed. 49 undergraduate majors. Federal methodology is used as a basis for awarding need-based institutional aid.

FRESHMAN FINANCIAL AID (Fall 2016, est.) 1,219 applied for aid; of those 100% were deemed to have need. 100% of freshmen with need received aid; of those 88% had need fully met. *Average percent of need met:* 90% (excluding resources awarded to replace EFC). *Average financial aid package:* $14,500 (excluding resources awarded to replace EFC).

UNDERGRADUATE FINANCIAL AID (Fall 2016, est.) 5,776 applied for aid; of those 100% were deemed to have need. 100% of undergraduates with need received aid; of those 90% had need fully met. *Average percent of need met:* 91% (excluding resources awarded to replace EFC). *Average financial aid package:* $15,818 (excluding resources awarded to replace EFC).

GIFT AID (NEED-BASED) *Total amount:* $34,982,566 (55% federal, 26% state, 16% institutional, 3% external sources). *Receiving aid:* Freshmen: 88% (1,073); all full-time undergraduates: 87% (5,001). *Average award:* Freshmen: $4205; Undergraduates: $5815. *Scholarships, grants, and awards:* Federal Pell, FSEOG, state, private, college/university gift aid from institutional funds, United Negro College Fund, Federal Nursing.

LOANS *Student loans:* $32,316,094 (100% need-based). 93% of past graduating class borrowed through all loan programs. *Average indebtedness per student:* $42,421. *Average need-based loan:* Freshmen: $3201. Undergraduates: $3794. *Parent loans:* $11,198,576 (100% need-based). *Programs:* Federal Direct (Subsidized and Unsubsidized Stafford, PLUS), state, college/university.

WORK-STUDY *Federal work-study:* Total amount: $479,824; 200 jobs averaging $4000. *State or other work-study/employment:* Total amount: $37,275 (100% need-based). 25 part-time jobs averaging $4000.

ATHLETIC AWARDS Total amount: $2,872,419 (100% need-based).

APPLYING FOR FINANCIAL AID *Required financial aid forms:* FAFSA, institution's own form. *Financial aid deadline (priority):* 4/15. *Notification date:* Continuous beginning 4/15.

CONTACT Office of Financial Aid, Texas Southern University, 3100 Cleburne Street, Houston, TX 77004-4584, 713-313-7011. *Fax:* 713-313-1858. *Website:* http://www.tsu.edu/.

TEXAS STATE UNIVERSITY
San Marcos, TX

Tuition & fees (TX res): $10,620	Average undergraduate aid package: $10,311

ABOUT THE INSTITUTION State-supported, coed. *Awards:* certificates, bachelor's, master's, and doctoral degrees. 92 undergraduate majors. *Total enrollment:* 38,808. Undergraduates: 34,244. Freshmen: 5,732. Federal methodology is used as a basis for awarding need-based institutional aid.

UNDERGRADUATE EXPENSES for 2017–2018 *Application fee:* $75. *Tuition, state resident:* full-time $8055; part-time $269 per credit hour. *Tuition, nonresident:* full-time $20,295; part-time $677 per credit hour. *Required fees:* full-time $2565; $50.63 per credit hour or $523 per term. Full-time tuition and fees vary according to course load and degree level. Part-time tuition and fees vary according to course load and degree level. *College room and board:* $9490; *Room only:* $6778. Room and board charges vary according to board plan and housing facility. *Payment plans:* Guaranteed tuition, tuition prepayment.

FRESHMAN FINANCIAL AID (Fall 2016, est.) 5,135 applied for aid; of those 69% were deemed to have need. 96% of freshmen with need received aid; of those 21% had need fully met. *Average percent of need met:* 66% (excluding resources awarded to replace EFC). *Average financial aid package:* $10,512 (excluding resources awarded to replace EFC). 5% of all full-time freshmen had no need and received non-need-based gift aid.

UNDERGRADUATE FINANCIAL AID (Fall 2016, est.) 23,799 applied for aid; of those 69% were deemed to have need. 97% of undergraduates with need received aid; of those 18% had need fully met. *Average percent of need met:* 63% (excluding resources awarded to replace EFC). *Average financial aid package:* $10,311 (excluding resources awarded to replace EFC). 2% of all full-time undergraduates had no need and received non-need-based gift aid.

GIFT AID (NEED-BASED) *Total amount:* $104,828,075 (50% federal, 46% state, 2% institutional, 2% external sources). *Receiving aid:* Freshmen: 51% (2,837); all full-time undergraduates: 48% (13,399). *Average award:* Freshmen: $7953; Undergraduates: $6993. *Scholarships, grants, and awards:* Federal Pell, FSEOG, state, private, college/university gift aid from institutional funds.

GIFT AID (NON-NEED-BASED) *Total amount:* $11,881,572 (2% federal, 38% institutional, 60% external sources). *Receiving aid:* Freshmen: 9% (474). Undergraduates: 5% (1,321). *Average award:* Freshmen: $4027. Undergraduates: $3770. *Scholarships, grants, and awards by category:* Academic interests/achievement: 967 awards ($3,572,678 total): agriculture, biological sciences, business, communication, computer science, education, engineering/technologies, English, foreign languages, general academic interests/achievements, health fields, home economics, humanities, international studies, mathematics, military science, physical sciences, social sciences. Creative arts/performance: 397 awards ($1,077,409 total): applied art and design, art/fine arts, dance, journalism/publications, music, theater/drama. Special achievements/activities: 81 awards ($115,300 total): leadership. Special characteristics: 1,583 awards ($7,195,537 total): international students, spouses of deceased or disabled public servants, veterans, veterans' children. *Tuition waivers:* Full or partial for employees or children of employees. *ROTC:* Army, Air Force.

LOANS *Student loans:* $115,939,058 (75% need-based, 25% non-need-based). 65% of past graduating class borrowed through all loan programs. *Average indebtedness per student:* $27,840. *Average need-based loan:* Freshmen: $3169. Undergraduates: $4043. *Parent loans:* $53,729,135 (25% need-based, 75% non-need-based). *Programs:* Federal Direct (Subsidized and Unsubsidized Stafford, PLUS), Perkins, state, college/university, short-term emergency loans.

WORK-STUDY *Federal work-study:* Total amount: $1,544,720; 443 jobs averaging $2958. *State or other work-study/employment:* Total amount: $327,678 (100% need-based). 122 part-time jobs averaging $3279.

ATHLETIC AWARDS Total amount: $3,693,321 (2% need-based, 98% non-need-based).

APPLYING FOR FINANCIAL AID *Required financial aid form:* FAFSA. *Financial aid deadline (priority):* 3/15. *Notification date:* Continuous beginning 5/1. Students must reply within 3 weeks of notification.

CONTACT Dr. Chris Murr, Director of Financial Aid, Texas State University, 601 University Drive, San Marcos, TX 78666-4602, 512-245-2315. *Fax:* 512-245-7920. *E-mail:* cm18@txstate.edu. *Website:* http://www.txstate.edu/.

TEXAS TECH UNIVERSITY
Lubbock, TX

Tuition & fees (TX res): $9781	Average undergraduate aid package: $14,932

ABOUT THE INSTITUTION State-supported, coed. *Awards:* certificates, bachelor's, master's, and doctoral degrees. 88 undergraduate majors. *Total enrollment:* 36,551. Undergraduates: 29,963. Freshmen: 4,762. Federal methodology is used as a basis for awarding need-based institutional aid.

UNDERGRADUATE EXPENSES for 2016–2017 *Application fee:* $75. *Tuition, state resident:* full-time $7050; part-time $235 per credit hour. *Tuition, nonresident:* full-time $19,290; part-time $643 per credit hour. *Required fees:* full-time $2731; $50.50 per credit hour or $608 per term. Full-time tuition and fees vary according to course level, course load, degree level, location, program, reciprocity agreements, and student level. Part-time tuition and fees vary according to course level, course load, degree level, location, program, reciprocity agreements, and student level. *College room and board:* $8505; *Room only:* $4510. Room and board charges vary according to board plan and housing facility.

FRESHMAN FINANCIAL AID (Fall 2015) 3,347 applied for aid; of those 73% were deemed to have need. 100% of freshmen with need received aid; of those 17% had need fully met. *Average percent of need met:* 70% (excluding resources awarded to replace EFC). *Average financial aid package:* $14,173 (excluding resources awarded to replace EFC). 14% of all full-time freshmen had no need and received non-need-based gift aid.

UNDERGRADUATE FINANCIAL AID (Fall 2015) 12,542 applied for aid; of those 83% were deemed to have need. 100% of undergraduates with need received aid; of those 7% had need fully met. *Average percent of need met:* 68% (excluding resources awarded to replace EFC). *Average financial aid package:* $14,932 (excluding resources awarded to replace EFC). 9% of all full-time undergraduates had no need and received non-need-based gift aid.

GIFT AID (NEED-BASED) *Total amount:* $86,548,280 (39% federal, 22% state, 28% institutional, 11% external sources). *Receiving aid:* Freshmen: 43% (2,175); all full-time undergraduates: 34% (8,877). *Average award:* Freshmen: $8411; Under-

---

graduates: $7579. *Scholarships, grants, and awards:* Federal Pell, FSEOG, state, private, college/university gift aid from institutional funds.

GIFT AID (NON-NEED-BASED) *Total amount:* $13,841,625 (77% institutional, 23% external sources). *Receiving aid:* Freshmen: 26% (1,334). Undergraduates: 11% (2,987). *Average award:* Freshmen: $3709. Undergraduates: $3495. *Scholarships, grants, and awards by category:* Academic interests/achievement: agriculture, architecture, biological sciences, business, communication, computer science, education, engineering/technologies, English, foreign languages, general academic interests/achievements, home economics, humanities, international studies, mathematics, military science, physical sciences, premedicine, social sciences. *Creative arts/performance:* applied art and design, art/fine arts, dance, journalism/publications, music, performing arts, theater/drama. *Special achievements/activities:* community service, general special achievements/activities, hobbies/interests, leadership, memberships, rodeo. *Special characteristics:* children of faculty/staff, first-generation college students, handicapped students, out-of-state students, veterans, veterans' children. *Tuition waivers:* Full or partial for employees or children of employees, senior citizens. *ROTC:* Army, Air Force.

LOANS *Student loans:* $120,633,895 (80% need-based, 20% non-need-based). 55% of past graduating class borrowed through all loan programs. *Average indebtedness per student:* $29,214. *Average need-based loan:* Freshmen: $4708. Undergraduates: $5338. *Parent loans:* $22,000,677 (74% need-based, 26% non-need-based). *Programs:* Federal Direct (Subsidized and Unsubsidized Stafford, PLUS), Perkins, state, college/university, private loans.

WORK-STUDY *Federal work-study:* 328 jobs averaging $2513. *State or other work-study/employment:* Part-time jobs available.

ATHLETIC AWARDS Total amount: $5,646,979 (48% need-based, 52% non-need-based).

APPLYING FOR FINANCIAL AID *Required financial aid form:* FAFSA. *Financial aid deadline (priority):* 3/15. *Notification date:* Continuous. Students must reply within 2 weeks of notification.

CONTACT Shannon Crossland, Interim Director of Student Financial Aid, Texas Tech University, PO Box 45011, Lubbock, TX 79409-5011, 806-742-3681. *Fax:* 806-742-0880.

Website: http://www.ttu.edu/.

TEXAS WESLEYAN UNIVERSITY
Fort Worth, TX

Tuition & fees: $27,684	Average undergraduate aid package: $24,260

ABOUT THE INSTITUTION Independent United Methodist, coed. *Awards:* bachelor's, master's, and doctoral degrees. 41 undergraduate majors. *Total enrollment:* 2,619. Undergraduates: 1,905. Freshmen: 301. Federal methodology is used as a basis for awarding need-based institutional aid.

UNDERGRADUATE EXPENSES for 2017–2018 *Comprehensive fee:* $37,314 includes full-time tuition ($24,178), mandatory fees ($3506), and room and board ($9630). *College room only:* $5646. Full-time tuition and fees vary according to course level, course load, degree level, program, and student level. Room and board charges vary according to housing facility. *Part-time tuition:* $828 per credit hour. *Part-time fees:* $120 per credit hour. Part-time tuition and fees vary according to course level, course load, degree level, program, and student level.

FRESHMAN FINANCIAL AID (Fall 2015) 212 applied for aid; of those 92% were deemed to have need. 100% of freshmen with need received aid; of those 19% had need fully met. *Average percent of need met:* 79% (excluding resources awarded to replace EFC). *Average financial aid package:* $26,785 (excluding resources awarded to replace EFC). 45% of all full-time freshmen had no need and received non-need-based gift aid.

UNDERGRADUATE FINANCIAL AID (Fall 2015) 1,059 applied for aid; of those 90% were deemed to have need. 100% of undergraduates with need received aid; of those 16% had need fully met. *Average percent of need met:* 72% (excluding resources awarded to replace EFC). *Average financial aid package:* $24,260 (excluding resources awarded to replace EFC). 27% of all full-time undergraduates had no need and received non-need-based gift aid.

GIFT AID (NEED-BASED) *Total amount:* $15,645,096 (22% federal, 16% state, 61% institutional, 1% external sources). *Receiving aid:* Freshmen: 53% (194); all full-time undergraduates: 60% (934). *Average award:* Freshmen: $19,964; Undergraduates: $16,801. *Scholarships, grants, and awards:* Federal Pell, FSEOG, state, private, college/university gift aid from institutional funds, Federal Nursing.

GIFT AID (NON-NEED-BASED) *Total amount:* $5,985,427 (1% federal, 3% state, 95% institutional, 1% external sources). *Receiving aid:* Freshmen: 19% (70). Undergraduates: 20% (311). *Average award:* Freshmen: $11,231. Undergraduates: $10,635. *Scholarships, grants, and awards by category:* Academic interests/achievement: 420 awards ($5,985,427 total): biological sciences, business, communication, education, English, foreign languages, general academic interests/achievements, health fields, humanities, international studies, mathematics, military science, physical sciences, premedicine, religion/biblical studies, social sciences. *Creative arts/performance:* 75 awards ($12,791 total): art/fine arts, creative writing, dance, debating, journalism/publications, music, performing arts, theater/drama. *Special achievements/activities:* 54 awards ($184,185 total): cheerleading/drum major, community service, leadership, memberships, religious involvement. *Special characteristics:* 77 awards ($247,500 total): adult students, children and siblings of alumni, children of current students, children of educators, children of faculty/staff, children of public servants, children of union members/company employees, children with a deceased or disabled parent, ethnic background, first-generation college students, general special characteristics, handicapped students, international students, local/state students, married students, members of minority groups, out-of-state students, parents of current students, previous college experience, public servants, relatives of clergy, religious affiliation, siblings of current students, spouses of current students, spouses of deceased or disabled public servants, twins, veterans, veterans' children. *Tuition waivers:* Full or partial for employees or children of employees. *ROTC:* Army cooperative, Air Force cooperative.

LOANS *Student loans:* $10,542,550 (87% need-based, 13% non-need-based). 57% of past graduating class borrowed through all loan programs. *Average indebtedness per student:* $12,164. *Average need-based loan:* Freshmen: $3098. Undergraduates: $3890. *Parent loans:* $933,554 (67% need-based, 33% non-need-based). *Programs:* Federal Direct (Subsidized and Unsubsidized Stafford, PLUS), state.

WORK-STUDY *Federal work-study:* 93 jobs averaging $4000. *State or other work-study/employment:* Total amount: $25,826 (94% need-based, 6% non-need-based). 7 part-time jobs averaging $4000.

ATHLETIC AWARDS Total amount: $1,718,659 (44% need-based, 56% non-need-based).

APPLYING FOR FINANCIAL AID *Required financial aid form:* FAFSA. *Financial aid deadline (priority):* 3/1. *Notification date:* Continuous beginning 3/1. Students must reply by 3/1.

CONTACT Laurie Rosenkrantz, Office of Financial Aid, Texas Wesleyan University, 1201 Wesleyan Street, Fort Worth, TX 76105-1536, 817-531-4420 or toll-free 800-580-8980. *Fax:* 817-531-4231. *E-mail:* financialaid@txwes.edu.

Website: http://www.txwes.edu/.

TEXAS WOMAN'S UNIVERSITY
Denton, TX

Tuition & fees (TX res): $8790	Average undergraduate aid package: $14,764

ABOUT THE INSTITUTION State-supported, coed, primarily women. *Awards:* certificates, bachelor's, master's, and doctoral degrees. 38 undergraduate majors. *Total enrollment:* 15,655. Undergraduates: 10,408. Freshmen: 1,317. Both federal and institutional methodology are used as a basis for awarding need-based institutional aid.

UNDERGRADUATE EXPENSES for 2017–2018 *Application fee:* $50. *Tuition, state resident:* full-time $6180; part-time $206.26 per credit hour. *Tuition, nonresident:* full-time $19,920; part-time $614.26 per credit hour. *Required fees:* full-time $2610; $78.06 per credit hour or $287 per term. Full-time tuition and fees vary according to course level, course load, program, and reciprocity agreements. Part-time tuition and fees vary according to course level, course load, program, and reciprocity agreements. *College room and board:* $7578; *Room only:* $4140. Room and board charges vary according to board plan and housing facility. *Payment plan:* Guaranteed tuition.

FRESHMAN FINANCIAL AID (Fall 2016, est.) 1,119 applied for aid; of those 82% were deemed to have need. 100% of freshmen with need received aid; of those 29% had need fully met. *Average percent of need met:* 84% (excluding resources awarded to replace EFC). *Average financial aid package:* $15,466 (excluding resources awarded to replace EFC). 10% of all full-time freshmen had no need and received non-need-based gift aid.

UNDERGRADUATE FINANCIAL AID (Fall 2016, est.) 5,368 applied for aid; of those 90% were deemed to have need. 100% of undergraduates with need received

aid; of those 29% had need fully met. **Average percent of need met:** 84% (excluding resources awarded to replace EFC). **Average financial aid package:** $14,764 (excluding resources awarded to replace EFC). 5% of all full-time undergraduates had no need and received non-need-based gift aid.

GIFT AID (NEED-BASED) Total amount: $42,637,293 (42% federal, 26% state, 29% institutional, 3% external sources). **Receiving aid:** Freshmen: 66% (857); all full-time undergraduates: 63% (4,431). **Average award:** Freshmen: $9318; Undergraduates: $7335. **Scholarships, grants, and awards:** Federal Pell, FSEOG, state, private, college/university gift aid from institutional funds, United Negro College Fund.

GIFT AID (NON-NEED-BASED) Total amount: $9,595,409 (100% institutional). **Receiving aid:** Freshmen: 24% (315). Undergraduates: 19% (1,304). **Average award:** Freshmen: $5341. Undergraduates: $5390. **Scholarships, grants, and awards by category:** Academic interests/achievement: biological sciences, business, communication, computer science, education, English, foreign languages, general academic interests/achievements, health fields, home economics, humanities, library science, mathematics, physical sciences, premedicine, social sciences. Creative arts/performance: applied art and design, art/fine arts, cinema/film/broadcasting, dance, journalism/publications, music, theater/drama. Special characteristics: international students. **Tuition waivers:** Full or partial for senior citizens. **ROTC:** Army cooperative, Naval cooperative, Air Force cooperative.

LOANS Student loans: $47,672,360 (100% need-based). 68% of past graduating class borrowed through all loan programs. Average indebtedness per student: $24,916. **Average need-based loan:** Freshmen: $5703. Undergraduates: $7334. **Parent loans:** $1,427,763 (100% need-based). **Programs:** Federal Direct (Subsidized and Unsubsidized Stafford, PLUS), Perkins, Federal Nursing, state, college/university, alternative loans.

WORK-STUDY Federal work-study: Total amount: $258,951; jobs available. **State or other work-study/employment:** Total amount: $1,389,435 (100% non-need-based). Part-time jobs available.

ATHLETIC AWARDS Total amount: $611,802 (100% need-based).

APPLYING FOR FINANCIAL AID Required financial aid forms: FAFSA, institution's own form. **Financial aid deadline (priority):** 3/1. **Notification date:** 5/1.

CONTACT Mr. Governor Jackson, Director of Financial Aid, Texas Woman's University, PO Box 425408, Denton, TX 76204-5408, 940-898-3051 or toll-free 866-809-6130. Fax: 940-898-3068. E-mail: gjackson@twu.edu.
Website: http://www.twu.edu/.

THEOLOGICAL UNIVERSITY OF THE CARIBBEAN
Saint Just, PR

Tuition & fees: $5168	Average undergraduate aid package: N/A

ABOUT THE INSTITUTION Independent Pentecostal, coed. **Awards:** certificates, diplomas, associate, bachelor's, master's, and doctoral degrees. 4 undergraduate majors. **Total enrollment:** 314. Undergraduates: 267. Freshmen: 53. Federal methodology is used as a basis for awarding need-based institutional aid.

UNDERGRADUATE EXPENSES for 2017–2018 Application fee: $45. **Comprehensive fee:** $7568 includes full-time tuition ($4168), mandatory fees ($1000), and room and board ($2400). **College room only:** $1200. Full-time tuition and fees vary according to course load. Room and board charges vary according to board plan. **Part-time tuition:** $18.27 per credit hour. **Part-time fees:** $137 per credit hour; $3288 per term. Part-time tuition and fees vary according to course load.

FRESHMAN FINANCIAL AID (Fall 2015) 45 applied for aid; of those 100% were deemed to have need. 100% of freshmen with need received aid.

UNDERGRADUATE FINANCIAL AID (Fall 2015) 243 applied for aid; of those 100% were deemed to have need. 100% of undergraduates with need received aid.

GIFT AID (NEED-BASED) Total amount: $928,432 (100% federal). **Receiving aid:** Freshmen: 100% (45); all full-time undergraduates: 100% (243). **Scholarships, grants, and awards:** Federal Pell.

GIFT AID (NON-NEED-BASED) Tuition waivers: Full or partial for employees or children of employees.

LOANS Student loans: $202,635 (100% need-based). 37% of past graduating class borrowed through all loan programs. **Programs:** Federal Direct (Subsidized and Unsubsidized Stafford).

APPLYING FOR FINANCIAL AID Required financial aid form: FAFSA. **Financial aid deadline:** 6/30 (priority: 1/1). **Notification date:** Continuous.

CONTACT Mrs. Claudia M. Rodriguez, Financial Aid Office, Theological University of the Caribbean, PO Box 901, Saint Just, PR 00978-0901, 787-761-0640 Ext. 224. Fax: 787-748-9220. E-mail: asistenciaeconomica@utcpr.edu.
Website: http://www.utcpr.edu/.

THIEL COLLEGE
Greenville, PA

Tuition & fees: $29,740	Average undergraduate aid package: $24,630

ABOUT THE INSTITUTION Independent Evangelical Lutheran Church in America, coed. **Awards:** associate and bachelor's degrees. 43 undergraduate majors. **Total enrollment:** 926. Undergraduates: 926. Freshmen: 207. Federal methodology is used as a basis for awarding need-based institutional aid.

UNDERGRADUATE EXPENSES for 2016–2017 Comprehensive fee: $41,440 includes full-time tuition ($27,910), mandatory fees ($1830), and room and board ($11,700). **College room only:** $5850. Full-time tuition and fees vary according to course load. Room and board charges vary according to housing facility. **Part-time tuition:** $900 per credit hour. **Part-time fees:** $915 per term. Part-time tuition and fees vary according to course load.

FRESHMAN FINANCIAL AID (Fall 2016, est.) 271 applied for aid; of those 96% were deemed to have need. 100% of freshmen with need received aid; of those 8% had need fully met. **Average percent of need met:** 66% (excluding resources awarded to replace EFC). **Average financial aid package:** $24,533 (excluding resources awarded to replace EFC). 7% of all full-time freshmen had no need and received non-need-based gift aid.

UNDERGRADUATE FINANCIAL AID (Fall 2016, est.) 800 applied for aid; of those 96% were deemed to have need. 100% of undergraduates with need received aid; of those 10% had need fully met. **Average percent of need met:** 68% (excluding resources awarded to replace EFC). **Average financial aid package:** $24,630 (excluding resources awarded to replace EFC). 7% of all full-time undergraduates had no need and received non-need-based gift aid.

GIFT AID (NEED-BASED) Total amount: $15,319,614 (12% federal, 8% state, 75% institutional, 5% external sources). **Receiving aid:** Freshmen: 86% (239); all full-time undergraduates: 92% (764). **Average award:** Freshmen: $21,084; Undergraduates: $20,722. **Scholarships, grants, and awards:** Federal Pell, FSEOG, state, private, college/university gift aid from institutional funds.

GIFT AID (NON-NEED-BASED) Total amount: $1,220,665 (2% state, 92% institutional, 6% external sources). **Receiving aid:** Freshmen: 7% (20). Undergraduates: 7% (60). **Average award:** Freshmen: $13,096. Undergraduates: $13,941. **Scholarships, grants, and awards by category:** Academic interests/achievement: biological sciences, business, communication, computer science, education, English, general academic interests/achievements, mathematics, physical sciences, religion/biblical studies. Creative arts/performance: 69 awards ($58,151 total): music, theater/drama. Special achievements/activities: 44 awards ($31,325 total): leadership. Special characteristics: 107 awards ($870,424 total): children and siblings of alumni, children of faculty/staff, international students, local/state students, relatives of clergy, religious affiliation, siblings of current students, veterans. **Tuition waivers:** Full or partial for employees or children of employees.

LOANS Student loans: $7,612,565 (79% need-based, 21% non-need-based). 88% of past graduating class borrowed through all loan programs. Average indebtedness per student: $37,932. **Average need-based loan:** Freshmen: $3956. Undergraduates: $4445. **Parent loans:** $2,818,052 (66% need-based, 34% non-need-based). **Programs:** Federal Direct (Subsidized and Unsubsidized Stafford, PLUS), Perkins.

WORK-STUDY Federal work-study: Total amount: $106,000; 76 jobs averaging $1395. **State or other work-study/employment:** Total amount: $570,538 (96% need-based, 4% non-need-based). 375 part-time jobs averaging $1456.

APPLYING FOR FINANCIAL AID Required financial aid forms: FAFSA, state aid form. **Financial aid deadline:** Continuous. **Notification date:** Continuous beginning 3/15. Students must reply within 2 weeks of notification.

CONTACT Ms. Cynthia H. Farrell, Director of Financial Aid, Thiel College, 75 College Avenue, Greenville, PA 16125-2181, 724-589-2178 or toll-free 800-248-4435. Fax: 724-589-2790. E-mail: cfarrell@thiel.edu.
Website: http://www.thiel.edu/.

THOMAS AQUINAS COLLEGE
Santa Paula, CA

Tuition & fees: $24,500	Average undergraduate aid package: $20,738

ABOUT THE INSTITUTION Independent Roman Catholic, coed. **Awards:** bachelor's degrees. 1 undergraduate major. **Total enrollment:** 389. Undergraduates: 389. Freshmen: 89. Both federal and institutional methodology are used as a basis for awarding need-based institutional aid.

UNDERGRADUATE EXPENSES for 2017–2018 Comprehensive fee: $32,450 includes full-time tuition ($24,500) and room and board ($7950). **Part-time tuition:** $681 per credit hour.

FRESHMAN FINANCIAL AID (Fall 2016, est.) 70 applied for aid; of those 93% were deemed to have need. 100% of freshmen with need received aid; of those 100% had need fully met. **Average percent of need met:** 100% (excluding resources awarded to replace EFC). **Average financial aid package:** $18,959 (excluding resources awarded to replace EFC).

UNDERGRADUATE FINANCIAL AID (Fall 2016, est.) 298 applied for aid; of those 97% were deemed to have need. 100% of undergraduates with need received aid; of those 100% had need fully met. **Average percent of need met:** 100% (excluding resources awarded to replace EFC). **Average financial aid package:** $20,738 (excluding resources awarded to replace EFC).

GIFT AID (NEED-BASED) Total amount: $3,541,960 (12% federal, 10% state, 77% institutional, 1% external sources). **Receiving aid:** Freshmen: 57% (50); all full-time undergraduates: 64% (249). **Average award:** Freshmen: $14,521; Undergraduates: $14,225. **Scholarships, grants, and awards:** Federal Pell, state, private, college/university gift aid from institutional funds, Canadian federal and provincial grants.

GIFT AID (NON-NEED-BASED) Total amount: $17,500 (100% external sources).

LOANS Student loans: $1,424,831 (85% need-based, 15% non-need-based). 85% of past graduating class borrowed through all loan programs. **Average indebtedness per student:** $16,901. **Average need-based loan:** Freshmen: $3238. Undergraduates: $4424. **Parent loans:** $251,572 (100% non-need-based). **Programs:** Federal Direct (Subsidized and Unsubsidized Stafford, PLUS), college/university, Canadian federal and provincial loans.

WORK-STUDY State or other work-study/employment: Total amount: $1,259,800 (100% need-based). 272 part-time jobs averaging $4632.

APPLYING FOR FINANCIAL AID Required financial aid forms: FAFSA, institution's own form, state aid form, federal income tax form(s), W-2 forms, institution's own Non-Custodial Parent Statement. **Financial aid deadline:** 3/2. **Notification date:** Continuous beginning 2/1. Students must reply by 5/1 or within 2 weeks of notification.

CONTACT Mr. Gregory Becher, Director of Financial Aid, Thomas Aquinas College, 10000 Ojai Road, Santa Paula, CA 93060-9980, 805-525-4419 Ext. 5936 or toll-free 800-634-9797. *Fax:* 805-525-9342. *E-mail:* gbecher@thomasaquinas.edu. *Website:* http://www.thomasaquinas.edu/.

THOMAS COLLEGE
Waterville, ME

Tuition & fees: $25,722	Average undergraduate aid package: $20,932

ABOUT THE INSTITUTION Independent, coed. **Awards:** associate, bachelor's, and master's degrees. 23 undergraduate majors. **Total enrollment:** 1,367. Undergraduates: 1,212. Freshmen: 257. Federal methodology is used as a basis for awarding need-based institutional aid.

UNDERGRADUATE EXPENSES for 2016–2017 Comprehensive fee: $35,950 includes full-time tuition ($24,468), mandatory fees ($1254), and room and board ($10,228). **College room only:** $4990. Room and board charges vary according to board plan and housing facility. **Part-time tuition:** $3059 per course. Part-time tuition and fees vary according to class time.

FRESHMAN FINANCIAL AID (Fall 2016, est.) 264 applied for aid; of those 94% were deemed to have need. 100% of freshmen with need received aid; of those 11% had need fully met. **Average percent of need met:** 85% (excluding resources awarded to replace EFC). **Average financial aid package:** $21,498 (excluding

resources awarded to replace EFC). 6% of all full-time freshmen had no need and received non-need-based gift aid.

UNDERGRADUATE FINANCIAL AID (Fall 2016, est.) 785 applied for aid; of those 94% were deemed to have need. 100% of undergraduates with need received aid; of those 10% had need fully met. **Average percent of need met:** 85% (excluding resources awarded to replace EFC). **Average financial aid package:** $20,932 (excluding resources awarded to replace EFC). 9% of all full-time undergraduates had no need and received non-need-based gift aid.

GIFT AID (NEED-BASED) Total amount: $11,018,821 (20% federal, 4% state, 76% institutional). **Receiving aid:** Freshmen: 91% (246); all full-time undergraduates: 87% (730). **Average award:** Freshmen: $16,849; Undergraduates: $15,927. **Scholarships, grants, and awards:** Federal Pell, FSEOG, state, private, college/university gift aid from institutional funds.

GIFT AID (NON-NEED-BASED) Total amount: $1,604,597 (73% institutional, 27% external sources). **Receiving aid:** Freshmen: 31% (84). Undergraduates: 17% (145). **Average award:** Freshmen: $11,144. Undergraduates: $9240. **Scholarships, grants, and awards by category:** Academic interests/achievement: 258 awards ($2,061,677 total): general academic interests/achievements. **Special characteristics:** children and siblings of alumni, children of current students, children of faculty/staff, international students, local/state students, out-of-state students, veterans, veterans' children. **Tuition waivers:** Full or partial for employees or children of employees.

LOANS Student loans: $7,336,626 (42% need-based, 58% non-need-based). 97% of past graduating class borrowed through all loan programs. **Average indebtedness per student:** $31,713. **Average need-based loan:** Freshmen: $4040. Undergraduates: $4547. **Parent loans:** $1,383,717 (100% non-need-based). **Programs:** Federal Direct (Subsidized and Unsubsidized Stafford, PLUS), Perkins.

WORK-STUDY Federal work-study: Total amount: $198,931; 102 jobs averaging $1950.

APPLYING FOR FINANCIAL AID Required financial aid form: FAFSA. **Financial aid deadline (priority):** 2/15. **Notification date:** Continuous beginning 1/15. Students must reply within 2 weeks of notification.

CONTACT Jeannine Bosse, Director of Student Financial Services, Thomas College, 180 West River Road, Waterville, ME 04901-5097, 800-339-7001. *Fax:* 207-859-1115. *E-mail:* sfsdir@thomas.edu. *Website:* http://www.thomas.edu/.

THOMAS EDISON STATE UNIVERSITY
Trenton, NJ

Tuition & fees (NJ res): $6350	Average undergraduate aid package: N/A

ABOUT THE INSTITUTION State-supported, coed. **Awards:** certificates, associate, bachelor's, master's, and doctoral degrees (offers only distance learning degree programs). 27 undergraduate majors. **Total enrollment:** 17,511. Undergraduates: 16,506. Federal methodology is used as a basis for awarding need-based institutional aid.

UNDERGRADUATE EXPENSES for 2016–2017 Application fee: $75. **Tuition, state resident:** full-time $6350; part-time $385 per credit hour. **Tuition, nonresident:** full-time $9352; part-time $499 per credit hour.

GIFT AID (NEED-BASED) Total amount: $54,975,684 (100% federal). **Scholarships, grants, and awards:** Federal Pell, state.

GIFT AID (NON-NEED-BASED) Tuition waivers: Full or partial for employees or children of employees.

LOANS Student loans: $18,793,000 (100% need-based). **Programs:** Federal Direct (Subsidized and Unsubsidized Stafford, PLUS), state, private loans.

APPLYING FOR FINANCIAL AID Required financial aid form: FAFSA. **Financial aid deadline:** Continuous. **Notification date:** Continuous. Students must reply within 4 weeks of notification.

CONTACT Mr. James Owens, Director of Financial Aid, Thomas Edison State University, 111 West State Street, Trenton, NJ 08608, 888-442-8372. *E-mail:* finaid@tesu.edu. *Website:* http://www.tesu.edu/.

THOMAS JEFFERSON UNIVERSITY
Philadelphia, PA

CONTACT Susan McFadden, University Director of Financial Aid, Thomas Jefferson University, 1015 Walnut Street, Suite 115, Philadelphia, PA 19107, 215-955-2867 or toll-free 877-533-3247. *Fax:* 215-923-6974. *E-mail:* financial.aid@jefferson.edu. *Website:* http://www.jefferson.edu/university.html.

THOMAS MORE COLLEGE
Crestview Hills, KY

Tuition & fees: $29,450	Average undergraduate aid package: $20,739

ABOUT THE INSTITUTION Independent Roman Catholic, coed. *Awards:* certificates, associate, bachelor's, and master's degrees. 48 undergraduate majors. *Total enrollment:* 1,959. Undergraduates: 1,821. Freshmen: 414. Federal methodology is used as a basis for awarding need-based institutional aid.

UNDERGRADUATE EXPENSES for 2016–2017 *Application fee:* $25. *One-time required fee:* $125. *Comprehensive fee:* $36,754 includes full-time tuition ($28,050), mandatory fees ($1400), and room and board ($7304). *College room only:* $2624. Room and board charges vary according to board plan and housing facility. *Part-time tuition:* $620 per semester hour. *Part-time fees:* $70 per semester hour.

FRESHMAN FINANCIAL AID (Fall 2016, est.) 394 applied for aid; of those 89% were deemed to have need. 100% of freshmen with need received aid; of those 27% had need fully met. *Average percent of need met:* 79% (excluding resources awarded to replace EFC). *Average financial aid package:* $23,134 (excluding resources awarded to replace EFC). 14% of all full-time freshmen had no need and received non-need-based gift aid.

UNDERGRADUATE FINANCIAL AID (Fall 2016, est.) 1,177 applied for aid; of those 89% were deemed to have need. 96% of undergraduates with need received aid; of those 26% had need fully met. *Average percent of need met:* 73% (excluding resources awarded to replace EFC). *Average financial aid package:* $20,739 (excluding resources awarded to replace EFC). 17% of all full-time undergraduates had no need and received non-need-based gift aid.

GIFT AID (NEED-BASED) *Total amount:* $16,138,665 (12% federal, 12% state, 75% institutional, 1% external sources). *Receiving aid:* Freshmen: 85% (350); all full-time undergraduates: 70% (962). *Average award:* Freshmen: $18,481; Undergraduates: $16,719. *Scholarships, grants, and awards:* Federal Pell, FSEOG, state, private, college/university gift aid from institutional funds, Federal Nursing.

GIFT AID (NON-NEED-BASED) *Total amount:* $5,095,065 (3% state, 95% institutional, 2% external sources). *Receiving aid:* Freshmen: 15% (61). Undergraduates: 13% (180). *Average award:* Freshmen: $15,766. Undergraduates: $15,432. *Scholarships, grants, and awards by category: Academic interests/achievement:* 948 awards ($10,534,855 total): biological sciences, business, communication, computer science, education, English, general academic interests/achievements, mathematics, physical sciences, premedicine, religion/biblical studies, social sciences. *Creative arts/performance:* 108 awards ($270,815 total): art/fine arts, music, theater/drama. *Special achievements/activities:* 72 awards ($156,750 total): cheerleading/drum major, community service, leadership, memberships, religious involvement. *Special characteristics:* 741 awards ($4,603,187 total): adult students, children and siblings of alumni, children of faculty/staff, children of union members/company employees, international students, members of minority groups, out-of-state students, religious affiliation, siblings of current students, veterans, veterans' children. *Tuition waivers:* Full or partial for employees or children of employees, senior citizens. *ROTC:* Army cooperative, Air Force cooperative.

LOANS *Student loans:* $7,417,623 (64% need-based, 36% non-need-based). 80% of past graduating class borrowed through all loan programs. *Average indebtedness per student:* $31,235. *Average need-based loan:* Freshmen: $3128. Undergraduates: $3748. *Parent loans:* $1,905,477 (45% need-based, 55% non-need-based). *Programs:* Federal Direct (Subsidized and Unsubsidized Stafford, PLUS), Perkins, Federal Nursing, college/university.

WORK-STUDY *Federal work-study:* Total amount: $126,307; 171 jobs averaging $739. *State or other work-study/employment:* 189 part-time jobs averaging $1031.

APPLYING FOR FINANCIAL AID *Required financial aid form:* FAFSA. *Financial aid deadline (priority):* 3/15. *Notification date:* Continuous beginning 3/1. Students must reply by 5/1.

CONTACT Mr. Mark Messingschlager, Director of Financial Aid, Thomas More College, 333 Thomas More Parkway, Crestview Hills, KY 41017-3495, 859-344-3506 or toll-free 800-825-4557. *Fax:* 859-344-4050. *E-mail:* messinm@thomasmore.edu. *Website:* http://www.thomasmore.edu/.

THOMAS MORE COLLEGE OF LIBERAL ARTS
Merrimack, NH

Tuition & fees: $20,400	Average undergraduate aid package: $14,269

ABOUT THE INSTITUTION Independent Roman Catholic Church, coed. 1 undergraduate major. Federal methodology is used as a basis for awarding need-based institutional aid.

UNDERGRADUATE EXPENSES for 2016–2017 *Comprehensive fee:* $30,100 includes full-time tuition ($20,400) and room and board ($9700). Full-time tuition and fees vary according to course load, program, and reciprocity agreements. Room and board charges vary according to board plan. *Part-time tuition:* $850 per credit hour. Part-time tuition and fees vary according to course load, program, and reciprocity agreements.

UNDERGRADUATE FINANCIAL AID (Fall 2015) 86 applied for aid; of those 98% were deemed to have need. 100% of undergraduates with need received aid. *Average financial aid package:* $14,269 (excluding resources awarded to replace EFC). 16% of all full-time undergraduates had no need and received non-need-based gift aid.

GIFT AID (NEED-BASED) *Receiving aid:* All full-time undergraduates: 97% (84). *Average award:* Undergraduates: $10,264. *Scholarships, grants, and awards:* Federal Pell, FSEOG, state, private, college/university gift aid from institutional funds.

GIFT AID (NON-NEED-BASED) *Receiving aid:* Undergraduates: 44% (38). *Average award:* Undergraduates: $8952. *Tuition waivers:* Full or partial for employees or children of employees.

LOANS *Student loans:* 65% of past graduating class borrowed through all loan programs. *Average indebtedness per student:* $23,452. *Average need-based loan:* Undergraduates: $6546. *Programs:* Federal Direct (Subsidized and Unsubsidized Stafford, PLUS).

WORK-STUDY *State or other work-study/employment:* Part-time jobs available.

APPLYING FOR FINANCIAL AID *Required financial aid form:* FAFSA. *Financial aid deadline:* Continuous. *Notification date:* Continuous beginning 2/15. Students must reply within 4 weeks of notification.

CONTACT Clinton A. Hanson Jr., Coordinator of Financial Aid, Thomas More College of Liberal Arts, 6 Manchester Street, Merrimack, NH 03054-4818, 603-880-8308 Ext. 23 or toll-free 800-880-8308. *Fax:* 603-880-9280. *E-mail:* chanson@thomasmorecollege.edu. *Website:* http://www.thomasmorecollege.edu/.

THOMAS UNIVERSITY
Thomasville, GA

Tuition & fees: $16,940	Average undergraduate aid package: N/A

ABOUT THE INSTITUTION Independent, coed. *Awards:* certificates, associate, bachelor's, and master's degrees. 23 undergraduate majors. *Total enrollment:* 1,156. Undergraduates: 769. Freshmen: 106. Federal methodology is used as a basis for awarding need-based institutional aid.

UNDERGRADUATE EXPENSES for 2017–2018 *Application fee:* $25. *Tuition:* full-time $15,940; part-time $630 per credit hour. *Required fees:* full-time $1000; $550 per year. Room and board charges vary according to housing facility.

FRESHMAN FINANCIAL AID (Fall 2016, est.) 62 applied for aid; of those 85% were deemed to have need. 100% of freshmen with need received aid. *Average* financial aid package: $83 (excluding resources awarded to replace EFC). 60% of all full-time freshmen had no need and received non-need-based gift aid.

UNDERGRADUATE FINANCIAL AID (Fall 2016, est.) 125 applied for aid; of those 58% were deemed to have need.

GIFT AID (NEED-BASED) Total amount: $2,283,478 (63% federal, 16% state, 21% institutional). **Receiving aid:** Freshmen: 53% (46). **Average award:** Freshmen: $87. **Scholarships, grants, and awards:** Federal Pell, FSEOG, state, private, college/university gift aid from institutional funds.

GIFT AID (NON-NEED-BASED) Receiving aid: Freshmen: 53% (46). **Average award:** Freshmen: $3249. **Scholarships, grants, and awards by category:** Academic interests/achievement: biological sciences, business, education, English, general academic interests/achievements, humanities, mathematics, physical sciences, social sciences. **Creative arts/performance:** art/fine arts, debating, music, theater/drama. **Special characteristics:** children and siblings of alumni, children of faculty/staff, ethnic background, out-of-state students, veterans.

LOANS Student loans: $5,095,109 (100% need-based). **Average need-based loan:** Freshmen: $87. **Parent loans:** $487,618 (100% need-based). **Programs:** Federal Direct (Subsidized and Unsubsidized Stafford, PLUS), state, alternative loans.

WORK-STUDY Federal work-study: Total amount: $43,512; 42 jobs averaging $1639.

ATHLETIC AWARDS Total amount: $2,302,331 (100% need-based).

APPLYING FOR FINANCIAL AID Required financial aid forms: FAFSA, state aid form. **Financial aid deadline:** Continuous. **Notification date:** Continuous beginning 1/1.

CONTACT Mr. Clifton L. Mitchell Jr., Director of Financial Aid, Thomas University, 1501 Millpond Road, Thomasville, GA 31792-7499, 229-226-1621 Ext. 1002 or toll-free 800-538-9784. *Fax:* 229-584-2400. *E-mail:* cmitchell@thomasu.edu. *Website:* http://www.thomasu.edu/.

TIFFIN UNIVERSITY
Tiffin, OH

Tuition & fees: $23,850	Average undergraduate aid package: $17,797

ABOUT THE INSTITUTION Independent, coed. **Awards:** certificates, associate, bachelor's, and master's degrees. 47 undergraduate majors. **Total enrollment:** 3,350. Undergraduates: 2,353. Freshmen: 458. Federal methodology is used as a basis for awarding need-based institutional aid.

UNDERGRADUATE EXPENSES for 2017–2018 Application fee: $20. **Comprehensive fee:** $34,750 includes full-time tuition ($23,700), mandatory fees ($150), and room and board ($10,900). **College room only:** $5900. Full-time tuition and fees vary according to course load, degree level, location, program, and reciprocity agreements. Room and board charges vary according to board plan and housing facility. **Part-time tuition:** $790 per credit hour. Part-time tuition and fees vary according to course load, degree level, location, program, and reciprocity agreements.

FRESHMAN FINANCIAL AID (Fall 2016, est.) 394 applied for aid; of those 93% were deemed to have need. 100% of freshmen with need received aid; of those 16% had need fully met. **Average percent of need met:** 68% (excluding resources awarded to replace EFC). **Average financial aid package:** $18,876 (excluding resources awarded to replace EFC).

UNDERGRADUATE FINANCIAL AID (Fall 2016, est.) 1,380 applied for aid; of those 92% were deemed to have need. 100% of undergraduates with need received aid; of those 18% had need fully met. **Average percent of need met:** 68% (excluding resources awarded to replace EFC). **Average financial aid package:** $17,797 (excluding resources awarded to replace EFC).

GIFT AID (NEED-BASED) Total amount: $18,463,462 (22% federal, 8% state, 69% institutional, 1% external sources). **Receiving aid:** Freshmen: 83% (365); all full-time undergraduates: 71% (1,226). **Average award:** Freshmen: $15,608; Undergraduates: $14,154. **Scholarships, grants, and awards:** Federal Pell, FSEOG, state, private, college/university gift aid from institutional funds, United Negro College Fund.

GIFT AID (NON-NEED-BASED) Receiving aid: Freshmen: 9% (38). Undergraduates: 7% (125). **Scholarships, grants, and awards by category:** Academic interests/achievement: 1,186 awards ($10,546,999 total): general academic interests/achievements. **Creative arts/performance:** 167 awards ($374,000 total): music, performing arts, theater/drama. **Special achievements/activities:** 18 awards ($17,500 total): cheerleading/drum major. **Special characteristics:** 13 awards ($164,502 total): children of faculty/staff. **Tuition waivers:** Full or partial for employees or children of employees, senior citizens. **ROTC:** Army cooperative, Air Force cooperative.

LOANS Student loans: $13,959,938 (100% need-based). 83% of past graduating class borrowed through all loan programs. *Average indebtedness per student:* $37,834. **Average need-based loan:** Freshmen: $3183. Undergraduates: $4066. **Parent loans:** $3,224,374 (100% need-based). **Programs:** Federal Direct (Subsidized and Unsubsidized Stafford, PLUS), Perkins, college/university, private loans.

WORK-STUDY Federal work-study: Total amount: $306,784; 199 jobs averaging $2095.

ATHLETIC AWARDS Total amount: $3,541,503 (100% need-based).

APPLYING FOR FINANCIAL AID Required financial aid form: FAFSA. **Financial aid deadline:** Continuous. **Notification date:** Continuous beginning 11/1. Students must reply within 2 weeks of notification.

CONTACT Ms. Cindy Little, Director of Financial Aid Operations, Tiffin University, 155 Miami Street, Tiffin, OH 44883, 419-448-3415 or toll-free 800-968-6446. *Fax:* 419-443-5006. *E-mail:* clittle@tiffin.edu. *Website:* http://www.tiffin.edu/.

TOCCOA FALLS COLLEGE
Toccoa Falls, GA

Tuition & fees: $22,034	Average undergraduate aid package: $18,393

ABOUT THE INSTITUTION Independent interdenominational, coed. **Awards:** certificates, associate, and bachelor's degrees. 30 undergraduate majors. **Total enrollment:** 1,254. Undergraduates: 1,254. Freshmen: 216. Federal methodology is used as a basis for awarding need-based institutional aid.

UNDERGRADUATE EXPENSES for 2017–2018 Application fee: $25. **Comprehensive fee:** $29,968 includes full-time tuition ($21,334), mandatory fees ($700), and room and board ($7934). Full-time tuition and fees vary according to location. Room and board charges vary according to board plan. **Part-time tuition:** $889 per credit hour. **Part-time fees:** $700 per year. Part-time tuition and fees vary according to location.

FRESHMAN FINANCIAL AID (Fall 2015) 176 applied for aid; of those 91% were deemed to have need. 100% of freshmen with need received aid; of those 13% had need fully met. **Average percent of need met:** 64% (excluding resources awarded to replace EFC). **Average financial aid package:** $17,959 (excluding resources awarded to replace EFC). 11% of all full-time freshmen had no need and received non-need-based gift aid.

UNDERGRADUATE FINANCIAL AID (Fall 2015) 591 applied for aid; of those 94% were deemed to have need. 100% of undergraduates with need received aid; of those 13% had need fully met. **Average percent of need met:** 67% (excluding resources awarded to replace EFC). **Average financial aid package:** $18,393 (excluding resources awarded to replace EFC). 9% of all full-time undergraduates had no need and received non-need-based gift aid.

GIFT AID (NEED-BASED) Total amount: $8,052,340 (18% federal, 11% state, 68% institutional, 3% external sources). **Receiving aid:** Freshmen: 89% (160); all full-time undergraduates: 90% (553). **Average award:** Freshmen: $15,075; Undergraduates: $14,645. **Scholarships, grants, and awards:** Federal Pell, FSEOG, state, private, college/university gift aid from institutional funds.

GIFT AID (NON-NEED-BASED) Total amount: $1,002,108 (21% state, 76% institutional, 3% external sources). **Receiving aid:** Freshmen: 11% (19). Undergraduates: 9% (55). **Average award:** Freshmen: $8736. Undergraduates: $10,529. **Scholarships, grants, and awards by category:** Academic interests/achievement: business, communication, education, general academic interests/achievements, religion/biblical studies. **Creative arts/performance:** music. **Special achievements/activities:** leadership. **Special characteristics:** children of faculty/staff, ethnic background, general special characteristics, international students, married students, relatives of clergy, religious affiliation, siblings of current students. **Tuition waivers:** Full or partial for employees or children of employees.

LOANS Student loans: $3,312,757 (84% need-based, 16% non-need-based). 81% of past graduating class borrowed through all loan programs. *Average indebtedness per student:* $27,567. **Average need-based loan:** Freshmen: $3195. Undergraduates: $3633. **Parent loans:** $1,166,469 (64% need-based, 36% non-need-based). **Programs:** Federal Direct (Subsidized and Unsubsidized Stafford, PLUS), state.

WORK-STUDY Federal work-study: jobs available. **State or other work-study/employment:** Part-time jobs available.

APPLYING FOR FINANCIAL AID *Required financial aid forms:* FAFSA, institution's own form. *Financial aid deadline (priority):* 5/1. *Notification date:* Continuous beginning 3/15. Students must reply within 2 weeks of notification.
CONTACT Wanda V. Pickens, Director of Student Financial Services, Toccoa Falls College, 107 Kincaid Drive, Box 800, Toccoa Falls, GA 30598, 706-886-7299 Ext. 5435 or toll-free 888-785-5624. *Fax:* 706-282-6041. *E-mail:* wpickens@tfc.edu. *Website:* http://www.tfc.edu/.

TORAH TEMIMAH TALMUDICAL SEMINARY
Brooklyn, NY

CONTACT Financial Aid Office, Torah Temimah Talmudical Seminary, 507 Ocean Parkway, Brooklyn, NY 11218-5913, 718-853-8500.

TOUGALOO COLLEGE
Tougaloo, MS

CONTACT Director of Financial Aid, Tougaloo College, 500 West County Line Road, Tougaloo, MS 39174, 601-977-6134 or toll-free 888-42GALOO. *Fax:* 601-977-6164.
Website: http://www.tougaloo.edu/.

TOURO COLLEGE
New York, NY

Tuition & fees: $16,980	Average undergraduate aid package: $12,164

ABOUT THE INSTITUTION Independent, coed. *Awards:* certificates, associate, bachelor's, master's, and doctoral degrees. 26 undergraduate majors. *Total enrollment:* 12,021. Undergraduates: 6,912. Freshmen: 626. Federal methodology is used as a basis for awarding need-based institutional aid.
**UNDERGRADUATE EXPENSES for 2016–2017 *Application fee:* $50. *Comprehensive fee:* $28,950 includes full-time tuition ($16,380), mandatory fees ($600), and room and board ($11,970). *College room only:* $8320. *Part-time tuition:* $680 per credit hour.
FRESHMAN FINANCIAL AID (Fall 2016, est.) 513 applied for aid; of those 81% were deemed to have need. 100% of freshmen with need received aid; of those 35% had need fully met. *Average percent of need met:* 40% (excluding resources awarded to replace EFC). *Average financial aid package:* $8231 (excluding resources awarded to replace EFC). 15% of all full-time freshmen had no need and received non-need-based gift aid.
UNDERGRADUATE FINANCIAL AID (Fall 2016, est.) 3,861 applied for aid; of those 81% were deemed to have need. 100% of undergraduates with need received aid; of those 9% had need fully met. *Average percent of need met:* 70% (excluding resources awarded to replace EFC). *Average financial aid package:* $12,164 (excluding resources awarded to replace EFC). 11% of all full-time undergraduates had no need and received non-need-based gift aid.
**GIFT AID (NEED-BASED) *Total amount:* $21,940,507 (63% federal, 37% state). *Receiving aid:* Freshmen: 68% (414); all full-time undergraduates: 47% (2,979). *Average award:* Freshmen: $8642; Undergraduates: $11,750. *Scholarships, grants, and awards:* Federal Pell, FSEOG, state, private, college/university gift aid from institutional funds.
**GIFT AID (NON-NEED-BASED) *Total amount:* $14,640,296 (1% state, 98% institutional, 1% external sources). *Receiving aid:* Freshmen: 31% (191). Undergraduates: 28% (1,799). *Average award:* Freshmen: $2428. Undergraduates: $2855. *Scholarships, grants, and awards by category:* Academic interests/achievement: general academic interests/achievements. *Special characteristics:* children of faculty/staff.
**LOANS *Average need-based loan:* Freshmen: $1402. Undergraduates: $2174. *Parent loans:* $626,163 (100% non-need-based). *Programs:* Federal Direct (Subsidized and Unsubsidized Stafford, PLUS), Perkins, alternative loans.

WORK-STUDY Federal work-study jobs available. *State or other work-study/employment:* Total amount: $17,930 (100% non-need-based). Part-time jobs available.
APPLYING FOR FINANCIAL AID *Required financial aid forms:* FAFSA, institution's own form. *Financial aid deadline:* 8/15 (priority: 5/15). *Notification date:* Continuous.
CONTACT Karyn Wright-Moore, Office of Financial Aid, Touro College, 27 West 23rd Street, New York, NY 10010, 212-463-0400 Ext. 5108. *E-mail:* karyn.wright-moore1@touro.edu.
Website: http://www.touro.edu/.

TOURO COLLEGE LOS ANGELES
West Hollywood, CA

CONTACT Financial Aid Office, Touro College Los Angeles, 1317 North Crescent Heights Boulevard, West Hollywood, CA 90046, 323-822-9700.
Website: http://www.touro.edu/losangeles/.

TOURO UNIVERSITY WORLDWIDE
Los Alamitos, CA

CONTACT Financial Aid Office, Touro University Worldwide, 10601 Calle Lee, Suite 179, Los Alamitos, CA 90720, 818-575-6800.
Website: http://www.tuw.edu/.

TOWSON UNIVERSITY
Towson, MD

Tuition & fees (MD res): $9408	Average undergraduate aid package: $10,201

ABOUT THE INSTITUTION State-supported, coed. *Awards:* certificates, bachelor's, master's, and doctoral degrees. 63 undergraduate majors. *Total enrollment:* 22,343. Undergraduates: 19,198. Freshmen: 2,755. Federal methodology is used as a basis for awarding need-based institutional aid.
**UNDERGRADUATE EXPENSES for 2016–2017 *Application fee:* $45. *Tuition, state resident:* full-time $6560; part-time $283 per credit hour. *Tuition, nonresident:* full-time $18,228; part-time $768 per credit hour. *Required fees:* full-time $2848; $124 per credit hour. Full-time tuition and fees vary according to course load and location. Part-time tuition and fees vary according to course load and location. *College room and board:* $11,754; *Room only:* $6748. Room and board charges vary according to board plan and housing facility.
FRESHMAN FINANCIAL AID (Fall 2016, est.) 2,331 applied for aid; of those 69% were deemed to have need. 94% of freshmen with need received aid; of those 10% had need fully met. *Average percent of need met:* 55% (excluding resources awarded to replace EFC). *Average financial aid package:* $10,131 (excluding resources awarded to replace EFC). 7% of all full-time freshmen had no need and received non-need-based gift aid.
UNDERGRADUATE FINANCIAL AID (Fall 2016, est.) 11,997 applied for aid; of those 77% were deemed to have need. 96% of undergraduates with need received aid; of those 10% had need fully met. *Average percent of need met:* 58% (excluding resources awarded to replace EFC). *Average financial aid package:* $10,201 (excluding resources awarded to replace EFC). 6% of all full-time undergraduates had no need and received non-need-based gift aid.
**GIFT AID (NEED-BASED) *Total amount:* $54,603,299 (44% federal, 21% state, 34% institutional, 1% external sources). *Receiving aid:* Freshmen: 30% (838); all full-time undergraduates: 34% (5,726). *Average award:* Freshmen: $9832; Undergraduates: $8715. *Scholarships, grants, and awards:* Federal Pell, FSEOG, state, private, college/university gift aid from institutional funds.
**GIFT AID (NON-NEED-BASED) *Total amount:* $14,521,360 (3% federal, 8% state, 74% institutional, 15% external sources). *Receiving aid:* Freshmen: 22% (593). Undergraduates: 14% (2,360). *Average award:* Freshmen: $4948. Undergraduates: $5362. *Scholarships, grants, and awards by category:* Academic interests/

achievement: 1,970 awards ($9,287,851 total): biological sciences, business, communication, computer science, education, English, foreign languages, general academic interests/achievements, home economics, mathematics, physical sciences. *Creative arts/performance:* 144 awards ($459,637 total): art/fine arts, cinema/film/broadcasting, dance, debating, music, performing arts, theater/drama. *Special achievements/activities:* 179 awards ($247,376 total): community service, memberships. *Special characteristics:* 491 awards ($1,878,452 total): adult students, children and siblings of alumni, children of faculty/staff, ethnic background, first-generation college students, handicapped students, international students, members of minority groups, previous college experience, veterans. *Tuition waivers:* Full or partial for employees or children of employees, senior citizens. *ROTC:* Army cooperative, Air Force cooperative.
LOANS *Student loans:* $75,194,371 (47% need-based, 53% non-need-based). 61% of past graduating class borrowed through all loan programs. *Average indebtedness per student:* $25,483. *Average need-based loan:* Freshmen: $3177. Undergraduates: $4096. *Parent loans:* $40,664,916 (1% need-based, 99% non-need-based). *Programs:* Federal Direct (Subsidized and Unsubsidized Stafford, PLUS), Perkins.
WORK-STUDY *Federal work-study:* Total amount: $1,067,397; 603 jobs averaging $1752.
ATHLETIC AWARDS Total amount: $6,173,740 (2% need-based, 98% non-need-based).
APPLYING FOR FINANCIAL AID *Required financial aid forms:* FAFSA, state aid form. *Financial aid deadline (priority):* 1/20. *Notification date:* Continuous beginning 3/21. Students must reply by 5/1 or within 2 weeks of notification.
CONTACT Mr. David Horne, Director of Financial Aid, Towson University, 8000 York Road, Towson, MD 21252-0001, 410-704-4236. *E-mail:* finaid@towson.edu. *Website:* http://www.towson.edu/.

TRANSYLVANIA UNIVERSITY
Lexington, KY

Tuition & fees: $37,290	Average undergraduate aid package: $28,085

ABOUT THE INSTITUTION Independent Christian Church (Disciples of Christ), coed. *Awards:* bachelor's degrees. 35 undergraduate majors. *Total enrollment:* 963. Undergraduates: 963. Freshmen: 242. Federal methodology is used as a basis for awarding need-based institutional aid.
UNDERGRADUATE EXPENSES for 2017–2018 *Comprehensive fee:* $47,450 includes full-time tuition ($35,770), mandatory fees ($1520), and room and board ($10,160). *College room only:* $5750. Room and board charges vary according to board plan and housing facility. *Part-time tuition:* $3980 per course. Part-time tuition and fees vary according to course load.
FRESHMAN FINANCIAL AID (Fall 2016, est.) 217 applied for aid; of those 80% were deemed to have need. 100% of freshmen with need received aid; of those 25% had need fully met. *Average percent of need met:* 78% (excluding resources awarded to replace EFC). *Average financial aid package:* $27,139 (excluding resources awarded to replace EFC). 28% of all full-time freshmen had no need and received non-need-based gift aid.
UNDERGRADUATE FINANCIAL AID (Fall 2016, est.) 731 applied for aid; of those 86% were deemed to have need. 100% of undergraduates with need received aid; of those 23% had need fully met. *Average percent of need met:* 81% (excluding resources awarded to replace EFC). *Average financial aid package:* $28,085 (excluding resources awarded to replace EFC). 33% of all full-time undergraduates had no need and received non-need-based gift aid.
GIFT AID (NEED-BASED) *Total amount:* $14,843,371 (7% federal, 16% state, 75% institutional, 2% external sources). *Receiving aid:* Freshmen: 72% (174); all full-time undergraduates: 66% (628). *Average award:* Freshmen: $24,019; Undergraduates: $24,196. *Scholarships, grants, and awards:* Federal Pell, FSEOG, state, private, college/university gift aid from institutional funds.
GIFT AID (NON-NEED-BASED) *Total amount:* $6,879,016 (8% state, 88% institutional, 4% external sources). *Receiving aid:* Freshmen: 15% (36). Undergraduates: 10% (91). *Average award:* Freshmen: $15,197. Undergraduates: $17,513. *Scholarships, grants, and awards by category: Academic interests/achievement:* $12,072,116 total: general academic interests/achievements. *Creative arts/performance:* $290,750 total: art/fine arts, music, theater/drama. *Special achievements/activities:* $3,789,490 total: general special achievements/activities. *Special characteristics:* $1,410,487 total: children of faculty/staff, members of minority groups, out-

of-state students, relatives of clergy, religious affiliation. *Tuition waivers:* Full or partial for employees or children of employees. *ROTC:* Army cooperative, Air Force cooperative.
LOANS *Student loans:* $4,910,782 (64% need-based, 36% non-need-based). 63% of past graduating class borrowed through all loan programs. *Average indebtedness per student:* $30,514. *Average need-based loan:* Freshmen: $3278. Undergraduates: $4284. *Parent loans:* $2,066,163 (33% need-based, 67% non-need-based). *Programs:* Federal Direct (Subsidized and Unsubsidized Stafford, PLUS), Perkins.
WORK-STUDY *Federal work-study:* Total amount: $349,230; 310 jobs averaging $1656. *State or other work-study/employment:* Total amount: $225,640 (36% need-based, 64% non-need-based). 40 part-time jobs averaging $5641.
APPLYING FOR FINANCIAL AID *Required financial aid form:* FAFSA. *Financial aid deadline (priority):* 10/31. *Notification date:* Continuous beginning 12/20. Students must reply within 2 weeks of notification.
CONTACT Ms. Jennifer Priest, Director of Financial Aid, Transylvania University, 300 North Broadway, Lexington, KY 40508-1797, 859-233-8239 or toll-free 800-872-6798. *Fax:* 859-281-3650. *E-mail:* jpriest@transy.edu. *Website:* http://www.transy.edu/.

TREVECCA NAZARENE UNIVERSITY
Nashville, TN

Tuition & fees: $25,100	Average undergraduate aid package: N/A

ABOUT THE INSTITUTION Independent Nazarene, coed. *Awards:* certificates, associate, bachelor's, master's, and doctoral degrees. 70 undergraduate majors. *Total enrollment:* 3,221. Undergraduates: 2,092. Freshmen: 414. Institutional methodology is used as a basis for awarding need-based institutional aid.
UNDERGRADUATE EXPENSES for 2017–2018 *Application fee:* $25. *Comprehensive fee:* $33,908 includes full-time tuition ($24,200), mandatory fees ($900), and room and board ($8808). *College room only:* $4404. Full-time tuition and fees vary according to course load and program. Room and board charges vary according to board plan. *Part-time tuition:* $935 per credit hour. Part-time tuition and fees vary according to course load and program. *Payment plan:* Tuition prepayment.
GIFT AID (NEED-BASED) *Total amount:* $3,671,217 (82% federal, 18% state). *Scholarships, grants, and awards:* Federal Pell, FSEOG, state, private, college/university gift aid from institutional funds, United Negro College Fund, Federal Nursing.
GIFT AID (NON-NEED-BASED) *Total amount:* $13,194,167 (13% state, 80% institutional, 7% external sources). *Scholarships, grants, and awards by category: Academic interests/achievement:* biological sciences, business, communication, education, English, general academic interests/achievements, physical sciences, religion/biblical studies, social sciences. *Creative arts/performance:* cinema/film/broadcasting, music, theater/drama. *Special achievements/activities:* general special achievements/activities, leadership. *Special characteristics:* children of faculty/staff, general special characteristics, relatives of clergy, religious affiliation, siblings of current students. *Tuition waivers:* Full or partial for employees or children of employees, senior citizens. *ROTC:* Army cooperative.
LOANS *Student loans:* $9,121,645 (45% need-based, 55% non-need-based). 72% of past graduating class borrowed through all loan programs. *Average indebtedness per student:* $29,291. *Parent loans:* $1,396,681 (100% non-need-based). *Programs:* Federal Direct (Subsidized and Unsubsidized Stafford, PLUS), Perkins.
WORK-STUDY *Federal work-study:* jobs available. *State or other work-study/employment:* Total amount: $645,481 (100% non-need-based). Part-time jobs available.
ATHLETIC AWARDS Total amount: $2,213,922 (100% non-need-based).
APPLYING FOR FINANCIAL AID *Required financial aid form:* FAFSA. *Financial aid deadline (priority):* 1/1. *Notification date:* Continuous beginning 12/1.
CONTACT Eddie White, Director of Financial Aid, Trevecca Nazarene University, 333 Murfreesboro Road, Nashville, TN 37210, 615-248-1242 or toll-free 888-210-4TNU. *Fax:* 615-248-7728. *E-mail:* ewhite@trevecca.edu. *Website:* http://www.trevecca.edu/.

TRIDENT UNIVERSITY INTERNATIONAL
Cypress, CA

CONTACT Taisha Azlin, Director of Financial Aid, Trident University International, 5665 Plaza Drive, Third Floor, Cypress, CA 90630, 800-375-9878 Ext. 1061. *Fax:* 714-484-7621. *E-mail:* financialaid@tuiu.edu. *Website:* http://www.trident.edu/.

TRINE UNIVERSITY
Peoria, AZ

CONTACT Financial Aid Office, Trine University, 14100 North 83rd. Avenue, Suite 100, Peoria, AZ 85381, 855-997-7701. *Website:* http://www.trine.edu/peoria/.

TRINE UNIVERSITY
Angola, IN

Tuition & fees: $31,540	Average undergraduate aid package: $27,021

ABOUT THE INSTITUTION Independent, coed. *Awards:* associate, bachelor's, master's, and doctoral degrees. 35 undergraduate majors. *Total enrollment:* 3,730. Undergraduates: 3,372. Freshmen: 461. Federal methodology is used as a basis for awarding need-based institutional aid.

UNDERGRADUATE EXPENSES for 2017–2018 *Comprehensive fee:* $42,110 includes full-time tuition ($31,080), mandatory fees ($460), and room and board ($10,570). Full-time tuition and fees vary according to degree level, location, and program. Room and board charges vary according to board plan and housing facility. *Part-time tuition:* $970 per credit hour. Part-time tuition and fees vary according to degree level, location, and program.

FRESHMAN FINANCIAL AID (Fall 2016, est.) 450 applied for aid; of those 91% were deemed to have need. 100% of freshmen with need received aid; of those 18% had need fully met. *Average percent of need met:* 81% (excluding resources awarded to replace EFC). *Average financial aid package:* $27,981 (excluding resources awarded to replace EFC). 11% of all full-time freshmen had no need and received non-need-based gift aid.

UNDERGRADUATE FINANCIAL AID (Fall 2016, est.) 1,496 applied for aid; of those 91% were deemed to have need. 100% of undergraduates with need received aid; of those 22% had need fully met. *Average percent of need met:* 82% (excluding resources awarded to replace EFC). *Average financial aid package:* $27,021 (excluding resources awarded to replace EFC). 14% of all full-time undergraduates had no need and received non-need-based gift aid.

GIFT AID (NEED-BASED) *Total amount:* $9,575,393 (25% federal, 22% state, 53% institutional). *Receiving aid:* Freshmen: 89% (411); all full-time undergraduates: 86% (1,353). *Average award:* Freshmen: $22,561; Undergraduates: $20,794. *Scholarships, grants, and awards:* Federal Pell, FSEOG, state, private, college/university gift aid from institutional funds.

GIFT AID (NON-NEED-BASED) *Total amount:* $24,110,251 (90% institutional, 10% external sources). *Receiving aid:* Freshmen: 10% (47). Undergraduates: 12% (185). *Average award:* Freshmen: $15,367. Undergraduates: $12,829. *Scholarships, grants, and awards by category: Academic interests/achievement:* 44 awards ($84,302 total): general academic interests/achievements, premedicine. *Creative arts/performance:* 117 awards ($146,646 total): dance, music. *Special achievements/activities:* 32 awards ($33,000 total): cheerleading/drum major. *Special characteristics:* 180 awards ($343,000 total): children and siblings of alumni, children of educators, children of faculty/staff, members of minority groups, siblings of current students, twins. *Tuition waivers:* Full or partial for employees or children of employees, senior citizens. *ROTC:* Air Force cooperative.

LOANS *Student loans:* $14,107,419 (32% need-based, 68% non-need-based). 82% of past graduating class borrowed through all loan programs. *Average indebtedness per student:* $38,161. *Average need-based loan:* Freshmen: $4239. Undergrad-

uates: $5413. *Parent loans:* $4,616,492 (100% non-need-based). *Programs:* Federal Direct (Subsidized and Unsubsidized Stafford, PLUS), alternative loans.

WORK-STUDY *Federal work-study:* Total amount: $280,000; jobs available. *State or other work-study/employment:* Part-time jobs available.

APPLYING FOR FINANCIAL AID *Required financial aid form:* FAFSA. *Financial aid deadline (priority):* 3/1. *Notification date:* Continuous beginning 3/10. Students must reply by 5/1.

CONTACT Kim Bennett, Assistant Vice President of Enrollment Management, Trine University, 1 University Avenue, Angola, IN 46703-1764, 260-665-4438 or toll-free 800-347-4878. *Fax:* 260-665-4511. *E-mail:* bennettk@trine.edu. *Website:* http://www.trine.edu/.

TRINITY BAPTIST COLLEGE
Jacksonville, FL

ABOUT THE INSTITUTION Independent Baptist, coed. *Awards:* associate, bachelor's, and master's degrees. 8 undergraduate majors. *Total enrollment:* 280. Undergraduates: 268.

GIFT AID (NEED-BASED) *Scholarships, grants, and awards:* Federal Pell, FSEOG, state, private, college/university gift aid from institutional funds.

GIFT AID (NON-NEED-BASED) *Scholarships, grants, and awards by category: Academic interests/achievement:* education, general academic interests/achievements, religion/biblical studies. *Special achievements/activities:* leadership, religious involvement. *Special characteristics:* relatives of clergy, religious affiliation, spouses of current students.

APPLYING FOR FINANCIAL AID *Required financial aid forms:* FAFSA, institution's own form, state aid form.

CONTACT Mr. Mark Elkins, Financial Aid Administrator, Trinity Baptist College, 800 Hammond Boulevard, Jacksonville, FL 32221, 904-596-2445 or toll-free 800-786-2206. *Fax:* 904-596-2531. *E-mail:* financialaid@tbc.edu. *Website:* http://www.tbc.edu/.

TRINITY BIBLE COLLEGE AND GRADUATE SCHOOL
Ellendale, ND

CONTACT Mary Anne Whitman, Director of Financial Aid, Trinity Bible College and Graduate School, 50 South 6th Avenue, Ellendale, ND 58436-7150, 701-349-5403 or toll-free 800-523-1603. *Fax:* 701-349-5786. *E-mail:* mwhitman@trinitybiblecollege.edu. *Website:* http://www.trinitybiblecollege.edu/.

TRINITY CHRISTIAN COLLEGE
Palos Heights, IL

Tuition & fees: $27,450	Average undergraduate aid package: $19,593

ABOUT THE INSTITUTION Independent Christian Reformed, coed. *Awards:* bachelor's and master's degrees. 47 undergraduate majors. *Total enrollment:* 1,286. Undergraduates: 1,193. Freshmen: 160. Federal methodology is used as a basis for awarding need-based institutional aid.

UNDERGRADUATE EXPENSES for 2016–2017 *Application fee:* $30. *One-time required fee:* $225. *Comprehensive fee:* $37,030 includes full-time tuition ($27,200), mandatory fees ($250), and room and board ($9580). Full-time tuition and fees vary according to course load and degree level. Room and board charges vary according to board plan and housing facility. *Part-time tuition:* $908 per credit hour. Part-time tuition and fees vary according to course load and degree level.

FRESHMAN FINANCIAL AID (Fall 2016, est.) 137 applied for aid; of those 92% were deemed to have need. 100% of freshmen with need received aid; of those 17% had need fully met. *Average percent of need met:* 76% (excluding resources awarded to replace EFC). *Average financial aid package:* $22,583 (excluding

resources awarded to replace EFC). 11% of all full-time freshmen had no need and received non-need-based gift aid.

UNDERGRADUATE FINANCIAL AID (Fall 2016, est.) 772 applied for aid; of those 92% were deemed to have need. 100% of undergraduates with need received aid; of those 14% had need fully met. *Average percent of need met:* 70% (excluding resources awarded to replace EFC). *Average financial aid package:* $19,593 (excluding resources awarded to replace EFC). 13% of all full-time undergraduates had no need and received non-need-based gift aid.

GIFT AID (NEED-BASED) *Total amount:* $9,983,660 (18% federal, 12% state, 69% institutional, 1% external sources). *Receiving aid:* Freshmen: 79% (126); all full-time undergraduates: 77% (694). *Average award:* Freshmen: $19,405; Undergraduates: $15,990. *Scholarships, grants, and awards:* Federal Pell, FSEOG, state, private, college/university gift aid from institutional funds, Federal Nursing.

GIFT AID (NON-NEED-BASED) *Total amount:* $1,759,366 (9% federal, 89% institutional, 2% external sources). *Receiving aid:* Freshmen: 13% (21). Undergraduates: 8% (72). *Average award:* Freshmen: $10,462. Undergraduates: $9420. *Scholarships, grants, and awards by category: Academic interests/achievement:* biological sciences, business, communication, computer science, education, engineering/technologies, English, general academic interests/achievements, humanities, international studies, mathematics, physical sciences, premedicine, religion/biblical studies, social sciences. *Creative arts/performance:* applied art and design, art/fine arts, general creative arts/performance, journalism/publications, music, performing arts, theater/drama. *Special achievements/activities:* community service, general special achievements/activities, leadership, religious involvement. *Special characteristics:* adult students, children and siblings of alumni, children of faculty/staff, ethnic background, first-generation college students, local/state students, members of minority groups, out-of-state students, religious affiliation, veterans. *Tuition waivers:* Full or partial for employees or children of employees.

LOANS *Student loans:* $7,227,713 (43% need-based, 57% non-need-based). 80% of past graduating class borrowed through all loan programs. *Average indebtedness per student:* $31,321. *Average need-based loan:* Freshmen: $3712. Undergraduates: $4640. *Parent loans:* $1,242,130 (100% non-need-based). *Programs:* Federal Direct (Subsidized and Unsubsidized Stafford, PLUS), Perkins, Federal Nursing.

WORK-STUDY *Federal work-study:* Total amount: $127,156; jobs available. *State or other work-study/employment:* Total amount: $484,480 (100% non-need-based). Part-time jobs available.

ATHLETIC AWARDS Total amount: $1,335,008 (92% need-based, 8% non-need-based).

APPLYING FOR FINANCIAL AID *Required financial aid form:* FAFSA. *Financial aid deadline (priority):* 2/15. *Notification date:* Continuous beginning 12/15. Students must reply by 5/1 or within 2 weeks of notification.

CONTACT Ryan P. Zantingh, Director of Financial Aid, Trinity Christian College, 6601 West College Drive, Palos Heights, IL 60463-0929, 708-239-4872 or toll-free 866-TRIN-4-ME. *Fax:* 708-239-4814. *E-mail:* ryan.zantingh@trnty.edu. *Website:* http://www.trnty.edu/.

TRINITY COLLEGE
Hartford, CT

ABOUT THE INSTITUTION Independent, coed. *Awards:* bachelor's and master's degrees. 48 undergraduate majors. *Total enrollment:* 2,397. Undergraduates: 2,289. Freshmen: 559.

GIFT AID (NEED-BASED) *Scholarships, grants, and awards:* Federal Pell, FSEOG, state, private, college/university gift aid from institutional funds, Academic Competitiveness Grants, National SMART Grants, Yellow Ribbon Grant Program.

GIFT AID (NON-NEED-BASED) *Scholarships, grants, and awards by category: Academic interests/achievement:* general academic interests/achievements. *Special achievements/activities:* leadership.

LOANS *Programs:* Federal Direct (PLUS), Perkins, college/university, alternative loans.

WORK-STUDY *Federal work-study:* 797 jobs averaging $1788. *State or other work-study/employment:* Part-time jobs available.

APPLYING FOR FINANCIAL AID *Required financial aid forms:* FAFSA, CSS Financial Aid PROFILE, noncustodial (divorced/separated) parent's statement, business/farm supplement, federal income tax form(s).

CONTACT Ms. Kelly O'Brien, Director of Financial Aid, Trinity College, 300 Summit Street, Hartford, CT 06106-3100, 860-297-2046. *Fax:* 860-987-6296. *E-mail:* financialaid@trincoll.edu. *Website:* http://www.trincoll.edu/.

TRINITY COLLEGE OF FLORIDA
Trinity, FL

Tuition & fees: $15,690	Average undergraduate aid package: $13,874

ABOUT THE INSTITUTION Independent nondenominational, coed. *Awards:* certificates, associate, and bachelor's degrees. 10 undergraduate majors. *Total enrollment:* 202. Undergraduates: 202. Freshmen: 26. Both federal and institutional methodology are used as a basis for awarding need-based institutional aid.

UNDERGRADUATE EXPENSES for 2017–2018 *Application fee:* $35. *Comprehensive fee:* $22,140 includes full-time tuition ($14,850), mandatory fees ($840), and room and board ($6450). Full-time tuition and fees vary according to course load and program. *Part-time tuition:* $495 per credit hour. *Part-time fees:* $420 per term. Part-time tuition and fees vary according to course load and program.

FRESHMAN FINANCIAL AID (Fall 2016, est.) 23 applied for aid; of those 96% were deemed to have need. 100% of freshmen with need received aid; of those 5% had need fully met. *Average percent of need met:* 82% (excluding resources awarded to replace EFC). *Average financial aid package:* $13,237 (excluding resources awarded to replace EFC). 4% of all full-time freshmen had no need and received non-need-based gift aid.

UNDERGRADUATE FINANCIAL AID (Fall 2016, est.) 154 applied for aid; of those 94% were deemed to have need. 100% of undergraduates with need received aid; of those 32% had need fully met. *Average percent of need met:* 74% (excluding resources awarded to replace EFC). *Average financial aid package:* $13,874 (excluding resources awarded to replace EFC). 5% of all full-time undergraduates had no need and received non-need-based gift aid.

GIFT AID (NEED-BASED) *Total amount:* $1,028,503 (55% federal, 8% state, 35% institutional, 2% external sources). *Receiving aid:* Freshmen: 77% (20); all full-time undergraduates: 81% (133). *Average award:* Freshmen: $7142; Undergraduates: $5348. *Scholarships, grants, and awards:* Federal Pell, FSEOG, state, college/university gift aid from institutional funds.

GIFT AID (NON-NEED-BASED) *Total amount:* $28,703 (11% state, 89% institutional). *Receiving aid:* Freshmen: 4% (1). Undergraduates: 2% (3). *Average award:* Freshmen: $3500. Undergraduates: $3262. *Scholarships, grants, and awards by category: Academic interests/achievement:* 33 awards ($32,493 total): general academic interests/achievements, religion/biblical studies. *Special achievements/activities:* 12 awards ($61,375 total): community service, leadership, religious involvement. *Special characteristics:* 5 awards ($5265 total): children of faculty/staff, relatives of clergy, spouses of current students. *Tuition waivers:* Full or partial for employees or children of employees, senior citizens.

LOANS *Student loans:* $1,174,856 (89% need-based, 11% non-need-based). 92% of past graduating class borrowed through all loan programs. *Average indebtedness per student:* $21,510. *Average need-based loan:* Freshmen: $7008. Undergraduates: $9138. *Parent loans:* $176,160 (45% need-based, 55% non-need-based). *Programs:* Federal Direct (Subsidized and Unsubsidized Stafford, PLUS), private loans.

WORK-STUDY *Federal work-study:* Total amount: $76,763; 27 jobs averaging $2599. *State or other work-study/employment:* Total amount: $3622 (100% need-based). 1 part-time job averaging $3622.

APPLYING FOR FINANCIAL AID *Required financial aid forms:* FAFSA, institution's own form. *Financial aid deadline:* Continuous. *Notification date:* Continuous beginning 1/1. Students must reply within 6 weeks of notification.

CONTACT Sue Wayne, Director of Financial Aid, Trinity College of Florida, 2430 Welbilt Boulevard, New Port Richey, FL 34655, 727-569-1413 or toll-free 800-388-0869. *Fax:* 727-376-0781. *E-mail:* swayne@trinitycollege.edu. *Website:* http://www.trinitycollege.edu/.

TRINITY COLLEGE OF NURSING AND HEALTH SCIENCES
Rock Island, IL

CONTACT Mrs. Christine Carol Christopherson, Financial Aid Specialist, Trinity College of Nursing and Health Sciences, 2122 25th Avenue, Rock Island, IL 61201, 309-779-7740. *Fax:* 309-779-7748. *E-mail:* c.christopherson@trinitycollegeqc.edu. *Website:* http://www.trinitycollegeqc.edu/.

TRINITY INTERNATIONAL UNIVERSITY
Deerfield, IL

CONTACT Pat Coles, Interim Director of Financial Aid, Trinity International University, 2065 Half Day Road, Deerfield, IL 60015-1284, 847-317-8060 or toll-free 800-822-3225. *Fax:* 847-317-7081. *E-mail:* finaid@tiu.edu.
Website: http://www.tiu.edu/.

TRINITY UNIVERSITY
San Antonio, TX

Tuition & fees: $41,344	Average undergraduate aid package: $36,123

ABOUT THE INSTITUTION Independent Presbyterian Church, coed. *Awards:* bachelor's and master's degrees. 60 undergraduate majors. *Total enrollment:* 2,502. Undergraduates: 2,334. Freshmen: 662. Both federal and institutional methodology are used as a basis for awarding need-based institutional aid.

UNDERGRADUATE EXPENSES for 2017–2018 *Comprehensive fee:* $54,480 includes full-time tuition ($40,728), mandatory fees ($616), and room and board ($13,136). *College room only:* $8478. Full-time tuition and fees vary according to course load. Room and board charges vary according to board plan. *Part-time tuition:* $1697 per credit hour. *Part-time fees:* $12.50 per credit hour. Part-time tuition and fees vary according to course load.

FRESHMAN FINANCIAL AID (Fall 2016, est.) 491 applied for aid; of those 68% were deemed to have need. 100% of freshmen with need received aid; of those 62% had need fully met. *Average percent of need met:* 97% (excluding resources awarded to replace EFC). *Average financial aid package:* $37,524 (excluding resources awarded to replace EFC). 49% of all full-time freshmen had no need and received non-need-based gift aid.

UNDERGRADUATE FINANCIAL AID (Fall 2016, est.) 1,287 applied for aid; of those 81% were deemed to have need. 100% of undergraduates with need received aid; of those 50% had need fully met. *Average percent of need met:* 93% (excluding resources awarded to replace EFC). *Average financial aid package:* $36,123 (excluding resources awarded to replace EFC). 48% of all full-time undergraduates had no need and received non-need-based gift aid.

GIFT AID (NEED-BASED) *Total amount:* $29,210,290 (8% federal, 6% state, 84% institutional, 2% external sources). *Receiving aid:* Freshmen: 50% (328); all full-time undergraduates: 45% (1,024). *Average award:* Freshmen: $30,334; Undergraduates: $28,826. *Scholarships, grants, and awards:* Federal Pell, FSEOG, state, private, college/university gift aid from institutional funds.

GIFT AID (NON-NEED-BASED) *Total amount:* $23,981,978 (95% institutional, 5% external sources). *Receiving aid:* Freshmen: 19% (128). Undergraduates: 11% (248). *Average award:* Freshmen: $20,388. Undergraduates: $19,042. *Scholarships, grants, and awards by category: Academic interests/achievement:* general academic interests/achievements. *Creative arts/performance:* art/fine arts, debating, music, theater/drama. *Special characteristics:* children and siblings of alumni, children of educators, international students, veterans, veterans' children. *Tuition waivers:* Full or partial for employees or children of employees. *ROTC:* Army cooperative, Air Force cooperative.

LOANS *Student loans:* $8,383,547 (54% need-based, 46% non-need-based). 45% of past graduating class borrowed through all loan programs. *Average indebtedness per student:* $38,605. *Average need-based loan:* Freshmen: $3406. Undergraduates: $5077. *Parent loans:* $2,232,082 (10% need-based, 90% non-need-based). *Programs:* Federal Direct (Subsidized and Unsubsidized Stafford, PLUS), Perkins, state, college/university.

WORK-STUDY *Federal work-study:* Total amount: $558,448; jobs available. *State or other work-study/employment:* Part-time jobs available.

APPLYING FOR FINANCIAL AID *Required financial aid forms:* FAFSA, CSS Financial Aid PROFILE. *Financial aid deadline (priority):* 2/15. *Notification date:* 3/15. Students must reply by 5/1.

CONTACT Office of Student Financial Services, Trinity University, One Trinity Place, San Antonio, TX 78212-7200, 210-999-8898 or toll-free 800-TRINITY. *Fax:* 210-999-8316. *E-mail:* studentfinancialservices@trinity.edu.
Website: http://www.trinity.edu/.

TRINITY WASHINGTON UNIVERSITY
Washington, DC

CONTACT Catherine H. Geier, Director of Student Financial Services, Trinity Washington University, 125 Michigan Avenue, NE, Washington, DC 20017-1094, 202-884-9530 or toll-free 800-IWANTTC. *Fax:* 202-884-9524. *E-mail:* financialaid@trinitydc.edu.
Website: http://www.trinitydc.edu/.

TRI-STATE BIBLE COLLEGE
South Point, OH

ABOUT THE INSTITUTION Independent nondenominational, coed. 3 undergraduate majors.
GIFT AID (NEED-BASED) *Scholarships, grants, and awards:* Federal Pell.
LOANS *Programs:* Federal Direct (Subsidized and Unsubsidized Stafford, PLUS).
APPLYING FOR FINANCIAL AID *Required financial aid form:* FAFSA.
CONTACT Mrs. Roberta Mercer, Financial Aid Director, Tri-State Bible College, 506 Margaret Street, PO Box 445, South Point, OH 45680, 740-377-2520 Ext. 23. *Fax:* 740-377-0001. *E-mail:* tsbc@zoominternet.net.
Website: http://www.tsbc.edu/.

TROY UNIVERSITY
Troy, AL

Tuition & fees (AL res): $11,199	Average undergraduate aid package: $4394

ABOUT THE INSTITUTION State-supported, coed. *Awards:* certificates, associate, bachelor's, master's, and doctoral degrees. 44 undergraduate majors. *Total enrollment:* 17,903. Undergraduates: 14,243. Freshmen: 1,834. Federal methodology is used as a basis for awarding need-based institutional aid.

UNDERGRADUATE EXPENSES for 2016–2017 *Application fee:* $30. *Tuition, state resident:* full-time $9632; part-time $301 per credit hour. *Tuition, nonresident:* full-time $19,264; part-time $602 per credit hour. *Required fees:* full-time $1567; $39 per credit hour or $50 per term. Full-time tuition and fees vary according to location and program. Part-time tuition and fees vary according to location and program. *College room and board:* $7853; *Room only:* $4635. Room and board charges vary according to board plan and housing facility.

FRESHMAN FINANCIAL AID (Fall 2016, est.) 1,380 applied for aid; of those 99% were deemed to have need. 100% of freshmen with need received aid. *Average financial aid package:* $3655 (excluding resources awarded to replace EFC). 29% of all full-time freshmen had no need and received non-need-based gift aid.

UNDERGRADUATE FINANCIAL AID (Fall 2016, est.) 6,455 applied for aid; of those 99% were deemed to have need. 100% of undergraduates with need received aid. *Average financial aid package:* $4394 (excluding resources awarded to replace EFC). 51% of all full-time undergraduates had no need and received non-need-based gift aid.

GIFT AID (NEED-BASED) *Total amount:* $33,771,636 (99% federal, 1% state). *Receiving aid:* Freshmen: 43% (773); all full-time undergraduates: 42% (3,956). *Average award:* Freshmen: $4718; Undergraduates: $4675. *Scholarships, grants, and awards:* Federal Pell, FSEOG, state, private, college/university gift aid from institutional funds.

GIFT AID (NON-NEED-BASED) *Total amount:* $62,818,681 (64% institutional, 36% external sources). *Receiving aid:* Freshmen: 44% (793). Undergraduates: 32% (3,020). *Average award:* Freshmen: $6719. Undergraduates: $7108. *Scholarships, grants, and awards by category: Academic interests/achievement:* general academic interests/achievements. *Creative arts/performance:* applied art and design, music, theater/drama. *Special achievements/activities:* 637 awards ($1,705,886 total): leadership. *Special characteristics:* general special characteristics. *Tuition waivers:* Full or partial for employees or children of employees. *ROTC:* Army, Air Force.

LOANS *Student loans:* $145,476,695 (100% need-based). 45% of past graduating class borrowed through all loan programs. *Average indebtedness per student:* $5475. *Average need-based loan:* Freshmen: $3367. Undergraduates: $4340. *Parent*

loans: $10,170,577 (100% need-based). **Programs:** Federal Direct (Subsidized and Unsubsidized Stafford, PLUS), Perkins.

WORK-STUDY *Federal work-study:* Total amount: $1,105,039; 4 jobs averaging $2876.

ATHLETIC AWARDS Total amount: $5,583,253 (100% non-need-based).

APPLYING FOR FINANCIAL AID *Required financial aid forms:* FAFSA, institution's own form. *Financial aid deadline (priority):* 3/1. *Notification date:* Continuous beginning 6/1. Students must reply within 2 weeks of notification.

CONTACT Ms. Carol Ballard, Associate Vice Chancellor of Financial Aid, Troy University, 131 Adams Administration Building, Troy, AL 36082, 334-670-3186 or toll-free 800-551-9716. *Fax:* 334-670-3702. *E-mail:* csupri@troy.edu. *Website:* http://www.troy.edu/.

TRUETT MCCONNELL UNIVERSITY
Cleveland, GA

Tuition & fees: $19,230	Average undergraduate aid package: $15,321

ABOUT THE INSTITUTION Independent Baptist, coed. **Awards:** bachelor's and master's degrees. 19 undergraduate majors. **Total enrollment:** 2,187. Undergraduates: 2,152. Freshmen: 222. Federal methodology is used as a basis for awarding need-based institutional aid.

UNDERGRADUATE EXPENSES for 2017–2018 *Comprehensive fee:* $26,630 includes full-time tuition ($18,570), mandatory fees ($660), and room and board ($7400). Full-time tuition and fees vary according to course load, degree level, location, and program. Room and board charges vary according to housing facility. *Part-time tuition:* $619 per credit hour. *Part-time fees:* $330 per term. Part-time tuition and fees vary according to course load, degree level, location, and program.

FRESHMAN FINANCIAL AID (Fall 2016, est.) 202 applied for aid; of those 90% were deemed to have need. 100% of freshmen with need received aid; of those 28% had need fully met. *Average percent of need met:* 71% (excluding resources awarded to replace EFC). *Average financial aid package:* $14,556 (excluding resources awarded to replace EFC). 14% of all full-time freshmen had no need and received non-need-based gift aid.

UNDERGRADUATE FINANCIAL AID (Fall 2016, est.) 644 applied for aid; of those 89% were deemed to have need. 99% of undergraduates with need received aid; of those 22% had need fully met. *Average percent of need met:* 68% (excluding resources awarded to replace EFC). *Average financial aid package:* $15,321 (excluding resources awarded to replace EFC). 14% of all full-time undergraduates had no need and received non-need-based gift aid.

GIFT AID (NEED-BASED) Total amount: $5,795,529 (24% federal, 22% state, 49% institutional, 5% external sources). *Receiving aid:* Freshmen: 83% (180); all full-time undergraduates: 82% (568). *Average award:* Freshmen: $12,076; Undergraduates: $11,975. *Scholarships, grants, and awards:* Federal Pell, FSEOG, state, private, college/university gift aid from institutional funds, Georgia Baptist Convention scholarships.

GIFT AID (NON-NEED-BASED) Total amount: $1,380,089 (37% state, 58% institutional, 5% external sources). *Receiving aid:* Freshmen: 20% (43). Undergraduates: 14% (95). *Average award:* Freshmen: $6426. Undergraduates: $6299. *Scholarships, grants, and awards by category: Academic interests/achievement:* $1,784,618 total: education, general academic interests/achievements, home economics, religion/biblical studies. *Creative arts/performance:* $156,220 total: music. *Special achievements/activities:* $1,979,866 total: community service, general special achievements/activities, leadership, religious involvement. *Special characteristics:* $1,066,222 total: children of current students, children of faculty/staff, general special characteristics, international students, local/state students, married students, out-of-state students, parents of current students, relatives of clergy, religious affiliation, siblings of current students, spouses of current students. *Tuition waivers:* Full or partial for employees or children of employees.

LOANS *Student loans:* $3,896,290 (77% need-based, 23% non-need-based). 66% of past graduating class borrowed through all loan programs. *Average indebtedness per student:* $23,222. *Average need-based loan:* Freshmen: $4121. Undergraduates: $4753. *Parent loans:* $671,005 (43% need-based, 57% non-need-based). *Programs:* Federal Direct (Subsidized and Unsubsidized Stafford, PLUS), state, private loans.

WORK-STUDY *Federal work-study:* Total amount: $48,587; 45 jobs averaging $1039.

ATHLETIC AWARDS Total amount: $1,438,777 (67% need-based, 33% non-need-based).

APPLYING FOR FINANCIAL AID *Required financial aid forms:* FAFSA, institution's own form. *Financial aid deadline:* Continuous. *Notification date:* Continuous beginning 1/3. Students must reply within 4 weeks of notification.

CONTACT Mrs. Trista Blankenship, Financial Aid Assistant, Truett McConnell University, 100 Alumni Drive, Cleveland, GA 30528, 706-865-2134 Ext. 4203 or toll-free 800-226-8621. *Fax:* 706-243-4642. *E-mail:* tblankenship@truett.edu. *Website:* http://www.truett.edu/.

TRUMAN STATE UNIVERSITY
Kirksville, MO

Tuition & fees (MO res): $7456	Average undergraduate aid package: $12,437

ABOUT THE INSTITUTION State-supported, coed. **Awards:** bachelor's and master's degrees. 37 undergraduate majors. **Total enrollment:** 6,379. Undergraduates: 6,039. Freshmen: 1,263. Federal methodology is used as a basis for awarding need-based institutional aid.

UNDERGRADUATE EXPENSES for 2016–2017 *One-time required fee:* $325. *Tuition, state resident:* full-time $7152; part-time $298 per credit hour. *Tuition, nonresident:* full-time $13,636; part-time $568 per credit hour. *Required fees:* full-time $304; $304 per year. Full-time tuition and fees vary according to course load, degree level, and program. Part-time tuition and fees vary according to course load, degree level, and program. *College room and board:* $8558; *Room only:* $5730. Room and board charges vary according to housing facility.

FRESHMAN FINANCIAL AID (Fall 2015) 1,054 applied for aid; of those 67% were deemed to have need. 100% of freshmen with need received aid; of those 39% had need fully met. *Average percent of need met:* 87% (excluding resources awarded to replace EFC). *Average financial aid package:* $13,540 (excluding resources awarded to replace EFC). 42% of all full-time freshmen had no need and received non-need-based gift aid.

UNDERGRADUATE FINANCIAL AID (Fall 2015) 3,732 applied for aid; of those 71% were deemed to have need. 100% of undergraduates with need received aid; of those 34% had need fully met. *Average percent of need met:* 84% (excluding resources awarded to replace EFC). *Average financial aid package:* $12,437 (excluding resources awarded to replace EFC). 37% of all full-time undergraduates had no need and received non-need-based gift aid.

GIFT AID (NEED-BASED) Total amount: $18,811,078 (28% federal, 16% state, 52% institutional, 4% external sources). *Receiving aid:* Freshmen: 56% (708); all full-time undergraduates: 49% (2,510). *Average award:* Freshmen: $8587; Undergraduates: $7636. *Scholarships, grants, and awards:* Federal Pell, FSEOG, state, private, college/university gift aid from institutional funds, TEACH Grants.

GIFT AID (NON-NEED-BASED) Total amount: $15,353,486 (1% federal, 11% state, 81% institutional, 7% external sources). *Receiving aid:* Freshmen: 56% (702). Undergraduates: 41% (2,101). *Average award:* Freshmen: $5573. Undergraduates: $5812. *Scholarships, grants, and awards by category: Academic interests/achievement:* 8,730 awards ($22,033,413 total): agriculture, biological sciences, business, communication, computer science, education, English, foreign languages, general academic interests/achievements, health fields, humanities, mathematics, military science, physical sciences, premedicine, social sciences. *Creative arts/performance:* 134 awards ($163,802 total): art/fine arts, debating, music, theater/drama. *Special achievements/activities:* 562 awards ($2,581,487 total): leadership. *Special characteristics:* 623 awards ($1,639,625 total): children and siblings of alumni, children of faculty/staff, ethnic background, first-generation college students, international students, out-of-state students, previous college experience. *Tuition waivers:* Full or partial for children of alumni, employees or children of employees, senior citizens. *ROTC:* Army.

LOANS *Student loans:* $25,113,806 (50% need-based, 50% non-need-based). 56% of past graduating class borrowed through all loan programs. *Average indebtedness per student:* $24,811. *Average need-based loan:* Freshmen: $3679. Undergraduates: $4479. *Parent loans:* $1,637,780 (13% need-based, 87% non-need-based). *Programs:* Federal Direct (Subsidized and Unsubsidized Stafford, PLUS), Perkins, Federal Nursing, college/university.

WORK-STUDY *Federal work-study:* 423 jobs averaging $1619. *State or other work-study/employment:* Total amount: $1,691,605 (3% need-based, 97% non-need-based). 1,437 part-time jobs averaging $1148.

ATHLETIC AWARDS Total amount: $1,481,375 (28% need-based, 72% non-need-based).

APPLYING FOR FINANCIAL AID *Required financial aid form:* FAFSA. *Financial aid deadline (priority):* 2/1. *Notification date:* Continuous beginning 1/1.

CONTACT Kathy Elsea, Director of Financial Aid, Truman State University, 103 McClain Hall, Kirksville, MO 63501-4221, 660-785-4130 or toll-free 800-892-7792. *Fax:* 660-785-7389. *E-mail:* kelsea@truman.edu.

Website: http://www.truman.edu/.

TUFTS UNIVERSITY
Medford, MA

Tuition & fees: $52,430	Average undergraduate aid package: $43,325

ABOUT THE INSTITUTION Independent, coed. *Awards:* certificates, bachelor's, master's, and doctoral degrees. 100 undergraduate majors. *Total enrollment:* 11,489. Undergraduates: 5,508. Freshmen: 1,336. Both federal and institutional methodology are used as a basis for awarding need-based institutional aid.

UNDERGRADUATE EXPENSES for 2016–2017 *Application fee:* $75. *Comprehensive fee:* $65,996 includes full-time tuition ($51,304), mandatory fees ($1126), and room and board ($13,566). *College room only:* $7392. Room and board charges vary according to board plan. *Payment plan:* Tuition prepayment.

FRESHMAN FINANCIAL AID (Fall 2016, est.) 664 applied for aid; of those 79% were deemed to have need. 98% of freshmen with need received aid; of those 100% had need fully met. *Average percent of need met:* 100% (excluding resources awarded to replace EFC). *Average financial aid package:* $43,518 (excluding resources awarded to replace EFC). 2% of all full-time freshmen had no need and received non-need-based gift aid.

UNDERGRADUATE FINANCIAL AID (Fall 2016, est.) 2,187 applied for aid; of those 88% were deemed to have need. 99% of undergraduates with need received aid; of those 100% had need fully met. *Average percent of need met:* 100% (excluding resources awarded to replace EFC). *Average financial aid package:* $43,325 (excluding resources awarded to replace EFC). 1% of all full-time undergraduates had no need and received non-need-based gift aid.

GIFT AID (NEED-BASED) *Total amount:* $80,447,066 (5% federal, 1% state, 92% institutional, 2% external sources). *Receiving aid:* Freshmen: 36% (481); all full-time undergraduates: 34% (1,800). *Average award:* Freshmen: $42,971; Undergraduates: $41,366. *Scholarships, grants, and awards:* Federal Pell, FSEOG, state, private, college/university gift aid from institutional funds.

GIFT AID (NON-NEED-BASED) *Total amount:* $853,573 (10% federal, 7% institutional, 83% external sources). *Receiving aid:* Freshmen: 2% (28). Undergraduates: 1% (72). *Average award:* Freshmen: $500. Undergraduates: $500. *Scholarships, grants, and awards by category:* Academic interests/achievement: general academic interests/achievements. *Tuition waivers:* Full or partial for employees or children of employees. *ROTC:* Army cooperative, Naval cooperative, Air Force cooperative.

LOANS *Student loans:* $10,449,397 (53% need-based, 47% non-need-based). 35% of past graduating class borrowed through all loan programs. *Average indebtedness per student:* $24,267. *Average need-based loan:* Freshmen: $2116. Undergraduates: $3122. *Parent loans:* $4,523,994 (100% non-need-based). *Programs:* Federal Direct (Subsidized and Unsubsidized Stafford, PLUS), Perkins, college/university.

WORK-STUDY *Federal work-study:* Total amount: $2,742,883; 1,432 jobs averaging $1894. *State or other work-study/employment:* Total amount: $306,500 (100% need-based). 160 part-time jobs averaging $1902.

APPLYING FOR FINANCIAL AID *Required financial aid forms:* FAFSA, CSS Financial Aid PROFILE, noncustodial (divorced/separated) parent's statement, federal income tax form(s). *Financial aid deadline:* 2/1. *Notification date:* 4/5. Students must reply by 5/1.

CONTACT Patricia C. Reilly, Director of Financial Aid, Tufts University, Dowling Hall, Medford, MA 02155, 617-627-2000. *Fax:* 617-627-3987. *E-mail:* patricia.reilly@tufts.edu.

Website: http://www.tufts.edu/.

TULANE UNIVERSITY
New Orleans, LA

Tuition & fees: $51,010	Average undergraduate aid package: $45,124

ABOUT THE INSTITUTION Independent, coed. *Awards:* certificates, bachelor's, master's, and doctoral degrees. 82 undergraduate majors. *Total enrollment:* 11,034. Undergraduates: 7,510. Freshmen: 1,856. Both federal and institutional methodology are used as a basis for awarding need-based institutional aid.

UNDERGRADUATE EXPENSES for 2016–2017 *Comprehensive fee:* $64,854 includes full-time tuition ($47,130), mandatory fees ($3880), and room and board ($13,844). *College room only:* $7942. Room and board charges vary according to board plan, housing facility, and student level. *Payment plan:* Tuition prepayment.

FRESHMAN FINANCIAL AID (Fall 2016, est.) 1,045 applied for aid; of those 59% were deemed to have need. 100% of freshmen with need received aid; of those 67% had need fully met. *Average percent of need met:* 98% (excluding resources awarded to replace EFC). *Average financial aid package:* $45,312 (excluding resources awarded to replace EFC). 36% of all full-time freshmen had no need and received non-need-based gift aid.

UNDERGRADUATE FINANCIAL AID (Fall 2016, est.) 2,942 applied for aid; of those 73% were deemed to have need. 100% of undergraduates with need received aid; of those 66% had need fully met. *Average percent of need met:* 96% (excluding resources awarded to replace EFC). *Average financial aid package:* $45,124 (excluding resources awarded to replace EFC). 36% of all full-time undergraduates had no need and received non-need-based gift aid.

GIFT AID (NEED-BASED) *Total amount:* $65,106,079 (4% federal, 2% state, 93% institutional, 1% external sources). *Receiving aid:* Freshmen: 33% (606); all full-time undergraduates: 31% (2,080). *Average award:* Freshmen: $32,702; Undergraduates: $33,003. *Scholarships, grants, and awards:* Federal Pell, FSEOG, state, private, college/university gift aid from institutional funds.

GIFT AID (NON-NEED-BASED) *Total amount:* $73,493,488 (4% state, 95% institutional, 1% external sources). *Receiving aid:* Freshmen: 13% (241). Undergraduates: 9% (590). *Average award:* Freshmen: $27,266. Undergraduates: $25,779. *Scholarships, grants, and awards by category:* Creative arts/performance: 97 awards ($200,600 total): music. *Special achievements/activities:* 38 awards ($568,175 total): community service. *Special characteristics:* 284 awards ($12,719,939 total): children of faculty/staff, international students, local/state students. *Tuition waivers:* Full or partial for employees or children of employees. *ROTC:* Army, Naval, Air Force.

LOANS *Student loans:* $27,791,090 (52% need-based, 48% non-need-based). 38% of past graduating class borrowed through all loan programs. *Average indebtedness per student:* $31,642. *Average need-based loan:* Freshmen: $7005. Undergraduates: $7753. *Parent loans:* $8,074,093 (4% need-based, 96% non-need-based). *Programs:* Federal Direct (Subsidized and Unsubsidized Stafford, PLUS), Perkins.

WORK-STUDY *Federal work-study:* Total amount: $3,135,343; 1,084 jobs averaging $2892. *State or other work-study/employment:* Total amount: $1,212,848 (20% need-based, 80% non-need-based). 114 part-time jobs averaging $8510.

ATHLETIC AWARDS Total amount: $13,019,726 (33% need-based, 67% non-need-based).

APPLYING FOR FINANCIAL AID *Required financial aid forms:* FAFSA, CSS Financial Aid PROFILE, noncustodial (divorced/separated) parent's statement, business/farm supplement. *Financial aid deadline (priority):* 2/15. *Notification date:* Continuous beginning 3/15. Students must reply by 5/1 or within 2 weeks of notification.

CONTACT Mr. Michael T. Goodman, Director of Financial Aid, Tulane University, 6823 St. Charles Avenue, New Orleans, LA 70118-5669, 504-865-5723 or toll-free 800-873-9283. *Fax:* 504-862-8750. *E-mail:* finaid@tulane.edu.

Website: http://www.tulane.edu/.

TUSCULUM COLLEGE
Greeneville, TN

Tuition & fees: $23,700	Average undergraduate aid package: $17,079

ABOUT THE INSTITUTION Independent Presbyterian, coed. *Awards:* associate, bachelor's, and master's degrees. 22 undergraduate majors. *Total enrollment:* 1,796. Undergraduates: 1,585. Freshmen: 324. Both federal and institutional methodology are used as a basis for awarding need-based institutional aid.

UNDERGRADUATE EXPENSES for 2017–2018 *Comprehensive fee:* $32,400 includes full-time tuition ($23,700) and room and board ($8700). *College room only:* $5810. *Part-time tuition:* $736 per credit hour.

FRESHMAN FINANCIAL AID (Fall 2016, est.) 303 applied for aid; of those 92% were deemed to have need. 97% of freshmen with need received aid; of those 12% had need fully met. *Average percent of need met:* 83% (excluding resources awarded to replace EFC). *Average financial aid package:* $20,594 (excluding resources awarded to replace EFC). 8% of all full-time freshmen had no need and received non-need-based gift aid.

UNDERGRADUATE FINANCIAL AID (Fall 2016, est.) 1,286 applied for aid; of those 93% were deemed to have need. 96% of undergraduates with need received aid; of those 9% had need fully met. *Average percent of need met:* 77% (excluding resources awarded to replace EFC). *Average financial aid package:* $17,079 (excluding resources awarded to replace EFC). 5% of all full-time undergraduates had no need and received non-need-based gift aid.

GIFT AID (NEED-BASED) *Total amount:* $9,431,090 (42% federal, 20% state, 38% institutional). *Receiving aid:* Freshmen: 68% (221); all full-time undergraduates: 64% (907). *Average award:* Freshmen: $10,882; Undergraduates: $9629. *Scholarships, grants, and awards:* Federal Pell, FSEOG, state, private, college/university gift aid from institutional funds.

GIFT AID (NON-NEED-BASED) *Total amount:* $8,136,373 (14% state, 84% institutional, 2% external sources). *Receiving aid:* Freshmen: 81% (262). Undergraduates: 62% (874). *Average award:* Freshmen: $10,019. Undergraduates: $8329. *Scholarships, grants, and awards by category:* Academic interests/achievement: general academic interests/achievements. Creative arts/performance: general creative arts/performance, music. Special achievements/activities: cheerleading/drum major, community service, leadership. Special characteristics: adult students, children of faculty/staff, local/state students. *Tuition waivers:* Full or partial for employees or children of employees.

LOANS *Student loans:* $8,119,793 (49% need-based, 51% non-need-based). 84% of past graduating class borrowed through all loan programs. *Average indebtedness per student:* $33,916. *Average need-based loan:* Freshmen: $3304. Undergraduates: $4098. *Parent loans:* $2,110,761 (100% non-need-based). *Programs:* Federal Direct (Subsidized and Unsubsidized Stafford, PLUS), Perkins.

WORK-STUDY *Federal work-study:* Total amount: $292,529; 293 jobs averaging $963. *State or other work-study/employment:* Part-time jobs available.

ATHLETIC AWARDS Total amount: $3,279,617 (100% non-need-based).

APPLYING FOR FINANCIAL AID *Required financial aid form:* FAFSA. *Financial aid deadline (priority):* 2/15. *Notification date:* Continuous beginning 3/1. Students must reply within 3 weeks of notification.

CONTACT Karen Sartain, Director of Financial Aid, Tusculum College, PO Box 5049, 60 Shiloh Road, Greeneville, TN 37743-9997, 423-636-7377 or toll-free 800-729-0256. *Fax:* 615-250-4968. *E-mail:* ksartain@tusculum.edu. *Website:* http://www.tusculum.edu/.

TUSKEGEE UNIVERSITY
Tuskegee, AL

Tuition & fees: $20,320	Average undergraduate aid package: $20,500

ABOUT THE INSTITUTION Independent, coed. *Awards:* bachelor's, master's, and doctoral degrees. 43 undergraduate majors. *Total enrollment:* 2,995. Undergraduates: 2,485. Freshmen: 595. Federal methodology is used as a basis for awarding need-based institutional aid.

UNDERGRADUATE EXPENSES for 2016–2017 *Application fee:* $25. *Comprehensive fee:* $29,640 includes full-time tuition ($18,560), mandatory fees ($1760), and room and board ($9320). *College room only:* $4300. Full-time tuition

and fees vary according to course load. Room and board charges vary according to board plan and housing facility. *Part-time tuition:* $5135 per term. Part-time tuition and fees vary according to course load.

FRESHMAN FINANCIAL AID (Fall 2015) 595 applied for aid; of those 97% were deemed to have need. 96% of freshmen with need received aid; of those 56% had need fully met. *Average percent of need met:* 85% (excluding resources awarded to replace EFC). *Average financial aid package:* $20,500 (excluding resources awarded to replace EFC). 26% of all full-time freshmen had no need and received non-need-based gift aid.

UNDERGRADUATE FINANCIAL AID (Fall 2015) 2,328 applied for aid; of those 94% were deemed to have need. 91% of undergraduates with need received aid; of those 63% had need fully met. *Average percent of need met:* 85% (excluding resources awarded to replace EFC). *Average financial aid package:* $20,500 (excluding resources awarded to replace EFC). 25% of all full-time undergraduates had no need and received non-need-based gift aid.

GIFT AID (NEED-BASED) *Total amount:* $9,445,946 (96% federal, 1% state, 3% institutional). *Receiving aid:* Freshmen: 49% (401); all full-time undergraduates: 64% (1,595). *Average award:* Freshmen: $950; Undergraduates: $950. *Scholarships, grants, and awards:* Federal Pell, FSEOG, state, private, college/university gift aid from institutional funds, United Negro College Fund.

GIFT AID (NON-NEED-BASED) *Total amount:* $4,594,118 (51% institutional, 49% external sources). *Receiving aid:* Freshmen: 26% (215). Undergraduates: 35% (868). *Average award:* Freshmen: $6500. Undergraduates: $6500. *Scholarships, grants, and awards by category:* Academic interests/achievement: 1,580 awards ($1,345,210 total): agriculture, architecture, business, computer science, engineering/technologies, general academic interests/achievements. Creative arts/performance: 150 awards ($220,000 total): music. Special characteristics: 21 awards ($408,200 total): children of faculty/staff, local/state students. *Tuition waivers:* Full or partial for employees or children of employees. *ROTC:* Army, Naval, Air Force.

LOANS *Student loans:* $4,950,628 (27% need-based, 73% non-need-based). 92% of past graduating class borrowed through all loan programs. *Average indebtedness per student:* $26,500. *Average need-based loan:* Freshmen: $5450. Undergraduates: $6000. *Parent loans:* $928,666 (100% non-need-based). *Programs:* Federal Direct (Subsidized and Unsubsidized Stafford, PLUS), Perkins.

WORK-STUDY *Federal work-study:* 625 jobs averaging $2610. *State or other work-study/employment:* Total amount: $644,250 (100% non-need-based). Part-time jobs available.

ATHLETIC AWARDS Total amount: $1,990,810 (100% non-need-based).

APPLYING FOR FINANCIAL AID *Required financial aid forms:* FAFSA, institution's own form. *Financial aid deadline (priority):* 2/1. *Notification date:* Continuous beginning 2/1. Students must reply within 2 weeks of notification.

CONTACT Mr. A. D. James Jr., Executive Director of Student Financial Services, Tuskegee University, Carnegie Hall, 2nd Floor, Tuskegee, AL 36088, 334-727-8088 or toll-free 800-622-6531. *Fax:* 334-724-4078. *E-mail:* ajames@tuskegee.edu. *Website:* http://www.tuskegee.edu/.

UNION COLLEGE
Barbourville, KY

Tuition & fees: $26,080	Average undergraduate aid package: $22,057

ABOUT THE INSTITUTION Independent United Methodist, coed. *Awards:* certificates, bachelor's, and master's degrees. 40 undergraduate majors. *Total enrollment:* 1,202. Undergraduates: 975. Freshmen: 264. Federal methodology is used as a basis for awarding need-based institutional aid.

UNDERGRADUATE EXPENSES for 2017–2018 *Application fee:* $10. *Comprehensive fee:* $33,480 includes full-time tuition ($24,590), mandatory fees ($1490), and room and board ($7400). *College room only:* $3350. Room and board charges vary according to housing facility. *Part-time tuition:* $345 per credit hour. *Part-time fees:* $25 per term. Part-time tuition and fees vary according to location.

FRESHMAN FINANCIAL AID (Fall 2015) 143 applied for aid; of those 94% were deemed to have need. 98% of freshmen with need received aid; of those 8% had need fully met. *Average percent of need met:* 68% (excluding resources awarded to replace EFC). *Average financial aid package:* $21,809 (excluding resources awarded to replace EFC). 19% of all full-time freshmen had no need and received non-need-based gift aid.

UNDERGRADUATE FINANCIAL AID (Fall 2015) 625 applied for aid; of those 94% were deemed to have need. 95% of undergraduates with need received aid; of those 16% had need fully met. *Average percent of need met:* 69% (excluding resources awarded to replace EFC). *Average financial aid package:* $22,057 (excluding resources awarded to replace EFC). 12% of all full-time undergraduates had no need and received non-need-based gift aid.

GIFT AID (NEED-BASED) *Total amount:* $11,448,861 (16% federal, 16% state, 65% institutional, 3% external sources). *Receiving aid:* Freshmen: 78% (132); all full-time undergraduates: 82% (557). *Average award:* Freshmen: $18,423; Undergraduates: $18,268. *Scholarships, grants, and awards:* Federal Pell, FSEOG, state, private, college/university gift aid from institutional funds.

GIFT AID (NON-NEED-BASED) *Total amount:* $2,113,490 (6% state, 89% institutional, 5% external sources). *Receiving aid:* Freshmen: 5% (9). Undergraduates: 10% (65). *Average award:* Freshmen: $14,777. Undergraduates: $15,481. *Scholarships, grants, and awards by category: Academic interests/achievement:* 463 awards ($4,473,527 total): general academic interests/achievements. *Creative arts/performance:* 58 awards ($102,950 total): music, theater/drama. *Special achievements/activities:* 152 awards ($431,488 total): cheerleading/drum major, community service, general special achievements/activities, hobbies/interests, leadership, memberships, religious involvement. *Special characteristics:* 98 awards ($246,339 total): adult students, children and siblings of alumni, children of current students, children of faculty/staff, members of minority groups, religious affiliation, siblings of current students, veterans, veterans' children. *Tuition waivers:* Full or partial for employees or children of employees.

LOANS *Student loans:* $4,386,394 (86% need-based, 14% non-need-based). 84% of past graduating class borrowed through all loan programs. *Average indebtedness per student:* $32,691. *Average need-based loan:* Freshmen: $3538. Undergraduates: $4203. *Parent loans:* $4,578,244 (87% need-based, 13% non-need-based). *Programs:* Federal Direct (Subsidized and Unsubsidized Stafford, PLUS), Perkins, college/university.

WORK-STUDY *Federal work-study:* jobs available. *State or other work-study/employment:* Total amount: $25,269 (100% need-based). Part-time jobs available.

ATHLETIC AWARDS Total amount: $3,586,040 (100% need-based).

APPLYING FOR FINANCIAL AID *Required financial aid form:* FAFSA. *Financial aid deadline:* Continuous. *Notification date:* Continuous beginning 2/25. Students must reply within 2 weeks of notification.

CONTACT Mrs. Andra Butler, Director of Financial Aid, Union College, 310 College Street, Barbourville, KY 40906-1499, 606-546-1224 or toll-free 800-489-8646. *Fax:* 606-546-1264. *E-mail:* abutler@unionky.edu. *Website:* http://www.unionky.edu/.

UNION COLLEGE
Lincoln, NE

Tuition & fees: $23,070	Average undergraduate aid package: $16,149

ABOUT THE INSTITUTION Independent Seventh-day Adventist, coed. *Awards:* associate, bachelor's, and master's degrees. 64 undergraduate majors. *Total enrollment:* 893. Undergraduates: 805. Freshmen: 156. Federal methodology is used as a basis for awarding need-based institutional aid.

UNDERGRADUATE EXPENSES for 2017–2018 *Comprehensive fee:* $29,996 includes full-time tuition ($21,970), mandatory fees ($1100), and room and board ($6926). *College room only:* $3980. Full-time tuition and fees vary according to course load, degree level, and program. Room and board charges vary according to board plan and housing facility. *Part-time tuition:* $916 per credit hour. Part-time tuition and fees vary according to program.

FRESHMAN FINANCIAL AID (Fall 2015) 142 applied for aid; of those 87% were deemed to have need. 100% of freshmen with need received aid; of those 21% had need fully met. *Average percent of need met:* 72% (excluding resources awarded to replace EFC). *Average financial aid package:* $18,067 (excluding resources awarded to replace EFC). 28% of all full-time freshmen had no need and received non-need-based gift aid.

UNDERGRADUATE FINANCIAL AID (Fall 2015) 590 applied for aid; of those 88% were deemed to have need. 100% of undergraduates with need received aid; of those 12% had need fully met. *Average percent of need met:* 62% (excluding resources awarded to replace EFC). *Average financial aid package:* $16,149 (excluding resources awarded to replace EFC). 27% of all full-time undergraduates had no need and received non-need-based gift aid.

GIFT AID (NEED-BASED) *Total amount:* $6,036,261 (24% federal, 1% state, 57% institutional, 18% external sources). *Receiving aid:* Freshmen: 72% (123); all full-time undergraduates: 71% (517). *Average award:* Freshmen: $14,632; Undergraduates: $11,588. *Scholarships, grants, and awards:* Federal Pell, FSEOG, state, private, college/university gift aid from institutional funds, United Negro College Fund.

GIFT AID (NON-NEED-BASED) *Total amount:* $2,022,340 (73% institutional, 27% external sources). *Receiving aid:* Freshmen: 13% (22). Undergraduates: 6% (16). *Average award:* Freshmen: $10,443. Undergraduates: $6746. *Scholarships, grants, and awards by category: Academic interests/achievement:* general academic interests/achievements. *Creative arts/performance:* music. *Special achievements/activities:* community service, leadership, religious involvement. *Tuition waivers:* Full or partial for employees or children of employees.

LOANS *Student loans:* $4,482,952 (84% need-based, 16% non-need-based). 65% of past graduating class borrowed through all loan programs. *Average indebtedness per student:* $35,893. *Average need-based loan:* Freshmen: $3924. Undergraduates: $4998. *Parent loans:* $1,012,813 (58% need-based, 42% non-need-based). *Programs:* Federal Direct (Subsidized and Unsubsidized Stafford, PLUS), Perkins, Federal Nursing, college/university.

WORK-STUDY *Federal work-study:* jobs available.

APPLYING FOR FINANCIAL AID *Required financial aid forms:* FAFSA, institution's own form. *Financial aid deadline:* Continuous. *Notification date:* Continuous beginning 12/1. Students must reply by 9/1.

CONTACT Mrs. Taryn A. Rouse, Director of Student Financial Services, Union College, 3800 South 48th Street, Lincoln, NE 68506-4300, 402-486-2600 Ext. 2505 or toll-free 800-228-4600. *Fax:* 402-486-2952. *E-mail:* sfs@ucollege.edu. *Website:* http://www.ucollege.edu/.

UNION COLLEGE
Schenectady, NY

Tuition & fees: $53,490	Average undergraduate aid package: $42,155

ABOUT THE INSTITUTION Independent, coed. *Awards:* bachelor's degrees. 40 undergraduate majors. *Total enrollment:* 2,203. Undergraduates: 2,203. Freshmen: 560. Both federal and institutional methodology are used as a basis for awarding need-based institutional aid.

UNDERGRADUATE EXPENSES for 2017–2018 *Comprehensive fee:* $66,609 includes full-time tuition ($53,019), mandatory fees ($471), and room and board ($13,119). *College room only:* $7194.

FRESHMAN FINANCIAL AID (Fall 2016, est.) 368 applied for aid; of those 80% were deemed to have need. 100% of freshmen with need received aid; of those 100% had need fully met. *Average percent of need met:* 100% (excluding resources awarded to replace EFC). *Average financial aid package:* $41,185 (excluding resources awarded to replace EFC). 27% of all full-time freshmen had no need and received non-need-based gift aid.

UNDERGRADUATE FINANCIAL AID (Fall 2016, est.) 1,195 applied for aid; of those 92% were deemed to have need. 100% of undergraduates with need received aid; of those 100% had need fully met. *Average percent of need met:* 100% (excluding resources awarded to replace EFC). *Average financial aid package:* $42,155 (excluding resources awarded to replace EFC). 30% of all full-time undergraduates had no need and received non-need-based gift aid.

GIFT AID (NEED-BASED) *Total amount:* $38,803,702 (5% federal, 2% state, 92% institutional, 1% external sources). *Receiving aid:* Freshmen: 51% (287); all full-time undergraduates: 49% (1,037). *Average award:* Freshmen: $36,393; Undergraduates: $36,748. *Scholarships, grants, and awards:* Federal Pell, FSEOG, state, private, college/university gift aid from institutional funds.

GIFT AID (NON-NEED-BASED) *Total amount:* $7,334,044 (3% federal, 1% state, 92% institutional, 4% external sources). *Receiving aid:* Freshmen: 5% (26). Undergraduates: 6% (117). *Average award:* Freshmen: $13,069. Undergraduates: $10,544. *Scholarships, grants, and awards by category: Academic interests/achievement:* 619 awards ($6,397,035 total): general academic interests/achievements. *Special achievements/activities:* 619 awards ($6,397,035 total). *Special characteristics:* 33 awards ($1,613,240 total): children of faculty/staff. *Tuition waivers:* Full or partial for employees or children of employees, senior citizens. *ROTC:* Army cooperative, Naval cooperative, Air Force cooperative.

LOANS *Student loans:* $10,485,979 (40% need-based, 60% non-need-based). 54% of past graduating class borrowed through all loan programs. *Average indebtedness per student:* $33,045. *Average need-based loan:* Freshmen: $3573. Undergraduates: $4940. *Parent loans:* $2,963,255 (100% non-need-based). *Programs:* Federal Direct (Subsidized and Unsubsidized Stafford, PLUS), Perkins, college/university.

WORK-STUDY *Federal work-study:* Total amount: $770,472; jobs available. *State or other work-study/employment:* Total amount: $315,000 (100% need-based). Part-time jobs available.

APPLYING FOR FINANCIAL AID *Required financial aid forms:* FAFSA, CSS Financial Aid PROFILE, state aid form, noncustodial (divorced/separated) parent's statement. *Financial aid deadline:* 1/15 (priority: 1/15). *Notification date:* 3/25. Students must reply by 5/1.

CONTACT Ms. Linda Parker, Director of Financial Aid, Union College, Grant Hall, 807 Union Street, Schenectady, NY 12308-2311, 518-388-6123 or toll-free 888-843-6688. *Fax:* 518-388-8052. *E-mail:* finaid@union.edu.
Website: http://www.union.edu/.

UNION INSTITUTE & UNIVERSITY
Cincinnati, OH

CONTACT Ms. Lisa Perdomo, Director of Financial Aid, Union Institute & University, 440 East McMillan Street, Cincinnati, OH 45206-1925, 513-861-6400 Ext. 1261 or toll-free 800-486-3116. *Fax:* 513-487-1078.
Website: http://www.myunion.edu/.

UNION UNIVERSITY
Jackson, TN

Tuition & fees: $31,780	Average undergraduate aid package: $26,410

ABOUT THE INSTITUTION Independent Southern Baptist, coed. *Awards:* certificates, associate, bachelor's, master's, and doctoral degrees. 66 undergraduate majors. *Total enrollment:* 3,339. Undergraduates: 2,214. Freshmen: 336. Federal methodology is used as a basis for awarding need-based institutional aid.

UNDERGRADUATE EXPENSES for 2017–2018 *Application fee:* $35. *Comprehensive fee:* $42,130 includes full-time tuition ($30,480), mandatory fees ($1300), and room and board ($10,350). *College room only:* $7800. Full-time tuition and fees vary according to class time, course load, degree level, location, and program. Room and board charges vary according to board plan and housing facility. *Part-time tuition:* $980 per semester hour. *Part-time fees:* $45 per credit hour. Part-time tuition and fees vary according to class time, course load, degree level, location, and program.

FRESHMAN FINANCIAL AID (Fall 2016, est.) 334 applied for aid; of those 77% were deemed to have need. 100% of freshmen with need received aid; of those 36% had need fully met. *Average percent of need met:* 79% (excluding resources awarded to replace EFC). *Average financial aid package:* $31,100 (excluding resources awarded to replace EFC). 18% of all full-time freshmen had no need and received non-need-based gift aid.

UNDERGRADUATE FINANCIAL AID (Fall 2016, est.) 1,504 applied for aid; of those 76% were deemed to have need. 100% of undergraduates with need received aid; of those 26% had need fully met. *Average percent of need met:* 68% (excluding resources awarded to replace EFC). *Average financial aid package:* $26,410 (excluding resources awarded to replace EFC). 9% of all full-time undergraduates had no need and received non-need-based gift aid.

GIFT AID (NEED-BASED) *Total amount:* $6,544,905 (35% federal, 18% state, 47% institutional). *Receiving aid:* Freshmen: 36% (122); all full-time undergraduates: 38% (677). *Average award:* Freshmen: $6801; Undergraduates: $6137. *Scholarships, grants, and awards:* Federal Pell, FSEOG, state, private, college/university gift aid from institutional funds, Federal Nursing.

GIFT AID (NON-NEED-BASED) *Total amount:* $20,390,295 (1% federal, 13% state, 84% institutional, 2% external sources). *Receiving aid:* Freshmen: 76% (256). Undergraduates: 54% (967). *Average award:* Freshmen: $16,379. Undergraduates: $15,077. *Scholarships, grants, and awards by category:* Academic interests/achievement: 1,170 awards ($11,537,417 total): biological sciences, business, communication, computer science, education, engineering/technologies, English, foreign languages, general academic interests/achievements, health fields, humanities,

international studies, mathematics, military science, physical sciences, premedicine, religion/biblical studies, social sciences. *Creative arts/performance:* 109 awards ($376,685 total): art/fine arts, cinema/film/broadcasting, debating, journalism/publications, music, theater/drama. *Special achievements/activities:* 659 awards ($1,329,002 total): cheerleading/drum major, community service, general special achievements/activities, leadership, memberships, religious involvement. *Special characteristics:* 924 awards ($3,580,961 total): children and siblings of alumni, children of current students, children of educators, children of faculty/staff, ethnic background, first-generation college students, general special characteristics, handicapped students, international students, members of minority groups, relatives of clergy, religious affiliation, siblings of current students, spouses of current students, twins, veterans, veterans' children. *Tuition waivers:* Full or partial for children of alumni, employees or children of employees. *ROTC:* Army cooperative.

LOANS *Student loans:* $11,398,331 (36% need-based, 64% non-need-based). 61% of past graduating class borrowed through all loan programs. *Average indebtedness per student:* $31,784. *Average need-based loan:* Freshmen: $3333. Undergraduates: $4470. *Parent loans:* $2,012,216 (100% non-need-based). *Programs:* Federal Direct (Subsidized and Unsubsidized Stafford, PLUS), Perkins, alternative loans.

WORK-STUDY *Federal work-study:* Total amount: $162,854; 55 jobs averaging $2906. *State or other work-study/employment:* Total amount: $156,500 (100% non-need-based). 56 part-time jobs averaging $2777.

ATHLETIC AWARDS Total amount: $2,626,738 (100% non-need-based).

APPLYING FOR FINANCIAL AID *Required financial aid forms:* FAFSA, institution's own form. *Financial aid deadline (priority):* 12/1. *Notification date:* 12/1. Students must reply by 5/1 or within 2 weeks of notification.

CONTACT Mr. John Windham, Director of Student Financial Planning, Union University, 1050 Union University Drive, Jackson, TN 38305-3697, 731-661-5015 or toll-free 800-33-UNION. *Fax:* 731-661-5570. *E-mail:* jwindham@uu.edu.
Website: http://www.uu.edu/.

UNITED STATES SPORTS ACADEMY
Daphne, AL

Tuition & fees: $10,280	Average undergraduate aid package: $4748

ABOUT THE INSTITUTION Independent, coed. *Awards:* certificates, diplomas, bachelor's, master's, and doctoral degrees. 4 undergraduate majors. *Total enrollment:* 476. Undergraduates: 270. Federal methodology is used as a basis for awarding need-based institutional aid.

UNDERGRADUATE EXPENSES for 2017–2018 *Application fee:* $50. *One-time required fee:* $50. *Tuition:* full-time $9480.

UNDERGRADUATE FINANCIAL AID (Fall 2016, est.) 31 applied for aid; of those 100% were deemed to have need. 100% of undergraduates with need received aid; of those 81% had need fully met. *Average percent of need met:* 29% (excluding resources awarded to replace EFC). *Average financial aid package:* $4748 (excluding resources awarded to replace EFC).

GIFT AID (NEED-BASED) *Total amount:* $239,481 (90% federal, 3% state, 7% external sources). *Receiving aid:* All full-time undergraduates: 71% (25). *Average award:* Undergraduates: $3978. *Scholarships, grants, and awards:* Federal Pell, FSEOG, state.

GIFT AID (NON-NEED-BASED) *Tuition waivers:* Full or partial for employees or children of employees.

LOANS *Student loans:* $501,697 (100% need-based). *Average need-based loan:* Undergraduates: $4758. *Parent loans:* $2750 (100% need-based). *Programs:* Federal Direct (Subsidized and Unsubsidized Stafford, PLUS).

APPLYING FOR FINANCIAL AID *Required financial aid form:* FAFSA. *Financial aid deadline:* Continuous. *Notification date:* Continuous.

CONTACT Office of Financial Aid, United States Sports Academy, One Academy Drive, Daphne, AL 36526, 800-223-2668. *E-mail:* financialaid@ussa.edu.
Website: http://www.ussa.edu/.

UNITED STATES UNIVERSITY
San Diego, CA

CONTACT Financial Aid Office, United States University, 7675 Mission Valley Road, San Diego, CA 92108, 619-477-6310 or toll-free 888-422-3381.
Website: http://www.usuniversity.edu/.

UNITED TALMUDICAL SEMINARY
Brooklyn, NY

CONTACT Financial Aid Office, United Talmudical Seminary, 82 Lee Avenue, Brooklyn, NY 11211-7900, 718-963-9770 Ext. 309.

UNITY COLLEGE
Unity, ME

Tuition & fees: $28,350	Average undergraduate aid package: $20,247

ABOUT THE INSTITUTION Independent, coed. *Awards:* bachelor's and master's degrees. 15 undergraduate majors. *Total enrollment:* 719. Undergraduates: 709. Freshmen: 216. Federal methodology is used as a basis for awarding need-based institutional aid.

UNDERGRADUATE EXPENSES for 2017–2018 *Comprehensive fee:* $38,750 includes full-time tuition ($27,150), mandatory fees ($1200), and room and board ($10,400). Room and board charges vary according to board plan and housing facility. *Part-time tuition:* $980 per credit.

FRESHMAN FINANCIAL AID (Fall 2016, est.) 210 applied for aid; of those 88% were deemed to have need. 100% of freshmen with need received aid; of those 11% had need fully met. *Average percent of need met:* 70% (excluding resources awarded to replace EFC). *Average financial aid package:* $21,209 (excluding resources awarded to replace EFC). 14% of all full-time freshmen had no need and received non-need-based gift aid.

UNDERGRADUATE FINANCIAL AID (Fall 2016, est.) 655 applied for aid; of those 90% were deemed to have need. 100% of undergraduates with need received aid; of those 12% had need fully met. *Average percent of need met:* 72% (excluding resources awarded to replace EFC). *Average financial aid package:* $20,247 (excluding resources awarded to replace EFC). 15% of all full-time undergraduates had no need and received non-need-based gift aid.

GIFT AID (NEED-BASED) *Total amount:* $8,066,372 (17% federal, 2% state, 77% institutional, 4% external sources). *Receiving aid:* Freshmen: 86% (185); all full-time undergraduates: 83% (587). *Average award:* Freshmen: $15,064; Undergraduates: $13,707. *Scholarships, grants, and awards:* Federal Pell, FSEOG, state, private, college/university gift aid from institutional funds.

GIFT AID (NON-NEED-BASED) *Total amount:* $1,251,635 (1% federal, 93% institutional, 6% external sources). *Receiving aid:* Freshmen: 7% (16). Undergraduates: 7% (49). *Average award:* Freshmen: $9800. Undergraduates: $9346. *Scholarships, grants, and awards by category: Academic interests/achievement:* 581 awards ($5,595,840 total): general academic interests/achievements. *Special achievements/activities:* 17 awards ($19,360 total): community service, general special achievements/activities, leadership. *Special characteristics:* 43 awards ($64,800 total): children of educators, general special characteristics, local/state students, members of minority groups. *Tuition waivers:* Full or partial for employees or children of employees.

LOANS *Student loans:* $6,253,041 (75% need-based, 25% non-need-based). *Average need-based loan:* Freshmen: $6013. Undergraduates: $6595. *Parent loans:* $2,203,846 (56% need-based, 44% non-need-based). *Programs:* Federal Direct (Subsidized and Unsubsidized Stafford, PLUS), Perkins.

WORK-STUDY *Federal work-study:* Total amount: $555,064; 468 jobs averaging $1186. *State or other work-study/employment:* Total amount: $31,650 (4% need-based, 96% non-need-based). 21 part-time jobs averaging $1271.

APPLYING FOR FINANCIAL AID *Required financial aid form:* FAFSA. *Financial aid deadline:* Continuous. *Notification date:* Continuous beginning 12/10.

CONTACT Mr. Rand E. Newell, Director of Financial Aid, Unity College, 90 Quaker Hill Road, Unity, ME 04988, 207-509-7201. *Fax:* 207-512-1168. *E-mail:* rnewell@unity.edu.
Website: http://www.unity.edu/.

UNIVERSIDAD ADVENTISTA DE LAS ANTILLAS
Mayagüez, PR

CONTACT Mrs. Awilda Matos, Director of Financial Aid, Universidad Adventista de las Antillas, Box 118, Mayaguez, PR 00681-0118, 787-834-9595 Ext. 2263. *Fax:* 787-834-9597. *E-mail:* amatos@uaa.edu .
Website: http://www.uaa.edu/.

UNIVERSIDAD DEL ESTE
Carolina, PR

CONTACT Mrs. Eigna De Jess Molinari, Director of Financial Aid , Universidad del Este, Apartado 2010, Carolina, PR 00928, 787-257-7373 Ext. 3301. *E-mail:* eidejesus@suagm.edu.
Website: http://www.suagm.edu/une/.

UNIVERSIDAD DEL TURABO
Gurabo, PR

CONTACT Ms. Carmen J. Rivera Lopez, Directora de la Oficina de Asistencia Economica, Universidad del Turabo, Apartado 3030, Gurabo, PR 00778-3030, 787-743-7979 Ext. 4352. *Fax:* 787-746-6777.
Website: http://www.suagm.edu/ut/.

UNIVERSIDAD METROPOLITANA
San Juan, PR

CONTACT Economic Assistant Director, Universidad Metropolitana, Call Box 21150, Rio Piedras, PR 00928-1150, 787-766-1717 Ext. 6586 or toll-free 800-747-8362 (out-of-state).
Website: http://www.suagm.edu/umet/.

UNIVERSIDAD PENTECOSTAL MIZPA
San Juan, PR

CONTACT Mrs. Myriam Juarbe, Director of Financial Aid, Universidad Pentecostal Mizpa, PO Box 20966, San Juan, PR 00928, 787-720-4476. *Fax:* 787-720-2012. *E-mail:* asistenciaeconomica@colmizpa.edu .
Website: http://www.mizpa.edu/.

UNIVERSITY AT ALBANY, STATE UNIVERSITY OF NEW YORK
Albany, NY

Tuition & fees (NY res): $9223	Average undergraduate aid package: $11,046

ABOUT THE INSTITUTION State-supported, coed. *Awards:* certificates, bachelor's, master's, and doctoral degrees. 60 undergraduate majors. *Total*

enrollment: 17,178. Undergraduates: 12,908. Freshmen: 2,590. Federal methodology is used as a basis for awarding need-based institutional aid.

UNDERGRADUATE EXPENSES for 2017–2018 *Application fee:* $50. *Tuition, state resident:* full-time $6470; part-time $270 per credit hour. *Tuition, nonresident:* full-time $21,550; part-time $898 per credit hour. *Required fees:* full-time $2753; $74.25 per credit hour or $216 per term. Part-time tuition and fees vary according to course load. *College room and board:* $12,942; *Room only:* $8042. Room and board charges vary according to board plan and housing facility.

FRESHMAN FINANCIAL AID (Fall 2016, est.) 2,411 applied for aid; of those 77% were deemed to have need. 95% of freshmen with need received aid; of those 6% had need fully met. *Average percent of need met:* 57% (excluding resources awarded to replace EFC). *Average financial aid package:* $11,352 (excluding resources awarded to replace EFC). 7% of all full-time freshmen had no need and received non-need-based gift aid.

UNDERGRADUATE FINANCIAL AID (Fall 2016, est.) 9,827 applied for aid; of those 83% were deemed to have need. 97% of undergraduates with need received aid; of those 6% had need fully met. *Average percent of need met:* 58% (excluding resources awarded to replace EFC). *Average financial aid package:* $11,046 (excluding resources awarded to replace EFC). 5% of all full-time undergraduates had no need and received non-need-based gift aid.

GIFT AID (NEED-BASED) *Total amount:* $52,466,892 (47% federal, 35% state, 16% institutional, 2% external sources). *Receiving aid:* Freshmen: 55% (1,502); all full-time undergraduates: 54% (6,724). *Average award:* Freshmen: $8794; Undergraduates: $7760. *Scholarships, grants, and awards:* Federal Pell, FSEOG, state, private, college/university gift aid from institutional funds, Excelsior Scholarship for qualified NY State Students.

GIFT AID (NON-NEED-BASED) *Total amount:* $4,084,098 (9% federal, 12% state, 70% institutional, 9% external sources). *Receiving aid:* Freshmen: 2% (43). Undergraduates: 1% (133). *Average award:* Freshmen: $4709. Undergraduates: $4414. *Scholarships, grants, and awards by category:* Academic interests/ achievement: 1,483 awards ($6,029,028 total): general academic interests/achievements. *ROTC:* Army, Air Force cooperative.

LOANS *Student loans:* $63,750,486 (47% need-based, 53% non-need-based). 67% of past graduating class borrowed through all loan programs. *Average indebtedness per student:* $21,217. *Average need-based loan:* Freshmen: $4108. Undergraduates: $4702. *Parent loans:* $20,445,828 (100% non-need-based). *Programs:* Federal Direct (Subsidized and Unsubsidized Stafford, PLUS), Perkins.

WORK-STUDY *Federal work-study:* Total amount: $87,500; 610 jobs averaging $1434. *State or other work-study/employment:* Total amount: $1,755,522 (74% need-based, 26% non-need-based). 234 part-time jobs averaging $7502.

ATHLETIC AWARDS Total amount: $6,741,527 (4% need-based, 96% non-need-based).

APPLYING FOR FINANCIAL AID *Required financial aid forms:* FAFSA, Tuition Assistance Program (TAP) for NY State residents. *Financial aid deadline (priority):* 12/1. *Notification date:* Continuous beginning 3/2.

CONTACT Stephen Kudzin, Director of Financial Aid, University at Albany, State University of New York, Student Financial Center, Campus Center G-26, 1400 Washington Avenue, Albany, NY 12222-0001, 518-442-3202. *Fax:* 518-442-5295. *E-mail:* sfc@albany.edu. *Website:* http://www.albany.edu/.

FRESHMAN FINANCIAL AID (Fall 2015) 2,934 applied for aid; of those 75% were deemed to have need. 94% of freshmen with need received aid; of those 8% had need fully met. *Average percent of need met:* 48% (excluding resources awarded to replace EFC). *Average financial aid package:* $10,577 (excluding resources awarded to replace EFC). 7% of all full-time freshmen had no need and received non-need-based gift aid.

UNDERGRADUATE FINANCIAL AID (Fall 2015) 13,712 applied for aid; of those 77% were deemed to have need. 95% of undergraduates with need received aid; of those 99% had need fully met. *Average percent of need met:* 50% (excluding resources awarded to replace EFC). *Average financial aid package:* $9246 (excluding resources awarded to replace EFC). 3% of all full-time undergraduates had no need and received non-need-based gift aid.

GIFT AID (NEED-BASED) *Total amount:* $74,324,643 (42% federal, 32% state, 22% institutional, 4% external sources). *Receiving aid:* Freshmen: 46% (1,676); all full-time undergraduates: 44% (8,047). *Average award:* Freshmen: $7952; Undergraduates: $7162. *Scholarships, grants, and awards:* Federal Pell, FSEOG, state, private, college/university gift aid from institutional funds, Federal Nursing.

GIFT AID (NON-NEED-BASED) *Total amount:* $4,771,793 (17% state, 71% institutional, 12% external sources). *Receiving aid:* Freshmen: 20% (736). Undergraduates: 12% (2,248). *Average award:* Freshmen: $4075. Undergraduates: $4361. *Tuition waivers:* Full or partial for minority students. *ROTC:* Army cooperative.

LOANS *Student loans:* $61,916,805 (82% need-based, 18% non-need-based). 58% of past graduating class borrowed through all loan programs. *Average indebtedness per student:* $26,046. *Average need-based loan:* Freshmen: $3282. Undergraduates: $4361. *Parent loans:* $14,289,930 (61% need-based, 39% non-need-based). *Programs:* Federal Direct (Subsidized and Unsubsidized Stafford, PLUS), Perkins, Federal Nursing, college/university.

WORK-STUDY *Federal work-study:* 1,059 jobs averaging $1075. *State or other work-study/employment:* Total amount: $19,650,538 (100% non-need-based). 978 part-time jobs averaging $14,795.

ATHLETIC AWARDS Total amount: $8,570,557 (88% need-based, 12% non-need-based).

APPLYING FOR FINANCIAL AID *Required financial aid form:* FAFSA. *Financial aid deadline (priority):* 3/1. *Notification date:* Continuous beginning 2/1. Students must reply by 5/1.

CONTACT John Gottardy, Director of Financial Aid, University at Buffalo, the State University of New York, 232 Capen Hall, Buffalo, NY 14260, 716-645-8232 or toll-free 888-UB-ADMIT. *Fax:* 716-645-6566. *E-mail:* johngott@buffalo.edu. *Website:* http://www.buffalo.edu/.

UNIVERSITY OF ADVANCING TECHNOLOGY
Tempe, AZ

CONTACT Financial Aid Office, University of Advancing Technology, 2625 West Baseline Road, Tempe, AZ 85283-1042, 602-383-8228 or toll-free 800-658-5744. *Fax:* 602-383-8222. *E-mail:* fa@uat.edu. *Website:* http://www.uat.edu/.

UNIVERSITY AT BUFFALO, THE STATE UNIVERSITY OF NEW YORK
Buffalo, NY

Tuition & fees (NY res): $9574	Average undergraduate aid package: $9246

ABOUT THE INSTITUTION State-supported, coed. *Awards:* certificates, bachelor's, master's, and doctoral degrees. 75 undergraduate majors. *Total enrollment:* 30,183. Undergraduates: 20,411. Freshmen: 4,103. Federal methodology is used as a basis for awarding need-based institutional aid.

UNDERGRADUATE EXPENSES for 2016–2017 *Application fee:* $50. *Tuition, state resident:* full-time $6470; part-time $270 per credit hour. *Tuition, nonresident:* full-time $23,710; part-time $988 per credit hour. *Required fees:* full-time $3104; $257.78 per credit hour. Part-time tuition and fees vary according to course load. *College room and board:* $13,548; *Room only:* $7798. Room and board charges vary according to board plan and housing facility.

THE UNIVERSITY OF AKRON
Akron, OH

Tuition & fees (OH res): $10,270	Average undergraduate aid package: $7517

ABOUT THE INSTITUTION State-supported, coed. *Awards:* certificates, associate, bachelor's, master's, and doctoral degrees. 153 undergraduate majors. *Total enrollment:* 21,099. Undergraduates: 17,416. Freshmen: 3,090. Federal methodology is used as a basis for awarding need-based institutional aid.

UNDERGRADUATE EXPENSES for 2017–2018 *Application fee:* $45. *Tuition, state resident:* full-time $8618; part-time $359 per credit hour. *Tuition, nonresident:* full-time $17,149; part-time $715 per credit hour. *Required fees:* full-time $1652. Full-time tuition and fees vary according to course load, degree level, location, and program. Part-time tuition and fees vary according to course load, degree level, location, and program. *College room and board:* $10,684; *Room only:* $7020. Room and board charges vary according to board plan and housing facility.

FRESHMAN FINANCIAL AID (Fall 2015) 3,602 applied for aid; of those 77% were deemed to have need. 100% of freshmen with need received aid; of those 13% had need fully met. *Average percent of need met:* 55% (excluding resources awarded to replace EFC). *Average financial aid package:* $8658 (excluding resources awarded to replace EFC). 18% of all full-time freshmen had no need and received non-need-based gift aid.

UNDERGRADUATE FINANCIAL AID (Fall 2015) 12,920 applied for aid; of those 79% were deemed to have need. 100% of undergraduates with need received aid; of those 10% had need fully met. *Average percent of need met:* 51% (excluding resources awarded to replace EFC). *Average financial aid package:* $7517 (excluding resources awarded to replace EFC). 13% of all full-time undergraduates had no need and received non-need-based gift aid.

GIFT AID (NEED-BASED) Total amount: $33,476,884 (85% federal, 15% state). *Receiving aid:* Freshmen: 40% (1,516); all full-time undergraduates: 38% (5,587). *Average award:* Freshmen: $5125; Undergraduates: $5068. *Scholarships, grants, and awards:* Federal Pell, FSEOG.

GIFT AID (NON-NEED-BASED) Total amount: $43,175,900 (4% state, 75% institutional, 21% external sources). *Receiving aid:* Freshmen: 67% (2,540). Undergraduates: 50% (7,307). *Average award:* Freshmen: $5261. Undergraduates: $4675. *Scholarships, grants, and awards by category: Academic interests/achievement:* 3,973 awards ($14,172,060 total): biological sciences, business, communication, computer science, education, engineering/technologies, English, foreign languages, general academic interests/achievements, health fields, home economics, humanities, international studies, mathematics, military science, physical sciences, premedicine, social sciences. *Creative arts/performance:* 124 awards ($174,647 total): applied art and design, art/fine arts, creative writing, dance, debating, general creative arts/performance, journalism/publications, music, performing arts, theater/drama. *Special achievements/activities:* 103 awards ($267,985 total): community service, general special achievements/activities, leadership, memberships. *Special characteristics:* 3,482 awards ($9,586,693 total): adult students, general special characteristics, handicapped students, international students, local/state students, members of minority groups, out-of-state students. *Tuition waivers:* Full or partial for employees or children of employees, senior citizens. *ROTC:* Army, Air Force cooperative.

LOANS Student loans: $72,039,294 (50% need-based, 50% non-need-based). 70% of past graduating class borrowed through all loan programs. *Average indebtedness per student:* $32,372. *Average need-based loan:* Freshmen: $3159. Undergraduates: $3886. *Parent loans:* $21,348,041 (100% non-need-based). *Programs:* Federal Direct (Subsidized and Unsubsidized Stafford, PLUS), Perkins, Federal Nursing, college/university.

WORK-STUDY Federal work-study: 424 jobs averaging $2608. *State or other work-study/employment:* Total amount: $15,164,826 (100% non-need-based). 3,460 part-time jobs averaging $4384.

ATHLETIC AWARDS Total amount: $6,489,224 (100% non-need-based).

APPLYING FOR FINANCIAL AID *Required financial aid forms:* FAFSA, institution's own form. *Financial aid deadline (priority):* 3/1. *Notification date:* Continuous beginning 3/15. Students must reply within 2 weeks of notification.

CONTACT Mrs. Jennifer E. Harpham, Director of Student Financial Aid, The University of Akron, 302 Buchtel Mall, Akron, OH 44325-6211, 330-972-5860 or toll-free 800-655-4884. *Fax:* 330-972-7139. *E-mail:* jharpham@uakron.edu. *Website:* http://www.uakron.edu/.

THE UNIVERSITY OF ALABAMA
Tuscaloosa, AL

Tuition & fees (AL res): $10,470	Average undergraduate aid package: $13,656

ABOUT THE INSTITUTION State-supported, coed. *Awards:* certificates, bachelor's, master's, and doctoral degrees. 72 undergraduate majors. *Total enrollment:* 37,663. Undergraduates: 32,563. Freshmen: 7,559. Federal methodology is used as a basis for awarding need-based institutional aid.

UNDERGRADUATE EXPENSES for 2016–2017 Application fee: $40. *Tuition, state resident:* full-time $10,470. *Tuition, nonresident:* full-time $26,950. *College room and board:* $9550; *Room only:* $6000. Room and board charges vary according to board plan, housing facility, and location.

FRESHMAN FINANCIAL AID (Fall 2015) 4,857 applied for aid; of those 72% were deemed to have need. 97% of freshmen with need received aid; of those 28% had need fully met. *Average percent of need met:* 58% (excluding resources awarded

to replace EFC). *Average financial aid package:* $15,376 (excluding resources awarded to replace EFC). 26% of all full-time freshmen had no need and received non-need-based gift aid.

UNDERGRADUATE FINANCIAL AID (Fall 2015) 15,770 applied for aid; of those 79% were deemed to have need. 98% of undergraduates with need received aid; of those 20% had need fully met. *Average percent of need met:* 53% (excluding resources awarded to replace EFC). *Average financial aid package:* $13,656 (excluding resources awarded to replace EFC). 24% of all full-time undergraduates had no need and received non-need-based gift aid.

GIFT AID (NEED-BASED) Total amount: $95,542,925 (33% federal, 4% state, 61% institutional, 2% external sources). *Receiving aid:* Freshmen: 39% (2,765); all full-time undergraduates: 32% (9,228). *Average award:* Freshmen: $13,777; Undergraduates: $11,597. *Scholarships, grants, and awards:* Federal Pell, FSEOG, state, private, college/university gift aid from institutional funds, Federal Nursing.

GIFT AID (NON-NEED-BASED) Total amount: $139,705,948 (6% federal, 8% state, 82% institutional, 4% external sources). *Receiving aid:* Freshmen: 31% (2,226). Undergraduates: 22% (6,208). *Average award:* Freshmen: $14,821. Undergraduates: $14,770. *Scholarships, grants, and awards by category: Academic interests/achievement:* area/ethnic studies, biological sciences, business, communication, computer science, education, engineering/technologies, English, foreign languages, general academic interests/achievements, home economics, library science, mathematics, military science, physical sciences, premedicine, social sciences. *Creative arts/performance:* art/fine arts, cinema/film/broadcasting, creative writing, dance, debating, journalism/publications, music, theater/drama. *Special achievements/activities:* cheerleading/drum major, community service, general special achievements/activities, hobbies/interests, junior miss. *Special characteristics:* children of union members/company employees, general special characteristics, international students, out-of-state students, spouses of deceased or disabled public servants. *ROTC:* Army, Air Force.

LOANS Student loans: $135,334,301 (65% need-based, 35% non-need-based). 47% of past graduating class borrowed through all loan programs. *Average indebtedness per student:* $33,816. *Average need-based loan:* Freshmen: $3450. Undergraduates: $4256. *Parent loans:* $70,132,291 (52% need-based, 48% non-need-based). *Programs:* Federal Direct (Subsidized and Unsubsidized Stafford, PLUS), Perkins, college/university, private loans.

WORK-STUDY Federal work-study: 618 jobs averaging $2725.

ATHLETIC AWARDS Total amount: $13,324,323 (4% need-based, 96% non-need-based).

APPLYING FOR FINANCIAL AID *Required financial aid form:* FAFSA. *Financial aid deadline (priority):* 3/1. *Notification date:* 4/1. Students must reply within 3 weeks of notification.

CONTACT Helen Allen, Director of Financial Aid, The University of Alabama, Box 870162, Tuscaloosa, AL 35487-0162, 205-348-6756 or toll-free 800-933-BAMA. *Fax:* 205-348-2989. *E-mail:* helen.leathers@ua.edu. *Website:* http://www.ua.edu/.

THE UNIVERSITY OF ALABAMA AT BIRMINGHAM
Birmingham, AL

Tuition & fees (AL res): $9936	Average undergraduate aid package: $10,369

ABOUT THE INSTITUTION State-supported, coed. *Awards:* certificates, bachelor's, master's, and doctoral degrees. 46 undergraduate majors. *Total enrollment:* 19,535. Undergraduates: 12,369. Freshmen: 2,021. Federal methodology is used as a basis for awarding need-based institutional aid.

UNDERGRADUATE EXPENSES for 2016–2017 Application fee: $30. *Tuition, state resident:* full-time $9936; part-time $305 per credit hour. *Tuition, nonresident:* full-time $22,844; part-time $717 per contact hour. Full-time tuition and fees vary according to course load, degree level, program, and reciprocity agreements. Part-time tuition and fees vary according to course load, degree level, program, and reciprocity agreements. *College room and board:* $9980; *Room only:* $6020. Room and board charges vary according to board plan and housing facility.

FRESHMAN FINANCIAL AID (Fall 2016, est.) 1,716 applied for aid; of those 74% were deemed to have need. 99% of freshmen with need received aid; of those 14% had need fully met. *Average percent of need met:* 56% (excluding resources awarded to replace EFC). *Average financial aid package:* $9923 (excluding

resources awarded to replace EFC). 26% of all full-time freshmen had no need and received non-need-based gift aid.

UNDERGRADUATE FINANCIAL AID (Fall 2016, est.) 6,626 applied for aid; of those 82% were deemed to have need. 98% of undergraduates with need received aid; of those 10% had need fully met. *Average percent of need met:* 50% (excluding resources awarded to replace EFC). *Average financial aid package:* $10,369 (excluding resources awarded to replace EFC). 20% of all full-time undergraduates had no need and received non-need-based gift aid.

GIFT AID (NEED-BASED) *Total amount:* $21,494,343 (98% federal, 1% institutional, 1% external sources). *Receiving aid:* Freshmen: 55% (1,066); all full-time undergraduates: 55% (4,879). *Average award:* Freshmen: $5087; Undergraduates: $5052. *Scholarships, grants, and awards:* Federal Pell, FSEOG, state, private, college/university gift aid from institutional funds, United Negro College Fund.

GIFT AID (NON-NEED-BASED) *Total amount:* $28,203,511 (94% institutional, 6% external sources). *Receiving aid:* Freshmen: 46% (897). Undergraduates: 27% (2,417). *Average award:* Freshmen: $7447. Undergraduates: $7582. *Scholarships, grants, and awards by category: Academic interests/achievement:* business, communication, computer science, engineering/technologies, general academic interests/achievements, health fields, mathematics. *Creative arts/performance:* art/fine arts, music, performing arts, theater/drama. *Special achievements/activities:* cheerleading/drum major, junior miss, leadership, memberships, religious involvement. *Special characteristics:* adult students, children and siblings of alumni, children of current students, children of educators, children of faculty/staff, children of public servants, children of union members/company employees, children of workers in trades, children with a deceased or disabled parent, ethnic background, first-generation college students, general special characteristics, handicapped students, international students, married students, members of minority groups, out-of-state students, parents of current students, previous college experience, public servants, relatives of clergy, siblings of current students, spouses of current students, spouses of deceased or disabled public servants, twins, veterans, veterans' children. *Tuition waivers:* Full or partial for employees or children of employees. *ROTC:* Army, Air Force cooperative.

LOANS *Student loans:* $49,099,201 (49% need-based, 51% non-need-based). 63% of past graduating class borrowed through all loan programs. *Average indebtedness per student:* $34,950. *Average need-based loan:* Freshmen: $4351. Undergraduates: $4574. *Parent loans:* $10,537,364 (100% non-need-based). *Programs:* Federal Direct (Subsidized and Unsubsidized Stafford, PLUS), Perkins, state, college/university.

WORK-STUDY *Federal work-study:* Total amount: $1,811,117; jobs available.

ATHLETIC AWARDS Total amount: $7,755,965 (100% non-need-based).

APPLYING FOR FINANCIAL AID *Required financial aid form:* FAFSA. *Financial aid deadline (priority):* 3/1. *Notification date:* Continuous beginning 3/15. Students must reply within 4 weeks of notification.

CONTACT Ms. Helen M. McIntyre, Office of Student Financial Aid, The University of Alabama at Birmingham, LHL 120, 1720 2nd Avenue South, Birmingham, AL 35294-0013, 205-934-8132 or toll-free 800-421-8743. *E-mail:* finaid@uab.edu. *Website:* http://www.uab.edu/.

THE UNIVERSITY OF ALABAMA IN HUNTSVILLE
Huntsville, AL

Tuition & fees (AL res): $9842	Average undergraduate aid package: $10,713

ABOUT THE INSTITUTION State-supported, coed. *Awards:* certificates, bachelor's, master's, and doctoral degrees. 35 undergraduate majors. *Total enrollment:* 8,468. Undergraduates: 6,507. Freshmen: 1,213. Both federal and institutional methodology are used as a basis for awarding need-based institutional aid.

UNDERGRADUATE EXPENSES for 2016–2017 *Application fee:* $30. *Tuition, state resident:* full-time $8996; part-time $382 per credit hour. *Tuition, nonresident:* full-time $19,766; part-time $841 per credit hour. *Required fees:* full-time $846. Full-time tuition and fees vary according to course load and program. Part-time tuition and fees vary according to course load and program. *College room and board:* $9603; *Room only:* $6553. Room and board charges vary according to board plan and housing facility.

FRESHMAN FINANCIAL AID (Fall 2016, est.) 1,203 applied for aid; of those 50% were deemed to have need. 100% of freshmen with need received aid; of those

34% had need fully met. *Average percent of need met:* 75% (excluding resources awarded to replace EFC). *Average financial aid package:* $13,165 (excluding resources awarded to replace EFC). 37% of all full-time freshmen had no need and received non-need-based gift aid.

UNDERGRADUATE FINANCIAL AID (Fall 2016, est.) 5,231 applied for aid; of those 51% were deemed to have need. 99% of undergraduates with need received aid; of those 17% had need fully met. *Average percent of need met:* 61% (excluding resources awarded to replace EFC). *Average financial aid package:* $10,713 (excluding resources awarded to replace EFC). 27% of all full-time undergraduates had no need and received non-need-based gift aid.

GIFT AID (NEED-BASED) *Total amount:* $16,735,839 (47% federal, 50% institutional, 3% external sources). *Receiving aid:* Freshmen: 45% (541); all full-time undergraduates: 42% (2,214). *Average award:* Freshmen: $9402; Undergraduates: $7486. *Scholarships, grants, and awards:* Federal Pell, FSEOG, state, private, college/university gift aid from institutional funds, Federal Nursing.

GIFT AID (NON-NEED-BASED) *Total amount:* $13,947,404 (96% institutional, 4% external sources). *Receiving aid:* Freshmen: 13% (157). Undergraduates: 5% (268). *Average award:* Freshmen: $10,118. Undergraduates: $8507. *Scholarships, grants, and awards by category: Academic interests/achievement:* biological sciences, business, communication, computer science, education, engineering/technologies, English, foreign languages, general academic interests/achievements, health fields, humanities, mathematics, physical sciences, social sciences. *Creative arts/performance:* art/fine arts, music. *Special achievements/activities:* cheerleading/drum major, community service, general special achievements/activities, junior miss, leadership. *Special characteristics:* general special characteristics, local/state students, members of minority groups. *Tuition waivers:* Full or partial for employees or children of employees. *ROTC:* Army cooperative.

LOANS *Student loans:* $24,826,313 (75% need-based, 25% non-need-based). 54% of past graduating class borrowed through all loan programs. *Average indebtedness per student:* $35,009. *Average need-based loan:* Freshmen: $5682. Undergraduates: $7218. *Parent loans:* $3,786,907 (49% need-based, 51% non-need-based). *Programs:* Federal Direct (Subsidized and Unsubsidized Stafford, PLUS).

WORK-STUDY *Federal work-study:* Total amount: $257,653; 66 jobs averaging $3904.

ATHLETIC AWARDS Total amount: $2,963,461 (21% need-based, 79% non-need-based).

APPLYING FOR FINANCIAL AID *Required financial aid form:* FAFSA. *Financial aid deadline:* 7/31 (priority: 4/1). *Notification date:* Continuous beginning 4/1. Students must reply within 2 weeks of notification.

CONTACT Mr. Patrick James, Director of Financial Aid, The University of Alabama in Huntsville, 301 Sparkman Drive, CTC Room 212, Huntsville, AL 35899, 256-824-6650 or toll-free 800-UAH-CALL. *Fax:* 256-824-6212. *E-mail:* finaid@uah.edu. *Website:* http://www.uah.edu/.

UNIVERSITY OF ALASKA ANCHORAGE
Anchorage, AK

Tuition & fees: N/R	Average undergraduate aid package: $9404

ABOUT THE INSTITUTION State-supported, coed. 107 undergraduate majors. Federal methodology is used as a basis for awarding need-based institutional aid.

FRESHMAN FINANCIAL AID (Fall 2016, est.) 1,127 applied for aid; of those 67% were deemed to have need. 97% of freshmen with need received aid; of those 20% had need fully met. *Average percent of need met:* 71% (excluding resources awarded to replace EFC). *Average financial aid package:* $9469 (excluding resources awarded to replace EFC). 8% of all full-time freshmen had no need and received non-need-based gift aid.

UNDERGRADUATE FINANCIAL AID (Fall 2016, est.) 3,698 applied for aid; of those 75% were deemed to have need. 95% of undergraduates with need received aid; of those 11% had need fully met. *Average percent of need met:* 62% (excluding resources awarded to replace EFC). *Average financial aid package:* $9404 (excluding resources awarded to replace EFC). 7% of all full-time undergraduates had no need and received non-need-based gift aid.

GIFT AID (NEED-BASED) *Total amount:* $28,100,861 (55% federal, 20% state, 13% institutional, 12% external sources). *Receiving aid:* Freshmen: 47% (619); all full-time undergraduates: 41% (2,150). *Average award:* Freshmen: $3330; Under-

graduates: $3220. **Scholarships, grants, and awards:** Federal Pell, FSEOG, state, private, college/university gift aid from institutional funds.
GIFT AID (NON-NEED-BASED) Total amount: $6,635,736 (47% state, 24% institutional, 29% external sources). **Average award:** Freshmen: $2606. Undergraduates: $2428. **Scholarships, grants, and awards by category:** Academic interests/achievement: biological sciences, business, communication, computer science, education, engineering/technologies, English, general academic interests/achievements, health fields, humanities, mathematics, social sciences. Creative arts/performance: art/fine arts, dance, debating, music, performing arts. Special achievements/activities: general special achievements/activities, leadership. Special characteristics: children and siblings of alumni, children of current students, children of educators, children of faculty/staff.
LOANS Student loans: $49,778,961 (75% need-based, 25% non-need-based). 51% of past graduating class borrowed through all loan programs. Average indebtedness per student: $26,951. **Average need-based loan:** Freshmen: $3298. Undergraduates: $4373. **Parent loans:** $8,039,646 (59% need-based, 41% non-need-based). **Programs:** Federal Direct (Subsidized and Unsubsidized Stafford, PLUS), state, private loans.
WORK-STUDY Federal work-study: Total amount: $458,101; jobs available.
ATHLETIC AWARDS Total amount: $1,588,828 (21% need-based, 79% non-need-based).
APPLYING FOR FINANCIAL AID Required financial aid form: FAFSA. **Financial aid deadline (priority):** 4/1. **Notification date:** Continuous beginning 2/1. Students must reply within 4 weeks of notification.
CONTACT Sonya F. Stein, Director of Student Financial Assistance, University of Alaska Anchorage, PO Box 141608, Anchorage, AK 99514-1608, 907-786-1517. Fax: 907-786-6122. E-mail: sfstein@alaska.edu.
Website: http://www.uaa.alaska.edu/.

UNIVERSITY OF ALASKA FAIRBANKS
Fairbanks, AK

Tuition & fees (AK res): $8144	Average undergraduate aid package: $8074

ABOUT THE INSTITUTION State-supported, coed. **Awards:** certificates, associate, bachelor's, master's, and doctoral degrees. 77 undergraduate majors. **Total enrollment:** 8,360. Undergraduates: 7,239. Freshmen: 846. Federal methodology is used as a basis for awarding need-based institutional aid.
UNDERGRADUATE EXPENSES for 2017–2018 Application fee: $50. **Tuition, state resident:** full-time $6690; part-time $202 per credit hour. **Tuition, nonresident:** full-time $22,080; part-time $715 per credit hour. **Required fees:** full-time $1454. Full-time tuition and fees vary according to course level, course load, location, program, and reciprocity agreements. Part-time tuition and fees vary according to course level, course load, location, program, and reciprocity agreements. **College room and board:** $8530; **Room only:** $4140. Room and board charges vary according to board plan, housing facility, and location.
FRESHMAN FINANCIAL AID (Fall 2015) 632 applied for aid; of those 57% were deemed to have need. 95% of freshmen with need received aid; of those 14% had need fully met. **Average percent of need met:** 56% (excluding resources awarded to replace EFC). **Average financial aid package:** $7882 (excluding resources awarded to replace EFC). 18% of all full-time freshmen had no need and received non-need-based gift aid.
UNDERGRADUATE FINANCIAL AID (Fall 2015) 2,741 applied for aid; of those 63% were deemed to have need. 96% of undergraduates with need received aid; of those 13% had need fully met. **Average percent of need met:** 53% (excluding resources awarded to replace EFC). **Average financial aid package:** $8074 (excluding resources awarded to replace EFC). 15% of all full-time undergraduates had no need and received non-need-based gift aid.
GIFT AID (NEED-BASED) Total amount: $12,040,043 (48% federal, 20% state, 20% institutional, 12% external sources). **Receiving aid:** Freshmen: 45% (313); all full-time undergraduates: 44% (1,450). **Average award:** Freshmen: $6898; Undergraduates: $6744. **Scholarships, grants, and awards:** Federal Pell, FSEOG, state, private, college/university gift aid from institutional funds.
GIFT AID (NON-NEED-BASED) Total amount: $6,036,211 (43% state, 34% institutional, 23% external sources). **Receiving aid:** Freshmen: 4% (31). Undergraduates: 4% (135). **Average award:** Freshmen: $4569. Undergraduates: $3929. **Scholarships, grants, and awards by category:** Academic interests/achievement:

biological sciences, business, computer science, education, engineering/technologies, general academic interests/achievements, mathematics, military science, physical sciences. Special achievements/activities: community service, general special achievements/activities, leadership. Special characteristics: local/state students. **Tuition waivers:** Full or partial for children of alumni, employees or children of employees, senior citizens. **ROTC:** Army.
LOANS Student loans: $13,460,570 (79% need-based, 21% non-need-based). 46% of past graduating class borrowed through all loan programs. Average indebtedness per student: $25,344. **Average need-based loan:** Freshmen: $2943. Undergraduates: $3793. **Parent loans:** $904,750 (59% need-based, 41% non-need-based). **Programs:** Federal Direct (Subsidized and Unsubsidized Stafford, PLUS), state.
WORK-STUDY Federal work-study: 35 jobs averaging $4210.
ATHLETIC AWARDS Total amount: $1,102,863 (22% need-based, 78% non-need-based).
APPLYING FOR FINANCIAL AID Required financial aid forms: FAFSA, institution's own form. **Financial aid deadline:** 7/1 (priority: 2/15). **Notification date:** Continuous beginning 3/1. Students must reply within 2 weeks of notification.
CONTACT Deanna Dieringer, Director of Financial Aid, University of Alaska Fairbanks, PO Box 756360, Fairbanks, AK 99775-6360, 907-474-7256 or toll-free 800-478-1823. Fax: 907-474-7065. E-mail: uaf-financialaid@alaska.edu.
Website: http://www.uaf.edu/.

UNIVERSITY OF ALASKA SOUTHEAST
Juneau, AK

Tuition & fees: N/R	Average undergraduate aid package: $4113

ABOUT THE INSTITUTION State-supported, coed. 27 undergraduate majors. Federal methodology is used as a basis for awarding need-based institutional aid.
FRESHMAN FINANCIAL AID (Fall 2015) 123 applied for aid; of those 74% were deemed to have need. 95% of freshmen with need received aid; of those 10% had need fully met. **Average percent of need met:** 59% (excluding resources awarded to replace EFC). **Average financial aid package:** $3205 (excluding resources awarded to replace EFC). 10% of all full-time freshmen had no need and received non-need-based gift aid.
UNDERGRADUATE FINANCIAL AID (Fall 2015) 517 applied for aid; of those 81% were deemed to have need. 97% of undergraduates with need received aid; of those 10% had need fully met. **Average percent of need met:** 54% (excluding resources awarded to replace EFC). **Average financial aid package:** $4113 (excluding resources awarded to replace EFC). 7% of all full-time undergraduates had no need and received non-need-based gift aid.
GIFT AID (NEED-BASED) Total amount: $3,476,802 (61% federal, 14% state, 12% institutional, 13% external sources). **Receiving aid:** Freshmen: 54% (79); all full-time undergraduates: 52% (335). **Average award:** Freshmen: $6869; Undergraduates: $6940. **Scholarships, grants, and awards:** Federal Pell, FSEOG, state, private, college/university gift aid from institutional funds.
GIFT AID (NON-NEED-BASED) Total amount: $755,853 (7% federal, 36% state, 33% institutional, 24% external sources). **Receiving aid:** Freshmen: 7% (11). Undergraduates: 6% (41). **Average award:** Freshmen: $2518. Undergraduates: $3287. **Scholarships, grants, and awards by category:** Academic interests/achievement: general academic interests/achievements. Creative arts/performance: general creative arts/performance. Special achievements/activities: leadership. Special characteristics: local/state students.
LOANS Student loans: $1,530,085 (95% need-based, 5% non-need-based). 46% of past graduating class borrowed through all loan programs. Average indebtedness per student: $25,090. **Average need-based loan:** Freshmen: $2904. Undergraduates: $4058. **Parent loans:** $1,940,709 (65% need-based, 35% non-need-based). **Programs:** Federal Direct (Subsidized and Unsubsidized Stafford, PLUS), state.
WORK-STUDY Federal work-study: jobs available.
APPLYING FOR FINANCIAL AID Required financial aid form: FAFSA. **Financial aid deadline (priority):** 4/15. **Notification date:** Continuous beginning 3/1. Students must reply within 3 weeks of notification.
CONTACT Ms. Corinne Soltis, Director of Financial Aid, University of Alaska Southeast, 11120 Glacier Highway, Juneau, AK 99801-8680, 907-796-6255 or toll-free 877-465-4827. Fax: 907-796-6250. E-mail: casoltis@uas.alaska.edu.
Website: http://www.uas.alaska.edu/.

UNIVERSITY OF ANTELOPE VALLEY
Lancaster, CA

CONTACT Financial Aid Office, University of Antelope Valley, 44055 North Sierra Highway, Lancaster, CA 93534, 661-726-1911.
Website: http://www.uav.edu/.

THE UNIVERSITY OF ARIZONA
Tucson, AZ

Tuition & fees (AZ res): $11,177	Average undergraduate aid package: $12,707

ABOUT THE INSTITUTION State-supported, coed. *Awards:* certificates, bachelor's, master's, and doctoral degrees. 111 undergraduate majors. *Total enrollment:* 43,625. Undergraduates: 34,072. Freshmen: 7,753. Both federal and institutional methodology are used as a basis for awarding need-based institutional aid.
UNDERGRADUATE EXPENSES for 2016–2017 *Application fee:* $50. *Tuition, state resident:* full-time $10,160; part-time $768 per credit hour. *Tuition, nonresident:* full-time $30,759; part-time $1415 per credit hour. *Required fees:* full-time $1017; $88.25 per credit hour. Full-time tuition and fees vary according to class time, course level, course load, degree level, location, program, reciprocity agreements, and student level. Part-time tuition and fees vary according to class time, course level, course load, degree level, location, program, reciprocity agreements, and student level. *College room and board:* $11,300; *Room only:* $7300. Room and board charges vary according to board plan and housing facility. *Payment plan:* Guaranteed tuition.
FRESHMAN FINANCIAL AID (Fall 2015) 4,996 applied for aid; of those 72% were deemed to have need. 97% of freshmen with need received aid; of those 13% had need fully met. *Average percent of need met:* 55% (excluding resources awarded to replace EFC). *Average financial aid package:* $12,542 (excluding resources awarded to replace EFC). 29% of all full-time freshmen had no need and received non-need-based gift aid.
UNDERGRADUATE FINANCIAL AID (Fall 2015) 18,907 applied for aid; of those 81% were deemed to have need. 97% of undergraduates with need received aid; of those 11% had need fully met. *Average percent of need met:* 56% (excluding resources awarded to replace EFC). *Average financial aid package:* $12,707 (excluding resources awarded to replace EFC). 21% of all full-time undergraduates had no need and received non-need-based gift aid.
GIFT AID (NEED-BASED) *Total amount:* $149,170,834 (35% federal, 53% institutional, 12% external sources). *Receiving aid:* Freshmen: 48% (3,322); all full-time undergraduates: 46% (13,622). *Average award:* Freshmen: $10,288; Undergraduates: $10,109. *Scholarships, grants, and awards:* Federal Pell, FSEOG, state, private, college/university gift aid from institutional funds, Federal Nursing.
GIFT AID (NON-NEED-BASED) *Total amount:* $75,399,901 (4% federal, 71% institutional, 25% external sources). *Receiving aid:* Freshmen: 6% (436). Undergraduates: 4% (1,272). *Average award:* Freshmen: $7703. Undergraduates: $8164. *Scholarships, grants, and awards by category: Academic interests/achievement:* agriculture, architecture, biological sciences, business, education, engineering/technologies, general academic interests/achievements, humanities, military science, physical sciences, religion/biblical studies. *Creative arts/performance:* art/fine arts, dance, music, performing arts, theater/drama. *Special characteristics:* children of faculty/staff, ethnic background, international students. *Tuition waivers:* Full or partial for employees or children of employees. *ROTC:* Army, Naval, Air Force.
LOANS *Student loans:* $109,754,212 (83% need-based, 17% non-need-based). 46% of past graduating class borrowed through all loan programs. *Average indebtedness per student:* $23,273. *Average need-based loan:* Freshmen: $3216. Undergraduates: $4146. *Parent loans:* $71,661,117 (78% need-based, 22% non-need-based). *Programs:* Federal Direct (Subsidized and Unsubsidized Stafford, PLUS), Perkins, Federal Nursing, college/university.
WORK-STUDY *Federal work-study:* jobs available. *State or other work-study/employment:* Total amount: $21,046,894 (65% need-based, 35% non-need-based). Part-time jobs available.
ATHLETIC AWARDS Total amount: $9,356,584 (41% need-based, 59% non-need-based).
APPLYING FOR FINANCIAL AID *Required financial aid form:* FAFSA. *Financial aid deadline:* Continuous. *Notification date:* Continuous beginning 2/1.

CONTACT Elizabeth Acree, Registrar, The University of Arizona, PO Box 210067, Tucson, AZ 85721-0067, 520-621-3432. *Fax:* 520-621-9473. *E-mail:* askaid@arizona.edu.
Website: http://www.arizona.edu/.

UNIVERSITY OF ARKANSAS
Fayetteville, AR

Tuition & fees (AR res): $8820	Average undergraduate aid package: $9440

ABOUT THE INSTITUTION State-supported, coed. *Awards:* certificates, bachelor's, master's, and doctoral degrees. 81 undergraduate majors. *Total enrollment:* 27,194. Undergraduates: 22,548. Freshmen: 4,967. Federal methodology is used as a basis for awarding need-based institutional aid.
UNDERGRADUATE EXPENSES for 2016–2017 *Application fee:* $40. *One-time required fee:* $140. *Tuition, state resident:* full-time $7204; part-time $240.12 per credit hour. *Tuition, nonresident:* full-time $21,552; part-time $718.39 per credit hour. *Required fees:* full-time $1616; $53.86 per credit hour. Full-time tuition and fees vary according to course load, location, and program. Part-time tuition and fees vary according to course load, location, and program. *College room and board:* $10,332; *Room only:* $6620. Room and board charges vary according to board plan, housing facility, and location.
FRESHMAN FINANCIAL AID (Fall 2016, est.) 3,872 applied for aid; of those 60% were deemed to have need. 96% of freshmen with need received aid; of those 13% had need fully met. *Average percent of need met:* 54% (excluding resources awarded to replace EFC). *Average financial aid package:* $8820 (excluding resources awarded to replace EFC). 16% of all full-time freshmen had no need and received non-need-based gift aid.
UNDERGRADUATE FINANCIAL AID (Fall 2016, est.) 12,366 applied for aid; of those 68% were deemed to have need. 95% of undergraduates with need received aid; of those 12% had need fully met. *Average percent of need met:* 56% (excluding resources awarded to replace EFC). *Average financial aid package:* $9440 (excluding resources awarded to replace EFC). 14% of all full-time undergraduates had no need and received non-need-based gift aid.
GIFT AID (NEED-BASED) *Total amount:* $44,152,058 (45% federal, 24% state, 24% institutional, 7% external sources). *Receiving aid:* Freshmen: 37% (1,836); all full-time undergraduates: 32% (6,349). *Average award:* Freshmen: $6482; Undergraduates: $7025. *Scholarships, grants, and awards:* Federal Pell, FSEOG, state, private, college/university gift aid from institutional funds.
GIFT AID (NON-NEED-BASED) *Total amount:* $33,775,528 (46% state, 47% institutional, 7% external sources). *Receiving aid:* Freshmen: 5% (248). Undergraduates: 4% (722). *Average award:* Freshmen: $4160. Undergraduates: $5035. *Scholarships, grants, and awards by category: Academic interests/achievement:* agriculture, architecture, area/ethnic studies, biological sciences, business, communication, computer science, education, engineering/technologies, English, foreign languages, general academic interests/achievements, health fields, home economics, humanities, international studies, mathematics, military science, physical sciences, pre-medicine, social sciences. *Creative arts/performance:* art/fine arts, journalism/publications, music, theater/drama. *Special achievements/activities:* cheerleading/drum major, community service, general special achievements/activities, leadership. *Special characteristics:* adult students, children and siblings of alumni, children of faculty/staff, children of union members/company employees, children of workers in trades, children with a deceased or disabled parent, ethnic background, first-generation college students, handicapped students, international students, local/state students, married students, members of minority groups, out-of-state students, previous college experience, veterans, veterans' children. *Tuition waivers:* Full or partial for employees or children of employees, senior citizens. *ROTC:* Army, Air Force.
LOANS *Student loans:* $74,280,138 (68% need-based, 32% non-need-based). 47% of past graduating class borrowed through all loan programs. *Average indebtedness per student:* $24,182. *Average need-based loan:* Freshmen: $4706. Undergraduates: $5059. *Parent loans:* $24,544,309 (35% need-based, 65% non-need-based). *Programs:* Federal Direct (Subsidized and Unsubsidized Stafford, PLUS), Perkins, state, college/university, alternative loans.
WORK-STUDY *Federal work-study:* Total amount: $2,833,695; 1,020 jobs averaging $2778.
ATHLETIC AWARDS Total amount: $7,150,219 (34% need-based, 66% non-need-based).

APPLYING FOR FINANCIAL AID *Required financial aid form:* FAFSA. *Financial aid deadline (priority):* 3/15. *Notification date:* Continuous beginning 4/1. Students must reply within 4 weeks of notification.

CONTACT Wendy Stouffer, Executive Director of Financial Aid and Academic Scholarships, University of Arkansas, 114 Silas H. Hunt Hall, Fayetteville, AR 72701-1201, 479-575-3806 or toll-free 800-377-8632. *Fax:* 479-575-7790. *E-mail:* wstouff@uark.edu.
Website: http://www.uark.edu/.

UNIVERSITY OF ARKANSAS AT LITTLE ROCK
Little Rock, AR

Tuition & fees: N/R	Average undergraduate aid package: $13,138

ABOUT THE INSTITUTION State-supported, coed. 57 undergraduate majors. Both federal and institutional methodology are used as a basis for awarding need-based institutional aid.

FRESHMAN FINANCIAL AID (Fall 2015) 759 applied for aid; of those 62% were deemed to have need. 100% of freshmen with need received aid. *Average financial aid package:* $13,731 (excluding resources awarded to replace EFC).

UNDERGRADUATE FINANCIAL AID (Fall 2015) 3,875 applied for aid; of those 65% were deemed to have need. 100% of undergraduates with need received aid. *Average financial aid package:* $13,138 (excluding resources awarded to replace EFC).

GIFT AID (NEED-BASED) *Total amount:* $14,387,862 (100% federal). *Receiving aid:* Freshmen: 58% (469); all full-time undergraduates: 54% (2,496). *Average award:* Freshmen: $4736; Undergraduates: $4482. *Scholarships, grants, and awards:* Federal Pell, FSEOG, state, private, college/university gift aid from institutional funds.

GIFT AID (NON-NEED-BASED) *Total amount:* $21,777,905 (2% federal, 31% state, 54% institutional, 13% external sources). *Receiving aid:* Freshmen: 49% (401). Undergraduates: 34% (1,572). *Scholarships, grants, and awards by category: Academic interests/achievement:* biological sciences, business, communication, computer science, education, engineering/technologies, English, foreign languages, general academic interests/achievements, health fields, humanities, international studies, mathematics, physical sciences, social sciences. *Creative arts/performance:* art/fine arts, music, theater/drama. *Special achievements/activities:* community service, leadership, memberships. *Special characteristics:* local/state students, members of minority groups, previous college experience.

LOANS *Student loans:* $33,642,626 (100% non-need-based). *Programs:* Federal Direct (Subsidized and Unsubsidized Stafford, PLUS).

WORK-STUDY *Federal work-study:* jobs available.

ATHLETIC AWARDS *Total amount:* $2,379,773 (100% non-need-based).

APPLYING FOR FINANCIAL AID *Required financial aid form:* FAFSA. *Financial aid deadline (priority):* 3/1. *Notification date:* 4/15.

CONTACT Financial Aid Office, University of Arkansas at Little Rock, 2801 South University Avenue, Little Rock, AR 72204-1099, 501-569-3035 or toll-free 800-482-8892. *E-mail:* financialaid@ualr.edu.
Website: http://www.ualr.edu/.

UNIVERSITY OF ARKANSAS AT MONTICELLO
Monticello, AR

CONTACT Susan Brewer, Director of Financial Aid, University of Arkansas at Monticello, PO Box 3470, Monticello, AR 71656, 870-460-1050 or toll-free 800-844-1826. *Fax:* 870-460-1450. *E-mail:* brewers@uamont.edu.
Website: http://www.uamont.edu/.

UNIVERSITY OF ARKANSAS AT PINE BLUFF
Pine Bluff, AR

CONTACT Mrs. Carolyn Iverson, Director of Financial Aid, University of Arkansas at Pine Bluff, 1200 North University Drive, PO Box 4985, Pine Bluff, AR 71601, 870-575-8303 or toll-free 800-264-6585. *Fax:* 870-575-4622. *E-mail:* iverson_c@uapb.edu.
Website: http://www.uapb.edu/.

UNIVERSITY OF ARKANSAS FOR MEDICAL SCIENCES
Little Rock, AR

ABOUT THE INSTITUTION State-supported, coed. *Awards:* certificates, associate, bachelor's, master's, and doctoral degrees (bachelor's degree is upper-level). 13 undergraduate majors. *Total enrollment:* 2,869. Undergraduates: 675.

GIFT AID (NEED-BASED) *Scholarships, grants, and awards:* Federal Pell, FSEOG, state, private, college/university gift aid from institutional funds.

LOANS *Programs:* Perkins, Federal Nursing.

CONTACT Ms. Gloria Kemp, Director of Student Financial Aid, University of Arkansas for Medical Sciences, 4301 West Markham Street, MS 601, Little Rock, AR 72205, 501-686-6936. *Fax:* 501-686-8798. *E-mail:* pvcarter@uams.edu.
Website: http://www.uams.edu/.

UNIVERSITY OF ARKANSAS–FORT SMITH
Fort Smith, AR

CONTACT Tammy Malone, Interim Financial Aid Director, University of Arkansas–Fort Smith, 5210 Grand Avenue, Fort Smith, AR 72913, 479-788-7099 or toll-free 888-512-5466. *Fax:* 479-788-7095. *E-mail:* tmalone@uafortsmith.edu.
Website: http://uafs.edu/.

UNIVERSITY OF BALTIMORE
Baltimore, MD

ABOUT THE INSTITUTION State-supported, coed. 29 undergraduate majors.

GIFT AID (NEED-BASED) *Scholarships, grants, and awards:* Federal Pell, FSEOG, state, private, college/university gift aid from institutional funds.

GIFT AID (NON-NEED-BASED) *Scholarships, grants, and awards by category: Academic interests/achievement:* business, English, general academic interests/achievements. *Special achievements/activities:* community service, memberships. *Special characteristics:* handicapped students.

LOANS *Programs:* Perkins, college/university.

APPLYING FOR FINANCIAL AID *Required financial aid form:* FAFSA.

CONTACT Financial Aid Office, University of Baltimore, 1420 North Charles Street, CH 123, Baltimore, MD 21201-5779, 410-837-4763. *Fax:* 410-837-5493. *E-mail:* financial-aid@ubalt.edu.
Website: http://www.ubalt.edu/.

UNIVERSITY OF BRIDGEPORT
Bridgeport, CT

Tuition & fees: $31,630	Average undergraduate aid package: $24,676

ABOUT THE INSTITUTION Independent, coed. *Awards:* certificates, associate, bachelor's, master's, and doctoral degrees. 40 undergraduate majors. *Total*

enrollment: 5,658. Undergraduates: 2,941. Freshmen: 487. Federal methodology is used as a basis for awarding need-based institutional aid.

UNDERGRADUATE EXPENSES for 2016–2017 *Application fee:* $25. *Comprehensive fee:* $44,950 includes full-time tuition ($29,550), mandatory fees ($2080), and room and board ($13,320). Full-time tuition and fees vary according to course load and program. Room and board charges vary according to board plan and housing facility. *Part-time tuition:* $985 per credit hour. *Part-time fees:* $210 per term. Part-time tuition and fees vary according to course load and program.

FRESHMAN FINANCIAL AID (Fall 2016, est.) 439 applied for aid; of those 97% were deemed to have need. 100% of freshmen with need received aid; of those 4% had need fully met. *Average percent of need met:* 61% (excluding resources awarded to replace EFC). *Average financial aid package:* $25,704 (excluding resources awarded to replace EFC). 18% of all full-time freshmen had no need and received non-need-based gift aid.

UNDERGRADUATE FINANCIAL AID (Fall 2016, est.) 1,798 applied for aid; of those 97% were deemed to have need. 100% of undergraduates with need received aid; of those 2% had need fully met. *Average percent of need met:* 59% (excluding resources awarded to replace EFC). *Average financial aid package:* $24,676 (excluding resources awarded to replace EFC). 13% of all full-time undergraduates had no need and received non-need-based gift aid.

GIFT AID (NEED-BASED) *Receiving aid:* Freshmen: 76% (365); all full-time undergraduates: 72% (1,535). *Average award:* Freshmen: $7988; Undergraduates: $8154. *Scholarships, grants, and awards:* Federal Pell, FSEOG, state, private, college/university gift aid from institutional funds.

GIFT AID (NON-NEED-BASED) *Receiving aid:* Freshmen: 88% (425). Undergraduates: 81% (1,744). *Average award:* Freshmen: $14,200. Undergraduates: $11,500. *Scholarships, grants, and awards by category:* Academic interests/achievement: biological sciences, business, engineering/technologies, general academic interests/achievements, mathematics. *Creative arts/performance:* applied art and design, music. *Special characteristics:* children of faculty/staff, international students, local/state students, previous college experience. *Tuition waivers:* Full or partial for employees or children of employees, senior citizens.

LOANS *Student loans:* 68% of past graduating class borrowed through all loan programs. *Average indebtedness per student:* $21,200. *Average need-based loan:* Freshmen: $3800. Undergraduates: $3950. *Programs:* Federal Direct (Subsidized and Unsubsidized Stafford, PLUS), Perkins.

WORK-STUDY Federal work-study jobs available. *State or other work-study/employment:* Part-time jobs available.

APPLYING FOR FINANCIAL AID *Required financial aid form:* FAFSA. *Financial aid deadline (priority):* 3/1. *Notification date:* Continuous beginning 3/1. Students must reply by 5/15 or within 4 weeks of notification.

CONTACT Ms. Christine E. Falzerano, Director of Student Financial Services, University of Bridgeport, 126 Park Avenue, Bridgeport, CT 06604, 203-576-4568 or toll-free 800-EXCEL-UB. *Fax:* 203-576-4570. *E-mail:* finaid@bridgeport.edu. *Website:* http://www.bridgeport.edu/.

UNIVERSITY OF CALIFORNIA, BERKELEY
Berkeley, CA

Tuition & fees (CA res): $13,509	Average undergraduate aid package: $20,066

ABOUT THE INSTITUTION State-supported, coed. *Awards:* certificates, bachelor's, master's, and doctoral degrees. 90 undergraduate majors. *Total enrollment:* 38,204. Undergraduates: 27,496. Freshmen: 5,550. Both federal and institutional methodology are used as a basis for awarding need-based institutional aid.

UNDERGRADUATE EXPENSES for 2016–2017 *Application fee:* $70. *Tuition, state resident:* full-time $11,220. *Tuition, nonresident:* full-time $37,902. *Required fees:* full-time $2289. *College room and board:* $16,042. Room and board charges vary according to board plan and housing facility.

FRESHMAN FINANCIAL AID (Fall 2016, est.) 4,363 applied for aid; of those 92% were deemed to have need. 99% of freshmen with need received aid; of those 56% had need fully met. *Average percent of need met:* 89% (excluding resources awarded to replace EFC). *Average financial aid package:* $17,284 (excluding resources awarded to replace EFC). 3% of all full-time freshmen had no need and received non-need-based gift aid.

UNDERGRADUATE FINANCIAL AID (Fall 2016, est.) 16,998 applied for aid; of those 95% were deemed to have need. 99% of undergraduates with need received aid; of those 44% had need fully met. *Average percent of need met:* 87% (excluding resources awarded to replace EFC). *Average financial aid package:* $20,066 (excluding resources awarded to replace EFC). 4% of all full-time undergraduates had no need and received non-need-based gift aid.

GIFT AID (NEED-BASED) *Total amount:* $284,650,172 (15% federal, 28% state, 54% institutional, 3% external sources). *Receiving aid:* Freshmen: 64% (3,949); all full-time undergraduates: 56% (15,847). *Average award:* Freshmen: $15,053; Undergraduates: $17,232. *Scholarships, grants, and awards:* Federal Pell, FSEOG, state, private, college/university gift aid from institutional funds.

GIFT AID (NON-NEED-BASED) *Total amount:* $20,391,209 (10% federal, 2% state, 60% institutional, 28% external sources). *Receiving aid:* Freshmen: 1% (41). Undergraduates: 104. *Average award:* Freshmen: $13,394. Undergraduates: $9390. *Scholarships, grants, and awards by category:* Academic interests/achievement: general academic interests/achievements. *ROTC:* Army, Naval, Air Force.

LOANS *Student loans:* $46,376,315 (69% need-based, 31% non-need-based). 37% of past graduating class borrowed through all loan programs. *Average indebtedness per student:* $18,789. *Average need-based loan:* Freshmen: $6666. Undergraduates: $6410. *Parent loans:* $24,566,070 (26% need-based, 74% non-need-based). *Programs:* Federal Direct (Subsidized and Unsubsidized Stafford, PLUS), Perkins.

WORK-STUDY *Federal work-study:* Total amount: $5,105,904; jobs available. *State or other work-study/employment:* Total amount: $3,712,290 (100% need-based). Part-time jobs available.

ATHLETIC AWARDS Total amount: $13,739,806 (29% need-based, 71% non-need-based).

APPLYING FOR FINANCIAL AID *Required financial aid forms:* FAFSA, noncustodial (divorced/separated) parent's statement, Cal Grant forms, GPA verification form (CA residents only). *Financial aid deadline:* 3/31. *Notification date:* 3/31. Students must reply by 5/1.

CONTACT Kathy Bradley, Administrative Specialist, University of California, Berkeley, 225 Sproul Hall, Berkeley, CA 94720-1960, 510-642-0649. *Fax:* 510-643-5526. *E-mail:* kbradley@berkeley.edu. *Website:* http://www.berkeley.edu/.

UNIVERSITY OF CALIFORNIA, DAVIS
Davis, CA

Tuition & fees (CA res): $14,100	Average undergraduate aid package: $21,194

ABOUT THE INSTITUTION State-supported, coed. *Awards:* certificates, bachelor's, master's, and doctoral degrees. 83 undergraduate majors. *Total enrollment:* 36,441. Undergraduates: 29,546. Freshmen: 5,778. Both federal and institutional methodology are used as a basis for awarding need-based institutional aid.

UNDERGRADUATE EXPENSES for 2017–2018 *Application fee:* $70. *Tuition, state resident:* full-time $11,220. *Tuition, nonresident:* full-time $39,516. *Required fees:* full-time $2880. *College room and board:* $16,136. Room and board charges vary according to board plan.

FRESHMAN FINANCIAL AID (Fall 2016, est.) 4,322 applied for aid; of those 78% were deemed to have need. 98% of freshmen with need received aid; of those 19% had need fully met. *Average percent of need met:* 82% (excluding resources awarded to replace EFC). *Average financial aid package:* $23,648 (excluding resources awarded to replace EFC). 5% of all full-time freshmen had no need and received non-need-based gift aid.

UNDERGRADUATE FINANCIAL AID (Fall 2016, est.) 20,393 applied for aid; of those 86% were deemed to have need. 98% of undergraduates with need received aid; of those 17% had need fully met. *Average percent of need met:* 79% (excluding resources awarded to replace EFC). *Average financial aid package:* $21,194 (excluding resources awarded to replace EFC). 4% of all full-time undergraduates had no need and received non-need-based gift aid.

GIFT AID (NEED-BASED) *Total amount:* $313,834,351 (20% federal, 34% state, 45% institutional, 1% external sources). *Receiving aid:* Freshmen: 57% (3,233); all full-time undergraduates: 59% (16,904). *Average award:* Freshmen: $20,328; Undergraduates: $18,271. *Scholarships, grants, and awards:* Federal Pell, FSEOG, state, private, college/university gift aid from institutional funds.

GIFT AID (NON-NEED-BASED) *Total amount:* $15,951,915 (17% federal, 4% state, 42% institutional, 37% external sources). *Receiving aid:* Freshmen: 1% (70). Undergraduates: 1% (247). *Average award:* Freshmen: $3472. Undergraduates: $5643. *Scholarships, grants, and awards by category:* Academic interests/ achievement: agriculture, area/ethnic studies, biological sciences, business, communication, computer science, engineering/technologies, English, foreign languages, general academic interests/achievements, health fields, home economics, humanities, international studies, mathematics, premedicine, religion/biblical studies, social sciences. **ROTC:** Army, Naval cooperative, Air Force cooperative.

LOANS *Student loans:* $60,010,899 (82% need-based, 18% non-need-based). 53% of past graduating class borrowed through all loan programs. *Average indebtedness per student:* $19,276. *Average need-based loan:* Freshmen: $5652. Undergraduates: $5558. *Parent loans:* $31,468,397 (21% need-based, 79% non-need-based). *Programs:* Federal Direct (Subsidized and Unsubsidized Stafford, PLUS), Perkins, state, college/university.

WORK-STUDY *Federal work-study:* Total amount: $1,579,575; jobs available. *State or other work-study/employment:* Total amount: $188,032 (100% need-based). Part-time jobs available.

ATHLETIC AWARDS Total amount: $7,292,043 (31% need-based, 69% non-need-based).

APPLYING FOR FINANCIAL AID *Required financial aid forms:* FAFSA, state aid form, noncustodial (divorced/separated) parent's statement. *Financial aid deadline (priority):* 3/2. *Notification date:* Continuous beginning 3/13.

CONTACT Deborah G. Agee, Director of Financial Aid and Scholarships, University of California, Davis, One Shields Avenue, 2116 Dutton Hall, Davis, CA 95616, 530-752-2396. *Fax:* 530-752-7339. *E-mail:* dgagee@ucdavis.edu.
Website: http://www.ucdavis.edu/.

UNIVERSITY OF CALIFORNIA, IRVINE
Irvine, CA

Tuition & fees (CA res): $15,035	Average undergraduate aid package: $23,022

ABOUT THE INSTITUTION State-supported, coed. *Awards:* certificates, bachelor's, master's, and doctoral degrees. 86 undergraduate majors. *Total enrollment:* 32,754. Undergraduates: 27,331. Freshmen: 6,552. Federal methodology is used as a basis for awarding need-based institutional aid.

UNDERGRADUATE EXPENSES for 2016–2017 *Application fee:* $70. *Tuition, state resident:* full-time $11,220. *Tuition, nonresident:* full-time $37,902. *Required fees:* full-time $3815. *College room and board:* $13,661. Room and board charges vary according to board plan and housing facility.

FRESHMAN FINANCIAL AID (Fall 2015) 4,700 applied for aid; of those 82% were deemed to have need. 98% of freshmen with need received aid; of those 24% had need fully met. *Average percent of need met:* 85% (excluding resources awarded to replace EFC). *Average financial aid package:* $24,400 (excluding resources awarded to replace EFC). 2% of all full-time freshmen had no need and received non-need-based gift aid.

UNDERGRADUATE FINANCIAL AID (Fall 2015) 19,466 applied for aid; of those 89% were deemed to have need. 98% of undergraduates with need received aid; of those 22% had need fully met. *Average percent of need met:* 82% (excluding resources awarded to replace EFC). *Average financial aid package:* $23,022 (excluding resources awarded to replace EFC). 2% of all full-time undergraduates had no need and received non-need-based gift aid.

GIFT AID (NEED-BASED) *Total amount:* $320,701,889 (18% federal, 43% state, 38% institutional, 1% external sources). *Receiving aid:* Freshmen: 57% (3,696); all full-time undergraduates: 62% (16,680). *Average award:* Freshmen: $20,049; Undergraduates: $19,149. *Scholarships, grants, and awards:* Federal Pell, FSEOG, state, private, college/university gift aid from institutional funds.

GIFT AID (NON-NEED-BASED) *Total amount:* $7,638,507 (5% federal, 10% state, 56% institutional, 29% external sources). *Receiving aid:* Freshmen: 1% (62). Undergraduates: 1% (228). *Average award:* Freshmen: $7118. Undergraduates: $7814. *Scholarships, grants, and awards by category:* Academic interests/ achievement: area/ethnic studies, biological sciences, business, communication, computer science, education, engineering/technologies, English, foreign languages, general academic interests/achievements, health fields, humanities, international studies, mathematics, physical sciences, premedicine, social sciences. *Creative arts/performance:* art/fine arts, cinema/film/broadcasting, creative writing, dance, general creative arts/

performance, music, performing arts, theater/drama. *Special achievements/activities:* community service, general special achievements/activities, leadership. *Special characteristics:* international students, out-of-state students. *Tuition waivers:* Full or partial for employees or children of employees. *ROTC:* Army, Air Force cooperative.

LOANS *Student loans:* $62,457,237 (84% need-based, 16% non-need-based). 59% of past graduating class borrowed through all loan programs. *Average indebtedness per student:* $20,628. *Average need-based loan:* Freshmen: $6795. Undergraduates: $6753. *Parent loans:* $36,664,596 (30% need-based, 70% non-need-based). *Programs:* Federal Direct (Subsidized and Unsubsidized Stafford, PLUS), Perkins, college/university, private loans.

WORK-STUDY *Federal work-study:* jobs available. *State or other work-study/employment:* Total amount: $4,202,072 (100% need-based). Part-time jobs available.

ATHLETIC AWARDS Total amount: $3,697,045 (33% need-based, 67% non-need-based).

APPLYING FOR FINANCIAL AID *Required financial aid forms:* FAFSA, state aid form. *Financial aid deadline:* 6/26 (priority: 3/2). *Notification date:* Continuous beginning 4/1. Students must reply within 2 weeks of notification.

CONTACT Ms. Lindsay Crowell, Senior Associate Director, University of California, Irvine, 102 Aldrich Hall, Irvine, CA 92697-2825, 949-824-4898. *Fax:* 949-824-2820. *E-mail:* finaid@uci.edu.
Website: http://www.uci.edu/.

UNIVERSITY OF CALIFORNIA, LOS ANGELES
Los Angeles, CA

Tuition & fees: N/R	Average undergraduate aid package: $22,998

ABOUT THE INSTITUTION State-supported, coed. *Awards:* bachelor's, master's, and doctoral degrees. 94 undergraduate majors. *Total enrollment:* 44,947. Undergraduates: 30,873. Freshmen: 6,545. Both federal and institutional methodology are used as a basis for awarding need-based institutional aid.

FRESHMAN FINANCIAL AID (Fall 2016, est.) 4,084 applied for aid; of those 87% were deemed to have need. 100% of freshmen with need received aid; of those 25% had need fully met. *Average percent of need met:* 83% (excluding resources awarded to replace EFC). *Average financial aid package:* $24,345 (excluding resources awarded to replace EFC). 3% of all full-time freshmen had no need and received non-need-based gift aid.

UNDERGRADUATE FINANCIAL AID (Fall 2016, est.) 18,067 applied for aid; of those 92% were deemed to have need. 100% of undergraduates with need received aid; of those 25% had need fully met. *Average percent of need met:* 83% (excluding resources awarded to replace EFC). *Average financial aid package:* $22,998 (excluding resources awarded to replace EFC). 3% of all full-time undergraduates had no need and received non-need-based gift aid.

GIFT AID (NEED-BASED) *Total amount:* $308,266,997 (15% federal, 37% state, 46% institutional, 2% external sources). *Receiving aid:* Freshmen: 53% (3,433); all full-time undergraduates: 52% (15,844). *Average award:* Freshmen: $21,100; Undergraduates: $19,577. *Scholarships, grants, and awards:* Federal Pell, FSEOG, state, private, college/university gift aid from institutional funds, United Negro College Fund, Federal Nursing.

GIFT AID (NON-NEED-BASED) *Total amount:* $8,697,140 (11% federal, 5% state, 61% institutional, 23% external sources). *Receiving aid:* Freshmen: 2% (105). Undergraduates: 1% (319). *Average award:* Freshmen: $4847. Undergraduates: $5000. *Scholarships, grants, and awards by category:* Academic interests/ achievement: general academic interests/achievements. *Creative arts/performance:* general creative arts/performance. *Special achievements/activities:* general special achievements/activities. *Special characteristics:* general special characteristics. **ROTC:** Army, Naval, Air Force.

LOANS *Student loans:* $70,881,033 (79% need-based, 21% non-need-based). 42% of past graduating class borrowed through all loan programs. *Average indebtedness per student:* $21,323. *Average need-based loan:* Freshmen: $7003. Undergraduates: $7242. *Parent loans:* $41,880,334 (28% need-based, 72% non-need-based). *Programs:* Federal Direct (Subsidized and Unsubsidized Stafford, PLUS), Perkins, Federal Nursing, state, college/university.

WORK-STUDY *Federal work-study:* Total amount: $5,834,540; 2,828 jobs averaging $2158. *State or other work-study/employment:* Total amount: $299,392 (100% need-based). 55 part-time jobs averaging $2487.

ATHLETIC AWARDS Total amount: $12,088,929 (33% need-based, 67% non-need-based).

APPLYING FOR FINANCIAL AID *Required financial aid form:* FAFSA. *Financial aid deadline (priority):* 3/2. *Notification date:* Continuous beginning 3/15.

CONTACT Ms. Carolyn Turpin, Budget Officer, University of California, Los Angeles, A-129 Murphy Hall, Los Angeles, CA 90095-1435, 310-206-0407. *E-mail:* finaid@saonet.ucla.edu.
Website: http://www.ucla.edu/.

UNIVERSITY OF CALIFORNIA, MERCED

Merced, CA

ABOUT THE INSTITUTION State-supported, coed. *Awards:* bachelor's, master's, and doctoral degrees. 24 undergraduate majors. *Total enrollment:* 6,685. Undergraduates: 6,237. Freshmen: 1,790.

GIFT AID (NEED-BASED) *Scholarships, grants, and awards:* Federal Pell, FSEOG, state, private, college/university gift aid from institutional funds.

GIFT AID (NON-NEED-BASED) *Scholarships, grants, and awards by category:* Academic interests/achievement: general academic interests/achievements.

LOANS *Programs:* Federal Direct (Subsidized and Unsubsidized Stafford, PLUS), alternative loans.

WORK-STUDY *Federal work-study:* jobs available.

APPLYING FOR FINANCIAL AID *Required financial aid form:* FAFSA.

CONTACT Ms. Diana M. Ralls, Director of Financial Aid, University of California, Merced, Kolligian Library, Room 122, 5200 North Lake Road, Merced, CA 95343, 209-228-7178. *Fax:* 209-228-7861. *E-mail:* finaid@ucmerced.edu.
Website: http://www.ucmerced.edu/.

UNIVERSITY OF CALIFORNIA, RIVERSIDE

Riverside, CA

Tuition & fees (CA res): $13,581	Average undergraduate aid package: $22,301

ABOUT THE INSTITUTION State-supported, coed. *Awards:* certificates, bachelor's, master's, and doctoral degrees. 56 undergraduate majors. *Total enrollment:* 22,921. Undergraduates: 19,799. Freshmen: 5,358. Federal methodology is used as a basis for awarding need-based institutional aid.

UNDERGRADUATE EXPENSES for 2016–2017 *Application fee:* $70. *Tuition, state resident:* full-time $11,220; part-time $5610 per year. *Tuition, nonresident:* full-time $37,902; part-time $18,951 per year. *Required fees:* full-time $2361. Full-time tuition and fees vary according to course load. Part-time tuition and fees vary according to course load. *College room and board:* $16,400. Room and board charges vary according to board plan and housing facility.

FRESHMAN FINANCIAL AID (Fall 2016, est.) 4,956 applied for aid; of those 89% were deemed to have need. 98% of freshmen with need received aid; of those 25% had need fully met. *Average percent of need met:* 85% (excluding resources awarded to replace EFC). *Average financial aid package:* $26,537 (excluding resources awarded to replace EFC). 1% of all full-time freshmen had no need and received non-need-based gift aid.

UNDERGRADUATE FINANCIAL AID (Fall 2016, est.) 17,057 applied for aid; of those 91% were deemed to have need. 98% of undergraduates with need received aid; of those 19% had need fully met. *Average percent of need met:* 78% (excluding resources awarded to replace EFC). *Average financial aid package:* $22,301 (excluding resources awarded to replace EFC). 1% of all full-time undergraduates had no need and received non-need-based gift aid.

GIFT AID (NEED-BASED) *Total amount:* $273,231,481 (19% federal, 46% state, 34% institutional, 1% external sources). *Receiving aid:* Freshmen: 79% (4,219); all full-time undergraduates: 76% (14,870). *Average award:* Freshmen: $22,241;

Undergraduates: $18,289. *Scholarships, grants, and awards:* Federal Pell, FSEOG, state, private, college/university gift aid from institutional funds.

GIFT AID (NON-NEED-BASED) *Total amount:* $5,270,471 (11% federal, 81% institutional, 8% external sources). *Receiving aid:* Freshmen: 1% (61). Undergraduates: 1% (218). *Average award:* Freshmen: $7088. Undergraduates: $5269. *Scholarships, grants, and awards by category:* Academic interests/achievement: agriculture, area/ethnic studies, biological sciences, business, education, engineering/technologies, English, general academic interests/achievements, humanities, mathematics, physical sciences, premedicine, social sciences. *Creative arts/performance:* art/fine arts, creative writing, dance, music, theater/drama. *Special characteristics:* religious affiliation, veterans, veterans' children. *ROTC:* Army cooperative, Air Force cooperative.

LOANS *Student loans:* $59,477,248 (87% need-based, 13% non-need-based). 68% of past graduating class borrowed through all loan programs. *Average indebtedness per student:* $21,838. *Average need-based loan:* Freshmen: $6171. Undergraduates: $6634. *Parent loans:* $25,361,939 (40% need-based, 60% non-need-based). *Programs:* Federal Direct (Subsidized and Unsubsidized Stafford, PLUS), Perkins, college/university.

WORK-STUDY *Federal work-study:* Total amount: $5,093,839; 3,196 jobs averaging $1540.

ATHLETIC AWARDS Total amount: $3,672,905 (32% need-based, 68% non-need-based).

APPLYING FOR FINANCIAL AID *Required financial aid forms:* FAFSA, state aid form. *Financial aid deadline:* 3/2. *Notification date:* Continuous beginning 3/1. Students must reply by 6/15 or within 3 weeks of notification.

CONTACT Mr. Jose A. Aguilar, Director of Financial Aid, University of California, Riverside, 2106 Student Services Building, Riverside, CA 92521-0209, 951-827-7249. *Fax:* 951-827-5619. *E-mail:* finaid@ucr.edu.
Website: http://www.ucr.edu/.

UNIVERSITY OF CALIFORNIA, SAN DIEGO

La Jolla, CA

Tuition & fees (CA res): $13,645	Average undergraduate aid package: $22,499

ABOUT THE INSTITUTION State-supported, coed. *Awards:* bachelor's, master's, and doctoral degrees. 68 undergraduate majors. *Total enrollment:* 34,979. Undergraduates: 28,127. Freshmen: 5,748. Both federal and institutional methodology are used as a basis for awarding need-based institutional aid.

UNDERGRADUATE EXPENSES for 2016–2017 *Application fee:* $60. *One-time required fee:* $165. *Tuition, state resident:* full-time $11,220. *Tuition, nonresident:* full-time $37,902. *Required fees:* full-time $2425. Room and board charges vary according to board plan and housing facility.

FRESHMAN FINANCIAL AID (Fall 2016, est.) 3,739 applied for aid; of those 77% were deemed to have need. 94% of freshmen with need received aid; of those 40% had need fully met. *Average percent of need met:* 87% (excluding resources awarded to replace EFC). *Average financial aid package:* $23,173 (excluding resources awarded to replace EFC). 2% of all full-time freshmen had no need and received non-need-based gift aid.

UNDERGRADUATE FINANCIAL AID (Fall 2016, est.) 17,287 applied for aid; of those 87% were deemed to have need. 97% of undergraduates with need received aid; of those 34% had need fully met. *Average percent of need met:* 86% (excluding resources awarded to replace EFC). *Average financial aid package:* $22,499 (excluding resources awarded to replace EFC). 2% of all full-time undergraduates had no need and received non-need-based gift aid.

GIFT AID (NEED-BASED) *Total amount:* $271,535,326 (18% federal, 38% state, 42% institutional, 2% external sources). *Receiving aid:* Freshmen: 48% (2,610); all full-time undergraduates: 52% (14,196). *Average award:* Freshmen: $19,028; Undergraduates: $18,412. *Scholarships, grants, and awards:* Federal Pell, FSEOG, state, private, college/university gift aid from institutional funds, TEACH Grants.

GIFT AID (NON-NEED-BASED) *Total amount:* $11,602,422 (19% federal, 6% state, 60% institutional, 15% external sources). *Receiving aid:* Freshmen: 1% (73). Undergraduates: 1% (259). *Average award:* Freshmen: $11,943. Undergraduates: $11,001. *Scholarships, grants, and awards by category:* Academic interests/achievement: biological sciences, business, communication, computer science, engineering/technologies, general academic interests/achievements, mathematics, physical sciences, premedicine, social sciences. *Creative arts/performance:* applied art and design, cinema/film/broadcasting, dance, journalism/publications, music, performing arts, theater/drama. *Special achievements/activities:* community service, leadership. *Special characteristics:* ethnic background, first-generation college students, handicapped students, members of minority groups, veterans' children. *ROTC:* Army cooperative, Naval cooperative, Air Force cooperative.

LOANS *Student loans:* $62,090,595 (79% need-based, 21% non-need-based). 53% of past graduating class borrowed through all loan programs. *Average indebtedness per student:* $21,830. *Average need-based loan:* Freshmen: $5319. Undergraduates: $5880. *Parent loans:* $14,125,378 (23% need-based, 77% non-need-based). *Programs:* Federal Direct (Subsidized and Unsubsidized Stafford, PLUS), Perkins, college/university, alternative loans.

WORK-STUDY *Federal work-study:* Total amount: $14,429,070; jobs available. *State or other work-study/employment:* Total amount: $70,734 (100% need-based). Part-time jobs available.

ATHLETIC AWARDS Total amount: $396,353 (48% need-based, 52% non-need-based).

APPLYING FOR FINANCIAL AID *Required financial aid forms:* FAFSA, state aid form. *Financial aid deadline (priority):* 3/2. *Notification date:* Continuous beginning 3/15.

CONTACT Ms. Vonda Garcia, Director of Financial Aid and Scholarships, University of California, San Diego, 9500 Gilman Drive, Mail Code 0013, La Jolla, CA 92093-0013, 858-534-4480. *Fax:* 858-534-5459. *E-mail:* vonda@ucsd.edu. *Website:* http://www.ucsd.edu/.

UNIVERSITY OF CALIFORNIA, SANTA BARBARA
Santa Barbara, CA

Tuition & fees (CA res): $14,069	Average undergraduate aid package: $22,544

ABOUT THE INSTITUTION State-supported, coed. *Awards:* certificates, bachelor's, master's, and doctoral degrees. 74 undergraduate majors. *Total enrollment:* 24,346. Undergraduates: 21,574. Freshmen: 4,996. Both federal and institutional methodology are used as a basis for awarding need-based institutional aid.

UNDERGRADUATE EXPENSES for 2016–2017 *Application fee:* $70. *Tuition, state resident:* full-time $11,220. *Tuition, nonresident:* full-time $37,902. *Required fees:* full-time $2849. *College room and board:* $13,605. Room and board charges vary according to board plan and housing facility.

FRESHMAN FINANCIAL AID (Fall 2016, est.) 3,807 applied for aid; of those 76% were deemed to have need. 96% of freshmen with need received aid; of those 22% had need fully met. *Average percent of need met:* 81% (excluding resources awarded to replace EFC). *Average financial aid package:* $24,479 (excluding resources awarded to replace EFC). 1% of all full-time freshmen had no need and received non-need-based gift aid.

UNDERGRADUATE FINANCIAL AID (Fall 2016, est.) 14,954 applied for aid; of those 85% were deemed to have need. 97% of undergraduates with need received aid; of those 19% had need fully met. *Average percent of need met:* 79% (excluding resources awarded to replace EFC). *Average financial aid package:* $22,544 (excluding resources awarded to replace EFC). 2% of all full-time undergraduates had no need and received non-need-based gift aid.

GIFT AID (NEED-BASED) *Total amount:* $226,145,927 (18% federal, 43% state, 38% institutional, 1% external sources). *Receiving aid:* Freshmen: 54% (2,699); all full-time undergraduates: 56% (11,879). *Average award:* Freshmen: $20,526; Undergraduates: $18,999. *Scholarships, grants, and awards:* Federal Pell, FSEOG, state, private, college/university gift aid from institutional funds, endowed and restricted scholarships and grants.

GIFT AID (NON-NEED-BASED) *Total amount:* $5,603,914 (13% federal, 8% state, 66% institutional, 13% external sources). *Receiving aid:* Freshmen: 1% (58). Undergraduates: 1% (180). *Average award:* Freshmen: $10,012. Undergraduates: $7952. *Scholarships, grants, and awards by category: Academic interests/achievement:* general academic interests/achievements. *ROTC:* Army, Air Force cooperative.

LOANS *Student loans:* $49,206,343 (79% need-based, 21% non-need-based). 53% of past graduating class borrowed through all loan programs. *Average indebtedness*

per student: $21,001. *Average need-based loan:* Freshmen: $6450. Undergraduates: $6477. *Parent loans:* $26,588,808 (24% need-based, 76% non-need-based). *Programs:* Federal Direct (Subsidized and Unsubsidized Stafford, PLUS), Perkins.

WORK-STUDY *Federal work-study:* Total amount: $5,677,769; jobs available. *State or other work-study/employment:* Total amount: $242,926 (100% need-based). Part-time jobs available.

ATHLETIC AWARDS Total amount: $4,611,088 (28% need-based, 72% non-need-based).

APPLYING FOR FINANCIAL AID *Required financial aid form:* FAFSA. *Financial aid deadline (priority):* 3/2. *Notification date:* Continuous beginning 3/15. Students must reply within 2 weeks of notification.

CONTACT Mike Miller, Office of Financial Aid, University of California, Santa Barbara, 2103 SAASB, Santa Barbara, CA 93106-3180, 805-893-2432. *Fax:* 805-893-8793. *Website:* http://www.ucsb.edu/.

UNIVERSITY OF CALIFORNIA, SANTA CRUZ
Santa Cruz, CA

Tuition & fees: N/R	Average undergraduate aid package: $24,821

ABOUT THE INSTITUTION State-supported, coed. *Awards:* certificates, bachelor's, master's, and doctoral degrees. 57 undergraduate majors. *Total enrollment:* 17,868. Undergraduates: 16,231. Freshmen: 3,620. Both federal and institutional methodology are used as a basis for awarding need-based institutional aid.

FRESHMAN FINANCIAL AID (Fall 2016, est.) 3,429 applied for aid; of those 74% were deemed to have need. 96% of freshmen with need received aid; of those 21% had need fully met. *Average percent of need met:* 83% (excluding resources awarded to replace EFC). *Average financial aid package:* $24,936 (excluding resources awarded to replace EFC). 8% of all full-time freshmen had no need and received non-need-based gift aid.

UNDERGRADUATE FINANCIAL AID (Fall 2016, est.) 12,677 applied for aid; of those 85% were deemed to have need. 97% of undergraduates with need received aid; of those 26% had need fully met. *Average percent of need met:* 84% (excluding resources awarded to replace EFC). *Average financial aid package:* $24,821 (excluding resources awarded to replace EFC). 7% of all full-time undergraduates had no need and received non-need-based gift aid.

GIFT AID (NEED-BASED) *Total amount:* $182,785,912 (17% federal, 41% state, 42% institutional). *Receiving aid:* Freshmen: 56% (2,359); all full-time undergraduates: 61% (10,020). *Average award:* Freshmen: $20,079; Undergraduates: $20,041. *Scholarships, grants, and awards:* Federal Pell, FSEOG, state, private, college/university gift aid from institutional funds.

GIFT AID (NON-NEED-BASED) *Total amount:* $11,397,180 (1% federal, 12% state, 64% institutional, 23% external sources). *Receiving aid:* Freshmen: 1% (47). Undergraduates: 1% (107). *Average award:* Freshmen: $5020. Undergraduates: $5064. *Scholarships, grants, and awards by category: Academic interests/achievement:* 190 awards ($756,882 total): computer science, general academic interests/achievements, humanities, mathematics, physical sciences, social sciences. *Creative arts/performance:* 72 awards ($75,104 total): art/fine arts, cinema/film/broadcasting, creative writing, music, theater/drama. *Special achievements/activities:* 21 awards ($10,500 total): leadership. *Special characteristics:* 1,025 awards ($4,841,350 total): first-generation college students, international students, out-of-state students, veterans. *ROTC:* Army cooperative, Naval cooperative, Air Force cooperative.

LOANS *Student loans:* $58,505,083 (57% need-based, 43% non-need-based). 68% of past graduating class borrowed through all loan programs. *Average indebtedness per student:* $22,582. *Average need-based loan:* Freshmen: $6375. Undergraduates: $6551. *Parent loans:* $26,297,812 (15% need-based, 85% non-need-based). *Programs:* Federal Direct (Subsidized and Unsubsidized Stafford, PLUS), Perkins.

WORK-STUDY *Federal work-study:* Total amount: $8,206,991; 1,086 jobs averaging $2649.

APPLYING FOR FINANCIAL AID *Required financial aid forms:* FAFSA, state aid form. *Financial aid deadline:* 3/2 (priority: 3/2). *Notification date:* 3/15. Students must reply by 5/1 or within 4 weeks of notification.

CONTACT John Patrick Register, Director of Financial Aid, University of California, Santa Cruz, 201 Hahn Student Services Building, Santa Cruz, CA 95064, 831-459-4404. *Fax:* 831-459-3628. *E-mail:* jpregis@ucsc.edu.
Website: http://www.ucsc.edu/.

UNIVERSITY OF CENTRAL ARKANSAS
Conway, AR

Tuition & fees (AR res): $8224	Average undergraduate aid package: N/A

ABOUT THE INSTITUTION State-supported, coed. *Awards:* certificates, bachelor's, master's, and doctoral degrees. 61 undergraduate majors. *Total enrollment:* 11,487. Undergraduates: 9,616. Freshmen: 1,880. Federal methodology is used as a basis for awarding need-based institutional aid.
UNDERGRADUATE EXPENSES for 2016–2017 *Application fee:* $25. *Tuition, state resident:* full-time $6223; part-time $207.43 per credit hour. *Tuition, nonresident:* full-time $12,446; part-time $414.86 per credit hour. *Required fees:* full-time $2001. Full-time tuition and fees vary according to course load. Part-time tuition and fees vary according to course load. *College room and board:* $6248. Room and board charges vary according to board plan and housing facility.
GIFT AID (NEED-BASED) *Scholarships, grants, and awards:* Federal Pell, FSEOG, state, private, college/university gift aid from institutional funds, Federal Nursing.
GIFT AID (NON-NEED-BASED) *Scholarships, grants, and awards by category:* Academic interests/achievement: general academic interests/achievements. *Tuition waivers:* Full or partial for employees or children of employees, senior citizens. *ROTC:* Army.
LOANS *Programs:* Perkins, Federal Nursing, state, alternative loans.
WORK-STUDY Federal work-study jobs available. *State or other work-study/employment:* Part-time jobs available.
APPLYING FOR FINANCIAL AID *Required financial aid form:* FAFSA. *Financial aid deadline:* 7/1 (priority: 4/15). *Notification date:* Continuous.
CONTACT Cheryl Lyons, Director of Student Aid, University of Central Arkansas, 201 Donaghey Avenue, Conway, AR 72035, 501-450-3140 or toll-free 800-243-8245. *Fax:* 501-450-5168. *E-mail:* clyons@uca.edu.
Website: http://www.uca.edu/.

UNIVERSITY OF CENTRAL FLORIDA
Orlando, FL

Tuition & fees (FL res): $6368	Average undergraduate aid package: $8744

ABOUT THE INSTITUTION State-supported, coed. *Awards:* certificates, associate, bachelor's, master's, and doctoral degrees. 83 undergraduate majors. *Total enrollment:* 64,321. Undergraduates: 55,776. Freshmen: 6,403. Federal methodology is used as a basis for awarding need-based institutional aid.
UNDERGRADUATE EXPENSES for 2016–2017 *Application fee:* $30. *Tuition, state resident:* full-time $6368; part-time $212.28 per credit hour. *Tuition, nonresident:* full-time $22,467; part-time $748.89 per credit hour. Full-time tuition and fees vary according to course load. Part-time tuition and fees vary according to course load. *College room and board:* $9554; *Room only:* $5400. Room and board charges vary according to board plan and housing facility. *Payment plan:* Tuition prepayment.
FRESHMAN FINANCIAL AID (Fall 2015) 5,543 applied for aid; of those 69% were deemed to have need. 96% of freshmen with need received aid; of those 9% had need fully met. *Average percent of need met:* 54% (excluding resources awarded to replace EFC). *Average financial aid package:* $8516 (excluding resources awarded to replace EFC). 8% of all full-time freshmen had no need and received non-need-based gift aid.
UNDERGRADUATE FINANCIAL AID (Fall 2015) 30,093 applied for aid; of those 79% were deemed to have need. 96% of undergraduates with need received aid; of those 7% had need fully met. *Average percent of need met:* 56% (excluding resources awarded to replace EFC). *Average financial aid package:* $8744

(excluding resources awarded to replace EFC). 4% of all full-time undergraduates had no need and received non-need-based gift aid.
GIFT AID (NEED-BASED) *Total amount:* $120,681,247 (71% federal, 8% state, 21% institutional). *Receiving aid:* Freshmen: 38% (2,395); all full-time undergraduates: 45% (16,878). *Average award:* Freshmen: $5824; Undergraduates: $5656. *Scholarships, grants, and awards:* Federal Pell, FSEOG, state, private, college/university gift aid from institutional funds.
GIFT AID (NON-NEED-BASED) *Total amount:* $53,180,442 (58% state, 30% institutional, 12% external sources). *Receiving aid:* Freshmen: 38% (2,385). Undergraduates: 28% (10,336). *Average award:* Freshmen: $3839. Undergraduates: $4180. *Scholarships, grants, and awards by category:* Academic interests/achievement: general academic interests/achievements. Creative arts/performance: cinema/film/broadcasting, music, theater/drama. Special achievements/activities: general special achievements/activities, leadership. Special characteristics: first-generation college students. *Tuition waivers:* Full or partial for employees or children of employees, senior citizens. *ROTC:* Army, Air Force.
LOANS *Student loans:* $173,386,405 (52% need-based, 48% non-need-based). 52% of past graduating class borrowed through all loan programs. *Average indebtedness per student:* $21,911. *Average need-based loan:* Freshmen: $3616. Undergraduates: $4667. *Parent loans:* $12,332,008 (100% non-need-based). *Programs:* Federal Direct (Subsidized and Unsubsidized Stafford, PLUS), Perkins.
WORK-STUDY *Federal work-study:* 719 jobs averaging $3529. *State or other work-study/employment:* Part-time jobs available.
ATHLETIC AWARDS Total amount: $3,517,325 (100% non-need-based).
APPLYING FOR FINANCIAL AID *Required financial aid form:* FAFSA. *Financial aid deadline:* 6/30 (priority: 12/1). *Notification date:* Continuous beginning 3/15. Students must reply within 3 weeks of notification.
CONTACT Ms. Alicia Keaton, Director of Student Financial Assistance, University of Central Florida, 4000 Central Florida Boulevard, Orlando, FL 32816-0113, 407-823-2827. *Fax:* 407-823-5241. *E-mail:* alicia.keaton@ucf.edu.
Website: http://www.ucf.edu/.

UNIVERSITY OF CENTRAL MISSOURI
Warrensburg, MO

Tuition & fees (MO res): $7322	Average undergraduate aid package: $8562

ABOUT THE INSTITUTION State-supported, coed. *Awards:* certificates, bachelor's, and master's degrees. 63 undergraduate majors. *Total enrollment:* 13,988. Undergraduates: 9,786. Freshmen: 1,605. Federal methodology is used as a basis for awarding need-based institutional aid.
UNDERGRADUATE EXPENSES for 2016–2017 *Application fee:* $30. *Tuition, state resident:* full-time $6446; part-time $214.85 per credit hour. *Tuition, nonresident:* full-time $12,891; part-time $429.70 per credit hour. *Required fees:* full-time $876; $29.20 per credit hour. Full-time tuition and fees vary according to course load and location. Part-time tuition and fees vary according to location. *College room and board:* $8318; *Room only:* $5288. Room and board charges vary according to board plan, housing facility, and student level.
FRESHMAN FINANCIAL AID (Fall 2015) 1,519 applied for aid; of those 72% were deemed to have need. 100% of freshmen with need received aid; of those 12% had need fully met. *Average percent of need met:* 65% (excluding resources awarded to replace EFC). *Average financial aid package:* $8907 (excluding resources awarded to replace EFC). 24% of all full-time freshmen had no need and received non-need-based gift aid.
UNDERGRADUATE FINANCIAL AID (Fall 2015) 6,670 applied for aid; of those 75% were deemed to have need. 100% of undergraduates with need received aid; of those 7% had need fully met. *Average percent of need met:* 62% (excluding resources awarded to replace EFC). *Average financial aid package:* $8562 (excluding resources awarded to replace EFC). 20% of all full-time undergraduates had no need and received non-need-based gift aid.
GIFT AID (NEED-BASED) *Total amount:* $26,662,225 (56% federal, 18% state, 26% external sources). *Receiving aid:* Freshmen: 40% (659); all full-time undergraduates: 39% (3,132). *Average award:* Freshmen: $4369; Undergraduates: $4284. *Scholarships, grants, and awards:* Federal Pell, FSEOG, state, private, college/university gift aid from institutional funds.
GIFT AID (NON-NEED-BASED) *Total amount:* $7,469,433 (8% federal, 4% state, 88% institutional). *Receiving aid:* Freshmen: 66% (1,079). Undergraduates:

60% (4,815). *Average award:* Freshmen: $3514. Undergraduates: $3338. *Tuition waivers:* Full or partial for employees or children of employees. *ROTC:* Army, Air Force cooperative.

LOANS *Student loans:* $42,965,731 (43% need-based, 57% non-need-based). 72% of past graduating class borrowed through all loan programs. *Average indebtedness per student:* $28,673. *Parent loans:* $6,930,838 (100% non-need-based). *Programs:* Federal Direct (Subsidized and Unsubsidized Stafford, PLUS), Perkins, private loans.

WORK-STUDY *Federal work-study:* 134 jobs averaging $1482. *State or other work-study/employment:* Total amount: $3,432,061 (100% non-need-based). 1,358 part-time jobs averaging $2165.

ATHLETIC AWARDS Total amount: $2,387,372 (100% non-need-based).

APPLYING FOR FINANCIAL AID *Required financial aid forms:* FAFSA, institution's own form. *Financial aid deadline (priority):* 4/1. *Notification date:* Continuous beginning 3/20. Students must reply within 3 weeks of notification.

CONTACT Ms. Angela Karlin, Director of Student Financial Assistance, University of Central Missouri, Ward Edwards Building 1100, Warrensburg, MO 64093, 660-543-4177 or toll-free 800-729-8266. *Fax:* 660-543-8080. *E-mail:* sfs@ucmo.edu. *Website:* http://www.ucmo.edu/.

UNIVERSITY OF CENTRAL OKLAHOMA
Edmond, OK

Tuition & fees (OK res): $6096	Average undergraduate aid package: $9879

ABOUT THE INSTITUTION State-supported, coed. *Awards:* certificates, associate, bachelor's, and master's degrees. 141 undergraduate majors. *Total enrollment:* 16,910. Undergraduates: 15,067. Freshmen: 2,474. Federal methodology is used as a basis for awarding need-based institutional aid.

UNDERGRADUATE EXPENSES for 2016–2017 *Application fee:* $90. *Tuition, state resident:* full-time $5157; part-time $171.90 per credit hour. *Tuition, nonresident:* full-time $14,033; part-time $467.75 per credit hour. *Required fees:* full-time $939; $31.30 per credit hour. Full-time tuition and fees vary according to course load, degree level, location, and program. Part-time tuition and fees vary according to course load, degree level, location, and program. *College room and board:* $7130; *Room only:* $3496. Room and board charges vary according to board plan and housing facility. *Payment plan:* Guaranteed tuition.

FRESHMAN FINANCIAL AID (Fall 2015) 1,542 applied for aid; of those 76% were deemed to have need. 97% of freshmen with need received aid; of those 16% had need fully met. *Average percent of need met:* 64% (excluding resources awarded to replace EFC). *Average financial aid package:* $11,430 (excluding resources awarded to replace EFC). 20% of all full-time freshmen had no need and received non-need-based gift aid.

UNDERGRADUATE FINANCIAL AID (Fall 2015) 6,754 applied for aid; of those 83% were deemed to have need. 96% of undergraduates with need received aid; of those 11% had need fully met. *Average percent of need met:* 54% (excluding resources awarded to replace EFC). *Average financial aid package:* $9879 (excluding resources awarded to replace EFC). 14% of all full-time undergraduates had no need and received non-need-based gift aid.

GIFT AID (NEED-BASED) *Total amount:* $31,869,285 (66% federal, 34% state). *Receiving aid:* Freshmen: 36% (820); all full-time undergraduates: 37% (3,890). *Average award:* Freshmen: $7259; Undergraduates: $6325. *Scholarships, grants, and awards:* Federal Pell, FSEOG, state, private, college/university gift aid from institutional funds.

GIFT AID (NON-NEED-BASED) *Total amount:* $13,464,354 (5% federal, 2% state, 9% institutional, 84% external sources). *Receiving aid:* Freshmen: 23% (529). Undergraduates: 20% (2,113). *Average award:* Freshmen: $2388. Undergraduates: $2699. *Scholarships, grants, and awards by category:* Academic interests/achievement: biological sciences, business, communication, computer science, education, English, foreign languages, general academic interests/achievements, health fields, home economics, humanities, mathematics, military science, physical sciences, social sciences. *Creative arts/performance:* applied art and design, art/fine arts, journalism/publications, music, theater/drama. *Special achievements/activities:* general special achievements/activities, junior miss, leadership. *Special characteristics:* children of faculty/staff, ethnic background, international students, members of minority groups.

Tuition waivers: Full or partial for employees or children of employees. *ROTC:* Army.

LOANS *Student loans:* $43,289,512 (45% need-based, 55% non-need-based). 56% of past graduating class borrowed through all loan programs. *Average indebtedness per student:* $26,335. *Average need-based loan:* Freshmen: $3372. Undergraduates: $4047. *Parent loans:* $3,702,475 (100% non-need-based). *Programs:* Federal Direct (Subsidized and Unsubsidized Stafford, PLUS).

WORK-STUDY *Federal work-study:* jobs available. *State or other work-study/employment:* Total amount: $4,400,000 (100% non-need-based). Part-time jobs available.

ATHLETIC AWARDS Total amount: $2,507,089 (100% non-need-based).

APPLYING FOR FINANCIAL AID *Required financial aid forms:* FAFSA, institution's own form. *Financial aid deadline:* Continuous. *Notification date:* Continuous beginning 5/1. Students must reply within 4 weeks of notification.

CONTACT Ms. Kerry Housley, Assistant Director of Technical Services, University of Central Oklahoma, 100 North University Drive, Edmond, OK 73034-5209, 405-974-5325. *Fax:* 405-340-7658. *E-mail:* khousley@uco.edu. *Website:* http://www.uco.edu/.

UNIVERSITY OF CHARLESTON
Charleston, WV

ABOUT THE INSTITUTION Independent, coed. *Awards:* associate, bachelor's, master's, and doctoral degrees. 31 undergraduate majors. *Total enrollment:* 2,425. Undergraduates: 1,761. Freshmen: 304.

GIFT AID (NEED-BASED) *Scholarships, grants, and awards:* Federal Pell, FSEOG, state, private, college/university gift aid from institutional funds.

GIFT AID (NON-NEED-BASED) *Scholarships, grants, and awards by category:* Academic interests/achievement: general academic interests/achievements. Creative arts/performance: music. *Special achievements/activities:* community service, general special achievements/activities, leadership. *Special characteristics:* international students.

LOANS *Programs:* Federal Direct (Subsidized and Unsubsidized Stafford, PLUS), Perkins, Federal Nursing, private loans.

WORK-STUDY Federal work-study jobs available. *State or other work-study/employment:* Part-time jobs available.

APPLYING FOR FINANCIAL AID *Required financial aid forms:* FAFSA, institution's own form, state aid form.

CONTACT Ms. Nina Morton, Director of Financial Aid, University of Charleston, 2300 MacCorkle Avenue SE, Charleston, WV 25304-1099, 304-357-4947 or toll-free 800-995-GOUC. *E-mail:* ninamorton@ucwv.edu. *Website:* http://www.ucwv.edu/.

UNIVERSITY OF CHICAGO
Chicago, IL

Tuition & fees: $52,491	Average undergraduate aid package: $49,967

ABOUT THE INSTITUTION Independent, coed. *Awards:* bachelor's, master's, and doctoral degrees. 48 undergraduate majors. *Total enrollment:* 13,322. Undergraduates: 5,941. Freshmen: 1,591. Both federal and institutional methodology are used as a basis for awarding need-based institutional aid.

UNDERGRADUATE EXPENSES for 2016–2017 *Application fee:* $75. *One-time required fee:* $1158. *Comprehensive fee:* $67,584 includes full-time tuition ($50,997), mandatory fees ($1494), and room and board ($15,093). Full-time tuition and fees vary according to course load. Room and board charges vary according to board plan and housing facility. Part-time tuition and fees vary according to course load.

FRESHMAN FINANCIAL AID (Fall 2016, est.) 893 applied for aid; of those 73% were deemed to have need. 100% of freshmen with need received aid; of those 100% had need fully met. *Average percent of need met:* 100% (excluding resources awarded to replace EFC). *Average financial aid package:* $52,659 (excluding resources awarded to replace EFC).

UNDERGRADUATE FINANCIAL AID (Fall 2016, est.) 3,058 applied for aid; of those 83% were deemed to have need. 100% of undergraduates with need received

aid; of those 100% had need fully met. **Average percent of need met:** 100% (excluding resources awarded to replace EFC). **Average financial aid package:** $49,967 (excluding resources awarded to replace EFC).

GIFT AID (NEED-BASED) Total amount: $116,168,039 (4% federal, 1% state, 95% institutional). **Receiving aid:** Freshmen: 41% (646); all full-time undergraduates: 42% (2,483). **Average award:** Freshmen: $47,321; Undergraduates: $43,792. **Scholarships, grants, and awards:** Federal Pell, FSEOG, state, private, college/university gift aid from institutional funds.

GIFT AID (NON-NEED-BASED) Total amount: $16,513,565 (81% institutional, 19% external sources). **Scholarships, grants, and awards by category:** *Academic interests/achievement:* general academic interests/achievements. *Special achievements/activities:* community service, leadership. **Tuition waivers:** Full or partial for employees or children of employees. **ROTC:** Army cooperative, Air Force cooperative.

LOANS Student loans: $6,235,747 (22% need-based, 78% non-need-based). 33% of past graduating class borrowed through all loan programs. *Average indebtedness per student:* $23,852. **Average need-based loan:** Undergraduates: $3858. **Parent loans:** $4,417,604 (100% non-need-based). **Programs:** Federal Direct (Subsidized and Unsubsidized Stafford, PLUS), Perkins.

WORK-STUDY Federal work-study: Total amount: $3,261,212; jobs available. *State or other work-study/employment:* Part-time jobs available.

APPLYING FOR FINANCIAL AID Required financial aid forms: FAFSA, institution's own form, CSS Financial Aid PROFILE, federal income tax form(s). **Financial aid deadline (priority):** 2/15. **Notification date:** 4/1. Students must reply by 5/1.

CONTACT Office of College Aid, University of Chicago, 1101 East 58th Street, Chicago, IL 60637, 773-702-8666. *Fax:* 773-834-4300. *E-mail:* college-aid@uchicago.edu. *Website:* http://www.uchicago.edu/.

UNIVERSITY OF CINCINNATI
Cincinnati, OH

Tuition & fees (OH res): $11,000	Average undergraduate aid package: $8489

ABOUT THE INSTITUTION State-supported, coed. **Awards:** certificates, associate, bachelor's, master's, and doctoral degrees. 107 undergraduate majors. **Total enrollment:** 36,637. Undergraduates: 25,860. Freshmen: 5,011. Federal methodology is used as a basis for awarding need-based institutional aid.

UNDERGRADUATE EXPENSES for 2016–2017 Application fee: $50. **Tuition, state resident:** full-time $9322; part-time $389 per credit hour. **Tuition, nonresident:** full-time $24,656; part-time $1028 per credit hour. **Required fees:** full-time $1678; $70 per credit hour. Full-time tuition and fees vary according to course load, location, program, and reciprocity agreements. Part-time tuition and fees vary according to course load, location, program, and reciprocity agreements. **College room and board:** $10,928; **Room only:** $6558. Room and board charges vary according to board plan and housing facility.

FRESHMAN FINANCIAL AID (Fall 2016, est.) 4,146 applied for aid; of those 71% were deemed to have need. 92% of freshmen with need received aid; of those 7% had need fully met. **Average percent of need met:** 46% (excluding resources awarded to replace EFC). **Average financial aid package:** $8558 (excluding resources awarded to replace EFC). 17% of all full-time freshmen had no need and received non-need-based gift aid.

UNDERGRADUATE FINANCIAL AID (Fall 2016, est.) 14,457 applied for aid; of those 77% were deemed to have need. 94% of undergraduates with need received aid; of those 5% had need fully met. **Average percent of need met:** 44% (excluding resources awarded to replace EFC). **Average financial aid package:** $8489 (excluding resources awarded to replace EFC). 16% of all full-time undergraduates had no need and received non-need-based gift aid.

GIFT AID (NEED-BASED) Total amount: $49,885,982 (50% federal, 9% state, 35% institutional, 6% external sources). **Receiving aid:** Freshmen: 21% (1,047); all full-time undergraduates: 22% (4,719). **Average award:** Freshmen: $6989; Undergraduates: $6192. **Scholarships, grants, and awards:** Federal Pell, FSEOG, state, private, college/university gift aid from institutional funds, United Negro College Fund, Federal Nursing, TEACH Grants.

GIFT AID (NON-NEED-BASED) Total amount: $20,964,817 (84% institutional, 16% external sources). **Receiving aid:** Freshmen: 28% (1,418). Undergrad-

uates: 19% (4,142). **Average award:** Freshmen: $5663. Undergraduates: $4847. **Tuition waivers:** Full or partial for employees or children of employees. **ROTC:** Army, Air Force.

LOANS Student loans: $92,280,568 (83% need-based, 17% non-need-based). 65% of past graduating class borrowed through all loan programs. *Average indebtedness per student:* $28,970. **Average need-based loan:** Freshmen: $3713. Undergraduates: $4424. **Parent loans:** $56,351,079 (78% need-based, 22% non-need-based). **Programs:** Federal Direct (Subsidized and Unsubsidized Stafford, PLUS), Perkins, Federal Nursing, state, college/university.

WORK-STUDY Federal work-study: Total amount: $4,090,662; 1,335 jobs averaging $3045.

ATHLETIC AWARDS Total amount: $5,858,079 (42% need-based, 58% non-need-based).

APPLYING FOR FINANCIAL AID Required financial aid form: FAFSA. **Financial aid deadline:** Continuous. **Notification date:** Continuous beginning 2/15. Students must reply within 2 weeks of notification.

CONTACT Mr. Randy Ulses, Director of Scholarships and Enrollment, University of Cincinnati, PO Box 210125, Cincinnati, OH 45221-0125, 513-556-1000. *Fax:* 513-556-9171. *E-mail:* financeaid@uc.edu. *Website:* http://www.uc.edu/.

UNIVERSITY OF COLORADO BOULDER
Boulder, CO

Tuition & fees (CO res): $11,531	Average undergraduate aid package: $16,838

ABOUT THE INSTITUTION State-supported, coed. **Awards:** certificates, bachelor's, master's, and doctoral degrees. 72 undergraduate majors. **Total enrollment:** 33,771. Undergraduates: 27,846. Freshmen: 6,439. Federal methodology is used as a basis for awarding need-based institutional aid.

UNDERGRADUATE EXPENSES for 2017–2018 Application fee: $50. **One-time required fee:** $182. **Tuition, state resident:** full-time $9768. **Tuition, nonresident:** full-time $32,346. **Required fees:** full-time $1763. Full-time tuition and fees vary according to program. Part-time tuition and fees vary according to course load and program. **College room and board:** $13,590. Room and board charges vary according to board plan, housing facility, and location. **Payment plan:** Guaranteed tuition.

FRESHMAN FINANCIAL AID (Fall 2016, est.) 4,955 applied for aid; of those 50% were deemed to have need. 98% of freshmen with need received aid; of those 46% had need fully met. **Average percent of need met:** 82% (excluding resources awarded to replace EFC). **Average financial aid package:** $16,237 (excluding resources awarded to replace EFC). 33% of all full-time freshmen had no need and received non-need-based gift aid.

UNDERGRADUATE FINANCIAL AID (Fall 2016, est.) 12,537 applied for aid; of those 72% were deemed to have need. 97% of undergraduates with need received aid; of those 41% had need fully met. **Average percent of need met:** 81% (excluding resources awarded to replace EFC). **Average financial aid package:** $16,838 (excluding resources awarded to replace EFC). 27% of all full-time undergraduates had no need and received non-need-based gift aid.

GIFT AID (NEED-BASED) Total amount: $78,528,571 (27% federal, 10% state, 58% institutional, 5% external sources). **Receiving aid:** Freshmen: 30% (1,879); all full-time undergraduates: 27% (6,844). **Average award:** Freshmen: $11,465; Undergraduates: $11,026. **Scholarships, grants, and awards:** Federal Pell, FSEOG, state, private, college/university gift aid from institutional funds.

GIFT AID (NON-NEED-BASED) Total amount: $37,661,366 (4% federal, 1% state, 65% institutional, 30% external sources). **Receiving aid:** Freshmen: 2% (135). Undergraduates: 1% (311). **Average award:** Freshmen: $8893. Undergraduates: $9205. **Scholarships, grants, and awards by category:** *Academic interests/achievement:* architecture, area/ethnic studies, biological sciences, business, communication, computer science, education, engineering/technologies, English, foreign languages, general academic interests/achievements, health fields, humanities, international studies, mathematics, military science, physical sciences, premedicine, social sciences. *Creative arts/performance:* art/fine arts, cinema/film/broadcasting, creative writing, dance, journalism/publications, music, performing arts, theater/drama. *Special achievements/activities:* community service, general special achievements/activities, leadership. *Special characteristics:* first-generation college students, general special characteristics, local/state students. *Tuition waivers:* Full or partial for employees or children of employees, senior citizens. *ROTC:* Army, Naval, Air Force.

LOANS *Student loans:* $89,933,734 (59% need-based, 41% non-need-based). 43% of past graduating class borrowed through all loan programs. *Average indebtedness per student:* $27,405. *Average need-based loan:* Freshmen: $5356. Undergraduates: $6490. *Parent loans:* $89,475,489 (33% need-based, 67% non-need-based). *Programs:* Federal Direct (Subsidized and Unsubsidized Stafford, PLUS), Perkins, college/university, private loans.

WORK-STUDY *Federal work-study:* Total amount: $1,079,200; 797 jobs averaging $1768. *State or other work-study/employment:* Total amount: $1,991,639 (97% need-based, 3% non-need-based). 1,014 part-time jobs averaging $2327.

ATHLETIC AWARDS Total amount: $9,368,273 (24% need-based, 76% non-need-based).

APPLYING FOR FINANCIAL AID *Required financial aid forms:* FAFSA, federal income tax form(s). *Financial aid deadline (priority):* 3/1. *Notification date:* Continuous beginning 3/15. Students must reply within 3 weeks of notification.

CONTACT Gwen E. Pomper, Director of Financial Aid, University of Colorado Boulder, 556 UCB, Boulder, CO 80309-0556, 303-492-5091. *Fax:* 303-492-0838. *E-mail:* finaid@colorado.edu.

Website: http://www.colorado.edu/.

UNIVERSITY OF COLORADO COLORADO SPRINGS
Colorado Springs, CO

Tuition & fees (CO res): $9863	Average undergraduate aid package: $8749

ABOUT THE INSTITUTION State-supported, coed. *Awards:* certificates, bachelor's, master's, and doctoral degrees. 33 undergraduate majors. *Total enrollment:* 12,258. Undergraduates: 10,414. Freshmen: 2,085. Federal methodology is used as a basis for awarding need-based institutional aid.

UNDERGRADUATE EXPENSES for 2016–2017 *Application fee:* $50. *One-time required fee:* $140. *Tuition, state resident:* full-time $8280; part-time $276 per credit hour. *Tuition, nonresident:* full-time $21,690; part-time $723 per credit hour. *Required fees:* full-time $1583. Full-time tuition and fees vary according to course load, degree level, location, program, reciprocity agreements, and student level. Part-time tuition and fees vary according to course load, degree level, location, program, reciprocity agreements, and student level. *College room and board:* $9800. Room and board charges vary according to board plan, housing facility, and student level.

FRESHMAN FINANCIAL AID (Fall 2015) 1,466 applied for aid; of those 71% were deemed to have need. 91% of freshmen with need received aid; of those 2% had need fully met. *Average percent of need met:* 43% (excluding resources awarded to replace EFC). *Average financial aid package:* $8049 (excluding resources awarded to replace EFC). 11% of all full-time freshmen had no need and received non-need-based gift aid.

UNDERGRADUATE FINANCIAL AID (Fall 2015) 6,113 applied for aid; of those 77% were deemed to have need. 92% of undergraduates with need received aid; of those 3% had need fully met. *Average percent of need met:* 44% (excluding resources awarded to replace EFC). *Average financial aid package:* $8749 (excluding resources awarded to replace EFC). 5% of all full-time undergraduates had no need and received non-need-based gift aid.

GIFT AID (NEED-BASED) *Total amount:* $28,184,612 (47% federal, 18% state, 25% institutional, 10% external sources). *Receiving aid:* Freshmen: 35% (552); all full-time undergraduates: 38% (2,846). *Average award:* Freshmen: $7255; Undergraduates: $6497. *Scholarships, grants, and awards:* Federal Pell, FSEOG, state, private, college/university gift aid from institutional funds.

GIFT AID (NON-NEED-BASED) *Receiving aid:* Freshmen: 29% (462). Undergraduates: 17% (1,235). *Average award:* Freshmen: $1493. Undergraduates: $2135. *Scholarships, grants, and awards by category:* Academic interests/achievement: general academic interests/achievements. *Tuition waivers:* Full or partial for employees or children of employees. *ROTC:* Army.

LOANS *Student loans:* $36,526,001 (100% need-based). 57% of past graduating class borrowed through all loan programs. *Average indebtedness per student:* $22,228. *Average need-based loan:* Freshmen: $3342. Undergraduates: $4252.

Parent loans: $13,284,823 (100% need-based). *Programs:* Federal Direct (Subsidized and Unsubsidized Stafford, PLUS), Perkins.

WORK-STUDY *Federal work-study:* 205 jobs averaging $2758. *State or other work-study/employment:* Total amount: $1,080,699 (100% need-based). 306 part-time jobs averaging $3532.

ATHLETIC AWARDS Total amount: $1,045,708 (100% need-based).

APPLYING FOR FINANCIAL AID *Required financial aid form:* FAFSA. *Financial aid deadline (priority):* 3/1. *Notification date:* Continuous beginning 1/15.

CONTACT Jevita Rogers, Executive Director of Financial Aid, University of Colorado Colorado Springs, 1420 Austin Bluffs Parkway, Colorado Springs, CO 80918, 719-255-3460 or toll-free 800-990-8227 Ext. 3383. *Fax:* 719-255-3650. *E-mail:* jrogers3@uccs.edu.

Website: http://www.uccs.edu/.

UNIVERSITY OF COLORADO DENVER
Denver, CO

Tuition & fees (CO res): $10,719	Average undergraduate aid package: $9995

ABOUT THE INSTITUTION State-supported, coed. *Awards:* certificates, bachelor's, master's, and doctoral degrees. 38 undergraduate majors. *Total enrollment:* 23,960. Undergraduates: 14,622. Federal methodology is used as a basis for awarding need-based institutional aid.

UNDERGRADUATE EXPENSES for 2017–2018 *Application fee:* $50. *Tuition, state resident:* full-time $9420; part-time $314 per credit hour. *Tuition, nonresident:* full-time $29,040; part-time $968 per credit hour. *Required fees:* full-time $1299; $1299 per year. Full-time tuition and fees vary according to course level, course load, degree level, location, program, reciprocity agreements, and student level. Part-time tuition and fees vary according to course level, course load, degree level, location, program, reciprocity agreements, and student level. Room and board charges vary according to board plan.

FRESHMAN FINANCIAL AID (Fall 2015) 1,128 applied for aid; of those 75% were deemed to have need. 91% of freshmen with need received aid; of those 3% had need fully met. *Average percent of need met:* 51% (excluding resources awarded to replace EFC). *Average financial aid package:* $8836 (excluding resources awarded to replace EFC). 5% of all full-time freshmen had no need and received non-need-based gift aid.

UNDERGRADUATE FINANCIAL AID (Fall 2015) 4,707 applied for aid; of those 87% were deemed to have need. 95% of undergraduates with need received aid; of those 3% had need fully met. *Average percent of need met:* 53% (excluding resources awarded to replace EFC). *Average financial aid package:* $9995 (excluding resources awarded to replace EFC). 5% of all full-time undergraduates had no need and received non-need-based gift aid.

GIFT AID (NEED-BASED) *Total amount:* $33,118,468 (45% federal, 22% state, 27% institutional, 6% external sources). *Receiving aid:* Freshmen: 49% (632); all full-time undergraduates: 39% (3,138). *Average award:* Freshmen: $7195; Undergraduates: $7497. *Scholarships, grants, and awards:* Federal Pell, FSEOG, state, private, college/university gift aid from institutional funds, College Access Challenge Grants, TEACH Grants, Armed Services Scholarships.

GIFT AID (NON-NEED-BASED) *Total amount:* $2,495,706 (5% state, 68% institutional, 27% external sources). *Receiving aid:* Freshmen: 3% (33). Undergraduates: 2% (150). *Average award:* Freshmen: $3501. Undergraduates: $2564. *Scholarships, grants, and awards by category:* Academic interests/achievement: 696 awards ($1,166,854 total): biological sciences, business, communication, education, engineering/technologies, English, general academic interests/achievements, home economics, humanities, international studies, mathematics, physical sciences, premedicine, social sciences. *Creative arts/performance:* 27 awards ($34,730 total): applied art and design, art/fine arts, cinema/film/broadcasting, general creative arts/performance, music, performing arts, theater/drama. *Special achievements/activities:* 10 awards ($3900 total): general special achievements/activities. *Special characteristics:* 442 awards ($1,111,527 total): children of faculty/staff, ethnic background, first-generation college students, general special characteristics, handicapped students, international students, members of minority groups, out-of-state students, veterans. *Tuition waivers:* Full or partial for employees or children of employees. *ROTC:* Army cooperative, Air Force cooperative.

LOANS *Student loans:* $36,955,742 (77% need-based, 23% non-need-based). 54% of past graduating class borrowed through all loan programs. *Average indebtedness*

per student: $19,378. *Average need-based loan:* Freshmen: $2652. Undergraduates: $3914. *Parent loans:* $9,161,790 (16% need-based, 84% non-need-based). *Programs:* Federal Direct (Subsidized and Unsubsidized Stafford, PLUS), Perkins, Federal Nursing.

WORK-STUDY *Federal work-study:* 382 jobs averaging $3614. *State or other work-study/employment:* Total amount: $1,642,928 (95% need-based, 5% non-need-based). 377 part-time jobs averaging $4358.

APPLYING FOR FINANCIAL AID *Required financial aid form:* FAFSA. *Financial aid deadline:* Continuous. *Notification date:* Continuous beginning 5/1.

CONTACT Justin Jaramillo, Interim Director of Financial Aid, University of Colorado Denver, PO Box 173364, Denver, CO 80217-3364, 303-315-1850. *Fax:* 303-315-1835. *E-mail:* financialaid@ucdenver.edu.
Website: http://www.ucdenver.edu/.

UNIVERSITY OF CONNECTICUT
Storrs, CT

CONTACT Mona L. Lucas, Director of Financial Aid, University of Connecticut, 233 Glenbrook Road, Unit 4116, Storrs, CT 06269-4116, 860-486-2819. *Fax:* 860-486-6629. *E-mail:* financialaid@uconn.edu.
Website: http://www.uconn.edu/.

UNIVERSITY OF DALLAS
Irving, TX

Tuition & fees: $37,230	Average undergraduate aid package: $30,907

ABOUT THE INSTITUTION Independent Roman Catholic, coed. *Awards:* certificates, bachelor's, master's, and doctoral degrees. 33 undergraduate majors. *Total enrollment:* 2,387. Undergraduates: 1,342. Freshmen: 393. Federal methodology is used as a basis for awarding need-based institutional aid.

UNDERGRADUATE EXPENSES for 2016–2017 *Application fee:* $50. *Comprehensive fee:* $48,770 includes full-time tuition ($34,650), mandatory fees ($2580), and room and board ($11,540). *College room only:* $6450. Full-time tuition and fees vary according to course load. Room and board charges vary according to board plan and housing facility. *Part-time tuition:* $1430 per credit. *Part-time fees:* $2580 per year. Part-time tuition and fees vary according to course load.

FRESHMAN FINANCIAL AID (Fall 2016, est.) 314 applied for aid; of those 85% were deemed to have need. 100% of freshmen with need received aid; of those 27% had need fully met. *Average percent of need met:* 83% (excluding resources awarded to replace EFC). *Average financial aid package:* $31,642 (excluding resources awarded to replace EFC). 27% of all full-time freshmen had no need and received non-need-based gift aid.

UNDERGRADUATE FINANCIAL AID (Fall 2016, est.) 962 applied for aid; of those 88% were deemed to have need. 100% of undergraduates with need received aid; of those 25% had need fully met. *Average percent of need met:* 79% (excluding resources awarded to replace EFC). *Average financial aid package:* $30,907 (excluding resources awarded to replace EFC). 35% of all full-time undergraduates had no need and received non-need-based gift aid.

GIFT AID (NEED-BASED) *Total amount:* $31,186,450 (4% federal, 3% state, 92% institutional, 1% external sources). *Receiving aid:* Freshmen: 71% (265); all full-time undergraduates: 61% (837). *Average award:* Freshmen: $28,424; Undergraduates: $26,016. *Scholarships, grants, and awards:* Federal Pell, FSEOG, state, private, college/university gift aid from institutional funds.

GIFT AID (NON-NEED-BASED) *Total amount:* $118,090 (3% federal, 97% institutional). *Average award:* Freshmen: $16,109. Undergraduates: $14,967. *Scholarships, grants, and awards by category:* Academic interests/achievement: biological sciences, business, education, foreign languages, general academic interests/achievements, mathematics, physical sciences, premedicine. *Creative arts/performance:* art/fine arts, theater/drama. *Special characteristics:* children of faculty/staff, ethnic background, religious affiliation, siblings of current students. *Tuition waivers:* Full or partial for employees or children of employees. *ROTC:* Army cooperative, Air Force cooperative.

LOANS *Student loans:* $7,096,248 (44% need-based, 56% non-need-based). 59% of past graduating class borrowed through all loan programs. *Average indebtedness per student:* $32,921. *Average need-based loan:* Freshmen: $3989. Undergraduates: $5621. *Parent loans:* $1,542,923 (100% non-need-based). *Programs:* Federal Direct (Subsidized and Unsubsidized Stafford, PLUS), Perkins, state.

WORK-STUDY *Federal work-study:* Total amount: $466,860; jobs available. *State or other work-study/employment:* Total amount: $37,614 (97% need-based, 3% non-need-based). Part-time jobs available.

APPLYING FOR FINANCIAL AID *Required financial aid form:* FAFSA. *Financial aid deadline (priority):* 3/1. *Notification date:* Continuous beginning 12/1. Students must reply by 5/1 or within 2 weeks of notification.

CONTACT Mrs. Taryn Anderson, Director of Financial Aid, University of Dallas, 1845 East Northgate Drive, Irving, TX 75062, 972-721-5266 or toll-free 800-628-6999. *Fax:* 972-721-5017. *E-mail:* ugadmis@udallas.edu.
Website: http://www.udallas.edu/.

UNIVERSITY OF DAYTON
Dayton, OH

Tuition & fees: $40,940	Average undergraduate aid package: $26,045

ABOUT THE INSTITUTION Independent Roman Catholic, coed. *Awards:* certificates, bachelor's, master's, and doctoral degrees. 74 undergraduate majors. *Total enrollment:* 10,803. Undergraduates: 8,330. Freshmen: 1,827. Federal methodology is used as a basis for awarding need-based institutional aid.

UNDERGRADUATE EXPENSES for 2016–2017 *Comprehensive fee:* $53,620 includes full-time tuition ($40,940) and room and board ($12,680). *College room only:* $7600. *Part-time tuition:* $1360 per credit hour.

FRESHMAN FINANCIAL AID (Fall 2015) 1,654 applied for aid; of those 71% were deemed to have need. 100% of freshmen with need received aid; of those 20% had need fully met. *Average percent of need met:* 78% (excluding resources awarded to replace EFC). *Average financial aid package:* $27,507 (excluding resources awarded to replace EFC). 35% of all full-time freshmen had no need and received non-need-based gift aid.

UNDERGRADUATE FINANCIAL AID (Fall 2015) 5,199 applied for aid; of those 71% were deemed to have need. 100% of undergraduates with need received aid; of those 38% had need fully met. *Average percent of need met:* 83% (excluding resources awarded to replace EFC). *Average financial aid package:* $26,045 (excluding resources awarded to replace EFC). 36% of all full-time undergraduates had no need and received non-need-based gift aid.

GIFT AID (NEED-BASED) *Total amount:* $101,991,527 (4% federal, 1% state, 94% institutional, 1% external sources). *Receiving aid:* Freshmen: 64% (1,173); all full-time undergraduates: 46% (3,626). *Average award:* Freshmen: $25,334; Undergraduates: $23,166. *Scholarships, grants, and awards:* Federal Pell, FSEOG, state, private, college/university gift aid from institutional funds.

GIFT AID (NON-NEED-BASED) *Total amount:* $50,143,677 (1% federal, 98% institutional, 1% external sources). *Receiving aid:* Freshmen: 5% (84). Undergraduates: 5% (380). *Average award:* Freshmen: $12,811. Undergraduates: $15,516. *Scholarships, grants, and awards by category:* Academic interests/achievement: biological sciences, business, communication, computer science, education, engineering/technologies, English, foreign languages, general academic interests/achievements, health fields, humanities, international studies, mathematics, military science, physical sciences, premedicine, religion/biblical studies, social sciences. *Creative arts/performance:* art/fine arts, music. *Special achievements/activities:* leadership. *Special characteristics:* children and siblings of alumni, children of faculty/staff, local/state students, members of minority groups, religious affiliation. *ROTC:* Army, Air Force cooperative.

LOANS *Student loans:* $53,794,451 (76% need-based, 24% non-need-based). 62% of past graduating class borrowed through all loan programs. *Average indebtedness per student:* $35,740. *Average need-based loan:* Freshmen: $2784. Undergraduates: $3032. *Parent loans:* $14,842,875 (54% need-based, 46% non-need-based). *Programs:* Federal Direct (Subsidized and Unsubsidized Stafford, PLUS), Perkins.

WORK-STUDY *Federal work-study:* jobs available. *State or other work-study/employment:* Total amount: $7,000,000 (29% need-based, 71% non-need-based). Part-time jobs available.

ATHLETIC AWARDS Total amount: $5,235,942 (46% need-based, 54% non-need-based).

APPLYING FOR FINANCIAL AID *Required financial aid form:* FAFSA. *Financial aid deadline (priority):* 3/1. *Notification date:* Continuous beginning 3/20. Students must reply within 2 weeks of notification.
CONTACT Catherine Mix, Director of Financial Aid, University of Dayton, 300 College Park, Dayton, OH 45469-1668, 937-229-4358 or toll-free 800-837-7433. *Fax:* 937-229-4338. *E-mail:* cmix01@udayton.edu.
Website: http://www.udayton.edu/.

APPLYING FOR FINANCIAL AID *Required financial aid form:* FAFSA. *Financial aid deadline:* 3/15 (priority: 1/15). *Notification date:* Continuous beginning 3/15. Students must reply by 5/1 or within 3 weeks of notification.
CONTACT Mr. James Holloway, Manager of Student Financial Services Compliance, University of Delaware, 140 Student Services Building, Newark, DE 19716, 302-831-0520. *Fax:* 302-831-4334. *E-mail:* holloway@udel.edu.
Website: http://www.udel.edu/.

UNIVERSITY OF DELAWARE
Newark, DE

Tuition & fees (DE res): $12,830	Average undergraduate aid package: $12,963

ABOUT THE INSTITUTION State-related, coed. *Awards:* associate, bachelor's, master's, and doctoral degrees. 126 undergraduate majors. *Total enrollment:* 21,463. Undergraduates: 18,374. Freshmen: 3,952. Federal methodology is used as a basis for awarding need-based institutional aid.
UNDERGRADUATE EXPENSES for 2016–2017 *Application fee:* $75. *Tuition, state resident:* full-time $11,540; part-time $481 per credit hour. *Tuition, nonresident:* full-time $30,960; part-time $1290 per credit hour. *Required fees:* full-time $1290. *College room and board:* $12,068; *Room only:* $7316. Room and board charges vary according to board plan and housing facility.
FRESHMAN FINANCIAL AID (Fall 2015) 3,366 applied for aid; of those 65% were deemed to have need. 98% of freshmen with need received aid; of those 13% had need fully met. *Average percent of need met:* 58% (excluding resources awarded to replace EFC). *Average financial aid package:* $13,812 (excluding resources awarded to replace EFC). 24% of all full-time freshmen had no need and received non-need-based gift aid.
UNDERGRADUATE FINANCIAL AID (Fall 2015) 11,547 applied for aid; of those 70% were deemed to have need. 98% of undergraduates with need received aid; of those 11% had need fully met. *Average percent of need met:* 56% (excluding resources awarded to replace EFC). *Average financial aid package:* $12,963 (excluding resources awarded to replace EFC). 20% of all full-time undergraduates had no need and received non-need-based gift aid.
GIFT AID (NEED-BASED) *Total amount:* $62,972,356 (16% federal, 13% state, 66% institutional, 5% external sources). *Receiving aid:* Freshmen: 49% (2,012); all full-time undergraduates: 40% (6,734). *Average award:* Freshmen: $10,142; Undergraduates: $9280. *Scholarships, grants, and awards:* Federal Pell, FSEOG, state, private, college/university gift aid from institutional funds.
GIFT AID (NON-NEED-BASED) *Total amount:* $32,212,028 (2% state, 88% institutional, 10% external sources). *Receiving aid:* Freshmen: 5% (200). Undergraduates: 3% (576). *Average award:* Freshmen: $7311. Undergraduates: $7568. *Scholarships, grants, and awards by category:* Academic interests/achievement: agriculture, biological sciences, business, communication, computer science, education, engineering/technologies, English, foreign languages, general academic interests/achievements, health fields, humanities, international studies, mathematics, military science, physical sciences, premedicine, religion/biblical studies, social sciences. Creative arts/performance: applied art and design, art/fine arts, music, theater/drama. Special achievements/activities: cheerleading/drum major, community service, general special achievements/activities, leadership. Special characteristics: children and siblings of alumni, children of faculty/staff, children of public servants, ethnic background, first-generation college students, general special characteristics, local/state students, members of minority groups. *Tuition waivers:* Full or partial for employees or children of employees, senior citizens. *ROTC:* Army, Air Force.
LOANS *Student loans:* $93,002,084 (57% need-based, 43% non-need-based). 59% of past graduating class borrowed through all loan programs. *Average indebtedness per student:* $33,150. *Average need-based loan:* Freshmen: $3674. Undergraduates: $4580. *Parent loans:* $32,153,475 (35% need-based, 65% non-need-based). *Programs:* Federal Direct (Subsidized and Unsubsidized Stafford, PLUS), Perkins, Federal Nursing.
WORK-STUDY *Federal work-study:* jobs available. *State or other work-study/employment:* Total amount: $154,551 (86% need-based, 14% non-need-based). Part-time jobs available.
ATHLETIC AWARDS Total amount: $11,146,786 (28% need-based, 72% non-need-based).

UNIVERSITY OF DENVER
Denver, CO

Tuition & fees: $48,669	Average undergraduate aid package: $37,109

ABOUT THE INSTITUTION Independent, coed. *Awards:* certificates, bachelor's, master's, and doctoral degrees. 79 undergraduate majors. *Total enrollment:* 11,614. Undergraduates: 5,754. Freshmen: 1,399. Institutional methodology is used as a basis for awarding need-based institutional aid.
UNDERGRADUATE EXPENSES for 2017–2018 *Application fee:* $65. *Comprehensive fee:* $61,281 includes full-time tuition ($47,520), mandatory fees ($1149), and room and board ($12,612). *College room only:* $7806. Full-time tuition and fees vary according to course load and program. Room and board charges vary according to board plan and housing facility. *Part-time tuition:* $1320 per credit hour. Part-time tuition and fees vary according to course load and program.
FRESHMAN FINANCIAL AID (Fall 2016, est.) 921 applied for aid; of those 67% were deemed to have need. 99% of freshmen with need received aid; of those 31% had need fully met. *Average percent of need met:* 84% (excluding resources awarded to replace EFC). *Average financial aid package:* $37,209 (excluding resources awarded to replace EFC). 38% of all full-time freshmen had no need and received non-need-based gift aid.
UNDERGRADUATE FINANCIAL AID (Fall 2016, est.) 2,923 applied for aid; of those 76% were deemed to have need. 99% of undergraduates with need received aid; of those 36% had need fully met. *Average percent of need met:* 84% (excluding resources awarded to replace EFC). *Average financial aid package:* $37,109 (excluding resources awarded to replace EFC). 40% of all full-time undergraduates had no need and received non-need-based gift aid.
GIFT AID (NEED-BASED) *Total amount:* $65,922,700 (6% federal, 2% state, 86% institutional, 6% external sources). *Receiving aid:* Freshmen: 45% (613); all full-time undergraduates: 40% (2,178). *Average award:* Freshmen: $30,469; Undergraduates: $30,824. *Scholarships, grants, and awards:* Federal Pell, FSEOG, state, private, college/university gift aid from institutional funds.
GIFT AID (NON-NEED-BASED) *Total amount:* $40,182,593 (94% institutional, 6% external sources). *Receiving aid:* Freshmen: 11% (157). Undergraduates: 10% (566). *Average award:* Freshmen: $19,861. Undergraduates: $16,702. *Scholarships, grants, and awards by category:* Academic interests/achievement: biological sciences, business, communication, computer science, engineering/technologies, English, general academic interests/achievements, humanities, international studies, mathematics, physical sciences, social sciences. Creative arts/performance: art/fine arts, debating, music, theater/drama. Special achievements/activities: community service, leadership. *Tuition waivers:* Full or partial for employees or children of employees, senior citizens. *ROTC:* Army cooperative, Air Force cooperative.
LOANS *Student loans:* $19,327,342 (51% need-based, 49% non-need-based). 44% of past graduating class borrowed through all loan programs. *Average indebtedness per student:* $31,077. *Average need-based loan:* Freshmen: $3347. Undergraduates: $4260. *Parent loans:* $10,935,864 (19% need-based, 81% non-need-based). *Programs:* Federal Direct (Subsidized and Unsubsidized Stafford, PLUS), Perkins, college/university.
WORK-STUDY *Federal work-study:* Total amount: $1,137,773; 398 jobs averaging $2929. *State or other work-study/employment:* Total amount: $471,266 (87% need-based, 13% non-need-based). 181 part-time jobs averaging $2920.
ATHLETIC AWARDS Total amount: $10,395,231 (16% need-based, 84% non-need-based).
APPLYING FOR FINANCIAL AID *Required financial aid forms:* FAFSA, institution's own form, CSS Financial Aid PROFILE, noncustodial (divorced/separated) parent's statement. *Financial aid deadline (priority):* 1/15. *Notification date:* 3/1. Students must reply by 5/1.

CONTACT Mr. John Gudvangen, Director of Financial Aid, University of Denver, University Hall, 2197 South University Boulevard, Denver, CO 80208, 303-871-4020 or toll-free 800-525-9495. *Fax:* 303-871-2341. *E-mail:* finaid@du.edu. *Website:* http://www.du.edu/.

UNIVERSITY OF DETROIT MERCY
Detroit, MI

Tuition & fees: $41,158	Average undergraduate aid package: $33,808

ABOUT THE INSTITUTION Independent Roman Catholic (Jesuit), coed. *Awards:* certificates, diplomas, bachelor's, master's, and doctoral degrees. 50 undergraduate majors. *Total enrollment:* 4,875. Undergraduates: 2,646. Freshmen: 532. Federal methodology is used as a basis for awarding need-based institutional aid.

UNDERGRADUATE EXPENSES for 2017–2018 *Comprehensive fee:* $50,610 includes full-time tuition ($41,158) and room and board ($9452). Full-time tuition and fees vary according to program. Room and board charges vary according to board plan and housing facility. *Part-time tuition:* $1049 per credit hour. Part-time tuition and fees vary according to location and program.

FRESHMAN FINANCIAL AID (Fall 2016, est.) 460 applied for aid; of those 78% were deemed to have need. 100% of freshmen with need received aid; of those 12% had need fully met. *Average percent of need met:* 84% (excluding resources awarded to replace EFC). *Average financial aid package:* $36,737 (excluding resources awarded to replace EFC). 31% of all full-time freshmen had no need and received non-need-based gift aid.

UNDERGRADUATE FINANCIAL AID (Fall 2016, est.) 1,822 applied for aid; of those 82% were deemed to have need. 100% of undergraduates with need received aid; of those 9% had need fully met. *Average percent of need met:* 76% (excluding resources awarded to replace EFC). *Average financial aid package:* $33,808 (excluding resources awarded to replace EFC). 29% of all full-time undergraduates had no need and received non-need-based gift aid.

GIFT AID (NEED-BASED) *Total amount:* $38,687,620 (12% federal, 6% state, 80% institutional, 2% external sources). *Receiving aid:* Freshmen: 68% (353); all full-time undergraduates: 68% (1,458). *Average award:* Freshmen: $30,565; Undergraduates: $26,032. *Scholarships, grants, and awards:* Federal Pell, FSEOG, state, private, college/university gift aid from institutional funds.

GIFT AID (NON-NEED-BASED) *Total amount:* $12,851,726 (99% institutional, 1% external sources). *Receiving aid:* Freshmen: 2% (13). Undergraduates: 1% (30). *Average award:* Freshmen: $22,176. Undergraduates: $20,196. *Scholarships, grants, and awards by category:* Academic interests/achievement: general academic interests/achievements. *Creative arts/performance:* 3 awards ($39,000 total): theater/drama. *Special achievements/activities:* 176 awards ($620,299 total): religious involvement. *Special characteristics:* 261 awards ($3,243,496 total): children and siblings of alumni, children of faculty/staff. *Tuition waivers:* Full or partial for children of alumni, employees or children of employees, senior citizens.

LOANS *Student loans:* $16,839,763 (89% need-based, 11% non-need-based). 69% of past graduating class borrowed through all loan programs. *Average indebtedness per student:* $33,631. *Average need-based loan:* Freshmen: $4424. Undergraduates: $5766. *Parent loans:* $5,902,848 (77% need-based, 23% non-need-based). *Programs:* Federal Direct (Subsidized and Unsubsidized Stafford, PLUS), Perkins, Federal Nursing, alternative loans.

WORK-STUDY *Federal work-study:* Total amount: $917,560; 397 jobs averaging $2500.

ATHLETIC AWARDS Total amount: $5,358,486 (40% need-based, 60% non-need-based).

APPLYING FOR FINANCIAL AID *Required financial aid form:* FAFSA. *Financial aid deadline (priority):* 3/1. *Notification date:* Continuous beginning 3/1.

CONTACT Jenny McAlonan, Director of Financial Aid and Scholarships, University of Detroit Mercy, 4001 West McNichols Road, Detroit, MI 48221-3038, 313-993-3350 or toll-free 800-635-5020. *Fax:* 313-993-3347. *E-mail:* mcalonjl@udmercy.edu. *Website:* http://www.udmercy.edu/.

UNIVERSITY OF DUBUQUE
Dubuque, IA

Tuition & fees: $28,700	Average undergraduate aid package: $24,370

ABOUT THE INSTITUTION Independent Presbyterian, coed. *Awards:* associate, bachelor's, master's, and doctoral degrees. 33 undergraduate majors. *Total enrollment:* 2,274. Undergraduates: 1,924. Freshmen: 441. Federal methodology is used as a basis for awarding need-based institutional aid.

UNDERGRADUATE EXPENSES for 2016–2017 *Application fee:* $25. *One-time required fee:* $100. *Comprehensive fee:* $38,050 includes full-time tuition ($27,400), mandatory fees ($1300), and room and board ($9350). *College room only:* $4510. Room and board charges vary according to board plan and housing facility. *Part-time tuition:* $775 per credit hour.

FRESHMAN FINANCIAL AID (Fall 2016, est.) 488 applied for aid; of those 92% were deemed to have need. 100% of freshmen with need received aid; of those 12% had need fully met. *Average percent of need met:* 73% (excluding resources awarded to replace EFC). *Average financial aid package:* $24,153 (excluding resources awarded to replace EFC). 13% of all full-time freshmen had no need and received non-need-based gift aid.

UNDERGRADUATE FINANCIAL AID (Fall 2016, est.) 1,462 applied for aid; of those 93% were deemed to have need. 100% of undergraduates with need received aid; of those 17% had need fully met. *Average percent of need met:* 59% (excluding resources awarded to replace EFC). *Average financial aid package:* $24,370 (excluding resources awarded to replace EFC). 11% of all full-time undergraduates had no need and received non-need-based gift aid.

GIFT AID (NEED-BASED) *Total amount:* $24,292,703 (16% federal, 9% state, 57% institutional, 18% external sources). *Receiving aid:* Freshmen: 84% (445); all full-time undergraduates: 87% (1,352). *Average award:* Freshmen: $16,490; Undergraduates: $17,301. *Scholarships, grants, and awards:* Federal Pell, FSEOG, state, private, college/university gift aid from institutional funds.

GIFT AID (NON-NEED-BASED) *Total amount:* $4,584,964 (1% state, 48% institutional, 51% external sources). *Receiving aid:* Freshmen: 9% (45). Undergraduates: 11% (170). *Average award:* Freshmen: $8552. Undergraduates: $9455. *Scholarships, grants, and awards by category:* Academic interests/achievement: 712 awards ($6,127,894 total): general academic interests/achievements. *Creative arts/performance:* 135 awards ($72,790 total): dance, music, performing arts, theater/drama. *Special characteristics:* 290 awards ($251,290 total): children and siblings of alumni, children of educators, children of faculty/staff, out-of-state students, relatives of clergy, religious affiliation, siblings of current students, spouses of current students. *Tuition waivers:* Full or partial for employees or children of employees. *ROTC:* Army.

LOANS *Student loans:* $15,675,334 (78% need-based, 22% non-need-based). 72% of past graduating class borrowed through all loan programs. *Average indebtedness per student:* $26,674. *Average need-based loan:* Freshmen: $7906. Undergraduates: $7620. *Parent loans:* $2,979,215 (57% need-based, 43% non-need-based). *Programs:* Federal Direct (Subsidized and Unsubsidized Stafford, PLUS), Perkins, college/university.

WORK-STUDY *Federal work-study:* Total amount: $1,183,352; 180 jobs averaging $2000. *State or other work-study/employment:* Total amount: $501,695 (49% need-based, 51% non-need-based). 175 part-time jobs averaging $2000.

APPLYING FOR FINANCIAL AID *Required financial aid form:* FAFSA. *Financial aid deadline (priority):* 4/1. *Notification date:* Continuous beginning 3/1. Students must reply within 3 weeks of notification.

CONTACT Teresa Brahm, Director of Student Financial Planning, University of Dubuque, 2000 University Avenue, Dubuque, IA 52001-5050, 563-589-3170 or toll-free 800-722-5583. *Fax:* 563-589-3690. *E-mail:* tbrahm@dbq.edu. *Website:* http://www.dbq.edu/.

UNIVERSITY OF EVANSVILLE
Evansville, IN

Tuition & fees: $35,396	Average undergraduate aid package: $28,569

ABOUT THE INSTITUTION Independent United Methodist Church, coed. *Awards:* associate, bachelor's, master's, and doctoral degrees. 72 undergraduate majors. **Total enrollment:** 2,514. Undergraduates: 2,348. Freshmen: 537. Institutional methodology is used as a basis for awarding need-based institutional aid.

UNDERGRADUATE EXPENSES for 2017–2018 Comprehensive fee: $47,556 includes full-time tuition ($34,300), mandatory fees ($1096), and room and board ($12,160). **College room only:** $6410. Room and board charges vary according to board plan and housing facility. Part-time tuition and fees vary according to course load.

FRESHMAN FINANCIAL AID (Fall 2016, est.) 441 applied for aid; of those 87% were deemed to have need. 100% of freshmen with need received aid; of those 30% had need fully met. **Average percent of need met:** 85% (excluding resources awarded to replace EFC). **Average financial aid package:** $31,560 (excluding resources awarded to replace EFC). 26% of all full-time freshmen had no need and received non-need-based gift aid.

UNDERGRADUATE FINANCIAL AID (Fall 2016, est.) 1,550 applied for aid; of those 89% were deemed to have need. 100% of undergraduates with need received aid; of those 28% had need fully met. **Average percent of need met:** 82% (excluding resources awarded to replace EFC). **Average financial aid package:** $28,569 (excluding resources awarded to replace EFC). 25% of all full-time undergraduates had no need and received non-need-based gift aid.

GIFT AID (NEED-BASED) Total amount: $28,655,399 (9% federal, 9% state, 78% institutional, 4% external sources). **Receiving aid:** Freshmen: 71% (383); all full-time undergraduates: 63% (1,371). **Average award:** Freshmen: $26,378; Undergraduates: $26,608. **Scholarships, grants, and awards:** FSEOG, state, private, college/university gift aid from institutional funds.

GIFT AID (NON-NEED-BASED) Total amount: $13,204,793 (1% federal, 93% institutional, 6% external sources). **Receiving aid:** Freshmen: 17% (92). Undergraduates: 13% (292). **Average award:** Freshmen: $22,868. Undergraduates: $19,026. **Scholarships, grants, and awards by category:** Academic interests/achievement: 2,403 awards ($24,454,870 total): biological sciences, business, communication, computer science, education, engineering/technologies, English, foreign languages, general academic interests/achievements, health fields, humanities, international studies, mathematics, physical sciences, premedicine, religion/biblical studies, social sciences. Creative arts/performance: 187 awards ($2,956,090 total): art/fine arts, music, performing arts, theater/drama. Special achievements/activities: 86 awards ($159,250 total): general special achievements/activities, leadership, memberships. Special characteristics: 613 awards ($6,218,618 total): children and siblings of alumni, children of faculty/staff, international students, members of minority groups, religious affiliation, siblings of current students, veterans. **Tuition waivers:** Full or partial for minority students, children of alumni, employees or children of employees, adult students, senior citizens. **ROTC:** Army cooperative.

LOANS Student loans: $10,423,009 (68% need-based, 32% non-need-based). 65% of past graduating class borrowed through all loan programs. Average indebtedness per student: $35,346. **Average need-based loan:** Freshmen: $3825. Undergraduates: $4790. **Parent loans:** $2,958,417 (41% need-based, 59% non-need-based). **Programs:** Federal Direct (Subsidized and Unsubsidized Stafford, PLUS), Perkins, Federal Nursing, college/university.

WORK-STUDY Federal work-study: Total amount: $370,853; 311 jobs averaging $1469. **State or other work-study/employment:** Total amount: $30,675 (10% need-based, 90% non-need-based). 37 part-time jobs averaging $1583.

ATHLETIC AWARDS Total amount: $4,931,952 (41% need-based, 59% non-need-based).

APPLYING FOR FINANCIAL AID Required financial aid form: FAFSA. **Financial aid deadline (priority):** 3/1. **Notification date:** Continuous beginning 12/1. Students must reply within 3 weeks of notification.

CONTACT Ms. Cathleen Wright, Director of Financial Aid, University of Evansville, 1800 Lincoln Avenue, Evansville, IN 47722, 812-488-2364 or toll-free 800-423-8633 Ext. 2468. Fax: 812-488-2028. E-mail: financialaid@evansville.edu. Website: http://www.evansville.edu/.

THE UNIVERSITY OF FINDLAY
Findlay, OH

Tuition & fees: $33,320	Average undergraduate aid package: $23,792

ABOUT THE INSTITUTION Independent Church of God, coed. **Awards:** certificates, associate, bachelor's, master's, and doctoral degrees. 71 undergraduate majors.

Total enrollment: 5,078. Undergraduates: 3,661. Freshmen: 544. Both federal and institutional methodology are used as a basis for awarding need-based institutional aid.

UNDERGRADUATE EXPENSES for 2017–2018 Comprehensive fee: $43,040 includes full-time tuition ($32,330), mandatory fees ($990), and room and board ($9720). **College room only:** $4850. Full-time tuition and fees vary according to program. Room and board charges vary according to board plan and housing facility. **Part-time tuition:** $715 per semester hour. **Part-time fees:** $430 per term. Part-time tuition and fees vary according to course load and program.

FRESHMAN FINANCIAL AID (Fall 2015) 672 applied for aid; of those 80% were deemed to have need. 100% of freshmen with need received aid; of those 20% had need fully met. **Average percent of need met:** 82% (excluding resources awarded to replace EFC). **Average financial aid package:** $24,531 (excluding resources awarded to replace EFC). 25% of all full-time freshmen had no need and received non-need-based gift aid.

UNDERGRADUATE FINANCIAL AID (Fall 2015) 2,205 applied for aid; of those 80% were deemed to have need. 100% of undergraduates with need received aid; of those 19% had need fully met. **Average percent of need met:** 73% (excluding resources awarded to replace EFC). **Average financial aid package:** $23,792 (excluding resources awarded to replace EFC). 36% of all full-time undergraduates had no need and received non-need-based gift aid.

GIFT AID (NEED-BASED) Total amount: $41,367,578 (9% federal, 2% state, 87% institutional, 2% external sources). **Receiving aid:** Freshmen: 75% (538); all full-time undergraduates: 64% (1,764). **Average award:** Freshmen: $20,654; Undergraduates: $19,065. **Scholarships, grants, and awards:** Federal Pell, FSEOG, state, college/university gift aid from institutional funds.

GIFT AID (NON-NEED-BASED) Total amount: $8,828,229 (2% federal, 4% state, 91% institutional, 3% external sources). **Receiving aid:** Freshmen: 75% (538). Undergraduates: 64% (1,764). **Average award:** Freshmen: $17,874. Undergraduates: $17,062. **Scholarships, grants, and awards by category:** Academic interests/achievement: general academic interests/achievements. Creative arts/performance: 203 awards ($213,164 total): music, theater/drama. Special characteristics: 205 awards ($2,544,927 total): children of faculty/staff. **Tuition waivers:** Full or partial for employees or children of employees, senior citizens. **ROTC:** Army cooperative, Air Force cooperative.

LOANS Student loans: $24,704,944 (84% need-based, 16% non-need-based). 85% of past graduating class borrowed through all loan programs. Average indebtedness per student: $36,249. **Average need-based loan:** Freshmen: $3248. Undergraduates: $4562. **Parent loans:** $7,298,710 (80% need-based, 20% non-need-based). **Programs:** Federal Direct (Subsidized and Unsubsidized Stafford, PLUS), Perkins, college/university.

WORK-STUDY Federal work-study: jobs available. **State or other work-study/employment:** Part-time jobs available.

ATHLETIC AWARDS Total amount: $4,704,540 (80% need-based, 20% non-need-based).

APPLYING FOR FINANCIAL AID Required financial aid form: FAFSA. **Financial aid deadline:** 9/1 (priority: 8/1). **Notification date:** Continuous beginning 11/1. Students must reply within 2 weeks of notification.

CONTACT Mr. Joseph F. Spencer, Interim Director of Financial Aid, The University of Findlay, 1000 North Main Street, Findlay, OH 45840-3695, 419-434-4659 or toll-free 800-548-0932. Fax: 419-434-4344. E-mail: spencer@findlay.edu. Website: http://www.findlay.edu/.

UNIVERSITY OF FLORIDA
Gainesville, FL

Tuition & fees (FL res): $6381	Average undergraduate aid package: $12,494

ABOUT THE INSTITUTION State-supported, coed. **Awards:** certificates, associate, bachelor's, master's, and doctoral degrees. 100 undergraduate majors. **Total enrollment:** 52,367. Undergraduates: 34,554. Freshmen: 6,833. Federal methodology is used as a basis for awarding need-based institutional aid.

UNDERGRADUATE EXPENSES for 2016–2017 Application fee: $30. **Tuition, state resident:** full-time $4477; part-time $149.24 per credit hour. **Tuition, nonresident:** full-time $26,755; part-time $856.45 per credit hour. **Required fees:** full-time $1904. **College room and board:** $9910; **Room only:** $5440.

FRESHMAN FINANCIAL AID (Fall 2015) 5,726 applied for aid; of those 59% were deemed to have need. 98% of freshmen with need received aid; of those 30% had need fully met. *Average percent of need met:* 99% (excluding resources awarded to replace EFC). *Average financial aid package:* $13,430 (excluding resources awarded to replace EFC). 5% of all full-time freshmen had no need and received non-need-based gift aid.

UNDERGRADUATE FINANCIAL AID (Fall 2015) 22,004 applied for aid; of those 73% were deemed to have need. 98% of undergraduates with need received aid; of those 25% had need fully met. *Average percent of need met:* 99% (excluding resources awarded to replace EFC). *Average financial aid package:* $12,494 (excluding resources awarded to replace EFC). 5% of all full-time undergraduates had no need and received non-need-based gift aid.

GIFT AID (NEED-BASED) *Total amount:* $73,998,402 (58% federal, 9% state, 33% institutional). *Receiving aid:* Freshmen: 30% (2,070); all full-time undergraduates: 31% (10,445). *Average award:* Freshmen: $7711; Undergraduates: $7083. *Scholarships, grants, and awards:* Federal Pell, FSEOG, state, private, college/university gift aid from institutional funds, United Negro College Fund.

GIFT AID (NON-NEED-BASED) *Total amount:* $100,621,511 (1% federal, 66% state, 20% institutional, 13% external sources). *Receiving aid:* Freshmen: 41% (2,817). Undergraduates: 35% (11,626). *Average award:* Freshmen: $2476. Undergraduates: $2531. *Scholarships, grants, and awards by category:* Academic interests/achievement: agriculture, architecture, business, communication, computer science, education, engineering/technologies, general academic interests/achievements, home economics, military science. *Creative arts/performance:* art/fine arts, dance, general creative arts/performance, journalism/publications, music, performing arts, theater/drama. *Special achievements/activities:* community service, general special achievements/activities, leadership. *Special characteristics:* children of faculty/staff, members of minority groups, out-of-state students. *ROTC:* Army, Naval, Air Force.

LOANS *Student loans:* $65,363,564 (50% need-based, 50% non-need-based). 41% of past graduating class borrowed through all loan programs. *Average indebtedness per student:* $21,645. *Average need-based loan:* Freshmen: $3545. Undergraduates: $4540. *Parent loans:* $16,955,343 (100% non-need-based). *Programs:* Federal Direct (Subsidized and Unsubsidized Stafford, PLUS), Perkins, college/university.

WORK-STUDY *Federal work-study:* 1,027 jobs averaging $2478. *State or other work-study/employment:* Total amount: $11,922,335 (1% need-based, 99% non-need-based). 4,720 part-time jobs averaging $1817.

ATHLETIC AWARDS Total amount: $10,922,587 (100% non-need-based).

APPLYING FOR FINANCIAL AID *Required financial aid form:* FAFSA. *Financial aid deadline (priority):* 3/15. *Notification date:* Continuous beginning 4/2.

CONTACT Mr. Richard D. Wilder, Director of Student Financial Affairs, University of Florida, S-107 Criser Hall, Gainesville, FL 32611-4025, 352-294-3220. *Fax:* 352-392-2861. *E-mail:* rwilder@ufl.edu. *Website:* http://www.ufl.edu/.

load, location, and program. Part-time tuition and fees vary according to course load, location, and program. *College room and board:* $9616; *Room only:* $5660. Room and board charges vary according to board plan and housing facility.

FRESHMAN FINANCIAL AID (Fall 2016, est.) 4,619 applied for aid; of those 56% were deemed to have need. 99% of freshmen with need received aid; of those 29% had need fully met. *Average percent of need met:* 77% (excluding resources awarded to replace EFC). *Average financial aid package:* $13,514 (excluding resources awarded to replace EFC). 3% of all full-time freshmen had no need and received non-need-based gift aid.

UNDERGRADUATE FINANCIAL AID (Fall 2016, est.) 18,463 applied for aid; of those 63% were deemed to have need. 98% of undergraduates with need received aid; of those 22% had need fully met. *Average percent of need met:* 71% (excluding resources awarded to replace EFC). *Average financial aid package:* $11,997 (excluding resources awarded to replace EFC). 5% of all full-time undergraduates had no need and received non-need-based gift aid.

GIFT AID (NEED-BASED) *Total amount:* $95,220,477 (28% federal, 65% state, 5% institutional, 2% external sources). *Receiving aid:* Freshmen: 47% (2,514); all full-time undergraduates: 40% (10,658). *Average award:* Freshmen: $10,337; Undergraduates: $9116. *Scholarships, grants, and awards:* Federal Pell, FSEOG, state, private, college/university gift aid from institutional funds.

GIFT AID (NON-NEED-BASED) *Total amount:* $97,200,038 (93% state, 4% institutional, 3% external sources). *Receiving aid:* Freshmen: 12% (640). Undergraduates: 7% (1,967). *Average award:* Freshmen: $3516. Undergraduates: $2418. *Scholarships, grants, and awards by category:* Academic interests/achievement: 26,215 awards ($163,801,909 total): agriculture, business, education, general academic interests/achievements. *Creative arts/performance:* 132 awards ($106,396 total): music. *Special characteristics:* 189 awards ($262,667 total): local/state students. *Tuition waivers:* Full or partial for senior citizens. *ROTC:* Army, Air Force.

LOANS *Student loans:* $74,061,697 (60% need-based, 40% non-need-based). 47% of past graduating class borrowed through all loan programs. *Average indebtedness per student:* $21,730. *Average need-based loan:* Freshmen: $3314. Undergraduates: $4232. *Parent loans:* $32,716,459 (28% need-based, 72% non-need-based). *Programs:* Federal Direct (Subsidized and Unsubsidized Stafford, PLUS), Perkins, state, college/university.

WORK-STUDY *Federal work-study:* Total amount: $983,420; 382 jobs averaging $2410.

ATHLETIC AWARDS Total amount: $10,230,925 (26% need-based, 74% non-need-based).

APPLYING FOR FINANCIAL AID *Financial aid deadline (priority):* 12/15. *Notification date:* Continuous beginning 12/1. Students must reply within 2 weeks of notification.

CONTACT Ms. Bonnie C. Joerschke, Director of Financial Aid, University of Georgia, 220 Holmes/Hunter Academic Building, Athens, GA 30602-6114, 706-542-6147. *Fax:* 706-542-8217. *E-mail:* osfa@uga.edu. *Website:* http://www.uga.edu/.

UNIVERSITY OF FORT LAUDERDALE
Lauderhill, FL

CONTACT Financial Aid Office, University of Fort Lauderdale, 4093 NW 16th Street, Lauderhill, FL 33313, 954-486-7728. *Website:* http://uftl.edu/.

UNIVERSITY OF GEORGIA
Athens, GA

Tuition & fees (GA res): $11,634	Average undergraduate aid package: $11,997

ABOUT THE INSTITUTION State-supported, coed. *Awards:* certificates, bachelor's, master's, and doctoral degrees. 185 undergraduate majors. *Total enrollment:* 36,574. Undergraduates: 27,951. Freshmen: 5,433. Federal methodology is used as a basis for awarding need-based institutional aid.

UNDERGRADUATE EXPENSES for 2016–2017 *Application fee:* $60. *Tuition, state resident:* full-time $9364. *Tuition, nonresident:* full-time $27,574. *Required fees:* full-time $2270. Full-time tuition and fees vary according to course

---

UNIVERSITY OF GREAT FALLS
Great Falls, MT

Tuition & fees: $25,050	Average undergraduate aid package: $20,083

ABOUT THE INSTITUTION Independent Roman Catholic, coed. *Awards:* certificates, associate, bachelor's, and master's degrees. 73 undergraduate majors. *Total enrollment:* 952. Undergraduates: 881. Freshmen: 95. Federal methodology is used as a basis for awarding need-based institutional aid.

UNDERGRADUATE EXPENSES for 2017–2018 *Application fee:* $35. *Comprehensive fee:* $33,550 includes full-time tuition ($24,400), mandatory fees ($650), and room and board ($8500). *College room only:* $4800. *Part-time tuition:* $789 per credit hour.

FRESHMAN FINANCIAL AID (Fall 2016, est.) 85 applied for aid; of those 85% were deemed to have need. 100% of freshmen with need received aid; of those 1% had need fully met. *Average percent of need met:* 67% (excluding resources awarded to replace EFC). *Average financial aid package:* $18,949 (excluding resources awarded to replace EFC). 9% of all full-time freshmen had no need and received non-need-based gift aid.

UNDERGRADUATE FINANCIAL AID (Fall 2016, est.) 415 applied for aid; of those 87% were deemed to have need. 100% of undergraduates with need received

aid; of those 2% had need fully met. **Average percent of need met:** 70% (excluding resources awarded to replace EFC). **Average financial aid package:** $20,083 (excluding resources awarded to replace EFC). 12% of all full-time undergraduates had no need and received non-need-based gift aid.

GIFT AID (NEED-BASED) Total amount: $3,404,657 (34% federal, 66% institutional). **Receiving aid:** Freshmen: 57% (53); all full-time undergraduates: 60% (289). **Average award:** Freshmen: $11,364; Undergraduates: $10,788. **Scholarships, grants, and awards:** Federal Pell, FSEOG, private, college/university gift aid from institutional funds.

GIFT AID (NON-NEED-BASED) Total amount: $2,459,748 (100% institutional). **Receiving aid:** Freshmen: 11% (10). Undergraduates: 8% (37). **Average award:** Freshmen: $3605. Undergraduates: $7724. **Scholarships, grants, and awards by category:** *Academic interests/achievement:* biological sciences, business, computer science, education, general academic interests/achievements, humanities, mathematics, physical sciences, premedicine, religion/biblical studies, social sciences. *Creative arts/performance:* dance, general creative arts/performance. *Special achievements/activities:* cheerleading/drum major, religious involvement. *Special characteristics:* children and siblings of alumni, children of current students, children of faculty/staff, ethnic background, first-generation college students, international students, local/state students, parents of current students, religious affiliation, siblings of current students, spouses of current students.

LOANS Student loans: $3,524,978 (75% need-based, 25% non-need-based). 73% of past graduating class borrowed through all loan programs. **Average indebtedness per student:** $30,118. **Average need-based loan:** Freshmen: $2983. Undergraduates: $3829. **Parent loans:** $390,165 (67% need-based, 33% non-need-based). **Programs:** Federal Direct (Subsidized and Unsubsidized Stafford, PLUS), Perkins.

WORK-STUDY Federal work-study: Total amount: $63,519; jobs available. **State or other work-study/employment:** Total amount: $147,000 (100% need-based). Part-time jobs available.

ATHLETIC AWARDS Total amount: $4,087,902 (65% need-based, 35% non-need-based).

APPLYING FOR FINANCIAL AID Required financial aid form: FAFSA. **Financial aid deadline (priority):** 3/1. **Notification date:** Continuous beginning 3/1.

CONTACT Kelli Engelhardt, Director of Financial Aid, University of Great Falls, 1301 20th Street South, Great Falls, MT 59405, 406-791-5237 or toll-free 800-856-9544. *Fax:* 406-791-5242. *E-mail:* kengelhardt01@ugf.edu. *Website:* http://www.ugf.edu/.

UNIVERSITY OF GUAM
Mangilao, GU

CONTACT Office of Financial Aid, University of Guam, UOG Station, Mangilao, GU 96923, 671-735-2288. *Fax:* 671-734-2907. *Website:* http://www.uog.edu/.

UNIVERSITY OF HARTFORD
West Hartford, CT

Tuition & fees: $38,970	Average undergraduate aid package: $25,950

ABOUT THE INSTITUTION Independent, coed. **Awards:** certificates, diplomas, associate, bachelor's, master's, and doctoral degrees. 80 undergraduate majors. **Total enrollment:** 6,714. Undergraduates: 5,150. Freshmen: 1,301. Federal methodology is used as a basis for awarding need-based institutional aid.

UNDERGRADUATE EXPENSES for 2017–2018 Application fee: $35. **Comprehensive fee:** $51,316 includes full-time tuition ($36,088), mandatory fees ($2882), and room and board ($12,346). **College room only:** $8008. Full-time tuition and fees vary according to program. Room and board charges vary according to board plan and housing facility. **Part-time tuition:** $556 per credit hour. Part-time tuition and fees vary according to course load and program. **Payment plan:** Tuition prepayment.

FRESHMAN FINANCIAL AID (Fall 2016, est.) 1,137 applied for aid; of those 90% were deemed to have need. 100% of freshmen with need received aid; of those

13% had need fully met. **Average percent of need met:** 66% (excluding resources awarded to replace EFC). **Average financial aid package:** $25,502 (excluding resources awarded to replace EFC). 16% of all full-time freshmen had no need and received non-need-based gift aid.

UNDERGRADUATE FINANCIAL AID (Fall 2016, est.) 3,602 applied for aid; of those 92% were deemed to have need. 99% of undergraduates with need received aid; of those 15% had need fully met. **Average percent of need met:** 68% (excluding resources awarded to replace EFC). **Average financial aid package:** $25,950 (excluding resources awarded to replace EFC). 19% of all full-time undergraduates had no need and received non-need-based gift aid.

GIFT AID (NEED-BASED) Total amount: $65,389,116 (10% federal, 1% state, 88% institutional, 1% external sources). **Receiving aid:** Freshmen: 80% (1,016); all full-time undergraduates: 72% (3,231). **Average award:** Freshmen: $21,397; Undergraduates: $20,600. **Scholarships, grants, and awards:** Federal Pell, FSEOG, state, private, college/university gift aid from institutional funds.

GIFT AID (NON-NEED-BASED) Total amount: $15,649,207 (99% institutional, 1% external sources). **Receiving aid:** Freshmen: 9% (112). Undergraduates: 7% (323). **Average award:** Freshmen: $17,147. Undergraduates: $15,431. **Scholarships, grants, and awards by category:** *Academic interests/achievement:* architecture, area/ethnic studies, biological sciences, business, communication, computer science, education, engineering/technologies, English, foreign languages, general academic interests/achievements, home economics, humanities, international studies, mathematics, premedicine, religion/biblical studies, social sciences. *Creative arts/performance:* applied art and design, art/fine arts, cinema/film/broadcasting, creative writing, dance, debating, general creative arts/performance, journalism/publications, music, performing arts, theater/drama. *Special achievements/activities:* community service, leadership. *Special characteristics:* adult students, children of current students, children of faculty/staff, children of union members/company employees, children with a deceased or disabled parent, ethnic background, first-generation college students, handicapped students, international students, local/state students, members of minority groups, parents of current students, previous college experience, religious affiliation, siblings of current students, spouses of current students, twins, veterans, veterans' children. **Tuition waivers:** Full or partial for employees or children of employees, senior citizens. **ROTC:** Army cooperative, Air Force cooperative.

LOANS Student loans: $39,772,643 (69% need-based, 31% non-need-based). **Average need-based loan:** Freshmen: $3568. Undergraduates: $4557. **Parent loans:** $16,074,351 (60% need-based, 40% non-need-based). **Programs:** Federal Direct (Subsidized and Unsubsidized Stafford, PLUS), Perkins.

WORK-STUDY Federal work-study: Total amount: $660,744; 449 jobs averaging $1472. **State or other work-study/employment:** Total amount: $1,556,220 (71% need-based, 29% non-need-based). Part-time jobs available.

ATHLETIC AWARDS Total amount: $5,347,316 (30% need-based, 70% non-need-based).

APPLYING FOR FINANCIAL AID Required financial aid form: FAFSA. **Financial aid deadline (priority):** 2/15. **Notification date:** Continuous beginning 3/1. Students must reply by 5/1 or within 2 weeks of notification.

CONTACT Victoria Hampton, Office of Financial Aid, University of Hartford, 200 Bloomfield Avenue, West Hartford, CT 06117-1599, 860-768-4296 or toll-free 800-947-4303. *Fax:* 860-768-4961. *E-mail:* finaid@hartford.edu. *Website:* http://www.hartford.edu/.

UNIVERSITY OF HAWAII AT HILO
Hilo, HI

CONTACT Financial Aid Office, University of Hawaii at Hilo, 200 West Kawili Street, Hilo, HI 96720-4091, 808-932-7449 or toll-free 800-897-4456. *Fax:* 808-932-7459. *E-mail:* uhhfao@hawaii.edu. *Website:* http://hilo.hawaii.edu/.

UNIVERSITY OF HAWAII AT MANOA
Honolulu, HI

Tuition & fees (HI res): $11,732	Average undergraduate aid package: $14,840

ABOUT THE INSTITUTION State-supported, coed. *Awards:* certificates, bachelor's, master's, and doctoral degrees. 90 undergraduate majors. *Total enrollment:* 18,056. Undergraduates: 13,132. Freshmen: 1,972. Federal methodology is used as a basis for awarding need-based institutional aid.

UNDERGRADUATE EXPENSES for 2017–2018 *Application fee:* $70. *Tuition, state resident:* full-time $10,872; part-time $453 per credit hour. *Tuition, nonresident:* full-time $32,904; part-time $1371 per credit hour. *Required fees:* full-time $860; $430 per term. Full-time tuition and fees vary according to class time, course level, course load, degree level, program, reciprocity agreements, and student level. Part-time tuition and fees vary according to class time, course level, course load, degree level, program, reciprocity agreements, and student level. Room and board charges vary according to board plan and housing facility.

FRESHMAN FINANCIAL AID (Fall 2016, est.) 1,521 applied for aid; of those 66% were deemed to have need. 98% of freshmen with need received aid; of those 32% had need fully met. *Average percent of need met:* 70% (excluding resources awarded to replace EFC). *Average financial aid package:* $14,723 (excluding resources awarded to replace EFC). 25% of all full-time freshmen had no need and received non-need-based gift aid.

UNDERGRADUATE FINANCIAL AID (Fall 2016, est.) 8,704 applied for aid; of those 68% were deemed to have need. 98% of undergraduates with need received aid; of those 30% had need fully met. *Average percent of need met:* 70% (excluding resources awarded to replace EFC). *Average financial aid package:* $14,840 (excluding resources awarded to replace EFC). 22% of all full-time undergraduates had no need and received non-need-based gift aid.

GIFT AID (NEED-BASED) *Total amount:* $42,975,752 (40% federal, 4% state, 50% institutional, 6% external sources). *Receiving aid:* Freshmen: 56% (970); all full-time undergraduates: 52% (5,609). *Average award:* Freshmen: $9831; Undergraduates: $9779. *Scholarships, grants, and awards:* Federal Pell, FSEOG, state, private, college/university gift aid from institutional funds.

GIFT AID (NON-NEED-BASED) *Total amount:* $16,567,407 (58% institutional, 42% external sources). *Receiving aid:* Freshmen: 14% (236). Undergraduates: 12% (1,309). *Average award:* Freshmen: $12,152. Undergraduates: $12,779. *Scholarships, grants, and awards by category:* Academic interests/achievement: general academic interests/achievements. Creative arts/performance: general creative arts/performance. Special achievements/activities: general special achievements/activities. Special characteristics: general special characteristics. *Tuition waivers:* Full or partial for minority students, employees or children of employees, adult students, senior citizens. *ROTC:* Army, Air Force.

LOANS *Student loans:* $38,710,584 (50% need-based, 50% non-need-based). 47% of past graduating class borrowed through all loan programs. *Average indebtedness per student:* $24,665. *Average need-based loan:* Freshmen: $3622. Undergraduates: $4601. *Parent loans:* $27,873,653 (100% non-need-based). *Programs:* Federal Direct (Subsidized and Unsubsidized Stafford, PLUS), Perkins, state.

WORK-STUDY *Federal work-study:* Total amount: $1,281,564; 553 jobs averaging $2317. *State or other work-study/employment:* Part-time jobs available.

ATHLETIC AWARDS Total amount: $8,100,294 (1% need-based, 99% non-need-based).

APPLYING FOR FINANCIAL AID *Required financial aid form:* FAFSA. *Financial aid deadline (priority):* 2/1. *Notification date:* Continuous beginning 12/1. Students must reply by 5/1 or within 4 weeks of notification.

CONTACT Jodie Kuba, Director of Financial Aid Services, University of Hawaii at Manoa, 2600 Campus Road, Suite 112, Honolulu, HI 96822, 808-956-7251 or toll-free 800-823-9771. *Fax:* 808-956-3985. *E-mail:* finaid@hawaii.edu. *Website:* http://manoa.hawaii.edu/.

UNIVERSITY OF HAWAII–WEST OAHU
Kapolei, HI

ABOUT THE INSTITUTION State-supported, coed. *Awards:* certificates and bachelor's degrees. 21 undergraduate majors. *Total enrollment:* 2,692. Undergraduates: 2,692. Freshmen: 254.

GIFT AID (NEED-BASED) *Scholarships, grants, and awards:* Federal Pell, FSEOG, state, private, college/university gift aid from institutional funds.

LOANS *Programs:* Federal Direct (Subsidized and Unsubsidized Stafford, PLUS).

APPLYING FOR FINANCIAL AID *Required financial aid form:* FAFSA.

CONTACT Lester Ishimoto, Office of Financial Aid, University of Hawaii–West Oahu, 91-1001 Farrington Highway, Kapolei, HI 96707, 808-689-2689 or toll-free 866-299-8656. *Fax:* 808-689-2691. *E-mail:* uhwo-finaid-l@lists.hawaii.edu. *Website:* http://www.uhwo.hawaii.edu/.

UNIVERSITY OF HOLY CROSS
New Orleans, LA

Tuition & fees: $11,632	Average undergraduate aid package: $7807

ABOUT THE INSTITUTION Independent Roman Catholic, coed. 17 undergraduate majors. Federal methodology is used as a basis for awarding need-based institutional aid.

UNDERGRADUATE EXPENSES for 2016–2017 *Tuition:* full-time $10,440; part-time $435 per credit hour. *Required fees:* full-time $1192; $535 per term. Full-time tuition and fees vary according to course load, degree level, and program. Part-time tuition and fees vary according to course load, degree level, and program.

FRESHMAN FINANCIAL AID (Fall 2015) 85 applied for aid; of those 84% were deemed to have need. 87% of freshmen with need received aid; of those 16% had need fully met. *Average percent of need met:* 36% (excluding resources awarded to replace EFC). *Average financial aid package:* $8107 (excluding resources awarded to replace EFC). 3% of all full-time freshmen had no need and received non-need-based gift aid.

UNDERGRADUATE FINANCIAL AID (Fall 2015) 500 applied for aid; of those 90% were deemed to have need. 92% of undergraduates with need received aid; of those 5% had need fully met. *Average percent of need met:* 27% (excluding resources awarded to replace EFC). *Average financial aid package:* $7807 (excluding resources awarded to replace EFC). 1% of all full-time undergraduates had no need and received non-need-based gift aid.

GIFT AID (NEED-BASED) *Total amount:* $2,470,609 (69% federal, 18% state, 3% institutional, 10% external sources). *Receiving aid:* Freshmen: 67% (58); all full-time undergraduates: 67% (337). *Average award:* Freshmen: $6360; Undergraduates: $5762. *Scholarships, grants, and awards:* Federal Pell, FSEOG, state, private, college/university gift aid from institutional funds, United Negro College Fund.

GIFT AID (NON-NEED-BASED) *Total amount:* $283,761 (71% state, 8% institutional, 21% external sources). *Receiving aid:* Freshmen: 6% (5). Undergraduates: 2% (11). *Average award:* Freshmen: $5972. Undergraduates: $3486. *Scholarships, grants, and awards by category:* Academic interests/achievement: biological sciences, business, education, English, general academic interests/achievements, health fields, home economics, humanities, premedicine, religion/biblical studies, social sciences. Special characteristics: children of faculty/staff, general special characteristics, relatives of clergy, religious affiliation. *Tuition waivers:* Full or partial for employees or children of employees.

LOANS *Student loans:* $5,060,391 (92% need-based, 8% non-need-based). 91% of past graduating class borrowed through all loan programs. *Average indebtedness per student:* $43,123. *Average need-based loan:* Freshmen: $2957. Undergraduates: $3561. *Parent loans:* $117,773 (48% need-based, 52% non-need-based). *Programs:* Federal Direct (Subsidized and Unsubsidized Stafford, PLUS), state.

WORK-STUDY *Federal work-study:* jobs available.

APPLYING FOR FINANCIAL AID *Required financial aid form:* FAFSA. *Financial aid deadline:* Continuous. *Notification date:* Continuous beginning 1/1.

CONTACT Ms. Hayden Wagar, Director of Financial Aid, University of Holy Cross, 4123 Woodland Drive, New Orleans, LA 70131-7399, 504-398-2133 or toll-free 800-259-7744. *Fax:* 504-394-1237. *E-mail:* hwagar@uhcno.edu. *Website:* http://www.uhcno.edu/.

UNIVERSITY OF HOUSTON
Houston, TX

Tuition & fees (TX res): $11,653	Average undergraduate aid package: $12,167

ABOUT THE INSTITUTION State-supported, coed. **Awards:** bachelor's, master's, and doctoral degrees. 87 undergraduate majors. **Total enrollment:** 43,774. Undergraduates: 35,871. Freshmen: 4,463. Federal methodology is used as a basis for awarding need-based institutional aid.

UNDERGRADUATE EXPENSES for 2016–2017 Application fee: $75. **Tuition, state resident:** full-time $10,671; part-time $356 per credit hour. **Tuition, nonresident:** full-time $25,911; part-time $864 per credit hour. **Required fees:** full-time $982. Full-time tuition and fees vary according to course level, course load, degree level, program, and student level. Part-time tuition and fees vary according to course level, course load, degree level, program, and student level. **College room and board:** $9830. Room and board charges vary according to board plan and housing facility. **Payment plan:** Guaranteed tuition.

FRESHMAN FINANCIAL AID (Fall 2016, est.) 3,329 applied for aid; of those 79% were deemed to have need. 95% of freshmen with need received aid; of those 18% had need fully met. **Average percent of need met:** 64% (excluding resources awarded to replace EFC). **Average financial aid package:** $12,922 (excluding resources awarded to replace EFC). 9% of all full-time freshmen had no need and received non-need-based gift aid.

UNDERGRADUATE FINANCIAL AID (Fall 2016, est.) 17,691 applied for aid; of those 88% were deemed to have need. 95% of undergraduates with need received aid; of those 14% had need fully met. **Average percent of need met:** 58% (excluding resources awarded to replace EFC). **Average financial aid package:** $12,167 (excluding resources awarded to replace EFC). 3% of all full-time undergraduates had no need and received non-need-based gift aid.

GIFT AID (NEED-BASED) Total amount: $117,955,596 (49% federal, 20% state, 25% institutional, 6% external sources). **Receiving aid:** Freshmen: 52% (2,205); all full-time undergraduates: 48% (12,223). **Average award:** Freshmen: $10,308; Undergraduates: $8121. **Scholarships, grants, and awards:** Federal Pell, FSEOG, state, private, college/university gift aid from institutional funds.

GIFT AID (NON-NEED-BASED) Total amount: $6,458,966 (1% state, 76% institutional, 23% external sources). **Receiving aid:** Freshmen: 4% (178). Undergraduates: 2% (520). **Average award:** Freshmen: $5924. Undergraduates: $5233. **Scholarships, grants, and awards by category:** Academic interests/achievement: architecture, area/ethnic studies, biological sciences, business, communication, computer science, education, engineering/technologies, English, foreign languages, general academic interests/achievements, health fields, humanities, international studies, library science, mathematics, military science, physical sciences, premedicine, social sciences. Creative arts/performance: art/fine arts, creative writing, dance, journalism/publications, music, performing arts, theater/drama. Special achievements/activities: cheerleading/drum major, community service, general special achievements/activities, hobbies/interests, leadership. Special characteristics: children and siblings of alumni, first-generation college students, handicapped students, international students, local/state students, out-of-state students, previous college experience. **ROTC:** Army, Naval cooperative, Air Force.

LOANS Student loans: $114,520,991 (84% need-based, 16% non-need-based). 51% of past graduating class borrowed through all loan programs. Average indebtedness per student: $23,665. **Average need-based loan:** Freshmen: $5475. Undergraduates: $7389. **Parent loans:** $10,303,199 (43% need-based, 57% non-need-based). **Programs:** Federal Direct (Subsidized and Unsubsidized Stafford, PLUS), Perkins, state.

WORK-STUDY Federal work-study: Total amount: $3,353,797; 858 jobs averaging $3909. **State or other work-study/employment:** Part-time jobs available.

ATHLETIC AWARDS Total amount: $6,266,950 (75% need-based, 25% non-need-based).

APPLYING FOR FINANCIAL AID Required financial aid form: FAFSA. **Financial aid deadline (priority):** 3/15. **Notification date:** Continuous beginning 2/1.

CONTACT Office of Scholarships and Financial Aid, University of Houston, 4800 Calhoun Road, Houston, TX 77204, 713-743-1010. Fax: 713-743-9098. Website: http://www.uh.edu/.

UNIVERSITY OF HOUSTON–CLEAR LAKE
Houston, TX

Tuition & fees: N/R	Average undergraduate aid package: $8122

ABOUT THE INSTITUTION State-supported, coed. **Awards:** certificates, bachelor's, master's, and doctoral degrees. 34 undergraduate majors. **Total enrollment:** 8,669. Undergraduates: 5,570. Freshmen: 196. Federal methodology is used as a basis for awarding need-based institutional aid.

FRESHMAN FINANCIAL AID (Fall 2015) 168 applied for aid; of those 73% were deemed to have need. 91% of freshmen with need received aid; of those 12% had need fully met. **Average percent of need met:** 58% (excluding resources awarded to replace EFC). **Average financial aid package:** $9815 (excluding resources awarded to replace EFC). 9% of all full-time freshmen had no need and received non-need-based gift aid.

UNDERGRADUATE FINANCIAL AID (Fall 2015) 1,928 applied for aid; of those 93% were deemed to have need. 95% of undergraduates with need received aid; of those 4% had need fully met. **Average percent of need met:** 44% (excluding resources awarded to replace EFC). **Average financial aid package:** $8122 (excluding resources awarded to replace EFC). 6% of all full-time undergraduates had no need and received non-need-based gift aid.

GIFT AID (NEED-BASED) Total amount: $12,621,963 (65% federal, 9% state, 24% institutional, 2% external sources). **Receiving aid:** Freshmen: 40% (69); all full-time undergraduates: 28% (1,250). **Average award:** Freshmen: $10,025; Undergraduates: $6097. **Scholarships, grants, and awards:** Federal Pell, FSEOG, state, private, college/university gift aid from institutional funds.

GIFT AID (NON-NEED-BASED) Total amount: $2,070,981 (9% federal, 72% institutional, 19% external sources). **Receiving aid:** Freshmen: 24% (41). Undergraduates: 14% (627). **Average award:** Freshmen: $7687. Undergraduates: $1229. **Scholarships, grants, and awards by category:** Academic interests/achievement: biological sciences, business, computer science, education, humanities, mathematics, social sciences. Creative arts/performance: art/fine arts. Special achievements/activities: community service, general special achievements/activities, leadership. Special characteristics: local/state students, veterans, veterans' children.

LOANS Student loans: $16,086,999 (46% need-based, 54% non-need-based). **Average need-based loan:** Freshmen: $3083. Undergraduates: $4317. **Parent loans:** $215,709 (100% non-need-based). **Programs:** Federal Direct (Subsidized and Unsubsidized Stafford, PLUS), Perkins, state, college/university.

WORK-STUDY Federal work-study: jobs available. **State or other work-study/employment:** Total amount: $49,628 (100% need-based). Part-time jobs available.

APPLYING FOR FINANCIAL AID Required financial aid form: FAFSA. **Financial aid deadline (priority):** 3/15. **Notification date:** Continuous beginning 4/1. Students must reply within 2 weeks of notification.

CONTACT Dr. Billy Satterfield, Executive Director of Student Financial Aid, University of Houston–Clear Lake, 2700 Bay Area Boulevard, Houston, TX 77058-1098, 281-283-2480. Fax: 281-283-2502. E-mail: satterfield@uhcl.edu. Website: http://www.uhcl.edu/.

UNIVERSITY OF HOUSTON–DOWNTOWN
Houston, TX

Tuition & fees: N/R	Average undergraduate aid package: $9191

ABOUT THE INSTITUTION State-supported, coed. **Awards:** certificates, bachelor's, and master's degrees. 37 undergraduate majors. **Total enrollment:** 14,251. Undergraduates: 11,865. Freshmen: 939. Federal methodology is used as a basis for awarding need-based institutional aid.

UNDERGRADUATE EXPENSES for 2017–2018 Application fee: $35. **Tuition, state resident:** part-time $202.50 per credit hour. **Tuition, nonresident:** part-time $610.50 per credit hour. Full-time tuition and fees vary according to course load and program. Part-time tuition and fees vary according to course load and program.

FRESHMAN FINANCIAL AID (Fall 2016, est.) 752 applied for aid; of those 85% were deemed to have need. 91% of freshmen with need received aid; of those 3% had need fully met. *Average percent of need met:* 61% (excluding resources awarded to replace EFC). *Average financial aid package:* $9035 (excluding resources awarded to replace EFC).

UNDERGRADUATE FINANCIAL AID (Fall 2016, est.) 5,080 applied for aid; of those 90% were deemed to have need. 100% of undergraduates with need received aid; of those 4% had need fully met. *Average percent of need met:* 57% (excluding resources awarded to replace EFC). *Average financial aid package:* $9191 (excluding resources awarded to replace EFC). 5% of all full-time undergraduates had no need and received non-need-based gift aid.

GIFT AID (NEED-BASED) *Total amount:* $32,504,741 (79% federal, 10% state, 11% institutional). *Receiving aid:* Freshmen: 68% (566); all full-time undergraduates: 72% (4,579). *Average award:* Freshmen: $12,002; Undergraduates: $4679. *Scholarships, grants, and awards:* Federal Pell, FSEOG, state, private, college/university gift aid from institutional funds.

GIFT AID (NON-NEED-BASED) *Total amount:* $4,526,541 (1% federal, 8% state, 81% institutional, 10% external sources). *Receiving aid:* Freshmen: 16% (133). Undergraduates: 21% (1,317). *Average award:* Undergraduates: $1987. *Scholarships, grants, and awards by category:* Academic interests/achievement: business, general academic interests/achievements. *Special achievements/activities:* community service, general special achievements/activities, leadership. *Special characteristics:* general special characteristics. *Tuition waivers:* Full or partial for senior citizens. *ROTC:* Army cooperative, Air Force cooperative.

LOANS *Student loans:* $39,962,909 (99% need-based, 1% non-need-based). 54% of past graduating class borrowed through all loan programs. *Average indebtedness per student:* $23,874. *Average need-based loan:* Freshmen: $4277. Undergraduates: $8177. *Parent loans:* $192,585 (100% need-based). *Programs:* Federal Direct (Subsidized and Unsubsidized Stafford, PLUS), state.

WORK-STUDY *Federal work-study:* Total amount: $846,117; jobs available. *State or other work-study/employment:* Total amount: $106,191 (100% need-based). Part-time jobs available.

APPLYING FOR FINANCIAL AID *Required financial aid form:* FAFSA. *Financial aid deadline (priority):* 4/1. *Notification date:* Continuous beginning 4/15. Students must reply within 4 weeks of notification.

CONTACT Office of Scholarships and Financial Aid, University of Houston–Downtown, One Main Street, Houston, TX 77002, 713-221-8041. *Fax:* 713-221-7483. *E-mail:* uhdfinaid@uhd.edu. *Website:* http://www.uhd.edu/.

UNIVERSITY OF HOUSTON–VICTORIA
Victoria, TX

Tuition & fees (TX res): $7368	Average undergraduate aid package: $9958

ABOUT THE INSTITUTION State-supported, coed. 16 undergraduate majors. Federal methodology is used as a basis for awarding need-based institutional aid.

UNDERGRADUATE EXPENSES for 2016–2017 *Tuition, state resident:* full-time $5720; part-time $190.70 per credit hour. *Tuition, nonresident:* full-time $17,960; part-time $598.70 per credit hour. *Required fees:* full-time $1648; $80.30 per credit hour. Full-time tuition and fees vary according to course level and course load. Part-time tuition and fees vary according to course level and course load. *College room and board:* $7664. Room and board charges vary according to board plan and housing facility.

UNDERGRADUATE FINANCIAL AID (Fall 2015) 1,248 applied for aid; of those 91% were deemed to have need. 98% of undergraduates with need received aid; of those 18% had need fully met. *Average percent of need met:* 71% (excluding resources awarded to replace EFC). *Average financial aid package:* $9958 (excluding resources awarded to replace EFC). 4% of all full-time undergraduates had no need and received non-need-based gift aid.

GIFT AID (NEED-BASED) *Total amount:* $8,485,305 (67% federal, 18% state, 15% institutional). *Receiving aid:* Entering class: 76% (213); all full-time undergraduates: 68% (1,037). *Average award:* Freshmen: $8548; Undergraduates: $5929. *Scholarships, grants, and awards:* Federal Pell, FSEOG, state, private, college/university gift aid from institutional funds.

GIFT AID (NON-NEED-BASED) *Total amount:* $1,119,672 (3% federal, 77% institutional, 20% external sources). *Receiving aid:* Freshmen: 72% (201). Undergraduates: 36% (550). *Average award:* Freshmen: $1352. Undergraduates: $1267. *Scholarships, grants, and awards by category:* Academic interests/achievement: biological sciences, business, communication, computer science, education, general academic interests/achievements, humanities, mathematics, social sciences. *Special achievements/activities:* community service, leadership, memberships. *Tuition waivers:* Full or partial for senior citizens.

LOANS *Student loans:* $11,747,442 (44% need-based, 56% non-need-based). *Average need-based loan:* Undergraduates: $3803. *Parent loans:* $236,074 (100% non-need-based). *Programs:* Federal Direct (Subsidized and Unsubsidized Stafford, PLUS), state.

WORK-STUDY *Federal work-study:* jobs available. *State or other work-study/employment:* Total amount: $21,053 (100% need-based). Part-time jobs available.

ATHLETIC AWARDS Total amount: $256,150 (100% non-need-based).

APPLYING FOR FINANCIAL AID *Required financial aid forms:* FAFSA, institution's own form. *Financial aid deadline (priority):* 3/15. *Notification date:* Continuous beginning 3/30. Students must reply within 3 weeks of notification.

CONTACT Carolyn Mallory, Director of Financial Aid, University of Houston–Victoria, 3007 North Ben Wilson, Victoria, TX 77901-5731, 361-570-4131 or toll-free 877-970-4848 Ext. 110. *Fax:* 361-580-5555. *E-mail:* malloryc@uhv.edu. *Website:* http://www.uhv.edu/.

UNIVERSITY OF IDAHO
Moscow, ID

Tuition & fees (ID res): $7232	Average undergraduate aid package: $13,811

ABOUT THE INSTITUTION State-supported, coed. *Awards:* certificates, bachelor's, master's, and doctoral degrees. 91 undergraduate majors. *Total enrollment:* 11,780. Undergraduates: 9,586. Freshmen: 1,660. Federal methodology is used as a basis for awarding need-based institutional aid.

UNDERGRADUATE EXPENSES for 2016–2017 *Application fee:* $60. *Tuition, state resident:* full-time $5162; part-time $302 per credit hour. *Tuition, nonresident:* full-time $19,970; part-time $1042 per credit hour. *Required fees:* full-time $2070; $60 per credit hour or $60 per credit hour. Full-time tuition and fees vary according to course load, program, and reciprocity agreements. Part-time tuition and fees vary according to program and reciprocity agreements. *College room and board:* $8354. Room and board charges vary according to board plan.

FRESHMAN FINANCIAL AID (Fall 2015) 1,422 applied for aid; of those 75% were deemed to have need. 99% of freshmen with need received aid; of those 36% had need fully met. *Average percent of need met:* 79% (excluding resources awarded to replace EFC). *Average financial aid package:* $13,894 (excluding resources awarded to replace EFC). 28% of all full-time freshmen had no need and received non-need-based gift aid.

UNDERGRADUATE FINANCIAL AID (Fall 2015) 6,228 applied for aid; of those 82% were deemed to have need. 98% of undergraduates with need received aid; of those 31% had need fully met. *Average percent of need met:* 76% (excluding resources awarded to replace EFC). *Average financial aid package:* $13,811 (excluding resources awarded to replace EFC). 21% of all full-time undergraduates had no need and received non-need-based gift aid.

GIFT AID (NEED-BASED) *Total amount:* $19,197,421 (75% federal, 11% state, 14% institutional). *Receiving aid:* Freshmen: 44% (718); all full-time undergraduates: 51% (3,721). *Average award:* Freshmen: $4727; Undergraduates: $4768. *Scholarships, grants, and awards:* Federal Pell, FSEOG, state, private, college/university gift aid from institutional funds.

GIFT AID (NON-NEED-BASED) *Total amount:* $12,254,563 (1% state, 80% institutional, 19% external sources). *Receiving aid:* Freshmen: 56% (910). Undergraduates: 40% (2,932). *Average award:* Freshmen: $5027. Undergraduates: $5058. *Scholarships, grants, and awards by category:* Academic interests/achievement: agriculture, architecture, biological sciences, business, communication, computer science, education, engineering/technologies, English, foreign languages, general academic interests/achievements, health fields, home economics, humanities, international studies, library science, mathematics, military science, physical sciences, premedicine, social sciences. *Creative arts/performance:* applied art and design, art/fine arts, creative writing, dance, general creative arts/performance, journalism/publications, music, performing arts, theater/drama. *Special achievements/activities:* cheerleading/drum major, general special achievements/activities, junior miss, leadership, rodeo. *Special characteristics:* adult students, children and siblings of alumni, children of faculty/staff, ethnic background, first-generation college students, general special characteristics, handicapped students, international students, local/state students, members of minority groups, out-of-state students, veterans, veterans' children. *Tuition waivers:* Full or partial for employees or children of employees. **ROTC:** Army, Naval, Air Force cooperative.

LOANS *Student loans:* $36,159,846 (50% need-based, 50% non-need-based). 64% of past graduating class borrowed through all loan programs. *Average indebtedness per student:* $26,539. *Average need-based loan:* Freshmen: $5286. Undergraduates: $6842. *Parent loans:* $9,422,060 (100% non-need-based). **Programs:** Federal Direct (Subsidized and Unsubsidized Stafford, PLUS), Perkins, college/university.

WORK-STUDY *Federal work-study:* 457 jobs averaging $1247. *State or other work-study/employment:* Total amount: $229,687 (100% need-based). 157 part-time jobs averaging $1463.

ATHLETIC AWARDS Total amount: $5,885,465 (100% non-need-based).

APPLYING FOR FINANCIAL AID *Required financial aid form:* FAFSA. *Financial aid deadline (priority):* 12/1. *Notification date:* Continuous beginning 12/22. Students must reply within 4 weeks of notification.

CONTACT Mr. Dan D. Davenport, Director of Student Financial Aid Services, University of Idaho, 875 Perimeter Drive, MS-4291, Moscow, ID 83844-4291, 208-885-6312 or toll-free 888-884-3246. *Fax:* 208-885-5592. *E-mail:* dand@uidaho.edu. *Website:* http://www.uidaho.edu/.

UNIVERSITY OF ILLINOIS AT CHICAGO
Chicago, IL

Tuition & fees (IL res): $13,664	Average undergraduate aid package: $14,546

ABOUT THE INSTITUTION State-supported, coed. *Awards:* certificates, bachelor's, master's, and doctoral degrees. 86 undergraduate majors. *Total enrollment:* 29,120. Undergraduates: 17,959. Freshmen: 3,307. Federal methodology is used as a basis for awarding need-based institutional aid.

UNDERGRADUATE EXPENSES for 2016–2017 *Application fee:* $50. *Tuition, state resident:* full-time $10,584. *Tuition, nonresident:* full-time $23,440. *Required fees:* full-time $3080. Full-time tuition and fees vary according to degree level and program. Part-time tuition and fees vary according to course load, degree level, and program. *College room and board:* $10,882; *Room only:* $7891. Room and board charges vary according to board plan and housing facility. *Payment plan:* Guaranteed tuition.

FRESHMAN FINANCIAL AID (Fall 2015) 3,150 applied for aid; of those 87% were deemed to have need. 95% of freshmen with need received aid; of those 11% had need fully met. *Average percent of need met:* 62% (excluding resources awarded to replace EFC). *Average financial aid package:* $14,896 (excluding resources awarded to replace EFC). 4% of all full-time freshmen had no need and received non-need-based gift aid.

UNDERGRADUATE FINANCIAL AID (Fall 2015) 13,536 applied for aid; of those 91% were deemed to have need. 97% of undergraduates with need received aid; of those 9% had need fully met. *Average percent of need met:* 61% (excluding resources awarded to replace EFC). *Average financial aid package:* $14,546 (excluding resources awarded to replace EFC). 3% of all full-time undergraduates had no need and received non-need-based gift aid.

GIFT AID (NEED-BASED) *Total amount:* $125,175,090 (33% federal, 26% state, 39% institutional, 2% external sources). *Receiving aid:* Freshmen: 68% (2,335); all full-time undergraduates: 63% (9,987). *Average award:* Freshmen: $13,899; Undergraduates: $13,099. *Scholarships, grants, and awards:* Federal Pell, FSEOG, state, private, college/university gift aid from institutional funds.

GIFT AID (NON-NEED-BASED) *Total amount:* $2,877,864 (15% state, 71% institutional, 14% external sources). *Receiving aid:* Freshmen: 4% (122). Undergraduates: 2% (310). *Average award:* Freshmen: $5926. Undergraduates: $5564. *Scholarships, grants, and awards by category:* Academic interests/achievement: 1,371 awards ($8,021,789 total): architecture, business, general academic interests/achievements. Creative arts/performance: 183 awards ($683,313 total): applied art and design, art/fine arts, creative writing, music, performing arts, theater/drama. *Tuition*

waivers: Full or partial for employees or children of employees, senior citizens. **ROTC:** Army, Naval cooperative, Air Force cooperative.

LOANS *Student loans:* $63,143,867 (89% need-based, 11% non-need-based). 63% of past graduating class borrowed through all loan programs. *Average indebtedness per student:* $24,601. *Average need-based loan:* Freshmen: $3258. Undergraduates: $4311. *Parent loans:* $17,938,837 (84% need-based, 16% non-need-based). **Programs:** Federal Direct (Subsidized and Unsubsidized Stafford, PLUS), Perkins, Federal Nursing, college/university, private loans.

WORK-STUDY *Federal work-study:* 883 jobs averaging $2500. *State or other work-study/employment:* Total amount: $8,159,067 (77% need-based, 23% non-need-based). 3,225 part-time jobs averaging $2500.

ATHLETIC AWARDS Total amount: $4,302,161 (41% need-based, 59% non-need-based).

APPLYING FOR FINANCIAL AID *Required financial aid form:* FAFSA. *Financial aid deadline (priority):* 2/15. *Notification date:* Continuous beginning 3/15. Students must reply by 5/1.

CONTACT Deidre Rush, Associate Director of Financial Aid, University of Illinois at Chicago, 1200 West Harrison, M/C 334, Suite 1800, Chicago, IL 60607-7128, 312-996-5563. *Fax:* 312-996-3385. *E-mail:* deidreb@uic.edu. *Website:* http://www.uic.edu/.

UNIVERSITY OF ILLINOIS AT SPRINGFIELD
Springfield, IL

Tuition & fees (IL res): $12,609	Average undergraduate aid package: $13,364

ABOUT THE INSTITUTION State-supported, coed. *Awards:* certificates, bachelor's, master's, and doctoral degrees. 27 undergraduate majors. *Total enrollment:* 5,428. Undergraduates: 2,959. Freshmen: 300. Federal methodology is used as a basis for awarding need-based institutional aid.

UNDERGRADUATE EXPENSES for 2017–2018 *Application fee:* $50. *Tuition, state resident:* full-time $9405; part-time $313.50 per credit hour. *Tuition, nonresident:* full-time $18,930; part-time $631 per credit hour. *Required fees:* full-time $3204; $18.40 per credit hour or $1106 per term. Full-time tuition and fees vary according to course load. Part-time tuition and fees vary according to course load. *College room and board:* $11,600; *Room only:* $7460. Room and board charges vary according to board plan and housing facility. *Payment plan:* Guaranteed tuition.

FRESHMAN FINANCIAL AID (Fall 2015) 244 applied for aid; of those 84% were deemed to have need. 97% of freshmen with need received aid; of those 23% had need fully met. *Average percent of need met:* 79% (excluding resources awarded to replace EFC). *Average financial aid package:* $16,348 (excluding resources awarded to replace EFC). 19% of all full-time freshmen had no need and received non-need-based gift aid.

UNDERGRADUATE FINANCIAL AID (Fall 2015) 1,527 applied for aid; of those 83% were deemed to have need. 98% of undergraduates with need received aid; of those 15% had need fully met. *Average percent of need met:* 69% (excluding resources awarded to replace EFC). *Average financial aid package:* $13,364 (excluding resources awarded to replace EFC). 16% of all full-time undergraduates had no need and received non-need-based gift aid.

GIFT AID (NEED-BASED) *Total amount:* $11,747,193 (39% federal, 25% state, 33% institutional, 3% external sources). *Receiving aid:* Freshmen: 73% (194); all full-time undergraduates: 59% (1,126). *Average award:* Freshmen: $13,815; Undergraduates: $10,582. *Scholarships, grants, and awards:* Federal Pell, FSEOG, state, private, college/university gift aid from institutional funds.

GIFT AID (NON-NEED-BASED) *Total amount:* $2,561,092 (9% federal, 18% state, 59% institutional, 14% external sources). *Receiving aid:* Freshmen: 14% (38). Undergraduates: 10% (187). *Average award:* Freshmen: $7615. Undergraduates: $7788. *Tuition waivers:* Full or partial for employees or children of employees, senior citizens.

LOANS *Student loans:* $11,498,264 (89% need-based, 11% non-need-based). 69% of past graduating class borrowed through all loan programs. *Average indebtedness per student:* $24,652. *Average need-based loan:* Freshmen: $3108. Undergraduates: $4264. *Parent loans:* $1,515,285 (78% need-based, 22% non-need-based).

Programs: Federal Direct (Subsidized and Unsubsidized Stafford, PLUS), Perkins, college/university.
WORK-STUDY *Federal work-study:* jobs available. *State or other work-study/employment:* Total amount: $1,245,397 (72% need-based, 28% non-need-based). Part-time jobs available.
ATHLETIC AWARDS Total amount: $1,046,994 (55% need-based, 45% non-need-based).
APPLYING FOR FINANCIAL AID *Required financial aid form:* FAFSA. *Financial aid deadline:* 11/15 (priority: 3/1). *Notification date:* Continuous beginning 1/1. Students must reply within 3 weeks of notification.
CONTACT Ms. Carolyn Schloemann, Acting Director of Financial Assistance, University of Illinois at Springfield, One University Plaza, MS UHB 1015, Springfield, IL 62703-5407, 217-206-6724 or toll-free 888-977-4847. Fax: 217-206-7376. E-mail: finaid@uis.edu.
Website: http://www.uis.edu/.

UNIVERSITY OF ILLINOIS AT URBANA–CHAMPAIGN
Champaign, IL

Tuition & fees (IL res): $15,698	Average undergraduate aid package: $16,395

ABOUT THE INSTITUTION State-supported, coed. 219 undergraduate majors. Federal methodology is used as a basis for awarding need-based institutional aid.
UNDERGRADUATE EXPENSES for 2016–2017 *Tuition, state resident:* full-time $12,036. *Tuition, nonresident:* full-time $27,658. *Required fees:* full-time $3662. Full-time tuition and fees vary according to program and student level. *College room and board:* $11,308. Room and board charges vary according to board plan, housing facility, and location. *Payment plan:* Guaranteed tuition.
FRESHMAN FINANCIAL AID (Fall 2015) 5,483 applied for aid; of those 69% were deemed to have need. 93% of freshmen with need received aid; of those 14% had need fully met. *Average percent of need met:* 67% (excluding resources awarded to replace EFC). *Average financial aid package:* $16,886 (excluding resources awarded to replace EFC). 11% of all full-time freshmen had no need and received non-need-based gift aid.
UNDERGRADUATE FINANCIAL AID (Fall 2015) 18,435 applied for aid; of those 100% were deemed to have need. 74% of undergraduates with need received aid; of those 12% had need fully met. *Average percent of need met:* 65% (excluding resources awarded to replace EFC). *Average financial aid package:* $16,395 (excluding resources awarded to replace EFC). 12% of all full-time undergraduates had no need and received non-need-based gift aid.
GIFT AID (NEED-BASED) *Total amount:* $150,881,395 (22% federal, 18% state, 55% institutional, 5% external sources). *Receiving aid:* Freshmen: 41% (3,070); all full-time undergraduates: 38% (11,865). *Average award:* Freshmen: $14,652; Undergraduates: $14,244. *Scholarships, grants, and awards:* Federal Pell, FSEOG, state, private, college/university gift aid from institutional funds, United Negro College Fund.
GIFT AID (NON-NEED-BASED) *Total amount:* $19,062,874 (3% federal, 3% state, 80% institutional, 14% external sources). *Receiving aid:* Freshmen: 8% (629). Undergraduates: 5% (1,467). *Average award:* Freshmen: $5013. Undergraduates: $5240. *Scholarships, grants, and awards by category:* Academic interests/achievement: agriculture, architecture, area/ethnic studies, biological sciences, business, communication, computer science, education, engineering/technologies, English, foreign languages, general academic interests/achievements, health fields, home economics, humanities, international studies, library science, mathematics, military science, physical sciences, premedicine, religion/biblical studies, social sciences. Creative arts/performance: applied art and design, art/fine arts, dance, general creative arts/performance, journalism/publications, music, performing arts, theater/drama. Special achievements/activities: general special achievements/activities, leadership. Special characteristics: children of faculty/staff, first-generation college students, general special characteristics, international students, local/state students, members of minority groups, veterans. *Tuition waivers:* Full or partial for employees or children of employees, senior citizens.
LOANS *Student loans:* $93,484,143 (83% need-based, 17% non-need-based). 47% of past graduating class borrowed through all loan programs. *Average indebtedness per student:* $25,222. *Average need-based loan:* Freshmen: $4405. Undergraduates: $4624. *Parent loans:* $73,520,249 (77% need-based, 23% non-need-based).

Programs: Federal Direct (Subsidized and Unsubsidized Stafford, PLUS), Perkins, college/university.
WORK-STUDY *Federal work-study:* jobs available. *State or other work-study/employment:* Total amount: $19,236,493 (52% need-based, 48% non-need-based). Part-time jobs available.
ATHLETIC AWARDS Total amount: $10,550,941 (37% need-based, 63% non-need-based).
APPLYING FOR FINANCIAL AID *Required financial aid form:* FAFSA. *Financial aid deadline (priority):* 3/15. *Notification date:* 3/15. Students must reply by 5/1 or within 3 weeks of notification.
CONTACT Daniel Mann, Director of Student Financial Aid, University of Illinois at Urbana–Champaign, Student Services Arcade Building, 620 East John Street, Champaign, IL 61820-5711, 217-333-0100.
Website: http://www.illinois.edu/.

UNIVERSITY OF INDIANAPOLIS
Indianapolis, IN

Tuition & fees: $28,390	Average undergraduate aid package: $18,471

ABOUT THE INSTITUTION Independent United Methodist Church, coed. *Awards:* associate, bachelor's, master's, and doctoral degrees. 62 undergraduate majors. *Total enrollment:* 5,711. Undergraduates: 4,346. Freshmen: 994. Federal methodology is used as a basis for awarding need-based institutional aid.
UNDERGRADUATE EXPENSES for 2017–2018 *Application fee:* $25. *Comprehensive fee:* $38,378 includes full-time tuition ($27,860), mandatory fees ($530), and room and board ($9988). Full-time tuition and fees vary according to class time. Room and board charges vary according to board plan and housing facility. Part-time tuition and fees vary according to class time and course load.
FRESHMAN FINANCIAL AID (Fall 2015) 881 applied for aid; of those 88% were deemed to have need. 100% of freshmen with need received aid; of those 15% had need fully met. *Average percent of need met:* 69% (excluding resources awarded to replace EFC). *Average financial aid package:* $19,900 (excluding resources awarded to replace EFC). 13% of all full-time freshmen had no need and received non-need-based gift aid.
UNDERGRADUATE FINANCIAL AID (Fall 2015) 3,253 applied for aid; of those 88% were deemed to have need. 99% of undergraduates with need received aid; of those 11% had need fully met. *Average percent of need met:* 64% (excluding resources awarded to replace EFC). *Average financial aid package:* $18,471 (excluding resources awarded to replace EFC). 14% of all full-time undergraduates had no need and received non-need-based gift aid.
GIFT AID (NEED-BASED) *Total amount:* $16,295,059 (37% federal, 42% state, 21% institutional). *Receiving aid:* Freshmen: 50% (481); all full-time undergraduates: 46% (1,844). *Average award:* Freshmen: $9558; Undergraduates: $8390. *Scholarships, grants, and awards:* Federal Pell, FSEOG, state, private, college/university gift aid from institutional funds.
GIFT AID (NON-NEED-BASED) *Total amount:* $27,874,789 (1% federal, 99% institutional). *Receiving aid:* Freshmen: 78% (750). Undergraduates: 58% (2,301). *Average award:* Freshmen: $12,232. Undergraduates: $10,214. *Scholarships, grants, and awards by category:* Academic interests/achievement: business, communication, general academic interests/achievements, health fields, physical sciences, religion/biblical studies. Creative arts/performance: art/fine arts, debating, music, theater/drama. Special achievements/activities: community service, religious involvement. Special characteristics: children of faculty/staff, international students, out-of-state students, relatives of clergy, religious affiliation, veterans. *Tuition waivers:* Full or partial for employees or children of employees, senior citizens. *ROTC:* Army cooperative.
LOANS *Student loans:* $38,232,928 (100% need-based). 75% of past graduating class borrowed through all loan programs. *Average indebtedness per student:* $36,304. *Average need-based loan:* Freshmen: $3270. Undergraduates: $4565. *Parent loans:* $8,681,011 (100% non-need-based). *Programs:* Federal Direct (Subsidized and Unsubsidized Stafford, PLUS), Perkins.
WORK-STUDY *Federal work-study:* 332 jobs averaging $881. *State or other work-study/employment:* Total amount: $1,226,072 (100% need-based). 165 part-time jobs averaging $7212.
ATHLETIC AWARDS Total amount: $6,288,410 (100% non-need-based).

APPLYING FOR FINANCIAL AID *Required financial aid forms:* FAFSA, institution's own form. *Financial aid deadline (priority):* 3/10. *Notification date:* Continuous beginning 3/1.

CONTACT Ms. Linda B. Handy, Associate Vice President of Financial Aid, University of Indianapolis, 1400 East Hanna Avenue, Indianapolis, IN 46227-3697, 317-788-3217 or toll-free 800-232-8634 Ext. 3216. *Fax:* 317-788-6136. *E-mail:* handy@uindy.edu. *Website:* http://www.uindy.edu/.

THE UNIVERSITY OF IOWA
Iowa City, IA

Tuition & fees: N/R	Average undergraduate aid package: $15,593

ABOUT THE INSTITUTION State-supported, coed. 138 undergraduate majors. Federal methodology is used as a basis for awarding need-based institutional aid.

FRESHMAN FINANCIAL AID (Fall 2015) 3,705 applied for aid; of those 66% were deemed to have need. 100% of freshmen with need received aid; of those 36% had need fully met. *Average percent of need met:* 70% (excluding resources awarded to replace EFC). *Average financial aid package:* $17,645 (excluding resources awarded to replace EFC). 31% of all full-time freshmen had no need and received non-need-based gift aid.

UNDERGRADUATE FINANCIAL AID (Fall 2015) 12,970 applied for aid; of those 72% were deemed to have need. 100% of undergraduates with need received aid; of those 29% had need fully met. *Average percent of need met:* 67% (excluding resources awarded to replace EFC). *Average financial aid package:* $15,593 (excluding resources awarded to replace EFC). 19% of all full-time undergraduates had no need and received non-need-based gift aid.

GIFT AID (NEED-BASED) *Total amount:* $67,780,048 (28% federal, 2% state, 66% institutional, 4% external sources). *Receiving aid:* Freshmen: 37% (1,787); all full-time undergraduates: 35% (6,822). *Average award:* Freshmen: $8225; Undergraduates: $7399. *Scholarships, grants, and awards:* Federal Pell, FSEOG, state, private, college/university gift aid from institutional funds.

GIFT AID (NON-NEED-BASED) *Total amount:* $42,249,340 (1% federal, 1% state, 90% institutional, 8% external sources). *Receiving aid:* Freshmen: 38% (1,855). Undergraduates: 25% (4,921). *Average award:* Freshmen: $5529. Undergraduates: $4768. *Scholarships, grants, and awards by category: Academic interests/achievement:* business, engineering/technologies, general academic interests/achievements, military science. *Creative arts/performance:* general creative arts/performance, music. *Special achievements/activities:* general special achievements/activities, leadership. *Special characteristics:* children and siblings of alumni, ethnic background, first-generation college students, handicapped students, local/state students, out-of-state students, veterans.

LOANS *Student loans:* $91,097,753 (68% need-based, 32% non-need-based). 53% of past graduating class borrowed through all loan programs. *Average indebtedness per student:* $27,715. *Average need-based loan:* Freshmen: $4139. Undergraduates: $4708. *Parent loans:* $44,034,487 (40% need-based, 60% non-need-based). *Programs:* Federal Direct (Subsidized and Unsubsidized Stafford, PLUS), Perkins, Federal Nursing, college/university.

WORK-STUDY *Federal work-study:* 1,068 jobs averaging $2479. *State or other work-study/employment:* Part-time jobs available.

ATHLETIC AWARDS Total amount: $11,461,082 (100% non-need-based).

APPLYING FOR FINANCIAL AID *Required financial aid form:* FAFSA. *Financial aid deadline (priority):* 12/1. *Notification date:* Continuous beginning 1/15. Students must reply by 5/1 or within 2 weeks of notification.

CONTACT Mark Warner, Director of Student Financial Aid, The University of Iowa, 208 Calvin Hall, Iowa City, IA 52242, 319-335-3127 or toll-free 800-553-4692. *E-mail:* mark-warner@uiowa.edu. *Website:* http://www.uiowa.edu/.

UNIVERSITY OF JAMESTOWN
Jamestown, ND

Tuition & fees: $21,158	Average undergraduate aid package: $15,775

ABOUT THE INSTITUTION Independent Presbyterian, coed. *Awards:* bachelor's, master's, and doctoral degrees, 45 undergraduate majors. *Total enrollment:* 1,134. Undergraduates: 955. Freshmen: 262. Federal methodology is used as a basis for awarding need-based institutional aid.

UNDERGRADUATE EXPENSES for 2017–2018 *Comprehensive fee:* $28,508 includes full-time tuition ($20,578), mandatory fees ($580), and room and board ($7350). *College room only:* $3466. Full-time tuition and fees vary according to course load, degree level, and program. Room and board charges vary according to housing facility. *Part-time tuition:* $435 per semester hour. Part-time tuition and fees vary according to course load, degree level, and program.

FRESHMAN FINANCIAL AID (Fall 2015) 244 applied for aid; of those 78% were deemed to have need. 100% of freshmen with need received aid; of those 26% had need fully met. *Average percent of need met:* 76% (excluding resources awarded to replace EFC). *Average financial aid package:* $16,219 (excluding resources awarded to replace EFC). 33% of all full-time freshmen had no need and received non-need-based gift aid.

UNDERGRADUATE FINANCIAL AID (Fall 2015) 691 applied for aid; of those 80% were deemed to have need. 100% of undergraduates with need received aid; of those 25% had need fully met. *Average percent of need met:* 75% (excluding resources awarded to replace EFC). *Average financial aid package:* $15,775 (excluding resources awarded to replace EFC). 33% of all full-time undergraduates had no need and received non-need-based gift aid.

GIFT AID (NEED-BASED) *Total amount:* $5,479,259 (21% federal, 7% state, 69% institutional, 3% external sources). *Receiving aid:* Freshmen: 65% (190); all full-time undergraduates: 64% (553). *Average award:* Freshmen: $13,361; Undergraduates: $12,412. *Scholarships, grants, and awards:* Federal Pell, FSEOG, state, private, college/university gift aid from institutional funds.

GIFT AID (NON-NEED-BASED) *Total amount:* $3,016,080 (5% state, 88% institutional, 7% external sources). *Receiving aid:* Freshmen: 14% (42). Undergraduates: 12% (103). *Average award:* Freshmen: $9167. Undergraduates: $8540. *Scholarships, grants, and awards by category: Academic interests/achievement:* 698 awards ($468,259 total): general academic interests/achievements, physical sciences. *Creative arts/performance:* 70 awards ($190,450 total): art/fine arts, music, theater/drama. *Special achievements/activities:* 67 awards ($107,734 total): community service, leadership. *Special characteristics:* 179 awards ($615,029 total): children and siblings of alumni, children of faculty/staff, relatives of clergy, religious affiliation, siblings of current students, spouses of current students, veterans. *Tuition waivers:* Full or partial for employees or children of employees.

LOANS *Student loans:* $5,403,146 (56% need-based, 44% non-need-based). 64% of past graduating class borrowed through all loan programs. *Average indebtedness per student:* $25,368. *Average need-based loan:* Freshmen: $3512. Undergraduates: $4174. *Parent loans:* $680,388 (44% need-based, 56% non-need-based). *Programs:* Federal Direct (Subsidized and Unsubsidized Stafford, PLUS), Perkins, alternative loans.

WORK-STUDY *Federal work-study:* 221 jobs averaging $841. *State or other work-study/employment:* Total amount: $39,929 (100% non-need-based). 76 part-time jobs averaging $526.

ATHLETIC AWARDS Total amount: $2,173,402 (57% need-based, 43% non-need-based).

APPLYING FOR FINANCIAL AID *Required financial aid forms:* FAFSA, noncustodial (divorced/separated) parent's statement. *Financial aid deadline:* Continuous. *Notification date:* Continuous beginning 11/15.

CONTACT Judy Hager, Director of Financial Aid, University of Jamestown, 6085 College Lane, Jamestown, ND 58405, 701-252-3467 Ext. 5548 or toll-free 800-336-2554. *Fax:* 701-253-4318. *E-mail:* jhager@uj.edu. *Website:* http://www.uj.edu/.

THE UNIVERSITY OF KANSAS
Lawrence, KS

Tuition & fees (KS res): $10,549	Average undergraduate aid package: $14,746

ABOUT THE INSTITUTION State-supported, coed. **Awards:** certificates, bachelor's, master's, and doctoral degrees (University of Kansas is a single institution with academic programs and facilities at two primary locations: Lawrence and Kansas City). 113 undergraduate majors. **Total enrollment:** 27,565. Undergraduates: 19,262. Freshmen: 4,233. Federal methodology is used as a basis for awarding need-based institutional aid.

UNDERGRADUATE EXPENSES for 2016–2017 Application fee: $40. **Tuition, state resident:** full-time $9579; part-time $319.30 per credit hour. **Tuition, nonresident:** full-time $24,962; part-time $832.05 per credit hour. **Required fees:** full-time $970; $77.83 per credit hour. Full-time tuition and fees vary according to program, reciprocity agreements, and student level. Part-time tuition and fees vary according to program, reciprocity agreements, and student level. **College room and board:** $9586; **Room only:** $5738. Room and board charges vary according to board plan and housing facility. **Payment plan:** Guaranteed tuition.

FRESHMAN FINANCIAL AID (Fall 2015) 3,152 applied for aid; of those 67% were deemed to have need. 97% of freshmen with need received aid; of those 43% had need fully met. **Average percent of need met:** 78% (excluding resources awarded to replace EFC). **Average financial aid package:** $15,269 (excluding resources awarded to replace EFC). 24% of all full-time freshmen had no need and received non-need-based gift aid.

UNDERGRADUATE FINANCIAL AID (Fall 2015) 11,075 applied for aid; of those 73% were deemed to have need. 97% of undergraduates with need received aid; of those 37% had need fully met. **Average percent of need met:** 75% (excluding resources awarded to replace EFC). **Average financial aid package:** $14,746 (excluding resources awarded to replace EFC). 19% of all full-time undergraduates had no need and received non-need-based gift aid.

GIFT AID (NEED-BASED) Total amount: $43,551,063 (44% federal, 4% state, 46% institutional, 6% external sources). **Receiving aid:** Freshmen: 44% (1,765); all full-time undergraduates: 36% (6,135). **Average award:** Freshmen: $7545; Undergraduates: $6855. **Scholarships, grants, and awards:** Federal Pell, FSEOG, state, private, college/university gift aid from institutional funds, Bureau of Indian Affairs Grants.

GIFT AID (NON-NEED-BASED) Total amount: $21,079,281 (92% institutional, 8% external sources). **Receiving aid:** Freshmen: 5% (207). Undergraduates: 3% (534). **Average award:** Freshmen: $5444. Undergraduates: $5267. **Scholarships, grants, and awards by category:** *Academic interests/achievement:* architecture, area/ethnic studies, biological sciences, business, communication, computer science, education, engineering/technologies, English, foreign languages, general academic interests/achievements, home economics, humanities, international studies, mathematics, military science, physical sciences, premedicine, religion/biblical studies, social sciences. *Creative arts/performance:* applied art and design, art/fine arts, cinema/film/broadcasting, creative writing, dance, debating, general creative arts/performance, journalism/publications, music, performing arts, theater/drama. *Special achievements/activities:* community service, general special achievements/activities, leadership. *Special characteristics:* adult students, children and siblings of alumni, children of faculty/staff, ethnic background, first-generation college students, general special characteristics, international students, local/state students, married students, members of minority groups, out-of-state students, previous college experience, veterans. *Tuition waivers:* Full or partial for employees or children of employees. **ROTC:** Army, Naval, Air Force.

LOANS Student loans: $71,811,498 (70% need-based, 30% non-need-based). 52% of past graduating class borrowed through all loan programs. *Average indebtedness per student:* $27,479. **Average need-based loan:** Freshmen: $3270. Undergraduates: $4253. **Parent loans:** $46,708,938 (38% need-based, 62% non-need-based). **Programs:** Federal Direct (Subsidized and Unsubsidized Stafford, PLUS), Perkins, Federal Nursing, college/university, Health Professions Student Loans (HPSL), Federal Loan for Disadvantaged Students, private loans.

WORK-STUDY Federal work-study: 652 jobs averaging $2326. **State or other work-study/employment:** Total amount: $219,647 (31% need-based, 69% non-need-based). 62 part-time jobs averaging $4447.

ATHLETIC AWARDS Total amount: $9,578,400 (27% need-based, 73% non-need-based).

APPLYING FOR FINANCIAL AID *Required financial aid form:* FAFSA. *Financial aid deadline (priority):* 3/1. *Notification date:* Continuous beginning 4/1. Students must reply within 4 weeks of notification.

CONTACT Ms. Brenda Maigaard, Director of Financial Aid and Scholarships, The University of Kansas, KU Visitor Center, 1502 Iowa Street, Lawrence, KS 66045-7576, 785-864-4700 or toll-free 888-686-7323 (in-state). *Fax:* 785-864-5469. *E-mail:* financialaid@ku.edu. *Website:* http://www.ku.edu/.

UNIVERSITY OF KENTUCKY
Lexington, KY

Tuition & fees (KY res): $11,483	Average undergraduate aid package: $12,245

ABOUT THE INSTITUTION State-supported, coed. **Awards:** certificates, bachelor's, master's, and doctoral degrees. 100 undergraduate majors. **Total enrollment:** 29,781. Undergraduates: 22,621. Freshmen: 5,117. Federal methodology is used as a basis for awarding need-based institutional aid.

UNDERGRADUATE EXPENSES for 2016–2017 Application fee: $50. **Tuition, state resident:** full-time $10,172; part-time $424 per credit hour. **Tuition, nonresident:** full-time $25,023; part-time $1042 per credit hour. **Required fees:** full-time $1311; $40.50 per credit hour. Full-time tuition and fees vary according to location, program, reciprocity agreements, and student level. Part-time tuition and fees vary according to course load, location, program, reciprocity agreements, and student level. **College room and board:** $12,184. Room and board charges vary according to board plan and housing facility.

FRESHMAN FINANCIAL AID (Fall 2016, est.) 4,122 applied for aid; of those 72% were deemed to have need. 99% of freshmen with need received aid; of those 19% had need fully met. **Average percent of need met:** 54% (excluding resources awarded to replace EFC). **Average financial aid package:** $12,873 (excluding resources awarded to replace EFC). 24% of all full-time freshmen had no need and received non-need-based gift aid.

UNDERGRADUATE FINANCIAL AID (Fall 2016, est.) 13,633 applied for aid; of those 79% were deemed to have need. 98% of undergraduates with need received aid; of those 17% had need fully met. **Average percent of need met:** 54% (excluding resources awarded to replace EFC). **Average financial aid package:** $12,245 (excluding resources awarded to replace EFC). 24% of all full-time undergraduates had no need and received non-need-based gift aid.

GIFT AID (NEED-BASED) Total amount: $158,944,261 (15% federal, 18% state, 62% institutional, 5% external sources). **Receiving aid:** Freshmen: 24% (1,227); all full-time undergraduates: 24% (4,886). **Average award:** Freshmen: $5708; Undergraduates: $5694. **Scholarships, grants, and awards:** Federal Pell, FSEOG, state, private, college/university gift aid from institutional funds.

GIFT AID (NON-NEED-BASED) Receiving aid: Freshmen: 56% (2,855). Undergraduates: 41% (8,451). **Average award:** Freshmen: $8819. Undergraduates: $9734. **Scholarships, grants, and awards by category:** *Academic interests/achievement:* agriculture, architecture, area/ethnic studies, biological sciences, business, communication, computer science, education, engineering/technologies, English, foreign languages, general academic interests/achievements, health fields, home economics, international studies, mathematics, military science, physical sciences. *Creative arts/performance:* applied art and design, art/fine arts, cinema/film/broadcasting, creative writing, dance, debating, general creative arts/performance, journalism/publications, music, performing arts, theater/drama. *Special achievements/activities:* cheerleading/drum major, general special achievements/activities, leadership. *Special characteristics:* adult students, children and siblings of alumni, children of educators, children of faculty/staff, children of public servants, children of union members/company employees, children of workers in trades, children with a deceased or disabled parent, ethnic background, first-generation college students, general special characteristics, handicapped students, international students, members of minority groups, out-of-state students, public servants, spouses of deceased or disabled public servants, veterans, veterans' children. *Tuition waivers:* Full or partial for employees or children of employees. **ROTC:** Army, Air Force.

LOANS Student loans: $92,853,968 (100% need-based). 51% of past graduating class borrowed through all loan programs. *Average indebtedness per student:* $32,571. **Average need-based loan:** Freshmen: $3655. Undergraduates: $4498. **Parent loans:** $373,055,548 (100% need-based). **Programs:** Federal Direct (Subsidized and Unsubsidized Stafford, PLUS), Perkins, college/university, private loans.

WORK-STUDY Federal work-study: Total amount: $338,406; 205 jobs averaging $1651. **State or other work-study/employment:** Part-time jobs available.

ATHLETIC AWARDS Total amount: $11,433,489 (100% need-based).

APPLYING FOR FINANCIAL AID *Required financial aid form:* FAFSA. *Financial aid deadline (priority):* 2/15. *Notification date:* Continuous beginning 4/1. Students must reply within 3 weeks of notification.

CONTACT Ms. Lynda S. George, Director of Financial Aid, University of Kentucky, 128 Funkhouser Building, Lexington, KY 40506-0054, 859-257-3172 Ext. 241 or toll-free 866-900-GO-UK. *Fax:* 859-257-4398. *E-mail:* lgeorge@email.uky.edu. *Website:* http://www.uky.edu/.

UNIVERSITY OF LA VERNE
La Verne, CA

Tuition & fees: $41,450	Average undergraduate aid package: $31,389

ABOUT THE INSTITUTION Independent, coed. *Awards:* certificates, bachelor's, master's, and doctoral degrees (also offers continuing education program with significant enrollment not reflected in profile). 51 undergraduate majors. *Total enrollment:* 4,873. Undergraduates: 2,809. Freshmen: 555. Federal methodology is used as a basis for awarding need-based institutional aid.

UNDERGRADUATE EXPENSES for 2017–2018 *Application fee:* $50. *Comprehensive fee:* $54,590 includes full-time tuition ($39,916), mandatory fees ($1534), and room and board ($13,140). *College room only:* $7030. Full-time tuition and fees vary according to location. Room and board charges vary according to board plan and housing facility. *Part-time tuition:* $1166 per credit hour. Part-time tuition and fees vary according to location.

FRESHMAN FINANCIAL AID (Fall 2016, est.) 500 applied for aid; of those 95% were deemed to have need. 100% of freshmen with need received aid; of those 7% had need fully met. *Average percent of need met:* 48% (excluding resources awarded to replace EFC). *Average financial aid package:* $31,855 (excluding resources awarded to replace EFC). 14% of all full-time freshmen had no need and received non-need-based gift aid.

UNDERGRADUATE FINANCIAL AID (Fall 2016, est.) 2,376 applied for aid; of those 95% were deemed to have need. 100% of undergraduates with need received aid; of those 9% had need fully met. *Average percent of need met:* 46% (excluding resources awarded to replace EFC). *Average financial aid package:* $31,389 (excluding resources awarded to replace EFC). 14% of all full-time undergraduates had no need and received non-need-based gift aid.

GIFT AID (NEED-BASED) *Total amount:* $60,454,564 (11% federal, 17% state, 72% institutional). *Receiving aid:* Freshmen: 78% (435); all full-time undergraduates: 55% (1,499). *Average award:* Freshmen: $16,820; Undergraduates: $10,505. *Scholarships, grants, and awards:* Federal Pell, FSEOG, state, private, college/university gift aid from institutional funds.

GIFT AID (NON-NEED-BASED) *Total amount:* $5,114,344 (98% institutional, 2% external sources). *Receiving aid:* Freshmen: 85% (474). Undergraduates: 83% (2,243). *Average award:* Freshmen: $19,451. Undergraduates: $21,784. *Scholarships, grants, and awards by category:* Academic interests/achievement: general academic interests/achievements. *Creative arts/performance:* 37 awards ($848,550 total): art/fine arts, cinema/film/broadcasting, journalism/publications, music, performing arts, theater/drama. *Special achievements/activities:* community service, leadership. *Tuition waivers:* Full or partial for employees or children of employees. *ROTC:* Army cooperative.

LOANS *Student loans:* $17,096,023 (94% need-based, 6% non-need-based). 83% of past graduating class borrowed through all loan programs. *Average indebtedness per student:* $31,445. *Average need-based loan:* Freshmen: $3810. Undergraduates: $4859. *Parent loans:* $10,473,879 (92% need-based, 8% non-need-based). *Programs:* Federal Direct (Subsidized and Unsubsidized Stafford, PLUS), Perkins, college/university.

WORK-STUDY *Federal work-study:* Total amount: $714,458; 281 jobs averaging $2530. *State or other work-study/employment:* Part-time jobs available.

APPLYING FOR FINANCIAL AID *Required financial aid forms:* FAFSA, state aid form. *Financial aid deadline (priority):* 3/2. *Notification date:* Continuous beginning 3/1. Students must reply by 5/1 or within 2 weeks of notification.

CONTACT Mr. David Busse, Interim Director of Financial Aid, University of La Verne, 1950 3rd Street, La Verne, CA 91750-4443, 800-649-0160 or toll-free 800-876-4858. *Fax:* 909-392-2751. *E-mail:* finaid@laverne.edu. *Website:* http://www.laverne.edu/.

UNIVERSITY OF LOUISIANA AT LAFAYETTE
Lafayette, LA

Tuition & fees: N/R	Average undergraduate aid package: $9903

ABOUT THE INSTITUTION State-supported, coed. *Awards:* certificates, bachelor's, master's, and doctoral degrees. 61 undergraduate majors. *Total enrollment:* 17,508. Undergraduates: 15,870. Freshmen: 3,179. Federal methodology is used as a basis for awarding need-based institutional aid.

FRESHMAN FINANCIAL AID (Fall 2015) 3,017 applied for aid; of those 66% were deemed to have need. 99% of freshmen with need received aid; of those 16% had need fully met. *Average percent of need met:* 62% (excluding resources awarded to replace EFC). *Average financial aid package:* $10,481 (excluding resources awarded to replace EFC). 15% of all full-time freshmen had no need and received non-need-based gift aid.

UNDERGRADUATE FINANCIAL AID (Fall 2015) 10,588 applied for aid; of those 71% were deemed to have need. 98% of undergraduates with need received aid; of those 11% had need fully met. *Average percent of need met:* 54% (excluding resources awarded to replace EFC). *Average financial aid package:* $9903 (excluding resources awarded to replace EFC). 9% of all full-time undergraduates had no need and received non-need-based gift aid.

GIFT AID (NEED-BASED) *Total amount:* $23,866,734 (91% federal, 9% state). *Receiving aid:* Freshmen: 61% (1,928); all full-time undergraduates: 52% (6,664). *Average award:* Freshmen: $8529; Undergraduates: $8002. *Scholarships, grants, and awards:* Federal Pell, FSEOG, state, college/university gift aid from institutional funds.

GIFT AID (NON-NEED-BASED) *Total amount:* $51,979,072 (69% state, 28% institutional, 3% external sources). *Receiving aid:* Freshmen: 10% (316). Undergraduates: 6% (762). *Average award:* Freshmen: $3492. Undergraduates: $3459. *Scholarships, grants, and awards by category:* Academic interests/achievement: general academic interests/achievements. *Creative arts/performance:* general creative arts/performance. *Special achievements/activities:* general special achievements/activities. *ROTC:* Army.

LOANS *Student loans:* $35,993,395 (48% need-based, 52% non-need-based). *Average need-based loan:* Freshmen: $3113. Undergraduates: $3707. *Parent loans:* $5,476,031 (100% non-need-based). *Programs:* Federal Direct (Subsidized and Unsubsidized Stafford, PLUS), Perkins, Federal Nursing.

WORK-STUDY *Federal work-study:* jobs available. *State or other work-study/employment:* Total amount: $509,396 (100% non-need-based). Part-time jobs available.

ATHLETIC AWARDS Total amount: $4,439,102 (100% non-need-based).

APPLYING FOR FINANCIAL AID *Required financial aid form:* FAFSA. *Financial aid deadline (priority):* 5/1. *Notification date:* Continuous beginning 4/1. Students must reply within 2 weeks of notification.

CONTACT Cindy S. Perez, Director of Financial Aid, University of Louisiana at Lafayette, PO Box 41206, Lafayette, LA 70504-1206, 337-482-6497 or toll-free 800-752-6553. *Fax:* 337-482-6502. *E-mail:* cperez@louisiana.edu. *Website:* http://www.louisiana.edu/.

UNIVERSITY OF LOUISIANA AT MONROE
Monroe, LA

Tuition & fees (LA res): $8282	Average undergraduate aid package: $15,431

ABOUT THE INSTITUTION State-supported, coed. *Awards:* certificates, associate, bachelor's, master's, and doctoral degrees. 44 undergraduate majors. *Total enrollment:* 8,645. Undergraduates: 7,276. Freshmen: 1,338. Federal methodology is used as a basis for awarding need-based institutional aid.

UNDERGRADUATE EXPENSES for 2016–2017 *Application fee:* $20. *Tuition, state resident:* full-time $5788; part-time $364.11 per credit hour. *Tuition, nonresident:* full-time $17,888; part-time $364.11 per credit hour. *Required fees:* full-time $2494; $304.80 per credit hour. Full-time tuition and fees vary according to course load, degree level, and program. Part-time tuition and fees vary according to course load, degree level, and program. **College room and board:** $7304; **Room only:** $4282. Room and board charges vary according to board plan and housing facility.

FRESHMAN FINANCIAL AID (Fall 2015) 1,328 applied for aid; of those 96% were deemed to have need. 100% of freshmen with need received aid. **Average financial aid package:** $18,616 (excluding resources awarded to replace EFC). 8% of all full-time freshmen had no need and received non-need-based gift aid.

UNDERGRADUATE FINANCIAL AID (Fall 2015) 7,506 applied for aid; of those 92% were deemed to have need. 100% of undergraduates with need received aid. **Average financial aid package:** $15,431 (excluding resources awarded to replace EFC). 6% of all full-time undergraduates had no need and received non-need-based gift aid.

GIFT AID (NEED-BASED) Total amount: $28,931,420 (41% federal, 59% state). **Receiving aid:** Freshmen: 81% (1,111); all full-time undergraduates: 55% (4,141). **Average award:** Freshmen: $6268; Undergraduates: $5629. **Scholarships, grants, and awards:** Federal Pell, FSEOG, state, private, college/university gift aid from institutional funds, Leveraging Educational Assistance Program (LEAP).

GIFT AID (NON-NEED-BASED) Total amount: $15,475,332 (95% institutional, 5% external sources). **Receiving aid:** Freshmen: 63% (858). Undergraduates: 33% (2,515). **Average award:** Freshmen: $10,557. Undergraduates: $11,365. **Scholarships, grants, and awards by category:** Academic interests/achievement: agriculture, biological sciences, business, communication, computer science, education, English, foreign languages, general academic interests/achievements, health fields, home economics, library science, mathematics, military science, physical sciences, social sciences. Creative arts/performance: art/fine arts, creative writing, debating, journalism/publications, music, performing arts, theater/drama. Special achievements/activities: cheerleading/drum major, community service, leadership. Special characteristics: children of faculty/staff, children with a deceased or disabled parent, international students, out-of-state students. **Tuition waivers:** Full or partial for employees or children of employees, senior citizens. **ROTC:** Army cooperative.

LOANS Student loans: $21,456,816 (100% non-need-based). **Programs:** Perkins, college/university, Federal Health Professions Student Loans.

WORK-STUDY Federal work-study: 605 jobs averaging $1373. **State or other work-study/employment:** Part-time jobs available.

ATHLETIC AWARDS Total amount: $10,099,001 (100% non-need-based).

APPLYING FOR FINANCIAL AID Required financial aid forms: FAFSA, institution's own form. **Financial aid deadline (priority):** 4/1. **Notification date:** Continuous beginning 6/15. Students must reply within 2 weeks of notification.

CONTACT Ms. Teresa Smith, Director of Financial Aid, University of Louisiana at Monroe, 700 University Avenue, Monroe, LA 71209, 318-342-5320 or toll-free 800-372-5127. Fax: 318-342-3539. E-mail: tsmith@ulm.edu.
Website: http://www.ulm.edu/.

of those 20% had need fully met. **Average percent of need met:** 59% (excluding resources awarded to replace EFC). **Average financial aid package:** $11,864 (excluding resources awarded to replace EFC). 15% of all full-time undergraduates had no need and received non-need-based gift aid.

GIFT AID (NEED-BASED) Total amount: $60,297,996 (31% federal, 20% state, 37% institutional, 12% external sources). **Receiving aid:** Freshmen: 64% (1,756); all full-time undergraduates: 54% (6,627). **Average award:** Freshmen: $9768; Undergraduates: $9166. **Scholarships, grants, and awards:** Federal Pell, FSEOG, state, private, college/university gift aid from institutional funds.

GIFT AID (NON-NEED-BASED) Total amount: $32,619,829 (23% state, 61% institutional, 16% external sources). **Receiving aid:** Freshmen: 12% (316). Undergraduates: 7% (888). **Average award:** Freshmen: $7751. Undergraduates: $8101. **Scholarships, grants, and awards by category:** Academic interests/achievement: biological sciences, business, education, engineering/technologies, English, foreign languages, general academic interests/achievements, health fields, mathematics, military science, premedicine. Creative arts/performance: art/fine arts, creative writing, dance, debating, general creative arts/performance, music, theater/drama. Special achievements/activities: cheerleading/drum major, community service, general special achievements/activities, hobbies/interests, junior miss, leadership, memberships. Special characteristics: adult students, children and siblings of alumni, children of faculty/staff, children of union members/company employees, children with a deceased or disabled parent, ethnic background, general special characteristics, local/state students, members of minority groups, out-of-state students, previous college experience, veterans, veterans' children. **Tuition waivers:** Full or partial for employees or children of employees, senior citizens. **ROTC:** Army, Air Force.

LOANS Student loans: $49,940,849 (69% need-based, 31% non-need-based). 54% of past graduating class borrowed through all loan programs. Average indebtedness per student: $23,553. Average need-based loan: Freshmen: $3350. Undergraduates: $4141. **Parent loans:** $10,221,353 (40% need-based, 60% non-need-based). **Programs:** Federal Direct (Subsidized and Unsubsidized Stafford, PLUS), Perkins, Federal Nursing.

WORK-STUDY Federal work-study: Total amount: $1,223,811; 398 jobs averaging $3356.

ATHLETIC AWARDS Total amount: $11,550,338 (31% need-based, 69% non-need-based).

APPLYING FOR FINANCIAL AID Required financial aid form: FAFSA. **Financial aid deadline (priority):** 3/15. **Notification date:** Continuous beginning 4/1. Students must reply by 5/1.

CONTACT Ms. Patricia O. Arauz, Director of Financial Aid, University of Louisville, 2301 South Third Street, Louisville, KY 40292-0001, 502-852-6145 or toll-free 800-334-8635. Fax: 502-852-0182. E-mail: finaid@louisville.edu.
Website: http://www.louisville.edu/.

UNIVERSITY OF LOUISVILLE
Louisville, KY

Tuition & fees (KY res): $11,264	Average undergraduate aid package: $11,864

ABOUT THE INSTITUTION State-supported, coed. **Awards:** certificates, associate, bachelor's, master's, and doctoral degrees. 54 undergraduate majors. **Total enrollment:** 21,579. Undergraduates: 15,827. Freshmen: 2,883. Federal methodology is used as a basis for awarding need-based institutional aid.

UNDERGRADUATE EXPENSES for 2017-2018 Application fee: $50. **Tuition, state resident:** full-time $11,068; part-time $462 per credit hour. **Tuition, nonresident:** full-time $26,090; part-time $1088 per credit hour. **Required fees:** full-time $196. Full-time tuition and fees vary according to reciprocity agreements. Part-time tuition and fees vary according to course load and reciprocity agreements. **College room and board:** $8560; **Room only:** $5776. Room and board charges vary according to board plan and housing facility.

FRESHMAN FINANCIAL AID (Fall 2016, est.) 2,419 applied for aid; of those 75% were deemed to have need. 99% of freshmen with need received aid; of those 24% had need fully met. **Average percent of need met:** 61% (excluding resources awarded to replace EFC). **Average financial aid package:** $12,815 (excluding resources awarded to replace EFC). 17% of all full-time freshmen had no need and received non-need-based gift aid.

UNDERGRADUATE FINANCIAL AID (Fall 2016, est.) 9,095 applied for aid; of those 81% were deemed to have need. 97% of undergraduates with need received aid;

UNIVERSITY OF MAINE
Orono, ME

Tuition & fees (ME res): $10,628	Average undergraduate aid package: $16,723

ABOUT THE INSTITUTION State-supported, coed. **Awards:** certificates, bachelor's, master's, and doctoral degrees. 85 undergraduate majors. **Total enrollment:** 11,219. Undergraduates: 9,323. Freshmen: 2,230. Federal methodology is used as a basis for awarding need-based institutional aid.

UNDERGRADUATE EXPENSES for 2016-2017 Application fee: $40. **Tuition, state resident:** full-time $8370; part-time $279 per credit hour. **Tuition, nonresident:** full-time $27,240; part-time $908 per credit hour. **Required fees:** full-time $2258. Full-time tuition and fees vary according to course load. Part-time tuition and fees vary according to course load. **College room and board:** $10,164; **Room only:** $5154. Room and board charges vary according to board plan and housing facility.

FRESHMAN FINANCIAL AID (Fall 2016, est.) 1,987 applied for aid; of those 77% were deemed to have need. 100% of freshmen with need received aid; of those 20% had need fully met. **Average percent of need met:** 85% (excluding resources awarded to replace EFC). **Average financial aid package:** $17,759 (excluding resources awarded to replace EFC). 29% of all full-time freshmen had no need and received non-need-based gift aid.

UNDERGRADUATE FINANCIAL AID (Fall 2016, est.) 6,789 applied for aid; of those 81% were deemed to have need. 99% of undergraduates with need received aid; of those 17% had need fully met. **Average percent of need met:** 83% (excluding resources awarded to replace EFC). *Average financial aid package:* $16,723 (excluding resources awarded to replace EFC). 18% of all full-time undergraduates had no need and received non-need-based gift aid.

GIFT AID (NEED-BASED) *Total amount:* $44,158,230 (32% federal, 7% state, 55% institutional, 6% external sources). *Receiving aid:* Freshmen: 70% (1,530); all full-time undergraduates: 59% (4,802). *Average award:* Freshmen: $9199; Undergraduates: $8495. *Scholarships, grants, and awards:* Federal Pell, FSEOG, state, private, college/university gift aid from institutional funds.

GIFT AID (NON-NEED-BASED) *Total amount:* $0,770,732 (85% institutional, 15% external sources). *Receiving aid:* Freshmen: 8% (181). Undergraduates: 5% (387). *Average award:* Freshmen: $6073. Undergraduates: $5495. *Scholarships, grants, and awards by category:* Academic interests/achievement: agriculture, biological sciences, business, communication, computer science, education, engineering/technologies, English, general academic interests/achievements, home economics, international studies, mathematics, military science, physical sciences, premedicine, social sciences. *Creative arts/performance:* art/fine arts, creative writing, dance, general creative arts/performance, journalism/publications, music, theater/drama. *Special achievements/activities:* community service, general special achievements/activities, leadership, memberships. *Special characteristics:* adult students, children and siblings of alumni, children of faculty/staff, children of union members/company employees, children of workers in trades, ethnic background, first-generation college students, general special characteristics, handicapped students, international students, local/state students, members of minority groups, out-of-state students, previous college experience, religious affiliation, spouses of current students, veterans, veterans' children. *Tuition waivers:* Full or partial for employees or children of employees, senior citizens. *ROTC:* Army, Naval.

LOANS *Student loans:* $57,455,432 (66% need-based, 34% non-need-based). 77% of past graduating class borrowed through all loan programs. *Average indebtedness per student:* $34,923. *Average need-based loan:* Freshmen: $3727. Undergraduates: $4523. *Parent loans:* $9,740,768 (44% need-based, 56% non-need-based). *Programs:* Federal Direct (Subsidized and Unsubsidized Stafford, PLUS), Perkins, state, college/university, private loans.

WORK-STUDY *Federal work-study:* Total amount: $3,834,147; 1,038 jobs averaging $2152. *State or other work-study/employment:* Part-time jobs available.

ATHLETIC AWARDS Total amount: $6,233,109 (33% need-based, 67% non-need-based).

APPLYING FOR FINANCIAL AID *Required financial aid form:* FAFSA. *Financial aid deadline:* 4/15 (priority: 3/1). *Notification date:* Continuous beginning 1/1. Students must reply by 5/1.

CONTACT Ms. Sarah Doheny, Director of Student Financial Aid, University of Maine, 5781 Wingate Hall, Orono, ME 04469-5781, 207-581-1324 or toll-free 877-486-2364. *Fax:* 207-581-3261. *E-mail:* sarah.doheny@maine.edu. *Website:* http://www.umaine.edu/.

UNIVERSITY OF MAINE AT AUGUSTA
Augusta, ME

Tuition & fees (ME res): $7448	Average undergraduate aid package: $9316

ABOUT THE INSTITUTION State-supported, coed. *Awards:* certificates, associate, and bachelor's degrees (also offers some graduate courses and continuing education programs with significant enrollment not reflected in profile). 28 undergraduate majors. *Total enrollment:* 4,683. Undergraduates: 4,683. Freshmen: 403. Federal methodology is used as a basis for awarding need-based institutional aid.

UNDERGRADUATE EXPENSES for 2016–2017 *Application fee:* $40. *Tuition, state resident:* full-time $6510; part-time $217 per credit. *Tuition, nonresident:* full-time $16,110; part-time $537 per credit. *Required fees:* full-time $938; $31.25 per credit hour. Full-time tuition and fees vary according to course load, location, program, and reciprocity agreements. Part-time tuition and fees vary according to course load, location, program, and reciprocity agreements.

FRESHMAN FINANCIAL AID (Fall 2016, est.) 167 applied for aid; of those 90% were deemed to have need. 99% of freshmen with need received aid; of those 5% had need fully met. *Average percent of need met:* 53% (excluding resources awarded to replace EFC). *Average financial aid package:* $7632 (excluding resources awarded to replace EFC). 1% of all full-time freshmen had no need and received non-need-based gift aid.

UNDERGRADUATE FINANCIAL AID (Fall 2016, est.) 1,364 applied for aid; of those 94% were deemed to have need. 97% of undergraduates with need received aid;

of those 4% had need fully met. *Average percent of need met:* 55% (excluding resources awarded to replace EFC). *Average financial aid package:* $9316 (excluding resources awarded to replace EFC). 1% of all full-time undergraduates had no need and received non-need-based gift aid.

GIFT AID (NEED-BASED) *Total amount:* $11,016,019 (72% federal, 21% state, 7% institutional). *Receiving aid:* Freshmen: 70% (129); all full-time undergraduates: 70% (1,046). *Average award:* Freshmen: $5718; Undergraduates: $6242. *Scholarships, grants, and awards:* Federal Pell, FSEOG, state, private, college/university gift aid from institutional funds.

GIFT AID (NON-NEED-BASED) *Total amount:* $14,473 (44% state, 56% institutional). *Receiving aid:* Freshmen: 4% (7). Undergraduates: 5% (69). *Average award:* Freshmen: $651. Undergraduates: $839. *Scholarships, grants, and awards by category:* Academic interests/achievement: biological sciences, business, general academic interests/achievements, mathematics. *Creative arts/performance:* music. *Special achievements/activities:* general special achievements/activities, leadership. *Special characteristics:* children of faculty/staff, ethnic background, international students, local/state students, veterans' children. *Tuition waivers:* Full or partial for minority students, employees or children of employees, senior citizens. *ROTC:* Army cooperative.

LOANS *Student loans:* $17,153,732 (86% need-based, 14% non-need-based). 78% of past graduating class borrowed through all loan programs. *Average indebtedness per student:* $30,457. *Average need-based loan:* Freshmen: $5711. Undergraduates: $7529. *Parent loans:* $98,490 (38% need-based, 62% non-need-based). *Programs:* Federal Direct (Subsidized and Unsubsidized Stafford, PLUS), Perkins, Federal Nursing.

WORK-STUDY *Federal work-study:* Total amount: $380,030; jobs available. *State or other work-study/employment:* Total amount: $41,000 (100% non-need-based). Part-time jobs available.

ATHLETIC AWARDS Total amount: $18,200 (69% need-based, 31% non-need-based).

APPLYING FOR FINANCIAL AID *Required financial aid form:* FAFSA. *Financial aid deadline (priority):* 3/1. *Notification date:* Continuous beginning 3/15. Students must reply within 2 weeks of notification.

CONTACT Financial Aid Office, University of Maine at Augusta, 46 University Drive, Augusta, ME 04330-9410, 207-621-3185 or toll-free 877-862-1234 Ext. 3185 (in-state), 877-862-1234 (out-of-state). *Fax:* 207-621-3116. *E-mail:* umafa@maine.edu. *Website:* http://www.uma.edu/.

UNIVERSITY OF MAINE AT FARMINGTON
Farmington, ME

ABOUT THE INSTITUTION State-supported, coed. *Awards:* certificates, bachelor's, and master's degrees. 43 undergraduate majors. *Total enrollment:* 2,000. Undergraduates: 1,782. Freshmen: 435.

GIFT AID (NEED-BASED) *Scholarships, grants, and awards:* Federal Pell, FSEOG, state, private, college/university gift aid from institutional funds.

GIFT AID (NON-NEED-BASED) *Scholarships, grants, and awards by category:* Academic interests/achievement: general academic interests/achievements. *Creative arts/performance:* music, theater/drama. *Special achievements/activities:* general special achievements/activities, leadership. *Special characteristics:* children of faculty/staff, general special characteristics, local/state students, members of minority groups, out-of-state students, veterans' children.

LOANS *Programs:* Federal Direct (Subsidized and Unsubsidized Stafford, PLUS), Perkins, state, college/university.

APPLYING FOR FINANCIAL AID *Required financial aid form:* FAFSA.

CONTACT Mr. Ronald P. Milliken, Director of Financial Aid, University of Maine at Farmington, 224 Main Street, Farmington, ME 04938-1990, 207-778-7105. *Fax:* 207-778-8178. *E-mail:* milliken@maine.edu. *Website:* http://www.umf.maine.edu/.

UNIVERSITY OF MAINE AT FORT KENT

Fort Kent, ME

Comprehensive fee: NR	Average undergraduate aid package: $11,403

ABOUT THE INSTITUTION State-supported, coed. *Awards:* associate and bachelor's degrees. 19 undergraduate majors. *Total enrollment:* 1,904. Undergraduates: 1,904. Freshmen: 172. Both federal and institutional methodology are used as a basis for awarding need-based institutional aid.

UNDERGRADUATE EXPENSES for 2017–2018 *Application fee:* $40. *College room only:* $4250. Room and board charges vary according to board plan and housing facility. *Part-time fees:* $65 per credit hour; $65 per credit hour.

FRESHMAN FINANCIAL AID (Fall 2016, est.) 108 applied for aid; of those 81% were deemed to have need. 100% of freshmen with need received aid; of those 60% had need fully met. *Average percent of need met:* 82% (excluding resources awarded to replace EFC). *Average financial aid package:* $11,421 (excluding resources awarded to replace EFC). 3% of all full-time freshmen had no need and received non-need-based gift aid.

UNDERGRADUATE FINANCIAL AID (Fall 2016, est.) 501 applied for aid; of those 85% were deemed to have need. 100% of undergraduates with need received aid; of those 57% had need fully met. *Average percent of need met:* 82% (excluding resources awarded to replace EFC). *Average financial aid package:* $11,403 (excluding resources awarded to replace EFC). 4% of all full-time undergraduates had no need and received non-need-based gift aid.

GIFT AID (NEED-BASED) *Total amount:* $3,297,050 (55% federal, 14% state, 24% institutional, 7% external sources). *Receiving aid:* Freshmen: 70% (84); all full-time undergraduates: 63% (363). *Average award:* Freshmen: $6068; Undergraduates: $6036. *Scholarships, grants, and awards:* Federal Pell, FSEOG, state, private, college/university gift aid from institutional funds, Federal Nursing.

GIFT AID (NON-NEED-BASED) *Total amount:* $63,172 (18% state, 82% institutional). *Receiving aid:* Freshmen: 2% (3). Undergraduates: 2% (10). *Average award:* Freshmen: $2500. Undergraduates: $1516. *Scholarships, grants, and awards by category:* Academic interests/achievement: biological sciences, business, communication, computer science, education, English, foreign languages, general academic interests/achievements, health fields, humanities, mathematics, social sciences. *Creative arts/performance:* general creative arts/performance, performing arts. *Special achievements/activities:* general special achievements/activities. *Special characteristics:* adult students, children of faculty/staff, ethnic background, general special characteristics, international students, members of minority groups. *Tuition waivers:* Full or partial for employees or children of employees, senior citizens.

LOANS *Student loans:* $4,302,709 (70% need-based, 30% non-need-based). 66% of past graduating class borrowed through all loan programs. *Average indebtedness per student:* $29,910. *Average need-based loan:* Freshmen: $5709. Undergraduates: $6479. *Parent loans:* $205,921 (39% need-based, 61% non-need-based). *Programs:* Federal Direct (Subsidized and Unsubsidized Stafford, PLUS), Perkins, Federal Nursing, state, college/university.

WORK-STUDY *Federal work-study:* Total amount: $177,518; 98 jobs averaging $1583. *State or other work-study/employment:* Part-time jobs available.

APPLYING FOR FINANCIAL AID *Required financial aid forms:* FAFSA, institution's own form, CSS Financial Aid PROFILE, state aid form. *Financial aid deadline (priority):* 3/1. *Notification date:* Continuous beginning 3/1.

CONTACT Lisa Fournier, Interim Director of Financial Aid, University of Maine at Fort Kent, 23 University Drive, Fort Kent, ME 04743-1292, 207-834-7607 or toll-free 888-TRY-UMFK. *Fax:* 207-834-7841. *E-mail:* lisafour@maine.edu. *Website:* http://www.umfk.maine.edu/.

UNIVERSITY OF MAINE AT MACHIAS

Machias, ME

Tuition & fees (ME res): $7480	Average undergraduate aid package: $13,982

ABOUT THE INSTITUTION State-supported, coed. *Awards:* certificates, associate, and bachelor's degrees. 37 undergraduate majors. *Total enrollment:* 786.

Undergraduates: 786. Freshmen: 131. Federal methodology is used as a basis for awarding need-based institutional aid.

UNDERGRADUATE EXPENSES for 2016–2017 *Application fee:* $40. *Tuition, state resident:* full-time $6660; part-time $222 per semester hour. *Tuition, nonresident:* full-time $18,480; part-time $616 per semester hour. *Required fees:* full-time $820. *College room and board:* $8466; *Room only:* $4140.

FRESHMAN FINANCIAL AID (Fall 2015) 114 applied for aid; of those 94% were deemed to have need. 100% of freshmen with need received aid; of those 57% had need fully met. *Average percent of need met:* 77% (excluding resources awarded to replace EFC). *Average financial aid package:* $13,125 (excluding resources awarded to replace EFC).

UNDERGRADUATE FINANCIAL AID (Fall 2015) 381 applied for aid; of those 92% were deemed to have need. 100% of undergraduates with need received aid; of those 63% had need fully met. *Average percent of need met:* 82% (excluding resources awarded to replace EFC). *Average financial aid package:* $13,982 (excluding resources awarded to replace EFC). 1% of all full-time undergraduates had no need and received non-need-based gift aid.

GIFT AID (NEED-BASED) *Total amount:* $3,597,821 (51% federal, 10% state, 30% institutional, 9% external sources). *Receiving aid:* Freshmen: 92% (107); all full-time undergraduates: 84% (340). *Average award:* Freshmen: $9050; Undergraduates: $8794. *Scholarships, grants, and awards:* Federal Pell, FSEOG, state, private, college/university gift aid from institutional funds.

GIFT AID (NON-NEED-BASED) *Total amount:* $13,621 (100% institutional). *Receiving aid:* Freshmen: 1% (1). Undergraduates: 1% (3). *Average award:* Undergraduates: $1420. *Scholarships, grants, and awards by category:* Academic interests/achievement: general academic interests/achievements. *Tuition waivers:* Full or partial for employees or children of employees, senior citizens.

LOANS *Student loans:* $2,258,588 (82% need-based, 18% non-need-based). 76% of past graduating class borrowed through all loan programs. *Average indebtedness per student:* $23,734. *Average need-based loan:* Freshmen: $4826. Undergraduates: $6093. *Parent loans:* $164,568 (28% need-based, 72% non-need-based). *Programs:* Federal Direct (Subsidized and Unsubsidized Stafford, PLUS), Perkins, state.

WORK-STUDY *Federal work-study:* jobs available. *State or other work-study/employment:* Part-time jobs available.

APPLYING FOR FINANCIAL AID *Required financial aid form:* FAFSA. *Financial aid deadline (priority):* 3/1. *Notification date:* Continuous.

CONTACT Ms. Stephanie Larrabee, Director of Financial Aid, University of Maine at Machias, 9 O'Brien Avenue, Machias, ME 04654, 207-255-1203 or toll-free 888-GOTOUMM (in-state), 888-468-6866 (out-of-state). *Fax:* 207-255-4864. *Website:* http://www.machias.edu/.

UNIVERSITY OF MAINE AT PRESQUE ISLE

Presque Isle, ME

Tuition & fees (ME res): $7884	Average undergraduate aid package: $11,665

ABOUT THE INSTITUTION State-supported, coed. *Awards:* certificates, associate, and bachelor's degrees. 27 undergraduate majors. *Total enrollment:* 1,326. Undergraduates: 1,326. Freshmen: 178. Federal methodology is used as a basis for awarding need-based institutional aid.

UNDERGRADUATE EXPENSES for 2017–2018 *Tuition, state resident:* full-time $6840; part-time $228 per credit hour. *Tuition, nonresident:* full-time $10,590; part-time $353 per credit hour. *Required fees:* full-time $1044. Full-time tuition and fees vary according to course load. Part-time tuition and fees vary according to course load. *College room and board:* $8264. Room and board charges vary according to board plan.

FRESHMAN FINANCIAL AID (Fall 2016, est.) 159 applied for aid; of those 87% were deemed to have need. 100% of freshmen with need received aid; of those 53% had need fully met. *Average percent of need met:* 82% (excluding resources awarded to replace EFC). *Average financial aid package:* $11,908 (excluding resources awarded to replace EFC). 5% of all full-time freshmen had no need and received non-need-based gift aid.

UNDERGRADUATE FINANCIAL AID (Fall 2016, est.) 574 applied for aid; of those 89% were deemed to have need. 100% of undergraduates with need received aid; of those 58% had need fully met. *Average percent of need met:* 85%

(excluding resources awarded to replace EFC). *Average financial aid package:* $11,665 (excluding resources awarded to replace EFC). 4% of all full-time undergraduates had no need and received non-need-based gift aid.

GIFT AID (NEED-BASED) *Total amount:* $3,915,844 (57% federal, 13% state, 22% institutional, 8% external sources). *Receiving aid:* Freshmen: 81% (138); all full-time undergraduates: 75% (504). *Average award:* Freshmen: $7523; Undergraduates: $6873. *Scholarships, grants, and awards:* Federal Pell, FSEOG, state, private, college/university gift aid from institutional funds.

GIFT AID (NON-NEED-BASED) *Total amount:* $148,504 (59% institutional, 41% external sources). *Receiving aid:* Freshmen: 2% (3). Undergraduates: 3% (20). *Average award:* Freshmen: $2222. Undergraduates: $2452. *Scholarships, grants, and awards by category:* Academic interests/achievement: general academic interests/achievements. Special achievements/activities: community service. Special characteristics: children of faculty/staff, ethnic background, international students, local/state students, out-of-state students, veterans' children. *Tuition waivers:* Full or partial for employees or children of employees, senior citizens.

LOANS *Student loans:* $2,630,801 (69% need-based, 31% non-need-based). 73% of past graduating class borrowed through all loan programs. *Average indebtedness per student:* $22,934. *Average need-based loan:* Freshmen: $4438. Undergraduates: $4537. *Parent loans:* $117,474 (28% need-based, 72% non-need-based). *Programs:* Federal Direct (Subsidized and Unsubsidized Stafford, PLUS), Perkins, state, college/university.

WORK-STUDY *Federal work-study:* Total amount: $701,245; jobs available.

APPLYING FOR FINANCIAL AID *Required financial aid form:* FAFSA. *Financial aid deadline (priority):* 4/1. *Notification date:* Continuous beginning 1/10. Students must reply within 2 weeks of notification.

CONTACT Christopher A.R. Bell, Director of Student Financial Services, University of Maine at Presque Isle, 181 Main Street, Presque Isle, ME 04769-2888, 207-768-9511. *Fax:* 207-768-9509. *E-mail:* chris@maine.edu.

Website: http://www.umpi.edu/.

UNIVERSITY OF MANAGEMENT AND TECHNOLOGY
Arlington, VA

ABOUT THE INSTITUTION Proprietary, coed. *Awards:* certificates, associate, bachelor's, master's, and doctoral degrees. 9 undergraduate majors. *Total enrollment:* 1,293. Undergraduates: 1,029.

GIFT AID (NEED-BASED) *Scholarships, grants, and awards:* Federal Pell.

LOANS *Programs:* Federal Direct (Subsidized and Unsubsidized Stafford, PLUS).

APPLYING FOR FINANCIAL AID *Required financial aid forms:* FAFSA, institution's own form.

CONTACT Financial Aid Administrator, University of Management and Technology, 1901 North Fort Myer Drive, Suite 700, Arlington, VA 22209, 703-516-0035 or toll-free 800-924-4883. *Fax:* 703-516-0985. *E-mail:* info@umtweb.edu.

Website: http://www.umtweb.edu/.

UNIVERSITY OF MARY
Bismarck, ND

ABOUT THE INSTITUTION Independent Roman Catholic, coed. *Awards:* bachelor's, master's, and doctoral degrees. 47 undergraduate majors. *Total enrollment:* 2,872. Undergraduates: 2,049. Freshmen: 405.

GIFT AID (NEED-BASED) *Scholarships, grants, and awards:* Federal Pell, FSEOG, state, private, college/university gift aid from institutional funds, TEACH Grants.

GIFT AID (NON-NEED-BASED) *Scholarships, grants, and awards by category:* Academic interests/achievement: general academic interests/achievements. Creative arts/performance: music. Special achievements/activities: general special achievements/activities. Special characteristics: children of faculty/staff, general special characteristics, local/state students, religious affiliation, veterans.

LOANS *Programs:* Federal Direct (Subsidized and Unsubsidized Stafford, PLUS), Perkins, Federal Nursing, private loans.

APPLYING FOR FINANCIAL AID *Required financial aid form:* FAFSA.

CONTACT Janell Thomas, Financial Assistance Director, University of Mary, 7500 University Drive, Bismarck, ND 58504-9652, 701-355-8244 or toll-free 800-288-6279. *Fax:* 701-255-7687. *E-mail:* jdthomas@umary.edu.

Website: http://www.umary.edu/.

UNIVERSITY OF MARY HARDIN-BAYLOR
Belton, TX

Tuition & fees: $25,860	Average undergraduate aid package: $17,171

ABOUT THE INSTITUTION Independent Southern Baptist, coed. *Awards:* certificates, bachelor's, master's, and doctoral degrees. 59 undergraduate majors. *Total enrollment:* 3,906. Undergraduates: 3,278. Freshmen: 750. Federal methodology is used as a basis for awarding need-based institutional aid.

UNDERGRADUATE EXPENSES for 2017–2018 *Application fee:* $35. *Comprehensive fee:* $33,452 includes full-time tuition ($23,660), mandatory fees ($2200), and room and board ($7592). Full-time tuition and fees vary according to course load and degree level. Room and board charges vary according to board plan and housing facility. *Part-time tuition:* $845 per credit hour. Part-time tuition and fees vary according to course load and degree level.

FRESHMAN FINANCIAL AID (Fall 2016, est.) 698 applied for aid; of those 84% were deemed to have need. 99% of freshmen with need received aid; of those 11% had need fully met. *Average percent of need met:* 64% (excluding resources awarded to replace EFC). *Average financial aid package:* $18,476 (excluding resources awarded to replace EFC). 17% of all full-time freshmen had no need and received non-need-based gift aid.

UNDERGRADUATE FINANCIAL AID (Fall 2016, est.) 2,635 applied for aid; of those 89% were deemed to have need. 100% of undergraduates with need received aid; of those 9% had need fully met. *Average percent of need met:* 57% (excluding resources awarded to replace EFC). *Average financial aid package:* $17,171 (excluding resources awarded to replace EFC). 14% of all full-time undergraduates had no need and received non-need-based gift aid.

GIFT AID (NEED-BASED) *Total amount:* $31,633,633 (18% federal, 16% state, 64% institutional, 2% external sources). *Receiving aid:* Freshmen: 81% (580); all full-time undergraduates: 83% (2,306). *Average award:* Freshmen: $15,322; Undergraduates: $13,293. *Scholarships, grants, and awards:* Federal Pell, FSEOG, state, private, college/university gift aid from institutional funds.

GIFT AID (NON-NEED-BASED) *Total amount:* $4,184,285 (1% state, 93% institutional, 6% external sources). *Receiving aid:* Freshmen: 7% (52). Undergraduates: 5% (145). *Average award:* Freshmen: $8112. Undergraduates: $8153. *Scholarships, grants, and awards by category:* Academic interests/achievement: biological sciences, business, communication, computer science, education, English, foreign languages, general academic interests/achievements, health fields, humanities, international studies, mathematics, physical sciences, premedicine, religion/biblical studies, social sciences. Creative arts/performance: art/fine arts, music. Special achievements/activities: cheerleading/drum major, community service, leadership, religious involvement. Special characteristics: children and siblings of alumni, children of faculty/staff, ethnic background, handicapped students, international students, local/state students, members of minority groups, out-of-state students, relatives of clergy, religious affiliation. *Tuition waivers:* Full or partial for employees or children of employees. *ROTC:* Army, Air Force cooperative.

LOANS *Student loans:* $20,443,524 (80% need-based, 20% non-need-based). 76% of past graduating class borrowed through all loan programs. *Average indebtedness per student:* $38,726. *Average need-based loan:* Freshmen: $3404. Undergraduates: $4467. *Parent loans:* $9,333,261 (49% need-based, 51% non-need-based). *Programs:* Federal Direct (Subsidized and Unsubsidized Stafford, PLUS), Perkins, state, private loans.

WORK-STUDY *Federal work-study:* Total amount: $721,754; jobs available. *State or other work-study/employment:* Total amount: $525,625 (38% need-based, 62% non-need-based). Part-time jobs available.

APPLYING FOR FINANCIAL AID *Required financial aid form:* FAFSA. *Financial aid deadline (priority):* 1/1. *Notification date:* Continuous beginning 11/1. Students must reply within 2 weeks of notification.

CONTACT Mr. David Orsag, Associate Director of Financial Aid, University of Mary Hardin-Baylor, 900 College Street, Box 8080, Belton, TX 76513, 254-295-4517 or toll-free 800-727-8642. *Fax:* 254-295-5009. *E-mail:* dorsag@umhb.edu. *Website:* http://www.umhb.edu/.

CONTACT Jane Hickey, Director, University of Maryland, Baltimore County, 1000 Hilltop Circle, Baltimore, MD 21250, 410-455-2387 or toll-free 800-UMBC-4U2 (in-state), 800-862-2402 (out-of-state). *Fax:* 410-455-3322. *Website:* http://www.umbc.edu/.

UNIVERSITY OF MARYLAND, BALTIMORE COUNTY
Baltimore, MD

Tuition & fees (MD res): $11,264	Average undergraduate aid package: $10,023

ABOUT THE INSTITUTION State-supported, coed. *Awards:* certificates, bachelor's, master's, and doctoral degrees. 53 undergraduate majors. *Total enrollment:* 13,640. Undergraduates: 11,142. Freshmen: 1,538. Federal methodology is used as a basis for awarding need-based institutional aid.

UNDERGRADUATE EXPENSES for 2016–2017 *Application fee:* $50. *One-time required fee:* $125. *Tuition, state resident:* full-time $8204; part-time $341 per credit hour. *Tuition, nonresident:* full-time $21,432; part-time $890 per credit hour. *Required fees:* full-time $3060; $134 per credit hour. Full-time tuition and fees vary according to location and program. Part-time tuition and fees vary according to location and program. *College room and board:* $11,218; *Room only:* $6796. Room and board charges vary according to board plan and housing facility.

FRESHMAN FINANCIAL AID (Fall 2016, est.) 1,201 applied for aid; of those 64% were deemed to have need. 91% of freshmen with need received aid; of those 18% had need fully met. *Average percent of need met:* 56% (excluding resources awarded to replace EFC). *Average financial aid package:* $10,253 (excluding resources awarded to replace EFC). 23% of all full-time freshmen had no need and received non-need-based gift aid.

UNDERGRADUATE FINANCIAL AID (Fall 2016, est.) 6,316 applied for aid; of those 80% were deemed to have need. 93% of undergraduates with need received aid; of those 10% had need fully met. *Average percent of need met:* 54% (excluding resources awarded to replace EFC). *Average financial aid package:* $10,023 (excluding resources awarded to replace EFC). 14% of all full-time undergraduates had no need and received non-need-based gift aid.

GIFT AID (NEED-BASED) *Total amount:* $30,665,215 (46% federal, 22% state, 28% institutional, 4% external sources). *Receiving aid:* Freshmen: 35% (531); all full-time undergraduates: 39% (3,648). *Average award:* Freshmen: $9373; Undergraduates: $8058. *Scholarships, grants, and awards:* Federal Pell, FSEOG, state, private, college/university gift aid from institutional funds.

GIFT AID (NON-NEED-BASED) *Total amount:* $12,085,071 (12% federal, 2% state, 65% institutional, 21% external sources). *Receiving aid:* Freshmen: 14% (212). Undergraduates: 5% (487). *Average award:* Freshmen: $7976. Undergraduates: $8666. *Scholarships, grants, and awards by category: Academic interests/achievement:* 2,613 awards ($16,139,460 total): biological sciences, computer science, education, engineering/technologies, English, foreign languages, general academic interests/achievements, humanities, mathematics, physical sciences, social sciences. *Creative arts/performance:* 31 awards ($33,950 total): art/fine arts, cinema/film/broadcasting, creative writing, dance, music, performing arts, theater/drama. *Tuition waivers:* Full or partial for employees or children of employees, senior citizens. *ROTC:* Army cooperative, Naval, Air Force cooperative.

LOANS *Student loans:* $37,920,201 (40% need-based, 60% non-need-based). 46% of past graduating class borrowed through all loan programs. *Average indebtedness per student:* $25,505. *Average need-based loan:* Freshmen: $3322. Undergraduates: $4334. *Parent loans:* $7,496,319 (75% need-based, 25% non-need-based). *Programs:* Federal Direct (Subsidized and Unsubsidized Stafford, PLUS), Perkins.

WORK-STUDY *Federal work-study:* Total amount: $369,570; 191 jobs averaging $1934. *State or other work-study/employment:* Total amount: $1,241,382 (55% need-based, 45% non-need-based). 119 part-time jobs averaging $10,431.

ATHLETIC AWARDS Total amount: $2,638,672 (35% need-based, 65% non-need-based).

APPLYING FOR FINANCIAL AID *Required financial aid form:* FAFSA. *Financial aid deadline (priority):* 2/14. *Notification date:* Continuous beginning 3/15.

UNIVERSITY OF MARYLAND, COLLEGE PARK
College Park, MD

Tuition & fees (MD res): $10,181	Average undergraduate aid package: $12,001

ABOUT THE INSTITUTION State-supported, coed. *Awards:* certificates, bachelor's, master's, and doctoral degrees. 90 undergraduate majors. *Total enrollment:* 39,083. Undergraduates: 28,472. Freshmen: 4,551. Federal methodology is used as a basis for awarding need-based institutional aid.

UNDERGRADUATE EXPENSES for 2016–2017 *Application fee:* $65. *Tuition, state resident:* full-time $8315; part-time $346 per credit hour. *Tuition, nonresident:* full-time $30,179; part-time $1258 per credit hour. *Required fees:* full-time $1866; $433 per term. Full-time tuition and fees vary according to location, program, and student level. Part-time tuition and fees vary according to course load, location, program, and student level. *College room and board:* $11,758; *Room only:* $6944. Room and board charges vary according to board plan and housing facility.

FRESHMAN FINANCIAL AID (Fall 2015) 3,102 applied for aid; of those 53% were deemed to have need. 100% of freshmen with need received aid; of those 23% had need fully met. *Average percent of need met:* 67% (excluding resources awarded to replace EFC). *Average financial aid package:* $12,005 (excluding resources awarded to replace EFC). 21% of all full-time freshmen had no need and received non-need-based gift aid.

UNDERGRADUATE FINANCIAL AID (Fall 2015) 15,359 applied for aid; of those 70% were deemed to have need. 100% of undergraduates with need received aid; of those 15% had need fully met. *Average percent of need met:* 66% (excluding resources awarded to replace EFC). *Average financial aid package:* $12,001 (excluding resources awarded to replace EFC). 13% of all full-time undergraduates had no need and received non-need-based gift aid.

GIFT AID (NEED-BASED) *Total amount:* $74,833,460 (31% federal, 21% state, 43% institutional, 5% external sources). *Receiving aid:* Freshmen: 33% (1,280); all full-time undergraduates: 33% (8,390). *Average award:* Freshmen: $10,072; Undergraduates: $9444. *Scholarships, grants, and awards:* Federal Pell, FSEOG, state, private, college/university gift aid from institutional funds.

GIFT AID (NON-NEED-BASED) *Total amount:* $30,902,422 (4% state, 79% institutional, 17% external sources). *Receiving aid:* Freshmen: 5% (197). Undergraduates: 3% (634). *Average award:* Freshmen: $6443. Undergraduates: $6671. *Scholarships, grants, and awards by category: Academic interests/achievement:* agriculture, architecture, biological sciences, business, communication, computer science, education, engineering/technologies, English, foreign languages, general academic interests/achievements, health fields, humanities, international studies, library science, mathematics, military science, physical sciences, premedicine, social sciences. *Creative arts/performance:* applied art and design, art/fine arts, dance, music, performing arts, theater/drama. *Special achievements/activities:* cheerleading/drum major. *Special characteristics:* adult students, out-of-state students. *Tuition waivers:* Full or partial for employees or children of employees. *ROTC:* Army, Naval cooperative, Air Force.

LOANS *Student loans:* $132,320,841 (49% need-based, 51% non-need-based). 43% of past graduating class borrowed through all loan programs. *Average indebtedness per student:* $27,559. *Average need-based loan:* Freshmen: $3492. Undergraduates: $4511. *Parent loans:* $27,026,192 (31% need-based, 69% non-need-based). *Programs:* Federal Direct (Subsidized and Unsubsidized Stafford, PLUS), Perkins, private loans.

WORK-STUDY *Federal work-study:* jobs available.

ATHLETIC AWARDS Total amount: $14,310,257 (35% need-based, 65% non-need-based).

APPLYING FOR FINANCIAL AID *Required financial aid form:* FAFSA. *Financial aid deadline (priority):* 2/15. *Notification date:* Continuous beginning 4/1. Students must reply by 5/1.

CONTACT Monique Boyd, Director of Financial Aid, University of Maryland, College Park, 0102 Lee Building, College Park, MD 20742, 301-314-9000 or toll-free 800-422-5867. *Fax:* 301-314-9265. *E-mail:* umfinaid@umd.edu.
Website: http://www.maryland.edu/.

UNIVERSITY OF MARYLAND EASTERN SHORE
Princess Anne, MD

Tuition & fees: N/R	Average undergraduate aid package: $4416

ABOUT THE INSTITUTION State-supported, coed. 51 undergraduate majors. Federal methodology is used as a basis for awarding need-based institutional aid.
FRESHMAN FINANCIAL AID (Fall 2015) 975 applied for aid; of those 89% were deemed to have need. 95% of freshmen with need received aid. *Average percent of need met:* 47% (excluding resources awarded to replace EFC). *Average financial aid package:* $4835 (excluding resources awarded to replace EFC). 2% of all full-time freshmen had no need and received non-need-based gift aid.
UNDERGRADUATE FINANCIAL AID (Fall 2015) 3,133 applied for aid; of those 86% were deemed to have need. 95% of undergraduates with need received aid; of those 1% had need fully met. *Average percent of need met:* 34% (excluding resources awarded to replace EFC). *Average financial aid package:* $4416 (excluding resources awarded to replace EFC). 3% of all full-time undergraduates had no need and received non-need-based gift aid.
GIFT AID (NEED-BASED) *Total amount:* $119,423,274 (93% federal, 4% state, 2% institutional, 1% external sources). *Receiving aid:* Freshmen: 64% (634); all full-time undergraduates: 62% (2,023). *Average award:* Freshmen: $3673; Undergraduates: $3337. *Scholarships, grants, and awards:* Federal Pell, FSEOG, state, private, college/university gift aid from institutional funds, United Negro College Fund.
GIFT AID (NON-NEED-BASED) *Total amount:* $19,935,829 (60% federal, 18% state, 15% institutional, 7% external sources). *Receiving aid:* Freshmen: 22% (215). Undergraduates: 19% (610). *Average award:* Freshmen: $3368. Undergraduates: $4545. *Scholarships, grants, and awards by category:* Academic interests/achievement: 228 awards ($442,168 total): agriculture, biological sciences, business, computer science, education, engineering/technologies, English, general academic interests/achievements, health fields, home economics, humanities, mathematics, physical sciences, social sciences. *Creative arts/performance:* 7 awards ($9533 total): applied art and design, art/fine arts. *Special achievements/activities:* 8 awards ($156,849 total): general special achievements/activities, memberships. *Special characteristics:* 419 awards ($1,024,592 total): children of faculty/staff, children of public servants, children of union members/company employees, general special characteristics, local/state students, public servants, veterans, veterans' children.
LOANS *Student loans:* $11,741,367 (52% need-based, 48% non-need-based). 62% of past graduating class borrowed through all loan programs. *Average indebtedness per student:* $9861. *Average need-based loan:* Freshmen: $3107. Undergraduates: $3996. *Parent loans:* $5,668,473 (100% non-need-based). *Programs:* Federal Direct (Subsidized and Unsubsidized Stafford, PLUS), Perkins.
WORK-STUDY *Federal work-study:* 88 jobs averaging $2955. *State or other work-study/employment:* Part-time jobs available.
ATHLETIC AWARDS Total amount: $1,786,041 (100% non-need-based).
APPLYING FOR FINANCIAL AID *Required financial aid form:* FAFSA. *Financial aid deadline (priority):* 3/1. *Notification date:* 4/16. Students must reply within 6 weeks of notification.
CONTACT Mr. Al J. Dorsett, Director of Financial Aid, University of Maryland Eastern Shore, 1 Backbone Road, SDC, Suite 1100, Princess Anne, MD 21853-1299, 410-651-6172. *Fax:* 410-651-7670. *E-mail:* ajdorsett@umes.edu.
Website: http://www.umes.edu/.

UNIVERSITY OF MARYLAND UNIVERSITY COLLEGE
Adelphi, MD

Tuition & fees (MD res): $7176	Average undergraduate aid package: $7217

ABOUT THE INSTITUTION State-supported, coed. *Awards:* certificates, associate, bachelor's, master's, and doctoral degrees (offers primarily part-time evening and weekend degree programs at more than 30 off-campus locations in Maryland and the Washington, DC area, and more than 180 military communities in Europe and Asia with military enrollment not reflected in this profile; associate of arts program available to military students only). 28 undergraduate majors. *Total enrollment:* 57,529. Undergraduates: 44,219. Freshmen: 990. Federal methodology is used as a basis for awarding need-based institutional aid.
UNDERGRADUATE EXPENSES for 2017–2018 *Application fee:* $50. *Tuition, state resident:* full-time $6816; part-time $284 per credit hour. *Tuition, nonresident:* full-time $11,976; part-time $499 per credit hour. *Required fees:* full-time $360.
FRESHMAN FINANCIAL AID (Fall 2015) 193 applied for aid; of those 92% were deemed to have need. 80% of freshmen with need received aid; of those 1% had need fully met. *Average percent of need met:* 27% (excluding resources awarded to replace EFC). *Average financial aid package:* $5534 (excluding resources awarded to replace EFC).
UNDERGRADUATE FINANCIAL AID (Fall 2015) 5,675 applied for aid; of those 95% were deemed to have need. 89% of undergraduates with need received aid; of those 1% had need fully met. *Average percent of need met:* 30% (excluding resources awarded to replace EFC). *Average financial aid package:* $7217 (excluding resources awarded to replace EFC).
GIFT AID (NEED-BASED) *Total amount:* $43,985,744 (87% federal, 5% state, 8% institutional). *Receiving aid:* Freshmen: 41% (120); all full-time undergraduates: 41% (3,631). *Average award:* Freshmen: $3686; Undergraduates: $4711. *Scholarships, grants, and awards:* Federal Pell, FSEOG, state, private, college/university gift aid from institutional funds.
GIFT AID (NON-NEED-BASED) *Total amount:* $5,430,751 (3% state, 96% institutional, 1% external sources). *Receiving aid:* Freshmen: 6% (17). Undergraduates: 13% (1,143). *Scholarships, grants, and awards by category:* Academic interests/achievement: general academic interests/achievements. Special achievements/activities: general special achievements/activities. *Tuition waivers:* Full or partial for employees or children of employees, senior citizens.
LOANS *Student loans:* $92,560,985 (42% need-based, 58% non-need-based). *Average need-based loan:* Freshmen: $3003. Undergraduates: $4254. *Parent loans:* $387,536 (100% non-need-based). *Programs:* Federal Direct (Subsidized and Unsubsidized Stafford, PLUS), Perkins.
WORK-STUDY Federal work-study jobs available. *State or other work-study/employment:* Part-time jobs available.
APPLYING FOR FINANCIAL AID *Required financial aid form:* FAFSA. *Financial aid deadline (priority):* 6/1. *Notification date:* Continuous beginning 5/1. Students must reply within 2 weeks of notification.
CONTACT Cheryl Storie, Associate Vice President of Financial Aid, University of Maryland University College, 3501 University Boulevard East, Adelphi, MD 20783, 301-985-7847 or toll-free 800-888-8682. *Fax:* 301-985-7462. *E-mail:* finaid@umuc.edu.
Website: http://www.umuc.edu/.

UNIVERSITY OF MARY WASHINGTON
Fredericksburg, VA

Tuition & fees (VA res): $11,570	Average undergraduate aid package: $9283

ABOUT THE INSTITUTION State-supported, coed. *Awards:* certificates, bachelor's, and master's degrees. 28 undergraduate majors. *Total enrollment:* 4,726. Undergraduates: 4,357. Freshmen: 972. Federal methodology is used as a basis for awarding need-based institutional aid.
UNDERGRADUATE EXPENSES for 2016–2017 *Application fee:* $50. *One-time required fee:* $60. *Tuition, state resident:* full-time $5772; part-time $248 per credit hour. *Tuition, nonresident:* full-time $20,362; part-time $853 per credit

hour. **Required fees:** full-time $5798; $165 per credit hour or $30 per term. Full-time tuition and fees vary according to course load, degree level, and location. Part-time tuition and fees vary according to course load, degree level, and location. **College room and board:** $11,118; **Room only:** $7326. Room and board charges vary according to board plan and housing facility.

FRESHMAN FINANCIAL AID (Fall 2015) 772 applied for aid; of those 60% were deemed to have need. 97% of freshmen with need received aid; of those 16% had need fully met. **Average percent of need met:** 46% (excluding resources awarded to replace EFC). **Average financial aid package:** $8868 (excluding resources awarded to replace EFC). 38% of all full-time freshmen had no need and received non-need-based gift aid.

UNDERGRADUATE FINANCIAL AID (Fall 2015) 2,449 applied for aid; of those 67% were deemed to have need. 96% of undergraduates with need received aid; of those 14% had need fully met. **Average percent of need met:** 49% (excluding resources awarded to replace EFC). **Average financial aid package:** $9283 (excluding resources awarded to replace EFC). 20% of all full-time undergraduates had no need and received non-need-based gift aid.

GIFT AID (NEED-BASED) Total amount: $7,544,119 (41% federal, 40% state, 19% institutional). **Receiving aid:** Freshmen: 33% (313); all full-time undergraduates: 28% (1,059). **Average award:** Freshmen: $3343; Undergraduates: $3352. **Scholarships, grants, and awards:** Federal Pell, FSEOG, state, private, college/university gift aid from institutional funds.

GIFT AID (NON-NEED-BASED) Total amount: $5,312,119 (80% institutional, 20% external sources). **Receiving aid:** Freshmen: 33% (316). Undergraduates: 17% (651). **Average award:** Freshmen: $2714. Undergraduates: $2825. **Scholarships, grants, and awards by category:** Academic interests/achievement: architecture, biological sciences, business, computer science, education, English, foreign languages, general academic interests/achievements, humanities, international studies, library science, mathematics, physical sciences, religion/biblical studies, social sciences. Creative arts/performance: art/fine arts, dance, journalism/publications, music, theater/drama. Special achievements/activities: leadership. Special characteristics: adult students, children and siblings of alumni, children of faculty/staff, local/state students. **Tuition waivers:** Full or partial for senior citizens. **ROTC:** Army cooperative.

LOANS Student loans: $12,558,795 (46% need-based, 54% non-need-based). 51% of past graduating class borrowed through all loan programs. Average indebtedness per student: $19,444. **Average need-based loan:** Freshmen: $3206. Undergraduates: $4145. **Parent loans:** $4,509,843 (100% need-based). **Programs:** Federal Direct (Subsidized and Unsubsidized Stafford, PLUS), Perkins.

WORK-STUDY Federal work-study: jobs available. **State or other work-study/employment:** Part-time jobs available.

APPLYING FOR FINANCIAL AID Required financial aid form: FAFSA. **Financial aid deadline:** 7/1 (priority: 2/1). **Notification date:** Continuous beginning 2/1. Students must reply by 5/1 or within 2 weeks of notification.

CONTACT Ms. Heidi Hunter-Goldsworthy, Director of Financial Aid, University of Mary Washington, 1301 College Avenue, Fredericksburg, VA 22401-5358, 540-654-2468 or toll-free 800-468-5614. Fax: 540-654-1858. E-mail: hhunterg@umw.edu. Website: http://www.umw.edu/.

FRESHMAN FINANCIAL AID (Fall 2015) 4,007 applied for aid; of those 64% were deemed to have need. 99% of freshmen with need received aid; of those 14% had need fully met. **Average percent of need met:** 86% (excluding resources awarded to replace EFC). **Average financial aid package:** $16,388 (excluding resources awarded to replace EFC). 19% of all full-time freshmen had no need and received non-need-based gift aid.

UNDERGRADUATE FINANCIAL AID (Fall 2015) 16,792 applied for aid; of those 71% were deemed to have need. 99% of undergraduates with need received aid; of those 14% had need fully met. **Average percent of need met:** 85% (excluding resources awarded to replace EFC). **Average financial aid package:** $16,749 (excluding resources awarded to replace EFC). 14% of all full-time undergraduates had no need and received non-need-based gift aid.

GIFT AID (NEED-BASED) Total amount: $93,543,963 (26% federal, 7% state, 63% institutional, 4% external sources). **Receiving aid:** Freshmen: 52% (2,427); all full-time undergraduates: 49% (10,356). **Average award:** Freshmen: $10,723; Undergraduates: $10,249. **Scholarships, grants, and awards:** Federal Pell, FSEOG, state, private, college/university gift aid from institutional funds.

GIFT AID (NON-NEED-BASED) Total amount: $19,599,640 (1% state, 83% institutional, 16% external sources). **Receiving aid:** Freshmen: 6% (277). Undergraduates: 4% (849). **Average award:** Freshmen: $6110. Undergraduates: $5132. **Scholarships, grants, and awards by category:** Academic interests/achievement: agriculture, architecture, biological sciences, business, communication, computer science, education, engineering/technologies, English, health fields, humanities, mathematics, military science, physical sciences, premedicine, social sciences. Creative arts/performance: art/fine arts, dance, journalism/publications, music, theater/drama. Special achievements/activities: cheerleading/drum major, general special achievements/activities, leadership. Special characteristics: children and siblings of alumni, children of faculty/staff, handicapped students, veterans. **Tuition waivers:** Full or partial for employees or children of employees, senior citizens. **ROTC:** Army, Air Force.

LOANS Student loans: $141,301,039 (59% need-based, 41% non-need-based). 68% of past graduating class borrowed through all loan programs. Average indebtedness per student: $31,397. **Average need-based loan:** Freshmen: $3396. Undergraduates: $4555. **Parent loans:** $30,824,288 (32% need-based, 68% non-need-based). **Programs:** Federal Direct (Subsidized and Unsubsidized Stafford, PLUS), Perkins, Federal Nursing.

WORK-STUDY Federal work-study: 2,026 jobs averaging $1248.

ATHLETIC AWARDS Total amount: $9,972,531 (32% need-based, 68% non-need-based).

APPLYING FOR FINANCIAL AID Required financial aid form: FAFSA. **Financial aid deadline (priority):** 3/1. **Notification date:** Continuous beginning 1/1. Students must reply by 5/1.

CONTACT Office of Financial Aid Services, University of Massachusetts Amherst, 255 Whitmore Administration Building, 181 Presidents Drive, Amherst, MA 01003, 413-545-0801. Fax: 413-545-1700. Website: http://www.umass.edu/.

UNIVERSITY OF MASSACHUSETTS AMHERST

Amherst, MA

Tuition & fees (MA res): $14,971	Average undergraduate aid package: $16,749

ABOUT THE INSTITUTION State-supported, coed. **Awards:** certificates, associate, bachelor's, master's, and doctoral degrees. 92 undergraduate majors. **Total enrollment:** 30,037. Undergraduates: 23,373. Freshmen: 4,690. Federal methodology is used as a basis for awarding need-based institutional aid.

UNDERGRADUATE EXPENSES for 2016–2017 Application fee: $75. **One-time required fee:** $185. **Tuition, state resident:** full-time $14,590; part-time $5110 per term. **Tuition, nonresident:** full-time $31,823; part-time $11,236 per term. **Required fees:** full-time $381; $191 per term. Full-time tuition and fees vary according to class time, location, program, reciprocity agreements, and student level. Part-time tuition and fees vary according to class time, course load, location, program, reciprocity agreements, and student level. **College room and board:** $11,897; **Room only:** $6659. Room and board charges vary according to board plan and housing facility.

UNIVERSITY OF MASSACHUSETTS BOSTON

Boston, MA

Tuition & fees (MA res): $13,435	Average undergraduate aid package: $15,856

ABOUT THE INSTITUTION State-supported, coed. **Awards:** certificates, bachelor's, master's, and doctoral degrees. 46 undergraduate majors. **Total enrollment:** 16,847. Undergraduates: 12,847. Freshmen: 1,651. Federal methodology is used as a basis for awarding need-based institutional aid.

UNDERGRADUATE EXPENSES for 2016–2017 Application fee: $60. **Tuition, state resident:** full-time $13,435; part-time $546.25 per credit hour. **Tuition, nonresident:** full-time $32,023; part-time $1320.75 per credit hour. **Required fees:** $13.50 per credit hour. Full-time tuition and fees vary according to program. Part-time tuition and fees vary according to program.

FRESHMAN FINANCIAL AID (Fall 2015) 1,212 applied for aid; of those 85% were deemed to have need. 100% of freshmen with need received aid; of those 39% had need fully met. **Average percent of need met:** 89% (excluding resources awarded to replace EFC). **Average financial aid package:** $14,989 (excluding

resources awarded to replace EFC). 8% of all full-time freshmen had no need and received non-need-based gift aid.

UNDERGRADUATE FINANCIAL AID (Fall 2015) 6,734 applied for aid; of those 90% were deemed to have need. 100% of undergraduates with need received aid; of those 39% had need fully met. *Average percent of need met:* 89% (excluding resources awarded to replace EFC). *Average financial aid package:* $15,856 (excluding resources awarded to replace EFC). 3% of all full-time undergraduates had no need and received non-need-based gift aid.

GIFT AID (NEED-BASED) *Total amount:* $56,560,122 (40% federal, 11% state, 47% institutional, 2% external sources). *Receiving aid:* Freshmen: 64% (989); all full-time undergraduates: 61% (5,637). *Average award:* Freshmen: $10,463; Undergraduates: $9448. *Scholarships, grants, and awards:* Federal Pell, FSEOG, state, private, college/university gift aid from institutional funds, TEACH Grants.

GIFT AID (NON-NEED-BASED) *Total amount:* $5,264,310 (2% state, 88% institutional, 10% external sources). *Receiving aid:* Freshmen: 5% (80). Undergraduates: 2% (172). *Average award:* Freshmen: $6830. Undergraduates: $5955. *Scholarships, grants, and awards by category:* Academic interests/achievement: general academic interests/achievements. Special achievements/activities: general special achievements/activities, leadership. Special characteristics: adult students, children of faculty/staff, children of union members/company employees, first-generation college students, local/state students, out-of-state students, veterans, veterans' children. **ROTC:** Army cooperative, Naval cooperative, Air Force cooperative.

LOANS *Student loans:* $50,192,981 (78% need-based, 22% non-need-based). 63% of past graduating class borrowed through all loan programs. *Average indebtedness per student:* $28,368. *Average need-based loan:* Freshmen: $5013. Undergraduates: $7025. *Parent loans:* $3,334,555 (34% need-based, 66% non-need-based). *Programs:* Federal Direct (Subsidized and Unsubsidized Stafford, PLUS), Perkins.

WORK-STUDY *Federal work-study:* jobs available.

APPLYING FOR FINANCIAL AID *Required financial aid form:* FAFSA. *Financial aid deadline (priority):* 3/1. *Notification date:* Continuous beginning 12/15.

CONTACT Judy L. Keyes, Director of Financial Aid Services, University of Massachusetts Boston, 100 Morrissey Boulevard, Boston, MA 02125-3393, 617-287-6300. *Fax:* 617-287-6323. *E-mail:* judy.keyes@umb.edu. *Website:* http://www.umb.edu/.

UNIVERSITY OF MASSACHUSETTS DARTMOUTH
North Dartmouth, MA

Tuition & fees (MA res): $13,188	Average undergraduate aid package: $17,213

ABOUT THE INSTITUTION State-supported, coed. *Awards:* certificates, bachelor's, master's, and doctoral degrees. 47 undergraduate majors. *Total enrollment:* 8,647. Undergraduates: 6,999. Freshmen: 1,367. Federal methodology is used as a basis for awarding need-based institutional aid.

UNDERGRADUATE EXPENSES for 2016–2017 *Application fee:* $60. *One-time required fee:* $100. *Tuition, state resident:* full-time $12,783; part-time $532.63 per credit. *Tuition, nonresident:* full-time $27,068; part-time $1127.83 per credit. *Required fees:* full-time $405; $25.88 per credit. Full-time tuition and fees vary according to class time, program, and reciprocity agreements. Part-time tuition and fees vary according to class time, course load, program, and reciprocity agreements. *College room and board:* $12,470; *Room only:* $4519. Room and board charges vary according to board plan and housing facility.

FRESHMAN FINANCIAL AID (Fall 2016, est.) 1,235 applied for aid; of those 82% were deemed to have need. 100% of freshmen with need received aid; of those 42% had need fully met. *Average percent of need met:* 85% (excluding resources awarded to replace EFC). *Average financial aid package:* $16,917 (excluding resources awarded to replace EFC). 13% of all full-time freshmen had no need and received non-need-based gift aid.

UNDERGRADUATE FINANCIAL AID (Fall 2016, est.) 5,028 applied for aid; of those 84% were deemed to have need. 100% of undergraduates with need received aid; of those 45% had need fully met. *Average percent of need met:* 87% (excluding resources awarded to replace EFC). *Average financial aid package:* $17,213 (excluding resources awarded to replace EFC). 7% of all full-time undergraduates had no need and received non-need-based gift aid.

GIFT AID (NEED-BASED) *Total amount:* $36,930,000 (32% federal, 11% state, 54% institutional, 3% external sources). *Receiving aid:* Freshmen: 70% (945); all full-time undergraduates: 63% (3,750). *Average award:* Freshmen: $10,070; Undergraduates: $10,181. *Scholarships, grants, and awards:* Federal Pell, FSEOG, state, private, college/university gift aid from institutional funds.

GIFT AID (NON-NEED-BASED) *Total amount:* $3,791,000 (2% state, 92% institutional, 6% external sources). *Receiving aid:* Freshmen: 6% (76). Undergraduates: 3% (208). *Average award:* Freshmen: $4396. Undergraduates: $4596. *Scholarships, grants, and awards by category:* Academic interests/achievement: biological sciences, business, computer science, education, engineering/technologies, foreign languages, general academic interests/achievements, home economics, humanities, mathematics, physical sciences, religion/biblical studies, social sciences. *Creative arts/performance:* applied art and design, art/fine arts. *Special achievements/activities:* community service. *Special characteristics:* adult students, children of faculty/staff, children of union members/company employees, children with a deceased or disabled parent, ethnic background, first-generation college students, local/state students, members of minority groups, previous college experience, public servants, veterans. *Tuition waivers:* Full or partial for employees or children of employees, senior citizens. *ROTC:* Army cooperative.

LOANS *Student loans:* $41,100,000 (68% need-based, 32% non-need-based). 78% of past graduating class borrowed through all loan programs. *Average indebtedness per student:* $32,099. *Average need-based loan:* Freshmen: $7915. Undergraduates: $8333. *Parent loans:* $11,100,000 (44% need-based, 56% non-need-based). *Programs:* Federal Direct (Subsidized and Unsubsidized Stafford, PLUS), Perkins, Federal Nursing, state.

WORK-STUDY *Federal work-study:* Total amount: $1,400,000; 933 jobs averaging $1300. *State or other work-study/employment:* Part-time jobs available.

APPLYING FOR FINANCIAL AID *Required financial aid form:* FAFSA. *Financial aid deadline (priority):* 3/1. *Notification date:* Continuous beginning 3/25. Students must reply within 3 weeks of notification.

CONTACT Ms. Korinne Peterson, Director of Financial Aid, University of Massachusetts Dartmouth, 285 Old Westport Road, North Dartmouth, MA 02747-2300, 508-999-8643. *Fax:* 508-999-8935. *E-mail:* financialaid@umassd.edu. *Website:* http://www.umassd.edu/.

UNIVERSITY OF MASSACHUSETTS LOWELL
Lowell, MA

Tuition & fees (MA res): $14,307	Average undergraduate aid package: $15,393

ABOUT THE INSTITUTION State-supported, coed. *Awards:* certificates, associate, bachelor's, master's, and doctoral degrees. 49 undergraduate majors. *Total enrollment:* 17,854. Undergraduates: 13,639. Freshmen: 1,685. Federal methodology is used as a basis for awarding need-based institutional aid.

UNDERGRADUATE EXPENSES for 2016–2017 *Application fee:* $60. *Tuition, state resident:* full-time $13,932; part-time $581 per credit hour. *Tuition, nonresident:* full-time $30,500; part-time $1271 per credit hour. *Required fees:* full-time $375; $16 per credit hour. Part-time tuition and fees vary according to course load. *College room and board:* $12,073; *Room only:* $7975. Room and board charges vary according to board plan and housing facility.

FRESHMAN FINANCIAL AID (Fall 2015) 1,345 applied for aid; of those 73% were deemed to have need. 100% of freshmen with need received aid; of those 52% had need fully met. *Average percent of need met:* 90% (excluding resources awarded to replace EFC). *Average financial aid package:* $16,108 (excluding resources awarded to replace EFC). 17% of all full-time freshmen had no need and received non-need-based gift aid.

UNDERGRADUATE FINANCIAL AID (Fall 2015) 7,331 applied for aid; of those 79% were deemed to have need. 100% of undergraduates with need received aid; of those 51% had need fully met. *Average percent of need met:* 90% (excluding resources awarded to replace EFC). *Average financial aid package:* $15,393 (excluding resources awarded to replace EFC). 9% of all full-time undergraduates had no need and received non-need-based gift aid.

GIFT AID (NEED-BASED) *Total amount:* $40,712,331 (37% federal, 11% state, 49% institutional, 3% external sources). *Receiving aid:* Freshmen: 57% (909); all full-time undergraduates: 53% (5,083). *Average award:* Freshmen: $9853; Undergrad-

uates: $8631. **Scholarships, grants, and awards:** Federal Pell, FSEOG, state, private, college/university gift aid from institutional funds.

GIFT AID (NON-NEED-BASED) Total amount: $7,142,138 (8% state, 84% institutional, 8% external sources). **Receiving aid:** Freshmen: 5% (72). Undergraduates: 3% (280). **Average award:** Freshmen: $4565. Undergraduates: $4648. **Scholarships, grants, and awards by category:** *Academic interests/achievement:* biological sciences, business, computer science, education, engineering/technologies, English, general academic interests/achievements, health fields, humanities, mathematics. *Creative arts/performance:* art/fine arts, music. *Special achievements/activities:* community service, general special achievements/activities. *Special characteristics:* children and siblings of alumni, children of faculty/staff, children of public servants, children of union members/company employees, general special characteristics, out-of-state students, veterans. **Tuition waivers:** Full or partial for employees or children of employees, senior citizens. **ROTC:** Army, Air Force.

LOANS Student loans: $70,335,989 (66% need-based, 34% non-need-based). 78% of past graduating class borrowed through all loan programs. *Average indebtedness per student:* $31,432. **Average need-based loan:** Freshmen: $3367. Undergraduates: $4410. **Parent loans:** $12,020,911 (30% need-based, 70% non-need-based). **Programs:** Federal Direct (Subsidized and Unsubsidized Stafford, PLUS), Perkins.

WORK-STUDY Federal work-study: jobs available. **State or other work-study/employment:** Total amount: $2,631,393 (96% need-based, 4% non-need-based). Part-time jobs available.

ATHLETIC AWARDS Total amount: $4,450,686 (36% need-based, 64% non-need-based).

APPLYING FOR FINANCIAL AID Required financial aid form: FAFSA. **Financial aid deadline (priority):** 3/1. **Notification date:** Continuous beginning 1/1.

CONTACT Joyce McLaughlin, Director of Financial Aid, University of Massachusetts Lowell, University Crossing, 220 Pawtucket Street, Suite 280, Lowell, MA 01854, 978-934-4220. *Fax:* 978-934-3009. *E-mail:* joyce_mclaughlin@uml.edu. *Website:* http://www.uml.edu/.

GIFT AID (NON-NEED-BASED) Total amount: $30,316,776 (57% state, 39% institutional, 4% external sources). **Receiving aid:** Freshmen: 49% (1,291). Undergraduates: 45% (5,612). **Average award:** Freshmen: $6030. Undergraduates: $6229. **Scholarships, grants, and awards by category:** *Academic interests/achievement:* biological sciences, business, communication, computer science, education, engineering/technologies, English, general academic interests/achievements, health fields, home economics, humanities, international studies, mathematics, military science, physical sciences, premedicine, social sciences. *Creative arts/performance:* art/fine arts, cinema/film/broadcasting, creative writing, dance, journalism/publications, music, theater/drama. *Special achievements/activities:* cheerleading/drum major, community service, general special achievements/activities, leadership. *Special characteristics:* adult students, children of educators, children of faculty/staff, children of public servants, handicapped students, members of minority groups, public servants. **Tuition waivers:** Full or partial for employees or children of employees, senior citizens. **ROTC:** Army, Naval, Air Force.

LOANS Student loans: $74,689,880 (47% need-based, 53% non-need-based). 67% of past graduating class borrowed through all loan programs. *Average indebtedness per student:* $27,155. **Average need-based loan:** Freshmen: $3241. Undergraduates: $4292. **Parent loans:** $9,929,953 (100% non-need-based). **Programs:** Federal Direct (Subsidized and Unsubsidized Stafford, PLUS), Perkins, college/university.

WORK-STUDY Federal work-study: Total amount: $346,299; 150 jobs averaging $2754. **State or other work-study/employment:** Total amount: $3,268,619 (100% non-need-based). Part-time jobs available.

ATHLETIC AWARDS Total amount: $7,287,192 (100% non-need-based).

APPLYING FOR FINANCIAL AID Required financial aid form: FAFSA. **Financial aid deadline (priority):** 3/1. **Notification date:** Continuous beginning 4/1. Students must reply by 8/1.

CONTACT Karen Smith, Interim Director of Financial Aid, University of Memphis, Wilder Tower 103, Memphis, TN 38152, 901-678-4825 or toll-free 800-669-2678. *Fax:* 901-678-3590. *E-mail:* kasmith@memphis.edu. *Website:* http://www.memphis.edu/.

UNIVERSITY OF MEMPHIS
Memphis, TN

Tuition & fees (TN res): $9497	Average undergraduate aid package: $9985

ABOUT THE INSTITUTION State-supported, coed. **Awards:** certificates, bachelor's, master's, and doctoral degrees. 67 undergraduate majors. **Total enrollment:** 20,585. Undergraduates: 16,639. Freshmen: 2,105. Federal methodology is used as a basis for awarding need-based institutional aid.

UNDERGRADUATE EXPENSES for 2016–2017 Application fee: $25. **Tuition, state resident:** full-time $7860; part-time $312 per credit hour. **Tuition, nonresident:** full-time $19,572; part-time $800 per credit hour. **Required fees:** full-time $1637. Full-time tuition and fees vary according to course load, degree level, program, and reciprocity agreements. Part-time tuition and fees vary according to course load, degree level, and program. **College room and board:** $9153; **Room only:** $5456. Room and board charges vary according to board plan, housing facility, and location.

FRESHMAN FINANCIAL AID (Fall 2016, est.) 2,599 applied for aid; of those 85% were deemed to have need. 87% of freshmen with need received aid; of those 6% had need fully met. **Average percent of need met:** 68% (excluding resources awarded to replace EFC). **Average financial aid package:** $10,501 (excluding resources awarded to replace EFC). 4% of all full-time freshmen had no need and received non-need-based gift aid.

UNDERGRADUATE FINANCIAL AID (Fall 2016, est.) 12,358 applied for aid; of those 84% were deemed to have need. 90% of undergraduates with need received aid; of those 15% had need fully met. **Average percent of need met:** 72% (excluding resources awarded to replace EFC). **Average financial aid package:** $9985 (excluding resources awarded to replace EFC). 11% of all full-time undergraduates had no need and received non-need-based gift aid.

GIFT AID (NEED-BASED) Total amount: $44,246,908 (79% federal, 20% state, 1% institutional). **Receiving aid:** Freshmen: 61% (1,606); all full-time undergraduates: 60% (7,426). **Average award:** Freshmen: $6909; Undergraduates: $6370. **Scholarships, grants, and awards:** Federal Pell, FSEOG, state, private, college/university gift aid from institutional funds.

UNIVERSITY OF MIAMI
Coral Gables, FL

Tuition & fees: $47,004	Average undergraduate aid package: $40,549

ABOUT THE INSTITUTION Independent, coed. **Awards:** certificates, bachelor's, master's, and doctoral degrees. 129 undergraduate majors. **Total enrollment:** 16,801. Undergraduates: 10,849. Freshmen: 2,065. Institutional methodology is used as a basis for awarding need-based institutional aid.

UNDERGRADUATE EXPENSES for 2016–2017 Application fee: $70. **Comprehensive fee:** $60,314 includes full-time tuition ($45,600), mandatory fees ($1404), and room and board ($13,310). **College room only:** $7720. Full-time tuition and fees vary according to course load. Room and board charges vary according to board plan and housing facility. **Part-time tuition:** $1900 per credit hour. Part-time tuition and fees vary according to course load and program.

FRESHMAN FINANCIAL AID (Fall 2016, est.) 1,275 applied for aid; of those 74% were deemed to have need. 98% of freshmen with need received aid; of those 98% had need fully met. **Average percent of need met:** 97% (excluding resources awarded to replace EFC). **Average financial aid package:** $42,187 (excluding resources awarded to replace EFC). 13% of all full-time freshmen had no need and received non-need-based gift aid.

UNDERGRADUATE FINANCIAL AID (Fall 2016, est.) 5,247 applied for aid; of those 86% were deemed to have need. 98% of undergraduates with need received aid; of those 94% had need fully met. **Average percent of need met:** 90% (excluding resources awarded to replace EFC). **Average financial aid package:** $40,549 (excluding resources awarded to replace EFC). 10% of all full-time undergraduates had no need and received non-need-based gift aid.

GIFT AID (NEED-BASED) Total amount: $131,443,160 (7% federal, 8% state, 80% institutional, 5% external sources). **Receiving aid:** Freshmen: 25% (518); all full-time undergraduates: 23% (2,307). **Average award:** Freshmen: $8925; Undergraduates: $10,616. **Scholarships, grants, and awards:** Federal Pell, FSEOG, state, private, college/university gift aid from institutional funds.

GIFT AID (NON-NEED-BASED) Total amount: $77,601,923 (9% state, 84% institutional, 7% external sources). **Receiving aid:** Freshmen: 44% (892). Undergraduates: 40% (4,085). **Average award:** Freshmen: $19,877. Undergraduates: $18,480.

Scholarships, grants, and awards by category: Academic interests/achievement: general academic interests/achievements, military science. *Creative arts/performance:* music, performing arts, theater/drama. *Special achievements/activities:* cheerleading/drum major, leadership. *Special characteristics:* children of faculty/staff, first-generation college students, international students, veterans, veterans' children. *Tuition waivers:* Full or partial for employees or children of employees. *ROTC:* Army, Air Force.

LOANS *Student loans:* $15,988,610 (74% need-based, 26% non-need-based). 37% of past graduating class borrowed through all loan programs. *Average indebtedness per student:* $21,500. *Average need-based loan:* Freshmen: $3425. Undergraduates: $4527. *Parent loans:* $13,880,086 (5% need-based, 95% non-need-based). *Programs:* Federal Direct (Subsidized and Unsubsidized Stafford, PLUS), Perkins, Federal Nursing, college/university, private loans.

WORK-STUDY *Federal work-study:* Total amount: $7,313,999; jobs available. *State or other work-study/employment:* Total amount: $2,095,654 (38% need-based, 62% non-need-based). Part-time jobs available.

ATHLETIC AWARDS Total amount: $14,399,501 (78% need-based, 22% non-need-based).

APPLYING FOR FINANCIAL AID *Required financial aid forms:* FAFSA, CSS Financial Aid PROFILE, noncustodial (divorced/separated) parent's statement, business/farm supplement, federal income tax form(s). *Financial aid deadline:* 4/15 (priority: 1/1). *Notification date:* Continuous beginning 1/20. Students must reply by 5/1.

CONTACT Mr. Raymond Nault-Hix, Executive Director for Financial Assistance Services, University of Miami, 1306 Stanford Drive, University Center, Suite 2275, Coral Gables, FL 33146, 305-284-5212. *Fax:* 305-284-8641. *E-mail:* rnaulthix@miami.edu.
Website: http://www.miami.edu/.

UNIVERSITY OF MICHIGAN
Ann Arbor, MI

Tuition & fees (MI res): $14,402	Average undergraduate aid package: $24,323

ABOUT THE INSTITUTION State-supported, coed. *Awards:* certificates, bachelor's, master's, and doctoral degrees. 127 undergraduate majors. *Total enrollment:* 44,718. Undergraduates: 28,983. Freshmen: 6,689. Both federal and institutional methodology are used as a basis for awarding need-based institutional aid.

UNDERGRADUATE EXPENSES for 2016–2017 *Application fee:* $75. *Tuition, state resident:* full-time $14,074; part-time $556 per credit hour. *Tuition, nonresident:* full-time $45,082; part-time $1848 per credit hour. *Required fees:* full-time $328; $164 per term. Full-time tuition and fees vary according to course load, degree level, program, and student level. Part-time tuition and fees vary according to course load, degree level, program, and student level. *College room and board:* $10,872. Room and board charges vary according to board plan and housing facility.

FRESHMAN FINANCIAL AID (Fall 2015) 4,123 applied for aid; of those 59% were deemed to have need. 96% of freshmen with need received aid; of those 81% had need fully met. *Average percent of need met:* 89% (excluding resources awarded to replace EFC). *Average financial aid package:* $24,025 (excluding resources awarded to replace EFC). 20% of all full-time freshmen had no need and received non-need-based gift aid.

UNDERGRADUATE FINANCIAL AID (Fall 2015) 14,276 applied for aid; of those 73% were deemed to have need. 97% of undergraduates with need received aid; of those 82% had need fully met. *Average percent of need met:* 87% (excluding resources awarded to replace EFC). *Average financial aid package:* $24,323 (excluding resources awarded to replace EFC). 15% of all full-time undergraduates had no need and received non-need-based gift aid.

GIFT AID (NEED-BASED) *Total amount:* $155,072,071 (13% federal, 87% institutional). *Receiving aid:* Freshmen: 32% (1,944); all full-time undergraduates: 32% (8,564). *Average award:* Freshmen: $17,410; Undergraduates: $17,673. *Scholarships, grants, and awards:* Federal Pell, FSEOG, state, private, college/university gift aid from institutional funds, TEACH Grants, Iraq and Afghanistan Service Grants, Michigan Competitive Scholarships.

GIFT AID (NON-NEED-BASED) *Total amount:* $71,499,284 (10% federal, 3% state, 66% institutional, 21% external sources). *Receiving aid:* Freshmen: 27% (1,661). Undergraduates: 23% (6,333). *Average award:* Freshmen: $5177. Undergraduates: $7442. *Scholarships, grants, and awards by category: Academic*

interests/achievement: architecture, area/ethnic studies, biological sciences, business, communication, computer science, education, engineering/technologies, English, foreign languages, general academic interests/achievements, health fields, humanities, international studies, library science, mathematics, military science, physical sciences, premedicine, social sciences. *Creative arts/performance:* art/fine arts, cinema/film/broadcasting, creative writing, dance, journalism/publications, music, performing arts, theater/drama. *Special achievements/activities:* community service, general special achievements/activities, leadership. *Special characteristics:* children of faculty/staff, children of workers in trades, handicapped students, international students, local/state students, members of minority groups, out-of-state students. *ROTC:* Army, Naval, Air Force.

LOANS *Student loans:* $69,515,491 (54% need-based, 46% non-need-based). 44% of past graduating class borrowed through all loan programs. *Average indebtedness per student:* $25,712. *Average need-based loan:* Freshmen: $4365. Undergraduates: $5401. *Parent loans:* $26,415,441 (100% non-need-based). *Programs:* Federal Direct (Subsidized and Unsubsidized Stafford, PLUS), Perkins, Federal Nursing, college/university, Health Professions Student Loans (HPSL).

WORK-STUDY *Federal work-study:* 2,451 jobs averaging $1550.

ATHLETIC AWARDS Total amount: $20,629,652 (100% non-need-based).

APPLYING FOR FINANCIAL AID *Required financial aid forms:* FAFSA, CSS Financial Aid PROFILE. *Financial aid deadline:* 4/30. *Notification date:* Continuous beginning 3/15.

CONTACT Office of Financial Aid, University of Michigan, 2500 Student Activities Building, 515 East Jefferson Street, Ann Arbor, MI 48109-1316, 734-763-6600. *Fax:* 734-647-3081. *E-mail:* financial.aid@umich.edu.
Website: http://www.umich.edu/.

UNIVERSITY OF MICHIGAN– DEARBORN
Dearborn, MI

Tuition & fees (MI res): $12,032	Average undergraduate aid package: $10,087

ABOUT THE INSTITUTION State-supported, coed. *Awards:* certificates, bachelor's, master's, and doctoral degrees. 69 undergraduate majors. *Total enrollment:* 9,131. Undergraduates: 7,141. Freshmen: 1,074. Federal methodology is used as a basis for awarding need-based institutional aid.

UNDERGRADUATE EXPENSES for 2016–2017 *Application fee:* $30. *Tuition, state resident:* full-time $11,310; part-time $447 per credit hour. *Tuition, nonresident:* full-time $23,550; part-time $937 per credit hour. *Required fees:* full-time $722; $293 per term. Full-time tuition and fees vary according to course level, course load, degree level, program, and student level. Part-time tuition and fees vary according to course level, course load, degree level, program, and student level.

FRESHMAN FINANCIAL AID (Fall 2015) 800 applied for aid; of those 77% were deemed to have need. 99% of freshmen with need received aid; of those 9% had need fully met. *Average percent of need met:* 63% (excluding resources awarded to replace EFC). *Average financial aid package:* $9940 (excluding resources awarded to replace EFC). 17% of all full-time freshmen had no need and received non-need-based gift aid.

UNDERGRADUATE FINANCIAL AID (Fall 2015) 3,784 applied for aid; of those 85% were deemed to have need. 100% of undergraduates with need received aid; of those 6% had need fully met. *Average percent of need met:* 55% (excluding resources awarded to replace EFC). *Average financial aid package:* $10,087 (excluding resources awarded to replace EFC). 13% of all full-time undergraduates had no need and received non-need-based gift aid.

GIFT AID (NEED-BASED) *Total amount:* $21,258,209 (60% federal, 2% state, 37% institutional, 1% external sources). *Receiving aid:* Freshmen: 49% (474); all full-time undergraduates: 49% (2,486). *Average award:* Freshmen: $6223; Undergraduates: $5776. *Scholarships, grants, and awards:* Federal Pell, FSEOG, state, private, college/university gift aid from institutional funds.

GIFT AID (NON-NEED-BASED) *Total amount:* $4,347,457 (96% institutional, 4% external sources). *Receiving aid:* Freshmen: 30% (286). Undergraduates: 23% (1,150). *Average award:* Freshmen: $4925. Undergraduates: $6018. *Scholarships, grants, and awards by category: Academic interests/achievement:* 2,167 awards ($7,235,144 total): biological sciences, business, communication, computer science, education, engineering/technologies, foreign languages, general academic interests/achievements, international studies, mathematics, physical sciences, social sciences.

Creative arts/performance: 50 awards ($37,430 total): art/fine arts, cinema/film/broadcasting, creative writing, debating, general creative arts/performance, journalism/publications. *Special achievements/activities:* 160 awards ($411,125 total): community service, general special achievements/activities, leadership, memberships. *Special characteristics:* 483 awards ($2,788,664 total): adult students, children and siblings of alumni, children of faculty/staff, ethnic background, general special characteristics, handicapped students, international students, members of minority groups, out-of-state students, previous college experience, public servants. **Tuition waivers:** Full or partial for employees or children of employees, senior citizens. **ROTC:** Army, Naval cooperative, Air Force cooperative.

LOANS *Student loans:* $27,432,537 (92% need-based, 8% non-need-based). 63% of past graduating class borrowed through all loan programs. *Average indebtedness per student:* $26,192. **Average need-based loan:** Freshmen: $3290. Undergraduates: $4424. **Parent loans:** $3,886,928 (39% need-based, 61% non-need-based). **Programs:** Federal Direct (Subsidized and Unsubsidized Stafford, PLUS), Perkins, alternative loans.

WORK-STUDY *Federal work-study:* 187 jobs averaging $1963. **State or other work-study/employment:** 709 part-time jobs averaging $3209.

ATHLETIC AWARDS Total amount: $192,700 (54% need-based, 46% non-need-based).

APPLYING FOR FINANCIAL AID *Required financial aid form:* FAFSA. *Financial aid deadline (priority):* 1/1. *Notification date:* Continuous beginning 12/10. Students must reply by 5/1 or within 4 weeks of notification.

CONTACT Ms. Katherine M. Allen, Director of Financial Aid and Scholarships, University of Michigan–Dearborn, 4901 Evergreen Road, 1183 University Center, Dearborn, MI 48128-2406, 313-593-5300. *Fax:* 313-593-5313. *E-mail:* umd.ask.ofa@umich.edu.
Website: http://www.umdearborn.edu/.

UNIVERSITY OF MICHIGAN–FLINT
Flint, MI

Tuition & fees (MI res): $10,884	Average undergraduate aid package: $12,767

ABOUT THE INSTITUTION State-supported, coed. **Awards:** certificates, bachelor's, master's, and doctoral degrees. 78 undergraduate majors. **Total enrollment:** 8,044. Undergraduates: 6,585. Freshmen: 640. Federal methodology is used as a basis for awarding need-based institutional aid.

UNDERGRADUATE EXPENSES for 2016–2017 *Application fee:* $30. *Tuition, state resident:* full-time $10,452; part-time $413 per credit hour. *Tuition, nonresident:* full-time $20,370; part-time $823.25 per credit hour. *Required fees:* full-time $432; $167 per term. Full-time tuition and fees vary according to course level, course load, degree level, program, and student level. Part-time tuition and fees vary according to course level, course load, degree level, program, and student level. *College room and board:* $8178; *Room only:* $5178. Room and board charges vary according to housing facility.

FRESHMAN FINANCIAL AID (Fall 2015) 504 applied for aid; of those 86% were deemed to have need. 94% of freshmen with need received aid; of those 1% had need fully met. *Average percent of need met:* 70% (excluding resources awarded to replace EFC). *Average financial aid package:* $12,080 (excluding resources awarded to replace EFC). 4% of all full-time freshmen had no need and received non-need-based gift aid.

UNDERGRADUATE FINANCIAL AID (Fall 2015) 3,189 applied for aid; of those 89% were deemed to have need. 97% of undergraduates with need received aid; of those 3% had need fully met. *Average percent of need met:* 69% (excluding resources awarded to replace EFC). *Average financial aid package:* $12,767 (excluding resources awarded to replace EFC). 2% of all full-time undergraduates had no need and received non-need-based gift aid.

GIFT AID (NEED-BASED) *Total amount:* $15,600,615 (72% federal, 2% state, 26% institutional). *Receiving aid:* Freshmen: 54% (315); all full-time undergraduates: 54% (2,136). *Average award:* Freshmen: $6781; Undergraduates: $5824. **Scholarships, grants, and awards:** Federal Pell, FSEOG, state, private, college/university gift aid from institutional funds.

GIFT AID (NON-NEED-BASED) *Total amount:* $3,738,772 (1% federal, 1% state, 82% institutional, 16% external sources). *Receiving aid:* Freshmen: 23% (133). Undergraduates: 15% (604). *Average award:* Freshmen: $2711. Undergraduates: $4114. **Scholarships, grants, and awards by category:** Academic interests/achievement: biological sciences, business, communication, computer science, education, engineering/technologies, English, foreign languages, general academic interests/achievements, humanities, international studies, mathematics, physical sciences, premedicine, social sciences. *Creative arts/performance:* art/fine arts, journalism/publications, music, performing arts, theater/drama. *Special achievements/activities:* community service, general special achievements/activities, hobbies/interests, leadership. *Special characteristics:* adult students, children and siblings of alumni, children of faculty/staff, children of union members/company employees, first-generation college students, general special characteristics, handicapped students, international students, local/state students, members of minority groups, veterans, veterans' children. **Tuition waivers:** Full or partial for senior citizens. **ROTC:** Army cooperative, Naval cooperative, Air Force cooperative.

LOANS *Student loans:* $31,841,874 (92% need-based, 8% non-need-based). 64% of past graduating class borrowed through all loan programs. *Average indebtedness per student:* $27,358. **Average need-based loan:** Freshmen: $3194. Undergraduates: $4157. **Parent loans:** $2,449,251 (100% non-need-based). **Programs:** Federal Direct (Subsidized and Unsubsidized Stafford, PLUS), Perkins.

WORK-STUDY *Federal work-study:* 189 jobs averaging $2341.

APPLYING FOR FINANCIAL AID *Required financial aid forms:* FAFSA, institution's own financial aid form (for spring and summer applicants only). *Financial aid deadline (priority):* 2/14. *Notification date:* Continuous beginning 3/15.

CONTACT Lori Vedder, Office of Financial Aid, University of Michigan–Flint, Room 277 Pavilion, 303 East Kearsley Street, Flint, MI 48502-1950, 810-762-3444 or toll-free 800-942-5636. *Fax:* 810-766-6757. *E-mail:* financialaid@umflint.edu. *Website:* http://www.umflint.edu/.

UNIVERSITY OF MINNESOTA, CROOKSTON
Crookston, MN

Tuition & fees (MN res): $11,700	Average undergraduate aid package: $11,692

ABOUT THE INSTITUTION State-supported, coed. **Awards:** bachelor's degrees. 43 undergraduate majors. **Total enrollment:** 2,823. Undergraduates: 2,823. Freshmen: 239. Federal methodology is used as a basis for awarding need-based institutional aid.

UNDERGRADUATE EXPENSES for 2016–2017 *Application fee:* $30. *Tuition, state resident:* full-time $10,180; part-time $391.54 per credit. *Tuition, nonresident:* full-time $10,180; part-time $391.54 per credit. *Required fees:* full-time $1520; $759.75 per term. *College room and board:* $7658; *Room only:* $3572. Room and board charges vary according to board plan and housing facility.

FRESHMAN FINANCIAL AID (Fall 2016, est.) 177 applied for aid; of those 79% were deemed to have need. 97% of freshmen with need received aid; of those 24% had need fully met. *Average percent of need met:* 79% (excluding resources awarded to replace EFC). *Average financial aid package:* $13,102 (excluding resources awarded to replace EFC). 12% of all full-time freshmen had no need and received non-need-based gift aid.

UNDERGRADUATE FINANCIAL AID (Fall 2016, est.) 911 applied for aid; of those 82% were deemed to have need. 98% of undergraduates with need received aid; of those 16% had need fully met. *Average percent of need met:* 73% (excluding resources awarded to replace EFC). *Average financial aid package:* $11,692 (excluding resources awarded to replace EFC). 7% of all full-time undergraduates had no need and received non-need-based gift aid.

GIFT AID (NEED-BASED) *Total amount:* $6,227,467 (36% federal, 28% state, 30% institutional, 6% external sources). *Receiving aid:* Freshmen: 64% (129); all full-time undergraduates: 59% (680). *Average award:* Freshmen: $10,221; Undergraduates: $8642. **Scholarships, grants, and awards:** Federal Pell, FSEOG, state, private, college/university gift aid from institutional funds, Academic Competitiveness Grants.

GIFT AID (NON-NEED-BASED) *Total amount:* $362,098 (5% state, 66% institutional, 29% external sources). *Receiving aid:* Freshmen: 6% (13). Undergraduates: 4% (44). *Average award:* Freshmen: $2746. Undergraduates: $2534. **Scholarships, grants, and awards by category:** Academic interests/achievement: agriculture, biological sciences, general academic interests/achievements. *Creative arts/performance:* general creative arts/performance. *Special achievements/activities:* leadership. *Special characteristics:* children and siblings of alumni, children of faculty/staff, ethnic background, first-generation college students, general special characteristics, local/

state students, members of minority groups. *Tuition waivers:* Full or partial for senior citizens. *ROTC:* Air Force cooperative.

LOANS *Student loans:* $8,658,582 (63% need-based, 37% non-need-based). 79% of past graduating class borrowed through all loan programs. *Average indebtedness per student:* $30,018. *Average need-based loan:* Freshmen: $3450. Undergraduates: $4098. *Parent loans:* $1,296,921 (22% need-based, 78% non-need-based). *Programs:* Federal Direct (Subsidized and Unsubsidized Stafford, PLUS), Perkins, state, private loans.

WORK-STUDY *Federal work-study:* Total amount: $218,114; jobs available. *State or other work-study/employment:* Total amount: $245,574 (100% need-based). Part-time jobs available.

ATHLETIC AWARDS Total amount: $1,328,623 (77% need-based, 23% non-need-based).

APPLYING FOR FINANCIAL AID *Required financial aid form:* FAFSA. *Financial aid deadline (priority):* 3/1. *Notification date:* Continuous beginning 3/1. Students must reply within 8 weeks of notification.

CONTACT Melissa Dingmann, Director of Financial Aid, University of Minnesota, Crookston, 170 Owen Hall, 2900 University Avenue, Crookston, MN 56716-5001, 218-281-8576 or toll-free 800-862-6466. *Fax:* 218-281-8575. *E-mail:* dingmann@umn.edu.
Website: http://www.umcrookston.edu/.

UNIVERSITY OF MINNESOTA, DULUTH
Duluth, MN

Tuition & fees (MN res): $13,082	Average undergraduate aid package: $12,275

ABOUT THE INSTITUTION State-supported, coed. *Awards:* certificates, bachelor's, master's, and doctoral degrees. 86 undergraduate majors. *Total enrollment:* 11,018. Undergraduates: 9,967. Freshmen: 2,138. Federal methodology is used as a basis for awarding need-based institutional aid.

UNDERGRADUATE EXPENSES for 2016–2017 *Application fee:* $40. *Tuition, state resident:* full-time $11,896; part-time $457.54 per credit. *Tuition, nonresident:* full-time $16,242; part-time $624.70 per credit. *Required fees:* full-time $1186. Full-time tuition and fees vary according to course load, program, and reciprocity agreements. Part-time tuition and fees vary according to course load, program, and reciprocity agreements. Room and board charges vary according to board plan and housing facility.

FRESHMAN FINANCIAL AID (Fall 2015) 1,794 applied for aid; of those 67% were deemed to have need. 98% of freshmen with need received aid; of those 27% had need fully met. *Average percent of need met:* 71% (excluding resources awarded to replace EFC). *Average financial aid package:* $12,396 (excluding resources awarded to replace EFC). 15% of all full-time freshmen had no need and received non-need-based gift aid.

UNDERGRADUATE FINANCIAL AID (Fall 2015) 6,844 applied for aid; of those 72% were deemed to have need. 98% of undergraduates with need received aid; of those 28% had need fully met. *Average percent of need met:* 71% (excluding resources awarded to replace EFC). *Average financial aid package:* $12,275 (excluding resources awarded to replace EFC). 14% of all full-time undergraduates had no need and received non-need-based gift aid.

GIFT AID (NEED-BASED) *Total amount:* $34,838,375 (27% federal, 32% state, 35% institutional, 6% external sources). *Receiving aid:* Freshmen: 53% (1,047); all full-time undergraduates: 49% (4,155). *Average award:* Freshmen: $8648; Undergraduates: $8124. *Scholarships, grants, and awards:* Federal Pell, FSEOG, state, private, college/university gift aid from institutional funds.

GIFT AID (NON-NEED-BASED) *Total amount:* $2,569,018 (3% state, 74% institutional, 23% external sources). *Receiving aid:* Freshmen: 10% (196). Undergraduates: 9% (754). *Average award:* Freshmen: $2070. Undergraduates: $2473. *Scholarships, grants, and awards by category: Academic interests/achievement:* general academic interests/achievements. *Tuition waivers:* Full or partial for children of alumni, employees or children of employees. *ROTC:* Air Force.

LOANS *Student loans:* $46,783,918 (75% need-based, 25% non-need-based). 73% of past graduating class borrowed through all loan programs. *Average indebtedness per student:* $30,579. *Average need-based loan:* Freshmen: $5593. Undergraduates: $6087. *Parent loans:* $15,658,115 (63% need-based, 37% non-need-based).

Programs: Federal Direct (Subsidized and Unsubsidized Stafford, PLUS), Perkins, state.

WORK-STUDY *Federal work-study:* 365 jobs averaging $1380. *State or other work-study/employment:* Total amount: $953,680 (100% need-based). 894 part-time jobs averaging $1067.

ATHLETIC AWARDS Total amount: $2,129,177 (83% need-based, 17% non-need-based).

APPLYING FOR FINANCIAL AID *Required financial aid form:* FAFSA. *Financial aid deadline (priority):* 3/1. *Notification date:* Continuous beginning 2/1.

CONTACT Ms. Brenda Herzig, Director of Financial Aid, University of Minnesota, Duluth, 10 University Drive, 184 Darland Administration Building, Duluth, MN 55812-2496, 218-726-8000 or toll-free 800-232-1339. *Fax:* 218-726-8219.
Website: http://www.d.umn.edu/.

UNIVERSITY OF MINNESOTA, MORRIS
Morris, MN

Tuition & fees (MN res): $12,846	Average undergraduate aid package: $12,633

ABOUT THE INSTITUTION State-supported, coed. *Awards:* bachelor's degrees. 39 undergraduate majors. *Total enrollment:* 1,771. Undergraduates: 1,771. Freshmen: 376. Federal methodology is used as a basis for awarding need-based institutional aid.

UNDERGRADUATE EXPENSES for 2016–2017 *Application fee:* $35. *Tuition, state resident:* full-time $11,896; part-time $457.54 per credit hour. *Tuition, nonresident:* full-time $13,896; part-time $534.47 per credit hour. *Required fees:* full-time $950. Full-time tuition and fees vary according to reciprocity agreements. Part-time tuition and fees vary according to course load and reciprocity agreements. *College room and board:* $7914; *Room only:* $3752. Room and board charges vary according to board plan and housing facility.

FRESHMAN FINANCIAL AID (Fall 2016, est.) 345 applied for aid; of those 78% were deemed to have need. 100% of freshmen with need received aid; of those 29% had need fully met. *Average percent of need met:* 77% (excluding resources awarded to replace EFC). *Average financial aid package:* $12,768 (excluding resources awarded to replace EFC). 17% of all full-time freshmen had no need and received non-need-based gift aid.

UNDERGRADUATE FINANCIAL AID (Fall 2016, est.) 1,256 applied for aid; of those 81% were deemed to have need. 99% of undergraduates with need received aid; of those 25% had need fully met. *Average percent of need met:* 75% (excluding resources awarded to replace EFC). *Average financial aid package:* $12,633 (excluding resources awarded to replace EFC). 12% of all full-time undergraduates had no need and received non-need-based gift aid.

GIFT AID (NEED-BASED) *Total amount:* $10,367,588 (29% federal, 26% state, 40% institutional, 5% external sources). *Receiving aid:* Freshmen: 71% (265); all full-time undergraduates: 60% (975). *Average award:* Freshmen: $10,266; Undergraduates: $10,095. *Scholarships, grants, and awards:* Federal Pell, FSEOG, state, private, college/university gift aid from institutional funds.

GIFT AID (NON-NEED-BASED) *Total amount:* $1,153,110 (1% state, 85% institutional, 14% external sources). *Receiving aid:* Freshmen: 6% (23). Undergraduates: 6% (90). *Average award:* Freshmen: $3483. Undergraduates: $4187. *Scholarships, grants, and awards by category: Academic interests/achievement:* general academic interests/achievements. *Creative arts/performance:* music. *Special achievements/activities:* general special achievements/activities. *Special characteristics:* ethnic background, international students, members of minority groups, veterans, veterans' children. *Tuition waivers:* Full or partial for senior citizens.

LOANS *Student loans:* $5,643,487 (58% need-based, 42% non-need-based). 67% of past graduating class borrowed through all loan programs. *Average indebtedness per student:* $25,732. *Average need-based loan:* Freshmen: $3045. Undergraduates: $3730. *Parent loans:* $344,527 (100% non-need-based). *Programs:* Federal Direct (Subsidized and Unsubsidized Stafford, PLUS), Perkins, state, non-federal education loans.

WORK-STUDY *Federal work-study:* Total amount: $938,724; 307 jobs averaging $1317. *State or other work-study/employment:* Total amount: $159,093 (100% need-based). 96 part-time jobs averaging $1515.

APPLYING FOR FINANCIAL AID *Required financial aid forms:* FAFSA, noncustodial (divorced/separated) parent's statement. *Financial aid deadline:*

Continuous. **Notification date:** Continuous beginning 3/1. Students must reply by 7/1 or within 3 weeks of notification.
CONTACT Ms. Jill Beauregard, Director of Financial Aid, University of Minnesota, Morris, 600 East 4th Street, Morris, MN 56267, 320-589-6046 or toll-free 888-866-3382. Fax: 320-589-1673. E-mail: morrisfa@morris.umn.edu.
Website: http://www.morris.umn.edu/.

UNIVERSITY OF MINNESOTA ROCHESTER
Rochester, MN

CONTACT Financial Aid Office, University of Minnesota Rochester, 111 South Broadway, Suite 300, Rochester, MN 55904, 877-280-4699.
Website: http://www.r.umn.edu/.

UNIVERSITY OF MINNESOTA, TWIN CITIES CAMPUS
Minneapolis, MN

Tuition & fees (MN res): $14,142	Average undergraduate aid package: $13,153

ABOUT THE INSTITUTION State-supported, coed. **Awards:** certificates, diplomas, bachelor's, master's, and doctoral degrees. 118 undergraduate majors. **Total enrollment:** 51,580. Undergraduates: 34,871. Freshmen: 5,880. Federal methodology is used as a basis for awarding need-based institutional aid.
UNDERGRADUATE EXPENSES for 2016–2017 Application fee: $55. **Tuition, state resident:** full-time $12,546; part-time $483 per credit hour. **Tuition, nonresident:** full-time $22,210; part-time $854 per credit hour. **Required fees:** full-time $1596. Full-time tuition and fees vary according to program and reciprocity agreements. Part-time tuition and fees vary according to course load, program, and reciprocity agreements. **College room and board:** $9377; **Room only:** $5270. Room and board charges vary according to board plan, housing facility, and location.
FRESHMAN FINANCIAL AID (Fall 2016, est.) 4,720 applied for aid; of those 62% were deemed to have need. 99% of freshmen with need received aid; of those 28% had need fully met. **Average percent of need met:** 77% (excluding resources awarded to replace EFC). **Average financial aid package:** $13,165 (excluding resources awarded to replace EFC). 13% of all full-time freshmen had no need and received non-need-based gift aid.
UNDERGRADUATE FINANCIAL AID (Fall 2016, est.) 19,218 applied for aid; of those 72% were deemed to have need. 99% of undergraduates with need received aid; of those 24% had need fully met. **Average percent of need met:** 73% (excluding resources awarded to replace EFC). **Average financial aid package:** $13,153 (excluding resources awarded to replace EFC). 8% of all full-time undergraduates had no need and received non-need-based gift aid.
GIFT AID (NEED-BASED) Total amount: $131,841,617 (24% federal, 27% state, 42% institutional, 7% external sources). **Receiving aid:** Freshmen: 43% (2,539); all full-time undergraduates: 40% (11,646). **Average award:** Freshmen: $10,456; Undergraduates: $10,140. **Scholarships, grants, and awards:** Federal Pell, FSEOG, state, private, college/university gift aid from institutional funds, Federal Nursing, ROTC Scholarships.
GIFT AID (NON-NEED-BASED) Total amount: $16,571,486 (1% state, 81% institutional, 18% external sources). **Receiving aid:** Freshmen: 5% (296). Undergraduates: 3% (978). **Average award:** Freshmen: $5031. Undergraduates: $4836. **Scholarships, grants, and awards by category:** Academic interests/achievement: agriculture, architecture, area/ethnic studies, biological sciences, business, communication, computer science, education, engineering/technologies, English, foreign languages, general academic interests/achievements, health fields, home economics, humanities, international studies, library science, mathematics, military science, physical sciences, premedicine, religion/biblical studies, social sciences. **Creative arts/performance:** art/fine arts, general creative arts/performance. **Special achievements/activities:** hobbies/interests, leadership. **Special characteristics:** general special characteristics, local/state students, members of minority groups. **Tuition waivers:** Full or partial for senior citizens. **ROTC:** Army, Naval, Air Force.

LOANS Student loans: $134,760,544 (60% need-based, 40% non-need-based). 56% of past graduating class borrowed through all loan programs. **Average indebtedness per student:** $26,644. **Average need-based loan:** Freshmen: $3659. Undergraduates: $4575. **Parent loans:** $94,463,452 (21% need-based, 79% non-need-based). **Programs:** Federal Direct (Subsidized and Unsubsidized Stafford, PLUS), Perkins, Federal Nursing, state, college/university, Health Professions Student Loans (HPSL).
WORK-STUDY Federal work-study: Total amount: $4,053,137; jobs available. **State or other work-study/employment:** Total amount: $11,686,203 (100% need-based). Part-time jobs available.
ATHLETIC AWARDS Total amount: $10,287,413 (89% need-based, 11% non-need-based).
APPLYING FOR FINANCIAL AID Required financial aid forms: FAFSA, institution's own form. **Financial aid deadline (priority):** 3/1. **Notification date:** Continuous beginning 2/15.
CONTACT Office of Student Finance, University of Minnesota, Twin Cities Campus, 200 Fraser Hall, 106 Pleasant Street SE, Minneapolis, MN 55455, 612-624-1111 or toll-free 800-752-1000. Fax: 612-624-9584. E-mail: onestop@umn.edu.
Website: http://www.umn.edu/tc/.

UNIVERSITY OF MISSISSIPPI
Oxford, MS

Tuition & fees (MS res): $7744	Average undergraduate aid package: $10,202

ABOUT THE INSTITUTION State-supported, coed. **Awards:** certificates, bachelor's, master's, and doctoral degrees. 73 undergraduate majors. **Total enrollment:** 23,212. Undergraduates: 18,785. Freshmen: 3,966. Federal methodology is used as a basis for awarding need-based institutional aid.
UNDERGRADUATE EXPENSES for 2016–2017 Tuition, state resident: full-time $7644; part-time $318.50 per credit hour. **Tuition, nonresident:** full-time $21,912; part-time $913 per credit hour. **Required fees:** full-time $100; $4.16 per credit hour. Full-time tuition and fees vary according to course load and program. Part-time tuition and fees vary according to course load and program. **College room and board:** $10,002. Room and board charges vary according to board plan and housing facility.
FRESHMAN FINANCIAL AID (Fall 2015) 2,790 applied for aid; of those 67% were deemed to have need. 97% of freshmen with need received aid; of those 18% had need fully met. **Average percent of need met:** 76% (excluding resources awarded to replace EFC). **Average financial aid package:** $12,549 (excluding resources awarded to replace EFC). 34% of all full-time freshmen had no need and received non-need-based gift aid.
UNDERGRADUATE FINANCIAL AID (Fall 2015) 10,859 applied for aid; of those 77% were deemed to have need. 97% of undergraduates with need received aid; of those 13% had need fully met. **Average percent of need met:** 73% (excluding resources awarded to replace EFC). **Average financial aid package:** $10,202 (excluding resources awarded to replace EFC). 25% of all full-time undergraduates had no need and received non-need-based gift aid.
GIFT AID (NEED-BASED) Total amount: $55,696,195 (38% federal, 10% state, 49% institutional, 3% external sources). **Receiving aid:** Freshmen: 42% (1,648); all full-time undergraduates: 42% (7,088). **Average award:** Freshmen: $9519; Undergraduates: $8561. **Scholarships, grants, and awards:** Federal Pell, FSEOG, state, private, college/university gift aid from institutional funds.
GIFT AID (NON-NEED-BASED) Total amount: $41,793,112 (7% state, 88% institutional, 5% external sources). **Receiving aid:** Freshmen: 8% (331). Undergraduates: 5% (894). **Average award:** Freshmen: $8036. Undergraduates: $8057. **Scholarships, grants, and awards by category:** Academic interests/achievement: 18,754 awards ($53,178,536 total): biological sciences, business, communication, computer science, education, engineering/technologies, English, foreign languages, general academic interests/achievements, health fields, home economics, humanities, international studies, mathematics, military science, physical sciences, premedicine, social sciences. **Creative arts/performance:** 987 awards ($1,439,368 total): art/fine arts, cinema/film/broadcasting, creative writing, debating, journalism/publications, music, performing arts, theater/drama. **Special achievements/activities:** 6,549 awards ($11,774,131 total): cheerleading/drum major, community service, general special achievements/activities, junior miss, leadership, memberships. **Special characteristics:** 6,157 awards ($20,575,061 total): adult students, children and siblings of alumni, children of faculty/staff, ethnic background, first-generation college students, general special characteristics, handicapped students, international students, local/state students, members of

minority groups, out-of-state students, previous college experience, spouses of current students, veterans, veterans' children. *Tuition waivers:* Full or partial for children of alumni, employees or children of employees, senior citizens. *ROTC:* Army, Naval, Air Force.

LOANS *Student loans:* $71,614,516 (68% need-based, 32% non-need-based). 48% of past graduating class borrowed through all loan programs. *Average indebtedness per student:* $28,162. *Average need-based loan:* Freshmen: $3404. Undergraduates: $4579. *Parent loans:* $31,341,720 (44% need-based, 56% non-need-based). *Programs:* Federal Direct (Subsidized and Unsubsidized Stafford, PLUS), Perkins, college/university, private loans, Health Professions Student Loans (HPSL).

WORK-STUDY *Federal work-study:* 397 jobs averaging $1378.

ATHLETIC AWARDS Total amount: $8,925,659 (47% need-based, 53% non-need-based).

APPLYING FOR FINANCIAL AID *Required financial aid form:* FAFSA. *Financial aid deadline (priority):* 3/1. *Notification date:* Continuous beginning 4/1. Students must reply within 4 weeks of notification.

CONTACT Ms. Laura Diven-Brown, Director of Financial Aid, University of Mississippi, 257 Martindale Center, University, MS 38677, 662-915-5788 or toll-free 800-653-6477 (in-state). *Fax:* 662-915-1164. *E-mail:* ldivenbr@olemiss.edu. *Website:* http://www.olemiss.edu/.

UNIVERSITY OF MISSISSIPPI MEDICAL CENTER
Jackson, MS

CONTACT Minetta Veazey, Administrative Secretary, University of Mississippi Medical Center, 2500 North State Street, Jackson, MS 39216, 601-984-1117. *Fax:* 601-984-6984. *E-mail:* mveazey@registrar.umsmed.edu. *Website:* http://www.umc.edu/.

UNIVERSITY OF MISSOURI
Columbia, MO

Tuition & fees (MO res): $9518	Average undergraduate aid package: $11,696

ABOUT THE INSTITUTION State-supported, coed. *Awards:* certificates, bachelor's, master's, and doctoral degrees. 115 undergraduate majors. *Total enrollment:* 35,448. Undergraduates: 27,812. Freshmen: 6,191. Federal methodology is used as a basis for awarding need-based institutional aid.

UNDERGRADUATE EXPENSES for 2016–2017 *Application fee:* $55. *Tuition, state resident:* full-time $8286; part-time $276.20 per credit hour. *Tuition, nonresident:* full-time $24,660; part-time $822 per credit hour. *Required fees:* full-time $1232. Full-time tuition and fees vary according to course load, program, and reciprocity agreements. Part-time tuition and fees vary according to course load, program, and reciprocity agreements. *College room and board:* $10,298; *Room only:* $7263. Room and board charges vary according to board plan and housing facility.

FRESHMAN FINANCIAL AID (Fall 2016, est.) 3,725 applied for aid; of those 67% were deemed to have need. 96% of freshmen with need received aid; of those 17% had need fully met. *Average percent of need met:* 60% (excluding resources awarded to replace EFC). *Average financial aid package:* $11,727 (excluding resources awarded to replace EFC). 24% of all full-time freshmen had no need and received non-need-based gift aid.

UNDERGRADUATE FINANCIAL AID (Fall 2016, est.) 15,683 applied for aid; of those 72% were deemed to have need. 97% of undergraduates with need received aid; of those 14% had need fully met. *Average percent of need met:* 59% (excluding resources awarded to replace EFC). *Average financial aid package:* $11,696 (excluding resources awarded to replace EFC). 18% of all full-time undergraduates had no need and received non-need-based gift aid.

GIFT AID (NEED-BASED) *Total amount:* $78,885,078 (29% federal, 13% state, 51% institutional, 7% external sources). *Receiving aid:* Freshmen: 45% (2,109); all full-time undergraduates: 38% (9,075). *Average award:* Freshmen: $10,495; Undergraduates: $9807. *Scholarships, grants, and awards:* Federal Pell, FSEOG, state, private, college/university gift aid from institutional funds, Federal Nursing.

GIFT AID (NON-NEED-BASED) *Total amount:* $33,473,914 (5% federal, 9% state, 65% institutional, 21% external sources). *Receiving aid:* Freshmen: 5% (216). Undergraduates: 3% (610). *Average award:* Freshmen: $6428. Undergraduates: $6104. *Scholarships, grants, and awards by category:* Academic interests/achievement: agriculture, area/ethnic studies, biological sciences, business, communication, computer science, education, engineering/technologies, English, foreign languages, general academic interests/achievements, health fields, home economics, humanities, international studies, library science, mathematics, physical sciences, premedicine, religion/biblical studies, social sciences. Creative arts/performance: art/fine arts, cinema/film/broadcasting, creative writing, journalism/publications, music, theater/drama. *Special achievements/activities:* cheerleading/drum major, general special achievements/activities, memberships. *Special characteristics:* adult students, children and siblings of alumni, children of faculty/staff, ethnic background, first-generation college students, international students, local/state students, members of minority groups, out-of-state students. *Tuition waivers:* Full or partial for employees or children of employees, senior citizens. *ROTC:* Army, Naval, Air Force.

LOANS *Student loans:* $92,077,111 (66% need-based, 34% non-need-based). 52% of past graduating class borrowed through all loan programs. *Average indebtedness per student:* $26,685. *Average need-based loan:* Freshmen: $3966. Undergraduates: $5032. *Parent loans:* $50,523,593 (47% need-based, 53% non-need-based). *Programs:* Federal Direct (Subsidized and Unsubsidized Stafford, PLUS), Perkins, Federal Nursing, state, college/university, alternative loans.

WORK-STUDY *Federal work-study:* Total amount: $1,234,350; jobs available.

ATHLETIC AWARDS Total amount: $8,681,883 (35% need-based, 65% non-need-based).

APPLYING FOR FINANCIAL AID *Required financial aid form:* FAFSA. *Financial aid deadline (priority):* 2/1. *Notification date:* Continuous beginning 12/15. Students must reply within 4 weeks of notification.

CONTACT Nicholas Prewett, Director of Student Financial Aid, University of Missouri, 11 Jesse Hall, Columbia, MO 65211, 573-882-7506 or toll-free 800-225-6075 (in-state). *Fax:* 573-884-5335. *E-mail:* finaidinfo@missouri.edu. *Website:* http://www.missouri.edu/.

UNIVERSITY OF MISSOURI–KANSAS CITY
Kansas City, MO

Tuition & fees (MO res): $9563	Average undergraduate aid package: $9810

ABOUT THE INSTITUTION State-supported, coed. *Awards:* certificates, bachelor's, master's, and doctoral degrees. 52 undergraduate majors. *Total enrollment:* 16,944. Undergraduates: 11,708. Freshmen: 1,212. Federal methodology is used as a basis for awarding need-based institutional aid.

UNDERGRADUATE EXPENSES for 2017–2018 *Application fee:* $45. *Tuition, state resident:* full-time $8169; part-time $272 per credit hour. *Tuition, nonresident:* full-time $23,362; part-time $832 per credit hour. *Required fees:* full-time $1394; $100 per credit hour. Full-time tuition and fees vary according to course load and program. Part-time tuition and fees vary according to course load and program. Room and board charges vary according to board plan and housing facility.

FRESHMAN FINANCIAL AID (Fall 2016, est.) 1,057 applied for aid; of those 78% were deemed to have need. 98% of freshmen with need received aid; of those 14% had need fully met. *Average percent of need met:* 64% (excluding resources awarded to replace EFC). *Average financial aid package:* $11,702 (excluding resources awarded to replace EFC). 20% of all full-time freshmen had no need and received non-need-based gift aid.

UNDERGRADUATE FINANCIAL AID (Fall 2016, est.) 5,942 applied for aid; of those 84% were deemed to have need. 96% of undergraduates with need received aid; of those 9% had need fully met. *Average percent of need met:* 54% (excluding resources awarded to replace EFC). *Average financial aid package:* $9810 (excluding resources awarded to replace EFC). 13% of all full-time undergraduates had no need and received non-need-based gift aid.

GIFT AID (NEED-BASED) *Total amount:* $27,409,920 (48% federal, 13% state, 31% institutional, 8% external sources). *Receiving aid:* Freshmen: 64% (770); all full-time undergraduates: 51% (4,000). *Average award:* Freshmen: $8378; Undergraduates: $7152. *Scholarships, grants, and awards:* Federal Pell, FSEOG, state, private, college/university gift aid from institutional funds, United Negro College Fund, Federal Nursing.

GIFT AID (NON-NEED-BASED) *Total amount:* $7,963,378 (6% state, 73% institutional, 21% external sources). *Receiving aid:* Freshmen: 4% (43). Undergraduates: 1% (100). *Average award:* Freshmen: $5131. Undergraduates: $5397. *Scholarships, grants, and awards by category: Academic interests/achievement:* 6,398 awards ($18,567,824 total): general academic interests/achievements. *Creative arts/performance:* 379 awards ($1,361,486 total): art/fine arts, debating, general creative arts/performance, music, performing arts. *Special achievements/activities:* 524 awards ($741,714 total): general special achievements/activities, leadership. *Special characteristics:* 753 awards ($6,560,071 total): children and siblings of alumni, ethnic background, local/state students, members of minority groups, out-of-state students. *Tuition waivers:* Full or partial for employees or children of employees. *ROTC:* Army, Air Force cooperative.
LOANS *Student loans:* $33,801,872 (83% need-based, 17% non-need-based). 61% of past graduating class borrowed through all loan programs. *Average indebtedness per student:* $25,912. *Average need-based loan:* Freshmen: $6272. Undergraduates: $7966. *Parent loans:* $9,415,799 (60% need-based, 40% non-need-based). *Programs:* Federal Direct (Subsidized and Unsubsidized Stafford, PLUS), Perkins, Federal Nursing, state, college/university.
WORK-STUDY *Federal work-study:* Total amount: $2,636,843; 632 jobs averaging $4144.
ATHLETIC AWARDS Total amount: $3,536,310 (34% need-based, 66% non-need-based).
APPLYING FOR FINANCIAL AID *Required financial aid form:* FAFSA. *Financial aid deadline (priority):* 3/1. *Notification date:* Continuous beginning 4/15. Students must reply within 2 weeks of notification.
CONTACT Scott Young, Director of Financial Aid and Scholarships, University of Missouri–Kansas City, 5100 Rockhill Road, Kansas City, MO 64110-2499, 816-235-1154 or toll-free 800-775-8652. *Fax:* 816-235-5511. *E-mail:* youngsc@umkc.edu. *Website:* http://www.umkc.edu/.

achievement: biological sciences, business, communication, computer science, education, engineering/technologies, English, foreign languages, general academic interests/achievements, home economics, humanities, international studies, mathematics, physical sciences, premedicine, social sciences. *Creative arts/performance:* art/fine arts, dance, music, theater/drama. *Special achievements/activities:* cheerleading/drum major, memberships. *Special characteristics:* adult students, children and siblings of alumni, children of faculty/staff, children with a deceased or disabled parent, ethnic background, first-generation college students, general special characteristics, international students, local/state students, members of minority groups, out-of-state students, previous college experience, spouses of deceased or disabled public servants, veterans, veterans' children. *Tuition waivers:* Full or partial for employees or children of employees, senior citizens. *ROTC:* Army, Air Force cooperative.
LOANS *Student loans:* $43,222,688 (80% need-based, 20% non-need-based). 61% of past graduating class borrowed through all loan programs. *Average indebtedness per student:* $24,186. *Average need-based loan:* Freshmen: $3232. Undergraduates: $4416. *Parent loans:* $1,888,199 (25% need-based, 75% non-need-based). *Programs:* Federal Direct (Subsidized and Unsubsidized Stafford, PLUS), Perkins, Federal Nursing, state.
WORK-STUDY *Federal work-study:* Total amount: $213,759; 50 jobs averaging $4275.
ATHLETIC AWARDS Total amount: $2,521,968 (42% need-based, 58% non-need-based).
APPLYING FOR FINANCIAL AID *Required financial aid form:* FAFSA. *Financial aid deadline (priority):* 2/1. *Notification date:* Continuous beginning 12/1. Students must reply within 2 weeks of notification.
CONTACT Ms. Svetlana Vejkovich, Associate Director, University of Missouri–St. Louis, One University Boulevard, 327 Millennium Student Center, St. Louis, MO 63121-4400, 314-516-5526 or toll-free 888-GO2-UMSL (in-state), 888-GO2-USML (out-of-state). *Fax:* 314-516-5408. *E-mail:* financialaid@umsl.edu. *Website:* http://www.umsl.edu/.

UNIVERSITY OF MISSOURI–ST. LOUIS
St. Louis, MO

Tuition & fees: N/R	Average undergraduate aid package: $11,633

ABOUT THE INSTITUTION State-supported, coed. *Awards:* certificates, bachelor's, master's, and doctoral degrees. 43 undergraduate majors. *Total enrollment:* 17,014. Undergraduates: 13,923. Freshmen: 441. Federal methodology is used as a basis for awarding need-based institutional aid.
UNDERGRADUATE EXPENSES for 2016–2017 *Application fee:* $35. *Tuition, state resident:* part-time $335.50 per credit hour. *Tuition, nonresident:* part-time $875.90 per credit hour. Full-time tuition and fees vary according to course level, course load, location, program, and reciprocity agreements. Part-time tuition and fees vary according to course level, course load, location, program, and reciprocity agreements. Room and board charges vary according to board plan and housing facility.
FRESHMAN FINANCIAL AID (Fall 2016, est.) 359 applied for aid; of those 84% were deemed to have need. 99% of freshmen with need received aid; of those 29% had need fully met. *Average percent of need met:* 75% (excluding resources awarded to replace EFC). *Average financial aid package:* $13,596 (excluding resources awarded to replace EFC). 8% of all full-time freshmen had no need and received non-need-based gift aid.
UNDERGRADUATE FINANCIAL AID (Fall 2016, est.) 4,272 applied for aid; of those 87% were deemed to have need. 98% of undergraduates with need received aid; of those 19% had need fully met. *Average percent of need met:* 66% (excluding resources awarded to replace EFC). *Average financial aid package:* $11,633 (excluding resources awarded to replace EFC). 7% of all full-time undergraduates had no need and received non-need-based gift aid.
GIFT AID (NEED-BASED) *Total amount:* $28,877,442 (48% federal, 13% state, 35% institutional, 4% external sources). *Receiving aid:* Freshmen: 63% (260); all full-time undergraduates: 58% (3,019). *Average award:* Freshmen: $11,101; Undergraduates: $8162. *Scholarships, grants, and awards:* Federal Pell, FSEOG, state, private, college/university gift aid from institutional funds, United Negro College Fund, Federal Nursing, TEACH Grants.
GIFT AID (NON-NEED-BASED) *Total amount:* $5,024,694 (4% federal, 4% state, 65% institutional, 27% external sources). *Receiving aid:* Freshmen: 14% (57). Undergraduates: 8% (411). *Average award:* Freshmen: $8195. Undergraduates: $5561. *Scholarships, grants, and awards by category: Academic interests/*

UNIVERSITY OF MOBILE
Mobile, AL

Tuition & fees: $21,400	Average undergraduate aid package: $17,739

ABOUT THE INSTITUTION Independent Southern Baptist, coed. *Awards:* associate, bachelor's, and master's degrees. 37 undergraduate majors. *Total enrollment:* 1,480. Undergraduates: 1,376. Freshmen: 225. Federal methodology is used as a basis for awarding need-based institutional aid.
UNDERGRADUATE EXPENSES for 2016–2017 *Application fee:* $25. *Comprehensive fee:* $31,000 includes full-time tuition ($20,200), mandatory fees ($1200), and room and board ($9600). *College room only:* $5400. Full-time tuition and fees vary according to course load. Room and board charges vary according to housing facility. *Part-time tuition:* $720 per credit hour. *Part-time fees:* $400 per year. Part-time tuition and fees vary according to course load.
FRESHMAN FINANCIAL AID (Fall 2016, est.) 199 applied for aid; of those 90% were deemed to have need. 100% of freshmen with need received aid; of those 100% had need fully met. *Average percent of need met:* 67% (excluding resources awarded to replace EFC). *Average financial aid package:* $19,353 (excluding resources awarded to replace EFC). 8% of all full-time freshmen had no need and received non-need-based gift aid.
UNDERGRADUATE FINANCIAL AID (Fall 2016, est.) 970 applied for aid; of those 92% were deemed to have need. 100% of undergraduates with need received aid; of those 100% had need fully met. *Average percent of need met:* 66% (excluding resources awarded to replace EFC). *Average financial aid package:* $17,739 (excluding resources awarded to replace EFC). 15% of all full-time undergraduates had no need and received non-need-based gift aid.
GIFT AID (NEED-BASED) *Total amount:* $10,662,750 (26% federal, 5% state, 64% institutional, 5% external sources). *Receiving aid:* Freshmen: 51% (114); all full-time undergraduates: 49% (547). *Average award:* Freshmen: $5553; Undergraduates: $5279. *Scholarships, grants, and awards:* Federal Pell, FSEOG, state, private, college/university gift aid from institutional funds, Federal Nursing.
GIFT AID (NON-NEED-BASED) *Receiving aid:* Freshmen: 78% (175). Undergraduates: 68% (752). *Average award:* Freshmen: $8488. Undergraduates: $10,158. *Scholarships, grants, and awards by category: Creative arts/performance:* art/fine arts, music, performing arts. *Special achievements/activities:* religious involvement. *Special characteristics:* children of faculty/staff, relatives of clergy.

Tuition waivers: Full or partial for employees or children of employees. **ROTC:** Army cooperative, Air Force cooperative.
LOANS Student loans: $11,236,194 (56% need-based, 44% non-need-based). 61% of past graduating class borrowed through all loan programs. *Average indebtedness per student:* $30,029. **Average need-based loan:** Freshmen: $2175. Undergraduates: $2175. **Parent loans:** $2,309,918 (100% non-need-based). **Programs:** Federal Direct (Subsidized and Unsubsidized Stafford, PLUS), Perkins, college/university.
WORK-STUDY Federal work-study: Total amount: $93,475; 55 jobs averaging $1575.
ATHLETIC AWARDS Total amount: $5,023,008 (100% non-need-based).
APPLYING FOR FINANCIAL AID Required financial aid forms: FAFSA, institution's own form, state aid form. **Financial aid deadline:** Continuous. **Notification date:** Continuous beginning 2/1.
CONTACT Mrs. Marie Thomas Batson, Associate Vice President for Enrollment, University of Mobile, 5735 College Parkway, Mobile, AL 36613, 251-442-2370 or toll-free 800-946-7267. *E-mail:* mbatson@umobile.edu.
Website: http://www.umobile.edu/.

UNIVERSITY OF MONTANA
Missoula, MT

Tuition & fees (MT res): $6446	Average undergraduate aid package: $14,092

ABOUT THE INSTITUTION State-supported, coed. **Awards:** certificates, associate, bachelor's, master's, and doctoral degrees. 117 undergraduate majors. **Total enrollment:** 13,044. Undergraduates: 10,778. Freshmen: 1,763. Federal methodology is used as a basis for awarding need-based institutional aid.
UNDERGRADUATE EXPENSES for 2016–2017 Application fee: $36. **Tuition, state resident:** full-time $4604; part-time $192 per credit hour. **Tuition, nonresident:** full-time $22,720; part-time $947 per credit hour. **Required fees:** full-time $1842. Full-time tuition and fees vary according to degree level, location, program, reciprocity agreements, and student level. Part-time tuition and fees vary according to course load, degree level, location, and student level. **College room and board:** $8826. Room and board charges vary according to board plan and housing facility.
FRESHMAN FINANCIAL AID (Fall 2016, est.) 1,244 applied for aid; of those 73% were deemed to have need. 98% of freshmen with need received aid; of those 12% had need fully met. **Average percent of need met:** 89% (excluding resources awarded to replace EFC). **Average financial aid package:** $14,821 (excluding resources awarded to replace EFC). 22% of all full-time freshmen had no need and received non-need-based gift aid.
UNDERGRADUATE FINANCIAL AID (Fall 2016, est.) 5,662 applied for aid; of those 80% were deemed to have need. 97% of undergraduates with need received aid; of those 10% had need fully met. **Average percent of need met:** 82% (excluding resources awarded to replace EFC). **Average financial aid package:** $14,092 (excluding resources awarded to replace EFC). 19% of all full-time undergraduates had no need and received non-need-based gift aid.
GIFT AID (NEED-BASED) Total amount: $22,165,795 (69% federal, 1% state, 24% institutional, 6% external sources). **Receiving aid:** Freshmen: 37% (546); all full-time undergraduates: 37% (2,903). **Average award:** Freshmen: $5068; Undergraduates: $4799. **Scholarships, grants, and awards:** Federal Pell, FSEOG, state, private, college/university gift aid from institutional funds.
GIFT AID (NON-NEED-BASED) Total amount: $4,844,678 (89% institutional, 11% external sources). **Receiving aid:** Freshmen: 33% (489). Undergraduates: 24% (1,838). **Average award:** Freshmen: $4114. Undergraduates: $3683. **Scholarships, grants, and awards by category:** *Academic interests/achievement:* biological sciences, business, computer science, education, English, foreign languages, general academic interests/achievements, health fields, humanities, international studies, mathematics, military science, physical sciences, premedicine, social sciences. *Creative arts/performance:* creative writing, dance, journalism/publications, music, performing arts, theater/drama. *Special achievements/activities:* cheerleading/drum major, leadership, rodeo. *Special characteristics:* children and siblings of alumni, children with a deceased or disabled parent, general special characteristics, international students, local/state students, out-of-state students, veterans. **Tuition waivers:** Full or partial for minority students, employees or children of employees, senior citizens. **ROTC:** Army.

THE UNIVERSITY OF MONTANA WESTERN
Dillon, MT

Tuition & fees (MT res): $4893	Average undergraduate aid package: $3423

ABOUT THE INSTITUTION State-supported, coed. **Awards:** certificates, associate, and bachelor's degrees. 27 undergraduate majors. **Total enrollment:** 1,505. Undergraduates: 1,505. Freshmen: 336. Federal methodology is used as a basis for awarding need-based institutional aid.
UNDERGRADUATE EXPENSES for 2016–2017 Application fee: $30. **Tuition, state resident:** full-time $3699; part-time $153 per credit hour. **Tuition, nonresident:** full-time $16,497; part-time $828.52 per credit hour. **Required fees:** full-time $1194. Full-time tuition and fees vary according to course load, location, program, reciprocity agreements, and student level. Part-time tuition and fees vary according to course load, location, program, reciprocity agreements, and student level. **College room and board:** $7482; **Room only:** $2752. Room and board charges vary according to housing facility.
FRESHMAN FINANCIAL AID (Fall 2016, est.) 314 applied for aid; of those 78% were deemed to have need. 91% of freshmen with need received aid. **Average percent of need met:** 14% (excluding resources awarded to replace EFC). **Average financial aid package:** $2959 (excluding resources awarded to replace EFC). 1% of all full-time freshmen had no need and received non-need-based gift aid.
UNDERGRADUATE FINANCIAL AID (Fall 2016, est.) 1,117 applied for aid; of those 83% were deemed to have need. 94% of undergraduates with need received aid; of those .1% had need fully met. **Average percent of need met:** 16% (excluding resources awarded to replace EFC). **Average financial aid package:** $3423 (excluding resources awarded to replace EFC). 1% of all full-time undergraduates had no need and received non-need-based gift aid.
GIFT AID (NEED-BASED) Total amount: $9,688,326 (49% federal, 5% state, 38% institutional, 8% external sources). **Receiving aid:** Freshmen: 52% (170); all full-time undergraduates: 50% (610). **Average award:** Freshmen: $3004; Undergraduates: $3514. **Scholarships, grants, and awards:** Federal Pell, FSEOG, state, private, college/university gift aid from institutional funds, Western Undergraduate Exchange (WUE) Scholarships.
GIFT AID (NON-NEED-BASED) Total amount: $4,035,411 (9% state, 76% institutional, 15% external sources). **Receiving aid:** Freshmen: 25% (81). Undergraduates: 22% (271). **Average award:** Freshmen: $1250. Undergraduates: $1261. **Scholarships, grants, and awards by category:** *Academic interests/achievement:* biological sciences, business, education, English, general academic interests/achievements, humanities, mathematics, physical sciences, premedicine, social sciences. *Creative arts/performance:* art/fine arts. *Special achievements/activities:* general special achievements/activities, rodeo. *Special characteristics:* children of faculty/staff, first-generation college students, international students, members of minority groups, out-of-state students, veterans. **Tuition waivers:** Full or partial for minority students, employees or children of employees, senior citizens.
LOANS Student loans: $12,250,744 (79% need-based, 21% non-need-based). 77% of past graduating class borrowed through all loan programs. *Average indebtedness*

LOANS Student loans: $39,459,568 (86% need-based, 14% non-need-based). 60% of past graduating class borrowed through all loan programs. *Average indebtedness per student:* $38,008. **Average need-based loan:** Freshmen: $3811. Undergraduates: $4347. **Parent loans:** $12,125,184 (68% need-based, 32% non-need-based). **Programs:** Federal Direct (Subsidized and Unsubsidized Stafford, PLUS), Perkins.
WORK-STUDY Federal work-study: Total amount: $3,775,309; jobs available. **State or other work-study/employment:** Total amount: $955,691 (64% need-based, 36% non-need-based). Part-time jobs available.
ATHLETIC AWARDS Total amount: $1,894,758 (100% non-need-based).
APPLYING FOR FINANCIAL AID Required financial aid forms: FAFSA, UM Supplemental Information Sheet. **Financial aid deadline (priority):** 2/16. **Notification date:** Continuous beginning 3/16. Students must reply within 4 weeks of notification.
CONTACT Mr. Kent McGowan, Director of Financial Aid, University of Montana, Lommasson Center 218, Missoula, MT 59812, 406-243-5373 or toll-free 800-462-8636. *Fax:* 406-243-4930. *E-mail:* faid@mso.umt.edu.
Website: http://www.umt.edu/.

per student: $29,779. **Average need-based loan:** Freshmen: $3467. Undergraduates: $3954. **Parent loans:** $1,886,577 (78% need-based, 22% non-need-based). **Programs:** Federal Direct (Subsidized and Unsubsidized Stafford, PLUS), Perkins, college/university.
WORK-STUDY Federal work-study: Total amount: $660,306; 107 jobs averaging $2000. **State or other work-study/employment:** Total amount: $267,955 (72% need-based, 28% non-need-based). 24 part-time jobs averaging $2000.
ATHLETIC AWARDS Total amount: $5,190,124 (43% need-based, 57% non-need-based).
APPLYING FOR FINANCIAL AID Required financial aid forms: FAFSA, Student Data Form. **Financial aid deadline (priority):** 3/1. **Notification date:** Continuous beginning 3/1. Students must reply by 7/1.
CONTACT Arlene Williams, Interim Director of Financial Aid, The University of Montana Western, 710 South Atlantic Street, Dillon, MT 59725, 406-683-7511 or toll-free 877-683-7331. Fax: 406-683-7510. E-mail: arlene.williams@umwestern.edu. Website: http://www.umwestern.edu/.

UNIVERSITY OF MONTEVALLO
Montevallo, AL

Tuition & fees (AL res): $12,040	Average undergraduate aid package: $11,100

ABOUT THE INSTITUTION State-supported, coed. **Awards:** certificates, bachelor's, and master's degrees. 26 undergraduate majors. **Total enrollment:** 2,800. Undergraduates: 2,409. Freshmen: 477. Federal methodology is used as a basis for awarding need-based institutional aid.
UNDERGRADUATE EXPENSES for 2016–2017 Application fee: $30. **Tuition, state resident:** full-time $11,370; part-time $379 per credit hour. **Tuition, nonresident:** full-time $23,640; part-time $788 per credit hour. **Required fees:** full-time $670. **College room and board:** $7462; **Room only:** $4762. Room and board charges vary according to housing facility.
FRESHMAN FINANCIAL AID (Fall 2016, est.) 393 applied for aid; of those 79% were deemed to have need. 99% of freshmen with need received aid; of those 27% had need fully met. **Average percent of need met:** 64% (excluding resources awarded to replace EFC). **Average financial aid package:** $11,870 (excluding resources awarded to replace EFC). 27% of all full-time freshmen had no need and received non-need-based gift aid.
UNDERGRADUATE FINANCIAL AID (Fall 2016, est.) 1,657 applied for aid; of those 86% were deemed to have need. 99% of undergraduates with need received aid; of those 21% had need fully met. **Average percent of need met:** 57% (excluding resources awarded to replace EFC). **Average financial aid package:** $11,100 (excluding resources awarded to replace EFC). 24% of all full-time undergraduates had no need and received non-need-based gift aid.
GIFT AID (NEED-BASED) Total amount: $11,030,036 (40% federal, 10% state, 45% institutional, 5% external sources). **Receiving aid:** Freshmen: 61% (288); all full-time undergraduates: 57% (1,237). **Average award:** Freshmen: $10,048; Undergraduates: $8588. **Scholarships, grants, and awards:** Federal Pell, FSEOG, state, private, college/university gift aid from institutional funds.
GIFT AID (NON-NEED-BASED) Total amount: $3,961,217 (11% state, 87% institutional, 2% external sources). **Receiving aid:** Freshmen: 14% (64). Undergraduates: 7% (159). **Average award:** Freshmen: $11,053. Undergraduates: $10,337. **Scholarships, grants, and awards by category:** Academic interests/achievement: 1,100 awards ($7,087,740 total): biological sciences, business, communication, education, English, foreign languages, general academic interests/achievements, health fields, humanities, mathematics, physical sciences, social sciences. Creative arts/performance: 107 awards ($273,589 total): art/fine arts, cinema/film/broadcasting, creative writing, journalism/publications, music, theater/drama. Special achievements/activities: 341 awards ($1,471,825 total): cheerleading/drum major, junior miss, leadership. Special characteristics: 203 awards ($2,238,363 total): children of faculty/staff, international students, out-of-state students. **Tuition waivers:** Full or partial for employees or children of employees. **ROTC:** Army cooperative, Air Force cooperative.
LOANS Student loans: $10,936,144 (43% need-based, 57% non-need-based). 62% of past graduating class borrowed through all loan programs. Average indebtedness per student: $28,848. **Average need-based loan:** Freshmen: $3155. Undergraduates: $4010. **Parent loans:** $21,513,959 (98% need-based, 2% non-need-based). **Programs:** Federal Direct (Subsidized and Unsubsidized Stafford, PLUS), Perkins.

WORK-STUDY Federal work-study: Total amount: $216,621; 134 jobs averaging $1649.
ATHLETIC AWARDS Total amount: $2,244,278 (43% need-based, 57% non-need-based).
APPLYING FOR FINANCIAL AID Required financial aid form: FAFSA. **Financial aid deadline (priority):** 3/1. **Notification date:** Continuous beginning 12/15.
CONTACT Mr. Bob Walker, Director of Student Aid, University of Montevallo, Station 6050, Montevallo, AL 35115, 205-665-6048 or toll-free 800-292-4349. Fax: 205-665-6047. E-mail: rwalker7@montevallo.edu.
Website: http://www.montevallo.edu/.

UNIVERSITY OF MOUNT OLIVE
Mount Olive, NC

Tuition & fees: N/R	Average undergraduate aid package: $14,100

ABOUT THE INSTITUTION Independent Free Will Baptist, coed. 24 undergraduate majors. Federal methodology is used as a basis for awarding need-based institutional aid.
FRESHMAN FINANCIAL AID (Fall 2015) 271 applied for aid; of those 86% were deemed to have need. 99% of freshmen with need received aid; of those 18% had need fully met. **Average percent of need met:** 74% (excluding resources awarded to replace EFC). **Average financial aid package:** $16,089 (excluding resources awarded to replace EFC). 13% of all full-time freshmen had no need and received non-need-based gift aid.
UNDERGRADUATE FINANCIAL AID (Fall 2015) 1,202 applied for aid; of those 89% were deemed to have need. 99% of undergraduates with need received aid; of those 18% had need fully met. **Average percent of need met:** 69% (excluding resources awarded to replace EFC). **Average financial aid package:** $14,100 (excluding resources awarded to replace EFC). 8% of all full-time undergraduates had no need and received non-need-based gift aid.
GIFT AID (NEED-BASED) Total amount: $15,789,915 (41% federal, 20% state, 20% institutional, 19% external sources). **Receiving aid:** Freshmen: 83% (226); all full-time undergraduates: 82% (984). **Average award:** Freshmen: $13,553; Undergraduates: $11,595. **Scholarships, grants, and awards:** Federal Pell, FSEOG, state, private, college/university gift aid from institutional funds.
GIFT AID (NON-NEED-BASED) Total amount: $1,297,482 (5% state, 59% institutional, 36% external sources). **Receiving aid:** Freshmen: 14% (39). Undergraduates: 15% (175). **Average award:** Freshmen: $4868. Undergraduates: $4957. **Scholarships, grants, and awards by category:** Academic interests/achievement: general academic interests/achievements. Creative arts/performance: art/fine arts, general creative arts/performance. Special achievements/activities: general special achievements/activities, leadership. Special characteristics: children of faculty/staff, local/state students, religious affiliation, veterans, veterans' children.
LOANS Student loans: $19,818,213 (85% need-based, 15% non-need-based). 78% of past graduating class borrowed through all loan programs. Average indebtedness per student: $31,273. **Average need-based loan:** Freshmen: $3000. Undergraduates: $3937. **Parent loans:** $869,341 (48% need-based, 52% non-need-based). **Programs:** Federal Direct (Subsidized and Unsubsidized Stafford, PLUS), Perkins, state.
WORK-STUDY Federal work-study: jobs available.
ATHLETIC AWARDS Total amount: $1,490,960 (57% need-based, 43% non-need-based).
APPLYING FOR FINANCIAL AID Required financial aid forms: FAFSA, institution's own form, state aid form. **Financial aid deadline:** Continuous. **Notification date:** Continuous beginning 2/15. Students must reply within 2 weeks of notification.
CONTACT Mrs. Katrina K. Lee, Director of Financial Aid, University of Mount Olive, 634 Henderson Street, Mount Olive, NC 28365, 919-658-2502 or toll-free 800-653-0854. Fax: 919-658-9816. E-mail: klee@umo.edu.
Website: http://www.umo.edu/.

UNIVERSITY OF MOUNT UNION
Alliance, OH

Tuition & fees: $29,890	Average undergraduate aid package: $22,577

ABOUT THE INSTITUTION Independent United Methodist, coed. *Awards:* bachelor's, master's, and doctoral degrees. 66 undergraduate majors. *Total enrollment:* 2,281. Undergraduates: 2,140. Freshmen: 642. Federal methodology is used as a basis for awarding need-based institutional aid.

UNDERGRADUATE EXPENSES for 2017–2018 *Comprehensive fee:* $39,990 includes full-time tuition ($29,560), mandatory fees ($330), and room and board ($10,100). Full-time tuition and fees vary according to course load and degree level. Room and board charges vary according to board plan and housing facility. *Part-time tuition:* $1260 per credit hour. Part-time tuition and fees vary according to course load. *Payment plan:* Tuition prepayment.

FRESHMAN FINANCIAL AID (Fall 2015) 526 applied for aid; of those 87% were deemed to have need. 100% of freshmen with need received aid; of those 12% had need fully met. *Average percent of need met:* 80% (excluding resources awarded to replace EFC). *Average financial aid package:* $23,612 (excluding resources awarded to replace EFC). 17% of all full-time freshmen had no need and received non-need-based gift aid.

UNDERGRADUATE FINANCIAL AID (Fall 2015) 1,778 applied for aid; of those 90% were deemed to have need. 100% of undergraduates with need received aid; of those 14% had need fully met. *Average percent of need met:* 78% (excluding resources awarded to replace EFC). *Average financial aid package:* $22,577 (excluding resources awarded to replace EFC). 18% of all full-time undergraduates had no need and received non-need-based gift aid.

GIFT AID (NEED-BASED) *Total amount:* $26,458,378 (11% federal, 4% state, 83% institutional, 2% external sources). *Receiving aid:* Freshmen: 74% (456); all full-time undergraduates: 77% (1,598). *Average award:* Freshmen: $18,139; Undergraduates: $16,946. *Scholarships, grants, and awards:* Federal Pell, FSEOG, state, private, college/university gift aid from institutional funds.

GIFT AID (NON-NEED-BASED) *Total amount:* $5,393,255 (1% federal, 96% institutional, 3% external sources). *Receiving aid:* Freshmen: 7% (45). Undergraduates: 8% (169). *Average award:* Freshmen: $12,863. Undergraduates: $12,016. *Scholarships, grants, and awards by category:* Academic interests/achievement: general academic interests/achievements. Creative arts/performance: 124 awards ($605,990 total): art/fine arts, journalism/publications, music, performing arts, theater/drama. Special characteristics: children and siblings of alumni, children of faculty/staff, ethnic background, international students, members of minority groups, relatives of clergy, religious affiliation, veterans. *Tuition waivers:* Full or partial for children of alumni, employees or children of employees, senior citizens. *ROTC:* Army, Air Force cooperative.

LOANS *Student loans:* $17,573,332 (66% need-based, 34% non-need-based). 86% of past graduating class borrowed through all loan programs. *Average indebtedness per student:* $32,680. *Average need-based loan:* Freshmen: $5534. Undergraduates: $5877. *Parent loans:* $5,739,773 (49% need-based, 51% non-need-based). *Programs:* Federal Direct (Subsidized and Unsubsidized Stafford, PLUS), Perkins, state, private loans.

WORK-STUDY *Federal work-study:* 1,257 jobs averaging $1074. *State or other work-study/employment:* Total amount: $473,678 (20% need-based, 80% non-need-based). 328 part-time jobs averaging $1487.

APPLYING FOR FINANCIAL AID *Required financial aid form:* FAFSA. *Financial aid deadline:* Continuous. *Notification date:* Continuous beginning 12/1. Students must reply by 8/1.

CONTACT Mrs. Emily J. Mattison, Director of Student Financial Services, University of Mount Union, 1972 Clark Avenue, Alliance, OH 44601-3993, 330-823-2674 or toll-free 800-334-6682. *Fax:* 330-829-2814. *E-mail:* mattisej@mountunion.edu. *Website:* http://www.mountunion.edu/.

UNIVERSITY OF NEBRASKA AT KEARNEY
Kearney, NE

Tuition & fees (NE res): $6953	Average undergraduate aid package: $10,368

ABOUT THE INSTITUTION State supported, coed. *Awards:* certificates, bachelor's, and master's degrees. 38 undergraduate majors. *Total enrollment:* 6,788. Undergraduates: 5,056. Freshmen: 1,008. Federal methodology is used as a basis for awarding need-based institutional aid.

UNDERGRADUATE EXPENSES for 2016–2017 *Application fee:* $45. *Tuition, state resident:* full-time $5460; part-time $182 per credit hour. *Tuition, nonresident:* full-time $11,888; part-time $396.25 per credit hour. *Required fees:* full-time $1493. Full-time tuition and fees vary according to course level, course load, degree level, location, and program. Part-time tuition and fees vary according to course level, course load, degree level, location, and program. *College room and board:* $9594; *Room only:* $4914. Room and board charges vary according to board plan and housing facility.

FRESHMAN FINANCIAL AID (Fall 2015) 825 applied for aid; of those 80% were deemed to have need. 99% of freshmen with need received aid; of those 27% had need fully met. *Average percent of need met:* 73% (excluding resources awarded to replace EFC). *Average financial aid package:* $11,564 (excluding resources awarded to replace EFC). 17% of all full-time freshmen had no need and received non-need-based gift aid.

UNDERGRADUATE FINANCIAL AID (Fall 2015) 3,391 applied for aid; of those 83% were deemed to have need. 98% of undergraduates with need received aid; of those 22% had need fully met. *Average percent of need met:* 67% (excluding resources awarded to replace EFC). *Average financial aid package:* $10,368 (excluding resources awarded to replace EFC). 18% of all full-time undergraduates had no need and received non-need-based gift aid.

GIFT AID (NEED-BASED) *Total amount:* $19,216,160 (36% federal, 6% state, 33% institutional, 25% external sources). *Receiving aid:* Freshmen: 67% (624); all full-time undergraduates: 55% (2,385). *Average award:* Freshmen: $8711; Undergraduates: $7801. *Scholarships, grants, and awards:* Federal Pell, FSEOG, state, private, college/university gift aid from institutional funds.

GIFT AID (NON-NEED-BASED) *Total amount:* $5,948,974 (1% state, 74% institutional, 25% external sources). *Receiving aid:* Freshmen: 12% (116). Undergraduates: 7% (325). *Average award:* Freshmen: $3914. Undergraduates: $4791. *Scholarships, grants, and awards by category:* Academic interests/achievement: communication, general academic interests/achievements, military science. Creative arts/performance: applied art and design, art/fine arts, debating, journalism/publications, music, theater/drama. Special achievements/activities: cheerleading/drum major, leadership. Special characteristics: children and siblings of alumni, children of faculty/staff, ethnic background, first-generation college students, international students, local/state students, members of minority groups, out-of-state students, veterans, veterans' children. *Tuition waivers:* Full or partial for employees or children of employees. *ROTC:* Army.

LOANS *Student loans:* $15,617,688 (71% need-based, 29% non-need-based). 54% of past graduating class borrowed through all loan programs. *Average indebtedness per student:* $23,879. *Average need-based loan:* Freshmen: $3570. Undergraduates: $4029. *Parent loans:* $4,250,363 (31% need-based, 69% non-need-based). *Programs:* Federal Direct (Subsidized and Unsubsidized Stafford, PLUS), Perkins, college/university.

WORK-STUDY *Federal work-study:* jobs available.

ATHLETIC AWARDS Total amount: $1,562,090 (39% need-based, 61% non-need-based).

APPLYING FOR FINANCIAL AID *Required financial aid forms:* FAFSA, institution's own form. *Financial aid deadline (priority):* 4/1. *Notification date:* Continuous beginning 3/15.

CONTACT Financial Aid Office, University of Nebraska at Kearney, Memorial Student Affairs Building, 905 West 25th Street, Kearney, NE 68849-0001, 308-865-8520 or toll-free 800-532-7639. *Fax:* 308-865-8096. *E-mail:* finaid1@unk.edu. *Website:* http://www.unk.edu/.

UNIVERSITY OF NEBRASKA AT OMAHA
Omaha, NE

Tuition & fees: N/R	Average undergraduate aid package: $9464

ABOUT THE INSTITUTION State-supported, coed. 84 undergraduate majors. Federal methodology is used as a basis for awarding need-based institutional aid.

FRESHMAN FINANCIAL AID (Fall 2015) 1,604 applied for aid; of those 80% were deemed to have need. 98% of freshmen with need received aid; of those 30% had need fully met. *Average percent of need met:* 65% (excluding resources awarded to replace EFC). *Average financial aid package:* $9306 (excluding resources awarded to replace EFC). 6% of all full-time freshmen had no need and received non-need-based gift aid.

UNDERGRADUATE FINANCIAL AID (Fall 2015) 6,657 applied for aid; of those 86% were deemed to have need. 94% of undergraduates with need received aid; of those 28% had need fully met. *Average percent of need met:* 67% (excluding resources awarded to replace EFC). *Average financial aid package:* $9464 (excluding resources awarded to replace EFC). 5% of all full-time undergraduates had no need and received non-need-based gift aid.

GIFT AID (NEED-BASED) *Total amount:* $42,384,531 (39% federal, 8% state, 24% institutional, 29% external sources). *Receiving aid:* Freshmen: 38% (758); all full-time undergraduates: 35% (3,478). *Average award:* Freshmen: $6517; Undergraduates: $6017. *Scholarships, grants, and awards:* Federal Pell, FSEOG, state, private, college/university gift aid from institutional funds.

GIFT AID (NON-NEED-BASED) *Receiving aid:* Freshmen: 6% (111). Undergraduates: 7% (655). *Average award:* Freshmen: $3698. Undergraduates: $2722. *Scholarships, grants, and awards by category:* Academic interests/achievement: biological sciences, business, communication, computer science, education, engineering/technologies, English, foreign languages, general academic interests/achievements, home economics, mathematics, physical sciences, premedicine, social sciences. *Creative arts/performance:* art/fine arts, creative writing, debating, journalism/publications, music, performing arts, theater/drama. *Special achievements/activities:* general special achievements/activities, leadership, memberships. *Special characteristics:* adult students, children and siblings of alumni, children of faculty/staff, ethnic background, first-generation college students, handicapped students, international students, members of minority groups, out-of-state students, veterans' children.

LOANS *Student loans:* $33,254,339 (44% need-based, 56% non-need-based). 61% of past graduating class borrowed through all loan programs. *Average indebtedness per student:* $26,728. *Average need-based loan:* Freshmen: $3128. Undergraduates: $3906. *Parent loans:* $8,564,592 (100% non-need-based). *Programs:* Perkins, college/university.

WORK-STUDY *Federal work-study:* jobs available.

ATHLETIC AWARDS Total amount: $1,432,593 (100% need-based).

APPLYING FOR FINANCIAL AID *Required financial aid form:* FAFSA. *Financial aid deadline (priority):* 4/1. *Notification date:* Continuous beginning 4/15. Students must reply within 2 weeks of notification.

CONTACT Marty Habrock, Office of Financial Aid, University of Nebraska at Omaha, 103 Eppley Administration Building, Omaha, NE 68182-0187, 402-554-2327 or toll-free 800-858-8648 (in-state). *Fax:* 402-554-3472. *E-mail:* finaid@unomaha.edu. *Website:* http://www.unomaha.edu/.

UNIVERSITY OF NEBRASKA–LINCOLN
Lincoln, NE

Tuition & fees (NE res): $8538	Average undergraduate aid package: $13,688

ABOUT THE INSTITUTION State-supported, coed. *Awards:* certificates, bachelor's, master's, and doctoral degrees. 119 undergraduate majors. *Total enrollment:* 25,260. Undergraduates: 20,182. Freshmen: 4,628. Both federal and institutional methodology are used as a basis for awarding need-based institutional aid.

UNDERGRADUATE EXPENSES for 2016–2017 *Application fee:* $45. *Tuition, state resident:* full-time $6758; part-time $225.25 per credit hour. *Tuition, nonresident:* full-time $21,278; part-time $709.25 per credit hour. *Required fees:* full-time $1780; $17.25 per credit hour or $380 per term. Full-time tuition and fees vary according to course load, program, and reciprocity agreements. Part-time tuition and fees vary according to course load, program, and reciprocity agreements. *College room and board:* $10,670. Room and board charges vary according to board plan and housing facility.

FRESHMAN FINANCIAL AID (Fall 2015) 3,557 applied for aid; of those 72% were deemed to have need. 98% of freshmen with need received aid; of those 24% had need fully met. *Average percent of need met:* 82% (excluding resources awarded to replace EFC). *Average financial aid package:* $14,543 (excluding resources awarded to replace EFC). 12% of all full-time freshmen had no need and received non-need-based gift aid.

UNDERGRADUATE FINANCIAL AID (Fall 2015) 11,147 applied for aid; of those 75% were deemed to have need. 97% of undergraduates with need received aid; of those 21% had need fully met. *Average percent of need met:* 78% (excluding resources awarded to replace EFC). *Average financial aid package:* $13,688 (excluding resources awarded to replace EFC). 7% of all full-time undergraduates had no need and received non-need-based gift aid.

GIFT AID (NEED-BASED) *Total amount:* $60,669,068 (29% federal, 5% state, 44% institutional, 22% external sources). *Receiving aid:* Freshmen: 46% (2,097); all full-time undergraduates: 34% (6,388). *Average award:* Freshmen: $7875; Undergraduates: $7479. *Scholarships, grants, and awards:* Federal Pell, FSEOG, state, private, college/university gift aid from institutional funds.

GIFT AID (NON-NEED-BASED) *Total amount:* $34,912,193 (1% federal, 89% institutional, 10% external sources). *Receiving aid:* Freshmen: 5% (228). Undergraduates: 3% (572). *Average award:* Freshmen: $6708. Undergraduates: $6821. *Scholarships, grants, and awards by category:* Academic interests/achievement: agriculture, architecture, biological sciences, business, computer science, education, engineering/technologies, English, foreign languages, general academic interests/achievements, health fields, home economics, humanities, international studies, mathematics, physical sciences, premedicine, social sciences. *Creative arts/performance:* art/fine arts, cinema/film/broadcasting, dance, journalism/publications, music, performing arts, theater/drama. *Special achievements/activities:* cheerleading/drum major, community service, leadership. *Special characteristics:* children and siblings of alumni, ethnic background, handicapped students, international students, members of minority groups, out-of-state students, veterans' children. *Tuition waivers:* Full or partial for employees or children of employees. *ROTC:* Army, Naval, Air Force.

LOANS *Student loans:* $53,344,168 (74% need-based, 26% non-need-based). 57% of past graduating class borrowed through all loan programs. *Average indebtedness per student:* $23,307. *Average need-based loan:* Freshmen: $4009. Undergraduates: $4642. *Parent loans:* $36,762,058 (52% need-based, 48% non-need-based). *Programs:* Federal Direct (Subsidized and Unsubsidized Stafford, PLUS), Perkins, college/university.

WORK-STUDY *Federal work-study:* 1,342 jobs averaging $2787.

ATHLETIC AWARDS Total amount: $9,232,035 (100% non-need-based).

APPLYING FOR FINANCIAL AID *Required financial aid form:* FAFSA. *Financial aid deadline (priority):* 4/1. *Notification date:* Continuous beginning 4/1.

CONTACT Ms. Jo Tederman, Assistant Director of Scholarships and Financial Aid, University of Nebraska–Lincoln, 12 Canfield Administration Building, Lincoln, NE 68588-0411, 402-472-2030 or toll-free 800-742-8800. *Fax:* 402-472-9826. *Website:* http://www.unl.edu/.

UNIVERSITY OF NEBRASKA MEDICAL CENTER
Omaha, NE

CONTACT Judy D. Walker, Director of Financial Aid, University of Nebraska Medical Center, 984265 Nebraska Medical Center, Omaha, NE 68198-4265, 402-559-6409 or toll-free 800-626-8431 Ext. 6468. *Fax:* 402-559-6796. *E-mail:* jdwalker@unmc.edu. *Website:* http://www.unmc.edu/.

UNIVERSITY OF NEVADA, LAS VEGAS
Las Vegas, NV

Tuition & fees (NV res): $7310	Average undergraduate aid package: $8335

ABOUT THE INSTITUTION State-supported, coed. *Awards:* certificates, bachelor's, master's, and doctoral degrees. 85 undergraduate majors. *Total enrollment:* 29,702. Undergraduates: 24,714. Freshmen: 3,859. Federal methodology is used as a basis for awarding need-based institutional aid.

UNDERGRADUATE EXPENSES for 2017–2018 *Application fee:* $60. *One-time required fee:* $120. *Tuition, state resident:* full-time $6764; part-time $215.50 per credit hour. *Tuition, nonresident:* full-time $20,952. *Required fees:* full-time $546; $9.97 per credit hour or $273 per term. Full-time tuition and fees vary according to course level, program, and reciprocity agreements. Part-time tuition and fees vary according to course level, program, and reciprocity agreements. *College room and board:* $10,806; *Room only:* $5880. Room and board charges vary according to board plan and housing facility.

FRESHMAN FINANCIAL AID (Fall 2016, est.) 3,334 applied for aid; of those 79% were deemed to have need. 97% of freshmen with need received aid; of those 8% had need fully met. *Average percent of need met:* 53% (excluding resources awarded to replace EFC). *Average financial aid package:* $10,987 (excluding resources awarded to replace EFC). 15% of all full-time freshmen had no need and received non-need-based gift aid.

UNDERGRADUATE FINANCIAL AID (Fall 2016, est.) 13,793 applied for aid; of those 84% were deemed to have need. 94% of undergraduates with need received aid; of those 8% had need fully met. *Average percent of need met:* 54% (excluding resources awarded to replace EFC). *Average financial aid package:* $8335 (excluding resources awarded to replace EFC). 8% of all full-time undergraduates had no need and received non-need-based gift aid.

GIFT AID (NEED-BASED) *Total amount:* $78,752,317 (54% federal, 20% state, 23% institutional, 3% external sources). *Receiving aid:* Freshmen: 46% (1,727); all full-time undergraduates: 43% (7,781). *Average award:* Freshmen: $5868; Undergraduates: $6006. *Scholarships, grants, and awards:* Federal Pell, FSEOG, state, private, college/university gift aid from institutional funds.

GIFT AID (NON-NEED-BASED) *Total amount:* $11,017,554 (31% federal, 28% state, 33% institutional, 8% external sources). *Receiving aid:* Freshmen: 54% (2,014). Undergraduates: 30% (5,491). *Average award:* Freshmen: $3659. Undergraduates: $3987. *Scholarships, grants, and awards by category:* Academic interests/achievement: architecture, biological sciences, business, communication, computer science, education, engineering/technologies, English, foreign languages, general academic interests/achievements, health fields, humanities, international studies, mathematics, physical sciences, premedicine, social sciences. *Creative arts/performance:* applied art and design, art/fine arts, cinema/film/broadcasting, creative writing, dance, debating, general creative arts/performance, journalism/publications, music, performing arts, theater/drama. *Special achievements/activities:* cheerleading/drum major, community service, general special achievements/activities, leadership, rodeo. *Special characteristics:* adult students, children and siblings of alumni, children of faculty/staff, children of public servants, children of union members/company employees, children with a deceased or disabled parent, ethnic background, first-generation college students, general special characteristics, handicapped students, international students, local/state students, members of minority groups, out-of-state students, previous college experience, veterans, veterans' children. *Tuition waivers:* Full or partial for employees or children of employees. *ROTC:* Army, Air Force.

LOANS *Student loans:* $105,024,908 (82% need-based, 18% non-need-based). 52% of past graduating class borrowed through all loan programs. *Average indebtedness per student:* $25,374. *Average need-based loan:* Freshmen: $3317. Undergraduates: $4218. *Parent loans:* $16,084,421 (63% need-based, 37% non-need-based). *Programs:* Federal Direct (Subsidized and Unsubsidized Stafford, PLUS), Perkins, Federal Nursing, state, college/university.

WORK-STUDY *Federal work-study:* Total amount: $1,100,000; jobs available. *State or other work-study/employment:* Total amount: $575,000 (100% need-based). Part-time jobs available.

ATHLETIC AWARDS Total amount: $7,100,918 (86% need-based, 14% non-need-based).

APPLYING FOR FINANCIAL AID *Required financial aid form:* FAFSA. *Financial aid deadline (priority):* 11/1. *Notification date:* Continuous beginning 4/1. Students must reply within 6 weeks of notification.

CONTACT Norm Bedford, Director of Financial Aid and Scholarships, University of Nevada, Las Vegas, 4505 South Maryland Parkway, Las Vegas, NV 89154-2016, 702-895-3424. *Fax:* 702-895-1353. *Website:* http://www.unlv.edu/.

UNIVERSITY OF NEVADA, RENO
Reno, NV

Tuition & fees (NV res): $7377	Average undergraduate aid package: $8756

ABOUT THE INSTITUTION State-supported, coed. *Awards:* certificates, bachelor's, master's, and doctoral degrees. 73 undergraduate majors. *Total enrollment:* 21,353. Undergraduates: 18,191. Freshmen: 3,353. Federal methodology is used as a basis for awarding need-based institutional aid.

UNDERGRADUATE EXPENSES for 2017–2018 *Application fee:* $60. *Tuition, state resident:* full-time $6735; part-time $224.50 per credit. *Tuition, nonresident:* full-time $20,923; part-time $461.50 per credit hour. *Required fees:* full-time $642; $282 per term. Full-time tuition and fees vary according to course level, course load, degree level, and program. Part-time tuition and fees vary according to course level, course load, degree level, and program. *College room and board:* $10,868; *Room only:* $6100. Room and board charges vary according to board plan and housing facility.

FRESHMAN FINANCIAL AID (Fall 2015) 3,051 applied for aid; of those 70% were deemed to have need. 100% of freshmen with need received aid; of those 10% had need fully met. *Average percent of need met:* 61% (excluding resources awarded to replace EFC). *Average financial aid package:* $8293 (excluding resources awarded to replace EFC). 23% of all full-time freshmen had no need and received non-need-based gift aid.

UNDERGRADUATE FINANCIAL AID (Fall 2015) 10,201 applied for aid; of those 78% were deemed to have need. 100% of undergraduates with need received aid; of those 9% had need fully met. *Average percent of need met:* 61% (excluding resources awarded to replace EFC). *Average financial aid package:* $8756 (excluding resources awarded to replace EFC). 13% of all full-time undergraduates had no need and received non-need-based gift aid.

GIFT AID (NEED-BASED) *Total amount:* $42,889,047 (49% federal, 21% state, 26% institutional, 4% external sources). *Receiving aid:* Freshmen: 40% (1,523); all full-time undergraduates: 41% (6,101). *Average award:* Freshmen: $5039; Undergraduates: $5080. *Scholarships, grants, and awards:* Federal Pell, FSEOG, state, private, college/university gift aid from institutional funds.

GIFT AID (NON-NEED-BASED) *Total amount:* $15,998,328 (55% state, 29% institutional, 16% external sources). *Receiving aid:* Freshmen: 45% (1,711). Undergraduates: 31% (4,656). *Average award:* Freshmen: $1770. Undergraduates: $2250. *Scholarships, grants, and awards by category:* Academic interests/achievement: agriculture, biological sciences, business, communication, computer science, education, engineering/technologies, English, foreign languages, general academic interests/achievements, health fields, mathematics, physical sciences. *Creative arts/performance:* art/fine arts, general creative arts/performance, journalism/publications, music, theater/drama. *Special characteristics:* adult students, children and siblings of alumni, ethnic background, first-generation college students, married students. *Tuition waivers:* Full or partial for employees or children of employees, senior citizens. *ROTC:* Army.

LOANS *Student loans:* $48,222,557 (65% need-based, 35% non-need-based). 52% of past graduating class borrowed through all loan programs. *Average indebtedness per student:* $23,110. *Average need-based loan:* Freshmen: $3342. Undergraduates: $4095. *Parent loans:* $14,663,391 (15% need-based, 85% non-need-based). *Programs:* Federal Direct (Subsidized and Unsubsidized Stafford, PLUS), Perkins, Federal Nursing, college/university, private loans.

WORK-STUDY *Federal work-study:* jobs available. *State or other work-study/employment:* Total amount: $372,281 (24% need-based, 76% non-need-based). Part-time jobs available.

ATHLETIC AWARDS Total amount: $6,455,660 (41% need-based, 59% non-need-based).

APPLYING FOR FINANCIAL AID *Required financial aid form:* FAFSA. *Financial aid deadline (priority):* 2/1. *Notification date:* Continuous beginning 3/1. Students must reply within 4 weeks of notification.

CONTACT Tim Wolfe, Director of Student Financial Aid, University of Nevada, Reno, Mail Stop 076, Reno, NV 89557, 775-784-4666 or toll-free 866-263-8232. *Fax:* 775-784-1025. *E-mail:* tawolfe@unr.edu. *Website:* http://www.unr.edu/.

UNIVERSITY OF NEW ENGLAND
Biddeford, ME

ABOUT THE INSTITUTION Independent, coed. *Awards:* certificates, bachelor's, master's, and doctoral degrees. 37 undergraduate majors. *Total enrollment:* 8,276. Undergraduates: 4,247. Freshmen: 722.

GIFT AID (NEED-BASED) *Scholarships, grants, and awards:* Federal Pell, FSEOG, state, private, college/university gift aid from institutional funds.

GIFT AID (NON-NEED-BASED) *Scholarships, grants, and awards by category:* Academic interests/achievement: general academic interests/achievements. *Special achievements/activities:* leadership. *Special characteristics:* children and siblings of alumni, siblings of current students.

LOANS *Programs:* Federal Direct (Subsidized and Unsubsidized Stafford, PLUS), Perkins, Federal Nursing, state.

APPLYING FOR FINANCIAL AID *Required financial aid form:* FAFSA.

CONTACT Paul Henderson, Director of Financial Aid, University of New England, 11 Hills Beach Road, Biddeford, ME 04005, 207-602-2342 or toll-free 800-477-4863. *Fax:* 207-602-5968. *E-mail:* finaid@une.edu. *Website:* http://www.une.edu/.

UNIVERSITY OF NEW HAMPSHIRE
Durham, NH

Tuition & fees (NH res): $17,624	Average undergraduate aid package: $23,451

ABOUT THE INSTITUTION State-supported, coed. *Awards:* certificates, associate, bachelor's, master's, and doctoral degrees. 82 undergraduate majors. *Total enrollment:* 15,236. Undergraduates: 12,871. Freshmen: 2,881. Federal methodology is used as a basis for awarding need-based institutional aid.

UNDERGRADUATE EXPENSES for 2016–2017 *Application fee:* $50. *Tuition, state resident:* full-time $14,410; part-time $600 per credit hour. *Tuition, nonresident:* full-time $28,210; part-time $1175 per credit hour. *Required fees:* full-time $3214; $1607 per year. Full-time tuition and fees vary according to program. Part-time tuition and fees vary according to course load and program. *College room and board:* $10,938; *Room only:* $6820. Room and board charges vary according to board plan and housing facility.

FRESHMAN FINANCIAL AID (Fall 2015) 2,758 applied for aid; of those 80% were deemed to have need. 98% of freshmen with need received aid; of those 16% had need fully met. *Average percent of need met:* 78% (excluding resources awarded to replace EFC). *Average financial aid package:* $24,031 (excluding resources awarded to replace EFC). 15% of all full-time freshmen had no need and received non-need-based gift aid.

UNDERGRADUATE FINANCIAL AID (Fall 2015) 9,991 applied for aid; of those 82% were deemed to have need. 99% of undergraduates with need received aid; of those 15% had need fully met. *Average percent of need met:* 76% (excluding resources awarded to replace EFC). *Average financial aid package:* $23,451 (excluding resources awarded to replace EFC). 16% of all full-time undergraduates had no need and received non-need-based gift aid.

GIFT AID (NEED-BASED) *Total amount:* $75,269,372 (20% federal, 71% institutional, 9% external sources). *Receiving aid:* Freshmen: 55% (1,684); all full-time undergraduates: 48% (5,850). *Average award:* Freshmen: $6686; Undergraduates: $5985. *Scholarships, grants, and awards:* Federal Pell, FSEOG, state, private, college/university gift aid from institutional funds, Veterans Education Benefits (GI Bill).

GIFT AID (NON-NEED-BASED) *Total amount:* $19,064,296 (100% institutional). *Receiving aid:* Freshmen: 6% (170). Undergraduates: 4% (468). *Average award:* Freshmen: $6022. Undergraduates: $6885. *Scholarships, grants, and awards by category:* Academic interests/achievement: agriculture, biological sciences, business, computer science, education, engineering/technologies, English, foreign languages, general academic interests/achievements, health fields, humanities, mathematics, military science, physical sciences. *Creative arts/performance:* art/fine

arts, dance, music, performing arts, theater/drama. *Special achievements/activities:* community service, leadership. *Special characteristics:* children and siblings of alumni, children of faculty/staff, handicapped students, international students, local/state students. *Tuition waivers:* Full or partial for employees or children of employees. *ROTC:* Army, Air Force.

LOANS *Student loans:* $112,362,055 (31% need-based, 69% non-need-based). 79% of past graduating class borrowed through all loan programs. *Average indebtedness per student:* $38,799. *Average need-based loan:* Freshmen: $2668. Undergraduates: $3296. *Parent loans:* $28,656,600 (100% non-need-based). *Programs:* Federal Direct (Subsidized and Unsubsidized Stafford, PLUS), Perkins, state, college/university.

WORK-STUDY *Federal work-study:* 5,807 jobs averaging $2491. *State or other work-study/employment:* Total amount: $7,641,213 (100% non-need-based). 4,016 part-time jobs averaging $1683.

ATHLETIC AWARDS Total amount: $9,022,614 (100% non-need-based).

APPLYING FOR FINANCIAL AID *Required financial aid form:* FAFSA. *Financial aid deadline (priority):* 3/1. *Notification date:* Continuous beginning 3/1.

CONTACT Mr. Joel B. Carstens, Director of Financial Aid, University of New Hampshire, 11 Garrison Avenue, Durham, NH 03824, 603-862-3600. *Fax:* 603-862-1947. *E-mail:* financial.aid@unh.edu. *Website:* http://www.unh.edu/.

UNIVERSITY OF NEW HAMPSHIRE AT MANCHESTER
Manchester, NH

Tuition & fees (NH res): $14,860	Average undergraduate aid package: $13,154

ABOUT THE INSTITUTION State-supported, coed. *Awards:* associate, bachelor's, and master's degrees. 21 undergraduate majors. *Total enrollment:* 1,045. Undergraduates: 762. Freshmen: 72. Federal methodology is used as a basis for awarding need-based institutional aid.

UNDERGRADUATE EXPENSES for 2017–2018 *Application fee:* $65. *Tuition, state resident:* full-time $14,430; part-time $437 per credit hour. *Tuition, nonresident:* full-time $28,990; part-time $481 per credit hour. *Required fees:* full-time $430. Full-time tuition and fees vary according to course load and program. Part-time tuition and fees vary according to course load and program. Room and board charges vary according to housing facility.

FRESHMAN FINANCIAL AID (Fall 2015) 53 applied for aid; of those 72% were deemed to have need. 84% of freshmen with need received aid; of those 19% had need fully met. *Average percent of need met:* 66% (excluding resources awarded to replace EFC). *Average financial aid package:* $11,895 (excluding resources awarded to replace EFC). 12% of all full-time freshmen had no need and received non-need-based gift aid.

UNDERGRADUATE FINANCIAL AID (Fall 2015) 543 applied for aid; of those 83% were deemed to have need. 98% of undergraduates with need received aid; of those 10% had need fully met. *Average percent of need met:* 58% (excluding resources awarded to replace EFC). *Average financial aid package:* $13,154 (excluding resources awarded to replace EFC). 5% of all full-time undergraduates had no need and received non-need-based gift aid.

GIFT AID (NEED-BASED) *Total amount:* $1,550,452 (56% federal, 33% institutional, 11% external sources). *Receiving aid:* Freshmen: 35% (20); all full-time undergraduates: 34% (234). *Average award:* Freshmen: $1109; Undergraduates: $1492. *Scholarships, grants, and awards:* Federal Pell, FSEOG, state, private, college/university gift aid from institutional funds.

GIFT AID (NON-NEED-BASED) *Total amount:* $499,429 (100% institutional). *Receiving aid:* Freshmen: 12% (7). Undergraduates: 4% (30). *Average award:* Freshmen: $2000. Undergraduates: $2233. *Scholarships, grants, and awards by category:* Academic interests/achievement: biological sciences, business, communication, computer science, engineering/technologies, English, general academic interests/achievements, humanities. *Special characteristics:* children of faculty/staff. *Tuition waivers:* Full or partial for employees or children of employees. *ROTC:* Army cooperative, Air Force cooperative.

LOANS *Student loans:* $4,096,344 (38% need-based, 62% non-need-based). 86% of past graduating class borrowed through all loan programs. *Average indebtedness per student:* $39,034. *Average need-based loan:* Freshmen: $2486. Undergrad-

uates: $3855. **Parent loans:** $299,653 (100% non-need-based). **Programs:** Federal Direct (Subsidized and Unsubsidized Stafford, PLUS), Perkins, state, college/university. **WORK-STUDY** Federal work-study: 197 jobs averaging $2477.

APPLYING FOR FINANCIAL AID **Required financial aid form:** FAFSA. **Financial aid deadline (priority):** 3/1. **Notification date:** Continuous beginning 4/1.

CONTACT Sharon Eaton, Associate Director of Financial Aid, University of New Hampshire at Manchester, 400 Commercial Street, Student Services Suite, 4th Floor, Manchester, NH 03101-1113, 603-641-4114. Fax: 603-641-1125.

Website: http://manchester.unh.edu/.

UNIVERSITY OF NEW HAVEN
West Haven, CT

Tuition & fees: $37,060	Average undergraduate aid package: $22,746

ABOUT THE INSTITUTION Independent, coed. **Awards:** certificates, associate, bachelor's, master's, and doctoral degrees. 62 undergraduate majors. **Total enrollment:** 6,835. Undergraduates: 4,936. Freshmen: 1,128. Federal methodology is used as a basis for awarding need-based institutional aid.

UNDERGRADUATE EXPENSES for 2016–2017 Application fee: $50. **Comprehensive fee:** $52,190 includes full-time tuition ($35,700), mandatory fees ($1360), and room and board ($15,130). **College room only:** $9580. Full-time tuition and fees vary according to course load, location, and program. Room and board charges vary according to board plan, housing facility, and location. **Part-time tuition:** $1190 per credit hour. **Part-time fees:** $65 per term. Part-time tuition and fees vary according to class time, course load, location, and program.

FRESHMAN FINANCIAL AID (Fall 2016, est.) 971 applied for aid; of those 92% were deemed to have need. 100% of freshmen with need received aid; of those 14% had need fully met. **Average percent of need met:** 58% (excluding resources awarded to replace EFC). **Average financial aid package:** $22,484 (excluding resources awarded to replace EFC). 15% of all full-time freshmen had no need and received non-need-based gift aid.

UNDERGRADUATE FINANCIAL AID (Fall 2016, est.) 3,697 applied for aid; of those 92% were deemed to have need. 100% of undergraduates with need received aid; of those 16% had need fully met. **Average percent of need met:** 60% (excluding resources awarded to replace EFC). **Average financial aid package:** $22,746 (excluding resources awarded to replace EFC). 14% of all full-time undergraduates had no need and received non-need-based gift aid.

GIFT AID (NEED-BASED) Total amount: $61,411,085 (10% federal, 1% state, 87% institutional, 2% external sources). **Receiving aid:** Freshmen: 80% (889); all full-time undergraduates: 75% (3,402). **Average award:** Freshmen: $19,621; Undergraduates: $19,147. **Scholarships, grants, and awards:** Federal Pell, FSEOG, state, private, college/university gift aid from institutional funds.

GIFT AID (NON-NEED-BASED) Total amount: $12,068,889 (100% institutional). **Receiving aid:** Freshmen: 10% (109). Undergraduates: 9% (410). **Average award:** Freshmen: $15,388. Undergraduates: $14,358. **Tuition waivers:** Full or partial for employees or children of employees, senior citizens. **ROTC:** Army, Air Force cooperative.

LOANS Student loans: $41,829,941 (69% need-based, 31% non-need-based). 80% of past graduating class borrowed through all loan programs. **Average indebtedness per student:** $46,449. **Average need-based loan:** Freshmen: $3428. Undergraduates: $4392. **Parent loans:** $21,166,920 (100% non-need-based). **Programs:** Federal Direct (Subsidized and Unsubsidized Stafford, PLUS), Perkins, state.

WORK-STUDY Federal work-study: Total amount: $330,065; jobs available.

ATHLETIC AWARDS Total amount: $2,848,790 (54% need-based, 46% non-need-based).

APPLYING FOR FINANCIAL AID **Required financial aid form:** FAFSA. **Financial aid deadline (priority):** 1/1. **Notification date:** Continuous beginning 1/15. Students must reply by 5/1 or within 2 weeks of notification.

CONTACT Karen Flynn, Associate Vice President for Financial Aid, University of New Haven, 300 Boston Post Road, West Haven, CT 06516-1916, 203-932-7315 or toll-free 800-342-5864. Fax: 203-931-6050. E-mail: financialaid@newhaven.edu.

Website: http://www.newhaven.edu/.

UNIVERSITY OF NEW MEXICO
Albuquerque, NM

CONTACT Brian Malone, Office of Student Financial Aid, University of New Mexico, MSC 11 6315, 1 University of New Mexico, Albuquerque, NM 87131, 505-277-8900 or toll-free 800-CALL-UNM. Fax: 505-277-6326. E-mail: finaid@unm.edu. Website: http://www.unm.edu/.

UNIVERSITY OF NEW ORLEANS
New Orleans, LA

Tuition & fees (LA res): $8694	Average undergraduate aid package: $10,007

ABOUT THE INSTITUTION State-supported, coed. **Awards:** certificates, bachelor's, master's, and doctoral degrees. 33 undergraduate majors. **Total enrollment:** 8,037. Undergraduates: 6,442. Freshmen: 876. Federal methodology is used as a basis for awarding need-based institutional aid.

UNDERGRADUATE EXPENSES for 2016–2017 Application fee: $20. **Tuition, state resident:** full-time $6090. **Tuition, nonresident:** full-time $19,907. **Required fees:** full-time $2604. Full-time tuition and fees vary according to course load and program. Part-time tuition and fees vary according to course load and program. **College room and board:** $9730. Room and board charges vary according to board plan and housing facility.

FRESHMAN FINANCIAL AID (Fall 2016, est.) 816 applied for aid; of those 83% were deemed to have need. 96% of freshmen with need received aid; of those 8% had need fully met. **Average percent of need met:** 62% (excluding resources awarded to replace EFC). **Average financial aid package:** $10,692 (excluding resources awarded to replace EFC). 11% of all full-time freshmen had no need and received non-need-based gift aid.

UNDERGRADUATE FINANCIAL AID (Fall 2016, est.) 3,991 applied for aid; of those 86% were deemed to have need. 92% of undergraduates with need received aid; of those 6% had need fully met. **Average percent of need met:** 58% (excluding resources awarded to replace EFC). **Average financial aid package:** $10,007 (excluding resources awarded to replace EFC). 7% of all full-time undergraduates had no need and received non-need-based gift aid.

GIFT AID (NEED-BASED) Total amount: $11,814,852 (85% federal, 5% state, 10% institutional). **Receiving aid:** Freshmen: 50% (423); all full-time undergraduates: 45% (2,085). **Average award:** Freshmen: $5838; Undergraduates: $5427. **Scholarships, grants, and awards:** Federal Pell, FSEOG, state, private, college/university gift aid from institutional funds.

GIFT AID (NON-NEED-BASED) Total amount: $11,202,982 (1% federal, 59% state, 36% institutional, 4% external sources). **Receiving aid:** Freshmen: 53% (448). Undergraduates: 37% (1,728). **Average award:** Freshmen: $2271. Undergraduates: $2374. **Tuition waivers:** Full or partial for employees or children of employees, senior citizens. **ROTC:** Army cooperative, Naval cooperative, Air Force cooperative.

LOANS Student loans: $17,195,135 (45% need-based, 55% non-need-based). 53% of past graduating class borrowed through all loan programs. **Average indebtedness per student:** $21,767. **Average need-based loan:** Freshmen: $3422. Undergraduates: $4221. **Parent loans:** $1,003,653 (100% non-need-based). **Programs:** Federal Direct (Subsidized and Unsubsidized Stafford, PLUS), Perkins.

WORK-STUDY Federal work-study: Total amount: $384,055; jobs available. **State or other work-study/employment:** Total amount: $602,102 (100% non-need-based). Part-time jobs available.

ATHLETIC AWARDS Total amount: $1,374,551 (55% need-based, 45% non-need-based).

APPLYING FOR FINANCIAL AID **Required financial aid form:** FAFSA. **Financial aid deadline (priority):** 1/15. **Notification date:** Continuous beginning 3/15.

CONTACT Ms. Ann Lockridge, Director of Financial Aid, Scholarships, and Veterans Services, University of New Orleans, Privateer Enrollment Center, 2000 Lakeshore Drive, 105 Earl K. Long Library, 1st Floor, New Orleans, LA 70148, 504-280-6603 or toll-free 888-514-4275. Fax: 504-280-3973. E-mail: finaid@uno.edu.

Website: http://www.uno.edu/.

UNIVERSITY OF NORTH ALABAMA
Florence, AL

Tuition & fees (AL res): $9920	Average undergraduate aid package: $7972

ABOUT THE INSTITUTION State-supported, coed. **Awards:** certificates, bachelor's, and master's degrees. 43 undergraduate majors. **Total enrollment:** 7,492. Undergraduates: 6,313. Freshmen: 1,196. Federal methodology is used as a basis for awarding need-based institutional aid.

UNDERGRADUATE EXPENSES for 2016–2017 Application fee: $25. **Tuition, state resident:** full-time $7920; part-time $264 per credit hour. **Tuition, nonresident:** full-time $15,840; part-time $528 per credit hour. **Required fees:** full-time $2000; $237 per credit hour. Full-time tuition and fees vary according to course load, program, and student level. Part-time tuition and fees vary according to course load and program. **College room and board:** $7284. Room and board charges vary according to board plan, housing facility, and student level.

FRESHMAN FINANCIAL AID (Fall 2015) 855 applied for aid; of those 88% were deemed to have need. 97% of freshmen with need received aid; of those 9% had need fully met. **Average percent of need met:** 53% (excluding resources awarded to replace EFC). **Average financial aid package:** $7334 (excluding resources awarded to replace EFC). 9% of all full-time freshmen had no need and received non-need-based gift aid.

UNDERGRADUATE FINANCIAL AID (Fall 2015) 2,893 applied for aid; of those 89% were deemed to have need. 98% of undergraduates with need received aid; of those 9% had need fully met. **Average percent of need met:** 54% (excluding resources awarded to replace EFC). **Average financial aid package:** $7972 (excluding resources awarded to replace EFC). 7% of all full-time undergraduates had no need and received non-need-based gift aid.

GIFT AID (NEED-BASED) Total amount: $10,445,167 (100% federal). **Receiving aid:** Freshmen: 44% (512); all full-time undergraduates: 35% (1,728). **Average award:** Freshmen: $4202; Undergraduates: $4254. **Scholarships, grants, and awards:** Federal Pell, FSEOG, state, private, Project OPEN.

GIFT AID (NON-NEED-BASED) Total amount: $6,878,052 (91% institutional, 9% external sources). **Receiving aid:** Freshmen: 31% (360). Undergraduates: 20% (992). **Average award:** Freshmen: $5068. Undergraduates: $4946. **Scholarships, grants, and awards by category:** Academic interests/achievement: 1,269 awards ($5,412,315 total): general academic interests/achievements, military science. Creative arts/performance: 336 awards ($827,460 total): art/fine arts, dance, journalism/publications, music, theater/drama. Special achievements/activities: 206 awards ($635,150 total): cheerleading/drum major, general special achievements/activities, leadership. Special characteristics: 33 awards ($54,950 total): children and siblings of alumni, first-generation college students, general special characteristics, international students, out-of-state students. **Tuition waivers:** Full or partial for employees or children of employees, senior citizens. **ROTC:** Army.

LOANS Student loans: $22,523,280 (47% need-based, 53% non-need-based). **Average need-based loan:** Freshmen: $2926. Undergraduates: $3646. **Parent loans:** $3,488,651 (100% non-need-based). **Programs:** Federal Direct (Subsidized and Unsubsidized Stafford, PLUS).

WORK-STUDY Federal work-study: 160 jobs averaging $2016. **State or other work-study/employment:** Total amount: $652,778 (100% non-need-based). 536 part-time jobs averaging $1759.

ATHLETIC AWARDS Total amount: $1,420,513 (100% non-need-based).

APPLYING FOR FINANCIAL AID Financial aid deadline (priority): 6/1. **Notification date:** Continuous beginning 3/30.

CONTACT Ms. Shauna L. James, Director of Student Financial Services, University of North Alabama, UNA Box 5014, Florence, AL 35632-0001, 256-765-4279 or toll-free 800-TALK-UNA. E-mail: sljames@una.edu.
Website: http://www.una.edu/.

UNIVERSITY OF NORTH CAROLINA AT ASHEVILLE
Asheville, NC

Tuition & fees (NC res): $6977	Average undergraduate aid package: $11,998

ABOUT THE INSTITUTION State-supported, coed. **Awards:** certificates, bachelor's, and master's degrees. 36 undergraduate majors. **Total enrollment:** 3,830. Undergraduates: 3,806. Freshmen: 666. Federal methodology is used as a basis for awarding need-based institutional aid.

UNDERGRADUATE EXPENSES for 2016–2017 Application fee: $75. **One-time required fee:** $150. **Tuition, state resident:** full-time $4041; part-time $168 per credit hour. **Tuition, nonresident:** full-time $20,436; part-time $852 per credit hour. **Required fees:** full-time $2936; $122 per credit hour. Full-time tuition and fees vary according to course load and degree level. Part-time tuition and fees vary according to course load and degree level. **College room and board:** $8746; **Room only:** $4890. Room and board charges vary according to board plan and housing facility.

FRESHMAN FINANCIAL AID (Fall 2015) 635 applied for aid; of those 66% were deemed to have need. 99% of freshmen with need received aid; of those 24% had need fully met. **Average percent of need met:** 77% (excluding resources awarded to replace EFC). **Average financial aid package:** $11,656 (excluding resources awarded to replace EFC). 7% of all full-time freshmen had no need and received non-need-based gift aid.

UNDERGRADUATE FINANCIAL AID (Fall 2015) 2,529 applied for aid; of those 73% were deemed to have need. 99% of undergraduates with need received aid; of those 27% had need fully met. **Average percent of need met:** 76% (excluding resources awarded to replace EFC). **Average financial aid package:** $11,998 (excluding resources awarded to replace EFC). 7% of all full-time undergraduates had no need and received non-need-based gift aid.

GIFT AID (NEED-BASED) Total amount: $12,218,060 (46% federal, 26% state, 28% institutional). **Receiving aid:** Freshmen: 54% (396); all full-time undergraduates: 54% (1,724). **Average award:** Freshmen: $7040; Undergraduates: $6778. **Scholarships, grants, and awards:** Federal Pell, FSEOG, state, private, college/university gift aid from institutional funds.

GIFT AID (NON-NEED-BASED) Total amount: $652,043 (1% federal, 2% state, 97% institutional). **Receiving aid:** Freshmen: 6% (44). Undergraduates: 7% (223). **Average award:** Freshmen: $2182. Undergraduates: $2434. **Scholarships, grants, and awards by category:** Academic interests/achievement: 594 awards ($201,889 total): area/ethnic studies, biological sciences, business, communication, computer science, education, engineering/technologies, English, foreign languages, general academic interests/achievements, health fields, home economics, humanities, international studies, mathematics, physical sciences, religion/biblical studies, social sciences. Creative arts/performance: 1 award ($400 total): art/fine arts, dance, general creative arts/performance, music, theater/drama. Special achievements/activities: community service, general special achievements/activities, leadership. **Tuition waivers:** Full or partial for employees or children of employees.

LOANS Student loans: $11,888,242 (71% need-based, 29% non-need-based). 53% of past graduating class borrowed through all loan programs. Average indebtedness per student: $22,026. **Average need-based loan:** Freshmen: $3600. Undergraduates: $4445. **Parent loans:** $1,874,096 (26% need-based, 74% non-need-based). **Programs:** Federal Direct (Subsidized and Unsubsidized Stafford, PLUS), Perkins, state, college/university.

WORK-STUDY Federal work-study: 53 jobs averaging $2700. **State or other work-study/employment:** 1,892 part-time jobs averaging $1135.

ATHLETIC AWARDS Total amount: $1,949,372 (42% need-based, 58% non-need-based).

APPLYING FOR FINANCIAL AID Required financial aid form: FAFSA. **Financial aid deadline (priority):** 3/1. **Notification date:** Continuous beginning 3/1. Students must reply within 2 weeks of notification.

CONTACT Financial Aid Office, University of North Carolina at Asheville, One University Heights, 215 Brown Hall, CPO 1330, Asheville, NC 28804, 828-251-6535 or toll-free 800-531-9842. Fax: 828-232-2294. E-mail: finaid@unca.edu.
Website: http://www.unca.edu/.

THE UNIVERSITY OF NORTH CAROLINA AT CHAPEL HILL
Chapel Hill, NC

Tuition & fees (NC res): $9005	Average undergraduate aid package: $19,310

ABOUT THE INSTITUTION State-supported, coed. *Awards:* certificates, bachelor's, master's, and doctoral degrees. 58 undergraduate majors. *Total enrollment:* 29,469. Undergraduates: 18,523. Freshmen: 4,228. Both federal and institutional methodology are used as a basis for awarding need-based institutional aid.

UNDERGRADUATE EXPENSES for 2017–2018 Application fee: $80. *Tuition, state resident:* full-time $7019. *Tuition, nonresident:* full-time $32,602. *Required fees:* full-time $1986. Full-time tuition and fees vary according to program. Part-time tuition and fees vary according to course load and program. *College room and board:* $11,556; *Room only:* $6482. Room and board charges vary according to board plan, housing facility, and location.

FRESHMAN FINANCIAL AID (Fall 2015) 2,948 applied for aid; of those 64% were deemed to have need. 100% of freshmen with need received aid; of those 83% had need fully met. *Average percent of need met:* 100% (excluding resources awarded to replace EFC). *Average financial aid package:* $19,081 (excluding resources awarded to replace EFC). 2% of all full-time freshmen had no need and received non-need-based gift aid.

UNDERGRADUATE FINANCIAL AID (Fall 2015) 10,311 applied for aid; of those 79% were deemed to have need. 100% of undergraduates with need received aid; of those 80% had need fully met. *Average percent of need met:* 100% (excluding resources awarded to replace EFC). *Average financial aid package:* $19,310 (excluding resources awarded to replace EFC). 4% of all full-time undergraduates had no need and received non-need-based gift aid.

GIFT AID (NEED-BASED) Total amount: $121,761,722 (15% federal, 10% state, 69% institutional, 6% external sources). *Receiving aid:* Freshmen: 42% (1,711); all full-time undergraduates: 41% (7,188). *Average award:* Freshmen: $17,240; Undergraduates: $17,260. *Scholarships, grants, and awards:* Federal Pell, FSEOG, state, private, college/university gift aid from institutional funds.

GIFT AID (NON-NEED-BASED) Total amount: $15,519,001 (3% state, 42% institutional, 55% external sources). *Receiving aid:* Freshmen: 4% (154). Undergraduates: 2% (383). *Average award:* Freshmen: $10,376. Undergraduates: $7679. *Scholarships, grants, and awards by category: Academic interests/achievement:* business, communication, education, English, general academic interests/achievements, health fields, mathematics. *Creative arts/performance:* applied art and design, art/fine arts, journalism/publications, music, theater/drama. *Special achievements/activities:* community service, general special achievements/activities, leadership. *Special characteristics:* children of faculty/staff, international students, out-of-state students, relatives of clergy, religious affiliation. *Tuition waivers:* Full or partial for employees or children of employees. *ROTC:* Army, Naval, Air Force.

LOANS Student loans: $44,323,008 (67% need-based, 33% non-need-based). 42% of past graduating class borrowed through all loan programs. *Average indebtedness per student:* $20,852. *Average need-based loan:* Freshmen: $4599. Undergraduates: $5246. *Parent loans:* $9,386,648 (8% need-based, 92% non-need-based). *Programs:* Federal Direct (Subsidized and Unsubsidized Stafford, PLUS), Perkins, state, college/university, alternative loans.

WORK-STUDY Federal work-study: 1,991 jobs averaging $1631.

ATHLETIC AWARDS Total amount: $14,247,916 (21% need-based, 79% non-need-based).

APPLYING FOR FINANCIAL AID Required financial aid forms: FAFSA, CSS Financial Aid PROFILE. *Financial aid deadline (priority):* 3/1. *Notification date:* Continuous beginning 3/15. Students must reply by 5/1.

CONTACT Ms. Shirley A. Ort, Director of Scholarships and Student Aid, The University of North Carolina at Chapel Hill, CB # 2300, 111 Pettigrew Hall, Chapel Hill, NC 27599, 919-962-8396. Fax: 919-962-2716. E-mail: aidinfo@unc.edu. *Website:* http://www.unc.edu/.

THE UNIVERSITY OF NORTH CAROLINA AT CHARLOTTE
Charlotte, NC

Tuition & fees (NC res): $6763	Average undergraduate aid package: $10,154

ABOUT THE INSTITUTION State-supported, coed. *Awards:* certificates, bachelor's, master's, and doctoral degrees. 65 undergraduate majors. *Total enrollment:* 28,721. Undergraduates: 23,404. Freshmen: 3,453. Federal methodology is used as a basis for awarding need-based institutional aid.

UNDERGRADUATE EXPENSES for 2016–2017 Application fee: $60. *Tuition, state resident:* full-time $3737. *Tuition, nonresident:* full-time $16,908. *Required fees:* full-time $3026. Full-time tuition and fees vary according to course load and program. Part-time tuition and fees vary according to course load and program. *College room and board:* $10,470; *Room only:* $5910. Room and board charges vary according to board plan and housing facility.

FRESHMAN FINANCIAL AID (Fall 2016, est.) 3,026 applied for aid; of those 71% were deemed to have need. 99% of freshmen with need received aid; of those 15% had need fully met. *Average percent of need met:* 62% (excluding resources awarded to replace EFC). *Average financial aid package:* $9875 (excluding resources awarded to replace EFC). 3% of all full-time freshmen had no need and received non-need-based gift aid.

UNDERGRADUATE FINANCIAL AID (Fall 2016, est.) 16,491 applied for aid; of those 82% were deemed to have need. 98% of undergraduates with need received aid; of those 14% had need fully met. *Average percent of need met:* 62% (excluding resources awarded to replace EFC). *Average financial aid package:* $10,154 (excluding resources awarded to replace EFC). 1% of all full-time undergraduates had no need and received non-need-based gift aid.

GIFT AID (NEED-BASED) Total amount: $73,516,325 (54% federal, 28% state, 14% institutional, 4% external sources). *Receiving aid:* Freshmen: 46% (1,641); all full-time undergraduates: 48% (10,298). *Average award:* Freshmen: $6837; Undergraduates: $6539. *Scholarships, grants, and awards:* Federal Pell, FSEOG, state, private, college/university gift aid from institutional funds.

GIFT AID (NON-NEED-BASED) Total amount: $3,914,245 (1% federal, 2% state, 95% institutional, 2% external sources). *Receiving aid:* Freshmen: 5% (186). Undergraduates: 3% (734). *Average award:* Freshmen: $5998. Undergraduates: $7148. *Scholarships, grants, and awards by category: Academic interests/achievement:* 204 awards ($344,362 total): architecture, biological sciences, business, computer science, education, engineering/technologies, foreign languages, general academic interests/achievements, health fields, home economics, international studies, mathematics, physical sciences, religion/biblical studies, social sciences. *Creative arts/performance:* 46 awards ($67,537 total): art/fine arts, dance, music, theater/drama. *Special characteristics:* 91 awards ($127,243 total): adult students, children of public servants, children of union members/company employees, first-generation college students, handicapped students, international students, local/state students, members of minority groups, veterans. *Tuition waivers:* Full or partial for employees or children of employees. *ROTC:* Army, Air Force.

LOANS Student loans: $141,110,868 (42% need-based, 58% non-need-based). 67% of past graduating class borrowed through all loan programs. *Average indebtedness per student:* $27,453. *Average need-based loan:* Freshmen: $3310. Undergraduates: $4326. *Parent loans:* $25,900,416 (100% non-need-based). *Programs:* Federal Direct (Subsidized and Unsubsidized Stafford, PLUS), Perkins, state, college/university.

WORK-STUDY Federal work-study: Total amount: $2,206,684; 920 jobs averaging $2399.

ATHLETIC AWARDS Total amount: $5,884,643 (100% non-need-based).

APPLYING FOR FINANCIAL AID Required financial aid form: FAFSA. *Financial aid deadline (priority):* 3/1. *Notification date:* Continuous beginning 3/29. Students must reply by 9/30.

CONTACT Mr. Bruce Blackmon, Office of Financial Aid, The University of North Carolina at Charlotte, 9201 University City Boulevard, Charlotte, NC 28223-0001, 704-687-7010. Fax: 704-687-1461. E-mail: ablackm8@uncc.edu. *Website:* http://www.uncc.edu/.

THE UNIVERSITY OF NORTH CAROLINA AT GREENSBORO
Greensboro, NC

Tuition & fees (NC res): $7042 | **Average undergraduate aid package: $11,315**

ABOUT THE INSTITUTION State-supported, coed. *Awards:* certificates, bachelor's, master's, and doctoral degrees. 88 undergraduate majors. *Total enrollment:* 19,653. Undergraduates: 16,281. Freshmen: 2,644. Federal methodology is used as a basis for awarding need-based institutional aid.

UNDERGRADUATE EXPENSES for 2016–2017 *Application fee:* $55. *Tuition, state resident:* full-time $4336; part-time $541.88 per credit hour. *Tuition, nonresident:* full-time $19,198; part-time $2399.63 per credit hour. *Required fees:* full-time $2706; $100.43 per credit hour. Part-time tuition and fees vary according to course load. *College room and board:* $8580; *Room only:* $5084. Room and board charges vary according to board plan and housing facility.

FRESHMAN FINANCIAL AID (Fall 2016, est.) 2,610 applied for aid; of those 99% were deemed to have need. 93% of freshmen with need received aid; of those 26% had need fully met. *Average percent of need met:* 80% (excluding resources awarded to replace EFC). *Average financial aid package:* $11,569 (excluding resources awarded to replace EFC). 5% of all full-time freshmen had no need and received non-need-based gift aid.

UNDERGRADUATE FINANCIAL AID (Fall 2016, est.) 11,682 applied for aid; of those 99% were deemed to have need. 96% of undergraduates with need received aid; of those 19% had need fully met. *Average percent of need met:* 74% (excluding resources awarded to replace EFC). *Average financial aid package:* $11,315 (excluding resources awarded to replace EFC). 2% of all full-time undergraduates had no need and received non-need-based gift aid.

GIFT AID (NEED-BASED) *Total amount:* $47,488,315 (73% federal, 2% state, 25% institutional). *Receiving aid:* Freshmen: 59% (1,671); all full-time undergraduates: 55% (7,714). *Average award:* Freshmen: $6623; Undergraduates: $5907. *Scholarships, grants, and awards:* Federal Pell, FSEOG, state, private, college/university gift aid from institutional funds.

GIFT AID (NON-NEED-BASED) *Total amount:* $26,302,295 (72% state, 16% institutional, 12% external sources). *Receiving aid:* Freshmen: 60% (1,713). Undergraduates: 52% (7,193). *Average award:* Freshmen: $4499. Undergraduates: $3804. *Scholarships, grants, and awards by category:* Academic interests/achievement: biological sciences, business, communication, computer science, education, English, foreign languages, general academic interests/achievements, health fields, home economics, humanities, international studies, library science, mathematics, physical sciences, premedicine, religion/biblical studies, social sciences. *Creative arts/performance:* art/fine arts, cinema/film/broadcasting, dance, music, performing arts, theater/drama. *Special achievements/activities:* community service, general special achievements/activities, junior miss, leadership, religious involvement. *Special characteristics:* adult students, children and siblings of alumni, children of faculty/staff, general special characteristics, handicapped students, international students, local/state students, out-of-state students, religious affiliation, veterans, veterans' children. *Tuition waivers:* Full or partial for employees or children of employees. *ROTC:* Army cooperative, Air Force cooperative.

LOANS *Student loans:* $65,018,502 (52% need-based, 48% non-need-based). 89% of past graduating class borrowed through all loan programs. *Average indebtedness per student:* $27,073. *Average need-based loan:* Freshmen: $3397. Undergraduates: $4213. *Parent loans:* $13,029,899 (100% non-need-based). *Programs:* Federal Direct (Subsidized and Unsubsidized Stafford, PLUS), Perkins, state, college/university.

WORK-STUDY *Federal work-study:* Total amount: $636,976; jobs available.

ATHLETIC AWARDS Total amount: $2,972,946 (100% non-need-based).

APPLYING FOR FINANCIAL AID *Required financial aid form:* FAFSA. *Financial aid deadline (priority):* 3/1. *Notification date:* Continuous beginning 3/15. Students must reply within 3 weeks of notification.

CONTACT Mr. Bruce Cabiness, Associate Director of Financial Aid, The University of North Carolina at Greensboro, PO Box 26170, Greensboro, NC 27402-6170, 336-334-5702. *Fax:* 336-334-3010. *E-mail:* finaid@uncg.edu. *Website:* http://www.uncg.edu/.

THE UNIVERSITY OF NORTH CAROLINA AT PEMBROKE
Pembroke, NC

Tuition & fees (NC res): $5816 | **Average undergraduate aid package: $10,204**

ABOUT THE INSTITUTION State-supported, coed. *Awards:* bachelor's and master's degrees. 43 undergraduate majors. *Total enrollment:* 6,268. Undergraduates: 5,514. Freshmen: 1,091. Federal methodology is used as a basis for awarding need-based institutional aid.

UNDERGRADUATE EXPENSES for 2016–2017 *Application fee:* $45. *Tuition, state resident:* full-time $3531. *Tuition, nonresident:* full-time $14,475. *Required fees:* full-time $2285. Full-time tuition and fees vary according to course load, location, and program. Part-time tuition and fees vary according to course load, location, and program. *College room and board:* $8572; *Room only:* $4890. Room and board charges vary according to board plan, housing facility, and location.

FRESHMAN FINANCIAL AID (Fall 2016, est.) 1,050 applied for aid; of those 87% were deemed to have need. 97% of freshmen with need received aid; of those 7% had need fully met. *Average percent of need met:* 61% (excluding resources awarded to replace EFC). *Average financial aid package:* $9653 (excluding resources awarded to replace EFC). 1% of all full-time freshmen had no need and received non-need-based gift aid.

UNDERGRADUATE FINANCIAL AID (Fall 2016, est.) 4,067 applied for aid; of those 90% were deemed to have need. 98% of undergraduates with need received aid; of those 6% had need fully met. *Average percent of need met:* 64% (excluding resources awarded to replace EFC). *Average financial aid package:* $10,204 (excluding resources awarded to replace EFC). 1% of all full-time undergraduates had no need and received non-need-based gift aid.

GIFT AID (NEED-BASED) *Total amount:* $24,068,849 (62% federal, 27% state, 11% institutional). *Receiving aid:* Freshmen: 72% (788); all full-time undergraduates: 68% (3,065). *Average award:* Freshmen: $6924; Undergraduates: $6932. *Scholarships, grants, and awards:* Federal Pell, FSEOG, state, college/university gift aid from institutional funds.

GIFT AID (NON-NEED-BASED) *Total amount:* $762,852 (2% institutional, 98% external sources). *Receiving aid:* Freshmen: 19% (212). Undergraduates: 14% (651). *Average award:* Freshmen: $1644. Undergraduates: $2005. *Scholarships, grants, and awards by category:* Academic interests/achievement: 257 awards ($188,698 total): education, general academic interests/achievements. *Creative arts/performance:* 2 awards ($590 total): art/fine arts. *Special characteristics:* 7 awards ($5904 total): children and siblings of alumni. *Tuition waivers:* Full or partial for employees or children of employees. *ROTC:* Army, Air Force.

LOANS *Student loans:* $30,955,525 (96% need-based, 4% non-need-based). 86% of past graduating class borrowed through all loan programs. *Average indebtedness per student:* $25,263. *Average need-based loan:* Freshmen: $3388. Undergraduates: $4214. *Parent loans:* $4,279,763 (68% need-based, 32% non-need-based). *Programs:* Federal Direct (Subsidized and Unsubsidized Stafford, PLUS), Perkins.

WORK-STUDY *Federal work-study:* Total amount: $156,000; 89 jobs averaging $1839.

ATHLETIC AWARDS Total amount: $1,546,495 (97% need-based, 3% non-need-based).

APPLYING FOR FINANCIAL AID *Required financial aid form:* FAFSA. *Financial aid deadline (priority):* 3/1. *Notification date:* Continuous beginning 4/15.

CONTACT Mildred Weber, Associate Director of Financial Aid, The University of North Carolina at Pembroke, PO Box 1510, Pembroke, NC 28372, 910-521-6612 or toll-free 800-949-UNCP. *Fax:* 910-775-4159. *E-mail:* mildred.weber@uncp.edu. *Website:* http://www.uncp.edu/.

UNIVERSITY OF NORTH CAROLINA SCHOOL OF THE ARTS
Winston-Salem, NC

Tuition & fees (NC res): $9211	Average undergraduate aid package: $13,596

ABOUT THE INSTITUTION State-supported, coed. *Awards:* certificates, bachelor's, and master's degrees. 5 undergraduate majors. *Total enrollment:* 1,040. Undergraduates: 907. Freshmen: 213. Federal methodology is used as a basis for awarding need-based institutional aid.

UNDERGRADUATE EXPENSES for 2017–2018 *Tuition, state resident:* full-time $6370; part-time $265 per credit hour. *Tuition, nonresident:* full-time $22,240; part-time $927 per credit hour. *Required fees:* full-time $2841; $118 per credit hour. *College room and board:* $8977; *Room only:* $4475. Room and board charges vary according to board plan and housing facility. *Payment plan:* Guaranteed tuition.

FRESHMAN FINANCIAL AID (Fall 2016, est.) 183 applied for aid; of those 74% were deemed to have need. 99% of freshmen with need received aid; of those 8% had need fully met. *Average percent of need met:* 61% (excluding resources awarded to replace EFC). *Average financial aid package:* $12,260 (excluding resources awarded to replace EFC). 6% of all full-time freshmen had no need and received non-need-based gift aid.

UNDERGRADUATE FINANCIAL AID (Fall 2016, est.) 672 applied for aid; of those 81% were deemed to have need. 99% of undergraduates with need received aid; of those 10% had need fully met. *Average percent of need met:* 63% (excluding resources awarded to replace EFC). *Average financial aid package:* $13,596 (excluding resources awarded to replace EFC). 4% of all full-time undergraduates had no need and received non-need-based gift aid.

GIFT AID (NEED-BASED) Total amount: $5,529,916 (23% federal, 45% state, 28% institutional, 4% external sources). *Receiving aid:* Freshmen: 54% (113); all full-time undergraduates: 53% (468). *Average award:* Freshmen: $8256; Undergraduates: $8575. *Scholarships, grants, and awards:* Federal Pell, FSEOG, state, private, college/university gift aid from institutional funds.

GIFT AID (NON-NEED-BASED) Total amount: $48,503 (87% institutional, 13% external sources). *Receiving aid:* Freshmen: 37% (78). Undergraduates: 34% (299). *Average award:* Freshmen: $2817. Undergraduates: $2070. *Scholarships, grants, and awards by category:* Creative arts/performance: applied art and design, cinema/film/broadcasting, dance, music, performing arts, theater/drama. *Tuition waivers:* Full or partial for employees or children of employees.

LOANS Student loans: $5,090,689 (92% need-based, 8% non-need-based). 64% of past graduating class borrowed through all loan programs. *Average indebtedness per student:* $28,551. *Average need-based loan:* Freshmen: $3554. Undergraduates: $4538. *Parent loans:* $2,273,950 (64% need-based, 36% non-need-based). *Programs:* Federal Direct (Subsidized and Unsubsidized Stafford, PLUS), Perkins.

WORK-STUDY Federal work-study: Total amount: $116,800; 146 jobs averaging $800.

APPLYING FOR FINANCIAL AID Required financial aid form: FAFSA. *Financial aid deadline (priority):* 3/1. *Notification date:* Continuous beginning 4/1. Students must reply within 2 weeks of notification.

CONTACT Jane C. Kamiab, Director of Financial Aid, University of North Carolina School of the Arts, 1533 South Main Street, Winston-Salem, NC 27127, 336-770-3297. *Fax:* 336-770-1489.
Website: http://www.uncsa.edu/.

THE UNIVERSITY OF NORTH CAROLINA WILMINGTON
Wilmington, NC

Tuition & fees (NC res): $6952	Average undergraduate aid package: $8932

ABOUT THE INSTITUTION State-supported, coed. *Awards:* certificates, bachelor's, master's, and doctoral degrees. 49 undergraduate majors. *Total enrollment:* 15,740. Undergraduates: 13,914. Freshmen: 2,223. Federal methodology is used as a basis for awarding need-based institutional aid.

UNDERGRADUATE EXPENSES for 2016–2017 *Application fee:* $75. *Tuition, state resident:* full-time $4356; part-time $158.73 per credit hour. *Tuition, nonresident:* full-time $18,324; part-time $667.80 per credit hour. *Required fees:* full-time $2596; $75.55 per credit hour. Full-time tuition and fees vary according to course load and location. Part-time tuition and fees vary according to course load and location. *College room and board:* $9489; *Room only:* $5879. Room and board charges vary according to board plan and housing facility.

FRESHMAN FINANCIAL AID (Fall 2015) 1,615 applied for aid; of those 71% were deemed to have need. 97% of freshmen with need received aid; of those 12% had need fully met. *Average percent of need met:* 62% (excluding resources awarded to replace EFC). *Average financial aid package:* $8252 (excluding resources awarded to replace EFC). 2% of all full-time freshmen had no need and received non-need-based gift aid.

UNDERGRADUATE FINANCIAL AID (Fall 2015) 8,234 applied for aid; of those 79% were deemed to have need. 97% of undergraduates with need received aid; of those 17% had need fully met. *Average percent of need met:* 60% (excluding resources awarded to replace EFC). *Average financial aid package:* $8932 (excluding resources awarded to replace EFC). 1% of all full-time undergraduates had no need and received non-need-based gift aid.

GIFT AID (NEED-BASED) Total amount: $21,311,278 (50% federal, 14% state, 35% institutional, 1% external sources). *Receiving aid:* Freshmen: 52% (1,047); all full-time undergraduates: 52% (5,987). *Average award:* Freshmen: $4794; Undergraduates: $5095. *Scholarships, grants, and awards:* Federal Pell, FSEOG, state, private, college/university gift aid from institutional funds, United Negro College Fund, Federal Nursing.

GIFT AID (NON-NEED-BASED) Total amount: $2,840,815 (59% institutional, 41% external sources). *Receiving aid:* Freshmen: 17% (343). Undergraduates: 10% (1,204). *Average award:* Freshmen: $3096. Undergraduates: $3584. *Scholarships, grants, and awards by category:* Academic interests/achievement: biological sciences, business, communication, computer science, education, engineering/technologies, English, foreign languages, general academic interests/achievements, health fields, humanities, international studies, mathematics, physical sciences, premedicine, social sciences. Creative arts/performance: art/fine arts, cinema/film/broadcasting, creative writing, music, theater/drama. Special achievements/activities: cheerleading/drum major, general special achievements/activities, leadership. Special characteristics: local/state students, married students. *Tuition waivers:* Full or partial for employees or children of employees.

LOANS Student loans: $42,481,185 (40% need-based, 60% non-need-based). 60% of past graduating class borrowed through all loan programs. *Average indebtedness per student:* $25,112. *Average need-based loan:* Freshmen: $3358. Undergraduates: $4309. *Parent loans:* $21,222,392 (100% non-need-based). *Programs:* Federal Direct (Subsidized and Unsubsidized Stafford, PLUS), Perkins, state, college/university, alternative loans.

WORK-STUDY Federal work-study: jobs available.

ATHLETIC AWARDS Total amount: $1,145,316 (100% non-need-based).

APPLYING FOR FINANCIAL AID Required financial aid forms: FAFSA, institution's own form. *Financial aid deadline (priority):* 3/1. *Notification date:* 4/1. Students must reply by 5/1 or within 3 weeks of notification.

CONTACT Mr. Frederick Holding, Director of the Office of Scholarships and Financial Aid, The University of North Carolina Wilmington, 601 South College Road, Wilmington, NC 28403-5951, 910-962-3177. *Fax:* 910-962-3851. *E-mail:* finaid@uncw.edu.
Website: http://www.uncw.edu/.

UNIVERSITY OF NORTH DAKOTA
Grand Forks, ND

CONTACT Janelle Kilgore, Interim Director of Student Financial Aid, University of North Dakota, 264 Centennial Drive Stop 8371, Grand Forks, ND 58202, 701-777-3121 or toll-free 800-CALL-UND. *Fax:* 701-777-2040. *E-mail:* janelle.kilgore@und.edu.
Website: http://www.und.edu/.

UNIVERSITY OF NORTHERN COLORADO
Greeley, CO

Tuition & fees (CO res): $8888	Average undergraduate aid package: $10,831

ABOUT THE INSTITUTION State-supported, coed. **Awards:** bachelor's, master's, and doctoral degrees. 45 undergraduate majors. **Total enrollment:** 12,260. Undergraduates: 9,503. Freshmen: 2,079. Federal methodology is used as a basis for awarding need-based institutional aid.

UNDERGRADUATE EXPENSES for 2017–2018 Application fee: $45. **One-time required fee:** $250. **Tuition, state resident:** full-time $6906; part-time $275.25 per credit hour. **Tuition, nonresident:** full-time $18,492; part-time $735.50 per credit hour. **Required fees:** full-time $1982; $91.60 per credit hour. Full-time tuition and fees vary according to location and program. Part-time tuition and fees vary according to location and program. **College room and board:** $10,770; **Room only:** $5100. Room and board charges vary according to board plan and housing facility.

FRESHMAN FINANCIAL AID (Fall 2015) 1,764 applied for aid; of those 71% were deemed to have need. 97% of freshmen with need received aid; of those 38% had need fully met. **Average percent of need met:** 81% (excluding resources awarded to replace EFC). **Average financial aid package:** $11,863 (excluding resources awarded to replace EFC). 14% of all full-time freshmen had no need and received non-need-based gift aid.

UNDERGRADUATE FINANCIAL AID (Fall 2015) 6,570 applied for aid; of those 76% were deemed to have need. 98% of undergraduates with need received aid; of those 32% had need fully met. **Average percent of need met:** 75% (excluding resources awarded to replace EFC). **Average financial aid package:** $10,831 (excluding resources awarded to replace EFC). 13% of all full-time undergraduates had no need and received non-need-based gift aid.

GIFT AID (NEED-BASED) Total amount: $34,765,560 (36% federal, 16% state, 36% institutional, 12% external sources). **Receiving aid:** Freshmen: 54% (1,054); all full-time undergraduates: 51% (4,135). **Average award:** Freshmen: $9348; Undergraduates: $7102. **Scholarships, grants, and awards:** Federal Pell, FSEOG, state, private, college/university gift aid from institutional funds.

GIFT AID (NON-NEED-BASED) Total amount: $6,850,372 (2% federal, 62% institutional, 36% external sources). **Receiving aid:** Freshmen: 35% (686). Undergraduates: 33% (2,685). **Average award:** Freshmen: $6381. Undergraduates: $5930. **Scholarships, grants, and awards by category:** Academic interests/achievement: biological sciences, business, communication, education, English, foreign languages, general academic interests/achievements, health fields, home economics, humanities, international studies, mathematics, military science, physical sciences, pre-medicine, social sciences. Creative arts/performance: applied art and design, art/fine arts, dance, journalism/publications, music, performing arts, theater/drama. Special achievements/activities: community service, general special achievements/activities, leadership, memberships. Special characteristics: adult students, children and siblings of alumni, children of faculty/staff, children of union members/company employees, children of workers in trades, ethnic background, first-generation college students, general special characteristics, handicapped students, international students, local/state students, married students, members of minority groups, out-of-state students, previous college experience, veterans. **Tuition waivers:** Full or partial for employees or children of employees. **ROTC:** Army, Air Force.

LOANS Student loans: $35,311,141 (71% need-based, 29% non-need-based). 60% of past graduating class borrowed through all loan programs. Average indebtedness per student: $27,393. **Average need-based loan:** Freshmen: $3216. Undergraduates: $3938. **Parent loans:** $17,667,268 (28% need-based, 72% non-need-based). **Programs:** Federal Direct (Subsidized and Unsubsidized Stafford, PLUS), Perkins, Federal Nursing.

WORK-STUDY Federal work-study: 197 jobs averaging $2206. **State or other work-study/employment:** Total amount: $1,471,878 (87% need-based, 13% non-need-based). 579 part-time jobs averaging $2589.

ATHLETIC AWARDS Total amount: $4,459,553 (41% need-based, 59% non-need-based).

APPLYING FOR FINANCIAL AID Required financial aid form: FAFSA. **Financial aid deadline (priority):** 3/1. **Notification date:** 3/15. Students must reply within 4 weeks of notification.

CONTACT Marty Somero, Director of Financial Aid, University of Northern Colorado, Carter Hall 1005, Greeley, CO 80639, 970-351-2502 or toll-free 888-700-4UNC. *Fax:* 970-351-3737. *E-mail:* ofa@unco.edu. *Website:* http://www.unco.edu/.

UNIVERSITY OF NORTHERN IOWA
Cedar Falls, IA

Tuition & fees (IA res): $8483	Average undergraduate aid package: $8363

ABOUT THE INSTITUTION State-supported, coed. **Awards:** bachelor's, master's, and doctoral degrees. 90 undergraduate majors. **Total enrollment:** 11,905. Undergraduates: 10,104. Freshmen: 2,000. Federal methodology is used as a basis for awarding need-based institutional aid.

UNDERGRADUATE EXPENSES for 2017–2018 Application fee: $40. **Tuition, state resident:** full-time $7240; part-time $302 per credit hour. **Tuition, nonresident:** full-time $17,782; part-time $741 per credit hour. **Required fees:** full-time $1243. Full-time tuition and fees vary according to course load and program. Part-time tuition and fees vary according to course load and program. **College room and board:** $8781; **Room only:** $4473. Room and board charges vary according to board plan and housing facility.

FRESHMAN FINANCIAL AID (Fall 2015) 1,612 applied for aid; of those 71% were deemed to have need. 97% of freshmen with need received aid; of those 19% had need fully met. **Average percent of need met:** 69% (excluding resources awarded to replace EFC). **Average financial aid package:** $8733 (excluding resources awarded to replace EFC). 20% of all full-time freshmen had no need and received non-need-based gift aid.

UNDERGRADUATE FINANCIAL AID (Fall 2015) 6,973 applied for aid; of those 78% were deemed to have need. 95% of undergraduates with need received aid; of those 16% had need fully met. **Average percent of need met:** 65% (excluding resources awarded to replace EFC). **Average financial aid package:** $8363 (excluding resources awarded to replace EFC). 11% of all full-time undergraduates had no need and received non-need-based gift aid.

GIFT AID (NEED-BASED) Total amount: $25,282,395 (47% federal, 4% state, 43% institutional, 6% external sources). **Receiving aid:** Freshmen: 35% (658); all full-time undergraduates: 33% (3,020). **Average award:** Freshmen: $4928; Undergraduates: $4714. **Scholarships, grants, and awards:** Federal Pell, FSEOG, state, private, college/university gift aid from institutional funds, TEACH Grants.

GIFT AID (NON-NEED-BASED) Total amount: $3,403,554 (11% federal, 4% state, 67% institutional, 18% external sources). **Receiving aid:** Freshmen: 43% (797). Undergraduates: 26% (2,349). **Average award:** Freshmen: $3342. Undergraduates: $3304. **Scholarships, grants, and awards by category:** Academic interests/achievement: biological sciences, business, communication, computer science, education, general academic interests/achievements, mathematics, physical sciences, social sciences. Creative arts/performance: applied art and design, art/fine arts, debating, music, theater/drama. Special achievements/activities: leadership. Special characteristics: general special characteristics, members of minority groups, veterans. **ROTC:** Army.

LOANS Student loans: $44,285,919 (43% need-based, 57% non-need-based). 69% of past graduating class borrowed through all loan programs. Average indebtedness per student: $24,325. **Average need-based loan:** Freshmen: $3681. Undergraduates: $4343. **Parent loans:** $11,331,663 (100% non-need-based). **Programs:** Federal Direct (Subsidized and Unsubsidized Stafford, PLUS), Perkins, private loans.

WORK-STUDY Federal work-study: 452 jobs averaging $1507. **State or other work-study/employment:** Part-time jobs available.

ATHLETIC AWARDS Total amount: $3,497,360 (88% need-based, 12% non-need-based).

APPLYING FOR FINANCIAL AID Required financial aid form: FAFSA. **Financial aid deadline:** Continuous. **Notification date:** Continuous beginning 3/15.

CONTACT Heather Soesbe, Associate Director of Student Financial Aid, University of Northern Iowa, 105 Gilchrist Hall, Cedar Falls, IA 50614-0024, 319-273-2701 or toll-free 800-772-2037. *Fax:* 319-273-6950. *E-mail:* heather.soesbe@uni.edu. *Website:* http://www.uni.edu/.

UNIVERSITY OF NORTH FLORIDA
Jacksonville, FL

Tuition & fees (FL res): $6394	Average undergraduate aid package: $8050

ABOUT THE INSTITUTION State-supported, coed. *Awards:* certificates, associate, bachelor's, master's, and doctoral degrees (doctoral degree in education only). 58 undergraduate majors. *Total enrollment:* 15,762. Undergraduates: 13,846. Freshmen: 1,978. Federal methodology is used as a basis for awarding need-based institutional aid.

UNDERGRADUATE EXPENSES for 2016–2017 Application fee: $30. *Tuition, state resident:* full-time $4281; part-time $142.70 per credit hour. *Tuition, nonresident:* full-time $17,999; part-time $599.97 per credit hour. *Required fees:* full-time $2113; $70.43 per credit hour. Full-time tuition and fees vary according to course load. Part-time tuition and fees vary according to course load. *College room and board:* $9772. Room and board charges vary according to board plan and housing facility.

FRESHMAN FINANCIAL AID (Fall 2016, est.) 1,522 applied for aid; of those 65% were deemed to have need. 94% of freshmen with need received aid; of those 18% had need fully met. *Average percent of need met:* 90% (excluding resources awarded to replace EFC). *Average financial aid package:* $8777 (excluding resources awarded to replace EFC). 11% of all full-time freshmen had no need and received non-need-based gift aid.

UNDERGRADUATE FINANCIAL AID (Fall 2016, est.) 6,673 applied for aid; of those 77% were deemed to have need. 93% of undergraduates with need received aid; of those 13% had need fully met. *Average percent of need met:* 89% (excluding resources awarded to replace EFC). *Average financial aid package:* $8050 (excluding resources awarded to replace EFC). 14% of all full-time undergraduates had no need and received non-need-based gift aid.

GIFT AID (NEED-BASED) Total amount: $31,858,438 (61% federal, 17% state, 20% institutional, 2% external sources). *Receiving aid:* Freshmen: 33% (615); all full-time undergraduates: 34% (3,265). *Average award:* Freshmen: $6515; Undergraduates: $5850. *Scholarships, grants, and awards:* Federal Pell, FSEOG, state, private, college/university gift aid from institutional funds.

GIFT AID (NON-NEED-BASED) Total amount: $6,987,521 (47% state, 49% institutional, 4% external sources). *Receiving aid:* Freshmen: 27% (511). Undergraduates: 18% (1,687). *Average award:* Freshmen: $3539. Undergraduates: $3331. *Scholarships, grants, and awards by category: Academic interests/achievement:* 304 awards ($912,782 total): business, computer science, education, engineering/technologies, general academic interests/achievements, health fields, international studies. *Creative arts/performance:* 46 awards ($129,370 total): art/fine arts, music. *Special achievements/activities:* 31 awards ($43,900 total): community service, general special achievements/activities, leadership. *Special characteristics:* 32 awards ($42,500 total): first-generation college students, general special characteristics, international students, members of minority groups, out-of-state students. *Tuition waivers:* Full or partial for employees or children of employees, senior citizens. *ROTC:* Army, Naval cooperative.

LOANS Student loans: $36,378,931 (82% need-based, 18% non-need-based). 50% of past graduating class borrowed through all loan programs. *Average indebtedness per student:* $18,685. *Average need-based loan:* Freshmen: $3351. Undergraduates: $4236. *Parent loans:* $3,302,133 (73% need-based, 27% non-need-based). *Programs:* Federal Direct (Subsidized and Unsubsidized Stafford, PLUS).

WORK-STUDY Federal work-study: Total amount: $467,734; 138 jobs averaging $3418.

ATHLETIC AWARDS Total amount: $2,110,209 (34% need-based, 66% non-need-based).

APPLYING FOR FINANCIAL AID Required financial aid form: FAFSA. *Financial aid deadline (priority):* 4/1. *Notification date:* Continuous beginning 3/15. Students must reply within 2 weeks of notification.

CONTACT Ms. Anissa Agne, Director of Financial Aid, University of North Florida, 1 UNF Drive, Jacksonville, FL 32224-7699, 904-620-5555. *E-mail:* anissa.agne@unf.edu. *Website:* http://www.unf.edu/.

UNIVERSITY OF NORTH GEORGIA
Dahlonega, GA

Tuition & fees (GA res): $7228	Average undergraduate aid package: $13,962

ABOUT THE INSTITUTION State-supported, coed. *Awards:* certificates, associate, bachelor's, master's, and doctoral degrees. 38 undergraduate majors. *Total enrollment:* 18,219. Undergraduates: 17,704. Freshmen: 3,958. Federal methodology is used as a basis for awarding need-based institutional aid.

UNDERGRADUATE EXPENSES for 2017–2018 Application fee: $30. *Tuition, state resident:* full-time $5352; part-time $178.40 per credit hour. *Tuition, nonresident:* full-time $18,894; part-time $629.80 per credit hour. *Required fees:* full-time $1876. Full-time tuition and fees vary according to course load, degree level, and location. Part-time tuition and fees vary according to course load, degree level, and location. *College room and board:* $9680; *Room only:* $5360. Room and board charges vary according to board plan and housing facility.

FRESHMAN FINANCIAL AID (Fall 2015) 3,334 applied for aid; of those 68% were deemed to have need. 100% of freshmen with need received aid; of those 62% had need fully met. *Average percent of need met:* 69% (excluding resources awarded to replace EFC). *Average financial aid package:* $9959 (excluding resources awarded to replace EFC). 8% of all full-time freshmen had no need and received non-need-based gift aid.

UNDERGRADUATE FINANCIAL AID (Fall 2015) 11,355 applied for aid; of those 66% were deemed to have need. 100% of undergraduates with need received aid; of those 61% had need fully met. *Average percent of need met:* 62% (excluding resources awarded to replace EFC). *Average financial aid package:* $13,962 (excluding resources awarded to replace EFC). 4% of all full-time undergraduates had no need and received non-need-based gift aid.

GIFT AID (NEED-BASED) Total amount: $32,118,606 (76% federal, 22% state, 1% institutional, 1% external sources). *Receiving aid:* Freshmen: 55% (2,021); all full-time undergraduates: 60% (7,368). *Average award:* Freshmen: $5906; Undergraduates: $5803. *Scholarships, grants, and awards:* Federal Pell, FSEOG, state, private, college/university gift aid from institutional funds.

GIFT AID (NON-NEED-BASED) Total amount: $22,325,878 (90% state, 5% institutional, 5% external sources). *Receiving aid:* Freshmen: 54% (1,991). Undergraduates: 59% (7,231). *Average award:* Freshmen: $1150. Undergraduates: $1292. *Scholarships, grants, and awards by category: Academic interests/achievement:* 687 awards ($892,997 total): biological sciences, business, education, English, general academic interests/achievements, health fields, humanities, mathematics, military science, physical sciences, premedicine. *Creative arts/performance:* applied art and design, general creative arts/performance, music. *Special achievements/activities:* 69 awards ($33,373 total): cheerleading/drum major, community service, general special achievements/activities, leadership. *Special characteristics:* 160 awards ($160,752 total): general special characteristics. *Tuition waivers:* Full or partial for employees or children of employees, senior citizens. *ROTC:* Army.

LOANS Student loans: $46,215,791 (50% need-based, 50% non-need-based). 46% of past graduating class borrowed through all loan programs. *Average indebtedness per student:* $10,062. *Average need-based loan:* Freshmen: $3808. Undergraduates: $5189. *Parent loans:* $2,617,353 (31% need-based, 69% non-need-based). *Programs:* Federal Direct (Subsidized and Unsubsidized Stafford, PLUS), Perkins, state, college/university.

WORK-STUDY Federal work-study: 94 jobs averaging $2425. *State or other work-study/employment:* Total amount: $1,111,438 (100% non-need-based). Part-time jobs available.

ATHLETIC AWARDS Total amount: $1,204,005 (17% need-based, 83% non-need-based).

APPLYING FOR FINANCIAL AID Required financial aid form: FAFSA. *Financial aid deadline (priority):* 2/20. *Notification date:* Continuous beginning 4/1. Students must reply within 2 weeks of notification.

CONTACT Jill Rayner, Director of Financial Aid, University of North Georgia, 82 College Circle, Dahlonega, GA 30597-1001, 706-864-1688 or toll-free 800-498-9581. *Fax:* 706-864-1411. *E-mail:* jill.rayner@ung.edu. *Website:* http://www.ung.edu/.

UNIVERSITY OF NORTH TEXAS
Denton, TX

Tuition & fees (TX res): $10,520	Average undergraduate aid package: $10,759

ABOUT THE INSTITUTION State-supported, coed. **Awards:** certificates, bachelor's, master's, and doctoral degrees. 87 undergraduate majors. **Total enrollment:** 37,979. Undergraduates: 31,209. Freshmen: 4,774. Federal methodology is used as a basis for awarding need-based institutional aid.

UNDERGRADUATE EXPENSES for 2016–2017 Application fee: $75. **Tuition, state resident:** full-time $7988; part-time $266.27 per credit hour. **Tuition, nonresident:** full-time $20,228; part-time $674.27 per credit hour. **Required fees:** full-time $2532. **College room and board:** $8679. Room and board charges vary according to board plan and housing facility. **Payment plan:** Guaranteed tuition.

FRESHMAN FINANCIAL AID (Fall 2016, est.) 3,815 applied for aid; of those 77% were deemed to have need. 95% of freshmen with need received aid; of those 11% had need fully met. **Average percent of need met:** 62% (excluding resources awarded to replace EFC). **Average financial aid package:** $12,387 (excluding resources awarded to replace EFC). 13% of all full-time freshmen had no need and received non-need-based gift aid.

UNDERGRADUATE FINANCIAL AID (Fall 2016, est.) 18,666 applied for aid; of those 83% were deemed to have need. 94% of undergraduates with need received aid; of those 11% had need fully met. **Average percent of need met:** 53% (excluding resources awarded to replace EFC). **Average financial aid package:** $10,759 (excluding resources awarded to replace EFC). 12% of all full-time undergraduates had no need and received non-need-based gift aid.

GIFT AID (NEED-BASED) Total amount: $123,605,322 (39% federal, 18% state, 28% institutional, 15% external sources). **Receiving aid:** Freshmen: 47% (2,097); all full-time undergraduates: 41% (10,550). **Average award:** Freshmen: $9579; Undergraduates: $7815. **Scholarships, grants, and awards:** Federal Pell, FSEOG, state, private, college/university gift aid from institutional funds.

GIFT AID (NON-NEED-BASED) Total amount: $6,525,175 (1% federal, 57% institutional, 42% external sources). **Receiving aid:** Freshmen: 25% (1,124). Undergraduates: 15% (3,938). **Average award:** Freshmen: $6255. Undergraduates: $5636. **Tuition waivers:** Full or partial for employees or children of employees, senior citizens. **ROTC:** Army, Air Force.

LOANS Student loans: $108,488,235 (86% need-based, 14% non-need-based). 63% of past graduating class borrowed through all loan programs. **Average indebtedness per student:** $25,249. **Average need-based loan:** Freshmen: $3092. Undergraduates: $4124. **Parent loans:** $62,515,708 (74% need-based, 26% non-need-based). **Programs:** Federal Direct (Subsidized and Unsubsidized Stafford, PLUS), Perkins, state.

WORK-STUDY Federal work-study: Total amount: $6,263,411; jobs available. **State or other work-study/employment:** Total amount: $1,390,724 (100% need-based). Part-time jobs available.

ATHLETIC AWARDS Total amount: $4,312,805 (42% need-based, 58% non-need-based).

APPLYING FOR FINANCIAL AID Required financial aid form: FAFSA. **Financial aid deadline (priority):** 3/15. **Notification date:** Continuous beginning 4/1.

CONTACT Mrs. Zelma DeLeon, Director of Student Financial Aid and Scholarships, University of North Texas, 1155 Union Circle #311370, Denton, TX 76203-5017, 940-565-2302 or toll-free 800-868-8211. *Fax:* 940-565-2738. *E-mail:* zelma.deleon@unt.edu.
Website: http://www.unt.edu/.

UNIVERSITY OF NORTH TEXAS AT DALLAS
Dallas, TX

Tuition & fees (TX res): $7848	Average undergraduate aid package: $8143

ABOUT THE INSTITUTION State-supported, coed. **Awards:** bachelor's, master's, and doctoral degrees. **Total enrollment:** 3,030. Undergraduates: 2,295.

Freshmen: 280. Federal methodology is used as a basis for awarding need-based institutional aid.

UNDERGRADUATE EXPENSES for 2016–2017 Application fee: $50. **Tuition, state resident:** full-time $7548; part-time $251.63 per credit hour. **Tuition, nonresident:** full-time $19,788; part-time $659.63 per credit hour. **Required fees:** full-time $300; $10 per credit hour or $10 per credit hour. Full-time tuition and fees vary according to degree level. Part-time tuition and fees vary according to degree level. Room and board charges vary according to board plan and housing facility. **Payment plan:** Guaranteed tuition.

FRESHMAN FINANCIAL AID (Fall 2016, est.) 189 applied for aid; of those 90% were deemed to have need. 99% of freshmen with need received aid; of those 8% had need fully met. **Average percent of need met:** 51% (excluding resources awarded to replace EFC). **Average financial aid package:** $8721 (excluding resources awarded to replace EFC). 99% of all full-time freshmen had no need and received non-need-based gift aid.

UNDERGRADUATE FINANCIAL AID (Fall 2016, est.) 958 applied for aid; of those 95% were deemed to have need. 97% of undergraduates with need received aid; of those 4% had need fully met. **Average percent of need met:** 40% (excluding resources awarded to replace EFC). **Average financial aid package:** $8143 (excluding resources awarded to replace EFC). 20% of all full-time undergraduates had no need and received non-need-based gift aid.

GIFT AID (NEED-BASED) Total amount: $6,522,993 (52% federal, 15% state, 25% institutional, 8% external sources). **Receiving aid:** Freshmen: 68% (145); all full-time undergraduates: 65% (736). **Average award:** Freshmen: $6688; Undergraduates: $5620. **Scholarships, grants, and awards:** Federal Pell, FSEOG, state, college/university gift aid from institutional funds, TEACH Grants.

GIFT AID (NON-NEED-BASED) Total amount: $1,026,491 (46% federal, 10% state, 19% institutional, 25% external sources). **Receiving aid:** Freshmen: 46% (99). Undergraduates: 26% (297). **Average award:** Freshmen: $1501. Undergraduates: $1924. **Tuition waivers:** Full or partial for employees or children of employees, senior citizens.

LOANS Student loans: $7,177,365 (81% need-based, 19% non-need-based). 79% of past graduating class borrowed through all loan programs. **Average indebtedness per student:** $6927. **Average need-based loan:** Freshmen: $2902. Undergraduates: $4110. **Parent loans:** $922,306 (78% need-based, 22% non-need-based). **Programs:** Federal Direct (Subsidized and Unsubsidized Stafford, PLUS), state, private loans.

APPLYING FOR FINANCIAL AID Notification date: Continuous.

CONTACT Office of Financial Aid and Scholarships, University of North Texas at Dallas, 7300 University Hills Boulevard, Dallas, TX 75241, 972-780-3662. *E-mail:* financialaid@untdallas.edu.
Website: http://untdallas.edu/.

UNIVERSITY OF NORTHWESTERN OHIO
Lima, OH

CONTACT Financial Aid Office, University of Northwestern Ohio, 1441 North Cable Road, Lima, OH 45805-1498, 419-227-3141.
Website: http://www.unoh.edu/.

UNIVERSITY OF NORTHWESTERN–ST. PAUL
St. Paul, MN

CONTACT Mr. Richard L. Blatchley, Director of Financial Aid, University of Northwestern–St. Paul, 3003 Snelling Avenue North, St. Paul, MN 55113-1598, 651-631-5321 or toll-free 800-827-6827. *Fax:* 651-628-3332. *E-mail:* rlb@nwc.edu.
Website: http://www.unwsp.edu/.

UNIVERSITY OF NOTRE DAME
Notre Dame, IN

Tuition & fees: $49,685	Average undergraduate aid package: $47,884

ABOUT THE INSTITUTION Independent Roman Catholic, coed. *Awards:* bachelor's, master's, and doctoral degrees. 64 undergraduate majors. *Total enrollment:* 12,393. Undergraduates: 8,530. Freshmen: 2,046. Both federal and institutional methodology are used as a basis for awarding need-based institutional aid.

UNDERGRADUATE EXPENSES for 2016–2017 *Application fee:* $75. *Comprehensive fee:* $64,043 includes full-time tuition ($49,178), mandatory fees ($507), and room and board ($14,358). *Part-time tuition:* $2049 per credit hour.

FRESHMAN FINANCIAL AID (Fall 2016, est.) 1,446 applied for aid; of those 73% were deemed to have need. 100% of freshmen with need received aid; of those 99% had need fully met. *Average percent of need met:* 100% (excluding resources awarded to replace EFC). *Average financial aid package:* $48,322 (excluding resources awarded to replace EFC). 2% of all full-time freshmen had no need and received non-need-based gift aid.

UNDERGRADUATE FINANCIAL AID (Fall 2016, est.) 4,898 applied for aid; of those 84% were deemed to have need. 100% of undergraduates with need received aid; of those 99% had need fully met. *Average percent of need met:* 100% (excluding resources awarded to replace EFC). *Average financial aid package:* $47,884 (excluding resources awarded to replace EFC). 5% of all full-time undergraduates had no need and received non-need-based gift aid.

GIFT AID (NEED-BASED) *Total amount:* $149,871,432 (5% federal, 92% institutional, 3% external sources). *Receiving aid:* Freshmen: 50% (1,021); all full-time undergraduates: 47% (3,997). *Average award:* Freshmen: $39,044; Undergraduates: $37,390. *Scholarships, grants, and awards:* Federal Pell, FSEOG, state, private, college/university gift aid from institutional funds.

GIFT AID (NON-NEED-BASED) *Total amount:* $18,634,494 (41% federal, 40% institutional, 19% external sources). *Receiving aid:* Freshmen: 9% (185). Undergraduates: 8% (652). *Average award:* Freshmen: $27,589. Undergraduates: $12,919. *Scholarships, grants, and awards by category:* Special characteristics: children of faculty/staff. *Tuition waivers:* Full or partial for employees or children of employees. *ROTC:* Army, Naval, Air Force.

LOANS *Student loans:* $32,908,034 (52% need-based, 48% non-need-based). 47% of past graduating class borrowed through all loan programs. *Average indebtedness per student:* $28,406. *Average need-based loan:* Freshmen: $3821. Undergraduates: $5017. *Parent loans:* $11,825,249 (3% need-based, 97% non-need-based). *Programs:* Federal Direct (Subsidized and Unsubsidized Stafford, PLUS), Perkins, college/university, private loans.

WORK-STUDY *Federal work-study:* Total amount: $2,016,792; jobs available. *State or other work-study/employment:* Total amount: $11,204,650 (21% need-based, 79% non-need-based). 3,376 part-time jobs averaging $3319.

ATHLETIC AWARDS Total amount: $21,613,177 (17% need-based, 83% non-need-based).

APPLYING FOR FINANCIAL AID *Required financial aid forms:* FAFSA, CSS Financial Aid PROFILE, noncustodial (divorced/separated) parent's statement, business/farm supplement, federal income tax form(s), W-2 forms, verification worksheet. *Financial aid deadline (priority):* 2/15. *Notification date:* Continuous beginning 3/28. Students must reply by 5/1.

CONTACT Mrs. Mary Nucciarone, Director, Financial Aid, University of Notre Dame, 115 Main Building, Notre Dame, IN 46556, 574-631-6436. *Fax:* 574-631-6899. *E-mail:* finaid@nd.edu. *Website:* http://www.nd.edu/.

UNIVERSITY OF OKLAHOMA
Norman, OK

Tuition & fees (OK res): $8631	Average undergraduate aid package: $12,746

ABOUT THE INSTITUTION State-supported, coed. *Awards:* certificates, bachelor's, master's, and doctoral degrees. 101 undergraduate majors. *Total enrollment:* 27,918. Undergraduates: 21,609. Freshmen: 4,198. Federal methodology is used as a basis for awarding need-based institutional aid.

UNDERGRADUATE EXPENSES for 2016–2017 *Application fee:* $40. *Tuition, state resident:* full-time $4575; part-time $152.50 per credit hour. *Tuition, nonresident:* full-time $18,897; part-time $629.90 per credit hour. *Required fees:* full-time $4056; $126.75 per credit hour or $126.50 per term. Full-time tuition and fees vary according to course load, location, program, and student level. Part-time tuition and fees vary according to course load, location, program, and student level. *College room and board:* $10,280; *Room only:* $6012. Room and board charges vary according to board plan and housing facility. *Payment plan:* Guaranteed tuition.

FRESHMAN FINANCIAL AID (Fall 2015) 2,842 applied for aid; of those 64% were deemed to have need. 98% of freshmen with need received aid; of those 80% had need fully met. *Average percent of need met:* 80% (excluding resources awarded to replace EFC). *Average financial aid package:* $13,032 (excluding resources awarded to replace EFC). 16% of all full-time freshmen had no need and received non-need-based gift aid.

UNDERGRADUATE FINANCIAL AID (Fall 2015) 10,536 applied for aid; of those 75% were deemed to have need. 98% of undergraduates with need received aid; of those 84% had need fully met. *Average percent of need met:* 84% (excluding resources awarded to replace EFC). *Average financial aid package:* $12,746 (excluding resources awarded to replace EFC). 14% of all full-time undergraduates had no need and received non-need-based gift aid.

GIFT AID (NEED-BASED) *Total amount:* $50,831,548 (40% federal, 27% state, 21% institutional, 12% external sources). *Receiving aid:* Freshmen: 22% (872); all full-time undergraduates: 25% (4,480). *Average award:* Freshmen: $6608; Undergraduates: $6098. *Scholarships, grants, and awards:* Federal Pell, FSEOG, state, private, college/university gift aid from institutional funds, United Negro College Fund.

GIFT AID (NON-NEED-BASED) *Total amount:* $14,128,116 (31% state, 44% institutional, 25% external sources). *Receiving aid:* Freshmen: 32% (1,252). Undergraduates: 25% (4,385). *Average award:* Freshmen: $2984. Undergraduates: $2625. *Scholarships, grants, and awards by category:* Academic interests/achievement: 7,224 awards ($44,830,821 total): architecture, area/ethnic studies, biological sciences, business, communication, computer science, education, engineering/technologies, English, foreign languages, general academic interests/achievements, humanities, international studies, mathematics, military science, physical sciences, social sciences. Creative arts/performance: 326 awards ($1,836,884 total): art/fine arts, cinema/film/broadcasting, dance, debating, journalism/publications, music, performing arts, theater/drama. Special achievements/activities: 219 awards ($357,456 total): leadership. Special characteristics: 703 awards ($1,180,318 total): children and siblings of alumni, children of faculty/staff, members of minority groups, previous college experience, public servants. *Tuition waivers:* Full or partial for employees or children of employees, senior citizens. *ROTC:* Army, Naval, Air Force.

LOANS *Student loans:* $64,051,898 (79% need-based, 21% non-need-based). 44% of past graduating class borrowed through all loan programs. *Average indebtedness per student:* $28,444. *Average need-based loan:* Freshmen: $3620. Undergraduates: $4229. *Parent loans:* $19,053,307 (72% need-based, 28% non-need-based). *Programs:* Federal Direct (Subsidized and Unsubsidized Stafford, PLUS), Perkins, college/university, alternative loans.

WORK-STUDY *Federal work-study:* 627 jobs averaging $2723. *State or other work-study/employment:* Total amount: $808,588 (55% need-based, 45% non-need-based). 101 part-time jobs averaging $7404.

ATHLETIC AWARDS Total amount: $11,848,765 (41% need-based, 59% non-need-based).

APPLYING FOR FINANCIAL AID *Required financial aid form:* FAFSA. *Financial aid deadline:* Continuous. *Notification date:* Continuous beginning 1/15. Students must reply within 6 weeks of notification.

CONTACT Office of Financial Aid, University of Oklahoma, 1000 Asp Avenue, Room 216, Norman, OK 73019-4078, 405-325-4521 or toll-free 800-234-6868. *Fax:* 405-325-0819. *E-mail:* financialaid@ou.edu. *Website:* http://www.ou.edu/.

UNIVERSITY OF OREGON
Eugene, OR

Tuition & fees (OR res): $10,762	Average undergraduate aid package: $10,879

ABOUT THE INSTITUTION State-supported, coed. *Awards:* certificates, bachelor's, master's, and doctoral degrees. 76 undergraduate majors. *Total*

enrollment: 23,608. Undergraduates: 20,047. Freshmen: 4,041. Federal methodology is used as a basis for awarding need-based institutional aid.

UNDERGRADUATE EXPENSES for 2016–2017 *Application fee:* $65. *One-time required fee:* $389. *Tuition, state resident:* full-time $8910; part-time $198 per credit hour. *Tuition, nonresident:* full-time $31,590; part-time $702 per credit hour. *Required fees:* full-time $1852. Full-time tuition and fees vary according to course load and program. Part-time tuition and fees vary according to course load and program. *College room and board:* $12,210. Room and board charges vary according to board plan and housing facility.

FRESHMAN FINANCIAL AID (Fall 2015) 3,037 applied for aid; of those 68% were deemed to have need. 94% of freshmen with need received aid; of those 7% had need fully met. *Average percent of need met:* 62% (excluding resources awarded to replace EFC). *Average financial aid package:* $10,812 (excluding resources awarded to replace EFC). 17% of all full-time freshmen had no need and received non-need-based gift aid.

UNDERGRADUATE FINANCIAL AID (Fall 2015) 10,783 applied for aid; of those 76% were deemed to have need. 95% of undergraduates with need received aid; of those 7% had need fully met. *Average percent of need met:* 63% (excluding resources awarded to replace EFC). *Average financial aid package:* $10,879 (excluding resources awarded to replace EFC). 14% of all full-time undergraduates had no need and received non-need-based gift aid.

GIFT AID (NEED-BASED) *Total amount:* $53,587,528 (43% federal, 12% state, 34% institutional, 11% external sources). *Receiving aid:* Freshmen: 37% (1,511); all full-time undergraduates: 33% (6,056). *Average award:* Freshmen: $9185; Undergraduates: $8320. *Scholarships, grants, and awards:* Federal Pell, FSEOG, state, private, college/university gift aid from institutional funds.

GIFT AID (NON-NEED-BASED) *Total amount:* $16,216,061 (100% institutional). *Receiving aid:* Freshmen: 3% (118). Undergraduates: 1% (217). *Average award:* Freshmen: $6133. Undergraduates: $5434. *Scholarships, grants, and awards by category:* Academic interests/achievement: 7,007 awards ($29,330,591 total): architecture, biological sciences, business, education, English, foreign languages, general academic interests/achievements, health fields, humanities, international studies, mathematics, military science, physical sciences, premedicine, social sciences. Creative arts/performance: 257 awards ($605,593 total): applied art and design, art/fine arts, creative writing, dance, debating, journalism/publications, music, performing arts, theater/drama. Special characteristics: 352 awards ($1,800,813 total): children of faculty/staff, general special characteristics, international students, local/state students, veterans, veterans' children. *Tuition waivers:* Full or partial for employees or children of employees. *ROTC:* Army, Air Force cooperative.

LOANS *Student loans:* $64,117,736 (63% need-based, 37% non-need-based). 47% of past graduating class borrowed through all loan programs. *Average indebtedness per student:* $25,542. *Average need-based loan:* Freshmen: $4045. Undergraduates: $4658. *Parent loans:* $57,352,828 (42% need-based, 58% non-need-based). *Programs:* Federal Direct (Subsidized and Unsubsidized Stafford, PLUS), Perkins, college/university.

WORK-STUDY *Federal work-study:* 2,420 jobs averaging $1765. *State or other work-study/employment:* Total amount: $208,000 (100% non-need-based). 79 part-time jobs averaging $2519.

ATHLETIC AWARDS Total amount: $10,965,341 (24% need-based, 76% non-need-based).

APPLYING FOR FINANCIAL AID *Required financial aid form:* FAFSA. *Financial aid deadline (priority):* 3/1. *Notification date:* Continuous beginning 4/15. Students must reply within 4 weeks of notification.

CONTACT Jim Brooks, Director of Financial Aid and Scholarships, University of Oregon, 1278 University of Oregon, 260 Oregon Hall, Eugene, OR 97403-1278, 800-760-6953 or toll-free 800-232-3825. *Fax:* 541-346-1175. *E-mail:* financialaid@uoregon.edu.
Website: http://www.uoregon.edu/.

UNIVERSITY OF PENNSYLVANIA
Philadelphia, PA

Tuition & fees: $53,534	Average undergraduate aid package: $46,707

ABOUT THE INSTITUTION Independent, coed. *Awards:* certificates, associate, bachelor's, master's, and doctoral degrees (also offers evening program with significant enrollment not reflected in profile). 96 undergraduate majors. *Total enrollment:*

21,826. Undergraduates: 10,019. Freshmen: 2,428. Both federal and institutional methodology are used as a basis for awarding need-based institutional aid.

UNDERGRADUATE EXPENSES for 2017–2018 *Application fee:* $75. *Comprehensive fee:* $68,600 includes full-time tuition ($47,416), mandatory fees ($6118), and room and board ($15,066). Room and board charges vary according to board plan and housing facility. Part-time tuition and fees vary according to course load. *Payment plan:* Tuition prepayment.

FRESHMAN FINANCIAL AID (Fall 2015) 1,367 applied for aid; of those 83% were deemed to have need. 100% of freshmen with need received aid; of those 100% had need fully met. *Average percent of need met:* 100% (excluding resources awarded to replace EFC). *Average financial aid package:* $47,992 (excluding resources awarded to replace EFC).

UNDERGRADUATE FINANCIAL AID (Fall 2015) 4,879 applied for aid; of those 92% were deemed to have need. 100% of undergraduates with need received aid; of those 100% had need fully met. *Average percent of need met:* 100% (excluding resources awarded to replace EFC). *Average financial aid package:* $46,707 (excluding resources awarded to replace EFC).

GIFT AID (NEED-BASED) *Total amount:* $200,162,187 (5% federal, 1% state, 92% institutional, 2% external sources). *Receiving aid:* Freshmen: 47% (1,112); all full-time undergraduates: 47% (4,445). *Average award:* Freshmen: $45,711; Undergraduates: $43,899. *Scholarships, grants, and awards:* Federal Pell, FSEOG, state, private, college/university gift aid from institutional funds.

GIFT AID (NON-NEED-BASED) *Total amount:* $5,460,967 (2% federal, 98% external sources). *Tuition waivers:* Full or partial for employees or children of employees. *ROTC:* Army cooperative, Naval, Air Force cooperative.

LOANS *Student loans:* $16,764,062 (6% need-based, 94% non-need-based). 31% of past graduating class borrowed through all loan programs. *Average indebtedness per student:* $24,536. *Average need-based loan:* Freshmen: $130. Undergraduates: $335. *Parent loans:* $9,603,607 (100% non-need-based). *Programs:* Federal Direct (Subsidized and Unsubsidized Stafford, PLUS), Perkins, Federal Nursing, college/university, supplemental third-party loans (guaranteed by institution).

WORK-STUDY *Federal work-study:* jobs available. *State or other work-study/employment:* Total amount: $3,627,276 (100% need-based). Part-time jobs available.

APPLYING FOR FINANCIAL AID *Required financial aid forms:* FAFSA, institution's own form, CSS Financial Aid PROFILE, noncustodial (divorced/separated) parent's statement, business/farm supplement, federal income tax form(s). *Financial aid deadline (priority):* 2/15. *Notification date:* 4/1. Students must reply by 5/1.

CONTACT Elaine Papas Varas, Director of Financial Aid, University of Pennsylvania, 3451 Walnut Streeet, 100 Franklin Building, Philadelphia, PA 19104-6270, 215-898-1988. *E-mail:* varas@upenn.edu.
Website: http://www.upenn.edu/.

UNIVERSITY OF PHOENIX–ATLANTA CAMPUS
Sandy Springs, GA

CONTACT ACS/AFS, University of Phoenix–Atlanta Campus, 875 West Elliot Road, Tempe, AZ 85284, 480-735-3000 or toll-free 866-766-0766. *Fax:* 480-940-2060.
Website: http://www.phoenix.edu/.

UNIVERSITY OF PHOENIX–BAY AREA CAMPUS
San Jose, CA

CONTACT ACS/AFS, University of Phoenix–Bay Area Campus, 875 West Elliot Road, Tempe, AZ 85284, 480-735-3000 or toll-free 866-766-0766. *Fax:* 480-940-2060.
Website: http://www.phoenix.edu/.

UNIVERSITY OF PHOENIX–CENTRAL FLORIDA CAMPUS
Orlando, FL

CONTACT ACS/AFS, University of Phoenix–Central Florida Campus, 875 West Elliot Road, Tempe, AZ 85284, 480-735-3000 or toll-free 866-766-0766. *Fax:* 480-940-2060.
Website: http://www.phoenix.edu/.

UNIVERSITY OF PHOENIX–CENTRAL VALLEY CAMPUS
Fresno, CA

CONTACT ACS/AFS, University of Phoenix–Central Valley Campus, 875 West Elliot Road, Tempe, AZ 85284, 480-735-3000 or toll-free 866-766-0766. *Fax:* 480-940-2060.
Website: http://www.phoenix.edu/.

UNIVERSITY OF PHOENIX–CHARLOTTE CAMPUS
Charlotte, NC

CONTACT ACS/AFS, University of Phoenix–Charlotte Campus, 875 West Elliot Road, Tempe, AZ 85284, 480-735-3000 or toll-free 866-766-0766. *Fax:* 480-940-2060.
Website: http://www.phoenix.edu/.

UNIVERSITY OF PHOENIX–COLORADO CAMPUS
Lone Tree, CO

CONTACT ACS/AFS, University of Phoenix–Colorado Campus, 875 West Elliot Road, Tempe, AZ 85284, 480-735-3000 or toll-free 866-766-0766. *Fax:* 480-940-2060.
Website: http://www.phoenix.edu/.

UNIVERSITY OF PHOENIX–COLORADO SPRINGS DOWNTOWN CAMPUS
Colorado Springs, CO

CONTACT ACS/AFS, University of Phoenix–Colorado Springs Downtown Campus, 875 West Elliot Road, Tempe, AZ 85284, 480-735-3000 or toll-free 866-766-0766. *Fax:* 480-940-2060.
Website: http://www.phoenix.edu/.

UNIVERSITY OF PHOENIX–COLUMBUS GEORGIA CAMPUS
Columbus, GA

CONTACT ACS/AFS, University of Phoenix–Columbus Georgia Campus, 875 West Elliot Road, Tempe, AZ 85284, 480-735-3000 or toll-free 866-766-0766. *Fax:* 480-940-2060.
Website: http://www.phoenix.edu/.

UNIVERSITY OF PHOENIX–DALLAS CAMPUS
Dallas, TX

CONTACT ACS/AFS, University of Phoenix–Dallas Campus, 875 West Elliot Road, Tempe, AZ 85284, 480-735-3000 or toll-free 866-766-0766. *Fax:* 480-940-2060.
Website: http://www.phoenix.edu/.

UNIVERSITY OF PHOENIX–DETROIT CAMPUS
Southfield, MI

CONTACT ACS/AFS, University of Phoenix–Detroit Campus, 875 West Elliot Road, Tempe, AZ 85284, 480-735-3000 or toll-free 866-766-0766. *Fax:* 480-940-2060.
Website: http://www.phoenix.edu/.

UNIVERSITY OF PHOENIX–HAWAII CAMPUS
Honolulu, HI

CONTACT ACS/AFS, University of Phoenix–Hawaii Campus, 875 West Elliot Road, Tempe, AZ 85284, 480-735-3000 or toll-free 866-766-0766. *Fax:* 480-940-2060.
Website: http://www.phoenix.edu/.

UNIVERSITY OF PHOENIX–HOUSTON CAMPUS
Houston, TX

CONTACT ACS/AFS, University of Phoenix–Houston Campus, 875 West Elliot Road, Tempe, AZ 85284, 480-735-3000 or toll-free 866-766-0766. *Fax:* 480-940-2060.
Website: http://www.phoenix.edu/.

UNIVERSITY OF PHOENIX–LAS VEGAS CAMPUS
Las Vegas, NV

CONTACT ACS/AFS, University of Phoenix–Las Vegas Campus, 875 West Elliot Road, Tempe, AZ 85284, 480-735-3000 or toll-free 866-766-0766. *Fax:* 480-940-2060.
Website: http://www.phoenix.edu/.

UNIVERSITY OF PHOENIX–NEW MEXICO CAMPUS
Albuquerque, NM

CONTACT ACS/AFS, University of Phoenix–New Mexico Campus, 875 West Elliot Road, Tempe, AZ 85284, 480-735-3000 or toll-free 866-766-0766. *Fax:* 480-940-2060.
Website: http://www.phoenix.edu/.

UNIVERSITY OF PHOENIX–NORTH FLORIDA CAMPUS
Jacksonville, FL

CONTACT ACS/AFS, University of Phoenix–North Florida Campus, 875 West Elliot Road, Tempe, AZ 85284, 480-735-3000 or toll-free 866-766-0766. *Fax:* 480-940-2060. *Website:* http://www.phoenix.edu/.

UNIVERSITY OF PHOENIX–ONLINE CAMPUS
Phoenix, AZ

CONTACT Office of Financial Aid, University of Phoenix–Online Campus, 3157 East Elwood Street, Phoenix, AZ 85034-7209, 866-766-0766. *Website:* http://www.phoenix.edu/.

UNIVERSITY OF PHOENIX–PHOENIX CAMPUS
Tempe, AZ

CONTACT Office of Financial Aid, University of Phoenix–Phoenix Campus, 1625 West Fountainhead Parkway, Tempe, AZ 85282-2371, 866-766-0766. *Website:* http://www.phoenix.edu/.

UNIVERSITY OF PHOENIX–SACRAMENTO VALLEY CAMPUS
Sacramento, CA

CONTACT ACS/AFS, University of Phoenix–Sacramento Valley Campus, 875 West Elliot Road, Tempe, AZ 85284, 480-735-3000 or toll-free 866-766-0766. *Fax:* 480-940-2060. *Website:* http://www.phoenix.edu/.

UNIVERSITY OF PHOENIX–SAN DIEGO CAMPUS
San Diego, CA

CONTACT ACS/AFS, University of Phoenix–San Diego Campus, 875 West Elliot Road, Tempe, AZ 85284, 480-735-3000 or toll-free 866-766-0766. *Fax:* 480-940-2060. *Website:* http://www.phoenix.edu/.

UNIVERSITY OF PHOENIX–SOUTHERN ARIZONA CAMPUS
Tucson, AZ

CONTACT ACS/AFS, University of Phoenix–Southern Arizona Campus, 875 West Elliot Road, Tempe, AZ 85284, 480-735-3000 or toll-free 866-766-0766. *Fax:* 480-940-2060. *Website:* http://www.phoenix.edu/.

UNIVERSITY OF PHOENIX–SOUTHERN CALIFORNIA CAMPUS
Costa Mesa, CA

CONTACT Office of Financial Aid, University of Phoenix–Southern California Campus, 3090 Bristol Street, Costa Mesa, CA 92626, 866-766-0766. *Website:* http://www.phoenix.edu/.

UNIVERSITY OF PHOENIX–SOUTH FLORIDA CAMPUS
Miramar, FL

CONTACT ACS/AFS, University of Phoenix–South Florida Campus, 875 West Elliot Road, Tempe, AZ 85284, 480-735-3000 or toll-free 866-766-0766. *Fax:* 480-940-2060. *Website:* http://www.phoenix.edu/.

UNIVERSITY OF PHOENIX–UTAH CAMPUS
Salt Lake City, UT

CONTACT ACS/AFS, University of Phoenix–Utah Campus, 875 West Elliot Road, Tempe, AZ 85284, 480-735-3000 or toll-free 866-766-0766. *Fax:* 480-940-2060. *Website:* http://www.phoenix.edu/.

UNIVERSITY OF PHOENIX–WASHINGTON D.C. CAMPUS
Washington, DC

CONTACT Financial Aid Office, University of Phoenix–Washington D.C. Campus, 25 Massachusetts Avenue NW, Suite 150, Washington, DC 20001 or toll-free 866-766-0766. *Website:* http://www.phoenix.edu/.

UNIVERSITY OF PHOENIX–WESTERN WASHINGTON CAMPUS
Tukwila, WA

CONTACT ACS/AFS, University of Phoenix–Western Washington Campus, 875 West Elliot Road, Tempe, AZ 85284, 480-735-3000 or toll-free 866-766-0766. *Fax:* 480-940-2060. *Website:* http://www.phoenix.edu/.

UNIVERSITY OF PIKEVILLE
Pikeville, KY

Tuition & fees: $20,200	Average undergraduate aid package: $18,612

ABOUT THE INSTITUTION Independent Presbyterian Church (U.S.A.), coed. *Awards:* associate, bachelor's, master's, and doctoral degrees. 20 undergraduate majors. *Total enrollment:* 2,366. Undergraduates: 1,658. Freshmen: 329. Federal methodology is used as a basis for awarding need-based institutional aid.
UNDERGRADUATE EXPENSES for 2017–2018 *Comprehensive fee:* $27,700 includes full-time tuition ($20,200) and room and board ($7500). Full-time tuition and fees vary according to course load. Room and board charges vary

according to housing facility. **Part-time tuition:** $842 per semester hour. Part-time tuition and fees vary according to course load.

FRESHMAN FINANCIAL AID (Fall 2016, est.) 323 applied for aid; of those 100% were deemed to have need. 100% of freshmen with need received aid; of those 58% had need fully met. **Average percent of need met:** 88% (excluding resources awarded to replace EFC). **Average financial aid package:** $19,414 (excluding resources awarded to replace EFC).

UNDERGRADUATE FINANCIAL AID (Fall 2016, est.) 1,062 applied for aid; of those 99% were deemed to have need. 100% of undergraduates with need received aid; of those 51% had need fully met. **Average percent of need met:** 86% (excluding resources awarded to replace EFC). **Average financial aid package:** $18,612 (excluding resources awarded to replace EFC).

GIFT AID (NEED-BASED) Total amount: $17,219,470 (22% federal, 26% state, 51% institutional, 1% external sources). **Receiving aid:** Freshmen: 98% (322); all full-time undergraduates: 93% (1,052). **Average award:** Freshmen: $18,882; Undergraduates: $18,234. **Scholarships, grants, and awards:** Federal Pell, FSEOG, state, private, college/university gift aid from institutional funds.

GIFT AID (NON-NEED-BASED) Receiving aid: Freshmen: 56% (183). Undergraduates: 43% (484). **Tuition waivers:** Full or partial for employees or children of employees, senior citizens. **ROTC:** Army cooperative.

LOANS Student loans: $7,146,437 (100% need-based). 79% of past graduating class borrowed through all loan programs. **Average indebtedness per student:** $26,013. **Average need-based loan:** Freshmen: $3468. Undergraduates: $4156. **Parent loans:** $536,310 (100% need-based). **Programs:** Federal Direct (Subsidized and Unsubsidized Stafford, PLUS), Perkins, college/university.

WORK-STUDY Federal work-study: Total amount: $400,550; 210 jobs averaging $1907.

ATHLETIC AWARDS Total amount: $2,604,011 (100% need-based).

APPLYING FOR FINANCIAL AID Required financial aid form: FAFSA. **Financial aid deadline (priority):** 2/1. **Notification date:** Continuous. Students must reply by 5/1.

CONTACT Mrs. Kristen Gast, Director of Student Financial Services, University of Pikeville, 147 Sycamore Street, Pikeville, KY 41501, 606-218-5254 or toll-free 866-232-7700. *Fax:* 606-218-5255. *E-mail:* kristengast@upike.edu. *Website:* http://www.upike.edu/.

UNIVERSITY OF PITTSBURGH
Pittsburgh, PA

Tuition & fees (PA res): $18,618	Average undergraduate aid package: $12,286

ABOUT THE INSTITUTION State-related, coed. **Awards:** certificates, bachelor's, master's, and doctoral degrees. 96 undergraduate majors. **Total enrollment:** 28,664. Undergraduates: 19,123. Freshmen: 3,954. Federal methodology is used as a basis for awarding need-based institutional aid.

UNDERGRADUATE EXPENSES for 2016–2017 Application fee: $45. **Tuition, state resident:** full-time $17,688; part-time $737 per credit hour. **Tuition, nonresident:** full-time $28,828; part-time $1201 per credit hour. **Required fees:** full-time $930; $274 per term. Full-time tuition and fees vary according to location and program. Part-time tuition and fees vary according to location and program. **College room and board:** $10,950; **Room only:** $6300. Room and board charges vary according to board plan, housing facility, and location.

FRESHMAN FINANCIAL AID (Fall 2015) 3,308 applied for aid; of those 66% were deemed to have need. 97% of freshmen with need received aid; of those 14% had need fully met. **Average percent of need met:** 54% (excluding resources awarded to replace EFC). **Average financial aid package:** $12,459 (excluding resources awarded to replace EFC). 7% of all full-time freshmen had no need and received non-need-based gift aid.

UNDERGRADUATE FINANCIAL AID (Fall 2015) 12,340 applied for aid; of those 77% were deemed to have need. 97% of undergraduates with need received aid; of those 12% had need fully met. **Average percent of need met:** 52% (excluding resources awarded to replace EFC). **Average financial aid package:** $12,286 (excluding resources awarded to replace EFC). 3% of all full-time undergraduates had no need and received non-need-based gift aid.

GIFT AID (NEED-BASED) Total amount: $56,796,721 (23% federal, 19% state, 46% institutional, 12% external sources). **Receiving aid:** Freshmen: 42% (1,684); all full-time undergraduates: 39% (7,011). **Average award:** Freshmen: $9960; Under-

graduates: $9289. **Scholarships, grants, and awards:** Federal Pell, FSEOG, state, private, college/university gift aid from institutional funds, Federal Nursing.

GIFT AID (NON-NEED-BASED) Total amount: $31,362,215 (1% state, 79% institutional, 20% external sources). **Receiving aid:** Freshmen: 7% (263). Undergraduates: 4% (764). **Average award:** Freshmen: $10,734. Undergraduates: $10,081. **Scholarships, grants, and awards by category:** Academic interests/achievement: general academic interests/achievements. **Special characteristics:** children of faculty/staff, children of union members/company employees. **Tuition waivers:** Full or partial for employees or children of employees. **ROTC:** Army, Naval cooperative, Air Force.

LOANS Student loans: $110,993,723 (61% need-based, 39% non-need-based). 65% of past graduating class borrowed through all loan programs. **Average indebtedness per student:** $38,612. **Average need-based loan:** Freshmen: $4047. Undergraduates: $5125. **Parent loans:** $34,535,888 (29% need-based, 71% non-need-based). **Programs:** Federal Direct (Subsidized and Unsubsidized Stafford, PLUS), Perkins, Federal Nursing, state, college/university.

WORK-STUDY Federal work-study: jobs available.

ATHLETIC AWARDS Total amount: $10,341,351 (32% need-based, 68% non-need-based).

APPLYING FOR FINANCIAL AID Required financial aid form: FAFSA. **Financial aid deadline (priority):** 3/1. **Notification date:** Continuous beginning 3/15.

CONTACT Mr. Marc Harding, Chief Enrollment Officer, University of Pittsburgh, 4227 Fifth Avenue, First Floor, Pittsburgh, PA 15260, 412-624-7488. *Fax:* 412-624-1817. *E-mail:* oafa@pitt.edu. *Website:* http://www.pitt.edu/.

UNIVERSITY OF PITTSBURGH AT BRADFORD
Bradford, PA

Tuition & fees (PA res): $13,608	Average undergraduate aid package: $16,539

ABOUT THE INSTITUTION State-related, coed. **Awards:** associate and bachelor's degrees. 35 undergraduate majors. **Total enrollment:** 1,476. Undergraduates: 1,476. Freshmen: 398. Federal methodology is used as a basis for awarding need-based institutional aid.

UNDERGRADUATE EXPENSES for 2016–2017 Application fee: $45. **One-time required fee:** $90. **Tuition, state resident:** full-time $12,688; part-time $528 per credit hour. **Tuition, nonresident:** full-time $23,710; part-time $987 per credit hour. **Required fees:** full-time $920; $155 per term. Full-time tuition and fees vary according to course load and program. Part-time tuition and fees vary according to course load and program. **College room and board:** $8794; **Room only:** $5330. Room and board charges vary according to board plan and housing facility.

FRESHMAN FINANCIAL AID (Fall 2016, est.) 335 applied for aid; of those 91% were deemed to have need. 99% of freshmen with need received aid; of those 14% had need fully met. **Average percent of need met:** 69% (excluding resources awarded to replace EFC). **Average financial aid package:** $17,581 (excluding resources awarded to replace EFC). 7% of all full-time freshmen had no need and received non-need-based gift aid.

UNDERGRADUATE FINANCIAL AID (Fall 2016, est.) 1,228 applied for aid; of those 92% were deemed to have need. 98% of undergraduates with need received aid; of those 17% had need fully met. **Average percent of need met:** 68% (excluding resources awarded to replace EFC). **Average financial aid package:** $16,539 (excluding resources awarded to replace EFC). 5% of all full-time undergraduates had no need and received non-need-based gift aid.

GIFT AID (NEED-BASED) Total amount: $10,110,268 (29% federal, 21% state, 45% institutional, 5% external sources). **Receiving aid:** Freshmen: 78% (276); all full-time undergraduates: 81% (1,105). **Average award:** Freshmen: $11,048; Undergraduates: $9968. **Scholarships, grants, and awards:** Federal Pell, FSEOG, state, private, college/university gift aid from institutional funds, Academic Competitiveness Grants, National SMART Grants.

GIFT AID (NON-NEED-BASED) Total amount: $1,254,608 (3% state, 88% institutional, 9% external sources). **Receiving aid:** Freshmen: 7% (25). Undergraduates: 5% (74). **Average award:** Freshmen: $6423. Undergraduates: $6339. **Scholarships, grants, and awards by category:** Academic interests/achievement: 162

awards ($152,500 total): biological sciences, business, communication, computer science, education, engineering/technologies, English, general academic interests/achievements, health fields, humanities, mathematics, physical sciences, premedicine, social sciences. *Creative arts/performance:* 7 awards ($2000 total): art/fine arts, cinema/film/broadcasting, creative writing, music, theater/drama. *Special characteristics:* 1,092 awards ($5,402,854 total): adult students, children of faculty/staff, children of union members/company employees, general special characteristics, international students, local/state students, members of minority groups, out-of-state students, veterans. *Tuition waivers:* Full or partial for employees or children of employees. *ROTC:* Army cooperative.

LOANS *Student loans:* $10,585,401 (75% need-based, 25% non-need-based). 88% of past graduating class borrowed through all loan programs. *Average indebtedness per student:* $32,816. *Average need-based loan:* Freshmen: $6891. Undergraduates: $7398. *Parent loans:* $3,158,045 (47% need-based, 53% non-need-based). *Programs:* Federal Direct (Subsidized and Unsubsidized Stafford, PLUS), Perkins.

WORK-STUDY *Federal work-study:* Total amount: $1,329,542; 180 jobs averaging $1980. *State or other work-study/employment:* 44 part-time jobs averaging $1857.

APPLYING FOR FINANCIAL AID *Required financial aid form:* FAFSA. *Financial aid deadline (priority):* 3/1. *Notification date:* Continuous beginning 4/1. Students must reply within 2 weeks of notification.

CONTACT Melissa Ibanez, Director of Financial Aid, University of Pittsburgh at Bradford, 300 Campus Drive, Bradford, PA 16701-2812, 814-362-7550 or toll-free 800-872-1787. *Fax:* 814-362-7578. *E-mail:* ibanez@pitt.edu. *Website:* http://www.upb.pitt.edu/.

UNIVERSITY OF PITTSBURGH AT GREENSBURG
Greensburg, PA

Tuition & fees (PA res): $13,618	Average undergraduate aid package: $10,873

ABOUT THE INSTITUTION State-related, coed. *Awards:* certificates and bachelor's degrees. 25 undergraduate majors. *Total enrollment:* 1,520. Undergraduates: 1,520. Freshmen: 467. Federal methodology is used as a basis for awarding need-based institutional aid.

UNDERGRADUATE EXPENSES for 2016–2017 *Application fee:* $45. *Tuition, state resident:* full-time $12,688; part-time $528 per credit hour. *Tuition, nonresident:* full-time $23,710; part-time $987 per credit hour. *Required fees:* full-time $930; $174 per term. *College room and board:* $9990; *Room only:* $6110. Room and board charges vary according to board plan and housing facility.

FRESHMAN FINANCIAL AID (Fall 2015) 375 applied for aid; of those 83% were deemed to have need. 98% of freshmen with need received aid; of those 9% had need fully met. *Average percent of need met:* 60% (excluding resources awarded to replace EFC). *Average financial aid package:* $11,436 (excluding resources awarded to replace EFC). 10% of all full-time freshmen had no need and received non-need-based gift aid.

UNDERGRADUATE FINANCIAL AID (Fall 2015) 1,266 applied for aid; of those 86% were deemed to have need. 97% of undergraduates with need received aid; of those 10% had need fully met. *Average percent of need met:* 59% (excluding resources awarded to replace EFC). *Average financial aid package:* $10,873 (excluding resources awarded to replace EFC). 5% of all full-time undergraduates had no need and received non-need-based gift aid.

GIFT AID (NEED-BASED) *Total amount:* $6,516,747 (38% federal, 31% state, 23% institutional, 8% external sources). *Receiving aid:* Freshmen: 67% (275); all full-time undergraduates: 60% (884). *Average award:* Freshmen: $9033; Undergraduates: $8221. *Scholarships, grants, and awards:* Federal Pell, FSEOG, state, private, college/university gift aid from institutional funds, United Negro College Fund.

GIFT AID (NON-NEED-BASED) *Total amount:* $744,072 (6% state, 75% institutional, 19% external sources). *Receiving aid:* Freshmen: 6% (25). Undergraduates: 5% (76). *Average award:* Freshmen: $3973. Undergraduates: $4301. *Tuition waivers:* Full or partial for employees or children of employees, senior citizens. *ROTC:* Army cooperative, Air Force cooperative.

LOANS *Student loans:* $9,557,802 (66% need-based, 34% non-need-based). 80% of past graduating class borrowed through all loan programs. *Average indebtedness per student:* $32,987. *Average need-based loan:* Freshmen: $3681. Undergrad-

uates: $4315. *Parent loans:* $1,984,303 (35% need-based, 65% non-need-based). *Programs:* Federal Direct (Subsidized and Unsubsidized Stafford, PLUS), Perkins.

WORK-STUDY *Federal work-study:* jobs available.

APPLYING FOR FINANCIAL AID *Required financial aid forms:* FAFSA, state aid form. *Financial aid deadline (priority):* 2/15. *Notification date:* Continuous beginning 3/15. Students must reply within 3 weeks of notification.

CONTACT Ms. Brandi S. Darr, Director of Financial Aid, University of Pittsburgh at Greensburg, 150 Finoli Drive, Greensburg, PA 15601-5898, 724-836-7167. *E-mail:* upgfnaid@pitt.edu. *Website:* http://www.greensburg.pitt.edu/.

UNIVERSITY OF PITTSBURGH AT JOHNSTOWN
Johnstown, PA

Tuition & fees (PA res): $13,388	Average undergraduate aid package: $10,567

ABOUT THE INSTITUTION State-related, coed. *Awards:* certificates, associate, and bachelor's degrees. 52 undergraduate majors. *Total enrollment:* 2,769. Undergraduates: 2,769. Freshmen: 715. Both federal and institutional methodology are used as a basis for awarding need-based institutional aid.

UNDERGRADUATE EXPENSES for 2017–2018 *Tuition, state resident:* full-time $12,452; part-time $518 per credit. *Tuition, nonresident:* full-time $23,268; part-time $969 per credit. *Required fees:* full-time $936; $127 per term. Full-time tuition and fees vary according to program. Part-time tuition and fees vary according to program. *College room and board:* $9684; *Room only:* $5470. Room and board charges vary according to board plan and housing facility.

FRESHMAN FINANCIAL AID (Fall 2015) 666 applied for aid; of those 84% were deemed to have need. 98% of freshmen with need received aid; of those 16% had need fully met. *Average percent of need met:* 58% (excluding resources awarded to replace EFC). *Average financial aid package:* $10,712 (excluding resources awarded to replace EFC). 9% of all full-time freshmen had no need and received non-need-based gift aid.

UNDERGRADUATE FINANCIAL AID (Fall 2015) 2,434 applied for aid; of those 85% were deemed to have need. 97% of undergraduates with need received aid; of those 16% had need fully met. *Average percent of need met:* 60% (excluding resources awarded to replace EFC). *Average financial aid package:* $10,567 (excluding resources awarded to replace EFC). 6% of all full-time undergraduates had no need and received non-need-based gift aid.

GIFT AID (NEED-BASED) *Total amount:* $10,535,632 (34% federal, 32% state, 27% institutional, 7% external sources). *Receiving aid:* Freshmen: 68% (489); all full-time undergraduates: 61% (1,673). *Average award:* Freshmen: $8367; Undergraduates: $7769. *Scholarships, grants, and awards:* Federal Pell, FSEOG, state, private, college/university gift aid from institutional funds, United Negro College Fund.

GIFT AID (NON-NEED-BASED) *Total amount:* $1,757,098 (3% state, 83% institutional, 14% external sources). *Receiving aid:* Freshmen: 8% (59). Undergraduates: 7% (185). *Average award:* Freshmen: $3053. Undergraduates: $3588. *Scholarships, grants, and awards by category:* Academic interests/achievement: biological sciences, business, communication, computer science, education, engineering/technologies, English, general academic interests/achievements, health fields, humanities, mathematics, physical sciences, premedicine, social sciences. *Creative arts/performance:* journalism/publications, theater/drama. *Special achievements/activities:* leadership. *Special characteristics:* children of faculty/staff. *Tuition waivers:* Full or partial for employees or children of employees.

LOANS *Student loans:* $19,475,570 (61% need-based, 39% non-need-based). 80% of past graduating class borrowed through all loan programs. *Average indebtedness per student:* $39,145. *Average need-based loan:* Freshmen: $3299. Undergraduates: $4301. *Parent loans:* $4,918,093 (30% need-based, 70% non-need-based). *Programs:* Federal Direct (Subsidized and Unsubsidized Stafford, PLUS), Perkins, college/university.

WORK-STUDY *Federal work-study:* jobs available. *State or other work-study/employment:* Part-time jobs available.

ATHLETIC AWARDS Total amount: $1,070,053 (59% need-based, 41% non-need-based).

APPLYING FOR FINANCIAL AID *Required financial aid forms:* FAFSA, state aid form. *Financial aid deadline (priority):* 4/1. *Notification date:* Continuous beginning 2/15. Students must reply by 5/1 or within 2 weeks of notification.

CONTACT Ms. Joni L. Trovato, Director of Student Financial Aid, University of Pittsburgh at Johnstown, 450 Schoolhouse Road, 114 Blackington Hall, Johnstown, PA 15904-2990, 814-269-7045 or toll-free 800-765-4875. *Fax:* 814-269-7061. *Website:* http://www.upj.pitt.edu/.

UNIVERSITY OF PORTLAND
Portland, OR

Tuition & fees: N/R	Average undergraduate aid package: $29,493

ABOUT THE INSTITUTION Independent Roman Catholic, coed. *Awards:* certificates, bachelor's, master's, and doctoral degrees. 38 undergraduate majors. *Total enrollment:* 4,338. Undergraduates: 3,770. Freshmen: 941. Federal methodology is used as a basis for awarding need-based institutional aid.
FRESHMAN FINANCIAL AID (Fall 2015) 796 applied for aid; of those 79% were deemed to have need. 100% of freshmen with need received aid; of those 10% had need fully met. *Average percent of need met:* 70% (excluding resources awarded to replace EFC). *Average financial aid package:* $27,296 (excluding resources awarded to replace EFC). 31% of all full-time freshmen had no need and received non-need-based gift aid.
UNDERGRADUATE FINANCIAL AID (Fall 2015) 2,702 applied for aid; of those 84% were deemed to have need. 100% of undergraduates with need received aid; of those 7% had need fully met. *Average percent of need met:* 73% (excluding resources awarded to replace EFC). *Average financial aid package:* $29,493 (excluding resources awarded to replace EFC). 34% of all full-time undergraduates had no need and received non-need-based gift aid.
GIFT AID (NEED-BASED) *Total amount:* $53,150,348 (7% federal, 1% state, 88% institutional, 4% external sources). *Receiving aid:* Freshmen: 51% (480); all full-time undergraduates: 48% (1,786). *Average award:* Freshmen: $22,709; Undergraduates: $22,439. *Scholarships, grants, and awards:* Federal Pell, FSEOG, state, private, college/university gift aid from institutional funds, United Negro College Fund, Federal Nursing, TEACH Grants.
GIFT AID (NON-NEED-BASED) *Total amount:* $21,418,964 (99% institutional, 1% external sources). *Receiving aid:* Freshmen: 64% (605). Undergraduates: 57% (2,108). *Average award:* Freshmen: $16,801. Undergraduates: $15,787. *Scholarships, grants, and awards by category: Academic interests/achievement:* 2,221 awards ($36,550,480 total): biological sciences, business, communication, computer science, education, engineering/technologies, English, foreign languages, general academic interests/achievements, health fields, humanities, mathematics, military science, physical sciences, premedicine, religion/biblical studies, social sciences. *Creative arts/performance:* 82 awards ($236,000 total): music, performing arts, theater/drama. *Special achievements/activities:* 31 awards ($26,629 total): general special achievements/activities. *Special characteristics:* 44 awards ($1,729,361 total): children of faculty/staff, relatives of clergy, religious affiliation. *ROTC:* Army, Air Force.
LOANS *Student loans:* $18,691,127 (89% need-based, 11% non-need-based). 59% of past graduating class borrowed through all loan programs. *Average indebtedness per student:* $28,307. *Average need-based loan:* Freshmen: $3603. Undergraduates: $5099. *Parent loans:* $25,237,976 (82% need-based, 18% non-need-based). *Programs:* Federal Direct (Subsidized and Unsubsidized Stafford, PLUS), Perkins, Federal Nursing, college/university, private loans.
WORK-STUDY *Federal work-study:* 444 jobs averaging $1030. *State or other work-study/employment:* Total amount: $2,257,425 (100% non-need-based). 1,437 part-time jobs averaging $1413.
ATHLETIC AWARDS Total amount: $5,059,531 (38% need-based, 62% non-need-based).
APPLYING FOR FINANCIAL AID *Required financial aid form:* FAFSA. *Financial aid deadline:* 3/1 (priority: 1/15). *Notification date:* Continuous beginning 11/15. Students must reply by 5/1.
CONTACT Ms. Janet Turner, Director of Financial Aid, University of Portland, 5000 North Willamette Boulevard, Portland, OR 97203-5798, 503-943-7311 or toll-free 888-627-5601. *Fax:* 503-943-7508. *E-mail:* turnerj@up.edu. *Website:* http://www.up.edu/.

UNIVERSITY OF PUERTO RICO IN AGUADILLA
Aguadilla, PR

CONTACT Director of Financial Aid, University of Puerto Rico in Aguadilla, PO Box 250-160, Aguadilla, PR 00604-0160, 787-890-2681 Ext. 273. *Website:* http://www.uprag.edu/.

UNIVERSITY OF PUERTO RICO IN ARECIBO
Arecibo, PR

CONTACT Myrta F. Salcedo-Ortiz, Director of Financial Aid, University of Puerto Rico in Arecibo, PO Box 4010, Arecibo, PR 00613, 787-878-2830 Ext. 2008. *E-mail:* myrta.ortiz@upr.edu. *Website:* http://www.upra.edu/.

UNIVERSITY OF PUERTO RICO IN BAYAMÓN
Bayamón, PR

Tuition & fees (PR res): $2048	Average undergraduate aid package: N/A

ABOUT THE INSTITUTION Commonwealth-supported, coed. *Awards:* associate and bachelor's degrees. 16 undergraduate majors. *Total enrollment:* 4,927. Undergraduates: 4,927. Freshmen: 1,246. Federal methodology is used as a basis for awarding need-based institutional aid.
UNDERGRADUATE EXPENSES for 2016–2017 *Application fee:* $30. *Tuition, state resident:* full-time $1904; part-time $56 per credit. *Tuition, non-resident:* full-time $3892; part-time $114 per credit. *Required fees:* full-time $144. Full-time tuition and fees vary according to class time, course load, and program. Part-time tuition and fees vary according to class time, course load, and program. *Payment plan:* Guaranteed tuition.
GIFT AID (NEED-BASED) *Total amount:* $15,902,630 (99% federal, 1% state). *Scholarships, grants, and awards:* Federal Pell, FSEOG, state, college/university gift aid from institutional funds.
GIFT AID (NON-NEED-BASED) *Scholarships, grants, and awards by category: Academic interests/achievement:* general academic interests/achievements. *Creative arts/performance:* 87 awards ($113,791 total): music, theater/drama. *Special achievements/activities:* cheerleading/drum major, community service. *Special characteristics:* 260 awards ($271,074 total): children of educators, children of faculty/staff, children of union members/company employees, handicapped students, veterans, veterans' children. *Tuition waivers:* Full or partial for employees or children of employees.
LOANS *Student loans:* $795,084 (100% need-based). *Programs:* Federal Direct (Unsubsidized Stafford, PLUS), Perkins.
WORK-STUDY *Federal work-study:* 238 jobs averaging $1473. *State or other work-study/employment:* Total amount: $39,540 (100% need-based). Part-time jobs available.
ATHLETIC AWARDS Total amount: $363,798 (100% need-based).
APPLYING FOR FINANCIAL AID *Required financial aid forms:* FAFSA, state income tax form(s). *Notification date:* Continuous.
CONTACT Mr. Marcos Cesar De Jesus Rosado, Financial Aid Director, University of Puerto Rico in Bayamón, Industrial Minillas Park 170 Road 174, Bayamon, PR 00959-1919, 787-993-8953 Ext. 4031. *Fax:* 787-993-8930. *E-mail:* marcos.dejesus@upr.edu. *Website:* http://www.uprb.edu/.

UNIVERSITY OF PUERTO RICO IN CAROLINA

Carolina, PR

CONTACT Financial Aid Office, University of Puerto Rico in Carolina, PO Box 4800, Carolina, PR 00984-4800, 787-257-0000.
Website: http://www.uprc.edu/.

UNIVERSITY OF PUERTO RICO IN CAYEY

Cayey, PR

CONTACT Mr. Hector Maldonado Otero, Director of Financial Aid, University of Puerto Rico in Cayey, Antonio Barcelo, Cayey, PR 00736, 787-738-2161. *Fax:* 787-263-0676.
Website: http://www.cayey.upr.edu/.

UNIVERSITY OF PUERTO RICO IN HUMACAO

Humacao, PR

CONTACT Alfredo Aponte Serrano, Director of Financial Aid, University of Puerto Rico in Humacao, HUC Station, Humacao, PR 00791-4300, 787-850-9362. *E-mail:* alfredo.aponte@upr.edu.
Website: http://www.uprh.edu/.

UNIVERSITY OF PUERTO RICO IN PONCE

Ponce, PR

CONTACT Carmelo Vega Montes, Director of Financial Aid, University of Puerto Rico in Ponce, Box 7186, Ponce, PR 00732-7186, 787-844-8181. *Fax:* 787-840-8108.
Website: http://www.uprp.edu/.

UNIVERSITY OF PUERTO RICO IN UTUADO

Utuado, PR

CONTACT Edgar Salv, Director of Financial Assistance, University of Puerto Rico in Utuado, PO Box 2500, Utuado, PR 00641, 787-894-2828 Ext. 2603. *Fax:* 787-894-3810. *E-mail:* esalva@uprutuado.edu.
Website: http://www.uprutuado.edu/.

UNIVERSITY OF PUERTO RICO, MAYAGÜEZ CAMPUS

Mayagüez, PR

Tuition & fees: N/R	Average undergraduate aid package: $5005

ABOUT THE INSTITUTION Commonwealth-supported, coed. 54 undergraduate majors. Federal methodology is used as a basis for awarding need-based institutional aid.
FRESHMAN FINANCIAL AID (Fall 2015) 2,230 applied for aid; of those 86% were deemed to have need. 85% of freshmen with need received aid. *Average*

percent of need met: 66% (excluding resources awarded to replace EFC).
Average financial aid package: $4979 (excluding resources awarded to replace EFC).
UNDERGRADUATE FINANCIAL AID (Fall 2015) 9,132 applied for aid; of those 92% were deemed to have need. 85% of undergraduates with need received aid; of those .1% had need fully met. *Average percent of need met:* 70% (excluding resources awarded to replace EFC). *Average financial aid package:* $5005 (excluding resources awarded to replace EFC).
GIFT AID (NEED-BASED) *Total amount:* $37,689,772 (98% federal, 1% state, 1% external sources). *Receiving aid:* Freshmen: 69% (1,624); all full-time undergraduates: 60% (7,109). *Average award:* Freshmen: $4979; Undergraduates: $5005. *Scholarships, grants, and awards:* Federal Pell, FSEOG, state, private, college/university gift aid from institutional funds.
GIFT AID (NON-NEED-BASED) *Total amount:* $189,017 (100% external sources).
LOANS *Student loans:* $8,045,775 (92% need-based, 8% non-need-based). 49% of past graduating class borrowed through all loan programs. *Average indebtedness per student:* $7550. *Average need-based loan:* Freshmen: $1087. Undergraduates: $1322. *Programs:* Federal Direct (Subsidized and Unsubsidized Stafford).
WORK-STUDY *Federal work-study:* jobs available. *State or other work-study/employment:* Total amount: $310,879 (100% need-based). Part-time jobs available.
ATHLETIC AWARDS Total amount: $576,925 (90% need-based, 10% non-need-based).
APPLYING FOR FINANCIAL AID *Required financial aid form:* FAFSA. *Financial aid deadline:* Continuous. *Notification date:* Continuous beginning 5/1. Students must reply within 2 weeks of notification.
CONTACT Ms. Miriam Barreto, Director of Financial Aid, University of Puerto Rico, Mayagüez Campus, PO Box 9000, Mayaguez, PR 00681, 787-265-3863. *Fax:* 787-265-1920. *E-mail:* miriam.barreto@upr.edu.
Website: http://www.uprm.edu/.

UNIVERSITY OF PUERTO RICO, MEDICAL SCIENCES CAMPUS

San Juan, PR

CONTACT Mrs. Zoraida Figueroa, Financial Aid Director, University of Puerto Rico, Medical Sciences Campus, Terreno Centro Medico-Edificio Decanato Farmacia y Estudiantes, San Juan, PR 00936-5067, 787-763-2525. *Fax:* 787-282-7117. *E-mail:* zoraida.figueroa@upr.edu.
Website: http://www.rcm.upr.edu/.

UNIVERSITY OF PUERTO RICO, RÍO PIEDRAS CAMPUS

San Juan, PR

CONTACT Mr. Efraim Williams, EDP Manager, University of Puerto Rico, Río Piedras Campus, PO Box 23300, San Juan, PR 00931-3300, 787-764-0000 Ext. 5573.
Website: http://www.uprrp.edu/.

UNIVERSITY OF PUGET SOUND

Tacoma, WA

Tuition & fees: $48,090	Average undergraduate aid package: $31,725

ABOUT THE INSTITUTION Independent, coed. *Awards:* bachelor's, master's, and doctoral degrees. 40 undergraduate majors. *Total enrollment:* 2,791. Undergraduates: 2,508. Freshmen: 674. Federal methodology is used as a basis for awarding need-based institutional aid.
UNDERGRADUATE EXPENSES for 2017–2018 *Application fee:* $50. *Comprehensive fee:* $60,210 includes full-time tuition ($47,840), mandatory fees ($250), and room and board ($12,120). *College room only:* $6620. Full-time tuition and

fees vary according to course load. Room and board charges vary according to board plan and housing facility. *Part-time tuition:* $6040 per unit. Part-time tuition and fees vary according to course load.

FRESHMAN FINANCIAL AID (Fall 2016, est.) 525 applied for aid; of those 74% were deemed to have need. 100% of freshmen with need received aid; of those 16% had need fully met. *Average percent of need met:* 77% (excluding resources awarded to replace EFC). *Average financial aid package:* $32,274 (excluding resources awarded to replace EFC). 42% of all full-time freshmen had no need and received non-need-based gift aid.

UNDERGRADUATE FINANCIAL AID (Fall 2016, est.) 1,506 applied for aid; of those 80% were deemed to have need. 100% of undergraduates with need received aid; of those 16% had need fully met. *Average percent of need met:* 76% (excluding resources awarded to replace EFC). *Average financial aid package:* $31,725 (excluding resources awarded to replace EFC). 50% of all full-time undergraduates had no need and received non-need-based gift aid.

GIFT AID (NEED-BASED) Total amount: $30,043,365 (7% federal, 2% state, 85% institutional, 6% external sources). *Receiving aid:* Freshmen: 57% (382); all full-time undergraduates: 48% (1,197). *Average award:* Freshmen: $26,770; Undergraduates: $24,456. *Scholarships, grants, and awards:* Federal Pell, FSEOG, state, private, college/university gift aid from institutional funds.

GIFT AID (NON-NEED-BASED) Total amount: $20,613,748 (94% institutional, 6% external sources). *Receiving aid:* Freshmen: 8% (54). Undergraduates: 6% (156). *Average award:* Freshmen: $16,832. Undergraduates: $15,870. *Scholarships, grants, and awards by category:* Academic interests/achievement: 1,290 awards ($17,841,102 total): biological sciences, business, communication, computer science, English, foreign languages, general academic interests/achievements, humanities, international studies, mathematics, physical sciences, premedicine, social sciences. Creative arts/performance: 75 awards ($734,891 total): art/fine arts, debating, music, theater/drama. Special achievements/activities: 3 awards ($7500 total): community service, leadership, religious involvement. Special characteristics: 26 awards ($545,841 total): children of faculty/staff, international students, veterans, veterans' children. *Tuition waivers:* Full or partial for employees or children of employees. *ROTC:* Army cooperative.

LOANS Student loans: $10,955,134 (87% need-based, 13% non-need-based). 50% of past graduating class borrowed through all loan programs. *Average indebtedness per student:* $34,140. *Average need-based loan:* Freshmen: $4805. Undergraduates: $6466. *Parent loans:* $5,999,978 (85% need-based, 15% non-need-based). *Programs:* Federal Direct (Subsidized and Unsubsidized Stafford, PLUS), Perkins.

WORK-STUDY Federal work-study: Total amount: $1,762,380; 528 jobs averaging $3092. *State or other work-study/employment:* Total amount: $2,469,118 (100% need-based). 841 part-time jobs averaging $2557.

APPLYING FOR FINANCIAL AID Required financial aid form: FAFSA. *Financial aid deadline (priority):* 1/15. *Notification date:* Continuous beginning 3/15. Students must reply by 5/1.

CONTACT Maggie A. Mittuch, Associate Vice President for Student Financial Services, University of Puget Sound, 1500 North Warner Street #1039, Tacoma, WA 98416-1039, 253-879-3214 or toll-free 800-396-7191. *Fax:* 253-879-8508. *E-mail:* mmittuch@pugetsound.edu. *Website:* http://www.pugetsound.edu/.

UNIVERSITY OF REDLANDS
Redlands, CA

Tuition & fees: $46,570	Average undergraduate aid package: $33,187

ABOUT THE INSTITUTION Independent, coed. *Awards:* certificates, diplomas, bachelor's, master's, and doctoral degrees. 45 undergraduate majors. *Total enrollment:* 5,215. Undergraduates: 3,493. Freshmen: 525. Institutional methodology is used as a basis for awarding need-based institutional aid.

UNDERGRADUATE EXPENSES for 2016–2017 Application fee: $30. *One-time required fee:* $150. *Comprehensive fee:* $60,050 includes full-time tuition ($46,220), mandatory fees ($350), and room and board ($13,480). Room and board charges vary according to board plan and housing facility. *Part-time tuition:* $1445 per credit hour. *Part-time fees:* $116 per year. Part-time tuition and fees vary according to course load.

FRESHMAN FINANCIAL AID (Fall 2015) 456 applied for aid; of those 86% were deemed to have need. 100% of freshmen with need received aid; of those 49% had

need fully met. *Average percent of need met:* 84% (excluding resources awarded to replace EFC). *Average financial aid package:* $34,212 (excluding resources awarded to replace EFC). 23% of all full-time freshmen had no need and received non-need-based gift aid.

UNDERGRADUATE FINANCIAL AID (Fall 2015) 2,342 applied for aid; of those 86% were deemed to have need. 100% of undergraduates with need received aid; of those 48% had need fully met. *Average percent of need met:* 83% (excluding resources awarded to replace EFC). *Average financial aid package:* $33,187 (excluding resources awarded to replace EFC). 20% of all full-time undergraduates had no need and received non-need-based gift aid.

GIFT AID (NEED-BASED) Total amount: $56,937,022 (8% federal, 11% state, 79% institutional, 2% external sources). *Receiving aid:* Freshmen: 75% (393); all full-time undergraduates: 74% (1,996). *Average award:* Freshmen: $29,047; Undergraduates: $27,847. *Scholarships, grants, and awards:* Federal Pell, FSEOG, state, private, college/university gift aid from institutional funds.

GIFT AID (NON-NEED-BASED) Total amount: $12,080,161 (97% institutional, 3% external sources). *Receiving aid:* Freshmen: 17% (90). Undergraduates: 16% (427). *Average award:* Freshmen: $18,075. Undergraduates: $15,733. *Scholarships, grants, and awards by category:* Academic interests/achievement: general academic interests/achievements. Creative arts/performance: art/fine arts, creative writing, debating, music. Special achievements/activities: general special achievements/activities. Special characteristics: international students. *Tuition waivers:* Full or partial for employees or children of employees. *ROTC:* Army cooperative, Air Force cooperative.

LOANS Student loans: $22,689,584 (59% need-based, 41% non-need-based). 68% of past graduating class borrowed through all loan programs. *Average indebtedness per student:* $32,662. *Average need-based loan:* Freshmen: $5935. Undergraduates: $6467. *Parent loans:* $7,618,723 (100% non-need-based). *Programs:* Perkins, college/university.

WORK-STUDY Federal work-study: jobs available. *State or other work-study/employment:* Total amount: $2,225,534 (56% need-based, 44% non-need-based). Part-time jobs available.

APPLYING FOR FINANCIAL AID Required financial aid forms: FAFSA, state aid form. *Financial aid deadline (priority):* 11/15. *Notification date:* Continuous beginning 2/28. Students must reply by 5/1.

CONTACT Alisha Aguilar, Director of Financial Aid, University of Redlands, 1200 East Colton Avenue, PO Box 3080, Redlands, CA 92373-0999, 909-748-8047 or toll-free 800-455-5064. *Fax:* 909-335-4089. *E-mail:* financialaid@redlands.edu. *Website:* http://www.redlands.edu/.

UNIVERSITY OF RHODE ISLAND
Kingston, RI

Tuition & fees (RI res): $12,884	Average undergraduate aid package: $15,768

ABOUT THE INSTITUTION State-supported, coed. *Awards:* certificates, bachelor's, master's, and doctoral degrees. 76 undergraduate majors. *Total enrollment:* 17,834. Undergraduates: 14,801. Freshmen: 3,257. Federal methodology is used as a basis for awarding need-based institutional aid.

UNDERGRADUATE EXPENSES for 2016–2017 Application fee: $65. *Tuition, state resident:* full-time $11,128; part-time $464 per credit hour. *Tuition, nonresident:* full-time $27,118; part-time $1130 per term. *Required fees:* full-time $1756; $44 per credit hour or $58 per term. Full-time tuition and fees vary according to course load, location, and reciprocity agreements. Part-time tuition and fees vary according to course load, location, and reciprocity agreements. *College room and board:* $7622; *Room only:* $4400. Room and board charges vary according to board plan and housing facility.

FRESHMAN FINANCIAL AID (Fall 2016, est.) 3,063 applied for aid; of those 79% were deemed to have need. 97% of freshmen with need received aid; of those 3% had need fully met. *Average percent of need met:* 64% (excluding resources awarded to replace EFC). *Average financial aid package:* $16,577 (excluding resources awarded to replace EFC). 11% of all full-time freshmen had no need and received non-need-based gift aid.

UNDERGRADUATE FINANCIAL AID (Fall 2016, est.) 12,459 applied for aid; of those 86% were deemed to have need. 92% of undergraduates with need received aid; of those 4% had need fully met. *Average percent of need met:* 57% (excluding resources awarded to replace EFC). *Average financial aid package:* $15,768

(excluding resources awarded to replace EFC). 8% of all full-time undergraduates had no need and received non-need-based gift aid.

GIFT AID (NEED-BASED) *Total amount:* $97,497,891 (17% federal, 3% state, 77% institutional, 3% external sources). *Receiving aid:* Freshmen: 70% (2,254); all full-time undergraduates: 74% (9,250). *Average award:* Freshmen: $10,594; Undergraduates: $10,125. *Scholarships, grants, and awards:* Federal Pell, FSEOG, state, private, college/university gift aid from institutional funds.

GIFT AID (NON-NEED-BASED) *Total amount:* $7,276,632 (1% federal, 93% institutional, 6% external sources). *Receiving aid:* Freshmen: 14% (465). Undergraduates: 9% (1,136). *Average award:* Freshmen: $7094. Undergraduates: $6683. *Scholarships, grants, and awards by category:* Academic interests/achievement: 1,134 awards ($1,598,266 total): agriculture, area/ethnic studies, biological sciences, business, communication, computer science, education, engineering/technologies, English, foreign languages, general academic interests/achievements, health fields, home economics, humanities, international studies, library science, mathematics, military science, physical sciences, premedicine, religion/biblical studies, social sciences. Creative arts/performance: 39 awards ($110,928 total): art/fine arts, journalism/publications, music, theater/drama. Special characteristics: 6 awards ($3307 total): children and siblings of alumni. *Tuition waivers:* Full or partial for minority students, employees or children of employees, senior citizens. *ROTC:* Army.

LOANS *Student loans:* $80,688,235 (76% need-based, 24% non-need-based). 77% of past graduating class borrowed through all loan programs. *Average indebtedness per student:* $32,750. *Average need-based loan:* Freshmen: $5786. Undergraduates: $6042. *Parent loans:* $34,386,181 (64% need-based, 36% non-need-based). *Programs:* Federal Direct (Subsidized and Unsubsidized Stafford, PLUS), Perkins, Federal Nursing, college/university.

WORK-STUDY *Federal work-study:* Total amount: $2,116,693; jobs available.

ATHLETIC AWARDS Total amount: $8,472,348 (92% need-based, 8% non-need-based).

APPLYING FOR FINANCIAL AID *Required financial aid form:* FAFSA. *Financial aid deadline (priority):* 3/1. *Notification date:* Continuous beginning 3/15. Students must reply by 5/1.

CONTACT Office of Enrollment Services, University of Rhode Island, Green Hall, 35 Campus Avenue, Kingston, RI 02881, 401-874-9500.
Website: http://www.uri.edu/.

UNIVERSITY OF RICHMOND
Richmond, VA

Tuition & fees: $50,910	Average undergraduate aid package: $45,784

ABOUT THE INSTITUTION Independent, coed. *Awards:* bachelor's, master's, and doctoral degrees. 52 undergraduate majors. *Total enrollment:* 3,570. Undergraduates: 3,036. Freshmen: 815. Institutional methodology is used as a basis for awarding need-based institutional aid.

UNDERGRADUATE EXPENSES for 2017–2018 *Application fee:* $50. *Comprehensive fee:* $62,730 includes full-time tuition ($50,910) and room and board ($11,820). *College room only:* $5440. Full-time tuition and fees vary according to course load. Room and board charges vary according to board plan and housing facility. *Part-time tuition:* $2546 per credit hour. Part-time tuition and fees vary according to course load.

FRESHMAN FINANCIAL AID (Fall 2016, est.) 500 applied for aid; of those 70% were deemed to have need. 100% of freshmen with need received aid; of those 88% had need fully met. *Average percent of need met:* 100% (excluding resources awarded to replace EFC). *Average financial aid package:* $46,348 (excluding resources awarded to replace EFC). 11% of all full-time freshmen had no need and received non-need-based gift aid.

UNDERGRADUATE FINANCIAL AID (Fall 2016, est.) 1,637 applied for aid; of those 82% were deemed to have need. 100% of undergraduates with need received aid; of those 83% had need fully met. *Average percent of need met:* 100% (excluding resources awarded to replace EFC). *Average financial aid package:* $45,784 (excluding resources awarded to replace EFC). 17% of all full-time undergraduates had no need and received non-need-based gift aid.

GIFT AID (NEED-BASED) *Total amount:* $49,338,760 (5% federal, 1% state, 92% institutional, 2% external sources). *Receiving aid:* Freshmen: 42% (341); all full-time undergraduates: 41% (1,308). *Average award:* Freshmen: $40,204; Undergraduates: $39,874. *Scholarships, grants, and awards:* Federal Pell, FSEOG, state, private, college/university gift aid from institutional funds.

GIFT AID (NON-NEED-BASED) *Total amount:* $15,946,605 (3% federal, 5% state, 85% institutional, 7% external sources). *Receiving aid:* Freshmen: 12% (94). Undergraduates: 8% (247). *Average award:* Freshmen: $33,299. Undergraduates: $22,658. *Scholarships, grants, and awards by category:* Academic interests/achievement: 169 awards ($7,833,040 total): biological sciences, computer science, general academic interests/achievements, mathematics, physical sciences, social sciences. Creative arts/performance: 36 awards ($1,230,240 total): art/fine arts, dance, music, performing arts, theater/drama. Special achievements/activities: 98 awards ($245,000 total): community service. *Tuition waivers:* Full or partial for employees or children of employees. *ROTC:* Army.

LOANS *Student loans:* $11,891,325 (35% need-based, 65% non-need-based). 40% of past graduating class borrowed through all loan programs. *Average indebtedness per student:* $27,670. *Average need-based loan:* Freshmen: $2871. Undergraduates: $3730. *Parent loans:* $4,484,051 (3% need-based, 97% non-need-based). *Programs:* Federal Direct (Subsidized and Unsubsidized Stafford, PLUS).

WORK-STUDY *Federal work-study:* Total amount: $903,880; 609 jobs averaging $1395.

ATHLETIC AWARDS Total amount: $10,380,820 (20% need-based, 80% non-need-based).

APPLYING FOR FINANCIAL AID *Required financial aid forms:* FAFSA, CSS Financial Aid PROFILE, noncustodial (divorced/separated) parent's statement, federal income tax form(s). *Financial aid deadline:* 2/1. *Notification date:* 4/1. Students must reply within 4 weeks of notification.

CONTACT Office of Financial Aid, University of Richmond, 28 Westhampton Way, University of Richmond, VA 23173, 804-289-8438 or toll-free 800-700-1662. *Fax:* 804-484-1650. *E-mail:* finaid@richmond.edu.
Website: http://www.richmond.edu/.

UNIVERSITY OF RIO GRANDE
Rio Grande, OH

CONTACT Ms. Meghann Fraley, Assistant Director of Financial Aid, University of Rio Grande, PO Box 500, 218 North College Avenue, Rio Grande, OH 45674, 740-245-7218 or toll-free 800-282-7201. *Fax:* 740-245-7102.
Website: http://www.rio.edu/.

UNIVERSITY OF ROCHESTER
Rochester, NY

Tuition & fees: $51,898	Average undergraduate aid package: $44,425

ABOUT THE INSTITUTION Independent, coed. *Awards:* certificates, bachelor's, master's, and doctoral degrees. 67 undergraduate majors. *Total enrollment:* 11,168. Undergraduates: 6,345. Freshmen: 1,461. Institutional methodology is used as a basis for awarding need-based institutional aid.

UNDERGRADUATE EXPENSES for 2017–2018 *Application fee:* $50. *Comprehensive fee:* $67,236 includes full-time tuition ($50,984), mandatory fees ($914), and room and board ($15,338). Room and board charges vary according to board plan and housing facility. *Part-time tuition:* $1593 per credit hour. Part-time tuition and fees vary according to course load.

FRESHMAN FINANCIAL AID (Fall 2016, est.) 1,023 applied for aid; of those 78% were deemed to have need. 100% of freshmen with need received aid; of those 91% had need fully met. *Average percent of need met:* 96% (excluding resources awarded to replace EFC). *Average financial aid package:* $44,623 (excluding resources awarded to replace EFC). 31% of all full-time freshmen had no need and received non-need-based gift aid.

UNDERGRADUATE FINANCIAL AID (Fall 2016, est.) 3,701 applied for aid; of those 83% were deemed to have need. 100% of undergraduates with need received aid; of those 90% had need fully met. *Average percent of need met:* 93% (excluding resources awarded to replace EFC). *Average financial aid package:* $44,425 (excluding resources awarded to replace EFC). 31% of all full-time undergraduates had no need and received non-need-based gift aid.

GIFT AID (NEED-BASED) *Total amount:* $116,225,143 (5% federal, 2% state, 90% institutional, 3% external sources). *Receiving aid:* Freshmen: 54% (798); all full-time undergraduates: 51% (3,062). *Average award:* Freshmen: $40,873; Undergraduates: $39,246. **Scholarships, grants, and awards:** Federal Pell, FSEOG, state, college/university gift aid from institutional funds.

GIFT AID (NON-NEED-BASED) Total amount: $33,500,558 (1% federal, 82% institutional, 17% external sources). **Receiving aid:** Freshmen: 9% (139). Undergraduates: 7% (404). **Average award:** Freshmen: $12,957. Undergraduates: $13,597. **Scholarships, grants, and awards by category:** Academic interests/achievement: engineering/technologies, general academic interests/achievements, military science. Creative arts/performance: general creative arts/performance, music, performing arts. Special achievements/activities: general special achievements/activities, leadership. Special characteristics: children and siblings of alumni, children of faculty/staff, general special characteristics, international students, veterans. **Tuition waivers:** Full or partial for employees or children of employees. **ROTC:** Army cooperative, Naval, Air Force cooperative.

LOANS Student loans: $24,458,775 (63% need-based, 37% non-need-based). 55% of past graduating class borrowed through all loan programs. Average indebtedness per student: $30,742. **Average need-based loan:** Freshmen: $3645. Undergraduates: $5246. **Parent loans:** $8,874,089 (17% need-based, 83% non-need-based). **Programs:** Federal Direct (Subsidized and Unsubsidized Stafford, PLUS), Perkins.

WORK-STUDY Federal work-study: Total amount: $6,589,147; jobs available. **State or other work-study/employment:** Total amount: $1,583,400 (42% need-based, 58% non-need-based). Part-time jobs available.

APPLYING FOR FINANCIAL AID Required financial aid forms: FAFSA, CSS Financial Aid PROFILE, state aid form, noncustodial (divorced/separated) parent's statement. **Financial aid deadline (priority):** 2/15. **Notification date:** 4/1. Students must reply by 5/1.

CONTACT Samantha Veeder, Director of Financial Aid, University of Rochester, Wallis Hall, PO Box 270261, Rochester, NY 14627-0250, 585-275-3226 or toll-free 888-822-2256. Fax: 585-756-7664. E-mail: samantha.veeder@rochester.edu. Website: http://www.rochester.edu/.

education, general academic interests/achievements, health fields, international studies, premedicine, social sciences. Creative arts/performance: 52 awards ($52,550 total): applied art and design, art/fine arts, general creative arts/performance, music, performing arts. Special achievements/activities: 581 awards ($4,729,956 total): cheerleading/drum major, community service, general special achievements/activities, leadership, religious involvement. Special characteristics: 364 awards ($890,940 total): adult students, children and siblings of alumni, children of educators, children of faculty/staff, ethnic background, first-generation college students, general special characteristics, religious affiliation, siblings of current students, veterans, veterans' children. **Tuition waivers:** Full or partial for children of alumni, employees or children of employees. **ROTC:** Army cooperative.

LOANS Student loans: $9,554,587 (67% need-based, 33% non-need-based). 79% of past graduating class borrowed through all loan programs. Average indebtedness per student: $31,506. **Average need-based loan:** Freshmen: $3514. Undergraduates: $4649. **Parent loans:** $3,837,498 (32% need-based, 68% non-need-based). **Programs:** Federal Direct (Subsidized and Unsubsidized Stafford, PLUS), Perkins, alternative loans.

WORK-STUDY Federal work-study: Total amount: $222,443; 156 jobs averaging $2484. **State or other work-study/employment:** Total amount: $396,000 (100% non-need-based). 300 part-time jobs averaging $2500.

ATHLETIC AWARDS Total amount: $4,430,625 (65% need-based, 35% non-need-based).

APPLYING FOR FINANCIAL AID Required financial aid forms: FAFSA, institution's own form. **Financial aid deadline (priority):** 11/15. **Notification date:** Continuous beginning 10/15. Students must reply within 8 weeks of notification.

CONTACT Mr. Bruce A. Foote, Executive Director of Financial Aid Services, University of St. Francis, 500 North Wilcox Street, Joliet, IL 60435-6188, 815-740-5097 or toll-free 800-735-7500. Fax: 815-740-3822. E-mail: bfoote@stfrancis.edu. Website: http://www.stfrancis.edu/.

UNIVERSITY OF ST. FRANCIS
Joliet, IL

Tuition & fees: $30,840	Average undergraduate aid package: $22,637

ABOUT THE INSTITUTION Independent Roman Catholic, coed. **Awards:** certificates, bachelor's, master's, and doctoral degrees. 54 undergraduate majors. **Total enrollment:** 2,578. Undergraduates: 1,362. Freshmen: 215. Federal methodology is used as a basis for awarding need-based institutional aid.

UNDERGRADUATE EXPENSES for 2016–2017 Comprehensive fee: $39,924 includes full-time tuition ($30,520), mandatory fees ($320), and room and board ($9084). Full-time tuition and fees vary according to degree level, location, and program. Room and board charges vary according to housing facility. **Part-time tuition:** $825 per credit hour. **Part-time fees:** $125 per term. Part-time tuition and fees vary according to degree level and program.

FRESHMAN FINANCIAL AID (Fall 2016, est.) 203 applied for aid; of those 92% were deemed to have need. 100% of freshmen with need received aid; of those 46% had need fully met. **Average percent of need met:** 86% (excluding resources awarded to replace EFC). **Average financial aid package:** $24,374 (excluding resources awarded to replace EFC). 7% of all full-time freshmen had no need and received non-need-based gift aid.

UNDERGRADUATE FINANCIAL AID (Fall 2016, est.) 1,197 applied for aid; of those 92% were deemed to have need. 100% of undergraduates with need received aid; of those 36% had need fully met. **Average percent of need met:** 80% (excluding resources awarded to replace EFC). **Average financial aid package:** $22,637 (excluding resources awarded to replace EFC). 7% of all full-time undergraduates had no need and received non-need-based gift aid.

GIFT AID (NEED-BASED) Total amount: $17,066,080 (14% federal, 14% state, 71% institutional, 1% external sources). **Receiving aid:** Freshmen: 87% (186); all full-time undergraduates: 84% (1,092). **Average award:** Freshmen: $20,660; Undergraduates: $18,534. **Scholarships, grants, and awards:** Federal Pell, FSEOG, state, private, college/university gift aid from institutional funds, Federal Nursing.

GIFT AID (NON-NEED-BASED) Total amount: $2,610,089 (11% federal, 84% institutional, 5% external sources). **Receiving aid:** Freshmen: 64% (137). Undergraduates: 83% (1,070). **Average award:** Freshmen: $12,745. Undergraduates: $10,115. **Scholarships, grants, and awards by category:** Academic interests/achievement: 1,133 awards ($9,591,128 total): biological sciences, communication,

UNIVERSITY OF SAINT FRANCIS
Fort Wayne, IN

CONTACT Office of Financial Aid, University of Saint Francis, 2701 Spring Street, Fort Wayne, IN 46808, 260-399-8003 or toll-free 800-729-4732. Fax: 260-399-8162. E-mail: finaid@sf.edu. Website: http://www.sf.edu/.

UNIVERSITY OF SAINT JOSEPH
West Hartford, CT

Tuition & fees: $38,033	Average undergraduate aid package: $25,455

ABOUT THE INSTITUTION Independent Roman Catholic, coed, primarily women. **Awards:** certificates, bachelor's, master's, and doctoral degrees. 25 undergraduate majors. **Total enrollment:** 2,467. Undergraduates: 894. Freshmen: 126. Federal methodology is used as a basis for awarding need-based institutional aid.

UNDERGRADUATE EXPENSES for 2017–2018 Application fee: $50. **Comprehensive fee:** $49,128 includes full-time tuition ($36,273), mandatory fees ($1760), and room and board ($11,095). **College room only:** $6250. Full-time tuition and fees vary according to course load, degree level, location, program, and student level. Room and board charges vary according to board plan and housing facility. **Part-time tuition:** $818 per credit hour. **Part-time fees:** $58 per credit hour. Part-time tuition and fees vary according to course load, degree level, location, program, and student level.

FRESHMAN FINANCIAL AID (Fall 2016, est.) 120 applied for aid; of those 92% were deemed to have need. 100% of freshmen with need received aid; of those 19% had need fully met. **Average percent of need met:** 75% (excluding resources awarded to replace EFC). **Average financial aid package:** $26,686 (excluding resources awarded to replace EFC). 10% of all full-time freshmen had no need and received non-need-based gift aid.

UNDERGRADUATE FINANCIAL AID (Fall 2016, est.) 674 applied for aid; of those 93% were deemed to have need. 100% of undergraduates with need received aid; of those 12% had need fully met. **Average percent of need met:** 69% (excluding resources awarded to replace EFC). **Average financial aid package:**

$25,455 (excluding resources awarded to replace EFC). 10% of all full-time undergraduates had no need and received non-need-based gift aid.

GIFT AID (NEED-BASED) *Total amount:* $12,544,435 (12% federal, 4% state, 75% institutional, 9% external sources). *Receiving aid:* Freshmen: 89% (110); all full-time undergraduates: 86% (602). *Average award:* Freshmen: $22,979; Undergraduates: $20,550. *Scholarships, grants, and awards:* Federal Pell, FSEOG, state, private, college/university gift aid from institutional funds, Federal Nursing.

GIFT AID (NON-NEED-BASED) *Total amount:* $1,406,574 (1% state, 89% institutional, 10% external sources). *Receiving aid:* Freshmen: 13% (16). Undergraduates: 7% (52). *Average award:* Freshmen: $19,384. Undergraduates: $13,871. *Scholarships, grants, and awards by category:* Academic interests/achievement: general academic interests/achievements. Special achievements/activities: leadership. Special characteristics: local/state students, members of minority groups, siblings of current students. *Tuition waivers:* Full or partial for employees or children of employees.

LOANS *Student loans:* $7,431,865 (78% need-based, 22% non-need-based). 25% of past graduating class borrowed through all loan programs. *Average indebtedness per student:* $29,028. *Average need-based loan:* Freshmen: $3830. Undergraduates: $5992. *Parent loans:* $2,117,146 (57% need-based, 43% non-need-based). *Programs:* Federal Direct (Subsidized and Unsubsidized Stafford, PLUS), Perkins.

WORK-STUDY *Federal work-study:* Total amount: $67,261; jobs available. *State or other work-study/employment:* Total amount: $225,891 (58% need-based, 42% non-need-based). Part-time jobs available.

APPLYING FOR FINANCIAL AID *Required financial aid form:* FAFSA. *Financial aid deadline (priority):* 3/1. *Notification date:* Continuous beginning 12/1. Students must reply by 5/1.

CONTACT Student Financial Services, University of Saint Joseph, 1678 Asylum Avenue, West Hartford, CT 06117, 860-231-5223 or toll-free 866-442-8752. *E-mail:* financialaid@usj.edu.
Website: http://www.usj.edu/.

UNIVERSITY OF SAINT MARY
Leavenworth, KS

CONTACT Mrs. Judy Wiedower, Financial Aid Director, University of Saint Mary, 4100 South Fourth Street, Leavenworth, KS 66048, 913-758-6314 or toll-free 800-752-7043. *Fax:* 913-758-6146. *E-mail:* wiedower@hub.smcks.edu.
Website: http://www.stmary.edu/.

UNIVERSITY OF ST. THOMAS
St. Paul, MN

Tuition & fees: $41,133	Average undergraduate aid package: $26,846

ABOUT THE INSTITUTION Independent Roman Catholic, coed. *Awards:* certificates, bachelor's, master's, and doctoral degrees. 69 undergraduate majors. *Total enrollment:* 9,983. Undergraduates: 6,111. Freshmen: 1,349. Federal methodology is used as a basis for awarding need-based institutional aid.

UNDERGRADUATE EXPENSES for 2017–2018 *Comprehensive fee:* $51,187 includes full-time tuition ($40,224), mandatory fees ($909), and room and board ($10,054). *College room only:* $6304. Room and board charges vary according to board plan and housing facility. *Part-time tuition:* $1257 per credit.

FRESHMAN FINANCIAL AID (Fall 2016, est.) 1,069 applied for aid; of those 76% were deemed to have need. 100% of freshmen with need received aid; of those 20% had need fully met. *Average percent of need met:* 87% (excluding resources awarded to replace EFC). *Average financial aid package:* $28,360 (excluding resources awarded to replace EFC). 18% of all full-time freshmen had no need and received non-need-based gift aid.

UNDERGRADUATE FINANCIAL AID (Fall 2016, est.) 3,965 applied for aid; of those 82% were deemed to have need. 100% of undergraduates with need received aid; of those 19% had need fully met. *Average percent of need met:* 84% (excluding resources awarded to replace EFC). *Average financial aid package:* $26,846 (excluding resources awarded to replace EFC). 11% of all full-time undergraduates had no need and received non-need-based gift aid.

GIFT AID (NEED-BASED) *Total amount:* $65,572,255 (8% federal, 9% state, 81% institutional, 2% external sources). *Receiving aid:* Freshmen: 60% (803); all full-time undergraduates: 55% (3,196). *Average award:* Freshmen: $22,127; Undergraduates: $20,378. *Scholarships, grants, and awards:* Federal Pell, FSEOG, state, private, college/university gift aid from institutional funds.

GIFT AID (NON-NEED-BASED) *Total amount:* $15,632,238 (94% institutional, 6% external sources). *Receiving aid:* Freshmen: 11% (154). Undergraduates: 8% (480). *Average award:* Freshmen: $18,888. Undergraduates: $17,372. *Scholarships, grants, and awards by category:* Academic interests/achievement: 2,009 awards ($36,005,149 total): biological sciences, business, education, English, general academic interests/achievements, humanities, international studies, mathematics, physical sciences, religion/biblical studies, social sciences. Creative arts/performance: 68 awards ($136,368 total): journalism/publications, music. Special characteristics: 193 awards ($5,864,925 total): children of educators, children of faculty/staff, general special characteristics. *Tuition waivers:* Full or partial for employees or children of employees, senior citizens. *ROTC:* Army cooperative, Naval cooperative, Air Force.

LOANS *Student loans:* $39,997,428 (60% need-based, 40% non-need-based). 64% of past graduating class borrowed through all loan programs. *Average indebtedness per student:* $40,307. *Average need-based loan:* Freshmen: $7860. Undergraduates: $8992. *Parent loans:* $4,606,095 (52% need-based, 48% non-need-based). *Programs:* Federal Direct (Subsidized and Unsubsidized Stafford, PLUS), Perkins, state, alternative loans.

WORK-STUDY *Federal work-study:* Total amount: $2,555,010; 860 jobs averaging $2971. *State or other work-study/employment:* Total amount: $5,223,632 (52% need-based, 48% non-need-based). 1,117 part-time jobs averaging $3044.

APPLYING FOR FINANCIAL AID *Required financial aid form:* FAFSA. *Financial aid deadline (priority):* 4/1. *Notification date:* Continuous beginning 3/1. Students must reply within 3 weeks of notification.

CONTACT Ms. Paula Benson, Associate Director of Student Financial Services, University of St. Thomas, 2115 Summit Avenue, MHC 152, St. Paul, MN 55105-1096, 651-962-6547 or toll-free 800-328-6819. *Fax:* 651-962-6599. *E-mail:* paula.benson@stthomas.edu.
Website: http://www.stthomas.edu/.

UNIVERSITY OF ST. THOMAS
Houston, TX

Tuition & fees: $32,660	Average undergraduate aid package: $24,458

ABOUT THE INSTITUTION Independent Roman Catholic, coed. *Awards:* diplomas, bachelor's, master's, and doctoral degrees. 37 undergraduate majors. *Total enrollment:* 3,312. Undergraduates: 1,814. Freshmen: 277. Federal methodology is used as a basis for awarding need-based institutional aid.

UNDERGRADUATE EXPENSES for 2017–2018 *Comprehensive fee:* $41,510 includes full-time tuition ($32,100), mandatory fees ($560), and room and board ($8850). *College room only:* $5360. Full-time tuition and fees vary according to course load. Room and board charges vary according to board plan and housing facility. *Part-time tuition:* $1070 per credit hour. Part-time tuition and fees vary according to course load.

FRESHMAN FINANCIAL AID (Fall 2016, est.) 226 applied for aid; of those 92% were deemed to have need. 100% of freshmen with need received aid; of those 13% had need fully met. *Average percent of need met:* 76% (excluding resources awarded to replace EFC). *Average financial aid package:* $28,300 (excluding resources awarded to replace EFC). 20% of all full-time freshmen had no need and received non-need-based gift aid.

UNDERGRADUATE FINANCIAL AID (Fall 2016, est.) 931 applied for aid; of those 95% were deemed to have need. 100% of undergraduates with need received aid; of those 10% had need fully met. *Average percent of need met:* 67% (excluding resources awarded to replace EFC). *Average financial aid package:* $24,458 (excluding resources awarded to replace EFC). 26% of all full-time undergraduates had no need and received non-need-based gift aid.

GIFT AID (NEED-BASED) *Total amount:* $19,223,665 (15% federal, 15% state, 69% institutional, 1% external sources). *Receiving aid:* Freshmen: 76% (208); all full-time undergraduates: 63% (869). *Average award:* Freshmen: $25,468; Undergraduates: $21,027. *Scholarships, grants, and awards:* Federal Pell, FSEOG, state, private, college/university gift aid from institutional funds, Academic Competitiveness Grants, National SMART Grants.

GIFT AID (NON-NEED-BASED) Total amount: $4,598,045 (97% institutional, 3% external sources). **Receiving aid:** Freshmen: 6% (17). Undergraduates: 4% (57). **Average award:** Freshmen: $12,426. Undergraduates: $11,769. **Scholarships, grants, and awards by category:** Academic interests/achievement: biological sciences, business, communication, computer science, education, English, foreign languages, general academic interests/achievements, health fields, humanities, international studies, mathematics, physical sciences, premedicine, religion/biblical studies, social sciences. Creative arts/performance: applied art and design, art/fine arts, general creative arts/performance, music, performing arts, theater/drama. Special achievements/activities: general special achievements/activities, leadership, religious involvement. Special characteristics: children of faculty/staff, general special characteristics, previous college experience, religious affiliation. **Tuition waivers:** Full or partial for employees or children of employees, senior citizens. **ROTC:** Army cooperative, Air Force cooperative.
LOANS Student loans: $5,164,413 (84% need-based, 16% non-need-based). 50% of past graduating class borrowed through all loan programs. Average indebtedness per student: $26,455. **Average need-based loan:** Freshmen: $3388. Undergraduates: $4778. **Parent loans:** $1,366,670 (40% need-based, 60% non-need-based). **Programs:** Federal Direct (Subsidized and Unsubsidized Stafford, PLUS), Perkins, state, private loans.
WORK-STUDY Federal work-study: Total amount: $384,000; 97 jobs averaging $3959. **State or other work-study/employment:** Total amount: $8000 (100% need-based). 2 part-time jobs averaging $4000.
ATHLETIC AWARDS Total amount: $506,526 (44% need-based, 56% non-need-based).
APPLYING FOR FINANCIAL AID Required financial aid form: FAFSA. **Financial aid deadline (priority):** 4/15. **Notification date:** Continuous beginning 2/15. Students must reply within 2 weeks of notification.
CONTACT Lynda McKendree, Dean of Scholarships and Financial Aid, University of St. Thomas, 3800 Montrose Boulevard, Houston, TX 77006-4696, 713-525-2170 or toll-free 800-856-8565. Fax: 713-525-2142. E-mail: finaid@stthom.edu. Website: http://www.stthom.edu/.

UNIVERSITY OF SAN DIEGO
San Diego, CA

Tuition & fees: $47,708	Average undergraduate aid package: $32,292

ABOUT THE INSTITUTION Independent Roman Catholic, coed. **Awards:** certificates, bachelor's, master's, and doctoral degrees. 43 undergraduate majors. **Total enrollment:** 8,508. Undergraduates: 5,711. Freshmen: 1,133. Federal methodology is used as a basis for awarding need-based institutional aid.
UNDERGRADUATE EXPENSES for 2017–2018 Application fee: $55. **Comprehensive fee:** $60,338 includes full-time tuition ($47,100), mandatory fees ($608), and room and board ($12,630). Room and board charges vary according to board plan and housing facility. **Part-time tuition:** $1625 per unit. **Part-time fees:** $524 per year. Part-time tuition and fees vary according to course load.
FRESHMAN FINANCIAL AID (Fall 2015) 788 applied for aid; of those 72% were deemed to have need. 98% of freshmen with need received aid; of those 14% had need fully met. **Average percent of need met:** 74% (excluding resources awarded to replace EFC). **Average financial aid package:** $32,725 (excluding resources awarded to replace EFC). 26% of all full-time freshmen had no need and received non-need-based gift aid.
UNDERGRADUATE FINANCIAL AID (Fall 2015) 3,283 applied for aid; of those 87% were deemed to have need. 98% of undergraduates with need received aid; of those 13% had need fully met. **Average percent of need met:** 70% (excluding resources awarded to replace EFC). **Average financial aid package:** $32,292 (excluding resources awarded to replace EFC). 17% of all full-time undergraduates had no need and received non-need-based gift aid.
GIFT AID (NEED-BASED) Total amount: $69,282,491 (15% federal, 7% state, 76% institutional, 2% external sources). **Receiving aid:** Freshmen: 50% (550); all full-time undergraduates: 51% (2,730). **Average award:** Freshmen: $26,943; Undergraduates: $25,655. **Scholarships, grants, and awards:** Federal Pell, FSEOG, state, private, college/university gift aid from institutional funds, Federal Nursing, TEACH Grants.
GIFT AID (NON-NEED-BASED) Total amount: $18,407,718 (17% federal, 81% institutional, 2% external sources). **Receiving aid:** Freshmen: 36% (397). Under-

graduates: 27% (1,436). **Average award:** Freshmen: $11,949. Undergraduates: $14,502. **Scholarships, grants, and awards by category:** Academic interests/achievement: 1,620 awards: general academic interests/achievements. Creative arts/performance: 19 awards: music. Special achievements/activities: 563 awards: leadership, religious involvement. Special characteristics: 97 awards: children of faculty/staff. **Tuition waivers:** Full or partial for employees or children of employees. **ROTC:** Army cooperative, Naval, Air Force cooperative.
LOANS Student loans: $22,167,341 (89% need-based, 11% non-need-based). 53% of past graduating class borrowed through all loan programs. Average indebtedness per student: $29,646. **Average need-based loan:** Freshmen: $5809. Undergraduates: $7061. **Parent loans:** $28,300,243 (49% need-based, 51% non-need-based). **Programs:** Federal Direct (Subsidized and Unsubsidized Stafford, PLUS), Perkins, college/university, non-federal loan programs.
WORK-STUDY Federal work-study: 514 jobs averaging $2098. **State or other work-study/employment:** Total amount: $2,870,229 (19% need-based, 81% non-need-based). Part-time jobs available.
ATHLETIC AWARDS Total amount: $7,011,435 (21% need-based, 79% non-need-based).
APPLYING FOR FINANCIAL AID Required financial aid form: FAFSA. **Financial aid deadline (priority):** 3/2. **Notification date:** Continuous beginning 3/1. Students must reply by 5/1 or within 3 weeks of notification.
CONTACT Judith Lewis Logue, Director of Financial Aid Services, University of San Diego, 5998 Alcala Park, San Diego, CA 92110-2492, 619-260-2700 or toll-free 800-248-4873. E-mail: jllogue@sandiego.edu. Website: http://www.sandiego.edu/.

UNIVERSITY OF SAN FRANCISCO
San Francisco, CA

Tuition & fees: $46,250	Average undergraduate aid package: $35,963

ABOUT THE INSTITUTION Independent Roman Catholic (Jesuit), coed. **Awards:** certificates, bachelor's, master's, and doctoral degrees. 100 undergraduate majors. **Total enrollment:** 11,018. Undergraduates: 6,745. Freshmen: 1,587. Federal methodology is used as a basis for awarding need-based institutional aid.
UNDERGRADUATE EXPENSES for 2017–2018 Application fee: $65. **Comprehensive fee:** $60,580 includes full-time tuition ($45,760), mandatory fees ($490), and room and board ($14,330). **College room only:** $9630. Full-time tuition and fees vary according to course load, degree level, location, program, and reciprocity agreements. Room and board charges vary according to board plan and housing facility. Part-time tuition and fees vary according to course load, degree level, location, program, and reciprocity agreements.
FRESHMAN FINANCIAL AID (Fall 2016, est.) 1,178 applied for aid; of those 83% were deemed to have need. 100% of freshmen with need received aid; of those 16% had need fully met. **Average percent of need met:** 55% (excluding resources awarded to replace EFC). **Average financial aid package:** $39,676 (excluding resources awarded to replace EFC). 20% of all full-time freshmen had no need and received non-need-based gift aid.
UNDERGRADUATE FINANCIAL AID (Fall 2016, est.) 3,971 applied for aid; of those 89% were deemed to have need. 100% of undergraduates with need received aid; of those 61% had need fully met. **Average percent of need met:** 77% (excluding resources awarded to replace EFC). **Average financial aid package:** $35,963 (excluding resources awarded to replace EFC). 16% of all full-time undergraduates had no need and received non-need-based gift aid.
GIFT AID (NEED-BASED) Total amount: $108,859,614 (8% federal, 10% state, 80% institutional, 2% external sources). **Receiving aid:** Freshmen: 51% (810); all full-time undergraduates: 46% (2,968). **Average award:** Freshmen: $24,144; Undergraduates: $21,451. **Scholarships, grants, and awards:** Federal Pell, FSEOG, state, private, college/university gift aid from institutional funds, Federal Nursing.
GIFT AID (NON-NEED-BASED) Total amount: $1,075,643 (89% institutional, 11% external sources). **Receiving aid:** Freshmen: 47% (747). Undergraduates: 34% (2,197). **Average award:** Freshmen: $14,636. Undergraduates: $13,208. **Scholarships, grants, and awards by category:** Academic interests/achievement: general academic interests/achievements. **Tuition waivers:** Full or partial for employees or children of employees. **ROTC:** Army, Air Force cooperative.
LOANS Student loans: $29,830,035 (100% need-based). 55% of past graduating class borrowed through all loan programs. Average indebtedness per student:

$34,114. *Average need-based loan:* Freshmen: $3472. Undergraduates: $4925. *Parent loans:* $17,691,797 (100% need-based). *Programs:* Federal Direct (Subsidized and Unsubsidized Stafford, PLUS), Perkins, Federal Nursing, college/university.
WORK-STUDY *Federal work-study:* Total amount: $4,558,300; 941 jobs averaging $4890. *State or other work-study/employment:* Total amount: $9,915,600 (100% need-based). 1,850 part-time jobs averaging $5361.
ATHLETIC AWARDS Total amount: $6,454,015 (100% need-based).
APPLYING FOR FINANCIAL AID *Required financial aid forms:* FAFSA, CSS Financial Aid PROFILE. *Financial aid deadline:* 2/15 (priority: 2/15). *Notification date:* Continuous beginning 4/1. Students must reply within 4 weeks of notification.
CONTACT Norman Caito, Director of Financial Aid Operations and Services, University of San Francisco, 2130 Fulton Street, LM 258, San Francisco, CA 94117-1080, 415-422-2624 or toll-free 800-CALL-USF. *E-mail:* caiton@usfca.edu. *Website:* http://www.usfca.edu/.

UNIVERSITY OF SCIENCE AND ARTS OF OKLAHOMA
Chickasha, OK

Tuition & fees: N/R	Average undergraduate aid package: $11,157

ABOUT THE INSTITUTION State-supported, coed. *Awards:* bachelor's degrees. 25 undergraduate majors. *Total enrollment:* 888. Undergraduates: 888. Freshmen: 223. Federal methodology is used as a basis for awarding need-based institutional aid.
UNDERGRADUATE EXPENSES for 2016–2017 *Application fee:* $40. *Tuition, state resident:* part-time $201 per credit hour. *Tuition, nonresident:* part-time $546 per credit hour. Room and board charges vary according to board plan and housing facility. *Payment plan:* Guaranteed tuition.
FRESHMAN FINANCIAL AID (Fall 2016, est.) 163 applied for aid; of those 84% were deemed to have need. 96% of freshmen with need received aid; of those 24% had need fully met. *Average percent of need met:* 73% (excluding resources awarded to replace EFC). *Average financial aid package:* $11,315 (excluding resources awarded to replace EFC). 10% of all full-time freshmen had no need and received non-need-based gift aid.
UNDERGRADUATE FINANCIAL AID (Fall 2016, est.) 589 applied for aid; of those 86% were deemed to have need. 97% of undergraduates with need received aid; of those 18% had need fully met. *Average percent of need met:* 68% (excluding resources awarded to replace EFC). *Average financial aid package:* $11,157 (excluding resources awarded to replace EFC). 13% of all full-time undergraduates had no need and received non-need-based gift aid.
GIFT AID (NEED-BASED) *Total amount:* $3,262,237 (51% federal, 27% state, 14% institutional, 8% external sources). *Receiving aid:* Freshmen: 61% (127); all full-time undergraduates: 59% (461). *Average award:* Freshmen: $10,007; Undergraduates: $9357. *Scholarships, grants, and awards:* Federal Pell, FSEOG, state, private, college/university gift aid from institutional funds, USAO Foundation Grants.
GIFT AID (NON-NEED-BASED) *Total amount:* $656,289 (1% federal, 24% state, 50% institutional, 25% external sources). *Receiving aid:* Freshmen: 11% (22). Undergraduates: 8% (59). *Average award:* Freshmen: $3112. Undergraduates: $3104. *Scholarships, grants, and awards by category:* Academic interests/achievement: 545 awards ($1,245,551 total): general academic interests/achievements. Creative arts/performance: 12 awards ($19,800 total): art/fine arts, music, theater/drama. Special achievements/activities: 9 awards ($7750 total): cheerleading/drum major. Special characteristics: 54 awards ($236,035 total): children of faculty/staff, international students, out-of-state students, previous college experience. *Tuition waivers:* Full or partial for employees or children of employees, senior citizens.
LOANS *Student loans:* $2,074,215 (74% need-based, 26% non-need-based). 63% of past graduating class borrowed through all loan programs. *Average indebtedness per student:* $22,760. *Average need-based loan:* Freshmen: $2678. Undergraduates: $3126. *Parent loans:* $191,316 (25% need-based, 75% non-need-based). *Programs:* Federal Direct (Subsidized and Unsubsidized Stafford, PLUS), college/university.
WORK-STUDY *Federal work-study:* Total amount: $215,402; 158 jobs averaging $1420.
ATHLETIC AWARDS Total amount: $2,031,117 (35% need-based, 65% non-need-based).

APPLYING FOR FINANCIAL AID *Financial aid deadline (priority):* 2/1. *Notification date:* Continuous beginning 11/1. Students must reply within 4 weeks of notification.
CONTACT Laura D. Coponiti, Director of Financial Aid, University of Science and Arts of Oklahoma, 1727 West Alabama, Chickasha, OK 73018-5322, 405-574-1350 or toll-free 800-933-8726. *Fax:* 405-574-1220. *E-mail:* lcoponiti@usao.edu. *Website:* http://www.usao.edu/.

THE UNIVERSITY OF SCRANTON
Scranton, PA

ABOUT THE INSTITUTION Independent Roman Catholic (Jesuit), coed. *Awards:* certificates, bachelor's, master's, and doctoral degrees. 66 undergraduate majors. *Total enrollment:* 5,380. Undergraduates: 3,867. Freshmen: 1,006.
GIFT AID (NEED-BASED) *Scholarships, grants, and awards:* Federal Pell, FSEOG, state, private, college/university gift aid from institutional funds.
GIFT AID (NON-NEED-BASED) *Scholarships, grants, and awards by category:* Academic interests/achievement: general academic interests/achievements, military science. Special characteristics: children of educators, children of faculty/staff, ethnic background, members of minority groups, religious affiliation, siblings of current students, veterans, veterans' children.
LOANS *Programs:* Federal Direct (Subsidized and Unsubsidized Stafford, PLUS), Perkins.
APPLYING FOR FINANCIAL AID *Required financial aid form:* FAFSA.
CONTACT Mr. William R. Burke, Director of Financial Aid, The University of Scranton, St. Thomas Hall, Scranton, PA 18510, 570-941-7701 or toll-free 888-SCRANTON. *Fax:* 570-941-4370. *E-mail:* finaid@scranton.edu. *Website:* http://www.scranton.edu/.

UNIVERSITY OF SIOUX FALLS
Sioux Falls, SD

Tuition & fees: $27,160	Average undergraduate aid package: $20,557

ABOUT THE INSTITUTION Independent American Baptist Churches in the USA, coed. 41 undergraduate majors. Federal methodology is used as a basis for awarding need-based institutional aid.
UNDERGRADUATE EXPENSES for 2016–2017 *Comprehensive fee:* $34,300 includes full-time tuition ($27,160) and room and board ($7140). Full-time tuition and fees vary according to course load, degree level, and program. Room and board charges vary according to board plan, housing facility, and student level. Part-time tuition and fees vary according to course load, degree level, and program.
FRESHMAN FINANCIAL AID (Fall 2016, est.) 247 applied for aid; of those 84% were deemed to have need. 100% of freshmen with need received aid; of those 29% had need fully met. *Average percent of need met:* 88% (excluding resources awarded to replace EFC). *Average financial aid package:* $22,150 (excluding resources awarded to replace EFC). 21% of all full-time freshmen had no need and received non-need-based gift aid.
UNDERGRADUATE FINANCIAL AID (Fall 2016, est.) 857 applied for aid; of those 86% were deemed to have need. 100% of undergraduates with need received aid; of those 24% had need fully met. *Average percent of need met:* 84% (excluding resources awarded to replace EFC). *Average financial aid package:* $20,557 (excluding resources awarded to replace EFC). 22% of all full-time undergraduates had no need and received non-need-based gift aid.
GIFT AID (NEED-BASED) *Total amount:* $10,865,979 (15% federal, 1% state, 80% institutional, 4% external sources). *Receiving aid:* Freshmen: 74% (201); all full-time undergraduates: 68% (696). *Average award:* Freshmen: $16,403; Undergraduates: $15,303. *Scholarships, grants, and awards:* Federal Pell, FSEOG, state, private, college/university gift aid from institutional funds.
GIFT AID (NON-NEED-BASED) *Total amount:* $3,740,384 (4% state, 89% institutional, 7% external sources). *Receiving aid:* Freshmen: 39% (105). Undergraduates: 29% (301). *Average award:* Freshmen: $13,527. Undergraduates: $12,385. *Scholarships, grants, and awards by category:* Academic interests/achievement: biological sciences, business, communication, computer science, education, engineering/technologies, English, general academic interests/achievements, humanities, mathematics, physical sciences, premedicine, religion/biblical studies, social

sciences. *Creative arts/performance:* art/fine arts, music, theater/drama. *Special achievements/activities:* cheerleading/drum major, leadership. *Special characteristics:* children and siblings of alumni, children of faculty/staff, international students, local/state students, out-of-state students, religious affiliation, siblings of current students, spouses of current students. *Tuition waivers:* Full or partial for employees or children of employees.

LOANS *Student loans:* $7,000,853 (68% need-based, 32% non-need-based). 83% of past graduating class borrowed through all loan programs. *Average indebtedness per student:* $31,148. *Average need-based loan:* Freshmen: $1926. Undergraduates: $5061. *Parent loans:* $612,594 (46% need-based, 54% non-need-based). *Programs:* Federal Direct (Subsidized and Unsubsidized Stafford, PLUS), Perkins, alternative loans.

WORK-STUDY *Federal work-study:* Total amount: $193,492; jobs available.

ATHLETIC AWARDS Total amount: $2,959,228 (50% need-based, 50% non-need-based).

APPLYING FOR FINANCIAL AID *Required financial aid form:* FAFSA. *Financial aid deadline (priority):* 1/1. *Notification date:* Continuous beginning 1/1. Students must reply within 4 weeks of notification.

CONTACT Rachel Gunn, Financial Aid Counselor, University of Sioux Falls, 1101 West 22nd Street, Sioux Falls, SD 57105-1699, 605-331-6623 or toll-free 800-888-1047. *Fax:* 605-331-6615. *E-mail:* rachel.gunn@usiouxfalls.edu.
Website: http://www.usiouxfalls.edu/.

UNIVERSITY OF SOUTH ALABAMA
Mobile, AL

Tuition & fees (AL res): $9060	Average undergraduate aid package: $9708

ABOUT THE INSTITUTION State-supported, coed. *Awards:* certificates, bachelor's, master's, and doctoral degrees. 52 undergraduate majors. *Total enrollment:* 16,443. Undergraduates: 11,755. Freshmen: 1,997. Federal methodology is used as a basis for awarding need-based institutional aid.

UNDERGRADUATE EXPENSES for 2016–2017 *Application fee:* $45. *Tuition, state resident:* full-time $9060; part-time $302 per credit hour. *Tuition, nonresident:* full-time $18,120; part-time $604 per credit hour. Full-time tuition and fees vary according to course load and program. Part-time tuition and fees vary according to course load and program. *College room and board:* $7340; *Room only:* $3850. Room and board charges vary according to board plan and housing facility.

FRESHMAN FINANCIAL AID (Fall 2015) 1,811 applied for aid; of those 76% were deemed to have need. 100% of freshmen with need received aid; of those 11% had need fully met. *Average percent of need met:* 54% (excluding resources awarded to replace EFC). *Average financial aid package:* $9894 (excluding resources awarded to replace EFC). 19% of all full-time freshmen had no need and received non-need-based gift aid.

UNDERGRADUATE FINANCIAL AID (Fall 2015) 7,167 applied for aid; of those 81% were deemed to have need. 100% of undergraduates with need received aid; of those 8% had need fully met. *Average percent of need met:* 50% (excluding resources awarded to replace EFC). *Average financial aid package:* $9708 (excluding resources awarded to replace EFC). 12% of all full-time undergraduates had no need and received non-need-based gift aid.

GIFT AID (NEED-BASED) *Total amount:* $21,213,984 (99% federal, 1% state). *Receiving aid:* Freshmen: 61% (1,261); all full-time undergraduates: 52% (4,892). *Average award:* Freshmen: $7184; Undergraduates: $6606. *Scholarships, grants, and awards:* Federal Pell, FSEOG, state, private, college/university gift aid from institutional funds.

GIFT AID (NON-NEED-BASED) *Total amount:* $12,915,494 (90% institutional, 10% external sources). *Receiving aid:* Freshmen: 61% (1,261). Undergraduates: 52% (4,892). *Average award:* Freshmen: $4923. Undergraduates: $5321. *Tuition waivers:* Full or partial for employees or children of employees. *ROTC:* Army, Air Force.

LOANS *Student loans:* $42,206,881 (44% need-based, 56% non-need-based). *Average need-based loan:* Freshmen: $3464. Undergraduates: $4348. *Parent loans:* $16,799,789 (100% non-need-based). *Programs:* Federal Direct (Subsidized and Unsubsidized Stafford, PLUS), Perkins, college/university.

WORK-STUDY *Federal work-study:* jobs available. *State or other work-study/employment:* Part-time jobs available.

ATHLETIC AWARDS Total amount: $5,151,289 (100% non-need-based).

APPLYING FOR FINANCIAL AID *Required financial aid form:* FAFSA. *Financial aid deadline (priority):* 5/31. *Notification date:* Continuous beginning 4/15.

CONTACT Financial Aid Office, University of South Alabama, 390 Alumni Circle, Meisler Hall, Suite 1200, Mobile, AL 36688-0001, 800-305-6828 or toll-free 800-872-5247. *Fax:* 251-460-6517. *E-mail:* finaid@southalabama.edu.
Website: http://www.southalabama.edu/.

UNIVERSITY OF SOUTH CAROLINA
Columbia, SC

Tuition & fees (SC res): $11,854	Average undergraduate aid package: $9400

ABOUT THE INSTITUTION State-supported, coed. *Awards:* certificates, associate, bachelor's, master's, and doctoral degrees. 76 undergraduate majors. *Total enrollment:* 34,099. Undergraduates: 25,556. Freshmen: 5,110. Federal methodology is used as a basis for awarding need-based institutional aid.

UNDERGRADUATE EXPENSES for 2016–2017 *Application fee:* $65. *Tuition, state resident:* full-time $11,454; part-time $477.25 per credit hour. *Tuition, nonresident:* full-time $30,882; part-time $1286.75 per credit hour. *Required fees:* full-time $400; $17 per term. Full-time tuition and fees vary according to program and reciprocity agreements. Part-time tuition and fees vary according to course load. *College room and board:* $9700; *Room only:* $6040. Room and board charges vary according to board plan, housing facility, and location.

FRESHMAN FINANCIAL AID (Fall 2016, est.) 4,125 applied for aid; of those 66% were deemed to have need. 97% of freshmen with need received aid; of those 31% had need fully met. *Average percent of need met:* 70% (excluding resources awarded to replace EFC). *Average financial aid package:* $8614 (excluding resources awarded to replace EFC). 38% of all full-time freshmen had no need and received non-need-based gift aid.

UNDERGRADUATE FINANCIAL AID (Fall 2016, est.) 16,266 applied for aid; of those 75% were deemed to have need. 97% of undergraduates with need received aid; of those 25% had need fully met. *Average percent of need met:* 75% (excluding resources awarded to replace EFC). *Average financial aid package:* $9400 (excluding resources awarded to replace EFC). 33% of all full-time undergraduates had no need and received non-need-based gift aid.

GIFT AID (NEED-BASED) *Total amount:* $74,277,483 (34% federal, 44% state, 16% institutional, 6% external sources). *Receiving aid:* Freshmen: 18% (947); all full-time undergraduates: 23% (5,392). *Average award:* Freshmen: $5453; Undergraduates: $5148. *Scholarships, grants, and awards:* Federal Pell, FSEOG, state, private, college/university gift aid from institutional funds, United Negro College Fund, Federal Nursing.

GIFT AID (NON-NEED-BASED) *Total amount:* $48,641,893 (53% state, 30% institutional, 17% external sources). *Receiving aid:* Freshmen: 47% (2,394). Undergraduates: 34% (7,882). *Average award:* Freshmen: $5886. Undergraduates: $6707. *Scholarships, grants, and awards by category: Academic interests/achievement:* area/ethnic studies, biological sciences, business, communication, computer science, education, engineering/technologies, English, foreign languages, general academic interests/achievements, health fields, humanities, international studies, library science, mathematics, military science, physical sciences, premedicine, religion/biblical studies, social sciences. *Creative arts/performance:* art/fine arts, dance, debating, journalism/publications, music, theater/drama. *Special achievements/activities:* cheerleading/drum major, community service, general special achievements/activities, leadership, memberships, religious involvement. *Special characteristics:* adult students, children and siblings of alumni, children of faculty/staff, children of union members/company employees, children of workers in trades, children with a deceased or disabled parent, ethnic background, first-generation college students, general special characteristics, handicapped students, international students, local/state students, members of minority groups, out-of-state students, religious affiliation, spouses of deceased or disabled public servants. *Tuition waivers:* Full or partial for employees or children of employees, senior citizens. *ROTC:* Army, Naval, Air Force.

LOANS *Student loans:* $113,064,055 (69% need-based, 31% non-need-based). 54% of past graduating class borrowed through all loan programs. *Average indebtedness per student:* $29,012. *Average need-based loan:* Freshmen: $3335. Undergraduates: $4351. *Parent loans:* $36,154,904 (51% need-based, 49% non-need-based).

Programs: Federal Direct (Subsidized and Unsubsidized Stafford, PLUS), Perkins, Federal Nursing.
WORK-STUDY *Federal work-study:* Total amount: $1,468,370; jobs available.
ATHLETIC AWARDS Total amount: $7,552,398 (40% need-based, 60% non-need-based).
APPLYING FOR FINANCIAL AID *Required financial aid form:* FAFSA. *Financial aid deadline (priority):* 4/1. *Notification date:* Continuous beginning 4/1.
CONTACT Joey C. Derrick, Director of Student Financial Aid and Scholarships, University of South Carolina, 1714 College Street, Columbia, SC 29208, 803-777-8134 or toll-free 800-868-5872. *Fax:* 803-777-0941. *E-mail:* jcderric@mailbox.sc.edu.
Website: http://www.sc.edu/.

UNIVERSITY OF SOUTH CAROLINA AIKEN
Aiken, SC

Tuition & fees (SC res): $10,196	Average undergraduate aid package: $10,964

ABOUT THE INSTITUTION State-supported, coed. *Awards:* bachelor's and master's degrees. 22 undergraduate majors. *Total enrollment:* 3,548. Undergraduates: 3,374. Freshmen: 623. Federal methodology is used as a basis for awarding need-based institutional aid.
UNDERGRADUATE EXPENSES for 2016–2017 *Application fee:* $45. *Tuition, state resident:* full-time $9882; part-time $411.75 per credit hour. *Tuition, nonresident:* full-time $19,788; part-time $824.50 per credit hour. *Required fees:* full-time $314; $11 per credit hour or $25 per term. Full-time tuition and fees vary according to reciprocity agreements. Part-time tuition and fees vary according to course load and reciprocity agreements. *College room and board:* $7466. Room and board charges vary according to board plan and housing facility.
FRESHMAN FINANCIAL AID (Fall 2015) 583 applied for aid; of those 73% were deemed to have need. 100% of freshmen with need received aid; of those 16% had need fully met. *Average percent of need met:* 63% (excluding resources awarded to replace EFC). *Average financial aid package:* $10,692 (excluding resources awarded to replace EFC). 4% of all full-time freshmen had no need and received non-need-based gift aid.
UNDERGRADUATE FINANCIAL AID (Fall 2015) 2,591 applied for aid; of those 72% were deemed to have need. 99% of undergraduates with need received aid; of those 17% had need fully met. *Average percent of need met:* 61% (excluding resources awarded to replace EFC). *Average financial aid package:* $10,964 (excluding resources awarded to replace EFC). 5% of all full-time undergraduates had no need and received non-need-based gift aid.
GIFT AID (NEED-BASED) *Total amount:* $11,264,172 (55% federal, 37% state, 6% institutional, 2% external sources). *Receiving aid:* Freshmen: 68% (398); all full-time undergraduates: 59% (1,534). *Average award:* Freshmen: $7426; Undergraduates: $6751. *Scholarships, grants, and awards:* Federal Pell, FSEOG, state, college/university gift aid from institutional funds.
GIFT AID (NON-NEED-BASED) *Total amount:* $4,367,709 (18% federal, 45% state, 7% institutional, 30% external sources). *Receiving aid:* Freshmen: 7% (42). Undergraduates: 6% (157). *Average award:* Freshmen: $1646. Undergraduates: $1866. *Scholarships, grants, and awards by category:* Academic interests/achievement: biological sciences, business, communication, computer science, education, engineering/technologies, English, general academic interests/achievements, health fields, humanities, mathematics, physical sciences, premedicine, social sciences. Creative arts/performance: art/fine arts, journalism/publications, music, theater/drama. Special achievements/activities: cheerleading/drum major, community service, hobbies/interests, leadership, memberships. Special characteristics: adult students, children and siblings of alumni, children of faculty/staff, children of public servants, ethnic background, first-generation college students, handicapped students, international students, local/state students, married students, members of minority groups, out-of-state students, previous college experience, veterans. *Tuition waivers:* Full or partial for employees or children of employees, senior citizens.
LOANS *Student loans:* $16,010,345 (74% need-based, 26% non-need-based). 75% of past graduating class borrowed through all loan programs. *Average indebtedness per student:* $31,289. *Average need-based loan:* Freshmen: $3189. Undergraduates: $4164. *Parent loans:* $2,746,222 (49% need-based, 51% non-need-based). *Programs:* Federal Direct (Subsidized and Unsubsidized Stafford, PLUS), Perkins.

WORK-STUDY *Federal work-study:* 78 jobs averaging $1776. *State or other work-study/employment:* Total amount: $614,765 (30% need-based, 70% non-need-based). 399 part-time jobs averaging $1469.
ATHLETIC AWARDS Total amount: $805,382 (37% need-based, 63% non-need-based).
APPLYING FOR FINANCIAL AID *Required financial aid form:* FAFSA. *Financial aid deadline (priority):* 3/15. *Notification date:* Continuous beginning 4/20. Students must reply within 2 weeks of notification.
CONTACT Mrs. Linda Aubrey-Higgins, Director of Financial Aid, University of South Carolina Aiken, 471 University Parkway, Aiken, SC 29801, 803-641-3476 or toll-free 888-WOW-USCA. *Fax:* 803-643-6840. *E-mail:* lindahi@usca.edu.
Website: http://www.usca.edu/.

UNIVERSITY OF SOUTH CAROLINA BEAUFORT
Bluffton, SC

ABOUT THE INSTITUTION State-supported, coed. *Awards:* associate and bachelor's degrees. 18 undergraduate majors. *Total enrollment:* 1,980. Undergraduates: 1,980. Freshmen: 517.
GIFT AID (NEED-BASED) *Scholarships, grants, and awards:* Federal Pell, FSEOG, state, private, college/university gift aid from institutional funds.
LOANS *Programs:* Federal Direct (Subsidized and Unsubsidized Stafford, PLUS).
WORK-STUDY *Federal work-study:* 21 jobs averaging $2800. *State or other work-study/employment:* Part-time jobs available.
APPLYING FOR FINANCIAL AID *Required financial aid form:* FAFSA.
CONTACT Heather Robinson, Financial Aid Administrative Assistant, University of South Carolina Beaufort, 801 Carteret Street, Beaufort, SC 29902, 843-521-3104. *Fax:* 843-521-3194. *E-mail:* uscbfina@uscb.edu.
Website: http://www.uscb.edu/.

UNIVERSITY OF SOUTH CAROLINA UPSTATE
Spartanburg, SC

Tuition & fees: N/R	Average undergraduate aid package: $9518

ABOUT THE INSTITUTION State-supported, coed. 31 undergraduate majors. Federal methodology is used as a basis for awarding need-based institutional aid.
FRESHMAN FINANCIAL AID (Fall 2016, est.) 643 applied for aid; of those 85% were deemed to have need. 99% of freshmen with need received aid; of those 6% had need fully met. *Average percent of need met:* 57% (excluding resources awarded to replace EFC). *Average financial aid package:* $10,329 (excluding resources awarded to replace EFC). 3% of all full-time freshmen had no need and received non-need-based gift aid.
UNDERGRADUATE FINANCIAL AID (Fall 2016, est.) 3,485 applied for aid; of those 88% were deemed to have need. 98% of undergraduates with need received aid; of those 5% had need fully met. *Average percent of need met:* 50% (excluding resources awarded to replace EFC). *Average financial aid package:* $9518 (excluding resources awarded to replace EFC). 3% of all full-time undergraduates had no need and received non-need-based gift aid.
GIFT AID (NEED-BASED) *Total amount:* $12,229,761 (89% federal, 11% state). *Receiving aid:* Freshmen: 55% (379); all full-time undergraduates: 52% (2,066). *Average award:* Freshmen: $5521; Undergraduates: $4969. *Scholarships, grants, and awards:* Federal Pell, FSEOG, state, private, college/university gift aid from institutional funds.
GIFT AID (NON-NEED-BASED) *Total amount:* $11,453,763 (81% state, 6% institutional, 13% external sources). *Receiving aid:* Freshmen: 72% (498). Undergraduates: 38% (1,495). *Average award:* Freshmen: $2458. Undergraduates: $1986. *Scholarships, grants, and awards by category:* Academic interests/achievement: 373 awards ($668,172 total): general academic interests/achievements. Special characteristics: first-generation college students.
LOANS *Student loans:* $27,607,432 (46% need-based, 54% non-need-based). 77% of past graduating class borrowed through all loan programs. *Average indebtedness*

per student: $27,338. **Average need-based loan:** Freshmen: $3253. Undergraduates: $4202. **Parent loans:** $4,605,738 (100% non-need-based). **Programs:** Federal Direct (Subsidized and Unsubsidized Stafford, PLUS), Perkins, state, private loans.
WORK-STUDY Federal work-study: Total amount: $42,651; 39 jobs averaging $1460.
ATHLETIC AWARDS Total amount: $1,495,031 (100% non-need-based).
APPLYING FOR FINANCIAL AID *Required financial aid form:* FAFSA. *Financial aid deadline (priority):* 3/1. *Notification date:* Continuous beginning 5/1. Students must reply within 2 weeks of notification.
CONTACT Bonnie Carson-Durham, Director of Financial Aid, University of South Carolina Upstate, 800 University Way, Spartanburg, SC 29303, 864-503-5340 or toll-free 800-277-8727. *Fax:* 864-503-5974. *E-mail:* bcarson@uscupstate.edu.
Website: http://www.uscupstate.edu/.

THE UNIVERSITY OF SOUTH DAKOTA
Vermillion, SD

Tuition & fees (SD res): $8457	Average undergraduate aid package: N/A

ABOUT THE INSTITUTION State-supported, coed. **Awards:** certificates, associate, bachelor's, master's, and doctoral degrees. 70 undergraduate majors. **Total enrollment:** 10,038. Undergraduates: 7,500. Freshmen: 1,243. Federal methodology is used as a basis for awarding need-based institutional aid.
UNDERGRADUATE EXPENSES for 2017–2018 *Application fee:* $20. *Tuition, state resident:* full-time $7155; part-time $238.50 per credit hour. *Tuition, nonresident:* full-time $10,386; part-time $346.20 per credit hour. *Required fees:* full-time $1302; $52.70 per term. Full-time tuition and fees vary according to course load. Part-time tuition and fees vary according to course load. *College room and board:* $7535; *Room only:* $4086. Room and board charges vary according to board plan and housing facility.
GIFT AID (NEED-BASED) *Scholarships, grants, and awards:* Federal Pell, FSEOG, state, private.
GIFT AID (NON-NEED-BASED) *Scholarships, grants, and awards by category:* Academic interests/achievement: biological sciences, business, communication, computer science, education, English, foreign languages, general academic interests/achievements, humanities, mathematics, military science, premedicine, social sciences. *Creative arts/performance:* art/fine arts, creative writing, debating, music, theater/drama. *Special achievements/activities:* leadership. *Special characteristics:* members of minority groups. **Tuition waivers:** Full or partial for children of alumni, employees or children of employees, senior citizens. **ROTC:** Army.
LOANS *Programs:* Federal Direct (Subsidized and Unsubsidized Stafford, PLUS), Perkins, Federal Nursing, college/university.
WORK-STUDY Federal work-study jobs available.
APPLYING FOR FINANCIAL AID *Required financial aid form:* FAFSA. *Financial aid deadline (priority):* 3/15. *Notification date:* Continuous beginning 3/1.
CONTACT Julie Pier, Director of Student Financial Aid, The University of South Dakota, Belbas Center, 414 East Clark Street, Vermillion, SD 57069, 605-677-5446 or toll-free 877-269-6837. *Fax:* 605-677-5238.
Website: http://www.usd.edu/.

UNIVERSITY OF SOUTHERN CALIFORNIA
Los Angeles, CA

Tuition & fees: $52,992	Average undergraduate aid package: $48,399

ABOUT THE INSTITUTION Independent, coed. **Awards:** certificates, bachelor's, master's, and doctoral degrees. 106 undergraduate majors. **Total enrollment:** 25,077. Undergraduates: 18,794. Freshmen: 3,068. Both federal and institutional methodology are used as a basis for awarding need-based institutional aid.
UNDERGRADUATE EXPENSES for 2016–2017 *Application fee:* $80. *One-time required fee:* $350. **Comprehensive fee:** $67,340 includes full-time tuition ($52,217), mandatory fees ($775), and room and board ($14,348). *College room only:* $8648. Full-time tuition and fees vary according to program. Room and board charges vary according to board plan and housing facility. **Part-time tuition:** $1733 per unit. Part-time tuition and fees vary according to course load and program. *Payment plan:* Tuition prepayment.
FRESHMAN FINANCIAL AID (Fall 2015) 1,701 applied for aid; of those 56% were deemed to have need. 100% of freshmen with need received aid; of those 80% had need fully met. **Average percent of need met:** 100% (excluding resources awarded to replace EFC). **Average financial aid package:** $51,311 (excluding resources awarded to replace EFC). 24% of all full-time freshmen had no need and received non-need-based gift aid.
UNDERGRADUATE FINANCIAL AID (Fall 2015) 9,013 applied for aid; of those 75% were deemed to have need. 100% of undergraduates with need received aid; of those 78% had need fully met. **Average percent of need met:** 100% (excluding resources awarded to replace EFC). **Average financial aid package:** $48,399 (excluding resources awarded to replace EFC). 19% of all full-time undergraduates had no need and received non-need-based gift aid.
GIFT AID (NEED-BASED) *Total amount:* $256,875,278 (8% federal, 8% state, 80% institutional, 4% external sources). **Receiving aid:** Freshmen: 28% (833); all full-time undergraduates: 34% (6,128). **Average award:** Freshmen: $36,995; Undergraduates: $35,011. **Scholarships, grants, and awards:** Federal Pell, FSEOG, state, private, college/university gift aid from institutional funds.
GIFT AID (NON-NEED-BASED) *Total amount:* $77,614,811 (87% institutional, 13% external sources). **Receiving aid:** Freshmen: 22% (636). Undergraduates: 18% (3,172). **Average award:** Freshmen: $21,761. Undergraduates: $19,665. **Scholarships, grants, and awards by category:** Academic interests/achievement: general academic interests/achievements. *Creative arts/performance:* art/fine arts, debating, music, theater/drama. *Special achievements/activities:* leadership. *Special characteristics:* children and siblings of alumni, children of faculty/staff. **Tuition waivers:** Full or partial for employees or children of employees. **ROTC:** Army, Naval, Air Force.
LOANS *Student loans:* $64,944,820 (63% need-based, 37% non-need-based). 41% of past graduating class borrowed through all loan programs. *Average indebtedness per student:* $27,882. **Average need-based loan:** Freshmen: $5058. Undergraduates: $6548. **Parent loans:** $63,484,223 (100% non-need-based). **Programs:** Federal Direct (Subsidized and Unsubsidized Stafford, PLUS), Perkins, college/university.
WORK-STUDY Federal work-study: jobs available.
ATHLETIC AWARDS Total amount: $19,873,092 (41% need-based, 59% non-need-based).
APPLYING FOR FINANCIAL AID *Required financial aid forms:* FAFSA, CSS Financial Aid PROFILE, noncustodial (divorced/separated) parent's statement, federal income tax form(s). *Financial aid deadline (priority):* 2/17. *Notification date:* 4/1. Students must reply by 5/1.
CONTACT Thomas McWhorter, Office of Financial Aid, University of Southern California, 700 Childs Way, Los Angeles, CA 90089-0914, 213-740-5445. *Fax:* 213-821-3796. *E-mail:* faodean@usc.edu.
Website: http://www.usc.edu/.

UNIVERSITY OF SOUTHERN INDIANA
Evansville, IN

Tuition & fees (IN res): $7165	Average undergraduate aid package: $9507

ABOUT THE INSTITUTION State-supported, coed. **Awards:** certificates, associate, bachelor's, master's, and doctoral degrees. 59 undergraduate majors. **Total enrollment:** 9,024. Undergraduates: 7,956. Freshmen: 1,685. Federal methodology is used as a basis for awarding need-based institutional aid.
UNDERGRADUATE EXPENSES for 2017–2018 *Application fee:* $40. *One-time required fee:* $500. *Tuition, state resident:* full-time $7105; part-time $236.82 per credit hour. *Tuition, nonresident:* full-time $17,347; part-time $578.22 per credit hour. *Required fees:* full-time $60; $22.75 per term. Full-time tuition and fees vary according to course level, course load, program, and reciprocity agreements. Part-time tuition and fees vary according to course level, course load, program, and reciprocity agreements. *College room and board:* $8896; *Room only:* $4856. Room and board charges vary according to board plan and housing facility.

FRESHMAN FINANCIAL AID (Fall 2016, est.) 1,545 applied for aid; of those 72% were deemed to have need. 100% of freshmen with need received aid; of those 11% had need fully met. *Average percent of need met:* 81% (excluding resources awarded to replace EFC). *Average financial aid package:* $9908 (excluding resources awarded to replace EFC). 27% of all full-time freshmen had no need and received non-need-based gift aid.

UNDERGRADUATE FINANCIAL AID (Fall 2016, est.) 6,108 applied for aid; of those 67% were deemed to have need. 99% of undergraduates with need received aid; of those 4% had need fully met. *Average percent of need met:* 74% (excluding resources awarded to replace EFC). *Average financial aid package:* $9507 (excluding resources awarded to replace EFC). 17% of all full-time undergraduates had no need and received non-need-based gift aid.

GIFT AID (NEED-BASED) *Total amount:* $24,741,372 (45% federal, 35% state, 17% institutional, 3% external sources). *Receiving aid:* Freshmen: 60% (990); all full-time undergraduates: 50% (3,348). *Average award:* Freshmen: $7997; Undergraduates: $7343. *Scholarships, grants, and awards:* Federal Pell, FSEOG, state, private, college/university gift aid from institutional funds, United Negro College Fund, Federal Nursing.

GIFT AID (NON-NEED-BASED) *Total amount:* $5,542,636 (80% institutional, 20% external sources). *Receiving aid:* Freshmen: 29% (484). Undergraduates: 27% (1,808). *Average award:* Freshmen: $3847. Undergraduates: $3449. *Scholarships, grants, and awards by category:* Academic interests/achievement: 2,129 awards ($3,960,319 total): biological sciences, business, education, engineering/technologies, general academic interests/achievements, health fields, humanities, mathematics, pre-medicine, social sciences. *Creative arts/performance:* 46 awards ($79,768 total): art/fine arts, creative writing, theater/drama. *Special achievements/activities:* leadership. *Special characteristics:* 658 awards ($3,582,712 total): adult students, children of faculty/staff, first-generation college students, general special characteristics, international students, members of minority groups, out-of-state students, veterans, veterans' children. *Tuition waivers:* Full or partial for employees or children of employees. *ROTC:* Army.

LOANS *Student loans:* $37,871,491 (84% need-based, 16% non-need-based). 69% of past graduating class borrowed through all loan programs. *Average indebtedness per student:* $24,762. *Average need-based loan:* Freshmen: $3238. Undergraduates: $4086. *Parent loans:* $3,777,379 (84% need-based, 16% non-need-based). *Programs:* Federal Direct (Subsidized and Unsubsidized Stafford, PLUS).

WORK-STUDY *Federal work-study:* Total amount: $213,874; 154 jobs averaging $1298.

ATHLETIC AWARDS Total amount: $1,270,403 (16% need-based, 84% non-need-based).

APPLYING FOR FINANCIAL AID *Required financial aid form:* FAFSA. *Financial aid deadline (priority):* 3/10. *Notification date:* Continuous beginning 4/1. Students must reply by 4/1.

CONTACT Mrs. Mary Harper, Financial Aid Office, University of Southern Indiana, 8600 University Boulevard, Evansville, IN 47712-3590, 812-464-1767 or toll-free 800-467-1965. *Fax:* 812-461-5305. *E-mail:* finaid@usi.edu. *Website:* http://www.usi.edu/.

UNIVERSITY OF SOUTHERN MAINE
Portland, ME

Tuition & fees (ME res): $8920	Average undergraduate aid package: $13,894

ABOUT THE INSTITUTION State-supported, coed. *Awards:* certificates, bachelor's, master's, and doctoral degrees. 48 undergraduate majors. *Total enrollment:* 7,855. Undergraduates: 6,189. Freshmen: 805. Federal methodology is used as a basis for awarding need-based institutional aid.

UNDERGRADUATE EXPENSES for 2016–2017 *Application fee:* $40. *Tuition, state resident:* full-time $7590; part-time $253 per credit hour. *Tuition, nonresident:* full-time $19,950; part-time $380 per credit hour. *Required fees:* full-time $1330; $1330 per year. Full-time tuition and fees vary according to course load, degree level, and reciprocity agreements. Part-time tuition and fees vary according to course load, degree level, and reciprocity agreements. *College room and board:* $9200; *Room only:* $5000. Room and board charges vary according to board plan and housing facility.

FRESHMAN FINANCIAL AID (Fall 2015) 623 applied for aid; of those 86% were deemed to have need. 100% of freshmen with need received aid; of those 47% had need fully met. *Average percent of need met:* 80% (excluding resources awarded

to replace EFC). *Average financial aid package:* $14,337 (excluding resources awarded to replace EFC). 9% of all full-time freshmen had no need and received non-need-based gift aid.

UNDERGRADUATE FINANCIAL AID (Fall 2015) 3,267 applied for aid; of those 85% were deemed to have need. 99% of undergraduates with need received aid; of those 59% had need fully met. *Average percent of need met:* 79% (excluding resources awarded to replace EFC). *Average financial aid package:* $13,894 (excluding resources awarded to replace EFC). 4% of all full-time undergraduates had no need and received non-need-based gift aid.

GIFT AID (NEED-BASED) *Total amount:* $22,545,454 (49% federal, 12% state, 31% institutional, 8% external sources). *Receiving aid:* Freshmen: 78% (514); all full-time undergraduates: 65% (2,400). *Average award:* Freshmen: $8477; Undergraduates: $7911. *Scholarships, grants, and awards:* Federal Pell, FSEOG, state, private, college/university gift aid from institutional funds.

GIFT AID (NON-NEED-BASED) *Total amount:* $1,104,850 (66% institutional, 34% external sources). *Receiving aid:* Freshmen: 5% (36). Undergraduates: 4% (135). *Average award:* Freshmen: $2865. Undergraduates: $3741. *Scholarships, grants, and awards by category:* Academic interests/achievement: general academic interests/achievements. *Creative arts/performance:* music, theater/drama. *Tuition waivers:* Full or partial for employees or children of employees. *ROTC:* Army cooperative, Air Force cooperative.

LOANS *Student loans:* $25,911,467 (75% need-based, 25% non-need-based). *Average need-based loan:* Freshmen: $5718. Undergraduates: $6939. *Parent loans:* $2,878,177 (30% need-based, 70% non-need-based). *Programs:* Federal Direct (Subsidized and Unsubsidized Stafford, PLUS), Perkins, Federal Nursing, college/university.

WORK-STUDY *Federal work-study:* jobs available.

APPLYING FOR FINANCIAL AID *Required financial aid form:* FAFSA. *Financial aid deadline (priority):* 2/15. *Notification date:* Continuous beginning 3/15.

CONTACT Mr. Keith P. Dubois, Director of Financial Aid, University of Southern Maine, 37 College Avenue, 107 Baily Hall, Gorham, ME 04038, 207-780-5122 or toll-free 800-800-4USM Ext. 5670. *Fax:* 207-780-5143. *E-mail:* dubois@maine.edu. *Website:* http://www.usm.maine.edu/.

UNIVERSITY OF SOUTHERN MISSISSIPPI
Hattiesburg, MS

Tuition & fees (MS res): $7854	Average undergraduate aid package: $13,604

ABOUT THE INSTITUTION State-supported, coed. *Awards:* certificates, bachelor's, master's, and doctoral degrees. 74 undergraduate majors. *Total enrollment:* 14,552. Undergraduates: 11,779. Freshmen: 1,558. Federal methodology is used as a basis for awarding need-based institutional aid.

UNDERGRADUATE EXPENSES for 2017–2018 *Application fee:* $40. *Tuition, state resident:* full-time $7854; part-time $305.59 per credit hour. *Tuition, nonresident:* full-time $9854; part-time $675.59 per credit hour. *Required fees:* $4.59 per credit hour or $55 per semester hour. Part-time tuition and fees vary according to course load and degree level. *College room and board:* $9012; *Room only:* $5222. Room and board charges vary according to board plan and housing facility.

FRESHMAN FINANCIAL AID (Fall 2015) 1,388 applied for aid; of those 84% were deemed to have need. 99% of freshmen with need received aid; of those 34% had need fully met. *Average percent of need met:* 74% (excluding resources awarded to replace EFC). *Average financial aid package:* $14,818 (excluding resources awarded to replace EFC). 11% of all full-time freshmen had no need and received non-need-based gift aid.

UNDERGRADUATE FINANCIAL AID (Fall 2015) 8,663 applied for aid; of those 88% were deemed to have need. 97% of undergraduates with need received aid; of those 24% had need fully met. *Average percent of need met:* 69% (excluding resources awarded to replace EFC). *Average financial aid package:* $13,604 (excluding resources awarded to replace EFC). 6% of all full-time undergraduates had no need and received non-need-based gift aid.

GIFT AID (NEED-BASED) *Total amount:* $36,914,804 (68% federal, 11% state, 17% institutional, 4% external sources). *Receiving aid:* Freshmen: 53% (809); all full-time undergraduates: 51% (5,218). *Average award:* Freshmen: $4999; Undergrad-

uates: $4671. **Scholarships, grants, and awards:** Federal Pell, FSEOG, state, private, college/university gift aid from institutional funds.

GIFT AID (NON-NEED-BASED) Total amount: $19,465,949 (14% federal, 13% state, 66% institutional, 7% external sources). **Receiving aid:** Freshmen: 53% (796). Undergraduates: 42% (4,217). **Average award:** Freshmen: $6732. Undergraduates: $5425. **Scholarships, grants, and awards by category:** Academic interests/achievement: general academic interests/achievements. Creative arts/performance: art/fine arts, dance, music, theater/drama. Special achievements/activities: cheerleading/drum major, leadership. Special characteristics: children and siblings of alumni, children of faculty/staff, ethnic background, local/state students, out-of-state students, veterans. **Tuition waivers:** Full or partial for children of alumni, employees or children of employees, senior citizens. **ROTC:** Army cooperative, Air Force.

LOANS Student loans: $57,995,118 (53% need-based, 47% non-need-based). 68% of past graduating class borrowed through all loan programs. Average indebtedness per student: $28,700. **Average need-based loan:** Freshmen: $3245. Undergraduates: $4714. **Parent loans:** $8,342,666 (52% need-based, 48% non-need-based). **Programs:** Federal Direct (Subsidized and Unsubsidized Stafford, PLUS).

WORK-STUDY Federal work-study: jobs available.

ATHLETIC AWARDS Total amount: $4,918,633 (47% need-based, 53% non-need-based).

APPLYING FOR FINANCIAL AID Required financial aid forms: FAFSA, institution's own form. **Financial aid deadline (priority):** 12/1. **Notification date:** Continuous beginning 12/15.

CONTACT Mr. David Williamson, Director of Financial Aid, University of Southern Mississippi, 118 College Drive #5101, Hattiesburg, MS 39406-0001, 601-266-4774. Fax: 601-266-5769. E-mail: financial.aid@usm.edu.
Website: http://www.usm.edu/.

UNIVERSITY OF SOUTH FLORIDA
Tampa, FL

Tuition & fees (FL res): $6410	Average undergraduate aid package: $11,240

ABOUT THE INSTITUTION State-supported, coed. **Awards:** associate, bachelor's, master's, and doctoral degrees. 80 undergraduate majors. **Total enrollment:** 42,861. Undergraduates: 31,461. Freshmen: 4,049. Federal methodology is used as a basis for awarding need-based institutional aid.

UNDERGRADUATE EXPENSES for 2017–2018 Application fee: $30. **Tuition, state resident:** full-time $6336; part-time $211.19 per credit hour. **Tuition, nonresident:** full-time $17,250; part-time $575.01 per credit hour. **Required fees:** full-time $74. **College room and board:** $9700.

FRESHMAN FINANCIAL AID (Fall 2015) 4,127 applied for aid; of those 76% were deemed to have need. 95% of freshmen with need received aid; of those 15% had need fully met. **Average percent of need met:** 65% (excluding resources awarded to replace EFC). **Average financial aid package:** $11,802 (excluding resources awarded to replace EFC). 16% of all full-time freshmen had no need and received non-need-based gift aid.

UNDERGRADUATE FINANCIAL AID (Fall 2015) 21,860 applied for aid; of those 83% were deemed to have need. 95% of undergraduates with need received aid; of those 10% had need fully met. **Average percent of need met:** 59% (excluding resources awarded to replace EFC). **Average financial aid package:** $11,240 (excluding resources awarded to replace EFC). 9% of all full-time undergraduates had no need and received non-need-based gift aid.

GIFT AID (NEED-BASED) Total amount: $114,254,918 (51% federal, 20% state, 26% institutional, 3% external sources). **Receiving aid:** Freshmen: 57% (2,726); all full-time undergraduates: 55% (15,171). **Average award:** Freshmen: $9005; Undergraduates: $7202. **Scholarships, grants, and awards:** Federal Pell, FSEOG, state, private, college/university gift aid from institutional funds, United Negro College Fund.

GIFT AID (NON-NEED-BASED) Total amount: $17,737,322 (51% state, 41% institutional, 8% external sources). **Receiving aid:** Freshmen: 4% (197). Undergraduates: 2% (628). **Average award:** Freshmen: $3070. Undergraduates: $2684. **Scholarships, grants, and awards by category:** Academic interests/achievement: 2,441 awards ($4,140,377 total): architecture, biological sciences, business, communication, computer science, education, engineering/technologies, English, foreign languages, general academic interests/achievements, health fields, home economics, humanities, international studies, library science, mathematics, military science,

physical sciences, premedicine, religion/biblical studies, social sciences. Creative arts/performance: 340 awards ($396,720 total): applied art and design, art/fine arts, cinema/film/broadcasting, creative writing, dance, music, performing arts, theater/drama. Special characteristics: 318 awards ($1,020,548 total): first-generation college students. **ROTC:** Army, Naval, Air Force.

LOANS Student loans: $112,247,872 (85% need-based, 15% non-need-based). 57% of past graduating class borrowed through all loan programs. Average indebtedness per student: $22,276. **Average need-based loan:** Freshmen: $4797. Undergraduates: $6579. **Parent loans:** $15,220,497 (44% need-based, 56% non-need-based). **Programs:** Federal Direct (Subsidized and Unsubsidized Stafford, PLUS), Perkins, college/university.

WORK-STUDY Federal work-study: 773 jobs averaging $3213. **State or other work-study/employment:** Total amount: $460,614 (100% need-based). 286 part-time jobs averaging $1611.

ATHLETIC AWARDS Total amount: $5,080,626 (42% need-based, 58% non-need-based).

APPLYING FOR FINANCIAL AID Required financial aid form: FAFSA. **Financial aid deadline (priority):** 1/1. **Notification date:** Continuous beginning 12/1.

CONTACT Ms. Billie Jo Hamilton, Director of Student Financial Aid, University of South Florida, 4202 East Fowler Avenue, SVC 1102, Tampa, FL 33620-6960, 813-974-4700. Fax: 813-974-5144. E-mail: bjhamilton@usf.edu.
Website: http://www.usf.edu/.

UNIVERSITY OF SOUTH FLORIDA, ST. PETERSBURG
St. Petersburg, FL

CONTACT Financial Aid Office, University of South Florida, St. Petersburg, 140 Seventh Ave S., St. Petersburg, FL 33701, 727-873-7748.
Website: http://www.stpt.usf.edu/.

UNIVERSITY OF SOUTH FLORIDA SARASOTA-MANATEE
Sarasota, FL

CONTACT Financial Aid Office, University of South Florida Sarasota-Manatee, 8350 N Tamiami Trail, Sarasota, FL 34243, 941-359-4200.
Website: http://www.usfsm.edu/.

THE UNIVERSITY OF TAMPA
Tampa, FL

Tuition & fees: $27,740	Average undergraduate aid package: $17,011

ABOUT THE INSTITUTION Independent, coed. **Awards:** certificates, bachelor's, and master's degrees. 61 undergraduate majors. **Total enrollment:** 8,235. Undergraduates: 7,382. Freshmen: 1,877. Federal methodology is used as a basis for awarding need-based institutional aid.

UNDERGRADUATE EXPENSES for 2016–2017 Application fee: $40. **One-time required fee:** $85. **Comprehensive fee:** $37,936 includes full-time tuition ($25,858), mandatory fees ($1882), and room and board ($10,196). **College room only:** $5384. Full-time tuition and fees vary according to class time, course load, and program. Room and board charges vary according to board plan and housing facility. **Part-time tuition:** $550 per credit hour. **Part-time fees:** $40 per term. Part-time tuition and fees vary according to class time, course load, and program.

FRESHMAN FINANCIAL AID (Fall 2016, est.) 1,588 applied for aid; of those 78% were deemed to have need. 100% of freshmen with need received aid; of those 10% had need fully met. **Average percent of need met:** 63% (excluding resources awarded to replace EFC). **Average financial aid package:** $17,039 (excluding

resources awarded to replace EFC). 29% of all full-time freshmen had no need and received non-need-based gift aid.

UNDERGRADUATE FINANCIAL AID (Fall 2016, est.) 5,133 applied for aid; of those 82% were deemed to have need. 100% of undergraduates with need received aid; of those 9% had need fully met. *Average percent of need met:* 61% (excluding resources awarded to replace EFC). *Average financial aid package:* $17,011 (excluding resources awarded to replace EFC). 29% of all full-time undergraduates had no need and received non-need-based gift aid.

GIFT AID (NEED-BASED) *Total amount:* $47,426,571 (15% federal, 9% state, 74% institutional, 2% external sources). *Receiving aid:* Freshmen: 63% (1,197); all full-time undergraduates: 58% (4,109). *Average award:* Freshmen: $14,237; Undergraduates: $13,377. *Scholarships, grants, and awards:* Federal Pell, FSEOG, state, private, college/university gift aid from institutional funds.

GIFT AID (NON-NEED-BASED) *Total amount:* $16,456,090 (10% state, 88% institutional, 2% external sources). *Receiving aid:* Freshmen: 61% (1,158). Undergraduates: 56% (4,019). *Average award:* Freshmen: $8364. Undergraduates: $7885. *Scholarships, grants, and awards by category:* Academic interests/achievement: 5,686 awards ($44,648,387 total): biological sciences, English, general academic interests/achievements, international studies, military science, physical sciences, premedicine, social sciences. *Creative arts/performance:* 147 awards ($305,000 total): art/fine arts, creative writing, dance, journalism/publications, music, performing arts, theater/drama. *Special achievements/activities:* 238 awards ($257,500 total): general special achievements/activities, leadership, memberships. *Special characteristics:* 507 awards ($3,293,735 total): children and siblings of alumni, children of faculty/staff, international students, veterans. *Tuition waivers:* Full or partial for employees or children of employees. *ROTC:* Army, Naval cooperative, Air Force cooperative.

LOANS *Student loans:* $35,843,334 (85% need-based, 15% non-need-based). 60% of past graduating class borrowed through all loan programs. *Average indebtedness per student:* $31,448. *Average need-based loan:* Freshmen: $3437. Undergraduates: $4358. *Parent loans:* $21,532,869 (88% need-based, 12% non-need-based). *Programs:* Federal Direct (Subsidized and Unsubsidized Stafford, PLUS), Perkins, college/university, private loans.

WORK-STUDY *Federal work-study:* Total amount: $235,420; 308 jobs averaging $2000. *State or other work-study/employment:* Total amount: $1,300,753 (3% need-based, 97% non-need-based). 212 part-time jobs averaging $2000.

ATHLETIC AWARDS Total amount: $2,433,934 (57% need-based, 43% non-need-based).

APPLYING FOR FINANCIAL AID *Required financial aid form:* FAFSA. *Financial aid deadline:* Continuous. *Notification date:* Continuous beginning 10/1. Students must reply by 5/1.

CONTACT Jacqueline M. LaTorella, Director of Financial Aid, The University of Tampa, 401 West Kennedy Boulevard, Box E, Tampa, FL 33606-1490, 813-253-6219 or toll-free 888-646-2738 (in-state), 888-MINARET (out-of-state). *Fax:* 813-258-7439. *E-mail:* finaid@ut.edu.
Website: http://www.ut.edu/.

THE UNIVERSITY OF TENNESSEE
Knoxville, TN

Tuition & fees (TN res): $12,724	Average undergraduate aid package: $13,012

ABOUT THE INSTITUTION State-supported, coed. *Awards:* certificates, bachelor's, master's, and doctoral degrees. 76 undergraduate majors. *Total enrollment:* 28,052. Undergraduates: 22,139. Freshmen: 4,851. Federal methodology is used as a basis for awarding need-based institutional aid.

UNDERGRADUATE EXPENSES for 2016–2017 *Application fee:* $50. *Tuition, state resident:* full-time $10,914; part-time $362 per credit hour. *Tuition, nonresident:* full-time $29,104; part-time $1121 per credit hour. *Required fees:* full-time $1810; $87 per credit hour. Full-time tuition and fees vary according to course level, location, program, reciprocity agreements, and student level. Part-time tuition and fees vary according to course level, location, program, reciprocity agreements, and student level. *College room and board:* $10,238. Room and board charges vary according to board plan and housing facility.

FRESHMAN FINANCIAL AID (Fall 2016, est.) 4,585 applied for aid; of those 63% were deemed to have need. 100% of freshmen with need received aid; of those 21% had need fully met. *Average percent of need met:* 61% (excluding resources awarded to replace EFC). *Average financial aid package:* $13,706 (excluding

---

resources awarded to replace EFC). 15% of all full-time freshmen had no need and received non-need-based gift aid.

UNDERGRADUATE FINANCIAL AID (Fall 2016, est.) 18,288 applied for aid; of those 66% were deemed to have need. 99% of undergraduates with need received aid; of those 19% had need fully met. *Average percent of need met:* 57% (excluding resources awarded to replace EFC). *Average financial aid package:* $13,012 (excluding resources awarded to replace EFC). 12% of all full-time undergraduates had no need and received non-need-based gift aid.

GIFT AID (NEED-BASED) *Total amount:* $139,768,107 (19% federal, 39% state, 39% institutional, 3% external sources). *Receiving aid:* Freshmen: 56% (2,726); all full-time undergraduates: 51% (10,557). *Average award:* Freshmen: $11,488; Undergraduates: $9760. *Scholarships, grants, and awards:* Federal Pell, FSEOG, state, private, college/university gift aid from institutional funds.

GIFT AID (NON-NEED-BASED) *Average award:* Freshmen: $5989. Undergraduates: $5348. *Scholarships, grants, and awards by category:* Academic interests/achievement: 2,269 awards ($7,032,581 total): agriculture, architecture, business, communication, computer science, education, engineering/technologies, general academic interests/achievements, home economics, humanities, international studies, library science, military science, social sciences. *Creative arts/performance:* 189 awards ($291,884 total): art/fine arts. *Tuition waivers:* Full or partial for employees or children of employees, senior citizens. *ROTC:* Army, Air Force.

LOANS *Student loans:* $80,540,337 (79% need-based, 21% non-need-based). 51% of past graduating class borrowed through all loan programs. *Average indebtedness per student:* $24,420. *Average need-based loan:* Freshmen: $5206. Undergraduates: $6755. *Parent loans:* $29,242,057 (100% need-based). *Programs:* Federal Direct (Subsidized and Unsubsidized Stafford, PLUS), Perkins, state, college/university.

WORK-STUDY *Federal work-study:* Total amount: $1,985,319; 772 jobs averaging $2502.

ATHLETIC AWARDS Total amount: $8,556,558 (100% need-based).

APPLYING FOR FINANCIAL AID *Required financial aid form:* FAFSA. *Financial aid deadline (priority):* 2/15. *Notification date:* Continuous beginning 3/15. Students must reply within 3 weeks of notification.

CONTACT Jeffery Gerkin, Office of Financial Aid and Scholarships, The University of Tennessee, 116 Student Services Building, Knoxville, TN 37996-0210, 865-974-1111. *Fax:* 865-974-2175. *E-mail:* finaid@utk.edu.
Website: http://www.utk.edu/.

THE UNIVERSITY OF TENNESSEE AT CHATTANOOGA
Chattanooga, TN

Tuition & fees (TN res): $8544	Average undergraduate aid package: $9747

ABOUT THE INSTITUTION State-supported, coed. *Awards:* certificates, bachelor's, master's, and doctoral degrees. 50 undergraduate majors. *Total enrollment:* 11,533. Undergraduates: 10,170. Freshmen: 2,080. Federal methodology is used as a basis for awarding need-based institutional aid.

UNDERGRADUATE EXPENSES for 2016–2017 *Application fee:* $30. *Tuition, state resident:* full-time $6768; part-time $282 per credit hour. *Tuition, nonresident:* full-time $22,886; part-time $954 per credit hour. *Required fees:* full-time $1776; $264 per credit hour. Full-time tuition and fees vary according to degree level. Part-time tuition and fees vary according to degree level. *College room and board:* $8676; *Room only:* $5226. Room and board charges vary according to board plan, housing facility, and location.

FRESHMAN FINANCIAL AID (Fall 2016, est.) 1,963 applied for aid; of those 65% were deemed to have need. 99% of freshmen with need received aid; of those 19% had need fully met. *Average percent of need met:* 72% (excluding resources awarded to replace EFC). *Average financial aid package:* $10,601 (excluding resources awarded to replace EFC). 13% of all full-time freshmen had no need and received non-need-based gift aid.

UNDERGRADUATE FINANCIAL AID (Fall 2016, est.) 7,926 applied for aid; of those 70% were deemed to have need. 99% of undergraduates with need received aid; of those 14% had need fully met. *Average percent of need met:* 64% (excluding resources awarded to replace EFC). *Average financial aid package:* $9747 (excluding resources awarded to replace EFC). 11% of all full-time undergraduates had no need and received non-need-based gift aid.

GIFT AID (NEED-BASED) *Total amount:* $34,313,192 (42% federal, 44% state, 13% institutional, 1% external sources). *Receiving aid:* Freshmen: 59% (1,215); all full-time undergraduates: 53% (4,671). *Average award:* Freshmen: $8382; Undergraduates: $7658. *Scholarships, grants, and awards:* Federal Pell, FSEOG, state, private, college/university gift aid from institutional funds.

GIFT AID (NON-NEED-BASED) *Total amount:* $11,697,922 (63% state, 32% institutional, 5% external sources). *Receiving aid:* Freshmen: 2% (49). Undergraduates: 2% (188). *Average award:* Freshmen: $3468. Undergraduates: $2994. *Scholarships, grants, and awards by category: Academic interests/achievement:* biological sciences, business, communication, education, engineering/technologies, English, general academic interests/achievements, home economics, mathematics, military science, physical sciences. *Creative arts/performance:* art/fine arts, cinema/film/broadcasting, journalism/publications, music, performing arts, theater/drama. *Special achievements/activities:* cheerleading/drum major, community service, memberships, religious involvement. *Special characteristics:* children and siblings of alumni, children of faculty/staff, children of union members/company employees, children with a deceased or disabled parent, ethnic background, handicapped students, religious affiliation. *Tuition waivers:* Full or partial for employees or children of employees, senior citizens. *ROTC:* Army.

LOANS *Student loans:* $51,647,012 (62% need-based, 38% non-need-based). 58% of past graduating class borrowed through all loan programs. *Average indebtedness per student:* $22,917. *Average need-based loan:* Freshmen: $3245. Undergraduates: $3998. *Parent loans:* $6,289,482 (39% need-based, 61% non-need-based). *Programs:* Federal Direct (Subsidized and Unsubsidized Stafford, PLUS), Perkins, private loans.

WORK-STUDY *Federal work-study:* Total amount: $385,593; jobs available. *State or other work-study/employment:* Total amount: $399,000 (26% need-based, 74% non-need-based). Part-time jobs available.

ATHLETIC AWARDS Total amount: $4,250,236 (42% need-based, 58% non-need-based).

APPLYING FOR FINANCIAL AID *Required financial aid forms:* FAFSA, institutional scholarship application form. *Financial aid deadline:* 5/1. *Notification date:* Continuous beginning 3/1. Students must reply within 4 weeks of notification.

CONTACT Jennifer Buckles, Director of Financial Aid, The University of Tennessee at Chattanooga, 615 McCallie Avenue, Chattanooga, TN 37403-2598, 423-425-4677 or toll-free 800-882-6627. *Fax:* 423-425-2292. *E-mail:* jennifer-buckles@utc.edu. *Website:* http://www.utc.edu/.

(excluding resources awarded to replace EFC). 5% of all full-time undergraduates had no need and received non-need-based gift aid.

GIFT AID (NEED-BASED) *Total amount:* $17,188,614 (75% federal, 23% state, 2% external sources). *Receiving aid:* Freshmen: 50% (470); all full-time undergraduates: 51% (2,511). *Average award:* Freshmen: $6905; Undergraduates: $6286. *Scholarships, grants, and awards:* Federal Pell, FSEOG, state, private, college/university gift aid from institutional funds.

GIFT AID (NON-NEED-BASED) *Total amount:* $15,183,114 (57% state, 23% institutional, 20% external sources). *Receiving aid:* Freshmen: 76% (710). Undergraduates: 74% (3,664). *Average award:* Freshmen: $1646. Undergraduates: $2024. *Scholarships, grants, and awards by category: Academic interests/achievement:* 213 awards ($187,074 total): agriculture, biological sciences, business, communication, computer science, education, engineering/technologies, English, foreign languages, general academic interests/achievements, health fields, home economics, humanities, international studies, mathematics, military science, physical sciences, premedicine, social sciences. *Creative arts/performance:* 15 awards ($13,750 total): art/fine arts, cinema/film/broadcasting, creative writing, journalism/publications, music, theater/drama. *Special achievements/activities:* 32 awards ($55,386 total): cheerleading/drum major, general special achievements/activities, junior miss, leadership, rodeo. *Special characteristics:* 248 awards ($571,970 total): adult students, children and siblings of alumni, children of educators, children of faculty/staff, children of public servants, children of union members/company employees, ethnic background, general special characteristics, local/state students, members of minority groups, out-of-state students, previous college experience. *Tuition waivers:* Full or partial for employees or children of employees, senior citizens. *ROTC:* Army.

LOANS *Student loans:* $23,142,352 (49% need-based, 51% non-need-based). 66% of past graduating class borrowed through all loan programs. *Average indebtedness per student:* $28,077. *Average need-based loan:* Freshmen: $3509. Undergraduates: $4396. *Parent loans:* $2,526,203 (100% non-need-based). *Programs:* Federal Direct (Subsidized and Unsubsidized Stafford, PLUS), Perkins.

WORK-STUDY *Federal work-study:* Total amount: $831,296; 324 jobs averaging $2566.

ATHLETIC AWARDS Total amount: $3,505,396 (100% non-need-based).

APPLYING FOR FINANCIAL AID *Required financial aid form:* FAFSA. *Financial aid deadline (priority):* 2/15. *Notification date:* Continuous beginning 3/15.

CONTACT Amy J. Mistric, Assistant Director, The University of Tennessee at Martin, 205 Administration Building, Martin, TN 38238-1000, 731-881-7031 or toll-free 800-829-8861. *Fax:* 731-881-7036. *E-mail:* amistric@utm.edu. *Website:* http://www.utm.edu/.

THE UNIVERSITY OF TENNESSEE AT MARTIN
Martin, TN

Tuition & fees (TN res): $9088	Average undergraduate aid package: $11,218

ABOUT THE INSTITUTION State-supported, coed. *Awards:* bachelor's and master's degrees. 85 undergraduate majors. *Total enrollment:* 6,705. Undergraduates: 6,279. Freshmen: 946. Federal methodology is used as a basis for awarding need-based institutional aid.

UNDERGRADUATE EXPENSES for 2016–2017 *Application fee:* $30. *Tuition, state resident:* full-time $7680; part-time $294 per credit hour. *Tuition, nonresident:* full-time $13,440; part-time $534 per credit hour. *Required fees:* full-time $1408; $59 per credit hour. Full-time tuition and fees vary according to student level. Part-time tuition and fees vary according to course level and course load. *College room and board:* $5788; *Room only:* $2600. Room and board charges vary according to board plan and housing facility.

FRESHMAN FINANCIAL AID (Fall 2016, est.) 902 applied for aid; of those 79% were deemed to have need. 100% of freshmen with need received aid; of those 21% had need fully met. *Average percent of need met:* 42% (excluding resources awarded to replace EFC). *Average financial aid package:* $12,298 (excluding resources awarded to replace EFC). 10% of all full-time freshmen had no need and received non-need-based gift aid.

UNDERGRADUATE FINANCIAL AID (Fall 2016, est.) 4,504 applied for aid; of those 82% were deemed to have need. 99% of undergraduates with need received aid; of those 18% had need fully met. *Average percent of need met:* 44% (excluding resources awarded to replace EFC). *Average financial aid package:* $11,218.

THE UNIVERSITY OF TEXAS AT ARLINGTON
Arlington, TX

Tuition & fees (TX res): $9616	Average undergraduate aid package: $10,350

ABOUT THE INSTITUTION State-supported, coed. 66 undergraduate majors. Federal methodology is used as a basis for awarding need-based institutional aid.

UNDERGRADUATE EXPENSES for 2016–2017 *Tuition, state resident:* full-time $7350. *Tuition, nonresident:* full-time $21,194. *Required fees:* full-time $2266. Full-time tuition and fees vary according to course load, degree level, location, program, and reciprocity agreements. Part-time tuition and fees vary according to course load, degree level, location, program, and reciprocity agreements. *College room and board:* $8397; *Room only:* $4649. Room and board charges vary according to board plan and housing facility.

FRESHMAN FINANCIAL AID (Fall 2015) 2,543 applied for aid; of those 85% were deemed to have need. 90% of freshmen with need received aid; of those 15% had need fully met. *Average percent of need met:* 65% (excluding resources awarded to replace EFC). *Average financial aid package:* $10,555 (excluding resources awarded to replace EFC). 7% of all full-time freshmen had no need and received non-need-based gift aid.

UNDERGRADUATE FINANCIAL AID (Fall 2015) 14,205 applied for aid; of those 92% were deemed to have need. 96% of undergraduates with need received aid; of those 11% had need fully met. *Average percent of need met:* 61% (excluding resources awarded to replace EFC). *Average financial aid package:* $10,350

(excluding resources awarded to replace EFC). 3% of all full-time undergraduates had no need and received non-need-based gift aid.

GIFT AID (NEED-BASED) *Total amount:* $98,613,880 (45% federal, 19% state, 27% institutional, 9% external sources). *Receiving aid:* Freshmen: 51% (1,388); all full-time undergraduates: 62% (10,160). *Average award:* Freshmen: $7427; Undergraduates: $7001. *Scholarships, grants, and awards:* Federal Pell, FSEOG, state, private, college/university gift aid from institutional funds, United Negro College Fund.

GIFT AID (NON-NEED-BASED) *Total amount:* $1,755,959 (81% institutional, 19% external sources). *Receiving aid:* Freshmen: 42% (1,144). Undergraduates: 32% (5,225). *Average award:* Freshmen: $5465. Undergraduates: $5139. *Scholarships, grants, and awards by category:* Academic interests/achievement: architecture, biological sciences, business, communication, computer science, education, engineering/technologies, English, foreign languages, general academic interests/achievements, health fields, humanities, international studies, mathematics, military science, physical sciences, social sciences. *Creative arts/performance:* journalism/publications, music, theater/drama. *Special achievements/activities:* cheerleading/drum major, community service, general special achievements/activities, leadership. *Special characteristics:* children with a deceased or disabled parent, first-generation college students, general special characteristics, handicapped students, public servants. *Tuition waivers:* Full or partial for senior citizens.

LOANS *Student loans:* $104,955,300 (92% need-based, 8% non-need-based). 83% of past graduating class borrowed through all loan programs. *Average indebtedness per student:* $15,559. *Average need-based loan:* Freshmen: $3587. Undergraduates: $4032. *Parent loans:* $4,576,115 (82% need-based, 18% non-need-based). *Programs:* Federal Direct (Subsidized and Unsubsidized Stafford, PLUS), Perkins, state.

WORK-STUDY *Federal work-study:* jobs available. *State or other work-study/employment:* Total amount: $148,890 (100% need-based). Part-time jobs available.

ATHLETIC AWARDS Total amount: $2,428,124 (97% need-based, 3% non-need-based).

APPLYING FOR FINANCIAL AID *Required financial aid form:* FAFSA. *Financial aid deadline (priority):* 4/17. *Notification date:* Continuous beginning 4/17. Students must reply within 3 weeks of notification.

CONTACT Karen Krause, Director of Financial Aid, The University of Texas at Arlington, UTA Box 19199, Arlington, TX 76019, 817-272-3561. *Fax:* 817-272-3555. *E-mail:* kkrause@uta.edu.

Website: http://www.uta.edu/.

THE UNIVERSITY OF TEXAS AT AUSTIN
Austin, TX

Tuition & fees (TX res): $10,144	Average undergraduate aid package: $12,283

ABOUT THE INSTITUTION State-supported, coed. *Awards:* certificates, bachelor's, master's, and doctoral degrees. 164 undergraduate majors. *Total enrollment:* 51,331. Undergraduates: 40,168. Freshmen: 8,719. Federal methodology is used as a basis for awarding need-based institutional aid.

UNDERGRADUATE EXPENSES for 2016–2017 *Application fee:* $75. *Tuition, state resident:* full-time $10,144. *Tuition, nonresident:* full-time $35,796. Full-time tuition and fees vary according to course load and program. Part-time tuition and fees vary according to course load and program. *College room and board:* $10,070. Room and board charges vary according to housing facility. *Payment plan:* Guaranteed tuition.

FRESHMAN FINANCIAL AID (Fall 2016, est.) 6,430 applied for aid; of those 54% were deemed to have need. 100% of freshmen with need received aid; of those 20% had need fully met. *Average percent of need met:* 68% (excluding resources awarded to replace EFC). *Average financial aid package:* $11,349 (excluding resources awarded to replace EFC). 1% of all full-time freshmen had no need and received non-need-based gift aid.

UNDERGRADUATE FINANCIAL AID (Fall 2016, est.) 21,887 applied for aid; of those 68% were deemed to have need. 100% of undergraduates with need received aid; of those 21% had need fully met. *Average percent of need met:* 70% (excluding resources awarded to replace EFC). *Average financial aid package:* $12,283 (excluding resources awarded to replace EFC). 1% of all full-time undergraduates had no need and received non-need-based gift aid.

GIFT AID (NEED-BASED) *Total amount:* $168,502,412 (26% federal, 17% state, 40% institutional, 17% external sources). *Receiving aid:* Freshmen: 31% (2,661); all full-time undergraduates: 32% (11,945). *Average award:* Freshmen: $9642; Undergraduates: $9587. *Scholarships, grants, and awards:* Federal Pell, FSEOG, state, private, college/university gift aid from institutional funds.

GIFT AID (NON-NEED-BASED) *Total amount:* $5,795,357 (7% institutional, 93% external sources). *Receiving aid:* Freshmen: 16% (1,365). Undergraduates: 9% (3,395). *Average award:* Freshmen: $2208. Undergraduates: $2502. *Scholarships, grants, and awards by category:* Academic interests/achievement: general academic interests/achievements. *Creative arts/performance:* art/fine arts, general creative arts/performance, music, theater/drama. *Special achievements/activities:* leadership. *Special characteristics:* local/state students. *Tuition waivers:* Full or partial for employees or children of employees, senior citizens. *ROTC:* Army, Naval, Air Force.

LOANS *Student loans:* $104,727,472 (67% need-based, 33% non-need-based). 45% of past graduating class borrowed through all loan programs. *Average indebtedness per student:* $25,338. *Average need-based loan:* Freshmen: $3406. Undergraduates: $4767. *Parent loans:* $724,374,125 (3% need-based, 97% non-need-based). *Programs:* Federal Direct (Subsidized and Unsubsidized Stafford, PLUS), Perkins, state.

WORK-STUDY *Federal work-study:* Total amount: $4,201,937; jobs available. *State or other work-study/employment:* Total amount: $52,676 (100% need-based). Part-time jobs available.

ATHLETIC AWARDS Total amount: $2,934,476 (100% non-need-based).

APPLYING FOR FINANCIAL AID *Required financial aid forms:* FAFSA, institution's own form. *Financial aid deadline (priority):* 3/15. *Notification date:* Continuous beginning 3/15. Students must reply by 5/1 or within 3 weeks of notification.

CONTACT Ms. Diane Sprague, Director of Student Financial Services, The University of Texas at Austin, PO Box 7758, Student Services Building, Suite 3.214, Austin, TX 78713-7758, 512-475-6282. *Fax:* 512-475-6296. *E-mail:* ask@finaid.utexas.edu.

Website: http://www.utexas.edu/.

THE UNIVERSITY OF TEXAS AT DALLAS
Richardson, TX

Tuition & fees (TX res): $12,162	Average undergraduate aid package: $12,888

ABOUT THE INSTITUTION State-supported, coed. *Awards:* certificates, bachelor's, master's, and doctoral degrees. 43 undergraduate majors. *Total enrollment:* 26,793. Undergraduates: 17,350. Freshmen: 3,229. Both federal and institutional methodology are used as a basis for awarding need-based institutional aid.

UNDERGRADUATE EXPENSES for 2016–2017 *Application fee:* $50. *Tuition, state resident:* full-time $12,162; part-time $405.40 per credit hour. *Tuition, nonresident:* full-time $33,654; part-time $1122 per credit hour. Full-time tuition and fees vary according to course load and degree level. Part-time tuition and fees vary according to course load and degree level. *College room and board:* $10,668. Room and board charges vary according to board plan and housing facility. *Payment plan:* Guaranteed tuition.

FRESHMAN FINANCIAL AID (Fall 2015) 1,931 applied for aid; of those 69% were deemed to have need. 97% of freshmen with need received aid; of those 23% had need fully met. *Average percent of need met:* 69% (excluding resources awarded to replace EFC). *Average financial aid package:* $13,429 (excluding resources awarded to replace EFC). 23% of all full-time freshmen had no need and received non-need-based gift aid.

UNDERGRADUATE FINANCIAL AID (Fall 2015) 8,095 applied for aid; of those 84% were deemed to have need. 97% of undergraduates with need received aid; of those 17% had need fully met. *Average percent of need met:* 65% (excluding resources awarded to replace EFC). *Average financial aid package:* $12,888 (excluding resources awarded to replace EFC). 21% of all full-time undergraduates had no need and received non-need-based gift aid.

GIFT AID (NEED-BASED) *Total amount:* $86,130,655 (24% federal, 10% state, 62% institutional, 4% external sources). *Receiving aid:* Freshmen: 44% (1,158); all full-time undergraduates: 48% (5,994). *Average award:* Freshmen: $10,535; Undergraduates: $9119. **Scholarships, grants, and awards:** Federal Pell, FSEOG, state, private, college/university gift aid from institutional funds.

GIFT AID (NON-NEED-BASED) Total amount: $9,793,822 (89% institutional, 11% external sources). **Receiving aid:** Freshmen: 6% (163). Undergraduates: 4% (463). **Average award:** Freshmen: $12,775. Undergraduates: $11,894. **Scholarships, grants, and awards by category:** Academic interests/achievement: biological sciences, business, computer science, engineering/technologies, general academic interests/achievements, mathematics, physical sciences. Special achievements/activities: general special achievements/activities, leadership. Special characteristics: adult students, children of public servants, general special characteristics, handicapped students, international students, local/state students, members of minority groups, out-of-state students, public servants, veterans, veterans' children. **Tuition waivers:** Full or partial for employees or children of employees, senior citizens. **ROTC:** Army cooperative, Air Force cooperative.

LOANS Student loans: $42,130,333 (78% need-based, 22% non-need-based). 35% of past graduating class borrowed through all loan programs. Average indebtedness per student: $20,432. **Average need-based loan:** Freshmen: $3328. Undergraduates: $4375. **Parent loans:** $3,805,275 (31% need-based, 69% non-need-based). **Programs:** Federal Direct (Subsidized and Unsubsidized Stafford, PLUS), Perkins, state, college/university.

WORK-STUDY Federal work-study: jobs available. **State or other work-study/employment:** Total amount: $107,481 (100% need-based). Part-time jobs available.

APPLYING FOR FINANCIAL AID Required financial aid form: FAFSA. **Financial aid deadline (priority):** 3/15. **Notification date:** Continuous beginning 3/15.

CONTACT M. Beth Tolan, Director of Financial Aid, The University of Texas at Dallas, 800 West Campbell Road, SS22, Richardson, TX 75080-3021, 972-883-2941 or toll-free 800-889-2443. Fax: 972-883-2947. E-mail: bnt031000@utdallas.edu. Website: http://www.utdallas.edu/.

THE UNIVERSITY OF TEXAS AT EL PASO
El Paso, TX

Tuition & fees (TX res): $7548	Average undergraduate aid package: $14,511

ABOUT THE INSTITUTION State-supported, coed. **Awards:** certificates, diplomas, bachelor's, master's, and doctoral degrees. 61 undergraduate majors. **Total enrollment:** 23,922. Undergraduates: 20,521. Freshmen: 3,040. Federal methodology is used as a basis for awarding need-based institutional aid.

UNDERGRADUATE EXPENSES for 2017–2018 Tuition, state resident: full-time $5769; part-time $192 per credit hour. **Tuition, nonresident:** full-time $18,744; part-time $625 per credit hour. **Required fees:** full-time $1779. **College room and board:** $9496; **Room only:** $4914. **Payment plan:** Guaranteed tuition.

FRESHMAN FINANCIAL AID (Fall 2015) 2,915 applied for aid; of those 86% were deemed to have need. 99% of freshmen with need received aid; of those 7% had need fully met. **Average percent of need met:** 66% (excluding resources awarded to replace EFC). **Average financial aid package:** $14,633 (excluding resources awarded to replace EFC). 3% of all full-time freshmen had no need and received non-need-based gift aid.

UNDERGRADUATE FINANCIAL AID (Fall 2015) 11,695 applied for aid; of those 89% were deemed to have need. 98% of undergraduates with need received aid; of those 7% had need fully met. **Average percent of need met:** 61% (excluding resources awarded to replace EFC). **Average financial aid package:** $14,511 (excluding resources awarded to replace EFC). 4% of all full-time undergraduates had no need and received non-need-based gift aid.

GIFT AID (NEED-BASED) Total amount: $93,619,379 (60% federal, 24% state, 15% institutional, 1% external sources). **Receiving aid:** Freshmen: 67% (2,036); all full-time undergraduates: 65% (8,542). **Average award:** Freshmen: $9521; Undergraduates: $8196. **Scholarships, grants, and awards:** Federal Pell, FSEOG, state, private, college/university gift aid from institutional funds, United Negro College Fund, Federal Nursing.

GIFT AID (NON-NEED-BASED) Total amount: $2,913,998 (4% state, 77% institutional, 19% external sources). **Receiving aid:** Freshmen: 7% (206). Undergrad-

uates: 9% (1,130). **Average award:** Freshmen: $5101. Undergraduates: $4391. **Scholarships, grants, and awards by category:** Academic interests/achievement: biological sciences, business, communication, computer science, education, engineering/technologies, English, general academic interests/achievements, health fields, humanities, international studies, mathematics, military science, physical sciences. Creative arts/performance: applied art and design, art/fine arts, journalism/publications, music, performing arts, theater/drama. Special achievements/activities: cheerleading/drum major, leadership. Special characteristics: ethnic background, international students, local/state students, members of minority groups, out-of-state students. **ROTC:** Army.

LOANS Student loans: $89,435,563 (99% need-based, 1% non-need-based). 60% of past graduating class borrowed through all loan programs. Average indebtedness per student: $21,840. **Average need-based loan:** Freshmen: $5241. Undergraduates: $6675. **Parent loans:** $22,695,621 (100% non-need-based). **Programs:** Federal Direct (Subsidized and Unsubsidized Stafford, PLUS), Perkins, Federal Nursing, state, college/university.

WORK-STUDY Federal work-study: 400 jobs averaging $3113. **State or other work-study/employment:** Total amount: $835,982 (98% need-based, 2% non-need-based). 103 part-time jobs averaging $2052.

ATHLETIC AWARDS Total amount: $5,508,895 (44% need-based, 56% non-need-based).

APPLYING FOR FINANCIAL AID Required financial aid forms: FAFSA, institution's own form. **Financial aid deadline (priority):** 3/15. **Notification date:** Continuous beginning 3/30. Students must reply within 2 weeks of notification.

CONTACT Mr. Ron Williams, Interim Director of Financial Aid, The University of Texas at El Paso, 500 West University Avenue, El Paso, TX 79968-0001, 915-747-5204 or toll-free 877-74MINER. Fax: 915-747-5631. E-mail: rwilliams@utep.edu. Website: http://www.utep.edu/.

THE UNIVERSITY OF TEXAS AT SAN ANTONIO
San Antonio, TX

Tuition & fees (TX res): $9044	Average undergraduate aid package: $9751

ABOUT THE INSTITUTION State-supported, coed. **Awards:** bachelor's, master's, and doctoral degrees. 71 undergraduate majors. **Total enrollment:** 28,959. Undergraduates: 24,724. Freshmen: 4,377. Federal methodology is used as a basis for awarding need-based institutional aid.

UNDERGRADUATE EXPENSES for 2016–2017 Application fee: $60. **Tuition, state resident:** full-time $6299; part-time $209.95 per credit hour. **Tuition, nonresident:** full-time $19,545; part-time $651.50 per credit hour. **Required fees:** full-time $2745. Full-time tuition and fees vary according to course load and degree level. Part-time tuition and fees vary according to course load and degree level. **College room and board:** $8074; **Room only:** $5190. Room and board charges vary according to board plan and housing facility. **Payment plan:** Guaranteed tuition.

FRESHMAN FINANCIAL AID (Fall 2015) 4,186 applied for aid; of those 78% were deemed to have need. 97% of freshmen with need received aid; of those 6% had need fully met. **Average percent of need met:** 57% (excluding resources awarded to replace EFC). **Average financial aid package:** $10,174 (excluding resources awarded to replace EFC). 7% of all full-time freshmen had no need and received non-need-based gift aid.

UNDERGRADUATE FINANCIAL AID (Fall 2015) 15,632 applied for aid; of those 85% were deemed to have need. 97% of undergraduates with need received aid; of those 5% had need fully met. **Average percent of need met:** 53% (excluding resources awarded to replace EFC). **Average financial aid package:** $9751 (excluding resources awarded to replace EFC). 4% of all full-time undergraduates had no need and received non-need-based gift aid.

GIFT AID (NEED-BASED) Total amount: $90,608,273 (49% federal, 19% state, 26% institutional, 6% external sources). **Receiving aid:** Freshmen: 57% (2,796); all full-time undergraduates: 56% (11,207). **Average award:** Freshmen: $8345; Undergraduates: $7147. **Scholarships, grants, and awards:** Federal Pell, FSEOG, state, private, college/university gift aid from institutional funds.

GIFT AID (NON-NEED-BASED) Total amount: $4,978,371 (7% federal, 1% state, 62% institutional, 30% external sources). **Receiving aid:** Freshmen: 2% (77).

Undergraduates: 1% (252). *Average award:* Freshmen: $2801. Undergraduates: $3418. *Scholarships, grants, and awards by category:* Academic interests/achievement: agriculture, architecture, area/ethnic studies, biological sciences, business, communication, computer science, education, engineering/technologies, English, foreign languages, general academic interests/achievements, humanities, international studies, mathematics, physical sciences, social sciences. *Creative arts/performance:* art/fine arts, creative writing, debating, music. *Special achievements/activities:* cheerleading/drum major, general special achievements/activities. *Special characteristics:* ethnic background, first-generation college students, general special characteristics, handicapped students, local/state students, members of minority groups, out-of-state students. *Tuition waivers:* Full or partial for employees or children of employees. *ROTC:* Army, Air Force.

LOANS *Student loans:* $83,354,644 (51% need-based, 49% non-need-based). 64% of past graduating class borrowed through all loan programs. *Average indebtedness per student:* $26,763. *Average need-based loan:* Freshmen: $3346. Undergraduates: $4109. *Parent loans:* $13,097,686 (100% non-need-based). *Programs:* Federal Direct (Subsidized and Unsubsidized Stafford, PLUS), Perkins, state, college/university.

WORK-STUDY *Federal work-study:* 366 jobs averaging $2877. *State or other work-study/employment:* Total amount: $1,806,042 (100% need-based). 900 part-time jobs averaging $2133.

ATHLETIC AWARDS Total amount: $4,528,438 (35% need-based, 65% non-need-based).

APPLYING FOR FINANCIAL AID *Required financial aid form:* FAFSA. *Financial aid deadline (priority):* 3/15. *Notification date:* Continuous beginning 3/1. Students must reply within 4 weeks of notification.

CONTACT Kim Canady, Associate Director of One Stop Enrollment Center, The University of Texas at San Antonio, One UTSA Circle, San Antonio, TX 78249, 210-458-8000 or toll-free 800-669-0919. *Fax:* 210-458-4638. *E-mail:* onestop@utsa.edu. *Website:* http://www.utsa.edu/.

THE UNIVERSITY OF TEXAS AT TYLER
Tyler, TX

CONTACT Candice A. Lindsey, Assistant Vice President for Enrollment Management, Marketing and Customer Relations, The University of Texas at Tyler, 3900 University Boulevard, Tyler, TX 75799, 903-566-7221 or toll-free 800-UTTYLER. *Fax:* 903-566-7183. *E-mail:* enroll@uttyler.edu. *Website:* http://www.uttyler.edu/.

THE UNIVERSITY OF TEXAS HEALTH SCIENCE CENTER AT HOUSTON
Houston, TX

Tuition & fees: N/R	Average undergraduate aid package: $9034

ABOUT THE INSTITUTION State-supported, coed. *Awards:* certificates, bachelor's, master's, and doctoral degrees. 2 undergraduate majors. *Total enrollment:* 4,811. Undergraduates: 677. Federal methodology is used as a basis for awarding need-based institutional aid.

UNDERGRADUATE FINANCIAL AID (Fall 2015) 660 applied for aid; of those 99% were deemed to have need. 100% of undergraduates with need received aid; of those 33% had need fully met. *Average percent of need met:* 42% (excluding resources awarded to replace EFC). *Average financial aid package:* $9034 (excluding resources awarded to replace EFC). 1% of all full-time undergraduates had no need and received non-need-based gift aid.

GIFT AID (NEED-BASED) *Total amount:* $2,163,190 (53% federal, 2% state, 39% institutional, 6% external sources). *Receiving aid:* All full-time undergraduates: 57% (381). *Average award:* Undergraduates: $5678. *Scholarships, grants, and awards:* Federal Pell, FSEOG, state, private, college/university gift aid from institutional funds.

GIFT AID (NON-NEED-BASED) *Average award:* Undergraduates: $3333. *Scholarships, grants, and awards by category:* Academic interests/achievement: home economics. *ROTC:* Army cooperative.

LOANS *Student loans:* $6,331,319 (100% need-based). *Average need-based loan:* Undergraduates: $6318. *Parent loans:* $696,005 (100% need-based). *Programs:* Federal Direct (Subsidized and Unsubsidized Stafford, PLUS), Perkins, Federal Nursing, state, college/university, alternative loans.

APPLYING FOR FINANCIAL AID *Financial aid deadline:* Continuous. *Notification date:* Continuous.

CONTACT Ms. Araceli Alvarez, Director of Student Financial Services, The University of Texas Health Science Center at Houston, PO Box 20036, Houston, TX 77225, 713-500-3860. *Fax:* 713-500-3863. *E-mail:* araceli.alvarez@uth.tmc.edu. *Website:* http://www.uthouston.edu/.

THE UNIVERSITY OF TEXAS HEALTH SCIENCE CENTER AT SAN ANTONIO
San Antonio, TX

CONTACT Robert T. Lawson, Financial Aid Administrator, The University of Texas Health Science Center at San Antonio, 7703 Floyd Curl Drive, MSC 7708, San Antonio, TX 78284, 210-567-0025. *Fax:* 210-567-6643. *Website:* http://www.uthscsa.edu/.

THE UNIVERSITY OF TEXAS MEDICAL BRANCH
Galveston, TX

CONTACT Mrs. Carol A. Cromie, University Financial Aid Officer, The University of Texas Medical Branch, 301 University Boulevard, Galveston, TX 77555-1305, 409-772-9795. *Fax:* 409-772-4466. *E-mail:* cacromie@umtb.edu. *Website:* http://www.utmb.edu/.

THE UNIVERSITY OF TEXAS OF THE PERMIAN BASIN
Odessa, TX

Tuition & fees (TX res): $7060	Average undergraduate aid package: $10,560

ABOUT THE INSTITUTION State-supported, coed. *Awards:* certificates, bachelor's, and master's degrees. 32 undergraduate majors. *Total enrollment:* 6,524. Undergraduates: 5,663. Freshmen: 427. Federal methodology is used as a basis for awarding need-based institutional aid.

UNDERGRADUATE EXPENSES for 2017–2018 *Application fee:* $40. *Tuition, state resident:* full-time $5598; part-time $186.30 per credit hour. *Tuition, nonresident:* full-time $18,078; part-time $602.60 per credit hour. *Required fees:* full-time $1462; $69.56 per credit hour. Full-time tuition and fees vary according to course load, degree level, and location. Part-time tuition and fees vary according to course load, degree level, and location. *College room and board:* $10,800; *Room only:* $7200. Room and board charges vary according to board plan and housing facility. *Payment plan:* Guaranteed tuition.

FRESHMAN FINANCIAL AID (Fall 2015) 328 applied for aid; of those 81% were deemed to have need. 95% of freshmen with need received aid; of those 83% had need fully met. *Average percent of need met:* 74% (excluding resources awarded to replace EFC). *Average financial aid package:* $12,060 (excluding resources awarded to replace EFC). 65% of all full-time freshmen had no need and received non-need-based gift aid.

UNDERGRADUATE FINANCIAL AID (Fall 2015) 1,946 applied for aid; of those 85% were deemed to have need. 95% of undergraduates with need received aid; of those 75% had need fully met. *Average percent of need met:* 65% (excluding resources awarded to replace EFC). *Average financial aid package:* $10,560 (excluding resources awarded to replace EFC). 42% of all full-time undergraduates had no need and received non-need-based gift aid.

GIFT AID (NEED-BASED) *Total amount:* $13,013,731 (49% federal, 10% state, 37% institutional, 4% external sources). *Receiving aid:* Freshmen: 52% (200); all full-

time undergraduates: 64% (1,380). *Average award:* Freshmen: $8650; Undergraduates: $7926. *Scholarships, grants, and awards:* Federal Pell, FSEOG, state, private, college/university gift aid from institutional funds.

GIFT AID (NON-NEED-BASED) *Total amount:* $2,754,239 (1% federal, 69% institutional, 30% external sources). *Receiving aid:* Freshmen: 43% (167). Undergraduates: 27% (578). *Average award:* Freshmen: $2862. Undergraduates: $2447. *Scholarships, grants, and awards by category:* Academic interests/achievement: 2,780 awards ($5,800,000 total): business, communication, education, engineering/technologies, general academic interests/achievements, home economics, humanities, physical sciences, social sciences. *Creative arts/performance:* 165 awards ($340,000 total): art/fine arts, dance, general creative arts/performance, music, performing arts, theater/drama. *Special achievements/activities:* 20 awards ($30,500 total): cheerleading/drum major, leadership. *Special characteristics:* 120 awards ($765,000 total): veterans, veterans' children.

LOANS *Student loans:* $9,839,993 (44% need-based, 56% non-need-based). 33% of past graduating class borrowed through all loan programs. *Average indebtedness per student:* $17,578. *Average need-based loan:* Freshmen: $3225. Undergraduates: $3750. *Parent loans:* $391,984 (100% non-need-based). *Programs:* Federal Direct (Subsidized and Unsubsidized Stafford, PLUS), state.

WORK-STUDY *Federal work-study:* jobs available. *State or other work-study/employment:* Total amount: $30,288 (100% need-based). Part-time jobs available.

ATHLETIC AWARDS Total amount: $774,092 (37% need-based, 63% non-need-based).

APPLYING FOR FINANCIAL AID *Required financial aid form:* FAFSA. *Financial aid deadline (priority):* 3/15. *Notification date:* Continuous beginning 3/15. Students must reply within 2 weeks of notification.

CONTACT Charles Edward Kerestly, Director of Financial Aid, The University of Texas of the Permian Basin, 4901 East University Boulevard, Odessa, TX 79762, 432-552-2620 or toll-free 866-552-UTPB. *Fax:* 432-552-2621. *E-mail:* finaid@utpb.edu. *Website:* http://www.utpb.edu/.

THE UNIVERSITY OF TEXAS RIO GRANDE VALLEY
Edinburg, TX

Tuition & fees (TX res): $7438	Average undergraduate aid package: $10,172

ABOUT THE INSTITUTION State-supported, coed. *Awards:* certificates, bachelor's, master's, and doctoral degrees. 53 undergraduate majors. *Total enrollment:* 27,560. Undergraduates: 24,433. Freshmen: 3,944. Federal methodology is used as a basis for awarding need-based institutional aid.

UNDERGRADUATE EXPENSES for 2016–2017 *Tuition, state resident:* full-time $5970; part-time $360.60 per credit hour. *Tuition, nonresident:* full-time $15,762; part-time $768.60 per credit hour. *Required fees:* full-time $1468; $184.93 per credit hour. Full-time tuition and fees vary according to course load, degree level, program, and student level. Part-time tuition and fees vary according to course load, degree level, program, and student level. *College room and board:* $7950; *Room only:* $4232. Room and board charges vary according to board plan, housing facility, and location. *Payment plan:* Guaranteed tuition.

FRESHMAN FINANCIAL AID (Fall 2015) 3,221 applied for aid; of those 94% were deemed to have need. 100% of freshmen with need received aid; of those 2% had need fully met. *Average percent of need met:* 68% (excluding resources awarded to replace EFC). *Average financial aid package:* $10,869 (excluding resources awarded to replace EFC). 3% of all full-time freshmen had no need and received non-need-based gift aid.

UNDERGRADUATE FINANCIAL AID (Fall 2015) 11,996 applied for aid; of those 96% were deemed to have need. 100% of undergraduates with need received aid; of those 3% had need fully met. *Average percent of need met:* 79% (excluding resources awarded to replace EFC). *Average financial aid package:* $10,172 (excluding resources awarded to replace EFC). 1% of all full-time undergraduates had no need and received non-need-based gift aid.

GIFT AID (NEED-BASED) *Total amount:* $128,984,654 (54% federal, 32% state, 13% institutional, 1% external sources). *Receiving aid:* Freshmen: 71% (2,984); all full-time undergraduates: 45% (11,082). *Average award:* Freshmen: $10,896;

Undergraduates: $10,688. *Scholarships, grants, and awards:* Federal Pell, FSEOG, state, private, college/university gift aid from institutional funds.

GIFT AID (NON-NEED-BASED) *Total amount:* $2,262,590 (5% federal, 1% state, 80% institutional, 14% external sources). *Receiving aid:* Freshmen: 1% (25). Undergraduates: 81. *Average award:* Freshmen: $3836. Undergraduates: $3357. *Scholarships, grants, and awards by category:* Academic interests/achievement: 1,807 awards ($4,641,971 total): biological sciences, business, communication, computer science, education, engineering/technologies, English, general academic interests/achievements, health fields, mathematics, military science, premedicine, social sciences. *Creative arts/performance:* 164 awards ($141,314 total): art/fine arts, dance, journalism/publications, music, theater/drama. *Special achievements/activities:* 20 awards ($16,550 total): cheerleading/drum major, community service, general special achievements/activities, leadership, memberships. *Special characteristics:* 101 awards ($203,889 total): general special characteristics, international students, local/state students, out-of-state students, veterans, veterans' children. *ROTC:* Army.

LOANS *Student loans:* $49,120,322 (91% need-based, 9% non-need-based). 58% of past graduating class borrowed through all loan programs. *Average indebtedness per student:* $15,731. *Average need-based loan:* Freshmen: $3041. Undergraduates: $4691. *Parent loans:* $662,124 (18% need-based, 82% non-need-based). *Programs:* Federal Direct (Subsidized and Unsubsidized Stafford, PLUS), Perkins, state.

WORK-STUDY *Federal work-study:* 749 jobs averaging $2640. *State or other work-study/employment:* Total amount: $764,687 (100% need-based). 406 part-time jobs averaging $1883.

ATHLETIC AWARDS Total amount: $1,818,169 (35% need-based, 65% non-need-based).

APPLYING FOR FINANCIAL AID *Required financial aid forms:* FAFSA, state aid form. *Financial aid deadline (priority):* 3/15. *Notification date:* Continuous beginning 3/15. Students must reply by 7/1 or within 2 weeks of notification.

CONTACT Mr. Elias Ozuna, Executive Director of Student Financial Services, The University of Texas Rio Grande Valley, 1201 West University Drive, Edinburg, TX 78539, 956-665-5372 or toll-free 888-882-4026 (in-state). *Fax:* 956-665-2396. *E-mail:* elias.ozuna@utrgv.edu. *Website:* http://www.utrgv.edu/.

THE UNIVERSITY OF THE ARTS
Philadelphia, PA

CONTACT Office of Financial Aid, The University of the Arts, 320 South Broad Street, Philadelphia, PA 19102-4944, 800-616-ARTS Ext. 6170 or toll-free 800-616-ARTS. *E-mail:* finaid@uarts.edu. *Website:* http://www.uarts.edu/.

UNIVERSITY OF THE CUMBERLANDS
Williamsburg, KY

ABOUT THE INSTITUTION Independent Kentucky Baptist, coed. *Awards:* certificates, associate, bachelor's, master's, and doctoral degrees. 39 undergraduate majors. *Total enrollment:* 7,693. Undergraduates: 3,082. Freshmen: 419.

GIFT AID (NEED-BASED) *Scholarships, grants, and awards:* Federal Pell, FSEOG, state, private, college/university gift aid from institutional funds.

GIFT AID (NON-NEED-BASED) *Scholarships, grants, and awards by category:* Academic interests/achievement: general academic interests/achievements. *Creative arts/performance:* music. *Special achievements/activities:* cheerleading/drum major, community service, leadership, religious involvement. *Special characteristics:* children and siblings of alumni, children of faculty/staff, general special characteristics, local/state students, relatives of clergy, religious affiliation, siblings of current students.

LOANS *Programs:* Federal Direct (Subsidized and Unsubsidized Stafford, PLUS), Perkins, college/university.

WORK-STUDY *Federal work-study:* 830 jobs averaging $1939. *State or other work-study/employment:* Total amount: $17,766 (100% non-need-based). 11 part-time jobs averaging $2095.

APPLYING FOR FINANCIAL AID *Required financial aid form:* FAFSA.

CONTACT Mr. Steve Allen, Vice President for Student Financial Planning, University of the Cumberlands, 6190 College Station Drive, Williamsburg, KY 40769-1372, 606-549-2200 or toll-free 800-343-1609. *Fax:* 606-539-4515. *E-mail:* finplan@ucumberlands.edu.
Website: http://www.ucumberlands.edu/.

UNIVERSITY OF THE DISTRICT OF COLUMBIA
Washington, DC

Tuition & fees: N/R	Average undergraduate aid package: $8618

ABOUT THE INSTITUTION District-supported, coed. 85 undergraduate majors. Federal methodology is used as a basis for awarding need-based institutional aid.
FRESHMAN FINANCIAL AID (Fall 2016, est.) 178 applied for aid; of those 92% were deemed to have need. 99% of freshmen with need received aid; of those 1% had need fully met. *Average financial aid package:* $9198 (excluding resources awarded to replace EFC). 1% of all full-time freshmen had no need and received non-need-based gift aid.
UNDERGRADUATE FINANCIAL AID (Fall 2016, est.) 1,156 applied for aid; of those 94% were deemed to have need. 99% of undergraduates with need received aid; of those 3% had need fully met. *Average financial aid package:* $8618 (excluding resources awarded to replace EFC). 1% of all full-time undergraduates had no need and received non-need-based gift aid.
GIFT AID (NEED-BASED) *Total amount:* $10,169,800 (95% federal, 4% state, 1% institutional). *Receiving aid:* Freshmen: 56% (135); all full-time undergraduates: 47% (839). *Average award:* Freshmen: $5557; Undergraduates: $5499. *Scholarships, grants, and awards:* Federal Pell, FSEOG, state, private, college/university gift aid from institutional funds, United Negro College Fund, Federal Nursing.
GIFT AID (NON-NEED-BASED) *Total amount:* $1,203,891 (45% institutional, 55% external sources). *Receiving aid:* Freshmen: 21% (51). Undergraduates: 13% (231). *Average award:* Freshmen: $3849. Undergraduates: $3086. *Scholarships, grants, and awards by category: Academic interests/achievement:* agriculture, education, health fields. *Special achievements/activities:* general special achievements/activities, junior miss. *Special characteristics:* children of faculty/staff.
LOANS *Student loans:* $15,361,140 (46% need-based, 54% non-need-based). 67% of past graduating class borrowed through all loan programs. *Average indebtedness per student:* $22,964. *Average need-based loan:* Freshmen: $3291. Undergraduates: $4146. *Parent loans:* $222,990 (100% non-need-based). *Programs:* Federal Direct (Subsidized and Unsubsidized Stafford, PLUS), private loans.
WORK-STUDY *Federal work-study:* Total amount: $40,811; 32 jobs averaging $1325. *State or other work-study/employment:* Part-time jobs available.
ATHLETIC AWARDS Total amount: $1,466,969 (100% non-need-based).
APPLYING FOR FINANCIAL AID *Required financial aid form:* FAFSA. *Financial aid deadline (priority):* 6/30. *Notification date:* Continuous beginning 5/20. Students must reply within 2 weeks of notification.
CONTACT Mrs. Nailah Williams, Director of Financial Aid, University of the District of Columbia, 4200 Connecticut Avenue NW, Washington, DC 20008-1175, 202-274-5618. *Fax:* 202-274-6060. *E-mail:* finaid@udc.edu.
Website: http://www.udc.edu/.

UNIVERSITY OF THE INCARNATE WORD
San Antonio, TX

Tuition & fees: $29,990	Average undergraduate aid package: $20,196

ABOUT THE INSTITUTION Independent Roman Catholic, coed. *Awards:* diplomas, associate, bachelor's, master's, and doctoral degrees. 72 undergraduate majors. *Total enrollment:* 8,906. Undergraduates: 6,423. Freshmen: 788. Federal methodology is used as a basis for awarding need-based institutional aid.
UNDERGRADUATE EXPENSES for 2017–2018 *Application fee:* $20. *Comprehensive fee:* $42,426 includes full-time tuition ($27,900), mandatory fees ($2090), and room and board ($12,436). Full-time tuition and fees vary according to course load, degree level, location, program, and reciprocity agreements. Room and board charges vary according to board plan and housing facility. *Part-time tuition:* $915 per credit hour. Part-time tuition and fees vary according to course load, degree level, location, program, and reciprocity agreements.
FRESHMAN FINANCIAL AID (Fall 2015) 768 applied for aid; of those 91% were deemed to have need. 100% of freshmen with need received aid; of those 21% had need fully met. *Average percent of need met:* 59% (excluding resources awarded to replace EFC). *Average financial aid package:* $21,365 (excluding resources awarded to replace EFC). 8% of all full-time freshmen had no need and received non-need-based gift aid.
UNDERGRADUATE FINANCIAL AID (Fall 2015) 3,376 applied for aid; of those 94% were deemed to have need. 100% of undergraduates with need received aid; of those 8% had need fully met. *Average percent of need met:* 76% (excluding resources awarded to replace EFC). *Average financial aid package:* $20,196 (excluding resources awarded to replace EFC). 22% of all full-time undergraduates had no need and received non-need-based gift aid.
GIFT AID (NEED-BASED) *Total amount:* $57,314,178 (21% federal, 11% state, 66% institutional, 2% external sources). *Receiving aid:* Freshmen: 80% (692); all full-time undergraduates: 74% (3,155). *Average award:* Freshmen: $19,046; Undergraduates: $16,738. *Scholarships, grants, and awards:* Federal Pell, FSEOG, state, private, college/university gift aid from institutional funds, Federal Nursing.
GIFT AID (NON-NEED-BASED) *Total amount:* $24,628 (53% federal, 47% institutional). *Receiving aid:* Undergraduates: 14. *Average award:* Freshmen: $5902. Undergraduates: $7979. *Scholarships, grants, and awards by category: Academic interests/achievement:* general academic interests/achievements. *Creative arts/performance:* art/fine arts, music, theater/drama. *Special achievements/activities:* leadership, religious involvement. *Special characteristics:* children and siblings of alumni, children of faculty/staff. *Tuition waivers:* Full or partial for employees or children of employees, senior citizens. *ROTC:* Army cooperative.
LOANS *Student loans:* $33,616,748 (86% need-based, 14% non-need-based). 69% of past graduating class borrowed through all loan programs. *Average indebtedness per student:* $19,243. *Average need-based loan:* Freshmen: $3266. Undergraduates: $3541. *Parent loans:* $9,539,233 (54% need-based, 46% non-need-based). *Programs:* Federal Direct (Subsidized and Unsubsidized Stafford, PLUS), Perkins, Federal Nursing, state, college/university, alternative loans.
WORK-STUDY *Federal work-study:* jobs available. *State or other work-study/employment:* Total amount: $51,041 (100% need-based). Part-time jobs available.
ATHLETIC AWARDS Total amount: $8,869,341 (18% need-based, 82% non-need-based).
APPLYING FOR FINANCIAL AID *Required financial aid form:* FAFSA. *Financial aid deadline (priority):* 4/1. *Notification date:* Continuous beginning 11/1. Students must reply within 2 weeks of notification.
CONTACT Ms. Amy Carcanagues, Director of Financial Assistance, University of the Incarnate Word, 4301 Broadway, San Antonio, TX 78209, 210-829-6008 or toll-free 800-749-WORD. *Fax:* 210-283-5053. *E-mail:* finaid@uiwtx.edu.
Website: http://www.uiw.edu/.

UNIVERSITY OF THE OZARKS
Clarksville, AR

CONTACT Ms. Jana D. Hart, Director of Financial Aid, University of the Ozarks, 415 North College Avenue, Clarksville, AR 72830-2880, 479-979-1221 or toll-free 800-264-8636. *Fax:* 479-979-1417. *E-mail:* jhart@ozarks.edu.
Website: http://www.ozarks.edu/.

UNIVERSITY OF THE PACIFIC
Stockton, CA

Tuition & fees: $44,588	Average undergraduate aid package: $32,595

ABOUT THE INSTITUTION Independent, coed. *Awards:* bachelor's, master's, and doctoral degrees. 54 undergraduate majors. *Total enrollment:* 6,128. Undergraduates: 3,483. Freshmen: 726. Federal methodology is used as a basis for awarding need-based institutional aid.

UNDERGRADUATE EXPENSES for 2016–2017 *Application fee:* $35. *Comprehensive fee:* $57,446 includes full-time tuition ($44,068), mandatory fees ($520), and room and board ($12,858). Room and board charges vary according to board plan and housing facility. *Part-time tuition:* $1520 per credit hour. Part-time tuition and fees vary according to course load.

FRESHMAN FINANCIAL AID (Fall 2016, est.) 618 applied for aid; of those 88% were deemed to have need. 100% of freshmen with need received aid; of those 20% had need fully met. *Average percent of need met:* 65% (excluding resources awarded to replace EFC). *Average financial aid package:* $32,756 (excluding resources awarded to replace EFC). 21% of all full-time freshmen had no need and received non-need-based gift aid.

UNDERGRADUATE FINANCIAL AID (Fall 2016, est.) 2,530 applied for aid; of those 92% were deemed to have need. 100% of undergraduates with need received aid; of those 13% had need fully met. *Average percent of need met:* 55% (excluding resources awarded to replace EFC). *Average financial aid package:* $32,595 (excluding resources awarded to replace EFC). 17% of all full-time undergraduates had no need and received non-need-based gift aid.

GIFT AID (NEED-BASED) *Total amount:* $57,606,672 (11% federal, 17% state, 72% institutional). *Receiving aid:* Freshmen: 74% (532); all full-time undergraduates: 67% (2,265). *Average award:* Freshmen: $27,538; Undergraduates: $25,217. *Scholarships, grants, and awards:* Federal Pell, FSEOG, state, private, college/university gift aid from institutional funds.

GIFT AID (NON-NEED-BASED) *Total amount:* $7,223,506 (100% institutional). *Average award:* Freshmen: $12,591. Undergraduates: $12,181. *Scholarships, grants, and awards by category:* Academic interests/achievement: general academic interests/achievements. Creative arts/performance: debating, music. Special achievements/activities: leadership, religious involvement. Special characteristics: religious affiliation. *Tuition waivers:* Full or partial for employees or children of employees. *ROTC:* Air Force cooperative.

LOANS *Student loans:* $22,672,077 (91% need-based, 9% non-need-based). 66% of past graduating class borrowed through all loan programs. *Average indebtedness per student:* $28,810. *Average need-based loan:* Freshmen: $6074. Undergraduates: $9224. *Parent loans:* $54,033,556 (86% need-based, 14% non-need-based). *Programs:* Federal Direct (Subsidized and Unsubsidized Stafford, PLUS), Perkins.

WORK-STUDY *Federal work-study:* Total amount: $2,105,531; jobs available.

ATHLETIC AWARDS Total amount: $8,719,470 (28% need-based, 72% non-need-based).

APPLYING FOR FINANCIAL AID *Required financial aid form:* FAFSA. *Financial aid deadline (priority):* 2/15. *Notification date:* Continuous beginning 3/1.

CONTACT Lynn Fox, Director of Financial Aid, University of the Pacific, 3601 Pacific Avenue, Stockton, CA 95211-0197, 209-946-2421.
Website: http://www.pacific.edu/.

UNIVERSITY OF THE POTOMAC
Washington, DC

CONTACT Phyllis Crews, Financial Aid Counselor, University of the Potomac, 4000 Chesapeake Street NW, Washington, DC 20016, 202-686-0876 or toll-free 888-686-0876. *Fax:* 202-686-0818. *E-mail:* pcrews@potomac.edu.
Website: http://www.potomac.edu/.

UNIVERSITY OF THE SACRED HEART
San Juan, PR

CONTACT Ms. Maria Torres, Director of Financial Aid, University of the Sacred Heart, PO Box 12383, San Juan, PR 00914-0383, 787-728-1515 Ext. 3605.
Website: http://www.sagrado.edu/.

UNIVERSITY OF THE SCIENCES
Philadelphia, PA

Tuition & fees: $38,850	Average undergraduate aid package: $22,387

ABOUT THE INSTITUTION Independent, coed. *Awards:* certificates, bachelor's, master's, and doctoral degrees. 18 undergraduate majors. *Total enrollment:* 2,664. Undergraduates: 2,246. Freshmen: 323. Federal methodology is used as a basis for awarding need-based institutional aid.

UNDERGRADUATE EXPENSES for 2016–2017 *Application fee:* $45. *Comprehensive fee:* $54,038 includes full-time tuition ($36,962), mandatory fees ($1888), and room and board ($15,188). *College room only:* $9280. Full-time tuition and fees vary according to program and student level. Room and board charges vary according to board plan and housing facility. *Part-time tuition:* $1540 per contact hour.

FRESHMAN FINANCIAL AID (Fall 2015) 383 applied for aid; of those 87% were deemed to have need. 100% of freshmen with need received aid; of those 60% had need fully met. *Average percent of need met:* 22% (excluding resources awarded to replace EFC). *Average financial aid package:* $18,444 (excluding resources awarded to replace EFC). 27% of all full-time freshmen had no need and received non-need-based gift aid.

UNDERGRADUATE FINANCIAL AID (Fall 2015) 1,900 applied for aid; of those 94% were deemed to have need. 100% of undergraduates with need received aid; of those 44% had need fully met. *Average percent of need met:* 16% (excluding resources awarded to replace EFC). *Average financial aid package:* $22,387 (excluding resources awarded to replace EFC). 20% of all full-time undergraduates had no need and received non-need-based gift aid.

GIFT AID (NEED-BASED) *Total amount:* $2,388,270 (23% federal, 14% state, 63% institutional). *Receiving aid:* Freshmen: 56% (256); all full-time undergraduates: 55% (1,218). *Average award:* Freshmen: $8015; Undergraduates: $7880. *Scholarships, grants, and awards:* Federal Pell, FSEOG, state, private, college/university gift aid from institutional funds.

GIFT AID (NON-NEED-BASED) *Total amount:* $5,674,490 (94% institutional, 6% external sources). *Receiving aid:* Freshmen: 64% (294). Undergraduates: 77% (1,716). *Average award:* Freshmen: $11,257. Undergraduates: $13,818. *Scholarships, grants, and awards by category:* Academic interests/achievement: general academic interests/achievements. Special achievements/activities: general special achievements/activities. *Tuition waivers:* Full or partial for employees or children of employees. *ROTC:* Army cooperative, Air Force cooperative.

LOANS *Student loans:* $3,746,428 (21% need-based, 79% non-need-based). 69% of past graduating class borrowed through all loan programs. *Average indebtedness per student:* $24,191. *Average need-based loan:* Freshmen: $3628. Undergraduates: $5129. *Parent loans:* $132,343 (100% non-need-based). *Programs:* Federal Direct (Subsidized and Unsubsidized Stafford, PLUS), Perkins, college/university, Health Professions Student Loans (HPSL), Loans for Disadvantaged Students.

WORK-STUDY *Federal work-study:* jobs available. *State or other work-study/employment:* Part-time jobs available.

ATHLETIC AWARDS Total amount: $270,532 (100% non-need-based).

APPLYING FOR FINANCIAL AID *Required financial aid form:* FAFSA. *Financial aid deadline (priority):* 3/15. *Notification date:* Continuous beginning 2/15. Students must reply by 5/1.

CONTACT Ms. Pamela Ramanathan, Director of Financial Aid, University of the Sciences, 600 South 43rd Street, Philadelphia, PA 19104, 215-596-8894 or toll-free 888-996-8747. *Fax:* 215-596-8554. *E-mail:* p.ramanathan@usciences.edu.
Website: http://www.usciences.edu/.

UNIVERSITY OF THE SOUTHWEST
Hobbs, NM

ABOUT THE INSTITUTION Independent Christian, coed. *Awards:* bachelor's and master's degrees. 20 undergraduate majors. *Total enrollment:* 1,059. Undergraduates: 450. Freshmen: 100.

GIFT AID (NEED-BASED) *Scholarships, grants, and awards:* Federal Pell, FSEOG, state, private, college/university gift aid from institutional funds.

GIFT AID (NON-NEED-BASED) *Scholarships, grants, and awards by category:* Academic interests/achievement: biological sciences, business, education,

English, general academic interests/achievements, humanities, mathematics, physical sciences, premedicine, religion/biblical studies, social sciences. *Creative arts/performance:* debating, music. *Special achievements/activities:* community service, general special achievements/activities, leadership, religious involvement. *Special characteristics:* children of faculty/staff.

LOANS *Programs:* Federal Direct (Subsidized and Unsubsidized Stafford, PLUS).

WORK-STUDY *Federal work-study:* 30 jobs averaging $750. *State or other work-study/employment:* Total amount: $7934 (100% need-based). 7 part-time jobs averaging $750.

APPLYING FOR FINANCIAL AID *Required financial aid form:* FAFSA.

CONTACT Dawny Kringel, Director of Financial Aid, University of the Southwest, 6610 North Lovington Highway, Hobbs, NM 88240-9129, 575-492-2114 or toll-free 800-530-4400. *Fax:* 575-392-6006. *E-mail:* dkringel@usw.edu. *Website:* http://www.usw.edu/.

UNIVERSITY OF THE VIRGIN ISLANDS
St. Thomas, VI

CONTACT Mavis M. Gilchrist, Director of Financial Aid, University of the Virgin Islands, RR #2, Box 10,000, Kingshill, St. Thomas, VI 00850, 340-692-4186 or toll-free 877-468-6884. *Fax:* 340-692-4145. *E-mail:* mgilchr@uvi.edu. *Website:* http://www.uvi.edu/.

UNIVERSITY OF THE WEST
Rosemead, CA

CONTACT Jamie Johnston, Financial Aid Officer, University of the West, 1409 Walnut Grove Avenue, Rosemead, CA 91770, 626-571-8811 Ext. 122. *Fax:* 626-571-1413. *E-mail:* jamiej@uwest.edu. *Website:* http://www.uwest.edu/.

THE UNIVERSITY OF TOLEDO
Toledo, OH

Tuition & fees (OH res): $9560	Average undergraduate aid package: $10,993

ABOUT THE INSTITUTION State-supported, coed. *Awards:* certificates, associate, bachelor's, master's, and doctoral degrees. 95 undergraduate majors. *Total enrollment:* 20,648. Undergraduates: 16,247. Freshmen: 3,392. Federal methodology is used as a basis for awarding need-based institutional aid.

UNDERGRADUATE EXPENSES for 2016–2017 *Application fee:* $40. *Tuition, state resident:* full-time $8052; part-time $335.49 per credit hour. *Tuition, nonresident:* full-time $17,390; part-time $724.57 per credit hour. *Required fees:* full-time $1508; $60.80 per credit hour or $6.50 per term. Full-time tuition and fees vary according to course load, program, reciprocity agreements, and student level. Part-time tuition and fees vary according to course load, program, reciprocity agreements, and student level. *College room and board:* $11,508; *Room only:* $7864. Room and board charges vary according to board plan and housing facility.

FRESHMAN FINANCIAL AID (Fall 2016, est.) 3,092 applied for aid; of those 78% were deemed to have need. 100% of freshmen with need received aid; of those 14% had need fully met. *Average percent of need met:* 64% (excluding resources awarded to replace EFC). *Average financial aid package:* $11,808 (excluding resources awarded to replace EFC). 25% of all full-time freshmen had no need and received non-need-based gift aid.

UNDERGRADUATE FINANCIAL AID (Fall 2016, est.) 10,597 applied for aid; of those 80% were deemed to have need. 99% of undergraduates with need received aid; of those 14% had need fully met. *Average percent of need met:* 57% (excluding resources awarded to replace EFC). *Average financial aid package:* $10,993 (excluding resources awarded to replace EFC). 23% of all full-time undergraduates had no need and received non-need-based gift aid.

GIFT AID (NEED-BASED) *Total amount:* $66,492,193 (35% federal, 8% state, 54% institutional, 3% external sources). *Receiving aid:* Freshmen: 71% (2,365); all full-time undergraduates: 57% (7,691). *Average award:* Freshmen: $9361; Undergraduates: $8711. *Scholarships, grants, and awards:* Federal Pell, FSEOG, state, private, college/university gift aid from institutional funds, TEACH Grants.

GIFT AID (NON-NEED-BASED) *Total amount:* $30,992,489 (1% federal, 2% state, 67% institutional, 30% external sources). *Receiving aid:* Freshmen: 19% (647). Undergraduates: 13% (1,697). *Average award:* Freshmen: $6052. Undergraduates: $6302. *Scholarships, grants, and awards by category: Academic interests/achievement:* biological sciences, business, communication, computer science, education, engineering/technologies, English, foreign languages, general academic interests/achievements, health fields, humanities, international studies, library science, mathematics, military science, physical sciences, premedicine, religion/biblical studies, social sciences. *Creative arts/performance:* art/fine arts, cinema/film/broadcasting, creative writing, general creative arts/performance, music, performing arts, theater/drama. *Special achievements/activities:* cheerleading/drum major, community service, general special achievements/activities, hobbies/interests, leadership, memberships, religious involvement. *Special characteristics:* adult students, children and siblings of alumni, children of faculty/staff, children of public servants, children of union members/company employees, ethnic background, first-generation college students, general special characteristics, handicapped students, international students, members of minority groups, out-of-state students, previous college experience, public servants, religious affiliation, siblings of current students, veterans, veterans' children. *Tuition waivers:* Full or partial for employees or children of employees. *ROTC:* Army, Air Force cooperative.

LOANS *Student loans:* $53,749,608 (89% need-based, 11% non-need-based). 66% of past graduating class borrowed through all loan programs. *Average indebtedness per student:* $24,437. *Average need-based loan:* Freshmen: $3637. Undergraduates: $4243. *Parent loans:* $18,972,734 (87% need-based, 13% non-need-based). *Programs:* Federal Direct (Subsidized and Unsubsidized Stafford, PLUS), Perkins, state, college/university, private loans, Primary Care Loans.

WORK-STUDY *Federal work-study:* Total amount: $826,713; jobs available.

ATHLETIC AWARDS Total amount: $7,058,370 (40% need-based, 60% non-need-based).

APPLYING FOR FINANCIAL AID *Required financial aid form:* FAFSA. *Financial aid deadline (priority):* 3/1. *Notification date:* Continuous beginning 4/1. Students must reply within 8 weeks of notification.

CONTACT Stephen Schissler, Director of Financial Aid, The University of Toledo, 2801 West Bancroft Street, MS-314, Toledo, OH 43606, 419-530-5812 or toll-free 800-5TOLEDO. *Fax:* 419-530-5835. *E-mail:* stephen.schissler@utoledo.edu. *Website:* http://www.utoledo.edu/.

THE UNIVERSITY OF TULSA
Tulsa, OK

Tuition & fees: $41,024	Average undergraduate aid package: $29,644

ABOUT THE INSTITUTION Independent, coed. *Awards:* certificates, bachelor's, master's, and doctoral degrees. 70 undergraduate majors. *Total enrollment:* 4,563. Undergraduates: 3,406. Freshmen: 717. Federal methodology is used as a basis for awarding need-based institutional aid.

UNDERGRADUATE EXPENSES for 2017–2018 *Application fee:* $50. *One-time required fee:* $485. *Comprehensive fee:* $52,140 includes full-time tuition ($40,484), mandatory fees ($540), and room and board ($11,116). *College room only:* $6394. Full-time tuition and fees vary according to course load and program. Room and board charges vary according to board plan and housing facility. *Part-time tuition:* $1453 per credit hour. Part-time tuition and fees vary according to course load and program.

FRESHMAN FINANCIAL AID (Fall 2016, est.) 547 applied for aid; of those 80% were deemed to have need. 100% of freshmen with need received aid; of those 46% had need fully met. *Average percent of need met:* 87% (excluding resources awarded to replace EFC). *Average financial aid package:* $32,073 (excluding resources awarded to replace EFC). 31% of all full-time freshmen had no need and received non-need-based gift aid.

UNDERGRADUATE FINANCIAL AID (Fall 2016, est.) 1,596 applied for aid; of those 86% were deemed to have need. 99% of undergraduates with need received aid; of those 43% had need fully met. *Average percent of need met:* 81% (excluding resources awarded to replace EFC). *Average financial aid package:* $29,644 (excluding resources awarded to replace EFC). 43% of all full-time undergraduates had no need and received non-need-based gift aid.

GIFT AID (NEED-BASED) *Total amount:* $7,359,325 (35% federal, 16% state, 47% institutional, 2% external sources). *Receiving aid:* Freshmen: 19% (132); all full-time undergraduates: 15% (492). *Average award:* Freshmen: $6417; Undergraduates: $5679. *Scholarships, grants, and awards:* Federal Pell, FSEOG, state, private, college/university gift aid from institutional funds.

GIFT AID (NON-NEED-BASED) *Total amount:* $51,936,026 (2% state, 95% institutional, 3% external sources). *Receiving aid:* Freshmen: 59% (423). Undergraduates: 40% (1,294). *Average award:* Freshmen: $23,514. Undergraduates: $19,520. *Scholarships, grants, and awards by category: Academic Interests/ achievement:* biological sciences, business, communication, computer science, education, engineering/technologies, English, foreign languages, general academic interests/ achievements, health fields, international studies, mathematics, physical sciences, pre-medicine, religion/biblical studies, social sciences. *Creative arts/performance:* art/fine arts, music, performing arts, theater/drama. *Special achievements/activities:* cheerleading/drum major, community service, leadership. *Special characteristics:* children and siblings of alumni, children of faculty/staff, relatives of clergy, religious affiliation, siblings of current students. *Tuition waivers:* Full or partial for employees or children of employees. *ROTC:* Air Force cooperative.

LOANS *Student loans:* $9,597,422 (46% need-based, 54% non-need-based). 48% of past graduating class borrowed through all loan programs. *Average indebtedness per student:* $37,136. *Average need-based loan:* Freshmen: $5429. Undergraduates: $6621. *Parent loans:* $5,607,720 (100% non-need-based). *Programs:* Federal Direct (Subsidized and Unsubsidized Stafford, PLUS), Perkins.

WORK-STUDY *Federal work-study:* Total amount: $863,131; 275 jobs averaging $2612. *State or other work-study/employment:* Part-time jobs available.

ATHLETIC AWARDS Total amount: $12,866,139 (100% non-need-based).

APPLYING FOR FINANCIAL AID *Required financial aid form:* FAFSA. *Financial aid deadline (priority):* 2/15. *Notification date:* Continuous beginning 2/15. Students must reply by 5/1 or within 2 weeks of notification.

CONTACT Ms. Vicki Hendrickson, Director of Student Financial Services, The University of Tulsa, 800 South Tucker Drive, Tulsa, OK 74104, 918-631-2526 or toll-free 800-331-3050. *Fax:* 918-631-5105. *E-mail:* finaid@utulsa.edu. *Website:* http://www.utulsa.edu/.

UNIVERSITY OF UTAH
Salt Lake City, UT

Tuition & fees (UT res): $8518	Average undergraduate aid package: $18,758

ABOUT THE INSTITUTION State-supported, coed. *Awards:* certificates, bachelor's, master's, and doctoral degrees. 85 undergraduate majors. *Total enrollment:* 31,860. Undergraduates: 23,789. Freshmen: 3,601. Federal methodology is used as a basis for awarding need-based institutional aid.

UNDERGRADUATE EXPENSES for 2016–2017 *Application fee:* $45. *Tuition, state resident:* full-time $7408; part-time $208.10 per credit hour. *Tuition, nonresident:* full-time $25,929; part-time $715.48 per credit hour. *Required fees:* full-time $1110; $455.36 per term. Full-time tuition and fees vary according to course level, course load, degree level, location, program, and student level. Part-time tuition and fees vary according to course level, course load, degree level, location, program, and student level. *College room and board:* $9406; *Room only:* $4874. Room and board charges vary according to board plan, housing facility, and location.

FRESHMAN FINANCIAL AID (Fall 2016, est.) 2,284 applied for aid; of those 68% were deemed to have need. 98% of freshmen with need received aid; of those 19% had need fully met. *Average percent of need met:* 68% (excluding resources awarded to replace EFC). *Average financial aid package:* $19,868 (excluding resources awarded to replace EFC). 52% of all full-time freshmen had no need and received non-need-based gift aid.

UNDERGRADUATE FINANCIAL AID (Fall 2016, est.) 10,102 applied for aid; of those 81% were deemed to have need. 97% of undergraduates with need received aid; of those 16% had need fully met. *Average percent of need met:* 65% (excluding resources awarded to replace EFC). *Average financial aid package:* $18,758 (excluding resources awarded to replace EFC). 27% of all full-time undergraduates had no need and received non-need-based gift aid.

GIFT AID (NEED-BASED) *Total amount:* $31,975,836 (88% federal, 2% state, 5% institutional, 5% external sources). *Receiving aid:* Freshmen: 41% (1,371); all full-time undergraduates: 39% (6,689). *Average award:* Freshmen: $8212; Undergrad-

---

uates: $7029. *Scholarships, grants, and awards:* Federal Pell, FSEOG, state, private, college/university gift aid from institutional funds, Federal Nursing.

GIFT AID (NON-NEED-BASED) *Total amount:* $52,849,769 (7% state, 66% institutional, 27% external sources). *Receiving aid:* Freshmen: 7% (239). Undergraduates: 3% (537). *Average award:* Freshmen: $7260. Undergraduates: $6212. *Scholarships, grants, and awards by category: Academic interests/achievement:* architecture, area/ethnic studies, biological sciences, business, communication, computer science, education, engineering/technologies, English, foreign languages, general academic interests/achievements, health fields, humanities, international studies, mathematics, military science, physical sciences, social sciences. *Creative arts/performance:* art/fine arts, cinema/film/broadcasting, creative writing, dance, journalism/publications, music, performing arts, theater/drama. *Special achievements/activities:* cheerleading/drum major, general special achievements/activities, leadership. *Special characteristics:* children of faculty/staff, children of public servants, children with a deceased or disabled parent, ethnic background, first-generation college students, handicapped students, out-of-state students, spouses of deceased or disabled public servants. *Tuition waivers:* Full or partial for employees or children of employees, senior citizens. *ROTC:* Army, Naval, Air Force.

LOANS *Student loans:* $72,743,685 (92% need-based, 8% non-need-based). 39% of past graduating class borrowed through all loan programs. *Average indebtedness per student:* $21,081. *Average need-based loan:* Freshmen: $3240. Undergraduates: $4235. *Parent loans:* $3,688,917 (100% need-based). *Programs:* Federal Direct (Subsidized and Unsubsidized Stafford, PLUS), Perkins, Federal Nursing, state, college/university.

WORK-STUDY *Federal work-study:* Total amount: $1,415,948; 320 jobs averaging $4194. *State or other work-study/employment:* Part-time jobs available.

ATHLETIC AWARDS Total amount: $10,228,641 (100% non-need-based).

APPLYING FOR FINANCIAL AID *Required financial aid form:* FAFSA. *Financial aid deadline (priority):* 3/1. *Notification date:* Continuous beginning 4/1. Students must reply within 6 weeks of notification.

CONTACT Office of Financial Aid, University of Utah, 201 South 1460 East, Room 105, Salt Lake City, UT 84112-9055, 801-581-6211 or toll-free 800-685-8856. *Fax:* 801-585-6350. *E-mail:* financialaid@sa.utah.edu. *Website:* http://www.utah.edu/.

UNIVERSITY OF VALLEY FORGE
Phoenixville, PA

Tuition & fees: $21,270	Average undergraduate aid package: $13,961

ABOUT THE INSTITUTION Independent Assemblies of God, coed. *Awards:* associate, bachelor's, and master's degrees. 28 undergraduate majors. *Total enrollment:* 877. Undergraduates: 810. Freshmen: 139. Federal methodology is used as a basis for awarding need-based institutional aid.

UNDERGRADUATE EXPENSES for 2017–2018 *Application fee:* $25. *Comprehensive fee:* $29,880 includes full-time tuition ($19,820), mandatory fees ($1450), and room and board ($8610). *College room only:* $4212. Full-time tuition and fees vary according to course load and location. Room and board charges vary according to board plan, housing facility, and location. *Part-time tuition:* $744 per credit hour. *Part-time fees:* $250 per semester hour. Part-time tuition and fees vary according to course load and location.

FRESHMAN FINANCIAL AID (Fall 2016, est.) 153 applied for aid; of those 92% were deemed to have need. 99% of freshmen with need received aid; of those 12% had need fully met. *Average percent of need met:* 55% (excluding resources awarded to replace EFC). *Average financial aid package:* $14,142 (excluding resources awarded to replace EFC). 11% of all full-time freshmen had no need and received non-need-based gift aid.

UNDERGRADUATE FINANCIAL AID (Fall 2016, est.) 640 applied for aid; of those 91% were deemed to have need. 99% of undergraduates with need received aid; of those 12% had need fully met. *Average percent of need met:* 56% (excluding resources awarded to replace EFC). *Average financial aid package:* $13,961 (excluding resources awarded to replace EFC). 10% of all full-time undergraduates had no need and received non-need-based gift aid.

GIFT AID (NEED-BASED) *Total amount:* $6,268,547 (31% federal, 9% state, 56% institutional, 4% external sources). *Receiving aid:* Freshmen: 86% (139); all full-time undergraduates: 86% (566). *Average award:* Freshmen: $11,395; Undergrad-

uates: $10,584. **Scholarships, grants, and awards:** Federal Pell, FSEOG, state, private, college/university gift aid from institutional funds.

GIFT AID (NON-NEED-BASED) Total amount: $832,691 (1% federal, 93% institutional, 6% external sources). **Receiving aid:** Freshmen: 7% (11). Undergraduates: 7% (45). **Average award:** Freshmen: $9428. Undergraduates: $8222. **Scholarships, grants, and awards by category:** Academic interests/achievement: 488 awards ($1,940,849 total): general academic interests/achievements. Creative arts/performance: 195 awards ($988,807 total): art/fine arts, music. Special achievements/activities: 105 awards ($199,741 total): community service, general special achievements/activities, leadership, religious involvement. Special characteristics: 338 awards ($950,140 total): children of current students, children of faculty/staff, general special characteristics, local/state students, married students, parents of current students, relatives of clergy, siblings of current students, spouses of current students. **Tuition waivers:** Full or partial for employees or children of employees, senior citizens.

LOANS Student loans: $5,579,508 (81% need-based, 19% non-need-based). 87% of past graduating class borrowed through all loan programs. Average indebtedness per student: $34,920. **Average need-based loan:** Freshmen: $3351. Undergraduates: $4059. **Parent loans:** $2,947,815 (64% need-based, 36% non-need-based). **Programs:** Federal Direct (Subsidized and Unsubsidized Stafford, PLUS), Perkins.

WORK-STUDY Federal work-study: Total amount: $48,078; 18 jobs averaging $2671.

APPLYING FOR FINANCIAL AID Required financial aid form: FAFSA. **Financial aid deadline (priority):** 5/1. **Notification date:** Continuous beginning 12/1. Students must reply within 2 weeks of notification.

CONTACT Mrs. Linda Stein, Director of Financial Aid, University of Valley Forge, 1401 Charlestown Road, Phoenixville, PA 19460-2399, 610-917-1416 or toll-free 800-432-8322. Fax: 610-917-2069. E-mail: llstein@vfcc.edu. Website: http://www.valleyforge.edu/.

UNIVERSITY OF VALLEY FORGE VIRGINIA CAMPUS
Woodbridge, VA

CONTACT Christiana Bruwaa-Frimpong, Student Accounts/Financial Aid Counselor, University of Valley Forge Virginia Campus, 13909 Smoketown Road, Woodbridge, VA 22192, 703-580-4810 Ext. 172 or toll-free 800-432-8322. Fax: 703-580-4806. Website: http://www.valleyforge.edu/.

UNIVERSITY OF VERMONT
Burlington, VT

Tuition & fees (VT res): $17,270	Average undergraduate aid package: $23,942

ABOUT THE INSTITUTION State-supported, coed. **Awards:** certificates, bachelor's, master's, and doctoral degrees. 101 undergraduate majors. **Total enrollment:** 13,105. Undergraduates: 11,159. Freshmen: 2,496. Federal methodology is used as a basis for awarding need-based institutional aid.

UNDERGRADUATE EXPENSES for 2016–2017 **Application fee:** $55. **Tuition, state resident:** full-time $15,096; part-time $611 per credit hour. **Tuition, nonresident:** full-time $38,160; part-time $1544 per credit hour. **Required fees:** full-time $2174. Part-time tuition and fees vary according to course load. **College room and board:** $11,608; **Room only:** $7788. Room and board charges vary according to board plan and housing facility.

FRESHMAN FINANCIAL AID (Fall 2015) 1,904 applied for aid; of those 76% were deemed to have need. 100% of freshmen with need received aid; of those 17% had need fully met. **Average percent of need met:** 69% (excluding resources awarded to replace EFC). **Average financial aid package:** $25,064 (excluding resources awarded to replace EFC). 33% of all full-time freshmen had no need and received non-need-based gift aid.

UNDERGRADUATE FINANCIAL AID (Fall 2015) 6,569 applied for aid; of those 81% were deemed to have need. 99% of undergraduates with need received aid; of those 14% had need fully met. **Average percent of need met:** 65% (excluding resources awarded to replace EFC). **Average financial aid package:** $23,942

(excluding resources awarded to replace EFC). 31% of all full-time undergraduates had no need and received non-need-based gift aid.

GIFT AID (NEED-BASED) Total amount: $79,051,830 (11% federal, 5% state, 80% institutional, 4% external sources). **Receiving aid:** Freshmen: 60% (1,436); all full-time undergraduates: 51% (4,966). **Average award:** Freshmen: $17,711; Undergraduates: $15,647. **Scholarships, grants, and awards:** Federal Pell, FSEOG, state, private, college/university gift aid from institutional funds, Federal Nursing.

GIFT AID (NON-NEED-BASED) Total amount: $29,321,332 (1% state, 92% institutional, 7% external sources). **Receiving aid:** Freshmen: 8% (188). Undergraduates: 5% (483). **Average award:** Freshmen: $13,360. Undergraduates: $10,950. **Scholarships, grants, and awards by category:** Academic interests/achievement: agriculture, area/ethnic studies, business, computer science, education, engineering/technologies, English, foreign languages, general academic interests/achievements, health fields, home economics, humanities, international studies, mathematics, military science, physical sciences, premedicine, social sciences. Creative arts/performance: debating, music, theater/drama. Special achievements/activities: community service, leadership, memberships. Special characteristics: adult students, ethnic background, first-generation college students. **Tuition waivers:** Full or partial for employees or children of employees. **ROTC:** Army.

LOANS Student loans: $45,028,749 (36% need-based, 64% non-need-based). 61% of past graduating class borrowed through all loan programs. Average indebtedness per student: $26,964. **Average need-based loan:** Freshmen: $3416. Undergraduates: $4454. **Parent loans:** $23,658,595 (100% non-need-based). **Programs:** Federal Direct (Subsidized and Unsubsidized Stafford, PLUS), Perkins, Federal Nursing, college/university.

WORK-STUDY Federal work-study: 1,415 jobs averaging $1600.

ATHLETIC AWARDS Total amount: $6,907,575 (24% need-based, 76% non-need-based).

APPLYING FOR FINANCIAL AID Required financial aid form: FAFSA. **Financial aid deadline (priority):** 2/1. **Notification date:** 3/15. Students must reply within 4 weeks of notification.

CONTACT Office of Student Financial Services, University of Vermont, 223 Waterman Building, Burlington, VT 05405-0160, 802-656-5700. Fax: 802-656-4076. E-mail: sfs@uvm.edu. Website: http://www.uvm.edu/.

UNIVERSITY OF VIRGINIA
Charlottesville, VA

Tuition & fees (VA res): $15,162	Average undergraduate aid package: $26,422

ABOUT THE INSTITUTION State-supported, coed. **Awards:** certificates, bachelor's, master's, and doctoral degrees. 50 undergraduate majors. **Total enrollment:** 23,883. Undergraduates: 16,736. Freshmen: 3,685. Both federal and institutional methodology are used as a basis for awarding need-based institutional aid.

UNDERGRADUATE EXPENSES for 2016–2017 **Application fee:** $60. **Tuition, state resident:** full-time $12,494; part-time $415 per credit hour. **Tuition, nonresident:** full-time $42,642; part-time $1420 per credit hour. **Required fees:** full-time $2668; $2654 per year. Full-time tuition and fees vary according to location, program, and student level. Part-time tuition and fees vary according to location, program, and student level. **College room and board:** $10,726; **Room only:** $5876. Room and board charges vary according to board plan and housing facility.

FRESHMAN FINANCIAL AID (Fall 2016, est.) 2,656 applied for aid; of those 48% were deemed to have need. 100% of freshmen with need received aid; of those 100% had need fully met. **Average percent of need met:** 100% (excluding resources awarded to replace EFC). **Average financial aid package:** $28,084 (excluding resources awarded to replace EFC). 3% of all full-time freshmen had no need and received non-need-based gift aid.

UNDERGRADUATE FINANCIAL AID (Fall 2016, est.) 8,961 applied for aid; of those 56% were deemed to have need. 100% of undergraduates with need received aid; of those 100% had need fully met. **Average percent of need met:** 100% (excluding resources awarded to replace EFC). **Average financial aid package:** $26,422 (excluding resources awarded to replace EFC). 4% of all full-time undergraduates had no need and received non-need-based gift aid.

GIFT AID (NEED-BASED) Total amount: $86,839,878 (13% federal, 7% state, 73% institutional, 7% external sources). **Receiving aid:** Freshmen: 30% (1,097); all full-time undergraduates: 27% (4,215). **Average award:** Freshmen: $21,517; Undergraduates: $20,980. *Scholarships, grants, and awards:* Federal Pell, FSEOG, state, private, college/university gift aid from institutional funds, Federal Nursing.

GIFT AID (NON-NEED-BASED) *Total amount:* $22,672,793 (9% federal, 21% institutional, 70% external sources). *Receiving aid:* Freshmen: 3% (97). Undergraduates: 2% (332). *Average award:* Freshmen: $7315. Undergraduates: $5966. *Scholarships, grants, and awards by category: Academic interests/achievement:* general academic interests/achievements. *Creative arts/performance:* music, theater/drama. *Special achievements/activities:* leadership. *Tuition waivers:* Full or partial for employees or children of employees, senior citizens. *ROTC:* Army, Naval, Air Force.

LOANS *Student loans:* $35,456,905 (51% need-based, 49% non-need-based). 33% of past graduating class borrowed through all loan programs. *Average indebtedness per student:* $24,598. *Average need-based loan:* Freshmen: $5314. Undergraduates: $5756. *Parent loans:* $11,968,856 (15% need-based, 85% non-need-based). *Programs:* Federal Direct (Subsidized and Unsubsidized Stafford, PLUS), Perkins, Federal Nursing, college/university, private loans.

WORK-STUDY *Federal work-study:* Total amount: $2,959,387; jobs available. *State or other work-study/employment:* Total amount: $131,373 (100% need-based). Part-time jobs available.

ATHLETIC AWARDS Total amount: $15,230,302 (19% need-based, 81% non-need-based).

APPLYING FOR FINANCIAL AID *Required financial aid forms:* FAFSA, CSS Financial Aid PROFILE. *Financial aid deadline (priority):* 3/1. *Notification date:* 4/5. Students must reply by 5/1.

CONTACT Mr. Scott Miller, Director of Financial Aid, University of Virginia, PO Box 400204, Charlottesville, VA 22904-4204, 434-982-6000. *Fax:* 434-924-0063. *E-mail:* faid@virginia.edu.

Website: http://www.virginia.edu/.

THE UNIVERSITY OF VIRGINIA'S COLLEGE AT WISE
Wise, VA

Tuition & fees (VA res): $9539	Average undergraduate aid package: $13,356

ABOUT THE INSTITUTION State-supported, coed. *Awards:* bachelor's degrees. 25 undergraduate majors. *Total enrollment:* 2,221. Undergraduates: 2,221. Freshmen: 334. Federal methodology is used as a basis for awarding need-based institutional aid.

UNDERGRADUATE EXPENSES for 2016–2017 *Application fee:* $25. *Tuition, state resident:* full-time $5210; part-time $222 per credit hour. *Tuition, nonresident:* full-time $21,278; part-time $900 per credit hour. *Required fees:* full-time $4329; $51 per credit hour or $51 per credit hour. Part-time tuition and fees vary according to course load. *College room and board:* $10,346. Room and board charges vary according to board plan and housing facility.

FRESHMAN FINANCIAL AID (Fall 2015) 315 applied for aid; of those 88% were deemed to have need. 100% of freshmen with need received aid; of those 34% had need fully met. *Average percent of need met:* 48% (excluding resources awarded to replace EFC). *Average financial aid package:* $15,285 (excluding resources awarded to replace EFC). 5% of all full-time freshmen had no need and received non-need-based gift aid.

UNDERGRADUATE FINANCIAL AID (Fall 2015) 1,192 applied for aid; of those 88% were deemed to have need. 100% of undergraduates with need received aid; of those 14% had need fully met. *Average percent of need met:* 88% (excluding resources awarded to replace EFC). *Average financial aid package:* $13,356 (excluding resources awarded to replace EFC). 2% of all full-time undergraduates had no need and received non-need-based gift aid.

GIFT AID (NEED-BASED) *Total amount:* $5,230,133 (69% federal, 7% state, 24% institutional). *Receiving aid:* Freshmen: 76% (244); all full-time undergraduates: 62% (807). *Average award:* Freshmen: $7606; Undergraduates: $4755. *Scholarships, grants, and awards:* Federal Pell, FSEOG, state, private, college/university gift aid from institutional funds.

GIFT AID (NON-NEED-BASED) *Total amount:* $2,684,672 (2% federal, 15% state, 52% institutional, 31% external sources). *Receiving aid:* Freshmen: 14% (46). Undergraduates: 56% (734). *Average award:* Freshmen: $4495. Undergraduates: $5483. *Scholarships, grants, and awards by category: Academic interests/*

achievement: agriculture, biological sciences, business, computer science, education, English, general academic interests/achievements, health fields, humanities, mathematics, physical sciences, premedicine, social sciences. *Creative arts/performance:* creative writing, general creative arts/performance, journalism/publications, music, performing arts, theater/drama. *Special achievements/activities:* community service, religious involvement. *Special characteristics:* children with a deceased or disabled parent, ethnic background, local/state students, veterans, veterans' children. *Tuition waivers:* Full or partial for employees or children of employees, senior citizens. *ROTC:* Army.

LOANS *Student loans:* $5,544,345 (49% need-based, 51% non-need-based). 58% of past graduating class borrowed through all loan programs. *Average indebtedness per student:* $14,478. *Average need-based loan:* Freshmen: $2278. Undergraduates: $3795. *Parent loans:* $942,172 (100% non-need-based). *Programs:* Perkins, state, college/university.

WORK-STUDY *Federal work-study:* jobs available.

ATHLETIC AWARDS Total amount: $1,245,545 (19% need-based, 81% non-need-based).

APPLYING FOR FINANCIAL AID *Required financial aid form:* FAFSA. *Financial aid deadline (priority):* 4/1. *Notification date:* Continuous. Students must reply within 4 weeks of notification.

CONTACT Mrs. Rebecca Huffman, Director of Financial Aid, The University of Virginia's College at Wise, 1 College Avenue, Wise, VA 24293, 276-328-0277 or toll-free 888-282-9324. *Fax:* 276-328-0251. *E-mail:* reg5a@uvawise.edu.

Website: http://www.uvawise.edu/.

UNIVERSITY OF WASHINGTON
Seattle, WA

Tuition & fees (WA res): $10,753	Average undergraduate aid package: $19,100

ABOUT THE INSTITUTION State-supported, coed. *Awards:* certificates, bachelor's, master's, and doctoral degrees. 147 undergraduate majors. *Total enrollment:* 45,591. Undergraduates: 30,933. Freshmen: 6,475. Federal methodology is used as a basis for awarding need-based institutional aid.

UNDERGRADUATE EXPENSES for 2017–2018 *Application fee:* $70. *Tuition, state resident:* full-time $9694; part-time $323 per credit. *Tuition, nonresident:* full-time $33,732; part-time $1124 per credit. *Required fees:* full-time $1059; $27 per credit or $84 per term. Full-time tuition and fees vary according to course load and location. Part-time tuition and fees vary according to course load and location. *College room and board:* $11,691. Room and board charges vary according to board plan and housing facility. *Payment plan:* Tuition prepayment.

FRESHMAN FINANCIAL AID (Fall 2016, est.) 4,664 applied for aid; of those 59% were deemed to have need. 83% of freshmen with need received aid; of those 48% had need fully met. *Average percent of need met:* 82% (excluding resources awarded to replace EFC). *Average financial aid package:* $17,800 (excluding resources awarded to replace EFC). 5% of all full-time freshmen had no need and received non-need-based gift aid.

UNDERGRADUATE FINANCIAL AID (Fall 2016, est.) 11,770 applied for aid; of those 99% were deemed to have need. 90% of undergraduates with need received aid; of those 30% had need fully met. *Average percent of need met:* 82% (excluding resources awarded to replace EFC). *Average financial aid package:* $19,100 (excluding resources awarded to replace EFC). 4% of all full-time undergraduates had no need and received non-need-based gift aid.

GIFT AID (NEED-BASED) *Total amount:* $167,800,000 (20% federal, 32% state, 45% institutional, 3% external sources). *Receiving aid:* Freshmen: 31% (2,050); all full-time undergraduates: 32% (9,000). *Average award:* Freshmen: $14,000; Undergraduates: $15,000. *Scholarships, grants, and awards:* Federal Pell, FSEOG, state, private, college/university gift aid from institutional funds.

GIFT AID (NON-NEED-BASED) *Total amount:* $25,000,000 (80% institutional, 20% external sources). *Receiving aid:* Freshmen: 5% (350). Undergraduates: 2% (650). *Average award:* Freshmen: $6000. Undergraduates: $6000. *Scholarships, grants, and awards by category: Academic interests/achievement:* architecture, business, computer science, education, engineering/technologies, general academic interests/achievements, health fields. *Creative arts/performance:* art/fine arts, general creative arts/performance, music, performing arts. *Special achievements/activities:* general special achievements/activities, leadership, memberships. *Tuition*

waivers: Full or partial for employees or children of employees, senior citizens. **ROTC:** Army, Naval, Air Force.
LOANS *Student loans:* $65,000,000 (72% need-based, 28% non-need-based). 40% of past graduating class borrowed through all loan programs. *Average indebtedness per student:* $21,900. *Average need-based loan:* Freshmen: $5500. Undergraduates: $7000. *Parent loans:* $46,000,000 (100% non-need-based). *Programs:* Federal Direct (Subsidized and Unsubsidized Stafford, PLUS), Perkins, Federal Nursing.
WORK-STUDY *Federal work-study:* Total amount: $1,800,000; 540 jobs averaging $4146. *State or other work-study/employment:* Total amount: $550,000 (100% need-based). 145 part-time jobs averaging $4841.
ATHLETIC AWARDS Total amount: $15,100,000 (100% non-need-based).
APPLYING FOR FINANCIAL AID *Required financial aid form:* FAFSA. *Financial aid deadline (priority):* 1/15. *Notification date:* 4/1. Students must reply by 5/1 or within 3 weeks of notification.
CONTACT Office of Student Financial Aid, University of Washington, Box 355880, Seattle, WA 98195-5880, 206-543-6101. *Fax:* 206-685-1338. *E-mail:* osfa@u.washington.edu.
Website: http://www.washington.edu/.

UNIVERSITY OF WASHINGTON, BOTHELL
Bothell, WA

Tuition & fees (WA res): $10,690	Average undergraduate aid package: $14,900

ABOUT THE INSTITUTION State-supported, coed. *Awards:* bachelor's and master's degrees. 32 undergraduate majors. *Total enrollment:* 5,734. Undergraduates: 5,112. Freshmen: 820. Federal methodology is used as a basis for awarding need-based institutional aid.
UNDERGRADUATE EXPENSES for 2017–2018 Application fee: $60. *Tuition, state resident:* full-time $9694; part-time $323 per credit. *Tuition, non-resident:* full-time $33,732; part-time $1124 per credit. *Required fees:* full-time $996; $33 per credit. Full-time tuition and fees vary according to course load. Part-time tuition and fees vary according to course load. *College room and board:* $10,833. Room and board charges vary according to board plan, housing facility, and location. *Payment plan:* Tuition prepayment.
FRESHMAN FINANCIAL AID (Fall 2016, est.) 632 applied for aid; of those 77% were deemed to have need. 93% of freshmen with need received aid; of those 24% had need fully met. *Average percent of need met:* 82% (excluding resources awarded to replace EFC). *Average financial aid package:* $13,100 (excluding resources awarded to replace EFC). 6% of all full-time freshmen had no need and received non-need-based gift aid.
UNDERGRADUATE FINANCIAL AID (Fall 2016, est.) 2,956 applied for aid; of those 84% were deemed to have need. 95% of undergraduates with need received aid; of those 27% had need fully met. *Average percent of need met:* 82% (excluding resources awarded to replace EFC). *Average financial aid package:* $14,900 (excluding resources awarded to replace EFC). 4% of all full-time undergraduates had no need and received non-need-based gift aid.
GIFT AID (NEED-BASED) *Total amount:* $31,015,200 (27% federal, 36% state, 36% institutional, 1% external sources). *Receiving aid:* Freshmen: 53% (420); all full-time undergraduates: 48% (2,105). *Average award:* Freshmen: $15,000; Undergraduates: $15,500. *Scholarships, grants, and awards:* Federal Pell, FSEOG, state, private, college/university gift aid from institutional funds.
GIFT AID (NON-NEED-BASED) *Total amount:* $1,150,000 (70% institutional, 30% external sources). *Receiving aid:* Freshmen: 6% (45). Undergraduates: 4% (170). *Average award:* Freshmen: $7300. Undergraduates: $7300. *Scholarships, grants, and awards by category: Academic interests/achievement:* general academic interests/achievements. *Tuition waivers:* Full or partial for employees or children of employees, senior citizens. *ROTC:* Army cooperative, Naval cooperative, Air Force cooperative.
LOANS *Student loans:* $14,000,000 (73% need-based, 27% non-need-based). 47% of past graduating class borrowed through all loan programs. *Average indebtedness per student:* $19,640. *Average need-based loan:* Freshmen: $5500. Undergraduates: $7000. *Parent loans:* $1,100,000 (100% need-based). *Programs:* Federal Direct (Subsidized and Unsubsidized Stafford, PLUS), Perkins, Federal Nursing.

WORK-STUDY *Federal work-study:* Total amount: $250,000; 70 jobs averaging $4187. *State or other work-study/employment:* Total amount: $200,000 (100% need-based). 22 part-time jobs averaging $4407.
APPLYING FOR FINANCIAL AID *Required financial aid form:* FAFSA. *Financial aid deadline (priority):* 1/15. *Notification date:* 4/1. Students must reply by 5/1 or within 3 weeks of notification.
CONTACT Office of Student Financial Aid, University of Washington, Bothell, Box 358500, 18115 Campus Way NE, Bothell, WA 98011-8246, 425-352-5240. *Fax:* 425-352-3217. *E-mail:* finaid@uwb.edu.
Website: http://www.uwb.edu/.

UNIVERSITY OF WASHINGTON, TACOMA
Tacoma, WA

Tuition & fees (WA res): $10,831	Average undergraduate aid package: $15,700

ABOUT THE INSTITUTION State-supported, coed. *Awards:* certificates, bachelor's, master's, and doctoral degrees. 36 undergraduate majors. *Total enrollment:* 4,987. Undergraduates: 4,285. Freshmen: 534. Federal methodology is used as a basis for awarding need-based institutional aid.
UNDERGRADUATE EXPENSES for 2017–2018 Application fee: $60. *Tuition, state resident:* full-time $9694; part-time $323 per credit. *Tuition, non-resident:* full-time $33,732; part-time $1124 per credit. *Required fees:* full-time $1137; $38 per credit. Full-time tuition and fees vary according to course load. Part-time tuition and fees vary according to course load. *College room and board:* $10,230. Room and board charges vary according to housing facility and location. *Payment plan:* Tuition prepayment.
FRESHMAN FINANCIAL AID (Fall 2016, est.) 460 applied for aid; of those 78% were deemed to have need. 91% of freshmen with need received aid; of those 33% had need fully met. *Average percent of need met:* 82% (excluding resources awarded to replace EFC). *Average financial aid package:* $13,400 (excluding resources awarded to replace EFC). 6% of all full-time freshmen had no need and received non-need-based gift aid.
UNDERGRADUATE FINANCIAL AID (Fall 2016, est.) 3,053 applied for aid; of those 88% were deemed to have need. 95% of undergraduates with need received aid; of those 31% had need fully met. *Average percent of need met:* 82% (excluding resources awarded to replace EFC). *Average financial aid package:* $15,700 (excluding resources awarded to replace EFC). 11% of all full-time undergraduates had no need and received non-need-based gift aid.
GIFT AID (NEED-BASED) *Total amount:* $36,359,000 (27% federal, 37% state, 35% institutional, 1% external sources). *Receiving aid:* Freshmen: 62% (311); all full-time undergraduates: 63% (2,356). *Average award:* Freshmen: $15,000; Undergraduates: $15,500. *Scholarships, grants, and awards:* Federal Pell, FSEOG, state, private, college/university gift aid from institutional funds.
GIFT AID (NON-NEED-BASED) *Total amount:* $910,000 (55% institutional, 45% external sources). *Receiving aid:* Freshmen: 6% (30). Undergraduates: 11% (400). *Average award:* Freshmen: $3000. Undergraduates: $3075. *Scholarships, grants, and awards by category: Academic interests/achievement:* general academic interests/achievements. *Tuition waivers:* Full or partial for employees or children of employees, senior citizens. *ROTC:* Army cooperative, Naval cooperative, Air Force cooperative.
LOANS *Student loans:* $14,231,000 (85% need-based, 15% non-need-based). 51% of past graduating class borrowed through all loan programs. *Average indebtedness per student:* $18,420. *Average need-based loan:* Freshmen: $5500. Undergraduates: $7000. *Parent loans:* $2,886,000 (26% need-based, 74% non-need-based). *Programs:* Federal Direct (Subsidized and Unsubsidized Stafford, PLUS), Perkins, Federal Nursing.
WORK-STUDY *Federal work-study:* Total amount: $295,000; 110 jobs averaging $4083. *State or other work-study/employment:* Total amount: $155,000 (100% need-based). 7 part-time jobs averaging $4386.
APPLYING FOR FINANCIAL AID *Required financial aid form:* FAFSA. *Financial aid deadline (priority):* 1/15. *Notification date:* 4/1. Students must reply by 5/1 or within 3 weeks of notification.

CONTACT Office of Student Financial Aid, University of Washington, Tacoma, 1900 Commerce Street, Box 358400, Tacoma, WA 98402-3100, 253-692-4374 or toll-free 800-736-7750. *Fax:* 253-692-4788. *E-mail:* uwtfa@uw.edu.
Website: http://www.tacoma.uw.edu/.

THE UNIVERSITY OF WEST ALABAMA
Livingston, AL

Tuition & fees (AL res): $8876	Average undergraduate aid package: $10,833

ABOUT THE INSTITUTION State-supported, coed. **Awards:** certificates, associate, bachelor's, and master's degrees. 28 undergraduate majors. **Total enrollment:** 3,986. Undergraduates: 1,978. Freshmen: 377. Federal methodology is used as a basis for awarding need-based institutional aid.
UNDERGRADUATE EXPENSES for 2017–2018 Application fee: $40. **Tuition, state resident:** full-time $7286; part-time $310 per hour. **Tuition, nonresident:** full-time $14,572; part-time $620 per hour. **Required fees:** full-time $1590. Full-time tuition and fees vary according to course load. Part-time tuition and fees vary according to course load. **College room and board:** $6640; **Room only:** $4040. Room and board charges vary according to board plan, housing facility, and student level.
FRESHMAN FINANCIAL AID (Fall 2015) 378 applied for aid; of those 89% were deemed to have need. 100% of freshmen with need received aid; of those 1% had need fully met. **Average percent of need met:** 23% (excluding resources awarded to replace EFC). **Average financial aid package:** $10,478 (excluding resources awarded to replace EFC). 7% of all full-time freshmen had no need and received non-need-based gift aid.
UNDERGRADUATE FINANCIAL AID (Fall 2015) 1,472 applied for aid; of those 88% were deemed to have need. 99% of undergraduates with need received aid; of those 7% had need fully met. **Average percent of need met:** 23% (excluding resources awarded to replace EFC). **Average financial aid package:** $10,833 (excluding resources awarded to replace EFC). 4% of all full-time undergraduates had no need and received non-need-based gift aid.
GIFT AID (NEED-BASED) Total amount: $4,471,951 (99% federal, 1% state). **Receiving aid:** Freshmen: 55% (231); all full-time undergraduates: 53% (908). **Average award:** Freshmen: $5116; Undergraduates: $5123. **Scholarships, grants, and awards:** Federal Pell, FSEOG, state, private, college/university gift aid from institutional funds, United Negro College Fund.
GIFT AID (NON-NEED-BASED) Total amount: $2,583,623 (89% institutional, 11% external sources). **Receiving aid:** Freshmen: 50% (208). Undergraduates: 33% (562). **Average award:** Freshmen: $4896. Undergraduates: $4844. **Scholarships, grants, and awards by category:** Academic interests/achievement: English, general academic interests/achievements. Creative arts/performance: dance, music, theater/drama. Special achievements/activities: cheerleading/drum major, general special achievements/activities, junior miss, leadership, memberships, rodeo. Special characteristics: children and siblings of alumni, children of faculty/staff, first-generation college students, previous college experience. **Tuition waivers:** Full or partial for employees or children of employees. **ROTC:** Air Force cooperative.
LOANS Student loans: $9,348,880 (47% need-based, 53% non-need-based). 76% of past graduating class borrowed through all loan programs. *Average indebtedness per student:* $24,449. **Parent loans:** $3,649,562 (100% non-need-based). **Programs:** Federal Direct (Subsidized and Unsubsidized Stafford, PLUS), Perkins.
WORK-STUDY Federal work-study: 99 jobs averaging $3338. **State or other work-study/employment:** 45 part-time jobs averaging $2300.
ATHLETIC AWARDS Total amount: $1,859,754 (100% non-need-based).
APPLYING FOR FINANCIAL AID Required financial aid form: FAFSA. **Financial aid deadline (priority):** 3/1. **Notification date:** Continuous beginning 4/15. Students must reply within 2 weeks of notification.
CONTACT Mr. Don Rainer, Director of Financial Aid, The University of West Alabama, Station 3, Livingston, AL 35470, 205-652-3576 or toll-free 888-636-8800. *Fax:* 205-652-3847. *E-mail:* drainer@uwa.edu.
Website: http://www.uwa.edu/.

UNIVERSITY OF WEST FLORIDA
Pensacola, FL

Tuition & fees (FL res): $6360	Average undergraduate aid package: $8006

ABOUT THE INSTITUTION State-supported, coed. **Awards:** certificates, associate, bachelor's, master's, and doctoral degrees. 56 undergraduate majors. **Total enrollment:** 12,798. Undergraduates: 10,200. Freshmen: 1,217. Federal methodology is used as a basis for awarding need-based institutional aid.
UNDERGRADUATE EXPENSES for 2016–2017 Application fee: $30. **Tuition, state resident:** full-time $6360; part-time $212 per credit hour. **Tuition, nonresident:** full-time $19,260; part-time $642 per credit hour. Full-time tuition and fees vary according to location and reciprocity agreements. Part-time tuition and fees vary according to location and reciprocity agreements. **College room and board:** $9580; **Room only:** $5800. Room and board charges vary according to board plan, housing facility, and student level. **Payment plan:** Tuition prepayment.
FRESHMAN FINANCIAL AID (Fall 2015) 1,001 applied for aid; of those 74% were deemed to have need. 97% of freshmen with need received aid; of those 13% had need fully met. **Average percent of need met:** 59% (excluding resources awarded to replace EFC). **Average financial aid package:** $7782 (excluding resources awarded to replace EFC). 2% of all full-time freshmen had no need and received non-need-based gift aid.
UNDERGRADUATE FINANCIAL AID (Fall 2015) 5,503 applied for aid; of those 84% were deemed to have need. 95% of undergraduates with need received aid; of those 10% had need fully met. **Average percent of need met:** 58% (excluding resources awarded to replace EFC). **Average financial aid package:** $8006 (excluding resources awarded to replace EFC). 3% of all full-time undergraduates had no need and received non-need-based gift aid.
GIFT AID (NEED-BASED) Total amount: $25,270,182 (62% federal, 18% state, 18% institutional, 2% external sources). **Receiving aid:** Freshmen: 60% (698); all full-time undergraduates: 55% (3,858). **Average award:** Freshmen: $5797; Undergraduates: $5798. **Scholarships, grants, and awards:** Federal Pell, FSEOG, state, private, college/university gift aid from institutional funds.
GIFT AID (NON-NEED-BASED) Total amount: $2,426,563 (61% state, 27% institutional, 12% external sources). **Receiving aid:** Freshmen: 2% (19). Undergraduates: 1% (71). **Average award:** Freshmen: $1380. Undergraduates: $2132. **Scholarships, grants, and awards by category:** Academic interests/achievement: biological sciences, business, communication, computer science, education, engineering/technologies, general academic interests/achievements, mathematics, military science, physical sciences, social sciences. Creative arts/performance: applied art and design, art/fine arts, music, theater/drama. Special achievements/activities: leadership. Special characteristics: children and siblings of alumni, children of faculty/staff, handicapped students, international students, out-of-state students, veterans. **Tuition waivers:** Full or partial for employees or children of employees, senior citizens. **ROTC:** Army, Air Force.
LOANS Student loans: $32,151,105 (83% need-based, 17% non-need-based). *Average need-based loan:* Freshmen: $3087. Undergraduates: $4022. **Parent loans:** $6,351,072 (13% need-based, 87% non-need-based). **Programs:** Federal Direct (Subsidized and Unsubsidized Stafford, PLUS), Perkins.
WORK-STUDY Federal work-study: 258 jobs averaging $1418. **State or other work-study/employment:** Part-time jobs available.
ATHLETIC AWARDS Total amount: $1,225,528 (42% need-based, 58% non-need-based).
APPLYING FOR FINANCIAL AID Required financial aid form: FAFSA. **Financial aid deadline:** Continuous. **Notification date:** Continuous beginning 3/1.
CONTACT Ms. Shana Gore, Coordinator of Financial Aid, University of West Florida, 11000 University Parkway, Pensacola, FL 32514-5750, 850-474-2398 or toll-free 800-263-1074. *E-mail:* sgore1@uwf.edu.
Website: http://www.uwf.edu/.

UNIVERSITY OF WEST GEORGIA
Carrollton, GA

Tuition & fees (GA res): $7188	Average undergraduate aid package: $8852

ABOUT THE INSTITUTION State-supported, coed. *Awards:* certificates, bachelor's, master's, and doctoral degrees. 39 undergraduate majors. *Total enrollment:* 13,308. Undergraduates: 11,155. Freshmen: 2,434. Federal methodology is used as a basis for awarding need-based institutional aid.

UNDERGRADUATE EXPENSES for 2017–2018 Application fee: $40. *Tuition, state resident:* full-time $5226; part-time $174.20 per semester hour. *Tuition, nonresident:* full-time $18,444; part-time $614.80 per semester hour. *Required fees:* full-time $1962. Full-time tuition and fees vary according to course load, degree level, location, and program. Part-time tuition and fees vary according to course load, degree level, location, and program. *College room and board:* $9652; *Room only:* $5300. Room and board charges vary according to board plan and housing facility.

FRESHMAN FINANCIAL AID (Fall 2016, est.) 2,296 applied for aid; of those 82% were deemed to have need. 99% of freshmen with need received aid; of those 60% had need fully met. *Average percent of need met:* 46% (excluding resources awarded to replace EFC). *Average financial aid package:* $8591 (excluding resources awarded to replace EFC). 8% of all full-time freshmen had no need and received non-need-based gift aid.

UNDERGRADUATE FINANCIAL AID (Fall 2016, est.) 8,162 applied for aid; of those 84% were deemed to have need. 98% of undergraduates with need received aid; of those 55% had need fully met. *Average percent of need met:* 47% (excluding resources awarded to replace EFC). *Average financial aid package:* $8852 (excluding resources awarded to replace EFC). 6% of all full-time undergraduates had no need and received non-need-based gift aid.

GIFT AID (NEED-BASED) Total amount: $25,893,350 (99% federal, 1% institutional). *Receiving aid:* Freshmen: 52% (1,235); all full-time undergraduates: 51% (4,602). *Average award:* Freshmen: $5002; Undergraduates: $4965. *Scholarships, grants, and awards:* Federal Pell, FSEOG, state, private, college/university gift aid from institutional funds, United Negro College Fund, Federal Nursing.

GIFT AID (NON-NEED-BASED) Total amount: $20,768,334 (89% state, 7% institutional, 4% external sources). *Receiving aid:* Freshmen: 14% (328). Undergraduates: 10% (901). *Average award:* Freshmen: $1675. Undergraduates: $2334. *Scholarships, grants, and awards by category: Academic interests/achievement:* biological sciences, business, communication, computer science, education, English, foreign languages, general academic interests/achievements, home economics, humanities, mathematics, physical sciences, premedicine, social sciences. *Creative arts/performance:* applied art and design, art/fine arts, debating, general creative arts/performance, journalism/publications, music, performing arts, theater/drama. *Special achievements/activities:* community service, leadership, memberships, religious involvement. *Special characteristics:* adult students, children and siblings of alumni, general special characteristics, handicapped students, international students, local/state students, members of minority groups. *Tuition waivers:* Full or partial for employees or children of employees, senior citizens. *ROTC:* Air Force cooperative.

LOANS Student loans: $48,247,786 (47% need-based, 53% non-need-based). 76% of past graduating class borrowed through all loan programs. *Average indebtedness per student:* $26,874. *Average need-based loan:* Freshmen: $3398. Undergraduates: $4058. *Parent loans:* $15,360,903 (100% non-need-based). *Programs:* Federal Direct (Subsidized and Unsubsidized Stafford, PLUS), Perkins, Federal Nursing, state.

WORK-STUDY Federal work-study: Total amount: $474,938; jobs available. *State or other work-study/employment:* Part-time jobs available.

ATHLETIC AWARDS Total amount: $1,358,311 (100% non-need-based).

APPLYING FOR FINANCIAL AID Required financial aid form: FAFSA. *Financial aid deadline:* 7/1 (priority: 4/1). *Notification date:* 5/1.

CONTACT Dr. Philip Hawkins, Director of Financial Aid, University of West Georgia, 1601 Maple Street, Aycock Hall, Carrollton, GA 30118, 678-839-6421. *Fax:* 678-839-6422. *E-mail:* finaid@westga.edu. *Website:* http://www.westga.edu/.

UNIVERSITY OF WISCONSIN–EAU CLAIRE
Eau Claire, WI

Tuition & fees (WI res): $8813	Average undergraduate aid package: $9403

ABOUT THE INSTITUTION State-supported, coed. *Awards:* certificates, associate, bachelor's, master's, and doctoral degrees. 52 undergraduate majors. *Total enrollment:* 10,629. Undergraduates: 9,981. Freshmen: 2,302. Federal methodology is used as a basis for awarding need-based institutional aid.

UNDERGRADUATE EXPENSES for 2016–2017 Application fee: $50. *Tuition, state resident:* full-time $7361; part-time $307 per credit. *Tuition, nonresident:* full-time $14,934; part-time $622 per credit. *Required fees:* full-time $1452; $61 per credit. Full-time tuition and fees vary according to program and reciprocity agreements. Part-time tuition and fees vary according to program and reciprocity agreements. *College room and board:* $6984; *Room only:* $4184. Room and board charges vary according to board plan and housing facility.

FRESHMAN FINANCIAL AID (Fall 2015) 1,909 applied for aid; of those 64% were deemed to have need. 99% of freshmen with need received aid; of those 21% had need fully met. *Average percent of need met:* 85% (excluding resources awarded to replace EFC). *Average financial aid package:* $9092 (excluding resources awarded to replace EFC). 7% of all full-time freshmen had no need and received non-need-based gift aid.

UNDERGRADUATE FINANCIAL AID (Fall 2015) 7,002 applied for aid; of those 70% were deemed to have need. 99% of undergraduates with need received aid; of those 21% had need fully met. *Average percent of need met:* 84% (excluding resources awarded to replace EFC). *Average financial aid package:* $9403 (excluding resources awarded to replace EFC). 5% of all full-time undergraduates had no need and received non-need-based gift aid.

GIFT AID (NEED-BASED) Total amount: $23,846,627 (45% federal, 22% state, 19% institutional, 14% external sources). *Receiving aid:* Freshmen: 46% (1,014); all full-time undergraduates: 44% (4,030). *Average award:* Freshmen: $5786; Undergraduates: $5872. *Scholarships, grants, and awards:* Federal Pell, FSEOG, state, private, college/university gift aid from institutional funds, Federal Nursing, Bureau of Indian Affairs Grants, Student Support Services Grants.

GIFT AID (NON-NEED-BASED) Total amount: $1,251,334 (10% state, 31% institutional, 59% external sources). *Receiving aid:* Freshmen: 2% (50). Undergraduates: 1% (130). *Average award:* Freshmen: $1804. Undergraduates: $2127. *Scholarships, grants, and awards by category: Academic interests/achievement:* area/ethnic studies, biological sciences, business, communication, computer science, education, English, foreign languages, general academic interests/achievements, health fields, humanities, international studies, library science, mathematics, physical sciences, premedicine, religion/biblical studies, social sciences. *Creative arts/performance:* art/fine arts, debating, journalism/publications, music, performing arts, theater/drama. *Special achievements/activities:* community service, general special achievements/activities, hobbies/interests, leadership, memberships. *Special characteristics:* adult students, ethnic background, first-generation college students, general special characteristics, international students, local/state students, members of minority groups, previous college experience. *ROTC:* Army.

LOANS Student loans: $41,440,047 (55% need-based, 45% non-need-based). 72% of past graduating class borrowed through all loan programs. *Average indebtedness per student:* $26,295. *Average need-based loan:* Freshmen: $3942. Undergraduates: $4363. *Parent loans:* $2,313,603 (67% need-based, 33% non-need-based). *Programs:* Federal Direct (Subsidized and Unsubsidized Stafford, PLUS), Perkins, college/university, private loans.

WORK-STUDY Federal work-study: 3,942 jobs averaging $1249.

APPLYING FOR FINANCIAL AID Required financial aid form: FAFSA. *Financial aid deadline (priority):* 4/15. *Notification date:* Continuous beginning 4/15.

CONTACT Ms. Kathleen Sahlhoff, Director of Financial Aid, University of Wisconsin–Eau Claire, Old Library 1123, Eau Claire, WI 54701, 715-836-3000. *E-mail:* sahlhoka@uwec.edu. *Website:* http://www.uwec.edu/.

UNIVERSITY OF WISCONSIN–GREEN BAY
Green Bay, WI

Tuition & fees (WI res): $7948	Average undergraduate aid package: $10,328

ABOUT THE INSTITUTION State-supported, coed. **Awards:** associate, bachelor's, and master's degrees. 47 undergraduate majors. **Total enrollment:** 7,030. Undergraduates: 6,758. Freshmen: 872. Federal methodology is used as a basis for awarding need-based institutional aid.

UNDERGRADUATE EXPENSES for 2017–2018 **Application fee:** $50. **One-time required fee:** $225. **Tuition, state resident:** full-time $6298; part-time $262 per credit hour. **Tuition, nonresident:** full-time $13,871; part-time $578 per credit hour. **Required fees:** full-time $1650; $57 per credit hour. Full-time tuition and fees vary according to course load and reciprocity agreements. Part-time tuition and fees vary according to reciprocity agreements. **College room and board:** $7200; **Room only:** $4300. Room and board charges vary according to board plan and housing facility.

FRESHMAN FINANCIAL AID (Fall 2016, est.) 723 applied for aid; of those 77% were deemed to have need. 100% of freshmen with need received aid; of those 27% had need fully met. **Average percent of need met:** 74% (excluding resources awarded to replace EFC). **Average financial aid package:** $9977 (excluding resources awarded to replace EFC). 10% of all full-time freshmen had no need and received non-need-based gift aid.

UNDERGRADUATE FINANCIAL AID (Fall 2016, est.) 3,282 applied for aid; of those 82% were deemed to have need. 100% of undergraduates with need received aid; of those 34% had need fully met. **Average percent of need met:** 76% (excluding resources awarded to replace EFC). **Average financial aid package:** $10,328 (excluding resources awarded to replace EFC). 4% of all full-time undergraduates had no need and received non-need-based gift aid.

GIFT AID (NEED-BASED) Total amount: $14,492,188 (51% federal, 30% state, 4% institutional, 15% external sources). **Receiving aid:** Freshmen: 52% (430); all full-time undergraduates: 50% (1,999). **Average award:** Freshmen: $6023; Undergraduates: $5976. **Scholarships, grants, and awards:** Federal Pell, FSEOG, state, private, college/university gift aid from institutional funds.

GIFT AID (NON-NEED-BASED) Total amount: $710,590 (4% state, 25% institutional, 71% external sources). **Receiving aid:** Freshmen: 3% (24). Undergraduates: 2% (88). **Average award:** Freshmen: $1457. Undergraduates: $1226. **Scholarships, grants, and awards by category:** Academic interests/achievement: area/ethnic studies, biological sciences, business, communication, education, engineering/technologies, general academic interests/achievements, health fields, humanities, physical sciences, premedicine, social sciences. Creative arts/performance: art/fine arts, dance, journalism/publications, music, theater/drama. Special achievements/activities: community service, general special achievements/activities, leadership. Special characteristics: adult students, children of public servants, ethnic background, handicapped students, members of minority groups, veterans. **Tuition waivers:** Full or partial for senior citizens. **ROTC:** Army cooperative.

LOANS Student loans: $23,481,369 (70% need-based, 30% non-need-based). 77% of past graduating class borrowed through all loan programs. Average indebtedness per student: $28,940. **Average need-based loan:** Freshmen: $5915. Undergraduates: $6565. **Parent loans:** $1,632,021 (24% need-based, 76% non-need-based). **Programs:** Federal Direct (Subsidized and Unsubsidized Stafford, PLUS), Perkins.

WORK-STUDY Federal work-study: Total amount: $431,348; 289 jobs averaging $1893.

ATHLETIC AWARDS Total amount: $2,453,885 (79% need-based, 21% non-need-based).

APPLYING FOR FINANCIAL AID Required financial aid form: FAFSA. **Financial aid deadline (priority):** 4/1. **Notification date:** Continuous beginning 1/1. Students must reply within 3 weeks of notification.

CONTACT Mr. James Rohan, Director of Financial Aid, University of Wisconsin–Green Bay, 2420 Nicolet Drive, Green Bay, WI 54311-7001, 920-465-2073. E-mail: rohanj@uwgb.edu.
Website: http://www.uwgb.edu/.

UNIVERSITY OF WISCONSIN–LA CROSSE
La Crosse, WI

Tuition & fees (WI res): $9091	Average undergraduate aid package: $7577

ABOUT THE INSTITUTION State-supported, coed. **Awards:** certificates, associate, bachelor's, master's, and doctoral degrees. 50 undergraduate majors. **Total enrollment:** 10,516. Undergraduates: 9,699. Freshmen: 2,086. Federal methodology is used as a basis for awarding need-based institutional aid.

UNDERGRADUATE EXPENSES for 2016–2017 **Application fee:** $50. **Tuition, state resident:** full-time $7585; part-time $370 per credit. **Tuition, nonresident:** full-time $16,106; part-time $725 per credit. **Required fees:** full-time $1506; $53.78 per credit. **College room and board:** $6156; **Room only:** $3606. Room and board charges vary according to board plan and housing facility.

FRESHMAN FINANCIAL AID (Fall 2015) 1,791 applied for aid; of those 60% were deemed to have need. 95% of freshmen with need received aid; of those 22% had need fully met. **Average percent of need met:** 70% (excluding resources awarded to replace EFC). **Average financial aid package:** $7593 (excluding resources awarded to replace EFC). 8% of all full-time freshmen had no need and received non-need-based gift aid.

UNDERGRADUATE FINANCIAL AID (Fall 2015) 6,902 applied for aid; of those 65% were deemed to have need. 97% of undergraduates with need received aid; of those 19% had need fully met. **Average percent of need met:** 70% (excluding resources awarded to replace EFC). **Average financial aid package:** $7577 (excluding resources awarded to replace EFC). 4% of all full-time undergraduates had no need and received non-need-based gift aid.

GIFT AID (NEED-BASED) Total amount: $13,910,547 (60% federal, 32% state, 1% institutional, 7% external sources). **Receiving aid:** Freshmen: 32% (666); all full-time undergraduates: 31% (2,793). **Average award:** Freshmen: $4476; Undergraduates: $4812. **Scholarships, grants, and awards:** Federal Pell, FSEOG, state, private, college/university gift aid from institutional funds.

GIFT AID (NON-NEED-BASED) Total amount: $6,055,324 (3% federal, 11% state, 31% institutional, 55% external sources). **Receiving aid:** Freshmen: 28% (584). Undergraduates: 15% (1,391). **Average award:** Freshmen: $2187. Undergraduates: $1733. **Scholarships, grants, and awards by category:** Academic interests/achievement: area/ethnic studies, biological sciences, business, communication, computer science, education, English, foreign languages, general academic interests/achievements, health fields, humanities, international studies, mathematics, military science, physical sciences, social sciences. Creative arts/performance: art/fine arts, music, theater/drama. Special achievements/activities: community service, leadership, memberships. Special characteristics: adult students, children and siblings of alumni, children of union members/company employees, ethnic background, first-generation college students, general special characteristics, international students, local/state students, members of minority groups, out-of-state students, veterans, veterans' children. **ROTC:** Army.

LOANS Student loans: $39,589,360 (38% need-based, 62% non-need-based). 69% of past graduating class borrowed through all loan programs. Average indebtedness per student: $26,487. **Average need-based loan:** Freshmen: $3388. Undergraduates: $4141. **Parent loans:** $4,818,428 (100% non-need-based). **Programs:** Federal Direct (Subsidized and Unsubsidized Stafford, PLUS), Perkins.

WORK-STUDY Federal work-study: 472 jobs averaging $1679. **State or other work-study/employment:** Total amount: $2,165,616 (100% non-need-based). 1,706 part-time jobs averaging $1401.

APPLYING FOR FINANCIAL AID Required financial aid form: FAFSA. **Financial aid deadline (priority):** 3/15. **Notification date:** Continuous beginning 4/1.

CONTACT Louise Janke, Director of Financial Aid, University of Wisconsin–La Crosse, 1725 State Street, La Crosse, WI 54601-3742, 608-785-8604. Fax: 608-785-8843. E-mail: finaid@uwlax.edu.
Website: http://www.uwlax.edu/.

UNIVERSITY OF WISCONSIN–MADISON
Madison, WI

Tuition & fees (WI res): $10,488	Average undergraduate aid package: $14,981

ABOUT THE INSTITUTION State-supported, coed. **Awards:** certificates, bachelor's, master's, and doctoral degrees. 120 undergraduate majors. **Total enrollment:** 43,336. Undergraduates: 31,710. Freshmen: 6,430. Federal methodology is used as a basis for awarding need-based institutional aid.

UNDERGRADUATE EXPENSES for 2016–2017 Application fee: $60. **Tuition, state resident:** full-time $9273; part-time $386.39 per credit hour. **Tuition, nonresident:** full-time $31,523; part-time $1313.46 per credit hour. **Required fees:** full-time $1215; $97.38 per credit hour. Full-time tuition and fees vary according to program and reciprocity agreements. Part-time tuition and fees vary according to course load, program, and reciprocity agreements. **College room and board:** $10,446. Room and board charges vary according to board plan and housing facility.

FRESHMAN FINANCIAL AID (Fall 2016, est.) 4,249 applied for aid; of those 58% were deemed to have need. 93% of freshmen with need received aid; of those 39% had need fully met. **Average percent of need met:** 77% (excluding resources awarded to replace EFC). **Average financial aid package:** $14,789 (excluding resources awarded to replace EFC). 7% of all full-time freshmen had no need and received non-need-based gift aid.

UNDERGRADUATE FINANCIAL AID (Fall 2016, est.) 15,028 applied for aid; of those 69% were deemed to have need. 96% of undergraduates with need received aid; of those 38% had need fully met. **Average percent of need met:** 79% (excluding resources awarded to replace EFC). **Average financial aid package:** $14,981 (excluding resources awarded to replace EFC). 7% of all full-time undergraduates had no need and received non-need-based gift aid.

GIFT AID (NEED-BASED) Total amount: $78,865,743 (22% federal, 13% state, 58% institutional, 7% external sources). **Receiving aid:** Freshmen: 29% (1,856); all full-time undergraduates: 27% (7,920). **Average award:** Freshmen: $10,922; Undergraduates: $10,943. **Scholarships, grants, and awards:** Federal Pell, FSEOG, state, private, college/university gift aid from institutional funds.

GIFT AID (NON-NEED-BASED) Total amount: $17,855,084 (16% state, 60% institutional, 24% external sources). **Receiving aid:** Freshmen: 4% (245). Undergraduates: 3% (935). **Average award:** Freshmen: $4365. Undergraduates: $4452. **Scholarships, grants, and awards by category:** Academic interests/achievement: general academic interests/achievements. Creative arts/performance: general creative arts/performance. Special achievements/activities: general special achievements/activities. Special characteristics: general special characteristics. **ROTC:** Army, Naval, Air Force.

LOANS Student loans: $91,167,308 (57% need-based, 43% non-need-based). 46% of past graduating class borrowed through all loan programs. **Average indebtedness per student:** $27,831. **Average need-based loan:** Freshmen: $5651. Undergraduates: $6130. **Parent loans:** $17,109,697 (28% need-based, 72% non-need-based). **Programs:** Federal Direct (Subsidized and Unsubsidized Stafford, PLUS), Perkins, Federal Nursing.

WORK-STUDY Federal work-study: Total amount: $6,973,264; jobs available. **State or other work-study/employment:** Part-time jobs available.

ATHLETIC AWARDS Total amount: $12,193,850 (13% need-based, 87% non-need-based).

APPLYING FOR FINANCIAL AID Required financial aid form: FAFSA. **Financial aid deadline (priority):** 12/1. **Notification date:** Continuous beginning 3/1. Students must reply within 3 weeks of notification.

CONTACT Office of Student Financial Aid, University of Wisconsin–Madison, 333 East Campus Mall #9701, Madison, WI 53715-1382, 608-262-3060. Fax: 608-262-9068. E-mail: finaid@wisc.edu. Website: http://www.wisc.edu/.

UNIVERSITY OF WISCONSIN–MILWAUKEE
Milwaukee, WI

Tuition & fees (WI res): $9534	Average undergraduate aid package: $7501

ABOUT THE INSTITUTION State-supported, coed. **Awards:** certificates, bachelor's, master's, and doctoral degrees. 83 undergraduate majors. **Total enrollment:** 26,011. Undergraduates: 21,375. Freshmen: 3,118. Federal methodology is used as a basis for awarding need-based institutional aid.

UNDERGRADUATE EXPENSES for 2017–2018 Application fee: $50. **Tuition, state resident:** full-time $8090. **Required fees:** full-time $1444. Full-time tuition and fees vary according to course load, degree level, location, program, and reciprocity agreements. Part-time tuition and fees vary according to course load, degree level, location, program, and reciprocity agreements. **College room and board:** $10,560; **Room only:** $6640. Room and board charges vary according to board plan, housing facility, and location.

FRESHMAN FINANCIAL AID (Fall 2015) 2,803 applied for aid; of those 78% were deemed to have need. 96% of freshmen with need received aid; of those 30% had need fully met. **Average percent of need met:** 40% (excluding resources awarded to replace EFC). **Average financial aid package:** $7086 (excluding resources awarded to replace EFC). 1% of all full-time freshmen had no need and received non-need-based gift aid.

UNDERGRADUATE FINANCIAL AID (Fall 2015) 18,560 applied for aid; of those 85% were deemed to have need. 84% of undergraduates with need received aid; of those 23% had need fully met. **Average percent of need met:** 45% (excluding resources awarded to replace EFC). **Average financial aid package:** $7501 (excluding resources awarded to replace EFC). 1% of all full-time undergraduates had no need and received non-need-based gift aid.

GIFT AID (NEED-BASED) Total amount: $56,623,615 (63% federal, 31% state, 3% institutional, 3% external sources). **Receiving aid:** Freshmen: 41% (1,267); all full-time undergraduates: 45% (8,961). **Average award:** Freshmen: $5995; Undergraduates: $5716. **Scholarships, grants, and awards:** Federal Pell, FSEOG, state, private, college/university gift aid from institutional funds, Federal Nursing.

GIFT AID (NON-NEED-BASED) Total amount: $19,260,649 (67% federal, 11% state, 6% institutional, 16% external sources). **Receiving aid:** Freshmen: 20% (615). Undergraduates: 13% (2,645). **Average award:** Freshmen: $2874. Undergraduates: $2310. **Scholarships, grants, and awards by category:** Academic interests/achievement: general academic interests/achievements. Creative arts/performance: general creative arts/performance. Special achievements/activities: general special achievements/activities. Special characteristics: general special characteristics. **Tuition waivers:** Full or partial for senior citizens. **ROTC:** Army cooperative, Naval cooperative, Air Force cooperative.

LOANS Student loans: $108,484,894 (43% need-based, 57% non-need-based). 76% of past graduating class borrowed through all loan programs. **Average indebtedness per student:** $36,945. **Average need-based loan:** Freshmen: $3447. Undergraduates: $4170. **Parent loans:** $14,605,379 (100% non-need-based). **Programs:** Federal Direct (Subsidized and Unsubsidized Stafford, PLUS), Perkins, Federal Nursing, state, alternative loans.

WORK-STUDY Federal work-study: jobs available.

ATHLETIC AWARDS Total amount: $622,672 (100% non-need-based).

APPLYING FOR FINANCIAL AID Required financial aid form: FAFSA. **Financial aid deadline (priority):** 3/1. **Notification date:** Continuous beginning 3/15. Students must reply within 2 weeks of notification.

CONTACT Tim Opgenorth, Director of Financial Aid, University of Wisconsin–Milwaukee, Mellencamp Hall 162, Milwaukee, WI 53201, 414-229-6300. E-mail: finaid@uwm.edu. Website: http://www.uwm.edu/.

UNIVERSITY OF WISCONSIN–OSHKOSH

Oshkosh, WI

Tuition & fees: N/R	Average undergraduate aid package: $8558

ABOUT THE INSTITUTION State-supported, coed. 56 undergraduate majors. Federal methodology is used as a basis for awarding need-based institutional aid.

FRESHMAN FINANCIAL AID (Fall 2016, est.) 1,279 applied for aid; of those 73% were deemed to have need. 98% of freshmen with need received aid; of those 41% had need fully met. **Average percent of need met:** 62% (excluding resources awarded to replace EFC). **Average financial aid package:** $6455 (excluding resources awarded to replace EFC). 6% of all full-time freshmen had no need and received non-need-based gift aid.

UNDERGRADUATE FINANCIAL AID (Fall 2016, est.) 6,769 applied for aid; of those 80% were deemed to have need. 99% of undergraduates with need received aid; of those 36% had need fully met. **Average percent of need met:** 71% (excluding resources awarded to replace EFC). **Average financial aid package:** $8558 (excluding resources awarded to replace EFC). 2% of all full-time undergraduates had no need and received non-need-based gift aid.

GIFT AID (NEED-BASED) Total amount: $24,516,801 (54% federal, 30% state, 7% institutional, 9% external sources). **Receiving aid:** Freshmen: 31% (455); all full-time undergraduates: 37% (3,085). **Average award:** Freshmen: $5973; Undergraduates: $6495. **Scholarships, grants, and awards:** Federal Pell, FSEOG, state, private, college/university gift aid from institutional funds, United Negro College Fund, Federal Nursing.

GIFT AID (NON-NEED-BASED) Total amount: $953,060 (12% federal, 13% state, 47% institutional, 28% external sources). **Receiving aid:** Freshmen: 33% (497). Undergraduates: 21% (1,750). **Average award:** Freshmen: $1702. Undergraduates: $2410. **Scholarships, grants, and awards by category:** Academic interests/achievement: general academic interests/achievements. Creative arts/performance: art/fine arts, general creative arts/performance. Special achievements/activities: leadership. Special characteristics: local/state students, members of minority groups.

LOANS Student loans: $52,336,216 (79% need-based, 21% non-need-based). 73% of past graduating class borrowed through all loan programs. **Average indebtedness per student:** $32,502. **Average need-based loan:** Freshmen: $3621. Undergraduates: $4827. **Parent loans:** $5,289,919 (62% need-based, 38% non-need-based). **Programs:** Federal Direct (Subsidized and Unsubsidized Stafford, PLUS), Perkins, Federal Nursing, state, college/university.

WORK-STUDY Federal work-study: Total amount: $1,946,613; jobs available. **State or other work-study/employment:** Part-time jobs available.

APPLYING FOR FINANCIAL AID Required financial aid form: FAFSA. **Financial aid deadline (priority):** 3/15. **Notification date:** 4/15.

CONTACT Ms. Stacy Drews, Financial Aid Counselor, University of Wisconsin–Oshkosh, 800 Algoma Boulevard, Oshkosh, WI 54901, 920-424-3379. *E-mail:* drewss@uwosh.edu.
Website: http://www.uwosh.edu/.

UNIVERSITY OF WISCONSIN–PARKSIDE

Kenosha, WI

Tuition & fees (WI res): $7367	Average undergraduate aid package: $9498

ABOUT THE INSTITUTION State-supported, coed. **Awards:** certificates, associate, bachelor's, and master's degrees. 49 undergraduate majors. **Total enrollment:** 4,399. Undergraduates: 4,276. Freshmen: 666. Federal methodology is used as a basis for awarding need-based institutional aid.

UNDERGRADUATE EXPENSES for 2017–2018 Application fee: $44. **One-time required fee:** $140. **Tuition, state resident:** full-time $6298; part-time $262.43 per credit hour. **Tuition, nonresident:** full-time $14,287; part-time $595.31 per credit hour. **Required fees:** full-time $1069; $44.55 per credit hour. Full-time tuition and fees vary according to course load and reciprocity agreements. Part-time tuition and fees vary according to course load and reciprocity agreements. **College**

room and board: $7736; **Room only:** $4406. Room and board charges vary according to board plan and housing facility.

FRESHMAN FINANCIAL AID (Fall 2015) 455 applied for aid; of those 78% were deemed to have need. 100% of freshmen with need received aid; of those 16% had need fully met. **Average percent of need met:** 67% (excluding resources awarded to replace EFC). **Average financial aid package:** $9353 (excluding resources awarded to replace EFC). 8% of all full-time freshmen had no need and received non-need-based gift aid.

UNDERGRADUATE FINANCIAL AID (Fall 2015) 2,510 applied for aid; of those 83% were deemed to have need. 100% of undergraduates with need received aid; of those 15% had need fully met. **Average percent of need met:** 66% (excluding resources awarded to replace EFC). **Average financial aid package:** $9498 (excluding resources awarded to replace EFC). 8% of all full-time undergraduates had no need and received non-need-based gift aid.

GIFT AID (NEED-BASED) Total amount: $11,918,170 (66% federal, 31% state, 3% external sources). **Receiving aid:** Freshmen: 45% (265); all full-time undergraduates: 49% (1,616). **Average award:** Freshmen: $6249; Undergraduates: $6126. **Scholarships, grants, and awards:** Federal Pell, FSEOG, state, private, college/university gift aid from institutional funds.

GIFT AID (NON-NEED-BASED) Total amount: $793,620 (11% state, 48% institutional, 41% external sources). **Receiving aid:** Freshmen: 21% (124). Undergraduates: 19% (621). **Average award:** Freshmen: $1877. Undergraduates: $2150. **Scholarships, grants, and awards by category:** Academic interests/achievement: biological sciences, business, communication, education, engineering/technologies, English, foreign languages, general academic interests/achievements, mathematics, physical sciences, premedicine, social sciences. Creative arts/performance: applied art and design, art/fine arts, music, theater/drama. Special achievements/activities: community service, leadership. Special characteristics: adult students, children of union members/company employees, children of workers in trades, ethnic background, general special characteristics, international students, local/state students, members of minority groups, out-of-state students. **Tuition waivers:** Full or partial for senior citizens. **ROTC:** Army cooperative, Air Force cooperative.

LOANS Student loans: $17,269,444 (45% need-based, 55% non-need-based). 76% of past graduating class borrowed through all loan programs. **Average indebtedness per student:** $29,362. **Average need-based loan:** Freshmen: $3659. Undergraduates: $4300. **Parent loans:** $2,322,934 (100% non-need-based). **Programs:** Federal Direct (Subsidized and Unsubsidized Stafford, PLUS), Perkins.

WORK-STUDY Federal work-study: 72 jobs averaging $1195. **State or other work-study/employment:** Total amount: $41,170 (100% need-based). Part-time jobs available.

ATHLETIC AWARDS Total amount: $45,734 (100% non-need-based).

APPLYING FOR FINANCIAL AID Required financial aid form: FAFSA. **Financial aid deadline (priority):** 3/15. **Notification date:** Continuous beginning 3/15.

CONTACT Kristina Klemens, Interim Director of Student Financial Aid, University of Wisconsin–Parkside, 900 Wood Road, Kenosha, WI 53141-2000, 262-595-2004. *Fax:* 262-595-2216. *E-mail:* klemens@uwp.edu.
Website: http://www.uwp.edu/.

UNIVERSITY OF WISCONSIN–PLATTEVILLE

Platteville, WI

CONTACT Elizabeth Tucker, Director of Financial Aid, University of Wisconsin–Platteville, 1 University Plaza, Platteville, WI 53818-3099, 608-342-1836 or toll-free 877-897-5288. *Fax:* 608-342-1281. *E-mail:* tucker@uwplatt.edu.
Website: http://www.uwplatt.edu/.

UNIVERSITY OF WISCONSIN–RIVER FALLS
River Falls, WI

Tuition & fees (WI res): $7981	Average undergraduate aid package: $6972

ABOUT THE INSTITUTION State-supported, coed. *Awards:* certificates, bachelor's, and master's degrees. 51 undergraduate majors. *Total enrollment:* 5,958. Undergraduates: 5,507. Freshmen: 1,033. Federal methodology is used as a basis for awarding need-based institutional aid.

UNDERGRADUATE EXPENSES for 2016–2017 *Application fee:* $44. *Tuition, state resident:* full-time $6428; part-time $267.85 per credit hour. *Tuition, nonresident:* full-time $14,401; part-time $583.39 per credit hour. *Required fees:* full-time $1553; $165.97 per credit hour. Full-time tuition and fees vary according to course load, degree level, program, and reciprocity agreements. Part-time tuition and fees vary according to course load, degree level, program, and reciprocity agreements. *College room and board:* $6576; *Room only:* $4136. Room and board charges vary according to board plan and housing facility.

FRESHMAN FINANCIAL AID (Fall 2015) 824 applied for aid; of those 72% were deemed to have need. 91% of freshmen with need received aid; of those 1% had need fully met. *Average percent of need met:* 52% (excluding resources awarded to replace EFC). *Average financial aid package:* $6828 (excluding resources awarded to replace EFC). 3% of all full-time freshmen had no need and received non-need-based gift aid.

UNDERGRADUATE FINANCIAL AID (Fall 2015) 3,888 applied for aid; of those 76% were deemed to have need. 93% of undergraduates with need received aid; of those 2% had need fully met. *Average percent of need met:* 52% (excluding resources awarded to replace EFC). *Average financial aid package:* $6972 (excluding resources awarded to replace EFC). 3% of all full-time undergraduates had no need and received non-need-based gift aid.

GIFT AID (NEED-BASED) *Total amount:* $9,171,519 (74% federal, 23% state, 3% external sources). *Receiving aid:* Freshmen: 40% (353); all full-time undergraduates: 37% (1,684). *Average award:* Freshmen: $4771; Undergraduates: $4678. *Scholarships, grants, and awards:* Federal Pell, FSEOG, state, private, college/university gift aid from institutional funds.

GIFT AID (NON-NEED-BASED) *Total amount:* $1,456,497 (6% state, 94% institutional). *Receiving aid:* Freshmen: 11% (97). Undergraduates: 15% (667). *Average award:* Freshmen: $2236. Undergraduates: $1908. *Scholarships, grants, and awards by category:* Academic interests/achievement: agriculture, area/ethnic studies, biological sciences, business, communication, computer science, education, English, foreign languages, general academic interests/achievements, health fields, humanities, international studies, mathematics, physical sciences, premedicine, social sciences. Creative arts/performance: art/fine arts, music, theater/drama. Special achievements/activities: leadership. Special characteristics: local/state students, members of minority groups. *ROTC:* Army.

LOANS *Student loans:* $24,705,783 (86% need-based, 14% non-need-based). 77% of past graduating class borrowed through all loan programs. *Average indebtedness per student:* $27,232. *Average need-based loan:* Freshmen: $3716. Undergraduates: $4139. *Parent loans:* $1,440,463 (100% need-based). *Programs:* Federal Direct (Subsidized and Unsubsidized Stafford, PLUS), Perkins, state, alternative loans.

WORK-STUDY *Federal work-study:* jobs available. *State or other work-study/employment:* Part-time jobs available.

APPLYING FOR FINANCIAL AID *Required financial aid form:* FAFSA. *Financial aid deadline:* Continuous. *Notification date:* Continuous beginning 4/15.

CONTACT Mr. Robert Bode, Director of Financial Aid, University of Wisconsin–River Falls, 410 South Third Street, River Falls, WI 54022-5001, 715-425-3141. *Fax:* 715-425-0708. *E-mail:* robert.bode@uwrf.edu. *Website:* http://www.uwrf.edu/.

UNIVERSITY OF WISCONSIN–STEVENS POINT
Stevens Point, WI

Tuition & fees (WI res): $9683	Average undergraduate aid package: $9069

ABOUT THE INSTITUTION State-supported, coed. *Awards:* associate, bachelor's, master's, and doctoral degrees. 72 undergraduate majors. *Total enrollment:* 8,626. Undergraduates: 8,296. Freshmen: 1,591. Federal methodology is used as a basis for awarding need-based institutional aid.

UNDERGRADUATE EXPENSES for 2017–2018 *Application fee:* $50. *Tuition, state resident:* full-time $7687; part-time $402.85 per credit. *Tuition, nonresident:* full-time $15,954; part-time $747.29 per credit. *Required fees:* full-time $1996. Full-time tuition and fees vary according to course load, location, program, reciprocity agreements, and student level. Part-time tuition and fees vary according to course load, location, program, reciprocity agreements, and student level. *College room and board:* $7180; *Room only:* $4240. Room and board charges vary according to board plan and housing facility.

FRESHMAN FINANCIAL AID (Fall 2015) 1,585 applied for aid; of those 66% were deemed to have need. 100% of freshmen with need received aid; of those 16% had need fully met. *Average percent of need met:* 67% (excluding resources awarded to replace EFC). *Average financial aid package:* $8177 (excluding resources awarded to replace EFC). 8% of all full-time freshmen had no need and received non-need-based gift aid.

UNDERGRADUATE FINANCIAL AID (Fall 2015) 6,953 applied for aid; of those 72% were deemed to have need. 100% of undergraduates with need received aid; of those 13% had need fully met. *Average percent of need met:* 72% (excluding resources awarded to replace EFC). *Average financial aid package:* $9069 (excluding resources awarded to replace EFC). 7% of all full-time undergraduates had no need and received non-need-based gift aid.

GIFT AID (NEED-BASED) *Total amount:* $20,325,967 (65% federal, 29% state, 3% institutional, 3% external sources). *Receiving aid:* Freshmen: 44% (780); all full-time undergraduates: 44% (3,728). *Average award:* Freshmen: $5122; Undergraduates: $5177. *Scholarships, grants, and awards:* Federal Pell, FSEOG, state, private, college/university gift aid from institutional funds.

GIFT AID (NON-NEED-BASED) *Total amount:* $1,729,877 (2% state, 59% institutional, 39% external sources). *Receiving aid:* Freshmen: 39% (690). Undergraduates: 39% (3,290). *Average award:* Freshmen: $1411. Undergraduates: $1483. *Scholarships, grants, and awards by category:* Academic interests/achievement: 21 awards ($8586 total): agriculture, architecture, biological sciences, business, communication, computer science, education, engineering/technologies, English, foreign languages, general academic interests/achievements, health fields, home economics, humanities, international studies, mathematics, military science, physical sciences, premedicine, social sciences. Creative arts/performance: applied art and design, creative writing, dance, music, performing arts, theater/drama. Special achievements/activities: general special achievements/activities, leadership. Special characteristics: adult students, ethnic background, general special characteristics, international students, members of minority groups, out-of-state students, veterans. *Tuition waivers:* Full or partial for senior citizens. *ROTC:* Army.

LOANS *Student loans:* $40,647,219 (62% need-based, 38% non-need-based). 77% of past graduating class borrowed through all loan programs. *Average indebtedness per student:* $25,646. *Average need-based loan:* Freshmen: $4414. Undergraduates: $5320. *Parent loans:* $4,202,505 (16% need-based, 84% non-need-based). *Programs:* Federal Direct (Subsidized and Unsubsidized Stafford, PLUS), Perkins.

WORK-STUDY *Federal work-study:* jobs available. *State or other work-study/employment:* Part-time jobs available.

APPLYING FOR FINANCIAL AID *Required financial aid form:* FAFSA. *Financial aid deadline:* 5/1 (priority: 3/15). *Notification date:* Continuous beginning 3/1. Students must reply within 4 weeks of notification.

CONTACT Ms. Mandy Slowinski, Director of Financial Aid, University of Wisconsin–Stevens Point, 106 Student Services Center, Stevens Point, WI 54481-3897, 715-346-4771. *Fax:* 715-346-3526. *E-mail:* finaid@uwsp.edu. *Website:* http://www.uwsp.edu/.

UNIVERSITY OF WISCONSIN–STOUT
Menomonie, WI

Tuition & fees (WI res): $9394	Average undergraduate aid package: $11,000

ABOUT THE INSTITUTION State-supported, coed. *Awards:* certificates, bachelor's, master's, and doctoral degrees. 13 undergraduate majors. *Total enrollment:* 9,619. Undergraduates: 8,398. Freshmen: 1,588. Federal methodology is used as a basis for awarding need-based institutional aid.

UNDERGRADUATE EXPENSES for 2016–2017 *Application fee:* $50. *Tuition, state resident:* full-time $7014; part-time $234 per credit hour. *Tuition, nonresident:* full-time $14,760; part-time $492 per credit hour. *Required fees:* full-time $2380. Full-time tuition and fees vary according to degree level and reciprocity agreements. Part-time tuition and fees vary according to degree level and reciprocity agreements. *College room and board:* $6624; *Room only:* $4040. Room and board charges vary according to board plan and housing facility.

FRESHMAN FINANCIAL AID (Fall 2016, est.) 1,378 applied for aid; of those 68% were deemed to have need. 96% of freshmen with need received aid; of those 13% had need fully met. *Average percent of need met:* 81% (excluding resources awarded to replace EFC). *Average financial aid package:* $10,611 (excluding resources awarded to replace EFC). 3% of all full-time freshmen had no need and received non-need-based gift aid.

UNDERGRADUATE FINANCIAL AID (Fall 2016, est.) 5,324 applied for aid; of those 71% were deemed to have need. 98% of undergraduates with need received aid; of those 18% had need fully met. *Average percent of need met:* 84% (excluding resources awarded to replace EFC). *Average financial aid package:* $11,000 (excluding resources awarded to replace EFC). 2% of all full-time undergraduates had no need and received non-need-based gift aid.

GIFT AID (NEED-BASED) Total amount: $14,196,832 (67% federal, 29% state, 4% external sources). *Receiving aid:* Freshmen: 43% (677); all full-time undergraduates: 41% (2,750). *Average award:* Freshmen: $4480; Undergraduates: $4719. *Scholarships, grants, and awards:* Federal Pell, FSEOG, state, private, college/university gift aid from institutional funds, Bureau of Indian Affairs Grants, GEAR UP Scholarships.

GIFT AID (NON-NEED-BASED) Total amount: $3,761,760 (11% state, 38% institutional, 51% external sources). *Receiving aid:* Freshmen: 20% (324). Undergraduates: 15% (993). *Average award:* Freshmen: $1852. Undergraduates: $1882. *Scholarships, grants, and awards by category: Academic interests/achievement:* 300 awards ($402,144 total): business, computer science, education, engineering/technologies, general academic interests/achievements, home economics, international studies, mathematics, physical sciences. *Creative arts/performance:* 14 awards ($15,150 total): applied art and design, art/fine arts, music. *Special achievements/activities:* 41 awards ($50,650 total): community service, general special achievements/activities, leadership, memberships, religious involvement. *Special characteristics:* 48 awards ($49,900 total): adult students, first-generation college students, handicapped students, international students, local/state students, members of minority groups, out-of-state students, previous college experience, veterans, veterans' children. *ROTC:* Army, Air Force cooperative.

LOANS Student loans: $43,867,198 (39% need-based, 61% non-need-based). 79% of past graduating class borrowed through all loan programs. *Average indebtedness per student:* $30,563. *Average need-based loan:* Freshmen: $4053. Undergraduates: $4596. *Parent loans:* $2,585,578 (100% non-need-based). *Programs:* Federal Direct (Subsidized and Unsubsidized Stafford, PLUS), Perkins, alternative loans.

WORK-STUDY Federal work-study: Total amount: $2,417,758; 1,399 jobs averaging $1592.

APPLYING FOR FINANCIAL AID Required financial aid form: FAFSA. *Financial aid deadline (priority):* 3/15. *Notification date:* Continuous beginning 3/31. Students must reply within 4 weeks of notification.

CONTACT Beth Boisen, Director of Financial Aid, University of Wisconsin–Stout, 712 South Broadway Street, Menomonie, WI 54751, 715-232-1363 or toll-free 800-HI-STOUT. *Fax:* 715-232-5246. *E-mail:* boisenb@uwstout.edu.
Website: http://www.uwstout.edu/.

UNIVERSITY OF WISCONSIN–SUPERIOR
Superior, WI

Tuition & fees (WI res): $8087	Average undergraduate aid package: $11,428

ABOUT THE INSTITUTION State-supported, coed. *Awards:* certificates, associate, bachelor's, and master's degrees. 68 undergraduate majors. *Total enrollment:* 2,487. Undergraduates: 2,365. Freshmen: 376. Federal methodology is used as a basis for awarding need-based institutional aid.

UNDERGRADUATE EXPENSES for 2016–2017 *Application fee:* $44. *Tuition, state resident:* full-time $6535; part-time $272.31 per credit hour. *Tuition, nonresident:* full-time $14,108; part-time $587.85 per credit hour. *Required fees:* full-time $1552. Full-time tuition and fees vary according to course load and reciprocity agreements. Part-time tuition and fees vary according to course load and reciprocity agreements. *College room and board:* $6520; *Room only:* $3490. Room and board charges vary according to board plan and housing facility.

FRESHMAN FINANCIAL AID (Fall 2016, est.) 293 applied for aid; of those 74% were deemed to have need. 99% of freshmen with need received aid; of those 19% had need fully met. *Average percent of need met:* 85% (excluding resources awarded to replace EFC). *Average financial aid package:* $10,276 (excluding resources awarded to replace EFC). 5% of all full-time freshmen had no need and received non-need-based gift aid.

UNDERGRADUATE FINANCIAL AID (Fall 2016, est.) 1,398 applied for aid; of those 81% were deemed to have need. 98% of undergraduates with need received aid; of those 17% had need fully met. *Average percent of need met:* 85% (excluding resources awarded to replace EFC). *Average financial aid package:* $11,428 (excluding resources awarded to replace EFC). 3% of all full-time undergraduates had no need and received non-need-based gift aid.

GIFT AID (NEED-BASED) Total amount: $5,849,241 (61% federal, 24% state, 13% institutional, 2% external sources). *Receiving aid:* Freshmen: 36% (134); all full-time undergraduates: 42% (759). *Average award:* Freshmen: $5033; Undergraduates: $5623. *Scholarships, grants, and awards:* Federal Pell, FSEOG, state, private, college/university gift aid from institutional funds.

GIFT AID (NON-NEED-BASED) Total amount: $666,143 (13% state, 17% institutional, 70% external sources). *Receiving aid:* Freshmen: 27% (101). Undergraduates: 18% (321). *Average award:* Freshmen: $1533. Undergraduates: $1789. *Scholarships, grants, and awards by category: Academic interests/achievement:* biological sciences, business, communication, computer science, education, English, general academic interests/achievements, health fields, humanities, mathematics, physical sciences, social sciences. *Creative arts/performance:* general creative arts/performance. *Special characteristics:* general special characteristics, international students, members of minority groups, veterans. *ROTC:* Air Force cooperative.

LOANS Student loans: $11,154,960 (41% need-based, 59% non-need-based). 74% of past graduating class borrowed through all loan programs. *Average indebtedness per student:* $27,382. *Average need-based loan:* Freshmen: $3704. Undergraduates: $4308. *Parent loans:* $509,671 (100% non-need-based). *Programs:* Federal Direct (Subsidized and Unsubsidized Stafford, PLUS), Perkins, state, college/university.

WORK-STUDY Federal work-study: Total amount: $377,600; jobs available. *State or other work-study/employment:* Total amount: $1,322,908 (8% need-based, 92% non-need-based). Part-time jobs available.

APPLYING FOR FINANCIAL AID Required financial aid form: FAFSA. *Financial aid deadline (priority):* 3/15. *Notification date:* Continuous beginning 4/1. Students must reply by 5/1 or within 4 weeks of notification.

CONTACT Tammi Reijo, Financial Aid Information Manager, University of Wisconsin–Superior, Belknap and Catlin, Old Main 110, PO Box 2000, Superior, WI 54880, 715-394-8148. *Fax:* 715-394-8027. *E-mail:* finaid@uwsuper.edu.
Website: http://www.uwsuper.edu/.

UNIVERSITY OF WISCONSIN–WHITEWATER
Whitewater, WI

Tuition & fees (WI res): $7650	Average undergraduate aid package: $8347

ABOUT THE INSTITUTION State-supported, coed. **Awards:** associate, bachelor's, master's, and doctoral degrees. 70 undergraduate majors. **Total enrollment:** 12,628. Undergraduates: 11,380. Freshmen: 2,163. Federal methodology is used as a basis for awarding need-based institutional aid.

UNDERGRADUATE EXPENSES for 2016–2017 Application fee: $50. **Tuition, state resident:** full-time $6519; part-time $272 per credit hour. **Tuition, nonresident:** full-time $15,092; part-time $628 per credit hour. **Required fees:** full-time $1131. Full-time tuition and fees vary according to course load, degree level, and reciprocity agreements. **College room and board:** $7204. Room and board charges vary according to board plan and housing facility.

FRESHMAN FINANCIAL AID (Fall 2016, est.) 2,002 applied for aid; of those 68% were deemed to have need. 94% of freshmen with need received aid; of those 41% had need fully met. **Average percent of need met:** 56% (excluding resources awarded to replace EFC). **Average financial aid package:** $7109 (excluding resources awarded to replace EFC). 6% of all full-time freshmen had no need and received non-need-based gift aid.

UNDERGRADUATE FINANCIAL AID (Fall 2016, est.) 8,026 applied for aid; of those 72% were deemed to have need. 96% of undergraduates with need received aid; of those 46% had need fully met. **Average percent of need met:** 63% (excluding resources awarded to replace EFC). **Average financial aid package:** $8347 (excluding resources awarded to replace EFC). 5% of all full-time undergraduates had no need and received non-need-based gift aid.

GIFT AID (NEED-BASED) Total amount: $23,106,000 (60% federal, 37% state, 3% external sources). **Receiving aid:** Freshmen: 33% (735); all full-time undergraduates: 35% (3,536). **Average award:** Freshmen: $5354; Undergraduates: $5466. **Scholarships, grants, and awards:** Federal Pell, FSEOG, state, private, college/university gift aid from institutional funds.

GIFT AID (NON-NEED-BASED) Total amount: $4,650,000 (3% federal, 3% state, 42% institutional, 52% external sources). **Receiving aid:** Freshmen: 18% (401). Undergraduates: 11% (1,085). **Average award:** Freshmen: $2357. Undergraduates: $2297. **Scholarships, grants, and awards by category:** Academic interests/achievement: biological sciences, business, communication, computer science, education, English, foreign languages, general academic interests/achievements, humanities, mathematics, physical sciences, premedicine, social sciences. Creative arts/performance: art/fine arts, cinema/film/broadcasting, creative writing, journalism/publications, music, theater/drama. Special achievements/activities: leadership. Special characteristics: adult students, ethnic background, handicapped students, international students, local/state students, members of minority groups, out-of-state students. **Tuition waivers:** Full or partial for senior citizens. **ROTC:** Army, Air Force.

LOANS Student loans: $52,500,000 (41% need-based, 59% non-need-based). 79% of past graduating class borrowed through all loan programs. **Average indebtedness per student:** $28,345. **Average need-based loan:** Freshmen: $3445. Undergraduates: $4223. **Parent loans:** $9,000,000 (100% non-need-based). **Programs:** Federal Direct (Subsidized and Unsubsidized Stafford, PLUS), Perkins.

WORK-STUDY Federal work-study: Total amount: $625,000; 542 jobs averaging $1296. **State or other work-study/employment:** Total amount: $4,700,000 (100% non-need-based). 2,468 part-time jobs averaging $1904.

APPLYING FOR FINANCIAL AID Required financial aid form: FAFSA. **Financial aid deadline (priority):** 3/1. **Notification date:** Continuous beginning 4/1. Students must reply within 3 weeks of notification.

CONTACT Ms. Carol Miller, Director of Financial Aid, University of Wisconsin–Whitewater, 800 West Main Street, Whitewater, WI 53190-1790, 262-472-1130. Fax: 262-472-5655. E-mail: millerc@uww.edu.
Website: http://www.uww.edu/.

UNIVERSITY OF WYOMING
Laramie, WY

Tuition & fees (WY res): $5055	Average undergraduate aid package: $9742

ABOUT THE INSTITUTION State-supported, coed. **Awards:** certificates, bachelor's, master's, and doctoral degrees. 83 undergraduate majors. **Total enrollment:** 12,648. Undergraduates: 10,045. Freshmen: 1,692. Federal methodology is used as a basis for awarding need-based institutional aid.

UNDERGRADUATE EXPENSES for 2016–2017 Application fee: $40. **One-time required fee:** $40. **Tuition, state resident:** full-time $3720; part-time $124 per credit hour. **Tuition, nonresident:** full-time $14,880; part-time $496 per credit hour. **Required fees:** full-time $1335; $321.33 per term. Full-time tuition and fees vary according to course load, location, and reciprocity agreements. Part-time tuition and fees vary according to course load, location, and reciprocity agreements. **College room and board:** $10,320; **Room only:** $4493. Room and board charges vary according to board plan and housing facility.

FRESHMAN FINANCIAL AID (Fall 2015) 1,342 applied for aid; of those 64% were deemed to have need. 98% of freshmen with need received aid; of those 24% had need fully met. **Average percent of need met:** 66% (excluding resources awarded to replace EFC). **Average financial aid package:** $10,788 (excluding resources awarded to replace EFC). 26% of all full-time freshmen had no need and received non-need-based gift aid.

UNDERGRADUATE FINANCIAL AID (Fall 2015) 5,349 applied for aid; of those 72% were deemed to have need. 97% of undergraduates with need received aid; of those 16% had need fully met. **Average percent of need met:** 59% (excluding resources awarded to replace EFC). **Average financial aid package:** $9742 (excluding resources awarded to replace EFC). 23% of all full-time undergraduates had no need and received non-need-based gift aid.

GIFT AID (NEED-BASED) Total amount: $17,602,777 (51% federal, 34% state, 11% institutional, 4% external sources). **Receiving aid:** Freshmen: 30% (499); all full-time undergraduates: 31% (2,545). **Average award:** Freshmen: $5261; Undergraduates: $5226. **Scholarships, grants, and awards:** Federal Pell, FSEOG, state, private, college/university gift aid from institutional funds.

GIFT AID (NON-NEED-BASED) Total amount: $28,854,533 (1% federal, 33% state, 56% institutional, 10% external sources). **Receiving aid:** Freshmen: 45% (758). Undergraduates: 31% (2,620). **Average award:** Freshmen: $4316. Undergraduates: $4821. **Scholarships, grants, and awards by category:** Academic interests/achievement: agriculture, architecture, area/ethnic studies, biological sciences, business, communication, computer science, education, engineering/technologies, English, foreign languages, general academic interests/achievements, health fields, home economics, humanities, international studies, mathematics, physical sciences, religion/biblical studies, social sciences. Creative arts/performance: applied art and design, art/fine arts, cinema/film/broadcasting, creative writing, dance, debating, general creative arts/performance, journalism/publications, music, performing arts, theater/drama. Special achievements/activities: cheerleading/drum major, community service, general special achievements/activities, hobbies/interests, junior miss, leadership, memberships, rodeo. Special characteristics: adult students, children and siblings of alumni, children of public servants, ethnic background, first-generation college students, general special characteristics, handicapped students, international students, local/state students, members of minority groups, out-of-state students, previous college experience, spouses of current students, veterans, veterans' children. **Tuition waivers:** Full or partial for children of alumni, employees or children of employees, senior citizens. **ROTC:** Army, Air Force.

LOANS Student loans: $28,558,816 (36% need-based, 64% non-need-based). 45% of past graduating class borrowed through all loan programs. **Average indebtedness per student:** $25,378. **Average need-based loan:** Freshmen: $3290. Undergraduates: $4139. **Parent loans:** $3,415,839 (100% non-need-based). **Programs:** Federal Direct (Subsidized and Unsubsidized Stafford, PLUS), Perkins, state, college/university, alternative loans.

WORK-STUDY Federal work-study: 289 jobs averaging $1972.

ATHLETIC AWARDS Total amount: $5,561,259 (76% need-based, 24% non-need-based).

APPLYING FOR FINANCIAL AID Required financial aid form: FAFSA. **Financial aid deadline (priority):** 3/1. **Notification date:** Continuous beginning 3/9.

CONTACT Kathy Bobbitt, Director of Student Financial Aid, University of Wyoming, Department 3335, 1000 East University Avenue, Laramie, WY 82071, 307-766-2116 or toll-free 800-342-5996. *Fax:* 307-766-3800. *E-mail:* finaid@uwyo.edu. *Website:* http://www.uwyo.edu/.

UPPER IOWA UNIVERSITY
Fayette, IA

Tuition & fees: $29,600	Average undergraduate aid package: $14,262

ABOUT THE INSTITUTION Independent, coed. *Awards:* certificates, associate, bachelor's, and master's degrees (enrollment figures include extended learning centers and online and distance education programs). 39 undergraduate majors. *Total enrollment:* 4,758. Undergraduates: 3,991. Freshmen: 214. Federal methodology is used as a basis for awarding need-based institutional aid.

UNDERGRADUATE EXPENSES for 2017–2018 *Comprehensive fee:* $37,970 includes full-time tuition ($28,850), mandatory fees ($750), and room and board ($8370). Full-time tuition and fees vary according to degree level, location, and program. Room and board charges vary according to board plan, housing facility, and location.

FRESHMAN FINANCIAL AID (Fall 2015) 159 applied for aid; of those 96% were deemed to have need. 99% of freshmen with need received aid; of those 6% had need fully met. *Average percent of need met:* 66% (excluding resources awarded to replace EFC). *Average financial aid package:* $21,039 (excluding resources awarded to replace EFC).

UNDERGRADUATE FINANCIAL AID (Fall 2015) 1,831 applied for aid; of those 94% were deemed to have need. 100% of undergraduates with need received aid; of those 8% had need fully met. *Average percent of need met:* 54% (excluding resources awarded to replace EFC). *Average financial aid package:* $14,262 (excluding resources awarded to replace EFC).

GIFT AID (NEED-BASED) *Total amount:* $19,307,344 (36% federal, 15% state, 46% institutional, 3% external sources). *Receiving aid:* Freshmen: 61% (145); all full-time undergraduates: 76% (1,464). *Average award:* Freshmen: $10,396; Undergraduates: $6285. *Scholarships, grants, and awards:* Federal Pell, FSEOG, state, private, college/university gift aid from institutional funds.

GIFT AID (NON-NEED-BASED) *Total amount:* $6,103,427 (1% federal, 4% state, 92% institutional, 3% external sources). *Receiving aid:* Freshmen: 2% (4). Undergraduates: 6% (117). *Scholarships, grants, and awards by category: Special achievements/activities:* 236 awards ($2,895,309 total): general special achievements/activities. *Special characteristics:* 25 awards ($13,000 total): children and siblings of alumni, children of current students, parents of current students, spouses of current students. *Tuition waivers:* Full or partial for employees or children of employees.

LOANS *Student loans:* $34,913,123 (85% need-based, 15% non-need-based). 56% of past graduating class borrowed through all loan programs. *Average indebtedness per student:* $34,123. *Average need-based loan:* Freshmen: $3208. Undergraduates: $4963. *Parent loans:* $4,923,103 (29% need-based, 71% non-need-based). *Programs:* Federal Direct (Subsidized and Unsubsidized Stafford, PLUS), Perkins, alternative loans.

WORK-STUDY *Federal work-study:* 218 jobs averaging $1975. *State or other work-study/employment:* Part-time jobs available.

ATHLETIC AWARDS Total amount: $2,895,309 (100% need-based).

APPLYING FOR FINANCIAL AID *Required financial aid form:* FAFSA. *Financial aid deadline (priority):* 3/1. *Notification date:* Continuous beginning 3/1. Students must reply within 3 weeks of notification.

CONTACT Rachael Ann Creque, Director of Financial Aid, Upper Iowa University, 605 Washington Street, Fayette, IA 52142-1859, 563-425-5170 or toll-free 800-553-4150. *Fax:* 563-425-5277. *E-mail:* crequer74@uiu.edu. *Website:* http://www.uiu.edu/.

URBANA UNIVERSITY
Urbana, OH

CONTACT Mrs. Amy M. Barnhart, Director of Financial Aid, Urbana University, 579 College Way, Urbana, OH 43078-2091, 937-484-1359 or toll-free 800-7-URBANA. *Fax:* 937-652-6870. *E-mail:* abarnhart@urbana.edu. *Website:* http://www.urbana.edu/.

URSINUS COLLEGE
Collegeville, PA

Tuition & fees: $50,360	Average undergraduate aid package: $36,770

ABOUT THE INSTITUTION Independent, coed. *Awards:* bachelor's degrees. 50 undergraduate majors. *Total enrollment:* 1,556. Undergraduates: 1,556. Freshmen: 382. Federal methodology is used as a basis for awarding need-based institutional aid.

UNDERGRADUATE EXPENSES for 2017–2018 *Comprehensive fee:* $62,920 includes full-time tuition ($50,360) and room and board ($12,560). *Part-time tuition:* $1574 per credit hour.

FRESHMAN FINANCIAL AID (Fall 2016, est.) 336 applied for aid; of those 87% were deemed to have need. 100% of freshmen with need received aid; of those 31% had need fully met. *Average percent of need met:* 84% (excluding resources awarded to replace EFC). *Average financial aid package:* $37,879 (excluding resources awarded to replace EFC). 19% of all full-time freshmen had no need and received non-need-based gift aid.

UNDERGRADUATE FINANCIAL AID (Fall 2016, est.) 1,316 applied for aid; of those 90% were deemed to have need. 100% of undergraduates with need received aid; of those 27% had need fully met. *Average percent of need met:* 83% (excluding resources awarded to replace EFC). *Average financial aid package:* $36,770 (excluding resources awarded to replace EFC). 23% of all full-time undergraduates had no need and received non-need-based gift aid.

GIFT AID (NEED-BASED) *Total amount:* $37,241,687 (4% federal, 3% state, 93% institutional). *Receiving aid:* Freshmen: 76% (292); all full-time undergraduates: 77% (1,183). *Average award:* Freshmen: $36,206; Undergraduates: $34,028. *Scholarships, grants, and awards:* Federal Pell, FSEOG, state, private, college/university gift aid from institutional funds.

GIFT AID (NON-NEED-BASED) *Total amount:* $10,964,898 (93% institutional, 7% external sources). *Receiving aid:* Freshmen: 19% (73). Undergraduates: 16% (240). *Average award:* Freshmen: $23,169. Undergraduates: $22,886. *Scholarships, grants, and awards by category: Academic interests/achievement:* general academic interests/achievements. *Creative arts/performance:* creative writing, dance, music, performing arts, theater/drama. *Special achievements/activities:* community service, general special achievements/activities, leadership. *Special characteristics:* children and siblings of alumni, children of faculty/staff, general special characteristics, international students, siblings of current students, veterans, veterans' children. *Tuition waivers:* Full or partial for employees or children of employees.

LOANS *Student loans:* $11,379,109 (34% need-based, 66% non-need-based). 74% of past graduating class borrowed through all loan programs. *Average indebtedness per student:* $38,537. *Average need-based loan:* Freshmen: $3089. Undergraduates: $4660. *Parent loans:* $5,192,995 (100% non-need-based). *Programs:* Federal Direct (Subsidized and Unsubsidized Stafford, PLUS), Perkins.

WORK-STUDY *Federal work-study:* Total amount: $1,227,700; jobs available. *State or other work-study/employment:* Part-time jobs available.

APPLYING FOR FINANCIAL AID *Required financial aid form:* FAFSA. *Financial aid deadline:* 2/1. *Notification date:* 2/1. Students must reply by 5/1.

CONTACT Ms. Suzanne Sparrow, Director of Scholarships and Financial Aid, Ursinus College, 601 East Main Street, Collegeville, PA 19426-1000, 610-409-3600. *Fax:* 610-409-3662. *E-mail:* finaid@ursinus.edu. *Website:* http://www.ursinus.edu/.

URSULINE COLLEGE
Pepper Pike, OH

Tuition & fees: $31,150	Average undergraduate aid package: $22,926

ABOUT THE INSTITUTION Independent Roman Catholic, coed, primarily women. *Awards:* certificates, bachelor's, master's, and doctoral degrees (applications from men are also accepted). 37 undergraduate majors. *Total enrollment:* 1,236. Undergraduates: 706. Federal methodology is used as a basis for awarding need-based institutional aid.

UNDERGRADUATE EXPENSES for 2017–2018 *Application fee:* $25. *Comprehensive fee:* $41,512 includes full-time tuition ($30,840), mandatory fees ($310), and room and board ($10,362). Full-time tuition and fees vary according to class time, course load, degree level, location, and program. Room and board charges vary according to housing facility. *Part-time tuition:* $1028 per credit hour. *Part-time fees:* $115 per term. Part-time tuition and fees vary according to class time, course load, degree level, location, and program.

FRESHMAN FINANCIAL AID (Fall 2016, est.) 97 applied for aid; of those 93% were deemed to have need. 100% of freshmen with need received aid; of those 16% had need fully met. *Average percent of need met:* 80% (excluding resources awarded to replace EFC). *Average financial aid package:* $26,348 (excluding resources awarded to replace EFC). 14% of all full-time freshmen had no need and received non-need-based gift aid.

UNDERGRADUATE FINANCIAL AID (Fall 2016, est.) 410 applied for aid; of those 93% were deemed to have need. 99% of undergraduates with need received aid; of those 12% had need fully met. *Average percent of need met:* 70% (excluding resources awarded to replace EFC). *Average financial aid package:* $22,926 (excluding resources awarded to replace EFC). 11% of all full-time undergraduates had no need and received non-need-based gift aid.

GIFT AID (NEED-BASED) *Total amount:* $6,161,044 (19% federal, 8% state, 70% institutional, 3% external sources). *Receiving aid:* Freshmen: 85% (90); all full-time undergraduates: 76% (352). *Average award:* Freshmen: $22,189; Undergraduates: $19,054. *Scholarships, grants, and awards:* Federal Pell, FSEOG, state, private, college/university gift aid from institutional funds, United Negro College Fund.

GIFT AID (NON-NEED-BASED) *Total amount:* $511,945 (98% institutional, 2% external sources). *Receiving aid:* Freshmen: 12% (13). Undergraduates: 8% (39). *Average award:* Freshmen: $7963. Undergraduates: $8531. *Scholarships, grants, and awards by category:* Academic interests/achievement: general academic interests/achievements. *Creative arts/performance:* general creative arts/performance. *Special achievements/activities:* community service, leadership. *Special characteristics:* children and siblings of alumni, children of faculty/staff, first-generation college students, relatives of clergy, religious affiliation, siblings of current students, veterans. *Tuition waivers:* Full or partial for employees or children of employees. *ROTC:* Army cooperative.

LOANS *Student loans:* $5,267,602 (81% need-based, 19% non-need-based). 81% of past graduating class borrowed through all loan programs. *Average indebtedness per student:* $32,375. *Average need-based loan:* Freshmen: $4191. Undergraduates: $5302. *Parent loans:* $874,685 (57% need-based, 43% non-need-based). *Programs:* Federal Direct (Subsidized and Unsubsidized Stafford, PLUS), Perkins, state, college/university.

WORK-STUDY *Federal work-study:* Total amount: $153,024; jobs available.

ATHLETIC AWARDS Total amount: $1,726,909 (56% need-based, 44% non-need-based).

APPLYING FOR FINANCIAL AID *Required financial aid form:* FAFSA. *Financial aid deadline:* Continuous. *Notification date:* Continuous beginning 1/1. Students must reply within 3 weeks of notification.

CONTACT Ms. Mary Lynn Perri, Director of Financial Aid and Enrollment Services, Ursuline College, 2550 Lander Road, Pepper Pike, OH 44124-4398, 440-646-8330 or toll-free 888-URSULINE. *Fax:* 440-684-6114. *E-mail:* mperri@ursuline.edu. *Website:* http://www.ursuline.edu/.

UTAH STATE UNIVERSITY
Logan, UT

Tuition & fees (UT res): $6869	Average undergraduate aid package: $9705

ABOUT THE INSTITUTION State-supported, coed. *Awards:* certificates, associate, bachelor's, master's, and doctoral degrees. 115 undergraduate majors. *Total enrollment:* 28,118. Undergraduates: 24,838. Freshmen: 4,466. Federal methodology is used as a basis for awarding need-based institutional aid.

UNDERGRADUATE EXPENSES for 2016–2017 *Application fee:* $50. *Tuition, state resident:* full-time $5817. *Tuition, nonresident:* full-time $18,720. *Required fees:* full-time $1052. Full-time tuition and fees vary according to course level, course load, program, and reciprocity agreements. Part-time tuition and fees vary according to course level, course load, program, and reciprocity agreements. *College room and board:* $5870; *Room only:* $2090. Room and board charges vary according to board plan and housing facility.

FRESHMAN FINANCIAL AID (Fall 2016, est.) 2,591 applied for aid; of those 75% were deemed to have need. 99% of freshmen with need received aid; of those 16% had need fully met. *Average percent of need met:* 64% (excluding resources awarded to replace EFC). *Average financial aid package:* $10,341 (excluding resources awarded to replace EFC). 22% of all full-time freshmen had no need and received non-need-based gift aid.

UNDERGRADUATE FINANCIAL AID (Fall 2016, est.) 10,972 applied for aid; of those 85% were deemed to have need. 99% of undergraduates with need received aid; of those 9% had need fully met. *Average percent of need met:* 57% (excluding resources awarded to replace EFC). *Average financial aid package:* $9705 (excluding resources awarded to replace EFC). 13% of all full-time undergraduates had no need and received non-need-based gift aid.

GIFT AID (NEED-BASED) *Total amount:* $37,813,135 (94% federal, 6% state). *Receiving aid:* Freshmen: 29% (1,205); all full-time undergraduates: 39% (6,657). *Average award:* Freshmen: $4377; Undergraduates: $4553. *Scholarships, grants, and awards:* Federal Pell, FSEOG, state, private.

GIFT AID (NON-NEED-BASED) *Total amount:* $17,104,824 (80% institutional, 20% external sources). *Receiving aid:* Freshmen: 32% (1,295). Undergraduates: 25% (4,174). *Average award:* Freshmen: $2672. Undergraduates: $3252. *Scholarships, grants, and awards by category:* Academic interests/achievement: agriculture, architecture, biological sciences, business, communication, computer science, education, engineering/technologies, English, foreign languages, general academic interests/achievements, health fields, home economics, humanities, international studies, library science, mathematics, physical sciences, premedicine, social sciences. *Creative arts/performance:* applied art and design, art/fine arts, general creative arts/performance, journalism/publications, music, performing arts, theater/drama. *Special achievements/activities:* leadership. *Special characteristics:* children and siblings of alumni, children of faculty/staff, international students, local/state students, members of minority groups, religious affiliation. *Tuition waivers:* Full or partial for minority students, children of alumni, employees or children of employees, adult students, senior citizens. *ROTC:* Army, Air Force.

LOANS *Student loans:* $64,393,351 (53% need-based, 47% non-need-based). 47% of past graduating class borrowed through all loan programs. *Average indebtedness per student:* $23,000. *Average need-based loan:* Freshmen: $3413. Undergraduates: $4282. *Parent loans:* $1,652,818 (100% non-need-based). *Programs:* Federal Direct (Subsidized and Unsubsidized Stafford, PLUS), Perkins, college/university.

WORK-STUDY *Federal work-study:* Total amount: $723,664; 465 jobs averaging $3567. *State or other work-study/employment:* Total amount: $758,015 (100% need-based). Part-time jobs available.

ATHLETIC AWARDS Total amount: $5,081,240 (100% non-need-based).

APPLYING FOR FINANCIAL AID *Required financial aid form:* FAFSA. *Financial aid deadline:* Continuous. *Notification date:* Continuous beginning 4/1. Students must reply within 4 weeks of notification.

CONTACT Office of Financial Aid, Utah State University, 1800 Old Main Hill, Logan, UT 84322-1800, 435-797-0173 or toll-free 800-488-8108. *Fax:* 435-797-0654. *E-mail:* finaid@usu.edu. *Website:* http://www.usu.edu/.

UTAH VALLEY UNIVERSITY
Orem, UT

Tuition & fees (UT res): $5530	Average undergraduate aid package: $7730

ABOUT THE INSTITUTION State-supported, coed. *Awards:* certificates, diplomas, associate, bachelor's, and master's degrees. 83 undergraduate majors. *Total enrollment:* 34,978. Undergraduates: 34,706. Freshmen: 3,962. Federal methodology is used as a basis for awarding need-based institutional aid.

UNDERGRADUATE EXPENSES for 2016–2017 *Application fee:* $35. *Tuition, state resident:* full-time $4840; part-time $207 per credit. *Tuition, nonresident:* full-time $15,000; part-time $640 per credit. *Required fees:* full-time $690; $345 per term or $345 per term.

FRESHMAN FINANCIAL AID (Fall 2016, est.) 1,894 applied for aid; of those 77% were deemed to have need. 95% of freshmen with need received aid; of those 15% had need fully met. *Average percent of need met:* 67% (excluding resources awarded to replace EFC). *Average financial aid package:* $7902 (excluding resources awarded to replace EFC). 2% of all full-time freshmen had no need and received non-need-based gift aid.

UNDERGRADUATE FINANCIAL AID (Fall 2016, est.) 11,403 applied for aid; of those 88% were deemed to have need. 97% of undergraduates with need received aid; of those 10% had need fully met. *Average percent of need met:* 65% (excluding resources awarded to replace EFC). *Average financial aid package:* $7730 (excluding resources awarded to replace EFC). 1% of all full-time undergraduates had no need and received non-need-based gift aid.

GIFT AID (NEED-BASED) *Total amount:* $53,336,524 (91% federal, 4% state, 4% institutional, 1% external sources). *Receiving aid:* Freshmen: 31% (964); all full-time undergraduates: 44% (7,475). *Average award:* Freshmen: $4826; Undergraduates: $4825. *Scholarships, grants, and awards:* Federal Pell, FSEOG, state, private, college/university gift aid from institutional funds.

GIFT AID (NON-NEED-BASED) *Total amount:* $4,400,528 (1% federal, 61% state, 25% institutional, 13% external sources). *Receiving aid:* Freshmen: 17% (514). Undergraduates: 12% (2,047). *Average award:* Freshmen: $1623. Undergraduates: $1788. *Tuition waivers:* Full or partial for employees or children of employees. *ROTC:* Army, Air Force cooperative.

LOANS *Student loans:* $140,077,096 (50% need-based, 50% non-need-based). 51% of past graduating class borrowed through all loan programs. *Average indebtedness per student:* $22,259. *Average need-based loan:* Freshmen: $2327. Undergraduates: $2927. *Parent loans:* $327,361 (54% need-based, 46% non-need-based). *Programs:* Federal Direct (Subsidized and Unsubsidized Stafford, PLUS), Perkins.

WORK-STUDY *Federal work-study:* Total amount: $817,738; jobs available. *State or other work-study/employment:* Part-time jobs available.

ATHLETIC AWARDS Total amount: $2,952,061 (24% need-based, 76% non-need-based).

APPLYING FOR FINANCIAL AID *Required financial aid form:* FAFSA. *Financial aid deadline:* Continuous. *Notification date:* Continuous beginning 1/1.

CONTACT John Curl, Director of Financial Aid and Scholarships, Utah Valley University, 800 West University Parkway, Orem, UT 84058, 801-863-8442. *Fax:* 801-863-8448. *E-mail:* jcurl@uvu.edu. *Website:* http://www.uvu.edu/.

U.T.A. MESIVTA OF KIRYAS JOEL
Monroe, NY

CONTACT Financial Aid Office, U.T.A. Mesivta of Kiryas Joel, 9 Nickelsburg Road, Unit 312, Monroe, NY 10950, 845-873-9901.

UTICA COLLEGE
Utica, NY

Tuition & fees: $19,996	Average undergraduate aid package: $13,588

ABOUT THE INSTITUTION Independent, coed. *Awards:* certificates, bachelor's, master's, and doctoral degrees. 47 undergraduate majors. *Total enrollment:* 5,119. Undergraduates: 3,550. Freshmen: 685. Federal methodology is used as a basis for awarding need-based institutional aid.

UNDERGRADUATE EXPENSES for 2016–2017 *Application fee:* $40. *Comprehensive fee:* $30,430 includes full-time tuition ($19,446), mandatory fees ($550), and room and board ($10,434). Full-time tuition and fees vary according to course load, degree level, and location. Room and board charges vary according to board plan. *Part-time tuition:* $648 per credit hour. *Part-time fees:* $50 per term. Part-time tuition and fees vary according to course load, degree level, and location.

FRESHMAN FINANCIAL AID (Fall 2016, est.) 653 applied for aid; of those 89% were deemed to have need. 100% of freshmen with need received aid; of those 6% had need fully met. *Average percent of need met:* 59% (excluding resources awarded to replace EFC). *Average financial aid package:* $14,292 (excluding resources awarded to replace EFC). 10% of all full-time freshmen had no need and received non-need-based gift aid.

UNDERGRADUATE FINANCIAL AID (Fall 2016, est.) 2,506 applied for aid; of those 90% were deemed to have need. 100% of undergraduates with need received aid; of those 7% had need fully met. *Average percent of need met:* 51% (excluding resources awarded to replace EFC). *Average financial aid package:* $13,588 (excluding resources awarded to replace EFC). 9% of all full-time undergraduates had no need and received non-need-based gift aid.

GIFT AID (NEED-BASED) *Total amount:* $21,672,314 (25% federal, 18% state, 53% institutional, 4% external sources). *Receiving aid:* Freshmen: 83% (569); all full-time undergraduates: 71% (1,969). *Average award:* Freshmen: $5486; Undergraduates: $4745. *Scholarships, grants, and awards:* Federal Pell, FSEOG, state, private, college/university gift aid from institutional funds.

GIFT AID (NON-NEED-BASED) *Total amount:* $1,722,801 (1% state, 84% institutional, 15% external sources). *Receiving aid:* Freshmen: 9% (59). Undergraduates: 7% (181). *Average award:* Freshmen: $4251. Undergraduates: $5450. *Scholarships, grants, and awards by category:* Academic interests/achievement: general academic interests/achievements. *Tuition waivers:* Full or partial for employees or children of employees. *ROTC:* Army, Air Force cooperative.

LOANS *Student loans:* $27,919,063 (90% need-based, 10% non-need-based). 85% of past graduating class borrowed through all loan programs. *Average indebtedness per student:* $33,336. *Average need-based loan:* Freshmen: $3411. Undergraduates: $4399. *Parent loans:* $6,432,911 (90% need-based, 10% non-need-based). *Programs:* Federal Direct (Subsidized and Unsubsidized Stafford, PLUS), Perkins.

WORK-STUDY *Federal work-study:* Total amount: $869,043; jobs available. *State or other work-study/employment:* Part-time jobs available.

APPLYING FOR FINANCIAL AID *Required financial aid form:* FAFSA. *Financial aid deadline (priority):* 2/15. *Notification date:* Continuous. Students must reply by 5/1 or within 4 weeks of notification.

CONTACT Laura Bedford, Director of Student Financial Services, Utica College, 1600 Burrstone Road, Utica, NY 13502-4892, 315-792-3179 or toll-free 800-782-8884. *Fax:* 315-792-3368. *E-mail:* lbedford@utica.edu. *Website:* http://www.utica.edu/.

VALDOSTA STATE UNIVERSITY
Valdosta, GA

Tuition & fees (GA res): $6297	Average undergraduate aid package: $15,919

ABOUT THE INSTITUTION State-supported, coed. *Awards:* certificates, associate, bachelor's, master's, and doctoral degrees. 51 undergraduate majors. *Total enrollment:* 11,375. Undergraduates: 8,780. Freshmen: 1,458. Both federal and institutional methodology are used as a basis for awarding need-based institutional aid.

UNDERGRADUATE EXPENSES for 2017–2018 *Application fee:* $40. *Tuition, state resident:* full-time $4181. *Tuition, nonresident:* full-time $14,755. *Required fees:* full-time $2116. Full-time tuition and fees vary according to course load, location, program, and reciprocity agreements. Part-time tuition and fees vary according to course load, location, program, and reciprocity agreements. **College room and board:** $7900; **Room only:** $4060. Room and board charges vary according to board plan and housing facility.

FRESHMAN FINANCIAL AID (Fall 2015) 1,320 applied for aid; of those 81% were deemed to have need. 99% of freshmen with need received aid; of those 19% had need fully met. **Average percent of need met:** 97% (excluding resources awarded to replace EFC). **Average financial aid package:** $16,340 (excluding resources awarded to replace EFC). 1% of all full-time freshmen had no need and received non-need-based gift aid.

UNDERGRADUATE FINANCIAL AID (Fall 2015) 6,194 applied for aid; of those 86% were deemed to have need. 100% of undergraduates with need received aid; of those 15% had need fully met. **Average percent of need met:** 78% (excluding resources awarded to replace EFC). **Average financial aid package:** $15,919 (excluding resources awarded to replace EFC). 1% of all full-time undergraduates had no need and received non-need-based gift aid.

GIFT AID (NEED-BASED) Total amount: $33,162,098 (61% federal, 37% state, 1% institutional, 1% external sources). **Receiving aid:** Freshmen: 70% (953); all full-time undergraduates: 71% (5,178). **Average award:** Freshmen: $6862; Undergraduates: $6361. **Scholarships, grants, and awards:** Federal Pell, FSEOG, state, private, college/university gift aid from institutional funds, United Negro College Fund, Federal Nursing.

GIFT AID (NON-NEED-BASED) Total amount: $4,059,230 (1% federal, 89% state, 5% institutional, 5% external sources). **Receiving aid:** Freshmen: 4% (58). Undergraduates: 3% (210). **Average award:** Freshmen: $2250. Undergraduates: $2478. **Scholarships, grants, and awards by category:** Academic interests/achievement: biological sciences, communication, education, general academic interests/achievements, health fields, library science, mathematics, physical sciences, social sciences. Creative arts/performance: art/fine arts, general creative arts/performance, journalism/publications, music, performing arts, theater/drama. Special achievements/activities: general special achievements/activities, religious involvement. Special characteristics: general special characteristics, local/state students, members of minority groups. **Tuition waivers:** Full or partial for employees or children of employees. **ROTC:** Air Force.

LOANS Student loans: $52,667,550 (80% need-based, 20% non-need-based). 75% of past graduating class borrowed through all loan programs. **Average indebtedness per student:** $29,607. **Average need-based loan:** Freshmen: $3310. Undergraduates: $3464. **Parent loans:** $50,846,467 (44% need-based, 56% non-need-based). **Programs:** Federal Direct (Subsidized and Unsubsidized Stafford, PLUS), state, college/university.

WORK-STUDY Federal work-study: jobs available. **State or other work-study/employment:** Part-time jobs available.

ATHLETIC AWARDS Total amount: $1,600,296 (47% need-based, 53% non-need-based).

APPLYING FOR FINANCIAL AID Required financial aid form: FAFSA. **Financial aid deadline (priority):** 4/1. **Notification date:** Continuous beginning 3/1.

CONTACT Mr. Douglas R. Tanner, Director of Financial Aid, Valdosta State University, 1500 North Patterson Street, Valdosta, GA 31698, 229-333-5935 or toll-free 800-618-1878. *Fax:* 229-333-5430. *Website:* http://www.valdosta.edu/.

VALENCIA COLLEGE
Orlando, FL

CONTACT College Answer Center Specialists, Valencia College, PO Box 3028, Orlando, FL 32802-3028, 407-299-5000.
Website: http://valenciacollege.edu/.

VALLEY CITY STATE UNIVERSITY
Valley City, ND

Tuition & fees (ND res): $7195	Average undergraduate aid package: $12,486

ABOUT THE INSTITUTION State-supported, coed. **Awards:** bachelor's and master's degrees. 45 undergraduate majors. **Total enrollment:** 1,452. Undergraduates: 1,295. Freshmen: 186. Federal methodology is used as a basis for awarding need-based institutional aid.

UNDERGRADUATE EXPENSES for 2016–2017 Application fee: $35. **Tuition, state resident:** full-time $5282; part-time $176.06 per semester hour. **Tuition, nonresident:** full-time $14,103; part-time $470.09 per semester hour. **Required fees:** full-time $1913; $79.70 per semester hour. Full-time tuition and fees vary according to course load, location, program, and reciprocity agreements. Part-time tuition and fees vary according to course load, location, program, and reciprocity agreements. **College room and board:** $6072; **Room only:** $3575. Room and board charges vary according to board plan and housing facility.

FRESHMAN FINANCIAL AID (Fall 2016, est.) 137 applied for aid; of those 69% were deemed to have need. 100% of freshmen with need received aid; of those 54% had need fully met. **Average percent of need met:** 89% (excluding resources awarded to replace EFC). **Average financial aid package:** $13,133 (excluding resources awarded to replace EFC). 37% of all full-time freshmen had no need and received non-need-based gift aid.

UNDERGRADUATE FINANCIAL AID (Fall 2016, est.) 591 applied for aid; of those 71% were deemed to have need. 99% of undergraduates with need received aid; of those 54% had need fully met. **Average percent of need met:** 86% (excluding resources awarded to replace EFC). **Average financial aid package:** $12,486 (excluding resources awarded to replace EFC). 19% of all full-time undergraduates had no need and received non-need-based gift aid.

GIFT AID (NEED-BASED) Total amount: $2,221,890 (55% federal, 24% state, 16% institutional, 5% external sources). **Receiving aid:** Freshmen: 59% (93); all full-time undergraduates: 54% (391). **Average award:** Freshmen: $7187; Undergraduates: $5937. **Scholarships, grants, and awards:** Federal Pell, FSEOG, state, private, college/university gift aid from institutional funds, United Negro College Fund.

GIFT AID (NON-NEED-BASED) Total amount: $596,648 (1% federal, 19% state, 61% institutional, 19% external sources). **Receiving aid:** Freshmen: 9% (14). Undergraduates: 6% (41). **Average award:** Freshmen: $2031. Undergraduates: $2224. **Scholarships, grants, and awards by category:** Academic interests/achievement: biological sciences, business, communication, computer science, education, engineering/technologies, English, general academic interests/achievements, humanities, library science, mathematics, physical sciences, social sciences. Creative arts/performance: applied art and design, art/fine arts, journalism/publications, music, theater/drama. Special achievements/activities: general special achievements/activities. Special characteristics: children and siblings of alumni, children of faculty/staff, ethnic background, general special characteristics, international students, members of minority groups. **Tuition waivers:** Full or partial for employees or children of employees.

LOANS Student loans: $4,656,367 (53% need-based, 47% non-need-based). 86% of past graduating class borrowed through all loan programs. **Average indebtedness per student:** $24,281. **Average need-based loan:** Freshmen: $4764. Undergraduates: $5831. **Parent loans:** $95,730 (16% need-based, 84% non-need-based). **Programs:** Federal Direct (Subsidized and Unsubsidized Stafford, PLUS), Perkins.

WORK-STUDY Federal work-study: Total amount: $99,356; 52 jobs averaging $2118. **State or other work-study/employment:** Part-time jobs available.

ATHLETIC AWARDS Total amount: $423,775 (62% need-based, 38% non-need-based).

APPLYING FOR FINANCIAL AID Required financial aid form: FAFSA. **Financial aid deadline (priority):** 3/15. **Notification date:** Continuous beginning 11/15. Students must reply within 4 weeks of notification.

CONTACT Ms. Betty Kuss Schumacher, Director of Student Financial Aid, Valley City State University, 101 College Street SW, Valley City, ND 58072, 701-845-7412 or toll-free 800-532-8641 Ext. 7101. *Fax:* 701-845-7410. *E-mail:* betty.schumacher@vcsu.edu. *Website:* http://www.vcsu.edu/.

VALPARAISO UNIVERSITY
Valparaiso, IN

Tuition & fees: $38,760	Average undergraduate aid package: $29,069

ABOUT THE INSTITUTION Independent Lutheran Church, coed. *Awards:* certificates, associate, bachelor's, master's, and doctoral degrees. 87 undergraduate majors. *Total enrollment:* 4,433. Undergraduates: 3,294. Freshmen: 862. Both federal and institutional methodology are used as a basis for awarding need-based institutional aid.

UNDERGRADUATE EXPENSES for 2017–2018 *Comprehensive fee:* $50,160 includes full-time tuition ($37,550), mandatory fees ($1210), and room and board ($11,400). *College room only:* $7000. Full-time tuition and fees vary according to course load and program. Room and board charges vary according to housing facility and student level. *Part-time tuition:* $1665 per credit hour. *Part-time fees:* $116 per term. Part-time tuition and fees vary according to course load and program. *Payment plan:* Tuition prepayment.

FRESHMAN FINANCIAL AID (Fall 2015) 695 applied for aid; of those 89% were deemed to have need. 100% of freshmen with need received aid; of those 59% had need fully met. *Average percent of need met:* 94% (excluding resources awarded to replace EFC). *Average financial aid package:* $31,139 (excluding resources awarded to replace EFC). 15% of all full-time freshmen had no need and received non-need-based gift aid.

UNDERGRADUATE FINANCIAL AID (Fall 2015) 2,536 applied for aid; of those 90% were deemed to have need. 100% of undergraduates with need received aid; of those 61% had need fully met. *Average percent of need met:* 93% (excluding resources awarded to replace EFC). *Average financial aid package:* $29,069 (excluding resources awarded to replace EFC). 20% of all full-time undergraduates had no need and received non-need-based gift aid.

GIFT AID (NEED-BASED) *Total amount:* $62,874,798 (8% federal, 3% state, 87% institutional, 2% external sources). *Receiving aid:* Freshmen: 83% (619); all full-time undergraduates: 74% (2,265). *Average award:* Freshmen: $28,968; Undergraduates: $26,100. *Scholarships, grants, and awards:* Federal Pell, FSEOG, state, private, college/university gift aid from institutional funds.

GIFT AID (NON-NEED-BASED) *Total amount:* $11,506,837 (94% institutional, 6% external sources). *Receiving aid:* Freshmen: 18% (130). Undergraduates: 12% (377). *Average award:* Freshmen: $17,669. Undergraduates: $15,226. *Scholarships, grants, and awards by category:* Academic interests/achievement: business, engineering/technologies, foreign languages, general academic interests/achievements, health fields, physical sciences, religion/biblical studies. *Creative arts/performance:* art/fine arts, music, performing arts, theater/drama. *Special characteristics:* children and siblings of alumni, children of faculty/staff, international students, relatives of clergy, religious affiliation. *Tuition waivers:* Full or partial for employees or children of employees. *ROTC:* Army cooperative, Air Force cooperative.

LOANS *Student loans:* $16,476,229 (87% need-based, 13% non-need-based). 71% of past graduating class borrowed through all loan programs. *Average indebtedness per student:* $37,294. *Average need-based loan:* Freshmen: $4210. Undergraduates: $4837. *Parent loans:* $4,326,623 (65% need-based, 35% non-need-based). *Programs:* Federal Direct (Subsidized and Unsubsidized Stafford, PLUS), Perkins, college/university, private loans.

WORK-STUDY *Federal work-study:* 570 jobs averaging $1440. *State or other work-study/employment:* Total amount: $1,237,150 (14% need-based, 86% non-need-based). 884 part-time jobs averaging $2145.

ATHLETIC AWARDS Total amount: $4,123,042 (53% need-based, 47% non-need-based).

APPLYING FOR FINANCIAL AID *Required financial aid form:* FAFSA. *Financial aid deadline (priority):* 3/1. *Notification date:* Continuous beginning 3/1.

CONTACT Ms. Karen Klimczyk, Director of Financial Aid, Valparaiso University, 1700 Chapel Drive, Valparaiso, IN 46383-6493, 219-464-5015 or toll-free 888-GO-VALPO. *Fax:* 219-464-5012. *E-mail:* karen.klimczyk@valpo.edu. *Website:* http://www.valpo.edu/.

VANDERBILT UNIVERSITY
Nashville, TN

Tuition & fees: $45,610	Average undergraduate aid package: $46,938

ABOUT THE INSTITUTION Independent, coed. *Awards:* bachelor's, master's, and doctoral degrees. 70 undergraduate majors. *Total enrollment:* 12,587. Undergraduates: 6,871. Freshmen: 1,601. Both federal and institutional methodology are used as a basis for awarding need-based institutional aid.

UNDERGRADUATE EXPENSES for 2016–2017 *Application fee:* $50. *Comprehensive fee:* $60,572 includes full-time tuition ($44,496), mandatory fees ($1114), and room and board ($14,962). *College room only:* $9772. Room and board charges vary according to board plan. *Part-time tuition:* $1854 per credit hour. *Payment plan:* Tuition prepayment.

FRESHMAN FINANCIAL AID (Fall 2016, est.) 1,048 applied for aid; of those 81% were deemed to have need. 100% of freshmen with need received aid; of those 100% had need fully met. *Average percent of need met:* 100% (excluding resources awarded to replace EFC). *Average financial aid package:* $47,712 (excluding resources awarded to replace EFC). 9% of all full-time freshmen had no need and received non-need-based gift aid.

UNDERGRADUATE FINANCIAL AID (Fall 2016, est.) 3,836 applied for aid; of those 89% were deemed to have need. 99% of undergraduates with need received aid; of those 100% had need fully met. *Average percent of need met:* 100% (excluding resources awarded to replace EFC). *Average financial aid package:* $46,938 (excluding resources awarded to replace EFC). 11% of all full-time undergraduates had no need and received non-need-based gift aid.

GIFT AID (NEED-BASED) *Total amount:* $145,737,417 (4% federal, 1% state, 94% institutional, 1% external sources). *Receiving aid:* Freshmen: 46% (741); all full-time undergraduates: 46% (3,121). *Average award:* Freshmen: $42,430; Undergraduates: $41,331. *Scholarships, grants, and awards:* Federal Pell, FSEOG, state, private, college/university gift aid from institutional funds.

GIFT AID (NON-NEED-BASED) *Total amount:* $21,728,423 (10% federal, 4% state, 80% institutional, 6% external sources). *Receiving aid:* Freshmen: 27% (431). Undergraduates: 21% (1,407). *Average award:* Freshmen: $21,873. Undergraduates: $22,357. *Scholarships, grants, and awards by category:* Academic interests/achievement: general academic interests/achievements. *Creative arts/performance:* general creative arts/performance. *Special achievements/activities:* community service, general special achievements/activities, leadership. *Special characteristics:* general special characteristics, local/state students, members of minority groups, veterans, veterans' children. *Tuition waivers:* Full or partial for employees or children of employees. *ROTC:* Army, Naval, Air Force cooperative.

LOANS *Student loans:* $7,992,758 (14% need-based, 86% non-need-based). 21% of past graduating class borrowed through all loan programs. *Average indebtedness per student:* $24,122. *Average need-based loan:* Freshmen: $3014. Undergraduates: $3375. *Parent loans:* $5,886,720 (100% non-need-based). *Programs:* Federal Direct (Subsidized and Unsubsidized Stafford, PLUS), Perkins, Federal Nursing.

WORK-STUDY *Federal work-study:* Total amount: $3,645,446; 1,466 jobs averaging $2383. *State or other work-study/employment:* Total amount: $980,486 (100% need-based). Part-time jobs available.

ATHLETIC AWARDS Total amount: $12,382,680 (22% need-based, 78% non-need-based).

APPLYING FOR FINANCIAL AID *Required financial aid forms:* FAFSA, CSS Financial Aid PROFILE. *Financial aid deadline (priority):* 2/1. *Notification date:* 4/1. Students must reply by 5/1.

CONTACT Mr. Brent Tener, Director of Financial Aid, Vanderbilt University, 2309 West End Avenue, Nashville, TN 37203, 615-322-3591 or toll-free 800-288-0432. *Fax:* 615-343-8512. *E-mail:* b.tener@vanderbilt.edu. *Website:* http://www.vanderbilt.edu/.

VANDERCOOK COLLEGE OF MUSIC
Chicago, IL

ABOUT THE INSTITUTION Independent, coed. *Awards:* bachelor's and master's degrees. 1 undergraduate major. *Total enrollment:* 298. Undergraduates: 155. Freshmen: 21.

GIFT AID (NEED-BASED) *Scholarships, grants, and awards:* Federal Pell, FSEOG, state, private, college/university gift aid from institutional funds.

GIFT AID (NON-NEED-BASED) *Scholarships, grants, and awards by category: Academic interests/achievement:* education, general academic interests/achievements. *Creative arts/performance:* music. *Special characteristics:* ethnic background, out-of-state students, religious affiliation.

LOANS *Programs:* Federal Direct (Subsidized and Unsubsidized Stafford, PLUS).

APPLYING FOR FINANCIAL AID *Required financial aid form:* FAFSA.

CONTACT Ms. Sirena Covington, Director of Financial Aid, VanderCook College of Music, 3140 South Federal Street, Chicago, IL 60616, 312-788-1146. *Fax:* 312-225-5211. *E-mail:* scovington@vandercook.edu.
Website: http://www.vandercook.edu/.

VANGUARD UNIVERSITY OF SOUTHERN CALIFORNIA
Costa Mesa, CA

Tuition & fees: N/R	Average undergraduate aid package: $14,537

ABOUT THE INSTITUTION Independent Assemblies of God, coed. *Awards:* certificates, associate, bachelor's, and master's degrees. 46 undergraduate majors. *Total enrollment:* 2,184. Undergraduates: 1,881. Freshmen: 374. Federal methodology is used as a basis for awarding need-based institutional aid.

UNDERGRADUATE EXPENSES for 2016–2017 *Application fee:* $45. *Tuition:* part-time $1290 per credit hour. Full-time tuition and fees vary according to course load, location, and program. Part-time tuition and fees vary according to course load and program. Room and board charges vary according to board plan and housing facility.

FRESHMAN FINANCIAL AID (Fall 2016, est.) 392 applied for aid; of those 100% were deemed to have need. 100% of freshmen with need received aid; of those 100% had need fully met. *Average financial aid package:* $15,449 (excluding resources awarded to replace EFC). 99% of all full-time freshmen had no need and received non-need-based gift aid.

UNDERGRADUATE FINANCIAL AID (Fall 2016, est.) 1,293 applied for aid; of those 100% were deemed to have need. 100% of undergraduates with need received aid; of those 100% had need fully met. *Average financial aid package:* $14,537 (excluding resources awarded to replace EFC). 93% of all full-time undergraduates had no need and received non-need-based gift aid.

GIFT AID (NEED-BASED) *Total amount:* $27,677,941 (13% federal, 17% state, 69% institutional, 1% external sources). *Receiving aid:* Freshmen: 58% (237); all full-time undergraduates: 55% (794). *Average award:* Freshmen: $6960; Undergraduates: $7047. *Scholarships, grants, and awards:* Federal Pell, FSEOG, state, private, college/university gift aid from institutional funds.

GIFT AID (NON-NEED-BASED) *Receiving aid:* Freshmen: 93% (380). Undergraduates: 80% (1,158). *Average award:* Freshmen: $8787. Undergraduates: $7759. *Scholarships, grants, and awards by category: Academic interests/achievement:* general academic interests/achievements. *Creative arts/performance:* debating, music, theater/drama. *Special characteristics:* children of faculty/staff, religious affiliation. *Tuition waivers:* Full or partial for employees or children of employees. *ROTC:* Air Force cooperative.

LOANS *Student loans:* $13,496,349 (100% need-based). 77% of past graduating class borrowed through all loan programs. *Average indebtedness per student:* $28,686. *Parent loans:* $7,932,316 (48% need-based, 52% non-need-based). *Programs:* Federal Direct (Subsidized and Unsubsidized Stafford, PLUS), Perkins.

WORK-STUDY *Federal work-study:* Total amount: $241,420; jobs available.

ATHLETIC AWARDS Total amount: $1,735,200 (100% need-based).

APPLYING FOR FINANCIAL AID *Required financial aid form:* FAFSA. *Financial aid deadline:* 3/2. *Notification date:* Continuous beginning 3/15. Students must reply within 3 weeks of notification.

CONTACT Financial Aid Office, Vanguard University of Southern California, 55 Fair Drive, Costa Mesa, CA 92626-6597, 714-619-5490 or toll-free 800-722-6279. *Fax:* 714-619-6655. *E-mail:* financialaid@vanguard.edu.
Website: http://www.vanguard.edu/.

VASSAR COLLEGE
Poughkeepsie, NY

Tuition & fees: $53,090	Average undergraduate aid package: $50,820

ABOUT THE INSTITUTION Independent, coed. *Awards:* bachelor's and master's degrees. 51 undergraduate majors. *Total enrollment:* 2,424. Undergraduates: 2,424. Freshmen: 659. Institutional methodology is used as a basis for awarding need-based institutional aid.

UNDERGRADUATE EXPENSES for 2016–2017 *Application fee:* $70. *One-time required fee:* $80. *Comprehensive fee:* $65,490 includes full-time tuition ($52,320), mandatory fees ($770), and room and board ($12,400). *College room only:* $6730. Room and board charges vary according to board plan and housing facility. *Part-time tuition:* $6230 per unit.

FRESHMAN FINANCIAL AID (Fall 2016, est.) 492 applied for aid; of those 83% were deemed to have need. 100% of freshmen with need received aid; of those 100% had need fully met. *Average percent of need met:* 100% (excluding resources awarded to replace EFC). *Average financial aid package:* $51,083 (excluding resources awarded to replace EFC).

UNDERGRADUATE FINANCIAL AID (Fall 2016, est.) 1,743 applied for aid; of those 89% were deemed to have need. 100% of undergraduates with need received aid; of those 100% had need fully met. *Average percent of need met:* 100% (excluding resources awarded to replace EFC). *Average financial aid package:* $50,820 (excluding resources awarded to replace EFC).

GIFT AID (NEED-BASED) *Total amount:* $68,862,413 (4% federal, 1% state, 92% institutional, 3% external sources). *Receiving aid:* Freshmen: 62% (408); all full-time undergraduates: 64% (1,548). *Average award:* Freshmen: $46,243; Undergraduates: $47,176. *Scholarships, grants, and awards:* Federal Pell, FSEOG, state, private, college/university gift aid from institutional funds.

GIFT AID (NON-NEED-BASED) *Total amount:* $308,725 (5% federal, 5% state, 90% external sources). *Tuition waivers:* Full or partial for employees or children of employees.

LOANS *Student loans:* $6,077,111 (52% need-based, 48% non-need-based). 44% of past graduating class borrowed through all loan programs. *Average indebtedness per student:* $18,462. *Average need-based loan:* Freshmen: $2631. Undergraduates: $3779. *Parent loans:* $3,029,469 (100% non-need-based). *Programs:* Federal Direct (Subsidized and Unsubsidized Stafford, PLUS), Perkins.

WORK-STUDY *Federal work-study:* Total amount: $2,678,814; 1,057 jobs averaging $2521. *State or other work-study/employment:* Total amount: $837,030 (100% need-based). 345 part-time jobs averaging $2471.

APPLYING FOR FINANCIAL AID *Required financial aid forms:* FAFSA, CSS Financial Aid PROFILE, noncustodial (divorced/separated) parent's statement. *Financial aid deadline:* 2/1. *Notification date:* 3/30. Students must reply by 5/1.

CONTACT Ms. Jessica L. Bernier, Director of Student Financial Services, Vassar College, 124 Raymond Avenue, Box 8, Poughkeepsie, NY 12604, 845-437-5320 or toll-free 800-827-7270. *Fax:* 845-437-5325. *E-mail:* jebernier@vassar.edu.
Website: http://www.vassar.edu/.

VAUGHN COLLEGE OF AERONAUTICS AND TECHNOLOGY
Flushing, NY

CONTACT Dorothy Martin, Director of Financial Aid, Vaughn College of Aeronautics and Technology, 86-01 23rd Avenue, Flushing, NY 11369, 718-429-6600 Ext. 187 or toll-free 866-6VAUGHN. *Fax:* 718-779-2231. *E-mail:* dorothy.martin@vaughn.edu.
Website: http://www.vaughn.edu/.

VERMONT TECHNICAL COLLEGE
Randolph Center, VT

Tuition & fees (VT res): $15,000	Average undergraduate aid package: $14,736

ABOUT THE INSTITUTION State-supported, coed. *Awards:* certificates, associate, bachelor's, and master's degrees. 24 undergraduate majors. *Total enrollment:* 1,632. Undergraduates: 1,625. Freshmen: 218. Federal methodology is used as a basis for awarding need-based institutional aid.

UNDERGRADUATE EXPENSES for 2017–2018 *Application fee:* $47. *Tuition, state resident:* full-time $13,512; part-time $563 per credit hour. *Tuition, nonresident:* full-time $25,824; part-time $1076 per credit hour. *Required fees:* full-time $1488; $47 per credit hour. Full-time tuition and fees vary according to course load and program. Part-time tuition and fees vary according to program. *College room and board:* $10,290; *Room only:* $6128. Room and board charges vary according to board plan.

FRESHMAN FINANCIAL AID (Fall 2016, est.) 205 applied for aid; of those 81% were deemed to have need. 100% of freshmen with need received aid; of those 8% had need fully met. *Average percent of need met:* 58% (excluding resources awarded to replace EFC). *Average financial aid package:* $12,492 (excluding resources awarded to replace EFC). 14% of all full-time freshmen had no need and received non-need-based gift aid.

UNDERGRADUATE FINANCIAL AID (Fall 2016, est.) 902 applied for aid; of those 90% were deemed to have need. 98% of undergraduates with need received aid; of those 9% had need fully met. *Average percent of need met:* 61% (excluding resources awarded to replace EFC). *Average financial aid package:* $14,736 (excluding resources awarded to replace EFC). 6% of all full-time undergraduates had no need and received non-need-based gift aid.

GIFT AID (NEED-BASED) *Total amount:* $6,417,418 (38% federal, 23% state, 29% institutional, 10% external sources). *Receiving aid:* Freshmen: 72% (153); all full-time undergraduates: 60% (662). *Average award:* Freshmen: $3080; Undergraduates: $5648. *Scholarships, grants, and awards:* Federal Pell, FSEOG, state, private, college/university gift aid from institutional funds.

GIFT AID (NON-NEED-BASED) *Total amount:* $498,203 (75% institutional, 25% external sources). *Receiving aid:* Freshmen: 39% (83). Undergraduates: 23% (253). *Average award:* Freshmen: $4620. Undergraduates: $4740. *Scholarships, grants, and awards by category:* Academic interests/achievement: 9 awards ($58,320 total): agriculture. *Tuition waivers:* Full or partial for employees or children of employees. *ROTC:* Army cooperative.

LOANS *Student loans:* $10,452,979 (92% need-based, 8% non-need-based). 86% of past graduating class borrowed through all loan programs. *Average indebtedness per student:* $29,988. *Average need-based loan:* Freshmen: $3340. Undergraduates: $3920. *Parent loans:* $1,404,441 (88% need-based, 12% non-need-based). *Programs:* Federal Direct (Subsidized and Unsubsidized Stafford, PLUS), Perkins.

WORK-STUDY *Federal work-study:* Total amount: $160,000; 177 jobs averaging $1260.

APPLYING FOR FINANCIAL AID *Required financial aid forms:* FAFSA, state aid form. *Financial aid deadline (priority):* 3/1. *Notification date:* Continuous beginning 11/20.

CONTACT Catherine R. McCullough, Director of Financial Aid, Vermont Technical College, PO Box 500, Randolph Center, VT 05061-0500, 802-728-1248 or toll-free 800-442-VTC1. *Fax:* 802-728-1436.
Website: http://www.vtc.edu/.

VILLA MARIA COLLEGE
Buffalo, NY

Tuition & fees: $20,770	Average undergraduate aid package: N/A

ABOUT THE INSTITUTION Independent Roman Catholic Church, coed. *Awards:* certificates, associate, and bachelor's degrees. 19 undergraduate majors. *Total enrollment:* 589. Undergraduates: 589. Freshmen: 148. Federal methodology is used as a basis for awarding need-based institutional aid.

UNDERGRADUATE EXPENSES for 2016–2017 *Tuition:* full-time $20,030; part-time $670 per credit hour. *Required fees:* full-time $740; $260 per year. Full-time tuition and fees vary according to program and reciprocity agreements. Part-time tuition and fees vary according to course load, program, and reciprocity agreements.

GIFT AID (NEED-BASED) *Scholarships, grants, and awards:* Federal Pell, FSEOG, state, private, college/university gift aid from institutional funds.

GIFT AID (NON-NEED-BASED) *Tuition waivers:* Full or partial for employees or children of employees.

LOANS *Student loans:* 91% of past graduating class borrowed through all loan programs. *Average indebtedness per student:* $22,658. *Programs:* Federal Direct (Subsidized and Unsubsidized Stafford, PLUS), private loans.

WORK-STUDY Federal work-study jobs available. *State or other work-study/employment:* Part-time jobs available.

APPLYING FOR FINANCIAL AID *Required financial aid forms:* FAFSA, state aid form. *Financial aid deadline:* Continuous. *Notification date:* Continuous beginning 5/1. Students must reply within 2 weeks of notification.

CONTACT Aimee Murch, Director of Financial Aid, Villa Maria College, 240 Pine Ridge Road, Buffalo, NY 14225, 716-961-1828. *Fax:* 716-896-0705. *E-mail:* murcha@villa.edu.
Website: http://www.villa.edu/.

VILLANOVA UNIVERSITY
Villanova, PA

Tuition & fees: $49,280	Average undergraduate aid package: $36,074

ABOUT THE INSTITUTION Independent Roman Catholic, coed. *Awards:* certificates, bachelor's, master's, and doctoral degrees. 51 undergraduate majors. *Total enrollment:* 10,842. Undergraduates: 6,999. Freshmen: 1,678. Both federal and institutional methodology are used as a basis for awarding need-based institutional aid.

UNDERGRADUATE EXPENSES for 2016–2017 *Application fee:* $80. *Comprehensive fee:* $62,373 includes full-time tuition ($48,610), mandatory fees ($670), and room and board ($13,093). Full-time tuition and fees vary according to degree level, location, and student level. Room and board charges vary according to board plan and housing facility. *Part-time tuition:* $2701 per credit hour. *Part-time fees:* $37 per credit hour. Part-time tuition and fees vary according to class time, course load, degree level, location, and program.

FRESHMAN FINANCIAL AID (Fall 2016, est.) 1,168 applied for aid; of those 69% were deemed to have need. 98% of freshmen with need received aid; of those 19% had need fully met. *Average percent of need met:* 81% (excluding resources awarded to replace EFC). *Average financial aid package:* $35,801 (excluding resources awarded to replace EFC). 7% of all full-time freshmen had no need and received non-need-based gift aid.

UNDERGRADUATE FINANCIAL AID (Fall 2016, est.) 3,859 applied for aid; of those 81% were deemed to have need. 97% of undergraduates with need received aid; of those 17% had need fully met. *Average percent of need met:* 79% (excluding resources awarded to replace EFC). *Average financial aid package:* $36,074 (excluding resources awarded to replace EFC). 8% of all full-time undergraduates had no need and received non-need-based gift aid.

GIFT AID (NEED-BASED) *Total amount:* $86,207,578 (7% federal, 1% state, 91% institutional, 1% external sources). *Receiving aid:* Freshmen: 44% (737); all full-time undergraduates: 44% (2,866). *Average award:* Freshmen: $31,433; Undergraduates: $30,497. *Scholarships, grants, and awards:* Federal Pell, FSEOG, state, private, college/university gift aid from institutional funds, endowed and restricted scholarships and grants.

GIFT AID (NON-NEED-BASED) *Total amount:* $12,077,412 (31% federal, 63% institutional, 6% external sources). *Receiving aid:* Freshmen: 5% (82). Undergraduates: 3% (170). *Average award:* Freshmen: $14,527. Undergraduates: $15,614. *Scholarships, grants, and awards by category:* Academic interests/achievement: 880 awards ($10,330,012 total): general academic interests/achievements, international studies, military science. *Special achievements/activities:* 25 awards ($22,750 total): general special achievements/activities. *Special characteristics:* 273 awards ($10,258,343 total): children of educators, children of faculty/staff, general special characteristics, religious affiliation. *Tuition waivers:* Full or partial for employees or children of employees, senior citizens. *ROTC:* Army, Naval, Air Force cooperative.

LOANS *Student loans:* $33,506,050 (83% need-based, 17% non-need-based). 53% of past graduating class borrowed through all loan programs. *Average indebtedness per student:* $35,545. *Average need-based loan:* Freshmen: $3820. Undergrad-

uates: $5064. *Parent loans:* $13,799,861 (76% need-based, 24% non-need-based). *Programs:* Federal Direct (Subsidized and Unsubsidized Stafford, PLUS), Perkins, Federal Nursing, alternative loans.

WORK-STUDY *Federal work-study:* Total amount: $6,557,121; 2,149 jobs averaging $2818. *State or other work-study/employment:* Total amount: $104,760 (100% need-based). 35 part-time jobs averaging $2852.

ATHLETIC AWARDS Total amount: $12,518,391 (27% need-based, 73% non-need-based).

APPLYING FOR FINANCIAL AID *Required financial aid forms:* FAFSA, CSS Financial Aid PROFILE, noncustodial (divorced/separated) parent's statement, federal income tax form(s), W-2 forms. *Financial aid deadline:* 1/15. *Notification date:* 4/1. Students must reply by 5/1.

CONTACT Bonnie Lee Behm, Director of Financial Assistance, Villanova University, 800 Lancaster Avenue, Villanova, PA 19085-1699, 610-519-4010. *Fax:* 610-519-7599. *E-mail:* bonnie.behm@villanova.edu. *Website:* http://www.villanova.edu/.

VIRGINIA BAPTIST COLLEGE
Fredericksburg, VA

CONTACT Financial Aid Office, Virginia Baptist College, 4111 Plank Road, Fredericksburg, VA 22407. *Website:* http://www.vbc.edu/.

VIRGINIA COLLEGE IN BIRMINGHAM
Birmingham, AL

CONTACT Vice President, Campus Administration, Virginia College in Birmingham, 65 Bagby Drive, Birmingham, AL 35209, 205-802-1200. *Fax:* 205-271-8273. *Website:* http://www.vc.edu/.

VIRGINIA COMMONWEALTH UNIVERSITY
Richmond, VA

Tuition & fees (VA res): $13,076	Average undergraduate aid package: $10,342

ABOUT THE INSTITUTION State-supported, coed. *Awards:* certificates, bachelor's, master's, and doctoral degrees. 58 undergraduate majors. *Total enrollment:* 31,242. Undergraduates: 24,212. Freshmen: 4,279. Federal methodology is used as a basis for awarding need-based institutional aid.

UNDERGRADUATE EXPENSES for 2016–2017 *Application fee:* $65. *Tuition, state resident:* full-time $10,846; part-time $374 per credit hour. *Tuition, nonresident:* full-time $29,378; part-time $1013 per credit hour. *Required fees:* full-time $2230. *College room and board:* $9919. Room and board charges vary according to board plan and housing facility.

FRESHMAN FINANCIAL AID (Fall 2015) 3,260 applied for aid; of those 78% were deemed to have need. 96% of freshmen with need received aid; of those 13% had need fully met. *Average percent of need met:* 53% (excluding resources awarded to replace EFC). *Average financial aid package:* $11,333 (excluding resources awarded to replace EFC). 16% of all full-time freshmen had no need and received non-need-based gift aid.

UNDERGRADUATE FINANCIAL AID (Fall 2015) 14,130 applied for aid; of those 82% were deemed to have need. 96% of undergraduates with need received aid; of those 11% had need fully met. *Average percent of need met:* 48% (excluding resources awarded to replace EFC). *Average financial aid package:* $10,342 (excluding resources awarded to replace EFC). 9% of all full-time undergraduates had no need and received non-need-based gift aid.

GIFT AID (NEED-BASED) *Total amount:* $71,859,955 (40% federal, 31% state, 17% institutional, 12% external sources). *Receiving aid:* Freshmen: 45% (1,884); all full-time undergraduates: 39% (7,862). *Average award:* Freshmen: $7205; Undergraduates: $6435. *Scholarships, grants, and awards:* Federal Pell, FSEOG, state, private, college/university gift aid from institutional funds, United Negro College Fund.

GIFT AID (NON-NEED-BASED) *Total amount:* $22,240,471 (1% state, 12% institutional, 87% external sources). *Receiving aid:* Freshmen: 17% (701). Undergraduates: 10% (2,087). *Average award:* Freshmen: $10,601. Undergraduates: $12,666. *Scholarships, grants, and awards by category:* Academic interests/achievement: biological sciences, business, computer science, education, engineering/technologies, foreign languages, general academic interests/achievements, health fields, humanities, mathematics, military science, physical sciences. *Creative arts/performance:* art/fine arts, dance, music, performing arts, theater/drama. *Special characteristics:* veterans' children. *Tuition waivers:* Full or partial for employees or children of employees. *ROTC:* Army cooperative.

LOANS *Student loans:* $114,495,460 (83% need-based, 17% non-need-based). 63% of past graduating class borrowed through all loan programs. *Average indebtedness per student:* $31,512. *Average need-based loan:* Freshmen: $3381. Undergraduates: $4236. *Parent loans:* $4,416,904 (42% need-based, 58% non-need-based). *Programs:* Federal Direct (Subsidized and Unsubsidized Stafford, PLUS), Perkins, Federal Nursing, college/university.

WORK-STUDY *Federal work-study:* 772 jobs averaging $1714. *State or other work-study/employment:* Total amount: $800 (62% need-based, 38% non-need-based). 8 part-time jobs averaging $100.

ATHLETIC AWARDS Total amount: $4,416,904 (42% need-based, 58% non-need-based).

APPLYING FOR FINANCIAL AID *Required financial aid form:* FAFSA. *Financial aid deadline (priority):* 3/1. *Notification date:* Continuous beginning 4/1. Students must reply within 2 weeks of notification.

CONTACT Financial Aid Office, Virginia Commonwealth University, PO Box 843026, 1015 Floyd Avenue, Richmond, VA 23284-3026, 804-828-1550 or toll-free 800-841-3638. *Fax:* 804-827-0060. *Website:* http://www.vcu.edu/.

VIRGINIA INTERNATIONAL UNIVERSITY
Fairfax, VA

CONTACT Financial Aid Office, Virginia International University, 4401 Village Drive, Fairfax, VA 22030, 703-591-7042 or toll-free 800-514-6848. *Website:* http://www.viu.edu/.

VIRGINIA MILITARY INSTITUTE
Lexington, VA

Tuition & fees (VA res): $17,492	Average undergraduate aid package: $24,611

ABOUT THE INSTITUTION State-supported, coed, primarily men. *Awards:* bachelor's degrees. 14 undergraduate majors. *Total enrollment:* 1,713. Undergraduates: 1,713. Freshmen: 454. Federal methodology is used as a basis for awarding need-based institutional aid.

UNDERGRADUATE EXPENSES for 2016–2017 *Application fee:* $40. *Tuition, state resident:* full-time $8461; part-time $328 per credit hour. *Tuition, nonresident:* full-time $32,770; part-time $1024 per credit hour. *Required fees:* full-time $9031. *College room and board:* $8968.

FRESHMAN FINANCIAL AID (Fall 2015) 334 applied for aid; of those 68% were deemed to have need. 99% of freshmen with need received aid; of those 25% had need fully met. *Average percent of need met:* 85% (excluding resources awarded to replace EFC). *Average financial aid package:* $22,640 (excluding resources awarded to replace EFC). 7% of all full-time freshmen had no need and received non-need-based gift aid.

UNDERGRADUATE FINANCIAL AID (Fall 2015) 1,134 applied for aid; of those 76% were deemed to have need. 99% of undergraduates with need received aid; of those 30% had need fully met. *Average percent of need met:* 85% (excluding resources awarded to replace EFC). *Average financial aid package:* $24,611 (excluding resources awarded to replace EFC). 5% of all full-time undergraduates had no need and received non-need-based gift aid.

GIFT AID (NEED-BASED) *Total amount:* $9,994,200 (9% federal, 10% state, 78% institutional, 3% external sources). *Receiving aid:* Freshmen: 49% (214); all full-time undergraduates: 41% (698). *Average award:* Freshmen: $12,953; Undergrad-

uates: $12,678. **Scholarships, grants, and awards:** Federal Pell, FSEOG, state, private, college/university gift aid from institutional funds.

GIFT AID (NON-NEED-BASED) Total amount: $9,255,235 (87% federal, 1% state, 11% institutional, 1% external sources). **Receiving aid:** Freshmen: 20% (85). Undergraduates: 26% (446). **Average award:** Freshmen: $3880. Undergraduates: $2791. **Scholarships, grants, and awards by category:** Academic interests/achievement: 205 awards ($997,562 total): biological sciences, business, computer science, engineering/technologies, English, foreign languages, general academic interests/achievements, humanities, international studies, mathematics, military science, physical sciences, premedicine. Creative arts/performance: 11 awards ($9450 total): music. Special achievements/activities: general special achievements/activities. Special characteristics: children and siblings of alumni, general special characteristics, local/state students, out-of-state students, veterans' children. **ROTC:** Army, Naval, Air Force.

LOANS Student loans: $7,439,647 (33% need-based, 67% non-need-based). 62% of past graduating class borrowed through all loan programs. Average indebtedness per student: $30,388. **Average need-based loan:** Freshmen: $2848. Undergraduates: $3861. **Parent loans:** $1,742,548 (100% non-need-based). **Programs:** Federal Direct (Subsidized and Unsubsidized Stafford, PLUS), Perkins, college/university.

ATHLETIC AWARDS Total amount: $184,564 (100% non-need-based).

APPLYING FOR FINANCIAL AID Required financial aid forms: FAFSA, institution's own form. **Financial aid deadline:** 3/1 (priority: 3/1). **Notification date:** Continuous beginning 4/1. Students must reply by 5/1.

CONTACT Capt. Brian Quisenerry, Director of Financial Aid, Virginia Military Institute, 302A Carroll Hall, Lexington, VA 24450, 540-464-7626 or toll-free 800-767-4207. Fax: 540-464-7629. E-mail: quisenberrybl@vmi.edu.

Website: http://www.vmi.edu/.

VIRGINIA POLYTECHNIC INSTITUTE AND STATE UNIVERSITY
Blacksburg, VA

Tuition & fees (VA res): $12,852	Average undergraduate aid package: $17,594

ABOUT THE INSTITUTION State-supported, coed. **Awards:** certificates, associate, bachelor's, master's, and doctoral degrees. 80 undergraduate majors. **Total enrollment:** 33,170. Undergraduates: 25,791. Freshmen: 5,929. Federal methodology is used as a basis for awarding need-based institutional aid.

UNDERGRADUATE EXPENSES for 2016–2017 Application fee: $60. **Tuition, state resident:** full-time $10,787. **Tuition, nonresident:** full-time $27,306. **Required fees:** full-time $2065. **College room and board:** $8564.

FRESHMAN FINANCIAL AID (Fall 2015) 4,788 applied for aid; of those 55% were deemed to have need. 94% of freshmen with need received aid; of those 21% had need fully met. **Average percent of need met:** 65% (excluding resources awarded to replace EFC). **Average financial aid package:** $17,742 (excluding resources awarded to replace EFC). 10% of all full-time freshmen had no need and received non-need-based gift aid.

UNDERGRADUATE FINANCIAL AID (Fall 2015) 15,848 applied for aid; of those 66% were deemed to have need. 95% of undergraduates with need received aid; of those 19% had need fully met. **Average percent of need met:** 65% (excluding resources awarded to replace EFC). **Average financial aid package:** $17,594 (excluding resources awarded to replace EFC). 12% of all full-time undergraduates had no need and received non-need-based gift aid.

GIFT AID (NEED-BASED) Total amount: $37,659,776 (49% federal, 41% state, 10% institutional). **Receiving aid:** Freshmen: 29% (1,805); all full-time undergraduates: 30% (7,493). **Average award:** Freshmen: $7550; Undergraduates: $7003. **Scholarships, grants, and awards:** Federal Pell, FSEOG, state, private, college/university gift aid from institutional funds, United Negro College Fund.

GIFT AID (NON-NEED-BASED) Total amount: $39,533,731 (38% federal, 29% institutional, 33% external sources). **Receiving aid:** Freshmen: 18% (1,126). Undergraduates: 14% (3,418). **Average award:** Freshmen: $3765. Undergraduates: $3808. **Scholarships, grants, and awards by category:** Academic interests/achievement: general academic interests/achievements, library science. Creative arts/performance: applied art and design, art/fine arts, cinema/film/broadcasting, creative writing, journalism/publications, music, performing arts, theater/drama. Special achievements/activities: cheerleading/drum major, community service, general special

achievements/activities, leadership, memberships, religious involvement. Special characteristics: children of faculty/staff, first-generation college students, local/state students, members of minority groups, out-of-state students, twins, veterans' children. **ROTC:** Army, Naval, Air Force.

LOANS Student loans: $98,436,743 (36% need-based, 64% non-need-based). 51% of past graduating class borrowed through all loan programs. Average indebtedness per student: $28,884. **Average need-based loan:** Freshmen: $3945. Undergraduates: $4655. **Parent loans:** $33,057,121 (100% non-need-based). **Programs:** Federal Direct (Subsidized and Unsubsidized Stafford, PLUS), Perkins, state, college/university.

WORK-STUDY Federal work-study: jobs available. **State or other work-study/employment:** Total amount: $12,951,998 (100% non-need-based). Part-time jobs available.

ATHLETIC AWARDS Total amount: $11,509,081 (100% non-need-based).

APPLYING FOR FINANCIAL AID Required financial aid form: FAFSA. **Financial aid deadline:** 1/1. **Notification date:** 4/1. Students must reply by 5/1 or within 4 weeks of notification.

CONTACT Miss Beth Armstrong, Director of Student Financial Services, Virginia Polytechnic Institute and State University, 300 Student Service Building, Blacksburg, VA 24061, 540-231-5179. Fax: 540-231-9139. E-mail: simmonsb@vt.edu. Website: http://www.vt.edu/.

VIRGINIA STATE UNIVERSITY
Petersburg, VA

Tuition & fees (VA res): $8472	Average undergraduate aid package: $11,586

ABOUT THE INSTITUTION State-supported, coed. **Awards:** certificates, bachelor's, master's, and doctoral degrees. 31 undergraduate majors. **Total enrollment:** 4,584. Undergraduates: 4,165. Freshmen: 1,024. Federal methodology is used as a basis for awarding need-based institutional aid.

UNDERGRADUATE EXPENSES for 2016–2017 Application fee: $25. **Tuition, state resident:** full-time $5172; part-time $369 per credit hour. **Tuition, nonresident:** full-time $14,992; part-time $817 per credit hour. **Required fees:** full-time $3300; $10 per credit hour. Full-time tuition and fees vary according to course load. Part-time tuition and fees vary according to course load. **College room and board:** $10,562; **Room only:** $6170. Room and board charges vary according to board plan and housing facility.

FRESHMAN FINANCIAL AID (Fall 2015) 703 applied for aid; of those 100% were deemed to have need. 100% of freshmen with need received aid; of those 34% had need fully met. **Average percent of need met:** 60% (excluding resources awarded to replace EFC). **Average financial aid package:** $10,985 (excluding resources awarded to replace EFC). 21% of all full-time freshmen had no need and received non-need-based gift aid.

UNDERGRADUATE FINANCIAL AID (Fall 2015) 3,817 applied for aid; of those 100% were deemed to have need. 100% of undergraduates with need received aid; of those 15% had need fully met. **Average percent of need met:** 58% (excluding resources awarded to replace EFC). **Average financial aid package:** $11,586 (excluding resources awarded to replace EFC). 10% of all full-time undergraduates had no need and received non-need-based gift aid.

GIFT AID (NEED-BASED) Total amount: $23,780,144 (56% federal, 30% state, 14% institutional). **Receiving aid:** Freshmen: 73% (562); all full-time undergraduates: 72% (3,054). **Average award:** Freshmen: $6485; Undergraduates: $6940. **Scholarships, grants, and awards:** Federal Pell, FSEOG, state, private, college/university gift aid from institutional funds, United Negro College Fund.

GIFT AID (NON-NEED-BASED) Total amount: $6,169,901 (38% state, 51% institutional, 11% external sources). **Receiving aid:** Freshmen: 31% (240). Undergraduates: 20% (839). **Average award:** Freshmen: $500. Undergraduates: $1000. **Scholarships, grants, and awards by category:** Academic interests/achievement: 125 awards ($1,000,000 total): biological sciences, computer science, engineering/technologies, mathematics, physical sciences, premedicine. Creative arts/performance: 15 awards ($30,000 total): applied art and design, art/fine arts, dance, music, performing arts. Special achievements/activities: 20 awards ($80,000 total): cheerleading/drum major, community service, hobbies/interests, leadership, religious involvement. **Tuition waivers:** Full or partial for senior citizens. **ROTC:** Army.

LOANS Student loans: $29,030,757 (93% need-based, 7% non-need-based). 92% of past graduating class borrowed through all loan programs. Average indebtedness per student: $28,250. **Average need-based loan:** Freshmen: $3500. Undergraduates: $5500. **Parent loans:** $10,734,109 (100% need-based). **Programs:** Federal Direct (Subsidized and Unsubsidized Stafford, PLUS), Perkins, college/university.

WORK-STUDY *Federal work-study:* 300 jobs averaging $2000. **State or other work-study/employment:** Total amount: $135,766 (100% need-based). 150 part-time jobs averaging $3000.

ATHLETIC AWARDS Total amount: $1,299,183 (100% need-based).

APPLYING FOR FINANCIAL AID *Required financial aid forms:* FAFSA, institution's own form. **Financial aid deadline (priority):** 3/31. **Notification date:** Continuous beginning 3/15. Students must reply within 2 weeks of notification.

CONTACT Mrs. Sheila Allen, Scholarship Manager, Virginia State University, PO Box 9031, Petersburg, VA 23806-2096, 800-823-7214 or toll-free 800-871-7611. *Fax:* 804-524-6818. *E-mail:* sallen@vsu.edu.
Website: http://www.vsu.edu/.

VIRGINIA UNION UNIVERSITY
Richmond, VA

ABOUT THE INSTITUTION Independent Baptist, coed. **Awards:** bachelor's, master's, and doctoral degrees. 35 undergraduate majors. **Total enrollment:** 1,922. Undergraduates: 1,509. Freshmen: 456.

GIFT AID (NEED-BASED) *Scholarships, grants, and awards:* Federal Pell, FSEOG, state, private, college/university gift aid from institutional funds.

GIFT AID (NON-NEED-BASED) *Scholarships, grants, and awards by category:* Academic interests/achievement: general academic interests/achievements. Creative arts/performance: music. Special characteristics: children of faculty/staff.

LOANS *Programs:* Federal Direct (Subsidized and Unsubsidized Stafford).

WORK-STUDY *Federal work-study:* 217 jobs averaging $2422.

APPLYING FOR FINANCIAL AID *Required financial aid forms:* FAFSA, state aid form.

CONTACT Mrs. Antoinette House, Director of Financial Aid, Virginia Union University, 1500 North Lombardy Street, Richmond, VA 23220-1170, 804-257-5854 or toll-free 800-368-3227. *E-mail:* athouse@vuu.edu.
Website: http://www.vuu.edu/.

VIRGINIA UNIVERSITY OF LYNCHBURG
Lynchburg, VA

CONTACT Mrs. Charlene P. Scruggs, Financial Aid Director, Virginia University of Lynchburg, 2058 Garfield Avenue, Lynchburg, VA 24572, 434-528-5276. *Fax:* 434-455-5958. *E-mail:* cscruggs@vul.edu.
Website: http://www.vul.edu/.

VIRGINIA WESLEYAN COLLEGE
Norfolk, VA

Tuition & fees: $36,660	Average undergraduate aid package: $24,802

ABOUT THE INSTITUTION Independent United Methodist, coed. **Awards:** certificates, bachelor's, and master's degrees. 50 undergraduate majors. **Total enrollment:** 1,374. Undergraduates: 1,374. Freshmen: 368. Federal methodology is used as a basis for awarding need-based institutional aid.

UNDERGRADUATE EXPENSES for 2017–2018 *One-time required fee:* $350. **Comprehensive fee:** $45,604 includes full-time tuition ($36,010), mandatory fees ($650), and room and board ($8944). Full-time tuition and fees vary according to course load. Room and board charges vary according to board plan and housing facility. **Part-time tuition:** $1500 per credit hour. Part-time tuition and fees vary according to course load.

FRESHMAN FINANCIAL AID (Fall 2015) 349 applied for aid; of those 87% were deemed to have need. 100% of freshmen with need received aid; of those 18% had need fully met. **Average percent of need met:** 69% (excluding resources awarded

to replace EFC). **Average financial aid package:** $25,256 (excluding resources awarded to replace EFC). 12% of all full-time freshmen had no need and received non-need-based gift aid.

UNDERGRADUATE FINANCIAL AID (Fall 2015) 1,336 applied for aid; of those 82% were deemed to have need. 100% of undergraduates with need received aid; of those 16% had need fully met. **Average percent of need met:** 69% (excluding resources awarded to replace EFC). **Average financial aid package:** $24,802 (excluding resources awarded to replace EFC). 18% of all full-time undergraduates had no need and received non-need-based gift aid.

GIFT AID (NEED-BASED) *Total amount:* $23,173,427 (16% federal, 9% state, 74% institutional, 1% external sources). **Receiving aid:** Freshmen: 87% (304); all full-time undergraduates: 81% (1,089). **Average award:** Freshmen: $21,595; Undergraduates: $21,149. **Scholarships, grants, and awards:** Federal Pell, FSEOG, state, private, college/university gift aid from institutional funds, United Negro College Fund.

GIFT AID (NON-NEED-BASED) *Total amount:* $6,118,438 (18% federal, 10% state, 71% institutional, 1% external sources). **Receiving aid:** Freshmen: 11% (38). Undergraduates: 15% (207). **Average award:** Freshmen: $21,889. Undergraduates: $20,584. **Scholarships, grants, and awards by category:** Academic interests/achievement: general academic interests/achievements. Special achievements/activities: religious involvement. Special characteristics: 17 awards ($423,667 total): children of faculty/staff, relatives of clergy, religious affiliation. **Tuition waivers:** Full or partial for employees or children of employees, adult students, senior citizens. **ROTC:** Army cooperative.

LOANS *Student loans:* $8,544,122 (77% need-based, 23% non-need-based). 76% of past graduating class borrowed through all loan programs. *Average indebtedness per student:* $36,255. **Average need-based loan:** Freshmen: $6165. Undergraduates: $7519. **Parent loans:** $5,233,480 (65% need-based, 35% non-need-based). **Programs:** Federal Direct (Subsidized and Unsubsidized Stafford, PLUS), Perkins, alternative loans.

WORK-STUDY *Federal work-study:* 187 jobs averaging $975.

APPLYING FOR FINANCIAL AID *Required financial aid forms:* FAFSA, state aid form. **Financial aid deadline (priority):** 3/1. **Notification date:** Continuous beginning 10/15. Students must reply by 5/1 or within 2 weeks of notification.

CONTACT Mrs. Teresa Rhyne, Director of Financial Aid, Virginia Wesleyan College, 1584 Wesleyan Drive, Norfolk, VA 23502-5599, 757-455-3345 or toll-free 800-737-8684. *Fax:* 757-455-6779. *E-mail:* finaid@vwc.edu.
Website: http://www.vwc.edu/.

VISIBLE MUSIC COLLEGE
Memphis, TN

CONTACT Financial Aid Office, Visible Music College, 200 Madison Avenue, Memphis, TN 38103, 901-381-3939.
Website: http://visible.edu/.

VITERBO UNIVERSITY
La Crosse, WI

Tuition & fees: $26,920	Average undergraduate aid package: N/A

ABOUT THE INSTITUTION Independent Roman Catholic, coed. **Awards:** certificates, associate, bachelor's, master's, and doctoral degrees. 71 undergraduate majors. **Total enrollment:** 1,875. Undergraduates: 1,875. Freshmen: 320. Both federal and institutional methodology are used as a basis for awarding need-based institutional aid.

UNDERGRADUATE EXPENSES for 2017–2018 **Comprehensive fee:** $35,680 includes full-time tuition ($26,230), mandatory fees ($690), and room and board ($8760). **College room only:** $3870. Full-time tuition and fees vary according to program. Room and board charges vary according to board plan and housing facility. Part-time tuition and fees vary according to program.

GIFT AID (NEED-BASED) *Scholarships, grants, and awards:* state, college/university gift aid from institutional funds.

GIFT AID (NON-NEED-BASED) *Tuition waivers:* Full or partial for employees or children of employees. **ROTC:** Army cooperative.

LOANS *Programs:* alternative loans.

WORK-STUDY Federal work-study jobs available. *State or other work-study/ employment:* Part-time jobs available.
APPLYING FOR FINANCIAL AID *Notification date:* Continuous.
CONTACT Terry Norman, Director of Financial Aid, Viterbo University, 900 Viterbo Drive, La Crosse, WI 54601-4797, 608-796-3900 or toll-free 800-VITERBO. *Fax:* 608-796-3050. *E-mail:* twnorman@viterbo.edu.
Website: http://www.viterbo.edu/.

VOORHEES COLLEGE
Denmark, SC

CONTACT Augusta L. Kitchen, Director of Financial Aid, Voorhees College, PO Box 678, Denmark, SC 29042, 803-703-7109 Ext. 7106 or toll-free 866-237-4570. *Fax:* 803-793-0831. *E-mail:* akitchen@voorhees.edu.
Website: http://www.voorhees.edu/.

WABASH COLLEGE
Crawfordsville, IN

Tuition & fees: $42,250	Average undergraduate aid package: $34,144

ABOUT THE INSTITUTION Independent, men only. *Awards:* bachelor's degrees. 25 undergraduate majors. *Total enrollment:* 842. Undergraduates: 842. Freshmen: 215. Both federal and institutional methodology are used as a basis for awarding need-based institutional aid.
UNDERGRADUATE EXPENSES for 2017–2018 *Application fee:* $50. *Comprehensive fee:* $52,100 includes full-time tuition ($41,600), mandatory fees ($650), and room and board ($9850). *College room only:* $5250. Room and board charges vary according to board plan and housing facility. *Part-time tuition:* $6933 per course. *Part-time fees:* $50 per term. Part-time tuition and fees vary according to course load. *Payment plan:* Tuition prepayment.
FRESHMAN FINANCIAL AID (Fall 2016, est.) 190 applied for aid; of those 89% were deemed to have need. 100% of freshmen with need received aid; of those 76% had need fully met. *Average percent of need met:* 94% (excluding resources awarded to replace EFC). *Average financial aid package:* $36,118 (excluding resources awarded to replace EFC). 20% of all full-time freshmen had no need and received non-need-based gift aid.
UNDERGRADUATE FINANCIAL AID (Fall 2016, est.) 792 applied for aid; of those 78% were deemed to have need. 100% of undergraduates with need received aid; of those 72% had need fully met. *Average percent of need met:* 92% (excluding resources awarded to replace EFC). *Average financial aid package:* $34,144 (excluding resources awarded to replace EFC). 26% of all full-time undergraduates had no need and received non-need-based gift aid.
GIFT AID (NEED-BASED) *Total amount:* $16,387,981 (6% federal, 6% state, 86% institutional, 2% external sources). *Receiving aid:* Freshmen: 78% (167); all full-time undergraduates: 72% (610). *Average award:* Freshmen: $30,243; Undergraduates: $26,374. *Scholarships, grants, and awards:* Federal Pell, FSEOG, state, private, college/university gift aid from institutional funds.
GIFT AID (NON-NEED-BASED) *Total amount:* $5,622,719 (91% institutional, 9% external sources). *Receiving aid:* Freshmen: 19% (40). Undergraduates: 13% (112). *Average award:* Freshmen: $21,990. Undergraduates: $19,928. *Scholarships, grants, and awards by category:* Academic interests/achievement: 769 awards ($11,897,085 total): general academic interests/achievements. Creative arts/performance: 55 awards ($195,000 total): art/fine arts, creative writing, journalism/publications, music, theater/drama. Special achievements/activities: 96 awards ($752,600 total): community service, leadership. Special characteristics: 10 awards ($383,800 total): children of faculty/staff. *Tuition waivers:* Full or partial for employees or children of employees.
LOANS *Student loans:* $6,195,084 (42% need-based, 58% non-need-based). 89% of past graduating class borrowed through all loan programs. *Average indebtedness per student:* $37,495. *Average need-based loan:* Freshmen: $3190. Undergraduates: $4913. *Parent loans:* $2,141,108 (19% need-based, 81% non-need-based). *Programs:* Federal Direct (Subsidized and Unsubsidized Stafford, PLUS), college/university.

WORK-STUDY *Federal work-study:* Total amount: $147,229; 57 jobs averaging $2691. *State or other work-study/employment:* Total amount: $938,962 (78% need-based, 22% non-need-based). 338 part-time jobs averaging $2872.
APPLYING FOR FINANCIAL AID *Required financial aid forms:* FAFSA, verification items such as federal income tax transcripts and W-2 forms. *Financial aid deadline (priority):* 1/15. *Notification date:* Continuous beginning 12/15. Students must reply by 5/1.
CONTACT Ms. Heidi Carl, Director of Financial Aid, Wabash College, PO Box 352, Crawfordsville, IN 47933-0352, 000-710-9710 or toll-free 800-345-5385. *Fax:* 765-361-6166. *E-mail:* financialaid@wabash.edu.
Website: http://www.wabash.edu/.

WAGNER COLLEGE
Staten Island, NY

Tuition & fees: $43,980	Average undergraduate aid package: $29,515

ABOUT THE INSTITUTION Independent, coed. *Awards:* certificates, bachelor's, master's, and doctoral degrees. 38 undergraduate majors. *Total enrollment:* 2,301. Undergraduates: 1,807. Freshmen: 442. Federal methodology is used as a basis for awarding need-based institutional aid.
UNDERGRADUATE EXPENSES for 2016–2017 *Comprehensive fee:* $57,240 includes full-time tuition ($43,500), mandatory fees ($480), and room and board ($13,260). Full-time tuition and fees vary according to program. *Part-time tuition:* $5438 per unit.
FRESHMAN FINANCIAL AID (Fall 2016, est.) 364 applied for aid; of those 89% were deemed to have need. 100% of freshmen with need received aid; of those 29% had need fully met. *Average percent of need met:* 76% (excluding resources awarded to replace EFC). *Average financial aid package:* $30,427 (excluding resources awarded to replace EFC). 16% of all full-time freshmen had no need and received non-need-based gift aid.
UNDERGRADUATE FINANCIAL AID (Fall 2016, est.) 1,324 applied for aid; of those 87% were deemed to have need. 100% of undergraduates with need received aid; of those 22% had need fully met. *Average percent of need met:* 70% (excluding resources awarded to replace EFC). *Average financial aid package:* $29,515 (excluding resources awarded to replace EFC). 24% of all full-time undergraduates had no need and received non-need-based gift aid.
GIFT AID (NEED-BASED) *Total amount:* $31,786,025 (6% federal, 31% state, 63% institutional). *Receiving aid:* Freshmen: 73% (324); all full-time undergraduates: 65% (1,138). *Average award:* Freshmen: $17,324; Undergraduates: $22,748. *Scholarships, grants, and awards:* Federal Pell, FSEOG, state, private, college/university gift aid from institutional funds.
GIFT AID (NON-NEED-BASED) *Total amount:* $10,440,650 (2% state, 98% institutional). *Average award:* Freshmen: $22,530. Undergraduates: $17,988. *Scholarships, grants, and awards by category:* Academic interests/achievement: general academic interests/achievements. Creative arts/performance: music, theater/drama. Special characteristics: children of faculty/staff, siblings of current students. *Tuition waivers:* Full or partial for employees or children of employees. *ROTC:* Army cooperative.
LOANS *Student loans:* $14,222,231 (84% need-based, 16% non-need-based). *Average need-based loan:* Freshmen: $2361. Undergraduates: $4937. *Parent loans:* $4,655,901 (85% need-based, 15% non-need-based). *Programs:* Federal Direct (Subsidized and Unsubsidized Stafford, PLUS), Perkins, Federal Nursing, alternative loans.
WORK-STUDY *Federal work-study:* Total amount: $650,202; jobs available.
ATHLETIC AWARDS Total amount: $7,663,540 (46% need-based, 54% non-need-based).
APPLYING FOR FINANCIAL AID *Required financial aid forms:* FAFSA, state aid form. *Financial aid deadline (priority):* 1/15. *Notification date:* 3/1. Students must reply within 3 weeks of notification.
CONTACT Ms. Theresa Weimer, Director of Financial Aid, Wagner College, One Campus Road, Staten Island, NY 10301, 718-390-3122 or toll-free 800-221-1010. *Fax:* 718-390-3203. *E-mail:* tweimer@wagner.edu.
Website: http://www.wagner.edu/.

WAKE FOREST UNIVERSITY
Winston-Salem, NC

Tuition & fees: $51,400	Average undergraduate aid package: $47,228

ABOUT THE INSTITUTION Independent, coed. **Awards:** certificates, bachelor's, master's, and doctoral degrees. 38 undergraduate majors. **Total enrollment:** 7,968. Undergraduates: 4,955. Freshmen: 1,306. Institutional methodology is used as a basis for awarding need-based institutional aid.

UNDERGRADUATE EXPENSES for 2017–2018 Application fee: $50. **Comprehensive fee:** $66,754 includes full-time tuition ($50,524), mandatory fees ($876), and room and board ($15,354). **College room only:** $9012. **Part-time tuition:** $2090 per credit hour.

FRESHMAN FINANCIAL AID (Fall 2016, est.) 613 applied for aid; of those 66% were deemed to have need. 100% of freshmen with need received aid; of those 100% had need fully met. **Average percent of need met:** 100% (excluding resources awarded to replace EFC). **Average financial aid package:** $46,337 (excluding resources awarded to replace EFC). 2% of all full-time freshmen had no need and received non-need-based gift aid.

UNDERGRADUATE FINANCIAL AID (Fall 2016, est.) 1,844 applied for aid; of those 82% were deemed to have need. 100% of undergraduates with need received aid; of those 100% had need fully met. **Average percent of need met:** 100% (excluding resources awarded to replace EFC). **Average financial aid package:** $47,228 (excluding resources awarded to replace EFC). 9% of all full-time undergraduates had no need and received non-need-based gift aid.

GIFT AID (NEED-BASED) Total amount: $56,705,106 (5% federal, 3% state, 89% institutional, 3% external sources). **Receiving aid:** Freshmen: 30% (386); all full-time undergraduates: 30% (1,449). **Average award:** Freshmen: $42,637; Undergraduates: $43,165. **Scholarships, grants, and awards:** Federal Pell, FSEOG, state, private, college/university gift aid from institutional funds, United Negro College Fund.

GIFT AID (NON-NEED-BASED) Total amount: $8,687,489 (15% federal, 65% institutional, 20% external sources). **Receiving aid:** Freshmen: 25% (324). Undergraduates: 19% (910). **Average award:** Freshmen: $30,453. Undergraduates: $12,582. **Scholarships, grants, and awards by category:** Academic interests/achievement: general academic interests/achievements. Creative arts/performance: art/fine arts, general creative arts/performance. Special achievements/activities: leadership. Special characteristics: children and siblings of alumni, local/state students, religious affiliation. ROTC: Army.

LOANS Student loans: $18,113,534 (76% need-based, 24% non-need-based). 39% of past graduating class borrowed through all loan programs. Average indebtedness per student: $33,797. **Average need-based loan:** Freshmen: $9264. Undergraduates: $9603. **Parent loans:** $6,295,623 (62% need-based, 38% non-need-based). **Programs:** Federal Direct (Subsidized and Unsubsidized Stafford, PLUS), Perkins, state, college/university.

WORK-STUDY Federal work-study: Total amount: $1,738,922; jobs available. **State or other work-study/employment:** Part-time jobs available.

ATHLETIC AWARDS Total amount: $13,905,238 (34% need-based, 66% non-need-based).

APPLYING FOR FINANCIAL AID Required financial aid forms: FAFSA, CSS Financial Aid PROFILE, state aid form, noncustodial (divorced/separated) parent's statement. **Financial aid deadline:** 1/1 (priority: 1/1). **Notification date:** Continuous beginning 4/1. Students must reply by 5/1 or within 4 weeks of notification.

CONTACT Bill Wells, Director of Student Financial Aid, Wake Forest University, PO Box 7246, Winston-Salem, NC 27109-7246, 336-758-5154. Fax: 336-758-4924. E-mail: financial-aid@wfu.edu.
Website: http://www.wfu.edu/.

WALDORF UNIVERSITY
Forest City, IA

Tuition & fees: $21,260	Average undergraduate aid package: $13,783

ABOUT THE INSTITUTION Independent Lutheran, coed. **Awards:** certificates, associate, bachelor's, and master's degrees. 32 undergraduate majors. **Total enrollment:** 2,388. Undergraduates: 2,058. Freshmen: 154. Federal methodology is used as a basis for awarding need-based institutional aid.

UNDERGRADUATE EXPENSES for 2016–2017 Comprehensive fee: $28,506 includes full-time tuition ($20,160), mandatory fees ($1100), and room and board ($7246). Full-time tuition and fees vary according to class time, course load, and program. Room and board charges vary according to board plan and housing facility.

FRESHMAN FINANCIAL AID (Fall 2015) 174 applied for aid; of those 93% were deemed to have need. 100% of freshmen with need received aid; of those 16% had need fully met. **Average percent of need met:** 72% (excluding resources awarded to replace EFC). **Average financial aid package:** $18,337 (excluding resources awarded to replace EFC). 15% of all full-time freshmen had no need and received non-need-based gift aid.

UNDERGRADUATE FINANCIAL AID (Fall 2015) 1,030 applied for aid; of those 93% were deemed to have need. 100% of undergraduates with need received aid; of those 10% had need fully met. **Average percent of need met:** 62% (excluding resources awarded to replace EFC). **Average financial aid package:** $13,783 (excluding resources awarded to replace EFC). 10% of all full-time undergraduates had no need and received non-need-based gift aid.

GIFT AID (NEED-BASED) Total amount: $6,955,118 (45% federal, 4% state, 41% institutional, 10% external sources). **Receiving aid:** Freshmen: 82% (158); all full-time undergraduates: 75% (836). **Average award:** Freshmen: $14,566; Undergraduates: $10,658. **Scholarships, grants, and awards:** Federal Pell, FSEOG, state, private, college/university gift aid from institutional funds.

GIFT AID (NON-NEED-BASED) Total amount: $1,081,927 (1% federal, 1% state, 81% institutional, 17% external sources). **Receiving aid:** Freshmen: 9% (18). Undergraduates: 4% (47). **Average award:** Freshmen: $6798. Undergraduates: $7090. **Scholarships, grants, and awards by category:** Academic interests/achievement: communication, general academic interests/achievements. Creative arts/performance: music, theater/drama. Special achievements/activities: cheerleading/drum major, junior miss, leadership. Special characteristics: children of faculty/staff, religious affiliation. **Tuition waivers:** Full or partial for employees or children of employees.

LOANS Student loans: $9,292,910 (82% need-based, 18% non-need-based). 100% of past graduating class borrowed through all loan programs. Average indebtedness per student: $33,494. **Average need-based loan:** Freshmen: $3978. Undergraduates: $4414. **Parent loans:** $2,725,790 (39% need-based, 61% non-need-based). **Programs:** Federal Direct (Subsidized and Unsubsidized Stafford, PLUS), Perkins, state, alternative loans.

WORK-STUDY Federal work-study: jobs available. **State or other work-study/employment:** Part-time jobs available.

ATHLETIC AWARDS Total amount: $2,818,911 (80% need-based, 20% non-need-based).

APPLYING FOR FINANCIAL AID Required financial aid forms: FAFSA, institution's own form. **Financial aid deadline (priority):** 3/1. **Notification date:** Continuous beginning 3/1. Students must reply within 2 weeks of notification.

CONTACT Duane Polsdofer, Director of Financial Aid, Waldorf University, 106 South 6th Street, Forest City, IA 50436, 641-585-8120 or toll-free 800-292-1903. Fax: 641-585-8125. E-mail: polsdofed@waldorf.edu.
Website: http://www.waldorf.edu/.

WALDEN UNIVERSITY
Minneapolis, MN

CONTACT Office of Financial Aid, Walden University, 100 Washington South, Suite 900, Minneapolis, MN 55401, 800-444-6795 or toll-free 866-492-5336. Fax: 410-843-6211. E-mail: finaid@waldenu.edu.
Website: http://www.waldenu.edu/.

WALLA WALLA UNIVERSITY
College Place, WA

Tuition & fees: $27,495	Average undergraduate aid package: $22,193

ABOUT THE INSTITUTION Independent Seventh-day Adventist, coed. **Awards:** associate, bachelor's, and master's degrees. 80 undergraduate majors. **Total enrollment:** 1,894. Undergraduates: 1,700. Freshmen: 387. Both federal and institutional methodology are used as a basis for awarding need-based institutional aid.

UNDERGRADUATE EXPENSES for 2017–2018 *Application fee:* $40. *Comprehensive fee:* $34,845 includes full-time tuition ($26,595), mandatory fees ($900), and room and board ($7350). *College room only:* $4185. *Part-time tuition:* $738 per quarter hour.

FRESHMAN FINANCIAL AID (Fall 2015) 311 applied for aid; of those 81% were deemed to have need. 100% of freshmen with need received aid; of those 39% had need fully met. *Average percent of need met:* 96% (excluding resources awarded to replace EFC). *Average financial aid package:* $21,879 (excluding resources awarded to replace EFC). 31% of all full-time freshmen had no need and received non-need-based gift aid.

UNDERGRADUATE FINANCIAL AID (Fall 2015) 1,138 applied for aid; of those 85% were deemed to have need. 99% of undergraduates with need received aid; of those 39% had need fully met. *Average percent of need met:* 92% (excluding resources awarded to replace EFC). *Average financial aid package:* $22,193 (excluding resources awarded to replace EFC). 29% of all full-time undergraduates had no need and received non-need-based gift aid.

GIFT AID (NEED-BASED) *Total amount:* $15,661,211 (17% federal, 5% state, 62% institutional, 16% external sources). *Receiving aid:* Freshmen: 49% (183); all full-time undergraduates: 52% (774). *Average award:* Freshmen: $5605; Undergraduates: $6334. *Scholarships, grants, and awards:* Federal Pell, FSEOG, state, private, college/university gift aid from institutional funds, Federal Nursing.

GIFT AID (NON-NEED-BASED) *Total amount:* $7,222,650 (3% federal, 58% institutional, 39% external sources). *Receiving aid:* Freshmen: 67% (249). Undergraduates: 59% (876). *Average award:* Freshmen: $10,457. Undergraduates: $8677. *Scholarships, grants, and awards by category:* Academic interests/achievement: biological sciences, business, communication, education, engineering/technologies, English, foreign languages, general academic interests/achievements, humanities, mathematics, religion/biblical studies. *Creative arts/performance:* general creative arts/performance, music, theater/drama. *Special achievements/activities:* leadership. *Special characteristics:* children of faculty/staff, veterans.

LOANS *Student loans:* $9,874,941 (69% need-based, 31% non-need-based). 63% of past graduating class borrowed through all loan programs. *Average indebtedness per student:* $33,018. *Average need-based loan:* Freshmen: $3421. Undergraduates: $4160. *Parent loans:* $1,061,740 (24% need-based, 76% non-need-based). *Programs:* Federal Direct (Subsidized and Unsubsidized Stafford, PLUS), Perkins, Federal Nursing, college/university.

WORK-STUDY *Federal work-study:* jobs available. *State or other work-study/employment:* Total amount: $146,153 (100% need-based). Part-time jobs available.

APPLYING FOR FINANCIAL AID *Required financial aid forms:* FAFSA, institution's own form. *Financial aid deadline (priority):* 4/30. *Notification date:* Continuous beginning 2/15.

CONTACT Ms. Cassie Ragenovich, Director of Student Financial Services, Walla Walla University, 204 South College Avenue, College Place, WA 99324-1198, 509-527-2315 or toll-free 800-541-8900. *Fax:* 509-527-2556. *E-mail:* financial.aid@wallawalla.edu.
Website: http://www.wallawalla.edu/.

WALSH COLLEGE OF ACCOUNTANCY AND BUSINESS ADMINISTRATION
Troy, MI

Tuition & fees: $16,590	Average undergraduate aid package: N/A

ABOUT THE INSTITUTION Independent, coed. *Awards:* certificates, bachelor's, and master's degrees. 7 undergraduate majors. *Total enrollment:* 2,423. Undergraduates: 935. Federal methodology is used as a basis for awarding need-based institutional aid.

UNDERGRADUATE EXPENSES for 2016–2017 *Application fee:* $35. *Tuition:* full-time $16,215; part-time $8295 per year. *Required fees:* full-time $375; $375 per year. Full-time tuition and fees vary according to course level and degree level. Part-time tuition and fees vary according to course level and degree level.

GIFT AID (NEED-BASED) *Total amount:* $1,590,280 (61% federal, 15% state, 24% institutional). *Scholarships, grants, and awards:* Federal Pell, FSEOG, state, private, college/university gift aid from institutional funds.

GIFT AID (NON-NEED-BASED) *Total amount:* $109,670 (100% institutional). *Scholarships, grants, and awards by category:* Academic interests/achievement: business, computer science. *Special characteristics:* previous college experience. *Tuition waivers:* Full or partial for employees or children of employees.

LOANS *Student loans:* $4,011,065 (52% need-based, 48% non-need-based). *Parent loans:* $34,974 (100% non-need-based). *Programs:* Federal Direct (Subsidized and Unsubsidized Stafford, PLUS), alternative loans.

APPLYING FOR FINANCIAL AID *Required financial aid forms:* FAFSA, institution's own form. *Financial aid deadline:* Continuous. *Notification date:* Continuous.

CONTACT Catherine Duff Berrahou, Director of Student Financial Resources, Walsh College of Accountancy and Business Administration, 3838 Livernois Road, PO Box 7006, Troy, MI 48007-7006, 248-823-1285 or toll-free 800-925-7401. *Fax:* 248-524-2520. *E-mail:* hthomas@walshcollege.edu.
Website: http://www.walshcollege.edu/.

WALSH UNIVERSITY
North Canton, OH

CONTACT Holly Van Gilder, Director of Financial Aid, Walsh University, 2020 East Maple NW, North Canton, OH 44720-3396, 330-490-7147 or toll-free 800-362-9846 (in-state), 800-362-8846 (out-of-state). *Fax:* 330-490-7372. *E-mail:* hvangilder@walsh.edu.
Website: http://www.walsh.edu/.

WARNER PACIFIC COLLEGE
Portland, OR

Tuition & fees: $22,710	Average undergraduate aid package: $18,736

ABOUT THE INSTITUTION Independent Church of God, coed. *Awards:* certificates, associate, bachelor's, and master's degrees. 30 undergraduate majors. *Total enrollment:* 554. Undergraduates: 552. Freshmen: 142. Federal methodology is used as a basis for awarding need-based institutional aid.

UNDERGRADUATE EXPENSES for 2016–2017 *Comprehensive fee:* $31,610 includes full-time tuition ($22,050), mandatory fees ($660), and room and board ($8900). *College room only:* $3680. Room and board charges vary according to board plan and housing facility. *Part-time tuition:* $1005 per semester hour. *Part-time fees:* $330 per term. Part-time tuition and fees vary according to course load.

FRESHMAN FINANCIAL AID (Fall 2016, est.) 85 applied for aid; of those 95% were deemed to have need. 100% of freshmen with need received aid; of those 17% had need fully met. *Average percent of need met:* 67% (excluding resources awarded to replace EFC). *Average financial aid package:* $18,992 (excluding resources awarded to replace EFC). 16% of all full-time freshmen had no need and received non-need-based gift aid.

UNDERGRADUATE FINANCIAL AID (Fall 2016, est.) 419 applied for aid; of those 92% were deemed to have need. 100% of undergraduates with need received aid; of those 19% had need fully met. *Average percent of need met:* 67% (excluding resources awarded to replace EFC). *Average financial aid package:* $18,736 (excluding resources awarded to replace EFC). 15% of all full-time undergraduates had no need and received non-need-based gift aid.

GIFT AID (NEED-BASED) *Total amount:* $3,623,628 (38% federal, 10% state, 48% institutional, 4% external sources). *Receiving aid:* Freshmen: 63% (62); all full-time undergraduates: 59% (285). *Average award:* Freshmen: $7239; Undergraduates: $6715. *Scholarships, grants, and awards:* Federal Pell, FSEOG, state, private, college/university gift aid from institutional funds.

GIFT AID (NON-NEED-BASED) *Total amount:* $579,583 (94% institutional, 6% external sources). *Receiving aid:* Freshmen: 73% (72). Undergraduates: 71% (342). *Average award:* Freshmen: $8594. Undergraduates: $7383. *Scholarships, grants, and awards by category:* Academic interests/achievement: 361 awards ($1,577,955 total): general academic interests/achievements. *Creative arts/performance:* 46 awards ($103,000 total): music, theater/drama. *Special achievements/activities:* 93 awards ($130,750 total): leadership, memberships. *Special characteristics:* 32

awards ($23,500 total): children and siblings of alumni, international students, local/state students, religious affiliation. **Tuition waivers:** Full or partial for children of alumni, employees or children of employees. **ROTC:** Air Force cooperative.

LOANS Student loans: $2,490,076 (85% need-based, 15% non-need-based). 80% of past graduating class borrowed through all loan programs. *Average indebtedness per student:* $36,916. **Average need-based loan:** Freshmen: $3449. Undergraduates: $4462. **Parent loans:** $827,588 (50% need-based, 50% non-need-based). **Programs:** Federal Direct (Subsidized and Unsubsidized Stafford, PLUS), Perkins.

WORK-STUDY Federal work-study: Total amount: $633,242; 319 jobs averaging $1985.

ATHLETIC AWARDS Total amount: $1,178,696 (76% need-based, 24% non-need-based).

APPLYING FOR FINANCIAL AID Required financial aid form: FAFSA. **Financial aid deadline:** Continuous. **Notification date:** Continuous beginning 12/1. Students must reply within 2 weeks of notification.

CONTACT Cynthia D. Pollard, Director of Financial Aid, Warner Pacific College, 2219 Southeast 68th Avenue, Portland, OR 97215-4099, 503-517-1018 or toll-free 800-804-1510. *Fax:* 503-517-1352. *E-mail:* cpollard@warnerpacific.edu.
Website: http://www.warnerpacific.edu/.

WARNER UNIVERSITY
Lake Wales, FL

Tuition & fees: $20,712	Average undergraduate aid package: N/A

ABOUT THE INSTITUTION Independent Church of God, coed. 24 undergraduate majors. Both federal and institutional methodology are used as a basis for awarding need-based institutional aid.

UNDERGRADUATE EXPENSES for 2016–2017 One-time required fee: $50. **Comprehensive fee:** $28,816 includes full-time tuition ($20,112), mandatory fees ($600), and room and board ($8104). **College room only:** $4200. Full-time tuition and fees vary according to class time, degree level, and program. Room and board charges vary according to board plan. **Part-time tuition:** $425 per credit hour. Part-time tuition and fees vary according to class time, degree level, and program.

GIFT AID (NEED-BASED) Total amount: $3,678,246 (84% federal, 7% state, 4% institutional, 5% external sources). **Scholarships, grants, and awards:** Federal Pell, FSEOG, state, private, college/university gift aid from institutional funds.

GIFT AID (NON-NEED-BASED) Total amount: $3,992,211 (61% state, 33% institutional, 6% external sources). **Scholarships, grants, and awards by category:** Academic interests/achievement: 737 awards ($5,759,636 total): agriculture, biological sciences, business, communication, education, English, general academic interests/achievements, home economics, humanities, physical sciences, social sciences. Creative arts/performance: 20 awards ($83,603 total): music. Special achievements/activities: 97 awards ($183,882 total): cheerleading/drum major, leadership, religious involvement. Special characteristics: 148 awards ($455,158 total): adult students, children and siblings of alumni, children of educators, children of faculty/staff, general special characteristics, international students, out-of-state students, previous college experience, relatives of clergy, siblings of current students, veterans, veterans' children. **Tuition waivers:** Full or partial for employees or children of employees.

LOANS Student loans: $9,679,747 (35% need-based, 65% non-need-based). 75% of past graduating class borrowed through all loan programs. *Average indebtedness per student:* $22,618. **Parent loans:** $967,391 (100% non-need-based). **Programs:** Federal Direct (Subsidized and Unsubsidized Stafford, PLUS), Perkins, alternative loans.

WORK-STUDY Federal work-study: 75 jobs averaging $2000. **State or other work-study/employment:** Total amount: $73,953 (100% need-based). 60 part-time jobs averaging $2000.

ATHLETIC AWARDS Total amount: $3,899,628 (1% need-based, 99% non-need-based).

APPLYING FOR FINANCIAL AID Required financial aid forms: FAFSA, state aid form, verification worksheet. **Financial aid deadline:** Continuous. **Notification date:** Continuous beginning 3/15. Students must reply within 4 weeks of notification.

CONTACT Lorrie Steedley, Student Financial Services, Warner University, 13895 Highway 27, Lake Wales, FL 33859, 863-638-7202 or toll-free 800-309-9563. *Fax:* 863-638-7603. *E-mail:* financialaid@warner.edu.
Website: http://www.warner.edu/.

WARREN WILSON COLLEGE
Swannanoa, NC

ABOUT THE INSTITUTION Independent Presbyterian Church (U.S.A.), coed. **Awards:** bachelor's and master's degrees. 19 undergraduate majors. **Total enrollment:** 812. Undergraduates: 753. Freshmen: 195.

GIFT AID (NEED-BASED) Scholarships, grants, and awards: Federal Pell, FSEOG, state, college/university gift aid from institutional funds.

GIFT AID (NON-NEED-BASED) Scholarships, grants, and awards by category: Academic interests/achievement: general academic interests/achievements. Creative arts/performance: art/fine arts, creative writing. Special achievements/activities: community service, leadership. Special characteristics: children of faculty/staff, general special characteristics, local/state students, previous college experience, relatives of clergy, religious affiliation.

LOANS Programs: Federal Direct (Subsidized and Unsubsidized Stafford, PLUS).

APPLYING FOR FINANCIAL AID Required financial aid forms: FAFSA, state aid form.

CONTACT Financial Aid Office, Warren Wilson College, PO Box 9000, Asheville, NC 28815-9000, 828-771-2082 or toll-free 800-934-3536. *Fax:* 828-771-2030. *E-mail:* finaid@warren-wilson.edu.
Website: http://www.warren-wilson.edu/.

WARTBURG COLLEGE
Waverly, IA

Tuition & fees: $39,730	Average undergraduate aid package: $27,932

ABOUT THE INSTITUTION Independent Lutheran, coed. **Awards:** bachelor's degrees. 60 undergraduate majors. **Total enrollment:** 1,482. Undergraduates: 1,482. Freshmen: 445. Federal methodology is used as a basis for awarding need-based institutional aid.

UNDERGRADUATE EXPENSES for 2017–2018 Comprehensive fee: $49,478 includes full-time tuition ($38,710), mandatory fees ($1020), and room and board ($9748). **College room only:** $4923. Room and board charges vary according to board plan and housing facility. **Part-time tuition:** $2030 per course. **Part-time fees:** $115 per year. Part-time tuition and fees vary according to course load.

FRESHMAN FINANCIAL AID (Fall 2015) 329 applied for aid; of those 89% were deemed to have need. 100% of freshmen with need received aid; of those 22% had need fully met. **Average percent of need met:** 82% (excluding resources awarded to replace EFC). **Average financial aid package:** $28,792 (excluding resources awarded to replace EFC). 19% of all full-time freshmen had no need and received non-need-based gift aid.

UNDERGRADUATE FINANCIAL AID (Fall 2015) 1,228 applied for aid; of those 88% were deemed to have need. 100% of undergraduates with need received aid; of those 20% had need fully met. **Average percent of need met:** 81% (excluding resources awarded to replace EFC). **Average financial aid package:** $27,932 (excluding resources awarded to replace EFC). 25% of all full-time undergraduates had no need and received non-need-based gift aid.

GIFT AID (NEED-BASED) Total amount: $25,047,526 (7% federal, 10% state, 72% institutional, 11% external sources). **Receiving aid:** Freshmen: 80% (292); all full-time undergraduates: 74% (1,074). **Average award:** Freshmen: $25,110; Undergraduates: $23,267. **Scholarships, grants, and awards:** Federal Pell, FSEOG, state, private, college/university gift aid from institutional funds.

GIFT AID (NON-NEED-BASED) Total amount: $11,830,992 (1% federal, 76% institutional, 23% external sources). **Receiving aid:** Freshmen: 17% (62). Undergraduates: 14% (208). **Average award:** Freshmen: $23,877. Undergraduates: $20,797. **Scholarships, grants, and awards by category:** Academic interests/achievement: 1,057 awards ($17,872,974 total): biological sciences, business, communication, computer science, education, engineering/technologies, English, foreign languages, general academic interests/achievements, humanities, mathematics, physical sciences, premedicine, religion/biblical studies, social sciences. Creative arts/performance: 332 awards ($1,124,984 total): art/fine arts, cinema/film/broadcasting, journalism/publications, music, performing arts, theater/drama. Special achievements/activities: 28 awards ($25,182 total): junior miss, leadership. Special characteristics: 681 awards ($5,028,703 total): children and siblings of alumni, children of faculty/staff, international students, previous college experience, religious affiliation, siblings of

current students. *Tuition waivers:* Full or partial for employees or children of employees.
LOANS *Student loans:* $11,915,282 (56% need-based, 44% non-need-based). 75% of past graduating class borrowed through all loan programs. *Average indebtedness per student:* $39,794. *Average need-based loan:* Freshmen: $4150. Undergraduates: $5260. *Parent loans:* $2,592,546 (66% need-based, 34% non-need-based). *Programs:* Federal Direct (Subsidized and Unsubsidized Stafford, PLUS), Perkins, college/university, private loans.
WORK-STUDY *Federal work-study:* 550 jobs averaging $1002. *State or other work-study/employment:* Total amount: $1,187,014 (100% non-need-based). 656 part-time jobs averaging $1270.
APPLYING FOR FINANCIAL AID *Required financial aid form:* FAFSA. *Financial aid deadline (priority):* 3/1. *Notification date:* Continuous beginning 3/1. Students must reply within 2 weeks of notification.
CONTACT Ms. Jennifer Sassman, Director of Financial Aid, Wartburg College, 100 Wartburg Boulevard, PO Box 1003, Waverly, IA 50677-0903, 319-352-8262 or toll-free 800-772-2085. *Fax:* 319-352-8514. *E-mail:* jennifer.sassman@wartburg.edu. *Website:* http://www.wartburg.edu/.

WASHBURN UNIVERSITY
Topeka, KS

Tuition & fees (KS res): $8300	Average undergraduate aid package: $9580

ABOUT THE INSTITUTION City-supported, coed. *Awards:* certificates, associate, bachelor's, master's, and doctoral degrees. 87 undergraduate majors. *Total enrollment:* 6,615. Undergraduates: 5,793. Freshmen: 813. Federal methodology is used as a basis for awarding need-based institutional aid.
UNDERGRADUATE EXPENSES for 2017–2018 *Application fee:* $20. *Tuition, state resident:* full-time $8190; part-time $273 per credit hour. *Tuition, nonresident:* full-time $18,510; part-time $617 per credit hour. *Required fees:* full-time $110. Full-time tuition and fees vary according to program. Part-time tuition and fees vary according to program. *College room and board:* $7527; *Room only:* $4287. Room and board charges vary according to board plan and housing facility.
FRESHMAN FINANCIAL AID (Fall 2016, est.) 785 applied for aid; of those 69% were deemed to have need. 100% of freshmen with need received aid; of those 15% had need fully met. *Average percent of need met:* 38% (excluding resources awarded to replace EFC). *Average financial aid package:* $9828 (excluding resources awarded to replace EFC). 17% of all full-time freshmen had no need and received non-need-based gift aid.
UNDERGRADUATE FINANCIAL AID (Fall 2016, est.) 3,366 applied for aid; of those 69% were deemed to have need. 100% of undergraduates with need received aid; of those 12% had need fully met. *Average percent of need met:* 37% (excluding resources awarded to replace EFC). *Average financial aid package:* $9580 (excluding resources awarded to replace EFC). 14% of all full-time undergraduates had no need and received non-need-based gift aid.
GIFT AID (NEED-BASED) *Total amount:* $11,308,283 (79% federal, 5% state, 12% institutional, 4% external sources). *Receiving aid:* Freshmen: 36% (307); all full-time undergraduates: 36% (1,358). *Average award:* Freshmen: $5263; Undergraduates: $5140. *Scholarships, grants, and awards:* Federal Pell, FSEOG, state, private, college/university gift aid from institutional funds.
GIFT AID (NON-NEED-BASED) *Total amount:* $4,224,707 (1% state, 72% institutional, 27% external sources). *Receiving aid:* Freshmen: 41% (347). Undergraduates: 31% (1,164). *Average award:* Freshmen: $3184. Undergraduates: $3331. *Scholarships, grants, and awards by category:* Academic interests/achievement: biological sciences, business, communication, computer science, education, engineering/technologies, English, foreign languages, general academic interests/achievements, health fields, humanities, international studies, mathematics, physical sciences, premedicine, religion/biblical studies, social sciences. *Creative arts/performance:* art/fine arts, cinema/film/broadcasting, debating, general creative arts/performance, journalism/publications, music, performing arts, theater/drama. *Special achievements/activities:* cheerleading/drum major, community service, leadership. *Special characteristics:* adult students, children and siblings of alumni, children of faculty/staff, ethnic background, international students, local/state students. *Tuition waivers:* Full or partial for employees or children of employees, senior citizens. *ROTC:* Army, Naval cooperative, Air Force cooperative.

LOANS *Student loans:* $19,613,164 (50% need-based, 50% non-need-based). 65% of past graduating class borrowed through all loan programs. *Average indebtedness per student:* $23,552. *Average need-based loan:* Freshmen: $3251. Undergraduates: $4128. *Parent loans:* $2,795,659 (23% need-based, 77% non-need-based). *Programs:* Federal Direct (Subsidized and Unsubsidized Stafford, PLUS), college/university.
WORK-STUDY *Federal work-study:* Total amount: $1,322,041; jobs available. *State or other work-study/employment:* Total amount: $65,531 (100% need-based). Part-time jobs available.
ATHLETIC AWARDS Total amount: $2,102,865 (47% need-based, 53% non-need-based).
APPLYING FOR FINANCIAL AID *Required financial aid form:* FAFSA. *Financial aid deadline (priority):* 2/15. *Notification date:* Continuous beginning 4/1. Students must reply within 4 weeks of notification.
CONTACT Dawn Boman, Associate Director of Financial Aid, Washburn University, 1700 SW College Avenue, Topeka, KS 66621, 785-670-1151 or toll-free 800-332-0291. *Fax:* 785-670-1079. *E-mail:* dawn.boman@washburn.edu. *Website:* http://www.washburn.edu/.

WASHINGTON ADVENTIST UNIVERSITY
Takoma Park, MD

CONTACT Sharon Conway, Director of Student Financial Services, Washington Adventist University, 7600 Flower Avenue, Takoma Park, MD 20912, 301-891-4005 or toll-free 800-835-4212. *Fax:* 301-891-4167. *E-mail:* sconway@wau.edu. *Website:* http://www.wau.edu/.

WASHINGTON & JEFFERSON COLLEGE
Washington, PA

Tuition & fees: $44,900	Average undergraduate aid package: $34,948

ABOUT THE INSTITUTION Independent, coed. *Awards:* certificates, bachelor's, and master's degrees. 33 undergraduate majors. *Total enrollment:* 1,406. Undergraduates: 1,396. Freshmen: 429. Both federal and institutional methodology are used as a basis for awarding need-based institutional aid.
UNDERGRADUATE EXPENSES for 2016–2017 *Application fee:* $25. *Comprehensive fee:* $56,754 includes full-time tuition ($44,320), mandatory fees ($580), and room and board ($11,854). *College room only:* $6956. Full-time tuition and fees vary according to reciprocity agreements. Room and board charges vary according to board plan and housing facility. *Part-time tuition:* $1112 per credit hour. Part-time tuition and fees vary according to course load. *Payment plan:* Tuition prepayment.
FRESHMAN FINANCIAL AID (Fall 2016, est.) 392 applied for aid; of those 89% were deemed to have need. 100% of freshmen with need received aid; of those 16% had need fully met. *Average percent of need met:* 79% (excluding resources awarded to replace EFC). *Average financial aid package:* $35,711 (excluding resources awarded to replace EFC). 18% of all full-time freshmen had no need and received non-need-based gift aid.
UNDERGRADUATE FINANCIAL AID (Fall 2016, est.) 1,187 applied for aid; of those 91% were deemed to have need. 100% of undergraduates with need received aid; of those 16% had need fully met. *Average percent of need met:* 80% (excluding resources awarded to replace EFC). *Average financial aid package:* $34,948 (excluding resources awarded to replace EFC). 20% of all full-time undergraduates had no need and received non-need-based gift aid.
GIFT AID (NEED-BASED) *Total amount:* $29,911,422 (6% federal, 6% state, 87% institutional, 1% external sources). *Receiving aid:* Freshmen: 66% (281); all full-time undergraduates: 67% (917). *Average award:* Freshmen: $10,406; Undergraduates: $13,627. *Scholarships, grants, and awards:* Federal Pell, FSEOG, state, private, college/university gift aid from institutional funds.

GIFT AID (NON-NEED-BASED) *Total amount:* $7,102,127 (97% institutional, 3% external sources). *Receiving aid:* Freshmen: 80% (345). Undergraduates: 72% (988). *Average award:* Freshmen: $22,925. Undergraduates: $19,612. *Scholarships, grants, and awards by category:* Academic interests/achievement: 1,195 awards ($22,374,609 total): business, general academic interests/achievements, humanities. *Special characteristics:* 117 awards ($2,474,550 total): children and siblings of alumni, children of faculty/staff, international students, local/state students, members of minority groups, veterans, veterans' children. *Tuition waivers:* Full or partial for employees or children of employees. *ROTC:* Army, Air Force cooperative.

LOANS *Student loans:* $11,961,998 (71% need-based, 29% non-need-based). 83% of past graduating class borrowed through all loan programs. *Average need-based loan:* Freshmen: $3622. Undergraduates: $4517. *Parent loans:* $4,310,704 (66% need-based, 34% non-need-based). *Programs:* Federal Direct (Subsidized and Unsubsidized Stafford, PLUS), Perkins, college/university.

WORK-STUDY *Federal work-study:* Total amount: $931,330; 594 jobs averaging $1568. *State or other work-study/employment:* Total amount: $305,000 (100% non-need-based). 130 part-time jobs averaging $1000.

APPLYING FOR FINANCIAL AID *Required financial aid form:* FAFSA. *Financial aid deadline (priority):* 2/15. *Notification date:* Continuous beginning 12/15. Students must reply by 5/1.

CONTACT Mrs. Michelle Duffy, Associate Vice President for Enrollment, Washington & Jefferson College, 60 South Lincoln Street, Washington, PA 15301-4801, 724-503-1001 Ext. 6019 or toll-free 888-WANDJAY. *Fax:* 724-250-3340. *E-mail:* manderson@washjeff.edu.
Website: http://www.washjeff.edu/.

WASHINGTON AND LEE UNIVERSITY
Lexington, VA

Tuition & fees: $49,254	Average undergraduate aid package: $48,392

ABOUT THE INSTITUTION Independent, coed. *Awards:* bachelor's, master's, and doctoral degrees. 37 undergraduate majors. *Total enrollment:* 2,160. Undergraduates: 1,830. Freshmen: 466. Both federal and institutional methodology are used as a basis for awarding need-based institutional aid.

UNDERGRADUATE EXPENSES for 2016–2017 *Application fee:* $60. *Comprehensive fee:* $60,634 includes full-time tuition ($48,267), mandatory fees ($987), and room and board ($11,380). *College room only:* $5250. Full-time tuition and fees vary according to degree level. Room and board charges vary according to board plan and housing facility. *Part-time tuition:* $1689 per credit hour. Part-time tuition and fees vary according to course load and degree level.

FRESHMAN FINANCIAL AID (Fall 2016, est.) 249 applied for aid; of those 85% were deemed to have need. 100% of freshmen with need received aid; of those 100% had need fully met. *Average percent of need met:* 100% (excluding resources awarded to replace EFC). *Average financial aid package:* $46,056 (excluding resources awarded to replace EFC). 7% of all full-time freshmen had no need and received non-need-based gift aid.

UNDERGRADUATE FINANCIAL AID (Fall 2016, est.) 832 applied for aid; of those 93% were deemed to have need. 100% of undergraduates with need received aid; of those 100% had need fully met. *Average percent of need met:* 100% (excluding resources awarded to replace EFC). *Average financial aid package:* $48,392 (excluding resources awarded to replace EFC). 8% of all full-time undergraduates had no need and received non-need-based gift aid.

GIFT AID (NEED-BASED) *Total amount:* $32,751,459 (3% federal, 97% institutional). *Receiving aid:* Freshmen: 45% (211); all full-time undergraduates: 42% (771). *Average award:* Freshmen: $40,072; Undergraduates: $42,292. *Scholarships, grants, and awards:* Federal Pell, FSEOG, state, private, college/university gift aid from institutional funds.

GIFT AID (NON-NEED-BASED) *Total amount:* $8,704,612 (4% federal, 9% state, 81% institutional, 6% external sources). *Receiving aid:* Freshmen: 22% (103). Undergraduates: 16% (296). *Average award:* Freshmen: $44,684. Undergraduates: $34,766. *Scholarships, grants, and awards by category:* Academic interests/achievement: 302 awards ($7,239,840 total): general academic interests/achievements. *Tuition waivers:* Full or partial for employees or children of employees. *ROTC:* Army cooperative.

LOANS *Student loans:* $2,910,984 (24% need-based, 76% non-need-based). 33% of past graduating class borrowed through all loan programs. *Average indebtedness*

per student: $26,397. *Average need-based loan:* Freshmen: $528. Undergraduates: $783. *Parent loans:* $4,359,839 (100% non-need-based). *Programs:* Federal Direct (Subsidized and Unsubsidized Stafford, PLUS), college/university.

WORK-STUDY *Federal work-study:* Total amount: $440,292; 222 jobs averaging $2000. *State or other work-study/employment:* Total amount: $714,532 (2% need-based, 98% non-need-based). 368 part-time jobs averaging $2000.

APPLYING FOR FINANCIAL AID *Required financial aid forms:* FAFSA, CSS Financial Aid PROFILE, noncustodial (divorced/separated) parent's statement, federal income tax form(s). *Financial aid deadline:* 2/15. *Notification date:* 4/1. Students must reply by 5/1.

CONTACT James D. Kaster, Director of Financial Aid, Washington and Lee University, 204 West Washington Street, Lexington, VA 24450, 540-458-8720. *Fax:* 540-458-8614. *E-mail:* financialaid@wlu.edu.
Website: http://www.wlu.edu/.

WASHINGTON COLLEGE
Chestertown, MD

Tuition & fees: $44,700	Average undergraduate aid package: $31,463

ABOUT THE INSTITUTION Independent, coed. *Awards:* bachelor's degrees. 35 undergraduate majors. *Total enrollment:* 1,479. Undergraduates: 1,479. Freshmen: 410. Federal methodology is used as a basis for awarding need-based institutional aid.

UNDERGRADUATE EXPENSES for 2017–2018 *Comprehensive fee:* $55,740 includes full-time tuition ($43,702), mandatory fees ($998), and room and board ($11,040). *College room only:* $5608. Room and board charges vary according to board plan, housing facility, and location. *Part-time tuition:* $1785 per credit hour. Part-time tuition and fees vary according to course load. *Payment plans:* Guaranteed tuition, tuition prepayment.

FRESHMAN FINANCIAL AID (Fall 2016, est.) 338 applied for aid; of those 87% were deemed to have need. 90% of freshmen with need received aid; of those 29% had need fully met. *Average percent of need met:* 84% (excluding resources awarded to replace EFC). *Average financial aid package:* $33,955 (excluding resources awarded to replace EFC). 24% of all full-time freshmen had no need and received non-need-based gift aid.

UNDERGRADUATE FINANCIAL AID (Fall 2016, est.) 1,006 applied for aid; of those 89% were deemed to have need. 93% of undergraduates with need received aid; of those 22% had need fully met. *Average percent of need met:* 80% (excluding resources awarded to replace EFC). *Average financial aid package:* $31,463 (excluding resources awarded to replace EFC). 29% of all full-time undergraduates had no need and received non-need-based gift aid.

GIFT AID (NEED-BASED) *Total amount:* $24,405,585 (6% federal, 4% state, 88% institutional, 2% external sources). *Receiving aid:* Freshmen: 64% (262); all full-time undergraduates: 57% (824). *Average award:* Freshmen: $29,513; Undergraduates: $26,221. *Scholarships, grants, and awards:* Federal Pell, FSEOG, state, private, college/university gift aid from institutional funds.

GIFT AID (NON-NEED-BASED) *Total amount:* $7,567,495 (95% institutional, 5% external sources). *Receiving aid:* Freshmen: 9% (35). Undergraduates: 6% (85). *Average award:* Freshmen: $16,854. Undergraduates: $17,039. *Scholarships, grants, and awards by category:* Academic interests/achievement: general academic interests/achievements. Creative arts/performance: art/fine arts, creative writing, music, performing arts, theater/drama. *Special characteristics:* 34 awards ($1,186,870 total): children of faculty/staff. *Tuition waivers:* Full or partial for employees or children of employees.

LOANS *Student loans:* $8,080,268 (38% need-based, 62% non-need-based). 61% of past graduating class borrowed through all loan programs. *Average indebtedness per student:* $35,957. *Average need-based loan:* Freshmen: $3219. Undergraduates: $4324. *Parent loans:* $5,944,521 (100% non-need-based). *Programs:* Federal Direct (Subsidized and Unsubsidized Stafford, PLUS).

WORK-STUDY *Federal work-study:* Total amount: $165,654; 125 jobs averaging $1527.

APPLYING FOR FINANCIAL AID *Required financial aid form:* FAFSA. *Financial aid deadline (priority):* 3/1. *Notification date:* Continuous beginning 2/1. Students must reply by 5/1.

CONTACT Mr. Cailean D. Leith, Associate Director of Financial Aid, Washington College, 300 Washington Avenue, Chestertown, MD 21620-1197, 410-778-7214 or toll-free 800-422-1782. *Fax:* 410-801-7160. *E-mail:* cleith2@washcoll.edu. *Website:* http://www.washcoll.edu/.

WASHINGTON STATE UNIVERSITY
Pullman, WA

Tuition & fees (WA res): $11,041	Average undergraduate aid package: $13,465

ABOUT THE INSTITUTION State-supported, coed. *Awards:* certificates, bachelor's, master's, and doctoral degrees. 142 undergraduate majors. *Total enrollment:* 20,382. Undergraduates: 17,716. Freshmen: 3,988. Federal methodology is used as a basis for awarding need-based institutional aid.

UNDERGRADUATE EXPENSES for 2016–2017 *Application fee:* $50. *Tuition, state resident:* full-time $9324; part-time $497 per credit. *Tuition, nonresident:* full-time $23,956; part-time $1226 per credit. *Required fees:* full-time $1717. Full-time tuition and fees vary according to course load, location, and reciprocity agreements. Part-time tuition and fees vary according to course load, location, and reciprocity agreements. *College room and board:* $11,356; *Room only:* $6858. Room and board charges vary according to board plan, housing facility, and location.

FRESHMAN FINANCIAL AID (Fall 2015) 3,873 applied for aid; of those 73% were deemed to have need. 98% of freshmen with need received aid; of those 15% had need fully met. *Average percent of need met:* 65% (excluding resources awarded to replace EFC). *Average financial aid package:* $13,745 (excluding resources awarded to replace EFC). 26% of all full-time freshmen had no need and received non-need-based gift aid.

UNDERGRADUATE FINANCIAL AID (Fall 2015) 16,012 applied for aid; of those 81% were deemed to have need. 97% of undergraduates with need received aid; of those 11% had need fully met. *Average percent of need met:* 64% (excluding resources awarded to replace EFC). *Average financial aid package:* $13,465 (excluding resources awarded to replace EFC). 14% of all full-time undergraduates had no need and received non-need-based gift aid.

GIFT AID (NEED-BASED) *Total amount:* $98,924,408 (38% federal, 52% state, 10% institutional). *Receiving aid:* Freshmen: 57% (2,634); all full-time undergraduates: 53% (11,197). *Average award:* Freshmen: $11,490; Undergraduates: $11,337. *Scholarships, grants, and awards:* Federal Pell, FSEOG, state, private, college/university gift aid from institutional funds, Federal Nursing.

GIFT AID (NON-NEED-BASED) *Total amount:* $20,613,939 (8% state, 57% institutional, 35% external sources). *Receiving aid:* Freshmen: 43% (1,998). Undergraduates: 27% (5,813). *Average award:* Freshmen: $3921. Undergraduates: $3935. *Scholarships, grants, and awards by category: Academic interests/ achievement:* agriculture, architecture, area/ethnic studies, biological sciences, business, communication, computer science, education, engineering/technologies, English, foreign languages, general academic interests/achievements, health fields, home economics, humanities, international studies, mathematics, military science, physical sciences, premedicine, social sciences. *Creative arts/performance:* applied art and design, art/fine arts, cinema/film/broadcasting, creative writing, general creative arts/ performance, journalism/publications, music, performing arts, theater/drama. *Special achievements/activities:* community service, general special achievements/activities, junior miss, leadership, memberships, religious involvement, rodeo. *Special characteristics:* children and siblings of alumni, children of faculty/staff, children of public servants, children with a deceased or disabled parent, first-generation college students, handicapped students, international students, local/state students, out-of-state students, previous college experience, public servants, religious affiliation, veterans, veterans' children. *Tuition waivers:* Full or partial for employees or children of employees, senior citizens. *ROTC:* Army, Naval cooperative, Air Force.

LOANS *Student loans:* $92,916,444 (45% need-based, 55% non-need-based). 58% of past graduating class borrowed through all loan programs. *Average indebtedness per student:* $25,874. *Average need-based loan:* Freshmen: $3740. Undergraduates: $4509. *Parent loans:* $39,576,483 (100% non-need-based). *Programs:* Federal Direct (Subsidized and Unsubsidized Stafford, PLUS), Perkins, Federal Nursing, private loans.

WORK-STUDY *Federal work-study:* jobs available. *State or other work-study/employment:* Total amount: $1,051,818 (100% need-based). Part-time jobs available.

ATHLETIC AWARDS Total amount: $9,304,954 (100% non-need-based).

APPLYING FOR FINANCIAL AID *Required financial aid form:* FAFSA. *Financial aid deadline:* 1/31. *Notification date:* Continuous beginning 2/1. Students must reply within 2 weeks of notification.

CONTACT Mr. Brian Dixon, Office of Financial Aid and Scholarships, Washington State University, PO Box 641068, Pullman, WA 99164-1068, 509-335-9711 or toll-free 888-468-6978. *Fax:* 509-335-1385. *E-mail:* finaid@wsu.edu. *Website:* http://www.wsu.edu/.

WASHINGTON STATE UNIVERSITY– GLOBAL CAMPUS
Pullman, WA

CONTACT Financial Aid Office, Washington State University–Global Campus, PO Box 645220, Washington State University, Pullman, WA 99164-5220 or toll-free 800-222-4978. *Website:* http://www.globalcampus.wsu.edu/.

WASHINGTON UNIVERSITY IN ST. LOUIS
St. Louis, MO

Tuition & fees: $51,533	Average undergraduate aid package: $43,722

ABOUT THE INSTITUTION Independent, coed. *Awards:* certificates, bachelor's, master's, and doctoral degrees. 174 undergraduate majors. *Total enrollment:* 15,032. Undergraduates: 7,540. Freshmen: 1,776. Institutional methodology is used as a basis for awarding need-based institutional aid.

UNDERGRADUATE EXPENSES for 2017–2018 *Application fee:* $75. *Comprehensive fee:* $67,539 includes full-time tuition ($50,650), mandatory fees ($883), and room and board ($16,006). *College room only:* $10,982. Room and board charges vary according to board plan and housing facility. *Payment plan:* Tuition prepayment.

FRESHMAN FINANCIAL AID (Fall 2016, est.) 895 applied for aid; of those 83% were deemed to have need. 99% of freshmen with need received aid; of those 100% had need fully met. *Average percent of need met:* 100% (excluding resources awarded to replace EFC). *Average financial aid package:* $46,548 (excluding resources awarded to replace EFC). 11% of all full-time freshmen had no need and received non-need-based gift aid.

UNDERGRADUATE FINANCIAL AID (Fall 2016, est.) 3,102 applied for aid; of those 92% were deemed to have need. 99% of undergraduates with need received aid; of those 100% had need fully met. *Average percent of need met:* 100% (excluding resources awarded to replace EFC). *Average financial aid package:* $43,722 (excluding resources awarded to replace EFC). 9% of all full-time undergraduates had no need and received non-need-based gift aid.

GIFT AID (NEED-BASED) *Total amount:* $113,338,378 (3% federal, 1% state, 92% institutional, 4% external sources). *Receiving aid:* Freshmen: 40% (708); all full-time undergraduates: 41% (2,781). *Average award:* Freshmen: $43,839; Undergraduates: $40,509. *Scholarships, grants, and awards:* Federal Pell, FSEOG, state, private, college/university gift aid from institutional funds.

GIFT AID (NON-NEED-BASED) *Total amount:* $3,940,455 (15% state, 52% institutional, 33% external sources). *Receiving aid:* Freshmen: 5% (81). Undergraduates: 2% (158). *Average award:* Freshmen: $12,824. Undergraduates: $6111. *Scholarships, grants, and awards by category: Academic interests/ achievement:* 1,046 awards ($23,706,616 total): architecture, biological sciences, business, communication, computer science, education, engineering/technologies, English, foreign languages, general academic interests/achievements, home economics, humanities, international studies, mathematics, military science, physical sciences, premedicine, religion/biblical studies, social sciences. *Creative arts/performance:* 45 awards ($343,402 total): applied art and design, art/fine arts, creative writing. *Tuition waivers:* Full or partial for employees or children of employees. *ROTC:* Army, Air Force cooperative.

LOANS *Student loans:* $10,155,657 (86% need-based, 14% non-need-based). 30% of past graduating class borrowed through all loan programs. *Average indebtedness per student:* $23,577. *Average need-based loan:* Freshmen: $3276. Undergraduates: $4901. *Parent loans:* $13,376,910 (13% need-based, 87% non-need-based). *Programs:* Federal Direct (Subsidized and Unsubsidized Stafford, PLUS), Perkins, state, college/university.

WORK-STUDY *Federal work-study:* Total amount: $2,736,219; 1,211 jobs averaging $2259.

APPLYING FOR FINANCIAL AID *Required financial aid forms:* institution's own form, CSS Financial Aid PROFILE, noncustodial (divorced/separated) parent's statement, FAFSA using IRS Data Retrieval Tool. *Financial aid deadline:* 2/1. *Notification date:* 4/1. Students must reply by 5/1.

CONTACT Mr. Michael Runiewicz, Director, Student Financial Services, Washington University in St. Louis, Campus Box 1041, St. Louis, MO 63130-4899, 314-935-5900 or toll-free 800-638-0700. *Fax:* 314-935-4037. *E-mail:* financial@wustl.edu. *Website:* http://www.wustl.edu/.

WATKINS COLLEGE OF ART, DESIGN, & FILM
Nashville, TN

ABOUT THE INSTITUTION Independent, coed. *Awards:* bachelor's and master's degrees. 6 undergraduate majors. *Total enrollment:* 251. Undergraduates: 246. Freshmen: 43.

GIFT AID (NEED-BASED) *Scholarships, grants, and awards:* Federal Pell, FSEOG, state, private, college/university gift aid from institutional funds, Academic Competitiveness Grants.

GIFT AID (NON-NEED-BASED) *Scholarships, grants, and awards by category:* Academic interests/achievement: general academic interests/achievements. Creative arts/performance: applied art and design, art/fine arts, cinema/film/broadcasting. Special achievements/activities: general special achievements/activities.

LOANS *Programs:* Federal Direct (Subsidized and Unsubsidized Stafford, PLUS), private loans.

APPLYING FOR FINANCIAL AID *Required financial aid forms:* FAFSA, institution's own form.

CONTACT Lyle Jones, Financial Aid Coordinator, Watkins College of Art, Design, & Film, 2298 Rosa L. Parks Boulevard, Nashville, TN 37228, 615-383-4848 Ext. 7421. *Fax:* 615-383-4849. *E-mail:* financialaid@watkins.edu. *Website:* http://www.watkins.edu/.

WAYLAND BAPTIST UNIVERSITY
Plainview, TX

Tuition & fees: $18,510	Average undergraduate aid package: $13,894

ABOUT THE INSTITUTION Independent Baptist, coed. *Awards:* associate, bachelor's, master's, and doctoral degrees (branch locations in Anchorage, AK; Amarillo, TX; Luke Air Force Base, AZ; Glorieta, NM; Aiea, HI; Lubbock, TX; San Antonio, TX; Wichita Falls, TX). 46 undergraduate majors. *Total enrollment:* 5,065. Undergraduates: 3,776. Freshmen: 342. Federal methodology is used as a basis for awarding need-based institutional aid.

UNDERGRADUATE EXPENSES for 2016–2017 *Application fee:* $35. *Comprehensive fee:* $25,686 includes full-time tuition ($17,250), mandatory fees ($1260), and room and board ($7176). *College room only:* $2900. Full-time tuition and fees vary according to course load and location. Room and board charges vary according to board plan and housing facility. *Part-time tuition:* $575 per credit hour. Part-time tuition and fees vary according to course load and location.

FRESHMAN FINANCIAL AID (Fall 2016, est.) 272 applied for aid; of those 92% were deemed to have need. 100% of freshmen with need received aid; of those 9% had need fully met. *Average percent of need met:* 60% (excluding resources awarded to replace EFC). *Average financial aid package:* $14,350 (excluding resources awarded to replace EFC). 9% of all full-time freshmen had no need and received non-need-based gift aid.

UNDERGRADUATE FINANCIAL AID (Fall 2016, est.) 879 applied for aid; of those 92% were deemed to have need. 100% of undergraduates with need received

aid; of those 10% had need fully met. *Average percent of need met:* 58% (excluding resources awarded to replace EFC). *Average financial aid package:* $13,894 (excluding resources awarded to replace EFC). 9% of all full-time undergraduates had no need and received non-need-based gift aid.

GIFT AID (NEED-BASED) *Total amount:* $10,596,783 (56% federal, 16% state, 16% institutional, 12% external sources). *Receiving aid:* Freshmen: 78% (246); all full-time undergraduates: 73% (778). *Average award:* Freshmen: $11,534; Undergraduates: $10,622. *Scholarships, grants, and awards:* Federal Pell, FSEOG, state, private, college/university gift aid from institutional funds.

GIFT AID (NON-NEED-BASED) *Total amount:* $992,451 (2% state, 72% institutional, 26% external sources). *Receiving aid:* Freshmen: 7% (22). Undergraduates: 6% (62). *Average award:* Freshmen: $5796. Undergraduates: $5344. *Scholarships, grants, and awards by category:* Academic interests/achievement: 540 awards ($1,595,971 total): biological sciences, business, communication, education, English, general academic interests/achievements, mathematics, physical sciences, religion/biblical studies, social sciences. Creative arts/performance: 198 awards ($396,666 total): art/fine arts, journalism/publications, music, theater/drama. Special achievements/activities: 80 awards ($98,920 total): cheerleading/drum major, leadership, memberships, religious involvement. Special characteristics: 286 awards ($1,052,869 total): children and siblings of alumni, children of faculty/staff, children of public servants, ethnic background, general special characteristics, international students, local/state students, members of minority groups, relatives of clergy, religious affiliation. *ROTC:* Army cooperative, Air Force cooperative.

LOANS *Student loans:* $15,287,464 (88% need-based, 12% non-need-based). 67% of past graduating class borrowed through all loan programs. *Average indebtedness per student:* $23,764. *Average need-based loan:* Freshmen: $3529. Undergraduates: $4245. *Parent loans:* $1,296,456 (53% need-based, 47% non-need-based). *Programs:* Federal Direct (Subsidized and Unsubsidized Stafford, PLUS), Perkins, state, private loans.

WORK-STUDY *Federal work-study:* Total amount: $164,910; 130 jobs averaging $1650. *State or other work-study/employment:* Total amount: $144,793 (40% need-based, 60% non-need-based). 351 part-time jobs averaging $1368.

ATHLETIC AWARDS Total amount: $2,718,247 (52% need-based, 48% non-need-based).

APPLYING FOR FINANCIAL AID *Required financial aid forms:* FAFSA, institution's own form. *Financial aid deadline (priority):* 5/1. *Notification date:* Continuous beginning 1/1. Students must reply within 3 weeks of notification.

CONTACT Karen LaQuey, Director of Financial Aid, Wayland Baptist University, 1900 West 7th Street, Plainview, TX 79072-6998, 806-291-3520 or toll-free 800-588-1928. *Fax:* 806-291-1956. *E-mail:* laquey@wbu.edu. *Website:* http://www.wbu.edu/.

WAYNESBURG UNIVERSITY
Waynesburg, PA

Tuition & fees: $22,800	Average undergraduate aid package: $18,776

ABOUT THE INSTITUTION Independent Presbyterian Church (U.S.A.), coed. *Awards:* bachelor's, master's, and doctoral degrees. 52 undergraduate majors. *Total enrollment:* 1,805. Undergraduates: 1,400. Freshmen: 401. Federal methodology is used as a basis for awarding need-based institutional aid.

UNDERGRADUATE EXPENSES for 2016–2017 *Application fee:* $20. *Comprehensive fee:* $32,290 includes full-time tuition ($22,380), mandatory fees ($420), and room and board ($9490). *College room only:* $4800. Full-time tuition and fees vary according to class time. Room and board charges vary according to board plan and housing facility. *Part-time tuition:* $930 per credit hour. *Part-time fees:* $16 per credit hour. Part-time tuition and fees vary according to class time, course load, and location.

FRESHMAN FINANCIAL AID (Fall 2016, est.) 393 applied for aid; of those 87% were deemed to have need. 100% of freshmen with need received aid; of those 32% had need fully met. *Average percent of need met:* 79% (excluding resources awarded to replace EFC). *Average financial aid package:* $18,999 (excluding resources awarded to replace EFC). 14% of all full-time freshmen had no need and received non-need-based gift aid.

UNDERGRADUATE FINANCIAL AID (Fall 2016, est.) 1,255 applied for aid; of those 89% were deemed to have need. 100% of undergraduates with need received aid; of those 33% had need fully met. *Average percent of need met:* 80% (excluding resources awarded to replace EFC). *Average financial aid package:*

$18,776 (excluding resources awarded to replace EFC). 15% of all full-time undergraduates had no need and received non-need-based gift aid.

GIFT AID (NEED-BASED) *Total amount:* $15,454,484 (13% federal, 13% state, 68% institutional, 6% external sources). *Receiving aid:* Freshmen: 81% (341); all full-time undergraduates: 80% (1,093). *Average award:* Freshmen: $14,699; Undergraduates: $14,082. *Scholarships, grants, and awards:* Federal Pell, FSEOG, state, private, college/university gift aid from institutional funds, United Negro College Fund.

GIFT AID (NON-NEED-BASED) *Total amount:* $3,142,521 (91% institutional, 9% external sources). *Receiving aid:* Freshmen: 11% (47). Undergraduates: 10% (137). *Average award:* Freshmen: $11,759. Undergraduates: $10,885. *Scholarships, grants, and awards by category: Academic interests/achievement:* 1,300 awards ($12,500,000 total): communication, general academic interests/achievements. *Creative arts/performance:* 10 awards ($25,000 total): art/fine arts, music, theater/drama. *Special achievements/activities:* 60 awards ($180,000 total): community service. *Special characteristics:* 55 awards ($650,000 total): children of faculty/staff, siblings of current students. *Tuition waivers:* Full or partial for employees or children of employees. *ROTC:* Army cooperative.

LOANS *Student loans:* $11,157,965 (56% need-based, 44% non-need-based). 84% of past graduating class borrowed through all loan programs. *Average indebtedness per student:* $30,850. *Average need-based loan:* Freshmen: $4316. Undergraduates: $5114. *Parent loans:* $3,175,075 (67% need-based, 33% non-need-based). *Programs:* Federal Direct (Subsidized and Unsubsidized Stafford, PLUS), Perkins, Federal Nursing, college/university.

WORK-STUDY *Federal work-study:* Total amount: $145,163; 600 jobs averaging $1500.

APPLYING FOR FINANCIAL AID *Required financial aid forms:* FAFSA, state aid form. *Financial aid deadline:* Continuous. *Notification date:* Continuous beginning 12/1. Students must reply within 2 weeks of notification.

CONTACT Matthew C. Stokan, Director of Financial Aid, Waynesburg University, 51 West College Street, Waynesburg, PA 15370-1222, 724-852-3208 or toll-free 800-225-7393. *Fax:* 724-852-6312. *E-mail:* mstokan@waynesburg.edu.

Website: http://www.waynesburg.edu/.

WAYNE STATE COLLEGE
Wayne, NE

Tuition & fees (NE res): $6427	Average undergraduate aid package: $9181

ABOUT THE INSTITUTION State-supported, coed. *Awards:* certificates, bachelor's, and master's degrees. 53 undergraduate majors. *Total enrollment:* 3,357. Undergraduates: 2,837. Freshmen: 579. Federal methodology is used as a basis for awarding need-based institutional aid.

UNDERGRADUATE EXPENSES for 2016–2017 *Tuition, state resident:* full-time $4800; part-time $160 per credit hour. *Tuition, nonresident:* full-time $9600; part-time $320 per credit hour. *Required fees:* full-time $1627; $62.85 per credit hour. Full-time tuition and fees vary according to course level and course load. Part-time tuition and fees vary according to course level and course load. *College room and board:* $7110; *Room only:* $3470. Room and board charges vary according to board plan and housing facility.

FRESHMAN FINANCIAL AID (Fall 2016, est.) 528 applied for aid; of those 79% were deemed to have need. 98% of freshmen with need received aid; of those 51% had need fully met. *Average percent of need met:* 52% (excluding resources awarded to replace EFC). *Average financial aid package:* $9388 (excluding resources awarded to replace EFC). 10% of all full-time freshmen had no need and received non-need-based gift aid.

UNDERGRADUATE FINANCIAL AID (Fall 2016, est.) 2,229 applied for aid; of those 77% were deemed to have need. 97% of undergraduates with need received aid; of those 45% had need fully met. *Average percent of need met:* 56% (excluding resources awarded to replace EFC). *Average financial aid package:* $9181 (excluding resources awarded to replace EFC). 6% of all full-time undergraduates had no need and received non-need-based gift aid.

GIFT AID (NEED-BASED) *Total amount:* $5,178,459 (80% federal, 17% state, 3% institutional). *Receiving aid:* Freshmen: 43% (249); all full-time undergraduates: 48% (1,179). *Average award:* Freshmen: $4789; Undergraduates: $4241. *Scholarships, grants, and awards:* Federal Pell, FSEOG, state, private, college/university gift aid from institutional funds.

GIFT AID (NON-NEED-BASED) *Total amount:* $3,665,041 (1% federal, 30% institutional, 69% external sources). *Receiving aid:* Freshmen: 53% (307). Undergraduates: 49% (1,211). *Average award:* Freshmen: $2448. Undergraduates: $2838. *Scholarships, grants, and awards by category: Academic interests/achievement:* biological sciences, business, communication, computer science, education, English, foreign languages, general academic interests/achievements, health fields, home economics, humanities, international studies, mathematics, physical sciences, premedicine, social sciences. *Creative arts/performance:* applied art and design, art/fine arts, creative writing, general creative arts/performance, journalism/publications, music, performing arts, theater/drama. *Special achievements/activities:* general special achievements/activities, leadership. *Special characteristics:* children of faculty/staff, ethnic background, general special characteristics, local/state students, members of minority groups, out-of-state students, veterans, veterans' children. *Tuition waivers:* Full or partial for employees or children of employees. *ROTC:* Army.

LOANS *Student loans:* $9,826,936 (43% need-based, 57% non-need-based). *Average need-based loan:* Freshmen: $3182. Undergraduates: $3875. *Parent loans:* $964,211 (100% non-need-based). *Programs:* Federal Direct (Subsidized and Unsubsidized Stafford, PLUS), Perkins.

WORK-STUDY *Federal work-study:* Total amount: $324,172; jobs available.

ATHLETIC AWARDS Total amount: $472,008 (100% non-need-based).

APPLYING FOR FINANCIAL AID *Required financial aid form:* FAFSA. *Financial aid deadline (priority):* 4/1. *Notification date:* Continuous beginning 2/1. Students must reply within 4 weeks of notification.

CONTACT Annette Kaus, Director of Financial Aid, Wayne State College, 1111 Main Street, Wayne, NE 68787, 402-375-7230 or toll-free 866-WSC-CATS. *Fax:* 402-375-7067. *E-mail:* ankaus1@wsc.edu.

Website: http://www.wsc.edu/.

WAYNE STATE UNIVERSITY
Detroit, MI

Tuition & fees: N/R	Average undergraduate aid package: $11,110

ABOUT THE INSTITUTION State-supported, coed. *Awards:* certificates, bachelor's, master's, and doctoral degrees. 83 undergraduate majors. *Total enrollment:* 27,298. Undergraduates: 17,280. Freshmen: 2,588. Federal methodology is used as a basis for awarding need-based institutional aid.

FRESHMAN FINANCIAL AID (Fall 2015) 1,994 applied for aid; of those 82% were deemed to have need. 99% of freshmen with need received aid; of those 13% had need fully met. *Average percent of need met:* 71% (excluding resources awarded to replace EFC). *Average financial aid package:* $13,659 (excluding resources awarded to replace EFC). 22% of all full-time freshmen had no need and received non-need-based gift aid.

UNDERGRADUATE FINANCIAL AID (Fall 2015) 9,519 applied for aid; of those 90% were deemed to have need. 98% of undergraduates with need received aid; of those 7% had need fully met. *Average percent of need met:* 52% (excluding resources awarded to replace EFC). *Average financial aid package:* $11,110 (excluding resources awarded to replace EFC). 16% of all full-time undergraduates had no need and received non-need-based gift aid.

GIFT AID (NEED-BASED) *Total amount:* $54,340,430 (65% federal, 35% institutional). *Receiving aid:* Freshmen: 54% (1,260); all full-time undergraduates: 55% (6,374). *Average award:* Freshmen: $9352; Undergraduates: $7032. *Scholarships, grants, and awards:* Federal Pell, FSEOG, state, private, college/university gift aid from institutional funds, United Negro College Fund.

GIFT AID (NON-NEED-BASED) *Total amount:* $31,215,611 (3% state, 93% institutional, 4% external sources). *Receiving aid:* Freshmen: 52% (1,195). Undergraduates: 45% (5,245). *Average award:* Freshmen: $6167. Undergraduates: $5273. *Scholarships, grants, and awards by category: Academic interests/achievement:* area/ethnic studies, biological sciences, business, communication, computer science, education, engineering/technologies, English, foreign languages, general academic interests/achievements, health fields, humanities, international studies, library science, mathematics, military science, physical sciences, premedicine, social sciences. *Creative arts/performance:* art/fine arts, dance, debating, general creative arts/performance, journalism/publications, music, performing arts, theater/drama. *Special achievements/activities:* leadership, memberships. *Special characteristics:* children of current students, children of faculty/staff, children with a deceased or disabled parent, ethnic background, international students, local/state students, out-of-state students, spouses of current students. *ROTC:* Army, Air Force cooperative.

LOANS *Student loans:* $75,069,021 (91% need-based, 9% non-need-based). 63% of past graduating class borrowed through all loan programs. *Average indebtedness per student:* $28,439. *Average need-based loan:* Freshmen: $3792. Undergraduates: $4291. *Parent loans:* $8,133,905 (100% non-need-based). *Programs:* Federal Direct (Subsidized and Unsubsidized Stafford, PLUS), Perkins, college/university.

WORK-STUDY *Federal work-study:* 559 jobs averaging $2259. *State or other work-study/employment:* Part-time jobs available.

ATHLETIC AWARDS Total amount: $3,636,550 (100% non-need-based).

APPLYING FOR FINANCIAL AID *Required financial aid forms:* FAFSA, federal income tax form(s), W-2 forms. *Financial aid deadline:* 6/30 (priority: 1/1). *Notification date:* Continuous beginning 3/31.

CONTACT Catherine Kay, Director of Financial Aid, Wayne State University, 42 West Warren Avenue, Detroit, MI 48202, 313-577-2100 or toll-free 877-WSU-INFO. *Fax:* 313-577-6648. *E-mail:* financialaid@wayne.edu.

Website: http://www.wayne.edu/.

WEBBER INTERNATIONAL UNIVERSITY
Babson Park, FL

Tuition & fees: $25,358	Average undergraduate aid package: $19,825

ABOUT THE INSTITUTION Independent, coed. *Awards:* associate, bachelor's, and master's degrees. 11 undergraduate majors. *Total enrollment:* 701. Undergraduates: 654. Freshmen: 177. Federal methodology is used as a basis for awarding need-based institutional aid.

UNDERGRADUATE EXPENSES for 2017–2018 *Application fee:* $35. *Comprehensive fee:* $34,052 includes full-time tuition ($22,770), mandatory fees ($2588), and room and board ($8694). *College room only:* $5512. Full-time tuition and fees vary according to class time, course load, and program. Room and board charges vary according to board plan, gender, and housing facility. *Part-time tuition:* $335 per credit hour. Part-time tuition and fees vary according to class time, course load, and program.

FRESHMAN FINANCIAL AID (Fall 2016, est.) 148 applied for aid; of those 97% were deemed to have need. 100% of freshmen with need received aid; of those 8% had need fully met. *Average percent of need met:* 59% (excluding resources awarded to replace EFC). *Average financial aid package:* $20,396 (excluding resources awarded to replace EFC). 17% of all full-time freshmen had no need and received non-need-based gift aid.

UNDERGRADUATE FINANCIAL AID (Fall 2016, est.) 475 applied for aid; of those 96% were deemed to have need. 100% of undergraduates with need received aid; of those 8% had need fully met. *Average percent of need met:* 60% (excluding resources awarded to replace EFC). *Average financial aid package:* $19,825 (excluding resources awarded to replace EFC). 21% of all full-time undergraduates had no need and received non-need-based gift aid.

GIFT AID (NEED-BASED) *Total amount:* $4,127,667 (37% federal, 33% state, 29% institutional, 1% external sources). *Receiving aid:* Freshmen: 80% (142); all full-time undergraduates: 72% (449). *Average award:* Freshmen: $17,496; Undergraduates: $16,287. *Scholarships, grants, and awards:* Federal Pell, FSEOG, state, private, college/university gift aid from institutional funds.

GIFT AID (NON-NEED-BASED) *Total amount:* $1,590,397 (8% state, 90% institutional, 2% external sources). *Receiving aid:* Freshmen: 6% (11). Undergraduates: 5% (29). *Average award:* Freshmen: $8300. Undergraduates: $10,851. *Scholarships, grants, and awards by category:* Academic interests/achievement: 413 awards ($1,524,027 total): business, general academic interests/achievements. Creative arts/performance: 16 awards ($30,500 total): journalism/publications, music. Special achievements/activities: 21 awards ($34,243 total): cheerleading/drum major, general special achievements/activities, leadership, memberships. Special characteristics: 89 awards ($1,322,157 total): children and siblings of alumni, children of faculty/staff, general special characteristics, international students, local/state students, siblings of current students, veterans. *Tuition waivers:* Full or partial for children of alumni, employees or children of employees, adult students, senior citizens.

LOANS *Student loans:* $3,418,149 (88% need-based, 12% non-need-based). 52% of past graduating class borrowed through all loan programs. *Average indebtedness per student:* $25,135. *Average need-based loan:* Freshmen: $3499. Undergrad-

uates: $4208. *Parent loans:* $1,796,993 (73% need-based, 27% non-need-based). *Programs:* Federal Direct (Subsidized and Unsubsidized Stafford, PLUS), Perkins.

WORK-STUDY *Federal work-study:* Total amount: $24,585; 35 jobs averaging $1704. *State or other work-study/employment:* Total amount: $50,145 (52% need-based, 48% non-need-based). 40 part-time jobs averaging $1247.

ATHLETIC AWARDS Total amount: $3,742,632 (83% need-based, 17% non-need-based).

APPLYING FOR FINANCIAL AID *Required financial aid forms:* FAFSA, state aid form. *Financial aid deadline:* 8/1 (priority: 4/1). *Notification date:* Continuous beginning 12/1. Students must reply within 4 weeks of notification.

CONTACT Ms. Kathleen Wilson, Vice President of Student Record Services, Webber International University, PO Box 96, 1201 Scenic Highway, Babson Park, FL 33827-0096, 863-638-2930 or toll-free 800-741-1844. *Fax:* 863-638-1513. *E-mail:* wilsonka@webber.edu.

Website: http://www.webber.edu/.

WEBB INSTITUTE
Glen Cove, NY

Tuition & fees: $48,775	Average undergraduate aid package: $50,710

ABOUT THE INSTITUTION Independent, coed. *Awards:* bachelor's degrees. 1 undergraduate major. *Total enrollment:* 92. Undergraduates: 92. Freshmen: 28. Both federal and institutional methodology are used as a basis for awarding need-based institutional aid.

UNDERGRADUATE EXPENSES for 2017–2018 *Application fee:* $60. *One-time required fee:* $3050. *Comprehensive fee:* $63,525 includes full-time tuition ($48,350), mandatory fees ($425), and room and board ($14,750). Webb provides scholarships that will fully cover the tuition expenses of U.S. citizens and permanent residents. One-time required fee is for a laptop charged in the first year only.

FRESHMAN FINANCIAL AID (Fall 2015) 8 applied for aid; of those 100% were deemed to have need. 100% of freshmen with need received aid. *Average percent of need met:* 89% (excluding resources awarded to replace EFC). *Average financial aid package:* $49,330 (excluding resources awarded to replace EFC). 54% of all full-time freshmen had no need and received non-need-based gift aid.

UNDERGRADUATE FINANCIAL AID (Fall 2015) 33 applied for aid; of those 100% were deemed to have need. 100% of undergraduates with need received aid. *Average percent of need met:* 89% (excluding resources awarded to replace EFC). *Average financial aid package:* $50,710 (excluding resources awarded to replace EFC). 64% of all full-time undergraduates had no need and received non-need-based gift aid.

GIFT AID (NEED-BASED) *Total amount:* $1,665,280 (2% federal, 93% institutional, 5% external sources). *Receiving aid:* Freshmen: 31% (8); all full-time undergraduates: 36% (33). *Average award:* Freshmen: $2000; Undergraduates: $2300. *Scholarships, grants, and awards:* Federal Pell, state, private, college/university gift aid from institutional funds.

GIFT AID (NON-NEED-BASED) *Receiving aid:* Freshmen: 31% (8). Undergraduates: 36% (33). *Average award:* Freshmen: $45,500. Undergraduates: $45,500. *Scholarships, grants, and awards by category:* Academic interests/achievement: 59 awards ($1,684,500 total): engineering/technologies, general academic interests/achievements. Special achievements/activities: 3 awards ($12,500 total): community service, leadership.

LOANS *Student loans:* $175,000 (100% need-based). 19% of past graduating class borrowed through all loan programs. *Average indebtedness per student:* $15,000. *Average need-based loan:* Freshmen: $3500. Undergraduates: $4100. *Parent loans:* $75,500 (100% need-based). *Programs:* Federal Direct (Subsidized and Unsubsidized Stafford, PLUS), college/university.

APPLYING FOR FINANCIAL AID *Required financial aid form:* FAFSA. *Financial aid deadline:* 5/1 (priority: 5/1). *Notification date:* Continuous beginning 5/1. Students must reply by 5/15 or within 2 weeks of notification.

CONTACT Jocelyn Wilson, Director of Financial Aid, Webb Institute, 298 Crescent Beach Road, Glen Cove, NY 11542-1398, 516-403-5928 Ext. 1108. *Fax:* 516-674-9838. *E-mail:* jwilson@webb.edu.

Website: http://www.webb.edu/.

WEBER STATE UNIVERSITY
Ogden, UT

Tuition & fees (UT res): $5525	Average undergraduate aid package: $5920

ABOUT THE INSTITUTION State-supported, coed. *Awards:* certificates, associate, bachelor's, and master's degrees. 163 undergraduate majors. *Total enrollment:* 26,809. Undergraduates: 26,112. Freshmen: 2,940. Both federal and institutional methodology are used as a basis for awarding need-based institutional aid.

UNDERGRADUATE EXPENSES for 2016–2017 *Application fee:* $30. *Tuition, state resident:* full-time $4611; part-time $2721 per year. *Tuition, non-resident:* full-time $13,837; part-time $8164 per year. *Required fees:* full-time $914; $560 per year. Full-time tuition and fees vary according to course level, course load, degree level, and program. Part-time tuition and fees vary according to course level, course load, degree level, and program. *College room and board:* $5400. Room and board charges vary according to board plan and housing facility.

FRESHMAN FINANCIAL AID (Fall 2016, est.) 1,520 applied for aid; of those 81% were deemed to have need. 83% of freshmen with need received aid; of those 60% had need fully met. *Average financial aid package:* $5183 (excluding resources awarded to replace EFC). 33% of all full-time freshmen had no need and received non-need-based gift aid.

UNDERGRADUATE FINANCIAL AID (Fall 2016, est.) 7,060 applied for aid; of those 86% were deemed to have need. 90% of undergraduates with need received aid; of those 72% had need fully met. *Average financial aid package:* $5920 (excluding resources awarded to replace EFC). 20% of all full-time undergraduates had no need and received non-need-based gift aid.

GIFT AID (NEED-BASED) *Total amount:* $40,301,333 (66% federal, 32% state, 2% external sources). *Receiving aid:* Freshmen: 35% (754); all full-time undergraduates: 39% (4,149). *Average award:* Freshmen: $3974; Undergraduates: $4112. *Scholarships, grants, and awards:* Federal Pell, FSEOG, state, private, college/university gift aid from institutional funds.

GIFT AID (NON-NEED-BASED) *Total amount:* $3,236,914 (100% institutional). *Receiving aid:* Freshmen: 7% (156). Undergraduates: 18% (1,873). *Average award:* Freshmen: $2403. Undergraduates: $3755. *Tuition waivers:* Full or partial for employees or children of employees, senior citizens. *ROTC:* Army, Naval cooperative, Air Force cooperative.

LOANS *Student loans:* $42,509,274 (46% need-based, 54% non-need-based). 44% of past graduating class borrowed through all loan programs. *Average indebtedness per student:* $22,029. *Average need-based loan:* Freshmen: $2571. Undergraduates: $3384. *Parent loans:* $299,868 (100% non-need-based). *Programs:* Federal Direct (Subsidized and Unsubsidized Stafford, PLUS), Perkins, college/university.

WORK-STUDY *Federal work-study:* Total amount: $850,052; jobs available. *State or other work-study/employment:* Total amount: $1,171,693 (100% need-based). Part-time jobs available.

ATHLETIC AWARDS Total amount: $5,739,373 (86% need-based, 14% non-need-based).

APPLYING FOR FINANCIAL AID *Required financial aid forms:* FAFSA, institution's own form. *Financial aid deadline (priority):* 3/1. *Notification date:* Continuous beginning 3/15. Students must reply within 2 weeks of notification.

CONTACT Mr. Jed Spencer, Financial Aid Director, Weber State University, Student Service Center, Suite 120, 3885 West Campus Drive, Department 1136, Ogden, UT 84408-1136, 801-626-7569 or toll-free 800-848-7700 (in-state), 800-848-7770 (out-of-state). *E-mail:* finaid@weber.edu.
Website: http://www.weber.edu/.

WEBSTER UNIVERSITY
St. Louis, MO

Tuition & fees: $26,300	Average undergraduate aid package: $25,521

ABOUT THE INSTITUTION Independent, coed. *Awards:* certificates, bachelor's, master's, and doctoral degrees. 68 undergraduate majors. *Total enrollment:* 4,222. Undergraduates: 2,621. Freshmen: 443. Federal methodology is used as a basis for awarding need-based institutional aid.

UNDERGRADUATE EXPENSES for 2016–2017 *Application fee:* $35. *One-time required fee:* $125. *Comprehensive fee:* $37,490 includes full-time tuition ($26,100), mandatory fees ($200), and room and board ($11,190). *College room only:* $6050. Full-time tuition and fees vary according to program. Room and board charges vary according to board plan and housing facility. *Part-time tuition:* $670 per credit hour.

FRESHMAN FINANCIAL AID (Fall 2016, est.) 414 applied for aid; of those 80% were deemed to have need. 100% of freshmen with need received aid; of those 5% had need fully met. *Average percent of need met:* 60% (excluding resources awarded to replace EFC). *Average financial aid package:* $26,788 (excluding resources awarded to replace EFC). 20% of all full-time freshmen had no need and received non-need-based gift aid.

UNDERGRADUATE FINANCIAL AID (Fall 2016, est.) 1,925 applied for aid; of those 84% were deemed to have need. 100% of undergraduates with need received aid; of those 12% had need fully met. *Average percent of need met:* 61% (excluding resources awarded to replace EFC). *Average financial aid package:* $25,521 (excluding resources awarded to replace EFC). 13% of all full-time undergraduates had no need and received non-need-based gift aid.

GIFT AID (NEED-BASED) *Total amount:* $28,432,547 (16% federal, 5% state, 77% institutional, 2% external sources). *Receiving aid:* Freshmen: 63% (283); all full-time undergraduates: 64% (1,427). *Average award:* Freshmen: $9387; Undergraduates: $8762. *Scholarships, grants, and awards:* Federal Pell, FSEOG, state, private, college/university gift aid from institutional funds.

GIFT AID (NON-NEED-BASED) *Total amount:* $4,917,766 (99% institutional, 1% external sources). *Receiving aid:* Freshmen: 69% (311). Undergraduates: 65% (1,453). *Average award:* Freshmen: $10,190. Undergraduates: $8870. *Scholarships, grants, and awards by category: Academic interests/achievement:* biological sciences, business, communication, computer science, education, English, foreign languages, general academic interests/achievements, humanities, international studies. *Creative arts/performance:* art/fine arts, creative writing, debating, music, theater/drama. *Special achievements/activities:* community service, leadership. *Special characteristics:* children and siblings of alumni, children of faculty/staff, ethnic background, international students, members of minority groups, out-of-state students, veterans' children. *Tuition waivers:* Full or partial for employees or children of employees. *ROTC:* Army cooperative, Air Force cooperative.

LOANS *Student loans:* $16,088,226 (94% need-based, 6% non-need-based). 47% of past graduating class borrowed through all loan programs. *Average indebtedness per student:* $28,479. *Average need-based loan:* Freshmen: $3280. Undergraduates: $4275. *Parent loans:* $3,492,955 (92% need-based, 8% non-need-based). *Programs:* Federal Direct (Subsidized and Unsubsidized Stafford, PLUS), Perkins, state, private loans.

WORK-STUDY *Federal work-study:* Total amount: $3,265,981; 1,214 jobs averaging $2760.

APPLYING FOR FINANCIAL AID *Required financial aid forms:* FAFSA, institution's own form. *Financial aid deadline (priority):* 3/1. *Notification date:* Continuous beginning 2/1.

CONTACT Office of Financial Aid, Webster University, 470 East Lockwood Avenue, St. Louis, MO 63119, 314-968-6992 or toll-free 800-753-6765. *Fax:* 314-968-7125. *E-mail:* financialaid@webster.edu.
Website: http://www.webster.edu/.

WELCH COLLEGE
Gallatin, TN

CONTACT Angie Edgmon, Financial Aid Coordinator, Welch College, 3606 West End Avenue, Nashville, TN 37205, 615-844-5000 Ext. 5249 or toll-free 800-763-9222. *Fax:* 615-269-6028. *E-mail:* finaid@fwbbc.edu.
Website: http://www.welch.edu/.

WELLESLEY COLLEGE
Wellesley, MA

Tuition & fees: $48,802	Average undergraduate aid package: $47,527

ABOUT THE INSTITUTION Independent, women only. *Awards:* bachelor's degrees (double bachelor's degree with Massachusetts Institute of Technology). 58 undergraduate majors. *Total enrollment:* 2,356. Undergraduates: 2,356. Both federal and institutional methodology are used as a basis for awarding need-based institutional aid.

UNDERGRADUATE EXPENSES for 2016–2017 *Comprehensive fee:* $63,916 includes full-time tuition ($48,510), mandatory fees ($292), and room and board ($15,114). *College room only:* $7672. *Part-time tuition:* $6064 per course. *Part-time fees:* $37 per course. Part-time tuition and fees vary according to course load. *Payment plan:* Tuition prepayment.

FRESHMAN FINANCIAL AID (Fall 2016, est.) 421 applied for aid; of those 84% were deemed to have need. 100% of freshmen with need received aid; of those 100% had need fully met. *Average percent of need met:* 100% (excluding resources awarded to replace EFC). *Average financial aid package:* $48,404 (excluding resources awarded to replace EFC).

UNDERGRADUATE FINANCIAL AID (Fall 2016, est.) 1,560 applied for aid; of those 90% were deemed to have need. 100% of undergraduates with need received aid; of those 100% had need fully met. *Average percent of need met:* 100% (excluding resources awarded to replace EFC). *Average financial aid package:* $47,527 (excluding resources awarded to replace EFC).

GIFT AID (NEED-BASED) *Total amount:* $61,488,189 (4% federal, 94% institutional, 2% external sources). *Receiving aid:* Freshmen: 57% (339); all full-time undergraduates: 62% (1,361). *Average award:* Freshmen: $47,355; Undergraduates: $45,178. *Scholarships, grants, and awards:* Federal Pell, FSEOG, state, private, college/university gift aid from institutional funds.

GIFT AID (NON-NEED-BASED) *Total amount:* $1,210,194 (100% external sources). *Tuition waivers:* Full or partial for employees or children of employees. *ROTC:* Army cooperative, Air Force cooperative.

LOANS *Student loans:* $4,129,328 (64% need-based, 36% non-need-based). 48% of past graduating class borrowed through all loan programs. *Average indebtedness per student:* $13,415. *Average need-based loan:* Freshmen: $2746. Undergraduates: $3728. *Parent loans:* $3,030,423 (100% non-need-based). *Programs:* Federal Direct (Subsidized and Unsubsidized Stafford, PLUS), Perkins, state, college/university.

WORK-STUDY *Federal work-study:* Total amount: $1,854,265; jobs available. *State or other work-study/employment:* Total amount: $688,187 (100% need-based). Part-time jobs available.

APPLYING FOR FINANCIAL AID *Required financial aid forms:* FAFSA, CSS Financial Aid PROFILE, noncustodial (divorced/separated) parent's statement, federal income tax form(s), W-2 forms. *Financial aid deadline (priority):* 2/15. *Notification date:* 4/1. Students must reply by 5/1.

CONTACT Mr. Scott J. Juedes, Director of Student Financial Services, Wellesley College, 106 Central Street, Wellesley, MA 02481-8203, 781-283-2360. *Fax:* 781-283-3946. *E-mail:* sfs@wellesley.edu.
Website: http://www.wellesley.edu/.

WELLS COLLEGE
Aurora, NY

Tuition & fees: $39,600	Average undergraduate aid package: $34,570

ABOUT THE INSTITUTION Independent, coed. *Awards:* bachelor's degrees. 36 undergraduate majors. *Total enrollment:* 515. Undergraduates: 515. Freshmen: 132. Federal methodology is used as a basis for awarding need-based institutional aid.

UNDERGRADUATE EXPENSES for 2017–2018 *Application fee:* $40. *Comprehensive fee:* $53,330 includes full-time tuition ($38,100), mandatory fees ($1500), and room and board ($13,730). *College room only:* $6865. Room and board charges vary according to housing facility. *Part-time tuition:* $1600 per credit hour. *Part-time fees:* $200 per term. Part-time tuition and fees vary according to course load.

FRESHMAN FINANCIAL AID (Fall 2015) 167 applied for aid; of those 97% were deemed to have need. 100% of freshmen with need received aid; of those 12% had

need fully met. *Average percent of need met:* 86% (excluding resources awarded to replace EFC). *Average financial aid package:* $37,677 (excluding resources awarded to replace EFC). 4% of all full-time freshmen had no need and received non-need-based gift aid.

UNDERGRADUATE FINANCIAL AID (Fall 2015) 551 applied for aid; of those 96% were deemed to have need. 99% of undergraduates with need received aid; of those 18% had need fully met. *Average percent of need met:* 84% (excluding resources awarded to replace EFC). *Average financial aid package:* $34,570 (excluding resources awarded to replace EFC). 6% of all full-time undergraduates had no need and received non-need-based gift aid.

GIFT AID (NEED-BASED) *Total amount:* $15,227,305 (9% federal, 6% state, 82% institutional, 3% external sources). *Receiving aid:* Freshmen: 95% (162); all full-time undergraduates: 92% (527). *Average award:* Freshmen: $33,255; Undergraduates: $29,867. *Scholarships, grants, and awards:* Federal Pell, FSEOG, state, private, college/university gift aid from institutional funds.

GIFT AID (NON-NEED-BASED) *Total amount:* $686,550 (1% state, 99% institutional). *Receiving aid:* Freshmen: 95% (162). Undergraduates: 92% (527). *Average award:* Freshmen: $23,826. Undergraduates: $20,606. *Scholarships, grants, and awards by category:* Academic interests/achievement: 447 awards ($8,302,886 total): general academic interests/achievements. *Special achievements/activities:* 68 awards ($680,000 total): leadership. *Special characteristics:* 15 awards ($60,250 total): children and siblings of alumni, international students. *Tuition waivers:* Full or partial for employees or children of employees, senior citizens.

LOANS *Student loans:* $4,824,180 (98% need-based, 2% non-need-based). 90% of past graduating class borrowed through all loan programs. *Average indebtedness per student:* $34,735. *Average need-based loan:* Freshmen: $2940. Undergraduates: $3649. *Parent loans:* $1,753,518 (99% need-based, 1% non-need-based). *Programs:* Federal Direct (Subsidized and Unsubsidized Stafford, PLUS), Perkins, state.

WORK-STUDY *Federal work-study:* 58 jobs averaging $1850. *State or other work-study/employment:* Total amount: $234,218 (93% need-based, 7% non-need-based). 235 part-time jobs averaging $1850.

APPLYING FOR FINANCIAL AID *Required financial aid form:* FAFSA. *Financial aid deadline (priority):* 2/15. *Notification date:* 3/1. Students must reply by 5/1.

CONTACT Ms. Laura Burns, Director of Financial Aid, Wells College, Route 90, Aurora, NY 13026, 315-364-3289 or toll-free 800-952-9355. *Fax:* 315-364-3445. *E-mail:* lburns@wells.edu.
Website: http://www.wells.edu/.

WENTWORTH INSTITUTE OF TECHNOLOGY
Boston, MA

Tuition & fees: $31,840	Average undergraduate aid package: $23,788

ABOUT THE INSTITUTION Independent, coed. *Awards:* certificates, associate, bachelor's, and master's degrees. 20 undergraduate majors. *Total enrollment:* 4,136. Undergraduates: 3,974. Freshmen: 961. Federal methodology is used as a basis for awarding need-based institutional aid.

UNDERGRADUATE EXPENSES for 2017–2018 *Application fee:* $50. *Comprehensive fee:* $44,410 includes full-time tuition ($31,840) and room and board ($12,570). Room and board charges vary according to board plan and housing facility. *Part-time tuition:* $995 per credit hour. Part-time tuition and fees vary according to course load.

FRESHMAN FINANCIAL AID (Fall 2016, est.) 843 applied for aid; of those 89% were deemed to have need. 100% of freshmen with need received aid; of those 7% had need fully met. *Average percent of need met:* 38% (excluding resources awarded to replace EFC). *Average financial aid package:* $22,272 (excluding resources awarded to replace EFC). 10% of all full-time freshmen had no need and received non-need-based gift aid.

UNDERGRADUATE FINANCIAL AID (Fall 2016, est.) 3,021 applied for aid; of those 90% were deemed to have need. 100% of undergraduates with need received aid; of those 7% had need fully met. *Average percent of need met:* 40% (excluding resources awarded to replace EFC). *Average financial aid package:* $23,788 (excluding resources awarded to replace EFC). 7% of all full-time undergraduates had no need and received non-need-based gift aid.

GIFT AID (NEED-BASED) *Total amount:* $42,013,127 (12% federal, 2% state, 86% institutional). *Receiving aid:* Freshmen: 68% (652); all full-time undergraduates: 58% (2,287). *Average award:* Freshmen: $5386; Undergraduates: $6352. *Scholarships, grants, and awards:* Federal Pell, FSEOG, state, private, college/university gift aid from institutional funds.

GIFT AID (NON-NEED-BASED) *Total amount:* $2,660,440 (100% institutional). *Receiving aid:* Freshmen: 77% (743). Undergraduates: 65% (2,556). *Average award:* Freshmen: $9483. Undergraduates: $8414. *Tuition waivers:* Full or partial for employees or children of employees. *ROTC:* Army cooperative, Air Force cooperative.

LOANS *Student loans:* $32,473,345 (93% need-based, 7% non-need-based). 81% of past graduating class borrowed through all loan programs. *Average need-based loan:* Freshmen: $3396. Undergraduates: $4279. *Parent loans:* $14,186,271 (95% need-based, 5% non-need-based). *Programs:* Federal Direct (Subsidized and Unsubsidized Stafford, PLUS), Perkins, state.

WORK-STUDY *Federal work-study:* Total amount: $1,653,038; 692 jobs averaging $820. *State or other work-study/employment:* Total amount: $1,508,651 (100% need-based). Part-time jobs available.

APPLYING FOR FINANCIAL AID *Required financial aid form:* FAFSA. *Financial aid deadline (priority):* 3/1. *Notification date:* Continuous beginning 3/15. Students must reply by 5/1 or within 2 weeks of notification.

CONTACT Anne-Marie Caruso, Director of Financial Aid, Wentworth Institute of Technology, 550 Huntington Avenue, Boston, MA 02115-5998, 617-989-4174 or toll-free 800-556-0610. *Fax:* 617-989-4201. *E-mail:* carusoa@wit.edu. *Website:* http://www.wit.edu/.

WESLEYAN COLLEGE
Macon, GA

Tuition & fees: $22,370	Average undergraduate aid package: $20,567

ABOUT THE INSTITUTION Independent United Methodist, undergraduate: women only; graduate: coed. *Awards:* bachelor's and master's degrees. 28 undergraduate majors. *Total enrollment:* 682. Undergraduates: 635. Freshmen: 104. Federal methodology is used as a basis for awarding need-based institutional aid.

UNDERGRADUATE EXPENSES for 2017–2018 *Application fee:* $30. *One-time required fee:* $250. *Comprehensive fee:* $31,940 includes full-time tuition ($21,370), mandatory fees ($1000), and room and board ($9570). Full-time tuition and fees vary according to class time, course load, program, and reciprocity agreements. Room and board charges vary according to housing facility. *Part-time tuition:* $510 per semester hour. *Part-time fees:* $40 per semester hour. Part-time tuition and fees vary according to class time, course load, and reciprocity agreements.

FRESHMAN FINANCIAL AID (Fall 2016, est.) 94 applied for aid; of those 90% were deemed to have need. 100% of freshmen with need received aid; of those 19% had need fully met. *Average percent of need met:* 76% (excluding resources awarded to replace EFC). *Average financial aid package:* $20,808 (excluding resources awarded to replace EFC). 12% of all full-time freshmen had no need and received non-need-based gift aid.

UNDERGRADUATE FINANCIAL AID (Fall 2016, est.) 345 applied for aid; of those 93% were deemed to have need. 99% of undergraduates with need received aid; of those 19% had need fully met. *Average percent of need met:* 74% (excluding resources awarded to replace EFC). *Average financial aid package:* $20,567 (excluding resources awarded to replace EFC). 21% of all full-time undergraduates had no need and received non-need-based gift aid.

GIFT AID (NEED-BASED) *Total amount:* $5,110,866 (25% federal, 14% state, 58% institutional, 3% external sources). *Receiving aid:* Freshmen: 87% (85); all full-time undergraduates: 77% (316). *Average award:* Freshmen: $16,980; Undergraduates: $15,880. *Scholarships, grants, and awards:* Federal Pell, FSEOG, state, private, college/university gift aid from institutional funds.

GIFT AID (NON-NEED-BASED) *Total amount:* $1,466,979 (1% federal, 17% state, 79% institutional, 3% external sources). *Receiving aid:* Freshmen: 15% (15). Undergraduates: 13% (54). *Average award:* Freshmen: $11,262. Undergraduates: $10,742. *Scholarships, grants, and awards by category:* Academic interests/achievement: biological sciences, business, communication, education, engineering/technologies, English, foreign languages, general academic interests/achievements, home economics, humanities, international studies, mathematics, premedicine, religion/biblical studies, social sciences. Creative arts/performance: art/fine arts, music,

theater/drama. *Special achievements/activities:* community service, general special achievements/activities, hobbies/interests, leadership, memberships, religious involvement. *Special characteristics:* adult students, children and siblings of alumni, children of current students, children of educators, children of faculty/staff, ethnic background, first-generation college students, general special characteristics, local/state students, parents of current students, previous college experience, relatives of clergy, religious affiliation, siblings of current students, spouses of current students, veterans. *Tuition waivers:* Full or partial for employees or children of employees. *ROTC:* Army cooperative

LOANS *Student loans:* $3,001,508 (85% need-based, 15% non-need-based). 57% of past graduating class borrowed through all loan programs. *Average indebtedness per student:* $35,392. *Average need-based loan:* Freshmen: $5319. Undergraduates: $5880. *Parent loans:* $512,804 (67% need-based, 33% non-need-based). *Programs:* Federal Direct (Subsidized and Unsubsidized Stafford, PLUS), Perkins, state, college/university.

WORK-STUDY *Federal work-study:* Total amount: $35,196; jobs available. *State or other work-study/employment:* Total amount: $218,990 (30% need-based, 70% non-need-based). Part-time jobs available.

APPLYING FOR FINANCIAL AID *Required financial aid forms:* FAFSA, institution's own form, state aid form. *Financial aid deadline:* 6/1 (priority: 3/15). *Notification date:* Continuous beginning 10/1. Students must reply within 2 weeks of notification.

CONTACT Courtney Haynes, Director of Financial Aid, Wesleyan College, 4760 Forsyth Road, Macon, GA 31210-4462, 478-757-5205 or toll-free 800-447-6610. *Fax:* 478-757-4030. *E-mail:* financialaid@wesleyancollege.edu. *Website:* http://www.wesleyancollege.edu/.

WESLEYAN UNIVERSITY
Middletown, CT

Tuition & fees: $52,474	Average undergraduate aid package: $47,077

ABOUT THE INSTITUTION Independent, coed. *Awards:* certificates, bachelor's, master's, and doctoral degrees. 45 undergraduate majors. *Total enrollment:* 3,206. Undergraduates: 2,971. Freshmen: 774. Institutional methodology is used as a basis for awarding need-based institutional aid.

UNDERGRADUATE EXPENSES for 2017–2018 *Application fee:* $55. *Comprehensive fee:* $66,940 includes full-time tuition ($52,174), mandatory fees ($300), and room and board ($14,466). Room and board charges vary according to board plan and student level.

FRESHMAN FINANCIAL AID (Fall 2016, est.) 356 applied for aid; of those 96% were deemed to have need. 100% of freshmen with need received aid; of those 100% had need fully met. *Average percent of need met:* 100% (excluding resources awarded to replace EFC). *Average financial aid package:* $44,344 (excluding resources awarded to replace EFC). 1% of all full-time freshmen had no need and received non-need-based gift aid.

UNDERGRADUATE FINANCIAL AID (Fall 2016, est.) 1,336 applied for aid; of those 97% were deemed to have need. 100% of undergraduates with need received aid; of those 100% had need fully met. *Average percent of need met:* 100% (excluding resources awarded to replace EFC). *Average financial aid package:* $47,077 (excluding resources awarded to replace EFC). 1% of all full-time undergraduates had no need and received non-need-based gift aid.

GIFT AID (NEED-BASED) *Total amount:* $52,755,433 (6% federal, 90% institutional, 4% external sources). *Receiving aid:* Freshmen: 40% (311); all full-time undergraduates: 41% (1,206). *Average award:* Freshmen: $41,149; Undergraduates: $42,457. *Scholarships, grants, and awards:* Federal Pell, FSEOG, state, private, college/university gift aid from institutional funds.

GIFT AID (NON-NEED-BASED) *Total amount:* $972,462 (76% institutional, 24% external sources). *Receiving aid:* Freshmen: 2% (12). Undergraduates: 1% (38). *Average award:* Freshmen: $36,406. Undergraduates: $31,571. *Scholarships, grants, and awards by category:* Special characteristics: 23 awards ($735,622 total): international students, veterans, veterans' children. *ROTC:* Air Force cooperative.

LOANS *Student loans:* $6,263,382 (57% need-based, 43% non-need-based). 43% of past graduating class borrowed through all loan programs. *Average indebtedness per student:* $22,495. *Average need-based loan:* Freshmen: $3020. Undergrad-

uates: $4153. **Parent loans:** $3,391,427 (100% non-need-based). **Programs:** Federal Direct (Subsidized and Unsubsidized Stafford, PLUS), Perkins, college/university.
WORK-STUDY *Federal work-study:* Total amount: $2,494,811; 1,008 jobs averaging $2513. *State or other work-study/employment:* Total amount: $363,019 (100% need-based). 156 part-time jobs averaging $2419.
APPLYING FOR FINANCIAL AID *Required financial aid forms:* FAFSA, CSS Financial Aid PROFILE, noncustodial (divorced/separated) parent's statement, parent and student tax forms, W-2s, business tax returns. *Financial aid deadline:* 2/15. *Notification date:* 4/1. Students must reply by 5/1.
CONTACT Robert Coughlin, Director of Financial Aid, Wesleyan University, 237 High Street, Middletown, CT 06459-0260, 860-685-2800. *Fax:* 860-685-2801. *E-mail:* finaid@wesleyan.edu.
Website: http://www.wesleyan.edu/.

WESLEY COLLEGE
Dover, DE

CONTACT Mr. Michael Hall, Director of Student Financial Planning, Wesley College, 120 North State Street, Dover, DE 19901-3875, 302-736-2334 or toll-free 800-937-5398. *Fax:* 302-736-2594. *E-mail:* halljmic@wesley.edu.
Website: http://www.wesley.edu/.

WEST CHESTER UNIVERSITY OF PENNSYLVANIA
West Chester, PA

Tuition & fees (PA res): $9720	Average undergraduate aid package: $7871

ABOUT THE INSTITUTION State-supported, coed. **Awards:** certificates, bachelor's, master's, and doctoral degrees. 52 undergraduate majors. **Total enrollment:** 17,006. Undergraduates: 14,398. Freshmen: 2,454. Federal methodology is used as a basis for awarding need-based institutional aid.
UNDERGRADUATE EXPENSES for 2016–2017 *Application fee:* $45. *Tuition, state resident:* full-time $7238; part-time $302 per credit hour. *Tuition, nonresident:* full-time $18,096; part-time $754 per credit hour. *Required fees:* full-time $2482; $103 per credit hour. Full-time tuition and fees vary according to course load and location. Part-time tuition and fees vary according to course load and location. *College room and board:* $8736; *Room only:* $5276. Room and board charges vary according to board plan and housing facility.
FRESHMAN FINANCIAL AID (Fall 2015) 2,146 applied for aid; of those 70% were deemed to have need. 100% of freshmen with need received aid; of those 8% had need fully met. *Average percent of need met:* 41% (excluding resources awarded to replace EFC). *Average financial aid package:* $7063 (excluding resources awarded to replace EFC). 2% of all full-time freshmen had no need and received non-need-based gift aid.
UNDERGRADUATE FINANCIAL AID (Fall 2015) 10,042 applied for aid; of those 75% were deemed to have need. 100% of undergraduates with need received aid; of those 9% had need fully met. *Average percent of need met:* 48% (excluding resources awarded to replace EFC). *Average financial aid package:* $7871 (excluding resources awarded to replace EFC). 2% of all full-time undergraduates had no need and received non-need-based gift aid.
GIFT AID (NEED-BASED) *Total amount:* $31,118,865 (48% federal, 33% state, 9% institutional, 10% external sources). *Receiving aid:* Freshmen: 32% (771); all full-time undergraduates: 34% (4,350). *Average award:* Freshmen: $5864; Undergraduates: $5587. *Scholarships, grants, and awards:* Federal Pell, FSEOG, state, private, college/university gift aid from institutional funds.
GIFT AID (NON-NEED-BASED) *Total amount:* $2,402,031 (2% state, 46% institutional, 52% external sources). *Receiving aid:* Freshmen: 15% (369). Undergraduates: 10% (1,223). *Average award:* Freshmen: $3737. Undergraduates: $4180. *Scholarships, grants, and awards by category:* Academic interests/achievement: business, general academic interests/achievements, mathematics, social sciences. Creative arts/performance: art/fine arts, music, theater/drama. Special achievements/activities: leadership. Special characteristics: children of faculty/staff. *Tuition waivers:* Full or partial for employees or children of employees, senior citizens. *ROTC:* Army, Air Force cooperative.

LOANS *Student loans:* $106,339,972 (77% need-based, 23% non-need-based). 74% of past graduating class borrowed through all loan programs. *Average indebtedness per student:* $33,814. *Average need-based loan:* Freshmen: $3194. Undergraduates: $4133. *Parent loans:* $22,912,221 (100% non-need-based). *Programs:* Federal Direct (Subsidized and Unsubsidized Stafford, PLUS), Perkins, Federal Nursing.
WORK-STUDY *Federal work-study:* 286 jobs averaging $1571. *State or other work-study/employment:* Part-time jobs available.
ATHLETIC AWARDS Total amount: $1,176,553 (81% need-based, 19% non-need-based).
APPLYING FOR FINANCIAL AID *Required financial aid form:* FAFSA. *Financial aid deadline (priority):* 2/15. *Notification date:* Continuous beginning 3/15. Students must reply within 4 weeks of notification.
CONTACT Mr. Dana Parker, Financial Aid Director, West Chester University of Pennsylvania, 25 University Avenue, Suite 030, West Chester, PA 19383, 610-436-2627 or toll-free 877-315-2165 (in-state). *Fax:* 610-436-2574. *E-mail:* finaid@wcupa.edu.
Website: http://www.wcupa.edu/.

WEST COAST UNIVERSITY
Anaheim, CA

CONTACT Financial Aid Office, West Coast University, 1477 S. Manchester Avenue, Anaheim, CA 92802, 714-782-1700.
Website: http://westcoastuniversity.edu/.

WEST COAST UNIVERSITY
North Hollywood, CA

CONTACT Financial Aid Office, West Coast University, 12215 Victory Boulevard, North Hollywood, CA 91606, 323-315-5207 or toll-free 866-508-2684.
Website: http://www.westcoastuniversity.edu/.

WEST COAST UNIVERSITY
Ontario, CA

CONTACT Financial Aid Office, West Coast University, 2855 E. Guasti Road, Ontario, CA 91761, 909-467-6100.
Website: http://westcoastuniversity.edu/.

WEST COAST UNIVERSITY
Doral, FL

CONTACT Financial Aid Office, West Coast University, 9250 NW 36th Street, Doral, FL 33178, 786-501-7070.
Website: http://westcoastuniversity.edu/.

WEST COAST UNIVERSITY
Dallas, TX

CONTACT Financial Aid Office, West Coast University, 8435 N. Stemmons Freeway, Dallas, TX 75247, 214-453-4533 or toll-free 866-508-2684.
Website: http://www.westcoastuniversity.edu/.

WESTERN CAROLINA UNIVERSITY
Cullowhee, NC

Tuition & fees (NC res): $7027	Average undergraduate aid package: $18,861

ABOUT THE INSTITUTION State-supported, coed. *Awards:* certificates, bachelor's, master's, and doctoral degrees. 70 undergraduate majors. *Total enrollment:* 10,805. Undergraduates: 9,171. Freshmen: 1,925. Federal methodology is used as a basis for awarding need-based institutional aid.

UNDERGRADUATE EXPENSES for 2016–2017 *Application fee:* $65. *Tuition, state resident:* full-time $3893. *Tuition, nonresident:* full-time $14,286. *Required fees:* full-time $3134. Full-time tuition and fees vary according to degree level. Part-time tuition and fees vary according to course load and degree level. *College room and board:* $8864; *Room only:* $4438. Room and board charges vary according to board plan and housing facility.

FRESHMAN FINANCIAL AID (Fall 2015) 1,493 applied for aid; of those 76% were deemed to have need. 98% of freshmen with need received aid; of those 69% had need fully met. *Average percent of need met:* 87% (excluding resources awarded to replace EFC). *Average financial aid package:* $18,707 (excluding resources awarded to replace EFC). 5% of all full-time freshmen had no need and received non-need-based gift aid.

UNDERGRADUATE FINANCIAL AID (Fall 2015) 6,614 applied for aid; of those 82% were deemed to have need. 98% of undergraduates with need received aid; of those 68% had need fully met. *Average percent of need met:* 87% (excluding resources awarded to replace EFC). *Average financial aid package:* $18,861 (excluding resources awarded to replace EFC). 5% of all full-time undergraduates had no need and received non-need-based gift aid.

GIFT AID (NEED-BASED) *Total amount:* $31,260,699 (46% federal, 28% state, 20% institutional, 6% external sources). *Receiving aid:* Freshmen: 64% (1,046); all full-time undergraduates: 62% (4,929). *Average award:* Freshmen: $11,349; Undergraduates: $10,922. *Scholarships, grants, and awards:* Federal Pell, FSEOG, state, private, college/university gift aid from institutional funds.

GIFT AID (NON-NEED-BASED) *Total amount:* $1,990,361 (9% state, 54% institutional, 37% external sources). *Receiving aid:* Freshmen: 19% (310). Undergraduates: 13% (1,059). *Average award:* Freshmen: $5031. Undergraduates: $4648. *Scholarships, grants, and awards by category:* Academic interests/achievement: biological sciences, business, communication, education, English, general academic interests/achievements, mathematics. *Creative arts/performance:* art/fine arts, music, theater/drama. *Special characteristics:* ethnic background, handicapped students, local/state students, members of minority groups.

LOANS *Student loans:* $35,524,135 (74% need-based, 26% non-need-based). 62% of past graduating class borrowed through all loan programs. *Average indebtedness per student:* $20,201. *Average need-based loan:* Freshmen: $6933. Undergraduates: $8447. *Parent loans:* $15,644,006 (27% need-based, 73% non-need-based). *Programs:* Federal Direct (Subsidized and Unsubsidized Stafford, PLUS), Perkins.

WORK-STUDY *Federal work-study:* jobs available.

ATHLETIC AWARDS Total amount: $3,020,961 (56% need-based, 44% non-need-based).

APPLYING FOR FINANCIAL AID *Required financial aid forms:* FAFSA, institution's own form. *Financial aid deadline (priority):* 3/15. *Notification date:* Continuous beginning 4/1.

CONTACT Ms. Trina F. Orr, Director of Financial Aid, Western Carolina University, 123 Killian Annex, Cullowhee, NC 28723, 828-227-7292 or toll-free 877-WCU4YOU. *Fax:* 828-227-7042. *E-mail:* torr@email.wcu.edu. *Website:* http://www.wcu.edu/.

WESTERN CONNECTICUT STATE UNIVERSITY
Danbury, CT

Tuition & fees (CT res): $10,017	Average undergraduate aid package: $8426

ABOUT THE INSTITUTION State-supported, coed. *Awards:* certificates, associate, bachelor's, master's, and doctoral degrees. 37 undergraduate majors. *Total enrollment:* 5,721. Undergraduates: 5,181. Freshmen: 836. Federal methodology is used as a basis for awarding need-based institutional aid.

UNDERGRADUATE EXPENSES for 2016–2017 *Application fee:* $50. *Tuition, state resident:* full-time $5216; part-time $217 per credit hour. *Tuition, nonresident:* full-time $16,882; part-time $223 per credit hour. *Required fees:* full-time $4801; $256 per credit hour. Full-time tuition and fees vary according to course load, program, and reciprocity agreements. *College room and board:* $11,884; *Room only:* $6829. Room and board charges vary according to board plan and housing facility.

FRESHMAN FINANCIAL AID (Fall 2015) 583 applied for aid; of those 83% were deemed to have need. 98% of freshmen with need received aid; of those 10% had need fully met. *Average percent of need met:* 32% (excluding resources awarded to replace EFC). *Average financial aid package:* $8443 (excluding resources awarded to replace EFC). 1% of all full-time freshmen had no need and received non-need-based gift aid.

UNDERGRADUATE FINANCIAL AID (Fall 2015) 3,436 applied for aid; of those 84% were deemed to have need. 97% of undergraduates with need received aid; of those 8% had need fully met. *Average percent of need met:* 45% (excluding resources awarded to replace EFC). *Average financial aid package:* $8426 (excluding resources awarded to replace EFC). 1% of all full-time undergraduates had no need and received non-need-based gift aid.

GIFT AID (NEED-BASED) *Total amount:* $14,408,289 (54% federal, 12% state, 30% institutional, 4% external sources). *Receiving aid:* Freshmen: 65% (437); all full-time undergraduates: 57% (2,407). *Average award:* Freshmen: $5810; Undergraduates: $5251. *Scholarships, grants, and awards:* Federal Pell, FSEOG, state, private, college/university gift aid from institutional funds, Federal Nursing.

GIFT AID (NON-NEED-BASED) *Receiving aid:* Freshmen: 2% (11). Undergraduates: 1% (40). *Average award:* Freshmen: $9546. Undergraduates: $10,195. *Scholarships, grants, and awards by category:* Academic interests/achievement: 103 awards ($744,803 total): general academic interests/achievements. *Tuition waivers:* Full or partial for employees or children of employees, senior citizens. *ROTC:* Army cooperative, Air Force cooperative.

LOANS *Student loans:* $24,668,549 (100% need-based). 77% of past graduating class borrowed through all loan programs. *Average indebtedness per student:* $31,229. *Average need-based loan:* Freshmen: $3150. Undergraduates: $4234. *Parent loans:* $5,137,209 (100% need-based). *Programs:* Federal Direct (Subsidized and Unsubsidized Stafford, PLUS), Perkins.

WORK-STUDY *Federal work-study:* 81 jobs averaging $2478. *State or other work-study/employment:* Part-time jobs available.

APPLYING FOR FINANCIAL AID *Required financial aid form:* FAFSA. *Financial aid deadline:* 3/15 (priority: 3/1). *Notification date:* Continuous beginning 3/20. Students must reply by 5/1 or within 2 weeks of notification.

CONTACT Melissa Stephens, Director of Student Financial Services, Western Connecticut State University, 181 White Street, Danbury, CT 06810-6860, 203-837-8582 or toll-free 877-837-WCSU. *Fax:* 203-837-8528. *E-mail:* stephensm@wcsu.edu. *Website:* http://www.wcsu.edu/.

WESTERN GOVERNORS UNIVERSITY
Salt Lake City, UT

CONTACT Robert Collins, Vice President of Financial Aid, Western Governors University, 4001 South 700 East, Suite 700, Salt Lake City, UT 84107, 877-435-7948 or toll-free 866-225-5948. *Fax:* 801-907-7727. *E-mail:* robert.collins@wgu.edu. *Website:* http://www.wgu.edu/.

WESTERN ILLINOIS UNIVERSITY
Macomb, IL

Tuition & fees (IL res): $11,245	Average undergraduate aid package: $11,646

ABOUT THE INSTITUTION State-supported, coed. *Awards:* certificates, bachelor's, master's, and doctoral degrees. 63 undergraduate majors. *Total enrollment:* 10,373. Undergraduates: 8,543. Freshmen: 1,527. Federal methodology is used as a basis for awarding need-based institutional aid.

UNDERGRADUATE EXPENSES for 2016–2017 *Application fee:* $30. *Tuition, state resident:* full-time $8541; part-time $284.70 per credit hour. *Tuition, nonresident:* full-time $12,812; part-time $427.05 per credit hour. *Required fees:* full-time $2704; $90.12 per credit hour. Full-time tuition and fees vary according to course load, location, and student level. Part-time tuition and fees vary according to course load, location, and student level. *College room and board:* $9580; *Room only:* $5880. Room and board charges vary according to board plan, housing facility, and student level. *Payment plan:* Guaranteed tuition.

FRESHMAN FINANCIAL AID (Fall 2016, est.) 1,367 applied for aid; of those 88% were deemed to have need. 99% of freshmen with need received aid; of those 25% had need fully met. *Average percent of need met:* 63% (excluding resources awarded to replace EFC). *Average financial aid package:* $12,676 (excluding resources awarded to replace EFC). 5% of all full-time freshmen had no need and received non-need-based gift aid.

UNDERGRADUATE FINANCIAL AID (Fall 2016, est.) 6,376 applied for aid; of those 88% were deemed to have need. 99% of undergraduates with need received aid; of those 27% had need fully met. *Average percent of need met:* 59% (excluding resources awarded to replace EFC). *Average financial aid package:* $11,646 (excluding resources awarded to replace EFC). 4% of all full-time undergraduates had no need and received non-need-based gift aid.

GIFT AID (NEED-BASED) Total amount: $41,396,724 (44% federal, 35% state, 19% institutional, 2% external sources). *Receiving aid:* Freshmen: 63% (926); all full-time undergraduates: 51% (3,823). *Average award:* Freshmen: $10,459; Undergraduates: $8952. *Scholarships, grants, and awards:* Federal Pell, FSEOG, state, private, college/university gift aid from institutional funds.

GIFT AID (NON-NEED-BASED) Total amount: $4,273,221 (27% state, 62% institutional, 11% external sources). *Receiving aid:* Freshmen: 46% (674). Undergraduates: 33% (2,497). *Average award:* Freshmen: $2024. Undergraduates: $3072. *Scholarships, grants, and awards by category: Academic interests/achievement:* 4,378 awards ($7,091,977 total): agriculture, area/ethnic studies, biological sciences, business, communication, computer science, education, engineering/technologies, English, foreign languages, general academic interests/achievements, health fields, home economics, international studies, library science, mathematics, military science, physical sciences, religion/biblical studies, social sciences. *Creative arts/performance:* 583 awards ($640,493 total): applied art and design, art/fine arts, cinema/film/broadcasting, creative writing, dance, debating, general creative arts/performance, journalism/publications, music, performing arts, theater/drama. *Special achievements/activities:* 199 awards ($159,505 total): community service, general special achievements/activities, leadership. *Special characteristics:* 1,584 awards ($2,863,533 total): children of faculty/staff, general special characteristics, international students, members of minority groups, veterans' children. *Tuition waivers:* Full or partial for employees or children of employees, senior citizens. *ROTC:* Army.

LOANS Student loans: $52,138,736 (40% need-based, 60% non-need-based). 83% of past graduating class borrowed through all loan programs. *Average indebtedness per student:* $30,721. *Average need-based loan:* Freshmen: $3382. Undergraduates: $4269. *Parent loans:* $9,108,834 (84% need-based, 16% non-need-based). *Programs:* Federal Direct (Subsidized and Unsubsidized Stafford, PLUS), Perkins, college/university, private loans.

WORK-STUDY Federal work-study: Total amount: $486,195; 183 jobs averaging $2508. *State or other work-study/employment:* Total amount: $1,660,263 (79% need-based, 21% non-need-based). 1,498 part-time jobs averaging $1528.

ATHLETIC AWARDS Total amount: $3,547,192 (41% need-based, 59% non-need-based).

APPLYING FOR FINANCIAL AID *Required financial aid form:* FAFSA. *Financial aid deadline (priority):* 2/15. *Notification date:* Continuous beginning 1/15.

CONTACT Office of Financial Aid, Western Illinois University, 1 University Circle, Macomb, IL 61455-1390, 309-298-2446 or toll-free 877-742-5948. *Fax:* 309-298-2353. *E-mail:* finaid@wiu.edu. *Website:* http://www.wiu.edu/.

WESTERN KENTUCKY UNIVERSITY
Bowling Green, KY

Tuition & fees (KY res): $9912	Average undergraduate aid package: $14,221

ABOUT THE INSTITUTION State-supported, coed. *Awards:* certificates, associate, bachelor's, master's, and doctoral degrees. 96 undergraduate majors. *Total enrollment:* 20,271. Undergraduates: 17,595. Freshmen: 3,192. Federal methodology is used as a basis for awarding need-based institutional aid.

UNDERGRADUATE EXPENSES for 2016–2017 *Application fee:* $45. *Tuition, state resident:* full-time $9912; part-time $413 per credit hour. *Tuition, nonresident:* full-time $24,792; part-time $1033 per credit hour. Full-time tuition and fees vary according to program and reciprocity agreements. Part-time tuition and fees vary according to course load, program, and reciprocity agreements. *College room and board:* $7713; *Room only:* $4463. Room and board charges vary according to board plan and housing facility.

FRESHMAN FINANCIAL AID (Fall 2015) 2,703 applied for aid; of those 75% were deemed to have need. 99% of freshmen with need received aid; of those 36% had need fully met. *Average percent of need met:* 36% (excluding resources awarded to replace EFC). *Average financial aid package:* $13,586 (excluding resources awarded to replace EFC). 14% of all full-time freshmen had no need and received non-need-based gift aid.

UNDERGRADUATE FINANCIAL AID (Fall 2015) 10,141 applied for aid; of those 79% were deemed to have need. 98% of undergraduates with need received aid; of those 33% had need fully met. *Average percent of need met:* 33% (excluding resources awarded to replace EFC). *Average financial aid package:* $14,221 (excluding resources awarded to replace EFC). 13% of all full-time undergraduates had no need and received non-need-based gift aid.

GIFT AID (NEED-BASED) Total amount: $30,088,220 (76% federal, 19% state, 5% institutional). *Receiving aid:* Freshmen: 39% (1,199); all full-time undergraduates: 39% (5,106). *Average award:* Freshmen: $5387; Undergraduates: $5165. *Scholarships, grants, and awards:* Federal Pell, FSEOG, state, private, college/university gift aid from institutional funds, United Negro College Fund.

GIFT AID (NON-NEED-BASED) Total amount: $42,257,094 (7% federal, 28% state, 59% institutional, 6% external sources). *Receiving aid:* Freshmen: 58% (1,783). Undergraduates: 42% (5,448). *Average award:* Freshmen: $6769. Undergraduates: $6745. *Scholarships, grants, and awards by category: Academic interests/achievement:* 4,001 awards ($17,515,118 total): agriculture, biological sciences, business, communication, education, engineering/technologies, English, foreign languages, general academic interests/achievements, health fields, home economics, mathematics, military science, physical sciences, premedicine, religion/biblical studies, social sciences. *Creative arts/performance:* 510 awards ($1,442,367 total): art/fine arts, cinema/film/broadcasting, dance, debating, general creative arts/performance, journalism/publications, music, theater/drama. *Special achievements/activities:* 760 awards ($2,123,891 total): general special achievements/activities, leadership, memberships. *Special characteristics:* 1,249 awards ($3,155,527 total): adult students, children of union members/company employees, ethnic background, general special characteristics, handicapped students, international students, local/state students, members of minority groups, out-of-state students, religious affiliation, veterans, veterans' children. *Tuition waivers:* Full or partial for employees or children of employees, senior citizens. *ROTC:* Army, Air Force cooperative.

LOANS Student loans: $57,444,858 (42% need-based, 58% non-need-based). 61% of past graduating class borrowed through all loan programs. *Average indebtedness per student:* $28,081. *Average need-based loan:* Freshmen: $3058. Undergraduates: $3847. *Parent loans:* $15,889,744 (100% non-need-based). *Programs:* Federal Direct (Subsidized and Unsubsidized Stafford, PLUS), Perkins.

WORK-STUDY Federal work-study: 583 jobs averaging $2050. *State or other work-study/employment:* Total amount: $4,462,501 (100% non-need-based). 1,825 part-time jobs averaging $2717.

ATHLETIC AWARDS Total amount: $5,796,821 (100% non-need-based).

APPLYING FOR FINANCIAL AID *Required financial aid form:* FAFSA. *Financial aid deadline (priority):* 2/15. *Notification date:* Continuous beginning 3/1.

CONTACT Cindy Burnette, Director of Student Financial Assistance, Western Kentucky University, Potter Hall, Room 317, Bowling Green, KY 42101-1018, 270-745-2758 or toll-free 800-495-8463. *Fax:* 270-745-6586. *E-mail:* cindy.burnette@wku.edu. *Website:* http://www.wku.edu/.

WESTERN MICHIGAN UNIVERSITY
Kalamazoo, MI

Tuition & fees (MI res): $11,493	Average undergraduate aid package: $13,577

ABOUT THE INSTITUTION State-supported, coed. *Awards:* certificates, bachelor's, master's, and doctoral degrees. 148 undergraduate majors. *Total enrollment:* 23,252. Undergraduates: 18,313. Freshmen: 2,930. Federal methodology is used as a basis for awarding need-based institutional aid.

UNDERGRADUATE EXPENSES for 2016–2017 *Application fee:* $40. *One-time required fee:* $300. *Tuition, state resident:* full-time $10,570; part-time $384.42 per credit hour. *Tuition, nonresident:* full-time $25,928; part-time $943.05 per credit hour. *Required fees:* full-time $923; $258.50 per term. Full-time tuition and fees vary according to course load, location, program, reciprocity agreements, and student level. Part-time tuition and fees vary according to course load, location, program, reciprocity agreements, and student level. *College room and board:* $9561; *Room only:* $4931. Room and board charges vary according to board plan and housing facility.

FRESHMAN FINANCIAL AID (Fall 2015) 2,547 applied for aid; of those 79% were deemed to have need. 98% of freshmen with need received aid; of those 30% had need fully met. *Average percent of need met:* 80% (excluding resources awarded to replace EFC). *Average financial aid package:* $15,083 (excluding resources awarded to replace EFC). 11% of all full-time freshmen had no need and received non-need-based gift aid.

UNDERGRADUATE FINANCIAL AID (Fall 2015) 13,633 applied for aid; of those 78% were deemed to have need. 97% of undergraduates with need received aid; of those 22% had need fully met. *Average percent of need met:* 75% (excluding resources awarded to replace EFC). *Average financial aid package:* $13,577 (excluding resources awarded to replace EFC). 9% of all full-time undergraduates had no need and received non-need-based gift aid.

GIFT AID (NEED-BASED) *Total amount:* $46,510,896 (62% federal, 3% state, 35% institutional). *Receiving aid:* Freshmen: 45% (1,334); all full-time undergraduates: 48% (7,426). *Average award:* Freshmen: $7104; Undergraduates: $5616. *Scholarships, grants, and awards:* Federal Pell, FSEOG, state, private, college/university gift aid from institutional funds.

GIFT AID (NON-NEED-BASED) *Total amount:* $25,871,748 (68% institutional, 32% external sources). *Receiving aid:* Freshmen: 35% (1,047). Undergraduates: 21% (3,237). *Average award:* Freshmen: $6060. Undergraduates: $5760. *Scholarships, grants, and awards by category: Academic interests/achievement:* general academic interests/achievements. *Creative arts/performance:* art/fine arts, dance, general creative arts/performance, music, theater/drama. *Special characteristics:* children and siblings of alumni, children of faculty/staff, international students, local/state students, out-of-state students, previous college experience, veterans. *Tuition waivers:* Full or partial for employees or children of employees, senior citizens. *ROTC:* Army.

LOANS *Student loans:* $101,892,294 (70% need-based, 30% non-need-based). 75% of past graduating class borrowed through all loan programs. *Average indebtedness per student:* $35,454. *Average need-based loan:* Freshmen: $3375. Undergraduates: $4471. *Parent loans:* $26,244,140 (50% need-based, 50% non-need-based). *Programs:* Federal Direct (Subsidized and Unsubsidized Stafford, PLUS), Perkins, private loans.

WORK-STUDY *Federal work-study:* jobs available. *State or other work-study/employment:* Part-time jobs available.

ATHLETIC AWARDS Total amount: $7,721,505 (100% non-need-based).

APPLYING FOR FINANCIAL AID *Required financial aid form:* FAFSA. *Financial aid deadline (priority):* 3/1. *Notification date:* Continuous beginning 12/10.

CONTACT Ms. Terrell Hodge, Interim Director of Financial Aid, Western Michigan University, Faunce Student Services, 1903 West Michigan Avenue, Kalamazoo, MI 49008-5337, 269-387-6000. *E-mail:* finaid-info@wmich.edu. *Website:* http://www.wmich.edu/.

WESTERN NEW ENGLAND UNIVERSITY
Springfield, MA

Tuition & fees: $34,874	Average undergraduate aid package: $25,735

ABOUT THE INSTITUTION Independent, coed. *Awards:* certificates, associate, bachelor's, master's, and doctoral degrees. 51 undergraduate majors. *Total enrollment:* 3,833. Undergraduates: 2,724. Freshmen: 723. Federal methodology is used as a basis for awarding need-based institutional aid.

UNDERGRADUATE EXPENSES for 2016–2017 *Application fee:* $40. *Comprehensive fee:* $48,088 includes full-time tuition ($32,524), mandatory fees ($2350), and room and board ($13,214). Full-time tuition and fees vary according to course load and program. Room and board charges vary according to board plan and housing facility. *Part-time tuition:* $613 per credit hour. Part-time tuition and fees vary according to course load and program. *Payment plan:* Tuition prepayment.

FRESHMAN FINANCIAL AID (Fall 2016, est.) 677 applied for aid; of those 90% were deemed to have need. 100% of freshmen with need received aid; of those 14% had need fully met. *Average percent of need met:* 74% (excluding resources awarded to replace EFC). *Average financial aid package:* $26,179 (excluding resources awarded to replace EFC). 16% of all full-time freshmen had no need and received non-need-based gift aid.

UNDERGRADUATE FINANCIAL AID (Fall 2016, est.) 2,201 applied for aid; of those 91% were deemed to have need. 100% of undergraduates with need received aid; of those 14% had need fully met. *Average percent of need met:* 74% (excluding resources awarded to replace EFC). *Average financial aid package:* $25,735 (excluding resources awarded to replace EFC). 16% of all full-time undergraduates had no need and received non-need-based gift aid.

GIFT AID (NEED-BASED) *Total amount:* $35,864,013 (10% federal, 1% state, 89% institutional). *Receiving aid:* Freshmen: 84% (606); all full-time undergraduates: 78% (2,006). *Average award:* Freshmen: $21,486; Undergraduates: $20,616. *Scholarships, grants, and awards:* Federal Pell, FSEOG, state, private, college/university gift aid from institutional funds.

GIFT AID (NON-NEED-BASED) *Total amount:* $7,629,417 (9% federal, 5% state, 81% institutional, 5% external sources). *Receiving aid:* Freshmen: 9% (65). Undergraduates: 7% (175). *Average award:* Freshmen: $13,535. Undergraduates: $13,110. *Scholarships, grants, and awards by category: Academic interests/achievement:* business, computer science, general academic interests/achievements, home economics. *Creative arts/performance:* music. *Special achievements/activities:* leadership. *Special characteristics:* children of faculty/staff, siblings of current students. *Tuition waivers:* Full or partial for employees or children of employees, senior citizens. *ROTC:* Army, Air Force cooperative.

LOANS *Student loans:* $22,599,820 (59% need-based, 41% non-need-based). 84% of past graduating class borrowed through all loan programs. *Average indebtedness per student:* $44,013. *Average need-based loan:* Freshmen: $3654. Undergraduates: $4663. *Parent loans:* $7,503,907 (50% need-based, 50% non-need-based). *Programs:* Federal Direct (Subsidized and Unsubsidized Stafford, PLUS), Perkins.

WORK-STUDY *Federal work-study:* Total amount: $2,138,299; 1,075 jobs averaging $1983. *State or other work-study/employment:* Total amount: $904,432 (100% need-based). Part-time jobs available.

APPLYING FOR FINANCIAL AID *Required financial aid forms:* FAFSA, FAFSA using IRS Data Retrieval Tool. *Financial aid deadline (priority):* 4/15. *Notification date:* Continuous beginning 3/1. Students must reply by 5/1 or within 2 weeks of notification.

CONTACT Ms. Kathy M. Chambers, Director of Financial Aid, Western New England University, 1215 Wilbraham Road, Springfield, MA 01119-2684, 413-796-2080 or toll-free 800-325-1122 Ext. 1321. *Fax:* 413-796-2081. *E-mail:* finaid@wne.edu. *Website:* http://www.wne.edu/.

WESTERN NEW MEXICO UNIVERSITY
Silver City, NM

ABOUT THE INSTITUTION State-supported, coed. 58 undergraduate majors.
GIFT AID (NEED-BASED) *Scholarships, grants, and awards:* Federal Pell, FSEOG, state, private, college/university gift aid from institutional funds.

GIFT AID (NON-NEED-BASED) *Scholarships, grants, and awards by category:* *Academic interests/achievement:* general academic interests/achievements. *Creative arts/performance:* performing arts. *Special achievements/activities:* general special achievements/activities. *Special characteristics:* general special characteristics, veterans.

LOANS *Programs:* Federal Direct (Subsidized and Unsubsidized Stafford, PLUS), Perkins, state, college/university.

APPLYING FOR FINANCIAL AID *Required financial aid forms:* FAFSA, institution's own form.

CONTACT Debra Reyes, Assistant Director, Western New Mexico University, PO Box 680, Silver City, NM 88062, 575-538-6173 or toll-free 800-872-WNMU. *Fax:* 575-538-6189. *E-mail:* reyesd@wnmu.edu.
Website: http://www.wnmu.edu/.

WESTERN OREGON UNIVERSITY
Monmouth, OR

Tuition & fees (OR res): $9285	Average undergraduate aid package: $9924

ABOUT THE INSTITUTION State-supported, coed. *Awards:* certificates, bachelor's, and master's degrees. 35 undergraduate majors. *Total enrollment:* 5,382. Undergraduates: 4,833. Freshmen: 886. Federal methodology is used as a basis for awarding need-based institutional aid.

UNDERGRADUATE EXPENSES for 2016–2017 *Application fee:* $60. *Tuition, state resident:* full-time $9285. *Tuition, nonresident:* full-time $23,445. Full-time tuition and fees vary according to course load. Part-time tuition and fees vary according to course load. *College room and board:* $9798; *Room only:* $8148. Room and board charges vary according to board plan and housing facility. *Payment plan:* Guaranteed tuition.

FRESHMAN FINANCIAL AID (Fall 2015) 724 applied for aid; of those 79% were deemed to have need. 100% of freshmen with need received aid; of those 9% had need fully met. *Average percent of need met:* 57% (excluding resources awarded to replace EFC). *Average financial aid package:* $9792 (excluding resources awarded to replace EFC). 20% of all full-time freshmen had no need and received non-need-based gift aid.

UNDERGRADUATE FINANCIAL AID (Fall 2015) 3,171 applied for aid; of those 85% were deemed to have need. 100% of undergraduates with need received aid; of those 8% had need fully met. *Average percent of need met:* 55% (excluding resources awarded to replace EFC). *Average financial aid package:* $9924 (excluding resources awarded to replace EFC). 9% of all full-time undergraduates had no need and received non-need-based gift aid.

GIFT AID (NEED-BASED) *Total amount:* $14,182,402 (59% federal, 18% state, 8% institutional, 15% external sources). *Receiving aid:* Freshmen: 74% (553); all full-time undergraduates: 73% (2,450). *Average award:* Freshmen: $7060; Undergraduates: $6807. *Scholarships, grants, and awards:* Federal Pell, FSEOG, state, private, college/university gift aid from institutional funds, United Negro College Fund, TEACH Grants.

GIFT AID (NON-NEED-BASED) *Total amount:* $978,543 (1% federal, 42% institutional, 57% external sources). *Receiving aid:* Freshmen: 3% (22). Undergraduates: 2% (74). *Average award:* Freshmen: $505. Undergraduates: $1212. *Scholarships, grants, and awards by category:* Academic interests/achievement: 1,693 awards ($1,365,315 total): biological sciences, business, communication, computer science, education, English, foreign languages, general academic interests/achievements, home economics, humanities, international studies, library science, mathematics, physical sciences, premedicine, social sciences. *Creative arts/performance:* 80 awards ($64,952 total): art/fine arts, dance, general creative arts/performance, music, performing arts, theater/drama. *Special achievements/activities:* 289 awards ($284,925 total): community service, general special achievements/activities, hobbies/interests, leadership. *Special characteristics:* 545 awards ($1,253,368 total): adult students, children of union members/company employees, ethnic background, first-generation college students, general special characteristics, handicapped students, international students, local/state students, members of minority groups, previous college experience, veterans, veterans' children. *ROTC:* Army cooperative.

LOANS *Student loans:* $21,262,325 (79% need-based, 21% non-need-based). 66% of past graduating class borrowed through all loan programs. *Average indebtedness per student:* $30,586. *Average need-based loan:* Freshmen: $3132. Undergraduates: $3966. *Parent loans:* $6,471,929 (36% need-based, 64% non-need-based). *Programs:* Federal Direct (Subsidized and Unsubsidized Stafford, PLUS), Perkins.

WORK-STUDY *Federal work-study:* 260 jobs averaging $1048.

ATHLETIC AWARDS *Total amount:* $686,820 (69% need-based, 31% non-need-based).

APPLYING FOR FINANCIAL AID *Required financial aid form:* FAFSA. *Financial aid deadline:* Continuous. *Notification date:* Continuous beginning 3/25.

CONTACT Ms. Kella Helyer, Director of Financial Aid, Western Oregon University, 345 Monmouth Avenue North, Monmouth, OR 97361, 503-838-8475 or toll-free 877-877-1593. *Fax:* 503-838-8200. *E-mail:* finaid@wou.edu.
Website: http://www.wou.edu/.

WESTERN STATE COLORADO UNIVERSITY
Gunnison, CO

Tuition & fees (CO res): $9193	Average undergraduate aid package: $9806

ABOUT THE INSTITUTION State-supported, coed. *Awards:* certificates, bachelor's, and master's degrees. 70 undergraduate majors. *Total enrollment:* 2,907. Undergraduates: 2,495. Freshmen: 469. Federal methodology is used as a basis for awarding need-based institutional aid.

UNDERGRADUATE EXPENSES for 2016–2017 *Application fee:* $30. *Tuition, state resident:* full-time $6312; part-time $263 per credit hour. *Tuition, nonresident:* full-time $17,616; part-time $734 per credit hour. *Required fees:* full-time $2881. Full-time tuition and fees vary according to course load and reciprocity agreements. Part-time tuition and fees vary according to course load and reciprocity agreements. *College room and board:* $9446; *Room only:* $4930. Room and board charges vary according to board plan and housing facility.

FRESHMAN FINANCIAL AID (Fall 2016, est.) 433 applied for aid; of those 64% were deemed to have need. 100% of freshmen with need received aid; of those 9% had need fully met. *Average percent of need met:* 60% (excluding resources awarded to replace EFC). *Average financial aid package:* $9105 (excluding resources awarded to replace EFC). 27% of all full-time freshmen had no need and received non-need-based gift aid.

UNDERGRADUATE FINANCIAL AID (Fall 2016, est.) 1,715 applied for aid; of those 63% were deemed to have need. 100% of undergraduates with need received aid; of those 7% had need fully met. *Average percent of need met:* 61% (excluding resources awarded to replace EFC). *Average financial aid package:* $9806 (excluding resources awarded to replace EFC). 25% of all full-time undergraduates had no need and received non-need-based gift aid.

GIFT AID (NEED-BASED) *Total amount:* $8,015,906 (31% federal, 11% state, 53% institutional, 5% external sources). *Receiving aid:* Freshmen: 54% (249); all full-time undergraduates: 51% (973). *Average award:* Freshmen: $7083; Undergraduates: $7399. *Scholarships, grants, and awards:* Federal Pell, FSEOG, state, private, college/university gift aid from institutional funds.

GIFT AID (NON-NEED-BASED) *Total amount:* $3,406,070 (1% state, 84% institutional, 15% external sources). *Receiving aid:* Freshmen: 54% (249). Undergraduates: 27% (506). *Average award:* Freshmen: $2465. Undergraduates: $4311. *Scholarships, grants, and awards by category:* Academic interests/achievement: general academic interests/achievements. *Creative arts/performance:* art/fine arts, music, performing arts. *Special achievements/activities:* leadership. *Special characteristics:* children and siblings of alumni. *Tuition waivers:* Full or partial for employees or children of employees, senior citizens.

LOANS *Student loans:* $10,987,521 (83% need-based, 17% non-need-based). 67% of past graduating class borrowed through all loan programs. *Average indebtedness per student:* $25,589. *Average need-based loan:* Freshmen: $3142. Undergraduates: $3846. *Parent loans:* $3,835,425 (71% need-based, 29% non-need-based). *Programs:* Federal Direct (Subsidized and Unsubsidized Stafford, PLUS), Perkins.

WORK-STUDY *Federal work-study:* Total amount: $123,892; 105 jobs averaging $1200. *State or other work-study/employment:* Total amount: $218,092 (43% need-based, 57% non-need-based). 150 part-time jobs averaging $1050.

ATHLETIC AWARDS *Total amount:* $2,198,651 (68% need-based, 32% non-need-based).

APPLYING FOR FINANCIAL AID *Required financial aid form:* FAFSA. *Financial aid deadline (priority):* 3/1. *Notification date:* Continuous beginning 3/1. Students must reply within 3 weeks of notification.

CONTACT Carrie Shaw, Director of Financial Aid, Western State Colorado University, Taylor Hall, Gunnison, CO 81231, 970-943-3026 or toll-free 800-876-5309. *Fax:* 970-943-3086. *E-mail:* cshaw@western.edu.
Website: http://www.western.edu/.

WESTERN WASHINGTON UNIVERSITY
Bellingham, WA

Tuition & fees (WA res): $7653	Average undergraduate aid package: $14,074

ABOUT THE INSTITUTION State-supported, coed. *Awards:* certificates, bachelor's, and master's degrees. 111 undergraduate majors. *Total enrollment:* 15,574. Undergraduates: 14,592. Freshmen: 2,888. Federal methodology is used as a basis for awarding need-based institutional aid.

UNDERGRADUATE EXPENSES for 2016–2017 Application fee: $55. *Tuition, state resident:* full-time $6116. *Tuition, nonresident:* full-time $20,060. *Required fees:* full-time $1537; $224 per credit hour. Full-time tuition and fees vary according to course load, location, and reciprocity agreements. Part-time tuition and fees vary according to course load, location, and reciprocity agreements. *College room and board:* $10,755. Room and board charges vary according to board plan, housing facility, and location.

FRESHMAN FINANCIAL AID (Fall 2016, est.) 2,353 applied for aid; of those 60% were deemed to have need. 97% of freshmen with need received aid; of those 20% had need fully met. *Average percent of need met:* 86% (excluding resources awarded to replace EFC). *Average financial aid package:* $13,714 (excluding resources awarded to replace EFC). 3% of all full-time freshmen had no need and received non-need-based gift aid.

UNDERGRADUATE FINANCIAL AID (Fall 2016, est.) 8,977 applied for aid; of those 72% were deemed to have need. 97% of undergraduates with need received aid; of those 16% had need fully met. *Average percent of need met:* 87% (excluding resources awarded to replace EFC). *Average financial aid package:* $14,074 (excluding resources awarded to replace EFC). 2% of all full-time undergraduates had no need and received non-need-based gift aid.

GIFT AID (NEED-BASED) Total amount: $38,550,085 (42% federal, 39% state, 14% institutional, 5% external sources). *Receiving aid:* Freshmen: 43% (1,229); all full-time undergraduates: 37% (4,977). *Average award:* Freshmen: $8614; Undergraduates: $8999. *Scholarships, grants, and awards:* Federal Pell, FSEOG, state, private, college/university gift aid from institutional funds.

GIFT AID (NON-NEED-BASED) Total amount: $2,543,298 (1% federal, 5% state, 43% institutional, 51% external sources). *Receiving aid:* Freshmen: 4% (118). Undergraduates: 2% (231). *Average award:* Freshmen: $2009. Undergraduates: $2068. *Scholarships, grants, and awards by category:* Academic interests/achievement: biological sciences, business, communication, computer science, education, engineering/technologies, English, foreign languages, general academic interests/achievements, health fields, humanities, library science, mathematics, physical sciences, premedicine, social sciences. *Creative arts/performance:* applied art and design, art/fine arts, cinema/film/broadcasting, creative writing, dance, general creative arts/performance, journalism/publications, music, performing arts, theater/drama. *Special achievements/activities:* community service, leadership, memberships. *Special characteristics:* children of public servants, children of union members/company employees, ethnic background, general special characteristics, international students, local/state students, members of minority groups, previous college experience, veterans. *Tuition waivers:* Full or partial for minority students, employees or children of employees, senior citizens.

LOANS Student loans: $50,306,013 (65% need-based, 35% non-need-based). 55% of past graduating class borrowed through all loan programs. *Average indebtedness per student:* $19,727. *Average need-based loan:* Freshmen: $3952. Undergraduates: $4490. *Parent loans:* $44,021,959 (24% need-based, 76% non-need-based). *Programs:* Federal Direct (Subsidized and Unsubsidized Stafford, PLUS), Perkins, college/university, alternative loans.

WORK-STUDY Federal work-study: Total amount: $835,424; 238 jobs averaging $3510. *State or other work-study/employment:* Total amount: $1,468,785 (100% need-based). 423 part-time jobs averaging $3472.

ATHLETIC AWARDS Total amount: $1,438,349 (36% need-based, 64% non-need-based).

APPLYING FOR FINANCIAL AID *Required financial aid form:* FAFSA. *Financial aid deadline (priority):* 2/15. *Notification date:* Continuous beginning 3/20. Students must reply by 5/1 or within 3 weeks of notification.
CONTACT Mrs. Christy Jensen, Associate Director of Financial Aid, Systems, Western Washington University, Old Main 260C, MS 9006, 516 High Street, Bellingham, WA 98225-9006, 360-650-4088. *E-mail:* christina.jensen@wwu.edu.
Website: http://www.wwu.edu/.

WESTFIELD STATE UNIVERSITY
Westfield, MA

Tuition & fees (MA res): $9275	Average undergraduate aid package: $8386

ABOUT THE INSTITUTION State-supported, coed. *Awards:* certificates, bachelor's, and master's degrees. 40 undergraduate majors. *Total enrollment:* 6,383. Undergraduates: 5,610. Freshmen: 1,068. Federal methodology is used as a basis for awarding need-based institutional aid.

UNDERGRADUATE EXPENSES for 2016–2017 Application fee: $50. *Tuition, state resident:* full-time $970; part-time $297 per credit hour. *Tuition, nonresident:* full-time $7050; part-time $297 per credit hour. *Required fees:* full-time $8305; $75 per term. Full-time tuition and fees vary according to program and reciprocity agreements. Part-time tuition and fees vary according to course load. *College room and board:* $10,396. Room and board charges vary according to board plan and housing facility.

FRESHMAN FINANCIAL AID (Fall 2015) 1,205 applied for aid; of those 77% were deemed to have need. 97% of freshmen with need received aid; of those 8% had need fully met. *Average percent of need met:* 58% (excluding resources awarded to replace EFC). *Average financial aid package:* $8371 (excluding resources awarded to replace EFC). 1% of all full-time freshmen had no need and received non-need-based gift aid.

UNDERGRADUATE FINANCIAL AID (Fall 2015) 4,076 applied for aid; of those 78% were deemed to have need. 96% of undergraduates with need received aid; of those 11% had need fully met. *Average percent of need met:* 62% (excluding resources awarded to replace EFC). *Average financial aid package:* $8386 (excluding resources awarded to replace EFC). 2% of all full-time undergraduates had no need and received non-need-based gift aid.

GIFT AID (NEED-BASED) Total amount: $14,598,049 (52% federal, 27% state, 16% institutional, 5% external sources). *Receiving aid:* Freshmen: 52% (672); all full-time undergraduates: 45% (2,208). *Average award:* Freshmen: $6242; Undergraduates: $5693. *Scholarships, grants, and awards:* Federal Pell, FSEOG, state, private, college/university gift aid from institutional funds.

GIFT AID (NON-NEED-BASED) Total amount: $722,883 (30% state, 36% institutional, 34% external sources). *Receiving aid:* Freshmen: 23% (301). Undergraduates: 16% (778). *Average award:* Freshmen: $4585. Undergraduates: $3904. *Scholarships, grants, and awards by category:* Academic interests/achievement: general academic interests/achievements. *Tuition waivers:* Full or partial for employees or children of employees, senior citizens. *ROTC:* Army cooperative, Air Force cooperative.

LOANS Student loans: $31,677,223 (65% need-based, 35% non-need-based). 83% of past graduating class borrowed through all loan programs. *Average indebtedness per student:* $29,602. *Average need-based loan:* Freshmen: $3205. Undergraduates: $4026. *Parent loans:* $6,313,061 (29% need-based, 71% non-need-based). *Programs:* Federal Direct (Subsidized and Unsubsidized Stafford, PLUS), Perkins.

WORK-STUDY Federal work-study: 333 jobs averaging $1461. *State or other work-study/employment:* Total amount: $1,833,502 (100% non-need-based). Part-time jobs available.

APPLYING FOR FINANCIAL AID *Required financial aid form:* FAFSA. *Financial aid deadline (priority):* 3/1. *Notification date:* 1/15.
CONTACT Catherine Ryan, Director of Financial Aid, Westfield State University, 333 Western Avenue, Westfield, MA 01086, 413-572-5218.
Website: http://www.westfield.ma.edu/.

WEST LIBERTY UNIVERSITY
West Liberty, WV

CONTACT Christ Taskalines, Financial Aid Manager, West Liberty University, PO Box 295, West Liberty, WV 26074-0295, 304-336-8016 or toll-free 800-732-6204 (in-state), 866-WESTLIB (out-of-state). *Fax:* 304-336-8088. *E-mail:* taskalic@westliberty.edu.
Website: http://www.westliberty.edu/.

WESTMINSTER COLLEGE
Fulton, MO

Tuition & fees: $24,540	Average undergraduate aid package: $22,459

ABOUT THE INSTITUTION Independent Presbyterian Church, coed. *Awards:* bachelor's degrees. 33 undergraduate majors. *Total enrollment:* 940. Undergraduates: 940. Freshmen: 239. Federal methodology is used as a basis for awarding need-based institutional aid.

UNDERGRADUATE EXPENSES for 2016–2017 *Comprehensive fee:* $34,020 includes full-time tuition ($23,200), mandatory fees ($1340), and room and board ($9480). *College room only:* $5120. Full-time tuition and fees vary according to reciprocity agreements. Room and board charges vary according to board plan and housing facility. *Part-time tuition:* $800 per credit hour.

FRESHMAN FINANCIAL AID (Fall 2016, est.) 209 applied for aid; of those 77% were deemed to have need. 100% of freshmen with need received aid; of those 53% had need fully met. *Average percent of need met:* 95% (excluding resources awarded to replace EFC). *Average financial aid package:* $23,607 (excluding resources awarded to replace EFC). 28% of all full-time freshmen had no need and received non-need-based gift aid.

UNDERGRADUATE FINANCIAL AID (Fall 2016, est.) 677 applied for aid; of those 81% were deemed to have need. 100% of undergraduates with need received aid; of those 49% had need fully met. *Average percent of need met:* 93% (excluding resources awarded to replace EFC). *Average financial aid package:* $22,459 (excluding resources awarded to replace EFC). 35% of all full-time undergraduates had no need and received non-need-based gift aid.

GIFT AID (NEED-BASED) *Total amount:* $14,868,648 (7% federal, 4% state, 78% institutional, 11% external sources). *Receiving aid:* Freshmen: 73% (161); all full-time undergraduates: 65% (548). *Average award:* Freshmen: $20,043; Undergraduates: $17,785. *Scholarships, grants, and awards:* Federal Pell, FSEOG, state, private, college/university gift aid from institutional funds.

GIFT AID (NON-NEED-BASED) *Total amount:* $198,132 (100% federal). *Average award:* Freshmen: $16,104. Undergraduates: $13,507. *Scholarships, grants, and awards by category: Academic interests/achievement:* general academic interests/achievements. *Creative arts/performance:* music. *Special achievements/activities:* general special achievements/activities, leadership. *Special characteristics:* children and siblings of alumni, children of faculty/staff, ethnic background, international students, local/state students, relatives of clergy, religious affiliation, siblings of current students, twins. *Tuition waivers:* Full or partial for children of alumni, employees or children of employees. *ROTC:* Army cooperative, Air Force cooperative.

LOANS *Student loans:* $5,114,500 (39% need-based, 61% non-need-based). 77% of past graduating class borrowed through all loan programs. *Average indebtedness per student:* $30,805. *Average need-based loan:* Freshmen: $3357. Undergraduates: $4463. *Parent loans:* $1,653,838 (100% non-need-based). *Programs:* Federal Direct (Subsidized and Unsubsidized Stafford, PLUS), Perkins.

WORK-STUDY *Federal work-study:* Total amount: $466,143; jobs available. *State or other work-study/employment:* Total amount: $308,514 (100% non-need-based). Part-time jobs available.

APPLYING FOR FINANCIAL AID *Required financial aid form:* FAFSA. *Financial aid deadline (priority):* 2/15. *Notification date:* Continuous beginning 3/15. Students must reply within 3 weeks of notification.

CONTACT Ms. Aimee Bristow, Senior Director of Student Financial Planning, Westminster College, 501 Westminster Avenue, Fulton, MO 65251-1299, 800-475-3361. *Fax:* 573-592-5255. *E-mail:* aimee.bristow@westminster-mo.edu.
Website: http://www.westminster-mo.edu/.

WESTMINSTER COLLEGE
New Wilmington, PA

Tuition & fees: $36,230	Average undergraduate aid package: $28,042

ABOUT THE INSTITUTION Independent Presbyterian Church (U.S.A.), coed. *Awards:* bachelor's and master's degrees. 50 undergraduate majors. *Total enrollment:* 1,252. Undergraduates: 1,168. Freshmen: 371. Federal methodology is used as a basis for awarding need-based institutional aid.

UNDERGRADUATE EXPENSES for 2017–2018 *Application fee:* $35. *Comprehensive fee:* $47,250 includes full-time tuition ($34,830), mandatory fees ($1400), and room and board ($11,020). Room and board charges vary according to board plan and housing facility. *Part-time tuition:* $1125 per credit hour.

FRESHMAN FINANCIAL AID (Fall 2015) 282 applied for aid; of those 91% were deemed to have need. 100% of freshmen with need received aid; of those 21% had need fully met. *Average percent of need met:* 83% (excluding resources awarded to replace EFC). *Average financial aid package:* $28,611 (excluding resources awarded to replace EFC). 13% of all full-time freshmen had no need and received non-need-based gift aid.

UNDERGRADUATE FINANCIAL AID (Fall 2015) 1,017 applied for aid; of those 93% were deemed to have need. 100% of undergraduates with need received aid; of those 21% had need fully met. *Average percent of need met:* 83% (excluding resources awarded to replace EFC). *Average financial aid package:* $28,042 (excluding resources awarded to replace EFC). 16% of all full-time undergraduates had no need and received non-need-based gift aid.

GIFT AID (NEED-BASED) *Total amount:* $21,860,930 (7% federal, 7% state, 82% institutional, 4% external sources). *Receiving aid:* Freshmen: 86% (256); all full-time undergraduates: 82% (930). *Average award:* Freshmen: $25,451; Undergraduates: $23,612. *Scholarships, grants, and awards:* Federal Pell, FSEOG, state, private, college/university gift aid from institutional funds.

GIFT AID (NON-NEED-BASED) *Total amount:* $3,260,381 (4% federal, 94% institutional, 2% external sources). *Receiving aid:* Freshmen: 86% (255). Undergraduates: 81% (914). *Average award:* Freshmen: $18,586. Undergraduates: $17,887. *Scholarships, grants, and awards by category: Academic interests/achievement:* 1,391 awards ($15,807,708 total): general academic interests/achievements, premedicine. *Creative arts/performance:* 105 awards ($97,860 total): cinema/film/broadcasting, general creative arts/performance, music, theater/drama. *Special characteristics:* 572 awards ($4,290,282 total): children and siblings of alumni, general special characteristics, religious affiliation. *Tuition waivers:* Full or partial for employees or children of employees. *ROTC:* Army cooperative.

LOANS *Student loans:* $8,540,031 (94% need-based, 6% non-need-based). 83% of past graduating class borrowed through all loan programs. *Average indebtedness per student:* $36,692. *Average need-based loan:* Freshmen: $3490. Undergraduates: $4600. *Parent loans:* $2,478,479 (99% need-based, 1% non-need-based). *Programs:* Federal Direct (Subsidized and Unsubsidized Stafford, PLUS), Perkins, alternative loans.

WORK-STUDY *Federal work-study:* 292 jobs averaging $1671. *State or other work-study/employment:* Total amount: $123,261 (60% need-based, 40% non-need-based). 80 part-time jobs averaging $1563.

APPLYING FOR FINANCIAL AID *Required financial aid forms:* FAFSA, W-2 forms. *Financial aid deadline (priority):* 5/1. *Notification date:* Continuous beginning 12/15. Students must reply by 5/1 or within 3 weeks of notification.

CONTACT Mrs. Cheryl A. Gerber, Director of Financial Aid, Westminster College, 319 South Market Street, New Wilmington, PA 16172-0001, 724-946-7102 or toll-free 800-942-8033. *Fax:* 724-946-6171. *E-mail:* gerberca@westminster.edu.
Website: http://www.westminster.edu/.

WESTMINSTER COLLEGE
Salt Lake City, UT

Tuition & fees: $32,104	Average undergraduate aid package: $26,199

ABOUT THE INSTITUTION Independent, coed. *Awards:* certificates, bachelor's, and master's degrees. 40 undergraduate majors. *Total enrollment:* 2,692. Undergraduates: 2,127. Freshmen: 434. Federal methodology is used as a basis for awarding need-based institutional aid.

UNDERGRADUATE EXPENSES for 2016–2017 *Application fee:* $50. *Comprehensive fee:* $41,722 includes full-time tuition ($31,584), mandatory fees ($520), and room and board ($9618). Full-time tuition and fees vary according to course load and program. Room and board charges vary according to board plan. *Part-time tuition:* $1316 per credit hour. Part-time tuition and fees vary according to course load and program.

FRESHMAN FINANCIAL AID (Fall 2016, est.) 337 applied for aid; of those 88% were deemed to have need. 100% of freshmen with need received aid; of those 24% had need fully met. *Average percent of need met.* 82% (excluding resources awarded to replace EFC). *Average financial aid package:* $27,834 (excluding resources awarded to replace EFC). 25% of all full-time freshmen had no need and received non-need-based gift aid.

UNDERGRADUATE FINANCIAL AID (Fall 2016, est.) 1,381 applied for aid; of those 87% were deemed to have need. 100% of undergraduates with need received aid; of those 23% had need fully met. *Average percent of need met:* 78% (excluding resources awarded to replace EFC). *Average financial aid package:* $26,199 (excluding resources awarded to replace EFC). 30% of all full-time undergraduates had no need and received non-need-based gift aid.

GIFT AID (NEED-BASED) *Total amount:* $23,456,791 (11% federal, 81% institutional, 8% external sources). *Receiving aid:* Freshmen: 69% (295); all full-time undergraduates: 59% (1,185). *Average award:* Freshmen: $22,738; Undergraduates: $20,755. *Scholarships, grants, and awards:* Federal Pell, FSEOG, state, private, college/university gift aid from institutional funds.

GIFT AID (NON-NEED-BASED) *Total amount:* $10,865,396 (85% institutional, 15% external sources). *Receiving aid:* Freshmen: 10% (43). Undergraduates: 8% (161). *Average award:* Freshmen: $14,729. Undergraduates: $13,402. *Tuition waivers:* Full or partial for employees or children of employees. *ROTC:* Army cooperative, Naval cooperative, Air Force cooperative.

LOANS *Student loans:* $12,568,182 (90% need-based, 10% non-need-based). 59% of past graduating class borrowed through all loan programs. *Average indebtedness per student:* $30,442. *Average need-based loan:* Freshmen: $3696. Undergraduates: $5123. *Parent loans:* $1,072,428 (90% need-based, 10% non-need-based). *Programs:* Federal Direct (Subsidized and Unsubsidized Stafford, PLUS), Perkins.

WORK-STUDY *Federal work-study:* Total amount: $1,470,576; 662 jobs averaging $2253. *State or other work-study/employment:* Total amount: $600,000 (100% non-need-based). Part-time jobs available.

ATHLETIC AWARDS Total amount: $1,077,559 (57% need-based, 43% non-need-based).

APPLYING FOR FINANCIAL AID *Required financial aid form:* FAFSA. *Financial aid deadline (priority):* 3/1. *Notification date:* Continuous beginning 12/1. Students must reply by 5/1 or within 3 weeks of notification.

CONTACT Jenny Ryan, Director of Financial Aid, Westminster College, 1840 South 1300 East, Salt Lake City, UT 84105, 801-832-2500 or toll-free 800-748-4753. *Fax:* 801-832-2501. *E-mail:* jryan@westminstercollege.edu. *Website:* http://www.westminstercollege.edu/.

WESTMONT COLLEGE
Santa Barbara, CA

Tuition & fees: $44,044	Average undergraduate aid package: $32,102

ABOUT THE INSTITUTION Independent nondenominational, coed. *Awards:* certificates and bachelor's degrees. 42 undergraduate majors. *Total enrollment:* 1,298. Undergraduates: 1,298. Freshmen: 347. Federal methodology is used as a basis for awarding need-based institutional aid.

UNDERGRADUATE EXPENSES for 2017–2018 *Application fee:* $50. *One-time required fee:* $300. *Comprehensive fee:* $57,930 includes full-time tuition ($42,890), mandatory fees ($1154), and room and board ($13,886). *College room only:* $8610. Room and board charges vary according to board plan and housing facility.

FRESHMAN FINANCIAL AID (Fall 2016, est.) 271 applied for aid; of those 91% were deemed to have need. 100% of freshmen with need received aid; of those 25% had need fully met. *Average percent of need met:* 83% (excluding resources awarded to replace EFC). *Average financial aid package:* $35,569 (excluding resources awarded to replace EFC). 24% of all full-time freshmen had no need and received non-need-based gift aid.

UNDERGRADUATE FINANCIAL AID (Fall 2016, est.) 929 applied for aid; of those 92% were deemed to have need. 100% of undergraduates with need received aid; of those 21% had need fully met. *Average percent of need met:* 79% (excluding resources awarded to replace EFC). *Average financial aid package:* $32,102 (excluding resources awarded to replace EFC). 25% of all full-time undergraduates had no need and received non-need-based gift aid.

GIFT AID (NEED-BASED) *Total amount:* $19,780,880 (6% federal, 10% state, 82% institutional, 2% external sources). *Receiving aid:* Freshmen: 71% (245); all full-time undergraduates: 66% (819). *Average award:* Freshmen: $28,676; Undergraduates: $24,806. *Scholarships, grants, and awards:* Federal Pell, FSEOG, state, private, college/university gift aid from institutional funds.

GIFT AID (NON-NEED-BASED) *Total amount:* $5,590,681 (1% federal, 94% institutional, 5% external sources). *Receiving aid:* Freshmen: 8% (28). Undergraduates: 7% (92). *Average award:* Freshmen: $17,726. Undergraduates: $14,186. *Scholarships, grants, and awards by category:* Academic interests/achievement: general academic interests/achievements. Creative arts/performance: art/fine arts, dance, music, theater/drama. Special achievements/activities: general special achievements/activities, leadership. Special characteristics: children of faculty/staff, ethnic background, international students. *Tuition waivers:* Full or partial for employees or children of employees. *ROTC:* Army cooperative, Air Force cooperative.

LOANS *Student loans:* $9,293,229 (69% need-based, 31% non-need-based). 51% of past graduating class borrowed through all loan programs. *Average indebtedness per student:* $31,609. *Average need-based loan:* Freshmen: $3891. Undergraduates: $5312. *Parent loans:* $4,153,429 (36% need-based, 64% non-need-based). *Programs:* Federal Direct (Subsidized and Unsubsidized Stafford, PLUS), Perkins, college/university, alternative loans.

WORK-STUDY *Federal work-study:* Total amount: $703,066; 349 jobs averaging $1806.

ATHLETIC AWARDS Total amount: $1,658,165 (57% need-based, 43% non-need-based).

APPLYING FOR FINANCIAL AID *Required financial aid forms:* FAFSA, institution's own form. *Financial aid deadline (priority):* 3/1. *Notification date:* Continuous beginning 12/1. Students must reply by 5/1 or within 2 weeks of notification.

CONTACT Mr. Sean Smith, Director of Financial Aid, Westmont College, 955 La Paz Road, Santa Barbara, CA 93108, 805-565-6063 or toll-free 800-777-9011. *Fax:* 805-565-7157. *E-mail:* finaid@westmont.edu. *Website:* http://www.westmont.edu/.

WEST TEXAS A&M UNIVERSITY
Canyon, TX

Tuition & fees (TX res): $7681	Average undergraduate aid package: $29,266

ABOUT THE INSTITUTION State-supported, coed. *Awards:* bachelor's, master's, and doctoral degrees. 61 undergraduate majors. *Total enrollment:* 9,901. Undergraduates: 7,389. Freshmen: 1,330. Federal methodology is used as a basis for awarding need-based institutional aid.

UNDERGRADUATE EXPENSES for 2016–2017 *Application fee:* $40. *Tuition, state resident:* full-time $5289; part-time $50 per credit hour. *Tuition, nonresident:* full-time $6279; part-time $80 per credit hour. *Required fees:* full-time $2392; $229.22 per credit hour or $237.85 per term. Full-time tuition and fees vary according to course load, degree level, program, and student level. Part-time tuition and fees vary according to course load, degree level, program, and student level. *College room and board:* $7196. Room and board charges vary according to board plan and housing facility. *Payment plan:* Guaranteed tuition.

FRESHMAN FINANCIAL AID (Fall 2015) 1,178 applied for aid; of those 76% were deemed to have need. 99% of freshmen with need received aid; of those 21% had need fully met. *Average percent of need met:* 69% (excluding resources awarded to replace EFC). *Average financial aid package:* $29,694 (excluding resources awarded to replace EFC). 9% of all full-time freshmen had no need and received non-need-based gift aid.

UNDERGRADUATE FINANCIAL AID (Fall 2015) 4,235 applied for aid; of those 81% were deemed to have need. 99% of undergraduates with need received aid; of those 18% had need fully met. *Average percent of need met:* 63% (excluding resources awarded to replace EFC). *Average financial aid package:* $29,266

(excluding resources awarded to replace EFC). 11% of all full-time undergraduates had no need and received non-need-based gift aid.

GIFT AID (NEED-BASED) *Total amount:* $19,950,208 (54% federal, 33% state, 8% institutional, 5% external sources). *Receiving aid:* Freshmen: 50% (690); all full-time undergraduates: 47% (2,665). *Average award:* Freshmen: $5589; Undergraduates: $4569. *Scholarships, grants, and awards:* Federal Pell, FSEOG, state, private, college/university gift aid from institutional funds.

GIFT AID (NON-NEED-BASED) *Total amount:* $2,659,356 (58% institutional, 42% external sources). *Receiving aid:* Freshmen: 31% (435). Undergraduates: 21% (1,217). *Average award:* Freshmen: $2070. Undergraduates: $2205. *Scholarships, grants, and awards by category:* Academic interests/achievement: 3,016 awards ($1,872,600 total): agriculture, business, communication, computer science, education, engineering/technologies, English, foreign languages, general academic interests/ achievements, home economics, humanities, mathematics, physical sciences, premedicine, social sciences. *Creative arts/performance:* 383 awards ($195,795 total): art/fine arts, cinema/film/broadcasting, creative writing, dance, debating, general creative arts/ performance, journalism/publications, music, theater/drama. *Special achievements/ activities:* 604 awards ($285,339 total): cheerleading/drum major, community service, general special achievements/activities, hobbies/interests, leadership, memberships, religious involvement, rodeo. *Special characteristics:* 451 awards ($269,501 total): children and siblings of alumni, children of faculty/staff, children of union members/ company employees, children of workers in trades, first-generation college students, general special characteristics, handicapped students, international students, local/state students, out-of-state students, public servants, religious affiliation, veterans, veterans' children. *Tuition waivers:* Full or partial for employees or children of employees.

LOANS *Student loans:* $31,887,324 (73% need-based, 27% non-need-based). 62% of past graduating class borrowed through all loan programs. *Average indebtedness per student:* $24,525. *Average need-based loan:* Freshmen: $2397. Undergraduates: $3341. *Parent loans:* $2,435,447 (16% need-based, 84% non-need-based). *Programs:* Federal Direct (Subsidized and Unsubsidized Stafford, PLUS), state.

WORK-STUDY *Federal work-study:* 143 jobs averaging $2643. *State or other work-study/employment:* Total amount: $59,115 (100% need-based). 41 part-time jobs averaging $1441.

ATHLETIC AWARDS Total amount: $1,955,270 (30% need-based, 70% non-need-based).

APPLYING FOR FINANCIAL AID *Required financial aid form:* FAFSA. *Financial aid deadline:* Continuous. *Notification date:* Continuous beginning 3/1. Students must reply within 2 weeks of notification.

CONTACT Marian Giesecke, Director of Financial Aid, West Texas A&M University, WTAMU Box 60939, Canyon, TX 79016-0001, 806-651-2055 or toll-free 800-99-WTAMU. *Fax:* 806-651-2924. *E-mail:* mgiesecke@mail.wtamu.edu. *Website:* http://www.wtamu.edu/.

WEST VIRGINIA STATE UNIVERSITY
Institute, WV

CONTACT Mrs. JoAnn L. Ross, Director of Student Financial Assistance, West Virginia State University, PO Box 1000, Ferrell Hall 324, Institute, WV 25112-1000, 304-204-4361 or toll-free 800-987-2112. *Website:* http://www.wvstateu.edu/.

WEST VIRGINIA UNIVERSITY
Morgantown, WV

Tuition & fees (WV res): $7992	Average undergraduate aid package: $6839

ABOUT THE INSTITUTION State-supported, coed. *Awards:* bachelor's, master's, and doctoral degrees. 74 undergraduate majors. *Total enrollment:* 28,488. Undergraduates: 22,350. Freshmen: 5,124. Federal methodology is used as a basis for awarding need-based institutional aid.

UNDERGRADUATE EXPENSES for 2016–2017 *Application fee:* $45. *Tuition, state resident:* full-time $7992; part-time $333 per credit hour. *Tuition, nonresident:* full-time $22,488; part-time $937 per credit hour. Full-time tuition and fees vary according to location, program, and reciprocity agreements. Part-time tuition and fees vary according to course load, location, program, and reciprocity agreements.

College room and board: $10,218. Room and board charges vary according to board plan, housing facility, and location.

FRESHMAN FINANCIAL AID (Fall 2015) 4,305 applied for aid; of those 68% were deemed to have need. 98% of freshmen with need received aid; of those 21% had need fully met. *Average percent of need met:* 72% (excluding resources awarded to replace EFC). *Average financial aid package:* $6616 (excluding resources awarded to replace EFC). 18% of all full-time freshmen had no need and received non-need-based gift aid.

UNDERGRADUATE FINANCIAL AID (Fall 2015) 15,727 applied for aid; of those 70% were deemed to have need. 99% of undergraduates with need received aid; of those 37% had need fully met. *Average percent of need met:* 75% (excluding resources awarded to replace EFC). *Average financial aid package:* $6839 (excluding resources awarded to replace EFC). 17% of all full-time undergraduates had no need and received non-need-based gift aid.

GIFT AID (NEED-BASED) *Total amount:* $40,586,154 (64% federal, 21% state, 15% institutional). *Receiving aid:* Freshmen: 41% (2,050); all full-time undergraduates: 39% (7,695). *Average award:* Freshmen: $4814; Undergraduates: $4790. *Scholarships, grants, and awards:* Federal Pell, FSEOG, state, private, college/ university gift aid from institutional funds, Federal Nursing.

GIFT AID (NON-NEED-BASED) *Total amount:* $43,271,030 (2% federal, 49% state, 40% institutional, 9% external sources). *Receiving aid:* Freshmen: 55% (2,707). Undergraduates: 47% (9,311). *Average award:* Freshmen: $2382. Undergraduates: $2437. *Scholarships, grants, and awards by category:* Academic interests/ achievement: agriculture, architecture, area/ethnic studies, biological sciences, business, communication, computer science, education, engineering/technologies, English, foreign languages, general academic interests/achievements, health fields, home economics, humanities, international studies, library science, mathematics, military science, physical sciences, premedicine, religion/biblical studies, social sciences. *Creative arts/performance:* art/fine arts, debating, music, theater/drama. *Special achievements/activities:* general special achievements/activities, leadership. *Special characteristics:* children of faculty/staff, children of union members/company employees, children of workers in trades, ethnic background, general special characteristics, international students, local/state students, members of minority groups. *Tuition waivers:* Full or partial for employees or children of employees, senior citizens. *ROTC:* Army, Air Force.

LOANS *Student loans:* $171,716,224 (24% need-based, 76% non-need-based). 64% of past graduating class borrowed through all loan programs. *Average indebtedness per student:* $27,993. *Average need-based loan:* Freshmen: $2826. Undergraduates: $3553. *Parent loans:* $58,220,286 (100% non-need-based). *Programs:* Federal Direct (Subsidized and Unsubsidized Stafford, PLUS), Perkins, Federal Nursing, college/university.

WORK-STUDY *Federal work-study:* 1,142 jobs averaging $1505. *State or other work-study/employment:* Total amount: $22,967,460 (100% non-need-based). Part-time jobs available.

ATHLETIC AWARDS Total amount: $8,262,176 (100% non-need-based).

APPLYING FOR FINANCIAL AID *Required financial aid forms:* FAFSA, state aid form. *Financial aid deadline:* 3/1. *Notification date:* Continuous beginning 3/15. Students must reply within 2 weeks of notification.

CONTACT Sandra Bennett, Executive Director of Financial Aid, West Virginia University, PO Box 6004, Morgantown, WV 26506-6004, 304-293-5242 or toll-free 800-344-9881. *Fax:* 304-293-4890. *E-mail:* sybennett@mail.wvu.edu. *Website:* http://www.wvu.edu/.

WEST VIRGINIA UNIVERSITY INSTITUTE OF TECHNOLOGY
Montgomery, WV

Tuition & fees (WV res): $6648	Average undergraduate aid package: $7200

ABOUT THE INSTITUTION State-supported, coed. *Awards:* certificates and bachelor's degrees. 31 undergraduate majors. *Total enrollment:* 1,347. Undergraduates: 1,347. Freshmen: 307. Federal methodology is used as a basis for awarding need-based institutional aid.

UNDERGRADUATE EXPENSES for 2016–2017 *Tuition, state resident:* full-time $6648; part-time $277 per credit hour. *Tuition, nonresident:* full-time $16,728; part-time $697 per credit hour. Full-time tuition and fees vary according to program. Part-time tuition and fees vary according to course load and program.

College room and board: $9814. Room and board charges vary according to board plan and housing facility.

FRESHMAN FINANCIAL AID (Fall 2015) 231 applied for aid; of those 78% were deemed to have need. 100% of freshmen with need received aid; of those 17% had need fully met. *Average percent of need met:* 72% (excluding resources awarded to replace EFC). *Average financial aid package:* $6706 (excluding resources awarded to replace EFC). 10% of all full-time freshmen had no need and received non-need-based gift aid.

UNDERGRADUATE FINANCIAL AID (Fall 2015) 829 applied for aid; of those 83% were deemed to have need. 100% of undergraduates with need received aid; of those 26% had need fully met. *Average percent of need met:* 75% (excluding resources awarded to replace EFC). *Average financial aid package:* $7200 (excluding resources awarded to replace EFC). 6% of all full-time undergraduates had no need and received non-need-based gift aid.

GIFT AID (NEED-BASED) Total amount: $3,114,412 (73% federal, 25% state, 2% institutional). *Receiving aid:* Freshmen: 57% (152); all full-time undergraduates: 56% (550). *Average award:* Freshmen: $5331; Undergraduates: $5341. *Scholarships, grants, and awards:* Federal Pell, FSEOG, state, private, college/university gift aid from institutional funds, Federal Nursing.

GIFT AID (NON-NEED-BASED) Total amount: $1,372,320 (2% federal, 57% state, 28% institutional, 13% external sources). *Receiving aid:* Freshmen: 30% (80). Undergraduates: 39% (382). *Average award:* Freshmen: $2619. Undergraduates: $2775. *Scholarships, grants, and awards by category: Academic interests/ achievement:* general academic interests/achievements. *Special achievements/activities:* cheerleading/drum major. *Special characteristics:* first-generation college students. *Tuition waivers:* Full or partial for senior citizens. *ROTC:* Army.

LOANS Student loans: $4,275,875 (45% need-based, 55% non-need-based). 68% of past graduating class borrowed through all loan programs. *Average indebtedness per student:* $27,364. *Average need-based loan:* Freshmen: $2284. Undergraduates: $2746. *Parent loans:* $1,099,462 (100% non-need-based). *Programs:* Federal Direct (Subsidized and Unsubsidized Stafford, PLUS), Perkins, college/university.

WORK-STUDY Federal work-study jobs available. *State or other work-study/ employment:* Part-time jobs available.

ATHLETIC AWARDS Total amount: $101,866 (100% non-need-based).

APPLYING FOR FINANCIAL AID *Required financial aid form:* FAFSA. *Financial aid deadline (priority):* 3/1. *Notification date:* Continuous beginning 3/15. Students must reply within 2 weeks of notification.

CONTACT Mr. Michael A. White, Director of Financial Aid Services, West Virginia University Institute of Technology, 405 Fayette Pike, Old Main, Room 206, Box 40, Montgomery, WV 25136, 304-442-3228 or toll-free 888-554-8324. *Fax:* 304-442-3052. *E-mail:* michael.white@mail.wvu.edu. *Website:* http://www.wvutech.edu/.

WEST VIRGINIA WESLEYAN COLLEGE
Buckhannon, WV

Tuition & fees: $29,952	Average undergraduate aid package: $27,645

ABOUT THE INSTITUTION Independent United Methodist Church, coed. *Awards:* certificates, bachelor's, and master's degrees. 61 undergraduate majors. *Total enrollment:* 1,542. Undergraduates: 1,396. Freshmen: 387. Federal methodology is used as a basis for awarding need-based institutional aid.

UNDERGRADUATE EXPENSES for 2016–2017 *Application fee:* $35. *Comprehensive fee:* $34,032 includes full-time tuition ($28,574), mandatory fees ($1378), and room and board ($4080). *College room only:* $4168. Full-time tuition and fees vary according to course load and student level. Room and board charges vary according to housing facility. Part-time tuition and fees vary according to course load.

FRESHMAN FINANCIAL AID (Fall 2016, est.) 350 applied for aid; of those 88% were deemed to have need. 100% of freshmen with need received aid; of those 29% had need fully met. *Average percent of need met:* 84% (excluding resources awarded to replace EFC). *Average financial aid package:* $28,400 (excluding resources awarded to replace EFC). 12% of all full-time freshmen had no need and received non-need-based gift aid.

UNDERGRADUATE FINANCIAL AID (Fall 2016, est.) 1,198 applied for aid; of those 90% were deemed to have need. 100% of undergraduates with need received aid; of those 28% had need fully met. *Average percent of need met:* 83%

(excluding resources awarded to replace EFC). *Average financial aid package:* $27,645 (excluding resources awarded to replace EFC). 13% of all full-time undergraduates had no need and received non-need-based gift aid.

GIFT AID (NEED-BASED) Total amount: $18,473,494 (12% federal, 5% state, 78% institutional, 5% external sources). *Receiving aid:* Freshmen: 79% (307); all full-time undergraduates: 79% (1,081). *Average award:* Freshmen: $25,954; Undergraduates: $24,490. *Scholarships, grants, and awards:* Federal Pell, FSEOG, private, college/university gift aid from institutional funds, Federal Nursing.

GIFT AID (NON-NEED-BASED) Total amount: $6,105,567 (1% federal, 32% state, 66% institutional, 1% external sources). *Receiving aid:* Freshmen: 19% (74). Undergraduates: 19% (253). *Average award:* Freshmen: $17,278. Undergraduates: $16,317. *Scholarships, grants, and awards by category: Academic interests/ achievement:* general academic interests/achievements. *Creative arts/performance:* art/fine arts, creative writing, dance, music, performing arts, theater/drama. *Special achievements/activities:* community service, leadership, religious involvement. *Special characteristics:* children and siblings of alumni, children of faculty/staff, general special characteristics, international students, relatives of clergy, religious affiliation, veterans. *Tuition waivers:* Full or partial for employees or children of employees.

LOANS Student loans: $5,094,049 (72% need-based, 28% non-need-based). 69% of past graduating class borrowed through all loan programs. *Average indebtedness per student:* $31,996. *Average need-based loan:* Freshmen: $3286. Undergraduates: $3827. *Parent loans:* $2,196,112 (100% non-need-based). *Programs:* Federal Direct (Subsidized and Unsubsidized Stafford, PLUS), Perkins, Federal Nursing.

WORK-STUDY *Federal work-study:* Total amount: $327,362; jobs available. *State or other work-study/employment:* Total amount: $89,526 (100% non-need-based). Part-time jobs available.

ATHLETIC AWARDS Total amount: $3,365,708 (65% need-based, 35% non-need-based).

APPLYING FOR FINANCIAL AID *Required financial aid form:* FAFSA. *Financial aid deadline (priority):* 3/1. *Notification date:* Continuous beginning 3/15. Students must reply within 3 weeks of notification.

CONTACT Susan George, Director of Financial Aid, West Virginia Wesleyan College, 59 College Avenue, Buckhannon, WV 26201, 304-473-8080 or toll-free 800-722-9933. *E-mail:* george_s@wvwc.edu. *Website:* http://www.wvwc.edu/.

WHEATON COLLEGE
Wheaton, IL

Tuition & fees: $34,050	Average undergraduate aid package: $24,946

ABOUT THE INSTITUTION Independent nondenominational, coed. *Awards:* certificates, bachelor's, master's, and doctoral degrees. 41 undergraduate majors. *Total enrollment:* 2,901. Undergraduates: 2,456. Freshmen: 588. Both federal and institutional methodology are used as a basis for awarding need-based institutional aid.

UNDERGRADUATE EXPENSES for 2016–2017 *Application fee:* $50. *Comprehensive fee:* $43,610 includes full-time tuition ($34,050) and room and board ($9560). *College room only:* $5650. Full-time tuition and fees vary according to program. Room and board charges vary according to board plan and housing facility. *Part-time tuition:* $1419 per credit hour. Part-time tuition and fees vary according to course load and program.

FRESHMAN FINANCIAL AID (Fall 2016, est.) 415 applied for aid; of those 82% were deemed to have need. 100% of freshmen with need received aid; of those 23% had need fully met. *Average percent of need met:* 86% (excluding resources awarded to replace EFC). *Average financial aid package:* $24,703 (excluding resources awarded to replace EFC). 26% of all full-time freshmen had no need and received non-need-based gift aid.

UNDERGRADUATE FINANCIAL AID (Fall 2016, est.) 1,504 applied for aid; of those 87% were deemed to have need. 99% of undergraduates with need received aid; of those 23% had need fully met. *Average percent of need met:* 85% (excluding resources awarded to replace EFC). *Average financial aid package:* $24,946 (excluding resources awarded to replace EFC). 22% of all full-time undergraduates had no need and received non-need-based gift aid.

GIFT AID (NEED-BASED) Total amount: $27,773,997 (8% federal, 2% state, 86% institutional, 4% external sources). *Receiving aid:* Freshmen: 58% (341); all full-time undergraduates: 54% (1,301). *Average award:* Freshmen: $20,671; Undergrad-

uates: $20,622. *Scholarships, grants, and awards:* Federal Pell, FSEOG, state, private, college/university gift aid from institutional funds.

GIFT AID (NON-NEED-BASED) *Total amount:* $4,080,425 (83% institutional, 17% external sources). *Receiving aid:* Freshmen: 17% (99). Undergraduates: 15% (361). *Average award:* Freshmen: $6247. Undergraduates: $6343. *Scholarships, grants, and awards by category:* Academic interests/achievement: 1,182 awards ($4,601,381 total): area/ethnic studies, biological sciences, business, communication, education, engineering/technologies, English, foreign languages, general academic interests/achievements, home economics, humanities, international studies, mathematics, military science, physical sciences, premedicine, religion/biblical studies, social sciences. *Creative arts/performance:* 171 awards ($593,410 total): applied art and design, art/fine arts, cinema/film/broadcasting, creative writing, debating, music. *Special achievements/activities:* 13 awards ($51,936 total): community service, general special achievements/activities, leadership, religious involvement. *Special characteristics:* 252 awards ($2,365,914 total): children and siblings of alumni, children of public servants, first-generation college students, general special characteristics, handicapped students, international students, members of minority groups, out-of-state students, relatives of clergy, veterans' children. *ROTC:* Army, Air Force cooperative.

LOANS *Student loans:* $9,716,487 (85% need-based, 15% non-need-based). 54% of past graduating class borrowed through all loan programs. *Average indebtedness per student:* $27,354. *Average need-based loan:* Freshmen: $4389. Undergraduates: $4929. *Parent loans:* $2,396,104 (71% need-based, 29% non-need-based). *Programs:* Federal Direct (Subsidized and Unsubsidized Stafford, PLUS), Perkins.

WORK-STUDY *Federal work-study:* Total amount: $207,453; 157 jobs averaging $1336. *State or other work-study/employment:* Total amount: $1,450,000 (100% non-need-based). Part-time jobs available.

APPLYING FOR FINANCIAL AID *Required financial aid forms:* FAFSA, institution's own form. *Financial aid deadline (priority):* 12/1. *Notification date:* Continuous beginning 1/15.

CONTACT Ms. Karen Belling, Director of Student Financial Services, Wheaton College, 501 College Avenue, Wheaton, IL 60187-5593, 630-752-5700 or toll-free 800-222-2419. *E-mail:* sfs@wheaton.edu.
Website: http://www.wheaton.edu/.

WHEATON COLLEGE
Norton, MA

Tuition & fees: $50,850	Average undergraduate aid package: $37,725

ABOUT THE INSTITUTION Independent, coed. *Awards:* bachelor's degrees. 44 undergraduate majors. *Total enrollment:* 1,651. Undergraduates: 1,651. Freshmen: 528. Both federal and institutional methodology are used as a basis for awarding need-based institutional aid.

UNDERGRADUATE EXPENSES for 2017–2018 *Application fee:* $60. *One-time required fee:* $50. *Comprehensive fee:* $63,818 includes full-time tuition ($50,520), mandatory fees ($330), and room and board ($12,968). *College room only:* $6918. *Part-time tuition:* $6315 per course.

FRESHMAN FINANCIAL AID (Fall 2016, est.) 411 applied for aid; of those 83% were deemed to have need. 100% of freshmen with need received aid; of those 61% had need fully met. *Average percent of need met:* 95% (excluding resources awarded to replace EFC). *Average financial aid package:* $41,456 (excluding resources awarded to replace EFC). 30% of all full-time freshmen had no need and received non-need-based gift aid.

UNDERGRADUATE FINANCIAL AID (Fall 2016, est.) 1,211 applied for aid; of those 86% were deemed to have need. 100% of undergraduates with need received aid; of those 48% had need fully met. *Average percent of need met:* 92% (excluding resources awarded to replace EFC). *Average financial aid package:* $37,725 (excluding resources awarded to replace EFC). 28% of all full-time undergraduates had no need and received non-need-based gift aid.

GIFT AID (NEED-BASED) *Total amount:* $35,229,915 (5% federal, 1% state, 92% institutional, 2% external sources). *Receiving aid:* Freshmen: 65% (341); all full-time undergraduates: 63% (1,036). *Average award:* Freshmen: $32,620; Undergraduates: $30,737. *Scholarships, grants, and awards:* Federal Pell, FSEOG, state, private, college/university gift aid from institutional funds.

GIFT AID (NON-NEED-BASED) *Total amount:* $9,534,873 (98% institutional, 2% external sources). *Receiving aid:* Freshmen: 13% (67). Undergraduates: 6% (106). *Average award:* Freshmen: $19,162. Undergraduates: $15,097. *Scholar-*

ships, grants, and awards by category: Academic interests/achievement: 490 awards ($7,206,328 total): general academic interests/achievements. *Tuition waivers:* Full or partial for employees or children of employees. *ROTC:* Army cooperative.

LOANS *Student loans:* $10,090,485 (90% need-based, 10% non-need-based). 67% of past graduating class borrowed through all loan programs. *Average indebtedness per student:* $33,040. *Average need-based loan:* Freshmen: $2806. Undergraduates: $4142. *Parent loans:* $3,019,425 (100% non-need-based). *Programs:* Federal Direct (Subsidized and Unsubsidized Stafford, PLUS), Perkins.

WORK-STUDY *Federal work-study:* Total amount: $1,116,024; 656 jobs averaging $1648. *State or other work-study/employment:* Total amount: $461,000 (63% need-based, 37% non-need-based). 332 part-time jobs averaging $1606.

APPLYING FOR FINANCIAL AID *Required financial aid forms:* FAFSA, CSS Financial Aid PROFILE, noncustodial (divorced/separated) parent's statement, business/farm supplement. *Financial aid deadline:* 2/1. *Notification date:* 4/1. Students must reply by 5/1.

CONTACT Ms. Susan Beard, Director, Student Financial Services, Wheaton College, 26 East Main Street, Norton, MA 02766, 508-286-8232 or toll-free 800-394-6003. *Fax:* 508-286-3787. *E-mail:* sfs@wheatoncollege.edu.
Website: http://www.wheatoncollege.edu/.

WHEELING JESUIT UNIVERSITY
Wheeling, WV

Tuition & fees: $28,110	Average undergraduate aid package: $25,276

ABOUT THE INSTITUTION Independent Roman Catholic (Jesuit), coed. *Awards:* certificates, bachelor's, master's, and doctoral degrees. 33 undergraduate majors. *Total enrollment:* 1,289. Undergraduates: 945. Freshmen: 222. Federal methodology is used as a basis for awarding need-based institutional aid.

UNDERGRADUATE EXPENSES for 2017–2018 *Application fee:* $25. *Comprehensive fee:* $37,106 includes full-time tuition ($27,000), mandatory fees ($1110), and room and board ($8996). *College room only:* $5006. Room and board charges vary according to board plan, housing facility, and student level. *Part-time tuition:* $735 per credit hour.

FRESHMAN FINANCIAL AID (Fall 2016, est.) 205 applied for aid; of those 91% were deemed to have need. 100% of freshmen with need received aid; of those 29% had need fully met. *Average percent of need met:* 84% (excluding resources awarded to replace EFC). *Average financial aid package:* $27,782 (excluding resources awarded to replace EFC). 16% of all full-time freshmen had no need and received non-need-based gift aid.

UNDERGRADUATE FINANCIAL AID (Fall 2016, est.) 688 applied for aid; of those 88% were deemed to have need. 100% of undergraduates with need received aid; of those 24% had need fully met. *Average percent of need met:* 80% (excluding resources awarded to replace EFC). *Average financial aid package:* $25,276 (excluding resources awarded to replace EFC). 22% of all full-time undergraduates had no need and received non-need-based gift aid.

GIFT AID (NEED-BASED) *Total amount:* $3,970,025 (34% federal, 7% state, 59% institutional). *Receiving aid:* Freshmen: 65% (144); all full-time undergraduates: 53% (416). *Average award:* Freshmen: $11,261; Undergraduates: $9454. *Scholarships, grants, and awards:* Federal Pell, FSEOG, state, private, college/university gift aid from institutional funds, Federal Nursing.

GIFT AID (NON-NEED-BASED) *Total amount:* $8,779,777 (4% state, 93% institutional, 3% external sources). *Receiving aid:* Freshmen: 84% (187). Undergraduates: 74% (582). *Average award:* Freshmen: $17,087. Undergraduates: $17,196. *Scholarships, grants, and awards by category:* Academic interests/achievement: 669 awards ($5,761,925 total): general academic interests/achievements, premedicine. *Creative arts/performance:* 38 awards ($132,500 total): music. *Special achievements/activities:* 65 awards ($338,406 total): community service, general special achievements/activities. *Special characteristics:* 223 awards ($1,406,497 total): children and siblings of alumni, children of faculty/staff, general special characteristics, religious affiliation. *Tuition waivers:* Full or partial for employees or children of employees.

LOANS *Student loans:* $4,186,154 (49% need-based, 51% non-need-based). 71% of past graduating class borrowed through all loan programs. *Average indebtedness per student:* $37,762. *Average need-based loan:* Freshmen: $4341. Undergrad-

uates: $4554. **Parent loans:** $857,573 (100% non-need-based). **Programs:** Federal Direct (Subsidized and Unsubsidized Stafford, PLUS), Perkins, alternative loans.

WORK-STUDY *Federal work-study:* Total amount: $200,725; 155 jobs averaging $2800. **State or other work-study/employment:** 93 part-time jobs averaging $2800.

ATHLETIC AWARDS Total amount: $2,684,670 (100% non-need-based).

APPLYING FOR FINANCIAL AID *Required financial aid form:* FAFSA. **Financial aid deadline:** 8/1 (priority: 11/1). **Notification date:** Continuous beginning 11/1. Students must reply within 2 weeks of notification.

CONTACT Christie Tomczyk, Director of Financial Aid, Wheeling Jesuit University, 316 Washington Avenue, Wheeling, WV 26003-6295, 304-243-2304 or toll-free 800-624-6992 Ext. 2359. *Fax:* 304-243-4397. *E-mail:* finaid@wju.edu.

Website: http://www.wju.edu/.

WHEELOCK COLLEGE
Boston, MA

Tuition & fees: $36,200	Average undergraduate aid package: $25,647

ABOUT THE INSTITUTION Independent, coed, primarily women. **Awards:** certificates, bachelor's, and master's degrees. 18 undergraduate majors. **Total enrollment:** 1,053. Undergraduates: 726. Freshmen: 158. Federal methodology is used as a basis for awarding need-based institutional aid.

UNDERGRADUATE EXPENSES for 2017–2018 Comprehensive fee: $51,175 includes full-time tuition ($34,950), mandatory fees ($1250), and room and board ($14,975). **Part-time tuition:** $1090 per credit hour.

FRESHMAN FINANCIAL AID (Fall 2016, est.) 143 applied for aid; of those 95% were deemed to have need. 100% of freshmen with need received aid; of those 10% had need fully met. **Average percent of need met:** 67% (excluding resources awarded to replace EFC). **Average financial aid package:** $26,673 (excluding resources awarded to replace EFC). 13% of all full-time freshmen had no need and received non-need-based gift aid.

UNDERGRADUATE FINANCIAL AID (Fall 2016, est.) 637 applied for aid; of those 94% were deemed to have need. 100% of undergraduates with need received aid; of those 11% had need fully met. **Average percent of need met:** 64% (excluding resources awarded to replace EFC). **Average financial aid package:** $25,647 (excluding resources awarded to replace EFC). 14% of all full-time undergraduates had no need and received non-need-based gift aid.

GIFT AID (NEED-BASED) Total amount: $12,636,590 (12% federal, 4% state, 80% institutional, 4% external sources). **Receiving aid:** Freshmen: 84% (136); all full-time undergraduates: 84% (598). **Average award:** Freshmen: $23,083; Undergraduates: $21,127. **Scholarships, grants, and awards:** Federal Pell, FSEOG, state, private, college/university gift aid from institutional funds.

GIFT AID (NON-NEED-BASED) Total amount: $1,786,661 (94% institutional, 6% external sources). **Receiving aid:** Freshmen: 7% (12). Undergraduates: 7% (47). **Average award:** Freshmen: $12,464. Undergraduates: $13,434. **Scholarships, grants, and awards by category:** Academic interests/achievement: general academic interests/achievements. Special achievements/activities: leadership. **Tuition waivers:** Full or partial for employees or children of employees.

LOANS Student loans: $7,169,284 (77% need-based, 23% non-need-based). 85% of past graduating class borrowed through all loan programs. **Average need-based loan:** Freshmen: $3278. Undergraduates: $4799. **Parent loans:** $2,046,821 (67% need-based, 33% non-need-based). **Programs:** Federal Direct (Subsidized and Unsubsidized Stafford, PLUS), Perkins, college/university.

WORK-STUDY *Federal work-study:* Total amount: $211,058; jobs available.

APPLYING FOR FINANCIAL AID *Required financial aid form:* FAFSA. **Financial aid deadline (priority):** 2/15. **Notification date:** Continuous beginning 3/1. Students must reply by 5/1.

CONTACT Elizabeth M. Gorra, Director of Financial Aid, Wheelock College, 200 Riverway, Boston, MA 02215-4176, 617-879-2443 or toll-free 800-734-5212. *E-mail:* egorra@wheelock.edu.

Website: http://www.wheelock.edu/.

WHITMAN COLLEGE
Walla Walla, WA

Tuition & fees: $49,766	Average undergraduate aid package: $37,926

ABOUT THE INSTITUTION Independent, coed. **Awards:** bachelor's degrees. 54 undergraduate majors. **Total enrollment:** 1,493. Undergraduates: 1,493. Freshmen: 405. Both federal and institutional methodology are used as a basis for awarding need-based institutional aid.

UNDERGRADUATE EXPENSES for 2017–2018 Application fee: $50. **Comprehensive fee:** $62,290 includes full-time tuition ($49,390), mandatory fees ($376), and room and board ($12,524). **College room only:** $5674. Room and board charges vary according to board plan and housing facility. **Part-time tuition:** $2057.92 per credit. Part-time tuition and fees vary according to course load.

FRESHMAN FINANCIAL AID (Fall 2016, est.) 311 applied for aid; of those 54% were deemed to have need. 100% of freshmen with need received aid; of those 20% had need fully met. **Average percent of need met:** 90% (excluding resources awarded to replace EFC). **Average financial aid package:** $36,324 (excluding resources awarded to replace EFC). 29% of all full-time freshmen had no need and received non-need-based gift aid.

UNDERGRADUATE FINANCIAL AID (Fall 2016, est.) 1,173 applied for aid; of those 57% were deemed to have need. 100% of undergraduates with need received aid; of those 30% had need fully met. **Average percent of need met:** 92% (excluding resources awarded to replace EFC). **Average financial aid package:** $37,926 (excluding resources awarded to replace EFC). 29% of all full-time undergraduates had no need and received non-need-based gift aid.

GIFT AID (NEED-BASED) Total amount: $22,794,638 (4% federal, 1% state, 92% institutional, 3% external sources). **Receiving aid:** Freshmen: 41% (168); all full-time undergraduates: 44% (668). **Average award:** Freshmen: $32,417; Undergraduates: $32,952. **Scholarships, grants, and awards:** Federal Pell, FSEOG, state, private, college/university gift aid from institutional funds.

GIFT AID (NON-NEED-BASED) Total amount: $4,782,684 (96% institutional, 4% external sources). **Receiving aid:** Freshmen: 13% (54). Undergraduates: 16% (244). **Average award:** Freshmen: $11,561. Undergraduates: $10,314. **Scholarships, grants, and awards by category:** Academic interests/achievement: general academic interests/achievements. Creative arts/performance: art/fine arts, debating, music, theater/drama. Special characteristics: ethnic background, first-generation college students, international students, veterans, veterans' children. **Tuition waivers:** Full or partial for employees or children of employees.

LOANS Student loans: $4,343,351 (59% need-based, 41% non-need-based). 38% of past graduating class borrowed through all loan programs. Average indebtedness per student: $18,089. **Average need-based loan:** Freshmen: $2443. Undergraduates: $3658. **Parent loans:** $1,477,758 (100% non-need-based). **Programs:** Federal Direct (Subsidized and Unsubsidized Stafford, PLUS), Perkins, private loans.

WORK-STUDY *Federal work-study:* Total amount: $604,725; jobs available. **State or other work-study/employment:** Total amount: $356,855 (100% need-based). Part-time jobs available.

APPLYING FOR FINANCIAL AID *Required financial aid forms:* FAFSA, CSS Financial Aid PROFILE, noncustodial (divorced/separated) parent's statement, federal income tax form(s), W-2 forms. **Financial aid deadline:** 2/1 (priority: 11/15). **Notification date:** 4/1. Students must reply by 5/1.

CONTACT Tyson Harlow, Assistant Director, Whitman College, 345 Boyer Avenue, Walla Walla, WA 99362-2046, 509-527-5178 or toll-free 877-462-9448. *Fax:* 509-527-4967.

Website: http://www.whitman.edu/.

WHITTIER COLLEGE
Whittier, CA

Tuition & fees: $46,110	Average undergraduate aid package: $35,665

ABOUT THE INSTITUTION Independent, coed. **Awards:** bachelor's, master's, and doctoral degrees. 36 undergraduate majors. **Total enrollment:** 2,074. Undergraduates: 1,615. Freshmen: 426. Federal methodology is used as a basis for awarding need-based institutional aid.

UNDERGRADUATE EXPENSES for 2017–2018 *Application fee:* $50. *Comprehensive fee:* $59,438 includes full-time tuition ($45,720), mandatory fees ($390), and room and board ($13,328). *College room only:* $7198. Full-time tuition and fees vary according to course load. Room and board charges vary according to board plan. *Part-time tuition:* $1905 per semester hour. Part-time tuition and fees vary according to course load.

FRESHMAN FINANCIAL AID (Fall 2016, est.) 383 applied for aid; of those 93% were deemed to have need. 100% of freshmen with need received aid; of those 17% had need fully met. *Average percent of need met:* 78% (excluding resources awarded to replace EFC). *Average financial aid package:* $36,933 (excluding resources awarded to replace EFC). 14% of all full-time freshmen had no need and received non-need-based gift aid.

UNDERGRADUATE FINANCIAL AID (Fall 2016, est.) 1,319 applied for aid; of those 93% were deemed to have need. 99% of undergraduates with need received aid; of those 16% had need fully met. *Average percent of need met:* 77% (excluding resources awarded to replace EFC). *Average financial aid package:* $35,665 (excluding resources awarded to replace EFC). 17% of all full-time undergraduates had no need and received non-need-based gift aid.

GIFT AID (NEED-BASED) *Total amount:* $30,211,948 (10% federal, 14% state, 75% institutional, 1% external sources). *Receiving aid:* Freshmen: 72% (305); all full-time undergraduates: 69% (1,079). *Average award:* Freshmen: $34,244; Undergraduates: $32,434. *Scholarships, grants, and awards:* Federal Pell, FSEOG, state, private, college/university gift aid from institutional funds.

GIFT AID (NON-NEED-BASED) *Total amount:* $16,101,570 (99% institutional, 1% external sources). *Receiving aid:* Freshmen: 12% (50). Undergraduates: 9% (139). *Average award:* Freshmen: $20,516. Undergraduates: $22,431. *Scholarships, grants, and awards by category:* Academic interests/achievement: general academic interests/achievements. Creative arts/performance: art/fine arts, music, theater/drama. Special characteristics: children and siblings of alumni, children of faculty/staff, international students. *Tuition waivers:* Full or partial for employees or children of employees. *ROTC:* Army cooperative.

LOANS *Student loans:* $10,463,645 (59% need-based, 41% non-need-based). 75% of past graduating class borrowed through all loan programs. *Average indebtedness per student:* $31,826. *Average need-based loan:* Freshmen: $5245. Undergraduates: $5676. *Parent loans:* $7,200,296 (40% need-based, 60% non-need-based). *Programs:* Federal Direct (Subsidized and Unsubsidized Stafford, PLUS), Perkins, college/university, alternative loans.

WORK-STUDY *Federal work-study:* Total amount: $337,363; 146 jobs averaging $2374. *State or other work-study/employment:* Total amount: $1,173,437 (82% need-based, 18% non-need-based). 572 part-time jobs averaging $1977.

APPLYING FOR FINANCIAL AID *Required financial aid form:* FAFSA. *Financial aid deadline:* 6/30 (priority: 3/1). *Notification date:* Continuous beginning 2/15. Students must reply within 2 weeks of notification.

CONTACT Mrs. Julie Aldama, Director of Financial Aid, Whittier College, 13406 East Philadelphia Street, Whittier, CA 90608-0634, 562-907-4285. *Fax:* 562-464-4560. *E-mail:* jaldama@whittier.edu. *Website:* http://www.whittier.edu/.

WHITWORTH UNIVERSITY
Spokane, WA

Tuition & fees: $42,186	Average undergraduate aid package: $34,546

ABOUT THE INSTITUTION Independent Presbyterian, coed. *Awards:* certificates, bachelor's, and master's degrees. 65 undergraduate majors. *Total enrollment:* 2,667. Undergraduates: 2,308. Freshmen: 595. Federal methodology is used as a basis for awarding need-based institutional aid.

UNDERGRADUATE EXPENSES for 2017–2018 *Comprehensive fee:* $53,682 includes full-time tuition ($41,086), mandatory fees ($1100), and room and board ($11,496). *College room only:* $6250. Room and board charges vary according to board plan and housing facility. *Part-time tuition:* $1712 per credit. *Part-time fees:* $490 per term. Part-time tuition and fees vary according to course load.

FRESHMAN FINANCIAL AID (Fall 2016, est.) 511 applied for aid; of those 84% were deemed to have need. 100% of freshmen with need received aid; of those 16% had need fully met. *Average percent of need met:* 80% (excluding resources awarded to replace EFC). *Average financial aid package:* $37,108 (excluding resources awarded to replace EFC). 26% of all full-time freshmen had no need and received non-need-based gift aid.

UNDERGRADUATE FINANCIAL AID (Fall 2016, est.) 1,731 applied for aid; of those 88% were deemed to have need. 100% of undergraduates with need received aid; of those 14% had need fully met. *Average percent of need met:* 79% (excluding resources awarded to replace EFC). *Average financial aid package:* $34,546 (excluding resources awarded to replace EFC). 29% of all full-time undergraduates had no need and received non-need-based gift aid.

GIFT AID (NEED-BASED) *Total amount:* $39,279,516 (6% federal, 8% state, 82% institutional, 4% external sources). *Receiving aid:* Freshmen: 72% (426); all full-time undergraduates: 68% (1,506). *Average award:* Freshmen: $28,026; Undergraduates: $25,948. *Scholarships, grants, and awards:* Federal Pell, FSEOG, state, private, college/university gift aid from institutional funds.

GIFT AID (NON-NEED-BASED) *Total amount:* $14,257,146 (2% federal, 1% state, 95% institutional, 2% external sources). *Receiving aid:* Freshmen: 8% (50). Undergraduates: 7% (150). *Average award:* Freshmen: $21,396. Undergraduates: $19,334. *Scholarships, grants, and awards by category:* Academic interests/achievement: 1,860 awards ($29,822,554 total): general academic interests/achievements, military science. Creative arts/performance: 229 awards ($911,703 total): art/fine arts, creative writing, debating, journalism/publications, music, theater/drama. Special achievements/activities: 31 awards ($30,500 total): religious involvement. Special characteristics: 700 awards ($2,083,601 total): children and siblings of alumni, ethnic background, international students, members of minority groups, religious affiliation, veterans, veterans' children. *Tuition waivers:* Full or partial for employees or children of employees, senior citizens. *ROTC:* Army cooperative.

LOANS *Student loans:* $11,343,679 (79% need-based, 21% non-need-based). 61% of past graduating class borrowed through all loan programs. *Average indebtedness per student:* $28,294. *Average need-based loan:* Freshmen: $3987. Undergraduates: $4737. *Parent loans:* $4,712,920 (48% need-based, 52% non-need-based). *Programs:* Federal Direct (Subsidized and Unsubsidized Stafford, PLUS), Perkins, college/university.

WORK-STUDY *Federal work-study:* Total amount: $2,123,830; 844 jobs averaging $2351. *State or other work-study/employment:* Total amount: $297,496 (100% need-based). 101 part-time jobs averaging $3195.

APPLYING FOR FINANCIAL AID *Required financial aid form:* FAFSA. *Financial aid deadline (priority):* 12/1. *Notification date:* Continuous beginning 1/17.

CONTACT Mrs. Traci L. Spoon Stensland, Director of Financial Aid, Whitworth University, 300 West Hawthorne Road, Spokane, WA 99251-0001, 509-777-4335 or toll-free 800-533-4668. *Fax:* 509-777-4601. *E-mail:* tstensland@whitworth.edu. *Website:* http://www.whitworth.edu/.

WICHITA STATE UNIVERSITY
Wichita, KS

Tuition & fees (KS res): $7895	Average undergraduate aid package: $5842

ABOUT THE INSTITUTION State-supported, coed. *Awards:* certificates, associate, bachelor's, master's, and doctoral degrees. 63 undergraduate majors. *Total enrollment:* 14,474. Undergraduates: 11,823. Freshmen: 1,476. Federal methodology is used as a basis for awarding need-based institutional aid.

UNDERGRADUATE EXPENSES for 2016–2017 *Application fee:* $30. *Tuition, state resident:* full-time $6385; part-time $212.84 per credit hour. *Tuition, nonresident:* full-time $15,124; part-time $504.16 per credit hour. *Required fees:* full-time $1510. Full-time tuition and fees vary according to course level, course load, degree level, program, and student level. Part-time tuition and fees vary according to course level, course load, degree level, program, and student level. *College room and board:* $10,980. Room and board charges vary according to board plan and housing facility.

FRESHMAN FINANCIAL AID (Fall 2015) 1,244 applied for aid; of those 39% were deemed to have need. 99% of freshmen with need received aid; of those 70% had need fully met. *Average percent of need met:* 52% (excluding resources awarded to replace EFC). *Average financial aid package:* $7347 (excluding resources awarded to replace EFC). 43% of all full-time freshmen had no need and received non-need-based gift aid.

UNDERGRADUATE FINANCIAL AID (Fall 2015) 7,784 applied for aid; of those 47% were deemed to have need. 99% of undergraduates with need received aid; of those 68% had need fully met. *Average percent of need met:* 63% (excluding resources awarded to replace EFC). *Average financial aid package:* $5842 (excluding resources awarded to replace EFC). 21% of all full-time undergraduates had no need and received non-need-based gift aid.

GIFT AID (NEED-BASED) *Total amount:* $19,552,007 (86% federal, 3% state, 10% institutional, 1% external sources). *Receiving aid:* Freshmen: 26% (330); all full-time undergraduates: 32% (2,706). *Average award:* Freshmen: $4340; Undergraduates: $4287. *Scholarships, grants, and awards:* Federal Pell, FSEOG, state, private, college/university gift aid from institutional funds, Bureau of Indian Affairs Grants.

GIFT AID (NON-NEED-BASED) *Total amount:* $9,239,444 (1% federal, 1% state, 83% institutional, 15% external sources). *Receiving aid:* Freshmen: 24% (306). Undergraduates: 14% (1,172). *Average award:* Freshmen: $1349. Undergraduates: $1499. *Scholarships, grants, and awards by category: Academic interests/ achievement:* biological sciences, business, communication, computer science, education, engineering/technologies, English, foreign languages, general academic interests/achievements, humanities, international studies, mathematics, physical sciences, premedicine, social sciences. *Creative arts/performance:* applied art and design, art/fine arts, creative writing, dance, general creative arts/performance, journalism/publications, music, performing arts, theater/drama. *Special achievements/activities:* general special achievements/activities, leadership, memberships. *Special characteristics:* adult students, children of faculty/staff, first-generation college students, international students, local/state students, members of minority groups, veterans. *Tuition waivers:* Full or partial for employees or children of employees, senior citizens.

LOANS *Student loans:* $43,873,995 (49% need-based, 51% non-need-based). 61% of past graduating class borrowed through all loan programs. *Average indebtedness per student:* $39,122. *Average need-based loan:* Freshmen: $2044. Undergraduates: $2564. *Parent loans:* $3,565,701 (100% non-need-based). *Programs:* Federal Direct (Subsidized and Unsubsidized Stafford, PLUS), Perkins.

WORK-STUDY *Federal work-study:* jobs available. *State or other work-study/employment:* Total amount: $81,999 (100% need-based). Part-time jobs available.

ATHLETIC AWARDS Total amount: $2,206,324 (100% non-need-based).

APPLYING FOR FINANCIAL AID *Required financial aid forms:* FAFSA, university department scholarship application(s). *Financial aid deadline (priority):* 3/1. *Notification date:* Continuous beginning 10/15. Students must reply by 5/1 or within 2 weeks of notification.

CONTACT Sheelu Surender, Director of Financial Aid, Wichita State University, 1845 Fairmount Street, Wichita, KS 67260-0024, 316-978-5337 or toll-free 800-362-2594. *Fax:* 316-978-3396. *E-mail:* sheelu.surender@wichita.edu. *Website:* http://www.wichita.edu/.

WIDENER UNIVERSITY
Chester, PA

Tuition & fees: $42,870	Average undergraduate aid package: $32,580

ABOUT THE INSTITUTION Independent, coed. *Awards:* certificates, associate, bachelor's, master's, and doctoral degrees. 74 undergraduate majors. *Total enrollment:* 6,402. Undergraduates: 3,591. Freshmen: 729. Both federal and institutional methodology are used as a basis for awarding need-based institutional aid.

UNDERGRADUATE EXPENSES for 2016–2017 *Comprehensive fee:* $56,486 includes full-time tuition ($42,034), mandatory fees ($836), and room and board ($13,616). *College room only:* $7088. Full-time tuition and fees vary according to class time, course load, and program. Room and board charges vary according to board plan and housing facility. *Part-time tuition:* $1400 per credit.

FRESHMAN FINANCIAL AID (Fall 2016, est.) 684 applied for aid; of those 90% were deemed to have need. 100% of freshmen with need received aid; of those 21% had need fully met. *Average percent of need met:* 81% (excluding resources awarded to replace EFC). *Average financial aid package:* $34,200 (excluding resources awarded to replace EFC). 8% of all full-time freshmen had no need and received non-need-based gift aid.

UNDERGRADUATE FINANCIAL AID (Fall 2016, est.) 2,593 applied for aid; of those 90% were deemed to have need. 100% of undergraduates with need received aid; of those 22% had need fully met. *Average percent of need met:* 80% (excluding resources awarded to replace EFC). *Average financial aid package:* $32,580 (excluding resources awarded to replace EFC). 7% of all full-time undergraduates had no need and received non-need-based gift aid.

GIFT AID (NEED-BASED) *Total amount:* $61,415,414 (7% federal, 4% state, 87% institutional, 2% external sources). *Receiving aid:* Freshmen: 83% (607); all full-time undergraduates: 77% (2,280). *Average award:* Freshmen: $29,160; Undergraduates: $26,700. *Scholarships, grants, and awards:* Federal Pell, FSEOG, state, private, college/university gift aid from institutional funds.

GIFT AID (NON-NEED-BASED) *Total amount:* $10,519,488 (97% institutional, 3% external sources). *Receiving aid:* Freshmen: 83% (604). Undergraduates: 73% (2,165). *Average award:* Freshmen: $26,500. Undergraduates: $23,800. *Scholarships, grants, and awards by category: Academic interests/achievement:* 2,555 awards ($55,259,293 total): biological sciences, business, communication, computer science, education, engineering/technologies, English, foreign languages, general academic interests/achievements, health fields, humanities, international studies, mathematics, military science, physical sciences, premedicine, social sciences. *Creative arts/performance:* 88 awards ($208,500 total): dance, music. *Special achievements/activities:* 47 awards ($235,000 total): community service, general special achievements/activities, leadership. *Special characteristics:* 86 awards ($2,297,000 total): adult students, children of faculty/staff, ethnic background, international students. *Tuition waivers:* Full or partial for employees or children of employees, senior citizens. *ROTC:* Army, Naval cooperative, Air Force cooperative.

LOANS *Student loans:* $29,334,092 (93% need-based, 7% non-need-based). *Average need-based loan:* Freshmen: $3850. Undergraduates: $4680. *Parent loans:* $8,477,138 (95% need-based, 5% non-need-based). *Programs:* Federal Direct (Subsidized and Unsubsidized Stafford, PLUS), Perkins, college/university.

WORK-STUDY *Federal work-study:* Total amount: $3,081,370; 1,565 jobs averaging $1960. *State or other work-study/employment:* Part-time jobs available.

APPLYING FOR FINANCIAL AID *Required financial aid form:* FAFSA. *Financial aid deadline (priority):* 2/15. *Notification date:* Continuous beginning 1/30. Students must reply within 4 weeks of notification.

CONTACT Thomas K. Malloy, Executive Director of Enrollment Management, Widener University, One University Place, Chester, PA 19013-5792, 610-499-4161 or toll-free 888-WIDENER. *Fax:* 610-499-4687. *E-mail:* finaidmc@mail.widener.edu. *Website:* http://www.widener.edu/.

WILBERFORCE UNIVERSITY
Wilberforce, OH

CONTACT Director of Financial Aid, Wilberforce University, 1055 North Bickett Road, Wilberforce, OH 45384, 937-708-5727 or toll-free 800-367-8568. *Fax:* 937-376-4752. *Website:* http://www.wilberforce.edu/.

WILEY COLLEGE
Marshall, TX

CONTACT Mr. Alan D. Jackson Jr., Director of Financial Aid, Wiley College, 711 Wiley Avenue, Marshall, TX 75670-5199, 903-927-3217 or toll-free 800-658-6889. *E-mail:* adjackson2@wileyc.edu. *Website:* http://www.wileyc.edu/.

WILKES UNIVERSITY
Wilkes-Barre, PA

Tuition & fees: $33,568	Average undergraduate aid package: $24,604

ABOUT THE INSTITUTION Independent, coed. *Awards:* bachelor's, master's, and doctoral degrees. 39 undergraduate majors. *Total enrollment:* 5,552. Undergraduates: 2,561. Freshmen: 664. Federal methodology is used as a basis for awarding need-based institutional aid.

UNDERGRADUATE EXPENSES for 2016–2017 *Application fee:* $40. *Comprehensive fee:* $47,314 includes full-time tuition ($31,946), mandatory fees ($1622), and room and board ($13,746). *College room only:* $8274. Room and board charges vary according to board plan and housing facility. **Part-time tuition:** $887 per credit hour. **Part-time fees:** $72 per credit hour.

FRESHMAN FINANCIAL AID (Fall 2016, est.) 614 applied for aid; of those 93% were deemed to have need. 100% of freshmen with need received aid; of those 10% had need fully met. **Average percent of need met:** 72% (excluding resources awarded to replace EFC). **Average financial aid package:** $25,938 (excluding resources awarded to replace EFC). 6% of all full-time freshmen had no need and received non-need-based gift aid.

UNDERGRADUATE FINANCIAL AID (Fall 2016, est.) 1,986 applied for aid; of those 93% were deemed to have need. 100% of undergraduates with need received aid; of those 11% had need fully met. **Average percent of need met:** 69% (excluding resources awarded to replace EFC). **Average financial aid package:** $24,604 (excluding resources awarded to replace EFC). 5% of all full-time undergraduates had no need and received non-need-based gift aid.

GIFT AID (NEED-BASED) Total amount: $37,595,292 (12% federal, 9% state, 78% institutional, 1% external sources). **Receiving aid:** Freshmen: 86% (570); all full-time undergraduates: 79% (1,807). **Average award:** Freshmen: $22,754; Undergraduates: $20,242. **Scholarships, grants, and awards:** Federal Pell, FSEOG, state, private, college/university gift aid from institutional funds.

GIFT AID (NON-NEED-BASED) Total amount: $3,345,226 (2% federal, 93% institutional, 5% external sources). **Receiving aid:** Freshmen: 67% (442). Undergraduates: 62% (1,430). **Average award:** Freshmen: $16,263. Undergraduates: $13,090. **Scholarships, grants, and awards by category:** Academic interests/achievement: general academic interests/achievements. Creative arts/performance: performing arts, theater/drama. Special achievements/activities: general special achievements/activities, leadership. Special characteristics: children of faculty/staff. **Tuition waivers:** Full or partial for employees or children of employees. **ROTC:** Army cooperative, Air Force.

LOANS Student loans: $20,213,804 (89% need-based, 11% non-need-based). 82% of past graduating class borrowed through all loan programs. Average indebtedness per student: $43,241. **Average need-based loan:** Freshmen: $3461. Undergraduates: $4405. **Parent loans:** $5,700,212 (85% need-based, 15% non-need-based). **Programs:** Federal Direct (Subsidized and Unsubsidized Stafford, PLUS), Perkins, Federal Nursing, state, college/university, Gulf Oil Loan Fund, Rulison Evans Loan Fund.

WORK-STUDY Federal work-study: Total amount: $1,130,141; jobs available. **State or other work-study/employment:** Part-time jobs available.

APPLYING FOR FINANCIAL AID Required financial aid form: FAFSA. **Financial aid deadline (priority):** 3/1. **Notification date:** Continuous beginning 3/1.

CONTACT Chanel Greene, Executive Director of Financial Aid, Wilkes University, 84 West South Street, Wilkes-Barre, PA 18766, 570-408-2000 or toll-free 800-945-5378 Ext. 4400. Fax: 570-408-4004. E-mail: financialaid@wilkes.edu. Website: http://www.wilkes.edu/.

WILLAMETTE UNIVERSITY
Salem, OR

Tuition & fees: $48,164	Average undergraduate aid package: $35,895

ABOUT THE INSTITUTION Independent United Methodist, coed. **Awards:** bachelor's, master's, and doctoral degrees. 56 undergraduate majors. **Total enrollment:** 2,665. Undergraduates: 2,002. Freshmen: 474. Federal methodology is used as a basis for awarding need-based institutional aid.

UNDERGRADUATE EXPENSES for 2017–2018 Application fee: $50. **Comprehensive fee:** $59,994 includes full-time tuition ($47,840), mandatory fees ($324), and room and board ($11,830). Full-time tuition and fees vary according to course load. Room and board charges vary according to board plan and housing facility. **Part-time tuition:** $5980 per credit. Part-time tuition and fees vary according to course load. **Payment plan:** Tuition prepayment.

FRESHMAN FINANCIAL AID (Fall 2016, est.) 419 applied for aid; of those 79% were deemed to have need. 100% of freshmen with need received aid; of those 26% had need fully met. **Average percent of need met:** 82% (excluding resources awarded to replace EFC). **Average financial aid package:** $37,016 (excluding resources awarded to replace EFC). 29% of all full-time freshmen had no need and received non-need-based gift aid.

UNDERGRADUATE FINANCIAL AID (Fall 2016, est.) 1,354 applied for aid; of those 86% were deemed to have need. 100% of undergraduates with need received

aid; of those 26% had need fully met. **Average percent of need met:** 80% (excluding resources awarded to replace EFC). **Average financial aid package:** $35,895 (excluding resources awarded to replace EFC). 36% of all full-time undergraduates had no need and received non-need-based gift aid.

GIFT AID (NEED-BASED) Total amount: $35,243,206 (7% federal, 1% state, 89% institutional, 3% external sources). **Receiving aid:** Freshmen: 68% (322); all full-time undergraduates: 62% (1,148). **Average award:** Freshmen: $31,229; Undergraduates: $29,689. **Scholarships, grants, and awards:** Federal Pell, FSEOG, state, private, college/university gift aid from institutional funds.

GIFT AID (NON-NEED-BASED) Total amount: $13,210,503 (99% institutional, 1% external sources). **Receiving aid:** Freshmen: 21% (99). Undergraduates: 11% (200). **Average award:** Freshmen: $22,438. Undergraduates: $21,056. **Scholarships, grants, and awards by category:** Academic interests/achievement: general academic interests/achievements. Creative arts/performance: general creative arts/performance. Special achievements/activities: general special achievements/activities. Special characteristics: general special characteristics. **Tuition waivers:** Full or partial for employees or children of employees. **ROTC:** Army cooperative, Air Force cooperative.

LOANS Student loans: $9,530,672 (91% need-based, 9% non-need-based). 62% of past graduating class borrowed through all loan programs. Average indebtedness per student: $29,958. **Average need-based loan:** Freshmen: $3497. Undergraduates: $5473. **Parent loans:** $3,910,123 (94% need-based, 6% non-need-based). **Programs:** Federal Direct (Subsidized and Unsubsidized Stafford, PLUS), Perkins.

WORK-STUDY Federal work-study: Total amount: $1,219,877; jobs available. **State or other work-study/employment:** Part-time jobs available.

APPLYING FOR FINANCIAL AID Required financial aid form: FAFSA. **Financial aid deadline (priority):** 2/1. **Notification date:** 3/15. Students must reply by 5/1 or within 2 weeks of notification.

CONTACT Patty Hoban, Director of Financial Aid, Willamette University, 900 State Street, Salem, OR 97301-3931, 503-370-6273 or toll-free 877-542-2787. Fax: 503-370-6588. E-mail: phoban@willamette.edu. Website: http://www.willamette.edu/.

WILLIAM CAREY UNIVERSITY
Hattiesburg, MS

CONTACT Ms. Brenda Pittman, Associate Director of Financial Aid, William Carey University, 498 Tuscan Avenue, Hattiesburg, MS 39401-5499, 601-318-6153 or toll-free 800-962-5991. Website: http://www.wmcarey.edu/.

WILLIAM JESSUP UNIVERSITY
Rocklin, CA

Tuition & fees: $28,700	Average undergraduate aid package: $21,232

ABOUT THE INSTITUTION Independent nondenominational, coed. **Awards:** certificates, associate, bachelor's, and master's degrees. 19 undergraduate majors. **Total enrollment:** 1,161. Undergraduates: 1,097. Freshmen: 147. Federal methodology is used as a basis for awarding need-based institutional aid.

UNDERGRADUATE EXPENSES for 2016–2017 Application fee: $45. **Comprehensive fee:** $39,350 includes full-time tuition ($28,300), mandatory fees ($400), and room and board ($10,650). Full-time tuition and fees vary according to course load. Room and board charges vary according to board plan and housing facility. **Part-time tuition:** $1190 per credit. Part-time tuition and fees vary according to course load.

FRESHMAN FINANCIAL AID (Fall 2016, est.) 186 applied for aid; of those 91% were deemed to have need. 100% of freshmen with need received aid; of those 18% had need fully met. **Average percent of need met:** 71% (excluding resources awarded to replace EFC). **Average financial aid package:** $23,226 (excluding resources awarded to replace EFC). 12% of all full-time freshmen had no need and received non-need-based gift aid.

UNDERGRADUATE FINANCIAL AID (Fall 2016, est.) 899 applied for aid; of those 92% were deemed to have need. 100% of undergraduates with need received aid; of those 14% had need fully met. **Average percent of need met:** 65%

(excluding resources awarded to replace EFC). *Average financial aid package:* $21,232 (excluding resources awarded to replace EFC). 14% of all full-time undergraduates had no need and received non-need-based gift aid.

GIFT AID (NEED-BASED) *Total amount:* $13,262,017 (17% federal, 20% state, 59% institutional, 4% external sources). *Receiving aid:* Freshmen: 84% (169); all full-time undergraduates: 82% (816). *Average award:* Freshmen: $20,936; Undergraduates: $17,973. *Scholarships, grants, and awards:* Federal Pell, FSEOG, state, private, college/university gift aid from institutional funds.

GIFT AID (NON-NEED-BASED) *Total amount:* $1,848,743 (83% institutional, 17% external sources). *Receiving aid:* Freshmen: 12% (25). Undergraduates: 7% (74). *Average award:* Freshmen: $12,098. Undergraduates: $9109. *Scholarships, grants, and awards by category:* Academic interests/achievement: 727 awards ($4,044,544 total): area/ethnic studies, biological sciences, business, computer science, education, English, general academic interests/achievements, humanities, international studies, mathematics, physical sciences, religion/biblical studies, social sciences. *Creative arts/performance:* 231 awards ($763,614 total): applied art and design, art/fine arts, general creative arts/performance, music, performing arts, theater/drama. *Special achievements/activities:* 419 awards ($1,279,549 total): general special achievements/activities, leadership, religious involvement. *Special characteristics:* 540 awards ($1,940,578 total): adult students, children of faculty/staff, ethnic background, first-generation college students, general special characteristics, international students, out-of-state students, previous college experience, relatives of clergy, siblings of current students, veterans, veterans' children. *Tuition waivers:* Full or partial for employees or children of employees. *ROTC:* Air Force cooperative.

LOANS *Student loans:* $7,168,977 (51% need-based, 49% non-need-based). 73% of past graduating class borrowed through all loan programs. *Average indebtedness per student:* $24,656. *Average need-based loan:* Freshmen: $3366. Undergraduates: $4520. *Parent loans:* $1,945,523 (55% need-based, 45% non-need-based). *Programs:* Federal Direct (Subsidized and Unsubsidized Stafford, PLUS).

WORK-STUDY *Federal work-study:* Total amount: $76,893; 148 jobs averaging $2313. *State or other work-study/employment:* Total amount: $450,000 (100% non-need-based). 125 part-time jobs averaging $2179.

ATHLETIC AWARDS Total amount: $2,149,184 (77% need-based, 23% non-need-based).

APPLYING FOR FINANCIAL AID *Required financial aid form:* FAFSA. *Financial aid deadline (priority):* 3/2. *Notification date:* Continuous beginning 3/2. Students must reply within 3 weeks of notification.

CONTACT Office of Financial Aid, William Jessup University, 2121 University Avenue, Rocklin, CA 95765, 916-577-2233. *Fax:* 916-577-2230. *E-mail:* finaid@jessup.edu.
Website: http://www.jessup.edu/.

WILLIAM JEWELL COLLEGE
Liberty, MO

Tuition & fees: $33,620	Average undergraduate aid package: $28,073

ABOUT THE INSTITUTION Independent, coed. *Awards:* certificates, bachelor's, and master's degrees (also offers evening program with significant enrollment not reflected in profile). 37 undergraduate majors. *Total enrollment:* 997. Undergraduates: 992. Freshmen: 241. Federal methodology is used as a basis for awarding need-based institutional aid.

UNDERGRADUATE EXPENSES for 2017–2018 *Comprehensive fee:* $43,260 includes full-time tuition ($32,850), mandatory fees ($770), and room and board ($9640). Full-time tuition and fees vary according to program. Room and board charges vary according to board plan and housing facility. *Part-time tuition:* $960 per credit hour.

FRESHMAN FINANCIAL AID (Fall 2016, est.) 226 applied for aid; of those 81% were deemed to have need. 100% of freshmen with need received aid; of those 40% had need fully met. *Average percent of need met:* 83% (excluding resources awarded to replace EFC). *Average financial aid package:* $31,216 (excluding resources awarded to replace EFC). 17% of all full-time freshmen had no need and received non-need-based gift aid.

UNDERGRADUATE FINANCIAL AID (Fall 2016, est.) 776 applied for aid; of those 87% were deemed to have need. 100% of undergraduates with need received aid; of those 27% had need fully met. *Average percent of need met:* 82% (excluding resources awarded to replace EFC). *Average financial aid package:*

$28,073 (excluding resources awarded to replace EFC). 30% of all full-time undergraduates had no need and received non-need-based gift aid.

GIFT AID (NEED-BASED) *Total amount:* $13,135,486 (12% federal, 4% state, 81% institutional, 3% external sources). *Receiving aid:* Freshmen: 76% (184); all full-time undergraduates: 63% (617). *Average award:* Freshmen: $22,930; Undergraduates: $21,406. *Scholarships, grants, and awards:* Federal Pell, FSEOG, state, college/university gift aid from institutional funds.

GIFT AID (NON-NEED-BASED) *Total amount:* $4,881,185 (1% state, 96% institutional, 3% external sources). *Receiving aid:* Freshmen: 76% (184). Undergraduates: 65% (632). *Average award:* Freshmen: $20,422. Undergraduates: $17,584. *Scholarships, grants, and awards by category:* Academic interests/achievement: 860 awards ($12,087,514 total): general academic interests/achievements. *Creative arts/performance:* 150 awards ($474,145 total): dance, debating, journalism/publications, music, theater/drama. *Special achievements/activities:* 16 awards ($33,500 total): cheerleading/drum major, religious involvement. *Special characteristics:* 159 awards ($866,330 total): children and siblings of alumni, children of faculty/staff, siblings of current students. *Tuition waivers:* Full or partial for employees or children of employees. *ROTC:* Army cooperative.

LOANS *Student loans:* $6,268,294 (72% need-based, 28% non-need-based). 69% of past graduating class borrowed through all loan programs. *Average indebtedness per student:* $31,183. *Average need-based loan:* Freshmen: $4152. Undergraduates: $4712. *Parent loans:* $1,615,720 (88% need-based, 12% non-need-based). *Programs:* Federal Direct (Subsidized and Unsubsidized Stafford, PLUS), Perkins, Federal Nursing, alternative loans.

WORK-STUDY *Federal work-study:* Total amount: $1,112,072; 408 jobs averaging $2341. *State or other work-study/employment:* 150 part-time jobs averaging $437.

ATHLETIC AWARDS Total amount: $4,298,849 (60% need-based, 40% non-need-based).

APPLYING FOR FINANCIAL AID *Required financial aid form:* FAFSA. *Financial aid deadline (priority):* 3/1. *Notification date:* Continuous beginning 11/1. Students must reply within 2 weeks of notification.

CONTACT Mr. Daniel Holt, Director of Financial Aid and Scholarship Services, William Jewell College, 500 College Hill, Liberty, MO 64068, 816-415-5977 or toll-free 888-2JEWELL. *Fax:* 816-415-5006. *E-mail:* holtd@william.jewell.edu. *Website:* http://www.jewell.edu/.

WILLIAM PATERSON UNIVERSITY OF NEW JERSEY
Wayne, NJ

Tuition & fees (NJ res): $12,574	Average undergraduate aid package: $10,524

ABOUT THE INSTITUTION State-supported, coed. *Awards:* certificates, bachelor's, master's, and doctoral degrees. 51 undergraduate majors. *Total enrollment:* 10,583. Undergraduates: 9,088. Freshmen: 1,376. Federal methodology is used as a basis for awarding need-based institutional aid.

UNDERGRADUATE EXPENSES for 2016–2017 *Application fee:* $50. *Tuition, state resident:* full-time $9976; part-time $319 per credit. *Tuition, non-resident:* full-time $17,868; part-time $579 per credit. *Required fees:* full-time $2598; $84 per credit. Full-time tuition and fees vary according to course load and location. Part-time tuition and fees vary according to course load and location. *College room and board:* $11,103; *Room only:* $6973. Room and board charges vary according to board plan and housing facility.

FRESHMAN FINANCIAL AID (Fall 2016, est.) 1,313 applied for aid; of those 80% were deemed to have need. 98% of freshmen with need received aid; of those 33% had need fully met. *Average financial aid package:* $10,798 (excluding resources awarded to replace EFC). 8% of all full-time freshmen had no need and received non-need-based gift aid.

UNDERGRADUATE FINANCIAL AID (Fall 2016, est.) 6,676 applied for aid; of those 83% were deemed to have need. 98% of undergraduates with need received aid; of those 27% had need fully met. *Average financial aid package:* $10,524 (excluding resources awarded to replace EFC). 7% of all full-time undergraduates had no need and received non-need-based gift aid.

GIFT AID (NEED-BASED) *Total amount:* $32,313,358 (59% federal, 40% state, 1% institutional). *Receiving aid:* Freshmen: 51% (700); all full-time undergraduates:

50% (3,747). *Average award:* Freshmen: $9222; Undergraduates: $8185. *Scholarships, grants, and awards:* Federal Pell, FSEOG, state, private, college/university gift aid from institutional funds.

GIFT AID (NON-NEED-BASED) *Total amount:* $9,410,589 (1% state, 95% institutional, 4% external sources). *Receiving aid:* Freshmen: 19% (258). Undergraduates: 19% (1,389). *Average award:* Freshmen: $7886. Undergraduates: $5273. *Scholarships, grants, and awards by category:* Academic interests/achievement: 1,878 awards ($8,314,510 total): general academic interests/achievements. *Creative arts/performance:* 93 awards ($331,580 total): art/fine arts, music. *Special characteristics:* 63 awards ($364,225 total): children of faculty/staff, veterans. *Tuition waivers:* Full or partial for employees or children of employees, senior citizens.

LOANS *Student loans:* $47,521,930 (44% need-based, 56% non-need-based). 74% of past graduating class borrowed through all loan programs. *Average indebtedness per student:* $32,949. *Average need-based loan:* Freshmen: $3397. Undergraduates: $4377. *Parent loans:* $8,616,348 (100% non-need-based). *Programs:* Federal Direct (Subsidized and Unsubsidized Stafford, PLUS), Federal Nursing, state.

WORK-STUDY *Federal work-study:* Total amount: $364,568; 199 jobs averaging $1832.

APPLYING FOR FINANCIAL AID *Required financial aid form:* FAFSA. *Financial aid deadline (priority):* 3/1. *Notification date:* Continuous beginning 2/15.

CONTACT Michael Corso, Director of Financial Aid, William Paterson University of New Jersey, 300 Pompton Road, Morris Hall, 1st Floor, Wayne, NJ 07470, 973-720-2202 or toll-free 877-WPU-EXCEL. *Fax:* 973-720-3133. *E-mail:* finaid@wpunj.edu. *Website:* http://www.wpunj.edu/.

WILLIAM PEACE UNIVERSITY
Raleigh, NC

Tuition & fees: $28,700	Average undergraduate aid package: $18,464

ABOUT THE INSTITUTION Independent Presbyterian Church (U.S.A.), coed. *Awards:* bachelor's degrees. 19 undergraduate majors. *Total enrollment:* 1,034. Undergraduates: 1,034. Freshmen: 190. Federal methodology is used as a basis for awarding need-based institutional aid.

UNDERGRADUATE EXPENSES for 2017–2018 *Application fee:* $35. *Comprehensive fee:* $39,500 includes full-time tuition ($28,500), mandatory fees ($200), and room and board ($10,800). *College room only:* $7200. Full-time tuition and fees vary according to class time and course load. Room and board charges vary according to board plan. *Part-time tuition:* $950 per credit hour. Part-time tuition and fees vary according to class time and course load.

FRESHMAN FINANCIAL AID (Fall 2016, est.) 194 applied for aid; of those 94% were deemed to have need. *Average percent of need met:* 60% (excluding resources awarded to replace EFC). *Average financial aid package:* $19,794 (excluding resources awarded to replace EFC). 4% of all full-time freshmen had no need and received non-need-based gift aid.

UNDERGRADUATE FINANCIAL AID (Fall 2016, est.) 828 applied for aid; of those 92% were deemed to have need. *Average percent of need met:* 64% (excluding resources awarded to replace EFC). *Average financial aid package:* $18,464 (excluding resources awarded to replace EFC). 7% of all full-time undergraduates had no need and received non-need-based gift aid.

GIFT AID (NEED-BASED) *Total amount:* $6,400,620 (43% federal, 21% state, 35% institutional, 1% external sources). *Receiving aid:* Freshmen: 86% (172); all full-time undergraduates: 78% (693). *Average award:* Freshmen: $9967; Undergraduates: $8612. *Scholarships, grants, and awards:* Federal Pell, FSEOG, state, private, college/university gift aid from institutional funds.

GIFT AID (NON-NEED-BASED) *Total amount:* $400,000 (100% institutional). *Average award:* Freshmen: $4563. Undergraduates: $3171. *Scholarships, grants, and awards by category:* Academic interests/achievement: general academic interests/achievements. *Creative arts/performance:* 19 awards ($21,500 total): art/fine arts, performing arts. *Special achievements/activities:* 268 awards ($608,250 total): community service, leadership. *Special characteristics:* 38 awards ($43,578 total): children of faculty/staff, siblings of current students. *Tuition waivers:* Full or partial for employees or children of employees. *ROTC:* Army cooperative, Naval cooperative, Air Force cooperative.

LOANS *Student loans:* $5,965,774 (97% need-based, 3% non-need-based). 66% of past graduating class borrowed through all loan programs. *Average indebtedness per student:* $20,921. *Average need-based loan:* Freshmen: $2983. Undergraduates: $4095. *Parent loans:* $5,488,772 (81% need-based, 19% non-need-based). *Programs:* Federal Direct (Subsidized and Unsubsidized Stafford, PLUS), state, alternative loans.

WORK-STUDY *Federal work-study:* Total amount: $179,365; 93 jobs averaging $2000.

APPLYING FOR FINANCIAL AID *Required financial aid form:* FAFSA. *Financial aid deadline (priority):* 3/15. *Notification date:* Continuous beginning 3/1.

CONTACT Miss Michelle Hemmer, Director of Financial Aid, William Peace University, 15 East Peace Street, Raleigh, NC 27604, 919-508-2284. *Fax:* 919-508-2325. *E-mail:* michelle.hemmer@peace.edu. *Website:* http://www.peace.edu/.

WILLIAM PENN UNIVERSITY
Oskaloosa, IA

CONTACT Cyndi Peiffer, Director of Financial Aid, William Penn University, 201 Trueblood Avenue, Oskaloosa, IA 52577-1799, 641-673-1060, *Fax:* 641-673-1115. *E-mail:* peifferc@wmpenn.edu. *Website:* http://www.wmpenn.edu/.

WILLIAMS BAPTIST COLLEGE
Walnut Ridge, AR

Tuition & fees: $17,320	Average undergraduate aid package: $19,240

ABOUT THE INSTITUTION Independent Southern Baptist, coed. *Awards:* associate, bachelor's, and master's degrees. 26 undergraduate majors. *Total enrollment:* 469. Undergraduates: 469. Freshmen: 113. Federal methodology is used as a basis for awarding need-based institutional aid.

UNDERGRADUATE EXPENSES for 2017–2018 *Comprehensive fee:* $24,920 includes full-time tuition ($16,200), mandatory fees ($1120), and room and board ($7600). Room and board charges vary according to board plan. *Part-time tuition:* $675 per credit hour. *Part-time fees:* $81 per term. Part-time tuition and fees vary according to course load.

FRESHMAN FINANCIAL AID (Fall 2015) 123 applied for aid; of those 72% were deemed to have need. 100% of freshmen with need received aid. *Average financial aid package:* $14,263 (excluding resources awarded to replace EFC).

UNDERGRADUATE FINANCIAL AID (Fall 2015) 432 applied for aid; of those 75% were deemed to have need. 100% of undergraduates with need received aid. *Average financial aid package:* $19,240 (excluding resources awarded to replace EFC).

GIFT AID (NEED-BASED) *Total amount:* $1,177,491 (97% federal, 3% state). *Receiving aid:* Freshmen: 52% (67); all full-time undergraduates: 45% (244). *Average award:* Freshmen: $4486; Undergraduates: $4656. *Scholarships, grants, and awards:* Federal Pell, FSEOG, state, private, college/university gift aid from institutional funds.

GIFT AID (NON-NEED-BASED) *Total amount:* $2,821,823 (29% state, 59% institutional, 12% external sources). *Receiving aid:* Freshmen: 70% (89). Undergraduates: 60% (324). *Scholarships, grants, and awards by category:* Academic interests/achievement: 399 awards ($1,544,164 total): biological sciences, business, education, general academic interests/achievements, humanities, religion/biblical studies. *Creative arts/performance:* 40 awards ($44,800 total): art/fine arts, music, theater/drama. *Special achievements/activities:* 13 awards ($7000 total): cheerleading/drum major. *Special characteristics:* 65 awards ($117,872 total): children of faculty/staff, international students, members of minority groups, relatives of clergy, religious affiliation. *Tuition waivers:* Full or partial for employees or children of employees. *ROTC:* Army cooperative.

LOANS *Student loans:* $2,058,245 (52% need-based, 48% non-need-based). 69% of past graduating class borrowed through all loan programs. *Average indebtedness per student:* $19,295. *Average need-based loan:* Freshmen: $3050. Undergrad-

uates: $3789. **Parent loans:** $464,554 (100% non-need-based). **Programs:** Federal Direct (Subsidized and Unsubsidized Stafford, PLUS).

WORK-STUDY *Federal work-study:* 181 jobs averaging $1417. *State or other work-study/employment:* Total amount: $31,422 (100% non-need-based). 20 part-time jobs averaging $1571.

ATHLETIC AWARDS Total amount: $1,819,945 (100% non-need-based).

APPLYING FOR FINANCIAL AID *Required financial aid form:* FAFSA. *Financial aid deadline:* Continuous. *Notification date:* Continuous beginning 4/1. Students must reply within 2 weeks of notification.

CONTACT Mrs. Barbara Turner, Director of Financial Aid, Williams Baptist College, 60 West Fulbright Avenue, Walnut Ridge, AR 72476, 870-759-4112 or toll-free 800-722-4434. *Fax:* 870-759-4209. *E-mail:* bturner@wbcoll.edu.
Website: http://www.wbcoll.edu/.

WILLIAMS COLLEGE
Williamstown, MA

Tuition & fees: $51,790	Average undergraduate aid package: $51,890

ABOUT THE INSTITUTION Independent, coed. **Awards:** bachelor's and master's degrees. 40 undergraduate majors. **Total enrollment:** 2,134. Undergraduates: 2,076. Freshmen: 553. Institutional methodology is used as a basis for awarding need-based institutional aid.

UNDERGRADUATE EXPENSES for 2016–2017 *Application fee:* $65. *Comprehensive fee:* $65,480 includes full-time tuition ($51,490), mandatory fees ($300), and room and board ($13,690). *College room only:* $6930. Room and board charges vary according to board plan.

FRESHMAN FINANCIAL AID (Fall 2016, est.) 358 applied for aid; of those 79% were deemed to have need. 100% of freshmen with need received aid; of those 100% had need fully met. *Average percent of need met:* 100% (excluding resources awarded to replace EFC). *Average financial aid package:* $52,512 (excluding resources awarded to replace EFC).

UNDERGRADUATE FINANCIAL AID (Fall 2016, est.) 1,164 applied for aid; of those 87% were deemed to have need. 100% of undergraduates with need received aid; of those 100% had need fully met. *Average percent of need met:* 100% (excluding resources awarded to replace EFC). *Average financial aid package:* $51,890 (excluding resources awarded to replace EFC).

GIFT AID (NEED-BASED) *Total amount:* $49,569,275 (4% federal, 93% institutional, 3% external sources). *Receiving aid:* Freshmen: 51% (282); all full-time undergraduates: 50% (1,014). *Average award:* Freshmen: $50,286; Undergraduates: $48,885. *Scholarships, grants, and awards:* Federal Pell, FSEOG, state, private, college/university gift aid from institutional funds.

GIFT AID (NON-NEED-BASED) *Total amount:* $982,082 (1% federal, 99% external sources). *ROTC:* Air Force cooperative.

LOANS *Student loans:* $2,654,147 (42% need-based, 58% non-need-based). 43% of past graduating class borrowed through all loan programs. *Average indebtedness per student:* $15,496. *Average need-based loan:* Freshmen: $2608. Undergraduates: $2852. *Parent loans:* $2,675,318 (100% non-need-based). *Programs:* Federal Direct (Subsidized and Unsubsidized Stafford, PLUS), Perkins, college/university.

WORK-STUDY *Federal work-study:* Total amount: $966,471; jobs available. *State or other work-study/employment:* Total amount: $2,487,750 (39% need-based, 61% non-need-based). Part-time jobs available.

APPLYING FOR FINANCIAL AID *Required financial aid forms:* FAFSA, CSS Financial Aid PROFILE, noncustodial (divorced/separated) parent's statement, federal income tax form(s). *Financial aid deadline:* 1/15. *Notification date:* 3/31. Students must reply by 5/1.

CONTACT Mr. Paul J. Boyer, Director of Financial Aid, Williams College, PO Box 37, Weston Hall, 995 Main Street, Williamstown, MA 01267, 413-597-4181. *Fax:* 413-597-2999. *E-mail:* paul.j.boyer@williams.edu.
Website: http://www.williams.edu/.

WILLIAMSON COLLEGE
Franklin, TN

CONTACT Jeanie Maguire, Director of Financial Aid, Williamson College, 200 Seaboard Lane, Franklin, TN 37067, 615-771-7821. *Fax:* 615-771-7810. *E-mail:* info@williamsoncc.edu.
Website: http://www.williamsoncc.edu/.

WILLIAM WOODS UNIVERSITY
Fulton, MO

Tuition & fees: $23,260	Average undergraduate aid package: $17,620

ABOUT THE INSTITUTION Independent Christian Church (Disciples of Christ), coed. **Awards:** certificates, associate, bachelor's, master's, and doctoral degrees. 35 undergraduate majors. **Total enrollment:** 2,074. Undergraduates: 971. Freshmen: 198. Federal methodology is used as a basis for awarding need-based institutional aid.

UNDERGRADUATE EXPENSES for 2017–2018 *Comprehensive fee:* $32,660 includes full-time tuition ($22,450), mandatory fees ($810), and room and board ($9400). *College room only:* $4900. Full-time tuition and fees vary according to degree level and program. Room and board charges vary according to board plan and housing facility. *Part-time tuition:* $400 per credit hour. *Part-time fees:* $50 per term. Part-time tuition and fees vary according to course load, degree level, and program.

FRESHMAN FINANCIAL AID (Fall 2016, est.) 198 applied for aid; of those 100% were deemed to have need. 99% of freshmen with need received aid; of those 24% had need fully met. *Average percent of need met:* 66% (excluding resources awarded to replace EFC). *Average financial aid package:* $16,313 (excluding resources awarded to replace EFC). 56% of all full-time freshmen had no need and received non-need-based gift aid.

UNDERGRADUATE FINANCIAL AID (Fall 2016, est.) 794 applied for aid; of those 86% were deemed to have need. 99% of undergraduates with need received aid; of those 25% had need fully met. *Average percent of need met:* 72% (excluding resources awarded to replace EFC). *Average financial aid package:* $17,620 (excluding resources awarded to replace EFC). 31% of all full-time undergraduates had no need and received non-need-based gift aid.

GIFT AID (NEED-BASED) *Total amount:* $7,100,919 (20% federal, 6% state, 71% institutional, 3% external sources). *Receiving aid:* Freshmen: 98% (194); all full-time undergraduates: 79% (662). *Average award:* Freshmen: $12,329; Undergraduates: $13,141. *Scholarships, grants, and awards:* Federal Pell, FSEOG, state, private, college/university gift aid from institutional funds.

GIFT AID (NON-NEED-BASED) *Total amount:* $2,960,004 (1% federal, 2% state, 93% institutional, 4% external sources). *Receiving aid:* Freshmen: 16% (32). Undergraduates: 13% (107). *Average award:* Freshmen: $9979. Undergraduates: $9191. *Scholarships, grants, and awards by category:* Academic interests/achievement: 219 awards ($1,613,545 total): general academic interests/achievements. Creative arts/performance: 14 awards ($46,500 total): art/fine arts, theater/drama. Special characteristics: 104 awards ($238,500 total): children and siblings of alumni, local/state students, siblings of current students. *Tuition waivers:* Full or partial for children of alumni, employees or children of employees, senior citizens. *ROTC:* Army cooperative, Naval cooperative, Air Force cooperative.

LOANS *Student loans:* $5,619,106 (69% need-based, 31% non-need-based). 82% of past graduating class borrowed through all loan programs. *Average indebtedness per student:* $27,729. *Average need-based loan:* Freshmen: $4239. Undergraduates: $5159. *Parent loans:* $2,981,739 (48% need-based, 52% non-need-based). *Programs:* Federal Direct (Subsidized and Unsubsidized Stafford, PLUS), Perkins, college/university.

WORK-STUDY *Federal work-study:* Total amount: $319,522; 186 jobs averaging $1625. *State or other work-study/employment:* Total amount: $121,794 (6% need-based, 94% non-need-based). 57 part-time jobs averaging $1989.

ATHLETIC AWARDS Total amount: $1,116,713 (40% need-based, 60% non-need-based).

APPLYING FOR FINANCIAL AID *Required financial aid forms:* FAFSA, institution's own form. *Financial aid deadline (priority):* 3/1. *Notification date:* Continuous beginning 3/15. Students must reply within 2 weeks of notification.

CONTACT Deana Ready, Director of Student Financial Services, William Woods University, One University Avenue, Fulton, MO 65251, 573-592-4236 or toll-free 800-995-3159 Ext. 4221. *Fax:* 573-592-1180. *E-mail:* deana.ready@williamwoods.edu. *Website:* http://www.williamwoods.edu/.

WILMINGTON COLLEGE
Wilmington, OH

CONTACT Donna Barton, Coordinator of Financial Aid, Wilmington College, Pyle Center Box 1184, Wilmington, OH 45177, 937-382-6661 Ext. 466 or toll-free 800-341-9318. *Fax:* 937-383-8564.
Website: http://www.wilmington.edu/.

WILMINGTON UNIVERSITY
New Castle, DE

CONTACT J. Lynn Iocono, Director of Financial Aid, Wilmington University, 320 DuPont Highway, New Castle, DE 19720, 302-328-9437 or toll-free 877-967-5464. *Fax:* 302-328-5902.
Website: http://www.wilmu.edu/.

WILSON COLLEGE
Chambersburg, PA

Tuition & fees: $24,430	Average undergraduate aid package: $21,589

ABOUT THE INSTITUTION Independent Presbyterian Church (U.S.A.), coed, primarily women. *Awards:* associate, bachelor's, and master's degrees. 23 undergraduate majors. *Total enrollment:* 662. Undergraduates: 571. Freshmen: 70. Federal methodology is used as a basis for awarding need-based institutional aid.
UNDERGRADUATE EXPENSES for 2017–2018 *Comprehensive fee:* $35,620 includes full-time tuition ($23,745), mandatory fees ($685), and room and board ($11,190). *College room only:* $5390. Full-time tuition and fees vary according to location and program. Room and board charges vary according to board plan and housing facility. *Part-time tuition:* $792 per credit hour. *Part-time fees:* $35 per credit hour. Part-time tuition and fees vary according to course load, location, and program.
FRESHMAN FINANCIAL AID (Fall 2015) 113 applied for aid; of those 81% were deemed to have need. 100% of freshmen with need received aid; of those 23% had need fully met. *Average percent of need met:* 77% (excluding resources awarded to replace EFC). *Average financial aid package:* $20,934 (excluding resources awarded to replace EFC). 3% of all full-time freshmen had no need and received non-need-based gift aid.
UNDERGRADUATE FINANCIAL AID (Fall 2015) 449 applied for aid; of those 94% were deemed to have need. 100% of undergraduates with need received aid; of those 16% had need fully met. *Average percent of need met:* 75% (excluding resources awarded to replace EFC). *Average financial aid package:* $21,589 (excluding resources awarded to replace EFC). 3% of all full-time undergraduates had no need and received non-need-based gift aid.
GIFT AID (NEED-BASED) *Total amount:* $6,676,312 (15% federal, 10% state, 69% institutional, 6% external sources). *Receiving aid:* Freshmen: 78% (91); all full-time undergraduates: 80% (396). *Average award:* Freshmen: $15,117; Undergraduates: $17,520. *Scholarships, grants, and awards:* Federal Pell, FSEOG, state, private, college/university gift aid from institutional funds.
GIFT AID (NON-NEED-BASED) *Total amount:* $328,818 (100% federal). *Receiving aid:* Freshmen: 63% (73). Undergraduates: 54% (267). *Average award:* Freshmen: $8250. Undergraduates: $9367. *Scholarships, grants, and awards by category: Academic interests/achievement:* biological sciences, business, communication, computer science, education, English, foreign languages, general academic interests/achievements, humanities, international studies, mathematics, physical sciences, premedicine, religion/biblical studies, social sciences. *Creative arts/performance:* music. *Special achievements/activities:* community service, general special achievements/activities, leadership. *Special characteristics:* adult students, children and siblings of alumni, children of current students, children of faculty/staff, international

students, local/state students, relatives of clergy, religious affiliation, veterans, veterans' children. *Tuition waivers:* Full or partial for employees or children of employees. *ROTC:* Army cooperative.
LOANS *Student loans:* $4,874,403 (38% need-based, 62% non-need-based). 72% of past graduating class borrowed through all loan programs. *Average indebtedness per student:* $31,613. *Average need-based loan:* Freshmen: $3435. Undergraduates: $4857. *Parent loans:* $1,552,836 (100% non-need-based). *Programs:* Federal Direct (Subsidized and Unsubsidized Stafford, PLUS), Perkins.
WORK-STUDY *Federal work-study:* 37 jobs averaging $2000. *State or other work-study/employment:* Total amount: $180,656 (44% need-based, 56% non-need-based). 140 part-time jobs averaging $2000.
APPLYING FOR FINANCIAL AID *Required financial aid forms:* FAFSA, institution's own form. *Financial aid deadline (priority):* 4/30. *Notification date:* Continuous beginning 11/7.
CONTACT Ms. Linda Brittain, Dean of Financial Aid/Senior Enrollment Associate, Wilson College, 1015 Philadelphia Avenue, Chambersburg, PA 17201-1285, 717-262-2002 or toll-free 800-421-8402. *Fax:* 717-262-2530. *E-mail:* finaid@wilson.edu. *Website:* http://www.wilson.edu/.

WINGATE UNIVERSITY
Wingate, NC

Tuition & fees: $31,120	Average undergraduate aid package: $24,280

ABOUT THE INSTITUTION Independent Baptist, coed. *Awards:* certificates, bachelor's, master's, and doctoral degrees. 39 undergraduate majors. *Total enrollment:* 3,193. Undergraduates: 2,084. Freshmen: 625. Federal methodology is used as a basis for awarding need-based institutional aid.
UNDERGRADUATE EXPENSES for 2017–2018 *Comprehensive fee:* $41,900 includes full-time tuition ($31,120) and room and board ($10,780). *Part-time tuition:* $1035 per credit hour. Part-time tuition and fees vary according to course load.
FRESHMAN FINANCIAL AID (Fall 2015) 592 applied for aid; of those 91% were deemed to have need. 95% of freshmen with need received aid; of those 33% had need fully met. *Average percent of need met:* 74% (excluding resources awarded to replace EFC). *Average financial aid package:* $24,556 (excluding resources awarded to replace EFC). 17% of all full-time freshmen had no need and received non-need-based gift aid.
UNDERGRADUATE FINANCIAL AID (Fall 2015) 1,731 applied for aid; of those 92% were deemed to have need. 96% of undergraduates with need received aid; of those 26% had need fully met. *Average percent of need met:* 75% (excluding resources awarded to replace EFC). *Average financial aid package:* $24,280 (excluding resources awarded to replace EFC). 20% of all full-time undergraduates had no need and received non-need-based gift aid.
GIFT AID (NEED-BASED) *Total amount:* $29,778,403 (11% federal, 14% state, 73% institutional, 2% external sources). *Receiving aid:* Freshmen: 79% (507); all full-time undergraduates: 75% (1,532). *Average award:* Freshmen: $22,223; Undergraduates: $20,912. *Scholarships, grants, and awards:* Federal Pell, FSEOG, state, private, college/university gift aid from institutional funds.
GIFT AID (NON-NEED-BASED) *Total amount:* $7,900,890 (96% institutional, 4% external sources). *Receiving aid:* Freshmen: 19% (124). Undergraduates: 13% (274). *Average award:* Freshmen: $17,350. Undergraduates: $15,467. *Scholarships, grants, and awards by category: Academic interests/achievement:* general academic interests/achievements. *Creative arts/performance:* art/fine arts, music, theater/drama. *Special characteristics:* children and siblings of alumni, relatives of clergy. *Tuition waivers:* Full or partial for employees or children of employees. *ROTC:* Army cooperative, Air Force cooperative.
LOANS *Student loans:* $12,487,047 (67% need-based, 33% non-need-based). 74% of past graduating class borrowed through all loan programs. *Average indebtedness per student:* $31,997. *Average need-based loan:* Freshmen: $3055. Undergraduates: $3914. *Parent loans:* $12,449,232 (34% need-based, 66% non-need-based). *Programs:* Federal Direct (Subsidized and Unsubsidized Stafford, PLUS).
WORK-STUDY *Federal work-study:* jobs available. *State or other work-study/employment:* Part-time jobs available.
ATHLETIC AWARDS Total amount: $5,061,534 (47% need-based, 53% non-need-based).

APPLYING FOR FINANCIAL AID *Required financial aid forms:* FAFSA, state aid form. *Financial aid deadline (priority):* 5/1. *Notification date:* Continuous beginning 3/15. Students must reply within 3 weeks of notification.

CONTACT Teresa G. Williams, Director of Student Financial Planning, Wingate University, Campus Box 3001, Wingate, NC 28174, 704-233-8209 or toll-free 800-755-5550. *Fax:* 704-233-9396. *E-mail:* tgwilliam@wingate.edu. *Website:* http://www.wingate.edu/.

WINONA STATE UNIVERSITY
Winona, MN

Tuition & fees (MN res): $9075	Average undergraduate aid package: $7785

ABOUT THE INSTITUTION State-supported, coed. *Awards:* certificates, associate, bachelor's, master's, and doctoral degrees. 64 undergraduate majors. *Total enrollment:* 8,126. Undergraduates: 7,656. Freshmen: 1,586. Federal methodology is used as a basis for awarding need-based institutional aid.

UNDERGRADUATE EXPENSES for 2016–2017 *Application fee:* $20. *Tuition, state resident:* full-time $7103; part-time $234.85 per credit hour. *Tuition, nonresident:* full-time $12,800; part-time $426.32 per credit hour. *Required fees:* full-time $1972; $37.83 per credit hour or $485 per term. Full-time tuition and fees vary according to location, program, and reciprocity agreements. Part-time tuition and fees vary according to course load, location, program, and reciprocity agreements. *College room and board:* $8460. Room and board charges vary according to board plan, housing facility, and location.

FRESHMAN FINANCIAL AID (Fall 2015) 1,432 applied for aid; of those 69% were deemed to have need. 98% of freshmen with need received aid; of those 10% had need fully met. *Average percent of need met:* 49% (excluding resources awarded to replace EFC). *Average financial aid package:* $7135 (excluding resources awarded to replace EFC). 22% of all full-time freshmen had no need and received non-need-based gift aid.

UNDERGRADUATE FINANCIAL AID (Fall 2015) 5,622 applied for aid; of those 73% were deemed to have need. 98% of undergraduates with need received aid; of those 11% had need fully met. *Average percent of need met:* 51% (excluding resources awarded to replace EFC). *Average financial aid package:* $7785 (excluding resources awarded to replace EFC). 13% of all full-time undergraduates had no need and received non-need-based gift aid.

GIFT AID (NEED-BASED) *Total amount:* $15,808,968 (53% federal, 27% state, 12% institutional, 8% external sources). *Receiving aid:* Freshmen: 45% (740); all full-time undergraduates: 40% (2,823). *Average award:* Freshmen: $5112; Undergraduates: $5432. *Scholarships, grants, and awards:* Federal Pell, FSEOG, state, private, college/university gift aid from institutional funds.

GIFT AID (NON-NEED-BASED) *Total amount:* $4,074,792 (10% federal, 52% institutional, 38% external sources). *Receiving aid:* Freshmen: 10% (170). Undergraduates: 6% (407). *Average award:* Freshmen: $2485. Undergraduates: $3270. *Scholarships, grants, and awards by category: Academic interests/achievement:* 1,543 awards ($1,562,375 total): general academic interests/achievements. *Creative arts/performance:* 76 awards ($107,300 total): art/fine arts, debating, music, theater/drama. *Special characteristics:* 327 awards ($1,754,518 total): children and siblings of alumni, children of faculty/staff, local/state students, members of minority groups, out-of-state students. *Tuition waivers:* Full or partial for employees or children of employees. *ROTC:* Army cooperative.

LOANS *Student loans:* $45,378,698 (57% need-based, 43% non-need-based). 76% of past graduating class borrowed through all loan programs. *Average indebtedness per student:* $35,221. *Average need-based loan:* Freshmen: $3164. Undergraduates: $3959. *Parent loans:* $4,202,997 (36% need-based, 64% non-need-based). *Programs:* Federal Direct (Subsidized and Unsubsidized Stafford, PLUS), Perkins, state, college/university.

WORK-STUDY *Federal work-study:* 160 jobs averaging $2226. *State or other work-study/employment:* Total amount: $834,360 (100% need-based). 353 part-time jobs averaging $2364.

ATHLETIC AWARDS Total amount: $856,333 (36% need-based, 64% non-need-based).

APPLYING FOR FINANCIAL AID *Required financial aid form:* FAFSA. *Financial aid deadline:* Continuous. *Notification date:* Continuous beginning 4/1. Students must reply within 3 weeks of notification.

CONTACT Mari Livingston, Associate Director of Financial Aid, Winona State University, PO Box 5838, Winona, MN 55987-5838, 507-457-5090 Ext. 2398 or toll-free 800-DIAL WSU. *Website:* http://www.winona.edu/.

WINSTON-SALEM STATE UNIVERSITY
Winston-Salem, NC

CONTACT Raymond Solomon, Director of Financial Aid Office, Winston-Salem State University, 601 Martin Luther King Jr. Drive, PO Box 19524, Winston-Salem, NC 27110-0003, 336-750-3299 or toll-free 800-257-4052. *Fax:* 336-750-3297. *Website:* http://www.wssu.edu/.

WINTHROP UNIVERSITY
Rock Hill, SC

Tuition & fees (SC res): $14,510	Average undergraduate aid package: $13,080

ABOUT THE INSTITUTION State-supported, coed. *Awards:* certificates, bachelor's, and master's degrees. 28 undergraduate majors. *Total enrollment:* 6,109. Undergraduates: 5,091. Freshmen: 1,072. Federal methodology is used as a basis for awarding need-based institutional aid.

UNDERGRADUATE EXPENSES for 2016–2017 *Application fee:* $40. *Tuition, state resident:* full-time $14,510; part-time $605 per credit hour. *Tuition, nonresident:* full-time $28,090; part-time $1170 per credit hour. Full-time tuition and fees vary according to degree level, reciprocity agreements, and student level. Part-time tuition and fees vary according to degree level and student level. *College room and board:* $8572; *Room only:* $5242. Room and board charges vary according to board plan and housing facility.

FRESHMAN FINANCIAL AID (Fall 2016, est.) 986 applied for aid; of those 87% were deemed to have need. 100% of freshmen with need received aid; of those 14% had need fully met. *Average percent of need met:* 60% (excluding resources awarded to replace EFC). *Average financial aid package:* $14,407 (excluding resources awarded to replace EFC). 12% of all full-time freshmen had no need and received non-need-based gift aid.

UNDERGRADUATE FINANCIAL AID (Fall 2016, est.) 3,891 applied for aid; of those 87% were deemed to have need. 100% of undergraduates with need received aid; of those 15% had need fully met. *Average percent of need met:* 56% (excluding resources awarded to replace EFC). *Average financial aid package:* $13,080 (excluding resources awarded to replace EFC). 12% of all full-time undergraduates had no need and received non-need-based gift aid.

GIFT AID (NEED-BASED) *Total amount:* $28,531,263 (33% federal, 35% state, 29% institutional, 3% external sources). *Receiving aid:* Freshmen: 79% (843); all full-time undergraduates: 68% (3,083). *Average award:* Freshmen: $9785; Undergraduates: $8744. *Scholarships, grants, and awards:* Federal Pell, FSEOG, state, private, college/university gift aid from institutional funds, TEACH Grants.

GIFT AID (NON-NEED-BASED) *Total amount:* $10,405,821 (1% federal, 46% state, 50% institutional, 3% external sources). *Receiving aid:* Freshmen: 12% (130). Undergraduates: 9% (414). *Average award:* Freshmen: $5244. Undergraduates: $5268. *Scholarships, grants, and awards by category: Academic interests/achievement:* general academic interests/achievements. *Creative arts/performance:* art/fine arts, dance, music, performing arts, theater/drama. *Special characteristics:* children of faculty/staff. *Tuition waivers:* Full or partial for employees or children of employees, senior citizens. *ROTC:* Army cooperative, Air Force cooperative.

LOANS *Student loans:* $28,917,807 (74% need-based, 26% non-need-based). 84% of past graduating class borrowed through all loan programs. *Average indebtedness per student:* $30,061. *Average need-based loan:* Freshmen: $3404. Undergraduates: $4361. *Parent loans:* $9,045,984 (60% need-based, 40% non-need-based). *Programs:* Federal Direct (Subsidized and Unsubsidized Stafford, PLUS), Perkins, alternative loans.

WORK-STUDY *Federal work-study:* Total amount: $324,093; 165 jobs averaging $1964. *State or other work-study/employment:* Part-time jobs available.

ATHLETIC AWARDS Total amount: $2,583,402 (36% need-based, 64% non-need-based).

APPLYING FOR FINANCIAL AID *Required financial aid form:* FAFSA. *Financial aid deadline (priority):* 3/1. *Notification date:* Continuous beginning 3/15.

CONTACT Michelle K. Hare, Director of Financial Aid, Winthrop University, Sykes House, 638 Oakland Avenue, Rock Hill, SC 29733, 803-323-2189 or toll-free 800-763-0230. *Fax:* 803-323-2557. *E-mail:* finaid@winthrop.edu. *Website:* http://www.winthrop.edu/.

WISCONSIN LUTHERAN COLLEGE
Milwaukee, WI

Tuition & fees: $27,984	Average undergraduate aid package: $20,867

ABOUT THE INSTITUTION Independent Wisconsin Evangelical Lutheran Synod, coed. 39 undergraduate majors. Federal methodology is used as a basis for awarding need-based institutional aid.

UNDERGRADUATE EXPENSES for 2016–2017 *Comprehensive fee:* $37,604 includes full-time tuition ($27,734), mandatory fees ($250), and room and board ($9620). Full-time tuition and fees vary according to program. Room and board charges vary according to housing facility. *Part-time tuition:* $720 per credit hour. Part-time tuition and fees vary according to program.

FRESHMAN FINANCIAL AID (Fall 2016, est.) 223 applied for aid; of those 91% were deemed to have need. 100% of freshmen with need received aid; of those 24% had need fully met. *Average percent of need met:* 81% (excluding resources awarded to replace EFC). *Average financial aid package:* $22,291 (excluding resources awarded to replace EFC). 11% of all full-time freshmen had no need and received non-need-based gift aid.

UNDERGRADUATE FINANCIAL AID (Fall 2016, est.) 831 applied for aid; of those 91% were deemed to have need. 100% of undergraduates with need received aid; of those 18% had need fully met. *Average percent of need met:* 78% (excluding resources awarded to replace EFC). *Average financial aid package:* $20,867 (excluding resources awarded to replace EFC). 15% of all full-time undergraduates had no need and received non-need-based gift aid.

GIFT AID (NEED-BASED) *Total amount:* $12,251,828 (10% federal, 6% state, 82% institutional, 2% external sources). *Receiving aid:* Freshmen: 89% (203); all full-time undergraduates: 80% (731). *Average award:* Freshmen: $18,901; Undergraduates: $17,109. *Scholarships, grants, and awards:* Federal Pell, FSEOG, state, private, college/university gift aid from institutional funds.

GIFT AID (NON-NEED-BASED) *Total amount:* $1,928,234 (1% federal, 94% institutional, 5% external sources). *Receiving aid:* Freshmen: 14% (33). Undergraduates: 8% (76). *Average award:* Freshmen: $12,100. Undergraduates: $10,677. *Scholarships, grants, and awards by category:* Academic interests/achievement: 926 awards ($8,518,200 total): biological sciences, business, communication, education, foreign languages, general academic interests/achievements, home economics, physical sciences, religion/biblical studies. *Creative arts/performance:* 58 awards ($70,500 total): art/fine arts, music, theater/drama. *Special achievements/activities:* 36 awards ($224,765 total): general special achievements/activities, leadership. *Special characteristics:* 794 awards ($1,270,499 total): adult students, children of faculty/staff, general special characteristics, international students, members of minority groups, out-of-state students, previous college experience, veterans, veterans' children. *Tuition waivers:* Full or partial for employees or children of employees.

LOANS *Student loans:* $7,020,141 (69% need-based, 31% non-need-based). 88% of past graduating class borrowed through all loan programs. *Average indebtedness per student:* $28,476. *Average need-based loan:* Freshmen: $3183. Undergraduates: $4067. *Parent loans:* $1,759,385 (30% need-based, 70% non-need-based). *Programs:* Federal Direct (Subsidized and Unsubsidized Stafford, PLUS), state, private loans.

WORK-STUDY *Federal work-study:* Total amount: $392,487; 167 jobs averaging $1925. *State or other work-study/employment:* Total amount: $193,065 (35% need-based, 65% non-need-based). 250 part-time jobs averaging $1781.

APPLYING FOR FINANCIAL AID *Required financial aid forms:* FAFSA, institution's own form. *Financial aid deadline (priority):* 12/1. *Notification date:* Continuous beginning 12/1. Students must reply by 5/1.

CONTACT Mrs. Linda Loeffel, Director of Financial Aid, Wisconsin Lutheran College, 8800 West Bluemound Road, Milwaukee, WI 53226-4699, 414-443-8856. *Fax:* 414-443-8514. *E-mail:* financial.aid@wlc.edu. *Website:* http://www.wlc.edu/.

WITTENBERG UNIVERSITY
Springfield, OH

Tuition & fees: $38,730	Average undergraduate aid package: $27,498

ABOUT THE INSTITUTION Independent Evangelical Lutheran Church, coed. *Awards:* bachelor's and master's degrees. 43 undergraduate majors. *Total enrollment:* 1,988. Undergraduates: 1,960. Freshmen: 553. Federal methodology is used as a basis for awarding need-based institutional aid.

UNDERGRADUATE EXPENSES for 2017–2018 *Application fee:* $40. *Comprehensive fee:* $48,856 includes full-time tuition ($37,930), mandatory fees ($800), and room and board ($10,126). *College room only:* $5158. Room and board charges vary according to board plan and housing facility. *Part-time tuition:* $1264 per credit hour. Part-time tuition and fees vary according to course load.

FRESHMAN FINANCIAL AID (Fall 2016, est.) 536 applied for aid; of those 88% were deemed to have need. 99% of freshmen with need received aid; of those 21% had need fully met. *Average percent of need met:* 80% (excluding resources awarded to replace EFC). *Average financial aid package:* $28,689 (excluding resources awarded to replace EFC). 15% of all full-time freshmen had no need and received non-need-based gift aid.

UNDERGRADUATE FINANCIAL AID (Fall 2016, est.) 1,664 applied for aid; of those 89% were deemed to have need. 98% of undergraduates with need received aid; of those 24% had need fully met. *Average percent of need met:* 80% (excluding resources awarded to replace EFC). *Average financial aid package:* $27,498 (excluding resources awarded to replace EFC). 19% of all full-time undergraduates had no need and received non-need-based gift aid.

GIFT AID (NEED-BASED) *Total amount:* $40,995,019 (8% federal, 2% state, 88% institutional, 2% external sources). *Receiving aid:* Freshmen: 84% (463); all full-time undergraduates: 78% (1,447). *Average award:* Freshmen: $27,073; Undergraduates: $25,281. *Scholarships, grants, and awards:* Federal Pell, FSEOG, state, private, college/university gift aid from institutional funds, United Negro College Fund.

GIFT AID (NON-NEED-BASED) *Total amount:* $3,823,284 (1% federal, 97% institutional, 2% external sources). *Average award:* Freshmen: $21,589. Undergraduates: $19,277. *Scholarships, grants, and awards by category:* Academic interests/achievement: general academic interests/achievements. *Creative arts/performance:* art/fine arts, dance, music, theater/drama. *Special achievements/activities:* community service, general special achievements/activities, leadership. *Special characteristics:* adult students, children and siblings of alumni, children of faculty/staff, ethnic background, international students, members of minority groups, relatives of clergy, religious affiliation. *Tuition waivers:* Full or partial for minority students, children of alumni, employees or children of employees, adult students, senior citizens. *ROTC:* Army cooperative, Air Force cooperative.

LOANS *Student loans:* $13,709,330 (92% need-based, 8% non-need-based). 71% of past graduating class borrowed through all loan programs. *Average indebtedness per student:* $35,034. *Average need-based loan:* Freshmen: $3427. Undergraduates: $4724. *Parent loans:* $5,425,058 (95% need-based, 5% non-need-based). *Programs:* Federal Direct (Subsidized and Unsubsidized Stafford, PLUS), Perkins, college/university.

WORK-STUDY *Federal work-study:* Total amount: $1,110,532; jobs available. *State or other work-study/employment:* Total amount: $1,387,317 (84% need-based, 16% non-need-based). Part-time jobs available.

APPLYING FOR FINANCIAL AID *Required financial aid form:* FAFSA. *Financial aid deadline (priority):* 3/1. *Notification date:* Continuous beginning 3/1. Students must reply by 5/1.

CONTACT Mr. J. Randy Green, Executive Director of Financial Aid, Wittenberg University, PO Box 720, Springfield, OH 45501-0720, 937-327-7321 or toll-free 800-677-7558 Ext. 6314. *Fax:* 937-327-6379. *E-mail:* jgreen@wittenberg.edu. *Website:* http://www.wittenberg.edu/.

WOFFORD COLLEGE
Spartanburg, SC

Tuition & fees: $41,955	Average undergraduate aid package: $34,662

ABOUT THE INSTITUTION Independent United Methodist Church, coed. *Awards:* bachelor's degrees. 26 undergraduate majors. *Total enrollment:* 1,622.

Undergraduates: 1,622. Freshmen: 440. Federal methodology is used as a basis for awarding need-based institutional aid.

UNDERGRADUATE EXPENSES for 2017–2018 *Application fee:* $35. *Comprehensive fee:* $54,095 includes full-time tuition ($41,955) and room and board ($12,140).

FRESHMAN FINANCIAL AID (Fall 2016, est.) 380 applied for aid; of those 73% were deemed to have need. 100% of freshmen with need received aid; of those 46% had need fully met. *Average percent of need met:* 91% (excluding resources awarded to replace EFC). *Average financial aid package:* $35,201 (excluding resources awarded to replace EFC). 26% of all full-time freshmen had no need and received non-need-based gift aid.

UNDERGRADUATE FINANCIAL AID (Fall 2016, est.) 1,224 applied for aid; of those 82% were deemed to have need. 100% of undergraduates with need received aid; of those 41% had need fully met. *Average percent of need met:* 89% (excluding resources awarded to replace EFC). *Average financial aid package:* $34,662 (excluding resources awarded to replace EFC). 27% of all full-time undergraduates had no need and received non-need-based gift aid.

GIFT AID (NEED-BASED) *Total amount:* $24,414,096 (5% federal, 18% state, 73% institutional, 4% external sources). *Receiving aid:* Freshmen: 63% (277); all full-time undergraduates: 64% (1,007). *Average award:* Freshmen: $31,055; Undergraduates: $30,783. *Scholarships, grants, and awards:* Federal Pell, FSEOG, state, private, college/university gift aid from institutional funds.

GIFT AID (NON-NEED-BASED) *Total amount:* $11,746,652 (18% state, 72% institutional, 10% external sources). *Receiving aid:* Freshmen: 22% (99). Undergraduates: 20% (317). *Average award:* Freshmen: $16,955. Undergraduates: $16,243. *Scholarships, grants, and awards by category: Academic interests/achievement:* general academic interests/achievements. *Creative arts/performance:* art/fine arts, music. *Special achievements/activities:* leadership. *Special characteristics:* children of faculty/staff, general special characteristics, local/state students, members of minority groups, relatives of clergy. *Tuition waivers:* Full or partial for employees or children of employees. *ROTC:* Army.

LOANS *Student loans:* $6,691,235 (62% need-based, 38% non-need-based). 49% of past graduating class borrowed through all loan programs. *Average indebtedness per student:* $31,102. *Average need-based loan:* Freshmen: $3199. Undergraduates: $4331. *Parent loans:* $2,974,957 (42% need-based, 58% non-need-based). *Programs:* Federal Direct (Subsidized and Unsubsidized Stafford, PLUS), Perkins.

WORK-STUDY *Federal work-study:* Total amount: $229,667; 138 jobs averaging $990.

ATHLETIC AWARDS Total amount: $8,722,920 (45% need-based, 55% non-need-based).

APPLYING FOR FINANCIAL AID *Required financial aid form:* FAFSA. *Financial aid deadline (priority):* 3/1. *Notification date:* 3/15. Students must reply by 5/1.

CONTACT Carolyn B. Sparks, Director of Financial Aid, Wofford College, 429 North Church Street, Spartanburg, SC 29303-3663, 864-597-4160. *Fax:* 864-597-4149. *E-mail:* finaid@wofford.edu. *Website:* http://www.wofford.edu/.

WOODBURY UNIVERSITY
Burbank, CA

Tuition & fees: $37,906	Average undergraduate aid package: $23,976

ABOUT THE INSTITUTION Independent, coed. *Awards:* bachelor's and master's degrees. 19 undergraduate majors. *Total enrollment:* 1,319. Undergraduates: 1,135. Freshmen: 137. Both federal and institutional methodology are used as a basis for awarding need-based institutional aid.

UNDERGRADUATE EXPENSES for 2016–2017 *Application fee:* $75. *Comprehensive fee:* $49,042 includes full-time tuition ($36,882), mandatory fees ($1024), and room and board ($11,136). *College room only:* $6868. Full-time tuition and fees vary according to course load, degree level, and program. Room and board charges vary according to board plan, housing facility, and location. *Part-time tuition:* $1201 per credit hour. *Part-time fees:* $500 per term. Part-time tuition and fees vary according to course load, degree level, and program.

FRESHMAN FINANCIAL AID (Fall 2016, est.) 111 applied for aid; of those 94% were deemed to have need. 99% of freshmen with need received aid; of those 2% had need fully met. *Average percent of need met:* 56% (excluding resources awarded

to replace EFC). *Average financial aid package:* $25,843 (excluding resources awarded to replace EFC). 5% of all full-time freshmen had no need and received non-need-based gift aid.

UNDERGRADUATE FINANCIAL AID (Fall 2016, est.) 639 applied for aid; of those 95% were deemed to have need. 99% of undergraduates with need received aid; of those 2% had need fully met. *Average percent of need met:* 51% (excluding resources awarded to replace EFC). *Average financial aid package:* $23,976 (excluding resources awarded to replace EFC). 14% of all full-time undergraduates had no need and received non-need-based gift aid.

GIFT AID (NEED-BASED) *Total amount:* $12,509,574 (18% federal, 18% state, 62% institutional, 2% external sources). *Receiving aid:* Freshmen: 75% (103); all full-time undergraduates: 83% (602). *Average award:* Freshmen: $22,946; Undergraduates: $19,919. *Scholarships, grants, and awards:* Federal Pell, FSEOG, state, private, college/university gift aid from institutional funds.

GIFT AID (NON-NEED-BASED) *Total amount:* $1,295,763 (2% state, 94% institutional, 4% external sources). *Receiving aid:* Freshmen: 1% (1). Undergraduates: 1% (8). *Average award:* Freshmen: $13,857. Undergraduates: $11,133. *Scholarships, grants, and awards by category: Academic interests/achievement:* architecture, business, general academic interests/achievements. *Tuition waivers:* Full or partial for employees or children of employees.

LOANS *Student loans:* $6,392,733 (92% need-based, 8% non-need-based). 83% of past graduating class borrowed through all loan programs. *Average indebtedness per student:* $41,211. *Average need-based loan:* Freshmen: $2954. Undergraduates: $4465. *Parent loans:* $4,230,165 (73% need-based, 27% non-need-based). *Programs:* Federal Direct (Subsidized and Unsubsidized Stafford, PLUS), Perkins, alternative loans.

WORK-STUDY *Federal work-study:* Total amount: $104,424; jobs available.

APPLYING FOR FINANCIAL AID *Required financial aid forms:* FAFSA, institution's own form, CSS Financial Aid PROFILE. *Financial aid deadline:* 2/1 (priority: 11/15). *Notification date:* Continuous beginning 12/1. Students must reply within 2 weeks of notification.

CONTACT Celeastia Williams, Director of Enrollment Services, Woodbury University, 7500 Glenoaks Boulevard, Burbank, CA 91510, 818-767-0888 Ext. 273 or toll-free 800-784-WOOD. *Fax:* 818-767-4816. *Website:* http://www.woodbury.edu/.

WORCESTER POLYTECHNIC INSTITUTE
Worcester, MA

Tuition & fees: $46,994	Average undergraduate aid package: $35,932

ABOUT THE INSTITUTION Independent, coed. *Awards:* certificates, bachelor's, master's, and doctoral degrees. 30 undergraduate majors. *Total enrollment:* 6,642. Undergraduates: 4,432. Freshmen: 1,120. Both federal and institutional methodology are used as a basis for awarding need-based institutional aid.

UNDERGRADUATE EXPENSES for 2016–2017 *Application fee:* $65. *One-time required fee:* $200. *Comprehensive fee:* $60,730 includes full-time tuition ($46,364), mandatory fees ($630), and room and board ($13,736). *College room only:* $7846. Room and board charges vary according to board plan and housing facility. *Part-time tuition:* $1288 per credit hour. Part-time tuition and fees vary according to course load. *Payment plan:* Tuition prepayment.

FRESHMAN FINANCIAL AID (Fall 2015) 910 applied for aid; of those 82% were deemed to have need. 100% of freshmen with need received aid; of those 53% had need fully met. *Average percent of need met:* 80% (excluding resources awarded to replace EFC). *Average financial aid package:* $36,113 (excluding resources awarded to replace EFC). 30% of all full-time freshmen had no need and received non-need-based gift aid.

UNDERGRADUATE FINANCIAL AID (Fall 2015) 3,015 applied for aid; of those 86% were deemed to have need. 99% of undergraduates with need received aid; of those 45% had need fully met. *Average percent of need met:* 83% (excluding resources awarded to replace EFC). *Average financial aid package:* $35,932 (excluding resources awarded to replace EFC). 34% of all full-time undergraduates had no need and received non-need-based gift aid.

GIFT AID (NEED-BASED) *Total amount:* $61,009,577 (5% federal, 1% state, 87% institutional, 7% external sources). *Receiving aid:* Freshmen: 68% (744); all full-

time undergraduates: 62% (2,518). *Average award:* Freshmen: $23,865; Undergraduates: $22,934. *Scholarships, grants, and awards:* Federal Pell, FSEOG, state, private, college/university gift aid from institutional funds.

GIFT AID (NON-NEED-BASED) *Total amount:* $26,414,581 (82% institutional, 18% external sources). *Receiving aid:* Freshmen: 24% (264). Undergraduates: 21% (846). *Average award:* Freshmen: $13,832. Undergraduates: $16,002. *Scholarships, grants, and awards by category: Academic interests/achievement:* 4,064 awards ($48,058,429 total): general academic interests/achievements. *Special achievements/activities:* leadership. *Special characteristics:* 30 awards ($236,215 total): children of workers in trades. *Tuition waivers:* Full or partial for employees or children of employees. *ROTC:* Army, Naval cooperative, Air Force.

LOANS *Student loans:* $29,673,429 (41% need-based, 59% non-need-based). *Average need-based loan:* Freshmen: $2866. Undergraduates: $2584. *Parent loans:* $10,451,543 (100% non-need-based). *Programs:* Federal Direct (Subsidized and Unsubsidized Stafford, PLUS), Perkins, state, college/university.

WORK-STUDY *Federal work-study:* 574 jobs averaging $973.

APPLYING FOR FINANCIAL AID *Required financial aid forms:* FAFSA, CSS Financial Aid PROFILE, noncustodial (divorced/separated) parent's statement. *Financial aid deadline:* 2/1. *Notification date:* 4/1. Students must reply by 5/1.

CONTACT Monica M. Blondin, Executive Director of Student Aid and Financial Literacy, Worcester Polytechnic Institute, 100 Institute Road, Worcester, MA 01609-2280, 508-831-5469. *Fax:* 508-831-5039. *E-mail:* finaid@wpi.edu. *Website:* http://www.wpi.edu/.

WORCESTER STATE UNIVERSITY
Worcester, MA

Tuition & fees (MA res): $9202	Average undergraduate aid package: $11,975

ABOUT THE INSTITUTION State-supported, coed. *Awards:* certificates, bachelor's, and master's degrees. 27 undergraduate majors. *Total enrollment:* 6,471. Undergraduates: 5,381. Freshmen: 789. Federal methodology is used as a basis for awarding need-based institutional aid.

UNDERGRADUATE EXPENSES for 2016–2017 *Application fee:* $50. *Tuition, state resident:* full-time $970; part-time $40.42 per credit hour. *Tuition, nonresident:* full-time $7050; part-time $293.75 per credit hour. *Required fees:* full-time $8232; $328.62 per credit hour. Full-time tuition and fees vary according to class time, course load, degree level, and reciprocity agreements. Part-time tuition and fees vary according to class time, course load, degree level, and reciprocity agreements. *College room and board:* $11,775; *Room only:* $8135. Room and board charges vary according to board plan and housing facility.

FRESHMAN FINANCIAL AID (Fall 2015) 757 applied for aid; of those 71% were deemed to have need. 98% of freshmen with need received aid; of those 37% had need fully met. *Average percent of need met:* 76% (excluding resources awarded to replace EFC). *Average financial aid package:* $12,541 (excluding resources awarded to replace EFC). 4% of all full-time freshmen had no need and received non-need-based gift aid.

UNDERGRADUATE FINANCIAL AID (Fall 2015) 3,523 applied for aid; of those 73% were deemed to have need. 99% of undergraduates with need received aid; of those 40% had need fully met. *Average percent of need met:* 80% (excluding resources awarded to replace EFC). *Average financial aid package:* $11,975 (excluding resources awarded to replace EFC). 3% of all full-time undergraduates had no need and received non-need-based gift aid.

GIFT AID (NEED-BASED) *Total amount:* $10,360,248 (63% federal, 21% state, 16% institutional). *Receiving aid:* Freshmen: 58% (471); all full-time undergraduates: 51% (2,076). *Average award:* Freshmen: $4934; Undergraduates: $4864. *Scholarships, grants, and awards:* Federal Pell, state, private, college/university gift aid from institutional funds.

GIFT AID (NON-NEED-BASED) *Total amount:* $2,087,236 (20% state, 53% institutional, 27% external sources). *Receiving aid:* Freshmen: 33% (270). Undergraduates: 23% (928). *Average award:* Freshmen: $3173. Undergraduates: $2593. *Tuition waivers:* Full or partial for employees or children of employees, senior citizens. *ROTC:* Army cooperative, Naval cooperative, Air Force cooperative.

LOANS *Student loans:* $22,750,414 (37% need-based, 63% non-need-based). 78% of past graduating class borrowed through all loan programs. *Average indebtedness per student:* $28,940. *Average need-based loan:* Freshmen: $2480. Undergraduates: $3188. *Parent loans:* $2,961,722 (100% non-need-based). *Programs:* Federal

Direct (Subsidized and Unsubsidized Stafford, PLUS), Perkins, Federal Nursing, state, college/university.

WORK-STUDY *Federal work-study:* 200 jobs averaging $1500.

APPLYING FOR FINANCIAL AID *Required financial aid form:* FAFSA. *Financial aid deadline:* 5/1 (priority: 3/1). *Notification date:* Continuous beginning 12/15. Students must reply within 3 weeks of notification.

CONTACT Ms. Jayne McGinn, Director of Financial Aid, Worcester State University, 486 Chandler Street, Worcester, MA 01602, 508-929-8058. *Fax:* 508-929-8194. *E-mail:* jayne.mcginn@worcester.edu. *Website:* http://www.worcester.edu/.

WORLD MISSION UNIVERSITY
Los Angeles, CA

CONTACT Financial Aid Office, World Mission University, 500 Shatto Place, Suite 600, Los Angeles, CA 90020, 213-385-2322. *Website:* http://www.wmu.edu/.

WRIGHT STATE UNIVERSITY
Dayton, OH

Tuition & fees (OH res): $8730	Average undergraduate aid package: $10,500

ABOUT THE INSTITUTION State-supported, coed. *Awards:* certificates, associate, bachelor's, master's, and doctoral degrees. 81 undergraduate majors. *Total enrollment:* 16,655. Undergraduates: 12,504. Freshmen: 2,174. Federal methodology is used as a basis for awarding need-based institutional aid.

UNDERGRADUATE EXPENSES for 2016–2017 *Application fee:* $30. *Tuition, state resident:* full-time $8730; part-time $394 per credit hour. *Tuition, nonresident:* full-time $17,098; part-time $791 per credit hour. Full-time tuition and fees vary according to course load, location, and reciprocity agreements. Part-time tuition and fees vary according to course load, location, and reciprocity agreements. *College room and board:* $11,376; *Room only:* $7104. Room and board charges vary according to board plan, housing facility, and location.

FRESHMAN FINANCIAL AID (Fall 2016, est.) 1,904 applied for aid; of those 80% were deemed to have need. 98% of freshmen with need received aid; of those 17% had need fully met. *Average percent of need met:* 62% (excluding resources awarded to replace EFC). *Average financial aid package:* $10,111 (excluding resources awarded to replace EFC). 12% of all full-time freshmen had no need and received non-need-based gift aid.

UNDERGRADUATE FINANCIAL AID (Fall 2016, est.) 7,340 applied for aid; of those 83% were deemed to have need. 98% of undergraduates with need received aid; of those 14% had need fully met. *Average percent of need met:* 58% (excluding resources awarded to replace EFC). *Average financial aid package:* $10,500 (excluding resources awarded to replace EFC). 17% of all full-time undergraduates had no need and received non-need-based gift aid.

GIFT AID (NEED-BASED) *Total amount:* $36,374,325 (54% federal, 16% state, 27% institutional, 3% external sources). *Receiving aid:* Freshmen: 61% (1,299); all full-time undergraduates: 55% (5,224). *Average award:* Freshmen: $6496; Undergraduates: $6182. *Scholarships, grants, and awards:* Federal Pell, FSEOG, state, private, college/university gift aid from institutional funds, United Negro College Fund, Federal Nursing, Choose Ohio First scholarships.

GIFT AID (NON-NEED-BASED) *Total amount:* $10,532,254 (1% federal, 15% state, 77% institutional, 7% external sources). *Receiving aid:* Freshmen: 6% (136). Undergraduates: 4% (412). *Average award:* Freshmen: $4892. Undergraduates: $4070. *Scholarships, grants, and awards by category: Academic interests/achievement:* 7,455 awards ($17,071,573 total): area/ethnic studies, biological sciences, business, communication, computer science, education, engineering/technologies, English, foreign languages, general academic interests/achievements, home economics, humanities, international studies, mathematics, military science, physical sciences, premedicine, religion/biblical studies, social sciences. *Creative arts/performance:* 268 awards ($389,230 total): applied art and design, art/fine arts, cinema/film/broadcasting, creative writing, dance, general creative arts/performance, music, performing arts, theater/drama. *Special achievements/activities:* 857 awards ($3,959,411 total): cheerleading/drum major, community service, general special achievements/activities, leadership, memberships. *Special characteristics:* 776 awards ($2,756,962 total): adult students, children and siblings of alumni, children of educators, children of faculty/staff, ethnic background, first-generation college students, handicapped students, international students, members of minority groups, out-of-state students. *Tuition waivers:* Full or partial for employees or children of employees, senior citizens. *ROTC:* Army, Air Force.

LOANS *Student loans:* $69,688,036 (77% need-based, 23% non-need-based). 68% of past graduating class borrowed through all loan programs. *Average indebtedness per student:* $30,061. *Average need-based loan:* Freshmen: $3615. Undergraduates: $4323. *Parent loans:* $6,451,637 (51% need-based, 49% non-need-based). *Programs:* Federal Direct (Subsidized and Unsubsidized Stafford, PLUS), Perkins, Federal Nursing, state, college/university, private loans.

WORK-STUDY *Federal work-study:* Total amount: $3,338,952; 757 jobs averaging $4371.

ATHLETIC AWARDS Total amount: $2,804,939 (38% need-based, 62% non-need-based).

APPLYING FOR FINANCIAL AID *Required financial aid form:* FAFSA. *Financial aid deadline (priority):* 12/1. *Notification date:* Continuous beginning 2/1.

CONTACT Raider Connect, Wright State University, 130 Student Union, 3640 Colonel Glenn Highway, Dayton, OH 45435, 937-775-4000 or toll-free 800-247-1770. *Fax:* 937-775-4410. *E-mail:* raiderconnect@wright.edu. *Website:* http://www.wright.edu/.

WRIGHT STATE UNIVERSITY–LAKE CAMPUS
Celina, OH

Tuition & fees (OH res): $5842	Average undergraduate aid package: $8676

ABOUT THE INSTITUTION State-supported, coed. *Awards:* certificates, associate, bachelor's, and master's degrees. 76 undergraduate majors. *Total enrollment:* 1,336. Undergraduates: 1,302. Freshmen: 284. Federal methodology is used as a basis for awarding need-based institutional aid.

UNDERGRADUATE EXPENSES for 2016–2017 *Application fee:* $30. *Tuition, state resident:* full-time $5842; part-time $265 per credit hour. *Tuition, nonresident:* full-time $14,210; part-time $662 per credit hour. Full-time tuition and fees vary according to course load, location, and reciprocity agreements. Part-time tuition and fees vary according to course load, location, and reciprocity agreements. *College room and board:* $9674; *Room only:* $4994. Room and board charges vary according to board plan, housing facility, and location.

FRESHMAN FINANCIAL AID (Fall 2016, est.) 233 applied for aid; of those 72% were deemed to have need. 98% of freshmen with need received aid; of those 23% had need fully met. *Average percent of need met:* 71% (excluding resources awarded to replace EFC). *Average financial aid package:* $7441 (excluding resources awarded to replace EFC). 14% of all full-time freshmen had no need and received non-need-based gift aid.

UNDERGRADUATE FINANCIAL AID (Fall 2016, est.) 702 applied for aid; of those 76% were deemed to have need. 97% of undergraduates with need received aid; of those 18% had need fully met. *Average percent of need met:* 64% (excluding resources awarded to replace EFC). *Average financial aid package:* $8676 (excluding resources awarded to replace EFC). 21% of all full-time undergraduates had no need and received non-need-based gift aid.

GIFT AID (NEED-BASED) *Total amount:* $2,408,811 (66% federal, 4% state, 27% institutional, 3% external sources). *Receiving aid:* Freshmen: 54% (145); all full-time undergraduates: 52% (464). *Average award:* Freshmen: $4269; Undergraduates: $4636. *Scholarships, grants, and awards:* Federal Pell, FSEOG, state, private, college/university gift aid from institutional funds, United Negro College Fund, Federal Nursing, Choose Ohio First scholarships.

GIFT AID (NON-NEED-BASED) *Total amount:* $741,680 (8% state, 80% institutional, 12% external sources). *Receiving aid:* Freshmen: 7% (18). Undergraduates: 5% (42). *Average award:* Freshmen: $3336. Undergraduates: $2749. *Scholarships, grants, and awards by category: Academic interests/achievement:* 565 awards ($916,086 total): area/ethnic studies, biological sciences, business, communication, computer science, education, engineering/technologies, English, foreign languages, general academic interests/achievements, home economics, humanities, international studies, mathematics, military science, physical sciences, premedicine, religion/biblical studies, social sciences. *Creative arts/performance:* 3 awards ($2500 total): applied art

and design, art/fine arts, cinema/film/broadcasting, creative writing, dance, general creative arts/performance, music, performing arts, theater/drama. *Special achievements/activities:* 131 awards ($341,534 total): cheerleading/drum major, community service, general special achievements/activities, leadership, memberships. *Special characteristics:* 26 awards ($101,243 total): adult students, children and siblings of alumni, children of educators, children of faculty/staff, ethnic background, first-generation college students, handicapped students, international students, members of minority groups, out-of-state students. *Tuition waivers:* Full or partial for employees or children of employees, senior citizens. *ROTC:* Army cooperative, Air Force cooperative.

LOANS *Student loans:* $5,757,966 (70% need-based, 30% non-need-based). 68% of past graduating class borrowed through all loan programs. *Average indebtedness per student:* $30,061. *Average need-based loan:* Freshmen: $3423. Undergraduates: $3976. *Parent loans:* $180,385 (57% need-based, 43% non-need-based). *Programs:* Federal Direct (Subsidized and Unsubsidized Stafford, PLUS), Perkins, Federal Nursing, state, college/university, private loans.

WORK-STUDY *Federal work-study:* Total amount: $207,222; 48 jobs averaging $4192. *State or other work-study/employment:* Part-time jobs available.

ATHLETIC AWARDS Total amount: $232,164 (35% need-based, 65% non-need-based).

APPLYING FOR FINANCIAL AID *Required financial aid form:* FAFSA. *Financial aid deadline:* Continuous. *Notification date:* Continuous beginning 2/1.

CONTACT Amy Barnhart, Assistant Vice President/Director of Financial Aid, Wright State University–Lake Campus, 3640 Colonel Glenn Highway, 216 Medical Sciences Building, Dayton, OH 45435, 937-775-5405 or toll-free 800-237-1477. *E-mail:* amy.barnhart@wright.edu. *Website:* http://www.wright.edu/lake/.

XAVIER UNIVERSITY
Cincinnati, OH

Tuition & fees: $36,150	Average undergraduate aid package: $22,866

ABOUT THE INSTITUTION Independent Roman Catholic, coed. 73 undergraduate majors. Federal methodology is used as a basis for awarding need-based institutional aid.

UNDERGRADUATE EXPENSES for 2016–2017 *Comprehensive fee:* $47,880 includes full-time tuition ($35,920), mandatory fees ($230), and room and board ($11,730). *College room only:* $6490. Full-time tuition and fees vary according to course load, location, and program. Room and board charges vary according to board plan and housing facility. *Part-time tuition:* $674 per credit hour. *Part-time fees:* $9 per credit hour. Part-time tuition and fees vary according to course load, location, and program.

FRESHMAN FINANCIAL AID (Fall 2015) 996 applied for aid; of those 78% were deemed to have need. 100% of freshmen with need received aid; of those 10% had need fully met. *Average percent of need met:* 68% (excluding resources awarded to replace EFC). *Average financial aid package:* $22,548 (excluding resources awarded to replace EFC). 31% of all full-time freshmen had no need and received non-need-based gift aid.

UNDERGRADUATE FINANCIAL AID (Fall 2015) 3,001 applied for aid; of those 82% were deemed to have need. 100% of undergraduates with need received aid; of those 25% had need fully met. *Average percent of need met:* 66% (excluding resources awarded to replace EFC). *Average financial aid package:* $22,866 (excluding resources awarded to replace EFC). 38% of all full-time undergraduates had no need and received non-need-based gift aid.

GIFT AID (NEED-BASED) *Total amount:* $33,258,591 (9% federal, 2% state, 87% institutional, 2% external sources). *Receiving aid:* Freshmen: 45% (513); all full-time undergraduates: 39% (1,658). *Average award:* Freshmen: $23,598; Undergraduates: $21,810. *Scholarships, grants, and awards:* Federal Pell, FSEOG, state, private, college/university gift aid from institutional funds.

GIFT AID (NON-NEED-BASED) *Total amount:* $41,198,562 (1% federal, 98% institutional, 1% external sources). *Receiving aid:* Freshmen: 21% (247). Undergraduates: 18% (739). *Average award:* Freshmen: $18,351. Undergraduates: $16,417. *Scholarships, grants, and awards by category: Academic interests/achievement:* foreign languages, general academic interests/achievements, mathematics, military science, physical sciences, social sciences. *Creative arts/performance:*

art/fine arts, music, performing arts, theater/drama. *Special characteristics:* children and siblings of alumni, international students, members of minority groups, siblings of current students. *Tuition waivers:* Full or partial for employees or children of employees, senior citizens.

LOANS *Student loans:* $25,613,534 (62% need-based, 38% non-need-based). 53% of past graduating class borrowed through all loan programs. *Average indebtedness per student:* $32,108. *Average need-based loan:* Freshmen: $3016. Undergraduates: $4123. *Parent loans:* $9,635,246 (50% need-based, 50% non-need-based). *Programs:* Federal Direct (Subsidized and Unsubsidized Stafford, PLUS), Perkins.

WORK-STUDY *Federal work-study:* jobs available. *State or other work-study/employment:* Part-time jobs available.

ATHLETIC AWARDS Total amount: $3,805,162 (9% need-based, 91% non-need-based).

APPLYING FOR FINANCIAL AID *Required financial aid form:* FAFSA. *Financial aid deadline (priority):* 2/15. *Notification date:* Continuous beginning 3/1. Students must reply by 5/1.

CONTACT Office of Financial Aid, Xavier University, 3800 Victory Parkway, Cincinnati, OH 45207-5111, 513-745-3142 or toll-free 877-XUADMIT. *Fax:* 513-745-2806.

Website: http://www.xavier.edu/.

XAVIER UNIVERSITY OF LOUISIANA
New Orleans, LA

Tuition & fees: $23,046	Average undergraduate aid package: $22,248

ABOUT THE INSTITUTION Independent Roman Catholic, coed. *Awards:* bachelor's, master's, and doctoral degrees. 49 undergraduate majors. *Total enrollment:* 2,997. Undergraduates: 2,327. Freshmen: 762. Federal methodology is used as a basis for awarding need-based institutional aid.

UNDERGRADUATE EXPENSES for 2016–2017 *Comprehensive fee:* $32,198 includes full-time tuition ($20,594), mandatory fees ($2452), and room and board ($9152). Room and board charges vary according to housing facility. *Part-time tuition:* $858 per credit hour. *Part-time fees:* $250 per term. Part-time tuition and fees vary according to course load.

FRESHMAN FINANCIAL AID (Fall 2015) 669 applied for aid; of those 88% were deemed to have need. 100% of freshmen with need received aid; of those .3% had need fully met. *Average financial aid package:* $22,835 (excluding resources awarded to replace EFC). 7% of all full-time freshmen had no need and received non-need-based gift aid.

UNDERGRADUATE FINANCIAL AID (Fall 2015) 2,078 applied for aid; of those 90% were deemed to have need. 100% of undergraduates with need received aid; of those .4% had need fully met. *Average financial aid package:* $22,248 (excluding resources awarded to replace EFC). 5% of all full-time undergraduates had no need and received non-need-based gift aid.

GIFT AID (NEED-BASED) *Total amount:* $3,975,530 (90% federal, 10% state). *Receiving aid:* Freshmen: 60% (411); all full-time undergraduates: 57% (1,250). *Average award:* Freshmen: $5773; Undergraduates: $5834. *Scholarships, grants, and awards:* Federal Pell, FSEOG, state, private, college/university gift aid from institutional funds, United Negro College Fund.

GIFT AID (NON-NEED-BASED) *Total amount:* $9,562,032 (21% state, 79% institutional). *Receiving aid:* Freshmen: 81% (554). Undergraduates: 71% (1,557). *Average award:* Freshmen: $12,833. Undergraduates: $13,048. *Scholarships, grants, and awards by category: Academic interests/achievement:* biological sciences, business, communication, computer science, education, engineering/technologies, English, foreign languages, general academic interests/achievements, health fields, humanities, mathematics, physical sciences, premedicine, religion/biblical studies, social sciences. *Creative arts/performance:* art/fine arts, music. *Special characteristics:* children of faculty/staff, spouses of current students. *Tuition waivers:* Full or partial for employees or children of employees. *ROTC:* Army cooperative, Naval cooperative, Air Force cooperative.

LOANS *Student loans:* $56,225,049 (98% need-based, 2% non-need-based). 82% of past graduating class borrowed through all loan programs. *Average indebtedness per student:* $22,142. *Average need-based loan:* Freshmen: $4698. Undergraduates: $5932. *Parent loans:* $5,195,135 (100% non-need-based). *Programs:* Federal Direct (Subsidized and Unsubsidized Stafford, PLUS), Perkins.

WORK-STUDY *Federal work-study:* jobs available.

ATHLETIC AWARDS Total amount: $690,101 (100% non-need-based).

APPLYING FOR FINANCIAL AID *Required financial aid form:* FAFSA. *Financial aid deadline (priority):* 1/1. *Notification date:* Continuous beginning 4/1. Students must reply within 2 weeks of notification.

CONTACT Mrs. Emily Jones, Financial Aid Director, Xavier University of Louisiana, One Drexel Drive, New Orleans, LA 70125-1098, 504-520-7517 or toll-free 877-XAVIERU. *E-mail:* ejones@xula.edu.

Website: http://www.xula.edu/.

YALE UNIVERSITY
New Haven, CT

Tuition & fees: $49,480	Average undergraduate aid package: $52,894

ABOUT THE INSTITUTION Independent, coed. *Awards:* certificates, bachelor's, master's, and doctoral degrees. 69 undergraduate majors. *Total enrollment:* 12,385. Undergraduates: 5,532. Freshmen: 1,363. Both federal and institutional methodology are used as a basis for awarding need-based institutional aid.

UNDERGRADUATE EXPENSES for 2016–2017 *Application fee:* $80. *Comprehensive fee:* $64,650 includes full-time tuition ($49,480) and room and board ($15,170). *College room only:* $8520. Room and board charges vary according to board plan.

FRESHMAN FINANCIAL AID (Fall 2016, est.) 763 applied for aid; of those 92% were deemed to have need. 100% of freshmen with need received aid; of those 100% had need fully met. *Average percent of need met:* 100% (excluding resources awarded to replace EFC). *Average financial aid package:* $54,590 (excluding resources awarded to replace EFC).

UNDERGRADUATE FINANCIAL AID (Fall 2016, est.) 2,891 applied for aid; of those 95% were deemed to have need. 100% of undergraduates with need received aid; of those 100% had need fully met. *Average percent of need met:* 100% (excluding resources awarded to replace EFC). *Average financial aid package:* $52,894 (excluding resources awarded to replace EFC).

GIFT AID (NEED-BASED) *Total amount:* $137,289,116 (4% federal, 93% institutional, 3% external sources). *Receiving aid:* Freshmen: 51% (701); all full-time undergraduates: 50% (2,732). *Average award:* Freshmen: $52,831; Undergraduates: $50,565. *Scholarships, grants, and awards:* Federal Pell, FSEOG, state, private, college/university gift aid from institutional funds, United Negro College Fund, Federal Nursing.

GIFT AID (NON-NEED-BASED) *Total amount:* $451,317 (100% external sources). *Tuition waivers:* Full or partial for employees or children of employees. *ROTC:* Army cooperative, Naval, Air Force.

LOANS *Student loans:* $2,646,859 (35% need-based, 65% non-need-based). 14% of past graduating class borrowed through all loan programs. *Average indebtedness per student:* $13,625. *Average need-based loan:* Freshmen: $2016. Undergraduates: $2725. *Programs:* Federal Direct (Subsidized and Unsubsidized Stafford, PLUS), Perkins, state, college/university.

WORK-STUDY *Federal work-study:* Total amount: $2,513,474; jobs available. *State or other work-study/employment:* Total amount: $2,930,645 (100% need-based). Part-time jobs available.

APPLYING FOR FINANCIAL AID *Required financial aid forms:* FAFSA, CSS Financial Aid PROFILE, noncustodial (divorced/separated) parent's statement, federal income tax form(s). *Financial aid deadline:* 3/1. *Notification date:* 4/1. Students must reply by 5/1 or within 1 week of notification.

CONTACT Mr. Caesar T. Storlazzi, University Director of Financial Aid, Yale University, PO Box 208288, New Haven, CT 06520-8288, 203-432-0371. *Fax:* 203-777-6100. *E-mail:* sfs@yale.edu.

Website: http://www.yale.edu/.

YESHIVA AND KOLEL BAIS MEDRASH ELYON
Monsey, NY

CONTACT Financial Aid Office, Yeshiva and Kolel Bais Medrash Elyon, 73 Main Street, Monsey, NY 10952, 845-356-7064.

YESHIVA AND KOLLEL HARBOTZAS TORAH
Brooklyn, NY

CONTACT Financial Aid Office, Yeshiva and Kollel Harbotzas Torah, 1049 East 15th Street, Brooklyn, NY 11230, 718-692-0208.

YESHIVA BETH MOSHE
Scranton, PA

CONTACT Financial Aid Office , Yeshiva Beth Moshe, 930 Hickory Street, Scranton, PA 18505-2124, 717-346-1747.

YESHIVA BETH YEHUDA–YESHIVA GEDOLAH OF GREATER DETROIT
Oak Park, MI

CONTACT Rabbi P. Rushnawitz, Executive Administrator , Yeshiva Beth Yehuda–Yeshiva Gedolah of Greater Detroit, 24600 Greenfield Road, Oak Park, MI 48237-1544, 810-968-3360. *Fax:* 810-968-8613.

YESHIVA COLLEGE OF THE NATION'S CAPITAL
Silver Spring, MD

CONTACT Financial Aid Office, Yeshiva College of the Nation's Capital, 1216 Arcola Avenue, Silver Spring, MD 20902, 301-593-2534. *Website:* http://www.yeshiva.edu/.

YESHIVA DERECH CHAIM
Brooklyn, NY

CONTACT Financial Aid Office, Yeshiva Derech Chaim, 1573 39th Street, Brooklyn, NY 11218, 718-438-5426.

YESHIVA D'MONSEY RABBINICAL COLLEGE
Monsey, NY

CONTACT Financial Aid Office, Yeshiva D'Monsey Rabbinical College, 2 Roman Boulevard, Monsey, NY 10952, 914-352-5852.

YESHIVA GEDOLAH IMREI YOSEF D'SPINKA
Brooklyn, NY

CONTACT Financial Aid Office, Yeshiva Gedolah Imrei Yosef D'Spinka, 1466 56th Street, Brooklyn, NY 11219, 718-851-8721.

YESHIVA GEDOLAH RABBINICAL COLLEGE
Miami Beach, FL

CONTACT Financial Aid Office, Yeshiva Gedolah Rabbinical College, 1140 Alton Road, Miami Beach, FL 33139, 305-673-5664.

YESHIVA GEDOLAH ZICHRON LEYMA
Linden, NJ

CONTACT Financial Aid Office, Yeshiva Gedolah Zichron Leyma, 1000 Orchard Terrace, Linden, NJ 07036, 908-587-0502.

YESHIVA KARLIN STOLIN RABBINICAL INSTITUTE
Brooklyn, NY

CONTACT Mr. Daniel Ross, Financial Aid Administrator, Yeshiva Karlin Stolin Rabbinical Institute, 1818 Fifty-fourth Street, Brooklyn, NY 11204, 718-232-7800 Ext. 116. *Fax:* 718-331-4833.

YESHIVA OF FAR ROCKAWAY DERECH AYSON RABBINICAL SEMINARY
Far Rockaway, NY

CONTACT Financial Aid Office, Yeshiva of Far Rockaway Derech Ayson Rabbinical Seminary, 802 Hicksville Road, Far Rockaway, NY 11691, 718-327-7600. *Website:* http://www.yofr.org/.

YESHIVA OF MACHZIKAI HADAS
Brooklyn, NY

CONTACT Financial Aid Office, Yeshiva of Machzikai Hadas, 1321 43rd Street, Brooklyn, NY 11219, 718-853-2442.

YESHIVA OF NITRA RABBINICAL COLLEGE
Mount Kisco, NY

CONTACT Mr. Yosef Rosen, Financial Aid Administrator , Yeshiva of Nitra Rabbinical College, 194 Division Avenue, Mount Kisco, NY 10549, 718-384-5460. *Fax:* 718-387-9400.

YESHIVA OF THE TELSHE ALUMNI
Riverdale, NY

CONTACT Financial Aid Office, Yeshiva of the Telshe Alumni, 4904 Independence Avenue, Riverdale, NY 10471, 718-601-3523.

YESHIVA OHR ELCHONON CHABAD/ WEST COAST TALMUDICAL SEMINARY
Los Angeles, CA

CONTACT Ms. Hendy Tauber, Director of Financial Aid , Yeshiva Ohr Elchonon Chabad/West Coast Talmudical Seminary, 7215 Waring Avenue, Los Angeles, CA 90046-7660, 213-937-3763. *Fax:* 213-937-9456.
Website: http://www.yoec.edu/.

YESHIVAS BE'ER YITZCHOK
Elizabeth, NJ

CONTACT Financial Aid Office, Yeshivas Be'er Yitzchok, 1391 North Avenue, Elizabeth, NJ 07208, 908-354-6057.
Website: http://www.elizabethkollel.org/.

YESHIVA SHAAREI TORAH OF ROCKLAND
Suffern, NY

CONTACT Financial Aid Office, Yeshiva Shaarei Torah of Rockland, 91 West Carlton Road, Suffern, NY 10901, 845-352-3431.

YESHIVA SHAAR HATORAH TALMUDIC RESEARCH INSTITUTE
Kew Gardens, NY

CONTACT Mr. Yoel Yankelewitz, Executive Director, Financial Aid, Yeshiva Shaar Hatorah Talmudic Research Institute, 117-06 84th Avenue, Kew Gardens, NY 11418-1469, 718-846-1940.

YESHIVAS NOVOMINSK
Brooklyn, NY

CONTACT Financial Aid Office, Yeshivas Novominsk, 1569 47th Street, Brooklyn, NY 11219, 718-438-2727.

YESHIVATH VIZNITZ
Monsey, NY

CONTACT Financial Aid Office, Yeshivath Viznitz, Phyllis Terrace, PO Box 446, Monsey, NY 10952, 914-356-1010.

YESHIVATH ZICHRON MOSHE
South Fallsburg, NY

CONTACT Ms. Miryom R. Miller, Director of Financial Aid , Yeshivath Zichron Moshe, Laurel Park Road, South Fallsburg, NY 12779, 914-434-5240. *Fax:* 914-434-1009. *E-mail:* lehus@aol.com.

YESHIVAT MIKDASH MELECH
Brooklyn, NY

CONTACT Financial Aid Office, Yeshivat Mikdash Melech, 1326 Ocean Parkway, Brooklyn, NY 11230-5601, 718-339-1090.

YESHIVA TORAS CHAIM
Lakewood, NJ

CONTACT Financial Aid Office, Yeshiva Toras Chaim, 999 Ridge Avenue, Lakewood, NJ 08701, 732-942-3090.

YESHIVA UNIVERSITY
New York, NY

ABOUT THE INSTITUTION Independent, coed. *Awards:* certificates, bachelor's, master's, and doctoral degrees (Yeshiva College and Stern College for Women are coordinate undergraduate colleges of arts and sciences for men and women, respectively. Sy Syms School of Business offers programs at both campuses). 36 undergraduate majors. *Total enrollment:* 6,203. Undergraduates: 2,744. Freshmen: 792.
GIFT AID (NEED-BASED) *Scholarships, grants, and awards:* Federal Pell, FSEOG, state, private, college/university gift aid from institutional funds.
GIFT AID (NON-NEED-BASED) *Scholarships, grants, and awards by category:* *Academic interests/achievement:* general academic interests/achievements.
LOANS *Programs:* Federal Direct (Subsidized and Unsubsidized Stafford, PLUS), Perkins, college/university.
APPLYING FOR FINANCIAL AID *Required financial aid form:* FAFSA.
CONTACT Marianela Cabral, Director of Student Aid Operations, Yeshiva University, 500 West 185th Street, Room 121, New York, NY 10033, 212-960-5399. *Fax:* 212-960-0037. *E-mail:* mcabral@yu.edu.
Website: http://www.yu.edu/.

YORK COLLEGE
York, NE

CONTACT Brien Alley, Director of Financial Aid, York College, 1125 East 8th Street, York, NE 68467, 402-363-5624 or toll-free 800-950-9675. *Fax:* 402-363-5623. *E-mail:* balley@york.edu.
Website: http://www.york.edu/.

YORK COLLEGE OF PENNSYLVANIA
York, PA

Tuition & fees: $18,780	Average undergraduate aid package: $12,240

ABOUT THE INSTITUTION Independent, coed. *Awards:* certificates, associate, bachelor's, master's, and doctoral degrees. 56 undergraduate majors. *Total enrollment:* 4,739. Undergraduates: 4,537. Freshmen: 896. Federal methodology is used as a basis for awarding need-based institutional aid.
UNDERGRADUATE EXPENSES for 2016–2017 *Comprehensive fee:* $29,240 includes full-time tuition ($16,970), mandatory fees ($1810), and room and board ($10,460). Full-time tuition and fees vary according to program. Room and board charges vary according to board plan and housing facility. *Part-time tuition:* $525 per credit hour.
FRESHMAN FINANCIAL AID (Fall 2016, est.) 814 applied for aid; of those 77% were deemed to have need. 100% of freshmen with need received aid; of those 17% had need fully met. *Average percent of need met:* 63% (excluding resources awarded to replace EFC). *Average financial aid package:* $13,354 (excluding resources awarded to replace EFC). 29% of all full-time freshmen had no need and received non-need-based gift aid.

UNDERGRADUATE FINANCIAL AID (Fall 2016, est.) 3,183 applied for aid; of those 80% were deemed to have need. 100% of undergraduates with need received aid; of those 15% had need fully met. **Average percent of need met:** 56% (excluding resources awarded to replace EFC). **Average financial aid package:** $12,240 (excluding resources awarded to replace EFC). 27% of all full-time undergraduates had no need and received non-need-based gift aid.

GIFT AID (NEED-BASED) Total amount: $21,555,219 (22% federal, 13% state, 62% institutional, 3% external sources). **Receiving aid:** Freshmen: 48% (427); all full-time undergraduates: 42% (1,618). **Average award:** Freshmen: $5591; Undergraduates: $5410. **Scholarships, grants, and awards:** Federal Pell, FSEOG, state, private, college/university gift aid from institutional funds.

GIFT AID (NON-NEED-BASED) Total amount: $5,899,410 (97% institutional, 3% external sources). **Receiving aid:** Freshmen: 70% (624). Undergraduates: 58% (2,214). **Average award:** Freshmen: $6308. Undergraduates: $5314. **Scholarships, grants, and awards by category:** Academic interests/achievement: engineering/technologies, general academic interests/achievements. Creative arts/performance: music. Special characteristics: children and siblings of alumni, children of union members/company employees, international students, members of minority groups. **Tuition waivers:** Full or partial for employees or children of employees.

LOANS Student loans: $32,253,821 (81% need-based, 19% non-need-based). 80% of past graduating class borrowed through all loan programs. **Average indebtedness per student:** $40,617. **Average need-based loan:** Freshmen: $3162. Undergraduates: $4112. **Parent loans:** $7,514,521 (87% need-based, 13% non-need-based). **Programs:** Federal Direct (Subsidized and Unsubsidized Stafford, PLUS), Perkins, Federal Nursing, college/university.

WORK-STUDY Federal work-study: Total amount: $537,938; jobs available. **State or other work-study/employment:** Total amount: $24,719 (84% need-based, 16% non-need-based). Part-time jobs available.

APPLYING FOR FINANCIAL AID Required financial aid form: FAFSA. **Financial aid deadline:** Continuous. **Notification date:** Continuous beginning 3/1. Students must reply within 4 weeks of notification.

CONTACT Calvin Williams, Director of Financial Aid, York College of Pennsylvania, 441 Country Club Road, York, PA 17403, 717-849-1682 or toll-free 800-455-8018. Fax: 717-849-1685. E-mail: financialaid@ycp.edu. Website: http://www.ycp.edu/.

YORK COLLEGE OF THE CITY UNIVERSITY OF NEW YORK
Jamaica, NY

Tuition & fees (NY res): $6747	Average undergraduate aid package: $7738

ABOUT THE INSTITUTION State and locally supported, coed. **Awards:** bachelor's and master's degrees. 46 undergraduate majors. **Total enrollment:** 8,360. Undergraduates: 8,258. Freshmen: 971. Federal methodology is used as a basis for awarding need-based institutional aid.

UNDERGRADUATE EXPENSES for 2016–2017 Application fee: $65. **Tuition, state resident:** full-time $6330; part-time $275 per credit hour. **Tuition, nonresident:** full-time $16,800; part-time $560 per credit hour. **Required fees:** full-time $417; $126.10 per term. Full-time tuition and fees vary according to degree level and student level. Part-time tuition and fees vary according to degree level and student level.

FRESHMAN FINANCIAL AID (Fall 2016, est.) 852 applied for aid; of those 100% were deemed to have need. 95% of freshmen with need received aid; of those 2% had need fully met. **Average percent of need met:** 56% (excluding resources awarded to replace EFC). **Average financial aid package:** $8441 (excluding resources awarded to replace EFC). 1% of all full-time freshmen had no need and received non-need-based gift aid.

UNDERGRADUATE FINANCIAL AID (Fall 2016, est.) 4,269 applied for aid; of those 100% were deemed to have need. 96% of undergraduates with need received aid; of those 2% had need fully met. **Average percent of need met:** 60% (excluding resources awarded to replace EFC). **Average financial aid package:** $7738 (excluding resources awarded to replace EFC). 1% of all full-time undergraduates had no need and received non-need-based gift aid.

GIFT AID (NEED-BASED) Total amount: $31,135,424 (56% federal, 44% state). **Receiving aid:** Freshmen: 79% (743); all full-time undergraduates: 77% (3,841).

Average award: Freshmen: $9191; Undergraduates: $8254. **Scholarships, grants, and awards:** Federal Pell, FSEOG, state, private, college/university gift aid from institutional funds, Federal Nursing.

GIFT AID (NON-NEED-BASED) Total amount: $819,087 (60% institutional, 40% external sources). **Receiving aid:** Freshmen: 3% (31). Undergraduates: 7% (338). **Average award:** Freshmen: $4182. Undergraduates: $4914. **Tuition waivers:** Full or partial for employees or children of employees, senior citizens. **ROTC:** Army.

LOANS Student loans: $4,237,291 (53% need-based, 17% non-need based). 6% of past graduating class borrowed through all loan programs. **Average indebtedness per student:** $4614. **Average need-based loan:** Freshmen: $2813. Undergraduates: $3931. **Parent loans:** $30,500 (100% non-need-based). **Programs:** Federal Direct (Subsidized and Unsubsidized Stafford, PLUS), Perkins.

WORK-STUDY Federal work-study: Total amount: $516,843; jobs available.

APPLYING FOR FINANCIAL AID Required financial aid forms: FAFSA, state aid form. **Financial aid deadline:** 6/30 (priority: 5/1). **Notification date:** Continuous beginning 2/15. Students must reply within 4 weeks of notification.

CONTACT Ms. Beverly Brown, Director of Student Financial Services, York College of the City University of New York, 94-20 Guy R. Brewer Boulevard, Jamaica, NY 11451-0001, 718-262-2240. E-mail: bbrown@york.cuny.edu. Website: http://www.york.cuny.edu/.

YOUNG HARRIS COLLEGE
Young Harris, GA

Tuition & fees: N/R	Average undergraduate aid package: $23,364

ABOUT THE INSTITUTION Independent United Methodist, coed. **Awards:** bachelor's degrees. 30 undergraduate majors. **Total enrollment:** 1,034. Undergraduates: 1,034. Freshmen: 388. Both federal and institutional methodology are used as a basis for awarding need-based institutional aid.

FRESHMAN FINANCIAL AID (Fall 2015) 363 applied for aid; of those 85% were deemed to have need. 100% of freshmen with need received aid; of those 20% had need fully met. **Average percent of need met:** 71% (excluding resources awarded to replace EFC). **Average financial aid package:** $22,731 (excluding resources awarded to replace EFC). 27% of all full-time freshmen had no need and received non-need-based gift aid.

UNDERGRADUATE FINANCIAL AID (Fall 2015) 931 applied for aid; of those 87% were deemed to have need. 100% of undergraduates with need received aid; of those 19% had need fully met. **Average percent of need met:** 73% (excluding resources awarded to replace EFC). **Average financial aid package:** $23,364 (excluding resources awarded to replace EFC). 29% of all full-time undergraduates had no need and received non-need-based gift aid.

GIFT AID (NEED-BASED) Total amount: $16,645,787 (12% federal, 12% state, 75% institutional, 1% external sources). **Receiving aid:** Freshmen: 72% (306); all full-time undergraduates: 70% (812). **Average award:** Freshmen: $20,333; Undergraduates: $20,363. **Scholarships, grants, and awards:** Federal Pell, FSEOG, state, private, college/university gift aid from institutional funds.

GIFT AID (NON-NEED-BASED) Total amount: $9,056,924 (13% state, 85% institutional, 2% external sources). **Receiving aid:** Freshmen: 14% (59). Undergraduates: 13% (147). **Average award:** Freshmen: $19,164. Undergraduates: $19,650. **Scholarships, grants, and awards by category:** Academic interests/achievement: 1,138 awards ($13,201,538 total): general academic interests/achievements. Creative arts/performance: 129 awards ($366,310 total): art/fine arts, music, performing arts, theater/drama. Special characteristics: 21 awards ($315,334 total): children of faculty/staff, religious affiliation.

LOANS Student loans: $5,424,043 (71% need-based, 29% non-need-based). 69% of past graduating class borrowed through all loan programs. **Average indebtedness per student:** $27,173. **Average need-based loan:** Freshmen: $3302. Undergraduates: $3709. **Parent loans:** $2,022,023 (51% need-based, 49% non-need-based). **Programs:** Federal Direct (Subsidized and Unsubsidized Stafford, PLUS), state, college/university.

WORK-STUDY Federal work-study: 116 jobs averaging $836. **State or other work-study/employment:** Total amount: $401,390 (42% need-based, 58% non-need-based). 377 part-time jobs averaging $1078.

APPLYING FOR FINANCIAL AID *Required financial aid forms:* FAFSA, state aid form. *Financial aid deadline (priority):* 5/1. *Notification date:* Continuous. Students must reply within 2 weeks of notification.

CONTACT Linda Adams, Director of Financial Aid, Young Harris College, 1 College Street, Young Harris, GA 30582, 706-379-5188 or toll-free 800-241-3754 (in-state). *Fax:* 706-379-4594. *E-mail:* leadams@yhc.edu. *Website:* http://www.yhc.edu/.

YOUNGSTOWN STATE UNIVERSITY
Youngstown, OH

Tuition & fees (OH res): $8317	Average undergraduate aid package: $9007

ABOUT THE INSTITUTION State-supported, coed. *Awards:* certificates, diplomas, associate, bachelor's, master's, and doctoral degrees. 141 undergraduate majors. *Total enrollment:* 12,751. Undergraduates: 11,391. Freshmen: 2,091. Federal methodology is used as a basis for awarding need-based institutional aid.

UNDERGRADUATE EXPENSES for 2016–2017 *Application fee:* $45. *Tuition, state resident:* full-time $7847; part-time $327 per credit hour. *Tuition, nonresident:* full-time $13,847; part-time $577 per credit hour. *Required fees:* full-time $470; $10 per credit hour or $115 per term. Full-time tuition and fees vary according to course load. Part-time tuition and fees vary according to course load. *College room and board:* $8990. Room and board charges vary according to board plan and housing facility.

FRESHMAN FINANCIAL AID (Fall 2015) 1,791 applied for aid; of those 85% were deemed to have need. 100% of freshmen with need received aid; of those 10% had need fully met. *Average percent of need met:* 34% (excluding resources awarded to replace EFC). *Average financial aid package:* $8750 (excluding resources awarded to replace EFC). 14% of all full-time freshmen had no need and received non-need-based gift aid.

UNDERGRADUATE FINANCIAL AID (Fall 2015) 7,315 applied for aid; of those 86% were deemed to have need. 99% of undergraduates with need received aid; of those 8% had need fully met. *Average percent of need met:* 32% (excluding resources awarded to replace EFC). *Average financial aid package:* $9007 (excluding resources awarded to replace EFC). 11% of all full-time undergraduates had no need and received non-need-based gift aid.

GIFT AID (NEED-BASED) *Total amount:* $30,183,184 (74% federal, 15% state, 1% institutional, 10% external sources). *Receiving aid:* Freshmen: 61% (1,174); all full-time undergraduates: 56% (4,761). *Average award:* Freshmen: $5324; Undergraduates: $5380. *Scholarships, grants, and awards:* Federal Pell, FSEOG, state, private, college/university gift aid from institutional funds, Advanced Education Nursing Scholarships.

GIFT AID (NON-NEED-BASED) *Total amount:* $11,463,962 (6% federal, 7% state, 25% institutional, 62% external sources). *Receiving aid:* Freshmen: 43% (838). Undergraduates: 31% (2,655). *Average award:* Freshmen: $3556. Undergraduates: $3165. *Scholarships, grants, and awards by category:* Academic interests/achievement: biological sciences, business, communication, computer science, education, engineering/technologies, English, foreign languages, general academic interests/achievements, health fields, humanities, mathematics, military science, physical sciences, premedicine, religion/biblical studies, social sciences. *Creative arts/performance:* art/fine arts, creative writing, journalism/publications, music, performing arts, theater/drama. *Special achievements/activities:* cheerleading/drum major, community service, leadership, memberships, religious involvement. *Special characteristics:* adult students, children and siblings of alumni, children of faculty/staff, children of union members/company employees, children of workers in trades, children with a deceased or disabled parent, ethnic background, handicapped students, international students, local/state students, members of minority groups, out-of-state students, public servants, religious affiliation, spouses of deceased or disabled public servants, veterans, veterans' children. *Tuition waivers:* Full or partial for employees or children of employees, senior citizens. *ROTC:* Army, Air Force cooperative.

LOANS *Student loans:* $55,556,804 (44% need-based, 56% non-need-based). 69% of past graduating class borrowed through all loan programs. *Average indebtedness per student:* $30,403. *Average need-based loan:* Freshmen: $3049. Undergraduates: $3791. *Parent loans:* $41,372,216 (100% non-need-based). *Programs:* Federal Direct (Subsidized and Unsubsidized Stafford, PLUS), Perkins, Charles E. Schell Foundation loans, George W. Wright Student Aid loans, Rogers student loans.

WORK-STUDY *Federal work-study:* jobs available. *State or other work-study/employment:* Total amount: $4,173,319 (100% non-need-based). Part-time jobs available.

ATHLETIC AWARDS Total amount: $4,688,054 (100% non-need-based).

APPLYING FOR FINANCIAL AID *Required financial aid form:* FAFSA. *Financial aid deadline (priority):* 12/1. *Notification date:* Continuous beginning 12/15. Students must reply within 2 weeks of notification.

CONTACT Barbara Greene, Associate Director of Financial Analysis and Reporting, Youngstown State University, One University Plaza, Youngstown, OH 44555, 330-941-3504 or toll-free 877-468-6978. *Fax:* 330-941-1659. *E-mail:* bgreene@ysu.edu. *Website:* http://www.ysu.edu/.

ZAYTUNA COLLEGE
Berkeley, CA

CONTACT Financial Aid Office, Zaytuna College, 2401 Le Conte Avenue, Berkeley, CA 94709, 510-356-4760. *Website:* http://www.zaytuna.edu/.

Appendix

State Scholarship and Grant Programs

Each state government has established one or more state-administered financial aid programs for qualified students. In many instances, these state programs are restricted to legal residents of the state. However, they often are available to out-of-state students who will be or are attending colleges or universities within the state. In addition to residential status, other qualifications frequently exist.

Gift aid and forgivable loan programs open to undergraduate students for all states and the District of Columbia are described on the following pages. They are arranged in alphabetical order, first by state name, then by program name. The annotation for each program provides information about the program, eligibility, and the contact addresses for applications or further information. Unless otherwise stated, this information refers to awards for 2015–16. Information is provided by the state-sponsoring agency in response to *Peterson's Annual Survey of Non-institutional Aid*, which was conducted between December 2015 and April 2016. Information is accurate when Peterson's receives it. However, it is always advisable to check with the sponsor to ascertain that the information remains correct.

You should write to the address given for each program to request that award details for 2017–18 be sent to you as soon as they are available. Descriptive information, brochures, and application forms for state scholarship programs are usually available from the financial aid offices of public colleges or universities within the specific state. High school guidance offices often have information and relevant forms for awards for which high school seniors may be eligible. Increasingly, state government agencies are putting state scholarship information on state government agency websites. In searching state government websites, however, you should be aware that the higher education agency in many states is separate from the state's general education office, which is often responsible only for elementary and secondary education. Also, the page at public university websites that provides information about student financial aid frequently has a list of state-sponsored scholarships and financial aid programs.

Names of scholarship programs are frequently used inconsistently or become abbreviated in popular usage. Many programs have variant names by which they are known. The program's sponsor has approved the title of the program that Peterson's uses in this guide, yet this name may differ from the program's official name or from its most commonly used name.

In addition to the grant aid and forgivable loan programs listed on the following pages, states may also offer internship or work-study programs, graduate fellowships and grants, or low-interest loans. If you are interested in learning more about these other kinds of programs, the state education office that supplies information or applications for the undergraduate scholarship programs listed here should be able to provide information about other kinds of higher education financial aid programs that are sponsored by the state.

ALABAMA

Air Force ROTC College Scholarship. Scholarship program provides three- and four-year scholarships in three different types to high school seniors. All scholarship cadets receive a nontaxable monthly allowance (stipend) during the academic year. For more details refer to web site http://www.afrotc.com/scholarships/hsschol/types.php. *Award:* Scholarship for use in freshman, sophomore, junior, or senior years; renewable. *Award amount:* $9000–$15,000. *Number of awards:* 2000–4000. *Eligibility Requirements:* Applicant must be age 17-30 and enrolled or expecting to enroll full-time at a two-year or four-year institution or university. Applicant must have 3.0 GPA or higher. Available to U.S. citizens. Applicant or parent must meet one or more of the following requirements: Air Force experience; retired from active duty; disabled or killed as a result of military service; prisoner of war; or missing in action. *Application Requirements:* Application form, interview, test scores, transcript. **Deadline:** December 1.

Contact Ty Christian, Chief Air Force ROTC Advertising Manager, Air Force Reserve Officer Training Corps, 551 East Maxwell Boulevard, Maxwell Air Force Base, AL 36112-6106. *E-mail:* ty.christian@maxwell.af.mil. *Phone:* 334-953-2278. *Fax:* 334-953-4384. *Website:* http://www.afrotc.com/.

Alabama G.I. Dependents Scholarship Program. Scholarship pays for tuition, textbooks and laboratory fees for eligible dependents of Alabama disabled, prisoner-of-war, or missing-in-action veterans. Child or stepchild must initiate training before 26th birthday; age 30 deadline may apply in certain situations. No age deadline for spouses or widows. The veteran and the step child's parent must have been married prior the child's 19th birthday. *Award:* Scholarship for use in freshman, sophomore, junior, or senior years; renewable. *Eligibility Requirements:* Applicant must be enrolled or expecting to enroll full- or part-time at a two-year or four-year or technical institution or university; resident of Alabama and studying in Alabama. Available to U.S. citizens. *Application Requirements:* Application form.

Contact Kayla Kyle, Department Operations Manager, Alabama Department of Veterans Affairs, PO Box 1509, Montgomery, AL 36102-1509. *Phone:* 334-242-5077. *Website:* http://www.va.alabama.gov/.

Alabama National Guard Educational Assistance Program. Renewable award aids Alabama residents who are members of the Alabama National Guard and are enrolled in a nationally recognized accredited college in Alabama. Forms must be signed by a representative of the Alabama Military Department and financial aid officer. Recipient must be in a degree-seeking program. *Award:* Scholarship for use in freshman, sophomore, junior, senior, or graduate years; not renewable. *Award amount:* $100–$2000. *Number of awards:* 400–800. *Eligibility Requirements:* Applicant must be enrolled or expecting to enroll full- or part-time at a two-year or four-year or technical institution or university; resident of Alabama and studying in Alabama. Available to U.S. citizens. Applicant must have national guard experience. *Application Requirements:* Application form, financial need analysis. **Deadline:** continuous.

Contact Cheryl Newton, Grants Coordinator. *E-mail:* cheryl.newton@ache.alabama.gov. *Phone:* 334-242-2273. *Fax:* 334-242-2269. *Website:* http://www.ache.alabama.gov/.

Alabama Student Assistance Program. Scholarship award of $300 to $5000 per academic year given to undergraduate students residing in the state of Alabama and attending a college or university in Alabama. *Award:* Grant for use in freshman, sophomore, junior, or senior years; not renewable. *Award amount:* $300–$5000. *Number of awards:* 3500–4500. *Eligibility Requirements:* Applicant must be enrolled or expecting to enroll full- or part-time at a two-year or four-year or technical institution or university; resident of Alabama and studying in Alabama. Available to U.S. citizens. *Application Requirements:* Application form, financial need analysis. **Deadline:** continuous.

Contact Cheryl Newton, Grants Coordinator. *E-mail:* cheryl.newton@ache.alabama.gov. *Phone:* 334-242-2273. *Fax:* 334-242-2269. *Website:* http://www.ache.alabama.gov/.

Alabama Student Grant Program. Nonrenewable awards available to Alabama residents for undergraduate study at certain independent colleges within the state. Both full and half-time students are eligible. Deadlines: September 15, January 15, and February 15. *Award:* Grant for use in freshman, sophomore, junior, or senior years; not renewable. *Award amount:* $200–$1200. *Number of awards:* 3500–5200. *Eligibility Requirements:* Applicant must be enrolled or expecting to enroll full- or part-time at a four-year institution or university; resident of Alabama and studying in Alabama. Available to U.S. citizens. *Application Requirements:* Application form.

Contact Cheryl Newton, Grants Coordinator. *E-mail:* cheryl.newton@ache.alabama.gov. *Phone:* 334-242-2273. *Fax:* 334-242-2269. *Website:* http://www.ache.alabama.gov/.

Police Officers and Firefighters Survivors Education Assistance Program-Alabama. Provides tuition, fees, books, and supplies to dependents of full-time police officers and firefighters killed or totally disabled in the line of duty. Must attend an Alabama public college as an undergraduate. Must be Alabama resident. *Award:* Scholarship for use in freshman, sophomore, junior, or senior years; renewable. *Award amount:* $1600–$12,000. *Number of awards:* 15–30. *Eligibility Requirements:* Applicant must be enrolled or expecting to enroll full- or part-time at a two-year or technical institution or university; resident of Alabama and studying in Alabama. Available to U.S. citizens. *Application Requirements:* Application form. **Deadline:** continuous.

Contact Cheryl Newton, Grants Coordinator. *E-mail:* cheryl.newton@ache.alabama.gov. *Phone:* 334-242-2273. *Fax:* 334-242-2269. *Website:* http://www.ache.alabama.gov/.

ALASKA

AlaskAdvantage Education Grant. The Alaska legislature created the AlaskAdvantage Education Grant Program (AEG) to provide need-based financial assistance to eligible Alaska students attending qualifying postsecondary educational institutions in Alaska. Students apply by completing the FAFSA annually. *Award:* Grant for use in freshman, sophomore, junior, or senior years; not renewable. *Award amount:* $500–$3000. *Eligibility Requirements:* Applicant must be enrolled or expecting to enroll full- or part-time at a two-year or four-year institution or university; resident of Alaska and studying in Alaska. Available to U.S. and non-U.S. citizens. *Application Requirements:* Completed FAFSA.

Contact Adam Weed, Special Programs Coordinator. *E-mail:* customer_service@acpe.state.ak.us. *Phone:* 907-465-6685. *Website:* http://www.acpe.alaska.gov.

Alaska Performance Scholarship. To qualify, students must take a specific, rigorous high school curriculum; earn a minimum 2.5 GPA; and do well on college or career readiness exam. Students apply by completing the FAFSA by the annual deadline. Awards can be used at any regionally accredited college or university in Alaska, or for approved career and technical education programs in the state. Students must use scholarship within 6 years of high school graduation. Students cannot receive award for more than 8 semesters. *Award:* Scholarship for use in freshman, sophomore, junior, senior, graduate, or postgraduate years; not renewable. *Award amount:* $500–$4755. *Eligibility Requirements:* Applicant must be enrolled or expecting to enroll full- or part-time at a two-year or four-year or technical institution or university; resident of Alaska and studying in Alaska. Applicant must have 2.5 GPA or higher. Available to U.S. and non-U.S. citizens. *Application Requirements:* FAFSA.

Contact Adam Weed, Special Programs Coordinator. *E-mail:* customer_service@acpe.state.ak.us. *Phone:* 907-465-6685. *Website:* http://www.acpe.alaska.gov.

ARIZONA

Leveraging Educational Assistance Partnership. Grants to financially needy students, who enroll in and attend post-secondary education or training in Arizona schools. Program was formerly known as the State Student Incentive Grant or SSIG Program. *Award:* Grant for use in freshman, sophomore, junior, senior, or graduate years; not renewable. *Award amount:* $100–$2500. *Eligibility Requirements:* Applicant must be enrolled or expecting to enroll full- or part-time at a two-year or four-year or technical institution or university; resident of Arizona and studying in Arizona. Available to U.S. citizens. *Application Requirements:* Application

form, financial need analysis, transcript. **Deadline:** April 30.

Contact Mila Zaporteza, Business Manager and LEAP Financial Aid Manager, Arizona Commission for Post-secondary Education, 2020 North Central Avenue, Suite 650, Phoenix, AZ 85004-4503. *E-mail:* mila@azhighered.gov. *Phone:* 602-258-2435 Ext. 102. *Fax:* 602-258-2483. *Website:* https://highered.az.gov/.

ARKANSAS

Arkansas Academic Challenge Scholarship Program. Awards for Arkansas residents who are graduating high school seniors, currently enrolled college students and nontraditional students to study at an approved Arkansas institution. Must have at least a 2.5 GPA or 19 ACT composite score (or the equivalent). Renewable up to three additional years. *Award:* Scholarship for use in freshman, sophomore, junior, or senior years; renewable. *Award amount:* $1250–$4500. *Number of awards:* 30,000–35,000. *Eligibility Requirements:* Applicant must be enrolled or expecting to enroll full- or part-time at a two-year or four-year institution or university; resident of Arkansas and studying in Arkansas. Applicant must have 2.5 GPA or higher. Available to U. S. citizens. *Application Requirements:* Application form, application form may be submitted online (http://www.adhe.edu), financial need analysis, test scores, transcript. **Deadline:** June 1.

Contact Philip Axelroth, Financial Aid Program Coordinator. *Phone:* 501-371-2000. *Website:* http://www.adhe.edu/.

Arkansas Governor's Scholars Program. Awards for outstanding Arkansas high school seniors. Must be an Arkansas resident and have a high school GPA of at least 3.5 or have scored at least 27 on the ACT. Award is $4000 per year for four years of full-time undergraduate study. Applicants who attain 32 or above on ACT, 1410 or above on SAT and have an academic 3.5 GPA, or are selected as National Merit or National Achievement finalists may receive an award equal to tuition, mandatory fees, room, and board up to $10,000 per year at any Arkansas institution. *Award:* Scholarship for use in freshman, sophomore, junior, senior, or graduate years; renewable. *Award amount:* $4000–$10,000. *Number of*

awards: 75–375. *Eligibility Requirements:* Applicant must be high school student; planning to enroll or expecting to enroll full-time at a two-year or four-year institution or university; resident of Arkansas and studying in Arkansas. Applicant must have 3.5 GPA or higher. Available to U.S. citizens. *Application Requirements:* Application form, application form may be submitted online (http://www.adhe.edu), community service, test scores, transcript. **Deadline:** February 1.

Contact Philip Axelroth, Financial Aid Program Coordinator. *Phone:* 501-371-2000. *Website:* http://www.adhe.edu/.

Arkansas Single Parent Scholarship Fund. Scholarships are awarded to economically disadvantaged single parents who live anywhere in Arkansas or in Bowie County, Texas. Applicants must have custodial care of at least one minor child. Generally, applicants who have not yet received a 4-year degree are preferred. In some cases, applications from students pursuing a Masters degree will be considered. Application forms, award values, deadlines, and other requirements will vary by county. Visit http://www.aspsf.org for more information. *Award:* Scholarship for use in freshman, sophomore, junior, or senior years; not renewable. *Award amount:* $200–$1800. *Number of awards:* 1–2000. *Eligibility Requirements:* Applicant must be enrolled or expecting to enroll full- or part-time at a two-year or four-year or technical institution or university; single and resident of Arkansas, Texas. Available to U.S. and non-U.S. citizens. *Application Requirements:* Application form, essay, financial need analysis, interview. **Deadline:** continuous.

Law Enforcement Officers' Dependents Scholarship–Arkansas. Scholarship for dependents, under 23 years old, of Arkansas law-enforcement officers killed or permanently disabled in the line of duty. Renewable award is a waiver of tuition, fees, and room at two- or four-year Arkansas institution. Submit birth certificate, death certificate, and claims commission report of findings of fact. Proof of disability from State Claims Commission may also be submitted. *Award:* Scholarship for use in freshman, sophomore, junior, or senior years; renewable. *Number of awards:* 27–32. *Eligibility Requirements:* Applicant must be enrolled or expecting to enroll full- or part-time at a two-year or four-year or technical institution or university; resident of Arkansas and studying in Arkansas. Available to U.S. citizens. *Application Requirements:* Application form. **Deadline:** continuous.

Contact Tara Smith, Director of Financial Aid, Arkansas Department of Higher Education, 114 East Capitol Avenue, Little Rock, AR 72201-3818. *E-mail:* taras@adhe.edu. *Phone:* 501-371-2000. *Fax:* 501-371-2001. *Website:* http://www.adhe.edu/.

Military Dependent's Scholarship Program. Renewable waiver of tuition, fees, room and board undergraduate students seeking a Bachelor's degree or certificate of completion at any public college, university or technical school in Arkansas who qualify as a spouse or dependent child of an Arkansas resident who has been declared to be missing in action, killed in action, a POW, or killed on ordnance delivery, or a veteran who has been declared to be 100 percent totally and permanently disabled during, or as a result of, active military service. *Award:* Scholarship for use in freshman, sophomore, junior, or senior years; renewable. *Number of awards:* 1–60. *Eligibility Requirements:* Applicant must be enrolled or expecting to enroll full-time at a two-year or four-year or technical institution or university; resident of Arkansas and studying in Arkansas. Available to U.S. citizens. Applicant or parent must meet one or more of the following requirements: general military experience; retired from active duty; disabled or killed as a result of military service; prisoner of war; or missing in action. *Application Requirements:* Application form, recommendations or references, report of casualty. **Deadline:** June 1.

Contact Tara Smith, Director of Financial Aid, Arkansas Department of Higher Education, 114 East Capitol Avenue, Little Rock, AR 72201-3818. *E-mail:* taras@adhe.edu. *Phone:* 501-371-2000. *Fax:* 501-371-2001. *Website:* http://www.adhe.edu/.

Second Effort Scholarship. Awarded to those scholars who achieved one of the 10 highest scores on the Arkansas High School Diploma Test (GED). Must be at least age 18 and not have graduated from high school. Students do not apply for this award, they are contacted by the Arkansas Department of Higher Edu-

cation. *Award:* Scholarship for use in freshman, sophomore, junior, or senior years; renewable. *Award amount:* up to $1000. *Number of awards:* 10. *Eligibility Requirements:* Applicant must be enrolled or expecting to enroll full- or part-time at a two-year or four-year institution or university; resident of Arkansas and studying in Arkansas. Available to U.S. citizens. *Application Requirements:* Application form, application form may be submitted online (http://www.adhe.edu). **Deadline:** varies.

Contact Philip Axelroth, Financial Aid Program Coordinator. *Phone:* 501-371-2000. *Website:* http://www.adhe.edu/.

CALIFORNIA

Cal Grant C. Award for California residents who are enrolled in a short-term vocational training program. Program must lead to a recognized degree or certificate. Course length must be a minimum of 4 months and no longer than 24 months. Students must be attending an approved California institution and show financial need. *Award:* Grant for use in freshman or sophomore years; renewable. *Award amount:* $576–$3168. *Number of awards:* up to 7761. *Eligibility Requirements:* Applicant must be enrolled or expecting to enroll full- or part-time at a two-year or technical institution; resident of California and studying in California. Available to U.S. citizens. *Application Requirements:* Application form, financial need analysis, GPA verification. **Deadline:** March 2.

Contact Catalina Mistler, Chief, Program Administration and Services Division, California Student Aid Commission, PO Box 419026, Rancho Cordova, CA 95741-9026. *E-mail:* studentsupport@csac.ca.gov. *Phone:* 916-464-7268. *Fax:* 916-526-8004. *Website:* http://www.csac.ca.gov/.

Child Development Teacher and Supervisor Grant Program. Award is for those students pursuing an approved course of study leading to a Child Development Permit issued by the California Commission on Teacher Credentialing. In exchange for each year funding is received, recipients agree to provide one year of service in a licensed childcare center. Child and Family Studies; Education. *Award:* Grant for

use in freshman, sophomore, junior, senior, or graduate years; renewable. *Award amount:* $1000–$2000. *Number of awards:* up to 300. *Eligibility Requirements:* Applicant must be enrolled or expecting to enroll full- or part-time at a two-year or four-year institution or university; resident of California and studying in California. Applicant or parent of applicant must have employment or volunteer experience in teaching/education. Available to U.S. citizens. *Application Requirements:* Application form, financial need analysis, GPA verification, recommendations or references. **Deadline:** April 16.

Contact Catalina Mistler, Chief, Program Administration and Services Division, California Student Aid Commission, PO Box 419026, Rancho Cordova, CA 95741-9026. *E-mail:* studentsupport@csac.ca.gov. *Phone:* 916-464-7268. *Fax:* 916-526-8004. *Website:* http://www.csac.ca.gov/.

Competitive Cal Grant A. Award for California residents who are not recent high school graduates attending an approved college or university within the state. Must show financial need and meet minimum 3.00 GPA requirement. *Award:* Grant for use in freshman, sophomore, junior, or senior years; renewable. *Award amount:* $5472–$12,192. *Number of awards:* 1000–2000. *Eligibility Requirements:* Applicant must be enrolled or expecting to enroll full- or part-time at a two-year or four-year institution or university; resident of California and studying in California. Applicant must have 3.0 GPA or higher. Available to U.S. citizens. *Application Requirements:* Application form, financial need analysis, GPA verification. **Deadline:** March 2.

Contact Catalina Mistler, Chief, Program Administration and Services Division, California Student Aid Commission, PO Box 419026, Rancho Cordova, CA 95741-9026. *E-mail:* studentsupport@csac.ca.gov. *Phone:* 916-464-7268. *Fax:* 916-526-8004. *Website:* http://www.csac.ca.gov/.

Entitlement Cal Grant B. Provide grant funds for access costs for low-income students in an amount not to exceed $1648 and tuition/fee expenses of up to $12,192. Must be California residents and enroll in an undergraduate academic program of not less than one academic year at a qualifying postsecondary institution. Must show financial need and meet the minimum 2.00 GPA requirement. *Award:* Grant for use in freshman, sophomore, junior, or senior years; renewable. *Award amount:* $700–$13,665. *Number of awards:* 61,340. *Eligibility Requirements:* Applicant must be enrolled or expecting to enroll full- or part-time at a two-year or four-year or technical institution or university; resident of California and studying in California. Available to U.S. citizens. *Application Requirements:* Application form, financial need analysis. **Deadline:** March 2.

Contact Catalina Mistler, Chief, Program Administration and Services Division, California Student Aid Commission, PO Box 419026, Rancho Cordova, CA 95741-9026. *E-mail:* studentsupport@csac.ca.gov. *Phone:* 916-464-7268. *Fax:* 916-526-8004. *Website:* http://www.csac.ca.gov/.

EOPS (Extended Opportunity Programs and Services)/CARE (Cooperative Agencies Resources for Education). Renewable award available to California residents and individuals who are exempt from paying nonresident tuition. Individuals must be enrolled as a full-time student at a two-year publicly-funded California community college. EOPS students must fulfill program-specific income and educational disadvantage eligibility requirements. CARE students must be in EOPS, currently receive CalWORKs/TANF, have at least one child under fourteen years of age at time of acceptance into CARE program, be a single head of household, and age 18 or older. EOPS students may also qualify for CARE if their dependent child(ren) receive CalWORKS/TANF cash aid even if the student (i.e., parent) is not a cash aid recipient. Contact local college EOPS/CARE office for an application and more information about supportive services and grants. To locate nearest community college campus, see http://www.cccco.edu/ *Award:* Grant for use in freshman or sophomore years; renewable. *Award amount:* $100–$1000. *Number of awards:* 10,000–85,000. *Eligibility Requirements:* Applicant must be enrolled or expecting to enroll full-time at a two-year institution; single; resident of California and studying in California. Available to U.S. citizens. *Application Requirements:* Application form, financial need analysis. **Deadline:** continuous.

Law Enforcement Personnel Dependents Scholarship. Provides college grants to needy dependents of California law enforcement officers, officers and employees of the Department of Corrections and Department of Youth Authority, and firefighters killed or disabled in the line of duty. *Award:* Grant for use in freshman, sophomore, junior, or senior years; renewable. *Award amount:* $100–$13,665. *Eligibility Requirements:* Applicant must be enrolled or expecting to enroll full- or part-time at a two-year or four-year institution or university; resident of California and studying in California. Applicant or parent of applicant must have employment or volunteer experience in police/firefighting. Available to U.S. citizens. *Application Requirements:* Application form, birth certificate, death certificate of parents or spouse, police report, financial need analysis, transcript. **Deadline:** continuous.

Contact Catalina Mistler, Chief, Program Administration and Services Division, California Student Aid Commission, PO Box 419026, Rancho Cordova, CA 95741-9026. *E-mail:* studentsupport@csac.ca.gov. *Phone:* 916-464-7268. *Fax:* 916-526-8004. *Website:* http://www.csac.ca.gov/.

COLORADO

Colorado Student Grant. Grants for Colorado residents attending eligible public, private, or vocational institutions within the state. Students must complete a Free Application for Federal Student Aid (FAFSA) and demonstrate need. Application deadlines vary by institution. Renewable award for undergraduates. Contact the financial aid office at the college/institution for application and more information. *Award:* Grant for use in freshman, sophomore, junior, or senior years; not renewable. *Award amount:* $300–$5000. *Eligibility Requirements:* Applicant must be enrolled or expecting to enroll full- or part-time at a two-year or four-year or technical institution; resident of Colorado and studying in Colorado. Available to U.S. citizens. *Application Requirements:* Application form, financial need analysis. **Deadline:** continuous.

Contact Celina Duran, Financial Aid Administrator, Colorado Commission on Higher Education, 1560 Broadway,

Suite 1600, Denver, CO 80202. *E-mail:* celina.duran@dhe.state.co.us. *Phone:* 303-866-2723. *Website:* http://highered.colorado.gov/cche/mission.html.

CONNECTICUT

AIFS-HACU Scholarships. Scholarships to outstanding Hispanic students to study abroad with AIFS. Available to students attending HACU member schools. Students will receive scholarships of up to 50 percent of the full program fee. Students must meet all standard AIFS eligibility requirements. Deadlines: April 15 for fall, October 1 for spring, and March 15 for summer. *Award:* Scholarship for use in freshman, sophomore, junior, or senior years; not renewable. *Award amount:* $6000–$8000. *Number of awards:* up to 1. *Eligibility Requirements:* Applicant must be Hispanic; enrolled or expecting to enroll full-time at a two-year or four-year institution or university and must have an interest in international exchange. Applicant must have 3.0 GPA or higher. Available to U.S. and non-U.S. citizens. *Application Requirements:* Application form, essay, personal photograph, recommendations or references, transcript. *Fee:* $95. **Deadline:** varies.

Contact David Mauro, Admissions Counselor, American Institute for Foreign Study, 1 High Ridge Park, Stamford, CT 06905. *E-mail:* dmauro@aifs.com. *Phone:* 800-727-2437 Ext. 5163. *Fax:* 203-399-5463. *Website:* http://www.aifsabroad.com/.

Connecticut Army National Guard 100% Tuition Waiver. Program is for any active member of the Connecticut Army National Guard in good standing. Must be a resident of Connecticut attending any Connecticut state (public) university, community-technical college or regional vocational-technical school. The total number of available awards is unlimited. *Award:* Scholarship for use in freshman, sophomore, junior, or senior years; not renewable. *Award amount:* $16,000. *Eligibility Requirements:* Applicant must be age 17-65; enrolled or expecting to enroll full- or part-time at a two-year or four-year or technical institution or university; resident of Connecticut and studying in Connecticut. Available to U.S. and non-U.S. citizens. Applicant or parent must meet one or more of the following requirements: national guard experience; retired from active duty; disabled or killed as a result of military service; prisoner of war; or missing in action. *Application Requirements:* Application form. **Deadline:** July 1.

Contact Capt. Jeremy Lingenfelser, Education Services Officer, Connecticut Army National Guard, 360 Broad Street, Hartford, CT 06105-3795. *E-mail:* education@ct.ngb.army.mil. *Phone:* 860-524-4816. *Fax:* 860-524-4904. *Website:* http://ct.ng.mil/Pages/default.aspx.

Governors Scholarship Program Academic Incentive Award. The Academic Incentive Award provides additional grant funds to Governor's Scholarship Program need-based aid recipients who are on track to complete their degree in the required time frame, 2 or 4 years. Eligible students must also demonstrate strong academic performance while in college. *Award:* Grant for use in sophomore, junior, or senior years; renewable. *Award amount:* $1000–$1200. *Number of awards:* 603. *Eligibility Requirements:* Applicant must be enrolled or expecting to enroll full-time at a two-year or four-year institution or university; resident of Connecticut and studying in Connecticut. Applicant must have 3.0 GPA or higher. Available to U. S. citizens. *Application Requirements:* Financial need analysis. **Deadline:** continuous.

Contact Ms. Lynne Little, Financial Aid Consultant, Connecticut Office of Higher Education, 61 Woodland Street, Hartford, CT 06105. *E-mail:* gsp@ctohe.org. *Phone:* 860-947-1855. *Website:* http://www.ctohe.org.

Governor's Scholarship Program— Need/Merit Scholarship. This program provides scholarships to eligible Connecticut residents attending eligible institutions of higher education in Connecticut. Eligibility is based on a minimum SAT score of 1800, or a minimum ACT score of 27 and/or top 20% ranking in the students junior year high school class. Applications must be filed through the students high school counseling office. In addition, all students must file a Free Application for Federal Student Aid (FAFSA) and, as a result, have an Expected Family Contribution (EFC) equal to or less than the annual allowable maximum EFC. Both the application and FAFSA must be processed by February 15th. *Award:* Scholarship for use in freshman, sophomore, junior, or senior years; renewable.

Award amount: $900–$5000. *Number of awards:* 2404. *Eligibility Requirements:* Applicant must be enrolled or expecting to enroll full- or part-time at a two-year or four-year institution or university; resident of Connecticut and studying in Connecticut. Applicant must have 3.5 GPA or higher. Available to U.S. citizens. *Application Requirements:* Application form, financial need analysis. **Deadline:** February 15.

Contact Ms. Lynne Goodwin, Student Financial Aid Consultant, Connecticut Office of Higher Education, 39 Woodland Street, Hartford, CT 06105. *E-mail:* sfa@ctohe.org. *Phone:* 860-947-1855. *Website:* http://www.ctohe.org.

Minority Teacher Incentive Grant Program. Program provides up to $5,000 a year for two years of full-time study in a teacher preparation program for the junior or senior year at a Connecticut college or university. Applicant must be African-American, Hispanic/Latino, Asian American or Native American heritage and be nominated by the Education Dean. Program graduates who teach in Connecticut public schools may be eligible for loan reimbursement stipends up to $2,500 per year for up to four years. Education. *Award:* Grant for use in junior or senior years; renewable. *Award amount:* $2500–$5000. *Number of awards:* 72. *Eligibility Requirements:* Applicant must be American Indian/Alaska Native, Asian/Pacific Islander, Black (non-Hispanic), Hispanic; enrolled or expecting to enroll full-time at a four-year institution or university and studying in Connecticut. Available to U.S. citizens. *Application Requirements:* Application form. **Deadline:** October 15.

Contact Ms. Lynne Goodwin, Executive Assistant, Connecticut Office of Higher Education, 39 Woodland Street, Hartford, CT 06105. *E-mail:* mtip@ctohe.org. *Phone:* 860-947-1855. *Website:* http://www.ctohe.org.

Roberta B. Willis Scholarship Program—Need-Based Grant. This program provides need-based grants to eligible Connecticut residents attending eligible institutions of higher education in Connecticut. Students must file a Free Application for Federal Student Aid (FAFSA) by their college's deadline, if applicable. Students, as a result of filing the FAFSA must have an Expected Family Contribution (EFC) equal to or

less than the allowable annual EFC. There is no application to fill out. *Award:* Grant for use in freshman, sophomore, junior, or senior years; renewable. *Award amount:* $650–$3000. *Eligibility Requirements:* Applicant must be Ukrainian citizen; enrolled or expecting to enroll full or part time at a two-year or four-year institution or university; resident of Connecticut and studying in Connecticut. Available to U. S. citizens. *Application Requirements:* Financial need analysis.

Contact Ms. Lynne Goodwin, Financial Aid Consultant, Connecticut Office of Higher Education, 39 Woodland Street, Hartford, CT 06105. *E-mail:* sfa@ctohe.org. *Phone:* 860-947-1855. *Website:* http://www.ctohe.org.

DELAWARE

Delaware Solid Waste Authority John P. "Pat" Healy Scholarship. Award for legal residents of Delaware who are U. S. citizens or eligible non-citizens. Must be high school seniors or full-time college students in their freshman or sophomore years. Must major in either environmental engineering or environmental sciences at a Delaware college. Selection based on financial need, academic performance, community and school involvement, and leadership ability. Engineering-Related Technologies; Environmental Science. *Award:* Scholarship for use in freshman or sophomore years; renewable. *Award amount:* $2000. *Number of awards:* 1. *Eligibility Requirements:* Applicant must be enrolled or expecting to enroll full-time at a two-year or four-year institution or university; resident of Delaware; studying in Delaware and must have an interest in leadership. Applicant or parent of applicant must have employment or volunteer experience in community service. Applicant must have 3.0 GPA or higher. Available to U. S. citizens. *Application Requirements:* Application form, FAFSA, Student Aid Report (SAR), financial need analysis. **Deadline:** March 14.

Contact Ms. Carylin Brinkley, Program Administrator, Delaware Higher Education Office, 401 Federal Street, Suite 2, Dover, DE 19901. *E-mail:* cbrinkley@doe.k12.de.us. *Phone:* 302-735-4120. *Fax:* 302-739-5894. *Website:* http://www.doe.k12.de.us.

Diamond State Scholarship. Award for legal residents of Delaware who are U. S. citizens or eligible non-citizens. Must be enrolled as a full-time student in a degree program at a nonprofit, regionally accredited institution. Minimum 3.0 GPA required. High school seniors should rank in upper quarter of class and have a combined score of at least 1800 on the SAT. *Award:* Scholarship for use in freshman year; renewable. *Award amount:* $1250. *Number of awards:* 50. *Eligibility Requirements:* Applicant must be high school student; planning to enroll or expecting to enroll full-time at a four-year institution or university and resident of Delaware. Applicant must have 3.0 GPA or higher. Available to U.S. citizens. *Application Requirements:* Application form, essay, test scores, transcript. **Deadline:** March 22.

Contact Ms. Carylin Brinkley, Program Administrator, Delaware Higher Education Office, 401 Federal Street, Suite 2, Dover, DE 19901. *E-mail:* cbrinkley@doe.k12.de.us. *Phone:* 302-735-4120. *Fax:* 302-739-5894. *Website:* http://www.doe.k12.de.us.

Educational Benefits for Children of Deceased Veterans. Award for children between the ages of 16 and 24 of deceased/MIA/POW veterans or state police officers. Must have been a resident of Delaware for 3 or more years prior to the date of application. If the applicant's parent is a member of the armed forces, the parent must have been a resident of Delaware at the time of death or declaration of missing in action or prisoner of war status. Award will not exceed tuition and fees at a Delaware public college. *Award:* Grant for use in freshman, sophomore, junior, or senior years; renewable. *Award amount:* $7479–$14,421. *Eligibility Requirements:* Applicant must be age 16-24; enrolled or expecting to enroll full-time at a two-year or four-year institution or university and resident of Delaware. Applicant or parent of applicant must have employment or volunteer experience in police/firefighting. Available to U.S. citizens. Applicant or parent must meet one or more of the following requirements: general military experience; retired from active duty; disabled or killed as a result of military service; prisoner of war; or missing in action. *Application Requirements:* Application form, verification of service-related death. **Deadline:** continuous.

Contact Ms. Carylin Brinkley, Program Administrator, Delaware Higher Education Office, 401 Federal Street, Suite 2, Dover, DE 19901. *E-mail:* cbrinkley@doe.k12.de.us. *Phone:* 302-735-4120. *Fax:* 302-739-5894. *Website:* http://www.doe.k12.de.us.

Governor's Education Grant for Unemployed Adults. Grants for unemployed part-time undergraduate students attending Delaware College of Art and Design, Delaware State University, Delaware Technical and Community College, Goldey-Beacom College, University of Delaware, Wesley College, Widener University (Delaware Campus), or PolyTech Adult division, Sussex Tech Adult division, or Wilmington College. Must be at least 18 years old, and a resident of Delaware. *Award:* Grant for use in freshman, sophomore, junior, or senior years; not renewable. *Award amount:* $2000. *Number of awards:* up to 1000. *Eligibility Requirements:* Applicant must be enrolled or expecting to enroll part-time at a two-year or four-year or technical institution or university. Available to U.S. citizens. *Application Requirements:* Application form. **Deadline:** continuous.

Contact Ms. Carylin Brinkley, Program Administrator, Delaware Higher Education Office, 401 Federal Street, Suite 2, Dover, DE 19901. *E-mail:* cbrinkley@doe.k12.de.us. *Phone:* 302-735-4120. *Fax:* 302-739-5894. *Website:* http://www.doe.k12.de.us.

Governor's Education Grant for Working Adults. Grants for part-time undergraduate students attending Delaware College of Art and Design, Delaware State University, Delaware Technical and Community College, Goldey-Beacom College, University of Delaware, Wesley College, Widener University (Delaware Campus), PolyTech Adult division, Sussex Tech Adult division, or Wilmington College. Must be at least 18 years old, a resident of Delaware, and employed by a company in Delaware that contributes to the Blue Collar Training Fund Program. *Award:* Grant for use in freshman, sophomore, junior, or senior years; not renewable. *Award amount:* $2000. *Number of awards:* up to 100. *Eligibility Requirements:* Applicant must be enrolled or expecting to enroll full- or part-time at a two-year or four-year or technical institution or university; resident of Delaware and studying in Delaware. Available to U.S. and non-U.S. citizens. *Application Requirements:* Application form. **Deadline:** varies.

Contact Ms. Carylin Brinkley, Program Administrator, Delaware Higher Education Office, 401 Federal Street, Suite 2, Dover, DE 19901. *E-mail:* cbrinkley@doe.k12.de.us. *Phone:* 302-735-4120. *Fax:* 302-739-5894. *Website:* http://www.doe.k12.de.us.

Scholarship Incentive Program (ScIP). Award for legal residents of Delaware who are U.S. citizens or eligible non-citizens. Must demonstrate substantial financial need and enroll full-time in an undergraduate degree program at a nonprofit, regionally accredited institution in Delaware or Pennsylvania. Minimum 2.5 GPA required. *Award:* Grant for use in freshman, sophomore, junior, senior, or graduate years; not renewable. *Award amount:* $700–$2200. *Number of awards:* 700–2200. *Eligibility Requirements:* Applicant must be enrolled or expecting to enroll full-time at a two-year or four-year institution or university; resident of Delaware and studying in Delaware, Pennsylvania. Applicant must have 2.5 GPA or higher. Available to U.S. citizens. *Application Requirements:* Application form, FAFSA, financial need analysis, transcript. **Deadline:** April 15.

Contact Ms. Carylin Brinkley, Program Administrator, Delaware Higher Education Office, 401 Federal Street, Suite 2, Dover, DE 19901. *E-mail:* cbrinkley@doe.k12.de.us. *Phone:* 302-735-4120. *Fax:* 302-739-5894. *Website:* http://www.doe.k12.de.us.

State Tuition Assistance. You must enlist in the Delaware Air or Army National Guard to be eligible for this scholarship award. Award providing tuition assistance for any member of the Air or Army National Guard attending a Delaware two-year or four-year college. Awards are renewable. Applicant's minimum GPA must be 2.0. *Award:* Scholarship for use in freshman, sophomore, junior, or senior years; renewable. *Award amount:* $1–$10,000. *Number of awards:* 1–200. *Eligibility Requirements:* Applicant must be enrolled or expecting to enroll full- or part-time at a two-year or four-year institution or university and studying in Delaware. Available to U.S. citizens. Applicant or parent must meet one or more of the following requirements:

national guard experience; retired from active duty; disabled or killed as a result of military service; prisoner of war; or missing in action. *Application Requirements:* Application form, transcript.

Contact Robert Csizmadia, State Tuition Assistance Manager, Delaware National Guard, 1st Regiment Road, Wilmington, DE 19808-2191. *E-mail:* robert.csizmadia@us.army.mil. *Phone:* 302-326-7012. *Fax:* 302-326-7029. *Website:* http://www.delawarenational-guard.com/.

DISTRICT OF COLUMBIA

American Indian Nurse Scholarship Program. The current goal is to grant a $1,500 scholarship each semester, as long as the student remains in academic good standing. The scholarship money is restricted to tuition and specific academic expenses. Health Administration; Nursing. *Award:* Scholarship for use in freshman, sophomore, junior, senior, graduate, or postgraduate years; renewable. *Award amount:* $500–$1500. *Number of awards:* 5–10. *Eligibility Requirements:* Applicant must be American Indian/Alaska Native and enrolled or expecting to enroll full-time at a two-year or four-year or technical institution or university. Applicant must have 2.5 GPA or higher. Available to U. S. citizens. *Application Requirements:* Application form, driver's license, financial need analysis, personal photograph, recommendations or references, transcript. **Deadline:** continuous.

Bureau of Indian Education Grant Program. Grants are provided to supplement financial assistance to eligible American Indian/Alaska Native students entering college seeking a Baccalaureate degree. A student must be a member of, or at least one-quarter degree Indian blood descendent of a member of an American Indian tribe who are eligible for the special programs and services provided by the United States through the Bureau of Indian Affairs to Indians because of their status as Indians. *Award:* Grant for use in freshman year; not renewable. *Eligibility Requirements:* Applicant must be American Indian/Alaska Native; high school student and planning to enroll or expecting to enroll full-time at a two-year or four-year institution or university. Available to U.S. citizens. *Application Requirements:* Application form, recommendations or references, test scores, transcript. **Deadline:** varies.

Contact Paulina Bell, Office Automation Assistant. *Phone:* 202-208-6123. *Fax:* 202-208-3312. *Website:* http://www.bie.edu/.

Costas G. Lemonopoulos Scholarship. Scholarships to children of NALC members attending public, four-year colleges or universities supported by the state of Florida or St. Petersburg Junior College. Scholarships are renewable one time. *Award:* Scholarship for use in freshman, sophomore, junior, or senior years; renewable. *Number of awards:* 1–20. *Eligibility Requirements:* Applicant must be enrolled or expecting to enroll full-time at a two-year or four-year institution or university and studying in Florida. Applicant or parent of applicant must be member of National Association of Letter Carriers. Available to U. S. citizens. *Application Requirements:* Application form, recommendations or references, transcript. **Deadline:** June 1.

Contact Ann Porch, Membership Committee. *E-mail:* nalcinf@nalc.org. *Phone:* 202-393-4695. *Website:* http://www.nalc.org/.

Harry S. Truman Scholarship. Scholarships for U.S. citizens or U.S. nationals who are college or university students with junior-level academic standing and who wish to attend professional or graduate school to prepare for careers in government or the nonprofit and advocacy sectors. Candidates must be nominated by their institution. Public service and leadership record considered. Visit web site http://www.truman.gov for further information and application. Political Science; Public Policy and Administration. *Award:* Scholarship for use in junior year; renewable. *Award amount:* $30,000. *Number of awards:* 65. *Eligibility Requirements:* Applicant must be enrolled or expecting to enroll full-time at a four-year institution or university and must have an interest in leadership. Available to U.S. citizens. *Application Requirements:* Application form, interview, policy proposal, recommendations or references. **Deadline:** February 5.

Contact Tonji Wade, Program Officer, Harry S. Truman Scholarship Foundation, 712 Jackson Place, NW, Washington, DC 20006. *E-mail:* office@truman.gov. *Phone:* 202-395-4831. *Fax:* 202-395-6995. *Website:* http://www.truman.gov/.

Montgomery GI Bill (Active Duty) Chapter 30. Award provides up to thirty-six months of education benefits to eligible veterans for college, business school, technical courses, vocational courses, correspondence courses, apprenticeships/job training, or flight training. Must be an eligible veteran with an Honorable Discharge and have high school diploma or GED before applying for benefits. *Award:* Scholarship for use in freshman, sophomore, junior, senior, or graduate years; renewable. *Eligibility Requirements:* Applicant must be enrolled or expecting to enroll full- or part-time at a two-year or four-year or technical institution or university. Available to U.S. citizens. Applicant or parent must meet one or more of the following requirements: general military experience; retired from active duty; disabled or killed as a result of military service; prisoner of war; or missing in action. *Application Requirements:* Application form. **Deadline:** continuous.

Contact Keith Wilson, Director, Education Service. *Phone:* 888-442-4551. *Website:* http://www.gibill.va.gov/.

Montgomery GI Bill (Selected Reserve). Educational assistance program for members of the selected reserve of the Army, Navy, Air Force, Marine Corps and Coast Guard, as well as the Army and Air National Guard. Available to all reservists and National Guard personnel who commit to a six-year obligation, and remain in the Reserve or Guard during the six years. Award is renewable. Monthly benefit is $309 for up to thirty-six months for full-time. *Award:* Scholarship for use in freshman, sophomore, junior, senior, or postgraduate years; renewable. *Eligibility Requirements:* Applicant must be enrolled or expecting to enroll full- or part-time at a two-year or four-year or technical institution or university. Available to U.S. citizens. Applicant or parent must meet one or more of the following requirements: general military experience; retired from active duty; disabled or killed as a result of military service; prisoner of war; or missing in action. *Application Requirements:* Application form. **Deadline:** continuous.

Contact Keith Wilson, Director, Education Service. *Phone:* 888-442-4551. *Website:* http://www.gibill.va.gov/.

Reserve Education Assistance Program. The program provides educational assistance to members of National Guard and reserve components. Selected Reserve and Individual Ready Reserve (IRR) who are called or ordered to active duty service in response to a war or national emergency as declared by the president or Congress are eligible. For further information see web site http://www.GIBILL.va.gov. *Award:* Scholarship for use in freshman, sophomore, junior, senior, graduate, or postgraduate years; renewable. *Eligibility Requirements:* Applicant must be enrolled or expecting to enroll full- or part-time at a two-year or four-year or technical institution or university. Available to U.S. citizens. Applicant or parent must meet one or more of the following requirements: general military experience; retired from active duty; disabled or killed as a result of military service; prisoner of war; or missing in action. *Application Requirements:* Application form. **Deadline:** continuous.

Contact Keith Wilson, Director, Education Service. *Phone:* 888-442-4551. *Website:* http://www.gibill.va.gov/.

Survivors and Dependents Educational Assistance (Chapter 35)-VA. Monthly $860 benefits for up to 45 months. Must be spouses or children under age 26 of current veterans missing in action or of deceased or totally and permanently disabled (service-related) service persons. For more information visit the following web site http://www.gibill.va.gov. *Award:* Scholarship for use in freshman, sophomore, junior, or senior years; renewable. *Eligibility Requirements:* Applicant must be enrolled or expecting to enroll full- or part-time at a two-year or four-year or technical institution or university. Available to U.S. and non-U.S. citizens. Applicant or parent must meet one or more of the following requirements: general military experience; retired from active duty; disabled or killed as a result of military service; prisoner of war; or missing in action. *Application Requirements:* Application form. **Deadline:** continuous.

Contact Keith Wilson, Director, Education Service. *Phone:* 888-442-4551. *Website:* http://www.gibill.va.gov/.

FLORIDA

Access to Better Learning and Education Grant. Grant program provides tuition assistance to Florida undergraduate students enrolled in degree programs at eligible private Florida colleges or universities. Must be a U.S. citizen or eligible non-citizen and must meet Florida residency requirements. The participating institution determines application procedures, deadlines, and student eligibility. An eligible student must complete and submit the FAFSA in order to receive program funding. For more details, visit the web site at http://www.FloridaStudentFinancialAid.org/SSFAD/home/uamain.htm. *Award:* Grant for use in freshman, sophomore, junior, or senior years; renewable. *Award amount:* up to $1500. *Eligibility Requirements:* Applicant must be enrolled or expecting to enroll full-time at a four-year institution or university; resident of Florida and studying in Florida. Available to U.S. citizens. *Application Requirements:* Application form.

First Generation Matching Grant Program. Need-based grants to Florida resident undergraduate students who are enrolled in state universities and community colleges in Florida and whose parents have not earned baccalaureate degrees. Available state funds are contingent upon matching contributions from private sources on a dollar-for-dollar basis. Institutions determine application procedures, deadlines, and student eligibility. For more details, visit the web site at http://www.FloridaStudentFinancialAid.org/SSFAD/home/uamain.htm. *Award:* Grant for use in freshman, sophomore, junior, or senior years; renewable. *Eligibility Requirements:* Applicant must be enrolled or expecting to enroll full- or part-time at a two-year or four-year institution or university; resident of Florida and studying in Florida. Available to U.S. citizens. *Application Requirements:* Application form, financial need analysis.

Florida Bright Futures Scholarship Program. Three lottery-funded scholarships reward Florida high school graduates for high academic achievement. Program is comprised of the following three awards: Florida Academic Scholars Award, Florida Medallion Scholars Award and Florida Gold Seal Vocational Scholars Award. An eligible student must complete and submit the FAFSA in order to receive program funding. For more details, visit the web site at http://www.FloridaStudentFinancialAid.org/SSFAD/home/uamain.htm. *Award:* Scholarship for use in freshman, sophomore, junior, or senior years; renewable. *Eligibility Requirements:* Applicant must be high school student; planning to enroll or expecting to enroll full- or part-time at a two-year or four-year or technical institution or university; resident of Florida and studying in Florida. Applicant must have 3.0 GPA or higher. Available to U.S. citizens. *Application Requirements:* Application form, application form may be submitted online, community service, test scores, transcript.

Florida Postsecondary Student Assistance Grant. Scholarships to degree-seeking, resident, undergraduate students who demonstrate substantial financial need and are enrolled in eligible degree-granting private colleges and universities not eligible under the Florida Private Student Assistance Grant. FSAG is a decentralized program, and each participating institution determines application procedures, deadlines and student eligibility. Number of awards varies. For more details, visit the web site at http://www.FloridaStudentFinancialAid.org/SSFAD/home/uamain.htm. *Award:* Grant for use in freshman, sophomore, junior, or senior years; renewable. *Award amount:* $200–$2610. *Eligibility Requirements:* Applicant must be enrolled or expecting to enroll full-time at a two-year or four-year institution or university; resident of Florida and studying in Florida. Available to U.S. citizens. *Application Requirements:* Financial need analysis.

Florida Private Student Assistance Grant. Grants for Florida residents who are U.S. citizens or eligible non-citizens attending eligible private, nonprofit, four-year colleges and universities in Florida. Must be a full-time student and demonstrate substantial financial need. For renewal, must have earned a minimum cumulative GPA of 2.0 at the last institution attended. For more details, visit the web site at http://www.FloridaStudentFinancialAid.org/SSFAD/home/uamain.htm. *Award:* Grant for use in freshman, sophomore, junior, or senior years; renewable. *Award amount:* $200–$2610. *Eligibility Requirements:* Applicant must be enrolled or expecting to enroll full-time at a four-year institution or university; resident of Florida and studying in Florida. Available to U.S. citizens. *Application Requirements:* Application form, financial need analysis.

Florida Public Student Assistance Grant. Grants for Florida residents, U.S. citizens or eligible non-citizens who attend state universities and public community colleges and demonstrate substantial financial need. For renewal, must have earned a minimum cumulative GPA of 2.0 at the last institution attended. For more details, visit the web site at http://www.FloridaStudentFinancialAid.org/SSFAD/home/uamain.htm. *Award:* Grant for use in freshman, sophomore, junior, or senior years; renewable. *Award amount:* $200–$2610. *Eligibility Requirements:* Applicant must be enrolled or expecting to enroll full- or part-time at a two-year or four-year institution or university; resident of Florida and studying in Florida. Available to U.S. citizens. *Application Requirements:* Application form, financial need analysis.

Florida Space Research Program. Grants for faculty researchers from Florida public and private universities and community colleges. One-time award for aerospace and technology research. Submit research proposal with budget. Aviation/Aerospace; Earth Science; Materials Science, Engineering, and Metallurgy; Mathematics; Mechanical Engineering. *Award:* Grant for use in junior, senior, graduate, or postgraduate years; not renewable. *Award amount:* $12,500–$25,000. *Number of awards:* 13–15. *Eligibility Requirements:* Applicant must be enrolled or expecting to enroll full- or part-time at a two-year or four-year institution or university; resident of Florida and studying in Florida. Available to U.S. citizens. *Application Requirements:* Application form. **Deadline:** June 17.

Contact Dr. Jaydeep Mukherjee, FSGC Director, NASA Florida Space Grant Consortium, PO Box 160650, 12354 Research Parkway, Room 218, Orlando, FL 32826. *E-mail:* fsgc@ucf.edu. *Phone:* 407-823-6177. *Website:* http://www.floridaspacegrant.org/.

Florida Student Assistance Grant-Career Education. Need-based grant program available to Florida residents enrolled in certificate programs of 450 or more clock hours at participating community colleges or career centers operated by district school boards. FSAG-CE is a decentralized state of Florida program, which means that each participating institution determines application procedures, deadlines, student eligibility, and award amounts. For more details, visit the web site at http://www.FloridaStudentFinancialAid.org/SSFAD/home/uamain.htm. *Award:* Grant for use in freshman, sophomore, junior, or senior years; renewable. *Award amount:* $200–$2610. *Eligibility Requirements:* Applicant must be enrolled or expecting to enroll full- or part-time at a two-year or technical institution; resident of Florida and studying in Florida. Available to U.S. citizens. *Application Requirements:* Application form may be submitted online, financial need analysis.

Florida Work Experience Program. Need-based program providing eligible Florida residents work experiences that will complement and reinforce their educational and career goals. Must maintain GPA of 2.0. Postsecondary institution will determine applicant's eligibility, number of hours to be worked per week, and the award amount. For more details, visit the web site at http://www.FloridaStudentFinancialAid.org/SSFAD/home/uamain.htm. *Award:* Grant for use in freshman, sophomore, junior, or senior years; renewable. *Eligibility Requirements:* Applicant must be enrolled or expecting to enroll full- or part-time at a two-year or four-year institution or university; resident of Florida and studying in Florida. Available to U.S. citizens. *Application Requirements:* Financial need analysis.

Jose Marti Scholarship Challenge Grant Fund. Award available to Hispanic-American students who were born in, or whose parent was born in a Hispanic country. Must be a Florida resident, be enrolled full-time in Florida at an eligible school, and have a GPA of 3.0 or above. Must be U.S. citizen or eligible non-citizen. FAFSA must be processed by May 15. For more details, visit the web site at http://www.FloridaStudentFinancialAid.org/SSFAD/home/uamain.htm. *Award:* Scholarship for use in freshman, sophomore, junior, or senior years; renewable. *Award amount:* $2000. *Eligibility Requirements:* Applicant must be of Hispanic heritage; high school student; planning to enroll or expecting to enroll full-time at a two-year or four-year institution or university; resident of Florida and studying in Florida. Applicant must have 3.0 GPA or higher. Available to U.S. citizens. *Application Requirements:* Application form, financial need analysis. **Deadline:** April 1.

Mary McLeod Bethune Scholarship. Renewable award to Florida residents with a GPA of 3.0 or above, who will attend Bethune-Cookman University, Edward Waters College, Florida A&M University, or Florida Memorial University. Must not have previously received a baccalaureate degree. Must demonstrate financial need as specified by the institution. For more details, visit the web site at http://www.FloridaStudentFinancialAid.org/SSFAD/home/uamain.htm. *Award:* Scholarship for use in freshman, sophomore, junior, or senior years; renewable. *Award amount:* $3000. *Eligibility Requirements:* Applicant must be enrolled or expecting to enroll full-time at a four-year institution or university; resident of Florida and studying in Florida. Applicant must have 3.0 GPA or higher. Available to U.S. citizens. *Application Requirements:* Financial need analysis.

Rosewood Family Scholarship Fund. Renewable award for eligible direct descendants of African-American Rosewood families affected by the incident of January 1923. Must not have previously received a baccalaureate degree. For more details, visit the web site at http://www.FloridaStudentFinancialAid.org/SSFAD/home/uamain.htm. *Award:* Scholarship for use in freshman, sophomore, junior, or senior years; renewable. *Award amount:* up to $6100. *Number of awards:* up to 50. *Eligibility Requirements:* Applicant must be enrolled or expecting to enroll full- or part-time at a two-year or four-year or technical institution or university and studying in Florida. Available to U.S. citizens. *Application Requirements:* Application form, documentation of Rosewood ancestry, financial need analysis. **Deadline:** April 1.

Scholarships for Children & Spouses of Deceased or Disabled Veterans. Renewable scholarships for children and spouses of deceased or disabled veterans. Children must be between the ages of 16 and 22, and attend an eligible

Florida postsecondary institution and enrolled at least part-time. Must ensure that the Florida Department of Veterans Affairs certifies the applicant's eligibility. Must maintain GPA of 2.0. For more details, visit the web site at http://www.FloridaStudentFinancialAid.org/SSFAD/home/uamain.htm. *Award:* Scholarship for use in freshman, sophomore, junior, or senior years; renewable. *Eligibility Requirements:* Applicant must be age 16-22; enrolled or expecting to enroll full- or part-time at a two-year or four-year or technical institution or university; resident of Florida and studying in Florida. Available to U.S. citizens. Applicant or parent must meet one or more of the following requirements: general military experience; retired from active duty; disabled or killed as a result of military service; prisoner of war; or missing in action. *Application Requirements:* Application form. **Deadline:** April 1.

William L. Boyd IV Florida Resident Access Grant. Renewable awards to Florida undergraduate residents attending an eligible private, nonprofit Florida college or university. Postsecondary institution will determine applicant's eligibility. Renewal applicant must have earned a minimum institutional GPA of 2.0. An eligible student must complete and submit the FAFSA in order to receive program funding. For more details, visit the web site at http://www.FloridaStudentFinancialAid.org/SSFAD/home/uamain.htm. *Award:* Grant for use in freshman, sophomore, junior, or senior years; renewable. *Award amount:* up to $3000. *Eligibility Requirements:* Applicant must be enrolled or expecting to enroll full-time at a four-year institution or university; resident of Florida and studying in Florida. Available to U.S. citizens. *Application Requirements:* Application form.

GEORGIA

Georgia HOPE Scholarship Program. Scholarship and Grant program for Georgia residents who are college undergraduates to attend an accredited two or four-year Georgia institution. Pays a percentage of actual undergraduate tuition charged at public postsecondary institutions. Percentage paid will vary from year to year. At private postsecondary institutions in Georgia, students may receive up to $3600 per

year for full-time study or $1800 per year for part-time. Minimum 3.0 GPA required. Renewable if student maintains grades. See http://www.GAcollege411.org for full details. *Award:* Scholarship for use in freshman, sophomore, junior, or senior years; renewable. *Award amount:* up to $6000. *Number of awards:* 200,000–230,000. *Eligibility Requirements:* Applicant must be enrolled or expecting to enroll full- or part-time at a two-year or four-year institution or university; resident of Georgia and studying in Georgia. Applicant must have 3.0 GPA or higher. Available to U.S. citizens. *Application Requirements:* Application form, high schools must report transcripts to GSFC. **Deadline:** continuous.

Contact Tracy Ireland, Vice President, Georgia Student Finance Commission, 2082 East Exchange Place, Suite 100, Tucker, GA 30084. *E-mail:* tracyi@gsfc.org. *Phone:* 800-505-4732. *Website:* http://www.GAcollege411.org/.

Georgia Public Safety Memorial Grant. Award for children of Georgia Public Safety Officers, prison guards, fire fighters, law enforcement officers or emergency medical technicians killed or permanently disabled in the line of duty. Must attend an accredited postsecondary Georgia school. Complete the Public Safety Memorial Grant application. *Award:* Grant for use in freshman, sophomore, junior, or senior years; not renewable. *Award amount:* $2000. *Number of awards:* 20–40. *Eligibility Requirements:* Applicant must be enrolled or expecting to enroll full-time at a two-year or four-year or technical institution or university; resident of Georgia and studying in Georgia. Available to U.S. citizens. *Application Requirements:* Application form, selective service registration. **Deadline:** continuous.

Contact Caylee French, Division Director, Georgia Student Finance Commission, 2082 East Exchange Place, Suite 100, Tucker, GA 30084. *E-mail:* cayleef@gsfc.org. *Phone:* 770-724-9244. *Website:* http://www.GAcollege411.org/.

Georgia Tuition Equalization Grant (GTEG). Award for Georgia residents pursuing undergraduate study at an accredited two- or four-year Georgia private postsecondary institution. *Award:* Grant for use in freshman, soph-

omore, junior, or senior years; not renewable. *Number of awards:* 1–35,000. *Eligibility Requirements:* Applicant must be learning disabled; Hispanic; enrolled or expecting to enroll full-time at a two-year or four-year institution or university; resident of Georgia and studying in Georgia. Applicant must be learning disabled. Available to U.S. citizens. *Application Requirements:* Application form, application form may be submitted online (http://www.gacollege411.org), social security number.

Contact Ms. Caylee French, Director, Student Aid Services, Georgia Student Finance Commission, 2082 East Exchange Place, Suite 100, Tucker, GA 30084. *E-mail:* cayleef@gsfc.org. *Phone:* 770-724-9244. *Fax:* 770-724-9249. *Website:* http://www.GAcollege411.org/.

Paper and Board Division Scholarships. Award to TAPPI student member or an undergraduate member of a TAPPI Student Chapter enrolled as a college or university undergraduate in an engineering or science program. Must be sophomore, junior, or senior and able to show a significant interest in the paper industry. Information can be found at http://www.tappi.org/s_tappi/sec.asp?CID=6101&DID=546695. Engineering/Technology; Paper and Pulp Engineering. *Award:* Scholarship for use in sophomore, junior, or senior years; not renewable. *Award amount:* $1000–$1500. *Number of awards:* 1–4. *Eligibility Requirements:* Applicant must be enrolled or expecting to enroll full-time at a four-year institution or university. Available to U.S. and non-U.S. citizens. *Application Requirements:* Application form. **Deadline:** February 15.

Contact Mr. Laurence Womack, Director of Standards and Awards, Technical Association of the Pulp & Paper Industry (TAPPI), 15 Technology Parkway South, Peachtree Corners, GA 30092. *E-mail:* standards@tappi.org. *Phone:* 770-209-7276. *Website:* http://www.tappi.org/.

Physicians for Rural Areas Assistance Program. Service repayable medical school scholarship for a maximum of $20,000 per year for four years available to Georgia residents enrolled in U.S. accredited medical school. Repay by practicing medicine for one year in rural

Georgia for each year that the scholarship is received. Service payment begins upon completion of residency training. Health and Medical Sciences. *Award:* Scholarship for use in freshman, sophomore, junior, or senior years; renewable. *Award amount:* up to $20,000. *Number of awards:* 20 25. *Eligibility Requirements:* Applicant must be enrolled or expecting to enroll full-time at an institution or university and resident of Georgia. Available to U.S. citizens. *Application Requirements:* Application form, essay, financial need analysis, interview, personal photograph, proof of GA residency, test scores, transcript. **Deadline:** June 1.

Contact Ms. Pamela Smith, Administration Manager, Georgia Board for Physician Workforce (GBPW), 2 Peachtree Street, NW, 36th Floor, Atlanta, GA 30303. *E-mail:* psmith@dch.ga.gov. *Phone:* 404-232-7972. *Website:* www.gbpw.georgia.gov.

HAWAII

Hawaii State Student Incentive Grant. Grants are given to residents of Hawaii who are enrolled in a participating Hawaiian state school. Funds are for undergraduate tuition only. Applicants must submit a financial need analysis. *Award:* Grant for use in freshman, sophomore, junior, or senior years; renewable. *Award amount:* $200–$2000. *Number of awards:* 470. *Eligibility Requirements:* Applicant must be enrolled or expecting to enroll full- or part-time at a two-year or four-year or technical institution or university; resident of Hawaii and studying in Hawaii. Available to U.S. citizens. *Application Requirements:* Application form, financial need analysis. **Deadline:** continuous.

Contact Janine Oyama, Financial Aid Specialist, Hawaii State Postsecondary Education Commission, University of Hawaii, Honolulu, HI 96822. *Phone:* 808-956-6066.

IDAHO

Idaho Opportunity Scholarship. The Idaho Opportunity Scholarship is an award open to Idaho citizens who have graduated from Idaho high schools. The application is open to any high school or college students who attended an Idaho high school, are Idaho residents, and are attending or who are planning on attending an eligible Idaho college or university. Students must be earning their first undergraduate degree. The required GPA is a 3.0 and applicants must show need by completing the FAFSA by March 1 each year. The award is renewable for a total of 4 years. *Award:* Scholarship for use in freshman, sophomore, junior, or senior years; renewable. *Award amount:* $1–$3000. *Number of awards:* 700–2000. *Eligibility Requirements:* Applicant must be enrolled or expecting to enroll full-time at a two-year or four-year or technical institution or university; resident of Idaho and studying in Idaho. Applicant must have 3.0 GPA or higher. Available to U.S. citizens. *Application Requirements:* Application form, financial need analysis. **Deadline:** March 1.

Contact Joy Miller, Scholarships Program Manager, Idaho State Board of Education, 650 West State Street, #307, Boise, ID 83720-0037. *E-mail:* joy.miller@osbe.idaho.gov. *Phone:* 208-332-1595. *Website:* http://www.boardofed.idaho.gov/.

ILLINOIS

Golden Apple Scholars of Illinois. Applicants must be between the ages of 16 and 21 and maintain a GPA of 2.5. Eligible applicants must be residents of Illinois studying education in Illinois. Recipients must agree to teach in an Illinois school school-of-need for 5 years. Education. *Award:* Scholarship for use in freshman, sophomore, junior, or senior years; renewable. *Award amount:* $23,000. *Number of awards:* 200. *Eligibility Requirements:* Applicant must be age 16-21; enrolled or expecting to enroll full-time at a two-year or four-year institution or university; resident of Illinois and studying in Illinois. Applicant must have 2.5 GPA or higher. Available to U.S. citizens. *Application Requirements:* Application form, essay, interview, personal photograph. **Deadline:** February 15.

Contact Ms. Patricia Kilduff, Director of Recruitment and Placement. *E-mail:* kilduff@goldenapple.org. *Phone:* 312-477-7515. *Website:* http://www.goldenapple.org/.

Grant Program for Dependents of Police, Fire, or Correctional Officers. Awards available to Illinois residents who are dependents of police, fire, and correctional officers killed or disabled in line of duty. Provides for tuition and fees at approved Illinois institutions. Number of grants and individual dollar amount awarded vary. *Award:* Grant for use in freshman, sophomore, junior, senior, graduate, or postgraduate years; renewable. *Eligibility Requirements:* Applicant must be enrolled or expecting to enroll full- or part-time at a two-year or four-year or technical institution or university; resident of Illinois and studying in Illinois. Available to U.S. citizens. *Application Requirements:* Application form. **Deadline:** October 1.

Higher Education License Plate Program-HELP. Grants for students who attend Illinois colleges for which the special collegiate license plates are available. The Illinois Secretary of State issues the license plates, and part of the proceeds are used for grants for undergraduate students attending these colleges, to pay tuition and mandatory fees. *Award:* Grant for use in freshman, sophomore, junior, or senior years; not renewable. *Eligibility Requirements:* Applicant must be enrolled or expecting to enroll full- or part-time at a two-year or four-year institution or university; resident of Illinois and studying in Illinois. Available to U.S. citizens. *Application Requirements:* Application form, financial need analysis. **Deadline:** continuous.

Illinois Monetary Award Program. Awards to Illinois residents enrolled in a minimum of 3 hours per term in a degree program at an approved Illinois institution. See web site for complete list of participating schools. Must demonstrate financial need, based on the information provided on the Free Application for Federal Student Aid. Number of grants and the individual dollar amount awarded vary. Deadline: As soon as possible after October 1 of the year before the student will enter college. *Award:* Grant for use in freshman, sophomore, junior, or senior years; not renewable. *Award amount:* $2987. *Eligibility Requirements:* Applicant must be enrolled or expecting to enroll full- or part-time at a two-year or four-year or technical institution or university; resident of Illinois and studying in Illinois. Available to U.S. citizens. *Application Requirements:* Financial need analysis. **Deadline:** June 30.

Illinois National Guard Grant Program. Active duty members of the Illinois National Guard, or who are within 12 months of discharge, and who have completed one full year of service are eligible. May be used for study at Illinois two- or four-year public colleges for a maximum of the equivalent of four academic years of full-time enrollment. Deadlines: October 1 of the academic year for full year, March 1 for second/third term, or June 15 for the summer term. *Award:* Grant for use in freshman, sophomore, junior, senior, or graduate years; not renewable. *Eligibility Requirements:* Applicant must be enrolled or expecting to enroll full- or part-time at a two-year or four-year institution or university; resident of Illinois and studying in Illinois. Available to U.S. citizens. Applicant or parent must meet one or more of the following requirements: national guard experience; retired from active duty; disabled or killed as a result of military service; prisoner of war; or missing in action. *Application Requirements:* Application form. **Deadline:** October 1.

Illinois Veteran Grant Program-IVG. Awards qualified veterans and pays eligible tuition and fees for study in Illinois public universities or community colleges. Program eligibility units are based on the enrolled hours for a particular term, not the dollar amount of the benefits paid. Applications are available at college financial aid office and can be submitted any time during the academic year for which assistance is being requested. *Award:* Grant for use in freshman, sophomore, junior, senior, or graduate years; renewable. *Eligibility Requirements:* Applicant must be enrolled or expecting to enroll full- or part-time at a two-year or four-year institution or university; resident of Illinois and studying in Illinois. Available to U.S. citizens. Applicant or parent must meet one or more of the following requirements: general military experience; retired from active duty; disabled or killed as a result of military service; prisoner of war; or missing in action. *Application Requirements:* Application form. **Deadline:** continuous.

Jill S. Tietjen P.E. Scholarship. $1750 award for a woman pursuing an ABET-accredited Baccalaureate program in preparation for a career in engineering, engineering technology, and computer science in the United States and Mexico. Must be a U.S. citizen and have minimum 3.0 GPA. Chemical Engineering; Civil Engineering; Computer Science/Data Processing; Electrical Engineering/Electronics; Energy and Power Engineering; Engineering/Technology; Marine/Ocean Engineering; Materials Science, Engineering, and Metallurgy; Mechanical Engineering; Paper and Pulp Engineering. *Award:* Scholarship for use in sophomore, junior, or senior years; not renewable. *Award amount:* $1750. *Number of awards:* 1. *Eligibility Requirements:* Applicant must be enrolled or expecting to enroll full-time at a four-year institution or university and female. Applicant must have 3.0 GPA or higher. Available to U.S. citizens. *Application Requirements:* Application form. **Deadline:** February 15.

MIA/POW Scholarship. Any Spouse, natural child, adopted child, or any step child of a veteran. Child must attend school prior to 26th birthday. No age limit for spouse. Veteran must be MIA, POW, died as the result of service connected disability determined by the U.S. Department of Veterans' Affairs or is 100% service connected disabled permanent and total established by the U.S. Department of Veterans' Affairs. Veteran must have been an Illinois resident at time of entry into service or became an Illinois resident within 6 months after entering service. Scholarship is equivalent to four full years of college, including summer terms. Based on a point system with 120 points as the maximum. Applicant has 12 years to utilize scholarship from the date they begin using it. *Award:* Scholarship for use in freshman, sophomore, junior, or senior years; renewable. *Eligibility Requirements:* Applicant must be enrolled or expecting to enroll full- or part-time at a two-year or four-year institution or university; married; resident of Illinois and studying in Illinois. Available to U.S. citizens. Applicant must have general military experience. *Application Requirements:* Application form. **Deadline:** continuous.

Contact Ms. Tracy Kimmel, Grants Section, Illinois Department of Veterans' Affairs, 833 South Spring Street, Springfield, IL 62794-9432. *Phone:* 217-782-3564. *Fax:* 217-782-4161. *Website:* https://www.illinois.gov/veterans/Pages/default.aspx.

Minority Teachers of Illinois Scholarship Program. Award for minority students intending to become school teachers; teaching commitment attached to receipt. Number of scholarships and the individual dollar amounts vary. Education. *Award:* Scholarship for use in freshman, sophomore, junior, senior, graduate, or postgraduate years; not renewable. *Eligibility Requirements:* Applicant must be American Indian/Alaska Native, Asian/Pacific Islander, Black (non-Hispanic), Hispanic; enrolled or expecting to enroll full- or part-time at a two-year or four-year institution or university; resident of Illinois and studying in Illinois. Available to U.S. citizens. *Application Requirements:* Application form. **Deadline:** March 1.

SWE Baltimore-Washington Section Scholarship. One $2000 award for a woman pursuing an ABET-accredited Baccalaureate or graduate program in preparation for a career in engineering, engineering technology, or computer science in the United States and Mexico. For use at a school in DC, MD, or VA. U.S. citizenship and SWE membership required. Chemical Engineering; Civil Engineering; Construction Engineering/Management; Electrical Engineering/Electronics; Energy and Power Engineering; Engineering/Technology; Marine/Ocean Engineering; Materials Science, Engineering, and Metallurgy; Mechanical Engineering; Paper and Pulp Engineering. *Award:* Scholarship for use in sophomore, junior, senior, or graduate years; not renewable. *Award amount:* $2000. *Number of awards:* 1. *Eligibility Requirements:* Applicant must be enrolled or expecting to enroll full-time at a four-year institution or university; female and studying in District of Columbia, Maryland, Virginia. Applicant or parent of applicant must be member of Society of Women Engineers. Applicant must have 3.0 GPA or higher. Available to U.S. citizens. *Application Requirements:* Application form. **Deadline:** February 15.

SWE Central New Mexico Pioneers Scholarship. Renewable $1500 scholarship for a woman pursuing an ABET-accredited Baccalaureate program in preparation for a career in engineering, engineering technology, or computer science in the United States and Mexico. Must attend a NM university or 4-year engineering/technology school. U.S. citizenship, SWE membership, and minimum 3.0 GPA required. Renewable up to three years. Availability dependent upon renewal. Chemical Engineering; Civil Engineering; Construction Engineering/Management; Electrical Engineering/Electronics; Energy and Power Engineering; Engineering/Technology; Marine/Ocean Engineering; Materials Science, Engineering, and Metallurgy; Mechanical Engineering; Paper and Pulp Engineering. *Award:* Scholarship for use in sophomore, junior, senior, or graduate years; renewable. *Award amount:* $1500. *Number of awards:* 1. *Eligibility Requirements:* Applicant must be enrolled or expecting to enroll full-time at a four-year institution or university; female and studying in New Mexico. Applicant or parent of applicant must be member of Society of Women Engineers. Applicant must have 3.0 GPA or higher. Available to U.S. citizens. *Application Requirements:* Application form. **Deadline:** February 15.

Veterans' Children Educational Opportunities. $250 award for each child aged 10 to 18 of a veteran who died or became totally disabled as a result of active duty. Must be Illinois resident studying in Illinois. Death must be service-connected. Disability must be rated 100 percent for two or more years. *Award:* Grant for use in freshman year; not renewable. *Award amount:* $250. *Eligibility Requirements:* Applicant must be age 10-18; enrolled or expecting to enroll full- or part-time at a two-year or four-year institution or university; single; resident of Illinois and studying in Illinois. Available to U.S. citizens. Applicant must have general military experience. *Application Requirements:* Application form. **Deadline:** June 30.

Contact Tracy Kimmel, Grants Section, Illinois Department of Veterans' Affairs, 833 South Spring Street, Springfield, IL 62794-9432. *Phone:* 217-782-3564. *Fax:* 217-782-4161. *Website:* https://www.illinois.gov/veterans/Pages/default.aspx.

INDIANA

Child of Disabled Veteran Grant or Purple Heart Recipient Grant. Free tuition at Indiana state-supported colleges or universities for children of disabled veterans or Purple Heart recipients. Must submit form DD214 or service record. Covers tuition and mandatory fees. *Award:* Grant for use in freshman, sophomore, junior, senior, graduate, or postgraduate years; renewable. *Eligibility Requirements:* Applicant must be enrolled or expecting to enroll full- or part-time at a two-year or four-year institution or university; resident of Indiana and studying in Indiana. Available to U.S. citizens. *Application Requirements:* Application form.

Contact Jon Brinkley, State Service Officer. *E-mail:* jbrinkley@dva.in.gov. *Phone:* 317-232-3910. *Fax:* 317-232-7721. *Website:* http://www.in.gov/dva.

Department of Veterans Affairs Free Tuition for Children of POW/MIA's in Vietnam. Renewable award for residents of Indiana who are the children of veterans declared missing in action or prisoner-of-war after January 1, 1960. Provides tuition at Indiana state-supported institutions for undergraduate study. *Award:* Grant for use in freshman, sophomore, junior, senior, graduate, or postgraduate years; renewable. *Eligibility Requirements:* Applicant must be enrolled or expecting to enroll full- or part-time at a two-year or four-year institution or university; resident of Indiana and studying in Indiana. Available to U.S. citizens. *Application Requirements:* Application form.

Contact Jon Brinkley, State Service Officer. *E-mail:* jbrinkley@dva.in.gov. *Phone:* 317-232-3910. *Fax:* 317-232-7721. *Website:* http://www.in.gov/dva.

Frank O'Bannon Grant Program. A need-based, tuition-restricted program for students attending Indiana public, private, or proprietary institutions seeking a first undergraduate degree. Students (and parents of dependent students) who are U.S. citizens and Indiana residents must file the FAFSA yearly by the March 10 deadline. *Award:* Grant for use in freshman, sophomore, junior, or senior years; not renewable. *Award amount:* $200–$10,992. *Number of awards:* 48,408–70,239. *Eligibility Requirements:* Applicant must be enrolled or expecting to enroll full-time at a two-year or four-year or technical institution or university; resident of Indiana and studying in Indiana. Available to U.S. citizens. *Application Requirements:* Application form, FAFSA, financial need analysis. **Deadline:** March 10.

Hoosier Scholar Award. A $500 nonrenewable award. Based on the size of the senior class, one to three scholars are selected by the guidance counselors of each accredited high school in Indiana. The award is based on academic merit and may be used for any educational expense at an eligible Indiana institution of higher education. *Award:* Scholarship for use in freshman year; not renewable. *Award amount:* $500. *Number of awards:* 666–840. *Eligibility Requirements:* Applicant must be high school student; planning to enroll or expecting to enroll full-time at a two-year or four-year institution or university; resident of Indiana and studying in Indiana. Applicant must have 3.5 GPA or higher. Available to U.S. citizens. *Application Requirements:* Application form, recommendations or references. **Deadline:** March 10.

Contact Ada Sparkman, Program Coordinator, State Student Assistance Commission of Indiana (SSACI), 150 West Market Street, Suite 500, Indianapolis, IN 46204-2805. *Phone:* 317-232-2350. *Fax:* 317-232-3260. *Website:* http://www.in.gov/ssaci.

Indiana National Guard Supplemental Grant. The award is a supplement to the Indiana Higher Education Grant program. Applicants must be members of the Indiana National Guard. All Guard paperwork must be completed prior to the start of each semester. The FAFSA must be received by March 10. Award covers certain tuition and fees at select public colleges. *Award:* Grant for use in freshman, sophomore, junior, or senior years; not renewable. *Award amount:* $20–$7110. *Number of awards:* 503–925. *Eligibility Requirements:* Applicant must be enrolled or expecting to enroll full- or part-time at a two-year or four-year institution or university; resident of Indiana and studying in Indiana. Available to U.S. citizens. Applicant or parent must meet one or more of the following requirements: national guard experience; retired from active duty; disabled or killed as a result of military service; prisoner of war; or missing in action. *Application Requirements:* Application form. **Deadline:** March 10.

Contact Kathryn Moore, Grants Counselor, State Student Assistance Commission of Indiana (SSACI), 150 West Market Street, Suite 500, Indianapolis, IN 46204-2805. *E-mail:*

kmoore@ssaci.in.gov. *Phone:* 317-232-2350. *Fax:* 317-232-2360. *Website:* http://www.in.gov/ssaci.

Indiana Nursing Scholarship Fund. Need-based tuition funding for nursing students enrolled full- or part-time at an eligible Indiana institution. Must be a U.S. citizen and an Indiana resident and have a minimum 2.0 GPA or meet the minimum requirements for the nursing program. Upon graduation, recipients must practice as a nurse in an Indiana health care setting for two years. Nursing. *Award:* Scholarship for use in freshman, sophomore, junior, or senior years; not renewable. *Award amount:* $200–$5000. *Number of awards:* 490–690. *Eligibility Requirements:* Applicant must be enrolled or expecting to enroll full- or part-time at a two-year or four-year institution or university; resident of Indiana and studying in Indiana. Available to U.S. citizens. *Application Requirements:* Application form, FAFSA, financial need analysis. **Deadline:** continuous.

Contact Yvonne Heflin, Director, Special Programs, State Student Assistance Commission of Indiana (SSACI), 150 West Market Street, Suite 500, Indianapolis, IN 46204-2805. *Phone:* 317-232-2350. *Fax:* 317-232-3260. *Website:* http://www.in.gov/ssaci.

National Guard Scholarship Extension Program. A scholarship extension applicant is eligible for a tuition scholarship under Indiana Code 21-13-5-4 for a period not to exceed the period of scholarship extension the applicant served on active duty as a member of the National Guard (mobilized and deployed). Must apply not later than one (1) year after the applicant ceases to be a member of the Indiana National Guard. Applicant should apply through the education officer of their last unit of assignment. *Award:* Grant for use in freshman, sophomore, junior, or senior years; renewable. *Eligibility Requirements:* Applicant must be enrolled or expecting to enroll full- or part-time at a two-year or four-year or technical institution or university and studying in Indiana. Available to U.S. citizens. Applicant must have national guard experience. *Application Requirements:* Application form.

Contact Pamela Moody, National Guard Education Officer, Indiana Department of Veterans Affairs, 302 West Washington Street, Room E-120, Indianapolis, IN 46204. *E-mail:* pamela.moody@in.ngb.army.mil. *Phone:* 317-964-7017. *Website:* http://www.in.gov/dva.

National Guard Tuition Supplement Program. Applicant must be a member of the Indiana National Guard, in active drilling status, who has not been AWOL during the last 12 months, does not possess a bachelor's degree, possesses the requisite academic qualifications, meets the requirements of the state-supported college or university, and meets all National Guard requirements. *Award:* Grant for use in freshman, sophomore, junior, or senior years; renewable. *Eligibility Requirements:* Applicant must be enrolled or expecting to enroll full- or part-time at a two-year or four-year or technical institution or university and studying in Indiana. Available to U.S. citizens. Applicant must have national guard experience. *Application Requirements:* Application form.

Contact Jon Brinkley, State Service Officer. *E-mail:* jbrinkley@dva.in.gov. *Phone:* 317-232-3910. *Fax:* 317-232-7721. *Website:* http://www.in.gov/dva.

Part-Time Grant Program. Program is designed to encourage part-time undergraduates to start and complete their Associate or Baccalaureate degrees or certificates by subsidizing part-time tuition costs. It is a term-based award that is based on need. State residency requirements must be met and a FAFSA must be filed. Eligibility is determined at the institutional level subject to approval by SSACI. *Award:* Grant for use in freshman, sophomore, junior, or senior years; not renewable. *Award amount:* $20–$4000. *Number of awards:* 4680–6700. *Eligibility Requirements:* Applicant must be enrolled or expecting to enroll part-time at a two-year or four-year or technical institution or university; resident of Indiana and studying in Indiana. Available to U.S. citizens. *Application Requirements:* Application form, financial need analysis. **Deadline:** continuous.

Resident Tuition for Active Duty Military Personnel. Applicant must be a nonresident of Indiana serving on active duty and stationed in Indiana and attending any state-supported college or university. Dependents remain eligible for the duration of their enrollment, even if the active duty person is no longer in Indiana. Entitlement is to the resident tuition rate. *Award:* Grant for use in freshman, sophomore, junior, senior, graduate, or postgraduate years; renewable. *Eligibility Requirements:* Applicant must be enrolled or expecting to enroll full- or part-time at a two-year or four-year or technical institution or university and studying in Indiana. Available to U.S. citizens. Applicant or parent must meet one or more of the following requirements: Air Force or Army experience; retired from active duty; disabled or killed as a result of military service; prisoner of war; or missing in action. *Application Requirements:* Application form.

Contact Jon Brinkley, State Service Officer. *E-mail:* jbrinkley@dva.in.gov. *Phone:* 317-232-3910. *Fax:* 317-232-7721. *Website:* http://www.in.gov/dva.

Tuition and Fee Remission for Children and Spouses of National Guard Members. Award to an individual whose father, mother or spouse was a member of the Indiana National Guard and suffered a service-connected death while serving on state active duty (which includes mobilized and deployed for federal active duty). The student must be eligible to pay the resident tuition rate at the state-supported college or university and must possess the requisite academic qualifications. *Award:* Grant for use in freshman, sophomore, junior, or senior years; renewable. *Eligibility Requirements:* Applicant must be enrolled or expecting to enroll full- or part-time at a two-year or four-year or technical institution or university and studying in Indiana. Available to U.S. citizens. Applicant or parent must meet one or more of the following requirements: national guard experience; retired from active duty; disabled or killed as a result of military service; prisoner of war; or missing in action. *Application Requirements:* Application form.

Contact R. Martin Umbarger, Adjutant General, Indiana Department of Veterans Affairs, 2002 South Holt Road, Indianapolis, IN 46241. *E-mail:* r.martin.umbarger@in.ngb.army.mil. *Phone:* 317-247-3559. *Website:* http://www.in.gov/dva.

Twenty-first Century Scholars Gear Up Summer Scholarship. Grant of up to $3000 that pays for summer school tuition and regularly assessed course fees (does not cover other costs such as textbooks or room and board). *Award:*

Scholarship for use in freshman, sophomore, junior, or senior years; not renewable. *Award amount:* up to $3000. *Number of awards:* 1. *Eligibility Requirements:* Applicant must be enrolled or expecting to enroll full-time at a two-year or four-year institution or university; resident of Indiana and studying in Indiana. Available to U.S. citizens. *Application Requirements:* Application form, must be in twenty-first century scholars program, high school diploma. **Deadline:** varies.

IOWA

Iowa National Guard Education Assistance Program. Program provides postsecondary grant assistance to members of Iowa National Guard Units. Must study at a postsecondary institution in Iowa. *Award:* Grant for use in freshman, sophomore, junior, or senior years; not renewable. *Eligibility Requirements:* Applicant must be enrolled or expecting to enroll full- or part-time at a two-year or four-year or technical institution or university; resident of Iowa and studying in Iowa. Available to U.S. citizens. Applicant must have national guard experience. *Application Requirements:* Application form. **Deadline:** July 1.

Contact Tracy Davis, Executive Officer 1, Iowa College Student Aid Commission, 430 E Grand Avenue, FL 3, Des Moines, IA 50309-1920. *Phone:* 877-272-4456. *Website:* http://www.iowacollegeaid.gov/.

Iowa Tuition Grant Program. Program assists students who attend independent postsecondary institutions in Iowa. Iowa residents currently enrolled, or planning to enroll, for at least 3 semester hours at one of the eligible Iowa postsecondary institutions may apply. Awards currently range from $100 to $5650. Grants may not exceed the difference between independent college and university tuition fees and the average tuition fees at the three public Regent universities. *Award:* Grant for use in freshman, sophomore, junior, or senior years; not renewable. *Award amount:* $100–$5650. *Number of awards:* 16,500–19,000. *Eligibility Requirements:* Applicant must be enrolled or expecting to enroll full- or part-time at a two-year or four-year institution or university; resident of Iowa and studying in Iowa. Available to U.S. citizens. *Application Require-

ments:* Financial need analysis. **Deadline:** July 1.

Contact Tristan Lynn, Executive Officer 1, Iowa College Student Aid Commission, 430 E Grand Avenue, FL 3, Des Moines, IA 50309-1920. *E-mail:* tristan.lynn@iowa.gov. *Phone:* 515-725-3409. *Website:* http://www.iowacollegeaid.gov/.

Iowa Vocational-Technical Tuition Grant Program. Program provides need-based financial assistance to Iowa residents enrolled in career education (vocational-technical), and career option programs at Iowa area community colleges. Grants range from $150 to $1200, depending on the length of the program, financial need, and available funds. *Award:* Grant for use in freshman or sophomore years; not renewable. *Award amount:* $150–$1200. *Number of awards:* 2500–3500. *Eligibility Requirements:* Applicant must be enrolled or expecting to enroll full- or part-time at a two-year or technical institution; resident of Iowa and studying in Iowa. Available to U.S. citizens. *Application Requirements:* Financial need analysis. **Deadline:** July 1.

Contact Tristan Lynn, Executive Officer 1, Iowa College Student Aid Commission, 430 E Grand Avenue, FL 3, Des Moines, IA 50309-1920. *E-mail:* tristan.lynn@iowa.gov. *Phone:* 515-725-3409. *Website:* http://www.iowacollegeaid.gov/.

KANSAS

Kansas Educational Benefits for Children of MIA, POW, and Deceased Veterans of the Vietnam War. Scholarship awarded to students who are children of veterans. Must show proof of parent's status as missing in action, prisoner-of-war, or killed in action in the Vietnam War. Kansas residence required of veteran at time of entry to service. Must attend a state-supported postsecondary school. *Award:* Scholarship for use in freshman, sophomore, junior, or senior years; not renewable. *Number of awards:* 1. *Eligibility Requirements:* Applicant must be enrolled or expecting to enroll full-time at a two-year or four-year or technical institution or university and studying in Kansas. Available to U.S. citizens. Applicant or parent must meet one or more of the following requirements: general military experience; retired from active duty; disabled

or killed as a result of military service; prisoner of war; or missing in action. *Application Requirements:* Application form, birth certificate, school acceptance letter, military discharge of veteran. **Deadline:** varies.

Contact Wayne Bollig, Program Director. *E-mail:* wbollig@kcva.org. *Phone:* 785-296-3976. *Fax:* 785-296-1462. *Website:* http://www.kcva.org/.

Kansas Ethnic Minority Scholarship. Scholarship program designed to assist financially needy, academically competitive students who are identified as members of any of the following ethnic/racial groups: African-American, American Indian or Alaskan Native, Asian or Pacific Islander, or Hispanic. Priority is given to applicants who are freshmen. Students must be Kansas residents attending postsecondary institutions in Kansas. For more details refer to web site http://www.kansasregents.org/students/student_financial_aid/scholarships_and_grants. *Award:* Scholarship for use in freshman, sophomore, junior, or senior years; renewable. *Award amount:* $50–$1850. *Number of awards:* 100–250. *Eligibility Requirements:* Applicant must be American Indian/Alaska Native, Asian/Pacific Islander, Black (non-Hispanic), Hispanic; enrolled or expecting to enroll full-time at a two-year or four-year institution or university; resident of Kansas and studying in Kansas. Applicant must have 3.0 GPA or higher. Available to U.S. citizens. *Application Requirements:* Application form, financial need analysis. *Fee:* $12. **Deadline:** May 1.

Contact Diane Lindeman, Director of Student Financial Assistance, Kansas Board of Regents, 1000 SW Jackson, Suite 520, Topeka, KS 66612. *E-mail:* dlindeman@ksbor.org. *Phone:* 785-430-4255. *Fax:* 785-430-4233. *Website:* http://www.kansasregents.org/.

Kansas Teacher Service Scholarship. Scholarship to encourage talented students to enter the teaching profession and teach in Kansas in specific curriculum areas or in underserved areas of Kansas. Students must be Kansas residents attending a postsecondary institution in Kansas. For more details, refer to web site http://www.kansasregents.org. Education. *Award:* Scholarship for use in junior, senior, or graduate years; renewable. *Award amount:* $2206–$5514. *Eligibility Requirements:* Applicant must be enrolled or expecting to enroll full- or part-time at a four-year institution or university; resident of Kansas and studying in Kansas. Applicant must have 3.0 GPA or higher. Available to U.S. citizens. *Application Requirements:* Application form, essay, financial need analysis. *Fee:* $12. **Deadline:** May 1.

Contact Diane Lindeman, Director of Student Financial Assistance, Kansas Board of Regents, 1000 SW Jackson, Suite 520, Topeka, KS 66612. *E-mail:* dlindeman@ksbor.org. *Phone:* 785-430-4255. *Fax:* 785-430-4233. *Website:* http://www.kansasregents.org/.

KENTUCKY

College Access Program (CAP) Grant. Award for U.S. citizens and Kentucky residents seeking their first undergraduate degree. Applicants enrolled in sectarian institutions are not eligible. Must submit Free Application for Federal Student Aid to demonstrate financial need. Funding is limited. Awards are made on a first-come, first-serve basis. *Award:* Grant for use in freshman, sophomore, junior, or senior years; not renewable. *Award amount:* $475–$1900. *Number of awards:* 44,900–45,000. *Eligibility Requirements:* Applicant must be enrolled or expecting to enroll full- or part-time at a two-year or four-year or technical institution or university; resident of Kentucky and studying in Kentucky. Available to U.S. citizens. *Application Requirements:* Application form. **Deadline:** continuous.

Contact Sheila Roe, Program Coordinator, Kentucky Higher Education Assistance Authority (KHEAA), PO Box 798, Frankfort, KY 40602-0798. *E-mail:* sroe@kheaa.com. *Phone:* 800-928-8926 Ext. 67393. *Website:* http://www.kheaa.com/.

Department of Veterans Affairs Tuition Waiver-KY KRS 164-507. Scholarship available to college students who are residents of Kentucky under the age of 26. *Award:* Scholarship for use in freshman, sophomore, junior, or senior years; not renewable. *Number of awards:* 400. *Eligibility Requirements:* Applicant must be enrolled or expecting to enroll full- or part-time at a two-year or four-year institution or university and resident of Kentucky. Available to U.S. citizens. *Application Requirements:* Application form. **Deadline:** varies.

Contact Barbara Sipek, Tuition Waiver Coordinator. *E-mail:* barbaraa.sipek@ky.gov. *Phone:* 502-595-4447. *Website:* http://www.veterans.ky.gov/.

Early Childhood Development Scholarship. Awards scholarship with conditional service commitment for part-time students currently employed by participating ECD facility or providing training in ECD for an approved organization. For more information, visit web site http://www.kheaa.com. *Award:* Scholarship for use in freshman, sophomore, junior, or senior years; not renewable. *Award amount:* $100–$1800. *Number of awards:* 500–800. *Eligibility Requirements:* Applicant must be enrolled or expecting to enroll part-time at a two-year or four-year institution or university; resident of Kentucky and studying in Kentucky. Available to U.S. citizens. *Application Requirements:* Application form. **Deadline:** continuous.

Contact Danny Prather, Program Coordinator, Kentucky Higher Education Assistance Authority (KHEAA), PO Box 798, Frankfort, KY 40602-0798. *E-mail:* danprather@kheaa.com. *Phone:* 800-928-8926 Ext. 67399. *Website:* http://www.kheaa.com/.

Environmental Protection Scholarship. Renewable awards for college juniors, seniors, and graduate students for in-state tuition, fees, room and board, and a book allowance at a Kentucky public university. Minimum 3.0 GPA required. Must work full-time for the Kentucky Department for Environmental Protection upon graduation (six months for each semester of scholarship support received). Interview required. Program not generally appropriate for non-residents. Biology; Chemical Engineering; Civil Engineering; Earth Science; Environmental Science; Hydrology; Mechanical Engineering; Natural Sciences. *Award:* Scholarship for use in junior, senior, or graduate years; renewable. *Award amount:* $10,000–$13,000. *Number of awards:* 1–4. *Eligibility Requirements:* Applicant must be enrolled or expecting to enroll full-time at a four-year institution or university; resident of Kentucky and studying in Kentucky. Applicant must have 3.0 GPA or higher. Available to U.S. citizens. *Application Requirements:* Application form, essay, interview. **Deadline:** February 15.

Contact James Kipp, Scholarship Program Coordinator, Kentucky Energy and Environment Cabinet, 233 Mining/Mineral Resources Building, Lexington, KY 40506-0107. *E-mail:* kipp@uky.edu. *Phone:* 859-257-1299. *Website:* http://dep.ky.gov.

Go Higher Grant. Need-based grant for adult students pursuing their first undergraduate degree. Completion of the FAFSA is required. *Award:* Grant for use in freshman year; not renewable. *Award amount:* $50–$1000. *Number of awards:* 100–300. *Eligibility Requirements:* Applicant must be enrolled or expecting to enroll full- or part-time at a two-year or four-year or technical institution or university; resident of Kentucky and studying in Kentucky. Available to U.S. citizens. *Application Requirements:* Application form. **Deadline:** continuous.

Contact Sheila Roe, Grant Program Coordinator, Kentucky Higher Education Assistance Authority (KHEAA), PO Box 798, Frankfort, KY 40206-0798. *E-mail:* sroe@kheaa.com. *Phone:* 800-928-8926 Ext. 67393. *Website:* http://www.kheaa.com/.

Kentucky Educational Excellence Scholarship (KEES). Annual award based on yearly high school GPA and highest ACT or SAT score received by high school graduation. Awards are renewable, if required cumulative GPA is maintained at a Kentucky postsecondary school. Must be a Kentucky resident, and a graduate of a Kentucky high school. Low-income students who qualify for the free/reduced lunch program at least one year of high school may receive supplemental awards for passing scores on Advanced Placement (AP) or International Baccalaureate (IB) exams. *Award:* Scholarship for use in freshman, sophomore, junior, or senior years; renewable. *Award amount:* $125–$2500. *Number of awards:* 65,000–75,000. *Eligibility Requirements:* Applicant must be enrolled or expecting to enroll full- or part-time at a two-year or four-year or technical institution or university; resident of Kentucky and studying in Kentucky. Available to U.S. citizens.

Contact Becky Gilpatrick, Director of Student Aid Services, Kentucky Higher Education Assistance Authority (KHEAA), PO Box 798, Frankfort, KY 40602. *E-mail:* rgilpatrick@kheaa.com.

Phone: 800-928-8926 Ext. 67394. *Website:* http://www.kheaa.com/.

Kentucky National Guard Tuition Award. Provides tuition assistance for active members of the Kentucky National Guard to attend a Kentucky college or university. Guard members may apply through their unit. *Award:* Grant for use in freshman, sophomore, junior, or senior years; not renewable. *Award amount:* $100–$11,500. *Number of awards:* 1000–1500. *Eligibility Requirements:* Applicant must be enrolled or expecting to enroll full- or part-time at a two-year or four-year or technical institution or university; resident of Kentucky and studying in Kentucky. Available to U.S. citizens. Applicant must have national guard experience. *Application Requirements:* Application form. **Deadline:** continuous.

Kentucky Office of Vocational Rehabilitation. Grant provides services necessary to secure employment. Eligible individual must possess physical or mental impairment that results in a substantial impediment to employment; benefit from vocational rehabilitation services in terms of an employment outcome; and require vocational rehabilitation services to prepare for, enter, or retain employment. *Award:* Grant for use in freshman, sophomore, junior, senior, graduate, or postgraduate years; renewable. *Eligibility Requirements:* Applicant must be enrolled or expecting to enroll full- or part-time at a two-year or four-year or technical institution or university. *Application Requirements:* Application form, eligibility for OVR services and in proper priority category, financial need analysis, interview, transcript. **Deadline:** continuous.

Contact Charles Puckett, Program Administrator, Kentucky Office of Vocational Rehabilitation, 600 West Cedar Street, Suite 2E, Louisville, KY 40202. *E-mail:* marianu.spencer@mail.state.ky.us. *Phone:* 502-595-4173. *Fax:* 502-564-2358. *Website:* http://www.ovr.ky.gov/.

Kentucky Transportation Cabinet Civil Engineering Scholarship Program. Scholarships awarded to qualified Kentucky residents who wish to study civil engineering at University of Kentucky, Western Kentucky University, University of Louisville or Kentucky State University. Applicant should be a graduate of an accredited Kentucky high school or a Kentucky resident. Scholarship recipients are given opportunities to work for the Cabinet during summers and job opportunities upon graduation within the state of KY. Civil Engineering. *Award:* Scholarship for use in freshman, sophomore, junior, or senior years; renewable. *Award amount:* $12,400–$51,200. *Number of awards:* 15–25. *Eligibility Requirements:* Applicant must be enrolled or expecting to enroll full-time at a four-year institution or university; resident of Kentucky and studying in Kentucky. Applicant must have 3.0 GPA or higher. Available to U.S. and non-U.S. citizens. *Application Requirements:* Application form, essay, interview. **Deadline:** February 1.

Contact Cherie Mertz, Scholarship Program Coordinator, Kentucky Transportation Cabinet, 200 Mero Street, 6th Floor West, Frankfort, KY 40622. *E-mail:* Cherie.Mertz@ky.gov. *Phone:* 502-564-4610. *Website:* http://transportation.ky.gov/Education/Pages/Scholarships.aspx.

Kentucky Tuition Grant (KTG). Grants available to Kentucky residents who are full-time undergraduates at an independent college within the state. Based on financial need. Must submit FAFSA. *Award:* Grant for use in freshman, sophomore, junior, or senior years; not renewable. *Award amount:* $200–$3000. *Number of awards:* 10,000–12,500. *Eligibility Requirements:* Applicant must be enrolled or expecting to enroll full-time at a two-year or four-year institution or university; resident of Kentucky and studying in Kentucky. Available to U.S. citizens. *Application Requirements:* Application form. **Deadline:** continuous.

Contact Sheila Roe, Grant Program Coordinator, Kentucky Higher Education Assistance Authority (KHEAA), PO Box 798, Frankfort, KY 40602-0798. *E-mail:* sroe@kheaa.com. *Phone:* 800-928-8926 Ext. 67393. *Website:* http://www.kheaa.com/.

Mary Jo Young Scholarship. Provides financial assistance for tuition and textbook expenses incurred by Kentucky high school students taking college/dual credit coursework. *Award:* Scholarship for use in freshman year; not renewable. *Award amount:* $125–$840. *Number of awards:* 700–1000.

Eligibility Requirements: Applicant must be high school student; planning to enroll or expecting to enroll part-time at a two-year or four-year or technical institution or university; resident of Kentucky and studying in Kentucky. Applicant must have 2.5 GPA or higher. Available to U.S. citizens. *Application Requirements:* Application form. **Deadline:** May 1.

Contact Danny Prather, Program Coordinator, Kentucky Higher Education Assistance Authority (KHEAA), PO Box 798, Frankfort, KY 40602-0798. *E-mail:* danprather@kheaa.com. *Phone:* 800-938-8926 Ext. 67399. *Website:* http://www.kheaa.com/.

Touchstone Energy All "A" Classic Scholarship. Award of $1000 for senior student in good standing at a Kentucky high school which is a member of the All Classic. Applicant must be a U.S. citizen and must plan to attend a postsecondary institution in Kentucky in the upcoming year as a full-time student and be drug free. *Award:* Scholarship for use in freshman year; not renewable. *Award amount:* $1000. *Number of awards:* 12. *Eligibility Requirements:* Applicant must be high school student; planning to enroll or expecting to enroll full-time at a two-year or four-year or technical institution or university; resident of Kentucky and studying in Kentucky. Available to U.S. citizens. *Application Requirements:* Application form, essay, personal photograph, recommendations or references, transcript. **Deadline:** December 3.

Contact David Cowden, Chairperson, Scholarship Committee, Kentucky Touchstone Energy Cooperatives, 1320 Lincoln Road, Lewisport, KY 42351. *E-mail:* allaclassic@alltel.net. *Phone:* 859-744-4812. *Website:* http://www.ekpc.coop.

LOUISIANA

Louisiana National Guard State Tuition Exemption Program. Renewable award for college undergraduates to receive tuition exemption upon satisfactory performance in the Louisiana National Guard. Applicant must attend a state-funded institution in Louisiana, be a resident and registered voter in Louisiana, meet the academic and residency requirements of the university attended, and provide documentation of Louisiana National Guard enlistment. The exemption can be used for up to 15 semesters. Minimum 2.5 GPA required. *Award:* Scholarship for use in freshman, sophomore, junior, or senior years; renewable. *Eligibility Requirements:* Applicant must be enrolled or expecting to enroll full- or part-time at a two-year or four-year or technical institution or university; resident of Louisiana and studying in Louisiana. Applicant must have 2.5 GPA or higher. Available to U.S. citizens. Applicant or parent must meet one or more of the following requirements: national guard experience; retired from active duty; disabled or killed as a result of military service; prisoner of war; or missing in action. *Application Requirements:* Application form, test scores, transcript. **Deadline:** continuous.

Contact Jona Hughes, Education Services Officer, Louisiana National Guard, Joint Task Force LA, Building 35, Jackson Barracks, JI-PD, New Orleans, LA 70146-0330. *E-mail:* hughesj@la-arng.ngb.army.mil. *Phone:* 504-278-8531 Ext. 8304. *Fax:* 504-278-8025. *Website:* http://geauxguard.com/organization/joint-force-headquarters-jfhq-la/.

Rockefeller State Wildlife Scholarship. For college undergraduates with a minimum of 60 credit hours who are majoring in Forestry, Wildlife, or Marine Science, and for college graduate students who are majoring in Forestry, Wildlife, or Marine Science. College undergraduates must have a grade point average of at least 2.50 to apply. College graduate students must have a grade point average of at least 3.00 in order to apply. Renewable up to three years as an undergraduate and two years as a graduate student. Biology; Marine Biology; Marine/Ocean Engineering; Natural Resources; Oceanography. *Award:* Scholarship for use in freshman, sophomore, junior, senior, graduate, or postgraduate years; renewable. *Award amount:* $2000–$3000. *Number of awards:* 20–30. *Eligibility Requirements:* Applicant must be enrolled or expecting to enroll full-time at a four-year institution or university; resident of Louisiana and studying in Louisiana. Applicant must have 2.5 GPA or higher. Available to U.S. citizens. *Application Requirements:* Application form, application form may be submitted online (http://www.osfa.la.gov for Rockefeller app), FAFSA, test scores, transcript. **Deadline:** July 1.

Contact Bonnie Lavergne, Public Information, Louisiana Office of Student Financial Assistance, PO Box 91202, Baton Rouge, LA 70821-9202. *E-mail:* custserv@osfa.la.gov. *Phone:* 800-259-5626 Ext. 7714. *Fax:* 225-612-6508. *Website:* http://www.osfa.la.gov/.

Taylor Opportunity Program for Students Honors Level. Program awards 8 semesters or 12 terms of tuition to any Louisiana State postsecondary institution plus $400 stipend per semester. Program awards 8 semesters or 12 terms of an amount equal to the weighted average public tuition to students attending a LAICU (Louisiana Association of Independent Colleges and Universities) institution plus $400 stipend per semester. Program awards 8 semesters or 12 terms of an amount equal to the weighted average public tuition to two out-of-state Institutions for Hearing Impaired Students: Gallaudet University and Rochester Institute of Technology plus $400 stipend per semester. Program awards $1744 per year to Approved Proprietary and Cosmetology schools plus a stipend of $800 per year. When you submit the FAFSA, you have automatically applied for all four levels of TOPS, for Federal Pell Grants and Go Grants and for Federal Student Loans. Please do not send separate letters of application to the TOPS office. *Award:* Scholarship for use in freshman, sophomore, junior, or senior years; renewable. *Award amount:* $836–$6736. *Number of awards:* 9661. *Eligibility Requirements:* Applicant must be enrolled or expecting to enroll full-time at a two-year or four-year or technical institution or university; resident of Louisiana and studying in Louisiana. Applicant must have 3.0 GPA or higher. Available to U.S. citizens. *Application Requirements:* Application form, application form may be submitted online (http://www.osfa.la.gov), FAFSA, test scores, transcript. **Deadline:** July 1.

Taylor Opportunity Program for Students Opportunity Level. Program awards 8 semesters or 12 terms of tuition to any Louisiana State postsecondary institution. Program awards 8 semesters or 12 terms of an amount equal to the weighted average public tuition to students attending a LAICU (Louisiana Association of Independent Colleges and Universities) institution. Program awards 8 semesters or 12 terms

of an amount equal to the weighted average public tuition to two out-of-state Institutions for Hearing Impaired Students: Gallaudet University and Rochester Institute of Technology. Program awards $1744 per year to Approved Proprietary and Cosmetology schools. When you submit the FAFSA, you have automatically applied for all four levels of TOPS, and for Federal Pell Grants and Go Grants. Please do not send separate letters of application to the TOPS office. *Award:* Scholarship for use in freshman, sophomore, junior, or senior years; renewable. *Award amount:* $436–$5936. *Number of awards:* 24,633. *Eligibility Requirements:* Applicant must be enrolled or expecting to enroll full-time at a two-year or four-year or technical institution or university; resident of Louisiana and studying in Louisiana. Applicant must have 2.5 GPA or higher. Available to U.S. citizens. *Application Requirements:* Application form, application form may be submitted online (http://www.osfa.la.gov), FAFSA, test scores, transcript. **Deadline:** July 1.

Taylor Opportunity Program for Students Performance Level. Program awards 8 semesters or 12 terms of tuition to any Louisiana State postsecondary institution plus $200 stipend per semester. Program awards 8 semesters or 12 terms of an amount equal to the weighted average public tuition to students attending a LAICU (Louisiana Association of Independent Colleges and Universities) institution plus $200 stipend per semester. Program awards 8 semesters or 12 terms of an amount equal to the weighted average public tuition to two out-of-state Institutions for Hearing Impaired Students: Gallaudet University and Rochester Institute of Technology plus $200 stipend per semester. Program awards $1744 plus $400 per year to Approved Proprietary and Cosmetology schools. When you submit the FAFSA, you have automatically applied for all four levels of TOPS, for Federal Pell Grants and Go Grants and for Federal Student Loans. Please do not send separate letters of application to the TOPS office. *Award:* Scholarship for use in freshman, sophomore, junior, or senior years; renewable. *Award amount:* $636–$6336. *Number of awards:* 11,928. *Eligibility Requirements:* Applicant must be enrolled or expecting to enroll full-time at a two-year or four-year or technical institution or university; resident of Louisiana and studying in Louisiana. Applicant must have 3.0 GPA or higher. Available to U.S. citizens. *Application Requirements:* Application form, application form may be submitted online (http://www.osfa.la.gov), FAFSA, test scores, transcript. **Deadline:** July 1.

Taylor Opportunity Program for Students Tech Level. Program awards an amount equal to tuition for up to 4 semesters and two summers of technical training at a Louisiana postsecondary institution that offers a vocational or technical education certificate or diploma program, or a non-academic degree program; or up to $1744 to an approved Proprietary or Cosmetology school. Must have completed the TOPS Opportunity core curriculum or the TOPS Tech core curriculum, must have achieved a 2.50 grade point average over the core curriculum only, and must have achieved an ACT score of 17 or an SAT score of 810. Program awards an amount equal to the weighted average public tuition for technical programs to students attending a LAICU private institution for technical training. When you submit the FAFSA, you have automatically applied for all four levels of TOPS, for Federal Pell Grants and Go Grants and Federal Student Loans. Please do not send separate letters of application to the TOPS office. *Award:* Scholarship for use in freshman or sophomore years; renewable. *Award amount:* $436–$3985. *Number of awards:* 1671. *Eligibility Requirements:* Applicant must be enrolled or expecting to enroll full-time at a technical institution; resident of Louisiana and studying in Louisiana. Applicant must have 2.5 GPA or higher. Available to U.S. citizens. *Application Requirements:* Application form, application form may be submitted online (http://www.osfa.la.gov), FAFSA, test scores, transcript. **Deadline:** July 1.

MAINE

American Legion Auxiliary Department of Maine Daniel E. Lambert Memorial Scholarship. Scholarships to assist young men and women in continuing their education beyond high school. Must demonstrate financial need, must be a resident of the State of Maine, U.S. citizen, and parent must be a veteran. *Award:* Scholarship

for use in freshman year; not renewable. *Award amount:* $1000. *Number of awards:* up to 2. *Eligibility Requirements:* Applicant must be high school student; planning to enroll or expecting to enroll full-time at a four-year institution or university and resident of Maine. Available to U.S. citizens. Applicant or parent must meet one or more of the following requirements: general military experience; retired from active duty; disabled or killed as a result of military service; prisoner of war; or missing in action. *Application Requirements:* Application form, financial need analysis. **Deadline:** May 1.

Contact Mary Wells, Education Chairman. *E-mail:* aladeptsecme@verizon.net. *Phone:* 207-532-6007. *Website:* http://www.mainelegion.org/.

American Legion Auxiliary Department of Maine Past Presidents' Parley Nurses Scholarship. One-time award for child, grandchild, sister, or brother of veteran. Must be resident of Maine and wishing to continue education at accredited school in medical field. Must submit photo, doctor's statement, and evidence of civic activity. Minimum 3.5 GPA required. Health and Medical Sciences; Nursing. *Award:* Scholarship for use in freshman, sophomore, junior, or senior years; not renewable. *Award amount:* $300. *Number of awards:* 1. *Eligibility Requirements:* Applicant must be enrolled or expecting to enroll full-time at a two-year or four-year or technical institution or university and resident of Maine. Applicant or parent of applicant must have employment or volunteer experience in community service. Applicant must have 2.5 GPA or higher. Available to U.S. citizens. Applicant or parent must meet one or more of the following requirements: general military experience; retired from active duty; disabled or killed as a result of military service; prisoner of war; or missing in action. *Application Requirements:* Application form, doctor's statement, personal photograph, recommendations or references, transcript. **Deadline:** March 31.

Contact Mary Wells, Education Chairman. *E-mail:* aladeptsecme@verizon.net. *Phone:* 207-532-6007. *Website:* http://www.mainelegion.org/.

Early College for ME. Scholarship for high school students who in their junior year have not made plans for college but

are academically capable of success in college. Recipients are selected by their school principal or Guidance Director. Students must be entering a Maine Community College. Refer to web site http://www.mccs.me.edu/our-programs/programs-for-high-school-students/early-college/ *Award:* Scholarship for use in freshman or sophomore years; renewable. *Award amount:* $2000. *Number of awards:* 400–500. *Eligibility Requirements:* Applicant must be high school student; planning to enroll or expecting to enroll full-time at a two-year institution; resident of Maine and studying in Maine. Available to U.S. citizens. *Application Requirements:* Application form, financial need analysis. **Deadline:** April 15.

Contact Mercedes Pour, State Director, Early College for ME, Maine Community College System, 6 Fundy Road, Suite 300, Falmouth, ME 04105. *E-mail:* mpour@mccs.me.edu. *Phone:* 207-699-4897. *Website:* http://www.mccs.me.edu/.

Maine Rural Rehabilitation Fund Scholarship Program. One-time scholarship open to Maine residents enrolled in or accepted by any school, college, or university. Must be full-time and demonstrate financial need. Those opting for a Maine institution given preference. Major must lead to an agricultural career. Minimum 3.0 GPA required. Agribusiness; Agriculture; Animal/Veterinary Sciences. *Award:* Scholarship for use in freshman, sophomore, junior, senior, graduate, or postgraduate years; not renewable. *Award amount:* $800–$2000. *Number of awards:* 10–20. *Eligibility Requirements:* Applicant must be enrolled or expecting to enroll full-time at a two-year or four-year or technical institution or university and resident of Maine. Applicant must have 3.0 GPA or higher. Available to U.S. citizens. *Application Requirements:* Application form, driver's license, financial need analysis, transcript. **Deadline:** June 15.

Contact Jane Aiudi, Director of Marketing. *E-mail:* jane.aiudi@maine.gov. *Phone:* 207-287-7628. *Fax:* 207-287-5576. *Website:* http://www.maine.gov/agriculture.

State of Maine Grant Program. Scholarship for residents of Maine, attending an eligible school in Maine, Connecticut, Massachusetts, New Hampshire, Rhode Island, or Vermont. Award based on need. Students attending out-of-state institutions must be participating in the New England Regional Tuition Break Program to be eligible. Students must apply annually. Complete free application for Federal Student Aid to apply. One-time award for undergraduate study. For further information see web site http://www.famemaine.com. *Award:* Grant for use in freshman, sophomore, junior, or senior years; not renewable. *Award amount:* $1500. *Number of awards:* 15,831. *Eligibility Requirements:* Applicant must be enrolled or expecting to enroll full- or part-time at a two-year or four-year or technical institution or university; resident of Maine and studying in Connecticut, Maine, Massachusetts, New Hampshire, Rhode Island, Vermont. Available to U.S. citizens. *Application Requirements:* Application form, financial need analysis. **Deadline:** May 1.

Contact Claude Roy, Education Services Officer, Finance Authority of Maine, 5 Community Drive, Augusta, ME 04332. *E-mail:* education@famemaine.com. *Phone:* 207-620-3507. *Website:* http://www.famemaine.com/.

Tuition Waiver Programs. Provides tuition waivers for children and spouses of EMS personnel, firefighters, and law enforcement officers who have been killed in the line of duty and for students who were foster children under the custody of the Department of Human Services when they graduated from high school. Waivers valid at the University of Maine System, the Maine Technical College System, and Maine Maritime Academy. Applicant must reside and study in Maine. *Award:* Grant for use in freshman, sophomore, junior, or senior years; renewable. *Number of awards:* 30. *Eligibility Requirements:* Applicant must be enrolled or expecting to enroll full- or part-time at a two-year or four-year institution or university; resident of Maine and studying in Maine. Applicant or parent of applicant must have employment or volunteer experience in police/firefighting. Available to U.S. citizens. *Application Requirements:* Application form. **Deadline:** continuous.

Contact Claude Roy, Education Services Officer, Finance Authority of Maine, 5 Community Drive, Augusta, ME 04332. *E-mail:* education@famemaine.com. *Phone:* 207-620-3507. *Website:* http://www.famemaine.com/.

Veterans Dependents Educational Benefits-Maine. Tuition waiver award for dependent children who have not reached their 22nd birthday or spouses of veterans permanently and totally disabled resulting from service-connected disability; died from a service-connected disability; at time of death was totally and permanently disabled due to service-connected disability, but whose death was not related to the service-connected disability; or member of the Armed Forces on active duty who has been listed for more than 90 days as missing in action, captured or forcibly detained or interned in the line of duty. Benefits apply only to the University of Maine System, Maine community colleges and Maine Maritime Academy. Must be high school graduate. Must submit with application proof of veteran's VA disability along with dependent verification paperwork such as birth, marriage, or adoption certificate and proof of enrollment in degree program. *Award:* Scholarship for use in freshman, sophomore, junior, or senior years; not renewable. *Eligibility Requirements:* Applicant must be enrolled or expecting to enroll full- or part-time at a two-year or four-year institution or university; resident of Maine and studying in Maine. Available to U.S. citizens. Applicant or parent must meet one or more of the following requirements: general military experience; retired from active duty; disabled or killed as a result of military service; prisoner of war; or missing in action. *Application Requirements:* Application form, see application.

Contact Mrs. Paula Gagnon, Office Associate II, Maine Veterans Services, State House Station 117, Augusta, ME 04333-0117. *E-mail:* mainebvs@maine.gov. *Phone:* 207-430-6035. *Fax:* 207-626-4471. *Website:* http://www.maine.gov/dvem/bvs.

MARYLAND

Charles W. Riley Fire and Emergency Medical Services Tuition Reimbursement Program. Award intended to reimburse members of rescue organizations serving Maryland communities for tuition costs of course work towards a degree or certificate in fire service or medical technology. Must attend a two- or four-year school in Maryland. Minimum 2.0 GPA. The scholarship is worth up to $6500. Fire Sciences;

Health and Medical Sciences; Trade/Technical Specialties. *Award:* Scholarship for use in freshman, sophomore, junior, or senior years; not renewable. *Award amount:* $1–$6500. *Number of awards:* 1–150. *Eligibility Requirements:* Applicant must be enrolled or expecting to enroll full- or part-time at a two-year or four-year institution or university; resident of Maryland and studying in Maryland. Applicant or parent of applicant must have employment or volunteer experience in police/firefighting. Available to U.S. citizens. *Application Requirements:* Application form. **Deadline:** June 1.

Contact Donna Thomas, Office of Student Financial Assistance, Maryland State Higher Education Commission, 6 North Liberty Street, Baltimore, MD 21202. *E-mail:* donnae.thomas@maryland.gov. *Phone:* 410-767-3109. *Website:* http://www.mhec.state.md.us/.

Delegate Scholarship Program-Maryland. Delegate scholarships help Maryland residents attending Maryland degree-granting institutions, certain career schools, or nursing diploma schools. May attend out-of-state institution if Maryland Higher Education Commission deems major to be unique and not offered at a Maryland institution. Free Application for Federal Student Aid may be required. Students interested in this program should apply by contacting their legislative district delegate. *Award:* Scholarship for use in freshman, sophomore, junior, or senior years; not renewable. *Award amount:* $200–$8650. *Number of awards:* up to 3500. *Eligibility Requirements:* Applicant must be enrolled or expecting to enroll full- or part-time at a two-year or four-year or technical institution or university; resident of Maryland and studying in Maryland. Available to U.S. citizens. *Application Requirements:* Application form, FAFSA. **Deadline:** continuous.

Contact Monica Wheatley, Office of Student Financial Assistance, Maryland State Higher Education Commission, 839 Bestgate Road, Suite 400, Annapolis, MD 21401-3013. *E-mail:* osfamail@mhec.state.md.us. *Phone:* 800-974-1024. *Fax:* 410-260-3200. *Website:* http://www.mhec.state.md.us/.

Edward T. Conroy Memorial Scholarship Program. Scholarship for dependents of deceased or 100 percent disabled U.S. Armed Forces personnel;

the son, daughter, or surviving spouse of a victim of the September 11, 2001 terrorist attacks who died as a result of the attacks on the World Trade Center in New York City, the attack on the Pentagon in Virginia, or the crash of United Airlines Flight 93 in Pennsylvania; a POW/MIA of the Vietnam Conflict or his/her son or daughter; the son, daughter or surviving spouse (who has not remarried) of a state or local public safety employee or volunteer who died in the line of duty; or a state or local public safety employee or volunteer who was 100 percent disabled in the line of duty. Must be Maryland resident at time of disability. Submit applicable VA certification. Must be at least 16 years of age and attend Maryland institution. *Award:* Scholarship for use in freshman, sophomore, junior, or senior years; renewable. *Award amount:* $7200–$9000. *Number of awards:* up to 121. *Eligibility Requirements:* Applicant must be age 16-24; enrolled or expecting to enroll full- or part-time at a two-year or four-year institution or university; resident of Maryland and studying in Maryland. Applicant or parent of applicant must have employment or volunteer experience in police/firefighting. Available to U.S. citizens. Applicant or parent must meet one or more of the following requirements: general military experience; retired from active duty; disabled or killed as a result of military service; prisoner of war; or missing in action. *Application Requirements:* Application form, birth and death certificate, disability papers. **Deadline:** July 15.

Contact Linda Asplin, Office of Student Financial Assistance, Maryland State Higher Education Commission, 839 Bestgate Road, Suite 400, Annapolis, MD 21401-3013. *E-mail:* lasplin@mhec.state.md.us. *Phone:* 410-260-4563. *Fax:* 410-260-3203. *Website:* http://www.mhec.state.md.us/.

Graduate and Professional Scholarship Program-Maryland. Graduate and professional scholarships provide need-based financial assistance to students attending a Maryland school of medicine, dentistry, law, pharmacy, social work, or nursing. Funds are provided to specific Maryland colleges and universities. Students must demonstrate financial need and be Maryland residents. Contact institution financial aid office for more information. Dental Health/Services; Health and Medical Sciences; Law/Legal Services; Nursing; Social Services. *Award:* Scholarship for use in freshman, sophomore, junior, or senior years; renewable. *Award amount:* $1000–$5000. *Number of awards:* up to 584. *Eligibility Requirements:* Applicant must be enrolled or expecting to enroll full- or part-time at a four-year institution or university; resident of Maryland and studying in Maryland. Available to U.S. citizens. *Application Requirements:* Application form, contact institution financial aid office, financial need analysis. **Deadline:** March 1.

Contact Monica Wheatley, Program Manager, Maryland State Higher Education Commission, 839 Bestgate Road, Suite 400, Annapolis, MD 21401. *E-mail:* mwheatle@mhec.state.md.us. *Phone:* 410-260-4560. *Fax:* 410-260-3202. *Website:* http://www.mhec.state.md.us/.

Howard P. Rawlings Educational Excellence Awards Educational Assistance Grant. Award for Maryland residents accepted or enrolled in a full-time undergraduate degree or certificate program at a Maryland institution or hospital nursing school. Must submit financial aid form by March 1. Must earn 2.0 GPA in college to maintain award. *Award:* Grant for use in freshman, sophomore, junior, or senior years; renewable. *Award amount:* $400–$2700. *Number of awards:* 15,000–30,000. *Eligibility Requirements:* Applicant must be enrolled or expecting to enroll full-time at a two-year or four-year institution or university; resident of Maryland and studying in Maryland. Available to U.S. citizens. *Application Requirements:* Application form, financial need analysis. **Deadline:** March 1.

Howard P. Rawlings Educational Excellence Awards Guaranteed Access Grant. Award for Maryland resident enrolling full-time in an undergraduate program at a Maryland institution. Must be under 21 at time of first award and begin college within one year of completing high school in Maryland with a minimum 2.5 GPA. Must have an annual family income less than 130 percent of the federal poverty level guideline. *Award:* Grant for use in freshman, sophomore, junior, or senior years; renewable. *Award amount:* $400–$14,800. *Number of awards:* up to 1000.

Eligibility Requirements: Applicant must be enrolled or expecting to enroll full-time at a two-year or four-year institution or university; resident of Maryland and studying in Maryland. Applicant must have 3.5 GPA or higher. Available to U.S. citizens. *Application Requirements:* Application form, financial need analysis, transcript. **Deadline:** March 1.

Contact Theresa Lowe, Office of Student Financial Assistance, Maryland State Higher Education Commission, 839 Bestgate Road, Suite 400, Annapolis, MD 21401-3013. *E-mail:* osfamail@mhec.state.md.us. *Phone:* 410-260-4555. *Fax:* 410-260-3200. *Website:* http://www.mhec.state.md.us/.

Janet L. Hoffmann Loan Assistance Repayment Program. Provides assistance for repayment of loan debt to Maryland residents working full-time in nonprofit organizations and state or local governments. Must submit Employment Verification Form and Lender Verification Form. Education; Law/Legal Services; Nursing; Social Services; Therapy/Rehabilitation. *Award:* Grant for use in freshman, sophomore, junior, or senior years; not renewable. *Award amount:* $1500–$10,000. *Number of awards:* up to 700. *Eligibility Requirements:* Applicant must be enrolled or expecting to enroll full-time at a four-year institution or university; resident of Maryland and studying in Maryland. Applicant or parent of applicant must have employment or volunteer experience in government/politics. Available to U.S. citizens. *Application Requirements:* Application form, IRS 1040 form, transcript. **Deadline:** September 30.

Contact Tamika McKelvin, Office of Student Financial Assistance, Maryland State Higher Education Commission, 839 Bestgate Road, Suite 400, Annapolis, MD 21401. *E-mail:* tmckelvin@mhec.state.md.us. *Phone:* 410-260-4546. *Fax:* 410-260-3203. *Website:* http://www.mhec.state.md.us/.

J.F. Tolbert Memorial Student Grant Program. Awards of $500 granted to Maryland residents attending a private career school in Maryland. The scholarship deadline continues. *Award:* Grant for use in freshman or sophomore years; not renewable. *Award amount:* $500. *Number of awards:* 522. *Eligibility Requirements:* Applicant must be enrolled or expecting to enroll full-time at a technical institution; resident of Maryland and studying in Maryland. Available to U.S. citizens. *Application Requirements:* Application form, financial need analysis. **Deadline:** continuous.

Contact Glenda Hamlet, Office of Student Financial Assistance, Maryland State Higher Education Commission, 839 Bestgate Road, Suite 400, Annapolis, MD 21401-3013. *E-mail:* osfamail@mhec.state.md.us. *Phone:* 800-974-1024. *Fax:* 410-260-3200. *Website:* http://www.mhec.state.md.us/.

Part-Time Grant Program-Maryland. Funds provided to Maryland colleges and universities. Eligible students must be enrolled on a part-time basis (6 to 11 credits) in an undergraduate degree program. Must demonstrate financial need and also be Maryland resident. Contact financial aid office at institution for more information. *Award:* Grant for use in freshman, sophomore, junior, or senior years; renewable. *Award amount:* $200–$1500. *Number of awards:* 1800–9000. *Eligibility Requirements:* Applicant must be enrolled or expecting to enroll part-time at a two-year or four-year institution or university; resident of Maryland and studying in Maryland. Available to U.S. citizens. *Application Requirements:* Application form, financial need analysis. **Deadline:** March 1.

Contact Monica Wheatley, Program Manager, Maryland State Higher Education Commission, 839 Bestgate Road, Suite 400, Annapolis, MD 21401. *E-mail:* mwheatle@mhec.state.md.us. *Phone:* 410-260-4560. *Fax:* 410-260-3202. *Website:* http://www.mhec.state.md.us/.

Senatorial Scholarships-Maryland. Renewable award for Maryland residents attending a Maryland degree-granting institution, nursing diploma school, or certain private career schools. May be used out-of-state only if Maryland Higher Education Commission deems major to be unique and not offered at Maryland institution. The scholarship value is $400 to $7000. *Award:* Scholarship for use in freshman, sophomore, junior, or senior years; renewable. *Award amount:* $400–$7000. *Number of awards:* up to 7000. *Eligibility Requirements:* Applicant must be enrolled or expecting to enroll full- or part-time at a two-year or four-year or technical institution or university; res-

ident of Maryland and studying in Maryland. Available to U.S. citizens. *Application Requirements:* Application form, financial need analysis, test scores. **Deadline:** March 1.

Contact Monica Wheatley, Office of Student Financial Assistance, Maryland State Higher Education Commission, 839 Bestgate Road, Suite 400, Annapolis, MD 21401-3013. *E-mail:* osfamail@mhec.state.md.us. *Phone:* 800-974-1024. *Fax:* 410-260-3200. *Website:* http://www.mhec.state.md.us/.

Tuition Reduction for Non-Resident Nursing Students. Available to nonresidents of Maryland who attend a two-year or four-year public institution in Maryland. It is renewable provided student maintains academic requirements designated by institution attended. Recipient must agree to serve as a full-time nurse in a hospital or related institution for two to four years. Nursing. *Award:* Scholarship for use in freshman, sophomore, junior, or senior years; renewable. *Eligibility Requirements:* Applicant must be enrolled or expecting to enroll full- or part-time at a two-year or four-year institution and studying in Maryland. Available to U.S. citizens. *Application Requirements:* Application form. **Deadline:** varies.

Contact Robert Parker, Director. *E-mail:* rparker@mhec.state.md.us. *Phone:* 410-260-4558. *Website:* http://www.mhec.state.md.us/.

Tuition Waiver for Foster Care Recipients. Applicant must be a high school graduate or GED recipient and under the age of 21. Must either have resided in a foster care home in Maryland at the time of high school graduation or GED reception, or until 14th birthday, and been adopted after 14th birthday. Applicant, if status approved, will be exempt from paying tuition and mandatory fees at a public college in Maryland. *Award:* Grant for use in freshman, sophomore, junior, senior, or graduate years; renewable. *Eligibility Requirements:* Applicant must be enrolled or expecting to enroll full- or part-time at a two-year or four-year institution or university; resident of Maryland and studying in Maryland. Available to U.S. citizens. *Application Requirements:* Application form, financial need analysis, must inquire at financial aid office of schools. **Deadline:** March 1.

Contact Robert Parker, Director. *E-mail:* rparker@mhec.state.md.us. *Phone:* 410-260-4558. *Website:* http://www.mhec.state.md.us/.

Veterans of the Afghanistan and Iraq Conflicts Scholarship Program. Provides financial assistance to Maryland resident U.S. Armed Forces personnel who served in Afghanistan or Iraq conflicts and their children or spouses who are attending Maryland institutions. *Award:* Scholarship for use in freshman, sophomore, junior, or senior years; renewable. *Award amount:* $8850. *Number of awards:* 123. *Eligibility Requirements:* Applicant must be enrolled or expecting to enroll full- or part-time at a two-year or four-year institution or university; resident of Maryland and studying in Maryland. Available to U.S. citizens. Applicant or parent must meet one or more of the following requirements: general military experience; retired from active duty; disabled or killed as a result of military service; prisoner of war; or missing in action. *Application Requirements:* Application form, birth certificate/marriage certificate, documentation of military order, financial need analysis. **Deadline:** March 1.

Contact Linda Asplin, Program Administrator, Maryland State Higher Education Commission, 839 Bestgate Road, Suite 400, Annapolis, MD 21401-3013. *E-mail:* lasplin@mhec.state.md.us. *Phone:* 410-260-4563. *Fax:* 410-260-3203. *Website:* http://www.mhec.state.md.us/.

Workforce Shortage Student Assistance Grant Program. Scholarship of $4000 available to students who will be required to major in specific areas and will be obligated to serve in the state of Maryland after completion of degree. *Award:* Scholarship for use in freshman, sophomore, junior, or senior years; renewable. *Award amount:* $4000. *Number of awards:* 1300. *Eligibility Requirements:* Applicant must be enrolled or expecting to enroll full- or part-time at a two-year or four-year institution or university; resident of Maryland and studying in Maryland. Available to U.S. citizens. *Application Requirements:* Application form, certain majors require additional documentation, essay, financial need analysis, recommendations or references, resume, transcript. **Deadline:** July 1.

Contact Maura Sappington, Program Manager, Maryland State Higher Education Commission, 839 Bestgate Road, Suite 400, Annapolis, MD 21401-3013. *E-mail:* msapping@mhec.state.md.us. *Phone:* 410-260-4569. *Fax:* 410-260-3203. *Website:* http://www.mhec.state.md.us/.

MASSACHUSETTS

Agnes M. Lindsay Scholarship. Scholarships for students with demonstrated financial need who are from rural areas of Massachusetts and attend public institutions of higher education in Massachusetts. Deadline varies. *Award:* Scholarship for use in freshman, sophomore, junior, or senior years; not renewable. *Eligibility Requirements:* Applicant must be enrolled or expecting to enroll full-time at a two-year or four-year institution or university; resident of Massachusetts and studying in Massachusetts. Available to U.S. citizens. *Application Requirements:* Application form, financial need analysis. **Deadline:** varies.

Contact Robert Brun, Director of Scholarships and Grants. *E-mail:* osfa@osfa.mass.edu. *Phone:* 617-727-9420. *Fax:* 617-727-0667. *Website:* http://www.osfa.mass.edu/.

Catherine E. Philbin Scholarship. One scholarship of up to $500 will be awarded to a graduate or undergraduate student studying public health. Eligible applicants will be residents of Massachusetts. Along with the application, students must send a personal statement of no more than 500 words addressing professional goals and financial need. Public Health. *Award:* Scholarship for use in freshman, sophomore, junior, senior, or graduate years; not renewable. *Award amount:* $500. *Number of awards:* 1. *Eligibility Requirements:* Applicant must be enrolled or expecting to enroll full-time at a four-year institution or university and resident of Massachusetts. Available to U.S. citizens. *Application Requirements:* Application form, essay. **Deadline:** March 1.

Christian A. Herter Memorial Scholarship. Renewable award for Massachusetts residents who are in the tenth and eleventh grades, and whose socio-economic backgrounds and environment may inhibit their ability to attain educational goals. Must exhibit severe personal or family-related difficulties, medical problems, or have overcome a personal obstacle. Provides up to 50 percent of the student's calculated need, as determined by federal methodology, at the college of their choice within the continental United States. *Award:* Scholarship for use in freshman, sophomore, junior, or senior years, renewable. *Award amount:* up to $15,000. *Number of awards:* 25. *Eligibility Requirements:* Applicant must be high school student; planning to enroll or expecting to enroll full-time at a two-year or four-year or technical institution or university and resident of Massachusetts. Applicant must have 2.5 GPA or higher. Available to U.S. citizens. *Application Requirements:* Application form, community service, financial need analysis, interview, recommendations or references. **Deadline:** February 1.

Contact Robert Brun, Director of Scholarships and Grants. *E-mail:* osfa@osfa.mass.edu. *Phone:* 617-727-9420. *Fax:* 617-727-0667. *Website:* http://www.osfa.mass.edu/.

Dorchester Women's Club Music Scholarship. Scholarship for undergraduate major in voice. Applicant must be a Massachusetts resident and an undergraduate currently enrolled in a four-year accredited college, university or school of music, majoring in voice. Music; Performing Arts. *Award:* Scholarship for use in sophomore, junior, or senior years; not renewable. *Award amount:* $500. *Number of awards:* 1. *Eligibility Requirements:* Applicant must be enrolled or expecting to enroll full-time at a four-year institution or university and resident of Massachusetts. Available to U.S. citizens. *Application Requirements:* Application form, driver's license, interview. **Deadline:** March 1.

DSS Adopted Children Tuition Waiver. Need-based tuition waiver for Massachusetts residents who are full-time undergraduate students. Must attend a Massachusetts public institution of higher education and be under 24 years of age. File the FAFSA after January 1. Contact school financial aid office for more information. *Award:* Scholarship for use in freshman, sophomore, junior, or senior years; renewable. *Eligibility Requirements:* Applicant must be enrolled or expecting to enroll full-time at a two-year or four-year institution and resident of Massachusetts. Available to U.S. and non-Canadian citizens. *Application Requirements:* Application form, FAFSA, financial need analysis. **Deadline:** varies.

Contact Robert Brun, Director of Scholarships and Grants. *E-mail:* osfa@osfa.mass.edu. *Phone:* 617-727-9420. *Fax:* 617-727-0667. *Website:* http://www.osfa.mass.edu/.

Early Childhood Educators Scholarship Program. Scholarship to provide financial assistance for currently employed early childhood educators and providers who enroll in an associate or bachelor degree program in Early Childhood Education or related programs. Awards are not based on financial need. Individuals taking their first college-level ECE course are eligible for 100 percent tuition, while subsequent ECE courses are awarded at 50 percent tuition. Can be used for one class each semester. Education. *Award:* Scholarship for use in freshman, sophomore, junior, or senior years; not renewable. *Award amount:* $150–$3600. *Eligibility Requirements:* Applicant must be enrolled or expecting to enroll full- or part-time at a four-year institution or university. Available to U.S. citizens. *Application Requirements:* Application form. **Deadline:** July 1.

Contact Robert Brun, Director of Scholarships and Grants. *E-mail:* osfa@osfa.mass.edu. *Phone:* 617-727-9420. *Fax:* 617-727-0667. *Website:* http://www.osfa.mass.edu/.

John and Abigail Adams Scholarship. Scholarship to reward and inspire student achievement, attract more high-performing students to Massachusetts public higher education, and provide families of college-bound students with financial assistance. Must be a U.S. citizen or an eligible non-citizen. There is no application process for the scholarship. Students who are eligible will be notified in the fall of their senior year in high school. *Award:* Scholarship for use in freshman year; not renewable. *Eligibility Requirements:* Applicant must be high school student; planning to enroll or expecting to enroll full-time at a two-year or four-year institution or university; resident of Massachusetts and studying in Massachusetts. Applicant must have 3.0 GPA or higher. Available to U.S. citizens. *Application Requirements:* **Deadline:** varies.

Contact Robert Brun, Director of Scholarships and Grants. *E-mail:* osfa@

osfa.mass.edu. *Phone:* 617-727-9420. *Fax:* 617-727-0667. *Website:* http://www.osfa.mass.edu/.

Massachusetts Assistance for Student Success Program. Provides need-based financial assistance to Massachusetts residents to attend undergraduate post-secondary institutions in Connecticut, Maine, Massachusetts, New Hampshire, Pennsylvania, Rhode Island, Vermont, and District of Columbia. High school seniors may apply. Expected Family Contribution (EFC) should be $3850. Timely filing of FAFSA required. *Award:* Grant for use in freshman, sophomore, junior, or senior years; not renewable. *Award amount:* $300–$1600. *Number of awards:* 50,000–57,000. *Eligibility Requirements:* Applicant must be enrolled or expecting to enroll full-time at a two-year or four-year or technical institution or university; resident of Massachusetts and studying in Connecticut, District of Columbia, Maine, Massachusetts, New Hampshire, Pennsylvania, Rhode Island, Vermont. Available to U.S. citizens. *Application Requirements:* FAFSA, financial need analysis. **Deadline:** May 1.

Contact Robert Brun, Director of Scholarships and Grants. *E-mail:* osfa@osfa.mass.edu. *Phone:* 617-727-9420. *Fax:* 617-727-0667. *Website:* http://www.osfa.mass.edu/.

Massachusetts Cash Grant Program. A need-based grant to assist with mandatory fees and non-state supported tuition. This supplemental award is available to Massachusetts residents, who are undergraduates at public two-year, four-year colleges and universities in Massachusetts. Must file FAFSA before May 1. Contact college financial aid office for information. *Award:* Grant for use in freshman, sophomore, junior, or senior years; not renewable. *Eligibility Requirements:* Applicant must be enrolled or expecting to enroll full-time at a two-year or four-year institution or university and resident of Massachusetts. Available to U.S. citizens. *Application Requirements:* Application form, FAFSA, financial need analysis. **Deadline:** continuous.

Contact Robert Brun, Director of Scholarships and Grants. *E-mail:* osfa@osfa.mass.edu. *Phone:* 617-727-9420. *Fax:* 617-727-0667. *Website:* http://www.osfa.mass.edu/.

Massachusetts Gilbert Matching Student Grant Program. Grants for permanent Massachusetts residents attending an independent, regionally accredited Massachusetts school or school of nursing full-time. Must be U.S. citizen and permanent legal resident of Massachusetts. File the Free Application for Federal Student Aid after January 1. Contact college financial aid office for complete details and deadlines. *Award:* Grant for use in freshman, sophomore, junior, or senior years; not renewable. *Award amount:* $200–$2500. *Eligibility Requirements:* Applicant must be enrolled or expecting to enroll full-time at a four-year institution or university; resident of Massachusetts and studying in Massachusetts. Available to U.S. citizens. *Application Requirements:* FAFSA, financial need analysis. **Deadline:** varies.

Contact Robert Brun, Director of Scholarships and Grants, Massachusetts Office of Student Financial Assistance, 454 Broadway, Suite 200, Revere, MA 02151. *E-mail:* rbrun@osfa.mass.edu. *Phone:* 617-727-9420. *Fax:* 617-727-0667. *Website:* http://www.osfa.mass.edu/.

Massachusetts Part-Time Grant Program. Award for permanent Massachusetts residents who have enrolled part-time for at least one year in a state-approved postsecondary school. The recipient must not have a Bachelor's degree. FAFSA must be filed before May 1. Contact college financial aid office for further information. *Award:* Grant for use in freshman, sophomore, junior, or senior years; not renewable. *Award amount:* $200–$1150. *Number of awards:* 200. *Eligibility Requirements:* Applicant must be enrolled or expecting to enroll part-time at a two-year or four-year or technical institution or university and resident of Massachusetts. Available to U.S. citizens. *Application Requirements:* Application form, FAFSA, financial need analysis. **Deadline:** varies.

Contact Robert Brun, Director of Scholarships and Grants. *E-mail:* osfa@osfa.mass.edu. *Phone:* 617-727-9420. *Fax:* 617-727-0667. *Website:* http://www.osfa.mass.edu/.

Massachusetts Public Service Grant Program. Scholarships for children and/or spouses of deceased members of fire, police, and corrections departments, who were killed in the line of duty. Awards Massachusetts residents attending Massachusetts institutions. Applicant should have not received a prior Bachelor's degree or its equivalent. *Award:* Grant for use in freshman, sophomore, junior, or senior years; not renewable. *Award amount:* $910–$1714. *Eligibility Requirements:* Applicant must be enrolled or expecting to enroll full-time at a four-year institution or university; resident of Massachusetts and studying in Massachusetts. Applicant or parent of applicant must have employment or volunteer experience in police/firefighting. Available to U.S. citizens. Applicant must have general military experience. *Application Requirements:* Application form, copy of birth certificate, copy of veteran's death certificate, financial need analysis. **Deadline:** May 1.

New England Regional Student Program-Tuition Break. Tuition discount for residents of six New England states (Connecticut, Maine, Massachusetts, New Hampshire, Rhode Island, Vermont). Students pay reduced out-of-state tuition at public colleges or universities in other New England states when enrolling in certain majors not offered at public institutions in home state. Details are available at http://www.nebhe.org/tuitionbreak. *Award:* Scholarship for use in freshman, sophomore, junior, senior, or graduate years; renewable. *Eligibility Requirements:* Applicant must be enrolled or expecting to enroll full- or part-time at a two-year or four-year institution or university; resident of Connecticut, Maine, Massachusetts, New Hampshire, Rhode Island, Vermont and studying in Connecticut, Maine, Massachusetts, New Hampshire, Rhode Island, Vermont. Available to U.S. citizens. *Application Requirements:* **Deadline:** continuous.

Contact Wendy Lindsay, Senior Director of Regional Student Program, New England Board of Higher Education, 45 Temple Place, Boston, MA 02111. *E-mail:* tuitionbreak@nebhe.org. *Phone:* 617-533-9511. *Website:* http://www.nebhe.org/.

Paraprofessional Teacher Preparation Grant. Grant providing financial aid assistance to Massachusetts residents, who are currently employed as paraprofessionals in Massachusetts public schools and wish to obtain higher education and become certified as full-time teachers. Education. *Award:* Grant for use in freshman, sophomore, junior, or senior years; not renewable. *Award amount:* $250–$7500. *Eligibility Requirements:* Applicant must be enrolled or expecting to enroll full- or part-time at a two-year or four-year institution or university and resident of Massachusetts. Available to U.S. citizens. *Application Requirements:* Application form, FAFSA. **Deadline:** August 1.

Contact Robert Brun, Director of Scholarships and Grants. *E-mail:* osfa@osfa.mass.edu. *Phone:* 617-727-9420. *Fax:* 617-727-0667. *Website:* http://www.osfa.mass.edu/.

MICHIGAN

American Legion Auxiliary Department of Michigan Medical Career Scholarship. Award for training in Michigan as registered nurse, licensed practical nurse, physical therapist, respiratory therapist, or in any medical career. Must be child, grandchild, great-grandchild, wife, or widow of honorably discharged or deceased veteran who has served during the eligibility dates for American Legion membership. Must be Michigan resident attending a Michigan school. Health and Medical Sciences; Nursing; Therapy/Rehabilitation. *Award:* Scholarship for use in freshman year; not renewable. *Award amount:* $500. *Number of awards:* 10–20. *Eligibility Requirements:* Applicant must be enrolled or expecting to enroll full-time at a two-year or four-year or technical institution or university; resident of Michigan and studying in Michigan. Applicant must have 3.5 GPA or higher. Available to U.S. citizens. Applicant must have general military experience. *Application Requirements:* Application form, financial need analysis. **Deadline:** March 15.

American Legion Auxiliary Department of Michigan Memorial Scholarship. Scholarship for daughter, granddaughter, and great-granddaughter of any honorably discharged or deceased veteran of U.S. wars or conflicts. Must be Michigan resident for minimum of one year, female between 16 and 21 years, and attend college in Michigan. Must include copy of military discharge and copy of parent or guardian's IRS 1040 form. *Award:* Scholarship for use in freshman or soph-omore years; not renewable. *Award amount:* $500. *Number of awards:* 10–20. *Eligibility Requirements:* Applicant must be age 16-21; enrolled or expecting to enroll full-time at a two-year or four-year or technical institution or university; female; resident of Michigan and studying in Michigan. Available to U.S. citizens. Applicant must have general military experience. *Application Requirements:* Application form, financial need analysis. **Deadline:** March 15.

American Legion Auxiliary Department of Michigan Scholarship for Non-Traditional Student. Applicant must be a dependent of a veteran. Must be one of the following: nontraditional student returning to classroom after some period of time in which their education was interrupted, student over the age of 22 attending college for the first time to pursue a degree, or student over the age of 22 attending a trade or vocational school. Applicants must be Michigan residents only and attend Michigan institution. Judging based on need, character/leadership, scholastic standing, and initiative/goal. *Award:* Scholarship for use in freshman, sophomore, junior, or senior years; renewable. *Award amount:* $500. *Number of awards:* 1. *Eligibility Requirements:* Applicant must be age 22-99; enrolled or expecting to enroll full- or part-time at a two-year or four-year or technical institution or university; resident of Michigan and studying in Michigan. Available to U.S. citizens. Applicant must have general military experience. *Application Requirements:* Application form, financial need analysis. **Deadline:** March 15.

Michigan Competitive Scholarship. Renewable awards for Michigan resident to pursue undergraduate study at a Michigan institution. Awards limited to tuition. Must maintain at least a 2.0 grade point average and meet the college's academic progress requirements. Must file Free Application for Federal Student Aid. http://www.michigan.gov/mistudentaid/0,4636,7-128-60969_61016-274563—,00.html *Award:* Scholarship for use in freshman, sophomore, junior, or senior years; renewable. *Eligibility Requirements:* Applicant must be enrolled or expecting to enroll full- or part-time at a two-year or four-year institution or university;

resident of Michigan and studying in Michigan. Available to U.S. citizens. *Application Requirements:* Application form, financial need analysis. **Deadline:** March 1.

Michigan Tuition Grant. Need-based program. Students must be Michigan residents and attend a Michigan private, nonprofit, degree-granting college. Must file the Free Application for Federal Student Aid and meet the college's academic progress requirements. http://www.michigan.gov/mistudentaid/0,4636,7-128-60969_61016-274564—,00.html *Award:* Grant for use in freshman, sophomore, junior, or senior years; renewable. *Eligibility Requirements:* Applicant must be enrolled or expecting to enroll full- or part-time at a four-year institution or university; resident of Michigan and studying in Michigan. Available to U.S. citizens. *Application Requirements:* Financial need analysis. **Deadline:** June 30.

Tuition Incentive Program. The Tuition Incentive Program (TIP) was established in 1987 under the Annual Higher Education Appropriations Act as an incentive program that encourages eligible students to complete high school by providing tuition assistance for the first two years of college and beyond. Students must be enrolled in courses leading to an associate degree or certificate. Certificate courses are defined as at least a one-year training program that leads to a certificate (or other recognized educational credential), which prepares students for gainful employment in a recognized occupation. Students must meet a Medicaid eligibility history requirement. Eligible students must apply prior to high school graduation (high school diploma or its recognized equivalent). The program targets students with financial need so students are encouraged to also complete the FAFSA. Funds are appropriated annually in the Higher Education Appropriations Act. This program is administered by the Student Scholarships and Grants Division. *Award:* Grant for use in freshman, sophomore, junior, or senior years; renewable. *Eligibility Requirements:* Applicant must be enrolled or expecting to enroll full- or part-time at a two-year or four-year institution or university; resident of Michigan and studying in Michigan. Available to U.S. citizens. *Application Requirements:* Application form.

MINNESOTA

Minnesota GI Bill Program. The Minnesota GI Bill program provides postsecondary financial assistance to eligible Minnesota veterans and service members as well as eligible spouses and children of deceased or severely disabled eligible Minnesota veterans. Full-time undergraduate or graduate students may be eligible to receive up to $1,000 per semester or term and part-time students may be eligible to receive up to $500 per semester or term. Eligible students may receive up to $3,000 per award year and up to the lifetime maximum of $10,000. *Award:* Grant for use in freshman, sophomore, junior, senior, graduate, or postgraduate years; not renewable. *Award amount:* $50–$3000. *Eligibility Requirements:* Applicant must be enrolled or expecting to enroll full- or part-time at a two-year or four-year or technical institution or university; resident of Minnesota and studying in Minnesota. Available to U.S. citizens. *Application Requirements:* Application form. **Deadline:** continuous.

Contact Meghan Flores, State Grant Manager. *E-mail:* meghan.flores@state.mn.us. *Phone:* 651-355-0610. *Website:* http://www.ohe.state.mn.us.

Minnesota Indian Scholarship. The Minnesota Indian Scholarship Program provides postsecondary financial assistance to eligible Minnesota resident students who are of one-fourth or more American Indian ancestry and demonstrate financial need for an award. Scholarships are available to eligible American Indian undergraduate students enrolled at least time and graduate students enrolled at least half time. The award amount is based on need up to $4,000 per year for undergraduate students and up to $6,000 for graduate students. *Award:* Scholarship for use in freshman, sophomore, junior, senior, graduate, or postgraduate years; not renewable. *Eligibility Requirements:* Applicant must be of Arumanian/Ulacedo-Romanian heritage; American Indian/Alaska Native; high school student; planning to enroll or expecting to enroll full- or part-time at a two-year or four-year or technical institution or university; resident of Minnesota and studying in Minnesota. Available to U.S. and Canadian citizens. *Application Requirements:* Application form,

financial need analysis. **Deadline:** continuous.

Contact Meghan Flores, State Grant Manager. *E-mail:* meghan.flores@state.mn.us. *Phone:* 651-355-0610. *Website:* http://www.ohe.state.mn.us.

Minnesota State Grant Program. Need-based grant program available for Minnesota residents attending Minnesota colleges. Student covers 50% of cost with remainder covered by Pell Grant, parent contribution and state grant. Students apply with FAFSA and colleges administer the program on campus. *Award:* Grant for use in freshman, sophomore, junior, or senior years; not renewable. *Award amount:* $100–$11,334. *Number of awards:* 71,000–120,000. *Eligibility Requirements:* Applicant must be enrolled or expecting to enroll full- or part-time at a two-year or four-year or technical institution or university; resident of Minnesota and studying in Minnesota. Available to U.S. citizens. *Application Requirements:* Application form, financial need analysis. **Deadline:** continuous.

Minnesota State Veterans' Dependents Assistance Program. Tuition assistance to dependents of persons considered to be prisoner-of-war or missing in action after August 1, 1958. Must be Minnesota resident attending Minnesota two- or four-year school. *Award:* Scholarship for use in freshman, sophomore, junior, or senior years; renewable. *Award amount:* $249–$250. *Number of awards:* 100–200. *Eligibility Requirements:* Applicant must be enrolled or expecting to enroll full- or part-time at a two-year or four-year institution; resident of Minnesota and studying in Minnesota. Available to U.S. citizens. *Application Requirements:* Application form. **Deadline:** continuous.

Contact Meghan Flores, State Grant Manager. *E-mail:* meghan.flores@state.mn.us. *Phone:* 651-355-0610. *Website:* http://www.ohe.state.mn.us.

Postsecondary Child Care Grant Program-Minnesota. Grant available for students who are not receiving MFIP (TANF) and have children in day care. Based on financial need. Cannot exceed actual child care costs or maximum award chart (based on income). Must be Minnesota resident. For use at Minnesota two- or four-year school, including public technical colleges.

Available until student has attended college for the equivalent of four full-time academic years. *Award:* Grant for use in freshman, sophomore, junior, or senior years; not renewable. *Award amount:* $100–$2800. *Number of awards:* 1–3500. *Eligibility Requirements:* Applicant must be enrolled or expecting to enroll full- or part-time at a two-year or four-year or technical institution or university; resident of Minnesota and studying in Minnesota. Available to U.S. citizens. *Application Requirements:* Application form, financial need analysis. **Deadline:** continuous.

Contact Brenda Larter, Program Administrator, Minnesota Office of Higher Education, 1450 Energy Park Drive, Suite 350, St. Paul, MN 55108-5227. *E-mail:* brenda.larter@state.mn.us. *Phone:* 651-355-0612. *Website:* http://www.ohe.state.mn.us.

Safety Officers' Survivor Grant Program. Grant for eligible survivors of Minnesota public safety officers killed in the line of duty. Safety officers who have been permanently or totally disabled in the line of duty are also eligible. Must be used at a Minnesota institution participating in State Grant Program. Write for details. Must submit proof of death or disability and Public Safety Officers Benefit Fund Certificate. Must apply for renewal each year. Five-year limit on awards. *Award:* Grant for use in freshman, sophomore, junior, senior, or graduate years; not renewable. *Award amount:* $1–$13,840. *Number of awards:* 1–10. *Eligibility Requirements:* Applicant must be enrolled or expecting to enroll full- or part-time at a two-year or four-year or technical institution or university; resident of Minnesota and studying in Minnesota. Applicant or parent of applicant must have employment or volunteer experience in police/firefighting. Available to U.S. citizens. *Application Requirements:* Application form. **Deadline:** continuous.

Contact Brenda Larter, Program Administrator. *E-mail:* brenda.larter@state.mn.us. *Phone:* 651-355-0612. *Website:* http://www.ohe.state.mn.us.

MISSISSIPPI

Higher Education Legislative Plan (HELP). Eligible applicant must be resident of Mississippi and apply for the first time as a freshman and/or sophomore student who graduated from high school within the immediate past two years. Must demonstrate need as determined by the results of the FAFSA, documenting an average family adjusted gross income of $36,500 or less over the prior two years. Must be enrolled full-time at a Mississippi college or university, have a GPA of 2.5, have completed a specific high school core curriculum, and have scored 20 on the ACT. *Award:* Grant for use in freshman, sophomore, junior, or senior years; renewable. *Award amount:* $340–$7344. *Number of awards:* 2661. *Eligibility Requirements:* Applicant must be enrolled or expecting to enroll full-time at a two-year or four-year institution or university; resident of Mississippi and studying in Mississippi. Applicant must have 3.0 GPA or higher. Available to U.S. citizens. *Application Requirements:* Application form, financial need analysis. **Deadline:** March 31.

Law Enforcement Officers/Firemen Scholarship. Financial assistance to dependent children and spouses of any Mississippi law enforcement officer, full-time fire fighter or volunteer fire fighter who has suffered fatal injuries or wounds or become permanently and totally disabled as a result of injuries or wounds which occurred in the performance of the official and appointed duties of his or her office. This financial assistance is offered as an eight semester tuition and room scholarship at any state-supported college or university in Mississippi. *Award:* Scholarship for use in freshman, sophomore, junior, or senior years; renewable. *Award amount:* $2010–$12,854. *Number of awards:* 1–30. *Eligibility Requirements:* Applicant must be enrolled or expecting to enroll full-time at a two-year or four-year institution or university; resident of Mississippi and studying in Mississippi. Applicant or parent of applicant must have employment or volunteer experience in police/firefighting. Applicant must have 2.5 GPA or higher. Available to U.S. citizens. *Application Requirements:* Application form. **Deadline:** continuous.

Mississippi Eminent Scholars Grant. Award for an entering freshmen or as a renewal for sophomore, junior or senior, who are residents of Mississippi. Applicants must achieve a GPA of 3.5 and must have scored 29 on the ACT. Must enroll full-time at an eligible Mississippi college or university. *Award:* Grant for

use in freshman, sophomore, junior, or senior years; not renewable. *Award amount:* $1157–$2500. *Eligibility Requirements:* Applicant must be enrolled or expecting to enroll full-time at a two-year or four-year institution or university; resident of Mississippi and studying in Mississippi. Applicant must have 3.5 GPA or higher. Available to U.S. citizens. *Application Requirements:* Application form. **Deadline:** September 15.

Mississippi Resident Tuition Assistance Grant. Must be a resident of Mississippi enrolled full-time at an eligible Mississippi college or university. Must maintain a minimum 2.5 GPA each semester. MTAG awards may be up to $500 per academic year for freshman and sophomores and $1000 per academic year for juniors and seniors. *Award:* Grant for use in freshman, sophomore, junior, or senior years; not renewable. *Award amount:* $17–$1000. *Eligibility Requirements:* Applicant must be enrolled or expecting to enroll full-time at a two-year or four-year institution or university; resident of Mississippi and studying in Mississippi. Applicant must have 2.5 GPA or higher. Available to U.S. citizens. *Application Requirements:* Application form. **Deadline:** September 15.

MISSOURI

Access Missouri Financial Assistance Program. Need-based program that provides awards to students who are enrolled full-time and have an expected family contribution (EFC) of $12,000 or less based on their Free Application for Federal Student Aid (FAFSA). Awards vary depending on EFC and the type of postsecondary school. *Award:* Grant for use in freshman, sophomore, junior, or senior years; not renewable. *Eligibility Requirements:* Applicant must be enrolled or expecting to enroll full-time at a two-year or technical institution or university; resident of Missouri and studying in Missouri. Applicant must have 2.5 GPA or higher. Available to U.S. citizens. *Application Requirements:* FAFSA on file by April 1.

Lillie Lois Ford Scholarship Fund. Two awards of $1000 each are given each year to one boy and one girl. Applicant must have attended a full session of Missouri Boys/Girls State or Missouri Cadet Patrol Academy. Must

be a Missouri resident below age 21, attending an accredited college/university as a full-time student. Must be an unmarried descendant of a veteran having served at least 90 days on active duty in the Army, Air Force, Navy, Marine Corps, or Coast Guard of the United States. *Award:* Scholarship for use in freshman year; not renewable. *Award amount:* $1000. *Number of awards:* 2. *Eligibility Requirements:* Applicant must be high school student; planning to enroll or expecting to enroll full-time at a two-year or four-year institution or university; single and resident of Missouri. Available to U.S. citizens. Applicant or parent must meet one or more of the following requirements: general military experience; retired from active duty; disabled or killed as a result of military service; prisoner of war; or missing in action. *Application Requirements:* Application form, copy of the veteran's discharge certificate, financial need analysis, test scores. **Deadline:** April 20.

Contact John Doane, Chairman, Education and Scholarship Committee, American Legion Department of Missouri, PO Box 179, Jefferson City, MO 65102-0179. *Phone:* 417-924-8186. *Website:* http://www.missourilegion.org/.

Marguerite Ross Barnett Memorial Scholarship. Scholarship was established for students who are employed while attending school part-time. Must be enrolled at least half-time but less than full-time at a participating Missouri postsecondary school, be employed and compensated for at least 20 hours per week, be 18 years of age, be a Missouri resident and a U.S. citizen or a permanent resident. *Award:* Scholarship for use in freshman, sophomore, junior, or senior years; renewable. *Eligibility Requirements:* Applicant must be enrolled or expecting to enroll part-time at a two-year or four-year or technical institution or university; resident of Missouri and studying in Missouri. Applicant must have 2.5 GPA or higher. Available to U.S. citizens. *Application Requirements:* FAFSA on file by August 1. **Deadline:** August 1.

Missouri Higher Education Academic Scholarship (Bright Flight). Program encourages top-ranked high school seniors to attend approved Missouri postsecondary schools. Must be a Missouri resident and a U.S. citizen or permanent resident. Must have a composite score on the ACT or SAT in the top 5 percent of all Missouri students taking those tests. Students with scores in the top 3 percent are eligible for an annual award of up to $3000 (up to $1500 each semester). Students with scores in the top 4% and 5% are eligible for an annual award of up to $1000 (up to $500 each semester). Award amounts, and the availability of the award for students in the 4% and 5%, are subject to change based on the amount of funding allocated for the program in the legislative session. *Award:* Scholarship for use in freshman, sophomore, junior, or senior years; renewable. *Award amount:* $1000–$3000. *Eligibility Requirements:* Applicant must be enrolled or expecting to enroll full-time at a two-year or four-year or technical institution or university; resident of Missouri and studying in Missouri. Applicant must have 2.5 GPA or higher. Available to U. S. citizens. *Application Requirements:* Test scores.

MONTANA

Montana Higher Education Opportunity Grant. This grant is awarded based on need to undergraduate students attending either part-time or full-time who are residents of Montana and attending participating Montana schools. Awards are limited to the most needy students. A specific major or program of study is not required. This grant does not need to be repaid, and students may apply each year. Apply by filing FAFSA by March 1 and contacting the financial aid office at the admitting college. *Award:* Grant for use in freshman, sophomore, junior, or senior years; not renewable. *Award amount:* $400–$600. *Number of awards:* up to 800. *Eligibility Requirements:* Applicant must be enrolled or expecting to enroll full- or part-time at a two-year or four-year institution or university; resident of Montana and studying in Montana. Available to U.S. citizens. *Application Requirements:* FAFSA, financial need analysis. **Deadline:** March 1.

Contact Jamie Dushin, Budget Analyst, Montana University System, Office of Commissioner of Higher Education, PO Box 203101, Helena, MT 59620-3101. *E-mail:* jdushin@mgslp. state.mt.us. *Phone:* 406-444-0638. *Fax:*

406-444-1869. *Website:* http://www. mus.edu.

Montana Tuition Assistance Program-Baker Grant. Need-based grant for Montana residents attending participating Montana schools who have earned at least $2575 during the previous calendar year. Must be enrolled full-time. Grant does not need to be repaid. Award covers the first undergraduate degree or certificate. Apply by filing FAFSA by March 1 and contacting the financial aid office at the admitting college. *Award:* Grant for use in freshman, sophomore, junior, or senior years; not renewable. *Award amount:* $100–$1000. *Number of awards:* 1000–3000. *Eligibility Requirements:* Applicant must be enrolled or expecting to enroll full-time at a two-year or four-year institution or university; resident of Montana and studying in Montana. Available to U.S. citizens. *Application Requirements:* Application form, FAFSA, financial need analysis, resume. **Deadline:** March 1.

Contact Jamie Dushin, Budget Analyst, Montana University System, Office of Commissioner of Higher Education, PO Box 203101, Helena, MT 59620-3101. *E-mail:* jdushin@mgslp. state.mt.us. *Phone:* 406-444-0638. *Fax:* 406-444-1869. *Website:* http://www. mus.edu.

Montana University System Honor Scholarship. Scholarship will be awarded annually to high school seniors graduating from accredited Montana high schools. The MUS Honor Scholarship is a four year renewable scholarship that waives the tuition and registration fee at one of the Montana University System campuses or one of the three community colleges (Flathead Valley in Kalispell, Miles in Miles City or Dawson in Glendive). The scholarship must be used within 9 months after high school graduation. Applicant must have a minimum GPA of 3.4. *Award:* Scholarship for use in freshman, sophomore, junior, or senior years; renewable. *Award amount:* $4000–$6000. *Number of awards:* up to 200. *Eligibility Requirements:* Applicant must be high school student; planning to enroll or expecting to enroll full-time at a two-year or four-year institution or university; resident of Montana and studying in Montana. Applicant must have 3.5 GPA or higher. Available to U.

S. citizens. *Application Requirements:* Application form, college acceptance letter, test scores, transcript. **Deadline:** March 15.

Contact Sheila Newlun, Grants and Scholarship Coordinator. *E-mail:* snewlun@montana.edu. *Phone:* 406-444-0638. *Fax:* 406-444-1869. *Website:* http://www.mus.edu.

NEBRASKA

Nebraska Opportunity Grant. Available to undergraduates attending a participating postsecondary institution in Nebraska. Must demonstrate financial need. Nebraska residency required. Awards determined by each participating institution. Student must complete the Free Application for Federal Student Aid (FAFSA) to apply. Contact financial aid office at institution for additional information. *Award:* Grant for use in freshman, sophomore, junior, or senior years; not renewable. *Award amount:* $100–$4270. *Eligibility Requirements:* Applicant must be enrolled or expecting to enroll full- or part-time at a two-year or four-year or technical institution or university; resident of Nebraska and studying in Nebraska. Available to U.S. citizens. *Application Requirements:* Application form, financial need analysis. **Deadline:** continuous.

Contact Mr. J. Ritchie Morrow, Financial Aid Officer, Nebraska's Coordinating Commission for Postsecondary Education, 140 North 8th Street, Suite 300, PO Box 95005, Lincoln, NE 68509-5005. *E-mail:* Ritchie.Morrow@ nebraska.gov. *Phone:* 402-471-2847. *Website:* https://ccpe.nebraska.gov/.

NEVADA

CouponChief.com Scholarship Program. We at CouponChief.com want to support young leaders that understand frugality and saving money, and how the skills and knowledge of using coupons can contribute to that end. We will award 1 scholarship winner with $1000 to put towards education every year. *Award:* Scholarship for use in freshman, sophomore, junior, senior, graduate, or postgraduate years; not renewable. *Award amount:* $1000. *Number of awards:* 1. *Eligibility Requirements:* Applicant must be enrolled or expecting to enroll full- or part-time at a two-year or four-year or technical institution or university. Available to U.S. citizens. *Application Requirements:* **Deadline:** July 31.

Governor Guinn Millennium Scholarship. Scholarship for Nevada residents. Student must graduate from a public or private high school within Nevada with a minimum GPA of 3.25. Must complete core curriculum. Maximum award is $10,000. Student must acknowledge award and use it within 6 years of high school graduation. *Award:* Scholarship for use in freshman, sophomore, junior, or senior years; renewable. *Award amount:* up to $10,000. *Number of awards:* 1. *Eligibility Requirements:* Applicant must be enrolled or expecting to enroll full-time at a two-year or four-year institution or university; resident of Nevada and studying in Nevada. Available to U.S. citizens. *Application Requirements:* Application form may be submitted online (http://nevadatreasurer.gov), high schools determine eligibility; student must accept award. **Deadline:** varies.

Contact Linda English, Executive Director. *E-mail:* info@nevadatreasurer. gov. *Phone:* 702-486-3889. *Fax:* 702-486-3246. *Website:* http://www.nevada-treasurer.gov/.

NEW HAMPSHIRE

Scholarships for Orphans of Veterans. Scholarship to provide financial assistance (room, board, books and supplies) to children of parents who served in World War II, Korean Conflict, Vietnam (Southeast Asian Conflict) or the Gulf Wars, or any other operation for which the armed forces expeditionary medal or theater of operations service medal was awarded to the veteran. Must be between the ages of 16 and 25 to qualify and be residents of New Hampshire studying at New Hampshire colleges and universities. *Award:* Scholarship for use in freshman, sophomore, junior, or senior years; renewable. *Award amount:* $1500–$2500. *Number of awards:* 1–10. *Eligibility Requirements:* Applicant must be age 16-25; enrolled or expecting to enroll full-time at a two-year or four-year institution or university; resident of New Hampshire and studying in New Hampshire. Available to U.S. citizens. Applicant or parent must meet one or more of the following requirements: general military experience; retired from active duty; disabled

or killed as a result of military service; prisoner of war; or missing in action. *Application Requirements:* Application form. **Deadline:** September 1.

Contact Mrs. Pat Moquin, Program Assistant, N.H. Department of Education, Division of Higher Education - Higher Education Commission, 101 Pleasant Street, Concord, NH 03301. *E-mail:* patricia.moquin@doe.nh.gov. *Phone:* 603-271-0289. *Fax:* 603-271-1953. *Website:* http://www.education. nh.gov/highered.

NEW JERSEY

Law Enforcement Officer Memorial Scholarship. Scholarships for full-time undergraduate study at approved New Jersey institutions for the dependent children of New Jersey law enforcement officers killed in the line of duty. Value of scholarship will be established annually. Deadline varies. *Award:* Scholarship for use in freshman, sophomore, junior, or senior years; not renewable. *Eligibility Requirements:* Applicant must be enrolled or expecting to enroll full-time at a two-year or four-year institution or university; resident of New Jersey and studying in New Jersey. Applicant or parent of applicant must have employment or volunteer experience in police/firefighting. Available to U.S. citizens. *Application Requirements:* Application form.

Contact Jean Hathoway, Assistant Director of Special Grants and Scholarships, New Jersey Higher Education Student Assistance Authority, PO Box 540, Trenton, NJ 08625. *Phone:* 609-588-3266. *Website:* http://www.hesaa. org/.

New Jersey Student Tuition Assistance Reward Scholarship II. Earn an associate degree from the home New Jersey county college as an NJ STARS recipient and graduate with a cumulative GPA of 3.25 or higher. Family income (taxable and untaxed income) must be less than $250,000 as derived from the FAFSA. NJ STARS II students may receive up to $1,250 per semester, paid completely by the State, after all other sources of federal and State grants and scholarships are applied to tuition charges. *Award:* Scholarship for use in junior or senior years; renewable. *Eligibility Requirements:* Applicant must be enrolled or expecting to enroll full-time at a four-year institution or university;

resident of New Jersey and studying in New Jersey. Applicant must have 3.0 GPA or higher. Available to U.S. citizens. *Application Requirements:* Application form.

Contact Jossette Greene, Program Officer. *E-mail:* jgreene@hesaa.org. *Phone:* 609-584-4480. *Website:* http://www.hesaa.org/.

New Jersey War Orphans Tuition Assistance. $500 scholarship to children of those service personnel who died while in the military or due to service-connected disabilities, or who are officially listed as missing in action by the U.S. Department of Defense. Must be a resident of New Jersey for at least one year immediately preceding the filing of the application and be between the ages of 16 and 21 at the time of application. *Award:* Scholarship for use in freshman, sophomore, junior, or senior years; renewable. *Award amount:* $500. *Eligibility Requirements:* Applicant must be age 16-21; enrolled or expecting to enroll full-time at a four-year institution or university and resident of New Jersey. Available to U.S. citizens. Applicant or parent must meet one or more of the following requirements: general military experience; retired from active duty; disabled or killed as a result of military service; prisoner of war; or missing in action. *Application Requirements:* Application form, transcript. **Deadline:** varies.

Contact Patricia Richter, Grants Manager, New Jersey Department of Military and Veterans Affairs, PO Box 340, Trenton, NJ 08625-0340. *E-mail:* patricia.richter@njdmava.state.nj.us. *Phone:* 609-530-6854. *Fax:* 609-530-6970. *Website:* http://www.state.nj.us/military.

New Jersey World Trade Center Scholarship. Scholarship was established by the legislature to aid the dependent children and surviving spouses of New Jersey residents who were killed in the terrorist attacks, or who are missing and officially presumed dead as a direct result of the attacks; applies to instate and out-of-state institutions for students seeking undergraduate degrees. *Award:* Scholarship for use in freshman, sophomore, junior, or senior years; not renewable. *Award amount:* $1–$6500. *Eligibility Requirements:* Applicant must be enrolled or expecting to enroll full-time at a two-year or four-year institution or university and resident of New

Jersey. Available to U.S. citizens. *Application Requirements:* Application form.

Contact Jean Hathaway, Assistant Director of Special Grants and Scholarships, New Jersey Higher Education Student Assistance Authority, PO Box 540, Trenton, NJ 08625. *E-mail:* jhathaway@hesaa.org. *Phone:* 609-588-3266. *Website:* http://www.hesaa.org/.

NJ Student Tuition Assistance Reward Scholarship. Students must enroll in a full time course of study at their home county colleges. The award covers tuition charges for up to 18 credit hours per term. *Award:* Scholarship for use in freshman or sophomore years; renewable. *Award amount:* $500–$2600. *Eligibility Requirements:* Applicant must be enrolled or expecting to enroll full-time at a two-year institution; resident of New Jersey and studying in New Jersey. Applicant must have 3.0 GPA or higher. Available to U.S. citizens. *Application Requirements:* Application form.

Contact Ms. Jossette Greene, Program Officer, New Jersey Higher Education Student Assistance Authority, PO Box 540, Trenton, NJ 08625. *E-mail:* jgreene@hessa.org. *Phone:* 609-584-4480. *Website:* http://www.hesaa.org/.

Part-Time Tuition Aid Grant for County Colleges. Provides financial aid to eligible part-time undergraduate students enrolled for 9 to 11 credits at New Jersey community colleges. *Award:* Grant for use in freshman or sophomore years; not renewable. *Award amount:* $500–$1900. *Eligibility Requirements:* Applicant must be enrolled or expecting to enroll part-time at a two-year institution; resident of New Jersey and studying in New Jersey. Available to U.S. citizens. *Application Requirements:* Application form.

Contact Jean Hathaway, AS of Grants and Scholarships, New Jersey Higher Education Student Assistance Authority, PO Box 540, Trenton, NJ 08625. *E-mail:* jhathaway@hesaa.org. *Phone:* 609-584-4480. *Website:* http://www.hesaa.org/.

POW-MIA Tuition Benefit Program. Free undergraduate college tuition provided to any child born or adopted before or during the period of time his or her parent was officially declared a prisoner of war or person missing in action after January 1, 1960. The POW-MIA must have been a New Jersey res-

ident at the time he or she entered the service. Child of veteran must attend either a public or private institution in New Jersey. A copy of DD 1300 must be furnished with the application. Minimum 2.5 GPA required. *Award:* Scholarship for use in freshman, sophomore, junior, or senior years; renewable. *Eligibility Requirements:* Applicant must be enrolled or expecting to enroll full-time at a two-year or four-year or technical institution or university; resident of New Jersey and studying in New Jersey. Applicant must have 2.5 GPA or higher. Available to U. S. citizens. Applicant or parent must meet one or more of the following requirements: general military experience; retired from active duty; disabled or killed as a result of military service; prisoner of war; or missing in action. *Application Requirements:* Application form, copy of DD 1300, transcript. **Deadline:** varies.

Contact Patricia Richter, Grants Manager, New Jersey Department of Military and Veterans Affairs, PO Box 340, Trenton, NJ 08625-0340. *E-mail:* patricia.richter@njdmava.state.nj.us. *Phone:* 609-530-6854. *Fax:* 609-530-6970. *Website:* http://www.state.nj.us/military.

Survivor Tuition Benefits Program. The scholarship provides tuition fees for spouses and dependents of law enforcement officers, fire, or emergency services personnel killed in the line of duty. Eligible recipients may attend any independent institution in the state; however, the annual value of the grant cannot exceed the highest tuition charged at a New Jersey public institution. *Award:* Scholarship for use in freshman, sophomore, junior, or senior years; renewable. *Eligibility Requirements:* Applicant must be enrolled or expecting to enroll full- or part-time at a two-year or four-year institution or university; resident of New Jersey and studying in New Jersey. Applicant or parent of applicant must have employment or volunteer experience in police/firefighting. Available to U.S. citizens. *Application Requirements:* Application form.

Contact Jean Hathaway, Assistant Director of Special Grants and Scholarships, New Jersey Higher Education Student Assistance Authority, PO Box 540, Trenton, NJ 08625. *E-mail:* jhathaway@hesaa.org. *Phone:* 609-588-3266. *Website:* http://www.hesaa.org/.

Tuition Aid Grant. The program provides grants to eligible undergraduate students attending participating in-state institutions. *Award:* Grant for use in freshman, sophomore, junior, or senior years; not renewable. *Award amount:* $1012–$12,190. *Eligibility Requirements:* Applicant must be enrolled or expecting to enroll full-time at a two-year or four-year institution or university; resident of New Jersey and studying in New Jersey. Available to U. S. citizens. *Application Requirements:* Application form, financial need analysis.

Contact Kathyrn Safran, Director of Grants and Scholarships, New Jersey Higher Education Student Assistance Authority, PO Box 540, Trenton, NJ 08625. *E-mail:* ksafran@hesaa.org. *Phone:* 609-584-4480. *Website:* http://www.hesaa.org/.

Veterans Tuition Credit Program-New Jersey. Award for New Jersey resident veterans who served in the armed forces between December 31, 1960, and May 7, 1975. Must have been a New Jersey resident at time of induction or discharge or for two years immediately prior to application. *Award:* Scholarship for use in freshman, sophomore, junior, or senior years; renewable. *Award amount:* $200–$400. *Eligibility Requirements:* Applicant must be enrolled or expecting to enroll full- or part-time at a two-year or four-year or technical institution or university and resident of New Jersey. Available to U. S. citizens. Applicant or parent must meet one or more of the following requirements: general military experience; retired from active duty; disabled or killed as a result of military service; prisoner of war; or missing in action. *Application Requirements:* Application form. **Deadline:** varies.

Contact Patricia Richter, Grants Manager, New Jersey Department of Military and Veterans Affairs, PO Box 340, Trenton, NJ 08625-0340. *E-mail:* patricia.richter@njdmava.state.nj.us. *Phone:* 609-530-6854. *Fax:* 609-530-6970. *Website:* http://www.state.nj.us/military.

NEW MEXICO

Children of Deceased Veterans Scholarship-New Mexico. Award for New Mexico residents who are children of veterans killed as a result of service, prisoner of war, or veterans missing in action. Must be between ages 16 and 26. For use at New Mexico schools for undergraduate study. Must submit parent's death certificate and DD form 214. *Award:* Scholarship for use in freshman, sophomore, junior, or senior years; not renewable. *Award amount:* $300. *Number of awards:* 49–50. *Eligibility Requirements:* Applicant must be age 16-26; enrolled or expecting to enroll full- or part-time at a two-year or four-year or technical institution or university; resident of New Mexico and studying in New Mexico. Available to U.S. citizens. *Application Requirements:* Application form.

Contact Mr. Dale Movius, Director, State Benefits, New Mexico Department of Veterans' Services, 407 Galisteo St, Room 142, Santa Fe, NM 87501. *E-mail:* dalej.movius@state.nm.us. *Phone:* 505-827-6300. *Website:* http://www.nmdvs.org.

College Affordability Grant. Grant available to New Mexico students with financial need who do not qualify for other state grants and scholarships to attend and complete educational programs at a New Mexico public college or university. Student must have unmet need after all other financial aid has been awarded. Student may not be receiving any other state grants or scholarships. Renewable upon satisfactory academic progress. *Award:* Grant for use in freshman, sophomore, junior, or senior years; renewable. *Award amount:* up to $1000. *Number of awards:* 1. *Eligibility Requirements:* Applicant must be enrolled or expecting to enroll full- or part-time at a two-year or four-year institution or university; resident of New Mexico and studying in New Mexico. Available to U.S. citizens. *Application Requirements:* Application form, FAFSA, financial need analysis. **Deadline:** continuous.

Contact Tashina Acker, Director of Financial Aid, New Mexico Commission on Higher Education, 1068 Cerrillos Road, Santa Fe, NM 87505-1650. *E-mail:* tashina.banks-moore@state.nm.us. *Phone:* 505-476-6549. *Fax:* 505-476-6511. *Website:* http://www.hed.state.nm.us/.

Legislative Endowment Scholarships. Renewable scholarships to provide aid for undergraduate students with substantial financial need who are attending public postsecondary institutions in New Mexico. Four-year schools may award up to $2500 per academic year, two-year schools may award up to $1000 per academic year. Deadlines varies. *Award:* Scholarship for use in freshman, sophomore, junior, or senior years; renewable. *Award amount:* $1000–$2500. *Number of awards:* 1. *Eligibility Requirements:* Applicant must be enrolled or expecting to enroll full- or part-time at a two-year or four-year institution or university; resident of New Mexico and studying in New Mexico. Available to U.S. citizens. *Application Requirements:* Application form, FAFSA, financial need analysis. **Deadline:** varies.

Contact Tashina Moore, Director of Financial Aid, New Mexico Commission on Higher Education, 1068 Cerrillos Road, Santa Fe, NM 87505-1650. *E-mail:* tashina.banks-moore@state.nm.us. *Phone:* 505-475-6549. *Fax:* 505-476-6511. *Website:* http://www.hed.state.nm.us/.

Legislative Lottery Scholarship. Renewable Scholarship for New Mexico high school graduates or GED recipients who plan to attend an eligible New Mexico public college or university. Must be enrolled full-time and maintain 2.5 GPA. *Award:* Scholarship for use in freshman year; renewable. *Number of awards:* 1. *Eligibility Requirements:* Applicant must be high school student; planning to enroll or expecting to enroll full-time at a four-year institution or university; resident of New Mexico and studying in New Mexico. Applicant must have 3.5 GPA or higher. Available to U.S. citizens. *Application Requirements:* Application form, FAFSA. **Deadline:** varies.

Contact Tashina Moore, Director of Financial Aid, New Mexico Commission on Higher Education, 1068 Cerrillos Road, Santa Fe, NM 87505. *E-mail:* tashina.banks-moore@state.nm.us. *Phone:* 505-476-6549. *Fax:* 505-476-6511. *Website:* http://www.hed.state.nm.us/.

New Mexico Competitive Scholarship. Scholarships for non-residents or non-citizens of the United States to encourage out-of-state students who have demonstrated high academic achievement in high school to enroll in public four-year universities in New Mexico. Renewable for up to four years. For details visit http://fin.hed.state.nm.us. *Award:* Scholarship for use in freshman year; renewable. *Eligibility Requirements:* Applicant must be high school student; planning to enroll or expecting to enroll full-time at a four-year institution or university and studying in New Mexico. Available to Canadian and non-U.S. citizens. *Application Requirements:* Application form, essay, recommendations or references, test scores. **Deadline:** varies.

Contact Tashina Moore, Director of Financial Aid, New Mexico Commission on Higher Education, 1068 Cerrillos Road, Santa Fe, NM 87505. *E-mail:* tashina.banks-moore@state.nm.us. *Phone:* 505-476-6549. *Fax:* 505-476-6511. *Website:* http://www.hed.state.nm.us/.

New Mexico Scholars' Program. Renewable award program created to encourage New Mexico high school students to attend public postsecondary institutions or the following private colleges in New Mexico: College of Santa Fe, St. John's College, College of the Southwest. For details visit http://fin.hed.state.nm.us. *Award:* Scholarship for use in freshman year; renewable. *Number of awards:* 1. *Eligibility Requirements:* Applicant must be high school student; planning to enroll or expecting to enroll full-time at a two-year or four-year institution; resident of New Mexico and studying in New Mexico. Available to U.S. citizens. *Application Requirements:* Application form, FAFSA, financial need analysis, test scores. **Deadline:** varies.

Contact Tashina Moore, Director of Financial Aid, New Mexico Commission on Higher Education, 1068 Cerrillos Road, Santa Fe, NM 87505-1650. *E-mail:* tashina.banks-moore@state.nm.us. *Phone:* 505-476-6549. *Fax:* 505-476-6511. *Website:* http://www.hed.state.nm.us/.

New Mexico Student Incentive Grant. Grant created to provide aid for undergraduate students with substantial financial need who are attending public colleges or universities or the following eligible colleges in New Mexico: College of Santa Fe, St. John's College, College of the Southwest, Institute of American Indian Art, Crownpoint Institute of Technology, Dine College and Southwestern Indian Polytechnic Institute. Part-time students are eligible for pro-rated awards. *Award:* Grant for use in freshman, sophomore, junior, or senior years; not renewable. *Award amount:* $200–$2500. *Number of* *awards:* 1. *Eligibility Requirements:* Applicant must be enrolled or expecting to enroll full- or part-time at a two-year or four-year or technical institution or university; resident of New Mexico and studying in New Mexico. Available to U.S. citizens. *Application Requirements:* Application form, FAFSA, financial need analysis. **Deadline:** varies.

Contact Tashina Moore, Director of Financial Aid, New Mexico Commission on Higher Education, 1068 Cerrillos Road, Santa Fe, NM 87505-1650. *E-mail:* tashina.banks-moore@state.nm. us. *Phone:* 505-476-6549. *Fax:* 505-476-6511. *Website:* http://www.hed. state.nm.us/.

New Mexico Vietnam Veteran Scholarship. Award for Vietnam veterans who have been New Mexico residents for a minimum of ten years and are attending state-funded postsecondary schools. Must have been awarded the Vietnam Campaign medal. Must submit DD 214 and discharge papers. *Award:* Scholarship for use in freshman, sophomore, junior, or senior years; renewable. *Award amount:* $3500–$4000. *Number of awards:* 100. *Eligibility Requirements:* Applicant must be enrolled or expecting to enroll full- or part-time at a two-year or four-year or technical institution or university; resident of New Mexico and studying in New Mexico. Available to U.S. citizens. *Application Requirements:* Application form.

Contact Mr. Dale Movius, Director, State Benefits, New Mexico Department of Veterans' Services, 407 Galisteo St, Room 142, Santa Fe, NM 87501. *E-mail:* Dalej.movius@state.nm.us. *Phone:* 505-827-6300. *Website:* http:// www.nmdvs.org.

New Mexico Wartime Veterans Scholarship. Award for Wartime Veterans who have been a New Mexico resident for a minimum of ten years and are attending state-funded postsecondary schools. Must have been awarded a campaign medal such as the Southwest Asia Service Medal, Global War on Terrorism Expeditionary Medal, Iraq Campaign Medal, Afghanistan Campaign Medal or any other medal issued for service in the Armed Forces of the United States in support of any US Military Campaign or armed conflict as defined by congress or presidential order or service after August 1, 1990.

Award: Scholarship for use in freshman, sophomore, junior, or senior years; renewable. *Award amount:* $3500–$4000. *Number of awards:* 100. *Eligibility Requirements:* Applicant must be enrolled or expecting to enroll full- or part-time at a two-year or four-year or technical institution or university; resident of New Mexico and studying in New Mexico. Available to U.S. citizens. Applicant must have general military experience.

Contact Mr. Dale Movius, Director, State Benefits, New Mexico Department of Veterans' Services, 407 Galisteo St, Room 142, Santa Fe, NM 87501. *E-mail:* dalej.movius@state.nm.us. *Phone:* 505-827-6374. *Website:* http:// www.nmdvs.org.

Vietnam Veterans' Scholarship Program. Renewable scholarship program created to provide aid for Vietnam veterans who are undergraduate and graduate students attending public postsecondary institutions or select private colleges in New Mexico. Private colleges include: College of Santa Fe, St. John's College and College of the Southwest. *Award:* Scholarship for use in freshman, sophomore, junior, or senior years; renewable. *Number of awards:* 1. *Eligibility Requirements:* Applicant must be enrolled or expecting to enroll full-time at a two-year or four-year institution; resident of New Mexico and studying in New Mexico. Available to U.S. citizens. Applicant or parent must meet one or more of the following requirements: general military experience; retired from active duty; disabled or killed as a result of military service; prisoner of war; or missing in action. *Application Requirements:* Application form, certification by the NM Veteran's commission. **Deadline:** varies.

Contact Tashina Moore, Director of Financial Aid, New Mexico Commission on Higher Education, 1068 Cerrillos Road, Santa Fe, NM 87505-1650. *E-mail:* tashina.banks-moore@state.nm. us. *Phone:* 505-476-6549. *Fax:* 505-476-6511. *Website:* http://www.hed. state.nm.us/.

NEW YORK

Alexander and Maude Hadden Scholarship. Youth Foundation offers exceptional students with financial need an award of $2500 to $4000 per year which is renewable for four years at the foun-

dation's discretion. Minimum GPA of 3. 5 required, community service and extra curricular activities expected. Must write Foundation for information and application request form. *Award:* Scholarship for use in freshman, sophomore, junior, or senior years; renewable. *Award amount:* $2500–$4000. *Number of awards:* 96–108. *Eligibility Requirements:* Applicant must be enrolled or expecting to enroll full-time at a four-year institution or university and resident of Yukon. Applicant or parent of applicant must have employment or volunteer experience in community service. Applicant must have 3.5 GPA or higher. Available to U.S. citizens. *Application Requirements:* Application form, community service, essay, financial need analysis, personal photograph. **Deadline:** February 28.

Contact Ms. Johanna Lee, Executive Administrator. *E-mail:* YouthFdn@aol. com. *Phone:* 212-840-6291. *Fax:* 212-840-6747. *Website:* http://fdnweb.org/ youthfdn.

DAAD University Summer Course Grant. Scholarships are awarded to full-time degree students of Canadian or US colleges, sophomore/2nd year and higher, for the pursuit of summer courses at universities in Germany. It is open to applicants of any major but there is a prerequisite of at least two years of college level German or the equivalent German language fluency. Courses are three to four weeks in duration, take place at many locations in Germany (universities), are taught in German, and topics include German language, literature, current affairs, political science, history, culture, arts, film and media, economics, linguistics, law, translation and interpretation, and test prep for German language proficiency examinations. Accommodations are arranged by the host institution. Foreign Language. *Award:* Grant for use in sophomore, junior, senior, or graduate years; not renewable. *Eligibility Requirements:* Applicant must be enrolled or expecting to enroll full-time at a four-year institution or university and must have an interest in German language/culture. Available to U.S. and non-U.S. citizens. *Application Requirements:* Application form, essay. **Deadline:** December 15.

New York Aid for Part-Time Study (APTS). Renewable scholarship provides tuition assistance to part-time undergraduate students who are New York residents, meet income eligibility requirements and are attending New York accredited institutions. Deadline varies. Must be U.S. citizen. *Award:* Grant for use in freshman, sophomore, junior, or senior years; renewable. *Award amount:* up to $2000. *Eligibility Requirements:* Applicant must be enrolled or expecting to enroll part-time at a two-year or four-year institution or university; resident of New York and studying in New York. Available to U.S. citizens. *Application Requirements:* Application form, financial need analysis. **Deadline:** varies.

New York Memorial Scholarships for Families of Deceased Police Officers, Fire Fighters, and Peace Officers. Renewable scholarship for children, spouses and financial dependents of deceased fire fighters, volunteer firefighters, police officers, peace officers and emergency medical service workers who died in the line of duty. Provides up to the cost of SUNY educational expenses. *Award:* Scholarship for use in freshman, sophomore, junior, or senior years; renewable. *Eligibility Requirements:* Applicant must be enrolled or expecting to enroll full-time at a four-year institution or university; resident of New York and studying in New York. Available to U.S. citizens. *Application Requirements:* Application form, financial need analysis, transcript. **Deadline:** May 1.

New York State Aid to Native Americans. Award for enrolled members of a New York State tribe and their children who are attending or planning to attend a New York State college and who are New York State residents. Deadlines: July 15 for the fall semester, December 31 for the spring semester, and May 20 for summer session. *Award:* Scholarship for use in freshman, sophomore, junior, or senior years; renewable. *Award amount:* $85–$2000. *Eligibility Requirements:* Applicant must be American Indian/Alaska Native; enrolled or expecting to enroll full- or part-time at a two-year or four-year or technical institution or university; resident of New York and studying in New York. Available to U.S. citizens. *Application Requirements:* Application form, financial need analysis, recommendations or references, transcript. **Deadline:** varies.

New York State Tuition Assistance Program. Award for New York state residents attending a New York postsecondary institution. Must be full-time student in approved program with tuition over $200 per year. Must show financial need and not be in default in any other state program. Renewable award of $500 to $5000 dependent on family income and tuition charged. *Award:* Grant for use in freshman, sophomore, junior, or senior years; renewable. *Award amount:* $500–$5000. *Number of awards:* 350,000–360,000. *Eligibility Requirements:* Applicant must be enrolled or expecting to enroll full-time at a two-year or four-year institution or university; resident of New York and studying in New York. Available to U.S. citizens. *Application Requirements:* Application form, financial need analysis. **Deadline:** May 1.

New York Vietnam/Persian Gulf/ Afghanistan Veterans Tuition Awards. Scholarship for veterans who served in Vietnam, the Persian Gulf, or Afghanistan. Must be a New York resident attending a New York institution. Must establish eligibility by September 1. *Award:* Scholarship for use in freshman, sophomore, junior, or senior years; renewable. *Eligibility Requirements:* Applicant must be enrolled or expecting to enroll full- or part-time at a two-year or four-year or technical institution or university; resident of New York and studying in New York. Available to U.S. citizens. Applicant or parent must meet one or more of the following requirements: general military experience; retired from active duty; disabled or killed as a result of military service; prisoner of war; or missing in action. *Application Requirements:* Application form, financial need analysis. **Deadline:** May 1.

Regents Award for Child of Veteran. Award for students whose parent, as a result of service in U.S. Armed Forces during war or national emergency, died; suffered a 40 percent or more disability; or is classified as missing in action or a prisoner of war. Veteran must be current New York State resident or have been so at time of death. Student must be a New York resident, attending, or planning to attend, college in New York State. Must establish eligibility before applying for payment. *Award:* Scholarship for use in freshman, sophomore, junior, or senior

years; not renewable. *Award amount:* up to $450. *Eligibility Requirements:* Applicant must be enrolled or expecting to enroll full-time at a two-year or four-year institution or university; resident of New York and studying in New York. Available to U.S. citizens. Applicant or parent must meet one or more of the following requirements: general military experience; retired from active duty; disabled or killed as a result of military service; prisoner of war; or missing in action. *Application Requirements:* Application form, proof of eligibility. **Deadline:** May 1.

Contact Rita McGivern, Student Information, New York State Higher Education Services Corporation, 99 Washington Avenue, Room 1320, Albany, NY 12255. *E-mail:* rmc-givern@hesc.com. *Website:* https://www.hesc.ny.gov/.

Scholarship for Academic Excellence. Renewable award for New York residents. Scholarship winners must attend a college or university in New York. 2000 scholarships are for $1500 and 6000 are for $500. The selection criteria used are based on Regents test scores or rank in class or local exam. Must be U.S. citizen or permanent resident. *Award:* Scholarship for use in freshman year; renewable. *Award amount:* $500–$1500. *Number of awards:* up to 8000. *Eligibility Requirements:* Applicant must be high school student; planning to enroll or expecting to enroll full-time at a two-year or four-year institution or university; resident of New York and studying in New York. Available to U.S. citizens. *Application Requirements:* Application form. **Deadline:** December 19.

Contact Lewis Hall, Supervisor. *E-mail:* scholar@mail.nysed.gov. *Phone:* 518-486-1319. *Fax:* 518-486-5346. *Website:* http://www.highered.nysed.gov/.

Scholarships for Academic Excellence. Renewable awards of up to $1500 for academically outstanding New York State high school graduates planning to attend an approved postsecondary institution in New York State. For full-time study only. Contact high school guidance counselor to apply. *Award:* Scholarship for use in freshman, sophomore, junior, or senior years; renewable. *Award amount:* $500–$1500. *Number of awards:* up to 8000. *Eligibility Requirements:* Applicant must be high school student; planning to enroll or expecting to enroll full-time at a four-year institution or university; resident of New York and studying in New York. Available to U.S. citizens. *Application Requirements:* Application form. **Deadline:** varies.

Contact Rita McGivern, Student Information, New York State Higher Education Services Corporation, 99 Washington Avenue, Room 1320, Albany, NY 12255. *E-mail:* scholarship@hesc.com. *Website:* https://www.hesc.ny.gov/.

World Trade Center Memorial Scholarship. Renewable awards of up to the cost of educational expenses at a State University of New York four-year college. Available to the children, spouses and financial dependents of victims who died or were severely disabled as a result of the September 11, 2001 terrorist attacks on the U.S. and the rescue and recovery efforts. *Award:* Scholarship for use in freshman, sophomore, junior, or senior years; renewable. *Eligibility Requirements:* Applicant must be enrolled or expecting to enroll full-time at a four-year institution or university and studying in New York. Available to U.S. and non-U.S. citizens. *Application Requirements:* Application form, financial need analysis, recommendations or references, transcript. **Deadline:** May 1.

NORTH CAROLINA

North Carolina Community College Grant Program. Grants are available to North Carolina residents who demonstrate financial need and are enrolled at NC community colleges. The applicant must be a N.C. resident for tuition purposes; enroll for at least six credit hours per semester in a curriculum program; and meet the Satisfactory Academic Progress requirements of the institution. Eligibility is determined based on the same criteria as the Federal Pell Grant; students not eligible for the Federal Pell Grant may be considered for the grant based on the expected family contribution (EFC). Student who have earned a Bachelor's degree already are ineligible. Applicants must complete the Free Application for Federal Student Aid (FAFSA). Consideration is automatic once the FAFSA is filed. Please contact the financial aid office at the local community college for more specific information regarding institutional

processes. *Award:* Grant for use in freshman or sophomore years; not renewable. *Award amount:* $150–$1150. *Number of awards:* 25,000. *Eligibility Requirements:* Applicant must be enrolled or expecting to enroll full- or part-time at a two-year or technical institution; resident of North Carolina and studying in North Carolina. Available to U.S. citizens. *Application Requirements:* Financial need analysis.

Contact Edna Williams, Manager, Award and Loan Origination Services, North Carolina State Education Assistance Authority, PO Box 13663, Research Triangle Park, NC 27709-3663. *E-mail:* ewilliams@ncseaa.edu. *Phone:* 919-248-4632. *Website:* http://www.ncseaa.edu/.

North Carolina Division of Services for the Blind Rehabilitation Services. Financial assistance is available for North Carolina residents who are blind or visually impaired and who require vocational rehabilitation to help find employment. Tuition and other assistance provided based on need. Open to U.S. citizens and legal residents of United States. Applicants goal must be to work after receiving vocational services. To apply, contact the local DSB office and apply for vocational rehabilitation services. *Award:* Scholarship for use in freshman, sophomore, junior, or senior years; renewable. *Eligibility Requirements:* Applicant must be visually impaired; enrolled or expecting to enroll full-time at a two-year or four-year or technical institution or university and resident of North Carolina. Applicant must be visually impaired. Available to U.S. citizens. *Application Requirements:* Application form, financial need analysis, interview, proof of eligibility. **Deadline:** continuous.

Contact JoAnn Strader, Chief of Rehabilitation Field Services, North Carolina Division of Services for the Blind, 2601 Mail Service Center, Raleigh, NC 27699-2601. *E-mail:* joann.strader@ncmail.net. *Phone:* 919-733-9700. *Fax:* 919-715-8771. *Website:* http://www.ncdhhs.gov/.

North Carolina National Guard Tuition Assistance Program. Scholarship for members of the North Carolina Air and Army National Guard who will remain in the service for two years following the period for which assistance is provided. Must reapply for each academic period. For use at approved

North Carolina institutions. *Award:* Grant for use in freshman, sophomore, junior, senior, or graduate years; not renewable. *Award amount:* $100–$3440. *Eligibility Requirements:* Applicant must be enrolled or expecting to enroll full- or part-time at a two-year or four-year or technical institution or university; resident of North Carolina and studying in North Carolina. Available to U.S. citizens. Applicant or parent must meet one or more of the following requirements: national guard experience; retired from active duty; disabled or killed as a result of military service; prisoner of war; or missing in action. *Application Requirements:* Application form. **Deadline:** continuous.

Contact Ms. Stacy Steinmetz, NCTAP Manager, North Carolina National Guard, 1636 Gold Star Drive, Raleigh, NC 27607. *E-mail:* stacy.m.steinmetz.nfg@mail.mil. *Phone:* 919-664-6272. *Website:* http://nc.ng.mil/Pages/default.aspx.

North Carolina Sheriffs' Association Undergraduate Criminal Justice Scholarships. One-time award for full-time North Carolina resident undergraduate students majoring in criminal justice at a University of North Carolina school. Priority given to child of any North Carolina law enforcement officer. Letter of recommendation from county sheriff required. Criminal Justice/Criminology; Law Enforcement/Police Administration. *Award:* Scholarship for use in freshman, sophomore, junior, or senior years; not renewable. *Award amount:* $1000–$2000. *Number of awards:* 10. *Eligibility Requirements:* Applicant must be enrolled or expecting to enroll full-time at a four-year institution or university; resident of North Carolina and studying in North Carolina. Applicant or parent of applicant must have employment or volunteer experience in police/firefighting. Available to U.S. citizens. *Application Requirements:* Application form, financial need analysis.

Contact Michele Goldston, Assistant, Scholarship and Grant Division, North Carolina State Education Assistance Authority, PO Box 13663, Research Triangle Park, NC 27709. *E-mail:* mgoldston@ncseaa.edu. *Phone:* 919-549-8614. *Website:* http://www.ncseaa.edu/.

North Carolina Veterans Scholarships Class I-A. Scholarships for children of certain deceased, disabled or POW/MIA veterans. Award value is $4500 per nine-month academic year in private colleges and junior colleges. No limit on number awarded each year. *Award:* Scholarship for use in freshman, sophomore, junior, or senior years; renewable. *Award amount:* $4500. *Eligibility Requirements:* Applicant must be enrolled or expecting to enroll full-time at a two-year or four-year or technical institution or university; resident of North Carolina and studying in North Carolina. Available to U.S. citizens. Applicant or parent must meet one or more of the following requirements: general military experience; retired from active duty; disabled or killed as a result of military service; prisoner of war; or missing in action. *Application Requirements:* Application form, financial need analysis, interview, transcript. **Deadline:** continuous.

Contact Charles Smith, Assistant Secretary. *E-mail:* charlie.smith@ncmail.net. *Phone:* 919-733-3851. *Fax:* 919-733-2834. *Website:* http://www.milvets.nc.gov/.

North Carolina Veterans Scholarships Class I-B. Awards for children of veterans rated by USDVA as 100 percent disabled due to wartime service as defined in the law, and currently or at time of death drawing compensation for such disability. Parent must have been a North Carolina resident at time of entry into service. Duration of the scholarship is four academic years (8 semesters) if used within 8 years. No limit on number awarded each year. *Award:* Scholarship for use in freshman, sophomore, junior, or senior years; renewable. *Award amount:* $1500. *Eligibility Requirements:* Applicant must be enrolled or expecting to enroll full- or part-time at a two-year or four-year or technical institution or university; resident of North Carolina and studying in North Carolina. Available to U.S. citizens. Applicant or parent must meet one or more of the following requirements: general military experience; retired from active duty; disabled or killed as a result of military service; prisoner of war; or missing in action. *Application Requirements:* Application form, financial need analysis, interview, transcript. **Deadline:** continuous.

Contact Charles Smith, Assistant Secretary. *E-mail:* charlie.smith@ncmail.net. *Phone:* 919-733-3851. *Fax:*

919-733-2834. *Website:* http://www.milvets.nc.gov/.

North Carolina Veterans Scholarships Class II. Awards for children of veterans rated by USDVA as much as 20 percent but less than 100 percent disabled due to wartime service as defined in the law, or awarded Purple Heart Medal for wounds received. Parent must have been a North Carolina resident at time of entry into service. Duration of the scholarship is four academic years (8 semesters) if used within 8 years. Free tuition and exemption from certain mandatory fees as set forth in the law in Public, Community and Technical Colleges. *Award:* Scholarship for use in freshman, sophomore, junior, or senior years; renewable. *Award amount:* $4500. *Number of awards:* up to 100. *Eligibility Requirements:* Applicant must be enrolled or expecting to enroll full- or part-time at a two-year or four-year or technical institution or university; resident of North Carolina and studying in North Carolina. Available to U.S. citizens. Applicant or parent must meet one or more of the following requirements: general military experience; retired from active duty; disabled or killed as a result of military service; prisoner of war; or missing in action. *Application Requirements:* Application form, financial need analysis, interview, transcript. **Deadline:** March 1.

Contact Charles Smith, Assistant Secretary. *E-mail:* charlie.smith@ncmail.net. *Phone:* 919-733-3851. *Fax:* 919-733-2834. *Website:* http://www.milvets.nc.gov/.

North Carolina Veterans Scholarships Class III. Awards for children of a deceased war veteran, who was honorably discharged and who does not qualify under any other provision within this synopsis or veteran who served in a combat zone or waters adjacent to a combat zone and received a campaign badge or medal and who does not qualify under any other provision within this synopsis. Duration of the scholarship is four academic years (8 semesters) if used within 8 years. *Award:* Scholarship for use in freshman, sophomore, junior, or senior years; renewable. *Award amount:* $4500. *Number of awards:* up to 100. *Eligibility Requirements:* Applicant must be enrolled or expecting to enroll full- or part-time at a two-year or four-year or technical institution or university; res-

ident of North Carolina and studying in North Carolina. Available to U.S. citizens. Applicant or parent must meet one or more of the following requirements: general military experience; retired from active duty; disabled or killed as a result of military service; prisoner of war; or missing in action. *Application Requirements:* Application form, financial need analysis, interview, transcript. **Deadline:** March 1.

Contact Charles Smith, Assistant Secretary. *E-mail:* charlie.smith@ncmail.net. *Phone:* 919-733-3851. *Fax:* 919-733-2834. *Website:* http://www.milvets.nc.gov/.

North Carolina Veterans Scholarships Class IV. Awards for children of veterans, who were prisoner of war or missing in action. Duration of the scholarship is four academic years (8 semesters) if used within 8 years. No limit on number awarded each year. Award value is $4500 per nine-month academic year in private colleges and junior colleges. *Award:* Scholarship for use in freshman, sophomore, junior, or senior years; renewable. *Award amount:* $4500. *Eligibility Requirements:* Applicant must be enrolled or expecting to enroll full- or part-time at a two-year or four-year or technical institution or university; resident of North Carolina and studying in North Carolina. Available to U.S. citizens. Applicant or parent must meet one or more of the following requirements: general military experience; retired from active duty; disabled or killed as a result of military service; prisoner of war; or missing in action. *Application Requirements:* Application form, financial need analysis, interview, transcript. **Deadline:** continuous.

Contact Charles Smith, Assistant Secretary. *E-mail:* charlie.smith@ncmail.net. *Phone:* 919-733-3851. *Fax:* 919-733-2834. *Website:* http://www.milvets.nc.gov/.

Training Support for Youth with Disabilities. Public service program that helps persons with disabilities obtain competitive employment. To qualify: student must have a mental, physical or learning disability that is an impediment to employment. A Rehabilitation Counselor along with the eligible student individually develops a rehabilitation program to achieve an employment outcome which requires post secondary training. Financial assistance is based on

NC Division of Vocational Rehabilitation demonstrated financial need and type of program in which the student enrolls. *Award:* Grant for use in freshman, sophomore, junior, senior, or graduate years; renewable. *Eligibility Requirements:* Applicant must be hearing impaired, learning disabled, physically disabled, or visually impaired; enrolled or expecting to enroll full- or part-time at a two-year or four-year or technical institution or university and resident of North Carolina. Applicant must be hearing impaired, learning disabled, physically disabled, or visually impaired. Available to U.S. citizens. *Application Requirements:* Application form, financial need analysis, interview. **Deadline:** continuous.

Contact Stephanie Hanes, Program Specialist for Transition. *E-mail:* stephanie.hanes@dhhs.nc.gov. *Phone:* 919-855-3576. *Website:* http://www.dhhs.state.nc.us/.

University of North Carolina Need-Based Grant. Applicants must be enrolled in at least 6 credit hours at one of sixteen UNC system universities. Eligibility based on need; award varies, consideration for grant automatic when FAFSA is filed. Late applications may be denied due to insufficient funds. *Award:* Grant for use in freshman, sophomore, junior, or senior years; renewable. *Eligibility Requirements:* Applicant must be enrolled or expecting to enroll full- or part-time at an institution or university; resident of North Carolina and studying in North Carolina. Available to U.S. citizens. *Application Requirements:* Application form, financial need analysis.

Contact Edna Williams, Manager, Award and Loan Origination Services, North Carolina State Education Assistance Authority, PO Box 13663, Research Triangle Park, NC 27709. *E-mail:* ewilliams@ncseaa.edu. *Phone:* 919-549-8614. *Website:* http://www.ncseaa.edu/.

NORTH DAKOTA

North Dakota Academic Scholarship. This scholarship rewards high schools students from ND for taking rigorous coursework in high school. Applicants must earn a cumulative high school GPA of 3.0 and have a minimum ACT score of 24. Full-time enrollment is required and is defined as 12 credits in the first two terms and 15 credits in subsequent terms. A minimum cumulative college GPA of 2.75 is required to renew the scholarship. This scholarship is based on merit. Awards are $750/sem. or $500/qtr. up to a total of $6,000. Students have up to 6 years following high school to utilize the scholarship. *Award:* Scholarship for use in freshman, sophomore, junior, senior, or graduate years; renewable. *Award amount:* $6000. *Number of awards:* 1–5000. *Eligibility Requirements:* Applicant must be high school student; planning to enroll or expecting to enroll full-time at a two-year or four-year institution or university; resident of North Dakota and studying in North Dakota. Applicant must have 3.0 GPA or higher. Available to U.S. citizens. *Application Requirements:* Application form. **Deadline:** June 2.

Contact Brenda Zastoupil, Director of Financial Aid, North Dakota University System, 600 E Boulevard Ave, Dept 21, Bismarck, ND 58505-0602. *E-mail:* ndfinaid@ndus.edu. *Phone:* 701-328-2906. *Fax:* 701-328-2979. *Website:* www.ndus.edu/.

North Dakota Career and Technical Education Scholarship. The ND Career and Technical Education Scholarship's goal is to reward students taking rigorous courses in high school, to increase awareness of career and technical programs, and to retain students within ND. The scholarship has an ACT or WorkKeys exam score requirement, a GPA requirement, and a specific high school course list that must be completed to qualify. Full-time enrollment is required and is defined as 12 credits in the first two terms and 15 credits in subsequent terms. A minimum cumulative college GPA of 2.75 is required to renew the scholarship. This scholarship is based on merit. Awards are $750/sem. or $500/qtr. up to a total of $6,000. Students have up to 6 years following high school to utilize the scholarship. *Award:* Scholarship for use in freshman, sophomore, junior, senior, or graduate years; renewable. *Award amount:* $6000. *Number of awards:* 1–4000. *Eligibility Requirements:* Applicant must be high school student; planning to enroll or expecting to enroll full-time at a two-year or four-year institution or university; resident of North Dakota and studying in North Dakota. Applicant must have 3.0 GPA or higher. Available to U.S. citizens. *Application Requirements:* Application form. **Deadline:** June 2.

Contact Brenda Zastoupil, Director of Financial Aid, North Dakota University System, 600 E Boulevard Ave, Dept 21, Bismarck, ND 58505-0602. *E-mail:* ndfinaid@ndus.edu. *Phone:* 701-328-2906. *Fax:* 701-328-2979. *Website:* www.ndus.edu/.

North Dakota Indian Scholarship Program. The North Dakota Indian Scholarship program was established to provide scholarship awards to Native American Students attending qualifying colleges or universities within North Dakota. Students must be ND residents as defined by the college, enrolled full-time (limited exceptions), and maintain a GPA of at least 2.0. Awards are available to both undergraduate and graduate students. Students who maintain a 3.50 GPA qualify for the scholarship based on merit. Students who have a GPA lower than 3.50 must show unmet need. The minimum required GPA is 2.0. The priority application date is July 15. Not all eligible applicants are awarded due to limited appropriations. *Award:* Scholarship for use in freshman, sophomore, junior, senior, graduate, or postgraduate years; not renewable. *Award amount:* $1–$2000. *Number of awards:* 230–270. *Eligibility Requirements:* Applicant must be American Indian/Alaska Native; enrolled or expecting to enroll full-time at a two-year or four-year or technical institution or university; resident of North Dakota and studying in North Dakota. Available to U.S. citizens. *Application Requirements:* Application form, financial need analysis. **Deadline:** July 15.

Contact Brenda Zastoupil, Director of Financial Aid, North Dakota University System, 600 E Boulevard Ave, Dept 21, Bismarck, ND 58505-0602. *E-mail:* ndfinaid@ndus.edu. *Phone:* 701-328-2906. *Fax:* 701-328-2979. *Website:* www.ndus.edu/.

North Dakota Scholars Program. The purpose of the ND Scholars Scholarship is to retain within ND, the brightest and best students who are pursuing post-secondary education. The scholarship amount equates to the tuition charged at the Scholar's eligible institution, not to exceed the highest regular resident undergraduate tuition rate in the NDUS system. This program provides merit-based, full-tuition scholarships to ND high school graduates who attend a qualifying college within ND. High school juniors who score in the top 95th percentile of all ND ACT test-takers prior to July 1 of the year preceding their freshman year of college will be considered as a candidate for this award. Not all eligible students will qualify due to limited appropriations. Students are ranked based on ACT test scores. This scholarship is renewable for up to three years. Recipients must be enrolled at qualifying institutions in ND at full-time status (12 cr. minimum per semester) and must maintain a cumulative GPA of 3.50. Only 40-50 new awards are made each year to new students. *Award:* Scholarship for use in freshman, sophomore, junior, or senior years; renewable. *Award amount:* $6652–$13,848. *Number of awards:* 40–50. *Eligibility Requirements:* Applicant must be high school student; planning to enroll or expecting to enroll full-time at a two-year or four-year institution or university; resident of North Dakota and studying in North Dakota. Available to U.S. citizens. *Application Requirements:* **Deadline:** June 30.

Contact Brenda Zastoupil, Director of Financial Aid, North Dakota University System, 600 E Boulevard Ave, Dept 21, Bismarck, ND 58505-0602. *E-mail:* ndfinaid@ndus.edu. *Phone:* 701-328-2906. *Fax:* 701-328-2979. *Website:* www.ndus.edu/.

North Dakota State Student Incentive Grant Program. The North Dakota State Grant is the premier need-based state grant in North Dakota. Maximum award of $975 per semester or $650 per quarter. The North Dakota State Grant supports ND residents attending an eligible college or university within North Dakota in a program of study that is at least one year in length. The FAFSA is required annually. Awards are available for up to 8 full-time equivalent semesters or 12 full-time equivalent quarters of undergraduate study. Students must meet the SAP guidelines of their institution and meet all title IV eligibility criteria, including having verification complete, if required. *Award:* Grant for use in freshman, sophomore, junior, or senior years; not renewable. *Award amount:* $1–$975. *Number of awards:* 7000–8000. *Eligibility Requirements:* Applicant must be enrolled or expecting to enroll full- or part-time at a two-year or four-year institution or uni-

versity; resident of North Dakota and studying in North Dakota. Available to U.S. citizens. *Application Requirements:* **Deadline:** continuous.

Contact Brenda Zastoupil, Director of Financial Aid, North Dakota University System, 600 E Boulevard Ave, Dept 21, Bismarck, ND 58505-0602. *E-mail:* ndfinaid@ndus.edu. *Phone:* 701-328-2906. *Fax:* 701-328-2979. *Website:* www.ndus.edu/.

OHIO

Ohio College Opportunity Grant. OCOG provides grant money to Ohio residents who demonstrate the highest levels of financial need (as determined by the results of the FAFSA) who are enrolled at Ohio public colleges or universities; Ohio private, non-profit colleges or universities; Ohio private, for-profit institutions; or eligible Pennsylvania institutions. *Award:* Grant for use in freshman, sophomore, junior, or senior years; not renewable. *Award amount:* $888–$2592. *Eligibility Requirements:* Applicant must be enrolled or expecting to enroll full- or part-time at a two-year or four-year institution or university; resident of Ohio and studying in Ohio, Pennsylvania. Available to U.S. citizens. *Application Requirements:* **Deadline:** October 1.

Contact Tamika Braswell, Director, Ohio Department of Higher Education, 25 South Front Street, Columbus, OH 43215. *E-mail:* ocog_admin@regents.state.oh.us. *Phone:* 614-728-8862. *Website:* www.ohiohighered.org.

Ohio Environmental Science & Engineering Scholarships. Merit-based, non-renewable, tuition-only scholarships awarded to undergraduate students admitted to Ohio state or private colleges and universities. Must be able to demonstrate knowledge of, and commitment to, careers in environmental sciences or environmental engineering. Environmental Science. *Award:* Scholarship for use in senior year; not renewable. *Award amount:* $1250–$2500. *Number of awards:* 18. *Eligibility Requirements:* Applicant must be enrolled or expecting to enroll full- or part-time at a two-year or four-year institution or university and studying in Ohio. Applicant must have 3.0 GPA or higher. Available to U.S. citizens. *Application Requirements:* Application form,

application form may be submitted online(https://mc04.manuscriptcentral.com/oas), community service, essay, recommendations or references, resume, self-addressed stamped envelope with application, transcript. **Deadline:** April 15.

Contact Dr. Stephen McConoughey, Chief Executive Officer, Ohio Academy of Science/Ohio Environmental Education Fund, 1500 West Third Avenue, Suite 228, Columbus, OH 43212-2817. *E-mail:* smcconoughey@ohiosci.org. *Phone:* 614-488-2228. *Fax:* 614-488-7629. *Website:* http://www.ohiosci.org/.

Ohio National Guard Scholarship Program. Scholarships are for undergraduate studies at an approved Ohio post-secondary institution. Applicants must enlist for six or three years of Selective Service Reserve Duty in the Ohio National Guard. Scholarship pays 100% instructional and general fees for public institutions and an average of cost of public universities is available for private schools. May reapply up to four years of studies (12 quarters or 8 semesters) for six year enlistment and two years of studies (6 quarters or 4 semesters) for three year enlistment. Deadlines: July 1 (fall), November 1 (winter quarter/spring semester), February 1 (spring quarter), April 1 (summer). *Award:* Scholarship for use in freshman, sophomore, junior, or senior years; not renewable. *Award amount:* up to $4006. *Number of awards:* up to 3500. *Eligibility Requirements:* Applicant must be enrolled or expecting to enroll full- or part-time at a two-year or four-year or technical institution or university; resident of Ohio and studying in Ohio. Available to U.S. citizens. Applicant must have national guard experience. *Application Requirements:* Application form. **Deadline:** varies.

Contact Mrs. Toni Davis, Grants Administrator, Ohio National Guard, 2825 West Dublin Granville Road, ONGSP, Columbus, OH 43235-2789. *E-mail:* toni.davis7@us.army.mil. *Phone:* 614-336-7143. *Fax:* 614-336-7318. *Website:* http://www.ong.ohio.gov/.

Ohio Safety Officers College Memorial Fund. Renewable award covering up to full tuition is available to children and surviving spouses of peace officers, other safety officers and fire fighters killed in the line of duty in any state. Children must be under 26 years of age. Dollar value of each award varies. Must be an Ohio resident and enroll full-time or part-time at an Ohio college or university. Any spouse/child of a member of the armed services of the U.S., who has been killed in the line duty during Operation Enduring Freedom, Operation Iraqi Freedom or a combat zone designated by the President of the United States. Dollar value of each award varies. *Award:* Scholarship for use in freshman, sophomore, junior, or senior years; renewable. *Eligibility Requirements:* Applicant must be enrolled or expecting to enroll full- or part-time at a two-year or four-year institution or university; resident of Ohio and studying in Ohio. Available to U.S. citizens. *Application Requirements:* **Deadline:** continuous.

Contact Ramah Church, Program Manager, Ohio Department of Higher Education, 25 South Front Street, Columbus, OH 43215. *E-mail:* osom_admin@regents.state.oh.us. *Phone:* 614-752-9528. *Website:* www.ohiohighered.org.

Ohio War Orphans Scholarship. Aids Ohio residents attending an eligible college in Ohio. Must be between the ages of 16 and 25, the child of a disabled or deceased veteran, and enrolled full-time. Must maintain a minimum GPA of 2.0. Renewable up to five years. Amount of award varies. Must include Form DD214. *Award:* Scholarship for use in freshman, sophomore, junior, or senior years; renewable. *Eligibility Requirements:* Applicant must be age 16-25; enrolled or expecting to enroll full-time at a two-year or four-year institution or university; resident of Ohio and studying in Ohio. Available to U.S. citizens. Applicant must have general military experience. *Application Requirements:* Application form. **Deadline:** May 15.

Contact Ramah Church, Program Manager, Ohio Department of Higher Education, 25 South Front Street, Columbus, OH 43215. *E-mail:* wo_admin@regents.state.oh.us. *Phone:* 614-752-9528. *Website:* www.ohio-highered.org.

OKLAHOMA

Academic Scholars Program. Awards for students of high academic ability to attend institutions in Oklahoma. Renewable up to four years. ACT or SAT scores must fall between 99.5 and 100th percentiles, or applicant must be designated as a National Merit scholar or finalist. Oklahoma public institutions can also select institutional nominees. *Award:* Scholarship for use in freshman, sophomore, junior, senior, or graduate years; renewable. *Award amount:* $1800–$5500. *Eligibility Requirements:* Applicant must be high school student; planning to enroll or expecting to enroll full-time at a two-year or four-year institution or university and studying in Oklahoma. Available to U.S. citizens. *Application Requirements:* Application form.

Future Teacher Scholarship-Oklahoma. Open to outstanding Oklahoma high school graduates who agree to teach in shortage areas. Must rank in top 15 percent of graduating class or score above 85th percentile on ACT or similar test, or be accepted in an educational program. Students nominated by institution. Reapply to renew. Must attend college/university in Oklahoma. Education. *Award:* Scholarship for use in freshman, sophomore, junior, senior, or graduate years; not renewable. *Award amount:* $500–$1500. *Eligibility Requirements:* Applicant must be enrolled or expecting to enroll full- or part-time at a two-year or four-year institution or university; resident of Oklahoma and studying in Oklahoma. Available to U.S. citizens. *Application Requirements:* Application form, essay.

Oklahoma Tuition Aid Grant. Award for Oklahoma residents enrolled at an Oklahoma institution at least part time each semester in a degree program. May be enrolled in two- or four-year or approved vocational-technical institution. Award for students attending public institutions or private colleges. Application is made through FAFSA. *Award:* Grant for use in freshman, sophomore, junior, or senior years; not renewable. *Award amount:* $1000–$1300. *Eligibility Requirements:* Applicant must be enrolled or expecting to enroll full- or part-time at a two-year or four-year or technical institution or university; resident of Oklahoma and studying in Oklahoma. Available to U.S. citizens. *Application Requirements:* Application form, financial need analysis.

Contact Mrs. Linette McMurtrey, Scholarship Programs Coordinator. *E-mail:* lmcmurtrey@osrhe.edu. *Phone:* 405-225-9131. *Website:* http://www.okhighered.org/.

Regional University Baccalaureate Scholarship. Renewable award for Oklahoma residents attending one of 11 participating Oklahoma public universities. Must have an ACT composite score of at least 30 or be a National Merit semifinalist or commended student. In addition to the award amount, each recipient will receive a resident tuition waiver from the institution. Must maintain a 3.25 GPA. Deadlines vary depending upon the institution attended. *Award:* Scholarship for use in freshman, sophomore, junior, or senior years; renewable. *Award amount:* $3000. *Eligibility Requirements:* Applicant must be enrolled or expecting to enroll full-time at an institution or university; resident of Oklahoma and studying in Oklahoma. Available to U.S. citizens. *Application Requirements:* Application form.

OREGON

American Legion Auxiliary Department of Oregon Department Grants. One-time award for educational use in the state of Oregon. Must be a resident of Oregon who is the child or widow of a veteran or the wife of a disabled veteran. *Award:* Scholarship for use in freshman year; not renewable. *Award amount:* $1000. *Number of awards:* 2. *Eligibility Requirements:* Applicant must be enrolled or expecting to enroll full- or part-time at a two-year or four-year or technical institution or university and resident of Oregon. Available to U.S. citizens. *Application Requirements:* Application form, essay, financial need analysis, interview. **Deadline:** February 10.

Contact Virginia Biddle, Secretary/Treasurer, American Legion Auxiliary Department of Oregon, PO Box 1730, Wilsonville, OR 97070. *E-mail:* alaor@pcez.com. *Phone:* 503-682-3162. *Website:* http://www.alaoregon.org/.

American Legion Auxiliary Department of Oregon Nurses Scholarship. One-time award for Oregon residents who are in their senior year of high school, who are the children of veterans who served during eligibility dates for American Legion membership. Must enroll in a nursing program. Contact local units for application. Nursing. *Award:* Scholarship for use in freshman year; not renewable. *Award amount:* $1500. *Number of awards:* 1. *Eligibility Requirements:* Applicant must be high school student; planning to enroll or expecting to enroll full- or part-time at a four-year institution or university and resident of Oregon. Available to U.S. citizens. *Application Requirements:* Application form, essay, financial need analysis, interview. **Deadline:** March 20.

Contact Virginia Biddle, Secretary/Treasurer, American Legion Auxiliary Department of Oregon, PO Box 1730, Wilsonville, OR 97070. *E-mail:* alaor@pcez.com. *Phone:* 503-682-3162. *Website:* http://www.alaoregon.org/.

Better A Life Scholarship. Scholarship award available to single parents age 17-25. High schools seniors must have at least 3.0 GPA and college students must have at least a 2.5 GPA or GED equivalent. For use at Oregon public and nonprofit colleges and universities. Applicants may not already possess a Bachelor's degree. May reapply for one additional year of funding. *Award:* Scholarship for use in freshman, sophomore, junior, or senior years; not renewable. *Eligibility Requirements:* Applicant must be age 17-25; enrolled or expecting to enroll full- or part-time at a two-year or four-year institution or university; single and studying in Oregon. Applicant must have 3.0 GPA or higher. Available to U.S. citizens. *Application Requirements:* Application form, financial need analysis. **Deadline:** March 1.

Contact Melissa Adams, Scholarship Processing Coordinator. *E-mail:* melissa.adams@hecc.oregon.gov. *Phone:* 541-687-7409. *Website:* http://www.GetCollegeFunds.org/.

Dorothy Campbell Memorial Scholarship. Renewable award for female Oregon high school graduates with a minimum 2.75 GPA. Must submit essay describing strong, continuing interest in golf and the contribution that sport has made to applicant's development. Preference for participation in high school golf team (including intramural), if available, and planning to enroll at a four-year Oregon public or nonprofit college. FAFSA required. *Award:* Scholarship for use in freshman year; renewable. *Eligibility Requirements:* Applicant must be enrolled or expecting to enroll full-time at a four-year institution or university; female; resident of Oregon; studying in Oregon and must have an interest in golf. Available to U. S. citizens. *Application Requirements:* Application form, essay, financial need analysis. **Deadline:** March 1.

Contact Melissa Adams, Scholarship Processing Coordinator. *E-mail:* melissa.adams@hecc.oregon.gov. *Phone:* 541-687-7409. *Website:* http://www.GetCollegeFunds.org/.

Glenn Jackson Scholars Scholarships. Renewable award for Oregon graduating high school seniors who are dependents of employees or retirees of Oregon Department of Transportation or Parks and Recreation Department. Employees must have worked in their department at least three years as of the March 1 scholarship deadline. Scholarship is automatically renewable if renewal criteria met. *Award:* Scholarship for use in freshman, sophomore, junior, or senior years; renewable. *Eligibility Requirements:* Applicant must be high school student; planning to enroll or expecting to enroll full- or part-time at a two-year or four-year institution or university and resident of Oregon. Applicant or parent of applicant must be affiliated with Oregon Department of Transportation Parks and Recreation. Available to U.S. citizens. *Application Requirements:* Application form, financial need analysis. **Deadline:** March 1.

Contact Melissa Adams, Scholarship Processing Coordinator. *E-mail:* melissa.adams@hecc.oregon.gov. *Phone:* 541-687-7409. *Website:* http://www.GetCollegeFunds.org/.

Laurence R. Foster Memorial Scholarship. One-time award to students enrolled or planning to enroll in a public health degree program. First preference given to those working in the public health field and those pursuing a graduate degree in public health. Undergraduates entering junior or senior year health programs may apply if seeking a public health career, and not private practice. Applicants from diverse environments preferred. Public Health. *Award:* Scholarship for use in junior, senior, or graduate years; not renewable. *Eligibility Requirements:* Applicant must be enrolled or expecting to enroll full- or part-time at a four-year institution or university. Available to U.S. citizens. *Application Requirements:* Application form, essay, financial need analysis. **Deadline:** March 1.

Contact Melissa Adams, Scholarship Processing Coordinator. *E-mail:* melissa.adams@hecc.oregon.gov. *Phone:* 541-687-7409. *Website:* http://www.GetCollegeFunds.org/.

Oregon Scholarship Fund Community College Student Award. Scholarship open to students enrolled or planning to enroll at least half time in Oregon community college programs. Recipients may reapply for one additional year. *Award:* Scholarship for use in freshman or sophomore years; renewable. *Eligibility Requirements:* Applicant must be enrolled or expecting to enroll full- or part-time at a two-year institution and studying in Oregon. Available to U.S. citizens. *Application Requirements:* Application form, financial need analysis. **Deadline:** March 1.

Contact Melissa Adams, Scholarship Processing Coordinator. *E-mail:* melissa.adams@hecc.oregon.gov. *Phone:* 541-687-7409. *Website:* http://www.GetCollegeFunds.org/.

Oregon Scholarship Fund Transfer Student Award. Award open to students who are currently enrolled in their second year at a community college and are planning to transfer to a four-year college in Oregon. Must enroll at least half-time. *Award:* Scholarship for use in junior or senior years; renewable. *Eligibility Requirements:* Applicant must be enrolled or expecting to enroll full- or part-time at a four-year institution or university and studying in Oregon. Available to U.S. citizens. *Application Requirements:* Application form, financial need analysis. **Deadline:** March 1.

Contact Melissa Adams, Scholarship Processing Coordinator. *E-mail:* melissa.adams@hecc.oregon.gov. *Phone:* 541-687-7409. *Website:* http://www.GetCollegeFunds.org/.

Oregon Trucking Association Safety Management Council Scholarship. One-time award available to a child of an Oregon Trucking Association member, or child of an employee of OTA member. Applicants must be graduating high school seniors planning to attend a public or nonprofit college or university. Oregon residency is not required. *Award:* Scholarship for use in freshman year; not renewable. *Eligibility Requirements:* Applicant must be high school student and planning to enroll or expecting to enroll full-time at a four-year institution. Applicant or parent of applicant must be affiliated with Oregon Trucking Association. Available to U.S. citizens. *Application Requirements:* Application form. **Deadline:** March 1.

Contact Melissa Adams, Scholarship Processing Coordinator. *E-mail:* melissa.adams@hecc.oregon.gov. *Phone:* 541-687-7409. *Website:* http://www.GetCollegeFunds.org/.

Oregon Veterans' Education Aid. To be eligible, veteran must have actively served in U.S. armed forces 90 days and been discharged under honorable conditions. Must be U.S. citizen and Oregon resident. Korean War veteran or received campaign or expeditionary medal or ribbon awarded by U.S. armed forces for services after June 30, 1958. Full-time students receive up to $150 per month, and part-time students receive up to $100 per month for a maximum of 36 months. Length of benefits depend on length of service. Payments contingent upon available funding. *Award:* Grant for use in freshman, sophomore, junior, senior, graduate, or postgraduate years; not renewable. *Award amount:* $3600–$5400. *Number of awards:* 1–200. *Eligibility Requirements:* Applicant must be enrolled or expecting to enroll full- or part-time at a two-year or four-year or technical institution or university; resident of Oregon and studying in Oregon. Available to U.S. citizens. Applicant must have general military experience. *Application Requirements:* Application form, certified copy of DD Form 214. **Deadline:** continuous.

Contact Loriann Sheridan, Veterans Programs Consultant, Oregon Department of Veterans' Affairs, 700 Summer Street, NE, Salem, OR 97301-1289. *E-mail:* sheridl@odva.state.or.us. *Phone:* 503-373-2264. *Fax:* 503-373-2393. *Website:* http://www.oregon.gov/odva.

Peter Connacher Memorial Scholarship. Renewable award for American prisoners-of-war and their descendants. Written proof of prisoner-of-war status and discharge papers from the U.S. Armed Forces must accompany application. Statement of relationship between applicant and former prisoner-of-war is required. Oregon residency preferred but not required. *Award:* Scholarship for use in freshman, sophomore, junior, senior, or graduate years;

renewable. *Eligibility Requirements:* Applicant must be enrolled or expecting to enroll full-time at a two-year or four-year institution. Available to U.S. citizens. *Application Requirements:* Application form. **Deadline:** March 1.

Contact Melissa Adams, Scholarship Processing Coordinator. *E-mail:* melissa.adams@hecc.oregon.gov. *Phone:* 541-687-7409. *Website:* http://www.GetCollegeFunds.org/.

PENNSYLVANIA

Blind or Deaf Beneficiary Grant Program. This state-funded program provides financial aid to blind or deaf students attending a postsecondary institution. This program awards funds on a first-come, first-served basis. *Award:* Grant for use in freshman, sophomore, junior, or senior years; not renewable. *Award amount:* $500. *Eligibility Requirements:* Applicant must be hearing impaired or visually impaired; enrolled or expecting to enroll full- or part-time at a two-year or four-year or technical institution or university and resident of Pennsylvania. Applicant must be hearing impaired or visually impaired. *Application Requirements:* Application form. **Deadline:** March 31.

Contact Keith New, Director of Public Relations. *E-mail:* knew@pheaa.org. *Phone:* 717-720-2509. *Website:* http://www.pheaa.org/.

Pennsylvania State Grant Program. Award for Pennsylvania residents attending an approved postsecondary institution as undergraduates in a program of at least two years duration. Renewable for up to eight semesters if applicants show continued need and academic progress. Must submit FAFSA. Number of awards granted varies annually. Scholarship value is $200 to $4340. Deadlines: May 1 and August 1. *Award:* Grant for use in freshman, sophomore, junior, or senior years; renewable. *Award amount:* $200–$4340. *Eligibility Requirements:* Applicant must be enrolled or expecting to enroll full- or part-time at a two-year or four-year or technical institution or university and resident of Pennsylvania. Available to U.S. citizens. *Application Requirements:* Application form, financial need analysis.

Contact Keith New, Director of Public Relations, Pennsylvania Higher Education Assistance Agency, 1200 North Seventh Street, Harrisburg, PA

17102-1444. *Phone:* 717-720-2509. *Website:* http://www.pheaa.org/.

Postsecondary Education Gratuity Program. The program offers waiver of tuition and fees for children of Pennsylvania police officers, firefighters, rescue or ambulance squad members, corrections facility employees, or National Guard members who died in line of duty after January 1, 1976. *Award:* Grant for use in freshman, sophomore, junior, or senior years; renewable. *Eligibility Requirements:* Applicant must be enrolled or expecting to enroll full-time at a two-year or four-year institution or university; resident of Pennsylvania and studying in Pennsylvania. Available to U.S. citizens. Applicant or parent must meet one or more of the following requirements: national guard experience; retired from active duty; disabled or killed as a result of military service; prisoner of war; or missing in action. *Application Requirements:* Application form. **Deadline:** July 1.

Contact Keith New, Director of Public Relations. *E-mail:* knew@pheaa.org. *Phone:* 717-720-2509. *Website:* http://www.pheaa.org/.

Ready to Succeed Scholarship Program. RTSS provides scholarships to high academic achievers that, in combination with the Pennsylvania State Grant Program, offer a total award up to $2,000 for full-time and $1,000 for part-time students. The minimum award is $500. Awards can be used to cover tuition, books, fees, supplies, and living expenses. Students must be nominated by their post-secondary institution for participation in the program. Funding is limited for the program and awards are made on a first-come, first-served basis. The program, which is funded by the Pennsylvania General Assembly, provides awards to high-achieving students whose annual family income does not exceed $110,000. *Award:* Scholarship for use in sophomore, junior, or senior years; not renewable. *Award amount:* $500–$2000. *Eligibility Requirements:* Applicant must be enrolled or expecting to enroll full- or part-time at a two-year or four-year or technical institution or university; resident of Pennsylvania and studying in Pennsylvania. Applicant must have 3.5 GPA or higher. *Application Requirements:* Application form, financial need analysis.

Contact Keith New, Director of Public Relations. *E-mail:* knew@pheaa.

org. *Phone:* 717-720-2509. *Website:* http://www.pheaa.org/.

SOUTH CAROLINA

Educational Assistance for Certain War Veterans Dependents Scholarship-South Carolina. Free tuition for South Carolina residents whose parent is a resident, wartime veteran, and meets one of these criteria. Must be awarded Purple Heart or Congressional Medal of Honor; permanently and totally disabled or killed as a result of military service; prisoner of war; or missing in action. Must be age 18 to 26 and enrolled or expecting to enroll full or part-time at a two-year or four-year technical institution or university in South Carolina. Complete information and qualifications for this award are on web site http://www.govoepp.state.sc.us. *Award:* Scholarship for use in freshman, sophomore, junior, or senior years; not renewable. *Eligibility Requirements:* Applicant must be age 18-26; enrolled or expecting to enroll full- or part-time at a two-year or four-year or technical institution or university; resident of South Carolina and studying in South Carolina. Available to U.S. citizens. Applicant or parent must meet one or more of the following requirements: general military experience; retired from active duty; disabled or killed as a result of military service; prisoner of war; or missing in action. *Application Requirements:* Application form, proof of qualification of veteran, transcript. **Deadline:** continuous.

Contact Adm. Dorian Sease-Phillips, Free Tuition Coordinator. *E-mail:* va@oepp.sc.gov. *Phone:* 803-647-2434. *Website:* http://www.govoepp.state.sc.us/vetaff.htm.

Palmetto Fellows Scholarship Program. Renewable award for qualified high school seniors in South Carolina to attend a four-year South Carolina institution. The scholarship must be applied directly towards the cost of attendance, less any other gift aid received. *Award:* Scholarship for use in freshman year; renewable. *Award amount:* $6700–$7500. *Number of awards:* 4846. *Eligibility Requirements:* Applicant must be high school student; planning to enroll or expecting to enroll full-time at a four-year institution or university; resident of South Carolina and studying in South Carolina.

Applicant must have 3.5 GPA or higher. Available to U.S. citizens. *Application Requirements:* Application form, test scores, transcript. **Deadline:** December 15.

Contact Dr. Karen Woodfaulk, Director of Student Services, South Carolina Commission on Higher Education, 1333 Main Street, Suite 200, Columbia, SC 29201. *E-mail:* kwoodfaulk@che.sc.gov. *Phone:* 803-737-2244. *Fax:* 803-737-3610. *Website:* http://www.che.sc.gov/.

South Carolina HOPE Scholarship. A merit-based scholarship for eligible first-time entering freshman attending a four-year South Carolina institution. Minimum GPA of 3.0 required. Must be a resident of South Carolina. *Award:* Scholarship for use in freshman year; not renewable. *Award amount:* $2800. *Number of awards:* 2605. *Eligibility Requirements:* Applicant must be high school student; planning to enroll or expecting to enroll full-time at a four-year institution or university; resident of South Carolina and studying in South Carolina. Applicant must have 3.0 GPA or higher. Available to U.S. citizens. *Application Requirements:* Transcript. **Deadline:** continuous.

Contact Gerrick Hampton, Scholarship Coordinator, South Carolina Commission on Higher Education, 1333 Main Street, Suite 200, Columbia, SC 29201. *E-mail:* ghampton@che.sc.gov. *Phone:* 803-737-4544. *Fax:* 803-737-3610. *Website:* http://www.che.sc.gov/.

South Carolina Need-Based Grants Program. Award based on FAFSA. A student may receive up to $2500 annually for full-time and up to $1250 annually for part-time study. The grant must be applied directly towards the cost of college attendance for a maximum of eight full-time equivalent terms. *Award:* Grant for use in freshman, sophomore, junior, senior, or graduate years; renewable. *Award amount:* $1250–$2500. *Number of awards:* 1–26,730. *Eligibility Requirements:* Applicant must be enrolled or expecting to enroll full- or part-time at a two-year or four-year or technical institution or university; resident of South Carolina and studying in South Carolina. Available to U.S. citizens. *Application Requirements:* Application form, financial need analysis. **Deadline:** continuous.

Contact Dr. Karen Woodfaulk, Director of Student Service, South Carolina Commission on Higher Education, 1333 Main Street, Suite 200, Columbia, SC 29201. *E-mail:* kwoodfaulk@che.sc.gov. *Phone:* 803-737-2244. *Fax:* 803-737-2297. *Website:* http://www.che.sc.gov/.

South Carolina Tuition Grants Program. Need-based grant set aside for students attending eligible independent colleges in South Carolina. Student must be a South Carolina resident. Must apply annually by submitting the Free Application for Federal Student Aid (FAFSA). Freshmen must graduate in top 75% of high school class OR score 900 on SAT/19 on ACT OR graduate with at least 2.0 on SC Uniform Grading Scale. Upperclassmen must pass a minimum of 24 credit hours annually. *Award:* Grant for use in freshman, sophomore, junior, or senior years; renewable. *Award amount:* $100–$3200. *Eligibility Requirements:* Applicant must be enrolled or expecting to enroll full-time at a two-year or four-year institution or university; resident of South Carolina and studying in South Carolina. Available to U.S. citizens. *Application Requirements:* Financial need analysis. **Deadline:** June 30.

Contact Zachary Christian, Financial Aid Counselor, South Carolina Tuition Grants Commission, 115 Atrium Way, Suite 102, Columbia, SC 29223. *E-mail:* zachary@sctuitiongrants.org. *Phone:* 803-896-1120. *Website:* http://www.sctuitiongrants.org/.

SOUTH DAKOTA

South Dakota Opportunity Scholarship. Renewable scholarship may be worth up to $5000 over four years to students who take a rigorous college-prep curriculum while in high school and stay in the state for their postsecondary education. *Award:* Scholarship for use in freshman, sophomore, junior, or senior years; renewable. *Award amount:* $1000. *Number of awards:* 1000. *Eligibility Requirements:* Applicant must be high school student; planning to enroll or expecting to enroll full-time at a two-year or four-year or technical institution or university; resident of South Dakota and studying in South Dakota. Applicant must have 3.0 GPA or higher. Available to U.S. citizens. *Application Requirements:* Application form, test scores, transcript. **Deadline:** September 1.

Contact Janelle Toman, Scholarship Committee, South Dakota Board of Regents, 306 East Capitol, Suite 200, Pierre, SD 57501-2545. *E-mail:* info@sdbor.edu. *Phone:* 605-773-3455. *Fax:* 605-773-2422. *Website:* http://www.sdbor.edu/.

TENNESSEE

Christa McAuliffe Scholarship Program. Scholarship to assist and support Tennessee students who have demonstrated a commitment to a career in educating the youth of Tennessee. Offered to college seniors for a period of one academic year. Must have a minimum college GPA of 3.5. Must have attained scores on either the ACT or SAT which meet or exceed the national norms. Must be enrolled full time and not be in default or owe repayment on a federal or state student loan. Award is made on a periodic basis as funding becomes available. Education. *Award:* Scholarship for use in senior year; not renewable. *Eligibility Requirements:* Applicant must be enrolled or expecting to enroll full-time at a four-year institution or university; resident of Tennessee and studying in Tennessee. Applicant must have 3.5 GPA or higher. Available to U.S. citizens. *Application Requirements:* Application form, essay. **Deadline:** April 1.

Contact Ms. Kathy Stripling, Grant and Scholarship Analyst, Tennessee Student Assistance Corporation, Parkway Towers, 404 James Robertson Parkway, Suite 1510, Nashville, TN 37243-0820. *E-mail:* kathy.stripling@tn.gov. *Phone:* 615-253-7480. *Website:* http://www.tn.gov/collegepays.

Dependent Children Scholarship Program. Scholarship for Tennessee residents who are dependent children of a Tennessee law enforcement officer, fireman, or an emergency medical service technician who have been killed or totally and permanently disabled while performing duties within the scope of such employment. The scholarship is awarded to full-time undergraduate students for a maximum of four academic years or the period required for the completion of the program of study. *Award:* Scholarship for use in freshman, sophomore, junior, or senior years; not renewable. *Award amount:* $3000–$30,000. *Eligibility*

Requirements: Applicant must be enrolled or expecting to enroll full-time at a two-year or four-year institution or university; resident of Tennessee and studying in Tennessee. Available to U.S. citizens. *Application Requirements:* Application form. **Deadline:** July 15.

Contact Ms. Kathy Stripling, Grant and Scholarship Analyst, Tennessee Student Assistance Corporation, Parkway Towers, 404 James Robertson Parkway, Suite 1510, Nashville, TN 37243-0820. *E-mail:* kathy.stripling@tn.gov. *Phone:* 615-253-7480. *Website:* http://www.tn.gov/collegepays.

Helping Heroes Grant. Provides assistance to Tennessee veterans who have been awarded the Iraq Campaign Medal, Afghanistan Campaign Medal, or Global War on Terrorism Expeditionary Medal (on or after 9/11/01) and who meet eligibility requirements for the program. Award is up to $1,000 per semester. For more information, visit http://www.TN.gov/collegepays. *Award:* Grant for use in freshman, sophomore, junior, or senior years; renewable. *Award amount:* $2000. *Eligibility Requirements:* Applicant must be enrolled or expecting to enroll full- or part-time at a two-year or four-year institution or university; resident of Tennessee and studying in Tennessee. Available to U.S. citizens. Applicant must have general military experience. *Application Requirements:* Application form. **Deadline:** September 1.

Contact Mr. Robert Biggers, Assistant Executive Director of Grant & Scholarship Programs, Tennessee Student Assistance Corporation, Parkway Towers, 404 James Robertson Parkway, Suite 1510, Nashville, TN 37243. *E-mail:* robert.biggers@tn.gov. *Phone:* 615-253-7453. *Website:* http://www.tn.gov/collegepays.

HOPE with ASPIRE. HOPE Scholarship of $2,000 per semester (four-year institution) or $1,000 per semester (two-year institution) with $750 supplement per semester. Must meet Tennessee HOPE Scholarship requirements and Adjusted Gross Income (AGI) attributable to the student must be $36,000 or less. *Award:* Scholarship for use in freshman, sophomore, junior, or senior years; renewable. *Award amount:* $5500. *Eligibility Requirements:* Applicant must be enrolled or expecting to enroll full- or part-time at a two-year or four-year institution or university;

resident of Tennessee and studying in Tennessee. Applicant must have 3.0 GPA or higher. Available to U.S. citizens. *Application Requirements:* **Deadline:** September 1.

Contact Mr. Robert Biggers, Assistant Executive Director of Grant & Scholarships Programs, Tennessee Student Assistance Corporation, Parkway Towers, 404 James Robertson Parkway, Suite 1510, Nashville, TN 37243-0820. *E-mail:* robert.biggers@tn.gov. *Phone:* 615-253-7453. *Website:* http://www.tn.gov/collegepays.

Ned McWherter Scholars Program. Award for Tennessee high school seniors with high academic ability. Must have minimum high school GPA of 3.5 and a score of 29 on the ACT or SAT equivalent. Must attend a college or university in Tennessee. Must be a Tennessee resident and U.S. citizen or permanent resident. For more information, visit web site http://tn.gov/collegepays. *Award:* Scholarship for use in freshman, sophomore, junior, or senior years; renewable. *Award amount:* $3000. *Eligibility Requirements:* Applicant must be enrolled or expecting to enroll full-time at a two-year or four-year or technical institution or university; resident of Tennessee and studying in Tennessee. Applicant must have 3.5 GPA or higher. Available to U.S. citizens. *Application Requirements:* Application form. **Deadline:** February 15.

Contact Ms. Kathy Stripling, Grants and Scholarship Analyst, Tennessee Student Assistance Corporation, 404 James Robertson Parkway, Suite 1510, Parkway Towers, Nashville, TN 37243-0820. *E-mail:* kathy.stripling@tn.gov. *Phone:* 615-253-7480. *Website:* http://www.tn.gov/collegepays.

TELS HOPE Access Grant. Nonrenewable award of $2,750 for students at four-year colleges or $1,750 for students at two-year colleges. Entering freshmen must have a minimum GPA of 2.75, ACT score of 18-20 (or SAT equivalent), and adjusted gross income attributable to the student must be $36,000 or less. Recipients will become eligible for Tennessee HOPE Scholarship by meeting HOPE Scholarship renewal criteria. *Award:* Grant for use in freshman, sophomore, junior, or senior years; not renewable. *Award amount:* $2750. *Eligibility Requirements:* Applicant must be enrolled or expecting to enroll full- or part-time at a two-year or four-year institution or university; resident of Tennessee and studying in Tennessee. Applicant must have 3.0 GPA or higher. Available to U.S. citizens. *Application Requirements:* **Deadline:** September 1.

Contact Mr. Robert Biggers, Assistant Executive Director of Grant & Scholarship Programs, Tennessee Student Assistance Corporation, Parkway Towers, 404 James Robertson Parkway, Suite 1510, Nashville, TN 37243-0820. *E-mail:* robert.biggers@tn. gov. *Phone:* 615-253-7453. *Website:* http://www.tn.gov/collegepays.

TELS -HOPE with General Assembly Merit Scholarship (GAMS). Students who qualify for the HOPE Scholarship can receive GAMS by earning a minimum 3.75 GPA and a 29 or above on the ACT (or SAT equivalent). The supplemental award is $500 per semester. Must be a Tennessee resident. For more information, visit www.tn.gov/collegepays. *Award:* Scholarship for use in freshman, sophomore, junior, or senior years; renewable. *Award amount:* $5000. *Eligibility Requirements:* Applicant must be enrolled or expecting to enroll full- or part-time at a two-year or four-year institution or university; resident of Tennessee and studying in Tennessee. Applicant must have 3.5 GPA or higher. Available to U.S. citizens. *Application Requirements:* **Deadline:** September 1.

Contact Mr. Robert Biggers, Assistant Executive Director of Grant & Scholarship Programs, Tennessee Student Assistance Corporation, Parkway Towers, 404 James Robertson Parkway, Suite 1510, Nashville, TN 37243-0820. *E-mail:* robert.biggers@tn. gov. *Phone:* 615-253-7453. *Website:* http://www.tn.gov/collegepays.

TELS - Tennessee HOPE Scholarship. Students must achieve a minimum 3.0 GPA or 21 or above on the ACT to qualify for the scholarship. Award amount is $1,750 for per semester at four-year institutions and $1,500 per semester at two-year institutions for entering freshmen who first received HOPE in fall 2015 and thereafter. Award amount is $2,000 per semester at four-year institutions and $1,000 per semester at two-year institutions for students who first received HOPE between fall 2009 and summer 2015. Must be a Tennessee resident

attending an eligible postsecondary institution in Tennessee. For more information, visit http://www.TN.gov/CollegePays. *Award:* Scholarship for use in freshman, sophomore, junior, or senior years; renewable. *Award amount:* $2000–$6000. *Eligibility Requirements:* Applicant must be enrolled or expecting to enroll full- or part-time at a two-year or four-year institution or university; resident of Tennessee and studying in Tennessee. Applicant must have 3.0 GPA or higher. Available to U. S. citizens. *Application Requirements:* **Deadline:** September 1.

Contact Mr. Robert Biggers, Assistant Executive Director of Grant & Scholarship Programs, Tennessee Student Assistance Corporation, Parkway Towers, 404 James Robertson Parkway, Suite 1510, Nashville, TN 37243-0820. *E-mail:* robert.biggers@tn. gov. *Phone:* 615-253-7453. *Website:* http://www.tn.gov/collegepays.

Tennessee Dual Enrollment Grant. Grant for study at an eligible Tennessee postsecondary institution awarded to juniors and seniors in a Tennessee high school who have been admitted to undergraduate study while still pursuing a high school diploma. For more information, visit web site http://www.tn.gov/collegepays. *Award:* Grant for use in freshman year; renewable. *Award amount:* $1200. *Eligibility Requirements:* Applicant must be high school student; planning to enroll or expecting to enroll part-time at a two-year or four-year or technical institution or university; resident of Tennessee and studying in Tennessee. Available to U.S. citizens. *Application Requirements:* Application form. **Deadline:** September 1.

Contact Mr. Robert Biggers, Assistant Executive Director of Grant & Scholarship Programs, Tennessee Student Assistance Corporation, Parkway Towers, 404 James Robertson Parkway, Suite 1510, Nashville, TN 37243-0820. *E-mail:* robert.biggers@tn. gov. *Phone:* 615-253-7453. *Website:* http://www.tn.gov/collegepays.

Tennessee Education Lottery Scholarship Program Wilder-Naifeh Technical Skills Grant. Award up to $2,000 for students enrolled in a certificate or diploma program at a Tennessee College of Applied Technology (TCAT). For more information, visit http://www.TN.gov/CollegePays. *Award:* Grant for use

in freshman or sophomore years; renewable. *Award amount:* $2000. *Eligibility Requirements:* Applicant must be enrolled or expecting to enroll full- or part-time at a technical institution; resident of Tennessee and studying in Tennessee. Available to U.S. citizens. *Application Requirements:* **Deadline:** November 1.

Contact Mr. Robert Biggers, Assistant Executive Director of Grant & Scholarship Programs, Tennessee Student Assistance Corporation, Parkway Towers, 404 James Robertson Parkway, Suite 1510, Nashville, TN 37243-0820. *E-mail:* robert.biggers@tn. gov. *Phone:* 615-253-7453. *Website:* http://www.tn.gov/collegepays.

Tennessee HOPE Foster Child Tuition Grant. Renewable tuition award available for recipients of the HOPE Scholarship or HOPE Access Grant. Student must have been in Tennessee state custody as a foster child for at least one year after reaching age 14. Award amount varies and shall not exceed the tuition and mandatory fees at an eligible Tennessee public postsecondary institution. For additional information, visit web site http://www.tn.gov/collegepays. *Award:* Scholarship for use in freshman, sophomore, junior, or senior years; renewable. *Eligibility Requirements:* Applicant must be enrolled or expecting to enroll full- or part-time at a two-year or four-year institution or university; resident of Tennessee and studying in Tennessee. Applicant must have 3.0 GPA or higher. Available to U.S. citizens. *Application Requirements:* **Deadline:** September 1.

Contact Mr. Robert Biggers, Assistant Executive Director of Grant & Scholarship Programs, Tennessee Student Assistance Corporation, Parkway Towers, 404 James Robertson Parkway, Suite 1510, Nashville, TN 37243-0820. *E-mail:* robert.biggers@tn. gov. *Phone:* 615-253-7453. *Website:* http://www.tn.gov/collegepays.

Tennessee Step Up Scholarship. Scholarship program designed to assist students with intellectual disabilities who have completed high school and enroll in up to a four-year individualized program at an eligible postsecondary institution. For entering students beginning with Fall 2015 and thereafter, students will receive $1,750 per semester. For students who first received the STEP UP Scholarship in

Fall 2012 through Summer 2015 students will continue to receive $2,000 per semester. *Award:* Scholarship for use in freshman, sophomore, junior, or senior years; not renewable. *Award amount:* $2000–$4000. *Eligibility Requirements:* Applicant must be enrolled or expecting to enroll full- or part-time at a four-year institution or university; resident of Tennessee and studying in Tennessee. Available to U.S. citizens. *Application Requirements:* Application form. **Deadline:** September 1.

Contact Ms. Tracy Biggers, Grant and Scholarship Analyst, Tennessee Student Assistance Corporation, Parkway Towers, 404 James Robertson Parkway, Suite 1510, Nashville, TN 37243. *E-mail:* Tracy.Biggers@tn.gov. *Phone:* 615-253-7460. *Website:* http://www.tn.gov/collegepays.

Tennessee Student Assistance Award. Award to assist financially-needy Tennessee residents attending an approved college or university within the state. Complete a Free Application for Federal Student Aid form. Students are encourage to complete the FAFSA as soon as possible after October 1 for priority consideration. To apply, go to http://www.fafsa.gov. For more information, go to www.tn.gov/collegepays *Award:* Grant for use in freshman, sophomore, junior, or senior years; not renewable. *Award amount:* $100–$4000. *Eligibility Requirements:* Applicant must be enrolled or expecting to enroll full- or part-time at a two-year or four-year or technical institution or university; resident of Tennessee and studying in Tennessee. Available to U.S. citizens. *Application Requirements:* **Deadline:** March 1.

Contact Mrs. Leah Louallen, Director of Grants and Scholarship Programs, Tennessee Student Assistance Corporation, Parkway Towers, 404 James Robertson Parkway, Suite 1510, Nashville, TN 37243-0820. *E-mail:* leah.louallen@tn.gov. *Phone:* 615-253-7478. *Website:* http://www.tn.gov/collegepays.

TEXAS

Conditional Grant Program. Renewable award to students who are considered economically disadvantaged based on federal guidelines. The maximum amount awarded per semester is $3000 not to exceed $6000 per academic year. Students already enrolled in an undergraduate program should have minimum GPA 2.5 and students newly enrolling should have minimum GPA 3.0. Civil Engineering; Computer Science/Data Processing; Occupational Safety and Health. *Award:* Grant for use in freshman, sophomore, junior, or senior years; renewable. *Award amount:* up to $6000. *Eligibility Requirements:* Applicant must be enrolled or expecting to enroll full-time at a four-year institution or university; resident of Texas and studying in Texas. Available to U.S. citizens. *Application Requirements:* Application form, essay, interview, recommendations or references, test scores, transcript. **Deadline:** March 1.

Contact Minnie Brown, Program Coordinator, Texas Department of Transportation, 125 East 11th Street, Austin, TX 78701-2483. *E-mail:* mbrown2@dot.state.tx.us. *Phone:* 512-416-4979. *Fax:* 512-416-4980. *Website:* http://www.txdot.gov/.

Texas Educational Opportunity Grant (TEOG). Provides grant aid to students with financial need attending public two-year colleges. For initial award, student must be enrolled at least half-time and awarded in the first 30 hours (or its equivalent) of an associate's degree or certificate program (excluding credits for dual enrollment or by examination). For renewal award, student must also maintain a minimum overall GPA of 2.50 and successfully complete a minimum of 75% of classes attempted during the school year. *Award:* Grant for use in freshman, sophomore, junior, or senior years; not renewable. *Award amount:* $1–$8000. *Eligibility Requirements:* Applicant must be enrolled or expecting to enroll full- or part-time at a two-year institution; resident of Texas and studying in Texas. Available to U.S. citizens. *Application Requirements:* FAFSA, financial need analysis.

Top 10% Scholarship Program. Encourage outstanding high school students who graduate within the top 10 percent of their high school graduating class to attend a public college or university in Texas. Students must demonstrate financial need and complete the FAFSA by the state priority deadline of March 15. Renewal award students must also maintain a minimum overall GPA of 3.25, successfully complete at least 30 SCH each year, and successfully complete at least 75% of the hours attempted each year. *Award:* Schol-arship for use in freshman, sophomore, junior, or senior years; renewable. *Award amount:* $1–$600. *Eligibility Requirements:* Applicant must be enrolled or expecting to enroll full-time at a two-year or four-year or technical institution or university; resident of Texas and studying in Texas. Available to U.S. citizens. *Application Requirements:* FAFSA, financial need analysis.

Toward EXcellence, Access, and Success (TEXAS) Grant. Renewable aid for students enrolled at least three-quarter time in a public four-year college or university in Texas within sixteen months of graduation from high school. Must demonstrate financial need and have completed the Foundation, Recommended, or DAP Curriculum in high school. For renewal awards, must also maintain a minimum GPA of 2.5 and complete a minimum of 24 SCH's each year. Amount of award is determined by the financial aid office of each school. Priority FAFSA completion deadline is March 15. Contact the college/university financial aid office for additional eligibility information. *Award:* Grant for use in freshman, sophomore, junior, or senior years; renewable. *Award amount:* $1–$8000. *Eligibility Requirements:* Applicant must be enrolled or expecting to enroll full- or part-time at a four-year institution or university; resident of Texas and studying in Texas. Available to U.S. citizens. *Application Requirements:* Financial need analysis, transcript.

Tuition Equalization Grant (TEG) Program. Renewable award for Texas residents enrolled at least three-quarter time at an independent college or university in Texas in a degree program that does not lead to ordination or licensure to preach. Non-residents who are National Merit Finalists and are receiving at least $1,000 in scholarships may also receive awards. Awards are based on financial need. Renewal awards also require the student to maintain a minimum overall college GPA of at least 2.5, complete at least 24 SCH's each year (18 SCH's for students in graduate programs), and complete a minimum of 75% of classes attempted each year. Priority deadline to complete the FAFSA is March 15. Must not be receiving athletic scholarship concurrently. Contact college/university financial aid office for application information. *Award:* Grant for use in freshman, sophomore, junior, senior, or graduate years; not renewable. *Award amount:* $1–$4875. *Eligibility Requirements:* Applicant must be enrolled or expecting to enroll full- or part-time at a two-year or four-year institution or university and studying in Texas. Available to U.S. citizens. *Application Requirements:* Financial need analysis.

The Urban Scholarships Fund. Eligibility - United States citizen or eligible non-citizen (permanent resident card I-551 front and back copy) Texas resident, graduate of high school from 29 urban cities: Abilene, Amarillo, Arlington, Austin, Beaumont, Brownsville, Carrollton, Corpus Christi, Dallas, Denton, El Paso, Fort Worth, Frisco, Garland, Grand Prairie, Houston, Irving, Killeen, Laredo, Lubbock, McAllen, McKinney, Mesquite, Midland, Pasadena, Plano, San Antonio, Waco and Wichita Falls *Award:* Scholarship for use in freshman, sophomore, junior, or senior years; not renewable. *Award amount:* $700–$1000. *Number of awards:* 450–500. *Eligibility Requirements:* Applicant must be age 16-65; enrolled or expecting to enroll full-time at a two-year or four-year or technical institution or university and resident of Texas. Available to U.S. citizens. *Application Requirements:* Financial need analysis. **Deadline:** July 10.

Contact Ms. Janice Jackson, Office Programs Administrator, Texas Association of Developing Colleges, 1140 Empire Central Drive 550, Dallas, TX 75247. *E-mail:* janice.jackson@txadc.org. *Phone:* 214-630-2511. *Website:* http://www.txadc.org.

UTAH

Higher Education Success Stipend Program. Award available to students with substantial financial need for use at any of the participating Utah institutions. The student must be a Utah resident. Contact the financial aid office of the participating institution for requirements and deadlines. *Award:* Grant for use in freshman, sophomore, junior, or senior years; not renewable. *Award amount:* $300–$5000. *Number of awards:* 495–8243. *Eligibility Requirements:* Applicant must be enrolled or expecting to enroll full- or part-time at a two-year or four-year or technical institution or university; resident of Utah and studying in Utah. Available to U.S. cit-

izens. *Application Requirements:* Financial need analysis. **Deadline:** continuous.

VERMONT

Vermont Incentive Grants. Renewable grants for Vermont residents based on financial need. Must meet needs test. Must be college undergraduate or graduate student enrolled full-time at an approved post secondary institution. Only available to Vermont residents. *Award:* Grant for use in freshman, sophomore, junior, or senior years; renewable. *Award amount:* $500–$10,800. *Eligibility Requirements:* Applicant must be enrolled or expecting to enroll full-time at a two-year or four-year or technical institution or university and resident of Vermont. Available to U.S. citizens. *Application Requirements:* Application form, FAFSA, financial need analysis. **Deadline:** continuous.

Vermont Non-Degree Student Grant Program. Need-based, renewable grants for Vermont residents enrolled in non-degree programs in a college, vocational school, or high school adult program, that will improve employability or encourage further study. Award amounts vary. *Award:* Grant for use in freshman, sophomore, junior, or senior years; renewable. *Eligibility Requirements:* Applicant must be enrolled or expecting to enroll full- or part-time at a two-year or four-year or technical institution or university and resident of Vermont. Available to U.S. citizens. *Application Requirements:* Application form, financial need analysis. **Deadline:** continuous.

Vermont Part-Time Student Grants. For undergraduates carrying less than twelve credits per semester who have not received a Bachelor's degree. Must be a Vermont resident. Based on financial need. Complete Vermont Financial Aid Packet to apply. May be used at any approved post-secondary institution. *Award:* Grant for use in freshman, sophomore, junior, or senior years; renewable. *Award amount:* $250–$8100. *Eligibility Requirements:* Applicant must be enrolled or expecting to enroll part-time at a four-year institution or university and resident of Vermont. Available to U.S. citizens. *Application Requirements:* Application form, financial need analysis. **Deadline:** continuous.

VIRGINIA

American Council of the Blind Scholarships. Merit-based award available to undergraduate students who are legally blind in both eyes. Submit certificate of legal blindness and proof of acceptance at an accredited postsecondary institution, as well as scholarship application, high school or college transcripts and other supporting documents (see directions on www.acb.org). Deadline: February 15. *Award:* Scholarship for use in freshman, sophomore, junior, senior, graduate, or postgraduate years; not renewable. *Award amount:* $1000–$3500. *Number of awards:* 16–20. *Eligibility Requirements:* Applicant must be visually impaired and enrolled or expecting to enroll full- or part-time at a two-year or four-year or technical institution or university. Applicant must be visually impaired. Applicant must have 3.5 GPA or higher. Available to U.S. citizens. *Application Requirements:* Application form, autobiography, driver's license, essay, interview. **Deadline:** February 15.

Mary Marshall Practical Nursing Scholarship (LPN). Awards for students who are accepted or enrolled as a full-time or part-time student in a practical school of nursing in the state of Virginia. Must be a Virginia resident for at least one year and have submitted a completed application form and a recommendation from the Director regarding scholastic attainment and financial need prior to June 30. Students pursuing a nursing degree not available in Virginia, are not eligible for the scholarship. Scholarship amount varies. Nursing. *Award:* Scholarship for use in freshman, sophomore, junior, or senior years; not renewable. *Award amount:* $600–$1200. *Number of awards:* 26–88. *Eligibility Requirements:* Applicant must be enrolled or expecting to enroll full- or part-time at a two-year or four-year or technical institution or university; resident of Virginia and studying in Virginia. Applicant must have 2.5 GPA or higher. Available to U.S. citizens. *Application Requirements:* Application form, driver's license, essay, financial need analysis, recommendations or references, transcript. **Deadline:** June 30.

Contact Miss Sarahbeth Jones, Communications Specialist, Virginia Department of Health, Office of

Minority Health and Health Equity, PO Box 2448, 109 Governor Street, Suite 1016-E, Richmond, VA 23218-2448. *E-mail:* IncentivePrograms@vdh.virginia. gov. *Phone:* 804-864-7422. *Fax:* 804-864-7440. *Website:* http://www.vdh.virginia.gov/.

Mary Marshall Registered Nursing Scholarships. Scholarship for Virginia residents who have been accepted or is enrollment as a full-time or part-time student in a school of nursing in the state of Virginia. Must demonstrate financial need, verified by the Financial Aid Office/authorized person at the applicant's nursing school. Must also be a resident of Virginia for at least one year and have a minimum 3.0 GPA in required courses. Must have submitted a completed application form and an official grade transcript to The Office of Minority Health and Public Health Policy prior to June 30. If no college courses attempted an official high school transcript or equivalent must be submitted. Nursing. *Award:* Scholarship for use in freshman, sophomore, junior, or senior years; not renewable. *Award amount:* $600–$2000. *Number of awards:* 28–95. *Eligibility Requirements:* Applicant must be enrolled or expecting to enroll full- or part-time at a two-year or four-year institution or university; resident of Virginia and studying in Virginia. Applicant must have 2.5 GPA or higher. Available to U.S. citizens. *Application Requirements:* Application form, driver's license, essay, financial need analysis, recommendations or references, transcript. **Deadline:** June 30.

Contact Miss. Sarahbeth Jones, Communications Specialist, Virginia Department of Health, Office of Minority Health and Health Equity, PO Box 2448, 109 Governor Street, Suite 1016-E, Richmond, VA 23218-2448. *E-mail:* IncentivePrograms@vdh.virginia. gov. *Phone:* 804-864-7422. *Fax:* 804-864-7440. *Website:* http://www.vdh.virginia.gov/.

State Department Federal Credit Union Annual Scholarship Program. Scholarships available to members who are currently enrolled in a degree program and have completed 12 credit hours of coursework at an accredited college or university. Must have own account in good standing with SDFCU, have a minimum 2.5 GPA, submit official cumulative transcripts, and describe need for financial assistance to continue their education. Scholarship only open to members of State Department Federal Credit Union. *Award:* Scholarship for use in sophomore, junior, senior, or graduate years; not renewable. *Award amount:* $2500. *Eligibility Requirements:* Applicant must be enrolled or expecting to enroll full-time at a four-year institution or university. Applicant must have 2.5 GPA or higher. Available to U.S. and non-U.S. citizens. *Application Requirements:* Application form, financial need analysis. **Deadline:** April 29.

Virginia Commonwealth Award. Need-based award for undergraduate or graduate study at a Virginia public two- or four-year college, or university. Undergraduates must be Virginia residents. The application and awards process are administered by the financial aid office at the Virginia public institution where the student is enrolled. Dollar value of each award varies. Contact college financial aid office for application and deadlines. *Award:* Grant for use in freshman, sophomore, junior, or senior years; not renewable. *Eligibility Requirements:* Applicant must be enrolled or expecting to enroll full- or part-time at a two-year or four-year institution or university; resident of Virginia and studying in Virginia. Available to U.S. citizens. *Application Requirements:* Financial need analysis.

Virginia Guaranteed Assistance Program. Awards to undergraduate students proportional to their need, up to full tuition, fees and book allowance. Must be a graduate of a Virginia high school. High school GPA of 2.5 required. Must be enrolled full-time in a public Virginia two- or four-year institution and demonstrate financial need. Must maintain minimum college GPA of 2.0 for renewal awards. *Award:* Grant for use in freshman, sophomore, junior, or senior years; not renewable. *Eligibility Requirements:* Applicant must be enrolled or expecting to enroll full-time at a two-year or four-year institution or university; resident of Virginia and studying in Virginia. Available to U.S. citizens. *Application Requirements:* Financial need analysis.

Virginia Military Survivors and Dependents Education Program. Scholarships for post-secondary students between ages 16 and 29 to attend Virginia state-supported institutions. Must be child or surviving spouse of veteran who has either been permanently or totally disabled due to war or other armed conflict; died as a result of war or other armed conflict; or been listed as a POW or MIA. Parent must also meet Virginia residency requirements. *Award:* Scholarship for use in freshman, sophomore, junior, senior, or graduate years; renewable. *Eligibility Requirements:* Applicant must be age 16-29; enrolled or expecting to enroll full-time at a two-year or four-year or technical institution or university; resident of Virginia and studying in Virginia. Available to U.S. citizens. Applicant or parent must meet one or more of the following requirements: general military experience; retired from active duty; disabled or killed as a result of military service; prisoner of war; or missing in action. *Application Requirements:* Application form, DD214 of service member, birth certificate of applicant, marriage certificate, acceptance letter from institution. **Deadline:** varies.

Contact Mrs. Doris Sullivan, Coordinator, Virginia Department of Veterans Services, 1351 Hershberger Road, Suite 220, Roanoke, VA 24012. *Phone:* 540-561-6625. *Fax:* 540-857-7573. *Website:* http://www.dvs.virginia.gov/.

Virginia Tuition Assistance Grant Program (Private Institutions). Awards for undergraduate students. Also available to graduate and first professional degree students pursuing a health-related degree program. Not to be used for religious study. Must be US citizen or eligible non-citizen, Virginia domiciled, and enrolled full-time at an approved private, nonprofit college within Virginia. Information and application available from participating Virginia colleges financial aid office. Visit http://www.schev.edu and click on Financial Aid. *Award:* Grant for use in freshman, sophomore, junior, senior, or graduate years; renewable. *Award amount:* $775–$3100. *Eligibility Requirements:* Applicant must be enrolled or expecting to enroll full-time at a four-year institution or university; resident of Virginia and studying in Virginia. Available to U.S. citizens. *Application Requirements:* Application form. **Deadline:** July 31.

WASHINGTON

WSCPA Foundation Scholarships. The Washington CPA Foundation is a 501(c)(3) not-for-profit foundation committed to ensuring that Washington's diverse communities have awareness of and access to both high quality accounting education and the resources required to make sound financial decisions. In order to make our vision a reality, the Foundation funds education and research in the field of accountancy, scholarships for accounting students, programs designed to improve accounting education and expand knowledge within the profession, and initiatives designed to improve the public's skills in personal financial management. *Award:* Scholarship for use in sophomore, junior, senior, graduate, or postgraduate years; not renewable. *Award amount:* $5000. *Number of awards:* 50–60. *Eligibility Requirements:* Applicant must be enrolled or expecting to enroll full- or part-time at a four-year institution or university. Applicant must have 3.0 GPA or higher. Available to U.S. and non-U.S. citizens. *Application Requirements:* Application form, essay. **Deadline:** February 14.

Contact Ms. Jocelyn Nystrom, Advocacy and Foundation Coordinator, Washington Society of Certified Public Accountants, 902 140th Ave NE, Bellevue, WA 98005. *E-mail:* Jnystrom@wscpa.org. *Phone:* 425-644-4800. *Website:* http://www.wscpa.org/.

WEST VIRGINIA

West Virginia Higher Education Grant Program. Award available for West Virginia resident for one year immediately preceding the date of application, high school graduate or the equivalent, demonstrate financial need, and enroll as a full-time undergraduate at an approved university or college located in West Virginia or Pennsylvania. *Award:* Grant for use in freshman, sophomore, junior, or senior years; not renewable. *Award amount:* $300–$2700. *Number of awards:* 18,000–21,000. *Eligibility Requirements:* Applicant must be enrolled or expecting to enroll full-time at a two-year or four-year institution or university; resident of West Virginia and studying in Pennsylvania, West Virginia. Available to U.S. citizens. *Application Requirements:* Financial need analysis. **Deadline:** April 15.

Contact Judy Smith, Senior Project Coordinator, West Virginia Higher Education Policy Commission-Student Services, 1018 Kanawha Boulevard East, Suite 700, Charleston, WV 25301-2827. *E-mail:* judy.kee@wvhepc.edu. *Phone:* 304-558-4618. *Website:* http://www.wvhepc.edu.

WISCONSIN

Handicapped Student Grant-Wisconsin. One-time award available to residents of Wisconsin who have severe or profound hearing or visual impairment. Must be enrolled at least half-time at a nonprofit institution. If the handicap prevents the student from attending a Wisconsin school, the award may be used out-of-state in a specialized college. Refer to web site for further details http://www.heab.state.wi.us. *Award:* Grant for use in freshman, sophomore, junior, or senior years; not renewable. *Award amount:* $250–$1800. *Eligibility Requirements:* Applicant must be hearing impaired or visually impaired; enrolled or expecting to enroll full- or part-time at a four-year institution or university and resident of Wisconsin. Applicant must be hearing impaired or visually impaired. Available to U.S. citizens. *Application Requirements:* Application form, financial need analysis. **Deadline:** continuous.

Contact Sandy Thomas, Program Coordinator, Wisconsin Higher Educational Aid Board, PO Box 7885, Madison, WI 53707-7885. *E-mail:* sandy.thomas@wi.gov. *Phone:* 608-266-0888. *Fax:* 608-267-2808. *Website:* http://www.heab.wi.gov/.

Minority Undergraduate Retention Grant-Wisconsin. The grant provides financial assistance to African-American, Native-American, Hispanic, and former citizens of Laos, Vietnam, and Cambodia, for study in Wisconsin. Must be Wisconsin resident, enrolled at least half-time in Wisconsin Technical College System schools, non-profit independent colleges and universities, and tribal colleges. Refer to web site for further details http://www.heab.state.wi.us. *Award:* Grant for use in sophomore, junior, or senior years; not renewable. *Award amount:* $250–$2500. *Eligibility Requirements:* Applicant must be American Indian/Alaska Native, Asian/Pacific Islander, Black (non-Hispanic), Hispanic; enrolled or expecting to enroll

full- or part-time at a two-year or four-year or technical institution or university; resident of Wisconsin and studying in Wisconsin. Available to U.S. and non-U.S. citizens. *Application Requirements:* Application form, financial need analysis. **Deadline:** continuous.

Contact Mary Lou Kuzdas, Program Coordinator, Wisconsin Higher Educational Aid Board, PO Box 7885, Madison, WI 53707-7885. *E-mail:* mary.kuzdas@wi.gov. *Phone:* 608-267-2212. *Fax:* 608-267-2808. *Website:* http://www.heab.wi.gov/.

Talent Incentive Program Grant. Grant assists residents of Wisconsin who are attending a nonprofit institution in Wisconsin, and who have substantial financial need. Must meet income criteria, be considered economically and educationally disadvantaged, and be enrolled at least half-time. Refer to web site for further details http://www.heab.state.wi.us. *Award:* Grant for use in freshman, sophomore, junior, or senior years; renewable. *Award amount:* $250–$1800. *Eligibility Requirements:* Applicant must be enrolled or expecting to enroll full- or part-time at a two-year or four-year or technical institution or university; resident of Wisconsin and studying in Wisconsin. Available to U.S. citizens. *Application Requirements:* Application form, financial need analysis, nomination by financial aid office. **Deadline:** continuous.

Contact Colette Brown, Program Coordinator, Wisconsin Higher Educational Aid Board, PO Box 7885, Madison, WI 53707-7885. *E-mail:* colette.brown@wi.gov. *Phone:* 608-266-1665. *Fax:* 608-267-2808. *Website:* http://www.heab.wi.gov/.

Veterans Education (VetEd) Reimbursement Grant. The grant is for eligible Wisconsin veterans enrolled at approved schools who have not yet earned a BS/BA. Reimburses up to 120 credits or eight semesters at the UW Madison rate for the same number of credits taken in one semester or term. The number of credits or semesters is based on length of time serving on active duty in the armed forces (active duty for training does not apply). Application is due no later than 60 days after the course start date. The student must earn a 2.0 or better for the semester. An eligible veteran will have entered active duty as a Wisconsin resident or lived in state for twelve consecutive months since entering active duty. *Award:* Grant for use in freshman, sophomore, junior, or senior years; renewable. *Award amount:* $1340–$4000. *Eligibility Requirements:* Applicant must be hearing impaired, learning disabled, physically disabled, or visually impaired; age 18-75; enrolled or expecting to enroll full- or part-time at a two-year or four-year or technical institution or university; resident of Wisconsin and studying in Minnesota, Wisconsin. Applicant must be hearing impaired, learning disabled, physically disabled, or visually impaired. Applicant must have 3.5 GPA or higher. Available to U.S. citizens. Applicant must have general military experience. *Application Requirements:* Application form. **Deadline:** July 15.

Contact Mrs. Leslie Busby-Amegashie, Analyst, Wisconsin Department of Veterans Affairs (WDVA), PO Box 7843, Madison, WI 53707-7843. *E-mail:* leslie.busby-amegashie@dva.wisconsin.gov. *Phone:* 800-947-8387. *Website:* http://www.dva.state.wi.us/.

Wisconsin Academic Excellence Scholarship. Renewable award for high school seniors with the highest GPA in graduating class. Must be a Wisconsin resident attending a nonprofit Wisconsin institution full-time. Scholarship value is $2250 toward tuition each year for up to four years. Must maintain 3.0 GPA for renewal. Refer to your high school counselor for more details. *Award:* Scholarship for use in freshman year; renewable. *Award amount:* up to $2250. *Eligibility Requirements:* Applicant must be high school student; planning to enroll or expecting to enroll full-time at a two-year or four-year or technical institution or university; resident of Wisconsin and studying in Wisconsin. Applicant must have 3.0 GPA or higher. Available to U.S. citizens. *Application Requirements:* Application form, test scores, transcript. **Deadline:** continuous.

Contact Nancy Wilkison, Program Coordinator, Wisconsin Higher Educational Aid Board, PO Box 7885, Madison, WI 53707-7885. *E-mail:* nancy.wilkison@wi.gov. *Phone:* 608-267-2213. *Fax:* 608-267-2808. *Website:* http://www.heab.wi.gov/.

Wisconsin Higher Education Grants (WHEG). Grants for residents of Wisconsin enrolled at least half-time in degree or certificate programs at a University of Wisconsin Institution, Wisconsin Technical College or an approved Tribal College. Must show financial need. Refer to web site for further details http://www.heab.wi.gov. *Award:* Grant for use in freshman, sophomore, junior, or senior years; not renewable. *Award amount:* $250–$3000. *Eligibility Requirements:* Applicant must be enrolled or expecting to enroll full- or part-time at a two-year or four-year or technical institution or university; resident of Wisconsin and studying in Wisconsin. Available to U.S. citizens. *Application Requirements:* Application form, financial need analysis. **Deadline:** continuous.

Contact Sandra Thomas, Program Coordinator, Wisconsin Higher Educational Aid Board, PO Box 7885, Madison, WI 53707-7885. *E-mail:* sandy.thomas@heab.state.wi.us. *Phone:* 608-266-0888. *Fax:* 608-267-2808. *Website:* http://www.heab.wi.gov/.

Wisconsin League for Nursing, Inc. Scholarship. One-time award for Wisconsin residents who have completed half of an accredited Wisconsin school of nursing program. Financial need of student must be demonstrated. Scholarship applications are mailed by WLN office ONLY to Wisconsin nursing schools in January for distribution to students. Students interested in obtaining an application must contact their nursing school and submit completed applications to their school. Applications sent directly to WLN office will be returned to applicant. For further information visit web site http://www.wisconsinwln.org/Scholarships.htm. Nursing. *Award:* Scholarship for use in junior or senior years; not renewable. *Award amount:* $500–$1000. *Number of awards:* 11–35. *Eligibility Requirements:* Applicant must be enrolled or expecting to enroll full-time at a two-year or four-year or technical institution or university; resident of Wisconsin and studying in Wisconsin. Available to U.S. citizens. *Application Requirements:* Application form, essay, financial need analysis. **Deadline:** March 1.

Contact Mary Ann Tanner, Administrative Secretary. *E-mail:* wln@wisconsinwln.org. *Phone:* 888-755-3329. *Website:* http://www.wisconsinwln.org/.

Wisconsin Native American/Indian Student Assistance Grant. Grants for Wisconsin residents who are at least one-quarter American Indian. Must be attending a college or university within the state. Refer to web site for further details, http://www.heab.state.wi.us. *Award:* Grant for use in freshman, sophomore, junior, or senior years; not renewable. *Award amount:* $250–$1100. *Eligibility Requirements:* Applicant must be American Indian/Alaska Native; enrolled or expecting to enroll full- or part-time at a two-year or four-year or technical institution or university; resident of Wisconsin and studying in Wisconsin. Available to U.S. citizens. *Application Requirements:* Application form, financial need analysis. **Deadline:** continuous.

Contact Sandra Thomas, Program Coordinator, Wisconsin Higher Educational Aid Board, PO Box 7885, Madison, WI 53707-7885. *E-mail:* sandy.thomas@wi.gov. *Phone:* 608-266-0888. *Fax:* 608-267-2808. *Website:* http://www.heab.wi.gov/.

WYOMING

Douvas Memorial Scholarship. Available to Wyoming residents who are first-generation Americans. Must be between 18 and 22 years old. Must be used at any Wyoming public institution of higher education for study in freshman year. *Award:* Scholarship for use in freshman year; not renewable. *Award amount:* $500. *Number of awards:* 2. *Eligibility Requirements:* Applicant must be age 18-22; enrolled or expecting to enroll full- or part-time at a two-year or four-year institution or university; resident of Wyoming and studying in Wyoming. Available to U.S. citizens. *Application Requirements:* Application form. **Deadline:** April 30.

Contact Stephanie Brady, Social Studies Consultant, Wyoming Department of Education, 2300 Capitol Avenue, Hathaway Building, 2nd Floor, Cheyenne, WY 82002. *E-mail:* stephanie.brady@wyo.gov. *Phone:* 307-777-3793. *Fax:* 307-777-6234. *Website:* http://edu.wyoming.gov/.

Hathaway Scholarship. Scholarship for Wyoming students to pursue postsecondary education within the state. Award ranges from $840 to $1680 per semester. Deadline varies. *Award:* Scholarship for use in freshman, sophomore, junior, senior, or graduate years; renewable. *Award amount:* $840–$1680. *Eligibility Requirements:* Applicant must be enrolled or expecting to enroll full- or part-time at a two-year or four-year institution or university; resident of Wyoming and studying in Wyoming. Applicant must have 2.5 GPA or higher. Available to U.S. citizens. *Application Requirements:* Application form. **Deadline:** continuous.

Contact Mr. Bradley Barker III, Hathaway Scholarship Consultant, Wyoming Department of Education, 2300 Capitol Avenue, Hathaway Building, 2nd Floor, Cheyenne, WY 82002. *E-mail:* hathawayscholarship@ wyo.gov. *Phone:* 307-777-6226. *Website:* http://edu.wyoming.gov/.

Superior Student in Education Scholarship-Wyoming. Scholarship available each year to sixteen Wyoming high school graduates who plan to teach in Wyoming. The award covers costs of undergraduate tuition at the University of Wyoming or any Wyoming community college. Education. *Award:* Scholarship for use in freshman, soph-omore, junior, or senior years; renewable. *Award amount:* $1000. *Number of awards:* 16–16. *Eligibility Requirements:* Applicant must be enrolled or expecting to enroll full-time at a two-year or four-year institution or university; resident of Wyoming and studying in Wyoming. Applicant must have 3.0 GPA or higher. Available to U. S. citizens. *Application Requirements:* Application form, recommendations or references, test scores, transcript. **Deadline:** October 31.

Contact Tammy Mack, Assistant Director, Scholarships, University of Wyoming, Department 3335, 1000 East University Avenue, Laramie, WY 82071. *E-mail:* FinAid@uwyo.edu. *Phone:* 307-766-2412. *Fax:* 307-766-3800. *Website:* http://www.uwyo.edu/ scholarships.

Vietnam Veterans Award-Wyoming. Scholarship available to Wyoming residents who served in the armed forces between August 5, 1964 and May 7, 1975, and received a Vietnam service medal. *Award:* Scholarship for use in freshman, sophomore, junior, or senior years; renewable. *Eligibility Requirements:* Applicant must be enrolled or expecting to enroll full- or part-time at a two-year or four-year institution or university and resident of Wyoming. Available to U.S. citizens. Applicant or parent must meet one or more of the following requirements: general military experience; retired from active duty; disabled or killed as a result of military service; prisoner of war; or missing in action. *Application Requirements:* Application form. **Deadline:** continuous.

Contact Tammy Mack, Assistant Director, Scholarships, University of Wyoming, Department 3335, 1000 East University Avenue, Laramie, WY 82071. *E-mail:* FinAid@uwyo.edu. *Phone:* 307-766-2412. *Fax:* 307-766-3800. *Website:* http://www.uwyo.edu/ scholarships.

Indexes

Non-Need Scholarships for Undergraduates

Academic Interests/Achievements

Agriculture

Abilene Christian University, TX
Angelo State University, TX
Arkansas Tech University, AR
Auburn University, AL
Austin Peay State University, TN
Berry College, GA
California Polytechnic State University, San Luis Obispo, CA
California State Polytechnic University, Pomona, CA
California State University, Bakersfield, CA
California State University, Chico, CA
California State University, Fresno, CA
Cameron University, OK
Clemson University, SC
Dickinson State University, ND
Dordt College, IA
Eastern Michigan University, MI
Ferris State University, MI
Florida Agricultural and Mechanical University, FL
Florida Southern College, FL
Fort Hays State University, KS
Iowa State University of Science and Technology, IA
Langston University, OK
Lincoln University, MO
Louisiana State University and Agricultural & Mechanical College, LA
Louisiana Tech University, LA
Lubbock Christian University, TX
Michigan State University, MI
Middle Tennessee State University, TN
Midway University, KY
Mississippi State University, MS
Montana State University, MT
Morehead State University, KY
Murray State University, KY
New Mexico State University, NM
North Carolina Agricultural and Technical State University, NC
North Carolina State University, NC
Northern State University, SD
Northwest Missouri State University, MO
The Ohio State University, OH
Oklahoma Panhandle State University, OK
Oklahoma State University, OK
Purdue University, IN
Sam Houston State University, TX
Southeast Missouri State University, MO
Southern Arkansas University–Magnolia, AR
Southern Illinois University Carbondale, IL
State University of New York College of Environmental Science and Forestry, NY
Stephen F. Austin State University, TX
Tennessee Technological University, TN
Texas A&M University, TX
Texas A&M University–Commerce, TX
Texas Christian University, TX
Texas State University, TX

Texas Tech University, TX
Truman State University, MO
Tuskegee University, AL
The University of Arizona, AZ
University of Arkansas, AR
University of California, Davis, CA
University of California, Riverside, CA
University of Delaware, DE
University of Florida, FL
University of Georgia, GA
University of Idaho, ID
University of Illinois at Urbana–Champaign, IL
University of Kentucky, KY
University of Louisiana at Monroe, LA
University of Maine, ME
University of Maryland, College Park, MD
University of Maryland Eastern Shore, MD
University of Massachusetts Amherst, MA
University of Minnesota, Crookston, MN
University of Minnesota, Twin Cities Campus, MN
University of Missouri, MO
University of Nebraska–Lincoln, NE
University of Nevada, Reno, NV
University of New Hampshire, NH
University of Rhode Island, RI
The University of Tennessee, TN
The University of Tennessee at Martin, TN
The University of Texas at San Antonio, TX
University of the District of Columbia, DC
University of Vermont, VT
The University of Virginia's College at Wise, VA
University of Wisconsin–River Falls, WI
University of Wisconsin–Stevens Point, WI
University of Wyoming, WY
Utah State University, UT
Vermont Technical College, VT
Warner University, FL
Washington State University, WA
Western Illinois University, IL
Western Kentucky University, KY
West Texas A&M University, TX
West Virginia University, WV

Architecture

Auburn University, AL
Ball State University, IN
Boise State University, ID
Boston Architectural College, MA
California Baptist University, CA
California Polytechnic State University, San Luis Obispo, CA
California State Polytechnic University, Pomona, CA
California State University, Bakersfield, CA
Calvin College, MI
City College of the City University of New York, NY
Clemson University, SC
Cooper Union for the Advancement of Science and Art, NY
Drury University, MO
Eastern Michigan University, MI

Fairmont State University, WV
Ferris State University, MI
Florida Agricultural and Mechanical University, FL
Florida International University, FL
Georgia Institute of Technology, GA
Hampton University, VA
Howard University, DC
Idaho State University, ID
Illinois Institute of Technology, IL
Iowa State University of Science and Technology, IA
James Madison University, VA
Kean University, NJ
Kent State University, OH
Lawrence Technological University, MI
Louisiana State University and Agricultural & Mechanical College, LA
Louisiana Tech University, LA
Marywood University, PA
Miami University, OH
Mississippi State University, MS
Missouri Western State University, MO
Montana State University, MT
New Jersey Institute of Technology, NJ
NewSchool of Architecture and Design, CA
North Carolina State University, NC
The Ohio State University, OH
Oklahoma State University, OK
Portland State University, OR
Robert Morris University Illinois, IL
Savannah College of Art and Design, GA
Southern California Institute of Architecture, CA
Southern Illinois University Carbondale, IL
State University of New York College of Environmental Science and Forestry, NY
Texas A&M University, TX
Texas Tech University, TX
Tuskegee University, AL
The University of Arizona, AZ
University of Arkansas, AR
University of Colorado Boulder, CO
University of Florida, FL
University of Hartford, CT
University of Houston, TX
University of Idaho, ID
University of Illinois at Chicago, IL
University of Illinois at Urbana–Champaign, IL
The University of Kansas, KS
University of Kentucky, KY
University of Maryland, College Park, MD
University of Mary Washington, VA
University of Massachusetts Amherst, MA
University of Michigan, MI
University of Minnesota, Twin Cities Campus, MN
University of Nebraska–Lincoln, NE
University of Nevada, Las Vegas, NV
The University of North Carolina at Charlotte, NC
University of Oklahoma, OK
University of Oregon, OR
University of South Florida, FL

The University of Tennessee, TN
The University of Texas at Arlington, TX
The University of Texas at San Antonio, TX
University of Utah, UT
University of Washington, WA
University of Wisconsin–Stevens Point, WI
University of Wyoming, WY
Utah State University, UT
Washington State University, WA
Washington University in St. Louis, MO
West Virginia University, WV
Woodbury University, CA

Area/Ethnic Studies
Augustana College, IL
Binghamton University, State University of
    New York, NY
Boise State University, ID
California State Polytechnic University,
    Pomona, CA
California State University, Chico, CA
California State University, Fresno, CA
California State University, Fullerton, CA
Calvin College, MI
City College of the City University of
    New York, NY
The College of New Rochelle, NY
College of Staten Island of the City
    University of New York, NY
Eastern Connecticut State University, CT
Eastern Washington University, WA
Edgewood College, WI
Florida Agricultural and Mechanical
    University, FL
Fort Hays State University, KS
Fort Lewis College, CO
Furman University, SC
Indiana State University, IN
Indiana University of Pennsylvania, PA
Iowa State University of Science and
    Technology, IA
Kean University, NJ
Kent State University, OH
Loyola Marymount University, CA
Middle Tennessee State University, TN
Mississippi State University, MS
Montana State University, MT
Moravian College, PA
New Jersey Institute of Technology, NJ
New Mexico State University, NM
Northern Illinois University, IL
The Ohio State University, OH
Ohio University, OH
Ohio University–Chillicothe, OH
Ohio University–Eastern, OH
Ohio University–Lancaster, OH
Ohio University–Southern Campus, OH
Ohio University–Zanesville, OH
Oklahoma State University, OK
Old Dominion University, VA
Ouachita Baptist University, AR
Portland State University, OR
Purchase College, State University
    of New York, NY
Saint Louis University, MO
San Diego State University, CA
Sonoma State University, CA
Southern Illinois University Carbondale, IL
State University of New York at
    New Paltz, NY
State University of New York at
    Oswego, NY
State University of New York at
    Plattsburgh, NY
State University of New York College
    at Geneseo, NY

Stetson University, FL
Stockton University, NJ
Stony Brook University, State University of
    New York, NY
The University of Alabama, AL
University of Arkansas, AR
University of California, Davis, CA
University of California, Irvine, CA
University of California, Riverside, CA
University of Colorado Boulder, CO
University of Hartford, CT
University of Houston, TX
University of Illinois at Urbana–
    Champaign, IL
The University of Kansas, KS
University of Kentucky, KY
University of Michigan, MI
University of Minnesota, Twin Cities
    Campus, MN
University of Missouri, MO
University of North Carolina
    at Asheville, NC
University of Oklahoma, OK
University of Rhode Island, RI
University of South Carolina, SC
The University of Texas at San Antonio, TX
University of Utah, UT
University of Vermont, VT
University of Wisconsin–Eau Claire, WI
University of Wisconsin–Green Bay, WI
University of Wisconsin–La Crosse, WI
University of Wisconsin–River Falls, WI
University of Wyoming, WY
Washington State University, WA
Wayne State University, MI
Western Illinois University, IL
West Virginia University, WV
Wheaton College, IL
William Jessup University, CA
Wright State University, OH
Wright State University–Lake Campus, OH

Biological Sciences
Abilene Christian University, TX
Alaska Pacific University, AK
Albertus Magnus College, CT
Alderson Broaddus University, WV
Alfred University, NY
Angelo State University, TX
Arkansas Tech University, AR
Armstrong State University, GA
Auburn University, AL
Augsburg College, MN
Augustana College, IL
Augustana University, SD
Austin College, TX
Austin Peay State University, TN
Averett University, VA
Ball State University, IN
Barton College, NC
Belhaven University, MS
Bellarmine University, KY
Belmont University, TN
Bemidji State University, MN
Bethel College, KS
Binghamton University, State University of
    New York, NY
Biola University, CA
Black Hills State University, SD
Bloomfield College, NJ
Bloomsburg University of Pennsylvania, PA
Blue Mountain College, MS
Bluffton University, OH
Boise State University, ID
Bowling Green State University, OH
Brenau University, GA

Briar Cliff University, IA
Bryan College, TN
Buena Vista University, IA
Butler University, IN
California Lutheran University, CA
California Polytechnic State University, San
    Luis Obispo, CA
California State Polytechnic University,
    Pomona, CA
California State University, Bakersfield, CA
California State University, Chico, CA
California State University, Fresno, CA
California State University, Fullerton, CA
California State University, Los Angeles, CA
California State University,
    San Bernardino, CA
Calvin College, MI
Cameron University, OK
Campbellsville University, KY
Carlow University, PA
Carroll University, WI
Carson-Newman University, TN
Case Western Reserve University, OH
Cedar Crest College, PA
Centenary College of Louisiana, LA
Central College, IA
Central Methodist University, MO
Central Michigan University, MI
Chapman University, CA
Christopher Newport University, VA
The Citadel, The Military College of South
    Carolina, SC
City College of the City University of New
    York, NY
Clarion University of Pennsylvania, PA
Clarkson University, NY
Clemson University, SC
Cleveland State University, OH
Coastal Carolina University, SC
The College at Brockport, State University
    of New York, NY
College of Charleston, SC
College of Coastal Georgia, GA
The College of Idaho, ID
The College of New Rochelle, NY
College of Saint Mary, NE
College of Staten Island of the City
    University of New York, NY
The Colorado College, CO
Colorado Mesa University, CO
Columbia College, MO
Columbus State University, GA
Concordia University Chicago, IL
Concordia University, Nebraska, NE
Concordia University Texas, TX
Dakota State University, SD
Dakota Wesleyan University, SD
Dallas Baptist University, TX
Davidson College, NC
Defiance College, OH
Delta State University, MS
Denison University, OH
DeSales University, PA
Dickinson State University, ND
Dordt College, IA
Drury University, MO
D'Youville College, NY
East Carolina University, NC
Eastern Connecticut State University, CT
Eastern Illinois University, IL
Eastern Mennonite University, VA
Eastern Michigan University, MI
Eastern Washington University, WA
East Stroudsburg University of
    Pennsylvania, PA
East Texas Baptist University, TX

Elizabethtown College, PA
Elmhurst College, IL
Elon University, NC
Emporia State University, KS
Evangel University, MO
Fairmont State University, WV
Ferris State University, MI
Fitchburg State University, MA
Florida Agricultural and Mechanical
    University, FL
Florida Gulf Coast University, FL
Florida International University, FL
Florida Southern College, FL
Fordham University, NY
Fort Hays State University, KS
Fort Lewis College, CO
Framingham State University, MA
Francis Marion University, SC
Frostburg State University, MD
Furman University, SC
Gannon University, PA
Gardner-Webb University, NC
George Fox University, OR
Georgia College & State University, GA
Georgia Institute of Technology, GA
Georgian Court University, NJ
Georgia Southern University, GA
Glenville State College, WV
Governors State University, IL
Grambling State University, LA
Grand View University, IA
Greenville College, IL
Grove City College, PA
Guilford College, NC
Hamline University, MN
Hampden-Sydney College, VA
Hampshire College, MA
Hampton University, VA
Hardin-Simmons University, TX
Harrisburg University of Science and
    Technology, PA
High Point University, NC
Hillsdale College, MI
Hood College, MD
Houghton College, NY
Howard Payne University, TX
Howard University, DC
Huntingdon College, AL
Husson University, ME
Idaho State University, ID
Illinois Institute of Technology, IL
Indiana State University, IN
Indiana University of Pennsylvania, PA
Indiana University–Purdue University
    Fort Wayne, IN
Indiana Wesleyan University, IN
Iowa State University of Science and
    Technology, IA
Jacksonville State University, AL
James Madison University, VA
John Carroll University, OH
Johnson C. Smith University, NC
Judson College, AL
Juniata College, PA
Kansas Wesleyan University, KS
Kean University, NJ
Kennesaw State University, GA
Kent State University, OH
Kenyon College, OH
King's College, PA
Kutztown University of Pennsylvania, PA
Lake Erie College, OH
Lawrence Technological University, MI
Lebanon Valley College, PA
Lees-McRae College, NC

Lee University, TN
Lewis-Clark State College, ID
Liberty University, VA
Lindenwood University, MO
Lindsey Wilson College, KY
Linfield College, OR
Lipscomb University, TN
Lock Haven University of Pennsylvania, PA
Longwood University, VA
Loras College, IA
Louisiana State University and Agricultural
    & Mechanical College, LA
Louisiana State University in
    Shreveport, LA
Louisiana Tech University, LA
Loyola Marymount University, CA
Lycoming College, PA
Lynn University, FL
Malone University, OH
Manhattan College, NY
Mansfield University of Pennsylvania, PA
Marquette University, WI
Marymount Manhattan College, NY
Marymount University, VA
Maryville University of Saint Louis, MO
Marywood University, PA
Massachusetts College of Liberal Arts, MA
The Master's University, CA
Mayville State University, ND
McKendree University, IL
Mercer University, GA
Meredith College, NC
Metropolitan State University of Denver, CO
Michigan State University, MI
Middle Georgia State University, GA
Middle Tennessee State University, TN
Midwestern State University, TX
Millersville University of Pennsylvania, PA
Millikin University, IL
Mills College, CA
Minnesota State University Moorhead, MN
Minot State University, ND
Mississippi State University, MS
Missouri University of Science and
    Technology, MO
Missouri Western State University, MO
Molloy College, NY
Monmouth University, NJ
Montana State University, MT
Montana State University Billings, MT
Montclair State University, NJ
Moravian College, PA
Morehead State University, KY
Morehouse College, GA
Murray State University, KY
Muskingum University, OH
Newberry College, SC
New England College, NH
New Jersey Institute of Technology, NJ
New Mexico Highlands University, NM
New Mexico State University, NM
North Carolina State University, NC
North Central College, IL
Northeastern Illinois University, IL
Northeastern State University, OK
Northern Illinois University, IL
Northern Kentucky University, KY
Northern Michigan University, MI
Northern State University, SD
Northwestern College, IA
Northwestern State University
    of Louisiana, LA
Northwest Missouri State University, MO
Northwest Nazarene University, ID
Ohio Northern University, OH

The Ohio State University, OH
Ohio University, OH
Ohio University–Chillicothe, OH
Ohio University–Eastern, OH
Ohio University–Lancaster, OH
Ohio University–Southern Campus, OH
Ohio University–Zanesville, OH
Oklahoma Baptist University, OK
Oklahoma Panhandle State University, OK
Oklahoma State University, OK
Oklahoma Wesleyan University, OK
Old Dominion University, VA
Oral Roberts University, OK
Ouachita Baptist University, AR
Pacific University, OR
Piedmont College, GA
Pittsburg State University, KS
Plymouth State University, NH
Point Loma Nazarene University, CA
Point Park University, PA
Purchase College, State University of New
    York, NY
Randolph College, VA
Regis University, CO
Rochester Institute of Technology, NY
Rockford University, IL
Rockhurst University, MO
Sacred Heart University, CT
Saginaw Valley State University, MI
St. Ambrose University, IA
Saint Augustine's University, NC
St. Edward's University, TX
St. John Fisher College, NY
St. John's University, NY
Saint Joseph's University, PA
Saint Louis University, MO
Saint Vincent College, PA
Samford University, AL
Sam Houston State University, TX
San Diego State University, CA
Savannah State University, GA
Schreiner University, TX
Shepherd University, WV
Shippensburg University of
    Pennsylvania, PA
Siena College, NY
Skidmore College, NY
Slippery Rock University of
    Pennsylvania, PA
Sonoma State University, CA
South Dakota School of Mines and
    Technology, SD
Southeastern Oklahoma
    State University, OK
Southeast Missouri State University, MO
Southern Adventist University, TN
Southern Arkansas University–
    Magnolia, AR
Southern Illinois University Carbondale, IL
Southern Oregon University, OR
Southwestern College, KS
Southwestern Oklahoma State
    University, OK
State University of New York
    at Fredonia, NY
State University of New York
    at New Paltz, NY
State University of New York
    at Oswego, NY
State University of New York
    at Plattsburgh, NY
State University of New York College
    at Geneseo, NY
State University of New York College
    at Potsdam, NY

State University of New York College of Environmental Science and Forestry, NY
Stephen F. Austin State University, TX
Stetson University, FL
Stockton University, NJ
Stony Brook University, State University of New York, NY
Tennessee Technological University, TN
Texas A&M University, TX
Texas A&M University–Commerce, TX
Texas Christian University, TX
Texas Lutheran University, TX
Texas State University, TX
Texas Tech University, TX
Texas Wesleyan University, TX
Texas Woman's University, TX
Thiel College, PA
Thomas More College, KY
Thomas University, GA
Towson University, MD
Trevecca Nazarene University, TN
Trinity Christian College, IL
Truman State University, MO
Union University, TN
The University of Akron, OH
The University of Alabama, AL
The University of Alabama in Huntsville, AL
University of Alaska Anchorage, AK
University of Alaska Fairbanks, AK
The University of Arizona, AZ
University of Arkansas, AR
University of Arkansas at Little Rock, AR
University of Bridgeport, CT
University of California, Davis, CA
University of California, Irvine, CA
University of California, Riverside, CA
University of California, San Diego, CA
University of Central Oklahoma, OK
University of Colorado Boulder, CO
University of Colorado Denver, CO
University of Dallas, TX
University of Dayton, OH
University of Delaware, DE
University of Denver, CO
University of Evansville, IN
University of Great Falls, MT
University of Hartford, CT
University of Holy Cross, LA
University of Houston, TX
University of Houston–Clear Lake, TX
University of Houston–Victoria, TX
University of Idaho, ID
University of Illinois at Urbana–Champaign, IL
The University of Kansas, KS
University of Kentucky, KY
University of Louisiana at Monroe, LA
University of Louisville, KY
University of Maine, ME
University of Maine at Augusta, ME
University of Maine at Fort Kent, ME
University of Mary Hardin-Baylor, TX
University of Maryland, Baltimore County, MD
University of Maryland, College Park, MD
University of Maryland Eastern Shore, MD
University of Mary Washington, VA
University of Massachusetts Amherst, MA
University of Massachusetts Dartmouth, MA
University of Massachusetts Lowell, MA
University of Memphis, TN
University of Michigan, MI
University of Michigan–Dearborn, MI
University of Michigan–Flint, MI
University of Minnesota, Crookston, MN

University of Minnesota, Twin Cities Campus, MN
University of Mississippi, MS
University of Missouri, MO
University of Missouri–St. Louis, MO
University of Montana, MT
The University of Montana Western, MT
University of Montevallo, AL
University of Nebraska at Omaha, NE
University of Nebraska–Lincoln, NE
University of Nevada, Las Vegas, NV
University of Nevada, Reno, NV
University of New Hampshire, NH
University of New Hampshire at Manchester, NH
University of North Carolina at Asheville, NC
The University of North Carolina at Charlotte, NC
The University of North Carolina at Greensboro, NC
The University of North Carolina Wilmington, NC
University of Northern Colorado, CO
University of Northern Iowa, IA
University of North Georgia, GA
University of Oklahoma, OK
University of Oregon, OR
University of Pittsburgh at Bradford, PA
University of Pittsburgh at Johnstown, PA
University of Portland, OR
University of Puget Sound, WA
University of Rhode Island, RI
University of Richmond, VA
University of St. Francis, IL
University of St. Thomas, MN
University of St. Thomas, TX
University of Sioux Falls, SD
University of South Carolina, SC
University of South Carolina Aiken, SC
The University of South Dakota, SD
University of Southern Indiana, IN
University of South Florida, FL
The University of Tampa, FL
The University of Tennessee at Chattanooga, TN
The University of Tennessee at Martin, TN
The University of Texas at Arlington, TX
The University of Texas at Dallas, TX
The University of Texas at El Paso, TX
The University of Texas at San Antonio, TX
The University of Texas Rio Grande Valley, TX
The University of Toledo, OH
The University of Tulsa, OK
University of Utah, UT
The University of Virginia's College at Wise, VA
University of West Florida, FL
University of West Georgia, GA
University of Wisconsin–Eau Claire, WI
University of Wisconsin–Green Bay, WI
University of Wisconsin–La Crosse, WI
University of Wisconsin–Parkside, WI
University of Wisconsin–River Falls, WI
University of Wisconsin–Stevens Point, WI
University of Wisconsin–Superior, WI
University of Wisconsin–Whitewater, WI
University of Wyoming, WY
Utah State University, UT
Valdosta State University, GA
Valley City State University, ND
Virginia Commonwealth University, VA
Virginia Military Institute, VA
Virginia State University, VA
Walla Walla University, WA

Warner University, FL
Wartburg College, IA
Washburn University, KS
Washington State University, WA
Washington University in St. Louis, MO
Wayland Baptist University, TX
Wayne State College, NE
Wayne State University, MI
Webster University, MO
Wesleyan College, GA
Western Carolina University, NC
Western Illinois University, IL
Western Kentucky University, KY
Western Oregon University, OR
Western Washington University, WA
West Virginia University, WV
Wheaton College, IL
Wichita State University, KS
Widener University, PA
William Jessup University, CA
Williams Baptist College, AR
Wilson College, PA
Wisconsin Lutheran College, WI
Wright State University, OH
Wright State University–Lake Campus, OH
Xavier University of Louisiana, LA
Youngstown State University, OH

Business
Abilene Christian University, TX
Adelphi University, NY
Alaska Pacific University, AK
Albertus Magnus College, CT
Alderson Broaddus University, WV
Alfred University, NY
Alliant International University–San Diego, CA
American Jewish University, CA
Anderson University, SC
Angelo State University, TX
Arkansas Tech University, AR
Asbury University, KY
Auburn University, AL
Augsburg College, MN
Augustana College, IL
Augustana University, SD
Augusta University, GA
Aurora University, IL
Austin College, TX
Austin Peay State University, TN
Averett University, VA
Babson College, MA
Ball State University, IN
Barton College, NC
Baylor University, TX
Belhaven University, MS
Bellarmine University, KY
Belmont Abbey College, NC
Belmont University, TN
Bemidji State University, MN
Berry College, GA
Bethel College, KS
Binghamton University, State University of New York, NY
Black Hills State University, SD
Bloomfield College, NJ
Bloomsburg University of Pennsylvania, PA
Blue Mountain College, MS
Boise State University, ID
Bowling Green State University, OH
Brenau University, GA
Briar Cliff University, IA
Bryan College, TN
Bucknell University, PA
Buena Vista University, IA
Butler University, IN

California Lutheran University, CA
California Polytechnic State University, San Luis Obispo, CA
California State Polytechnic University, Pomona, CA
California State University, Bakersfield, CA
California State University, Chico, CA
California State University, Fresno, CA
California State University, Fullerton, CA
California State University, Los Angeles, CA
California State University Maritime Academy, CA
California State University, Monterey Bay, CA
California State University, Northridge, CA
California State University, San Bernardino, CA
Calvin College, MI
Cameron University, OK
Campbellsville University, KY
Carlow University, PA
Carroll University, WI
Carson-Newman University, TN
Case Western Reserve University, OH
Catawba College, NC
Centenary College of Louisiana, LA
Central College, IA
Central Methodist University, MO
Central Michigan University, MI
Champlain College, VT
Christopher Newport University, VA
The Citadel, The Military College of South Carolina, SC
Clarion University of Pennsylvania, PA
Clarkson University, NY
Clemson University, SC
Cleveland State University, OH
Coastal Carolina University, SC
The College at Brockport, State University of New York, NY
College of Charleston, SC
College of Coastal Georgia, GA
The College of Idaho, ID
The College of New Rochelle, NY
The College of Saint Rose, NY
College of Staten Island of the City University of New York, NY
Colorado Mesa University, CO
Colorado School of Mines, CO
Columbia College, MO
Columbus State University, GA
Concordia University Ann Arbor, MI
Concordia University Chicago, IL
Concordia University, Nebraska, NE
Concordia University Texas, TX
Concord University, WV
Cornerstone University, MI
Creighton University, NE
Dakota State University, SD
Dakota Wesleyan University, SD
Dallas Baptist University, TX
Davidson College, NC
Defiance College, OH
Delta State University, MS
DeSales University, PA
Dickinson State University, ND
Dordt College, IA
Drury University, MO
D'Youville College, NY
East Carolina University, NC
Eastern Connecticut State University, CT
Eastern Illinois University, IL
Eastern Mennonite University, VA
Eastern Michigan University, MI
Eastern University, PA

Eastern Washington University, WA
East Stroudsburg University of Pennsylvania, PA
East Texas Baptist University, TX
ECPI University, VA
Elizabethtown College, PA
Elmhurst College, IL
Elon University, NC
Emmanuel College, GA
Emory University, GA
Emporia State University, KS
Endicott College, MA
Evangel University, MO
Fairmont State University, WV
Felician University, NJ
Ferris State University, MI
Fitchburg State University, MA
Flagler College, FL
Florida Agricultural and Mechanical University, FL
Florida Atlantic University, FL
Florida College, FL
Florida Gulf Coast University, FL
Florida Institute of Technology, FL
Florida International University, FL
Florida Southern College, FL
Fordham University, NY
Fort Hays State University, KS
Fort Lewis College, CO
Francis Marion University, SC
Fresno Pacific University, CA
Frostburg State University, MD
Furman University, SC
Gannon University, PA
Gardner-Webb University, NC
George Fox University, OR
Georgia College & State University, GA
Georgian Court University, NJ
Georgia Southern University, GA
Glenville State College, WV
Gonzaga University, WA
Goshen College, IN
Governors State University, IL
Grambling State University, LA
Grand Valley State University, MI
Grand View University, IA
Grove City College, PA
Hamline University, MN
Hampton University, VA
Hardin-Simmons University, TX
Harrisburg University of Science and Technology, PA
Hawai`i Pacific University, HI
High Point University, NC
Hillsdale College, MI
Hood College, MD
Houghton College, NY
Howard Payne University, TX
Howard University, DC
Husson University, ME
Idaho State University, ID
Illinois Institute of Technology, IL
Indiana State University, IN
Indiana University of Pennsylvania, PA
Indiana Wesleyan University, IN
Iowa State University of Science and Technology, IA
Iowa Wesleyan University, IA
Jacksonville State University, AL
James Madison University, VA
John Carroll University, OH
John Wesley University, NC
Juniata College, PA
Kansas Wesleyan University, KS
Kean University, NJ

Kennesaw State University, GA
Kent State University, OH
Kent State University at Geauga, OH
Kent State University at Stark, OH
King's College, PA
Kutztown University of Pennsylvania, PA
Lake Erie College, OH
Langston University, OK
Lawrence Technological University, MI
Lee University, TN
Lehigh University, PA
Lewis-Clark State College, ID
Liberty University, VA
Lindenwood University, MO
Lindsey Wilson College, KY
Linfield College, OR
Lipscomb University, TN
Lock Haven University of Pennsylvania, PA
Long Island University–LIU Post, NY
Longwood University, VA
Loras College, IA
Louisiana State University and Agricultural & Mechanical College, LA
Louisiana State University in Shreveport, LA
Louisiana Tech University, LA
Loyola Marymount University, CA
Lubbock Christian University, TX
Lycoming College, PA
Lynn University, FL
Lyon College, AR
Malone University, OH
Manhattan College, NY
Maranatha Baptist University, WI
Marquette University, WI
Marymount University, VA
Maryville University of Saint Louis, MO
Marywood University, PA
Massachusetts College of Liberal Arts, MA
The Master's University, CA
Mayville State University, ND
McKendree University, IL
Mercer University, GA
Mercy College, NY
Meredith College, NC
Methodist University, NC
Metropolitan State University of Denver, CO
Michigan State University, MI
Michigan Technological University, MI
Middle Georgia State University, GA
Middle Tennessee State University, TN
Midway University, KY
Midwestern State University, TX
Millersville University of Pennsylvania, PA
Millikin University, IL
Millsaps College, MS
Milwaukee School of Engineering, WI
Minnesota State University Moorhead, MN
Minot State University, ND
Mississippi State University, MS
Missouri University of Science and Technology, MO
Missouri Western State University, MO
Molloy College, NY
Monmouth University, NJ
Montana State University, MT
Montana State University Billings, MT
Montana Tech of The University of Montana, MT
Montclair State University, NJ
Moravian College, PA
Morehead State University, KY
Morehouse College, GA
Mount Mary University, WI
Murray State University, KY

Newberry College, SC
New England College, NH
New Jersey Institute of Technology, NJ
New Mexico Highlands University, NM
New Mexico State University, NM
North Carolina Agricultural and Technical State University, NC
North Carolina State University, NC
North Central College, IL
Northeastern Illinois University, IL
Northeastern State University, OK
Northern Illinois University, IL
Northern Kentucky University, KY
Northern Michigan University, MI
Northern State University, SD
Northwestern College, IA
Northwestern State University of Louisiana, LA
Northwest Missouri State University, MO
Northwest Nazarene University, ID
Ohio Northern University, OH
The Ohio State University, OH
Ohio University, OH
Ohio University–Chillicothe, OH
Ohio University–Eastern, OH
Ohio University–Lancaster, OH
Ohio University–Southern Campus, OH
Ohio University–Zanesville, OH
Ohio Valley University, WV
Ohio Wesleyan University, OH
Oklahoma Baptist University, OK
Oklahoma City University, OK
Oklahoma Panhandle State University, OK
Oklahoma State University, OK
Oklahoma Wesleyan University, OK
Old Dominion University, VA
Olivet College, MI
Oral Roberts University, OK
Ouachita Baptist University, AR
Pacific University, OR
Peirce College, PA
Piedmont College, GA
Pittsburg State University, KS
Point Loma Nazarene University, CA
Point Park University, PA
Portland State University, OR
Providence College, RI
Queens University of Charlotte, NC
Randall University, OK
Robert Morris University Illinois, IL
Rochester Institute of Technology, NY
Rockford University, IL
Rockhurst University, MO
Rogers State University, OK
Sacred Heart University, CT
The Sage Colleges, NY
Saginaw Valley State University, MI
St. Andrews University, NC
St. Bonaventure University, NY
St. Edward's University, TX
St. John Fisher College, NY
St. John's University, NY
Saint Louis University, MO
Saint Martin's University, WA
St. Thomas Aquinas College, NY
Saint Vincent College, PA
Salem International University, WV
Salisbury University, MD
Samford University, AL
Sam Houston State University, TX
San Diego State University, CA
Santa Clara University, CA
Savannah State University, GA
Schreiner University, TX
Shenandoah University, VA
Shepherd University, WV

Shippensburg University of Pennsylvania, PA
Siena College, NY
Simpson University, CA
Slippery Rock University of Pennsylvania, PA
Sonoma State University, CA
Southeastern Louisiana University, LA
Southeastern Oklahoma State University, OK
Southeast Missouri State University, MO
Southern Adventist University, TN
Southern Arkansas University–Magnolia, AR
Southern Illinois University Carbondale, IL
Southern Illinois University Edwardsville, IL
Southern New Hampshire University, NH
Southern Oregon University, OR
Southwestern College, KS
Southwestern Oklahoma State University, OK
Southwestern University, TX
State University of New York at Fredonia, NY
State University of New York at New Paltz, NY
State University of New York at Oswego, NY
State University of New York at Plattsburgh, NY
State University of New York College at Geneseo, NY
State University of New York College at Potsdam, NY
Stephen F. Austin State University, TX
Stetson University, FL
Stevens Institute of Technology, NJ
Stockton University, NJ
Stony Brook University, State University of New York, NY
Suffolk University, MA
Susquehanna University, PA
Tennessee Technological University, TN
Texas A&M International University, TX
Texas A&M University, TX
Texas A&M University–Commerce, TX
Texas A&M University–Texarkana, TX
Texas Christian University, TX
Texas Lutheran University, TX
Texas State University, TX
Texas Tech University, TX
Texas Wesleyan University, TX
Texas Woman's University, TX
Thiel College, PA
Thomas More College, KY
Thomas University, GA
Toccoa Falls College, GA
Towson University, MD
Trevecca Nazarene University, TN
Trinity Christian College, IL
Truman State University, MO
Tuskegee University, AL
Union University, TN
The University of Akron, OH
The University of Alabama, AL
The University of Alabama at Birmingham, AL
The University of Alabama in Huntsville, AL
University of Alaska Anchorage, AK
University of Alaska Fairbanks, AK
The University of Arizona, AZ
University of Arkansas, AR
University of Arkansas at Little Rock, AR
University of Bridgeport, CT

University of California, Davis, CA
University of California, Irvine, CA
University of California, Riverside, CA
University of California, San Diego, CA
University of Central Oklahoma, OK
University of Colorado Boulder, CO
University of Colorado Denver, CO
University of Dallas, TX
University of Dayton, OH
University of Delaware, DE
University of Denver, CO
University of Evansville, IN
University of Florida, FL
University of Georgia, GA
University of Great Falls, MT
University of Hartford, CT
University of Holy Cross, LA
University of Houston, TX
University of Houston–Clear Lake, TX
University of Houston–Downtown, TX
University of Houston–Victoria, TX
University of Idaho, ID
University of Illinois at Chicago, IL
University of Illinois at Urbana–Champaign, IL
University of Indianapolis, IN
The University of Iowa, IA
The University of Kansas, KS
University of Kentucky, KY
University of Louisiana at Monroe, LA
University of Louisville, KY
University of Maine, ME
University of Maine at Augusta, ME
University of Maine at Fort Kent, ME
University of Mary Hardin-Baylor, TX
University of Maryland, College Park, MD
University of Maryland Eastern Shore, MD
University of Mary Washington, VA
University of Massachusetts Amherst, MA
University of Massachusetts Dartmouth, MA
University of Massachusetts Lowell, MA
University of Memphis, TN
University of Michigan, MI
University of Michigan–Dearborn, MI
University of Michigan–Flint, MI
University of Minnesota, Twin Cities Campus, MN
University of Mississippi, MS
University of Missouri, MO
University of Missouri–St. Louis, MO
University of Montana, MT
The University of Montana Western, MT
University of Montevallo, AL
University of Nebraska at Omaha, NE
University of Nebraska–Lincoln, NE
University of Nevada, Las Vegas, NV
University of Nevada, Reno, NV
University of New Hampshire, NH
University of New Hampshire at Manchester, NH
University of North Carolina at Asheville, NC
The University of North Carolina at Chapel Hill, NC
The University of North Carolina at Charlotte, NC
The University of North Carolina at Greensboro, NC
The University of North Carolina Wilmington, NC
University of Northern Colorado, CO
University of Northern Iowa, IA
University of North Florida, FL
University of North Georgia, GA
University of Oklahoma, OK
University of Oregon, OR

University of Pittsburgh at Bradford, PA
University of Pittsburgh at Johnstown, PA
University of Portland, OR
University of Puget Sound, WA
University of Rhode Island, RI
University of St. Thomas, MN
University of St. Thomas, TX
University of Sioux Falls, SD
University of South Carolina, SC
University of South Carolina Aiken, SC
The University of South Dakota, SD
University of Southern Indiana, IN
University of South Florida, FL
The University of Tennessee, TN
The University of Tennessee at
    Chattanooga, TN
The University of Tennessee at Martin, TN
The University of Texas at Arlington, TX
The University of Texas at Dallas, TX
The University of Texas at El Paso, TX
The University of Texas at San Antonio, TX
The University of Texas of the Permian
    Basin, TX
The University of Texas Rio
    Grande Valley, TX
The University of Toledo, OH
The University of Tulsa, OK
University of Utah, UT
University of Vermont, VT
The University of Virginia's
    College at Wise, VA
University of Washington, WA
University of West Florida, FL
University of West Georgia, GA
University of Wisconsin–Eau Claire, WI
University of Wisconsin–Green Bay, WI
University of Wisconsin–La Crosse, WI
University of Wisconsin–Parkside, WI
University of Wisconsin–River Falls, WI
University of Wisconsin–Stevens Point, WI
University of Wisconsin–Stout, WI
University of Wisconsin–Superior, WI
University of Wisconsin–Whitewater, WI
University of Wyoming, WY
Utah State University, UT
Valley City State University, ND
Valparaiso University, IN
Virginia Commonwealth University, VA
Virginia Military Institute, VA
Walla Walla University, WA
Walsh College of Accountancy and Business
    Administration, MI
Warner University, FL
Wartburg College, IA
Washburn University, KS
Washington & Jefferson College, PA
Washington State University, WA
Washington University in St. Louis, MO
Wayland Baptist University, TX
Wayne State College, NE
Wayne State University, MI
Webber International University, FL
Webster University, MO
Wesleyan College, GA
West Chester University of Pennsylvania, PA
Western Carolina University, NC
Western Illinois University, IL
Western Kentucky University, KY
Western New England University, MA
Western Oregon University, OR
Western Washington University, WA
West Texas A&M University, TX
West Virginia University, WV
Wheaton College, IL
Wichita State University, KS

Widener University, PA
William Jessup University, CA
Williams Baptist College, AR
Wilson College, PA
Wisconsin Lutheran College, WI
Woodbury University, CA
Wright State University, OH
Wright State University–Lake Campus, OH
Xavier University of Louisiana, LA
Youngstown State University, OH

Communication
Abilene Christian University, TX
Adelphi University, NY
Alaska Pacific University, AK
Albertus Magnus College, CT
Albion College, MI
Alderson Broaddus University, WV
Alfred University, NY
Alliant International University–
    San Diego, CA
Angelo State University, TX
Arkansas Tech University, AR
Auburn University, AL
Augsburg College, MN
Augustana College, IL
Augustana University, SD
Austin College, TX
Austin Peay State University, TN
Ball State University, IN
Barton College, NC
Baylor University, TX
Belhaven University, MS
Bemidji State University, MN
Berry College, GA
Bethel College, KS
Biola University, CA
Black Hills State University, SD
Bloomfield College, NJ
Bloomsburg University of Pennsylvania, PA
Boise State University, ID
Bowling Green State University, OH
Brenau University, GA
Briar Cliff University, IA
Bryan College, TN
Butler University, IN
California Lutheran University, CA
California Polytechnic State University, San
    Luis Obispo, CA
California State Polytechnic University,
    Pomona, CA
California State University, Bakersfield, CA
California State University, Chico, CA
California State University, Fresno, CA
California State University, Fullerton, CA
California State University, Los Angeles, CA
California State University, Northridge, CA
Calvin College, MI
Cameron University, OK
Campbellsville University, KY
Carlow University, PA
Carroll University, WI
Case Western Reserve University, OH
Cedar Crest College, PA
Centenary College of Louisiana, LA
Central Methodist University, MO
Central Michigan University, MI
Champlain College, VT
Christopher Newport University, VA
City College of the City University of
    New York, NY
Clarion University of Pennsylvania, PA
Clarkson University, NY
Clemson University, SC
Cleveland State University, OH

Coastal Carolina University, SC
The College at Brockport, State University
    of New York, NY
College of Charleston, SC
The College of New Rochelle, NY
The College of Saint Rose, NY
College of Staten Island of the City
    University of New York, NY
Colorado Mesa University, CO
Columbia College, MO
Columbus State University, GA
Concordia University Chicago, IL
Concordia University, Nebraska, NE
Concordia University Texas, TX
Concord University, WV
Cornerstone University, MI
Dakota State University, SD
Dallas Baptist University, TX
Defiance College, OH
DeSales University, PA
Dickinson State University, ND
Dordt College, IA
Drury University, MO
East Carolina University, NC
East Central University, OK
Eastern Connecticut State University, CT
Eastern Illinois University, IL
Eastern Michigan University, MI
Eastern Washington University, WA
East Stroudsburg University of
    Pennsylvania, PA
East Texas Baptist University, TX
Elizabethtown College, PA
Elmhurst College, IL
Elon University, NC
Emmanuel College, GA
Emporia State University, KS
Evangel University, MO
Ferris State University, MI
Fitchburg State University, MA
Flagler College, FL
Florida Agricultural and Mechanical
    University, FL
Florida College, FL
Florida International University, FL
Florida Southern College, FL
Fordham University, NY
Fort Hays State University, KS
Fort Lewis College, CO
Francis Marion University, SC
Franklin Pierce University, NH
Frostburg State University, MD
Furman University, SC
Gardner-Webb University, NC
George Fox University, OR
Georgia Southern University, GA
Goshen College, IN
Governors State University, IL
Grambling State University, LA
Grand Valley State University, MI
Grand View University, IA
Grove City College, PA
Hamline University, MN
Hampton University, VA
Harding University, AR
Hardin-Simmons University, TX
Hillsdale College, MI
Hofstra University, NY
Hood College, MD
Houghton College, NY
Howard Payne University, TX
Howard University, DC
Huntington University, IN
Husson University, ME
Idaho State University, ID

Illinois Institute of Technology, IL
Indiana State University, IN
Indiana University of Pennsylvania, PA
Indiana Wesleyan University, IN
Iowa State University of Science and
    Technology, IA
Ithaca College, NY
Jacksonville State University, AL
John Carroll University, OH
Juniata College, PA
Kansas Wesleyan University, KS
Kean University, NJ
Kennesaw State University, GA
Kent State University, OH
Kent State University at Stark, OH
King's College, PA
Kutztown University of Pennsylvania, PA
Lake Erie College, OH
Lawrence Technological University, MI
Lee University, TN
Lehigh University, PA
Lewis-Clark State College, ID
Liberty University, VA
Lindenwood University, MO
Linfield College, OR
Lipscomb University, TN
Lock Haven University of Pennsylvania, PA
Loras College, IA
Loyola Marymount University, CA
Lubbock Christian University, TX
Lycoming College, PA
Lynn University, FL
Malone University, OH
Mansfield University of Pennsylvania, PA
Maria College, NY
Marquette University, WI
Marymount University, VA
Marywood University, PA
Massachusetts College of Liberal Arts, MA
The Master's University, CA
Mayville State University, ND
Metropolitan State University of Denver, CO
Michigan State University, MI
Middle Georgia State University, GA
Middle Tennessee State University, TN
Midwestern State University, TX
Millersville University of Pennsylvania, PA
Millikin University, IL
Milwaukee School of Engineering, WI
Minnesota State University Moorhead, MN
Minot State University, ND
Mississippi State University, MS
Missouri University of Science and
    Technology, MO
Missouri Western State University, MO
Molloy College, NY
Monmouth University, NJ
Montana State University, MT
Montana State University Billings, MT
Montclair State University, NJ
Moravian College, PA
Morehead State University, KY
Mount Mary University, WI
Murray State University, KY
Newberry College, SC
New England College, NH
New Jersey Institute of Technology, NJ
New Mexico Highlands University, NM
New Mexico State University, NM
North Central College, IL
Northeastern Illinois University, IL
Northeastern State University, OK
Northern Illinois University, IL
Northern Kentucky University, KY
Northern Michigan University, MI
Northern State University, SD

Northwestern College, IA
Northwestern State University of
    Louisiana, LA
Northwest Missouri State University, MO
Northwest Nazarene University, ID
Ohio Northern University, OH
The Ohio State University, OH
Ohio University, OH
Ohio University–Chillicothe, OH
Ohio University–Eastern, OH
Ohio University–Lancaster, OH
Ohio University–Southern Campus, OH
Ohio University–Zanesville, OH
Oklahoma City University, OK
Oklahoma State University, OK
Old Dominion University, VA
Olivet College, MI
Oral Roberts University, OK
Ouachita Baptist University, AR
Pacific University, OR
Piedmont College, GA
Pittsburg State University, KS
Point Loma Nazarene University, CA
Point Park University, PA
Queens University of Charlotte, NC
Rochester Institute of Technology, NY
Rockhurst University, MO
St. Ambrose University, IA
St. Edward's University, TX
St. John's University, NY
Saint Louis University, MO
St. Thomas Aquinas College, NY
Salisbury University, MD
Sam Houston State University, TX
San Diego State University, CA
Schreiner University, TX
Shepherd University, WV
Shippensburg University of
    Pennsylvania, PA
Siena College, NY
Simpson University, CA
Slippery Rock University of
    Pennsylvania, PA
Sonoma State University, CA
Southeastern Louisiana University, LA
Southeastern Oklahoma State
    University, OK
Southeastern University, FL
Southeast Missouri State University, MO
Southern Adventist University, TN
Southern Illinois University Carbondale, IL
Southwestern College, KS
Southwestern Oklahoma
    State University, OK
State University of New York at
    Fredonia, NY
State University of New York at
    New Paltz, NY
State University of New York at
    Oswego, NY
State University of New York at
    Plattsburgh, NY
State University of New York College at
    Geneseo, NY
State University of New York College at
    Potsdam, NY
Stephen F. Austin State University, TX
Stetson University, FL
Stockton University, NJ
Tennessee Technological University, TN
Texas A&M International University, TX
Texas A&M University–Commerce, TX
Texas Christian University, TX
Texas Lutheran University, TX
Texas State University, TX
Texas Tech University, TX

Texas Wesleyan University, TX
Texas Woman's University, TX
Thiel College, PA
Thomas More College, KY
Toccoa Falls College, GA
Towson University, MD
Trevecca Nazarene University, TN
Trinity Christian College, IL
Truman State University, MO
Union University, TN
The University of Akron, OH
The University of Alabama, AL
The University of Alabama at
    Birmingham, AL
The University of Alabama in
    Huntsville, AL
University of Alaska Anchorage, AK
University of Arkansas, AR
University of Arkansas at Little Rock, AR
University of California, Davis, CA
University of California, Irvine, CA
University of California, San Diego, CA
University of Central Oklahoma, OK
University of Colorado Boulder, CO
University of Colorado Denver, CO
University of Dayton, OH
University of Delaware, DE
University of Denver, CO
University of Evansville, IN
University of Florida, FL
University of Hartford, CT
University of Houston, TX
University of Houston–Victoria, TX
University of Idaho, ID
University of Illinois at Urbana–
    Champaign, IL
University of Indianapolis, IN
The University of Kansas, KS
University of Kentucky, KY
University of Louisiana at Monroe, LA
University of Maine, ME
University of Maine at Fort Kent, ME
University of Mary Hardin-Baylor, TX
University of Maryland, College Park, MD
University of Massachusetts Amherst, MA
University of Memphis, TN
University of Michigan, MI
University of Michigan–Dearborn, MI
University of Michigan–Flint, MI
University of Minnesota, Twin Cities
    Campus, MN
University of Mississippi, MS
University of Missouri, MO
University of Missouri–St. Louis, MO
University of Montevallo, AL
University of Nebraska at Kearney, NE
University of Nebraska at Omaha, NE
University of Nevada, Las Vegas, NV
University of Nevada, Reno, NV
University of New Hampshire at
    Manchester, NH
University of North Carolina at
    Asheville, NC
The University of North Carolina at Chapel
    Hill, NC
The University of North Carolina at
    Greensboro, NC
The University of North Carolina
    Wilmington, NC
University of Northern Colorado, CO
University of Northern Iowa, IA
University of Oklahoma, OK
University of Pittsburgh at Bradford, PA
University of Pittsburgh at Johnstown, PA
University of Portland, OR
University of Puget Sound, WA

University of Rhode Island, RI
University of St. Francis, IL
University of St. Thomas, TX
University of Sioux Falls, SD
University of South Carolina, SC
University of South Carolina Aiken, SC
The University of South Dakota, SD
University of South Florida, FL
The University of Tennessee, TN
The University of Tennessee at
    Chattanooga, TN
The University of Tennessee at Martin, TN
The University of Texas at Arlington, TX
The University of Texas at El Paso, TX
The University of Texas at San Antonio, TX
The University of Texas of the Permian
    Basin, TX
The University of Texas Rio
    Grande Valley, TX
The University of Toledo, OH
The University of Tulsa, OK
University of Utah, UT
University of West Florida, FL
University of West Georgia, GA
University of Wisconsin–Eau Claire, WI
University of Wisconsin–Green Bay, WI
University of Wisconsin–La Crosse, WI
University of Wisconsin–Parkside, WI
University of Wisconsin–River Falls, WI
University of Wisconsin–Stevens Point, WI
University of Wisconsin–Superior, WI
University of Wisconsin–Whitewater, WI
University of Wyoming, WY
Utah State University, UT
Valdosta State University, GA
Valley City State University, ND
Waldorf University, IA
Walla Walla University, WA
Warner University, FL
Wartburg College, IA
Washburn University, KS
Washington State University, WA
Washington University in St. Louis, MO
Wayland Baptist University, TX
Waynesburg University, PA
Wayne State College, NE
Wayne State University, MI
Webster University, MO
Wesleyan College, GA
Western Carolina University, NC
Western Illinois University, IL
Western Kentucky University, KY
Western Oregon University, OR
Western Washington University, WA
West Texas A&M University, TX
West Virginia University, WV
Wheaton College, IL
Wichita State University, KS
Widener University, PA
Wilson College, PA
Wisconsin Lutheran College, WI
Wright State University, OH
Wright State University–Lake Campus, OH
Xavier University of Louisiana, LA
Youngstown State University, OH

Computer Science
Adelphi University, NY
Albertus Magnus College, CT
Alderson Broaddus University, WV
Alliant International University–
    San Diego, CA
Angelo State University, TX
Arkansas Tech University, AR
Armstrong State University, GA

Auburn University, AL
Augsburg College, MN
Augustana College, IL
Augustana University, SD
Augusta University, GA
Austin Peay State University, TN
Baylor University, TX
Bemidji State University, MN
Binghamton University, State University of
    New York, NY
Black Hills State University, SD
Bloomfield College, NJ
Bloomsburg University of Pennsylvania, PA
Boise State University, ID
Bowling Green State University, OH
Briar Cliff University, IA
Bryan College, TN
Buena Vista University, IA
Butler University, IN
California Lutheran University, CA
California Polytechnic State University, San
    Luis Obispo, CA
California State Polytechnic University,
    Pomona, CA
California State University, Chico, CA
California State University, Fullerton, CA
California State University, Los Angeles, CA
California State University, Northridge, CA
California State University,
    San Bernardino, CA
Calvin College, MI
Cameron University, OK
Campbellsville University, KY
Carlow University, PA
Carroll University, WI
Case Western Reserve University, OH
Central College, IA
Central Methodist University, MO
Central Michigan University, MI
Champlain College, VT
Christopher Newport University, VA
City College of the City University of
    New York, NY
Clarion University of Pennsylvania, PA
Clarkson University, NY
Clemson University, SC
Cleveland State University, OH
Coastal Carolina University, SC
The College at Brockport, State University
    of New York, NY
College of Charleston, SC
College of Saint Benedict, MN
College of Staten Island of the City
    University of New York, NY
Colorado Mesa University, CO
Colorado School of Mines, CO
Columbia College, MO
Columbus State University, GA
Concordia University Chicago, IL
Concordia University, Nebraska, NE
Concordia University Texas, TX
Dakota State University, SD
Dallas Baptist University, TX
Delta State University, MS
DeSales University, PA
Dickinson State University, ND
DigiPen Institute of Technology, WA
Dordt College, IA
Drury University, MO
East Carolina University, NC
Eastern Connecticut State University, CT
Eastern Illinois University, IL
Eastern Michigan University, MI
Eastern Washington University, WA

East Stroudsburg University of
    Pennsylvania, PA
ECPI University, VA
Elizabeth City State University, NC
Elizabethtown College, PA
Elmhurst College, IL
Elon University, NC
Emporia State University, KS
Evangel University, MO
Fairmont State University, WV
Ferris State University, MI
Fitchburg State University, MA
Florida Agricultural and Mechanical
    University, FL
Florida International University, FL
Fort Hays State University, KS
Francis Marion University, SC
Frostburg State University, MD
Furman University, SC
Gardner-Webb University, NC
George Fox University, OR
Georgia College & State University, GA
Georgia Institute of Technology, GA
Georgian Court University, NJ
Georgia Southern University, GA
Graceland University, IA
Grambling State University, LA
Grand Valley State University, MI
Hampton University, VA
Harding University, AR
Hardin-Simmons University, TX
Harrisburg University of Science and
    Technology, PA
Hood College, MD
Howard University, DC
Huntingdon College, AL
Husson University, ME
Idaho State University, ID
Illinois Institute of Technology, IL
Indiana State University, IN
Indiana Tech, IN
Indiana University of Pennsylvania, PA
Indiana Wesleyan University, IN
Iowa State University of Science and
    Technology, IA
Jacksonville State University, AL
James Madison University, VA
John Carroll University, OH
Johnson C. Smith University, NC
Juniata College, PA
Kansas Wesleyan University, KS
Kean University, NJ
Kennesaw State University, GA
Kent State University, OH
Kenyon College, OH
King's College, PA
Kutztown University of Pennsylvania, PA
Lawrence Technological University, MI
Liberty University, VA
Lindenwood University, MO
Linfield College, OR
Lock Haven University of Pennsylvania, PA
Longwood University, VA
Loras College, IA
Louisiana State University and Agricultural
    & Mechanical College, LA
Louisiana State University in
    Shreveport, LA
Louisiana Tech University, LA
Lubbock Christian University, TX
Lycoming College, PA
Manhattan College, NY
Maryville University of Saint Louis, MO
Marywood University, PA
Massachusetts College of Liberal Arts, MA

The Master's University, CA
Mayville State University, ND
Meredith College, NC
Metropolitan State University of Denver, CO
Michigan State University, MI
Middle Tennessee State University, TN
Midwestern State University, TX
Millersville University of Pennsylvania, PA
Mills College, CA
Milwaukee School of Engineering, WI
Minnesota State University Moorhead, MN
Minot State University, ND
Mississippi State University, MS
Missouri University of Science and Technology, MO
Missouri Western State University, MO
Monmouth University, NJ
Montana State University, MT
Montana State University Billings, MT
Montana Tech of The University of Montana, MT
Montreat College, NC
Moravian College, PA
Morehouse College, GA
Morningside College, IA
Murray State University, KY
Muskingum University, OH
New England College, NH
New Jersey Institute of Technology, NJ
New Mexico Highlands University, NM
New Mexico State University, NM
North Carolina State University, NC
North Central College, IL
Northeastern Illinois University, IL
Northeastern State University, OK
Northern Illinois University, IL
Northern Kentucky University, KY
Northern Michigan University, MI
Northern State University, SD
Northwestern College, IA
Northwest Missouri State University, MO
Northwest Nazarene University, ID
Ohio Northern University, OH
The Ohio State University, OH
Ohio University, OH
Ohio University–Chillicothe, OH
Ohio University–Eastern, OH
Ohio University–Lancaster, OH
Ohio University–Southern Campus, OH
Ohio University–Zanesville, OH
Ohio Valley University, WV
Oklahoma Baptist University, OK
Oklahoma Panhandle State University, OK
Oklahoma State University, OK
Oklahoma Wesleyan University, OK
Old Dominion University, VA
Ouachita Baptist University, AR
Peirce College, PA
Pittsburg State University, KS
Plymouth State University, NH
Point Park University, PA
Portland State University, OR
Purchase College, State University of New York, NY
Purdue University, IN
Robert Morris University Illinois, IL
Rochester Institute of Technology, NY
Rockford University, IL
Rockhurst University, MO
Rollins College, FL
Sacred Heart University, CT
Saginaw Valley State University, MI
St. Edward's University, TX
St. John's University, NY
Saint Joseph's University, PA
Saint Louis University, MO

St. Thomas Aquinas College, NY
Salisbury University, MD
Samford University, AL
Sam Houston State University, TX
San Diego State University, CA
Savannah State University, GA
Shepherd University, WV
Shippensburg University of Pennsylvania, PA
Siena College, NY
Skidmore College, NY
Slippery Rock University of Pennsylvania, PA
Sonoma State University, CA
South Dakota School of Mines and Technology, SD
Southeastern Louisiana University, LA
Southeastern Oklahoma State University, OK
Southeast Missouri State University, MO
Southern Adventist University, TN
Southern Arkansas University–Magnolia, AR
Southern Illinois University Carbondale, IL
Southern New Hampshire University, NH
Southwestern College, KS
Southwestern Oklahoma State University, OK
State University of New York at Fredonia, NY
State University of New York at Oswego, NY
State University of New York at Plattsburgh, NY
State University of New York College at Geneseo, NY
State University of New York College at Potsdam, NY
Stephen F. Austin State University, TX
Stetson University, FL
Stevens Institute of Technology, NJ
Stockton University, NJ
Stony Brook University, State University of New York, NY
Tennessee Technological University, TN
Texas A&M University, TX
Texas A&M University–Commerce, TX
Texas Lutheran University, TX
Texas State University, TX
Texas Tech University, TX
Texas Woman's University, TX
Thiel College, PA
Thomas More College, KY
Towson University, MD
Trinity Christian College, IL
Truman State University, MO
Tuskegee University, AL
Union University, TN
The University of Akron, OH
The University of Alabama, AL
The University of Alabama at Birmingham, AL
The University of Alabama in Huntsville, AL
University of Alaska Anchorage, AK
University of Alaska Fairbanks, AK
University of Arkansas, AR
University of Arkansas at Little Rock, AR
University of California, Davis, CA
University of California, Irvine, CA
University of California, San Diego, CA
University of California, Santa Cruz, CA
University of Central Oklahoma, OK
University of Colorado Boulder, CO
University of Dayton, OH
University of Delaware, DE

University of Denver, CO
University of Evansville, IN
University of Florida, FL
University of Great Falls, MT
University of Hartford, CT
University of Houston, TX
University of Houston–Clear Lake, TX
University of Houston–Victoria, TX
University of Idaho, ID
University of Illinois at Urbana–Champaign, IL
The University of Kansas, KS
University of Kentucky, KY
University of Louisiana at Monroe, LA
University of Maine, ME
University of Maine at Fort Kent, ME
University of Mary Hardin-Baylor, TX
University of Maryland, Baltimore County, MD
University of Maryland, College Park, MD
University of Maryland Eastern Shore, MD
University of Mary Washington, VA
University of Massachusetts Amherst, MA
University of Massachusetts Dartmouth, MA
University of Massachusetts Lowell, MA
University of Memphis, TN
University of Michigan, MI
University of Michigan–Dearborn, MI
University of Michigan–Flint, MI
University of Minnesota, Twin Cities Campus, MN
University of Mississippi, MS
University of Missouri, MO
University of Missouri–St. Louis, MO
University of Montana, MT
University of Nebraska at Omaha, NE
University of Nebraska–Lincoln, NE
University of Nevada, Las Vegas, NV
University of Nevada, Reno, NV
University of New Hampshire, NH
University of New Hampshire at Manchester, NH
University of North Carolina at Asheville, NC
The University of North Carolina at Charlotte, NC
The University of North Carolina at Greensboro, NC
The University of North Carolina Wilmington, NC
University of Northern Iowa, IA
University of North Florida, FL
University of Oklahoma, OK
University of Pittsburgh at Bradford, PA
University of Pittsburgh at Johnstown, PA
University of Portland, OR
University of Puget Sound, WA
University of Rhode Island, RI
University of Richmond, VA
University of St. Thomas, TX
University of Sioux Falls, SD
University of South Carolina, SC
University of South Carolina Aiken, SC
The University of South Dakota, SD
University of South Florida, FL
The University of Tennessee, TN
The University of Tennessee at Martin, TN
The University of Texas at Arlington, TX
The University of Texas at Dallas, TX
The University of Texas at El Paso, TX
The University of Texas at San Antonio, TX
The University of Texas Rio Grande Valley, TX
The University of Toledo, OH
The University of Tulsa, OK
University of Utah, UT

University of Vermont, VT
The University of Virginia's
    College at Wise, VA
University of Washington, WA
University of West Florida, FL
University of West Georgia, GA
University of Wisconsin–Eau Claire, WI
University of Wisconsin–La Crosse, WI
University of Wisconsin–River Falls, WI
University of Wisconsin–Stevens Point, WI
University of Wisconsin–Stout, WI
University of Wisconsin–Superior, WI
University of Wisconsin–Whitewater, WI
University of Wyoming, WY
Utah State University, UT
Valley City State University, ND
Virginia Commonwealth University, VA
Virginia Military Institute, VA
Virginia State University, VA
Walsh College of Accountancy and Business
    Administration, MI
Wartburg College, IA
Washburn University, KS
Washington State University, WA
Washington University in St. Louis, MO
Wayne State College, NE
Wayne State University, MI
Webster University, MO
Western Illinois University, IL
Western New England University, MA
Western Oregon University, OR
Western Washington University, WA
West Texas A&M University, TX
West Virginia University, WV
Wichita State University, KS
Widener University, PA
William Jessup University, CA
Wilson College, PA
Wright State University, OH
Wright State University–Lake Campus, OH
Xavier University of Louisiana, LA
Youngstown State University, OH

Education
Abilene Christian University, TX
Alaska Pacific University, AK
Albertus Magnus College, CT
Alderson Broaddus University, WV
Alfred University, NY
Alliant International University–
    San Diego, CA
Anderson University, SC
Angelo State University, TX
Arkansas Tech University, AR
Armstrong State University, GA
Auburn University, AL
Augsburg College, MN
Augustana College, IL
Augustana University, SD
Augusta University, GA
Aurora University, IL
Austin College, TX
Austin Peay State University, TN
Averett University, VA
Ball State University, IN
The Baptist College of Florida, FL
Barclay College, KS
Barton College, NC
Baylor University, TX
Belhaven University, MS
Bellarmine University, KY
Belmont Abbey College, NC
Bemidji State University, MN
Berklee College of Music, MA
Berry College, GA

Binghamton University, State University of
    New York, NY
Black Hills State University, SD
Bloomfield College, NJ
Bloomsburg University of Pennsylvania, PA
Blue Mountain College, MS
Boise State University, ID
Bowling Green State University, OH
Brenau University, GA
Briar Cliff University, IA
Bryan College, TN
Buena Vista University, IA
Butler University, IN
California Lutheran University, CA
California Polytechnic State University, San
    Luis Obispo, CA
California State Polytechnic University,
    Pomona, CA
California State University, Bakersfield, CA
California State University, Chico, CA
California State University, Fresno, CA
California State University, Fullerton, CA
California State University, Los Angeles, CA
California State University, Northridge, CA
California State University,
    San Bernardino, CA
Calvin College, MI
Cameron University, OK
Campbellsville University, KY
Carlow University, PA
Carroll University, WI
Carson-Newman University, TN
Catawba College, NC
Centenary College of Louisiana, LA
Central College, IA
Central Methodist University, MO
Central Michigan University, MI
Champlain College, VT
Charlotte Christian College and Theological
    Seminary, NC
Christopher Newport University, VA
Cincinnati Christian University, OH
City College of the City University of New
    York, NY
Clarion University of Pennsylvania, PA
Clarks Summit University, PA
Clemson University, SC
Cleveland State University, OH
Coastal Carolina University, SC
The College at Brockport, State University
    of New York, NY
College of Charleston, SC
College of Coastal Georgia, GA
The College of Idaho, ID
The College of New Rochelle, NY
College of Saint Mary, NE
The College of Saint Rose, NY
College of Staten Island of the City
    University of New York, NY
Colorado Mesa University, CO
Columbia College, MO
Columbus State University, GA
Concordia University Ann Arbor, MI
Concordia University Chicago, IL
Concordia University, Nebraska, NE
Concordia University Texas, TX
Concord University, WV
Cornerstone University, MI
Creighton University, NE
Daemen College, NY
Dakota State University, SD
Dakota Wesleyan University, SD
Dallas Baptist University, TX
Davidson College, NC
Defiance College, OH

Delta State University, MS
DeSales University, PA
Dickinson State University, ND
Dominican College, NY
Dordt College, IA
Drury University, MO
Duquesne University, PA
D'Youville College, NY
East Carolina University, NC
Eastern Connecticut State University, CT
Eastern Illinois University, IL
Eastern Mennonite University, VA
Eastern Michigan University, MI
Eastern Washington University, WA
East Stroudsburg University of
    Pennsylvania, PA
East Texas Baptist University, TX
Elizabeth City State University, NC
Elizabethtown College, PA
Elmhurst College, IL
Elon University, NC
Emmanuel College, GA
Emporia State University, KS
Endicott College, MA
Evangel University, MO
Fairmont State University, WV
Felician University, NJ
Ferris State University, MI
Fitchburg State University, MA
Flagler College, FL
Florida Agricultural and Mechanical
    University, FL
Florida College, FL
Florida Gulf Coast University, FL
Florida International University, FL
Florida Southern College, FL
Fort Hays State University, KS
Fort Lewis College, CO
Framingham State University, MA
Francis Marion University, SC
Frostburg State University, MD
Furman University, SC
Gannon University, PA
Gardner-Webb University, NC
George Fox University, OR
Georgia College & State University, GA
Georgian Court University, NJ
Georgia Southern University, GA
Glenville State College, WV
Goshen College, IN
Governors State University, IL
Grambling State University, LA
Grand Valley State University, MI
Grand View University, IA
Grove City College, PA
Hamline University, MN
Hampden-Sydney College, VA
Hampton University, VA
Hardin-Simmons University, TX
Hawai'i Pacific University, HI
High Point University, NC
Hillsdale College, MI
Hood College, MD
Houghton College, NY
Houston Baptist University, TX
Howard Payne University, TX
Howard University, DC
Husson University, ME
Idaho State University, ID
Indiana State University, IN
Indiana Tech, IN
Indiana University of Pennsylvania, PA
Indiana Wesleyan University, IN
Iowa State University of Science and
    Technology, IA

Iowa Wesleyan University, IA
Jacksonville State University, AL
James Madison University, VA
John Carroll University, OH
John Wesley University, NC
Juniata College, PA
Kansas Wesleyan University, KS
Kean University, NJ
Kennesaw State University, GA
Kent State University, OH
Kent State University at Geauga, OH
Kent State University at Stark, OH
Keuka College, NY
King's College, PA
Kutztown University of Pennsylvania, PA
LaGrange College, GA
Lake Erie College, OH
Langston University, OK
Lawrence Technological University, MI
Lees-McRae College, NC
Lee University, TN
Lewis-Clark State College, ID
Liberty University, VA
Lindenwood University, MO
Lindsey Wilson College, KY
Linfield College, OR
Lipscomb University, TN
Lock Haven University of Pennsylvania, PA
Longwood University, VA
Loras College, IA
Louisiana State University and Agricultural
 & Mechanical College, LA
Louisiana State University in
 Shreveport, LA
Louisiana Tech University, LA
Loyola Marymount University, CA
Lubbock Christian University, TX
Lycoming College, PA
Malone University, OH
Mansfield University of Pennsylvania, PA
Marquette University, WI
Maryville University of Saint Louis, MO
Marywood University, PA
Massachusetts College of Liberal Arts, MA
The Master's University, CA
Mayville State University, ND
Mercer University, GA
Meredith College, NC
Methodist University, NC
Metropolitan State University of Denver, CO
Miami University, OH
Michigan State University, MI
Middle Georgia State University, GA
Middle Tennessee State University, TN
Midwestern State University, TX
Millersville University of Pennsylvania, PA
Millikin University, IL
Minnesota State University Moorhead, MN
Minot State University, ND
Mississippi State University, MS
Missouri University of Science and
 Technology, MO
Missouri Western State University, MO
Molloy College, NY
Monmouth University, NJ
Montana State University, MT
Montana State University Billings, MT
Montclair State University, NJ
Moravian College, PA
Morehead State University, KY
Mount Mary University, WI
Murray State University, KY
Newberry College, SC
New England College, NH
New Jersey Institute of Technology, NJ
New Mexico Highlands University, NM

New Mexico State University, NM
North Carolina State University, NC
North Central College, IL
Northeastern Illinois University, IL
Northeastern State University, OK
Northern Illinois University, IL
Northern Kentucky University, KY
Northern Michigan University, MI
Northern State University, SD
Northwestern College, IA
Northwestern State University of
 Louisiana, LA
Northwest Missouri State University, MO
Northwest Nazarene University, ID
Ohio Northern University, OH
The Ohio State University, OH
Ohio University, OH
Ohio University–Chillicothe, OH
Ohio University–Eastern, OH
Ohio University–Lancaster, OH
Ohio University–Southern Campus, OH
Ohio University–Zanesville, OH
Ohio Valley University, WV
Ohio Wesleyan University, OH
Oklahoma Baptist University, OK
Oklahoma City University, OK
Oklahoma Panhandle State University, OK
Oklahoma State University, OK
Oklahoma Wesleyan University, OK
Old Dominion University, VA
Olivet College, MI
Oral Roberts University, OK
Ouachita Baptist University, AR
Pacific Union College, CA
Pacific University, OR
Piedmont College, GA
Pittsburg State University, KS
Point Loma Nazarene University, CA
Point Park University, PA
Portland State University, OR
Purdue University, IN
Queens University of Charlotte, NC
Randall University, OK
Randolph College, VA
Rockford University, IL
Rockhurst University, MO
Sacred Heart University, CT
The Sage Colleges, NY
Saginaw Valley State University, MI
St. Bonaventure University, NY
St. Edward's University, TX
St. John's University, NY
Saint Louis University, MO
Saint Martin's University, WA
St. Mary's College of Maryland, MD
St. Thomas Aquinas College, NY
Salem International University, WV
Salisbury University, MD
Samford University, AL
Sam Houston State University, TX
San Diego State University, CA
Schreiner University, TX
Shasta Bible College, CA
Shepherd University, WV
Shippensburg University of
 Pennsylvania, PA
Siena College, NY
Slippery Rock University of
 Pennsylvania, PA
Sonoma State University, CA
Southeastern Louisiana University, LA
Southeastern Oklahoma State
 University, OK
Southeastern University, FL
Southeast Missouri State University, MO
Southern Adventist University, TN

Southern Arkansas University–
 Magnolia, AR
Southern Illinois University Carbondale, IL
Southern Illinois University
 Edwardsville, IL
Southern New Hampshire University, NH
Southern Oregon University, OR
Southwestern College, KS
Southwestern Oklahoma State
 University, OK
State University of New York at
 Fredonia, NY
State University of New York at
 New Paltz, NY
State University of New York at
 Oswego, NY
State University of New York at
 Plattsburgh, NY
State University of New York College at
 Cortland, NY
State University of New York College at
 Geneseo, NY
State University of New York College at
 Potsdam, NY
Stephen F. Austin State University, TX
Stetson University, FL
Stockton University, NJ
Tennessee Technological University, TN
Texas A&M International University, TX
Texas A&M University, TX
Texas A&M University–Commerce, TX
Texas A&M University–Texarkana, TX
Texas Christian University, TX
Texas Lutheran University, TX
Texas State University, TX
Texas Tech University, TX
Texas Wesleyan University, TX
Texas Woman's University, TX
Thiel College, PA
Thomas More College, KY
Thomas University, GA
Toccoa Falls College, GA
Towson University, MD
Trevecca Nazarene University, TN
Trinity Christian College, IL
Truett McConnell University, GA
Truman State University, MO
Union University, TN
The University of Akron, OH
The University of Alabama, AL
The University of Alabama in
 Huntsville, AL
University of Alaska Anchorage, AK
University of Alaska Fairbanks, AK
The University of Arizona, AZ
University of Arkansas, AR
University of Arkansas at Little Rock, AR
University of California, Irvine, CA
University of California, Riverside, CA
University of Central Oklahoma, OK
University of Colorado Boulder, CO
University of Colorado Denver, CO
University of Dallas, TX
University of Dayton, OH
University of Delaware, DE
University of Evansville, IN
University of Florida, FL
University of Georgia, GA
University of Great Falls, MT
University of Hartford, CT
University of Holy Cross, LA
University of Houston, TX
University of Houston–Clear Lake, TX
University of Houston–Victoria, TX
University of Idaho, ID

University of Illinois at Urbana–
  Champaign, IL
The University of Kansas, KS
University of Kentucky, KY
University of Louisiana at Monroe, LA
University of Louisville, KY
University of Maine, ME
University of Maine at Fort Kent, ME
University of Mary Hardin Baylor, TX
University of Maryland,
  Baltimore County, MD
University of Maryland, College Park, MD
University of Maryland Eastern Shore, MD
University of Mary Washington, VA
University of Massachusetts Amherst, MA
University of Massachusetts Dartmouth, MA
University of Massachusetts Lowell, MA
University of Memphis, TN
University of Michigan, MI
University of Michigan–Dearborn, MI
University of Michigan–Flint, MI
University of Minnesota, Twin Cities
  Campus, MN
University of Mississippi, MS
University of Missouri, MO
University of Missouri–St. Louis, MO
University of Montana, MT
The University of Montana Western, MT
University of Montevallo, AL
University of Nebraska at Omaha, NE
University of Nebraska–Lincoln, NE
University of Nevada, Las Vegas, NV
University of Nevada, Reno, NV
University of New Hampshire, NH
University of North Carolina at
  Asheville, NC
The University of North Carolina at
  Chapel Hill, NC
The University of North Carolina at
  Charlotte, NC
The University of North Carolina at
  Greensboro, NC
The University of North Carolina at
  Pembroke, NC
The University of North Carolina
  Wilmington, NC
University of Northern Colorado, CO
University of Northern Iowa, IA
University of North Florida, FL
University of North Georgia, GA
University of Oklahoma, OK
University of Oregon, OR
University of Pittsburgh at Bradford, PA
University of Pittsburgh at Johnstown, PA
University of Portland, OR
University of Rhode Island, RI
University of St. Francis, IL
University of St. Thomas, MN
University of St. Thomas, TX
University of Sioux Falls, SD
University of South Carolina, SC
University of South Carolina Aiken, SC
The University of South Dakota, SD
University of Southern Indiana, IN
University of South Florida, FL
The University of Tennessee, TN
The University of Tennessee at
  Chattanooga, TN
The University of Tennessee at Martin, TN
The University of Texas at Arlington, TX
The University of Texas at El Paso, TX
The University of Texas at San Antonio, TX
The University of Texas of the Permian
  Basin, TX

The University of Texas Rio
  Grande Valley, TX
University of the District of Columbia, DC
The University of Toledo, OH
The University of Tulsa, OK
University of Utah, UT
University of Vermont, VT
The University of Virginia's
  College at Wise, VA
University of Washington, WA
University of West Florida, FL
University of West Georgia, GA
University of Wisconsin–Eau Claire, WI
University of Wisconsin–Green Bay, WI
University of Wisconsin–La Crosse, WI
University of Wisconsin–Parkside, WI
University of Wisconsin–River Falls, WI
University of Wisconsin–Stevens Point, WI
University of Wisconsin–Stout, WI
University of Wisconsin–Superior, WI
University of Wisconsin–Whitewater, WI
University of Wyoming, WY
Utah State University, UT
Valdosta State University, GA
Valley City State University, ND
Virginia Commonwealth University, VA
Walla Walla University, WA
Warner University, FL
Wartburg College, IA
Washburn University, KS
Washington State University, WA
Washington University in St. Louis, MO
Wayland Baptist University, TX
Wayne State College, NE
Wayne State University, MI
Webster University, MO
Wesleyan College, GA
Western Carolina University, NC
Western Illinois University, IL
Western Kentucky University, KY
Western Oregon University, OR
Western Washington University, WA
West Texas A&M University, TX
West Virginia University, WV
Wheaton College, IL
Wichita State University, KS
Widener University, PA
William Jessup University, CA
Williams Baptist College, AR
Wilson College, PA
Wisconsin Lutheran College, WI
Wright State University, OH
Wright State University–Lake Campus, OH
Xavier University of Louisiana, LA
Youngstown State University, OH

Engineering/Technologies
Abilene Christian University, TX
Alfred University, NY
Arkansas Tech University, AR
Armstrong State University, GA
Auburn University, AL
Austin College, TX
Averett University, VA
Ball State University, IN
Baylor University, TX
Bemidji State University, MN
Berklee College of Music, MA
Binghamton University, State University of
  New York, NY
Bluefield State College, WV
Boise State University, ID
Boston University, MA
Bowling Green State University, OH
Bucknell University, PA

Butler University, IN
California Baptist University, CA
California Polytechnic State University, San
  Luis Obispo, CA
California State Polytechnic University,
  Pomona, CA
California State University, Chico, CA
California State University, Fresno, CA
California State University, Fullerton, CA
California State University, Los Angeles, CA
California State University Maritime
  Academy, CA
California State University, Northridge, CA
Calvin College, MI
Cameron University, OK
Case Western Reserve University, OH
Centenary College of Louisiana, LA
Central College, IA
Central Michigan University, MI
Christian Brothers University, TN
Christopher Newport University, VA
The Citadel, The Military College of South
  Carolina, SC
City College of the City University
  of New York, NY
Clarkson University, NY
Clemson University, SC
Cleveland State University, OH
College of Charleston, SC
College of Saint Benedict, MN
The College of Saint Rose, NY
College of Staten Island of the City
  University of New York, NY
Colorado Mesa University, CO
Colorado School of Mines, CO
Cooper Union for the Advancement of
  Science and Art, NY
DigiPen Institute of Technology, WA
Dordt College, IA
East Carolina University, NC
Eastern Illinois University, IL
Eastern Michigan University, MI
Eastern University, PA
Eastern Washington University, WA
ECPI University, VA
Elizabethtown College, PA
Elon University, NC
Emporia State University, KS
Evangel University, MO
Fairmont State University, WV
Ferris State University, MI
Fitchburg State University, MA
Florida Agricultural and Mechanical
  University, FL
Florida Atlantic University, FL
Florida Gulf Coast University, FL
Florida International University, FL
Fort Hays State University, KS
Framingham State University, MA
Francis Marion University, SC
Frostburg State University, MD
Furman University, SC
Gannon University, PA
George Fox University, OR
Georgia Institute of Technology, GA
Georgia Southern University, GA
Gonzaga University, WA
Graceland University, IA
Grambling State University, LA
Grand Valley State University, MI
Greenville College, IL
Grove City College, PA
Hampton University, VA
Harding University, AR
Hillsdale College, MI

Hofstra University, NY
Howard University, DC
Idaho State University, ID
Illinois Institute of Technology, IL
Indiana State University, IN
Indiana Tech, IN
Indiana University of Pennsylvania, PA
Indiana University–Purdue University Fort
　Wayne, IN
Iowa State University of Science and
　Technology, IA
James Madison University, VA
Johnson C. Smith University, NC
Kean University, NJ
Kennesaw State University, GA
Kent State University, OH
King's College, PA
Langston University, OK
Lawrence Technological University, MI
Lehigh University, PA
Lewis-Clark State College, ID
Liberty University, VA
Lindenwood University, MO
Lipscomb University, TN
Loras College, IA
Louisiana State University and Agricultural
　& Mechanical College, LA
Louisiana Tech University, LA
Loyola Marymount University, CA
Manhattan College, NY
Marquette University, WI
Mercer University, GA
Metropolitan State University of Denver, CO
Miami University, OH
Michigan State University, MI
Middle Georgia State University, GA
Middle Tennessee State University, TN
Midwestern State University, TX
Milwaukee School of Engineering, WI
Minnesota State University Moorhead, MN
Mississippi State University, MS
Missouri University of Science and
　Technology, MO
Missouri Western State University, MO
Montana State University, MT
Montana State University Billings, MT
Montana Tech of The University of
　Montana, MT
Moravian College, PA
Morehead State University, KY
Morehouse College, GA
Murray State University, KY
Muskingum University, OH
New Jersey Institute of Technology, NJ
New Mexico Highlands University, NM
New Mexico State University, NM
North Carolina Agricultural and Technical
　State University, NC
North Carolina State University, NC
Northern Illinois University, IL
Northern Kentucky University, KY
Northern Michigan University, MI
Northwestern State University of
　Louisiana, LA
Northwest Nazarene University, ID
Ohio Northern University, OH
The Ohio State University, OH
Ohio University, OH
Ohio University–Chillicothe, OH
Ohio University–Eastern, OH
Ohio University–Lancaster, OH
Ohio University–Southern Campus, OH
Ohio University–Zanesville, OH
Oklahoma Christian University, OK
Oklahoma State University, OK
Old Dominion University, VA

Oral Roberts University, OK
Ouachita Baptist University, AR
Philadelphia University, PA
Pittsburg State University, KS
Plymouth State University, NH
Point Loma Nazarene University, CA
Point Park University, PA
Portland State University, OR
Purdue University, IN
Rice University, TX
Rochester Institute of Technology, NY
Rockhurst University, MO
Rollins College, FL
Saginaw Valley State University, MI
St. Ambrose University, IA
Saint Louis University, MO
Saint Martin's University, WA
St. Thomas Aquinas College, NY
Sam Houston State University, TX
San Diego State University, CA
Santa Clara University, CA
Savannah State University, GA
Seattle Pacific University, WA
Shepherd University, WV
Slippery Rock University of
　Pennsylvania, PA
Sonoma State University, CA
South Dakota School of Mines and
　Technology, SD
Southeastern Oklahoma State
　University, OK
Southeast Missouri State University, MO
Southern Illinois University Carbondale, IL
Southwestern Oklahoma State
　University, OK
State University of New York at
　New Paltz, NY
State University of New York at
　Plattsburgh, NY
State University of New York College at
　Potsdam, NY
State University of New York College of
　Environmental Science and Forestry, NY
Stevens Institute of Technology, NJ
Stony Brook University, State University of
　New York, NY
Suffolk University, MA
Tennessee Technological University, TN
Texas A&M International University, TX
Texas A&M University, TX
Texas A&M University–Commerce, TX
Texas A&M University–Texarkana, TX
Texas Christian University, TX
Texas State University, TX
Texas Tech University, TX
Trinity Christian College, IL
Tuskegee University, AL
Union University, TN
The University of Akron, OH
The University of Alabama, AL
The University of Alabama at
　Birmingham, AL
The University of Alabama in
　Huntsville, AL
University of Alaska Anchorage, AK
University of Alaska Fairbanks, AK
The University of Arizona, AZ
University of Arkansas, AR
University of Arkansas at Little Rock, AR
University of Bridgeport, CT
University of California, Davis, CA
University of California, Irvine, CA
University of California, Riverside, CA
University of California, San Diego, CA
University of Colorado Boulder, CO
University of Colorado Denver, CO

University of Dayton, OH
University of Delaware, DE
University of Denver, CO
University of Evansville, IN
University of Florida, FL
University of Hartford, CT
University of Houston, TX
University of Idaho, ID
University of Illinois at Urbana–
　Champaign, IL
The University of Iowa, IA
The University of Kansas, KS
University of Kentucky, KY
University of Louisville, KY
University of Maine, ME
University of Maryland,
　Baltimore County, MD
University of Maryland, College Park, MD
University of Maryland Eastern Shore, MD
University of Massachusetts Amherst, MA
University of Massachusetts Dartmouth, MA
University of Massachusetts Lowell, MA
University of Memphis, TN
University of Michigan, MI
University of Michigan–Dearborn, MI
University of Michigan–Flint, MI
University of Minnesota, Twin Cities
　Campus, MN
University of Mississippi, MS
University of Missouri, MO
University of Missouri–St. Louis, MO
University of Nebraska at Omaha, NE
University of Nebraska–Lincoln, NE
University of Nevada, Las Vegas, NV
University of Nevada, Reno, NV
University of New Hampshire, NH
University of New Hampshire at
　Manchester, NH
University of North Carolina at
　Asheville, NC
The University of North Carolina at
　Charlotte, NC
The University of North Carolina
　Wilmington, NC
University of North Florida, FL
University of Oklahoma, OK
University of Pittsburgh at Bradford, PA
University of Pittsburgh at Johnstown, PA
University of Portland, OR
University of Rhode Island, RI
University of Rochester, NY
University of Sioux Falls, SD
University of South Carolina, SC
University of South Carolina Aiken, SC
University of Southern Indiana, IN
University of South Florida, FL
The University of Tennessee, TN
The University of Tennessee at
　Chattanooga, TN
The University of Tennessee at Martin, TN
The University of Texas at Arlington, TX
The University of Texas at Dallas, TX
The University of Texas at El Paso, TX
The University of Texas at San Antonio, TX
The University of Texas of the Permian
　Basin, TX
The University of Texas Rio
　Grande Valley, TX
The University of Toledo, OH
The University of Tulsa, OK
University of Utah, UT
University of Vermont, VT
University of Washington, WA
University of West Florida, FL
University of Wisconsin–Green Bay, WI
University of Wisconsin–Parkside, WI

University of Wisconsin–Stevens Point, WI
University of Wisconsin–Stout, WI
University of Wyoming, WY
Utah State University, UT
Valley City State University, ND
Valparaiso University, IN
Virginia Commonwealth University, VA
Virginia Military Institute, VA
Virginia State University, VA
Walla Walla University, WA
Wartburg College, IA
Washburn University, KS
Washington State University, WA
Washington University in St. Louis, MO
Wayne State University, MI
Webb Institute, NY
Wesleyan College, GA
Western Illinois University, IL
Western Kentucky University, KY
Western Washington University, WA
West Texas A&M University, TX
West Virginia University, WV
Wheaton College, IL
Wichita State University, KS
Widener University, PA
Wright State University, OH
Wright State University–Lake Campus, OH
Xavier University of Louisiana, LA
York College of Pennsylvania, PA
Youngstown State University, OH

English
Abilene Christian University, TX
Alaska Pacific University, AK
Albertus Magnus College, CT
Alfred University, NY
Alliant International University–
    San Diego, CA
Angelo State University, TX
Arkansas Tech University, AR
Armstrong State University, GA
Auburn University, AL
Augsburg College, MN
Augustana College, IL
Augustana University, SD
Austin College, TX
Austin Peay State University, TN
Averett University, VA
Ball State University, IN
Barton College, NC
Baylor University, TX
Belhaven University, MS
Bemidji State University, MN
Berry College, GA
Binghamton University, State University of
    New York, NY
Black Hills State University, SD
Bloomfield College, NJ
Bloomsburg University of Pennsylvania, PA
Blue Mountain College, MS
Boise State University, ID
Bowling Green State University, OH
Brenau University, GA
Briar Cliff University, IA
Bryan College, TN
Butler University, IN
California Lutheran University, CA
California Polytechnic State University, San
    Luis Obispo, CA
California State Polytechnic University,
    Pomona, CA
California State University, Chico, CA
California State University, Fresno, CA
California State University, Fullerton, CA
California State University, Los Angeles, CA

California State University, Northridge, CA
Calvin College, MI
Cameron University, OK
Campbellsville University, KY
Carlow University, PA
Case Western Reserve University, OH
Cedar Crest College, PA
Centenary College of Louisiana, LA
Central Methodist University, MO
Central Michigan University, MI
Christopher Newport University, VA
City College of the City University of New
    York, NY
Clarion University of Pennsylvania, PA
Clemson University, SC
Cleveland State University, OH
Coastal Carolina University, SC
The College at Brockport, State University
    of New York, NY
College of Charleston, SC
The College of Idaho, ID
The College of New Rochelle, NY
The College of Saint Rose, NY
College of Staten Island of the City
    University of New York, NY
Colorado Mesa University, CO
Columbia College, MO
Columbus State University, GA
Concordia University Chicago, IL
Concordia University, Nebraska, NE
Concordia University Texas, TX
Concord University, WV
Cornerstone University, MI
Dakota State University, SD
Dallas Baptist University, TX
Defiance College, OH
Delta State University, MS
Denison University, OH
DeSales University, PA
Dickinson State University, ND
Dordt College, IA
Drury University, MO
D'Youville College, NY
East Carolina University, NC
Eastern Connecticut State University, CT
Eastern Illinois University, IL
Eastern Mennonite University, VA
Eastern Michigan University, MI
Eastern Washington University, WA
East Stroudsburg University of
    Pennsylvania, PA
East Texas Baptist University, TX
Elizabethtown College, PA
Elmhurst College, IL
Emmanuel College, GA
Emporia State University, KS
Evangel University, MO
Fairmont State University, WV
Felician University, NJ
Fitchburg State University, MA
Flagler College, FL
Florida Agricultural and Mechanical
    University, FL
Florida College, FL
Florida International University, FL
Fort Hays State University, KS
Fort Lewis College, CO
Framingham State University, MA
Francis Marion University, SC
Frostburg State University, MD
Furman University, SC
Gannon University, PA
Gardner-Webb University, NC
George Fox University, OR
Georgian Court University, NJ

Georgia Southern University, GA
Glenville State College, WV
Governors State University, IL
Grambling State University, LA
Grand Valley State University, MI
Grand View University, IA
Grove City College, PA
Hamline University, MN
Hampshire College, MA
Harding University, AR
Hardin-Simmons University, TX
High Point University, NC
Hillsdale College, MI
Hood College, MD
Houghton College, NY
Howard Payne University, TX
Howard University, DC
Husson University, ME
Idaho State University, ID
Indiana State University, IN
Indiana University of Pennsylvania, PA
Indiana Wesleyan University, IN
Iowa State University of Science and
    Technology, IA
Iowa Wesleyan University, IA
Jacksonville State University, AL
James Madison University, VA
John Carroll University, OH
Kansas Wesleyan University, KS
Kean University, NJ
Kennesaw State University, GA
Kent State University, OH
King's College, PA
Kutztown University of Pennsylvania, PA
Lake Erie College, OH
Lebanon Valley College, PA
Lewis-Clark State College, ID
Liberty University, VA
Lindenwood University, MO
Lindsey Wilson College, KY
Linfield College, OR
Lipscomb University, TN
Lock Haven University of Pennsylvania, PA
Longwood University, VA
Loras College, IA
Louisiana State University and Agricultural
    & Mechanical College, LA
Louisiana State University in
    Shreveport, LA
Louisiana Tech University, LA
Loyola Marymount University, CA
Lubbock Christian University, TX
Lycoming College, PA
Marquette University, WI
Marymount University, VA
Maryville University of Saint Louis, MO
Marywood University, PA
Massachusetts College of Liberal Arts, MA
Mayville State University, ND
Mercer University, GA
Meredith College, NC
Methodist University, NC
Metropolitan State University of Denver, CO
Michigan State University, MI
Middle Tennessee State University, TN
Midwestern State University, TX
Millersville University of Pennsylvania, PA
Millikin University, IL
Minnesota State University Moorhead, MN
Minot State University, ND
Mississippi State University, MS
Missouri University of Science and
    Technology, MO
Missouri Western State University, MO
Molloy College, NY

Monmouth University, NJ
Montana State University, MT
Montana State University Billings, MT
Montclair State University, NJ
Moravian College, PA
Mount Mary University, WI
Murray State University, KY
New Mexico Highlands University, NM
New Mexico State University, NM
North Central College, IL
Northeast Catholic College, NH
Northeastern Illinois University, IL
Northeastern State University, OK
Northern Illinois University, IL
Northern Kentucky University, KY
Northern Michigan University, MI
Northern State University, SD
Northwestern College, IA
Northwestern State University of
　Louisiana, LA
Northwest Missouri State University, MO
Northwest Nazarene University, ID
Ohio Northern University, OH
The Ohio State University, OH
Ohio University, OH
Ohio University–Chillicothe, OH
Ohio University–Eastern, OH
Ohio University–Lancaster, OH
Ohio University–Southern Campus, OH
Ohio University–Zanesville, OH
Ohio Valley University, WV
Oklahoma Baptist University, OK
Oklahoma Panhandle State University, OK
Oklahoma State University, OK
Old Dominion University, VA
Olivet College, MI
Ouachita Baptist University, AR
Pacific University, OR
Piedmont College, GA
Pittsburg State University, KS
Point Park University, PA
Purchase College, State University of New
　York, NY
Randall University, OK
Randolph College, VA
Rockford University, IL
Rockhurst University, MO
Sacred Heart University, CT
The Sage Colleges, NY
St. Edward's University, TX
St. John Fisher College, NY
St. John's University, NY
Saint Louis University, MO
St. Thomas Aquinas College, NY
Samford University, AL
Sam Houston State University, TX
San Diego State University, CA
Savannah State University, GA
Schreiner University, TX
Shepherd University, WV
Shippensburg University of
　Pennsylvania, PA
Siena College, NY
Slippery Rock University of
　Pennsylvania, PA
Sonoma State University, CA
Southeastern Louisiana University, LA
Southeastern Oklahoma State
　University, OK
Southeast Missouri State University, MO
Southern Adventist University, TN
Southern Arkansas University–
　Magnolia, AR
Southern Illinois University Carbondale, IL
Southern Oregon University, OR

Southwestern Oklahoma State
　University, OK
State University of New York at
　Fredonia, NY
State University of New York at
　New Paltz, NY
State University of New York at
　Oswego, NY
State University of New York at
　Plattsburgh, NY
State University of New York College at
　Geneseo, NY
State University of New York College at
　Potsdam, NY
Stephens College, MO
Stetson University, FL
Stony Brook University, State University of
　New York, NY
Tennessee Technological University, TN
Texas A&M International University, TX
Texas A&M University–Commerce, TX
Texas A&M University–Texarkana, TX
Texas Christian University, TX
Texas Lutheran University, TX
Texas State University, TX
Texas Tech University, TX
Texas Wesleyan University, TX
Texas Woman's University, TX
Thiel College, PA
Thomas More College, KY
Thomas University, GA
Towson University, MD
Trevecca Nazarene University, TN
Trinity Christian College, IL
Truman State University, MO
Union University, TN
The University of Akron, OH
The University of Alabama, AL
The University of Alabama in
　Huntsville, AL
University of Alaska Anchorage, AK
University of Arkansas, AR
University of Arkansas at Little Rock, AR
University of California, Davis, CA
University of California, Irvine, CA
University of California, Riverside, CA
University of Central Oklahoma, OK
University of Colorado Boulder, CO
University of Colorado Denver, CO
University of Dayton, OH
University of Delaware, DE
University of Denver, CO
University of Evansville, IN
University of Hartford, CT
University of Holy Cross, LA
University of Houston, TX
University of Idaho, ID
University of Illinois at Urbana–
　Champaign, IL
The University of Kansas, KS
University of Kentucky, KY
University of Louisiana at Monroe, LA
University of Louisville, KY
University of Maine, ME
University of Maine at Fort Kent, ME
University of Mary Hardin-Baylor, TX
University of Maryland,
　Baltimore County, MD
University of Maryland, College Park, MD
University of Maryland Eastern Shore, MD
University of Mary Washington, VA
University of Massachusetts Amherst, MA
University of Massachusetts Lowell, MA
University of Memphis, TN
University of Michigan, MI
University of Michigan–Flint, MI

University of Minnesota, Twin Cities
　Campus, MN
University of Mississippi, MS
University of Missouri, MO
University of Missouri–St. Louis, MO
University of Montana, MT
The University of Montana Western, MT
University of Montevallo, AL
University of Nebraska at Omaha, NE
University of Nebraska–Lincoln, NE
University of Nevada, Las Vegas, NV
University of Nevada, Reno, NV
University of New Hampshire, NH
University of New Hampshire at
　Manchester, NH
University of North Carolina at
　Asheville, NC
The University of North Carolina at Chapel
　Hill, NC
The University of North Carolina at
　Greensboro, NC
The University of North Carolina
　Wilmington, NC
University of Northern Colorado, CO
University of North Georgia, GA
University of Oklahoma, OK
University of Oregon, OR
University of Pittsburgh at Bradford, PA
University of Pittsburgh at Johnstown, PA
University of Portland, OR
University of Puget Sound, WA
University of Rhode Island, RI
University of St. Thomas, MN
University of St. Thomas, TX
University of Sioux Falls, SD
University of South Carolina, SC
University of South Carolina Aiken, SC
The University of South Dakota, SD
University of South Florida, FL
The University of Tampa, FL
The University of Tennessee at
　Chattanooga, TN
The University of Tennessee at Martin, TN
The University of Texas at Arlington, TX
The University of Texas at El Paso, TX
The University of Texas at San Antonio, TX
The University of Texas Rio
　Grande Valley, TX
The University of Toledo, OH
The University of Tulsa, OK
University of Utah, UT
University of Vermont, VT
The University of Virginia's
　College at Wise, VA
The University of West Alabama, AL
University of West Georgia, GA
University of Wisconsin–Eau Claire, WI
University of Wisconsin–La Crosse, WI
University of Wisconsin–Parkside, WI
University of Wisconsin–River Falls, WI
University of Wisconsin–Stevens Point, WI
University of Wisconsin–Superior, WI
University of Wisconsin–Whitewater, WI
University of Wyoming, WY
Utah State University, UT
Valley City State University, ND
Virginia Military Institute, VA
Walla Walla University, WA
Warner University, FL
Wartburg College, IA
Washburn University, KS
Washington State University, WA
Washington University in St. Louis, MO
Wayland Baptist University, TX
Wayne State College, NE
Wayne State University, MI

Webster University, MO
Wesleyan College, GA
Western Carolina University, NC
Western Illinois University, IL
Western Kentucky University, KY
Western Oregon University, OR
Western Washington University, WA
West Texas A&M University, TX
West Virginia University, WV
Wheaton College, IL
Wichita State University, KS
Widener University, PA
William Jessup University, CA
Wilson College, PA
Wright State University, OH
Wright State University–Lake Campus, OH
Xavier University of Louisiana, LA
Youngstown State University, OH

Foreign Languages
Abilene Christian University, TX
Adelphi University, NY
Albertus Magnus College, CT
Alfred University, NY
Alliant International University–
    San Diego, CA
Angelo State University, TX
Arkansas Tech University, AR
Armstrong State University, GA
Auburn University, AL
Augsburg College, MN
Augustana College, IL
Augustana University, SD
Austin College, TX
Austin Peay State University, TN
Averett University, VA
Ball State University, IN
Baylor University, TX
Belhaven University, MS
Bemidji State University, MN
Binghamton University, State University of
    New York, NY
Black Hills State University, SD
Bloomsburg University of Pennsylvania, PA
Boise State University, ID
Bowling Green State University, OH
Briar Cliff University, IA
Bryan College, TN
Butler University, IN
California Lutheran University, CA
California Polytechnic State University, San
    Luis Obispo, CA
California State Polytechnic University,
    Pomona, CA
California State University, Bakersfield, CA
California State University, Chico, CA
California State University, Fresno, CA
California State University, Fullerton, CA
California State University, Los Angeles, CA
California State University,
    San Bernardino, CA
Calvin College, MI
Cameron University, OK
Case Western Reserve University, OH
Centenary College of Louisiana, LA
Central College, IA
Central Methodist University, MO
Central Michigan University, MI
Centre College, KY
Charlotte Christian College and Theological
    Seminary, NC
Christopher Newport University, VA
City College of the City University of
    New York, NY
Clarion University of Pennsylvania, PA

Clemson University, SC
Coastal Carolina University, SC
The College at Brockport, State University
    of New York, NY
College of Charleston, SC
The College of Idaho, ID
The College of Saint Rose, NY
College of Staten Island of the City
    University of New York, NY
Colorado Mesa University, CO
Concordia University Chicago, IL
Concordia University Texas, TX
Cornerstone University, MI
Davidson College, NC
Delta State University, MS
Denison University, OH
DeSales University, PA
Dickinson State University, ND
Dordt College, IA
Drury University, MO
East Carolina University, NC
Eastern Connecticut State University, CT
Eastern Illinois University, IL
Eastern Mennonite University, VA
Eastern Michigan University, MI
Eastern Washington University, WA
East Stroudsburg University of
    Pennsylvania, PA
Edgewood College, WI
Elizabethtown College, PA
Elmhurst College, IL
Emporia State University, KS
Evangel University, MO
Fitchburg State University, MA
Flagler College, FL
Florida Agricultural and Mechanical
    University, FL
Florida International University, FL
Fordham University, NY
Fort Hays State University, KS
Francis Marion University, SC
Frostburg State University, MD
Furman University, SC
Gannon University, PA
Gardner-Webb University, NC
George Fox University, OR
Georgian Court University, NJ
Georgia Southern University, GA
Grambling State University, LA
Grand Valley State University, MI
Grove City College, PA
Hamline University, MN
Hardin-Simmons University, TX
High Point University, NC
Hillsdale College, MI
Hood College, MD
Howard University, DC
Idaho State University, ID
Indiana State University, IN
Indiana University of Pennsylvania, PA
Indiana Wesleyan University, IN
Iowa State University of Science and
    Technology, IA
John Carroll University, OH
Juniata College, PA
Kansas Wesleyan University, KS
Kean University, NJ
Kennesaw State University, GA
Kent State University, OH
Kent State University at Stark, OH
King's College, PA
Kutztown University of Pennsylvania, PA
Lake Erie College, OH
Lindenwood University, MO
Linfield College, OR

Lock Haven University of Pennsylvania, PA
Louisiana State University and Agricultural
    & Mechanical College, LA
Louisiana Tech University, LA
Loyola Marymount University, CA
Lubbock Christian University, TX
Lycoming College, PA
Manhattan College, NY
Marquette University, WI
Marywood University, PA
Mercer University, GA
Meredith College, NC
Methodist University, NC
Metropolitan State University of Denver, CO
Michigan State University, MI
Middle Tennessee State University, TN
Midwestern State University, TX
Millersville University of Pennsylvania, PA
Millikin University, IL
Minot State University, ND
Mississippi State University, MS
Missouri Western State University, MO
Monmouth College, IL
Monmouth University, NJ
Montana State University, MT
Montana State University Billings, MT
Montclair State University, NJ
Moravian College, PA
Newberry College, SC
New Mexico Highlands University, NM
New Mexico State University, NM
North Central College, IL
Northeastern Illinois University, IL
Northeastern State University, OK
Northern Illinois University, IL
Northern Kentucky University, KY
Northern Michigan University, MI
Northern State University, SD
Northwestern College, IA
Northwest Missouri State University, MO
Ohio Northern University, OH
The Ohio State University, OH
Ohio University, OH
Ohio University–Chillicothe, OH
Ohio University–Eastern, OH
Ohio University–Lancaster, OH
Ohio University–Southern Campus, OH
Ohio University–Zanesville, OH
Oklahoma Baptist University, OK
Oklahoma State University, OK
Old Dominion University, VA
Olivet College, MI
Ouachita Baptist University, AR
Pacific University, OR
Piedmont College, GA
Pittsburg State University, KS
Portland State University, OR
Rockford University, IL
Rockhurst University, MO
St. Ambrose University, IA
St. Edward's University, TX
St. John Fisher College, NY
St. John's University, NY
Saint Louis University, MO
St. Thomas Aquinas College, NY
Samford University, AL
Sam Houston State University, TX
San Diego State University, CA
Shippensburg University of
    Pennsylvania, PA
Siena College, NY
Slippery Rock University of
    Pennsylvania, PA
Sonoma State University, CA
Southeastern Louisiana University, LA

Southeast Missouri State University, MO
Southern Adventist University, TN
Southern Arkansas University–
Magnolia, AR
Southern Illinois University Carbondale, IL
Southern Oregon University, OR
Southwestern Oklahoma State
University, OK
State University of New York at
Fredonia, NY
State University of New York at
New Paltz, NY
State University of New York at
Oswego, NY
State University of New York College at
Geneseo, NY
State University of New York College at
Potsdam, NY
Stetson University, FL
Stony Brook University, State University of
New York, NY
Suffolk University, MA
Tennessee Technological University, TN
Texas A&M International University, TX
Texas A&M University–Commerce, TX
Texas Christian University, TX
Texas Lutheran University, TX
Texas State University, TX
Texas Tech University, TX
Texas Wesleyan University, TX
Texas Woman's University, TX
Towson University, MD
Truman State University, MO
Union University, TN
The University of Akron, OH
The University of Alabama, AL
The University of Alabama in
Huntsville, AL
University of Arkansas, AR
University of Arkansas at Little Rock, AR
University of California, Davis, CA
University of California, Irvine, CA
University of Central Oklahoma, OK
University of Colorado Boulder, CO
University of Dallas, TX
University of Dayton, OH
University of Delaware, DE
University of Evansville, IN
University of Hartford, CT
University of Houston, TX
University of Idaho, ID
University of Illinois at Urbana–
Champaign, IL
The University of Kansas, KS
University of Kentucky, KY
University of Louisiana at Monroe, LA
University of Louisville, KY
University of Maine at Fort Kent, ME
University of Mary Hardin-Baylor, TX
University of Maryland,
Baltimore County, MD
University of Maryland, College Park, MD
University of Mary Washington, VA
University of Massachusetts Dartmouth, MA
University of Michigan, MI
University of Michigan–Dearborn, MI
University of Michigan–Flint, MI
University of Minnesota, Twin Cities
Campus, MN
University of Mississippi, MS
University of Missouri, MO
University of Missouri–St. Louis, MO
University of Montana, MT
University of Montevallo, AL
University of Nebraska at Omaha, NE
University of Nebraska–Lincoln, NE

University of Nevada, Las Vegas, NV
University of Nevada, Reno, NV
University of New Hampshire, NH
University of North Carolina at
Asheville, NC
The University of North Carolina at
Charlotte, NC
The University of North Carolina at
Greensboro, NC
The University of North Carolina
Wilmington, NC
University of Northern Colorado, CO
University of Oklahoma, OK
University of Oregon, OR
University of Portland, OR
University of Puget Sound, WA
University of Rhode Island, RI
University of St. Thomas, TX
University of South Carolina, SC
The University of South Dakota, SD
University of South Florida, FL
The University of Tennessee at Martin, TN
The University of Texas at Arlington, TX
The University of Texas at San Antonio, TX
The University of Toledo, OH
The University of Tulsa, OK
University of Utah, UT
University of Vermont, VT
University of West Georgia, GA
University of Wisconsin–Eau Claire, WI
University of Wisconsin–La Crosse, WI
University of Wisconsin–Parkside, WI
University of Wisconsin–River Falls, WI
University of Wisconsin–Stevens Point, WI
University of Wisconsin–Whitewater, WI
University of Wyoming, WY
Utah State University, UT
Valparaiso University, IN
Virginia Commonwealth University, VA
Virginia Military Institute, VA
Walla Walla University, WA
Wartburg College, IA
Washburn University, KS
Washington State University, WA
Washington University in St. Louis, MO
Wayne State College, NE
Wayne State University, MI
Webster University, MO
Wesleyan College, GA
Western Illinois University, IL
Western Kentucky University, KY
Western Oregon University, OR
Western Washington University, WA
West Texas A&M University, TX
West Virginia University, WV
Wheaton College, IL
Wichita State University, KS
Widener University, PA
Wilson College, PA
Wisconsin Lutheran College, WI
Wright State University, OH
Wright State University–Lake Campus, OH
Xavier University, OH
Xavier University of Louisiana, LA
Youngstown State University, OH

Health Fields

Alaska Pacific University, AK
Alderson Broaddus University, WV
Allen College, IA
Arkansas Tech University, AR
Armstrong State University, GA
Auburn University, AL
Augsburg College, MN
Augustana University, SD
Austin Peay State University, TN

Averett University, VA
Ball State University, IN
Baylor University, TX
Belmont University, TN
Bemidji State University, MN
Black Hills State University, SD
Bloomfield College, NJ
Bloomsburg University of Pennsylvania, PA
Boise State University, ID
Bowling Green State University, OH
Briar Cliff University, IA
California Polytechnic State University, San
Luis Obispo, CA
California State University, Bakersfield, CA
California State University, Chico, CA
California State University, Fresno, CA
California State University, Fullerton, CA
California State University, Los Angeles, CA
California State University,
San Bernardino, CA
Calvin College, MI
Campbellsville University, KY
Carroll University, WI
Case Western Reserve University, OH
Central College, IA
Central Methodist University, MO
Central Michigan University, MI
Clarion University of Pennsylvania, PA
Clemson University, SC
College of Charleston, SC
The College of New Rochelle, NY
Colorado Mesa University, CO
Columbus State University, GA
Concordia University, Nebraska, NE
Davidson College, NC
Delta State University, MS
DeSales University, PA
Dickinson State University, ND
Drury University, MO
D'Youville College, NY
East Carolina University, NC
Eastern Illinois University, IL
Eastern Michigan University, MI
Eastern Washington University, WA
East Stroudsburg University of
Pennsylvania, PA
East Texas Baptist University, TX
ECPI University, VA
Elizabethtown College, PA
Elmhurst College, IL
Emmanuel College, GA
Emporia State University, KS
Endicott College, MA
Fairmont State University, WV
Felician University, NJ
Ferris State University, MI
Fitchburg State University, MA
Florida Agricultural and Mechanical
University, FL
Florida Gulf Coast University, FL
Florida International University, FL
Florida Southern College, FL
Fort Hays State University, KS
Frostburg State University, MD
Furman University, SC
Gardner-Webb University, NC
George Fox University, OR
Georgia Southern University, GA
Governors State University, IL
Grambling State University, LA
Grand Valley State University, MI
Hampton University, VA
Harding University, AR
Hardin-Simmons University, TX
Howard University, DC
Husson University, ME

Indiana State University, IN
Indiana University of Pennsylvania, PA
Indiana Wesleyan University, IN
Iowa State University of Science and
    Technology, IA
Iowa Wesleyan University, IA
Jacksonville State University, AL
James Madison University, VA
John Carroll University, OH
Kean University, NJ
Kennesaw State University, GA
Kent State University, OH
King's College, PA
Langston University, OK
Lewis-Clark State College, ID
Lindenwood University, MO
Lock Haven University of Pennsylvania, PA
Louisiana State University and Agricultural
    & Mechanical College, LA
Louisiana Tech University, LA
Loyola Marymount University, CA
Lycoming College, PA
Malone University, OH
Mansfield University of Pennsylvania, PA
Marymount University, VA
Maryville University of Saint Louis, MO
Marywood University, PA
Massachusetts College of Liberal Arts, MA
Mayville State University, ND
Michigan State University, MI
Middle Georgia State University, GA
Middle Tennessee State University, TN
Midwestern State University, TX
Minot State University, ND
Mississippi State University, MS
Monmouth University, NJ
Montana State University, MT
Montana State University Billings, MT
Montana Tech of The University of
    Montana, MT
Moravian College, PA
Morehead State University, KY
Murray State University, KY
New Mexico Highlands University, NM
New Mexico State University, NM
Northeastern State University, OK
Northern Illinois University, IL
Northern Kentucky University, KY
Northern Michigan University, MI
Northwestern State University
    of Louisiana, LA
Northwest Missouri State University, MO
Ohio Northern University, OH
The Ohio State University, OH
Ohio University, OH
Ohio University–Chillicothe, OH
Ohio University–Eastern, OH
Ohio University–Lancaster, OH
Ohio University–Southern Campus, OH
Ohio University–Zanesville, OH
Oklahoma Baptist University, OK
Oklahoma Panhandle State University, OK
Oklahoma Wesleyan University, OK
Old Dominion University, VA
Oral Roberts University, OK
Ouachita Baptist University, AR
Pacific University, OR
Peirce College, PA
Piedmont College, GA
Pittsburg State University, KS
Point Loma Nazarene University, CA
Point Park University, PA
Purdue University, IN
Randall University, OK
Research College of Nursing, MO

Robert Morris University Illinois, IL
Rockhurst University, MO
Sacred Heart University, CT
Saginaw Valley State University, MI
St. Ambrose University, IA
Saint Francis Medical Center College of
    Nursing, IL
St. John's University, NY
Samford University, AL
Sam Houston State University, TX
San Diego State University, CA
Shepherd University, WV
Siena College, NY
Sonoma State University, CA
Southeast Missouri State University, MO
Southern Adventist University, TN
Southern Arkansas University–
    Magnolia, AR
Southern Illinois University Carbondale, IL
Southern Oregon University, OR
Southwestern College, KS
State University of New York at
    Plattsburgh, NY
Stephen F. Austin State University, TX
Stockton University, NJ
Stony Brook University, State University of
    New York, NY
Tennessee Technological University, TN
Texas A&M International University, TX
Texas A&M University, TX
Texas A&M University–Commerce, TX
Texas Christian University, TX
Texas Lutheran University, TX
Texas State University, TX
Texas Wesleyan University, TX
Texas Woman's University, TX
Truman State University, MO
Union University, TN
The University of Akron, OH
The University of Alabama at
    Birmingham, AL
The University of Alabama in
    Huntsville, AL
University of Alaska Anchorage, AK
University of Arkansas, AR
University of Arkansas at Little Rock, AR
University of California, Davis, CA
University of California, Irvine, CA
University of Central Oklahoma, OK
University of Colorado Boulder, CO
University of Dayton, OH
University of Delaware, DE
University of Evansville, IN
University of Holy Cross, LA
University of Houston, TX
University of Idaho, ID
University of Illinois at Urbana–
    Champaign, IL
University of Indianapolis, IN
University of Kentucky, KY
University of Louisiana at Monroe, LA
University of Louisville, KY
University of Maine at Fort Kent, ME
University of Mary Hardin-Baylor, TX
University of Maryland, College Park, MD
University of Maryland Eastern Shore, MD
University of Massachusetts Amherst, MA
University of Massachusetts Lowell, MA
University of Memphis, TN
University of Michigan, MI
University of Minnesota, Twin Cities
    Campus, MN
University of Mississippi, MS
University of Missouri, MO
University of Montana, MT

University of Montevallo, AL
University of Nebraska–Lincoln, NE
University of Nevada, Las Vegas, NV
University of Nevada, Reno, NV
University of New Hampshire, NH
University of North Carolina at
    Asheville, NC
The University of North Carolina at
    Chapel Hill, NC
The University of North Carolina at
    Charlotte, NC
The University of North Carolina at
    Greensboro, NC
The University of North Carolina
    Wilmington, NC
University of Northern Colorado, CO
University of North Florida, FL
University of North Georgia, GA
University of Oregon, OR
University of Pittsburgh at Bradford, PA
University of Pittsburgh at Johnstown, PA
University of Portland, OR
University of Rhode Island, RI
University of St. Francis, IL
University of St. Thomas, TX
University of South Carolina, SC
University of South Carolina Aiken, SC
University of Southern Indiana, IN
University of South Florida, FL
The University of Tennessee at Martin, TN
The University of Texas at Arlington, TX
The University of Texas at El Paso, TX
The University of Texas Rio Grande
    Valley, TX
University of the District of Columbia, DC
The University of Toledo, OH
The University of Tulsa, OK
University of Utah, UT
University of Vermont, VT
The University of Virginia's College at
    Wise, VA
University of Washington, WA
University of Wisconsin–Eau Claire, WI
University of Wisconsin–Green Bay, WI
University of Wisconsin–La Crosse, WI
University of Wisconsin–River Falls, WI
University of Wisconsin–Stevens Point, WI
University of Wisconsin–Superior, WI
University of Wyoming, WY
Utah State University, UT
Valdosta State University, GA
Valparaiso University, IN
Virginia Commonwealth University, VA
Washburn University, KS
Washington State University, WA
Wayne State College, NE
Wayne State University, MI
Western Illinois University, IL
Western Kentucky University, KY
Western Washington University, WA
West Virginia University, WV
Widener University, PA
Xavier University of Louisiana, LA
Youngstown State University, OH

Home Economics
Arkansas Tech University, AR
Auburn University, AL
Augustana University, SD
Austin College, TX
Averett University, VA
Baylor University, TX
Binghamton University, State University of
    New York, NY
Bloomfield College, NJ

Boise State University, ID
Bowling Green State University, OH
Brenau University, GA
Butler University, IN
Caldwell University, NJ
California Baptist University, CA
California Polytechnic State University, San
    Luis Obispo, CA
California State University, Fullerton, CA
Cameron University, OK
Carson-Newman University, TN
Case Western Reserve University, OH
Cedar Crest College, PA
Central Michigan University, MI
Cleveland State University, OH
The College at Brockport, State University
    of New York, NY
College of Coastal Georgia, GA
College of Staten Island of the City
    University of New York, NY
Concordia University Texas, TX
Cox College, MO
Daemen College, NY
Dakota State University, SD
Dominican University, IL
East Carolina University, NC
Eastern Connecticut State University, CT
Eastern Illinois University, IL
Eastern Michigan University, MI
East Texas Baptist University, TX
ECPI University, VA
Evangel University, MO
Fort Hays State University, KS
Framingham State University, MA
Francis Marion University, SC
George Fox University, OR
Georgian Court University, NJ
Georgia Southern University, GA
Grambling State University, LA
Hampden-Sydney College, VA
Husson University, ME
Idaho State University, ID
Indiana University of Pennsylvania, PA
Iowa State University of Science and
    Technology, IA
Jacksonville State University, AL
Juniata College, PA
Kansas Wesleyan University, KS
Kean University, NJ
Kent State University at Geauga, OH
Kent State University at Stark, OH
Lewis-Clark State College, ID
Lipscomb University, TN
Long Island University–LIU Brooklyn, NY
Long Island University–LIU Post, NY
Loras College, IA
Louisiana Tech University, LA
Maria College, NY
Marquette University, WI
Maryville University of Saint Louis, MO
Marywood University, PA
Medical University of South Carolina, SC
Mercy College of Ohio, OH
Metropolitan State University of Denver, CO
Michigan State University, MI
Middle Tennessee State University, TN
Millersville University of Pennsylvania, PA
Millikin University, IL
Milwaukee School of Engineering, WI
Minnesota State University Moorhead, MN
Minot State University, ND
Mississippi State University, MS
Missouri Western State University, MO
Monmouth University, NJ
Montana State University, MT
Montclair State University, NJ

Moravian College, PA
Murray State University, KY
Nebraska Methodist College, NE
New Mexico State University, NM
Northeastern State University, OK
Northern Kentucky University, KY
Northern Michigan University, MI
Northwest Missouri State University, MO
Northwest Nazarene University, ID
The Ohio State University, OH
Ohio University, OH
Ohio University–Chillicothe, OH
Ohio University–Eastern, OH
Ohio University–Lancaster, OH
Ohio University–Southern Campus, OH
Ohio University–Zanesville, OH
Oklahoma City University, OK
Oklahoma Panhandle State University, OK
Oklahoma State University, OK
Oregon Health & Science University, OR
Ouachita Baptist University, AR
Pittsburg State University, KS
Point Loma Nazarene University, CA
Queens University of Charlotte, NC
Rochester Institute of Technology, NY
The Sage Colleges, NY
St. Edward's University, TX
Saint Louis University, MO
Saint Vincent College, PA
Salisbury University, MD
Samford University, AL
Sam Houston State University, TX
San Diego State University, CA
Shepherd University, WV
Slippery Rock University of
    Pennsylvania, PA
Southeast Missouri State University, MO
Southern Adventist University, TN
Southern Illinois University Carbondale, IL
Southern Illinois University
    Edwardsville, IL
State University of New York at
    Plattsburgh, NY
Stephen F. Austin State University, TX
Stockton University, NJ
Tennessee Technological University, TN
Texas State University, TX
Texas Tech University, TX
Texas Woman's University, TX
Towson University, MD
Truett McConnell University, GA
The University of Akron, OH
The University of Alabama, AL
University of Arkansas, AR
University of California, Davis, CA
University of Central Oklahoma, OK
University of Colorado Denver, CO
University of Florida, FL
University of Hartford, CT
University of Holy Cross, LA
University of Idaho, ID
University of Illinois at Urbana–
    Champaign, IL
The University of Kansas, KS
University of Kentucky, KY
University of Louisiana at Monroe, LA
University of Maine, ME
University of Maryland Eastern Shore, MD
University of Massachusetts Dartmouth, MA
University of Memphis, TN
University of Minnesota, Twin Cities
    Campus, MN
University of Mississippi, MS
University of Missouri, MO
University of Missouri–St. Louis, MO
University of Nebraska at Omaha, NE

University of Nebraska–Lincoln, NE
University of North Carolina at
    Asheville, NC
The University of North Carolina at
    Charlotte, NC
The University of North Carolina at
    Greensboro, NC
University of Northern Colorado, CO
University of Rhode Island, RI
University of South Florida, FL
The University of Tennessee, TN
The University of Tennessee at
    Chattanooga, TN
The University of Tennessee at Martin, TN
The University of Texas Health Science
    Center at Houston, TX
The University of Texas of the Permian
    Basin, TX
University of Vermont, VT
University of West Georgia, GA
University of Wisconsin–Stevens Point, WI
University of Wisconsin–Stout, WI
University of Wyoming, WY
Utah State University, UT
Warner University, FL
Washington State University, WA
Washington University in St. Louis, MO
Wayne State College, NE
Wesleyan College, GA
Western Illinois University, IL
Western Kentucky University, KY
Western New England University, MA
Western Oregon University, OR
West Texas A&M University, TX
West Virginia University, WV
Wheaton College, IL
Wisconsin Lutheran College, WI
Wright State University, OH
Wright State University–Lake Campus, OH

Humanities
Alaska Pacific University, AK
Albertus Magnus College, CT
Alfred University, NY
Alliant International University–
    San Diego, CA
Angelo State University, TX
Arkansas Tech University, AR
Armstrong State University, GA
Auburn University, AL
Augustana College, IL
Augustana University, SD
Austin College, TX
Austin Peay State University, TN
Averett University, VA
Ball State University, IN
Barton College, NC
Baylor University, TX
Belhaven University, MS
Belmont Abbey College, NC
Bemidji State University, MN
Berry College, GA
Binghamton University, State University of
    New York, NY
Black Hills State University, SD
Bloomfield College, NJ
Bloomsburg University of Pennsylvania, PA
Blue Mountain College, MS
Boise State University, ID
Bowling Green State University, OH
Brenau University, GA
Briar Cliff University, IA
Bryan College, TN
Buena Vista University, IA
Butler University, IN
California Lutheran University, CA

California Polytechnic State University, San Luis Obispo, CA
California State Polytechnic University, Pomona, CA
California State University, Bakersfield, CA
California State University, Chico, CA
California State University, Fresno, CA
California State University, Fullerton, CA
Calvin College, MI
Campbellsville University, KY
Carlow University, PA
Carroll University, WI
Case Western Reserve University, OH
Centenary College of Louisiana, LA
Central College, IA
Central Methodist University, MO
Central Michigan University, MI
Christopher Newport University, VA
The Citadel, The Military College of South Carolina, SC
City College of the City University of New York, NY
Clarion University of Pennsylvania, PA
Clarkson University, NY
Clemson University, SC
Cleveland State University, OH
Coastal Carolina University, SC
The College at Brockport, State University of New York, NY
College of Charleston, SC
The College of Idaho, ID
The College of New Rochelle, NY
The College of Saint Rose, NY
College of Staten Island of the City University of New York, NY
College of the Holy Cross, MA
Colorado Mesa University, CO
Columbia College, MO
Columbus State University, GA
Concordia University, Nebraska, NE
Cornerstone University, MI
Dallas Baptist University, TX
Defiance College, OH
Delta State University, MS
DeSales University, PA
Dickinson State University, ND
Dominican University of California, CA
Dordt College, IA
Drury University, MO
D'Youville College, NY
East Carolina University, NC
Eastern Illinois University, IL
Eastern Mennonite University, VA
Eastern Michigan University, MI
Eastern Washington University, WA
East Texas Baptist University, TX
Elizabethtown College, PA
Elmhurst College, IL
Emory University, GA
Emporia State University, KS
Evangel University, MO
Fairmont State University, WV
Flagler College, FL
Florida Agricultural and Mechanical University, FL
Florida Gulf Coast University, FL
Florida International University, FL
Fort Hays State University, KS
Fort Lewis College, CO
Francis Marion University, SC
Fresno Pacific University, CA
Frostburg State University, MD
Furman University, SC
Gannon University, PA
Gardner-Webb University, NC

George Fox University, OR
Georgia College & State University, GA
Georgian Court University, NJ
Georgia Southern University, GA
Grambling State University, LA
Grand Valley State University, MI
Hamline University, MN
Hampshire College, MA
Hardin Simmons University, TX
High Point University, NC
Hood College, MD
Howard University, DC
Husson University, ME
Idaho State University, ID
Illinois Institute of Technology, IL
Indiana State University, IN
Indiana University of Pennsylvania, PA
Iowa State University of Science and Technology, IA
Jacksonville State University, AL
James Madison University, VA
Juniata College, PA
Kansas Wesleyan University, KS
Kean University, NJ
Kennesaw State University, GA
Kent State University, OH
Kent State University at Geauga, OH
Kenyon College, OH
King's College, PA
Kutztown University of Pennsylvania, PA
Lake Erie College, OH
Lawrence Technological University, MI
Lees-McRae College, NC
Lewis-Clark State College, ID
Lindenwood University, MO
Linfield College, OR
Longwood University, VA
Louisiana State University and Agricultural & Mechanical College, LA
Louisiana State University in Shreveport, LA
Loyola Marymount University, CA
Lubbock Christian University, TX
Lycoming College, PA
Massachusetts College of Liberal Arts, MA
Messiah College, PA
Metropolitan State University of Denver, CO
Middle Tennessee State University, TN
Midwestern State University, TX
Millersville University of Pennsylvania, PA
Millikin University, IL
Minot State University, ND
Mississippi State University, MS
Missouri University of Science and Technology, MO
Missouri Western State University, MO
Molloy College, NY
Monmouth University, NJ
Montana State University, MT
Montana State University Billings, MT
Montclair State University, NJ
Moravian College, PA
Mount Mary University, WI
Murray State University, KY
Newberry College, SC
New England College, NH
New Jersey Institute of Technology, NJ
New Mexico Highlands University, NM
New Mexico State University, NM
North Carolina State University, NC
North Central College, IL
Northeast Catholic College, NH
Northeastern State University, OK
Northern Illinois University, IL
Northern Michigan University, MI

Northern State University, SD
Northwestern College, IA
Northwestern State University of Louisiana, LA
Northwest Missouri State University, MO
Oakland University, MI
Ohio Northern University, OH
The Ohio State University, OH
Ohio University, OH
Ohio University–Chillicothe, OH
Ohio University–Eastern, OH
Ohio University–Lancaster, OH
Ohio University–Southern Campus, OH
Ohio University–Zanesville, OH
Oklahoma Baptist University, OK
Oklahoma State University, OK
Old Dominion University, VA
Ouachita Baptist University, AR
Pacific University, OR
Piedmont College, GA
Point Loma Nazarene University, CA
Point Park University, PA
Portland State University, OR
Purchase College, State University of New York, NY
Purdue University, IN
Queens University of Charlotte, NC
Rensselaer Polytechnic Institute, NY
Rochester Institute of Technology, NY
Rockhurst University, MO
Sacred Heart University, CT
St. Edward's University, TX
St. John Fisher College, NY
St. John's University, NY
Saint Louis University, MO
St. Thomas Aquinas College, NY
Salem International University, WV
Salisbury University, MD
Samford University, AL
Sam Houston State University, TX
San Diego State University, CA
Savannah State University, GA
Shepherd University, WV
Shippensburg University of Pennsylvania, PA
Siena College, NY
Sonoma State University, CA
Southeastern Louisiana University, LA
Southeast Missouri State University, MO
Southern Adventist University, TN
Southern Illinois University Carbondale, IL
Southwestern University, TX
State University of New York at Fredonia, NY
State University of New York at Oswego, NY
State University of New York at Plattsburgh, NY
State University of New York College at Geneseo, NY
State University of New York College at Potsdam, NY
Stetson University, FL
Stevens Institute of Technology, NJ
Stockton University, NJ
Tennessee Technological University, TN
Texas A&M University–Commerce, TX
Texas Christian University, TX
Texas State University, TX
Texas Tech University, TX
Texas Wesleyan University, TX
Texas Woman's University, TX
Thomas University, GA
Trinity Christian College, IL
Truman State University, MO

Union University, TN
The University of Akron, OH
The University of Alabama in
    Huntsville, AL
University of Alaska Anchorage, AK
The University of Arizona, AZ
University of Arkansas, AR
University of Arkansas at Little Rock, AR
University of California, Davis, CA
University of California, Irvine, CA
University of California, Riverside, CA
University of California, Santa Cruz, CA
University of Central Oklahoma, OK
University of Colorado Boulder, CO
University of Colorado Denver, CO
University of Dayton, OH
University of Delaware, DE
University of Denver, CO
University of Evansville, IN
University of Great Falls, MT
University of Hartford, CT
University of Holy Cross, LA
University of Houston, TX
University of Houston–Clear Lake, TX
University of Houston–Victoria, TX
University of Idaho, ID
University of Illinois at Urbana–
    Champaign, IL
The University of Kansas, KS
University of Maine at Fort Kent, ME
University of Mary Hardin-Baylor, TX
University of Maryland,
    Baltimore County, MD
University of Maryland, College Park, MD
University of Maryland Eastern Shore, MD
University of Mary Washington, VA
University of Massachusetts Amherst, MA
University of Massachusetts Dartmouth, MA
University of Massachusetts Lowell, MA
University of Memphis, TN
University of Michigan, MI
University of Michigan–Flint, MI
University of Minnesota, Twin Cities
    Campus, MN
University of Mississippi, MS
University of Missouri, MO
University of Missouri–St. Louis, MO
University of Montana, MT
The University of Montana Western, MT
University of Montevallo, AL
University of Nebraska–Lincoln, NE
University of Nevada, Las Vegas, NV
University of New Hampshire, NH
University of New Hampshire at
    Manchester, NH
University of North Carolina at
    Asheville, NC
The University of North Carolina at
    Greensboro, NC
The University of North Carolina
    Wilmington, NC
University of Northern Colorado, CO
University of North Georgia, GA
University of Oklahoma, OK
University of Oregon, OR
University of Pittsburgh at Bradford, PA
University of Pittsburgh at Johnstown, PA
University of Portland, OR
University of Puget Sound, WA
University of Rhode Island, RI
University of St. Thomas, MN
University of St. Thomas, TX
University of Sioux Falls, SD
University of South Carolina, SC
University of South Carolina Aiken, SC
The University of South Dakota, SD

University of Southern Indiana, IN
University of South Florida, FL
The University of Tennessee, TN
The University of Tennessee at Martin, TN
The University of Texas at Arlington, TX
The University of Texas at El Paso, TX
The University of Texas at San Antonio, TX
The University of Texas of the Permian
    Basin, TX
The University of Toledo, OH
University of Utah, UT
University of Vermont, VT
The University of Virginia's College at
    Wise, VA
University of West Georgia, GA
University of Wisconsin–Eau Claire, WI
University of Wisconsin–Green Bay, WI
University of Wisconsin–La Crosse, WI
University of Wisconsin–River Falls, WI
University of Wisconsin–Stevens Point, WI
University of Wisconsin–Superior, WI
University of Wisconsin–Whitewater, WI
University of Wyoming, WY
Utah State University, UT
Valley City State University, ND
Virginia Commonwealth University, VA
Virginia Military Institute, VA
Walla Walla University, WA
Warner University, FL
Wartburg College, IA
Washburn University, KS
Washington & Jefferson College, PA
Washington State University, WA
Washington University in St. Louis, MO
Wayne State College, NE
Wayne State University, MI
Webster University, MO
Wesleyan College, GA
Western Oregon University, OR
Western Washington University, WA
West Texas A&M University, TX
West Virginia University, WV
Wheaton College, IL
Wichita State University, KS
Widener University, PA
William Jessup University, CA
Williams Baptist College, AR
Wilson College, PA
Wright State University, OH
Wright State University–Lake Campus, OH
Xavier University of Louisiana, LA
Youngstown State University, OH

International Studies
Albertus Magnus College, CT
Alfred University, NY
Alliant International University–
    San Diego, CA
Angelo State University, TX
Armstrong State University, GA
Augsburg College, MN
Augustana University, SD
Austin College, TX
Austin Peay State University, TN
Ball State University, IN
Baylor University, TX
Belhaven University, MS
Bemidji State University, MN
Binghamton University, State University of
    New York, NY
Bloomsburg University of Pennsylvania, PA
Boise State University, ID
Bowling Green State University, OH
Buena Vista University, IA
Butler University, IN
California Lutheran University, CA

California Polytechnic State University, San
    Luis Obispo, CA
California State Polytechnic University,
    Pomona, CA
California State University, Chico, CA
California State University, Fullerton, CA
California State University,
    San Bernardino, CA
Calvin College, MI
Carroll University, WI
Case Western Reserve University, OH
Central College, IA
Central Michigan University, MI
City College of the City University
    of New York, NY
Clarion University of Pennsylvania, PA
Clemson University, SC
Coastal Carolina University, SC
The College at Brockport, State University
    of New York, NY
College of Staten Island of the City
    University of New York, NY
Columbus State University, GA
Concordia University Texas, TX
Davidson College, NC
Defiance College, OH
Drury University, MO
D'Youville College, NY
East Carolina University, NC
Eastern Connecticut State University, CT
Eastern Illinois University, IL
Eastern Washington University, WA
Elizabethtown College, PA
Elmhurst College, IL
Evangel University, MO
Fairmont State University, WV
Fort Hays State University, KS
Frostburg State University, MD
Furman University, SC
Gannon University, PA
George Fox University, OR
Georgia College & State University, GA
Georgian Court University, NJ
Georgia Southern University, GA
Glenville State College, WV
Grand Valley State University, MI
Grand View University, IA
Grove City College, PA
Hampden-Sydney College, VA
Hampshire College, MA
High Point University, NC
Houghton College, NY
Howard University, DC
Idaho State University, ID
Indiana University of Pennsylvania, PA
Indiana Wesleyan University, IN
Iowa State University of Science and
    Technology, IA
James Madison University, VA
Juniata College, PA
Kean University, NJ
Kennesaw State University, GA
Kent State University, OH
Kutztown University of Pennsylvania, PA
Lake Erie College, OH
Lawrence Technological University, MI
Lehigh University, PA
Lindenwood University, MO
Linfield College, OR
Lock Haven University of Pennsylvania, PA
Long Island University–LIU Brooklyn, NY
Long Island University–LIU Post, NY
Longwood University, VA
Louisiana Tech University, LA
Loyola Marymount University, CA
Lycoming College, PA

Lynn University, FL
Maryville University of Saint Louis, MO
Mercer University, GA
Methodist University, NC
Michigan State University, MI
Middle Tennessee State University, TN
Midwestern State University, TX
Millikin University, IL
Minnesota State University Moorhead, MN
Mississippi State University, MS
Missouri University of Science and
      Technology, MO
Molloy College, NY
Montclair State University, NJ
Moravian College, PA
Morehead State University, KY
Murray State University, KY
New England College, NH
New Jersey Institute of Technology, NJ
North Central College, IL
Northern Illinois University, IL
Northern Kentucky University, KY
Northern Michigan University, MI
Northern State University, SD
Ohio Northern University, OH
The Ohio State University, OH
Ohio University, OH
Ohio University–Chillicothe, OH
Ohio University–Eastern, OH
Ohio University–Lancaster, OH
Ohio University–Southern Campus, OH
Ohio University–Zanesville, OH
Oklahoma State University, OK
Old Dominion University, VA
Ouachita Baptist University, AR
Point Park University, PA
Portland State University, OR
Rochester Institute of Technology, NY
Rockhurst University, MO
St. Ambrose University, IA
St. Edward's University, TX
Saint Louis University, MO
Saint Martin's University, WA
Salisbury University, MD
Samford University, AL
San Diego State University, CA
Siena College, NY
Southeast Missouri State University, MO
Southern Illinois University Carbondale, IL
Southwestern University, TX
State University of New York at
      Fredonia, NY
State University of New York at
      New Paltz, NY
State University of New York at
      Oswego, NY
State University of New York at
      Plattsburgh, NY
State University of New York College at
      Cortland, NY
State University of New York College at
      Geneseo, NY
Stony Brook University, State University of
      New York, NY
Tennessee Technological University, TN
Texas A&M International University, TX
Texas A&M University–Commerce, TX
Texas Christian University, TX
Texas Lutheran University, TX
Texas State University, TX
Texas Tech University, TX
Texas Wesleyan University, TX
Trinity Christian College, IL
Union University, TN
The University of Akron, OH

University of Arkansas, AR
University of Arkansas at Little Rock, AR
University of California, Davis, CA
University of California, Irvine, CA
University of Colorado Boulder, CO
University of Colorado Denver, CO
University of Dayton, OH
University of Delaware, DE
University of Denver, CO
University of Evansville, IN
University of Hartford, CT
University of Houston, TX
University of Idaho, ID
University of Illinois at Urbana–
      Champaign, IL
The University of Kansas, KS
University of Kentucky, KY
University of Maine, ME
University of Mary Hardin-Baylor, TX
University of Maryland, College Park, MD
University of Mary Washington, VA
University of Memphis, TN
University of Michigan, MI
University of Michigan–Dearborn, MI
University of Michigan–Flint, MI
University of Minnesota, Twin Cities
      Campus, MN
University of Mississippi, MS
University of Missouri, MO
University of Missouri–St. Louis, MO
University of Montana, MT
University of Nebraska–Lincoln, NE
University of Nevada, Las Vegas, NV
University of North Carolina at
      Asheville, NC
The University of North Carolina at
      Charlotte, NC
The University of North Carolina at
      Greensboro, NC
The University of North Carolina
      Wilmington, NC
University of Northern Colorado, CO
University of North Florida, FL
University of Oklahoma, OK
University of Oregon, OR
University of Puget Sound, WA
University of Rhode Island, RI
University of St. Francis, IL
University of St. Thomas, MN
University of St. Thomas, TX
University of South Carolina, SC
University of South Florida, FL
The University of Tampa, FL
The University of Tennessee, TN
The University of Tennessee at Martin, TN
The University of Texas at Arlington, TX
The University of Texas at El Paso, TX
The University of Texas at San Antonio, TX
The University of Toledo, OH
The University of Tulsa, OK
University of Utah, UT
University of Vermont, VT
University of Wisconsin–Eau Claire, WI
University of Wisconsin–La Crosse, WI
University of Wisconsin–River Falls, WI
University of Wisconsin–Stevens Point, WI
University of Wisconsin–Stout, WI
University of Wyoming, WY
Utah State University, UT
Villanova University, PA
Virginia Military Institute, VA
Washburn University, KS
Washington State University, WA
Washington University in St. Louis, MO
Wayne State College, NE

Wayne State University, MI
Webster University, MO
Wesleyan College, GA
Western Illinois University, IL
Western Oregon University, OR
West Virginia University, WV
Wheaton College, IL
Wichita State University, KS
Widener University, PA
William Jessup University, CA
Wilson College, PA
Wright State University, OH
Wright State University–Lake Campus, OH

Library Science
Alverno College, WI
Bluefield College, VA
California Polytechnic State University, San
      Luis Obispo, CA
Clarion University of Pennsylvania, PA
East Carolina University, NC
Iowa State University of Science and
      Technology, IA
Kent State University, OH
Kutztown University of Pennsylvania, PA
Lindenwood University, MO
Lock Haven University of Pennsylvania, PA
Mayville State University, ND
Mississippi State University, MS
Moravian College, PA
Northeastern State University, OK
Northern Illinois University, IL
Old Dominion University, VA
Sam Houston State University, TX
Southern Arkansas University–
      Magnolia, AR
Texas Woman's University, TX
The University of Alabama, AL
University of Houston, TX
University of Idaho, ID
University of Illinois at Urbana–
      Champaign, IL
University of Louisiana at Monroe, LA
University of Maryland, College Park, MD
University of Mary Washington, VA
University of Michigan, MI
University of Minnesota, Twin Cities
      Campus, MN
University of Missouri, MO
The University of North Carolina at
      Greensboro, NC
University of Rhode Island, RI
University of South Carolina, SC
University of South Florida, FL
The University of Tennessee, TN
The University of Toledo, OH
University of Wisconsin–Eau Claire, WI
Utah State University, UT
Valdosta State University, GA
Valley City State University, ND
Virginia Polytechnic Institute and State
      University, VA
Wayne State University, MI
Western Illinois University, IL
Western Oregon University, OR
Western Washington University, WA
West Virginia University, WV

Mathematics
Abilene Christian University, TX
Adelphi University, NY
Alaska Pacific University, AK
Albertus Magnus College, CT
Alderson Broaddus University, WV
Alfred University, NY
Angelo State University, TX

Arkansas Tech University, AR
Armstrong State University, GA
Auburn University, AL
Augsburg College, MN
Augustana College, IL
Augustana University, SD
Augusta University, GA
Austin Peay State University, TN
Averett University, VA
Ball State University, IN
Barton College, NC
Baylor University, TX
Belhaven University, MS
Bemidji State University, MN
Bethel College, KS
Binghamton University, State University of
 New York, NY
Black Hills State University, SD
Bloomfield College, NJ
Bloomsburg University of Pennsylvania, PA
Blue Mountain College, MS
Bluffton University, OH
Boise State University, ID
Bowling Green State University, OH
Briar Cliff University, IA
Bryan College, TN
Bucknell University, PA
Buena Vista University, IA
Butler University, IN
California Lutheran University, CA
California Polytechnic State University, San
 Luis Obispo, CA
California State Polytechnic University,
 Pomona, CA
California State University, Bakersfield, CA
California State University, Chico, CA
California State University, Fresno, CA
California State University, Fullerton, CA
California State University, Los Angeles, CA
California State University, Northridge, CA
California State University,
 San Bernardino, CA
California State University, San Marcos, CA
Calvin College, MI
Cameron University, OK
Campbellsville University, KY
Carlow University, PA
Carroll University, WI
Carson-Newman University, TN
Case Western Reserve University, OH
Cedar Crest College, PA
Centenary College of Louisiana, LA
Central College, IA
Central Methodist University, MO
Central Michigan University, MI
Christian Brothers University, TN
Christopher Newport University, VA
City College of the City University of New
 York, NY
Clarion University of Pennsylvania, PA
Clarkson University, NY
Clemson University, SC
Cleveland State University, OH
Coastal Carolina University, SC
The College at Brockport, State University
 of New York, NY
College of Charleston, SC
College of Coastal Georgia, GA
The College of Idaho, ID
The College of New Rochelle, NY
College of Saint Benedict, MN
College of Saint Mary, NE
The College of Saint Rose, NY
College of Staten Island of the City
 University of New York, NY
The Colorado College, CO

Colorado Mesa University, CO
Colorado School of Mines, CO
Columbia College, MO
Columbus State University, GA
Concordia University Chicago, IL
Concordia University, Nebraska, NE
Concordia University Texas, TX
Concord University, WV
Cornerstone University, MI
Dakota State University, SD
Dakota Wesleyan University, SD
Dallas Baptist University, TX
Davidson College, NC
Defiance College, OH
Delta State University, MS
Denison University, OH
DeSales University, PA
Dickinson State University, ND
DigiPen Institute of Technology, WA
Dordt College, IA
Drury University, MO
Duke University, NC
D'Youville College, NY
East Carolina University, NC
Eastern Connecticut State University, CT
Eastern Illinois University, IL
Eastern Mennonite University, VA
Eastern Michigan University, MI
Eastern Washington University, WA
East Stroudsburg University of
 Pennsylvania, PA
East Texas Baptist University, TX
Elizabeth City State University, NC
Elizabethtown College, PA
Elmhurst College, IL
Elon University, NC
Emporia State University, KS
Evangel University, MO
Fairmont State University, WV
Ferris State University, MI
Fitchburg State University, MA
Florida Agricultural and Mechanical
 University, FL
Florida Gulf Coast University, FL
Florida International University, FL
Fort Hays State University, KS
Fort Lewis College, CO
Framingham State University, MA
Francis Marion University, SC
Frostburg State University, MD
Furman University, SC
Gannon University, PA
Gardner-Webb University, NC
George Fox University, OR
Georgian Court University, NJ
Georgia Southern University, GA
Glenville State College, WV
Governors State University, IL
Grambling State University, LA
Grand Valley State University, MI
Grand View University, IA
Greenville College, IL
Grove City College, PA
Hamline University, MN
Hampshire College, MA
Hardin-Simmons University, TX
High Point University, NC
Hillsdale College, MI
Hood College, MD
Houghton College, NY
Howard Payne University, TX
Howard University, DC
Huntingdon College, AL
Idaho State University, ID
Illinois Institute of Technology, IL
Indiana State University, IN

Indiana University of Pennsylvania, PA
Indiana Wesleyan University, IN
Iowa State University of Science and
 Technology, IA
Jacksonville State University, AL
James Madison University, VA
John Carroll University, OH
Johnson C. Smith University, NC
Juniata College, PA
Kansas Wesleyan University, KS
Kean University, NJ
Kennesaw State University, GA
Kent State University, OH
Kenyon College, OH
King's College, PA
Knox College, IL
Kutztown University of Pennsylvania, PA
Lake Erie College, OH
Lawrence Technological University, MI
Lebanon Valley College, PA
Lees-McRae College, NC
Lewis-Clark State College, ID
Liberty University, VA
Lindenwood University, MO
Lindsey Wilson College, KY
Linfield College, OR
Lipscomb University, TN
Lock Haven University of Pennsylvania, PA
Longwood University, VA
Loras College, IA
Louisiana State University and Agricultural
 & Mechanical College, LA
Louisiana Tech University, LA
Loyola Marymount University, CA
Lycoming College, PA
Malone University, OH
Manhattan College, NY
Mansfield University of Pennsylvania, PA
Marquette University, WI
Marymount University, VA
Maryville University of Saint Louis, MO
Marywood University, PA
Massachusetts College of Liberal Arts, MA
The Master's University, CA
Mayville State University, ND
Meredith College, NC
Metropolitan State University of Denver, CO
Michigan State University, MI
Middle Tennessee State University, TN
Midwestern State University, TX
Millersville University of Pennsylvania, PA
Millikin University, IL
Mills College, CA
Milwaukee School of Engineering, WI
Minnesota State University Moorhead, MN
Minot State University, ND
Mississippi State University, MS
Missouri University of Science and
 Technology, MO
Missouri Western State University, MO
Molloy College, NY
Monmouth University, NJ
Montana State University, MT
Montana State University Billings, MT
Montana Tech of The University of
 Montana, MT
Montclair State University, NJ
Moravian College, PA
Morehouse College, GA
Mount Mary University, WI
Murray State University, KY
Muskingum University, OH
Newberry College, SC
New Jersey Institute of Technology, NJ
New Mexico Highlands University, NM
New Mexico State University, NM

North Carolina State University, NC
North Central College, IL
Northeastern Illinois University, IL
Northeastern State University, OK
Northern Illinois University, IL
Northern Kentucky University, KY
Northern Michigan University, MI
Northern State University, SD
Northwestern College, IA
Northwestern State University of
    Louisiana, LA
Northwest Missouri State University, MO
Northwest Nazarene University, ID
Ohio Northern University, OH
The Ohio State University, OH
Ohio University, OH
Ohio University–Chillicothe, OH
Ohio University–Eastern, OH
Ohio University–Lancaster, OH
Ohio University–Southern Campus, OH
Ohio University–Zanesville, OH
Ohio Valley University, WV
Oklahoma Baptist University, OK
Oklahoma Panhandle State University, OK
Oklahoma State University, OK
Old Dominion University, VA
Ouachita Baptist University, AR
Pacific University, OR
Piedmont College, GA
Pittsburg State University, KS
Plymouth State University, NH
Point Loma Nazarene University, CA
Point Park University, PA
Purchase College, State University of
    New York, NY
Purdue University, IN
Randolph College, VA
Regis University, CO
Rensselaer Polytechnic Institute, NY
Rochester Institute of Technology, NY
Rockford University, IL
Rockhurst University, MO
Rollins College, FL
Sacred Heart University, CT
Saginaw Valley State University, MI
St. Edward's University, TX
St. John Fisher College, NY
St. John's University, NY
Saint Joseph's University, PA
Saint Louis University, MO
Saint Michael's College, VT
St. Thomas Aquinas College, NY
Saint Vincent College, PA
Samford University, AL
Sam Houston State University, TX
San Diego State University, CA
Savannah State University, GA
Schreiner University, TX
Shepherd University, WV
Shippensburg University of
    Pennsylvania, PA
Siena College, NY
Skidmore College, NY
Slippery Rock University of
    Pennsylvania, PA
Sonoma State University, CA
South Dakota School of Mines and
    Technology, SD
Southeastern Louisiana University, LA
Southeastern Oklahoma State
    University, OK
Southeast Missouri State University, MO
Southern Adventist University, TN
Southern Arkansas University–
    Magnolia, AR

Southern Illinois University Carbondale, IL
Southern Oregon University, OR
Southwestern Oklahoma State
    University, OK
Southwestern University, TX
State University of New York at
    Fredonia, NY
State University of New York at
    New Paltz, NY
State University of New York at
    Oswego, NY
State University of New York at
    Plattsburgh, NY
State University of New York College at
    Cortland, NY
State University of New York College at
    Geneseo, NY
State University of New York College at
    Potsdam, NY
Stephen F. Austin State University, TX
Stetson University, FL
Stevens Institute of Technology, NJ
Stockton University, NJ
Stony Brook University, State University of
    New York, NY
Suffolk University, MA
Tennessee Technological University, TN
Texas A&M International University, TX
Texas A&M University, TX
Texas A&M University–Commerce, TX
Texas A&M University–Texarkana, TX
Texas Christian University, TX
Texas Lutheran University, TX
Texas State University, TX
Texas Tech University, TX
Texas Wesleyan University, TX
Texas Woman's University, TX
Thiel College, PA
Thomas More College, KY
Thomas University, GA
Towson University, MD
Trinity Christian College, IL
Truman State University, MO
Union University, TN
The University of Akron, OH
The University of Alabama, AL
The University of Alabama at
    Birmingham, AL
The University of Alabama in
    Huntsville, AL
University of Alaska Anchorage, AK
University of Alaska Fairbanks, AK
University of Arkansas, AR
University of Arkansas at Little Rock, AR
University of Bridgeport, CT
University of California, Davis, CA
University of California, Irvine, CA
University of California, Riverside, CA
University of California, San Diego, CA
University of California, Santa Cruz, CA
University of Central Oklahoma, OK
University of Colorado Boulder, CO
University of Colorado Denver, CO
University of Dallas, TX
University of Dayton, OH
University of Delaware, DE
University of Denver, CO
University of Evansville, IN
University of Great Falls, MT
University of Hartford, CT
University of Houston, TX
University of Houston–Clear Lake, TX
University of Houston–Victoria, TX
University of Idaho, ID

University of Illinois at Urbana–
    Champaign, IL
The University of Kansas, KS
University of Kentucky, KY
University of Louisiana at Monroe, LA
University of Louisville, KY
University of Maine, ME
University of Maine at Augusta, ME
University of Maine at Fort Kent, ME
University of Mary Hardin-Baylor, TX
University of Maryland, Baltimore
    County, MD
University of Maryland, College Park, MD
University of Maryland Eastern Shore, MD
University of Mary Washington, VA
University of Massachusetts Amherst, MA
University of Massachusetts Dartmouth, MA
University of Massachusetts Lowell, MA
University of Memphis, TN
University of Michigan, MI
University of Michigan–Dearborn, MI
University of Michigan–Flint, MI
University of Minnesota, Twin Cities
    Campus, MN
University of Mississippi, MS
University of Missouri, MO
University of Missouri–St. Louis, MO
University of Montana, MT
The University of Montana Western, MT
University of Montevallo, AL
University of Nebraska at Omaha, NE
University of Nebraska–Lincoln, NE
University of Nevada, Las Vegas, NV
University of Nevada, Reno, NV
University of New Hampshire, NH
University of North Carolina at
    Asheville, NC
The University of North Carolina at Chapel
    Hill, NC
The University of North Carolina at
    Charlotte, NC
The University of North Carolina at
    Greensboro, NC
The University of North Carolina
    Wilmington, NC
University of Northern Colorado, CO
University of Northern Iowa, IA
University of North Georgia, GA
University of Oklahoma, OK
University of Oregon, OR
University of Pittsburgh at Bradford, PA
University of Pittsburgh at Johnstown, PA
University of Portland, OR
University of Puget Sound, WA
University of Rhode Island, RI
University of Richmond, VA
University of St. Thomas, MN
University of St. Thomas, TX
University of Sioux Falls, SD
University of South Carolina, SC
University of South Carolina Aiken, SC
The University of South Dakota, SD
University of Southern Indiana, IN
University of South Florida, FL
The University of Tennessee at
    Chattanooga, TN
The University of Tennessee at Martin, TN
The University of Texas at Arlington, TX
The University of Texas at Dallas, TX
The University of Texas at El Paso, TX
The University of Texas at San Antonio, TX
The University of Texas Rio
    Grande Valley, TX
The University of Toledo, OH
The University of Tulsa, OK

University of Utah, UT
University of Vermont, VT
The University of Virginia's College
    at Wise, VA
University of West Florida, FL
University of West Georgia, GA
University of Wisconsin–Eau Claire, WI
University of Wisconsin–La Crosse, WI
University of Wisconsin–Parkside, WI
University of Wisconsin–River Falls, WI
University of Wisconsin–Stevens Point, WI
University of Wisconsin–Stout, WI
University of Wisconsin–Superior, WI
University of Wisconsin–Whitewater, WI
University of Wyoming, WY
Utah State University, UT
Valdosta State University, GA
Valley City State University, ND
Virginia Commonwealth University, VA
Virginia Military Institute, VA
Virginia State University, VA
Walla Walla University, WA
Wartburg College, IA
Washburn University, KS
Washington State University, WA
Washington University in St. Louis, MO
Wayland Baptist University, TX
Wayne State College, NE
Wayne State University, MI
Wesleyan College, GA
West Chester University of Pennsylvania, PA
Western Carolina University, NC
Western Illinois University, IL
Western Kentucky University, KY
Western Oregon University, OR
Western Washington University, WA
West Texas A&M University, TX
West Virginia University, WV
Wheaton College, IL
Wichita State University, KS
Widener University, PA
William Jessup University, CA
Wilson College, PA
Wright State University, OH
Wright State University–Lake Campus, OH
Xavier University, OH
Xavier University of Louisiana, LA
Youngstown State University, OH

Military Science

Angelo State University, TX
Arkansas Tech University, AR
Armstrong State University, GA
Austin Peay State University, TN
Ball State University, IN
Baylor University, TX
Black Hills State University, SD
Boise State University, ID
Boston College, MA
Boston University, MA
Bowling Green State University, OH
California Polytechnic State University, San
    Luis Obispo, CA
California State University, Fullerton, CA
Cameron University, OK
Carson-Newman University, TN
Central Michigan University, MI
Christopher Newport University, VA
The Citadel, The Military College of South
    Carolina, SC
Claremont McKenna College, CA
Clarion University of Pennsylvania, PA
Clarkson University, NY
Clemson University, SC
The College at Brockport, State University
    of New York, NY

College of Saint Benedict, MN
College of the Holy Cross, MA
Colorado School of Mines, CO
Columbus State University, GA
Creighton University, NE
Dickinson College, PA
East Carolina University, NC
Eastern Washington University, WA
Elizabeth City State University, NC
Elon University, NC
Florida Agricultural and Mechanical
    University, FL
Florida Institute of Technology, FL
Fort Hays State University, KS
Furman University, SC
Georgia Southern University, GA
Gonzaga University, WA
Grambling State University, LA
Howard University, DC
Idaho State University, ID
Indiana University of Pennsylvania, PA
Iowa State University of Science and
    Technology, IA
Jacksonville State University, AL
James Madison University, VA
John Carroll University, OH
Kent State University, OH
Lawrence Technological University, MI
Lehigh University, PA
Lincoln University, MO
Lindenwood University, MO
Longwood University, VA
Louisiana Tech University, LA
Manhattan College, NY
Mercer University, GA
Methodist University, NC
Michigan State University, MI
Middle Tennessee State University, TN
Mississippi State University, MS
Missouri University of Science and
    Technology, MO
Missouri Western State University, MO
Montana State University, MT
Moravian College, PA
Morehead State University, KY
Morehouse College, GA
Murray State University, KY
New Mexico State University, NM
North Carolina State University, NC
Northern Illinois University, IL
Northern Michigan University, MI
Northwestern State University of
    Louisiana, LA
Northwest Nazarene University, ID
The Ohio State University, OH
Ohio University, OH
Ohio University–Chillicothe, OH
Ohio University–Eastern, OH
Ohio University–Lancaster, OH
Ohio University–Southern Campus, OH
Ohio University–Zanesville, OH
Oklahoma State University, OK
Old Dominion University, VA
Olivet Nazarene University, IL
Pittsburg State University, KS
Providence College, RI
Purdue University, IN
Rensselaer Polytechnic Institute, NY
Rochester Institute of Technology, NY
Rogers State University, OK
Saint Augustine's University, NC
St. Edward's University, TX
St. John's University, NY
Saint Louis University, MO
St. Mary's University, TX
Sam Houston State University, TX

San Diego State University, CA
Santa Clara University, CA
Savannah State University, GA
Siena College, NY
Slippery Rock University of
    Pennsylvania, PA
South Dakota School of Mines and
    Technology, SD
Southeast Missouri State University, MO
Southern Illinois University Carbondale, IL
Stephen F. Austin State University, TX
Stetson University, FL
Tennessee Technological University, TN
Texas Christian University, TX
Texas State University, TX
Texas Tech University, TX
Texas Wesleyan University, TX
Truman State University, MO
Union University, TN
The University of Akron, OH
The University of Alabama, AL
University of Alaska Fairbanks, AK
The University of Arizona, AZ
University of Arkansas, AR
University of Central Oklahoma, OK
University of Colorado Boulder, CO
University of Dayton, OH
University of Delaware, DE
University of Florida, FL
University of Houston, TX
University of Idaho, ID
University of Illinois at Urbana–
    Champaign, IL
The University of Iowa, IA
The University of Kansas, KS
University of Kentucky, KY
University of Louisiana at Monroe, LA
University of Louisville, KY
University of Maine, ME
University of Maryland, College Park, MD
University of Massachusetts Amherst, MA
University of Memphis, TN
University of Miami, FL
University of Michigan, MI
University of Minnesota, Twin Cities
    Campus, MN
University of Mississippi, MS
University of Montana, MT
University of Nebraska at Kearney, NE
University of New Hampshire, NH
University of North Alabama, AL
University of Northern Colorado, CO
University of North Georgia, GA
University of Oklahoma, OK
University of Oregon, OR
University of Portland, OR
University of Rhode Island, RI
University of Rochester, NY
University of South Carolina, SC
The University of South Dakota, SD
University of South Florida, FL
The University of Tampa, FL
The University of Tennessee, TN
The University of Tennessee at
    Chattanooga, TN
The University of Tennessee at Martin, TN
The University of Texas at Arlington, TX
The University of Texas at El Paso, TX
The University of Texas Rio
    Grande Valley, TX
The University of Toledo, OH
University of Utah, UT
University of Vermont, VT
University of West Florida, FL
University of Wisconsin–La Crosse, WI
University of Wisconsin–Stevens Point, WI

Villanova University, PA
Virginia Commonwealth University, VA
Virginia Military Institute, VA
Washington State University, WA
Washington University in St. Louis, MO
Wayne State University, MI
Western Illinois University, IL
Western Kentucky University, KY
West Virginia University, WV
Wheaton College, IL
Whitworth University, WA
Widener University, PA
Wright State University, OH
Wright State University–Lake Campus, OH
Xavier University, OH
Youngstown State University, OH

Physical Sciences
Abilene Christian University, TX
Adelphi University, NY
Alaska Pacific University, AK
Albertus Magnus College, CT
Alderson Broaddus University, WV
Alfred University, NY
Angelo State University, TX
Arkansas Tech University, AR
Armstrong State University, GA
Auburn University, AL
Augsburg College, MN
Augustana College, IL
Augustana University, SD
Austin College, TX
Austin Peay State University, TN
Averett University, VA
Ball State University, IN
Barton College, NC
Baylor University, TX
Bellarmine University, KY
Bemidji State University, MN
Binghamton University, State University of
    New York, NY
Black Hills State University, SD
Bloomfield College, NJ
Bloomsburg University of Pennsylvania, PA
Blue Mountain College, MS
Bluffton University, OH
Boise State University, ID
Bowling Green State University, OH
Briar Cliff University, IA
Bryan College, TN
Bucknell University, PA
Butler University, IN
California Lutheran University, CA
California Polytechnic State University, San
    Luis Obispo, CA
California State Polytechnic University,
    Pomona, CA
California State University, Bakersfield, CA
California State University, Chico, CA
California State University, Fresno, CA
California State University, Fullerton, CA
California State University, Los Angeles, CA
California State University,
    San Bernardino, CA
Calvin College, MI
Cameron University, OK
Campbellsville University, KY
Carroll University, WI
Case Western Reserve University, OH
Catawba College, NC
Centenary College of Louisiana, LA
Central College, IA
Central Methodist University, MO
Central Michigan University, MI
Chapman University, CA

Christopher Newport University, VA
Clarion University of Pennsylvania, PA
Clarkson University, NY
Clemson University, SC
Cleveland State University, OH
Coastal Carolina University, SC
The College at Brockport, State University
    of New York, NY
College of Charleston, SC
The College of Idaho, ID
The College of New Rochelle, NY
College of Saint Benedict, MN
College of Staten Island of the City
    University of New York, NY
The Colorado College, CO
Colorado Mesa University, CO
Colorado School of Mines, CO
Columbia College, MO
Columbus State University, GA
Concordia University, Nebraska, NE
Concordia University Texas, TX
Concord University, WV
Cornerstone University, MI
Dakota State University, SD
Dallas Baptist University, TX
Davidson College, NC
Defiance College, OH
Delta State University, MS
Denison University, OH
DeSales University, PA
Dickinson State University, ND
Dordt College, IA
Drury University, MO
East Carolina University, NC
Eastern Connecticut State University, CT
Eastern Illinois University, IL
Eastern Mennonite University, VA
Eastern Michigan University, MI
Eastern Washington University, WA
East Stroudsburg University of
    Pennsylvania, PA
East Texas Baptist University, TX
Elizabethtown College, PA
Elmhurst College, IL
Elon University, NC
Emory University, GA
Emporia State University, KS
Evangel University, MO
Fairmont State University, WV
Flagler College, FL
Florida Agricultural and Mechanical
    University, FL
Florida Atlantic University, FL
Florida Gulf Coast University, FL
Florida International University, FL
Florida Southern College, FL
Fort Hays State University, KS
Fort Lewis College, CO
Framingham State University, MA
Francis Marion University, SC
Frostburg State University, MD
Furman University, SC
Gardner-Webb University, NC
George Fox University, OR
Georgia College & State University, GA
Georgia Institute of Technology, GA
Georgian Court University, NJ
Governors State University, IL
Grambling State University, LA
Grand Valley State University, MI
Grand View University, IA
Greenville College, IL
Grove City College, PA
Hamline University, MN
Hampshire College, MA

Hampton University, VA
Hardin-Simmons University, TX
Harrisburg University of Science and
    Technology, PA
High Point University, NC
Hillsdale College, MI
Houghton College, NY
Howard Payne University, TX
Howard University, DC
Husson University, ME
Idaho State University, ID
Indiana State University, IN
Indiana University of Pennsylvania, PA
Indiana Wesleyan University, IN
Iowa State University of Science and
    Technology, IA
Jacksonville State University, AL
James Madison University, VA
John Carroll University, OH
Juniata College, PA
Kansas Wesleyan University, KS
Kean University, NJ
Kennesaw State University, GA
Kent State University, OH
Kenyon College, OH
King's College, PA
Kutztown University of Pennsylvania, PA
Lake Erie College, OH
Lawrence Technological University, MI
Lebanon Valley College, PA
Lewis-Clark State College, ID
Lindenwood University, MO
Linfield College, OR
Lock Haven University of Pennsylvania, PA
Loras College, IA
Louisiana State University and Agricultural
    & Mechanical College, LA
Louisiana State University in
    Shreveport, LA
Louisiana Tech University, LA
Loyola Marymount University, CA
Lubbock Christian University, TX
Lycoming College, PA
Mansfield University of Pennsylvania, PA
Marquette University, WI
Massachusetts College of Liberal Arts, MA
The Master's University, CA
Mayville State University, ND
Meredith College, NC
Metropolitan State University of Denver, CO
Michigan State University, MI
Middle Tennessee State University, TN
Midwestern State University, TX
Millersville University of Pennsylvania, PA
Millikin University, IL
Mills College, CA
Minnesota State University Moorhead, MN
Mississippi State University, MS
Missouri University of Science and
    Technology, MO
Missouri Western State University, MO
Monmouth University, NJ
Montana State University, MT
Montana State University Billings, MT
Montana Tech of The University of
    Montana, MT
Montclair State University, NJ
Moravian College, PA
Morehead State University, KY
Murray State University, KY
Muskingum University, OH
Newberry College, SC
New Jersey Institute of Technology, NJ
New Mexico Highlands University, NM
New Mexico State University, NM

North Carolina State University, NC
North Central College, IL
Northeastern Illinois University, IL
Northeastern State University, OK
Northern Illinois University, IL
Northern Kentucky University, KY
Northern Michigan University, MI
Northern State University, SD
Northwestern College, IA
Northwest Missouri State University, MO
Northwest Nazarene University, ID
Oberlin College, OH
Ohio Northern University, OH
The Ohio State University, OH
Ohio University, OH
Ohio University–Chillicothe, OH
Ohio University–Eastern, OH
Ohio University–Lancaster, OH
Ohio University–Southern Campus, OH
Ohio University–Zanesville, OH
Oklahoma Baptist University, OK
Oklahoma Panhandle State University, OK
Oklahoma State University, OK
Old Dominion University, VA
Ouachita Baptist University, AR
Pacific University, OR
Piedmont College, GA
Pittsburg State University, KS
Point Park University, PA
Portland State University, OR
Purdue University, IN
Randolph College, VA
Regis University, CO
Rhodes College, TN
Rochester Institute of Technology, NY
Rockford University, IL
Rockhurst University, MO
Rollins College, FL
Sacred Heart University, CT
Saginaw Valley State University, MI
St. Edward's University, TX
St. John Fisher College, NY
St. John's University, NY
Saint Joseph's University, PA
Saint Louis University, MO
Saint Vincent College, PA
Salisbury University, MD
Samford University, AL
Sam Houston State University, TX
San Diego State University, CA
Savannah State University, GA
Schreiner University, TX
Shepherd University, WV
Shippensburg University of
    Pennsylvania, PA
Siena College, NY
Skidmore College, NY
Slippery Rock University of
    Pennsylvania, PA
Sonoma State University, CA
South Dakota School of Mines and
    Technology, SD
Southeastern Oklahoma State
    University, OK
Southeast Missouri State University, MO
Southern Adventist University, TN
Southern Arkansas University–
    Magnolia, AR
Southern Illinois University Carbondale, IL
Southern Oregon University, OR
Southwestern College, KS
Southwestern Oklahoma State
    University, OK
State University of New York at
    Fredonia, NY

State University of New York at
    New Paltz, NY
State University of New York at
    Oswego, NY
State University of New York at
    Plattsburgh, NY
State University of New York College at
    Cortland, NY
State University of New York College at
    Geneseo, NY
State University of New York College at
    Potsdam, NY
State University of New York College of
    Environmental Science and Forestry, NY
Stephen F. Austin State University, TX
Stetson University, FL
Stevens Institute of Technology, NJ
Stockton University, NJ
Stony Brook University, State University of
    New York, NY
Tennessee Technological University, TN
Texas A&M International University, TX
Texas A&M University, TX
Texas A&M University–Commerce, TX
Texas Christian University, TX
Texas Lutheran University, TX
Texas State University, TX
Texas Tech University, TX
Texas Wesleyan University, TX
Texas Woman's University, TX
Thiel College, PA
Thomas More College, KY
Thomas University, GA
Towson University, MD
Trevecca Nazarene University, TN
Trinity Christian College, IL
Truman State University, MO
Union University, TN
The University of Akron, OH
The University of Alabama, AL
The University of Alabama in
    Huntsville, AL
University of Alaska Fairbanks, AK
The University of Arizona, AZ
University of Arkansas, AR
University of Arkansas at Little Rock, AR
University of California, Irvine, CA
University of California, Riverside, CA
University of California, San Diego, CA
University of California, Santa Cruz, CA
University of Central Oklahoma, OK
University of Colorado Boulder, CO
University of Colorado Denver, CO
University of Dallas, TX
University of Dayton, OH
University of Delaware, DE
University of Denver, CO
University of Evansville, IN
University of Great Falls, MT
University of Houston, TX
University of Idaho, ID
University of Illinois at Urbana–
    Champaign, IL
University of Indianapolis, IN
University of Jamestown, ND
The University of Kansas, KS
University of Kentucky, KY
University of Louisiana at Monroe, LA
University of Maine, ME
University of Mary Hardin-Baylor, TX
University of Maryland, Baltimore
    County, MD
University of Maryland, College Park, MD
University of Maryland Eastern Shore, MD
University of Mary Washington, VA
University of Massachusetts Amherst, MA

University of Massachusetts Dartmouth, MA
University of Memphis, TN
University of Michigan, MI
University of Michigan–Dearborn, MI
University of Michigan–Flint, MI
University of Minnesota, Twin Cities
    Campus, MN
University of Mississippi, MS
University of Missouri, MO
University of Missouri–St. Louis, MO
University of Montana, MT
The University of Montana Western, MT
University of Montevallo, AL
University of Nebraska at Omaha, NE
University of Nebraska–Lincoln, NE
University of Nevada, Las Vegas, NV
University of Nevada, Reno, NV
University of New Hampshire, NH
University of North Carolina at
    Asheville, NC
The University of North Carolina at
    Charlotte, NC
The University of North Carolina at
    Greensboro, NC
The University of North Carolina
    Wilmington, NC
University of Northern Colorado, CO
University of Northern Iowa, IA
University of North Georgia, GA
University of Oklahoma, OK
University of Oregon, OR
University of Pittsburgh at Bradford, PA
University of Pittsburgh at Johnstown, PA
University of Portland, OR
University of Puget Sound, WA
University of Rhode Island, RI
University of Richmond, VA
University of St. Thomas, MN
University of St. Thomas, TX
University of Sioux Falls, SD
University of South Carolina, SC
University of South Carolina Aiken, SC
University of South Florida, FL
The University of Tampa, FL
The University of Tennessee at
    Chattanooga, TN
The University of Tennessee at Martin, TN
The University of Texas at Arlington, TX
The University of Texas at Dallas, TX
The University of Texas at El Paso, TX
The University of Texas at San Antonio, TX
The University of Texas of the Permian
    Basin, TX
The University of Toledo, OH
The University of Tulsa, OK
University of Utah, UT
University of Vermont, VT
The University of Virginia's College at
    Wise, VA
University of West Florida, FL
University of West Georgia, GA
University of Wisconsin–Eau Claire, WI
University of Wisconsin–Green Bay, WI
University of Wisconsin–La Crosse, WI
University of Wisconsin–Parkside, WI
University of Wisconsin–River Falls, WI
University of Wisconsin–Stevens Point, WI
University of Wisconsin–Stout, WI
University of Wisconsin–Superior, WI
University of Wisconsin–Whitewater, WI
University of Wyoming, WY
Utah State University, UT
Valdosta State University, GA
Valley City State University, ND
Valparaiso University, IN
Virginia Commonwealth University, VA

Virginia Military Institute, VA
Virginia State University, VA
Warner University, FL
Wartburg College, IA
Washburn University, KS
Washington State University, WA
Washington University in St. Louis, MO
Wayland Baptist University, TX
Wayne State College, NE
Wayne State University, MI
Western Illinois University, IL
Western Kentucky University, KY
Western Oregon University, OR
Western Washington University, WA
West Texas A&M University, TX
West Virginia University, WV
Wheaton College, IL
Wichita State University, KS
Widener University, PA
William Jessup University, CA
Wilson College, PA
Wisconsin Lutheran College, WI
Wright State University, OH
Wright State University–Lake Campus, OH
Xavier University, OH
Xavier University of Louisiana, LA
Youngstown State University, OH

Premedicine

Albertus Magnus College, CT
Alderson Broaddus University, WV
Alfred University, NY
American Jewish University, CA
Angelo State University, TX
Arkansas Tech University, AR
Auburn University, AL
Augustana University, SD
Austin College, TX
Averett University, VA
Baylor University, TX
Belhaven University, MS
Bemidji State University, MN
Bethel College, KS
Binghamton University, State University of New York, NY
Bloomfield College, NJ
Blue Mountain College, MS
Bluffton University, OH
Boise State University, ID
Bryan College, TN
Butler University, IN
California State University, Bakersfield, CA
Calvin College, MI
Campbellsville University, KY
Carroll University, WI
Case Western Reserve University, OH
Centenary College of Louisiana, LA
Central College, IA
Central Methodist University, MO
Central Michigan University, MI
Christopher Newport University, VA
City College of the City University of New York, NY
Clarion University of Pennsylvania, PA
Clemson University, SC
Cleveland State University, OH
The College at Brockport, State University of New York, NY
College of Charleston, SC
The College of Idaho, ID
The College of New Rochelle, NY
The College of Saint Rose, NY
College of Staten Island of the City University of New York, NY
Concordia University, Nebraska, NE

Concord University, WV
Dakota Wesleyan University, SD
Dallas Baptist University, TX
Davidson College, NC
Defiance College, OH
Delta State University, MS
DeSales University, PA
Dickinson State University, ND
Dordt College, IA
Drury University, MO
D'Youville College, NY
Eastern Illinois University, IL
Eastern Mennonite University, VA
Eastern Washington University, WA
Elizabethtown College, PA
Elmhurst College, IL
Elon University, NC
Emporia State University, KS
Evangel University, MO
Florida Agricultural and Mechanical University, FL
Fort Hays State University, KS
Francis Marion University, SC
Frostburg State University, MD
Furman University, SC
Gannon University, PA
Gardner-Webb University, NC
Georgian Court University, NJ
Grambling State University, LA
Grand Valley State University, MI
Hamline University, MN
Hampden-Sydney College, VA
Hardin-Simmons University, TX
High Point University, NC
Hillsdale College, MI
Hobart and William Smith Colleges, NY
Howard Payne University, TX
Howard University, DC
Husson University, ME
Idaho State University, ID
Illinois Institute of Technology, IL
Indiana State University, IN
Indiana University of Pennsylvania, PA
Indiana University–Purdue University Fort Wayne, IN
Indiana Wesleyan University, IN
Iowa State University of Science and Technology, IA
James Madison University, VA
John Carroll University, OH
Judson College, AL
Juniata College, PA
Kansas Wesleyan University, KS
Kean University, NJ
Kennesaw State University, GA
Kent State University, OH
King's College, PA
Lawrence Technological University, MI
Liberty University, VA
Lindenwood University, MO
Lindsey Wilson College, KY
Lipscomb University, TN
Lock Haven University of Pennsylvania, PA
Loras College, IA
Louisiana State University in Shreveport, LA
Lycoming College, PA
Malone University, OH
Mayville State University, ND
Mercy College of Ohio, OH
Middle Tennessee State University, TN
Midway University, KY
Midwestern State University, TX
Millikin University, IL
Mills College, CA

Minnesota State University Moorhead, MN
Mississippi State University, MS
Missouri University of Science and Technology, MO
Missouri Western State University, MO
Montana State University Billings, MT
Moravian College, PA
Murray State University, KY
Muskingum University, OH
New Jersey Institute of Technology, NJ
North Central College, IL
Northeastern State University, OK
Northern Kentucky University, KY
Northern Michigan University, MI
Northwestern College, IA
Northwest Nazarene University, ID
Ohio Northern University, OH
The Ohio State University, OH
Ohio University, OH
Ohio University–Chillicothe, OH
Ohio University–Eastern, OH
Ohio University–Lancaster, OH
Ohio University–Southern Campus, OH
Ohio University–Zanesville, OH
Oklahoma Baptist University, OK
Oklahoma State University, OK
Ouachita Baptist University, AR
Pacific University, OR
Piedmont College, GA
Plymouth State University, NH
Point Park University, PA
Providence College, RI
Randolph College, VA
Rochester Institute of Technology, NY
Rockford University, IL
Rockhurst University, MO
Rogers State University, OK
Sacred Heart University, CT
St. Edward's University, TX
St. John's University, NY
Saint Joseph's University, PA
Saint Louis University, MO
Saint Martin's University, WA
Samford University, AL
Schreiner University, TX
Shepherd University, WV
Siena College, NY
Sonoma State University, CA
Southeastern Louisiana University, LA
Southeast Missouri State University, MO
Southern Adventist University, TN
Southern Illinois University Carbondale, IL
Southwestern University, TX
State University of New York at Oswego, NY
State University of New York at Plattsburgh, NY
State University of New York College at Geneseo, NY
State University of New York College of Environmental Science and Forestry, NY
Stephen F. Austin State University, TX
Stetson University, FL
Stevens Institute of Technology, NJ
Sweet Briar College, VA
Tennessee Technological University, TN
Texas A&M International University, TX
Texas A&M University, TX
Texas A&M University–Commerce, TX
Texas Christian University, TX
Texas Lutheran University, TX
Texas Tech University, TX
Texas Wesleyan University, TX
Texas Woman's University, TX
Thomas More College, KY

Trine University, IN
Trinity Christian College, IL
Truman State University, MO
Union University, TN
The University of Akron, OH
The University of Alabama, AL
University of Arkansas, AR
University of California, Davis, CA
University of California, Irvine, CA
University of California, Riverside, CA
University of California, San Diego, CA
University of Colorado Boulder, CO
University of Colorado Denver, CO
University of Dallas, TX
University of Dayton, OH
University of Delaware, DE
University of Evansville, IN
University of Great Falls, MT
University of Hartford, CT
University of Holy Cross, LA
University of Houston, TX
University of Idaho, ID
University of Illinois at Urbana–
  Champaign, IL
The University of Kansas, KS
University of Louisville, KY
University of Maine, ME
University of Mary Hardin-Baylor, TX
University of Maryland, College Park, MD
University of Massachusetts Amherst, MA
University of Memphis, TN
University of Michigan, MI
University of Michigan–Flint, MI
University of Minnesota, Twin Cities
  Campus, MN
University of Mississippi, MS
University of Missouri, MO
University of Missouri–St. Louis, MO
University of Montana, MT
The University of Montana Western, MT
University of Nebraska at Omaha, NE
University of Nebraska–Lincoln, NE
University of Nevada, Las Vegas, NV
The University of North Carolina at
  Greensboro, NC
The University of North Carolina
  Wilmington, NC
University of Northern Colorado, CO
University of North Georgia, GA
University of Oregon, OR
University of Pittsburgh at Bradford, PA
University of Pittsburgh at Johnstown, PA
University of Portland, OR
University of Puget Sound, WA
University of Rhode Island, RI
University of St. Francis, IL
University of St. Thomas, TX
University of Sioux Falls, SD
University of South Carolina, SC
University of South Carolina Aiken, SC
The University of South Dakota, SD
University of Southern Indiana, IN
University of South Florida, FL
The University of Tampa, FL
The University of Tennessee at Martin, TN
The University of Texas Rio
  Grande Valley, TX
The University of Toledo, OH
The University of Tulsa, OK
University of Vermont, VT
The University of Virginia's College at
  Wise, VA
University of West Georgia, GA
University of Wisconsin–Eau Claire, WI
University of Wisconsin–Green Bay, WI
University of Wisconsin–Parkside, WI

University of Wisconsin–River Falls, WI
University of Wisconsin–Stevens Point, WI
University of Wisconsin–Whitewater, WI
Utah State University, UT
Virginia Military Institute, VA
Virginia State University, VA
Wartburg College, IA
Washburn University, KS
Washington State University, WA
Washington University in St. Louis, MO
Wayne State College, NE
Wayne State University, MI
Wesleyan College, GA
Western Kentucky University, KY
Western Oregon University, OR
Western Washington University, WA
Westminster College, PA
West Texas A&M University, TX
West Virginia University, WV
Wheaton College, IL
Wheeling Jesuit University, WV
Wichita State University, KS
Widener University, PA
Wilson College, PA
Wright State University, OH
Wright State University–Lake Campus, OH
Xavier University of Louisiana, LA
Youngstown State University, OH

Religion/Biblical Studies
Abilene Christian University, TX
Alaska Bible College, AK
Alaska Pacific University, AK
Albertus Magnus College, CT
Alderson Broaddus University, WV
Anderson University, SC
Augsburg College, MN
Augustana College, IL
Augustana University, SD
Austin College, TX
Austin Graduate School of Theology, TX
Averett University, VA
The Baptist College of Florida, FL
Barclay College, KS
Barton College, NC
Baylor University, TX
Belhaven University, MS
Belmont University, TN
Berry College, GA
Bloomfield College, NJ
Bloomsburg University of Pennsylvania, PA
Blue Mountain College, MS
Boise State University, ID
Briar Cliff University, IA
Bryan College, TN
Butler University, IN
California Baptist University, CA
California Lutheran University, CA
California State University, Bakersfield, CA
California State University, Fullerton, CA
Calvary University, MO
Calvin College, MI
Campbellsville University, KY
Carolina Christian College, NC
Carson-Newman University, TN
Case Western Reserve University, OH
Centenary College of Louisiana, LA
Central College, IA
Central Methodist University, MO
Central Michigan University, MI
Charlotte Christian College and Theological
  Seminary, NC
Cincinnati Christian University, OH
The Citadel, The Military College of South
  Carolina, SC
Clarks Summit University, PA

The College of Idaho, ID
The College of New Rochelle, NY
Columbia College, MO
Concordia University Ann Arbor, MI
Concordia University Chicago, IL
Concordia University, Nebraska, NE
Concordia University, St. Paul, MN
Concordia University Texas, TX
Concordia University Wisconsin, WI
Cornerstone University, MI
Criswell College, TX
Crossroads Bible College, IN
Dallas Baptist University, TX
Davidson College, NC
Davis College, NY
Defiance College, OH
DeSales University, PA
Dordt College, IA
Eastern Mennonite University, VA
Eastern Michigan University, MI
Eastern University, PA
East Texas Baptist University, TX
Elizabethtown College, PA
Elmhurst College, IL
Elon University, NC
Emmanuel College, GA
Evangel University, MO
Faulkner University, AL
Felician University, NJ
Flagler College, FL
Florida College, FL
Florida Gulf Coast University, FL
Florida Southern College, FL
Furman University, SC
Gannon University, PA
Gardner-Webb University, NC
George Fox University, OR
Georgian Court University, NJ
Grand View University, IA
Grove City College, PA
Hamline University, MN
Harding University, AR
Hardin-Simmons University, TX
Hellenic College, MA
Heritage Bible College, NC
High Point University, NC
Hood College, MD
Houghton College, NY
Howard Payne University, TX
Howard University, DC
Indiana University of Pennsylvania, PA
Indiana Wesleyan University, IN
James Madison University, VA
John Carroll University, OH
John Wesley University, NC
Kansas Wesleyan University, KS
Kent State University, OH
King's College, PA
Lebanon Valley College, PA
Lee University, TN
Liberty University, VA
Lindenwood University, MO
Lindsey Wilson College, KY
Linfield College, OR
Lipscomb University, TN
Loras College, IA
Loyola Marymount University, CA
Lubbock Christian University, TX
Lycoming College, PA
Malone University, OH
Maranatha Baptist University, WI
Marymount University, VA
Marywood University, PA
The Master's University, CA
McKendree University, IL
Mercer University, GA

Meredith College, NC
Methodist University, NC
Mid-Atlantic Christian University, NC
Mississippi State University, MS
Missouri Baptist University, MO
Missouri Western State University, MO
Montclair State University, NJ
Moravian College, PA
Newberry College, SC
North Central College, IL
Northeast Catholic College, NH
Northwest Christian University, OR
Northwestern College, IA
Northwest Nazarene University, ID
Ohio Northern University, OH
Ohio Valley University, WV
Oklahoma Baptist University, OK
Oklahoma Christian University, OK
Oklahoma City University, OK
Oklahoma Wesleyan University, OK
Oral Roberts University, OK
Ouachita Baptist University, AR
Pacific Union College, CA
Piedmont College, GA
Point Loma Nazarene University, CA
Randall University, OK
Randolph-Macon College, VA
Rockhurst University, MO
St. Ambrose University, IA
St. Edward's University, TX
Saint Louis University, MO
St. Thomas Aquinas College, NY
Samford University, AL
San Diego State University, CA
Schreiner University, TX
Siena College, NY
Southeastern University, FL
Southeast Missouri State University, MO
Southern Adventist University, TN
Southwestern College, KS
Stetson University, FL
Texas Christian University, TX
Texas Lutheran University, TX
Texas Wesleyan University, TX
Thiel College, PA
Thomas More College, KY
Toccoa Falls College, GA
Trevecca Nazarene University, TN
Trinity Christian College, IL
Trinity College of Florida, FL
Truett McConnell University, GA
Union University, TN
The University of Arizona, AZ
University of California, Davis, CA
University of Dayton, OH
University of Delaware, DE
University of Evansville, IN
University of Great Falls, MT
University of Hartford, CT
University of Holy Cross, LA
University of Illinois at Urbana–
    Champaign, IL
University of Indianapolis, IN
The University of Kansas, KS
University of Mary Hardin-Baylor, TX
University of Mary Washington, VA
University of Massachusetts Dartmouth, MA
University of Minnesota, Twin Cities
    Campus, MN
University of Missouri, MO
University of North Carolina at
    Asheville, NC
The University of North Carolina at
    Charlotte, NC

The University of North Carolina at
    Greensboro, NC
University of Portland, OR
University of Rhode Island, RI
University of St. Thomas, MN
University of St. Thomas, TX
University of Sioux Falls, SD
University of South Carolina, SC
University of South Florida, FL
The University of Toledo, OH
The University of Tulsa, OK
University of Wisconsin–Eau Claire, WI
University of Wyoming, WY
Valparaiso University, IN
Walla Walla University, WA
Wartburg College, IA
Washburn University, KS
Washington University in St. Louis, MO
Wayland Baptist University, TX
Wesleyan College, GA
Western Illinois University, IL
Western Kentucky University, KY
West Virginia University, WV
Wheaton College, IL
William Jessup University, CA
Williams Baptist College, AR
Wilson College, PA
Wisconsin Lutheran College, WI
Wright State University, OH
Wright State University–Lake Campus, OH
Xavier University of Louisiana, LA
Youngstown State University, OH

Social Sciences
Abilene Christian University, TX
Alaska Pacific University, AK
Albertus Magnus College, CT
Alderson Broaddus University, WV
Alfred University, NY
Alliant International University–
    San Diego, CA
Angelo State University, TX
Arkansas Tech University, AR
Auburn University, AL
Augsburg College, MN
Augustana College, IL
Augustana University, SD
Austin College, TX
Austin Peay State University, TN
Ball State University, IN
Barton College, NC
Baylor University, TX
Belhaven University, MS
Belmont University, TN
Bemidji State University, MN
Bethel College, KS
Binghamton University, State University of
    New York, NY
Black Hills State University, SD
Bloomfield College, NJ
Bloomsburg University of Pennsylvania, PA
Blue Mountain College, MS
Boise State University, ID
Bowling Green State University, OH
Briar Cliff University, IA
Bryan College, TN
Butler University, IN
California Lutheran University, CA
California Polytechnic State University, San
    Luis Obispo, CA
California State Polytechnic University,
    Pomona, CA
California State University, Bakersfield, CA
California State University, Chico, CA
California State University, Fresno, CA

California State University, Fullerton, CA
California State University, Los Angeles, CA
California State University, Northridge, CA
California State University,
    San Bernardino, CA
Calvin College, MI
Cameron University, OK
Campbellsville University, KY
Carlos Albizu University, PR
Carlow University, PA
Carroll University, WI
Case Western Reserve University, OH
Centenary College of Louisiana, LA
Central College, IA
Central Methodist University, MO
Central Michigan University, MI
Champlain College, VT
Christopher Newport University, VA
City College of the City University of
    New York, NY
Clarion University of Pennsylvania, PA
Clarkson University, NY
Clemson University, SC
Cleveland State University, OH
Coastal Carolina University, SC
The College at Brockport, State University
    of New York, NY
College of Charleston, SC
The College of Idaho, ID
The College of New Rochelle, NY
The College of Saint Rose, NY
College of Staten Island of the City
    University of New York, NY
Colorado Mesa University, CO
Columbia College, MO
Concordia University, Nebraska, NE
Concordia University Texas, TX
Concord University, WV
Cornerstone University, MI
Dallas Baptist University, TX
Davidson College, NC
Defiance College, OH
Delta State University, MS
DeSales University, PA
Dickinson State University, ND
Dordt College, IA
Drury University, MO
D'Youville College, NY
East Carolina University, NC
Eastern Connecticut State University, CT
Eastern Illinois University, IL
Eastern Mennonite University, VA
Eastern Michigan University, MI
Eastern Washington University, WA
East Stroudsburg University of
    Pennsylvania, PA
East Texas Baptist University, TX
Elizabethtown College, PA
Elmhurst College, IL
Elon University, NC
Emporia State University, KS
Evangel University, MO
Fairmont State University, WV
Fitchburg State University, MA
Flagler College, FL
Florida Agricultural and Mechanical
    University, FL
Florida Atlantic University, FL
Florida Gulf Coast University, FL
Florida International University, FL
Florida Southern College, FL
Fort Hays State University, KS
Fort Lewis College, CO
Francis Marion University, SC
Fresno Pacific University, CA

Frostburg State University, MD
Furman University, SC
Gannon University, PA
Gardner-Webb University, NC
George Fox University, OR
Georgia College & State University, GA
Georgian Court University, NJ
Georgia Southern University, GA
Glenville State College, WV
Governors State University, IL
Grambling State University, LA
Grand Valley State University, MI
Grand View University, IA
Grove City College, PA
Hamline University, MN
Hampshire College, MA
Hardin-Simmons University, TX
Hillsdale College, MI
Hood College, MD
Howard Payne University, TX
Howard University, DC
Husson University, ME
Idaho State University, ID
Illinois Institute of Technology, IL
Indiana State University, IN
Indiana University of Pennsylvania, PA
Indiana Wesleyan University, IN
Iowa State University of Science and
    Technology, IA
Iowa Wesleyan University, IA
Jacksonville State University, AL
James Madison University, VA
John Carroll University, OH
Juniata College, PA
Kansas Wesleyan University, KS
Kean University, NJ
Kennesaw State University, GA
Kent State University, OH
Kent State University at Stark, OH
King's College, PA
Lake Erie College, OH
Lebanon Valley College, PA
Lewis-Clark State College, ID
Lindenwood University, MO
Linfield College, OR
Lock Haven University of Pennsylvania, PA
Longwood University, VA
Louisiana State University in
    Shreveport, LA
Louisiana Tech University, LA
Loyola Marymount University, CA
Lubbock Christian University, TX
Lycoming College, PA
Malone University, OH
Marymount University, VA
Maryville University of Saint Louis, MO
Marywood University, PA
Massachusetts College of Liberal Arts, MA
The Master's University, CA
Mayville State University, ND
Metropolitan State University of Denver, CO
Michigan State University, MI
Middle Georgia State University, GA
Middle Tennessee State University, TN
Midwestern State University, TX
Millersville University of Pennsylvania, PA
Minnesota State University Moorhead, MN
Minot State University, ND
Mississippi State University, MS
Missouri University of Science and
    Technology, MO
Missouri Western State University, MO
Molloy College, NY
Monmouth University, NJ
Montana State University, MT
Montana State University Billings, MT

Montclair State University, NJ
Moravian College, PA
Morehead State University, KY
Mount Mary University, WI
Murray State University, KY
Newberry College, SC
New England College, NH
New Mexico Highlands University, NM
New Mexico State University, NM
North Carolina State University, NC
North Central College, IL
Northeastern Illinois University, IL
Northeastern State University, OK
Northern Illinois University, IL
Northern Kentucky University, KY
Northern Michigan University, MI
Northern State University, SD
Northwestern College, IA
Northwestern State University of
    Louisiana, LA
Northwest Missouri State University, MO
Northwest Nazarene University, ID
Ohio Northern University, OH
The Ohio State University, OH
Ohio University, OH
Ohio University–Chillicothe, OH
Ohio University–Eastern, OH
Ohio University–Lancaster, OH
Ohio University–Southern Campus, OH
Ohio University–Zanesville, OH
Oklahoma Baptist University, OK
Oklahoma State University, OK
Old Dominion University, VA
Ouachita Baptist University, AR
Pacific University, OR
Paul Smith's College, NY
Piedmont College, GA
Pittsburg State University, KS
Point Loma Nazarene University, CA
Point Park University, PA
Portland State University, OR
Purchase College, State University of New
    York, NY
Queens University of Charlotte, NC
Randolph College, VA
Rochester Institute of Technology, NY
Rockford University, IL
Rockhurst University, MO
St. Edward's University, TX
St. John Fisher College, NY
St. John's University, NY
Saint Louis University, MO
St. Thomas Aquinas College, NY
Salisbury University, MD
Samford University, AL
Sam Houston State University, TX
San Diego State University, CA
Savannah State University, GA
Schreiner University, TX
Shepherd University, WV
Shippensburg University of
    Pennsylvania, PA
Siena College, NY
Slippery Rock University of
    Pennsylvania, PA
Sonoma State University, CA
Southeastern Louisiana University, LA
Southeastern Oklahoma State
    University, OK
Southeast Missouri State University, MO
Southern Arkansas University–
    Magnolia, AR
Southern Illinois University Carbondale, IL
Southern New Hampshire University, NH
Southern Oregon University, OR
Southwestern College, KS

Southwestern Oklahoma State
    University, OK
Southwestern University, TX
State University of New York at
    Fredonia, NY
State University of New York at
    Oswego, NY
State University of New York at
    Plattsburgh, NY
State University of New York College at
    Geneseo, NY
State University of New York College at
    Potsdam, NY
Stetson University, FL
Stockton University, NJ
Stony Brook University, State University of
    New York, NY
Tennessee Technological University, TN
Texas A&M International University, TX
Texas A&M University–Commerce, TX
Texas A&M University–Texarkana, TX
Texas Christian University, TX
Texas Lutheran University, TX
Texas State University, TX
Texas Tech University, TX
Texas Wesleyan University, TX
Texas Woman's University, TX
Thomas More College, KY
Thomas University, GA
Trevecca Nazarene University, TN
Trinity Christian College, IL
Truman State University, MO
Union University, TN
The University of Akron, OH
The University of Alabama, AL
The University of Alabama in
    Huntsville, AL
University of Alaska Anchorage, AK
University of Arkansas, AR
University of Arkansas at Little Rock, AR
University of California, Davis, CA
University of California, Irvine, CA
University of California, Riverside, CA
University of California, San Diego, CA
University of California, Santa Cruz, CA
University of Central Oklahoma, OK
University of Colorado Boulder, CO
University of Colorado Denver, CO
University of Dayton, OH
University of Delaware, DE
University of Denver, CO
University of Evansville, IN
University of Great Falls, MT
University of Hartford, CT
University of Holy Cross, LA
University of Houston, TX
University of Houston–Clear Lake, TX
University of Houston–Victoria, TX
University of Idaho, ID
University of Illinois at Urbana–
    Champaign, IL
The University of Kansas, KS
University of Louisiana at Monroe, LA
University of Maine, ME
University of Maine at Fort Kent, ME
University of Mary Hardin-Baylor, TX
University of Maryland, Baltimore
    County, MD
University of Maryland, College Park, MD
University of Maryland Eastern Shore, MD
University of Mary Washington, VA
University of Massachusetts Amherst, MA
University of Massachusetts Dartmouth, MA
University of Memphis, TN
University of Michigan, MI
University of Michigan–Dearborn, MI

University of Michigan–Flint, MI
University of Minnesota, Twin Cities Campus, MN
University of Mississippi, MS
University of Missouri, MO
University of Missouri–St. Louis, MO
University of Montana, MT
The University of Montana Western, MT
University of Montevallo, AL
University of Nebraska at Omaha, NE
University of Nebraska–Lincoln, NE
University of Nevada, Las Vegas, NV
University of North Carolina at Asheville, NC
The University of North Carolina at Charlotte, NC
The University of North Carolina at Greensboro, NC
The University of North Carolina Wilmington, NC
University of Northern Colorado, CO
University of Northern Iowa, IA
University of Oklahoma, OK
University of Oregon, OR
University of Pittsburgh at Bradford, PA
University of Pittsburgh at Johnstown, PA
University of Portland, OR
University of Puget Sound, WA
University of Rhode Island, RI
University of Richmond, VA
University of St. Francis, IL
University of St. Thomas, MN
University of St. Thomas, TX
University of Sioux Falls, SD
University of South Carolina, SC
University of South Carolina Aiken, SC
The University of South Dakota, SD
University of Southern Indiana, IN
University of South Florida, FL
The University of Tampa, FL
The University of Tennessee, TN
The University of Tennessee at Martin, TN
The University of Texas at Arlington, TX
The University of Texas at San Antonio, TX
The University of Texas of the Permian Basin, TX
The University of Texas Rio Grande Valley, TX
The University of Toledo, OH
The University of Tulsa, OK
University of Utah, UT
University of Vermont, VT
The University of Virginia's College at Wise, VA
University of West Florida, FL
University of West Georgia, GA
University of Wisconsin–Eau Claire, WI
University of Wisconsin–Green Bay, WI
University of Wisconsin–La Crosse, WI
University of Wisconsin–Parkside, WI
University of Wisconsin–River Falls, WI
University of Wisconsin–Stevens Point, WI
University of Wisconsin–Superior, WI
University of Wisconsin–Whitewater, WI
University of Wyoming, WY
Utah State University, UT
Valdosta State University, GA
Valley City State University, ND
Warner University, FL
Wartburg College, IA
Washburn University, KS
Washington State University, WA
Washington University in St. Louis, MO
Wayland Baptist University, TX
Wayne State College, NE

Wayne State University, MI
Wesleyan College, GA
West Chester University of Pennsylvania, PA
Western Illinois University, IL
Western Kentucky University, KY
Western Oregon University, OR
Western Washington University, WA
West Texas A&M University, TX
West Virginia University, WV
Wheaton College, IL
Wichita State University, KS
Widener University, PA
William Jessup University, CA
Wilson College, PA
Wright State University, OH
Wright State University–Lake Campus, OH
Xavier University, OH
Xavier University of Louisiana, LA
Youngstown State University, OH

Creative Arts/Performance

Applied Art and Design

Alderson Broaddus University, WV
Arcadia University, PA
Art Academy of Cincinnati, OH
Auburn University, AL
Belhaven University, MS
Belmont University, TN
Bemidji State University, MN
Brenau University, GA
Butler University, IN
California Baptist University, CA
California Institute of the Arts, CA
California Polytechnic State University, San Luis Obispo, CA
California State University, Chico, CA
Calvin College, MI
Central Michigan University, MI
Chatham University, PA
City College of the City University of New York, NY
Claflin University, SC
Clemson University, SC
College of Staten Island of the City University of New York, NY
Concordia University, Nebraska, NE
Converse College, SC
Defiance College, OH
Dominican University, IL
East Carolina University, NC
Eastern Illinois University, IL
Eastern Michigan University, MI
East Stroudsburg University of Pennsylvania, PA
Emmanuel College, GA
Ferris State University, MI
Flagler College, FL
Florida Agricultural and Mechanical University, FL
Fort Hays State University, KS
Georgian Court University, NJ
Grand Valley State University, MI
Grand View University, IA
Greenville College, IL
Hamline University, MN
Hardin-Simmons University, TX
Hofstra University, NY
Howard University, DC
Huntington University, IN
Illinois Institute of Technology, IL
Indiana State University, IN
Indiana University of Pennsylvania, PA

Iowa State University of Science and Technology, IA
Kansas Wesleyan University, KS
Kean University, NJ
Keene State College, NH
Kent State University, OH
Kutztown University of Pennsylvania, PA
Lafayette College, PA
Laguna College of Art & Design, CA
Lindenwood University, MO
Lindsey Wilson College, KY
Louisiana State University and Agricultural & Mechanical College, LA
Louisiana Tech University, LA
Loyola Marymount University, CA
Lycoming College, PA
Marymount California University, CA
Maryville University of Saint Louis, MO
Massachusetts College of Liberal Arts, MA
Memphis College of Art, TN
Meredith College, NC
Mississippi State University, MS
Morehead State University, KY
Mount Ida College, MA
Mount Mary University, WI
Muskingum University, OH
New England College, NH
New Jersey Institute of Technology, NJ
New Mexico State University, NM
Northeastern State University, OK
Northern Illinois University, IL
Northern Michigan University, MI
Northwest College of Art & Design, WA
Ohio Northern University, OH
Ohio University, OH
Ohio University–Chillicothe, OH
Ohio University–Eastern, OH
Ohio University–Lancaster, OH
Ohio University–Southern Campus, OH
Ohio University–Zanesville, OH
Ohio Wesleyan University, OH
Oklahoma Baptist University, OK
Oklahoma Christian University, OK
Oklahoma City University, OK
Old Dominion University, VA
Oral Roberts University, OK
Piedmont College, GA
Rhode Island School of Design, RI
Ringling College of Art and Design, FL
Robert Morris University Illinois, IL
Rochester Institute of Technology, NY
Sacred Heart University, CT
Saint Mary-of-the-Woods College, IN
San Diego State University, CA
Savannah College of Art and Design, GA
Schreiner University, TX
Seton Hill University, PA
Shepherd University, WV
Slippery Rock University of Pennsylvania, PA
Sonoma State University, CA
Southern Illinois University Carbondale, IL
Southwestern Oklahoma State University, OK
State University of New York at Fredonia, NY
State University of New York College at Geneseo, NY
Stetson University, FL
Stockton University, NJ
Texas A&M University–Commerce, TX
Texas Christian University, TX
Texas State University, TX
Texas Tech University, TX
Texas Woman's University, TX

Trinity Christian College, IL
Troy University, AL
The University of Akron, OH
University of Bridgeport, CT
University of California, San Diego, CA
University of Central Oklahoma, OK
University of Colorado Denver, CO
University of Delaware, DE
University of Hartford, CT
University of Idaho, ID
University of Illinois at Chicago, IL
University of Illinois at Urbana–
    Champaign, IL
The University of Kansas, KS
University of Kentucky, KY
University of Maryland, College Park, MD
University of Maryland Eastern Shore, MD
University of Massachusetts Dartmouth, MA
University of Nebraska at Kearney, NE
University of Nevada, Las Vegas, NV
The University of North Carolina at Chapel
    Hill, NC
University of North Carolina School of the
    Arts, NC
University of Northern Colorado, CO
University of Northern Iowa, IA
University of North Georgia, GA
University of Oregon, OR
University of St. Francis, IL
University of St. Thomas, TX
University of South Florida, FL
The University of Texas at El Paso, TX
University of West Florida, FL
University of West Georgia, GA
University of Wisconsin–Parkside, WI
University of Wisconsin–Stevens Point, WI
University of Wisconsin–Stout, WI
University of Wyoming, WY
Utah State University, UT
Valley City State University, ND
Virginia Polytechnic Institute and State
    University, VA
Virginia State University, VA
Washington State University, WA
Washington University in St. Louis, MO
Wayne State College, NE
Western Illinois University, IL
Western Washington University, WA
Wheaton College, IL
Wichita State University, KS
William Jessup University, CA
Wright State University, OH
Wright State University–Lake Campus, OH

Art/Fine Arts

Abilene Christian University, TX
Adelphi University, NY
Alaska Pacific University, AK
Albertus Magnus College, CT
Albion College, MI
Albright College, PA
Alfred University, NY
Alma College, MI
Alverno College, WI
Anderson University, SC
Arcadia University, PA
Arizona State University at the
    Tempe campus, AZ
Arkansas Tech University, AR
Armstrong State University, GA
Art Academy of Cincinnati, OH
Asbury University, KY
Auburn University, AL
Augsburg College, MN
Augustana College, IL
Augustana University, SD

Augusta University, GA
Aurora University, IL
Austin College, TX
Austin Peay State University, TN
Averett University, VA
Baker University, KS
Barclay College, KS
Barton College, NC
Baylor University, TX
Belhaven University, MS
Bellarmine University, KY
Belmont University, TN
Bemidji State University, MN
Berry College, GA
Bethany Lutheran College, MN
Bethel College, IN
Bethel College, KS
Bethel University, MN
Binghamton University, State University of
    New York, NY
Black Hills State University, SD
Bloomfield College, NJ
Bluefield College, VA
Blue Mountain College, MS
Bluffton University, OH
Boise State University, ID
Boston University, MA
Bowling Green State University, OH
Bradley University, IL
Brenau University, GA
Brescia University, KY
Brevard College, NC
Briar Cliff University, IA
Brigham Young University, UT
Bucknell University, PA
Buena Vista University, IA
Butler University, IN
Caldwell University, NJ
California Baptist University, CA
California Institute of the Arts, CA
California Lutheran University, CA
California Polytechnic State University, San
    Luis Obispo, CA
California State University, Bakersfield, CA
California State University, Chico, CA
California State University, Fresno, CA
California State University, Fullerton, CA
California State University, Los Angeles, CA
California State University,
    San Bernardino, CA
California State University, San Marcos, CA
Calumet College of Saint Joseph, IN
Calvin College, MI
Cameron University, OK
Campbellsville University, KY
Campbell University, NC
Canisius College, NY
Cardinal Stritch University, WI
Carroll College, MT
Carroll University, WI
Carson-Newman University, TN
Case Western Reserve University, OH
Cedar Crest College, PA
Centenary College of Louisiana, LA
Central College, IA
Central Michigan University, MI
Central Washington University, WA
Chapman University, CA
Chatham University, PA
Christian Brothers University, TN
Christopher Newport University, VA
City College of the City University of
    New York, NY
Claflin University, SC
Clarion University of Pennsylvania, PA
Clarke University, IA

Clemson University, SC
Cleveland State University, OH
Coastal Carolina University, SC
Coe College, IA
The College at Brockport, State University
    of New York, NY
College of Charleston, SC
The College of Idaho, ID
The College of New Jersey, NJ
The College of New Rochelle, NY
College of Saint Benedict, MN
College of Saint Mary, NE
The College of Saint Rose, NY
College of Staten Island of the City
    University of New York, NY
Colorado Mesa University, CO
Colorado State University, CO
Columbia College, MO
Columbus College of Art & Design, OH
Columbus State University, GA
Concordia College, MN
Concordia University Ann Arbor, MI
Concordia University, Nebraska, NE
Concord University, WV
Cooper Union for the Advancement of
    Science and Art, NY
Cornell College, IA
Creighton University, NE
Culver-Stockton College, MO
Daemen College, NY
Dakota Wesleyan University, SD
Dallas Baptist University, TX
Davidson College, NC
Delta State University, MS
DePaul University, IL
Dickinson State University, ND
DigiPen Institute of Technology, WA
Doane University, NE
Dominican University, IL
Drake University, IA
Drew University, NJ
Drury University, MO
East Carolina University, NC
Eastern Connecticut State University, CT
Eastern Illinois University, IL
Eastern Mennonite University, VA
Eastern Michigan University, MI
Eastern Oregon University, OR
Eastern Washington University, WA
East Stroudsburg University of
    Pennsylvania, PA
Eckerd College, FL
Edgewood College, WI
Elizabethtown College, PA
Elmhurst College, IL
Elon University, NC
Emmanuel College, GA
Emory & Henry College, VA
Emory University, GA
Emporia State University, KS
Endicott College, MA
Eureka College, IL
Evangel University, MO
Fairmont State University, WV
Ferris State University, MI
Flagler College, FL
Florida Agricultural and Mechanical
    University, FL
Florida Gulf Coast University, FL
Florida International University, FL
Florida Southern College, FL
Fort Hays State University, KS
Fort Lewis College, CO
Francis Marion University, SC
Franklin College, IN
Friends University, KS

Frostburg State University, MD
Furman University, SC
Gardner-Webb University, NC
George Fox University, OR
Georgia College & State University, GA
Georgian Court University, NJ
Georgia Southern University, GA
Georgia Southwestern State University, GA
Glenville State College, WV
Goddard College, VT
Gordon College, MA
Goucher College, MD
Graceland University, IA
Grand Valley State University, MI
Grand View University, IA
Greenville College, IL
Gustavus Adolphus College, MN
Hamline University, MN
Harding University, AR
Hardin-Simmons University, TX
Hartwick College, NY
Hendrix College, AR
High Point University, NC
Hillsdale College, MI
Hobart and William Smith Colleges, NY
Hofstra University, NY
Hood College, MD
Hope College, MI
Houghton College, NY
Houston Baptist University, TX
Howard Payne University, TX
Howard University, DC
Huntington University, IN
Idaho State University, ID
Illinois College, IL
Illinois Wesleyan University, IL
Indiana State University, IN
Indiana University of Pennsylvania, PA
Indiana University–Purdue University Fort
   Wayne, IN
Indiana Wesleyan University, IN
Iowa State University of Science and
   Technology, IA
Iowa Wesleyan University, IA
Jacksonville State University, AL
Jacksonville University, FL
James Madison University, VA
John Brown University, AR
Judson College, AL
Judson University, IL
Juniata College, PA
Kalamazoo College, MI
Kansas City Art Institute, MO
Kansas Wesleyan University, KS
Kean University, NJ
Keene State College, NH
Kennesaw State University, GA
Kent State University, OH
Kentucky State University, KY
Kentucky Wesleyan College, KY
Kenyon College, OH
King University, TN
Knox College, IL
Kutztown University of Pennsylvania, PA
Lafayette College, PA
LaGrange College, GA
Laguna College of Art & Design, CA
Lake Erie College, OH
Lewis-Clark State College, ID
Lewis University, IL
Lincoln University, MO
Lindenwood University, MO
Lipscomb University, TN
Lock Haven University of Pennsylvania, PA
Long Island University–LIU Brooklyn, NY

Long Island University–LIU Post, NY
Longwood University, VA
Louisiana State University and Agricultural
   & Mechanical College, LA
Louisiana Tech University, LA
Loyola Marymount University, CA
Loyola University Chicago, IL
Loyola University New Orleans, LA
Lubbock Christian University, TX
Lycoming College, PA
Lynchburg College, VA
Lyon College, AR
Manhattanville College, NY
Mansfield University of Pennsylvania, PA
Marietta College, OH
Marlboro College, VT
Marshall University, WV
Marygrove College, MI
Marymount Manhattan College, NY
Maryville College, TN
Maryville University of Saint Louis, MO
Marywood University, PA
Massachusetts College of Liberal Arts, MA
McPherson College, KS
Memphis College of Art, TN
Mercer University, GA
Meredith College, NC
Messiah College, PA
Miami University, OH
Michigan State University, MI
Michigan Technological University, MI
Midwestern State University, TX
Millersville University of Pennsylvania, PA
Milligan College, TN
Millikin University, IL
Millsaps College, MS
Minnesota State University Mankato, MN
Minnesota State University Moorhead, MN
Minot State University, ND
Mississippi State University, MS
Missouri Western State University, MO
Molloy College, NY
Monmouth College, IL
Montana State University, MT
Montana State University Billings, MT
Montclair State University, NJ
Moravian College, PA
Morehead State University, KY
Morehouse College, GA
Morningside College, IA
Mount Ida College, MA
Mount Marty College, SD
Mount Mary University, WI
Mount Mercy University, IA
Mount St. Joseph University, OH
Mount St. Mary's University, MD
Mount Vernon Nazarene University, OH
Muhlenberg College, PA
Murray State University, KY
Muskingum University, OH
Nazareth College of Rochester, NY
New England College, NH
New Jersey Institute of Technology, NJ
New Mexico Highlands University, NM
New Mexico State University, NM
North Central College, IL
Northeastern Illinois University, IL
Northeastern State University, OK
Northern Arizona University, AZ
Northern Illinois University, IL
Northern Kentucky University, KY
Northern State University, SD
Northland College, WI
Northwest College of Art & Design, WA
Northwestern College, IA

Northwestern State University of
   Louisiana, LA
Northwest Missouri State University, MO
Oakland City University, IN
Oglethorpe University, GA
Ohio Northern University, OH
Ohio University, OH
Ohio University–Chillicothe, OH
Ohio University–Eastern, OH
Ohio University–Lancaster, OH
Ohio University–Southern Campus, OH
Ohio University–Zanesville, OH
Ohio Wesleyan University, OH
Oklahoma Baptist University, OK
Oklahoma City University, OK
Oklahoma Panhandle State University, OK
Oklahoma State University, OK
Old Dominion University, VA
Olivet College, MI
Olivet Nazarene University, IL
O'More College of Design, TN
Oral Roberts University, OK
Oregon College of Art and Craft, OR
Otterbein University, OH
Ouachita Baptist University, AR
Pacific Union College, CA
Pacific University, OR
Piedmont College, GA
Point Loma Nazarene University, CA
Portland State University, OR
Purchase College, State University of New
   York, NY
Queens University of Charlotte, NC
Rhode Island College, RI
Rhode Island School of Design, RI
Rhodes College, TN
Rice University, TX
Ringling College of Art and Design, FL
Roanoke College, VA
Roberts Wesleyan College, NY
Rochester Institute of Technology, NY
Rockford University, IL
Rogers State University, OK
Rollins College, FL
Rosemont College, PA
Sacred Heart University, CT
The Sage Colleges, NY
Saginaw Valley State University, MI
St. Ambrose University, IA
St. Edward's University, TX
St. Gregory's University, OK
Saint John's University, MN
St. John's University, NY
Saint Louis University, MO
Saint Mary-of-the-Woods College, IN
Saint Mary's University of Minnesota, MN
Saint Michael's College, VT
St. Norbert College, WI
St. Olaf College, MN
Salisbury University, MD
Salve Regina University, RI
Sam Houston State University, TX
San Diego State University, CA
San Francisco Art Institute, CA
San Jose State University, CA
Savannah College of Art and Design, GA
School of the Art Institute of Chicago, IL
School of Visual Arts, NY
Schreiner University, TX
Seattle Pacific University, WA
Seattle University, WA
Seton Hill University, PA
Shepherd University, WV
Shippensburg University of
   Pennsylvania, PA

Simpson College, IA
Slippery Rock University of
  Pennsylvania, PA
Sonoma State University, CA
Southeastern Louisiana University, LA
Southeastern Oklahoma State
  University, OK
Southeastern University, FL
Southern Adventist University, TN
Southern Arkansas University–
  Magnolia, AR
Southern Illinois University Carbondale, IL
Southern Illinois University
  Edwardsville, IL
Southern Oregon University, OR
Southern Utah University, UT
Southwest Baptist University, MO
Southwestern Oklahoma State
  University, OK
Southwestern University, TX
Spring Arbor University, MI
State University of New York at Fredonia,
  NY
State University of New York at New Paltz,
  NY
State University of New York at Plattsburgh,
  NY
State University of New York College at
  Cortland, NY
State University of New York College at
  Geneseo, NY
State University of New York College at
  Potsdam, NY
Sterling College, KS
Stetson University, FL
Stevens Institute of Technology, NJ
Stevenson University, MD
Stockton University, NJ
Syracuse University, NY
Temple University, PA
Tennessee Technological University, TN
Texas A&M International University, TX
Texas A&M University–Commerce, TX
Texas A&M University–Corpus Christi, TX
Texas Christian University, TX
Texas Lutheran University, TX
Texas State University, TX
Texas Tech University, TX
Texas Wesleyan University, TX
Texas Woman's University, TX
Thomas More College, KY
Thomas University, GA
Towson University, MD
Transylvania University, KY
Trinity Christian College, IL
Trinity University, TX
Truman State University, MO
Union University, TN
The University of Akron, OH
The University of Alabama, AL
The University of Alabama at
  Birmingham, AL
The University of Alabama in
  Huntsville, AL
University of Alaska Anchorage, AK
The University of Arizona, AZ
University of Arkansas, AR
University of Arkansas at Little Rock, AR
University of California, Irvine, CA
University of California, Riverside, CA
University of California, Santa Cruz, CA
University of Central Oklahoma, OK
University of Colorado Boulder, CO
University of Colorado Denver, CO
University of Dallas, TX
University of Dayton, OH

University of Delaware, DE
University of Denver, CO
University of Evansville, IN
University of Florida, FL
University of Hartford, CT
University of Houston, TX
University of Houston–Clear Lake, TX
University of Idaho, ID
University of Illinois at Chicago, IL
University of Illinois at Urbana–
  Champaign, IL
University of Indianapolis, IN
University of Jamestown, ND
The University of Kansas, KS
University of Kentucky, KY
University of La Verne, CA
University of Louisiana at Monroe, LA
University of Louisville, KY
University of Maine, ME
University of Mary Hardin-Baylor, TX
University of Maryland,
  Baltimore County, MD
University of Maryland, College Park, MD
University of Maryland Eastern Shore, MD
University of Mary Washington, VA
University of Massachusetts Amherst, MA
University of Massachusetts Dartmouth, MA
University of Massachusetts Lowell, MA
University of Memphis, TN
University of Michigan, MI
University of Michigan–Dearborn, MI
University of Michigan–Flint, MI
University of Minnesota, Twin Cities
  Campus, MN
University of Mississippi, MS
University of Missouri, MO
University of Missouri–Kansas City, MO
University of Missouri–St. Louis, MO
University of Mobile, AL
The University of Montana Western, MT
University of Montevallo, AL
University of Mount Olive, NC
University of Mount Union, OH
University of Nebraska at Kearney, NE
University of Nebraska at Omaha, NE
University of Nebraska–Lincoln, NE
University of Nevada, Las Vegas, NV
University of Nevada, Reno, NV
University of New Hampshire, NH
University of North Alabama, AL
University of North Carolina at
  Asheville, NC
The University of North Carolina at Chapel
  Hill, NC
The University of North Carolina at
  Charlotte, NC
The University of North Carolina at
  Greensboro, NC
The University of North Carolina at
  Pembroke, NC
The University of North Carolina
  Wilmington, NC
University of Northern Colorado, CO
University of Northern Iowa, IA
University of North Florida, FL
University of Oklahoma, OK
University of Oregon, OR
University of Pittsburgh at Bradford, PA
University of Puget Sound, WA
University of Redlands, CA
University of Rhode Island, RI
University of Richmond, VA
University of St. Francis, IL
University of St. Thomas, TX
University of Science and Arts of
  Oklahoma, OK

University of Sioux Falls, SD
University of South Carolina, SC
University of South Carolina Aiken, SC
The University of South Dakota, SD
University of Southern California, CA
University of Southern Indiana, IN
University of Southern Mississippi, MS
University of South Florida, FL
The University of Tampa, FL
The University of Tennessee, TN
The University of Tennessee at
  Chattanooga, TN
The University of Tennessee at Martin, TN
The University of Texas at Austin, TX
The University of Texas at El Paso, TX
The University of Texas at San Antonio, TX
The University of Texas of the Permian
  Basin, TX
The University of Texas Rio
  Grande Valley, TX
University of the Incarnate Word, TX
The University of Toledo, OH
The University of Tulsa, OK
University of Utah, UT
University of Valley Forge, PA
University of Washington, WA
University of West Florida, FL
University of West Georgia, GA
University of Wisconsin–Eau Claire, WI
University of Wisconsin–Green Bay, WI
University of Wisconsin–La Crosse, WI
University of Wisconsin–Oshkosh, WI
University of Wisconsin–Parkside, WI
University of Wisconsin–River Falls, WI
University of Wisconsin–Stout, WI
University of Wisconsin–Whitewater, WI
University of Wyoming, WY
Utah State University, UT
Valdosta State University, GA
Valley City State University, ND
Valparaiso University, IN
Virginia Commonwealth University, VA
Virginia Polytechnic Institute and State
  University, VA
Virginia State University, VA
Wabash College, IN
Wake Forest University, NC
Wartburg College, IA
Washburn University, KS
Washington College, MD
Washington State University, WA
Washington University in St. Louis, MO
Wayland Baptist University, TX
Waynesburg University, PA
Wayne State College, NE
Wayne State University, MI
Webster University, MO
Wesleyan College, GA
West Chester University of Pennsylvania, PA
Western Carolina University, NC
Western Illinois University, IL
Western Kentucky University, KY
Western Michigan University, MI
Western Oregon University, OR
Western State Colorado University, CO
Western Washington University, WA
Westmont College, CA
West Texas A&M University, TX
West Virginia University, WV
West Virginia Wesleyan College, WV
Wheaton College, IL
Whitman College, WA
Whittier College, CA
Whitworth University, WA
Wichita State University, KS
William Jessup University, CA

William Paterson University of New Jersey, NJ
William Peace University, NC
Williams Baptist College, AR
William Woods University, MO
Wingate University, NC
Winona State University, MN
Winthrop University, SC
Wisconsin Lutheran College, WI
Wittenberg University, OH
Wofford College, SC
Wright State University, OH
Wright State University–Lake Campus, OH
Xavier University, OH
Xavier University of Louisiana, LA
Young Harris College, GA
Youngstown State University, OH

Cinema/Film/Broadcasting

Adelphi University, NY
Arkansas Tech University, AR
Auburn University, AL
Baker University, KS
Ball State University, IN
Baylor University, TX
Belhaven University, MS
Belmont University, TN
Bemidji State University, MN
Binghamton University, State University of New York, NY
Biola University, CA
Bloomfield College, NJ
Bowling Green State University, OH
Butler University, IN
California Baptist University, CA
California Institute of the Arts, CA
California Polytechnic State University, San Luis Obispo, CA
California State University, Chico, CA
California State University, Fullerton, CA
Calvin College, MI
Cameron University, OK
Central Michigan University, MI
Chapman University, CA
City College of the City University of New York, NY
The College at Brockport, State University of New York, NY
College of Staten Island of the City University of New York, NY
DeSales University, PA
Eastern Illinois University, IL
Eastern Michigan University, MI
Eastern Washington University, WA
Emory University, GA
Flagler College, FL
Florida Agricultural and Mechanical University, FL
Florida State University, FL
Fort Hays State University, KS
George Fox University, OR
Georgia Southern University, GA
Grand Valley State University, MI
Harding University, AR
Hofstra University, NY
Howard University, DC
Huntington University, IN
Husson University, ME
Ithaca College, NY
James Madison University, VA
Kansas Wesleyan University, KS
Kean University, NJ
Keene State College, NH
Kent State University, OH
Lafayette College, PA

Liberty University, VA
Lindenwood University, MO
Long Island University–LIU Brooklyn, NY
Long Island University–LIU Post, NY
Loyola Marymount University, CA
Massachusetts College of Liberal Arts, MA
Milligan College, TN
Minnesota State University Moorhead, MN
Minot State University, ND
Mississippi State University, MS
Missouri Western State University, MO
Montana State University, MT
Montclair State University, NJ
Morningside College, IA
Muhlenberg College, PA
New Mexico State University, NM
North Central College, IL
Northwestern State University of Louisiana, LA
Northwest Missouri State University, MO
Ohio University, OH
Ohio University–Chillicothe, OH
Ohio University–Eastern, OH
Ohio University–Lancaster, OH
Ohio University–Southern Campus, OH
Ohio University–Zanesville, OH
Old Dominion University, VA
Oral Roberts University, OK
Point Park University, PA
Purchase College, State University of New York, NY
Rhode Island College, RI
Ringling College of Art and Design, FL
Rochester Institute of Technology, NY
Sacred Heart University, CT
St. John's University, NY
Sam Houston State University, TX
San Diego State University, CA
Savannah College of Art and Design, GA
Sonoma State University, CA
Southeastern University, FL
Southern Illinois University Carbondale, IL
Southwestern College, KS
Sterling College, KS
Stony Brook University, State University of New York, NY
Texas Christian University, TX
Texas Lutheran University, TX
Texas Woman's University, TX
Towson University, MD
Trevecca Nazarene University, TN
Union University, TN
The University of Alabama, AL
University of California, Irvine, CA
University of California, San Diego, CA
University of California, Santa Cruz, CA
University of Central Florida, FL
University of Colorado Boulder, CO
University of Colorado Denver, CO
University of Hartford, CT
The University of Kansas, KS
University of Kentucky, KY
University of La Verne, CA
University of Maryland, Baltimore County, MD
University of Memphis, TN
University of Michigan, MI
University of Michigan–Dearborn, MI
University of Mississippi, MS
University of Missouri, MO
University of Montevallo, AL
University of Nebraska–Lincoln, NE
University of Nevada, Las Vegas, NV
The University of North Carolina at Greensboro, NC

University of North Carolina School of the Arts, NC
The University of North Carolina Wilmington, NC
University of Oklahoma, OK
University of Pittsburgh at Bradford, PA
University of South Florida, FL
The University of Tennessee at Chattanooga, TN
The University of Tennessee at Martin, TN
The University of Toledo, OH
University of Utah, UT
University of Wisconsin–Whitewater, WI
University of Wyoming, WY
Virginia Polytechnic Institute and State University, VA
Wartburg College, IA
Washburn University, KS
Washington State University, WA
Western Illinois University, IL
Western Kentucky University, KY
Western Washington University, WA
Westminster College, PA
West Texas A&M University, TX
Wheaton College, IL
Wright State University, OH
Wright State University–Lake Campus, OH

Creative Writing

Arkansas Tech University, AR
Auburn University, AL
Augustana College, IL
Augustana University, SD
Austin Peay State University, TN
Belhaven University, MS
Belmont University, TN
Bemidji State University, MN
Binghamton University, State University of New York, NY
Bloomfield College, NJ
Bowling Green State University, OH
Brenau University, GA
Brescia University, KY
Bucknell University, PA
California Institute of the Arts, CA
California Lutheran University, CA
California Polytechnic State University, San Luis Obispo, CA
California State University, Chico, CA
Calumet College of Saint Joseph, IN
Calvin College, MI
Cameron University, OK
Campbell University, NC
Carroll College, MT
Case Western Reserve University, OH
Central College, IA
Central Michigan University, MI
Chapman University, CA
City College of the City University of New York, NY
Cleveland State University, OH
Coe College, IA
The College at Brockport, State University of New York, NY
The College of New Rochelle, NY
College of Staten Island of the City University of New York, NY
Colorado Mesa University, CO
Colorado State University, CO
Columbia College, MO
Davidson College, NC
Delta State University, MS
Dickinson State University, ND
Drury University, MO
Eastern Illinois University, IL

Eastern Michigan University, MI
Eastern Washington University, WA
Eckerd College, FL
Edgewood College, WI
Emmanuel College, GA
Emporia State University, KS
Fairmont State University, WV
Flagler College, FL
Florida Agricultural and Mechanical
     University, FL
Fort Hays State University, KS
Frostburg State University, MD
Furman University, SC
Goddard College, VT
Graceland University, IA
Grove City College, PA
Hamline University, MN
Hampshire College, MA
Hardin-Simmons University, TX
Hobart and William Smith Colleges, NY
Hollins University, VA
Hope College, MI
Huntington University, IN
Kent State University, OH
Kentucky Wesleyan College, KY
Kenyon College, OH
Knox College, IL
Lafayette College, PA
Lewis-Clark State College, ID
Long Island University–LIU Brooklyn, NY
Long Island University–LIU Post, NY
Louisiana Tech University, LA
Loyola Marymount University, CA
Lycoming College, PA
Malone University, OH
Manhattanville College, NY
Meredith College, NC
Michigan State University, MI
Middle Tennessee State University, TN
Midwestern State University, TX
Millikin University, IL
Minnesota State University Moorhead, MN
Mississippi State University, MS
Missouri Western State University, MO
Molloy College, NY
Morningside College, IA
Mount Mercy University, IA
New England College, NH
New Mexico State University, NM
Northeastern Illinois University, IL
Northern Illinois University, IL
Northland College, WI
Northwestern State University of
     Louisiana, LA
Ohio Northern University, OH
The Ohio State University, OH
Ohio University, OH
Ohio University–Chillicothe, OH
Ohio University–Eastern, OH
Ohio University–Lancaster, OH
Ohio University–Southern Campus, OH
Ohio University–Zanesville, OH
Oklahoma State University, OK
Old Dominion University, VA
Plymouth State University, NH
Purchase College, State University of New
     York, NY
Rockhurst University, MO
Sacred Heart University, CT
St. John's University, NY
Saint Mary-of-the-Woods College, IN
St. Thomas Aquinas College, NY
San Diego State University, CA
Savannah College of Art and Design, GA
Siena College, NY
Sonoma State University, CA

Southern Illinois University Carbondale, IL
Southern Oregon University, OR
State University of New York College at
     Geneseo, NY
Sterling College, KS
Stockton University, NJ
Susquehanna University, PA
Texas Christian University, TX
Texas Wesleyan University, TX
The University of Akron, OH
The University of Alabama, AL
University of California, Irvine, CA
University of California, Riverside, CA
University of California, Santa Cruz, CA
University of Colorado Boulder, CO
University of Hartford, CT
University of Houston, TX
University of Idaho, ID
University of Illinois at Chicago, IL
The University of Kansas, KS
University of Kentucky, KY
University of Louisiana at Monroe, LA
University of Louisville, KY
University of Maine, ME
University of Maryland,
     Baltimore County, MD
University of Memphis, TN
University of Michigan, MI
University of Michigan–Dearborn, MI
University of Mississippi, MS
University of Missouri, MO
University of Montana, MT
University of Montevallo, AL
University of Nebraska at Omaha, NE
University of Nevada, Las Vegas, NV
The University of North Carolina
     Wilmington, NC
University of Oregon, OR
University of Pittsburgh at Bradford, PA
University of Redlands, CA
The University of South Dakota, SD
University of Southern Indiana, IN
University of South Florida, FL
The University of Tampa, FL
The University of Tennessee at Martin, TN
The University of Texas at San Antonio, TX
The University of Toledo, OH
University of Utah, UT
The University of Virginia's College
     at Wise, VA
University of Wisconsin–Stevens Point, WI
University of Wisconsin–Whitewater, WI
University of Wyoming, WY
Ursinus College, PA
Virginia Polytechnic Institute and State
     University, VA
Wabash College, IN
Washington College, MD
Washington State University, WA
Washington University in St. Louis, MO
Wayne State College, NE
Webster University, MO
Western Illinois University, IL
Western Washington University, WA
West Texas A&M University, TX
West Virginia Wesleyan College, WV
Wheaton College, IL
Whitworth University, WA
Wichita State University, KS
Wright State University, OH
Wright State University–Lake Campus, OH
Youngstown State University, OH

Dance
Adelphi University, NY
Alma College, MI

Arizona State University at the Tempe
     campus, AZ
Augustana University, SD
Baker University, KS
Ball State University, IN
Belhaven University, MS
Belmont University, TN
Benedictine College, KS
Binghamton University, State University of
     New York, NY
Boise State University, ID
Bowling Green State University, OH
Brenau University, GA
Bucknell University, PA
Butler University, IN
California Institute of the Arts, CA
California Polytechnic State University, San
     Luis Obispo, CA
California State University, Bakersfield, CA
California State University, Chico, CA
California State University, Fullerton, CA
Case Western Reserve University, OH
Cedar Crest College, PA
Centenary College of Louisiana, LA
Central Michigan University, MI
Chapman University, CA
Cleveland State University, OH
The College at Brockport, State University
     of New York, NY
College of Staten Island of the City
     University of New York, NY
The College of Wooster, OH
Colorado Mesa University, CO
Colorado State University, CO
Columbus State University, GA
Concordia University, Nebraska, NE
Creighton University, NE
Culver-Stockton College, MO
DeSales University, PA
Dominican University of California, CA
Drexel University, PA
Duquesne University, PA
East Carolina University, NC
Eastern Michigan University, MI
Eastern University, PA
Emmanuel College, GA
Florida Agricultural and Mechanical
     University, FL
Florida International University, FL
Florida State University, FL
Fordham University, NY
Fort Hays State University, KS
Friends University, KS
Georgian Court University, NJ
Goddard College, VT
Goucher College, MD
Graceland University, IA
Grambling State University, LA
Grand Valley State University, MI
Grand View University, IA
Gustavus Adolphus College, MN
Hawai`i Pacific University, HI
Hendrix College, AR
Hobart and William Smith Colleges, NY
Hofstra University, NY
Hollins University, VA
Hope College, MI
Howard University, DC
Huntingdon College, AL
Idaho State University, ID
Indiana University of Pennsylvania, PA
Ithaca College, NY
James Madison University, VA
The Juilliard School, NY
Kansas Wesleyan University, KS
Kean University, NJ

Keene State College, NH
Kennesaw State University, GA
Kent State University, OH
Knox College, IL
Kutztown University of Pennsylvania, PA
Lafayette College, PA
Lake Erie College, OH
Lees-McRae College, NC
Lindenwood University, MO
Long Island University–LIU Brooklyn, NY
Long Island University–LIU Post, NY
Loyola Marymount University, CA
Manhattanville College, NY
Marygrove College, MI
Marymount Manhattan College, NY
McKendree University, IL
Messiah College, PA
Methodist University, NC
Middle Tennessee State University, TN
Milligan College, TN
Millikin University, IL
Mississippi State University, MS
Missouri Western State University, MO
Montana State University, MT
Montclair State University, NJ
Morningside College, IA
Muhlenberg College, PA
Murray State University, KY
New Mexico State University, NM
Nicholls State University, LA
Northeastern Illinois University, IL
Northeastern State University, OK
Northern Illinois University, IL
Northwestern College, IA
Northwestern State University of
    Louisiana, LA
Northwest Missouri State University, MO
Ohio Northern University, OH
The Ohio State University, OH
Ohio University, OH
Ohio University–Chillicothe, OH
Ohio University–Eastern, OH
Ohio University–Lancaster, OH
Ohio University–Southern Campus, OH
Ohio University–Zanesville, OH
Ohio Wesleyan University, OH
Oklahoma City University, OK
Old Dominion University, VA
Palm Beach Atlantic University, FL
Plymouth State University, NH
Point Park University, PA
Purchase College, State University of New
    York, NY
Rhode Island College, RI
Robert Morris University Illinois, IL
Rockford University, IL
Rogers State University, OK
Sacred Heart University, CT
St. Ambrose University, IA
St. Gregory's University, OK
St. John's University, NY
Saint Mary-of-the-Woods College, IN
St. Olaf College, MN
Sam Houston State University, TX
San Diego State University, CA
Santa Clara University, CA
Savannah College of Art and Design, GA
Seton Hill University, PA
Shenandoah University, VA
Slippery Rock University of
    Pennsylvania, PA
Sonoma State University, CA
Southeastern Oklahoma State
    University, OK
Southeast Missouri State University, MO

Southern Arkansas University–
    Magnolia, AR
Southern Illinois University Carbondale, IL
Southern Illinois University
    Edwardsville, IL
Southwestern College, KS
State University of New York at
    Fredonia, NY
State University of New York College at
    Geneseo, NY
State University of New York College at
    Potsdam, NY
Stephens College, MO
Stockton University, NJ
Temple University, PA
Texas A&M International University, TX
Texas Christian University, TX
Texas State University, TX
Texas Tech University, TX
Texas Wesleyan University, TX
Texas Woman's University, TX
Towson University, MD
Trine University, IN
The University of Akron, OH
The University of Alabama, AL
University of Alaska Anchorage, AK
The University of Arizona, AZ
University of California, Irvine, CA
University of California, Riverside, CA
University of California, San Diego, CA
University of Colorado Boulder, CO
University of Dubuque, IA
University of Florida, FL
University of Great Falls, MT
University of Hartford, CT
University of Houston, TX
University of Idaho, ID
University of Illinois at Urbana–
    Champaign, IL
The University of Kansas, KS
University of Kentucky, KY
University of Louisville, KY
University of Maine, ME
University of Maryland, Baltimore
    County, MD
University of Maryland, College Park, MD
University of Mary Washington, VA
University of Massachusetts Amherst, MA
University of Memphis, TN
University of Michigan, MI
University of Missouri–St. Louis, MO
University of Montana, MT
University of Nebraska–Lincoln, NE
University of Nevada, Las Vegas, NV
University of New Hampshire, NH
University of North Alabama, AL
University of North Carolina at
    Asheville, NC
The University of North Carolina at
    Charlotte, NC
The University of North Carolina at
    Greensboro, NC
University of North Carolina School of the
    Arts, NC
University of Northern Colorado, CO
University of Oklahoma, OK
University of Oregon, OR
University of Richmond, VA
University of South Carolina, SC
University of Southern Mississippi, MS
University of South Florida, FL
The University of Tampa, FL
The University of Texas of the Permian
    Basin, TX

The University of Texas Rio
    Grande Valley, TX
University of Utah, UT
The University of West Alabama, AL
University of Wisconsin–Green Bay, WI
University of Wisconsin–Stevens Point, WI
University of Wyoming, WY
Ursinus College, PA
Virginia Commonwealth University, VA
Virginia State University, VA
Wayne State University, MI
Western Illinois University, IL
Western Kentucky University, KY
Western Michigan University, MI
Western Oregon University, OR
Western Washington University, WA
Westmont College, CA
West Texas A&M University, TX
West Virginia Wesleyan College, WV
Wichita State University, KS
Widener University, PA
William Jewell College, MO
Winthrop University, SC
Wittenberg University, OH
Wright State University, OH
Wright State University–Lake Campus, OH

Debating
Abilene Christian University, TX
Alderson Broaddus University, WV
Augustana College, IL
Austin Peay State University, TN
Baker University, KS
Ball State University, IN
Baylor University, TX
Berry College, GA
Bethany Lutheran College, MN
Bethel College, KS
Bethel University, MN
Boise State University, ID
Bowling Green State University, OH
California Baptist University, CA
California Polytechnic State University, San
    Luis Obispo, CA
California State University, Chico, CA
Cameron University, OK
Carroll College, MT
Carson-Newman University, TN
Cedarville University, OH
Clarion University of Pennsylvania, PA
The College of Idaho, ID
College of Saint Mary, NE
College of Staten Island of the City
    University of New York, NY
Concordia College, MN
Concordia University Irvine, CA
Concordia University, Nebraska, NE
Culver-Stockton College, MO
Doane University, NE
Dordt College, IA
Drury University, MO
Eastern Illinois University, IL
Eastern Michigan University, MI
Emory University, GA
Emporia State University, KS
Evangel University, MO
Fairmont State University, WV
Ferris State University, MI
George Fox University, OR
Gonzaga University, WA
Gustavus Adolphus College, MN
Harding University, AR
Hawai`i Pacific University, HI
Hillsdale College, MI
Idaho State University, ID

Kansas Wesleyan University, KS
Lewis & Clark College, OR
Lewis-Clark State College, ID
Liberty University, VA
Lindenwood University, MO
Linfield College, OR
Louisiana Tech University, LA
Loyola University Chicago, IL
Malone University, OH
Marist College, NY
McKendree University, IL
Mercer University, GA
Methodist University, NC
Michigan State University, MI
Middle Tennessee State University, TN
Mississippi State University, MS
Monmouth College, IL
Muskingum University, OH
North Central College, IL
Northeastern State University, OK
Northern Illinois University, IL
Northwest Missouri State University, MO
Northwest Nazarene University, ID
Northwest University, WA
Ohio University, OH
Ohio University–Chillicothe, OH
Ohio University–Eastern, OH
Ohio University–Lancaster, OH
Ohio University–Southern Campus, OH
Ohio University–Zanesville, OH
Oklahoma City University, OK
Oklahoma Panhandle State University, OK
Pacific University, OR
Patrick Henry College, VA
Piedmont College, GA
Point Loma Nazarene University, CA
Regis University, CO
St. John's University, NY
Saint Joseph's University, PA
Samford University, AL
San Diego State University, CA
Santa Clara University, CA
Savannah College of Art and Design, GA
Simpson College, IA
Southeastern Oklahoma State
    University, OK
Southern Illinois University Carbondale, IL
Southwest Baptist University, MO
Sterling College, KS
Tennessee Technological University, TN
Texas Wesleyan University, TX
Thomas University, GA
Towson University, MD
Trinity University, TX
Truman State University, MO
Union University, TN
The University of Akron, OH
The University of Alabama, AL
University of Alaska Anchorage, AK
University of Denver, CO
University of Hartford, CT
University of Indianapolis, IN
The University of Kansas, KS
University of Kentucky, KY
University of Louisiana at Monroe, LA
University of Louisville, KY
University of Michigan–Dearborn, MI
University of Mississippi, MS
University of Missouri–Kansas City, MO
University of Nebraska at Kearney, NE
University of Nebraska at Omaha, NE
University of Nevada, Las Vegas, NV
University of Northern Iowa, IA
University of Oklahoma, OK
University of Oregon, OR
University of Puget Sound, WA

University of Redlands, CA
University of South Carolina, SC
The University of South Dakota, SD
University of Southern California, CA
The University of Texas at San Antonio, TX
University of the Pacific, CA
University of Vermont, VT
University of West Georgia, GA
University of Wisconsin–Eau Claire, WI
University of Wyoming, WY
Vanguard University of
    Southern California, CA
Washburn University, KS
Wayne State University, MI
Webster University, MO
Western Illinois University, IL
Western Kentucky University, KY
West Texas A&M University, TX
West Virginia University, WV
Wheaton College, IL
Whitman College, WA
Whitworth University, WA
William Jewell College, MO
Winona State University, MN

Journalism/Publications

Abilene Christian University, TX
Alaska Pacific University, AK
Albright College, PA
Alderson Broaddus University, WV
Arkansas Tech University, AR
Auburn University, AL
Augustana University, SD
Austin Peay State University, TN
Averett University, VA
Baker University, KS
Ball State University, IN
Baylor University, TX
Belhaven University, MS
Belmont University, TN
Bemidji State University, MN
Benedictine College, KS
Berry College, GA
Bethany Lutheran College, MN
Binghamton University, State University of
    New York, NY
Biola University, CA
Bloomfield College, NJ
Boise State University, ID
Bowling Green State University, OH
Brenau University, GA
Brescia University, KY
Bryan College, TN
Butler University, IN
California Baptist University, CA
California Lutheran University, CA
California Polytechnic State University, San
    Luis Obispo, CA
California State University, Chico, CA
California State University, Fresno, CA
California State University, Fullerton, CA
California State University, Los Angeles, CA
California State University, Northridge, CA
California State University,
    San Bernardino, CA
Calvin College, MI
Cameron University, OK
Campbellsville University, KY
Campbell University, NC
Carroll University, WI
Carson-Newman University, TN
Central Michigan University, MI
The Citadel, The Military College of South
    Carolina, SC
Cleveland State University, OH

The College at Brockport, State University
    of New York, NY
The College of New Rochelle, NY
College of Staten Island of the City
    University of New York, NY
Colorado Mesa University, CO
Concord University, WV
Cornerstone University, MI
Delta State University, MS
Dickinson State University, ND
Dordt College, IA
Eastern Illinois University, IL
Eastern Washington University, WA
Elon University, NC
Emmanuel College, GA
Fairmont State University, WV
Faulkner University, AL
Ferris State University, MI
Florida Agricultural and Mechanical
    University, FL
Florida International University, FL
Fort Hays State University, KS
Francis Marion University, SC
Franklin College, IN
Frostburg State University, MD
Georgia College & State University, GA
Glenville State College, WV
Grand Valley State University, MI
Hamline University, MN
Harding University, AR
Hardin-Simmons University, TX
Hawai`i Pacific University, HI
Hillsdale College, MI
Hofstra University, NY
Howard University, DC
Huntington University, IN
Husson University, ME
Idaho State University, ID
Indiana University of Pennsylvania, PA
Iowa State University of Science and
    Technology, IA
Ithaca College, NY
Jacksonville State University, AL
James Madison University, VA
John Brown University, AR
Kansas Wesleyan University, KS
Kent State University, OH
Kent State University at Stark, OH
Lees-McRae College, NC
Lehigh University, PA
Liberty University, VA
Lincoln University, MO
Lindenwood University, MO
Lipscomb University, TN
Lock Haven University of Pennsylvania, PA
Long Island University–LIU Brooklyn, NY
Long Island University–LIU Post, NY
Louisiana State University and Agricultural
    & Mechanical College, LA
Louisiana Tech University, LA
Loyola Marymount University, CA
Loyola University Chicago, IL
Lubbock Christian University, TX
Malone University, OH
Mansfield University of Pennsylvania, PA
Massachusetts College of Liberal Arts, MA
Michigan State University, MI
Middle Georgia State University, GA
Middle Tennessee State University, TN
Midwestern State University, TX
Mississippi State University, MS
Missouri Western State University, MO
Morehead State University, KY
Morningside College, IA
Murray State University, KY
Muskingum University, OH

New Jersey Institute of Technology, NJ
New Mexico State University, NM
North Central College, IL
Northeastern Illinois University, IL
Northeastern State University, OK
Northern Illinois University, IL
Northwest Missouri State University, MO
Oglethorpe University, GA
Ohio Northern University, OH
The Ohio State University, OH
Ohio University, OH
Ohio University–Chillicothe, OH
Ohio University–Eastern, OH
Ohio University–Lancaster, OH
Ohio University–Southern Campus, OH
Ohio University–Zanesville, OH
Ohio Valley University, WV
Oklahoma Christian University, OK
Oklahoma State University, OK
Old Dominion University, VA
Olivet College, MI
Oral Roberts University, OK
Ouachita Baptist University, AR
Pacific University, OR
Patrick Henry College, VA
Piedmont College, GA
Rhode Island College, RI
Robert Morris University Illinois, IL
St. Ambrose University, IA
St. Bonaventure University, NY
St. Edward's University, TX
St. John's University, NY
Saint Mary-of-the-Woods College, IN
Samford University, AL
Sam Houston State University, TX
San Diego State University, CA
Savannah College of Art and Design, GA
Schreiner University, TX
Siena College, NY
Sonoma State University, CA
Southeastern University, FL
Southern Adventist University, TN
Southern Illinois University Carbondale, IL
Southern Oregon University, OR
Southwestern College, KS
State University of New York at
    Plattsburgh, NY
State University of New York College at
    Geneseo, NY
Stephen F. Austin State University, TX
Sterling College, KS
Stevens Institute of Technology, NJ
Stockton University, NJ
Stony Brook University, State University of
    New York, NY
Suffolk University, MA
Texas A&M University, TX
Texas A&M University–Commerce, TX
Texas Christian University, TX
Texas Lutheran University, TX
Texas State University, TX
Texas Tech University, TX
Texas Wesleyan University, TX
Texas Woman's University, TX
Trinity Christian College, IL
Union University, TN
The University of Akron, OH
The University of Alabama, AL
University of Arkansas, AR
University of California, San Diego, CA
University of Central Oklahoma, OK
University of Colorado Boulder, CO
University of Florida, FL
University of Hartford, CT
University of Houston, TX

University of Idaho, ID
University of Illinois at Urbana–
    Champaign, IL
The University of Kansas, KS
University of Kentucky, KY
University of La Verne, CA
University of Louisiana at Monroe, LA
University of Maine, ME
University of Mary Washington, VA
University of Massachusetts Amherst, MA
University of Memphis, TN
University of Michigan, MI
University of Michigan–Dearborn, MI
University of Michigan–Flint, MI
University of Mississippi, MS
University of Missouri, MO
University of Montana, MT
University of Montevallo, AL
University of Mount Union, OH
University of Nebraska at Kearney, NE
University of Nebraska at Omaha, NE
University of Nebraska–Lincoln, NE
University of Nevada, Las Vegas, NV
University of Nevada, Reno, NV
University of North Alabama, AL
The University of North Carolina at Chapel
    Hill, NC
University of Northern Colorado, CO
University of Oklahoma, OK
University of Oregon, OR
University of Pittsburgh at Johnstown, PA
University of Rhode Island, RI
University of St. Thomas, MN
University of South Carolina, SC
University of South Carolina Aiken, SC
The University of Tampa, FL
The University of Tennessee at
    Chattanooga, TN
The University of Tennessee at Martin, TN
The University of Texas at Arlington, TX
The University of Texas at El Paso, TX
The University of Texas Rio
    Grande Valley, TX
University of Utah, UT
The University of Virginia's College
    at Wise, VA
University of West Georgia, GA
University of Wisconsin–Eau Claire, WI
University of Wisconsin–Green Bay, WI
University of Wisconsin–Whitewater, WI
University of Wyoming, WY
Utah State University, UT
Valdosta State University, GA
Valley City State University, ND
Virginia Polytechnic Institute and State
    University, VA
Wabash College, IN
Wartburg College, IA
Washburn University, KS
Washington State University, WA
Wayland Baptist University, TX
Wayne State College, NE
Wayne State University, MI
Webber International University, FL
Western Illinois University, IL
Western Kentucky University, KY
Western Washington University, WA
West Texas A&M University, TX
Whitworth University, WA
Wichita State University, KS
William Jewell College, MO
Youngstown State University, OH

Music

Abilene Christian University, TX
Adelphi University, NY
Agnes Scott College, GA
Alabama State University, AL
Alaska Bible College, AK
Alaska Pacific University, AK
Albion College, MI
Albright College, PA
Alcorn State University, MS
Alderson Broaddus University, WV
Allegheny Wesleyan College, OH
Alma College, MI
Alverno College, WI
Anderson University, SC
Andrews University, MI
Arizona State University at the Tempe
    campus, AZ
Arkansas Tech University, AR
Armstrong State University, GA
Asbury University, KY
Auburn University, AL
Augsburg College, MN
Augustana College, IL
Augustana University, SD
Augusta University, GA
Aurora University, IL
Austin College, TX
Austin Peay State University, TN
Ave Maria University, FL
Averett University, VA
Baker University, KS
Baldwin Wallace University, OH
Ball State University, IN
The Baptist College of Florida, FL
Barclay College, KS
Barton College, NC
Baylor University, TX
Belhaven University, MS
Bellarmine University, KY
Belmont University, TN
Beloit College, WI
Bemidji State University, MN
Benedictine College, KS
Benedictine University, IL
Berklee College of Music, MA
Berry College, GA
Bethany College, WV
Bethany Lutheran College, MN
Bethel College, IN
Bethel College, KS
Bethel University, MN
Binghamton University, State University of
    New York, NY
Biola University, CA
Black Hills State University, SD
Bluefield College, VA
Blue Mountain College, MS
Bluffton University, OH
Boise State University, ID
Boston University, MA
Bowling Green State University, OH
Bradley University, IL
Brenau University, GA
Brescia University, KY
Brevard College, NC
Briar Cliff University, IA
Bridgewater College, VA
Brigham Young University, UT
Bryan College, TN
Bucknell University, PA
Buena Vista University, IA
Butler University, IN
Cairn University, PA
Caldwell University, NJ

California Baptist University, CA
California Institute of the Arts, CA
California Lutheran University, CA
California Polytechnic State University, San
    Luis Obispo, CA
California State University, Bakersfield, CA
California State University, Chico, CA
California State University, East Bay, CA
California State University, Fresno, CA
California State University, Fullerton, CA
California State University, Los Angeles, CA
California State University, Northridge, CA
California State University,
    San Bernardino, CA
Calvin College, MI
Cameron University, OK
Campbellsville University, KY
Campbell University, NC
Canisius College, NY
Capital University, OH
Cardinal Stritch University, WI
Carleton College, MN
Carroll College, MT
Carroll University, WI
Carson-Newman University, TN
Case Western Reserve University, OH
Catawba College, NC
The Catholic University of America, DC
Cedarville University, OH
Centenary College of Louisiana, LA
Central College, IA
Central Methodist University, MO
Central Michigan University, MI
Central Washington University, WA
Centre College, KY
Chapman University, CA
Chatham University, PA
Chestnut Hill College, PA
Chowan University, NC
Christopher Newport University, VA
Cincinnati Christian University, OH
The Citadel, The Military College of South
    Carolina, SC
City College of the City
    University of New York, NY
Claflin University, SC
Clarion University of Pennsylvania, PA
Clark Atlanta University, GA
Clarke University, IA
Clarks Summit University, PA
Clear Creek Baptist Bible College, KY
Cleveland Institute of Music, OH
Cleveland State University, OH
Coastal Carolina University, SC
Coe College, IA
The Colburn School
    Conservatory of Music, CA
The College at Brockport, State University
    of New York, NY
College of Charleston, SC
The College of Idaho, ID
The College of New Jersey, NJ
The College of New Rochelle, NY
College of Saint Benedict, MN
College of Saint Mary, NE
The College of Saint Rose, NY
The College of St. Scholastica, MN
College of Staten Island of the City
    University of New York, NY
College of the Holy Cross, MA
The College of William and Mary, VA
The College of Wooster, OH
Colorado Mesa University, CO
Colorado State University, CO
Columbia College, MO
Columbus State University, GA

Concordia College, MN
Concordia University Ann Arbor, MI
Concordia University Chicago, IL
Concordia University Irvine, CA
Concordia University, Nebraska, NE
Concordia University, St. Paul, MN
Concordia University Texas, TX
Concordia University Wisconsin, WI
Concord University, WV
Converse College, SC
Corban University, OR
Cornell College, IA
Cornerstone University, MI
Covenant College, GA
Creighton University, NE
Crown College, MN
Culver-Stockton College, MO
Dakota Wesleyan University, SD
Dallas Baptist University, TX
Davidson College, NC
Davis College, NY
Defiance College, OH
Delta State University, MS
DePaul University, IL
Dickinson State University, ND
Doane University, NE
Dominican University of California, CA
Dordt College, IA
Drake University, IA
Drew University, NJ
Drexel University, PA
Drury University, MO
Duquesne University, PA
East Carolina University, NC
East Central University, OK
Eastern Connecticut State University, CT
Eastern Illinois University, IL
Eastern Kentucky University, KY
Eastern Mennonite University, VA
Eastern Michigan University, MI
Eastern University, PA
Eastern Washington University, WA
East Stroudsburg University of
    Pennsylvania, PA
East Texas Baptist University, TX
Eckerd College, FL
Edgewood College, WI
Elizabeth City State University, NC
Elizabethtown College, PA
Elmhurst College, IL
Elon University, NC
Emmanuel College, GA
Emory & Henry College, VA
Emory University, GA
Emporia State University, KS
Endicott College, MA
Eureka College, IL
Evangel University, MO
Fairmont State University, WV
Faulkner University, AL
Ferris State University, MI
Florida Agricultural and Mechanical
    University, FL
Florida Atlantic University, FL
Florida College, FL
Florida Gulf Coast University, FL
Florida Institute of Technology, FL
Florida International University, FL
Florida Southern College, FL
Florida State University, FL
Fordham University, NY
Fort Hays State University, KS
Fort Lewis College, CO
Francis Marion University, SC
Franklin & Marshall College, PA
Franklin College, IN

Fresno Pacific University, CA
Friends University, KS
Frostburg State University, MD
Furman University, SC
Gannon University, PA
Gardner-Webb University, NC
Geneva College, PA
George Fox University, OR
Georgia College & State University, GA
Georgia Southern University, GA
Georgia Southwestern State University, GA
Gettysburg College, PA
Glenville State College, WV
Gonzaga University, WA
Gordon College, MA
Goshen College, IN
Goucher College, MD
Graceland University, IA
Grambling State University, LA
Grand Valley State University, MI
Grand View University, IA
Greenville College, IL
Grove City College, PA
Guilford College, NC
Gustavus Adolphus College, MN
Hamline University, MN
Hampden-Sydney College, VA
Hampton University, VA
Harding University, AR
Hardin-Simmons University, TX
Harris-Stowe State University, MO
Hartwick College, NY
Hawai`i Pacific University, HI
Heidelberg University, OH
Hendrix College, AR
High Point University, NC
Hillsdale College, MI
Hobart and William Smith Colleges, NY
Hofstra University, NY
Hollins University, VA
Hood College, MD
Hope College, MI
Hope International University, CA
Houghton College, NY
Houston Baptist University, TX
Howard Payne University, TX
Howard University, DC
Huntingdon College, AL
Huntington University, IN
Huston-Tillotson University, TX
Idaho State University, ID
Illinois College, IL
Illinois Wesleyan University, IL
Indiana State University, IN
Indiana University of Pennsylvania, PA
Indiana University–Purdue University Fort
    Wayne, IN
Indiana Wesleyan University, IN
Iona College, NY
Iowa State University of Science and
    Technology, IA
Iowa Wesleyan University, IA
Ithaca College, NY
Jackson State University, MS
Jacksonville State University, AL
Jacksonville University, FL
James Madison University, VA
John Brown University, AR
Johnson C. Smith University, NC
John Wesley University, NC
Judson College, AL
Judson University, IL
The Juilliard School, NY
Juniata College, PA
Kalamazoo College, MI
Kansas Wesleyan University, KS

Kean University, NJ
Keene State College, NH
Kennesaw State University, GA
Kent State University, OH
Kent State University at Stark, OH
Kentucky Mountain Bible College, KY
Kentucky State University, KY
Kentucky Wesleyan College, KY
Kenyon College, OH
King University, TN
Knox College, IL
Kutztown University of Pennsylvania, PA
Kuyper College, MI
Lafayette College, PA
LaGrange College, GA
Lake Erie College, OH
Lancaster Bible College, PA
Langston University, OK
Lawrence University, WI
Lebanon Valley College, PA
Lee University, TN
Lehigh University, PA
Le Moyne College, NY
Lenoir-Rhyne University, NC
Lewis & Clark College, OR
Lewis-Clark State College, ID
Lewis University, IL
Liberty University, VA
Lincoln Memorial University, TN
Lincoln University, MO
Lincoln University, PA
Lindenwood University, MO
Lindsey Wilson College, KY
Linfield College, OR
Lipscomb University, TN
Lock Haven University of Pennsylvania, PA
Long Island University–LIU Brooklyn, NY
Long Island University–LIU Post, NY
Longwood University, VA
Loras College, IA
Louisiana State University and Agricultural
    & Mechanical College, LA
Louisiana Tech University, LA
Loyola Marymount University, CA
Loyola University Chicago, IL
Lubbock Christian University, TX
Luther College, IA
Lycoming College, PA
Lynchburg College, VA
Lynn University, FL
Lyon College, AR
Malone University, OH
Manchester University, IN
Manhattan College, NY
Manhattanville College, NY
Mansfield University of Pennsylvania, PA
Maranatha Baptist University, WI
Marian University, WI
Marietta College, OH
Marist College, NY
Martin Luther College, MN
Marygrove College, MI
Maryville College, TN
Maryville University of Saint Louis, MO
Marywood University, PA
Massachusetts College of Liberal Arts, MA
The Master's University, CA
Mayville State University, ND
McKendree University, IL
McNally Smith College of Music, MN
McPherson College, KS
Mercer University, GA
Meredith College, NC
Messiah College, PA
Methodist University, NC

Metropolitan State University of Denver, CO
Miami University, OH
Michigan State University, MI
Middle Tennessee State University, TN
Midway University, KY
Midwestern State University, TX
Millersville University of Pennsylvania, PA
Milligan College, TN
Millikin University, IL
Millsaps College, MS
Mills College, CA
Minnesota State University Moorhead, MN
Minot State University, ND
Mississippi State University, MS
Missouri Baptist University, MO
Missouri University of Science and
    Technology, MO
Missouri Western State University, MO
Molloy College, NY
Monmouth College, IL
Montana State University, MT
Montana State University Billings, MT
Montclair State University, NJ
Montreat College, NC
Moravian College, PA
Morehead State University, KY
Morehouse College, GA
Morningside College, IA
Mount Aloysius College, PA
Mount Marty College, SD
Mount Mary University, WI
Mount Mercy University, IA
Mount St. Joseph University, OH
Mount Saint Mary's University, CA
Mount Vernon Nazarene University, OH
Muhlenberg College, PA
Murray State University, KY
Muskingum University, OH
Nazareth College of Rochester, NY
Newberry College, SC
New England Conservatory of Music, MA
New Mexico Highlands University, NM
New Mexico State University, NM
Nicholls State University, LA
North Carolina Agricultural and Technical
    State University, NC
North Central College, IL
Northeastern Illinois University, IL
Northeastern State University, OK
Northern Arizona University, AZ
Northern Illinois University, IL
Northern Kentucky University, KY
Northern Michigan University, MI
Northern State University, SD
Northland College, WI
Northwest Christian University, OR
Northwestern College, IA
Northwestern State University of
    Louisiana, LA
Northwestern University, IL
Northwest Missouri State University, MO
Northwest Nazarene University, ID
Northwest University, WA
Oakland City University, IN
Oberlin College, OH
Occidental College, CA
Oglethorpe University, GA
Ohio Northern University, OH
The Ohio State University, OH
Ohio University, OH
Ohio University–Chillicothe, OH
Ohio University–Eastern, OH
Ohio University–Lancaster, OH
Ohio University–Southern Campus, OH
Ohio University–Zanesville, OH

Ohio Valley University, WV
Ohio Wesleyan University, OH
Oklahoma Baptist University, OK
Oklahoma Christian University, OK
Oklahoma City University, OK
Oklahoma Panhandle State University, OK
Oklahoma State University, OK
Oklahoma Wesleyan University, OK
Old Dominion University, VA
Olivet College, MI
Olivet Nazarene University, IL
Oral Roberts University, OK
Otterbein University, OH
Ouachita Baptist University, AR
Pacific Union College, CA
Pacific University, OR
Palm Beach Atlantic University, FL
Patrick Henry College, VA
Paul Quinn College, TX
Peabody Conservatory of The Johns Hopkins
    University, MD
Philander Smith College, AR
Piedmont College, GA
Pittsburg State University, KS
Plymouth State University, NH
Point Loma Nazarene University, CA
Portland State University, OR
Presbyterian College, SC
Purchase College, State University of New
    York, NY
Purdue University, IN
Queens College of the City University of
    New York, NY
Queens University of Charlotte, NC
Randall University, OK
Regis University, CO
Rhode Island College, RI
Rhodes College, TN
Rice University, TX
Roanoke College, VA
Robert Morris University Illinois, IL
Roberts Wesleyan College, NY
Rockford University, IL
Rockhurst University, MO
Rocky Mountain College, MT
Rogers State University, OK
Rollins College, FL
Rowan University, NJ
Sacred Heart University, CT
Saginaw Valley State University, MI
St. Ambrose University, IA
Saint Augustine's University, NC
St. Bonaventure University, NY
St. Gregory's University, OK
Saint John's University, MN
St. John's University, NY
Saint Louis University, MO
Saint Martin's University, WA
Saint Mary-of-the-Woods College, IN
St. Mary's University, TX
Saint Mary's University of Minnesota, MN
St. Norbert College, WI
St. Olaf College, MN
Salem College, NC
Salisbury University, MD
Samford University, AL
Sam Houston State University, TX
San Diego Christian College, CA
San Diego State University, CA
San Francisco Conservatory of Music, CA
San Jose State University, CA
Santa Clara University, CA
Savannah College of Art and Design, GA
Schreiner University, TX
Seattle University, WA

Seton Hill University, PA
Shasta Bible College, CA
Shenandoah University, VA
Shepherd University, WV
Shippensburg University of
 Pennsylvania, PA
Siena College, NY
Simpson College, IA
Simpson University, CA
Skidmore College, NY
Slippery Rock University of
 Pennsylvania, PA
Sonoma State University, CA
Southeastern Louisiana University, LA
Southeastern Oklahoma State
 University, OK
Southeastern University, FL
Southeast Missouri State University, MO
Southern Adventist University, TN
Southern Arkansas University–
 Magnolia, AR
Southern Illinois University Carbondale, IL
Southern Illinois University
 Edwardsville, IL
Southern New Hampshire University, NH
Southern Oregon University, OR
Southern Utah University, UT
Southwest Baptist University, MO
Southwestern College, KS
Southwestern Oklahoma
 State University, OK
Southwestern University, TX
Spelman College, GA
State University of New York at Fredonia,
 NY
State University of New York at New Paltz,
 NY
State University of New York at Plattsburgh,
 NY
State University of New York College at
 Cortland, NY
State University of New York College at
 Geneseo, NY
State University of New York College at
 Potsdam, NY
Stephen F. Austin State University, TX
Stephens College, MO
Sterling College, KS
Stetson University, FL
Stevens Institute of Technology, NJ
Stockton University, NJ
Stony Brook University, State University of
 New York, NY
Susquehanna University, PA
Sweet Briar College, VA
Syracuse University, NY
Tarleton State University, TX
Taylor University, IN
Temple University, PA
Tennessee State University, TN
Tennessee Technological University, TN
Tennessee Wesleyan University, TN
Texas A&M International University, TX
Texas A&M University–Commerce, TX
Texas Christian University, TX
Texas Lutheran University, TX
Texas State University, TX
Texas Tech University, TX
Texas Wesleyan University, TX
Texas Woman's University, TX
Thiel College, PA
Thomas More College, KY
Thomas University, GA
Tiffin University, OH
Toccoa Falls College, GA
Towson University, MD

Transylvania University, KY
Trevecca Nazarene University, TN
Trine University, IN
Trinity Christian College, IL
Trinity University, TX
Troy University, AL
Truett McConnell University, GA
Truman State University, MO
Tulane University, LA
Tusculum College, TN
Tuskegee University, AL
Union College, KY
Union College, NE
Union University, TN
The University of Akron, OH
The University of Alabama, AL
The University of Alabama at
 Birmingham, AL
The University of Alabama
 in Huntsville, AL
University of Alaska Anchorage, AK
The University of Arizona, AZ
University of Arkansas, AR
University of Arkansas at Little Rock, AR
University of Bridgeport, CT
University of California, Irvine, CA
University of California, Riverside, CA
University of California, San Diego, CA
University of California, Santa Cruz, CA
University of Central Florida, FL
University of Central Oklahoma, OK
University of Colorado Boulder, CO
University of Colorado Denver, CO
University of Dayton, OH
University of Delaware, DE
University of Denver, CO
University of Dubuque, IA
University of Evansville, IN
The University of Findlay, OH
University of Florida, FL
University of Georgia, GA
University of Hartford, CT
University of Houston, TX
University of Idaho, ID
University of Illinois at Chicago, IL
University of Illinois at Urbana–
 Champaign, IL
University of Indianapolis, IN
The University of Iowa, IA
University of Jamestown, ND
The University of Kansas, KS
University of Kentucky, KY
University of La Verne, CA
University of Louisiana at Monroe, LA
University of Louisville, KY
University of Maine, ME
University of Maine at Augusta, ME
University of Mary Hardin-Baylor, TX
University of Maryland,
 Baltimore County, MD
University of Maryland, College Park, MD
University of Mary Washington, VA
University of Massachusetts Amherst, MA
University of Massachusetts Lowell, MA
University of Memphis, TN
University of Miami, FL
University of Michigan, MI
University of Michigan–Flint, MI
University of Minnesota, Morris, MN
University of Mississippi, MS
University of Missouri, MO
University of Missouri–Kansas City, MO
University of Missouri–St. Louis, MO
University of Mobile, AL
University of Montana, MT
University of Montevallo, AL

University of Mount Union, OH
University of Nebraska at Kearney, NE
University of Nebraska at Omaha, NE
University of Nebraska–Lincoln, NE
University of Nevada, Las Vegas, NV
University of Nevada, Reno, NV
University of New Hampshire, NH
University of North Alabama, AL
University of North Carolina at
 Asheville, NC
The University of North Carolina at Chapel
 Hill, NC
The University of North Carolina at
 Charlotte, NC
The University of North Carolina at
 Greensboro, NC
University of North Carolina School of the
 Arts, NC
The University of North Carolina
 Wilmington, NC
University of Northern Colorado, CO
University of Northern Iowa, IA
University of North Florida, FL
University of North Georgia, GA
University of Oklahoma, OK
University of Oregon, OR
University of Pittsburgh at Bradford, PA
University of Portland, OR
University of Puerto Rico in Bayamón, PR
University of Puget Sound, WA
University of Redlands, CA
University of Rhode Island, RI
University of Richmond, VA
University of Rochester, NY
University of St. Francis, IL
University of St. Thomas, MN
University of St. Thomas, TX
University of San Diego, CA
University of Science and Arts of
 Oklahoma, OK
University of Sioux Falls, SD
University of South Carolina, SC
University of South Carolina Aiken, SC
The University of South Dakota, SD
University of Southern California, CA
University of Southern Maine, ME
University of Southern Mississippi, MS
University of South Florida, FL
The University of Tampa, FL
The University of Tennessee at
 Chattanooga, TN
The University of Tennessee at Martin, TN
The University of Texas at Arlington, TX
The University of Texas at Austin, TX
The University of Texas at El Paso, TX
The University of Texas at San Antonio, TX
The University of Texas of the Permian
 Basin, TX
The University of Texas Rio
 Grande Valley, TX
University of the Incarnate Word, TX
University of the Pacific, CA
The University of Toledo, OH
The University of Tulsa, OK
University of Utah, UT
University of Valley Forge, PA
University of Vermont, VT
University of Virginia, VA
The University of Virginia's
 College at Wise, VA
University of Washington, WA
The University of West Alabama, AL
University of West Florida, FL
University of West Georgia, GA
University of Wisconsin–Eau Claire, WI
University of Wisconsin–Green Bay, WI

University of Wisconsin–La Crosse, WI
University of Wisconsin–Parkside, WI
University of Wisconsin–River Falls, WI
University of Wisconsin–Stevens Point, WI
University of Wisconsin–Stout, WI
University of Wisconsin–Whitewater, WI
University of Wyoming, WY
Ursinus College, PA
Utah State University, UT
Valdosta State University, GA
Valley City State University, ND
Valparaiso University, IN
Vanguard University of
    Southern California, CA
Virginia Commonwealth University, VA
Virginia Military Institute, VA
Virginia Polytechnic Institute and State
    University, VA
Virginia State University, VA
Wabash College, IN
Wagner College, NY
Waldorf University, IA
Walla Walla University, WA
Warner Pacific College, OR
Warner University, FL
Wartburg College, IA
Washburn University, KS
Washington College, MD
Washington State University, WA
Wayland Baptist University, TX
Waynesburg University, PA
Wayne State College, NE
Wayne State University, MI
Webber International University, FL
Webster University, MO
Wesleyan College, GA
West Chester University of Pennsylvania, PA
Western Carolina University, NC
Western Illinois University, IL
Western Kentucky University, KY
Western Michigan University, MI
Western New England University, MA
Western Oregon University, OR
Western State Colorado University, CO
Western Washington University, WA
Westminster College, MO
Westminster College, PA
Westmont College, CA
West Texas A&M University, TX
West Virginia University, WV
West Virginia Wesleyan College, WV
Wheaton College, IL
Wheeling Jesuit University, WV
Whitman College, WA
Whittier College, CA
Whitworth University, WA
Wichita State University, KS
Widener University, PA
William Jessup University, CA
William Jewell College, MO
William Paterson University of
    New Jersey, NJ
Williams Baptist College, AR
Wilson College, PA
Wingate University, NC
Winona State University, MN
Winthrop University, SC
Wisconsin Lutheran College, WI
Wittenberg University, OH
Wofford College, SC
Wright State University, OH
Wright State University–Lake Campus, OH
Xavier University, OH
Xavier University of Louisiana, LA
York College of Pennsylvania, PA

Young Harris College, GA
Youngstown State University, OH

Performing Arts
Adelphi University, NY
Albertus Magnus College, CT
Albion College, MI
Alma College, MI
Anderson University, SC
Auburn University, AL
Augsburg College, MN
Augustana University, SD
Austin Peay State University, TN
Ball State University, IN
Belhaven University, MS
Belmont University, TN
Bemidji State University, MN
Binghamton University, State University of
    New York, NY
Bloomfield College, NJ
Bluefield College, VA
Bluffton University, OH
Boise State University, ID
Bowling Green State University, OH
Brenau University, GA
Bryan College, TN
Bucknell University, PA
Butler University, IN
California Institute of the Arts, CA
California Lutheran University, CA
California Polytechnic State University, San
    Luis Obispo, CA
California State University, Chico, CA
California State University, Fullerton, CA
Calvin College, MI
Cameron University, OK
Capital University, OH
Carroll College, MT
Carroll University, WI
Case Western Reserve University, OH
Cedar Crest College, PA
Centenary College of Louisiana, LA
Central Michigan University, MI
Chapman University, CA
Christian Brothers University, TN
Christopher Newport University, VA
City College of the City
    University of New York, NY
Clemson University, SC
Cleveland State University, OH
Coastal Carolina University, SC
Coe College, IA
College of Charleston, SC
The College of Idaho, ID
College of Staten Island of the City
    University of New York, NY
Colorado Mesa University, CO
Colorado State University, CO
Columbus State University, GA
Concordia University Ann Arbor, MI
Corban University, OR
Cornell College, IA
Creighton University, NE
Davidson College, NC
Delta State University, MS
DeSales University, PA
Doane University, NE
Drew University, NJ
Drexel University, PA
East Carolina University, NC
East Central University, OK
Eastern Connecticut State University, CT
Eastern Illinois University, IL
Eastern Michigan University, MI
Edgewood College, WI

Elizabeth City State University, NC
Elizabethtown College, PA
Elon University, NC
Emerson College, MA
Emmanuel College, GA
Endicott College, MA
Eureka College, IL
Flagler College, FL
Florida Agricultural and Mechanical
    University, FL
Florida Atlantic University, FL
Florida International University, FL
Fort Hays State University, KS
Fort Lewis College, CO
Francis Marion University, SC
Franklin College, IN
Franklin Pierce University, NH
Fresno Pacific University, CA
Friends University, KS
Frostburg State University, MD
Gannon University, PA
Goddard College, VT
Goucher College, MD
Grambling State University, LA
Greenville College, IL
Hardin-Simmons University, TX
Hawai`i Pacific University, HI
Heidelberg University, OH
Hobart and William Smith Colleges, NY
Hofstra University, NY
Houghton College, NY
Howard University, DC
Huntingdon College, AL
Huntington University, IN
Idaho State University, ID
Indiana State University, IN
Indiana University of Pennsylvania, PA
Ithaca College, NY
The Juilliard School, NY
Juniata College, PA
Kalamazoo College, MI
Kansas Wesleyan University, KS
Kean University, NJ
Kennesaw State University, GA
Kent State University, OH
Kent State University at Stark, OH
Kentucky State University, KY
Kentucky Wesleyan College, KY
King University, TN
Lafayette College, PA
Lake Erie College, OH
Lawrence University, WI
Lees-McRae College, NC
Lehigh University, PA
Liberty University, VA
Lincoln University, MO
Lindenwood University, MO
Lock Haven University of Pennsylvania, PA
Long Island University–LIU Brooklyn, NY
Long Island University–LIU Post, NY
Louisiana State University and Agricultural
    & Mechanical College, LA
Louisiana Tech University, LA
Loyola Marymount University, CA
Lubbock Christian University, TX
Manhattanville College, NY
Marietta College, OH
Marymount Manhattan College, NY
Massachusetts College of Liberal Arts, MA
McPherson College, KS
Metropolitan State University of Denver, CO
Michigan State University, MI
Michigan Technological University, MI
Middle Tennessee State University, TN
Minot State University, ND

Mississippi State University, MS
Missouri Western State University, MO
Molloy College, NY
Montclair State University, NJ
Mount Aloysius College, PA
Mount Marty College, SD
Muhlenberg College, PA
New Jersey Institute of Technology, NJ
New Mexico Highlands University, NM
New Mexico State University, NM
Northeastern Illinois University, IL
Northeastern State University, OK
Northern Illinois University, IL
Northwestern College, IA
Northwestern State University
    of Louisiana, LA
Oglethorpe University, GA
Ohio Northern University, OH
The Ohio State University, OH
Ohio University, OH
Ohio University–Chillicothe, OH
Ohio University–Eastern, OH
Ohio University–Lancaster, OH
Ohio University–Southern Campus, OH
Ohio University–Zanesville, OH
Ohio Valley University, WV
Ohio Wesleyan University, OH
Oklahoma Baptist University, OK
Oklahoma City University, OK
Oklahoma Panhandle State University, OK
Old Dominion University, VA
Olivet Nazarene University, IL
Ouachita Baptist University, AR
Paul Quinn College, TX
Piedmont College, GA
Point Park University, PA
Purchase College, State
    University of New York, NY
Robert Morris University Illinois, IL
Rockford University, IL
Rockhurst University, MO
Sacred Heart University, CT
The Sage Colleges, NY
St. Andrews University, NC
Saint Augustine's University, NC
St. Bonaventure University, NY
Saint Louis University, MO
Saint Mary-of-the-Woods College, IN
Saint Michael's College, VT
Samford University, AL
Sam Houston State University, TX
San Diego Christian College, CA
San Diego State University, CA
Savannah College of Art and Design, GA
Seattle Pacific University, WA
Seton Hill University, PA
Shenandoah University, VA
Shepherd University, WV
Siena College, NY
Slippery Rock University of
    Pennsylvania, PA
Sonoma State University, CA
Southeastern Oklahoma
    State University, OK
Southeastern University, FL
Southeast Missouri State University, MO
Southern Illinois University Carbondale, IL
Southwestern College, KS
State University of New
    York at Fredonia, NY
State University of New York College at
    Geneseo, NY
State University of New York College at
    Potsdam, NY
Stephens College, MO
Sterling College, KS

Stevens Institute of Technology, NJ
Stockton University, NJ
Temple University, PA
Texas A&M International University, TX
Texas A&M University, TX
Texas A&M University–Commerce, TX
Texas Christian University, TX
Texas Lutheran University, TX
Texas Tech University, TX
Texas Wesleyan University, TX
Tiffin University, OH
Towson University, MD
Trinity Christian College, IL
The University of Akron, OH
The University of Alabama at
    Birmingham, AL
University of Alaska Anchorage, AK
The University of Arizona, AZ
University of California, Irvine, CA
University of California, San Diego, CA
University of Colorado Boulder, CO
University of Colorado Denver, CO
University of Dubuque, IA
University of Evansville, IN
University of Florida, FL
University of Hartford, CT
University of Houston, TX
University of Idaho, ID
University of Illinois at Chicago, IL
University of Illinois at Urbana–
    Champaign, IL
The University of Kansas, KS
University of Kentucky, KY
University of La Verne, CA
University of Louisiana at Monroe, LA
University of Maine at Fort Kent, ME
University of Maryland,
    Baltimore County, MD
University of Maryland, College Park, MD
University of Miami, FL
University of Michigan, MI
University of Michigan–Flint, MI
University of Mississippi, MS
University of Missouri–Kansas City, MO
University of Mobile, AL
University of Montana, MT
University of Mount Union, OH
University of Nebraska at Omaha, NE
University of Nebraska–Lincoln, NE
University of Nevada, Las Vegas, NV
University of New Hampshire, NH
The University of North Carolina at
    Greensboro, NC
University of North Carolina
    School of the Arts, NC
University of Northern Colorado, CO
University of Oklahoma, OK
University of Oregon, OR
University of Portland, OR
University of Richmond, VA
University of Rochester, NY
University of St. Francis, IL
University of St. Thomas, TX
University of South Florida, FL
The University of Tampa, FL
The University of Tennessee at
    Chattanooga, TN
The University of Texas at El Paso, TX
The University of Texas of the Permian
    Basin, TX
The University of Toledo, OH
The University of Tulsa, OK
University of Utah, UT
The University of Virginia's College at
    Wise, VA
University of Washington, WA

University of West Georgia, GA
University of Wisconsin–Eau Claire, WI
University of Wisconsin–Stevens Point, WI
University of Wyoming, WY
Ursinus College, PA
Utah State University, UT
Valdosta State University, GA
Valparaiso University, IN
Virginia Commonwealth University, VA
Virginia Polytechnic Institute and State
    University, VA
Virginia State University, VA
Wartburg College, IA
Washburn University, KS
Washington College, MD
Washington State University, WA
Wayne State College, NE
Wayne State University, MI
Western Illinois University, IL
Western Oregon University, OR
Western State Colorado University, CO
Western Washington University, WA
West Virginia Wesleyan College, WV
Wichita State University, KS
Wilkes University, PA
William Jessup University, CA
William Peace University, NC
Winthrop University, SC
Wright State University, OH
Wright State University–Lake Campus, OH
Xavier University, OH
Young Harris College, GA
Youngstown State University, OH

Theater/Drama

Abilene Christian University, TX
Adelphi University, NY
Alabama State University, AL
Alaska Pacific University, AK
Albertus Magnus College, CT
Albion College, MI
Albright College, PA
Alma College, MI
Anderson University, SC
Arcadia University, PA
Arizona State University at the Tempe
    campus, AZ
Arkansas Tech University, AR
Asbury University, KY
Auburn University, AL
Augsburg College, MN
Augustana College, IL
Augustana University, SD
Aurora University, IL
Austin College, TX
Austin Peay State University, TN
Averett University, VA
Baker University, KS
Ball State University, IN
Barton College, NC
Baylor University, TX
Belhaven University, MS
Belmont Abbey College, NC
Belmont University, TN
Benedictine College, KS
Berry College, GA
Bethany Lutheran College, MN
Bethel College, IN
Bethel College, KS
Bethel University, MN
Binghamton University, State University of
    New York, NY
Biola University, CA
Black Hills State University, SD
Bluefield College, VA
Blue Mountain College, MS

Boise State University, ID
Boston University, MA
Bowling Green State University, OH
Bradley University, IL
Brenau University, GA
Brevard College, NC
Briar Cliff University, IA
Brigham Young University, UT
Bryan College, TN
Bucknell University, PA
Buena Vista University, IA
Butler University, IN
California Baptist University, CA
California Institute of the Arts, CA
California Lutheran University, CA
California Polytechnic State University, San
    Luis Obispo, CA
California State University, Bakersfield, CA
California State University, Chico, CA
California State University, Fresno, CA
California State University, Fullerton, CA
California State University, Los Angeles, CA
California State University,
    San Bernardino, CA
Calumet College of Saint Joseph, IN
Calvin College, MI
Cameron University, OK
Campbellsville University, KY
Campbell University, NC
Cardinal Stritch University, WI
Carroll College, MT
Carroll University, WI
Case Western Reserve University, OH
Catawba College, NC
The Catholic University of America, DC
Cedar Crest College, PA
Centenary College of Louisiana, LA
Central College, IA
Central Methodist University, MO
Central Michigan University, MI
Central Washington University, WA
Centre College, KY
Chapman University, CA
Christopher Newport University, VA
Clarion University of Pennsylvania, PA
Clarke University, IA
Clemson University, SC
Cleveland State University, OH
Coastal Carolina University, SC
Coe College, IA
The College at Brockport, State University
    of New York, NY
College of Charleston, SC
The College of Idaho, ID
College of Saint Benedict, MN
College of Staten Island of the City
    University of New York, NY
The College of William and Mary, VA
The College of Wooster, OH
Colorado Mesa University, CO
Colorado State University, CO
Columbus State University, GA
Concordia College, MN
Concordia University Ann Arbor, MI
Concordia University Irvine, CA
Concordia University, Nebraska, NE
Concordia University, St. Paul, MN
Concord University, WV
Converse College, SC
Corban University, OR
Cornell College, IA
Creighton University, NE
Culver-Stockton College, MO
Dakota Wesleyan University, SD
Davidson College, NC

DePaul University, IL
DeSales University, PA
Dickinson State University, ND
Doane University, NE
Dordt College, IA
Drake University, IA
Drew University, NJ
Drexel University, PA
Drury University, MO
East Central University, OK
Eastern Connecticut State University, CT
Eastern Illinois University, IL
Eastern Michigan University, MI
Eastern Washington University, WA
East Stroudsburg University of
    Pennsylvania, PA
East Texas Baptist University, TX
Eckerd College, FL
Edgewood College, WI
Elizabethtown College, PA
Elmhurst College, IL
Elon University, NC
Emmanuel College, GA
Emory & Henry College, VA
Emory University, GA
Emporia State University, KS
Eureka College, IL
Evangel University, MO
Fairmont State University, WV
Faulkner University, AL
Ferris State University, MI
Flagler College, FL
Florida Agricultural and Mechanical
    University, FL
Florida International University, FL
Florida Southern College, FL
Florida State University, FL
Fort Hays State University, KS
Fort Lewis College, CO
Francis Marion University, SC
Franklin College, IN
Franklin Pierce University, NH
Fresno Pacific University, CA
Friends University, KS
Frostburg State University, MD
Furman University, SC
Gannon University, PA
Gardner-Webb University, NC
George Fox University, OR
Georgia Southern University, GA
Georgia Southwestern State University, GA
Goddard College, VT
Gordon College, MA
Goshen College, IN
Goucher College, MD
Graceland University, IA
Grambling State University, LA
Grand Valley State University, MI
Grand View University, IA
Guilford College, NC
Gustavus Adolphus College, MN
Hamline University, MN
Hardin-Simmons University, TX
Harris-Stowe State University, MO
Hendrix College, AR
Hillsdale College, MI
Hofstra University, NY
Hollins University, VA
Hope College, MI
Howard Payne University, TX
Howard University, DC
Huntington University, IN
Husson University, ME
Idaho State University, ID
Illinois College, IL

Illinois Wesleyan University, IL
Indiana State University, IN
Indiana University of Pennsylvania, PA
Indiana University–Purdue University Fort
    Wayne, IN
Indiana Wesleyan University, IN
Iowa State University of Science and
    Technology, IA
Ithaca College, NY
Jacksonville State University, AL
Jacksonville University, FL
James Madison University, VA
John Brown University, AR
Judson University, IL
The Juilliard School, NY
Juniata College, PA
Kansas Wesleyan University, KS
Kean University, NJ
Keene State College, NH
Kennesaw State University, GA
Kent State University, OH
Kent State University at Stark, OH
Kentucky Mountain Bible College, KY
King University, TN
Knox College, IL
Lafayette College, PA
LaGrange College, GA
Lake Erie College, OH
Lawrence University, WI
Lees-McRae College, NC
Lee University, TN
Lehigh University, PA
Lewis-Clark State College, ID
Lewis University, IL
Lincoln University, MO
Lindenwood University, MO
Linfield College, OR
Lipscomb University, TN
Long Island University–LIU Brooklyn, NY
Long Island University–LIU Post, NY
Longwood University, VA
Louisiana State University and Agricultural
    & Mechanical College, LA
Louisiana Tech University, LA
Loyola Marymount University, CA
Loyola University Chicago, IL
Lubbock Christian University, TX
Lycoming College, PA
Lynchburg College, VA
Lyon College, AR
Malone University, OH
Manhattanville College, NY
Marietta College, OH
Marist College, NY
Marquette University, WI
Maryville College, TN
Massachusetts College of Liberal Arts, MA
Mayville State University, ND
McPherson College, KS
Mercer University, GA
Messiah College, PA
Methodist University, NC
Metropolitan State University of Denver, CO
Miami University, OH
Michigan State University, MI
Michigan Technological University, MI
Middle Tennessee State University, TN
Midwestern State University, TX
Milligan College, TN
Millikin University, IL
Millsaps College, MS
Minnesota State University Moorhead, MN
Minot State University, ND
Mississippi State University, MS
Missouri Baptist University, MO

Missouri University of Science and Technology, MO
Missouri Western State University, MO
Molloy College, NY
Monmouth College, IL
Montana State University, MT
Montana State University Billings, MT
Montclair State University, NJ
Morehead State University, KY
Morningside College, IA
Mount Marty College, SD
Mount Mercy University, IA
Muhlenberg College, PA
Murray State University, KY
Muskingum University, OH
Nazareth College of Rochester, NY
Newberry College, SC
New England College, NH
New Jersey Institute of Technology, NJ
New Mexico State University, NM
Niagara University, NY
North Central College, IL
Northeastern Illinois University, IL
Northeastern State University, OK
Northern Arizona University, AZ
Northern Illinois University, IL
Northern Kentucky University, KY
Northern Michigan University, MI
Northern State University, SD
Northwestern College, IA
Northwestern State University of Louisiana, LA
Northwest Missouri State University, MO
Northwest Nazarene University, ID
Oglethorpe University, GA
Ohio Northern University, OH
The Ohio State University, OH
Ohio University, OH
Ohio University–Chillicothe, OH
Ohio University–Eastern, OH
Ohio University–Lancaster, OH
Ohio University–Southern Campus, OH
Ohio University–Zanesville, OH
Ohio Valley University, WV
Ohio Wesleyan University, OH
Oklahoma Baptist University, OK
Oklahoma Christian University, OK
Oklahoma City University, OK
Oklahoma Panhandle State University, OK
Oklahoma State University, OK
Old Dominion University, VA
Olivet Nazarene University, IL
Otterbein University, OH
Ouachita Baptist University, AR
Pacific Union College, CA
Pacific University, OR
Palm Beach Atlantic University, FL
Piedmont College, GA
Plymouth State University, NH
Point Loma Nazarene University, CA
Point Park University, PA
Portland State University, OR
Providence College, RI
Purchase College, State University of New York, NY
Queens College of the City University of New York, NY
Queens University of Charlotte, NC
Randall University, OK
Rhode Island College, RI
Rhodes College, TN
Rider University, NJ
Robert Morris University Illinois, IL
Rockford University, IL
Rockhurst University, MO
Rogers State University, OK

Rollins College, FL
Sacred Heart University, CT
The Sage Colleges, NY
Saginaw Valley State University, MI
St. Ambrose University, IA
St. Andrews University, NC
St. Edward's University, TX
St. Gregory's University, OK
Saint John's University, MN
Saint Joseph's University, PA
Saint Louis University, MO
Saint Martin's University, WA
Saint Mary-of-the-Woods College, IN
Saint Mary's University of Minnesota, MN
Saint Michael's College, VT
St. Norbert College, WI
St. Olaf College, MN
Salisbury University, MD
Samford University, AL
Sam Houston State University, TX
San Diego Christian College, CA
San Diego State University, CA
San Jose State University, CA
Santa Clara University, CA
Savannah College of Art and Design, GA
Schreiner University, TX
Seattle University, WA
Seton Hill University, PA
Shenandoah University, VA
Shepherd University, WV
Shippensburg University of Pennsylvania, PA
Siena College, NY
Simpson College, IA
Slippery Rock University of Pennsylvania, PA
Sonoma State University, CA
Southeastern Louisiana University, LA
Southeastern Oklahoma State University, OK
Southeast Missouri State University, MO
Southern Adventist University, TN
Southern Arkansas University–Magnolia, AR
Southern Illinois University Carbondale, IL
Southern Illinois University Edwardsville, IL
Southern Oregon University, OR
Southern Utah University, UT
Southwest Baptist University, MO
Southwestern College, KS
Southwestern Oklahoma State University, OK
Southwestern University, TX
Spelman College, GA
State University of New York at Fredonia, NY
State University of New York at New Paltz, NY
State University of New York at Plattsburgh, NY
State University of New York College at Geneseo, NY
State University of New York College at Potsdam, NY
Stephen F. Austin State University, TX
Stephens College, MO
Sterling College, KS
Stetson University, FL
Stevens Institute of Technology, NJ
Stockton University, NJ
Susquehanna University, PA
Syracuse University, NY
Tarleton State University, TX
Taylor University, IN
Temple University, PA

Texas A&M University, TX
Texas A&M University–Commerce, TX
Texas Christian University, TX
Texas Lutheran University, TX
Texas State University, TX
Texas Tech University, TX
Texas Wesleyan University, TX
Texas Woman's University, TX
Thiel College, PA
Thomas More College, KY
Thomas University, GA
Tiffin University, OH
Towson University, MD
Transylvania University, KY
Trevecca Nazarene University, TN
Trinity Christian College, IL
Trinity University, TX
Troy University, AL
Truman State University, MO
Union College, KY
Union University, TN
The University of Akron, OH
The University of Alabama, AL
The University of Alabama at Birmingham, AL
The University of Arizona, AZ
University of Arkansas, AR
University of Arkansas at Little Rock, AR
University of California, Irvine, CA
University of California, Riverside, CA
University of California, San Diego, CA
University of California, Santa Cruz, CA
University of Central Florida, FL
University of Central Oklahoma, OK
University of Colorado Boulder, CO
University of Colorado Denver, CO
University of Dallas, TX
University of Delaware, DE
University of Denver, CO
University of Detroit Mercy, MI
University of Dubuque, IA
University of Evansville, IN
The University of Findlay, OH
University of Florida, FL
University of Hartford, CT
University of Houston, TX
University of Idaho, ID
University of Illinois at Chicago, IL
University of Illinois at Urbana–Champaign, IL
University of Indianapolis, IN
University of Jamestown, ND
The University of Kansas, KS
University of Kentucky, KY
University of La Verne, CA
University of Louisiana at Monroe, LA
University of Louisville, KY
University of Maine, ME
University of Maryland, Baltimore County, MD
University of Maryland, College Park, MD
University of Mary Washington, VA
University of Massachusetts Amherst, MA
University of Memphis, TN
University of Miami, FL
University of Michigan, MI
University of Michigan–Flint, MI
University of Mississippi, MS
University of Missouri, MO
University of Missouri–St. Louis, MO
University of Montana, MT
University of Montevallo, AL
University of Mount Union, OH
University of Nebraska at Kearney, NE
University of Nebraska at Omaha, NE
University of Nebraska–Lincoln, NE

University of Nevada, Las Vegas, NV
University of Nevada, Reno, NV
University of New Hampshire, NH
University of North Alabama, AL
University of North Carolina at Asheville, NC
The University of North Carolina at Chapel Hill, NC
The University of North Carolina at Charlotte, NC
The University of North Carolina at Greensboro, NC
University of North Carolina School of the Arts, NC
The University of North Carolina Wilmington, NC
University of Northern Colorado, CO
University of Northern Iowa, IA
University of Oklahoma, OK
University of Oregon, OR
University of Pittsburgh at Bradford, PA
University of Pittsburgh at Johnstown, PA
University of Portland, OR
University of Puerto Rico in Bayamón, PR
University of Puget Sound, WA
University of Rhode Island, RI
University of Richmond, VA
University of St. Thomas, TX
University of Science and Arts of Oklahoma, OK
University of Sioux Falls, SD
University of South Carolina, SC
University of South Carolina Aiken, SC
The University of South Dakota, SD
University of Southern California, CA
University of Southern Indiana, IN
University of Southern Maine, ME
University of Southern Mississippi, MS
University of South Florida, FL
The University of Tampa, FL
The University of Tennessee at Chattanooga, TN
The University of Tennessee at Martin, TN
The University of Texas at Arlington, TX
The University of Texas at Austin, TX
The University of Texas at El Paso, TX
The University of Texas of the Permian Basin, TX
The University of Texas Rio Grande Valley, TX
University of the Incarnate Word, TX
The University of Toledo, OH
The University of Tulsa, OK
University of Utah, UT
University of Vermont, VT
University of Virginia, VA
The University of Virginia's College at Wise, VA
The University of West Alabama, AL
University of West Florida, FL
University of West Georgia, GA
University of Wisconsin–Eau Claire, WI
University of Wisconsin–Green Bay, WI
University of Wisconsin–La Crosse, WI
University of Wisconsin–Parkside, WI
University of Wisconsin–River Falls, WI
University of Wisconsin–Stevens Point, WI
University of Wisconsin–Whitewater, WI
University of Wyoming, WY
Ursinus College, PA
Utah State University, UT
Valdosta State University, GA
Valley City State University, ND
Valparaiso University, IN

Vanguard University of Southern California, CA
Virginia Commonwealth University, VA
Virginia Polytechnic Institute and State University, VA
Wabash College, IN
Wagner College, NY
Waldorf University, IA
Walla Walla University, WA
Warner Pacific College, OR
Wartburg College, IA
Washburn University, KS
Washington College, MD
Washington State University, WA
Wayland Baptist University, TX
Waynesburg University, PA
Wayne State College, NE
Wayne State University, MI
Webster University, MO
Wesleyan College, GA
West Chester University of Pennsylvania, PA
Western Carolina University, NC
Western Illinois University, IL
Western Kentucky University, KY
Western Michigan University, MI
Western Oregon University, OR
Western Washington University, WA
Westminster College, PA
Westmont College, CA
West Texas A&M University, TX
West Virginia University, WV
West Virginia Wesleyan College, WV
Whitman College, WA
Whittier College, CA
Whitworth University, WA
Wichita State University, KS
Wilkes University, PA
William Jessup University, CA
William Jewell College, MO
Williams Baptist College, AR
William Woods University, MO
Wingate University, NC
Winona State University, MN
Winthrop University, SC
Wisconsin Lutheran College, WI
Wittenberg University, OH
Wright State University, OH
Wright State University–Lake Campus, OH
Xavier University, OH
Young Harris College, GA
Youngstown State University, OH

Special Achievements/Activities

Cheerleading/Drum Major
Abilene Christian University, TX
Anderson University, SC
Arkansas Tech University, AR
Auburn University, AL
Augustana University, SD
Baker University, KS
Belhaven University, MS
Bellarmine University, KY
Belmont Abbey College, NC
Belmont University, TN
Benedictine College, KS
Bethel College, KS
Bluefield College, VA
Bluefield State College, WV
Blue Mountain College, MS
Boise State University, ID
Brenau University, GA
Brevard College, NC
California Baptist University, CA

Cameron University, OK
Campbellsville University, KY
Campbell University, NC
Carroll College, MT
Catawba College, NC
Central Methodist University, MO
Claflin University, SC
Cleveland State University, OH
Coastal Carolina University, SC
Columbus State University, GA
Concordia University, Nebraska, NE
Culver-Stockton College, MO
Dakota Wesleyan University, SD
Delta State University, MS
Dickinson State University, ND
Drexel University, PA
Drury University, MO
East Central University, OK
Eastern Kentucky University, KY
East Texas Baptist University, TX
Emmanuel College, GA
Evangel University, MO
Fairmont State University, WV
Faulkner University, AL
Florida Agricultural and Mechanical University, FL
Florida Institute of Technology, FL
Fort Hays State University, KS
Francis Marion University, SC
Friends University, KS
Gardner-Webb University, NC
Georgia Institute of Technology, GA
Georgia Southern University, GA
Glenville State College, WV
Graceland University, IA
Grambling State University, LA
Grand View University, IA
Greenville College, IL
Harding University, AR
Hawai`i Pacific University, HI
Hofstra University, NY
Hope International University, CA
Houston Baptist University, TX
Howard University, DC
Huntingdon College, AL
Huntington University, IN
Idaho State University, ID
Indiana Wesleyan University, IN
James Madison University, VA
Kansas Wesleyan University, KS
Kentucky State University, KY
Langston University, OK
Lawrence Technological University, MI
Lees-McRae College, NC
Lee University, TN
Lenoir-Rhyne University, NC
Lewis University, IL
Liberty University, VA
Lincoln Memorial University, TN
Lincoln University, MO
Lindenwood University, MO
Lindsey Wilson College, KY
Lipscomb University, TN
Long Island University–LIU Brooklyn, NY
Long Island University–LIU Post, NY
Louisiana Tech University, LA
Lyon College, AR
Malone University, OH
Maryville University of Saint Louis, MO
McKendree University, IL
McPherson College, KS
Methodist University, NC
Middle Tennessee State University, TN
Midway University, KY
Midwestern State University, TX

Milligan College, TN
Mississippi State University, MS
Missouri Baptist University, MO
Missouri Western State University, MO
Montana State University Billings, MT
Morehead State University, KY
Morehouse College, GA
Morningside College, IA
Newberry College, SC
New Mexico State University, NM
Nicholls State University, LA
North Carolina State University, NC
Northeastern State University, OK
Northern Illinois University, IL
Northern Kentucky University, KY
Northern Michigan University, MI
Northwestern State University of
     Louisiana, LA
Northwest Missouri State University, MO
The Ohio State University, OH
Oklahoma Baptist University, OK
Oklahoma Christian University, OK
Oklahoma Panhandle State University, OK
Oklahoma State University, OK
Old Dominion University, VA
Olivet Nazarene University, IL
Oral Roberts University, OK
Ouachita Baptist University, AR
Queens University of Charlotte, NC
Robert Morris University Illinois, IL
Rocky Mountain College, MT
Rogers State University, OK
St. Ambrose University, IA
St. Edward's University, TX
St. John's University, NY
Saint Louis University, MO
St. Mary's University, TX
Samford University, AL
San Diego State University, CA
Seton Hill University, PA
Southeastern Louisiana University, LA
Southeastern Oklahoma State
     University, OK
Southeastern University, FL
Southeast Missouri State University, MO
Southern Arkansas University–
     Magnolia, AR
Southern Illinois University Carbondale, IL
Southwestern College, KS
Southwestern Oklahoma State
     University, OK
Stephen F. Austin State University, TX
Sterling College, KS
Stetson University, FL
Temple University, PA
Tennessee Technological University, TN
Tennessee Wesleyan University, TN
Texas A&M University–Commerce, TX
Texas Wesleyan University, TX
Thomas More College, KY
Tiffin University, OH
Trine University, IN
Tusculum College, TN
Union College, KY
Union University, TN
The University of Alabama, AL
The University of Alabama at
     Birmingham, AL
The University of Alabama in
     Huntsville, AL
University of Arkansas, AR
University of Delaware, DE
University of Great Falls, MT
University of Houston, TX
University of Idaho, ID
University of Kentucky, KY

University of Louisiana at Monroe, LA
University of Louisville, KY
University of Mary Hardin-Baylor, TX
University of Maryland, College Park, MD
University of Massachusetts Amherst, MA
University of Memphis, TN
University of Miami, FL
University of Mississippi, MS
University of Missouri, MO
University of Missouri–St. Louis, MO
University of Montana, MT
University of Montevallo, AL
University of Nebraska at Kearney, NE
University of Nebraska–Lincoln, NE
University of Nevada, Las Vegas, NV
University of North Alabama, AL
The University of North Carolina
     Wilmington, NC
University of North Georgia, GA
University of Puerto Rico in Bayamón, PR
University of St. Francis, IL
University of Science and Arts
     of Oklahoma, OK
University of Sioux Falls, SD
University of South Carolina, SC
University of South Carolina Aiken, SC
University of Southern Mississippi, MS
The University of Tennessee at
     Chattanooga, TN
The University of Tennessee at Martin, TN
The University of Texas at Arlington, TX
The University of Texas at El Paso, TX
The University of Texas at San Antonio, TX
The University of Texas of the Permian
     Basin, TX
The University of Texas Rio
     Grande Valley, TX
The University of Toledo, OH
The University of Tulsa, OK
University of Utah, UT
The University of West Alabama, AL
University of Wyoming, WY
Virginia Polytechnic Institute and State
     University, VA
Virginia State University, VA
Waldorf University, IA
Warner University, FL
Washburn University, KS
Wayland Baptist University, TX
Webber International University, FL
West Texas A&M University, TX
West Virginia University Institute of
     Technology, WV
William Jewell College, MO
Williams Baptist College, AR
Wright State University, OH
Wright State University–Lake Campus, OH
Youngstown State University, OH

Community Service
Adelphi University, NY
Agnes Scott College, GA
Alaska Pacific University, AK
Albertus Magnus College, CT
Allen College, IA
Alliant International University–
     San Diego, CA
Alvernia University, PA
Alverno College, WI
Arcadia University, PA
Armstrong State University, GA
Augsburg College, MN
Augustana University, SD
Austin College, TX
Ball State University, IN
Baylor University, TX

Bellarmine University, KY
Belmont University, TN
Beloit College, WI
Benedictine University, IL
Bentley University, MA
Berry College, GA
Bethany College, WV
Bethel University, MN
Binghamton University, State University of
     New York, NY
Biola University, CA
Bloomfield College, NJ
Boise State University, ID
Bradley University, IL
Brenau University, GA
Brevard College, NC
Bryan College, TN
Caldwell University, NJ
California Lutheran University, CA
California Polytechnic State University, San
     Luis Obispo, CA
California State University, Bakersfield, CA
California State University, Chico, CA
California State University, Fresno, CA
California State University, Los Angeles, CA
California State University,
     San Bernardino, CA
Calvin College, MI
Cedar Crest College, PA
Centenary College of Louisiana, LA
Central College, IA
Centre College, KY
Chaminade University of Honolulu, HI
Christopher Newport University, VA
The Citadel, The Military College of South
     Carolina, SC
City College of the City University of New
     York, NY
Clarion University of Pennsylvania, PA
Clemson University, SC
Coe College, IA
The College at Brockport, State University
     of New York, NY
The College of New Rochelle, NY
College of Saint Mary, NE
The College of Saint Rose, NY
College of Staten Island of the City
     University of New York, NY
The College of Wooster, OH
Columbia College, MO
Columbus State University, GA
Concord University, WV
Creighton University, NE
Dallas Baptist University, TX
Davidson College, NC
Defiance College, OH
DePaul University, IL
DePauw University, IN
Dominican University of California, CA
Dordt College, IA
Drew University, NJ
Eastern Connecticut State University, CT
Eastern University, PA
ECPI University, VA
Edgewood College, WI
Elon University, NC
Endicott College, MA
Eureka College, IL
Flagler College, FL
Florida Agricultural and Mechanical
     University, FL
Florida Gulf Coast University, FL
Florida Southern College, FL
Francis Marion University, SC
Frostburg State University, MD
Furman University, SC

Gannon University, PA
Georgian Court University, NJ
Georgia Southern University, GA
Goshen College, IN
Grand View University, IA
Grove City College, PA
Hamline University, MN
Hampshire College, MA
Hawai`i Pacific University, HI
Hendrix College, AR
Hillsdale College, MI
Hobart and William Smith Colleges, NY
Hollins University, VA
Houghton College, NY
Howard Payne University, TX
Huntingdon College, AL
Illinois Institute of Technology, IL
Indiana University of Pennsylvania, PA
Indiana Wesleyan University, IN
Iona College, NY
Iowa State University of Science
    and Technology, IA
John Carroll University, OH
Juniata College, PA
Kean University, NJ
Kennesaw State University, GA
Kent State University, OH
Kent State University at Stark, OH
Keuka College, NY
King's College, PA
Knox College, IL
Kutztown University of Pennsylvania, PA
Lake Erie College, OH
La Salle University, PA
Lawrence University, WI
Lewis & Clark College, OR
Lewis-Clark State College, ID
Lewis University, IL
Lindenwood University, MO
Linfield College, OR
Lipscomb University, TN
Lock Haven University of Pennsylvania, PA
Longwood University, VA
Loyola Marymount University, CA
Loyola University Chicago, IL
Lycoming College, PA
Manhattan College, NY
Manhattanville College, NY
Marymount University, VA
Maryville College, TN
Maryville University of Saint Louis, MO
Marywood University, PA
McKendree University, IL
Mercer University, GA
Meredith College, NC
Michigan State University, MI
Millersville University of Pennsylvania, PA
Milligan College, TN
Millikin University, IL
Millsaps College, MS
Minnesota State University Moorhead, MN
Misericordia University, PA
Missouri Western State University, MO
Molloy College, NY
Montana Tech of The University of
    Montana, MT
Montclair State University, NJ
Moravian College, PA
Morehead State University, KY
Morehouse College, GA
Mount Carmel College of Nursing, OH
Mount Ida College, MA
Mount Marty College, SD
Mount St. Joseph University, OH
Mount Saint Mary's University, CA

Muskingum University, OH
New England College, NH
New Jersey Institute of Technology, NJ
Niagara University, NY
Nichols College, MA
North Central College, IL
Northeastern State University, OK
Northern Illinois University, IL
Northern Kentucky University, KY
Northwest Christian University, OR
Oglethorpe University, GA
Ohio Northern University, OH
Ohio Valley University, WV
Oklahoma State University, OK
Old Dominion University, VA
Olivet College, MI
Oral Roberts University, OK
Otterbein University, OH
Pacific Union College, CA
Pacific University, OR
Patrick Henry College, VA
Philander Smith College, AR
Piedmont College, GA
Point Park University, PA
Portland State University, OR
Principia College, IL
Providence College, RI
Queens University of Charlotte, NC
Randolph College, VA
Ringling College of Art and Design, FL
Robert Morris University Illinois, IL
Rochester Institute of Technology, NY
Rockford University, IL
Rockhurst University, MO
Sacred Heart University, CT
The Sage Colleges, NY
Saginaw Valley State University, MI
St. Andrews University, NC
St. Edward's University, TX
St. John Fisher College, NY
St. John's University, NY
St. Joseph's College, Long Island
    Campus, NY
St. Joseph's College, New York, NY
Saint Joseph's University, PA
St. Lawrence University, NY
St. Louis College of Pharmacy, MO
Saint Louis University, MO
Saint Martin's University, WA
Saint Mary-of-the-Woods College, IN
St. Olaf College, MN
St. Thomas Aquinas College, NY
Schreiner University, TX
Shippensburg University of
    Pennsylvania, PA
Siena College, NY
Simmons College, MA
Simpson College, IA
Simpson University, CA
Slippery Rock University of
    Pennsylvania, PA
Sonoma State University, CA
Southern Adventist University, TN
Southern Illinois University Carbondale, IL
Southern New Hampshire University, NH
Southern Oregon University, OR
Southern Vermont College, VT
Southwestern College, KS
Spring Hill College, AL
State University of New York at
    Plattsburgh, NY
State University of New York College at
    Cortland, NY
State University of New York College at
    Geneseo, NY

State University of New York College at
    Potsdam, NY
State University of New York College of
    Environmental Science and Forestry, NY
State University of New York College of
    Technology at Delhi, NY
Stetson University, FL
Stockton University, NJ
Stony Brook University, State University of
    New York, NY
Suffolk University, MA
Texas A&M University, TX
Texas A&M University–Texarkana, TX
Texas Christian University, TX
Texas Tech University, TX
Texas Wesleyan University, TX
Thomas More College, KY
Towson University, MD
Trinity Christian College, IL
Trinity College of Florida, FL
Truett McConnell University, GA
Tulane University, LA
Tusculum College, TN
Union College, KY
Union College, NE
Union University, TN
Unity College, ME
The University of Akron, OH
The University of Alabama, AL
The University of Alabama in
    Huntsville, AL
University of Alaska Fairbanks, AK
University of Arkansas, AR
University of Arkansas at Little Rock, AR
University of California, Irvine, CA
University of California, San Diego, CA
University of Chicago, IL
University of Colorado Boulder, CO
University of Delaware, DE
University of Denver, CO
University of Florida, FL
University of Hartford, CT
University of Houston, TX
University of Houston–Clear Lake, TX
University of Houston–Downtown, TX
University of Houston–Victoria, TX
University of Indianapolis, IN
University of Jamestown, ND
The University of Kansas, KS
University of La Verne, CA
University of Louisiana at Monroe, LA
University of Louisville, KY
University of Maine, ME
University of Maine at Presque Isle, ME
University of Mary Hardin-Baylor, TX
University of Massachusetts Dartmouth, MA
University of Massachusetts Lowell, MA
University of Memphis, TN
University of Michigan, MI
University of Michigan–Dearborn, MI
University of Michigan–Flint, MI
University of Mississippi, MS
University of Nebraska–Lincoln, NE
University of Nevada, Las Vegas, NV
University of New Hampshire, NH
University of North Carolina at
    Asheville, NC
The University of North Carolina at Chapel
    Hill, NC
The University of North Carolina at
    Greensboro, NC
University of Northern Colorado, CO
University of North Florida, FL
University of North Georgia, GA
University of Puerto Rico in Bayamón, PR

University of Puget Sound, WA
University of Richmond, VA
University of St. Francis, IL
University of South Carolina, SC
University of South Carolina Aiken, SC
The University of Tennessee at
    Chattanooga, TN
The University of Texas at Arlington, TX
The University of Texas Rio
    Grande Valley, TX
The University of Toledo, OH
The University of Tulsa, OK
University of Valley Forge, PA
University of Vermont, VT
The University of Virginia's
    College at Wise, VA
University of West Georgia, GA
University of Wisconsin–Eau Claire, WI
University of Wisconsin–Green Bay, WI
University of Wisconsin–La Crosse, WI
University of Wisconsin–Parkside, WI
University of Wisconsin–Stout, WI
University of Wyoming, WY
Ursinus College, PA
Ursuline College, OH
Vanderbilt University, TN
Virginia Polytechnic Institute and State
    University, VA
Virginia State University, VA
Wabash College, IN
Washburn University, KS
Washington State University, WA
Waynesburg University, PA
Webb Institute, NY
Webster University, MO
Wesleyan College, GA
Western Illinois University, IL
Western Oregon University, OR
Western Washington University, WA
West Texas A&M University, TX
West Virginia Wesleyan College, WV
Wheaton College, IL
Wheeling Jesuit University, WV
Widener University, PA
William Peace University, NC
Wilson College, PA
Wittenberg University, OH
Wright State University, OH
Wright State University–Lake Campus, OH
Youngstown State University, OH

Hobbies/Interests
Bethany College, WV
California State Polytechnic University,
    Pomona, CA
California State University, Chico, CA
California State University,
    San Bernardino, CA
Capital University, OH
Centenary College of Louisiana, LA
The College at Brockport, State University
    of New York, NY
The College of New Rochelle, NY
College of Staten Island of the City
    University of New York, NY
Colorado Mesa University, CO
Emmanuel College, GA
Florida Institute of Technology, FL
Francis Marion University, SC
Graceland University, IA
Hawai`i Pacific University, HI
Hollins University, VA
Illinois Institute of Technology, IL
Indiana University of Pennsylvania, PA
Indiana Wesleyan University, IN
Lake Erie College, OH

Michigan State University, MI
Middle Tennessee State University, TN
Millsaps College, MS
Montana Tech of The University of
    Montana, MT
New Jersey Institute of Technology, NJ
New Mexico State University, NM
The Ohio State University, OH
Sacred Heart University, CT
St. John's University, NY
Saint Martin's University, WA
San Diego State University, CA
Siena College, NY
Southern New Hampshire University, NH
Southern Oregon University, OR
State University of New York College at
    Cortland, NY
Stephen F. Austin State University, TX
Texas Tech University, TX
Union College, KY
The University of Alabama, AL
University of Houston, TX
University of Louisville, KY
University of Michigan–Flint, MI
University of Minnesota, Twin Cities
    Campus, MN
University of South Carolina Aiken, SC
The University of Toledo, OH
University of Wisconsin–Eau Claire, WI
University of Wyoming, WY
Virginia State University, VA
Wesleyan College, GA
Western Oregon University, OR
West Texas A&M University, TX

Junior Miss
Arkansas Tech University, AR
Augsburg College, MN
Belhaven University, MS
Bluefield State College, WV
Campbellsville University, KY
Carroll University, WI
Cedar Crest College, PA
Concordia University Texas, TX
DeSales University, PA
Georgia Southern University, GA
Goshen College, IN
Grambling State University, LA
Grand View University, IA
Gustavus Adolphus College, MN
Huntingdon College, AL
Kansas Wesleyan University, KS
Kentucky Wesleyan College, KY
Lawrence Technological University, MI
Lewis-Clark State College, ID
Lindenwood University, MO
Lindsey Wilson College, KY
Louisiana Tech University, LA
McDaniel College, MD
Midway University, KY
Mississippi State University, MS
Morehead State University, KY
Muskingum University, OH
New Mexico State University, NM
Northeastern State University, OK
Ohio Northern University, OH
Oklahoma City University, OK
Roberts Wesleyan College, NY
Rogers State University, OK
Spring Arbor University, MI
Stetson University, FL
Tennessee Wesleyan University, TN
Texas A&M University–Commerce, TX
Texas Lutheran University, TX
The University of Alabama, AL

The University of Alabama at
    Birmingham, AL
The University of Alabama in
    Huntsville, AL
University of Central Oklahoma, OK
University of Idaho, ID
University of Louisville, KY
University of Mississippi, MS
University of Montevallo, AL
The University of North Carolina at
    Greensboro, NC
The University of Tennessee at Martin, TN
University of the District of Columbia, DC
The University of West Alabama, AL
University of Wyoming, WY
Waldorf University, IA
Wartburg College, IA
Washington State University, WA

Leadership
Abilene Christian University, TX
Adelphi University, NY
Agnes Scott College, GA
Alabama State University, AL
Alaska Pacific University, AK
Albertus Magnus College, CT
Alcorn State University, MS
Alderson Broaddus University, WV
Allen College, IA
Alliant International University–
    San Diego, CA
Alvernia University, PA
American Jewish University, CA
American University, DC
Anderson University, SC
Andrews University, MI
Aquinas College, MI
Arcadia University, PA
Arizona State University at the Downtown
    Phoenix campus, AZ
Arizona State University at the Polytechnic
    campus, AZ
Arizona State University at the Tempe
    campus, AZ
Arizona State University at the West campus,
    AZ
Asbury University, KY
Auburn University, AL
Augsburg College, MN
Augustana College, IL
Augustana University, SD
Augusta University, GA
Aurora University, IL
Austin College, TX
Austin Peay State University, TN
Ave Maria University, FL
Averett University, VA
Babson College, MA
Baker University, KS
Baldwin Wallace University, OH
Ball State University, IN
Barclay College, KS
Barton College, NC
Baylor University, TX
Belhaven University, MS
Bellarmine University, KY
Belmont Abbey College, NC
Belmont University, TN
Beloit College, WI
Bemidji State University, MN
Benedictine College, KS
Benedictine University, IL
Bentley University, MA
Berry College, GA
Bethany College, WV
Bethel College, IN

Bethel University, MN
Binghamton University, State University of New York, NY
Biola University, CA
Bloomfield College, NJ
Bluefield State College, WV
Blue Mountain College, MS
Bluffton University, OH
Boise State University, ID
Bowdoin College, ME
Bowling Green State University, OH
Bradley University, IL
Brenau University, GA
Brescia University, KY
Brevard College, NC
Briar Cliff University, IA
Brigham Young University, UT
Bryan College, TN
Bryn Mawr College, PA
Bucknell University, PA
Buena Vista University, IA
Caldwell University, NJ
California Lutheran University, CA
California Polytechnic State University, San Luis Obispo, CA
California State Polytechnic University, Pomona, CA
California State University, Bakersfield, CA
California State University, Chico, CA
California State University, Fresno, CA
California State University, Fullerton, CA
California State University, Monterey Bay, CA
California State University, Northridge, CA
California State University, San Marcos, CA
Calumet College of Saint Joseph, IN
Calvin College, MI
Cameron University, OK
Campbellsville University, KY
Campbell University, NC
Capital University, OH
Carlow University, PA
Carroll College, MT
Carroll University, WI
Carson-Newman University, TN
Case Western Reserve University, OH
Catawba College, NC
Cedarville University, OH
Central Methodist University, MO
Central Michigan University, MI
Central Penn College, PA
Central Washington University, WA
Champlain College, VT
Chatham University, PA
Chowan University, NC
Christian Brothers University, TN
Christopher Newport University, VA
Cincinnati Christian University, OH
The Citadel, The Military College of South Carolina, SC
City College of the City University of New York, NY
Claremont McKenna College, CA
Clarion University of Pennsylvania, PA
Clark Atlanta University, GA
Clarke University, IA
Clarkson University, NY
Clarks Summit University, PA
Clemson University, SC
Cleveland Institute of Art, OH
The College at Brockport, State University of New York, NY
College of Coastal Georgia, GA
The College of Idaho, ID
The College of New Rochelle, NY

College of Saint Mary, NE
College of Staten Island of the City University of New York, NY
Colorado Mesa University, CO
Columbia College, MO
Columbia International University, SC
Columbus State University, GA
Concordia University Texas, TX
Concord University, WV
Corban University, OR
Covenant College, GA
Creighton University, NE
Crown College, MN
Culver-Stockton College, MO
Daemen College, NY
Dallas Baptist University, TX
Davidson College, NC
Davis College, NY
Defiance College, OH
Delta State University, MS
DePaul University, IL
DeSales University, PA
Dickinson State University, ND
DigiPen Institute of Technology, WA
Dominican University of California, CA
Dordt College, IA
Drury University, MO
Duke University, NC
Eastern Connecticut State University, CT
Eastern Illinois University, IL
Eastern Michigan University, MI
Eastern Oregon University, OR
Eastern University, PA
East Stroudsburg University of Pennsylvania, PA
East Texas Baptist University, TX
Elmira College, NY
Elon University, NC
Embry-Riddle Aeronautical University–Daytona, FL
Emmanuel College, GA
Emory University, GA
Emporia State University, KS
Endicott College, MA
Eureka College, IL
Evangel University, MO
Fairmont State University, WV
Faulkner University, AL
Fitchburg State University, MA
Flagler College, FL
Florida Agricultural and Mechanical University, FL
Florida Gulf Coast University, FL
Florida Institute of Technology, FL
Florida Southern College, FL
Fort Hays State University, KS
Fort Lewis College, CO
Francis Marion University, SC
Franklin College, IN
Franklin Pierce University, NH
Friends University, KS
Frostburg State University, MD
Furman University, SC
Gallaudet University, DC
Gannon University, PA
Geneva College, PA
George Fox University, OR
Georgia Institute of Technology, GA
Georgian Court University, NJ
Georgia Southern University, GA
Georgia Southwestern State University, GA
Gonzaga University, WA
Gordon College, MA
Goucher College, MD
Graceland University, IA

Grambling State University, LA
Greenville College, IL
Grove City College, PA
Hamline University, MN
Hampden-Sydney College, VA
Hampshire College, MA
Hampton University, VA
Harding University, AR
Hawai'i Pacific University, HI
Hendrix College, AR
Heritage Bible College, NC
Hilbert College, NY
Hillsdale College, MI
Hobart and William Smith Colleges, NY
Hofstra University, NY
Hollins University, VA
Hood College, MD
Hope International University, CA
Houghton College, NY
Howard Payne University, TX
Howard University, DC
Husson University, ME
Illinois Institute of Technology, IL
Indiana University of Pennsylvania, PA
Indiana University–Purdue University Fort Wayne, IN
Iowa State University of Science and Technology, IA
Ithaca College, NY
Jackson State University, MS
Jacksonville State University, AL
Jacksonville University, FL
James Madison University, VA
John Carroll University, OH
John Wesley University, NC
Judson University, IL
Juniata College, PA
Kalamazoo College, MI
Kean University, NJ
Keene State College, NH
Kennesaw State University, GA
Kent State University, OH
Kentucky Wesleyan College, KY
Keuka College, NY
The King's College, NY
King's College, PA
Kutztown University of Pennsylvania, PA
Kuyper College, MI
LaGrange College, GA
Lancaster Bible College, PA
Langston University, OK
Lawrence Technological University, MI
Lawrence University, WI
Lee University, TN
Le Moyne College, NY
Lenoir-Rhyne University, NC
Lewis & Clark College, OR
Lewis-Clark State College, ID
Lewis University, IL
Liberty University, VA
Life University, GA
LIM College, NY
Lindenwood University, MO
Lindsey Wilson College, KY
Linfield College, OR
Lipscomb University, TN
Lock Haven University of Pennsylvania, PA
Longwood University, VA
Loyola Marymount University, CA
Loyola University Chicago, IL
Loyola University New Orleans, LA
Lubbock Christian University, TX
Lycoming College, PA
Lynn University, FL
MacMurray College, IL

Malone University, OH
Manhattan College, NY
Mansfield University of Pennsylvania, PA
Marlboro College, VT
Marygrove College, MI
Marymount Manhattan College, NY
Marymount University, VA
Maryville College, TN
Maryville University of Saint Louis, MO
Marywood University, PA
Massachusetts College of Liberal Arts, MA
Massachusetts Maritime Academy, MA
The Master's University, CA
McDaniel College, MD
McKendree University, IL
Mercer University, GA
Meredith College, NC
Merrimack College, MA
Messiah College, PA
Methodist University, NC
Metropolitan State University of Denver, CO
Miami University, OH
Michigan State University, MI
Middle Tennessee State University, TN
Midway University, KY
Midwestern State University, TX
Millikin University, IL
Millsaps College, MS
Mills College, CA
Minnesota State University Mankato, MN
Misericordia University, PA
Mississippi State University, MS
Missouri State University, MO
Missouri Western State University, MO
Molloy College, NY
Monmouth University, NJ
Montana State University, MT
Montana Tech of The University of
    Montana, MT
Montclair State University, NJ
Montreat College, NC
Moravian College, PA
Morehead State University, KY
Morehouse College, GA
Morningside College, IA
Morrisville State College, NY
Mount Aloysius College, PA
Mount Ida College, MA
Mount Marty College, SD
Mount Mary University, WI
Mount St. Joseph University, OH
Mount Saint Mary College, NY
Mount Saint Mary's University, CA
Muskingum University, OH
National University, CA
Nazareth College of Rochester, NY
Nebraska Methodist College, NE
New England College, NH
New Jersey Institute of Technology, NJ
New Mexico State University, NM
Nicholls State University, LA
Nichols College, MA
North Carolina State University, NC
Northeastern Illinois University, IL
Northeastern State University, OK
Northern Arizona University, AZ
Northern Illinois University, IL
Northern Kentucky University, KY
Northern Michigan University, MI
Northern State University, SD
Northland College, WI
Northwest Christian University, OR
Northwestern State University of
    Louisiana, LA
Northwest Missouri State University, MO
Northwest Nazarene University, ID

Northwest University, WA
Occidental College, CA
Ohio Northern University, OH
The Ohio State University, OH
Ohio Valley University, WV
Ohio Wesleyan University, OH
Oklahoma Baptist University, OK
Oklahoma City University, OK
Oklahoma State University, OK
Oklahoma Wesleyan University, OK
Old Dominion University, VA
Olivet College, MI
O'More College of Design, TN
Oral Roberts University, OK
Oregon State University, OR
Otterbein University, OH
Pacific Union College, CA
Palm Beach Atlantic University, FL
Patrick Henry College, VA
Paul Smith's College, NY
Peirce College, PA
Philander Smith College, AR
Piedmont College, GA
Portland State University, OR
Presbyterian College, SC
Prescott College, AZ
Principia College, IL
Purdue University, IN
Queens University of Charlotte, NC
Randolph College, VA
Regent University, VA
Regis University, CO
Rice University, TX
Robert Morris University Illinois, IL
Rochester Institute of Technology, NY
Rockford University, IL
Rockhurst University, MO
Rogers State University, OK
Sacred Heart University, CT
The Sage Colleges, NY
Saginaw Valley State University, MI
St. Ambrose University, IA
St. Andrews University, NC
St. Edward's University, TX
St. John's University, NY
St. Joseph's College, Long
    Island Campus, NY
St. Joseph's College, New York, NY
St. Lawrence University, NY
St. Louis College of Pharmacy, MO
Saint Louis University, MO
Saint Martin's University, WA
Saint Mary-of-the-Woods College, IN
Saint Mary's University of Minnesota, MN
Saint Peter's University, NJ
St. Thomas Aquinas College, NY
St. Thomas University, FL
Salem College, NC
Salisbury University, MD
Samford University, AL
Sam Houston State University, TX
San Diego Christian College, CA
San Diego State University, CA
San Jose State University, CA
Schreiner University, TX
Seattle University, WA
Shepherd University, WV
Shippensburg University of
    Pennsylvania, PA
Siena College, NY
Simpson College, IA
Simpson University, CA
Slippery Rock University of
    Pennsylvania, PA
Soka University of America, CA
Sonoma State University, CA

Southeastern Louisiana University, LA
Southeastern Oklahoma
    State University, OK
Southeastern University, FL
Southeast Missouri State University, MO
Southern Adventist University, TN
Southern Arkansas University–
    Magnolia, AR
Southern Illinois University Carbondale, IL
Southern New Hampshire University, NH
Southern Oregon University, OR
Southern Utah University, UT
Southern Vermont College, VT
Southwestern College, KS
Southwestern Oklahoma
    State University, OK
Southwestern University, TX
State University of New York at
    Fredonia, NY
State University of New York at
    Plattsburgh, NY
State University of New York College at
    Cortland, NY
State University of New York College at
    Geneseo, NY
State University of New York College at
    Potsdam, NY
State University of New York College of
    Agriculture and Technology at
    Cobleskill, NY
State University of New York College of
    Environmental Science and Forestry, NY
State University of New York Maritime
    College, NY
Stephen F. Austin State University, TX
Stephens College, MO
Stetson University, FL
Stockton University, NJ
Stony Brook University, State University of
    New York, NY
Suffolk University, MA
Susquehanna University, PA
Taylor University, IN
Texas A&M University, TX
Texas A&M University–Commerce, TX
Texas A&M University–Texarkana, TX
Texas Christian University, TX
Texas Lutheran University, TX
Texas State University, TX
Texas Tech University, TX
Texas Wesleyan University, TX
Thiel College, PA
Thomas More College, KY
Toccoa Falls College, GA
Trevecca Nazarene University, TN
Trinity Christian College, IL
Trinity College of Florida, FL
Troy University, AL
Truett McConnell University, GA
Truman State University, MO
Tusculum College, TN
Union College, KY
Union College, NE
Union University, TN
Unity College, ME
The University of Akron, OH
The University of Alabama at
    Birmingham, AL
The University of Alabama in
    Huntsville, AL
University of Alaska Anchorage, AK
University of Alaska Fairbanks, AK
University of Alaska Southeast, AK
University of Arkansas, AR
University of Arkansas at Little Rock, AR
University of California, Irvine, CA

University of California, San Diego, CA
University of California, Santa Cruz, CA
University of Central Florida, FL
University of Central Oklahoma, OK
University of Chicago, IL
University of Colorado Boulder, CO
University of Dayton, OH
University of Delaware, DE
University of Denver, CO
University of Evansville, IN
University of Florida, FL
University of Hartford, CT
University of Houston, TX
University of Houston–Clear Lake, TX
University of Houston–Downtown, TX
University of Houston–Victoria, TX
University of Idaho, ID
University of Illinois at Urbana–
  Champaign, IL
The University of Iowa, IA
University of Jamestown, ND
The University of Kansas, KS
University of Kentucky, KY
University of La Verne, CA
University of Louisiana at Monroe, LA
University of Louisville, KY
University of Maine, ME
University of Maine at Augusta, ME
University of Mary Hardin-Baylor, TX
University of Mary Washington, VA
University of Massachusetts Amherst, MA
University of Massachusetts Boston, MA
University of Memphis, TN
University of Miami, FL
University of Michigan, MI
University of Michigan–Dearborn, MI
University of Michigan–Flint, MI
University of Minnesota, Crookston, MN
University of Minnesota, Twin Cities
  Campus, MN
University of Mississippi, MS
University of Missouri–Kansas City, MO
University of Montana, MT
University of Montevallo, AL
University of Mount Olive, NC
University of Nebraska at Kearney, NE
University of Nebraska at Omaha, NE
University of Nebraska–Lincoln, NE
University of Nevada, Las Vegas, NV
University of New Hampshire, NH
University of North Alabama, AL
University of North Carolina at
  Asheville, NC
The University of North Carolina at Chapel
  Hill, NC
The University of North Carolina at
  Greensboro, NC
The University of North Carolina
  Wilmington, NC
University of Northern Colorado, CO
University of Northern Iowa, IA
University of North Florida, FL
University of North Georgia, GA
University of Oklahoma, OK
University of Pittsburgh at Johnstown, PA
University of Puget Sound, WA
University of Rochester, NY
University of St. Francis, IL
University of Saint Joseph, CT
University of St. Thomas, TX
University of San Diego, CA
University of Sioux Falls, SD
University of South Carolina, SC
University of South Carolina Aiken, SC
The University of South Dakota, SD

University of Southern California, CA
University of Southern Indiana, IN
University of Southern Mississippi, MS
The University of Tampa, FL
The University of Tennessee at Martin, TN
The University of Texas at Arlington, TX
The University of Texas at Austin, TX
The University of Texas at Dallas, TX
The University of Texas at El Paso, TX
The University of Texas of the Permian
  Basin, TX
The University of Texas Rio
  Grande Valley, TX
University of the Incarnate Word, TX
University of the Pacific, CA
The University of Toledo, OH
The University of Tulsa, OK
University of Utah, UT
University of Valley Forge, PA
University of Vermont, VT
University of Virginia, VA
University of Washington, WA
The University of West Alabama, AL
University of West Florida, FL
University of West Georgia, GA
University of Wisconsin–Eau Claire, WI
University of Wisconsin–Green Bay, WI
University of Wisconsin–La Crosse, WI
University of Wisconsin–Oshkosh, WI
University of Wisconsin–Parkside, WI
University of Wisconsin–River Falls, WI
University of Wisconsin–Stevens Point, WI
University of Wisconsin–Stout, WI
University of Wisconsin–Whitewater, WI
University of Wyoming, WY
Ursinus College, PA
Ursuline College, OH
Utah State University, UT
Vanderbilt University, TN
Virginia Polytechnic Institute and State
  University, VA
Virginia State University, VA
Wabash College, IN
Wake Forest University, NC
Waldorf University, IA
Walla Walla University, WA
Warner Pacific College, OR
Warner University, FL
Wartburg College, IA
Washburn University, KS
Washington State University, WA
Wayland Baptist University, TX
Wayne State College, NE
Wayne State University, MI
Webber International University, FL
Webb Institute, NY
Webster University, MO
Wells College, NY
Wesleyan College, GA
West Chester University of Pennsylvania, PA
Western Illinois University, IL
Western Kentucky University, KY
Western New England University, MA
Western Oregon University, OR
Western State Colorado University, CO
Western Washington University, WA
Westminster College, MO
Westmont College, CA
West Texas A&M University, TX
West Virginia University, WV
West Virginia Wesleyan College, WV
Wheaton College, IL
Wheelock College, MA
Wichita State University, KS
Widener University, PA

Wilkes University, PA
William Jessup University, CA
William Peace University, NC
Wilson College, PA
Wisconsin Lutheran College, WI
Wittenberg University, OH
Wofford College, SC
Worcester Polytechnic Institute, MA
Wright State University, OH
Wright State University–Lake Campus, OH
Youngstown State University, OH

Memberships
Adelphi University, NY
Albright College, PA
Alvernia University, PA
American University, DC
Anderson University, SC
Arcadia University, PA
Auburn University, AL
Austin Peay State University, TN
Averett University, VA
Benedictine University, IL
Blue Mountain College, MS
Boston University, MA
Caldwell University, NJ
California State University, Chico, CA
California State University,
  San Bernardino, CA
Carroll University, WI
Carson-Newman University, TN
Central Penn College, PA
Chaminade University of Honolulu, HI
Charlotte Christian College and Theological
  Seminary, NC
Christian Brothers University, TN
The College of New Rochelle, NY
Corban University, OR
Dallas Baptist University, TX
Delta State University, MS
Eastern Michigan University, MI
Eastern University, PA
Emmanuel College, GA
Emporia State University, KS
Ferris State University, MI
Flagler College, FL
Florida Institute of Technology, FL
Francis Marion University, SC
Franklin College, IN
Georgian Court University, NJ
Georgia Southern University, GA
Gonzaga University, WA
Grand View University, IA
Greenville College, IL
Grove City College, PA
Hamline University, MN
Hawai`i Pacific University, HI
Houghton College, NY
Howard University, DC
Illinois Institute of Technology, IL
Kean University, NJ
Kennesaw State University, GA
Lewis-Clark State College, ID
Lewis University, IL
LIM College, NY
Lock Haven University of Pennsylvania, PA
Longwood University, VA
Loyola Marymount University, CA
Loyola University Chicago, IL
Marymount University, VA
Massachusetts College of Liberal Arts, MA
Michigan State University, MI
Middle Tennessee State University, TN
Mississippi State University, MS
Missouri Baptist University, MO

Missouri Western State University, MO
Molloy College, NY
Montana Tech of The University of
    Montana, MT
Morrisville State College, NY
Murray State University, KY
Nebraska Methodist College, NE
New Mexico State University, NM
Northern Illinois University, IL
Northern Michigan University, MI
Northwestern State University of
    Louisiana, LA
Northwest Missouri State University, MO
The Ohio State University, OH
Oklahoma State University, OK
Old Dominion University, VA
Olivet College, MI
O'More College of Design, TN
Oral Roberts University, OK
Pacific University, OR
Patrick Henry College, VA
Paul Smith's College, NY
Peirce College, PA
Point Park University, PA
Portland State University, OR
Queens University of Charlotte, NC
Regent University, VA
Sacred Heart University, CT
Saint Louis University, MO
Saint Mary-of-the-Woods College, IN
San Diego Christian College, CA
San Diego State University, CA
Schreiner University, TX
Siena College, NY
Sonoma State University, CA
Southeastern Louisiana University, LA
Southeast Missouri State University, MO
Southern New Hampshire University, NH
Southern Oregon University, OR
Southwestern College, KS
State University of New York College at
    Geneseo, NY
State University of New York College of
    Environmental Science and Forestry, NY
Stephens College, MO
Tennessee Wesleyan University, TN
Texas A&M University, TX
Texas A&M University–Texarkana, TX
Texas Christian University, TX
Texas Lutheran University, TX
Texas Tech University, TX
Texas Wesleyan University, TX
Thomas More College, KY
Towson University, MD
Union College, KY
Union University, TN
The University of Akron, OH
The University of Alabama at
    Birmingham, AL
University of Arkansas at Little Rock, AR
University of Evansville, IN
University of Houston–Victoria, TX
University of Louisville, KY
University of Maine, ME
University of Maryland Eastern Shore, MD
University of Michigan–Dearborn, MI
University of Mississippi, MS
University of Missouri, MO
University of Missouri–St. Louis, MO
University of Nebraska at Omaha, NE
University of Northern Colorado, CO
University of South Carolina, SC
University of South Carolina Aiken, SC
The University of Tampa, FL
The University of Tennessee at
    Chattanooga, TN

The University of Texas
    Rio Grande Valley, TX
The University of Toledo, OH
University of Vermont, VT
University of Washington, WA
The University of West Alabama, AL
University of West Georgia, GA
University of Wisconsin–Eau Claire, WI
University of Wisconsin–La Crosse, WI
University of Wisconsin–Stout, WI
University of Wyoming, WY
Virginia Polytechnic Institute and State
    University, VA
Warner Pacific College, OR
Washington State University, WA
Wayland Baptist University, TX
Wayne State University, MI
Webber International University, FL
Wesleyan College, GA
Western Kentucky University, KY
Western Washington University, WA
West Texas A&M University, TX
Wichita State University, KS
Wright State University, OH
Wright State University–Lake Campus, OH
Youngstown State University, OH

Religious Involvement

Alaska Bible College, AK
Alaska Pacific University, AK
Albright College, PA
Alma College, MI
Alvernia University, PA
Amridge University, AL
Andrews University, MI
Augsburg College, MN
Augustana College, IL
Augustana University, SD
Austin College, TX
Austin Graduate School of Theology, TX
Averett University, VA
Baker University, KS
Barton College, NC
Baylor University, TX
Bellarmine University, KY
Belmont Abbey College, NC
Belmont University, TN
Berry College, GA
Bethany College, WV
Bethel University, MN
Blue Mountain College, MS
Briar Cliff University, IA
Brigham Young University, UT
Bryan College, TN
Caldwell University, NJ
California Lutheran University, CA
Calvary University, MO
Calvin College, MI
Campbellsville University, KY
Campbell University, NC
Capital University, OH
Carlow University, PA
Carroll College, MT
Carroll University, WI
Cedar Crest College, PA
Centenary College of Louisiana, LA
Central College, IA
Central Methodist University, MO
Chaminade University of Honolulu, HI
Charlotte Christian College and Theological
    Seminary, NC
Cincinnati Christian University, OH
The Citadel, The Military College of South
    Carolina, SC
Clarke University, IA
Clarks Summit University, PA

The College at Brockport, State University
    of New York, NY
The College of New Rochelle, NY
College of Saint Mary, NE
The College of Wooster, OH
Columbia College, MO
Columbia International University, SC
Concordia University Texas, TX
Criswell College, TX
Crossroads Bible College, IN
Dallas Baptist University, TX
Davidson College, NC
Defiance College, OH
Drury University, MO
Earlham College, IN
Eastern Mennonite University, VA
Eastern Michigan University, MI
East Texas Baptist University, TX
Edgewood College, WI
Elizabethtown College, PA
Elon University, NC
Emmanuel College, GA
Emory & Henry College, VA
Endicott College, MA
Eureka College, IL
Evangel University, MO
Faulkner University, AL
Flagler College, FL
Franciscan University of Steubenville, OH
Franklin College, IN
Friends University, KS
Furman University, SC
Gardner-Webb University, NC
George Fox University, OR
Georgian Court University, NJ
Georgia Southern University, GA
Graceland University, IA
Grand View University, IA
Greenville College, IL
Grove City College, PA
Harding University, AR
Hawai`i Pacific University, HI
Hellenic College, MA
Hendrix College, AR
Heritage Bible College, NC
Houghton College, NY
Houston Baptist University, TX
Howard Payne University, TX
Howard University, DC
Indiana Wesleyan University, IN
Kutztown University of Pennsylvania, PA
Lancaster Bible College, PA
Lee University, TN
Lewis University, IL
Lindsey Wilson College, KY
Lipscomb University, TN
Loyola Marymount University, CA
MacMurray College, IL
Malone University, OH
Maryville University of Saint Louis, MO
Methodist University, NC
Mid-Atlantic Christian University, NC
Midway University, KY
Millsaps College, MS
Missouri Baptist University, MO
Missouri Western State University, MO
Molloy College, NY
Monmouth College, IL
Moravian College, PA
Morehouse College, GA
Mount Marty College, SD
Mount St. Mary's University, MD
Mount Vernon Nazarene University, OH
Newberry College, SC
New Jersey Institute of Technology, NJ
North Central College, IL

Northwest Christian University, OR
Northwest Nazarene University, ID
Northwest University, WA
Oakland City University, IN
Oglethorpe University, GA
Ohio Valley University, WV
Oklahoma Baptist University, OK
Oklahoma City University, OK
Oklahoma Wesleyan University, OK
Oral Roberts University, OK
Pacific Union College, CA
Pacific University, OR
Patrick Henry College, VA
Philander Smith College, AR
Piedmont College, GA
Presbyterian College, SC
Principia College, IL
Queens University of Charlotte, NC
Randall University, OK
Randolph-Macon College, VA
Regent University, VA
Roberts Wesleyan College, NY
Sacred Heart University, CT
St. Gregory's University, OK
St. John's University, NY
Saint Louis University, MO
Saint Martin's University, WA
Saint Mary-of-the-Woods College, IN
St. Olaf College, MN
San Diego Christian College, CA
Schreiner University, TX
Shenandoah University, VA
Siena College, NY
Simpson College, IA
Simpson University, CA
Southeastern University, FL
Southern Adventist University, TN
Southwest Baptist University, MO
Southwestern College, KS
Sterling College, KS
Stetson University, FL
Texas Christian University, TX
Texas Lutheran University, TX
Texas Wesleyan University, TX
Thomas More College, KY
Trinity Christian College, IL
Trinity College of Florida, FL
Truett McConnell University, GA
Union College, KY
Union College, NE
Union University, TN
The University of Alabama at Birmingham, AL
University of Detroit Mercy, MI
University of Great Falls, MT
University of Indianapolis, IN
University of Mary Hardin-Baylor, TX
University of Mobile, AL
The University of North Carolina at Greensboro, NC
University of Puget Sound, WA
University of St. Francis, IL
University of St. Thomas, TX
University of San Diego, CA
University of South Carolina, SC
The University of Tennessee at Chattanooga, TN
University of the Incarnate Word, TX
University of the Pacific, CA
The University of Toledo, OH
University of Valley Forge, PA
The University of Virginia's College at Wise, VA
University of West Georgia, GA
University of Wisconsin–Stout, WI

Valdosta State University, GA
Virginia Polytechnic Institute and State University, VA
Virginia State University, VA
Virginia Wesleyan College, VA
Warner University, FL
Washington State University, WA
Wayland Baptist University, TX
Wesleyan College, GA
West Texas A&M University, TX
West Virginia Wesleyan College, WV
Wheaton College, IL
Whitworth University, WA
William Jessup University, CA
William Jewell College, MO
Youngstown State University, OH

Rodeo
Boise State University, ID
California Polytechnic State University, San Luis Obispo, CA
Dickinson State University, ND
East Texas Baptist University, TX
Fort Hays State University, KS
Lewis-Clark State College, ID
Michigan State University, MI
Murray State University, KY
New Mexico State University, NM
Oklahoma Panhandle State University, OK
Oklahoma State University, OK
Sam Houston State University, TX
Southeastern Oklahoma State University, OK
Southern Arkansas University–Magnolia, AR
Southwestern Oklahoma State University, OK
Stephen F. Austin State University, TX
Texas A&M University, TX
Texas A&M University–Commerce, TX
Texas A&M University–Kingsville, TX
Texas Tech University, TX
University of Idaho, ID
University of Montana, MT
The University of Montana Western, MT
University of Nevada, Las Vegas, NV
The University of Tennessee at Martin, TN
The University of West Alabama, AL
University of Wyoming, WY
Washington State University, WA
West Texas A&M University, TX

Special Characteristics

Adult Students
Adelphi University, NY
Agnes Scott College, GA
Alaska Pacific University, AK
Allegheny College, PA
American University, DC
Augustana University, SD
Averett University, VA
Ball State University, IN
Barton College, NC
Bay Path University, MA
Bellarmine University, KY
Berry College, GA
Binghamton University, State University of New York, NY
Bluefield College, VA
Blue Mountain College, MS
Caldwell University, NJ
California Baptist University, CA
California Lutheran University, CA
California State University, Chico, CA

Calvin College, MI
Campbellsville University, KY
Carroll University, WI
Christian Brothers University, TN
Christopher Newport University, VA
Claflin University, SC
Coe College, IA
The College at Brockport, State University of New York, NY
College of Saint Elizabeth, NJ
The College of Saint Rose, NY
College of Staten Island of the City University of New York, NY
Colorado Mesa University, CO
Columbia College, MO
Concordia University Texas, TX
Dominican University of California, CA
East Carolina University, NC
Eastern Connecticut State University, CT
Eastern Washington University, WA
East Stroudsburg University of Pennsylvania, PA
East Texas Baptist University, TX
ECPI University, VA
Elon University, NC
Emmanuel College, GA
Evangel University, MO
The Evergreen State College, WA
Fairmont State University, WV
Faulkner University, AL
Ferris State University, MI
Fitchburg State University, MA
Florida Gulf Coast University, FL
Fordham University, NY
Fort Hays State University, KS
Fort Lewis College, CO
Francis Marion University, SC
Franklin Pierce University, NH
Frostburg State University, MD
Gannon University, PA
Georgia College & State University, GA
Georgian Court University, NJ
Georgia Southern University, GA
Graceland University, IA
Grand Valley State University, MI
Grand View University, IA
Hampton University, VA
Hollins University, VA
Houghton College, NY
Howard University, DC
Indiana University of Pennsylvania, PA
Iowa State University of Science and Technology, IA
Kean University, NJ
Kent State University, OH
Kent State University at Stark, OH
Kentucky State University, KY
Lawrence Technological University, MI
Lewis-Clark State College, ID
Lincoln University, MO
Lipscomb University, TN
Lock Haven University of Pennsylvania, PA
Loyola Marymount University, CA
Loyola University Chicago, IL
Maryville University of Saint Louis, MO
Mercer University, GA
Meredith College, NC
Messiah College, PA
Metropolitan State University of Denver, CO
Middle Tennessee State University, TN
Midway University, KY
Millsaps College, MS
Minnesota State University Moorhead, MN
Mississippi State University, MS
Missouri Baptist University, MO

Missouri Western State University, MO
Monmouth University, NJ
Montana State University Billings, MT
Moravian College, PA
Morehead State University, KY
Mount St. Joseph University, OH
Murray State University, KY
New Jersey Institute of Technology, NJ
New Mexico State University, NM
North Central College, IL
Northeastern Illinois University, IL
Northern Illinois University, IL
Northern Kentucky University, KY
Northern State University, SD
Northwestern State University of
    Louisiana, LA
The Ohio State University, OH
Ohio Valley University, WV
Oklahoma Baptist University, OK
Oklahoma State University, OK
Palm Beach Atlantic University, FL
Piedmont College, GA
Portland State University, OR
Queens University of Charlotte, NC
Randolph College, VA
Regis University, CO
Robert Morris University Illinois, IL
Rogers State University, OK
Sacred Heart University, CT
The Sage Colleges, NY
Saginaw Valley State University, MI
St. Ambrose University, IA
St. Edward's University, TX
Saint Mary-of-the-Woods College, IN
Salisbury University, MD
San Diego State University, CA
Siena College, NY
Simpson College, IA
Sonoma State University, CA
South Dakota School of Mines and
    Technology, SD
Southeastern Louisiana University, LA
Southern Arkansas University–
    Magnolia, AR
Southern Oregon University, OR
Spring Arbor University, MI
State University of New York College at
    Cortland, NY
State University of New York College at
    Geneseo, NY
State University of New York College at
    Potsdam, NY
Stephen F. Austin State University, TX
Stockton University, NJ
Texas A&M University–Commerce, TX
Texas Christian University, TX
Texas Wesleyan University, TX
Thomas More College, KY
Towson University, MD
Trinity Christian College, IL
Tusculum College, TN
Union College, KY
The University of Akron, OH
The University of Alabama at
    Birmingham, AL
University of Arkansas, AR
University of Hartford, CT
University of Idaho, ID
The University of Kansas, KS
University of Kentucky, KY
University of Louisville, KY
University of Maine, ME
University of Maine at Fort Kent, ME
University of Maryland, College Park, MD
University of Mary Washington, VA
University of Massachusetts Boston, MA

University of Massachusetts Dartmouth, MA
University of Memphis, TN
University of Michigan–Dearborn, MI
University of Michigan–Flint, MI
University of Mississippi, MS
University of Missouri, MO
University of Missouri–St. Louis, MO
University of Nebraska at Omaha, NE
University of Nevada, Las Vegas, NV
University of Nevada, Reno, NV
The University of North Carolina at
    Charlotte, NC
The University of North Carolina at
    Greensboro, NC
University of Northern Colorado, CO
University of Pittsburgh at Bradford, PA
University of St. Francis, IL
University of South Carolina, SC
University of South Carolina Aiken, SC
University of Southern Indiana, IN
The University of Tennessee at Martin, TN
The University of Texas at Dallas, TX
The University of Toledo, OH
University of Vermont, VT
University of West Georgia, GA
University of Wisconsin–Eau Claire, WI
University of Wisconsin–Green Bay, WI
University of Wisconsin–La Crosse, WI
University of Wisconsin–Parkside, WI
University of Wisconsin–Stevens Point, WI
University of Wisconsin–Stout, WI
University of Wisconsin–Whitewater, WI
University of Wyoming, WY
Warner University, FL
Washburn University, KS
Wesleyan College, GA
Western Kentucky University, KY
Western Oregon University, OR
Wichita State University, KS
Widener University, PA
William Jessup University, CA
Wilson College, PA
Wisconsin Lutheran College, WI
Wittenberg University, OH
Wright State University, OH
Wright State University–Lake Campus, OH
Youngstown State University, OH

Children and Siblings of Alumni
Adelphi University, NY
Alaska Pacific University, AK
Albion College, MI
Albright College, PA
Alderson Broaddus University, WV
Alliant International University–
    San Diego, CA
Alma College, MI
Alvernia University, PA
American University, DC
Aquinas College, MI
Arcadia University, PA
Asbury University, KY
Auburn University, AL
Augsburg College, MN
Augustana College, IL
Augustana University, SD
Aurora University, IL
Averett University, VA
Baker University, KS
Baldwin Wallace University, OH
Barclay College, KS
Barton College, NC
Belhaven University, MS
Bellarmine University, KY
Belmont University, TN
Bemidji State University, MN

Benedictine University, IL
Berklee College of Music, MA
Bethany College, WV
Bethel College, KS
Bethel University, MN
Binghamton University, State University of
    New York, NY
Bloomfield College, NJ
Blue Mountain College, MS
Bluffton University, OH
Boston University, MA
Bowling Green State University, OH
Bradley University, IL
Brenau University, GA
Briar Cliff University, IA
Bryan College, TN
Cabrini University, PA
Caldwell University, NJ
California Lutheran University, CA
California Polytechnic State University, San
    Luis Obispo, CA
California State Polytechnic University,
    Pomona, CA
California State University,
    Monterey Bay, CA
Calumet College of Saint Joseph, IN
Calvary University, MO
Calvin College, MI
Canisius College, NY
Capital University, OH
Cardinal Stritch University, WI
Carlow University, PA
Carroll University, WI
Carson-Newman University, TN
The Catholic University of America, DC
Cedar Crest College, PA
Centenary College of Louisiana, LA
Central College, IA
Central Methodist University, MO
Central Michigan University, MI
Central Washington University, WA
Centre College, KY
Chapman University, CA
Chatham University, PA
Christian Brothers University, TN
The Citadel, The Military College of South
    Carolina, SC
City College of the City University of New
    York, NY
Clarke University, IA
Clarkson University, NY
Coe College, IA
The College at Brockport, State University
    of New York, NY
The College of Idaho, ID
The College of New Rochelle, NY
College of Saint Benedict, MN
College of Saint Elizabeth, NJ
The College of Saint Rose, NY
The College of St. Scholastica, MN
College of Staten Island of the City
    University of New York, NY
Columbia College, MO
Columbia International University, SC
Concordia University Ann Arbor, MI
Concordia University Chicago, IL
Concordia University, Nebraska, NE
Concordia University Texas, TX
Converse College, SC
Corban University, OR
Cornell College, IA
Crown College, MN
Culver-Stockton College, MO
Curry College, MA
Davis College, NY
Defiance College, OH

Delta State University, MS
DePauw University, IN
Dickinson College, PA
Doane University, NE
Dominican University, IL
Dominican University of California, CA
Dordt College, IA
Drake University, IA
Drexel University, PA
Drury University, MO
Duke University, NC
Duquesne University, PA
D'Youville College, NY
East Carolina University, NC
Eastern Kentucky University, KY
Eastern Mennonite University, VA
Eastern Michigan University, MI
Eastern University, PA
Eastern Washington University, WA
East Stroudsburg University of
    Pennsylvania, PA
East Texas Baptist University, TX
ECPI University, VA
Edgewood College, WI
Elmhurst College, IL
Elmira College, NY
Emory & Henry College, VA
Emporia State University, KS
Endicott College, MA
Eureka College, IL
Evangel University, MO
Fairfield University, CT
Fairmont State University, WV
Faulkner University, AL
Ferris State University, MI
Fitchburg State University, MA
Florida Institute of Technology, FL
Florida Southern College, FL
Fordham University, NY
Fort Hays State University, KS
Fort Lewis College, CO
Francis Marion University, SC
Franklin College, IN
Franklin Pierce University, NH
Friends University, KS
George Fox University, OR
Georgian Court University, NJ
Georgia Southern University, GA
Georgia Southwestern State University, GA
Gonzaga University, WA
Gordon College, MA
Graceland University, IA
Grambling State University, LA
Grand Valley State University, MI
Grand View University, IA
Greenville College, IL
Gustavus Adolphus College, MN
Gwynedd Mercy University, PA
Hamline University, MN
Hanover College, IN
Hardin-Simmons University, TX
Hartwick College, NY
Heidelberg University, OH
Hilbert College, NY
Hobart and William Smith Colleges, NY
Hofstra University, NY
Hollins University, VA
Hood College, MD
Houghton College, NY
Howard Payne University, TX
Huntingdon College, AL
Huntington University, IN
Husson University, ME
Illinois Institute of Technology, IL
Indiana State University, IN

Indiana University–Purdue University Fort
    Wayne, IN
Indiana Wesleyan University, IN
Iona College, NY
Iowa State University of Science and
    Technology, IA
Iowa Wesleyan University, IA
Ithaca College, NY
Jackson State University, MS
Jacksonville State University, AL
James Madison University, VA
Juniata College, PA
Kalamazoo College, MI
Kansas Wesleyan University, KS
Keene State College, NH
Kennesaw State University, GA
Kent State University, OH
Kent State University at Stark, OH
Kentucky Wesleyan College, KY
Keuka College, NY
The King's College, NY
King's College, PA
Kuyper College, MI
Lancaster Bible College, PA
Lasell College, MA
Lawrence Technological University, MI
Lawrence University, WI
Lebanon Valley College, PA
Le Moyne College, NY
Lenoir-Rhyne University, NC
Lewis-Clark State College, ID
Lewis University, IL
Life University, GA
Lincoln Memorial University, TN
Lincoln University, PA
Lindenwood University, MO
Lindsey Wilson College, KY
Long Island University–LIU Brooklyn, NY
Long Island University–LIU Post, NY
Longwood University, VA
Louisiana Tech University, LA
Loyola Marymount University, CA
Loyola University New Orleans, LA
Luther College, IA
Lynn University, FL
Lyon College, AR
MacMurray College, IL
Malone University, OH
Manchester University, IN
Mansfield University of Pennsylvania, PA
Maranatha Baptist University, WI
Marietta College, OH
Marshall University, WV
Maryville College, TN
Maryville University of Saint Louis, MO
The Master's University, CA
McKendree University, IL
McPherson College, KS
Methodist University, NC
Michigan State University, MI
Michigan Technological University, MI
Mid-Atlantic Christian University, NC
Middle Tennessee State University, TN
Midway University, KY
Midwestern State University, TX
Millikin University, IL
Minot State University, ND
Misericordia University, PA
Mississippi State University, MS
Missouri Baptist University, MO
Missouri State University, MO
Missouri University of Science and
    Technology, MO
Missouri Western State University, MO
Monmouth University, NJ

Montana State University, MT
Montana State University Billings, MT
Montana Tech of The University of
    Montana, MT
Montclair State University, NJ
Montreat College, NC
Moravian College, PA
Morehead State University, KY
Morehouse College, GA
Morningside College, IA
Mount Mary University, WI
Mount St. Joseph University, OH
Mount Saint Mary's University, CA
Muskingum University, OH
Nazareth College of Rochester, NY
Newberry College, SC
New England College, NH
New Mexico State University, NM
Nichols College, MA
North Carolina State University, NC
Northeastern State University, OK
Northern Arizona University, AZ
Northern Illinois University, IL
Northern Kentucky University, KY
Northern Michigan University, MI
Northland College, WI
Northwestern College, IA
Northwest Missouri State University, MO
Northwest Nazarene University, ID
Oakland City University, IN
Ohio Northern University, OH
The Ohio State University, OH
Ohio University, OH
Ohio University–Chillicothe, OH
Ohio University–Eastern, OH
Ohio University–Lancaster, OH
Ohio University–Southern Campus, OH
Ohio University–Zanesville, OH
Ohio Wesleyan University, OH
Oklahoma Baptist University, OK
Oklahoma Panhandle State University, OK
Oklahoma State University, OK
Oklahoma Wesleyan University, OK
Olivet College, MI
Oral Roberts University, OK
Oregon State University, OR
Otterbein University, OH
Ouachita Baptist University, AR
Pacific Union College, CA
Pacific University, OR
Palm Beach Atlantic University, FL
Peirce College, PA
Penn State Abington, PA
Penn State Altoona, PA
Penn State Beaver, PA
Penn State Berks, PA
Penn State Brandywine, PA
Penn State Erie, The Behrend College, PA
Penn State Harrisburg, PA
Penn State Hazleton, PA
Penn State New Kensington, PA
Penn State York, PA
Pittsburg State University, KS
Principia College, IL
Queens University of Charlotte, NC
Randall University, OK
Randolph-Macon College, VA
Regent University, VA
Rensselaer Polytechnic Institute, NY
Research College of Nursing, MO
Rhode Island College, RI
Roberts Wesleyan College, NY
Rockford University, IL
Sacred Heart University, CT
The Sage Colleges, NY

St. Ambrose University, IA
St. John Fisher College, NY
St. Joseph's College, Long
    Island Campus, NY
St. Joseph's College, New York, NY
Saint Joseph's University, PA
St. Lawrence University, NY
Saint Martin's University, WA
Saint Mary-of-the-Woods College, IN
Saint Mary's University of Minnesota, MN
Salisbury University, MD
Salve Regina University, RI
San Diego Christian College, CA
San Diego State University, CA
San Francisco Art Institute, CA
Santa Clara University, CA
Seattle Pacific University, WA
Seattle University, WA
Seton Hill University, PA
Shippensburg University of
    Pennsylvania, PA
Siena College, NY
Simmons College, MA
Simpson College, IA
Simpson University, CA
Slippery Rock University of
    Pennsylvania, PA
Sonoma State University, CA
Southeastern Louisiana University, LA
Southeastern Oklahoma State
    University, OK
Southern Adventist University, TN
Southern Arkansas University–
    Magnolia, AR
Southern Illinois University Carbondale, IL
Southern New Hampshire University, NH
Southern Utah University, UT
Southwestern Oklahoma State
    University, OK
Springfield College, MA
State University of New York at
    Fredonia, NY
State University of New York College at
    Potsdam, NY
State University of New York College of
    Agriculture and Technology at
    Cobleskill, NY
State University of New York College of
    Environmental Science and Forestry, NY
Stephen F. Austin State University, TX
Sterling College, KS
Stetson University, FL
Stevens Institute of Technology, NJ
Suffolk University, MA
Susquehanna University, PA
Taylor University, IN
Tennessee Technological University, TN
Tennessee Wesleyan University, TN
Texas A&M University–Commerce, TX
Texas Lutheran University, TX
Texas Wesleyan University, TX
Thiel College, PA
Thomas College, ME
Thomas More College, KY
Thomas University, GA
Towson University, MD
Trine University, IN
Trinity Christian College, IL
Trinity University, TX
Truman State University, MO
Union College, KY
Union University, TN
The University of Alabama at
    Birmingham, AL
University of Alaska Anchorage, AK
University of Arkansas, AR

University of Dayton, OH
University of Delaware, DE
University of Detroit Mercy, MI
University of Dubuque, IA
University of Evansville, IN
University of Great Falls, MT
University of Houston, TX
University of Idaho, ID
The University of Iowa, IA
University of Jamestown, ND
The University of Kansas, KS
University of Kentucky, KY
University of Louisville, KY
University of Maine, ME
University of Mary Hardin-Baylor, TX
University of Mary Washington, VA
University of Massachusetts Amherst, MA
University of Massachusetts Lowell, MA
University of Michigan–Dearborn, MI
University of Michigan–Flint, MI
University of Minnesota, Crookston, MN
University of Mississippi, MS
University of Missouri, MO
University of Missouri–Kansas City, MO
University of Missouri–St. Louis, MO
University of Montana, MT
University of Mount Union, OH
University of Nebraska at Kearney, NE
University of Nebraska at Omaha, NE
University of Nebraska–Lincoln, NE
University of Nevada, Las Vegas, NV
University of Nevada, Reno, NV
University of New Hampshire, NH
University of North Alabama, AL
The University of North Carolina at
    Greensboro, NC
The University of North Carolina at
    Pembroke, NC
University of Northern Colorado, CO
University of Oklahoma, OK
University of Rhode Island, RI
University of Rochester, NY
University of St. Francis, IL
University of Sioux Falls, SD
University of South Carolina, SC
University of South Carolina Aiken, SC
University of Southern California, CA
University of Southern Mississippi, MS
The University of Tampa, FL
The University of Tennessee at
    Chattanooga, TN
The University of Tennessee at Martin, TN
University of the Incarnate Word, TX
The University of Toledo, OH
The University of Tulsa, OK
The University of West Alabama, AL
University of West Florida, FL
University of West Georgia, GA
University of Wisconsin–La Crosse, WI
University of Wyoming, WY
Upper Iowa University, IA
Ursinus College, PA
Ursuline College, OH
Utah State University, UT
Valley City State University, ND
Valparaiso University, IN
Virginia Military Institute, VA
Wake Forest University, NC
Warner Pacific College, OR
Warner University, FL
Wartburg College, IA
Washburn University, KS
Washington & Jefferson College, PA
Washington State University, WA
Wayland Baptist University, TX
Webber International University, FL

Webster University, MO
Wells College, NY
Wesleyan College, GA
Western Michigan University, MI
Western State Colorado University, CO
Westminster College, MO
Westminster College, PA
West Texas A&M University, TX
West Virginia Wesleyan College, WV
Wheaton College, IL
Wheeling Jesuit University, WV
Whittier College, CA
Whitworth University, WA
William Jewell College, MO
William Woods University, MO
Wilson College, PA
Wingate University, NC
Winona State University, MN
Wittenberg University, OH
Wright State University, OH
Wright State University–Lake Campus, OH
Xavier University, OH
York College of Pennsylvania, PA
Youngstown State University, OH

Children of Current Students
Augustana University, SD
Aurora University, IL
Barclay College, KS
Bethel College, KS
Bloomfield College, NJ
Blue Mountain College, MS
Bryan College, TN
Caldwell University, NJ
California State Polytechnic University,
    Pomona, CA
Cardinal Stritch University, WI
Carroll University, WI
Central College, IA
College of Staten Island of the City
    University of New York, NY
Columbia College, MO
Curry College, MA
ECPI University, VA
Elmhurst College, IL
Emmanuel College, GA
Franklin College, IN
Franklin Pierce University, NH
Indiana Tech, IN
Kansas Wesleyan University, KS
Lancaster Bible College, PA
Long Island University–LIU Brooklyn, NY
Long Island University–LIU Post, NY
Marymount University, VA
Misericordia University, PA
Missouri Baptist University, MO
Mount Aloysius College, PA
Mount Marty College, SD
New Mexico State University, NM
Northwest University, WA
Palm Beach Atlantic University, FL
Queens University of Charlotte, NC
Rockford University, IL
Sacred Heart University, CT
Saint Mary-of-the-Woods College, IN
Springfield College, MA
Texas Wesleyan University, TX
Thomas College, ME
Truett McConnell University, GA
Union College, KY
Union University, TN
The University of Alabama at
    Birmingham, AL
University of Alaska Anchorage, AK
University of Great Falls, MT
University of Hartford, CT

University of Valley Forge, PA
Upper Iowa University, IA
Wayne State University, MI
Wesleyan College, GA
Wilson College, PA

Children of Educators
Agnes Scott College, GA
Alfred University, NY
Allegheny College, PA
Amridge University, AL
Austin Peay State University, TN
Bard College, NY
Bridgewater College, VA
Bryan College, TN
Caldwell University, NJ
Calvary University, MO
Campbellsville University, KY
Canisius College, NY
Carlow University, PA
Centenary College of Louisiana, LA
Chestnut Hill College, PA
Chowan University, NC
Coe College, IA
The College of Idaho, ID
College of Staten Island of the City
    University of New York, NY
The College of Wooster, OH
Columbia College, MO
Columbus College of Art & Design, OH
Concordia University, Nebraska, NE
Davis College, NY
Emmanuel College, GA
Emory & Henry College, VA
Endicott College, MA
Evangel University, MO
Flagler College, FL
Franklin Pierce University, NH
Goshen College, IN
Governors State University, IL
Grand View University, IA
Hampden-Sydney College, VA
Hardin-Simmons University, TX
Hillsdale College, MI
Jacksonville University, FL
John Carroll University, OH
Judson College, AL
Kansas Wesleyan University, KS
King's College, PA
Lipscomb University, TN
Long Island University–LIU Brooklyn, NY
Long Island University–LIU Post, NY
Lycoming College, PA
Lynn University, FL
Maranatha Baptist University, WI
Mary Baldwin University, VA
McDaniel College, MD
Mississippi State University, MS
Moravian College, PA
Mount St. Mary's University, MD
New England College, NH
Northwest University, WA
Occidental College, CA
Oklahoma Wesleyan University, OK
Palm Beach Atlantic University, FL
Research College of Nursing, MO
Rockford University, IL
St. Ambrose University, IA
Saint Anselm College, NH
Salem College, NC
Seattle University, WA
Simpson College, IA
Sonoma State University, CA
Southeastern University, FL
Southern Illinois University Carbondale, IL

Southern New Hampshire University, NH
Stevens Institute of Technology, NJ
Tarleton State University, TX
Tennessee Technological University, TN
Texas Christian University, TX
Texas Wesleyan University, TX
Trine University, IN
Trinity University, TX
Union University, TN
Unity College, ME
The University of Alabama at
    Birmingham, AL
University of Alaska Anchorage, AK
University of Dubuque, IA
University of Kentucky, KY
University of Memphis, TN
University of Puerto Rico in Bayamón, PR
University of St. Francis, IL
University of St. Thomas, MN
The University of Tennessee at Martin, TN
Villanova University, PA
Warner University, FL
Wesleyan College, GA
Wright State University, OH
Wright State University–Lake Campus, OH

Children of Faculty/Staff
Abilene Christian University, TX
Adelphi University, NY
Agnes Scott College, GA
Alaska Bible College, AK
Alaska Pacific University, AK
Alcorn State University, MS
Alderson Broaddus University, WV
Alfred University, NY
Allegheny College, PA
Allen College, IA
Alliant International University–
    San Diego, CA
Alvernia University, PA
Alverno College, WI
American University, DC
Amridge University, AL
Anderson University, SC
Andrews University, MI
Aquinas College, MI
Arizona State University at the Downtown
    Phoenix campus, AZ
Arizona State University at the Polytechnic
    campus, AZ
Arizona State University at the
    Tempe campus, AZ
Arizona State University at the
    West campus, AZ
Arkansas Tech University, AR
Asbury University, KY
Auburn University, AL
Augustana College, IL
Augustana University, SD
Aurora University, IL
Austin College, TX
Austin Peay State University, TN
Ave Maria University, FL
Baker University, KS
Ball State University, IN
Barclay College, KS
Bard College, NY
Barton College, NC
Baylor University, TX
Bay Path University, MA
Belhaven University, MS
Bellarmine University, KY
Belmont Abbey College, NC
Belmont University, TN
Bemidji State University, MN

Benedictine College, KS
Benedictine University, IL
Berklee College of Music, MA
Berry College, GA
Bethany College, WV
Bethany Lutheran College, MN
Bethel College, IN
Bethel College, KS
Bethel University, MN
Binghamton University, State University of
    New York, NY
Biola University, CA
Bloomsburg University of Pennsylvania, PA
Bluefield College, VA
Blue Mountain College, MS
Bluffton University, OH
Boston University, MA
Bowdoin College, ME
Bowling Green State University, OH
Bradley University, IL
Brenau University, GA
Brevard College, NC
Bridgewater College, VA
Bryan College, TN
Buena Vista University, IA
Cairn University, PA
Caldwell University, NJ
California Baptist University, CA
California Lutheran University, CA
California State University, Bakersfield, CA
California State University, Chico, CA
Calumet College of Saint Joseph, IN
Calvary University, MO
Calvin College, MI
Cameron University, OK
Campbellsville University, KY
Campbell University, NC
Canisius College, NY
Capital University, OH
Cardinal Stritch University, WI
Carlos Albizu University, Miami
    Campus, FL
Carlow University, PA
Carroll College, MT
Carroll University, WI
Case Western Reserve University, OH
Catawba College, NC
The Catholic University of America, DC
Cedarville University, OH
Centenary College of Louisiana, LA
Central College, IA
Central Methodist University, MO
Central Michigan University, MI
Central Washington University, WA
Centre College, KY
Chaminade University of Honolulu, HI
Chatham University, PA
Chestnut Hill College, PA
Chowan University, NC
Cincinnati Christian University, OH
Claflin University, SC
Clarion University of Pennsylvania, PA
Clarke University, IA
Clarkson University, NY
Clarks Summit University, PA
Clemson University, SC
Cleveland Institute of Music, OH
Cleveland State University, OH
Coastal Carolina University, SC
Coe College, IA
The College at Brockport, State University
    of New York, NY
The College of Idaho, ID
The College of New Rochelle, NY
College of Saint Mary, NE

The College of Saint Rose, NY
The College of St. Scholastica, MN
College of Staten Island of the City
  University of New York, NY
College of the Holy Cross, MA
The College of Wooster, OH
The Colorado College, CO
Colorado State University, CO
Columbia College, MO
Columbia International University, SC
Columbus College of Art & Design, OH
Concordia University Ann Arbor, MI
Concordia University Chicago, IL
Concordia University Irvine, CA
Concordia University, Nebraska, NE
Concordia University, St. Paul, MN
Concordia University Texas, TX
Concord University, WV
Converse College, SC
Corban University, OR
Cornell College, IA
Cornerstone University, MI
Covenant College, GA
Crossroads Bible College, IN
Crown College, MN
Culver-Stockton College, MO
Curry College, MA
Daemen College, NY
Dakota Wesleyan University, SD
Dallas Baptist University, TX
Davis College, NY
Defiance College, OH
Delta State University, MS
Denison University, OH
DePaul University, IL
Dickinson College, PA
Dickinson State University, ND
Doane University, NE
Dominican College, NY
Dominican University, IL
Dominican University of California, CA
Dordt College, IA
Drury University, MO
Duquesne University, PA
D'Youville College, NY
East Carolina University, NC
East Central University, OK
Eastern Kentucky University, KY
Eastern Mennonite University, VA
Eastern University, PA
East Texas Baptist University, TX
Eckerd College, FL
ECPI University, VA
Edgewood College, WI
Elizabethtown College, PA
Elmira College, NY
Elms College, MA
Elon University, NC
Embry-Riddle Aeronautical University–
  Worldwide, FL
Emmanuel College, GA
Emmanuel College, MA
Emory & Henry College, VA
Emory University, GA
Emporia State University, KS
Eureka College, IL
Evangel University, MO
Fairfield University, CT
Fairmont State University, WV
Faulkner University, AL
Felician University, NJ
Flagler College, FL
Florida College, FL
Florida Institute of Technology, FL
Florida Southern College, FL
Fordham University, NY

Fort Hays State University, KS
Fort Lewis College, CO
Framingham State University, MA
Franciscan University of Steubenville, OH
Francis Marion University, SC
Franklin College, IN
Franklin Pierce University, NH
Fresno Pacific University, CA
Friends University, KS
Furman University, SC
Gardner-Webb University, NC
Geneva College, PA
George Fox University, OR
Georgetown University, DC
Georgia College & State University, GA
Georgian Court University, NJ
Glenville State College, WV
Gonzaga University, WA
Gordon College, MA
Goshen College, IN
Graceland University, IA
Grambling State University, LA
Grand Valley State University, MI
Grand View University, IA
Greenville College, IL
Guilford College, NC
Gwynedd Mercy University, PA
Hampden-Sydney College, VA
Hampshire College, MA
Hampton University, VA
Hanover College, IN
Harding University, AR
Hardin-Simmons University, TX
Hartwick College, NY
Heidelberg University, OH
Hendrix College, AR
Hillsdale College, MI
Hofstra University, NY
Hollins University, VA
Hood College, MD
Hope International University, CA
Houghton College, NY
Houston Baptist University, TX
Howard Payne University, TX
Huntingdon College, AL
Huntington University, IN
Husson University, ME
Idaho State University, ID
Illinois College, IL
Illinois Institute of Technology, IL
Illinois Wesleyan University, IL
Indiana State University, IN
Indiana Tech, IN
Indiana University of Pennsylvania, PA
Indiana Wesleyan University, IN
Iowa Wesleyan University, IA
Ithaca College, NY
Jackson State University, MS
Jacksonville University, FL
James Madison University, VA
John Carroll University, OH
Johnson C. Smith University, NC
John Wesley University, NC
Judson College, AL
Juniata College, PA
Kansas Wesleyan University, KS
Kent State University, OH
Kent State University at Geauga, OH
Kent State University at Stark, OH
Kentucky Mountain Bible College, KY
Kentucky State University, KY
Kentucky Wesleyan College, KY
Keuka College, NY
King's College, PA
King University, TN
Knox College, IL

Kutztown University of Pennsylvania, PA
Kuyper College, MI
LaGrange College, GA
Lake Erie College, OH
Lancaster Bible College, PA
La Salle University, PA
Lasell College, MA
Lawrence Technological University, MI
Lebanon Valley College, PA
Lees-McRae College, NC
Lee University, TN
Lehigh University, PA
Lenoir-Rhyne University, NC
Lewis & Clark College, OR
Lewis-Clark State College, ID
Lewis University, IL
Liberty University, VA
LIM College, NY
Lincoln Christian University, IL
Lincoln Memorial University, TN
Lincoln University, MO
Lincoln University, PA
Lindenwood University, MO
Lindsey Wilson College, KY
Linfield College, OR
Lipscomb University, TN
Long Island University–LIU Brooklyn, NY
Long Island University–LIU Post, NY
Louisiana Tech University, LA
Loyola Marymount University, CA
Loyola University New Orleans, LA
Lubbock Christian University, TX
Lycoming College, PA
Lynn University, FL
Lyon College, AR
MacMurray College, IL
Manchester University, IN
Manhattan College, NY
Manhattanville College, NY
Maranatha Baptist University, WI
Marian University, WI
Marquette University, WI
Marshall University, WV
Mary Baldwin University, VA
Marygrove College, MI
Marymount University, VA
Maryville College, TN
Massachusetts College of
  Art and Design, MA
The Master's University, CA
Mayville State University, ND
McKendree University, IL
McNally Smith College of Music, MN
McPherson College, KS
Memphis College of Art, TN
Mercer University, GA
Mercy College, NY
Meredith College, NC
Merrimack College, MA
Messiah College, PA
Methodist University, NC
Miami University, OH
Michigan State University, MI
Michigan Technological University, MI
Mid-Atlantic Christian University, NC
Midway University, KY
Midwestern State University, TX
Milligan College, TN
Millikin University, IL
Millsaps College, MS
Milwaukee School of Engineering, WI
Minnesota State University Moorhead, MN
Minot State University, ND
Misericordia University, PA
Mississippi State University, MS
Missouri Baptist University, MO

Missouri University of Science and
   Technology, MO
Monmouth University, NJ
Montana State University Billings, MT
Montana Tech of The University of
   Montana, MT
Montreat College, NC
Moravian College, PA
Morehouse College, GA
Morningside College, IA
Morrisville State College, NY
Mount Carmel College of Nursing, OH
Mount Marty College, SD
Mount Mary University, WI
Mount St. Joseph University, OH
Mount Saint Mary College, NY
Mount St. Mary's University, MD
Mount Vernon Nazarene University, OH
Murray State University, KY
Nazareth College of Rochester, NY
Nebraska Methodist College, NE
Newberry College, SC
New England College, NH
New Jersey Institute of Technology, NJ
New Mexico State University, NM
NewSchool of Architecture and Design, CA
New York Institute of Technology, NY
Niagara University, NY
Nicholls State University, LA
Nichols College, MA
North Carolina State University, NC
North Central College, IL
Northeastern Illinois University, IL
Northeastern State University, OK
Northern Illinois University, IL
Northern Kentucky University, KY
Northern Michigan University, MI
Northwest Christian University, OR
Northwestern College, IA
Northwestern State University of
   Louisiana, LA
Northwest Missouri State University, MO
Northwest Nazarene University, ID
Northwest University, WA
Nova Southeastern University, FL
Oakland City University, IN
Occidental College, CA
Oglethorpe University, GA
Ohio Northern University, OH
The Ohio State University, OH
Ohio University, OH
Ohio University–Chillicothe, OH
Ohio University–Eastern, OH
Ohio University–Lancaster, OH
Ohio University–Southern Campus, OH
Ohio University–Zanesville, OH
Ohio Valley University, WV
Oklahoma Baptist University, OK
Oklahoma Christian University, OK
Oklahoma City University, OK
Oklahoma Panhandle State University, OK
Oklahoma Wesleyan University, OK
Old Dominion University, VA
Olivet College, MI
Olivet Nazarene University, IL
O'More College of Design, TN
Oral Roberts University, OK
Otterbein University, OH
Ouachita Baptist University, AR
Our Lady of the Lake University, TX
Pacific University, OR
Palm Beach Atlantic University, FL
Patrick Henry College, VA
Peirce College, PA
Philander Smith College, AR

Piedmont College, GA
Piedmont International University, NC
Plymouth State University, NH
Point Park University, PA
Presbyterian College, SC
Principia College, IL
Purdue University, IN
Queens University of Charlotte, NC
Quinnipiac University, CT
Ramapo College of New Jersey, NJ
Randall University, OK
Randolph College, VA
Randolph-Macon College, VA
Regent University, VA
Regis University, CO
Rensselaer Polytechnic Institute, NY
Research College of Nursing, MO
Rhode Island School of Design, RI
Rhodes College, TN
Robert Morris University, PA
Robert Morris University Illinois, IL
Roberts Wesleyan College, NY
Rochester Institute of Technology, NY
Rockford University, IL
Rockhurst University, MO
Sacred Heart University, CT
St. Ambrose University, IA
Saint Anselm College, NH
Saint Augustine's University, NC
St. Bonaventure University, NY
St. Edward's University, TX
St. John Fisher College, NY
St. John's College, NM
St. John's University, NY
St. Joseph's College, Long
   Island Campus, NY
St. Joseph's College, New York, NY
Saint Joseph's University, PA
Saint Leo University, FL
St. Louis College of Pharmacy, MO
Saint Louis University, MO
Saint Martin's University, WA
Saint Mary-of-the-Woods College, IN
St. Mary's College of Maryland, MD
St. Mary's University, TX
Saint Mary's University of Minnesota, MN
St. Norbert College, WI
Saint Peter's University, NJ
Saint Vincent College, PA
Salem College, NC
Samford University, AL
San Diego Christian College, CA
San Diego State University, CA
Santa Clara University, CA
Schreiner University, TX
Seattle Pacific University, WA
Seattle University, WA
Seton Hill University, PA
Shawnee State University, OH
Shenandoah University, VA
Siena College, NY
Simpson College, IA
Simpson University, CA
Skidmore College, NY
Slippery Rock University of
   Pennsylvania, PA
Soka University of America, CA
Sonoma State University, CA
Southeastern Louisiana University, LA
Southeastern University, FL
Southeast Missouri State University, MO
Southern Arkansas
   University–Magnolia, AR
Southern Connecticut State University, CT
Southern Illinois University Carbondale, IL

Southern Illinois University
   Edwardsville, IL
Southern Vermont College, VT
Southwestern College, KS
Southwestern Oklahoma
   State University, OK
Southwestern University, TX
Spring Arbor University, MI
Springfield College, MA
Spring Hill College, AL
State University of New York at
   New Paltz, NY
State University of New York College at
   Potsdam, NY
Stephen F. Austin State University, TX
Stephens College, MO
Sterling College, KS
Stetson University, FL
Stevens Institute of Technology, NJ
Stockton University, NJ
Stonehill College, MA
Suffolk University, MA
Susquehanna University, PA
Tarleton State University, TX
Taylor University, IN
Temple University, PA
Tennessee Technological University, TN
Tennessee Wesleyan University, TN
Texas A&M University, TX
Texas Christian University, TX
Texas Lutheran University, TX
Texas Tech University, TX
Texas Wesleyan University, TX
Thiel College, PA
Thomas College, ME
Thomas More College, KY
Thomas University, GA
Tiffin University, OH
Toccoa Falls College, GA
Touro College, NY
Towson University, MD
Transylvania University, KY
Trevecca Nazarene University, TN
Trine University, IN
Trinity Christian College, IL
Trinity College of Florida, FL
Truett McConnell University, GA
Truman State University, MO
Tulane University, LA
Tusculum College, TN
Tuskegee University, AL
Union College, KY
Union College, NY
Union University, TN
The University of Alabama at
   Birmingham, AL
University of Alaska Anchorage, AK
The University of Arizona, AZ
University of Arkansas, AR
University of Bridgeport, CT
University of Central Oklahoma, OK
University of Colorado Denver, CO
University of Dallas, TX
University of Dayton, OH
University of Delaware, DE
University of Detroit Mercy, MI
University of Dubuque, IA
University of Evansville, IN
The University of Findlay, OH
University of Florida, FL
University of Great Falls, MT
University of Hartford, CT
University of Holy Cross, LA
University of Idaho, ID

University of Illinois at Urbana–
Champaign, IL
University of Indianapolis, IN
University of Jamestown, ND
The University of Kansas, KS
University of Kentucky, KY
University of Louisiana at Monroe, LA
University of Louisville, KY
University of Maine, ME
University of Maine at Augusta, ME
University of Maine at Fort Kent, ME
University of Maine at Presque Isle, ME
University of Mary Hardin-Baylor, TX
University of Maryland Eastern Shore, MD
University of Mary Washington, VA
University of Massachusetts Amherst, MA
University of Massachusetts Boston, MA
University of Massachusetts Dartmouth, MA
University of Massachusetts Lowell, MA
University of Memphis, TN
University of Miami, FL
University of Michigan, MI
University of Michigan–Dearborn, MI
University of Michigan–Flint, MI
University of Minnesota, Crookston, MN
University of Mississippi, MS
University of Missouri, MO
University of Missouri–St. Louis, MO
University of Mobile, AL
The University of Montana Western, MT
University of Montevallo, AL
University of Mount Olive, NC
University of Mount Union, OH
University of Nebraska at Kearney, NE
University of Nebraska at Omaha, NE
University of Nevada, Las Vegas, NV
University of New Hampshire, NH
University of New Hampshire at
Manchester, NH
The University of North Carolina at
Chapel Hill, NC
The University of North Carolina at
Greensboro, NC
University of Northern Colorado, CO
University of Notre Dame, IN
University of Oklahoma, OK
University of Oregon, OR
University of Pittsburgh, PA
University of Pittsburgh at Bradford, PA
University of Pittsburgh at Johnstown, PA
University of Portland, OR
University of Puerto Rico in Bayamón, PR
University of Puget Sound, WA
University of Rochester, NY
University of St. Francis, IL
University of St. Thomas, MN
University of St. Thomas, TX
University of San Diego, CA
University of Science and Arts of
Oklahoma, OK
University of Sioux Falls, SD
University of South Carolina, SC
University of South Carolina Aiken, SC
University of Southern California, CA
University of Southern Indiana, IN
University of Southern Mississippi, MS
The University of Tampa, FL
The University of Tennessee at
Chattanooga, TN
The University of Tennessee at Martin, TN
University of the District of Columbia, DC
University of the Incarnate Word, TX
The University of Toledo, OH
The University of Tulsa, OK
University of Utah, UT
University of Valley Forge, PA

The University of West Alabama, AL
University of West Florida, FL
Ursinus College, PA
Ursuline College, OH
Utah State University, UT
Valley City State University, ND
Valparaiso University, IN
Vanguard University of
Southern California, CA
Villanova University, PA
Virginia Polytechnic Institute and State
University, VA
Virginia Wesleyan College, VA
Wabash College, IN
Wagner College, NY
Waldorf University, IA
Walla Walla University, WA
Warner University, FL
Wartburg College, IA
Washburn University, KS
Washington & Jefferson College, PA
Washington College, MD
Washington State University, WA
Wayland Baptist University, TX
Waynesburg University, PA
Wayne State College, NE
Wayne State University, MI
Webber International University, FL
Webster University, MO
Wesleyan College, GA
West Chester University of Pennsylvania, PA
Western Illinois University, IL
Western Michigan University, MI
Western New England University, MA
Westminster College, MO
Westmont College, CA
West Texas A&M University, TX
West Virginia University, WV
West Virginia Wesleyan College, WV
Wheeling Jesuit University, WV
Whittier College, CA
Wichita State University, KS
Widener University, PA
Wilkes University, PA
William Jessup University, CA
William Jewell College, MO
William Paterson University of
New Jersey, NJ
William Peace University, NC
Williams Baptist College, AR
Wilson College, PA
Winona State University, MN
Winthrop University, SC
Wisconsin Lutheran College, WI
Wittenberg University, OH
Wofford College, SC
Wright State University, OH
Wright State University–Lake Campus, OH
Xavier University of Louisiana, LA
Young Harris College, GA
Youngstown State University, OH

Children of Public Servants
California State University,
San Bernardino, CA
Central Washington University, WA
Chowan University, NC
College of Staten Island of the City
University of New York, NY
Framingham State University, MA
Georgia Southern University, GA
Governors State University, IL
Grambling State University, LA
Illinois Institute of Technology, IL
Louisiana Tech University, LA
Mercer University, GA

Mississippi State University, MS
Missouri Western State University, MO
Monmouth University, NJ
New Mexico State University, NM
Northern Kentucky University, KY
Northwestern State University
of Louisiana, LA
The Ohio State University, OH
Patrick Henry College, VA
Peirce College, PA
Regent University, VA
Robert Morris University Illinois, IL
Siena College, NY
Sonoma State University, CA
Southern Illinois University Carbondale, IL
Tennessee Technological University, TN
Texas Wesleyan University, TX
The University of Alabama
at Birmingham, AL
University of Delaware, DE
University of Kentucky, KY
University of Maryland Eastern Shore, MD
University of Massachusetts Lowell, MA
University of Memphis, TN
University of Nevada, Las Vegas, NV
The University of North Carolina at
Charlotte, NC
University of South Carolina Aiken, SC
The University of Tennessee at Martin, TN
The University of Texas at Dallas, TX
The University of Toledo, OH
University of Utah, UT
University of Wisconsin–Green Bay, WI
University of Wyoming, WY
Washington State University, WA
Wayland Baptist University, TX
Western Washington University, WA
Wheaton College, IL

Children of Union Members/Company Employees
Auburn University, AL
Averett University, VA
California State University, Bakersfield, CA
Calvin College, MI
Carroll College, MT
Chowan University, NC
Clarion University of Pennsylvania, PA
The College of New Rochelle, NY
The College of Saint Rose, NY
College of Staten Island of the City
University of New York, NY
Columbia College, MO
Eastern Connecticut State University, CT
Eastern Washington University, WA
Emporia State University, KS
Framingham State University, MA
Francis Marion University, SC
Frostburg State University, MD
Grand Valley State University, MI
Hofstra University, NY
Husson University, ME
Kennesaw State University, GA
Kent State University, OH
Kentucky State University, KY
Kutztown University of Pennsylvania, PA
Lindenwood University, MO
Marian University, WI
Massachusetts College of
Art and Design, MA
Michigan State University, MI
Midwestern State University, TX
Millersville University of Pennsylvania, PA
Millikin University, IL
Missouri University of Science and
Technology, MO
Missouri Western State University, MO

Montana State University Billings, MT
Moravian College, PA
New Jersey Institute of Technology, NJ
New Mexico State University, NM
Northeastern Illinois University, IL
Northern Michigan University, MI
The Ohio State University, OH
Sacred Heart University, CT
St. Gregory's University, OK
Sam Houston State University, TX
Siena College, NY
Slippery Rock University of
    Pennsylvania, PA
Sonoma State University, CA
Stephen F. Austin State University, TX
Stephens College, MO
Stockton University, NJ
Stonehill College, MA
Texas Christian University, TX
Texas Wesleyan University, TX
Thomas More College, KY
The University of Alabama, AL
The University of Alabama at
    Birmingham, AL
University of Arkansas, AR
University of Hartford, CT
University of Kentucky, KY
University of Louisville, KY
University of Maine, ME
University of Maryland Eastern Shore, MD
University of Massachusetts Boston, MA
University of Massachusetts Dartmouth, MA
University of Massachusetts Lowell, MA
University of Michigan–Flint, MI
University of Nevada, Las Vegas, NV
The University of North Carolina at
    Charlotte, NC
University of Northern Colorado, CO
University of Pittsburgh, PA
University of Pittsburgh at Bradford, PA
University of Puerto Rico in Bayamón, PR
University of South Carolina, SC
The University of Tennessee at
    Chattanooga, TN
The University of Tennessee at Martin, TN
The University of Toledo, OH
University of Wisconsin–La Crosse, WI
University of Wisconsin–Parkside, WI
Western Kentucky University, KY
Western Oregon University, OR
Western Washington University, WA
West Texas A&M University, TX
West Virginia University, WV
York College of Pennsylvania, PA
Youngstown State University, OH

Children of Workers in Trades

Calvin College, MI
The College of New Rochelle, NY
College of Staten Island of the City
    University of New York, NY
Grand Valley State University, MI
Huntingdon College, AL
Kennesaw State University, GA
Midwestern State University, TX
Missouri Western State University, MO
New Mexico State University, NM
The Ohio State University, OH
San Diego State University, CA
Siena College, NY
Sonoma State University, CA
Texas Christian University, TX
The University of Alabama at
    Birmingham, AL
University of Arkansas, AR

University of Kentucky, KY
University of Maine, ME
University of Michigan, MI
University of Northern Colorado, CO
University of South Carolina, SC
University of Wisconsin–Parkside, WI
West Texas A&M University, TX
West Virginia University, WV
Worcester Polytechnic Institute, MA
Youngstown State University, OH

Children with a Deceased or Disabled Parent

The Baptist College of Florida, FL
Bay Path University, MA
California State University,
    San Bernardino, CA
Calvin College, MI
The Citadel, The Military College of South
    Carolina, SC
Clarion University of Pennsylvania, PA
The College of New Jersey, NJ
College of Staten Island of the City
    University of New York, NY
Dickinson State University, ND
Elmhurst College, IL
Fairfield University, CT
Fordham University, NY
Georgia Institute of Technology, GA
Harding University, AR
Idaho State University, ID
Kentucky State University, KY
Lees-McRae College, NC
Lipscomb University, TN
Louisiana State University and Agricultural
    & Mechanical College, LA
Marian University, WI
Midwestern State University, TX
Millikin University, IL
New Mexico State University, NM
Northeastern State University, OK
Northern Illinois University, IL
Northern Kentucky University, KY
Santa Clara University, CA
Siena College, NY
Southern Illinois University Carbondale, IL
Texas Wesleyan University, TX
The University of
    Alabama at Birmingham, AL
University of Arkansas, AR
University of Hartford, CT
University of Kentucky, KY
University of Louisiana at Monroe, LA
University of Louisville, KY
University of Massachusetts Dartmouth, MA
University of Missouri–St. Louis, MO
University of Montana, MT
University of Nevada, Las Vegas, NV
University of South Carolina, SC
The University of Tennessee at
    Chattanooga, TN
The University of Texas at Arlington, TX
University of Utah, UT
The University of Virginia's
    College at Wise, VA
Washington State University, WA
Wayne State University, MI
Youngstown State University, OH

Ethnic Background

Abilene Christian University, TX
Alaska Pacific University, AK
Albright College, PA
Alderson Broaddus University, WV
Alverno College, WI
American University, DC
Anderson University, SC

Armstrong State University, GA
Asbury University, KY
Auburn University, AL
Augustana College, IL
Augustana University, SD
Austin Peay State University, TN
Baker University, KS
Ball State University, IN
Bellarmine University, KY
Berry College, GA
Bethel College, KS
Binghamton University, State University of
    New York, NY
Biola University, CA
Boise State University, ID
Buena Vista University, IA
California State University, Bakersfield, CA
California State University, Chico, CA
California University of Pennsylvania, PA
Calvin College, MI
Capital University, OH
Cedarville University, OH
Centenary College of Louisiana, LA
Central Michigan University, MI
Centre College, KY
Chaminade University of Honolulu, HI
Christian Brothers University, TN
Claflin University, SC
Clemson University, SC
Coe College, IA
The College at Brockport, State University
    of New York, NY
The College of Saint Rose, NY
College of Staten Island of the City
    University of New York, NY
Columbia College, MO
Columbia International University, SC
Concordia University Ann Arbor, MI
Cornerstone University, MI
DeSales University, PA
Dickinson State University, ND
Drury University, MO
Duke University, NC
Duquesne University, PA
Earlham College, IN
East Carolina University, NC
Eastern Connecticut State University, CT
Eastern Mennonite University, VA
Eastern Michigan University, MI
Eastern Washington University, WA
Elizabeth City State University, NC
Elmhurst College, IL
Elon University, NC
The Evergreen State College, WA
Fairfield University, CT
Fairmont State University, WV
Ferris State University, MI
Fitchburg State University, MA
Flagler College, FL
Florida Agricultural and Mechanical
    University, FL
Florida Gulf Coast University, FL
Fort Lewis College, CO
Franklin College, IN
Furman University, SC
Gannon University, PA
George Fox University, OR
Georgian Court University, NJ
Goshen College, IN
Grambling State University, LA
Grand View University, IA
Grove City College, PA
Gustavus Adolphus College, MN
Hampden-Sydney College, VA
Hardin-Simmons University, TX

Hawai`i Pacific University, HI
Hood College, MD
Hope College, MI
Howard University, DC
Huntington University, IN
Husson University, ME
Idaho State University, ID
Indiana University of Pennsylvania, PA
Iowa State University of Science and
Technology, IA
Johnson C. Smith University, NC
Juniata College, PA
Kennesaw State University, GA
Kent State University, OH
Kentucky State University, KY
Kenyon College, OH
LaGrange College, GA
Langston University, OK
Lawrence University, WI
Lenoir-Rhyne University, NC
Lesley University, MA
Lewis-Clark State College, ID
Lock Haven University of Pennsylvania, PA
Loyola Marymount University, CA
Lyon College, AR
Macalester College, MN
Maryville University of Saint Louis, MO
Massachusetts Maritime Academy, MA
Medical University of South Carolina, SC
Meredith College, NC
Methodist University, NC
Middle Tennessee State University, TN
Millsaps College, MS
Minot State University, ND
Molloy College, NY
Montana State University Billings, MT
Morehead State University, KY
Muskingum University, OH
Nazareth College of Rochester, NY
New England College, NH
New Jersey Institute of Technology, NJ
New Mexico State University, NM
Northern Illinois University, IL
Northern State University, SD
Northland College, WI
Northwestern College, IA
Oakland City University, IN
Ohio Northern University, OH
The Ohio State University, OH
Ohio Valley University, WV
Oklahoma State University, OK
Ouachita Baptist University, AR
Pacific University, OR
Piedmont International University, NC
Portland State University, OR
Randolph-Macon College, VA
Rensselaer Polytechnic Institute, NY
Sacred Heart University, CT
The Sage Colleges, NY
St. John Fisher College, NY
Saint Martin's University, WA
Saint Mary-of-the-Woods College, IN
Saint Mary's University of Minnesota, MN
Sam Houston State University, TX
Shepherd University, WV
Siena College, NY
Simpson College, IA
Simpson University, CA
Slippery Rock University of
Pennsylvania, PA
Sonoma State University, CA
South Dakota School of Mines and
Technology, SD
Southwestern University, TX
State University of New York at
Fredonia, NY

State University of New York at
New Paltz, NY
State University of New York College at
Geneseo, NY
State University of New York College at
Potsdam, NY
Stetson University, FL
Stockton University, NJ
Stony Brook University, State University of
New York, NY
Taylor University, IN
Tennessee Technological University, TN
Texas Christian University, TX
Texas Wesleyan University, TX
Thomas University, GA
Toccoa Falls College, GA
Towson University, MD
Trinity Christian College, IL
Truman State University, MO
Union University, TN
The University of Alabama at
Birmingham, AL
The University of Arizona, AZ
University of Arkansas, AR
University of California, San Diego, CA
University of Central Oklahoma, OK
University of Colorado Denver, CO
University of Dallas, TX
University of Delaware, DE
University of Great Falls, MT
University of Hartford, CT
University of Idaho, ID
The University of Iowa, IA
The University of Kansas, KS
University of Kentucky, KY
University of Louisville, KY
University of Maine, ME
University of Maine at Augusta, ME
University of Maine at Fort Kent, ME
University of Maine at Presque Isle, ME
University of Mary Hardin-Baylor, TX
University of Massachusetts Dartmouth, MA
University of Michigan–Dearborn, MI
University of Minnesota, Crookston, MN
University of Minnesota, Morris, MN
University of Mississippi, MS
University of Missouri, MO
University of Missouri–Kansas City, MO
University of Missouri–St. Louis, MO
University of Mount Union, OH
University of Nebraska at Kearney, NE
University of Nebraska at Omaha, NE
University of Nebraska–Lincoln, NE
University of Nevada, Las Vegas, NV
University of Nevada, Reno, NV
University of Northern Colorado, CO
University of St. Francis, IL
University of South Carolina, SC
University of South Carolina Aiken, SC
University of Southern Mississippi, MS
The University of Tennessee at
Chattanooga, TN
The University of Tennessee at Martin, TN
The University of Texas at El Paso, TX
The University of Texas at San Antonio, TX
The University of Toledo, OH
University of Utah, UT
University of Vermont, VT
The University of Virginia's College at
Wise, VA
University of Wisconsin–Eau Claire, WI
University of Wisconsin–Green Bay, WI
University of Wisconsin–La Crosse, WI
University of Wisconsin–Parkside, WI
University of Wisconsin–Stevens Point, WI
University of Wisconsin–Whitewater, WI

University of Wyoming, WY
Valley City State University, ND
Washburn University, KS
Wayland Baptist University, TX
Wayne State College, NE
Wayne State University, MI
Webster University, MO
Wesleyan College, GA
Western Carolina University, NC
Western Kentucky University, KY
Western Oregon University, OR
Western Washington University, WA
Westminster College, MO
Westmont College, CA
West Virginia University, WV
Whitman College, WA
Whitworth University, WA
Widener University, PA
William Jessup University, CA
Wittenberg University, OH
Wright State University, OH
Wright State University–Lake Campus, OH
Youngstown State University, OH

First-Generation College Students
Abilene Christian University, TX
American University, DC
Austin College, TX
Averett University, VA
Berry College, GA
Binghamton University, State University of
New York, NY
Bluefield College, VA
Boise State University, ID
Brenau University, GA
Briar Cliff University, IA
Cabarrus College of Health Sciences, NC
California State Polytechnic University,
Pomona, CA
California State University, Bakersfield, CA
California State University, Chico, CA
California State University,
San Bernardino, CA
Calvin College, MI
Centenary College of Louisiana, LA
Centre College, KY
Champlain College, VT
Chowan University, NC
Christopher Newport University, VA
Claflin University, SC
Clarion University of Pennsylvania, PA
The College at Brockport, State University
of New York, NY
The College of Idaho, ID
College of Saint Mary, NE
College of Staten Island of the City
University of New York, NY
Colorado Mesa University, CO
Colorado State University, CO
Columbia College, MO
Concordia University Irvine, CA
Creighton University, NE
Culver-Stockton College, MO
Davidson College, NC
Eastern Washington University, WA
Elon University, NC
Emmanuel College, GA
Emporia State University, KS
The Evergreen State College, WA
Fairfield University, CT
Fairmont State University, WV
Flagler College, FL
Florida Agricultural and Mechanical
University, FL
Florida International University, FL
Fort Lewis College, CO

Franklin College, IN
Georgian Court University, NJ
Georgia Southern University, GA
Glenville State College, WV
Graceland University, IA
Grand View University, IA
Grove City College, PA
Guilford College, NC
Gustavus Adolphus College, MN
Hamline University, MN
Hood College, MD
Howard University, DC
Idaho State University, ID
Iowa State University of Science and
    Technology, IA
Juniata College, PA
Kean University, NJ
Kent State University, OH
Kent State University at Stark, OH
Kenyon College, OH
Keuka College, NY
Kutztown University of Pennsylvania, PA
LaGrange College, GA
Lewis-Clark State College, ID
Loyola Marymount University, CA
Lyon College, AR
MacMurray College, IL
Mercy College of Ohio, OH
Meredith College, NC
Metropolitan State University of Denver, CO
Michigan State University, MI
Middle Tennessee State University, TN
Midwestern State University, TX
Millsaps College, MS
Minnesota State University Moorhead, MN
Mississippi State University, MS
Missouri Baptist University, MO
Missouri Western State University, MO
Monmouth University, NJ
Montana State University Billings, MT
Montana Tech of The University of
    Montana, MT
Montreat College, NC
Moravian College, PA
New Jersey Institute of Technology, NJ
Northern Illinois University, IL
Northwestern College, IA
Ohio University, OH
Ohio University–Chillicothe, OH
Ohio University–Eastern, OH
Ohio University–Lancaster, OH
Ohio University–Southern Campus, OH
Ohio University–Zanesville, OH
Oklahoma State University, OK
Ouachita Baptist University, AR
Pacific University, OR
Paul Quinn College, TX
Queens University of Charlotte, NC
The Sage Colleges, NY
St. John Fisher College, NY
Saint Louis University, MO
Saint Mary-of-the-Woods College, IN
Saint Vincent College, PA
Salisbury University, MD
Sam Houston State University, TX
San Diego State University, CA
San Francisco Art Institute, CA
Sonoma State University, CA
Southeastern Louisiana University, LA
Southeast Missouri State University, MO
Southern Illinois University Carbondale, IL
State University of New York at
    New Paltz, NY
State University of New York College at
    Geneseo, NY

Stephen F. Austin State University, TX
Stetson University, FL
Stockton University, NJ
Tennessee Technological University, TN
Texas A&M University, TX
Texas A&M University–Commerce, TX
Texas A&M University–Corpus Christi, TX
Texas Lutheran University, TX
Texas Tech University, TX
Texas Wesleyan University, TX
Towson University, MD
Trinity Christian College, IL
Truman State University, MO
Union University, TN
The University of Alabama at
    Birmingham, AL
University of Arkansas, AR
University of California, San Diego, CA
University of California, Santa Cruz, CA
University of Central Florida, FL
University of Colorado Boulder, CO
University of Colorado Denver, CO
University of Delaware, DE
University of Great Falls, MT
University of Hartford, CT
University of Houston, TX
University of Idaho, ID
University of Illinois at Urbana–
    Champaign, IL
The University of Iowa, IA
The University of Kansas, KS
University of Kentucky, KY
University of Maine, ME
University of Massachusetts Boston, MA
University of Massachusetts Dartmouth, MA
University of Miami, FL
University of Michigan–Flint, MI
University of Minnesota, Crookston, MN
University of Mississippi, MS
University of Missouri, MO
University of Missouri–St. Louis, MO
The University of Montana Western, MT
University of Nebraska at Kearney, NE
University of Nebraska at Omaha, NE
University of Nevada, Las Vegas, NV
University of Nevada, Reno, NV
University of North Alabama, AL
The University of North Carolina at
    Charlotte, NC
University of Northern Colorado, CO
University of North Florida, FL
University of St. Francis, IL
University of South Carolina, SC
University of South Carolina Aiken, SC
University of South Carolina Upstate, SC
University of Southern Indiana, IN
University of South Florida, FL
The University of Texas at Arlington, TX
The University of Texas at San Antonio, TX
The University of Toledo, OH
University of Utah, UT
University of Vermont, VT
The University of West Alabama, AL
University of Wisconsin–Eau Claire, WI
University of Wisconsin–La Crosse, WI
University of Wisconsin–Stout, WI
University of Wyoming, WY
Ursuline College, OH
Virginia Polytechnic Institute and State
    University, VA
Washington State University, WA
Wesleyan College, GA
Western Oregon University, OR
West Texas A&M University, TX

West Virginia University Institute of
    Technology, WV
Wheaton College, IL
Whitman College, WA
Wichita State University, KS
William Jessup University, CA
Wright State University, OH
Wright State University–Lake Campus, OH

Handicapped Students

Bemidji State University, MN
Binghamton University, State University of
    New York, NY
Boise State University, ID
Bryan College, TN
California State University, Chico, CA
California State University, Fresno, CA
California State University,
    San Bernardino, CA
Calvin College, MI
Central College, IA
Chowan University, NC
Clear Creek Baptist Bible College, KY
The College of St. Scholastica, MN
College of Staten Island of the City
    University of New York, NY
Dordt College, IA
East Carolina University, NC
Eastern Connecticut State University, CT
Eastern Washington University, WA
East Stroudsburg University of
    Pennsylvania, PA
Elizabeth City State University, NC
Emporia State University, KS
Fairmont State University, WV
Florida Gulf Coast University, FL
Fordham University, NY
Fort Lewis College, CO
Francis Marion University, SC
Franklin College, IN
Gardner-Webb University, NC
Georgia Southern University, GA
Grand Valley State University, MI
Grove City College, PA
Hardin-Simmons University, TX
Hofstra University, NY
Houghton College, NY
Howard University, DC
Idaho State University, ID
James Madison University, VA
Kennesaw State University, GA
Kent State University, OH
Kutztown University of Pennsylvania, PA
Kuyper College, MI
Lock Haven University of Pennsylvania, PA
Louisiana Tech University, LA
Loyola Marymount University, CA
Malone University, OH
Michigan State University, MI
Mid-Atlantic Christian University, NC
Middle Tennessee State University, TN
Midwestern State University, TX
Mississippi State University, MS
Morehead State University, KY
New Jersey Institute of Technology, NJ
New Mexico State University, NM
Northern Illinois University, IL
Northern Kentucky University, KY
Northern State University, SD
Northwestern College, IA
The Ohio State University, OH
Oklahoma State University, OK
Ouachita Baptist University, AR
Portland State University, OR
Sacred Heart University, CT

San Diego State University, CA
Santa Clara University, CA
Shepherd University, WV
Shippensburg University of
    Pennsylvania, PA
Sonoma State University, CA
Southern Illinois University Carbondale, IL
Southern New Hampshire University, NH
Southwest Baptist University, MO
State University of New York College at
    Geneseo, NY
State University of New York College at
    Potsdam, NY
Texas Christian University, TX
Texas Tech University, TX
Texas Wesleyan University, TX
Towson University, MD
Union University, TN
The University of Akron, OH
The University of Alabama at
    Birmingham, AL
University of Arkansas, AR
University of California, San Diego, CA
University of Colorado Denver, CO
University of Hartford, CT
University of Houston, TX
University of Idaho, ID
The University of Iowa, IA
University of Kentucky, KY
University of Maine, ME
University of Mary Hardin-Baylor, TX
University of Massachusetts Amherst, MA
University of Memphis, TN
University of Michigan, MI
University of Michigan–Dearborn, MI
University of Michigan–Flint, MI
University of Mississippi, MS
University of Nebraska at Omaha, NE
University of Nebraska–Lincoln, NE
University of Nevada, Las Vegas, NV
University of New Hampshire, NH
The University of North Carolina at
    Charlotte, NC
The University of North Carolina at
    Greensboro, NC
University of Northern Colorado, CO
University of Puerto Rico in Bayamón, PR
University of South Carolina, SC
University of South Carolina Aiken, SC
The University of Tennessee at
    Chattanooga, TN
The University of Texas at Arlington, TX
The University of Texas at Dallas, TX
The University of Texas at San Antonio, TX
The University of Toledo, OH
University of Utah, UT
University of West Florida, FL
University of West Georgia, GA
University of Wisconsin–Green Bay, WI
University of Wisconsin–Stout, WI
University of Wisconsin–Whitewater, WI
University of Wyoming, WY
Washington State University, WA
Western Carolina University, NC
Western Kentucky University, KY
Western Oregon University, OR
West Texas A&M University, TX
Wheaton College, IL
Wright State University, OH
Wright State University–Lake Campus, OH
Youngstown State University, OH

International Students
Agnes Scott College, GA
Alaska Pacific University, AK
Albion College, MI

Alderson Broaddus University, WV
Allegheny College, PA
Alliant International University–
    San Diego, CA
Alverno College, WI
Anderson University, SC
Andrews University, MI
Arizona State University at the Downtown
    Phoenix campus, AZ
Arizona State University at the Polytechnic
    campus, AZ
Arizona State University at the Tempe
    campus, AZ
Arizona State University at the
    West campus, AZ
Arkansas Tech University, AR
Armstrong State University, GA
Asbury University, KY
Augsburg College, MN
Augustana College, IL
Augustana University, SD
Austin College, TX
Averett University, VA
Baker University, KS
Ball State University, IN
Barclay College, KS
Barton College, NC
Bay Path University, MA
Belhaven University, MS
Bellarmine University, KY
Bemidji State University, MN
Benedictine University, IL
Bentley University, MA
Berry College, GA
Bethany College, WV
Bethel College, IN
Bethel College, KS
Binghamton University, State University of
    New York, NY
Biola University, CA
Bloomfield College, NJ
Bloomsburg University of Pennsylvania, PA
Bluffton University, OH
Boise State University, ID
Bowling Green State University, OH
Brenau University, GA
Brevard College, NC
Briar Cliff University, IA
Bridgewater College, VA
Bryan College, TN
Buena Vista University, IA
California Baptist University, CA
California Lutheran University, CA
California State University, Chico, CA
California University of Pennsylvania, PA
Calvin College, MI
Cameron University, OK
Campbellsville University, KY
Campbell University, NC
Canisius College, NY
Capital University, OH
Cardinal Stritch University, WI
Carlow University, PA
Carroll College, MT
Carroll University, WI
Centenary College of Louisiana, LA
Central College, IA
Central Methodist University, MO
Central Michigan University, MI
Champlain College, VT
Chestnut Hill College, PA
Chowan University, NC
Cincinnati Christian University, OH
Claflin University, SC
Clarkson University, NY
Clear Creek Baptist Bible College, KY

Coastal Carolina University, SC
Coe College, IA
The College at Brockport, State University
    of New York, NY
College of Coastal Georgia, GA
The College of Idaho, ID
College of Saint Benedict, MN
College of Saint Mary, NE
The College of St. Scholastica, MN
College of Staten Island of the City
    University of New York, NY
The College of Wooster, OH
Colorado State University, CO
Columbia College, MO
Columbia International University, SC
Concordia College, MN
Concordia University Chicago, IL
Concordia University, Nebraska, NE
Concordia University Texas, TX
Corban University, OR
Cornerstone University, MI
Covenant College, GA
Crown College, MN
Culver-Stockton College, MO
Daemen College, NY
Davis College, NY
Defiance College, OH
DeSales University, PA
Dickinson State University, ND
Dominican University of California, CA
Dordt College, IA
Drake University, IA
Drury University, MO
Duke University, NC
Duquesne University, PA
East Central University, OK
Eastern Mennonite University, VA
Eastern Michigan University, MI
Eastern University, PA
East Stroudsburg University of
    Pennsylvania, PA
East Texas Baptist University, TX
Eckerd College, FL
Edgewood College, WI
Elizabeth City State University, NC
Elizabethtown College, PA
Elmira College, NY
Elon University, NC
Emmanuel College, GA
Emporia State University, KS
Endicott College, MA
Fairmont State University, WV
Ferris State University, MI
Flagler College, FL
Florida Gulf Coast University, FL
Florida Institute of Technology, FL
Fort Hays State University, KS
Fort Lewis College, CO
Franciscan University of Steubenville, OH
Francis Marion University, SC
Franklin Pierce University, NH
Frostburg State University, MD
Furman University, SC
Gannon University, PA
George Fox University, OR
Gonzaga University, WA
Gordon College, MA
Goshen College, IN
Graceland University, IA
Grambling State University, LA
Grand Valley State University, MI
Grand View University, IA
Greenville College, IL
Gustavus Adolphus College, MN
Hamline University, MN
Hampden-Sydney College, VA

Hampton University, VA
Hanover College, IN
Harding University, AR
Hartwick College, NY
Harvey Mudd College, CA
Hawai`i Pacific University, HI
Hendrix College, AR
Hillsdale College, MI
Hollins University, VA
Hood College, MD
Houghton College, NY
Howard University, DC
Huntingdon College, AL
Huntington University, IN
Husson University, ME
Idaho State University, ID
Illinois College, IL
Illinois Institute of Technology, IL
Illinois Wesleyan University, IL
Indiana University of Pennsylvania, PA
Iowa State University of Science and
    Technology, IA
Iowa Wesleyan University, IA
Jacksonville University, FL
James Madison University, VA
Johnson C. Smith University, NC
Juniata College, PA
Kansas Wesleyan University, KS
Kennesaw State University, GA
Kent State University, OH
Keuka College, NY
King's College, PA
Kuyper College, MI
Lancaster Bible College, PA
Lawrence Technological University, MI
Lawrence University, WI
Lebanon Valley College, PA
Lees-McRae College, NC
Liberty University, VA
Life University, GA
Lincoln Christian University, IL
Lincoln University, MO
Lincoln University, PA
Linfield College, OR
Lipscomb University, TN
Lock Haven University of Pennsylvania, PA
Long Island University–LIU Brooklyn, NY
Long Island University–LIU Post, NY
Louisiana Tech University, LA
Loyola Marymount University, CA
Malone University, OH
Manchester University, IN
Marymount Manhattan College, NY
Marymount University, VA
Mayville University of Saint Louis, MO
The Master's University, CA
Mayville State University, ND
McKendree University, IL
McPherson College, KS
Mercer University, GA
Meredith College, NC
Merrimack College, MA
Michigan State University, MI
Mid-Atlantic Christian University, NC
Middle Tennessee State University, TN
Midwestern State University, TX
Millersville University of Pennsylvania, PA
Millikin University, IL
Minot State University, ND
Missouri Western State University, MO
Monmouth College, IL
Monmouth University, NJ
Montclair State University, NJ
Montreat College, NC
Moravian College, PA

Morehead State University, KY
Morningside College, IA
Mount Marty College, SD
Mount Vernon Nazarene University, OH
Muskingum University, OH
Newberry College, SC
New England College, NH
New Jersey Institute of Technology, NJ
New Mexico State University, NM
NewSchool of Architecture and Design, CA
North Central College, IL
Northern Illinois University, IL
Northern Michigan University, MI
Northern State University, SD
Northwest Christian University, OR
Northwestern College, IA
Northwestern State University of
    Louisiana, LA
Northwestern University, IL
Northwest Nazarene University, ID
Northwest University, WA
Oakland City University, IN
Ohio Northern University, OH
Ohio Valley University, WV
Ohio Wesleyan University, OH
Oklahoma Baptist University, OK
Oklahoma Christian University, OK
Oklahoma State University, OK
Oklahoma Wesleyan University, OK
Old Dominion University, VA
Olivet College, MI
O'More College of Design, TN
Oral Roberts University, OK
Otterbein University, OH
Ouachita Baptist University, AR
Pacific University, OR
Peirce College, PA
Piedmont College, GA
Piedmont International University, NC
Plymouth State University, NH
Point Park University, PA
Portland State University, OR
Queens University of Charlotte, NC
Quinnipiac University, CT
Ramapo College of New Jersey, NJ
Randolph College, VA
Roberts Wesleyan College, NY
Rockford University, IL
Sacred Heart University, CT
St. Ambrose University, IA
St. Gregory's University, OK
Saint John's University, MN
Saint Louis University, MO
Saint Martin's University, WA
Saint Mary-of-the-Woods College, IN
Saint Mary's University of Minnesota, MN
St. Norbert College, WI
Schreiner University, TX
Seattle Pacific University, WA
Seton Hill University, PA
Simpson College, IA
Sonoma State University, CA
South Dakota School of Mines and
    Technology, SD
Southeastern University, FL
Southeast Missouri State University, MO
Southern Adventist University, TN
Southern Illinois University Carbondale, IL
Southern New Hampshire University, NH
Southern Oregon University, OR
Southwest Baptist University, MO
Southwestern College, KS
Spring Arbor University, MI
State University of New York at
    Fredonia, NY

State University of New York at
    Plattsburgh, NY
State University of New York College at
    Geneseo, NY
State University of New York College of
    Environmental Science and Forestry, NY
Stetson University, FL
Stevens Institute of Technology, NJ
Stockton University, NJ
Taylor University, IN
Texas A&M University, TX
Texas A&M University–Corpus Christi, TX
Texas Christian University, TX
Texas State University, TX
Texas Wesleyan University, TX
Texas Woman's University, TX
Thiel College, PA
Thomas College, ME
Thomas More College, KY
Toccoa Falls College, GA
Towson University, MD
Trinity University, TX
Truett McConnell University, GA
Truman State University, MO
Tulane University, LA
Union University, TN
The University of Akron, OH
The University of Alabama, AL
The University of Alabama at
    Birmingham, AL
The University of Arizona, AZ
University of Arkansas, AR
University of Bridgeport, CT
University of California, Irvine, CA
University of California, Santa Cruz, CA
University of Central Oklahoma, OK
University of Colorado Denver, CO
University of Evansville, IN
University of Great Falls, MT
University of Hartford, CT
University of Houston, TX
University of Idaho, ID
University of Illinois at Urbana–
    Champaign, IL
University of Indianapolis, IN
The University of Kansas, KS
University of Kentucky, KY
University of Louisiana at Monroe, LA
University of Maine, ME
University of Maine at Augusta, ME
University of Maine at Fort Kent, ME
University of Maine at Presque Isle, ME
University of Mary Hardin-Baylor, TX
University of Miami, FL
University of Michigan, MI
University of Michigan–Dearborn, MI
University of Michigan–Flint, MI
University of Minnesota, Morris, MN
University of Mississippi, MS
University of Missouri, MO
University of Missouri–St. Louis, MO
University of Montana, MT
The University of Montana Western, MT
University of Montevallo, AL
University of Mount Union, OH
University of Nebraska at Kearney, NE
University of Nebraska at Omaha, NE
University of Nebraska–Lincoln, NE
University of Nevada, Las Vegas, NV
University of New Hampshire, NH
University of North Alabama, AL
The University of North Carolina at Chapel
    Hill, NC
The University of North Carolina at
    Charlotte, NC

The University of North Carolina at
Greensboro, NC
University of Northern Colorado, CO
University of North Florida, FL
University of Oregon, OR
University of Pittsburgh at Bradford, PA
University of Puget Sound, WA
University of Redlands, CA
University of Rochester, NY
University of Science and Arts of
Oklahoma, OK
University of Sioux Falls, SD
University of South Carolina, SC
University of South Carolina Aiken, SC
University of Southern Indiana, IN
The University of Tampa, FL
The University of Texas at Dallas, TX
The University of Texas at El Paso, TX
The University of Texas Rio
Grande Valley, TX
The University of Toledo, OH
University of West Florida, FL
University of West Georgia, GA
University of Wisconsin–Eau Claire, WI
University of Wisconsin–La Crosse, WI
University of Wisconsin–Parkside, WI
University of Wisconsin–Stevens Point, WI
University of Wisconsin–Stout, WI
University of Wisconsin–Superior, WI
University of Wisconsin–Whitewater, WI
University of Wyoming, WY
Ursinus College, PA
Utah State University, UT
Valley City State University, ND
Valparaiso University, IN
Warner Pacific College, OR
Warner University, FL
Wartburg College, IA
Washburn University, KS
Washington & Jefferson College, PA
Washington State University, WA
Wayland Baptist University, TX
Wayne State University, MI
Webber International University, FL
Webster University, MO
Wells College, NY
Wesleyan University, CT
Western Illinois University, IL
Western Kentucky University, KY
Western Michigan University, MI
Western Oregon University, OR
Western Washington University, WA
Westminster College, MO
Westmont College, CA
West Texas A&M University, TX
West Virginia University, WV
West Virginia Wesleyan College, WV
Wheaton College, IL
Whitman College, WA
Whittier College, CA
Whitworth University, WA
Wichita State University, KS
Widener University, PA
William Jessup University, CA
Williams Baptist College, AR
Wilson College, PA
Wisconsin Lutheran College, WI
Wittenberg University, OH
Wright State University, OH
Wright State University–Lake Campus, OH
Xavier University, OH
York College of Pennsylvania, PA
Youngstown State University, OH

Local/State Students
Abilene Christian University, TX
Agnes Scott College, GA
Alaska Pacific University, AK
Albertus Magnus College, CT
Albright College, PA
Allen College, IA
Alliant International University–
San Diego, CA
Alvernia University, PA
American University, DC
Arizona State University at the Downtown
Phoenix campus, AZ
Arizona State University at the
Polytechnic campus, AZ
Arizona State University at the
Tempe campus, AZ
Arizona State University at the
West campus, AZ
Auburn University, AL
Augustana University, SD
Augusta University, GA
Austin College, TX
Averett University, VA
Ball State University, IN
Barclay College, KS
Barton College, NC
Belhaven University, MS
Bellarmine University, KY
Belmont University, TN
Benedictine University, IL
Berry College, GA
Bethany College, WV
Bethel College, KS
Binghamton University, State University of
New York, NY
Bloomfield College, NJ
Bluefield College, VA
Boise State University, ID
Boston University, MA
Brevard College, NC
Bridgewater State University, MA
Brigham Young University, UT
Bryan College, TN
Caldwell University, NJ
California Polytechnic State University, San
Luis Obispo, CA
California State University, Bakersfield, CA
California State University, Chico, CA
California State University, Fresno, CA
California State University,
Monterey Bay, CA
California State University, San Marcos, CA
Calvin College, MI
Campbell University, NC
Centenary College of Louisiana, LA
Central College, IA
Central Michigan University, MI
Central Washington University, WA
Chowan University, NC
Christian Brothers University, TN
Christopher Newport University, VA
The Citadel, The Military College of South
Carolina, SC
City College of the City University
of New York, NY
Claflin University, SC
Clarion University of Pennsylvania, PA
Clarkson University, NY
Clemson University, SC
Coastal Carolina University, SC
College of Coastal Georgia, GA
The College of Idaho, ID
The College of St. Scholastica, MN
College of Staten Island of the City
University of New York, NY

Colorado Mesa University, CO
Colorado Mountain College, CO
Columbia College, MO
Columbia International University, SC
Columbus College of Art & Design, OH
Concordia University, Nebraska, NE
Culver-Stockton College, MO
Davidson College, NC
DePaul University, IL
Dordt College, IA
Duke University, NC
Eastern Connecticut State University, CT
Eastern Oregon University, OR
Eastern Washington University, WA
East Stroudsburg University of
Pennsylvania, PA
Eckerd College, FL
Elizabethtown College, PA
Elmira College, NY
Emmanuel College, GA
Emory University, GA
Endicott College, MA
Everglades University, FL
The Evergreen State College, WA
Fairmont State University, WV
Faulkner University, AL
Ferris State University, MI
Fitchburg State University, MA
Flagler College, FL
Florida Agricultural and Mechanical
University, FL
Florida Gulf Coast University, FL
Florida Southern College, FL
Florida State University, FL
Fort Lewis College, CO
Franciscan University of Steubenville, OH
Francis Marion University, SC
Franklin College, IN
Franklin Pierce University, NH
Frostburg State University, MD
Furman University, SC
Gardner-Webb University, NC
Georgia College & State University, GA
Georgia Institute of Technology, GA
Georgian Court University, NJ
Georgia Southwestern State University, GA
Graceland University, IA
Grambling State University, LA
Grand Valley State University, MI
Greenville College, IL
Guilford College, NC
Hamline University, MN
Hawai`i Pacific University, HI
Hofstra University, NY
Hollins University, VA
Hood College, MD
Houghton College, NY
Howard Payne University, TX
Howard University, DC
Huntingdon College, AL
Huntington University, IN
Idaho State University, ID
Illinois Institute of Technology, IL
Indiana Tech, IN
Indiana University–Purdue University Fort
Wayne, IN
Iowa State University of Science and
Technology, IA
Jacksonville State University, AL
James Madison University, VA
John Carroll University, OH
Juniata College, PA
Kansas Wesleyan University, KS
Kean University, NJ
Kennesaw State University, GA
Kent State University, OH

Kentucky State University, KY
Kentucky Wesleyan College, KY
Kutztown University of Pennsylvania, PA
Lawrence Technological University, MI
Lees-McRae College, NC
Lee University, TN
Lenoir-Rhyne University, NC
Liberty University, VA
Life University, GA
LIM College, NY
Lincoln Memorial University, TN
Lipscomb University, TN
Lock Haven University of Pennsylvania, PA
Longwood University, VA
Loyola Marymount University, CA
Lycoming College, PA
Lyon College, AR
Malone University, OH
Mansfield University of Pennsylvania, PA
Marian University, WI
Marist College, NY
Marshall University, WV
Marymount Manhattan College, NY
Marymount University, VA
Mayville State University, ND
McDaniel College, MD
Medical University of South Carolina, SC
Messiah College, PA
Methodist University, NC
Metropolitan State University of Denver, CO
Miami University, OH
Michigan State University, MI
Middle Georgia State University, GA
Middle Tennessee State University, TN
Millsaps College, MS
Minot State University, ND
Mississippi State University, MS
Missouri State University, MO
Missouri Western State University, MO
Monmouth University, NJ
Montana State University, MT
Montana State University Billings, MT
Montana Tech of The University of
    Montana, MT
Montreat College, NC
Morehead State University, KY
Morehouse College, GA
Morningside College, IA
Morrisville State College, NY
Murray State University, KY
Muskingum University, OH
Newberry College, SC
New England College, NH
New Jersey Institute of Technology, NJ
New Mexico State University, NM
Nicholls State University, LA
North Carolina State University, NC
Northeastern State University, OK
Northern Arizona University, AZ
Northern Kentucky University, KY
Northern Michigan University, MI
Northern State University, SD
Ohio Valley University, WV
Ohio Wesleyan University, OH
Oklahoma Baptist University, OK
Oklahoma Panhandle State University, OK
Oklahoma State University, OK
Old Dominion University, VA
Oral Roberts University, OK
Oregon State University, OR
Ouachita Baptist University, AR
Paul Quinn College, TX
Queens College of the City University of
    New York, NY
Randall University, OK

Randolph College, VA
Regis University, CO
Rice University, TX
Robert Morris University Illinois, IL
Sacred Heart University, CT
Saginaw Valley State University, MI
Saint Augustine's University, NC
St. Bonaventure University, NY
St. Edward's University, TX
St. John Fisher College, NY
St. John's University, NY
Saint Leo University, FL
Saint Martin's University, WA
Saint Mary-of-the-Woods College, IN
Saint Mary's University of Minnesota, MN
San Diego State University, CA
San Jose State University, CA
Schreiner University, TX
Shenandoah University, VA
Shepherd University, WV
Shippensburg University of
    Pennsylvania, PA
Siena College, NY
Slippery Rock University of
    Pennsylvania, PA
Smith College, MA
Sonoma State University, CA
South Dakota School of Mines and
    Technology, SD
Southern Adventist University, TN
Southern Illinois University Carbondale, IL
Southern New Hampshire University, NH
Southern Utah University, UT
Southwest Baptist University, MO
Southwestern Oklahoma State
    University, OK
State University of New York at
    Fredonia, NY
State University of New York at
    New Paltz, NY
State University of New York College at
    Cortland, NY
State University of New York College at
    Geneseo, NY
State University of New York College at
    Potsdam, NY
State University of New York College of
    Agriculture and Technology at
    Cobleskill, NY
State University of New York College of
    Environmental Science and Forestry, NY
State University of New York Polytechnic
    Institute, NY
Stephen F. Austin State University, TX
Stetson University, FL
Stevens Institute of Technology, NJ
Stockton University, NJ
Swarthmore College, PA
Tennessee State University, TN
Tennessee Technological University, TN
Texas A&M University, TX
Texas Christian University, TX
Texas Wesleyan University, TX
Thiel College, PA
Thomas College, ME
Trinity Christian College, IL
Truett McConnell University, GA
Tulane University, LA
Tusculum College, TN
Tuskegee University, AL
Unity College, ME
The University of Akron, OH
The University of Alabama in
    Huntsville, AL
University of Alaska Fairbanks, AK

University of Alaska Southeast, AK
University of Arkansas, AR
University of Arkansas at Little Rock, AR
University of Bridgeport, CT
University of Colorado Boulder, CO
University of Dayton, OH
University of Delaware, DE
University of Georgia, GA
University of Great Falls, MT
University of Hartford, CT
University of Houston, TX
University of Houston–Clear Lake, TX
University of Idaho, ID
University of Illinois at Urbana–
    Champaign, IL
The University of Iowa, IA
The University of Kansas, KS
University of Louisville, KY
University of Maine, ME
University of Maine at Augusta, ME
University of Maine at Presque Isle, ME
University of Mary Hardin-Baylor, TX
University of Maryland Eastern Shore, MD
University of Mary Washington, VA
University of Massachusetts Boston, MA
University of Massachusetts Dartmouth, MA
University of Michigan, MI
University of Michigan–Flint, MI
University of Minnesota, Crookston, MN
University of Minnesota, Twin Cities
    Campus, MN
University of Mississippi, MS
University of Missouri, MO
University of Missouri–Kansas City, MO
University of Missouri–St. Louis, MO
University of Montana, MT
University of Mount Olive, NC
University of Nebraska at Kearney, NE
University of Nevada, Las Vegas, NV
University of New Hampshire, NH
The University of North Carolina at
    Charlotte, NC
The University of North Carolina at
    Greensboro, NC
The University of North Carolina
    Wilmington, NC
University of Northern Colorado, CO
University of Oregon, OR
University of Pittsburgh at Bradford, PA
University of Saint Joseph, CT
University of Sioux Falls, SD
University of South Carolina, SC
University of South Carolina Aiken, SC
University of Southern Mississippi, MS
The University of Tennessee at Martin, TN
The University of Texas at Austin, TX
The University of Texas at Dallas, TX
The University of Texas at El Paso, TX
The University of Texas at San Antonio, TX
The University of Texas Rio
    Grande Valley, TX
University of Valley Forge, PA
The University of Virginia's
    College at Wise, VA
University of West Georgia, GA
University of Wisconsin–Eau Claire, WI
University of Wisconsin–La Crosse, WI
University of Wisconsin–Oshkosh, WI
University of Wisconsin–Parkside, WI
University of Wisconsin–River Falls, WI
University of Wisconsin–Stout, WI
University of Wisconsin–Whitewater, WI
University of Wyoming, WY
Utah State University, UT
Valdosta State University, GA

Vanderbilt University, TN
Virginia Military Institute, VA
Virginia Polytechnic Institute and State
  University, VA
Wake Forest University, NC
Warner Pacific College, OR
Washburn University, KS
Washington & Jefferson College, PA
Washington State University, WA
Wayland Baptist University, TX
Wayne State College, NE
Wayne State University, MI
Webber International University, FL
Wesleyan College, GA
Western Carolina University, NC
Western Kentucky University, KY
Western Michigan University, MI
Western Oregon University, OR
Western Washington University, WA
Westminster College, MO
West Texas A&M University, TX
West Virginia University, WV
Wichita State University, KS
William Woods University, MO
Wilson College, PA
Winona State University, MN
Wofford College, SC
Youngstown State University, OH

Married Students

Alaska Bible College, AK
Auburn University, AL
Barclay College, KS
Binghamton University, State University of
  New York, NY
Blue Mountain College, MS
California State University, Chico, CA
Clarks Summit University, PA
The College at Brockport, State University
  of New York, NY
The College of Idaho, ID
College of Staten Island of the City
  University of New York, NY
Crossroads Bible College, IN
Davis College, NY
Eastern Washington University, WA
Emmanuel College, GA
Franklin Pierce University, NH
Georgian Court University, NJ
Georgia Southern University, GA
Howard University, DC
Indiana Tech, IN
John Wesley University, NC
Lawrence Technological University, MI
Lock Haven University of Pennsylvania, PA
Mid-Atlantic Christian University, NC
Montana Tech of The University of
  Montana, MT
New Mexico State University, NM
Northwestern State University of
  Louisiana, LA
Northwest University, WA
Ouachita Baptist University, AR
Sonoma State University, CA
South Dakota School of Mines and
  Technology, SD
Texas Wesleyan University, TX
Toccoa Falls College, GA
Truett McConnell University, GA
The University of Alabama at
  Birmingham, AL
University of Arkansas, AR
The University of Kansas, KS
University of Nevada, Reno, NV
The University of North Carolina
  Wilmington, NC

University of Northern Colorado, CO
University of South Carolina Aiken, SC
University of Valley Forge, PA

Members of Minorities

Abilene Christian University, TX
Alabama State University, AL
Alaska Pacific University, AK
Alice Lloyd College, KY
Allen College, IA
American University, DC
Anderson University, SC
Assumption College, MA
Augsburg College, MN
Augustana College, IL
Augustana University, SD
Augusta University, GA
Austin Peay State University, TN
Baker University, KS
Baldwin Wallace University, OH
Ball State University, IN
Bellarmine University, KY
Belmont University, TN
Bemidji State University, MN
Bentley University, MA
Berry College, GA
Bethel College, IN
Binghamton University, State University of
  New York, NY
Biola University, CA
Bluffton University, OH
Boise State University, ID
Boston University, MA
Bowling Green State University, OH
Brenau University, GA
Briar Cliff University, IA
Bridgewater College, VA
Bridgewater State University, MA
Brigham Young University, UT
Bryan College, TN
California State Polytechnic University,
  Pomona, CA
California State University, Chico, CA
California University of Pennsylvania, PA
Calvin College, MI
Cameron University, OK
Capital University, OH
Carson-Newman University, TN
Centenary College of Louisiana, LA
Central College, IA
Central Connecticut State University, CT
Central Washington University, WA
Champlain College, VT
Christopher Newport University, VA
Cincinnati Christian University, OH
Clarion University of Pennsylvania, PA
Clarkson University, NY
Clemson University, SC
Coe College, IA
The College at Brockport, State University
  of New York, NY
The College of Idaho, ID
The College of New Jersey, NJ
The College of Saint Rose, NY
College of Staten Island of the City
  University of New York, NY
The College of Wooster, OH
Colorado State University, CO
Columbia College, MO
Columbia International University, SC
Concordia University, Nebraska, NE
Cornerstone University, MI
Covenant College, GA
Creighton University, NE
Crown College, MN
Defiance College, OH

Dickinson State University, ND
Dominican University of California, CA
Dordt College, IA
Drury University, MO
Duquesne University, PA
East Central University, OK
Eastern Connecticut State University, CT
Eastern Kentucky University, KY
Eastern Michigan University, MI
Eastern Oregon University, OR
East Stroudsburg University of
  Pennsylvania, PA
Elizabeth City State University, NC
Elizabethtown College, PA
Elmhurst College, IL
Elon University, NC
Emporia State University, KS
Fairfield University, CT
Fairmont State University, WV
Ferris State University, MI
Fitchburg State University, MA
Flagler College, FL
Florida Gulf Coast University, FL
Francis Marion University, SC
Franklin College, IN
Fresno Pacific University, CA
Friends University, KS
Gallaudet University, DC
Gannon University, PA
Gardner-Webb University, NC
George Fox University, OR
Georgia Institute of Technology, GA
Georgian Court University, NJ
Georgia Southern University, GA
Gonzaga University, WA
Goshen College, IN
Governors State University, IL
Graceland University, IA
Grambling State University, LA
Grove City College, PA
Gustavus Adolphus College, MN
Hamline University, MN
Hampden-Sydney College, VA
Hampton University, VA
Hanover College, IN
Hilbert College, NY
Hofstra University, NY
Howard University, DC
Husson University, ME
Idaho State University, ID
Indiana State University, IN
Iowa State University of Science and
  Technology, IA
Ithaca College, NY
James Madison University, VA
Kennesaw State University, GA
Kent State University, OH
Kent State University at Stark, OH
Keuka College, NY
Lawrence Technological University, MI
Lehigh University, PA
Le Moyne College, NY
Lenoir-Rhyne University, NC
Lewis-Clark State College, ID
Life University, GA
Lincoln Memorial University, TN
Linfield College, OR
Lipscomb University, TN
Lock Haven University of Pennsylvania, PA
Louisiana Tech University, LA
Loyola Marymount University, CA
Luther College, IA
Lyon College, AR
Malone University, OH
Manchester University, IN
Mansfield University of Pennsylvania, PA

Marietta College, OH
Marshall University, WV
Maryville College, TN
Maryville University of Saint Louis, MO
Massachusetts Maritime Academy, MA
Mayville State University, ND
Medical University of South Carolina, SC
Meredith College, NC
Methodist University, NC
Miami University, OH
Middle Tennessee State University, TN
Midway University, KY
Midwestern State University, TX
Minnesota State University Mankato, MN
Minnesota State University Moorhead, MN
Minot State University, ND
Misericordia University, PA
Missouri State University, MO
Missouri University of Science and
Technology, MO
Molloy College, NY
Monmouth University, NJ
Montana State University, MT
Montana State University Billings, MT
Morehead State University, KY
Morrisville State College, NY
Mount Carmel College of Nursing, OH
Mount St. Mary's University, MD
Mount Vernon Nazarene University, OH
Murray State University, KY
Muskingum University, OH
New Jersey Institute of Technology, NJ
New Mexico State University, NM
Nicholls State University, LA
Northeastern State University, OK
Northern Arizona University, AZ
Northern Illinois University, IL
Northern Kentucky University, KY
Northern Michigan University, MI
Northern State University, SD
Northland College, WI
Northwest Missouri State University, MO
Oakland City University, IN
The Ohio State University, OH
Ohio Wesleyan University, OH
Oklahoma Baptist University, OK
Oregon State University, OR
Otterbein University, OH
Ouachita Baptist University, AR
Portland State University, OR
Rensselaer Polytechnic Institute, NY
Rhodes College, TN
Rice University, TX
Rider University, NJ
Sacred Heart University, CT
The Sage Colleges, NY
Saginaw Valley State University, MI
St. Ambrose University, IA
St. Bonaventure University, NY
St. John Fisher College, NY
Saint Joseph's University, PA
Saint Louis University, MO
Saint Martin's University, WA
Saint Mary-of-the-Woods College, IN
Saint Mary's University of Minnesota, MN
Saint Michael's College, VT
Samford University, AL
Sam Houston State University, TX
Seattle University, WA
Shepherd University, WV
Simpson College, IA
Simpson University, CA
Slippery Rock University of
Pennsylvania, PA
Sonoma State University, CA

South Dakota School of Mines and
Technology, SD
Southeast Missouri State University, MO
Southern Adventist University, TN
Southern Illinois University Carbondale, IL
Southern Oregon University, OR
Southern Utah University, UT
Southwestern College, KS
Spring Arbor University, MI
State University of New York at
Fredonia, NY
State University of New York at
New Paltz, NY
State University of New York College at
Cortland, NY
State University of New York College at
Geneseo, NY
State University of New York College at
Potsdam, NY
State University of New York College of
Agriculture and Technology at
Cobleskill, NY
State University of New York College of
Environmental Science and Forestry, NY
State University of New York Polytechnic
Institute, NY
Stetson University, FL
Stevens Institute of Technology, NJ
Stockton University, NJ
Tennessee State University, TN
Tennessee Technological University, TN
Texas Christian University, TX
Texas Wesleyan University, TX
Thomas More College, KY
Towson University, MD
Transylvania University, KY
Trine University, IN
Trinity Christian College, IL
Union College, KY
Union University, TN
Unity College, ME
The University of Akron, OH
The University of Alabama at
Birmingham, AL
The University of Alabama in
Huntsville, AL
University of Arkansas, AR
University of Arkansas at Little Rock, AR
University of California, San Diego, CA
University of Central Oklahoma, OK
University of Colorado Denver, CO
University of Dayton, OH
University of Delaware, DE
University of Evansville, IN
University of Florida, FL
University of Hartford, CT
University of Idaho, ID
University of Illinois at Urbana–
Champaign, IL
The University of Kansas, KS
University of Kentucky, KY
University of Louisville, KY
University of Maine, ME
University of Maine at Fort Kent, ME
University of Mary Hardin-Baylor, TX
University of Massachusetts Dartmouth, MA
University of Memphis, TN
University of Michigan, MI
University of Michigan–Dearborn, MI
University of Michigan–Flint, MI
University of Minnesota, Crookston, MN
University of Minnesota, Morris, MN
University of Minnesota, Twin Cities
Campus, MN
University of Mississippi, MS

University of Missouri, MO
University of Missouri–Kansas City, MO
University of Missouri–St. Louis, MO
The University of Montana Western, MT
University of Mount Union, OH
University of Nebraska at Kearney, NE
University of Nebraska at Omaha, NE
University of Nebraska–Lincoln, NE
University of Nevada, Las Vegas, NV
The University of North Carolina at
Charlotte, NC
University of Northern Colorado, CO
University of Northern Iowa, IA
University of North Florida, FL
University of Oklahoma, OK
University of Pittsburgh at Bradford, PA
University of Saint Joseph, CT
University of South Carolina, SC
University of South Carolina Aiken, SC
The University of South Dakota, SD
University of Southern Indiana, IN
The University of Tennessee at Martin, TN
The University of Texas at Dallas, TX
The University of Texas at El Paso, TX
The University of Texas at San Antonio, TX
The University of Toledo, OH
University of West Georgia, GA
University of Wisconsin–Eau Claire, WI
University of Wisconsin–Green Bay, WI
University of Wisconsin–La Crosse, WI
University of Wisconsin–Oshkosh, WI
University of Wisconsin–Parkside, WI
University of Wisconsin–River Falls, WI
University of Wisconsin–Stevens Point, WI
University of Wisconsin–Stout, WI
University of Wisconsin–Superior, WI
University of Wisconsin–Whitewater, WI
University of Wyoming, WY
Utah State University, UT
Valdosta State University, GA
Valley City State University, ND
Vanderbilt University, TN
Virginia Polytechnic Institute and State
University, VA
Washington & Jefferson College, PA
Wayland Baptist University, TX
Wayne State College, NE
Webster University, MO
Western Carolina University, NC
Western Illinois University, IL
Western Kentucky University, KY
Western Oregon University, OR
Western Washington University, WA
West Virginia University, WV
Wheaton College, IL
Whitworth University, WA
Wichita State University, KS
Williams Baptist College, AR
Winona State University, MN
Wisconsin Lutheran College, WI
Wittenberg University, OH
Wofford College, SC
Wright State University, OH
Wright State University–Lake Campus, OH
Xavier University, OH
York College of Pennsylvania, PA
Youngstown State University, OH

Out-of-State Students
Abilene Christian University, TX
Alaska Pacific University, AK
Albion College, MI
Allen College, IA
Anderson University, SC

Arizona State University at the Downtown
   Phoenix campus, AZ
Arizona State University at the Polytechnic
   campus, AZ
Arizona State University at the Tempe
   campus, AZ
Arizona State University at the
   West campus, AZ
Arkansas Tech University, AR
Asbury University, KY
Auburn University, AL
Augustana College, IL
Aurora University, IL
Austin College, TX
Averett University, VA
Baker University, KS
Ball State University, IN
Bellarmine University, KY
Bemidji State University, MN
Benedictine University, IL
Berry College, GA
Bethany College, WV
Bethel University, MN
Binghamton University, State University of
   New York, NY
Bluefield College, VA
Bluffton University, OH
Boise State University, ID
Brenau University, GA
Bridgewater College, VA
Buena Vista University, IA
Cabrini University, PA
California State University, Chico, CA
Calvin College, MI
Cameron University, OK
Campbell University, NC
Capital University, OH
Centenary College of Louisiana, LA
Central College, IA
Central Michigan University, MI
Central Penn College, PA
Central Washington University, WA
Chowan University, NC
Christian Brothers University, TN
The Citadel, The Military College of South
   Carolina, SC
Cleveland State University, OH
Coastal Carolina University, SC
The College of Idaho, ID
The College of New Rochelle, NY
College of Saint Benedict, MN
The College of Saint Rose, NY
College of Staten Island of the City
   University of New York, NY
Colorado Mesa University, CO
Concordia University Ann Arbor, MI
Concordia University Wisconsin, WI
Davidson College, NC
Davis College, NY
Delta State University, MS
Dordt College, IA
East Central University, OK
Eastern Michigan University, MI
East Texas Baptist University, TX
Elmira College, NY
Emory & Henry College, VA
Evangel University, MO
The Evergreen State College, WA
Fairmont State University, WV
Faulkner University, AL
Fitchburg State University, MA
Flagler College, FL
Florida Agricultural and Mechanical
   University, FL
Florida Gulf Coast University, FL
Florida Southern College, FL

Fort Lewis College, CO
Francis Marion University, SC
Franklin College, IN
Frostburg State University, MD
Gardner-Webb University, NC
George Fox University, OR
Georgia College & State University, GA
Georgia Institute of Technology, GA
Georgian Court University, NJ
Glenville State College, WV
Grambling State University, LA
Grand Valley State University, MI
Grand View University, IA
Greenville College, IL
Gustavus Adolphus College, MN
Hamline University, MN
Hampden-Sydney College, VA
Hanover College, IN
Hardin-Simmons University, TX
Hawai`i Pacific University, HI
Heidelberg University, OH
Hollins University, VA
Hood College, MD
Husson University, ME
Idaho State University, ID
Iowa State University of Science and
   Technology, IA
Iowa Wesleyan University, IA
James Madison University, VA
Johnson C. Smith University, NC
Kent State University, OH
Kent State University at Geauga, OH
Kent State University at Stark, OH
Kentucky Wesleyan College, KY
King University, TN
Lewis-Clark State College, ID
Lincoln University, MO
Lipscomb University, TN
Louisiana State University and Agricultural
   & Mechanical College, LA
Louisiana Tech University, LA
Loyola Marymount University, CA
Lynn University, FL
MacMurray College, IL
Manchester University, IN
Marian University, WI
Marygrove College, MI
Marymount Manhattan College, NY
Marymount University, VA
Maryville University of Saint Louis, MO
Mayville State University, ND
Meredith College, NC
Miami University, OH
Michigan State University, MI
Minnesota State University Moorhead, MN
Minot State University, ND
Misericordia University, PA
Mississippi State University, MS
Missouri University of Science and
   Technology, MO
Missouri Western State University, MO
Monmouth University, NJ
Montana State University Billings, MT
Montana Tech of The University of
   Montana, MT
Moravian College, PA
Morehead State University, KY
Morningside College, IA
Morrisville State College, NY
Murray State University, KY
Nazareth College of Rochester, NY
New College of Florida, FL
New Jersey Institute of Technology, NJ
New Mexico State University, NM
Nicholls State University, LA
Northeastern State University, OK

Northern Michigan University, MI
Northland College, WI
Northwestern State University of
   Louisiana, LA
Northwest Missouri State University, MO
Ohio Northern University, OH
The Ohio State University, OH
Oklahoma Baptist University, OK
Oklahoma Panhandle State University, OK
Oklahoma State University, OK
Ouachita Baptist University, AR
Piedmont College, GA
Portland State University, OR
Ramapo College of New Jersey, NJ
Randolph-Macon College, VA
Robert Morris University Illinois, IL
Roberts Wesleyan College, NY
Rockford University, IL
Rogers State University, OK
Sacred Heart University, CT
St. Ambrose University, IA
St. Bonaventure University, NY
St. Edward's University, TX
Saint John's University, MN
Saint Martin's University, WA
Saint Mary-of-the-Woods College, IN
Saint Michael's College, VT
Saint Vincent College, PA
Salem International University, WV
San Diego Christian College, CA
Shawnee State University, OH
Shepherd University, WV
Siena College, NY
Simpson University, CA
Slippery Rock University of
   Pennsylvania, PA
Sonoma State University, CA
South Dakota School of Mines and
   Technology, SD
Southeastern Louisiana University, LA
Southeastern Oklahoma State
   University, OK
Southeast Missouri State University, MO
Southern Adventist University, TN
Southern Arkansas University–
   Magnolia, AR
Southern Oregon University, OR
Southwestern Oklahoma State
   University, OK
State University of New York at
   Fredonia, NY
State University of New York at
   Plattsburgh, NY
State University of New York College of
   Environmental Science and Forestry, NY
Stetson University, FL
Tennessee Technological University, TN
Tennessee Wesleyan University, TN
Texas A&M University–Commerce, TX
Texas Tech University, TX
Texas Wesleyan University, TX
Thomas College, ME
Thomas More College, KY
Thomas University, GA
Transylvania University, KY
Trinity Christian College, IL
Truett McConnell University, GA
Truman State University, MO
The University of Akron, OH
The University of Alabama, AL
The University of Alabama at
   Birmingham, AL
University of Arkansas, AR
University of California, Irvine, CA
University of California, Santa Cruz, CA
University of Colorado Denver, CO

University of Dubuque, IA
University of Florida, FL
University of Houston, TX
University of Idaho, ID
University of Indianapolis, IN
The University of Iowa, IA
The University of Kansas, KS
University of Kentucky, KY
University of Louisiana at Monroe, LA
University of Louisville, KY
University of Maine, ME
University of Maine at Presque Isle, ME
University of Mary Hardin-Baylor, TX
University of Maryland, College Park, MD
University of Massachusetts Boston, MA
University of Massachusetts Lowell, MA
University of Michigan, MI
University of Michigan–Dearborn, MI
University of Mississippi, MS
University of Missouri, MO
University of Missouri–Kansas City, MO
University of Missouri–St. Louis, MO
University of Montana, MT
The University of Montana Western, MT
University of Montevallo, AL
University of Nebraska at Kearney, NE
University of Nebraska at Omaha, NE
University of Nebraska–Lincoln, NE
University of Nevada, Las Vegas, NV
University of North Alabama, AL
The University of North Carolina at Chapel
  Hill, NC
The University of North Carolina at
  Greensboro, NC
University of Northern Colorado, CO
University of North Florida, FL
University of Pittsburgh at Bradford, PA
University of Science and Arts of
  Oklahoma, OK
University of Sioux Falls, SD
University of South Carolina, SC
University of South Carolina Aiken, SC
University of Southern Indiana, IN
University of Southern Mississippi, MS
The University of Tennessee at Martin, TN
The University of Texas at Dallas, TX
The University of Texas at El Paso, TX
The University of Texas at San Antonio, TX
The University of Texas Rio
  Grande Valley, TX
The University of Toledo, OH
University of Utah, UT
University of West Florida, FL
University of Wisconsin–La Crosse, WI
University of Wisconsin–Parkside, WI
University of Wisconsin–Stevens Point, WI
University of Wisconsin–Stout, WI
University of Wisconsin–Whitewater, WI
University of Wyoming, WY
Virginia Military Institute, VA
Virginia Polytechnic Institute and State
  University, VA
Warner University, FL
Washington State University, WA
Wayne State College, NE
Wayne State University, MI
Webster University, MO
Western Kentucky University, KY
Western Michigan University, MI
West Texas A&M University, TX
Wheaton College, IL
William Jessup University, CA
Winona State University, MN
Wisconsin Lutheran College, WI
Wright State University, OH

Wright State University–Lake Campus, OH
Youngstown State University, OH

Parents of Current Students
Arkansas Tech University, AR
Aurora University, IL
Barclay College, KS
Blue Mountain College, MS
Caldwell University, NJ
Cincinnati Christian University, OH
The College of New Rochelle, NY
College of Staten Island of the City
  University of New York, NY
Columbia College, MO
ECPI University, VA
Emerson College, MA
Emmanuel College, GA
Franklin Pierce University, NH
Manchester University, IN
Marygrove College, MI
Maryville University of Saint Louis, MO
Millikin University, IL
Missouri Baptist University, MO
Mount Aloysius College, PA
Mount Marty College, SD
New England College, NH
Northwest University, WA
Rockford University, IL
St. Joseph's College, Long Island
  Campus, NY
St. Joseph's College, New York, NY
Saint Mary-of-the-Woods College, IN
State University of New York at
  Fredonia, NY
Stephens College, MO
Texas Wesleyan University, TX
Truett McConnell University, GA
The University of Alabama at
  Birmingham, AL
University of Great Falls, MT
University of Hartford, CT
University of Valley Forge, PA
Upper Iowa University, IA
Wesleyan College, GA

Previous College Experience
Abilene Christian University, TX
Alaska Pacific University, AK
American University, DC
Austin College, TX
Bellarmine University, KY
Bemidji State University, MN
Bethel College, KS
Bloomfield College, NJ
Boise State University, ID
Brevard College, NC
Bridgewater College, VA
Caldwell University, NJ
Calumet College of Saint Joseph, IN
Central College, IA
Clarion University of Pennsylvania, PA
The College at Brockport, State University
  of New York, NY
The College of New Rochelle, NY
The College of St. Scholastica, MN
College of Staten Island of the City
  University of New York, NY
Columbia College, MO
Eastern Michigan University, MI
East Texas Baptist University, TX
Elmira College, NY
Fairmont State University, WV
Ferris State University, MI
Fitchburg State University, MA
Florida Institute of Technology, FL
Gardner-Webb University, NC

Georgian Court University, NJ
Graceland University, IA
Hamline University, MN
Hawai`i Pacific University, HI
Hendrix College, AR
Hollins University, VA
Hood College, MD
Howard University, DC
Illinois College, IL
Illinois Institute of Technology, IL
Indiana State University, IN
Kansas Wesleyan University, KS
Kean University, NJ
Kent State University, OH
Lawrence Technological University, MI
Lees-McRae College, NC
Lewis-Clark State College, ID
Linfield College, OR
Lock Haven University of Pennsylvania, PA
Loyola Marymount University, CA
Manhattanville College, NY
McDaniel College, MD
Memphis College of Art, TN
Meredith College, NC
Midway University, KY
Millikin University, IL
Misericordia University, PA
Mississippi State University, MS
Missouri Western State University, MO
Monmouth University, NJ
Morehead State University, KY
Mount Mercy University, IA
Muskingum University, OH
New Mexico State University, NM
New York Institute of Technology, NY
Nicholls State University, LA
Northwest Missouri State University, MO
The Ohio State University, OH
Oklahoma State University, OK
Old Dominion University, VA
Otterbein University, OH
Ouachita Baptist University, AR
Palm Beach Atlantic University, FL
Point Park University, PA
St. Ambrose University, IA
St. John's University, NY
Saint Louis University, MO
Saint Vincent College, PA
Salisbury University, MD
San Diego State University, CA
Shepherd University, WV
Siena College, NY
Slippery Rock University of
  Pennsylvania, PA
Sonoma State University, CA
Southeast Missouri State University, MO
Southern New Hampshire University, NH
Southern Oregon University, OR
State University of New York at
  Fredonia, NY
State University of New York College at
  Potsdam, NY
State University of New York Polytechnic
  Institute, NY
Stephen F. Austin State University, TX
Stockton University, NJ
Texas A&M University–Commerce, TX
Texas Christian University, TX
Texas Wesleyan University, TX
Towson University, MD
Truman State University, MO
The University of Alabama at
  Birmingham, AL
University of Arkansas, AR
University of Arkansas at Little Rock, AR

University of Bridgeport, CT
University of Hartford, CT
University of Houston, TX
The University of Kansas, KS
University of Louisville, KY
University of Maine, ME
University of Massachusetts Dartmouth, MA
University of Michigan–Dearborn, MI
University of Mississippi, MS
University of Missouri–St. Louis, MO
University of Nevada, Las Vegas, NV
University of Northern Colorado, CO
University of Oklahoma, OK
University of St. Thomas, TX
University of Science and Arts of
   Oklahoma, OK
University of South Carolina Aiken, SC
The University of Tennessee at Martin, TN
The University of Toledo, OH
The University of West Alabama, AL
University of Wisconsin–Eau Claire, WI
University of Wisconsin–Stout, WI
University of Wyoming, WY
Walsh College of Accountancy and Business
   Administration, MI
Warner University, FL
Wartburg College, IA
Washington State University, WA
Wesleyan College, GA
Western Michigan University, MI
Western Oregon University, OR
Western Washington University, WA
William Jessup University, CA
Wisconsin Lutheran College, WI

Public Servants
Arkansas Tech University, AR
Caldwell University, NJ
Central Washington University, WA
Chowan University, NC
College of Staten Island of the City
   University of New York, NY
Francis Marion University, SC
Georgia College & State University, GA
Grambling State University, LA
Grand Valley State University, MI
Hardin-Simmons University, TX
Hofstra University, NY
Kent State University at Stark, OH
Kentucky State University, KY
Lindenwood University, MO
Missouri Baptist University, MO
Missouri Western State University, MO
New Mexico State University, NM
Nicholls State University, LA
Northwestern State University of
   Louisiana, LA
Patrick Henry College, VA
Peirce College, PA
Regent University, VA
Regis University, CO
St. John's University, NY
St. Joseph's College, Long Island
   Campus, NY
St. Joseph's College, New York, NY
Southern Illinois University Carbondale, IL
Sterling College, KS
Tennessee Technological University, TN
Texas Wesleyan University, TX
The University of Alabama at
   Birmingham, AL
University of Kentucky, KY
University of Maryland Eastern Shore, MD
University of Massachusetts Dartmouth, MA
University of Memphis, TN
University of Michigan–Dearborn, MI

University of Oklahoma, OK
The University of Texas at Arlington, TX
The University of Texas at Dallas, TX
The University of Toledo, OH
Washington State University, WA
West Texas A&M University, TX
Youngstown State University, OH

Relatives of Clergy
Abilene Christian University, TX
Albion College, MI
American University, DC
Arcadia University, PA
Asbury University, KY
Augsburg College, MN
Austin College, TX
Averett University, VA
Baker University, KS
Barclay College, KS
Barton College, NC
Benedictine University, IL
Bethany College, WV
Bethel College, KS
Bethel University, MN
Biola University, CA
Bloomfield College, NJ
Blue Mountain College, MS
Boston University, MA
Bryan College, TN
Cairn University, PA
Caldwell University, NJ
California Baptist University, CA
California Lutheran University, CA
Calvary University, MO
Campbellsville University, KY
Capital University, OH
Carson-Newman University, TN
Cedar Crest College, PA
Centenary College of Louisiana, LA
Central Methodist University, MO
Chowan University, NC
Claflin University, SC
Clarke University, IA
Corban University, OR
Cornerstone University, MI
Crown College, MN
Dallas Baptist University, TX
Davidson College, NC
Davis College, NY
Dominican College, NY
Drury University, MO
Duquesne University, PA
Eastern University, PA
Elon University, NC
Emmanuel College, GA
Eureka College, IL
Evangel University, MO
Faulkner University, AL
Florida Southern College, FL
Franklin College, IN
Fresno Pacific University, CA
Friends University, KS
Furman University, SC
Gardner-Webb University, NC
George Fox University, OR
Gordon College, MA
Hamline University, MN
Harding University, AR
Hardin-Simmons University, TX
Hawai'i Pacific University, HI
Heidelberg University, OH
Hendrix College, AR
High Point University, NC
Hobart and William Smith Colleges, NY
Houghton College, NY
Houston Baptist University, TX

Howard Payne University, TX
Huntington University, IN
Indiana Wesleyan University, IN
Judson College, AL
Kentucky Wesleyan College, KY
King's College, PA
Kuyper College, MI
LaGrange College, GA
Lancaster Bible College, PA
La Salle University, PA
Lees-McRae College, NC
Lenoir-Rhyne University, NC
Lincoln Christian University, IL
Lindsey Wilson College, KY
Lipscomb University, TN
Lycoming College, PA
Malone University, OH
Maranatha Baptist University, WI
The Master's University, CA
Mercer University, GA
Merrimack College, MA
Methodist University, NC
Midway University, KY
Millikin University, IL
Misericordia University, PA
Missouri Baptist University, MO
Montreat College, NC
Moravian College, PA
Mount Vernon Nazarene University, OH
Muskingum University, OH
Newberry College, SC
New Jersey Institute of Technology, NJ
Niagara University, NY
North Central College, IL
Northwest Christian University, OR
Northwest Nazarene University, ID
Northwest University, WA
Ohio Northern University, OH
Ohio Valley University, WV
Ohio Wesleyan University, OH
Oklahoma Baptist University, OK
Oklahoma City University, OK
Oklahoma Wesleyan University, OK
Olivet Nazarene University, IL
Oral Roberts University, OK
Otterbein University, OH
Ouachita Baptist University, AR
Pacific University, OR
Patrick Henry College, VA
Piedmont International University, NC
Presbyterian College, SC
Queens University of Charlotte, NC
Randall University, OK
Randolph College, VA
Randolph-Macon College, VA
Rhodes College, TN
Roberts Wesleyan College, NY
St. Bonaventure University, NY
St. John's University, NY
Saint Peter's University, NJ
Salem College, NC
Samford University, AL
San Diego Christian College, CA
Schreiner University, TX
Seattle Pacific University, WA
Shasta Bible College, CA
Shenandoah University, VA
Siena College, NY
Simpson College, IA
Simpson University, CA
Southwest Baptist University, MO
Southwestern University, TX
Spring Arbor University, MI
Stonehill College, MA
Susquehanna University, PA
Tennessee Wesleyan University, TN

Texas Christian University, TX
Texas Wesleyan University, TX
Thiel College, PA
Toccoa Falls College, GA
Transylvania University, KY
Trevecca Nazarene University, TN
Trinity College of Florida, FL
Truett McConnell University, GA
Union University, TN
The University of Alabama at
    Birmingham, AL
University of Dubuque, IA
University of Holy Cross, LA
University of Indianapolis, IN
University of Jamestown, ND
University of Mary Hardin-Baylor, TX
University of Mobile, AL
University of Mount Union, OH
The University of North Carolina
    at Chapel Hill, NC
University of Portland, OR
The University of Tulsa, OK
University of Valley Forge, PA
Ursuline College, OH
Valparaiso University, IN
Virginia Wesleyan College, VA
Warner University, FL
Wayland Baptist University, TX
Wesleyan College, GA
Westminster College, MO
West Virginia Wesleyan College, WV
Wheaton College, IL
William Jessup University, CA
Williams Baptist College, AR
Wilson College, PA
Wingate University, NC
Wittenberg University, OH
Wofford College, SC

Religious Affiliation

Abilene Christian University, TX
Agnes Scott College, GA
Alaska Pacific University, AK
Albertus Magnus College, CT
Alderson Broaddus University, WV
Alverno College, WI
Anderson University, SC
Arcadia University, PA
Armstrong State University, GA
Augustana College, IL
Augustana University, SD
Augusta University, GA
Aurora University, IL
Austin College, TX
Ave Maria University, FL
Averett University, VA
Baker University, KS
Baldwin Wallace University, OH
The Baptist College of Florida, FL
Barclay College, KS
Barton College, NC
Belhaven University, MS
Bellarmine University, KY
Bethany College, WV
Bethel College, KS
Bluefield College, VA
Blue Mountain College, MS
Bluffton University, OH
Boston University, MA
Bridgewater College, VA
Brigham Young University, UT
Buena Vista University, IA
Cabrini University, PA
Caldwell University, NJ
California Baptist University, CA

California Lutheran University, CA
Calumet College of Saint Joseph, IN
Calvary University, MO
Calvin College, MI
Campbellsville University, KY
Canisius College, NY
Capital University, OH
Cardinal Stritch University, WI
Carlow University, PA
Carroll College, MT
The Catholic University of America, DC
Cedarville University, OH
Centenary College of Louisiana, LA
Central College, IA
Central Methodist University, MO
Chaminade University of Honolulu, HI
Charlotte Christian College and Theological
    Seminary, NC
Chowan University, NC
Christopher Newport University, VA
Claflin University, SC
Coe College, IA
The College at Brockport, State University
    of New York, NY
The College of St. Scholastica, MN
Columbia College, MO
Concordia University Ann Arbor, MI
Concordia University Chicago, IL
Concordia University Irvine, CA
Concordia University, Nebraska, NE
Concordia University, St. Paul, MN
Concordia University Texas, TX
Covenant College, GA
Culver-Stockton College, MO
Dakota Wesleyan University, SD
Dallas Baptist University, TX
Davidson College, NC
Defiance College, OH
Doane University, NE
Dordt College, IA
Drury University, MO
Duquesne University, PA
Eastern Connecticut State University, CT
Eastern Mennonite University, VA
Eastern Michigan University, MI
East Texas Baptist University, TX
Eckerd College, FL
Elizabethtown College, PA
Elmhurst College, IL
Elms College, MA
Emmanuel College, GA
Emory University, GA
Emporia State University, KS
Endicott College, MA
Eureka College, IL
Evangel University, MO
Faulkner University, AL
Florida Southern College, FL
Franciscan University of Steubenville, OH
Franklin College, IN
Fresno Pacific University, CA
Friends University, KS
Furman University, SC
Gannon University, PA
Geneva College, PA
George Fox University, OR
Georgian Court University, NJ
Georgia Southern University, GA
Graceland University, IA
Grand View University, IA
Greenville College, IL
Hamline University, MN
Hanover College, IN
Hardin-Simmons University, TX
Hawai`i Pacific University, HI

Heidelberg University, OH
Hood College, MD
Houghton College, NY
Houston Baptist University, TX
Howard Payne University, TX
Howard University, DC
Huntingdon College, AL
Huntington University, IN
Indiana Wesleyan University, IN
Iona College, NY
Judson College, AL
Kansas Wesleyan University, KS
Kennesaw State University, GA
Kentucky Wesleyan College, KY
Keuka College, NY
LaGrange College, GA
Lees-McRae College, NC
Lenoir-Rhyne University, NC
Lewis University, IL
Liberty University, VA
Lindsey Wilson College, KY
Lipscomb University, TN
Loyola Marymount University, CA
Loyola University Chicago, IL
Luther College, IA
Lyon College, AR
Malone University, OH
Manchester University, IN
Mansfield University of Pennsylvania, PA
Marymount University, VA
Maryville College, TN
McKendree University, IL
McPherson College, KS
Meredith College, NC
Merrimack College, MA
Messiah College, PA
Methodist University, NC
Midway University, KY
Millsaps College, MS
Missouri Baptist University, MO
Missouri Western State University, MO
Molloy College, NY
Montreat College, NC
Moravian College, PA
Mount Aloysius College, PA
Mount Marty College, SD
Mount Vernon Nazarene University, OH
Muskingum University, OH
Nebraska Methodist College, NE
Newberry College, SC
New Jersey Institute of Technology, NJ
Northeastern State University, OK
Northwest Christian University, OR
Northwestern College, IA
Northwest Nazarene University, ID
Northwest University, WA
Oakland City University, IN
Ohio Northern University, OH
Ohio Valley University, WV
Ohio Wesleyan University, OH
Oklahoma Baptist University, OK
Oklahoma City University, OK
Oklahoma Wesleyan University, OK
Olivet College, MI
Olivet Nazarene University, IL
Ouachita Baptist University, AR
Our Lady of the Lake University, TX
Presbyterian College, SC
Queens University of Charlotte, NC
Randall University, OK
Randolph College, VA
Regent University, VA
Rhodes College, TN
Roberts Wesleyan College, NY
Sacred Heart University, CT

St. Ambrose University, IA
St. Bonaventure University, NY
St. Edward's University, TX
St. John's University, NY
Saint Louis University, MO
Saint Mary-of-the-Woods College, IN
Saint Peter's University, NJ
Saint Vincent College, PA
Salem International University, WV
San Diego Christian College, CA
Schreiner University, TX
Seattle Pacific University, WA
Seattle University, WA
Shenandoah University, VA
Siena College, NY
Simpson College, IA
Simpson University, CA
Southeastern University, FL
Southwest Baptist University, MO
Southwestern College, KS
Southwestern University, TX
Spring Arbor University, MI
State University of New York College at
    Geneseo, NY
Taylor University, IN
Tennessee Wesleyan University, TN
Texas Christian University, TX
Texas Lutheran University, TX
Texas Wesleyan University, TX
Thiel College, PA
Thomas More College, KY
Toccoa Falls College, GA
Transylvania University, KY
Trevecca Nazarene University, TN
Trinity Christian College, IL
Truett McConnell University, GA
Union College, KY
Union University, TN
University of California, Riverside, CA
University of Dallas, TX
University of Dayton, OH
University of Dubuque, IA
University of Evansville, IN
University of Great Falls, MT
University of Hartford, CT
University of Holy Cross, LA
University of Indianapolis, IN
University of Jamestown, ND
University of Maine, ME
University of Mary Hardin-Baylor, TX
University of Mount Olive, NC
University of Mount Union, OH
The University of North Carolina at
    Chapel Hill, NC
The University of North Carolina at
    Greensboro, NC
University of Portland, OR
University of St. Francis, IL
University of St. Thomas, TX
University of Sioux Falls, SD
University of South Carolina, SC
The University of Tennessee at
    Chattanooga, TN
University of the Pacific, CA
The University of Toledo, OH
The University of Tulsa, OK
Ursuline College, OH
Utah State University, UT
Valparaiso University, IN
Vanguard University of Southern
    California, CA
Villanova University, PA
Virginia Wesleyan College, VA
Wake Forest University, NC
Waldorf University, IA
Warner Pacific College, OR

Wartburg College, IA
Washington State University, WA
Wayland Baptist University, TX
Wesleyan College, GA
Western Kentucky University, KY
Westminster College, MO
Westminster College, PA
West Texas A&M University, TX
West Virginia Wesleyan College, WV
Wheeling Jesuit University, WV
Whitworth University, WA
Williams Baptist College, AR
Wilson College, PA
Wittenberg University, OH
Young Harris College, GA
Youngstown State University, OH

Siblings of Current Students
Albertus Magnus College, CT
Albright College, PA
Alliant International University–
    San Diego, CA
Alma College, MI
Alvernia University, PA
Asbury University, KY
Augsburg College, MN
Augustana College, IL
Augustana University, SD
Aurora University, IL
Ave Maria University, FL
Baldwin Wallace University, OH
Barclay College, KS
Barton College, NC
Bay Path University, MA
Belhaven University, MS
Belmont University, TN
Beloit College, WI
Benedictine University, IL
Bethel College, KS
Bloomfield College, NJ
Blue Mountain College, MS
Buena Vista University, IA
Cabrini University, PA
Caldwell University, NJ
California Baptist University, CA
Calvary University, MO
Campbell University, NC
Capital University, OH
Cardinal Stritch University, WI
Carlow University, PA
Carroll College, MT
Carroll University, WI
Carson-Newman University, TN
Catawba College, NC
The Catholic University of America, DC
Cedar Crest College, PA
Centenary College of Louisiana, LA
Central College, IA
Central Methodist University, MO
Chaminade University of Honolulu, HI
Chatham University, PA
Christendom College, VA
Cincinnati Christian University, OH
Clarke University, IA
Coe College, IA
The College of Idaho, ID
The College of New Rochelle, NY
The College of Saint Rose, NY
The College of St. Scholastica, MN
College of Staten Island of the City
    University of New York, NY
Columbia College, MO
Concordia University Ann Arbor, MI
Concordia University Texas, TX
Corban University, OR
Crossroads Bible College, IN

Crown College, MN
Culver-Stockton College, MO
Curry College, MA
Davis College, NY
DeSales University, PA
Doane University, NE
Dominican University, IL
Drexel University, PA
Eastern University, PA
Elizabethtown College, PA
Elmhurst College, IL
Elmira College, NY
Elms College, MA
Emmanuel College, GA
Emory & Henry College, VA
Eureka College, IL
Faulkner University, AL
Felician University, NJ
Florida Institute of Technology, FL
Florida Southern College, FL
Franciscan University of Steubenville, OH
Franklin College, IN
Franklin Pierce University, NH
Georgian Court University, NJ
Gonzaga University, WA
Greenville College, IL
Gustavus Adolphus College, MN
Gwynedd Mercy University, PA
Hanover College, IN
Harding University, AR
Hardin-Simmons University, TX
Hartwick College, NY
Hilbert College, NY
Hood College, MD
Houghton College, NY
Howard Payne University, TX
Indiana Tech, IN
Indiana Wesleyan University, IN
Iona College, NY
Iowa Wesleyan University, IA
Ithaca College, NY
James Madison University, VA
Johnson C. Smith University, NC
Juniata College, PA
Kansas Wesleyan University, KS
Keuka College, NY
King's College, PA
Kuyper College, MI
Lancaster Bible College, PA
Lasell College, MA
Lawrence University, WI
Lees-McRae College, NC
Lee University, TN
Lenoir-Rhyne University, NC
LIM College, NY
Long Island University–LIU Brooklyn, NY
Long Island University–LIU Post, NY
Lynn University, FL
Manchester University, IN
Marian University, WI
Marygrove College, MI
Marymount University, VA
McDaniel College, MD
Mercer University, GA
Merrimack College, MA
Methodist University, NC
Millikin University, IL
Misericordia University, PA
Missouri Baptist University, MO
Molloy College, NY
Moravian College, PA
Mount Aloysius College, PA
Mount Marty College, SD
Mount Mary University, WI
Mount St. Mary's University, MD
Muskingum University, OH

Nazareth College of Rochester, NY
Newberry College, SC
New England College, NH
New Jersey Institute of Technology, NJ
Nichols College, MA
Northwest Christian University, OR
Northwestern College, IA
Northwest University, WA
Oglethorpe University, GA
Ohio Northern University, OH
Oklahoma Wesleyan University, OK
Olivet College, MI
Oral Roberts University, OK
Otterbein University, OH
Pacific Union College, CA
Peirce College, PA
Piedmont College, GA
Point Park University, PA
Providence College, RI
Queens University of Charlotte, NC
Quinnipiac University, CT
Randolph-Macon College, VA
Regent University, VA
Research College of Nursing, MO
Rockford University, IL
Rockhurst University, MO
Sacred Heart University, CT
Saint Anselm College, NH
St. Bonaventure University, NY
St. Joseph's College, Long Island
    Campus, NY
St. Joseph's College, New York, NY
Saint Joseph's University, PA
St. Lawrence University, NY
Saint Louis University, MO
Saint Martin's University, WA
Saint Mary-of-the-Woods College, IN
Saint Michael's College, VT
St. Thomas Aquinas College, NY
Samford University, AL
San Diego Christian College, CA
Schreiner University, TX
Seton Hill University, PA
Simpson College, IA
Simpson University, CA
Southern Adventist University, TN
Southern New Hampshire University, NH
Springfield College, MA
Spring Hill College, AL
Stephens College, MO
Sterling College, KS
Stonehill College, MA
Suffolk University, MA
Tennessee Wesleyan University, TN
Texas Wesleyan University, TX
Thiel College, PA
Thomas More College, KY
Toccoa Falls College, GA
Trevecca Nazarene University, TN
Trine University, IN
Truett McConnell University, GA
Union College, KY
Union University, TN
The University of Alabama at
    Birmingham, AL
University of Dallas, TX
University of Dubuque, IA
University of Evansville, IN
University of Great Falls, MT
University of Hartford, CT
University of Jamestown, ND
University of St. Francis, IL
University of Saint Joseph, CT
University of Sioux Falls, SD
The University of Toledo, OH

The University of Tulsa, OK
University of Valley Forge, PA
Ursinus College, PA
Ursuline College, OH
Wagner College, NY
Warner University, FL
Wartburg College, IA
Waynesburg University, PA
Webber International University, FL
Wesleyan College, GA
Western New England University, MA
Westminster College, MO
William Jessup University, CA
William Jewell College, MO
William Peace University, NC
William Woods University, MO
Xavier University, OH

Spouses of Current Students
Alaska Bible College, AK
Alliant International University–
    San Diego, CA
American University, DC
Augustana University, SD
Aurora University, IL
The Baptist College of Florida, FL
Barclay College, KS
Bethel College, KS
Bloomfield College, NJ
Blue Mountain College, MS
Boise State University, ID
Bryan College, TN
Caldwell University, NJ
Calvary University, MO
Cardinal Stritch University, WI
Carroll College, MT
Carroll University, WI
Central Methodist University, MO
Cincinnati Christian University, OH
Clarion University of Pennsylvania, PA
The College of New Rochelle, NY
The College of St. Scholastica, MN
College of Staten Island of the City
    University of New York, NY
Columbia College, MO
Columbia International University, SC
Crossroads Bible College, IN
Curry College, MA
Davis College, NY
Elmhurst College, IL
Emmanuel College, GA
Emmanuel College, MA
Franklin College, IN
Franklin Pierce University, NH
Fresno Pacific University, CA
Huntingdon College, AL
Indiana Tech, IN
John Wesley University, NC
Kansas Wesleyan University, KS
Lee University, TN
Long Island University–LIU Brooklyn, NY
Long Island University–LIU Post, NY
Manchester University, IN
Maranatha Baptist University, WI
Marygrove College, MI
Mid-Atlantic Christian University, NC
Missouri Baptist University, MO
Mount Aloysius College, PA
Mount Marty College, SD
New Mexico State University, NM
Northwest University, WA
Pacific Union College, CA
Piedmont International University, NC
Regent University, VA

St. Joseph's College,
    Long Island Campus, NY
St. Joseph's College, New York, NY
Saint Louis University, MO
Saint Mary-of-the-Woods College, IN
St. Thomas Aquinas College, NY
Samford University, AL
Simpson University, CA
Southern Adventist University, TN
Texas Wesleyan University, TX
Trinity College of Florida, FL
Truett McConnell University, GA
Union University, TN
The University of Alabama at
    Birmingham, AL
University of Dubuque, IA
University of Great Falls, MT
University of Hartford, CT
University of Jamestown, ND
University of Maine, ME
University of Mississippi, MS
University of Sioux Falls, SD
University of Valley Forge, PA
University of Wyoming, WY
Upper Iowa University, IA
Wayne State University, MI
Wesleyan College, GA
Xavier University of Louisiana, LA

Spouses of Deceased or Disabled Public Servants
The College of New Rochelle, NY
College of Staten Island of the City
    University of New York, NY
Eastern Washington University, WA
Francis Marion University, SC
Grand Valley State University, MI
Louisiana Tech University, LA
Michigan State University, MI
Mississippi State University, MS
New Mexico State University, NM
Northeastern State University, OK
Northern Kentucky University, KY
Southern Illinois University Carbondale, IL
Texas State University, TX
Texas Wesleyan University, TX
The University of Alabama, AL
The University of Alabama at
    Birmingham, AL
University of Kentucky, KY
University of Missouri–St. Louis, MO
University of South Carolina, SC
University of Utah, UT
Youngstown State University, OH

Twins
Blue Mountain College, MS
Caldwell University, NJ
Calvin College, MI
The Catholic University of America, DC
Central College, IA
The College of New Rochelle, NY
The College of Saint Rose, NY
Drexel University, PA
Emmanuel College, GA
Lake Erie College, OH
Long Island University–LIU Brooklyn, NY
Long Island University–LIU Post, NY
Mount Aloysius College, PA
Ohio Wesleyan University, OH
Ouachita Baptist University, AR
Randolph College, VA
Sacred Heart University, CT
St. Joseph's College,
    Long Island Campus, NY
St. Joseph's College, New York, NY
St. Thomas Aquinas College, NY

Simpson College, IA
Southern New Hampshire University, NH
Sterling College, KS
Texas Wesleyan University, TX
Trine University, IN
Union University, TN
The University of Alabama at
    Birmingham, AL
University of Hartford, CT
Virginia Polytechnic Institute and State
    University, VA
Westminster College, MO

Veterans
Adelphi University, NY
Agnes Scott College, GA
Alliant International University–
    San Diego, CA
American University, DC
Amridge University, AL
Anderson University, SC
Arkansas Tech University, AR
Augustana University, SD
Augusta University, GA
Aurora University, IL
Austin College, TX
Austin Peay State University, TN
Babson College, MA
Ball State University, IN
Barton College, NC
Baylor University, TX
Belhaven University, MS
Belmont University, TN
Beloit College, WI
Benedictine University, IL
Berry College, GA
Bethel University, MN
Binghamton University, State University of
    New York, NY
Bloomfield College, NJ
Bluefield College, VA
Boise State University, ID
Boston University, MA
Brown University, RI
Butler University, IN
Caldwell University, NJ
California Baptist University, CA
California Lutheran University, CA
California State University, Bakersfield, CA
California State University,
    San Bernardino, CA
California University of Pennsylvania, PA
Calvin College, MI
Cameron University, OK
Campbellsville University, KY
Campbell University, NC
Canisius College, NY
Carroll College, MT
The Catholic University of America, DC
Cedarville University, OH
Centenary College of Louisiana, LA
Central College, IA
Central Washington University, WA
Chestnut Hill College, PA
Chowan University, NC
Christian Brothers University, TN
The Citadel, The Military College of
    South Carolina, SC
Claflin University, SC
Claremont McKenna College, CA
Clarion University of Pennsylvania, PA
Clarkson University, NY
Clemson University, SC
Coe College, IA
Colgate University, NY

The College at Brockport, State University
    of New York, NY
The College of New Rochelle, NY
College of Staten Island of the City
    University of New York, NY
Colorado State University, CO
Columbia College, MO
Columbia International University, SC
Concordia University, Nebraska, NE
Concordia University, St. Paul, MN
Concordia University Texas, TX
Concord University, WV
Corban University, OR
Culver-Stockton College, MO
Daemen College, NY
Dakota State University, SD
Dallas Baptist University, TX
Defiance College, OH
Denison University, OH
DePaul University, IL
Dickinson College, PA
Dickinson State University, ND
Dominican University of California, CA
Drury University, MO
Duquesne University, PA
D'Youville College, NY
East Central University, OK
Eastern Connecticut State University, CT
Eastern Washington University, WA
East Texas Baptist University, TX
ECPI University, VA
Elizabeth City State University, NC
Elmhurst College, IL
Elmira College, NY
Elon University, NC
Emmanuel College, MA
Emory University, GA
Emporia State University, KS
Everglades University, FL
The Evergreen State College, WA
Fairfield University, CT
Fairmont State University, WV
Ferris State University, MI
Fitchburg State University, MA
Florida International University, FL
Fort Hays State University, KS
Framingham State University, MA
Francis Marion University, SC
Franklin College, IN
Frostburg State University, MD
Furman University, SC
Gannon University, PA
Georgia Institute of Technology, GA
Georgian Court University, NJ
Glenville State College, WV
Gordon College, MA
Governors State University, IL
Grambling State University, LA
Grand Valley State University, MI
Grand View University, IA
Gwynedd Mercy University, PA
Hamline University, MN
Hampden-Sydney College, VA
Hampton University, VA
Hardin-Simmons University, TX
Hartwick College, NY
Hillsdale College, MI
Hofstra University, NY
Hollins University, VA
Hood College, MD
Hope International University, CA
Houghton College, NY
Huntingdon College, AL
Huntington University, IN
Illinois Institute of Technology, IL
Indiana State University, IN

Indiana Tech, IN
Indiana Wesleyan University, IN
Iona College, NY
Iowa State University of Science and
    Technology, IA
John Carroll University, OH
Kansas Wesleyan University, KS
Kean University, NJ
Kennesaw State University, GA
Kent State University, OH
Kent State University at Stark, OH
Kentucky State University, KY
Kentucky Wesleyan College, KY
Keuka College, NY
King's College, PA
King University, TN
Knox College, IL
Lake Erie College, OH
La Salle University, PA
Lasell College, MA
Lawrence Technological University, MI
Lawrence University, WI
Lebanon Valley College, PA
Lees-McRae College, NC
Lewis University, IL
Liberty University, VA
Lindenwood University, MO
Linfield College, OR
Long Island University–LIU Brooklyn, NY
Long Island University–LIU Post, NY
Louisiana State University and Agricultural
    & Mechanical College, LA
Louisiana Tech University, LA
Loyola Marymount University, CA
Lynn University, FL
MacMurray College, IL
Malone University, OH
Manhattanville College, NY
Marian University, WI
Marygrove College, MI
Marymount Manhattan College, NY
Marymount University, VA
Maryville College, TN
Massachusetts College of
    Art and Design, MA
The Master's University, CA
McDaniel College, MD
McKendree University, IL
McNally Smith College of Music, MN
Merrimack College, MA
Methodist University, NC
Metropolitan State University of Denver, CO
Michigan State University, MI
Michigan Technological University, MI
Midway University, KY
Midwestern State University, TX
Millikin University, IL
Minot State University, ND
Missouri Baptist University, MO
Molloy College, NY
Monmouth College, IL
Monmouth University, NJ
Montana State University Billings, MT
Montana Tech of The University of
    Montana, MT
Montreat College, NC
Moravian College, PA
Morehead State University, KY
Mount Mary University, WI
Nazareth College of Rochester, NY
New England College, NH
New Jersey Institute of Technology, NJ
New Mexico State University, NM
NewSchool of Architecture and Design, CA
New York Institute of Technology, NY
Nicholls State University, LA

Northern Illinois University, IL
Northern Kentucky University, KY
Northwestern College, IA
Northwestern State University
of Louisiana, LA
Nova Southeastern University, FL
Occidental College, CA
Ohio Northern University, OH
Oklahoma Baptist University, OK
Oklahoma Panhandle State University, OK
Olivet Nazarene University, IL
Otterbein University, OH
Pacific Union College, CA
Pacific University, OR
Patrick Henry College, VA
Paul Smith's College, NY
Peirce College, PA
Piedmont College, GA
Piedmont International University, NC
Portland State University, OR
Queens University of Charlotte, NC
Randall University, OK
Randolph-Macon College, VA
Regent University, VA
Robert Morris University, PA
Robert Morris University Illinois, IL
Rochester Institute of Technology, NY
Rogers State University, OK
Sacred Heart University, CT
The Sage Colleges, NY
Saginaw Valley State University, MI
St. Ambrose University, IA
St. Edward's University, TX
St. John's College, NM
St. John's University, NY
Saint Joseph's University, PA
Saint Louis University, MO
Saint Martin's University, WA
St. Mary's University, TX
Saint Michael's College, VT
St. Thomas Aquinas College, NY
Samford University, AL
Sam Houston State University, TX
San Diego Christian College, CA
San Diego State University, CA
Savannah College of Art and Design, GA
Schreiner University, TX
Seattle Pacific University, WA
Shasta Bible College, CA
Shawnee State University, OH
Simpson College, IA
Simpson University, CA
Sonoma State University, CA
Southeastern Louisiana University, LA
Southeast Missouri State University, MO
Southern Connecticut State University, CT
Southern Illinois University Carbondale, IL
Southern New Hampshire University, NH
Southern Oregon University, OR
Southwestern College, KS
State University of New York
College at Geneseo, NY
Stephen F. Austin State University, TX
Stephens College, MO
Stetson University, FL
Stonehill College, MA
Suffolk University, MA
Susquehanna University, PA
Tarleton State University, TX
Texas A&M University, TX
Texas A&M University–Commerce, TX
Texas A&M University–Texarkana, TX
Texas Christian University, TX
Texas Lutheran University, TX
Texas State University, TX

Texas Tech University, TX
Texas Wesleyan University, TX
Thiel College, PA
Thomas College, ME
Thomas More College, KY
Thomas University, GA
Towson University, MD
Trinity Christian College, IL
Trinity University, TX
Union College, KY
Union University, TN
The University of Alabama at
Birmingham, AL
University of Arkansas, AR
University of California, Riverside, CA
University of California, Santa Cruz, CA
University of Colorado Denver, CO
University of Evansville, IN
University of Hartford, CT
University of Houston–Clear Lake, TX
University of Idaho, ID
University of Illinois at Urbana–
Champaign, IL
University of Indianapolis, IN
The University of Iowa, IA
University of Jamestown, ND
The University of Kansas, KS
University of Kentucky, KY
University of Louisville, KY
University of Maine, ME
University of Maryland Eastern Shore, MD
University of Massachusetts Amherst, MA
University of Massachusetts Boston, MA
University of Massachusetts Dartmouth, MA
University of Massachusetts Lowell, MA
University of Miami, FL
University of Michigan–Flint, MI
University of Minnesota, Morris, MN
University of Mississippi, MS
University of Missouri–St. Louis, MO
University of Montana, MT
The University of Montana Western, MT
University of Mount Olive, NC
University of Mount Union, OH
University of Nebraska at Kearney, NE
University of Nevada, Las Vegas, NV
The University of North Carolina at
Charlotte, NC
The University of North Carolina at
Greensboro, NC
University of Northern Colorado, CO
University of Northern Iowa, IA
University of Oregon, OR
University of Pittsburgh at Bradford, PA
University of Puerto Rico in Bayamón, PR
University of Puget Sound, WA
University of Rochester, NY
University of St. Francis, IL
University of South Carolina Aiken, SC
University of Southern Indiana, IN
University of Southern Mississippi, MS
The University of Tampa, FL
The University of Texas at Dallas, TX
The University of Texas of the Permian
Basin, TX
The University of Texas
Rio Grande Valley, TX
The University of Toledo, OH
The University of Virginia's
College at Wise, VA
University of West Florida, FL
University of Wisconsin–Green Bay, WI
University of Wisconsin–La Crosse, WI
University of Wisconsin–Stevens Point, WI
University of Wisconsin–Stout, WI

University of Wisconsin–Superior, WI
University of Wyoming, WY
Ursinus College, PA
Ursuline College, OH
Vanderbilt University, TN
Walla Walla University, WA
Warner University, FL
Washington & Jefferson College, PA
Washington State University, WA
Wayne State College, NE
Webber International University, FL
Wesleyan College, GA
Wesleyan University, CT
Western Kentucky University, KY
Western Michigan University, MI
Western Oregon University, OR
Western Washington University, WA
West Texas A&M University, TX
West Virginia Wesleyan College, WV
Whitman College, WA
Whitworth University, WA
Wichita State University, KS
William Jessup University, CA
William Paterson University of
New Jersey, NJ
Wilson College, PA
Wisconsin Lutheran College, WI
Youngstown State University, OH

Veterans' Children
Agnes Scott College, GA
Alliant International University–
San Diego, CA
American University, DC
Anderson University, SC
Arkansas Tech University, AR
Aurora University, IL
Ball State University, IN
Baylor University, TX
Belhaven University, MS
Belmont University, TN
Benedictine University, IL
Berry College, GA
Bethel University, MN
Binghamton University, State University of
New York, NY
Bluefield College, VA
Boise State University, ID
Boston University, MA
Brevard College, NC
Brown University, RI
Butler University, IN
Caldwell University, NJ
California Baptist University, CA
California Lutheran University, CA
California State University,
San Bernardino, CA
Calvin College, MI
Cameron University, OK
The Catholic University of America, DC
Centenary College of Louisiana, LA
Central College, IA
Central Washington University, WA
Chestnut Hill College, PA
Chowan University, NC
Christian Brothers University, TN
The Citadel, The Military College of South
Carolina, SC
Claflin University, SC
Claremont McKenna College, CA
Clarion University of Pennsylvania, PA
Coastal Carolina University, SC
Coe College, IA
Colgate University, NY
The College of Idaho, ID

The College of New Rochelle, NY
College of Staten Island of the City
   University of New York, NY
Columbia College, MO
Columbia International University, SC
Concordia University, Nebraska, NE
Concordia University, St. Paul, MN
Concordia University Texas, TX
Concord University, WV
Corban University, OR
Culver-Stockton College, MO
Dallas Baptist University, TX
Defiance College, OH
DePaul University, IL
DeSales University, PA
Dickinson College, PA
Dickinson State University, ND
Dominican University of California, CA
Duquesne University, PA
East Central University, OK
Eastern Washington University, WA
ECPI University, VA
Elizabeth City State University, NC
Elmhurst College, IL
Emory University, GA
Emporia State University, KS
The Evergreen State College, WA
Fairfield University, CT
Fairmont State University, WV
Florida International University, FL
Fort Hays State University, KS
Fort Lewis College, CO
Francis Marion University, SC
Franklin College, IN
Frostburg State University, MD
Georgia Institute of Technology, GA
Glenville State College, WV
Gordon College, MA
Grambling State University, LA
Grand Valley State University, MI
Gwynedd Mercy University, PA
Hampden-Sydney College, VA
Hampton University, VA
Hardin-Simmons University, TX
Hobart and William Smith Colleges, NY
Hofstra University, NY
Hood College, MD
Huntingdon College, AL
Huntington University, IN
Illinois Institute of Technology, IL
Indiana Tech, IN
Iona College, NY
Iowa State University of Science and
   Technology, IA
John Carroll University, OH
Kansas Wesleyan University, KS
Kennesaw State University, GA
Kent State University, OH
Keuka College, NY
King University, TN
Lake Erie College, OH
Lasell College, MA
Lawrence University, WI
Lees-McRae College, NC
Lewis University, IL
Lindenwood University, MO
Long Island University–LIU Brooklyn, NY
Long Island University–LIU Post, NY
Louisiana Tech University, LA
Loyola Marymount University, CA

Loyola University New Orleans, LA
Marygrove College, MI
Marymount Manhattan College, NY
Marymount University, VA
The Master's University, CA
Mayville State University, ND
McKendree University, IL
McNally Smith College of Music, MN
Michigan Technological University, MI
Midwestern State University, TX
Minot State University, ND
Missouri Baptist University, MO
Monmouth University, NJ
Montreat College, NC
Moravian College, PA
Morehead State University, KY
New England College, NH
New Jersey Institute of Technology, NJ
New Mexico State University, NM
Northern Illinois University, IL
Northern Kentucky University, KY
Northwestern State University
   of Louisiana, LA
Occidental College, CA
Oklahoma Panhandle State University, OK
Old Dominion University, VA
Paul Smith's College, NY
Peirce College, PA
Piedmont College, GA
Queens University of Charlotte, NC
Randall University, OK
Randolph-Macon College, VA
Regent University, VA
Sacred Heart University, CT
Saginaw Valley State University, MI
St. Edward's University, TX
St. John's University, NY
Saint Joseph's University, PA
St. Lawrence University, NY
Saint Leo University, FL
Saint Martin's University, WA
St. Mary's University, TX
Saint Michael's College, VT
San Diego Christian College, CA
San Diego State University, CA
Savannah College of Art and Design, GA
Seattle Pacific University, WA
Siena College, NY
Simpson College, IA
Simpson University, CA
Southeastern Louisiana University, LA
Southern Illinois University Carbondale, IL
Southern Oregon University, OR
Stephen F. Austin State University, TX
Stephens College, MO
Sterling College, KS
Stetson University, FL
Stonehill College, MA
Tarleton State University, TX
Texas A&M University, TX
Texas A&M University–Commerce, TX
Texas A&M University–Texarkana, TX
Texas Christian University, TX
Texas Lutheran University, TX
Texas State University, TX
Texas Tech University, TX
Texas Wesleyan University, TX
Thomas College, ME
Thomas More College, KY
Trinity University, TX

Union College, KY
Union University, TN
The University of Alabama
   at Birmingham, AL
University of Arkansas, AR
University of California, Riverside, CA
University of California, San Diego, CA
University of Hartford, CT
University of Houston–Clear Lake, TX
University of Idaho, ID
University of Kentucky, KY
University of Louisville, KY
University of Maine, ME
University of Maine at Augusta, ME
University of Maine at Presque Isle, ME
University of Maryland Eastern Shore, MD
University of Massachusetts Boston, MA
University of Miami, FL
University of Michigan–Flint, MI
University of Minnesota, Morris, MN
University of Mississippi, MS
University of Missouri–St. Louis, MO
University of Mount Olive, NC
University of Nebraska at Kearney, NE
University of Nebraska at Omaha, NE
University of Nebraska–Lincoln, NE
University of Nevada, Las Vegas, NV
The University of North Carolina at
   Greensboro, NC
University of Oregon, OR
University of Puerto Rico in Bayamón, PR
University of Puget Sound, WA
University of St. Francis, IL
University of Southern Indiana, IN
The University of Texas at Dallas, TX
The University of Texas of the Permian
   Basin, TX
The University of Texas
   Rio Grande Valley, TX
The University of Toledo, OH
The University of Virginia's
   College at Wise, VA
University of Wisconsin–La Crosse, WI
University of Wisconsin–Stout, WI
University of Wyoming, WY
Ursinus College, PA
Vanderbilt University, TN
Virginia Commonwealth University, VA
Virginia Military Institute, VA
Virginia Polytechnic Institute and State
   University, VA
Warner University, FL
Washington & Jefferson College, PA
Washington State University, WA
Wayne State College, NE
Webster University, MO
Wesleyan University, CT
Western Illinois University, IL
Western Kentucky University, KY
Western Oregon University, OR
West Texas A&M University, TX
Wheaton College, IL
Whitman College, WA
Whitworth University, WA
William Jessup University, CA
Wilson College, PA
Wisconsin Lutheran College, WI
Youngstown State University, OH

Athletic Grants for Undergraduates

Archery

Campbellsville University, KY	M,W
Emmanuel College, GA	M,W
Union College, KY	M,W

Baseball

Abilene Christian University, TX	M
Academy of Art University, CA	M
Adams State University, CO	M
Adelphi University, NY	M
Alabama State University, AL	M
Alcorn State University, MS	M
Alderson Broaddus University, WV	M
Alice Lloyd College, KY	M
Anderson University, SC	M
Angelo State University, TX	M
Appalachian State University, NC	M
Aquinas College, MI	M
Arizona State University at the Downtown Phoenix campus, AZ	M
Arizona State University at the Polytechnic campus, AZ	M
Arizona State University at the Tempe campus, AZ	M
Arizona State University at the West campus, AZ	M
Arkansas Tech University, AR	M
Armstrong State University, GA	M
Asbury University, KY	M
Auburn University, AL	M
Auburn University at Montgomery, AL	M
Augustana University, SD	M
Augusta University, GA	M
Austin Peay State University, TN	M
Azusa Pacific University, CA	M
Baker University, KS	M
Ball State University, IN	M
Barry University, FL	M
Barton College, NC	M
Baylor University, TX	M
Belhaven University, MS	M
Bellarmine University, KY	M
Belmont Abbey College, NC	M
Belmont University, TN	M
Bemidji State University, MN	M
Benedictine College, KS	M
Bethel College, IN	M
Bethune-Cookman University, FL	M
Binghamton University, State University of New York, NY	M
Biola University, CA	M
Bloomfield College, NJ	M
Bloomsburg University of Pennsylvania, PA	M
Bluefield College, VA	M
Bluefield State College, WV	M
Blue Mountain College, MS	M
Boston College, MA	M
Bowling Green State University, OH	M
Bradley University, IL	M
Brescia University, KY	M
Briar Cliff University, IA	M
Brigham Young University, UT	M

Bryan College, TN	M
Butler University, IN	M
Caldwell University, NJ	M
California Baptist University, CA	M
California Polytechnic State University, San Luis Obispo, CA	M
California State Polytechnic University, Pomona, CA	M
California State University, Chico, CA	M
California State University, Dominguez Hills, CA	M
California State University, Fresno, CA	M
California State University, Fullerton, CA	M
California State University, Long Beach, CA	M
California State University, Monterey Bay, CA	M
California State University, Northridge, CA	M
California State University, Sacramento, CA	M
California State University, San Bernardino, CA	M
Calumet College of Saint Joseph, IN	M
Cameron University, OK	M
Campbellsville University, KY	M
Canisius College, NY	M
Carson-Newman University, TN	M
Catawba College, NC	M
Cedarville University, OH	M
Central Connecticut State University, CT	M
Central Methodist University, MO	M
Central Michigan University, MI	M
Central Washington University, WA	M
Chestnut Hill College, PA	M
Chowan University, NC	M
Christian Brothers University, TN	M
The Citadel, The Military College of South Carolina, SC	M
Clarion University of Pennsylvania, PA	M
Clark Atlanta University, GA	M
Clarke University, IA	M
Clemson University, SC	M
Coastal Carolina University, SC	M
College of Charleston, SC	M
The College of Idaho, ID	M
The College of Saint Rose, NY	M
College of the Ozarks, MO	M
The College of William and Mary, VA	M
Colorado Mesa University, CO	M
Colorado School of Mines, CO	M
Columbia College, MO	M
Columbus State University, GA	M
Concordia University Irvine, CA	M
Concordia University, Nebraska, NE	M
Concordia University, St. Paul, MN	M
Concord University, WV	M
Corban University, OR	M

Cornerstone University, MI	M
Creighton University, NE	M
Culver-Stockton College, MO	M
Dakota State University, SD	M
Dallas Baptist University, TX	M
Davidson College, NC	M
Dickinson State University, ND	M
Dixie State University, UT	M
Doane University, NE	M
Dominican College, NY	M
Drury University, MO	M
East Carolina University, NC	M
East Central University, OK	M
Eastern Illinois University, IL	M
Eastern Michigan University, MI	M
East Stroudsburg University of Pennsylvania, PA	M
Eckerd College, FL	M
Elizabeth City State University, NC	M
Elon University, NC	M
Embry-Riddle Aeronautical University–Daytona, FL	M
Emmanuel College, GA	M
Emporia State University, KS	M
Evangel University, MO	M
Fairfield University, CT	M
Faulkner University, AL	M
Felician University, NJ	M
Flagler College, FL	M
Florida Agricultural and Mechanical University, FL	M
Florida Atlantic University, FL	M
Florida Gulf Coast University, FL	M
Florida Institute of Technology, FL	M
Florida International University, FL	M
Florida Southern College, FL	M
Florida State University, FL	M
Fordham University, NY	M
Francis Marion University, SC	M
Franklin Pierce University, NH	M
Freed-Hardeman University, TN	M
Fresno Pacific University, CA	M
Friends University, KS	M
Furman University, SC	M
Gannon University, PA	M
Gardner-Webb University, NC	M
Georgetown University, DC	M
The George Washington University, DC	M
Georgia College & State University, GA	M
Georgia Institute of Technology, GA	M
Georgia Southern University, GA	M
Georgia Southwestern State University, GA	M
Georgia State University, GA	M
Gonzaga University, WA	M
Goshen College, IN	M
Graceland University, IA	M
Grambling State University, LA	M
Grand Valley State University, MI	M
Grand View University, IA	M
Harding University, AR	M

Harris-Stowe State University, MO	M	Midland College, TX	M	Robert Morris University Illinois, IL	M
Hawai`i Pacific University, HI	M	Millersville University of Pennsylvania, PA	M	Rockhurst University, MO	M
High Point University, NC	M	Milligan College, TN	M	Rogers State University, OK	M
Hillsdale College, MI	M	Minnesota State University Mankato, MN	M	Rollins College, FL	M
Hofstra University, NY	M	Minot State University, ND	M	Sacred Heart University, CT	M
Houston Baptist University, TX	M	Mississippi State University, MS	M	Saginaw Valley State University, MI	M
Huntington University, IN	M	Missouri Baptist University, MO	M	St. Ambrose University, IA	M
Huston-Tillotson University, TX	M	Missouri State University, MO	M	St. Andrews University, NC	M
Indiana State University, IN	M	Missouri University of Science and Technology, MO	M	Saint Augustine's University, NC	M
Indiana University Bloomington, IN	M	Missouri Western State University, MO	M	St. Bonaventure University, NY	M
Indiana University of Pennsylvania, PA	M	Molloy College, NY	M	St. Edward's University, TX	M
Indiana University Southeast, IN	M	Monmouth University, NJ	M	St. Gregory's University, OK	M
Inter American University of Puerto Rico, Bayamón Campus, PR	M	Morehead State University, KY	M	St. John's University, NY	M
Iona College, NY	M	Morehouse College, GA	M	Saint Joseph's University, PA	M
Jackson State University, MS	M	Morningside College, IA	M	Saint Leo University, FL	M
Jacksonville State University, AL	M	Mount Marty College, SD	M	Saint Louis University, MO	M
Jacksonville University, FL	M	Mount Mercy University, IA	M	Saint Martin's University, WA	M
James Madison University, VA	M	Mount St. Mary's University, MD	M	St. Petersburg College, FL	M
Judson University, IL	M	Mount Vernon Nazarene University, OH	M	Saint Peter's University, NJ	M
Kansas State University, KS	M	Murray State University, KY	M	St. Thomas Aquinas College, NY	M
Kansas Wesleyan University, KS	M	Newberry College, SC	M	St. Thomas University, FL	M
Kennesaw State University, GA	M	New Mexico Highlands University, NM	M	Samford University, AL	M
Kent State University, OH	M	New Mexico State University, NM	M	Sam Houston State University, TX	M
Kentucky State University, KY	M	New York Institute of Technology, NY	M	San Diego State University, CA	M
Kentucky Wesleyan College, KY	M	Niagara University, NY	M	San Francisco State University, CA	M
King University, TN	M	North Carolina State University, NC	M	Santa Clara University, CA	M
Kutztown University of Pennsylvania, PA	M	Northeastern State University, OK	M	Seton Hill University, PA	M
Lake Erie College, OH	M	Northeastern University, MA	M	Shawnee State University, OH	M
Lamar University, TX	M	Northern Illinois University, IL	M	Shepherd University, WV	M
Lane College, TN	M	Northern Kentucky University, KY	M	Shippensburg University of Pennsylvania, PA	M
La Salle University, PA	M	Northern State University, SD	M	Siena College, NY	M
Lee University, TN	M	Northwestern College, IA	M	Simpson University, CA	M
Le Moyne College, NY	M	Northwestern State University of Louisiana, LA	M	Slippery Rock University of Pennsylvania, PA	M
Lenoir-Rhyne University, NC	M	Northwest Missouri State University, MO	M	Sonoma State University, CA	M
Lewis University, IL	M	Nova Southeastern University, FL	M	Southeastern Louisiana University, LA	M
Liberty University, VA	M	Oakland City University, IN	M	Southeastern Oklahoma State University, OK	M
Lincoln Christian University, IL	M	The Ohio State University, OH	M	Southeastern University, FL	M
Lincoln University, PA	M	Ohio University, OH	M	Southeast Missouri State University, MO	M
Lindenwood University, MO	M	Ohio Valley University, WV	M	Southern Arkansas University–Magnolia, AR	M
Lindsey Wilson College, KY	M	Oklahoma Baptist University, OK	M	Southern Connecticut State University, CT	M
Lipscomb University, TN	M	Oklahoma Christian University, OK	M	Southern Illinois University Carbondale, IL	M
Lock Haven University of Pennsylvania, PA	M	Oklahoma City University, OK	M	Southern Illinois University Edwardsville, IL	M
Longwood University, VA	M	Oklahoma State University, OK	M	Southern New Hampshire University, NH	M
Louisiana State University and Agricultural & Mechanical College, LA	M	Old Dominion University, VA	M	Southwest Baptist University, MO	M
Louisiana Tech University, LA	M	Olivet Nazarene University, IL	M	Southwestern College, KS	M
Loyola Marymount University, CA	M	Oral Roberts University, OK	M	Southwestern Oklahoma State University, OK	M
Lubbock Christian University, TX	M	Oregon State University, OR	M	Spring Hill College, AL	M
Lynn University, FL	M	Ouachita Baptist University, AR	M	Stanford University, CA	M
Lyon College, AR	M	Our Lady of the Lake University, TX	M	Stephen F. Austin State University, TX	M
Malone University, OH	M	Palm Beach Atlantic University, FL	M	Sterling College, KS	M
Manhattan College, NY	M	Penn State University Park, PA	M	Stonehill College, MA	M
Mansfield University of Pennsylvania, PA	M	Pepperdine University, CA	M	Stony Brook University, State University of New York, NY	M
Marist College, NY	M	Pittsburg State University, KS	M	Tarleton State University, TX	M
Marshall University, WV	M	Point Loma Nazarene University, CA	M	Taylor University, IN	M
Marymount California University, CA	M	Point Park University, PA	M	Tennessee Wesleyan University, TN	M
Maryville University of Saint Louis, MO	M	Prairie View A&M University, TX	M	Texas A&M International University, TX	M
The Master's University, CA	M	Presbyterian College, SC	M	Texas A&M University, TX	M
McKendree University, IL	M	Purdue University, IN	M		
Mercer University, GA	M	Queens College of the City University of New York, NY	M		
Mercy College, NY	M	Quinnipiac University, CT	M		
Merrimack College, MA	M	Radford University, VA	M		
Metropolitan State University of Denver, CO	M	Regis University, CO	M		
Miami University, OH	M	Research College of Nursing, MO	M		
Michigan State University, MI	M	Rice University, TX	M		

Texas A&M University–Corpus Christi, TX	M
Texas Christian University, TX	M
Texas State University, TX	M
Texas Tech University, TX	M
Texas Wesleyan University, TX	M
Thomas University, GA	M
Tiffin University, OH	M
Towson University, MD	M
Trevecca Nazarene University, TN	M
Trinity Christian College, IL	M
Troy University, AL	M
Truett McConnell University, GA	M
Truman State University, MO	M
Tulane University, LA	M
Tusculum College, TN	M
Union College, KY	M
Union University, TN	M
University at Albany, State University of New York, NY	M
University at Buffalo, the State University of New York, NY	M
The University of Alabama, AL	M
The University of Alabama at Birmingham, AL	M
The University of Alabama in Huntsville, AL	M
The University of Arizona, AZ	M
University of Arkansas, AR	M
University of Bridgeport, CT	M
University of California, Davis, CA	M
University of California, Irvine, CA	M
University of California, Los Angeles, CA	M
University of California, Riverside, CA	M
University of California, Santa Barbara, CA	M
University of Central Arkansas, AR	M
University of Central Florida, FL	M
University of Central Missouri, MO	M
University of Cincinnati, OH	M
University of Colorado Colorado Springs, CO	M
University of Dayton, OH	M
University of Delaware, DE	M
University of Evansville, IN	M
The University of Findlay, OH	M
University of Florida, FL	M
University of Georgia, GA	M
University of Hartford, CT	M
University of Hawaii at Manoa, HI	M
University of Houston, TX	M
University of Illinois at Chicago, IL	M
University of Illinois at Springfield, IL	M
University of Indianapolis, IN	M
University of Jamestown, ND	M
The University of Kansas, KS	M
University of Kentucky, KY	M
University of Louisiana at Monroe, LA	M
University of Louisville, KY	M
University of Maine, ME	M
University of Maryland, Baltimore County, MD	M
University of Maryland, College Park, MD	M
University of Massachusetts Amherst, MA	M

University of Massachusetts Lowell, MA	M
University of Miami, FL	M
University of Michigan, MI	M
University of Minnesota, Crookston, MN	M
University of Minnesota, Duluth, MN	M
University of Minnesota, Twin Cities Campus, MN	M
University of Missouri–St. Louis, MO	M
University of Mobile, AL	M
University of Montevallo, AL	M
University of Nebraska at Kearney, NE	M
University of Nevada, Las Vegas, NV	M
University of Nevada, Reno, NV	M
University of New Haven, CT	M
University of New Orleans, LA	M
University of North Alabama, AL	M
University of North Carolina at Asheville, NC	M
The University of North Carolina at Chapel Hill, NC	M
The University of North Carolina at Charlotte, NC	M
The University of North Carolina at Greensboro, NC	M
The University of North Carolina at Pembroke, NC	M
The University of North Carolina Wilmington, NC	M
University of Northern Colorado, CO	M
University of North Florida, FL	M
University of North Georgia, GA	M
University of Notre Dame, IN	M
University of Oklahoma, OK	M
University of Oregon, OR	M
University of Pikeville, KY	M
University of Pittsburgh, PA	M
University of Pittsburgh at Johnstown, PA	M
University of Rhode Island, RI	M
University of Richmond, VA	M
University of St. Francis, IL	M
University of San Diego, CA	M
University of San Francisco, CA	M
University of Science and Arts of Oklahoma, OK	M
University of South Alabama, AL	M
University of South Carolina, SC	M
University of South Carolina Aiken, SC	M
University of Southern California, CA	M
University of Southern Indiana, IN	M
University of Southern Mississippi, MS	M
University of South Florida, FL	M
The University of Tampa, FL	M
The University of Tennessee, TN	M
The University of Tennessee at Martin, TN	M
The University of Texas at Austin, TX	M
The University of Texas at San Antonio, TX	M
The University of Texas of the Permian Basin, TX	M
The University of Texas Rio Grande Valley, TX	M
University of the Incarnate Word, TX	M

University of the Pacific, CA	M
The University of Toledo, OH	M
University of Utah, UT	M
University of Virginia, VA	M
The University of Virginia's College at Wise, VA	M
University of Washington, WA	M
The University of West Alabama, AL	M
University of West Georgia, GA	M
University of Wisconsin–Milwaukee, WI	M
University of Wisconsin–Parkside, WI	M
Upper Iowa University, IA	M
Utah Valley University, UT	M
Valdosta State University, GA	M
Valley City State University, ND	M
Valparaiso University, IN	M
Vanderbilt University, TN	M
Villanova University, PA	M
Virginia Commonwealth University, VA	M
Virginia Military Institute, VA	M
Virginia State University, VA	M
Viterbo University, WI	M
Wagner College, NY	M
Wake Forest University, NC	M
Waldorf University, IA	M
Washburn University, KS	M
Washington State University, WA	M
Wayland Baptist University, TX	M
Wayne State College, NE	M
Wayne State University, MI	M
Webber International University, FL	M
West Chester University of Pennsylvania, PA	M
Western Carolina University, NC	M
Western Illinois University, IL	M
Western Kentucky University, KY	M
Western Michigan University, MI	M
Western Oregon University, OR	M
Westmont College, CA	M
West Texas A&M University, TX	M
West Virginia University, WV	M
West Virginia University Institute of Technology, WV	M
West Virginia Wesleyan College, WV	M
Wheeling Jesuit University, WV	M
Wichita State University, KS	M
William Jewell College, MO	M
Williams Baptist College, AR	M
William Woods University, MO	M
Wingate University, NC	M
Winona State University, MN	M
Winthrop University, SC	M
Wofford College, SC	M
Wright State University, OH	M
Youngstown State University, OH	M

Basketball

Abilene Christian University, TX	M,W
Academy of Art University, CA	M,W
Adams State University, CO	M,W
Adelphi University, NY	M,W
Alabama State University, AL	M,W
Alcorn State University, MS	M,W
Alderson Broaddus University, WV	M,W
Alice Lloyd College, KY	M,W
American University, DC	M,W
Anderson University, SC	M,W
Angelo State University, TX	M,W
Appalachian State University, NC	M,W
Aquinas College, MI	M,W

Arizona State University at the Downtown Phoenix campus, AZ	M,W	California State University, Long Beach, CA	M,W	Dixie State University, UT	M,W
Arizona State University at the Polytechnic campus, AZ	M,W	California State University Maritime Academy, CA	M,W	Doane University, NE	M,W
Arizona State University at the Tempe campus, AZ	M,W	California State University, Monterey Bay, CA	M,W	Dominican College, NY	M,W
Arizona State University at the West campus, AZ		California State University, Northridge, CA	M,W	Dominican University of California, CA	M,W
Arkansas Tech University, AR	M,W	California State University, Sacramento, CA		Drake University, IA	M,W
Armstrong State University, GA	M,W	California State University, San Bernardino, CA	M,W	Drexel University, PA	M,W
Asbury University, KY	M,W	Calumet College of Saint Joseph, IN	M,W	Drury University, MO	M,W
Assumption College, MA	M,W	Cameron University, OK	M,W	Duquesne University, PA	M,W
Auburn University, AL	M,W	Campbellsville University, KY	M,W	East Carolina University, NC	M,W
Auburn University at Montgomery, AL	M,W	Canisius College, NY	M,W	East Central University, OK	
Augustana University, SD	M,W	Cardinal Stritch University, WI	M,W	Eastern Illinois University, IL	
Augusta University, GA	M,W	Carlow University, PA	M,W	Eastern Michigan University, MI	
Austin Peay State University, TN	M,W	Carroll College, MT	M,W	Eastern Oregon University, OR	M,W
Azusa Pacific University, CA	M,W	Carson-Newman University, TN	M,W	Eastern Washington University, WA	M,W
Baker University, KS	M,W	Catawba College, NC	M,W	East Stroudsburg University of Pennsylvania, PA	M,W
Ball State University, IN	M,W	Cedarville University, OH	M,W	Eckerd College, FL	M,W
Barry University, FL	M,W	Central Connecticut State University, CT	M,W	Elizabeth City State University, NC	M,W
Barton College, NC	M,W	Central Methodist University, MO	M,W	Elon University, NC	M,W
Baylor University, TX	M,W	Central Michigan University, MI	M,W	Embry-Riddle Aeronautical University–Daytona, FL	M,W
Belhaven University, MS	M,W	Central Washington University, WA	M,W	Embry-Riddle Aeronautical University–Prescott, AZ	M,W
Bellarmine University, KY	M,W	Chaminade University of Honolulu, HI	M,W	Emmanuel College, GA	M,W
Belmont Abbey College, NC	M,W	Chestnut Hill College, PA	M,W	Emporia State University, KS	M,W
Belmont University, TN	M,W	Chowan University, NC	M,W	Evangel University, MO	M,W
Bemidji State University, MN	M,W	Christian Brothers University, TN	M,W	The Evergreen State College, WA	M,W
Benedictine College, KS	M,W	The Citadel, The Military College of South Carolina, SC	M	Fairfield University, CT	M,W
Bentley University, MA	M,W	Clarion University of Pennsylvania, PA	M,W	Faulkner University, AL	M,W
Bethel College, IN	M,W	Clark Atlanta University, GA	M,W	Felician University, NJ	M,W
Bethel College, KS	M,W	Clarke University, IA	M,W	Ferris State University, MI	M,W
Bethune-Cookman University, FL	M,W	Clayton State University, GA	M,W	Flagler College, FL	M,W
Binghamton University, State University of New York, NY	M,W	Clemson University, SC	M,W	Florida Agricultural and Mechanical University, FL	M,W
Biola University, CA	M,W	Cleveland State University, OH	M,W	Florida Atlantic University, FL	M,W
Black Hills State University, SD	M,W	Coastal Carolina University, SC	M,W	Florida College, FL	M
Bloomfield College, NJ	M,W	Colgate University, NY	M,W	Florida Gulf Coast University, FL	M,W
Bloomsburg University of Pennsylvania, PA	M,W	College of Charleston, SC	M,W	Florida Institute of Technology, FL	M,W
Bluefield College, VA	M,W	College of Coastal Georgia, GA	M,W	Florida International University, FL	M,W
Bluefield State College, WV	M,W	The College of Idaho, ID	M,W	Florida National University, FL	M
Blue Mountain College, MS	M,W	College of Saint Mary, NE	W	Florida Southern College, FL	M,W
Boise State University, ID	M,W	The College of Saint Rose, NY	M,W	Florida State University, FL	M,W
Boston College, MA	M,W	College of the Holy Cross, MA	M,W	Fordham University, NY	M,W
Boston University, MA	M,W	College of the Ozarks, MO	M,W	Fort Lewis College, CO	M,W
Bowling Green State University, OH	M,W	The College of William and Mary, VA	M,W	Francis Marion University, SC	M,W
Bradley University, IL	M,W	Colorado Mesa University, CO	M,W	Franklin Pierce University, NH	M,W
Brenau University, GA	W	Colorado School of Mines, CO	M,W	Freed-Hardeman University, TN	M,W
Brescia University, KY	M,W	Colorado State University, CO	M,W	Fresno Pacific University, CA	M,W
Briar Cliff University, IA	M,W	Columbia College, MO	M,W	Friends University, KS	M,W
Brigham Young University, UT	M,W	Columbia International University, SC	M,W	Furman University, SC	M,W
Bryan College, TN	M,W	Columbus State University, GA	M,W	Gannon University, PA	M,W
Bucknell University, PA	M,W	Concordia University Irvine, CA	M,W	Gardner-Webb University, NC	M,W
Butler University, IN	M,W	Concordia University, Nebraska, NE	M,W	Georgetown University, DC	M,W
Caldwell University, NJ	M,W	Concordia University, St. Paul, MN	M,W	The George Washington University, DC	M,W
California Baptist University, CA	M,W	Concord University, WV	M,W	Georgia College & State University, GA	M,W
California Polytechnic State University, San Luis Obispo, CA	M,W	Converse College, SC	W	Georgia Institute of Technology, GA	M,W
California State Polytechnic University, Pomona, CA	M,W	Corban University, OR	M,W	Georgian Court University, NJ	M,W
California State University, Bakersfield, CA	M	Cornerstone University, MI	M,W	Georgia Southern University, GA	M,W
California State University, Chico, CA	M,W	Creighton University, NE	M,W	Georgia Southwestern State University, GA	M,W
California State University, Dominguez Hills, CA	M,W	Culver-Stockton College, MO	M,W	Georgia State University, GA	M,W
California State University, Fresno, CA	M,W	Daemen College, NY	M,W	Gonzaga University, WA	M,W
California State University, Fullerton, CA	M,W	Dakota State University, SD	M,W	Goshen College, IN	M,W
		Dallas Baptist University, TX	M	Governors State University, IL	M,W
		Davidson College, NC	M,W	Graceland University, IA	M,W
		Dickinson State University, ND	M,W	Grambling State University, LA	M,W
				Grand Valley State University, MI	M,W
				Grand View University, IA	M,W
				Hampton University, VA	M,W

Harding University, AR	M,W
Harris-Stowe State University, MO	M,W
Hawai`i Pacific University, HI	M,W
High Point University, NC	M,W
Hillsdale College, MI	M,W
Hofstra University, NY	M,W
Holy Family University, PA	M,W
Hope International University, CA	M,W
Houston Baptist University, TX	M,W
Humboldt State University, CA	M,W
Huntington University, IN	M,W
Huston-Tillotson University, TX	M,W
Idaho State University, ID	M,W
Indiana State University, IN	M,W
Indiana University Bloomington, IN	M,W
Indiana University Northwest, IN	M,W
Indiana University of Pennsylvania, PA	M,W
Indiana University–Purdue University Indianapolis, IN	M,W
Indiana University South Bend, IN	M,W
Indiana University Southeast, IN	M,W
Inter American University of Puerto Rico, Bayamón Campus, PR	M,W
Inter American University of Puerto Rico, Guayama Campus, PR	M,W
Iona College, NY	M,W
Iowa State University of Science and Technology, IA	M,W
Jackson State University, MS	M,W
Jacksonville State University, AL	M,W
Jacksonville University, FL	M,W
James Madison University, VA	M,W
John Brown University, AR	M,W
Johnson C. Smith University, NC	M,W
Judson University, IL	M,W
Kansas State University, KS	M,W
Kansas Wesleyan University, KS	M,W
Kennesaw State University, GA	M,W
Kent State University, OH	M,W
Kentucky State University, KY	M,W
Kentucky Wesleyan College, KY	M,W
King University, TN	M,W
Kutztown University of Pennsylvania, PA	M,W
Lake Erie College, OH	M,W
Lamar University, TX	M,W
Lane College, TN	M,W
Langston University, OK	M,W
La Salle University, PA	M,W
Lawrence Technological University, MI	M,W
Lees-McRae College, NC	M,W
Lee University, TN	M,W
Lehigh University, PA	M,W
Le Moyne College, NY	M,W
Lenoir-Rhyne University, NC	M,W
Lewis University, IL	M,W
Liberty University, VA	M,W
Life University, GA	M,W
Lincoln Christian University, IL	M,W
Lincoln University, MO	M,W
Lincoln University, PA	M,W
Lindenwood University, MO	M,W
Lindsey Wilson College, KY	M,W
Lipscomb University, TN	M,W
Lock Haven University of Pennsylvania, PA	M,W
Longwood University, VA	M,W
Louisiana State University and Agricultural & Mechanical College, LA	M,W
Louisiana Tech University, LA	M,W
Loyola Marymount University, CA	M,W
Loyola University Chicago, IL	M,W
Loyola University Maryland, MD	M,W
Loyola University New Orleans, LA	M,W
Lubbock Christian University, TX	M,W
Lynn University, FL	M,W
Lyon College, AR	M,W
Malone University, OH	M,W
Manhattan College, NY	M,W
Mansfield University of Pennsylvania, PA	M,W
Marist College, NY	M,W
Marquette University, WI	M,W
Marshall University, WV	M,W
Maryville University of Saint Louis, MO	M,W
The Master's University, CA	M,W
McKendree University, IL	M,W
Mercer University, GA	M,W
Mercy College, NY	M,W
Merrimack College, MA	M,W
Metropolitan State University of Denver, CO	M,W
Miami University, OH	M,W
Michigan State University, MI	M,W
Michigan Technological University, MI	M,W
Midland College, TX	M,W
Millersville University of Pennsylvania, PA	M,W
Milligan College, TN	M,W
Minnesota State University Mankato, MN	M,W
Minnesota State University Moorhead, MN	M,W
Minot State University, ND	M,W
Mississippi State University, MS	M,W
Missouri Baptist University, MO	M,W
Missouri State University, MO	M,W
Missouri University of Science and Technology, MO	M,W
Missouri Western State University, MO	M,W
Molloy College, NY	M,W
Monmouth University, NJ	M,W
Montana State University, MT	M,W
Montana State University Billings, MT	M,W
Montana Tech of The University of Montana, MT	M,W
Morehead State University, KY	M,W
Morehouse College, GA	M
Morningside College, IA	M,W
Mount Marty College, SD	M,W
Mount Mercy University, IA	M,W
Mount St. Mary's University, MD	M,W
Mount Vernon Nazarene University, OH	M,W
Murray State University, KY	M,W
Newberry College, SC	M,W
New Mexico Highlands University, NM	M,W
New Mexico State University, NM	M,W
New York Institute of Technology, NY	M,W
Niagara University, NY	M,W
North Carolina State University, NC	M,W
Northeastern State University, OK	M,W
Northeastern University, MA	M,W
Northern Arizona University, AZ	M,W
Northern Illinois University, IL	M,W
Northern Kentucky University, KY	M,W
Northern State University, SD	M,W
Northwest Christian University, OR	M,W
Northwestern College, IA	M,W
Northwestern State University of Louisiana, LA	M,W
Northwest Missouri State University, MO	M,W
Northwest University, WA	M,W
Nova Southeastern University, FL	M,W
Oakland City University, IN	M,W
The Ohio State University, OH	M,W
Ohio University, OH	M,W
Ohio Valley University, WV	M,W
Oklahoma Baptist University, OK	M,W
Oklahoma Christian University, OK	M,W
Oklahoma City University, OK	M,W
Oklahoma State University, OK	M,W
Old Dominion University, VA	M,W
Olivet Nazarene University, IL	M,W
Oral Roberts University, OK	M,W
Oregon State University, OR	M,W
Ouachita Baptist University, AR	M,W
Our Lady of the Lake University, TX	M,W
Palm Beach Atlantic University, FL	M,W
Penn State University Park, PA	M,W
Pepperdine University, CA	M,W
Philander Smith College, AR	M,W
Pittsburg State University, KS	M,W
Point Loma Nazarene University, CA	M,W
Point Park University, PA	M,W
Prairie View A&M University, TX	M,W
Presbyterian College, SC	M,W
Providence College, RI	M,W
Purdue University, IN	M,W
Queens College of the City University of New York, NY	M,W
Quinnipiac University, CT	M,W
Radford University, VA	M,W
Regis University, CO	M,W
Research College of Nursing, MO	M,W
Rice University, TX	M,W
Robert Morris University, PA	M,W
Robert Morris University Illinois, IL	M,W
Roberts Wesleyan College, NY	M,W
Rockhurst University, MO	M,W
Rocky Mountain College, MT	M,W
Rogers State University, OK	M,W
Rollins College, FL	M,W
Sacred Heart University, CT	M,W
Saginaw Valley State University, MI	M,W
St. Ambrose University, IA	M,W
St. Andrews University, NC	M,W
Saint Augustine's University, NC	M,W
St. Bonaventure University, NY	M,W
St. Edward's University, TX	M,W
St. Gregory's University, OK	M,W
St. John's University, NY	M,W
Saint Joseph's University, PA	M,W
Saint Leo University, FL	M,W
St. Louis College of Pharmacy, MO	M,W
Saint Louis University, MO	M,W
Saint Martin's University, WA	M,W
Saint Mary-of-the-Woods College, IN	W
Saint Michael's College, VT	M,W
St. Petersburg College, FL	M,W
Saint Peter's University, NJ	M,W
St. Thomas Aquinas College, NY	M,W
St. Thomas University, FL	M,W

Samford University, AL	M,W	Trinity Christian College, IL	M,W	University of Michigan–	
Sam Houston State University, TX	M,W	Troy University, AL	M,W	Dearborn, MI	M,W
San Diego State University, CA	M,W	Truett McConnell University, GA	M,W	University of Minnesota,	
San Francisco State University, CA	M,W	Truman State University, MO	M,W	Crookston, MN	M,W
Santa Clara University, CA	M,W	Tulane University, LA	M,W	University of Minnesota, Duluth, MN	M,W
Seattle Pacific University, WA	M,W	Tusculum College, TN	M,W	University of Minnesota, Twin	
Seattle University, WA	M,W	Union College, KY	M,W	Cities Campus, MN	M,W
Seton Hill University, PA	M,W	Union University, TN	M,W	University of Missouri–	
Shawnee State University, OH	M,W	University at Albany, State		Kansas City, MO	M,W
Shepherd University, WV	M,W	University of New York, NY	M,W	University of Missouri–St.	
Shippensburg University of		University at Buffalo, the State		Louis, MO	M,W
Pennsylvania, PA	M,W	University of New York, NY	M,W	University of Mobile, AL	M,W
Siena College, NY	M,W	The University of Akron, OH	M,W	The University of Montana	
Simpson University, CA	M,W	The University of Alabama, AL	M,W	Western, MT	M,W
Slippery Rock University of		The University of Alabama at		University of Montevallo, AL	M,W
Pennsylvania, PA	M,W	Birmingham, AL	M,W	University of Nebraska at	
Sonoma State University, CA	M,W	The University of Alabama in		Kearney, NE	M,W
South Dakota School of Mines and		Huntsville, AL	M,W	University of Nevada, Las Vegas, NV	M,W
Technology, SD	M,W	University of Alaska Fairbanks, AK	M,W	University of Nevada, Reno, NV	M,W
Southeastern Louisiana		The University of Arizona, AZ	M,W	University of New Hampshire, NH	M,W
University, LA	M,W	University of Arkansas, AR	M,W	University of New Haven, CT	M,W
Southeastern Oklahoma State		University of Bridgeport, CT	M,W	University of New Orleans, LA	M,W
University, OK	M,W	University of California, Davis, CA	M,W	University of North Alabama, AL	M,W
Southeastern University, FL	M,W	University of California,		University of North Carolina at	
Southeast Missouri State		Irvine, CA	M,W	Asheville, NC	M,W
University, MO	M,W	University of California, Los		The University of North Carolina	
Southern Arkansas		Angeles, CA	M,W	at Chapel Hill, NC	M,W
University–Magnolia, AR	M,W	University of California,		The University of North Carolina	
Southern Connecticut State		Riverside, CA	M,W	at Charlotte, NC	M,W
University, CT	M,W	University of California, Santa		The University of North Carolina	
Southern Illinois University		Barbara, CA	M,W	at Greensboro, NC	M,W
Carbondale, IL	M,W	University of Central Arkansas, AR	M,W	The University of North Carolina	
Southern Illinois University		University of Central Florida, FL	M,W	at Pembroke, NC	M,W
Edwardsville, IL	M,W	University of Central Missouri, MO	M,W	The University of North Carolina	
Southern Methodist University, TX	M,W	University of Cincinnati, OH	M,W	Wilmington, NC	M,W
Southern New Hampshire		University of Colorado Boulder, CO	M,W	University of Northern Colorado, CO	M,W
University, NH	M,W	University of Colorado Colorado		University of Northern Iowa, IA	M,W
Southern Oregon University, OR	M,W	Springs, CO	M,W	University of North Florida, FL	M,W
Southern Utah University, UT	M,W	University of Dayton, OH	M,W	University of North Georgia, GA	M,W
Southwest Baptist University, MO	M,W	University of Delaware, DE	M,W	University of North Texas, TX	M,W
Southwestern College, KS	M,W	University of Denver, CO	M,W	University of Notre Dame, IN	M,W
Southwestern Oklahoma State		University of Detroit Mercy, MI	M,W	University of Oklahoma, OK	M,W
University, OK	M,W	University of Evansville, IN	M,W	University of Oregon, OR	M,W
Spring Hill College, AL	M,W	The University of Findlay, OH	M,W	University of Pikeville, KY	M,W
Stanford University, CA	M,W	University of Florida, FL	M,W	University of Pittsburgh, PA	M,W
Stephen F. Austin State		University of Georgia, GA	M,W	University of Pittsburgh at	
University, TX	M,W	University of Great Falls, MT	M,W	Johnstown, PA	M,W
Stephens College, MO	W	University of Hartford, CT	M,W	University of Puerto Rico in	
Sterling College, KS	M,W	University of Hawaii at Manoa, HI	M,W	Bayamón, PR	M,W
Stonehill College, MA	M,W	University of Houston, TX	M,W	University of Rhode Island, RI	M
Stony Brook University, State		University of Idaho, ID	M,W	University of Richmond, VA	M,W
University of New York, NY	M,W	University of Illinois at		University of St. Francis, IL	M,W
Syracuse University, NY	M,W	Chicago, IL	M,W	University of St. Thomas, TX	M,W
Tarleton State University, TX	M,W	University of Illinois at		University of San Diego, CA	M,W
Taylor University, IN	M,W	Springfield, IL	M,W	University of San Francisco, CA	M,W
Temple University, PA	M,W	University of Indianapolis, IN	M,W	University of Science and Arts	
Tennessee State University, TN	M,W	University of Jamestown, ND	M,W	of Oklahoma, OK	M,W
Tennessee Wesleyan University, TN	M,W	The University of Kansas, KS	M,W	University of South Alabama, AL	M,W
Texas A&M International		University of Kentucky, KY	M,W	University of South Carolina, SC	M,W
University, TX		University of Louisiana at		University of South Carolina	
Texas A&M University, TX	M,W	Monroe, LA	M,W	Aiken, SC	M,W
Texas A&M University–		University of Louisville, KY	M,W	The University of South Dakota, SD	M,W
Commerce, TX	M,W	University of Maine, ME	M,W	University of Southern	
Texas A&M University–		University of Maryland,		California, CA	M,W
Corpus Christi, TX	M,W	Baltimore County, MD	M,W	University of Southern Indiana, IN	M,W
Texas Christian University, TX	M,W	University of Maryland, College		University of Southern	
Texas State University, TX	M,W	Park, MD	M,W	Mississippi, MS	M,W
Texas Tech University, TX	M,W	University of Massachusetts		University of South Florida, FL	M,W
Texas Wesleyan University, TX	M,W	Amherst, MA	M,W	The University of Tampa, FL	M,W
Texas Woman's University, TX	W	University of Massachusetts		The University of Tennessee, TN	M,W
Tiffin University, OH	M,W	Lowell, MA	M,W	The University of Tennessee at	
Towson University, MD	M,W	University of Miami, FL	M,W	Chattanooga, TN	M,W
Trevecca Nazarene University, TN	M,W	University of Michigan, MI	M,W		

The University of Tennessee at Martin, TN	M,W
The University of Texas at Austin, TX	M,W
The University of Texas at El Paso, TX	M,W
The University of Texas at San Antonio, TX	M,W
The University of Texas of the Permian Basin, TX	M,W
The University of Texas Rio Grande Valley, TX	M,W
University of the Incarnate Word, TX	M,W
University of the Pacific, CA	M,W
The University of Toledo, OH	M,W
The University of Tulsa, OK	M,W
University of Utah, UT	M,W
University of Vermont, VT	M,W
University of Virginia, VA	M,W
The University of Virginia's College at Wise, VA	M,W
University of Washington, WA	M,W
The University of West Alabama, AL	M,W
University of West Georgia, GA	M,W
University of Wisconsin–Green Bay, WI	M,W
University of Wisconsin–Madison, WI	M,W
University of Wisconsin–Milwaukee, WI	M,W
University of Wisconsin–Parkside, WI	M,W
Upper Iowa University, IA	M,W
Ursuline College, OH	W
Utah State University, UT	M,W
Utah Valley University, UT	M,W
Valdosta State University, GA	M,W
Valley City State University, ND	M,W
Valparaiso University, IN	M,W
Vanderbilt University, TN	M,W
Villanova University, PA	M,W
Virginia Commonwealth University, VA	M,W
Virginia Military Institute, VA	M
Virginia State University, VA	M,W
Viterbo University, WI	M,W
Wagner College, NY	M,W
Wake Forest University, NC	M,W
Waldorf University, IA	M,W
Washburn University, KS	M,W
Washington State University, WA	M,W
Wayland Baptist University, TX	M,W
Wayne State College, NE	M,W
Wayne State University, MI	M,W
Webber International University, FL	M,W
Weber State University, UT	M,W
West Chester University of Pennsylvania, PA	M,W
Western Carolina University, NC	M,W
Western Illinois University, IL	M,W
Western Kentucky University, KY	M,W
Western Michigan University, MI	M,W
Western Oregon University, OR	M,W
Western State Colorado University, CO	M,W
Western Washington University, WA	M,W
Westminster College, UT	M,W
Westmont College, CA	M,W
West Texas A&M University, TX	M,W
West Virginia University, WV	M,W
West Virginia University Institute of Technology, WV	M,W

West Virginia Wesleyan College, WV	M,W
Wheeling Jesuit University, WV	M,W
Wichita State University, KS	M,W
William Jewell College, MO	M,W
Williams Baptist College, AR	M,W
William Woods University, MO	M,W
Wingate University, NC	M,W
Winona State University, MN	M,W
Winthrop University, SC	M,W
Wofford College, SC	M,W
Wright State University, OH	M,W
Xavier University of Louisiana, LA	M,W
Youngstown State University, OH	M,W

Bowling

Adelphi University, NY	W
Alabama State University, AL	W
Aquinas College, MI	M,W
Baker University, KS	W
Bethune-Cookman University, FL	W
Blue Mountain College, MS	M,W
Caldwell University, NJ	W
Calumet College of Saint Joseph, IN	M,W
Campbellsville University, KY	M,W
Chestnut Hill College, PA	W
Chowan University, NC	W
Clarke University, IA	M,W
Cornerstone University, MI	M,W
Culver-Stockton College, MO	M,W
Daemen College, NY	W
Duquesne University, PA	W
Elizabeth City State University, NC	W
Emmanuel College, GA	M,W
Felician University, NJ	W
Florida Agricultural and Mechanical University, FL	W
Grambling State University, LA	W
Grand View University, IA	M,W
Hampton University, VA	W
Huntington University, IN	M,W
Jackson State University, MS	W
Johnson C. Smith University, NC	W
Judson University, IL	M,W
Kansas Wesleyan University, KS	M,W
Kentucky Wesleyan College, KY	W
Kutztown University of Pennsylvania, PA	W
Lawrence Technological University, MI	M,W
Lincoln University, MO	W
Lindenwood University, MO	M,W
Lindsey Wilson College, KY	M,W
Maryville University of Saint Louis, MO	W
McKendree University, IL	W
Missouri Baptist University, MO	M,W
Molloy College, NY	W
Monmouth University, NJ	W
Olivet College, MI	M,W
Prairie View A&M University, TX	W
Robert Morris University Illinois, IL	M,W
Roberts Wesleyan College, NY	W
Sacred Heart University, CT	W
St. Ambrose University, IA	M,W
Saint Augustine's University, NC	W
Sam Houston State University, TX	W
Savannah College of Art and Design, GA	M,W
Stephen F. Austin State University, TX	W
Tennessee Wesleyan University, TN	M,W

Union College, KY	M,W
The University of Alabama at Birmingham, AL	W
University of Central Missouri, MO	M,W
University of Pikeville, KY	M,W
University of St. Francis, IL	M,W
Ursuline College, OH	W
Valparaiso University, IN	W
Vanderbilt University, TN	W
Virginia State University, VA	W
Viterbo University, WI	M,W
Waldorf University, IA	M,W
Webber International University, FL	M,W
West Texas A&M University, TX	M,W
Wichita State University, KS	M,W

Cheerleading

Adelphi University, NY	W
Alabama State University, AL	M,W
Alderson Broaddus University, WV	M,W
Anderson University, SC	W
Aquinas College, MI	M,W
Arkansas Tech University, AR	M,W
Auburn University at Montgomery, AL	M,W
Austin Peay State University, TN	M,W
Baker University, KS	M,W
Baylor University, TX	M,W
Bellarmine University, KY	M,W
Benedictine College, KS	W
Bethel College, IN	M,W
Biola University, CA	W
Bluefield College, VA	M,W
Blue Mountain College, MS	W
Brenau University, GA	W
Brescia University, KY	M,W
Briar Cliff University, IA	W
Brigham Young University, UT	M,W
Bryan College, TN	M,W
California Baptist University, CA	W
Cameron University, OK	M,W
Campbellsville University, KY	M,W
Carroll College, MT	M,W
Clayton State University, GA	W
Columbus State University, GA	M,W
Concordia University Irvine, CA	M,W
Concordia University, Nebraska, NE	W
Cornerstone University, MI	W
Culver-Stockton College, MO	M,W
Doane University, NE	W
Drake University, IA	M,W
Drury University, MO	M,W
Eastern Oregon University, OR	W
East Texas Baptist University, TX	W
Emporia State University, KS	M,W
Faulkner University, AL	M,W
Freed-Hardeman University, TN	W
Friends University, KS	M,W
Gannon University, PA	W
Gardner-Webb University, NC	M,W
Graceland University, IA	M,W
Grambling State University, LA	M,W
Grand View University, IA	M,W
Harris-Stowe State University, MO	M,W
Hofstra University, NY	M,W
Houston Baptist University, TX	M,W
John Brown University, AR	W
Judson University, IL	M,W
Kansas Wesleyan University, KS	M,W
Kentucky State University, KY	W
King University, TN	M,W
Lee University, TN	M,W
Lenoir-Rhyne University, NC	M,W

Lewis University, IL	W	University of Idaho, ID	M,W	Saint Joseph's University, PA	M,W
Liberty University, VA	M,W	University of Illinois at		Seattle Pacific University, WA	W
Lincoln University, MO	W	Springfield, IL	M,W	Southern Methodist University, TX	W
Lincoln University, PA	W	University of Louisville, KY	M,W	Stanford University, CA	M,W
Lindenwood University, MO	M,W	University of Michigan, MI	M,W	Syracuse University, NY	M,W
Lindsey Wilson College, KY	M,W	University of Mobile, AL	W	Temple University, PA	M,W
Lipscomb University, TN	W	The University of Montana		University at Buffalo, the State	
Loyola University New Orleans, LA	M,W	Western, MT	M,W	University of New York, NY	W
Maryville University of Saint		University of Nevada, Las Vegas, NV	M,W	The University of Alabama, AL	W
Louis, MO	M,W	University of North Alabama, AL	M,W	University of California,	
McKendree University, IL	M,W	The University of North Carolina		Los Angeles, CA	W
Midland College, TX	M,W	at Charlotte, NC	M,W	University of Central Florida, FL	W
Millersville University of		University of Oklahoma, OK	M,W	University of Delaware, DE	W
Pennsylvania, PA	M,W	University of Pikeville, KY	M,W	The University of Kansas, KS	W
Mississippi State University, MS	M,W	University of Rhode Island, RI	M,W	University of Massachusetts	
Missouri Baptist University, MO	M,W	University of St. Francis, IL	M,W	Amherst, MA	W
Montana State University, MT	M,W	University of Science and Arts		University of Miami, FL	W
Morehead State University, KY	M,W	of Oklahoma, OK	M,W	University of Michigan, MI	W
Newberry College, SC	M,W	University of South Carolina, SC	M,W	The University of North Carolina	
North Carolina State University, NC	M,W	University of Southern Indiana, IN	M,W	at Chapel Hill, NC	W
Northern Kentucky University, KY	M,W	The University of Tennessee at		University of Notre Dame, IN	W
Northwestern College, IA	M,W	Martin, TN	W	University of Oklahoma, OK	W
Northwest Missouri State		The University of Texas of the		University of Rhode Island, RI	M
University, MO	M,W	Permian Basin, TX	M,W	University of San Diego, CA	W
Oakland City University, IN	W	University of the Incarnate Word, TX	W	University of Southern	
Oklahoma City University, OK	M,W	University of Utah, UT	M,W	California, CA	W
Oklahoma State University, OK	M,W	University of Washington, WA	M,W	The University of Tampa, FL	W
Old Dominion University, VA	M,W	The University of West Alabama, AL	M,W	The University of Tennessee, TN	W
Olivet College, MI	M,W	University of West Georgia, GA	W	The University of Texas at Austin, TX	W
Olivet Nazarene University, IL	M,W	Waldorf University, IA	M,W	The University of Tulsa, OK	W
Pittsburg State University, KS	M,W	Washburn University, KS	M,W	University of Virginia, VA	W
Presbyterian College, SC	M,W	Wayland Baptist University, TX	M,W	University of Washington, WA	M,W
Robert Morris University		Wayne State University, MI	M,W	Washington State University, WA	W
Illinois, IL	M,W	Webber International University, FL	M,W	Western Washington University, WA	M,W
Rocky Mountain College, MT	M,W	Weber State University, UT	M,W	West Virginia University, WV	W
Rogers State University, OK	M,W	Westminster College, UT	M,W		
St. Ambrose University, IA	M,W	William Jewell College, MO	M,W	**Cross-country running**	
Saint Augustine's		Williams Baptist College, AR	W	Abilene Christian University, TX	M,W
University, NC	W	William Woods University, MO	W	Academy of Art University, CA	M,W
St. Thomas University, FL	W	Wright State University, OH	M,W	Adams State University, CO	M,W
Sam Houston State University, TX	M,W			Adelphi University, NY	M,W
Southeastern Louisiana		**Crew**		Alabama State University, AL	M,W
University, LA	M,W	Barry University, FL	W	Alcorn State University, MS	M,W
Southeast Missouri State		Boston College, MA	W	Alderson Broaddus University, WV	M,W
University, MO	M,W	Boston University, MA	M,W	American University, DC	M,W
Southern Arkansas		California State University,		Anderson University, SC	M,W
University–Magnolia, AR	M,W	Sacramento, CA	M,W	Angelo State University, TX	M,W
Southern Methodist University, TX	M,W	Clemson University, SC	W	Appalachian State University, NC	M,W
Southern Utah University, UT	M,W	College of the Holy Cross, MA	W	Aquinas College, MI	M,W
Southwestern College, KS	M,W	Creighton University, NE	W	Arizona State University at the	
Southwestern Oklahoma State		Drexel University, PA	M,W	Downtown Phoenix campus, AZ	M,W
University, OK	M,W	Duquesne University, PA	W	Arizona State University at the	
Stephen F. Austin State		Eastern Michigan University, MI	W	Polytechnic campus, AZ	M,W
University, TX	M,W	Fairfield University, CT	M,W	Arizona State University at the	
Sterling College, KS	M,W	Florida Institute of Technology, FL	M,W	Tempe campus, AZ	M,W
Tarleton State University, TX	M,W	Fordham University, NY	W	Arizona State University at the	
Tennessee Wesleyan University, TN	M,W	Georgetown University, DC	M,W	West campus, AZ	M,W
Texas A&M University–		The George Washington		Arkansas Tech University, AR	W
Commerce, TX	M,W	University, DC	M,W	Armstrong State University, GA	W
Texas Wesleyan University, TX	M,W	Indiana University Bloomington, IN	W	Asbury University, KY	M,W
Tiffin University, OH	M,W	Jacksonville University, FL	M,W	Auburn University, AL	M,W
Tusculum College, TN	M,W	Kansas State University, KS	W	Auburn University at	
Union College, KY	M,W	La Salle University, PA	M,W	Montgomery, AL	M,W
Union University, TN	W	Lehigh University, PA	W	Augustana University, SD	M,W
The University of Alabama, AL	M,W	Loyola Marymount University, CA	W	Augusta University, GA	M,W
The University of Alabama in		Loyola University Maryland, MD	M,W	Austin Peay State University, TN	M,W
Huntsville, AL	M,W	Marist College, NY	W	Azusa Pacific University, CA	M,W
University of Central Arkansas, AR	M,W	Merrimack College, MA	W	Baker University, KS	M,W
University of Central Florida, FL	M,W	Michigan State University, MI	W	Ball State University, IN	W
University of Delaware, DE	M,W	Northeastern University, MA	M,W	Barton College, NC	W
University of Detroit Mercy, MI	M,W	Nova Southeastern University, FL	W	Baylor University, TX	M,W
University of Florida, FL	M,W	Oklahoma City University, OK	M,W	Belhaven University, MS	M,W
University of Great Falls, MT	M,W	Old Dominion University, VA	W	Bellarmine University, KY	M,W
		Robert Morris University, PA	W	Belmont Abbey College, NC	M,W

Belmont University, TN	M,W	Clarke University, IA	M,W	Friends University, KS	M,W
Bemidji State University, MN	W	Clayton State University, GA	M,W	Furman University, SC	M,W
Benedictine College, KS	M,W	Clemson University, SC	M,W	Gannon University, PA	M,W
Bethel College, IN	M,W	Cleveland State University, OH	W	Gardner-Webb University, NC	M,W
Bethel College, KS	M,W	Coastal Carolina University, SC	M,W	Georgetown University, DC	M,W
Bethune-Cookman University, FL	M,W	College of Charleston, SC	M,W	The George Washington	
Binghamton University, State		The College of Idaho, ID	M,W	University, DC	M,W
University of New York, NY	M,W	College of Saint Mary, NE	W	Georgia College & State	
Biola University, CA	M,W	The College of Saint Rose, NY	M,W	University, GA	M,W
Black Hills State University, SD	M,W	College of the Holy Cross, MA	W	Georgia Institute of Technology, GA	M,W
Bloomfield College, NJ	M,W	The College of William and Mary, VA	M,W	Georgian Court University, NJ	M,W
Bloomsburg University of		Colorado Mesa University, CO	M,W	Georgia Southern University, GA	W
Pennsylvania, PA	M,W	Colorado School of Mines, CO	M,W	Georgia Southwestern State	
Bluefield College, VA	M,W	Colorado State University, CO	M,W	University, GA	W
Bluefield State College, WV	M,W	Columbia College, MO	M,W	Georgia State University, GA	W
Blue Mountain College, MS	M,W	Columbia International		Gonzaga University, WA	M,W
Boise State University, ID	M,W	University, SC	M,W	Goshen College, IN	M,W
Boston College, MA	M,W	Columbus State University, GA	M,W	Governors State University, IL	M,W
Boston University, MA	M,W	Concordia University Irvine, CA	M,W	Graceland University, IA	M,W
Bowling Green State University, OH	M,W	Concordia University, Nebraska, NE	M,W	Grand Valley State University, MI	M,W
Bradley University, IL	M,W	Concordia University, St. Paul, MN	M,W	Grand View University, IA	M,W
Brenau University, GA	W	Concord University, WV	M,W	Hampton University, VA	M,W
Brescia University, KY	M,W	Converse College, SC	W	Harding University, AR	M,W
Briar Cliff University, IA	M,W	Corban University, OR	M,W	Hawai`i Pacific University, HI	M,W
Brigham Young University, UT	M,W	Cornerstone University, MI	M,W	High Point University, NC	M,W
Bryan College, TN	M,W	Creighton University, NE	M,W	Hillsdale College, MI	M,W
Bucknell University, PA	W	Culver-Stockton College, MO	M,W	Hofstra University, NY	M,W
Butler University, IN	M,W	Daemen College, NY	M,W	Holy Family University, PA	M,W
Caldwell University, NJ	M,W	Dakota State University, SD	M,W	Hope International University, CA	M,W
California Baptist University, CA	M,W	Dallas Baptist University, TX	W	Houston Baptist University, TX	M,W
California Polytechnic State		Davidson College, NC	M,W	Humboldt State University, CA	M,W
University, San Luis Obispo, CA	M,W	Dickinson State University, ND	M,W	Huntington University, IN	M,W
California State Polytechnic		Dixie State University, UT	M,W	Huston-Tillotson University, TX	M
University, Pomona, CA	M,W	Doane University, NE	M,W	Idaho State University, ID	M,W
California State University,		Dominican College, NY	M,W	Indiana State University, IN	M,W
Chico, CA	M,W	Dominican University of		Indiana University Bloomington, IN	M,W
California State University,		California, CA	M,W	Indiana University of	
Fresno, CA	M,W	Drake University, IA	M,W	Pennsylvania, PA	M,W
California State University,		Drury University, MO	M,W	Indiana University–Purdue	
Fullerton, CA	M,W	Duquesne University, PA	M,W	University Indianapolis, IN	M,W
California State University,		East Carolina University, NC	M,W	Inter American University of	
Long Beach, CA	M,W	East Central University, OK	M,W	Puerto Rico, Bayamón	
California State University,		Eastern Illinois University, IL	M,W	Campus, PR	M,W
Monterey Bay, CA	M,W	Eastern Michigan University, MI	M,W	Inter American University of	
California State University,		Eastern Oregon University, OR	M,W	Puerto Rico, Guayama	
Northridge, CA	M,W	Eastern Washington University, WA	M,W	Campus, PR	M,W
California State University,		East Stroudsburg University of		Iona College, NY	M,W
Sacramento, CA	M,W	Pennsylvania, PA	M,W	Iowa State University of Science	
Calumet College of Saint Joseph, IN	M,W	Elon University, NC	M,W	and Technology, IA	M,W
Cameron University, OK	M	Embry-Riddle Aeronautical		Jackson State University, MS	M,W
Campbellsville University, KY	M,W	University–Daytona, FL	M,W	Jacksonville State University, AL	M,W
Canisius College, NY	M,W	Embry-Riddle Aeronautical		Jacksonville University, FL	W
Cardinal Stritch University, WI	M,W	University–Prescott, AZ		James Madison University, VA	W
Carlow University, PA	M,W	Emmanuel College, GA	M,W	John Brown University, AR	M,W
Carroll College, MT	M,W	Emporia State University, KS	M,W	Johnson C. Smith University, NC	M,W
Carson-Newman University, TN	M,W	Evangel University, MO	M,W	Judson University, IL	M,W
Catawba College, NC	M,W	Fairfield University, CT	M,W	Kansas State University, KS	M,W
Cedarville University, OH	M,W	Felician University, NJ	M,W	Kansas Wesleyan University, KS	M,W
Central Connecticut State		Ferris State University, MI	M,W	Kennesaw State University, GA	M,W
University, CT	M,W	Flagler College, FL	M,W	Kent State University, OH	M,W
Central Methodist University, MO	M,W	Florida Agricultural and		Kentucky State University, KY	M,W
Central Michigan University, MI	M,W	Mechanical University, FL	M,W	Kentucky Wesleyan College, KY	M,W
Central Washington University, WA	M,W	Florida Gulf Coast University, FL	M,W	King University, TN	M,W
Chaminade University of		Florida Institute of Technology, FL	M,W	Kutztown University of	
Honolulu, HI	M,W	Florida International		Pennsylvania, PA	M,W
Chestnut Hill College, PA	M,W	University, FL	M,W	Lake Erie College, OH	M,W
Chowan University, NC	M,W	Florida Southern College, FL	M,W	Lamar University, TX	M,W
Christian Brothers University, TN	M,W	Florida State University, FL	M,W	Lane College, TN	M,W
The Citadel, The Military		Fordham University, NY	M,W	La Salle University, PA	M,W
College of South Carolina, SC	M,W	Fort Lewis College, CO	M,W	Lawrence Technological	
Clarion University of		Francis Marion University, SC	M,W	University, MI	M,W
Pennsylvania, PA	W	Freed-Hardeman University, TN	M,W	Lees-McRae College, NC	M,W
Clark Atlanta University, GA	M,W	Fresno Pacific University, CA	M,W	Lee University, TN	M,W

Lehigh University, PA	M,W	New Mexico Highlands		San Diego State University, CA	W
Le Moyne College, NY	M,W	University, NM	M,W	San Francisco State University, CA	M,W
Lenoir-Rhyne University, NC	M,W	New Mexico State University, NM	M,W	Santa Clara University, CA	M,W
Lewis University, IL	M,W	New York Institute of		Savannah College of Art and	
Liberty University, VA	M,W	Technology, NY	M,W	Design, GA	M,W
Life University, GA	W	Niagara University, NY	M,W	Seattle Pacific University, WA	M,W
Lincoln University, MO	W	North Carolina State University, NC	M,W	Seattle University, WA	M,W
Lincoln University, PA	M	Northeastern University, MA	M,W	Seton Hill University, PA	M,W
Lindenwood University, MO	M,W	Northern Arizona University, AZ	M,W	Shawnee State University, OH	M,W
Lindsey Wilson College, KY	M,W	Northern Kentucky University, KY	M,W	Shippensburg University of	
Lipscomb University, TN	M,W	Northern State University, SD	M,W	Pennsylvania, PA	
Lock Haven University of		Northwest Christian University, OR	M,W	Siena College, NY	M,W
Pennsylvania, PA	M,W	Northwestern College, IA	M,W	Simpson University, CA	M,W
Longwood University, VA	M,W	Northwestern State University of		Slippery Rock University of	
Louisiana State University and		Louisiana, LA	M,W	Pennsylvania, PA	M,W
Agricultural &		Northwest Missouri State		Soka University of America, CA	M,W
Mechanical College, LA	M,W	University, MO	M,W	South Dakota School of Mines and	
Louisiana Tech University, LA	M,W	Northwest University, WA	M,W	Technology, SD	M,W
Loyola Marymount University, CA	M,W	Nova Southeastern University, FL	M,W	Southeastern Louisiana	
Loyola University Chicago, IL	M,W	Oakland City University, IN	M,W	University, LA	M,W
Loyola University Maryland, MD	M,W	The Ohio State University, OH	M,W	Southeastern Oklahoma State	
Loyola University New Orleans, LA	M,W	Ohio University, OH	M,W	University, OK	W
Lubbock Christian University, TX	M,W	Ohio Valley University, WV	M,W	Southeastern University, FL	M,W
Lynn University, FL	W	Oklahoma Baptist University, OK	M,W	Southeast Missouri State	
Lyon College, AR	M,W	Oklahoma Christian University, OK	M,W	University, MO	M,W
Malone University, OH	M,W	Oklahoma State University, OK	M,W	Southern Arkansas	
Manhattan College, NY	M,W	Olivet Nazarene University, IL	M,W	University–Magnolia, AR	M,W
Mansfield University of		Oral Roberts University, OK	M,W	Southern Connecticut State	
Pennsylvania, PA	M,W	Oregon State University, OR	W	University, CT	M,W
Marist College, NY	M,W	Ouachita Baptist University, AR	W	Southern Illinois University	
Marquette University, WI	M,W	Our Lady of the Lake University, TX	M,W	Carbondale, IL	M,W
Marshall University, WV	M,W	Palm Beach Atlantic University, FL	W	Southern Illinois University	
Maryville University of Saint		Penn State University Park, PA	M,W	Edwardsville, IL	M,W
Louis, MO	M,W	Pepperdine University, CA	M,W	Southern Methodist University, TX	W
The Master's University, CA	M,W	Pittsburg State University, KS	M,W	Southern New Hampshire	
McKendree University, IL	M,W	Point Loma Nazarene University, CA	W	University, NH	M,W
Mercer University, GA	M,W	Point Park University, PA	M,W	Southern Utah University, UT	M,W
Merrimack College, MA	M,W	Prairie View A&M University, TX	M,W	Southwest Baptist University, MO	M,W
Miami University, OH	M,W	Presbyterian College, SC	M,W	Southwestern College, KS	M,W
Michigan State University, MI	M,W	Providence College, RI	M,W	Southwestern Oklahoma State	
Michigan Technological		Purdue University, IN	M,W	University, OK	W
University, MI	M,W	Queens College of the City		Spring Hill College, AL	M,W
Millersville University of		University of New York, NY	M,W	Stanford University, CA	M,W
Pennsylvania, PA	W	Quinnipiac University, CT	M,W	Stephen F. Austin State	
Milligan College, TN	M,W	Radford University, VA	M,W	University, TX	M,W
Minnesota State University		Regis University, CO	M,W	Stephens College, MO	W
Mankato, MN	M,W	Rice University, TX	M,W	Sterling College, KS	M,W
Minnesota State University		Robert Morris University, PA	W	Stonehill College, MA	M,W
Moorhead, MN	M,W	Robert Morris University		Stony Brook University, State	
Minot State University, ND	M,W	Illinois, IL	M,W	University of New York, NY	M,W
Mississippi State University, MS	W	Roberts Wesleyan College, NY	M,W	Syracuse University, NY	M,W
Missouri Baptist University, MO	M,W	Rockhurst University, MO	W	Tarleton State University, TX	M,W
Missouri State University, MO	W	Rocky Mountain College, MT	M,W	Taylor University, IN	M,W
Missouri University of Science		Rogers State University, OK	M,W	Temple University, PA	M,W
and Technology, MO	M,W	Sacred Heart University, CT	M,W	Tennessee State University, TN	M,W
Missouri Western State		Saginaw Valley State University, MI	M,W	Tennessee Wesleyan University, TN	M,W
University, MO	M,W	St. Ambrose University, IA	M,W	Texas A&M International	
Molloy College, NY	M,W	St. Andrews University, NC	M,W	University, TX	M,W
Monmouth University, NJ	M,W	Saint Augustine's		Texas A&M University–	
Montana State University, MT	M,W	University, NC	M,W	Commerce, TX	M,W
Montana State University		St. Bonaventure University, NY	M,W	Texas A&M University–	
Billings, MT	M,W	St. John's University, NY	W	Corpus Christi, TX	M,W
Morehead State University, KY	M,W	Saint Joseph's University, PA	M,W	Texas Christian University, TX	M,W
Morehouse College, GA	M	Saint Leo University, FL	M,W	Texas State University, TX	M,W
Morningside College, IA	M,W	St. Louis College of Pharmacy, MO	M,W	Texas Tech University, TX	M,W
Mount Marty College, SD	M,W	Saint Louis University, MO	M,W	Texas Wesleyan University, TX	M,W
Mount Mercy University, IA	M,W	Saint Martin's University, WA	M,W	Tiffin University, OH	M,W
Mount St. Mary's		Saint Mary-of-the-Woods College, IN	W	Towson University, MD	W
University, MD	M,W	Saint Peter's University, NJ	W	Trevecca Nazarene University, TN	M,W
Mount Vernon Nazarene		St. Thomas Aquinas College, NY	M,W	Trinity Christian College, IL	M,W
University, OH	M,W	St. Thomas University, FL	M,W	Troy University, AL	M,W
Murray State University, KY	W	Samford University, AL	M,W	Truett McConnell University, GA	M,W
Newberry College, SC	M,W	Sam Houston State University, TX	M,W	Truman State University, MO	M,W

Tulane University, LA	M,W	University of Mobile, AL	M,W	University of Utah, UT	W
Tusculum College, TN	M,W	The University of Montana		University of Vermont, VT	M,W
Union College, KY	M,W	Western, MT	M,W	University of Virginia, VA	M,W
Union University, TN	W	University of Nebraska at		The University of Virginia's	
University at Albany, State		Kearney, NE	M,W	College at Wise, VA	M,W
University of New York, NY	M,W	University of Nevada, Las Vegas, NV	W	University of Washington, WA	M,W
University at Buffalo, the State		University of Nevada, Reno, NV	W	The University of West Alabama, AL	M,W
University of New York, NY	M,W	University of New Hampshire, NH	M,W	University of West Georgia, GA	M,W
The University of Akron, OH	M,W	University of New Haven, CT	M,W	University of Wisconsin–	
The University of Alabama, AL	M,W	University of New Orleans, LA	M,W	Green Bay, WI	M,W
The University of Alabama at		University of North Alabama, AL	M,W	University of Wisconsin–	
Birmingham, AL	W	University of North Carolina at		Madison, WI	M,W
The University of Alabama in		Asheville, NC	M,W	University of Wisconsin–	
Huntsville, AL	M,W	The University of North Carolina		Milwaukee, WI	M,W
University of Alaska Fairbanks, AK	M,W	at Chapel Hill, NC	M,W	University of Wisconsin–	
The University of Arizona, AZ	M,W	The University of North Carolina		Parkside, WI	M,W
University of Arkansas, AR	M,W	at Charlotte, NC	M,W	Upper Iowa University, IA	W
University of Bridgeport, CT	M,W	The University of North Carolina		Ursuline College, OH	W
University of California, Davis, CA	M,W	at Greensboro, NC	M,W	Utah State University, UT	M,W
University of California,		The University of North Carolina		Utah Valley University, UT	M,W
Irvine, CA	M,W	at Pembroke, NC	M,W	Valdosta State University, GA	M,W
University of California, Los		The University of North Carolina		Valley City State University, ND	M,W
Angeles, CA	M,W	Wilmington, NC	M,W	Valparaiso University, IN	M,W
University of California,		University of Northern Colorado, CO	M,W	Vanderbilt University, TN	M,W
Riverside, CA	M,W	University of Northern Iowa, IA	M,W	Villanova University, PA	M,W
University of California, Santa		University of North Florida, FL	M,W	Virginia Commonwealth	
Barbara, CA	M,W	University of North Georgia, GA	W	University, VA	M,W
University of Central Arkansas, AR	M,W	University of North Texas, TX	M,W	Virginia Military Institute, VA	M,W
University of Central Florida, FL	W	University of Notre Dame, IN	M,W	Virginia State University, VA	M,W
University of Central Missouri, MO	M,W	University of Oklahoma, OK	M,W	Viterbo University, WI	M,W
University of Cincinnati, OH	M,W	University of Oregon, OR	M,W	Wagner College, NY	M,W
University of Colorado Boulder, CO	M,W	University of Pikeville, KY	M,W	Wake Forest University, NC	M,W
University of Colorado Colorado		University of Pittsburgh, PA	M,W	Waldorf University, IA	M,W
Springs, CO	M,W	University of Pittsburgh at		Washington State University, WA	M,W
University of Dayton, OH	M,W	Johnstown, PA	M,W	Wayland Baptist University, TX	M,W
University of Delaware, DE	W	University of Puerto Rico in		Wayne State College, NE	M,W
University of Detroit Mercy, MI	M,W	Bayamón, PR	M,W	Wayne State University, MI	M,W
University of Evansville, IN	M,W	University of Rhode Island, RI	M,W	Webber International University, FL	M,W
The University of Findlay, OH	M,W	University of Richmond, VA	W	West Chester University of	
University of Florida, FL	M,W	University of St. Francis, IL	M,W	Pennsylvania, PA	M,W
University of Georgia, GA	M,W	University of San Diego, CA	M,W	Western Carolina University, NC	M,W
University of Hartford, CT	M,W	University of San Francisco, CA	M,W	Western Illinois University, IL	M,W
University of Houston, TX	M,W	University of South Alabama, AL	M,W	Western Kentucky University, KY	M,W
University of Idaho, ID	M,W	University of South Carolina, SC	W	Western Michigan University, MI	W
University of Illinois at		University of South Carolina		Western Oregon University, OR	M,W
Chicago, IL	M,W	Aiken, SC	W	Western State Colorado	
University of Illinois at		The University of South Dakota, SD	M,W	University, CO	M,W
Springfield, IL	M,W	University of Southern		Western Washington University, WA	M,W
University of Indianapolis, IN	M,W	California, CA	W	Westminster College, UT	M,W
University of Jamestown, ND	M,W	University of Southern Indiana, IN	M,W	Westmont College, CA	M,W
The University of Kansas, KS	M,W	University of Southern		West Texas A&M University, TX	M,W
University of Kentucky, KY	M,W	Mississippi, MS	W	West Virginia University, WV	W
University of Louisiana at		University of South Florida, FL	M,W	West Virginia University	
Monroe, LA	M,W	The University of Tampa, FL	M,W	Institute of Technology, WV	M,W
University of Louisville, KY	M,W	The University of Tennessee at		West Virginia Wesleyan College, WV	M,W
University of Maine, ME	M,W	Chattanooga, TN	M,W	Wheeling Jesuit University, WV	M,W
University of Maryland,		The University of Tennessee at		Wichita State University, KS	M,W
Baltimore County, MD	M,W	Martin, TN	M,W	William Jewell College, MO	M,W
University of Maryland, College		The University of Texas at		Williams Baptist College, AR	M,W
Park, MD	W	Austin, TX	M,W	William Woods University, MO	M,W
University of Massachusetts		The University of Texas at El		Wingate University, NC	M,W
Amherst, MA	M,W	Paso, TX	M,W	Winona State University, MN	M,W
University of Massachusetts		The University of Texas at San		Winthrop University, SC	M,W
Lowell, MA	M,W	Antonio, TX	M,W	Wofford College, SC	M,W
University of Miami, FL	M,W	The University of Texas of the		Wright State University, OH	M,W
University of Michigan, MI	M,W	Permian Basin, TX	M,W	Youngstown State University, OH	M,W
University of Michigan–		The University of Texas Rio			
Dearborn, MI	M,W	Grande Valley, TX	M,W	**Equestrian sports**	
University of Minnesota, Duluth, MN	M,W	University of the Incarnate		Auburn University, AL	W
University of Minnesota, Twin		Word, TX	M,W	Baylor University, TX	W
Cities Campus, MN	M,W	University of the Pacific, CA	W	California State University,	
University of Missouri–		The University of Toledo, OH	M,W	Fresno, CA	W
Kansas City, MO	M,W	The University of Tulsa, OK	M,W	Converse College, SC	W

New Mexico State University, NM	W
Oklahoma State University, OK	W
St. Andrews University, NC	M,W
Saint Mary-of-the-Woods College, IN	W
Savannah College of Art and Design, GA	M,W
Seton Hill University, PA	W
Southern Methodist University, TX	W
Southwestern Oklahoma State University, OK	M,W
Texas A&M University, TX	W
Texas Christian University, TX	W
Tiffin University, OH	M,W
University of Georgia, GA	W
University of Great Falls, MT	M,W
University of Minnesota, Crookston, MN	W
University of South Carolina, SC	W
The University of Tennessee at Martin, TN	W
West Texas A&M University, TX	W

Fencing

Cleveland State University, OH	M,W
The Ohio State University, OH	M,W
Penn State University Park, PA	M,W
Queens College of the City University of New York, NY	W
St. John's University, NY	M,W
Stanford University, CA	M,W
Temple University, PA	W
University of Detroit Mercy, MI	M,W
The University of North Carolina at Chapel Hill, NC	M,W
University of Notre Dame, IN	M,W
Wagner College, NY	W
Wayne State University, MI	M,W

Field hockey

Adelphi University, NY	W
American University, DC	W
Appalachian State University, NC	W
Ball State University, IN	W
Bellarmine University, KY	W
Bloomsburg University of Pennsylvania, PA	W
Boston College, MA	W
Boston University, MA	W
Bucknell University, PA	W
Central Michigan University, MI	W
Colgate University, NY	W
College of the Holy Cross, MA	W
The College of William and Mary, VA	W
Davidson College, NC	W
Drexel University, PA	W
East Stroudsburg University of Pennsylvania, PA	W
Fairfield University, CT	W
Franklin Pierce University, NH	W
Georgetown University, DC	W
Hofstra University, NY	W
Indiana University of Pennsylvania, PA	W
James Madison University, VA	W
Kent State University, OH	W
Kutztown University of Pennsylvania, PA	W
La Salle University, PA	W
Lehigh University, PA	W
Liberty University, VA	W
Lindenwood University, MO	W
Lock Haven University of Pennsylvania, PA	W
Longwood University, VA	W

Mansfield University of Pennsylvania, PA	W
Mercy College, NY	W
Merrimack College, MA	W
Miami University, OH	W
Michigan State University, MI	W
Millersville University of Pennsylvania, PA	W
Missouri State University, MO	W
Molloy College, NY	W
Monmouth University, NJ	W
Newberry College, SC	W
Northeastern University, MA	W
The Ohio State University, OH	W
Ohio University, OH	W
Old Dominion University, VA	W
Penn State University Park, PA	W
Providence College, RI	W
Quinnipiac University, CT	W
Sacred Heart University, CT	W
Saint Joseph's University, PA	W
Saint Louis University, MO	W
Seton Hill University, PA	W
Shippensburg University of Pennsylvania, PA	W
Siena College, NY	W
Slippery Rock University of Pennsylvania, PA	W
Southern Connecticut State University, CT	W
Southern New Hampshire University, NH	W
Stanford University, CA	W
Stonehill College, MA	W
Syracuse University, NY	W
Temple University, PA	W
Towson University, MD	W
University at Albany, State University of New York, NY	W
University of California, Davis, CA	W
University of Delaware, DE	W
University of Louisville, KY	W
University of Maine, ME	W
University of Maryland, College Park, MD	W
University of Massachusetts Amherst, MA	W
University of Massachusetts Lowell, MA	W
University of Michigan, MI	W
University of New Hampshire, NH	W
University of New Haven, CT	W
The University of North Carolina at Chapel Hill, NC	W
University of Richmond, VA	W
University of the Pacific, CA	W
University of Vermont, VT	W
University of Virginia, VA	W
Villanova University, PA	W
Virginia Commonwealth University, VA	W
Wake Forest University, NC	W
West Chester University of Pennsylvania, PA	W

Football

Abilene Christian University, TX	M
Adams State University, CO	M
Alabama State University, AL	M
Alcorn State University, MS	M
Alderson Broaddus University, WV	M
Angelo State University, TX	M
Appalachian State University, NC	M

Arizona State University at the Downtown Phoenix campus, AZ	M
Arizona State University at the Polytechnic campus, AZ	M
Arizona State University at the Tempe campus, AZ	M
Arizona State University at the West campus, AZ	M
Arkansas Tech University, AR	M
Auburn University, AL	M
Augustana University, SD	M
Austin Peay State University, TN	M
Azusa Pacific University, CA	M
Baker University, KS	M
Ball State University, IN	M
Baylor University, TX	M
Belhaven University, MS	M
Bemidji State University, MN	M
Benedictine College, KS	M
Bethel College, KS	M
Bethune-Cookman University, FL	M
Black Hills State University, SD	M
Bloomsburg University of Pennsylvania, PA	M
Bluefield College, VA	M
Boise State University, ID	M
Boston College, MA	M
Bowling Green State University, OH	M
Briar Cliff University, IA	M
Brigham Young University, UT	M
Bucknell University, PA	M
California Polytechnic State University, San Luis Obispo, CA	M
California State University, Fresno, CA	M
California State University, Northridge, CA	M
California State University, Sacramento, CA	M
Campbellsville University, KY	M
Carroll College, MT	M
Carson-Newman University, TN	M
Catawba College, NC	M
Central Methodist University, MO	M
Central Michigan University, MI	M
Central Washington University, WA	M
Chestnut Hill College, PA	M
Chowan University, NC	M
The Citadel, The Military College of South Carolina, SC	M
Clarion University of Pennsylvania, PA	M
Clark Atlanta University, GA	M
Clemson University, SC	M
Coastal Carolina University, SC	M
Colgate University, NY	M
College of the Holy Cross, MA	M
The College of William and Mary, VA	M
Colorado Mesa University, CO	M
Colorado School of Mines, CO	M
Colorado State University, CO	M
Concordia University, Nebraska, NE	M
Concordia University, St. Paul, MN	M
Concord University, WV	M
Culver-Stockton College, MO	M
Dakota State University, SD	M
Davidson College, NC	M
Dickinson State University, ND	M
Dixie State University, UT	M
Doane University, NE	M
Duquesne University, PA	M
East Carolina University, NC	M
East Central University, OK	M

Eastern Illinois University, IL	M	Lyon College, AR	M	Shippensburg University of	
Eastern Michigan University, MI	M	Malone University, OH	M	Pennsylvania, PA	M
Eastern Oregon University, OR	M	Marshall University, WV	M	Slippery Rock University of	
Eastern Washington University, WA	M	McKendree University, IL	M	Pennsylvania, PA	M
East Stroudsburg University of		Mercer University, GA	M	South Dakota School of Mines and	
Pennsylvania, PA	M	Merrimack College, MA	M	Technology, SD	M
Elizabeth City State University, NC	M	Miami University, OH	M	Southeastern Louisiana	
Elon University, NC	M	Michigan State University, MI	M	University, LA	M
Emporia State University, KS	M	Michigan Technological		Southeastern Oklahoma State	
Evangel University, MO	M	University, MI		University, OK	M
Faulkner University, AL	M	Millersville University of		Southeastern University, FL	M
Ferris State University, MI	M	Pennsylvania, PA	M	Southeast Missouri State	
Florida Agricultural and		Minnesota State University		University, MO	M
Mechanical University, FL	M	Mankato, MN	M	Southern Arkansas	
Florida Atlantic University, FL	M	Minnesota State University		University–Magnolia, AR	M
Florida Institute of Technology, FL	M	Moorhead, MN	M	Southern Connecticut State	
Florida International		Minot State University, ND	M	University, CT	M
University, FL	M	Mississippi State University, MS	M	Southern Illinois University	
Florida State University, FL	M	Missouri Baptist University, MO	M	Carbondale, IL	M
Fordham University, NY	M	Missouri State University, MO	M	Southern Methodist University, TX	M
Fort Lewis College, CO	M	Missouri University of Science		Southern Oregon University, OR	M
Friends University, KS	M	and Technology, MO	M	Southern Utah University, UT	M
Furman University, SC	M	Missouri Western State		Southwest Baptist University, MO	M
Gannon University, PA	M	University, MO	M	Southwestern College, KS	M
Gardner-Webb University, NC	M	Monmouth University, NJ	M	Southwestern Oklahoma State	
Georgia Institute of Technology, GA	M	Montana State University, MT	M	University, OK	M
Georgia Southern University, GA	M	Montana Tech of The University		Stanford University, CA	M
Georgia State University, GA	M	of Montana, MT	M	Stephen F. Austin State	
Graceland University, IA	M	Morehouse College, GA	M	University, TX	M
Grambling State University, LA	M	Morningside College, IA	M	Sterling College, KS	M
Grand Valley State University, MI	M	Murray State University, KY	M	Stonehill College, MA	M
Grand View University, IA	M	Newberry College, SC	M	Stony Brook University, State	
Hampton University, VA	M	New Mexico Highlands University, NM	M	University of New York, NY	M
Harding University, AR	M	New Mexico State University, NM	M	Syracuse University, NY	M
Hillsdale College, MI	M	North Carolina State University, NC	M	Tarleton State University, TX	M
Houston Baptist University, TX	M	Northeastern State University, OK	M	Taylor University, IN	M
Humboldt State University, CA	M	Northern Arizona University, AZ	M	Temple University, PA	M
Idaho State University, ID	M	Northern Illinois University, IL	M	Tennessee State University, TN	M
Indiana State University, IN	M	Northern State University, SD	M	Texas A&M University, TX	M
Indiana University Bloomington, IN	M	Northwestern College, IA	M	Texas A&M University–	
Indiana University of		Northwestern State University of		Commerce, TX	M
Pennsylvania, PA	M	Louisiana, LA	M	Texas Christian University, TX	M
Iowa State University of Science		Northwest Missouri State		Texas State University, TX	M
and Technology, IA	M	University, MO	M	Texas Tech University, TX	M
Jackson State University, MS	M	The Ohio State University, OH	M	Texas Wesleyan University, TX	M
Jacksonville State University, AL	M	Ohio University, OH	M	Tiffin University, OH	M
James Madison University, VA	M	Oklahoma Baptist University, OK	M	Towson University, MD	M
Johnson C. Smith University, NC	M	Oklahoma State University, OK	M	Troy University, AL	M
Kansas State University, KS	M	Old Dominion University, VA	M	Truman State University, MO	M
Kansas Wesleyan University, KS	M	Olivet Nazarene University, IL	M	Tulane University, LA	M
Kennesaw State University, GA	M	Oregon State University, OR	M	Tusculum College, TN	M
Kent State University, OH	M	Ouachita Baptist University, AR	M	Union College, KY	M
Kentucky State University, KY	M	Penn State University Park, PA	M	University at Albany, State	
Kentucky Wesleyan College, KY	M	Pittsburg State University, KS	M	University of New York, NY	M
Kutztown University of		Prairie View A&M University, TX	M	University at Buffalo, the State	
Pennsylvania, PA	M	Presbyterian College, SC	M	University of New York, NY	M
Lake Erie College, OH	M	Purdue University, IN	M	The University of Akron, OH	M
Lamar University, TX	M	Rice University, TX	M	The University of Alabama, AL	M
Lane College, TN	M	Robert Morris University, PA	M	The University of Alabama at	
Langston University, OK	M	Robert Morris University		Birmingham, AL	M
Lehigh University, PA	M	Illinois, IL	M	The University of Arizona, AZ	M
Lenoir-Rhyne University, NC	M	Rocky Mountain College, MT	M	University of Arkansas, AR	M
Liberty University, VA	M	Sacred Heart University, CT	M	University of California, Davis, CA	M
Lincoln University, MO	M	Saginaw Valley State University, MI	M	University of California, Los	
Lincoln University, PA	M	St. Ambrose University, IA	M	Angeles, CA	M
Lindenwood University, MO	M	Saint Augustine's		University of Central Arkansas, AR	M
Lindsey Wilson College, KY	M,W	University, NC	M	University of Central Florida, FL	M
Lock Haven University of		Samford University, AL	M	University of Central Missouri, MO	M
Pennsylvania, PA	M	Sam Houston State University, TX	M	University of Cincinnati, OH	M
Louisiana State University and		San Diego State University, CA	M	University of Colorado Boulder, CO	M
Agricultural &		Seton Hill University, PA	M	University of Delaware, DE	M
Mechanical College, LA	M	Shepherd University, WV	M	The University of Findlay, OH	M
Louisiana Tech University, LA	M			University of Florida, FL	M

University of Georgia, GA	M
University of Hawaii at Manoa, HI	M
University of Houston, TX	M
University of Idaho, ID	M
University of Indianapolis, IN	M
University of Jamestown, ND	M
The University of Kansas, KS	M
University of Kentucky, KY	M
University of Louisiana at Monroe, LA	M
University of Louisville, KY	M
University of Maine, ME	M
University of Maryland, College Park, MD	M
University of Massachusetts Amherst, MA	M
University of Miami, FL	M
University of Michigan, MI	M
University of Minnesota, Crookston, MN	M
University of Minnesota, Duluth, MN	M
University of Minnesota, Twin Cities Campus, MN	M
The University of Montana Western, MT	M
University of Nebraska at Kearney, NE	M
University of Nevada, Las Vegas, NV	M
University of Nevada, Reno, NV	M
University of New Hampshire, NH	M
University of New Haven, CT	M
University of North Alabama, AL	M
The University of North Carolina at Chapel Hill, NC	M
The University of North Carolina at Charlotte, NC	M
The University of North Carolina at Pembroke, NC	M
University of Northern Colorado, CO	M
University of Northern Iowa, IA	M
University of North Texas, TX	M
University of Notre Dame, IN	M
University of Oklahoma, OK	M
University of Oregon, OR	M
University of Pikeville, KY	M
University of Pittsburgh, PA	M
University of Rhode Island, RI	M
University of Richmond, VA	M
University of St. Francis, IL	M
University of South Alabama, AL	M
University of South Carolina, SC	M
The University of South Dakota, SD	M
University of Southern California, CA	M
University of Southern Mississippi, MS	M
University of South Florida, FL	M
The University of Tennessee, TN	M
The University of Tennessee at Chattanooga, TN	M
The University of Tennessee at Martin, TN	M
The University of Texas at Austin, TX	M
The University of Texas at El Paso, TX	M
The University of Texas at San Antonio, TX	M
The University of Texas of the Permian Basin, TX	M
University of the Incarnate Word, TX	M
The University of Toledo, OH	M
The University of Tulsa, OK	M

University of Utah, UT	M
University of Virginia, VA	M
The University of Virginia's College at Wise, VA	M
University of Washington, WA	M
The University of West Alabama, AL	M
University of West Georgia, GA	M
University of Wisconsin–Madison, WI	M
Upper Iowa University, IA	M
Utah State University, UT	M
Valdosta State University, GA	M
Valley City State University, ND	M
Vanderbilt University, TN	M
Villanova University, PA	M
Virginia Military Institute, VA	M
Virginia Polytechnic Institute and State University, VA	M
Virginia State University, VA	M
Wagner College, NY	M
Wake Forest University, NC	M
Waldorf University, IA	M
Washburn University, KS	M
Washington State University, WA	M
Wayland Baptist University, TX	M
Wayne State College, NE	M
Wayne State University, MI	M
Webber International University, FL	M
Weber State University, UT	M
West Chester University of Pennsylvania, PA	M
Western Carolina University, NC	M
Western Illinois University, IL	M
Western Kentucky University, KY	M
Western Michigan University, MI	M
Western Oregon University, OR	M
Western State Colorado University, CO	M
West Texas A&M University, TX	M
West Virginia University, WV	M
West Virginia Wesleyan College, WV	M
William Jewell College, MO	M
Wingate University, NC	M
Winona State University, MN	M
Wofford College, SC	M
Youngstown State University, OH	M

Golf

Abilene Christian University, TX	M
Academy of Art University, CA	M,W
Adams State University, CO	M,W
Adelphi University, NY	M,W
Alabama State University, AL	M,W
Alcorn State University, MS	M,W
Alderson Broaddus University, WV	M,W
Anderson University, SC	M,W
Angelo State University, TX	W
Appalachian State University, NC	M,W
Aquinas College, MI	M,W
Arizona State University at the Downtown Phoenix campus, AZ	M,W
Arizona State University at the Polytechnic campus, AZ	M,W
Arizona State University at the Tempe campus, AZ	M,W
Arizona State University at the West campus, AZ	M,W
Arkansas Tech University, AR	M,W
Armstrong State University, GA	M,W
Asbury University, KY	M,W
Auburn University, AL	M,W
Augustana University, SD	M,W
Augusta University, GA	M,W
Austin Peay State University, TN	M,W

Baker University, KS	M,W
Ball State University, IN	M,W
Barry University, FL	M,W
Barton College, NC	M,W
Baylor University, TX	M,W
Belhaven University, MS	M,W
Bellarmine University, KY	M,W
Belmont Abbey College, NC	M,W
Belmont University, TN	M,W
Bemidji State University, MN	M,W
Bethel College, IN	M,W
Bethel College, KS	M,W
Bethune-Cookman University, FL	M,W
Binghamton University, State University of New York, NY	M
Biola University, CA	M,W
Bluefield College, VA	M
Bluefield State College, WV	M
Blue Mountain College, MS	M
Boise State University, ID	M,W
Boston College, MA	M,W
Boston University, MA	W
Bowling Green State University, OH	M,W
Bradley University, IL	M,W
Brenau University, GA	W
Brescia University, KY	M,W
Briar Cliff University, IA	M,W
Brigham Young University, UT	M,W
Bryan College, TN	M,W
Butler University, IN	M,W
California Baptist University, CA	M,W
California Polytechnic State University, San Luis Obispo, CA	M,W
California State University, Bakersfield, CA	M
California State University, Chico, CA	M,W
California State University, Dominguez Hills, CA	M
California State University, Fresno, CA	M,W
California State University, Fullerton, CA	M,W
California State University, Long Beach, CA	M,W
California State University Maritime Academy, CA	M
California State University, Monterey Bay, CA	M,W
California State University, Northridge, CA	M
California State University, Sacramento, CA	M
California State University, San Bernardino, CA	M
Calumet College of Saint Joseph, IN	M,W
Cameron University, OK	M,W
Campbellsville University, KY	M,W
Canisius College, NY	M
Cardinal Stritch University, WI	M,W
Carroll College, MT	M,W
Carson-Newman University, TN	M
Catawba College, NC	M,W
Cedarville University, OH	M
Central Connecticut State University, CT	M,W
Central Michigan University, MI	W
Chaminade University of Honolulu, HI	M
Chestnut Hill College, PA	M
Chowan University, NC	M,W
Christian Brothers University, TN	M,W

The Citadel, The Military College of South Carolina, SC	W	Furman University, SC	W	Loyola University Maryland, MD	M
Clarion University of Pennsylvania, PA	M,W	Gannon University, PA	M,W	Loyola University New Orleans, LA	M,W
		Gardner-Webb University, NC	M,W	Lubbock Christian University, TX	M,W
		Georgetown University, DC	M,W	Lynn University, FL	M,W
Clarke University, IA	M,W	The George Washington University, DC	M	Lyon College, AR	M,W
Clayton State University, GA	M			Malone University, OH	M,W
Clemson University, SC	M	Georgia College & State University, GA	M	Manhattan College, NY	M
Cleveland State University, OH	M	Georgia Institute of Technology, GA	M	Marquette University, WI	M
Coastal Carolina University, SC	M,W	Georgia Southern University, GA	M	Marshall University, WV	M,W
College of Charleston, SC	M,W	Georgia Southwestern State University, GA	M	Marymount California University, CA	M,W
College of Coastal Georgia, GA	M,W			Maryville University of Saint Louis, MO	M,W
The College of Idaho, ID	M,W	Georgia State University, GA	M,W	The Master's University, CA	M
College of Saint Mary, NE	W	Gonzaga University, WA	M,W	McKendree University, IL	M,W
The College of Saint Rose, NY	M,W	Governors State University, IL	M,W	Mercer University, GA	M,W
The College of William and Mary, VA	M,W	Graceland University, IA	M,W	Merrimack College, MA	W
Colorado Mesa University, CO	M,W	Grand Valley State University, MI	M,W	Metropolitan State University of Denver, CO	W
Colorado School of Mines, CO	M	Grand View University, IA	M,W	Miami University, OH	M
Colorado State University, CO	M,W	Hampton University, VA	M,W	Michigan State University, MI	M,W
Columbia College, MO	M,W	Harding University, AR	M,W	Midland College, TX	M
Columbus State University, GA	M,W	Hawai`i Pacific University, HI	M,W	Millersville University of Pennsylvania, PA	M,W
Concordia University, Nebraska, NE	M,W	High Point University, NC	M,W	Milligan College, TN	M,W
Concordia University, St. Paul, MN	M,W	Hillsdale College, MI	M	Minnesota State University Mankato, MN	M,W
Concord University, WV	M,W	Hofstra University, NY	M,W		
Converse College, SC	W	Hope International University, CA	M,W	Minnesota State University Moorhead, MN	W
Corban University, OR	M,W	Houston Baptist University, TX	M,W		
Cornerstone University, MI	M,W	Huntington University, IN	M	Mississippi State University, MS	M,W
Creighton University, NE	M,W	Idaho State University, ID	W	Missouri Baptist University, MO	M,W
Culver-Stockton College, MO	M,W	Indiana State University, IN	W	Missouri State University, MO	M,W
Daemen College, NY	M	Indiana University Bloomington, IN	M,W	Missouri Western State University, MO	M,W
Dallas Baptist University, TX	W	Indiana University of Pennsylvania, PA	M	Monmouth University, NJ	M,W
Davidson College, NC	M			Montana State University, MT	W
Dickinson State University, ND	M,W	Indiana University–Purdue University Indianapolis, IN	M,W	Montana Tech of The University of Montana, MT	M,W
Dixie State University, UT	M,W	Iona College, NY	M		
Doane University, NE	M,W	Iowa State University of Science and Technology, IA	M,W	Morehead State University, KY	M,W
Dominican College, NY	M			Morningside College, IA	M,W
Dominican University of California, CA	M,W	Jackson State University, MS	M,W	Mount Marty College, SD	M,W
Drake University, IA	M	Jacksonville State University, AL	M,W	Mount Mercy University, IA	M,W
Drexel University, PA	M	Jacksonville University, FL	M,W	Mount Vernon Nazarene University, OH	M,W
Drury University, MO	M,W	James Madison University, VA	M,W		
East Carolina University, NC	M,W	Johnson C. Smith University, NC	M	Murray State University, KY	M,W
Eastern Illinois University, IL	M,W	Judson University, IL	M,W	Newberry College, SC	M,W
Eastern Michigan University, MI	M,W	Kansas State University, KS	M,W	New Mexico State University, NM	M,W
Eastern Washington University, WA	W	Kansas Wesleyan University, KS	M,W	Niagara University, NY	M,W
Eckerd College, FL	M,W	Kennesaw State University, GA	M,W	North Carolina State University, NC	M,W
Elizabeth City State University, NC	M	Kent State University, OH	M,W	Northeastern State University, OK	M,W
Elon University, NC	M,W	Kentucky State University, KY	M	Northern Arizona University, AZ	W
Embry-Riddle Aeronautical University–Daytona, FL	M,W	Kentucky Wesleyan College, KY	M,W	Northern Illinois University, IL	M,W
		King University, TN	M,W	Northern Kentucky University, KY	M,W
Embry-Riddle Aeronautical University–Prescott, AZ	M,W	Kutztown University of Pennsylvania, PA	W	Northwest Christian University, OR	M,W
Emmanuel College, GA	M,W	Lamar University, TX	M,W	Northwestern College, IA	M,W
Evangel University, MO	M,W	La Salle University, PA	M,W	Northwest Missouri State University, MO	W
Fairfield University, CT	M,W	Lawrence Technological University, MI	M,W		
Faulkner University, AL	M,W			Nova Southeastern University, FL	M,W
Felician University, NJ	M	Lee University, TN	M,W	Oakland City University, IN	M,W
Ferris State University, MI	M,W	Lehigh University, PA	M,W	The Ohio State University, OH	M,W
Flagler College, FL	M,W	Le Moyne College, NY	M,W	Ohio University, OH	M,W
Florida Agricultural and Mechanical University, FL	M,W	Lenoir-Rhyne University, NC	M,W	Ohio Valley University, WV	M,W
		Lewis University, IL	M,W	Oklahoma Baptist University, OK	M,W
Florida Atlantic University, FL	M,W	Liberty University, VA	M	Oklahoma Christian University, OK	M,W
Florida Gulf Coast University, FL	M,W	Lincoln University, MO	M,W	Oklahoma City University, OK	M,W
Florida Institute of Technology, FL	M,W	Lindenwood University, MO	M,W	Oklahoma State University, OK	M,W
Florida International University, FL	W	Lindsey Wilson College, KY	M,W	Old Dominion University, VA	M,W
		Lipscomb University, TN	M,W	Olivet Nazarene University, IL	M
Florida Southern College, FL	M,W	Longwood University, VA	M,W	Oral Roberts University, OK	M,W
Florida State University, FL	M,W	Louisiana State University and Agricultural & Mechanical College, LA	M,W	Oregon State University, OR	M,W
Fordham University, NY	M			Our Lady of the Lake University, TX	M
Fort Lewis College, CO	M			Palm Beach Atlantic University, FL	M,W
Francis Marion University, SC	M	Louisiana Tech University, LA	M	Penn State University Park, PA	M,W
Freed-Hardeman University, TN	M,W	Loyola Marymount University, CA	M	Pepperdine University, CA	M,W
Friends University, KS	W	Loyola University Chicago, IL	M,W		

Pittsburg State University, KS	M	Temple University, PA	M	University of Maryland, College Park, MD	M,W
Point Loma Nazarene University, CA	W	Tennessee State University, TN	M	University of Miami, FL	W
Point Park University, PA	M,W	Tennessee Wesleyan University, TN	M,W	University of Michigan, MI	M,W
Prairie View A&M University, TX	M,W	Texas A&M International University, TX	M,W	University of Minnesota, Crookston, MN	M,W
Presbyterian College, SC	M,W	Texas A&M University, TX	M,W	University of Minnesota, Twin Cities Campus, MN	M,W
Purdue University, IN	M,W	Texas A&M University– Commerce, TX	M,W	University of Missouri– Kansas City, MO	M,W
Quinnipiac University, CT	W	Texas A&M University–		University of Missouri–St.	
Radford University, VA	M,W	Corpus Christi, TX	W	Louis, MO	M,W
Regis University, CO	M,W	Texas Christian University, TX	M,W	University of Mobile, AL	M,W
Research College of Nursing, MO	M,W	Texas State University, TX	M,W	University of Montevallo, AL	M,W
Rice University, TX	M	Texas Tech University, TX	M,W	University of Nebraska at	
Robert Morris University, PA	M	Texas Wesleyan University, TX	M,W	Kearney, NE	M,W
Robert Morris University		Thomas University, GA	M	University of Nevada, Las Vegas, NV	M
Illinois, IL	M,W	Tiffin University, OH	M,W	University of Nevada, Reno, NV	M,W
Roberts Wesleyan College, NY	M	Towson University, MD	M,W	University of New Orleans, LA	M
Rockhurst University, MO	M,W	Trevecca Nazarene University, TN	M,W	University of North Alabama, AL	M
Rocky Mountain College, MT	M,W	Trinity Christian College, IL	M	University of North Carolina at	
Rogers State University, OK	M,W	Troy University, AL	M,W	Asheville, NC	W
Rollins College, FL	M,W	Truett McConnell University, GA	M,W	The University of North Carolina	
Sacred Heart University, CT	M,W	Truman State University, MO	W	at Chapel Hill, NC	M,W
Saginaw Valley State University, MI	M	Tulane University, LA	W	The University of North Carolina	
St. Ambrose University, IA	M,W	Tusculum College, TN	M	at Charlotte, NC	M,W
St. Andrews University, NC	M,W	Union College, KY	M,W	The University of North Carolina	
Saint Augustine's		Union University, TN	M	at Greensboro, NC	M,W
University, NC	M	University at Albany, State		The University of North Carolina	
St. Bonaventure University, NY	M	University of New York, NY	W	at Pembroke, NC	W
St. Edward's University, TX	M,W	The University of Akron, OH	M,W	The University of North Carolina	
St. John's University, NY	M,W	The University of Alabama, AL	M,W	Wilmington, NC	M,W
Saint Joseph's University, PA	M	The University of Alabama at		University of Northern Colorado, CO	M,W
Saint Leo University, FL	M,W	Birmingham, AL	M,W	University of Northern Iowa, IA	M,W
Saint Martin's University, WA	M,W	The University of Arizona, AZ	M,W	University of North Florida, FL	M
Saint Mary-of-the-Woods College, IN	W	University of Arkansas, AR	M,W	University of North Georgia, GA	M,W
Saint Peter's University, NJ	M	University of California, Davis, CA	M,W	University of North Texas, TX	M,W
St. Thomas University, FL	M,W	University of California,		University of Notre Dame, IN	M,W
Samford University, AL	M,W	Irvine, CA	M,W	University of Oklahoma, OK	M,W
Sam Houston State University, TX	M,W	University of California, Los		University of Oregon, OR	M,W
San Diego State University, CA	M,W	Angeles, CA	M,W	University of Pikeville, KY	M,W
Santa Clara University, CA	M,W	University of California,		University of Pittsburgh at	
Savannah College of Art and		Riverside, CA	M	Johnstown, PA	M
Design, GA	M,W	University of California, Santa		University of Rhode Island, RI	M
Seattle University, WA	M,W	Barbara, CA	M	University of Richmond, VA	M,W
Seton Hill University, PA	W	University of Central Arkansas, AR	M,W	University of St. Francis, IL	M,W
Shawnee State University, OH	M,W	University of Central Florida, FL	M,W	University of St. Thomas, TX	M,W
Shepherd University, WV	M	University of Central Missouri, MO	M,W	University of San Diego, CA	M
Siena College, NY	M,W	University of Cincinnati, OH	M,W	University of San Francisco, CA	M,W
Simpson University, CA	M,W	University of Colorado Boulder, CO	M,W	University of South Alabama, AL	M,W
South Dakota School of Mines and		University of Colorado Colorado		University of South Carolina, SC	M,W
Technology, SD	M,W	Springs, CO	M,W	University of South Carolina	
Southeastern Louisiana		University of Dayton, OH	M	Aiken, SC	M
University, LA	M	University of Delaware, DE	M,W	The University of South Dakota, SD	W
Southeastern Oklahoma State		University of Denver, CO	M,W	University of Southern	
University, OK	M	University of Detroit Mercy, MI	M,W	California, CA	M,W
Southeastern University, FL	M,W	University of Evansville, IN	M,W	University of Southern Indiana, IN	M,W
Southern Illinois University		The University of Findlay, OH	M,W	University of Southern	
Carbondale, IL	M,W	University of Florida, FL	M	Mississippi, MS	M,W
Southern Illinois University		University of Georgia, GA	M,W	University of South Florida, FL	M,W
Edwardsville, IL	M,W	University of Great Falls, MT	M,W	The University of Tampa, FL	M,W
Southern Methodist University, TX	M,W	University of Hartford, CT	M,W	The University of Tennessee, TN	M,W
Southern New Hampshire		University of Hawaii at Manoa, HI	M,W	The University of Tennessee at	
University, NH	M,W	University of Houston, TX	M,W	Chattanooga, TN	M,W
Southern Utah University, UT	M,W	University of Idaho, ID	M,W	The University of Tennessee at	
Southwest Baptist University, MO	M,W	University of Illinois at		Martin, TN	M
Southwestern College, KS	M,W	Springfield, IL	M,W	The University of Texas at	
Southwestern Oklahoma State		University of Indianapolis, IN	M,W	Austin, TX	M,W
University, OK	M,W	University of Jamestown, ND	M,W	The University of Texas at El	
Spring Hill College, AL	M,W	The University of Kansas, KS	M,W	Paso, TX	M
Stanford University, CA	M,W	University of Kentucky, KY	M,W	The University of Texas at San	
Stephen F. Austin State		University of Louisiana at		Antonio, TX	M,W
University, TX	M,W	Monroe, LA	M,W		
Stephens College, MO	W	University of Louisville, KY	M,W		
Sterling College, KS	M,W				
Tarleton State University, TX	W				
Taylor University, IN	M,W				

The University of Texas of the
Permian Basin, TX — M,W
The University of Texas Rio
Grande Valley, TX — M,W
University of the Incarnate
Word, TX — M,W
University of the Pacific, CA — M
The University of Toledo, OH — M,W
The University of Tulsa, OK — W
University of Utah, UT — M
University of Virginia, VA — M,W
University of Washington, WA — M,W
The University of West Alabama, AL — M,W
University of West Georgia, GA — M,W
University of Wisconsin–
Green Bay, WI — M,W
University of Wisconsin–
Madison, WI — M,W
University of Wisconsin–
Parkside, WI — M
Upper Iowa University, IA — M,W
Ursuline College, OH — W
Utah State University, UT — M
Utah Valley University, UT — M,W
Valdosta State University, GA — M
Valley City State University, ND — M,W
Valparaiso University, IN — M,W
Vanderbilt University, TN — M,W
Virginia Commonwealth
University, VA — M
Virginia Military Institute, VA — M
Virginia Polytechnic Institute
and State University, VA — M
Virginia State University, VA — M,W
Viterbo University, WI — M,W
Wagner College, NY — M,W
Wake Forest University, NC — M,W
Waldorf University, IA — M,W
Washburn University, KS — M
Washington State University, WA — M,W
Wayland Baptist University, TX — M,W
Wayne State University, MI — M,W
Webber International University, FL — M,W
Weber State University, UT — M,W
West Chester University of
Pennsylvania, PA — M,W
Western Carolina University, NC — M,W
Western Illinois University, IL — M
Western Kentucky University, KY — M,W
Western Michigan University, MI — W
Western Washington University, WA — M,W
Westminster College, UT — M,W
West Texas A&M University, TX — M,W
West Virginia University, WV — M
West Virginia University
Institute of Technology, WV — M
West Virginia Wesleyan College, WV — M,W
Wheeling Jesuit University, WV — M,W
Wichita State University, KS — M,W
William Jewell College, MO — M,W
Williams Baptist College, AR — M,W
William Woods University, MO — M,W
Wingate University, NC — M,W
Winona State University, MN — M,W
Winthrop University, SC — M,W
Wofford College, SC — M,W
Wright State University, OH — M
Youngstown State University, OH — M,W

Gymnastics

Alderson Broaddus University, WV — W
Arizona State University at the
Downtown Phoenix campus, AZ — W

Arizona State University at the
Polytechnic campus, AZ — W
Arizona State University at the
Tempe campus, AZ — W
Arizona State University at the
West campus, AZ — W
Auburn University, AL — W
Azusa Pacific University, CA — W
Ball State University, IN — W
Boise State University, ID — W
Bowling Green State University, OH — W
Brigham Young University, UT — W
California State University,
Sacramento, CA — W
Central Michigan University, MI — W
The College of William and Mary,
VA — M,W
Eastern Michigan University, MI — W
Gannon University, PA — W
The George Washington
University, DC — W
Hawai`i Pacific University, HI — W
Iowa State University of Science
and Technology, IA — W
Kent State University, OH — W
King University, TN — M,W
Lindenwood University, MO — W
Louisiana State University and
Agricultural &
Mechanical College, LA — W
Michigan State University, MI — W
North Carolina State University,
NC — W
Northern Illinois University, IL — W
The Ohio State University, OH — M,W
Oregon State University, OR — W
Penn State University Park, PA — M,W
Quinnipiac University, CT — W
Seattle Pacific University, WA — W
Southeast Missouri State
University, MO — W
Southern Connecticut State
University, CT — W
Southern Utah University, UT — W
Stanford University, CA — M,W
Temple University, PA — W
Texas Woman's University, TX — W
Towson University, MD — W
The University of Alabama, AL — W
The University of Arizona, AZ — W
University of Arkansas, AR — W
University of Bridgeport, CT — W
University of California, Davis, CA — W
University of California, Los
Angeles, CA — W
University of California, Santa
Barbara, CA — M,W
University of Denver, CO — W
University of Florida, FL — W
University of Georgia, GA — W
University of Illinois at
Chicago, IL — M,W
University of Kentucky, KY — W
University of Maryland, College
Park, MD — W
University of Michigan, MI — M,W
University of Minnesota, Twin
Cities Campus, MN — M,W
University of New Hampshire, NH — W
The University of North Carolina
at Chapel Hill, NC — W
University of Oklahoma, OK — M,W
University of Pittsburgh, PA — W

University of Utah, UT — W
University of Washington, WA — W
Utah State University, UT — W
West Chester University of
Pennsylvania, PA — W
Western Michigan University, MI — W
West Virginia University, WV — W

Ice hockey

Arizona State University at the
Downtown Phoenix campus, AZ — M
Arizona State University at the
Polytechnic campus, AZ — M
Arizona State University at the
Tempe campus, AZ — M
Arizona State University at the
West campus, AZ — M
Bemidji State University, MN — M,W
Bentley University, MA — M
Boston College, MA — M,W
Boston University, MA — M,W
Bowling Green State University, OH — M
Canisius College, NY — M
Clarkson University, NY — M,W
Colgate University, NY — M,W
College of the Holy Cross, MA — M
The Colorado College, CO — M
Ferris State University, MI — M
Life University, GA — M
Lindenwood University, MO — M,W
Merrimack College, MA — M,W
Miami University, OH — M
Michigan State University, MI — M
Michigan Technological
University, MI — M
Minnesota State University
Mankato, MN — M,W
Niagara University, NY — M
Northeastern University, MA — M,W
The Ohio State University, OH — M,W
Penn State University Park, PA — M,W
Providence College, RI — M,W
Quinnipiac University, CT — M,W
Rensselaer Polytechnic
Institute, NY — M,W
Robert Morris University, PA — M
Sacred Heart University, CT — M
Syracuse University, NY — W
The University of Alabama in
Huntsville, AL — M
University of Alaska Fairbanks, AK — M
University of Denver, CO — M
University of Maine, ME — M,W
University of Massachusetts
Amherst, MA — M
University of Massachusetts
Lowell, MA — M
University of Michigan, MI — M
University of Minnesota, Duluth,
MN — M,W
University of Minnesota, Twin
Cities Campus, MN — M,W
University of New Hampshire, NH — M,W
University of Notre Dame, IN — M
University of Vermont, VT — M,W
University of Wisconsin–
Madison, WI — M,W
Western Michigan University, MI — M

Lacrosse

Adams State University, CO — M,W
Adelphi University, NY — M,W
Alderson Broaddus University, WV — M,W

American University, DC	W	Kutztown University of		Slippery Rock University of	
Aquinas College, MI	M,W	Pennsylvania, PA	W	Pennsylvania, PA	W
Arizona State University at the		Lake Erie College, OH	M,W	Southern Connecticut State	
Downtown Phoenix campus, AZ	W	La Salle University, PA	W	University, CT	W
Arizona State University at the		Lawrence Technological		Southern New Hampshire	
Polytechnic campus, AZ	W	University, MI	M,W	University, NH	M,W
Arizona State University at the		Lees-McRae College, NC	M,W	Stanford University, CA	W
Tempe campus, AZ	W	Lee University, TN	W	Stonehill College, MA	W
Arizona State University at the		Lehigh University, PA	M,W	Stony Brook University, State	
West campus, AZ	W	Le Moyne College, NY	M,W	University of New York, NY	M,W
Asbury University, KY	M,W	Lenoir-Rhyne University, NC	M,W	Syracuse University, NY	M,W
Barton College, NC	W	Liberty University, VA	W	Temple University, PA	W
Bellarmine University, KY	M	Lindenwood University, MO	M,W	Tennessee Wesleyan University, TN	M,W
Belmont Abbey College, NC	M,W	Lock Haven University of		Tiffin University, OH	W
Bethel College, IN	W	Pennsylvania, PA	W	Towson University, MD	M,W
Binghamton University, State		Longwood University, VA	W	Truett McConnell University, GA	W
University of New York, NY	M,W	Loyola University Maryland, MD	M,W	Tusculum College, TN	M,W
Bloomsburg University of		Lynn University, FL	M	Union College, KY	M
Pennsylvania, PA	W	Manhattan College, NY	M,W	University at Albany, State	
Boston College, MA	W	Marist College, NY	M,W	University of New York, NY	M,W
Boston University, MA	M,W	Marquette University, WI	M,W	University of Bridgeport, CT	W
Bucknell University, PA	M,W	Marymount California		University of California, Davis, CA	W
Butler University, IN	W	University, CA	M,W	University of Cincinnati, OH	W
Caldwell University, NJ	W	Maryville University of Saint		University of Colorado Boulder, CO	W
California State University, Fresno, CA	W	Louis, MO	M	University of Colorado	
Canisius College, NY	M,W	McKendree University, IL	W	Colorado Springs, CO	W
Catawba College, NC	M,W	Mercer University, GA	M,W	University of Delaware, DE	M,W
Central Connecticut State		Mercy College, NY	M,W	University of Denver, CO	M,W
University, CT	W	Merrimack College, MA	M,W	University of Detroit Mercy, MI	M,W
Central Michigan University, MI	W	Millersville University of		The University of Findlay, OH	W
Chestnut Hill College, PA	M,W	Pennsylvania, PA	W	University of Florida, FL	W
Chowan University, NC	M,W	Missouri Baptist University, MO	M,W	University of Hartford, CT	M
Clarke University, IA	M,W	Molloy College, NY	M,W	University of Louisville, KY	W
Coastal Carolina University, SC	W	Monmouth University, NJ	M,W	University of Maryland,	
Colgate University, NY	M,W	Mount St. Mary's		Baltimore County, MD	M,W
The College of Saint Rose, NY	M	University, MD	M,W	University of Maryland, College	
College of the Holy Cross, MA	W	Newberry College, SC	W	Park, MD	M,W
The College of William and Mary, VA	W	New York Institute of		University of Massachusetts	
Colorado Mesa University, CO	M,W	Technology, NY	M,W	Amherst, MA	M,W
Concordia University Irvine, CA	M,W	Niagara University, NY	W	University of Massachusetts	
Concordia University, St. Paul, MN	W	The Ohio State University, OH	M,W	Lowell, MA	M,W
Converse College, SC	W	Ohio Valley University, WV	M	University of Michigan, MI	M,W
Davidson College, NC	W	Oklahoma Baptist University, OK	W	University of Michigan–	
Dominican College, NY	M,W	Old Dominion University, VA	W	Dearborn, MI	M
Dominican University of		Penn State University Park, PA	M,W	University of New Hampshire, NH	W
California, CA	M	Presbyterian College, SC	W	University of New Haven, CT	W
Drexel University, PA	M,W	Providence College, RI	M	The University of North Carolina	
Duquesne University, PA	W	Queens College of the City		at Chapel Hill, NC	M,W
East Stroudsburg University of		University of New York, NY	W	University of Notre Dame, IN	M,W
Pennsylvania, PA	W	Quinnipiac University, CT	M,W	University of Oregon, OR	W
Elon University, NC	W	Radford University, VA	W	University of Richmond, VA	M,W
Embry-Riddle Aeronautical		Regis University, CO	W	University of Southern	
University–Daytona, FL	M,W	Robert Morris University, PA	M	California, CA	W
Emmanuel College, GA	M,W	Robert Morris University		The University of Tampa, FL	M,W
Fairfield University, CT	M	Illinois, IL	M,W	University of Vermont, VT	M,W
Florida Institute of Technology, FL	M,W	Roberts Wesleyan College, NY	M,W	University of Virginia, VA	M,W
Florida Southern College, FL	M,W	Rockhurst University, MO	M,W	The University of Virginia's	
Fort Lewis College, CO	W	Sacred Heart University, CT	M,W	College at Wise, VA	W
Gannon University, PA	W	St. Ambrose University, IA	M	Ursuline College, OH	W
Gardner-Webb University, NC	W	St. Andrews University, NC	M,W	Vanderbilt University, TN	W
Georgetown University, DC	M,W	St. Bonaventure University, NY	W	Villanova University, PA	M,W
Georgian Court University, NJ	M,W	St. John's University, NY	M	Virginia Commonwealth	
Hampton University, VA	M	Saint Joseph's University, PA	M,W	University, VA	W
High Point University, NC	M,W	Saint Leo University, FL	M,W	Virginia Military Institute, VA	M
Hofstra University, NY	M,W	San Diego State University, CA	W	Virginia Polytechnic Institute	
Holy Family University, PA	W	Savannah College of Art and		and State University, VA	W
Indiana University of		Design, GA	M,W	Wagner College, NY	M,W
Pennsylvania, PA	W	Seton Hill University, PA	M,W	West Chester University of	
Iona College, NY	W	Shepherd University, WV	W	Pennsylvania, PA	W
Jacksonville University, FL	M,W	Shippensburg University of		Westminster College, UT	M,W
James Madison University, VA	W	Pennsylvania, PA	W	West Virginia Wesleyan College, WV	W
Judson University, IL	M	Siena College, NY	M,W	Wheeling Jesuit University, WV	M,W
Kennesaw State University, GA	W				

Wingate University, NC — M,W
Wofford College, SC — W

Riflery
The Citadel, The Military
  College of South Carolina, SC — M,W
Concordia University, Nebraska, NE — M,W
Emmanuel College, GA — M,W
Georgia Southern University, GA — W
Grand View University, IA — M,W
Hillsdale College, MI — M,W
Jacksonville State University, AL — M,W
Lindenwood University, MO — M,W
Morehead State University, KY — M,W
Murray State University, KY — M,W
North Carolina State University, NC — M,W
Texas Christian University, TX — W
The University of Akron, OH — W
The University of Alabama at
  Birmingham, AL — W
University of Alaska Fairbanks, AK — M,W
University of Kentucky, KY — M,W
University of Nevada, Reno, NV — M,W
University of North Georgia, GA — M,W
The University of Tennessee at
  Martin, TN — M,W
Virginia Military Institute, VA — M,W
West Virginia University, WV — M,W
Wofford College, SC — M,W

Rowing
Boston University, MA — M,W
Embry-Riddle Aeronautical
  University–Daytona, FL — M,W
Gonzaga University, WA — M,W
Indiana University Bloomington, IN — W
Michigan State University, MI — W
Robert Morris University, PA — W
San Diego State University, CA — W
Stanford University, CA — M,W
University of Louisville, KY — W
University of Oklahoma, OK — W
University of Washington, WA — M,W

Rugby
Bethel College, IN — M
Central Washington University, WA — M,W
East Texas Baptist University, TX — M,W
Lee University, TN — M,W
Life University, GA — M,W
Lindenwood University, MO — M,W
Molloy College, NY — W
Quinnipiac University, CT — W
The University of North Carolina
  at Pembroke, NC — M
West Chester University of
  Pennsylvania, PA — W
Wheeling Jesuit University, WV — M

Sailing
Hampton University, VA — M,W

Sand volleyball
Arizona State University at the
  Downtown Phoenix campus, AZ — W
Arizona State University at the
  Polytechnic campus, AZ — W
Arizona State University at the
  Tempe campus, AZ — W
Arizona State University at the
  West campus, AZ — W
Coastal Carolina University, SC — W
Colorado Mesa University, CO — W
Georgia State University, GA — W
Mercer University, GA — W

St. Thomas University, FL — W
Texas Christian University, TX — W
University of Louisiana at
  Monroe, LA — W
The University of Tennessee at
  Martin, TN — W
Webber International University, FL — M,W

Skiing (cross-country)
Bluefield College, VA — M,W
Michigan Technological
  University, MI — M,W
Montana State University, MT — M,W
University of Alaska Fairbanks, AK — M,W
University of Colorado Boulder, CO — M,W
University of Denver, CO — M,W
University of New Hampshire, NH — M,W
University of Utah, UT — M,W
University of Vermont, VT — M,W
University of Wisconsin–
  Green Bay, WI — M,W

Skiing (downhill)
The College of Idaho, ID — M,W
Montana State University, MT — M,W
Rocky Mountain College, MT — M,W
University of Colorado Boulder, CO — M,W
University of Denver, CO — M,W
University of New Hampshire, NH — M,W
University of Utah, UT — M,W
University of Vermont, VT — M,W
Westminster College, UT — M,W

Soccer
Abilene Christian University, TX — W
Academy of Art University, CA — M,W
Adams State University, CO — M,W
Adelphi University, NY — M,W
Alabama State University, AL — W
Alcorn State University, MS — W
Alderson Broaddus University, WV — M,W
American University, DC — M,W
Anderson University, SC — M,W
Angelo State University, TX — W
Appalachian State University, NC — M,W
Aquinas College, MI — M,W
Arizona State University at the
  Downtown Phoenix campus, AZ — W
Arizona State University at the
  Polytechnic campus, AZ — W
Arizona State University at the
  Tempe campus, AZ — W
Arizona State University at the
  West campus, AZ — W
Armstrong State University, GA — W
Asbury University, KY — M,W
Auburn University, AL — W
Auburn University at
  Montgomery, AL — M,W
Augustana University, SD — W
Austin Peay State University, TN — W
Azusa Pacific University, CA — M,W
Baker University, KS — M,W
Ball State University, IN — W
Barry University, FL — M,W
Barton College, NC — M,W
Baylor University, TX — W
Belhaven University, MS — M,W
Bellarmine University, KY — M,W
Belmont Abbey College, NC — M,W
Belmont University, TN — M,W
Bemidji State University, MN — W
Benedictine College, KS — M,W
Bethel College, IN — M,W

Bethel College, KS — M,W
Binghamton University, State
  University of New York, NY — M,W
Biola University, CA — M,W
Bloomfield College, NJ — M,W
Bloomsburg University of
  Pennsylvania, PA — M,W
Bluefield College, VA — M,W
Boise State University, ID — W
Boston College, MA — M,W
Boston University, MA — M,W
Bowling Green State University, OH — M,W
Bradley University, IL — M
Brenau University, GA — W
Brescia University, KY — M,W
Briar Cliff University, IA — M,W
Brigham Young University, UT — W
Bryan College, TN — M,W
Bucknell University, PA — M
Butler University, IN — M,W
Caldwell University, NJ — M,W
California Baptist University, CA — M,W
California Polytechnic State
  University, San Luis Obispo, CA — M,W
California State Polytechnic
  University, Pomona, CA — M,W
California State University,
  Bakersfield, CA — M
California State University,
  Chico, CA — M,W
California State University,
  Dominguez Hills, CA — M,W
California State University,
  Fresno, CA — W
California State University,
  Fullerton, CA — M,W
California State University,
  Long Beach, CA — W
California State University
  Maritime Academy, CA — M
California State University,
  Monterey Bay, CA — M,W
California State University,
  Northridge, CA — M
California State University,
  Sacramento, CA — M,W
California State University, San
  Bernardino, CA — M,W
Calumet College of
  Saint Joseph, IN — M,W
Campbellsville University, KY — M,W
Canisius College, NY — M,W
Cardinal Stritch University, WI — M,W
Carlow University, PA — W
Carroll College, MT — M,W
Carson-Newman University, TN — M,W
Catawba College, NC — M,W
Cedarville University, OH — M,W
Central Connecticut State
  University, CT — M,W
Central Methodist University, MO — M,W
Central Michigan University, MI — W
Central Washington University, WA — W
Chaminade University of
  Honolulu, HI — M,W
Chestnut Hill College, PA — M,W
Chowan University, NC — M,W
Christian Brothers University, TN — M,W
The Citadel, The Military
  College of South Carolina, SC — W
Clarion University of
  Pennsylvania, PA — W
Clarke University, IA — M,W

Clayton State University, GA	M,W	Francis Marion University, SC	M,W	Life University, GA	M,W
Clemson University, SC	M,W	Franklin Pierce University, NH	M,W	Lincoln Christian University, IL	M,W
Cleveland State University, OH	M	Freed-Hardeman University, TN	M,W	Lincoln University, PA	W
Coastal Carolina University, SC	M,W	Fresno Pacific University, CA	M,W	Lindenwood University, MO	M,W
Colgate University, NY	M,W	Friends University, KS	M,W	Lindsey Wilson College, KY	M,W
College of Charleston, SC	M,W	Furman University, SC	M,W	Lipscomb University, TN	M,W
The College of Idaho, ID	M,W	Gannon University, PA	M,W	Lock Haven University of	
College of Saint Mary, NE	W	Gardner-Webb University, NC	M,W	Pennsylvania, PA	M,W
The College of Saint Rose, NY	M,W	Georgetown University, DC	M,W	Longwood University, VA	M,W
College of the Holy Cross, MA	M,W	The George Washington		Louisiana State University and	
The College of William		University, DC	M,W	Agricultural &	
and Mary, VA	M,W	Georgia College & State		Mechanical College, LA	
The Colorado College, CO	W	University, GA	W	Loyola Marymount University, CA	M,W
Colorado Mesa University, CO	M,W	Georgian Court University, NJ	M,W	Loyola University Chicago, IL	M,W
Colorado School of Mines, CO	M,W	Georgia Southern University, GA	M,W	Loyola University Maryland, MD	M,W
Colorado State University, CO	W	Georgia Southwestern State		Lubbock Christian University, TX	M,W
Columbia College, MO	M,W	University, GA	M,W	Lynn University, FL	M,W
Columbia International		Georgia State University, GA	M,W	Lyon College, AR	M,W
University, SC	M,W	Gonzaga University, WA	M,W	Malone University, OH	M,W
Columbus State University, GA	W	Goshen College, IN	M,W	Manhattan College, NY	M,W
Concordia University Irvine, CA	M,W	Graceland University, IA	M,W	Mansfield University of	
Concordia University, Nebraska, NE	M,W	Grand Valley State University, MI	W	Pennsylvania, PA	W
Concordia University, St. Paul, MN	W	Grand View University, IA	M,W	Marist College, NY	M,W
Concord University, WV	M,W	Harding University, AR	M,W	Marquette University, WI	M,W
Converse College, SC	W	Harris-Stowe State University, MO	M,W	Marshall University, WV	M,W
Corban University, OR	M,W	Hartwick College, NY	M	Marymount California	
Cornerstone University, MI	M,W	Hawai`i Pacific University, HI	M,W	University, CA	M,W
Creighton University, NE	M,W	High Point University, NC	M,W	Maryville University of Saint	
Culver-Stockton College, MO	M,W	Hofstra University, NY	M,W	Louis, MO	M,W
Daemen College, NY	M,W	Holy Family University, PA	M,W	The Master's University, CA	M,W
Dallas Baptist University, TX	W	Hope International University, CA	M,W	McKendree University, IL	M,W
Davidson College, NC	M,W	Houston Baptist University, TX	M,W	Mercer University, GA	M,W
Dixie State University, UT	M,W	Humboldt State University, CA	M,W	Mercy College, NY	M,W
Doane University, NE	M,W	Huntington University, IN	M,W	Merrimack College, MA	M,W
Dominican College, NY	M,W	Huston-Tillotson University, TX	M,W	Metropolitan State University of	
Dominican University of		Idaho State University, ID	W	Denver, CO	M,W
California, CA	M,W	Indiana State University, IN	W	Miami University, OH	W
Drake University, IA	M,W	Indiana University Bloomington, IN	M,W	Michigan State University, MI	M,W
Drexel University, PA	M,W	Indiana University of		Michigan Technological	
Drury University, MO	M,W	Pennsylvania, PA	W	University, MI	W
Duquesne University, PA	M,W	Indiana University–Purdue		Millersville University of	
East Carolina University, NC	W	University Indianapolis, IN	M,W	Pennsylvania, PA	M,W
East Central University, OK	W	Inter American University of		Milligan College, TN	M,W
Eastern Illinois University, IL	M,W	Puerto Rico, Guayama Campus, PR	M	Minnesota State University	
Eastern Michigan University, MI	W	Iona College, NY	M,W	Mankato, MN	W
Eastern Oregon University, OR	M,W	Iowa State University of Science		Minnesota State University	
Eastern Washington University, WA	W	and Technology, IA	W	Moorhead, MN	
East Stroudsburg University of		Jackson State University, MS	W	Mississippi State University, MS	W
Pennsylvania, PA	M,W	Jacksonville State University, AL	W	Missouri Baptist University, MO	M,W
Eckerd College, FL	M,W	Jacksonville University, FL	M,W	Missouri State University, MO	M,W
Elon University, NC	M,W	James Madison University, VA	M,W	Missouri University of Science	
Embry-Riddle Aeronautical		John Brown University, AR	M,W	and Technology, MO	M,W
University–Daytona, FL	M,W	John Wesley University, NC	M,W	Missouri Western State	
Embry-Riddle Aeronautical		Judson University, IL	M,W	University, MO	W
University–Prescott, AZ	M,W	Kansas Wesleyan University, KS	M,W	Molloy College, NY	M,W
Emmanuel College, GA	M,W	Kennesaw State University, GA	W	Monmouth University, NJ	M,W
Emporia State University, KS	W	Kent State University, OH	W	Montana State University	
The Evergreen State College, WA	M,W	Kentucky Wesleyan College, KY	M,W	Billings, MT	M,W
Fairfield University, CT	M,W	King University, TN	M,W	Morehead State University, KY	W
Faulkner University, AL	M,W	Kutztown University of		Morningside College, IA	M,W
Felician University, NJ	M,W	Pennsylvania, PA	W	Mount Marty College, SD	M,W
Ferris State University, MI	W	Lake Erie College, OH	M,W	Mount Mercy University, IA	M,W
Flagler College, FL	M,W	Lamar University, TX	W	Mount St. Mary's	
Florida College, FL	M,W	La Salle University, PA	M,W	University, MD	W
Florida Gulf Coast University, FL	M,W	Lawrence Technological		Mount Vernon Nazarene	
Florida Institute of Technology, FL	M,W	University, MI	M,W	University, OH	M,W
Florida International		Lees-McRae College, NC	M,W	Murray State University, KY	W
University, FL	M,W	Lee University, TN	M,W	Newberry College, SC	M,W
Florida National University, FL	M	Lehigh University, PA	M,W	New Mexico Highlands University,	
Florida Southern College, FL	M,W	Le Moyne College, NY	M,W	NM	W
Florida State University, FL	W	Lenoir-Rhyne University, NC	M,W	New Mexico State University, NM	W
Fordham University, NY	M,W	Lewis University, IL	M,W	New York Institute of	
Fort Lewis College, CO	M,W	Liberty University, VA	M,W	Technology, NY	M,W

Niagara University, NY	M,W	San Francisco State University, CA	M,W	University at Albany, State	
North Carolina State University, NC	M,W	Santa Clara University, CA	M,W	University of New York, NY	M,W
Northeastern State University, OK	M,W	Savannah College of Art and		University at Buffalo, the State	
Northeastern University, MA	M,W	Design, GA	M,W	University of New York, NY	M,W
Northern Arizona University, AZ	W	Seattle Pacific University, WA	M,W	The University of Akron, OH	M,W
Northern Illinois University, IL	M,W	Seattle University, WA	M,W	The University of Alabama, AL	W
Northern Kentucky University, KY	M,W	Seton Hill University, PA	M,W	The University of Alabama at	
Northern State University, SD	W	Shawnee State University, OH	M,W	Birmingham, AL	M,W
Northwest Christian University, OR	M,W	Shepherd University, WV	M,W	The University of Alabama in	
Northwestern College, IA	M,W	Shippensburg University of		Huntsville, AL	M,W
Northwestern State University of		Pennsylvania, PA	M,W	The University of Arizona, AZ	W
Louisiana, LA	W	Siena College, NY	M,W	University of Arkansas, AR	W
Northwest Missouri State		Simpson University, CA	M,W	University of Bridgeport, CT	M,W
University, MO	W	Slippery Rock University of		University of California, Davis, CA	M,W
Northwest University, WA	M,W	Pennsylvania, PA	M,W	University of California, Irvine, CA	M,W
Nova Southeastern University, FL	M,W	Soka University of America, CA	M,W	University of California, Los	
Oakland City University, IN	M,W	Sonoma State University, CA	M,W	Angeles, CA	M,W
The Ohio State University, OH	M,W	Southeastern Louisiana		University of California,	
Ohio University, OH	W	University, LA	W	Riverside, CA	M,W
Ohio Valley University, WV	M,W	Southeastern University, FL	M,W	University of California, Santa	
Oklahoma Baptist University, OK	M,W	Southeast Missouri State		Barbara, CA	M,W
Oklahoma Christian University, OK	M,W	University, MO	W	University of Central Arkansas, AR	M,W
Oklahoma City University, OK	M,W	Southern Connecticut State		University of Central Florida, FL	M,W
Oklahoma State University, OK	W	University, CT	M,W	University of Central Missouri, MO	W
Old Dominion University, VA	M,W	Southern Illinois University		University of Cincinnati, OH	M,W
Olivet Nazarene University, IL	M,W	Edwardsville, IL	M,W	University of Colorado Boulder, CO	W
Oral Roberts University, OK	M,W	Southern Methodist University, TX	M,W	University of Colorado Colorado	
Oregon State University, OR	M,W	Southern New Hampshire		Springs, CO	M,W
Ouachita Baptist University, AR	M,W	University, NH	M,W	University of Dayton, OH	M,W
Our Lady of the Lake University, TX	M,W	Southern Oregon University, OR	W	University of Delaware, DE	M,W
Palm Beach Atlantic University, FL	M,W	Southern Utah University, UT	W	University of Denver, CO	M,W
Penn State University Park, PA	M,W	Southwest Baptist University, MO	W	University of Detroit Mercy, MI	M,W
Pepperdine University, CA	W	Southwestern College, KS	M,W	University of Evansville, IN	M,W
Point Loma Nazarene University, CA	M,W	Southwestern Oklahoma State		The University of Findlay, OH	M,W
Point Park University, PA	M,W	University, OK	W	University of Florida, FL	W
Prairie View A&M University, TX	W	Spring Hill College, AL	M,W	University of Georgia, GA	W
Presbyterian College, SC	M,W	Stanford University, CA	M,W	University of Great Falls, MT	M,W
Providence College, RI	M,W	Stephen F. Austin State		University of Hartford, CT	M,W
Purdue University, IN	W	University, TX	W	University of Hawaii at Manoa, HI	W
Queens College of the City		Stephens College, MO	W	University of Houston, TX	W
University of New York, NY	M,W	Sterling College, KS	M,W	University of Idaho, ID	W
Quinnipiac University, CT	M,W	Stonehill College, MA	M,W	University of Illinois at Chicago, IL	M
Radford University, VA	M,W	Stony Brook University, State		University of Illinois at	
Regis University, CO	M,W	University of New York, NY	M,W	Springfield, IL	M,W
Research College of Nursing, MO	M,W	Syracuse University, NY	M,W	University of Indianapolis, IN	M,W
Rice University, TX	W	Taylor University, IN	M,W	University of Jamestown, ND	M,W
Robert Morris University, PA	M,W	Temple University, PA	M,W	The University of Kansas, KS	W
Robert Morris University Illinois, IL	M,W	Tennessee Wesleyan University, TN	M,W	University of Kentucky, KY	M,W
Roberts Wesleyan College, NY	M,W	Texas A&M International		University of Louisiana at	
Rockhurst University, MO	M,W	University, TX	M,W	Monroe, LA	W
Rocky Mountain College, MT	M,W	Texas A&M University, TX	W	University of Louisville, KY	M,W
Rogers State University, OK	M,W	Texas A&M University–		University of Maine, ME	W
Rollins College, FL	M,W	Commerce, TX	W	University of Maryland,	
Sacred Heart University, CT	M,W	Texas A&M University–		Baltimore County, MD	M,W
Saginaw Valley State University, MI	M,W	Corpus Christi, TX	W	University of Maryland, College	
St. Ambrose University, IA	M,W	Texas Christian University, TX	W	Park, MD	M,W
St. Andrews University, NC	M,W	Texas State University, TX	W	University of Massachusetts	
St. Bonaventure University, NY	M,W	Texas Tech University, TX	W	Amherst, MA	M,W
St. Edward's University, TX	M,W	Texas Wesleyan University, TX	M,W	University of Massachusetts	
St. Gregory's University, OK	M,W	Texas Woman's University, TX	W	Lowell, MA	M,W
St. John's University, NY	M,W	Thomas University, GA	M,W	University of Miami, FL	W
Saint Joseph's University, PA	M,W	Tiffin University, OH	M,W	University of Michigan, MI	M,W
Saint Leo University, FL	M,W	Towson University, MD	W	University of Michigan–	
St. Louis College of Pharmacy, MO	M,W	Trevecca Nazarene University, TN	M,W	Dearborn, MI	M
Saint Louis University, MO	M,W	Trinity Christian College, IL	M,W	University of Minnesota,	
Saint Martin's University, WA	W	Troy University, AL	W	Crookston, MN	W
Saint Mary-of-the-Woods College, IN	W	Truett McConnell University, GA	M,W	University of Minnesota, Duluth, MN	W
Saint Peter's University, NJ	M,W	Truman State University, MO	M,W	University of Minnesota, Twin	
St. Thomas Aquinas College, NY	M,W	Tulane University, LA	W	Cities Campus, MN	W
St. Thomas University, FL	M,W	Tusculum College, TN	M,W	University of Missouri–	
Samford University, AL	W	Union College, KY	M,W	Kansas City, MO	M,W
Sam Houston State University, TX	W	Union University, TN	M,W	University of Missouri–St.	
San Diego State University, CA	M,W			Louis, MO	M,W

University of Mobile, AL	M,W
University of Montevallo, AL	M,W
University of Nebraska at Kearney, NE	W
University of Nevada, Las Vegas, NV	M,W
University of Nevada, Reno, NV	W
University of New Hampshire, NH	M,W
University of New Haven, CT	M,W
University of North Alabama, AL	W
University of North Carolina at Asheville, NC	M,W
The University of North Carolina at Chapel Hill, NC	M,W
The University of North Carolina at Charlotte, NC	M,W
The University of North Carolina at Greensboro, NC	M,W
The University of North Carolina at Pembroke, NC	M,W
The University of North Carolina Wilmington, NC	M,W
University of Northern Colorado, CO	W
University of Northern Iowa, IA	W
University of North Florida, FL	M,W
University of North Georgia, GA	M,W
University of North Texas, TX	W
University of Notre Dame, IN	M,W
University of Oklahoma, OK	W
University of Oregon, OR	W
University of Pikeville, KY	M,W
University of Pittsburgh, PA	M,W
University of Pittsburgh at Johnstown, PA	M,W
University of Rhode Island, RI	M,W
University of Richmond, VA	W
University of St. Francis, IL	M,W
University of St. Thomas, TX	M,W
University of San Diego, CA	M,W
University of San Francisco, CA	M,W
University of Science and Arts of Oklahoma, OK	M,W
University of South Alabama, AL	W
University of South Carolina, SC	M,W
University of South Carolina Aiken, SC	M,W
The University of South Dakota, SD	W
University of Southern California, CA	W
University of Southern Indiana, IN	M,W
University of Southern Mississippi, MS	W
University of South Florida, FL	M,W
The University of Tampa, FL	M,W
The University of Tennessee, TN	W
The University of Tennessee at Chattanooga, TN	W
The University of Tennessee at Martin, TN	W
The University of Texas at Austin, TX	W
The University of Texas at San Antonio, TX	W
The University of Texas of the Permian Basin, TX	M,W
University of the Incarnate Word, TX	M,W
University of the Pacific, CA	W
The University of Toledo, OH	W
The University of Tulsa, OK	M,W
University of Utah, UT	W
University of Vermont, VT	M,W
University of Virginia, VA	M,W
University of Washington, WA	M,W

The University of West Alabama, AL	M,W
University of West Georgia, GA	W
University of Wisconsin–Green Bay, WI	M,W
University of Wisconsin–Madison, WI	M,W
University of Wisconsin–Milwaukee, WI	M,W
University of Wisconsin–Parkside, WI	M,W
Upper Iowa University, IA	M,W
Ursuline College, OH	W
Utah State University, UT	W
Utah Valley University, UT	W
Valdosta State University, GA	W
Valparaiso University, IN	M,W
Vanderbilt University, TN	W
Villanova University, PA	M,W
Virginia Commonwealth University, VA	M,W
Virginia Military Institute, VA	M
Virginia Polytechnic Institute and State University, VA	M,W
Viterbo University, WI	M,W
Wagner College, NY	W
Wake Forest University, NC	M,W
Waldorf University, IA	M,W
Washburn University, KS	W
Washington State University, WA	W
Wayland Baptist University, TX	M,W
Wayne State College, NE	W
Webber International University, FL	M,W
Weber State University, UT	W
West Chester University of Pennsylvania, PA	M,W
Western Carolina University, NC	W
Western Illinois University, IL	M,W
Western Michigan University, MI	M,W
Western Oregon University, OR	W
Western State Colorado University, CO	W
Western Washington University, WA	M,W
Westminster College, UT	M,W
Westmont College, CA	M,W
West Texas A&M University, TX	M,W
West Virginia University, WV	M,W
West Virginia University Institute of Technology, WV	M,W
West Virginia Wesleyan College, WV	M,W
Wheeling Jesuit University, WV	M,W
William Jewell College, MO	M,W
Williams Baptist College, AR	M,W
William Woods University, MO	M,W
Wingate University, NC	M,W
Winona State University, MN	W
Winthrop University, SC	M,W
Wofford College, SC	M,W
Wright State University, OH	M,W
Youngstown State University, OH	W

Softball

Abilene Christian University, TX	W
Academy of Art University, CA	W
Adams State University, CO	W
Adelphi University, NY	W
Alabama State University, AL	W
Alcorn State University, MS	M
Alderson Broaddus University, WV	W
Anderson University, SC	W
Angelo State University, TX	W
Appalachian State University, NC	W
Aquinas College, MI	W
Arizona State University at the Downtown Phoenix campus, AZ	W

Arizona State University at the Polytechnic campus, AZ	W
Arizona State University at the Tempe campus, AZ	W
Arizona State University at the West campus, AZ	W
Arkansas Tech University, AR	W
Armstrong State University, GA	W
Asbury University, KY	W
Auburn University, AL	W
Auburn University at Montgomery, AL	W
Augustana University, SD	W
Augusta University, GA	W
Austin Peay State University, TN	W
Azusa Pacific University, CA	W
Baker University, KS	W
Ball State University, IN	W
Barry University, FL	W
Barton College, NC	W
Baylor University, TX	W
Belhaven University, MS	W
Bellarmine University, KY	W
Belmont Abbey College, NC	W
Belmont University, TN	W
Bemidji State University, MN	W
Benedictine College, KS	W
Bethel College, IN	W
Bethune-Cookman University, FL	W
Binghamton University, State University of New York, NY	W
Biola University, CA	W
Bloomfield College, NJ	W
Bloomsburg University of Pennsylvania, PA	W
Bluefield College, VA	W
Bluefield State College, WV	W
Blue Mountain College, MS	W
Boise State University, ID	W
Boston College, MA	W
Boston University, MA	W
Bowling Green State University, OH	W
Bradley University, IL	W
Brenau University, GA	W
Brescia University, KY	W
Briar Cliff University, IA	W
Brigham Young University, UT	W
Bryan College, TN	W
Bucknell University, PA	W
Butler University, IN	W
Caldwell University, NJ	W
California Baptist University, CA	W
California Polytechnic State University, San Luis Obispo, CA	W
California State University, Bakersfield, CA	W
California State University, Chico, CA	W
California State University, Dominguez Hills, CA	W
California State University, Fresno, CA	W
California State University, Fullerton, CA	W
California State University, Long Beach, CA	W
California State University, Monterey Bay, CA	W
California State University, Northridge, CA	W
California State University, Sacramento, CA	W
California State University, San Bernardino, CA	W

Calumet College of Saint Joseph, IN	W
Cameron University, OK	W
Campbellsville University, KY	W
Canisius College, NY	W
Cardinal Stritch University, WI	W
Carlow University, PA	W
Carroll College, MT	W
Carson-Newman University, TN	W
Catawba College, NC	W
Cedarville University, OH	W
Central Connecticut State University, CT	W
Central Methodist University, MO	W
Central Michigan University, MI	W
Central Washington University, WA	W
Chaminade University of Honolulu, HI	W
Chestnut Hill College, PA	W
Chowan University, NC	W
Christian Brothers University, TN	W
Clarion University of Pennsylvania, PA	W
Clark Atlanta University, GA	W
Clarke University, IA	W
Cleveland State University, OH	W
Coastal Carolina University, SC	W
Colgate University, NY	W
College of Charleston, SC	W
College of Coastal Georgia, GA	W
The College of Idaho, ID	W
College of Saint Mary, NE	W
The College of Saint Rose, NY	W
College of the Holy Cross, MA	W
Colorado Mesa University, CO	W
Colorado School of Mines, CO	W
Colorado State University, CO	W
Columbia College, MO	W
Columbus State University, GA	W
Concordia University Irvine, CA	W
Concordia University, Nebraska, NE	W
Concordia University, St. Paul, MN	W
Concord University, WV	W
Corban University, OR	W
Cornerstone University, MI	W
Creighton University, NE	W
Culver-Stockton College, MO	W
Dakota State University, SD	W
Dickinson State University, ND	W
Dixie State University, UT	W
Doane University, NE	W
Dominican College, NY	W
Dominican University of California, CA	W
Drake University, IA	W
Drexel University, PA	W
Drury University, MO	W
East Carolina University, NC	W
East Central University, OK	W
Eastern Illinois University, IL	W
Eastern Michigan University, MI	W
Eastern Oregon University, OR	W
East Stroudsburg University of Pennsylvania, PA	W
Eckerd College, FL	W
Elizabeth City State University, NC	W
Elon University, NC	M,W
Embry-Riddle Aeronautical University–Daytona, FL	W
Embry-Riddle Aeronautical University–Prescott, AZ	W
Emmanuel College, GA	W
Emporia State University, KS	W
Evangel University, MO	W
Fairfield University, CT	W
Faulkner University, AL	W
Felician University, NJ	W
Ferris State University, MI	W
Flagler College, FL	W
Florida Agricultural and Mechanical University, FL	W
Florida Atlantic University, FL	W
Florida Gulf Coast University, FL	W
Florida Institute of Technology, FL	W
Florida International University, FL	W
Florida Southern College, FL	W
Florida State University, FL	W
Fordham University, NY	W
Fort Lewis College, CO	W
Francis Marion University, SC	W
Franklin Pierce University, NH	W
Freed-Hardeman University, TN	W
Friends University, KS	W
Furman University, SC	W
Gannon University, PA	W
Gardner-Webb University, NC	W
Georgetown University, DC	W
Georgia College & State University, GA	W
Georgia Institute of Technology, GA	W
Georgian Court University, NJ	W
Georgia Southern University, GA	W
Georgia Southwestern State University, GA	W
Georgia State University, GA	W
Goshen College, IN	W
Graceland University, IA	W
Grambling State University, LA	W
Grand Valley State University, MI	W
Grand View University, IA	W
Hampton University, VA	W
Harding University, AR	W
Harris-Stowe State University, MO	W
Hawai`i Pacific University, HI	W
Hillsdale College, MI	W
Hofstra University, NY	W
Holy Family University, PA	W
Hope International University, CA	W
Houston Baptist University, TX	W
Humboldt State University, CA	W
Huntington University, IN	W
Huston-Tillotson University, TX	W
Idaho State University, ID	W
Indiana State University, IN	W
Indiana University Bloomington, IN	W
Indiana University of Pennsylvania, PA	W
Indiana University–Purdue University Indianapolis, IN	W
Inter American University of Puerto Rico, Bayamón Campus, PR	M,W
Inter American University of Puerto Rico, Guayama Campus, PR	M,W
Iona College, NY	W
Iowa State University of Science and Technology, IA	W
Jackson State University, MS	W
Jacksonville State University, AL	W
Jacksonville University, FL	W
James Madison University, VA	W
Johnson C. Smith University, NC	W
John Wesley University, NC	W
Judson University, IL	W
Kansas Wesleyan University, KS	W
Kennesaw State University, GA	W
Kent State University, OH	W
Kentucky State University, KY	W
Kentucky Wesleyan College, KY	W
King University, TN	W
Kutztown University of Pennsylvania, PA	W
Lake Erie College, OH	W
Lane College, TN	W
La Salle University, PA	W
Lees-McRae College, NC	W
Lee University, TN	W
Lehigh University, PA	W
Le Moyne College, NY	W
Lenoir-Rhyne University, NC	W
Lewis University, IL	W
Liberty University, VA	W
Lincoln University, MO	W
Lincoln University, PA	W
Lindenwood University, MO	W
Lindsey Wilson College, KY	W
Lipscomb University, TN	W
Lock Haven University of Pennsylvania, PA	W
Longwood University, VA	W
Louisiana State University and Agricultural & Mechanical College, LA	W
Louisiana Tech University, LA	W
Loyola Marymount University, CA	W
Loyola University Chicago, IL	W
Lubbock Christian University, TX	W
Lynn University, FL	W
Lyon College, AR	W
Malone University, OH	W
Manhattan College, NY	W
Mansfield University of Pennsylvania, PA	W
Marist College, NY	W
Marshall University, WV	W
Maryville University of Saint Louis, MO	W
McKendree University, IL	W
Mercer University, GA	W
Mercy College, NY	W
Merrimack College, MA	W
Metropolitan State University of Denver, CO	W
Miami University, OH	W
Michigan State University, MI	W
Midland College, TX	W
Millersville University of Pennsylvania, PA	W
Milligan College, TN	W
Minnesota State University Mankato, MN	W
Minnesota State University Moorhead, MN	W
Minot State University, ND	W
Mississippi State University, MS	W
Missouri Baptist University, MO	W
Missouri State University, MO	W
Missouri University of Science and Technology, MO	W
Missouri Western State University, MO	W
Molloy College, NY	W
Monmouth University, NJ	W
Morehead State University, KY	W
Morningside College, IA	W
Mount Marty College, SD	W
Mount Mercy University, IA	W

Mount St. Mary's University, MD	W
Mount Vernon Nazarene University, OH	W
Murray State University, KY	W
Newberry College, SC	W
New Mexico Highlands University, NM	W
New Mexico State University, NM	W
New York Institute of Technology, NY	W
Niagara University, NY	W
North Carolina State University, NC	W
Northeastern State University, OK	W
Northern Illinois University, IL	W
Northern Kentucky University, KY	W
Northern State University, SD	W
Northwest Christian University, OR	W
Northwestern College, IA	W
Northwestern State University of Louisiana, LA	W
Northwest Missouri State University, MO	W
Northwest University, WA	W
Nova Southeastern University, FL	W
Oakland City University, IN	W
The Ohio State University, OH	W
Ohio University, OH	W
Ohio Valley University, WV	W
Oklahoma Baptist University, OK	W
Oklahoma Christian University, OK	W
Oklahoma City University, OK	W
Oklahoma State University, OK	W
Olivet Nazarene University, IL	W
Oregon State University, OR	W
Ouachita Baptist University, AR	W
Our Lady of the Lake University, TX	W
Palm Beach Atlantic University, FL	W
Penn State Hazleton, PA	W
Penn State University Park, PA	W
Pittsburg State University, KS	W
Point Park University, PA	W
Prairie View A&M University, TX	W
Presbyterian College, SC	W
Providence College, RI	W
Purdue University, IN	W
Queens College of the City University of New York, NY	W
Quinnipiac University, CT	W
Radford University, VA	W
Regis University, CO	W
Research College of Nursing, MO	W
Robert Morris University, PA	W
Robert Morris University Illinois, IL	
Rockhurst University, MO	W
Rogers State University, OK	W
Rollins College, FL	W
Sacred Heart University, CT	W
Saginaw Valley State University, MI	W
St. Ambrose University, IA	W
St. Andrews University, NC	W
Saint Augustine's University, NC	W
St. Bonaventure University, NY	W
St. Edward's University, TX	W
St. Gregory's University, OK	W
St. John's University, NY	W
Saint Joseph's University, PA	W
Saint Leo University, FL	W
St. Louis College of Pharmacy, MO	W
Saint Louis University, MO	W
Saint Martin's University, WA	W
Saint Mary-of-the-Woods College, IN	W
St. Petersburg College, FL	W

Saint Peter's University, NJ	W
St. Thomas Aquinas College, NY	W
St. Thomas University, FL	W
Samford University, AL	W
Sam Houston State University, TX	W
San Diego State University, CA	W
San Francisco State University, CA	W
Santa Clara University, CA	W
Seattle University, WA	W
Seton Hill University, PA	W
Shawnee State University, OH	W
Shepherd University, WV	W
Shippensburg University of Pennsylvania, PA	W
Siena College, NY	W
Simpson University, CA	W
Slippery Rock University of Pennsylvania, PA	W
Sonoma State University, CA	W
Southeastern Louisiana University, LA	W
Southeastern Oklahoma State University, OK	W
Southeastern University, FL	W
Southeast Missouri State University, MO	W
Southern Arkansas University–Magnolia, AR	W
Southern Connecticut State University, CT	W
Southern Illinois University Carbondale, IL	W
Southern Illinois University Edwardsville, IL	W
Southern New Hampshire University, NH	W
Southern Oregon University, OR	W
Southern Utah University, UT	W
Southwest Baptist University, MO	W
Southwestern College, KS	W
Southwestern Oklahoma State University, OK	W
Spring Hill College, AL	W
Stanford University, CA	W
Stephen F. Austin State University, TX	W
Stephens College, MO	W
Sterling College, KS	W
Stonehill College, MA	W
Stony Brook University, State University of New York, NY	W
Syracuse University, NY	W
Tarleton State University, TX	W
Taylor University, IN	W
Tennessee Wesleyan University, TN	W
Texas A&M International University, TX	W
Texas A&M University, TX	W
Texas A&M University–Corpus Christi, TX	W
Texas State University, TX	W
Texas Tech University, TX	W
Texas Wesleyan University, TX	W
Texas Woman's University, TX	W
Thomas University, GA	W
Tiffin University, OH	W
Towson University, MD	W
Trevecca Nazarene University, TN	W
Trinity Christian College, IL	W
Troy University, AL	W
Truett McConnell University, GA	W
Truman State University, MO	W
Tusculum College, TN	W

Union College, KY	W
Union University, TN	W
University at Albany, State University of New York, NY	W
University at Buffalo, the State University of New York, NY	W
The University of Akron, OH	W
The University of Alabama, AL	W
The University of Alabama at Birmingham, AL	W
The University of Alabama in Huntsville, AL	W
The University of Arizona, AZ	W
University of Arkansas, AR	W
University of Bridgeport, CT	W
University of California, Davis, CA	W
University of California, Los Angeles, CA	W
University of California, Riverside, CA	W
University of California, Santa Barbara, CA	W
University of Central Arkansas, AR	W
University of Central Florida, FL	W
University of Central Missouri, MO	W
University of Colorado Colorado Springs, CO	W
University of Dayton, OH	W
University of Delaware, DE	W
University of Detroit Mercy, MI	W
University of Evansville, IN	W
The University of Findlay, OH	W
University of Florida, FL	W
University of Georgia, GA	W
University of Hartford, CT	W
University of Hawaii at Manoa, HI	W
University of Houston, TX	W
University of Illinois at Chicago, IL	W
University of Illinois at Springfield, IL	W
University of Indianapolis, IN	W
University of Jamestown, ND	W
The University of Kansas, KS	W
University of Kentucky, KY	W
University of Louisiana at Monroe, LA	W
University of Louisville, KY	W
University of Maine, ME	W
University of Maryland, Baltimore County, MD	W
University of Maryland, College Park, MD	W
University of Massachusetts Amherst, MA	W
University of Massachusetts Lowell, MA	W
University of Michigan, MI	W
University of Michigan–Dearborn, MI	W
University of Minnesota, Crookston, MN	W
University of Minnesota, Duluth, MN	W
University of Minnesota, Twin Cities Campus, MN	W
University of Missouri–Kansas City, MO	W
University of Missouri–St. Louis, MO	W
University of Mobile, AL	W
University of Nebraska at Kearney, NE	W
University of Nevada, Las Vegas, NV	W

University of Nevada, Reno, NV	W
University of New Haven, CT	W
University of North Alabama, AL	W
The University of North Carolina at Chapel Hill, NC	W
The University of North Carolina at Charlotte, NC	W
The University of North Carolina at Greensboro, NC	W
The University of North Carolina at Pembroke, NC	W
The University of North Carolina Wilmington, NC	W
University of Northern Colorado, CO	W
University of Northern Iowa, IA	W
University of North Florida, FL	W
University of North Georgia, GA	W
University of North Texas, TX	W
University of Notre Dame, IN	W
University of Oklahoma, OK	W
University of Oregon, OR	W
University of Pikeville, KY	W
University of Pittsburgh, PA	W
University of Pittsburgh at Johnstown, PA	W
University of Rhode Island, RI	W
University of St. Francis, IL	W
University of San Diego, CA	W
University of Science and Arts of Oklahoma, OK	W
University of South Alabama, AL	W
University of South Carolina, SC	W
University of South Carolina Aiken, SC	W
The University of South Dakota, SD	W
University of Southern Indiana, IN	W
University of Southern Mississippi, MS	W
University of South Florida, FL	W
The University of Tampa, FL	W
The University of Tennessee, TN	W
The University of Tennessee at Chattanooga, TN	W
The University of Tennessee at Martin, TN	W
The University of Texas at Austin, TX	W
The University of Texas at San Antonio, TX	W
The University of Texas of the Permian Basin, TX	W
University of the Incarnate Word, TX	W
University of the Pacific, CA	W
The University of Toledo, OH	W
The University of Tulsa, OK	W
University of Utah, UT	W
University of Virginia, VA	W
The University of Virginia's College at Wise, VA	W
University of Washington, WA	W
The University of West Alabama, AL	W
University of West Georgia, GA	W
University of Wisconsin–Green Bay, WI	W
University of Wisconsin–Madison, WI	W
University of Wisconsin–Parkside, WI	W
Upper Iowa University, IA	W
Ursuline College, OH	W
Utah State University, UT	W
Utah Valley University, UT	W
Valdosta State University, GA	W
Valley City State University, ND	W
Valparaiso University, IN	W

Villanova University, PA	W
Virginia State University, VA	W
Viterbo University, WI	W
Wagner College, NY	W
Waldorf University, IA	W
Washburn University, KS	W
Wayne State College, NE	W
Wayne State University, MI	W
Webber International University, FL	W
Weber State University, UT	W
West Chester University of Pennsylvania, PA	W
Western Carolina University, NC	W
Western Illinois University, IL	W
Western Kentucky University, KY	W
Western Michigan University, MI	W
Western Oregon University, OR	W
Western Washington University, WA	W
West Texas A&M University, TX	W
West Virginia University Institute of Technology, WV	W
West Virginia Wesleyan College, WV	W
Wheeling Jesuit University, WV	W
Wichita State University, KS	W
William Jewell College, MO	W
Williams Baptist College, AR	W
William Woods University, MO	W
Wingate University, NC	W
Winona State University, MN	W
Winthrop University, SC	W
Wright State University, OH	W
Youngstown State University, OH	W

Squash

Drexel University, PA	M,W
Fordham University, NY	M
Stanford University, CA	W
University of Great Falls, MT	W
University of Rochester, NY	M

Swimming and diving

Adams State University, CO	M,W
Adelphi University, NY	M,W
Alderson Broaddus University, WV	M,W
Arizona State University at the Downtown Phoenix campus, AZ	M,W
Arizona State University at the Polytechnic campus, AZ	M,W
Arizona State University at the Tempe campus, AZ	M,W
Arizona State University at the West campus, AZ	M,W
Asbury University, KY	M,W
Auburn University, AL	M,W
Augustana University, SD	W
Azusa Pacific University, CA	W
Ball State University, IN	M,W
Barton College, NC	M,W
Bellarmine University, KY	M,W
Binghamton University, State University of New York, NY	M,W
Biola University, CA	M,W
Bloomsburg University of Pennsylvania, PA	M,W
Boise State University, ID	W
Boston College, MA	M,W
Boston University, MA	M,W
Bowling Green State University, OH	W
Brenau University, GA	W
Brigham Young University, UT	M,W
Bucknell University, PA	M
California Baptist University, CA	M,W

California Polytechnic State University, San Luis Obispo, CA	M,W
California State University, Bakersfield, CA	M,W
California State University, Fresno, CA	W
California State University, Northridge, CA	M,W
Campbellsville University, KY	M,W
Canisius College, NY	M,W
Carson-Newman University, TN	M,W
Catawba College, NC	M,W
Central Connecticut State University, CT	W
Chowan University, NC	W
Clarion University of Pennsylvania, PA	M,W
Cleveland State University, OH	M,W
The College of Idaho, ID	M,W
College of Saint Mary, NE	W
The College of Saint Rose, NY	M,W
College of the Holy Cross, MA	W
Colorado Mesa University, CO	M,W
Colorado School of Mines, CO	M,W
Colorado State University, CO	W
Concordia University Irvine, CA	M,W
Converse College, SC	W
Davidson College, NC	M,W
Drexel University, PA	M,W
Drury University, MO	M,W
Duquesne University, PA	W
East Carolina University, NC	M,W
Eastern Illinois University, IL	M,W
Eastern Michigan University, MI	M,W
East Stroudsburg University of Pennsylvania, PA	W
Emmanuel College, GA	M,W
Fairfield University, CT	M,W
Florida Agricultural and Mechanical University, FL	M,W
Florida Gulf Coast University, FL	W
Florida Institute of Technology, FL	M,W
Florida International University, FL	W
Florida Southern College, FL	M,W
Florida State University, FL	M,W
Fordham University, NY	M,W
Fresno Pacific University, CA	M,W
Gannon University, PA	M,W
Gardner-Webb University, NC	M,W
Georgetown University, DC	W
The George Washington University, DC	M,W
Georgia Institute of Technology, GA	M,W
Georgia Southern University, GA	W
Grand Valley State University, MI	M,W
Hillsdale College, MI	W
Indiana State University, IN	W
Indiana University Bloomington, IN	M,W
Indiana University of Pennsylvania, PA	M,W
Indiana University–Purdue University Indianapolis, IN	M,W
Inter American University of Puerto Rico, Bayamón Campus, PR	M,W
Iona College, NY	M,W
Iowa State University of Science and Technology, IA	M,W
James Madison University, VA	W
King University, TN	M,W
Kutztown University of Pennsylvania, PA	W

La Salle University, PA	M,W	Seattle University, WA	M,W	University of North Florida, FL	W
Lehigh University, PA	M,W	Shippensburg University of		University of North Texas, TX	W
Le Moyne College, NY	M,W	Pennsylvania, PA	M,W	University of Notre Dame, IN	M,W
Lenoir-Rhyne University, NC	M,W	Siena College, NY	W	University of Pittsburgh, PA	M,W
Lewis University, IL	M,W	Soka University of America, CA	M,W	University of Rhode Island, RI	W
Liberty University, VA	W	Southern Connecticut State		University of Richmond, VA	W
Life University, GA	W	University, CT	M,W	University of San Diego, CA	W
Lindenwood University, MO	M,W	Southern Illinois University		University of South Carolina, SC	M,W
Lindsey Wilson College, KY	M,W	Carbondale, IL	M,W	The University of South Dakota, SD	M,W
Lock Haven University of		Southern Methodist University, TX	M,W	University of Southern	
Pennsylvania, PA	W	Stanford University, CA	M,W	California, CA	M,W
Louisiana State University and		Stony Brook University, State		The University of Tampa, FL	M,W
Agricultural &		University of New York, NY	W	The University of Tennessee, TN	M,W
Mechanical College, LA	M,W	Texas A&M University, TX	M,W	The University of Texas at	
Loyola Marymount University, CA	W	Texas Christian University, TX	M,W	Austin, TX	M,W
Loyola University Maryland, MD	M,W	Tiffin University, OH	M,W	The University of Texas of the	
Loyola University New Orleans, LA	M,W	Towson University, MD	M,W	Permian Basin, TX	M,W
Lynn University, FL	W	Truman State University, MO	W	University of the Incarnate	
Malone University, OH	M,W	Tulane University, LA	W	Word, TX	M,W
Manhattan College, NY	M,W	Union College, KY	M,W	University of the Pacific, CA	M,W
Marist College, NY	M,W	University at Buffalo, the State		The University of Toledo, OH	W
Marshall University, WV	W	University of New York, NY	M,W	University of Utah, UT	M,W
Maryville University of Saint		The University of Akron, OH	W	University of Vermont, VT	W
Louis, MO	M,W	The University of Alabama, AL	M,W	University of Virginia, VA	M,W
McKendree University, IL	M,W	University of Alaska Fairbanks, AK	W	University of Wisconsin–	
Merrimack College, MA	W	The University of Arizona, AZ	M,W	Green Bay, WI	M,W
Miami University, OH	M,W	University of Arkansas, AR	W	University of Wisconsin–	
Michigan State University, MI	M,W	University of Bridgeport, CT	M,W	Madison, WI	M,W
Millersville University of		University of California, Davis, CA	W	University of Wisconsin–	
Pennsylvania, PA	W	University of California, Los		Milwaukee, WI	M,W
Milligan College, TN	M,W	Angeles, CA	W	Ursuline College, OH	W
Minnesota State University		University of California, Santa		Valparaiso University, IN	M,W
Mankato, MN	W	Barbara, CA	M,W	Vanderbilt University, TN	W
Minnesota State University		University of Cincinnati, OH	M,W	Villanova University, PA	W
Moorhead, MN	W	University of Delaware, DE	W	Virginia Military Institute, VA	M
Missouri State University, MO	M,W	University of Denver, CO	M,W	Virginia Polytechnic Institute	
Missouri University of Science		University of Evansville, IN	M,W	and State University, VA	M,W
and Technology, MO	M	The University of Findlay, OH	M,W	Wagner College, NY	W
Morningside College, IA	M,W	University of Florida, FL	M,W	Washington State University, WA	W
Mount St. Mary's		University of Georgia, GA	M,W	Wayne State University, MI	M,W
University, MD	M,W	University of Hawaii at Manoa, HI	M,W	West Chester University of	
New Mexico State University, NM	W	University of Houston, TX	W	Pennsylvania, PA	M,W
Niagara University, NY	M,W	University of Idaho, ID	W	Western Illinois University, IL	M,W
North Carolina State University,		University of Illinois at		Western State Colorado	
NC	M,W	Chicago, IL	M,W	University, CO	W
Northeastern University, MA	W	University of Indianapolis, IN	M,W	West Virginia University, WV	M,W
Northern Arizona University, AZ	W	The University of Kansas, KS	W	West Virginia University	
Northern Illinois University, IL	M,W	University of Kentucky, KY	M,W	Institute of Technology, WV	M,W
Northern State University, SD	W	University of Louisville, KY	M,W	West Virginia Wesleyan College, WV	M,W
Nova Southeastern University, FL	M,W	University of Maine, ME	W	Wheeling Jesuit University, WV	M,W
The Ohio State University, OH	M,W	University of Maryland,		William Jewell College, MO	M,W
Ohio University, OH	W	Baltimore County, MD	M,W	Williams Baptist College, AR	M,W
Oklahoma Baptist University, OK	M,W	University of Massachusetts		Wingate University, NC	M,W
Oklahoma Christian University, OK	M,W	Amherst, MA	M,W	Wright State University, OH	M,W
Old Dominion University, VA	M,W	University of Miami, FL	M,W	Youngstown State University, OH	W
Oregon State University, OR	W	University of Michigan, MI	M,W		
Ouachita Baptist University, AR	M,W	University of Minnesota, Twin		**Table tennis**	
Penn State University Park, PA	M,W	Cities Campus, MN	M,W	Inter American University of	
Pepperdine University, CA	W	University of Missouri–St.		Puerto Rico, Bayamón	
Purdue University, IN	W	Louis, MO	M,W	Campus, PR	M,W
Queens College of the City		University of Nebraska at		Lindenwood University, MO	M,W
University of New York, NY	M,W	Kearney, NE	W	Texas Wesleyan University, TX	M,W
Rice University, TX	W	University of Nevada, Las Vegas, NV	M,W		
Roberts Wesleyan College, NY	M,W	University of Nevada, Reno, NV	W	**Tennis**	
Sacred Heart University, CT	W	University of New Hampshire, NH	W	Abilene Christian University, TX	M,W
Saginaw Valley State University, MI	M,W	University of North Carolina at		Academy of Art University, CA	W
St. Bonaventure University, NY	M,W	Asheville, NC		Adelphi University, NY	M,W
Saint Leo University, FL	M,W	The University of North Carolina		Alabama State University, AL	M,W
Saint Louis University, MO	M,W	at Chapel Hill, NC	M,W	Alcorn State University, MS	M,W
Saint Peter's University, NJ	M,W	The University of North Carolina		Alderson Broaddus University, WV	W
San Diego State University, CA	W	Wilmington, NC	M,W	Anderson University, SC	M,W
Savannah College of Art and		University of Northern Colorado, CO	W	Appalachian State University, NC	M,W
Design, GA	M,W	University of Northern Iowa, IA	W	Aquinas College, MI	M,W

Arizona State University at the Downtown Phoenix campus, AZ	M,W
Arizona State University at the Polytechnic campus, AZ	M,W
Arizona State University at the Tempe campus, AZ	M,W
Arizona State University at the West campus, AZ	M,W
Arkansas Tech University, AR	W
Armstrong State University, GA	M,W
Asbury University, KY	M,W
Auburn University, AL	M,W
Auburn University at Montgomery, AL	M,W
Augustana University, SD	M,W
Augusta University, GA	M,W
Austin Peay State University, TN	M,W
Azusa Pacific University, CA	M,W
Baker University, KS	M,W
Ball State University, IN	M,W
Barry University, FL	M,W
Barton College, NC	M,W
Baylor University, TX	M,W
Belhaven University, MS	M,W
Bellarmine University, KY	M,W
Belmont Abbey College, NC	M,W
Belmont University, TN	M,W
Bemidji State University, MN	W
Bethel College, IN	M,W
Bethel College, KS	M,W
Bethune-Cookman University, FL	M,W
Binghamton University, State University of New York, NY	M,W
Biola University, CA	M,W
Bloomfield College, NJ	M
Bloomsburg University of Pennsylvania, PA	M,W
Bluefield College, VA	M,W
Bluefield State College, WV	M,W
Boise State University, ID	M,W
Boston College, MA	M,W
Boston University, MA	W
Bowling Green State University, OH	W
Bradley University, IL	W
Brenau University, GA	W
Briar Cliff University, IA	M,W
Brigham Young University, UT	M,W
Butler University, IN	M,W
Caldwell University, NJ	M,W
California Polytechnic State University, San Luis Obispo, CA	M,W
California State University, Bakersfield, CA	W
California State University, Fresno, CA	M,W
California State University, Fullerton, CA	W
California State University, Long Beach, CA	W
California State University, Northridge, CA	W
California State University, Sacramento, CA	M,W
Calumet College of Saint Joseph, IN	M,W
Cameron University, OK	M,W
Campbellsville University, KY	M,W
Cardinal Stritch University, WI	M,W
Carlow University, PA	W
Carson-Newman University, TN	M,W
Catawba College, NC	M,W
Cedarville University, OH	M,W
Chaminade University of Honolulu, HI	W

Chestnut Hill College, PA	M,W
Chowan University, NC	M,W
Christian Brothers University, TN	M,W
The Citadel, The Military College of South Carolina, SC	M
Clarion University of Pennsylvania, PA	W
Clark Atlanta University, GA	W
Clayton State University, GA	W
Clemson University, SC	M,W
Cleveland State University, OH	W
Coastal Carolina University, SC	M,W
College of Charleston, SC	M,W
College of Coastal Georgia, GA	M,W
The College of Idaho, ID	W
College of Saint Mary, NE	W
The College of Saint Rose, NY	W
The College of William and Mary, VA	M,W
Colorado Mesa University, CO	M,W
Colorado State University, CO	W
Columbus State University, GA	M,W
Concordia University Irvine, CA	M,W
Concordia University, Nebraska, NE	M,W
Concord University, WV	M,W
Converse College, SC	W
Creighton University, NE	M,W
Daemen College, NY	M,W
Dallas Baptist University, TX	W
Davidson College, NC	M,W
Dixie State University, UT	W
Dominican University of California, CA	W
Drake University, IA	M,W
Drexel University, PA	M,W
Drury University, MO	M,W
Duquesne University, PA	M,W
East Carolina University, NC	M,W
Eastern Illinois University, IL	M,W
Eastern Michigan University, MI	W
Eastern Washington University, WA	M,W
East Stroudsburg University of Pennsylvania, PA	W
Eckerd College, FL	M,W
Elizabeth City State University, NC	W
Elon University, NC	M,W
Embry-Riddle Aeronautical University–Daytona, FL	M,W
Emmanuel College, GA	M,W
Emporia State University, KS	M,W
Evangel University, MO	M,W
Fairfield University, CT	M,W
Ferris State University, MI	M,W
Flagler College, FL	M,W
Florida Agricultural and Mechanical University, FL	M,W
Florida Gulf Coast University, FL	M,W
Florida Institute of Technology, FL	M,W
Florida International University, FL	W
Florida Southern College, FL	M,W
Florida State University, FL	M,W
Fordham University, NY	M,W
Francis Marion University, SC	M,W
Franklin Pierce University, NH	M,W
Friends University, KS	M,W
Furman University, SC	M,W
Gardner-Webb University, NC	M,W
Georgetown University, DC	W
The George Washington University, DC	M,W
Georgia College & State University, GA	M,W

Georgia Institute of Technology, GA	M,W
Georgia Southern University, GA	M,W
Georgia Southwestern State University, GA	M,W
Georgia State University, GA	M,W
Gonzaga University, WA	M,W
Goshen College, IN	M,W
Grambling State University, LA	W
Grand Valley State University, MI	M,W
Grand View University, IA	M,W
Hampton University, VA	M,W
Harding University, AR	M,W
Hawai`i Pacific University, HI	M,W
Hillsdale College, MI	M,W
Hofstra University, NY	M,W
Holy Family University, PA	W
Hope International University, CA	M,W
Huntington University, IN	M,W
Idaho State University, ID	M,W
Indiana University Bloomington, IN	M,W
Indiana University of Pennsylvania, PA	W
Indiana University–Purdue University Indianapolis, IN	M,W
Iowa State University of Science and Technology, IA	W
Jackson State University, MS	M,W
Jacksonville State University, AL	M,W
James Madison University, VA	M,W
John Brown University, AR	M,W
Johnson C. Smith University, NC	M,W
Judson University, IL	M,W
Kansas State University, KS	W
Kansas Wesleyan University, KS	M,W
Kennesaw State University, GA	M,W
Kentucky Wesleyan College, KY	W
King University, TN	M,W
Kutztown University of Pennsylvania, PA	M,W
Lamar University, TX	M,W
Lane College, TN	M,W
La Salle University, PA	M,W
Lawrence Technological University, MI	M,W
Lees-McRae College, NC	M,W
Lee University, TN	M,W
Lehigh University, PA	M,W
Le Moyne College, NY	M,W
Lenoir-Rhyne University, NC	M,W
Lewis University, IL	M,W
Liberty University, VA	M,W
Lindenwood University, MO	M,W
Lindsey Wilson College, KY	M,W
Lipscomb University, TN	M,W
Longwood University, VA	M,W
Louisiana State University and Agricultural & Mechanical College, LA	M,W
Louisiana Tech University, LA	W
Loyola Marymount University, CA	M,W
Loyola University Maryland, MD	M,W
Loyola University New Orleans, LA	M,W
Lynn University, FL	M,W
Manhattan College, NY	W
Marist College, NY	M,W
Marquette University, WI	M,W
Marshall University, WV	W
Maryville University of Saint Louis, MO	W
McKendree University, IL	M,W
Mercer University, GA	M,W
Merrimack College, MA	M,W

Metropolitan State University of Denver, CO	M,W	St. Ambrose University, IA	M,W	Union College, KY	M,W
Miami University, OH	W	St. Andrews University, NC	M,W	University at Albany, State University of New York, NY	W
Michigan State University, MI	M,W	St. Bonaventure University, NY	M,W		
Michigan Technological University, MI	M,W	St. Edward's University, TX	M,W	University at Buffalo, the State University of New York, NY	M,W
		St. John's University, NY	M,W	The University of Akron, OH	W
Millersville University of Pennsylvania, PA	M,W	Saint Joseph's University, PA	M,W	The University of Alabama, AL	M,W
		Saint Leo University, FL	M,W	The University of Alabama at Birmingham, AL	M,W
Milligan College, TN	M,W	St. Louis College of Pharmacy, MO	M,W		
Minnesota State University Mankato, MN	M,W	Saint Louis University, MO	M,W	The University of Alabama in Huntsville, AL	M,W
		St. Petersburg College, FL	W		
Minnesota State University Moorhead, MN	W	Saint Peter's University, NJ	M,W	The University of Arizona, AZ	M,W
		St. Thomas University, FL	M,W	University of Arkansas, AR	M,W
Mississippi State University, MS	M,W	Samford University, AL	M,W	University of California, Davis, CA	M,W
Missouri Baptist University, MO	M,W	Sam Houston State University, TX	W	University of California, Irvine, CA	M,W
Missouri Western State University, MO	W	San Diego State University, CA	M,W		
		Santa Clara University, CA	M,W	University of California, Los Angeles, CA	M,W
Molloy College, NY	W	Savannah College of Art and Design, GA	M,W		
Monmouth University, NJ	M,W			University of California, Santa Barbara, CA	M,W
Montana State University, MT	M,W	Seton Hill University, PA	W		
Morehead State University, KY	M,W	Shawnee State University, OH	M,W	University of Central Arkansas, AR	W
Morehouse College, GA	M	Shepherd University, WV	M,W	University of Central Florida, FL	M,W
Morningside College, IA	M,W	Shippensburg University of Pennsylvania, PA	W	University of Cincinnati, OH	W
Mount Marty College, SD	W			University of Colorado Boulder, CO	W
Mount St. Mary's University, MD	M,W	Siena College, NY	M,W	University of Dayton, OH	M,W
		Slippery Rock University of Pennsylvania, PA	W	University of Delaware, DE	M,W
Mount Vernon Nazarene University, OH	M,W	Sonoma State University, CA	M,W	University of Denver, CO	M,W
		Southeastern Louisiana University, LA	W	University of Detroit Mercy, MI	M,W
Murray State University, KY	W			University of Evansville, IN	W
Newberry College, SC	M,W	Southeastern Oklahoma State University, OK	M,W	The University of Findlay, OH	M,W
New Mexico State University, NM	M,W			University of Florida, FL	M,W
New York Institute of Technology, NY	M,W	Southeastern University, FL	M,W	University of Georgia, GA	M,W
		Southeast Missouri State University, MO	W	University of Hawaii at Manoa, HI	M,W
Niagara University, NY	M,W			University of Houston, TX	W
North Carolina State University, NC	M,W	Southern Arkansas University–Magnolia, AR	W	University of Idaho, ID	M,W
Northeastern State University, OK	W			University of Illinois at Chicago, IL	M,W
Northern Arizona University, AZ	M,W	Southern Illinois University Carbondale, IL	M,W	University of Illinois at Springfield, IL	M,W
Northern Illinois University, IL	M,W				
Northern Kentucky University, KY	M,W	Southern Illinois University Edwardsville, IL	M,W	University of Indianapolis, IN	M,W
Northwestern College, IA	W			The University of Kansas, KS	W
Northwestern State University of Louisiana, LA	W	Southern Methodist University, TX	M,W	University of Kentucky, KY	M,W
		Southern New Hampshire University, NH	M,W	University of Louisiana at Monroe, LA	W
Northwest Missouri State University, MO	M,W	Southern Utah University, UT	M,W	University of Louisville, KY	M,W
		Southwest Baptist University, MO	M,W		
Nova Southeastern University, FL	W	Southwestern College, KS	M,W	University of Maryland, Baltimore County, MD	M,W
Oakland City University, IN	M,W	Spring Hill College, AL	M,W		
The Ohio State University, OH	M,W	Stanford University, CA	M,W	University of Massachusetts Amherst, MA	W
Oklahoma Baptist University, OK	M,W	Stephen F. Austin State University, TX	W		
Oklahoma State University, OK	M,W			University of Miami, FL	M,W
Old Dominion University, VA	M,W	Stephens College, MO	W	University of Michigan, MI	M,W
Olivet Nazarene University, IL	M,W	Stonehill College, MA	M,W	University of Minnesota, Crookston, MN	W
Oral Roberts University, OK	M,W	Stony Brook University, State University of New York, NY	W		
Ouachita Baptist University, AR	M,W			University of Minnesota, Duluth, MN	W
Our Lady of the Lake University, TX	M,W	Syracuse University, NY	W	University of Minnesota, Twin Cities Campus, MN	M,W
		Tarleton State University, TX	W		
Palm Beach Atlantic University, FL	M,W	Taylor University, IN	M,W	University of Missouri– Kansas City, MO	M,W
Penn State University Park, PA	M,W	Temple University, PA	M,W		
Pepperdine University, CA	M,W	Tennessee State University, TN	M,W	University of Missouri–St. Louis, MO	M,W
Point Loma Nazarene University, CA	M,W	Tennessee Wesleyan University, TN	M&W		
		Texas A&M University, TX	M,W	University of Mobile, AL	M,W
Prairie View A&M University, TX	M,W	Texas A&M University– Corpus Christi, TX	M,W	University of Montevallo, AL	W
Presbyterian College, SC	M,W			University of Nebraska at Kearney, NE	M,W
Purdue University, IN	M,W	Texas Christian University, TX	M,W		
Queens College of the City University of New York, NY	M,W	Texas State University, TX	W	University of Nevada, Las Vegas, NV	M,W
		Texas Tech University, TX	M,W		
Quinnipiac University, CT	M,W	Thomas University, GA	W	University of Nevada, Reno, NV	M,W
Radford University, VA	M,W	Tiffin University, OH	M,W	University of New Haven, CT	W
Research College of Nursing, MO	M,W	Towson University, MD	W	University of New Orleans, LA	M,W
Rice University, TX	M,W	Troy University, AL	M,W	University of North Alabama, AL	M,W
Roberts Wesleyan College, NY	M,W	Truman State University, MO	M,W	University of North Carolina at Asheville, NC	M,W
Rockhurst University, MO	M,W	Tulane University, LA	M,W		
Rollins College, FL	M,W	Tusculum College, TN	M,W	The University of North Carolina at Chapel Hill, NC	M,W
Sacred Heart University, CT	M,W				
Saginaw Valley State University, MI	W				

The University of North Carolina at Charlotte, NC — M,W

The University of North Carolina at Greensboro, NC — M,W

The University of North Carolina Wilmington, NC — M,W

University of Northern Colorado, CO — M,W

University of Northern Iowa, IA — W

University of North Florida, FL — M,W

University of North Georgia, GA — M,W

University of Notre Dame, IN — M,W

University of Oklahoma, OK — M,W

University of Oregon, OR — M,W

University of Pikeville, KY — M,W

University of Pittsburgh, PA — W

University of Puerto Rico in Bayamón, PR — M,W

University of Rhode Island, RI — W

University of Richmond, VA — M,W

University of St. Francis, IL — M,W

University of San Diego, CA — M,W

University of San Francisco, CA — M,W

University of South Alabama, AL — M,W

University of South Carolina, SC — M,W

University of South Carolina Aiken, SC — M,W

The University of South Dakota, SD — W

University of Southern California, CA — M,W

University of Southern Indiana, IN — M,W

University of Southern Mississippi, MS — M,W

University of South Florida, FL — M,W

The University of Tampa, FL — W

The University of Tennessee, TN — M,W

The University of Tennessee at Chattanooga, TN — M,W

The University of Tennessee at Martin, TN — W

The University of Texas at Austin, TX — M,W

The University of Texas at El Paso, TX — W

The University of Texas at San Antonio, TX — M,W

The University of Texas of the Permian Basin, TX — M,W

The University of Texas Rio Grande Valley, TX — M,W

University of the Incarnate Word, TX — M,W

University of the Pacific, CA — M,W

The University of Toledo, OH — M,W

The University of Tulsa, OK — M,W

University of Utah, UT — M,W

University of Virginia, VA — M,W

The University of Virginia's College at Wise, VA — M,W

University of Washington, WA — M,W

The University of West Alabama, AL — M,W

University of West Georgia, GA — W

University of Wisconsin–Green Bay, WI — M,W

University of Wisconsin–Madison, WI — M,W

University of Wisconsin–Milwaukee, WI — W

Upper Iowa University, IA — W

Ursuline College, OH — W

Utah State University, UT — M,W

Valdosta State University, GA — M,W

Valparaiso University, IN — M,W

Vanderbilt University, TN — M,W

Virginia Commonwealth University, VA — M,W

Virginia Military Institute, VA — M

Virginia Polytechnic Institute and State University, VA — M,W

Virginia State University, VA — M,W

Wagner College, NY — M,W

Wake Forest University, NC — M,W

Washburn University, KS — M,W

Washington State University, WA — W

Wayne State University, MI — M,W

Webber International University, FL — M,W

Weber State University, UT — M,W

West Chester University of Pennsylvania, PA — M,W

Western Carolina University, NC — W

Western Illinois University, IL — M,W

Western Kentucky University, KY — M,W

Western Michigan University, MI — M,W

Westmont College, CA — M,W

West Virginia University, WV — W

West Virginia Wesleyan College, WV — M,W

Wichita State University, KS — M,W

William Jewell College, MO — M,W

William Woods University, MO — M,W

Wingate University, NC — M,W

Winona State University, MN — W

Winthrop University, SC — M,W

Wofford College, SC — M,W

Wright State University, OH — M,W

Xavier University of Louisiana, LA — M,W

Youngstown State University, OH — M,W

Track and field

Abilene Christian University, TX — M,W

Academy of Art University, CA — M,W

Adams State University, CO — M,W

Adelphi University, NY — M,W

Alabama State University, AL — M,W

Alcorn State University, MS — M,W

Alderson Broaddus University, WV — M,W

American University, DC — M,W

Anderson University, SC — M,W

Angelo State University, TX — M,W

Appalachian State University, NC — M,W

Aquinas College, MI — M,W

Arizona State University at the Downtown Phoenix campus, AZ — M,W

Arizona State University at the Polytechnic campus, AZ — M,W

Arizona State University at the Tempe campus, AZ — M,W

Arizona State University at the West campus, AZ — M,W

Asbury University, KY — M,W

Auburn University, AL — M,W

Augustana University, SD — M,W

Augusta University, GA — M,W

Austin Peay State University, TN — W

Azusa Pacific University, CA — M,W

Baker University, KS — M,W

Ball State University, IN — W

Barton College, NC — M,W

Baylor University, TX — M,W

Bellarmine University, KY — M,W

Belmont Abbey College, NC — M,W

Belmont University, TN — M,W

Bemidji State University, MN — W

Benedictine College, KS — M,W

Bethel College, IN — M,W

Bethel College, KS — M,W

Bethune-Cookman University, FL — M,W

Binghamton University, State University of New York, NY — M,W

Biola University, CA — M,W

Black Hills State University, SD — M,W

Bloomsburg University of Pennsylvania, PA — M,W

Boise State University, ID — M,W

Boston College, MA — M,W

Boston University, MA — M,W

Bowling Green State University, OH — W

Bradley University, IL — M,W

Brenau University, GA — W

Brescia University, KY — W

Briar Cliff University, IA — M,W

Brigham Young University, UT — M,W

Bryan College, TN — M,W

Bucknell University, PA — W

Butler University, IN — M,W

Caldwell University, NJ — M,W

California Baptist University, CA — M,W

California Polytechnic State University, San Luis Obispo, CA — M,W

California State Polytechnic University, Pomona, CA — M,W

California State University, Bakersfield, CA — M,W

California State University, Chico, CA — M,W

California State University, Dominguez Hills, CA — W

California State University, Fresno, CA — M,W

California State University, Fullerton, CA — M,W

California State University, Long Beach, CA — M,W

California State University, Northridge, CA — M,W

California State University, Sacramento, CA — M,W

Calumet College of Saint Joseph, IN — M,W

Campbellsville University, KY — M,W

Cardinal Stritch University, WI — M,W

Carroll College, MT — M,W

Carson-Newman University, TN — M,W

Cedarville University, OH — M,W

Central Connecticut State University, CT — M,W

Central Methodist University, MO — M,W

Central Michigan University, MI — M,W

Central Washington University, WA — M,W

Chestnut Hill College, PA — M,W

Christian Brothers University, TN — M,W

The Citadel, The Military College of South Carolina, SC — M,W

Clarion University of Pennsylvania, PA — W

Clark Atlanta University, GA — M,W

Clarke University, IA — M,W

Clayton State University, GA — M,W

Clemson University, SC — M,W

Cleveland State University, OH — W

Coastal Carolina University, SC — M,W

The College of Idaho, ID — M,W

The College of Saint Rose, NY — M,W

College of the Holy Cross, MA — W

The College of William and Mary, VA — M,W

Colorado Mesa University, CO — M,W

Colorado School of Mines, CO — M,W

Colorado State University, CO — M,W

Columbus State University, GA — M,W

Concordia University Irvine, CA — M,W

Concordia University, Nebraska, NE	M,W
Concordia University, St. Paul, MN	M,W
Concord University, WV	M,W
Converse College, SC	W
Corban University, OR	M,W
Cornerstone University, MI	M,W
Culver-Stockton College, MO	M,W
Daemen College, NY	M,W
Dakota State University, SD	M,W
Dallas Baptist University, TX	W
Davidson College, NC	M,W
Dickinson State University, ND	M,W
Doane University, NE	M,W
Dominican College, NY	M,W
Drake University, IA	M,W
Drury University, MO	M,W
Duquesne University, PA	M,W
East Carolina University, NC	M,W
Eastern Illinois University, IL	M,W
Eastern Michigan University, MI	M,W
Eastern Oregon University, OR	M,W
Eastern Washington University, WA	M,W
East Stroudsburg University of Pennsylvania, PA	M,W
Elon University, NC	W
Embry-Riddle Aeronautical University–Daytona, FL	M,W
Embry-Riddle Aeronautical University–Prescott, AZ	M,W
Emmanuel College, GA	M,W
Emporia State University, KS	M,W
Evangel University, MO	M,W
The Evergreen State College, WA	M,W
Ferris State University, MI	M,W
Flagler College, FL	M,W
Florida Agricultural and Mechanical University, FL	M,W
Florida Institute of Technology, FL	M,W
Florida International University, FL	M,W
Florida State University, FL	M,W
Fordham University, NY	M,W
Freed-Hardeman University, TN	M,W
Fresno Pacific University, CA	M,W
Friends University, KS	M,W
Furman University, SC	M,W
Gardner-Webb University, NC	M,W
Georgetown University, DC	M,W
Georgia Institute of Technology, GA	M,W
Georgian Court University, NJ	M,W
Georgia Southern University, GA	W
Georgia State University, GA	W
Gonzaga University, WA	M,W
Goshen College, IN	M,W
Graceland University, IA	M,W
Grambling State University, LA	M,W
Grand Valley State University, MI	M,W
Grand View University, IA	M,W
Hampton University, VA	M,W
Harding University, AR	M,W
High Point University, NC	M,W
Hillsdale College, MI	M,W
Holy Family University, PA	M,W
Hope International University, CA	M,W
Houston Baptist University, TX	M,W
Humboldt State University, CA	M,W
Huntington University, IN	M,W
Huston-Tillotson University, TX	M,W
Idaho State University, ID	M,W
Indiana State University, IN	M,W
Indiana University Bloomington, IN	M,W
Indiana University of Pennsylvania, PA	M,W

Inter American University of Puerto Rico, Bayamón Campus, PR	M,W
Inter American University of Puerto Rico, Guayama Campus, PR	M,W
Iona College, NY	M,W
Iowa State University of Science and Technology, IA	M,W
Jackson State University, MS	M,W
Jacksonville University, FL	W
James Madison University, VA	W
Johnson C. Smith University, NC	M,W
Judson University, IL	M,W
Kansas State University, KS	M,W
Kansas Wesleyan University, KS	M,W
Kennesaw State University, GA	M,W
Kent State University, OH	M,W
Kentucky State University, KY	M,W
Kentucky Wesleyan College, KY	M,W
King University, TN	M,W
Kutztown University of Pennsylvania, PA	M,W
Lake Erie College, OH	M,W
Lamar University, TX	M,W
Lane College, TN	M,W
Langston University, OK	M,W
La Salle University, PA	M,W
Lees-McRae College, NC	M,W
Lee University, TN	M,W
Lehigh University, PA	M,W
Le Moyne College, NY	M,W
Lenoir-Rhyne University, NC	M,W
Lewis University, IL	M,W
Liberty University, VA	M,W
Life University, GA	W
Lincoln University, MO	M,W
Lincoln University, PA	M,W
Lindenwood University, MO	M,W
Lindsey Wilson College, KY	M,W
Lipscomb University, TN	M,W
Lock Haven University of Pennsylvania, PA	M,W
Louisiana State University and Agricultural & Mechanical College, LA	M,W
Louisiana Tech University, LA	M,W
Loyola University Chicago, IL	M,W
Loyola University Maryland, MD	W
Loyola University New Orleans, LA	M,W
Malone University, OH	M,W
Manhattan College, NY	M,W
Mansfield University of Pennsylvania, PA	M,W
Marist College, NY	M,W
Marquette University, WI	M,W
Marshall University, WV	M,W
Marymount California University, CA	M
Maryville University of Saint Louis, MO	M,W
The Master's University, CA	M,W
McKendree University, IL	M,W
Mercer University, GA	W
Merrimack College, MA	M,W
Miami University, OH	M,W
Michigan State University, MI	M,W
Michigan Technological University, MI	M,W
Millersville University of Pennsylvania, PA	W
Milligan College, TN	M,W
Minnesota State University Mankato, MN	M,W

Minnesota State University Moorhead, MN	M,W
Minot State University, ND	M,W
Mississippi State University, MS	M,W
Missouri Baptist University, MO	M,W
Missouri State University, MO	W
Missouri University of Science and Technology, MO	M,W
Missouri Western State University, MO	M,W
Molloy College, NY	M,W
Monmouth University, NJ	M,W
Montana State University, MT	M,W
Morehead State University, KY	M,W
Morehouse College, GA	M
Morningside College, IA	M,W
Mount Marty College, SD	M,W
Mount Mercy University, IA	M,W
Mount St. Mary's University, MD	M,W
Mount Vernon Nazarene University, OH	M,W
Murray State University, KY	W
New Mexico State University, NM	W
Niagara University, NY	W
North Carolina State University, NC	M,W
Northeastern University, MA	M,W
Northern Arizona University, AZ	M,W
Northern Kentucky University, KY	M,W
Northern State University, SD	M,W
Northwest Christian University, OR	M,W
Northwestern College, IA	M,W
Northwestern State University of Louisiana, LA	M,W
Northwest Missouri State University, MO	M,W
Northwest University, WA	M,W
Nova Southeastern University, FL	M,W
The Ohio State University, OH	M,W
Ohio University, OH	W
Oklahoma Baptist University, OK	M,W
Oklahoma Christian University, OK	M,W
Oklahoma City University, OK	M,W
Oklahoma State University, OK	M,W
Olivet Nazarene University, IL	M,W
Oral Roberts University, OK	M,W
Oregon State University, OR	W
Our Lady of the Lake University, TX	M,W
Penn State University Park, PA	M,W
Pepperdine University, CA	M,W
Philander Smith College, AR	M,W
Pittsburg State University, KS	M,W
Point Loma Nazarene University, CA	W
Prairie View A&M University, TX	M,W
Providence College, RI	M,W
Purdue University, IN	M,W
Queens College of the City University of New York, NY	M,W
Quinnipiac University, CT	W
Radford University, VA	W
Rice University, TX	M,W
Robert Morris University, PA	W
Robert Morris University Illinois, IL	M,W
Roberts Wesleyan College, NY	M,W
Rocky Mountain College, MT	M,W
Rogers State University, OK	M,W
Sacred Heart University, CT	M,W
Saginaw Valley State University, MI	M,W
St. Ambrose University, IA	M,W
Saint Augustine's University, NC	M,W
St. Gregory's University, OK	M,W
St. John's University, NY	W

Saint Joseph's University, PA	M,W
Saint Leo University, FL	M,W
St. Louis College of Pharmacy, MO	M,W
Saint Louis University, MO	M,W
Saint Martin's University, WA	M,W
Saint Peter's University, NJ	M,W
St. Thomas University, FL	M,W
Samford University, AL	M,W
Sam Houston State University, TX	M,W
San Diego State University, CA	W
San Francisco State University, CA	W
Santa Clara University, CA	M,W
Seattle Pacific University, WA	M,W
Seattle University, WA	M,W
Seton Hill University, PA	M,W
Shawnee State University, OH	M,W
Shippensburg University of Pennsylvania, PA	M,W
Slippery Rock University of Pennsylvania, PA	M,W
Soka University of America, CA	M,W
South Dakota School of Mines and Technology, SD	M,W
Southeastern Louisiana University, LA	M,W
Southeast Missouri State University, MO	M,W
Southern Arkansas University–Magnolia, AR	M,W
Southern Connecticut State University, CT	M,W
Southern Illinois University Carbondale, IL	M,W
Southern Illinois University Edwardsville, IL	M,W
Southern New Hampshire University, NH	W
Southern Oregon University, OR	M,W
Southern Utah University, UT	M,W
Southwest Baptist University, MO	M,W
Southwestern College, KS	M,W
Spring Hill College, AL	M,W
Stanford University, CA	M,W
Stephen F. Austin State University, TX	M,W
Sterling College, KS	M,W
Stonehill College, MA	M,W
Stony Brook University, State University of New York, NY	M,W
Syracuse University, NY	M,W
Tarleton State University, TX	M,W
Taylor University, IN	M,W
Temple University, PA	W
Tennessee State University, TN	M,W
Tennessee Wesleyan University, TN	M,W
Texas A&M University, TX	M,W
Texas A&M University–Commerce, TX	M,W
Texas A&M University–Corpus Christi, TX	M,W
Texas Christian University, TX	M,W
Texas State University, TX	M,W
Texas Tech University, TX	M,W
Texas Wesleyan University, TX	M,W
Tiffin University, OH	M,W
Towson University, MD	W
Trevecca Nazarene University, TN	M,W
Trinity Christian College, IL	M,W
Troy University, AL	M,W
Truman State University, MO	M,W
Tulane University, LA	W
Tusculum College, TN	M,W
Union College, KY	M,W
University at Albany, State University of New York, NY	M,W
University at Buffalo, the State University of New York, NY	M,W
The University of Akron, OH	M,W
The University of Alabama, AL	M,W
The University of Alabama at Birmingham, AL	W
The University of Alabama in Huntsville, AL	M,W
The University of Arizona, AZ	M,W
University of Arkansas, AR	M,W
University of California, Davis, CA	M,W
University of California, Irvine, CA	M,W
University of California, Los Angeles, CA	M,W
University of California, Santa Barbara, CA	M,W
University of Central Arkansas, AR	M,W
University of Central Florida, FL	W
University of Central Missouri, MO	M,W
University of Cincinnati, OH	M,W
University of Colorado Boulder, CO	M,W
University of Colorado Colorado Springs, CO	M,W
University of Dayton, OH	W
University of Delaware, DE	W
University of Detroit Mercy, MI	M,W
The University of Findlay, OH	M,W
University of Florida, FL	M,W
University of Georgia, GA	M,W
University of Great Falls, MT	M,W
University of Hawaii at Manoa, HI	W
University of Houston, TX	M,W
University of Idaho, ID	M,W
University of Illinois at Chicago, IL	M,W
University of Illinois at Springfield, IL	M,W
University of Indianapolis, IN	M,W
University of Jamestown, ND	M,W
The University of Kansas, KS	M,W
University of Kentucky, KY	M,W
University of Louisiana at Monroe, LA	M,W
University of Louisville, KY	M,W
University of Maine, ME	M,W
University of Maryland, Baltimore County, MD	M,W
University of Maryland, College Park, MD	W
University of Massachusetts Amherst, MA	M,W
University of Massachusetts Lowell, MA	M,W
University of Miami, FL	M,W
University of Michigan, MI	M,W
University of Minnesota, Twin Cities Campus, MN	M,W
University of Missouri–Kansas City, MO	M,W
University of Mobile, AL	M,W
The University of Montana Western, MT	M,W
University of Nebraska at Kearney, NE	M,W
University of Nevada, Las Vegas, NV	W
University of Nevada, Reno, NV	W
University of New Hampshire, NH	M,W
University of New Haven, CT	M,W
University of New Orleans, LA	M,W
University of North Alabama, AL	W
University of North Carolina at Asheville, NC	M,W
The University of North Carolina at Chapel Hill, NC	M,W
The University of North Carolina at Charlotte, NC	M,W
The University of North Carolina at Greensboro, NC	M,W
The University of North Carolina at Pembroke, NC	M,W
The University of North Carolina Wilmington, NC	M,W
University of Northern Colorado, CO	M,W
University of Northern Iowa, IA	M,W
University of North Florida, FL	M,W
University of North Texas, TX	M,W
University of Notre Dame, IN	M,W
University of Oklahoma, OK	M,W
University of Oregon, OR	M,W
University of Pikeville, KY	M,W
University of Pittsburgh, PA	M,W
University of Pittsburgh at Johnstown, PA	M,W
University of Puerto Rico in Bayamón, PR	M,W
University of Rhode Island, RI	M,W
University of Richmond, VA	W
University of St. Francis, IL	M,W
University of San Diego, CA	W
University of San Francisco, CA	W
University of South Alabama, AL	M,W
University of South Carolina, SC	M,W
The University of South Dakota, SD	M,W
University of Southern California, CA	M,W
University of Southern Indiana, IN	M,W
University of Southern Mississippi, MS	M,W
University of South Florida, FL	M,W
The University of Tampa, FL	M,W
The University of Tennessee, TN	M,W
The University of Tennessee at Chattanooga, TN	M,W
The University of Texas at Austin, TX	M,W
The University of Texas at El Paso, TX	M,W
The University of Texas at San Antonio, TX	M,W
The University of Texas Rio Grande Valley, TX	M,W
University of the Incarnate Word, TX	M,W
The University of Toledo, OH	W
The University of Tulsa, OK	M,W
University of Utah, UT	W
University of Vermont, VT	M,W
University of Virginia, VA	M,W
University of Washington, WA	M,W
The University of West Alabama, AL	M,W
University of West Georgia, GA	W
University of Wisconsin–Madison, WI	M,W
University of Wisconsin–Milwaukee, WI	M,W
University of Wisconsin–Parkside, WI	M,W
Upper Iowa University, IA	W
Ursuline College, OH	W
Utah State University, UT	M,W
Utah Valley University, UT	M,W
Valley City State University, ND	M,W
Valparaiso University, IN	M,W

Vanderbilt University, TN	W
Villanova University, PA	M,W
Virginia Commonwealth University, VA	M,W
Virginia Military Institute, VA	M,W
Virginia Polytechnic Institute and State University, VA	M,W
Virginia State University, VA	M,W
Wagner College, NY	M,W
Wake Forest University, NC	M,W
Waldorf University, IA	M,W
Washington State University, WA	M,W
Wayland Baptist University, TX	M,W
Wayne State College, NE	M,W
Wayne State University, MI	W
Webber International University, FL	M,W
Weber State University, UT	M,W
West Chester University of Pennsylvania, PA	M,W
Western Carolina University, NC	M,W
Western Illinois University, IL	M,W
Western Kentucky University, KY	M,W
Western Michigan University, MI	W
Western Oregon University, OR	M,W
Western State Colorado University, CO	M,W
Western Washington University, WA	M,W
Westminster College, UT	M,W
Westmont College, CA	M,W
West Texas A&M University, TX	M,W
West Virginia University, WV	W
West Virginia Wesleyan College, WV	M,W
Wheeling Jesuit University, WV	M,W
Wichita State University, KS	M,W
William Jewell College, MO	M,W
Williams Baptist College, AR	M,W
William Woods University, MO	M,W
Wingate University, NC	M,W
Winona State University, MN	W
Winthrop University, SC	M,W
Wofford College, SC	M,W
Wright State University, OH	W
Youngstown State University, OH	M,W

Triathlon

Arizona State University at the Downtown Phoenix campus, AZ	W
Arizona State University at the Polytechnic campus, AZ	W
Arizona State University at the Tempe campus, AZ	W
Arizona State University at the West campus, AZ	W
The University of West Alabama, AL	W
Webber International University, FL	M,W

Volleyball

Abilene Christian University, TX	W
Academy of Art University, CA	W
Adams State University, CO	W
Adelphi University, NY	W
Alabama State University, AL	W
Alcorn State University, MS	W
Alderson Broaddus University, WV	M,W
American University, DC	W
Anderson University, SC	W
Angelo State University, TX	W
Appalachian State University, NC	W
Aquinas College, MI	W
Arizona State University at the Downtown Phoenix campus, AZ	W
Arizona State University at the Polytechnic campus, AZ	

Arizona State University at the Tempe campus, AZ	W
Arizona State University at the West campus, AZ	W
Arkansas Tech University, AR	W
Armstrong State University, GA	W
Asbury University, KY	W
Auburn University, AL	W
Augustana University, SD	W
Austin Peay State University, TN	W
Azusa Pacific University, CA	W
Baker University, KS	W
Ball State University, IN	M,W
Barry University, FL	W
Barton College, NC	M,W
Baylor University, TX	W
Belhaven University, MS	W
Bellarmine University, KY	W
Belmont Abbey College, NC	M,W
Belmont University, TN	W
Bemidji State University, MN	W
Benedictine College, KS	W
Bethel College, IN	W
Bethel College, KS	W
Bethune-Cookman University, FL	W
Binghamton University, State University of New York, NY	W
Biola University, CA	W
Black Hills State University, SD	W
Bloomfield College, NJ	W
Bluefield College, VA	M,W
Boise State University, ID	W
Boston College, MA	W
Bowling Green State University, OH	W
Bradley University, IL	W
Brenau University, GA	W
Brescia University, KY	W
Briar Cliff University, IA	W
Brigham Young University, UT	M,W
Bryan College, TN	M,W
Bucknell University, PA	W
Butler University, IN	W
Caldwell University, NJ	W
California Baptist University, CA	M,W
California Polytechnic State University, San Luis Obispo, CA	W
California State Polytechnic University, Pomona, CA	W
California State University, Bakersfield, CA	W
California State University, Chico, CA	W
California State University, Dominguez Hills, CA	W
California State University, Fresno, CA	W
California State University, Fullerton, CA	W
California State University, Long Beach, CA	M,W
California State University Maritime Academy, CA	W
California State University, Monterey Bay, CA	W
California State University, Northridge, CA	M,W
California State University, Sacramento, CA	W
California State University, San Bernardino, CA	W
Calumet College of Saint Joseph, IN	M,W
Cameron University, OK	W
Campbellsville University, KY	M,W
Canisius College, NY	W
Cardinal Stritch University, WI	M,W

Carlow University, PA	W
Carroll College, MT	W
Carson-Newman University, TN	W
Catawba College, NC	W
Cedarville University, OH	W
Central Connecticut State University, CT	W
Central Methodist University, MO	W
Central Michigan University, MI	W
Central Washington University, WA	W
Chaminade University of Honolulu, HI	W
Chestnut Hill College, PA	W
Chowan University, NC	W
Christian Brothers University, TN	W
The Citadel, The Military College of South Carolina, SC	W
Clark Atlanta University, GA	W
Clarke University, IA	M,W
Clemson University, SC	W
Cleveland State University, OH	W
Coastal Carolina University, SC	W
Colgate University, NY	W
College of Charleston, SC	W
College of Coastal Georgia, GA	W
The College of Idaho, ID	W
College of Saint Mary, NE	W
The College of Saint Rose, NY	W
College of the Holy Cross, MA	W
College of the Ozarks, MO	W
The College of William and Mary, VA	W
Colorado Mesa University, CO	W
Colorado School of Mines, CO	W
Colorado State University, CO	W
Columbia College, MO	W
Columbus State University, GA	W
Concordia University Irvine, CA	M,W
Concordia University, Nebraska, NE	W
Concordia University, St. Paul, MN	W
Concord University, WV	W
Converse College, SC	W
Corban University, OR	W
Cornerstone University, MI	W
Creighton University, NE	W
Culver-Stockton College, MO	M,W
Daemen College, NY	W
Dakota State University, SD	W
Dallas Baptist University, TX	W
Davidson College, NC	W
Dickinson State University, ND	W
Dixie State University, UT	W
Doane University, NE	W
Dominican College, NY	W
Dominican University of California, CA	W
Drake University, IA	W
Drury University, MO	W
Duquesne University, PA	W
East Carolina University, NC	W
East Central University, OK	W
Eastern Illinois University, IL	W
Eastern Michigan University, MI	W
Eastern Oregon University, OR	W
Eastern Washington University, WA	W
East Stroudsburg University of Pennsylvania, PA	W
Eckerd College, FL	W
Elizabeth City State University, NC	W
Elon University, NC	M,W
Embry-Riddle Aeronautical University–Daytona, FL	W
Embry-Riddle Aeronautical University–Prescott, AZ	W

Emmanuel College, GA	M,W
Emporia State University, KS	W
Evangel University, MO	W
The Evergreen State College, WA	W
Fairfield University, CT	W
Faulkner University, AL	W
Felician University, NJ	W
Ferris State University, MI	W
Flagler College, FL	W
Florida Agricultural and Mechanical University, FL	W
Florida Atlantic University, FL	W
Florida College, FL	W
Florida Gulf Coast University, FL	W
Florida Institute of Technology, FL	W
Florida International University, FL	W
Florida National University, FL	W
Florida Southern College, FL	W
Florida State University, FL	W
Fordham University, NY	W
Fort Lewis College, CO	W
Francis Marion University, SC	W
Franklin Pierce University, NH	W
Freed-Hardeman University, TN	W
Fresno Pacific University, CA	W
Friends University, KS	W
Furman University, SC	W
Gannon University, PA	W
Gardner-Webb University, NC	W
Georgetown University, DC	W
The George Washington University, DC	W
Georgia College & State University, GA	W
Georgia Institute of Technology, GA	W
Georgian Court University, NJ	W
Georgia Southern University, GA	W
Georgia State University, GA	W
Gonzaga University, WA	W
Goshen College, IN	W
Governors State University, IL	M,W
Graceland University, IA	M,W
Grambling State University, LA	W
Grand Valley State University, MI	W
Grand View University, IA	M,W
Hampton University, VA	W
Harding University, AR	W
Harris-Stowe State University, MO	W
Hawai`i Pacific University, HI	W
High Point University, NC	W
Hillsdale College, MI	W
Hofstra University, NY	W
Holy Family University, PA	W
Hope International University, CA	M,W
Houston Baptist University, TX	W
Humboldt State University, CA	W
Huntington University, IN	W
Huston-Tillotson University, TX	W
Idaho State University, ID	W
Indiana State University, IN	W
Indiana University Bloomington, IN	W
Indiana University of Pennsylvania, PA	W
Indiana University–Purdue University Indianapolis, IN	W
Indiana University Southeast, IN	W
Inter American University of Puerto Rico, Bayamón Campus, PR	M,W
Iona College, NY	W
Iowa State University of Science and Technology, IA	W

Jackson State University, MS	W
Jacksonville State University, AL	W
Jacksonville University, FL	W
James Madison University, VA	W
John Brown University, AR	W
Johnson C. Smith University, NC	W
John Wesley University, NC	W
Judson University, IL	W
Kansas State University, KS	W
Kansas Wesleyan University, KS	W
Kennesaw State University, GA	W
Kent State University, OH	W
Kentucky State University, KY	W
Kentucky Wesleyan College, KY	W
King University, TN	M,W
Kutztown University of Pennsylvania, PA	W
Lake Erie College, OH	W
Lamar University, TX	W
Lane College, TN	W
La Salle University, PA	W
Lawrence Technological University, MI	M,W
Lees-McRae College, NC	M,W
Lee University, TN	W
Lehigh University, PA	W
Le Moyne College, NY	W
Lenoir-Rhyne University, NC	W
Lewis University, IL	M,W
Liberty University, VA	W
Life University, GA	W
Lincoln Christian University, IL	W
Lincoln University, PA	W
Lindenwood University, MO	M,W
Lindsey Wilson College, KY	W
Lipscomb University, TN	W
Lock Haven University of Pennsylvania, PA	W
Louisiana State University and Agricultural & Mechanical College, LA	W
Louisiana Tech University, LA	W
Loyola Marymount University, CA	W
Loyola University Chicago, IL	M,W
Loyola University Maryland, MD	W
Loyola University New Orleans, LA	W
Lubbock Christian University, TX	W
Lynn University, FL	W
Lyon College, AR	W
Malone University, OH	W
Manhattan College, NY	W
Marist College, NY	W
Marquette University, WI	W
Marshall University, WV	W
Maryville University of Saint Louis, MO	W
The Master's University, CA	W
McKendree University, IL	M,W
Mercer University, GA	W
Mercy College, NY	W
Merrimack College, MA	W
Metropolitan State University of Denver, CO	W
Miami University, OH	W
Michigan State University, MI	W
Michigan Technological University, MI	W
Midland College, TX	W
Millersville University of Pennsylvania, PA	W
Milligan College, TN	W
Minnesota State University Mankato, MN	W

Minnesota State University Moorhead, MN	W
Minot State University, ND	W
Mississippi State University, MS	W
Missouri Baptist University, MO	M,W
Missouri State University, MO	W
Missouri University of Science and Technology, MO	W
Missouri Western State University, MO	W
Molloy College, NY	W
Montana State University, MT	W
Montana State University Billings, MT	W
Montana Tech of The University of Montana, MT	W
Morehead State University, KY	W
Morningside College, IA	W
Mount Marty College, SD	W
Mount Mercy University, IA	W
Mount Vernon Nazarene University, OH	W
Murray State University, KY	W
Newberry College, SC	W
New Mexico Highlands University, NM	W
New Mexico State University, NM	W
New York Institute of Technology, NY	W
Niagara University, NY	W
North Carolina State University, NC	W
Northeastern University, MA	W
Northern Arizona University, AZ	W
Northern Illinois University, IL	W
Northern Kentucky University, KY	W
Northern State University, SD	W
Northwest Christian University, OR	W
Northwestern College, IA	W
Northwestern State University of Louisiana, LA	W
Northwest Missouri State University, MO	W
Northwest University, WA	W
Nova Southeastern University, FL	W
Oakland City University, IN	W
The Ohio State University, OH	M,W
Ohio University, OH	W
Ohio Valley University, WV	W
Oklahoma Baptist University, OK	W
Oklahoma City University, OK	W
Olivet Nazarene University, IL	W
Oral Roberts University, OK	W
Oregon State University, OR	W
Ouachita Baptist University, AR	W
Our Lady of the Lake University, TX	W
Palm Beach Atlantic University, FL	W
Penn State University Park, PA	M,W
Pepperdine University, CA	M,W
Philander Smith College, AR	W
Pittsburg State University, KS	W
Point Loma Nazarene University, CA	W
Point Park University, PA	W
Prairie View A&M University, TX	W
Presbyterian College, SC	W
Providence College, RI	W
Purdue University, IN	W
Queens College of the City University of New York, NY	W
Quinnipiac University, CT	W
Radford University, VA	W
Regis University, CO	W
Research College of Nursing, MO	W
Rice University, TX	W
Robert Morris University, PA	W

Robert Morris University Illinois, IL	M,W
Roberts Wesleyan College, NY	W
Rockhurst University, MO	W
Rocky Mountain College, MT	W
Rollins College, FL	W
Sacred Heart University, CT	W
Saginaw Valley State University, MI	W
St. Ambrose University, IA	M,W
Saint Augustine's University, NC	W
St. Edward's University, TX	W
St. Gregory's University, OK	W
St. John's University, NY	W
Saint Leo University, FL	W
St. Louis College of Pharmacy, MO	W
Saint Louis University, MO	W
Saint Martin's University, WA	W
St. Petersburg College, FL	W
Saint Peter's University, NJ	W
St. Thomas Aquinas College, NY	W
St. Thomas University, FL	W
Samford University, AL	W
Sam Houston State University, TX	W
San Diego State University, CA	W
San Francisco State University, CA	W
Santa Clara University, CA	W
Seattle Pacific University, WA	W
Seattle University, WA	W
Seton Hill University, PA	W
Shawnee State University, OH	W
Shepherd University, WV	W
Shippensburg University of Pennsylvania, PA	W
Siena College, NY	W
Simpson University, CA	W
Slippery Rock University of Pennsylvania, PA	W
Sonoma State University, CA	W
South Dakota School of Mines and Technology, SD	W
Southeastern Louisiana University, LA	W
Southeastern Oklahoma State University, OK	W
Southeastern University, FL	W
Southeast Missouri State University, MO	W
Southern Arkansas University–Magnolia, AR	W
Southern Connecticut State University, CT	W
Southern Illinois University Carbondale, IL	W
Southern Illinois University Edwardsville, IL	W
Southern Methodist University, TX	W
Southern New Hampshire University, NH	W
Southern Oregon University, OR	W
Southern Utah University, UT	W
Southwest Baptist University, MO	W
Southwestern College, KS	W
Southwestern Oklahoma State University, OK	W
Spring Hill College, AL	W
Stanford University, CA	M,W
Stephen F. Austin State University, TX	W
Stephens College, MO	W
Sterling College, KS	W
Stonehill College, MA	W

Stony Brook University, State University of New York, NY	W
Syracuse University, NY	W
Tarleton State University, TX	W
Taylor University, IN	W
Temple University, PA	W
Tennessee Wesleyan University, TN	W
Texas A&M International University, TX	W
Texas A&M University, TX	W
Texas A&M University– Commerce, TX	W
Texas A&M University– Corpus Christi, TX	W
Texas Christian University, TX	W
Texas State University, TX	W
Texas Tech University, TX	W
Texas Wesleyan University, TX	W
Texas Woman's University, TX	W
Tiffin University, OH	W
Towson University, MD	W
Trevecca Nazarene University, TN	W
Trinity Christian College, IL	W
Troy University, AL	W
Truett McConnell University, GA	W
Truman State University, MO	W
Tulane University, LA	W
Tusculum College, TN	W
Union College, KY	W
Union University, TN	W
University at Albany, State University of New York, NY	W
University at Buffalo, the State University of New York, NY	W
The University of Akron, OH	W
The University of Alabama, AL	W
The University of Alabama at Birmingham, AL	W
The University of Alabama in Huntsville, AL	W
University of Alaska Fairbanks, AK	W
The University of Arizona, AZ	W
University of Arkansas, AR	W
University of Bridgeport, CT	W
University of California, Davis, CA	W
University of California, Irvine, CA	M,W
University of California, Los Angeles, CA	M,W
University of California, Riverside, CA	W
University of California, Santa Barbara, CA	M,W
University of Central Arkansas, AR	W
University of Central Florida, FL	W
University of Central Missouri, MO	W
University of Cincinnati, OH	W
University of Colorado Boulder, CO	W
University of Colorado Colorado Springs, CO	W
University of Dayton, OH	W
University of Delaware, DE	W
University of Denver, CO	W
University of Evansville, IN	W
The University of Findlay, OH	W
University of Florida, FL	W
University of Georgia, GA	W
University of Great Falls, MT	W
University of Hartford, CT	W
University of Hawaii at Manoa, HI	M,W
University of Houston, TX	W
University of Idaho, ID	W

University of Illinois at Chicago, IL	W
University of Illinois at Springfield, IL	W
University of Indianapolis, IN	W
University of Jamestown, ND	W
The University of Kansas, KS	W
University of Kentucky, KY	W
University of Louisiana at Monroe, LA	W
University of Louisville, KY	W
University of Maine, ME	W
University of Maryland, Baltimore County, MD	W
University of Maryland, College Park, MD	W
University of Massachusetts Lowell, MA	W
University of Miami, FL	W
University of Michigan, MI	W
University of Michigan– Dearborn, MI	W
University of Minnesota, Crookston, MN	W
University of Minnesota, Duluth, MN	W
University of Minnesota, Twin Cities Campus, MN	W
University of Missouri– Kansas City, MO	W
University of Missouri–St. Louis, MO	W
University of Mobile, AL	W
The University of Montana Western, MT	W
University of Montevallo, AL	W
University of Nebraska at Kearney, NE	W
University of Nevada, Las Vegas, NV	W
University of Nevada, Reno, NV	W
University of New Hampshire, NH	W
University of New Haven, CT	W
University of New Orleans, LA	W
University of North Alabama, AL	W
University of North Carolina at Asheville, NC	W
The University of North Carolina at Chapel Hill, NC	W
The University of North Carolina at Charlotte, NC	W
The University of North Carolina at Greensboro, NC	W
The University of North Carolina at Pembroke, NC	W
The University of North Carolina Wilmington, NC	W
University of Northern Colorado, CO	W
University of Northern Iowa, IA	W
University of North Florida, FL	W
University of North Texas, TX	W
University of Notre Dame, IN	W
University of Oklahoma, OK	W
University of Oregon, OR	W
University of Pikeville, KY	W
University of Pittsburgh, PA	W
University of Pittsburgh at Johnstown, PA	W
University of Puerto Rico in Bayamón, PR	M,W
University of Rhode Island, RI	W
University of St. Francis, IL	W
University of St. Thomas, TX	W
University of San Diego, CA	W
University of San Francisco, CA	W
University of South Alabama, AL	W

University of South Carolina, SC	W	
University of South Carolina Aiken, SC	W	
The University of South Dakota, SD	W	
University of Southern California, CA	M,W	
University of Southern Indiana, IN	W	
University of Southern Mississippi, MS	W	
University of South Florida, FL	W	
The University of Tampa, FL	W	
The University of Tennessee, TN	W	
The University of Tennessee at Chattanooga, TN	W	
The University of Tennessee at Martin, TN	W	
The University of Texas at Austin, TX	W	
The University of Texas at El Paso, TX	W	
The University of Texas at San Antonio, TX	W	
The University of Texas of the Permian Basin, TX	W	
The University of Texas Rio Grande Valley, TX	W	
University of the Incarnate Word, TX	W	
University of the Pacific, CA	M,W	
The University of Toledo, OH	W	
The University of Tulsa, OK	W	
University of Utah, UT	W	
University of Virginia, VA	W	
The University of Virginia's College at Wise, VA	W	
University of Washington, WA	W	
The University of West Alabama, AL	W	
University of West Georgia, GA	W	
University of Wisconsin–Green Bay, WI	W	
University of Wisconsin–Madison, WI	W	
University of Wisconsin–Milwaukee, WI	W	
University of Wisconsin–Parkside, WI	W	
Upper Iowa University, IA	W	
Ursuline College, OH	W	
Utah State University, UT	W	
Utah Valley University, UT	W	
Valdosta State University, GA	W	
Valley City State University, ND	W	
Valparaiso University, IN	W	
Villanova University, PA	W	
Virginia Commonwealth University, VA	W	
Virginia State University, VA	W	
Viterbo University, WI	W	
Wake Forest University, NC	W	
Waldorf University, IA	W	
Washburn University, KS	W	
Washington State University, WA	W	
Wayland Baptist University, TX	W	
Wayne State College, NE	W	
Wayne State University, MI	W	
Webber International University, FL	M,W	
Weber State University, UT	W	
West Chester University of Pennsylvania, PA	W	
Western Carolina University, NC	W	
Western Illinois University, IL	W	
Western Kentucky University, KY	W	
Western Michigan University, MI	W	

Western Oregon University, OR	W	
Western State Colorado University, CO	W	
Western Washington University, WA	W	
Westminster College, UT	W	
Westmont College, CA	W	
West Texas A&M University, TX	W	
West Virginia University, WV	W	
West Virginia University Institute of Technology, WV	W	
West Virginia Wesleyan College, WV	W	
Wheeling Jesuit University, WV	W	
Wichita State University, KS	W	
William Jewell College, MO	W	
Williams Baptist College, AR	W	
William Woods University, MO	W	
Wingate University, NC	W	
Winona State University, MN	W	
Winthrop University, SC	W	
Wofford College, SC	W	
Wright State University, OH	W	
Youngstown State University, OH	W	

Water polo

Arizona State University at the Downtown Phoenix campus, AZ	W	
Arizona State University at the Polytechnic campus, AZ	W	
Arizona State University at the Tempe campus, AZ	W	
Arizona State University at the West campus, AZ	W	
California Baptist University, CA	M,W	
California State University, Bakersfield, CA	W	
California State University, Long Beach, CA	M,W	
California State University, Monterey Bay, CA	W	
Concordia University Irvine, CA	M,W	
Fordham University, NY	M	
Fresno Pacific University, CA	M,W	
Gannon University, PA	M,W	
The George Washington University, DC	M	
Hartwick College, NY	W	
Indiana University Bloomington, IN	W	
Iona College, NY	W	
La Salle University, PA	M,W	
Lindenwood University, MO	M,W	
Loyola Marymount University, CA	M,W	
Marist College, NY	W	
McKendree University, IL	M,W	
Pepperdine University, CA	M	
San Diego State University, CA	W	
Santa Clara University, CA	M,W	
Siena College, NY	W	
Stanford University, CA	M,W	
University of California, Davis, CA	M,W	
University of California, Irvine, CA	M,W	
University of California, Los Angeles, CA	M,W	
University of California, Santa Barbara, CA	M,W	
University of Hawaii at Manoa, HI	W	
University of Maryland, College Park, MD	W	
University of Michigan, MI	W	
University of Southern California, CA	M,W	
University of the Pacific, CA	M,W	
Wagner College, NY	M,W	

Weight lifting

Inter American University of Puerto Rico, Bayamón Campus, PR	M	
Lindenwood University, MO	M,W	

Wrestling

Adams State University, CO	M	
Alderson Broaddus University, WV	M,W	
American University, DC	M	
Appalachian State University, NC	M	
Arizona State University at the Downtown Phoenix campus, AZ	M	
Arizona State University at the Polytechnic campus, AZ	M	
Arizona State University at the Tempe campus, AZ	M	
Arizona State University at the West campus, AZ	M	
Augustana University, SD	M	
Baker University, KS	M	
Bellarmine University, KY	M	
Belmont Abbey College, NC	M	
Benedictine College, KS	M	
Binghamton University, State University of New York, NY	M	
Bloomsburg University of Pennsylvania, PA	M	
Boise State University, ID	M	
Briar Cliff University, IA	M	
Bucknell University, PA	M	
California Baptist University, CA	M	
California Polytechnic State University, San Luis Obispo, CA	M	
California State University, Bakersfield, CA	M	
Calumet College of Saint Joseph, IN	M	
Campbellsville University, KY	M,W	
Central Michigan University, MI	M	
The Citadel, The Military College of South Carolina, SC	M	
Clarion University of Pennsylvania, PA	M	
Cleveland State University, OH	M	
Colorado Mesa University, CO	M	
Colorado School of Mines, CO	M	
Concordia University, Nebraska, NE	M	
Davidson College, NC	M	
Dickinson State University, ND	M	
Drexel University, PA	M	
Eastern Michigan University, MI	M	
East Stroudsburg University of Pennsylvania, PA	M	
Embry-Riddle Aeronautical University–Prescott, AZ	M	
Emmanuel College, GA	M,W	
Gannon University, PA	M	
Gardner-Webb University, NC	M	
Graceland University, IA	M	
Grand View University, IA	M	
Hofstra University, NY	M	
Indiana University Bloomington, IN	M	
Iowa State University of Science and Technology, IA	M	
Kansas Wesleyan University, KS	M	
Kent State University, OH	M	
King University, TN	M,W	
Kutztown University of Pennsylvania, PA	M	
Lake Erie College, OH	M	
Lehigh University, PA	M	
Life University, GA	M,W	
Lindenwood University, MO	M,W	
Lindsey Wilson College, KY	M	

Lock Haven University of Pennsylvania, PA	M
Lyon College, AR	M,W
Maryville University of Saint Louis, MO	M
McKendree University, IL	M,W
Michigan State University, MI	M
Millersville University of Pennsylvania, PA	M
Minnesota State University Mankato, MN	M
Minnesota State University Moorhead, MN	M
Missouri Baptist University, MO	M,W
Morningside College, IA	M
Newberry College, SC	M
North Carolina State University, NC	M
Northern Illinois University, IL	M
Northern State University, SD	M
Northwestern College, IA	M
The Ohio State University, OH	M
Ohio University, OH	M
Ohio Valley University, WV	M
Oklahoma City University, OK	M,W
Oklahoma State University, OK	M
Old Dominion University, VA	M
Oregon State University, OR	M
Ouachita Baptist University, AR	M
Penn State University Park, PA	M
Purdue University, IN	M
Sacred Heart University, CT	M
San Francisco State University, CA	M
Seton Hill University, PA	M
Shippensburg University of Pennsylvania, PA	M
Simpson University, CA	M
Southeastern University, FL	M
Southern Illinois University Edwardsville, IL	M
Southern Oregon University, OR	M
Stanford University, CA	M
Tiffin University, OH	M
Truett McConnell University, GA	M
Truman State University, MO	M
University at Buffalo, the State University of New York, NY	M
University of Central Missouri, MO	M
The University of Findlay, OH	M
University of Great Falls, MT	M
University of Indianapolis, IN	M
University of Jamestown, ND	M,W
University of Maryland, College Park, MD	M
University of Michigan, MI	M
University of Minnesota, Twin Cities Campus, MN	M
University of Nebraska at Kearney, NE	M
The University of North Carolina at Chapel Hill, NC	M
The University of North Carolina at Pembroke, NC	M
University of Northern Colorado, CO	M
University of Northern Iowa, IA	M
University of Oklahoma, OK	M
University of Pittsburgh, PA	M
University of Pittsburgh at Johnstown, PA	M
The University of Tennessee at Chattanooga, TN	M
University of Virginia, VA	M
University of Wisconsin–Madison, WI	M
University of Wisconsin–Parkside, WI	M
Upper Iowa University, IA	M
Utah Valley University, UT	M
Virginia Military Institute, VA	M
Waldorf University, IA	M,W
Wayland Baptist University, TX	M,W
Western State Colorado University, CO	M
West Virginia University, WV	M
West Virginia University Institute of Technology, WV	M
Wheeling Jesuit University, WV	M
Williams Baptist College, AR	M

Co-Op Programs

Academy College, MN
Adams State University, CO
Adelphi University, NY
Alabama State University, AL
Alcorn State University, MS
Alfred University, NY
Allen College, IA
Alma College, MI
American University, DC
Anderson University, SC
Andrews University, MI
Aquinas College, MI
Arcadia University, PA
Arizona State University at the Downtown Phoenix campus, AZ
Arizona State University at the Polytechnic campus, AZ
Arizona State University at the Tempe campus, AZ
Arizona State University at the West campus, AZ
Armstrong State University, GA
Athens State University, AL
Auburn University, AL
Auburn University at Montgomery, AL
Augsburg College, MN
Austin Peay State University, TN
Averett University, VA
Azusa Pacific University, CA
Ball State University, IN
Bates College, ME
Bay Path University, MA
Bellarmine University, KY
Belmont Abbey College, NC
Belmont University, TN
Benedictine College, KS
Bethany Lutheran College, MN
Bethel College, KS
Bethune-Cookman University, FL
Biola University, CA
Black Hills State University, SD
Bloomsburg University of Pennsylvania, PA
Bluefield College, VA
Boise State University, ID
Boston University, MA
Bowling Green State University, OH
Bradley University, IL
Butler University, IN
Cabarrus College of Health Sciences, NC
Cabrini University, PA
Caldwell University, NJ
California Christian College, CA
California Institute of Technology, CA
California Lutheran University, CA
California Polytechnic State University, San Luis Obispo, CA
California State Polytechnic University, Pomona, CA
California State University, Chico, CA
California State University, Dominguez Hills, CA
California State University, East Bay, CA
California State University, Fresno, CA
California State University, Fullerton, CA
California State University, Monterey Bay, CA
California State University, San Bernardino, CA
California University of Pennsylvania, PA
Calumet College of Saint Joseph, IN

Calvary University, MO
Campbellsville University, KY
Canisius College, NY
Capital University, OH
Cardinal Stritch University, WI
Carlow University, PA
Carnegie Mellon University, PA
Carroll College, MT
Case Western Reserve University, OH
The Catholic University of America, DC
Cedarville University, OH
Central Connecticut State University, CT
Central Methodist University, MO
Central Washington University, WA
Centre College, KY
Champlain College, VT
Chatham University, PA
Chestnut Hill College, PA
Chowan University, NC
Christendom College, VA
Christian Brothers University, TN
The Citadel, The Military College of South Carolina, SC
Clarion University of Pennsylvania, PA
Clark Atlanta University, GA
Clarke University, IA
Clarkson University, NY
Clayton State University, GA
Clemson University, SC
Cleveland State University, OH
Coastal Carolina University, SC
Cogswell Polytechnical College, CA
The College at Brockport, State University of New York, NY
College of Charleston, SC
The College of Idaho, ID
College of the Atlantic, ME
Colorado School of Mines, CO
Colorado State University, CO
Columbia College, MO
Columbia College Chicago, IL
Columbia International University, SC
Columbus State University, GA
Concordia College, MN
Concord University, WV
Converse College, SC
Corban University, OR
Cornell University, NY
Dakota State University, SD
Davis College, NY
Dean College, MA
DePauw University, IN
DeSales University, PA
Dickinson State University, ND
Dixie State University, UT
Doane University, NE
Dominican College, NY
Drake University, IA
Drexel University, PA
Drury University, MO
East Carolina University, NC
Eastern Michigan University, MI
Eastern Oregon University, OR
Eastern Washington University, WA
Edgewood College, WI
Elizabeth City State University, NC
Embry-Riddle Aeronautical University–Daytona, FL
Embry-Riddle Aeronautical University–Prescott, AZ

Embry-Riddle Aeronautical University–Worldwide, FL
Emory & Henry College, VA
Emory University, GA
Emporia State University, KS
Endicott College, MA
Eureka College, IL
Farmingdale State College, NY
Felician University, NJ
Ferris State University, MI
Flagler College, FL
Florida Agricultural and Mechanical University, FL
Florida Atlantic University, FL
Florida Gulf Coast University, FL
Florida Institute of Technology, FL
Florida International University, FL
Florida National University, FL
Florida State University, FL
Framingham State University, MA
Franciscan University of Steubenville, OH
Franklin College, IN
Freed-Hardeman University, TN
Fresno Pacific University, CA
Friends University, KS
Frostburg State University, MD
Gannon University, PA
Gardner-Webb University, NC
Geneva College, PA
The George Washington University, DC
Georgia Institute of Technology, GA
Georgia Southern University, GA
Georgia State University, GA
Gordon College, MA
Graceland University, IA
Grambling State University, LA
Grand Valley State University, MI
Grand View University, IA
Greenville College, IL
Guilford College, NC
Gwynedd Mercy University, PA
Hampden-Sydney College, VA
Hampton University, VA
Hanover College, IN
Harding University, AR
Harris-Stowe State University, MO
Hawai`i Pacific University, HI
Heidelberg University, OH
Hendrix College, AR
High Point University, NC
Hilbert College, NY
Hofstra University, NY
Holy Family University, PA
Houghton College, NY
Humboldt State University, CA
Husson University, ME
Huston-Tillotson University, TX
Idaho State University, ID
Indiana State University, IN
Indiana University Bloomington, IN
Indiana University East, IN
Indiana University Northwest, IN
Indiana University of Pennsylvania, PA
Indiana University–Purdue University Indianapolis, IN
Inter American University of Puerto Rico, Bayamón Campus, PR
Inter American University of Puerto Rico, Guayama Campus, PR

Iowa State University of Science and
    Technology, IA
Iowa Wesleyan University, IA
Jackson State University, MS
Jacksonville State University, AL
Jacksonville University, FL
John Jay College of Criminal Justice of the
    City University of New York, NY
Johnson C. Smith University, NC
Kansas State University, KS
Kean University, NJ
Keene State College, NH
Kennesaw State University, GA
Kent State University, OH
Kentucky Mountain Bible College, KY
Kentucky State University, KY
Kentucky Wesleyan College, KY
Keuka College, NY
King University, TN
Kuyper College, MI
Lamar University, TX
Lane College, TN
Langston University, OK
La Salle University, PA
Lasell College, MA
Lawrence Technological University, MI
Lees-McRae College, NC
Lee University, TN
Lehigh University, PA
Lehman College of the City University
    of New York, NY
LeTourneau University, TX
Liberty University, VA
Life University, GA
LIM College, NY
Lincoln Christian University, IL
Lincoln University, MO
Lindsey Wilson College, KY
Lock Haven University of Pennsylvania, PA
Logan University, MO
Loras College, IA
Louisiana State University and Agricultural
    & Mechanical College, LA
Loyola University Chicago, IL
Loyola University Maryland, MD
Loyola University New Orleans, LA
Lubbock Christian University, TX
Lycoming College, PA
Lynn University, FL
Manhattan College, NY
Marian University, WI
Marist College, NY
Marquette University, WI
Marshall University, WV
Marymount California University, CA
Maryville University of Saint Louis, MO
Massachusetts College of Liberal Arts, MA
Massachusetts Institute of Technology, MA
Massachusetts Maritime Academy, MA
The Master's University, CA
McKendree University, IL
MCPHS University, MA
Medgar Evers College of the City University
    of New York, NY
Mercer University, GA
Mercy College, NY
Meredith College, NC
Merrimack College, MA
Messiah College, PA
Metropolitan College of New York, NY
Metropolitan State University of Denver, CO
Miami University, OH
Michigan State University, MI
Michigan Technological University, MI
Midland College, TX
Millersville University of Pennsylvania, PA

Milligan College, TN
Mills College, CA
Minnesota State University Mankato, MN
Minot State University, ND
Misericordia University, PA
Mississippi State University, MS
Missouri State University, MO
Missouri University of Science and
    Technology, MO
Monmouth University, NJ
Montana State University Billings, MT
Montana Tech of The University of
    Montana, MT
Montclair State University, NJ
Moravian College, PA
Morehead State University, KY
Morehouse College, GA
Morrisville State College, NY
Mount Ida College, MA
Mount Marty College, SD
Mount St. Joseph University, OH
Mount Saint Mary College, NY
Mount Saint Mary's University, CA
Murray State University, KY
National University, CA
Nazareth College of Rochester, NY
Nebraska Methodist College, NE
Neumann University, PA
New Jersey City University, NJ
New Mexico Highlands University, NM
New Mexico Institute of Mining and
    Technology, NM
New Mexico State University, NM
New York Institute of Technology, NY
Niagara University, NY
Nichols College, MA
North Carolina State University, NC
Northeastern Illinois University, IL
Northeastern State University, OK
Northeastern University, MA
Northern Arizona University, AZ
Northern Illinois University, IL
Northern Kentucky University, KY
Northern State University, SD
Northwest Christian University, OR
Northwestern College, IA
Northwestern State University of
    Louisiana, LA
Northwestern University, IL
Northwest University, WA
The Ohio State University, OH
Ohio University, OH
Oklahoma Baptist University, OK
Oklahoma City University, OK
Old Dominion University, VA
Olivet College, MI
Olivet Nazarene University, IL
O'More College of Design, TN
Oregon State University, OR
Otterbein University, OH
Ouachita Baptist University, AR
Our Lady of the Lake University, TX
Patrick Henry College, VA
Peirce College, PA
Penn State University Park, PA
Pennsylvania College of Technology, PA
Philander Smith College, AR
Piedmont College, GA
Pitzer College, CA
Point Park University, PA
Portland State University, OR
Prairie View A&M University, TX
Purdue University, IN
Queens College of the City University of
    New York, NY
Ramapo College of New Jersey, NJ

Reed College, OR
Regis University, CO
Rensselaer Polytechnic Institute, NY
Rhodes College, TN
Robert Morris University, PA
Roberts Wesleyan College, NY
Rochester Institute of Technology, NY
Rockhurst University, MO
Rogers State University, OK
Roger Williams University, RI
Rose-Hulman Institute of Technology, IN
Rowan University, NJ
Rutgers University–Camden, NJ
Rutgers University–Newark, NJ
Rutgers University–New Brunswick, NJ
Sacred Heart University, CT
The Sage Colleges, NY
Saginaw Valley State University, MI
St. Ambrose University, IA
Saint Augustine's University, NC
St. Gregory's University, OK
Saint Joseph's University, PA
Saint Louis University, MO
Saint Martin's University, WA
St. Mary's College of Maryland, MD
Saint Mary's University of Minnesota, MN
St. Petersburg College, FL
Saint Peter's University, NJ
Saint Vincent College, PA
Salisbury University, MD
Samuel Merritt University, CA
San Francisco Conservatory of Music, CA
San Francisco State University, CA
Santa Clara University, CA
Savannah College of Art and Design, GA
School of the Art Institute of Chicago, IL
Schreiner University, TX
Shepherd University, WV
Shippensburg University
    of Pennsylvania, PA
Siena College, NY
Simpson College, IA
Soka University of America, CA
Sonoma State University, CA
South Dakota School of Mines and
    Technology, SD
Southeastern University, FL
Southern Connecticut State University, CT
Southern Illinois University Carbondale, IL
Southern Illinois
    University Edwardsville, IL
Southern Methodist University, TX
Southern New Hampshire University, NH
Southern Oregon University, OR
Southern Utah University, UT
Southwest Baptist University, MO
Southwestern Oklahoma
    State University, OK
Spelman College, GA
State University of New York at
    New Paltz, NY
State University of New York at
    Oswego, NY
State University of New York at
    Plattsburgh, NY
State University of New York College of
    Agriculture and Technology at
    Cobleskill, NY
State University of New York College of
    Environmental Science and Forestry, NY
State University of New York College of
    Technology at Canton, NY
State University of New York Polytechnic
    Institute, NY
Stephen F. Austin State University, TX
Stephens College, MO

Stevens Institute of Technology, NJ
Stevenson University, MD
Stony Brook University, State University of New York, NY
Suffolk University, MA
Syracuse University, NY
Tarleton State University, TX
Taylor University, IN
Temple University, PA
Tennessee State University, TN
Texas A&M University, TX
Texas A&M University–Commerce, TX
Texas A&M University–Corpus Christi, TX
Texas Tech University, TX
Texas Woman's University, TX
Thomas Aquinas College, CA
Thomas More College, KY
Thomas University, GA
Towson University, MD
Trine University, IN
Trinity Christian College, IL
Trinity College of Florida, FL
Truman State University, MO
Tufts University, MA
Tulane University, LA
Union College, NE
Union University, TN
Unity College, ME
University at Buffalo, the State University of New York, NY
The University of Akron, OH
The University of Alabama, AL
The University of Alabama at Birmingham, AL
The University of Alabama in Huntsville, AL
University of Alaska Fairbanks, AK
The University of Arizona, AZ
University of Arkansas, AR
University of Bridgeport, CT
University of California, San Diego, CA
University of California, Santa Barbara, CA
University of Central Arkansas, AR
University of Central Florida, FL
University of Cincinnati, OH
University of Colorado Boulder, CO
University of Colorado Colorado Springs, CO
University of Colorado Denver, CO
University of Dayton, OH
University of Denver, CO
University of Detroit Mercy, MI
University of Evansville, IN
The University of Findlay, OH
University of Florida, FL
University of Georgia, GA
University of Hartford, CT
University of Hawaii at Manoa, HI
University of Houston, TX
University of Houston–Clear Lake, TX
University of Idaho, ID
University of Illinois at Chicago, IL
University of Illinois at Springfield, IL
University of Indianapolis, IN
University of Jamestown, ND
The University of Kansas, KS
University of Kentucky, KY
University of Louisiana at Monroe, LA
University of Louisville, KY
University of Maine at Fort Kent, ME
University of Maine at Presque Isle, ME
University of Maryland, Baltimore County, MD
University of Maryland, College Park, MD

University of Maryland University College, MD
University of Massachusetts Amherst, MA
University of Massachusetts Boston, MA
University of Massachusetts Dartmouth, MA
University of Massachusetts Lowell, MA
University of Miami, FL
University of Michigan, MI
University of Michigan–Dearborn, MI
University of Michigan–Flint, MI
University of Minnesota, Crookston, MN
University of Minnesota, Duluth, MN
University of Minnesota, Twin Cities Campus, MN
University of Missouri–Kansas City, MO
University of Missouri–St. Louis, MO
The University of Montana Western, MT
University of Mount Union, OH
University of Nevada, Las Vegas, NV
University of New Hampshire, NH
University of New Hampshire at Manchester, NH
University of New Haven, CT
University of New Orleans, LA
University of North Alabama, AL
University of North Carolina at Asheville, NC
The University of North Carolina at Charlotte, NC
The University of North Carolina at Pembroke, NC
The University of North Carolina Wilmington, NC
University of Northern Colorado, CO
University of Northern Iowa, IA
University of North Florida, FL
University of North Georgia, GA
University of North Texas, TX
University of North Texas at Dallas, TX
University of Oklahoma, OK
University of Oregon, OR
University of Pennsylvania, PA
University of Pittsburgh, PA
University of Pittsburgh at Bradford, PA
University of Pittsburgh at Johnstown, PA
University of Puerto Rico in Bayamón, PR
University of Puget Sound, WA
University of Rhode Island, RI
University of Rochester, NY
University of St. Thomas, MN
University of San Francisco, CA
University of South Alabama, AL
University of South Carolina, SC
University of South Carolina Aiken, SC
The University of South Dakota, SD
University of Southern California, CA
University of Southern Indiana, IN
University of Southern Maine, ME
University of Southern Mississippi, MS
University of South Florida, FL
The University of Tampa, FL
The University of Tennessee, TN
The University of Tennessee at Chattanooga, TN
The University of Tennessee at Martin, TN
The University of Texas at Austin, TX
The University of Texas at Dallas, TX
The University of Texas at El Paso, TX
The University of Texas at San Antonio, TX
The University of Texas of the Permian Basin, TX
The University of Texas Rio Grande Valley, TX
University of the Incarnate Word, TX
University of the Pacific, CA

The University of Toledo, OH
University of Utah, UT
University of Vermont, VT
University of Virginia, VA
The University of Virginia's College at Wise, VA
University of Washington, WA
University of Washington, Bothell, WA
The University of West Alabama, AL
University of West Georgia, GA
University of Wisconsin–Eau Claire, WI
University of Wisconsin–La Crosse, WI
University of Wisconsin–Madison, WI
University of Wisconsin–Milwaukee, WI
University of Wisconsin–Parkside, WI
University of Wisconsin–Stevens Point, WI
University of Wisconsin–Stout, WI
University of Wisconsin–Superior, WI
University of Wisconsin–Whitewater, WI
Upper Iowa University, IA
Ursinus College, PA
Utah State University, UT
Utah Valley University, UT
Utica College, NY
Valdosta State University, GA
Valley City State University, ND
Valparaiso University, IN
Vanderbilt University, TN
Vassar College, NY
Vermont Technical College, VT
Villa Maria College, NY
Villanova University, PA
Virginia Commonwealth University, VA
Virginia Polytechnic Institute and State University, VA
Virginia State University, VA
Wagner College, NY
Waldorf University, IA
Walla Walla University, WA
Washburn University, KS
Washington State University, WA
Washington University in St. Louis, MO
Wayne State College, NE
Wayne State University, MI
Webber International University, FL
Weber State University, UT
Webster University, MO
Wentworth Institute of Technology, MA
Wesleyan College, GA
Western Carolina University, NC
Western Connecticut State University, CT
Western Kentucky University, KY
Western Michigan University, MI
Western Washington University, WA
Westminster College, UT
West Texas A&M University, TX
West Virginia University Institute of Technology, WV
Wheaton College, MA
Whitman College, WA
Wichita State University, KS
Widener University, PA
Wilkes University, PA
William Jewell College, MO
William Peace University, NC
Winthrop University, SC
Wittenberg University, OH
Worcester Polytechnic Institute, MA
Wright State University, OH
Wright State University–Lake Campus, OH
Xavier University of Louisiana, LA
York College of Pennsylvania, PA
York College of the City University of New York, NY
Youngstown State University, OH

ROTC Programs

Air Force
Adelphi University, NY*
Agnes Scott College, GA*
Alabama State University, AL
Alaska Pacific University, AK*
Alverno College, WI*
American University, DC*
Amherst College, MA*
Anderson University, SC*
Angelo State University, TX
Arizona State University at the Downtown Phoenix campus, AZ*
Arizona State University at the Polytechnic campus, AZ*
Arizona State University at the Tempe campus, AZ
Arizona State University at the West campus, AZ*
Asbury University, KY*
Assumption College, MA*
Auburn University, AL
Auburn University at Montgomery, AL*
Augsburg College, MN*
Augustana University, SD*
Austin Peay State University, TN*
Azusa Pacific University, CA*
Baker University, KS*
Baldwin Wallace University, OH*
Barnard College, NY*
Barry University, FL*
Baylor University, TX
Bay Path University, MA*
Belhaven University, MS*
Bellarmine University, KY*
Belmont University, TN*
Bentley University, MA*
Bethel College, IN*
Bethel University, MN*
Bethune-Cookman University, FL*
Binghamton University, State University of New York, NY*
Biola University, CA*
Bloomsburg University of Pennsylvania, PA*
Boston College, MA*
Boston University, MA
Bowling Green State University, OH
Brandeis University, MA*
Bridgewater State University, MA*
Brigham Young University, UT
Brown University, RI*
Bryn Mawr College, PA*
Butler University, IN*
Cabrini University, PA*
Cairn University, PA*
California Baptist University, CA*
California Institute of Technology, CA*
California Lutheran University, CA*
California State University, Dominguez Hills, CA*
California State University, Fresno, CA
California State University, Long Beach, CA*
California State University Maritime Academy, CA*
California State University, Northridge, CA*
California State University, Sacramento, CA
California State University, San Bernardino, CA
California State University, San Marcos, CA*
Capital University, OH*

Carlow University, PA*
Carnegie Mellon University, PA*
Case Western Reserve University, OH*
Catawba College, NC*
The Catholic University of America, DC*
Cazenovia College, NY*
Cedarville University, OH*
Central Connecticut State University, CT*
Central Methodist University, MO*
Central Michigan University, MI*
Central Washington University, WA
Centre College, KY*
Chaminade University of Honolulu, HI*
Chapman University, CA*
Chatham University, PA*
Christian Brothers University, TN*
The Citadel, The Military College of South Carolina, SC
Claremont McKenna College, CA*
Clarkson University, NY
Clark University, MA*
Clayton State University, GA*
Clemson University, SC
Cleveland State University, OH*
Coe College, IA*
The College at Brockport, State University of New York, NY*
College of Charleston, SC*
The College of New Jersey, NJ*
College of Saint Mary, NE*
The College of Saint Rose, NY*
The College of St. Scholastica, MN*
College of the Holy Cross, MA*
Colorado School of Mines, CO
Colorado State University, CO
Columbia College, MO*
Columbia University, NY*
Columbia University, School of General Studies, NY*
Concordia College, MN*
Concordia University, Nebraska, NE*
Concordia University, St. Paul, MN*
Corban University, OR*
Cornell University, NY
Creighton University, NE*
Dakota State University, SD*
Dallas Baptist University, TX*
Davidson College, NC*
DePauw University, IN*
Doane University, NE*
Drake University, IA*
Drexel University, PA*
Duquesne University, PA*
East Carolina University, NC
Eastern Michigan University, MI*
Eastern University, PA*
East Stroudsburg University of Pennsylvania, PA*
Eckerd College, FL*
Edgewood College, WI*
Elmira College, NY*
Elms College, MA*
Elon University, NC*
Embry-Riddle Aeronautical University–Daytona, FL
Embry-Riddle Aeronautical University–Prescott, AZ
Emory University, GA*
Fairfield University, CT*

Farmingdale State College, NY
Faulkner University, AL*
Felician University, NJ*
Florida Agricultural and Mechanical University, FL*
Florida Atlantic University, FL*
Florida College, FL*
Florida International University, FL
Florida Southern College, FL*
Florida State University, FL
Fordham University, NY*
Franciscan University of Steubenville, OH*
Franklin Pierce University, NH*
Gardner-Webb University, NC*
George Fox University, OR*
Georgetown University, DC*
The George Washington University, DC*
Georgia Institute of Technology, GA
Georgia State University, GA*
Goucher College, MD*
Grambling State University, LA*
Grand View University, IA*
Guilford College, NC*
Hamilton College, NY*
Hamline University, MN*
Harvard University, MA
Harvey Mudd College, CA
Hawai`i Pacific University, HI*
Heidelberg University, OH*
High Point University, NC*
Hobart and William Smith Colleges, NY*
Houston Baptist University, TX*
Huntingdon College, AL*
Indiana State University, IN
Indiana University Bloomington, IN
Indiana University–Purdue University Indianapolis, IN*
Indiana University South Bend, IN*
Indiana University Southeast, IN*
Iona College, NY*
Iowa State University of Science and Technology, IA
Ithaca College, NY*
Jackson State University, MS
James Madison University, VA*
John Brown University, AR*
Kansas State University, KS
Kean University, NJ*
Keene State College, NH*
Kennesaw State University, GA*
Kent State University, OH
Kent State University at Stark, OH*
Kentucky State University, KY*
King's College, PA*
Lamar University, TX*
La Roche College, PA*
La Salle University, PA*
Lawrence Technological University, MI*
Le Moyne College, NY*
Lewis University, IL*
Liberty University, VA*
Lindenwood University, MO*
Linfield College, OR*
Lipscomb University, TN*
Louisiana State University and Agricultural & Mechanical College, LA
Louisiana Tech University, LA
Loyola Marymount University, CA
Loyola University Chicago, IL*

* program is offered at another college's campus

Loyola University Maryland, MD*
Loyola University New Orleans, LA*
Lubbock Christian University, TX*
Lynn University, FL*
Macalester College, MN*
Manhattan College, NY
Maranatha Baptist University, WI*
Maria College, NY*
Marquette University, WI
Mary Baldwin University, VA*
Marywood University, PA*
Massachusetts Institute of Technology, MA
The Master's University, CA*
McKendree University, IL*
Mercy College, NY*
Meredith College, NC*
Merrimack College, MA*
Metropolitan State University
    of Denver, CO*
Miami University, OH
Michigan State University, MI
Michigan Technological University, MI
Millsaps College, MS*
Milwaukee School of Engineering, WI*
Minnesota State University Moorhead, MN*
Misericordia University, PA*
Mississippi State University, MS
Missouri University of Science and
    Technology, MO
Monmouth University, NJ*
Montana State University, MT
Morehead State University, KY
Morehouse College, GA*
Morrisville State College, NY*
Mount Carmel College of Nursing, OH*
Mount Holyoke College, MA*
National University, CA*
Nazareth College of Rochester, NY*
Nebraska Methodist College, NE*
Neumann University, PA*
New England College, NH*
New Mexico State University, NM
New York Institute of Technology, NY*
North Carolina State University, NC
North Central College, IL*
Northeastern Illinois University, IL*
Northeastern University, MA*
Northern Arizona University, AZ
Northern Illinois University, IL*
Northern Kentucky University, KY*
Northwestern State University
    of Louisiana, LA*
Northwestern University, IL*
Northwest University, WA*
Occidental College, CA*
The Ohio State University, OH
Ohio University, OH
Ohio Wesleyan University, OH*
Oklahoma Baptist University, OK*
Oklahoma Christian University, OK*
Oklahoma City University, OK*
Oklahoma State University, OK
Olivet College, MI*
Oral Roberts University, OK*
Oregon State University, OR
Otterbein University, OH*
Penn State Abington, PA*
Penn State Altoona, PA
Penn State Brandywine, PA*
Penn State Hazleton, PA*
Penn State New Kensington, PA*
Penn State University Park, PA
Penn State Wilkes-Barre, PA*
Penn State Worthington Scranton, PA*
Pepperdine University, CA*

Pitzer College, CA*
Plymouth State University, NH*
Point Loma Nazarene University, CA*
Point Park University, PA*
Pomona College, CA*
Portland State University, OR*
Prairie View A&M University, TX*
Princeton University, NJ*
Purdue University, IN
Queens College of the City University
    of New York, NY*
Quinnipiac University, CT*
Ramapo College of New Jersey, NJ*
Regis University, CO*
Rensselaer Polytechnic Institute, NY
Rhodes College, TN*
Rice University, TX*
Robert Morris University, PA*
Roberts Wesleyan College, NY*
Rochester Institute of Technology, NY
Rose-Hulman Institute of Technology, IN
Rutgers University–Camden, NJ*
Rutgers University–Newark, NJ
Rutgers University–New Brunswick, NJ
Sacred Heart University, CT*
The Sage Colleges, NY*
Saint Augustine's University, NC*
St. Edward's University, TX*
St. John Fisher College, NY*
Saint Joseph's University, PA
Saint Leo University, FL
St. Louis College of Pharmacy, MO*
Saint Louis University, MO
Saint Martin's University, WA*
Saint Mary's College, IN*
Saint Michael's College, VT*
Saint Peter's University, NJ*
St. Thomas Aquinas College, NY*
Saint Vincent College, PA*
Salisbury University, MD*
Samford University, AL
San Diego State University, CA
San Francisco State University, CA*
Santa Clara University, CA*
Sarah Lawrence College, NY*
Scripps College, CA*
Seattle Pacific University, WA*
Seattle University, WA*
Shepherd University, WV*
Siena College, NY*
Skidmore College, NY*
Smith College, MA*
Sonoma State University, CA*
Southeast Missouri State University, MO
Southern Connecticut State University, CT*
Southern Illinois University Carbondale, IL
Southern Illinois University
    Edwardsville, IL*
Southern Methodist University, TX*
Southern New Hampshire University, NH*
Southwestern University, TX*
Spelman College, GA*
Spring Hill College, AL*
Stanford University, CA*
State University of New York
    at Oswego, NY*
State University of New York College at
    Cortland, NY*
State University of New York College at
    Geneseo, NY*
State University of New York College at
    Potsdam, NY*
State University of New York College of
    Environmental Science and Forestry, NY*

State University of New York College of
    Technology at Canton, NY*
State University of New York Polytechnic
    Institute, NY*
Stephens College, MO*
Stevens Institute of Technology, NJ*
Stevenson University, MD*
Stony Brook University, State University of
    New York, NY*
Swarthmore College, PA*
Syracuse University, NY
Temple University, PA*
Tennessee State University, TN
Texas A&M University, TX
Texas A&M University–Commerce, TX*
Texas Christian University, TX
Texas Lutheran University, TX*
Texas State University, TX
Texas Tech University, TX
Texas Wesleyan University, TX*
Texas Woman's University, TX*
Thomas More College, KY*
Tiffin University, OH*
Towson University, MD*
Transylvania University, KY*
Trine University, IN*
Trinity University, TX*
Troy University, AL
Tufts University, MA*
Tulane University, LA
Union College, NY*
University at Albany, State University
    of New York, NY*
The University of Akron, OH*
The University of Alabama, AL
The University of Alabama at
    Birmingham, AL*
The University of Arizona, AZ
University of Arkansas, AR
University of California, Davis, CA*
University of California, Irvine, CA*
University of California, Los Angeles, CA
University of California, Riverside, CA*
University of California, San Diego, CA*
University of California, Santa Barbara, CA*
University of Central Florida, FL
University of Central Missouri, MO*
University of Chicago, IL*
University of Cincinnati, OH
University of Colorado Boulder, CO
University of Colorado Denver, CO*
University of Dayton, OH*
University of Delaware, DE
University of Denver, CO*
The University of Findlay, OH*
University of Florida, FL
University of Georgia, GA
University of Hartford, CT*
University of Hawaii at Manoa, HI
University of Houston, TX
University of Houston–Downtown, TX*
University of Idaho, ID*
University of Illinois at Chicago, IL*
The University of Kansas, KS
University of Kentucky, KY
University of Louisville, KY
University of Mary Hardin-Baylor, TX*
University of Maryland, Baltimore
    County, MD*
University of Maryland, College Park, MD
University of Massachusetts Amherst, MA
University of Massachusetts Boston, MA*
University of Massachusetts Lowell, MA
University of Miami, FL
University of Michigan, MI

---

* program is offered at another college's campus

University of Michigan–Dearborn, MI*
University of Michigan–Flint, MI*
University of Minnesota, Crookston, MN*
University of Minnesota, Duluth, MN
University of Minnesota, Twin Cities
Campus, MN
University of Missouri–Kansas City, MO*
University of Missouri–St. Louis, MO*
University of Mobile, AL*
University of Montevallo, AL*
University of Mount Union, OH*
University of Nevada, Las Vegas, NV
University of New Hampshire, NH
University of New Hampshire
at Manchester, NH*
University of New Haven, CT*
University of New Orleans, LA*
The University of North Carolina at Chapel
Hill, NC
The University of North Carolina at
Charlotte, NC
The University of North Carolina at
Greensboro, NC*
The University of North Carolina at
Pembroke, NC
University of Northern Colorado, CO
University of North Texas, TX
University of Notre Dame, IN
University of Oklahoma, OK
University of Oregon, OR*
University of Pennsylvania, PA*
University of Pittsburgh, PA
University of Pittsburgh at Greensburg, PA*
University of Rochester, NY*
University of St. Thomas, MN
University of St. Thomas, TX*
University of San Diego, CA*
University of San Francisco, CA*
University of South Alabama, AL
University of South Carolina, SC
University of Southern California, CA
University of Southern Maine, ME*
University of Southern Mississippi, MS
University of South Florida, FL
The University of Tampa, FL*
The University of Tennessee, TN
The University of Texas at Austin, TX
The University of Texas at Dallas, TX*
The University of Texas at San Antonio, TX
University of the Pacific, CA*
The University of Toledo, OH*
The University of Tulsa, OK*
University of Utah, UT
University of Virginia, VA
University of Washington, WA
University of Washington, Bothell, WA*
University of Washington, Tacoma, WA*
The University of West Alabama, AL*
University of West Georgia, GA*
University of Wisconsin–Madison, WI
University of Wisconsin–Milwaukee, WI*
University of Wisconsin–Parkside, WI*
University of Wisconsin–Stout, WI*
University of Wisconsin–Superior, WI*
University of Wisconsin–Whitewater, WI
Utah State University, UT
Utah Valley University, UT*
Utica College, NY*
Valdosta State University, GA
Valparaiso University, IN*
Vanderbilt University, TN*
Villanova University, PA*
Virginia Military Institute, VA
Virginia Polytechnic Institute and State
University, VA

Washburn University, KS*
Washington & Jefferson College, PA*
Washington State University, WA
Washington University in St. Louis, MO*
Wayland Baptist University, TX*
Wayne State University, MI*
Weber State University, UT*
Webster University, MO*
Wentworth Institute of Technology, MA*
Wesleyan University, CT*
West Chester University
of Pennsylvania, PA*
Western Connecticut State University, CT*
Western Kentucky University, KY*
Western New England University, MA*
Westfield State University, MA*
Westminster College, UT*
Westmont College, CA*
West Virginia University, WV
Wheaton College, IL*
Widener University, PA*
Wilkes University, PA
Willamette University, OR*
William Peace University, NC*
Williams College, MA*
William Woods University, MO*
Wingate University, NC*
Winthrop University, SC*
Wittenberg University, OH*
Worcester Polytechnic Institute, MA
Worcester State University, MA*
Wright State University, OH
Wright State University–Lake Campus, OH*
Xavier University of Louisiana, LA*
Youngstown State University, OH*

Army

Adelphi University, NY*
Agnes Scott College, GA*
Alabama State University, AL*
Albright College, PA*
Alcorn State University, MS
Alfred University, NY*
Allen College, IA*
Alma College, MI*
Alvernia University, PA*
Alverno College, WI*
American University, DC*
Amherst College, MA*
Anderson University, SC*
Appalachian State University, NC
Arizona State University at the Downtown
Phoenix campus, AZ*
Arizona State University at the
Polytechnic campus, AZ*
Arizona State University at the Tempe
campus, AZ
Arizona State University at the
West campus, AZ*
Arkansas Tech University, AR*
Armstrong State University, GA
Asbury University, KY*
Assumption College, MA*
Auburn University, AL
Auburn University at Montgomery, AL
Augsburg College, MN*
Augustana University, SD*
Augusta University, GA
Aurora University, IL*
Austin Peay State University, TN
Azusa Pacific University, CA
Baker University, KS*
Baldwin Wallace University, OH*
Ball State University, IN
Barnard College, NY*

Barry University, FL*
Baruch College of the City University
of New York, NY*
Baylor University, TX
Bay Path University, MA*
Belhaven University, MS*
Bellarmine University, KY*
Belmont University, TN*
Benedictine College, KS*
Bentley University, MA*
Bethany Lutheran College, MN*
Bethel College, IN*
Bethel University, MN*
Bethune-Cookman University, FL*
Binghamton University, State
University of New York, NY*
Biola University, CA*
Black Hills State University, SD
Bloomfield College, NJ*
Bloomsburg University of Pennsylvania, PA
Boise State University, ID
Boston College, MA*
Boston University, MA
Bowling Green State University, OH
Bradley University, IL
Brandeis University, MA*
Briar Cliff University, IA*
Bridgewater State University, MA*
Brigham Young University, UT
Brown University, RI*
Bucknell University, PA
Buena Vista University, IA
Butler University, IN*
Cabrini University, PA*
Caldwell University, NJ*
California Baptist University, CA
California Institute of Technology, CA*
California Lutheran University, CA*
California Polytechnic State University, San
Luis Obispo, CA
California State Polytechnic University,
Pomona, CA
California State University,
Dominguez Hills, CA
California State University, Fresno, CA
California State University, Fullerton, CA
California State University, Long Beach, CA
California State University, Northridge, CA*
California State University, Sacramento, CA*
California State University,
San Bernardino, CA
California State University, San Marcos, CA
California University of Pennsylvania, PA
Calvary University, MO*
Calvin College, MI*
Cameron University, OK
Campbellsville University, KY*
Canisius College, NY
Capital University, OH
Carlow University, PA*
Carnegie Mellon University, PA*
Carroll College, MT
Carson-Newman University, TN
Case Western Reserve University, OH
Catawba College, NC*
The Catholic University of America, DC*
Cazenovia College, NY*
Cedar Crest College, PA*
Cedarville University, OH*
Central Connecticut State University, CT*
Central Methodist University, MO*
Central Michigan University, MI
Central Washington University, WA
Centre College, KY*
Chaminade University of Honolulu, HI*

---

* program is offered at another college's campus

Champlain College, VT*
Chapman University, CA*
Chatham University, PA*
Christian Brothers University, TN*
Christopher Newport University, VA
The Citadel, The Military College of South Carolina, SC
City College of the City University of New York, NY
Claremont McKenna College, CA
Clarion University of Pennsylvania, PA
Clark Atlanta University, GA*
Clarke University, IA*
Clarkson University, NY
Clark University, MA*
Clayton State University, GA*
Clemson University, SC
Cleveland State University, OH*
Coastal Carolina University, SC
Coe College, IA
Colby College, ME*
Colgate University, NY*
The College at Brockport, State University of New York, NY
The College of Idaho, ID*
The College of New Jersey, NJ*
College of Saint Benedict, MN*
College of Saint Mary, NE*
The College of Saint Rose, NY*
College of the Holy Cross, MA*
College of the Ozarks, MO
The College of William and Mary, VA
The Colorado College, CO*
Colorado School of Mines, CO
Colorado State University, CO
Columbia College, MO*
Columbia University, NY*
Columbia University, School of General Studies, NY*
Columbus State University, GA
Concordia College, MN*
Concordia University, Nebraska, NE*
Concordia University, St. Paul, MN*
Converse College, SC*
Cooper Union for the Advancement of Science and Art, NY*
Corban University, OR*
Cornell University, NY
Cornerstone University, MI*
Creighton University, NE
Curry College, MA*
Daemen College, NY*
Dakota State University, SD*
Dallas Baptist University, TX*
Dartmouth College, NH*
Davidson College, NC
Denison University, OH*
DePauw University, IN*
DeSales University, PA*
Dickinson College, PA
Dixie State University, UT
Doane University, NE*
Drake University, IA*
Drew University, NJ*
Drexel University, PA
Drury University, MO*
Duquesne University, PA
D'Youville College, NY*
East Carolina University, NC
Eastern Illinois University, IL
Eastern Michigan University, MI
Eastern Oregon University, OR
Eastern University, PA*
Eastern Washington University, WA

East Stroudsburg University of Pennsylvania, PA
Eckerd College, FL*
Edgewood College, WI*
Elizabeth City State University, NC
Elmira College, NY
Elms College, MA*
Elon University, NC
Embry-Riddle Aeronautical University–Daytona, FL
Embry-Riddle Aeronautical University–Prescott, AZ
Emmanuel College, MA*
Emory University, GA*
Endicott College, MA*
Evangel University, MO*
Fairfield University, CT*
Farmingdale State College, NY*
Faulkner University, AL*
Felician University, NJ*
Ferris State University, MI*
Fisher College, MA*
Fitchburg State University, MA
Florida Agricultural and Mechanical University, FL
Florida Atlantic University, FL
Florida College, FL*
Florida Institute of Technology, FL
Florida International University, FL
Florida Southern College, FL
Florida State University, FL
Fordham University, NY
Franciscan University of Steubenville, OH
Francis Marion University, SC
Franklin & Marshall College, PA*
Franklin College, IN*
Franklin Pierce University, NH*
Furman University, SC
Gannon University, PA
Gardner-Webb University, NC
Geneva College, PA*
Georgetown University, DC
The George Washington University, DC*
Georgia College & State University, GA*
Georgia Institute of Technology, GA
Georgia Southern University, GA
Georgia State University, GA
Gettysburg College, PA*
Gonzaga University, WA
Gordon College, MA*
Goucher College, MD*
Grambling State University, LA
Grand View University, IA*
Guilford College, NC*
Hamilton College, NY*
Hamline University, MN*
Hampden-Sydney College, VA*
Hampshire College, MA*
Hampton University, VA
Harris-Stowe State University, MO*
Harvard University, MA
Harvey Mudd College, CA*
Hawai`i Pacific University, HI*
Heidelberg University, OH*
Hendrix College, AR*
High Point University, NC*
Hilbert College, NY*
Hobart and William Smith Colleges, NY*
Hofstra University, NY
Holy Family University, PA*
Hood College, MD
Hope College, MI*
Hope International University, CA*
Houghton College, NY*
Houston Baptist University, TX*

Huntingdon College, AL*
Husson University, ME
Idaho State University, ID
Illinois Wesleyan University, IL*
Indiana State University, IN
Indiana University Bloomington, IN
Indiana University Kokomo, IN
Indiana University Northwest, IN
Indiana University of Pennsylvania, PA
Indiana University–Purdue University Indianapolis, IN
Indiana University South Bend, IN*
Indiana University Southeast, IN*
Inter American University of Puerto Rico, Bayamón Campus, PR*
Inter American University of Puerto Rico, Guayama Campus, PR*
Iona College, NY*
Iowa State University of Science and Technology, IA
Ithaca College, NY*
Jackson State University, MS
Jacksonville State University, AL
Jacksonville University, FL
James Madison University, VA
John Brown University, AR*
John Carroll University, OH
Judson University, IL*
Kalamazoo College, MI*
Kansas State University, KS
Kean University, NJ*
Keene State College, NH*
Kennesaw State University, GA*
Kent State University, OH
Kent State University at Stark, OH*
Kentucky State University, KY*
Kentucky Wesleyan College, KY*
The King's College, NY*
King's College, PA
Kutztown University of Pennsylvania, PA*
Kuyper College, MI*
Lafayette College, PA*
Lane College, TN
Langston University, OK*
La Roche College, PA*
La Salle University, PA*
Lehigh University, PA
Lehman College of the City University of New York, NY*
Le Moyne College, NY*
Lewis & Clark College, OR*
Lewis University, IL*
Liberty University, VA
Lincoln University, MO
Lincoln University, PA*
Lindenwood University, MO*
Lipscomb University, TN*
Lock Haven University of Pennsylvania, PA
Longwood University, VA
Loras College, IA*
Louisiana State University and Agricultural & Mechanical College, LA
Louisiana Tech University, LA*
Loyola Marymount University, CA*
Loyola University Chicago, IL
Loyola University Maryland, MD
Loyola University New Orleans, LA*
Lubbock Christian University, TX*
Lycoming College, PA*
Macalester College, MN*
Manhattan College, NY*
Mansfield University of Pennsylvania, PA*
Maranatha Baptist University, WI
Marian University, WI*
Marist College, NY

---

* program is offered at another college's campus

Marquette University, WI
Marshall University, WV
Mary Baldwin University, VA*
Marymount University, VA*
Maryville University of Saint Louis, MO*
Marywood University, PA*
Massachusetts Institute of Technology, MA
Massachusetts Maritime Academy, MA*
The Master's University, CA*
McDaniel College, MD
McKendree University, IL*
Mercer University, GA
Mercy College, NY*
Meredith College, NC*
Metropolitan State University of Denver, CO
Miami University, OH*
Michigan State University, MI
Michigan Technological University, MI
Mid-Atlantic Christian University, NC*
Middlebury College, VT*
Millersville University of Pennsylvania, PA
Millsaps College, MS*
Mills College, CA*
Milwaukee School of Engineering, WI*
Minnesota State University Mankato, MN
Minnesota State University Moorhead, MN*
Misericordia University, PA*
Mississippi State University, MS
Missouri Baptist University, MO*
Missouri State University, MO
Missouri University of Science and
    Technology, MO
Missouri Western State University, MO
Molloy College, NY*
Monmouth College, IL*
Monmouth University, NJ*
Montana State University, MT
Montana State University Billings, MT
Moravian College, PA*
Morehead State University, KY
Morehouse College, GA
Morningside College, IA*
Morrisville State College, NY*
Mount Carmel College of Nursing, OH*
Mount Holyoke College, MA*
Mount Marty College, SD*
Mount St. Joseph University, OH*
Mount Saint Mary College, NY*
Mount St. Mary's University, MD*
Muhlenberg College, PA*
Murray State University, KY
National University, CA*
Nazareth College of Rochester, NY*
Neumann University, PA*
Newberry College, SC
New England College, NH*
New Mexico State University, NM
New York Institute of Technology, NY*
Niagara University, NY
North Carolina State University, NC
North Central College, IL*
Northeastern Illinois University, IL*
Northeastern State University, OK
Northeastern University, MA
Northern Arizona University, AZ
Northern Illinois University, IL
Northern Kentucky University, KY*
Northwestern State University
    of Louisiana, LA
Northwestern University, IL*
Northwest Missouri State University, MO*
Northwest University, WA*
Occidental College, CA*
The Ohio State University, OH
Ohio University, OH

Ohio Wesleyan University, OH*
Oklahoma Christian University, OK*
Oklahoma City University, OK*
Oklahoma State University, OK
Old Dominion University, VA
Olivet Nazarene University, IL
Oregon State University, OR
Otterbein University, OH*
Ouachita Baptist University, AR
Our Lady of the Lake University, TX*
Palm Beach Atlantic University, FL*
Penn State Abington, PA*
Penn State Altoona, PA
Penn State Berks, PA*
Penn State Brandywine, PA*
Penn State Erie, The Behrend College, PA
Penn State Harrisburg, PA*
Penn State Lehigh Valley, PA*
Penn State University Park, PA
Penn State Wilkes-Barre, PA*
Penn State Worthington Scranton, PA*
Pennsylvania College of Technology, PA
Pepperdine University, CA*
Philander Smith College, AR*
Pittsburg State University, KS
Pitzer College, CA*
Plymouth State University, NH*
Point Loma Nazarene University, CA*
Point Park University, PA*
Polytechnic University of Puerto Rico, PR*
Pomona College, CA*
Portland State University, OR*
Prairie View A&M University, TX
Presbyterian College, SC
Princeton University, NJ
Providence College, RI
Purdue University, IN
Queens College of the City University of
    New York, NY*
Quinnipiac University, CT*
Radford University, VA
Ramapo College of New Jersey, NJ*
Randolph-Macon College, VA*
Regent University, VA*
Regis University, CO*
Rensselaer Polytechnic Institute, NY
Research College of Nursing, MO*
Rhode Island College, RI*
Rhode Island School of Design, RI*
Rhodes College, TN*
Rice University, TX*
Robert Morris University, PA
Robert Morris University Illinois, IL*
Roberts Wesleyan College, NY*
Rochester Institute of Technology, NY
Rockhurst University, MO*
Rocky Mountain College, MT*
Roger Williams University, RI
Rose-Hulman Institute of Technology, IN
Rowan University, NJ*
Rutgers University–Camden, NJ*
Rutgers University–Newark, NJ
Rutgers University–New Brunswick, NJ
The Sage Colleges, NY*
Saint Anselm College, NH*
Saint Augustine's University, NC
St. Bonaventure University, NY
St. Edward's University, TX*
St. John Fisher College, NY*
Saint John's University, MN
St. John's University, NY
Saint Joseph's University, PA*
Saint Leo University, FL
St. Louis College of Pharmacy, MO*
Saint Louis University, MO*

Saint Martin's University, WA*
Saint Mary's College, IN*
Saint Mary's University of Minnesota, MN*
Saint Michael's College, VT*
St. Norbert College, WI
St. Petersburg College, FL*
Saint Peter's University, NJ*
Saint Vincent College, PA*
Salisbury University, MD
Salve Regina University, RI*
Samford University, AL*
Sam Houston State University, TX
San Diego State University, CA
San Francisco State University, CA*
Santa Clara University, CA
Scripps College, CA*
Seattle Pacific University, WA*
Seattle University, WA
Seton Hill University, PA*
Shippensburg University of Pennsylvania, PA
Siena College, NY
Simmons College, MA*
Skidmore College, NY*
Slippery Rock University of
    Pennsylvania, PA
Smith College, MA*
Sonoma State University, CA*
South Dakota School of Mines and
    Technology, SD
Southeastern Louisiana University, LA
Southeastern University, FL*
Southern Connecticut State University, CT*
Southern Illinois University Carbondale, IL
Southern Illinois University Edwardsville, IL
Southern Methodist University, TX
Southern New Hampshire University, NH*
Southern Oregon University, OR
Southern Utah University, UT
Southwest Baptist University, MO*
Spelman College, GA*
Spring Hill College, AL*
Stanford University, CA*
State University of New York
    at Oswego, NY*
State University of New York College at
    Cortland, NY*
State University of New York College at
    Geneseo, NY*
State University of New York College at
    Potsdam, NY*
State University of New York College of
    Environmental Science and Forestry, NY*
State University of New York College of
    Technology at Canton, NY*
State University of New York Maritime
    College, NY*
State University of New York Polytechnic
    Institute, NY*
Stephen F. Austin State University, TX
Stephens College, MO*
Stevens Institute of Technology, NJ*
Stevenson University, MD*
Stockton University, NJ*
Stonehill College, MA
Stony Brook University, State University of
    New York, NY
Suffolk University, MA*
Susquehanna University, PA*
Swarthmore College, PA*
Syracuse University, NY
Tarleton State University, TX
Temple University, PA
Tennessee State University, TN*
Texas A&M International University, TX
Texas A&M University, TX

* program is offered at another college's campus

Peterson's® How to Get Money for College 2018

Texas A&M University–Corpus Christi, TX
Texas A&M University–Kingsville, TX
Texas Christian University, TX
Texas Lutheran University, TX*
Texas State University, TX
Texas Tech University, TX
Texas Wesleyan University, TX*
Texas Woman's University, TX*
Thomas More College, KY*
Tiffin University, OH*
Towson University, MD*
Transylvania University, KY*
Trevecca Nazarene University, TN*
Trinity University, TX*
Troy University, AL
Truman State University, MO
Tufts University, MA*
Tulane University, LA
Union College, NY*
Union University, TN*
University at Albany, State University
    of New York, NY
University at Buffalo, the State University of
    New York, NY*
The University of Akron, OH
The University of Alabama, AL
The University of Alabama at
    Birmingham, AL
The University of Alabama in
    Huntsville, AL*
University of Alaska Fairbanks, AK
The University of Arizona, AZ
University of Arkansas, AR
University of California, Davis, CA
University of California, Irvine, CA
University of California, Los Angeles, CA
University of California, Riverside, CA*
University of California, San Diego, CA*
University of California, Santa Barbara, CA
University of Central Arkansas, AR
University of Central Florida, FL
University of Central Missouri, MO
University of Chicago, IL*
University of Cincinnati, OH
University of Colorado Boulder, CO
University of Colorado Colorado Springs, CO
University of Colorado Denver, CO*
University of Dayton, OH
University of Delaware, DE
University of Denver, CO*
University of Dubuque, IA
University of Evansville, IN*
The University of Findlay, OH*
University of Florida, FL
University of Georgia, GA
University of Hartford, CT*
University of Hawaii at Manoa, HI
University of Houston, TX
University of Houston–Downtown, TX*
University of Idaho, ID
University of Illinois at Chicago, IL
University of Indianapolis, IN*
The University of Kansas, KS
University of Kentucky, KY
University of La Verne, CA*
University of Louisiana at Monroe, LA*
University of Louisville, KY
University of Maine, ME
University of Mary Hardin-Baylor, TX
University of Maryland,
    Baltimore County, MD*
University of Maryland, College Park, MD
University of Mary Washington, VA*
University of Massachusetts Amherst, MA
University of Massachusetts Boston, MA*

University of Massachusetts
    Dartmouth, MA*
University of Massachusetts Lowell, MA
University of Miami, FL
University of Michigan, MI
University of Michigan–Dearborn, MI
University of Michigan–Flint, MI*
University of Minnesota, Twin Cities
    Campus, MN
University of Missouri–Kansas City, MO
University of Missouri–St. Louis, MO
University of Mobile, AL*
University of Montevallo, AL*
University of Mount Union, OH
University of Nebraska at Kearney, NE
University of Nevada, Las Vegas, NV
University of Nevada, Reno, NV
University of New Hampshire, NH
University of New Hampshire
    at Manchester, NH*
University of New Haven, CT
University of New Orleans, LA*
University of North Alabama, AL
The University of North Carolina
    at Chapel Hill, NC
The University of North Carolina at
    Charlotte, NC
The University of North Carolina at
    Greensboro, NC*
The University of North Carolina at
    Pembroke, NC
University of Northern Colorado, CO
University of Northern Iowa, IA
University of North Florida, FL
University of North Georgia, GA
University of North Texas, TX
University of Notre Dame, IN
University of Oklahoma, OK
University of Oregon, OR
University of Pennsylvania, PA*
University of Pikeville, KY*
University of Pittsburgh, PA
University of Pittsburgh at Bradford, PA*
University of Pittsburgh at Greensburg, PA*
University of Puget Sound, WA*
University of Rhode Island, RI
University of Richmond, VA
University of Rochester, NY*
University of St. Francis, IL*
University of St. Thomas, MN*
University of St. Thomas, TX*
University of San Diego, CA*
University of San Francisco, CA
University of South Alabama, AL
University of South Carolina, SC
The University of South Dakota, SD
University of Southern California, CA
University of Southern Indiana, IN
University of Southern Maine, ME*
University of Southern Mississippi, MS*
University of South Florida, FL
The University of Tampa, FL
The University of Tennessee, TN
The University of Tennessee
    at Chattanooga, TN
The University of Tennessee at Martin, TN
The University of Texas at Austin, TX
The University of Texas at Dallas, TX*
The University of Texas at El Paso, TX
The University of Texas at San Antonio, TX
The University of Texas Rio Grande
    Valley, TX
University of the Incarnate Word, TX*
The University of Toledo, OH
University of Utah, UT

University of Vermont, VT
University of Virginia, VA
The University of Virginia's
    College at Wise, VA
University of Washington, WA
University of Washington, Bothell, WA*
University of Washington, Tacoma, WA*
University of Wisconsin–Eau Claire, WI
University of Wisconsin–Green Bay, WI*
University of Wisconsin–La Crosse, WI
University of Wisconsin–Madison, WI
University of Wisconsin–Milwaukee, WI*
University of Wisconsin–Parkside, WI*
University of Wisconsin–Stevens Point, WI
University of Wisconsin–Stout, WI
University of Wisconsin–Whitewater, WI
Ursuline College, OH*
Utah State University, UT
Utah Valley University, UT
Utica College, NY
Valparaiso University, IN*
Vanderbilt University, TN
Vermont Technical College, VT*
Villanova University, PA
Virginia Commonwealth University, VA*
Virginia Military Institute, VA
Virginia Polytechnic Institute and State
    University, VA
Virginia State University, VA
Virginia Wesleyan College, VA*
Viterbo University, WI*
Wagner College, NY*
Wake Forest University, NC
Washburn University, KS
Washington & Jefferson College, PA
Washington and Lee University, VA*
Washington State University, WA
Washington University in St. Louis, MO
Wayland Baptist University, TX*
Waynesburg University, PA*
Wayne State College, NE
Wayne State University, MI
Weber State University, UT
Webster University, MO*
Wentworth Institute of Technology, MA*
Wesleyan College, GA*
West Chester University of Pennsylvania, PA
Western Connecticut State University, CT*
Western Illinois University, IL
Western Kentucky University, KY
Western Michigan University, MI
Western New England University, MA
Western Oregon University, OR*
Westfield State University, MA*
Westminster College, PA*
Westminster College, UT*
Westmont College, CA*
West Virginia University, WV
West Virginia University Institute of
    Technology, WV
Wheaton College, IL
Wheaton College, MA*
Whittier College, CA*
Whitworth University, WA*
Widener University, PA
Wilkes University, PA*
Willamette University, OR*
William Jewell College, MO*
William Peace University, NC*
Williams Baptist College, AR*
William Woods University, MO*
Wilson College, PA*
Wingate University, NC*
Winona State University, MN*
Winthrop University, SC*

* program is offered at another college's campus

Wittenberg University, OH*
Wofford College, SC
Worcester Polytechnic Institute, MA
Worcester State University, MA*
Wright State University, OH
Wright State University–Lake Campus, OH*
Xavier University of Louisiana, LA*
York College of the City University
of New York, NY
Youngstown State University, OH

Naval
Arizona State University at the Downtown
Phoenix campus, AZ*
Arizona State University at the Polytechnic
campus, AZ*
Arizona State University at the Tempe
campus, AZ
Arizona State University at the
West campus, AZ*
Armstrong State University, GA*
Auburn University, AL
Augsburg College, MN*
Barnard College, NY*
Belmont University, TN*
Boston College, MA*
Boston University, MA
Brown University, RI*
Cabrini University, PA*
California State University
Maritime Academy, CA*
California State University, San Marcos, CA*
Carlow University, PA*
Carnegie Mellon University, PA
The Catholic University of America, DC*
Chatham University, PA*
Christian Brothers University, TN*
The Citadel, The Military College of South
Carolina, SC
Clark Atlanta University, GA*
Clayton State University, GA*
The College at Brockport, State University of
New York, NY*
The College of Saint Rose, NY*
College of the Holy Cross, MA
Columbia College, MO*
Columbia University, NY
Columbia University, School of
General Studies, NY
Cornell University, NY
Drexel University, PA*
Duquesne University, PA*
Eastern Michigan University, MI*
Edgewood College, WI*
Embry-Riddle Aeronautical University–
Daytona, FL
Emory University, GA*
Farmingdale State College, NY*
Florida Agricultural and Mechanical
University, FL
Florida State University, FL*
Fordham University, NY*

Georgetown University, DC*
The George Washington University, DC
Georgia Institute of Technology, GA
Georgia State University, GA*
Hampton University, VA
Harvard University, MA
Houston Baptist University, TX*
Husson University, ME*
Indiana University South Bend, IN*
Iowa State University of Science and
Technology, IA
Jacksonville University, FL
Louisiana State University and Agricultural &
Mechanical College, LA*
Loyola University Chicago, IL*
Loyola University New Orleans, LA*
Macalester College, MN*
Marquette University, WI
Mary Baldwin University, VA*
Massachusetts Institute of Technology, MA
Miami University, OH
Milwaukee School of Engineering, WI*
Molloy College, NY*
Morehouse College, GA
Mount Carmel College of Nursing, OH*
North Carolina State University, NC
Northeastern University, MA*
Northwestern University, IL
The Ohio State University, OH
Old Dominion University, VA
Oregon State University, OR
Penn State University Park, PA
Point Loma Nazarene University, CA*
Prairie View A&M University, TX
Princeton University, NJ*
Purdue University, IN
Regent University, VA*
Regis University, CO*
Rensselaer Polytechnic Institute, NY
Rhodes College, TN*
Rice University, TX
Robert Morris University, PA*
Rochester Institute of Technology, NY*
Rutgers University–Newark, NJ
Rutgers University–New Brunswick, NJ
St. John Fisher College, NY*
Saint Joseph's University, PA*
St. Louis College of Pharmacy, MO*
Saint Mary's College, IN*
San Diego State University, CA
Seattle Pacific University, WA*
Seattle University, WA*
Spelman College, GA*
Stanford University, CA*
State University of New York Maritime
College, NY
Stephens College, MO*
Swarthmore College, PA*
Temple University, PA*
Tennessee State University, TN*
Texas A&M University, TX
Texas Woman's University, TX*

Tufts University, MA*
Tulane University, LA
Union College, NY*
The University of Arizona, AZ
University of California, Davis, CA*
University of California, Los Angeles, CA
University of California, San Diego, CA*
University of Colorado Boulder, CO
University of Florida, FL
University of Houston, TX*
University of Idaho, ID
University of Illinois at Chicago, IL*
The University of Kansas, KS
University of Maine, ME
University of Maryland,
Baltimore County, MD
University of Maryland, College Park, MD*
University of Massachusetts Boston, MA*
University of Michigan, MI
University of Michigan–Dearborn, MI*
University of Michigan–Flint, MI*
University of Minnesota, Twin Cities
Campus, MN
University of New Orleans, LA*
The University of North Carolina at Chapel
Hill, NC
University of North Florida, FL*
University of Notre Dame, IN
University of Oklahoma, OK
University of Pennsylvania, PA
University of Pittsburgh, PA*
University of Rochester, NY
University of St. Thomas, MN*
University of San Diego, CA
University of South Carolina, SC
University of Southern California, CA
University of South Florida, FL
The University of Tampa, FL*
The University of Texas at Austin, TX
University of Utah, UT
University of Virginia, VA
University of Washington, WA
University of Washington, Bothell, WA*
University of Washington, Tacoma, WA*
University of Wisconsin–Madison, WI
University of Wisconsin–Milwaukee, WI*
Vanderbilt University, TN
Villanova University, PA
Virginia Military Institute, VA
Virginia Polytechnic Institute and State
University, VA
Washburn University, KS*
Washington State University, WA*
Weber State University, UT*
Westminster College, UT*
Widener University, PA*
William Peace University, NC*
William Woods University, MO*
Worcester Polytechnic Institute, MA*
Worcester State University, MA*
Xavier University of Louisiana, LA*

---

* program is offered at another college's campus

Tuition Waivers

Adult Students
Albright College, PA
Barton College, NC
Bluefield State College, WV
Caldwell University, NJ
Campbellsville University, KY
Carlow University, PA
Cedarville University, OH
Coe College, IA
Creighton University, NE
DeSales University, PA
Faulkner University, AL
Hilbert College, NY
Judson University, IL
Lane College, TN
Lewis University, IL
Lipscomb University, TN
Lynchburg College, VA
Marist College, NY
Messiah College, PA
Montreat College, NC
New England College, NH
Piedmont College, GA
Randolph College, VA
Roanoke College, VA
St. Andrews University, NC
St. John's University, NY
Southeastern Oklahoma State
　University, OK
Sweet Briar College, VA
University of Evansville, IN
University of Hawaii at Manoa, HI
Utah State University, UT
Virginia Wesleyan College, VA
Webber International University, FL
Wittenberg University, OH

Children of Alumni
Adelphi University, NY
Alliant International University–
　San Diego, CA
Aquinas College, MI
Aurora University, IL
Baldwin Wallace University, OH
Barton College, NC
Bethel College, KS
Black Hills State University, SD
Cabrini University, PA
Caldwell University, NJ
Calumet College of Saint Joseph, IN
Carlow University, PA
The Catholic University of America, DC
Central Methodist University, MO
Central Michigan University, MI
College of Saint Elizabeth, NJ
Columbia College, MO
Concordia University Chicago, IL
Concordia University Texas, TX
Corban University, OR
Curry College, MA
Drake University, IA
Drexel University, PA
Drury University, MO
D'Youville College, NY
Eastern University, PA
Emmanuel College, MA
Florida Southern College, FL
Georgian Court University, NJ
Grambling State University, LA
Grand View University, IA

Hilbert College, NY
Hillsdale College, MI
Huntingdon College, AL
Iona College, NY
Ithaca College, NY
Jackson State University, MS
Kansas Wesleyan University, KS
Kentucky Wesleyan College, KY
Langston University, OK
Lasell College, MA
Lewis University, IL
Lincoln University, PA
Louisiana Tech University, LA
MacMurray College, IL
Manhattanville College, NY
Marshall University, WV
McKendree University, IL
McPherson College, KS
Michigan Technological University, MI
Mid-Atlantic Christian University, NC
Minot State University, ND
Mississippi State University, MS
Missouri Baptist University, MO
Missouri State University, MO
Morehead State University, KY
Morningside College, IA
Morrisville State College, NY
Murray State University, KY
Muskingum University, OH
Nazareth College of Rochester, NY
New England College, NH
Northern State University, SD
Northwest College of Art & Design, WA
Ohio Northern University, OH
Oklahoma State University, OK
Palm Beach Atlantic University, FL
Peirce College, PA
Randall University, OK
Saint Augustine's University, NC
Saint Louis University, MO
Saint Martin's University, WA
Simpson College, IA
South Dakota School of Mines and
　Technology, SD
Southeastern Oklahoma State
　University, OK
Southern Illinois University Carbondale, IL
Southern Utah University, UT
Southwestern Oklahoma State
　University, OK
Stetson University, FL
Suffolk University, MA
Texas Lutheran University, TX
Truman State University, MO
Union University, TN
University of Alaska Fairbanks, AK
University of Detroit Mercy, MI
University of Evansville, IN
The University of Findlay, OH
University of Minnesota, Duluth, MN
University of Mississippi, MS
University of Mount Union, OH
University of St. Francis, IL
The University of South Dakota, SD
University of Southern Mississippi, MS
University of Wyoming, WY
Utah State University, UT
Warner Pacific College, OR
Webber International University, FL
Westminster College, MO

William Woods University, MO
Wittenberg University, OH

Minority Students
Bethel College, KS
Drury University, MO
Fort Lewis College, CO
Hilbert College, NY
Lock Haven University of Pennsylvania, PA
Mayville State University, ND
Minot State University, ND
Montana State University, MT
Montana Tech of The University of
　Montana, MT
Morehead State University, KY
Morrisville State College, NY
Nazareth College of Rochester, NY
Ohio Northern University, OH
Shepherd University, WV
Slippery Rock University
　of Pennsylvania, PA
Southeastern Oklahoma State
　University, OK
University at Buffalo, the State University of
　New York, NY
University of Evansville, IN
University of Hawaii at Manoa, HI
University of Maine at Augusta, ME
University of Montana, MT
The University of Montana Western, MT
University of Rhode Island, RI
Utah State University, UT
Western Washington University, WA
Wittenberg University, OH

Senior Citizens
Adams State University, CO
Adelphi University, NY
Alaska Bible College, AK
Albertus Magnus College, CT
Albright College, PA
Alvernia University, PA
Andrews University, MI
Arkansas Tech University, AR
Armstrong State University, GA
Asbury University, KY
Athens State University, AL
Auburn University at Montgomery, AL
Augusta University, GA
Austin Peay State University, TN
Averett University, VA
Baker University, KS
Ball State University, IN
Barton College, NC
Baruch College of the City University of
　New York, NY
Belmont University, TN
Bemidji State University, MN
Benedictine College, KS
Berry College, GA
Bethany Lutheran College, MN
Bethel College, KS
Black Hills State University, SD
Bloomfield College, NJ
Bloomsburg University of Pennsylvania, PA
Bluefield College, VA
Bluefield State College, WV
Boise State University, ID
Bowling Green State University, OH
Bradley University, IL
Brescia University, KY

Bridgewater State University, MA
Cabrini University, PA
Caldwell University, NJ
California State University, Bakersfield, CA
California State University, Chico, CA
California State University, Dominguez Hills, CA
California State University, East Bay, CA
California State University, Fullerton, CA
California State University, Long Beach, CA
California State University, Northridge, CA
California State University, San Bernardino, CA
California State University, San Marcos, CA
Calumet College of Saint Joseph, IN
Cameron University, OK
Campbellsville University, KY
Capital University, OH
Carroll College, MT
Carson-Newman University, TN
Cedarville University, OH
Central Connecticut State University, CT
Central Michigan University, MI
Central Washington University, WA
Chestnut Hill College, PA
Chowan University, NC
Christopher Newport University, VA
The Citadel, The Military College of South Carolina, SC
City College of the City University of New York, NY
Clayton State University, GA
Clemson University, SC
Cleveland State University, OH
Coastal Carolina University, SC
Coe College, IA
College of Charleston, SC
College of Coastal Georgia, GA
The College of New Jersey, NJ
The College of New Rochelle, NY
College of Saint Elizabeth, NJ
College of Saint Mary, NE
The College of St. Scholastica, MN
College of Staten Island of the City University of New York, NY
The College of William and Mary, VA
Columbia College, MO
Concordia University Chicago, IL
Corban University, OR
Covenant College, GA
Creighton University, NE
Culver-Stockton College, MO
Daemen College, NY
Dakota State University, SD
Dakota Wesleyan University, SD
Delta State University, MS
DeSales University, PA
Dickinson College, PA
Dixie State University, UT
Doane University, NE
Dominican College, NY
Dordt College, IA
Drake University, IA
Duquesne University, PA
D'Youville College, NY
East Central University, OK
Eastern Illinois University, IL
Eastern Kentucky University, KY
Eastern Oregon University, OR
East Stroudsburg University of Pennsylvania, PA
Elmhurst College, IL
Elms College, MA
Emmanuel College, GA
Emporia State University, KS
Eureka College, IL

The Evergreen State College, WA
Fitchburg State University, MA
Florida Agricultural and Mechanical University, FL
Florida Atlantic University, FL
Florida Institute of Technology, FL
Florida State University, FL
Framingham State University, MA
Francis Marion University, SC
Franklin College, IN
Franklin Pierce University, NH
Friends University, KS
Frostburg State University, MD
Gannon University, PA
George Fox University, OR
George Mason University, VA
Georgia College & State University, GA
Georgia Institute of Technology, GA
Georgian Court University, NJ
Georgia Southern University, GA
Georgia Southwestern State University, GA
Georgia State University, GA
Glenville State College, WV
Gonzaga University, WA
Governors State University, IL
Graceland University, IA
Grambling State University, LA
Grand View University, IA
Greenville College, IL
Hanover College, IN
Harding University, AR
Hilbert College, NY
Holy Family University, PA
Hood College, MD
Houghton College, NY
Houston Baptist University, TX
Husson University, ME
Idaho State University, ID
Indiana State University, IN
Indiana University of Pennsylvania, PA
Indiana University–Purdue University Fort Wayne, IN
John Carroll University, OH
Judson University, IL
Juniata College, PA
Kansas Wesleyan University, KS
Kean University, NJ
Keene State College, NH
Kennesaw State University, GA
Kent State University, OH
Kent State University at Geauga, OH
Kent State University at Stark, OH
Kentucky State University, KY
Kentucky Wesleyan College, KY
King's College, PA
King University, TN
Kutztown University of Pennsylvania, PA
LaGrange College, GA
Lake Erie College, OH
Lamar University, TX
La Roche College, PA
Lebanon Valley College, PA
Lee University, TN
Lenoir-Rhyne University, NC
Lewis-Clark State College, ID
Lincoln Christian University, IL
Lincoln University, MO
Lindenwood University, MO
Lindsey Wilson College, KY
Linfield College, OR
Lock Haven University of Pennsylvania, PA
Longwood University, VA
Louisiana Tech University, LA
Loyola University Chicago, IL
Loyola University New Orleans, LA
Lynchburg College, VA

MacMurray College, IL
Malone University, OH
Mansfield University of Pennsylvania, PA
Marian University, WI
Marquette University, WI
Marshall University, WV
Marymount California University, CA
Marymount Manhattan College, NY
Marymount University, VA
Maryville University of Saint Louis, MO
Marywood University, PA
Massachusetts College of Art and Design, MA
Massachusetts College of Liberal Arts, MA
Mayville State University, ND
Mercy College, NY
Merrimack College, MA
Messiah College, PA
Metropolitan State University of Denver, CO
Michigan Technological University, MI
Mid-Atlantic Christian University, NC
Middle Georgia State University, GA
Midland College, TX
Millersville University of Pennsylvania, PA
Minnesota State University Mankato, MN
Minot State University, ND
Mississippi State University, MS
Missouri Baptist University, MO
Missouri State University, MO
Missouri Western State University, MO
Molloy College, NY
Monmouth University, NJ
Montana State University, MT
Montana State University Billings, MT
Montana Tech of The University of Montana, MT
Montclair State University, NJ
Morehead State University, KY
Morningside College, IA
Morrisville State College, NY
Mount Mary University, WI
Mount St. Joseph University, OH
Mount Vernon Nazarene University, OH
Murray State University, KY
New England College, NH
New Jersey City University, NJ
New Mexico Highlands University, NM
New Mexico Institute of Mining and Technology, NM
New Mexico State University, NM
New York Institute of Technology, NY
Nicholls State University, LA
North Central College, IL
Northeastern Illinois University, IL
Northern Illinois University, IL
Northern Kentucky University, KY
Northern State University, SD
Northwest Missouri State University, MO
Oakland University, MI
The Ohio State University, OH
Ohio University, OH
Ohio University–Eastern, OH
Ohio University–Zanesville, OH
Oklahoma Baptist University, OK
Oklahoma Panhandle State University, OK
Oklahoma State University, OK
Old Dominion University, VA
Penn State Abington, PA
Penn State Altoona, PA
Penn State Beaver, PA
Penn State Berks, PA
Penn State Brandywine, PA
Penn State Erie, The Behrend College, PA
Penn State Greater Allegheny, PA
Penn State Harrisburg, PA
Penn State Hazleton, PA

Penn State Lehigh Valley, PA
Penn State New Kensington, PA
Penn State Schuylkill, PA
Penn State University Park, PA
Penn State Wilkes-Barre, PA
Penn State Worthington Scranton, PA
Penn State York, PA
Plymouth State University, NH
Point Loma Nazarene University, CA
Portland State University, OR
Prairie View A&M University, TX
Presbyterian College, SC
Purdue University, IN
Queens College of the City University of New York, NY
Radford University, VA
Ramapo College of New Jersey, NJ
Randall University, OK
Research College of Nursing, MO
Roanoke College, VA
Roberts Wesleyan College, NY
Rockhurst University, MO
Rogers State University, OK
St. Andrews University, NC
St. Bonaventure University, NY
St. John's University, NY
St. Mary's College of Maryland, MD
St. Olaf College, MN
Salisbury University, MD
San Francisco State University, CA
Savannah State University, GA
Seattle Pacific University, WA
Shawnee State University, OH
Shepherd University, WV
Shippensburg University of Pennsylvania, PA
Simpson College, IA
Skidmore College, NY
Slippery Rock University of Pennsylvania, PA
South Dakota School of Mines and Technology, SD
Southeastern Oklahoma State University, OK
Southeast Missouri State University, MO
Southern Adventist University, TN
Southern Connecticut State University, CT
Southern Illinois University Carbondale, IL
Southern Illinois University Edwardsville, IL
Southern New Hampshire University, NH
Southern Oregon University, OR
Southern Utah University, UT
Southwestern College, KS
Southwestern Oklahoma State University, OK
State University of New York College of Agriculture and Technology at Cobleskill, NY
Stephen F. Austin State University, TX
Sterling College, KS
Stockton University, NJ
Suffolk University, MA
Sweet Briar College, VA
Taylor University, IN
Texas A&M International University, TX
Texas A&M University–Commerce, TX
Texas A&M University–Corpus Christi, TX
Texas A&M University–Kingsville, TX
Texas Tech University, TX
Texas Woman's University, TX

Thomas More College, KY
Tiffin University, OH
Towson University, MD
Trevecca Nazarene University, TN
Trine University, IN
Trinity College of Florida, FL
Truman State University, MO
Union College, NY
The University of Akron, OH
University of Alaska Fairbanks, AK
University of Arkansas, AR
University of Bridgeport, CT
University of Central Arkansas, AR
University of Central Florida, FL
University of Colorado Boulder, CO
University of Delaware, DE
University of Denver, CO
University of Detroit Mercy, MI
University of Evansville, IN
The University of Findlay, OH
University of Georgia, GA
University of Hartford, CT
University of Hawaii at Manoa, HI
University of Houston–Downtown, TX
University of Houston–Victoria, TX
University of Illinois at Chicago, IL
University of Illinois at Springfield, IL
University of Illinois at Urbana–Champaign, IL
University of Indianapolis, IN
University of Louisiana at Monroe, LA
University of Louisville, KY
University of Maine, ME
University of Maine at Augusta, ME
University of Maine at Fort Kent, ME
University of Maine at Machias, ME
University of Maine at Presque Isle, ME
University of Maryland, Baltimore County, MD
University of Maryland University College, MD
University of Mary Washington, VA
University of Massachusetts Amherst, MA
University of Massachusetts Dartmouth, MA
University of Massachusetts Lowell, MA
University of Memphis, TN
University of Michigan–Dearborn, MI
University of Michigan–Flint, MI
University of Minnesota, Crookston, MN
University of Minnesota, Morris, MN
University of Minnesota, Twin Cities Campus, MN
University of Mississippi, MS
University of Missouri, MO
University of Missouri–St. Louis, MO
University of Montana, MT
The University of Montana Western, MT
University of Mount Union, OH
University of Nevada, Reno, NV
University of New Hampshire at Manchester, NH
University of New Haven, CT
University of New Orleans, LA
University of North Alabama, AL
University of North Florida, FL
University of North Georgia, GA
University of North Texas, TX
University of North Texas at Dallas, TX
University of Oklahoma, OK
University of Pikeville, KY
University of Pittsburgh at Greensburg, PA

University of Rhode Island, RI
University of St. Thomas, MN
University of St. Thomas, TX
University of Science and Arts of Oklahoma, OK
University of South Carolina, SC
University of South Carolina Aiken, SC
The University of South Dakota, SD
University of Southern Mississippi, MS
The University of Tennessee, TN
The University of Tennessee at Chattanooga, TN
The University of Tennessee at Martin, TN
The University of Texas at Arlington, TX
The University of Texas at Austin, TX
The University of Texas at Dallas, TX
University of the Incarnate Word, TX
University of Utah, UT
University of Valley Forge, PA
University of Virginia, VA
The University of Virginia's College at Wise, VA
University of Washington, WA
University of Washington, Bothell, WA
University of Washington, Tacoma, WA
University of West Florida, FL
University of West Georgia, GA
University of Wisconsin–Green Bay, WI
University of Wisconsin–Milwaukee, WI
University of Wisconsin–Parkside, WI
University of Wisconsin–Stevens Point, WI
University of Wisconsin–Whitewater, WI
University of Wyoming, WY
Utah State University, UT
Villanova University, PA
Virginia State University, VA
Virginia Wesleyan College, VA
Washburn University, KS
Washington State University, WA
Webber International University, FL
Weber State University, UT
Wells College, NY
West Chester University of Pennsylvania, PA
Western Connecticut State University, CT
Western Illinois University, IL
Western Kentucky University, KY
Western Michigan University, MI
Western New England University, MA
Western State Colorado University, CO
Western Washington University, WA
Westfield State University, MA
West Virginia University, WV
West Virginia University Institute of Technology, WV
Whitworth University, WA
Wichita State University, KS
Widener University, PA
William Paterson University of New Jersey, NJ
William Woods University, MO
Winthrop University, SC
Wittenberg University, OH
Worcester State University, MA
Wright State University, OH
Wright State University–Lake Campus, OH
Xavier University, OH
York College of the City University of New York, NY
Youngstown State University, OH

Tuition Payment Alternatives

College	
Abilene Christian University, TX	I,P
Academy College, MN	I
Academy of Art University, CA	I
Adams State University, CO	D,G,I
Adelphi University, NY	D,I,P
Agnes Scott College, GA	I
Alabama State University, AL	D
Alaska Pacific University, AK	D,I
Albertus Magnus College, CT	I
Albion College, MI	D,I
Albright College, PA	I
Alcorn State University, MS	I
Alderson Broaddus University, WV	I
Alfred University, NY	I
Alice Lloyd College, KY	I
Allegheny College, PA	I
Allen College, IA	D
Alliant International University–San Diego, CA	D
Alma College, MI	D,I
Alvernia University, PA	I
Alverno College, WI	D,I
American University, DC	I,P
Amherst College, MA	I
Amridge University, AL	G,I,P
Anderson University, SC	I
Andrews University, MI	I
Angelo State University, TX	G,I
Appalachian State University, NC	I
Aquinas College, MI	D,I
Arcadia University, PA	I
Arizona State University at the Downtown Phoenix campus, AZ	I
Arizona State University at the Polytechnic campus, AZ	I
Arizona State University at the Tempe campus, AZ	I
Arizona State University at the West campus, AZ	I
Arkansas Tech University, AR	D,I
Armstrong State University, GA	I
Asbury University, KY	I
Assumption College, MA	G
Athens State University, AL	I
Auburn University, AL	I
Auburn University at Montgomery, AL	I
Augsburg College, MN	I
Augustana College, IL	I,P
Augustana University, SD	I
Augusta University, GA	I
Aurora University, IL	D,I
Austin College, TX	I
Austin Graduate School of Theology, TX	I
Austin Peay State University, TN	I
Averett University, VA	I
Azusa Pacific University, CA	I
Baker University, KS	I
Baldwin Wallace University, OH	D,I
Ball State University, IN	I
Baptist University of the Americas, TX	I
Barclay College, KS	I
Bard College, NY	I,P
Barnard College, NY	D,I,P
Barry University, FL	D,I
Barton College, NC	I
Baruch College of the City University of New York, NY	D,I
Bates College, ME	I,P
Baylor University, TX	I
Bay Path University, MA	I
Belhaven University, MS	I
Bellarmine University, KY	I
Belmont Abbey College, NC	D,G,I
Belmont University, TN	D,I
Beloit College, WI	I
Bemidji State University, MN	I
Benedictine College, KS	I
Bennington College, VT	I
Bentley University, MA	I
Berklee College of Music, MA	D,P
Berry College, GA	I
Bethany College, WV	I
Bethany Lutheran College, MN	I
Bethel College, IN	I
Bethel College, KS	D,I
Bethel University, MN	I,P
Bethune-Cookman University, FL	I
Binghamton University, State University of New York, NY	I
Biola University, CA	I
Black Hills State University, SD	I
Blessing-Rieman College of Nursing & Health Sciences, IL	I
Bloomfield College, NJ	D,I
Bloomsburg University of Pennsylvania, PA	I
Bluefield College, VA	I
Bluefield State College, WV	I
Blue Mountain College, MS	D,I
Bluffton University, OH	I
Boise State University, ID	I
Boston Architectural College, MA	I
Boston College, MA	I
Boston University, MA	I,P
Bowdoin College, ME	D,I
Bowling Green State University, OH	I
Bradley University, IL	D,I
Brandeis University, MA	I
Brenau University, GA	I
Brescia University, KY	I
Briar Cliff University, IA	D,I
Bridgewater College, VA	I
Bridgewater State University, MA	I
Brown University, RI	I
Bryan College, TN	I
Bryn Mawr College, PA	I
Bucknell University, PA	I,P
Buena Vista University, IA	I
Butler University, IN	I
Cabarrus College of Health Sciences, NC	I
Cabrini University, PA	I
Cairn University, PA	I
Caldwell University, NJ	I
California Baptist University, CA	I
California Christian College, CA	I
California College of the Arts, CA	I
California Institute of Technology, CA	D,I
California Lutheran University, CA	I
California Polytechnic State University, San Luis Obispo, CA	I
California State Polytechnic University, Pomona, CA	D,I
California State University, Chico, CA	D,I
California State University, Dominguez Hills, CA	I
California State University, East Bay, CA	I
California State University, Fullerton, CA	D,I
California State University, Long Beach, CA	I
California State University Maritime Academy, CA	I
California State University, Northridge, CA	I
California State University, San Bernardino, CA	I
California University of Pennsylvania, PA	I
Calumet College of Saint Joseph, IN	D,G
Calvary University, MO	I
Calvin College, MI	I,P
Cameron University, OK	I
Campbellsville University, KY	I
Campbell University, NC	I
Canisius College, NY	D,I
Capital University, OH	I
Cardinal Stritch University, WI	I
Carleton College, MN	I
Carlos Albizu University, Miami Campus, FL	I
Carlow University, PA	I
Carnegie Mellon University, PA	I
Carolina Christian College, NC	I
Carroll College, MT	I
Carroll University, WI	I
Carson-Newman University, TN	D,I
Case Western Reserve University, OH	I
Catawba College, NC	I
The Catholic University of America, DC	I
Cazenovia College, NY	I
Cedar Crest College, PA	D,I
Cedarville University, OH	I
Centenary College of Louisiana, LA	I
Central College, IA	I
Central Connecticut State University, CT	I
Central Methodist University, MO	I
Central Michigan University, MI	I
Central Penn College, PA	I
Central Washington University, WA	I
Centre College, KY	I
Chaminade University of Honolulu, HI	I
Champlain College, VT	I,P
Chapman University, CA	D,I,P
Charter Oak State College, CT	I
Chatham University, PA	I
Chestnut Hill College, PA	D,I
Christendom College, VA	I
Christian Brothers University, TN	I
Christopher Newport University, VA	I
The Citadel, The Military College of South Carolina, SC	I
City College of the City University of New York, NY	D
Claflin University, SC	D,I
Claremont McKenna College, CA	I
Clark Atlanta University, GA	I
Clarke University, IA	D,I
Clarkson University, NY	I
Clark University, MA	I,P

D = deferred payment system; *G* = guaranteed tuition rate; *I* = installment payments; *P* = prepayment locks in tuition rate

Clemson University, SC	I	Delta State University, MS	I	Fordham University, NY	I
Cleveland Institute of Art, OH	I	Denison University, OH	I	Fort Lewis College, CO	I
Cleveland State University, OH	I	DePaul University, IL	D,I	Framingham State University, MA	I,P
Coastal Carolina University, SC	I	DePauw University, IN	I	Franciscan University of	
Coe College, IA	I	DeSales University, PA	D,I	Steubenville, OH	I
Cogswell Polytechnical College, CA	D	Dickinson College, PA	I	Francis Marion University, SC	I
The Colburn School Conservatory of		Dickinson State University, ND	I	Franklin & Marshall College, PA	D,I
Music, CA	I	DigiPen Institute of Technology, WA	I	Franklin College, IN	I
Colby College, ME	I	Dixie State University, UT	I	Franklin Pierce University, NH	I
Colgate University, NY	D,I,P	Doane University, NE	I	Franklin W. Olin College of	
The College at Brockport, State		Dominican College, NY	D,I	Engineering, MA	I
University of New York, NY	D,I	Dominican University, IL	D	Freed-Hardeman University, TN	I
College of Charleston, SC	I	Dominican University of		Friends University, KS	I
College of Coastal Georgia, GA	I	California, CA	I	Frostburg State University, MD	D,I
The College of Idaho, ID	I	Dordt College, IA	I	Furman University, SC	I
The College of New Jersey, NJ	I	Drake University, IA	I	Gallaudet University, DC	D,I
The College of New Rochelle, NY	I	Drew University, NJ	D,I,P	Gannon University, PA	D,I
College of Saint Benedict, MN	I	Drexel University, PA	I	Gardner-Webb University, NC	I
College of Saint Elizabeth, NJ	I	Drury University, MO	D,I	Geneva College, PA	I
College of Saint Mary, NE	D,I	Duquesne University, PA	D,I	George Fox University, OR	I
The College of Saint Rose, NY	I	D'Youville College, NY	D,G,I	George Mason University, VA	D,I
The College of St. Scholastica, MN	I	Earlham College, IN	D,I,P	Georgetown University, DC	I
College of Staten Island of the		East Carolina University, NC	D,I	The George Washington University, DC	G,I
City University of New York, NY	I	East Central University, OK	G	Georgia College & State	
College of the Atlantic, ME	I	Eastern Connecticut State		University, GA	I
College of the Holy Cross, MA	I	University, CT	I	Georgia Institute of Technology, GA	D
College of the Ozarks, MO	I	Eastern Illinois University, IL	G,I	Georgian Court University, NJ	I
The College of William and Mary, VA	I	Eastern Kentucky University, KY	I	Georgia Southern University, GA	I
The College of Wooster, OH	I	Eastern Mennonite University, VA	I	Gettysburg College, PA	I
The Colorado College, CO	I	Eastern Michigan University, MI	I	Glenville State College, WV	I
Colorado Mesa University, CO	I	Eastern Oregon University, OR	D,I	Goldfarb School of Nursing at	
Colorado School of Mines, CO	I	Eastern University, PA	I	Barnes-Jewish College, MO	I
Columbia College, MO	D,G,I	Eastern Washington University, WA	I	Gonzaga University, WA	D,I
Columbia College Chicago, IL	I	East Stroudsburg University of		Gordon College, MA	I
Columbia International		Pennsylvania, PA	I	Goshen College, IN	I
University,		East Texas Baptist University, TX	I	Goucher College, MD	I,P
SC	I	Eckerd College, FL	I	Governors State University, IL	D,G,I
Columbia University, NY	I,P	Edgewood College, WI	I	Graceland University, IA	I
Columbia University, School of		Elizabeth City State University, NC	I	Grambling State University, LA	D,I
General Studies, NY	I,P	Elizabethtown College, PA	I	Grand Valley State University, MI	D,I
Columbus College of Art & Design, OH	D,I	Elmhurst College, IL	I	Grand View University, IA	I
Concordia College, MN	I	Elmira College, NY	I,P	Grinnell College, IA	I
Concordia University Ann Arbor, MI	I	Elms College, MA	I	Guilford College, NC	I
Concordia University Chicago, IL	I	Elon University, NC	I	Gustavus Adolphus College, MN	I,P
Concordia University Irvine, CA	I	Embry-Riddle Aeronautical		Gwynedd Mercy University, PA	I
Concordia University, Nebraska, NE	I	University–Daytona, FL	I	Hamilton College, NY	I
Concordia University, St. Paul, MN	I	Emerson College, MA	I	Hamline University, MN	I
Concordia University Texas, TX	I	Emmanuel College, GA	I	Hampden-Sydney College, VA	I
Concord University, WV	I	Emory & Henry College, VA	D,G,I	Hampshire College, MA	I
Connecticut College, CT	I	Emory University, GA	I	Hampton University, VA	D,I
Converse College, SC	I	Emporia State University, KS	D,I	Hanover College, IN	I
Cooper Union for the Advancement		Endicott College, MA	I,P	Harding University, AR	I,P
of Science and Art, NY	I	Eureka College, IL	I	Hardin-Simmons University, TX	G,I
Corban University, OR	I	Evangel University, MO	I	Harrisburg University of Science	
Cornell College, IA	I	Everglades University, FL	I	and Technology, PA	D,I
Cornell University, NY	I	The Evergreen State College, WA	I	Harris-Stowe State University, MO	I
Cornerstone University, MI	I	Excelsior College, NY	I	Hartwick College, NY	I
Covenant College, GA	I	Fairfield University, CT	I	Harvard University, MA	I,P
Cox College, MO	D,I	Fairmont State University, WV	I	Harvey Mudd College, CA	I
Creighton University, NE	I	Farmingdale State College, NY	I	Haverford College, PA	I,P
Criswell College, TX	I	Faulkner University, AL	D,I	Hawai'i Pacific University, HI	I
The Culinary Institute of		Felician University, NJ	I	Heidelberg University, OH	I
America, NY	I	Ferris State University, MI	I	Hellenic College, MA	I
Culver-Stockton College, MO	I	Fisher College, MA	I	Hendrix College, AR	I
Curry College, MA	I	Fitchburg State University, MA	I	High Point University, NC	I
Daemen College, NY	D,I	Flagler College, FL	I	Hilbert College, NY	I
Dakota State University, SD	I	Florida Agricultural and		Hillsdale College, MI	I
Dakota Wesleyan University, SD	I	Mechanical University, FL	P	Hobart and William Smith	
Dallas Baptist University, TX	D,I	Florida Atlantic University, FL	D,I,P	Colleges, NY	I,P
Dartmouth College, NH	I,P	Florida College, FL	I	Hofstra University, NY	G,I
Davidson College, NC	I	Florida Institute of Technology, FL	I	Hollins University, VA	I,P
Davis College, NY	I	Florida International University, FL	I	Holy Family University, PA	D,I
Dean College, MA	I	Florida National University, FL	G,I,P	Hood College, MD	I
Defiance College, OH	I	Florida Southern College, FL	I	Hope College, MI	I
Delaware Valley University, PA	I	Florida State University, FL	I,P	Hope International University, CA	I

D = deferred payment system; *G* = guaranteed tuition rate; *I* = installment payments; *P* = prepayment locks in tuition rate

College		College		College	
Houghton College, NY	I	Lane College, TN	D,I	Maryville College, TN	I
Houston Baptist University, TX	I	Langston University, OK	G,I,P	Maryville University of Saint Louis, MO	D,I
Howard Payne University, TX	I	La Roche College, PA	I		
Humboldt State University, CA	I	La Salle University, PA	D,I	Marywood University, PA	D,I
Huntingdon College, AL	D,G,I	Lasell College, MA	I	Massachusetts College of Art and Design, MA	I
Husson University, ME	I,P	Lawrence Technological University, MI	I	Massachusetts College of Liberal Arts, MA	I
Huston-Tillotson University, TX	D,I	Lawrence University, WI	I		
Idaho State University, ID	G,I	Lebanon Valley College, PA	I	Massachusetts Institute of Technology, MA	I
Illinois College, IL	I	Lees-McRae College, NC	G,I	Massachusetts Maritime Academy, MA	I
Illinois Institute of Technology, IL	I	Lee University, TN	D	The Master's University, CA	I
Illinois Wesleyan University, IL	I	Lehigh University, PA	I,P	Mayville State University, ND	I
Indiana State University, IN	D,I	Le Moyne College, NY	D,I	McDaniel College, MD	I
Indiana Tech, IN	D,G,I	Lesley University, MA	I	McKendree University, IL	D,I
Indiana University Bloomington, IN	D,I	LeTourneau University, TX	I	McPherson College, KS	I
Indiana University East, IN	D,I	Lewis & Clark College, OR	I	MCPHS University, MA	I
Indiana University Kokomo, IN	D,I	Lewis-Clark State College, ID	D	Medgar Evers College of the City University of New York, NY	D,I
Indiana University Northwest, IN	D,I	Lewis University, IL	I		
Indiana University of Pennsylvania, PA	D,I	Liberty University, VA	I	Memphis College of Art, TN	I,P
		Life University, GA	I	Mercer University, GA	I
Indiana University–Purdue University Fort Wayne, IN	D,I	LIM College, NY	I	Mercy College, NY	D,I
		Lincoln Christian University, IL	I	Mercy College of Ohio, OH	D,I
Indiana University–Purdue University Indianapolis, IN	D	Lincoln University, MO	D,I	Merrimack College, MA	I
		Lincoln University, PA	D,G,I	Messiah College, PA	I
Indiana University South Bend, IN	D,I	Lindenwood University, MO	D,I	Metropolitan College of New York, NY	D,G,I
Indiana University Southeast, IN	D,I	Lindsey Wilson College, KY	I		
Indiana Wesleyan University, IN	D,I	Linfield College, OR	I	Metropolitan State University of Denver, CO	D,I
Inter American University of Puerto Rico, Bayamón Campus, PR	D	Lipscomb University, TN	I		
		Lock Haven University of Pennsylvania, PA	I	Miami University, OH	G,I
Inter American University of Puerto Rico, Guayama Campus, PR	D			Michigan State University, MI	D
		Long Island University–LIU Brooklyn, NY	I	Michigan Technological University, MI	D,I
Iona College, NY	I				
Iowa State University of Science and Technology, IA	D,I	Long Island University–LIU Post, NY	I	Mid-Atlantic Christian University, NC	D
		Longwood University, VA	I	Middlebury College, VT	P
Iowa Wesleyan University, IA	D,I	Loras College, IA	I	Middle Georgia State University, GA	I
Ithaca College, NY	I	Louisiana State University and Agricultural & Mechanical College, LA	D	Middle Tennessee State University, TN	I
Jackson State University, MS	I				
Jacksonville State University, AL	I				
Jacksonville University, FL	D	Louisiana State University in Shreveport, LA	I	Midland College, TX	I
John Brown University, AR	I			Millersville University of Pennsylvania, PA	I
John Carroll University, OH	I	Louisiana Tech University, LA	D,I		
John Paul the Great Catholic University, CA	G	Loyola Marymount University, CA	D,I	Milligan College, TN	I
		Loyola University Chicago, IL	D,I	Millikin University, IL	I
Johnson C. Smith University, NC	I	Loyola University Maryland, MD	I	Mills College, CA	I
John Wesley University, NC	I	Loyola University New Orleans, LA	I	Milwaukee School of Engineering, WI	I
Judson College, AL	D,I	Lubbock Christian University, TX	I	Minnesota State University Mankato, MN	I
Judson University, IL	D	Luther College, IA	I		
The Juilliard School, NY	I	Lycoming College, PA	I	Minot State University, ND	I
Juniata College, PA	I	Lynchburg College, VA	I,P	Misericordia University, PA	D,I
Kalamazoo College, MI	I	Lynn University, FL	D,I	Mississippi State University, MS	I,P
Kansas City Art Institute, MO	I	Lyon College, AR	I	Missouri Baptist University, MO	I
Kansas State University, KS	D,I	Macalester College, MN	I	Missouri State University, MO	D
Kansas Wesleyan University, KS	I	MacMurray College, IL	D	Missouri University of Science and Technology, MO	I
Kean University, NJ	I	Malone University, OH	I		
Keene State College, NH	I	Manchester University, IN	I	Missouri Western State University, MO	I
Kent State University, OH	I	Manhattan College, NY	D,I	Molloy College, NY	D,I
Kent State University at Geauga, OH	I	Manhattanville College, NY	D,I	Monmouth College, IL	I
Kent State University at Stark, OH	I	Mansfield University of Pennsylvania, PA	D,I	Monmouth University, NJ	I
Kentucky Mountain Bible College, KY	I			Montana State University, MT	D,I
Kentucky State University, KY	I	Maranatha Baptist University, WI	I	Montana State University Billings, MT	I
Kentucky Wesleyan College, KY	D,I	Maria College, NY	I		
Kenyon College, OH	I	Marian University, WI	I	Montana Tech of The University of Montana, MT	I
Keuka College, NY	I	Marietta College, OH	I		
The King's College, NY	D,I	Marist College, NY	I	Montclair State University, NJ	I
King's College, PA	I	Marlboro College, VT	I	Montreat College, NC	I
King University, TN	I	Marquette University, WI	I	Moravian College, PA	I
Knox College, IL	I	Marshall University, WV	I	Morehead State University, KY	D,I
Kutztown University of Pennsylvania, PA	D,I	Martin Luther College, MN	I	Morehouse College, GA	I
		Mary Baldwin University, VA	I	Morgan State University, MD	D,I
Kuyper College, MI	D,I	Marygrove College, MI	D,I	Morningside College, IA	I
Lafayette College, PA	G	Marylhurst University, OR	I	Morrisville State College, NY	D,I
LaGrange College, GA	I	Marymount California University, CA	I	Mount Carmel College of Nursing, OH	I
Laguna College of Art & Design, CA	I	Marymount Manhattan College, NY	I	Mount Holyoke College, MA	I
Lake Erie College, OH	I	Marymount University, VA	I		
Lamar University, TX	G,I				

D = deferred payment system; *G* = guaranteed tuition rate; *I* = installment payments; *P* = prepayment locks in tuition rate

Mount Ida College, MA	I	Oregon College of Art and Craft, OR	I	Rochester Institute of	
Mount Marty College, SD	I	Ouachita Baptist University, AR	D,I	Technology, NY	D,I,P
Mount Mary University, WI	I	Our Lady of the Lake University, TX	D,I	Rockford University, IL	I
Mount Mercy University, IA	I	Pacific University, OR	D,I	Rockhurst University, MO	D,I
Mount St. Joseph University, OH	D,I	Palm Beach Atlantic University, FL	I	Rocky Mountain College, MT	I
Mount Saint Mary College, NY	I	Patrick Henry College, VA	D,I	Rogers State University, OK	I
Mount Saint Mary's		Peabody Conservatory of The Johns		Roger Williams University, RI	D,G
University, CA	I	Hopkins University, MD	I	Rollins College, FL	I
Mount St. Mary's University, MD	I	Peirce College, PA	D,I	Rose-Hulman Institute of	
Mount Vernon Nazarene University, OH	I	Penn State Abington, PA	D,I	Technology, IN	I,P
Muhlenberg College, PA	I	Penn State Altoona, PA	D,I	Rosemont College, PA	I
Murray State University, KY	I	Penn State Beaver, PA	D	Rowan University, NJ	D,I
Muskingum University, OH	I	Penn State Berks, PA	D	Rutgers University–Camden, NJ	I
National University, CA	D	Penn State Brandywine, PA	D	Rutgers University–Newark, NJ	I
Nazareth College of Rochester, NY	D,I	Penn State Erie, The Behrend		Rutgers University–New	
Nebraska Methodist College, NE	I	College, PA	D	Brunswick, NJ	I
Neumann University, PA	D,I	Penn State Greater Allegheny, PA	D	Sacred Heart University, CT	I
Newberry College, SC	G,I	Penn State Harrisburg, PA	D	The Sage Colleges, NY	I
New College of Florida, FL	I	Penn State Hazleton, PA	D	Saginaw Valley State University, MI	I
New England College, NH	I	Penn State Lehigh Valley, PA	D	St. Ambrose University, IA	D,I
New Jersey City University, NJ	D	Penn State New Kensington, PA	D	St. Andrews University, NC	I
New Jersey Institute of		Penn State Schuylkill, PA	D	Saint Anselm College, NH	I
Technology, NJ	D,I	Penn State University Park, PA	D	Saint Augustine's University, NC	D
New Mexico Highlands University, NM	I	Penn State Wilkes-Barre, PA	D,I	St. Edward's University, TX	I
New Mexico State University, NM	D,I	Penn State Worthington Scranton, PA	D,I	Saint Francis Medical Center	
New York Institute of Technology, NY	I	Penn State York, PA	D,I	College of Nursing, IL	I
New York School of Interior		Pennsylvania College of		St. Gregory's University, OK	G,I,P
Design, NY	I	Technology, PA	D	St. John Fisher College, NY	D,I
New York University, NY	D,I,P	Pepperdine University, CA	I	St. John's College, MD	I,P
Niagara University, NY	D,I	Philadelphia University, PA	D,I	St. John's College, NM	I
Nicholls State University, LA	D,I	Piedmont College, GA	I	Saint John's University, MN	I
Nichols College, MA	I	Piedmont International		St. John's University, NY	I
North Carolina State University, NC	G,I	University, NC	I	St. Joseph's College, Long	
North Central College, IL	I	Plymouth State University, NH	I	Island Campus, NY	I
Northeastern Illinois University, IL	D,G	Point Loma Nazarene University, CA	I	St. Joseph's College, New York, NY	I
Northeastern State University, OK	G,I	Point Park University, PA	D,I	Saint Joseph's University, PA	I
Northeastern University, MA	I	Polytechnic University of Puerto		St. Lawrence University, NY	I,P
Northern Arizona University, AZ	G,I	Rico, PR	D	Saint Leo University, FL	D,I
Northern Illinois University, IL	I	Pomona College, CA	I	St. Louis College of Pharmacy, MO	D
Northern Kentucky University, KY	I	Portland State University, OR	I	Saint Louis University, MO	I
Northern State University, SD	I	Prairie View A&M University, TX	G,I	Saint Martin's University, WA	I
Northland College, WI	I	Presbyterian College, SC	I	Saint Mary-of-the-Woods College, IN	G,I
Northwest Christian University, OR	I	Prescott College, AZ	I	Saint Mary's College, IN	I
Northwest College of Art		Princeton University, NJ	D,I	St. Mary's College of	
& Design, WA	D,I	Principia College, IL	I	Maryland, MD	I
Northwestern College, IA	I,P	Providence College, RI	I	Saint Mary's University of	
Northwestern University, IL	I	Purchase College, State University		Minnesota, MN	I
Northwest Missouri State		of New York, NY	I	Saint Michael's College, VT	I
University, MO	D,I	Purdue University, IN	I	St. Norbert College, WI	D,I
Northwest Nazarene University, ID	I	Queens College of the City		St. Olaf College, MN	I
Northwest University, WA	I	University of New York, NY	I	St. Thomas Aquinas College, NY	I
Nova Southeastern University, FL	D,I	Queens University of Charlotte, NC	I	St. Thomas University, FL	D,I
Oakland City University, IN	D	Quinnipiac University, CT	I	Saint Vincent College, PA	I
Oakland University, MI	D,I	Radford University, VA	I	Salem College, NC	I
Oberlin College, OH	I	Ramapo College of New Jersey, NJ	I	Salisbury University, MD	I
Occidental College, CA	I,P	Randall University, OK	I	Salve Regina University, RI	I
Oglethorpe University, GA	I,P	Randolph College, VA	I	Samford University, AL	I
Ohio Northern University, OH	I	Randolph-Macon College, VA	I	Sam Houston State University, TX	G,I
The Ohio State University, OH	I	Reed College, OR	I	San Diego Christian College, CA	I
Ohio University, OH	G,I	Regent University, VA	I	San Diego State University, CA	I
Ohio University–Eastern, OH	I	Regis University, CO	D,I	San Francisco Art Institute, CA	I
Ohio University–Zanesville, OH	I	Rensselaer Polytechnic Institute, NY	I	San Francisco Conservatory of	
Ohio Valley University, WV	I	Research College of Nursing, MO	D,I	Music, CA	I
Ohio Wesleyan University, OH	I	Rhode Island College, RI	I	San Francisco State University, CA	I
Oklahoma Baptist University, OK	I	Rhode Island School of Design, RI	I	San Jose State University, CA	D,I
Oklahoma Christian University, OK	I,P	Rhodes College, TN	I	Santa Clara University, CA	I
Oklahoma City University, OK	D,I	Rice University, TX	I	Sarah Lawrence College, NY	I
Oklahoma Panhandle State		Rider University, NJ	I	Savannah College of Art and	
University, OK	G,I	Ringling College of Art and		Design, GA	I
Oklahoma State University, OK	G,I	Design, FL	I	Savannah State University, GA	I
Old Dominion University, VA	D,I	Roanoke College, VA	I	School of the Art Institute of	
Olivet College, MI	I	Robert Morris University, PA	D,I	Chicago, IL	I
Olivet Nazarene University, IL	I	Robert Morris University Illinois, IL	I	Schreiner University, TX	I
O'More College of Design, TN	I	Roberts Wesleyan College, NY	I	Scripps College, CA	I,P
Oral Roberts University, OK	I			Seattle Pacific University, WA	D,I

D = deferred payment system; *G* = guaranteed tuition rate; *I* = installment payments; *P* = prepayment locks in tuition rate

Seattle University, WA	D,I	State University of New York Polytechnic Institute, NY	I	University of Alaska Fairbanks, AK	D,I
Seton Hill University, PA	I	Stephen F. Austin State		The University of Arizona, AZ	G,I
Sewanee: The University of the South, TN	G,I	University, TX	G,I	University of Arkansas, AR	I
Shasta Bible College, CA	I	Sterling College, KS	I	University of Bridgeport, CT	D,I
Shawnee State University, OH	I	Stetson University, FL	I	University of California, Berkeley, CA	I
Shenandoah University, VA	I	Stevens Institute of Technology, NJ	I	University of California, Irvine, CA	I
Shepherd University, WV	I	Stevenson University, MD	I	University of California,	
Shippensburg University of Pennsylvania, PA	I	Stockton University, NJ	D,I	Riverside, CA	D
Siena College, NY	I	Stonehill College, MA	I,P	University of California, Santa Barbara, CA	I
Simmons College, MA	I	Stony Brook University, State University of New York, NY	I	University of Central Arkansas, AR	I
Simpson College, IA	I	Suffolk University, MA	D,I	University of Central Florida, FL	D,P
Simpson University, CA	D	Susquehanna University, PA	I,P	University of Central Missouri, MO	D,I
Skidmore College, NY	I,P	Swarthmore College, PA	I	University of Central Oklahoma, OK	D,G
Slippery Rock University of Pennsylvania, PA	I	Sweet Briar College, VA	I	University of Chicago, IL	I
Smith College, MA	I,P	Syracuse University, NY	I,P	University of Cincinnati, OH	I
Soka University of America, CA	D,I	Tarleton State University, TX	G,I	University of Colorado Boulder, CO	D,G
Sonoma State University, CA	I	Taylor University, IN	I	University of Colorado Colorado	
South Dakota School of Mines and Technology, SD	I	Temple University, PA	I	Springs, CO	I
Southeastern Louisiana University, LA	I	Tennessee Wesleyan University, TN	I	University of Colorado Denver, CO	D,I
Southeastern Oklahoma State		Texas A&M International		University of Dallas, TX	I
University, OK	G,I	University, TX	I	University of Delaware, DE	I
Southeastern University, FL	I	Texas A&M University, TX	G,I	University of Denver, CO	D,I
Southeast Missouri State		Texas A&M University–		University of Detroit Mercy, MI	D,I
University, MO	D,I	Commerce, TX	G,I	University of Dubuque, IA	I
Southern Adventist University, TN	I	Texas A&M University–Corpus		University of Evansville, IN	I
Southern Connecticut State		Christi, TX	G,I	The University of Findlay, OH	I
University, CT	D,I	Texas A&M University–		University of Hartford, CT	I,P
Southern Illinois University		Kingsville, TX	G,I	University of Hawaii at Manoa, HI	I
Carbondale, IL	G,I	Texas Christian University, TX	I	University of Holy Cross, LA	I
Southern Illinois University		Texas Lutheran University, TX	I	University of Houston, TX	D,G,I
Edwardsville, IL	G,I	Texas State University, TX	G,I,P	University of Houston–	
Southern Methodist University, TX	I,P	Texas Tech University, TX	I	Downtown, TX	I
Southern New Hampshire		Texas Wesleyan University, TX	D,I	University of Houston–	
University, NH	D,I	Texas Woman's University, TX	G,I	Victoria, TX	D,I
Southern Oregon University, OR	D,I	Theological University of the		University of Idaho, ID	I
Southern Utah University, UT	I	Caribbean, PR	D	University of Illinois at Chicago, IL	G,I
Southwest Baptist University, MO	I	Thiel College, PA	I	University of Illinois at	
Southwestern College, KS	I	Thomas Aquinas College, CA	I	Springfield, IL	G,I
Southwestern Oklahoma State		Thomas College, ME	D	University of Illinois at	
University, OK	D,I	Thomas Edison State University, NJ	I	Urbana–Champaign, IL	G,I
Southwestern University, TX	I	Thomas More College, KY	D,I	University of Indianapolis, IN	I
Spelman College, GA	D,I	Thomas More College of Liberal		University of Jamestown, ND	I
Spring Arbor University, MI	I	Arts, NH	I	The University of Kansas, KS	G,I
Spring Hill College, AL	I	Thomas University, GA	I	University of Kentucky, KY	I
Stanford University, CA	I	Tiffin University, OH	D,I	University of La Verne, CA	D,I
State University of New York at		Toccoa Falls College, GA	I	University of Louisiana at Monroe, LA	I
Fredonia, NY	I	Towson University, MD	I	University of Louisville, KY	I
State University of New York at		Transylvania University, KY	I	University of Maine, ME	I
New Paltz, NY	I	Trevecca Nazarene University, TN	I,P	University of Maine at Augusta, ME	I
State University of New York at		Trine University, IN	I	University of Maine at Fort Kent, ME	I
Oswego, NY	I	Trinity Christian College, IL	I	University of Maine at Machias, ME	I
State University of New York at		Trinity College of Florida, FL	I	University of Maine at Presque	
Plattsburgh, NY	D,I	Trinity University, TX	I	Isle, ME	I
State University of New York		Troy University, AL	I	University of Mary Hardin-Baylor, TX	I
College at Cortland, NY	I	Truett McConnell University, GA	I	University of Maryland, Baltimore	
State University of New York		Truman State University, MO	I	County, MD	I
College at Geneseo, NY	D,I	Tufts University, MA	I,P	University of Maryland, College	
State University of New York		Tulane University, LA	I,P	Park, MD	D,I
College at Potsdam, NY	I	Tusculum College, TN	I	University of Maryland University	
State University of New York College of Agriculture and Technology		Tuskegee University, AL	I	College, MD	I
at Cobleskill, NY	D,I	Union College, KY	I	University of Mary Washington, VA	I
State University of New York College of Environmental Science and		Union College, NE	I	University of Massachusetts	
		Union College, NY	I	Amherst, MA	I
Forestry, NY	D,I	Union University, TN	D,I	University of Massachusetts	
State University of New York		United States Sports Academy, AL	I	Dartmouth, MA	I
College of Technology at Canton, NY	D,I	Unity College, ME	I	University of Massachusetts	
State University of New York		University at Buffalo, the State		Lowell, MA	I
College of Technology at Delhi, NY	I	University of New York, NY	I	University of Memphis, TN	I
State University of New York		The University of Akron, OH	I	University of Miami, FL	I
Maritime College, NY	I	The University of Alabama at		University of Michigan, MI	I
		Birmingham, AL	I	University of Michigan–	
		The University of Alabama in		Dearborn, MI	I
		Huntsville, AL	I		

D = deferred payment system; *G* = guaranteed tuition rate; *I* = installment payments; *P* = prepayment locks in tuition rate

University of Michigan–Flint, MI — I
University of Minnesota, Crookston, MN — I
University of Minnesota, Duluth, MN — I
University of Minnesota, Morris, MN — I
University of Minnesota, Twin Cities Campus, MN — I
University of Missouri, MO — I
University of Missouri–Kansas City, MO — I
University of Missouri–St. Louis, MO — I
University of Mobile, AL — I
University of Montana, MT — I
The University of Montana Western, MT — D,I
University of Montevallo, AL — I
University of Mount Union, OH — I,P
University of Nebraska at Kearney, NE — I
University of Nebraska–Lincoln, NE — I
University of Nevada, Las Vegas, NV — D
University of Nevada, Reno, NV — I
University of New Hampshire, NH — I
University of New Hampshire at Manchester, NH — I
University of New Haven, CT — I
University of North Alabama, AL — I
University of North Carolina at Asheville, NC — D,I
The University of North Carolina at Chapel Hill, NC — I
The University of North Carolina at Charlotte, NC — I
The University of North Carolina at Greensboro, NC — I
The University of North Carolina at Pembroke, NC — I
University of North Carolina School of the Arts, NC — G
The University of North Carolina Wilmington, NC — I
University of Northern Colorado, CO — I
University of Northern Iowa, IA — I
University of North Florida, FL — I
University of North Georgia, GA — I
University of North Texas, TX — G,I
University of North Texas at Dallas, TX — G
University of Notre Dame, IN — I
University of Oklahoma, OK — G,I
University of Oregon, OR — I
University of Pennsylvania, PA — I,P
University of Pikeville, KY — I
University of Pittsburgh, PA — D,I
University of Pittsburgh at Bradford, PA — I
University of Pittsburgh at Greensburg, PA — I
University of Pittsburgh at Johnstown, PA — I
University of Puerto Rico in Bayamón, PR — D,G
University of Puget Sound, WA — D,I
University of Redlands, CA — I
University of Rhode Island, RI — I
University of Richmond, VA — I
University of Rochester, NY — I
University of St. Francis, IL — D,I
University of Saint Joseph, CT — I
University of St. Thomas, MN — D,I
University of St. Thomas, TX — D,I
University of San Diego, CA — I
University of San Francisco, CA — I

University of Science and Arts of Oklahoma, OK — G,I
University of Sioux Falls, SD — I
University of South Alabama, AL — I
University of South Carolina, SC — D
University of South Carolina Aiken, SC — D
The University of South Dakota, SD — D
University of Southern California, CA — I,P
University of Southern Indiana, IN — I
University of Southern Maine, ME — I
University of Southern Mississippi, MS — I
University of South Florida, FL — D
The University of Tampa, FL — I
The University of Tennessee, TN — I
The University of Tennessee at Chattanooga, TN — I
The University of Tennessee at Martin, TN — D,I
The University of Texas at Arlington, TX — I
The University of Texas at Austin, TX — G,I
The University of Texas at Dallas, TX — G,I
The University of Texas at El Paso, TX — G,I
The University of Texas at San Antonio, TX — D,G,I
The University of Texas of the Permian Basin, TX — G,I
The University of Texas Rio Grande Valley, TX — G,I
University of the Incarnate Word, TX — I
University of the Pacific, CA — D
University of the Sciences, PA — I
The University of Toledo, OH — I
The University of Tulsa, OK — I
University of Utah, UT — D,I
University of Valley Forge, PA — I
University of Vermont, VT — I
University of Virginia, VA — I
The University of Virginia's College at Wise, VA — D,I
University of Washington, WA — P
University of Washington, Bothell, WA — I,P
University of Washington, Tacoma, WA — I,P
The University of West Alabama, AL — I
University of West Florida, FL — D,P
University of West Georgia, GA — I
University of Wisconsin–Eau Claire, WI — I
University of Wisconsin–Green Bay, WI — I
University of Wisconsin–La Crosse, WI — I
University of Wisconsin–Milwaukee, WI — I
University of Wisconsin–Parkside, WI — I
University of Wisconsin–Stevens Point, WI — D,I
University of Wisconsin–Superior, WI — I
University of Wisconsin–Whitewater, WI — D,I
University of Wyoming, WY — I
Upper Iowa University, IA — I
Ursuline College, OH — I
Utah State University, UT — D
Utah Valley University, UT — D
Valdosta State University, GA — I
Valley City State University, ND — I
Valparaiso University, IN — I,P
Vanderbilt University, TN — I,P

Vanguard University of Southern California, CA — I
Vassar College, NY — I
Vermont Technical College, VT — I
Villa Maria College, NY — I
Villanova University, PA — I
Virginia Commonwealth University, VA — I
Virginia Military Institute, VA — I
Virginia State University, VA — I
Virginia Wesleyan College, VA — I
Wabash College, IN — I,P
Wagner College, NY — I
Waldorf University, IA — D,I
Walsh College of Accountancy and Business Administration, MI — D
Warner Pacific College, OR — D,I
Warner University, FL — I
Wartburg College, IA — I
Washburn University, KS — I
Washington & Jefferson College, PA — I,P
Washington and Lee University, VA — I
Washington College, MD — G,I,P
Washington University in St. Louis, MO — I,P
Wayland Baptist University, TX — I
Waynesburg University, PA — I
Wayne State College, NE — I
Webber International University, FL — I
Weber State University, UT — I
Webster University, MO — D
Wellesley College, MA — I,P
Wells College, NY — I
Wentworth Institute of Technology, MA — I
Wesleyan College, GA — I
Wesleyan University, CT — I
West Chester University of Pennsylvania, PA — I
Western Connecticut State University, CT — I
Western Illinois University, IL — G,I
Western Kentucky University, KY — I
Western Michigan University, MI — I
Western New England University, MA — I,P
Western Oregon University, OR — G
Western State Colorado University, CO — D,I
Western Washington University, WA — I
Westfield State University, MA — I
Westminster College, MO — I
Westminster College, PA — I
Westminster College, UT — D,I
Westmont College, CA — I
West Texas A&M University, TX — G,I
West Virginia University, WV — I
West Virginia University Institute of Technology, WV — I
West Virginia Wesleyan College, WV — I
Wheaton College, IL — D,I
Wheaton College, MA — I
Wheelock College, MA — I
Whitman College, WA — D
Whittier College, CA — I
Whitworth University, WA — I
Wichita State University, KS — I
Widener University, PA — I
Wilkes University, PA — D,I
Willamette University, OR — I,P
William Jessup University, CA — D
William Jewell College, MO — I
William Paterson University of New Jersey, NJ — I
William Peace University, NC — I
Williams Baptist College, AR — I
Williams College, MA — I
William Woods University, MO — I
Wilson College, PA — I

D = deferred payment system; *G* = guaranteed tuition rate; *I* = installment payments; *P* = prepayment locks in tuition rate

Wingate University, NC	I	Worcester Polytechnic Institute, MA	D,I,P	Yale University, CT	I
Winona State University, MN	I	Worcester State University, MA	I	York College of Pennsylvania, PA	I
Winthrop University, SC	I	Wright State University, OH	I		
Wisconsin Lutheran College, WI	I	Wright State University–Lake		York College of the City	
Wittenberg University, OH	I	Campus, OH	I	University of New York, NY	I
Wofford College, SC	I	Xavier University, OH	D,I		
Woodbury University, CA	D	Xavier University of Louisiana, LA	I	Youngstown State University, OH	I

D = deferred payment system; *G* = guaranteed tuition rate; *I* = installment payments; *P* = prepayment locks in tuition rate

NOTES

NOTES